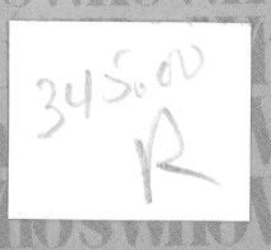

Who'sWho in the Midwest®

Who'sWho in the Midwest®

2009

35th Edition

Including Illinois, Indiana, Iowa, Kansas, Michigan, Minnesota, Missouri, Nebraska, North Dakota, Ohio, South Dakota, and Wisconsin, and in Canada: Manitoba and western Ontario

MARQUIS
Who'sWho®

890 Mountain Avenue, Suite 300
New Providence, NJ 07974 U.S.A.
www.marquiswhoswho.com

Who's Who in the Midwest®

Marquis Who's Who®

For information, contact: Marquis Who's Who
890 Mountain Avenue, Suite 300
New Providence, New Jersey 07974
1-800-473-7020
midwest@marquiswhoswho.com
www.marquiswhoswho.com

Library of Congress Catalog Card Number 50-289
International Standard Book Number 978-0-8379-0738-3
International Standard Serial Number 0083-9787

Manufactured in the United States of America.

Table of Contents

Preface

Marquis Who's Who is proud to present the 2009 Edition of *Who's Who in the Midwest,* our 35th compilation of biographical information on men and women of distinction whose influence is concentrated in the midwest region of North America, but may also be felt nationally and internationally.

This volume contains more than 16,000 biographies of people working in Illinois, Indiana, Iowa, Kansas, Michigan, Minnesota, Missouri, Nebraska, North Dakota, Ohio, South Dakota, and Wisconsin in the United States, and from Manitoba and western Ontario in Canada. Some individuals listed are not residents of this region; however, the professional activities of these listees have been widely influential in the midwest.

The persons sketched in this volume represent virtually every important field of endeavor. Included are executives and officials in government, business, education, religion, the press, law, civic activities, and many other fields. Also included are leaders in the fields of science, healthcare, engineering, and notable people involved in the arts and cultural affairs.

Factors such as position, noteworthy accomplishments, visibility, and prominence in a field are all taken into account in making selections for the book. Final decisions concerning inclusion or exclusion are made following extensive discussion, evaluation, and deliberation.

Biographical information is gathered in a variety of manners. In most cases, we invite our biographees to submit their biographical details. In many cases, though, the information is collected independently by our editorial staff who use a wide assortment of tools to gather complete, accurate, and up-to-date information. Sketches researched by Marquis Who's Who will be followed by an asterisk (*).

While the Marquis Who's Who editors exercise the utmost care in preparing each biographical sketch for publication, in a publication involving so many profiles, occasional errors may appear. Users of this publication are urged to notify the publisher of any issues so that adjustments can be made.

All of the profiles featured in *Who's Who in the Midwest* are available on *Who's Who on the Web* (www.marquiswhoswho.com) through a subscription. At the present time, subscribers to *Who's Who on the Web* have access to all of the names included in all of the Marquis Who's Who publications, as well as many new biographies that will appear in upcoming publications.

We sincerely hope that this volume will be an indispensable reference tool for you. We are always looking for ways to better serve you and welcome your ideas for improvements. In addition, we continue to welcome your Marquis Who's Who nominations. *Who's Who in the Midwest* and all Marquis Who's Who publications pay tribute to those individuals who make significant contributions to our society. It is our honor and privilege to present their profiles to you.

Key to Information

[1] STEELE, FLETCHER DAVID, [2] mechanical engineer; **[3]** b. Normal, Ill., Jan. 20, 1939; **[4]** s. Thomas William and Susan (Shobe) S.; **[5]** m. Julie Ann Walsh, Sept. 8, 1964; **[6]** children: Elizabeth Carter, Michael Thomas. **[7]** BSME, Purdue U., 1961; MS, U. Ill., 1965. **[8]** Registered profl. engr., Ill., Iowa. **[9]** Asst. engr. Kelly, Kitching, Berendes & Brault, Engrs., Chgo., 1966-67, engr., 1967-71; sr. engr. Kelly, Kitching, Berendes & Brault, Internat., Des Moines, 1971-78, mgr. fluids divsn. 1979-84, v.p. R & D, 1985-90, exec. v.p. 1990—. **[10]** Lectr. Drake U., 1995-97. **[11]** Contbr. articles to Jour. Biomech. Engring., Jour. Fluids Engring. **[12]** Asst. troop leader Des Moines coun. Boy Scouts Am., 1992—. **[13]** Lt. US Army, 1961-63. **[14]** Recipient Nat. Engring. award, 1975; Fulbright scholar, 1965. **[15]** Mem. ASME, NSPE, Iowa Mech. Engrs. Assn., Big Sand Lake Club. **[16]** Republican. **[17]** Roman Catholic. **[18]** Achievements include design of L16500 Workhorse rotar; patent for internal piston lock for hydraulic cylinders; research in linear regression analysis for large-lot engine data comparisons. **[19]** Avocations: cooking, running. **[20]** Home: 733 N Ottawa Rd Ankeny IA 50021 **[21]** Office: 1245 34th St Des Moines IA 50311*

KEY

[1] Name
[2] Occupation
[3] Vital statistics
[4] Parents
[5] Marriage
[6] Children
[7] Education
[8] Professional certifications
[9] Career
[10] Career-related
[11] Writings and creative works
[12] Civic and political activities
[13] Military
[14] Awards and fellowships
[15] Professional and association memberships, clubs and lodges
[16] Political affiliation
[17] Religion
[18] Achievements information
[19] Avocations
[20] Home address
[21] Office address
[*] Researched by Marquis Who's Who

Table of Abbreviations

The following is a list of some frequently used Marquis abbreviations:

A

A Associate (used with academic degrees)
AA Associate in Arts
AAAL American Academy of Arts and Letters
AAAS American Association for the Advancement of Science
AACD American Association for Counseling and Development
AACN American Association of Critical Care Nurses
AAHA American Academy of Health Administrators
AAHP American Association of Hospital Planners
AAHPERD American Alliance for Health, Physical Education, Recreation, and Dance
AAS Associate of Applied Science
AASL American Association of School Librarians
AASPA American Association of School Personnel Administrators
AAU Amateur Athletic Union
AAUP American Association of University Professors
AAUW American Association of University Women
AB Arts, Bachelor of
AB Alberta
ABA American Bar Association
AC Air Corps
acad. academy
acct. accountant
acctg. accounting
ACDA Arms Control and Disarmament Agency
ACHA American College of Hospital Administrators
ACLS Advanced Cardiac Life Support
ACLU American Civil Liberties Union
ACOG American College of Ob-Gyn
ACP American College of Physicians
ACS American College of Surgeons
ADA American Dental Association
adj. adjunct, adjutant
adm. admiral
adminstr. administrator
adminstrn. administration
adminstrv. administrative
ADN Associate's Degree in Nursing
ADP Automatic Data Processing
adv. advocate, advisory
advt. advertising
AE Agricultural Engineer
AEC Atomic Energy Commission
aero. aeronautical, aeronautic
aerodyn. aerodynamic
AFB Air Force Base
AFTRA American Federation of Television and Radio Artists
agr. agriculture
agrl. agricultural
agt. agent
AGVA American Guild of Variety Artists
agy. agency
A&I Agricultural and Industrial
AIA American Institute of Architects
AIAA American Institute of Aeronautics and Astronautics
AIChE American Institute of Chemical Engineers
AICPA American Institute of Certified Public Accountants
AID Agency for International Development
AIDS Acquired Immune Deficiency Syndrome
AIEE American Institute of Electrical Engineers
AIME American Institute of Mining, Metallurgy, and Petroleum Engineers
AK Alaska
AL Alabama
ALA American Library Association
Ala. Alabama
alt. alternate
Alta. Alberta
A&M Agricultural and Mechanical
AM Arts, Master of
Am. American, America
AMA American Medical Association
amb. ambassador
AME African Methodist Episcopal
Amtrak National Railroad Passenger Corporation
AMVETS American Veterans
ANA American Nurses Association
anat. anatomical
ANCC American Nurses Credentialing Center
ann. annual
anthrop. anthropological
AP Associated Press
APA American Psychological Association
APHA American Public Health Association
APO Army Post Office
apptd. appointed
Apr. April
apt. apartment
AR Arkansas
ARC American Red Cross
arch. architect
archeol. archeological
archtl. architectural
Ariz. Arizona
Ark. Arkansas
ArtsD Arts, Doctor of
arty. artillery
AS Associate in Science, American Samoa
ASCAP American Society of Composers, Authors and Publishers
ASCD Association for Supervision and Curriculum Development
ASCE American Society of Civil Engineers
ASME American Society of Mechanical Engineers
ASPA American Society for Public Administration
ASPCA American Society for the Prevention of Cruelty to Animals
assn. association
assoc. associate
asst. assistant
ASTD American Society for Training and Development
ASTM American Society for Testing and Materials
astron. astronomical
astrophys. astrophysical
ATLA Association of Trial Lawyers of America
ATSC Air Technical Service Command
atty. attorney
Aug. August
aux. auxiliary
Ave. Avenue
AVMA American Veterinary Medical Association
AZ Arizona

B

B Bachelor
b. born
BA Bachelor of Arts
BAgr Bachelor of Agriculture
Balt. Baltimore
Bapt. Baptist
BArch Bachelor of Architecture
BAS Bachelor of Agricultural Science
BBA Bachelor of Business Administration
BBB Better Business Bureau
BC British Columbia
BCE Bachelor of Civil Engineering
BChir Bachelor of Surgery
BCL Bachelor of Civil Law
BCS Bachelor of Commercial Science
BD Bachelor of Divinity
bd. board
BE Bachelor of Education
BEE Bachelor of Electrical Engineering
BFA Bachelor of Fine Arts
bibl. biblical
bibliog. bibliographical
biog. biographical
biol. biological
BJ Bachelor of Journalism
Bklyn. Brooklyn
BL Bachelor of Letters
bldg. building
BLS Bachelor of Library Science
Blvd. Boulevard

BMI Broadcast Music, Inc.
bn. battalion
bot. botanical
BPE Bachelor of Physical Education
BPhil Bachelor of Philosophy
br. branch
BRE Bachelor of Religious Education
brig. gen. brigadier general
Brit. British
Bros. Brothers
BS Bachelor of Science
BSA Bachelor of Agricultural Science
BSBA Bachelor of Science in Business Administration
BSChemE Bachelor of Science in Chemical Engineering
BSD Bachelor of Didactic Science
BSEE Bachelor of Science in Electrical Engineering
BSN Bachelor of Science in Nursing
BST Bachelor of Sacred Theology
BTh Bachelor of Theology
bull. bulletin
bur. bureau
bus. business
BWI British West Indies

C

CA California
CAD-CAM Computer Aided Design–Computer Aided Model
Calif. California
Can. Canada, Canadian
CAP Civil Air Patrol
capt. captain
cardiol. cardiological
cardiovasc. cardiovascular
Cath. Catholic
cav. cavalry
CBI China, Burma, India Theatre of Operations
CC Community College
CCC Commodity Credit Corporation
CCNY City College of New York
CCRN Critical Care Registered Nurse
CCU Cardiac Care Unit
CD Civil Defense
CE Corps of Engineers, Civil Engineer
CEN Certified Emergency Nurse
CENTO Central Treaty Organization
CEO chief executive officer
CERN European Organization of Nuclear Research
cert. certificate, certification, certified
CETA Comprehensive Employment Training Act
CFA Chartered Financial Analyst
CFL Canadian Football League
CFO chief financial officer
CFP Certified Financial Planner
ch. church
ChD Doctor of Chemistry
chem. chemical
ChemE Chemical Engineer
ChFC Chartered Financial Consultant
Chgo. Chicago
chirurg., der surgeon
chmn. chairman
chpt. chapter
CIA Central Intelligence Agency
Cin. Cincinnati
cir. circle, circuit
CLE Continuing Legal Education
Cleve. Cleveland
climatol. climatological
clin. clinical
clk. clerk
CLU Chartered Life Underwriter
CM Master in Surgery
CM Northern Mariana Islands
cmty. community
CO Colorado
Co. Company
COF Catholic Order of Foresters
C. of C. Chamber of Commerce
col. colonel
coll. college
Colo. Colorado
com. committee
comd. commanded
comdg. commanding
comdr. commander
comdt. commandant
comm. communications
commd. commissioned
comml. commercial
commn. commission
commr. commissioner
compt. comptroller
condr. conductor
conf. Conference
Congl. Congregational, Congressional
Conglist. Congregationalist
Conn. Connecticut
cons. consultant, consulting
consol. consolidated
constl. constitutional
constn. constitution
constrn. construction
contbd. contributed
contbg. contributing
contbn. contribution
contbr. contributor
contr. controller
Conv. Convention
COO chief operating officer
coop. cooperative
coord. coordinator
corp. corporation, corporate
corr. correspondent, corresponding, correspondence
coun. council
CPA Certified Public Accountant
CPCU Chartered Property and Casualty Underwriter
CPH Certificate of Public Health
cpl. corporal
CPR Cardio-Pulmonary Resuscitation
CS Christian Science
CSB Bachelor of Christian Science
CT Connecticut
ct. court
ctr. center
ctrl. central

D

D Doctor
d. daughter of
DAgr Doctor of Agriculture
DAR Daughters of the American Revolution
dau. daughter
DAV Disabled American Veterans
DC District of Columbia
DCL Doctor of Civil Law
DCS Doctor of Commercial Science
DD Doctor of Divinity
DDS Doctor of Dental Surgery
DE Delaware
Dec. December
dec. deceased
def. defense
Del. Delaware
del. delegate, delegation
Dem. Democrat, Democratic
DEng Doctor of Engineering
denom. denomination, denominational
dep. deputy
dept. department
dermatol. dermatological
desc. descendant
devel. development, developmental
DFA Doctor of Fine Arts
DHL Doctor of Hebrew Literature
dir. director
dist. district
distbg. distributing
distbn. distribution
distbr. distributor
disting. distinguished
div. division, divinity, divorce
divsn. division
DLitt Doctor of Literature
DMD Doctor of Dental Medicine
DMS Doctor of Medical Science
DO Doctor of Osteopathy
docs. documents
DON Director of Nursing
DPH Diploma in Public Health
DPhil, Doctor of Philosophy
DR Daughters of the Revolution
Dr. Drive, Doctor
DRE Doctor of Religious Education
DrPH Doctor of Public Health
DSc Doctor of Science
DSChemE Doctor of Science in Chemical Engineering
DSM Distinguished Service Medal
DST Doctor of Sacred Theology
DTM Doctor of Tropical Medicine
DVM Doctor of Veterinary Medicine
DVS Doctor of Veterinary Surgery

E

E East
ea. eastern
Eccles. Ecclesiastical
ecol. ecological

econ. economic
ECOSOC UN Economic and Social Council
ED Doctor of Engineering
ed. educated
EdB Bachelor of Education
EdD Doctor of Education
edit. edition
editl. editorial
EdM Master of Education
edn. education
ednl. educational
EDP Electronic Data Processing
EdS Specialist in Education
EE Electrical Engineer
EEC European Economic Community
EEG Electroencephalogram
EEO Equal Employment Opportunity
EEOC Equal Employment Opportunity Commission
EKG electrocardiogram
elec. electrical
electrochem. electrochemical
electrophys. electrophysical
elem. elementary
EM Engineer of Mines
EMT Emergency Medical Technician
ency. encyclopedia
Eng. England
engr. engineer
engring. engineering
entomol. entomological
environ. environmental
EPA Environmental Protection Agency
epidemiol. epidemiological
Episc. Episcopalian
ERA Equal Rights Amendment
ERDA Energy Research and Development Administration
ESEA Elementary and Secondary Education Act
ESL English as Second Language
ESSA Environmental Science Services Administration
ethnol. ethnological
ETO European Theatre of Operations
EU European Union
Evang. Evangelical
exam. examination, examining
Exch. Exchange
exec. executive
exhbn. exhibition
expdn. expedition
expn. exposition
expt. experiment
exptl. experimental
Expy. Expressway
Ext. Extension

F

FAA Federal Aviation Administration
FAO UN Food and Agriculture Organization
FBA Federal Bar Association
FBI Federal Bureau of Investigation
FCA Farm Credit Administration
FCC Federal Communications Commission
FCDA Federal Civil Defense Administration
FDA Food and Drug Administration
FDIA Federal Deposit Insurance Administration
FDIC Federal Deposit Insurance Corporation
FEA Federal Energy Administration
Feb. February
fed. federal
fedn. federation
FERC Federal Energy Regulatory Commission
fgn. foreign
FHA Federal Housing Administration
fin. financial, finance
FL Florida
Fl. Floor
Fla. Florida
FMC Federal Maritime Commission
FNP Family Nurse Practitioner
FOA Foreign Operations Administration
found. foundation
FPC Federal Power Commission
FPO Fleet Post Office
frat. fraternity
FRS Federal Reserve System
FSA Federal Security Agency
Ft. Fort
FTC Federal Trade Commission
Fwy. Freeway

G

GA, Ga. Georgia
GAO General Accounting Office
gastroent. gastroenterological
GATT General Agreement on Tariffs and Trade
GE General Electric Company
gen. general
geneal. genealogical
geog. geographic, geographical
geol. geological
geophys. geophysical
geriat. geriatrics
gerontol. gerontological
GHQ General Headquarters
gov. governor
govt. government
govtl. governmental
GPO Government Printing Office
grad. graduate, graduated
GSA General Services Administration
Gt. Great
GU Guam
gynecol. gynecological

H

hdqs. headquarters
HEW Department of Health, Education and Welfare
HHD Doctor of Humanities
HHFA Housing and Home Finance Agency
HHS Department of Health and Human Services
HI Hawaii
hist. historical, historic
HM Master of Humanities
homeo. homeopathic
hon. honorary, honorable
House of Dels. House of Delegates
House of Reps. House of Representatives
hort. horticultural
hosp. hospital
HS High School
HUD Department of Housing and Urban Development
Hwy. Highway
hydrog. hydrographic

I

IA Iowa
IAEA International Atomic Energy Agency
IBRD International Bank for Reconstruction and Development
ICA International Cooperation Administration
ICC Interstate Commerce Commission
ICCE International Council for Computers in Education
ICU Intensive Care Unit
ID Idaho
IEEE Institute of Electrical and Electronics Engineers
IFC International Finance Corporation
IL, Ill. Illinois
illus. illustrated
ILO International Labor Organization
IMF International Monetary Fund
IN Indiana
Inc. Incorporated
Ind. Indiana
ind. independent
Indpls. Indianapolis
indsl. industrial
inf. infantry
info. information
ins. insurance
insp. inspector
inst. institute
instl. institutional
instn. institution
instr. instructor
instrn. instruction
instrnl. instructional
internat. international
intro. introduction
IRE Institute of Radio Engineers
IRS Internal Revenue Service

J

JAG Judge Advocate General
JAGC Judge Advocate General Corps
Jan. January
Jaycees Junior Chamber of Commerce
JB Jurum Baccalaureus
JCB Juris Canoni Baccalaureus
JCD Juris Canonici Doctor, Juris Civilis Doctor
JCL Juris Canonici Licentiatus
JD Juris Doctor

jg. junior grade
jour. journal
jr. junior
JSD Juris Scientiae Doctor
JUD Juris Utriusque Doctor
jud. judicial

K

Kans. Kansas
KC Knights of Columbus
KS Kansas
KY, Ky. Kentucky

L

LA, La. Louisiana
LA Los Angeles
lab. laboratory
L.Am. Latin America
lang. language
laryngol. laryngological
LB Labrador
LDS Latter Day Saints
lectr. lecturer
legis. legislation, legislative
LHD Doctor of Humane Letters
LI Long Island
libr. librarian, library
lic. licensed, license
lit. literature
litig. litigation
LittB Bachelor of Letters
LittD Doctor of Letters
LLB Bachelor of Laws
LLD Doctor of Laws
LLM Master of Laws
Ln. Lane
LPGA Ladies Professional Golf Association
LPN Licensed Practical Nurse
lt. lieutenant
Ltd. Limited
Luth. Lutheran
LWV League of Women Voters

M

M Master
m. married
MA Master of Arts
MA Massachusetts
MADD Mothers Against Drunk Driving
mag. magazine
MAgr Master of Agriculture
maj. major
Man. Manitoba
Mar. March
MArch Master in Architecture
Mass. Massachusetts
math. mathematics, mathematical
MB Bachelor of Medicine, Manitoba
MBA Master of Business Administration
MC Medical Corps
MCE Master of Civil Engineering
mcht. merchant
mcpl. municipal
MCS Master of Commercial Science
MD Doctor of Medicine
MD, Md. Maryland
MDiv Master of Divinity
MDip Master in Diplomacy
mdse. merchandise
MDV Doctor of Veterinary Medicine
ME Mechanical Engineer
ME Maine
M.E.Ch. Methodist Episcopal Church
mech. mechanical
MEd. Master of Education
med. medical
MEE Master of Electrical Engineering
mem. member
meml. memorial
merc. mercantile
met. metropolitan
metall. metallurgical
MetE Metallurgical Engineer
meteorol. meteorological
Meth. Methodist
Mex. Mexico
MF Master of Forestry
MFA Master of Fine Arts
mfg. manufacturing
mfr. manufacturer
mgmt. management
mgr. manager
MHA Master of Hospital Administration
MI Military Intelligence, Michigan
Mich. Michigan
micros. microscopic
mid. middle
mil. military
Milw. Milwaukee
Min. Minister
mineral. mineralogical
Minn. Minnesota
MIS Management Information Systems
Miss. Mississippi
MIT Massachusetts Institute of Technology
mktg. marketing
ML Master of Laws
MLA Modern Language Association
MLitt Master of Literature, Master of Letters
MLS Master of Library Science
MME Master of Mechanical Engineering
MN Minnesota
mng. managing
MO, Mo. Missouri
moblzn. mobilization
Mont. Montana
MP Member of Parliament
MPA Master of Public Administration
MPE Master of Physical Education
MPH Master of Public Health
MPhil Master of Philosophy
MPL Master of Patent Law
Mpls. Minneapolis
MRE Master of Religious Education
MRI Magnetic Resonance Imaging
MS Master of Science
MS, Ms. Mississippi
MSc Master of Science
MSChemE Master of Science in Chemical Engineering
MSEE Master of Science in Electrical Engineering
MSF Master of Science of Forestry
MSN Master of Science in Nursing
MST Master of Sacred Theology
MSW Master of Social Work
MT Montana
Mt. Mount
mus. museum, musical
MusB Bachelor of Music
MusD Doctor of Music
MusM Master of Music
mut. mutual
MVP Most Valuable Player
mycol. mycological

N

N. North
NAACOG Nurses Association of the American College of Obstetricians and Gynecologists
NAACP National Association for the Advancement of Colored People
NACA National Advisory Committee for Aeronautics
NACDL National Association of Criminal Defense Lawyers
NACU National Association of Colleges and Universities
NAD National Academy of Design
NAE National Academy of Engineering, National Association of Educators
NAESP National Association of Elementary School Principals
NAFE National Association of Female Executives
N.Am. North America
NAM National Association of Manufacturers
NAMH National Association for Mental Health
NAPA National Association of Performing Artists
NARAS National Academy of Recording Arts and Sciences
NAREB National Association of Real Estate Boards
NARS National Archives and Record Service
NAS National Academy of Sciences
NASA National Aeronautics and Space Administration
NASP National Association of School Psychologists
NASW National Association of Social Workers
nat. national
NATAS National Academy of Television Arts and Sciences
NATO North Atlantic Treaty Organization

nav. navigation
NB, N.B. New Brunswick
NBA National Basketball Association
NC North Carolina
NCAA National College Athletic Association
NCCJ National Conference of Christians and Jews
ND North Dakota
NDEA National Defense Education Act
NE Nebraska
NE Northeast
NEA National Education Association
Nebr. Nebraska
NEH National Endowment for Humanities
neurol. neurological
Nev. Nevada
NF Newfoundland
NFL National Football League
Nfld. Newfoundland
NG National Guard
NH New Hampshire
NHL National Hockey League
NIH National Institutes of Health
NIMH National Institute of Mental Health
NJ New Jersey
NLRB National Labor Relations Board
NM, N.Mex. New Mexico
No. Northern
NOAA National Oceanographic and Atmospheric Administration
NORAD North America Air Defense
Nov. November
NOW National Organization for Women
nr. near
NRA National Rifle Association
NRC National Research Council
NS Nova Scotia
NSC National Security Council
NSF National Science Foundation
NSTA National Science Teachers Association
NSW New South Wales
nuc. nuclear
numis. numismatic
NV Nevada
NW Northwest
NWT Northwest Territories
NY New York
NYC New York City
NYU New York University
NZ New Zealand

O

ob-gyn obstetrics-gynecology
obs. observatory
obstet. obstetrical
occupl. occupational
oceanog. oceanographic
Oct. October
OD Doctor of Optometry
OECD Organization for Economic Cooperation and Development
OEEC Organization of European Economic Cooperation
OEO Office of Economic Opportunity
ofcl. official
OH Ohio
OK, Okla. Oklahoma
ON, Ont. Ontario
oper. operating
ophthal. ophthalmological
ops. operations
OR Oregon
orch. orchestra
Oreg. Oregon
orgn. organization
orgnl. organizational
ornithol. ornithological
orthop. orthopedic
OSHA Occupational Safety and Health Administration
OSRD Office of Scientific Research and Development
OSS Office of Strategic Services
osteo. osteopathic
otol. otological
otolaryn. otolaryngological

P

PA, Pa. Pennsylvania
paleontol. paleontological
path. pathological
pediat. pediatrics
PEI Prince Edward Island
PEN Poets, Playwrights, Editors, Essayists and Novelists
penol. penological
pers. personnel
PGA Professional Golfers' Association of America
PHA Public Housing Administration
pharm. pharmaceutical
PharmD Doctor of Pharmacy
PharmM Master of Pharmacy
PhB Bachelor of Philosophy
PhD Doctor of Philosophy
PhDChemE Doctor of Science in Chemical Engineering
PhM Master of Philosophy
Phila. Philadelphia
philharm. philharmonic
philol. philological
philos. philosophical
photog. photographic
phys. physical
physiol. physiological
Pitts. Pittsburgh
Pk. Park
Pky. Parkway
Pl. Place
Plz. Plaza
PO Post Office
polit. political
poly. polytechnic, polytechnical
PQ Province of Quebec
PR Puerto Rico
prep. preparatory
pres. president
Presbyn. Presbyterian
presdl. presidential
prin. principal
procs. proceedings
prod. produced
prodn. production
prodr. producer
prof. professor
profl. professional
prog. progressive
propr. proprietor
pros. prosecuting
pro tem. pro tempore
psychiat. psychiatric
psychol. psychological
PTA Parent-Teachers Association
ptnr. partner
PTO Pacific Theatre of Operations, Parent Teacher Organization
pub. publisher, publishing, published, public
publ. publication
pvt. private

Q

quar. quarterly
qm. quartermaster
Que. Quebec

R

radiol. radiological
RAF Royal Air Force
RCA Radio Corporation of America
RCAF Royal Canadian Air Force
Rd. Road
R&D Research & Development
REA Rural Electrification Administration
rec. recording
ref. reformed
regt. regiment
regtl. regimental
rehab. rehabilitation
rels. relations
Rep. Republican
rep. representative
Res. Reserve
ret. retired
Rev. Reverend
rev. review, revised
RFC Reconstruction Finance Corporation
RI Rhode Island
Rlwy. Railway
Rm. Room
RN Registered Nurse
roentgenol. roentgenological
ROTC Reserve Officers Training Corps
RR rural route, railroad
rsch. research
rschr. researcher
Rt. Route

S

S. South
s. son
SAC Strategic Air Command
SAG Screen Actors Guild
S.Am. South America
san. sanitary

SAR Sons of the American Revolution
Sask. Saskatchewan
savs. savings
SB Bachelor of Science
SBA Small Business Administration
SC South Carolina
ScB Bachelor of Science
SCD Doctor of Commercial Science
ScD Doctor of Science
sch. school
sci. science, scientific
SCV Sons of Confederate Veterans
SD South Dakota
SE Southeast
SEC Securities and Exchange Commission
sec. secretary
sect. section
seismol. seismological
sem. seminary
Sept. September
s.g. senior grade
sgt. sergeant
SI Staten Island
SJ Society of Jesus
SJD Scientiae Juridicae Doctor
SK Saskatchewan
SM Master of Science
SNP Society of Nursing Professionals
So. Southern
soc. society
sociol. sociological
spkr. speaker
spl. special
splty. specialty
Sq. Square
SR Sons of the Revolution
sr. senior
SS Steamship
St. Saint, Street
sta. station
stats. statistics
statis. statistical
STB Bachelor of Sacred Theology
stblzn. stabilization
STD Doctor of Sacred Theology
std. standard
Ste. Suite
subs. subsidiary
SUNY State University of New York
supr. supervisor
supt. superintendent
surg. surgical
svc. service
SW Southwest
sys. system

T

Tb. tuberculosis
tchg. teaching
tchr. teacher
tech. technical, technology
technol. technological
tel. telephone
telecom. telecommunications
temp. temporary
Tenn. Tennessee
TESOL Teachers of English to Speakers of Other Languages
Tex. Texas
ThD Doctor of Theology
theol. theological
ThM Master of Theology
TN Tennessee
tng. training
topog. topographical
trans. transaction, transferred
transl. translation, translated
transp. transportation
treas. treasurer
TV television
twp. township
TX Texas
typog. typographical

U

U. University
UAW United Auto Workers
UCLA University of California at Los Angeles
UK United Kingdom
UN United Nations
UNESCO United Nations Educational, Scientific and Cultural Organization
UNICEF United Nations International Children's Emergency Fund
univ. university
UNRRA United Nations Relief and Rehabilitation Administration
UPI United Press International
urol. urological
US, USA United States of America
USAAF United States Army Air Force
USAF United States Air Force
USAFR United States Air Force Reserve
USAR United States Army Reserve
USCG United States Coast Guard
USCGR United States Coast Guard Reserve
USES United States Employment Service
USIA United States Information Agency
USMC United States Marine Corps
USMCR United States Marine Corps Reserve
USN United States Navy
USNG United States National Guard
USNR United States Naval Reserve
USO United Service Organizations
USPHS United States Public Health Service
USS United States Ship
USSR Union of the Soviet Socialist Republics
USTA United States Tennis Association
UT Utah

V

VA Veterans Administration
VA, Va. Virginia
vet. veteran, veterinary
VFW Veterans of Foreign Wars
VI Virgin Islands
vis. visiting
VISTA Volunteers in Service to America
vocat. vocational
vol. volunteer, volume
v.p. vice president
vs. versus
VT, Vt. Vermont

W

W West
WA, Wash. Washington (state)
WAC Women's Army Corps
WAVES Women's Reserve, US Naval Reserve
WCTU Women's Christian Temperance Union
we. western
WHO World Health Organization
WI Wisconsin, West Indies
Wis. Wisconsin
WV, W.Va. West Virginia
WY, Wyo. Wyoming

X, Y, Z

YK Yukon Territory
YMCA Young Men's Christian Association
YMHA Young Men's Hebrew Association
YM & YWHA Young Men's and Young Women's Hebrew Association
yr. year
YT Yukon Territory
YWCA Young Women's Christian Association

Alphabetical Practices

Names are arranged alphabetically according to the surnames, and under identical surnames according to the first given name. If both surname and first given name are identical, names are arranged alphabetically according to the second given name.

Surnames beginning with De, Des, Du, however capitalized or spaced, are recorded with the prefix preceding the surname and arranged alphabetically under the letter D.

Surnames beginning with Mac and Mc are arranged alphabetically under M.

Surnames beginning with Saint or St. appear after names that begin Sains, and are arranged according to the second part of the name, e.g., St. Clair before Saint Dennis.

Surnames beginning with Van, Von, or von are arranged alphabetically under the letter V.

Compound surnames are arranged according to the first member of the compound.

Many hyphenated Arabic names begin Al-, El-, or al-. These names are alphabetized according to each biographee's designation of last name. Thus Al-Bahar, Neta may be listed either under Al- or under Bahar, depending on the preference of the listee.

Also, Arabic names have a variety of possible spellings when transposed to English. Spelling of these names is always based on the practice of the biographee. Some biographees use a Western form of word order, while others prefer the Arabic word sequence.

Similarly, Asian names may have no comma between family and given names, but some biographees have chosen to add the comma. In each case, punctuation follows the preference of the biographee.

Parentheses used in connection with a name indicate which part of the full name is usually omitted in common usage. Hence, Chambers, E(lizabeth) Anne indicates that the first name, Elizabeth, is generally recorded as an initial. In such a case, the parentheses are ignored in alphabetizing and the name would be arranged as Chambers, Elizabeth Anne.

However, if the entire first name appears in parentheses, for example, Chambers, (Elizabeth) Anne, the first name is not commonly used, and the alphabetizing is therefore arranged as though the name were Chambers, Anne.

If the entire middle name is in parentheses, it is still used in alphabetical sorting. Hence, Belamy, Katherine (Lucille) would sort as Belamy, Katherine Lucille. The same occurs if the entire last name is in parentheses, e.g., (Brandenberg), Howard Keith would sort as Brandenberg, Howard Keith.

For visual clarification:

Smith, H(enry) George: Sorts as Smith, Henry George
Smith, (Henry) George: Sorts as Smith, George
Smith, Henry (George): Sorts as Smith, Henry George
(Smith), Henry George: Sorts as Smith, Henry George

Who'sWho in the Midwest®

Biographees

AAMOTH, GORDON M., medical association administrator; b. Apr. 12, 1940; MD, Northwestern U., 1966. Intern U. Calif., San Francisco, 1966—67, fellow, 1968—69, residency, 1969—73; clinical prof. of orthopaedic surgery U. Minn.; dir. private rotation in dept. orthopaedic surgery Abbott Northwestern Hosp., pres., med. staf; faculty mem. Hennepin County Gen. Hosp., Mpls.; pres., CEO Robin Found., Mpls. Spkr. in field; vis. prof. for several universities. Assoc. editor Clinical Orthopaedics and Related Research, consulting reviewer Journal of Bone and Joint Surgery. Recipient Charles Bowles-Bowles Rogers award, Hennepin County Med. Soc., 2004. Mem.: Am. Bd. Med. Specialties, Am. Orthopaedic Assn., Assn. Bone and Joint Surgeons, Am. Acad. Orthopaedic Surgeons (mem-at-large bd. dirs. 2005—), Am. Bd. of Orthopaedic Surgery (past pres., bd. dir.). Office: U Minn Depart of Orthopaedic Surgery 2512 S 7th St R200 Minneapolis MN 55454 Office Phone: 612-273-9400. E-mail: gaamoth@msn.com.*

AARSVOLD, OLE, state legislator; m. Marilyn Haugen; 3 children. BS, Mayville State U., 1963; MS, U. ND, 1969. Tchr., prin. secondary sch.; instr. Univ.; farmer; mem. N.D. Ho. of Reps. from 20th dist., 1989—. Appt. com. budget sect. Edn. Svcs. Com.; bd. dirs. Farmers Union Oil Co., Clifco Energy. Bd. dirs. Traill County Econ. Devel. Commn.; clerk-treas. Greenfield (N.D.) Twp.; commr., v.p. N.D. Tchrs. Practices Commn.; field dir. No. Plains Indian Tchr. Corps. Recipient Outstanding Young Educator award, Outstanding Agriculturist award, Disting. Alumni award Mayville State U. Mem. Traill County Crop Improvement Assn. (past bd. dirs., past pres.), Traill County Farmers Union (bd. dirs.). Democrat.

ABBETT, WILLIAM S., former dean; Dean Mich. State U. Coll. Human Medicine, East Lansing, 2000—00. Office: Mich State U Office Dean A110 E Fee Hall East Lansing MI 48824

ABBEY, G(EORGE) MARSHALL, lawyer, retired health facility administrator; b. Dunkirk, NY, July 24, 1933; s. Ralph Ambrose and Grace A. (Fisher) A.; m. Sue Carroll, July 13, 1974; children: Mark, Steven, Michael, Lincoln. BA with high distinction, U. Rochester, 1954; JD with distinction, Cornell U., 1957. Bar: N.H. 1957, Ill. 1965. Atty. McLane, Carleton, Graf, Greene & Brown, Manchester, N.H., 1957-65, Baxter Internat. Inc., Deerfield, Ill., 1965-69, gen. counsel, 1969-72, sec., gen. counsel, 1972-75, v.p., sec., gen. counsel, 1975-82, sr. v.p., gen. counsel, 1985-90, sr. v.p., sec., gen. counsel, 1990-93; of counsel Bell Boyd & Lloyd, Chgo., 1997—2000; pvt. practice, 1993-97, 2000—. Editor Cornell Law Rev., 1956-57. Mem. vis. com. Law Sch., U. Chgo., 1978-81; dir. Coun. Puerto Rico-U.S. Affairs, 1988-92; mem. indsl. adv. coun. U. P.R.; dir. P.R.-USA Found., 1975-93, B.U.I.L.D., Chgo., 1980-84, bus. adv. com. B.U.I.L.D. Inc.; bd. dirs. Hundred Club of Lake County, Ill., 1976-86; dir. Food and Drug Law Inst., 1975-93; bd. dirs. Evanston Inventure, 1986-88; former trustee Winnetka Congl. Ch.; dir. Nat. Com. for Quality Health Care, 1988-93; mem. Northwestern U. Corp. Coun. adv. bd., 1976-93; dir. P.R. Cmty. Found., 1986-94; bd. dirs. Better Bus. Bur. Chgo. and No. Ill., 1991-93; mem. Conf. Bd's. Coun. Chief Legal Officers and Legal Quality Coun., 1991-93. Mem. ABA, Ill. Bar Assn., Lake County Bar Assn., Chgo. Bar Assn., Health Industry Mfrs. Assn. (chmn. legal/regulatory affairs 1976-78, bd. dirs. 1978-80, chmn. govt. affairs com. 1980-81), Univ. Club, Exmoor Country Club, Bankers Club (P.R.), Order of the Coif, Phi Beta Kappa. Office: 836 Skokie Blvd orthbrook IL 60062-4001

ABBOTT, BILL, radio personality; b. Kansas City, Jan. 12; children: Brett, Suzette, Tony. Radio host WDAF, Westwood, Kans., 1977—. Office: WDAF 4935 Belinder Rd Westwood KS 66205

ABBOTT, DAVID HENRY, manufacturing executive; b. Milton, Ky., July 6, 1936; s. Carl and Rachael (Miles) A.; m. Joan Shefchik, Aug. 14, 1976; children— Kristine, Gina, Beth, Linsey BS, U. Ky., 1960, MBA, 1961. With Ford Motor Co., Louisville, Mpls. and Dearborn, Mich., 1961-69; div. controller J I Case Co., Racine, Wis., 1970-73, gen. mgr. service parts supply div., 1973-75, v.p., 1975, v.p. and gen. mgr. constrn. equipment div., 1975-77, v.p., gen. mgr. Drott div. Wausau, Wis., 1977-79, exec. v.p. worldwide constrn. equipment, 1979-81; pres., chief operating officer Portec, Inc., Oak Brook, Ill., 1981-87, also dir.; pres., chief exec. officer, dir. E.D. Etnyre & Co., Oregon, Ill., 1988—2002, ret., 2002. Dir. Oak Brook Bank, 1982-88. Served with U.S. Army, 1958 Mem. Constrn. Industry Mfrs. Assn. (bd. dirs. 1979-81, 82-2002, chmn. 1992), Am. Rd. and Transpn. Builders Assn. (dir. 1988—2002). Republican. Home: 2461 Saddlewood Ct Lanark IL 61046

ABBOTT, DAVID L., agricultural products executive; BS, Univ. Vt. CEO Purina Mills, St. Louis; pres., CEO E-markets Inc., Ames, Iowa. Mem.: Nat. FFA Found. (bd. mem.), Am. Feed Ind. Assn. (past pres.). Office: E-markets Inc Ste 108 1606 Golden Aspen Dr Ames IA 50010-8011

ABBOUD, ALFRED ROBERT, banker, investor, consultant, director; b. Boston, May 29, 1929; s. Alfred and Victoria (Karam) A.; m. Joan Grover, June 11, 1955; children: Robert G., Jeanne Frances, Katherine Jane. BS cum laude, Harvard U., 1951, LL.B., 1956, MBA, 1958. Bar: Mass. 1957, Ill. 1959. Asst. cashier First Nat. Bank of Chgo., 1960-62, asst. v.p., 1962-64, v.p., 1964-69, sr. v.p., 1969-72, exec. v.p., 1972-73, vice chmn. bd., 1973-74, dep. chmn. bd., 1974-75, chmn. bd., CEO, 1975-80; pres., COO Occidental Petroleum Corp., LA, 1980-84; pres. A. Robert Abboud & Co., Fox River Grove, Ill., 1984—; chmn., CEO First City Bancorp. of Tex. Inc., Houston, 1988-91. Co-chmn., lead dir. Ivanhoe Energy, Inc., 2006—. Author: Money in the Bank: How Safe Is It?, 1988. Capt. USMC, 1951-53. Decorated Purple Heart, Bronze Star; Baker scholar, 1958. Mem. Econ. Comml. Club, The Chgo. Club, Harvard Club Chgo., Harvard Club N.Y.C., Barrington Hills Country Club. Home: 209 Braeburn Rd Barrington IL 60010-9637 Office: PO Box 33 212 Stone Hill Ctr Fox River Grove IL 60021-0033 Home Phone: 847-658-4808; Office Phone: 847-639-0101.

ABBOUD, FRANCOIS MITRY, physician, educator; b. Cairo, Jan. 5, 1931; arrived in U.S., 1955, naturalized, 1963; s. Mitry Y. and Asma (Habac) Abboud; m. Doris Evelyn Khal, June 5, 1955; children: Mary Agnese, Susan Marie, Nancy Louise, Anthony Lawrence. Student, U. Cairo, 1948—52; MBBCh, Ains Chams U., 1955; D (hon.), U. Lyon, France, 1991; DSc (hon.), Med. Coll. Wis., 1994. Diplomate Am. Bd. Internal Medicine, Am. Bd. Cardiovasc. Disease (bd. govs. 1987-93). Intern Demerdash Govt. Hosp., Cairo, 1955; resident Milw. County Hosp., 1955—58; Am. Heart Assn. rsch. fellow cardiovasc. labs. Marquette U., 1958—60; Am. Heart Assn. advanced rsch. fellow U. Iowa, 1960—62, asst. prof., 1961—65, assoc. prof. medicine, 1965—68, prof. medicine, 1968—, prof. molecular physiology and biophysics, 1975—, Edith King Pearson chair of cardiovascular rsch., 1988—, dir. cardiovasc. divsn., 1970—76, chmn. dept. internal medicine, 1976—2002, dir. cardiovasc. rsch. ctr., 1974—, assoc. v.p. for rsch., 2003—. Attending physician U. Iowa Hosps., 1961—, VA Hosp., Iowa City, 1963—; chmn. rsch. rev. com. Nat. Heart, Lung and Blood Inst., 1978—80, adv. coun., 1995—99. Editor Circulation Rsch., 1981—86, Procs. Assn. Am. Physicians, 1995—2000, assoc. editor Advances in Internal Medicine, 1991—95, Physiology in Medicine, 2002—, editl. bd. Medicine, 1992—. Recipient European Traveling fellowship, French govt., 1948, NIH Career Devel. award, 1962—71, Disting. Rsch. award, Assn. Am. Med. Colls., 2006. Master: ACP (award for outstanding work in sci. related to medicine 2000); mem.: AMA, Procs. Assn. Am. Physicians (editor-in-chief 1995—99), World Congress Cardiology (mem. adv. bd. 2001—02), Clin. and Translational Sci. (editl. bd. 2007—), Am. Coll. Cardiology (Disting. Scientist award 2004), Assn. Patient Oriented Rsch. (founding mem.), Am. Acad. Arts and Scis., Internat. Soc. Hypertension (Merck Sharp & Dohme Internat. award for rsch. in hypertension 1994), Am. Soc. Pharmacology and Exptl. Therapeutics (award exptl. therapeutics 1972), Am. Clin. and Climatol. Assn. (councillor 1993—96), Am. Physiol. Soc. (chmn. clin. physiology sect. 1979—83, chmn. circulation group 1980, publ. com. 1987—90, Wiggers award 1988, Carl Ludwig lecture award 2000), Assn. Am. Physicians (treas. 1979—84, councillor 1984—89, pres.-elect 1989—90, pres. 1990—91), Assn. Profs. Medicine (bd. dirs. 1993—97, Robert H. Williams Disting. Chmn. of Medicine award 1993), Assn. Univ. Cardiologists, Am. Fedn. Clin. Rsch. (pres. 1971—72), Am. Heart Assn. (bd. dirs. 1977—80, 1988—91, pres.-elect 1989—90, pres. 1990—91, past chmn. rsch. coms., award of merit 1982, Disting. Achievement award 1987, CIBA award for hypertension rsch. 1990, Gold Heart award 1995, Rsch. Achievement award 1999, Disting. Scientist award 2007), Soc. Exptl. Biology and Medicine (councilor 2003—07), Ctrl. Soc. for Clin. Rsch. (pres. elect 1984—85, pres. 1985—86), Am. Soc. Clin. Investigation, Inst. Medicine NAS, Alpha Omega Alpha (bd. dirs. 1989—92), Sigma Xi. Achievements include research and publications in cardiovascular physiology on neurohumoral control of circulation and molecular mechanisms and gene regulation of baroreceptor activation. Home: 24 Kennedy Pky Iowa City IA 52246-2780 Office: Carver Coll Medicine U Iowa Assoc Vice pres Rsch 318 CMAB Iowa City IA 52242-1101

ABCARIAN, HERAND, surgeon, educator; b. Ahvaz, Iran, Jan. 23, 1941; arrived in U.S., 1966; s. Joseph and Stella (Banki) A.; m. Karen Jane Berger, May 10, 1969; children: Gregory, Ariane, Margot. MD, Teheran U., 1965. Intern Cook County Hosp., Chgo., 1966—67, resident in gen. surgery, 1967—71, resident in colon and rectal surgery, 1971—72, chmn. colon and rectal surgery, 1972—93; head dept. surgery, Turi Josefson prof. U. Ill. Coll. Med., Chgo., 1989—; exec. dir./sec. treas. Am. Bd. Colon & Rectal Surgery, Taylor, Mich. Assoc. editor: Diseases of Colon and Rectum, 1981—95. Fellow ACS (various coms. and offices), Am. Soc. Colon and Rectal Surgeons (sec. 1985-87, pres. 1988-89), Can. Soc. Colon and Rectal Surgeons (hon.); mem. Am. Surg. Assn., Soc. Am. Gastroendoscopic Surgeons (founder), Sydney Soc. Colon and Rectal Surgeons (hon.), Assn. Coloprotology of Gt. Britain (hon. fellow). Republican. Roman Catholic. Avocations: visual arts, music, philately. Office: U Ill 840 S Wood St 518 Chicago IL 60612-7317 Address: Am Bd Colon & Rectal Surgery 20600 Eureka Rd Ste 713 Taylor MI 48180-5376 Home Phone: 708-366-5065; Office Phone: 312-996-2061. Business E-Mail: abcarian@uic.edu.

ABDOU, NABIH I., physician, educator; b. Cairo, Oct. 11, 1934; came to U.S., 1962, naturalized, 1972; m. Nancy L. Layle, Aug. 26, 1939; children— Mark L., Marie L. MD, Cairo U., 1958; PhD, McGill U., 1969. Intern then resident Cairo Univ. Hosp., 1959-62; resident, fellow in allergy and immunology Hosp. U. Pa., 1963-65, Mayo Clinic, 1965-67, Royal Victoria Hosp., Montreal, Que., Can., 1967-69; asst., assoc. prof. U. Pa., 1969-75; assoc. prof. medicine U. Kans. Med. Ctr., Kansas City, 1975-78, prof. medicine, 1978-89; pvt. practice Ctr. for Rheumatic Disease and Ctr. for Allergy Immunology, Kansas City, 1989—. Clin. prof. medicine U. Mo., 1989—. Fulbright scholar, 1962-65 Fellow ACP, Am. Acad. Allergy, Asthma & Immunology, Am. Coll. Rheumatology; mem. Am. Assn. Immunologists, Cen. Soc. Clin. Rsch., Clin. Immunology Soc. Office: Ctr for Rheumatic Disease and Ctr Allergy Immunology 4330 Wornall Rd Ste 40 Kansas City MO 64111-3217 Home Phone: 913-383-3782; Office Phone: 816-531-0930. Business E-Mail: niabdou@centerforrheumatic.com.

ABEL, GREGORY E., utilities company executive; b. 1962; B in Commerce with honors, U. Alberta, Can., 1984. Chartered acct., Can. With Price Waterhouse, San Francisco, Calif. Energy Co., Inc., 1992, sr. v.p.; pres., COO MidAmerican Energy Holdings Co., Des Moines, 1997—2008, pres., CEO, 2008—. CEO CE Electric UK, MidAmerican Funding, LLC; bd. dirs. Kern River Gas Transmission Co., Northern Natural Gas Co., MidAmerican Energy Holdings Co., HomeServices America, Inc., Edison Electric Inst. Bd., exec. com. Greater Des Moines Partnership; Iowa Bus. Coun.; bd. dirs. Wells Fargo Iowa Community, Iowa; exec. bd. Mid-Iowa Coun. Boy Scouts Am. Mem.: Alberta Inst. Chartered Accts., Canadian Inst. Chartered Accts. Office: Mid American Energy Holdings Co 666 Grand Ave Des Moines IA 50309 E-mail: geabel@midamerican.com.

ABEL, MARK ROGERS, federal judge; b. 1944; BA, Ohio U., 1966; JD, Ohio State U., 1969. Bar: Ohio 1969, U.S. Dist. Ct. (so. dist.) Ohio 1971. Law clk. to Hon. Judge Joseph Kinneary U.S. Dist. Ct. (so. dist.) Ohio, 1969-71, magistrate judge Columbus, 1971—. Mem. FBA, Ohio Bar Assn., Columbus Bar Assn. Office: US Dist Ct So Dist Ohio 208 US Courthouse 85 Marconi Blvd Columbus OH 43215-2823 Fax: (614) 719-3505.

ABELES, NORMAN, psychologist, educator; came to U.S., 1939, naturalized, 1944; s. Felix and Bertha (Gronich) A.; m. Jeanette Bueller, Apr. 14, 1957; children: Linda, Mark. BA, NYU, 1949; MA, U. Tex., 1952, PhD, 1958. Diplomate: Am. Bd. Profl. Psychology (Midwest regional bd. 1972-78, chmn. regional bd. 1975-77; nat. trustee 1975-77). Fellow in counseling U. Tex., Austin, 1956-57; instr. Mich. State U., East Lansing, 1957-59, asst. prof., 1959-64, asso. prof., 1964-67, prof. psychology, 1968—, dir. psychol. clinic, 1978—2004, co-dir. clin. tng., 1981-96, asst. dir. counseling center, 1965-71. U.S. State Dept. ednl. exch. prof. U. Utrecht, Netherlands, 1969, vis. prof., 1975; cons. Peace Corps, 1965-69; vocat. cons. Social Security Office of Hearings and Appeals, 1962—; med. advisor Social Security Office of Hearings and Appeals, 1986—; mem. Mich. Commn. Cert. of Psychologists, 1962-77, chmn., 1966-68; mem. coun. Nat. Register Health Svc. Providers in Psychology, 1974—, vice chmn., 1975-80, bd. dirs. 2005—; del. White House Conf. on Aging, 1995, 2005; mem. geriatric and gerontology adv. com. to Sec. of VA, 2002—. Editor: Acad. Psychology bull., 1978-82; cons. editor Am. Jour. Alzheimers Disease and other Dementias, Jour. Personality Assessment, 1988-2005, Clin. Psychology: Sci. and Practice, 1994-2004, Clin. Psychology Rev., 1995-98, Profl. Psychology: Rsch. and Practice, 1979-81, 89—, editor, 1983-88; contbr. articles to profl. jours. Served with U.S. Army, 1954-56. Fulbright-Hays grantee, 1969; recipient Disting. Psychologist award Mich. Soc. Clin. Psychologists, 1984; Disting. Practitioner, Nat. Acad. Practice, 1982; Arthur Furst Ethics Lectureship medal Pacific Grad. Sch. Psychology, 1996; Dept. Vets. Affairs Spl. Contbns. award, Battle Creek Mich., 1997. Fellow APA (coun. reps. 1972-75, 77-79, 89-91, 93-95, 99-2001, 06-07, 08—, policy and planning bd. 1975-79, chmn. 1976, rec. sec. 1980-86, chmn. edn. and tng. bd. 1988, bd. ednl. affairs 1999-2001, com. on internat. rels. in psychology 2002-04, pres. divsn. psychotherapy and divsn. clin. psychology 1990, publs. and comm. bd. 1990-96, 2008—, chmn. 1995, pres.-elect 1996, pres. 1997, bd. dirs. divsn. psychotherapy 2000-2005, pres. divsn. 7 geropsychology/internat. psychology 2005, pres. sect. IX assessment divsn. clin. psychology 2004, ethics com. 2005-07, bd. dirs., 2008—), Am. Psychol. Found. (sec. 2002-07), Coun. Sci. Socs. Pres.; mem. Midwestern Psychol. Assn., Mich. Psychol. Assn. (legis. chmn. 1964-72, pres. 1971-72, Disting. Psychologist 1974), Internat. Union Psychol. Scis. (U.S. com. 1999-2005), Sigma Xi. Home: 953 Rosewood Ave East Lansing MI 48823-3126 Office: Mich State U Dept Psychology 110C Psychology Bldg East Lansing MI 48824-1117 Home Phone: 517-337-0853; Office Phone: 517-353-7274. Business E-Mail: abeles@msu.edu.

ABELL, DAVID ROBERT, lawyer; b. Raleigh, NC, Nov. 24, 1934; s. De Witt Sterling and Edna Renilde (Doughty) A.; children: David Charles, Elizabeth A. Harrington, Kimberly A. Creasman, Hilary Ayres, Glenn Bryan; m. Ellen Penrod Hackmann, July 27, 1985. BA, Denison U., 1956; JD (Internat. fellow), Columbia U., 1963. Bar: Pa. 1963, Ill. 1973. Assoc. Ballard, Spahr, Andrews & Ingersoll, Phila., 1963-68; sec., counsel Hurst Performance, Inc., Warminster, Pa., 1969-70; sec., gen. counsel STP Corp., Des Plaines, Ill., 1970-72; ptnr. David R. Abell Ltd., Winnetka, Ill., 1974-96, Rooks, Pitts & Poust, Chgo., 1996-2000, Schuyler, Roche & Zwirner, Chgo. and Evanston, Ill., 2000—03, Rooks Pitts, Chgo., 2003—. Author: Residential Real Estate System, 1977, 2d edit., 1990. Trustee Music Inst. Chgo., 1988-96, Village of Winnetka, 2003-; bd. govs. Winnetka Cmty. House, 1993-96. Aviator USMCR, 1956-60. Mem. ABA, Ill. Bar Assn., Chgo. Bar Assn., Rotary (pres. Winnetka 1977-78). Episcopalian. Home: 740 Oak St Winnetka IL 60093-2521 Office: 560 Green Bay Rd Ste 203 Winnetka IL 60093 Business E-Mail: dabell@rookspitts.com.

ABELSON, HERBERT TRAUB, pediatrician, educator; b. St. Louis, Feb. 19, 1941; s. Benjamin J. and Ann (Traub) Abelson; m. Constance Faye Caldwell, May 17, 1968; children: Matthew, Rebecca, Jonathan, Daniel. AB with high honors, U. Ill., 1962; MD, Washington U., St. Louis, 1966. Diplomate Am. Bd. Pediat., Am. Bd. Pediatric Hematology-Oncology. Intern pediat. U Colo. Med. Ctr., Denver, 1966—67; resident Boston Children's Hosp., 1969—71; staff assoc. Nat. Cancer Inst. NIH, Bethesda, Md., 1967—69; Jane Childs Meml. Fund for Med. Rsch. fellow NIH, 1971, spl. postdoctoral fellow, 1972; teaching fellow Med. Sch. Harvard Coll., Boston, 1970—71, instr. pediat., 1973—74, asst. prof., 1974—79; tutor in med. scis., 1977—79; assoc. prof. Harvard Coll., Boston, 1979—83; vis. prof., Ctr. for Cancer Rsch. MIT, Cambridge, 1982—83; prof., chmn. dept. pediat. Med. Sch. U. Wash., Seattle, 1983—95; prof., chmn., physician-in-chief dept. pediat. U. Chgo., 1995—2004, assoc. dean. admissions Pritzker Sch. Medicine, 2005—. Rsch. fellow in hematology Children's Hosp. Med. Ctr., Boston, 1971—73; rsch. assoc. in biology MIT, 1971—73; mem. exec. com. Am. Med. Sch. Pediatric Dept. Chairmen, 1989—91; lectr. U. Wash., 1990; mem. pediatric residency rev. com. Accreditation Coun. for Grad. Med. Edn., 1992—97; examiner Am. Bd. Pediatrics, 1988—, bd. dirs., 1992—97, sec.-treas., 1995, chmn. elect., 1995—96, chmn., 1996—97; endowed chair U. Chgo., 2004. Contbr. articles to profl. jours. Lt. comdr. USPHS, 1967—69. Recipient Rsch. Career Devel. award, NIH, 1975—80, Alumni achievement award, Washington U., 2001. Fellow: Am. Acad. Pediat.; mem.: Am. Soc. Pediat. Hematology (fin. com.), Am. Bd. Med. Spltys. (fin. com.), Am. Pediatric Soc., Soc. Pediatric Rsch., Am. Soc. Clin. Oncology, Am. Assn. Cancer Rsch., Am. Soc. Hematology (mem. sci. subcom. on pediatric hematology 1987—91). Avocations: aviation, squash, cooking. Office: Univ Chgo Office Medical Edn 924 E 57th St BSLC104 MC1000 Chicago IL 60637-1455 Office Phone: 773-702-3650. Business E-Mail: habelson@bsd.uchicago.edu.

ABERLE, ELTON DAVID, retired dean; b. Sabetha, Kans., Aug. 30, 1940; s. Alphia Henry and Irene Judith A.; n. Carrie Rae Campbell, Sept. 11, 1965; children; Krista Kaye, Barbara Ann. BS, Kans. State U., 1962; MS, Mich. State U., 1965, DPhil, 1967. Asst. prof. Purdue U., West Lafayette, Ind., 1967-71, assoc. prof., 1971-76, prof., 1976-83; prof., dept. head U. Nebr., Lincoln, 1983-98; dean Coll. Agrl. and Life Scis. U. Wis., Madison, 1998—2005, dean emeritus, 2005—. Author: Principles of Meat Science, 1975, 4th edit., 2001; contbr. articles to profl. jours. Fellow AAAS, Am. Soc. Animal Sci. (pres. 1994-95, Meat Rsch. award 1982, Signal Svc. award 1998); mem. Am. Meat Sci. Assn. (dir. 1979-80, pres. 1985-86, Disting. Teaching award 1983, Disting. Rsch. award 1986), Inst. Food Tech., Coun. Agrl. Sci. and Tech. (dir. 1996-99), Kiwanis. Avocations: golf, fishing, hunting. Home: 5810 Windsona Cir Madison WI 53711-5853 E-mail: eda@cals.wisc.edu.

ABHYANKAR, SHREERAM SHANKAR, mathematics professor; b. Ujjain, India, July 22, 1930; came to U.S., 1951, naturalized, 1989; s. Shankar Keshav and Uma (Tamhankar) A.; m. Yvonne Margit Kraft, June 5, 1958; children: Hari Shreeram, Kashi Shreeram. BSc, Bombay U., 1951; AM, Harvard U., 1952, PhD, 1955; DHD (hon.), U. Angers, 1998. Rsch. instr. Columbia U., NYC, 1955-56, vis. asst. prof., 1956-57; asst. prof. Cornell U., Ithaca, NY, 1957-58; vis. asst. prof. Princeton (N.J.) U., 1958-59; assoc. prof. Johns Hopkins U., Balt., 1959-63; pres. math. Purdue U., West Lafayette, Ind., 1963-67, Marshall disting. prof. math., 1967—, prof. indsl. engring., 1987—, prof. computer scis., 1988—. Vis. lectr. Harvard U., 1960-61; vis. prof. Munster U., Erlangen U., summer 1963, Matsci., Madras, India, fall 1963, Tata Inst., Bombay, 1969-70, 75-76, spring 1974, Kyoto U., fall 1976, U. Ky., fall 1978, U. Paris, spring 1980, ENS St. Cloud, France, spring 1982, U. Nice, spring 1983, U. Sydney, spring 1986, U. Strasbourg, spring 1991, Ohio State U., spring 1995; vis. assoc. prof. Yale U., spring 1963; spkr. numerous profl. meetings, univ., insts., symposia, confs., and congresses, 1960—. Author: Ramification Theoretic Methods in Algebraic Geometry, 1959, Local Analytic Geometry, 1964, Resolution of Singularities of Embedded Algebraic Surfaces, 1966, 2d enlarged edit. 1998, A Glimpse of Algebraic Geometry, 1971, Algebraic Space Curves, 1971, Lectures on Expansion Techniques in Algebraic Geometry, 1977, Weighted Expansions for Canonical Desingularization, 1982, Enumerative Combinatorics of Young Tableaux, 1988, Algebraic Geometry for Scientists and Engineers, 1990; also over 150 articles. Recipient Herbert Newby McCoy award Purdue U., 1973, Medal of Honor, U. Valliadolid, Spain, 1990; grantee NSF, 1960-87, 89-91, 89-2002, Office Naval Rsch., 1986-90, Army Rsch. Office, 1988-90, Nat. Security Agy., 1992-99; rsch. fellow Alfred P. Sloan Found., 1958-60. Fellow Indian Nat. Sci. Acad., Indian Acad. Scis.; mem. Am. Math. Soc., Math. Assn. Am. (Lester R. Ford prize 1977, Chauvenet award 1978), Phi Beta Kappa. Achievements include research in algebraic geometry, commutative and local algebra, theory of functions of several complex variables, quantum electrodynamics, circuit and invariant theory, combinatorics, computer aided design, and robotics. Home: 111 Waldron St West Lafayette IN 47906-2836 Office: Purdue U Div Math Sci West Lafayette IN 47907 Business E-Mail: ram@cs.purdue.edu.

ABID, ANN B., art librarian; b. St. Louis, Mar. 17, 1942; d. Clarence Frederick and Luella (Niehaus) Bartelsmeyer; m. Amor Abid (div. 1969); children: Rod, Kady; m. Cleon R. Yohe, Aug. 10, 1974 (div.); m. Roldo S. Bartimole, Feb. 1, 1991. Cert. in Librarianship, Washington U., St. Louis, 1976. Asst. to libr. St. Louis Art Mus., 1963-68, libr., 1968-85; head libr. Cleve. Mus. Art, 1985—2004; ret., 2004. Vis. com. univ. librs. Case We. Res.U., 1987-90, co-chairperson, 1990. Author: Introduction, Art Museum Libraries and Librarianship, 2007; co-author: Documents of Surrealism, 1918-1942, 1981, Planning for Automation of the Slide and Photograph Collections at the Cleveland Museum of Art: A Draft Marc Visual Materials Record, 1998; contbr. articles to profl. jours. Grantee Mo. Coun. Arts, 1978, Mo. Com. Humanities, 1980, Nat. Hist. Pubs. and Records Commn., 1981, Reinberger Found., 1987, Japan Found., 1996. Mem. ALA, Art Librs. Soc. N.Am. (chmn. mus.-type-of-libr. group nat. chpt. 1979-81, chmn. New Orleans 1980, nominating com. 1980, 84, Wittenborn awards com. 1981, 90, v.p., pres.-elect 1987-88, pres. 1988-89, past pres. 1989-90, chmn. N.Am. art libr. resources com. 1991-93, search com. new exec. dir. 1993-94. chmn. fin. com. 1996-98, presenter numerous papers, chmn. nominating com. 1999-2000, co-chair conf. program com. 1999-2000), Soc. Am. Archivists, Midwest Mus. Conf. (co-chmn. program com. ann. meeting 1982), Spl. Librs. Assn., Rsch. Librs. Group (shares exec. group 1996-98, shares participation com. 1997-99). Personal E-mail: annaoh@adelphia.net.

ABLE, WARREN WALTER, natural resource company executive, physician; b. Seymour, Ind., Mar. 3, 1932; s. Walter Cudwith and Edith (Harmon) A.; m. Joan Graham, May 6, 1956; children: Susan, Nancy, Cynthia, Wally. AB, Ind. U., 1953, MD, 1956, JD, 1968. Bar: Ind. 1968. Intern Indpls. Gen. Hosp., 1956-57; surgeon USPHS, 1957-59; pres. Able Ventures, Inc., Columbus, Ind., 1968—. Bd. dirs. Salin Bank & Trust. Editor: Lawyer's Medical Cyclopedia, 1967-68. Bd. dirs. Bartholomew Consol. Sch. Corp., Columbus, 1970-74; trustee Christian Theol. Sem., 1991—2003. Mem. AMA, Ind. Med. Soc., ABA, Ind. Bar Soc., Nat. Benevolent Assn. (bd. dirs. 1983-90). Democrat. Mem. Christian Ch. (Disciples Of Christ). Avocations: aviation, farming. Home and Office: 4253 E Windsor Ln Columbus IN 47201-9681

ABLER, RONALD FRANCIS, geography educator; b. Milw., May 30, 1939; s. Ambrose Francis and Lucille Bernice A.; m. Barbara Ruth Bailey, Apr. 23, 1983; children: Frederick F., Kenneth J. BA, U. Minn., Mpls., 1963, MA, 1966, PhD, 1968. Prof. Pa. State U., University Park, 1967-95; exec. dir. Assn. Am. Geographers, Washington, 1990—2002; sr. scientist Nat. Acad. Sci., Nat. Rsch. Coun., 2003—. Dir. geography program NSF, Washington, 1984-88; vis. prof. Stockholm Sch. Econs., 1982-83, U. Minn., Mpls., 1972-74, U. B.C., Vancouver, 1971; sec. gen., treas. Internat. Geographical Union, 2000-06, v.p. 2007-. Editor:

A Comparative Atlas of America's Great Cities, 1976; co-editor: Atlas of Pennsylvania, 1989, Geography's Inner Worlds, 1992, Global Change and Local Places: Estimating, Understanding, and Reducing Greenhouse Gases, 2003. Councilman State College (Pa.) Borough, 1978-82. Recipient Publ. award Geog. Soc. Chgo., 1976, Centenary medal Royal Scottish Geog. Soc., 1990, Spl. Recognition award NSF, Washington, 1988, Victoria medal Royal Geog. Soc./Inst. Brit. Geographers, 1996, Samuel Finley Breese Morse medal Am. Geog. Soc., 2004. Fellow AAAS, Assn. Am. Geographers (pres. 1985-86, exec. dir. 1990—2002, Honors 1995), Cosmos Club. Avocation: beekeeping. Office: Internat Geog Union 525 Pennsylvania Ave Unit 301 Sheboygan WI 53081-4666 Home: 525Pennsylvania Ave Unit 301 Sheboygan WI 53081-4666 Home Phone: 920-208-3452.

ABNEE, A. VICTOR, trade association executive; b. Lexington, Ky., June 12, 1923; s. A. Victor and Irene Sarah (Brogle) A.; m. Doris Heuck, Dec. 28, 1946 (deceased); children: Janice Lee Abnee Williams, A. Victor III. BA, U. Cin., 1948. With U.S. Gypsum Co., Chgo., 1948-63, dir. advt. and promotion, 1961-64; with Gypsum Assn., Evanston, Ill., 1964—, exec. v.p., 1964-83, pres., 1983-88; cons., 1988—. Served to capt. C.E., AUS, 1943-46, PTO. Named Alumna of Yr., U. Cin., 1967, Constrn. Industry Man of Yr. Wall and Ceiling Industries Assn., 1980. Mem. Nat. Assn. Mfrs. (councilman 1983—), Am. Soc. Assn. Execs., Ariz. Econ. Soc. Assn. Execs., Exec. Svc. Corps, Internat. Exec. Svc. Corps., Economic, Ariz., Chgo. Soc. Assn. Execs. (hon. life), Les Cheneaux Islands Assn. (pres. 1986-87), Bohemian Club, Sigma Chi (Significant Sig award 1986). Clubs: Les Cheneaux Yacht (bd. dirs. 1982-85), Foundation (Chgo.) (pres. 1985), University (Chgo.) (pres. 1981-83), Adventurers (Chgo.), University (Evanston) (pres. 1984-85), Skokie Country (Glencoe, Ill.), Skyline Country (Tucson), Gyro Internat. Lodges: Shriners, Masons.

ABOLINS, MARIS ARVIDS, physicist, educator; b. Liepaja, Latvia, Feb. 5, 1938; came to U.S., 1949, naturalized, 1956; s. Arvids Gustavs and Olga Elizabete (Grintals) A.; m. Frances Delano, Dec. 19, 1959 BS magna cum laude, U. Wash., 1960; MS, U. Calif.-San Diego, 1962, PhD, 1965. Research asst. U. Calif.-San Diego, 1960-65; physicist Lawrence Berkeley Lab., 1965-68; assoc. prof. physics Mich. State U., East Lansing, 1968-73, prof. physics, 1973—. Cons. U.S. Dept. Energy; sci. assoc. CERN, Geneva, 1976-77; vis. research scientist, Saclay, France, 1977, Fermi Nat. Accelerator Lab., 1990-92, Saclay, France, 1997; mem. tech. adv. com. Argonne Nat. Lab., 1971-72; mem. prep. com. Fermilab, 1978-79; chmn. Fermilab Users' Exec. Com., 1982-83; mem. SSC Users Exec. Com., 1988-91; chmn. bd. dirs. ATLAS Trigger/DAQ Instnl., 1997-99. NSF research grantee, 1971—; Disting. Faculty award 1998. Fellow Am. Phys. Soc. (exec. com. div. particles and fields 1984-86); mem. AAAS, Patria, Phi Beta Kappa, Sigma Xi. Home: 1430 Fairoaks Ct East Lansing MI 48823-1812 Office: Mich State U Dept Physics And Astro East Lansing MI 48824 Home Phone: 517-351-7376; Office Phone: 517-355-9200 x2121. Business E-Mail: abolins@pa.msu.edu.

ABRAHAM, WILLIAM JOHN, JR., lawyer; b. Jan. 17, 1948; s. William John and Constance (Dudley) A.; m. Linda Omeis, Aug. 31, 1968; children: Richard W., Heidi K. BA with honors, U. Ill., 1969; JD magna cum laude, U. Mich., Ann Arbor, 1972. Bar: Wis. 1973, U.S. Supreme Ct. 1975. Jud. clk. U.S. Ct. Appeals (D.C. cir.), Washington, 1972-73; ptnr. Foley & Lardner, Milw., 1973—. Former mem. mgmt. com., former chmn. bus. law dept; bd. dirs. The Vollrath Co., Windway Capital Corp., Phillips Plastics Corp., Quad/Graphics, Inc., Park Bank, L'eft Bank Wine Co., Ltd., Proliance, Inc.; Hi-Liter, LLC lectr. MBA program U. Wis.; prin. Lakeview Equity Ptnrs. LLC; prin. Lakeview Eqity Ptrs. Mem. adv. bd. Wis. Policy Rsch. Inst.; mem. Greater Milw. Com.; chmn. Children's Rsch. Inst.; bd. dirs. Children's Health Sys. of Milw.; past bd. dirs. United Way of Greater Milw., Family Svc. of Milw., Milw. Zool. Soc.; bd. dirs., former chmn. Children's Hosp. Found. Named All-Am. Big 10 Fencing Champion, 1968—69. Mem. ABA, State Bar of Wis. (former chmn. legis. com.), Milw. Bar Assn., Barristers, Tripoli Country Club (bd. dirs., pres.), Milw. Athletic Club, Milw. Club, Desert Mountain Country Club. Office: Foley & Lardner 777 E Wisconsin Ave Ste 3800 Milwaukee WI 53202-5367 Office Phone: 414-297-5667. Business E-Mail: wabraham@foley.com.

ABRAHAMSON, SHIRLEY SCHLANGER, state supreme court chief justice; b. NYC, Dec. 17, 1933; d. Leo and Ceil (Sauerteig) Schlanger; m. Seymour Abrahamson, Aug. 26, 1953; 1 son, Daniel Nathan. AB, NYU, 1953; JD, Ind. U., 1956; SJD, U. Wis., 1962. Bar: Ind. 1956, N.Y. 1961, Wis. 1962. Asst. dir. Legis. Drafting Research Fund, Columbia U. Law Sch., 1957-60; since practiced in Madison, Wis., 1962-76; mem. firm LaFollette, Sinykin, Anderson & Abrahamson, 1962-76; justice Wis. Supreme Ct., Madison, 1976-96, chief justice, 1996—. Bd. visitors Ind. U. Sch. Law, 1972-02, U. Miami Sch. Law, 1982-97, U. Chgo. Law Sch., 1988-92, Brigham Young U., Sch. Law, 1986-88, Northwestern U. Law Sch., 1989-94; chmn. Wis. Rhodes Scholarship Com., 1992-95; chmn. nat. adv. com. on ct.-adjudicated and ct.-ordered health care George Washington U. Ctr. Health Policy, Washington, 1993-95; mem. DNA adv. bd. FBI, U.S. Dept. Justice, 1995-2001; bd. dirs. Inst. Jud. Adminstrn., Inc., NYU Sch. Law; chair Nat. Inst. Justice's Commn. Future DNA Evidence, 1997-2001; prof. U. Wis. Sch. Law, 1966-92; v.p. Conference of Chief Justices, 2002-. Editor: Constitutions of the United States (National and State) 2 vols, 1962. Mem. study group program of rsch., mental health and the law John D. and Catherine T. MacArthur Found., 1988-96; mem. coun. fund for rsch. on dispute resolution Ford Found., 1987-91; bd. dirs. Wis. Civil Liberties Union, 1968-72; mem. ct. reform adv. panel Internat. Human Rights Law Group Cambodia Project, 1995-97. Recipient Dwight D. Opperman award, Am. Judicature Soc., 2004. Mem. ABA (coun., sect. legal edn. and admissions to bar 1976-86, mem. commn. on undergrad. edn. in law and the humanities 1978-79, standing com. on pub. edn. 1991-95, mem. commn. on access to justice/2000 1993-02, mem. adv. bd. Ctrl. and East European law initiative 1994-99, mem. consortium on legal svcs. and the public 1995-2001, vice-chair ABA Coalition for Justice 1997-2000), Wis. Bar Assn., Dane County Bar Assn., 7th Cir. Bar Assn., Nat. Assn. Women Judges, Am. Law Inst. (mem. coun. 1985-), Am. Philos. Soc., Am. Acad. Arts and Scis. Office: Wis Supreme Ct PO Box 1688 Madison WI 53702-1688

ABRAMS, GERALD DAVID, pathologist, educator; b. Detroit, Apr. 27, 1932; s. Arthur and Esther (Kushner) A.; m. Gloria Sandra Turner, June 6, 1954; children— Kathryn, ancy AB, Wayne U., 1951; MD, U. Mich., 1955. Diplomate Am. Bd. Pathology. House officer pathology U. Mich., Ann Arbor, 1955-59, instr. pathology, 1959-60, asst. prof. pathology, 1963-66, assoc. prof. Ann Arbor, Mich., 1966-69, prof., 1969—2002, prof. emeritus, 2002—, dir. anatomic pathology, 1985-89; asst. chief dept. exptl. pathology Walter Reed Army Inst. Rsch., 1961-62. Dep. med. examiner Washtenaw County, Mich., 1963—; cons. physician Ann Arbor VA Hosp., 1970—2002. Served to capt. M.C., US Army, 1961-62 Markle scholar John and Mary Markle Found., 1963-68; recipient Elizabeth Crosby Teaching award U. Mich., 1969, 87, 96, Kaiser-Permanente Teaching award U. Mich., 1978, Lifetime Achievement award in Med. Edn., 2002, Disting. Svc. award U. Mich. Med. Ctr. Alumni Soc., 2005. Mem. AAAS, US-Can. Acad. Pathology, Mich. Soc. Pathologists Office: U Mich Dept Pathology Ann Arbor MI 48109 Home Phone: 734-663-5433; Office Phone: 734-936-6770. Business E-Mail: gabrams@umich.edu.

ABRAMS, LEE NORMAN, lawyer; b. Chgo., Feb. 28, 1935; s. Saul E. and Evelyn (Cohen) A.; m. Myrna Parker, Dec. 26, 1965; 1 dau., Elana Shira. AB, U. Mich., 1955, JD, 1957. Bar: Ill. 1957, U.S. Supreme Ct. 1961, U.S. Tax Ct. 1972. Assoc. firm Mayer, Brown, Rowe & Maw and predecessors, Chgo., 1957-66, ptnr., 1966—. Mem. visitors com. U. Mich. Law Sch., 1970—; bd. assocs. Nat. Coll. Edn., Chgo., 1973-80. Recipient Gold medal AICPA, 1958. Mem. ABA (coun. antitrust sect. 1975-77, fin. officer 1977-81, program chair antitrust sect. 1988-91, vice chair antitrust sect. 1991-92, chmn. forum on franchising 1982-85, chmn. antitrust com. sect. bus. law 1995-99), Chgo. Bar Assn. (antitrust law com. 1970-85), Ill. State Bar Assn. (antitrust section coun. 1994-2001), U.S. C. of C. (antitrust and trade regulation com. 1974-80), Briarwood Country Club, Royal and Ancient Golf Club of St. Andrews (Scotland). Office: Mayer Brown Rowe & Maw & predecessors 71 S Wacker Dr Chicago IL 60606 Home Phone: 847-256-6262; Office Phone: 312-701-7083. Business E-Mail: labrams@mayerbrown.com.

ABRAMS, RONALD LAWRENCE, state legislator; b. Apr. 1952; m. Joanne Abrams; two children. BA summa cum laude, U. Minn., 1974; JD, Harvard U., 1977. Atty. Briggs and Morgan, St. Paul, 1977—80; atty. and area mgr. Grp. W. Cable TV, Mpls., 1980—84; asst. minority leader Minn. Ho. of Reps., 1992-99, state rep. Dist. 45A, 1989—2006; judge Minn. Jud. Ctr., St. Paul, 2006—. Mem. Fin. Instn. & Ins. Com., Gen. Legislation Com., Vet. Affairs & Elections Com., Rules & Legis. Adminstrn. Com., Ways & Means & Taxes Coms.; chair tax com. 1999—; spkr. pro tem Minn. Ho. of Reps., 1999—. Office: Minn Jud Ctr 25 Rev Dr Martin Luther King Jr Blvd Saint Paul MN 55155 Office Phone: 651-297-7650.

ABRAMS, SYLVIA FLECK, religious studies educator; b. Buffalo, Apr. 5, 1942; d. Abraham and Ann (Hanf) Fleck; m. Ronald M. Abrams, June 30, 1963; children: Ruth, Sharon. BA magna cum laude, Western Res. U., 1963, MA, 1964, PhD, 1988; BHL, Cleve. Coll. Jewish Studies, 1976, MHL, 1983; postgrad., U. Haifa, 1975, Yad Va Shem Summer Inst., Hebrew U., 1983. Hebrew tchr. The Temple, 1959-77, Hebrew coord., 1973-77; tchr. Beachwood H.S., 1964-66; tchr. Hebrew and social studies Agnon Sch., Cleve., 1975-77, social studies resource tchr., 1976-77; ednl. dir. Temple Emanu El, Cleve., 1977-85; asst. dir. Cleve. Bur. Jewish Edn., 1985-92, acting exec. v.p., 1993-94; exec. dir. ednl. svcs. Jewish Edn. Ctr. Cleve., 1994-99; dean Siegal Coll. of Judaic Studies, 1999—. Chmn. ednl. dirs. coun. Cleve. Bd. Jewish Edn., 1982-85. Editor: You and Your Schools, 1972. Appointed to Ohio Coun. Holocaust Edn., 1986; co-chair Cmty. Holocaust Remembrance Com., 1999-2001, bd. dirs. 2001. Recipient Elbert J. Benton award Western Res. U., 1963; Fred and Rose Rosenwasser Bible award Coll. Jewish Studies, 1974; Emmanuel Gamoran Meml. Curriculum award Nat. Assn. Temple Educator, 1978; Samuel Lipson Meml. award Coll. Jewish Studies, 1981, Bingham fellow Case Western Res. U., 1984-86. Mem. ASCD, Nat. Assn. Temple Educators (bd. dirs. 1984-88), Coun. Jewish Edn. (bd. dirs. 1991—, v.p. 1995), Assn. Dirs. Ctrl. Agys. (sec.-treas. 1995-98), Coalition for Advancement of Jewish Edn. (bd. mem. at large 1989-93, pres. 1996-2000, bd. dirs. 2000-03), Union Am. Hebrew Congregations (Israel curriculum task force), Cleve. Bur. Jewish Edn. (chmn. ednl. dirs. coun. 1982-85), Nat. Coun. Jewish Women (life), Hadassah (life), Phi Beta Kappa. Jewish. Office: Siegal Coll of Judaic Studies 26500 Shaker Blvd Cleveland OH 44122-7197 Office Phone: 888-336-2257.

ABRAMSON, HANLEY NORMAN, pharmacy educator; b. Detroit, June 10, 1940; s. Frederick Jacob and Lillian (Kampner) A.; m. Young Hee Kim, Aug. 4, 1967; children: Nathaniel, Deborah, Stephen. BS in Pharmacy, Wayne State U., 1962; MS in Pharm. Chemistry, U. Mich., 1963, PhD in Pharm. Chemistry, 1966. Registered pharmacist. Rsch. assoc. The Hebrew U., Jerusalem, 1966-67; asst. prof. Wayne State U., Detroit, 1967-73, assoc. prof., 1973-78, prof., 1978—, chmn. dept. pharm. sci., 1986-95, interim dean Eugene Applebaum Coll. of Pharmacy and Health Scis., 1987—88, assoc. provost, 1991-95, assoc. dean, 1996-99, dep. dean pharmacy, 2000—02. Author numerous published articles in field of medicinal chemistry. Bd. trustees 1st Bapt. Ch. of Oak Park, Mich., 1974-78; deacon Bloomfield Hills (Mich.) Bapt. Ch., 1986-89; dir. Met. Detroit Alliance for Minority Participation, 1994-2000. Recipient rsch. grants Mich. Heart Assn., Detroit, 1967-76, Nat. Cancer Inst., Bethesda, Md., 1982-91. Mem. AAAS, Am. Chem. Soc., Am. Pharm. Assn., Am. Assn. Colls. Pharmacy. Baptist. Avocations: astronomy, coin collecting/numismatics, baseball history, classical music. Home: 5530 Hammersmith Dr West Bloomfield MI 48322-1452 Office: Wayne State U 3607 Applebaum Bldg Detroit MI 48201 Home Phone: 248-661-0419; Office Phone: 313-577-1711. Business E-Mail: ac2531@wayne.edu.

ABRAMSON, MARC A., dentist; Degree, Mich. State U.; DDS, U. Mich. Sch. Dentistry, Ann Arbor, 1977. Gen. practice residency St. Vincent's Med. Ctr., Toledo; solo dental practice Garden City, Mich.; dentist Exceptional Dental, Cambridge Dental Group, Dearborn Heights, Mich., 2002—. Office: Exceptional Dental Cambridge Dental Group 27188 W Warren Dearborn Heights MI 48127 Office Phone: 313-274-4040, 313-278-8800. Office Fax: 313-274-8080.

ABRAMSON, NORMAN M., lawyer; b. Mpls. BA cum laude, Boston U., 1990; JD cum laude, U. Minn. Sch. Law, 1993. Bar: Minn. 1993, US Dist. Ct. (dist. Minn.) 1993. Law clk. to Hon. Margaret M. Marrinan Ramsey County Dist. Ct.; assoc. Doherty, Rumble & Butler; ptnr. Patterson, Thuente, Skaar & Christensen, P.A., Mpls.; atty. Gray, Plant & Mooty, Mpls. Named a Rising Star, Minn. Super Lawyers mag., 2006. Mem.: Minn. State Bar Assn., Ramsey County Bar Assn. Office: Gray Plant Mooty 500 IDS Ctr 80 S 8th St Minneapolis MN 55402 Office Phone: 612-632-3342. Office Fax: 612-632-4342. E-mail: norman.abramson@gpmlaw.com.

ABRAMSON, PAUL ROBERT, political scientist, educator; b. St. Louis, Nov. 28, 1937; s. Harry Benjamin and Hattie Abramson; m. Janet Carolyn Schwartz, Sept. 11, 1966; children: Lee Jacob, Heather Lyn. BA, Washington U., St. Louis, 1959; MA, U. Calif.-Berkeley, 1961, PhD, 1967. Asst. prof. polit. sci. Mich. State U., East Lansing, 1967-71, assoc. prof. polit. sci., 1971-77, prof. polit. sci., 1977—. Lady Davis vis. prof. Hebrew U. Jerusalem, 1994. Author: Generational Change in American Politics, 1975, The Political Socialization of Black Americans, 1977, Political Attitudes in America, 1983; co-author: Change and Continuity in the 1980 Elections, 1982, rev. edit., 1983, Change and Continuity in the 1984 Elections, 1986, rev. edit., 1987, Change and Continuity in the 1988 Elections, 1990, rev. edit., 1991, Change and Continuity in the 1992 Elections, 1994, rev. edit., 1995, Value Change in Global Perspective, 1995, Change and Continuity in the 1996 Elections, 1998, Change and Continuity in the 1996 and 1998 Elections, 1999, Change and Continuity in the 2000 Elections, 2002, Change and Continuity in the 2000 and 2002 Elections, 2003, Change and Continuity in the 2004 Elections, 2006, Change and Continuity in the 2004 and 2006 Elections, 2007; contbr. articles to profl. jours. Served to lt. US Army, 1960—62. Woodrow Wilson fellow, 1959-60; Ford Found. faculty research fellow, 1972-73; Fulbright grantee sr. lectr. Hebrew U. of Jerusalem, 1987-88. Mem. Am. Polit. Sci. Assn., Midwest Polit. Sci. Assn., So. Polit. Sci. Assn., Am. Sociol. Assn., Internat. Polit. Sci. Assn., Phi Beta Kappa Home: 2830 Turtlecreek Dr East Lansing MI 48823-6333 Office: Mich State U Dept Polit Sci East Lansing MI 48824-1032 Office Phone: 517-353-3285. E-mail: abramson@msu.edu.

ABRIKOSOV, ALEXEI ALEXEYEVICH, physicist; b. Moscow, June 25, 1928; s. Aleksey Ivanovich and Fanny Davidovna (Vulf) Abrikosov; m. Svetlana Yuriyevna Bun-kova, 1977; 3 children. Degree, Moscow U., 1948; DS in Physics and Math., Inst. Phys. Problems, Moscow, 1955; DS (hon.), U. Lausanne, 1975, U. Bordeaux, 2003, U. Laughborough, 2004, U. Tsukuba, 2005, U. Hong Kong, 2005, U. Orleans, 2006; DS, Slovak Acad. Scis., 2007. Rsch. assoc., sr. scientist Inst. Phys. Problems USSR Acad. Scis., Moscow, 1948-65, head dept. L.D. Landau Inst. Theoretical Physics, 1965-88; dir. Inst. High Pressure Physics, Moscow, 1988-91; disting. sci. Argonne Nat. Lab., Ill., 1991—. Prof. Moscow Univ, 1951—68, Gorky Univ, 1971—72, Moscow Physical Eng Inst, 1974—75; head chair theoretical physics Moscow Inst Steel and Alloys, 1976—92. Author: Quantum Field Theory Methods in Statistical Physics, 1962, Introduction to the Theory of Normal Metals, 1972, Fundamentals of the Theory of Metals, 1987; contbr. articles to profl jours. Recipient Lenin Prize, 1966, Fritz London Award, 1972, State Prize, 1982, Landau Prize, Acad Sci USSR, 1989, Int John Bardeen Award, 1991, Nobel prize in physics, 2003, Golden Plate award, Acad. Achievement, 2004. Fellow: Am. Acad. Arts and Scis., Am. Physics Soc.; mem.: NAS, Royal Soc. London (fgn.), Hungarian Acad. Scis. (hon.), Russian Acad. Scis. Office: Argonne Nat Lab 9700 Cass Ave Argonne IL 60439-4803 Home Phone: 630-257-0742; Office Phone: 630-252-5482. E-mail: abrikosov@anl.gov.

ABROMOWITZ, HERMAN I., family physician, occupational medicine physician; m. Joyce Abromowitz; children: Leslie M., David M. MD, Ohio State U., 1958. Clin. prof. Wright State U. Sch. of Medicine. Past pres., v.p. Montgomery County Combined Health Dist. Fellow Am. Acad. of Family Physicians; mem. AMA (bd. trustees 1997, coun. med. svc. 1990-96, exec. com., chair, mem. couns. subcom. on health care rev., svc. and chairmanship reference coms., forum for med. affairs, 1989—, sec.-treasurer, 2003-04), Am. Med. Polit. Action Com., AMA Found. (sec.-treas. 1998-99), Am. Coll. Occupl. and Environtl. Medicine, Ohio State Med. Assn. (county del., pres. 1985-86), Western Ohio Occupational & Environmental Med. Assn. (pres. 1988-92), Orgn. of State Med. Assn. Pres. (past pres. 1991). Office: Wright State U Sch Medicine PO Box 927 3640 Colonel Glenn Hwy Dayton OH 45401-0927

ABT, JEFFREY, art educator, art historian, artist, writer; b. Kansas City, Mo., Feb. 27, 1949; s. Arthur and Lottie (Weinman) A.; m. Mary Kathleen Paquette, July 16, 1972; children: Uriel, Danya. BFA, Drake U., 1971, MFA, 1977. Curator collections Wichita (Kans.) Art Mus., 1977-78; gen. mgr. Billy Hork Galleries, Ltd., Chgo., 1978-80; exhbns. coordinator U. Chgo. Libr., 1980-86; asst. dir. Smart Mus. of Art, U. Chgo., 1986—87, acting dir., 1987—89; assoc. prof. dept. art and art history Wayne State U., Detroit, 1989—, dept. chair, 1989-94, mem. adv. bd. Humanities Ctr., 1993-95; interim asst. dean Coll. Fine Performing Comm. Arts, 2007—08. Author: A Museum on the Verge: A Socioeconomic History of the Detroit Institute of Arts, 1882-2000, 001; exhbn. catalogues The Printer's Craft, 1982, The Book Made Art, 1986; one-man shows include Cliff Dwellers, 1997, Cary Gallery, 1998, Wayne State U., 1999, 2003, Worthington Arts Coun. Gallery, 2000; editor ann. Book and Paper Group Am. Inst. for Conservation, 1985-86; editor exhbn. catalogue Up From the Streets: Detroit Art from the Duffy Warehouse Collection, 2001; mem. editl. bd. Wayne State U. Press, 1990-96, 2002—, chmn. editl. bd., 1996—2001; mem. editl. bd. Museum History Jour., 2006-; illustrator: Water: Sheba's Story, 1997; contbr. articles and book revs. to profl. jours., chpts. to books and encys. Bd. dir. Hyde Pk. Jewish Cmty. Ctr., Chgo., 1988-89, Detroit Artists Market, 1994—, sec., 1996-99, pres., chmn. bd. dir., 1999-2001, hon. dir., 2004—; trustee Ragdale Found., Lake Forest, Ill., 1985-96, nat. adv. coun., 1996—; intercultural programs com., 1990-92, libr. adv. com., 1990-96, edn. adv. com., 1992-95, Detroit Inst. Arts; visual arts com. Detroit Festival of the Arts, 1989-92; juror art exhbns., 1986—; dir. Reva and David Logan Found., Chgo., 2003—. Recipient numerous purchase prizes, awards and commns. for artistic work, 1974—, award of merit Mich. Hist. Soc., 2002, Benard L. Mass. prize, 2007, Bd. Govs. award Wayne State U., 2003; Hebrew Union Coll.-Jewish Inst. Religion fellow, Jerusalem, 1971-72; grantee IMS, NEA, NEH, Rockefeller Archive Ctr., Rockefeller U., Logan Found., Wayne State U. Humanities Ctr., Kaufman Meml. Trust, Woodrow Wilson Nat. Fellowship Found. Mem. Am. Assn. Mus., Coll. Art Assn., Assn. Mus. History (co-founder), Mus. and Galleries History Group. Office: Wayne State U Dept Art and Art History 150 Art Bldg Detroit MI 48202 Office Phone: 313-993-6785. Business E-Mail: j_abt@wayne.edu.

ACHELPOHL, STEVEN EDWARD, lawyer; b. Wichita, Kans., July 15, 1950; s. Ray Edward and Juanita J. (Barnes); m. Shelley R. Kiel (div. Sept. 1987); m. Sara K. Nabity, Nov. 24, 1989; children: Joseph E., Samuel B., Raechel A., Ryan Sullivan, Peter Sullivan. BA, U. Nebr., 1972, JD with distinction, 1975. Bar: Nebr. 1975, US Dist. Ct. Nebr. 1975, US Ct. Appeals (8th cir.) 1981. Law clk. hon. Donald R. Ross US Ct. Appeals (8th cir.), 1975-77; atty. McGrath, North, O'Mally, Kratz, Omaha, 1977-80, Dwyer, O'Leary & Martin, Omaha, 1980-83; ptnr. Schumacher & Achelpohl, Omaha, 1983-92, Smith Peterson, Omaha, 1992-93; pvt. practice Omaha, 1994—. Mem. Dem. Nat. Com., 2001—; chair Neb. Dem. Party, 2001—. Recipient Robert M. Spire Pub. Svc. award, Omaha Bar Assn., 2006. Fellow: eb. State Bar Found., Am. Coll. Trial Lawyers. Avocations: golf, baseball, politics. Home: 6420 Underwood Ave Omaha NE 68132-1812 Office: 1823 Harney St Ste 1010 Omaha NE 68102-1900 Office Phone: 402-346-1900. Personal E-mail: achelpohl@usa.net.

ACHENBACH, JAN DREWES, engineering scientist; b. Leeuwarden, Netherlands, Aug. 20, 1935; arrived in U.S., 1959, naturalized, 1978; s. Johannes and Elizabeth (Schipper) Achenbach; m. Marcia Graham Fee, July 15, 1961. Candidate engr., Tech. U. Delft, 1959; PhD, Stanford U., Calif., 1962. Preceptor Columbia U., 1962-63; asst. prof. Northwestern U., Evanston, Ill., 1963, assoc. prof., 1966-69, prof. dept. civil engring., 1969—, Walter P. Murphy prof. civil engring., mech. engring. and applied math., 1981—, dir. Ctr. for Quality Engring. and Failure Prevention, 1986—2006; vis. assoc. prof. U. Calif., San Diego, 1969; vis. prof. Tech. U. Delft, 1970-71; prof. Huazhong Inst. Sci. and Tech., 1981. Mem. at large US Nat. Com. Theoretical and Applied Mechanics, 1972—78, 1986—. Author: Wave Propagation in Elastic Solids, 1973, A Theory of Elasticity with Microstructure for Directionally Reinforced Composites, 1975; author: (with A. K. Gautesen and H. McMaken) Ray Methods for Waves in Elastic Solids, 1982; author: (with Y. Rajapakse) Solid Mechanics Research for Quantitative on-Destructive Evaluation, 1987, Reciprocity in Elastodynamics, 2004; editor (with J. Miklowitz): Modern Problems in Elastic Wave Propagation, 1978; editor: (with S. K. Datta and Y. S. Rajapakse) Elastic Waves and Ultrasonic Nondestructive Testing, 1990; editor-in-chief: Wave Motion, 1979—. Named to Tempo All-Prof. Team Scis., Chgo. Tribune, 1993; recipient award, C. Gelderman Found., 1970, C. W. McGraw Rsch. award, Am. Soc. Engring. Edn., 1975, Model of Excellence award, McDonnell-Douglas, 1996, DSM, Am. Acad. Mechanics, 1997, Nat. medal Tech., 2003, Ultrasonics Lifetime Achievement award, SPIE, 2005, at. Medal Sci., 2007. Fellow: AAAS, ASME (hon. Timoshenko medal 1992), Soc. Engring. Sci., Acoustical Soc. Am., Soc. Engring. Sci. (Prager medal 2001), Am. Acad. Arts Scis.; mem.: Am. Soc. Nondestructive Testing (Tutorial citation 2004), US Nat. Acad. Engring., Royal Dutch Acad. Scis. (corr.), US Nat. Acad. Scis. Home: 711 Roslyn Ter Evanston IL 60201-1721 Office: Northwestern U Room 324 2137 N Sheridan Catalysis Bldg Evanston IL 60208 Office Phone: 847-491-5527. Business E-Mail: achenbach@northwestern.edu.

ACHGILL, RALPH KENNETH, retired research scientist; b. Indpls., June 17, 1938; s. Kenneth and Lois Ann (Philips) A.; m. Virginia Ann Swisher, July 21, 1956 (dec. Nov. 1992); children: Kenneth Edward, Douglas Alan, Kerry Wayne, Bridget Marie; m. Diane K. McCauley, Dec. 26, 1993. Student, Purdue U., 1956-60. Rsch. scientist Eli Lilly & Co., Indpls., 1956-93, internat. tech. coord., 1974-93; ret., 1993. Patentee in field. Mem. Masons (past master), Optimist Club (charter pres.). Republican. Avocation: philatelic dealer and auctioneer. Office Phone: 765-477-1032. Personal E-mail: rka@rkacovers.com.

ACKER, ALAN SCOTT, lawyer; b. Chgo., Mar. 14, 1953; s. Isreal and Loretta (Alter) A.; m. Lillian Grace Kacyn, Aug. 12, 1973; children: Steven, Kenneth, Jennifer, Daniel. BS, U. Ill., 1974; JD, Chgo.-Kent Coll. Law, 1977. Bar: Ill. 1977, Va. 1986, Ohio 1990. 2nd v.p. AM. Nat. and Trust Co., Chgo., 1978-81; assoc. Reuben & Procter, Chgo., 1981-86, Hofheimer, Nusbaum, McPhaul & Samuels, Norfolk, Va.; ptnr. Schottenstein, Zox & Dunn, Columbus, Ohio; sole practice atty. Columbus. Adj. prof. law DePaul U., Chgo., 1984-85; adj. prof. income taxation of trusts and estates, Capital Law Sch., Columbus, Ohio, 1992-2003. Contbr. articles to profl. jours. Named one of Top 100 Attys., Worth mag., 2005. Fellow Am. Coll. Trusts and Estates Counsel; mem. ABA, Ill. State Bar Assn., Chgo. Bar Assn. (David C. Hilliard award 1985), Va. Bar Assn., Norfolk-Portsmouth Bar Assn., Tidewater Estate Planning Coun., Va. CPA Soc., AICPA, Ill. CPA Soc., Columbus Bar Assn., Ohio State Bar Assn., Ohio Soc. CPA. Jewish. Office: 145 E Rich St 4th Fl Columbus OH 43215 Office Phone: 614-220-8877. Office Fax: 614-220-8876. E-mail: alansacker@aol.com.

ACKER, ANN E., lawyer; b. Chgo., July 21, 1948; BA magna cum laude, St. Mary's Coll., 1970; JD cum laude, Loyola U., 1973. Bar: Ill. 1973. Asst. corp. counsel City of Chgo.; partner Chapman and Cutler, Chgo. Fellow: Am. Bar Found.; mem.: Nat. Assoc. of Bond Lawyers, Chicago Bar Assoc., Amer. Bar Assoc. Office: Chapman and Cutler 111 W Monroe St Ste 1700 Chicago IL 60603-4006 Office Phone: 312-845-3710. Office Fax: 312-701-2361. Business E-Mail: acker@chapman.com.

ACKER, FREDERICK GEORGE, lawyer; b. Defiance, Ohio, May 7, 1934; s. Julius William and Orah Louise (Dowler) A.; m. Cynthia Ann Wayne, Dec. 1, 1962; children: Frederick Wayne, Mary Katherine, Richard Hoghton, Jennifer Ruth. Student, Ind. U., 1952-54; BA, Valparaiso U., 1956; MA, Harvard U., 1957, JD, 1961; postgrad., U. Manchester, Eng., 1957-58. Bar: Ill. 1961, Ind. 1961. Ptnr. Winston & Strawn, Chgo., 1961-88, McDermott, Will & Emery, Chgo., 1988—2003, counsel, 2003—. Co-chmn. Joint Prin. and Income Act. com., Chgo., 1976-81. Co-author: (portfolio) Generation-Skipping Tax, 1991; contbr. articles to profl. jours. Bd. dirs. Max McGraw Wildlife Found., Dundee, Ill., 1984-03, chmn., pres. 1997-01; trustee L.S. Wood Ednl. Trust, Chgo., 1975—, Ill. chpt. The Nature Conservancy, Chgo., 1981-90, chmn., 1986-90. Danforth Found. fellow, 1956; Fulbright scholar, 1957. Mem. Trout Unlimited, Fulbright Assn. (bd. dirs. 1994-2000, pres. 2000), Met. Chgo. Club, Anglers Club, Coleman Lake Club. Lutheran. Avocations: hunting, fishing. Home: 543 N Madison St Hinsdale IL 60521-3213 Office: McDermott Will & Emery 227 W Monroe St Ste 3100 Chicago IL 60606-5096

ACKERMAN, EUGENE, biophysics professor; b. Bklyn., July 8, 1920; s. Saul Benton and Dorothy (Salwen) A.; m. Dorothy Hopkirk, June 5, 1943; children— Francis H., Emmanuel T., Amy R. Ackerman de Canésie. BA, Swarthmore Coll., 1941; Sc.M., Brown U., 1943; PhD, U. Wis., 1949; postgrad., U. Pa., 1949-51, fellow, 1957-58. Instr. Brown U., 1943; from asst. prof. to prof. biophysics Pa. State U., 1951-60; mem. faculty U. Minn. Mayo Grad. Sch. Medicine, 1960-67, prof. biophysics, 1965-91, Hill Family Found. prof. biomed. computing, prof. biometry also computer scis. Mpls., 1967-79, prof. dept. lab. medicine and pathology, 1969-91, prof. emeritus, 1991—, dir. div. health computer sci.,

1969-79; staff cons. biophysics Mayo Found. and Mayo Clinic, 1960-67; dir. computer facility Mayo Found., 1964-65. Cons. bioacoustics USAF, 1957-62; mem. epidemiology and biometry tng. com. NIH, 1963-67, spl. study sect. ultrasonic applications, 1965-67, spl. study sect. lab. med. scis., 1967-69, computer and biomath. sci. study sect., 1969-73; dir. nat. resource for simulation of stochastic micropopulation models, 1983-90 Author: Biophysical Science, 1962, (with L. Ellis and L. Williams), 2d edit., 1979; (with L. Gatewood) Math Models in the Health Sciences, 1979, (with L. Elveback and J. Fox) Infectious Disease: Simulation of Epidemics and Vaccination Strategies, 1984; editor Biophys. Jour., 1983-87; also articles, tech. reports, chpts. in books. Rsch. grantee Am. Cancer Soc., 1953-56, NSF, 1958-64, NIH, 1954-90 Mem. Biophys. Soc., Am. Physiol. Soc., Assn. Computing Machinery, IEEE, Phi Beta Kappa, Sigma Xi, Gamma Alpha. Mem. Soc. Of Friends. Home: 11301 Park Ridge Dr W Minnetonka MN 55305-2551 Office: U Minn Health Ctr Box 511 MMC 420 Delaware St SE Minneapolis MN 55455-0374 Business E-Mail: acker004@umn.edu.

ACKERMAN, F. KENNETH, JR., health facility administrator; b. Mansfield, Ohio, Apr. 2, 1939; m. Patricia Ackerman, Dec. 17, 1960; children: Franklin Kenneth III, Robert Christian, Peter Jonathan. BS in Biology, Denison U., 1961; MHA, U. Mich., 1963. Adminstrv. resident Henry Ford Hosp., Detroit, 1963—64; from asst. adminstrv. dir. to pres. Geisinger Med. Ctr., Danville, Pa., 1964—94; sr. v.p. adminstrv. affairs Geisinger Found., Danville, Pa., 1981—94; prin. assoc. McManis Assocs., Washington, 1994—97, v.p., 1991—2001; pres. Clark Consulting-Healthcare Group, Mpls., 2001—, ptnr., sr. cons., 2001—02. Bd. dirs. Pa. Millers Mut. Ins. Co., Wilkes-Barre. Mem. Nat. Adv. Com. on Rural Health, Washington, 1988—94; bd. trustees Suburban Hosp. and Health Sys., Bethesda, Md., 1995—2000; Bd. dirs. Nat. Com. for Quality Healthcare, Washington, 1985—, Pa. Chamber of Bus. and Industry, Harrisburg, 1977—90, Healthcare R&D Inst., Pensacola, Fla., 1990—95. Recipient Adminstr. Yr. award Am. Group Practice Assn., 1988, Polit. Action Com. award Hosp. Assn. Pa., 1982, 85, 86, 88, 90, 91, Nat. Merit award Duke U. Hosp. and Health Adminstrn. Alumni Assn., 1991, Harry Harwick award for Excellence, 1994, Article of Yr. award Am. Coll. Med. Practice Execs., 1994. Mem. Am. Coll. Healthcare Execs. (regents adv. coun. 1989—, Hudgens' Meml. Award 1975). Office: Clark Consulting Healthcare Group 225 S 6th St 1200 Minneapolis MN 55402-5624 Office Phone: 612-339-0919. Office Fax: 612-339-2569. Business E-Mail: ken.ackerman@clarkconsulting.com.

ACKERMAN, JOHN HENRY, health services consultant, physician; b. Fond du Lac, Wis., Feb. 27, 1925; s. Henry Theodore and Clara Frances (Voss) A.; m. Eugenia Ellen Mulligan, May 22, 1948 (dec. 1996); children: H. John, Mary, Lisa, Paul. Student, Cornell U., 1943-44, Ind. U., 1944; MD, Marquette U., 1948; M.P.H., Johns Hopkins U., 1955. Intern St. Agnes Hosp., Fond du Lac, 1948-49; family practice medicine Clarksville, Iowa, 1949-51; commd. officer USPHS, 1951-70; dep. chief tng. program Center Disease Control, Atlanta, 1970, ret. as capt., 1970; dep. dir. Ohio Dept. Health, Columbus, 1970-75, dir., 1975-83; utilization rev. cons. Grant Med. Ctr., Columbus, Ohio, 1985-88; med. dir. Ohio Health Choice Plan, 1985-88; dir. med. affairs CRT, Inc., 1988-92; med. dir. Co. Rehab. Svcs.; med. cons. EBMC, 1991-95. Clin. prof. preventive medicine Ohio State U.; cons. WHO; med. cons. EBMC, Inc., ACMS, Inc., 1989-95. Served with AUS, 1943-46. Fellow APHA, Am. Coll. Preventive Medicine, Royal Soc. Health; mem. Commd. Officers Assn., N.Y. Acad. Sci., Ohio Med. Assn., Columbus Acad. Medicine, Alpha Kappa Kappa. Roman Catholic. E-mail: RDMassie@aol.com.

ACKERS, GARY KEITH, biophysical chemistry educator, researcher; b. Dodge City, Kans., Oct. 25, 1939; s. Leo Finley and Mabel Ida (Hostetler) A.; children: Lisa, Sandra, Keith. BS in Chemistry and Math., Harding Coll., Searcy, Ark., 1961; PhD in Physiol. Chemistry, Johns Hopkins U., 1964. Instr. physiol. chemistry Johns Hopkins U. Sch. Medicine, Balt., 1965-66, prof. biology and biophysics, 1977-89, dir. Inst. Biophys. Rsch., 1987-89; asst. prof. biochemistry U. Va. Sch. Medicine, Charlottesville, 1966-67, assoc. prof., 1967-72, prof. biochemistry and biophysics, 1972-77; prof. biochemistry and molecular biophysics Washington U., St. Louis, 1989—, head dept. biochemistry and molecular biophysics, 1989-96. Instr. physiology Marine Biol. Labs., Woods Hole, Mass., 1974-76; chmn. Gordon Conf. on Proteins, 1985; disting. lectr. Red Cell Club, 1997—. Mem. editorial bd. Analytical Biochemistry, 1970-79, Biophys. Chemistry, 1973-78, Proteins, Structures, Functional Genetics, 1991—; contbr. over 150 articles to sci. jours. Guggenheim fellow, 1972-73; recipient NIH Merit award, 1987. Fellow Biophys. Soc. (coun. 1972-74, 80-83, pres. 1984-85, Cole rsch. award 1994); mem. Am. Chem. Soc. (program chair biol. chem. divsn. 1994), Am. Soc. Biochem. Molecular Biology. Office: Washington U Med Sch Dept Biochem and Molecular Biophysics 660 S Euclid Ave Saint Louis MO 63110-1010

ACKLIE, DUANE WILLIAM, transportation company executive; s. William R. and Irene (Bove) A.; m. Phyllis Ann Osborn, Dec. 19, 1933; children: Dodie Acklie Nakajima, Laura Acklie Schumacher, Holly Acklie Ostergard. BS, U. Nebr., 1953, LLB, 1955, JD, 1959; cert., Army Intelligence Ctr., Balt., 1956; LLD (hon.), Nebr. Wesleyan U., 1988. Lt., spl. agt. Counter Intelligence Corps—Investigations, Europe, 1955-57; pvt. practice Acklie & Peterson, 1958-71; pres., chief exec. officer Crete Carrier Corp., Lincoln, Nebr., 1971-92, chmn., 1992—. Mem. Nebr. State Highway Commn., 1981—, State of Nebr. Econ. Devel. Commn., 1986-88; bd. dirs. Exec. Com. Interstate Carriers Conf., Alexandria, Va.; bd. dirs., Nebr. State v.p. Am. Trucking Assns.; Nebr. adv. bd. Peoples Natural Gas, Omaha. Mem. exec. com. Nebr. State Rep. Party, 1963—, nat. committeeman, 1984—; chmn. bd., chmn. exec. com. Lincoln Found. Inc., 1986-90; vice chair RNC, 1989—; adv. coun. U. Nebr.-Lincoln Food Processing Ctr., 1988-90; world bd. govs. USO, 1987—. Recipient Disting. Alumnus award U. Nebr., Lincoln, 1985, Outstanding Bus. Leader award U. Nebr. Coll. Bus., 1986, Outstanding Alumnus award Norfolk (Nebr.) Jr. Coll., 1987; named Entrepreneur of the Yr. U. Nebr. Coll. Bus. Adminstrn. Mem. ABA, Nebr. Bar Assn., Lincoln Bar Assn., Transp. Lawyers Assn., Chief Execs. Orgn., World Bus. Council Inc. Republican. Methodist. Office: Crete Carrier Corp PO Box 81228 Lincoln NE 68501-1228

ACTON, ELIZABETH S., corporate financial executive; b. 1952; V.p. multinational banking group Continental Bank, Chgo.; exec. v.p. fin., CFO Ford Motor Credit Co., Dearborn, Mich.; v.p., treas. Ford Motor Co., Dearborn, Mich., 2000—02; exec. v.p., CFO Coamerica Inc., Detroit, 2002—. Office: Coamerica Tower at Detroit Ctr MC 3391 500 Woodward Ave Detroit MI 48226

ADAM, KARL, political organization administrator, bank executive; m. Joan Adam; 5 children. B in Pub. Adminstrn., U. SD, 1987, MPA, 1989. With US dept. commerce George H.W. Bush adminstrn., Washington, 1989—91; with office econ. devel. Govt. SD, 1991—95; CEO Dakota State Bank; chmn. SD Rep. Party, 2007—. Mem. bd. dirs. SD Housing Devel. Authority, 2004—, SD Bankers, SD Bankers Insurance Svcs. Mem. bd. dirs. St. Mary's Found.; trustee U. SD Found.; chmn. Rawlins Mcpl. Libr. Bd. Republican. Office: SD Rep Party PO Box 1099 415 S Pierre St Pierre SD 57501 Office Phone: 605-224-7347.*

ADAM, PATRICIA ANN, legislative aide; b. Mobridge, SD, May 22, 1936; d. George T. and Madge Mickelson; m. Thomas C. Adam, Aug. 28, 1959; children: Kathleen Bykowski, Paula Adam-Burchill, Karlton Adam, Sarah Adam Axtman. BA in Speech Pathology, U. S.D., 1958, MA in Speech Pathology, 1961. Dir. 1st Nat. Bank, Selby, S.D.; sec. S.D. State Senate. Bd. dirs. Cmty. 1st Bancshares. Bd. dirs. AAUW Nursery Sch., 1965—, YMCA, Children's Care Hosp. and Sch., Sioux Falls, S.D., U. S.D. Found., Vermillion, Oahe Found., S.D., Pierre Sch. Found.; pres. Pierre Sch. Bd., 1977-86; bd. dirs. Sch. Bd. Assn., pres.; mem. City of Pierre Pk. and Recreation Bd.; pres. bd. trustees S.D. State Hist. Soc. Office: State Capitol Pierre SD 57501

ADAMAK, M. JEANELLE, broadcast executive; b. Odessa, Tex., Aug. 18, 1952; d. E.W. and Jo Martin; m. Russell J. Adamak, July 19, 1973; children: Aaron, Ashley. BS in Mgmt./Telecom., Ind. Wesleyan U., 1995. Dir. devel. Odessa Coll., 1986-90; exec. v.p. WFYI TelePlex, Indpls., 1990—. Chair Exec. Women's Leadership Program, Indpls., 1994-96, Vol. Action Ctr. Com., Indpls., 1996—. Mem. Vol. Action Ctr., United Way, 1996-98; bd. dirs. YWCA, Indpls., 1995-99, Cmty. Svc. Coun.-United Way, Indpls., 1996—, Prevent Blindness, Ind., 1996-2000. Recipient Devel. award So. Ednl. Comm. Assn., 1988. Office: WFYI TelePlex 1401 N Meridian St Indianapolis IN 46202-2304 E-mail: jadamak@wfyi.org.

ADAMLE, MIKE, sports commentator; b. Oct. 4, 1949; Grad., Northwestern U., 1971. Fullback Kansas City Chiefs, 1971-72, N.Y. Jets, 1973-74, Chgo. Bears, 1975-77; host SportsWorld, reporter NBC Sports, 1977-83; sports anchor WLS TV, Chgo., 1983-89; host Am. Gladiators, 1989-95; studio host ESPN, 1996-98; sports edit. WMAQ TV, Chgo., 1998—. Office: WMAQ 454 N Columbus Dr Fl 1 Chicago IL 60611-5555

ADAMO, KENNETH ROBERT, lawyer; b. SI, NY, Sept. 27, 1950; BS, ChE, Rensselaer Polytech. Inst., 1972; JD, Union U., Albany, 1975; LLM, John Marshall Law Sch., 1989. Bar: Ill. 1975, N.Y. 1976, Ohio 1984, Tex. 1988, U.S. Patent and Trademark Office. Ptnr. Jones, Day, Reavis & Pogue, Cleve. Mem.: Internat. Bar Assn. Office: Jones Day Reavis & Pogue N Point 901 Lakeside Ave Cleveland OH 44114 Address: 2727 N Harwood Dallas TX 75201 Office Phone: 216-586-7120, 214-969-4856. Business E-Mail: kradamo@jonesday.com.

ADAMS, ALBERT T., lawyer; b. Cleve., Dec. 20, 1950; BA, Harvard Coll., 1973; MBA, Harvard Bus. Sch., 1977; JD, Harvard Law Sch., 1977. Bar: Ohio 1977, US Tax Ct., 1977. Ptnr. Baker & Hostetler, Cleve., chmn. Cleve. office, 1996—, mem. policy com. Mem.: ABA (mem. bus. law section, mem. com. on developments in bus. financing), Cleve. Bar Assn., Ohio Bar Assn. Office: Baker & Hostetler 3200 Nat City Ctr 1900 E 9th St Ste 3200 Cleveland OH 44114-3475 Office Phone: 261-861-7499. Office Fax: 216-696-0740. Business E-Mail: aadams@bakerlaw.com.

ADAMS, ALBERT WILLIE, JR., lubrication company executive; b. Detroit, Nov. 22, 1948; s. Albert Willie and Goldie Inez (Davis) A.; m. Linda Maureen North, Sept. 2, 1972; children— Nichole Leahna, Albert Willie III, Melanie Rachel, Kimberly Monet. BA in Elem. Edn., Harris Tchrs. Coll., St. Louis, 1970; MBA, So. Ill. U., Edwardsville, 1974. Recreation leader City of St. Louis, 1967-69; recreation supr. Mo. Hills Home for Boys, 1969-70; tchr. spl. edn. St. Louis Bd. Edn., 1968-71; personnel asst. Equal Opportunity Adminstrn., Seven-Up Co., St. Louis, 1971-75, corporate equal opportunity adminstr., 1975-80, sr. employee relations adminstr., 1980-81, personnel mgr., 1981-82, mgr. indsl. relations, 1982-83, mgr. personnel programs and services, 1983-85, mgr. personnel ops., 1985-87; regional mgr. A. L. Williams, St. Louis, 1987-89; staff v.p. human resources Citicorp Mortgage Inc., St. Louis, 1989-91; v.p. human resources and quality Lincoln Indsl., Pentair Co., 1991—. Residence counselor Magdala Found., halfway house, 1971-77 Community-at-large mem. Affirmative Action Commn. Minorities St. Louis U., 1974-76; chmn. St. Louis corp. solicitation United Negro Coll. Fund, 1972; mem. adv. com. Statewide Job Placement Svc., 1979-84, Project Search, 1980-85; mem. Family and Children's Svc. N.W. Community Adv. Coun., 1982-85; mem. allocations com. United Way, 1985-90, bd. dirs., 1989-93; apptd. commr. St. Louis Civil Rights Enforcement Agy., 1988; bd. dirs. Vanderschmidt Sch., 1989-98, Habitat for Humanity, St. Louis, 1996-98, Pentair Found., 1998-01, Gateway Eagles of Mo., 2000--; statewide adv. bd. Internat. Student Internship, 2001--. U.S. Naval Acad. nominee, 1965; St. Louis Post-Dispatch scholar, 1971; Parsons-Blewett Meml. scholar tchrs., 1971; recipient Jr. Achievement scholarship award, 1966, St. Louis Sales and Mktg. Execs. award, 1966, St. Louis Sentinel achiever award, 1980 Mem.: AAIM (bd. dirs. 1998—2001), Black Pilots Am., Assn. MBA Execs., St. Louis Indsl. Rels. Assn., Kappa Alpha Psi. Baptist. Home: 2331 Albion Pl Saint Louis MO 63104-2524

ADAMS, AUSTIN A., bank executive; b. NC, 1943; Grad., Appalachian State Univ., 1965. Head of operations and automation First Union Corp., 1985—2001; exec. v.p., head of technology and operation Bank One Corp., 2001, exec. v.p., chief info. officer, 2001—04, JPMorgan Chase (acquired Bank One), 2004—. Named a Premier 100 IT Leader, Computerworld mag., 2004; recipient Disting. Alumni award, Appalachian State Univ., 1996. Office: JPMorgan Chase 1 Bank One Plz Chicago IL 60670

ADAMS, CHARLES GILCHRIST, theology studies educator, pastor; b. Detroit, Dec. 13, 1936; Student, Fisk U., 1954-56; BA with honors, U. Mich., 1958; MDiv. with honors, Harvard U., 1964; DD (hon.), Birmingham Bapt. Coll., 1976, Shaw Coll., Detroit, 1980, Morris Coll., 1980, Morehouse Coll., 1984; LHD (hon.), Marygrove Coll., 1985; LLD (hon.), Dillard U., 1985; D Hum (hon.), U. Mich., 1986; DD (hon.), Edward Waters Coll., 1987; LHD (hon.), Kalamazoo Coll., 1994. Pastor Concord Bapt. Ch., Boston, 1962-69, Hartford Meml. Bapt. Ch., Detroit, 1970—; Williams and Lucille Nickerson prof. of practice of ethics and ministry Harvard Div. Sch., 2007—. Instr. theology Boston U., Andover Newton Sch. Theology, Ctrl. Bapt. Sem., Kansas City, Iliff Sch. Theology, Denver; invited speaker UN, 1989, World Congress of Bapt. World Alliance, Seoul, Korea, 1990, 7th Gen. assembly of World Coun. Chs., Canberra, Australia, 1991, Evian, France, 1992; conf. preacher Hampton (Va.) U. Ministers Conf., 1993-94. Doctoral fellow Union Theol. Sem., N.Y.C.; named One of Ebony's Top 100 Influential Black Ams., 1990-94, One of 15 Greatest Black Preachers, 1993-94. Office: Harvard Div Sch Andover Hall 45 Francis Ave Cambridge MA 02138

ADAMS, CHERYL, newscaster; Grad., Marquette U. Coll. Journalism. Creator weekly news setment The Parent Place Sta. WXIN-TV, Indpls., anchor, 1994—. Nominee Emmy awards (5); recipient Outstanding Journalist award, Luth. Child and Family Svcs.; fellow, Casey Journalism Ctr. Children and Families, U. Md., 1997. Mem.: Indpls. Assn. Black Journalists.

ADAMS, EDMUND JOHN, lawyer; b. Lansing, Mich., June 6, 1938; s. John Edmund and Helen Kathryn (Pavlick) A.; m. Mary Louise Riegler, Aug. 11, 1962 (dec. May 2004); m. Cynthia A.Howell, May 20, 2006. BA, Xavier U., 1960; LLB, U. Notre Dame, 1963; LHD (hon.), Coll. Mt. St. Joseph, 2006. Bar: Ohio 1963. Assoc. Paxton & Seasongood, Cin., 1965-70, Frost & Jacobs (now Frost Brown Todd), 1970-71, ptnr., 1971-2000, mem. exec. com., 1985-88, 90-96, mng. ptnr., 1994-96, chmn., 1996-2000, of counsel, 2000—; tournament counsel Western & Southern Fin. Group Tennis Masters Tournament, 2003—05. Author: Catholic Trails West, The Founding Catholic Families of Pennsylvania, Vol. 1, 1988, Vol. 2, 1989. Mem. Ohio Bd. Regents, 1999—, sec., 2002-03, vice-chmn., 2003-04, chmn. 2005-06; mem., com. co-chair Ohio Gov.'s Commn. on Higher Edn. and the Economy, 2003-04; mem. Gov.'s Partnership for Continued Learning, 2005-07; trustee Jewish Hosp., 1995-2001, Cin. Internat. Visitors Ctr., 1989-91, Japan Am. Soc. Greater Cin., 1988-96, Ursuline Acad., 1992-94; trustee S.W. Ohio Regional Transit Authority, 1980-91, pres., 1983, 88; trustee Sister Cities Assn. Greater Cin., 1984-91, chmn., 1984-90; trustee Econ. Ctr. for Edn. and Rsch., 1996—, exec. com., 1999-, vice-chmn., 2002-04, chmn., 2005-06; chmn. USTA Nat. Father and Son Clay Ct. Tennis Championships, 1990-92; exec. com. Hamilton County Rep., 1982—, fin. com., 1990-04, chmn., 1992-94, ctrl. com., 2000—, adv. bd. Elder HS, 2002—, Ohio Coll. Access Network, 2005-07; mem. adv. bd. Global Ctr., 2007—; bd. dirs. Elder HS Altiora Found., 2007—. 1st lt. U.S. Army, 1963-65. Recipient Gt. Ctr. Notre Dame Club award of Yr., 2004. Fellow Am. Coll. Bankruptcy; mem. ABA, Ohio Bar Assn., Cin. Bar Assn., Cin. Tennis Club (trustee 1990-98, treas. 1992-93, sec. 1994-95, pres. 1996-98, historian 2001—), Met. Club. (bd. dirs. 1996-2001), Friendly Sons St. Patrick of Cin. (historian 2006—). Roman Catholic. Home: 3210 Columbia Pky Cincinnati OH 45226-1042 Office: Frost Brown Todd 2500 PNC Ctr 201 E 5th St Cincinnati OH 45202-4182 E-mail: eadams@fbtlaw.com.

ADAMS, HENRY, art educator; b. Boston, May 12, 1949; s. Thomas Boylston and Ramelle (Cochrane) A.; m. Marianne Berardi, Apr. 12, 1989. BA, Harvard U., 1971; MA, Yale U., 1977, PhD, 1980. Asst. prof. U. Ill., Champaign, 1981-82; curator fine arts Carnegie Mus., Pitts., 1982-84; Samuel Sosland curator Am. Art elson-Atkins Mus. Art, Kansas City, Mo., 1984-93; dir. Cummer Mus. Art, Jacksonville, Fla., 1994—95; interim dir. Kemper Mus. Art, Kansas City, Mo., 1996; curator, Am. Art Cleve. Mus. Art, 1996; prof., Am. Art Case Western Reserve Univ., Cleve., 1997—. Adj. prof. U. Kans., U. Mo., Kans. Author: Thomas Hart Benton: An American Original, 1989, Thomas Hart Benton: Drawing from Life, 1990, Andrew Wyeth: Master Drawings, 1996, Albert Bloch: The American Blue Rider, 1997, Eakins Revealed: The Secret Life of an American Artist, 2005, American Da Vinci: Viktor Schreckengost and Modern Design, 2006, (with others) John La Farge, 1989; contbr. articles to jours. in field. Recipient Arthur Kingsley Porter prize Coll. Art Assn., 1985, William F. Yates Disting. Svc. medal William Jewell Coll., 1989, Frances Blanshard prize Yale U., Inst. of Mus. Svcs. Nat. Mus. Svc. award for Cummer Mus., 1994. Office: Mather House Case Western Reserve Univ 11201 Euclid Ave Cleveland OH 44106-7110 Office Phone: 216-368-4119. E-mail: henry.adams@case.edu.

ADAMS, JENNIFER, medical products executive; MBA, Northwestern Univ. Kellogg Sch. Mgmt., 1998. Office supplies sales; with Deerfield Med. Supplies, Chgo., Baxter Internat. Inc., Chgo., 1994—, v.p. sales, transfusion therapies, 2002—. Named one of 40 Under Forty, Crain's Bus. Chgo., 2005. Avocations: running sprint triathlons, running marathons.

ADAMS, JOHN MARSHALL, lawyer; b. Columbus, Ohio, Dec. 6, 1930; s. H.F. and Ada Margaret (Gregg) A.; m. Janet Hawk, June 28, 1952; children: John Marshall, Susan Lynn, William Alfred. BA, Ohio State U., 1952; JD summa cum laude, 1954. Bar: Ohio 1954. Mem. Cowan & Adams, Columbus, 1954—55; asst. city atty. City of Columbus, 1955—56; mem. Knepper, White, Richards & Miller, 1956-63; practiced in Columbus, 1963—74; ptnr. Porter, Wright, Morris & Arthur, Columbus, 1975—91, of counsel, 1992—. Vice chmn. Ohio Bar Liability Ins. Co., 1990-93, chmn., 1994-2002, chair emeritus, 2002—; trustee Ohio Legal Ctr. Inst., 1976-81, Ohio Lawpac, 1980-89. Fellow Am. Coll. Trial Lawyers, Am. Bar Found., Ohio Bar Found. (trustee 1975-84); mem. ABA, Ohio State Bar Assn. (exec. com. 1975-80, pres. 1978-79, Ohio Bar medal 1994), Columbus Bar Assn. (bd. govs. 1970-76, pres. 1974-75), Lawyers Club (pres. 1968-69), 6th Cir. Jud. Conf. (life), Am. Contract Bridge League (life master), Order of Coif, Grey Oaks Country Club (Naples, Fla.), Scioto Country Club, Delta Upsilon, Phi Delta Phi. Republican. Home: 1566 A Oyster Catcher Point Naples FL 34105

ADAMS, JOHN S., insurance company executive; V.p., corp. fin. and svcs. Old Republic Internat. Corp., Chgo., sr. v.p., chief fin. officer, 2001—04, v.p., fin., 2004—. Office: Old Rep Internat Corp 307 N Michigan Ave Chicago IL 60601 Office Phone: 312-346-8100 ext. 205. Office Fax: 312-726-0309.

ADAMS, JOHN STEPHEN, geography educator; b. Mpls., Sept. 7, 1938; s. Edward Francis and Ellen Cecilia (Cullen) A.; m. Judith Estelle Nielsen, Sept. 1, 1962; children: John D., Ellen Anastasia, Martin Francis, David Joseph Cullen. BA, U. St. Thomas, 1960; MA, U. Minn., 1962, PhD, 1966. Rsch. asst., rsch. fellow Upper Midwest Econ. Study, Mpls., 1960-64; teaching asst. dept. geography U. Minn., Mpls., 1964-66, from assoc. prof. to prof. emeritus geography, 1970—2007, prof. emeritus geography, 2007—, assoc. dean H.H. Humphrey Inst. Pub. Affairs, 2007—; asst. prof. geography Pa. State U., State College, 1966-70. Rsch. asst. N. Star Rsch. and Devel., Inc., Mpls., 1964; Fulbright prof. geog. Econ. U. Vienna, Austria, 1975-76; vis. prof. geography U. Wash., Seattle, 1979; vis. prof. geography and environ. engring. U.S. Mil. Acad., West Point, N.Y., 1990-91; vis. prof. geography and earth scis. Marie Curie-Sklodowska U., Lublin, Poland, 1997; mem. nat. adv. com. H.H. Humphrey N.-S. Fellowship Program, Inst. Internat. Edn., N.Y.C., 1979-81, coord. at U. Minn., 1981-87, 89-90; econ. geographer in residence Bank of Am., San Francisco, 1980-81; mem. exec. com. Nat. Com. Rsch. on 1980 census Social Sci. Rsch. Coun., N.Y.C., 1981-88; bd. dirs. Consortium of Social Sci. Assns., Washington, 1983-85, FVB Energy Inc.; mem. geography panel Coun. for Internat. Exchange of Scholars, Washington, 1983-85, chair, 1986, mem. Soviet-Eastern European panel, 1990-93; mem. geography div. adv. com. U.S. Bur. Census, Washington, 1985; Bush sabbatical fellow, 1987-88, Fulbright prof. geography Moscow State U., 1988. Author: (with R. Abler and P. Gould) Spatial Organization, 1971, (with Abler and K. Lee) A Comparative Atlas of America's Great Cities, 1976 (Geog. Soc. Chgo. award 1977), Housing America in the 1980s, 1987); editor: Contemporary Metropolitan America, 4 vols., 1976, Urban Policy Making and Metropolitan Dynamics, 1976, (with B. Van Drasek) Minneapolis-St. Paul People, Place and Public Life, 1993; mem. editl. bd. Geographia Polonica, Govt. and Policy, Urban Geography, Eurasian Geography and Economics. Bd. dirs. Newman Ctr., Mpls., 1983—88, 1994—2002. Sr. Scientist Rsch. fellow NSF, Berkeley, Calif., 1980-81. Mem. Assn. Am. Geographers (nat. sec. 1975-78, v.p. 1981-82, pres. 1982-83, honors award 1988), Nat. Coun. Geog. Edn., Mpls. Com. Fgn. Rels. Democrat. Roman Catholic. Avocations: photography, coin collecting/numismatics, gardening. Home: 2611 W 49th St Minneapolis MN 55410-1902 Office: U Minn Dept Geography 267 19th Ave S Minneapolis MN 55455-0499 Home Phone: 612-925-1340; Office Phone: 612-625-0571. Business E-Mail: adams004@umn.edu.

ADAMS, KENT J., state legislator; b. Warsaw, Ind., Aug. 6, 1936; m. Nancy Adams. BS, Manchester Coll.; MA, Ball State U.; EdD, Walden U. Asst. supt. Goshen Cmty. Sch., 1973—85, Mishawaka City Sch., 1985—88; trustee German Twp. Marshall County, 1978-88; spl. agt. FBI; Ind. state rep. Dist. 22, 1988-92; mem. pub. health, urban affairs and ways and means coms. Ind. Ho. Reps.; mem. Ind. Senate from dist. 9, 1992—; mem. agrl. and small bus. edn. Ind. Senate; environ. affairs coms. Ind. State Senate; mem. Ind. state pension mgmt. oversight commn. Ind. Senate, gov.'s state adv. com. on child mental health; dir. fin. Warsaw Cmty. Sch., 1988—90; state police trooper; pub. sch. adminstr. Pvt. cons. Dalton Foundries Inc.; bd. dirs. Warsaw Cmty. Develop Corp., Bowen Ctr. Human Svcs., 1998--. Mem. Ind. Twp. Trustees Assn., Ind. Assn. Pub. Sch. Supts., Ins. Assn. Sch. Bus. Offcls., Bashor Home Bd. Home: 1303 Lakewood Hills Dr Warsaw IN 46580-2163

ADAMS, MARTY E., diversified financial services company executive; BS, West Liberty State U. Pres., CEO Citizens Bancshares, Inc., 1987—98; pres., COO Sky Fin. Group, Inc., 1998—99, pres., CEO, 1999—2000, chmn., pres., CEO, 2000—07; pres., COO Huntington Bancshares Inc., Columbus, Ohio, 2007—. Office: Huntington Bancshares Inc 41 S High St Columbus OH 43287

ADAMS, R. TINY, state representative; b. Muncie, Ind., June 27, 1945; married; 4 children. Cmty. svc. liaison AFL0-CIO, Ind.; state rep. dist. 34 Ind. Ho. of Reps., Indpls., 1996—, chmn., higher edn. subcom., mem. human affairs, local govt., and ways and means coms. Mem.: Children's Mus., Eagles. Democrat. Office: Ind Ho of Reps 200 W Washington St Indianapolis IN 46204-2786

ADAMS, RICHARD C., information technology executive; B in Econs., Millersville State U., 1975; M in Econs., Wash. State U., 1977; DSc in Tech. Policy, George Mason U., 1995. Rsch. scientist Battelle Meml. Inst., Columbus, Ohio, 1977, various positions including energy sys. ept. mgr., tech. planning and analysis ctr. mgr., mgr. Tech. Planning and Analysis Ctr., human resources dir.; dir. human resources Dept. Energy's Pacific N.W. Nat. Lab., 1996—98; sr. v.p., chief tech. officer Battelle Meml. Inst., Columbus, Ohio, 1998—. Bd. dirs. Brookhaven Sci. Assocs. Office: Battelle Meml Inst 505 King Ave Columbus OH 43201

ADAMS, ROBERT T., lawyer; b. Kansas City, Mo., 1961; BA, U. Kans., 1984; JD, U. Mo., 1987. Bar: Mo. 1987, US Dist. Ct., We. Dist. of Mo., US Dist. Ct., Dist. of Kans., US Ct. Appeals, Fourth and Eighth Cirs. Ptnr. Shook, Hardy & Bacon LLP, Kansas City, Mo., mem. Exec. Com., 2000—. Mem.: Mo. Orgn. of Defense Lawyers, Fedn. of Defense and Corp. Counsel (bd. dirs.), Mo. Bar Found. (Lon O. Hocker Trial Lawyer Award). Office: Shook, Hardy & Bacon LLP 2555 Grand Blvd Kansas City MO 64108 Office Phone: 816-559-2230. Office Fax: 816-421-5547. E-mail: radams@shb.com.

ADAMS, W. RANDOLPH, JR., retired management consultant, performing company executive; b. Cleve., Aug. 5, 1944; s. William Randolph and Virginia (Fulcher) A.; m. Margaret Montgomery, Sept. 1, 1968; children: William Duff, Jessica Montgomery. BA, Dartmouth Coll., 1967, MBA, 1974; M in Pub. Adminstrn., Syracuse U., 1972. Cons. Towers Perrin Co. (formerly Cresap, McCormick and Paget), Chgo., 1974-78; prin. Cresap, McCormick and Paget, Chgo., 1978-82, v.p., 1982—, dir. cons. services to fin. insts., 1984—2001; exec. dir. St. Louis Symphony Orch., 2002—. Contbr. articles to Bankers mag. Active task force on fin. services Chgo. Civic Com. Served as lt. USN, 1968-71. Mem.: University (Chgo.); Indian Hill (Winnetka, Ill.); Dartmouth of N.Y. Office: St Louis Symphony Orch 718 N Grand Blvd Saint Louis MO 63103-3414 Home: 210 Parkhurst Ter Saint Louis MO 63119-3631

ADAMSON, JOHN WILLIAM, hematologist; b. Oakland, Calif., Dec. 28, 1936; s. John William and Florence Jean Adamson; m. Susan Elizabeth Wood, June 16, 1960; children: Cairn Elizabeth, Loch Rachael; m. Christine Fenyvest, Sept. 1, 1989. BA, U. Calif., Berkeley, 1958; MD, UCLA, 1962. Intern, resident in medicine U. Wash. Med. Ctr., Seattle, 1962-64, clin. and rsch. fellow hematology, 1964-67, faculty, 1969-90, prof. hematology, 1978-90, head divsn. hematology, 1981-89; pres. N.Y. Blood Ctr., NYC, 1989-97; dir. Lindsley F. Kimball Rsch. Inst., NYC, 1989-98; exec. v.p. rsch., dir. Blood Rsch. Inst. Blood

Ctr./Southeastern Wis., Milw., 1998—. Josiah Macy Jr. Found. scholar, vis. scientist Nuffield dept. clin. medicine, U. Oxford, Eng., faculty medicine, 1976-77. Author papers in field, chpts. in books. With USPHS, 1967-69. Recipient Rsch. Career Devel. award NIH, 1972-77, Rsch. grant, 1976-95. Fellow AAAS; mem. Am. Soc. Hematology (pres. 1995-96), Assn. Am. Physicians, Am. Soc. Clin. Investigation, Western Assn. Physicians.

ADAWI, IBRAHIM HASAN, physics professor; b. Palestine, Apr. 18, 1930; came to U.S., 1951, naturalized, 1961; s. Hasan and Dabella (Miari) A.; children: Omar, Nadia, Yasmin, Rhonda, Tariq. BS in Engring. Physics, Washington U., St. Louis, 1953; PhD in Engring. Physics, Cornell U., 1957. Mem. tech. staff RCA Labs., Princeton, NJ, 1956-60; research cons. Battelle Meml. Inst., Columbus, Ohio, 1960-68; adj. prof. elec. engring. Ohio State U., 1965-68; prof. physics U. Mo., Rolla, 1968-97, emeritus prof. physics, 1997—. Vis. prof. U. Hamburg, W.Ger., winter 1977, Sch. Math. and Physics, U. East Anglia, Norwich, Eng., fall 1982; Fulbright lectr. Rabat, Morocco, 1982; sr. scientist Motorola, Phoenix, summer 1979; rsch. leader Internat. Ctr. Theoretical Physics, Trieste, Italy, summers 1982, 83, 85. Jr. fellow Cornell U., 1953-54; J. McMullen scholar, 1954-55; Sigma Xi fellow, 1955-56 Mem. Am. Phys. Soc Home: 10540 County Road 3010 Rolla MO 65401-7754 Office: U Mo-Rolla Dept Physics Rolla MO 65401 Business E-Mail: adawi@mst.edu.

ADDAI, JOSEPH, professional football player; b. Houston, Tex., May 3, 1983; BA in gen. studies, LSU, 2005. Running back Ind. Colts, 2006—. Achievements include being mem. BCS Nat. Championship team, 2003-2004; holding record for post-season reception and yards by rookie, 2007; leading all rookies in rushing yards, 2006-2007. Office: Ind Colts 7001 W 56th St Indianapolis IN 46254

ADDERLEY, TERENCE EDWARD, human resources executive; b. 1933; BBA, U. Mich., 1955, MBA, 1956. Fin. analyst Standard Oil Co. NJ, 1956-57; with Kelly Svcs., Inc., Troy, Mich., 1958—61, v.p., 1961-65, exec. v.p., 1965-67, pres., COO, 1967—87, pres., CEO, 1987—98, chmn., CEO, 1998—2006, chmn., 2006—. Mem. vis. com. Ross Sch. Bus., Univ. Mich.; mem. health sys. adv. group Univ. Mich.; bd. mem. Detroit Renaissance Found., Oakland County Bus. Roundtable, Detroit County Day Sch., William Beaumont Hosp., Citizens Rsch. Council Mich., Detroit Econ. Club. Office: Kelly Svcs Inc 999 W Big Beaver Rd Troy MI 48084-4716

ADDIS, LAIRD CLARK, JR., philosopher, educator, musician; b. Bath, NY, Mar. 25, 1937; s. Laird Clark and Dora Ersel (Webber) A.; m. Patricia Karen Peterson, Dec. 20, 1962; children— Kristin, Karin. BA, U. Iowa, 1959, PhD, 1964; MA (Woodrow Wilson fellow), Brown U., 1960. Instr. U. Iowa, Iowa City, 1963-64, asst. prof., 1964-68, asso. prof., 1968-74, prof. philosophy, 1974—2004, chmn. dept. philosophy., 1977-85, emeritus, 2004—. Sr. Fulbright lectr. State U. Groningen, etherlands, 1970-71 Author: (with Douglas Lewis) Moore and Ryle: Two Ontologists, 1965, The Logic of Society, 1975, Natural Signs, 1989, Of Mind and Music, 1999; contbr. articles to profl. jours. Mem. Am. Philos. Assn., Philosophy of Sci. Assn., Am. Soc. for Aesthetics, Am. Fedn. Musicians, Quad City Symphony Orch. (ret.), Soc. Humanist Philosophers. Home: 20 W Park Rd Iowa City IA 52246-2304 Office: U Iowa Dept Philosophy Iowa City IA 52242 Office Phone: 319-335-0021. Business E-Mail: laird-addis@uiowa.edu.

ADDIS, PAUL D., utilities executive; Pres. Am. Electric Power Co., Inc., Columbus, Ohio, 1999—. Office: Am Electric Power Co Inc 1 Riverside Plz Columbus OH 43215-2355

ADDUCCI, JOSEPH EDWARD, obstetrician, gynecologist; b. Chgo., Dec. 1, 1934; s. Dominee Edward and Harriet Evelyn (Kneppreth) A.; m. Mary Ann Tiertje, 1958; children: Christopher, Gregory, Steven, Jessica, Tobias. BS, U. Ill., 1955; MD, Loyola U., Chgo., 1959. Diplomate Am. Bd. Ob-Gyn., Nat. Bd. Med. Examiners. Intern Cook County Hosp, Chgo., 1959-60; resident in ob-gyn Mt. Carmel Hosp., Detroit, 1960-64; practice medicine specializing in obstetrics and gynecology Williston, ND, 1996—; chmn. dept. ob-gyn. Mercy Hosp., 1994—2004; councillor ND Med. Assn., 2004—. Chief staff, chmn. obstetrics dept. Mercy Hosp., Williston, gov. bd., 1996, chmn. dept. surgery; clin. prof. U. ND Med. Sch., 1973—; gov. bd. Mercy Hosp. Cath. Health Corp.; mem. coun. Accreditation Coun. for Gynecologic Endoscopy, 1999—. Mem. ND Bd. Med. Examiners, 1974—, past chmn.; project dir. Tri County Family Planning Svc.; past pres. Tri County Health Planning Coun.; governing bd. Mercy Hosp., Williston, ND With Med. Corps, AUS, 1964-66. Fellow Am. Soc. Abdominal Surgeons, ACS (regent ND 1990—), Am. Coll. Obstetrics and Gynecologists (sect. chmn. ND), Internat. Coll. Surgeons (regent 1972-74, 88-89), Am. Fertility Soc., Am. Assn. Internat. Lazar Soc., Gynecol. Lataropists, ND Obstetricians and Gynecologists Soc. (pres. 1966, 76); mem. Am. Soc. for Colopscopy and Colpomicroscopy, Am. Soc. Cryosurgery, Am. Soc. Contemporary Medicine and Surgery, Am. Assn. Profl. Ob-Gyn., Pan Am. Med. Assn., ND State Med. Assn. (coun. 2004-05), Kotana Med. Soc. (pres. 2003—), Elks. Home: 1717 Main St Williston ND 58801-4244 Office: Med Ctr Dept Ob-Gyn Williston ND 58801 Office Phone: 701-572-0316. Personal E-mail: jadducci@prodigy.net.

ADDY, ALVA LEROY, mechanical engineer; b. Dallas, SD, Mar. 29, 1936; s. Alva Isaac and Nellie Amelia (Brumbaugh) A.; m. Sandra Ruth Turney, June 8, 1958 BS, S.D. Sch. Mines and Tech., 1958; MS, U. Cin., 1960; PhD, U. Ill., 1963. Engr. Gen. Electric Co., Cin., also Lancaster, Calif., 1958-60; prof. mech. engring. U. Ill., Urbana, 1963-98, prof. emeritus, 1998—, dir. mech. engring. lab., 1965-97, assoc. head mech. engring. dept., 1980-87, head, 1987-98. Aerodynamics cons. U.S. Army Missile Command, Redstone Arsenal, Ala., summers 1965-98; cons. U.S. Army Research Office, 1964—; cons. in high-speed fluid dynamics to indsl. firms, 1963—; vis. research prof. U.S. Army, 1976; lectr. Von Karman Inst. Fluid Dynamics, Brussels, 1968, 75, 76 Fellow ASME (hon. fellow award 2006), AIAA (assoc.), Am. Soc. for Engring. Edn. (Ralph Coates Roe award 1990); mem. Sigma Xi, Pi Tau Sigma, Sigma Tau. Home: 726 Elk Run Rd Spearfish SD 57783

ADELBERG, ARNOLD MELVIN, mathematics professor, researcher; b. Bklyn., Mar. 17, 1936; s. David and Evelyn (Brass) A.; m. Harriet Diamond, June 30, 1962; children: Danielle Hamill, Erica. BA, Columbia U., 1956; MA, Princeton U., 1959, PhD, 1996. Instr. Columbia U., NYC, 1959-62; instr., asst. prof., assoc. prof., prof. Grinnell (Iowa) Coll., 1962—, Myra Steele prof. math., 1991—. Chair math. dept., sci. div. several times, chmn. faculty Grinnell Coll., 1974-76. Contbr. articles to profl. jours. Mem. Math. Assn. Am., Am. Math. Soc. Avocations: bridge, chess. Home: 1930 Manor Cir Grinnell IA 50112-1136 Office: Grinnell Coll Math Dept PO Box 805 Grinnell IA 50112-0805 Office Phone: 641-269-4201. Business E-Mail: adelbe@math.grinnell.edu.

ADELMAN, LYNN, federal judge; b. Milw., Oct. 1, 1939; s. Albert B. and Edith Margoles Adelman; m. Elizabeth Halmbacher, 1976; children: Lisa, Mia. AB, Princeton U., 1961; LLB, Columbia U., 1965. State senator dist. 28 State of Wis., Milw., 1977-97; judge U.S. Dist. Ct. (Ea. Dist.) Wis., Milw., 1997—. Chmn. judiciary and consumer affairs com. Wis. State Senate; pvt. practice as atty. Democrat. also: US Cthse & Fed Bldg 517 E Wisconsin Ave Milwaukee WI 53202-4500

ADELMAN, RICHARD CHARLES, gerontologist, educator; b. Newark, Mar. 10, 1940; s. Morris and Elanor (Wachman) A.; m. Lynn Betty Richman, Aug. 18, 1963; children: Mindy Robin, Nicole Ann AB, Kenyon Coll., 1962; MA, Temple U., 1965, PhD, 1967. Postdoctoral fellow Albert Einstein Coll. Medicine, Bronx, N.Y., 1967-69; from asst. prof. to prof. Temple U., Phila., 1969-82, dir. Inst. Aging, 1978-82; prof. biol. chemistry U. Mich., Ann Arbor, 1982-2000, dir. Inst. Gerontology, 1982-97, prof. emeritus, 2001—; dir. univ. rels. University Assisted Living, Ann Arbor, 2002—. Mem. study sect. NIH, 1975-78; adv. coun. VA, 1981-85; chmn. Gordon Rsch. Conf. Biol. Aging, 1976; adv. com. VA, 1981-91; chmn. VA Geriatrics and Gerontology Adv. Com., 1987-91; dir. univ. rels. Univ. Living, Inc., 2001—. Mem. various editorial bds. biomed. research jours., 1972—. Bd. dirs. Botsford Continuing Care Ctrs., Inc., Farmington Hills, Mich., 1984-88. Recipient Medalist award Intrasci. Research Found., 1977; grantee NIH, 1970—; established investigator Am. Heart Assn., 1975-78 Fellow Gerontol. Soc. Am. (v.p. 1976-77, pres. elect 1986-87, Kent award 1990); mem. Am. Soc. Biol. Chemists, Gerontol. Soc. Am. (pres. 1986-87), Am. Chem. Soc., AAAS, Phila. Biochemists (pres.), Practictioners in Aging. Jewish. Home Phone: 734-995-1303; Office Phone: 734-764-3715.

ADELMAN, STANLEY JOSEPH, lawyer; b. Devils Lake, ND, May 20, 1942; s. Isadore Russell Adelman and Eva Claire (Robins) Stoller; m. Mary Beth Petchaft, Jan. 30, 1972; children: Laura E., Sarah A. BS, U. Wis., 1964, JD, 1967. Bar: Ill. 1967, U.S. Dist. Ct. (no. dist.) Ill. 1967, Wis. 1968, U.S. Ct. Appeals (7th cir.), U.S. Dist. Ct. (ea. dist.) Wis. 1979, U.S. Supreme Ct. 1982, U.S. Ct. Appeals (10th cir.) 1984, U.S. Ct. Appeals (fed. cir.) 1987. Assoc. Sonnenchein, Carlin, Nath & Rosenthal, Chgo., 1967-75, ptnr., 1975-85, DLA Piper US LLP, Chgo., 1985—, co-chmn. litigation dept., 1985-91, 96-97, profl. responsibility ptnr., 1992-94, mem. mgmt. com., 1985-97, co-chmn. complex litigation practice group, 1997-98, pro bono ptnr., 2003—. Bd. dirs. Legal Assistance Found., Chgo., 1982—83. Fellow Nat. Inst. Trial Advocacy; mem. Chgo. Bar Assn., Chgo. Coun. Lawyers, Am. Inns of Ct. (pres. Markey/Wigmore chpt. 1998-99), Lawyers Club Chgo., Order of Coif. Jewish. Home: 115 Crescent Dr Glencoe IL 60022-1303 Office: DLA Piper US LLP 203 N La Salle St Ste 1900 Chicago IL 60601-1210 Home Phone: 847-835-1343; Office Phone: 312-368-4095. Business E-Mail: stanley.adelman@dlapiper.com.

ADELMAN, STEVEN ALLEN, chemist, educator; b. Chgo., July 4, 1945; s. Hyman and Sarah Adelman; m. Barbara Stolberg, May 13, 1974 BS, Ill. Inst. Tech., 1967; PhD, Harvard U., 1972. Postdoctoral fellow MIT, Cambridge, 1972-73; postdoctoral fellow U. Chgo., 1973-74; asst. prof. chemistry Purdue U., West Lafayette, Ind., 1975-77, assoc. prof., 1977-82, prof., 1982—. Cons. Exxon Rsch. Co., Los Alamos Nat. Lab.; vis. prof. U. Paris, 1985; nominator 1994 Nobel Prize in Chemistry, Royal Swedish Acad. Scis.; Renaissance Weekend Participant, 2003. Contbr. articles to profl. jours.and chapters to books. Vol. U.S. Peace Corp., Ankara, Turkey, 1969-70. Fellow Alfred P. Sloan Found., 1976-78, Guggenheim Found., 1982-83; NSF grantee, 1976—; named Outstanding Sr. in Chemistry, Am. Inst. Chemistry, 1967. Fellow Am. Phys. Soc.; mem. AAAS, Am. Chem. Soc., Am. Statis. Assn., Math. Assn. Am., Sigma Xi. Achievements include creating the mathematical and physical foundation for studying chemical reaction dynamics on solid surfaces and in liquid solution; developing the theory of fast variable/slow bath irreversible motion; making basic contributions to the theory of friction on molecules and to the theory of liquid phase vibrational energy relaxation. Avocations: long-distance running, strength training, turkish language and literature. Home: 3037 Courthouse Dr W Apt 2C West Lafayette IN 47906-1035 Office: Purdue U Dept Chemistry 560 Oval Dr West Lafayette IN 47907-2084 Office Phone: 765-494-5277. Business E-Mail: saa@purdue.edu.

ADELMAN, STEVEN HERBERT, lawyer; b. Dec. 21, 1945; s. Irving and Sylvia (Cohen) A.; m. Pamela Bernice Kozoll, June 30, 1968; children: David, Robert. BS, U. Wis., Madison, 1967; JD, DePaul U., 1970. Bar: Ill. 1970, U.S. Dist. Ct. (no. dist.) Ill. 1970, U.S. Ct. Appeals (7th cir.) 1975. Ptnr. Keck, Mahin & Cate, Chgo., 1970-93, Lord, Bissell & Brook, Chgo., 1993—. Bd. dirs. Bur. Jewish Employment Problems, Chgo., 1983-2006, pres. 1991, 92; employment relations com. Chgo. Assn. Commerce and Industry, 1982-90. Contbr. chpts. to books, articles to profl. jours. Bd. dirs. Victory Gardens Theater, 2004—. Named one of leading labor and employment lawyers in Ill., Leading Lawyers Network; recipient, Leading Atty. Network. Fellow Coll. Labor and Employment Lawyers; mem. ABA (Silver key award 1969), Chgo. Bar Assn. (chmn. labor and employment law com. 1988-89), Ill. State Bar Assn., Chgo. Coun. Lawyers, Decalogue Soc. Office: Locke Lord Bissell & Liddell LLC 111 S Wacker Dr Chicago IL 60606 E-mail: sadelman@lockelord.com.

ADELMAN, WILLIAM JOHN, retired academic administrator, industrial relations specialist; b. Chgo., July 26, 1932; s. William Sidney and Annie Teresa (Goan) A.; m. Nora Jill Walters, June 26, 1952; children: Michelle, Marguerite, Marc, Michael, Jessica. Student, Lafayette Coll., 1952; BA, Elmhurst Coll., 1956; MA, U. Chgo., 1964. Tchr. Whitecross Sch., Hereford, Eng., 1956-57, Jefferson Sch., Berwyn, Ill., 1957-60, Morton High Sch., Berwyn, 1960-66; mem. faculty dept. labor and indsl. relations U. Ill., Chgo., 1966-91, prof., 1978-91, prof. emeritus, 1991—; coordinator Chgo. Labor Edn. Program, 1981-87. Lectr. Road Scholar Program, Ill. Humanities Coun., 1997. Author: Touring Pullman, 1972, Haymarket Revisited, 1976, Pilsen and the West Side, 1981; writer: film Packingtown U.S.A., 1968; narrator: Palace Cars and Paradise: Pullman's Model Town, 1983' appeared on PBS Am. Experience, City of the Century, 2003, PBS History Detective, 2007. Bd. dirs. Chgo. Regional Blood Program, 1977-80; mem. Ill. State Employment Security Adv. Bd., 1974-75; Democratic candidate U.S. Ho. of Reps. from 14th dist. Ill., 1970; organizer Haymarket Centennial Events, 1986; chmn. adv. bd. Jane Addams' Hull House, 1991-99; mem. adv. bd. Maxwell St. Mus., 2001—; mem. Haymarket Monument Adv. Panel, 2002-04. Ill. Humanities Council grantee, 1977; German Marshall Fund U.S. grantee, 1977; recipient Tradition of Excellence award Oak Park/River Forest H.S., 1993, Eugene V. Debs award Midwest Labor Press assn., 1995. Mem. Ill. Labor History Soc. (founding mem., v.p., Union Hall of Honor 1993), Am. Fedn. Tchrs., Doris Humphrey Soc. (v.p. 1990—). Unitarian Universalist. Home and Office: 613 S Highland Ave Oak Park IL 60304-1524

ADELSON, LAWRENCE SETH, electronics executive, lawyer; b. San Francisco, Mar. 28, 1950; s. Joseph Bernard Adelson and Edna Sylvia (Kamener) Fraiberg; m. Pamela Joan Williams, Dec. 1, 1984; 1 child, Emily. BA, U. Mich., 1972; JD, Harvard U., 1975. Bar: Ill. 1977, U.S. Dist. Ct. (no. dist.) Ill. 1977, U.S. Ct. Appeals (7th cir.) 1980. Law clk. to judge U.S. Ct. Appeals for 9th Cir., Honolulu, 1975-76; assoc. Isham Lincoln & Beale, Chgo., 1976-85; gen. counsel CMC Real Estate Corp., Chgo., 1985-90, v.p., 1987-90, v.p., gen. counsel, 1988-90, CMC Heartland Ptnrs., Chgo., 1990—. V.p. and gen. counsel Chgo.-Milw. Corp., 1988—, Heartland Tech., Inc., 1998—; chmn., CEO Heartland Tech., Inc., 2002—; CEO Heartland Ptnrs., 2002—. Editor Harvard Law Rev., 1973-75. Pres., bd. dirs. Gus Giordano Jazz Dance; pres. West Ctrl. Assn., 1997-2000. Mem. Chgo. Bar Assn. (chmn. law week subcom. 1982, neighborhood outreach project 1983-84, membership com. 1987-88), Lawyers Club. Jewish. Office: Heartland Tech Inc 303 N Jefferson Ct, Ste 305 Chicago IL 60661

ADESS, MELVIN SIDNEY, lawyer; b. Chgo., May 9, 1944; s. Samuel and Evelyn E. (Bromberg) A.; m. Roberta L. Kaplan, Aug. 14, 1966; children: Jason, Stefanie, Matthew. BS with highest distinction, Northwestern U., 1966; JD cum laude, U. Chgo., 1969. CPA Ill., 1996; bar: Ill. 1969. Assoc. Kirkland & Ellis, Chgo., 1969-74, ptnr., 1974—99, KPMG LLP, 1999—. Lectr. Northwestern U. Sch. Law, Chgo., DePaul U. Sch. Law, Chgo., DePaul U. Sch. Bus. Trustee Chgo. City Ballet. State Farm Exceptional Student fellow. Mem. ABA (com. fgn. activities of U.S. taxpayers), Ill. Bar Assn., Chgo. Bar Assn. (former vice chmn. corp. distributions, reorgns. and fgn. tax com.), Am. Law Inst. (cons. fed. income tax project on internat. aspects of U.S. income taxation), Phi Eta Sigma, Beta Gamma Sigma, Beta Alpha Psi, Order of Coif. Office: KPMG 303 East Wacker Drive Chicago IL 60601

ADKINS, GREGORY D., higher education administrator; b. Charleston, W.Va., May 20, 1941; s. Wondel Lafayette and Corda Christenia (Carnes) A.; m. Dolores June Lowe, Sept. 9, 1961; children: Christenia Lea, Angela Dawn BS, U. Charleston, 1962; MEd, Fla. Atlantic U., 1966; M.C.S., U. Miss., 1968, EdD, 1970. Assoc. prof. edn. Palm Beach Atlantic Coll., West Palm Beach, Fla., 1972-74, chair dept. edn., 1972-73, chair div. profl. studies, dir. tchr. edn., 1973-74; assoc. dean career edn. W.Va. No. Community Coll., Wheeling, 1974-75, dean acad. affairs, 1975-79; coordinator instrn. and planning Colo. State Bd. C.C.s. and Occupational Edn., Denver, 1979-81; pres. So. W.Va. Community Coll., Logan, 1981-88, Bluefield (W.Va.) State Coll., 1988-93, Franklin County Schs., Frankfort, Ky., 1993-94, Jefferson Coll., Hillsboro, Mo., 1994—. Vice chmn. adv. coun. of pres. W.Va. Bd. Regents, 1986-87; chair legis. affairs com., 1986-87; bd. dirs. Missourians for Higher Edn., Mo. Coordinating Bd. for Higher Edn. Com. on Transfer and Articulation, 1997—, Jefferson Coll. Found. Inc. Mem. Gov.'s Labor/Mgmt. Coun., Charleston, 1986-93, W.Va. Enterprise Zone Authority, Charleston, 1987-93, Mercer County Econ. Devel. Authority, 1989-93; bd. dirs. Bluefield Regional Med. Ctr., 1988-89, W.Va. Joint Commn. for Vocat. and Occupational Edn., 1989-93, Missourians for Higher Edn., 1996—; mem. coms. on transfer and articulation Mo. Coordinating Bd. for Higher Edn., 1996—. Recipient Alumnus of Yr. award U. Charleston, 1984, award VFW, Chapmanville, 1987; NSF grad. fellow 1967-68, Richard Weaver fellow Intercollegiate Studies Inst., 1969-70. Mem. W.Va. Assn. Coll. and Univ. Pres. (pres. 1984-85), W.Va. C.C. Assn. (pres. 1985-86), Mo. C.C. Assn. (bd. dirs. 1995-97, adv. coun. of pres. 1994—), North Ctrl. Assn. (cons., evaluator 1984—, commr.-at-large 1984-90), Kiwanis, Rotary Internat., Chi Beta Phi (pres.). Mem. Ch. of Christ. Avocations: outdoor sports, gardening. Office: Jefferson Coll 1000 Viking Dr Hillsboro MO 63050-2440

ADLER, JULIUS, biochemist, educator, biologist; b. Edelfingen, Germany, Apr. 30, 1930; came to U.S., 1938, naturalized, 1943; s. Adolf and Irma (Stern) A.; m. Hildegard Wohl, Oct. 15, 1963; children: David Paul, Jean Susan. AB, Harvard U., 1952; MS, U. Wis., 1954, PhD, 1957; postdoctoral fellow, Washington U., St. Louis, 1957-59, Stanford U., 1959-60; doctorate (hon.), U. Tübingen, Germany, 1987, U. Regensburg, 1995. Asst. prof. biochemistry and genetics U. Wis., Madison, 1960-63, assoc. prof., 1963-66, prof., 1966-96; prof. emeritus U.Wis., Madison, 1996—; Edwin Bret Hart prof. biochemistry and genetics U. Wis., Madison, 1972, Steenbock prof. microbiol. scis., 1982-92. Recipient hon. symposium on behavior and signaling in microorganisms, 1995. Research, publs. in field. Recipient Otto-Warburg medal German Soc. Biol. Chemistry, 1986, R.H. Wright award Simon Fraser U., 1988, Hilldale award U. Wis., 1988, Abbott-Am. Soc. Microbiology Lifetime Achievment award, 1995, William C. Rose award Am. Soc. Biochemistry and Molecular Biology, 1996. Mem. NAS (Selman A. Waksman Microbiology award 1980), Am. Acad. Arts and Scis., Am. Philos. Soc., Wis. Acad. Scis., Arts and Letters. Home: 1234 Wellesley Rd Madison WI 53705-2232 Office: U Wis Dept Biochemistry Madison WI 53706 Business E-Mail: adler@biochem.wisc.edu.

ADLER, SOLOMON STANLEY, internist, hematologist, oncologist; b. Bronx, NY, May 26, 1945; MD, Albert Einstein Coll. Medicine, 1970. Diplomate Am. Bd. Internal Medicine, Am. Bd. Oncology, Am. Bd. Hematology. Intern Brookdale Hosp. Med. Ctr., NYC, 1970-71, resident in internal medicine, 1971-72, resident in hematology-oncology, 1972-73; fellow in hematology Rush-Presbyn., St. Luke's Hosp., Chgo., 1973-75; internist, hematologist, oncologist Rush-Presbyn. St Luke's Med. Ctr., Chgo., 1975—. Adj. prof. medicine Rush Med. Coll. Mem. ACP, Am. Fedn. for Clin. Rsch., Am. Soc. Clin. Oncology, Am. Soc. Hematology, Ctrl. Soc. Clin. Rsch., Internat. Soc. Hematology, Internat. Soc. Exptl. Hematology. E-mail: solomon_adler@rush.edu.

ADOLPH, ROBERT J., medical educator; b. Chgo., May 12, 1927; s. Abe and Ina Adolph; m. IvaDean Lair-Adolph, July 12, 1986. PhB, U. Chgo., 1947; BS, U. Ill., 1950, MD, 1952. Instr., then asst. prof. medicine U. Ill. Med. Sch., 1958-60, asst. dir. med. clinics, Rsch. and Edn. Hosps., 1958-60; spl. rsch. fellow NIH U. Wash. Med. Sch., Seattle, 1960-62; mem. faculty U. Cin. Med. Sch., 1962—, prof. medicine, 1970—, prof. emeritus, dir. div. cardiology, 1986-90. Cons. VA Hosp., U. Cin. Hosp., dir., Cardiac Clinic. Author: papers, abstracts in field; editl. bd. Am. Jour. Cardiology, 1980—, Jour. of Am. Coll. Cardiology, 1980—93. Fellow: ACP, Am. Coll. Cardiology (gov. Ohio chpt. 1982—85, chmn. bd. gov. 1984—85, trustee 1986—91); mem.: Am. Bd. Internal Medicine (chmn. com. cardiovascular diseases 1979—81), Laennec Soc. (pres. 1978—79), Cin. Soc. Internal Med. (pres. 1982—83), Assn. Univ. Cardiologists, Am. Heart Assn. (adv. bd., trustee Southwest Ohio chpt.), AAAS, Pi Kappa Epsilon, Alpha Omega Alpha, Sigma Xi. Office: 231 Bethesda Ave Cincinnati OH 45229-2827 also: U Cin Med Sch 8024 Witts Mill Ln Cincinnati OH 45255 Office Phone: 513-558-3074. E-mail: robert.adolph@uc.edu.

ADRAY, DEBORAH, retail executive; Pres. Adray Appliance & Photo Ctr., Dearborn, Mich. Office: Adray Appliance/Photo Ctr 20219 Carlysle St Dearborn MI 48124-3898 Fax: 313-274-6874.

AFIFI, ADEL KASSIM, physician; b. Akka, Palestine, Oct. 19, 1930; came to U.S., 1984; naturalized, 1988; s. Kassim and Zeinnab (Akki) A.; m. Larryanna Patten, June 17, 1960; children: Rema, Walid. MD, Am. U., Beirut, 1957; MS, U. Iowa, 1965. Intern Am. U. of Beirut, 1956-57, resident in internal medicine, 1959-61; resident in neurology U. Iowa, 1962-64, fellow in neuroanatomy, 1961-62; fellow in neurology N.Y. Neurol. Inst., 1964-65; fellow in electron microscopy Johns Hopkins U., Balt., 1967-68; asst. prof. Am. U., Beirut, 1965-69, assoc. prof., 1969-74, prof., 1974-84, asst. dean Coll. Medicine, 1969-78, chmn. Dept. Human Morphology, 1969-84; prof. U. Iowa, Iowa City, 1984—. Author: Atlas of Microscopic Anatomy, 1974, 89, Basic Neuroscience, 1980, 86, Compendium of Anatomical Variation, 1988, Atlas of Human Anatomy, 1991; contbr. articles to jours. in field. Trustee Diana Tamari Sabbagh Found., Beirut, 1979—, Med. Welfare Fund, Switzerland, 1991—; mem. King Faisal Internat. Prize in Medicine, Riyadh, Saudi Arabia, 1981-85. Fulbright scholar U. Iowa, 1980-81. Mem. Am. Neurol. Assn., Am. Acad. Neurology, Child Neurology Soc., Soc. for Neurosci., Alpha Omega Alpha. Home: 1147 Penkridge Dr Iowa City IA 52246-4933 Office: U Iowa Coll Medicine Dept Anatomy Iowa City IA 52242

AGARWAL, GYAN CHAND, engineering educator; b. Bhagwanpur, India, Apr. 22, 1940; came to U.S., 1960; s. Hari Chand and Ramrati (Jindal) A.; m. Sadhna Garg, July 7, 1965; children: Monika, Mudita. BS, Agra U., India, 1957; BE with honors, U. Roorkee, India, 1960; MSEE, Purdue U., Ind., 1962, PhD, 1965. Lic. profl. engr. Ill., Wis. Asst. prof. engring. U. Ill., Chgo., 1965-69, assoc. prof. engring., 1969-73, prof. engring., 1973-99, prof. emeritus, 1999—, dir. grad. studies, 1975-79, 82-85, 91-99; vis. prof. Rush Med. Coll., Chgo., 1976—. Vis. prof. Indian Inst. Sci., Bangalore, 1971, Indian Inst. Tech., Kanpur, 1972, Rush Med. Coll., Chgo., 1976—; cons. FDA, Washington, 1979—; mem. study sect. NIH, 1990-94. Co-editor: Biomaterials, 1969; cons. editor Jour. Motor Behavior, 1981-93; assoc. editor IEEE Transactions on Biomed. Engring., 1988-96, Jour. Electromyography and Kinesiology, 1994—; contbr. articles to profl. jours. U. Roorkee merit scholar, 1958-60; NSF, NIH, NASA, VA, Wright-Patterson AFB rsch. grantee. Fellow AAAS, IEEE, Am. Inst. for Med. and Biol. Engring. (founding); mem. Soc. Neurosci., Sigma Xi, Phi Kappa Phi, Eta Kappa Nu. Home: 947 Lathrop Ave River Forest IL 60305-1448 Office: U Ill Coll Engring Dept Elec Engring 851 S Morgan St Rm 1120 SEO Chicago IL 60607-7042

AGARWAL, RAMESH KUMAR, aeronautical scientist, researcher, educator; b. Mainpuri, India, Jan. 4, 1947; came to U.S., 1968; s. Radhakishan and Parkashvati (Goel) A.; m. Sugita Goel, Oct. 26, 1976; children: Vivek, Gautam. BS, U. Allahabad, 1965; BTech, Indian Inst. Tech., 1968; MS, U. Minn., 1969; PhD, Stanford U., Calif., 1975. Rsch. assoc. NASA Ames Rsch. Ctr., Moffett Field, Calif., 1976-78; McDonnell Douglas fellow, program dir. McDonnell Douglas Aerospace, St. Louis, 1978-94; Bloomfield disting. prof., chair aerospace engring. Wichita State U., 1994-96, Bloomfield disting prof., exec. dir. Nat. Inst. Aviatn Rsch., 1997—2001; William Palm prof. engring., dir. Aerospace Rsch. and Edn. Ctr. Washington U., St. Louis, 2001—. Affiliate prof. Washington U., St. Louis, 1986-95. Contbr. more than 200 articles to profl. jours. Fellow AIAA, AAAS, ASME, SME, IEEE, Soc. Automotive Engring., Royal Aero. Soc., Am. Phys. Soc.; mem. Am. Helicopter Soc., World Innovation Found., Tau Beta Pi, Sigma Gamma Tau, Pi Tau Sigma. Office: Washington U Dept Mech Engring Saint Louis MO 63130 Office Phone: 314-935-6091. Business E-Mail: rka@me.wustl.edu.

AGARWAL, SUMAN KUMAR, editor; b. Bolpur, India, Jan. 21, 1945; came to U.S., 1980; s. Hari Prasad and Rukmini (Modi) A.; children: Tripti, Samantha Rani. BSc with honors, Visva-Bharati, Santiniketan, India, 1966; MSc, Delhi U., India, 1971; PhD, U. Paris, 1975, DSc, 1979. Rsch. scholar Atomic Energy Commn. of France, Saclay, 1976-80; rsch. assoc. Purdue U., West Lafayette, Ind., 1980-82; sr. sci. info. analyst Chem. Abstracts Svc., Columbus, Ohio, 1982—; pres. Commodities Internat. Ltd. Inc., Columbus, Ohio, 1992—2002, Concrete Machines, Inc., Hilliard, Ohio, 2006—. Contbr. articles to profl. jours. Vol. Columbus Schs., 1984-85, Ohio State U. TV, Columbus, 1986-88. Scholar Govt. of France, 1973-76. Mem. Am. Chem. Soc. Avocations: bridge, photography, tennis. Personal E-mail: suman_agarwal33@yahoo.com.

AGEMA, GERALD WALTON, publishing executive; b. Rockford, Ill., Sept. 9, 1947; s. Samuel W. and Lillian (Walton) A.; m. Marcia L. Vander Meer, June 14, 1969; children: Jerry, Matt and Mike (twins). BS in Acctg., No. Ill. U., 1970; MBA, U. Chgo., 1984. CPA, Ill. Staff/sr. auditor Price Waterhouse, Chgo., 1971—76, audit mgr., 1976—79, Tribune Co., 1979—80, asst. contr., 1980—85; dir., CFO Tribune Broadcasting Co., 1985—86, v.p., CFO, 1986—88, v.p. ops., CFO, 1988—97, v.p. adminstrn., CFO, 1997—2001, Tribune Pub. Co., 2001—. Bd. dirs. Mus. of Broadcast Comms., Chgo., 1986—, treas., 1986-97. Mem. AICPA, Ill. Soc. CPAs, Internat. Newspapers Fin. Exec. Assn. Avocations: reading, boating, fishing, travel. Office: Tribune Pub Co 435 N Michigan Ave Ste 1900 Chicago IL 60611-4066

AGLER, BRIAN, professional basketball coach; m. Robin Agler; children: Bryce, Taylor. BA, Wittenberg U.; MEd, Pitts. State U., Kans. Profl. basketball player, Blackpool, England, 1980-81; coach Northeastern Okla. A&M U., 1984—88, U. Mo., Kansas City, 1988—93; head women's basketball coach Kans. State U., 1993—96; head coach Columbus Quest, 1996—99; head coach, gen. mgr. Minn. Lynx, Mpls., 1999—2002; asst. coach Phoenix Mercury, Ariz., 2004—. Inductee Wittenberg U. Athletic Hall of Honor, 1995; named ABL Ea. Conf. All-Star head coach, 1997, 98, ABL Coach of the Yr., 1996-97. Mem. Women's Basketball Coaches Assn. Office: Phoenix Mercury 201 E Jefferson St Phoenix AZ 85004

AGNELLO, GINO J., federal court administrator; BS, U. Ill.; JD, Ill. Inst. Tech. Pvt. practice; with U.S. Bankruptcy Ct. (no. dist.) Ill., Chgo.; dep. cir. exec.; clk. of ct. U.S. Ct. Appeals (7th cir.), Chgo., 1997—. Office: US Ct Appeals (7th cir) 219 S Dearborn St Ste 2710A Chicago IL 60604-1803

AGNEW, GARY, professional hockey coach; b. Niagara Falls, Ont., Can., May 24, 1960; m. Barbara Agnew; children: Brett, Lindsay. Grad., U. NB, 1982; M in Coaching, U. We. Ont. Asst. coach U. New Brunswick Hockey Team, 1985—87; head coach London Knights (Ont. Hockey League), 1990—94, 1997—2000, Kingston Frontenacs, 1994—97, Syracuse Crunch (Am. Hockey League), 2000—06; asst. coach Columbus Blue Jackets, 2006—, interim head coach, 2006. Recipient Matt Leyden Trophy as Coach of Yr., Ont. Hockey League, 1993, 1998. Office: Columbus Blue Jackets Nationwide Arena 200 W Nationwide Blvd, Ste Level Columbus OH 43215

AGOOS, JEFF, professional soccer player; b. Geneva, May 2, 1968; Grad., U. Va., 1989. Defender Maryland Bays, A-League, 1991, Dallas Sidekicks (indoor), 1992, SV Wehen, Germany, 1994—95, DC United, Herndon, Va., 1996—2000, San Jose Earthquakes, 2000—04, MetroStars, 2004—. Mem. U.S. Under-15, Under-17, Under-20, World Univ. and Indoor Nat. Teams; vol. asst. coach Bruce Arena, U. Va., 1995. Named Soccer Am.'s co-freshman of yr., 1986, MLS Defender of Yr., 2001; named one of Soccer Am.'s 11 most valuable players, 1989, MLS Best XI, 1997, 1999, 2001. Achievements include competitor 13 international matches in 1996; scoring winning goal in 2d international appearance, Guatemala; mem. silver-medal U.S. Futsai Nat. Team, Hong Kong, 1992; helped lead DC United to inaugural MLS Cup title and 1996 U.S. Open Cup championship. Office: US Soccer Fedn 1801-1811 S Prairie Ave Chicago IL 60616 and: DC United 13832 Redstein Dr Herndon VA 20171

AGRANOFF, BERNARD WILLIAM, biochemist, educator; b. Detroit, June 26, 1926; s. William and Phyllis (Pelavin) A.; m. Raquel Betty Schwartz, Sept. 1, 1957; children: William, Adam. MD, Wayne State U., 1950; BS, U. Mich., 1954. Intern Robert Packer Hosp., Sayre, Pa., 1950-51; commd. surgeon USPHS, 1954-60; biochemist at. Inst. Neurol. Diseases and Blindness, NIH, Bethesda, Md., 1954-60; mem. faculty U. Mich., Ann Arbor, 1960—, prof. biochemistry, 1965—; R.W. Gerard prof. of neurosci. in psychiatry, 1991. Rsch. biochemist Mental Health Rsch. Inst., 1960—, assoc. dir., 1977-83, dir. 1983-95, dir. neurosci. lab., 1983-2000; vis. scientist Max Planck Inst. Zellchemie, Munich, 1957-58, Nat. Inst. Med. Rsch., Mill Hill, Eng., 1974-75; Henry Russel lectr. U. Mich., 1987; cons. pharm. industry, govt. Contbr. articles to profl. jours. Fogarty scholar-in-residence NIH, Bethesda, Md., 1989-95; named Mich. Scientist of Yr. Mus. of Sci., Lansing, 1992. Fellow AAAS, Am. Acad. Arts and Scis., N.Y. Acad. Sci., Am. Coll. Neuropsychopharmacology; mem. Am. Soc. Biochemistry and Molecular Biology, Am. Chem. Soc., Inst. Medicine of NAS, Internat. Soc. Neurochemistry (treas. 1985-89, chmn. 1989-91), Am. Soc. Neurochemistry (pres. 1973-75). Achievements include research in brain lipids, biochem. basis of learning, memory and regeneration in the nervous system, human brain imaging. Office: U Mich Molecular and Behavior Rsch Inst 205 Zina Pitcher Pl Ann Arbor MI 48109-5720 Personal E-mail: agranoff@umich.edu.

AGRAWAL, DHARMA PRAKASH, engineering educator; b. Balod, India, Apr. 12, 1945; arrived in US, 1976; s. Saryoo Prasad and Chandra K. Agrawal; m. Purnima Agrawal, June 7, 1971; children: Sonali, Braj. BE, Ravishankar U., Raipur, India, 1966; ME with honors, Roorkee U., India, 1968; DSc, Fed. Inst. Tech., Lausanne, Switzerland, 1975. Lectr. M.N.R. Engrng. Coll., Allahabad, India, 1968-72, Roorkee U., 1972-73; asst. Fed. Inst. Tech., Lausanne, 1973-75; instr., postdoctoral work So. Meth. U., Dallas, 1976-77; asst. prof., then assoc. prof. Wayne State U., Detroit, 1977-82; assoc. prof. N.C. State U., Raleigh, 1982-84, prof., 1984-98; OBR Disting. prof. U. Cin., 1998—. Gen. co-chair Advanced Computing Conf., 1997—2000; Fulbright sr. specialist, 2002—; keynote spkr. Internat. Conf. on Parallel and Distributed Sys., 1997; presenter in field. Co-author: Introduction to Wireless and Mobile Systems, 2003, Ad Hoc and Sesor Networks, 2006; editor: Advanced Computer Architecture, 1986, Advances in Distributed System Reliability, 1990, Distributed Computing Network Reliability, 1990; editor: Jour. Parallel and Distg. Computing, 1984, Computer mag., 1986-91. Fellow AAAS, IEEE (chair tech. com. on computer architecture, IEEE Computer Soc. 1991-94, chair McDowell Award and Harry Grode Award coms. 1991-99, chair Eckerdt Mauchley award in computer architecture, program chair internat. conf. on parallel processing 1994, chair disting. visitor program, workshop chair internat. conf. on parallel processing 1995, gen. chair 4th internat. workshop on modeling analysis and simulation of computer and telecom. sys. 1996, 2001, editor jour. 1992-96), Assn. Computing Machinery, World Innovation Found.; mem. AIM, Internat. Conf. on Mobile Adhoc Sensor Sys. (gen. chair), Sigma Xi. Office: U Cin CS Dept PO Box 210030 Cincinnati OH 45221-0030 Business E-Mail: dpa@ececs.uc.edu.

AGRE, JAMES COURTLAND, physiatrist; b. Northfield, Minn., May 2, 1950; s. Courtland Leverne and Ellen Violet (Swedberg) A.; m. Patti Dee Soderberg, Aug. 6, 1982. MD, U. Minn., 1976, PhD, 1985. Cert. diplomate Nat. Bd. Med. Examiners, bd. cert. Am. Bd. Phys. Medicine and Rehab. Rsch. fellow dept. phys. medicine and rehab. U. Minn., Mpls., 1979-80, instr. dept. phys. medicine and rehab., 1980-84; asst. prof. dept. phys. medicine and rehab. U. Wis., Madison, 1984-90, assoc. prof. dept. rehab. medicine, 1990-93, chmn. dept. rehab. medicine, 1991-97, prof. dept. rehab. medicine, 1993-97; practitioner in svc. Ministry Health Care, Rhinelander and Eagle River, Wis., 1997—. Mem. editorial bd. and contbr. articles to Archives of Phys. Medicine and Rehab., 1988-2000. Ski coord. Wis. Ski for Light, Madison, 1985-95. Fellow Am. Acad. Phys. Medicine and Rehab. (Elizabeth and Sidney Licht award 1989, Excellence in Sci. Writing award 1990), Am. Coll. Sports Medicine (New Investigator award 1991). Office: Ministry Health Care 930 E Wall St Eagle River WI 54521 Office Phone: 715-477-3000. Business E-Mail: jagre@shsmh.org.

AGRUSS, NEIL STUART, cardiologist; b. Chgo., June 2, 1939; s. Meyer and Frances (Spector) A.; m. Janyce Zucker; children: David, Lauren, Michael, Joshua, Susan, Robyn, Bryan. BS, U. Ill., 1960, MD, 1963. Diplomate Am. Bd. Internal Medicine. Resident in internal medicine Cin. Gen. Hosp., 1964-65, 67-68, fellow in cardiology, 1968-70, dir. coronary care unit, 1971-74, dir. echocardiography lab., 1972-74; asst. prof. medicine U. Cin., 1970-74; dir. cardiac diagnostic labs. Ctr. DuPage Hosp., Winfield, Ill., 1974—; asst. prof. medicine Rush Med. Coll., 1976—. Chmn. coronary care com. Heart Assn. DuPage County, 1974-76. Author, co-author publs. in field. Active Congregation Beth Shalom, Naperville, Ill. Capt. M.C. U.S. Army, 1965-67. Fellow ACP, Am. Coll. Cardiology, Am. Coll. Chest Physicians, Coun. Clin. Cardiology, Am. Heart Assn.; mem. AMA, DuPage County Med. Soc., Ill. Med. Soc., Am. Fedn. Clin. Rsch., Chgo. Heart Assn. Office: 454 Pennsylvania Ave Glen Ellyn IL 60137-4418 Business E-Mail: hrtdoctor729@msn.com.

AGUILAR, RAYMOND M., state legislator; b. Grand Island, Nebr., Oct. 24, 1947; m. Susan Ann, Dec. 14, 1973; children: Toni, Polly, Scott, Dean, T.C., Ali, Shelly, Audra, Jason. Undergrad., Central Cmty. Coll. Bldg., grounds dir. Grand Island Ctrl.; constrn. Chief Industries; prodn. mgr. Merrick Machine Co.; mem. ebr. Legislature from 35th dist., Lincoln, 1999—. Mem. Grand Island City Coun., Lincoln Sch. PTA (pres.), Mayor's Youth Coun., Mayor's Cmty. Crime Commn., Am. Red Cross, lectr., eucharistic min., religious edn. com. St. Mary's Cath. Ch. Mem. Hall Cty. Leadership Tomorrow, Grand Island Little Theatre; minority adv. mem. Nebr. Coordinating Commn. for Postsecondary Edn. Roman Catholic. Office: State Capitol (Dist 35) Room 1008 PO Box 94604 Lincoln NE 68509-4604

AGUILERA, JOHN, state representative; Grad., Calumet Coll. St. Joseph, 1984, U. Indpls., 1979. Ops. mgr., info. tech. dept. ISPAT Inland; councilman Lake County (Ind.) Coun., 1994—2000; state rep. dist. 12 Ind. Ho. of Reps., Indpls., 2000—, vice chmn., local govt. com., mem. rds. and transp., and ways and means coms. Mem.: Hispanic Coordinating Coun., United Way, Boys and Girls Club. Democrat. Office: Ind Ho of Reps 200 W Washington St Indianapolis IN 46204-2786

AGUIRRE, FERNANDO, food products executive; b. Mex. BSBA, So. Ill. U. With Procter & Gamble, 1980—2004, pres., gen. mgr. P&G Brazil, 1992—96, pres. P&G Mex., 1996—99, v.p. global and U.S. snacks and food products, 1999—2000, pres. global feminine care, 2000—04; chmn., pres., CEO Chiquita Brands Internat., Inc., Cin., 2004—. Bd. dirs. Univision Comm., Inc.; chmn. emeritus corp. adv. bd. Marshall Sch. Bus. U. So. Calif. Office: Chiquita Brands Internat 250 E 5th St Cincinnati OH 45202

AHERN, MARY ANN, reporter; m. Thomas Ahern; 3 children. BA, John Carroll U., 1976; MEd, Northeastern Ill. U., 1979; M Journalism, Northwestern U., 1982. Tchr. 2 Chgo. area H.S., 1976—79; reporter, weekend anchor Sta. WEEK-TV, Peoria, Ill., 1982—85; polit. reporter Sta. WXIA-TV, Atlanta, 1985—89; gen. assignment reporter NBC 5, Chgo., 1989—. Office: NBC 454 N Columbus Dr Chicago IL 60611

AHERN, MIKE, newscaster; b. Jan. 13, 1939; m. Sherry Ahern. Degree in Comm. Arts, Notre Dame U. Sports dir. WSND, South Bend, Ind.; news reporter, sports dir. WIRE, Indpls.; reporter coverage Indpls. 500 Race Speedway Radio Network, 1961—73; feature column Sunday edit. Indpls. Star, 1963; anchor Sta. WISH-TV, 1967—. Co-author: Festerwood at Five, 1998. Named Best News Anchor; recipient Casper awards (4). Office: WISH-TV 1950 N Meridian St Indianapolis IN 46207

AHLERICH, STAN, farmer, farm association administrator; m. Molly Ahlerich; children: Alexis, Nicholas. Degree in agrl. econs., Kans. State U. Farmer, Cowley County, Kans.; pres. Kans. Farm Bur., Manhattan, 1999—. Pres. bd. Cowley County Farm Bur., v.p.; chmn. Young Farmers and Ranchers; polit. edn. chmn., policy chmn., info. chmn., voting del. state conv. Young Farmers and Ranchers; chmn. Young Farmers and Ranchers state com. Kans. Farm Bur., 1983—84, chmn., 1984; bd. dirs. Am. Farm Bur., Commerce Bank of Wichita, Kans. Charter mem. state bd., chmn. Kans. Agr. and Rural Leadership, 1992—93; mem. Kans. Inc., Walnut River Basin Adv. Bd.; mem. farm and ranch adv. bd. Sen. Bob Dole, 1986. Office: Kans Farm Bur 2627 KFB Plz Manhattan KS 66503

AHLERS, LINDA L., retail executive; BA, U. Wisc. Buyer, Target Stores Dayton Hudson Corp., 1977-83, divsn. mdse. mgr., Target Stores, 1983-85, dir. mdse. planning and control, 1985-88, v.p. mdse. planning and control, 1988, sr. v.p. Target Stores, 1988-95, exec. v.p. merchandising, dept. store divsn., 1995-96; pres., dept. store divsn. Dayton Hudson Corp. (now Marshall Field's), 1996—; bd. dirs. Dayton Hudson Corp., 1997—. Dir. Guthrie Theatre; mem. Com. of 200, Detroit Renaissance Bd., Minn. Women's Econ. Roundtable. Office: Target Corp 1000 Nicollet Mall Minneapolis MN 55403-2467

AHLQUIST, PAUL GERALD, molecular biology researcher, educator; b. Des Moines, Jan. 9, 1954; s. Irving Elmer and Signun Evelyn (Eidbo) A. BS in Physics, Iowa State U., 1976; PhD in Biophysics, U. Wis., 1981. Asst. sci. in biophysics U. Wis., Madison, 1981-84, asst. prof. biophysics and plant pathology, 1984-87, assoc. prof. molecular virology and plant pathology, 1987-91, prof., 1991—, prof. molecular virology, oncology and plant pathology, 1997—, chmn. molecular virology, 1996-97, Paul J. Kaesberg prof., 2000—; investigator Howard Hughes Med. Inst., 1997—. Mem. exec. com. Internat. Commn. Taxonomy of Viruses, 1987-93; van Arkel hon. faculty chair in biochemistry Leiden (The Netherlands) U., 1995. Editor: RNA Genetics, vols. I, II, III, 1988, Molecular Biology of Plant-Microbe Interactions, 1989; assoc. editor Virology, 1988-93, Molecular Plant-Microbe Interactions, 1988-95, Plant Molecular Biology, 1987-90; contbr. articles to profl. jours. Recipient Presdl. Young Investigator award NSF, 1985-90, Romnes Faculty Fellowship award, 1988, Shaw Faculty Scholar award Milw. Found., 1985-90, Allen Rsch. award Am. Phytopathology Soc., 1988, Pound Rsch. award, 1987, WARF Mid-Career Rsch. award, 1995, NIH Merit award, 1995—. Mem. NAS, Am. Soc. Virology (mem. exec. coun. 1993-96), Internat. Soc. Plant Molecular Biology (bd. dirs. 1989-93), Am. Soc. for Microbiology, Genetics Soc. Am.

AHMANN, JOHN STANLEY, retired psychologist; b. Struble, Iowa, Oct. 17, 1921; s. Henry Francis and Philomine (Wictor) Ahmann; children: Sandi Ann, Sheri Kay, Gregory Steven, Shelly Joan. BA, Trinity Coll., 1943; BS, Iowa State U., Ames, 1947, MS, 1949, PhD, 1951. Instr. profl. studies Iowa State U., 1949-51, prof. edn. and psychology Ames, 1975—, disting. prof. edn., 1981—, chmn. dept. profl. studies, 1975-84; asst. prof. div. ednl. psychology and psychol. measurement Cornell U., 1951-54, asso. prof., 1954-58, prof., 1958-60; prof. psychology Colo. State U., 1960-75; assoc. dir. Human Factors Rsch. Lab., 1969-71, asst. to pres., 1961-64, head dept. psychology, 1962-64, acad. v.p., 1964-69; retired. Adj. prof. psychology and edn. U. Denver, 1971—76; vis. prof. Colo. State U., 1951, Wash. State U., 1960, Western Wash. U., 1970; cons. rsch. programs U.S. Dept. Edn.; cons. evaluation ednl. programs, Colo., NY, La., Tex., Ark., Hawaii, Ga., Ariz., Ohio, Minn., Iowa; project dir. Nat. Assessment Ednl. Progress, 1971—75; dir. various fed. and state sponsored rsch. projects; hon. lectr. Mid-Am. State U. Assn., 1976—77. Author: (book) Statistical Methods in Educational and Psychological Research, 1954, Evaluating Student Progress, 6th edit., 1981, Evaluating Elementary School Pupils, 1960, Testing Student Achievement and Aptitudes, 1962, Measuring and Evaluating Educational Achievement, 2d edit., 1975, How Much Are Our Young People Learning?, 1976, Needs Assessment for Program Planning in Vocational Education, 1979, Academic Achievements of Young Americans, 1983; assoc. editor: Ednl. Studies, 1975—79. With USNR, 1943—46, PTO. Recipient Laureate award, Iowa State U., 1975. Fellow: APA, AAAS; mem.: Nat. Coun. Measurement Edn., Am. Ednl. Rsch. Assn., Psi Chi, Alpha Chi Sigma, Phi Lambda Upsilon, Phi Delta Kappa, Phi Kappa Phi, Sigma Xi. Home: 5055 S Lemay Ave Unit 1 201 Fort Collins CO 80525-9401

AHOY, CHRISTOPHER KEEN, educational association administrator, architect; b. Kalimpong, India, May 29, 1939; came to US, 1964; s. King Nam (Lai) and Chun Oi (Tham) A.; m. Breena E. D'Silva (div.); m. E. Ruth Lynn, Nov. 6, 1981; stepchildren: Gregorio, Deborah, Claudette Altomirono. Student, St. Xavier's Coll., Calcutta, India, 1959; BArch, Indian Inst. Tech., Kharagpur, India, 1964; MArch, U. Calif., Berkeley, 1965; postgraduate student, U. So. Calif. Registered arch., Calif., Alaska. Arch. Joseph Esherick & Assocs., San Francisco, 1965—73; project mgr. M. Arthur Gensler & Assocs., San Francisco, 1973; chief arch., mgr. atkin and Weber, San Francisco, 1973—74; assoc. arch. to asst. dir. design svcs. U. Calif., Berkeley, 1974—77, campus arch., sr. mgr. tech. svcs. dept. facilities mgmt., 1977—81; dir. statewide office facilities planning and constrn. U. Alaska, 1981—87; pres., CEO Comprehensive Facilities Mgmt., Berkeley, 1987—94; asst. v.p. bus. and fin., dir. facilities planning and mgmt. U. Nebr. sys., Lincoln, 1994—97; assoc. v.p. facilities Iowa State U., Ames, 1997—. Conductor seminars; spkr. in field. Author: Manual for Selection Consultants, 1988. Commr. Urban Beautification Commn., Fairbanks, Alaska, 1982-85, chmn. 1983-85. Mem. AIA (Cert. of Appreciation, 1974), Assn. Univ. Architects (Resolution Appreciation award, 1987, bd. regents U. Alaska 1987), Soc. Coll. Univ. Planners, Am. Planning Assn., Assn. Phys. Plant Adminstrs., Nat. Assn. Coll. Univ. Bus. Officers, Internat. Facility Mgmt. Assn., MIT Office of Facilities Mgmt. Systems (mem. bd. tech. adv. group), Assn. Higher Edn. Facilities Officers (pres.), Toastmasters, Rotary. Office: Facilities Planning and Mgmt Iowa State U Gen Serv Rm 108 Ames IA 50011-4001 Office Phone: 515-294-8079. Office Fax: 515-294-4593. E-mail: ckahoy@iastate.edu.

AHRENS, FRANKLIN ALFRED, veterinary pharmacology educator; b. Leigh, Nebr., Apr. 27, 1936; s. Alfred Henry and Agnes Elizabeth (Higgins) A.; m. Katherine Aldene Henning, May 8, 1960; children— Jeffrey, Gregory, Matthew, Kristin D.V.M., Kans. State U., 1959; MS, Cornell U., 1965, PhD, 1968. Instr. U. Minn.-St. Paul, 1959-60; asst. prof. pharmacology Coll. Vet. Medicine, Iowa State U., Ames, 1968-70, assoc. prof. pharmacology, 1970-75, prof. pharmacology, 1975—2001, chmn. dept. vet. physiology and pharmacology, 1982-90; prof. emeritus Coll. Vet. Medicine Iowa State U., 2001—. Served as capt. USAF, 1960-63, lt. col. Air N.G., 1971-91. Recipient Norden Disting. Tchr. award Iowa State U., 1981; NIH spl. research fellow Cornell U., 1967-68 Mem. AVMA, N.Y. Acad. Scis., Assn. Mil. Surgeons U.S., Sigma Xi Democrat. Lutheran.

AHRENS, KENT, museum director, art historian; b. Martinsburg, W.Va. s. Fred E. and Mary C. (Routzahn) A. AB, Dartmouth Coll., 1961; MA, U. Md., 1966; PhD, U. Del., 1972. Mem. faculty Fla. State U., Tallahassee, 1971-74, Randolph-Macon Woman's Coll., Lynchburg, Va., 1974-77; mem. curatorial staff Wadsworth Atheneum, Hartford, Conn., 1977-78; mem. faculty Georgetown U., Washington, 1979-82; dir. Everhart Mus., Scranton, Pa., 1982-90, Rockwell Mus., Corning, Y, 1990-95, Civic Fine Arts Ctr., Sioux Falls, SD, 1996-97, Kennedy Mus. of Art, Ohio U., Athens, 1997—2000; mus. cons., 2000—; dir. devel. Cmty. Action, Athens, 2002—06. Mem. task force on art activities Lynchburg Bicentennial Commn., 1975-76; project evaluator Md. Com. Humanities, 1980-82; adv. panel Lucan Ctr., Scranton, Pa., 1983-84; mus. adv. com. Pa. Hist. and Mus. Commn., 1984-86; trustee Williamstown (Mass.) Regional Art Conservation Lab., Inc., 1984-92; art mus. adv. panel Pa. Coun. on Arts, 1984-87; adv. panel Pa. Fedn. Mus. and Hist. Orgns., 1989-90; adv. com. on exhbns. at Pa. Gov.'s residence, 1987-90; juror Regional Art '89, Marywood Coll. Art Galleries, Scranton, 1989, Regional 1991, Arnot Art Mus., Elmira, 1991, Cmty. Cultural Ctr,. Brookings, SD, 1996; juror Fiber and Textile Exhibn. Civic Fine Arts Ctr., Sioux Falls, SD, 1996, Wilbur Stilwell Student Awards Exhibn., U. SD, Vermillion, 1997, Zanesville (Ohio) Art Ctr., 2000; adj. prof. Sch. Art, Ohio U., Athens, 1997-2000, percent for art com., 1997-99. Author: (with others) Rembrandt in the National Gallery of Art, 1969; author: The Drawings and Watercolors by Truman Seymour (1824-1891), Everhart Mus. 1986; co-author: Frederic C. Knight (1898-1979), Everhart Mus., 1987; author: The Oils and Watercolors by Edward D. Boit (1840-1915), Everhart Mus., 1990, Cyrus E. Dallin: His Small Bronzes and Plasters, Rockwell Mus., 1995, others; contbg. author: American Paintings and Sculpture: Illustrated Catalogue, Nat. Gallery of Art, 1970, Wadsworth Atheneum Paintings: The Netherlands and German-speaking Countries, 1978, Dictionary of Women Artists, 1997, Allgemeines Künsterlexikon, 1999—; author: Currier & Ives: Selection from the Nationwide Collection, Kennedy Mus. Art, 2000; Small Bronzes by Harriet W. Frishmuth, Kennedy Mus. of Art, 2001. Vol. Bosnia-Herzegovina Heritage Rescue, London, 1995-2001; trustee, bd. dirs. Bosnia-Herzegovina Heritage Rescue, Inc., USA, 2001-03; trustee Cmty. Shares of Mid Ohio, 2004-2005, v.p., 2005. 1st lt. US Army, 1962—64. Recipient grant-in-aid Am. Philos. Soc., 1975; Samuel H. Kress fellow Nat. Gallery of Art, 1968-69; Chester Dale fellow Nat. Gallery Art, 1970-71; NEH fellow, 1973-74, Mus. Mgmt. Inst., J. Paul Getty Trust, 1991, award for superior vol. svc. Am. Assn. Mus., 1999, award The Fund Raising Sch., Ctr. on Philanthropy, Ind. U., Indpls., 2004. Mem. Coll. Art Assn., Am. Assn. Mus. (on-site surveyor mus. assessment program 1984-89, 92—, accreditation com. 1986, 1990-2007), Mus. Assn. Pa. (chmn. 1984-90), Mid-Atlantic Assn. Mus., Ohio Assn. Non-profit Orgns.(peer rev., standards on excellence, 2005-06), Am. Vets., Rotary, Elks. Business E-Mail: kenta@frognet.net.

AIKEN, MICHAEL THOMAS, former academic administrator; b. El Dorado, Ark., Aug. 20, 1932; s. William Floyd and Mary (Gibbs) Aiken; m. Catherine Comet, Mar. 28, 1969; 1 child, Caroline R. BA, U. Miss., 1954; MA, U. Mich., 1955, PhD, 1964. Asst. prof. U. Wis., Madison, 1963—67, assoc. prof., 1967—70, prof., 1970—84, assoc. dean coll. arts and scis., 1980—82; prof. U. Pa., Phila., 1984—93, dean sch. arts and scis., 1985—87, provost, 1987—93; chancellor U. Ill., Urbana, 1993—2001, Champaign/Urbana, 1993—2001. Co-author: The Dynamics of Idealism, 1971, Economic Failure, Alienation, and Extremism, 1968; co-editor: Complex Organizations: Critical Perspectives, 1981, The Structures of Community Power, 1970. Mem.: Am. Sociol. Assn. (sec. 1986—89). Office Phone: 307-587-7506. E-mail: windymt22@aol.com.

AINSWORTH, JOHN HENRY, state legislator; b. Sept. 21, 1940; Grad. high sch. State assemblyman dist. 4 State of Wis., 1990-92, state assemblyman dist. 6, 1993—. Mem. agrl. adv. com. Wis. State Assmebly; dairy farmer. Mem. Shawano County Rep. Com. Mem. Shawano County Farm Bur. (former pres.). Republican. Office: W6382 Waukechon Rd Shawano WI 54166-7042

AINSWORTH, LOUIS LYNDE, lawyer, manufacturing executive; b. Moline, Ill., Aug. 31, 1947; s. Calvin and Elizabeth (Carney) A.; m. Susan H. Hopper, Mar. 22, 1969; children: Katherine E., Lucy A. BA summa cum laude, Seattle U., 1972; JD cum laude, William Mitchell Coll., St. Paul, 1977. Bar: Minn. 1977, U.S. Dist. Ct. Minn. 1977, U.S. Ct. Appeals (8th cir.) 1981. Assoc., ptnr. Wiese & Cox Ltd., Mpls., 1977-84; ptnr. Henson & Efron, P.A., Mpls., 1984-97; sr. v.p. and gen. counsel Pentair, Inc., St. Paul, 1997—, sec., 2002—. Office: Pentair Inc 5500 Wayzata Blvd Golden Valley MN 55416-1259

AITAY, VICTOR, concert violinist, music educator; b. Budapest, Hungary; came to U.S., 1946, naturalized, 1952; s. Sigmund and Irma (Fazekas) A.; m. Eva Vera Kellner; 1 child, Ava Georgianna. Pvt. studies with father; entered, Royal Acad. Music at age 7; studies with Bela Bartok, studies with Ernest von Dohnanyi, studies with Leo Weiner, studies with Zoltan Kodaly; artist diploma, Franz Liszt Royal Acad. Music, Budapest, 1939; DFA, Lake Forest Coll., 1986. Prof. 1st Internat. String Congress; prof. violin DePaul U., Chgo., 1962—. Organizer, leader Aitay String Quartet, European tour, recitals; also solo symphony orchs.; concertmaster Met. Opera Assn., N.Y.C., 948-54, Chgo. Symphony Orch., 1954—; leader Chgo. Symphony String Quartet; condr., music dir. Lake Forest (Ill.) Symphony Orch.; numerous performances Casals Festival by invitation of Pablo Casals. Office: Chgo Symphony Assn 220 S Michigan Ave Chicago IL 60604-2596

AKCASU, AHMET ZIYAEDDIN, nuclear engineer, educator; b. Aydin, Turkey, Aug. 26, 1924; s. Osman Nuri and Faika (Egel) Akcasu; m. Melahat Turksal, July 16, 1954; children: ur, Feza, Aydin. BS, MS, Tech. U. Istanbul, 1948; PhD, U. Mich., 1963. From asst. prof. to assoc. prof. Tech. U. Istanbul, 1948-58; resident research asso. Argonne (Ill.) Nat. Lab., 1959-61; mem. faculty U. Mich., Ann Arbor, 1963—, prof. nuc. engring., 1968-95, emeritus, 1995—. Co-author: Mathematical Methods in Nuclear Reactor Dynamics, 1971; contbr. articles to profl. jours. Recipient Glenn Murphy award, Am. Soc. Engring. Edn., 1986, Rsch. award for. Sr. U.S. Scientist, Alexander von Humboldt, 1991, Sci. award, Turkish Sci. and Tech. Rsch. Coun., 1992, Excellence in Rsch. award, U. Mich. Coll. Engring., 1995. Fellow: Am. Phys. Soc., Am. Nuc. Soc.; mem.: Turkish Phys. Soc., Sigma Xi. Home: 2820 Pebble Creek Dr Ann Arbor MI 48108-1728 Office: U Mich Dept Nuc Engring and Radiol Scis Ann Arbor MI 48109-2104 Office Phone: 734-764-5535. Business E-Mail: ziya@umich.edu.

AKEEL, HADI ABU, robotics executive; b. Cairo, Apr. 9, 1938; came to U.S., 1961; s. Kobaisi Aly Abu-Akeel and Zeinab Makhlouf; children: Shereef, Nezar; m. aglaa Mostafa. BS in Mech. Engring., Cairo U., 1959; MS in Applied Mechanics, UCLA, 1963; PhD in Mech. Engring., U. Calif., Berkeley, 1966. Cert. mfg. engr. Acting instr. U. Calif., Berkeley, 1963-66; analytical specialist Bendix Corp., South Bend, Ind., 1966-69; assoc. prof. Ain Shams U., Cairo, 1969-74; sr. staff engr. GM Mfg., Warren, Mich., 1974-76; program mgr. GM Corp., Warren, 1976-78; dept. head mfg. staff GM, Warren, 1978-80, chief engr. flexible automation systems, 1980-82; v.p., chief engr. GMFanuc Robotics Corp., Auburn Hills, Mich., 1982-92; sr. v.p. Fanuc U.S.A., 1992-96, also bd. dirs., vice chmn., 1992-98; gen. mgr. Berkeley Lab. Fanuc Am. Corp., Union City, Calif., 1992—2001; sr. v.p. Fanuc Robotics Am., Inc., 1996—99. Tech. advisor FANUC Ltd., Japan, 1992—; advisor Mgmt. of Tech. Program U. Calif., Berkeley, 1988-92; chmn. bd. dirs. Robotics Internat. of SME, Dearborn, Mich., 1992-93; pres. Amteng Corp., 1996—. Author: Machine Design, 1972; contbr. articles to profl. jours.; holds over 60 U.S. and fgn. patents. Soccer coach Am. Youth Soccer Orgn.; mem. bd. advisors Sch. Engring., U. Mich., Dearborn, 1991-2006; chmn. bd. visitors Sch. Engring., Oakland U., 1991-92. Recipient Joseph F. Engleberger award Robotic Industries Assn., 1989, Mich. Sci. Trailblazer award State Mich., 1989. Fellow ASME, Soc. Mfg. Engrs. (internat. dir. 1998-2003); mem. IEEE, Nat. Acad. Engring. Independent. Muslim. Avocations: tennis, swimming, camping, travel, machine shop. Office: Fanuc Robotics Corp 3900 W Hamlin Rd Rochester Hills MI 48309-3253 Home: 1735 Dell Rose Dr Bloomfield Hills MI 48302 Personal E-mail: majesticct-who@yahoo.com.

AKEMANN, DAVID R., lawyer; b. Elgin, Ill., Oct. 31, 1951; s. Theodore H. and Lois (Marr) A.; m. Vickie C. Skala, Aug. 5, 1978; children— Carrie, Julie, Collin. B.S., Brigham Young U., 1972; J.D., Lewis U., 1978. Bar: Ill. 1978, U.S. Dist. Ct. (no. dist.) Ill. 1978, U.S. Ct. Appeals (7th cir.) 1979, U.S. Supreme Ct. 1981. Clk. States Atty. Office, Kane County, Geneva, Ill., 1977-78; asst. states atty., 1978-79, chief civil divsn., 1979—87; sole practice, Elgin, 1978—92; elected states atty., 1992-2000; asst. atty. gen., 2000-03; Apptd. commnr. Ill. Industrial Commn., 2003. Recipient Am. Jurisprudence Constn. Law award

Lawyers Coop. Pub. Co., 1978. Mem. ABA, Ill. Bar Assn., Kane County Bar Assn., Ill. Pub. Employers Labor Relations Assn. (prin.). Methodist. Home: 420 Hoxie Ct Elgin IL 60123-3220 E-mail: dakemann@mail.state.il.us.

AKER, ALAN D., state legislator; Logging contractor, Rapid City, S.D.; senator Senate of S.D., Pierre, 1995-99; pres., homebuilder Aker Woods Co., Piedmont, S.D., 1999—. Mem. agr. and natural resources com., edn. and local govt. coms. S.D. State Senate.

AKERLOF, CARL WILLIAM, physics professor; b. New Haven, Mar. 5, 1938; s. Gosta Carl and Rosalie Clara (Hirschfelder) A.; m. Carol Irene Ruska, Sept. 4, 1965; children— Karen Louise, William Gustav BA, Yale U., 1960; PhD, Cornell U., 1967. Research assoc. U. Mich., Ann Arbor, 1966-68, asst. prof., 1968-72, assoc. prof., 1972-78, prof. physics, 1978—. Contbr. articles to profl. jours. Incorporator Ann Arbor Hands-On Mus. Fellow Am. Phys. Soc.; mem. Am. Astron. Soc. Office: U Mich Randall Lab Physics Dept Physics Ann Arbor MI 48109 Home Phone: 734-973-9579.

AKERS, MICHELLE ANNE, professional soccer player; b. Santa Clara, Calif., Feb. 1, 1966; m. Roby Stahl, Apr. 1990 (div. 1994). BS in Liberal Studies and Health, U. Ctrl. Fla., 1989. Forward Tyreso Football Club, Sweden, 1990, 1992, 1994, Orlando (Fla.) Calibre Soccer Club, 1993, US Women's Nat. Soccer Team, Chgo., 1985—2000; retired from US Nat. team on Aug. 24, 2000; founding player Women's United Soccer Assn., 2001. Author (with Tim Nash): Standing Fast; author: (with Judith A. Nelson) Face to Face; author: The Game and the Glory; columnist: Soccer Jr. mag., 1995—, Sidekicks mag., 1994—. Founder Soccer Outreach Internat., 1998. Named All-Am., Ctrl. Fla. Athlete of Yr., 1988—89, MVP, CONCACAF Qualifying Championship, 1994, U.S. Soccer Female Athlete of Yr., 1990, 1991, ESPN Athlete of Yr., 1985; recipient Hermann Trophy, Golden Boot award, FIFA Women's World Championship, 1991, Silver Ball award, 1991, Gold medal, Atlanta Olympics, 1996. Mem.: Women's Sports Found. (adv. bd. 1992—), U.S. Soccer Fedn. (nat. bd. dirs. 1990—95), Soccer Outreach Internat. (founder 1998). Office: US Soccer Fedn US Soccer House 1801 S Prairie Ave Chicago IL 60616-1319

AKIL, HUDA, neuroscientist, educator, researcher; b. Damascus, Syria, May 19, 1945; came to U.S., 1968; d. Fakher and Widad (Al-Imam) A.; m. Stanley Jack Watson Jr., Dec. 21, 1972; children: Brendon Omar, Kathleen Tamara. BA, Am. U., Beirut, Lebanon, 1966, MA, 1968; PhD, UCLA, 1972. Postdoctoral fellow Stanford U., Palo Alto, Calif., 1974-78; from asst. prof. to Disting. Univ. Prof. and Quarton Prof. Neurosciences, Dept. Psychiatry U. Mich., Ann Arbor, 1979—, co-dir., rsch. prof., Molecular and Behavioral Neuroscience Inst. Mem. adv. bd. Neurex Corp., Menlo Park, Calif., 1986—, Neurobiol. Techs., Inc., 1994-97; sec. Internat. Narcotics Rsch. Conf., 1990-94. Editor: (jour.) Pain and Headache: Neurochemistry of Pain, 1990; contbr. articles over 300 articles to profl. jours., 1971—2001. Recipient Pacesetter award Nat. Inst. Drug Abuse, 1993, Pasarow award Pasarow Found., 1994, Bristol-Myers Squibb award, 1998, Edward Sachar award Columbia U., 1998; Rockefeller scholar, Beirut, 1963-66; Alfred P. Sloan fellow, Stanford, Calif., 1974-78; grantee Nat. Inst. Drug Abuse, Washington, 1978—, NIMH, Washington, 1980—, Markey Found., U. Mich., 1988-97. Fellow Am. Acad. Arts & Scis., Am. Coll. europsychopharmacology (pres. 1997-98), U. Mich. Soc. Fellows; mem. Inst. Medicine (coun. mem. 2006), NAS, Soc.for Neuroscience (pres. 2002-03, Mika Salpeter Lifetime Achievement award, 2007). Achievements include first to produce physiological evidence for existence of naturally occurring opiate-like substances (endorphins) in brain; described phenomenon of stress-induced analgesia; described functions and regulation of endorphins in brain and pituitary gland; contributed to understanding of biological mechanisms of morphine tolerance and physical dependence; (with colleagues) cloned two main types of opiate receptors, described critical brain circuits relevant to stress and depression. Office: Univ Michigan Molecular & Behavioral Neuroscience Inst 4137 Undergraduate Research Bldg 205 Zina Pitcher Pl 2064 MBNI Bldg Ann Arbor MI 48109-0720 Office Phone: 734-763-3770. E-mail: akil@umich.edu.*

AKIN, TODD (WILLIAM TODD AKIN), congressman, former state legislator; b. NYC, July 5, 1947; m. Lulli Boe, 1971; 6 children. BS in Mgmt. Engring., Worcester Poly. Inst., Mass., 1971; MDiv, Covenant Theol. Sem., St. Louis, 1984. Mktg. mgr. IBM Computer Systems, 1973—77; corp. mgr. Laclede Steel Co., 1977—82; internat. mktg. educator, 1985—92; mem. Mo. State Ho. Reps. from Dist. 86, 1988—2001, US Congress from 2nd Mo. dist., 2001—. Mem. armed svcs. com. US Congress, mem. small bus. com., mem. sci. and tech. com., ranking mem. oversight & investigations subcommittee. Bd. dirs. Mission Gate Prison Ministry. Officer to 2nd lt. Army Combat Engrs. US Army, 1971—80. Recipient Award, Mfg. Legis. Excellence, NAM, 2003, Lawmaker award, Independent Elec. Contractors, Inc., 2004, Taxpayers' Friend award, Nat. Taxpayers Union, Hero of the Taxpayer award, Ams. for Tax Reform. Republican. Office: US House Reps 117 Cannon Ho Office Bldg Washington DC 20515-2502 Office Phone: 202-225-2561. Office Fax: 202-225-2563.

AKINS, CINDY S., human resources professional; BS, U. Ill.; MS in Labor and Indsl. Rels., Loyola U., Chgo. Various supervisory positions pub. sector; mgr. human resources Zurich Life Ins., Schaumburg, Ill.; dir. human resources Morningstar Inc., Chgo., from 1996, v.p. human resources. Mem. Am. Compensation Assn. (cert. compensation profl.). Office: Morningstar Inc 225 W Wacker Dr Chicago IL 60606-1224 Fax: 312-696-6001.

AKOS, FRANCIS, retired violinist, conductor; b. Budapest, Hungary, Mar. 30, 1922; came to U.S., 1954; s. Karoly and Rose (Reti) Weinberg; m. Phyllis Malvin Sommers, June 7, 1981; children from previous marriage: Katherine Elizabeth, Judith Margaret. Baccalaureate, Budapest, 1941; MA, Franz Liszt Acad. Music, Budapest, 1940, PhD, 1941. Concertmaster, Budapest Symphony Orch., 1945-46, Royal Opera and Philharmonic Soc., Budapest, 1947-48, Gothenburg (Sweden) Symphony Orch., 1948-50, Municipal Opera (now Deutsche Oper), West Berlin, Ger., 1950-54, Mpls. Symphony Orch., 1954, asst. concertmaster, Chgo. Symphony Orch., 1955—, ret., 2003, concertmaster emeritus, 1997-, also performed as soloist; performed at Salzburg Festival, 1948, Scandinavian Festival, Helsinki, Finland, 1950, Berlin Festival, 1951, Prades Festival, 1953, Bergen Festival, 1962, Vienna Festival, 1962, founder, condr., Chgo. Strings, chamber orch., 1961, condr., Fox River Valley Symphony, Aurora, Ill., 1965-73, Chicago Heights Symphony, Ill., 1975-79, Highland Park Strings, 1979—. Prizewinner Hubay competition, Budapest, 1939, Remenyi competition, Budapest, 1939 Personal E-mail: violak1310@yahoo.com.

AKRE, DONALD J., school system administrator; Supt. Selby (S.D.) Area Sch. Dist. State finalist Nat. Supt. Yr., 1992. Office: PO Box 222 Selby SD 57472-0222

ALAPONT, JOSÉ MARIA, automotive executive; b. Spain; Degree in Indsl. Engring., Tech. Sch. Valencia, Spain; degree in Philology, U. Valencia, Spain. With Ford Motor Corp., 1974—90; ops. dir. through group v.p. Valeo Group, 1990—97; exec. dir., through pres. internat. ops. Delphi Automotive Sys., 1997—2003; CEO, dir. IVECO S.p.A., Torino, Italy, 2003—05; chmn., pres., CEO Federal-Mogul Corp., Southfield, Mich., 2005—08, pres., CEO, 2008—. Office: Federal-Mogul Corp 26555 Northwestern Hwy Southfield MI 48034

ALBAIN, KATHY S., oncologist; b. Monroe, Mich., June 4, 1952; d. James Jay and Elizabeth G. (Jakscy) A. BS in Chemistry summa cum laude, Wheaton Coll., 1974; MD, U. Mich., 1978. Diplomate Am. Bd. Internal Medicine, Am. Bd. Oncology. Instr. physical diagnosis U. Mich. Med. Sch., 1978; intern U. Ill. Med. Ctr., Chgo., 1978-79, resident in internal medicine, 1979-81, clin. instr. medicine, 1980-81; instr. in medicine U. Ill. Hosps. and Clinics, 1980-81; fellow dept. medicine sect. hematology/oncology U. Chgo. Med. Ctr./U. Chgo. Hosps. and Clinics, 1981-84; asst. prof. medicine Loyola U. Chgo. Strich Sch. Medicine, 1984-91, assoc. prof. medicine divsn. hematology/oncology, prof. medicine, hematology/oncology; attending physician Hines (Ill.) VA Hosp., 1984—, Loyola U. Chgo. Foster G. McGaw Hosp., 1994—. Co-investigator multidisciplinary lung cancer staging and rsch. group U. Chgo. and Michael Reese Hosp. Med. Ctrs., 1982-84; coord. ann. breast cancer screening program Sr. Ctr. LaGrange, Ill., 1985-91; mem. med. adv. bd. Y-Me Nat. Breast Cancer Orgn., 1987—; co-dir. Multidisciplinary Breast Care Ctr. Loyola U. Med. Ctr., 1991—, dir. Multidisciplinary Lung Cancer Evaluation Ctr., 1994—; mem. oncology med. adv. bd. Eli Lilly and Co., 1993—; co-investigator nat. surg. adjuvant breast and bowel project U. Chgo., 1982-84; mem. breast cancer com., breast cancer working group, lung cancer com., lung cancer working group S.W. Oncology Group, 1986—, mem. gynecol. cancer com. and working group, 1989—, sarcoma and brain coms., 1990—, chair com. on women's health, 1992—; mem. intergroup lung cancer working cadre Nat. Cancer Inst., 1993—, mem. breast cancer intergroup com. on correlative scis. Nat. Cancer Inst., 1995, mem. breast cancer intergroup chairs com., 1994—; clin. trials co-chair Sec. of HHS Nat. Breast Cancer Action Plan, 1993-94; mem. adv. panel State of Ill. Breast and Cervical Cancer Rsch. Fund, 1994—; charter mem. adv. com. on rsch. in women's health NIH, 1995—; mem. Early Breast Cancer Trialists' Collaborative Group, 1995—; mem. clin. trials working group Sec. of Health Nat. Breast Cancer Action Plan, 1995—; mem. adv. bd. cancerandcareers.org; rschr., lectr., presenter in field. Reviewer jours. Cytometry, Breast Cancer Rsch. and Treatment, Cancer Rsch., Jour. Clin. Oncology, Cancer, Chest; contbr. articles to profl. publs. Mem. sr. choir Grace Luth. Ch., River Forest, Ill. Nat. Cancer Inst. fellowship tng. grantee, 1981-84, grantee Bristol-Myers, 1988-93, Squibb Mark Co., 1989, UpJohn Co., 1990, 92, Office Rsch. on Women's Health/Nat. Cancer Inst., 1992, 93-95, Nat. Cancer Inst., 1993—. Mem. ACP, Am. Assn. Cancer Rsch., Am. Fedn. Clin. Rsch., Am. Soc. Clin. Oncology, Internat. Assn. for Study of Lung Cancer, Christian Med. and Dental Soc. Avocations: classical music, travel, bicycling, reading, hiking, singing, exercise, pipe organ. Office: Loyola U Med Ctr Divsn Hematology/Oncology 2160 S 1st Ave Maywood IL 60153-3304

ALBANO, MICHAEL SANTO JOHN, lawyer; b. Bklyn., Jan. 13, 1944; s. Alexander Joseph and Josephine (Giannetto) A.; m. Grace Alma Hoelzel, Mar. 14, 1944; children: Christine Grace, Sarah Michelle. BA, U. Mo., Kansas City, 1965, JD, 1968. Bar: Mo. 1968, U.S. Dist. Ct. (we. dist.) Mo. 1968. From assoc. to shareholder Welch, Martin & Albano LLC, Independence, Mo., 1968—. Contbr. articles to profl. jours. Recipient Practitioner of Yr. award U. Mo. Kansas City Law Alumni, 2001, Presdl. Alumni Svc. citation U. Mo., Kansas City, 2003, Best Friend award U. Mo. Law Sch., Kansas City, 2006; named one of Top 100 Lawyers Mo. and Kans. Super Lawyers, 2007, Top 50 Family Law Attys. in Mo. and Kans., Top Family Law Attorney in Kansas City area Mo. Lawyer's Weekly, named Best of Best KC Bus. Jour.; scholar Tchrs. Assn., 1963-64, U. Mo., Kansas City, 1963-66. Mem. ABA (chmn. family law sect. 1984-85), Am. Acad. Matrimonial Lawyers (pres. 1993-94), Mo. Bar Assn.(Practitioner of Yr. 2004), Kansas City Bar Assn., Am. Coll. Family Trial Lawyers (diplomate, exec. com. 1994-2007), U. Mo. Kansas City All Alumni Assn. (pres. 2001-03), Phi Delta Phi. Democrat. Lutheran. Office: 311 W Kansas Ave Independence MO 64050-3715 Office Phone: 816-836-8000. E-mail: mjalbano@wmamlaw.com.

ALBER, JOHN I., lawyer; AB, Ind. U., Bloomington, 1974; JD, So. Ill. U., Edwardsville, 1979. Bar: Ill. 1979, Mo. 1979, US Dist. Ct., Ea. Dist. Mo. 1981. Assoc. to ptnr. Bryan Cave LLP, St. Louis, 1980—88, tech. ptnr., 1999—; CEO database, software company, 1988—99. Named one of Top 25 Chief Tech. Officers, InfoWorld mag., 2007. Office: Bryan Cave LLP One Metropolitan Square 211 North Broadway, Ste 3600 Saint Louis MO 63102 Office Phone: 314-259-2144. E-mail: jialber@bryancave.com.

ALBERS, JAMES WILSON, neurologist; b. Detroit, Oct. 28, 1943; s. James Milton and Willa Jean (Wilson) A.; m. Janet Mary Rakocy, May 10, 1968; children— Jeffrey, Matthew, Katherine, Elizabeth BS in E.E., U. Mich., 1965, MS, 1966, MS, 1968, PhD, 1970, MD, 1972. Diplomate Am. Bd. Neurology. Instr. neurology Mayo Clinic, Rochester, Minn., 1976; asst. prof. neurology Med. Coll. Wis., Milw., 1976-79; assoc. prof. neurology U. Mich., Ann Arbor, 1979-83, prof., 1983—, dir. neuromuscular program, 1979—. Contbr. articles to profl. jours. Recipient Henry W. Woltman award Neurology Dept. Mayo Clinic, 1978 Fellow Am. Acad. eurology; mem. Am. Assn. Electromyography and Electrodiagnosis (bd. dirs. 1984—), Mich. Neurologic Assn. (sec. treas. 1985—), Sigma Xi, Eta Kappa Nu, Tau Beta Pi Home: 3889 Waldenwood Dr Ann Arbor MI 48105-3006 Office: Univ Mich Med Ctr Dept Neurology B4952 CFOB Ann Arbor MI 48109

ALBERS, SHERYL KAY, state legislator; b. Sauk County, Wis., Sept. 9, 1954; d. Marcus J. and Norma Gumz; 1 child, Joel Albert. BA, Ripon Coll., 1976; JD, U. Wis., 2004. Mem. children and families com. Wis. State Assembly, chmn. property rights/land mgmt. com. Assembly Rep. Caucus Wis., 1987-91; mem. Local Emergency Planning Com. Juneau County; mem. Joint Com. on Fin., 1996-2000; mem. Sauey Foun. Scholarship Com. Recipient Campbell award Sauk County Rep. Com., 1981, 90, Top 10 County award Wis. State Rep. Party, 1982, Pacesetter award Wis. Forage Coun., 1983, Bovay award Rep. Party Wis., 1990; named one of Outstanding Farmers Sauk County Farm Bur., 1982. Mem. Sauk County Farm Bur. (dir., treas. 1977-82), Sauk County Hist. Soc., Agrl. Bus. Coun. Wis., Kiwanis. Republican. Office: Hazelbaker and Assoc SC 3240 University Ave Ste 3 Madison WI 53704 Office Phone: 608-266-8531. Business E-Mail: Rep.Albers@legis.state.wi.us.

ALBERT, DANIEL MYRON, ophthalmologist, educator; b. Newark, Dec. 19, 1936; s. Maurice I. and Flora Albert; m. Eleanor Kagle, June 26, 1960; children: B. Steven, Michael. BS, Franklin and Marshall Coll., Lancaster, Pa., 1958; MD, U. Pa., 1962; MA (hon.), Harvard U., Cambridge, Mass., 1976; D honoris causa, Louis Pasteur U., Strasbourg, 1992; MS, U. Wis., Madison, 1997. Diplomate Am. Bd. Ophthalmology. Intern Hosp. U. Pa., 1962-63, resident, 1963-66; surgeon USPHS, 1966-68; NIH spl. fellow in ophthalmic pathology Armed Forces Inst. Pathology, 1968-69; asst. prof. ophthalmology Yale U. Sch. Medicine, 1969-70, assoc. prof., 1970-75, prof., 1975-76; practice medicine specializing in ophthalmology; assoc. surgeon Mass. Eye and Ear Infirmary, 1976-86, surgeon, 1986-92, dir. David G. Cogan eye pathology lab., 1979-92; prof. ophthalmic pathology Harvard U. Med. Sch., 1976-84, David G. Cogan prof. ophthalmology, 1984-92; Frederick Allison Davis prof., dept. ophthalmology U. Wis., Madison, 1992—, chmn. dept. ophthalmology, 1992—2002, emeritus chmn., 2002—, Lorenz E. Zimmerman prof. dept. ophthalmology emeritus chmn., 1999—, dir. Eye Rsch. Inst., 2002—. Author: (with Scheie) A History of Ophthalmology at the University of Pennsylvania, 1965, Textbook of Ophthalmology, 8th edit. 1969, 9th edit. 1977; co-author: Jaegar's Atlas of Ophthalmology, 1972, (with Puliafito) Foundations of Ophthalmology, 1979, Men of Vision, 1993, (with Jakobiec) Atlas of Clinical Ophthalmology, 1996; editor: Archives of Ophthalmology, 1994—, (with Edwards) The History of Ophthalmology, 1996, John Jeffres' Lectures on the Diseases of the Eye, 1998, Ophthalmic Surgery: Principles and Techniques, 1998, A Physician's Guide to Health Care Management, 2002, (with Polans) Ocular Oncology, 2003, (with Lucarelli) Clinical Atlas of Procedures in Ophthalic Surgery, 2003; co-editor (with Jakobiec) Principles and Practice of Ophthalmology, 1994, 2d edit., 1999, A Physician's Guide to Healthcare Management, 2002, Dates in Ophthalmology, 2002, (with Lucarelli) Clinical Atlas of Procedures in Ophthalmic Surgery, 2003, (with Polans) Ocular Oncology, 2003, (with Miller, Azar, and Blodi) Albert & Jakobiec's Principles and Practice of Ophthalmology, 3rd edit., 2007; contbr. articles to profl. jours. Recipient Oliver Meml. medal, U. Pa., 1962, Friedenwald award, Assn. for Rsch. in Vision and Opthamology, 1981, Von Sallmann award in vision and ophthalmology, Internat. Conf. for Eye Rsch., 1988, award, Humboldt Found., 1991, MacKenzie medal, Scottish Ophthal. Soc., 1992, Lighthouse Pisart Vision award, The Lighthouse Inc., 1997, Lorenz E. Zimmerman (WARF) professorship, 1999, Disting. Alumni award, U. Pa. Sch. Medicine, 2001, Weisenfeld award, Fight for Sight, 2003; William and Mary Greve scholar, 1978—79, Alcon Rsch. Inst. scholar, 1984—85. Fellow ACS; mem. Am. Assn. Ophthalmic Pathology (Zimmerman medal 1993), Am. Acad. Ophthalmology (Jackson Meml. lectr. 1996), Am. Bd. Ophthalmology (dir. 1997-2005), Macula Soc. (W. Richard Green award 2003), Fight for Sight, New Eng. Ophthal. Soc. (Taylor Smith Gold medal 2004), Midwest Glaucoma Soc. (Albert C. Muse award 2006), Am. Ophthalmological Soc. (Howe medal 2007). Jewish. Home: 1106 Wellesley Rd Madison WI 53705-2230 Office: Univ Wis Sch Medicine and Pub Health Dept Ophthalmology K6/412 CSC 600 Highland Ave Madison WI 53792-4673 Office Phone: 608-263-9798.

ALBERTS, BARRY S., lawyer; b. Chgo., Feb. 2, 1946; s. Irving and Evelyn Alberts; m. Susan Weinstein, Apr. 28, 1974; 1 child, Jaime Eliana. BA cum laude, Miami U., 1968; JD, U. Chgo., 1971. Bar: Ill. 1971, US Dist. Ct. (no. dist.) Ill. 1971, US Ct. Appeals (7th cir.) 1989, US Ct. Appeals (6th cir.) 1996, US Ct. Appeals (2d cir.) 1997. Ptnr. Schiff Hardin LLP, Chgo. Adj. prof. law Northwestern U. Law Sch., Chgo., 1991—98, Chgo., 2003; lectr. law U. Chgo. Law Sch., 1995—2007. Contbr. articles to profl. jours. Mem. bd. dirs. Chgo. Children's Choir, 2002—07. Mem. Am. Law Inst. (hon.), ABA (co-chair ethics and professionalism sect. litig. 1998-2002, trial evidence com., 1995-98, task force ethical guidelines settlement negotiations 2001-2002), Acad. Laureates Ill. Lawyers (hon., bd. regents), Ill. State Bar Assn. (hon.), Chgo. Bar Assn., Chgo. Coun. Lawyers, Lincoln-Am. Inn of Ct., Phi Beta Kappa. Office: Schiff Hardin LLP 6600 Sears Tower Chicago IL 60606-6473 Home: 200 Dempster St Evanston IL 60202-1406 Office Phone: 312-258-5611. Business E-Mail: balberts@schiffhardin.com.

ALBERTY, WILLIAM EDWIN, lawyer; b. Quincy, Ill., Jan. 3, 1944; s. Edwin Harry and Elizabeth May (Barth) A.; m. Carol Ellen Pinion, June 27, 1970; children: Wade Dixson, Anne Elizabeth. BA, Culver-Stockton Coll., Canton, Mo.; JD, U. Mo., 1969. Bar: Mo. 1969. Asst. prosecutor Buchanan County Prosecutor's Office, St. Joseph, Mo., 1969-70; asst. city atty. City of St. Joseph, 1970-71; pvt. practice Edina, Mo., 1971-82; ptnr. Alberty & Deveny, Edina, 1982—. Avocation: golf.

ALBRECHT, CHRIS, talent agency executive, former broadcast executive; b. Queens, NY, July 24, 1952; BA in Dramatic Lit., Hofstra U., 1973. Co-owner Improvisation nightclub, NYC, 1975—80; talent mgmt. consultant ABC, NYC, 1975; talent agent Internat. Creative Mgmt., L.A., Calif., 1980—85; sr. v.p. original programming, West Coast Home Box Office, Inc. (HBO), L.A., Calif., 1985—90, pres. original programming NYC, 1995—2002, chmn., CEO, 2002—07, pres. HBO Independent Productions L.A., Calif., 1990—95; pres. IMG Global Media, Cleve., 2007—; spl. limited ptnr. Forstmann Little & Co., 2007—. Bd. dirs. Museum TV & Radio, 2003—. Recipient Television Showmanship award, Union Publicists, 2001. Mem.: Am. Film Inst. (bd. trustees). Office: IMG 1360 E 9th St Ste 100 Cleveland OH 44114*

ALBRECHT, RONALD FRANK, anesthesiologist; b. Chgo., Apr. 17, 1937; s. Frank William and Mabel Dorothy (Cassens) A.; children: Ronald Frank II, Mark Burchfield, Meredith Ann. AB, U. Ill., 1958, BS, 1959, MD, 1961. Diplomate Am. Bd. Anesthesiology. Intern U. Cin. Hosp., 1961-62; resident in anesthesiology U. Ill. Hosp., Chgo., 1962-64, attending physician, 1966-73, 89—, chief dept. anesthesiology, 1989—2007, pres. med. staff, 1999-2001; clin. assoc. NIH, Bethesda, Md., 1964-66; practice medicine specializing in anesthesiology Chgo., 1966—; asst. prof. anesthesiology U. Ill., Chgo., 1966-70, clin. assoc. prof., 1970-73, prof. anesthesiology, 1989—, head dept. Coll. Medicine, 1989—2007, chief dept. anesthesiology, 1989—2007. Chmn. dept. anesthesiology Michael Reese Med. Ctr., Chgo., 1971-2005; prof. anesthesiology U. Chgo., 1973-89. Contbr. articles to profl. jours. Served to lt. comdr. USPHS, 1964-66. Fellow Am. Coll. Anesthesiologists; mem. AMA, Internat. Anesthesia Rsch. Soc., Am. Soc. Anesthesiologists, Assn. Anesthesists Gt. Britain and Ireland, Am. Physiol. Soc., Soc. Acad. Anesthesiology Chairs, Assn. Anesthesiology Program Dirs. (pres. 1991-93), Ill. Soc. Anesthesiologists (pres. 1980-81), Ill. State Med. Soc., Chgo. Med. Soc., Chgo. Soc. Anesthesiologists (pres. 1986-90), Assn. Univ. Anesthesiologists. Presbyterian. Home: 1020 Chestnut Ave Wilmette IL 60091-1732 Office: U Ill Chgo Coll Medicine Dept Anesthesiology MC/515 1740 W Taylor St Ste 3200 Chicago IL 60612-7239 Home Phone: 847-256-1955; Office Phone: 312-996-4020. Business E-Mail: ralbrech@uic.edu.

ALBRECHT, THOMAS W., lawyer; b. Coral Gables, Fla., July 6, 1954; BA summa cum laude, U. Dayton, 1975; JD cum laude, U. Chgo., 1979. Bar: Ill. 1979. Ptnr. Sidley Austin Brown & Wood, Chgo., co-head, global securitization and structured fin. practice group, mng. ptnr. Chgo. office, and mem. mgmt. and exec. committees. Contbr. articles to profl. journals. Recipient Hinton Moot Ct. Cup. Mem. ABA, Chgo. Bar Assn., Am. Coll. of Comml. Fin. Lawyers, Order Coif. Office: Sidley Austin Brown & Wood LLP Bank One Plz 10 S Dearborn St Chicago IL 60603 Office Phone: 312-853-7213. Office Fax: 312-853-7036. Business E-Mail: talbrecht@sidley.com.

ALBRECHT, WILLIAM PRICE, economist, educator, government official; b. Pitts., Jan. 7, 1935; s. William Price and Jane Lanier (Moses) A.; m. Alice Annette Cooper, June 14, 1956 (div. Nov. 1975); children— William, Alison, Jonathan, Jeffrey; m. Fran Jaecques, July 4, 1976 AB, Princeton U., 1956; MA, U. S.C., 1962, Yale U., 1963, PhD, 1965. Asst. prof. U. Iowa, Iowa City, 1965-70, assoc. prof., 1970-82, prof. econs., 1982-88, assoc. dean Coll. Bus. Adminstrn., 1984-88; self-employed antitrust cons., 1978-88; commr. Commodity Futures Trading Commn., Washington, 1988-93; prof. econs. U. Iowa, Iowa City, 1993—, dir. Inst. for Internat. Bus., 1998—2003, Justice prof. Internat. Bus., 2000—. TV fin. advisor. Author: Economics, 1974, 4th edit., 1986, Black Employment, 1970, Microeconomic Principles, 1979, Macroeconomic Principles, 1979 Candidate U.S. Ho. of Reps., 1970; legis. asst. U.S. Senator Dick Clark, 1974; mem. nat. adv. coun. US Small Bus. Adminstrn., 2003—. Served to lt. USN, 1956-61. Mem. Am. Econ. Assn., Midwest Econ. Assn. (v.p. 1981-82). Avocations: tennis, farming. Home: 5770 NE Morse Rd Solon IA 52333-8806 Office: U Iowa Dept Econs Iowa City IA 52242 Office Phone: 319-335-3125. Business E-Mail: william-albrecht@uiowa.edu.

ALBRIGHT, CHRISTINE L., lawyer; b. June 21, 1951; BA with high distinction, U. Mich., 1973, JD magna cum laude, 1976. Bar: Ill. 1976, U.S. Dist. Ct. Ill. (no. dist.) 1976, Fla. 1985. Ptnr. Winston & Strawn LLP, Chgo., 1993—, head trusts and estates dept. Adj. prof. Northwestern U.; mem. charitable advisory coun. Ill. Atty. Gen.; mem. Estate Planning Coun., Chgo. Past dir. YWCA Met. Chgo. Fellow: Am. Coll. Trust and Estate Counsel (regent); mem.: ABA (chair real property, probate and trust law sects.), Fla. Bar Assn., DC Bar Assn., Chgo. Bar Assn. (past chair trust law com.), Order of Coif. Office: Winston & Strawn LLP 35 W Wacker Dr Chicago IL 60601-9703 Office Phone: 312-558-5585. Office Fax: 312-558-5700. Business E-Mail: calbrigh@winston.com.

ALBRIGHT, JACK LAWRENCE, animal science and veterinary educator; b. San Francisco, Mar. 14, 1930; s. George Clarence and Elizabeth Ann (Murphy) A.; m. Lorraine Aylmer Hughes, Aug. 17, 1957; children: Maryann A. Williams, Amy Elizabeth Schalk. BS with honors, Calif. State Poly. U., 1952; MS, Wash. State U., 1954, PhD, 1957. Rsch. asst. Wash. State U., 1952-54, 55-57, acting instr., 1954-55; instr. Calif. State Poly. U., 1955, 57-59; asst. prof. U. Ill., Urbana, 1959-63; assoc. prof. Purdue U., West Lafayette, Ind., 1963-66, prof. animal sci. Sch. Agr., 1966-96, prof. animal mgmt. and behavior Sch. Vet. Medicine, 1974-96, prof. emeritus animal sci. and vet. medicine, 1996—. Mem. Ctr. Applied Ethology and Human-Animal Interactions, Human/Animal Bond Purdue U., 1982-96, Purdue Interdisciplinary Undergrad. Program in Animal Welfare and Societal Concerns, 1992-96, Purdue Animal Care and Use com., 1989-92, Ctr. for Rsch. on Livestock Behavior and Well-Being in Food Animals, 1992-96; vis. prof. U. Ariz., Tucson, 1995, N.Mex. State U., Las Cruces, 1995, U. Ill., Urbana, 1988-89; vis. prof. pure and applied zoology U. Reading, Eng., 1977-78; vis. scientist N.Z. Dept. Agr., Ruakura, Hamilton, 1971-72, Dairy Shrine, Ft. Atkinson, Wis., 1958—; cons., lectr. in field, animal mgmt., behavior, care and welfare; mem. Ind. Commn. Farm Animal Care, 1981-99; numerous invited lectures worldwide. Author more than 900 papers, revs., chpts., guidelines, and books; reviewer sci. jours. Vestryman St. John's Episcopal Ch., Lafayette, Ind., 1979-82; bellringer Salvation Army, 1964—; mem. judging teams Cal Poly Dairy Cattle, Dairy Products and Livestock; vol. Ind. Livestock Care Assistance Project Helpline, 1999—, Heifer Project Internat., Hoofed Animal Humane Soc. Fulbright scholar, N.Z., 1971-72; NSF Animal Behavior grantee, summer 1964; USDA/FAS/ICD Sci. and Tech. Exch. Program awardee to Rep. of Ireland, 1994; recipient Guardian award Ind. Vet. Med. Assn., 1995, Sci., Edn. and Tech. award dept. animal scis. Washington State U., 1996; one of 7 named to inaugural Renaissance Acad. Hall of Fame, Paso Robles H.S., 1998. Fellow AAAS, Am. Dairy Sci. Assn., Ind. Acad. Sci.; mem. Am. Dairy Sci. Assn. (sec. 1972-73, chmn. profl. coun. 1973-74, Dairy Mgmt. Rsch. award 1986, invited lectrs. ann. meeting, 1982, 86-87, 92, 94, found. charter 1992), Animal Behavior Soc. (charter), Am. Soc. Animal Sci. (chmn. animal behavior com. 1970, 76, 85, Animal Mgmt. Rsch. award 1988, Found. charter 1993, animal care com. 1994-96), Am. Registry Profl. Animal Sci. (dairy and animal behavior 1993—), Humane Slaughter Assn., Am. Coll. Animal Behavior Sci. (cert., charter, diplomate 1995), Am. Soc. Vet. Ethology (charter), Internat. Soc. Applied Ethology, Chillingham Wild Cattle Assn. (life), Soc. Study Ethics and Animals, Scientist's Ctr. Animal Welfare (corr.), Univs. Fedn. for Animal Welfare, Hooved Animal Humane Soc., Los Lecheros Dairy Club Calif. State Poly. U. (hon.), Kiwanis (pres. Lafayette Noon club 1969-70, bd. dirs. 1971-75, 2004—, treas. found. 1971-75, sec. found. 1976-77, Tablet of Honor Internat. Kiwanis Found. 2000), Blue Key, Delta Soc., Sigma Xi, Alpha Zeta, Gamma Sigma Delta, Farm House. Home: 188 Blueberry Ln West Lafayette IN 47906-4810 Office: Purdue Univ Poul Bldg Dept Animal Scis West Lafayette IN 47907-1026 Personal E-mail: jackalbrig@aol.com.

ALBRIGHT, LYLE FREDERICK, chemical engineering educator; b. Bay City, Mich., May 3, 1921; s. William Edward and Isabella (Sidebotham) A.; m. Jeanette Van Belle, Mar. 4, 1950; children: Christine, Diane. BS in Chem. Engring, U. Mich., 1943, MS in Chem. Engring, 1944, PhD in Chem. Engring, 1950. Lab. technician Dow Chem. Co., Midland, Mich., 1939-41; chem. engr. Manhattan Project E.I. duPont de Nemours & Co., Hanford, Wash., 1944-46; research chem. engr. Colgate-Palmolive Co., Jersey City, 1950-51; asst. prof. U. Okla., Norman, 1951-54, assoc. prof., 1954-55, Purdue U., West Lafayette, Ind., 1955-58, prof. chem. engring., 1958—. Cons. to numerous chem. petroleum cos., 1960— Author: Industrial and Laboratory Pyrolyses, 1976, Industrial and Laboratory Alkylations, 1977, Coke Formation on Metals, 1982, Pyrolysis: Theory and Industrial Practice, 1983, Processes for Major Addition Type Plastics and Their Monomers, 2d edit., 1985, ovel Production Methods for Ethylene, Light Hydrocarbons, and Aromatics, 1992, Nitrations: Recent Laboratory and Industrial Developments, 1996, Albright's Chemical Engineering Handbook, 2008. Recipient Shreve prize Purdue U., 1960, 70, 88, Potter award for best instr. Schs. of Engring. Purdue U., 1988. Fellow AIChE (dir. 1982-84, Van Antwerpen award 2003); mem. Am. Chem. Soc., Internat. Brotherhood Magicians, Sigma Xi, Tau Beta Pi. Methodist. Home: 4750N N 250 W West Lafayette IN 47906-5525 Office: Purdue Univ Sch Chem Engring West Lafayette IN 47907 Office Phone: 765-494-4087. E-mail: albright@ecn.purdue.edu.

ALBRIGHT, TERRILL D., lawyer; b. Lebanon, Ind., June 23, 1938; s. David Henry and Georgia Pauline (Doty) A.; m. Judith Ann Stoelting, June 2, 1962; children: Robert T., Elizabeth A. AB, Ind. U., 1960, JD, 1965. Bar: Ind. 1965, US Dist. Ct. (so. dist.) Ind. 1965, US Dist. Ct. (no. dist.) Ind. 1980, US Ct. Appeals (7th cir.) 1981, US Ct. Appeals (3d and DC cirs.) 1982, US Supreme Ct. 1972; cert. arbitrator for large complex cse program constrn. and internat. comml. cases; cert. mediator; on constrn. master arbitrator roster, Am. Arbitration Assn. Assoc. Baker and Daniels Law Firm, Indpls., 1965-72, ptnr., 1972—. Mem. panel of disting. neutrals. nat. panel for constrn. and regional comml. panel CPR Inst. for Dispute Resolution, NYC. Pres. Christamore House, Indpls., 1979-86; bd. dirs. Greater Indpls. YMCA, 1980-82; chmn. Jordan YMCA, Indpls., 1982; pres. Community Ctrs. Indpls., 1987-90. 1st lt. US Army, 1960—62. amed Disting. Barrister, Ind. Lawyer, 2006. Fellow: Acad. Law Alumni, Ind. U. Sch. of Law (bd. dirs. 1974—80, pres. 1979—80), Am. Coll. Trial Lawyers, Ind. Bar Found, Indpls. Bar Found., Am. Bar Found.; mem.: Am. Arbitration Assn., Ind. State Bar Assn. (chmn. young lawyers sect. 1971—72, rep. 11th dist. 1983—85, bd. dirs., v.p. 1991—92, pres.-elect 1992—93, pres. 1993—94), Nat. Conf. Bar. Pres. (exec. coun. 1995—98). Democrat. Office: Baker & Daniels 300 Meridian St Ste 2700 Indianapolis IN 46204-1782 Office Phone: 317-237-1262. Business E-Mail: terry.albright@bakerd.com.

ALDAG, RAMON JOHN, management and organization educator; b. Beccles, Suffolk, Eng., Feb. 11, 1945; came to U.S., 1947; s. Melvin Frederick and Joyce Evelyn (Butcher) A.; children: Elizabeth, Katherine BS, Mich. State U., 1966, MBA, 1968, PhD, 1974. Thermal engr. Bendix Aerospace divsn., Ann Arbor, Mich., 1968—70; tchg. asst., instr. Mich. State U., East Lansing, 1968—73; asst. prof. mgmt. U. Wis., Madison, 1973—78, assoc. prof., 1978—82, prof. mgmt. and orgn., 1982—, chmn. dept. mgmt., 1986—88, assoc. dir. Indsl. Rels. Rsch. Inst., 1977—83, co-dir. Ctr. for Study of Orgnl. Performance, 1982—, faculty senator, 1980—84, Pyle Bascom prof. leadership, 1982—, student advisor, 1979—, Glen A. Skillrud Family chair in bus., 2001—, chmn. dept. mgmt. and human resources Sch. Bus., 1995—, co-dir. Weinert Ctr. for Entrepreneurship, 2000—, exec. dir. Weinert Ctr. Entrepreneurship, 2002—. Mgmt. cons. various businesses and industries, 1973-Author: Task Design and Employee Motivation, 1979, Managing Organizational Behavior, 1981, Introduction to Business, 1984, (now titled Business in a Changing World), 3d edit., 1993, 4th edit., 1996, Management, 1987, 2d edit., 1991, Leadership and Vision, 2000, Organizational Behavior and Management, 2002, Mastering Management Skills, 2005; contbr. articles to profl. jours.; cons. editor for mgmt. South-Western Pub. Co., 1987—; assoc. editor Jour. Bus. Rsch., 1988—, Decision Scis., 2002-; essays co-editor Jour. Mgmt. Inquiry. Bd. dirs. Family Enhancement Program, Madison Grantee U. Wis., HEW, 1975-85; recipient Adminstrv. Rsch. Inst. award, 1976, Jerred Disting. Svc. award, 1993, NSF, 2000—; U. Wis. faculty rsch. fellow, 1985-88 Fellow. Acad. of Mgmt. (divsn. chmn. 1971—, bd. govs. 1986—, v.p. and program chair 1989—, pres. elect 1990, pres. 1991, past pres. 1992—, dep. dean 2003-05, dean 2005—, recipient Disting Svc. award, 1995); mem. Midwest Acad. Mgmt. (pres. 1973-), Decision Scis. Inst. (track chmn. 1975-), Indsl. Rels. Rsch. Assn. (elections commn. 1980—), Found. Administrn. Rsch. (pres. 1992—), Pi Tau Sigma, Tau Beta Pi, Sigma Iota Epsilon, Beta Gamma Sigma, Alpha Iota Delta Avocations: bicycling, gardening, reading, fishing. Office: U Wis 3112 Grainger Hall 975 University Ave Madison WI 53706-1323 Home: 19 Halite Way Madison WI 53711 Office Phone: 608-263-3771. Business E-Mail: raldag@bus.wisc.edu.

ALDERMAN, AMY KATHLEEN, plastic surgeon, educator; b. Apr. 27, 1970; BA in Sociology, Birmingham-So. Coll., Ala., 1992; MD with honors, U. Ala. Sch. Medicine, Birmingham, 1996; MPH, U. Mich. Sch. Pub. Health, Ann Arbor, 2001. Lic. Mich., 1996, cert. Am. Bd. Plastic Surgery, 2005. Postdoctoral tng., clin. tng., plastic surgery integrated resident U. Mich., 1996—2000, 2002—04; rsch. tng., Robert Wood Johnson Clin. Scholar U. Mich. Sch. Medicine, 2000—02; asst. prof., dept. surgery, sect. plastic surgery U. Mich., Ann Arbor, 2004—; practicing plastic surgeon, health svcs. researcher U. Mich. Health Sys.; asst. prof., rsch. investigator Ann Arbor Veterans Adminstrn. Health Svcs. R&D. Fellow: ACS; mem.: Am. Soc. Plastic Surgeons (candidate), Alpha Omega Alpha Soc. Office: 2130 Taubman Ctr 1500 E Medical Center Dr Ann Arbor MI 48109-0340 Office Phone: 734-998-6022. Office Fax: 734-763-5354.*

ALDERMAN, ROBERT K., state legislator; b. Nov. 14, 1942; m. Susan M. Toycen. Student, Ind. U. Ind. state rep. Dist. 19, 1976-91, Dist. 83, 1991—; chmn. housing aged and aging com. Ind. Ho. Reps., Vet. Affairs com., pub. safety com., human affairs and interstate coop. coms., ranking minority mem., pub. policy com., ethics com., rules and legis. procedures com., local govt. com. Capt. Allen County Police Dept., Ft. Wayne. With U.S. Army Nat. Guard. Recipient Acad. Achievement award Ind. Law Enforcement Acad., 1971; named Top 10 Legislators Am. Nat. Assembly Govt. Employee, 1983. Republican. Home: 5715 Kroemer Rd Fort Wayne IN 46818-9328

ALDINGER, WILLIAM F., III, diversified financial services company executive; b. 1947; BA, CUNY, 1969. With U.S. Trust Co., NYC, 1969-75, Citibank Corp., NYC, 1975-76; exec. v.p. Wells Fargo Bank NA, San Francisco, 1986-98; CEO HSBC N. Am. Inc. (Formerly Household Internat., Inc.), Prospect Heights, Ill., 1994—, chmn. bd. dirs., 1996—. Office: HSBC N America Inc 2700 Sanders Rd Prospect Heights IL 60070-2701

ALDRICH, ANN, judge; b. Providence, June 28, 1927; d. Allie C. and Ethel M. (Carrier) A.; m. Chester Aldrich, 1960 (dec.); children: Martin, William; children by previous marriage: James, Allen; m. John H. McAllister III, 1986 (dec. May, 2004). BA cum laude, Columbia U., 1948; LLB cum laude, NYU, 1950, LLM, 1964, JSD, 1967. Bar: DC, NY 1952, Conn. 1966, Ohio 1973, US Supreme Ct. 1956. Rsch. asst. to mem. faculty NYU Sch. Law; atty. IBRD, 1952; atty., rsch. asst. Samuel Nakasian, Esq., Washington, 1952—53; gen. counsel's staff FCC, Washington, 1953—60; US del. to Internat. Radio Conf., Geneva, 1959; practicing atty. Darien, Conn., 1961—68; assoc. prof. law Cleve. State U., 1968—71, prof., 1971—80; judge US Dist. Ct. (no. dist.) Ohio, Cleve., 1980—. Instrn. com. Sixth Cir. Pattern Criminal Jury, 1986—. Mem. Fed. Bar Assn., Nat. Assn. of Women Judges, Fed. Communications Bar Assn., Fed. Judge Assn. Episcopalian. Office: US District Court Ste 17B 801 W Superior Ave Cleveland OH 44113-1829 Home Phone: 216-761-1112; Office Phone: 216-357-7200. Business E-Mail: ann_aldrich@ohnd.uscourts.gov.

ALDRIDGE, DONALD O'NEAL, military officer; b. Solo., Mo., July 22, 1932; BA in History, U. Nebr., Omaha, 1974; postgrad., Creighton U., 1975. Commd. 2d lt. USAF, 1958, advanced through grades to lt. gen., 1988, asst. dir. plans Washington, 1978-79; spl. asst. to dir. Joinr Chiefs of Staff, Washington, 1979-80; dep. dir. Def. Mapping Agy., Washington, 1980-81; dep. U.S. rep. NATO Mil. Com., Brussels, 1981-83; rep. Joint Chiefs of Staff, Geneva, 1983-86; comdr. 1st Strat. Aerospace Divsn. USAF, Vanderberg AFB, Calif., 1986-88, vice-CINC Strategic Air Command Offutt AFB, Nebr., 1988—91; mgmt. cons. Sacramento, 1991—. Chmn. bd. dir. Octus, Inc., 1995—98, Ceracon, Inc., 1996—2005. Office Phone: 402-293-0543. Personal E-mail: daldridge@cox.net.

ALDRIDGE, SANDRA, civic volunteer; b. Iowa, Apr. 22, 1939; d. Maurice D. and Maureen M. (Bennett) Anderson; m. Guy E. Seymour, Jan. 8, 1960 (div. Oct. 1966); m. Victor E. Aldridge, Jr., Nov. 11, 1970 (dec. May 1995); 1 child, Victor E. III. Student, Millikin U., Decatur, Ill., 1957—58. Pres. Crawford Sch. PTA, 1976-78, Terre Haute Lawyers Aux., 1979; pres., dir. Wabash Valley Assn. for Gifted and Talented Children, 1981-83, Vigo County Task Force for Alcohol and Drug Abuse, 1983-84; treas., dir. Union Hosp. Svc. League; bd. dirs. YWCA Terre Haute, Inc., 1987-89; v.p., fin. chair, mem. exec. coun. Wabash Valley coun. Boy Scouts Am., Inc.; active Vigo County Tax Adjustment Bd., 1986-88, Class IX Leadership Terre Haute, 1985; bd. trustees Vigo County Sch. Corp., Terre Haute, 1985-97, v.p., 1992-93, 96; sec. Ernie Pyle Chpt., Ret. Officers Assn., 1998-2006; active Children's Theatre, United Way Wabash Valley Mem. Ind. Assn. Gifted Children, Swope Art Gallery, Vigo County Hist. Soc., Women's Dept. Club, Arts Illiana, Elks Women's Golf League Episcopalian. Home: 2929 Winthrop Rd Terre Haute IN 47802-3443

ALEXA, WILLIAM E., state legislator; b. June 20, 1941; m. Joyce Ann Alexa. JD, Valparaiso U. Atty. Valparaiso Planning Commn. and Bd. Zoning Appeals, 1974; dep. and chief prosecuting atty. Porter County, 1975-79; pres. Valparaiso Park Bd.; mem. Ind. Senate from 5th dist., 1988—2002; criminal and civil procedures and fin. coms.; ranking minority mem., judiciary and pub. policy coms.; judge Porter Superior Ct. II, 2002—; chair Criminal Law Study Commn. Bd. dirs. Porter county Assn. for Retarded Citizens, 1975-76; past pres. Valparaiso Park Bd.; mem. Thunderhouse Campus Ministry Ctr.; mem. United Way Budget and Allocation Com. Mem. Valparaiso Univ. Law Alumnae Assn., Porter County and Ind. State Bar Assn., Valparaiso C. of C. Democrat. Home: 337 Deerfield Rd Valparaiso IN 46383-6954

ALEXANDER, ANTHONY J., electric power industry executive; m. Becky Alexander; 4 children. BS, U. Akron, 1972, JD, 1975. Bar: Ohio 1976. Sr. tax acct. Ohio Edison Co., Akron, 1972-76, atty., 1976-83, sr. atty., 1984-87, assoc. gen. counsel, 1987-89, sr. v.p., gen. counsel, 1898-91; exec. v.p., gen. counsel Ohio Edison Co. (merged with Centerior Energy to form FirstEnergy), Akron, 1996—97, FirstEnergy Corp., Akron, 1997—2000, pres., 2000—, COO, 2001—04, CEO, 2004—. Bd. dir. Ohio Electric Utility Inst., Assn. of Edison Illuminating Companies, Inc; bd. dir., mem. exec. com. Nuclear Energy Inst. Bd. trustees Akron Gen. Health System, The NEOUCOM Found., Playhouse Square Found., Green Schools Found., U. Akron Found.; vice chmn. Greater Akron Chamber. Recipient Dr. Frank L. Simonetti Dist. Bus. Alumni award, U. Akron. Mem.: Nat. Assn. of Manufacturers (dir.-at-large). Office: FirstEnergy Corp 76 S Main St 18th Fl Akron OH 44308-1812

ALEXANDER, BUZZ (WILLIAM), literature and language professor; BA, Harvard U., PhD, 1967; BA, U. Cambridge. Prof. English and lit. U. Mich., Ann Arbor, 1971—, Arthur F. Thurnau prof., 2003—, founder Prison Creative Arts Project. Contbr. articles to profl. jours. Recipient US Professors of Yr. Award for Outstanding Doctoral and Rsch. Universities Prof., Carnegie Found. for Advancement of Tchg. and Coun. for Advancement and Support of Edn., 2005. Office: U Mich Dept English 435 S State St 3187 Angell Hall Ann Arbor MI 48109-1003 Office Phone: 734-764-2393. E-mail: alexi@umich.edu.

ALEXANDER, JAMES WESLEY, surgeon, educator; b. El Dorado, Kans., May 23, 1934; s. Rossiter Wells and Merle Lydia Alexander; m. Maureen L. Strohofer; children: Joseph, Judith, Elizabeth, Randolph, John Charles, Lori, Molly. Student, Tex. Technol. Coll., 1951-53; MD, U. Tex., 1957; ScD, U. Cin., 1958-64; postgrad., U. Minn., 1966-67. Diplomate Am. Bd. Surgery, Am. Bd. Thoracic Surgery, lic. physician Ohio. Intern Cin. Gen. Hosp., 1957-58; resident U. Cin.-Cin. Gen. Hosp., 1958-64; mem. faculty Coll. Medicine, U. Cin., 1962-64, 66—, prof. surgery, 1975—, dir. transplantation div., dept. surgery, 1967-99, dir. surg. immunology lab., 1967—2000; dir. research Shriners Burns Inst., 1979-90; practice medicine and surgery Cin., 1966—; dir. Ctr. for Surg. Weight Loss, 2001—. Mem. staff U. Cin. Hosp., Christ Hosp., Good Samaritan Hosp., Jewish Hosp.; mem. study sect. NIH, 1983—87, 1989—93, chmn, 1990—93, mem. ad hoc com., 1990—. Author (with R.A. Good): (immuno biology for surgeons) Fundamentals of Clinical Immunology, 1977; mem. editl. bd. Annals of Surgery, 1975—, Jour. Burn Care and Rehab., 1979—99, Burns, Including Thermal Injury, 1985—98, Graft, 1998—, Jour. Parenteral and Enteral Nutrition, 1991—99, Nutrition, 1991—2000, Transplantation Sci., 1991—94, (transplantation), 1994—98, Jour. Trauma, 1998—2005, (stock), 1994—2000; contbr. more than 670 articles to sci. jours. Capt. M.C. US Army, 1964—66. Mem.: ACS, AAAS, Am. Soc. Metabolic and Bariatric Surgeons, Mont Reid Surg. Soc., Shock Soc., Transplantation Soc., Surg. Infection Soc. (sec. 1981—84, pres.-elect 1985—86, pres. 1986—87), Soc. Univ. Surgeons, Ohio State Med. Assn., St. Paul Surg. Soc., Internat. Soc. Surgery, Halsted Soc., Am. Surg. Assn., Am. Soc. Parenteral and Enteral Nutrition, Am. Soc. Transplant Surgeons (sec. 1985—87, pres.-elect 1987—88, pres. 1988—89), Am. Burn Assn. (pres.-elect 1983—84, pres. 1984—85), Am. Assn. for Surgery of Trauma, Peruvian Acad. Surgery (hon.), Colombian Coll. Surgeons (hon.), Surg. Biology Club, Phi Eta Sigma, Alpha Epsilon Delta, Alpha Chi, Alpha Omega Alpha. Home: 757 Riverwatch Dr Crescent Springs KY 41017-4480 Office: 2123 Auburn Ave Ste 315 Cincinnati OH 45219 Office Phone: 513-558-6006, 513-585-2434. Business E-Mail: jwesley.alexander@uc.edu.

ALEXANDER, JEFFREY, performing company executive; Grad., New Eng. Conservatory of Music, Boston. Gen. mgr. Grapa Concerts, U.S.A., New York, 1980-82, Laredo Philharm. Orch., Laredo, Tex., 1982-84; dir. Cin. Symphony Orch., 1984-88, mgr., 1988-93, gen. mgr., 1993—; also gen. mgr. Cin. May Festival. Office: Cincinnati Symphony Orch 1241 Elm St Cincinnati OH 45210-2231

ALEXANDER, JOHN THORNDIKE, historian, educator; b. Cooperstown, NY, Jan. 18, 1940; s. Edward Porter and Alice Wagner (Bolton) A.; m. Maria Kovalak Hreha, June 13, 1964; children— Michal Porter, Darya Ann BA, Wesleyan U., Middletown, Conn., 1961; cert. regional specialization Russian Inst., Ind. U., 1963, MA, 1963, PhD, 1966. Asst. prof. U. Kans., Lawrence, 1966-70, assoc. prof., 1970-74, prof. history, 1974—. Fellow Inter-Univ. Com. on Travel Grants, 1964-65, Internat. Research and Exchanges Bd., 1971, 75, 96. Author: Autocratic Politics, 1969, Emperor of the Cossacks, 1973, Bubonic Plague in Russia, 1980, 2003, Catherine the Great, 1989 (Byron Caldwell Smith award for best book by a Kans. author pub. in 1987-88), reissued luxury edit., 1999; translator, editor: Platonov, Time of Troubles, 1970, Anisimov, Reforms of Peter the Great, 1993, Anisimov, Empress Elisabeth, 1995. Recipient Balfour Jeffrey Higuchi Endowment Rsch. Achievement award, 1992. Mem. Am. Assn. for Advancement Slavic Studies, Brit. Study Group on 18th Century Russia, So. Conf. on Slavic Studies (ann. sr. scholar award 2001). Democrat. Roman Catholic. Avocation: sports. Home: 2216 Orchard Ln Lawrence KS 66049-2706 Office: U Kans Dept History Wescoe Hall Rm 3001 1445 Jayhawk Blvd Lawrence KS 66045-7590 E-mail: jatalex@ku.edu.

ALEXANDER, KAREN, museum staff member; m. Walter Alexander. Vice chmn. bd. trustees Art Inst. Chgo., vol. Dept. European Decorative Arts and Sculpture and Ancient Art. Office: Art Inst Chgo 111 S Michigan Ave Chicago IL 60603

ALEXANDER, MARTHA SUE, retired librarian; b. Washington, June 8, 1945; d. Lyle Thomas and Helen (Goodwin) Alexander; m. David Henry Bowman, June 11, 1965 (div. 1982); 1 child, Elaine BA, U. Md., 1967; MS in Library Sci., Cath. U. Am., 1969. Librarian U. Md., College Park, 1969-72, head acquisitions, 1973-75; asst. univ. librarian George Washington U., Washington, 1975-78, assoc. univ. librarian, 1978-82; univ. librarian U. Louisville, 1983-90; dir. libraries U. Mo., Columbia, 1990—2002; ret., 2002. Chmn. bd. dirs. SOLINET (Southeastern Library Network), 1987-88. Coord. U. Louisville United Way, 1987; bd. dirs. Mo. Libr. Network Corp., 1990-2002; coord. United Way campaign U. Mo., 2002. Mem. ALA (chmn. poster sessions 1983-85, co-chmn. nat. conf. in Cin. 1989), Am. Assn. Higher Edn., Athletic Assn. U. Louisville (vice chmn., bd. dirs. 1989-90), D.C. Library Assn. (pres. 1981-82), Women Acad. Libr. Dirs. Exch. etwork. Episcopalian. Home: 100 Mumford Dr Columbia MO 65203-0226

ALEXANDER, RALPH WILLIAM, JR., physics professor; b. Phila., May 17, 1941; s. Ralph William and Gladys (Robin) A.; m. Janet Erdien Bradley, Sept. 4, 1965; children: Ralph III, Margaret. BA, Wesleyan U., Middletown, Conn., 1963; PhD, Cornell U., Ithaca, NY, 1968; postdoctoral study, U. of Freiburg, Fed. Republic Germany, 1968-70. From asst. to assoc. prof. physics U. Mo., Rolla, 1970-80, prof., 1980—, chmn. dept., 1983-92. Contbr. articles to profl. jours. Mem. Am. Phys. Soc., Assn. Am. Physics Tchrs. Office: Mo Univ Sci and Tech Dept Physics Rolla MO 65409-0640 Home Phone: 573-364-1512; Office Phone: 573-341-4796. Business E-Mail: ralexand@mst.edu.

ALEXANDER, RICHARD DALE, zoology educator; b. White Heath, Ill., Nov. 18, 1929; m. 1950; two children. BSc, Ill. State U., 1950; MSc, The Ohio State U., 1951, PhD in Entomology, 1956; LHD, Ill. State U. Rsch. assoc. Rockefeller Found., NYC, 1956-57; from instr. to assoc. prof. U. Mich., Ann Arbor, 1957-69; curator Insects U. Mich. Mus. Zoology, Ann Arbor, 1957—, prof. Zoology, 1969—, Hubbell Dist. U. Prof. Evolutionary Biol., 1990—. Recipient Daniel Giraud Elliot medal, 1971; Newcomb Cleveland prize, AAAS, 1961. Mem. Fellow AAAS, Animal Behavior Soc., mem. Nat. Acad. Scis. Office: Mus Zool U Mich 1109 Geddes Ave Ann Arbor MI 48109-1079 E-mail: rdalex@umich.edu.

ALEXANDER, ROBERTA SUE, history professor; b. NYC, Mar. 19, 1943; d. Bernard Milton and Dorothy (Linn) Cohn; m. John Kurt Alexander, 1966 (div. Sept. 1972); m. Ronald Burett Fost, May 7, 1977. BA, UCLA, 1964; MA, U. Chgo., 1966, PhD, 1974; JD, U. Dayton, 2000. Instr. Roosevelt U., Chgo., 1967-68; prof. U. Dayton, Ohio, 1969—. Author: North Carolina Faces the Freedman: Race Relations During Presidential Reconstruction, 1985; mem. editl. bd. Cin. Hist. Soc., 1973—; contbr. chpt. to book and articles to law revs. Recipient summer stipend NEH, Washington, 1975, Tchg. Excellence and Campus Leadership award Sears-Roebuck Found, 1990, Tchg. Excellence in History award Ohio Acad. History, 1991, Michael and Elissa Cohen Writing award, 1999; fellow in residence NEH, 1976-77, fellow Inst. for Legal Studies, NEH, 1982, summer rsch. fellow U. Dayton, 1972, 74, 76, 80. Mem. Am. Hist. Assn., Orgn. Am. Historians, Am. Soc. Legal History, Midwest Assn. Prelaw Advisors (pres.), So. Hist. Soc., Mortar Bd., Am. Contract Bridge Assn. (life master 1983), Phi Beta Kappa, Phi Alpha Theta. Avocations: bridge, golf. Office: U Dayton Dept History Dayton OH 45469-0310 Home: 701 Ocean Club Pl Fernandina Beach FL 32034-6565 Fax: (937) 229-4298. E-mail: roberta.alexander@notes.udayton.edu.

ALGEO, JOHN THOMAS, association executive, retired educator; b. St. Louis, Nov. 12, 1930; s. Thomas George and Julia Winifred (Wathen) A.; m. Adele Marie Silbereisen, Sept. 6, 1958; children: Thomas John, Catherine Marie. EdB cum laude, U. Miami, Coral Gables, 1955; MA, U. Fla., Gainesville, 1957, PhD, 1960. Instr. Fla. State U., Tallahassee, 1959-61; from asst. to full prof. U. Fla., Gainesville, 1961-71, asst. dean grad. sch., 1969-71, dir. program in linguistics, 1969-71; prof. U. Ga., Athens, 1971-88, dir. program in linguistics, 1974-79, head dept. English, 1975-79, alumni found. disting. prof., 1988-94; nat. pres. Theosophical Soc. in Am., Wheaton, Ill., 1993—2002; internat. v.p. Theosophical Soc., Adyar, India, 2002—. Mem. gen. coun. Theosophical Soc., Adyar, India, 1993—; dir. Manor Found. Ltd., Sydney, Australia, 1995—; accreditation cons. So. Assn. Colls. and Schs., Atlanta, 1967-90; cons. NEH, Washington, 1974-94; dir. Commn. on the English Lang., Nat. Coun. Tchrs. of English, Urbana, Ill., 1976-82; del. Am. Coun. Learned Socs., NYC, 1984-87; cons. in lang. and lexicography Cambridge Univ. Press, NYC, 1989-93; cons. in English Language Cambridge U. Press, Cambridge Eng., 1987-; cons. in Am. usage Kenkyusha Ltd., Tokyo, 1991-99; cons. Webster's New World Dictionary, 4th edit., Cleve., 1993-95. Author: Problems in the Origins and Development of the English Language, 1966, 6th edit., 2008, On Defining the Proper Name, 1973, Exercises in Contemporary English, 1974, The Origins and Development of the English Language, 1982, 6th edit., 2008, Reincarnation Explored, 1987, Reincarnatie in Kaart gebracht, 1990, Fifty Years "Among the New Words": A Dictionary of Neologisms, 1941-91, 1991, 1993, Eigo no kigen to hattatsu, 1991, Reinkarnation: Evolution der Seele, 1991, 96, Reinkarnation i ny belysning, 1994, Investigando a reencarnacao, 1995, Unlocking the Door: Studies in The Key to Theosophy, 2001, British or American English? A Handbook of Word and Grammar Patterns, 2006; co-author: English: An Introduction to Language, 1970, Spelling: Sound to Letter, 1971, Elements of Literature, Sixth Course: Literature of Britain, 1989, The Power of Thought, 2001, Pensamento: O que e e como usar, 2003, British or American English?, 2006; editor: American Speech, 1972-81, Thomas Pyles: Selected Essays on English Usage, 1979, Among the New Words, American Speech, 1987-97, Cambridge History of the English Language, vol. 6, English in North America, 2001, 02, The Quest, 1997-03, The Letters of H.P. Blavatsky, vol. 1, 2003, Echoes From the Gnosis, 2006; assoc. editor: The Oxford Companion to the English Language, 1992; mem. editl. bd. Jour. of English Linguistics, 1970—, Internat. Jour. Lexicography, 1990-93, World Englishes, 1996—, Names, 1997—, Language Problems Language Planning, 1997-99, Studies in English Language, 1987—. Sgt. US Army, 1951-54, Korea. Fellow Guggenheim Found., London, 1986-87; Fulbright scholar U. Coll. London, Eng., 1986-87. Mem. Am. Dialect Soc. (pres. 1979), Am. ame Soc. (pres. 1984), Internat. Assn. Univ. Profs. English, Internat. Linguistic Assn., Ea. Order Internat. Co-Freemasonry, Internat. Phonetic Assn., Linguistic Assn. of the U.S. and Can., Linguistic Soc. Am., Modern Lang. Assn. Am., Philological Soc., Southeastern Conf. on Linguistics (pres. 1970-71), Dictionary Soc. N.Am. (pres. 1995-97), Theosophical Soc. (nat. pres. 1993-2002, internat. v.p. 2002-), Ea. Order Internat. Co-Freemasonry (adminstr. 2002—). Democrat. Home: PO Box 80206 Athens GA 30608-0206 Personal E-mail: jalgeo@jalgeo.com.

ALGER, CHADWICK FAIRFAX, political scientist, educator; b. Chambersburg, Pa., Oct. 9, 1924; s. Herbert and Thelma (Drawbaugh) A.; m. Elinor Reynolds, Aug. 28, 1948; children: Mark, Scott, Laura, Craig. BA, Ursinus Coll., 1949, LLD, 1979; MA, Johns Hopkins U., 1950; PhD, Princeton, 1958. Internat. relations specialist Dept. Navy, 1950-54; instr. Swarthmore Coll., 1957; faculty Northwestern U., Evanston, Ill., 1958-71, prof. polit. sci., 1966-71, dir. internat. relations program, 1967-71; Mershon prof. polit. sci. and pub. policy Ohio State U., 1971-95, emeritus prof., 1995—, dir. transnat. intellectual cooperation program, 1971-80, dir. world affairs program, Mershon Ctr., 1980-88, coord. working group on global rels. and peace studies, 1988-95, acting dir. univ. ctr. for internat. studies, 1990-91. Vis. prof. UN affairs NYU, 1962-63 Author: Internationalization from Local Areas: Beyond Interstate Relations, 1987, Perceiving, Understanding and Coping with World Relations in Everyday Life, 1993, The United Nations System: Potential for the Twenty-First Century, 1998, The United Nations System: A Reference Handbook, 2006; co-author: Simulation in International Relations, 1963, You and Your Community in the World, 1978, Conflicts and Crisis of International Order: New Tasks for Peace Research, 1985, A Just Peace Through Transformation: Cultural, Economic and Political Foundations for Change, 1988, The United Nations System: The Policies of Member States, 1995; contbr. articles to profl. jours. Mem. Trade Coun., State of Ohio, 1984-87; adv. com. Global Issues Ctr. Cuyahoga C.C., 2005—; mem. adv. coun. Ams. for UNESCO, 2006—. Served with USNR, 1943-46. Recipient Disting. Scholar award Internat. Soc. for Ednl., Cultural and Sci. Interchanges, 1980, Golden Apple award Am. Forum for Global Edn., 1993. Mem. Am. Polit. Sci. Assn. (coun. 1970-72), Internat. Polit. Sci. Assn., Internat. Studies Assn. (pres. 1978-79), Internat. Studies Assn. Midwest (Quincy Wright disting. scholar award 2000), Internat. Peace Rsch. Assn. (coun. 1971-77, sec.-gen. 1983-87), Internat. Peace Rsch. Assn. Found. (v.p. 1998—), Midwest Conf. Polit. Scis. (recipient prize 1966), Consortium on Peace Rsch., Edn. and Devel. (exec. com. 1971-77, chmn. 1976-77), Hunger and Devel. Coalition of Cen. Ohio (bd. dirs. 1983-90), Columbus Coun. on World Affairs (bd. dirs. 1974-88), UN Assn. (pres. Columbus chpt. 1991-93). Home: 2674 Westmont Blvd Columbus OH 43221-3354 Office: Ohio State U Mershon Ctr 1501 Neil Ave Columbus OH 43201-2602 E-mail: Alger1@osu.edu.

ALI, JEFFER, lawyer; b. Buffalo, Mar. 17, 1966; PharmD, U. Mich., 1990; JD cum laude, U. Minn., 1994. Bar: Minn. 1994, US Dist. Ct. (dist. Minn.) 1995. Hiring ptnr. Merchant & Gould, P.C., Mpls. Adj. prof. U. Minn. Law Sch. Intellectual Property Moot Ct. Named a Rising Star, Minn. Super Lawyers mag., 2006; recipient Pro Bono Atty. of Yr. award, Vol. Lawyers Network, 2000. Mem.: Minn. State Bar Assn., Minn. Intellectual Property Law Assn., Am. Intellectual Property Law Assn. Office: Merchant & Gould PC 3200 IDS Ctr 80 S 8th St Minneapolis MN 55402 Office Phone: 612-371-5351. E-mail: jali@merchant-gould.com.

ALI, MIR MASOOM, retired statistician, educator; b. Bangladesh, Feb. 1, 1937; arrived in U.S., 1969; s. Mir Muazzam and Azifa Khatoon (Chowdhury) Ali; m. Firoza Chowdhury, June 25, 1959; children: Naheed, Fahima, Farah, Mir Ishtiaque. BSc, U. Dhaka, 1956, MSc, 1957, U. Toronto, 1967, PhD, 1969. Rsch. officer, Ministry of Food and Agr., Ministry of Commerce, Ctrl. Pub. Svc.

Commn. Govt. of Pakistan, 1958—66; tchg. asst. U. Toronto, Ont., Canada, 1966—69; asst. prof. math. scis. Ball State U., Muncie, Ind., 1969—74, assoc. prof., 1974—78, prof., 1978—2000, George and Frances Ball disting. prof. stats., 2000—07, George and Frances Ball Disting. Prof. Emeritus of Stats., 2007. Vis. prof. U. Windsor, Canada, 1972—73, U. Dhaka, 1983—84, Purdue U., 1978, Jahangirnagar U., 1991, Indian Stats. Inst., Calcutta, 1991, Yeungnam U., Republic of Korea, 1993, King Saud U., 1999. Assoc. editor Jour. Statis. Rsch., Aligarh Jour. Stats., Pakistan Jour. Stats., Jour. Statis Mgmt. Systems, overseas exec. editor Jour. Statis. Studies; contbr. articles to profl. jours. Named Sagamore of the Wabash, State of Ind., 2002; recipient Q.M. Husain Gold medal, Bangladesh Stats. Assn., 1990. Fellow: Bangladesh Acad. Sci., Inst. Statisticians, Royal Statis. Soc., Am. Statis. Assn. (Meritorious Svc. award biopharm. sect. 1987, 1997, 2002); mem.: Islamic Statis. Soc., Inst. Math. Stats., Internat. Statis. Inst. (Gold medal 2005). Muslim. Home: 5200 W Deerbrook Dr Muncie IN 47304-3475 Office: Ball State U Dept Math Scis Muncie IN 47306-0490 Office Phone: 765-285-8670. Business E-Mail: mali@bsu.edu.

ALI, SANDRA, announcer; b. Queens, NY; Grad. cum laude, Syracuse U.; M in Journalism, Northwestern U. Weekend anchor, reporter WTAJ-TV 10, Altoona, Pa.; anchor 6pm and 10pm WJBK Fox 2, Detroit, 2000—. Avocations: attending plays, reading. Office: WJBK Fox 2 PO Box 2000 Southfield MI 48037-2000

ALIBER, ROBERT Z., economist, educator; b. Keene, NH, Sept. 19, 1930; s. Norman H. and Sophie (Becker) A.; m. Deborah Baltzly, Sept. 9, 1955; children: Jennifer, Rachel, Michael. BA, Williams Coll., Williamstown, Mass., 1952, Cambridge U., 1954, MA, 1957; PhD, Yale U., New Haven, Conn., 1962. Staff economist Commn. Money and Credit, NYC, 1959-61, Com. on Econ. Devel., Washington, 1961-64; sr. econ. advisor AID, Dept. State, Washington, 1964-65; assoc. prof., then prof. internat. econs. and fin. U. Chgo., 1965—2004; pres. Dorchester Capital Mgmt., 1990—2007. Vis. prof. Brandeis U., 1987-93; vis. Bundesbank prof. Free U. Berlin, 1999; Houblon-Norman fellow, Bank of Eng., 1996, J.P. Morgan Internat. prize fellow, Am. Academy in Berlin, 2002. Author: The International Money Game, 1973, 76, 79, 83, 87, 2001, Exchange Risk and Corporate International Finance, 1978, Your Money and Your Life, 1982; co-author: Money, Banking, and the Economy, 1981, 84, 87, 90, 93, The Multinational Paradigm, 1993; co-author Manias, Panics, and Crashes, 2005; editor: National Monetary Policies and the International Financial System, 1974, The Political Economy of Monetary Reform, 1976, The Reconstruction of International Monetary Arrangements, 1987, The Handbook of International Financial Management, 1989; co-editor Global Portfolios, 1991, Readings in International Business: A Decision Approach, 1993. With US Army, 1954—56. Fulbright fellow, 1952-54. Fellow Woodrow Wilson Internat. Ctr. Scholars, 2004-05; mem. Am. Econs. Assn., Acad. Internat. Bus., Quadrangle Club, Williams Club of NY, Post Mills Soaring Club. Office Phone: 603-643-0107. Business E-Mail: rza@chicagogsb.edu.

ALIEV, ELDAR, former artistic director, choreographer, educator; b. Azerbaijan; Grad. (hon.), Baku Choreographic Acad. CEO, artistic dir. Ballet Internationale, Indpls., 1994—2005. Former prin. ballet dancer with the Kirov Ballet appearing in more than 30 countries; guest star Bolshoi Ballet and the Australian Ballet; choreographer ballets 1001 Nights, 1995, The Nutcracker, 1996, The Firebird, 1999; choreographer operas Eugene Onegin, 1999, Samson and Deliah, 2000, Anoush, 2001; classics restaged Don Quixote, Giselle, La Sylphide, Paquita, Les Sylphides.

ALJETS, CURTIS J., federal agency administrator; b. Carrington, ND, May 21, 1946; m. Catherine Seil, Nov. 18, 1967; 3 children. BS in Math. Edn., N.D. State U., 1968. Tchr. sci. Dunseith (N.D.) Pub. Schs., 1970-72; immigration inspector, port dir. U.S. Immigration & Naturalization, Dept. Justice, 1972-87, asst. regional commr. examination & adjudication, 1987-92, staff asst. field ops. No. Regional Office, 1992-95, assoc. regional dir. Ctrl. Regional Office, 1995-97, dist. dir. Bloomington, Minn., 1997—. 2d lt. U.S. Army, 1968-70. Mem. Hennepin County (Minn.) Chiefs of Police Assn., Minn. State Sheriffs Assn. Evangelical. Avocations: reading, jogging, computers, photography. Office: US Dept Immigration & Naturalization Dept Justice 2901 Metro Dr Ste 100 Bloomington MN 55425-1555

ALLDREDGE, WILLIAM T., metal products executive; BA, Mich. St. U., 1961, MBA, 1962. Pres., CEO Mirro Corp.; v.p., finance Newell Rubbermaid Inc., Freeport, Ill., 1983, CFO, pres. corp. devel., 2001—03; ret., 2003. Office: Newell Ctr 29 E Stephenson St Freeport IL 61032-0943

ALLDRITT, RICHARD, state legislator; m. Carmen Alldritt. Mem. from dist. 105 Kans. Ho. of Reps., Topeka. Mem. calendar and printing com., utilities com., info. tech. com., Kans. 2000 select com., legis. post audit com. Kans. Ho. of Reps., also minority whip. Democrat. Home: 613 W 15th St Harper KS 67058-1514 E-mail: alldritt@house.state.ks.us, alldritt@attica.net.

ALLEGRUCCI, DONALD LEE, state supreme court justice; b. Pittsburg, Kans., Sept. 19, 1936; s. Nello and Josephine Marie (Funaro) A.; m. Joyce Ann Thompson, Nov. 30, 1963; children: Scott David, Bowen Jay. AB, Pittsburg State U., 1959; JD, Washburn U., 1963. Bar: Kans. 1963. Asst. county atty. Butler County, El Dorado, Kans., 1963-67; state senator Kans. Legislature, Topeka, 1976-80; mem. Kans. Pub. Relations Bd., 1981-82; dist. judge Kans. 11th Jud. Dist., Pittsburg, 1982-87, adminstrv. judge, 1983-87; justice Kans. Supreme Ct., Topeka, 1987—. Instr. Pittsburg State U., 1969-72; exec. dir. Mid-Kans. Community Action Program, Inc.; mem. exec. com. Kansas Dist. Judges Assn., 1982-87; chmn. KDJA Legislative Coordinating Com., 1982-86; mem. Judicial Council Ct. Unification Advisory Com., 1984-85. Mem. Dem. State Com., 1974-80; candidate 5th Congl. Dist., 1978; past pres. Heart Assn.; bd. dirs. YMCA. Served in USAF, 1959—66. Mem. Kans. Bar Assn.; former mem. Crawford County Bar Assn. (past pres.), Butler County Bar Assn. (past pres.). Democrat. Office: Kansas Supreme Court 374 Kansas Judicial Ctr 301 SW 10th Ave Fl 3 Topeka KS 66612-1507

ALLEMANG, ARNOLD A., chemicals executive; B in Chemistry, Sam Houston State U. Unit mgr. Dow Chem. Co., 1981—84, prodn. mgr. Terneuzen, Netherlands, 1984—88, mgr. hydrocarbon prodn. Freeport, Tex., 1988—89, dir. tech. ctrs. Midland, Mich., 1989—92, mfg. gen. mgr. Dow Benelux, 1992—93, regional v.p. mfg. and adminstrn. Dow Benelux, 1993, v.p. mfg. ops. Dow Europe, 1993—95, VP ops. Midland, 1995—, exec. v.p., 2000—04, bd. dir., sr. advisor, 2004—. Bd. dirs. Dow Corning Corp., Liana Ltd., Dorinco Reinsurance Co., Mems. Com. of Dupont Dow Elastomers LLC, Cargill Dow, LLC. Adv. bd. President's Cir. of Sam Houston State. U.; adv. bd. Coll. Engring. Kans. State U. Mem.: Nat. Assn. Mfrs. (bd. dirs.), Am. Chem. Soc., Ctr. Chem. Process Safety (advisory bd.).

ALLEN, BARBARA, state legislator; Atty.; mem. Kans. Ho. of Reps. from 21st dist., 1987-2000, Kans. Senate from 8th dist., Topeka, 2001—. Mem. appropriations com., fiscal oversight com., social svcs. budget com., chairperson tourism com. Kans. Ho. of Reps. Republican. Office: Kansas Senate State Capitol Topeka KS 66612 Home: 9851 Ash Dr Overland Park KS 66207-3226 Office Fax: 913 498 8488; Home Fax: 913 384 5400. E-mail: allen@house.state.ks.us.

ALLEN, BELLE, management consulting firm and communications executive; b. Chgo. d. Isaac and Clara (Friedman) Allen., U. Chgo. Cert. conf. mgr. Internat. Inst. Conf. Planning and Mgmt., 1989. Reporter, spl. corr. The Leader Newspapers, Chgo., Washington, 1960—64; cons., v.p., treas., dir. William Karp Cons. Co. Inc., Chgo., 1961—79, chmn. bd., pres., treas., 1979—; pres. Belle Allen Comm., Chgo., 1961—; nat. corr. CCA Press, 1990—. Apptd. pub. mem., com. on judicial evaluation Chgo. Bar Assn., 1998—; v.p., treas., bd. dirs. Cultural Arts Survey Inc., Chgo., 1965-79; cons., bd. dirs. Am. Diversified Rsch. Corp., Chgo., 1967-70; v.p., sec., bd. dirs. Mgmt. Performance Sys. Inc., 1976-77; cons. City Club Chgo., 1962-65, Ill. Commn. on Tech. Progress, 1965-67; hearing mem. Ill. Gov.'s Grievance Panel for State Employees, 1979—; hearing mem. grievance panel Ill. Dept. Transp., 1985—; mem. adv. governing bd. Ill. Coalition on Employment of Women, 1980-88; advisor, spl. program The President's Project Partnership, Washington, DC, 1980-88; bd. govs. fed. res. com., nominee consumer adv. coun. FRS, 1979-82; reporter CCA Press, 1990—; panel mem. Free Press vs. Fair Trial Nat. Ctr. Freedom of Info. Studies Loyola U. Law Sch., 1993, mem. planning com. Freedom of Info. awards, 1993; conf. chair The Swedish Inst. Press Ethics: How to Handle, 1993. Editor: Operations Research and the Management of Mental Health Systems, 1968; contbr. articles to profl. jours. Mem. campaign staff Adlai E. Stevenson II, 1952, 56, John F. Kennedy, 1960; founding mem. women's bd. United Cerebral Palsy Assn., Chgo., 1954, bd. dirs., 1954-58; pres. Dem. Fedn. Ill., 1958-61; pres. conf. staff Eleanor Roosevelt, 1960; mem. Welfare Pub. Rels. Forum, 1960-61; bd. dirs., mem. exec. com., chmn. pub. rels. com. Regional Ballet Ensemble, Chgo., 1961-63; bd. dirs. Soc. Chgo. Strings, 1963-64; mem. Ind. Dem. Coalition, 1968-69; bd. dirs. Citizens for Polit. Change, 1969; campaign mgr. aldermanic election 42d ward Chgo. City Coun., 1969; mem. selection com. Robert Aragon Scholarship, 1991; mem. planning com. mem. Hutchins Era reunion U. Chgo., 1995, 2000. Recipient Outstanding Svc. award United Cerebral Palsy Assn., Chgo., 1954, 55, Chgo. Lighthouse for Blind, 1986, Spl. Comms. award The White House, 1961, cert. of appreciation Ill. Dept. Human Rights, 1985, Internat. Assn. Ofcl. Human Rights Agys., 1985; selected as reference source Am. Bicentennial Rsch. Inst. Libr. Human Resources, 1973; named Hon. Citizen, City of Alexandria, Va., 1985; selected to be photographed by Bachrach nat. exhibit for Faces of Chicago, 1990. Mem. AAAS, NOW, AAAU, Affirmative Action Assn. (bd. dirs. 1981-85, chmn. mem. and programs com. 1981-85, pres. 1983—), Fashion Group (bd. dirs. 1981-83, chmn. Restrospective View of an Hist. Decade 1960-70, editor The Bull. 1981), Indsl. Rels. Rsch. Assn. (bd. dirs., chmn. pers. placement com. 1960-61), Sarah Siddons Soc., Soc. Pers. Adminstrs., Women's Equity Action League, Nat. Assn. Inter-Group Rels. Ofcls. (nat. conf. program 1959), Publicity Club Chgo. (chmn. inter-city rels. com. 1960-61, Disting. Svc. award 1968), Ill. C. of C. (cmty. rels. com., alt. mem. labor rels. com. 1971-74), Chgo. C. of C. and Industry (merit employment com. 1961-63), Internat. Press Club Chgo. (charter 1992—, bd. dirs. 1992—), Chgo. Press Club (chmn. women's activities 1969-71), U. Chgo. Club of Met. Chgo. (program com. 1993—, chair summer quarter programs 1994), Soc. Profl. Journalists (Chgo. Headline Club 1992—, regional conf. planning com. 1993, co-chair Peter Lisagor awards 1993, program com. 1992—), Assn. Women Journalists, Nat. Trust for Historic Preservation. Office: 111 E Chestnut St Ste 29J Chicago IL 60611

ALLEN, BENJAMIN J., academic administrator; b. Jan. 5, 1947; BS in Bus. Econs., Ind. U., 1969; MA in Econs., U. Ill., 1973, PhD in Econs., 1974. Asst. prof. Wash. State U., 1974—79, mem. grad. faculty, 1976—79, Iowa State U., 1979—90, Iowa, 1991—, acting head transp. and logistics area, 1982—83, prof., 1984—88, Iowa, 1991—, dir. Midwest Transp. Ctr., 1988—90, dean Coll. Bus. Iowa, 1994—2001, interim v.p. external affairs Iowa, 2001—02, provost Iowa, 2002—; prof. U. Ark., 1990—91, mem. grad. faculty, 1990—91. Bd. dirs. Heartland Express, INc.; pres. Midwest Bus. Deans Assn., 1998—99. Mem. editl. rev. bd.: Jour. Bus. Logistics, 1986—94, Transp. Jour., 1988—, Jour. Advanced Transp., 1990—92, Transport Logistics, 1995—, Jour. Transp. Rsch. Forum, 1996—; contbr. articles to profl. jours. Bd. dirs. Ames (Iowa) C. of C., 1995—2000, pres.-elect bd. dirs., 1996, pres. bd. dirs., 1998; mem. exec. com., bd. dirs. Greater DesMoines C. of C. Fedn., 1998. Recipient Disting. Transp. Rsch. award, Transp. Rsch. Forum, 1996; NSF fellow, U. Ill., 1969—70, Univ. fellow, 1972—73, Brookings Econ. Policy fellow, 1976—77, Twin City Barge fellow in transp., 1980—81. Mem.: Transp. and Pub. Utilities Group, Am. Soc. Transp. and Logistics, Am. Econ. Assn., Golden Key Nat. Honor Soc., Phi Kappa Phi. Office: Iowa State Univ Office of the Provost 1550 Beardshear Hall Ames IA 50011-2021

ALLEN, BRUCE TEMPLETON, retired economics professor; b. Oak Park, Ill., Jan. 27, 1938; s. William Hendry and Harriet (Iverson) A.; m. Virginia Elizabeth Peterson, June 16, 1962; children: Elizabeth Rachel, Catherine Grace. AB, De Pauw U., 1960; MBA, U. Chgo., 1961; PhD, Cornell U., 1965. Asst. prof. econs. Mich. State U., East Lansing, 1965-75, assoc. prof., 1975-80, prof., 1980—2003; ret., 2003. Mem. Am. Econ. Assn., Indsl. Orgn. Soc. Avocations: railroads, choral singing. Personal E-mail: allenb@msu.edu.

ALLEN, CHARLES EUGENE, university administrator, agriculturist, educator; b. Burley, Idaho, Jan. 25, 1939; s. Charles W. and Elsie P. (Fowler) A.; m. Connie J. Block, June 19, 1960; children: Kerry J., Tamara S. BS, U. Idaho, 1961; MS, U. Wis., 1963, PhD, 1965. NSF postdoctoral fellow, Sydney, Australia, 1966-67; asst. prof. agr. U. Minn., St. Paul, 1967-69, assoc. prof., 1969-72, prof., 1972—, dean Coll. Agr., assoc. dir. Agrl. Expt. Sta., 1984-88, acting v.p., 1988-90, v.p. agriculture, forestry and home econs., dir. Minn. Agr. Expt. Sta., 1990-95, provost profl. studies, dir. Minn. Agr. Expt. Sta., 1995-97, dir. global outreach, 1997-98, exec. dir. internat. programs, 1998—2004, assoc. v.p. for internat. programs, 2004—06. Vis. prof. Pa. State U., 1978; cons. to industry; C. Glen King lectr. Wash. State U., 1981; Univ. lectr. U. Wyo., Laramie, 1984; adj. prof. Hassan II U., Rabat, Morocco, 1984. Recipient Horace T. Morse-Amoco Found. award U. Minn., 1984, Disting. Tchr. award U. Minn. Coll. Agr., 1984, Disting. Alumni award U. Idaho, 1989. Fellow AAAS, Inst. Food Tech.; mem. Am. Meat Sci. Assn. (bd. dirs. 1970-72, Rsch. award 1980, Signal Svc. award, 1985), Am. Soc. Animal Sci. (Exceptional Rsch. Achievement award 1972, Rsch. award 1977). Avocations: photography, reading, outdoor sports, golf. Business E-Mail: ceallen@umn.edu.

ALLEN, DANIELLE S., political science and classics educator; AB, Princeton U., 1993; MPhil, U. Cambridge, 1994, PhD, 1996; MA, Harvard U., 1998, PhD, 2001. Asst. prof. U. Chgo., 1997—2000, assoc. prof., 1997—2003, prof. dept. politics and com. on social thought and dept. classical lang. and lit., 2003—07, dean humanities div.; UPS found. prof. Sch. Social Sci., Institute for Advanced Study, Princeton, NJ, 2007—. Adj. lectr. Suffolk Univ., 1996—97, Tufts Univ., 1997; bd. dir. Franke Inst. for the Humanities, 2002—, Ill. Humanities Council, 2003—; mem. editl. bd. Classical Philology, 1998—, Critical Inquiry, 2002—. Author: The World of Prometheus: the politics of punishing in democratic Athens, 2000, Talking to Strangers: Anxieties of Citizenship Since Brown vs. the Board of Education, 2004; contbr. articles to profl. jours. Fellow, NSF, 1997, Frank Inst. for Humanities fellow, U. Chgo., 1999, Mac Arthur Fellow, 2002. Mem.: Am. Philological Assn., Am. Polit. Sci. Assn., Chgo. Polit. Theory Group. Office: Inst for Advanced Study Einstein Dr Princeton NJ 08540 Office Phone: 609-734-8000.

ALLEN, DAVID JAMES, lawyer; b. East Chicago, Ind. BS, Ind. U., 1957, MA, 1959, JD, 1965. Bar: Ind. 1965, U.S. Dist. Ct. (so. dist.) Ind. 1965, U.S. Ct. Appeals 1965, U.S. Tax Ct. 1965, U.S. Supreme Ct. 1965, U.S. Ct. Appeals (fed. and 7th cirs.) 1983. Of counsel Hagemier, Allen and Smith, Indpls., 1975—. Adminstrv. asst. Gov. of Ind. Mathew E. Welsh, 1961—65; counsel Ind. Gov. Roger D. Branigin, 1965—69; asst. to Gov. Edgar D. Whitcomb, 1969; univ. counsel Ind. State U., Terre Haute, 1969—70; legis. counsel Ind. Gov. Evan Bayh, 1989—90; spl. counsel Gov. Frank O'Bannon State of Ind., 1999—2002; mem. Spl. Commn. on Ind. Exec. Reorgn., 1967—69; commr. Ind. Utility Regulatory Commn., 1970—75; mem. Ind. Law Enforcement Acad. Bd. and Adv. Coun., 1968—85, Ind. State Police Bd., 1968—2008; commr. for revision Ind. Commn. Recommend Changes Ind. Legis. Process, 1990—2002; commr. Ind. Criminal Code Revision Study Commn., 1998—2002; nat. judge adv. Acacia Frat., 1980—86, 1992—2002, internat. pres., 2002—; chief counsel Ind. Ho. Reps., 1975—76, spl. counsel, 1979—89, Ind. Senate, 1990—97; adj. prof. pub. law Sch. Pub. and Environ. Affairs, Ind. U., Bloomington, 1976—. Author: (book) New Governor in Indiana: Transition of Executive Power, 1965. Mem.: ABA, Indpls. Bar Assn., Ind. State Bar Assn. (criminal justice law exec. com. 1966—72, mem. adminstrv. law com. 1968—77, chmn. adminstrv. law com. 1973—76, mem. law sch. liaison com. 1977—78). Office: Hagemier Allen & Smith 1170 Market Tower 10 W Market St Ste 1170 Indianapolis IN 46204-5924

ALLEN, DIXIE J., state representative; b. 1935; married; 3 children. BSBA, Ctrl. Ohio State U.; postgrad., Nat. U., LA; DHL (hon.), Ctrl. Ohio State U. Civilian employee USAF; state rep. dist. 39 Ohio Ho. of Reps., Columbus, 1998—, ranking minority mem. banking, pensions and securities com., mem. fin. and appropriations, and homeland security engring. and archtl. design coms., mem. human svcs. subcom. Adv. bd. Women in Leadership; personnel adv. bd. Daybreak; adv. bd. Coll. Arts and Scis., Ctrl. State U. Mem.: NAACP, SCLC, Miami Valley Mil. Affairs Assn., Delta Sigma Theta. Office: 77 S High St 10th fl Columbus OH 43215-6111

ALLEN, GARLAND EDWARD, biologist, professor, writer; b. Louisville, Feb. 13, 1936; s. Garland Edward and Virginia (Blandford) A.; children: Tania Leigh, Carin Tove. AB, U. Louisville, 1957; AMT, Harvard U., 1958, AM, 1963, PhD, 1966. Programmer, announcer WFPL-WFPK, Louisville, 1956—58; tchr. Mt. Hermon (Mass.) Sch., 1958—61; Allston-Burr sr. tutor, instr. history of sci. Harvard, 1965—67; asst. prof. biology Washington U., St. Louis, 1967—72, assoc. prof., 1972—80, prof., 1980—. Cons. Ednl. Rsch. Corp., Cleve., 1967-85; commr. Commn. Undergrad. Edn. in Biol. Scis., 1967-70; mem. NSF Panel for Social Scis., 1968-71; mem. ELSI rev. panel NIH, 2002; trustee Marine Biol. Lab., Woods Hole, Mass., 1985-93; Sigma Xi nat. lectr., 1973-74, bicentennial lectr., 1974-77; Watkins vis. prof. Wichita State U., 1984; vis. prof. dept. history of sci. Harvard U., 1989-91, Sarton Award Lecture, AAAS, 1998. Author: Life Sciences in the Twentieth Century, 1975, 1978, T.H. Morgan: The Man and His Science, 1978; author: (with J.J.W. Baker) Matter, Energy and Life, 1965, 1970, 1975, 1981; author: The Study of Biology, 1967, The Study of Biology, 4th edit., 1982, Hypothesis, Prediction and Implication, 1969, The Process of Biology, 1970, Biology: Scientific Process and Social Issues, 2001; co-editor: Mendel Newsletter, 1989—92, Jour. History of Biology, 1996—2006; mem. editl. bd.: San Josè Studies, —, Jour. History of Biology, 1968—91, Folia Medeliana, History and Philosophy of the Life Scis., 1993—; co-editor: Science, History, and Social Activism: A Tribute to Everett Mendelsohn, 2002, Centennial History of the Carnegie Institution of Washington's Department of Embryology, 2005. Adv. bd. Holocaust Meml. Mus., 2000—01, Human Genome Sequencing Ctr. Outreach Washington U., 2003—06, Beach Ctr. for Disability U. Kans., 2003—07. Fellow Charles Warren Ctr. for Studies in Am. History, Harvard U., 1981-82; sr. fellow Dibner Inst. for the History of Sci. and Tech., MIT, 2002, Humanities Ctr., Washington U., 2008. Mem. AAAS (coun., sect. L exec. com. 1975, Sarton award lectr. 1998), History Sci. Soc. (chmn. Schumann Prize com. 1972, Pfizer prize com. 1977, 80, 91-94, HSS coun. 1994-96, nominating com. 2006—, vis. lectr. program 1985-87), Internat. Soc. for the History, Philosophy and Social Studies of Biology (pres.-elect 2003-05, pres. 05-07), Sigma Xi. Home: 1526 Mississippi Ave Saint Louis MO 63104-2512 Office: Washington U Biology Dept Saint Louis MO 63130 Office Phone: 314-935-6808. Business E-Mail: allen@biology2.wustl.edu.

ALLEN, GARY, radio personality; m. Laurie Allen; children: Michael, Patrick. With WTIQ-AM, Manistique, Mich., WTOC-AF/FM, Savannah, Ga., WBIA-AM, Augusta, Ga., KBZB-AM, Odessa/Midland, Tex., WCUZ-AM, Grand Rapids, Mich., WOOD 1300, Grand Rapids, Mich., 1981—, co-host Grand Rapids First News. Active Heal the Children-Mich., Mich.; vol. pub. TV auction WGVU-TV; active West Mich. coun. Boy Scouts Am., Mich. Office: Newsradio WOOD 1300 777 Monroe Center Ste 100 Grand Rapids MI 49503

ALLEN, GEMMA B., lawyer; b. Chgo., June 28, 1948; BS magna cum laude, Loyola U. Chgo., 1966; JD, U. Mich., 1969. Bar: Fla. 1970, Ill. 1972. With Pretzel & Stouffer, Chgo., 1990—99; ptnr., co-founder Ladden & Allen, Chgo., 2000—. Apptd. mem. Gov.'s Task Force on Child Support, Task Force on Attys. for Children, 1997—98; spkr. in field. Contbr. articles to profl. jours. Named one of 100 Most Influential Women, Crain's Chgo. Bus., 2004. Mem.: ABA (mem. family law sect.), Ill. State Bar Assn. (past chmn. family law com. mediation alternative dispute resolution, apptd. mem. family law sect. coun. 1996—99, co-chair model mediation act subcom.). Office: Ladden & Allen 55 W Monroe St Ste 3950 Chicago IL 60603 Office Phone: 312-853-3000. Office Fax: 312-201-1436.

ALLEN, HENRY SERMONES, JR., lawyer; b. Bronxville, NY, Aug. 26, 1947; s. Henry S. and Cecelia Marie (Chartrand) A.; m. Patricia Stromberger, Nov. 26, 1988; children: David Beckman, Amy Louise, Jeffrey Roy. AB magna cum laude, Washington U., St. Louis, 1969; MPA, Cornell U., 1973, JD, 1974. Adminstrv. resident Montefiore Hosp. and Med. Ctr., Bronx, NY, 1971; rsch. trainee Nat. Ctr. Health Svcs. Rsch. HEW, 1974—75; assoc. Vedder, Price, Kaufman & Kammholz, Chgo., 1975—79; pvt. practice Springfield, 1979—81; ptnr. Allen & Reed, Chgo., 1981—86, McBride, Baker & Coles, 1986—2002, Holland & Knight LLC, Chgo., 2002—. Adj. asst. prof. hosp. law Ithaca (NY) Coll., 1974-75; adj. prof. Cornell U., 1995—, Northwestern U. Sch. Law, 2003—, Northwestern U. Kellogg Sch. Mgmt., 2003—. HUD fellow, 1969-71. Mem. Am. Health Lawyers Assn., Ill. Soc. Hosp. Attys., Nat. Health Lawyers Assn., Cornell U. Club Chgo., Phi Beta Kappa, Omicron Delta Epsilon Office: Holland and Knight LLC 131 S Dearborn St Chicago IL 60603-5506 Business E-Mail: henry.allen@hklaw.com.

ALLEN, JARED SCOT, professional football player; b. Dallas, Apr. 3, 1982; Grad., Idaho State U., Pocatello, 2004. Def. end. Kans. City Chiefs, 2004—08, Minn. Vikings, 2008—. Advocate Juvenile Diabetes Rsch. Found. Named NFL All-Pro, 2007—08; named to Am. Football Conf. Pro Bowl Team, 2008; recipient Buck Buchanan award, Football Championship Subdivison, 2003, Mack Allen award, Kansas City Chiefs, 2005. Office: Minn Vikings 9520 Viking Dr Eden Prairie MN 55344*

ALLEN, JOHN L., JR., journalist, writer; m. Shannon Allen. Degree in Philosophy, Fort Hays State U., 1989; MA in Scripture, U. Kans. Opinion editor Nat. Cath. Reporter, 1997—2000, Rome corr., 2000—, author weekly internet column The Word from Rome, 2001—. Contbr. FOX News Channel; Vatican analyst CNN, NPR. Author: Cardinal Ratzinger: The Vatican's Enforcer of the Faith, 2000, Conclave: The Politics, Personalities and Process of the Next Papal Election, 2002, All the Pope's Men: The Inside Story of How the Vatican Really Thinks, 2004, The Rise of Benedict XVI: The Inside Story of How the Pope Was Elected and Where He Will Take the Catholic Church, 2005; Has contbd. to The Tablet, Jesus, Second Opinion, The Nation, The Miami Herald, Die Furche, The Irish Examiner. Office: Nat Cath Reporter Pub Co 115 E Armour Blvd Kansas City MO 64111-1203 Business E-Mail: jallen@natcath.org.

ALLEN, JON G., psychologist; BS, U. Conn.; D in Clin. Psychology, U. Rochester. Clin. psychology fellowship Karl Menninger Sch. of Psychiatry and Mental Health Scis., faculty, Washburn U., U. Kans., Kans. State U. Author: Coping With Trauma: A Guide to Self-Understanding; editor: (with others) Diagnosis and Treatment of Dissociative Disorders, Contemporary Treatment of Psychosis: Healing Relationships in the Decade of the Brain; co-author: Borderline Personality Disorder: Tailoring the Therapy to the Patient; past editor Bull. of the Menninger Clinic; cons. editor Psychiatry; contbr. chpts. to books and numerous articles to profl. publs. Recipient I. Arthur Marshall Disting. Alumnus award Menninger Alumni Assn. Address: Menningers PO Box 809045 Houston TX 77280

ALLEN, JULIE O'DONNELL, lawyer; BA, Stanford U., 1980; JD, U. Iowa, 1983. Bar: Iowa 1983, Ill. 1985, U.S. Dist. Ct. (no. dist.) Ill., U.S. Ct. Appeals (8th and 7th cirs.). Jud. clk. to Chief Judge Donald P. Lay, U.S. Ct. Appeals for 8th Circuit, 1983-84; assoc. Sidley & Austin, Chgo., 1985—, ptnr. Contbr. articles to law publs. Office: Sidley & Austin 1 S First National Plz Chicago IL 60603-2000 Fax: 323-853-7036. E-mail: jallen@sidley.com.

ALLEN, LAYMAN EDWARD, law educator, research scientist; b. Turtle Creek, Pa., June 9, 1927; s. Layman Grant and Viola Iris (Williams) A.; m. Christine R. Patmore, Mar. 29, 1950 (dec.); children: Layman G., Patricia R.; m. Emily C. Hall, Oct. 3, 1981 (div. 1992); children: Phyllip A. Hall, Kelly C. Hairston; m. Leslie A. Olsen, June 10, 1995. Student, Washington and Jefferson Coll., 1945-46; AB, Princeton U., 1951; MPA, Harvard U., 1952; LLB, Yale U., 1956. Bar: Conn. 1956. Fellow Ctr. for Advanced Study in Behavioral Scis., 1961-62; sr. fellow Yale Law Sch., 1956-57, lectr., 1957-58, instr., 1958-59, asst. prof., 1959-63, assoc. prof., 1963-66; assoc. prof. law U. Mich. Law Sch., Ann Arbor, 1966-71, prof., 1971—2006, prof. emeritus, 2006; disting. vis prof. Detroit Mercy Law Sch., 2006—. Chmn. bd. trustees Accelerated Learning Found., 1998—; sr. rsch. scientist Mental Health Rsch. Inst., U. Mich., 1966-99; cons. legal drafting Nat. Life Ins. Co., Mich. Blue Cross & Blue Shield (various law firms); mem. electronic data retrieval com. Am. Bar Assn.; ops. rsch. analyst McKinsey & Co.; orgn. and methods analyst Office of Sec. Air Force.; trustee Ctr. for Study of Responsive Law. Founding editor: Jurimetrics Jour.; editor: Games and Simulations, Artificial Intelligence and Law Jour., Theoria, Simulation/Gaming/News, Jour. Legal Edn., Jour. of Conflict Resolutiion; author: WFF 'N Proof: The Game of Modern Logic, 1961, rev. edit., 1990, (with Robin B.S. Brooks, Patricia A. James) Automatic Retrieval of Legal Literature: Why and How, 1962, WFF: The Beginner's Game of Modern Logic, 1962, rev. edit., 1973, Equations: The Game of Creative Mathematics, 1963, rev. edit., 1994, (with Mary E. Caldwell) Reflections of the Communications Sciences and Law: The Jurimetrics Conference, 1965, (with J. Ross and P. Kugel) Queries 'N Theories: The Game of Science and Language, 1970, rev. edit., 1973, (with F. Goodman, D. Humphrey and J. Ross), On-Words: The Game of Word Structures, 1971, rev. edit., 1973; contbr. articles to profl. jours.; co-author/designer: (with J. Ross and C. Stratton) DIG (Diagnostic Instrnl. Gaming) Math; (with Charles Saxon) Normalizer Clear Legal Drafting Program, 1986, MINT System for

Generating Dynamically Multiple-Interpretation Legal Decision-Assistance Systems, 1991, The Legal Argument Game of Legal Relations, 1997, (with Sandra Bartlett) LawToe: the Game to Learn the Game Rules of The Legal Argument Game of Legal Relations, 2003, (with Sandra Bartlett) The New Legal Argument Game of Legal Relations, 2003, (with Adam Trury) New MINT System for Dynamically Generating Multiple Interpretation Legal Analysis Systems, 2004, (with Sandra Bartlett) A Learning Program for the Legal Relations Language. With USNR, 1945—46. Mem. ABA (coun. sect. sci. and tech.), AAAS, ACLU, Assn. Symbolic Logic, Nat. Coun. Tchrs. Math. Democrat. Unitarian Universalist. Home: 5353 Red Fox Run Ann Arbor MI 48105 Office: U Mich Sch Law 808 Legal Rsch Ann Arbor MI 48109-1215 Office Phone: 734-764-9339. Business E-Mail: laymanal@umich.edu.

ALLEN, LEATRICE DELORICE, psychologist; b. Chgo., July 15, 1948; d. Burt and Mildred Floy (Taylor) Hawkins; m. Allen Jr. Moore, July 30, 1965 (div. Oct. 1975); children: Chandra, Valarie, Allen; m. Armstead Allen, May 11, 1978 (div. May 1987). AA in Bus. Edn., Olive Harvey Coll., Chgo., 1975; BA in Psychology, Chgo. State U., 1977; M in Clin. Psychology, Roosevelt U., 1980; MS in Health Care Adminstrn., Coll. St. Francis, Joliet, Ill., 1993. Lic. clin. profl. counselor. Clk. U.S. Post Office, Chgo., 1967—72; clin. therapist Bobby Wright Mental Health Ctr., Chgo., 1979—80, Cmty. Mental Health Coun., Chgo., 1980—83, assoc. dir., 1983—2006; sr. program dir. Nat. Able Network, 2006—. Cons. Edgewater Mental Health, Chgo., 1984—, Project Price, Chgo., 1980—83; victim svcs. coord. Cmty. Mental Health Coun., Chgo., 1986—87; mgr. youth family svcs. Mile Sq. Health Ctr., Chgo., 1987—88; coord. Evang. Health Sys., Oakbrook, Ill., 1988—93; adminstr. Human Enrichment Devel. Assn., Hazel Crest, Ill., 1993—96; bd. dirs. Ada S. McKinley, Chgo., Nat. Able Network, Chgo.; mem. faculty Prairie State Coll., 2004—, U. Phoenix, 2006—. Fellow, Menninger Found., 1985; scholar, Chgo. State U., 1976, Roosevelt U., 1978. Mem.: Chgo. Coun. Fgn. Rels., Chgo. Sexual Assault Svcs. Network (vice-chair, bd. dirs.), Soc. Traumatic Stress Studies (treatment innovations task force), Ill. Coalition Against Sexual Assault (el. 1985—), Nat. Orgn. for Victim Assistance, Am. Profl. Soc. on Abuse of Children. Avocations: aerobics, reading, theater, dining, making and collecting dolls. Home Phone: 708-333-8144. Personal E-mail: leatriceallen@sbcglobal.net.

ALLEN, LYLE WALLACE, lawyer; b. Chillicothe, Ill., June 17, 1924; s. Donald M. and Mary Ellen (McEvoy) A.; m. Helen Kolar, Aug. 16, 1947; children: Mary Elizabeth Watkins, Bryan James. Student, N.C. State Coll., 1943-44; BS, Northwestern U., 1947; postgrad., Columbia Law Sch., 1947-48; JD, U. Wis., 1950. Bar: Ill. 1950, Wis. 1950. Of counsel Heyl Royster Voelker & Allen, Peoria, Ill., 1951—. Served with 87th Inf. Div. U.S. Army, World War II. Decorated Purple Heart, Bronze star, Combat Infantry badge, Presdl. Unit Citation. Mem. ABA, Ill. State Bar Assn. (pres. 1972-73), Assn. of Ins. Attys. (pres. 1965-66), Illinois Valley Yacht Club. Democrat. Presbyterian. Office: 124 SW Adams St Ste 600 Peoria IL 61602-1392 Office Phone: 309-676-0400.

ALLEN, MARC KEVIN, emergency physician, educator; b. Bedford, Ind., Sept. 2, 1956; s. Robert Edward and Edna Ruth (Little) A.; m. Marita Ann Volk, May 13, 1995. AB, Washington U., St. Louis, 1978; MD, Wright State U., 1982. Diplomate Am. Bd. Emergency Medicine. Intern Mt. Sinai Med. Ctr., Cleve., 1982-83, chief resident in emergency medicine, 1984-85, rsch. dir. emergency med. residency, 1986-96; attending physician Worcester (Mass.) City Hosp., 1985-86; flight physician Metro Lifeflight, Cleve., 1984—2006; attending physician Summa Health Sys., Akron, Ohio, 1999—2005, Lake County Hosp., Willoughby, Ohio, 2005—. Co-author: A Practical Approach Emergency Medicine, 1987. Co-chmn. Washington U. YWCA-YMCA, 1977—78; med. dir. Aurora (Ohio) Fire Dept., 1997—, Six Flags Worlds of Adventure, 2001—03. Fellow Am. Coll. Emergency Physicians (councillor 1996-98, Star of Life Ohio chpt. 2005); mem. Ohio Assn. Emergency Med. Svcs. (med. dirs. 2004—), South Ea. Area Law Enforcement (med. dir. 2004-05), Phi Rho Sigma. Avocations: skiing, golf, cooking. Home: 485 Club Dr Aurora OH 44202-8564 Personal E-mail: ermarc@aol.com.

ALLEN, MARCUS, retired professional football player; b. San Diego, Mar. 26, 1960; Student, U. So. Calif. Running back with Los Angeles Raiders, NFL, El Segundo, Calif., 1982-92; with Kansas City Chiefs, NFL, 1993-97; nat. analyst, broadcaster CBS Sports, NYC, 1998; co-host Marcus Allen Show KCTV 5, Kansas City, Mo., 1997-98; features/sideline reporter CBS Sports, 1999—. Co-owner Pro Ball Beverage Corp.; v.p. Marcus Allen's Broadway Ford, Kansas City, Mo. Author: (with Carlton Stowers) Marcus: The Autobiography of Marcus Allen, 1997. Recipient Heisman Trophy Downtown Athletic Club of N.Y.C., 1981; named Coll. Football Player of Yr., Sporting News, 1981, The Sporting News NFL Rookie of Yr., 1982, Player of Yr., 1985; named to Sporting News Coll. All-Am. Team, 1981. Achievements include playing in NFL championship game, 1984, Pro Bowl, 1983, 85, 86, 88; establishing NFL season record for most combined yards, 1985; holds NFL record for most consecutive games with 100 or more yards rushing (11), 1986. Office: Marcus Allen's Ford 3401 Broadway St Kansas City MO 64111-2403

ALLEN, MAURICE BARTELLE, JR., architect; b. Lansing, Mich., Mar. 20, 1926; s. Maurice Bartelle and Marguerite Rae (Stahl) A.; m. Nancy Elizabeth Huff, June 29, 1951; children— Robert (dec.), Katherine, David. Student, Western Mich. U., 1944, Notre Dame U., 1944-46; BArch, U. Mich., 1950. Registered profl. architect, Mich. Draftsman, designer Smith, Hinchman & Grylls (architects), Detroit, 1950-51; designer, assoc. Eero Saarinen & Assocs., Bloomfield Hills, Mich., 1951-61; v.p. design and planning TMP Assos. (architects, engrs. and planners), Bloomfield Hills, 1961-92, emeritus, 1993; design critic, lectr. Coll. Architecture and Urban Planning, U. Mich., 1958—. Cons. arch. Camelback Bible Ch., Paradise Valley, Ariz. Prin. archtl. works include Gen. Motors Inst. campus devel. and bldgs, Flint, Mich., Mackinac and Manitou halls, Grand Valley State Coll, O'Dowd Hall, Oakland U, Prototype Regional Correctional Facilities, Mich. Dept. Corrections, Fine Arts Ctr. and Theater, Allied Scis. Bldg., Macomb Community Coll., Scheide Music Ctr., Coll. of Wooster, Towsley Ctr. Sch. of Music, U. Mich., Performing Arts Ctr. and Student Ctr., Lake Superior State U., Art Music Humanities Ctr., Wabash Coll., Univ. Community Ctr., U. Western Ont., Drama Theater and Arts Bldg., Concordia Coll., St. Paul. Active Detroit Area council Boy Scouts Am., 1969—, Detroit Inst. Arts, Detroit Symphony; mem. environmental arts com. Mich. Council for Arts, 1970; vice chmn. Mich. Gov.'s Spl. Commn. on Architecture, 1971. Served with USNR, 1944-47. Recipient honor awards Detroit chpt. AIA, 1970-71, Gold medal, 1994, citation for design high rise structures Am. Iron and Steel Inst., 1971, citation of excellence Architecture for Justice Exhbn., 1982. Mem. Coll. of Fellows AIA (co-chair urban priorities Detroit chpt. 1995—), Mich. Soc. Architects (honor awards 1970-71), Sr. Men's Club Birmingham, Masons, Alpha Tau Omega. Republican. Episcopalian. Home and Office: 4325 Derry Rd Bloomfield Hills MI 48302-1835

ALLEN, RENEE, principal; Prin. Villa Duchesne Sch., St. Louis, 1988—. Recipient Blue Ribbon Sch. award U.S. Dept. Edn., 1990-91. Office: Villa Duchesne Oakhill Sch 801 S Spoede Rd Saint Louis MO 63131-2606

ALLEN, RONALD JAY, law educator; b. Chgo., July 14, 1948; s. J. Matteson and Carolyn L. (Latchum) A.; m. Debra Jane Livingston, May 25, 1974 (div. 1982); children: Sarah, Adrienne; m. Julie O'Donnell, Sept. 2, 1984; children: Michael, Conor. BS, Marshall U., 1970; JD, U. Mich., 1973. Bar: Nebr. 1974, Iowa 1979, US Ct. Appeals (8th cir.) 1980, US Supreme Ct. 1981, Ill. 1986. Prof. law SUNY, Buffalo, 1974-79, U. Iowa, Iowa City, 1979-82, 83-84, Duke U., Durham, NC, 1982-83, Northwestern U., Chgo., 1984—, John Henry Wigmore prof., 1992—. Pres. faculty senate U. Iowa, 1980-81. Author: Constitutional Criminal Procedure, 1985, 3rd edit., 1995, An Analytical Approach to Evidence, 1989, Evidence: Text, Cases and Problems, 1997, Arthritis of the Hip and Knee: The Active Person's Guide to Taking Charge, 1998, Comprehensive Criminal Procedure, 2d edit., 2005, Evidence: Text, Problems, Cases, 2002, 4th edit., 2006, Criminal Procedure: Investigation and Right to Counsel, 2005; contbr. articles to profl. jours. Bd. dirs. Constnl. Rights Found., 1992—, Joffrey Ballet, 2003. Mem. ABA (rules com. criminal justice sect.), Am. Law Inst. Office: Northwestern U Sch Law 357 E Chicago Ave Chicago IL 60611-3059 Office Phone: 312-503-8372.

ALLEN, STEPHEN D(EAN), pathologist, microbiologist; b. Linton, Ind., Sept. 8, 1943; s. Wilburn and Betty Allen; m. Vally C. Autrey, June 17, 1964; children: Christopher D., Amy C. BA, Ind. U., 1965, MA, 1967; MD, Ind. U., Indpls., 1970. Diplomate Am. Bd. Pathology Anatomic and Clin. Pathology and Med. Microbiology. Intern in pathology Vanderbilt U. Hosp., Nashville, 1970-71, resident in pathology, 1971-74; clin. asst. prof. pathology Emory U., Atlanta, 1974-77; asst. prof. clin. pathology Ind. U., Indpls., 1977-79, asst. prof. pathology, 1979-81, assoc. prof. pathology, 1981-86, prof. pathology, 1986-92, prof. pathology and lab. medicine, 1992—, James Warren Smith prof. clin. microbiology, 2006—, assoc. dir. div. clin. microbiology, dept. pathology 1977-92, dir. grad. progam pathology, 1986—, sr. assoc. chmn. dept. pathology, 1990-91, dir. divsn. clin. microbiology dept. pathology/lab. medicine, 1992-98, assoc. chair dept. pathology and lab. medicine & dir. labs., 1996-99; dir. disease control lab. divsn. Ind. State Dept. Health, Indpls., 1994—2004; dir. divsn. clin. microbiology dept. pathology/lab. medicine Clarian-Meth.-Ind U.-Riley Hosps., 1998—. Mem. residency rev. com. for pathology Accreditation Coun. for Grad. Med. Edn., 1996—2004, mem. residency rev. com. for molecular genetic pathology, 1999—2004, vice chmn., 2003—04, mem. molecular genetic pathology policy com., 1999—; trustee Am. Bd. Pathology, 1995—2006, life trustee, 2007—, chmn. microbiology test devel. and adv. com., 1995—2006, sec. bd., 2001—02, v.p., 2002, pres., 03, immediate past pres., 04. Co-author: Introduction to Diagnostic Microbiology, 1994, Color Atlas and Textbook of Diagnostic Microbiology, 1997, 2006, Direct Smear Atlas, A Monograph of Gram-Stained Smear Preparations of Clinical Specimens, 2001, (CD-ROM) Direct Smear Atlas, 1998, Parasitology Image Atlas, 2003, Mycology Image Atlas, 2004, Bacteriology I Image Atlas, 2005; contbr. With USPHS, 1974—77. Fellow: Binford-Dammin Soc. Infectious Disease Pathologists, Infectious Diseases Soc. Am., Am. Acad. Microbiology, Coll. Am. Pathologists; mem.: Anaerobe Soc. Ams. (mem. coun. 1994—2002, pres. 2002—04), Am. Soc. Clin. Pathologists (coun. microbiology 1983—89), Masons (32d deg.), Shriners, Sigma Xi. Avocations: musicial instruments, fly fishing. Office: Ind U Sch Medicine Clarian Pathology Bldg Rm 6027 350 West 11th St Rm 6027 Indianapolis IN 46202

ALLEN, THOMAS DRAPER, lawyer; b. Detroit, June 25, 1926; s. Draper and Florence (Jones) A.; m. Joyce M. Johnson, July 18, 1953; children— Nancy A. Bowser, Robert D., Rebecca A. Hubbard. BS, Northwestern U., 1949; JD, U. Mich., 1952. Bar: Ill. 1952, U.S. Supreme Ct. 1971. Assoc. Kirkland & Ellis, Chgo., 1952-60, ptnr., 1961-67, Wildman, Harrold, Allen & Dixon, Chgo., 1967-96, of counsel, 1997—. Chmn. Community Caucus, Hinsdale, Ill., 1960-61; mem. Hinsdale Bd. Edn., 1965-71, pres., 1970-71; pres. West Suburban coun. Boy Scouts Am., 1980-82, mem. nat. exec. bd., 1986-2006, chmn. internat. com., 1995-99, chmn. resolutions com., 1995-2006, mem. world program com., 1983-93, mem. nat. adv. coun. 2006—; moderator Union Ch., Hinsdale, 1983-84; trustee Chgo. Theol. Sem., 1988-97, chair, 1990-96, life trustee, 1997—. With USN, 1944-46. Recipient Silver Beaver award Boy Scouts Am., 1964, Silver Buffalo award, 1997, Bronze Wolf award World Scout Orgn., 1993. Fellow Am. Coll. Trial Lawyers (state chair 1984-85, chair internat. com. 1997-99); mem. ABA, Ill. Bar Assn., Chgo. Bar Assn. (bd. of mgrs 1989-91), Law Club of Chgo., Legal Club of Chgo., Jaycees Internat. (senator, 1965), Internat. Bar Assn., Hinsdale Golf Club. Mem. United Ch. of Christ. Home: 505 N Lake Shore Dr Chicago IL 60611-3427 Office: Wildman Harrold Allen & Dixon 225 W Wacker Dr Chicago IL 60606-1224 Office Phone: 312-201-2630. Business E-Mail: allen@wildman.com.

ALLER, HUGH DUNCAN, astronomer, educator; Prof. astronomy, dir. obs., chmn. dept. astronomy U. Mich., Ann Arbor. Office: 810 Dennison 500 Church St Ann Arbor MI 48104-2514

ALLISON, JOHN ROBERT, lawyer; b. San Antonio, Feb. 9, 1945; s. Lyle (stepfather) and Beatrice (Kaliner) Forehand; m. Rebecca M. Picard; 1 child, Katharine. BS, Stanford U., 1966; JD, U. Wash., 1969. Bar: Wash. 1969, DC 1973, Minn. 1994, US Supreme Ct. 1973. Assoc. Garvey, Schubert & Barer, Seattle, 1969-73; ptnr., 1973-86; prin. Betts, Patterson & Mines, P.S., 1986-94; sr. counsel 3M Co., 1994-2000, asst. gen. counsel, 2000—. Bd. dirs. So. Minn. Regional Legal Svcs.; pres. Jewish Family Svc., St. Paul, 2005-07; lectr. bus. law Seattle U., 1970, U. Wash., 1970-73; judge pro tem, King County Superior Ct., 1983-94 Mem. ABA (vice chmn. toxic and hazardous substances and environ. law com. 1986-91, chair elect 1991-92, chair 1992-93), Minn. Bar Assn., Seattle-King County Bar Assn. (chmn. jud. evaln. polling com. 1982-83), Wash. State Bar Assn. (bd. bar examiners 1984-94), DC Bar Assn., Nat. Inst. Pollution Liability (co-chmn. 1988), Order of the Coif. Office: 3M Co 3 M Ctr Saint Paul MN 55144-1000 Office Phone: 651-736-3993. Business E-Mail: jrallison@mmm.com.

ALLISON, JON B., lawyer; b. Dayton, Ohio, Oct. 25, 1970; BA, U. Mich., 1994; JD, U. Cin. Coll. of Law, 2001. Bar: Ohio 2001, Ct. of Appeals, Sixth Cir., Ct. of Appeals, Eleventh Cir., USDC Southern Dist. Ohio, USDC Eastern Dist. Wis., USDC Southern Dist. Ind. Assoc. Dinsmore & Shohl LLP, Cin. Named one of Ohio's Rising Stars, Super Lawyers, 2006. Mem.: Cin. Bar Assn., Ohio State Bar Assn. Office: Dinsmore & Shohl LLP 255 E 5th St Ste 1900 Cincinnati OH 45202 Office Phone: 513-977-8410. Office Fax: 513-977-8141.

ALLISON, MARK S., trust company executive; BSBA, U. Kans.; MBA, U. Tex. Exec. v.p., chief investment officer Midwest Trust Co., Overland Park, Kans. Office: Midwest Trust Company 5901 College Blvd Ste 100 Leawood KS 66211-1834

ALMEIDA, RICHARD JOSEPH, finance company administrator; b. NYC, Apr. 29, 1942; s. Caetano Escudero and Grace (Maya) A.; m. Jill Farris, Mar. 17, 1979; 1 child, Alexis Farris. BA in Internat. Affairs, George Washington U., 1963; MA in Internat. Adminstrn., Maxwell Sch. Syracuse U., 1965. Comml. and internat. banker Citibank, NY, S.Am., 1966; area head comml. and internat. banking Citicorp/Citibank, Chgo., 1976, LA, 1978-84, dep. strategic planning NYC, 1984; head fin. inst. and investment banking origination Citicorp Investment Bank, 1985-87; CFO Heller Fin., Inc., Chgo., 1987—2002, chmn., CEO, 1995—2002. Bd. dirs. Corn Products Internat., E-funds Corp., United Airlines, Care-USA, Marmon Group. With USCG, 1966—72. Mem.: Chgo. Coun. Global Affairs, Comml. Club Chgo, Econ. Club. Chgo, Racquet Club, Casino, Chgo. Club. Roman Catholic. Office Phone: 312-214-3969.

ALMEN, LOWELL GORDON, church official; b. Grafton, ND, Sept. 25, 1941; s. Paul Orville and Helen Eunice (Johnson) A.; m. Sally Arlyn Clark, Aug. 14, 1965; children: Paul Simon, Cassandra Gabrielle. BA, Concordia Coll., Moorhead, Minn., 1963; MDiv, Luther Theol. Sem., St. Paul, 1967; LittD (hon.), Capital U., 1981; DD (hon.), Carthage Coll., 1989, Concordia Coll., 1994. Ordained to ministry Luth. Ch., 1967. Pastor St. Peter's Luth. Ch., Dresser, Wis., 1967-69; asso. campus pastor, dir. communications Concordia Coll., Moorhead, Minn., 1969-74; mng. editor Luth. Standard ofcl. publ. Am. Luth. Ch., Mpls., 1974-78; editor Luth. Standard, 1979-87; sec., officer Evangelical Luth. Ch. Am., Chgo., 1987—. Author: Old Songs for a New Journey, 1990, One Great Cloud of Witnesses, 1997; author, co-editor: The Many Faces of Pastoral Ministry, 1989; editor: World Religions and Christian Mission, 1967, Our Neighbor's Faith, 1968. Recipient Disting. Alumnus award Concordia Coll., 1982; Bush Found. grantee, 1972 Lutheran. Office: Evang Luth Ch 8765 W Higgins Rd Chicago IL 60631-4101

ALMONY, ROBERT ALLEN, JR., librarian; b. Charleston, W.Va., Oct. 14, 1945; s. Robert Allen and Margaret Elizabeth A.; m. Carol A. Krzeminski, May 6, 1972; children— Rob, Michael, Chandra, Rachel. AA, Grossmont Coll., 1965; BA, San Diego State U., 1968; M.L.S., U. Calif.-Berkeley, 1977. Sr. div. clk. San Diego State U. Library, 1965-68; acct. Calif. Tchrs. Fin. Services, Orange County, 1968-70, v.p., gen. mgr., 1971-76; research asst. library sch. U. Calif.-Berkeley, 1976-77; reference librarian Oberlin Coll. Library, Ohio, 1977-79; asst. dir. libraries U. Mo., Columbia, 1980—; owner Almony & Assocs. Tax and Fin. Planning, Columbia, 1980—; distbr. USA Today, Columbia, 1984-88. Guest lectr. libr. budgeting, personal fin. planning; spkr. on fin. planning, U. Mo. HR seminars, 1999—; cons. libr. copy svcs.; faculty coun. exec. bd., 1994-2000, recorder Mo. U., 1994-98, chair fiscal affairs, 1998-2000, learning strategies tchr., 1986—, adj. faculty Libr. Sch., 1997—. Contbr. articles to profl. jours. Treas. Bahai's of Columbia, 1982-86, 95-97, 2003-, sec., 1987-89, 93-95, 1998-2001, 2001-2002, chmn., 1989-93; coach Columbia Youth Soccer League, 1981-92; cubmaster Boy Scouts Am., Columbia, 1983-85; asst. scoutmaster, 1985-91; hon. warrior Mic-O-Say, 1986-, treas. Mo. U. Soccer Boosters, 1996—2003; mem. Daniel Boone Regional Libr. Devel. Bd., 1999-2000. Mem. ALA, Mo. Libr. Assn. (treas. 1996-97, 98-99), Assn. Coll. and Rsch. Librs. (exec. com. 1983-86), Libr. Adminstrn. and Mgmt. Assn. (chmn. mem. 1991-93, 2000-01, Outstanding Svc. award 1994, B & F Officers Group Libr. Adminstrn. and Mgmt. (chmn. 1987-91), Nat. Commn. on Ednl. Stats. Integrated Post-Secondary Edn. Data Sys. Acad. Librs. (coord. Mo. 1992-, Mo. Assn. Coll. and Rsch. Librs. (vice chmn., chmn. 1982-84), Hickman Athletic Boosters (pres. 1991-94), Maplewood Barn Theater (bd. dirs. 1993-00, sec., treas. 1998-00), COE Coll. Parents (bd. dirs. 1993-95). Home: 301 Rothwell Dr Columbia MO 65203-0257 Office: U Mo 104 Ellis Libr Columbia MO 65201-5149 Office Phone: 573-882-4701. Personal E-mail: ralmony@aol.com. Business E-Mail: almonyr@missouri.edu.

ALONS, DWAYNE, state representative; b. Boyden, Iowa, Sept. 1946; s. Gerrit and Hattie Alons; m. Clarice Ahlers; children: Dwayne, Kyle, Kristin. BS in Math., orthwestern Coll., 1968; M in Mgmt., U. Ark., 1974. Mem. Iowa Ho. Reps., DesMoines, 1999—, chair govt. oversight com., mem. agr. com., mem. appropriations com., mem. pub. safety com., mem. transp. com. Vice-comdr. Iowa Air Nat. Guard Hdqrs.; active Sioux County Farm Bur., Lincoln twp. dir., mem. legis. com. Brig. gen. USAF, 1975—. Mem.: Iowa Corn Growers Assn., Am. Soybean Assn., Gideons Internat. Home: 1314 7th St Hull IA 51239 Office: State Capitol East 12th and Grand Des Moines IA 50319

ALPERS, DAVID HERSHEL, gastroenterologist, educator; b. Phila., May 9, 1935; s. Bernard Jacob and Lillian (Sher) A.; m. Melanie Goldman, Aug. 12, 1977; children: Ann, Ruth, Barbara. BA, Harvard U., 1956, MD, 1960. Cert. Am. Bd. Internal Medicine, 1967. Intern Mass. Gen. Hosp., Boston, 1960-61, resident in internal medicine, 1961-62; instr. medicine Harvard U., 1965-67, assoc. in medicine, 1967-68, asst. prof., 1968-69; asst. prof. medicine Washington U., St. Louis, 1969-72, assoc. prof., 1972-73, prof., 1973—, William B. Kountz prof., 1997—, dir. gastrointestinal divsn., 1969-97, asst. dir. clin. nutrition rsch. unit, 1999—; sr. cons. R&D GlaxoSmithKline, 1999—. Author: (with others) Manual of Nutritional Therapeutics, 4th edit., 2002; assoc. editor: Textbook of Gastroenterology, 4th edit., 2003, Physiology of the Gastrointestinal Tract, 4th edit., 1997; assoc. editor: Jour. Clin. Investigation, 1977-82, Encyclopedia of Gastroenterology, 2003; editor: Am. Jour. Physiology, Gastrointestinal and Liver Physiology, 1991-97; mem. editl. bd.: Jour. Biol. Chemistry, 1998-2003; editor, Curr Opin Gastroenterol, sect. Small Intestine and Nutrition, 1995-; contbr. articles and revs. to profl. jours., chpts. to books. With USPHS, 1962—64. Fellow, Am. Soc. Nutritional Scis., 2003; David H. Alpers Ann. lectureship, Wash. U., Sch. Medicine, 1999. Fellow Am. Soc. utritional Scis.; mem. Am. Soc. Clin. Investigation, Assn. Am. Physicians, Am. Gastroent. Assn. (chmn. tng. and edn. com. 1974-78, dir. undergrad. tchg. project 1974-99, pres. 1990-91, Julius Friedenwald medal 1997), Am. Soc. Biochem. Molecular Biology (editl. bd. 1998-2003), Am. Fedn. Clin. Rsch., Am. Soc. Clin. Nutrition, Am. Psychol. Assn. (mem. gastrointestinal sect. steering com. 1991-97, Disting. Gastrointestinal Physiology Rsch. award 1998, mem. pubs. com. 1999-2001). Avocation: music. Office: Washington U Med Sch Dept Internal Medicine PO Box 8031 Saint Louis MO 63110-1010 Business E-Mail: dalpers@im.wustl.edu.

ALPERT, DANIEL, broadcast executive; b. Chgo., June 20, 1952; s. Herbert and Miriam Florence (Nemiroff) A.; m. Doreen Marie Podolski, Apr. 30, 1976; children: Hilary Marie, Neil Andrew. BA, Mich. State U., 1973, postgrad., 1974-76. News reporter, disk jockey Sta. WITL-AM-FM, Lansing, Mich., 1973; audio producer Instructional Media Ctr. Mich. State U., East Lansing, 1973-74; dir. pub. info. Sta. WKAR-TV, East Lansing, 1974-76; v.p., dir. pub. info. Sta. WTVS Detroit Pub. TV, 1976-82, sr. v.p., acting gen. mgr., 1983, sr. v.p., asst. gen. mgr., 1983-96, sr. v.p. sta. mgr., 1996-2000, COO, Sta. mgr., 2000—, interim gen. mgr., 2007—. Contbr. articles on travel and sci. local newspapers. Trustee Karmanos Cancer Inst., Detroit, 1984-2004. Recipient Devel. award Corp. for Pub. Broadcasting, 1976, Promotion award Broadcast Promotion Assn., 1978, Pub. Broadcasting Svc., 1981, Govt. Rels. awards Nat. Assn. Pub. TV Stas., 1989, 96, ACE award Mich. Assn. Broadcasters, 1991. Mem. NATAS (gov. Detroit chpt. 1980-97, Silver Circle award Mich. chpt. 2000), Mich. Assn. Broadcasters, Mich. Pub. Broadcasters (exec. com. 1995—). Office: Sta WTVS Klover Ct Wixom MI 48393 Business E-Mail: alpert@dptv.org.

ALSCHULER, ALBERT W., law educator; b. Aurora, Ill, Sept. 24, 1940; s. Sam and Winifred (King) Alschuler; m. Louise Evans Alschuler, Mar. 21, 1970 (div.); 1 child, Samuel Jonathan. AB in History, cum laude, Harvard U., 1962, LLB magna cum laude, 1965. Bar: Ill. 1965. Law clk. to Hon. Walter V. Schaefer Ill. Supreme Ct., 1965—66; fellow Ctr. for Studies in Criminal Justice U. Chgo., 1967—68; spl. asst. to Hon. Fred M. Vinson, Jr. Asst. Atty. Gen. criminal divsn., 1968—69; asst. prof. law U. Tex., Austin, 1966—67, assoc. prof., 1969—70, prof., 1970—76, U. Colo., Boulder, Colo., 1976—84, U Pa., Phila., 1984, U. Chgo. Law Sch., 1985—88, Wilson-Dickinson prof., 1988—2002, Julius Kreeger prof. law and criminology, 2002—. Author: Law Without Values: The Life, Work and Legacy of Justice Holmes, 2000; co-author: The Privilege Against Self-Incrimination: Its Origins and Development, 1997. Fellow: Am. Bar Found. Office: U Chgo Law Sch 1111 E 60th St Chicago IL 60637-2776 Office Phone: 773-702-3586. E-mail: awaa@midway.uchicago.edu.

ALSOP, DONALD DOUGLAS, federal judge; b. Duluth, Minn., Aug. 28, 1927; s. Robert Alvin and Mathilda (Aaseng) A.; m. Jean Lois Tweeten, Aug. 16, 1952; children: David, Marcia, Robert. BS, U. Minn., 1950, LLB, 1952. Bar: Minn. 1952. Pvt. practice, New Ulm, Minn.; ptnr. Gislason, Alsop, Dosland & Hunter, 1954-75; judge U.S. Dist. Ct. Minn., St. Paul, 1975—, chief dist. judge, 1985-92, sr. dist. judge, 1992—. Mem. 8th cir. jud. coun., 1987-92, Jud. Conf. Com. to Implement Criminal Justice Act, 1979-87; mem. exec. com. Nat. Conf. Fed. Trial Judges, 1990-94. Chmn. Brown County (Minn.) Republican Com., 1960-64, 2d Congl. Dist. Rep. Com., 1968-72, Brown County chpt. ARC, 1968-74. Served with AUS, 1945-46. Mem. 8th Cir. Dist. Judges Assn. (pres. 1982-84), New Ulm C. of C. (pres. 1974-75), Order of Coif. Office: US Dist Ct 754 Fed Bldg 316 Robert St N Saint Paul MN 55101-1495

ALSTROM, SVEN ERIK, architect; b. Emporia, Kans., July 27, 1951; s. William E. and Willa M. (Russell) A.; m. Lynn M. Mathews, June 22, 1974 (div. June 1983). B in Gen. Studies, U. Kans., 1975; postgrad., U. Denver, 1984. Registered Calif., Colo., Kans., Mo., NC, N. Mex., cert. Nat. Coun. Archtl. Registration Bds. Arch. PGAV Archs., Kansas City, Mo., 1972-74, Horner Blessing, Kansas City, 1977-79, MSFS Archs., Kansas City, 1979-80, Urban Design, Denver, 1981-82, Dominck Assocs., Denver, 1983-84; with C. Welton Anderson & Assocs., Aspen, Colo., 1989-90; arch. Ecol. Archs., Aspen, 1999—; pvt. practice Ecol. Architecture PC, Aspen, 1990—2008. Mem. City of Lawrence Kans. Historic Resources Commn., 2004—. Mem.: AIA. Presbyterian. Office: 842 W 21st St Lawrence KS 66046 Office Phone: 785-749-1018. E-mail: alstrom@sbcglobal.net.

ALTAN, TAYLAN, engineering educator, director; b. Trabzon, Turkey, Feb. 12, 1938; arrived in US, 1962; s. Seref and Sadife (Baysal) Kadioglu; m. Susan Borah, July 18, 1964; children: Peri Michele, Aylin Elisabeth Diploma in engring., Tech. U., Hannover, Fed. Republic Germany, 1962; MS in Mech. Engring., U. Calif.-Berkeley, 1964, PhD in Mech. Engring., 1966. Rsch. engr. DuPont Co., Wilmington, Del., 1966-68; rsch. scientist Battelle Columbus Labs., Ohio, 1968-72, rsch. fellow Ohio, 1972-75, sr. rsch. leader Ohio, 1975-86; prof. mech. engring., dir. engring. rsch. ctr. Ohio State U., Columbus, 1985—. Chmn. sci. com. N.Am. Mfg. Rsch. Inst. Soc. Mfg. Engrs., Detroit, 1982-86, pres., 1987; dir. Ctr. for Net Shape Mfg. Co-author: Forging Equipment, 1973, Metal Forming, 1983, Metal Forming and the Finite Element Method, 1989, Cold, Warm and Hot Forging, 2004; contbr. more than 400 tech. articles to profl. jours. Fellow: ASME, Am. Soc. Metals (chmn. forging com. 1978—87), Soc. Mfg. Engrs. (Gold medal 1985). Avocations: languages, travel. Office: Ohio State U 210 Baker Bldg 1971 Neil Ave Columbus OH 43210-1210 Office Phone: 614-292-5063. Business E-Mail: altan.1@osu.edu.

ALTER, WILLIAM, state legislator; b. Iowa City, May 15, 1944; m. Merijo Robinson, 1963; children: Angela, William Brett (dec.). Student, Jefferson Coll. Law, Enforcement Tng. Ctr., 1982-84. mem. consumer protection com., elections com., criminal law com. Mo. State rep. Dist. 90, 1988-2000; owner, mgr. sml. bus.; sales v.p. Nat. Co.; police officer small municipality, Mo.; pres. Alter Mgmt., 1977—. Founder N. Jefferson C. of C., Mo; treas. High Ridge Ch. of Christ. Mem. NRA (life), Hist. Soc. and Rep. Club, Rotary (past pres.). Home: 1800 Gravois Rd High Ridge MO 63049-2610

ALTERMAN, IRWIN MICHAEL, lawyer; b. Vineland, NJ, Mar. 4, 1941; s. Joseph and Rose A.; m. Susan Simon, Aug. 6, 1972 (dec. Apr. 1997); 1 son, Owen. AB, Princeton U., 1962; LLB, Columbia U., 1965. Bar: N.Y. 1966, Mich. 1967. Law clk. to chief judge Theodore Levin U.S. Dist. Ct. (ea. dist.) Mich.,

1965-67; assoc. Kaye Scholer, NYC, 1967—70, Hyman, Gurwin, Nachman, Friedman & Winkelman, Southfield, Mich., 1970-74, ptnr., 1974—88, Kaufman and Payton, Farmington Hills, 1988—89, Kemp Klein, Troy, 1989—. Author: Plain and Accurate Style in Court Papers, 1987; founding editor: Mich. Antitrust, 1975—92; editor: Mich. Antitrust Digest, 3d edit., 2001; contbr. articles to profl. jours. Bd. gov. Jewish Fedn. Detroit, 1990—; nat. young leadership cabinet United Jewish Appeal, 1978-79, nat. exec. com., 1980; past pres. Adat Shalom Synagogue, Farmington Hills, Mich., Jewish Cmty. Ctr., West Bloomfield, Mich. Mem. ABA, Am. Law Inst., State Bar Mich. (past chmn. com. on plain English, past. chmn. antitrust sect.), Princeton Club (past pres. Mich.). Office: Kemp Klein Ste 600 201 W Big Beaver Rd Troy MI 48084-4136 Office Phone: 248-528-1111. Business E-Mail: irwin.alterman@kkue.com.

ALTHAVER, LAMBERT EWING, manufacturing executive; b. Kansas City, Mo., May 18, 1931; s. Edward William and Dorothy Lambert (Ewing) A.; m. Holly Elizabeth Walpole, Feb. 28, 1953; children: Brian, Lauren BA, Principia Coll, 1952; LLD honoris causa, Northwood U., 2003. Account exec. Walbro Corp., Cass City, Mich., 1954-58, asst. to pres., 1958-65, v.p. fin., 1965-70, exec. v.p., 1970-77, pres., chief ops. officer, 1977-82, pres., CEO, 1982-87, chmn., pres., CEO, 1987-96, also bd. dirs., chmn., CEO, 1996-98, chmn. emeritus, 1998-2000. Councilman Village of Cass City, 1963—65, pres., 1965—84, 1987—2000, 2004—; mem. Tuscola County Planning Commn., Caro, Mich., 1966—94; chmn. Cass City Econ. Devel. Corp., 1983—96, Tuscola Area Airport Authority, 1994—2004; co-founder, v.p. Village Bach Festival, 1979—; mem. Mich. Jobs Commn., 1996—99; bd. dirs. Tuscola Econ. Devel. Corp., 1985—2004; vice-chmn., sec., dir. Artrain, Inc., 1975—96, chmn., 1996—2003; v.p., bd. dirs. Lake Huron area Boy Scouts Am., 1988—94; dir. Am. Bus. Conf. Found., Washington, 1998—, Mich. Mcpl. League Found., Ann Arbor, 1999—2002; trustee Jordan Coll., 1990—95, Northwood U., 2000—, Hills & Dales Hosp., Cass City, 1998—. With US Army, 1952—54. Named Citizen of Yr., Case City C. of C., 1978, Outstanding Bus. Leader, Northwood U., 1997; recipient Silver Beaver award, Boy Scouts Am., 1995, Disting. Eagle Scout award, 1989; Paul Harris fellow, Rotary Internat., Evanston, Ill., 1979, 1994, 1999, 2002, 2004, 2005, 2006. Mem.: Mich. C. of C. (bd. dirs. 1986—92), Cass City C. of C. (bd. dirs. 1985—2004), Detroit Athletic Club, Rotary. Avocation: golf. Office: PO Box 27 Cass City MI 48726-0027 Office Phone: 989-872-8183. E-mail: althaver@tband.net.

ALTING, RONNIE JOE, state legislator, restaurateur; b. Lafayette, Ind., Mar. 15, 1956; s. Frank and Estell (Buschong) A., m. Elizabeth; two children, Ronnie Jr., Ashley. BS, Purdue U., 1977. Program dir. Lafayette YMCA, 1977-80; pres. Price Properties, Inc., Lafayette, 1980-83; v.p. Shook Mgmt., Inc., Lafayette, 1983-84; property mgr. U.S. region R.W.B. Realty, New Orleans, 1984-86; co-owner, gen. mgr. Patout's Restaurant, New Orleans, 1986—; mem. Ind. Senate, 1998—. Pub. relations chmn., bd. dirs. Big Bros., New Orleans, 1987—; bd. dirs. New Orleans YMCA, 1987—. Named One of Outstanding Young Men of Am., 1985. Mem. Sons of Am. Legion. Republican. Methodist. Avocations: running, assisting youth charities, racquetball. Office: Ind State Senate 200 W Washington St Indianapolis IN 46204-2785 also: 3600 Cedar Ln Lafayette IN 47905-3914

ALTMAN, JIM, newscaster; married; 1 child. Grad., Syracuse U. Reporter Sta. WAMI-TV, Miami; with ABC Newsmagazine, 20/20; anchor Sta. WSYX/WTTE-TV, Columbus, Ohio. Recipient Emmy awards, Cine Golden Eagle awards (2). Office: WSYX/WTTE-TV 1261 Dublin Rd Columbus OH 43215

ALTOSE, MURRAY DAVID, critical care physician, educator; b. Winnipeg, Man., Can., Oct. 1, 1941; came to U.S., 1969; m. Connie Jean Tesmer, Jan. 14, 1973; children: Michael Dov, Aaron Judah, Benjamin Isaac. BSc, MD, U. Man., 1965. Diplomate Am. Bd. Internal medicine, Am. Bd. Pulmonary Disease. Rotating intern Winnipeg Gen. Hosp., 1965-66, asst. resident in medicine, 1966-67, resident in critical care medicine, 1968-69; asst. resident medicine Cleve. Met. Gen. Hosp., 1969-70, resident-in-charge pulmonary disease sect., 1970-71, chief pulmonary divsn. dept. medicine, 1977-88, assoc. dir. dept. medicine, 1981-88; fellow pulmonary disease sect. Hosp. U. Pa., Phila., 1971-73, co-dir. respiratory ICU, 1973-74, dir. diagnostic svcs., 1973-77; assoc. in medicine U. Pa. Sch. Medicine, Phila., 1973, asst. prof. medicine, 1973-77; assoc. prof. medicine Case Western Res. U. Sch. Medicine, Cleve., 1977-84, prof. medicine, 1984—; chief of staff Dept. Vets. Affairs Med. Ctr., Cleve., 1988—96; mgr. med.-surg. specialties care line Vets. Healthcare Sys. Ohio, 1996—. Assoc. dean Vets. Hosp. Affairs, 1988—; attending physician pulmonary in-patient svc. med. ICU and Pulmonary Cons. Svc. Cleve. Met. Gen. Hosp., 1977-78, med. dir. respiratory therapy dept., 1977-88, dir. respiratory ICU, 1977-81, attending physician med. ICU Univ. Hosps., Cleve., 1978—; mem. med. rsch. svc. rev. bd. for respiration VA, 1986-89; spl. reviewer NIH Clin. Sci., 1985, 88; cons. spl. emphasis panel NIH Nat. Heart, Lung and Blood Inst., 1996; temp. mem. NIH Respiratory and Applied Physiology Study Sect., 1996; attending physician respiratory ICU VA Med. Ctr., Cleve., 1988—, attending physician med. svc., 1988; lectr. in field. Mem. editl. bd. Jour. Applied Physiology, 1984-93, editl. referee, 1980—; contbr. articles to profl. publs., chpts. to books, abstracts. Trustee Northeast Ohio affiliate Am. Heart Assn., 1993-98, mem. rsch. allocation com., 1989-93. Mem. Am. Fedn. Clin. Rsch. (mem. program 1982, steering com. sect. on respiratory pathophysiology 1981-82, chmn. sect. 1982-84, mem. program and awards coms. ann. sci. assembly 1985), Am. Thoracic Soc. (program com. sci. assembly on respiratory structure and function 1989-90), Ohio Thoracic Soc., Am. Coll. Chest Physicians (gov. Ohio 2001-03, program com., awards com. ann. sci. assembly 1985), Am. Physiol. Soc., Am. Coll. Physician Execs., Am. Heart Assn., Nat. Assn. VA Chiefs of Staff (pres. elect 1996, pres. 1997-98). Office: Cleve VA Med Ctr 10701 East Blvd Cleveland OH 44106-1702

ALTSCHAEFFL, ADOLPH GEORGE, retired civil engineering educator; b. Passaic, NJ, July 20, 1930; s. Ludwig and Crescenz (Liebl) A.; m. Martha Anne Filiatreau, Aug. 6, 1966. BSC.E., Purdue U., 1952, MSC.E., 1955, PhD, 1960. Instr. civil engring. Purdue U., West Lafayette, Ind., 1952-60, asst. prof. civil engring., 1960-64, assoc. prof., 1964-74, prof., 1974-2000, asst. head dept., 1983-91, head geotech. engring., 1994-2000; with Waterways Expt. Sta., C.E., Vicksburg, Miss., 1955, U.S. Geol. Survey, Indpls., 1956; ret., 2000. Cons. civil engring. with various architect and contractor firms. Contbr. articles to profl. jours. Trustee West Lafayette Pub. Libr., Ind., 2005—, v.p. bd. trustees, 2007—. With USAR, 1950—61. Mem.: NSPE, ASCE, Am. Soc. Engring. Edn. Personal E-mail: altsch@ecn.purdue.edu.

ALUMBAUGH, JOANN MCCALLA, magazine editor; b. Ann Arbor, Mich., Sept. 16, 1952; d. William Samuel and Jean Arliss (Guy) McCalla; m. Lyle Ray Alumbaugh, Apr. 27, 1974; children: Brent William, Brandon Jess, Brooke Louise. BA, Ea. Mich. U., 1974. Cert. elem. tch., Mich. Assoc. editor Chester White Swine Record Assn., Rochester, Ind., 1974-77; prodn. editor United Duroc Swine Registry, Peoria, Ill., 1977-79; dir., pres. Nat. Assn. Swine Records, Macomb, Ill., 1979-82; free-lance writer, artist Ill. and Nat. Specific Pathogen Free Assn., Ind. producers, Good Hope, Emden, Ill., 1982-85; editor The Hog Producer Farm Progress Publs., Urbandale, Iowa, 1985-99; exec. editor Nebr. Farmer, Kans. Farmer, Mo. Ruralist, We. Beef Prodr., Beef Prodr., Farm & Fireside, 1999—2003; dir. comms. Farms.Com, 2003—. Family Living Program, Farm Progress Show, 1985-2004, Master Farm Homemaker Program, 1989-99; mem. U.S. Agrl. Export Devel. Coun., Washington, 1979-82, apptd. mem. Blue Ribbon Com. on Agr., 1980-81. Contbr. numerous articles to profl. jours. Precinct chmn. Rep. Party, Linden, Iowa, 1988; mem. Keep Improving Dist. Schs., Panora, Iowa, 1990-91; v.p. Sunday sch. com. Sunset Circle, United Meth. Ch., Linden, 1990-91; pres. PTA, Panorama Schs., Panora, 1993-94; coach Odyssey of Mind Program World Competition, 1994—. Mem.: Iowa Master Farm Homemakers (chair nat. farm homemakers planning com. 2005—06), Guthrie County Prok Prodrs., McDonough County and Ill. Porkettes (county pres. 1978—79, Belleringer award 1979), Nat. Pork Prodrs. Coun., Iowa Pork Prodrs. Assn. (legis. com. 1990—95, hon. master pork prodr.), U.S. Animal Health Assn., Am. Agrl. Editors Assn. (chmn. dist. svc. com. 1991, master writer 1997, pres.-elect 1998, pres. 1999, chmn. adv. coun. 1999—2002, trustee 2002—, chmn. internat. com. 2005—, co-chmn. comm. clinic, chmn. comms. clinic, chmn. agrl. media summit, chmn. steering com., World of Difference award 1995, Oscar in Agr. 1999), Internat. Platform Assn. Avocations: reading, painting, gardening. Home: 2644 Amarillo Ave Linden IA 50146-8029 Office: PigChamp Aspen Business Park 426 S 17th Ames IA 50010 Office Phone: 641-744-2114. Business E-Mail: joann.alumbaugh@farms.com.

ALUTTO, JOSEPH ANTHONY, academic administrator, former dean, management educator; b. Bronx, NY, June 3, 1941; s. Anthony and Concetta (Del Prete) Alutto; m. Carol ewcomb, Sept. 9, 1948; children: Patricia, Christina, Kerrie, Heather. BBA, Manhattan Coll., Riverdale, NY, 1962; MA in Indsl. Relations, U. Ill., 1965; PhD in Orgnl. Behavior, Cornell U., 1968. Asst. prof. orgnl. behavior SUNY, Buffalo, 1966-72, assoc. prof., 1972-75, prof., 1975-91, dean Sch. Mgmt., 1976-91, Clarence S. Marsh chair mgmt., 1991; dean Max M. Fisher Coll. of Bus. Ohio State U., Columbus, 1991—2007, exec. dean for profl. colleges, 1998—2007, John W. Berry sr. chmn. bus., 1999—2007, interim pres., 2007, interim exec. v.p. and provost, 2007—. Bd. dirs. United Retail Group, Inc., ationwide Fin. Svcs.; pres., bd. dirs. M/I Homes. Author: (with others) Theory Testing in Organizational Behavior: The Varient Approach, 1983; contbr. 65 articles to profl. jours. United Way, Buffalo, 1982—91; pres. Amherst Cen. Sch. Bd., 1982—86. Mem. APA, AAAS, Acad. Mgmt. (pres. Ea. divsn. 1980-81), Am. Sociol. Assn., Am. Assembly of Collegiate Schools Bus. -Internat. Assn. Mgmt. Edn. (pres. 1996-98), Capital Club, Athletic Club. Business E-Mail: alutto.1@osu.edu.

ALVARADO, SERAFIN, wine connoisseur; m. Soyoung Alvarado; 3 children. Grad. in Chemistry, U. Puerto Rico. Master sommelier 2005. Room svc. waiter Hilton Hotels, PR; head wine sch. Cadierno Corp., PR, 1994; wine steward Charlie Trotter's, Chgo., 2001—05; dir. wine edn. So. Wine & Spirits of Ill., 2005—. Wine columnist El Nuevo Dia, PR. Named one of Top 40 Under 40, Crain's Chgo. Bus., 2006; recipient Bill Rice Disting. Sommelier of Yr. award, 2005. Mem.: Ct. Master Sommeliers. Achievements include being the first Puerto Rican named a master sommelier. Avocation: jazz. Mailing: Southern Wine & Spirits of Ill 300 E Crossroads Pky Bolingbrook IL 60440

ALVAREZ, RALPH, food products executive; b. Cuba; BBA cum laude, U. Miami, 1976. Various pos., including mng. dir. Burger King Spain, pres. Burger King Can., regional v.p. Fla. region Burger King Corp., 1977—89; divsn. v.p.-Fla. to corp. v.p. Wendy's Internat. Inc., 1990—94; dir. devel. for No. Calif. McDonald's Corp., 1994, regional v.p., Sacramento region, regional dir., Chipotle Mex. Grill, 1999—2000, pres. McDonald's Mex., 2000—01, pres., ctrl. divsn., McDonald's USA, 2001—03; COO, exec. v.p. McDonald's USA, Oak Brook, Ill., 2003—04, pres., 2004—05, McDonald's N. Am., 2005—06; pres., COO McDonald's Corp., 2006—. Bd. dirs. McDonald's Corp., 2008—. Named one of 50 Most Important Hispanics in Tech. & Bus., Hispanic Engr. & Info. Tech. mag., 2005. Office: McDonald's Corp 1 McDonald's Plz 2915 Jorie Blvd Oak Brook IL 60523*

ALVERSON, WILLIAM H., lawyer; b. Rockford, Ill., July 23, 1933; AB, Princeton U., 1955; LL.B., U. Wis., 1960. Bar: Wis. 1960. Currently mem. firm Godfrey & Kahn. Pres. Milw. Profl. Sports and Services, 1972-76; chmn. Houston Rockets basketball team, 1977-79; chmn. bd. govs. Nat. Basketball Assn., 1975-76. Mem. Milw., Am. bar assns., State Bar Wis., Phi Delta Phi. Office: 780 N Water St Milwaukee WI 53202-3512

AMACK, REX, state agency administrator; Dir. Nebr. Games and Pks. Commn., Lincoln, 1998—. Office: Nebr Games & Pks Commn 2200 N 33rd St Lincoln NE 68503-1417

AMAN, ALFRED CHARLES, JR., law educator; b. Rochester, NY, July 7, 1945; s. Alfred Charles Sr. and Jeannette Mary (Czebatul) Aman; m. Carol Jane Greenhouse, Sept. 23, 1976. AB, U. Rochester, 1967; JD, U. Chgo., 1970. Bar: DC 1971, Ga. 1972, NY 1980, Ind. 1993. Law clk. U.S. Ct. Appeals, Atlanta, 1970—72; assoc. Sutherland, Asbill & Brennan, Atlanta, 1972—75, Washington, 1975—77; assoc. prof. Sch. Law, Cornell U., Ithaca, NY, 1977—82, prof. law, 1983—91, exec. dir. Internat. Legal Studies Program, 1988—90; dean Sch. Law, Ind. U., Bloomington, 1991—2002, prof. law, 1991—2007, Roscoe C. O'Byrne chair in law, 1999—2007, disting. Fulbright chair in comparative constitutional law, 1998; vis. prof. law U. Paris II, 1998; vis. fellow law and pub. affairs program Princeton U., 2002—03; dean, prof. Suffolk U. Law Sch., Boston, 2007—. Cons. U.S. Adminstrv. Conf., Washington, 1978—80, Washington, 1986—; trustee U. Rochester, 1980—; vis. fellow Wolfson Coll., Cambridge U., 1983—84, 1990—91. Author: Energy and Natural Resources, 1983, Administrative Law in a Global Era, 1992, Administrative Law Treatise, 1992, 2d edit., 2001. Chmn. Ithaca Bd. Zoning Appeals, 1980—82. Mem.: ABA, N.Y. State Bar Assn., Ga. Bar Assn., D.C. Bar Assn., Am. Assn. Law Schs., Phi Beta Kappa. Avocations: music, piano. Office: Ind U Sch Law 211 S Indiana Ave Bloomington IN 47405-7001 Office Phone: 617-573-8155. Personal E-mail: aaman@suffolk.edu.

AMAN, MOHAMMED MOHAMMED, dean, library and information science professor; b. Alexandria, Egypt, Jan. 3, 1940; came to U.S., 1963, naturalized, 1975; s. Mohammed Aman and Fathia Ali (al-Maghrabi) Mohammed; m. Mary Jo Parker, Sept. 15, 1972; 1 son, David. BA, Cairo U., 1961; MS, Columbia U., 1965; PhD, U. Pitts., 1968. Libr. Egyptian Nat. Libr., 1961-63, Duquesne U., Pitts., 1966-68; asst. prof. libr. sci. Pratt Inst., NYC, 1968-69; from asst. prof. to assoc. prof. St. John's U., Jamaica, NY, 1969-73, prof., dir. divsn. libr. and info. sci., 1973-76; prof. libr. sci., dean Palmer Grad. Libr. Sch., C.W. Post Ctr., L.I. U., 1976-79; dean Sch. Info. Studies U. Wis., 1979—2003, prof., dean, interim dean Sch. Edn. Milw., 2001—02, dean emeritus, prof. Sch. Info. Scis., 2003—. Cons. UNESCO, U.S., AID and UNIDO; USIA acad. specialist, Germany, 1989; Fulbright lectr. Cairo U., 1990-91; USIA-sponsored lectr. Mohamed V. Univ., Rabat, Morocco, 1997. Author: Librarianship and the Third World, 1976, Cataloging and Classifications of Non-Western Library Material: Issues, Trends and Practices, 1980, Arab Serials and Periodicals: A Subject Bibliography, 1979, Online Access to Databases, 1983, On Developing Computer-Based Library Systems (Arabic), 1984, Information Services (Arabic), 1985, Trends in Urban Library Management, 1989, The Bibliotheca Alexandrina: A Link in the Chain of Cultural Continuity, 1991, Information Technology Use in Libraries (Arabic), 1998, Internet Use in Libraries, 2000, The Gulf War in World Literature, 2002; editor-in-chief: Digest of Middle East Studies, 1991-. Chmn. Black Faculty Coun., U. Wis., Milw.; mktg. com. Milw. Art Mus.; bd. dirs. Clara Mohammed Sch., 2001-. Recipient Outstanding Achievement award, Egyptian Libr. Assn., 1997. Mem. NAACP, ALA (chmn. internat. rels. com. 1984-86, standing com. on libr. edn., internat. subcom. 1990-91, chmn. 1991-93, internat. rels. Round Table 1993-94, John Ames Humphry/Online Computer Libr. Ctr. Outstanding Contbn. award 1989, Leadership award black caucus 1994, Excellence award black caucus 1995), Assn. Libr. and Sci. (Svc. award 1988), Am. Soc. for Info. Sci. (chmn. spl. interest group in internat. info. issues, internat. rels. com.), Egyptian Libr. Assn. (life, Outstanding Achievement award 1997), Arab/Jewish Dialogue, Egyptian-Am. Scholars Assn., Assn. for Libr. and Info. Sci. Edn. (chmn. internat. rels. com. 1983-85), Wis. Libr. Assn. (Svc. award 1992, P.N. Kaula Internat. award and medal 1996, Wis. Libr. of Yr. 1998), Libr. Svcs. and Constrn. Act. (adv. com. 1986-89), Internat. Archtl. Jury for Bibliotheca Alexandrina, Internat. Fedn. Libr. Assns. and Insts. (sec. on edn. and tng. 1983-92), Coun. on Egyptian Am. Rels., The Gamaliel Chair (bd. dirs. 1995-97), Leaders Forum (bd. dirs. 1995—), America's Black Holocaust Mus. (bd. dirs. 1999—), Islamic Social Family Svcs. (bd. dirs. 1999—), Milw. Tchr.'s Edn. Ctr. (bd. dirs.). Democrat. Muslim. Office: U Wis-Milw Sch Info Studies PO Box 413 Milwaukee WI 53201-0413 Home Phone: 262-242-9031; Office Phone: 414-229-3315. Business E-Mail: aman@sois.uwn.edu, aman@uwm.edu.

AMANN, CHARLES ALBERT, mechanical engineer, researcher; b. Thief River Falls, Minn., Apr. 21, 1926; s. Charles Alois and Bertha Ann (Oetting) Amann; m. Marilynn Ann Reis, Aug. 26, 1950; children: Richard, Barbara, Nancy, Julie. BS, U. Minn., 1946, MSME, 1948. Instr. U. Minn., Mpls., 1946-49; rsch. engr. GM Rsch. Labs., Detroit, 1949-54, supervisory rsch. engr. Warren, Mich., 1954-71, asst. dept. head, 1971-73, dept. head, 1973-89, rsch. fellow, 1989-91; prin. engr. KAB Engring., 1991—. Spl. instr. Wayne State U., Detroit, 1952—55; guest lectr. Mich. State U., 1980—2006; outside prof. U. Ariz., 1983; mem. adv. com. Gas Rsch. Inst., 1992—98, Oak Ridge Nat. Lab., 1996—98; invited lectr. Inst. Advanced Engring., Seoul, Republic of Korea, 1994. Author (with others): Automotive Engine Alternatives, 1986, Advanced Diesel Engineering and Operations, 1988, Marks' Standard Handbook for Mechanical Engineers, 2007; co-editor: Combustion Modeling in Reciprocating Engines, 1980. Lt. (j.g.) USNR, 1944—46. Recipient James Clayton prize, Inst. Mech. Engrs., 1975, Oustanding Achievement award, U. Minn., 1991. Fellow: Soc. Automotive Engrs. (Arch T. Colwell merit award 1972, Disting. Spkr. award 1981, Arch T. Colwell merit award 1984, Disting. Spkr. award 1991, Forest R. McFarland award 2001); mem.: ASME (Richard S. Woodbury award 1989, Soichiro Honda lectr. 1992, Spkr. award Internal Combustion Engine Divsn. 1997, Internal Combustion Engine award 2000, Disting. lectr. 2002—04), NAE, Tau Beta Pi, Tau Omega, Sigma Xi. Presbyterian. Achievements include patents in field. Avocation: music. Home Phone: 248-646-0198. E-mail: mcamann@juno.com.

AMBERG, DEBORAH ANN, lawyer; b. 1965; BA, U. Minn., 1987, JD cum laude, 1990. Bar: Minn. 1990. Staff atty. Allete, Inc., Duluth, Minn., 1990—98, sr. atty., 1998—2004, gen. counsel, v.p., corp. legal svcs. corp. sec., 2004—. Mem.: ABA, Minn. State Bar Assn., Minn. Women Lawyers. Office: Allete Inc 30 W Superior St Duluth MN 55802-2093 Office Phone: 218-723-3930. Office Fax: 218-723-3996. E-mail: damberg@allete.com.

AMBERG, THOMAS L., public relations executive; b. Glen Cove, NY, Apr. 13, 1948; s. Richard Hiller Amberg and Janet Law Volkman; m. Tauna Urban, June 19, 1971 (div. Jan. 1980); children: Edward, Robert; m. Kathy Stewart, Oct. 9, 1982; 1 child, Thomas Jr. BA, Colgate U., 1971; MBA, U. Mo., St. Louis, 1980. Reporter, editor St. Louis Globe-Democrat, 1971-83; pres., coo Aaron D. Cushman and Assocs., Chgo., 1991—; pres. Cushman Amberg Comms., Chgo. Mem. adv. bd. Salvation Army, St. Louis, 1986-91, Chgo., 1992—, pres., 1995-2003; bd. dirs. Wishing Well Found., St. Louis, 1985-91, Hope Ctr., St. Louis, 1985-91; bd. trustees St. Patrick's Sch., Chgo., 1994-2001. Recipient Disting. Achievement award Inland Daily Press Assn., 1978, 82, Frank Kelly Meml. award, 1980, Gavel award ABA, 1983, Unity awards in Media Lincoln U., 1984. Mem. Mental Health Assn. St. Louis (pres. 1987-88), Pub. Rels. Soc. Am., Press. Club Met. St. Louis (pres. 1981-83), Internat. Assn. Bus. Communicators, Soc. Am. Travel Writers. Presbyterian. Home: 1783 Bowling Green Dr Lake Forest IL 60045-3559 Office: Cushman Amberg Comms 180 N Michigan Ave Ste 1600 Chicago IL 60601-7478

AMBOIAN, JOHN PETER, JR., investment company executive; b. 1961; m. Ann Amboian; 3 children. BS in Econs., U. Chgo., 1983, MBA, 1984. Various fin. positions Philip Morris Cos., Kraft Foods, Inc.; CFO, sr. v.p. fin., strategy & sys. Miller Brewing Co.; exec. v.p., CFO Nuveen Investments, Inc., Chgo., 1995—98, pres., 1999—2007, CEO, 2007—. Mem. fin. com. Chgo. Humanities Festival, bd. governance and mem. nominating com.; bd. dirs. Boys and Girls Clubs Chgo., N. Shore Country Day Sch., Children's Meml. Hosp. Office: Nuveen Investments Inc 333 W Wacker Dr Chicago IL 60606

AMDURSKY, SAUL JACK, library director; b. Rochester, NY, Aug. 11, 1945; s. Harry S. and Eva (Forman) A.; m. Marion Susan Arndt, May 30, 1969; 1 child, Jacob Arthur. BA, St. John Fisher Coll., 1969; MSLS, U. Ky., 1971. Asst. mgr. Lincoln First Banks, Rochester, 1966-70; supervising libr. Prince William County Pub. Libr., Manassas, Va., 1971-75; dir. Albion (Mich.) Pub. Libr., 1975-79; adminstr. Racine (Wis.) County Libr. Sys., 1979-82; libr. dir. Bloomington (Ill.) Pub. Libr., 1982-87, Kalamazoo (Mich.) Pub. Libr., 1987—. Interim part-time adminstr. Woodlands Libr. Coop., Albion, 1978-79; instr. Ill. State U., ormal, 1984. Contbr. articles to Libr. Jour., Ill. Librs., Va. Libr., book revs. to Libr. Jour., Sch. Libr. Jour., Am. Reference Books Ann. Mem. ALA, Mich. Libr. Assn. (pub. policy com.), Ill. Libr. Assn. (legis. com.), Pi Gamma Mu (lifetime). Office: Kalamazoo Pub Libr 315 S Rose St Kalamazoo MI 49007-5201

AMEND, JAMES MICHAEL, lawyer; b. Chgo., July 19, 1942; s. Nathan and Edith (Greenberg) A.; m. Sheila Rae Cohen, Apr. 4, 1971; children: Allison, Anthony. BSE, U. Mich., 1964, JD, 1967. Bar: Ill. 1968, U.S. Dist. Ct. (no. dist.) Ill. 1968, U.S. Ct. Appeals (7th cir.) 1969, U.S. Supreme Ct. 1970, U.S. Ct. Appeals (9th cir.) 1985. Ptnr. Kirkland & Ellis, Chgo., 1968—. Prof. Stanford U. Law Sch., 1996-97. Editor U. Mich. Law Rev., 1966, Patent Law: A Primer for Federal District Court Judges, 1998; author: Intellectual Property Law, 1982. Chmn. Chgo. Lawyers Com. for Civil Rights Under Law, 1985-86. Fulbright scholar, 1967. Mem. ABA, U.S. Trademark Assn., Mid-Am. Club (Chgo.). Jewish. Avocations: running, skiing, golf. Office: Kirkland & Ellis 200 E Randolph St Fl 54 Chicago IL 60601-6636 Office Phone: 312-861-2154. E-mail: jamend@kirkland.com.

AMEND, JOSEPH H., III, military officer; BS in Civil Engring., Va. Poly. Inst. and State U., 1971, MS in Civil Engring., 1972, PhD in Civil Engring., 1973. Commd. 2d lt. USAF, 1971, advanced through grades to col., 1996; assoc. prof. civil engring., vice commandant and dean Civil Engr. and Svcs. Sch., Air Force Inst. Tech., 1997—98, assoc. prof. civil engring., dean Civil Engr. and Svcs. Sch., 1998—2001, vice commandant, 2001—. Decorated Meritorious Svc. medal with 4 oak leaf clusters, Commendation medal with one oak leaf cluster, Achievement medal, Outstanding Unit award with 3 oak leaf clusters, Organizational Excellence award with 3 oak leaf clusters, Def. Svc. medal with svc. star, Armed Forces Expeditionary medal; named Air Force Mil. Engr. of Yr., Nat. Soc. Profl. Engrs., 1984. Fellow: ASCE; mem.: Chi Epsilon, Tau Beta Pi, Phi Kappa Phi. Office: Air Force Inst Tech Office of Pub Affairs Wright Patterson AFB OH 45433-7765

AMERI, ANAN, museum director; b. Palestine; PhD in Sociology, Wayne State U. Cultural arts dir. Arab Cmty. Ctr. for Econ. and Social Services (ACCESS), Dearborn, Mich.; founding dir. Arab Am. Nat. Mus., Dearborn, Mich., 2005—. Vis. scholar Ctr. for Middle Eastern Studies Harvard U.; fellow Bunting Inst. Radcliffe Coll., Cambridge, Mass. Author: Arab Americans in Metro Detroit: A Pictorial History, (articles) Can I At Least Have My Scarf?, 2000, many others. Mem.: Palestine Aid Soc. (founding pres.). Office: Arab American National Museum 13624 Michigan Ave Dearborn MI 48126 Office Phone: 313-624-0200. Office Fax: 313-582-1086. E-mail: aameri@accesscommunity.org.

AMES, DONALD PAUL, retired air research director; b. Brandon, Man., Canada, Sept. 13, 1922; came to U.S., 1932; s. Paul M. and Della Johanna (Hebel) A.; m. Doris Elizabeth Ubbelohde, Dec. 30, 1949; children: Elizabeth Carol Ames Herbert, Barbara Louise Ames Jones. BS in Chemistry, U. Wis., 1944, PhD in Phys. Chemistry, 1949; LLD (hon.), U. Mo., St. Louis, 1978. AEC postdoctoral fellow, 1949—50; staff chemist Los Alamos Sci. Lab., 1950—52; asst. prof. phys. chemistry U. Ky., Lexington, 1952—54; staff chemist DuPont Co., Aiken, SC, 1954—56; sr. rsch. chemist, scientist/fellow Monsanto, St. Louis, 1956—61; from scientist to sr. scientist rsch. div. McDonnell Aircraft Co., St. Louis, 1961—68; from dep. dir. rsch. to dir. rsch. McDonnell Douglas Rsch. Labs., St. Louis, 1968—71, dir., 1971—76, staff v.p., 1976—86, staff v.p., gen. mgr., disting. fellow, 1986—89, cons., 1989—; pres. Fluotech Inc., 1991—. Adj. prof. physics U. Mo., St. Louis, 1989—2000, Washington U., St. Louis, 1989-99; mem. vis. com. dept. mech. engring. Lehigh U., 1984-90; mem. adv. bd. Coll. Engring., U. Ill., Urbana, 1986-89; mem. spl. com. U. Chgo. 7 GeV Synchrotron Light Source, 1984-89; adv. com. U. Mo. Rsch. Reactor, Columbia, 1985-92; mem. indsl. adv. coun. dept. chemistry U. Mo., St. Louis, 1985-95; mem. subcom. on materials sci. and engring. needs and opportunities in aerospace industry NAS, 1985-86; bd. dirs. St. Louis Tech. Ctr., 1983-95; participant Manhattan Project U.S. Army, 1944-46. Contbr. articles to profl. jours.; patentee in field. Special engr. detachment US Army, 1944—46. Recipient Civic award St. Louis sect. AIAA, 1985, James B. Eads award Acad. Sci. St. Louis, 2003; Wis. Alumni Rsch. fellow, 1946-48, AEC fellow, 1948-49, Monsanto fellow, 1959-61, McDonnell Douglas Disting. fellow, 1986-89. Fellow Acad. Sci. St. Louis; mem. Am. Phys. Soc., Am. Chem. Soc., Soc. Engring Sci., Combustion Inst., Mo. Acad. Sci., Phi Beta Kappa, Sigma Xi, Phi Eta Sigma, Phi Kappa Phi, Phi Lambda Upsilon, Gamma Alpha, Alpha Chi Sigma. Office Phone: 314-984-8846. E-mail: ames922@sbcglobal.net.

AMIDON, PAUL CHARLES, publishing executive; b. St. Paul, July 23, 1932; s. Paul Samuel and Eleanor Ruth (Simons) A.; m. Patricia Jean Winjum, May 7, 1960; children: Karen, Michael, Susan. BA, U. Minn., 1954. Bus. mgr. Paul S. Amidon & Assocs., Inc., St. Paul, 1956-66, pres., 1966—. Served with AUS, 1954-56. Home: 1582 Hillcrest Ave Saint Paul MN 55116-2147 Office: 1966 Benson Ave Saint Paul MN 55116-3214 Business E-Mail: paul@amidongraphics.com.

AMIGONI, MICHAEL, information technology executive; MBA, U. Ill., Chgo. Cons. in field for small co. including ARO Inc., Kansas City, Mo.; managed operations and info. tech. ARO's Contact Ctr., Kansas City, 1992—; head architect remote bus. model ARO, Inc., Kansas City, 1997, CIO, COO. Office: ARO Contact Ctr 3100 Broadway Ste 100 Kansas City MO 64111

AMIRIKIA, HASSAN, obstetrician, gynecologist; b. Tehran, Iran, Dec. 10, 1937; came to U.S., 1966; d. Ahmad and Showkat (Asgari) Cheftsaz; m. Minoo Vassigh Amirikia, Apr. 4, 1964; children: Arezo, Omid. MD, Tehran U., 1964. Cert. Am. Bd. Ob-Gyn. Intern Cook County Hosp., Chgo., 1966—67; resident Wayne State U., Detroit, 1967—71, fellow, 1971—72; practice reproductive endocrine specializing in infertility Detroit, 1972—; asst. prof. Wayne State U., Detroit, 1972—, dir. ob-gyn. tng. dept. family medicine, 1979—; dir. infertility and reproductive endocrinology St. Joseph's Hosp., Pontiac, Mich., 1990—93; chief staff Detroit Med. Ctr., 1993—, pres. med. staff, 1997—; chief staff Hutzel Hosp., 1996—2002. Pres. med. staff Detroit Med. Ctr., 1998-2004, bd. trustees, 2002-2004, chair med. exec. com., 1997—, pres. Pvt. Practice Physician Corp.; alt. del. AMA 2003. Contbr. articles to profl. jours. Fellow ACS, ACOG (Mich. sect.), Royal Coll. Physicians and Surgeons, Wayne County Med. Soc. (pres. 1995-96); mem. AMA (life), Mich. State Med. Soc. (bd. dirs. 1996—, pres. 2003). Achievements include research in effects of androgens on the ovary. Home: 1435 Lone Pine Rd Bloomfield Hills MI 48302-2632 Office: 4727 Saint Antoine St Ste 408 Detroit MI 48201-1461 also: 29877 Telegraph Rd Southfield MI 48034-1332 Office Phone: 313-832-0766. Personal E-mail: h.amirikia@hotmail.com. Business E-Mail: hamiriki@dmc.org.

AMLADI, PRASAD GANESH, management consulting executive, health care consultant, researcher; b. Mudhol, India, Sept. 12, 1941; arrived in U.S., 1969, permanent resident, 1992; s. Ganesh L. and Sundari G. Amladi; m. Chitra G. Panje, Dec. 20, 1970; children: Amita, Amol. BTech with honors in Mech. Engring., Indian Inst. Tech., India, 1963; MBA with high distinction, U. Mich., 1975. Sr. rsch. engr. Ford Motor Co., Dearborn, Mich., 1968-75; mgr. strategic planning Mich. Consol. Gas Co., Detroit, 1975-78; mgr. planning svcs. The Resources Group, Bloomfield Hills, Mich., 1978-80; project mgr., sr. cons. Mediflex Systems Corp., Bloomfield Hills, 1980-85; mgr. strategic planning svcs. Mersco Corp., Bloomfield Hills, 1985-86; mgr. corp. planning and rsch. Diversified Techs., Inc., New Hudson, Mich., 1986-87; mgr. planning and rsch. Blue Cross & Blue Shield of Mich., Detroit, 1987—2007; exec. dir. Decision Analytics Co. LLC, 2007—. Contbr. papers to profl. publs. Recipient Kodama Meml. Gold medal, 1957; Govt. India Merit scholar, 1959-63, K.C. Mahindra Ednl. Trust scholar, 1967, R.D. Sethna Grad. scholar, 1968. Mem. Inst. Indsl. Engrs. (sr.), N.Am. Soc. Corp. Planning, Econ. Club Detroit, Beta Gamma Sigma. Office: Decision Analytics Co 2439 Worcester Rd West Bloomfield MI 48323 Personal E-mail: pamladi@stanfordalumni.org. Business E-Mail: pamladi@umich.edu.

AMMAR, RAYMOND GEORGE, physicist, researcher; b. Kingston, Jamaica, July 15, 1932; arrived in US, 1950, naturalized, 1965; s. Elias George and Nellie (Khaleel) A.; m. Carroll Ikerd, June 17, 1961 (dec. 2004); children: Elizabeth, Robert (dec.), David. AB, Harvard U., 1953; PhD, U. Chgo., 1959. Rsch. assoc. Enrico Fermi Inst., U. Chgo., 1959-60; asst. prof. physics Northwestern U., Evanston, Ill., 1960-64, assoc. prof., 1964-69; prof. physics U. Kans., Lawrence, 1969—, chmn. dept. physics and astronomy, 1989—2003; (on sabbatical leave Fermilab and Deutsches Elektronen Synchrotron, 1984-85). Cons. Argonne (Ill.) Nat. Lab., 1965-69, vis. scientist, 1971-72; vis. scientist Fermilab, Batavia, Ill., summers 1976-81, Deutsches Elektronen Synchroton, Hamburg, Germany, summers 1982-88, lab. of nuclear studies Cornell U., summers 1989-98; project dir. NSF grant for rsch. in high energy physics, 1962-2001. Contbr. articles to sci. jours. Fellow Am. Phys. Soc.; mem. AAUP. Home: 1651 Hillcrest Rd Lawrence KS 66044-4525 Office: U Kans Dept Physics And Astronomy Lawrence KS 66045-7582 Home Phone: 785-842-4285; Office Phone: 785-864-4626. Business E-Mail: ammar@ku.edu.

AMMON, HARRY, history professor; b. Waterbury, Conn., Sept. 4, 1917; s. Grover and Lena Mary (Pyne) Amman. BS, Georgetown U., 1939, MA, 1940; PhD, U. Va., 1948. Editor Md. Hist. Mag., Balt., 1948-50; asst. prof. So. Ill. U., Carbondale, 1950-57, assoc. prof., 1957-66, prof. history, 1967—, prof. emeritus, 1984—, chmn. dept., 1977-1983. Fulbright lectr. U. Vienna, Austria, 1954-55, Seoul Nat. U., Korea, 1984-85; vis. prof. U. Va., Charlottesville, 1968-69; guest lectr. Northeast Normal and Liaoning Univs., People's Republic of China, 1986, 88. Author: James Monroe: The Quest for National Identity, 1971, new edit. 1990, The Genet Mission, 1973, James Monroe A Bibliography, 1991. Mem.: Phi Beta Kappa. Office: So Ill U History Dept Carbondale IL 62901 Home: 2950 Westridge Pl Apt 222 Carbondale IL 62901-1090 E-mail: harryam@verizon.net.

AMOS, MARTIN JOHN, bishop; b. Cleve., Dec. 8, 1941; s. William and Mary Amos. BA, Borromeo Sem. Coll., Wickliffe, Ohio, 1964; STB, St. Mary Seminary, Cleve., 1968; MS, St. John Coll., 1975. Ordained priest Diocese of Cleve., 1968; asst. prin. Borromeo Sem. HS; pastor St. Dominic Parish, Shaker Heights; ordained bishop, 2001; aux. bishop Diocese of Cleve., 2001—06; bishop Diocese of Davenport, Iowa, 2006—. Roman Catholic. Office: Diocese Davenport St Vincent Ctr 2706 N Gaines St Davenport IA 52804 Office Phone: 563-324-1911. Office Fax: 563-324-5842.*

AMSDEN, TED THOMAS, lawyer; b. Cleve., Dec. 11, 1950; s. Richard Thomas and Mary Agnes (Hendricks) A.; m. Ruth Anna Rydstedt, May 1, 1982; children: Jennifer Rydstedt, Matthew Lars, Alexis Linnea. BA in econs., Wayne State U., 1972; JD, Harvard U., 1975; Grad. in orgn. devel., Ea. Mich. U., 2005. Bar: Mich. 1975, U.S. Dist. Ct. (ea. dist.) Mich. 1975, U.S. Ct. Appeals (6th cir.) 1975, U.S. Supreme Ct. 1979. Assoc. Dykema Gossett PLLC, Detroit, 1975—83, ptnr., 1983—2006; sr. cons. The Leadership Grp. LLC, Grosse Pointe Shores, Mich., 2005—, NCCJ, 2000, 2007, Seda Consulting. Contbr. articles to profl jours. Chmn. Baha'i Justice Soc., 1986-88, corr. sec., 1988-92, bd. dirs., 1986-93, 95—; bd. dirs. Internat. Inst., Detroit, 1989-97, 99-2006, v.p. legal affairs, 1991-94, v.p., 1994-95, pres.-elect 1995-96, pres., 1996-97, co-chair Ethnic Summit '96; bd. dirs. Racial Justice Ctr., Grosse Pointe, Mich., 1992-94, Greater Detroit Interfaith Roundtable, 1994—, bd. dirs. Model of Racial Unity, Inc., 1995-97, treas., 1997—, chmn., 1998—, vice chmn.; mem. Mich. Bar Rep. Assembly, 1988-94, comml. mediator, Wayne Circuit Ct., 1996-2004. Recipient Detroit Principles award of Race Relations Coun. of Metropolitan Detroit, 1993, Spirit of Detroit award City of Detroit Common Coun., 1996, 97, Diversity Champion award Birmingham-Bloomfield Task Force on Race Rels., 2002, Best Project Cons., 2004-. Mem. ABA, Mich. Bar Assn., Wolverine Bar Assn., Detroit Bar Assn., Detroit Bar Assn. Found. (bd. dirs. 1992-98, sec., 1993-95, pres. 1995-97), Macomb County Bar Assn., Assn. Def. Counsel, Civic Searchlight (Macomb County steering com., jud. com. 1990-91, Wayne County jud. com. 1992-95). Office: The Leadership LLC 987 Lake Shore Rd Grosse Pointe MI 48236 Office Phone: 313-506-2550. Office Fax: 313-885-3777. Business E-Mail: amsdener@yahoo.com.

AMSLER, JANA, chef; Grad., CHIC; student, Las Belles Artes, Elmhurst, Ill. Pastry, soup and salad chef Salbute, Hinsdale, Ill., 1997—. Office: Salbute 20 E 1st St Hinsdale IL 60521

AMSTUTZ, HAROLD EMERSON, veterinarian, educator; b. Barrs Mill, Ohio, June 21, 1919; s. Nelson David and Viola Emma (Schnitzer) A.; m. Mabelle Josephine Bower, June 26, 1949; children: Suzanne Marie, Cynthia Lou, Patricia Lynn, David Bruce. BS in Agr, Ohio State U., 1942, DVM, 1945. Diplomate Am. Coll. Vet. Internal Medicine (pres. 1972-73, chmn. bd. regents 1973-74); hon. diplomate Am. Coll. Theriogenology. Pvt. practice vet. medicine, Orrville, Ohio, 1946-47; instr. vet. medicine Ohio State U., 1947-52, asst. prof., 1952-54, asso. prof., 1954-56, prof., 1957-61, prof., head dept. vet. medicine, 1956-61; head dept. vet. clinics Purdue U., West Lafayette, Ind., 1961-75, prof. large animal clinics, 1975-89, prof. emeritus, 1989—. Editor: Bovine Medicine and Surgery Book, 1979; contbg. editor: Modern Veterinary Practice, 1979-84; mem. editorial bd. The Merck Vet. Manual, 6th, 7th and 8th edits.; contbr. to books on diseases of large domestic animals. Mem. exec. bd. Ind.-Ky. synod Luth. Ch. Am., 1986-88; pres. World Assn. for Buiatrics, 1972-84. Served with U.S. Army, 1945-46. Recipient Borden award for outstanding research in diseases of dairy cattle, 1978; named Disting. Alumnus Ohio State U. Coll. Vet. Medicine, 1974; recipient Alumni Faculty award Sch. Vet. Medicine, Purdue U., 1989, Sagamore of the Wabash Ind. Gov., 1990, Ark. Traveler award Ark. Gov., 1969, Gustav Rosenberger Meml. award Dutch Veterinary Assn., 1992, Alumni Recognition award Vet. Medicine Alumni Soc. Ohio State U., 1998. Mem. AVMA (12th Internat. Congress prize for contributing to internat. understanding of vet. medicine 1995), Am. Assn. Vet. Clinicians (pres. 1972), Am. Assn. Bovine Practitioners (exec. sec. 1971-89, exec. v.p. 1989-93, hon. mem. 1993), World Assn. Buiatrics (pres. 1972-84), Am. Coll. of Theriogenologists (hon. diplomate 1993), Sigma Xi, Phi Zeta, Gamma Sigma Delta (award of merit), Omega Tau Sigma (nat. Gamma award). Republican. Avocations: tennis, gardening. Office: Purdue Univ Dept Veterinary Sci West Lafayette IN 47907 Office Phone: 765-494-8560. Business E-Mail: amstutzh@purdue.edu.

AMSTUTZ, RONALD, state legislator; b. Wooster, Ohio, June 2, 1961; m. Joanne Amstutz; children: Julianne, Jefferson. BA, Capitol U.; postgrad., Kent State U.; BA, Malone Coll.; postgrad., Goshen Coll. Mem. Ohio Ho. of Reps., Columbus, 1981-2000; vice chmn. policy com.; mem. Ohio Senate from 22nd dist, Columbus, 2001—. Chair tech. and elections com., fin. and appropriations com., primary and secondary edn. subcom., ethics and stds. com., ways and means com. Ohio Ho. of Reps. Mem. Orrville (Ohio) City Charter Commn., 1974-75; mayor City of Orrville, 1976-80; mem. Wayne County Rep. Exec. Com., past pres. and chmn.; bd. dirs. United Conservatives Ohio. Mem. Farm Bur., Am. Legis. Exch. Coun., Nat. Tax Payers Union Ohio, Orrville Jaycees (past pres. and chmn.), Rotary. Office: 4456 Wood Lake Trl Wooster OH 44691-8582

AMUNDSON, ROBERT A., state supreme court justice; m. Katherine Amundson; children: Robert, Beth, Amy. BBA, Augustana Coll., 1961; JD, U. S.D., 1964. Asst. atty. gen. Atty. Gen's. Office, 1965-69; mem. firm Belle Fourche and Lead, 1970-89; cir. judge 2d Jud. Cir., 1989-91; justice Supreme Ct. of S.D., Vermillion, 1991—2003.

AMY, JONATHAN WEEKES, chemist, educator; b. Delaware, Ohio, Mar. 3, 1923; s. Ernest Francis and Theresa Louise (Say) A.; m. Ruthanna Borden, Dec. 20, 1947 (dec. Apr. 1999); m. Betty Joy Flood, July 2, 2000; children— Joseph Wilbur, James Borden, Theresa BA, Ohio Wesleyan U., 1948; MS, Purdue U., 1950, PhD, 1955. Rsch. assoc. dept. chemistry Purdue U., West Lafayette, Ind., 1954-60, assoc. prof., 1960-70, prof., 1970—, assoc. dir. labs., 1960—, dir. instrumentation, 1970-84, emeritus, 1988. Cons. chem. instrumentation; sec.-treas. Technometrics, Inc., 1968-2001; mem. adv. panels AAAS, Assn. Am. Univs., NSF, Am. Chem. Soc.; vis. scholar Stanford U., 1992. Assoc. editor Ind. Chem. News; patentee elec. measuring equipment and chem. instrumentation Pres. Wabash Twp. Vol. Fire Dept., 1970-86. Served with U.S. Maritime Service, 1943-46. Recipient George award Lafayette Jour. and Courier, 1978, Sagamore of the Wabash award State of Ind., 1999. Mem. AAAS, Am. Chem. Soc. (Chem. Instrumentation award), Sigma Xi, Sigma Chi. Episcopalian.

ANDERHALTER, OLIVER FRANK, educational organization executive; b. Trenton, Ill., Feb. 14, 1922; s. Oliver Valentine and Catherine (Vollet) A.; m. Elizabeth Fritz, Apr. 30, 1945; children: Sharon, Stephen, Dennis. B.Ed., Eastern Ill. State Tchrs. Coll., 1943, Ped.D. (hon.), 1956; A.M., St. Louis U., 1947, PhD, 1949. Mem. faculty St. Louis U., 1947—, prof. edn., 1957—; dir. Bur. Instl. Research, 1949-65, 1949-65, Univ. Computer Center, 1961-69, chmn. research methodology dept., 1968-76; v.p. Scholastic Testing Service, Chgo., 1951-89; pres. Scholastic Testing Svc., Chgo. and St. Louis, 1989—. Chmn. finance com. Greater St. Louis Campfire Girls Orgn., 1958-59 Author, editor standardized tests. Served as pilot USNR, 1943-46. Mem. Am. Ednl. Research Assn., Nat. Council Measurement, Am. Statis. Assn., N.E.A. Home: 12756 Whispering Hills Ln Saint Louis MO 63146-4449 Office: Scholastic Testing Svc 4320 Green Ash Dr Earth City MO 63045-1208 Office Phone: 314-739-3650. E-mail: budbetty@sbcglobal.net.

ANDERSEN, BURTON ROBERT, immunologist, educator, medical historian; b. Chgo., Aug. 27, 1932; s. Burton R. and Alice C. (Mara) A.; children: Ellen C., Julia A., Brian E. Student, Northwestern U., Evanston, Ill., 1950—51; BS, U. Ill., Chgo., 1953, MS, MD, U. Ill., Chgo., 1957. Intern Mpls. Gen. Hosp., 1957-58; resident and fellow U. Ill. Hosp., 1958-61; clin. assoc. NIH, Bethesda, Md., 1961-64; asst. prof. U. Rochester, NY, 1964-67; assoc. prof. Northwestern U., 1967-70; prof. medicine and microbiology U. Ill., Chgo., 1970—, chief infectious diseases, 1986-99, West Side VA Med. Ctr., 1970-90. Contbr. sci. rsch. articles to profl. jours. Served as sr. surgeon USPHS, 1961-63. Grantee Rsch. grantee, NEH, 2000—03. Fellow ACP; mem. Am. Assn. Immunologists, Am. Soc. for Clin. Investigation, Ctrl. Soc. for Clin. Rsch. Achievements include research in infectious diseases, white blood cells and ancient Mesopotamian medicine. Office: U Ill Sect Infectious Diseases 808 S Wood St Chicago IL 60612-7300 Business E-Mail: branders@uic.edu.

ANDERSEN, KENNETH ELDON, speech communication educator, consultant; b. Harlan, Iowa, Dec. 28, 1933; s. Edward and Anna Christina (Christiansen) A.; m. Mary Ann Klaaren, Aug. 20, 1964; 1 child, Erik LaMont. BA, U. No. Iowa, 1954, MA, 1955; PhD (Merchant scholar, Knapp fellow), U. Wis., 1961. Instr. U. Colo., Boulder, 1955-56, U. Mich., Ann Arbor, 1961-63, asst. prof., 1963-67, assoc. prof., 1967-70, U. Ill., Urbana, 1970-73, prof. speech comm., 1973-95, prof. emeritus, 1995—, assoc. head dept., 1971-78, assoc. dean Liberal Arts and Scis., 1981-87, dep. vice chancellor for acad. affairs, 1988-92, chmn. senate council, 1981— 84, chmn. univ. senate conf., vis. prof. Chgo., 1966, faculty adv. coun. mem. Ill. Bd. Higher Edn., 2000—, chair, 2001—03; vis. prof. U. So. Calif., Los Angeles, 1968. Author textbooks; editor: Jour. Am. Forensic Assn, 1968-71; editorial bd., 1964-68; editor: Speaker and Gavel, 1975-78; contbr. articles profl. jours. Mem. bd. visitors Def. Info. Sch., 1983-96; treas. State Univ. Annuitants Assn., 2000-04. Served with AUS, 1956-58. Mem. AAUP (nat. coun. 1988-91, chpt. pres., Ill. Conf. pres., Tacey award 1998), Nat. Comm. Assn. (fin. bd. 1974-76, adminstrv. com. 1974-76, 80-84, 2d v.p. 1980-81, 1st v.p. 1981-82, pres. 1982-83, Disting. Svc. award 1994), Rhetoric Soc., Ctrl. States Communication Assn. (exec. sec., conv. mgr. 1969-72, editl. bd. 1967-70, pres. 1974-75, Outstanding Young Tchrs. Speech award 1962), Am. Forensic Assn., Assn. Comm. Adminstrn. (pres. 1994, exec. com. 1992-95), Ill. Speech and Theatre Assn., Assn. Edn. in Journalism and Mass Comm., Internat. Comm. Assn., Delta Sigma Rho-Tau Kappa Alpha (Svc. award 1979, Disting. Alumni award 1983), Assn. Applied and Profl. Ethics. Home: 2002 Galen Dr Champaign IL 61821-6010 Office: Univ Ill 702 S Wright St Ste 244 Urbana IL 61801-3629 Business E-Mail: keanders@uiuc.edu.

ANDERSEN, WAYNE R., federal judge; b. Chgo., July 30, 1945; m. Sheila M. O'Brien, Jan. 5, 1991. BA with honors, Harvard Coll., 1967; JD, U. Ill., 1970. Adminstrv. asst. Henry J. Hyde, majority leader Ill. House Reps., 1970-72; assoc. Burditt & Calkins, Chgo., 1972-76, ptnr., 1977-80; dep. sec. state Ill., 1981-84; judge Cir. Ct. Cook County, 1984-91; supr. judge traffic divsn. First Municipal Dist., 1989-91; dist. judge No. U.S. Courthouse, Ill., 1991—. Dir. Rehab. Inst. Chgo.; interviewer schs. com. Harvard Club Chgo. Contbr. articles to profl. jours. Pres., dir., precinct capt. Maine Township Regular Rep. Orgn.; alt. del. Rep. Nat. Conv., Sixth Congrl. Dist. Ill., 1984; Rep. candidate for treas. Cook County, 1974. Mem. Ill. Judges Assn., Chgo. Bar Assn., Fed. Judges Assn. Office: US Courthouse 1486 Dirksen Bldg 219 S Dearborn St Chicago IL 60604-1702

ANDERSLAND, ORLANDO BALDWIN, retired engineering educator; b. Albert Lea, Minn., Aug. 15, 1929; s. Ole Larsen and Brita Kristine (Okland) A.; m. Phyllis Elaine Burgess, Aug. 15, 1958; children: Mark, John, Ruth BCE, U. Minn., 1952; MSCE, Purdue U., 1956, PhD, 1960. Registered profl. engr., Minn., Mich. Staff engr. NAS, Am. Assn. State Hwy. Ofcls. Road Test, Ottawa, Ill., 1956-57; rsch. engr. Purdue U., West Lafayette, Ind., 1957-59; mem. faculty Mich. State U., East Lansing, 1960—, prof. civil engring., 1968—, prof. emeritus, 1994—. Co-author: Geotechnical Software for the IBM, PC, 1987, Geotechnical Engineering and Soil Testing, 1992, An Introduction to Frozen Ground Engineering, 1994, 2d edit., 2004; sr. editor: Geotechnical Engineering for Cold Regions, 1978; contbr. chpt. Ground Engineer's Handbook, 1987; contbr. articles to profl. jours.; patentee in field. 1st lt. C.E., U.S. Army, 1952-55. Decorated Nat. Def. Svc. medal; UN Svc. medal; Korean Svc. medal; recipient Best Paper award Assn. Asphalt Paving Technologists, 1956; postdoctoral fellow Norwegian Geotech. Inst., 1966; grantee NSF, EPA, Dept. of Energy. Fellow ASCE (best paper award Cold Regions Engring. Jour. 1991); mem. ASTM (sr.), Internat. Soc. Soil Mechanics and Found. Engring., Am. Soc. Engring. Edn. (life), Sigma Xi, Chi Epsilon, Tau Beta Pi. Lutheran. Office: Mich State U Dept Civil/Environ Engring East Lansing MI 48824

ANDERSON, AUSTIN GOTHARD, lawyer, consultant, academic administrator; b. Calumet, Minn., June 30, 1931; s. Hugo Gothard and Turna Marie (Johnson) A.; m. Catherine Antoinette Spellacy, Jan. 2. 1954; children: Todd, Susan, Timothy, Linda, Mark. BA, U. Minn., Mpls., 1954, JD, 1958. Bar: Minn. 1958, Ill. 1962, Mich. 1974. Assoc. Spellacy, Spellacy, Lano & Anderson, Marble, Minn., 1958-62; dir. Ill. Inst. Continuing Legal Edn., Springfield, 1962-64; dir. dept. continuing legal edn. U. Minn., Mpls., 1964-70, assoc. dean gen. extension divsn., 1968-70; ptnr. Dorsey, Marquart, Windhorst, West & Halladay, Mpls., 1970-73; assoc. dir. Nat. Ctr. State Cts., St. Paul, 1973-74; dir. Inst. CLE U. Mich., Ann Arbor, 1973-92; dir. Inst. on Law Firm Mgmt., 1992-95; prin. Anderson Boyer Group, Ann Arbor, 1995—; pres. Network of Leading Law Firms, 1995—. Adj. faculty U. Minn., 1974, Wayne State U., 1974-75; mem. adv. bd. Ctr. for Law Firm Mgmt. Nottingham Trent U., Eng.; draftsman ABA Guidelines for Approval of Legal Asst. Programs, 1973, Model Guidelines for Minimum CLE, 1988; chair law practice mgmt. sect. State Bar Mich., 2000-01; mem. Task Force on Court Filing, State Bar of Mich., 2000—; mem. Com. on Quality of Life, 2000-01; cons. in field. Author 3 books 1971; co-editor, contbg. author: Lawyer's Handbook, 1975, co-editor 3d edit., 1992; author: A Plan for Lawyer Development, 1986, Marketing Your Practice: A Practical Guide to Client Development, 1986; cons. editor, contbg. author: Webster's Legal Secretaries Handbook, 1981; cons. editor Merriam Webster's Legal Secretarial Handbook, 2d edit., 1996; co-author: The Effective Associate Training Program-Improving Firm Performance, Profits and Prospective Partners, 2000, Associate Retention: Keeping Our Best and Brightest, 2002; author, co-editor: The Effective Training and Development Program, 2005; contbr. chpt. to book and articles to profl. jours. Chmn. City of Bloomington Park and Recreation Adv. Commn., Minn., 1967-72; chmn. Ann Arbor Citizens Recreation Adv. Com., 1981-89, Ann Arbor Parks Adv. Com., 1983-92, chair, 1991-92; rep. Class of '58 U. Minn. Law Sch., 1996-2004. Recipient Excellence award CLE sect. Assn. of Am. Law Schs., 1992. Fellow Am. Bar Found. (Mich. chmn. 2002—), State Bar Mich. Found.; mem. ABA (vice chmn. CLE com. sect. legal edn. and admission to bar 1988-93, standing com. continuing edn. of bar 1984-90, 00—, chmn. law practice mgmt. sect. 1981-82, Am. Law Inst.-ABA com. on continuing profl. edn. 1993-96, Am. Law Inst.-ABA com. on continuing profl. edn. 1999-02, spl. com. on rsch. on future of legal profession 1998-2000, sec. Coll. of Law Practice Mgmt. 1993-97, house of dels. 1993-99, commn. on lawyer advt. 1994-97, mem. task force Lawyer Ctr. on pers. legal svcs. and client devel. 2002-03, spl. advisor to standing com. on continuing edn. of the bar 2002—, chair cmty. on econ. of law practices, 2002-04, torts, trial and ins. practice sect., mem. sr. lawyers sect. 2005—07, instr. ABA/CLE and bus. devel. workshops, Bahrain 2006), Internat. Bar Assn., Mich. Bar Assn., Ill. Bar Assn., State Bar of Mich. (chair law practice mgmt. sect. 2000-01, vice chair 2007-08, disting. lawyer com. 2005-07, mem. e-filing task force), Minn. Bar Assn., Internat. Bar Assn., Assn. Continuing Legal Edn. Adminstrs. (pres. 1969-70), Laurel Gardens Condominium Assn. (pres. 2004-07). Home: 4660 Bayberry Cir Ann Arbor MI 48105-9762 Office: AndersonBoyer Group 3135 S State St Ste 360 H Ann Arbor MI 48108 Office Phone: 734-929-6943, 734-352-7301. Business E-Mail: aga@andersonboyer.com.

ANDERSON, BRADBURY H., retail executive; b. Sheridan, Wyo., 1949; m. Janet Anderson; 2 children. AA, Waldorf Coll., 1969; BA, U. Denver, 1971. Salesman Sound of Music, 1973—81, store mgr., 1981—86; exec. v.p. Best Buy Co., Inc., Richfield, Minn., 1986—91, pres., COO, 1991—2002, vice chmn., 2001—, CEO, 2002—. Bd. dirs. Best Buy Co., 1986—, General Mills, 2007—, Minn. Public Radio, Am. Film Inst., Best Buy Children's Found., Internat. Mass Retail Assn., Waldorf Coll. Bd. Regents. Bd. dirs. Am. Film Inst., Best Buy Children's Found., Internat. Mass Retail Assn.; bd. regents Waldorf Coll. Recipient Alumni Disting. Svc. award, Waldorf Coll., 1997, Retail Exec. of the Yr., Retail Merchandiser mag., 2002. Office: Best Buy Co Inc 7601 Penn Ave S Richfield MN 55423-3645

ANDERSON, CAROLE ANN, nursing educator, academic administrator; b. Chgo., Feb. 21, 1938; d. Robert and Marian (Harrity) Irving; m. Clark Anderson, Feb. 14, 1973; 1 child, Julie. Diploma, St. Francis Hosp., 1958; BS, U. Colo., 1962, MS, 1963, PhD, 1977. Group psychotherapist Dept. Vocat. Rehab., Denver, 1963-72; psychotherapist Prof. Psychiatry and Guidance Clinic, Denver, 1970-71; asst. prof., chmn. nursing sch. U. Colo., Denver, 1971-75; therapist, coordinator The Genessee Mental Health, Rochester, N.Y., 1977-78; assoc. dean U. Rochester, N.Y., 1978-86; dean, prof. Coll. Nursing Ohio State U., Columbus, 1986-2001, prof., 2001—, vice provost acad. and faculty offices, 2001—, interim dean grad. sch., 2005. Lectr. nursing sch. U. Colo., Denver, 1970-71; prin. investigator biomed. rsch. support grant, 1986-93, clin. rsch. facilitation grant, 1981-82; program dir. profl. nurse traineeship, 1978-86, advanced nurse tng. grant, 1982-85. Author: (with others) Women as Victims, 1986, Violence Toward Women, 1982, Substance Abuse of Women, 1982; editor Nursing Outlook, 1993-2002. Pres., bd. dirs. Health Assn., Rochester, 1984-86; mem. north sub area council Finger Lakes Health Systems Agy., 1983-86, longrange planning com., 1981-82; mem. Columbus Bd. Health; dir. Netcare Mental Health Ctr. Am. Acad. Nursing fellow. Mem. ANA, Ohio Nurses Assn., Am. Assn. Colls. ursing (bd. dirs. 1992-94, pres.-elect 1994-96, pres. 1996-98), Sigma Theta Tau. Home: 406 W 6th Ave Columbus OH 43201-3137 Office: The OH State U Office Acad Affairs 203 Bricker Hall 190 N Oval Mall Columbus OH 43210-1358 Business E-Mail: anderson.32@osu.edu.

ANDERSON, CATHY C., lawyer; BA, U. Mich.; JD, Loyola U. Dir. comml. law svcs. The Nutrasweet Co., 1986—92, dep. gen. counsel, asst. sec., 1992—95; exec. v.p., gen. counsel, sec. Alliant Foodservice, Inc., Deerfield, Ill., 1995—2003; sr. v.p., gen. counsel, sec. True Value Co. (formerly TruServ Corp.), Chgo., 2003—. Affiliated with Georgetown U. Corp. Coun. Inst. Bd. dirs. Evanston-Northwestern Healthcare. Mem.: ABA, Chgo. Bar Assn. Office: True Value Co 8600 W Bryn Mawr Ave Chicago IL 60631-3505 Office Phone: 773-695-5000.

ANDERSON, CHRISTOPHER, astronomy educator; b. Las Cruces, N.Mex., Feb. 21, 1941; m. Dorothy Nemec, Mar. 7, 1970; twins. BS in Astronomy, U. Ariz., 1963; PhD in Astronomy, Calif. Inst. Tech., 1968. Asst. prof. astronomy dept. U. Wis., Madison, 1968-74, assoc. prof. astronomy dept., 1974-79, prof. astronomy dept., 1979—. Mem. facility definition team STARLAB, 1975-85; STARLAB rep. Instrument Control and Data Handling Working Group for Spacelab Facilities, 1976-78; co-investigator Wis. Ultraviolet Photo-Polarimeter Experiment, 1978—; mem. observers com. Kitt Peak Nat. Obs., 1977-78; prin. investigator for devel. Midwestern Astron. Data Reduction and Analysis Facility, NSF, 1978-80. Contbr. articles to profl. jours. Mem. Internat. Astron. Union, Am. Astron. Soc., Phi Beta Kappa. Office: U Wis Madison Dept Astronomy 475 N Charter St Madison WI 53706

ANDERSON, CHRISTOPHER JAMES, lawyer; b. Chgo., Nov. 26, 1950; s. James M. and Margaret E. (Anderson) A.; m. Lyn R. Buckley, Jan. 3, 1976; children: Vaughn Buckley, Weston Buckley. BA, Grinnell Coll., 1972; JD with highest distinction, U. Iowa, 1975. Bar: Mo. 1975. From assoc. to ptnr. Armstrong Teasdale LLP, Kansas City, Mo., 1975—. Mem. ABA, Mo. Bar Assn., Kans. City Bar Assn., Lawyers Assn. Kansas City, Estate Planning Soc. Office: Armstrong Teasdale, et al 2345 Grand Blvd Ste 2000 Kansas City MO 64108-2617 Office Phone: 816-221-3420. E-mail: canderso@armstrongteasdale.com.

ANDERSON, DAVID GASKILL, JR., Spanish language educator; b. Tarboro, NC, Feb. 21, 1945; s. David G. Sr. and Lucile (Gammon) A.; m. Jonetta Gentemann, Jan. 29, 1968; children: Allene Q., David III, James H., John G. AB, U. N.C., 1967; MA, Vanderbilt U., 1974, PhD, 1985. Instr. of langs. Union U., Tenn., 1975-76; instr. Spanish Ouachita Bapt. U., Ark., 1976-85; asst. prof. fgn. langs. N.E. La. U., 1985-87; asst. prof. Spanish, John Carroll U., Cleve., 1987-93, assoc. prof., 1993—, acting chmn. dept. classical and modern langs., 1996, chmn., 1997—2005, George Grauel faculty fellow rsch. sabbatical, spring 1997. Tchg. fellow Vanderbilt U., 1983-84, NEH summer seminar on poetry, 1990; presenter in field. Author: On Elevating the Commonplace: A Structuralist Analysis of The Odas of Pablo Neruda, 1987; contbr. articles to profl. jours. Vol. ESL Peace Corps, Colombia, 1968-70. Named Outstanding Young Men of Am., 1979. Mem. Am. Assn. Tchrs. Spanish and Portuguese, Modern Lang. Assn., Cleve. Diocesan Fgn. Lang. Assn. (bd. mem. 1988-93), Cleve. Assn., Phi Beta Kappa. Democrat. Home: 2573 Dysart Rd Cleveland OH 44118-4446 Office: John Carroll Univ Classical & Modern Langs Cleveland OH 44118 Personal E-mail: unc67@msn.com.

ANDERSON, DAVID R., insurance company executive; m. Mary Anderson; 5 children. B, M, U. Wis. Budget dir. Am. Family Mut. Ins. Co., Madison, Wis., 1975, fin. planning dir., acctg. dir., v.p. info. svcs., 1996-98, pres., COO, 1998—2006, chmn., CEO, 2007—. Office: Am Family Ins Group 6000 American Pky Madison WI 53783

ANDERSON, DAVID WAYNE, entrepreneur, former federal agency administrator; b. Chgo. married. MPA, Harvard U., 1986; Ph.D (hon.), Northland Coll., 2004. Chmn., CEO Famous Dave's of Am., Inc., Eden Prairie, Minn., 1994—2003, chmn. emeritus, 2003—; asst. sec. for Indian affairs US Dept. Interior, Washington, 2004—05. Mem. National Task Force on Reservation Gaming, Bur. Indian Affairs, 1983, Am. Indian Edn. Found., 2003; mem. Presdl. Adv. Coun. Tribal Colls. and Univs., 2001; founder LifeSkills Ctr. for Leadership, 2001—. Author: Life Skills for Success, Backroads & Sidestreets. Named Emerging Entrepreneurof Yr., Ernst and Young, NASDAQ, USA Today, Restaurateur of Yr., Mpls.-St. Paul (Minn.) Mag., 1998, Olympic Torch Carrier, 2002. Office: Famous Dave's America Inc 12701 Whitewater Dr Ste 200 Minnetonka MN 55343

ANDERSON, DAVIN CHARLES, business representative, labor consultant; b. Mpls., July 26, 1955; s. Roland Lawrence Anderson and Merlyne (Aldrich) Bissell; m. Diane Elmshauser, Aug. 14, 1982; children: Kiersten Janel, Matilda Rae. Student, St. Cloud State U., Minn., 1973-76; BS, U. Minn., 1979. Technician Northwest Cinema, Mpls., 1976-78, Mann Cinemas, Mpls., 1978-81, Gen. Cinema Corp., Mpls., 1981-99, Tacora Theatre, 1999—; account exec. Van Clemens & Co., Mpls., 1987—. Sec. Assn. Entertainment Industries Unions, St. Paul, 1987—. Mem. AFL-CIO (del.), Internat Alliance Theatrical and Stage Employees (bus. rep. Local 219 1986—), Nat. Assn. Investors Clubs, Trades and Labor Council (del.), Cen. Labor Union Council (del.), Toastmasters. Lutheran. Avocations: fishing, boating, skiing, hiking, flying. Home: 201 3d Ave S PO Box 626 Biwabik MN 55708-0626

ANDERSON, DONALD KENNEDY, JR., language educator; b. Evanston, Ill., Mar. 18, 1922; s. Donald Kennedy and Kathryn Marie (Shields) A.; m. Kathleen Elizabeth Hughes, Sept. 11, 1949; children: David J., Lawrence W. AB, Yale U., 1943; MA, Northwestern U., 1947; PhD, Duke U., 1957. Instr. Geneva Coll., Beaver Falls, Pa., 1947-49; from instr. to asst. prof. Rose Poly. Inst., Terre Haute, Ind., 1952-58; asst. prof., assoc. prof. Butler U., Indpls., 1958-65; assoc. prof. U. Mo., Columbia, 1965-67, prof. dept. English, 1967-92, prof. emeritus Columbia, 1992—, assoc. dean Grad. Sch. Columbia, 1970-74. Author: John Ford, 1972; editor: John Ford's Perkin Warbeck, 1965, John Ford's The Broken Heart, 1968, Concord in Discord, The Plays of John Ford, 1586-1986, 1987. Served to lt. (j.g.) USNR, 1943-46. Folger fellow, 1965; U. Mo. Summer Research fellow, 1966, 68, 76, 79, 84 Mem. MLA (midwest regional del. 1972-75), AAUP (sec.-treas. 1962-63) Democrat. Methodist. Home: 1800 Riverside Dr Apt 221 Columbus OH 43212-1804

ANDERSON, DYKE A., former medical association administrator; Dir. Nat. Assn. Bds. Pharmacy, Park Ridge, Ill., 2000—01.

ANDERSON, EDGAR RATCLIFFE, JR., career officer, physician, health facility administrator; b. Baton Rouge, Mar. 13, 1940; m. Sandra Caston; children: Melisa, Edward, Mark. MD, La. State U., 1964; grad., Industrial Coll. Armed Forces, 1972, Air War Coll., 1982. Diplomate Am. Bd. Family Practice, Am. Bd. Dermatology, Am. Bd. Preventive Medicine. Commd. 2d lt. USAF, 1965, advanced through grades to lt. gen., 1994, flight surgeon 464th Troop Carrier Wing Pope AFB, N.C., 1965-68, chief aerospace medicine 33d Tactical Fighter Wing Eglin AFB, Fla., 1968-69, undergrad. pilot tng. Williams AFB, Ariz., 1969-71, completed F-4 combat crew tng. MacDill AFB, Fla., 1971, aircraft comdr. 336th Tactical Fighter Squadron Seymour Johnson AFB, N.C., 1971, asst. ops. officer Ubon Royal Thai AFB, chief aeromed. svcs. USAF Regional Hosp. MacDill AFB, 1973-75, comdr. USAF Hosp. Seymour Johnson AFB, 1975-77, staff dermatologist USAF Med. Ctr. Keesler AFB, Miss., 1980-81, chief flight test ops. USAF-RAF exchange program Royal Air Force Station, Farnborough, Eng., 1981-83, comdr. USAF Regional Hosp. Langley AFB, Va., 1983-84, dir. profl. svcs. Office of Command Surgeon Tactical Air Command, 1984, command surgeon HQ Pacific Air Forces Hickam AFB, Hawaii, 1984-86, command surgeon SAC Offutt AFB, Nebr., 1986-90, comdr. Wilford Hall USAF Med. Ctr. Lackland AFB, Tex., 1990, surgeon general Washington, ret., 1996; CEO Truman Health Sys., Kansas City, Mo., 1996-98. Dean, prof. Sch. Med. U. Mo., Kansas City, 1996-97; exec. v.p., CEO AMA, Chgo., 1998-2001; pres., CEO Anderson Med. Consulting, LLC, 2001-; prof. medicine Loyola U. Med. Ctr., Chgo., 2002-. Decorated D.S.M. with oak leaf cluster, Legion of Merit with oak leaf cluster, D.F.C. with oak leaf cluster, Meritorious Svc. Medal with two oak leaf clusters, Air medal with nine oak leaf clusters, Air Force Commendation Medal.

ANDERSON, ELLEN RUTH, state legislator; b. Gary, Ind., Nov. 25, 1959; d. John Ernest Anderson and Marion Jane (Reeves) Martin; m. Andrew J. Dawkins. BA in History, Carleton Coll., 1982; JD, U. Minn., 1986. Bar: Minn., 1987, U.S. Dist. Ct. Minn. 1988. Jud. law clk. Minn. Ct. Appeals, St. Paul, 1987-88; atty. Hennepin County Pub. Defender, Mpls., 1988-91; staff atty. Minn. Edn. Assn., St. Paul, 1991-92; mem. Minn. Senate from 66th dist., St. Paul, 1993—. Democrat. Office: State of Minn G-24 Capitol 75 Constitution Ave Saint Paul MN 55155-1601

ANDERSON, ERIC SCOTT, lawyer; b. Grand Forks, ND, Aug. 26, 1949; s. Lyle William and Norma Sylvia (Lundeby) A.; children: Peter Scott, Nathan William. BSChemE, U. Wis., 1971, JD, 1977. Bar: Wis. 1977, Minn. 1977, U.S. Dist. Ct. (we. dist.) Wis. 1977, U.S. Dist. Ct. Minn. 1978. Assoc. Fredrikson & Byron, P.A., Mpls., 1977-83, shareholder, 1983—. Mem. Wis. Bar Assn., Minn. Bar Assn., Hennepin County Bar Assn., Phi Eta Sigma, Tau Beta Pi, Phi Kappa Phi, Order of Coif. Avocations: golf, running, music. Office: Fredrikson & Byron PA 200 S 6th St Ste 4000 Minneapolis MN 55402-1425 Office Phone: 612-492-7030. E-mail: eanderson@fredlaw.com.

ANDERSON, G. BARRY, state supreme court justice; b. Mankato, Minn., Oct. 24, 1954; m. Louise Helleoid, June 30, 1884; 3 children. BA magna cum laude, Gustavus Adolphus Coll., 1976; JD, U. Minn., 1979. Bar: Minn. 1979, U.S. Dist. Ct. Minn. 1979, U.S. Ct. Appeals (8th cir.) 1980; cert. civil trial specialist. Partner Arnold, Anderson & Dove; city atty. City of Hutchinson, Minn., 1987-88; gen. counsel Minn. Rep. Party, 1987-97; chair Minn. Ethical Practices Bd., 1997-98; judge Minn. Ct. Appeals, St. Paul, 1998—2004; justice Minn. Supreme Ct., 2004—. Bd. dirs. Hutchinson Cmty. Video Network, pres., 1984-98. Mem. Alpha Kappa Psi, Rotary (pres. Hutchinson chpt. 1997-98). Lutheran. Avocations: golf, historical and biographical works. Office: Minn Supreme Ct 305 Minn Jud Ctr 25 Rev Dr Martin Luther King Jr Blvd Saint Paul MN 55155

ANDERSON, GERARD M., energy executive; b. Toledo, Ohio; BS in Civil Engring., Notre Dame U.; MBA, U. of Mich., M. in Public Policy. Sr. cons. McKinsey & Co., 1988—93; v.p. non-utility bus. Detroit Edison DTE Energy Co., Detroit, 1993, CEO DTE Biomass Energy, exec. v.p., 1997, pres., COO energy resources bus. unit, 1998, pres., 2004—, COO, 2005—. Vice chmn. Nature Conservancy, Mich. Chap., Mich. Greenway Initiative. Office: DTE Energy Co 2000 2d Ave Detroit MI 48226-1279

ANDERSON, HAROLD E., trucking company executive; married Jeanette Anderson. Pres., founder Anderson Trucking Svc., St. Cloud, Minn., 1955—. Served to capt. USAF, WWII. Decorated Air medal, Disting. Flying Cross. Office: Anderson Trucking Svc 203 Cooper Ave N Saint Cloud MN 56303-4446

ANDERSON, HARRISON CLARKE, pathologist, educator, biomedical researcher; b. Louisville, Sept. 2, 1932; married, 1961. BA in Zoology, U. Louisville, 1954, MD, 1958. Diplomate Am. Bd. Pathology. Pathology intern Mass. Gen. Hosp., Boston, 1958-59; NIH rsch. trainee U. Louisville, Ky., 1959-60; resident in pathology Sloan Kettering Meml. Hosp, NYC, 1960-62; postdoctoral fellow Sloan Kettering Inst., Rye, NY, 1962-63; from asst. prof., assoc. prof. to prof. pathology SUNY Downstate Med. Ctr., Bklyn., 1963-78; prof. pathology, chmn. dept. U. Kans. Med. Ctr., Kansas City, Mo., 1978-90, Harrington prof. orthopedic rsch., 1990—; prof. emeritus pathology, 2002. Mem. study sect. NIH, Bethesda, Md., 1977—81, Bethesda, 1999—2005; chmn. Gordon Rsch. Conf. on Bone, Meriden, NH, 1981. Edit. bd. Am. Jour. Pathology, others, 1981—; contbr. articles to profl. jours. Recipient Biol. Mineralization Research award Internat. Assn. Dental Research, 1985, Sr. Faulty Research award U. Kans. Med. Ctr., 1986, Kappa Delta Orthopedic Rsch. award Orthopedic Rsch. Soc., 1982, Higuchi Biomed. Rsch. award U. Kansas, 1991; NIH rsch. fellow Strangeways Lab., Cambridge, Eng., 1971-72, NIH sr. rsch. fellow in cell biology Yale U., New Haven,, 1984-85; grantee NIH, 1967-2007. Mem. Am. Soc. Investigative Pathologists, Assn. Pathology Chmn. (pres. 1988-90), Am. Soc. Cell Biology, Am. Soc. Bone and Mineral Research, Orthopaedic Research Soc. Clubs: Am. Yacht (Rye); Carriage (Kansas City). Avocations: tennis, skiing, sailing. Office: U Kansas Med Center Dept Pathology 39th & Rainbow Kansas City KS 66160-0001 Home Phone: 913-262-8203; Office Phone: 913-588-7474. Business E-Mail: handerso@kumc.edu.

ANDERSON, HARRY FREDERICK, JR., architect; b. Chgo., Feb. 4, 1927; s. Harry Frederick and Sarah Matilda (Anderson) A.; m. Frances Annette Zeilstra, Jan. 27, 1951 (dv. Jan. 1979); children: Scott H., Mark S., Robert R., Grant Alan; m. Elizabeth Jane Elden, Jan. 17, 1979 (dec. Apr. 1982); m. Joanell Vivian Mangan, Mar. 22, 1983. B.Arch., Ill. Inst. Tech., 1953. Chief draftsman Stade & Cooley, Chgo., 1953-55; ptnr. Stade, Dolan & Anderson, Chgo., 1955-65; project architect Perkins & Will Partnership, Chgo., 1965-67, ptnr., v.p., 1967-85, sr. v.p., 1973-74, exec. v.p., 1974-75, pres., chief exec. officer, 1975-85, chmn. bd., 1982-85; chmn., chief exec. officer Anderson, Mikos Architects Ltd., Oak Brook, Ill., 1985—. Bd. dirs. Chgo. Bldg. Congress. Prin. works include Rockford (Ill.) Coll. Library, 1967, Sci. Bldg, 1968, Arts Complex, 1970, Women's Dormitory, 1969, Silver Cross Hosp, Joliet, Ill., 1971, Westlake Hosp, Melrose Park, Ill., 1970, Am. Soc. Clin. Pathologists bldg., Chgo., 1971, Ingalls Hosp, 1974, St. Mary of Nazareth Hosp, 1975, Childrens Meml. Hosp., Chgo., 1980, U. Chgo. Hosp, 1980, Northwestern Meml. Hosp., Chgo., 1987, Michael Reese Hosp., Chgo., 1987, Ctrl. Dupage Hosp., Winfield, Ill., 1998, Advocate Health Care Sys., Chgo., 1998. Chmn. adv. council Booth Meml. Hosp., Chgo., 1969-81; adv. bd. Chgo. Salvation Army, 1969-81. Served with USN, 1944-47. Fellow AIA; Mem. Internat. Hosp. Fedn., Am. Pub. Health Assn., Soc. Hosp. Planning and Mktg., Hinsdale Golf Club. Home: 721 W Walnut St Hinsdale IL 60521-3062 Office: Anderson Mikos Architects Ltd 1420 Kensington Rd Ste 306 Hinsdale IL 60523-2147

ANDERSON, HUGH GEORGE, bishop; b. LA, Mar. 10, 1932; s. Reuben Leroy and Frances Sophia (Nielsen) A.; m. Synnøve Anna Hella, Nov. 3, 1956 (dec. Apr. 1982); 1 child, Erik; m. Jutta Ilse Fischer, July 2, 1983; children: Lars, Niels; 1 child, Kristi. AB, Yale U., 1953; BD, Luth. Theol. Sem., Phila., 1956, STM, 1958; MA, U. Pa., 1957, PhD, 1962; LittD, Lenoir Rhyne Coll., 1971; DD, Roanoke Coll., 1971, Wagner Coll., 1987, Gen. Theol. Sem., NYC, 1996, Luther Coll., Decorah, Iowa, 1996; LHD, Newberry Coll., 1979, Columbia Coll., SC, 1981. Ordained Luth. min. Tchg. fellow Luth. Theol. Sem., Phila., 1956—58; prof. ch. history Luth. Theol. So. Sem., Columbia, SC, 1958—70, dir. grad. studies, pres., 1970—82, Luther Coll., Decorah, Iowa, 1982—95; presiding bishop Evang. Luth. Ch. Am., Chgo., 1995—2001; ret., 2001. Chair Pub. House of the Evang. Luth. Ch. Am., 1987—93; co-chmn. U.S. Luth.-Roman Cath. Dialogue, 1979—90; mem. Commn. for a New Luth. Ch., 1982—86; v.p. Luth. World Fedn., 1996—. Author: Lutheranism in the Southeastern States, 1969, A Good Time to be the Church, 1997; co-author: Lutherans in North America, 1975; translator: I Believe (H. Thielicke), 1968, Historical Commentary on the Augsburg Confession (W. Maurer), 1986. Bd. dirs. Minn. Pub. Radio, St. Paul, 1983—91. Mem.: Luth. World Fedn. (commn. on studies 1984—90). Lutheran. Avocations: astronomy, sailing.

ANDERSON, J. TRENT, lawyer; b. Indpls., July 22, 1939; s. Robert C. and Charlotte M. (Pfeifer) Anderson; m. Judith J. Zimmerman, Sept. 8, 1962; children: Evan M., Molly K. BS, Purdue U., 1961; LLB, U. Va., 1964. Bar: Ill. 1965, Ind. 1965. Tchg. asst. Law Sch. U. Calif., Berkeley, 1964-65; assoc. Mayer, Brown & Platt, Chgo., 1965-72; ptnr. Mayer, Brown, Rowe & Maw LLP, Chgo., 1972—2007, sr. counsel, 2007—. Instr. Loyola U. Law Sch., Chgo., 1985. Mem.: Mich. Shores Club, Union League Club, Law Club. Home: 3037 Iroquois Rd Wilmette IL 60091-1106 Office: Mayer Brown Rowe & Maw LLP 71 S Wacker Dr Chicago IL 60606-4637 Office Phone: 312-701-7365. Business E-Mail: janderson@mayerbrown.com.

ANDERSON, JAMES GEORGE, sociologist, educator, communications educator; b. Balt., July 24, 1936; s. Clair Sherrill and Kathryn Ann (Plovanich) A.; m. Marilyn Anderson, 1984; children: Robin Marie, James Brian, Melissa Lee, Derek Clair. B in Engring. Scis. in Chem. Engring, Johns Hopkins U., 1957, MSE in Ops. Rsch. and Indsl. Engring., 1959, MAT in Chemistry and Math., 1960, PhD in Edn. and Sociology, 1964. Adminstrv. asst. to dean Eve. Coll., Johns Hopkins U., 1964-65, dir. divsn. engring., 1965-66; rsch. prof. ednl. adminstrn. N.Mex. State U., 1966-70; mem. faculty Purdue U., Lafayette, Ind., 1970—, prof. sociology, 1974—, prof. com., 2004—; asst. dean for analytical studies Sch. Humanities, Social Sci. and Edn., Lafayette, Ind., 1975-78. Assoc. dir. AIDS Rsch. Ctr., Purdue U., 1991—, co-dir. Rural Ctr. for AIDS/STD Prevention, 1993-2006; adj. prof. med. sociology grad. med. edn. program Meth. Hosp. Ind., 1991—; dir. Social Rsch. Inst., Purdue U., 1995-98; cons. in field. Guest editor spl. issue on simulation in health sci.; spl. issues on modeling epidemics: spl. issue on simulation in med. informatics, Jour. the Am. Med. Informatics Assn., 2002, issue on simulation in health care mgmt., Health Care Mgmt. Sci., 2002, 07, issue on performance modeling and simulation in healthcare information systems, Simulation, 2007. Mem. Am. Assn. for Med. Systems and Informatics Del. to the Peoples Republic of China, 1985; mem., citizens amb. People to People Med. Informatics Del. to Hungary and Russia, 1993. USPHS grant; recipient award for outstanding paper Am. Assn. Med. Sys. and Informatics, 1983, Gov. award State of Ind., 1987, T. Hale New Investigators award Assn. Am. Med. Coll., 1988, Wyeth-Ayerst/William Campbell Felch, MD award Alliance for Continuing Med. Edn., 1995, Seeds of Excellence award, Purdue U., 2005. Fellow: Am. Coll. Med. Informatics; mem.: APHA, AAUP, AAAS (rep. soc. for computer simulation biol. scis. sect. 1992—99), Social Sci. Computing Assn. (chair life scis. 1991—), Am. Sociol. Assn. (chair sect. sociology and computers 2000—01), Internat. Soc. Sys. Sci. in Health Care, Internat. etwork for Social Network Analysis (chair life scis. 1997—), Soc. Modeling and Computer Simulation (sr.; assoc. v.p. simulation in health care 1992—), Am. Med. Informatics Assn. (internat. affairs com. 1993—96, chmn. sect. ethical, legal and social issues 1997—2000, sci. program com. ann. conf. 1999, mem. editl. bd. 2000—, chmn. sect. on quality improvement 2002—04, guest editor 2002, Best Theoretical Paper award 1997), Am. Ednl. Rsch. Assn. (treas. spl. interest group 1969—71), Am. Sociol. Assn., Assn. for Computing Machinery. Business E-Mail: andersonj@purdue.edu.

ANDERSON, JAMES MILTON, lawyer, hospital administrator; b. Chgo., Dec. 29, 1941; s. Milton H. and Eunice (Carlson) A.; m. Marjorie Henry Caldwell, Jan. 22, 1966; children: James Milton, Joseph H., Hilding F., Marjorie II. BA, Yale U., New Haven, Conn., 1963; JD, Vanderbilt U., Nashville, 1966. Bar: Ohio 1967. Assoc. rifm Taft, Stettinius & Hollister, Cin., 1968-75, ptnr., 1975-77, 82-96, mem. exec. com., 1975-77, 91-96; pres. US ops., dir. Xomox Corp., Cin., 1977-81; sec. Access Corp., 1984-96; asst. sec. Carlisle Cos., 1985-90; bd. dirs. Nat. Stock Exch., 1978—, chmn., 1980-89, 2007—. Bd. dirs. Command Sys. Inc., 1986—2002; trustee, chmn. Monarch Found., 1988—; assoc. sr. v.p. med. affairs U. Cin., 1997—; bd. adminstrs. Coun. Tchg. Hosps., 2000—04; dir. Nat. Assn. Children's Hosps. and Related Instns., 2002—; bd. dirs. 3CDC Inc., 2003—, Uptown Consortium, 2004—, Union Ctrl. Life Ins. Co., 2002—06; chmn. bd. dirs. Cin. br. Fed. Res. Bank Cleve., 2005—; mem. US Medicaid Commn., 2005—06; bd. dirs. UNIFI Mutual Holding Co., 2006—, Inst. for Healthcare Improvement, 2007—. Mem. Indian Hill Coun., 1981-89, vice-mayor, 1985-87, mayor, 1987-89; mem. Hamilton County Airport Authority, 1980-85; trustee Children's Hosp. Med. Ctr., Cin., 1979—, chmn. bd. trustees, 1991-96, pres., CEO, 1996—; trustee The Children's Hosp. Found., 1990—, chmn. bd. trustees, 1990-93; trustee Cin. Ctr. for Devel. Disorders, 1969—, pres., 1974-80; trustee Dan Beard coun. Boy Scouts Am., 1982—, chmn., 1984-87, area pres. Ea. Ctrl. Region, 1989-91; trustee Cin. Mus. Natural History, 1984-87, Coll. Mt. St. Joseph, 1990-98; trustee Joy Outdoor Edn. Ctr., 1984-2000, pres., 1991-93, chmn., 1993-95. Capt. AUS, 1966-68. Decorated Bronze Star with two oak leaf clusters, Air medal. Mem. ABA, Ohio Bar Assn., Cin. Bar Assn., Valve Mfrs. Assn., Young Pres. Orgn., Camargo Club, Queen City Club, Commonwealth Club, Yale Club of N.Y., Cin. Yale Club, Order of Coif, Comml. Club. Avocation: sailing. Office: 3333 Burnet Ave Cincinnati OH 45229-3026

ANDERSON, JERRY WILLIAM, JR., diversified financial services company executive, educator; b. Stow, Mass., Jan. 14, 1926; s. Jerry William and Heda Charlotte (Petersen) A.; m. Joan Hukill Balyeat, Sept. 13, 1947; children: Katheleen, Diane. BS in Physics, U. Cin., 1949, PhD in Econs., 1976; MBA, Xavier U., 1959. Rsch. and test project engr. Wright-Patterson AFB, Ohio, 1949-53; project engr., electronics divsn. AVCO Corp., Cin., 1953-70, program mgr., 1970-73; program dir. Cin. Electronics Corp., 1973-78; pres. Anderson Industries Unltd., 1978—. Chmn. dept. mgmt. and mgmt. info. svcs. Xavier U., 1980-89, prof. mgmt., 1989-94, prof. emeritus, 1994—; lectr. No. Ky. U., 1977-78; tech. adviser Cin. Tech. Coll., 1971-80; co-founder, exec. v.p. Loving God Complete Bible Christian Ministries, 1988—. Contbr. articles on radars, lasers, infrared detection equipment, air pollution to govt. pubs. and prof. jours.; author: 3 books in field; reviewer, referee: Internat. Jour. Energy Sys., 1985—86. Mem. Madeira City Planning Commn., Ohio, 1962-80; founder, pres. Grassroots, Inc., 1964; active United Appeal, Heart Fund, Multiple Sclerosis Fund. With USNR, 1943-46. Named Man of Yr., City of Madeira, 1964. Mem. MADD, VFW (life), Am. Mgmt. Assn., Assn. Energy Engrs. (charter), Internat. Acad. Mgmt. and Mktg., Nat. Right to Life, Assn. Cogeneration Engrs. (charter), Assn. Environ. Engrs. (charter), Am. Legion (past comdr.), Acad. Mgmt., Madeira Civic Assn. (past v.p.), Cin. Art Mus., Cin. Zoo, Colonial Williamsburg Found., Omicron Delta Epsilon. Republican. Home and Office: 7208 Sycamorehill Ln Cincinnati OH 45243-2101 Office Phone: 513-561-7685.

ANDERSON, JOHN ROBERT, retired mathematics professor; b. Stromsburg, Nebr., Aug. 1, 1928; s. Norris Merton and Violet Charlotte (Stromberg) A.; m. Bertha Margery Nore, Aug. 27, 1950; children: Eric Jon, Mary Lynn. Student, Midland Coll., 1945-46; AA, Luther Jr. Coll., 1949; BS (Regents scholar), U. Nebr., Lincoln, 1951, MA in Math, 1954; PhD, Purdue U., 1970. Tchr. math., coach Bloomfield (Nebr.) High Sch., 1951-52; control systems analyst, Allison div. Gen. Motors Corp., Indpls., 1954-60; prof. math. Depauw U., Greencastle, Ind., 1960, asst. dean, dir. grad. studies, 1973-76, dir. grad. studies, 1976-84, chmn. math. dept., 1984-90, prof. math., 1990-92, ret., 1992; adj. prof. math. IVTC, Greencastle, 1996—; resident dir. W. European studies program Depauw U., Germany, 1975, resident dir. Mediterranean Studies program Athens, Greece, 1982, 1990; dir. NSF Coop. Coll. Sch., Sci. Inst., 1969-70; instr. NSF summer inst., 1972; instr. Challenge sci. and math. program U.S. Students in Europe, 1976, 77, 78, 80, 82. Bd. dir. Law Focused Edn., Indpls., 1975-77, Ind. Regional Math. Consortium, 1977-92. Bd. dir. Luth. Brotherhood br. 8746, 1967-2002, pres. Thrivent Luth. chpt. 30903, 2002-06, United Way of Greencastle, Ind., 1992-98, treas., Putnam Co. Food Pantry, 1993-98; officer, elder Peace Evangel. Luth. Ch., 1960—. Served with U.S. Army, 1946-48. Danforth Tchr. fellow, 1963-64; SF sci. faculty fellow, 1964-65; Lilly Found. edn. grantee, summers 1961-63 Mem. Math. Assn. Am., Nat. Council Tchrs. Math., North Central Assn. (commr. 1974-78), Sigma Xi, Pi Mu Epsilon, Kappa Delta Pi, Beta Sigma Psi. Clubs: Rotary Internat. (sec. 1976-77, v.p. 1977-78, pres. 1978-79, 1998-99). Home: 1560 S Bloomington St Greencastle IN 46135-2212 E-mail: johnanderson@depauw.edu, jranderson28@hotmail.com.

ANDERSON, JON STEPHEN, newswriter; b. Montreal, Que., Can., Mar. 13, 1936; arrived in U.S., 1963; s. William Howard and Dorothy Beatrice (Ryan) A.; m. Gail Rutherford, Feb. 20, 1960 (div. 1966); 1 child, Jon Gregory (dec.); m. Abra Prentice, Sept. 14, 1968 (div. 1976); children: Ashley Prentice Norton, Abra Cantrill Williams, Anthony Ryan; m. Pamela Sherrod, Sept. 23, 2001. BA, Mt. Allison U., Sackville, Can., 1955; BCL, McGill U., Montreal, 1959; MAW, U. Iowa, 1991. Reporter Montreal Gazette, 1957-60; chief bur. Time Mag., Montreal, 1960-63, staff corr. Chgo., 1963-66; staff writer Chgo. Sun-Times, 1967-69; columnist Chgo. Daily News, 1969-72; pub. Chicagoan Mag., 1972-74; staff writer Chgo. Tribune, 1978—2006; writing instr. U. Iowa, 1989—2002; freelance writer, 2006—. Author: City Watch: Discovering the Uncommon Chicago, 2000; contbr. articles to Readers Digest, 1977-85, Chgo. Mag., 1977, Clothesline Rev., 1986. Gen. mgr. Second City Ctr. Pub. Arts, 1966-67; bd. dirs. Chgo. Internat. Film Festival, 1975-78 Recipient Stick o' Type award, Newspaper Guild Am., 1969, Studs Terkel Journalism award, 1999. Mem.: Order Ky. Cols. Roman Catholic. Personal E-mail: jonanderson99@aol.com.

ANDERSON, JOSHUA M., speech educator; BS in Edn., Emporia State Univ., 1997; MA in Sch. Leadership, Baker Univ., 2001. Lang. arts tchr. Basehor-Linwood H.S., 1997—2003, Olathe (Kans.) Northwest H.S., 2003—. Finalist Nat. Tchr. of Yr., 2007; named Kans. Tchr. of Yr., 2007. Mem.: Internat. Thespian Soc., Nat. Forensics League (Diamond Key Award for Excellence in Edn. 2005), Assn Supervision and Curriculum Devel., E. Kans. Nat. Forensics League, Nat. Cath. Forensics League, Kans. Speech Comm. Assn., Kans. NEA, NEA, ACLU. Office: Olathe Northwest High Sch 21300 College Blvd Olathe KS 66061 Business E-Mail: jandersonnw@olatheschools.com.

ANDERSON, JUDITH HELENA, English language educator; b. Worcester, Mass., Apr. 21, 1940; d. Oscar William and Beatrice Marguerite (Beaudry) A.; m. E. Talbot Donaldson, May 18, 1971 (dec. Apr. 1987). AB magna cum laude, Radcliffe Coll., 1961; MA, Yale U., 1962, PhD, 1965. Instr. English Cornell U., Ithaca, NY, 1964-66, asst. prof. English, 1966-72; vis. lectr. Coll. Seminar Program, Yale U., New Haven, 1973; vis. asst. prof. English U. Mich., Ann Arbor, 1973-74; assoc. prof. Ind. U., Bloomington, 1974-79, prof., 1979—, Chancellor's prof., 1999—, dir. grad. studies, 1986-90, 93, mem. governing bd. univ. Inst. for Advanced Study, 1983-85, 86-88. Morris W. Croll lectr. Gettysburg Coll., 1988, Kathleen Williams lectr., 89, 95; dir. Folger Inst. Sem., 1991; adv. bd. Textbase of Women Writers, Brown U., 1989—2000. Author: The Growth of a Personal Voice, 1976, Biographical Truth, 1984, Words that Matter, 1996, Translating Investments, 2005, Reading The Allegorical Intertect, 2008; editor: (with Elizabeth D. Kirk) Piers Plowman, 1990; (with Donald Cheney and David A. Richardson) Spenser's Life and the Subject of Biography, 1996, (with Christine R. Farris) Integrating Literature and Writing Instruction, 2007; mem. editl. bd. Spenser Ency., 1979-90, Duquesne Studies in Lang. and Lit., 1976-2004, Spenser Studies, 1986—, Medieval and Renaissance Literary Studies, 2004—; contbr. articles to profl. jours. Rsch. grant Huntington Libr., 1978, 97; Woodrow Wilson fellow, 1961-64, NEH summer fellow and sr. rsch. fellow, 1979, 81-82, NEH-Huntington fellow, 1985-86, Mayers Found. fellow, 1990-91, Dulin fellow Folger Libr., 1991, Nat. Humanities Ctr. fellow, 1995-96, EH-Newberry fellow, 2002-03; recipient Outstanding Scholar award Office of Women's Affairs Ind. U., 1996 Mem. MLA (exec. com. Renaissance divsn. 1973-78, 86-90, del. to assembly 1991-93, publs. com. 1999-2002), AAUP, internat. Spenser Soc. (pres. 1980, 88, Lifetime Achievement award 2004, exec. com. 2007-09), Renaissance Soc. Am. (rep. for English to coun. 1991-93), Milton Soc., Donne Soc. (exec. com. 2004-06), Shakespeare Assn., Chaucer Soc., Phi Beta Kappa. Home: 2525 E 8th St Bloomington IN 47408-4214 Office: Ind U Dept English Bloomington IN 47405 Office Phone: 812-855-8224. Business E-Mail: anders@indiana.edu.

ANDERSON, KARL STEPHEN, editor; b. Chgo., Nov. 10, 1933; s. Karl William and Eleanore (Grell) a.; m. Saralee Hegland, Nov. 5, 1977; children by previous marriage: Matthew, Douglas, Eric. BS in Editl. Journalism, U. Ill., 1955. Successively advt. mgr., asst. to pub., plant mgr. Pioneer Press, Oak Park, St. Charles, Ill., 1955-71; asst. to pub., then pub. Crescent Newspapers, Downers Grove, Ill., 1971-73; assoc. pub., editor Chronicle Pub. Co., St. Charles, 1973-80; assoc. pub. Chgo. Daily Law Bull., 1981-88; dir. comm., editor Ill. State Bar Assn., 1988—. Past pres. Chgo. Pub. Rels. Forum. Trustee emeritus Chi Psi Ednl. Trust; trustee Leo Sowerby Found.; bd. dirs. Ill. Press Found., Swedish Am. Hist. Soc., Ill. First Amendment Ctr. Recipient C.V. Amenoff award No. Ill. U. Dept. Journalism, 1976, Bd. Govs. award Ill. State Bar, 1987, Print Media Humanitarian award Coalition Sub Bar Assns., 1987, Robert C. Preble, Jr. award Chi Psi, 1991, Asian-Am. Bar Media Sensitivity award, 1991, Liberty Bell award DuPage County Bar Assn., 1993, Glass Ceiling Busters award DuPage Women Lawyers, 1993, Disting. Svc. award Chgo. Vol. Legal Svcs. Found., 1993, Gratitude award Lawyers Assistance Program, 1993, Outstanding Achievement in Comm. award Justinian Soc., 1994, Communicator of Yr. award, 1999, 3rd prize Nat. Libr. Poetry, 1995, Svc. award Women's Bar Assn. Ill., 1998, Peoria County Bar Assn., 1998 Mem. Nat. Assn. Bar Execs., Baltic Bar Assn., Chgo. Journalists Assn., Ill. Press Assn. (Will Loomis award 1977, 80), Kane County Bar Assn., DuPage Women Lawyers Assn., West Suburban Bar Assn., North Suburban Bar Assn. (Pub. Svc. award 1997), N.W. Suburban Bar Assn. (Svc. award 2005), Bohemian Lawyers Assn. (Liberty award 1999), No. Ill. Newspaper Assn. (past pres.), Pub. Rels. Soc. Ctrl. Ill. (Master Communicator award of achievement 1997), Soc. Profl. Journalists, Headline Club (past pres.), Nordic Law Club, Nellie Fox Soc., Union League Club Chgo., Chgo. Illini Club (bd. dirs.), Chi Psi. Home: 3180 N Lake Shore Dr Apt 14D Chicago IL 60657-4851 Office: Ill State Bar Assn 20 S Clark St Ste 900 Chicago IL 60603-1885 Office Phone: 312-726-8775.

ANDERSON, KERRII B., food service executive; b. 1957; BS, Elon Coll., 1978; MBA, Duke U., 1987. CPA. With Peat, Marwick, Mitchell & Co., Greensboro, NC, 1978-84, RJ Reynolds Corp., Winston-Salem, NC, 1984-85, Key Co., Greensboro, NC, 1985-87; sec. M/I Schottenstein Homes Inc.,

Columbus, 1987—94, sr. v.p., CFO, chmn. bd., 1987—2000, asst. sec., 1994—2000; exec. v.p., CFO Wendy's Internat. Inc., Dublin, Ohio, 2000—06, interim CEO, 2006, pres., CEO, 2006—. Bd. dirs. The Lancaster Colony Corp., M/I Schottenstein Homes, Inc., Wendy's Internat. Inc., 2000—. Mem. fin. com. The Columbus Found.; bd. mem. Grant-Riverside Hosp.; mem. dean's adv. com. Fisher Coll. Bus., Ohio State U. Office: Wendys Internat Inc One Dave Thomas Blvd Dublin OH 43017 also: 4288 W Dublin-Granville Rd Dublin OH 43017-0256

ANDERSON, KIMBALL RICHARD, lawyer; b. San Antonio, Aug. 20, 1952; s. Richard John and Martha (Bishop) A.; m. Karen Gatsis, Aug. 18, 1974; children: Alexis Katrina, Melissa Martha, Sophia Diane. BA, U. Ill., 1974, JD, 1977. Bar: Ill. 1977, U.S. Ct. Appeals (7th cir.) 1979, U.S. Supreme Ct. 1987; CPA, Ill. 1974. Assoc. Winston & Strawn LLP, Chgo., 1977-84, ptnr., 1984—, chmn. pro bono com., 1984—, mem. exec. com., 1994—, gen. counsel, 2000—. Disting. neutral CPR Inst. for Dispute Resolution; adj. prof. trial advocacy Northwestern U; pres. CBA TV Prodns., Inc., 1989-1991, CBA Ins. Adminstrs., 1993-; spkr. in field. Contbr. articles to profl. jours. V.p. Pub. Interest Law Initiative, 2002—05, pres., 2006—; chmn. bd. AIDS Legal Coun. Chgo.; bd. dirs. De Paul U. Coll. Law Ctr. Justice in Capital Cases, pres., 2003—. Named Person of Yr. 1996 Chgo. Lawyer Mag., laureate Ill. Acad. Lawyers, 2005. Fellow Am. Coll. Trial Lawyers, Am. Bar Found.; mem. ABA (mem. ethics 2000 adv. coun. 1998-, mem. Ctr. Profl. responsibility, Pro Bono Publico award 2003), Ill. Bar Assn., Chgo. Bar Assn. (bd. mgrs. 1990-92), Ill. CPA Soc., Chgo. Bar Found. (2d v.p. 2001-02, 1st v.p. 2003-05, pres. 2005—). Home: 2045 N Seminary Ave Chicago IL 60614-4109 Office: Winston & Strawn 35 W Wacker Dr Ste 4200 Chicago IL 60601-1695 Office Phone: 312-558-5858. Business E-Mail: kanderson@winston.com.

ANDERSON, LESLIE J., lawyer; b. 1953; BA in English Lit. magna cum laude, Allegheny Coll., 1975; MA in English and Comparative Lit., Columbia Univ., 1976, MPhil, 1979; JD cum laude, Univ. Mich., 1983. Bar: Minn. 1983. Assoc. Dorsey & Whitney LLP, Mpls, 1984—91; ptnr., litig. group Dorsey & Whitney, Mpls., 1991, now ptnr., co-chair, employee benefits group. Staff mem. Mich.Yearbook of Internat. Legal Studies, 1981—82, editor-in-chief, 1982—83. Bd. dir. Greater Twin Cities Youth Symphonies, 2003—. Mem.: Minn. Women Lawyers, Minn. Advocates for Human Rights, Phi Beta Kappa. Office: Dorsey & Whitney LLP Ste 1500 50 S Sixth St Minneapolis MN 55402-1498 Office Phone: 612-343-7960. Office Fax: 612-340-2868. Business E-Mail: anderson.leslie@dorsey.com.

ANDERSON, LOUIS WILMER, JR., physicist, researcher; b. Houston, Dec. 24, 1933; s. Louis Wilmer and Margaret Quarles (Brockett) A.; m. Marguerite Gillespie, Aug. 30; children— Margaret Mary, Louis Charles, Elizabeth Brockett BA, Rice U., 1956; A.M., Harvard U., 1957, PhD, 1960. Asst. prof. U. Wis.-Madison, 1960-63, assoc. prof., 1963-68, prof. physics, 1968-94, Julian E. Mack prof. physics, 1994—. Cons. U. Calif.-Berkeley Lawrence Lab. Author 2 textbooks. Contbr. articles to profl. jours. Patentee type of N2 laser, collisional pumping ion source. Fellow U. Wis. Tchg. Acad.; co-recipient IEEE Particle Accelerator Conf. Tech. award for invention and devel. of optically pumped polarized H-Ion source, 1993. Fellow Am. Phys. Soc.; mem. Sigma Xi Avocation: painting. Home: 1818 Chadbourne Ave Madison WI 53726 Office: U Wis Dept Physics Madison WI 53706 Office Phone: 608-262-8962. Business E-Mail: lwanders@wisc.edu.

ANDERSON, LYLE ARTHUR, retired manufacturing executive; b. Jewell, Kans., Dec. 29, 1931; s. Arvid Herman and Clara Vera (Herman) A.; m. Harriet Virginia Robson, June 12, 1953; children— Brian, Karen, Eric. BS, U. Kans., 1953; MS, Butler U., 1961. C.P.A., Mo., Kans. Mgmt. trainee, internal auditor RCA, Camden, N.J. and Indpls., 1955-59; auditor Ernst & Ernst (C.P.A.'s), Kansas City, Mo., 1959-63; v.p. fin. and adminstrn., treas., dir. Affiliated Hosp. Products, Inc., St. Louis, 1963-71; sr. v.p. Sara Lee Corp., Deerfield, Ill., 1971-74; exec. v.p. fin. Consol. Foods Corp., Chgo., 1974-76. Pres. Autotrol Corp., Crystal Lake, Ill. Bd. dirs. Crystal Lake Civic Ctr. Authority. With U.S. Army, 1953-55. Mem. Omicron Delta Kappa. Republican. Methodist. Home: 9804 Partridge Ln Crystal Lake IL 60014-6627

ANDERSON, MIKE, newscaster; Student, La. State U., Career Acad. Journalism and Broadcasting Sch. Radio journalist, Birmingham, Ala.; with Sta. WISN TV, Milw., 1981—, anchorman 12 News This Morning and 12 News at Noon. Avocations: exercising, writing songs. Office: WISN PO Box 402 Milwaukee WI 53201-0402

ANDERSON, MILTON ANDREW, chemicals executive; b. Fond du Lac, Wis., Oct. 22, 1927; s. Andrew Andreas and Bertha Victoria (Almquist) A.; m. Dorothy Mae Verke, Nov. 27, 1954; children: Edward, Victoria. BS, U. Wis., Madison, 1954; MS in Mgmt., Lake Forest Grad. Sch. Mgmt., 1980. Registered profl. engr., Calif. Specification engr. Johns-Manville, Waukegan, Ill., 1955-59, supr., 1959-64, chemist, 1964-70, devel. engr., 1970-73; supr. Abbott Labs., North Chicago, 1973-74, quality engr., 1974-77, cons., auditing., 1977-81, mgr. rsch. auditing good lab. practices/good clin. practices, 1981-92; pres. Rsch. Compliance Svcs. Ltd., Lake Villa, Ill., 1992—. Author: GLP Quality Audit Manual, 1987, 3rd edit., 2000, GLP Essentials, 1995, 2d edit., 2002. Pres. Millburn Elem. Sch. Bd., 1971—73; elected trustee Village of Old Mill Creek, Ill., 2005—. Lt. naval aviator, 1948—52. Mem. Soc. Quality Assurance, Am. Soc. for Quality Control (chmn. Northea. Ill. sect. 1980-82, sect. bd. dirs. 1982—85). Republican. Home and Office: Rsch Compliance Svcs Ltd 19176 W Grass Lake Rd Lake Villa IL 60046-9242 Home Phone: 847-356-8767. E-mail: miltseen@aol.com.

ANDERSON, MOSES BOSCO, bishop emeritus; b. Selma, Ala., Sept. 9, 1928; Student, St. Michael's Coll., St. Edmunds Sem., U. Legon, Ghana. Ordained priest Soc. of St. Edmund, 1958; aux. bishop Archdiocese of Detroit, 1982—2003; ordained bishop, 1983. Roman Catholic. Office: Diocese of Detroit 1234 Washington Blvd Detroit MI 48226-1825 Office Phone: 313-237-5816.*

ANDERSON, PAUL HOLDEN, state supreme court justice; b. May 14, 1943; m. Janice M. Anderson; 2 children. BA cum laude, Macalester Coll., 1965; JD, U. Minn., 1968. Atty. Vols. in Svc. to Am., 1968—69; spl. asst. atty. gen. criminal divsn. dept. pub. safety Office Minn. Atty. Gen., 1970—71; assoc., ptnr. LeVander, Gillen & Miller, South St. Paul, Minn., 1971—92; chief judge Minn. Ct. Appeals, 1992—94; assoc. justice Minn. Supreme Ct., 1994—. Mem. PER coms. Ind. Sch. Dist. 199, 1982—84, chmn. cmty. svcs. adv. com., bd. dirs., chmn. bd.; deacon, ruling elder, clk. of session House of Hope Presbyn. Ch., St. Paul. Mem.: Dakota County Bar Assn. (bd. dirs., pres.), South St. Paul/Inver Grove Heights C. of C. (bd. dirs., exec. com.). Avocations: tennis, gourmet cooking, bike riding. Office: 425 Minn Judicial Ctr 25 Rev Dr Martin Luther King Jr Blvd Saint Paul MN 55155-0001 Office Phone: 651-296-3314. Fax: 651-282-5115. Business E-Mail: paul.anderson@courts.state.mn.us.

ANDERSON, RICHARD CHARLES, geology educator; b. Moline, Ill., Apr. 22, 1930; s. Edgar Oscar and Sarah Albertina (Olson) A.; m. Ethel Irene Cada, June 27, 1953; children: Eileen Ruth, Elizabeth Sarah, Penelope Cada. AB, Augustana Coll., Rock Island, Ill., 1952; SM, U. Chgo., 1953, PhD, 1955. Geologist Geophoto Svcs., Denver, 1955-57; from asst. prof. to prof. geology Augustana Coll., Rock Island, 1957-96; prof. emeritus, 1996—. Rsch. affiliate Ill. State Geol. Survey, Champaign, 1959—. Editor: Earth Interpreters, 1992; author reports. Recipient Neil Miner award Nat. Assn. Geology Tchrs., 1992. Fellow Geol. Soc. Am. (sect. co-chair 1990). Lutheran. Home: 2012 24th St Rock Island IL 61201-4533 Office: Augustana Coll Dept Geology 639 38th St Rock Island IL 61201-2210 E-mail: glanderson@augustana.edu.

ANDERSON, RICHARD H., air transportation executive; b. Galveston, Tex., 1956; m. Susan Anderson. BS, U. Houston, 1977; JD, South Tex. Coll. Law, 1981. Various positions Harris County Dist. Atty.'s office, Houston, 1978—87; staff v.p., dep. gen. counsel Continental Airlines, 1987—90; v.p., dep. gen. counsel orthwest Airlines Corp., Eagan, Minn., 1990—94, sr. v.p. labor rels., state affairs, law, 1994—96, sr. v.p. tech. ops. and airport affairs, 1997—98, exec. v.p. tech. ops. and airport affairs, 1998, exec. v.p., COO Eagan, Minn., 1998—2001, CEO, 2001—04; exec. v.p., CEO Ingenix subs. UnitedHealth Group, Mpls., 2005—06, exec. v.p., pres. comml. svc. group, 2006—07; CEO Delta Air Lines, Inc., Atlanta, 2007—. Bd. dirs. Mesaba Holdings, Inc., 1999—2003, orthwest Airlines Corp., 2001—05, Medtronic, Inc., 2002—, Xcel Energy, Inc., 2004—06, Cargill, Inc., 2006—, Delta Airlines, Inc., 2007—, Minn. Life Ins. Co., Mpls. Inst. Arts, Mpls. Downtown Coun.; chmn. Min. Bus. Leadership Network. Mailing: Delta Air Lines Inc PO Box 20706 Atlanta GA 30320-6001 Office: Delta Air Lines 1030 Delta Blvd Atlanta GA 30320*

ANDERSON, RICHARD J., lawyer; BA summa cum laude, Coll. St. Thomas, 1984; PhD, U. Minn., 1988, JD magna cum laude, 1991. Bar: Minn. 1991, US Patent and Trademark Office. Law clk. to Hon. Daniel M. Friedman US Ct. Appeals, Fed. Cir., 1991—92; prin. Fish & Richardson PC, Minneapolis. Office: Fish & Richardson PC 60 So Sixth St 3300 Dain Rauscher Plaza Minneapolis MN 55402 Office Phone: 612-337-2501. Office Fax: 612-288-9696. E-mail: anderson@fr.com.

ANDERSON, RICHARD PAUL, agricultural company executive; b. Toledo, Apr. 10, 1929; s. Harold and Margaret Mary (Meilink) A.; m. Frances Mildred Heilman, Nov. 28, 1953; children— Christopher, Daniel, James, Martha, Jennifer, Timothy. BS magna cum laude, Mich. State U., 1953. With The Andersons, Maumee, Ohio, 1946—, gen. ptnr., 1951—, gen. mgr., 1980-82, mng. ptnr., 1983—, pres., CEO, 1986-96, chmn., CEO, 1996-98, chmn., 1999—. Bd. dirs. Chemfirst. Pres. Toledo Area council Boy Scouts Am., 1966-69; gen. chmn. Crusade of Mercy, Toledo, 1972; bd. dirs. Childrens Services, St. Luke's Hosp.; chmn. support council Ohio Agrl. Research and Devel. Ctr.; trustee U. Toledo Corp., 1985-98, chmn. bd. trustees, 1986—; bd. dirs. Pub. Broadcasting Found. NW Ohio, 1983—, chmn. bd. dirs., 1986-92. Served with AUS, 1954-56. Named Toledo Area Citizen of Yr. Toledo Bd. Realtors, 1974, Outstanding Lay Leader N.W. Ohio chpt. Nat. Assn. Social Workers, 1971; recipient Disting. Service award Ohio State U., 1986. Mem. Com. 100 (bd. dirs. exec. com. 1987-92). Clubs: Rotary (Toledo.) (pres. 1976-77). Republican. Roman Catholic. Home: 1833 S Holland Sylvania Rd Maumee OH 43537-1380 Office: The Andersons 480 W Dussel Dr Maumee OH 43537-1690

ANDERSON, RICHARD TODD, college president; BSc in Indsl. Edn., U. Wis., Stout, 1957; MEd, Marquette U., 1963, PhD in Edn., 1975. Tchr. Waukesha Vocat. Sch., Pewaukee, Wis., 1957-62; various adminstrv. positions Waukesha County Tech. Coll., Pewaukee, Wis., 1962-68, asst. dist. dir., 1968-73, pres., 1973—. Co-chair Waukesha County VTAE/DPI Articulation Com. (chair certification hearing bd. 1978-79), Waukesha County Tech Prep Advisory Council; mem. Wis. Hispanic Council Higher Edn.; bd. dirs. Public Policy Com., Special Transportation Com. Recipient Eagle award Wisc. Instructional Svcs. Assn., 1984, Distinguished Svc. award Am. Assn. Women Cmty. Jr. Colls., 1985, Outstanding Corp. Leadership award Waukesha YWCA, 1991; Fulbright scholar India, 1986. Mem. Nat. Assn. Pub. Sch. Adult Edn., Am. Mgmt. Assn., Am. Tech. Edn. Assn., Am. Vocat. Assn., USAF Assn., U.S. Apprenticeship Assn., Cmty. Colls. Internat. Dev. (bd. dirs.), Council Occupl. Edn., Wis. Assn. Vocat. Adult Edn., U. Wis. Alumni Assn., Kiwanis Early Risers, Phi Delta Kappa, Phi Sigma Epsilon. Office: Waukesha County Technical College Office of the President 800 Main St Pewaukee WI 53072-4601

ANDERSON, RICHARD VERNON, ecology educator, researcher; b. Julesburg, Colo., Sept. 9, 1946; s. Vernon Franklin and Charolett Iona (Jeppesen) A.; m. Arline June Rosentreter, Jan. 23, 1971; children: Rustle R., Michael C., Theodore F. Student, Chadron State Coll., 1964-66, Western State Coll., 1970; BS, No. Ill. U., 1974, MS, 1975; PhD, Colo. State U., 1978. Grad. teaching asst. No. Ill. U., DeKalb, 1974-75; grad. rsch. asst. Colo. State U., 1975-78, postdoctoral fellow Nat. Resource Ecology Lab., 1978-79; asst. prof. Western Ill. U., Macomb, 1979-82, assoc. prof., 1982-87, prof., dir. Kibbe Life Scis. Field Sta., 1987-2001, chmn. dept. biol. scis., 2001—. Vis. asst. prof. inst. for. environ. studies Water Resources Ctr., U. Ill., 1980; mem. assoc. faculty Argonne at. Lab., 1985—; assoc. supportive scientist Ill. Natural History Survey, 1985—; proposal reviewer ecology, ecosystem studies, regulatory biology, divsn. internat. programs NSF, 1981—, mem. proposal panel for equipment and facilities grants, 1987; proposal reviewer U.S./Israel Binational Sci. Found., 1981-82, Natural Environ. Rsch. Coun., Eng., 1983-84; environ. cons. aquatic sect. Environ. Cons. and Planners, DeKalb, 1974; program chmn. Internat. Conf. on Ecological Integrity of Large Floodplain Rivers, 1994. Reviewer Natural Resource Ecology Lab., 1977-81, Jour. Nematology, 1977-81, Archives Environ. Contamination and Toxicology, 1978-81, Ecology, 1978-85, Argonne Nat. Lab., 1980—, Pedobiologia, 1982-87, Jour. Freshwater Ecology, 1982—, Freshwater Invertebrate Ecology, 1982—; contbr. over 250 sci. articles, reports, papers and abstracts; presenter papers in field. Grantee NSF, 1972, 73, 82, 83, 84, 85, (two grants), 86, (two grants), 87, 88, 99, 2002, Western Ill. U., 1980, (two grants), 81, Upper Miss. River Basin Comm./U. Ill., 1980, Abbott Labs., 1981, Ill. Dept. Transp., 1981, 85, Ctrl. Ill. Light Co., 1981, 82, 83, 84, Nat. Fish and Wildlife Svc., 1983, Ill. Dept. Conservation, 1985, 87, 88, 89, 91, U.S. Fish and Wildlife Svc./Ill. Dept. Conservation, 1988, 89, 90, 91, Environ. Cons. and Planners, Inc., 1988, 89, 91, Booker Assocs., Inc., 1989, (two grants), Ill. Natural History Survey, 1989, Wetlands Rsch., Inc., 1989, 90, 91, 92, 95, 98, 2002, USDA, U. Ill., 1991, 92, Hey and Assocs., Inc. Biotic Surveys, yearly from 1992-2004. Mem. Entomol. Soc. Am., N.Am. Benthological Soc. (program com. 1982-83, reviewer jour. 1990—), Ecol. Soc., Soc. Nematologists (ecology com. 1981-82, systematic resources com. 1981-82), Internat. Congress Ecologists, Ill. State Acad. Sci., Miss. River Rsch. Consortium (mem. exec. bd. 1981-82, v.p. bd. dirs. 1991-92, pres. bd. dirs. 1992-93, 99-2000), Internat. Conf. on Integrity of Large Floodplain River (program chmn. 1994), Xerces Soc., Sigma Xi (Rsch. of Yr. award 1984), Phi Kappa Phi. Achievements include research in invertebrate ecology, aquatic biology with an emphasis on large river ecosystems, aquatic invertebrates and freeliving nematodes, the effects of invertebrates on nutrient cycling. Home: 704 S Randolph St Macomb IL 61455-2966 Office: Western Ill U Dept Biol Scis Macomb IL 61455 Home Phone: 309-836-6536; Office Phone: 309-298-2408. Business E-Mail: r-anderson1@wiu.edu.

ANDERSON, ROBERT MORRIS, JR., electrical engineer; b. Crookston, Minn., Feb. 15, 1939; s. Robert Morris and Eleanor Elaine (Huotte) A.; m. Janice Ilene Pendell, Sept. 3, 1960; children— Erik Martin, Kristi Lynn. BEE, U. Mich., 1961, MEE, 1963, MS in Physics, 1965, PhD in Elec. Engring, 1967. Asst. research engr. U. Mich., Ann Arbor, 1963-67; research engr. Conductron Corp., Ann Arbor, summer 1967; asst. prof. elec. engring. Purdue U., West Lafayette, Ind., 1967-71, assoc. prof., 1971-79, prof., 1979, engring. coordinator for continuing edn., 1973-79, Ball Bros. prof., 1976-79; mgr. engring. edn. and tng., corp. cons. services GE, Bridgeport, Conn., 1979-82, mgr. tech. edn. operation, corp. engring. and mfg., 1982-88; mgr. tech. edn., corp. mgmt. devel. Gen. Electric Co., Bridgeport, Conn., 1988-90; vice provost, dir. coop. extension Iowa State U., Ames, 1990-95, prof. elec. engring., 1990-2000, prof. emeritus, elec. engring., 2000—. Author: (multi-media learning packagE) Fundamentals of Vacuum Technology, 1973; author: (with others) Divided Loyalties, 1980; contbr. with others articles to profl. jours. Chmn. bd. dirs. Lincoln Way Chapter, Am. Red Cross, 2003—04; bd. trustees Ames Pub. Libr., 2005—. Recipient Dow Outstanding Young Faculty award, 1974, Ky. Col. award, Jullian M. Carroll, Gov., Commonwealth Ky., 1977. Fellow Am. Soc. Engring. Edn. (cert. of merit 1977, Joseph M. Biedenbach Disting. Svc. award 1986), IEEE (Meritorious Achievement award in continuing edn. activities 1987), Rotary Club (pres. 2005-06, Unsung Hero award 2002). Conservative. Lutheran. Office: Iowa State U 2218 Coover Hall Ames IA 50011-0001 Home: 4038 Stone Brook Rd Ames IA 50010-2900 Personal E-mail: bobsoldmr2@aol.com.

ANDERSON, ROGER GORDON, minister; b. Milw., Feb. 1, 1937; s. Arthur Gordon and Dorothy K. (Junger) A.; m. Margery V. Burleson; children: Jonathan P., Nancy L., Leslie J., Kristi A. BA, Grace Bible Coll., Grand Rapids, Mich., 1958; postgrad., Purdue U., U. Minn. Ordained to ministry Grace Gospel Fellowship, 1960. Pastor Grace Bible Ch., Lafayette, Ind., 1958-60, Preakness Bible Ch., Wayne, N.J., 1960-69, Bethesda Free Ch., Mpls., 1969-86, Grace Community Ch., Salinas, Calif., 1986-91; pres. Grace Gospel Fellowship, Grand Rapids, Mich., 1991—. Pres. Evang. Ministers' Fellowship, Mpls., 1972-85; trainer Evangelism Explosion, Mpls., 1980-89. Bd. dirs. Goodwill Home and Rescue Mission, Newark, 1962-69; bd. dirs. Grace Bible Coll., Grand Rapids, 1975—, chmn. bd., 1984-91; bd. dirs. Grace Missions Inc., Grand Rapids, 1966-75; chaplain Police Dept., Mpls., 1975-80. Recipient Meritorious Svc. award City of Mpls., 1977. Mem. Grace Gospel Fellowship (bd. dirs. 1966-68). Republican. Office: Grace Gospel Fellowship 2125 Martindale Ave SW Grand Rapids MI 49509-1837

ANDERSON, RUSSELL A., state supreme court chief justice; b. Bemidji, Minn., May 28, 1942; m. Kristin Anderson; children: Rebecca, John, Sarah. BA, St. Olaf Coll., 1964; JD, U. Minn., 1968; LLM, George Washington U., 1977. Pvt. practice, 1976-82; county atty. Beltrami County, 1978-82; dist. ct. judge 9th Jud. Dist., 1982-98; assoc. justice Minn. Supreme Ct., 1998—, chief justice, 2006—. Chair Jud. Coun. Lt. comdr. USN, 1968—76. Mem.: Minn. Dist. Judges Assn., Minn. State Bar Assn. Office: Minn Supreme Ct 424 Minn Judicial Ctr 25 Rev Martin Luther King Jr Blvd Saint Paul MN 55155

ANDERSON, SCOTT ROBBINS, hospital administrator; b. Fargo, ND, Mar. 25, 1940; BA, U. N.D., 1962; M Health Adminstrn., U. Iowa, 1964. Adminstrn. res. St. Luke's Methodist Hosp., Veteran's Adminstrn. Med. Ctr., Cedar Rapids, Iowa City, 1963-64; adminstrv. asst. North Meml. Med. Ctr., Robbinsdale, Minn., 1964-65, asst. dir., 1965-69, adminstr., 1969-76, v.p., 1976-81, pres., 1981—; pres., ceo North Meml. Med. Ctr. (now North Meml. Health Care), Robbinsdale, Minn., 1981—. Adj. prof. in field. Office: N Meml Health Care 3300 Oakdale Ave N Robbinsdale MN 55422-2926

ANDERSON, STEFAN STOLEN, retired banker; b. Madison, Wis., Apr. 15, 1934; s. Theodore M. and Siri (Stolen) A.; m. Joan Timmermann, Sept. 19, 1959; children: Sharon Jill, Theodore Peter. AB magna cum laude, Harvard, 1956; MBA, U. Chgo., 1960; PhD (hon.), Ball State U., 1993. With Am. Nat. Bank & Trust Co. of Chgo., 1960—74, exec. v.p., 1969—74, 1st Mchts. Bank, Muncie, Ind., 1974, pres., 1979—98, chmn. bd. dirs., 1987—2005; pres., dir. First Mchts. Corp., Muncie, 1983—98, chmn. bd. dirs., 1987—2005; dir. Fed. Res. Bank of Chgo., 1991—97; ret., 2003. Bd. dirs. Maxon Corp., 1985-2004, Techpoint Inc., Pub. Radio Capital Fund, 2000-03. Past pres. Delaware County United Way, Muncie Symphony Orch.; trustee Roosevelt U., 1970-74, George Francis Ball Found., Ball State U. Found., BMH Found., Ziegler Found., Ind. State Mus. Found.; trustee, chmn. Minnitrista Cultural Found.; past chair Ind. Nature Conservancy; past pres. Cmty. Found. of Muncie and Delaware County. Mem. Ind. Acad., Skyline Club (Indpls.), Rotary (past pres.), Phi Beta Kappa, Beta Gamma Sigma. Home and Office: 2705 W Twickingham Dr Muncie IN 47304-1050

ANDERSON, TIM, airport terminal executive; Dir. of airports Mpls. St. Paul Internat. Airport, 1996, dep. exec. dir. of ops., 1998—; now ops. dir. Metropolitan Airports Commn. Office: Metropolitan Airports Commn 6040 28th Ave S Minneapolis MN 55450-2701

ANDERSON, TIMOTHY, pharmaceutical executive; B.Acctg., Northwestern U.; M. Fin. and Internat. Bus., Stanford U. Mktg. planning analyst Baxter Internat., Inc., Deerfield, Ill., 1972—80, v.p. Asian ops., 1980—85, v.p. corp. devel., 1985—86, pres. of Fenwal, 1986—91, pres. biotherapy, 1991—92, corp. v.p. and pres. Biotech Group, 1992—98, sr. v.p., 1998—. Bd. dirs. TECAN AG. Bd. dirs. Lake Forest Hosp.

ANDERSON, WARREN, distribution company executive; BA in Polit. Sci., U. Mich., 1974, M in Journalism, 1977. CEO Anderson-DuBose Co., Cleve. Office: Anderson-DuBose Co 6575 Davis Industrial Pkwy Cleveland OH 44139-3549 Fax: (440) 248-6208.

ANDERSON, WILLIAM CORNELIUS, III, lawyer; b. Haddonfield, NJ, Dec. 1, 1947; s. William Cornelius Jr. and Madelyn Anna (Penny) A.; m. Christine Joan Keck, June 20, 1970; children: William C. IV, Teresa, Stephen, Geoffrey, Thomas, Matthew. BA, Georgetown U., 1969; JD, Villanova U., 1975. Bar: Del. 1975, Ill. 1979. Atty. Morris, ichols, Arsht & Tunnell, Wilmington, Del., 1975-77, Biggs & Battaglia, Wilmington, 1978, Lord, Bissell & Brook, Chgo., 1979-85, ptnr., 1985-2000; founding ptnr. Anderson, Bennett & Ptnrs., Chgo., 2000—. Contbr. chpt. to book, articles to law jours. Capt. USAR, 1969-72. Fellow Am. Coll. Trial Lawyers; mem. ABA, Internat. Assn. Def. Counsel, Am. Acad. Healthcare Attys., Soc. Trial Attys., North Shore Country Club, Kenilworth Club. Home: 717 Kent Rd Kenilworth IL 60043-1031 Office: Anderson Rasor & Ptnrs 55 E Monroe St Ste 3650 Chicago IL 60603-5713 E-mail: w.anderson@arandpartners.com.

ANDERSON, WILLIAM R., botanist, educator, curator; BS Botany, Duke U., 1964; MS Systematic Botany, U. Mich., 1965, PhD, 1971. Assoc. curator N.Y. Botanical Garden, 1971-74; from asst. prof. to prof., dept. Biology U. Mich., 1974—, also assoc. curator, 1974-86, curator, 1986—, dir. Herbarium, 1986-99. Field work in Jamaica, 1963, 66, Hawaii, 1964, Mexico, 1965, 66, 68, 70, 81, 83, 88, 94, 95, 98, Costa Rica, 1969, 90, Brazil, 1972-76, 78, 82, 90, Argentina, 1982, 90, Venezuela, 1984, 96. Gen. editor numerous vols., chpts. in field; contbr. articles in field to profl. jours. Office: U of Mich Herbarium N University Building Ann Arbor MI 48109-1057

ANDOLINO, ROSEMARIE S., airport terminal executive; b. 1967; BS in Mktg., DePaul Univ., Chgo. With City of Chgo., 1990—, with dept. planning and devel., 1999—, first dep. commr. planning devel. dept.; asst. to dir. Mayor of Chgo., 1995—99; exec. dir. O'Hare Modernization Program, 2005—. Named one of 40 Under Forty, Crain's Bus. Chgo., 2005. Office: O'Hare Modernization Project c/o Mayor's Office 121 N LaSalle St Chicago IL 60602

ANDORKA, FRANK HENRY, lawyer; b. Lorain, Ohio, July 25, 1946; s. Frank Henry and Sue (Parham) A.; m. M. Jean Deliman, Aug. 10, 1968; children: Frank Henry Jr., Claire E. AB, Ohio U., 1968; postgrad., Ind. U., 1968-69; JD, Cornell U., 1975. Bar: Ohio 1975, U.S. Dist. Ct. (no. dist.) Ohio 1975. From assoc. to ptnr. Baker & Hostetler, Cleve., 1975—. Author: A Practical Guide to Copyrights and Trademarks, 1989, What is a Copyright?, 1992. Served to 1st lt. U.S. Army, 1969-72. Mem. ABA (chmn. internat. copyright laws and treaties com. 1984-86, chmn. govt. rels. to copyright com. 1986-88, chmn. broadcasting, sound rec. and performing artists com. 1988-90, chmn. divsn. III copyrights 1990-92, chmn. divsn. IX publs. 1992-93), Ohio Bar Assn., Greater Cleve. Bar Assn. Avocations: bowling, tennis. Home: 31000 Clinton Dr Cleveland OH 44140-1500 Office: Baker & Hostetler 3200 Nat City Ctr 1900 E 9th St Ste 3200 Cleveland OH 44114-3475 E-mail: fandorka@bakerlaw.com.

ANDREAS, DAVID LOWELL, retired banker; b. St. Paul, Mar. 1, 1949; s. Lowell Willard and Nadine B. (Hamilton) A.; m. Debra Kelley, June 20, 1985; 2 children. BA, U. Denver, 1971; MA, Mankato State U., 1976. Credit mgmt. trainee United Calif. Bank, Los Angeles, 1976-77; comml. loan officer Nat. City Bank of Mpls., 1977-80; from v.p., sr. vp., to chmn., chief exec. officer to pres. & CEO Nat. City Bancorp., Mpls., 1980—2001. Chmn. ADAPA, Inc., Mpls., 1986-93; chmn. bd. Nat. City Bank, Mpls., 1991-94; pres., CEO Nat. City Bank, Mpls., 1994-2001. Bd. mem. Minn. Ctr. Victims of Torture, Marshall & Ilsley Corp., Milwaukee; mem. exec. com., dir. Children's Heart Link, 1988—, Ctr. Ethical Bus. Cultures, Minn. State U., Mankato Coll. Bus. Adv. Coun., Bus. Adv. Coun.; mem. Minn. State U. Mankato Coll. bus. adv. coun.; mem. Coll. of Social and Behavioral Scis. adv. bd.; trustee Breck Sch., Golden Valley, Minn., 1997, Mpls. Coll. Art and Design. With U.S. Army, 1971-73. Mem.: Golden Valley Golf & Country Club. Avocations: swimming, snowboarding. E-mail: 5033@us-internet.com.

ANDREAS, DWAYNE ORVILLE, agricultural products executive; b. Worthington, Minn., Mar. 4, 1918; s. Reuben P. and Lydia (Stoltz) A.; m. Bertha Benedict, 1938 (div.); 1 dau., Sandra Ann Andreas McMurtie; m. Dorothy Inez Snyder, Dec. 21, 1947; children: TerryLynn, Michael D. Student, Wheaton Coll., Ill., 1935-36; degree (hon.), Barry U. V.p., dir. Honeymead Products Co., Cedar Rapids, Iowa, 1936-46; chmn. bd., chief exec. officer Honeymead Products Co. (now Nat. City Bancorp.), Mankato, Minn., 1952-72; v.p. Cargill, Inc., Mpls., 1946-52; exec. v.p. Farmers Union Grain Terminal Assn., St. Paul, 1960-66; chmn. bd., chief exec. officer Archer-Daniels-Midland Co., Decatur, Ill., 1970-97, chmn. bd., 1997-98, chmn. emeritus, 1999. Mem. Pres.'s Gen. Adv. Comm. of Fgn. Assistance Programs, 1965-68, Pres.'s Adv. Coun. on Mgmt. Improvement, 1969-73; chmn. Pres.'s Task Force on Internat. Pvt. Enterprise.

Nat. bd. dirs. Boys' Club Am.; former chmn. U.S.-USSR Trade and Econ. Coun.; former chmn. Exec. Coun. on Fgn. Diplomats; former trustee Hoover Inst. on War, Revolution and Peace; former vice chmn. Woodrow Wilson Internat. Ctr. for Scholars; former mem. Trilateral Commn.; chmn. Found. for Commemoration of the U.S. Constitution, 1986. Mem. Fgn. Policy Assn. N.Y. (dir.), Indian Creek Country Club (Miami Beach, Fla.), Blind Brook Country Club (Purchase, N.Y.), Links, Knickerbocker, Friars (N.Y.C.). Office Phone: 217-424-5515.

ANDREAS, G(LENN) ALLEN, JR., former agricultural company executive; b. Cedar Rapids, Iowa, June 22, 1943; s. Glenn Allen and Vera Irene (Yates) A.; m. Toni Kay Hibma, June 19, 1964; children: Bronwyn Denise, Glenn Allen III, Shannon Tori. BA, Valparaiso U., 1965, JD, 1968. Bar: Colo. 1969. Atty. U.S. Dept. Treasury, Denver, 1969-73, Archer Daniels Midland Co., Decatur, Ill., 1973-75, asst. treas., 1975-86, treas., 1986—89, v.p., CFO Europe, 1989—94, v.p., counsel to chief exec., 1994-96, mem. Office of Chief Exec., 1996-97, pres., CEO, 1997-99, chmn., CEO, 1999—2006, pres., 2005—06, chmn., 2006—07. Bd. dirs. Nat. City Bancorp., Mpls., Oelmühle Hamburg A.G, Hamburg, Federal Republic of Germany. Mem. ABA, Colo. State Bar Assn., Decatur Bar Assn. Clubs: Country of Decatur, Decatur. Democrat. Avocation: golf.

ANDREASEN, JAMES HALLIS, retired state supreme court judge; b. Mpls., May 16, 1931; s. John A. and Alice M. Andreasen; m. Janet Andreasen, June 25, 1961 (dec. July 1985); children: Jon A., Amy E., Steven J.; m. Marilyn McGuire, May 17, 1987. BS in Commerce, U. Iowa, 1953, JD, 1958. Bar: Iowa 1958. Pvt. practice law, Algona, Iowa, 1958-75; with Algona City Coun., 1961-68; judge 3d Jud. Dist. Ct., 1975-87, Supreme Ct. Iowa, Des Moines, 1987-98, ret., sr. judge, 1998—. Lt. col. USAFR, 1954-75. Mem. ABA, Iowa State Bar Assn., Kossuth County Bar Assn. Methodist. Office: Kossuth County Courthouse Algona IA 50511

ANDREASEN, NANCY COOVER, psychiatrist, educator, neuroscientist; d. John A. Sr. and Pauline G. Coover; children: Robin, Susan. BA summa cum laude, U. Nebr., 1958, PhD, 1963; MA, Radcliffe Coll., 1959; MD, U. Iowa, 1970. Instr. English Nebr. Wesleyan Coll., 1960—61, U. Nebr., Lincoln, 1962—63; asst. prof. English U. Iowa, Iowa City, 1963—66, resident, 1970—73, asst. prof. psychiatry, 1973—77, assoc. prof., 1977—81, prof. psychiatry, 1981—82, Andrew H. Woods prof. psychiatry, 1992—97, Andrew H. Woods chair psychiatry, 1997—. Sr. cons. Northwick Park Hosp., London, 1983; acad. visitor Maudsley Hosp., London, 1986; dir. Mental Health Clin. Rsch. Ctr., 1987—. Author: The Broken Brain, 1984, Introductory Psychiatry Textbook, 1991; editor: Can Schizophrenia be Localized to the Brain?, 1986, Brain Imaging: Applications in Psychiatry, 1988, Brave New Brain: Conquering Mental Illness in the Era of the Genome, 2001, The Creating Brain: The Neuroscience of Genius, 2005, Am. Jour. Psychiat., 1988—, 1989—93; editor-in-chief:, 1993—2005; contbr. articles to profl. jours. Recipient Rhonda and Bernard Sarnat award NAS, 1999, C. Charles Burlingame award, 1999, Arthur P. Noyes award in schizophrenia, 1999, Lieber prize Nat. Alliance for Rsch. on Schizophrenia and Depression, 2000, Pres.'s Nat. Medal Sci., 2000, Interbrew Baillet-Latour Health prize, 2003, William K. Warren award Internat. Schizophrenia Congress, 2005, Vanderbilt prize in Biomedical Sci., Vanderbilt U. Sch. Medicine, 2006; Woodrow Wilson fellow, 1958-59, Fulbright fellow Oxford U., London, 1959-60. Fellow Royal Coll. Physicians Surgeons Can. (hon.), Am. Psychiat. Assn. (Adolf Meyer award 1999, Disting. Svc. award 2004, Judd Marmor award, 2007), Am. Coll. Neuropharmacologists, Royal Soc. Medicine; mem. Am. Acad. Arts and Scis., Am. Psychopathol. Assn. (pres. 1989-90), Inst. Medicine of NAS (coun. 1996—). Office: U Iowa Hosps and Clinics 200 Hawkins Dr Iowa City IA 52242-1057

ANDREASEN, NIELS-ERIK ALBINUS, religious educator; b. Asminderod, Denmark, May 14, 1941; came to U.S., 1963; s. Caleb A. and Erna E. (Pedersen) A.; m. Demetra Lougani, Sept. 5, 1965; 1 child, Michael. BA, Newbold Coll., England, 1963; MA, Andrews U., Mich., 1965, BD, 1966; PhD, Vanderbilt U., 1971. From asst. to assoc. prof. Pacific Union Coll., Calif., 1970-75; vis. lectr. Avondale Coll., Australia, 1975-77; prof., dean of religion Loma Linda (Calif.) U., 1977-90; pres. Walla Walla (Wash.) Coll., 1990-94, Andrews (Mich.) U., 1994—. Author: The Old Testament Sabbath, 1972, Rest and Redemption, 1978, The Christian Use of Time, 1978. Mem. Soc. Bibl. Lit. Seventh Day Adventist. Office: Andrews University Office Of The President Berrien Springs MI 49104-0001 Office Phone: 269-471-3100. E-mail: NEAA@Andrews.edu.

ANDREKOPOULOS, WILLIAM, school system administrator; married; 3 children. BA, Marquette Univ., 1970; MA, Cardinal Stritch Univ., 1985. Cert. supt. Univ. Wis.-Milw. Prin. Fritsche Middle Sch., Milw., 1988—2002; supt. Milwaukee Pub. Schools, 2002—. Office: Milwaukee Public Schools 5225 W Vliet St Milwaukee WI 53208 Office Phone: 414-475-8393.

ANDREOLI, KATHLEEN GAINOR, nurse, educator, dean; b. Albany, NY, Sept. 22, 1935; d. John Edward and Edmunda Elizabeth (Ringlemann) Gainor; children: Paula Kathleen, Thomas Anthony, Karen Marie. BSN, Georgetown U., 1957; MSN, Vanderbilt U., 1959; DSN, U. Ala., Birmingham, 1979. Staff nurse Albany Hosp. Med. Ctr., 1957; instr. St. Thomas Hosp. Sch. Nursing, Nashville, 1958—59, Georgetown U. Sch. Nursing, 1959—60, Duke U. Sch. Nursing, 1960—61, Bon Secours Hosp. Sch. Nursing, Balt., 1962—64; ednl. coordinator, physician asst. program, instr. coronary care unit nursing inservice edn. Duke U. Med. Ctr., Durham, NC, 1965—70; ednl. dir. physician asst. program dept. medicine U. Ala. Med. Ctr., Birmingham, 1970—75, clin. assoc. prof. cardiovasc. nursing Sch. Nursing, 1970—77, asst. prof. nursing dept. medicine, 1971, assoc. prof., 1972—, assoc. prof. nursing Sch. Pub. and Allied Health, 1973—; assoc. dir. Family Nurse Practitioner Program, 1976, assoc. prof. cmty. health nursing Grad. Program, 1977—79, assoc. prof. dept. pub. health, 1978—79; prof. nursing, spl. asst. to pres. for ednl. affairs U. Tex. Health Sci. Ctr., Houston, 1979—82, acting dean Sch. Allied Health Scis., 1981, v.p. for ednl. svcs., interdisciplinary edn., internat. programs, 1983—87; v.p. nursing affairs Rush-Presbyn.-St. Lukes's Med. Ctr., Chgo., 1987—; dean Rush U. Coll. Nursing, 1987—2005, Kellogg emeritus dean, 2005—. Mem. nat. adv. nursing coun. VHA, 1992; adv. bd. Nursing Spectrum, midwest region, 1995—; cons. in field. Editor: Heart and Lung, Jour. of Total Care, 1971; editl. bd. Nursing Consult, Elsevier Publs., 2004—05; contbr. articles to profl. jours.; author, editor: Comprehensive Cardiac Care, 1983. Active Internat. Nursing Coalition for Mass Casualty Edn., 2002—05; mem. adv. bd. Robert Wood Johnson Clin. Nurse Sch. Program; mem. vis. com. Vanderbilt U. Sch. Nursing; mem. Leadership Ill., 1991; mem. nat. nursing asdv. com. Voluntary Hosp. Am., 1991; mem. governing coun. Inst. for Hosp. Clin. ursing Edn., Am. Hosp. Assn., 1993; bd. dirs. Ill. League for Nursing, 1994, Lyric Opera Chgo. Guild; bd. dirs., chair rsch. and edn. com. Rehab. Inst. Chgo., 2005—; adv. bd. Hospice Ptnrs. Recipient Founder's award, N.C. Heart Assn., 1970, Disting. Alumni award, Vanderbilt U. Sch. Nursing, 1985, Leadership Tex. award, 1985, Disting. Alumni award, U. Ala. Sch. Nursing, 1991, Henry Betts MD Employment Advocacy award, 2004, Sage Mentor award, Ill. ursing Leadership Annual Conf., 2005. Fellow: Am. Acad. Nursing; mem.: ACNA, ANA, Internat. Nursing Coalition for Mass Casualty Edn., Inst. Medicine Chgo. (bd. govs. 2004—, sec. bd. 2005—), Nat. Nursing Adv. Coun. Hosps. Am., Am. Heart Assn. Coun. Cardiovasc. Nursing, Coun. Family Nurse Practitioners and Clinicians, Ala. Heart Assn., Nat. League Nursing, Inst. Medicine of NAS, Am. Assn. Colls. Nursing (dean emeritus 2005—), Rotary One Club Chgo., Phi Kappa Phi, Alpha Eta, Sigma Theta Tau (Dreher Outstanding Dean award 2003, Rehab. Inst. of Chgo. Henry Setts Disability Advocacy award 2004, U. Ill. Power uring Nursing Mentor award 2005, Sage Membership award Ill. Nursing Leadership Conf. 2005). Roman Catholic. Home: 1212 N Lake Shore Dr Apt 10AN Chicago IL 60610-2359 Office: 1212 N Lake Shore Dr Chicago IL 60610-2359 Office Phone: 312-266-8338. Business E-Mail: kathleen_g_andreoli@rush.edu.

ANDREOZZI, BRADLEY JOSEPH, lawyer; b. NYC, Oct. 9, 1958; BA magna cum laude, Yale U., 1980; JD, U. Chgo., 1983. Bar: NY 1984, Ill. 1999, admitted to practice: US Dist. Ct. (So. Dist.) NY 1985, US Dist. Ct. (Ea. Dist.) NY 1985, US Ct. Appeals (1st Cir.) 1986, US Ct. Appeals (2nd Cir.) 1990, US Ct. Appeals (3rd Cir.) 2003, US Ct. Appeals (6th Cir.) 2002, US Ct. Appeals (7th Cir.) 1999, US Supreme Ct. 1991, US Dist. Ct. (No. Dist.) Ill. 1999. Assoc. Hughes Hubbard & Reed, NYC, 1983-86, Reboul, MacMurray, Hewitt, Maynard & Kristol, NYC, 1986-91, Mayer, Brown & Platt, NYC, 1991—98, ptnr. Chgo., 1998—. Mem.: NY County Lawyers Assn., ABA. Office: Mayer Brown Rowe & Maw LLP 71 S Wacker Dr Chicago IL 60606 Office Phone: 312-701-8564. Office Fax: 312-706-8757. E-mail: bandreozzi@mayerbrown.com.

ANDREOZZI, LOUIS JOSEPH, lawyer; b. NJ, 1959; m. Lisa Marie Clark, Apr. 12, 1987. BS in Bus. Adminstrn. with hons., Rutgers U., 1981; JD, Seton Hall U., 1984. Bar: N.J. 1984. Asst. gen. counsel Gordon Pub., Inc., Randolph, NJ, 1984—93; dep. gen. counsel Elsevier U.S. Holdings, Morris Plains, NJ, 1985—93; v.p., sec., gen. counsel Reed Elsevier Med. Pub., Belle Mead, NJ, 1994—95; v.p., gen. counsel, sec., head ops. support and svcs., purchasing, sales force homeworking project, customer svc. integration project Lexis-Nexis, Miamisburg, Ohio, 1994—97; pub. Martindale-Hubbell, 1996; chief legal counsel Lexis-Nexis, 1997—98; COO Martindale-Hubbell, New Providence, NJ, 1997—99, Marquis, NRP, New Providence, NJ, 1998—99; vice-chmn. Reed Tech. and Info. Svcs., Inc., 1999—2000; pres., CEO Martindale-Hubbell, Marquis, NRP, New Providence, 1999—2000, LexisNexis North American Legal Markets, 2000—05; global officer, mktg. and technology LexisNexis Group, 2001—05. Mem. legal adv. bd. Lexis-Nexis, 1994—2005, exec. bd., 1994—2005; mem. Friends of the Law Libr. of Congress; bd. dirs. Am. Assn. of Pub. Named to Dept. Distinction in Bus., Rutgers U., 1981, Nat. Honor Soc. in Econs. and Bus., 1981. Mem.: ABA, N.J. Employment Law Assn., Am. Corp. Counsel Assn., Internat. Bar Assn., N.J. Bar Assn. Roman Catholic.

ANDRES, RONALD PAUL, chemical engineer, educator; b. Chgo., Jan. 9, 1938; s. Harold William and Amanda Ann (Breuhaus) A.; m. Jean Mills Elwood, July 15, 1961; children: Douglas, Jennifer, Mark. BS, Northwestern U., 1959; PhD, Princeton U., 1962. Asst. prof. Princeton U., 1962-68, assoc. prof., 1968-76, prof. chem. engring., 1976-81, Purdue U., West Lafayette, Ind., 1981—, head Sch. Chem. Engring., 1981-87, engring. rsch. prof., 1987—2004, emeritus prof. chem. engring., 2004—. Mem. Sigma Xi, Tau Beta Pi, Pi Mu Epsilon, Phi Lambda Upsilon, Phi Eta Sigma. Office: Purdue U Sch Chem Engring West Lafayette IN 47907-2100 Home Phone: 765-449-7041; Office Phone: 765-494-4047. Business E-Mail: ronald@ecn.purdue.edu.

ANDRETTI, MICHAEL MARIO, racing company executive, retired professional race car driver; b. Bethlehem, Pa., Oct. 5, 1962; s. Mario Andretti and Dee Ann (Hoch); m. Sandra Spinozzi, 1985 (div. 1996); children: Marco, Marissa; m. Leslie Andretti, Dec. 24, 1997 (div.); 1 child, Lucca; m. Jodi Ann Paterson, Oct. 7, 2006. HS diploma, Nazareth, Pa. Profl. race car driver Bertil Roos, 1980-81, Carl Haas Racing, Arciero Racing, GTC Racing, Garvin Brown Racing, 1982, Ralt Am., Preston Henn Racing, 1983, Kraco Racing, 1983-88, Alfa Romeo, Hendrick Motorsports, Conte Racing, 1987, Newman/Haas Racing, 1989-92, McLaren Internat. Ltd., 1993, Chip Ganassi Racing Teams, 1994, Newman/Haas Racing, 1995-2000, Team Motorola, 2001—03, Andretti Racing, 2003—07; ret., 2007. V.p. Andretti Enterprises Inc., Nazareth, 1986—, Andretti Devel. Co. Inc., Nazareth, 1987—, Andretti/Piazza Sports Cafes, Race Rock Theme Restaurants; owner Andretti Toyota, Andretti Scion, Andretti Ford, Andretti Chrysler-Dodge-Jeep, Andretti Indoor Karting and Games, Andretti Global Devel.; pres. Michael Andretti Powersports, 1999—; CEO Andretti Green Racing, chmn., 2006-. Founder Michael Andretti Found., 2003—. N.E. divsn. Formula Ford champion, 1981; Sports Car Club Am. Pro Rookie of Yr., 1982; Super Vee nat. champion, 1982; Formula Atlantic nat. champion, 1983; Indy 500 Co-Rookie of Yr., 1984; Indy Car nat. champion, 1991; Driver of Yr., 1991. Roman Catholic. Achievements include holding the record for career racing victories with 42; won more races, more poles, and led more laps than any other active Championship Auto Racing Teams Champ car driver; came out of retirement in 2006 to place third at the Indianapolis 500 just behind his son Marco. Office: Andretti Green Racing 7615 Zionsville Rd Indianapolis IN 46268

ANDREWS, CAESAR, editor; BA, Grambling State U., La., 1979. Sr. mgr. Florida Today, Melbourne, Fla., The Reporter, Lansdale, Pa., Rockland Jour.-News, West yack, NY, Gannett Suburban Newspapers, White Plains, NY; various positions, including dep. mng. editor, spl. sect. and chief states editor USA Today, 1982—86; editor Gannett News Svc., Arlington, Va., 1997—2005; exec. editor Detroit Free Press, 2005—. Lectr. Am. Press Inst. Mem.: Am. Soc. Newspaper Editors, Nat. Assn. Minority Media Exec., Nat. Assn. Black Journalists, AP Mng. Editors (mem. bd., v.p.). Office: Detroit Free Press 600 W Fort St Detroit MI 48226 Office Phone: 313-222-6821. E-mail: candrews@freepress.com.

ANDREWS, FRANK LEWIS, lawyer; b. Rhinebeck, NY, June 8, 1950; s. William Fisher and Merna Louise (Lewis) A.; m. Barbara Della Chapman, Aug. 30, 1980; children: William Chapman, S. Ross Chapman. Student, U. Vienna, Austria, 1971; BS magna cum laude, Mich. State U., 1973; JD cum laude, Harvard U., 1976. Bar: Mich. 1976. Sr. prin. Miller, Canfield, Paddock & Stone PLC, Troy, Mich., 1983—. Avocations: skiing, sailing.

ANDREWS, OAKLEY V., lawyer; b. Cleve., Apr. 15, 1940; BA, Yale U., 1962; JD, Western Reserve U., 1965. Bar: Ohio 1965, U.S. Tax Ct. 1968, U.S. Dist. Ct. (no. dist.) Ohio 1968, U.S. Ct. Appeals (6th cir.) 1968. Ptnr. Baker & Hostetler, LLP, Cleve. Fellow Am. Coll. Trust and Estate Coun.; mem. Ohio State Bar Assn., Estate Planning Coun. Cleve. (pres. 1982-83), Cleve. Bar Assn. (chmn. Estate Planning, Probate and Trust law sect. 1984-85), Phi Delta Phi Office: Baker & Hostetler LLP 3200 Nat City Ctr 1900 E 9th St Ste 3200 Cleveland OH 44114-3475 Office Phone: 216-861-7568. E-mail: oandrews@bakerlaw.com.

ANDREWS, RICHARD VINCENT, physiologist, educator; b. Arapahoe, Nebr., Jan. 9, 1932; s. Wilber Vincent and Fern (Clawson) A.; m. Elizabeth Williams, June 1, 1954 (dec. Dec. 1994); children: Thomas, William, Robert, Catherine, James, John; m. Wyoma Upward, Oct. 18, 1997. BS, Creighton U., 1958, MS, 1959; PhD, U. Iowa, 1963. Instr. biology Creighton U., Omaha, 1958-60; instr. physiology U. Iowa, 1960-63; asst. prof. Creighton U., Omaha, 1963-65, assoc. prof., 1965-68, prof. physiology, 1968-97, asst. med. dean, 1972-75, dean grad. studies, 1975-85, dean emeritus, 1995—, prof. emeritus, 1997—. Vis. prof. Naval Arctic Rsch. Lab., 1963-72, U. B.C., 1985-86, U. Tasmania, 1993-94; cons. VA, NSF, NRC, ARS; plenary speaker USSR Symposium on Environment, 1970, Internat. Soc. Biomet., 1972. Contbr. articles to profl. jours. Mem. Gov.'s task force on fatigue State Nebr. Served with M.C. U.S. Army, 1951-54. NSF fellow, 1962-63; SF-NIH-ONR-AINA grantee, 1963— Fellow Explorers Club, Arctic Inst. N.Am.; mem. Am. Physiol. Soc., Am. Mammal Soc., Endocrine Soc., Soc. Exptl. Biology and Medicine, Internat. Soc. for Biometeorology, Sigma Xi. E-mail: randwandrews@aol.com.

ANDREWS, STEVEN R., lawyer; b. 1953; BA, JD, U. Nebraska. Clerk to Judge Donald R. Ross U.S. Ct. of Appeals Eighth Circuit; special asst. to dir. FBI; various positions including interim pres., CEO, v.p., gen. counsel & sec. Multigraphics, Inc. (formerly AM Internat., Inc.), Mt. Prospect, Ill., 1994—99; sr. v.p., gen. counsel, sec. PepsiAmericas, Inc. (formerly Whitman Corp.), Rolling Meadows, Ill., 1999—2001; sr. v.p., gen. counsel Shopko Stores, Green Bay, Wis., 2002—03, sr. v.p. law & human resources, 2003—. Office: ShopKo Stores Inc PO Box 19060 Green Bay WI 54307-9060

ANDRIST, JOHN M., state senator; b. Crosby, ND, Aug. 1, 1931; s. Calvin L. and Lela G. (Revis) A.; m. Elaine G. Thvedt, June 17, 1951; children: Pamela, Paula, Steve, Stan, Penny. Pub. Crosby (N.D.) Jour., 1958-91; mem. ND Senate from 2nd dist., 1993—; mem. appropriations com. ND Senate, 1997—2003. Mem. N.D. ewspaper Assn. (past pres.), Nat. Newspaper Assn. (N.D. state chmn. 1970-82, bd. dirs., representing Iowa, N.D., S.D., Minn. 1982-87, treas. 1988, v.p. 1989, pres. 1990), Crosby Bus. Builders (pres.), Crosby Jaycees (past pres.), N.D. Jaycees (state sec.), N.D. Profl. chpt. Soc. Profl. Journalists (past pres.). Lodges: Kiwanis, Moose. Presbyterian. Avocations: golf, running, bicycling. Office: PO Box E Crosby ND 58730-0660

ANGADIATH, JACOB, bishop; b. Periappuram, Kerala, India, Oct. 26, 1945; s. Ulahannan and Mariam Angadiath. BA, U. Kerala, 1978; M. Th., Univ. of Dallas, 1995. Ordained priest Diocese of Palai (Syro-Malabarese), India, 1972; asst. vicar St. Joseph's Ch. Kudakkachira, 1972—73, St. George Forane Ch. Aruvithura, 1973—77; vicar St. John's Ch. Amparanirappel, 1977—80; vice rector Minor Sem., 1980—84; dir. Syro-Malabar Cath. Mission Dallas, 1984—99, Syro-Malabar Cath. Mission Chgo., 1999—2001; ordained bishop, 2001; bishop Eparchy of St. Thomas the Apostle of Chgo. (Syro-Malabarese), 2001—. Asst. pastor St. Pius X Ch. Dallas, 1984—97, St. Michael the Archangel Ch. Garland, Tex., 1997—99. Roman Catholic. Office: St Thomas Syro-Malabar Cath Diocese Chgo 372 S Prairie Ave Elmhurst IL 60126 Office Phone: 630-279-1383. Office Fax: 630-279-1479.*

ANGELO, JEFF M., state legislator; b. St. Louis, Dec. 5, 1964; m. Debbie. Chair Union County Rep. Ctrl. Com.; mem. Iowa Senate from 44th dist., 1996—. Mem. Univ. Ext. Coun.; stewardship, fin. chair First Congl. Ch., Creston, Iowa. Republican. Office: State Capitol Dist 44 3 9th And Grand Des Moines IA 50319-0001 Home: PO Box 604 Creston IA 50801-0604 E-mail: jeff_angelo@legis.state.ia.us.

ANGELO, JERRY, professional sports team executive; m. Bernie Angelo; children: Leisa Rice, Sutton. Part-time defensive line coach Colo. State U., 1972; defensive line coach, recruiting coord. U. Tampa, Tampa, Fla., 1973—74; defensive line coach Syracuse, 1975—79; dir. player personnel Tampa Bay Buccaneers, Fla.; gen. mgr. Chgo. Bears. Office: 1000 Football Drive Lake Forest IL 60045

ANGER, PAUL, newspaper editor; m. Vickie Dahlman-Anger. Graduate, Univ. Wis., Oshkosh. Sports copy editor, page designer Miami Herald, 1972—77, sports editor, 1977—95, page 1A duty officer, 1989—95, Broward editor Hollywood, Fla., 1995—98, v.p., pub., Broward edition, 1998—2001; v.p., editor Des Moines Register, Iowa, 2002—05; Washington bur. news editor Knight Ridder, 2001; editor Detroit Free Press, 2005—. Office: Detroit Free Press 600 W Fort St Detroit MI 48226 Office Phone: 313-222-6606.*

ANGINO, ERNEST EDWARD, retired geology and engineering educator; b. Winsted, Conn., Feb. 16, 1932; s. Alfred and Filomena Mabel (Serluco) A.; m. Margaret Mary Lachat, June 26, 1954; children— Cheryl Ann, Kimberly Ann. BS in Mining Engring., Lehigh U., Bethlehem, Pa., 1954; MS in Geology, U. Kans., 1958, PhD in Geology, 1961. Instr. geology U. Kans., Lawrence, 1961-62, prof. civil engring., 1971-99, prof. geology, 1972-99, prof. emeritus, 1999—, chmn. dept. geology, 1972-86, dir. water resources ctr., 1990-99; asst. prof. Tex. A&M U., College Station, 1962-65; chief geochemist Kans. Geol. Survey, Lawrence, 1965-70, assoc. state geologist, 1970-72. Cons. on water chemistry and pollution to various cos. and govt. agys. including Dow Chem. Co., Ocean Mining Inc., Envicon, Oak Ridge Lab., Fisheries Rsch. Bd. Can., Midwest Rsch. Inst., Coast and Geodetic Survey, U.S. Geol. Survey. Author: (with G.K. Billings) Atomic Absorption Spectrometry in Geology, 1967; author, editor: (with D.T. Long) Geochemistry of Bismuth, 1979; editor: (with R.K. Hardy) Proc. 3d Forum Geol. Industrial Minerals, 1967, (with G.K. Billings) Geochemistry Subsurface Brines, 1969; contbr. more than 125 articles to sci. and profl. jours. Sec. Geochem. Soc., 1970-76; mem. Lawrence City Police Rels. Commn., 1970-76, Lawrence City Commn., 1983-87, mayor, 1984-85; pres. Soc. Environ. Geochemistry and Health, 1978-79; treas. Internat. Assn. Geochemistry and Cosmochemistry, 1980-94; mem. Lawrence 2020 Planning Commn., 1992-94, Police Adv. Coun., 1994-06, Crimestoppers Bd., 1994-03, Lawrence Tax Abatement Commn., 2001-02, Lawrence-Douglas County Planning Commn. 2002-05, Health Care Access Bd., 1997-02, Lawrence-Douglas County Econ. Devel. Commn., 2006—. With U.S. Army, 1955-57. NSF fellow Oak Ridge Lab., 1963; recipient Antarctic Service medal Dept. Def., 1969; Angino Buttress in Antarctica named in his honor, 1967. Mem. Am. Philatelist Soc., Meter Stamp Soc., Forum Club (Factotum 1978-79), Rotary (pres. 1993-95). Republican. Roman Catholic. Avocations: philately, Western history, Indian lore. Home: 4605 Grove Dr Lawrence KS 66049-3777 Office: U Kans Dept Geology Lindley 120 1475 Jayhawk Blvd Lawrence KS 66045-0001 Personal E-mail: rockdoc@sunflower.com.

ANGST, GERALD L., lawyer; b. Chgo., Dec. 29, 1950; s. Gerald L. Sr. and Audrey M. (Hides) A.; m. Candace Simning, Jan. 29, 1983. BA magna cum laude, Loyola U., Chgo., 1972, JD cum laude, 1975. Assoc. Sidley Austin, Chgo., 1975-82, ptnr., 1982—. Mem.: ABA (constrn. litigation com. litigation sect.), Chgo. Bar Assn. (civil practice com.). Office: Sidley Austin One S Dearborn St Fl 34 Chicago IL 60603 Office Phone: 312-853-7757. Business E-Mail: gangst@sidley.com.

ANGUS, JOHN COTTON, chemical engineering educator; b. Grand Haven, Mich., Feb. 22, 1934; s. Francis Clark and Margaret (Cotton) A.; m. Caroline Helen Gezon, June 25, 1960; children: Lorraine Margaret, Charles Thomas. BSChemE, U. Mich., 1956, MS, 1958, PhD in Engring, 1960; DSc (hon.), Ohio U., 1998. Registered profl. engr., Ohio. Research engr. Minn. Mining & Mfg. Co., St. Paul, 1960-63; prof. Case Inst. Tech. (now Case Western Res. U.), Cleve., 1963-67, prof. chem. engring., 1967—2004, prof. emeritus, 2004—, chmn. dept., 1974-80, interim dean engring., 1986-87. Vis. lectr. U. Edinburgh, Scotland, 1972-73; vis. prof. Northwestern U., 1980-81. Trustee Ohio Scottish Games. NSF fellow, 1956-57; NATO sr. fellow, 1972-73 Fellow AIChE, Electrochem. Soc. (Pioneer award); mem. NAE, Am. Chem. Soc., Sigma Xi, Tau Beta Pi, Phi Lambda Upsilon. Achievements include research in fields of crystal growth, diamond synthesis, conducting diamond, electrochemical devices, thermodynamics. Office: Case Western Res U Dept Chem Engring Cleveland OH 44106-7217

ANNEXSTAD, ALBERT T., insurance company executive; b. Sept. 17, 1940; s. Alice Annexstad. BA, Mankato State Univ., 1967; DHL (hon.), Gustavus Adolphus Coll., 2005. Mktg. & mgmt. positions Federated Mutual Ins., Owatonna, Minn., 1965—86, dir. mktg, 1986—99, pres., CEO, 1999—, chmn., 2000—. Bd. gov. Property Casualty Insurers Assn. Am. Trustee Gustavus Adolphus Coll.; mem. exec. com. Minn. Bus. Partnership. Recipient Connecting with Youth Lifetime Achievement award, Minn. Bus. Partnership. Office: Federated Mutual Insurance PO Box 328 121 E Park Sq Owatonna MN 55060-0328

ANSBACHER, RUDI, physician; b. Sidney, NY, Oct. 11, 1934; s. Stefan and Beatrice (Michel) A.; m. Elisabeth Cornelia Vellenga, Nov. 19, 1965; children— R. Todd, Jeffrey N. Grad., Harvard Coll., 1951; BA, Va. Mil. Inst., 1955; MD, U. Va., 1959; MS, U. Mich., 1970. Diplomate Am. Bd. Ob-Gyn. Staff ob-gyn, chief clin. investigation Brooke Med. Ctr., San Antonio, 1971-75, asst. chief ob-gyn, 1975-77; chief dept. ob-gyn Letterman Army Med. Ctr., San Francisco, 1977-80; from prof. ob-gyn to prof. emeritus U. Mich., Ann Arbor, 1980—2001, prof. emeritus, 2002—. Cons. Biomed. Adv. Com. Population Resource Ctr., 1978-81; bd. dirs. Health Policy Internat. Contbr. articles to profl. jours., chpts to books; mem. editorial bds., reviewer jours. Served to col. U.S. Army, 1960-80. amed Disting. Mil. Grad. Va. Mil. Inst., Lexington, Va., 1955; NIH grantee, 1973-78 Fellow ACOG (Chmn.'s award 1970), AAAS; mem. Am. Fertility Soc. (dir. 1979-82), Am. Soc. Andrology (sec. 1978-80, pres. 1984-85), Central Assn. Ob-Gyn, Assn. Mil. Surgeons U.S., Soc. for Study Reprodn., Mich. State Med. Soc. (bd. dirs. 1995-2005, sec. 2005-06), Mich. State Med. Soc. Found. (bd. dirs. 2003—), Physicians Rev. Orgn. Mich. (bd. dirs. 2000-), U. Mich. Med. Ctr. Alumni Soc. (bd. dirs. 2004—). Republican. Presbyterian. Avocations: tennis, softball, gardening, skiing. Home: 3755 Tremont Ln Ann Arbor MI 48105-3022 Home Phone: 734-665-2396; Office Phone: 734-763-4344. Business E-Mail: ansbache@med.umich.edu.

ANSHAW, CAROL, writer; b. Grosse Pointe Shores, Mich., Mar. 22, 1946; d. Henry G. and Virginia (Anshaw) Stanley; m. Charles J. White III, Mar. 15, 1969. BA, Mich. State U., 1968. Book reviewer, Voice Literary Supplement, prof. Creative Writing Art Inst. Chgo. Author: They Do It All With Mirrors, 1978, Aquamarine, 1992, Seven Moves, 1996. Tutor Literacy Council of Chgo., 1989—. Recipient Nat. Book Critics Circle citation for excellence in reviewing, 1989. Mem. Nat. Book Critics Cir., Nat. Writers Union. Democrat. Achievements include Stories included in Best Am. Short Stories 1994, 1998. Avocation: swimming.

ANSTAETT, JENNIFER GRIFFIN, lawyer; b. Sikeston, Mo., Dec. 14, 1975; m. Patrick Anstaett. BA in Eng., Ctr. Coll. Ky., 1998, BA in Hist., 1998; JD, Washington & Lee U. Sch. of Law, 2001. Bar: Ohio 2001, US Dist. Ct., Southern Dist. Ohio, US Supreme Ct. Assoc. Beckman Weil Shepardson LLC, Cin., 2004—. Planned giving com. Alzheimer's Assn., Ky., exec. com., Young Professionals, Ky.; bd. dir. Franciscan Haircuts from the Heart. Named one of Ohio's Rising Stars, Super Lawyers, 2005, 2006. Mem.: Assn. Professionals in Aging, Am. Health Lawyers Assn., Ohio Bar Assn., Cin. Bar Assn. (Basic Estate Planning Seminar Com.). Office: Beckman Weil Shepardson LLC American Book Bldg 300 Pike St Ste 400 Cincinnati OH 45202 Office Phone: 513-621-2100. Office Fax: 513-621-0106.

ANTHONY, CAROLYN ADDITON, librarian; b. Pitts., Nov. 27, 1949; d. Elwood Prince and Elizabeth Martha (Gruginskis) Additon; m. William W. Anthony, III, July 7, 1973; children: Margaret Susan, Lauren Elizabeth. AB, Colby Coll., 1971; MLS, U. R.I., 1973. Reference libr. Enoch Pratt Free Lib., Balt., 1973-75, head info. and referral svc., 1975-78; head info. svcs. Balt. County Pub. Libr., Towson, Md., 1978-80, head, info. and program svcs., 1980-85; dir. Skokie (Ill.) Pub. Libr., 1985—. Pres. Libr. Adminstr. Conf. No. Ill., 1988—89; chair adv. bd. Pub. Librs., 1986—89; bd. mem. Rush North Shore Med. Ctr., 2004—06, pres. women's bd., 2004—06. Recipient Libr. of Yr., North Suburban Libr. Sys., 2004. Mem.: ALA (mem. coun. 1993—97), Ill. Libr. Assn. (pres. 1999—2000, award, Libr. of the Yr. 2003), Am. Libr. Trustee Assn. (bd. dirs.), Pub. Libr. Assn. (new stds. task force com. 1984—87, bd. dirs. 1987—89, 2005—), Met. Libr. Assn. (exec. com. 1990—93), Chgo. Libr. Club (pres. 1991—92), Rotary (pres. Skokie chpt. 1992—93). Democrat. Soc. Of Friends. Office: Skokie Pub Libr 5215 Oakton St Skokie IL 60077-3680 Office Phone: 847-673-7774. Business E-Mail: canthony@skokielibrary.info.

ANTHONY, DONALD BARRETT, engineering executive; b. Kansas City, Kans., Jan. 28, 1948; s. Donald W. and Marjorie (Lifsey) A.; m. Darla S. Donovan, Dec. 16, 1972; children: Jennifer L., Danielle S. BSChemE, U. Toledo, 1970; MS, MIT, 1971, DSc, 1974. Asst. prof., practice sch. dir. dept. chem. engring. MIT, Cambridge, Mass., 1974-75; group supr. coal R&D Std. Oil Co. Ohio, Cleve., 1976-77, mgr. marine planning, 1978-79, mgr. synthetic fuels devel., 1980-83, v.p., gen. mgr. Pfaudler Divsn. Rochester, NY, 1983-85; v.p. R&D Std. Oil Co., Cleve., 1985-87, BP Am., Inc., Cleve., 1987-88, BP Exploration, Inc., Cleve., 1989-90; v.p. tech. Bechtel, Inc., Houston, 1990-94, v.p. ops., 1994-95, v.p. reference, 1995-96; pres. Bailey Controls Co., 1996-98, Process Ind. Group, ABB Automation, 1999—2000; pres., CEO NineSigma, Inc., Cleve., 2001—03; pres. Coun. for Chem. Rsch., Wash., DC, 2004—07; chief tech. officer Great Point Energy, Ill., 2007—. Contbr. articles to profl. jours.; patentee in field. Capt. AUS, 1970-78. MIT Esso fellow, 1970-71, Little rsch.-devel. fellow, 1971-72, Procter & Gamble fellow, 1972-73, Bechtel fellow, 1992. Mem. AIChE, Am. Chem. Soc., Sigma Xi, Phi Kappa Phi, Tau Beta Pi, Pi Mu Epsilon, Phi Eta Sigma. Lutheran. Home: 122 Portofino Dr North Venice FL 34275 Office: Great Point Energy 1700 South Mount Prospect Rd Des Plaines IL 60018 Office Phone: 202-429-3971. Business E-Mail: danthony@greatpointenergy.com.

ANTHONY, LEONARD MORRIS, steel company administrator, consultant; b. Allentown, Pa., July 28, 1954; s. Leonard M. and Gladys (Davies) A.; m. Pamela Ann Leon, Nov. 3, 1976; 1 child, Lindsay C. BS in Acctg., Pa. State U., 1976; MBA in Fin., U. Pa., 1993. Comml. lender Meridian Bancorp., Allentown, 1977-78; credit analyst Bethlehem Steel Corp., Bethlehem, Pa., 1979-82, adminstrv. mgr. credit, 1982-84, treasury analyst, 1984-85, credit mgr., 1985-86, dir. fin. svcs., 1986-90, dir. risk mgmt., 1990-93, mgr. fin. planning, 1993—95, asst. treasurer, 1995—99, treasurer, 1999—2001, senior vice president finance, CFO, 2001—03; CFO Internat. Steel Group, Richfield, Ohio, 2003—. Prin. MMC Cons., Phila., 1993—. Avocations: scuba, golf, personal investing, wine collecting. Home: 2224 Summit Dr Hellertown PA 18055-2948 Office: International Steel Group 3250 Interstate Dr Richfield OH 44286

ANTHONY, MICHAEL FRANCIS, lawyer; b. Chgo., Dec. 19, 1950; s. Rudolph A. and Margaret M. (Shea) Anthony; m. Megan P. O'Connell; children: Erin Christine, Ian O'Connell, Connor Cullerton, Madeline Shea, McKenzie Galligan. BS cum laude, Xavier U., Cin., 1972, MHA, 1974; JD, U. Balt., 1978. Bar: Md. 1978, Fla. 1979, Ill. 1980, DC 1989. Various adminstrv. positions Johns Hopkins Hosp., Balt., 1973-78; assoc. Ober Kaler Grimes & Shriver, Balt., 1978-80; from assoc. to ptnr. McDermott, Will & Emery, Chgo., 1980-87, 1989—91, nat. head health law dept., 1991—2001, 2006—; sr. v.p. for legal affairs Am. Hosp. Assn., Chgo., 1987-89. Contbr. articles to profl. jours. Mem. adv. bd. De Paul Inst. Health Law. Fellow: Am. Health Lawyers Assn. (past pres.), Am. Coll. Healthcare Execs. (various coms.). Office: McDermott Will & Emery 227 W Monroe St Ste 5300 Chicago IL 60606-5096 Office Phone: 312-984-7635. Business E-Mail: manthony@mwe.com.

ANTHONY, THOMAS DALE, lawyer; b. Cleve., July 23, 1952; m. Susan Shelly; children: Lara, Elizabeth. BS, Miami U., Oxford, Ohio, 1974; JD, Case Western Res. U., 1977. Bar: Ohio 1977. Tax specialist Ernst & Young, Cleve., 1977—79; ptnr. Benesch, Friedlander, Coplan and Aronoff, Cin., 1979—89, Frost and Jacobs, Cin., 1989—98; exec. v.p., chief legal officer, sec. Choice Care, 1996—98; pres., CEO PacifiCare of Ohio, 1998—2002; mem., vice chair corp. dept. Frost Brown Todd LLC, 2001—. Speaker various orgns. Mem. Cin. Coun. on World Affairs, 1980-82; vol. fundraising drive Sta. WVIZ, 1978-79, Sta. WCET, 1980-82; legal counsel Children's Internat. Summer Villages, 1979—; account capt. United Way of Hamilton County, 1986-88, cabinet mem., 1993; pres. State Libr. Bd., Ohio, 1987-89; mem. bus. adv. coun., subcom. ednl. legis. Mariemont City Schs. and Bd. of Edn.; bd. dirs. Greater Cin. Ctr. for Econ. Edn., Am. Heart Assn. (Cin. chpt.), Juvenile Diabetes Found.; bd. mem. Cin. Playhouse in the Park; exec. com., v.p. strategic planning Cin. Nature Ctr. Named one of Best Lawyer in Am. Health Care. Mem. ABA (taxation sect., tax acctg. problems com., tax shelter subcom., small bus. com., mem. health law forum), Ohio State Bar Assn. (health law com., ins. sect.), Assn. Corp. Growth (bd. dirs. Cin. chpt.), Cin. Bar Assn. (chmn. tax. inst. com. 1990, adminstrn. and fin. com. 1991-93, chmn. tax sect. 1993, health law com.), Cin. C. of C., Miami U. Alumni Assn. (bd. dirs., treas. 1989-91, v.p. 1991-92), Nat. Health Lawyers Assn., Rotary (co-chair youth in city govt. program), Omicron Delta Kappa, Sigma Phi Epsilon. Home: 4337 Ashley Oaks Dr Cincinnati OH 45227-3947 Office: PacifiCare 11260 Chester Rd Ste 800 Cincinnati OH 45246-4096 Office Phone: 513-651-6191. Business E-Mail: tanthony@fbtlaw.com.

ANTICH-CARR, ROSE ANN, state legislator; b. Apr. 11, 1938; married John Carr; 1 son, Marc Antich. Grad., Hammond Bus. Coll.; postgrad., Ind. U. N.W. Radio and TV personality, lectr. positive mental attitude and stress control, astrologist; mem. Ind. Senate from 4th dist., 1991—, asst. caucus chair, 1996—. Mem. town coun., 1983-87. Democrat. Roman Catholic. Home: 5401 Lincoln St Merrillville IN 46410-1926 Office: Ind State House 200 W Washington St Indianapolis IN 46204-2728 E-mail: roseann@urisp.com.

ANTOINE, RICHARD L., human resources specialist, consumer products company executive; m. Dorothy O'Brien; 1 child. BS, U. Wis., 1969. Various positions including soap process supr. and plant mgr. Procter & Gamble Co., mgr. N.Am. supply sys., engring., and purchasing divsn., 1992—99, dir. global supply sys., 1999—2001, global human resources officer, 2001—. Bd. dirs. Cinn. Ballet Co. Avocations: travel, golf. Office: Procter & Gamble Co 1 Procter & Gamble Plz Cincinnati OH 45202 Office Phone: 513-983-1100. Office Fax: 513-983-9369.

ANTONSEN, ELMER HAROLD, Germanic languages and linguistics educator; b. Glens Falls, NY, Nov. 17, 1929; s. Haakon and Astrid Caroline Emilie (Sommer) A.; m. Hannelore Gertrude Adam, Mar. 24, 1956; children: Ingrid Carol, Christopher Walter. BA, Union Coll., Schenectady, NY, 1951; postgrad., U. Vienna, 1951-52, U. Goettingen, 1956; MA, U. Ill., 1957, PhD, 1961. Instr. German, Northwestern U., Evanston, Ill., 1959-61; asst. prof. U. Iowa, Iowa City, 1961-64, assoc. prof., 1964-67, U. Ill., Urbana, 1967-70, prof. Germanic langs. and linguistics, 1970—, head dept. Germanic langs., 1973-82, head dept. linguistics, 1990-96, assoc. Ctr. for Advanced Studies, 1984. Vis. prof. U. N.C., Chapel Hill, 1972-73, U. Goettingen, 1988. Author: A Concise Grammar of the Older Runic Inscriptions, 1975, Runes and Germanic Linguistics, 2002, Elements of German, 2007; editor: The Grimm Brothers and the Germanic Past, 1989, Studies in the Linguistic Sciences, 1995—2002; co-editor: Staefcraeft: Studies in Germanic Linguistics, 1991; contbr. articles to profl. jours. Served with AUS, 1953-56. Fulbright scholar, 1951—52. Mem. Linguistic Soc. Am., Royal Norwegian Soc. Scis. and Letters, Soc. Advancement of Scandinavian Study, Institut für Deutsche Sprache (corr. mem.), Selskab for nordisk filologi, Soc. for Germanic Linguistics, Phi Beta Kappa. Home: 2210 Plymouth Dr Champaign IL 61821-6542 Personal E-mail: elmer.antonsen@insightbb.com.

ANUZIS, SAUL See ANUZIS, SAULIUS

ANUZIS, SAULIUS (SAUL ANUZIS), political organization administrator; b. Detroit, Mar. 6, 1959; s. Ceslovas and Elena Vilnionis Anuzis; m. Lina Anuzis, 1985; children: Matas, Tadas, Vytis, Marius. BA, U. Mich., Dearborn, 1981. Comm. specialist Mich. House Representatives, Lansing, 1981—82; third vice chmn. Mich. State Rep. Com., 1981—83; pres. Data Base Enterprises, Ltd., 1982—85, Fin. Devel. Group, 1985; adminstrv. asst. Senator Dick Posthumus, 1983—91; mem. exec. com. Eaton County Rep., 1985—86; chmn. 3rd Congl. Dist. Rep., 1986—90; chief of staff Senate Majority Leader Dick Posthumus, 1991—92; co-founder, v.p. Coast to Coast Telecom., 1992—94, chmn., 1995—2001; co-founder, chmn. Quick Connect USA, 2001—; chmn. Mich. Rep. Party, 2005—; mem. Rep. Nat. Com., 2005—. Del. Rep. Nat. Conv., 1980, 88; mem. bd. dirs. Phone Bank Syst, Inc., 1982—92, Real Group Inc., 1988—89; bd. mem. Mich. Export Devel. Authority, 1991—94, Mich. Internat. Trade Authority, 1994—95, Mich. Jobs Commn., 1996, Lithuanian Found. Inc., 2004—, US Baltic Found. Inc., 2005—; co-chmn. Senate Rep. Campaign Com., 1992—96. Vol. scoutmaster Boy Scouts, Troop 100, 1976—; bd. mem. Greater Lansing Cath. Edn. Found., 2005—. Republican. Home: 5 Locust Ln Lansing MI 48911 Office: Mich Rep Party Secchia-Weiser Mich Rep Ctr 520 Seymour St Lansing MI 48933 Office Phone: 517-487-5413. Office Fax: 517-487-0080. Business E-Mail: sanuzis@migop.org.*

ANVARIPOUR, M. A., lawyer; b. Tehran, Iran, Jan. 23, 1935; arrived in U.S., 1957; s. Ahmed and Monir (Georgi) A.; m. Patricia Matson Lynch (div. 1971); 1 dau., Sandra M.; m. Guilda Eshtehardi, Mar. 31, 1978 (div. 1984); 1 son, Cyrus Ramsey; m. Tess Temel, May 15, 1995 (div. 2002). LLB, U. Tehran, 1956; BS, U. San Francisco, 1959; student, U. Calif. Hastings Coll. Law, San Francisco, JD, 1973. Bar: Ill. 1973, Fed. cts. Asst. field dir. Am. Friends of Middle East, Inc., Iran, 1962-64, field dir., 1964-66; asst. dean students, dean internat. students and faculty affairs Ill. Inst. Tech., Chgo., 1966-81; practiced in Chgo., 1973—, in San Francisco, 1985—; ednl. and legal adviser Consulate Gen. Iran, Chgo., 1973-79; aux. lawyer NAACP, Chgo., 1973-74. Lectr. immigration and law seminar Ill. Inst. Tech.-Chgo.-Kent Coll. Law Sch., 1974 Mem. Am., Iran-Am. (sec.-gen. 1964-66), Chgo. Bar Assn. (chmn. immigration com. 1982-83), Iran Am. Alumni Assn. (sec. 1964-66), Nat. Assn. Fgn. Student Affairs (Ill. chmn. 1968-69), U. Tehran, U. San Francisco, Idaho State U. (hon.), Ill. Inst. Tech., Chgo.-Kent Coll. Law alumni assns., Am. Immigration Lawyers Assn. (sec.-treas. Chgo. chpt. 1976-78, v.p. 1978-80, pres. 1980-81), Armour Faculty Club (pres. 1977-78), Phi Delta Phi. Office: 180 N La Salle St Chicago IL 60601-2501 Office Phone: 312-750-0558. Personal E-mail: anvaripourlaw@yahoo.com.

APELBAUM, PHYLLIS L., delivery messenger service executive; 1 child, Mark. Instr. Am. United Cab Co., Chgo., 1957-65; gen. mgr. City Bonded Messenger Svc., Chgo., 1960-74; founder, pres. Arrow Messenger Svc., Inc., Chgo., 1974—. 1st chair Affirmative Action Adv. Bd. of Chgo., 1991-92; chair Variety Club Children's Carnival, Chgo., 1990-94; mem. bicycle com. City of Chgo., 1992-95, parking task force, 1993-95; gov. Ill. Coun. on Econ. Edn., Chgo., 1995—; mem. Lakefront SRO Adv. Bd., Chgo., 1989-94; mem. Chgo. Police bd., 1995—. Recipient Small Bus. Innovative Mgmt. award Bank of Am., 1994; named Entrepreneur of the Yr., Ernst & Young, 1992, Nat. Small Bus. Person of the Yr., Small Bus. Assn., 1990; named to Entrepreneurship Hall of Fame, U. Ill., Chgo., 1993. Mem. Messenger Courier Assn. of Am. (bd. dirs. 1989—), Messenger Svc. Assn. Ill. (co-founder, pres.), Nat. Assn. Women Bus. Owners, The Chgo. Network. Office: Arrow Messenger Svc Inc 1322 W Walton St Chicago IL 60622-5340

APICELLA, MICHAEL ALLEN, microbiologist, educator; b. Bklyn., Apr. 4, 1938; s. Anthony D. and Fay (Kahn) A.; m. Agnes Dengler, Aug. 19, 1961; children: Michael P., Christopher A., Peter N. AB, Holy Cross Coll., 1959; MD, SUNY, Bklyn., 1963. Diplomate Am. Bd. Internal Medicine, Am. Bd. Infectious Disease. Postdoctoral fellow Johns Hopkins Hosp., Balt., 1966-68; asst. prof. microbiology SUNY, Buffalo, 1970-74, assoc. prof., 1974-78, prof., 1981-92; prof., chmn. dept. microbiology Coll. Medicine U. Iowa, Iowa City, 1993—. Contbr. over 150 articles to profl. jours. Maj. USAF, 1968-70. Office: U Iowa Coll Medicine Dept Microbiology Coll Medicine 3-403 Science Bldg Iowa City IA 52242 E-mail: michael.apicella@uiowa.edu.

APPEL, NINA SCHICK, law educator, dean, academic administrator; b. Feb. 17, 1936; d. Leo and Nora Schick; m. Alfred Appel Jr.; children: Karen Oshman, Richard. Student, Cornell U.; JD, Columbia U., 1959. Instr. Columbia Law Sch., 1959-60; adminstr. Stanford U., mem. faculty, prof. law, 1973—, assoc. dean, 1976-83; dean Sch. Law Loyola U., 1983—2004, dean emerita, prof. law, 2004—. Mem. Am. Bar Found., Ill. Bar Found., Chgo. Bar Found., Chgo. Legal Club, Chgo. Network. Jewish. Office: Loyola U Sch Law 25 E Pearson St Chicago IL 60611-2055 Home Phone: 847-256-5458; Office Phone: 312-915-7128. E-mail: nappel@luc.edu.

APPEL, WILLIAM FRANK, pharmacist; b. Mpls., Oct. 8, 1924; s. William Ignatius and Elna Antonia (Mulzahn) A.; m. Louise D. Altman, Sept. 24, 1949; children— Nancy, Peggy, James, Elizabeth. BS in Pharmacy, U. Minn., 1949; D.Sc. (hon.), Phila. Coll. Pharmacy and Sci., 1978. Intern in pharmacy Northwestern Hosp., Mpls.; pres., pharmacist, mgr. Appel Com-Pharm, Inc., Mpls., 1949—; pres. Pharm. Cons. Services, P.A., St. Paul, 1960—. Mem. Minn. Bd. Pharmacy, 1960-65, pres., 1965; preceptor internship requirement program; chmn. Minn. Gov.'s Commn. on Drug Abuse, 1971-73; mem. Mpls. Health Dept. Task Force on Pub. Health Approaches to Chem. Dependency; clin. instr. U. Minn. Coll. Pharmacy, 1970—; cons. HEW; long term care facilities; rep. Nat. Pharmacy/Industry Com. on at. Health Ins.; mem. revision com. U.S. Pharmacopeial Conv., 1980— Served with USN, 1942-46. Recipient Good Neighbor award, Sta. WCCO, Mpls., 1973. Mem. Twin City Met. Drug Assn., Minn. Pharm. Assn. (v.p., Harold R. Popp award 1974, mem. continuing edn. faculty 1970—), Am. Pharm. Assn. (pres. N.W. br., nat. pres. 1976-77, Daniel B. Smith award 1970, treas. 1979—) pharm. assns), Minn. Gerontol. Soc., U. Minn. Coll. Pharmacy Alumni Assn. (v.p., Distinguished Pharmacist award 1971) Office: Preferred Choice Pharmacy 900 Long Lake Rd #150 New Brighton MN 55112 Home: 5251 Ashlar Dr Minneapolis MN 55437-3360

APPLEBAUM, EDWARD LEON, otolaryngologist, educator; b. Detroit, Jan. 14, 1940; s. M. Lawrence and Frieda Applebaum; m. Eva Redei; children: Daniel Ira, Rachel Anne. AB, Wayne State U., 1961, MD, 1964. Diplomate: Am. Bd. Otolaryngology. Intern Univ. Hosp., Ann Arbor, Mich., 1964-65; resident Mass. Eye and Ear Infirmary Harvard Med. Sch., Boston, 1966-69; practice medicine specializing in otolaryngology Chgo., 1972—2007; assoc. prof. Northwestern U. Med. Sch., 1972-79, prof. Chgo., 2000—06, chmn. dept. otolaryngology, 2000—06, prof. emeritus, 2007—; prof., head dept. otolaryngology, head and neck surgery Coll. Medicine, U. Ill., 1979-2000, prof. emeritus, 1979—. Mem. staff Northwestern Meml. Hosp. Author: Tracheal Intubation, 1976; editor: Am. Jour. Otolaryngology, 1982-87; mem. editl. bd. Am. Jour. Otolaryngology, Laryngoscope. Served as maj. U.S. Army, 1969-71. Recipient Anna Albert Keller Rsch. award Wayne State U. Coll. Medicine, 1964, Disting. Alumni award, 1989, William Beaumont Soc. Original Rsch. award, 1964, Disting. Faculty award, U. Ill. Coll. Medicine, 1996. Fellow ACS, Am. Soc. for Head and Neck Surgery, Surgery, Am. Acad. Otolaryngology, Head and Neck Surgery, Am. Laryngol., Rhinol. and Otol. Soc. (v.p. 1993, pres. 2000), Am. Laryngol. Assn., Am. Otol. Soc., Soc. Univ. Otolaryngologists, Head and Neck Surgeons (pres. 1988), Assn. Acad. Depts. Otolaryngology-Head and Neck Surgery (pres. 1995-96). E-mail: eapple@northwestern.edu.

APPLEBY, R(OBERT) SCOTT, history educator; b. Shreveport, La., Dec. 3, 1956; s. John and Joanne (Jackson) A.; m. Margaret Calhoun; children: Benjamin, Paul, Clare, Tony. BA, U. Notre Dame, 1978; MA, U. Chgo., 1979, PhD, 1985. Asst. prof., chair dept. religious studies St. Xavier Coll., Chgo., 1985-87; rsch. assoc. U. Chgo., 1988-94; assoc. dir. The Fundamentalism Project Am. Acad. Arts and Scis., Chgo., 1988—; dir. Cushwa Ctr. for Study of Am. Catholicism U. Notre Dame, Ind., 1994—, assoc. prof. history Ind., 1994—. Cons. Lilly Endowment, 1994—, William Benton Broadcast Project, U. Chgo., 1989-92. Editor: (with Martin E. Marty) Fundamentalisms Observed, 1991. Mem. Am. Acad. Religion, Am. Hist. Assn., Am. Cath. Hist. Assn., Am. Soc. Ch. History, Coll. Theology Soc., Religious Rsch. Assn. (nominations com. 1993—). Office: U Notre Dame 614 Hesburgh Ctr Notre Dame IN 46556-5677

APPLETON, R. O., JR., lawyer; b. San Francisco, Aug. 17, 1945; s. Robert Oser and Leslie Jeanne (Roth) A.; m. Susan Frelich, June 3, 1971; children: Jesse David, Seth Daniel. AB, Stanford U., 1967; JD, U. Calif., San Francisco, 1970; postgrad., NYU, 1971. Bar: Calif. 1971, U.S. Dist. Calif. (no. dist.) Calif. 1971, Mo. 1973, U.S. Dist. Ct. (ea. dist.) Mo. 1974, U.S. Ct. Appeals (8th cir.) 1975, U.S. Ct. Internat. Trade, 1980. Assoc. Dinkelspiel & Dinkelspiel, San Francisco, 1971-73, Schramm & Morganstern, St. Louis, 1973-75; pvt. practice, 1975-77; ptnr. Braun, Newman, Stewart & Appleton, St. Louis, 1977-82, Appleton, Newman & Kretmar, St. Louis, 1982-84, Appleton, Newman & Gerson, St. Louis, 1984-89, Appleton & Kretmar, St. Louis, 1989—, Appleton, Kretmar & Beatty. Adj. prof. pre-trial litigation Washington U. Sch. Law, St. Louis, 1985-88. Arbitrator, vol. Better Bus. Bur. of St. Louis, 1980—; St. Louis Gymnastic Centre, 1984—; bd. dirs. St. Louis Friends of Tibet, 1991-94. Mem. ABA, Calif. Bar Assn., Met. Bar Assn. of St. Louis, St. Louis County Bar Assn., Am. Arbitration Assn. (arbitrator comml. panel, arbitrator mass claims appeals com. 1999), Stanford Club (pres. 1991—), Stanford Assocs. (bd of gov., 2007-) Democrat. Jewish. Avocations: jogging, swimming, cooking, model trains, reading. Home: 8317 Cornell Ave Saint Louis MO 63132-5025 Office: Appleton Kretmar Beatty & Stolze 8000 Maryland Ave Ste 900 Saint Louis MO 63105-3911 Office Phone: 314-721-8685. Personal E-mail: roajratty1@aol.com.

APPLEYARD, DAVID FRANK, retired mathematics professor; b. South Haven, Mich., July 13, 1939; s. Edwin Ray and Hortense Ruth (Guilford) A.; m. Joey Hierlmeier, Aug. 5, 1967; children: David Wayne, Gregory Jay, Robert James. BA, Carleton Coll., 1961; MS, U. Wis., 1963, PhD, 1970. Teaching asst. in math. U. Wis., Madison, 1961-66; prof. math. and computer science Carleton Coll., Northfield, Minn., 1966—2007, Lloyd P. Johnson Norwest Found. prof. liberal arts, 1993—2007, dean students, 1977—83, faculty pres., 1988-91; ret., 2007. Carleton Coll. faculty athletic rep. to Midwest Collegiate Athletic Conf., 1975-83, pres., 1982-83 Trustee United Ch. Christ, Northfield, 1969—72. Recipient Cowling Cup for career achievement, 2002; NSF fellow, 1964, grantee prin. investigator, 1993—97; NASA traineeship, 1965-66; Sloan Found. grantee, 1969, 73, 84. Mem.: Nat. Coun. Tchrs. Math., Math. Assn. Am. (N. Ctrl. sect., award for disting. coll. or univ. tchg. 2006), Sigma Xi. Avocations: canoeing, vintage baseball. Home: 6450 134th St E Northfield MN 55057-4611 Personal E-mail: dappleya@carleton.edu.

APRISON, MORRIS HERMAN, retired experimental and theoretical neurobiology educator; b. Milw., Oct. 6, 1923; s. Henry and Ethel Aprison; m. Shirley Reder, Aug. 21, 1949; children— Barry, Robert. BS in Chemistry, U. Wis., 1945, tchrs. cert., 1947, MS in Physics, 1949, PhD in Biochemistry, 1952. Grad. teaching asst. in physics U. Wis., Madison, 1947-49; grad. research asst. in pathology Sch. Medicine, 1950-51, grad. research asst. in biochemistry, 1951-52; tech. asst. in physics Inst. Paper Chemistry, Appleton, Wis., 1949-50; biochemist, prin. investigator, head biophysics sect. Galesburg (Ill.) State Research Hosp., 1952-56; prin. research investigator in biochemistry Inst. Psychiat. Research; asst. prof. depts. biochemistry and psychiatry Ind. U. Med. Sch., Indpls., 1956-60, asso. prof., 1960-64, prof. biochemistry, 1964-78, distinguished prof. neurobiology and biochemistry, 1978-93, disting. prof. emeritus, 1993—, chief neurobiology sect., 1969-74. Mem. exec. com. dept. psychiatry, exec. adminstr. Inst. Psychiat. Rsch., 1973-74, dir. inst., 1974-78, chief sect. applied and theoretical neurobiology, 1978-93; co-chmn. session on neurotransmitters 23d Internat. Physiol. Congress, 1965; chmn. session neurochemistry and neuropharmacology 25th Congress, 1971; ad hoc mem. study sect. psychopharmacology NIMH, 1967-71, mem. neuropsychology study sect., 1970-74; mem. molecular and cellular neurobiology program adv. panel NSF, 1984-86; mem. com. recommendations U.S. Army sci. rsch. Nat. Rsch. Coun. Bd. Physics and Astronomy, 1987-89; mem. gov. bd. Inst. for Advanced Study Ind. U., Bloomington, 1989-92; vis. prof. 4th ASPET Workshop, Vanderbilt U., 1972; guest scholar Grad. Sch., Kans. State U., 1973. Adv. editor Neurosci. Rsch., 1968-73, Jour. Biol. Psychiatry, 1968-83, Neuropharmacology, 1969-93, Jour. eurochemistry, 1972-75, Pharmacology, Biochemistry and Behavior, 1973-89, Jour. Comparative and General Pharmacology, 1974-75, Jour. Gen. Pharmacology, 1975-93, Jour. Developmental Psychobiology, 1974-77; regional editor Life Scis., 1970-73; co-editor Advances in Neurochemistry, 1973-92; mem. editorial bd. Jour. Neurochemistry, 1975-79, dep. chief editor, 1980-83; mem. editorial bd. Neurochem. Rsch., 1975-82, Jour. Neurosci. Rsch., 1984-92; co-editor 10 books; contbr. more than 355 rsch. articles and abstracts to profl. jours., chpts. to books, including one in History of Neuroscience in Autobiography, vol. 3, 2001. Mem. Ind. regional adv. bd. Anti-Defamation League, 1973-76; bd. overseers St. Meinrad Sem., 1974-77. Served with USNR, 1944-46. Recipient First 50th Univ. award, Inst. Psychiat. Rsch., 2007. Mem. Am. Physiol. Soc., Biophys. Soc., Soc. Biol. Psychiatry (program com. 1974-75, co-chmn. 1975-76, gold medal 1975), Internat. Brain Rsch. Orgn., Internat. Soc. Neurochemistry (co-chmn. session 1st internat. meeting Strasbourg, France 1967, 4th meeting Tokyo 1973, 7th meeting Jerusalem 1979, coun. 1973-75, sec. 1975-79, chmn. 1979-81, publicity com. 1975-83, nominating com. 1983-87, policy adv. com. 1985-98, ad hoc and founding rules com. 1998-2000, standing rules com., 2000—), Am. Soc. Neurochemistry (co-chmn. sci. program com. 1972, mem. 1973), Soc. for Neurosci. (pres. Indpls. chpt. 1970-71), Sigma Xi. Achievements include development of the Morris Aprison lecture in biological psychiatry 2006-; having the department of psychiatry at Indiana Universities School of Medicine create awards in his honor from 1999-2005 for the best research towards a PhD in medical neurobiology. Home: 9268 Spring Forest Dr Indianapolis IN 46260-1266

ARAKAWA, KASUMI, physician, educator; b. Toyohashi, Japan, Feb. 19, 1926; came to U.S., 1954, naturalized, 1963; s. Masumi and Fayuko (Hattori) A.; m. Juen Hope Takahara, Aug. 27, 1956; children: Jane Riet, Kenneth Luke, Amy Kathryn. MD, Tokyo Med. Coll., 1953; PhD, Showa U., 1984. Diplomate Am. Bd. Anesthesiology. Intern Iowa Meth. Hosp., Des Moines, 1954—56; resident in internal medicine U. Kans. Med. Ctr., Kansas City, 1956—58, instr. anesthesiology, 1961—64, from asst. prof. to prof., 1964—94; prof. emeritus, 1994—; Arakawa Disting. prof. anesthesiology U. Kans. Med. Ctr., Kansas City, 1990, Kasumi Arakawa professorship, 1994. Clin. assoc. prof. U. Mo.-Kans. City Sch. Dentistry, 1973—; dir. Kansas City Health Care, Inc. Fulbright scholar, 1954; nat. cons. to surgeon gen., USAF, 1990—. Recipient Outstanding Faculty award Student AMA, 1970 Fellow Am. Coll. Anesthesiology; mem. Assn. Univ. Anesthetists, Acad. Anesthesiology (pres. 1986-87), Japan-Am. Soc. Midwest (v.p. 1965, 71). Office: Univ Med Ctr 3901 Rainbow Blvd Kansas City KS 66160-0001 Home: 2190 Rosa Vista Terr Camarillo CA 93012 Personal E-mail: kcarakawamdphdca@verizon.net.

ARAND, FREDERICK FRANCIS, accountant, finance company executive; b. Chgo., Mar. 14, 1954; s. Bernard Anthony and Millicent Catherine (Schweizer) A.; m. Judith Mary Utz, May 22, 1982; children: Joseph, Diana, Thomas, Amanda, Laura. AB, Dartmouth Coll., 1976; MBA, U. Mich., 1978. CPA Mich. Staff acct. Ernst & Young, Chgo., 1978-79, advanced staff acct., 1979-80, sr. staff acct., 1980-82, supr., 1982-85, sr. mgr., 1985—94; contr. Ancilla Sys., Inc., Hobart, Ind., 1994—97, v.p. fin. svcs., 1997—. Bd. dirs. Simmons Ambulance Co., treas., 2004—, Ancilla Domini Sisters; bd. dirs. L. Gilbraith SPC Ltd. Leader Jr. Achievement, Wheaton, Ill., 1981—83; mgr., coach Niles Baseball and Soccer Leagues, 1989—94, Park Ridge Softball and Soccer Leagues, 1993—94, Schererville Soccer League, 1994—2004, St. John Softball League, 1996, CYO Soccer League, 1997—2004; adv. bd. St. John Evangelist Sch.; bd. dirs. Schererville Soccer Club, treas., 1998—99; bd. dirs. Gary Citywide Devel. Corp., treas., 2004—07; bd. dirs. PHJC Cmty. Support Trust, St. Joseph Med. Ctr. of Ft. Wayne, St. Mary's Hosp. Health Found., Sisters of Providence Cmty. Support Trust, Gary Cmty. Health Found., Ancilla Ins. Trust, Catherine Kasper Life Ctr., treas., 2004—07; bd. dirs. Linden Ho. of Mishawaka, treas., 2004—; bd. dirs. Simmons Ambulance Co., treas., 2004—; bd. dirs. Advantage Health Solutions. Mem. AICPA (grassroots panel, 2003-), Math. Assn. Am., Ill. CPA Soc., Ind. CPA Soc. (leadership cabinet, 2003-), Fin. Mgr. Soc. (mem. fin. mgmt. com. 1986-91, vice chmn. 1987-88, chmn. 1988-90, mem. accounting issues com. 1991-92), Healthcare Fin. Mgmt. Assn., Fin. Execs. Internat., Dartmouth Alumni Club, Met. Club, Toastmasters (area gov. 1985-86). Avocations: soccer, golf, tennis, softball. Home: 9123 Olcott Ave Saint John IN 46373-9729 Office: Ancilla Systems Inc 1419 S Lake Park Ave Hobart IN 46342

ARAQUE, JOHAN ALEXANDER SANTANA See SANTANA, JOHAN

ARBIT, BRUCE, direct marketing executive, consultant; b. Milw., Nov. 16, 1954; s. Saul B. and Naomi (Chase) A.; m. Tanya Arbit; children: Oren, Carmiel, Eugene. Student, U. Haifa, Israel, U. Wis. Founder, co-mgr., dir. A B Data, Ltd., Milw., 1977—. Chmn., bd. dirs. Integrated Mail Industries Ltd., Asset Devel. Group, Inc.; bd. dirs. Integrated Mail Industries Israel, Ltd.; chmn. Fox Point Capital, LLC, Fox Point Credit Corp Pres., gen. campaign chmn., bd. dirs., pres. Milw. Jewish Fedn. Keshet, Milw. Jewish Day Sch., Habonim Dror Found.; mem. United Jewish Appeal Young Leadership Cabinet; mem. Wexner Heritage Found., Non-profit Mailers Fedn., Campaign Cabinet Devel. Corp. for Israel; trustee United Israel Appeal, sec.; bd. dirs., sec. Jewish Telegraphic Agy.; bd. govs. Jewish Agy. for Israel, co-chmn. ednl. resources devel. com.; mem. nom.

exec. com. United Jewish Communities. Recipient Benjamin E. Nickoll Young Leadership award Milw. Jewish Fedn., 1989. Mem. Direct Mktg. Assn., Israel Direct Mktg., Wis. Direct Mktg. Assn. (Direct Marketer of Yr. award 1997), Am. Assn. Polit. Cons. Office: AB Data Ltd 8050 N Port Washington Rd Milwaukee WI 53217-2600 Business E-Mail: barbit@abdata.com.

ARBUCKLE, JOSEPH W., military officer; b. Lincoln, Ill., Feb. 28, 1946; married; 2 children. BA in Psychology, Western State Coll., Colo.; MS in Sys. Mgmt., U. So. Calif.; grad., Command and Gen. Staff Coll., Army War Coll. Commd. 2d lt. U.S. Army, 1970, advanced through grades to maj. gen., various assignments; dep. chief of staff for ammunition U.S. Army Material Command, Alexandria, Va.; comdr. armament rsch., devel. and engring. ctr. U.S. Army Tank-automotive and Armament Command, Rock Island; commdg. gen. U.S. Army Indsl. Ops. Command, Rock Island, Ill., 1998—. Decorated Legion of Merit with 5 oak leaf clusters, Bronze Star with 2 oak leaf clusters, Meritorious Svc. medal with 3 oak leaf clusters, Vietnamese Cross of Gallantry with 2 Silver stars, Vietnamese Svc. medal.

ARCHABAL, NINA M(ARCHETTI), historic site director; b. Long Branch, NJ, Apr. 11, 1940; d. John William and Santina Matilda (Giuffre) Marchetti; m. John William Archabal, Aug. 8, 1964; 1 child, John Fidel. BA in Music History cum laude, Radcliffe Coll., 1962; MAT in Music History, Harvard U., 1963; PhD in Music History, U. Minn., 1979. Asst. dir. humanities art mus. U. Minn., Mpls., 1975-77; asst. supr. edn. divsn. Minn. Hist. Soc., St. Paul, 1977-78, dep. dir. for program mgmt., 1978-86, acting dir., 1986-87, dir., 1987—, sec. governing bd. Bd. dirs. US nat. com. Internat. Coun. Mus.; mem. Nat. Coun. on Humanities, 2000. V.p. Friends of St. Paul Pub. Libr., 1983-93; Minn. state hist. preservation officer, 1987—; chair State Hist. Records Adv. Bd., 1987—, St. Anthony Falls Heritage Bd., 1988—; trustee, bd. dirs. Am. Folklife Ctr., Libr. of Congress, 1989-98; bd. dirs. N.W. Area Found., 1989-98, St. Paul Acad. and Summit Sch., 1993-2002, St. Paul Riverfront Corp., 2000-03, Rsch. Librs. Group, 2004—; bd. regents St. John's U., Collegeville, Minn., 1997-2004; overseer Harvard Coll., Cambridge, Mass., 1997—; mem. bd. overseers Hill Mus. and Manuscript Libr., 2004—. NDEA fellow U. Minn., 1969-72, U. Minn. grad. fellow, 1974-75; recipient Nat. Humanities medal The White House, 1997. Mem. Am. Assn. State and Local History (sec. 1986-88), Am. Assn. Museums (v.p. 1991-94, chair bd. dirs. 1994-96; named to Centennial Honor Roll, 2006). Office: Minn Hist Soc 345 Kellogg Blvd W Saint Paul MN 55102-1906 Office Phone: 651-296-6126.

ARCHER, DENNIS WAYNE, lawyer, former mayor; b. Detroit, Jan. 1, 1942; s. Ernest James and Frances (Carroll) A.; m. Trudy Ann DunCombe, June 17, 1967; children: Dennis Wayne, Vincent DunCombe BS, Western Mich. U., 1965; JD, Detroit Coll. Law, 1970; LLD (hon.), Western Mich. U., 1987, Detroit Coll. Law, 1988, U. Detroit, 1988, John Marshall Law Sch., 1991, Gonzaga U., 1991, U. Mich., 1994; D in Pub. Svc. (hon.), Ea. Mich. U., 1994; LLD (hon.), Aquinos Coll., 1996, Marygrove Coll., 1997, Hamline U., 2001, Wayne State U., 2002, U. Balt., 2002, Stetson U., 2003, Temple U., 2004, U. Conn., 2004. Bar: Mich. 1970. Tchr. spl. edn. Detroit Bd. Edn., 1965-70; assoc. Gragg & Gardner, 1970-71; ptnr. Hall, Stone, Allen, Archer & Glenn, P.C., 1971-73, Charfoos, Christensen & Archer, P.C., 1973-85; assoc. justice Mich. Supreme Ct., 1986-90; ptnr. Dickinson, Wright, Moon, Van Dusen & Freeman, Detroit, 1991-93; chmn. Dickinson Wright PLLC, 2001—, Detroit, 2002—; mayor City of Detroit, 1994—2001. Assoc. prof. Detroit Coll. Law, 1972-78; adj. prof. Wayne State U. Law Sch., Detroit, 1984-85; mem. Mich. Bd. Ethics, 1979-83; mem. adv. bd. U.S. Conf. Mayors, 1994—; bd. dirs. Nat. Conf. Black Mayors, 1994—; mem. intergovtl. policy adv. com. U.S. Trade Rep.; bd. dirs. Compuware, Johnson Controls, Inc. Contbr. articles to legal jours. Bd. dirs. Legal Aid and Defenders Assn., Detroit, 1980-82, Nat. Conf. Black Mayors, 1994, CATCH, Henry Ford Health Sys.; co-chmn. Met. Detroit Cmty. Coalition for Dems., 1979-80; bd. trustees Olivet Coll., 1991-93; active numerous local Dem. campaigns, 1970-85; host local pub. svc. radio programs; co-chair platform com. Dem. Conv., 1996; pres. at. Conf. Dem. Mayors, 1996; mem. Nat. Com. on Crime Control and Prevention, 1995. Named Most Respected Judge in Mich. Mich. Lawyers Weekly Jour., 1990. Mem. ABA (ho. dels. 1979-93, chmn. drafting com. 1986-88, com. on scope and correlation of work sect. officers liaison 1987-90, chmn. gen. practice sect. 1987-88, chair commn. on opportunities for minorities in the profession 1987-91, sect. legal edn. and admissions to the bar, coun. mem. 1989-95, task force on profl. skills instrn. 1989-91, task force on law schs. and the profession, Narrowing The Gap, 1989-91, chmn. spl. com. prepaid legal svcs. 1981-83, chmn. sect. officers conf. 1988-90, resource devel. coun. 1988-91, bd. editors ABA Jour. 1988-94, bd. editors The Practical Litigator 1989-94, chmn. rules and calendar com. 1990-92, state del. 1990-96, pres. 2003-2004), ATLA, Nat. Bar Assn. (pres. 1983-84), Am. Judicature Soc. (bd. dirs 1977-81), State Bar Mich. (pres. 1984-85), Wolverine Bar Assn. (pres. 1979-80), Detroit Bar Assn. (bd. dirs. 1973-75), Mich. Trial Lawyers Assn. (exec. bd. 1973-74), Econ. Club, Alpha Phi Alpha. Roman Catholic. Office: Dickinson Wright Ste 4000 500 Woodward Ave Detroit MI 48226-3425 Office Phone: 313-223-3500. Office Fax: 313-223-3598. Business E-Mail: darcher@dickinsonwright.com.

ARCHER, J(OHN) BARRY, municipal official; b. Ft. Jackson, SC, Mar. 21, 1946; BS in Civil Engring., Va. Mil. Inst., 1968; MA in Engring. Adminstrn., George Washington U., 1979; student, JFK Ctr. Spl. Warfare. Registered profl. engr.; cert. bldg. ofcl.; cert. profl. codes adminstr. Engr. trainee Va. Dept. of Transp.; project mgr. George Hyman Constrn. Co.; asst. city engr. Fairfax City, Va.; structural engr. Fairfax County, 1974-78; county bldg. ofcl., dep. dir. devel. adminstrn./pub. works Prince William County, Va., 1978-94; dir. dept. codes adminstrn. City of Kansas City, 1994—. Chmn. Manufactured Homes Constrn. and Safety Stds. Code Change Com.; mem. manufactured home adv. com. U.S. Dept. HUD. Mem. rev. bd. Va. State Tech. Maj. U.S. Army Green Berets, 1969-70, Vietnam. Decorated Bronze Star with 1 oak leaf cluster, Combat Infantrymans Badge, Master Parachutist Wings, Vietnamese Spl. Forces Parachutist Wings; named Local Ofcl. of Yr. Northeastern Region Nat. Assn. Home Builders, 1992, Codes Adminstr. of Yr. Gtr. Kansas City Automatic Sprinkler Contractors Assn., 1997; recipient Meritorius Svc. award Va. Bldg. and Code Ofcls. Assn., 1994. Mem. NSPE, Am. Concrete Inst. Internat., Mo. Assn. Code Adminstrs., Internat. Conf. Bldg. Ofcls., Mo. Assn. Bldg. Ofcls. and Insps. Spl. Forces Assn. (life), Spl. Ops. Assn., Vietnam Vets. Assn. Am., VFW. Office: City of Kansas City Codes Adminstrn Dept City Hall 18th Fl 414 E 12th St Kansas City MO 64106-2702 E-mail: archer@kcmo.org.

ARDINGER, ROBERT HALL, JR., physician, educator; b. Corona, Calif., Dec. 4, 1956; s. Robert Hall Sr. and Alice Marie (Schaal) A.; m. Holly Hutchison, Nov. 6, 1982; children: Andrew, Patrick. BS, Calif. State Polytech. U., 1979; MD, U. Calif., San Diego, 1983. Diplomate Am. Bd. Pediats. Intern U. Iowa, Iowa City, 1983-84, resident, 1984-86, fellow, 1986-89; instr. U. Rochester, N.Y., 1989-90; asst. prof. U. Kans., Kansas City, 1990-96, assoc. prof., 1996-2001, U. Mo., Kansas City, 2001—. Fellow Am. Acad. Pediats., Am. Coll. Cardiology. Office: Children's Mercy Hosp Cardiology 2401 Gillham Rd Kansas City MO 64108

ARENA, BRUCE, professional soccer coach; b. Bklyn., Sept. 21, 1951; m. Phyllis Arena; 1 child. Student, Nassau CC, NY, 1969-71; BS in Bus., Cornell U., 1973. Asst. lacrosse coach, asst. soccer coach Cornell U., Ithaca, NY, 1973-76; head soccer coach U. Puget Sound, Tacoma, 1976-78; head soccer coach, asst. men's lacrosse coach U. Va., Charlottesville, 1978-95; head coach DC United, Washington, 1995-98, US Nat. Soccer Team, Chgo., 1998—2006; sporting dir., head coach NY Red Bulls, 2006—07. Mem. U.S. nat. teams in both soccer and lacrosse and competed professionally in both sports; past chmn. ACC soccer coaches, ISAA Divsn. I nat. poll; "A" coaching lic. from U.S. Soccer Fedn.; mem. NCAA Divsn. I soccer com., 1989-95; head coach U.S. Olympic team 1996, U.S. World Cup Team 2002, 2006. Named ACC Coach of Yr., 1979, 84, 86, 88, 89, 91, South Atlantic Region Coach of Yr., 1982, 83, 87, nat. Coach of Yr. by Lanzera, 1993. Inducted into Cornell Athletic Field Hall of Fame, 1986, Long Island Lacrosse Hall of Fame, 1990. Named MLS Coach of Year, 1997. Achievements include career record of 295-58-32 (.808) in 18 yrs. at U. Va., leading U. Va. to NCAA titles in 1989, 91, 92, 93, 94, taking U. Va. to 6 of the last 7 NCAA semi-finals and 8 straight quarter finals, directing U. Va. to 15 straight NCAA tournament appearances (longest active streak in U.S.), Major League Soccer Cup Championships, 1996, 97, U.S. Open Cup Championship, 1996, World Cup quarterfinals 2002.

ARENDS, HERMAN JOSEPH, former insurance company executive; b. 1945; M of Math., Mich. State U., 1967. Tchr. Laningsburg (Mich.) H.S., 1967-72; chmn., CEO Auto-Owners Ins. Co., Lansing, Mich., 1972—2004. Office: Auto-Owners Insurance Co 6101 Anacapri Dr Lansing MI 48917-3994

ARENS, ALVIN ARMOND, accountant, educator; b. Marshall, Minn., Nov. 24, 1935; married, 3 children. BBA, U. Minn., 1960, M, 1967, PhD, 1970. CPA, Minn., 1963. Staff auditor Boulay, Anderson, Waldo & Co., Mpls., 1960-63, Ernst & Ernst, Mpls., 1963-64; lectr. U. Minn., Mpls., 1962-66; instr. Augsburg Coll., Mpls., 1966-67; asst. prof. Mich. State U., East Lansing, Mich., 1968-72, assoc. prof., 1972-77, acting dept. chmn. acctg., 1976-77, prof., 1977—, dir. acad. initiatives for Ctr. for Internat. Bus. Edn., 1990-91, Price Waterhouse Auditing prof., 1978—, chmn. dept. acctg., 1994—. Tchr. auditing to local grain officials in China, June, 1986; lectr. at Univs. in Beijing, Shanghai, Wuhan, Chengdu, China; Jackarta, Jojakarta, Indonesia; Singapore; Bangkok, Thailand; Kuala Lumpur, Malaysia, 1988; guest spkr. Young Accts. Meeting, Kolding, Denmark, 1989, Copenhagen, Denmark, 1991, U. Denmark, Aarhus and Kolding, 1989, Oslo Sch. of Bus., 1989; tchr. Norwegian Sch. of Econs. and Bus. Adminstrn., Bergen, Norway, 1989; guest spkr. Conv. of Nat. Changchi U. and Fedn. of CPAs in Republic of China, Tapei, Taiwan, June, 1991, at Erasmus U., Rotterdam, the Netherlands, 1992; mem. evaluation team bus. sch. United Arab Emirates U., Al Ain, 1989, 90, 92; mem. vis. team to Bus. Sch. DeLaSalle U., Manila, 1993; co-chair Price Waterhouse Auditing Conf., 1988, Auditing Symposium, San Francisco, 1993; seminar leader Arthur Anderson's Symposium, St. Charles, Ill., 1992, 94; mem. Nat. Assn. State Bds. of Accountancy, 1988-89, Auditing Standards Bd. Attestation Compliance Guidance Task Force, 1991-94, Going Concern Task Force, 1992-94, Agreed Upon Procedures Task Force, 1994; mem. acad. adv. bd. Deloitte & Touche, 1991-97. Author: Auditing (CPA Rev. Manual), 1972, Statistical Sampling for Small Audit Clients, 1974, Statistical Sampling: Attributes for Small Audit Clients, 1976, CPA Review Manual, 1979, The Use of Attributes Sampling for Small Audit Clients, 1982; co-author: (with James K. Loebbecke) Auditing: An Integrated Approach, 1976, 6th rev. edit., 1994 (also Canadian, French-Canadian, Singaporean, Australian and Russian versions), Applications of Statistical Sampling to Auditing, 1981; (with D. Dewey Ward) Systems Understanding Aids for Auditing and Financial Accounting, 4th edit., 1995, Systems Understanding Aid-Microcomputer Version, 1985, 3d edit. 1989, (with David S. Kerr) Integrated Audit Practice Case, 1993; contbr. articles to profl. jours and chpts. to books. With U.S. Army, 1955-57. Named Price Waterhouse Auditing Prof., 1978—, Alumnus of Yr., 1993, Beta Alpha Psi, U. Minn., 1993; fellow Arthur Young & Co., 1965, Price Waterhouse & Co, 1966, Ernst & Whinney Dissertation 1967-68; grantee: Ford Found., 1967. Mem. AICPA (mem. statistical sampling in auditing com. 1974-76, sole acad. mem. auditing standards bd. 1992-94, founding ptnr., mng. ptnr. AHI Assocs., 1975—, joint venture with AICPA, 1990—, Educator of Yr. 1993), Am. Acctg Assn. (numerous coms. and offices including pres. auditing sect. 1977-78, mem. exec. com. and sec.-treas. 1983-85, pres. elect 1989-90, pres. 1990-91, Disting. Internat. Visiting Lectr. 1987-88), Mich. Assn. Cert. Pub. Accts. (mem. com. on profl. edn. 1971-74, mandatory continuing edn. com. 1974-75, accounting and auditing com., and industry govt. edn. com. 1975-76, Outstanding Acctg. Educator award 1992, 93), Mich. Soc. Cert. Pub. Accts., Beta Alpha Psi (acct. of yr. award 1995). Office: Mich State U Eli Broad Coll Bus Dept Acctg East Lansing MI 48824-1121

ARLE, JOHN P., electronics executive; B, Colgate U., 1969; MBA, Harvard U., 1975. Various pos., including sr. analyst, dir. overseas fin. analysis, dir. employee benefit plans, dir. compensaion and benefit plans analysis GM Treas.'s Office, NYC, 1975—82; dir. fin. GM de Venezuela, Venezuela, 1982—86; v.p., CFO GM Hughes Electronics, 1986—88; gen. mgr., comptroller GM/Toyota NUMMI, Calif., 1988—92; v.p., fin. mgr. GM of Can., Ltd., 1992—93; v.p., CFO Saab Automobile AB, 1993—98; exec. dir. planning Delphi Corp., Troy, Mich., 1998, v.p. mergers, acquisitions and planning, 1998—2002, v.p. corp. audit svcs., 2002—. Office: World Hdqrs Adelphi Corp 5725 Delphi Dr Troy MI 28098-2815

ARMARIO, JOSE M., food products executive; b. Cuba, Apr. 22, 1959; m. Mary Armario; 3 children. MA in Profl. Mgmt., U. Miami. Joined McDonald's Corp., 1996, sr. v.p. & internat. rels. ptnr., group pres. McDonald's Can. & Latin Am., 2008—; pres. McDonald's Latin Am., 2003—08. Bd. dirs. Internat. Adv. Bd., Mex. C. of C, Pres. Coun. U. Miami, Chgo. Coun. Global Affairs. Office: McDonalds Corp McDonalds Plaza Oak Brook IL 60523*

ARMBRUSTER, BOB, radio personality; b. Louisiana, Mo. m. Trila Fugman. BA, Principia Coll.; MA, Lindenwood U. Announcer, traffic manager Classic 99, St. Louis. Avocation: kite flying. Office: Classic 99 85 Founders Ln Saint Louis MO 63105

ARMBRUSTER, JEFFRY J., state legislator; b. Normal, OH, Aug. 30, 1947; BS, Milliken U., 1969. Mayor North Ridgeville (OH); pres. Pinzone-Armbruster, Inc.; mem. Ohio Senate from 13th dist., Columbus, 1999—, North Ridgeville City Coun. Mem. Westlake C. of C., North Ridgeville C. of C., Greater Cleveland Growth Assn. (COSE). Recipient Shell Inner Cir. of Success. Mem. OH Assn. Retail Mchts., Loraine County Farm Bur. Office: Senate Bldg 13th Dist State House Room 142 1st Fl Columbus OH 43215

ARMES, ROY V., manufacturing executive; married; 2 children. BSME, U. Toledo. Mgmt. positions Whirlpool Corp., 1975—2006; corp. v.p., gen. dir. Whirlpool Mexico; pres., mng. dir. Whirlpool Greater China; corp. v.p., global procurement ops. Whirlpool Corp., sr. v.p., project mgmt.; pres., CEO Cooper Tire & Rubber Co., Findlay, Ohio, 2007—. Office: Cooper Tire & Rubber Co 701 Lima Ave Findlay OH 45840 Office Phone: 419-423-1321. Office Fax: 419-424-4108. E-mail: cooperinfo@coopertire.com.

ARMITAGE, JAMES O., medical educator; b. LA, Dec. 19, 1946; m. Nancy Elaine Roker, Aug. 12, 1967; children: Amy Jolane, Gregory Olen, Anne Marie, Joel Donald. BS, U. Nebr., Lincoln, 1969; MD, U. Nebr., Omaha, 1973. Diplomate in internal medicine, med. oncology and hematology Am. Bd. Internal Medicine. Med. intern U. ebr. Med. Ctr., Omaha, 1973-74, resident in internal medicine, 1974-75; fellow hematology/oncology U. Iowa Hosps. and Clinics, Iowa City, 1975-77; clin. asst. prof. medicine U. Nebr. Coll. Medicine, Omaha, 1977-79, assoc. prof., 1982-87, vice chmn. dept. internal medicine, 1982-90; from assoc. prof. to Joe Shapiro prof. internal medicine Epley Inst. for Rsch. in Cancer and Allied Diseases, Omaha, 1985—; chief sect. oncology/hematology U. Nebr. Coll. Medicine, Omaha, 1986-89, prof. internal medicine, 1987—, chmn. dept. internal medicine, 1990-99, dean, 2000—03; pvt. practice hematology/oncology Omaha, 1977-79. Contbr. articles to profl. jours. Recipient Sir William Osler Teaching award, 1988, Arnold Ungerman-Robert Lubin Cancer Rsch. award, 1993, Richard and Hinda Rosenthal Found. award, 1996, numerous others. Fellow ACP, Am. Assn. Cancer Rsch., Am. Soc. Blood and Marrow Transplantation, Am. Soc. Clin. Oncology, Am. Soc. Hematology, Am. Fedn. for Clin. Rsch., Assn. Profs. Medicine, Ctrl. Soc. for Clin. Rsch., European Soc. Med. Oncology, Internat. Soc. Exptl. Hematology, Nebr. Med. Assn., Met. Omaha Med. Soc., Midwest Blood Club, Royal Coll. Physicians Edinburgh, Internat. Soc. for Hematotherapy and Graft Engring., European Hematology Soc., Phi Beta Kappa, Sigma Xi, Alpha Omega Alpha, others. Office: U Nebr Med Ctr Dept Internal Medicine 987680 Nebr Med Ctr Omaha NE 68198-0001

ARMITAGE, KENNETH BARCLAY, retired biology professor; b. Steubenville, Ohio, Apr. 18, 1925; s. Albert Kenneth and Virginia Ethel (Barclay) A.; m. Katie Lou Hart, June 5, 1953; children: Karole, Keith, Kevin BS summa cum laude, Bethany Coll., W.Va., 1949; MS, U. Wis.-Madison, 1951, PhD, 1954. Instr. U. Wis.-Green Bay, 1954-55; instr. U. Wis.-Wausau, 1955-56; asst. prof. biology U. Kans., Lawrence, 1956-62, assoc. prof., 1962-66, prof., 1966-96, William J. Baumgartner disting. prof., 1987-96, chmn. dept. systematics & ecology, 1982-88, dir. environ. studies program, 1976-82, dir. exptl. and applied ecology program, 1974-94, prof. emeritus, 1996—. Vis. prof. U. Modena, Italy, 1989; mem. com. examiners Grad. Record Exam. Biology Test, 1986—92, chmn., 1988—92; sr. investigator Rocky Mountain Biol. Lab, Gothic, Colo., 1962—2004, trustee, 1969—86, pres. bd. trustees, 1985—86; cons. Vancouver Island Marmot Recovery Program; vis. rschr. Queen Mary Coll., London, 1972—73. Author: (lab. manual) Investigations in General Biology, (with others) Principles of Modern Biology; contbr. articles to profl. jours.; co-editor: Holarctic Marmots as a Factor of Biodiversity, 3d Internat. Marmot Conf. proceedings; mem. editl. bd.: Ethology, Ecology and Evolution, 1989—, Ibex Jour. Mountain Ecology, 1994—, Oecologia Montana, 1996—; sci. editor: Die Murmeltiere der Welt. Pres. Douglas County chpt. Zero Population Growth, 1969-71; bd. dirs. Children's Hour, Inc., Lawrence, 1969-70; v.p. Hist. Mt. Oread, Lawrence, 1998-2004, pres., 2004—. Recipient Antarctic medal NSF, 1968, Edn. Service award U. Kans., 1979, Alumni Achievement award Bethany Coll., 1989; Knapp House fellow U. Wis., Madison, 1952-53, NSF fellow, 1952-53, 58. Fellow AAAS, Animal Behavior Soc.; mem. Am. Soc. Naturalists (treas. 1984-86), Am. Inst. Biol. Scis. (mem. task force for 90s), Ecol. Soc. Am., Am. Soc. Zoologists, Am. Soc. Mammalogists (C. Hart Merriam award 1997), Orgn. Biol. Field Stations (v.p. 1986-87, pres. 1988-89), Sigma Xi, Phi Beta Kappa, Beta Beta Beta, Gamma Sigma Kappa. Avocations: stamp collecting/philately, gardening, natural history, western history. Home: 505 Ohio St Lawrence KS 66044-2245 Office: U Kans Dept Ecology & Evolutionary Biology Lawrence KS 66045-7534 Home Phone: 785-841-3303; Office Phone: 785-864-3236. E-mail: marmots@ku.edu.

ARMITAGE, ROBERT ALLEN, lawyer, pharmaceutical executive; b. Port Huron, Mich., June 16, 1948; s. George Robert and Deloris Alene (Fitz) A.; m. Deborah Ann Wismer, Dec. 29, 1973; children: Aimee Elizabeth, Emily Ann. BA with highest honors, Albion Coll., Mich., 1970; MS in Physics, U. Mich., 1971, JD with honors, 1973. Bar: Mich. 1974, US Ct. Appeals (fed. cir.) 1983, US Supreme Ct. 1993, DC 1994. Patent atty. The Upjohn Co., Kalamazoo, 1974-78, mgr. patent law dept., 1979-83, patent counsel, exec. dir. patent law, 1983—87, v.p. corp. patents and trademarks, 1987—93, asst. sec., 1988—93; ptnr. Vinson & Elkins, LLP, Washington, 1993—99; v.p., gen. patent counsel Lilly Rsch. Labs., 1999—2003; sr. v.p., gen. counsel Eli Lilly and Co., 2003—. Past bd. dirs. Human Genome Scis. Inc. Pres. Hospice of Kalamazoo, 1985-87. Fellow Woodrow Wilson Nat. Fellowship Found., Princeton, NJ, 1971. Mem. Mich. Bar Assn. (chair intellectual property law sect. 1986), Am. Intellectual Property Law Assn. (pres. 1994), Intellectual Property Owners Inc. (bd. dirs. 1985-93), Assn. Corp. Patent Counsel (pres. 1993), Phi Beta Kappa. Office: Eli Lilly and Co Lilly Corp Ctr Indianapolis IN 46285 Office Phone: 317-276-2000.

ARMITAGE, THOMAS EDWARD, library director; b. Torrington, Wyo., Dec. 11, 1946; s. Ross Eugene Armitage and Mary Kathleen (Donley) Wieland; m. Linda Lou Theisen, May 23, 1987; children: Anne, Nicholas, Rachel. AA in History, Santa Ana CC, Calif., 1971; BA in History, Kans. State U., Pittsburg, 1973; MLS, U. Mo., 1974. Asst. dir. Ottumwa (Iowa) Pub. Libr., 1975-77; libr. dir. Ft. Dodge (Iowa) Pub. Libr., 1977-86, Cedar Rapids (Iowa) Pub. Libr., 1987—. With USN, 1967-69. Mem. ALA, Iowa Libr. Assn., Iowa Urban Pub. Libr. Assn. (pres. 1999—, sec. 1995-98), Linn County Libr. Assn. (v.p. 1993—), Linn County Libr. Consortium (sec. 1995—), Rotary, Greater Cedar Rapids C. of C. Office: Cedar Rapids Pub Libr 500 1st St SE Cedar Rapids IA 52401-2002 Home Phone: 319-393-0675; Office Phone: 319-739-0401. E-mail: armitage@mail.crlibrary.org.

ARMSTRONG, DANIEL WAYNE, chemist, educator; b. Ft. Wayne, Ind., Nov. 2, 1949; s. Robert Eugene and Nila Louise (Koeneman) A.; m. Linda Marilyn Todd, June 11, 1972; children: Lincoln Thomas, Ross Alexander, Colleen Victoria. BS, Washington and Lee U., 1972; MS in Chem. Oceanography, Tex. A&M U., 1974, PhD in Chemistry, 1977. Prof. Bowdoin Coll., Brunswick, Maine, 1978-79, Georgetown U., Washington, 1980-83, Tex. Tech. U., Lubbock, 1983-87; Curators' disting. prof., head ctr. environ. sci. and tech.; head dept. analytical chemistry U. Mo., Rolla, 1987-2000; Caldwell prof. chemistry Iowa State U., 2000—06; Robert A. Welch prof. chemistry and biochemistry U. Tex., Arlington, Tex., 2006—. Bd dirs. Advanced Separations Techs., Whippany, NJ; Moreton lectr. Millsaps Coll., 2001, R.A. Welch lectr., 2002, Dow lectr., 2003; lectr. Columbia U., 2003. Host Univ. Forum Radio Show, Washington, 1981-83; writer, host weekly radio show We're Sci. Nat. Pub. Radio, 1993—; author film, radio shows; contbr. articles to profl. jours. Recipient Tchg. Excellence award U. Mo., 1985, 88-89, 92, 94, Faculty Excellence award U. Mo., 1988-89, Martin medal, 1991, EAS Chromatography award, 1990, Isco award, 1992, Presdl. award, 1993, Perkin Elmer award, 1994, R&D 100 award R&D Mag., 1995, Benedetti-Pichler award Am. Microchem. Soc. 1996, Helen M. Free award, 1998, CLDG Merit award, 2001, Weber medal, 2001, Kenneth A. Spencer award for agr. and food chemistry, 2002, Chirality medal, 2003, Dal Nogre award for separation sci., 2005. Slovak Med. Soc. medal. 2007; named Disting. Scholar Hope Coll., 1999; grantee Rsch. Corp., 1979, Petroleum Rsch. Fund, 1979, 91, NSF, 1981; Rsch. grantee Whatman Corp., 1981, Dept. Energy, 1984, 87, 91, 94, Dow Chem., 1985-90, NIH, 1986, 91, 95, 2000, 03, 05, EPA, 1995, Shell Co., 1989-92. Fellow Am. Assn. Pharm. Scientists; mem. Am. Chem. Soc. (49th Midwest award for chemistry 1993, award in chromatography 1999), Slovak Pharm. Soc. (hon., Vladimir J. Zuffu medal 2004), Sigma Xi, Phi Lambda Upsilon. Achievements include patents in field. Office: Iowa State U Dept Chemistry Gilman Hall Ames IA 50011 Business E-Mail: sec4dwa@iastate.edu.

ARMSTRONG, DOUGLAS DEAN, journalist; b. Wichita, Kans., Mar. 12, 1945; s. H. Glenn and Emma F. (Starkey) A.; m. Paige Prillaman, Jan. 3, 1967 (div. Sept. 1982); children: David Douglas, Christine Elizabeth; m. Mary Alyce Dooley, Mar. 8, 1987; children: Patrick Glenn, Gillian Marie. BA, U. Minn., 1967. Entertainment writer Milw. Jour. Sentinel, 1967-72, editl. writer, 1972-74, consumer writer, 1974-81, movie critic, 1981-95, bus. writer, 1995-2000, personal fin. columnist, 1995-2000. Guest lectr. U. Wis., Milw., 1982-89; movie reviewer WISN-TV, Milw., 1984-85; movie critic WKTI-FM, Milw., 1989-97; pres. Lexington Software Corp., 1996—2003; mem. faculty studies com. Whitefish Bay Schs. Contbr. short fiction to Ellery Queen's Mystery Mag., Alfred Hitchcock's Mystery Mag., Boys' Life. Recipient Pub. Interest award Ctr. for Pub. Representation, 1978. Mem. Mystery Writers Am., Allied Authors, Coun. Wis. Writers, Milw. Press Club. Avocations: video, piano, golf. E-mail: doug@douglasarmstrong.com.

ARMSTRONG, EDWIN RICHARD, lawyer; b. Chgo., Sept. 25, 1921; BA, Knox Coll., 1942; JD, Northwestern U., 1948. Ptnr. Reimers & Armstrong, 1949-55; assoc. Friedman & Friedman, 1957-62; ptnr. Friedman, Armstrong & Donnelly, 1962-78, Armstrong & Donnelly, Chgo., 1978—. Home: 860 N Lake Shore Dr Apt 17M Chicago IL 60611-1788 Office: 77 W Washington St Ste 515 Chicago IL 60602-2802 Office Phone: 312-372-3215.

ARMSTRONG, J. HORD, III, pharmaceutical company executive; Chmn. bd., CEO D&K Healthcare Resources, Inc., Saint Louis, 1993—. Office: D&K Healthcare Resources Inc PO Box 16989 Saint Louis MO 63105-1389

ARMSTRONG, NEIL ALDEN, retired astronaut; b. Wapakoneta, Ohio, Aug. 5, 1930; s. Stephen A.; children: Eric, Mark. BS In Aero. Engring., Purdue U., 1955; MS in Aero. Engring., U. So. Calif. With Lewis Flight Propulsion Lab., NACA, 1955; then aero. research pilot for NACA (later NASA, High Speed Flight Sta.), Edwards, Calif.; astronaut Manned Spacecraft Center, NASA, Houston, 1962-70; command pilot Gemini 8; comdr. Apollo 11; dep. assoc. adminstr. for aeros. Office Advanced Research and Tech., Hdqrs. NASA, Washington, 1970-71; prof. aerospace engring. U. Cin., 1971-79; chmn. AIL Sys., Inc., 1989-2000, EDO Corp., 2000—02. Mem. Pres.'s Commn. on Space Shuttle, 1986, Nat. Commn. on Space, 1985-86. Served as naval aviator USN, 1949-52, Korea. Recipient numerous awards, including Octave Chanute award Inst. Aero. Scis., 1962, Presdl. Medal for Freedom, 1969, Exceptional Service medal NASA, Hubbard Gold medal Nat. Geog. Soc., 1970, Kitty Hawk Meml. award, 1969, Pere Marquette medal, 1969, Arthur S. Fleming award, 1970, Congl. Space Medal of Honor, Explorers Club medal. Fellow AIAA (hon., Astronautics award 1966), Internat. Astronautical Fedn. (hon.), Soc. Exptl. Test Pilots; mem. Nat. Acad. Engring. Achievements include being the first man to walk on the Moon, July 20, 1969. Office: Edo Corporation 60 E 42nd St New York NY 10165-0006

ARMSTRONG, THEODORE MORELOCK, corporate financial executive; b. St. Louis, July 22, 1939; s. Theodore Roosevelt and Vassar Fambrough (Morelock) A.; m. Carol Mercer Robert, Sept. 7, 1963 (div. 2006); children: Evelyn Anne, Robert Theodore; m. Kathryn Sibbald, Apr. 27, 2007. BA, Yale U., New Haven, Conn., 1961; LLB, Duke U., Durham, NC, 1964. Bar: Mo. 1964. With Miss. River Transmission Corp. and affiliated cos., 1964-85; corp. sec. Mo. Pacific Corp., 1971-75, River Cement Co., 1968-75; asst. v.p. Miss. River Transmission Corp., 1974-75, v.p. gas supply, 1975-79, exec. v.p., 1979-83, pres., chief exec. officer, 1983-85; exec. v.p. Natural Gas Pipeline of Am., 1985; sr. v.p. fin. and adminstrn., CFO Angelica Corp., St. Louis, 1986—2004; pvt. practice fin. cons. St. Louis, 2004—. Bd. dirs. UMB Fin. Corp., Custom Cuts,

Inc., Cabela's, Inc., World's Foremost Bank. Bd. dirs., past pres. Boys and Girls Town Mo.; past pres. Tenn. Soc. St. Louis; mem. St. Louis County Boundary Commn.; former alderman, former mem. bd. adjustment City of Frontenac; bd. dirs., pres. Ctrl. Inst. Deaf; mem. fin. com. City of Creve Coeur. Mem. Mo. Bar Assn., Bellerive Country Club (treas., bd. dirs.), Saint Louis Club (past pres. bd. dirs.), Yale Club (St. Louis, NYC), Phi Alpha Delta. Republican. Presbyterian. Office: 7730 Carondelet Ste 103 Saint Louis MO 63105 Home: 424 Twin Creek Rd Saint Louis MO 63141 Office Phone: 314-862-4224. Personal E-mail: tmarmstrong@sbcglobal.net.

ARNOLD, ALLEN D., academic administrator; b. Lebanon, Pa., Apr. 4, 1943; s. Henry J. and Mary (Heisey) A.; m. Judith Moreland, Aug. 1, 1970; children: Caroline, David. BA in English and Philosophy, U. Scranton, 1965; MA in English, Vanderbilt U., 1971; EdD, Va. Poly. Inst. and State U., 1980. Instr. English Lebanon Valley Coll., Annville, Pa., 1967-68, Cath. U. Puerto Rico, Ponce, 1969-71; assoc. prof. English Dabney Lancaster Community Coll., Clifton Forge, Va., 1973-77, asst. chmn. devel. studies, dir. spl. svcs., 1977-79, div. chair humanities and sponsored programs, 1979-83; dir. humanities div. Lakeland Community Coll., Mentor, Ohio, 1983-85, dean, 1986-87; v.p. acad. affairs Triton Coll., River Grove, Ill., 1987-88, exec. v.p., 1988-95; pres., dean Charles S. Mott C.C., Flint, Mich., 1995—. Editor: New Directions for Community Colleges: Alternative Funding Sources, 1989, (newsletter) Fusions, 1989-90. Bd. dirs. Oak Park (Ill.) Housing Ctr., 1989-90. Mem. Rotary. Office: Charles S Mott CC 1401 E Court St Flint MI 48503-6208

ARNOLD, GARY L., retail executive; b. Ft. Wayne, Ind. married; 5 children. Mgr. mktg. svcs. firm; various positions Hollywood Records, Trans World Music Corp., Disc Records; merchandise mgr. music Best Buy Co., 1994-96, v.p. mktg., 1996—2001; pres. Redline Entertainment, 2001—. Avocations: cooking, gardening.

ARNOLD, JEROME GILBERT, lawyer; s. Edward F. and Annastacia (Thielen) A.; m. Judith Lindor, Dec. 18, 1971; children: Thomas, Mark, John, Jason, Maria. BS, U. Minn., 1964; LLB, U. N.D., 1967. Bar: Minn. 1967, S.D. 1967, U.S. Dist. Ct. S.D. 1967, U.S. Dist. Ct. Minn. 1973, U.S. Ct. Appeals (8th cir.) 1986. Law clk. U.S. Dist. Ct., Aberdeen, SD, 1967-68; asst. city atty. City of Duluth, Minn., 1968-69; asst. county atty. St. Louis County, Duluth, 1969-70, chief criminal prosecutor, 1970-71; spl. asst. to county atty. County of Carlton, Minn., 1971; ptnr. Hunt & Arnold, Duluth, Minn., 1971—86; U.S. atty. U.S. Dist. Ct. Minn., Mpls., 1986—91; ptnr. Larson, Husby, Brodin & Arnold, Duluth, 1992—93; compensation judge State of Minn., Duluth, 1993—2004, 2005—; mem. Falsani, Balmer, Peterson, Quinn and Beyer, Duluth, Minn., 2004—05; compensation judge State of Minn., 2005—. Mem. adv. com. Supreme Ct. Appointments, St. Paul, 1980; chmn. selection com. 6th Jud. Dist., Duluth, 1978-83. Chmn. St. Louis City (Minn.) Bd. Adjustment, 1978-82; Rep. nominee 8th Congl. Dist, Minn., 1974; mem. state steering com. Reagan for Pres., 1976, 80, 84. Mem. Fed. Bar Assn. (bd. dirs. 1986-91), Minn. Bar Assn., Minn. Trial Lawyers Assn. Roman Catholic. Avocations: fishing, hunting. Office Fax: 218-723-1931.

ARNOLD, JOHN FOX, lawyer; b. St. Louis, Sept. 17, 1937; s. John Anderson and Mildred Chapin (Fox) Arnold; m. Martha Ann Freeman, June 29, 1963 (div. Oct. 1993); children: Lisa A. Galena, Laura Wray, Lynne A. Binder, Lesli Johnston; m. Ann Ruwitch, Mar. 3, 2003. AB, U. Mo., Columbia, 1959, LLB, 1961. Bar: Mo. 1961, US Dist. Ct. (ea. dist.) Mo. 1961, US Ct. Appeals (8th cir.) 1961, US Supreme Ct. 1971. Ptnr. Green, Hennings, Henry & Arnold, St. Louis, 1963-70; mem. Lashly & Baer, P.C., St. Louis, 1970—, chmn., 1987—. Mem. St. Louis County Charter Revision Com., 1968, Mo. State Governance Rev. Com., 2005; chmn. St. Louis County Bd. Election Commrs., 1981—86; chmn. bd. dirs. Downtown St. Louis Inc., 1996—98, Downtown St. Louis Partnership, Inc., 1997—99; chmn. bd. overseers Lindenwood U., 1992—93, bd. dir., 1993—95. Lt. USAR, 1961—63. Recipient citation of merit U. Mo. Law Sch., Columbia, 1984, Mo. Bar Pres.'s award, 2005, Best Lawyers in Am., 2005, 06, 07, 08, Found. award St. Louis Bar Found., 2006. Fellow Am. Bar Found.; mem. ABA (mem. house of dels. 1986-90), Bar Assn. Met. St. Louis (pres. 1975-76), Mo. Bar (pres. 1984-85), Nat. Conf. Commrs. on Uniform State Laws (life, drafting com. Securities Act, Partnership Act, article 2 sales, 2A leases and 8 investment securities of Uniform Comml. Code), Am. Law Inst. (life). Republican. Office: Lashly & Baer 714 Locust St Saint Louis MO 63101-1699 Office Phone: 314-621-2939. Business E-Mail: jfarnold@lashlybaer.com.

ARNOLD, NEAL E., corporate financial executive; BA, MBA, U. ND. CFO First Nat. Bank N.D., Grand Forks, 1980—90; treas. divsn. Fifth Third Bancorp., Cin., 1990—98, CFO, exec. v.p., 1998—. Office: Fifth Third Bancorp Fifth Third Ctr 38 Fountain Square Plaza Cincinnati OH 45263

ARNOLD, PERI ETHAN, political scientist; b. Chgo., Sept. 21, 1942; s. Joseph Evon and Eve (Jacobs) A.; m. Beverly Ann Kessler, Aug. 22, 1965; children: Emma, Rachel. BA, Roosevelt U., Chgo., 1964; MA, U. Chgo., 1967, PhD, 1972. Lectr. Roosevelt U., Chgo., 1966-68; instr. polit. sci. Western Mich. U., Kalamazoo, 1970-71; asst. prof. polit. sci. U. Notre Dame, Ind., 1971-76, assoc. prof. govt. Ind., 1976-86, prof. of govt. and internat. studies Ind., 1986; chair dept. govt., 1986-92. Compton vis. prof. of world politics Miller Ctr., U. Va., 1993-94; dir. Hesburgh Program in Pub. Svc., 1995-2001; dir. Notre Dame Semester in Washington, 1997-2001. Author: Making the Managerial Presidency, 1986 (Louis Brownlow Book award 1987), 2nd rev. ed., 1998; mem. editl. bd. Am. Jour. Polit. Sci., 1991-94, Polity, 1995—2004, Presdl. Studies Quar., 1997—2005; co-editor Jour. of Policy History, 1987-88; mem. editl. adv. bd. Hughes Leadership Series, Tex. A&M U. Press, 1999—; contbr. articles to profl. jours. and edited vols. Bd. dirs. South Bend Hebrew Day Sch., Mishawaka, Ind., 1985—88; chair Cmty. Rels. Coun. of Jewish Fedn. of St. Joseph Valley, South Bend, Ind., 1990—94; mem. acquisitions com. Snite Mus. Art, Notre Dame, Ind., 1994—99; mem. adv. com. Coll. Arts and Scis., Roosevelt U., 2006; trustee Congregation Beth El, South Bend, 1994—2000, sec., exec. com., 2000—02; bd. dirs. Jewish Fedn. of St. Joseph Valley, 1999—2002, v.p., 2001—03. Recipient Spl. Presdl. award U. Notre Dame, 1993, Marshall Dimock award Am. Soc. Pub. Adminstrn., 1996; grantee Am. Coun. Learned Socs., 1974; rsch. grantee Herbert Hoover Libr. Assn., 1993-94; Ford Found. fellow, 1978-81. Fellow Nat. Acad. Pub. Adminstrn.; mem. Am. Polit. Sci. Assn. (program chmn., exec. com. presidency sect.), Midwest Polit. Sci. Assn., The Cliff Dwellers Club (Chgo.). Democrat. Jewish. Avocations: literature, music, drama. Home: 1419 E Colfax Ave South Bend IN 46617-3307 Office: U Notre Dame Dept Polit Sci otre Dame IN 46556 Home Phone: 574-233-9535; Office Phone: 574-631-7430. Business E-Mail: peri.e.arnold.1@nd.edu.

ARNOLD, RICHARD, state official; b. Russell, Iowa, Feb. 9, 1945; m. Cheryl Arnold. Student, Iowa State U. Mem.: Iowa Cattlemen's Assn., Farm Bur., Pheasants Forever, Ducks Unltd. Republican. Office: State Capitol E 12th and Grand Des Moines IA 50319

ARNOLD, SUSAN E., consumer products company executive; b. Pitts., Mar. 8, 1954; 2 children. BA, U. Pa., 1976; MBA, U. Pitts., 1980. Joined Procter & Gamble Co., Cin., 1980, brand asst., Dawn/Ivory Snow, 1980, sales tng. Phila., 1981, asst. brand mgr., Oxydol Cin., 1981—83, asst. brand mgr., Cascade, 1983—84, brand mgr., Gain/Spl. Assignment, 1984—85, brand mgr., Tide Sheets, 1985—86, brand mgr., Dawn, 1986—87, assoc. advertising mgr., PS& D Advertising, 1987, assoc. advertising mgr., laundry products, PS&D Divsn., 1987—88, assoc. advertising mgr., laundry specialty products, PS&D Divsn., 1988—89, advertising mgr., fabric softeners, BS&HCP Divsn., 1989—90, mgr., Noxell Products, Internat. Divsn. Canada, 1990—92, gen. mgr., deodorants/Old Spice (U.S.A.), 1993—96; v.p., gen. mgr., deodorants/Old Spice and Skin Products-US Procter & Gamble Co. N.Am., 1997—97, v.p., gen. mgr., laundry products-US, 1997—99; v.p., N.Am. Fabric Care Procter & Gamble Co., Cin., 1999, pres., global skin care, 1999—2000, pres., global cosmetics & skin care, 2000, pres., personal beauty care, 2000—02, pres., global personal beauty care & global feminine care, 2002—04, vice chmn. global beauty care, 2004—, vice-chmn., beauty & health (oral care, personal health and pharm. businesses), 2006—07, pres. global bus. units, 2007—. Bd. dir. Reflect.com, Cin. Zoo, Walt Disney Co., 2007—, Goodyear Tire & Rubber Co., 2003—05. Named Top Marketer and One of the 21 to Watch in the 21st Century, Advt. Age, Career Woman of Achievement, YWCA, 2000; named one of 50 Most Powerful Women in Bus., Fortune mag., 2002—, 50 Women to Watch, Wall Street Jour., 2004, 2005, 100 Most Powerful Women, Forbes Mag., 2006—07, 50 Most Powerful Women in Bus., Fortune mag., 2006; recipient Best Boss award, Cosmetic Exec. Women, 2003. Achievements include first women to reach a president-level position at Procter & Gamble Co; first women to be named to the vice chairman position at Procter & Gamble Co. Avocation: surfing. Office: Procter & Gamble Co 1 Procter & Gamble Plz Cincinnati OH 45202

ARNOLD, VALERIE DOWNING, lawyer; b. Istanbul, Turkey, Jan. 6, 1967; BA in French, U. Minn., 1988; student, Universite de Savoir, Chambery, France, 1990; MA in French, U. Minn., 1992, JD, 1997. Bar: Minn. 1997, US Dist. Ct. (dist. Minn.) 2004. Shareholder Tuft & Arnold, P.L.L.C., Maplewood, Minn. Named a Rising Star, Minn. Super Lawyers mag., 2006. Mem.: Warren E. Burger Inn of Ct., Minn. Women Lawyers, Ramsey County Bar Assn., Minn. State Bar Assn. Office: Tuft & Arnold PLLC 2109 County Rd D East Ste A Saint Paul MN 55109 Office Phone: 651-771-0050. E-mail: val@tuftarnoldlaw.com.

ARNOULD, RICHARD JULIUS, economist, educator, consultant, dean; b. Rochelle, Ill., Nov. 18, 1941; s. Elliott and Blanch (Colwell) A.; m. Carol Foster, Aug. 27, 1960; children: Debra, Laura. BS, Iowa State U., 1963, MS, 1965, PhD, 1968. Instr. Iowa State U., Ames, 1963-65; asst. prof. econs. and bus. adminstrn. U. Ill., Champaign, 1967-72, assoc. prof., 1973-82, prof., 1982—2003, prof. emeritus, 2003—, dir. Coll. Rsch. Office, 1995-96, assoc. dean for acad. affairs, Coll. Commerce and Bus. Adminstrn., 1979-87, prof. econs., Coll. Medicine, 1984—, adj. prof. Inst. of Govt. and Pub. Affairs, 1987—, dir. Program in Health Econs., Mgmt. & Policy, 1989—, head dept. econs., 1996—2003; exec. dir. Am. Soc. Health Economists, 2003—. Acting dir. Exec. Devel. Ctr., part-time 1982, 84, mem. Med. Scholars Steering Com., active numerous other univ., coll. and dept. coms.; rsch. economist pricing and competition grp., USDA, 1965-67; vice chmn. Dept. Econs., U. Ill., 1970-73; vis. economist Econ. Policy Office, U.S. Justice Dept., 1973-74; regional economist U.S. Comptroller of Currency, 1976-79; vis. rsch. prof. Duke U., 1977-78; vis. rsch. scholar York (Eng.) U.; cons. Carle Found., chmn. bd., 1989-91; mem. Gov's. Task Force on Health Care Reform, 1992-95; cons. Auditor Gen. State of Ill., GAO, Health Care Financing Adminstrn., Anti-trust div. U.S. Justice Dept., ABA, AMA, Prepaid Legal Svcs. Inst., others; bd. dirs. First Busey Trust & Investment Co.; expert witness numerous law firms; speaker profl. meetings. Author: Extra Territorial Application and Effects of Certain U.S. and Canadian Laws, 1978, (monograph) Blue Shield Fee Setting in the Physicians' Service Market: A Theoretical and Empirical Analysis, (pamphlets) Diversification and Profitability Among Large Food Processing Firms, USDA, 1970, (with R. Resek) A Comparative Cost Study of Staff Panel and Participating Attorney Panel Prepaid Legal Servcie Plans, ABA, 1982; editor spl. issue Quar. Rev. of Econs. and Bus., 1990, also book chpts. and revs.; co-editor: (with R. Rich and W. White) Competitive Approaches to Health Care Reform, 1993; contbr. numerous articles to profl. jours. Bd. dirs. City Bank Champaign, First Basey Trust and Investment Co.; trustee Carle Found., 1981-93, chmn. fin. com., 1982-86, chmn. bd., 1989-91; elder 1st Presbyn. Ch., Champaign; mem. Gov.'s Task Force on Health Care Reform; mem. U.S. Govt. Study of Econ. Underpinning of Vaccine Markets. Brookings Inst. Econ. Policy fellow, 1973; recipient Outstanding Service award, U.S. Justice Dept., 1974; grantee Internat. Bur. Edn., 1979, Carle Found., 1982-83, Grad. Research Bd., 1983-86; named Outstanding Tchr. U. Ill. various yrs. Mem. Am. Econ. Assn., So. Econ. Assn., Internat. Health Econs. Assn., Midwest Econ. Assn. Avocation: golf. Office: U Ill 1206 S 6th St Champaign IL 61820-6978 Business E-Mail: rarnould@uiuc.edu.

ARNOVE, ROBERT FREDERICK, education educator; b. Chgo. s. Isadore and Julie (Zeplowitz) A.; m. Toby Strout; 1 child, Anthony Keats BA, U. Mich., 1969; MA, Tufts U., 1961; PhD, Stanford U., 1969. Vol. tchr. Peace Corps, Venezuela, 1962-64; Ford Found. edn. advisor Bogota, Colombia, 1969-71; prof. comparative edn. Ind. U., Bloomington, 1969—, Ind. U.-Hangzhou, People's Rep. China, 1983; vis. prof. Stanford U., McGill U. Edn. cons. to Latin Am. ministries and agys.; dir. Overseas Study Program of Ind., Purdue, and Wis. univs. in Madrid, 1989—; USIA Exch. scholar, Ryazan, Russia, 1996, Yaounde, Cameroon, 1997, Salamanca, Spain, 2001; UNESCO-chair vis. scholar U. Palermo, Buenos Aires, 1997-2002; adv. prof. Hong Kong Inst. Edn. Author, editor, co-editor: Student Alienation, Educational Television, Education and American Culture Comparative Education, Philanthropy and Cultural Imperialism, Education and Revolution in icaragua, National Literacy Campaign: Historical and Comparative Perspectives, Emergent Issues in Education: Comparative Perspectives, Education as Contested Terrain: Nicaragua 1979-93, 1994, Comparative education: The Dialectic of the Global and the Local, 1999, 07, Civil Society or Shadow State: State NGO Education Relations, 2004; prodr. (documentary) Alternative Public Schools, 1978, Asi Fue: Election Time Nicaragua, 1984; contbr. articles to profl. jours. Citizens Party candidate for U.S. Congress, 8th dist. Ind., 1982 Fulbright grantee, India, 1982; Fulbright lectr. Fed. U. Bahai, Brazil, 1995; Fulbright sr. scholar U. Iberoamericana, Dominican Republic, 2003. Mem. Comparative and Internat. Edn. Soc. (pres. 2001, hon. fellow), Latin Am. Studies Assn., Am. Ednl. Rsch. Assn. Phi Delta Kappa. Office: Ind U Sch Edn Bloomington IN 47405 Office Phone: 812-856-8374. Business E-Mail: arnove@indiana.edu.

ARNSTEIN, WALTER LEONARD, retired historian; b. Stuttgart, Germany, May 14, 1930; arrived in U.S., 1939, naturalized, 1944; s. Richard and Charlotte (Heymann) Arnstein; m. Charlotte Culver Sutphen, June 8, 1952; children: Sylvia, Peter. BSS., CCNY, 1951; MA, Columbia U., 1954; PhD, Northwestern U., 1961; postgrad., U. London, Eng., 1956-57. Asst. prof. history Roosevelt U., Chgo., 1957-62, assoc. prof., 1962-66, prof., acting dean grad. divsn., 1966-67; prof. history U. Ill., Urbana, 1968-98, LAS Jubilee prof. history, 1989-98, prof. history and LAS Jubilee prof. history emeritus, 1998—, chmn. dept., 1974-78, assoc. Ctr. for Advanced Study, 1972-73. Vis. assoc. prof. history Northwestern U., 1963—64; vis. fellow Clare Hall, Cambridge U., 1982; hon. fellow U. Edinburgh, 1989. Author: The Bradlaugh Case: A Study in Late Victorian Opinion and Politics, 1965, 2d edit., 1984, Britain Yesterday and Today, 1966, 8th edit., 2001, Protestant Versus Catholic in Mid-Victorian England, 1982, (with William B. Willcox) The Age of Aristocracy, 3d edit., 1976, 8th edit., 2001, Queen Victoria, 2003; editor: The Past Speaks: Sources and Problems in British History Since 1688, 1981, 2d edit. 1993; editor: Recent Historians of Great Britain, 1990; bd. editors The Historian, 1976-2000, Am. Hist. Rev., 1982-85, Albion, 1988-93; mem. bd. advisers: Victorian Studies, 1966-75; contbr. articles profl. jours. Vice chmn. Ill. Humanities Coun., 1983-84. Served with AUS, 1951-53, Korea. Fellow, Am. Coun. Learned Socs., 1967—68; Fulbright scholar, 1956—57. Fellow Royal Hist. Soc.; mem. Am. Hist. Assn., Brit. Hist. Assn., N.Am. Conf. Brit. Studies (exec. com. 1971-76, v.p. 1993-95, pres. 1995-97), Midwest Conf. on Brit. Studies (pres. 1980-82), Midwest Victorian Studies Assn. (pres. 1977-80, annual Walter L. Arnstein Dissertation prize awarded in his name 1992—), Phi Beta Kappa, Phi Alpha Theta. Home: 804 W Green St Champaign IL 61820-5017 Office: U Ill Dept History 309 Gregory Hall 810 S Wright St Urbana IL 61801-3644 Business E-Mail: warnstei@uiuc.edu.

ARONOWITZ, DAVID M., lawyer, chemicals executive; BA, Haverford Coll.; JD, Yale U. Assoc. Skadden, Arps, Slate, Meagher and Flom; v.p., gen. counsel, sec. Grimes Aerospace Co., Columbus, Ohio; asst. gen. counsel Taylor Pub. Co., Insilco Corp., Dublin; v.p., asst. gen. counsel The Scotts Miracle-Gro Co., Marysville, 1998—2000, sr. v.p., asst. gen. counsel, asst. sec., 2000—01, exec. v.p., gen. counsel, sec., 2001—. Office: Scotts Miracle-Gro Co 14111 Scottslawn Rd Marysville OH 43041 Office Phone: 937-644-0011.

ARONSON, HOWARD ISAAC, linguist, educator; b. Chgo., Mar. 5, 1936; s. Abe and Jean A. BA, U. Ill., 1956; MA, Ind. U., 1958, PhD, 1961. Asst. prof. Slavic langs. and lit. U. Wis., Madison, 1961-62; asst. prof. Slavic linguistics U. Chgo., 1962-65, asso. prof. depts. slavic langs. and lit. and linguistics, 1965-73, prof., 1973—2002, chmn. dept. linguistics, 1972-80, prof. emeritus, 2002—, chmn. dept. Slavic langs. and lits., 1983-91, 2000-01. Editor: Annual of the Society for the Study of Caucasia, 1989—. Mem. Am. Assn. Advancement Slavic Studies. Jewish. Home: 415 W Aldine Ave Apt 7B Chicago IL 60657-3601 Office: U Chgo Dept Slavic Langs and Lit Chicago IL 60637 Home Phone: 773-935-7535. Personal E-mail: hia5@rcn.com. Business E-Mail: hia5@uchicago.edu.

ARONSON, VIRGINIA L., lawyer; b. Bremerton, Wash., June 4, 1947; m. Simon Aronson. BA, U. Chgo., 1969, MA, 1973, JD, 1975. Bar: Ill. 1975. Ptnr. Sidley Austin LLP, Chgo. Mem. U. Chgo. Law Review, 1974—75; mem. exec. and mgmt. com. Sidley Austin LLP. Contbr. articles to profl. jours. Mem. leadership coun. Chgo. Pub. Edn. Fund; bd. dirs. Chgo. Civic Alliance; mem. bd. dirs. Chgo. Ctrl. Area Com. Mem. Am. Coll. Real Estate Lawyers, Chgo. Mortgage Attys. Assn., The Chgo. etwork. Office: Sidley Austin LLP 1 South Dearborn St Chicago IL 60603 Office Phone: 312-853-7741. Office Fax: 312-853-7036. Business E-Mail: varonson@sidley.com.

ARORA, JASBIR SINGH, engineering educator; b. Tarn-Taran, India, 1943; came to U.S., 1965; naturalized 1977; m. Rita Arora, 1972. BS in Engring. with honors, Punjab U., India, 1964; MS, Kans. State U., 1967; PhD, U. Iowa, 1971. Asst. prof. G.N. Engring Coll., Ludhiana, India, 1964-65; from asst. prof. to prof. U. Iowa, Iowa City, 1972—2002, F. Wendell Miller disting. prof. engring., 2002—. Author: Introduction to Optimum Design, 1989, 2nd edit., 2004; co-author: Applied Optimal Design, 1979; contbr. articles to profl. jours. Fellow: ASCE, ASME; mem.: AIAA (sr.). Office: U Iowa # 4110 SC Iowa City IA 52242

ARPINO, GERALD PETER, performing company executive; b. SI, NY, Jan. 14, 1928; s. Luigi and Anna (Santanastasio) A. Student, Wagner Coll., PhD (hon.), 1980; student ballet under Mary Ann Wells, student modern dance under May O'Donnell and Gertrude Shurr. Dancer Ballet Russe, 1951-52; co-founder Joffrey Ballet, 1956, dancer, to 1962, former assoc. artistic dir., now artistic dir. Chgo., resident choreographer, until 1990, artistic dir.; with faculty Joffrey Ballet Sch., NYC, from 1953, now artistic dir., 1988—, assoc. dir., 1988—, prin. choreographer, 1988—. Bd. dirs. Dance Notation Bur., Dancers in Transition; mem. adv. coun. to dept. dance Calif. State U., Long Beach, also mem. Disting. Artists Forum. Choreographer ballets including Incubus, 1962, Viva Vivaldi!, 1965, Olympics, Nightwings, both 1966, Cello Concerto, Arcs and Angels, Elegy, all 1967, Secret Places, The Clowns, Fanfarita, A Light Fantastic, 1968, Animus, The Poppet, 1969, Confetti, Solarwind, Trinity, all 1970, Reflections, Valentine, Kettentanz, all 1971, Chabriesque, Sacred Grove on Mount Talmalpais, both 1972, Jackpot, 1973, The Relativity of Icarus, 1974, Drums, Dreams on Banjos, 1975, Orpheus Times Light 2, 1976, Touch Me, 1977, Choura, L'Air d 'Esprit, Suite Saint-Saens, all 1978, Epode, 1979, Celebration, 1980, Ropes, Partita for Four, Sea Shadow, Diverdissement, 1980, Light Rain, 1981, Round of Angels, 1982, Italian Suite, Quarter-Tones, 1983, Jamboree (commd. by City of San Antonio) Adv. Sportsmedicine Edn. & Rsch. Found., L.A.; mem. adv. com. N.Y. Internat. Festival of the Arts; mem. nat. adv. coun. ITI/USA Internat. Ballet Competition; mem. hon. com. The Yard Benefit-Vineyard Celebration, 1989; mng. dir., bd. dirs. Found. for Joffrey Balllet, Inc. Served with USCG, 1945-48. Recipient Dancemagazine award, 1974, Bravo award San Antonio Performing Arts Assn., 1984, Disting. Achievement award Nat. Orgn. Italian-Am. Women, 1987, Tiffany award Internat. Soc. Performing Arts Adminstrs., 1989, Outstanding Artistic Achievement award Staten Island Coun. on Arts, 1990, Ammy award Am. Express Corp. Office: Joffrey Ballet Chgo 70 E Lake St Fl 1300 Chicago IL 60601-5917

ARRINGTON, MICHAEL BROWNE, foundation administrator; b. Chgo., Mar. 24, 1943; s. W. Russell and Ruth Marian (Browne) Arrington; m. DeEtta Jane Watson, Dec. 15, 1966 (div. 1969); m. Trudi Jeanne Robertson, Dec. 4, 1971 (div. 1992); children: Jennifer Lorraine, Patrick Browne; m. Catherine L. Swainbank, July 14, 2006 (div. 2008). AA, Kendall Coll., Evanston, Ill.; BA in Polit. Sci., U. Ill. Adminstrv. asst. to Senate Majority Leader State of Ill., Springfield, 1966-67; dir. pub. affairs Union League Club of Chgo., 1967-68; exec. dir. South Loop Improvement Orgn., Chgo., 1968-69; pres., chief exec. officer The Arrington Found., Chgo., 1979—, Arrington Travel Ctr., Inc., Chgo., 1969-99, Recon Mgmt Svcs., Evanston, Ill., 1999—. Mem. Nat. White House Conf. Travel and Tourism, Disting. Entrepreneurship Bd., U. Ill., Chgo. Bd. dirs. Robert R. McCormick Chgo. Boys & Girls Club, 1982—, Friends of Prentice Hosp., Chgo., 1986—; mem. chancellor's adv. bd. U. Ill., Chgo. Cpl. USMC, 1962-64. Named finalist Entrepreneur of Yr., 1989, 1990, Man of Yr., Ill. Vietnam Vets Leadership Program, 1993; named to Hall of Fame, Nat. Assn. Trade and Tech. Schs., 1988, Entrepreneurship Hall of Fame, 1994; recipient Excellence in Phys. Fitness award, USMC, 1962, Significant Contbn. to Dental Health award, Ill. Dental Health Soc., 1967, Alumni Achievement award, U. Ill., 2001. Mem. World Pres.'s Orgn., Econ. Club of Chgo., Chgo. Club, Westmoreland Country Club, 100 Club Cook County, Chief Execs. Orgn. Republican. Episcopalian. Avocations: golf, boating, skiing, scuba diving. Office: Recon Mgmt Svcs Inc 929 Edgemere Ct Evanston IL 60202-1428 Home Phone: 847-869-1336; Office Phone: 312-726-1800. E-mail: arringtonusa@aol.com.

ARTH, LAWRENCE JOSEPH, insurance executive; b. Lincoln, Nebr., July 8, 1943; s. William John and Josephine Marie (Willie) A.; children: Laura, Susan, William. BBA, U. ebr., 1965, MA in Bus. Adminstrn., 1969. Asst. v.p. securities Bankers Life Ins. Co. Nebr., Lincoln, 1973-78, 2nd v.p. fin., 1978-83, v.p. fin., 1983, v.p. fin. treas., 1983-85, sr. v.p. investments, treas., 1985-88; chmn. Ameritas Investment Advisors, Inc., Lincoln, 1986—; pres., COO Ameritas Life Ins. Corp., Lincoln, 1988-94, chmn., CEO, 1995—, Ameritas Acacia Mutual Holding Co., Lincoln, 1999—. Fellow Fin. Analysts Fedn.; mem. Omaha/Lincoln Soc. Fin. Analysts (bd. dirs. 1978-84, pres. 1983-84), Lincoln C. of C. (chmn. 1997), Lincoln Country Club (bd. dirs. 1984-87). Republican. Roman Catholic. Avocations: hunting, fishing, golf, tennis. Office: Ameritas Life Ins Corp PO Box 81889 Lincoln NE 68501-1889

ARTNER, ALAN GUSTAV, art critic, journalist; b. Chgo., May 14, 1947; s. Gustav and Katherine Rose (Lucas) A. BA, Northwestern U., 1968, MA, 1969. Apprentice music critic Chgo. Tribune, 1972-73, art critic, 1973—; contbg. editor The Art Gallery Mag., 1975-76; corr. Artnews Mag., 1977-80. Contbr. to Playbill, 1994—. Decorated Chevalier de l'ordre des Arts et des Lettres; Rockefeller Found. grantee, 1971-72 Office: Chgo Tribune Co 435 N Michigan Ave Chicago IL 60611-4066

ARTZT, EDWIN LEWIS, consumer products company executive; b. NYC, Apr. 15, 1930; s. William and Ida A.; m. Ruth Nadine Martin, May 12, 1950; children: Wendy Anne, Karen Susan, William M., Laura Grace, Elizabeth Louise. BS, U. Oreg., 1951. Account exec. Glasser Gailey Advt. Agy., LA, 1952-53; with Procter & Gamble Co., Cin., 1953-95, brand mgr. advt. dept., 1955-58, assoc. brand promotion mgr., 1958-60, brand promotion mgr., 1960, 62-65, copy mgr., 1960-62, mgr. advt. dept. paper products div., 1965-68, mgr. food products divsn., 1968-69, v.p. food products divsn., 1969-70, v.p., acting mgr. coffee div., 1970, v.p., group exec., 1970-75, bd. dirs., 1972-75, 80-95, exec. v.p. then vice chmn. internat. ops., 1980-89, group v.p. European ops. Europe, Belgium, 1975-80; pres. Procter & Gamble Internat., 1984-89, chmn., chief exec. officer, 1995-99. Bd. dir. GTE Corp., Delta Air Lines, Am. Express Co., Spalding Holdings Corp., Barilla G.e R.F.lli S.p.A., Italy, Am. Inst. for Contemporary German Studies, Am. Enterprise Inst. for Public Policy Rsch. Bd.; mem. Internat. Adv. Bd. Babson Coll. Internat. councilor Ctr. for Strategic and Internat. Studies, Washington; mem. Coun. on Fgn. Rels., The Jackson Hole Land Trust; bd. trustees Cin. Inst. of Fine Arts; mem. exec. com. The Business Coun.; past chmn. residential div. United Appeal; past chmn. Public Library Capital Funds campaign; past dist. chmn. Capital Fund Raising dr. Boy Scouts Am., past leadership tng. chmn.; past chmn. advt. com. Sch. Tax Levy, County Govt. Issue; past trustee Kansas City Philharmonic, Nutrition Found., Boys' Clubs Greater Cin.; past bd. dirs. Kansas City Lyric Theater; past bd. govs. Kansas City Art Inst. Recipient Martin Luther King, Jr. Salute to Greatness award, 1995, Leadership Conf. on Civil Rights Private Sector Leadership award, 1995; inducted to Nat. Sales Hall of Fame, 1995, Advt. Hall of Fame, 1996. Mem. Am. C. of C. Belgium (v.p.), Conf. Bd. Europe (adv. council), Internat. C. of C. (exec. com. U.S. council), Nat. Fgn. Trade Council, Queen City Club, Commercial Club, Camargo Club, Teton Pines Club. Clubs: Queen City (Cin.), Cin. Country (Cin.), Comml. (Cin.). Office: Procter & Gamble Co 1 Procter And Gamble Plz Cincinnati OH 45202-3393 Home: 3849 Hedgewood Dr Lawrenceburg IN 47025-8047

ARUFFO, ALEJANDRO, pharmaceutical executive; PhD in Biophysics, Harvard U. Postdoctoral rsch. fellow Harvard Med. Sch.; v.p. cardiovasc. and metabolic drug discovery Bristol-Myers Squibb; pres. Abbott Bioresearch Ctr., 2002—; divsnl. v.p. Abbott Labs., 2002—. Office: Abbott Laboratories 100 Abbott Park Rd Abbott Park IL 60064-6400

ARVIA, ANNE L., bank executive; m. Jack Arvia; 2 children. BS in Acctg., Mich. State Univ. CPA. Acctg. mgr. Crowe, Chizekand Co. LLP; asst. controller ShoreBank Corp., Chgo., 1991—93, v.p., controller, 1993—96, sr. v.p., 1996—98, CFO, 1998—2001, pres., 2001—06, CEO, 2003—06, Nationwide Bank, Columbus, Ohio, 2006—. Bd. dir. Cmty. Investment Corp., Cmty. Initiatives Inc. Mem. Leadership Chgo. Named one of 100 Most Influential Women, Crain's Chgo. Bus., 2004, 25 Most Powerful Women in Banking, US Banker mag., 2005; named to 40 Under 40, Crain's Chgo. Bus., 2002. Mem.: Ill.

CPA (Fin. Inst. Com.), Ill. Bankers Assn., Chgo. Fin. Exchange, Leadership Ill. Office: Nationwide Bank One Nationwide Plz Columbus OH 43215 Office Phone: 773-288-1000. Office Fax: 773-493-6609.

ARZBAECHER, ROBERT C(HARLES), research institute executive, electrical engineer, researcher; b. Chgo., Oct. 28, 1931; s. Hugo L. and Caroline G. A.; m. Joan Collins, June 16, 1956; children: Carolyn, Robert, Mary Beth, Jean, Thomas. BS, Fournier Inst., 1953; MS, U. Ill., 1958; PhD, 1960. Asst. prof. elec. engring. Christian Bros. Coll., Memphis, 1960-63, assoc. prof., 1963-67; assoc. prof. elec. engring. U. Ill.-Chgo., 1967-70, prof., 1970-76; chmn. dept. elec. engring. U. Iowa, Iowa City, 1976-81; dir. Pritzker Inst. Med. Engring., Ill. Inst. Tech., Chgo., 1981—; v.p. U. Iowa Research Found., 1978-81; pres. Arzco. Inc., Chgo., 1980-87. Contbr. articles to profl. jours.; inventor Arzco pill electrode. Trustee Ill. Cancer Coun., Chgo., 1981-92. Fellow IEEE, Am. Coll. Cardiology, Am. Inst. Med. Biol. Engring. Home: 5757 N Sheridan Rd Chicago IL 60660-4746 Office: Ill Inst Tech Pritzker Inst Med Engr 10 E 32nd St Chicago IL 60616-3813

ASCH, SUSAN MCCLELLAN, pediatrician; b. Cleve., Dec. 31, 1945; d. William Alton and Alice Lonore (Heide) McClellan; m. Marc Asch, Sept. 10, 1966; children: Marc William, Sarah Susan, Rebecca Janney. AB, Oberlin Coll., Ohio, 1967; MA, Mich. State U., 1968, PhD, 1975; MD, Case Western Res., 1977. Diplomate Nat. Bd. Med. Examiners, Am. Bd. Pediatrics, Am. Bd. Emergency Pediatrics. Instr. sociology Mich. State U., East Lansing, 1971-73; resident in pediatrics Children's Nat. Med. Ctr., Washington, 1977-80, chief resident in ambulatory and emergency pediatrics, 1979-80; asst. to dir. Office for Med. Applications of Rsch. NIH, Bethesda, 1980-81; pvt. practice in pediatrics Millinocket (Maine) Regional Hosp., 1981-84; assoc. dir. emergency Akron (Ohio) Children's Hosp., 1984-87; asst. prof. pediatrics Northeastern Ohio U. Coll. Medicine, 1984-87; dir. emergency St. Paul Children's Hosp., 1987-91; asst. prof. pediatrics U. Minn., 1987-93, clin. asst. prof., 1993—; pvt. practice pediatrics Stillwater, Minn., 1992—; sec. exec. com. med. staff Lakeview Meml. Hosp., 1999—2001, vice chief of staff, 2001—03, chief of staff, 2003—05, past chief of staff, 2005—07, chair pediatrics, 2005—07. Nat. faculty PALS Am. Heart Assn., Mpls., Dallas, 1987—94, regional PALS faculty, 1994—, state bd. dirs. Minn. affiliate, 1988—92; mem. task force, sub-bd. emergency pediat. Am. Bd. Pediat., 1987—91, mem. sub-bd. emergency pediat., 1991—93; chmn. SIDS task force Minn. Dept. Maternal and Child Health, St. Paul, 1990—92. Assoc. editor Pediatric Emergency Medicine, 1992, contbr., 1992, 96; author various publs., 1970—. Mem.: Minn. Med. Assn. (emergency svcs. com. 1990, ho. of dels. 1994), Am. Acad. Pediat. (exec. com. sect. on emergency pediat. 1988—90, chair Minn. emergency pediat. com. 1989—91, nat. faculty advanced pediat. life support 1989—, regional faculty neonatal resuscitation program 1994—, nat. svc. commendation 1991), Alpha Omega Alpha. Democrat. Mem. Soc. Of Friends. Avocations: travel, cutting horses. Home: 34 N Oaks Rd North Oaks MN 55127-6325 Office: Stillwater Med Group 921 Greeley St S Stillwater MN 55082-5935 Office Phone: 651-439-1234.

ASCHAUER, CHARLES JOSEPH, JR., retired health products executive; b. Decatur, Ill., July 23, 1928; s. Charles Joseph and Beulah Diehl (Kniple) A.; m. Elizabeth Claire Meagher, Apr. 28, 1962; children: Karen A. Vorwald, Thomas Arthur, Susan A. Baisley, Karl Andrew. BBA, Northwestern U., 1950. Cert. internat. bus. adminstr. Centre d'Etudes Industrielles, 1951. Prin. McKinsey & Co., Chgo., 1955-62; v.p. mktg. Mead Johnson Labs. div. Mead Johnson & Co., Evansville, Ind., 1962-67; v.p., pres. automotive group Maremont Corp., Chgo., 1967-70; v.p., group exec. Whittaker Corp., Los Angeles, 1970-71; v.p., pres. hosp. products div. Abbott Labs., North Chicago, Ill., 1971-76, v.p., group exec., 1976-79, exec. v.p., dir., 1979-89, ret., 1989. Lt. Supply Corps. USNR, 1951—55. Mem.: Shadow Wood Country Club, Sunset Ridge Country Club, Econs. Club Chgo., Univ. Club Chgo.

ASH, GEORGE W., lawyer; b. Highland Park, Mich., Apr. 16, 1950; s. Charles R. and Frances I. (Hipes) A.; m. Angel Gale Smith, June 10, 1972; 1 child, Allison. BS, USAF Acad., 1972; JD, U. Denver, 1975; diploma air and space law, London Inst. World Affairs, 1985; LLM, U. London, 1985. Bar: Iowa 1976, U.S. Ct. Mil. Appeals 1976. Commd. 2d lt. USAF, 1972, advanced through grades to lt. col.; asst. staff judge advocate Wurtsmith AFB, Mich., 1976-78; assoc. prof. law USAF Acad., Colo., 1978-81; staff judge advocate RAF Fairford, Eng., 1981-84; asst. gen. counsel Strategic Def. Initiative, Washington, 1985-89; staff judge advocate McChord AFB, Wash., 1989-92, ret., 1992; of counsel Dykema Gossett, Detroit, 1992—; ptnr. Foley & Lardner LLP, Detroit, gen. regulatory practice group. Advisor U.S. Arms Delegation, Def. and Space Talks, Geneva, Switzerland, 1984. Recipient Def. Superior Svc. medal Sec. of Def., 1989, Dirs. award Dir SDIO, 1989. Mem. ABA, Iowa Bar Assn., Nat. Contract Mgmt. Assn. Avocation: fly fishing. Office: Foley & Lardner LLP 150 Jefferson Ave Ste 1000 Detroit MI 48226-4443 Office Phone: 313-442-6463. Business E-Mail: gash@foley.com.

ASH, J. MARSHALL, mathematician, educator; b. NYC, Feb. 18, 1940; s. Barney and Rosalyn (Hain) A.; m. Alison Igo, Nov. 24, 1977; children: Michael A., Garrett A., Andrew A. SB, U. Chgo., 1961, SM, 1963, PhD, 1966. Joseph Fels Ritt instr. Columbia U., NYC, 1966-69; asst. prof. math. DePaul U., Chgo., 1970-72, assoc. prof., 1972-74, prof., 1974—. Vis. prof. Stanford U., 1977. Author: Studies in Harmonic Analysis, 1976, Harmonic Analysis: Calderon-Zygmund and Beyond, 2006; co-author: (with R. Jones) Human Analysis: Colderon-Zygmund and Beyond, 2006; contbr. articles to profl. jours. George Westinghouse fellow, 1961, SF fellow, 1962-66. Mem. AAUP, Am. Math. Soc., Math. Assn. Am., Sigma Xi. Office: De Paul U Math Dept Chicago IL 60614 Home: 2314 N Lincoln Pk W #3S Chicago IL 60614 Office Phone: 773-325-4216. Business E-Mail: mash@math.depaul.edu.

ASHE, ARTHUR JAMES, III, chemistry professor; b. NYC, Aug. 5, 1940; s. Arthur James and Helen Louise (Hawelka) A.; m. Penelope Guerard Vaughan, Aug. 25, 1962; children: Arthur J., Christopher V. BA, Yale U., 1962, MS, 1965, PhD, 1966; postgrad., Cambridge U., 1962-63. Asst. prof. chemistry U. Mich., Ann Arbor, 1966-71, assoc. prof., 1971-76, prof., 1976—, chmn. dept., 1983-86, prof. macromolecular sci. and engring., 2000—. Vis. scientist Phys. Chemistry Inst., U. Basle, Switzerland, 1974 Mem. editorial avd. bds. profl. jours, 1984—. Alfred P. Sloan fellow, 1972-76 Mem. Am. Chem. Soc. Office: U Mich Dept Chemistry Ann Arbor MI 48109 Business E-Mail: ajashe@umich.edu.

ASHENFELTER, DAVID LOUIS, reporter; b. Toledo, Oct. 20, 1948; s. Duaine Louis and Betty Jean A.; m. Barbara Ann Dinwiddie, Feb. 22, 1974. BS in Edn., Ind. U., 1971. Reporter Kokomo Morning Times, Ind., 1966-67, Bloomington Daily Herald-Telephone, Ind., 1968-69, Bloomington Courier-Tribune, 1970-71, Detroit News, 1971-82, Detroit Free Press, 1982—. Recipient Disting. Svc. award Soc. Profl. Journalists, 1981, 83, 85, Pulitzer prize for meritorious pub. service Columbia U., 1982, Silver Gavel award ABA, 1986, Worth Bingham Prize, 1986, and more than 40 local, state and nat. newswriting awards; named to Mich. Journalism Hall of Fame. Mem. Sigma Chi. Office: Detroit Free Press 600 W Fort St Detroit MI 48226-2706 Business E-Mail: dashenfelter@freepress.com.

ASHER, FREDERICK M., art educator, art historian; Prof., chmn. dept art history U. Minn., Mpls. Mem.: Am. Inst. Indian Studies (pres.), Coll. Art Assn. (mem. program com.). Office: U Minn Dept Art History 340 Heller Hall 271 19th Ave S Minneapolis MN 55455

ASHLEY, RENEE, writer, creative writing educator, consultant; b. Palo Alto, Calif., Aug. 10, 1949; BA in English with honors, San Francisco State U., 1979, BA in French, 1979, BA in World and Comparative Lit., 1979, MA, 1981. Instr. creative writing West Milford (N.J.) Cmty. Sch., 1983-85; instr. creative writing, cons. artist residencies Rockland Ctr. for Arts, West Nyack, NY, 1985—; mem. MFA in Creative Writing faculty Fairleigh Dickinson U., 2001—. Author: Salt, 1991 (Brittingham prize in Poetry 1991), The Various Reasons of Light, 1998, The Revisionist's Dream, 2001, Someplace Like This, 2003; contbr. to anthologies including Touching Fire: Erotic Writings by Women, 1989, What's a Nice Girl Like You?, 1992, Breaking Up Is Hard to Do, 1994, Dog Music, 1996, (textbook) Writing Poems, 1995, The Breath of Parted Lips, Vol. II, 2004; contbr. to American Voice, Antioch Rev., Harvard Rev., Kenyon Rev., Poetry. Fellow N.J. State Coun. Arts, 1985, 89, 94, 2003, Yaddo, Saratoga Springs, N.Y., 1990, McDowell Colony, Peterborogh, N.H., 1993-94, NEA, 1997-98; grantee Poets and Writers, Inc., 1986, N.Y. State Coun. Arts, 1986; recipient Washington prize in poetry Word Works, Inc., 1986, Lit. Excellence award, Kenyon Review, 1990, 92, Pushcart prize, 2000. Mem. MLA, Acad. Am. Poets, Poetry Soc. Am. (Ruth Lake Meml. award 1987, Robert H. Winner award 1989). E-mail: reneea@verizion.net.

ASHMAN, CHARLES H., retired minister; b. Johnstown, Pa., June 1, 1924; s. Charles H. Sr. and Flora A.; m. Frances Marie Bradley, July 12, 1946; children: Kenneth W., Judy Ashman Fairman, Karl W. BA cum laude, Westmont Coll., 1947; MDiv magna cum laude, Grace Theol. Seminary, Winona Lake, Ind., 1950. Ordained to ministry Grace Brethren Ch., 1950. Sr. pastor Grace Brethren Ch., Rittman, Ohio, 1950-55, Phoenix, 1955-62, Winona Lake, Ind., 1962-89, pastor emeritus, 1989—; asst. coord. Fellowship of Grace Brethren Chs., Winona Lake, Ind., 1979—. Prof. Grace Theol. Sem., 1969-89. Mem. Nat. Fellowship Grace Brethren Ministers (pres. 1984, Pastor of Yr. 1989, moderator nat. conf. 1973-74), Kiwanis (pres. 1991-92). Office: Fellowship Grace Brethren PO Box 386 Winona Lake IN 46590-0386 Home: 1413 Avalon Ct Winona Lake IN 46590-5601 E-mail: charlesashman@fgbc.org.

ASHMAN, MARTIN C., federal judge; b. 1931; m. Betty Ashman; two children. JD, DePaul U., 1953. Bar: Ill. 1953, U.S. Supreme Ct. 1959. Atty. Ashman & Jaffe, 1954-70, Martin C. Ashman, Ltd., 1970-87; commr. Ill. Ct. Claims, 1974-87; corp. counsel Village of Morton Grove, Ill., 1977-87; cir. judge domestic rels. divsn., law divsn. State of Ill., 1987-95; magistrate judge U.S. Dist. Ct. (no. dist.) Ill., 1995—. Vol. Legal Svcs. Found., Chgo. Recipient Spl. Tribute award Ill. Coun. Against Handgun Violence; Outstanding Svc. to Legal Profession award, DePaul U. Law Sch., 2001. Mem. ABA, Fed. Bar Assn., Fed. Magistrate Judges Assn., Ill. State Bar Assn., Decalogue Soc. Lawyers, Chgo. Bar Assn. (Cert. of Appreciation). Office: US Dist Ct 1366 Dirksen Bldg 219 S Dearborn St Chicago IL 60604-1800 Office Phone: 312-435-5624. Business E-Mail: martin_ashman@uscourts.gov.

ASHMUS, KEITH ALLEN, lawyer; b. Cleve., Aug. 19, 1949; s. Richard A. and Rita (Petti) A.; m. Marie Sachiko Matsuoka, Dec. 15, 1973; children: Emmy Marie, Christopher Todd. BA in Policy Sci., Mich. State U., 1971, MA in Econs., 1972; JD, Yale U., 1974. Bar: Ohio 1974, Calif. 1991, US Dist. Ct. (no. dist.) Ohio 1975, US Dist. Ct. (no., so. and ctrl. dists.) Calif. 1991, US Dist. Ct. (so. dist.) Ohio 2000, US Ct. Appeals (6th cir.) 1975, US Ct. Appeals (11th cir.) 2005, US Supreme Ct. 1980. Assoc. Thompson Hine & Flory LLP, Cleve., 1974-82, ptnr., 1982—2000, ptnr.-in-charge Cleve. office, 1996-99, dept. chmn., 1999-2000; founding ptnr. Frantz Ward LLP, Cleve., 2000—. Mediator/arbitrator Am. Arbitration Assn. Comml. Employment Panels, 1995—, Nat. Complex Case Panel, 2007-; mem. employment panel CPR Internat. Inst. Conflict Prevention and Resolution, 2006-. Co-author: Public Sector Collective Bargaining: The Ohio System, 1984. Trustee cmty. arts Baycrafters, Bay Village, Ohio, 1981-84, Hospice Coun. No. Ohio, 1982-84, Inst. for Personal Health Skills, Cleve. 1985-90, Coun. Smaller Enterprises, 1990-96, 98—, 1st vice chmn., 2000-01, chmn., 2001-03, Village Found., 1997—, pres. 2005-07; Vocat. Guidance Svcs. 1999-02, Youth Opportunities Unlimited, 2000-04, Cleve. Saves, 2001—, Greater Cleve. Partnership, 2004—, exec. com., 2006—; sec. George W. Codrington Charitable Found., 1994-2000; chmn. job placement for older persons Skills Available, Cleve., 1980-87; gov.'s appointee to Health Care Quality Adv. Coun., 1996; mem. adv. bd. Greater Cleve. Salvation Army, 1997—, treas., 2000-01, vice chmn., 2001-04, chmn. 2004-06; exec. com. Fund Econ. Future, 2004—07, funders com., 2004-07. Named one of Outstanding Vols. award Nat. Hospice Orgn., 1982, Vol. of Yr. Vocat. Guidance and Rehab. Services, 1985, 86.; recipient Others award, Salvation Army, 2007. Fellow Am. Bar. Found., Ohio State Bar found. (bd. dirs. 2002—); mem. State Bar Calif., Ohio State Bar Assn. (coun. dels. 1995—, bd. govs. 1998-01, pres. 2003-04), Cleve. Bar Assn. (trustee 1985-88, 98-2001, chmn. labor law sect. 1983-84), ABA (ho. delegates 2004—); Def. Rsch. Inst., Pub. Sector Labor Rels. Assn. (exec. com. 1989-93), Am. Arbitration Assn. (chmn. comml. adv. panel 2004-05), Yale Law Alumni Assn. (mem. exec. coun. 2003—), Nat. Small Bus. Assn. (bd. dirs. 2001—, vice chair advocacy 2005-07, treas. 2007—). Avocations: golf, fishing. Office: Frantz Ward LLP 127 Public Sq 2500 Key Ctr Cleveland OH 44114-1230 Home Phone: 440-835-3393; Office Phone: 216-515-1660. Business E-Mail: kashmus@frantzward.com.

ASHWORTH, JULIE, elementary school educator; Tchr. Hawthorne Elem. Sch., Sioux Falls, SD, 1990—. Participant Internat. Space Camp, Huntsville, Ala., 1993; S.D. tchr. participant Goals 2000 Forum, U.S. Dept. Edn., Washington, 1993; mem. S.D. Gov.'s Adv. Coun. on Cert. for Tchrs., 1994—; mem. exceptional needs standards com. Nat. Bd. for Profl. Tchg. Stds., Washington, 1994—; initiator, organizer S.D. Tchrs. Forum, 1994. Named S.D. Tchr. of Yr., Sioux Falls Sch. Dist., 1992, S.D. Elem. Tchr. of Yr., 1993. Home: 2015 Pendar Ln Sioux Falls SD 57105-3022 Office: Hawthorne Elem Sch 601 N Spring Ave Sioux Falls SD 57104-2721

ASHWORTH, RONALD BROUGHTON, health facility executive, accountant; b. San Francisco, Apr. 19, 1945; s. Robert William and Tracy Marie (Parks) Ashworth; m. Carol Lynn Heaps, Oct. 2, 1970; 1 child, Christina Ann. BBA, U. Mo., Columbia, 1967; MA, U. Mo., 1968. CPA Mo., NC, Ill., La. With Peat Marwick Mitchell & Co., 1968—91, ptnr., 1975—91, in charge St. Louis Office health care practice, 1975—77, nat. dir. health care practice, 1978—91, Chgo., 1979—91; exec. v.p., COO Sisters of Mercy Health Sys., 1991—99, pres., CEO, 1999—. Bd. dirs. Chgo. Lung Assn., Mid-Am. chpt. ARC. Recipient Haskins and Sells award, 1967, award, Fin. Execs. Inst., 1967; scholar, Alpha Kappa Psi, 1967. Mem.: Ill. Soc. CPAs, Am. Hosp. Assn., Fedn. Am. Hosps., Am. Inst. CPAs, Healthcare Fin. Mgmt. Assn., Country Club Mo., Medinah Country Club, Tavern Club. Office: Sisters of Mercy Health System 14528 S Outer Forty Chesterfield MO 63017

ASKEY, RICHARD ALLEN, mathematician, educator; b. St. Louis, June 4, 1933; s. Philip Edwin and Bessie May (Yates) Askey; m. Elizabeth Ann Hill, June 14, 1958; children: James, Suzanne. BA, Washington U., St. Louis, 1955; MA, Harvard U., Cambridge, Mass., 1956; PhD, Princeton U., NJ, 1961. Instr. in math. Washington U., St. Louis, 1958-61; instr. U. Chgo., Chgo., 1961-63; asst. prof. U. Wis., Madison, 1963-65, asso. prof., 1965-68, prof., 1968-86, Gabor Szego prof., 1986-95, John Bascom prof., 1995—2003, prof. emeritus, 2003—. Author: (book) Orthogonal Polynomials and Special Functions, 1975; author: (with G. E. Andrews and R. Roy) Special Functions, 1999; editor: Theory and Application of Special Functions, 1975, Collected Papers of Gabor Szego, 1982. Recipient Edyth May Sliffe award; fellow Guggenheim, 1969—70. Fellow: AAAS, Am. Acad. Arts and Scis., Indian Acad. Sci. (hon.); mem.: Soc. Indsl. and Applied Math., Math. Assn. Am., Nat. Acad. Sci., Am. Math. Soc. Home: 2105 Regent St Madison WI 53726-3941 Office: U Wis Van Vleck Hall Madison WI 53706

ASKREN, STAN A., manufacturing executive; BA Business Administration, U. of Northern Iowa; MBA, Washington U. Group v.p. The HON Co., 1998—99; Pres. Allsteel Inc., 1999—2003; exec. v.p. HNI Corp., Muscatine, Iowa, 2001—03, pres., 2003—04, chmn., pres., CEO, 2004—. Office: HNI Corp PO Box 1109 408 E 2d St Muscatine IA 52761-0071

ASLANIDES, JAMES, state representative; b. Massilon, Ohio, Jan. 3, 1960; married; 2 children. Student in engring., Kent State U. Instrument rated pilot, complex aircraft Aircraft Owners and Pilots Assn. Small bus. owner; state rep. dist. 94 Ohio Ho. of Reps., Columbus, 1999—, chair, agr. and natural resources com., mem. econ. devel. and tech., energy and environment, and transp. and pub. safety coms., mem. regulatory reform subcom. Mem. Nat. Rep. Congl. Com. Mem.: Ohio Energy Edn. Program, Ind. Petroleum Assn. Am., Southeastern Ohio Oil and Gas Assn., Ohio Oil and Gas Assn., Nat. Fedn. Ind. Bus., Ohio Twp. Assn. (assoc.), NRA, Aircraft Owners and Pilots Assn., Farm Bur., Coshocton, HOlmes, Muskingum, and Hocking County Cs. of C., Ohio C. of C. Republican. Office: 77 S High St 12th fl Columbus OH 43215-6111

ASP, WILLIAM GEORGE, librarian; b. Hutchinson, Minn., July 4, 1943; s. George William and Blanche Irene (Mattson) A. BA, U. Minn., 1966, MA, 1970; postgrad., U. Iowa, 1972-75. Dir. East Cen. Regional Libr., Cambridge, Minn., 1967-70; asst. prof. Sch. Libr. Sci. U. Iowa, 1970-75; dir. Minn. Office Libr. Devel. and Svcs., St. Paul, 1975-96, Dakota County Libr., Eagan, Minn., 1996—2003. Mem. Nat. Coun. Quality Continuing Edn. for Info., Libr. and Media Pers., 1979-85; bd. dirs. Bakken Libr. Electricity and Life, 1976-2007, Mpls.; vice chmn. White House Conf. on Libr. and Info. Svcs. Task Force, 1980-81, chmn., 1982, mem. adv. com., 1989-91; pres. Continuing Libr. Edn. Network and Exch., 1986-87. Mem. Minn. Regional Network Bd., 1992-96. Mem. ALA (mem. coun. 1985-88, 00-02), Minn. Libr. Assn., Chief Officers State Libr. Agys. (chmn. 1979-80), Minn. Ednl. Media Orgn., Minn. Assn. Continuing and Adult Edn., Assn. Specialized and Coop. Libr. Agys. (pres. 1989-90), Am. Field Svc. Home: 2095 Batello Dr Venice FL 34292

ASPEN, MARVIN EDWARD, federal judge; b. Chgo., July 11, 1934; s. George Abraham and Helen (Adelson) A.; m. Susan Alona Tubbs, Dec. 18, 1966; children: Jennifer Marion, Jessica Maile, Andrew Joseph. BS in Sociology, Loyola Univ., 1956; JD, Northwestern U., 1958. Bar: Ill. 1958. Individual practice, Chgo., 1958-59; draftsman joint com. to draft new Ill. criminal code Chgo. Bar Assn.-Ill. Bar Assn., 1959-60; asst. state's atty. Cook County, Ill., 1960-63; asst. corp. counsel City of Chgo., 1963-71; pvt. practice law, 1971; judge Cir. Ct. Cook County, Ill., 1971-79; judge ea. divsn. U.S. Dist. Ct. (no. dist.) Ill., Chgo., 1979-95, chief judge, 1995—2002. Edward Avery Harriman adj. prof. law Northwestern U. Law Sch.; past chmn. new judges, recent devels. in criminal law, and evidence coms. Ill. Judicial Conf., past chmn., adv. bd. Inst. Criminal Justice, John Marshall Sch. Law; past mem. Ill. Law Enforcement Commn., Gov. Ill. Adv. Commn. Criminal Justice, Cook County Bd. Corrections; past chmn. assoc. rules com. Ill. Supreme Ct., com. on ordinance violation problems; past vice chmn. com. on pattern jury instrns. in criminal cases; lectr. at judicial confs. and trial advocacy programs nationally and internationally; planner, participant in legal seminars at numerous schools including Harvard U., Emory U., U. Fla., Oxford U. (Eng.), U. Bologna, Nuremberg (Germany) U., U. Cairo, Egypt, U. Zimbabwe, U. Malta, U. The Philippines, U. Madrid; past mem. Georgetown U. Law Ctr. Project on Plea Bargaining in U.S., spl. faculty ITA advanced Trial Advocacy Program introducing Brit. trial techniques to experienced Am. litigators, spl. faculty of ABA designed to acquaint Scottish lawyers with modern litigation and tech.; frequent faculty mem. Nat. Judiciary Coll., Fed. Judicial Ctr., U. Nev. (Reno), Nat. Inst. for Trial Advocacy, Colo.; bd. dir. Fed. Judicial Ctr., past chair dir. search com.; past mem. Judicial Conf. Com. on Adminstrn. of the Bankruptcy System, Trial Bar Implementation Com. on Civility of the 7th Fed. Cir.; mem. Northwestern U. Law Bd. Co-author Criminal Law for the Layman-A Citizen's Guide, 2d edit., 1977, Criminal Evidence for the Police, 1972, Protective Security Law, 1983; contbr. over two dozen articles to legal publs. Past mem. vis. com. orthwestern U. Sch. Law, chmn. adv. com. for short courses (post law sch. ednl. program), mem. law bd.; past mem. vis. com. U. Chgo. Law Sch.; mem. vis. com. No. Ill. U. Sch. Law; organizer, past pres. Northwestern Univ. Sch. of Law chpt. Amincourt Program U.S. Judicial Conf; past mem. Cook County Bd. Corrections, John Howard Assn.; active CEELI programs in Bulgaria and Yugoslavia Ford Found. Jud. Tng. Program in China. With USAF, 1958-59; trustee Am. Inns Ct. Recipient Nat. Ctr. Freedom of Info. Studies award, Ctr. for Pub. Resources award, Merit award Northwestern U. Alumni Assn., Herbert Harley award Am. Judicature Soc.; named Person of Yr. Chgo. Lawyer, 1995. Mem. Am. Bar Found. (bd. dirs.), Judicature Soc. Ill. (past chmn. coms.), Chgo. Bar Assn. (bd. mgrs. 1978-79, past chmn. criminal law com., past bd. editors Chgo. Bar Record, mem. commn. on criminal justice. coms. on cont. legal edn., devel. of law, civil disorder and others), Ill. State Bar Assn. (past chmn. pub. rels., corrections, fair trial/free press, criminal law coms., mem. others), orthwestern U. Law Alumni Assn. (past pres., Merit award), ABA (co-chair, sec. of litigation Inst. for Trial practical task force, mem. standing com. on fed. jud. improvements, pres. ABA mus., mem. bd. Am. Bar Fedn., past mem. ABA bd. govs., mem. house dels., past chmn. exec com., mem. bd. editors ABA Jour.), Nat. Conf. Fed. Trial Judges (past mem. coun. sect., past chmn. exec. com. litigation, past chmn., coun. sect. criminal justice, mem. edn. bd. sect. criminal justice mag., past co-chmn. liason jud. com. sect. litigation, mem. jury comprehension study com., ho. dels., standing com. fed. jud. improvements, co-chmn. sect. litigation Inst. Trial Practice Task Force), Am. Inns Ct. Office: US Dist Ct 2578 US Courthouse 219 S Dearborn St Chicago IL 60604-1800 E-mail: aspen@ilnd.uscourts.gov.

ASSANIS, DENNIS N. (DIONISSIOS), mechanical engineering educator; b. Athens, Greece, Feb. 9, 1959; came to U.S., 1980; s. Nicholas and Kyriaki Assanis; m. Helen Stavrianos, Aug. 25, 1984; children: Nicholas, Dimitris. BSc in Marine Engring. with distinction, Newcastle U., UK, 1980; SMME, SM in Naval Arch. Marine Engring., MIT, 1982, PhD in Power and Propulsion, 1985, SM in Mgmt., 1986. Asst. prof. mech. engring. U. Ill., Urbana-Champaign, 1985-90, assoc. prof. mech. engring., 1990-94; prof. mech. engring. U. Mich., Ann Arbor, 1994—, dir. program automotive engring., 1995—2002, Arthur F. Thurnau prof., Jon R. and Beverly S. Holt prof. engring., 2000—, chair mech. engring., 2002—07, dir. Automotive Rsch. Ctr., 2000—; co-dir. Gen. Motors Collaborative Rsch. Lab., 2002—. Adj. rsch. staff energy and environ. systems divsn. Argonne Nat. Lab., 1978—; cons. in field. Assoc. editor ASME Transactions, Jour. Engring. for Gas Turbines and Power, 1996-2005; contbr. over 250 articles to profl. jours. and conf. proceedings. Univ. scholar, 1991-94, Athens Coll. Acad. scholar, 1967-77; recipient IBM Rsch. award, 1991, NSF Presdl. Young Investigator award, 1988-93, NSF Engring. Initiation award, 1987, NASA Cert. of Recognition for Creative Devel. of a Tech. Innovation, 1987; Lilly Endowment Teaching fellow, 1988. Fellow Soc. Automotive Engrs. (faculty advisor U. Mich. student sect. 1997-2003, Ralph Teetor award 1987, Russell Springer Best Paper award 1991, award for rsch. on automotive lubricants 2002); mem. NAE, ASME (faculty advisor U. Ill. student sect. 1989-91, ASME/Pi Tau Sigma Gold Medal award 1990, Internal Combustion Engine Divsn. Speaker awards 1993, 94, Meritorious Svc. award 1997), Am. Soc. for Engring. Edn., Combustion Inst., Sigma Xi. Achievements include development of comprehensive models of internal combustion engine processes and systems. Office: U Mich Dept Mech Engring 2045 WE Lay Automotive Lab Ann Arbor MI 48109-2121 Office Phone: 734-763-7880. Business E-Mail: assanis@umich.edu.

ASTRACHAN, BORIS MORTON, psychiatry educator, consultant; b. NYC, Dec. 1, 1931; s. Isaac and Ethel (Kahn) A.; m. Batja Sanders, June 17, 1956; children: David Isaac, Joseph Henry, Michael Sanders, Ellen Beth Astrachan-Fletcher. BA cum laude, Alfred U., NY, 1952; MD, Albany Med. Coll., 1956. Lic. Ill.; bd. cert. in psychiatry. Intern, resident USN Hosp., St. Albans and Phila., N.Y., 1956-57, 57-58; asst. depot psychiatrist recruitment tng. depot USMC, Parris Island, S.C., 1958-61; resident in psychiatry dept. psychiatry Yale U., New Haven, 1961-63, from asst. prof. to assoc. prof. dept. psychiatry, 1963-71; dir. Conn. Mental Health Ctr., New Haven, 1971-87; prof. dept. psychiatry Yale U., New Haven, 1971-90; prof., head dept. psychiatry U. Ill., Chgo., 1990-98, disting. prof. psychiatry, 1998—2001, disting. prof. emeritus psychiatry, 2001—. Mem. NIMH Initial Rev. Group, Rockville, Md., 1987-90, chmn., 1989-91; mem. IBM Mental Health Adv. Bd., White Plains, N.Y., 1990—; mem. adv. bd. Alcohol, Drug Addiction, Mental Health Adminstrn., Washington, 1985-86; mem. rsch. task force Pres. Commn. on Mental Health and Illness, Washington, 1977-78; vis. prof. U. Rotterdam, Amsterdam, 1986, Boston U., 1996. Co-author: (with Tischler) Quality Assurance in Mental Health, 1983; contbr. articles to profl. jours. (Citation classic 1986). Mem. State Health Clin. Coordinating Com., Hartford, Conn., 1980s; mem. clin. adv. com. Ill. Dept. Mental Health and Devel. Disabilities, Chgo., 1995-97; chair mental health task force Ill. Dept. Children and Family Svcs., Chgo., 1993-97; chair Mental Health Svc. Sys. Adv. Coun., Springfield and Chgo., Ill., 1992-95. Lt. comdr. USN, 1955-61. Recipient Disting. Faculty award U. Ill., Chgo., 1997; named Alumnus of Yr., Albany Med. Coll., 1999. Fellow Am. Coll. Psychiatrists, Am. Psychiat. Assn. (life, trustee-at-large, Adminstrv. Psychiatry award 1995), Am. Assn. Psychiat. Adminstrs. (Past. Pres. award 1992); mem. AMA. Jewish. Avocations: time with family, listening to music, reading. Home: 333 E Ontario St Apt 2902B Chicago IL 60611-4882 Office: Dept Psychiatry M/C 913 912 S Wood St Chicago IL 60612-7325

ATCHISON, CHRISTOPHER GEORGE, public health director; AB in Pol. Sci., Loyola U., Chgo., 1971; MPA, U. Ill., Springfield, 1990; student, Harvard U., 1996. Chief staff Office Lt. Gov., Springfield, Ill., 1978-81; exec. dir. Ill. Rep. State Com., Springfield, Ill., 1981-85; spl. asst. to dir. Ill. Dept. Pub. Health, Springfield, Ill., 1985-87, acting chief epidemiological studies, 1987, asst. dir., 1987-91; dir. Iowa Dept. Pub. Health, Des Moines, 1991-99, Ctr. Pub. Health Practice, U. Iowa, Iowa City, 1999—. Chair One Gift Campaign, Iowa, 1993, Health Data Commn., Iowa, 1993-96, Health Regulation Task Force, Iowa, 1996—; sec. Prospective Minor Parent Program Adv. Commn., Iowa, 1996—; vice chair Long Term Care Coord. Unit, Iowa, 1993—; mem. Iowa Leadership Consortium, 1991-92, Govs. Health Care Reform Council, Iowa, 1993-94. Pub. Health scholar Pub. Health Leadership Inst., 1992-93. Mem. AMA, Am. Pub. Health Assn. (pres. Iowa chpt. 1994-95, Ill. chpt., pub. health medicine steering com. 1995—), Assn. State Territorial Health Ofcls. (pres. 1994-95, chair nominations com. 1995—, exec. com. 1992—, chair primary care com. 1992-93, chair joint council official pub. health agys. 1994-95), N.Y. Acad. Med.

(medicine pub. health panel 1996—), Milbank Found. (reforming states group 1995—), Pub. Health Leadership Inst., Am. Soc. Pub. Adminstrn. (Iowa chpt., pres. ctrl. Ill. chpt. 1990-91, exec. council Ill. 1987-91). Office: U Iowa College of Public Health 2700 Steinsler Building Iowa City IA 52242-1008

ATCHISON, STEVEN, real estate company executive; b. 1969; Internal auditor Pulte Homes Inc., 1995, v.p., fin., Las Vegas divsn., pres. Tucson, Houston, Mich., 2005—. Named one of 40 Under 40, Crain's Detroit Bus., 2006. Office: Pulte Homes Incorporated 450 W Fourth St Royal Oak MI 48067-0956 Office Phone: 248-546-2300. Office Fax: 248-541-5533.

ATHAS, GUS JAMES, lawyer; b. Chgo., Aug. 6, 1936; s. James G. and Pauline (Parhas) A.; m. Marilyn Carres, July 12, 1964; children: Paula C. Vlahakos, James G., Christopher G. BS, U. Ill., 1958; JD cum laude, Loyola U., Chgo., 1965. Bar: Ill. 1965, U.S. Dist. Ct. (no. dist.) Ill. 1965, U.S. Ct. Appeals (7th cir.) 1970. With Isham, Lincoln & Beale, Chgo., 1965-69; group gen. counsel, asst. sec. ITT, Skokie, Ill., 1969-87; assoc. gen. counsel Itel Corp., Chgo., 1987; sr. v.p., gen. counsel, sec. Eagle Industries, Inc., Chgo., 1987-97; exec. v.p. adminstrn., gen. counsel, sec. Falcon Bldg. Products, Inc., Chgo., 1994-99; sr. v.p., gen. counsel Great Am. Mgmt. and Investment, Inc., Chgo., 1995-97; ptnr. Stamos & Trucco, Chgo., 2000—. Contbr. articles to profl. jours. 1st lt. U.S. Army, 1958-62. Mem. ABA, Ill. Bar Assn., Chgo. Bar Assn. Greek Orthodox. Home: 1240 Hawthorne Ln Downers Grove IL 60515-4503 Office: Stamos & Trucco 30 W Monroe Ste 1600 Chicago IL 60603 Office Phone: 312-630-7979. Business E-Mail: gathas@stamostrucco.com.

ATHAS, RITA REAGEN, municipal official; b. Chgo., Sept. 29, 1947; d. Joseph Daniel and Mary Ellen R.; m. Gregory Richard Athas, June 17, 1967; children: Gregory JOseph, Heather Hillman. BA in Urban Studies, Elmhurst Coll., Ill., 1976; MPA, No. Ill. U., DeKalb, 1978. Asst. to mgr. Village of Streamwood (Ill.), 1978, asst. village mgr., 1979—81; cmty. devel. dir. Village of Hannover Park (Ill.), 1981—85; asst. dir. N.W. Mcpl. Conf., Des Plaines, Ill., 1985—89, creative dir., 1989—97; asst. to mayor, dir. regional programs City of Chgo., 1997—2001, dep. chief of staff for external affairs, 2001—07; exec. dir. World Bus. Chgo., 2007—. V.p. Northwestern Ill. Planning Commn., Chgo., 1998—; mem. coun. Chgo. Metropolis 2020, 2000—. Bd. dirs. Leadership Greater Chgo., 1998—; mem. adv. bd. No. Ill. U. Pub. Adminstrn. Bd., DeKalb, 1999—. Named Alumni of Yr., Elmhurst Coll., 2000; fellow Leadership Greater Chgo., 1989, 1990. Democrat. Roman Catholic. Avocations: walking, cooking, reading. Office: World Business Chicago 177 N State St Chicago IL 60601*

ATKINS, STEVEN, construction executive, contractor; CFO Hunt Constrn. Group, Indpls. Office: Hunt Construction Group PO Box 128 Indianapolis IN 46206 Office Fax: (317) 227-7810.

ATKINSON, BARBARA F., dean, medical educator, executive vice chancellor; b. Mpls., Oct. 19, 1942; MD, Jefferson Med. Coll., Thomas Jefferson Univ., 1974. Diplomate Am. Bd. Anatomic and Clin. Pathology, Am. Bd. Cytopathology. Intern Hosp. U. Pa., Phila., 1974—75, resident in pathology, 1975—78; mem. faculty U. Kans., Kansas City; dir. resident program U. Kans. Med. Ctr., Kansas City, exec. vice chancellor, dean Sch. Medicine. Assoc. scientist Wistar Inst. Anatomy and Biology, 1983—87; mem. staff dept. pathology Hosp. of U. Pa., 1978—87, dir. cytopathology, 1978—87, med. program dir. Sch. Cytotech., 1978—86; chmn. dept. pathology and lab. medicine Med. Coll. Pa., 1987—94; dir. Delaware Valley Regional Lab. Svcs., Med. Coll. Hosps. and St. Christopher's Hosp. for Children, 1991—96; chmn. dept. pathology and lab. medicine Med. Coll. Pa. and Hahnemann U., 1994—96; trustee Am. Bd. Pathology, 1992—95, pres., 1998—. Mem. editl. bd. Lab. Investigation, 1988—94, Modern Pathology, 1990—94, Human Pathology, 1992—94, manuscript reviewer Cancer, Diagnostic Cytopathology, Modern Pathology, 1988—94, abstract rev. bd. U.S. and Can. Acad. Pathology, 1989—92, rev. panel Am. Soc. Clin. Pathology Abstract, 1991—96; contbr. articles to profl. jours., chapters to books. Bd. dirs., treas. Laennec Soc. Phila., 1979—81; bd. dirs. Thyroid Soc. Phila., 1982—84; exec. com., bd. dirs. Med. Coll. Pa., 1994—96; bd. trustees Hahnemann U., 1994—96. Recipient Golden Apple Tchg. award for excellent sci. tchg., 1994; grantee, NIH, 1985—88, Takeda-Abbott R&D, 1989—94, NIA, 1991—94. Fellow: ASIM, Coll. Am. Pathologists; mem.: NAS (mem. Inst. Medicine), U.S. and Can. Acad. Pathology, Am. Soc. Clin. Pathology (Janet M. Glasgow Meml. scholarship 1974), Am. Soc. Cytopathology. Office: U Kans Med Ctr Mail Stop 2015 3901 Rainbow Blvd Kansas City KS 66160 Office Phone: 913-588-1440. Business E-Mail: batkinson@kumc.edu.

ATKINSON, THOMAS P., environmental engineer; Commd. 2d lt. USAF. Named Fed. Engrs. of Yr., 1998. Mem. NSPE. Office: Minot AFB 5th Svcs Squad 5 SVS/SVtl 201 Summit Dr Minot AFB ND 58705

ATREYA, SUSHIL KUMAR, planetary-space science educator, astrophysicist; b. Apr. 15, 1946; came to U.S., 1966, naturalized, 1975; s. Harvansh Lal and Kailash Vati (Sharma) A.; 1 child, Chloë E. ScB, U. Rajasthan, India, 1963, MSc, 1965; MS, Yale U., 1968; PhD, U. Mich., 1973. Rsch. assoc. physics U. Pitts., 1973-74; asst., then assoc. rsch. scientist U. Mich., Ann Arbor, 1974-78, asst. prof., 1978-81, assoc. prof. atmospheric sci., 1981-87, prof. atmospheric and space sci., 1987—, dir. planetary sci. lab. Assoc. prof. U. Paris, 1984-85, vis. prof., 2000-01; vis. sr. rsch. scientist Imperial Coll., London, 1984; vis. astronomer Paris Observatory, 2006-; disting. vis. scientist Jet Propulsion Lab, Calif. Inst. Tech., 2006-; mem. sci. expt. and investigation team Mars Sci. Lab., Sample Analysis Mars Ste., Juno-Jupiter Polar Orbiter, Cassini-Huygens Probe to Saturn-Titan, Galileo Jupiter Probe; dep. US lead scientist Mars Express and Venus Express Missions, Russian Mars '96 and Soviet Phobos missions, Voyager spacecraft missions to the giant planets, Comet Rendezvous/Asteroid Flyby, 1986-92, Japanese Mars Mission-Nozomi, 1999-2004, and SpaceLab 1; guest observer/investigator on Spitzer Telescope, Hubble Space Telescope, Internat. Ultraviolet Spectrometer and Copernicus Orbiting Astron. Obs.; sci. working groups, adv. coms. NASA, Jet Propulsion Lab., European Space Agy. Author: Atmospheres and Ionospheres of the Outer Planets and their Satellites, 1986; editor: Planetary Aeronomy and Astronomy, 1981, Outer Planets, 1989, Cometary Environments, 1989, Origin and Evolution of Planetary and Satellite Atmospheres, 1989; contbr. numerous articles to books and profl. jours. Recipient NASA award for exceptional sci. contbns. Voyager Project, 1981, NASA Group Achievement award for Voyager Ultraviolet Spectrometer Investigations, 1981, 86, 90, NASA Group Achievement awards for Galileo Probe Mass Spectrometer experiment, and for Significant Outstanding Contbns. to the Galileo Probe and Orbiter to Jupiter, Excellence in Rsch. award U. Mich. Coll. Engring., 1995, Disting. Faculty award U. Mich., 2007. Fellow AAAS; mem. Internat. Assn. Meteorology and Atmospheric Scis. (pres. commn. planetary atmospheres and their evolution 1987-95, sec. 1983-87, pres. emeritus, 1995—), Am. Geophys. Union (assoc. editor Geophys. Rsch. Letters jour. 1986-89), Internat. Astron. Union, Am. Astron. Soc., Internat. Acad. Astronautics (academician 1993—). Office: Space Rsch Bldg Univ Mich Ann Arbor MI 48109-2143

ATWATER, JOHN, news correspondent; b. Chgo. Grad. Journalism and Econs., Northwestern U. Internship Sta. WUWM-FM, Milw., Sta. WISN-TV, Milw.; with pub. rels. dept. Hadley Sch. for the Blind; gen. assignment reporter Sta. WKYT-TV, Lexington, Ky., Sta. WISN-TV, Milw., 2001—. Avocations: being outdoors, biking in summer, snowboarding. Office: Sta WISN PO Box 420 Milwaukee WI 53201-0402

ATWOOD, HOLLYE STOLZ, lawyer; b. St. Louis, Dec. 25, 1945; d. Robert George and Elise (Sauselle) Stolz; m. Frederick Howard Atwood III, Aug. 12, 1978 (div.); children: Katherine Stolz, Jonathan Robert. BA, Washington U., St. Louis, 1968; JD, Washington U., 1973. Bar: Mo. 1973. Jr. ptnr. Bryan Cave, St. Louis, 1973-82, ptnr., 1983—2001, mem. exec. com., 1995-2000, of counsel, 2002—. Bd. dirs. St. Louis coun. Girl Scouts U.S., 1976-86; trustee John Burroughs Sch., St. Louis, 1983-86. Mem. ABA, Met. St. Louis Bar Assn., Washington U. Law Sch. Alumni Assn. (pres. 1983-84), Noonday (St. Louis) (bd. govs. 1983-86). Office: Bryan Cave One Metropolitan Sq 211 N Broadway Saint Louis MO 63102-2733 E-mail: hsatwood@bryancave.com.

ATWOOD, JOHN BRIAN, dean; b. Wareham, Mass., July 25, 1942; s. Ellsworth Savary and Bernice Anita (Perkins) A.; m. Susan Johnson, Aug. 3, 1991; children: John, Deborah, Michelle. BA, Boston U., 1964; postgrad., Am. U., 1970, LLD (hon.), 1995. Mgmt. intern Nat. Security Agy., Washington, 1964-66; fgn. svc. officer U.S. Dept. State, Washington, 1966-71; legis. asst. to Senator Thomas F. Eagleton, 1971-77; dep. asst. sec. for congl. rels. U.S. Dept. State, Washington, 1977-79, asst. sec., 1979-81; dean, profl. studies and acad. affairs Fgn. Svc. Inst., Washington, 1981-82; v.p. Internat. Reporting and Info. Systems, Washington, 1982—; exec. dir. Dem. Senatorial Campaign Com., Washington, 1982-84; pres. Nat. Dem. Inst. for Internat. Affairs, Washington, 1985-93; adminstr. U.S. AID, Washington, 1993-99; pres. Citizens Internat., Boston, 1999—2002; prof. Harvard U., Cambridge, Mass., 1999—2002; dean prof.Hubert H. Humphrey Inst. Pub. Affairs U. Minn., Mpls., 2002—. Mem. Coun. Fgn. Rels., UN Assn. Bd. dirs. Nat. Dem. Inst., World Peace Found., Acad. Ednl. Devel. Recipient Harvard Prize Book award, 1959, Sec. of State Disting. Svc. award. Office: Hubert H Humphrey Inst for Public Affairs 300 Humphrey Ctr 301 19th Ave Minneapolis MN 55455 Home Phone: 952-935-5443; Office Phone: 612-625-0669. E-mail: jbatwood@hhh.umn.edu.

AUER, RON, state legislator; b. St. Louis, Jan. 24, 1950; s. Lawrence J. and Loretta B. Goettler A.; m. Ann Marie Hoelscher, 1980; children: Amanda Marie, Lindsey Marie, Neal Collins, Tracy Collins. BS, S.E. Mo. State U., 1972. Mo. State rep. Dist. 59, 1977—; educator, 1972-77; real estate and ins. agt., 1979-83; mktg. acct. rep. Health Maintenance Orgn. HMO, 1983—. Office: 3120 S Compton Ave Saint Louis MO 63118-2110

AUFDERHEIDE, ARTHUR CARL, pathologist; b. New Ulm, Minn., Sept. 9, 1922; s. Herman John and Esther (Sannwald) A.; m. Mary Lillian Buryk, Jan. 26, 1946; children: Patricia Ann, Tom Paul, Walter Herman. MD, U. Minn., 1946; DSc (hon.), Coll. of St. Scholastica, 1983. Chief dept. pathology Mpls. VA Hosp., 1952-53, St. Mary's Hosp., Duluth, Minn., 1953-57; chief dept. pathology Sch. Medicine U. Minn., Duluth, 1970-87, dean Sch. Medicine, 1974-75, dir. paleobiology lab. Sch. Medicine, 1977—. Mem. Plaisted Polar Expdn., 1968; rsch. cons. anthropology lab. U. Colombia, Bogota, 1989—, Pigorini Mus., Rome, 1988, Archeol. Mus. of Tenerife, Canary Islands, 1989-90; chmn. sci. com. Cronos Rsch Project, Santa Cruz, Tenerife, 1991—. Author: Cambridge Ency. Author: Scientific Study of Mummies 2002 Human Paleopathology, 1998; co-editor: Paleopathology, 1991; author: (documentary film) Copper Eskimo, 1970; contbr. numerous articles to profl. publs. Chmn. civil com. to devel. a degree-granting med. sch., Duluth, 1988. Capt. U.S. Army, 1947-49. Fellow AAAS; mem. Paleopathology Assn., .Y. Acad. Scis. Democrat. Lutheran. Achievements include research in soft tissue paleopathology. Home: 4711 Colorado St Duluth MN 55804-1512 Office: U Minn 10 University Dr Duluth MN 55812-2403 Home Phone: 218-525-2572; Office Phone: 218-726-7911. Business E-Mail: aaufderh@d.umn.edu.

AUGELLI, JOHN PAT, geographer, educator, writer, consultant, rancher; b. Celenza, Italy, Jan. 30, 1921; s. Pat John and M. Antoinette (Iacaruso) A.; divorced; children: John, Robert. BA, Clark U., 1943; MA, Harvard U., 1949, PhD, 1951. Teaching fellow Harvard U., Cambridge, Mass., 1948—49; from asst. to assoc. prof. geography U. P.R., Rio Piedras, 1949—51; assoc. prof. U. Md., College Park, 1952—61; prof. U. Kans., Lawrence, 1961—70, 1971—91; prof. geography, dir. Ctr. Latin Am. Studies U. Ill., Champaign-Urbana, 1970—71. Lectr., travel cons. Mediterranean and Latin Am. cruises, 1991-95; mem. Bd. Fgn. Scholarships, Washington, 1967-70; cons. Nat. Geographic Soc., Washington, 1984-87; del. U.S. Acad. Scis., New Delhi, 1968; sec. Coun. of Inter-Am. Affairs, Washington, 1959-60. Author: Carribean Lands, 1965, Puerto Rico, 1973, Middle America, 3d edit., 1989; cons.: (atlas) World & North America, 1984; contbr. 76 articles to profl. jours. Served to lst lt. U.S. Army, 1943-46, PTO, Res., 1949-51. Recipient Fulbright research grant, 1982. Fellow Am. Geog. Soc.; mem. Assn. Am. Geographers (sec. 1966-69), Latin Am. Studies Assn. (pres. 1969), Nat. Council Geographic Edn. (master tchr. 1979), Conf. of Latin Americanist Geographers (outstanding contbn. to research and teaching award 1982). Democrat. Roman Catholic. Avocations: travel, fishing. Address: 35 Mediterranean Blvd E Port Saint Lucie FL 34952-8557

AULT, JOHN L., manufacturing executive, accountant; b. Findlay, Ohio, Mar. 5, 1946; s. Herman Cedric and Janice J. (Steegman) A.; m. Sean J. Locklear, Dec. 17, 1979; children: John Scott, Jamie Fawn, Wendy Dawn Rogers, Edward H. Rogers III. BS, Miami U., Oxford, Ohio, 1968. CPA, Ohio. Audit supr. Ernst & Whinney, Cleve., 1968-76; fin. analyst Sherwin-Williams Co., Cleve., 1976-78, dir. acctg., 1978-81, asst. contr., 1981-87, v.p., corp. contr., 1987—. Mem. AICPA, Ohio Soc. CPA's, Nat. Assn. Accts., Fin. Execs. Inst. Methodist. Home: 1491 Adelaide St Cleveland OH 44145-2469 Office: Sherwin-Williams Co 101 Prospect Ave NW Cleveland OH 44115

AUMILLER, WENDY L., utilities executive; BS, MBA, Miami U. CPA. Tchr. acctg. Miami U.; with Coopers and Lybrand; various positions in treasury strategic planning Cincinnati Gas & Electric Co., 1980—, asst. treas., gen. mgr. strategic planning, acting treas.; treas. Cinergy Corp., Cincinnati, 2002—. Office: Cinergy Corp 139 E 4th St Cincinnati OH 45202

AUNE, DEBRA BJURQUIST, lawyer; b. Rochester, Minn., June 13, 1956; d. Alton Herbert and Violet Lucille (Dutcher) Bjurquist; m. Gary ReMine, June 6, 1981 (div. June 1993); children: Jessica Bjurquist ReMine, Melissa Bjurquist ReMine; m. David Aune, Jan. 1, 1995. BA, Augsburg Coll., 1978; JD, Hamline U., 1981. Bar: Minn. 1981. Assoc. Hvistendahl & Moersch, Northfield, Minn., 1981-82; adjuster Federated Ins. Cos., Owatonna, 1982-84; advanced life markets advisor Federated Life Ins. Co., Owatonna, 1984-87; mktg. svcs. advisor Federated Ins. Cos., Owatonna, 1987-89, 2d v.p., corp. legal counsel, 1989-92, v.p. gen. counsel, 1992-95, 1st v.p., gen. counsel, 1996-99; ind. cons., 1999—. Mem. Hamline Law Rev., 1979-80. Pres. Owatonna Ins. Women, 1983-84; charter commr. City of Owatonna, 1992—. Mem. ABA, Minn. State Bar Assn., 5th Dist. Bar Assn., Steele County Bar Assn. (sec. 1986-87, v.p. 1987-88, pres. 1988-89), Assn. Life Ins. Counsel, Alliance Am. Insurers (legal com. 1989—). Lutheran. Office Phone: 952-250-9587. E-mail: db.aune@gmail.com.

AUPPERLE, ERIC MAX, engineering educator, research scientist; b. Batavia, NY, Apr. 14, 1935; s. Max Karl and Hedwig Elise (Haas) A.; m. Nancy Ann Jach, June 21, 1958; children: Bryan, Lisa. BSEE, U. Mich., 1957, BSE in Math, 1957, MSE in Nuclear Engring., 1958, Instm.E., 1964. Registered profl. engr., Mich. Lectr. dept. electrical engring. U. Mich., 1972, lectr. dept. indsl. & ops. engring., 1973-74, 1963—, from asst. rsch. engr. to rsch. engr. Cooley Electronics Lab., 1957-69, rsch. engr. Inst. Sci. & Tech., 1969-74, rsch. scientist Inst. Sci. & Tech., 1974—; project leader Merit Computer Network of Inst. Sci. & Tech., U. Mich., 1969-73, assoc. dir., 1973-74, dir., 1974-78; assoc. dir. comm. Computing Ctr. U. Mich., 1981-89, interim dir. Info. Tech. Divsn. Network Systems, 1990-92, pres. Merit Network, Inc. Info. Tech. Divsn. Network Systems, 1988—. Alt. mem. senate assembly U. Mich., 1975, coll. engring. rep. senate assembly, 1976-79, mem. univ. hierarchical computing study com., 1978-79, mem. univ. com. computer policy and utilization, 1979-80, chmn., 1980-84; guest lectr. computer sci. sect. dept. math. Wayne State U., 1975; cons. Cholette, Perkins & Buchanan, Computer Tech. Mgmt. Svcs., Reliance Electric Co., Votrax, Prentice Hall, IMB, Owens-Ill., Donnelly Mirror, Inc., others; panelist instructional sci. equipment program NSF, 1978; mem. program com. Nat. Electronic Conf., 1962-65, 70-73, chmn. student activities com., 1966, chmn. intensive refresher seminar com. 1967, faculty mem. profl. growth seminar series, 1969-74. Editorial bd. Spectrum, 1975-80. Mem. IEEE (sr., dir. Southeastern Mich. sect. 1963-64, 65-67, mem. aid to Apelscor com. 1967-76, mem. Jackson ednl. com. 1967—, Southeastern Mich. sect. treas., 1972, Southeastern Mich. sect. sec. 1973, Southeastern Mich. sect. vice chmn. 1974, Southeastern Mich. sect. chmn. 1975, jr. past chmn. 1976, sr. past chmn. 1977), U. Mich. Sci. Rsch. Club, Phi Eta Sigma, Eta Kappa Nu, Tau Beta Pi, Sigma Xi, Pi Kappa Phi. Office: Merit Network Inc U Mich 4251 Plymouth Rd Ann Arbor MI 48105-2789

AURIN, ROBERT JAMES, entrepreneur; b. St. Louis; m. Kathryn L. Engel, 1998. B in Journalism, U. Mo., 1965. Copywriter Leo Burnett Co., Chgo., 1971-72, Young & Rubicam, Inc., Chgo., 1972-73; from copywriter to v.p., creative dir. Foote, Cone & Belding, Inc., Chgo., 1973-79; exec. v.p., dir. creative services Grey-North Inc., Chgo., 1979-82; pres. Robert Aurin Assocs., Chgo., 1982—; owner ROMAR Investments Co., Chgo., 1984-99. Exec. creative dir. DraftWorldwide, Inc., 1996-99. Lt. USN, 1965—70, Vietnam.

AUSMAN, ROBERT K., surgeon, research and development company executive; b. Milw., Jan. 31, 1933; s. Donald Charles and Mildred (Shafrin) A.; m. Christine McCann, 1992. Student, Kenyon Coll., 1953; MD, Marquette U., 1957. Damon Runyon cancer fellow U. Minn., 1958-61; dir. Health Research Inc. Roswell Park Meml. Inst., 1961-69; dep. dir. Fla. Regional Med. Assn., 1969-70; v.p. clin. research Baxter Travenol Labs., 1970-82, pres. advanced devel. group, 1982-90; pres. Mildon Corp., 1985—, Citation Pub. Co., 1991—. Clin. prof. surgery Med. Coll. Wis., 1972—. Named Outstanding Young Man in N.Y. Buffalo Evening News, 1966, Citizen of Year, 1967 Mem.: Am. Assn. Cancer Rsch., Am. Soc. Clin. Oncology, Masons. Home: PO Box 3538 Long Grove IL 60047 Office: Willow Valley Rd Long Grove IL 60047

AUSTIN, ARTHUR DONALD, II, lawyer, educator; b. Staunton, Va., Dec. 2, 1932; s. George Milnes and Mae (Eichner) A.; m. Irene Clara Wittenberg, June 12, 1960; 1 son, Brian Carl. BS in Commerce, U. Va., 1958; JD, Tulane U., 1963. Bar: Va. 1964, D.C. 1970. Asst. prof. Coll. of William and Mary, Williamsburg, Va., 1963-64, Bowling Green State U., Ohio, 1964-66; asst. prof. law Cleve. State U., 1966-68; prof. law Case Western Res. U., Cleve., 1968-70, 72-78, Edgar A. Hahn prof. jurisprudence, 1978—. Atty. Dept. Justice, Washington, 1970-71 Author: Antitrust: Law, Economics, Policy, 1976, Complex Litigation Confronts the Jury System, 1984, The Empire Strikes Back: Outsiders and the Struggle Over Legal Education, 1998; contbr. articles to law revs. Served with U.S. Army, 1952-54. Decorated Bronze Star medal with V, Purple Heart. Home: 1174 Stony Hill Rd Hinckley OH 44233-9538 Office: 11075 East Blvd Cleveland OH 44106-5409 Office Phone: 216-368-3289.

AUSTIN, JAMES H(OWARD), JR., healthcare executive; b. Durham, NC, June 6, 1951; s. James Howard and Constance E. (Shaw) A.; m. Susan Conger, Sept. 6, 1986; children: James Tanner, Samuel Conger. BA, Yale U., 1976; M.Pub. Policy, M. Urban & Regional Plan., Princeton U., 1982. Economist Govt. of Botswana, 1976-80; cons. Arthur D. Little, Inc., Cambridge, Mass., 1982-86; dir. strategy Anchor HMO, Chgo., 1986-88; cons. Baxter Healthcare, Deerfield, Ill., 1988-90; dir. strategy devel. Renal div. Baxter Healthcare, Deerfield, Ill., 1990—. Mem. Planning Forum (internat. bd. dirs. 1991—), Univ. Club of Chgo. (bd. dirs. 1991-93).

AUSTIN, JOAN KESSNER, mental health nurse; b. Tell City, Ind., Sept. 24, 1944; d. Edward E. and Dorothy A. (Ziegelgraber) Kessner; m. David Ross Austin, Dec. 18, 1965; 1 child, Janet Lynn. Diploma, Deaconess Hosp., Evansville, Ind., 1965; BS in Nursing, Tex. Woman's U., 1975; MS in Nursing, Ind. U., 1978, DNS, 1981. Clin. instr. Tex. Woman's U., Denton, Tex.; with Ind U. Sch. Nursing, Indpls., 1981—, dist. prof. dept. environ. health, 1999—, disting. prof. nursing, 1999—; dir. Ctr. for Enhancing the Quality of Life in Chronic Illness, Indpls., 2000—. Adj. prof. depts. psychiatry & neurology Ind. U. Sch. Medicine, Indpls.; adj. prof. psychology Ind. U. Purdue Sch. Sci.; pres. Am. Epilepsy Soc., 2005—; mem. rsch. commn. Internat. Bur. Epilepsy; profl. adv. bd. Epilepsy Found. Contbr. articles for profl. jours. Grantee Nat. Inst. Neurol. Disorders and Stroke., Distinguished Contribution to Nursing Research in the Midwest award, Midwest Nursing Rsch. Soc., 1993, Clin. Investigator award, Am. Epilepsy Soc., 1993, Spl. Recognition award, Epilepsy Found. Am., 1995, Social Accomplishment award, 1999, Jacob Javits Neurosci. award, NIH, 2000, Disting. Contbn. to Nursing Sci. award, Am. Nurses Found., 2004, Clemens award, Epilepsy Found. St. Louis, 2004. Fellow Am. Acad. Nursing, 1990; mem. Epilepsy Found. Am. (profl. adv. bd. 1987-95), Internat. League Against Epilepsy, Ind. State Nurses Assn., Inst. Medicine Home: 3040 N Ramble Rd W Bloomington IN 47408-1052 Office Phone: 317-274-8254. E-mail: joausti@iupui.edu.

AUSTIN, SAM M., physicist, educator; b. Columbus, Wis., June 6, 1933; s. A. Wright and Mildred G. (Reinhard) A.; m. Mary E. Herb, Aug. 15, 1959; children: Laura Gail, Sara Kay. BS in Physics, U. Wis., 1955, MS, 1957, PhD, 1960. Rsch. assoc. U. Wis., Madison, 1960; NSF postdoctoral fellow Oxford U., Eng., 1960-61; asst. prof. Stanford U., Calif., 1961-65; assoc. prof. physics Mich. State U., East Lansing, 1965-69, prof., 1969-90, univ. disting. prof., 1990-2000, univ. disting. prof. emeritus, 2000—, chmn. dept., 1980-83, acting dean Coll. Natural Sci., 1994, assoc. dir. Cyclotron Lab., 1976-79, rsch. dir., 1983-85, co-dir., 1985-89, dir., 1989-92. Guest Niels Bohr Inst., 1970; guest prof. U. Munich, 1972-73; sci. collaborator Saclay and Lab. Rene Bernas, 1979-80; vis. scientist Triumf-U. B.C., 1993-94; invited prof. U. Paris, Orsay, 1996; mem. grant selection com. sub-atomic physics, NSERC (Can.), 1996-99; mem. com. nuc. physics NRC, 1996-99; mem. steering com. Nuc. Physics Summer Sch.; mem. internat. adv. com. and exec. com. NSF Joint Inst. Nuc. Astrophysics, 2003-. Author, editor: The Two Body Force in Nuclei, 1972, The (p,n) Reaction and Nucleon-Nucleon Force, 1980; editor: Phys. Rev. C., 1988—2002, Virtual Jour. Nuc. Astrophysics, 2003—; editor: (assoc.) Atomic Data and Nuc. Data Tables, 1990—; contbr. over 125 pubs. to profl. jours. Fellow NSF, 1960-61, Alfred P. Sloan Found., 1963-66; recipient Mich. Assn. of Governing Bds. Disting. Prof., 1992 Fellow AAAS (chair nominating com.), Am. Phys. Soc. (vice chmn. nuc. physics divsn. 1981-82, chmn. 1982-83, exec. com. 1983-84, 86-89, coun. 1986-89, coun. exec. com. 1987-88, panel on pub. affairs 1996-98); mem. APS, Sigma Xi (Sr. rsch. award 1977). Achievements include research in nuclear physics, nuclear astrophysics and nitrogen fixation. Home: 1201 Woodwind Trl Haslett MI 48840-8994 Office: Mich State U Nat Supercondr Cyclotron Lab East Lansing MI 48824 Business E-Mail: austin@nscl.msu.edu.

AUSTIN, TERRI JO, state representative; b. Elwood, Ind., May 17, 1955; m. Michael Austin; 2 children. B in Elem. Edn., Ball State U., M in Spl. Edn.; degree in Ednl. Adminstrn. and Supervision, Butler U. Classroom tchr., dist. administr. Anderson Cmty. Sch. Corp., 1983—; nat. cons. U.S. Dept. Edn.; dir. Madison County Cmty. Alliances to Promote Edn.; state rep. dist. 36 Ind. Ho. of Reps., Indpls., 2002—, vice chair, commerce and econ. devel. com., mem. ways and means, pub. policy, ethics and vets. affairs, and tech. R & D coms. Asst. prof. Anderson U.; vice chair econ. trade and cultural affairs NCSL; pub. policy and vets. affairs RMM. Candidate Ind. Ho. of Reps., 2000; mem. alumni bd. Ball State Tchrs. Coll. Mem.: United Way of Madison County, AAUW, LWV, Anderson Area C. of C., Anderson Rotary Club. Democrat. Episcopalian. Office: Ind Ho of Reps 200 W Washington St Indianapolis IN 46204-2786 Home Phone: 765-649-2911; Office Phone: 800-382-9842. E-mail: h36@in.gov.

AUSTRIA, STEVE, state legislator; BA in Polit. Sci., Marquette U. Mem. Ohio Ho. Reps. from 76th dist., Columbus, 1998-2000, Ohio Senate from 10th dist., Columbus, 2001—. Recipient Great Am. Family of the Yr. award Reagan Adminstrn. Mem. KC (Family of the Yr. award), Miami Valley Mil. Affairs Assn., Ohio Twp. Assn., Beavercreek C. of C., Fairborn C. of C., Xenia C. of C., Rotary. Office: Rm # 034 Senate Bldg Columbus OH 43215

AUTTONBERRY, SHERI E., lawyer; BA, La. Tech U., 1996; JD, Vanderbilt U. Law Sch., 1999. Bar: Ohio 1999. Assoc. Katz, Teller, Brant & Hild, Cin., dir., Fine Arts Fund. Mem. Vol. Lawyers for the Poor. Named one of Ohio's Rising Stars, Super Lawyers, 2006. Mem.: Cin. Bar Assn. (legal adv.), Class X, Cin. Acad. Leadership for Lawyers. Avocations: reading, gardening, sports. Office: Katz Teller Brant & Hild 255 E 5th St Ste 2400 Cincinnati OH 45202-4724 Office Phone: 513-721-4532. Office Fax: 513-762-0012.

AUWERS, STANLEY JOHN, motor carrier executive; b. Grand Rapids, Mich., Mar. 22, 1923; s. Joseph T. and Cornelia (Moelhoek) A.; m. Elizabeth Kruis, Apr. 6, 1946; children— Ellen (Mrs. William Northway), Stanley John, Thomas. Student, Calvin Coll., 1940-41; BBA, U. Mich., 1943. C.P.A., Mich. With Ernst & Ernst, Detroit, 1943-51; controller Interstate Motor Freight System, Grand Rapids, Mich., 1951-61, v.p., controller, 1961-65, v.p. finance, 1965-69, exec. v.p., 1969-72; also dir.; pres. Transam. Freight Lines, Detroit, 1973—. Chmn. cost com. Mich. Trucking Adv. Bd. to Mich. Pub. Service Commn., 1958-63; mem. citizens com. to study Mich. tax structure advisory Mich. Ho. Reps., 1958 Mem. Am. Motor Carriers Central Freight Assn. (gov. regular common carrier conf.), Mich. Motor Carriers Central Freight Assn. (v.p., gov.), Tax Execs. Inst., Am. Inst. C.P.A.s, Trucking Employers. Presbyterian. Home: 3099 Lakeshore Dr Douglas MI 49406 Office: 3684 28th St SE Grand Rapids MI 49512-1606 E-mail: sauwers@umich.edu.

AVELLA, JOSEPH RALPH, university professor; b. NYC, Nov. 13, 1942; s. Salvatore Ralph and Bianca (Artoni) A.; m. Felicia Robinson Kauffmann, Oct. 13, 2007, Elizabeth Theresa Eberhardt, Aug. 12, 1967 (dec. Aug. 2000); children: Edward Jay, James Joseph. BS in Chemistry, Rensselaer Poly. Inst., Troy, NY, 1964; MA, Cath. U. Am., Washington, 1992, PhD, 1995; MBA, Capella U., Washington, 2001. Mgr. Md. ops. Great Atlantic and Pacific Tea Co., Inc., 1978-83; program mgr. Honeywell Fed. Sys., Inc., McLean, Va., 1984-86, mgr. integration svcs., 1987-89; dep. dir. mobilization Office Sec. Def., Washington, 1990-92, dir. internat. programs, 1992-93; sr. fellow global strategy program Potomac Found., McLean, 1995-98; prof. and acad. dean Am. Mil. U., Manassas, Va., 1995-98; exec. v.p. Capella U., 1998—2001, prof. bus., 2001—. Seminar moderator US Naval War Coll., Newport, RI, 1989-91; sec. NATO Forces Com., Brussels, Belgium, 1992-94; cons. Masi Rsch. Cons., Inc., Boston, 1995-; pres. Delphic Consulting Inc., 1998; mem. faculty TUI U., 2004-. Contbr. articles to profl. jours. With USNR, 1964—95. Recipient Achievement award No. Va. Navy League, 1989, Cert. of Apprecation Sec. of Navy, 1986, 88, Award of Appreciation U.S. Naval Sea Cadet Corps, 1986. Mem. Assn. Naval Aviation (past chpt. sec.), Navy League US (former mem. bd. dirs.), Pi Sigma Alpha. Roman Catholic. Office: Capella Univ 225 S 6th St Fl 9 Minneapolis MN 55402 Home: 313 Pine Glen Way Englewood FL 34223 Office Phone: 941-460-0247. Personal E-mail: javella@aol.com.

AVENT, SHARON L. HOFFMAN, manufacturing company executive; b. St. Paul, Feb. 7, 1946; d. Ebba and Harold Hoffman; m. Terry Avent; 2 children. Student, Hamline U., St. Paul. With Smead Mfg. Co., Hastings, Minn., 1965—, pres., CEO, 1998—; acquired The Atlanta Group (now Smead-Europe), Hoogezand, Netherlands, 1998—. Bd. dirs. Hastings Public Sch. Found. Named Minn. World Trader of the Year, World Trade Week, Inc., 2002; recipient Spirit of Life honoree, City of Hope, 2003. Office: Smead Mfg Co 600 Smead Blvd Hastings MN 55033-2219

AVERILL, BRUCE ALAN, chemistry professor; b. Bucyrus, Ohio, May 19, 1948; s. Kenneth L. Averill and Mildred (Reid) Krug; m. Patricia Ann Eldredge, Aug. 23, 1986; children: Lindsay Patricia, Alan Eldredge, Ryan Eldredge. BS, Mich. State U., 1969; PhD, MIT, 1973. Asst. prof. chemistry Mich. State U., East Lansing, 1976-81, assoc. prof. chemistry, 1981-82, U. Va., Charlottesville, 1982-88, prof. chemistry, 1988-94; prof. biochemistry U. of Amsterdam, 1994-2001; disting. univ. prof. chemistry U. Toledo, 2001—; Jefferson Sci. fellow U.S. Dept. State, 2004—05, William C. Foster fellow, 2006—. Mem. biophysics adv. panel NSF, Washington, 1985-88; mem. faculty forum for sci. rsch. U. Va., Charlottesville, 1984-88; group leader protein rsch. and coord. chemistry working parties Dutch Found. Chem. Rsch., 1995-2001, mem. exec. com. protein rsch. working party, 1996-99. Acquisitions editor ChemTracts-Inorganic Chemistry, 2002—; contbr. more than 140 articles to sci. jours. A.P. Sloan fellow, 1981-83; recipient creativity award NSF, 1991. Mem. AAAS, Am. Soc. Biochemistry and Molecular Biology, Am. Chem. Soc., Royal Soc. Chemistry, Soc. Biol. Inorganic Chemistry, Sigma Xi. Office: U Toledo Dept Chemistry 2801 W Bancroft Rd Toledo OH 43606-3390 Business E-Mail: baa@utoledo.edu.

AVERY, DENNIS THEODORE, state legislator; b. Evansville, Ind., Sept. 28, 1946; 1 child, Jessica. BS, U. Evansville, 1969. Ind. state rep. Dist. 75, 1974—; mem. environ. affairs, cts. and criminal code com. Ind. Ho. Reps.; ways and means com. Coord. adult mktg. U. So. Ind. Mem. adv. com. Evansville State Hosp.; active Vanderburgh County Arts Coun., Beacon Group, Vanderburgh County Soil Water Conservation Dist. Mem. Med. Sch. Adv. Coun. Address: 11400 Big Cynthiana Rd Evansville IN 47720-7303 E-mail: davery@usi.edu, hts@ai.org.

AVERY, ROBERT DEAN, lawyer; b. Youngstown, Ohio, Apr. 23, 1944; s. Donald and Alta Belle (Simon) Avery; m. Ann Mitchell Lashen, May 16, 1993; 1 child from previous marriage, Benjamin Robert. BA, Northwestern U., 1966; JD, Columbia U., 1969. Bar: Ohio 1971, Calif. 1973, Ill. 2001. Law clk. to Hon. Robert P. Anderson U.S. Ct. Appeals 2d Cir., NYC, 1969-70; assoc. lawyer Jones Day, Cleve., 1970-74, LA, 1974-76, ptnr., 1977-98, adminstrv. ptnr., 1990-92, ptnr. Chgo., 1999—. Editor: Columbia Law Rev., 1968—69. Dir. Wilshire YMCA, LA, 1981—88; mem. bd. govs. Northwstern U. Libr., 2004—. Harlan Fiske Stone scholar. Home: 45 E Division St Chicago IL 60610-2316 Office: Jones Day 77 W Wacker Dr Chicago IL 60601-1662 Office Phone: 312-269-4103. Business E-Mail: rdavery@jonesday.com.

AVIS, ROBERT GRIER, investment company executive, civil engineer; b. St. Louis, June 23, 1931; s. Clarence W. Avis and Mary (Grier) Edwards; m. Ann Y. Freedman, June 12, 1954; children— Lisa Avis Savage, Mary L. Avis Bolin, Stephen G. BSc in Civil Engring., U. Mo., Columbia, 1958. Dept. mgr. Proctor & Gamble Co., Cin., 1958-65; various positions A. G. Edwards, St. Louis, 1965-89; vice chmn. A.G. Edwards, St. Louis, 1989—; chmn. A.G. Edwards Trust Co., 1989—. Bd. govs. Am. Stock Exchange, 1992—. Served to lt. USN, 1952-56 Mem. Securities Industry Assn. (bd. dirs. 1989-92), Chi Epsilon, Tau Beta Pi. Clubs: Old Warson Country (St. Louis); Royal Poinciana Country (Naples, Fla.); Port Royal (Naples, Fla.). Presbyterian. Avocation: sports. Office: A G Edwards & Sons Inc 1 N Jefferson Ave Saint Louis MO 63103-2205

AWAIS, GEORGE MUSA, obstetrician, gynecologist; b. Ajloun, Jordan, Dec. 15, 1929; arrived in U.S., 1951; s. Musa and Meha (Koury) A.; m. Nabila Rizk, June 24, 1970 AB, Hope Coll., 1955; MD, U. Toronto, 1960. Diplomate Am. Bd. Obstetrics and Gynecology. Intern U. Toronto Hosps., Ont., Canada, 1960—61, resident in ob-gyn, 1961—64, chief resident, 1965, Harlem Hosp., Columbia U., NYC, 1966; asst. ob-gyn Cleve. Met. Gen. Hosp., 1967, assoc. ob-gyn, 1969; instr. ob-gyn Case We. Res. U., Cleve., 1967—70, asst. ob-gyn MacDonald House, 1970, asst. prof., 1970, asst. clin. prof. dept. reproductive biology, 1971, asst. ob-gyn Univ. Hosps., 1971; mem. staff, dept. gynecology Cleve. Clinic Found., 1971—91. Chmn. dept. ob-gyn. King Faisal Specialist Hosp. and Rsch. Ctr., Riyadh, 1975-76; cons. panel mem. Internat. Corr. Soc. Obstetricians and Gynecologists, 1971; emeritus staff Cleve. Clinic Found., 1991; pres. Task Force on Humanitarian Aid and Relief Inc., 1997. Contbr. articles to publs. in field, papers, reports to confs., TV appearances, Saudi Arabia Named Grand Officer of Order of Independence His Majesty King Hussein of Jordan, 1992. Fellow ACS, Am. Coll. Obstetricians and Gynecologists, Royal Coll. Surgeons Can.; mem. AMA, AAAS, Am. Infertility Soc., Arab Am. Med. Assn. (pres. 1991—, chmn. humanities relief 1996), Acad. Medicine of Cleve. Office: Cleve Clinic Found Emeritus Office EE/40 9500 Euclid Ave Cleveland OH 44195-0001 Office Phone: 216-444-6814. Business E-Mail: emeritus@ccf.org.

AXE, JOHN RANDOLPH, lawyer, finance company executive; b. Grand Rapids, Mich., Apr. 30, 1938; s. John Jacob and Elizabeth Katherine (Lynott) A.; m. Linda Sadlier Stroh, June 1, 1989; children from previous marriage: Catherine, Peter, Meredith, Sara, Jay, stepchildren: Suzanne Stroh, Greg Stroh. AB, U. Mich., 1960; LLB, Harvard U., 1963. Bar: Mich. 1964. Ptnr. Dickinson, Wright, McKean, Cudlip, Detroit, 1972-80, Martin, Axe, Buhl & Schwartz, Bloomfield Hills, Mich., 1981-82, Axe & Schwartz, Bloomfield Hills, 1983-85, Dykema, Gossett, Spencer, Goodnow, Detroit, 1985-89; prin. John R. Axe and Assocs., Detroit, 1989—2000; shareholder Axe & Ecklund, P.C., Detroit, 2001—. Pres. Mcpl. Fin. Cons., Inc., Gross Pointe Farms, 1982-2005, chmn., 2006-; adj. prof. Wayne State U. Law Sch., 1992-. Mem. Mich. Higher Edn. Assistance Authority, Lansing, Mich., 1977-83. Lt. USNR, 1965—69. Mem. Nat. Assn. Bond Lawyers (steering com. 1981-83, 86, bd. dirs. 1987-90), Mich. Assn. County Treas. (gen. counsel 1977-88), Downtown Assn. Club (N.Y.C.), Doubles Club (N.Y.C.), Mill Reef Club (Antigua). Office: Axe & Ecklund PC 21 Kercheval Ave Ste 360 Grosse Pointe Farms MI 48236-3633 E-mail: johna@mfci.com.

AXELROD, LEONARD, management consultant; b. Oct. 27; s. Morris and Doris S. A. BA, Ind. U., 1972; MPA, U. So. Calif., 1974; JD, Hamline U., 1982. Asst. dir. Ind. Jud. Ctr. Ind. U. Sch. Law, Indpls., 1974-76; cons. Booz, Allen & Hamilton, Washington, 1976-77; staff assoc. Nat. Ctr. State Cts., St. Paul, 1977-82; ptnr. Ct. Mgmt. Cons., Mpls., Va., 1982-87, Friedman, Farrar & Axelrod, Mpls., 1984-86; prin. Ct. Mgmt. Cons., Mpls., 1987-94; v.p. CMC Justice Svcs., Inc., Mpls., 1994—; project mgr. Legal Rsch. Ctr., Mpls., 1996-97; ct. adminstr. U.S. Bankruptcy Ct., Mpls., 1997—2005; govt. acct. mgr. Thomson-West, Mpls., 2005—. Cons. Ctr. Jury Studies, Vienna, Va., 1979-82, Calif. Atty. Gen., 1972-73, Control Data Bus. Advisers, Mpls., 1982-88; arbitrator BBB, 2002—; adj. prof. Coll. Mgmt. Met. State U., 1998— Author: North Dakota Bench Book, 1982; contbr. articles to profl. jours.; assoc. editor Law Rev. Digest, 1982. Mem. presdl. search com. Hamline U., 1980-81; reporter Minn. Citizen Conf. on Cts., 1980; appointed to The Petrofund Bd., 1994. Samuel Miller scholar, 1981. Mem. ABA, ASPA, So. Calif. Soc. Pub. Adminstrn., Booz, Allen & Hamilton Alumni (pres. Minn. 1980), The Brandeis Soc. (exec. dir. Mpls. 1980), U. so. Calif. Midwest Alumni (exec. bd. Chgo. 1974), Phi Alpha Alpha, Phi Alpha Delta. Office: PO Box 11967 Saint Paul MN 55111-0967 Office Phone: 651-398-7345. E-mail: cmc@justice.com.

AXINN, GEORGE HAROLD, rural sociology educator; b. Jamaica, NY, Feb. 1, 1926; s. Hyman and Celia (Schneider) A.; m. Nancy Kathryn Wigsten, Feb. 17, 1945; children: Catherine, Paul, Martha, William. BS, Cornell U., 1947; MS, U. Wis., 1952, PhD, 1958. Editorial asst. Cornell U. Geneva, N.Y., 1947; bull. editor U. Md., College Park, 1949; chmn. dept. rural communication U. Del., Newark, 1950; mem. faculty Mich. State U., East Lansing, 1953—, assoc. dir. coop. extension service, 1955-60; coordinator U. Nigeria program, 1961-65, prof. agrl. econs., 1970-85, prof. resource devel., 1985-95, prof. emeritus, 1996—, asst. dean internat. studies and programs, 1964-85; pres., exec. dir. Midwest Univs. Consortium for Internat. Activities, Inc., 1969-76, 1969-76. FAO rep. to Nepal, 1983-85, India and Bhutan, 1989-91; cons. World Bank, 1973-74, Ford Found., 1968, UNICEF, 1978, FAO, 1974, 87, 89, Govt. of India, 1988; vis. prof. Cornell U., Ithaca, N.Y., 1958-60, U. Ill., Urbana, 1969-70 Author: Modernizing World Agriculture: A Comparative Study of Agricultural Extension Education Systems, 1972, New Strategies for Rural Development, Rural Life Associates, 1978, FAO Guide Alternative Approaches to Agricultural Extension, 1988, Collaboration in International Rural Development -A Practitioner's Handbook (with Nancy W. Axinn), 1997; contbr. articles to various publs. Served with USNR, 1944-46. Recipient Outstanding Alumni award Cornell U. Coll. Agrl. and Life Sci., 1993; W.K. Kellogg Found. fellow, 1956-57. Home: The Fountains at La Cholla 2001 W Rudasill Rd #5211 Tucson AZ 85704 Personal E-mail: axinn@msu.edu.

AXLEY, DIXIE L., insurance company executive; B in Social Welfare, Ill. Wesleyan U. Chartered property casualty underwriter. Pers. devel. specialist State Farm Mutual Automobile Ins. Co., Bloomington, Ill., 1987-88, supt., 1988-91, dir. mgmt. planning and info., 1991-93, mgr. pub. affairs, 1993-94, asst. divsn. mgr., 1994-95, asst. dir.-pub. affairs, then dir.-pub. affairs, 1995-96, asst. v.p.-pub. affairs, 1996-97, v.p. pub. affairs, 1997—. Office: State Farm Ins Cos Pub Affairs Dept 1 State Farm Plz Bloomington IL 61710-0001

AXLEY, FREDERICK WILLIAM, lawyer; b. Chgo., June 23, 1941; s. Frederick R. and Elena (Hoffman-Pinther) A.; m. Cinda Jane Russell, Mar. 29, 1969; children: Sarah Elizabeth, Elizabeth Jane. BA, Holy Cross Coll., 1963; MA, U. Wis., 1966; JD, U. Chgo., 1969. Bar: Ill. 1969, U.S. Dist. Ct. (no. dist.) Ill. 1969, U.S. Ct. Appeals (7th cir.) 1970. Assoc. McDermott, Will & Emery, Chgo., 1969-74, jr. ptnr., 1974-80, sr. ptnr., 1980—. Trustee Wilmette Elem. Sch. Dist. #39, Ill., 1976-81, Ill. chpt. Nature Conservancy, 1983-91; bd. dirs. Bus. and Profl. People for the Pub. Interest, Chgo., 1984—; bd. dirs. Friends of the Chgo. River, 1994—, pres., 1998—; bd. dirs. Shore Line Place, 1994—, pres. 2001—, Interfaith Housing Devel. Corp., 1997—, 1st. v.p., 2000—. Served to lt. USN, 1963-65. Mem. Mich. Shores Club (Wilmette). Democrat. Roman Catholic. Office: McDermott Will & Emery 227 W Monroe St Ste 3100 Chicago IL 60606-5096 E-mail: faxley@msn.com.

AXTELL, JOHN DAVID, genetics educator, researcher, agronomist; b. Mpls., Feb. 5, 1934; s. Maynard J. and Caroline (Kolstad) A.; m. Susan Dee Kent, Aug. 17, 1957; children— Catherine Dee, John D. Jr., Laura Jean BS, U. Minn., St. Paul, 1957, MS, 1965; PhD, U. Wis., Madison, 1967. Research asst. U. Minn., St. Paul, 1957-59; research assoc. U. Wis., Madison, 1959-67; prof. agronomy Purdue U., West Lafayette, Ind., 1967-84, Lynn Disting. prof., 1984—. Mem. Research Adv. com. AID, Washington, 1983—, sci. liaison officer, 1984— Contbr. chpts. to books, articles to profl. jours. Recipient Cert. of Appreciation award U.S. AID, 1975; Alexander Von Humboldt award, 1976; Rsch. award Crop Sci. Soc. Am., 1977; Internat. award Disting. Svc. to Agr., 1984; Sigma Xi Purdue Faculty Rsch. award, 1975; Nat. Inst. Gen. Med. Scis. fellow. Fellow AAAS, Am. Soc. Agronomy; mem. NAS, Am. Soc. Agronomy, Crop Sci. Soc. Agronomy, Sigma Xi, Gamma Sigma Delta, Alpha Zeta Home: 1824 Sheridan Rd West Lafayette IN 47906-2226

AXTELL, ROGER E., writer, retired marketing professional; m. Mitzi Axtell. Degree, U. Wis., 1953. With Parker Pen Co., v.p.; ret. Author: Do's & Taboos Around the World: A Guide to International Behavior, Do's & Taboos of International Trade: A Small Business Primer, Do's & Taboos of Hosting International Visitors, Do's & Taboos of Preparing for Your Trip Aborad, Gestures: Do's & Taboos of Body Language Around the World, LINDO: The Do's & Taboos of Using American/English. Mem. bd. regents U. Wis., 1999—; vice chmn. Gov.'s Task Force on Internat. Edn.; mem. Gov.'s Commn. on U. Wis. Sys. Compensation, Wis., 1992. Named one of 25 most influential people in internat. trade, World Mag., 1998. Office: One Parker Pl Ste 360 Janesville WI 53545

AYALA, MICHAEL, newscaster; b. NY, Aug. 26, 1962; BS in TV and Radio, Ithaca Coll., NYC, 1985; JD with honors, N.Y. Law Sch., 1988. Pvt. practice atty., NYC; bus. and legal affairs atty. Warner-Music Internat., 1990—93; reporter and prodr. Court-TV, 1995—99, anchor Open Court, 1999—2001; co-anchor 5am and 7am news and reporter WBBM-TV, Chgo., 2001—. Prodr.(reporter and prodr.): (TV series) The Sys., 1995—96, Inside Am.'s Courts, 1996—97; TV journalist (documentaries) Hot Guns, CBS FRONTLINE (Emmy, 1997). Avocations: reading, coaching baseball, martial arts.

AYARS, PATTI, human resources specialist, health products executive; B in Bus. Adminstrn. with highest distinction, U. Neb. Various internat. and domestic human resources positions Monsanto Corp./Pharmacia, 1981—2001; sr. v.p. human resources Roche Diagnostic Corp., Indpls., 2001—. Co-author: (book) Mastering Momentum: A Practical and Powerful Approach for Successful Change. Office: Roche Diagnostics Corp 9115 Hague Rd Indianapolis IN 46256-1025 Office Phone: 317-521-2000. Office Fax: 317-845-2221. Personal E-mail: payars01@aol.com.

AYLWARD, RONALD LEE, lawyer; b. St. Louis, May 30, 1930; s. John Thomas and Edna (Ketcherside) A.; m. Margaret Cecilia Hellweg, Aug. 10, 1963; children: Susan Marie Jotte, Stephen Ronald, Carolyn Ann Dolan. AB, Washington U., St. Louis, 1952, JD, 1954; student, U. Va., Charlottesville, 1955. Bar: Mo. 1954, Ill. 1961, US Supreme Ct. 1968. Assoc. Heneghan, Roberts & Cole, St. Louis, 1958-59; asst. counsel Olin Corp., East Alton, Ill., 1960-64; asst. gen. counsel INTERCO, Inc., St. Louis, 1964-66, assoc. gen. counsel, mgr. law dept., 1966-69, asst. sec., 1966-74, gen. counsel, 1969-81, mem. oper. bd., 1970-92, v.p., 1971-81, mem. exec. com., dir., 1975-92, exec. v.p., 1981-85, vice chmn. bd. dirs., 1985-92; chmn., pres. Aylward & Assocs., Inc., St. Louis, 1992—. Mem. dist. export coun. US Dept. Commerce, 1974-77; dir., mem. exec. com. Boatmen's Nat. Bank St. Louis, 1982-91, trust estates com., 1982-85, chmn. audit com., 1986-91; bd. dirs. Boatmen's Bancshares, Inc., mem. audit com., 1984-91, mem. compensation com., 1986-91; trustee Maryville U., 1989-92, chmn. bd., 1991-92. Trustee St. Louis Coun. World Affairs, sec., 1977—84; chmn. lay bd. DePaul Health Ctr., 1979—81; mem. exec. com. lay bd., 1981—89; mem. lay adv. bd. Chaminade Coll. Prep. Sch., 1980—84, chmn. bd. trustees, 1981—84; mem. lay bd. Acad. of the Visitation, 1981—85; bd. dirs. Cath. Charities of St. Louis, 1994—2001, vice chmn., 1995—97, chmn., 1997—99; mem. coun. Archdiocesan Devel. Appeal, 1994—97, chmn., 1996—97, vice chmn., 1995—97, mem. exec. com., 1995—97, chmn. rev./planning com., 1995—96, chmn., 1996—, hon. life mem.; mem. fin. coun. Archdiocese of St. Louis, 1995—98, mem. investment com., 1995—97; bd. dirs. St. Louis chpt. Nat. Found. March of Dimes, 1974—84, sec., 1976—78, chmn., 1979—82; bd. dirs. Cardinal Ritter Inst., 1975—90, chmn. pers. com., 1986—90; bd. dirs. St. Louis chpt. ARC, 1977—82, Linda Vista Montessori Sch., 1975—77, BBB Greater St. Louis, 1978—81, YMCA Greater St. Louis, 1981—2001, adv. dir., 2001—, NCCJ, 1992—93; bd. dirs. Carindal Glennon Children's Hosp., 1991—96, mem. exec. com., 1992—96, bd. dirs. Found., 1996—2001, dir.emeritus, 2001—; bd. dirs., fin. United Way Greater St. Louis, 1986—2001; mem. investment com. St. Louis Cmty. Found., 1993—95. With US Army, 1955—58. Recipient of Order of St. Louis's King, Archdiocese of St. Louis. Mem.: NAM (taxation com. 1970—76, pub. affairs com. 1973—76, govt. ops./expenditures com. 1973—78), St. Louis Bar Assn., Mo. Bar Assn. (sr. counselor), Innsbrook Resort, Am. Soc. Corp. Secs. (pres. St. Louis regional group 1972—73), Am. Apparel Mfrs. Assn. (bd. dirs. 1983—85), Am. Footwear Industries Assn. (nat. affairs vice chmn. 1970, chmn. 1971—75), Assoc. Industries Mo. (bd. dirs. 1973—80, 2d v.p. 1974—76, exec. com. 1974—80, pres. 1976—78), Serra Internat., St. Louis C. of C. (legis. and tax com. 1966—74, vice-chmn. 1970—71), Old Kinderhood Golf Club, Bellerive Country Club, Mo. Athletic Club, Rotary (bd. dirs. St. Louis Club 1976—79), Bellerive Country Club (bd. dirs. 1981—84), Serra Club (trustee 2004—05), Order of St. Louis King, Knights of Malta (hospitaller), Knights of Holy Sepulcher, Delta Theta Phi (pres. St. Louis Alumni 1963, dist. chancellor Mo. 1970—79). Home: 55 Muirfield Saint Louis MO 63141-7372 Office: Aylward and Assoc Inc 55 Muirfield Ct Saint Louis MO 63141

AYRES, RALPH DONALD, state legislator; b. Sept. 12, 1948; BS, Ind. U., 1970, MS, 1975. Coun. mem., Porter County, Ind., 1978-80; state rep. dist. 4 Ind. Ho. of Reps., Indpls., 1980—, mem. cts. and criminal code com., mem. ways and means com.; educator Duneland Sch. Corp., Chesterton, Ind., ret. Named Outstanding Young Hoosier; recipient Elvis J. Stahr Outstanding Tchr. award. Mem. NEA, Ind. Tchrs. Assn., Phi Delta Kappa. Republican. Home: 520 Park Ave Chesterton IN 46304-2929 Business E-Mail: R4@ai.org.

BABB, RALPH W., JR., bank executive; b. Sherman, Tex., Feb. 4, 1949; s. Ralph Wheeler and Billie Margaret (Odneal) B.; m. Barbara Louise Alexander, Aug. 30, 1970; children: Dana P., Derek R. BS in Acctg., U. Mo., Columbia, 1971. CPA, Mo. Audit mgr. Peat, Marwick, Mitchell & Co., CPA's, St. Louis, 1971-78; contr., sr. v.p. Mercantile Bancorp. Inc., St. Louis, 1978-83, treas., sr. v.p., 1979-83, CFO, exec. v.p., 1983-94, vice chmn., 1987-95; EVP, CFO Comerica Bank, Comercia Inc., Detroit, 1995—99, vice chmn., CFO, 1999—2001, CFO, 2002, chmn., pres., CEO, dir., 2002—. Mem. Fin. Execs. Inst. (pres. St. Louis chpt. 1986-87). Methodist. Office: Comerica Inc PO Box 75000 Detroit MI 48275-0001

BABCOCK, CHARLES LUTHER, classics educator; b. Whittier, Calif., May 26, 1924; s. Robert Louis and Margarette Estelle (Fuller) B.; m. Mary Ayer Taylor, Aug. 6, 1955; children: Robert Sherburne, Jennie Rownd Chapman, Jonathan Taylor. AB in Latin, U. Calif., Berkeley, 1948, MA in Latin, 1949, PhD in Classics, 1953. Asst. in classics U. Utah, Salt Lake City, 1949-50; instr. classics Cornell U., Ithaca, N.Y., 1955-57; acting. instr. Stanford U., Calif., summer 1956; asst. prof. classical studies U. Pa., Phila., 1957-62, assoc. prof., 1962-66, asst. dean, vice dean of coll., 1960-62, 62-64, acting dean, spring 1964; prof. classics Ohio State U., Columbus, 1966-92, prof. emeritus, 1992—, chmn. dept., 1966-68, 80-88, dean Coll. of Humanities, 1968-70. Prof.-in-charge summer sch. Am. Acad. in Rome, 1966, resident in classical studies, 1986, acting Mellon prof.-in-charge sch. classical studies, 1988-89, chmn. adv. coun. sch. classical studies, 1992-94; Latin exam. com. Advanced Placement Program, 1967-74, chmn., 1972-74; prof.-in-charge Intercollegiate Ctr. Classical Studies, Rome, 1974, chair mng. com., 1975-82; scholar in residence Hope Coll., 1993. Co-author: Aspects of Roman Civilization, humanftes, 1980; contbr. articles on Latin lit. (especially Horace), Latin epigraphy, Roman civilization. Served to capt. inf. US Army, 1943—47, ETO. Univ. fellow in classics U. Calif., Berkeley, 1951-53; Fulbright scholar in classics, Rome, 1953-55; AAR fellowship, 1953-55. Fellow Am. Acad. in Rome (trustee 1981-83, trustee emeritus 1994—); mem. Am. Philol. Assn. (bd. dirs. 1968-72), Classical Assn. of Mid. West and South (Ovatio award 1982, pres. 1977-78), Vergilian Soc. Am. (pres. 1975-76), Assn. Depts. Fgn. Langs. (pres. 1986), Archeol. Inst. Am., Ohio Classical Conf., Phi Beta Kappa (pres. Epsilon of Ohio 1969-70), Phi Kappa Phi, Phi Sigma Kappa (chpt. pres. U. Calif., regional dep. 1949-51), Scabbard and Blade Club (Pa., hon.), Philomathean Soc. (Pa. hon.), Greater Columbus Latin Club. Home: 969 Village Brook Way Columbus OH 43235-5039 Office: Ohio State U Dept Greek & Latin 230 N Oval Mall Columbus OH 43210-1319 Office Phone: 614-292-3280. E-mail: babcock.2@osu.edu.

BABCOCK, LYNDON ROSS, JR., environmental engineer, educator; b. Detroit, Apr. 8, 1934; s. Lyndon Ross and Lucille Kathryn (Miller) B.; m. Betty Irene Immonen, June 21, 1957; children: Lyndon Ross III, Sheron Lucille Babcock Fruehauf, Susan Elizabeth Babcock Williams, Andrew Dag BSChemE, Mich. Tech. U., 1956; MSChemE, U. Washington, 1958, PhD in Environ. Engring., 1970. Chem. engr. polymers Shell Chem. Co., Calif., N.J., N.Y., 1958-67; assoc. prof. environ. engring., geography, pub. health U. Ill., Chgo., 1970-75, prof. environ. engring., geography, pub. health, 1975-90, prof. emeritus, 1990—, dir. environ. health scis. program Sch. Pub. Health, 1978-79, dir. environ. and occupational health scis. program Sch. Pub. Health, 1979-84, assoc. dean Sch. Pub. Health, 1984-85. Cons. WHO, 1985, Interam. Devel. Bank, 1990-91, Environ. Secretariat Fed. Dist., Mexico City, 1995-97; USA coord. air quality project for Gestión de la Calidad del Aire, Mexico City, 1986-92; environ. cons./lectr. Tech. Instns., Mexican Secretariat of Pub. Edn., 1993-95; vis. prof. El Colegio de Mexico, Mexico City, 1996-2000. Mem. editorial bd. The Environ. Profl., 1979-90; contbr. environ. articles to profl jours.; patentee plastics composition and processing. Bd. dirs. Chgo. Lung Assn., 1981-92. Fulbright lectr., Turkey and India, 1975-76, Mexico, 1986-87, 1992-93; fed. and state environ. research and ednl. grantee Mem. Air and Waste Mgmt. Assn. (chmn. Lake Michigan sect. 1977-78), UN Assn.-USA, League Am. Bicyclists, League Mich. Bicyclists, Chicagoland Bicycle Fedn. (v.p. 1985-86). Office: U Ill Sch Pub Health EOHS MC922 2121 W Taylor St Chicago IL 60612-7260 Office Phone: 517-455-7532. E-mail: lyndonrb@comcast.net.

BABCOCK, SANDRA L., lawyer, educator; BA in Internat. Rels., Johns Hopkins U., Balt., 1986; JD, Harvard U., 1991. Pub. defender Hennepin County, Minn.; dir. Mex. Capital Legal Assistance Prog., 2000; clin. assoc. prof. law, clin. dir. Ctr. Internat. Human Rights Northwestern U. Sch. Law, Chgo., 2006—. Adj. law prof. South Tex. Coll. Law; of counsel Govt. of Mex.; cons. Human Rights Com., Inter-Am. Commn. Human Rights, Inter-Am. Ct. Human Rights. Recipient Aguila Azteca, Govt. of Mex., 2003. Office: Bluhm Legal Clinic Northwestern U Sch Law 357 E Chgo Ave Chicago IL 60611-3069 Office Phone: 312-503-0114. E-mail: s-babcock@law.northwestern.edu, sandrababcock@earthlink.net.

BABINGTON, CHARLES MARTIN, III, lawyer; b. St. Louis, Mar. 15, 1944; s. Charles Martin Jr. and Sarah Elizabeth (Karraker) B.; m. Ann Baker, July 6, 1974; children: Martin, Anthony, Liza. AB, Dartmouth Coll., 1965; JD, U. Mich., 1968; LLM in Tax, Washington U., St. Louis, 1975. Bar: Mo. 1968, U.S. Dist. Ct. (ea. dist.) Mo. 1968, U.S. Ct. Appeals (8th cir.) 1973, U.S. Ct. Claims 1974, U.S. Tax Ct. 1975. Judge adv. USAF, Beale AFB, Calif., 1968-72; assoc. Thompson & Mitchell, St. Louis, 1972-77, ptnr., 1978-95; of counsel Thompson Coburn, 1996-98; ret., 1999. Bd. dirs., sec. St. Louis Steam Train Assn., 1986-2002; bd. dirs. Ecumenical Housing Prodn. Corp., 1992-97. Capt. USAF, 1968-72. Mem. Mo. Bar Assn. (mem. staff benefits com. 1979-96), Univ. Club St. Louis (bd. dirs. 1994-98, sec. 2002—). Republican. Episcopalian. Avocations: steam locomotive restoration, photography. Home: 25 Warson Ter Saint Louis MO 63124-1680 E-mail: cbabing3@swbell.net.

BABLER, JAMES CARL, lawyer; b. Antigo, Wis. Oct. 13, 1955; s. Carl Leo and Barbara Ruth (Hoppe) B. B.A., U. Wis., 1976, J.D., 1979. Bar: Wis. 1979, U.S. Dist. Ct. (we. dist.) Wis. 1979. Asst. dist. atty Barron County, Barron, Wis., 1979-80; asst. dist. atty. Polk County, Balsam Lake, Wis., 1980-83; dist. atty. Barron County, 1983—; instr. Wis. Indianhead Tech. Inst., Rice Lake, Wis., 1981—. Mem. Wis. Dist. Attys. Assn., Wis. Law Enforcement Officers Assn. Democrat. United Methodist. Home: 266 W Monroe Ave Barron WI 54812-1327

BABLER, WAYNE E., JR., lawyer; b. Detroit, Apr. 29, 1942; s. Wayne E. and Mary E. (Blome) Babler; m. Patricia A. Ward, Feb. 5, 1972; children: Dean W., Anne E. BA, Wittenberg U., 1964; JD, U. Wis., 1967. Bar: Wis. 1967, US Dist. Ct. (ea. and we. dists.) Wis. 1967, US Ct. Appeals (7th cir.) 1971, US Supreme Ct. 1980, US Ct. Appeals (9th and 10th cirs.) 1981, US Ct. Appeals (DC cir.) 1983, US Dist. Ct. (ctrl. and no. dists.) Ill. 1987, US Dist. Ct. (ea. and we. dists.) Mich. 1990. Assoc. Quarles, Herriott, Clemons, Teschner & Noelke, Milw., 1971-74, Quarles & Brady, Milw., 1974-76, ptnr., 1976—. Rep. of chief justice Wis. Supreme Ct. to Wis. Jud. Compensation Com., 1983—84. Author (with others): Business and Commercial Litigation in Federal Court, 1998, 2005; rsch. editor: Wis. Law Rev., 1966—67, Antitrust, Federal Civil Litigation, State Civil Litigation. Campaign cabinet United Performing Arts Fund, Inc., Milw., 1977—78; bd. dirs. Milw. Bar Found., 1976—79, Wis. Bar Found., 1983—2000, pres., 1985—87; bd. dirs. Legal Aid Soc., Milw., 1997—2006; mem. U. Wis. Benchers Soc. With JAGC USN, 1967—71. Fellow: Wis. Law Found., Am. Coll. Trial Lawyers (state chair 2002—04), Am. Bar Found.; mem.: ABA (ho. of dels. 1984—96), Bar Assn. 7th Fed. Cir., State Bar Wis. (bd. govs. 1983—87), Milw. Bar Assn. (bd. dirs. 1976—83, pres. 1981—82), Delreay Dunes Country Club, Order of Coif. Office: Quarles & Brady 411 E Wisconsin Ave Milwaukee WI 53202-4497 Home: 2 Acacia Dr Boynton Beach FL 33436 Office Phone: 414-277-5529. Business E-Mail: web@quarles.com.

BABLITCH, WILLIAM A., lawyer, retired state supreme court justice; b. Stevens Point, Wis., Mar. 1, 1941; BS, U. Wis., Madison, 1963, JD, 1968; MA,

U. of Virginia, 1987. Bar: Wis. 1968. Pvt. practice law, Stevens Point, Wis.; dist. atty. Portage County, Wis., 1969-72; mem. Wis. Senate, 1972-85, senate majority leader, 1976-82; justice Wis. Supreme Ct., Madison, 1983—2003; atty. Michael Best & Friedrich, Madison, 2003—. Volunteer US Peace Corp., Liberia, 1963—65. Mem.: Nat. Conf. State Legislators (exec. com. 1979). Office: Michael Best & Friedrich One S Pinckney St Ste 700 Madison WI 53703 Office Phone: 608-283-0100. Office Fax: 608-283-2275. E-mail: wabablitch@michaelbest.com.

BABROWSKI, CLAIRE HARBECK, retail executive; b. Ottawa, Ill., July 25, 1957; d. John Clayton Harbeck and Corrine Ann (Lavender) French; m. David Lee Babrowski, July 3, 1982; 2 stepdaughters. Student, U. Ill., 1975-77; MBA, U. NC, 1995. Dental asst., Ottawa, 1975-76; crew person McDonald's Corp., Ottawa, 1974-76, mem. restaurant mgmt. Champaign, Ill., 1976-80, ops. and tng. cons. St. Louis, 1980-84, ops. mgr., 1984-86, dir. nat. ops. Oak Brook, Ill., 1986-88, dir. ops. Phila., 1988-89, sr. regional mgr. Raleigh, NC, 1989—92, regional v.p., 1992—95, corp. v.p. ops., 1995—97, sr. v.p. ops., 1997—98, exec. v.p. U.S. Restaurant Sys., 1998—99, exec. v.p. Worldwide Restaurant Sys., 1999—2001, pres. McDonald's Asia/Pacific/the Middle East and Africa, 2001—03, chief restaurant ops. officer, 2003—04; exec. v.p., COO RadioShack Corp., Fort Worth, Tex., 2005—06, acting CEO, 2006; exec. v.p., COO Toys "R" Us, Inc., Wayne, J, 2007—. Chmn. NC Ronald McDonald's Children's Charities, Raleigh, 1989-95; relationship ptnr. Donatos Pizza, Pret A Manger, Chipotle Mexican Grill, chmn. bd. dirs.; mem. Com. of 200.; bd. dir. Delhaize Group, 2006-. Author: (manual) Training Consultants Development Program, 1987. Named one of Named one of Next 20 Female CEOs, Pink Mag. & Forté Found., 2006; recipient Emerging Leader award, US Women's Svc. Forum. Mem. NC Restaurant Assn. (bd. dirs. 1992-95). Republican. Roman Catholic. Avocations: tennis, gardening. Office: Toys R Us Inc 1 Geoffrey Way Wayne NJ 07470

BACA, STACEY, newscaster; married. BA in Broadcast News, U. Colo., Boulder, 1991. Staff writer Brighton Std.-Blade, Colo., 1991—92, Denver Post, 1992—96; anchor weekend am news WTKR-TV, Norfolk, Va., 1996—98, KNSD-TV, San Diego, 1999—2002, reporter, 1999—2002; co-anchor Sunday Morning News and reporter WLS-TV, Chgo., 2002—. Mem.: Nat. Assn. of Hispanic Journalists. Office: WLS-TV 190 N State St Chicago IL 60601

BACH, JAN MORRIS, composer, educator; b. Forrest, Ill., Dec. 11, 1937; s. John Nicholas and Anne (Morris) B.; m. Dalia Zakaras; children: Dawn, Eva. MusB, U. Ill., 1959, MusM, 1961, MusD, 1971; postgrad., U. Va., Arlington, 1963—65, Yale U., 1960, Berkshire Music Ctr., 1961. Instr. music U. Tampa, Fla., 1965—66; prof. music No. Ill. U., DeKalb, 1966—2002, Presdl. Rsch. prof. Dekalb, 1982—86, Disting. Rsch. prof., 1986—; composer-in-residence Institut de Hautes Etudes Musicales, Montreux, Switzerland, 1976; editor for brass compositions M.M. Cole, Chgo., 1968—72. Mem. Ill. Arts Coun., 1986-89, Ind. Arts Coun., 1992. Composer: Skizzen, 1967, Woodwork, 1970, Eisteddfod, 1972, Turkish Music, 1968, Four Two-Bit Contraptions, 1971, The System, 1973, Dirge for a Minstrel, 1974, Three Choral Dances, 1975, Laudes, 1975, Piano Concerto, 1975, Three Bagatelles, 1978, Hair Today, 1978, The Happy Prince, 1978, My Wilderness, 1979, Student from Salamanca, 1979, Rounds and Dances, 1980, Horn Concerto, 1982, Helix, 1984, Escapade, 1984, Dompes & Jompes, 1986, Harp Concerto, 1986, Trumpet Concerto, 1987, A Solemn Music, 1987, Triptych, 1989, Euphonium Concerto, 1990, With Trumpet and Drum, 1991, Anachronisms String Quartet, 1991, People of Note, 1993, Concerto for Steelpan and Orchestra, 1994, The Last Flower, 1995, Foliations, 1995, Bassoon Concertino, 1996, Pilgrimage, 1997, Variations on a Theme of Brahms, 1997, Kimberly's Song, 1998, Dear God, 1998, NIU MIUSIC, 1999, In the Hands of the Tongue, 1999, The Duel, 1999, Songs of the Streetwise, 2000, Music for a Low Budget Epic, 2001, If Music be the Food of Love, 2001, Tuba Concerto, 2003, Choral Fanfare, 2003, The Haunted Palace, 2004, Penny Poems, 2004, A Prayer of Intercession, 2004, A Little Knight Music, 2005, The Song of Simeon, 2005, Triple Play, 2005, Oompah Suite, 2006, Baptism of Christ, 2006, Duologue, 2007, Berceuse, 2007, Blowout, 2007 (CDs) The Happy Prince, 1980, Laudes: The NY Brass Quintet, 1980, Rounds and Dances: Premieres, 1984, Four Two-Bit Contraptions: Is This the Way to Carnegie Hall?, 1986, Introducing the Bowie Brass Quintet, 1989, Skizzen: American Wind Music, 1990, Eisteddfod: Chamber Music for Flute, Harp, and Strings, 1990, Meridian Arts Ensemble, 1991, Heavy Metal, 1993, 20th Century Wind Chamber Music, 1994, Clockworks, 1995, Concert Variations: Eu-Fish, 1995, Fanfare and Fugue: Contrasts for Trumpets, 1995, Eisteddfod: In the Shadow of a Miracle, 1996, Triptych: Premier, 1996, Praetorius Suite: Jubilee, 1997, Eisteddfod: Garten von Freuden und Traurigkeit, 2000, The Duel: Spring Flowers, 2000, Concert Variations: Obsessions, 2002, Steelpan Concerto: Paul Freeman Introduces Exotic Concertos, 2002, My Very First Solo: My Very First Solo, 2003, Concert Variations: Everyone But Me, 2003, Gala fanfare, Concerto for Horn and Orch., French Suite, Helix, Four Two-Bit Contraptions: The Music of Jan Bach, 2006, Concert Variations: The Real Euphonium, II, 2007; commns. include Tuba Brotherhood, 1977, Internat. Trumpet Guild, 1978, 86, Internat. Brass Congress, 1980, Greenwich Philharmonia, 1981, Orch. of Ill., 1982, NACWPI, 1982, Minot Symphony, 1984, Am. Brass Quintet-Chamber Music Am., 1988, Sacramento Symphony-N.C. Symphony, 1989, Camarata Singers, 1991, WFMT-Vermeer Quartet, 1991, Woodstock Chimes Fund, 1994, Ronen Chamber Ensemble, 1994, Stockholm Chamber Brass, 1994, Eileen Gress-N.C. Symphony, 1995, Elmhurst Symphony, 1996, Ramon Parcells, 1996, Palos Park Cmty. Chorale, 1997, Cantori of Hobart and William Smith Colls., 1998, No. Ill. Children's Chorus, 1999, South Bend Chamber Singers, 1999, Robert Sims, 1999, Regina H. Helcher, 2000, Jeff Nesseth, 2001, Jay Hunsberger-Fla. West Coast Symphony, 2002, Gloria Musicae, 2003, Diane Ragains, 2004, Kaneland Cmty. Schs., 2005, Zephyr Brass Trio, 2005, Walker Bowman, 2005, Internat. Double Reed Soc., Nebr. Brass, others. With US Army, 1962—65. Recipient BMI student composers 1st prize, 1957, Koussevitsky composition award, 1961, Harvey Gaul composition award, 1973, Mannes Opera award, 1973, Pulitzer prize nomination, 1973, 81, 82, 84, 92, SAI composition award, 1974, Excellence in Tchg. award No. Ill. U., 1978, choral composition award Brown U., 1978, Nebr. Sinfonia Chamber Orch. contest, 1979, N.Y.C. Opera contest, 1980; named to Fox Valley Arts Hall of Fame, 2004. Mem. Broadcast Music, Phi Eta Sigma, Phi Mu Alpha, Phi Kappa Phi, Pi Kappa Lambda, Omicron Delta Kappa. Business E-Mail: janbach@janbach.com.

BACHE, ROBERT JAMES, physician, educator; MD, Harvard U. Diplomate Am. Bd. Internal Medicine, Am. Bd. Cardiovasc. Disease. Resident in internal medicine Duke U., Durham, NC, assoc. prof. medicine; prof. medicine U. Minn., Mpls. Contbr. articles to profl. jours. Fellow Am. Coll. Cardiology; mem. Am. Soc. for Clin. Investigation, Assn. of Am. Physicians, Assn. Univ. Cardiologists, Am. Heart Assn. Office: U Minn Med Sch Med Box 508 Mayo 420 Delaware St SE Minneapolis MN 55455-0374 Office Phone: 612-624-8970. Business E-Mail: bache001@umn.edu.

BACHELDER, CHERYL ANNE, former food service company executive; b. Columbus, Ohio, May 4, 1956; d. Max Edwin and Margaret Anne Stanton; m. Christopher Frank Bachelder, June 13, 1981; 2 children. BS, Ind. U., 1977, MBA, 1978. Asst. product mgr. Procter & Gamble Co., Cin., 1978-81; product mgr. The Gillette Co., Boston, 1981-84; sr. product mgr. R.J.R. Nabisco, Planters Life Savers Co., Parsippany, N.J., 1984, group product mgr., 1985-87, dir. mktg. Winston-Salem, NC, 1987, v.p. mktg., 1988-91; v.p., gen. mgr. Life Savers Div., Nabisco Foods Group, 1991-92; pres. Bachelder & Assoc., 1992-95; v.p. mktg. & product devel. Domino's Pizza, Inc., Ann Arbor, Mich., 1995—2001; pres., chief concept officer KFC Corp., divsn. Yum! Brands, 2001—03. Bd. dirs. True Value Co., 2006—, AFC Enterprises, Inc., 2006—. Named one of 100 Best and Brightest Women in Advt. Advt. Age mag., Chgo., 1988; featured in Fortune Mag. People to Watch column, 1990. Home: 41 Glendale Ave Hillsdale MI 49242-1524

BACHER, ROBERT NEWELL, church official; b. Houston; m. Shirley Ann Good; children: Carol Lynn March, Laurie Ann Andrews, Joy Marie. BA in English, BS in Indsl. Engring., Tex. A&M U., 1957; MDiv, Luth. Sch. Theology, Chgo., 1961; MEd in Edn. Psychology, Temple U., 1970; MPA, DPA, U. So. Calif., 1981. ordained, 1961. Pastor St. Mark Luth. Ch., Lakewood, Colo., 1961-66; assoc. youth dir. Commn. Youth Ministry Luth. Ch. in Am., Phila., 1966-72; project mgr. action rsch., dept. rsch. and planning Divsn. for Parish Svcs., Luth. Ch. in Am., Phila., 1972-75, asst. dir. dept. rsch. and planning, 1975-77, asst. exec. dir. planning and budgeting, 1977-85, exec. dir., 1985-87; exec. for adminstrn., asst. to bishop Evang. Luth. Ch. in Am., 1987—. Contbr. articles to profl. jours. Office: Evang Luthern Church in Am 8765 W Higgins Rd Chicago IL 60631-4101

BACHMAN, SISTER JANICE, healthcare executive, religious order administrator; b. Coshocton, Ohio, Oct. 25, 1945; d. Edward Michael and Kathryn Elizabeth (Norris) B. Student, Ohio Dominican Coll., 1963-67; BS in Pharmacy, Ohio State U., 1971; MBA in Mgmt., Xavier U., 1976; MA in Christian Spirituality, Creighton U., 1989. Joined Dominican Sisters, 1963. Staff pharmacist St. George Hosp., Cin., 1971-73, dir. pharmacy svcs., 1973-76; instr. pharmacology and related courses Coll. Mt. St. Joseph, Cin., 1973-74; instr. pharmacology Sch. Nursing Bethesda Hosp., Cin., 1975; adminstrv. resident St. Joseph Hosp., Mt. Clemens, Mich., 1976-77, adminstrv. asst., 1977-78, asst. adminstr., 1978-79; corp. dir. religious programs St. Francis-St. George Hosp., Inc., Cin., 1979-80, asst. v.p. hosp. support svcs., 1980-82, v.p. therapeutic and diagnostic svcs., 1983-89; dir. exec. affairs Benedictine Health Sys., Inc., Duluth, Minn., 1989-90; vicaress Dominican Sisters St. Mary of the Springs, Columbus, Ohio, 1990-96. Editor: Guidelines for Developing an IV Admixture, 1976. Trustee Ohio Dominican Coll., 1980-96, mem. devel. com., 1984-94, physical facilities com., 1994-96; mem. radiologic tech. adv. bd. Xavier U., Cin., 1983-89; mem. MLT adv. bd. Coll. Mt. St. Joseph, 1983-85; trustee Program for Medically Underserved dba Health Moms and Babes, 1986-91, co-founder, chair, 1986-89; bd. dirs. Franciscan Health Sys. Cin., 1990-92; chmn. bd. dirs. Nazareth Towers, Columbus, 1990-94; bd. dirs. Dominican Acad., N.Y.C., 1990-95; trustee St. Mary of the Springs Montessori Sch., Columbus, 1990-95; trustee Milford (Ohio) Spiritual Ctr., 1993-99, vice chair, 1993-94, chair, 1994-98; mem. fin. com. Dominican Leadership Conf., 1994-96; bd. dirs. Westwood Civic Assn., Cin., 1979-86, past sec., past 1st v.p., past pres.; mem. steering com. Cong. Neighborhood Groups, Cin., treas., 1981-84; mem. planning divsn. bd. Cmty. Chest and Coun., Cin., 1981-88, chair single parent task force study, 1983-85; mem. rev. bd. City of Cin. Commercial/Indsl. Revolving Loan Fund, 1982-84; bd. dirs. Cin. Area Chpt. ARC, 1982-89, chair nursing and health com., 1983-87, bd. exec. com., 1987-89; bd. dirs. SW Ohio Residences, Cin., 1983-89, vice chair, 1984-87, chair, 1987-89; trustee Providence Fund, Franciscan Sisters of Stella, Niagara, N.Y., 1996—, C.G. Jung Assn. Ctrl. Ohio, co-chair program com., 1996-99; trustee Las Casas (Ministry to Cheyenne and Arapaho Native Ams.), Canton, Okla., 1996-2003, treas., 1997—2002. Recipient Cmty. Leadership award United Appeal and Cmty. Chest, 1985, 9th Ann. Living Faith award Columbus Met. Area Ch. Coun., 2000. Fellow Am. Coll. Healthcare Execs.; mem. Spiritual Dirs. Internat. Avocations: swimming, cross country skiing, biking. Office: St Mary of the Springs 2320 Airport Dr Columbus OH 43219-2098 Personal E-mail: janbachman@aol.com.

BACHMANN, JOHN WILLIAM, security firm executive; b. Centralia, Ill., Nov. 16, 1938; s. George Adam and Helen (Johnston) B.; m. Katharine I. Butler; children: John C., Kristene Ellen Bachmann. AB, Wabash Coll., 1960; MBA, Northwestern U., 1962; LLD (hon.), Wabash Coll., 1990. Rschr. Edward Jones, St. Louis, 1962-63, investment rep., 1963-70, gen. ptnr., 1970-80, mng. ptnr., 1980—2003, sr. ptnr., 2004—. Bd. dirs. Am. Airlines, Inc., The Monsanto Co. Emeritus Trustee Wabash Coll., Crawfordsville, Ind., 2007-; chmn. bd. visitors Drucker Ctr. Claremont (Calif.) Grad. Sch., 1987—; past chmn., bd. dirs. Arts and Edn. Coun. Greater St. Louis; commr. St. Louis Art Mus.; chmn. St. Louis Symphony Soc.; past chmn. St. Louis Regional Chamber and Growth Assn.; past chmn. US C. of C., 2004-05, chmn. exec. com. 2005-06. Mem. Nat. Assn. Securities Dealers (past dist. chmn., bd. dirs.), Securities Industry Assn. (bd. dirs., chmn. 1976-79), Securities Industry Found. for Econ. Edn. (chmn. trustees 1988-92), St. Louis Club, Bogey Club. Office: Edward Jones 12555 Manchester Rd Saint Louis MO 63131

BACHMANN, MICHELE, congresswoman, former state legislator; b. Waterloo, Iowa, Apr. 6, 1956; m. Marcus Bachmann; 5 children. BA, Winona State U., 1978; JD, Coburn Sch. Law, 1986; LLM, Coll. William & Mary, 1988. Tax litigation atty. US Fed. Tax Ct., St. Paul, 1988—93; mem. Minn. State Senate from Dist. 52, 2000—07, asst. minority leader, 2004—05, mem. capital investment com., edn. com., taxes com., jobs, housing and cmty. devel. com., E-12 edn. budget divsn. com.,property tax budget divsn. com; mem. US Congress from 6th Minn. dist., 2007—, mem. fin. svcs. com. Named a Friend of the Taxpayer, Taxpayers League Minn., 2001—02; named Best Friend of the Taxpayer, 2003—04. Republican. Wis. Evangelical Lutheran Synod. Office: 412 Cannon House Office Bldg Washington DC 20515

BACIGALUPI, DON, museum director; BA summa cum laude, U. Houston; MA, U. Tex., Austin, PhD in Art Hist. Tchr. art hist. U. Tex., U. Houston; dir., chief curator Blaffer Gallery, U. Houston; curator contemporary art San Antonio Mus. Art; exec. dir. San Diego Mus. Art, 1999—2003; pres., dir., CEO Toledo Mus. Art, 2003—. Named one of 50 People to Watch, San Diego Mag., 2000. Office: Toledo Museum Art PO Box 1013 Toledo OH 43697

BACKER, GRACIA YANCEY, state legislator; b. Jefferson City, Mo., Jan. 25, 1950; m. F. Mike Backer; 1 child, Justin. Student, S.W. Mo. State Coll. Mem. from dist. 20 Mo. Ho. of Reps., 1983—2000; majority floor leader, 1996-98; dep. chief of staff Gov. Roger Wilson, Mo., 2000; dir. divsn. employment security Mo. Dept. Labor, 2001—. Active NAACP. Democrat. Baptist. Home: 2885 State Road Tt New Bloomfield MO 65063-1643 Office: Divsn Employment Security Dept Labor 421 E Dunklin St PO Box 59 Jefferson City MO 65104-0059

BACKMAN, VADIM, biomedical engineer, educator; b. St. Petersburg, Russia, May 7, 1973; arrived in U.S., 1996, naturalized, 2002; s. Yuri and Galina Backman. MS, St. Petersburg Technical U., 1996, MIT, 1998; PhD, Harvard U., 2001. Rsch. asst. Ioffe Phys. Tech. Inst. Russian Acad. Sci., St. Petersburg, 1993—96; rsch. asst. MIT, Cambridge, Mass., 1996—2000, rsch. assoc., 2000—01; asst. prof., dir. biomed. optical imaging & spectroscopy lab. Northwestern U., Evanston, Ill., 2001—. Cons. MIT, Cambridge, 2001—. Author: Handbook of Optical Biomedical Diagnostics, 2002, Biomedical Optical Engineering, 2002; contbr. articles to profl. jours. Named one of 100 Most Innovative People Under 35, Tech. Rev. Mag., 2005; recipient Best Paper award in New Techs. in Biomedical Optics and Med. Imaging, Nat. Sci. Found., 2002, Nat. Sci. Found. Career award, 2003, Translational Rsch. award, Coulter Found., 2006; fellow, George Soros Internat. Sci. Found., 1995, Lester Wolfe fellow, 1999, Poitras fellow, 2000; scholar, GM Cancer Rsch. Found., 2002. Mem.: Am. Physical Soc., Optical Soc. Am. Achievements include invention of light scattering spectroscopy; tri-modal spectroscopy of tissue. Office: BME Dept Northwestern Univ 2145 Sheridan Rd Evanston IL 60208 Home Phone: 773 404-8219; Office Phone: 847-491-3536. Office Fax: 847-491-4928. Business E-Mail: v-backman@northwestern.edu.

BACKSTROM, NIKLAS, professional hockey player; b. Helsinki, Finland, Feb. 13, 1978; Goalie Karpat Oulu (Finnish Elite League), 2002—06, Minn. Wild, 2006—. Co-recipient William M. Jennings Trophy, 2007; recipient Roger Crozier Saving Grace Award, 2007. Office: c/o Minn Wild 317 Washington St Saint Paul MN 55102

BACON, BRETT KERMIT, lawyer; b. Perry, Iowa, Aug. 8, 1947; s. Royden S. and Aldeen A. (Zuker) B.; m. Bonnie Jeanne Hall; children: Jeffrey Brett, Scott Michael. BA, U. Dubuque, 1969; JD, Northwestern U., 1972. Bar: Ohio 1972, U.S. Ct. Appeals (6th cir.) 1972, U.S. Supreme Ct. 1980. Assoc. Thompson, Hine & Flory, Cleve., 1972-80, ptnr., 1980-2000; founding ptnr. Frantz Ward, Cleve., 2000—. Spkr. in field. Author: Computer Law, 1982, 84. V.p. profl. sect. United Way, Cleve., 1982-86; pres. Shaker Heights Youth Ctr., Inc., Ohio, 1984-86; elder Ch. of Western Res., 1996—. Mem. Fedn. Ins. and Corp. Counsel, Bar Assn. Greater Cleve., Cleve. Play House Club (officer 1986-94, pres. 1991-93, pres. men's com. 1993-96), Pepper Pike Civic League (trustee and treas. 1994-97). Home: 8190 Devon Ct Chagrin Falls OH 44023 Office: Frantz Ward LLP Key Ctr Ste 2500 127 Public Sq Cleveland OH 44114 Office Phone: 216-515-1613. Business E-Mail: bbacon@frantzward.com.

BACON, BRUCE RAYMOND, physician; b. Amherst, Ohio, Nov. 7, 1949; s. Raymond Clifford and Cathryn E. (Fowell) B.; children: Jeffrey Dale, Laurie Katherine. BA in Chemistry, Coll. Wooster, 1971; MD, Case We. Res. U., 1975. Diplomate Am. Bd. Internal Medicine and Gastroenterology. Asst. prof. medicine Case We. Res. U., Cleve., 1982—87, assoc. prof. medicine, 1987—88; assoc. prof. medicine, chief gastroenterology sect. La. State U., Shreveport, 1988—90; prof. internal medicine, dir. gastroenterology divsn. St. Louis U. Sch. Medicine, 1990—. Chair subsplty. bd. gasteroenterology Am. Bd. Internal Medicine, 1999-2003, chair subsplty. bd. transplant hepatology, 2004-. Co-author: Essentials of Clinical Hepatology, 1993; co-editor: Liver Disease: Diagnosis and Management, 2000, Comprehensive Clinical Hepatology, 2006; contbr. numerous articles to profl. jours. Fellow ACP, Am. Coll. Gastroenterology, Am. Soc. Clin. Investigation; mem. Am. Assn. Study Liver Disease (pres. 2004). Presbyterian. Avocation: photography. Office: St Louis U Health Sci Ctr 3635 Vista Ave PO Box 15250 Saint Louis MO 63110-0250 Office Phone: 314-577-8764. Business E-Mail: baconbr@slu.edu.

BACON, GEORGE EDGAR, pediatrician; b. NYC, Apr. 13, 1932; s. Edgar and Margaret Priscilla (Anderson) B.; m. Grace Elizabeth Graham, June 30, 1956; children: Nancy, George, John BA, Wesleyan U., 1953; MD, Duke U., 1957; MS in Pharmacology, U. Mich., 1967. Diplomate Am. Bd. Pediatrics, subsplty. Bd. Pediatric Endocrinology. Intern in pediatrics Duke Hosp., Durham, NC, 1957-58; resident in pediatrics Columbia-Presbyn. Med. Ctr., NYC, 1961-63; from instr. to prof. emeritus U. Mich., Ann Arbor, 1963—86, prof. emeritus, 1986—, chief pediatric endocrinology svc., dept. pediatrics, 1970-83, dir. house officer programs, dept. pediatrics, 1981-86, assoc. chmn. dept. pediatrics, 1983-86, mem. senate assembly, 1978-80; vice chmn. dir.'s adv. coun. Univ. Hosp., Ann Arbor, 1981-82; prof. pediatrics Tex. Tech U., Lubbock, 1986—90, chmn. dept., 1986—90, chmn. med. practice income plan, 1989; chief staff pediatrics Lubbock Gen. Hosp., 1986—90; dir. med. edn. and rsch. Butterworth Hosp., Grand Rapids, Mich., 1990-91, med. dir. dept. pediatrics, 1991—95; prof. pediatrics Mich. State U., East Lansing, 1990—95; pediatric endocrinologist Univ. Mich. Hosp., Ann Arbor, 1995—2007, Detroit Med. Ctr., Southfield, Mich., 1996—2001. Coord. profl. svc. C.S. Mott Children's Hosp., 1973-83, mem. exec. com. for clin. affairs, 1975-76, 77-79, assoc. vice chmn. med. staff, 1978-79; chmn. exec. com. Women's Hosp., Holden Hosp., Ann Arbor, 1973-82. Author: A Practical Approach to Pediatric Endocrinology, 1975, 3d edit., 1990; contbr. articles to profl. jours. Capt. U.S. Army, 1958-61. Fellow Am. Acad. Pediatrics (treas. Mich. chpt. 1983-86, alt.-at-large 1995-2001, coun. Tex. chpt. 1986-89, Pediatrician of Yr. Mich. chpt. 2002); mem. Am. Pediatric Soc., Pediatric Endocrine Soc. Home: 3911 Waldenwood Dr Ann Arbor MI 48105-3008 Office: U MIch Med Ctr Dept Pediatrics PO Box 718 Ann Arbor MI 48109-0718 Office Phone: 734-764-5175. E-mail: gbacon4999@aol.com.

BACON, JENNIFER GILLE, lawyer; b. Kansas City, Kansas, Dec. 26, 1949; BA with honors, U. Kansas, 1971, JD, 1976; MA, Ohio State U., 1973. Bar: Mo. Ptnr. Shughart, Thompson & Kilroy, Kansas City, Mo. Contbr. articles to profl. jours. Mem. ABA, Mo. Bar (pres.), Kansas City Metro. Bar Assn., Lawyers Assn. Kansas City. Office: Shughart Thompson & Kilroy 12 Wyandotte Plz 120 W 12th St Ste 1600 Kansas City MO 64105-1924

BADALAMENT, ROBERT ANTHONY, urologist, oncologist; b. Detroit, Mar. 20, 1954; s. Louis F. and Grace D. (Costello) B.; m. Providence F. Vitale, Nov. 9, 1980; children: Louis F., Peter P., Grace F. BS in Biology, So. Meth. U., 1976; MD, Emory U., 1980. Diplomate Am. Bd. Urology. Surg. intern Henry Ford Hosp., Detroit, 1980-81, surg. resident, 1981-82, urologic resident, 1982-85; fellow in urologic oncology Meml. Sloan Kettering Cancer Ctr., NYC, 1985-87; asst. prof. Ohio State U., Columbus, 1987-92, assoc. prof., 1992-95, prof. Sch. Pub. Health, 1995—; mem. attending staff Arthur James Cancer Ctr., Columbus, 1990-95, Crittenton Hosp., Rochester Hills, Mich., 1995—, chief dept. surgery, 2007—. Contbr. chpt. to book, articles to profl. jours. Fellow ACS; mem. AMA, Soc. Urologic Oncology. Office: Rochester Urology PC 1135 W University Dr Ste 420 Rochester Hills MI 48307-1893

BADALAMENTI, ANTHONY, financial planner; b. St. Louis, Apr. 1, 1940; s. Sebastino and Grace (Orlando) B.; 1 child, Annette Marie. BS in Acctg., Washington U., 1970. CPA, Mo.; registered investment advisor. Staff acct. Fischer & Fischer, CPAs, St. Louis, 1959-63; acct. McDonnell Aircraft Corp., St. Louis, 1963-65; asst. chief acct. Dempsey Tegler, Inc., St. Louis, 1965-66; contr. Cummins Mo. Diesel, Inc., St. Louis, 1966-67; sr. acct. Elmer Fox & Co., CPAs, St. Louis, 1967-71; pvt. practice St. Louis, 1972-94; fin. planner Asset Builders Fin. Planners, St. Louis, 1995—. Tchr. Meramec C.C., St. Louis, 1973—. Mem. Mo. Soc. CPAs, Crestwood-Sunset Hills C. of C. (pres. 1980-81, Bus. Profl. Month award 1986, 91), Rotary (pres. Crestwood-Sunset Hills chpt. 1982-83). Republican. Roman Catholic. Avocations: basketball, softball, dance. Home: 1865 Locks Mill Dr Fenton MO 63026-2662 Office: 4901 S Lindbergh Blvd Saint Louis MO 63126 E-mail: abtp@sbcglobal.net.

BADAWY, ALY AHMED, automotive parts manufacturing company executive; b. Alexandria, Egypt, Aug. 10, 1948; s. Ahmed K. and Aziza A. (Luxor) B.; m. Barbara Linn Badawy; children: Meral, Mike. M in Marine Engring., McMaster U., Can., 1977; PhD, McMaster U., 1980. Prin. rsch. scientist Battelle, Columbus, Ohio, 1980-85; supt. mfg. engring. New Departure Hyatt, Sandusky, Ohio, 1985-89; dir. R&D, chief engr., electric power sys. Delphi Saginaw Steering Systems, GM, Saginaw, Mich., 1989—99; v.p. engring. TRW Automotive, Mich., 1999—. Contbr. articles to profl. jours. Office: TRW Automotive 24175 Research Dr Farmington MI 48335

BADEER, HENRY SARKIS, physiology educator; b. Mersine, Turkey, Jan. 31, 1915; arrived in US, 1965, naturalized, 1971; s. Sarkis and Persape Hagop (Koundakjian) B.; m. Mariam Mihran Kassarjian, July 12, 1948; children: Gilbert H., Daniel H. MD, Am. U., Beirut, Lebanon, 1938. Gen. practice medicine, Beirut, 1940—51; asst. instr. Am. U. Sch. Medicine, Beirut, 1938—45, adj. prof., 1945—51, assoc. prof., 1951—62, prof. physiology, 1962—65, acting chmn. dept., 1951—56, chmn., 1956—65; rsch. fellow Harvard U. Med. Sch., Boston, 1948—49; prof. physiology Creighton U. Med. Sch., Omaha, 1967—91, emeritus prof., 1991—, acting chmn. dept., 1971—72. Vis. prof. U. Iowa, Iowa City, 1957-58, Downstate Med. Center, Bklyn., 1965-67; mem. med. com. Azounieh Sanatorium, Beirut, 1961-65; mem. research com. Nebr. Heart Assn., 1967-70, 85-88. Author textbook Spanish translation; contbr. chpts. to books, articles to profl. jours. Recipient Golden Apple award Students of AMA, 1975, Disting. Prof. award, 1992; Rockefeller fellow., 1948-49; grantee med. research com. Am. U. Beirut, 1956-65 Mem. Internat. Soc. Heart Rsch., Am. Physiol. Soc., Internat. Soc. for Adaptive Medicine (founding mem.). Home: 2808 S 99th Ave Omaha NE 68124-2603 Office: Creighton U Med Sch 2500 California Plz Omaha NE 68178-0001

BADEL, JULIE, lawyer; b. Chgo., Sept. 14, 1946; d. Charles and Saima (Hrykas) Badel. Student, Knox Coll., 1963—65; BA, Columbia Coll., Chgo., 1967; JD, DePaul U., 1977. Bar: Ill. 1977, U.S. Dist. Ct. (no. dist.) Ill. 1977, U.S. Ct. Appeals (7th and D.C. cirs.) 1981, U.S. Supreme Ct. 1985, U.S. Dist. Ct. (ea. dist.) Mich. 1989, U.S. Dist. Ct. (no. dist.) Ind. 2002, U.S. Dist. Ct. (we. dist.) Mich. 2005. Hearings referee State of Ill., Chgo., 1974-78; assoc. Cohn, Lambert, Ryan & Schneider, Chgo., 1978-80, McDermott, Will & Emery, Chgo., 1980-84, ptnr., 1985-2001, Epstein, Becker & Green, PC, Chgo., 2001—. Legal counsel, mem. adv. bd. Health Evaluation Referral Svc. Chgo., 1980-89; mem. Finnish Coun. Finlandia U., 2006—. Author: Hospital Restructuring: Employment Law Pitfalls, 1985; editor DePaul U. Law Rev., 1976-77. Bd. dirs. Alternatives, Inc., 1990—2002, Chgo. chpt. Asthma and Allergy Found., 1993—94, Glenwood Sch.; mem. bus. adv. coun. Lake Forest Grad. Sch. Mgmt. Mem.: ABA, Finnish Am. Lawyers Assn., Chgo. Bar Assn., Labor and Employment and Animal Law (vice chair 2005—06, chair 2006—07), Columbia Coll. Alumni Assn. (1st v.p., bd. dirs. 1981—86), Pi Gamma Mu. Office: Epstein Becker & Green 150 Michigan Ave 35th Fl Chicago IL 60601-7553 Business E-Mail: jbadel@ebglaw.com.

BADEN, MARK, meteorologist; m. Heather Baden; 1 child, Grace Marie. BS in Meteorology, Western Ill. U. Meteorologist KMOV-TV, St. Louis, KCAU-TV, Sious City, Iowa, KMIZ-TV, Columbia, Mo.; chief meteorologist WOI-TV, Des Moines, WISN, Milw., 1997—. Recipient Seal of Approval, Am. Meteorol. Soc., 1993. Office: WISN PO Box 402 Milwaukee WI 53201-0402

BADER, ALFRED ROBERT, chemist; b. Vienna, Apr. 28, 1924; came to U.S., 1947, naturalized, 1964; s. Alfred and Elizabeth Maria (Serenyi) B.; m. Isabel Overton, Jan. 26, 1982; children from previous marriage: David, Daniel. BS in Engring. Chemistry, Queens U., Can., 1945, BA in History, 1946, MS in Organic Chemistry, 1947, LLD (hon.), 1986; MA, Harvard U., 1949, PhD, 1950; DS (hon.), U. Wis.-Milw., 1980, Purdue U., 1984, U. Wis.-Madison, 1984, Northwestern U., 1990; D.Univ. (hon.), U. Sussex, Eng., 1989; DSc (hon.), U. Edinburgh, 1998, Glasgow U., 1999, Masaryk U., 2000, Simon Fraser U., 2005,

U. Ottawa, 2006. Rsch. chemist PPG Co., Milw., 1950-53, group leader, 1953-54; chief chemist Aldrich Chem. Co., Milw., 1954-55, pres., 1955-81, chmn., 1981-91; pres. Sigma-Aldrich Corp., 1975-80, chmn., 1980-91, chmn. emeritus, 1991-92; pres. Alfred Bader Fine Arts, Milw., 1991—. Author: Adventures of a Chemist Collector, 1995; patentee in field. Guest curator Milw. Art Mus., 1976, 89. Recipient Winthrop-Sears medal Chem. Industry Assn., 1980, J.E. Purkyne medal Acad. Scis., Czech Republic, 1994, Gold medal Am. Inst. Chemists, 1997, Boron USA award, 1997; named Entrepreneur of Yr. Rsch. Dirs. Assn., 1980, Hon. Citizen, U. Vienna, 1995, Comdr. of the Brit. Empire, 1998. Fellow: Royal Soc. Arts, Royal Soc. Chemistry (hon.); mem.: Appraisers Assn. Am., Am. Chem. Soc. (award Milw. sect. 1971, Parsons' award 1995, named one of the top 75 disting. contbrs. to the chem. enterprise in the last 75 years 1998). Jewish. Office: Alfred Bader Fine Arts 924 E Juneau Ave Ste 622 Milwaukee WI 53202-2748 Office Phone: 414-277-0730. Fax: 414-277-0709. E-mail: alfred@alfredbader.com, baderfa@execpc.com.

BADER, KATHLEEN M., chemicals executive; B in Liberal Arts, Notre Dame; MBA, U. Calif., Berkeley. Joined Dow Chem. Co., Chgo., 1973—2005, corp. v.p. Quality and Business Excellence, 1999, pres. bus. group styrenics and engineered products, corp. v.p., quality and bus. excellence Zurich, Switzerland, 2000—04; chmn., pres., CEO Dow Cargill, Minnetonka, Minn., 2004—05; pres., CEO NatureWorks LLC (formerly known as Cargill Dow LLC), Mpls., 2005—. Chair dept. pvt. sector sr. advisory com. Homeland Security; adv. coun. US Homeland Security, 2002—; bd. dirs. Textron Inc., Providence, 2004—. Internat. bd. dir. Habitat for Humanity; dean's coun. Harvard Sch. Govt. Named One of 50 Most Powerful Women in Internat. Bus., Fortune Mag., 2001—03; recipient Henry Laurence Gantt medal, ASME, 2005. Office: NatureWorks LLC PO Box 5830 Minneapolis MN 55440-5830 Office Phone: 877-423-7659.

BADER, RONALD L., advertising executive; b. 1931; With Amana (Iowa) Refrigeration, 1949-55, Gittens Co., Milw., 1955-60, Brady Co., Milw., 1961-70, Hoffman, York, Baker & Johnson, Milw., 1971-74, Bader Rutter & Assocs., Inc., Brookfield, Wis., 1975—, now pres, sec., treas., CEO. Office: Bader Rutter & Assocs 13845 Bishops Dr Brookfield WI 53005-6604

BADER, SAMUEL DAVID, physicist; b. NYC, Feb. 4, 1947; s. Fred and Norma (Blake) Bader; m. Karen Deborah Natal, Dec. 23, 1971 (dec. Aug. 1994); children: Ari, Danya. BS, U. Calif., Berkeley, 1967, PhD, 1974. Postdoctoral fellow Argonne Nat. Lab., Ill., 1974-76, asst. physicist materials sci. divsn., 1976-79, physicist, 1979-90, group leader, 1987—, sr. physicist, 1990—. Chair editl. bd. Jour. Vacuum Sci. and Tech., Argonne, 1988-91. Assoc. editor Applied Physics Letters, 1986—; adv. editor Jour. of Magnetism and Magnetic Materials, 1990-97, editor, 1998—; contbr. numerous articles to profl. jours. Recipient Material Sci. Rsch. Competition award for outstanding sci. achievement in solid state physics US Dept. Energy, 1992, U. Chgo. Award for Disting. Performance at Argonne at. Lab., 1994. Fellow Am. Phys. Soc. (mem. exec. com. divsn. materials physics 1992-95, sec.-treas. 1996—, David Adler Lectureship award in Field of Materials Physics); mem. Am. Vacuum Soc. (chmn. publ. com. 1988-91). Achievements include 1 patent in magneto-optical storage materials. Office: Argonne at Lab MSD-223 9700 Cass Ave Argonne IL 60439-4803 E-mail: Bader@ANL.gov.

BADGER, DAVID HARRY, lawyer; b. Indpls., June 16, 1931; s. David Henry and Mayme Pearl (Wright) B.; m. Donna Lee Bailey, June 24, 1954; children: David Mark, Lee Ann, Steven Michael. BEE, Rose Poly. Inst., 1953; JD, Ind. U., 1964. Bar: Ind. 1964, U.S. Dist. Ct. (so and no. dists.) Ind. 1964, U.S. Patent Office 1964, U.S. Ct. Customs and Patent Appeals 1971, U.S. Ct. Appeals (fed. cir.) 1982. Engr. GE, 1953-56, Ransburg Corp., Indpls., 1956-62; chief elec. engr. Rex Metal Craft, Inc., Indpls., 1963-64; patent counsel, corp. sec. Ransburg Corp., Indpls., 1964—76; legal counsel Ball Corp., Muncie, Ind., 1976-77; ptnr. Jenkins, Coffey, Hyland, Badger & Conard, Indpls., 1977-82; mng. ptnr. Brinks, Hofer, Gilson & Lione, Indpls., 1982-98. Contbr. articles to profl. jours.; patentee in U.S. and fgn. countries. With USN, 1953-55, lt. comdr. USNR. Named Hon. Alumnus Rose Hulman Inst. Tech., 1987. Mem. ABA (various coms.), IEEE, Ind. Bar Assn. (various coms.), Am. Intellectual Property Law Assn. (various coms.), Licensing Execs. Soc. (various coms.), Indpls. Bar Assn., Internat. Assn. Intellectual Property Law, Indpls. Jazz Club (bd. dirs. 1983-85, 95-97), Junto of Indpls. (bd. dirs. 1997-99). Office: Brinks Hofer Gilson & Lione 1 Indiana Sq Ste 1600 Indianapolis IN 46204-2045 Home Phone: 317-876-7556; Office Phone: 317-636-0886. Personal E-mail: badger938@aol.com.

BADGEROW, JOHN NICHOLAS, lawyer; b. Macon, Mo., Apr. 7, 1951; s. Harry Leroy Badgerow and Barbara Raines (Buell) Novaria; m. Teresa Ann Zvolanek, Aug. 7, 1976; children: Anthony Thornton, Andrew Cameron, James Terrill. BA in Bus. and English with honors, Principia Coll., 1972; JD, U. Mo., Kansas City, 1975. Bar: Kans. 1976, US Dist. Ct. Kans. 1976, US Ct. Appeals (10th cir.) 1977, US Ct. Appeals (4th cir.) 1979, US Supreme Ct. 1982, US Ct. Appeals (fed. cir.) 1985, US Ct. Appeals (8th cir.) 1986, Mo. 1986, US Dist. Ct. (we. dist.) Mo. 1986, Civil Lit., Nat. Bd. Trial Advocates, 1994. Ptnr. McAnany, VanCleave & Phillips, P.A., Kansas City, Kans., 1975-85; ptnr.-in-charge Spencer, Fane, Britt & Browne, Kansas City, Mo. and Overland Park, Kans., 1986—. Chmn. ethics grievance com. Johnson County, 1988—; mem. Kans. Jud. Coun., 1995—, Kans. Bd. Discipline for Attys., 2000—, chmn. Ethics 2000 Commn., 2002—, chmn. Kans. ethics adv. opinion com., 2005—. Co-author: Kansas Employment Law, 1992, 2d edit., 2001; co-author, co-editor Kansas Lawyer Ethics, 1996; contbr. articles to jour. Co-chmn. Civil Justice Reform Act Commn., Dist. of Kans., 1995-96; chmn. Kans. Ethics Adv. Opinion Com., 2005-. Mem.: ABA, Earl O'Connor Am. Inn of Ct. (pres. 1996), Kans. Assn. Def. Counsel, Kans. Bar Assn. (ethics adv. opinion com. 1997—, Outstanding Svc. award 1995), Kans. Jud. Coun., Mission Valley Hunt Club (Stilwell, Kans.). Republican. Christian Scientist. Avocations: horseback riding, carpentry, reading. Office: Spencer Fane Britt & Browne 9401 Indian Creek Pkwy Ste 700 Shawnee Mission KS 66210-2038 Office Phone: 913-345-8100. Business E-Mail: nbadgerow@spencerfane.com.

BADO, KENNETH STEVE, automotive company administrator; b. Amherst, Ohio, Mar. 13, 1941; s. Steve and Hildegarde Paulene (Gutosky) B.; m. Linda Bonita Crabtree, May 30, 1962 (div. Oct. 1989); children: Bradley Steve, Cheryl Lynn Smith, John Robert; m. Polly Ann Steele, Nov. 28, 1989. Student, Ohio U., 1958-60, Lorain County CC, 1960-62. Mfg. planning specialist Ford Motor Co., Lorain, Ohio, 1960—97; farmer Henrietta, Ohio, 1972—; owner, mgr. The Galleon, Lorain, Ohio, 1986—. Leader Sub-System Group (Group Tng.), Lorain, 1987-92. Advisor Lorain County Steer Club (4-H), Lorain County, 1977-93, Henrietta Hazers Club (4-H), Lorain County, 1976-88. Mem. Am. Quarter Horse Assn., Ohio Quarter Horse Assn., Moose, Masons (32 degree), Scottish Rite Soc. Republican. Lutheran. Avocations: boating, fishing, horseback riding, computer work. Home: 12359 Baird Rd # 2 Oberlin OH 44074-9632 Office: The Galleon 4875 W Erie Ave Lorain OH 44053-1331 E-mail: Galleon@aol.com.

BADRA, ROBERT GEORGE, theology studies and humanities educator; b. Lansing, Mich., Dec. 8, 1933; s. Razouk Anthony and Anna (Paul) Badra; m. Maria Theresa Beer, Oct. 25, 1968 (div. 1973); m. Kristen Lillie Stuckey, Dec. 30, 1977 (div. 2001); children: Rachal Jennifer, Danielle Elizabeth Jane. BA, Sacred Heart Sem., 1957; MA, Western Mich. U., 1968; MDiv, St. John's Provincial Sem., 1985. Ordained priest Roman Cath. Ch., 1961. Mem. faculty Kalamazoo Valley CC, 1968—, prof. philosophy, religion and humanities, 1968—. Adj. prof. Nazareth Coll., 1985—91, Siena Heights U., 1993—; mem. faculty ministry formation Cath. Diocese Kalamazoo, 1999—2003. Bd. dirs. Kalamazoo Coun. Humanities, 1983—86, Van Buren Youth Camp, 1993—2007, v.p. bd. dirs., 2002—07. Recipient Edn. award, Exxon, 1996; grantee NEH, 1991—. Mem.: Assn. Religion and Intellectual Life. Office: Kalamazoo Valley CC PO Box 4070 Kalamazoo MI 49003-4070 Personal E-mail: bbadra1579@aol.com.

BAEHREN, JAMES W., lawyer; b. Toledo, June 11, 1950; BS, Ohio State U., 1972, MBA, 1974; JD, U. Toledo, 1978. Assoc. Fuller & Henry, 1978—85, ptnr., 1985—92; asst. gen. counsel Owens-Illinois Inc., Toledo, 1992, sec., 1998, dir. fin., sr. v.p., gen. counsel, corp. sec. Mem.: ABA, Ohio State Bar Assn., Toledo Bar Assn. Office: Owens-Illinois 1 Michael Owens Way Perrysburg OH 43551-2999 Office Phone: 419-247-5000. Office Fax: 419-247-7107. E-mail: jim.baehren@owens-ill.com.

BAER, ERIC, engineering and science educator; b. Nieder-Weisel, Germany, July 18, 1932; came to U.S., 1947, naturalized, 1952; s. Arthur and Erna (Kraemer) B.; m. Ana Golender, Aug. 5, 1956; children: Lisa, Michelle. MA, Johns Hopkins, 1953, D. of Engring., 1957. Research engr., polychems. dept. E.I. du Pont de Nemours & Co., Inc., 1957-60; asst. prof. chemistry and chem. engring. U. Ill., 1960-62; assoc. prof. engring. Case Inst. Tech., 1962-66; prof., head dept. polymer sci. Case Western Res. U., 1966-78; dean Case Inst. Tech., 1978-83, Leonard Case prof. macromolecular sci., 1984-89, Herbert Henry Dow prof. sci. and engring., 1989—. Cons. to industry, 1961—, Edison Polymer Innovations Corp. Author articles in field.; Editor: Engineering Design for Plastics, 1963, Polymer Engineering and Science, 1967-90, Journal of Applied Polymer Science, 1988—. Recipient Curtis W. McGraw award ASEE, 1968 Mem. Am. Chem. Soc. (Borden award 1981), Am. Phys. Soc., Am. Inst. Chem. Engring., Soc. Plastics Engring. (internat. award 1980), Plastics Inst. Am. (trustee) Home: 2 Mornington Ln Cleveland Heights OH 44106 Office: Case Western Reserve Univ Engring Dept Cleveland OH 44106

BAER, ROBERT J., retired transportation company executive; b. St. Louis, Oct. 25, 1937; s. Charles A. and Angeline Baer; m. Jo Baer, Aug. 27, 1960; children: Bob Jr., Angie, Tim, Cathy. BA, So. Ill. U., 1962, MS, 1964; LLD (hon.), Maryville Univ., St. Louis, 1992. Regional supr. div. recreation City of St. Louis, 1957-64; dep. dir. Human Devel. Corp., St. Louis, 1964-70; chief to staff to co. exec. St. Louis County Govt., 1970-74; exec. dir. Bi-State Devel. Agy., St. Louis, 1974-77; v.p., gen. mgr. United Van Lines Inc. and subs., Fenton, Mo., 1977-80, exec. v.p., 1980-82; pres. COO, 1982-95; CEO United Van Lines, Fenton, 1995—2002, Vanliner Ins. Co., Fenton, Total Transp. Svcs. Inc., Mayflower Transit, Fenton, 1995—2002, UniGroup Worldwide, Inc., Fenton, 1998—2002; pres., COO UniGroup Inc., Fenton, Mo., 1987—2002; pres. emeritus UniGroup, Inc., 2002—. Bd. dirs. Firstar-St. Louis (now US Bancorp), United Van Lines, Vanliner Ins. Co., Inc., Kellwood Co., 2004-. Pres. St. Louis Bd. Police Commn., 1984-89; chmn. St. Louis Regional Conv. and Sports Conv. and Sports Complex Authority, 1990-96; mem. Civic Progress, Inc., 1996—2002. Office: Bd Dir Kellwood Co 600 Kellwood Pkwy Chesterfield MO 63017

BAER, WERNER, economist, educator; b. Offenbach, Germany, Dec. 14, 1931; came to U.S., 1945, naturalized, 1952; s. Richard and Grete (Herz) B. 58776, CUNY, YC, 1953; MA, Harvard U., 1955, PhD, 1958; D honoris causa, Fed. U. Pernambuco, Brazil, 1988, New U. Lisbon, Portugal, 2000; D honoris causa (hon.), Fed. U. Ceara, Brazil, 1993. Instr. Harvard U., 1958-61; asst. prof. Yale U., New Haven, 1961-65; assoc. prof. Vanderbilt U., Nashville, 1965-69, prof., 1969-74; prof. econs. U. Ill., Urbana, 1974—. Vis. prof. U. São Paulo, Brazil, 1966-68, Vargas Found., Brazil, 1966-68; Rhodes fellow St. Antony's Coll., Oxford (Eng.) U., 1975. Author: The Brazilian Economy: Growth and Development, 6th edit., 2008, Privatization in Latin America, vol. 17, 1994, The Changing Role of International Capital in Latin America, 1998; co-author: (with P. Elosegui and A. Gallo) The Achievements and Failures of Argentina's eo-Liberal Policies, 2002, (with J. Bang) Privatization and Equity in Brazil and Russia, 2002, (with E. Amann) Anchors Away: The Costs and Benefits of Brazil's Devaluation, 2003; co-editor: Latin America-Privatization, Property Rights and Deregulation, 1993, (with W. Maloney) Neo-Liberalism and Income Distribution in Latin America, 1997, (with W. Miles, A. Moran) The End of the Asian Myth, 1999, The State and Industry in the Development Process, 1999 (with E. Amann) Neoliberalism and it's Consequences in Brazil, 2002; contbr. articles to profl. jours. Decorated Order So. Cross (Brazil). Mem. Am. Econ. Assn., Latin Am. Studies Assn. Home: 1703 Devonshire Dr Champaign IL 61821-5901 Office: U Ill 1407 W Gregory Dr Urbana IL 61801-3606 Office Phone: 217-333-8388. Business E-Mail: wbaer@uiuc.edu.

BAERENKLAU, ALAN H., hotel executive; b. NYC; Grad., Cornell U. V.p. ops. Howard Johnson Co.; pres., COO MOA Hospitality; also bd. dirs. Founder, pres. Fla. Hospitality Group; lectr. Cornell U., Hillsborough Cmty. Coll; mem. Howard Johnson Internat. Operators Coun. Mem. Walt Disney Hotel Assn Office: MOA Hospitality Inc 701 Lee St Ste 1000 Des Plaines IL 60016-4555

BAERNSTEIN, ALBERT, II, mathematician, educator; b. Birmingham, Ala., Apr. 25, 1941; s. Albert and Kathryn (Wiesel) B.; m. Judith Haynes, June 14, 1962; children— P. Renée, Amy. Student, U. Ala., 1958-59; AB, Cornell U., 1962; MA, U. Wis., 1964, PhD, 1968. Instr. math. U. Wis., Whitewater, 1966-68; asst. prof. math. Syracuse U., NY, 1968-72; assoc. prof. math. Washington U., St. Louis, 1972-74, prof. math., 1974—. Fulbright sr. research scholar Imperial Coll., London, 1976-77 Mem. Am. Math. Soc., Math. Assn. Am. Office: Washington U Dept Math Saint Louis MO 63130

BAETZ, W. TIMOTHY, lawyer; b. Cin., Aug. 5, 1944; s. William G. and Virginia (Fauntleroy) Baetz. BA, Harvard U., 1966; JD, U. Mich., 1969. Bar: Ill. 1969, D.C. 1980. Assoc. McDermott, Will & Emery, Chgo., 1969-74, income ptnr., 1975-78, capital ptnr., 1979—2001. Mem. mgmt. com. McDermott, Will & Emery, 1987-92, 95-2001. With U.S. Army, 1969-75. Fellow Am. Coll. Trust and Estate Counsel. Episcopalian. Home: 940 Golfview Rd Glenview IL 60025-3116

BAGAN, GRANT ALAN, lawyer; b. Chgo., Dec. 27, 1953; s. Seymour Jack and Joyce (Klass) B. m. Laurie Beth Weiss, Aug. 19, 1978; children: Stacy, Michelle, Ashley. BA cum laude, Tulane U., 1976; JD magna cum laude, U. Ill., 1979. Bar: Ill. 1979. Assoc. McDermott, Will & Emery, Chgo., 1979-85, ptnr., mem. firm exec. mgmt. com., chmn. corp. dept., 1985—. ABA.

BAGLEY, BRIAN G., materials science educator, researcher; b. Racine, Wis., Nov. 20, 1934; s. Wesley John and Ethel (Rasmussen) B.; m. Dorothy Elizabeth Olson, Nov. 20, 1959 (div. Aug. 1993); children: Brian John, James David, Kristin Marie. BS, U. Wis., 1958, MS, 1959; AM, Harvard U., 1964, PhD, 1968. Mem. tech. staff Bell Telephone Labs., Inc., Murray Hill, N.J., 1967-83, Bell Communications Rsch. Inc., Red Bank, N.J., 1984-91; NEG endowed chair, dir. Eitel Inst., prof. physics U. Toledo, 1991—. Served to 1st lt. AUS, 1960-61. Xerox predoctoral fellow Harvard U., 1964-66, Robert J. Painter predoctoral fellow Harvard U., 1966-67. Mem. Am. Phys. Soc., Am. Vacuum Soc. (chpt. chmn. 1991), Materials Rsch. Soc., Sigma Xi, Sigma Pi Sigma. Home: 16474 W River Rd Bowling Green OH 43402-9469 Office: U Toledo Eitel Inst for Silicate Rsch McMaster Hall Rm 4004 Toledo OH 43606-3328

BAHADUR, BIRENDRA, displays research specialist; b. Gorakhpur, India, July 1, 1949; came to Can., 1981; s. Bijai Bahadur and Shakuntala Srivastva; m. Urmila Bahadur, May 29, 1970; children: Shivendra, Shachindra. BS in Physics, Chemistry and Math., Gorakhpur U., 1967, MS in Physics, 1969, PhD, 1976. Rsch. scholar physics dept. Gorakhpur U., 1969-76, asst. prof. physics dept., 1976-77; sr. sci. officer Nat. Phys. Lab. India, New Delhi, 1977-81; v.p. R&D Data Images, Ottawa, Ont., Canada, 1981-85; mgr. R&D Litton Data Images, Ottawa, 1985-91; engr. mgr. liquid crystal display material and process Litton Systems, Can., Toronto, 1988-97; prin. engr. Display Ctr. Rockwell Collins Inc., 1997—. Adj. prof. dept. computers and elec. engring. Waterloo (Can.) U., 1995; active various Internat. Confs. on Liquid Crystals; participant numerous profl. meetings; mem. liquid crystal tech. com. SID, 1993—. Author: Liquid Crystal Displays, 1984; editor: Liquid Crystals--Applications and Uses, vol. I, 1990, vol. II, 1991, vol. III, 1992; mem. editl. bd. Displays, 1993-2006, Liquid Crystal Today, 1995—; abstracting panel Liquid Crystal Abstracts, 1978-80; contbr. articles to profl. jours. V.p. nat. capitol region India Can. Assn., 1989-90, pres., 1990-91. Grantee Indsl. Rsch. Assistance Program, NRC Can., 1982-85, 84-87, 88-91, Wright Patterson AFB, 1991-94. Mem. Internat. Liquid Crystal Soc., Soc. Info. Displays (dir. Upper Midwest chpt. 2003-, Spl. Recognition award 1993, LC tech. com. 1993—, chmn. 1997), Inst. Physics, Soc. de Chimie Physique. Achievements include patent for Process for Production of Printed Electrode Pattern for Use in Electro-Optical Display Devices (India); co-development of technology of various liquid crystal displays; patent for wide viewing angle dye doped TN LCDs with retardation sheets. Home: 935 71st St NE Cedar Rapids IA 52402-7295 Office: Rockwell Collins Inc Mail Sta 106-191 400 Collins Rd Cedar Rapids IA 52498-0001 Home Phone: 319-294-8891; Office Phone: 319-295-9251. E-mail: bbahadur@rockwellcollins.com.

BAHAR, EZEKIEL, electrical engineering educator; US citizen; s. Silas and Hannah Bahar; m. Ophira Rodoff; children: Zillah, Ruth Iris, Ron Jonathan. BS, Technion IIT, Haifa, Israel, 1958, MS, 1960; PhD, U. Colo., Boulder, 1964. Instr. Technion, Haifa, Israel, 1960—62; rsch. assoc. U. Colo., Boulder, 1962—64, asst. prof., 1964—67; assoc. prof. U. Nebr., Lincoln, 1967—71, prof., 1971—80, Durham prof., 1981—89, George Holmes disting. prof., 1989—, u. disting. prof., 1999—, dir. program revs., 1981—83. Vis. prof. NOAA, Boulder, 1979. Pres. faculty senate U. Nebr., Lincoln, 1980. Recipient Outstanding Rsch. and Creative Activities award U. Nebr., Lincoln, 1980, Scholarship citation U. Colo., Boulder, 1964 Fellow IEEE (life); mem. Internat. Union Radio Sci. (rep. 1978, 81, 84, 87, 90, 93, 96, 99, 2002). Achievements include research in radio wave propagation in complex media, metamaterials with chiral properties, remote sensing, nanotechnology rsch; Mueller matrix detection and identification of optical activity. Avocation: swimming. Home: 2431 Bretigne Dr Lincoln NE 68512-1913 Office: U Nebr WSEC 218 N Lincoln NE 68588-0511 Office Phone: 402-472-1966. Business E-Mail: ebahar@unl.edu.

BAHL, TRACY L., healthcare executive; b. Apr. 10, 1962; Student, Whittier Coll. Sch. Law; grad. in Bus. and Health, Gustavus Adolphus Coll.; diplomat, Am. Coll. Healthcare Exec. With UniHealth Am., Calif., Maxicare Healthplans, Calif.; dir. provider rels. CIGNA HealthCare Calif., Calif.; v.p., exec. dir. CIGNA HealthCare NY; pres., gen. mgr. CIGNA HealthCare Mid-Atlantic; pres. strategic bus. svcs. United HealthCare Corp., Hartford, Conn., 1998; pres. Uniprise Strategic Solutions, 1998—2002; sr. v.p. comml. health plan CIGNA HealthCare; sr. v.p., chief mktg. officer UnitedHealth Grp., Minnetonka, Minn., 2003—04; CEO Uniprise, 2004—07; spl. adv. healthcare sector General Atlantic LLC, 2007—.

BAHLMAN, WILLIAM THORNE, JR., retired lawyer; b. Cin., Jan. 9, 1920; s. William Thorne and Janet (Rhodes) B.; m. Nancy W. DeCamp, Mar. 21, 1953; children: Charles R., William Ward, Baker D. BA, Yale U., 1941, LL.B., 1947. Bar: Ohio 1947. Prin. Paxton & Seasongood, L.P.A., Cin., 1947-67, 73-88; ptnr. Paxton & Seasongood, Cin., 1954-67, Thompson Hine, LLP, Cin., 1989-94; prof. law U. Cin. Coll. Law, 1967-73, lectr., 1965-67, 73-77; ret., 1994. Served with USAAF, 1942-46. Mem. Am. Law Inst., ABA, Ohio State Bar Assn., Cin. Bar Assn. Office: Thompson Hine LLP 312 Walnut St Fl 14 Cincinnati OH 45202-4024 Office Phone: 513-352-6716. E-mail: WilliamBahlman@ThompsonHine.com.

BAHLS, STEVEN CARL, academic administrator, educator; b. Des Moines, Sept. 4, 1954; s. Carl Robert and Dorothy Rose (Jensen) B.; m. Jane Emily Easter, June 18, 1977; children: Daniel David, Timothy Carl, Angela Emily. BBA, U. Iowa, 1976; JD, Northwestern U., Chgo., 1979. Bar: Wis. 1979, Mont. 1989; CPA, Iowa. Assoc. Frisch, Dudek & Slattery, Milw., 1979-84, dir., 1985; assoc. dean and prof. U. Mont. Sch. of Law, Missoula, 1985-94; dean., prof. law sch. Capital U. Law Sch., Columbus, Ohio, 1994—2003; pres. Augustana Coll., Rock Island, Ill., 2003—. Coordinating exec. editor Northwestern U. Law Rev., 1979. Pres. Illowa coun. Boy Scouts Am.; bd. dirs. Quad Cities United Way, 2004—; treas. Ill. Quad Cities C. of C., 2007, Quad Cities Symphony Orch.; vice chmn., bd. dirs. Putnam Mus., 2007; bd. visitors U. Mont. Sch. Law, 2006—. Mem. ABA, Nat. Assn. Ind. Colls. (bd. dirs.), Am. Agrl. Law Assn. (pres. 2000), Wis. Bar Assn., Mont. Bar Assn., Order of Coif. Avocations: photography, travel, hiking. Office: Augustana College 639 38th Street Rock Island IL 61201-2296

BAILAR, BARBARA ANN, retired statistician; b. Monroe, Mich., Nov. 24, 1935; d. Malcolm Laurie and Clara Florence (Parent) Dezendorf; m. John Francis Powell (div. 1966); 1 child, Pamela; m. John Christian Bailar; 1 child, Melissa. BA, SUNY, 1956; MS, Va. Poly. Inst., 1965; PhD, Am. U., 1972. With Bur. of Census, Washington, 1958-88, chief Ctr. Rsch. Measurement Methods, 1973-79, assoc. dir. for statis. standards and methodology, 1979-88; exec. dir. Am. Statis. Assn., Alexandria, Va., 1988-95; sr. v.p. for survey rsch. Nat. Opinion Rsch. Ctr., Chgo., 1995—2001. Instr. George Washington U., 1984-85; head dept. math. and stats. USDA Grad. Sch., Washington, 1972-87. Contbr. articles, book chpts. to profl. publs. Pres. bd. dirs. Harbour Sq. Coop., Washington, 1988-89. Recipient Silver medal U.S. Dept. Commerce, 1980. Fellow Am. Statis. Assn. (pres. 1987); mem. AAAS (chair sect. stats. 1984-85), Internat. Assn. Survey Statisticians (pres. 1989-91), Internat. Statis. Inst. (Pres.'s invited speaker 1983, v.p. 1993-95), Cosmos Club. Personal E-mail: babailar@aol.com.

BAILAR, JOHN CHRISTIAN, III, retired public health educator, physician, statistician; b. Urbana, Ill., Oct. 9, 1932; married; 4 children. BA, U. Colo., 1953; MD, Yale U., 1955; PhD in Stats., Am. U., 1973. Intern U. Colo. Med. Ctr., Denver, 1955-56; field investigator, biometry br. Nat Cancer Inst., NIH, Bethesda, Md., 1956-62, head demography sect., 1962-70, dir. 3d nat. cancer survey, 1967-70, dep. assoc. dir. for cancer control, 1972-74; editor-in-chief JNCI, 1974-80; dir. research service VA, Washington, 1970-72; lectr. in biostats. Harvard U., Cambridge, Mass., 1980-87; prof. McGill U., Montreal, 1987-95, chair dept. epidemiology and biostats., 1993—95; sr. scientist Office Disease Prevention and Health Promotion, Dept. HHS, Washington, 1983-92; chair dept. health studies U. Chgo., 1995—99, prof. dept. health studies, 1995—2001, assoc. faculty Harris Sch. Pub. Policy, 1999-2000, prof. emeritus, 2001—. Sr. scientist health and environ. rev. divsn. EPA, 1980-83; lectr. epidemiology and pub. health Yale U., New Haven, Conn., 1958-63; mem. faculty math. and stats. USDA Grad. Sch., Washington, 1966-76; vis. prof. stats. SUNY, Buffalo, 1974-80; professorial lectr. George Washington U., Washington, 1975-80; cons. in biostats. and epidemiology Dana-Farber Cancer Inst., Boston, 1977-83; vis. prof. Harvard U., 1977-79; spl. appointment grad. faculty U. Colo. Med. Ctr., Denver, 1979-81; scholar in residence NAS, 1992-96, 2002—. Mem. editl. adv. bd. Cancer Rsch., 1968-72; statis. cons. New Eng. Jour. Medicine, 1980-91; mem. bd. editors New Eng. Jour. Medicine, 1992-96; contbr. numerous articles to profl. jours.; editor JNCI, 1974-80. John D. and Catherine T. MacArthur Found. fellow, 1990-95. Fellow AAAS (chair sect. U 2000-01), Am. Coll. Epidemiology, Am. Statis. Assn. (chair-elect and chair biometric sect. 1979-81, founding chair sect. stats. and environment 1990); mem. Am. Med. Writer's Assn. (hon.), Inst. of Medicine, Internat. Statis. Inst., Coun. Biology Editors (chair publishing policy com. 1983-89, pres.-elect, pres., past pres. 1986-89), Soc. Risk Analysis (founding chair Boston chpt. 1985-86). Office: Apt 8 2101 Connecticut Ave NW Washington DC 20008 Office Phone: 202-334-3784. Business E-Mail: jcbailar@midway.uchicago.edu.

BAILEY, DANIEL ALLEN, lawyer; b. Pitts., Aug. 31, 1953; s. Richard A. and Virginia (Henry) B.; m. Janice Abraham, Oct. 10, 1981; children: Jeffrey, Megan. BBA, Bowling Green State U., 1975; JD, Ohio State U., 1978. Bar: Ohio 1978, U.S. Dist. Ct. (so. dist.) Ohio 1978, U.S. Tax Ct. 1979. Ptnr. Arter & Hadden, Columbus, Ohio, 1978—2003, chair exec. com., 2000—03; mem. Baily Cavalieri LLC, Columbus, 2003—, chair bd. mgrs., 2003—. Co-author: Handbook for Corporate Directors, 1985, Liability of Corporate Officers and Directors, 7th edit., 2002. Bd. dirs. Columbus Met. Community Action Orgn., 1979-80, Franklin County Head Start, Columbus, 1979-80, Faith Luth. Ch., Whitehall, Ohio, 1985-90, Luth. Social Svcs. Ctrl Ohio, 1991-2000, 2006—, Concorde Counseling Svcs., 2000—. Mem. ABA, Ohio Bar Assn., Columbus Bar Assn., Phi Kappa Phi, Beta Gamma Sigma, Omicron Delta Kappa. Office: Bailey Cavalieri LLC 10 W Broad St Ste 2100 Columbus OH 43215-3422 Office Phone: 614-229-3213.

BAILEY, GLENN E., wholesale distribution executive; b. Scranton, Pa., July 17, 1954; s. Harry E. and Naomi K. (Lee) B.; m. Karan Clover Thomasson, July 16, 1982; children: Virginia, Lee. BSBA, Oral Roberts, 1976; MBA, Harvard U., 1978. Chief fin. officer Spring Arbor Distributors, Belleville, Mich., 1986-87, chief exec. officer, 1987—, also bd. dirs. V.p. planning Word, Inc., Waco, Tex., 1978-82, chief fin. officer, Waco, 1982-86; bd. advisors M Bank, Waco, 1984-86. Founding bd. mem. Habitat for Humanity of Waco, 1985-86. Mem. Am. Wholesale Booksellers Assn. (bd. trustees 1990—). Office: Spring Arbor Distbrs 10885 Textile Rd Belleville MI 48111-2315 Home: 222 Jackson St Chelsea MI 48118-1018

BAILEY, JUDITH IRENE, academic administrator, educator, consultant; b. Winston-Salem, NC, Aug. 24, 1946; d. William Edward Hege Jr. and Julia (Hedrick) Hege; m. Brendon Stinson Bailey, Jr, June 8, 1968. BA, Coker Coll., 1968; MEd, Va. Tech., 1973, EdD, 1976; postgrad., Harvard U., 1994, 1994—95. Tchr. Chariho Regional H.S., Wood River Junction, RI, 1969—70, Prince William County Pub. Schs., Woodbridge, Va., 1968—72; asst. prin. Osbourn H.S., Manassas, Va., 1973; secondary sch. coord. Stafford (Va.) County Schs., 1973—74; middle sch. coord. Stafford County Schs., 1975—76; human rels. coord. Coop. Extension Svc. U. Md., College Park, 1976—79; dep. dir. Coop. Extension Svc. U. D.C., Washington, 1980-88; asst. v.p., dir. Coop. Extension U. Maine, Orono, 1988—92, interim v.p. for rsch. and pub. svc., 1992—93, v.p. rsch. and pub. svc., 1993—95, v.p. acad. affairs, provost, 1995—97; pres. No. Mich. U., Marquette, 1997—2003, Western Mich. U.,

Kalamazoo, 2003—06, prof. ednl. leadership, 2006—. Adj. prof. George Mason U., Fairfax, Va., 1978; grad. student adv. U. Md., 1979—80; spkr. and cons. in field; trustee Bronson Healthcare Group, Kalamazoo, 2003—; mem. steering com. Mich. Tri-Tech. Corridor, 2003—05; mem. governing bd. Bioscis. Rsch. and Commercialization Ctr., 2003—06; pres. Western Mich. U. Rsch. Found., 2006—06; mem. Mich. Strategic Econ. Investment and Commercialization Bd., 2006. Co-author: Contingency Planning for a Unitary School System; contbr. articles to profl. jours. Co-vice chmn. Lake Superior Cmty. Partnership, 1997—2003; bd. trustees Marquette (Mich.) Gen. Health Sys., 1998—2003; mem. Mich. Humanities Coun., 1999—2002, sec., treas., 2002; mem. adv. bd. Huntington Bank, 2003—; apptd. by gov. to Mich. Quarter Commn., 2004; mem. Am. Coun. Edn. Commn. on Women, 2004; trustee Southwest Mich. First; vice chmn. Greater Kalamazoo United Way, 2006; bd. dirs. Pine Tree State 4-H Found., 1988—97, Maine Toxicology Inst., 1992—95, Bangor (Maine) Symphony Orch, 1991—97, Shorebank, 1997—2003, Gilmore Keyboard Festival, 2003—. Recipient Disting. Alumni Achievement award, Coker Coll., 1998, Northwoods Woman Educator of Yr. award, 1999, Case V Chief Exec. Leadership award, 2002, Disting. Grad. Alumni Achievement award, Va. Tech., 2005; fellow Susan Coker Watson fellow, 1967. Mem.: AAUW, Grand Rapids Econ. Club, Econ. Club Marquette County (bd. dirs. 1997—2003), Rotary (Paul Harris fellow 2004), Epsilon Sigma Phi (sec. Mu chpt. 1987, v.p. 1988, State Disting. Svc. award), Phi Kappa Phi, Phi Delta Kappa. Republican. Avocations: cooking, hiking. Home: 1201 Short Rd Kalamazoo MI 49008 Office: Western Mich U Coll Edn 1903 W MIchigan Kalamazoo MI 49008-5202 Business E-Mail: judi.bailey@wmich.edu.

BAILEY, MICHAEL J., manufacturing executive; CFO JohnsonDiversey, Sturtevant, Wis., 1999—2004, exec. v.p. corp. develop., 2004—. Office: JohnsonDiversey 8310 16th St Sturtevant WI 53177 Office Fax: (262) 260-4282.

BAILEY, REEVE MACLAREN, museum curator; b. Fairmont, W.Va., May 2, 1911; s. Joseph Randall and Elizabeth Weston (Maclaren) B.; m. Marian Alvinette Kregel, Aug. 13, 1939; children— Douglas M., David R., Thomas G., Susan Helen. Student, Toledo U., 1929-30; AB, U. Mich., 1933, PhD, 1938. Instr. zoology Iowa State Coll. (now univ.), 1938-42, asst. prof., 1942-44; asst. prof. zoology U. Mich., 1944-50, asso. prof., 1950-59, prof., 1959-81, prof. emeritus, 1981—. Assoc. curator Mus. Zoology, 1944-48, curator, 1948—; rsch. assoc. Am. Mus. Nat. History, 1964—. Contbr. over 160 articles, bulls., revs. to profl. jours. on ichthyology and herpetology. Fellow Iowa Acad. Sci.; mem. Am. Soc. Ichthyologists and Herpetologists (editl. bd., v.p. 1954, pres. 1959, Robert H. Gibbs Jr. Meml. award 1995), Am. Fisheries Soc. (pres. 1974, hon. mem. 1979—, recipient Award of Excellence 1980, Meritorious Svc. award 1989, Justin W. Leonard award of excellence Mich. chpt. 1985), Am. Inst. Fisheries Rsch. Biologists (Outstanding Achievement award 1996), AAAS (coun. 1968-72), Ecol. Soc. Am., Soc. Study Evolution, Soc. Systematic Biologists, Soc. Limnology and Oceanography, Mich. Acad. Sci., Arts and Letters. Avocation: ichthyology expeditions in US, Bermuda, Bolivia, Guatemala, Paraguay, and Zambia. Home: 4001 Glacier Hills Dr Apt 325 Ann Arbor MI 48105-3652 Office: Univ Mich Museum Zoology Ann Arbor MI 48109 Home Phone: 313-769-0493. E-mail: reevemarian@yahoo.com.

BAILEY, RICHARD, food company executive; Exec. v.p. ops. Kraft Foods N.Am., 1988-96; exec. v.p. worldwide food ops. Phillip Morris Cos. Inc., 1996-98; pres., COO Dean Foods Co., Franklin Park, Ill., 1998—. Office: 3600 River Rd Franklin Park IL 60131-2152

BAILEY, ROBERT, JR., advertising executive; b. Kansas City, Kans., Apr. 27, 1945; s. Robert and Sarah (Morgan) B.; m. Rita Carol Burdinie, June 26, 1971; children: Rebecca, Sarah. AB, U. Kans., 1967; MA, Northwestern U., 1968, PhD, 1972, MBA, 1979. Rsch. supr. Energy BBDO, Chgo., 1973-78, v.p. rsch. dir., 1978-82, sr. v.p., mktg. svcs. dir., 1982-85, exec. v.p., rsch. dir., 1985—. Author: Radicals In Urban Politics, 1974; contbr. articles to profl. jours. Mem. Am. Mktg. Assn. Office: Energy BBDO 410 N Michigan Ave Ste 8 Chicago IL 60611-4273

BAILEY, ROBERT L., finance company executive; CEO State Auto Fin. Corp., 1989—, pres., 1991-96, also chmn. bd. dirs. Office: State Auto Fin Corp 518 E Broad St Columbus OH 43215-3901

BAILEY, ROBERT SHORT, retired lawyer; b. Bklyn., Oct. 17, 1931; s. Cecil Graham and Mildred (Short) B.; m. Doris Furlow, Aug. 29, 1953 (dec. 2001); children: Elizabeth Jane Goldentyer, Robert F., Barbara A. Jongbloed. AB, Wesleyan U., Middletown, Conn., 1953; JD, U. Chgo., 1956. Bar: Ill. 1965, U.S. Dist. Ct. D.C. 1956, U.S. Supreme Ct. 1960. Atty. criminal divsn. U.S. Dept. Justice, 1956-61, asst. U.S. atty. No. dist. Ill., 1961-65; ptnr. LeFevour & Bailey, Oak Park, Ill., 1965-68; pvt. practice, Chgo., 1968—. Panel atty. Fed. Defender Program, 1965—. Mem. NACDL (faculty 1976-78, legis. chmn. 1976-78). Home: 17 Timber Trail Streamwood IL 60107-1353 Personal E-mail: bobsbailey@comcast.net.

BAILEY, WILLIAM L., communications executive; b. Bay City, Mich., Mar. 23, 1952; s. Benjamin E. and Kathryn Ann (Kehoe) B.; m. Penny Kay Weber, Feb. 28, 1988; children: Mike, Ryan. BS, Western Mich. U., 1975; postgrad., Saginaw Valley State U., 1976-78. Journalist Booth Newspaper, TV, Radio, Mich., 1978-82; publisher Glovebox Guidebooks Am., Saginaw, 1988—; dir. comm. City of Saginaw, Mich., 1997—. Comm., pub. rels. cons. Bailey & Assoc., Saginaw, 1985—. Prodr., host: Dateline Radio and TV Talk Show, 1995—; contbr. articles to profl. jours. Mem. Outdoor Writer Am. Avocations: reading, writing. Home and Office: 3523 N Gleaner Rd Freeland MI 48623-8829

BAILEY, WILLIAM W., state legislator, realtor; b. Mayfield, Ky., Aug. 1, 1948; m. Donna R. Bailey. BS, Murray State U., 1970; postgrad., Ind. U. City councilman, Seymour, Ind., 1976-80; mayor, 1983-90; Ind. state rep. Dist. 66, 1990—; mem. com. rules and legis. procedures and human affairs com. Ind. Ho. Reps., ranking minority mem., local govt. com., chmn. cities and towns. Mem. Ind. Job Tng. Coord. Coun.; chief offcl. So. Ctrl. Ind. Pvt. Industry Coun. Democrat. Home: 715 Wendemere Dr Seymour IN 47274-2701

BAILIS, DAVID PAUL, lawyer; b. Dec. 19, 1955; B in Commerce, McGill U., 1977; JD, Washington U., 1981; LLM in Taxation, NYU, 1985. Bar: Mo. 1981, N.C. 1990, Nebr. 1991. Atty. Peper, Martin, Jensen, Maichel and Hetlage, St. Louis, Mo., 1981-89; gen. counsel Health Sys. Group First Data Corp., Omaha, 1989-91, gen. counsel First Data Resources, 1991-92, gen. counsel, 1992—. Contbr. articles to profl. jours. Office: First Data Corp 212 N 117th Ave # 30 Omaha NE 68154-2211

BAILLIE, JAMES LEONARD, lawyer; b. Mpls., Aug. 27, 1942; s. Leonard Thompson and Sylvia Alfreda (Fundberg) B.; m. Jacqueline McGlamery; children: Jennifer, Craig, John. AB in History, 1964; JD, U. Chgo., 1967. Bar: Minn. 1967, U.S. Dist. Ct. Minn. 1968, U.S. Ct. Appeals (8th cir.) 1969, U.S. Ct. Appeals (5th cir.) 1980. Law clk. to presiding justice U.S. Dist. Ct., Mpls., 1967-68; assoc. Fredrikson & Byron, P.A., Mpls., 1968-73, shareholder, 1973—. Mem. ABA (litigation sect. co-editor Bankruptcy Litigation 1998, bus. law sect. editl. bd. Bus. Law Today 1993-98, bus. sect. chair pro bono com. 1999-2003, section coun 2003—, standing com. on lawyer pub. svc. responsibility 1991-96, chmn. 1993-96, nat. pro bono award 1984, John Minor Wisdom award 1999), Minn. State Bar Assn. (chmn. bankruptcy sect. 1985-88, sec. 2000-01, treas. 2001-02, pres. elect., 2003-03, pres. 2003-04), Hennepin County Bar Assn. (sec. 1992-93, treas. 1993-95, pres. elect., 1995-96, pres. 1996-97). Office: Fredrikson & Byron PA 200 S 6th St # 4000 Minneapolis MN 55402 Office Phone: 612-492-7013. Business E-Mail: jbaillie@fredlaw.com.

BAIN, DOUGLAS G., retired aerospace transportation executive, lawyer; b. Charlottesville, Va., Mar. 12, 1949; m. Cindy Bain; children: Tyler, Emily, Allison. BA, U. Va., 1971, JD, 1974. Bar: Calif. 1974, Wash. 1982, Ill. 2005. Atty. Office Gen. Counsel USAF, Washington, 1975—77; atty. Pillsbury, Madison & Sutro; various positions in legal dept. including sr. counsel & asst. gen. counsel The Boeing Co., Chgo., 1982—96, v.p. legal, contracts, ethics and govt. rels. comml. airplanes group, 1996—99, v.p., gen. counsel, 1999—2000, sr. v.p., gen. counsel, 2000—06.

BAINES, DON A., manufacturing executive; BBA in Acctg., St. Edward's U., Austin. CPA. Various positions including contr. process/transport divsn. Trade Co. (predecessor ALTEC), 1976-85; v.p., mgr. of fin. ALTEC, 1986-89; CFO HIS, 1989—; CFO, treas. Chart Industries, 1992—. Office: 5885 Landerbrook Dr Ste 150 Mayfield Heights OH 44124-4031

BAIR, GERALD D., state government official; BS in Bus. Adminstrn., Morningside Coll., 1965. From corp. auditor to dir. revenue and finance Department of Revenue, Des Moines, 1965-75, dir. revenue and finance, 1975—. Mem. Fedn. Tax Adminstrs. (exec. bd.), Legislative Interstate Coop. com., Ankeny Rotary (internat. bd.), Drake U. adv. council. Office: Iowa Revenue and Finance Dept Hoover State Office Bldg Des Moines IA 50319-0001

BAIRD, DOUGLAS GORDON, law educator, dean; b. Phila., July 10, 1953; s. Henry Welles and Eleanora (Gordon) B. BA in English summa cum laude, Yale U., 1975; JD, Stanford U., 1979; LLD (hon.), U. Rochester, 1994. Law clk. to Hon. Shirley M. Hufstedler US Ct. Appeals 9th Cir., 1979, law clk. to Hon. Dorothy W. elson, 1980; asst. prof. law U. Chgo. Law Sch., 1980-83, prof., 1984—87, Harry A. Bigelow prof. law, 1988—96, Harry A. Bigelow disting. svc. prof. law, 1996—, assoc. dean, 1984-87, dean, 1994-99. Vis. prof. law Stanford U., 1987—88, Yale U., 2000; Robert Braucher vis. prof. law Harvard U., 1993. Author: The Elements of Bankruptcy, 1992, 4th edit., 2006; co-author:(with Gertner & and Picker) Game Theory and the Law, 1994. Fellow: Am. Coll. Bankruptcy, Am. Acad. Arts and Scis. Office: U Chgo Sch Law 1111 E 60th St Chicago IL 60637-2776 Office Phone: 773-702-9571.

BAIRD, ROBERT DAHLEN, retired theology studies educator; b. Phila., June 29, 1933; s. Jesse Dahlen and Clara (Sonntag) Baird; m. Patty Jo Lutz, Dec. 18, 1954; children: Linda Sue, Stephen Robert, David Bryan, Janna Ann. BA, Houghton Coll., 1954; BD, Fuller Theol. Sem., 1957; STM, So. Meth. U., 1959; PhD, U. Iowa, 1964. Instr. philosophy and religion U. Omaha, 1962-65; fellow Asian religions Soc. Religion in Higher Edn., 1965-66; asst. prof. religion U. Iowa, Iowa City, 1966-69, assoc. prof., 1969-74, prof., 1974-2001, prof. emeritus, 2001—, acting dir. Sch. Religion, 1985, dir., Sch. Religion, 1995—2000; Leonard S. Florsheim Sr. Eminent Scholar's chair New Coll., U. South Fla., Sarasota, 1988-89. Vis. prof. Grinnell Coll., 1983; Goodwin-Philpot Eminent chair in religion Auburn U., 2001—03; adj. prof. Ripon (Wis.) Coll., 2005—. Author: Category Formation and the History of Religions, 1971, 2d paperback edit., 1991; author: (with W. R. Comstock et al) Religion and Man: An Introduction, 1971, Indian and Far Eastern Religious Traditions, 1972; editor: Methodological Issues in Religious Studies, 1975, Religion in Modern India, 1981, 4th edit., 2001, Essays in History of Religions, 1991, Religion and Law in Independent India, 1993, 2d edit., 2005; book rev. editor: Jour. Am. Acad. Religion, 1979—84; contbr. articles to profl. jours. Ford Found. fellow, 1965—66, Sr. fellow, Am. Inst. Indian Studies, 1972, 1992, Faculty Devel. grantee, U. Iowa, 1979, 1986, 1992. Mem.: N.Am. Assn. Study Religion, Assn. Asian Studies, Am. Acad. Religion. Democrat. Presbyterian. Office: 113 Glenn Dr Cottage Grove WI 53527 Home Phone: 608-839-1509. E-mail: robert-baird@uiowa.edu.

BAIRD, ROBERT DEAN, mission director; b. Hereford, Tex., Aug. 12, 1933; s. Kay and Maybelle (Witherspoon) B.; m. Margaret Ann Roberts, Aug. 27, 1953; children: Sandy, Deana Young. AA, Amarillo Jr. Coll., 1953; BTh., Bapt. Bible Coll., 1970, DD (hon.), 1986, Atlantic Bapt. Bible Coll., 1986; HHD (hon.), La. Bapt. Univ. Theol. Sem., 2002. Ordained to ministry Bapt. Ch., 1969. Asst. pastor High St. Bapt. Ch., Springfield, Mo., 1969-72; missionary Bapt. Bible Fellowship Internat., Jamaica, 1972-77, asst. mission dir. Springfield, 1977-81; pastor Hallmark Bapt. Ch., Fort Worth, 1981-86; mission dir. Bapt. Bible Fellowship Internat., Springfield, Mo., 1986—. Co-author (with Alfred Bloom): (books) Religion and Man: Indian and Far Eastern Religious Traditions, 1972; editor: Religion in Modern India, 1982; author: Category Formation and the History of Religions, 1991, Essays in the History of Religions, 1991, Religion and Law in Independent India, 1993. Mem. Internat. Conf. on World Evangelism (steering com. 1990—). Office: Bapt Bible Fellowship Internat PO Box 191 Springfield MO 65801-0191

BAIRD, SAMUEL P., state finance director; b. Superior, Nebr. Grad. U. Nebr. Coll. Law, Lincoln. V.p. to pres., CEO FSB, Inc.; pres., CEO KL&DM, Inc.; dir. Nebr. Dept. Banking & Fin., Lincoln, 1999—. Bd. dirs. 10th Fed. Res. Bank, Kansas City, 1996—98. Trustee, mem. investment com. U. Nebr. Found. Mem.: Nebr. Bankers Assn. (pres. 1989—90). Office: Nebr Dept Banking & Fin PO Box 95006 Lincoln NE 68509-5006

BAISLEY, JAMES MAHONEY, retired lawyer; b. Dec. 21, 1932; s. Charles Thomas and Katherine (Mahoney) B.; m. Barbara Brosnan, Sept. 7, 1960; children— Mary Elizabeth, Katherine, Barbara, Paul, Genevieve, Charles, James BS, Fordham U., 1954, LLB, 1961. Bar: N.Y. 1961, Ill. 1969. Assoc. Naylon, Aronson, Huber & Magill, YC, 1961-66; asst. counsel GTE Corp, 1966-69; v.p., gen. counsel GTE Automatic Electric Inc., Northlake, Ill., 1969-81; gen. counsel, v.p. W. W. Grainger Inc., Skokie, Ill., 1981-92, corp. sec., 1991-2000, ret., 2000. Bd. dirs. EAC, Inc. Served with USMC, 1954-57 Mem. ABA, Chgo. Bar Assn., Union League Club Chgo., North Shore Country Club. Republican. Roman Catholic. Home: 2936 Iroquois Rd Wilmette IL 60091-1105

BAKER, CARL LEROY, lawyer; b. Woodland, Calif., Nov. 9, 1943; s. Elmer L. and Lucea G. (Tickner) B.; m. Suzon L. Lockhart, June 13, 1966; children: Michele S., Eric L. BA, Sacramento State Coll., 1965; JD, Ind. U., 1968. Bar: Ind. 1968, U.S. Dist. Ct. (no. and so. dists.) Ind. 1968, U.S. Supreme Ct. 1978. Atty. Lincoln Nat. Corp., Ft. Wayne, Ind., 1968-74, asst. gen. counsel, 1974-77, assoc. gen. counsel, 1977-81, 2d v.p., 1979-85, v.p., 1985—, v.p., deputy gen. counsel, 1992—. Mem. assoc. faculty Ind.-Purdue U. at Ft. Wayne, 1976—. Mem. staff Law Jour. Ind. U. Sch. Law, 1966-67. Bd. dirs., v.p. Garrett (Ind.) Pub. Libr., Ch. Builders, Inc., Ft. Wayne, 1986—, pres., 1994; pro bono atty. indigent clients, Ft. Wayne, 1968—; mem. adv. bd. Lincoln Mus. Mem. Ind. Bar Assn. (conf. speaker 1988), Am. Coun. Life Ins. (legal sect. 1972—), Assn. Life Ins. Counsel, Am. Judicature Soc., Ind. Trial Lawyers Assn., Am. Corp. Counsel Assn., Nat. Lawyers Club (Washington), Delta Theta Phi, Sigma Phi Epsilon. Avocations: trout fishing, splitting firewood, hiking, Indiana U. basketball. Office: Lincoln Nat Corp 1300 S Clinton St Fort Wayne IN 46802-3506

BAKER, DAVID HIRAM, nutritionist, educator; b. DeKalb, Ill., Feb. 26, 1939; s. Vernon T. and Lucille M. (Severson) B.; m. Norraine A. Baker; children: Barbara G., Michael D., Susan G., Debora A., Luann C., Beth A. BS, U. Ill., 1961, MS, 1963, PhD, 1965. Sr. scientist Eli Lilly & Co., Greenfield, Ind., 1965-67; mem. faculty U. Ill., Champaign-Urbana, 1967—, prof. nutrition, dept. animal sci., nutritional biochemist, 1974—, dept. head, 1988-90. Author: Sulfur in onruminant Nutrition, 1977, Bioavailability of Nutrients for Animals, 1995; mem. editorial bd. Jour. Animal Sci., 1969-73, Jour. Nutrition, 1975-79, 89-99, Poultry Sci., 1978-84, Nutrition Revs., 1983-92; contbr. numerous articles to sci. jours. Chmn. bd. Champaign-Urbana Teen Challenge Drug Rehab. Program, 1977-80. Recipient Disting. Svc. award USDA, 1987; Univ. Scholar award. 1986; Nutrition Rsch. award, 1986; Am. Feed Mfrs., 1973; Merck award, 1977; Paul A. Funk award, 1977; H. H. Mitchell Tchg. award, 1979, 85; Broiler Rsch. award, 1983. Mem. NAS, Am. Soc. Animal Sci. (Young Scientist award 1971, Gustaf Bohstedt award 1985, Hoffman LaRoche award 1985, Morrison award 1994, Frontiers in Animal Nutrition award 2006, Charles A. Black award 2007), Poultry Sci. Assn., Am. Soc. Nutritional Sci. (Borden award 1986, Dannon award 2003), Fedn. Am. Socs. Exptl. Biology, Sigma Xi, Phi Kappa Phi, Alpha Zeta, Gamma Sigma Delta. Home: 2609 Wadsworth Ln Urbana IL 61802-9403 Office: U Ill Nutrition Dept Urbana IL 61801 Office Phone: 217-333-0243. Business E-Mail: dhbaker@uiuc.edu.

BAKER, DOUGLAS FINLEY, library director; b. Highland, Ill., July 21, 1950; s. Elmer Eugene and Winifred Ilona (Timmons) B.; children: Gretchen, Richard, Charles. BA with distinction, U. Iowa, 1972, MA in Libr. Sci., 1973. Libr. West Side Br., Des Moines Libr., 1974; I-LITE coord. State Libr. of Iowa, 1974-77, dir. office in interlibr. cooperation, 1977-78; dir. N.W. Wis. Libr. System (now No. Waters Libr. Svc.), Ashland, 1978-86, Kenosha (Wis.) Pub. Libr., 1986—. Mem. ALA, System and Resource Libr. Adminstrs. Assn. of Wis., Wis. Libr. Assn., Wis. Assn. of Pub. Librs. Office: Kenosha Pub Libr PO Box 1414 812 56th St Kenosha WI 53140-3735

BAKER, DOUGLAS M., JR., service industry executive; Various mktg. and mgmt. positions Proctor & Gamble Co.; with Ecolab Inc., St. Paul, 1989, sr. v.p. inst. sector, 2001—02, pres., COO, 2002—04, pres., CEO, bd. dir., 2004—, chmn., 2006—. Bd. dir. U.S. Bancorp, 2008—. Office: Ecolab 370 Wabasha St N Saint Paul MN 55102*

BAKER, DUSTY (JOHNNIE B. BAKER JR.), professional baseball team manager, retired professional baseball player; b. Riverside, Calif., June 15, 1949; s. Johnnie B. Baker Sr. and Christine Baker; m. Melissa Baker; children: Natosha, Darren. Student, Am. River Coll. Outfielder Atlanta Braves, 1968-75, LA Dodgers, 1976-83, San Francisco Giants, 1984, Oakland A's, 1985-86; mgr. San Francisco Giants, 1993—2002, Chgo. Cubs, 2002—06, Cin. Reds, 2008—. Mem. Nat. League All-Star Team, 1981, 82. Baseball analyst ESPN, 2006. Named MVP, Nat. League Championship Series, 1977, Nat. League Mgr. of Yr., 1993, 1997, 2000; recipient Silver Slugger award, 1980, 1981, Golden Glove award, 1981. Office: Cin Reds Great Am Ball Pk 100 Main St Cincinnati OH 45202-4109 Office Phone: 513-765-7000.

BAKER, EDWARD MARTIN, engineering and industrial psychologist; s. Harold H. and Paula B.; m. Shige Jajiki; 1 son, Evan Keith. BA, CCNY, 1962, MBA, 1964; PhD (Research fellow), Bowling Green State U., 1972. Human factors research engr. environ. and safety engring. staff Ford Motor Co., Dearborn, Mich., 1972-77, tech. tng. assoc. mgmt. and tech. tng. dept. Detroit, 1977-79, orgn. devel. cons., personnel and orgn. staff, 1979-81, statis. assoc., ops. support product quality office, 1981-83, statis methods mgr. Asia-Pacific and Latin-Am. automotive ops., 1983-87, dir. total quality planning, cons. and statis. methods corp. quality office, 1987—, dir. quality strategy and ops. support, 1990-92; sr. fellow Aspen Inst., Wye, Md., 1992-95. Deming scholars MBA program adv. bd. Fordham U., 1992—, adj. faculty MBA program, 1994—; cons. in field. Author: Scoring a Whole in One, 1999; contbr. articles to profl. jours.; editorial referee: Jour. Quality Tech, 1974-75, 77-81. Trustee W. Edwards Deming Inst., Washington, 1993-2003. Capt. US Army, 1964—67. Fellow Am. Soc. Quality (Brumbaugh award 1975, Craig award 1976, 79, 86, 88, Ishikawa medal 1995, Deming medal 1997). Home and Office: PO Box 5797 Scottsdale AZ 85261-5797 Personal E-mail: lifemap@ix.netcom.com.

BAKER, FRANK C. (BUZZ BAKER), advertising executive; m. Terry Baker; 1 child, Scott. BA in History and Econs., Harvard U., postgrad. With Fletcher/Mayo Assocs., St. Joseph, Mo., 1976-81; pres. & mng. dir. Cedar Rapids unit, dir. acct. mgmt. Creswel Munsell Fultz & Zirbel, Cedar Rapids, Iowa, 1981-90, pres., CEO, 1990—2002; sr. cons. Alexander Marketing Svcs., Grand Rapids, Mich., 2002—. Bd. dir. United Way, Hugh O'Brien Found., March of Dimes, Young Parent's Network. Mem.: Ad Club West Mich. (program chair), Cedar Rapids Advt. Fedn. (named to Hall of Fame 1991), Nat. AgriMktg. Assn. Avocation: sports. Office: Alexander Marketing Services 277 Crahen Ave NE Grand Rapids MI 49546 Mailing: Alexander Marketing Services PO Box 601 Grand Rapids MI 49516-0601 E-mail: bbaker@alexandermarketing.com.

BAKER, FREDERICK MILTON, JR., lawyer; b. Flint, Mich., Nov. 2, 1949; s. Frederick Milton Baker and Mary Jean (Hallitt) Rarig; m. Irene Taylor; children: Jessica, Jordan. BA, U. Mich., 1971; JD, Washington U., St. Louis, 1975. Bar: Mich. 1975, U.S. Dist. Ct. (we. dist.) Mich. 1980, U.S. Dist. Ct. (ea. dist.) Mich. 1981, U.S. Ct. Appeals (6th cir.) 1983, U.S. Supreme Ct. 1986. Instr. law Wayne State U., Detroit, 1975-76; rsch. atty. Mich. Ct. Appeals, Lansing, 1976-77, law clk. to chief judge, 1977; asst. prof. T.M. Cooley Law Sch., Lansing, 1978-80; ptnr. Willingham & Cote, Lansing, 1980-86, Honigman, Miller, Schwartz & Cohn, Lansing, 1986—2004; commr. Mich. Supreme Ct., 2005—. Adj. prof. T.M. Cooley Law Sch., 1980—86, 1995—96, Detroit Coll. Law Mich. State U., East Lansing, 2001—. Author: Michigan Bar Appeal Manual, 1982; editor Mich. Bar Jour., 1984—; contbr. articles to profl. jours. Founder, pres. Sixty Plus Law Ctr., Lansing, 1978-87, bd. dirs., 1987—; mem. cmty. adv. bd. Lansing Jr. League, 1983-90; co-founder, dir., sec.-treas. John D. Voelker Found., 1989—; bd. dirs. Greater Lansing chpt., ACLU 1997-2004; treas. Kehillat Israel, 1996-98; trustee Thoman Found., 2000-, Lansing Area Cmty. Trust, 2003—; pres. Gerald Beckwith Fund, 2002-04. Recipient Disting. Brief award T.M. Cooley Law Rev., 1988, 99. Fellow Mich. State Bar Found.; mem. ABA (Outstanding Single Project award 1980), Mich. Bar Assn. (vice chmn. jour. adv. bd. 1984-87, chmn. jour. adv. bd. 1987—, young lawyers sect. coun. 1980-84, grievance com. 1982-84, John W. Cummiskey award 1984), Ingham County Bar Assn. (Disting. Vol. award 2000), Big Oak Club (Baldwin, Mich.). Unitarian Universalist. Avocations: photography, fishing, running, frisbee, writing. Home: 5127 Barton Rd Williamston MI 48895-9304 Office: Mich Supreme Ct PO Box 30104 Lansing MI 48909 Home Phone: 517-655-5501; Office Phone: 517-373-0260. E-mail: bakerf@courts.mi.gov.

BAKER, HAROLD ALBERT, federal judge; b. Mt. Kisco, NY, Oct. 4, 1929; s. John Shirley and Ruth (Sarmiento) B.; m. Dorothy Ida Armstrong, June 24, 1951; children: Emily, Nancy, Peter. AB, U. Ill., 1951, JD, 1956. Bar: Ill. 1956. Practiced in, Champaign, Ill., 1956-78; partner firm Hatch & Baker, 1960-78; chief judge U.S. Dist. Ct. (cen. dist.) Ill., Danville, 1978-94, sr. judge, 1994—. Adj. mem. faculty Coll. Law, U. Ill., 1972-78; sr. counsel Presdl. Commn. on CIA Activities within U.S., 1975 Pres. Champaign Bd. Edn., 1967-76, pres., 1967-76. Served to lt. j.g. USN, 1951-53. Mem. ABA, Ill. Bar Assn. Democrat. Episcopalian. Office: US Dist Ct 201 S Vine St Rm 338 Urbana IL 61802-3369

BAKER, HOLLIS MACLURE, furniture manufacturing company executive; b. Allegan, Mich., Apr. 27, 1916; s. Hollis Siebe and Ruth (MacClure) B.; m. Betty Jane Brown, Aug. 2, 1947; children: Tomelyn Ann, Susan MacClure; m. Elsie Margarite Leigh, Aug. 27, 2003. Student, U. Va., 1935-37. With Baker Furniture, Inc., Holland, Mich., 1938-40, 45-73, v.p., treas., 1959-61, pres., 1961-70, chmn. bd., 1970-73; v.p., gen. mgr. Grand Rapids Chair Co., Mich., 1959-61, pres., 1961-70. V.p., dir. Manor House, Inc., N.Y.C., 1958-70; pres. Boyne City R.R. Co., Mich., 400 Bldg. Corp., Palm Beach, Fla.; dir. Mich. Nat. Bank, Lansing, 1968-83, Am. Seating Co., Grand Rapids, 1973-83, Mich. Nat. Bank, Grand Rapids, 1959-84, Norton Gallery, Palm Beach, 1984-91. Author: A Brief History of Schloss Branzoll, 1975, A History of the Chateau de Caussade, 1980, A History of the Chateau de la Roque, 1985, Five Castles Are Enough, 1989. Bd. dirs. USCG Found., 1981-91. Lt. (s.g.) USNR, 1941-45. Mem. Nat. Assn. Furniture Mfrs. (dir.), Furniture Mfrs. Assn. Grand Rapids (dir., past pres 1970-84), Zeta Psi. Clubs: Brook (N.Y.C.), River (N.Y.C.), New York Yacht (N.Y.C.), Leash (N.Y.C.); Kent Country (Grand Rapids), University (Grand Rapids), Indian (Grand Rapids), Peninsular (Grand Rapids); Everglades (Palm Beach), Bath and Tennis (Palm Beach); Buck's (London). Episcopalian. Home: 301 Chapel Hill Rd Palm Beach FL 33480-4124 Office: 2220 Wealthy St Grand Rapids MI 49506

BAKER, JACK SHERMAN, retired architect; b. Champaign, Ill., Aug. 8, 1920; s. Clyde Lee and Jane Cecilia (Walker) B. BA with honors, U Ill., 1943, MS, 1949; cert., .Y. Beaux Art Inst. Design, 1943. Aero engr., designer Boeing Aircraft, Seattle, 1943-44; assoc. Atkins, Barrow & Lasswith, Urbana, 1947-50; pvt. practice architecture Champaign, 1947—; mem. faculty U. Ill. Sch. Architecture, Urbana, 1947—, prof. architecture, 1950-90, acting prof. emeritus, 1990—97, Disting. prof. emeritus, 1997—, former mem. exec. com.; ret. Hon. bd. dirs. Gerhart Music Festival, Guntersville, Ala., Stravinsky awards, Champaign, Conservatory of Cen. Ill.; hon. bd. dirs. Ruth Hindman Found., Huntsville, Ala.; dir., performer personal performance loft space for Interaction of the Arts and Architecture, 1960—; participant U. Ill. Exploring the Arts course (Act-NCEA award), 1970—, campus honors program, 1995—; former mem. Chancellor's com. on graphic design and art acquisition and installation, former mem. adv. bd., designer of exhbn., Krannert Mus., U. Ill., engr. basic, Ft. Leonard Wood, Mo., topog. engr., Ft. Blevoir, Va. Exhibitions include watercolors, archtl. drawings and photography, Monograph and Retrospective Arch. Exhibit: "I" Space Gallery, Chgo., 1997, U. Ill. Temple Buell Arch. Gallery, 1998, Temple Buell Hall Gallery, 2000, Japanese House Drawings Exhibit, Krannert Art Mus., U. Ill., 1998; contbr. articles to numerous jours. and confs. Mem. U. Ill. Pres.'s Coun., U. Ill. Bronze Cir., 1986; mem. mus. bd. and affiliate World Heritage Mus.; former mem. adv. bd. Krannert Ctr. for Performing Arts, Assembly Hall U. Ill.; exhbn. designer World Heritage Mus., U. Ill. Served with U.S. Army, AFH, 1945-46, Caserta, Italy, ETO. Recipient "prix d'Emulation Societe des Architectes Diplomes par le Gouvernment" Beaux-Arts medal, 1942, cert. for dedicated and disting. svc., Nat. AIA Com. on Environ. and Design, 1955, Decade of Achievement award, World Heritage Mus., 1992, Art and Humanities award, 1981, 1982, Honor award for advancing profession architecture, CIC/AIA, 1983, Excellence in Edn. award and medal, IC/AIA, 1989,

Heritage award, PACA, 1997, numerous other honors and design excellence awards in field, Recognition award, U. Ill. Found., 2001, U. Ill. Sch. Arch., 2006. Fellow: AIA (medal 1977), Nat. Coun. Archtl. Registration Bds. (cert.); mem.: Soc. Archtl. Historians, Ill. Coun./AIA, The Nature Conservancy, Nat. Resources Def. Coun., Gargoyle, Scarab, Cliff Dwellers Club (Chgo.), Alpha Rho Chi. Home: 71 1/2 E Chester St Champaign IL 61820-4149

BAKER, JERRY L., police chief; m. Elaine Baker; 3 children. Student, Ind. U.; B in Criminal Justice, Ind. U.-Purdue U., 1978; grad., FBI Nat. Acad. Joined Indpls. Police Dept., 1969, sgt., 1975, comdr. auto theft br., asst. comdr. vice br., lt., comdr. Spl. Ops. and Response/SWAT Team, dep. chief West Dist., 1994—2000, chief of police, 2000—. With US Army, Vietnam. Mem.: VFW, FBI Nat. Acad. Ind., Mil. Order Purple Heart, Vietnam Vets. Am., Am. Legion. Office: Inpls Police Dept Ste E211 50 N Alabama St Indianapolis IN 46204-5305

BAKER, JOHN, electronics executive; Pres. Micro Electronics, Columbus, Ohio; founder, Micro Center, 1979. Office: Micro Electronics Inc PO Box 1143 Hilliard OH 43026-6143

BAKER, JOHN RUSSELL, utilities executive; b. Lexington, Mo., July 21, 1926; s. William Frederick and Flora Anne (Dunford) B.; m. Elizabeth Jane Torrence, June 16, 1948; children— John Russell, Burton T. BS, U. Mo., 1948, MBA, 1962. With Mo. Public Service Co., Kansas City, 1948—, treas., 1966-68, v.p. fin., 1968-71, sr. v.p., 1971-73, exec. v.p., 1973—, also dir. Lectr. fin. U. Mo.; vice-chmn. Aquila Inc., 1991—. Vice-pres. Mid-Continent coun. Girl Scouts U.S., 1981; mem. adv. coun. Sch. Acctg., U. Mo., Columbia. Recipient Outstanding alumnus award Sch. Adminstrn. U. Mo., Kansas City, 1965; citation of merit U. Mo., 1995. Mem. Tax Execs. Inst. (pres. Kansas City 1968), U. Mo. Sch. Adminstrn. Alumni Assn. (pres. 1965). Clubs: Kansas City. Republican. Methodist. Home: 205 NW Oxford Ln Lees Summit MO 64063-2118 Office: Aquila Inc 20 W 9th St Kansas City MO 64105-1704

BAKER, KENDALL L., academic administrator; b. Clearwater, Fla., Nov. 1, 1942; s. Robert B. and Anne E. Baker; m. Tobin Ratliff McGough, Apr. 12, 1981; children: Kraig, Kris, John, Shannon, Brian. BA with honors, U. Md., 1963; MA, Georgetown U., 1967, PhD, 1979. Instr., Dept. Polit. Sci. U. Wyo., Laramie, 1967-69, asst. prof., 1969-73, assoc. prof., 1973-77, prof., 1977-82, chmn., 1979-82, asst. v.p. for Acad. Affairs, 1976-77; dean, Coll. Arts & Scis., Bowling Green State U., Ohio, 1982-87; v.p., provost No. Ill. U., DeKalb, 1987-92; pres. U. N. D., 1992-99, Ohio Northern U, 1999—. Cons. survey rsch. to various agys. and polit. candidates, 1967—; panel chmn. Rocky Mt. Social Sci. Conv., 1973, We. Social Sci. Conv., 1975, Coun. Colls. Arts and Scis., 1983, 86; guest participant study trip to Germany, 77. Author: The Wyoming Legislature: Lawmakers, the Public, and the Press, 1973; author: (with R. Dalton and K. Hildebrandt) Germany Tranformed: Political Culture and the New Politics, 1981; contbr. articles to profl. jours. Coach Laramie Soccer Assn., 1978—81; election observer Germany, 1980. Mem.: Conf. Group German Politics (mem. exec. com. 1984—87, co-editor newsletter 1985—91), Midwest Polit. Sci. Assn. (chmn. panel ann. conv. 1985, 1986), Am. Polit. Sci. Assn. (chmn. panel ann. conv. 1983), Pi Sigma Alpha, Omicron Delta Kappa, Phi Kappa Phi. Home: 920 West Lima Ada OH 45810 Office: President's Office 525 S Main St Ada OH 45810-1599 Office Phone: 419-772-2030. Business E-Mail: k-baker@onu.edu.

BAKER, KENNETH R., energy company executive; Various mgmt. positions GM Corp., 1969-99; former vice-chmn., chief operating officer Energy Conversion Devices, Inc., 1999; pres., CEO Environmental Rsch. Inst. of Mich., Ann Arbor, 1999—. Bd. dirs. Energy Conversion Devices. Recipient award for outstanding engring. contbn. to environment, City of Los angeles, 1996; named to World's Top 25 R&D Mgrs., A.D. Little, 1997. Office: ECD Inc 2956 Waterview Dr Rochester MI 48309-3484

BAKER, LAURENCE HOWARD, oncology educator; b. Bklyn., Jan. 14, 1943; s. Jacob and Sylvia (Tannenbaum) B.; m. Maxine V. Friedman, July 25, 1964; children: Mindy, Jennifer. BA, Bklyn. Coll. of CUNY, 1962; DO, U. Osteo. Medicine and Surgery, Des Moines, 1966. Diplomate Am. Bd. Internal Medicine. Rotating intern Flint Osteo. Hosp., Flint, Mich., 1966-67; med. resident Detroit Osteo. Hosp., 1967-69; fellow in oncology Wayne State U., Detroit, 1970-72; asst. prof. medicine, dept. oncology Wayne State U. Sch. Medicine, Detroit, 1972-76, assoc. prof. medicine, dept. oncology, 1976-79, prof. medicine, dept. oncology, 1979-82, assoc. chmn., dept. oncology, 1980-82, prof. medicine, dir. div. med. oncology, dept. internal medicine, 1982-86, prof. medicine, dir. div. hematology and oncology, dept. internal medicine, 1986-93, asst. dean for cancer programs, 1988-94; dir. Meyer L. Prentis Comprehensive Ctr. Met. Detroit; now prof. internal med. U. Mich. Sch. Medicine, Ann Arbor, dep., dir. clin. rsch. Comprehensive Cancer Ctr., 1994—. Bd. dirs. Mich. Cancer Consortium, Dept. Pub. Health, Mich. Cancer Found., U.S. Bioscis. Sci. Bd.; assoc. chmn. S.W. Oncology Group; presenter in field. Author or co-author over 150 articles, 28 books, 15 case reports, over 90 abstracts in field; mem. editl. adv. bd. Primary Care and Cancer; assoc. editor New Agents and Pharmacology; reviewer Cancer Rsch., Cancer Treatment Reports, Cancer, Am. Jour. Clin. Oncology, JAMA, Investigational New Drugs. Major U.S. Army, 1968-70, Vietnam; USAR, 1970-74. Recipient Faculty Ednl. Devel. award bur. Health Manpower NIH, 1973; grantee S.W. Oncology Group, 1974—, Intergroup Sarcoma Contract, 1986-89, Cancer Ctr., 1989-90, Clin. Therapeutics, Kasle Trust, 1988-89, Marilyn J. Smith Breast Cancer Rsch. Fund, 1986—, Program Project, New Drug Devel., 1989-94. Mem. Am. Soc. Cancer Rsch., Am. Soc. Clin. Oncology, Am. Soc. for Clin. Pharmacology and Therapeutics, Am. Assn. Clin. Rsch., Am. Assn. Cancer Edn., Am. Coll. Osteo. Internists, Cen. Soc. Clin. Rsch. Office: U Mich 1904 Taubman Ctr Box 0312 1500 E Medical Center Dr Ann Arbor MI 48109-0005

BAKER, MARK, television newscaster; b. Hannibal, Mo., Feb. 21, 1959; m. Jacqueline Christine Baker; 2 children. BA, U. Mo., 1981. Rep. candidate 17th dist. Ill. U.S. House of Reps., 1996. Methodist. Office: 1804 Tulip Ln Wausau WI 54401-6504

BAKER, MARK, food service executive; Chef Seasons Restaurant, Four Seasons Hotel, Chgo. Recipient award, James Beard Found., 2001. Office: Seasons Restaurant Four Seasons Hotel 120 Delaware Pl Chicago IL 60611

BAKER, NANNETTE A., lawyer, city official; b. Tuscaloosa, Ala., Oct. 3, 1957; BS, U. Tenn., 1978; JD, St. Louis U., 1994. Bar: Mo., Ill. TV journalist, St. Louis, Memphis, Knoxville; law clk. to Odell Horton U.S. Dist. Judge, Memphis, 1994-95; with firm Lashley & Baer, P.C., 1995-96; assoc. firm Schlichter, Bogard & Denton, St. Louis, 1996-99; chair Bd. Election Commrs. for City of St. Louis, 1997-99; judge State of Mo. (22d jud. cir.), 1999—. Bd. dirs. St. Patrick's Ctr., Nat. Mus. Transport, Coll. for Living; mem. adv. bd. SSM Rehab. Inst. Mem. ABA, ATLA, Mo. Trial Lawyer Orgn., Ill. Trial Lawyer Orgn., Nat. Bar Assn., Mound City Bar Assn. Office: 100 S 4th St Ste 900 Saint Louis MO 63102-1823

BAKER, PAMELA, lawyer; b. Detroit, Apr. 6, 1951; d. William D. and Lois (Tukey) Baker; m. Jay R. Franke, June 10, 1972; children: Baker Eugene, Alexandra Britell. AB, Smith Coll., 1972; JD, U. Wis. Madison, 1976. Bar: Ill. 1976, Wis. 1976. Ptnr. Sonnenschein, Nath & Rosenthal, Chgo.; chair nat. employee benefits and exec. compensation practice group. Contbr. articles to profl. jour. Fellow Am. Coll. Employee Benefits Counsel (charter), Am. Bar Found.; mem. ABA (mem. employee benefits com. 1984—, chair-elect 1998-99, chair 1999-2000, mem. plan mergers and acquisitions com. 1985— mem. fed. regulation of securities com. 1989—, chair 1989-95), Ill. State Bar Assn. (sec. employee benefits sect. coun. 1989-90, vice chair 1990-91, chair 1991-92), Chgo. Bar Assn. (employee benefits com. 1978—, sec. 1984-85, vice chair 1985-86, chair 1986-87, fed. taxation com. 1980—, exec. coun. 1982-85). Office: Sonnenschein ath & Rosenthal Sears Tower 233 S Wacker Dr Ste 7800 Chicago IL 60606-6491

BAKER, RICHARD LEE, book publishing company executive; b. Grand Rapids, Mich., July 27, 1935; s. Herman and Angeline (Sterkenberg) B.; m. Frances Leona Gesink, June 10, 1957; children: Dawn, Dwight, David, Daniel. Student, Calvin Coll., Grand Rapids, 1954-56. Pres. Baker Book House, Grand Rapids, 1957-97, chmn. bd. dirs., 1997—. Bd. dirs. Christian Schs. Internat., 1981-86; pres. bd. dirs. Christian Schs. Internat. Found., 1988—. Mem. Christian Booksellers Assn. (bd. dirs. 1985-93), Evang. Christian Pubs. Assn. (bd. dirs. 1981-84). Republican. Mem. Christian Reformed Ch. Avocations: golf, skiing, racquetball. Home: 2240 Shawnee Dr SE Grand Rapids MI 49506-5335 Office: Baker Book House PO Box 6287 Grand Rapids MI 49516-6287

BAKER, ROBERT I., manufacturing executive; b. Bridgeport, Conn., Sept. 28, 1940; s. Irwin Henry and Anna (Keane) B.; m. Patricia Turoczi, Nov. 28, 1968; children: Scott Allen, Christopher Keane. BA, U. Conn., 1962; postgrad., Syracuse U., 1975, U. Pa., 1978. With U.S. Electric Motors div. Emerson, Milford, Conn., 1963-66; with Henry G. Thompson div. Vt. Am., Branford, Conn., 1966-75, pres., gen. mgr. Magna div. Elizabethtown, Ky., 1977-84, corp. v.p., 1982-84, pres., CEO, Louisville, 1984-91; pres., owner Distbrs. Source, Portsmouth, N.H., 1991-92; CEO The Chamberlain Group, Inc., Elmhurst, Ill., 1992-96, The Chamberlain Group, Elmhurst, 1996—2000; ret., 2000. Cons. in field; bd. dirs. Chamberlain, Durasol, Brinkmann. Mem. Medinah Country Club, Abenaqui Country Club. Avocations: skiing, golf, woodworking. Home: 56 Old Bay Rd PO Box 2164 New Castle NH 03854

BAKER, ROBERT J(OHN), hospital administrator; b. Detroit, Feb. 2, 1944; s. Wesley Ries and Irma Louise (Richards) B.; m. Priscilla Horschak, Sept. 10, 1966; children: Scott, Katherine. BA, Kalamazoo Coll., 1966; MBA, U. Chgo., 1968. Adminstr. Indian Hosp., Sells, Ariz., 1968-70; asst. dir. U. Minn. Hosp., Mpls., 1970-73, assoc. dir., 1973-74, assoc. dir. ops., 1974-77, sr. assoc. dir., 1977; dir. U. Nebr. Hosp. and Clinic, Omaha, 1977-86; pres., chief exec. officer U. Health Sys. Consortium, Oak Brook, Ill., 1986—. Served with USPHS, 1968-70. Recipient Mary H. Bachmeyer award U. Chgo., 1968; Carl A. Erickson fellow, 1966 Mem. Council Teaching Hosps., Omaha-Council Bluffs Hosp. Assn. (pres. 1983) Office: U Health Systems Consortium 2001 Spring Rd Ste 700 Oak Brook IL 60523-1890

BAKER, RONALD LEE, folklore educator; b. Indpls., June 30, 1937; m. Catherine Anne Neal, Oct. 21, 1960; children: Susannah Jill, Jonathan Kemp. BS, Ind. State U., Terre Haute, 1960; MA, Ind. State U., 1961; postgrad., U. Ill., 1963-65; PhD, Ind U., 1969. Instr. English U. Ill., Urbana, 1963-65; teaching assoc. Ind. U., Ft. Wayne, 1965-66; prof. English Ind State U., Terre Haute, 1966—2006, chmn. dept., 1980—2006, chair and prof. emeritus, 2006—; vis. lectr. U. Ill., 1972-73; vis. assoc. prof. Ind. U., Bloomington, 1975, vis. prof., 1978, 84. Author: Folklore in the Writings of Rowland E. Robinson, 1973, Hoosier Folk Legends, 1982, Jokelore, 1986, French Folklife in Old Vincennes, 1989, The Study of Place Names, 1991, From Needmore to Prosperity: Hoosier Place Names in Folklore and History, 1995, Homeless, Friendless, and Penniless: The WPA Interviews with Former Slaves Living in Indiana, 2000, Jesse Stuart and the Hoosier Schoolmasters, 2007; (with others) Indiana Place Names, 1975. Fellow Am. Folklore Soc.; mem. MLA, Am. Name Soc. (v.p. 1981-82), Hoosier Folklore Soc. (pres. 1970-79, exec. sec.-treas. 1988-2000). Home: 3688 N Randall St Terre Haute IN 47805-9736 Office: Indiana State University Terre Haute IN 47809-9989 Home Phone: 812-877-9627; Office Phone: 812-237-3163. E-mail: ronbaker@indstate.edu.

BAKER, SHIRLEY KISTLER, academic administrator, university librarian; b. Lehighton, Pa., Mar. 16, 1943; d. Harvey Daniel and Miriam Grace (Osenbach) Kistler; m. Richard Christopher Baker, Oct. 22, 1966; children: Nicholas Christopher, India Jane. BA in Economics, Muhlenberg Coll., 1965; MA in Libr. Sci., U. Chgo., 1974, MA in South Asian Languages and Civilizations, 1974. Undergrad. libr. Northwestern U., Evanston, Ill., 1974-76; access libr. Johns Hopkins U., Balt., 1976-82; assoc. dir. librs. MIT, Cambridge, 1982-89; dean univ. librs. Washington U., St. Louis, 1989—, vice chancellor for info. tech., 1995—. Contbr. articles to profl. jours. Mem. ALA, Nat. Info. Standards Orgn. (bd. dirs. 1990-94), Assn. Rsch. Librs. (bd. dirs. 1996-2002, pres. 2000-01), Coalition for etworked Info. (steering com. 1999—), Mo. Libr. Network Corp. (bd. dirs. 1990-00). Democrat. Avocations: reading, travel. Home: 6310 Alexander Dr Saint Louis MO 63105-2223 Office: Washington Univ Campus Box 1061 1 Brookings Dr Saint Louis MO 63130-4899 E-mail: baker@wustl.edu.

BAKER, THOMAS C., state legislator; b. McCook, Nebr., Aug. 24, 1948; m. Patricia L. Anderson, Aug. 30, 1969; children: Kimberly Peterson, Jeff Baker, Mike Baker. BS in Agronomy, U. Nebr., 1971. Cert. secondary sci. edn. Owner Trails West Convenience Store and Truck Stop; mem. Nebr. Legislature from 44th dist., Lincoln, 1998—. Treas. B and A Enterprises Inc. Mem. Trenton Rural Fire Bd.; bd. trustees St. James Cath. Ch., Nebr. Farm Bur., Nebr. Cattlemen; former mem. Nebr. Oil and Gas Commn., Trenton Sch. Bd., Hitchcock County Ext. Bd.; bd. dirs. Trenton Ambulance Svc.; former bd. dirs. Nebr. Leadership Coun. Mem. Elks Club, KC. Home: HC 2 Box 140 Trenton NE 69044-9754 Office: State Capitol Dist 44 PO Box 94604 Rm 1101 Lincoln NE 68509

BAKER, VERNON G., II, lawyer, automotive executive; BA, Dartmouth Coll.; JD, Am. U. Assoc. Schnader, Harrison, Segal & Lewis, 1978—80; counsel Scott Paper Co.; assoc. gen. counsel Advanced Material Group; v.p., gen. counsel, Corp. Rsch. Tech. Hoechst Celanese Corp; sr. v.p., gen. counsel, sect. Meritor (now ArvinMeritor), 1999—. Recipient Trailblazer award, Minority Corp. Counsel Assn. Office: Arvin Meritor Inc 2135 W Maple Inc Troy MI 48084

BAKER, W. RANDOLPH, brewery company executive; With Anheuser-Busch Cos. Inc., St. Louis, 1970—, various positions to chief exec. and chmn. Busch Entertainment Corp., 1983—96, v.p., CFO, 1996—. Bd. dirs. St. Louis Chpt. of the Asthma and Allergy Found. Am. Office: Anheuser-Busch Cos Inc One Busch Pl Saint Louis MO 63118 Office Phone: 314-577-2000.

BAKK, THOMAS, state legislator; b. June 8, 1954; 2 children. BBA in Labor Mgmt. Rels., U. Minn., Duluth. Labor rep.; rep. Dist. 6A Minn. Ho. of Reps., 1994—. Mem. commerce com., environment and natura resources policy com., environment and natural resources finance com. Minn. Ho. of Reps. Office: 345 State Office Bldg Saint Paul MN 55155 also: 307 1st St N Virginia MN 55792 E-mail: rep.Thomas.Bakk@house.leg.state.mn.us.

BAKKEN, DOUGLAS ADAIR, foundation executive; b. Breckenridge, Minn., Mar. 12, 1939; s. John and Marie (Folstad) B.; m. Jacquelyn Ann Nielsen, July 8, 1962; children: Amy Michelle, Wendy Kay. BS, N.D. State U., 1961; cert. archives adminstrn., Am. U., 1966; MA in History, U. Nebr., 1967. Archivist Nebr. State Hist. Soc., Lincoln, 1966-67; assoc. archivist Cornell U., Ithaca, N.Y., 1967-71; archivist adminstr. Anheuser Busch Cos., St. Louis, 1971-77; dir. archives and library Henry Ford Mus., Dearborn, Mich., 1977-83; exec. dir. Ball Bros. Found., Muncie, Ind., 1983—. Pres. Ind. Donors Alliance Found., 1993—; mem. Minn. Cultural Found., 1989—. Served to 1st lt. Intelligence Corps U.S. Army, 1962-64. Sagamore of the Wabash, 1992. Fellow Soc. Am. Archivists; mem. Muncie Rotary Club, Ind. Colls. of Ind., Sports and Hobby Devel. Group Inc., Ind. Donors Alliance (founding mem.) Republican. Lutheran. Home: 4801 N Everett Rd Muncie IN 47304-1092 Office: Ball Bros Found 222 S Mulberry St Muncie IN 47305-2802

BAKKEN, EARL ELMER, electrical engineer, bioengineering company executive; b. Mpls., Jan. 10, 1924; s. Osval Elmer and Florence (Hendricks) B.; m. Constance L. Olson, Sept. 11, 1948 (div. May 1979); children: Wendy, Jeff, Brad, Pam; m. Doris Jane Marshall, Oct. 21, 1982. BEE, U. Minn., 1948, postgrad. in elec. engring., DSc (hon.), 1988, Tulane U., 1988. Ptnr. Medtronic, Inc., Mpls., 1949-57, pres., 1957-74, chmn., CEO, 1974-76, founder, sr. chmn., 1976-85, sr. chmn., 1985-89, dir., 1989-94, founder, dir. emeritus, 1994—. Contbr. articles to profl. jours.; developer first wearable, external, battery-powered heart pacemaker. Pres., bd. dirs. Bakken Libr. and Mus. Electricity in Life, Mpls., 1975-94, v.p., 1994—; pres. North Hawaii Cmty. Hosp., 1990-2000, Five Mtn. Med. Cmty., Waimea, Hawaii, 1997—; vice chmn. Pavek Mus. Broadcasting, Mpls., 1989—; chmn. bd. dirs. Archaeus Project, Waimea, Hawaii, 1985—. Staff sgt. USAAF, 1942-46. Decorated royal officer Order of Orange-Nassau (Netherlands); recipient Minn. Bus. Hall of Fame award, 1978, Outstanding Achievement award U. Minn., Mpls., 1981, Med.-Tech. Outstanding Achievement award Wale Securities, 1984, Engring. for Gold award NASPE, 1984, Achievement award Sci. Mus. Minn., 1988, Govs. award Minn. Med. Alley Assn., 1988, Centennial medal Coll. St. Thomas, 1986; named Outstanding Minnesotan of Yr. Minn. Broadcasters Assn., 1988, Lifetime Achievement award Entrepreneur of the Yr. program, 1991, Entrepreneur of Yr. award Minn. Entrepreneur's Club, 1993, Spl. Svc. award Richard Smart Big Island Cmty. Achievement, Waimea, Hawaii, 1995, Am. Creativity Assn. Lifetime Creative Achievement award, 1996, Lifetime Achievement award Minn. High Tech. Coun., 1996, Am. Heart Assn. Heart Ball honoree, Hawaii, 1996, Found. Laufman-Greatbatch prize, 1998, Spl. award Cardiostim XX Anniversary for Engrs. and Industry Founders, 1998, Honpa Hongwanji Mission of Hawaii Living Treasure of Hawaii award, 1998, Heart Inst. Innovator award, 1998, NASPE Pioneering award, 1999, Gold medal European Soc. Cardiology, 1999, Tex. Heart Inst. Innovator awrd, 1999, Outstanding Philanthropist of Yr., at. Philanthropy Soc., 2000, Russ prize Nat. Acad. Engring., 2001, Trailblazer award Scripps Ctr. for Integrative Medicine, 2002, others; named to Minn. Inventors Hall of Fame, 1995, Am. Heart Assn. West Hawaii Hall of Fame, 1998. Fellow IEEE (Centennial medal 1984, Eli Lilly award in med. and biol. engring. 1994), Bakken Soc., Instrument soc. Am., Am. Coll. Cardiology (hon.), Internat. Coll. Surgeons (hon.); mem. N.Am. Soc. Pacing and Electrophysiology (assoc., Disting. Svc. award 1985), Assn. Advancement Med. Instrumentation (Tex. Heart Inst. Innovator award 1998), Am. Antiquarian Soc., Minn. Med. Alley Assn. (bd. dirs. 1985-94), NAE, 1990—. Lutheran. Achievements include development of first wearable, external, battery-powered, transistorized pacemaker, 1957. Avocations: history of medical electrical technology, future studies, ballroom dancing. Office: Medtronic Inc MS LC110 710 Medtronic Pkwy Minneapolis MN 55432-5604

BAKKEN, ERIC ALLEN, lawyer; b. June 22, 1967; BS, St. Mary's U.; JD, William Mitchell Coll. Law. Bar: 1994. With Regis Corp., Edina, Minn., 1994—, v.p. law, 1998—2004, v.p., gen. counsel, sec., 2004—, sr. v.p. and gen. counsel, 2006—. Mem.: ABA, Beauty Industry Fund, Minn. Bar Assn., Hennepin County Bar Assn. Office: Regis Corp 7201 Metro Blvd Edina MN 55439 Office Phone: 952-947-7777.

BAKWIN, EDWARD MORRIS, banker; b. NYC, May 13, 1928; s. Harry and Ruth (Morris) B BA, Hamilton Coll., 1950; MBA, U. Chgo., 1961. With Nat. Stock Yards Nat. Bank, ational City, Ill., 1953—55; with Mid-City Nat. Bank Chgo., 1955—2001, pres., 1962—72, chmn. bd., CEO, 1967—2001, Darling-Del. Corp., Chgo., 1972—86, Mid-City Fin. Corp., 1982—2001, Nat. Stock Yards Co., 1985—93; chmn. bd. MBFI, Chgo., 2001—06. Bd. dirs. Duncan-Med. YMCA, 1963-72, Northwestern Meml. Hosp., 1980-88, West Ctrl. Assn., 1962-67, pres., 1962-65; mem. global bd. U. Chgo.; trustee Am. Mus. Fly Fishing, 1990—, Art Inst. Chgo. With AUS, 1951-52 Mem. Am. Bankers Assn., Ill. Bankers Assn. (bd. govs. 1966-69), Explorers Club, Adventurers Club (Chgo.), Chgo. Yacht Club, Mid-Am. Club, N.Y. Yacht Club Home: 0433 W US Hwy 20 La Porte IN 46350

BALANOFF, CLEM, county election director; b. Chgo., Apr. 14, 1953; m. Virginia Balanoff; 2 children. Student, Ripon Coll., 1971-73. Mem. Ill. House, 1989-95; Dem. candidate U.S. House, 1994, 96. Home: 5606 S Blackstone #3 Chicago IL 60637 Office: Cook County Clerk 69 W Washington 5th flr Chicago IL 60602 Office Phone: 312-603-0925. Business E-Mail: cbalan@cookcountygov.com.

BALASI, MARK GEOFFREY, architect; b. Chgo., Feb. 29, 1952; s. Alfred Victor and Betty Lou (Biggs) B.; m. Barbara Jane Ritt, May 25, 1985; children: Geoffrey Adam, Maria Elizabeth. Student, Ecole-des-Beaux-Arts, Versailles, France, 1974—75; BS in Archtl. Studies, U. Ill., 1975; postgrad., U. Wis., 1986, postgrad., 1989, postgrad., 1992. Lic. arch., Ill., Mich., Ohio. Arch. Davy McKee, Chgo., 1976-80, Perkins & Will, Chgo., 1980-82; prin. Hansen Lind Meyer Inc., Chgo., 1982-95; v.p. Phillips Swager Assocs., Naperville, Ill., 1995—2003, HDR Architecture, Inc., Chgo., 2003—. Lectr. Italian Nat. Ctr. Hosp. Bldg. and Technique. Editor: Balasi Archives, U. Iowa Librs. Spl. Collections; author: Sgt. Balasic WWI Album-Austro-Hungarian Army, 1996, Balasic Family Vaudeville Album, 1994; contbr.: (with Paul F. Stevens) Low Level Liberators in World War II, 1998; contbr. articles to profl. jours.; prin. works include Villa Schaefer, Mattoon, Ill., Nunamaker House, Mattoon, Mary Brown Stephenson Radiation Oncology Ctr., Zion, Ill. Active Hist. Preservation Commn., McHenry County, Ill. Mem. AIA (Nat. Coun. Archtl. Registration Bds. cert.), Am. Soc. Hosp. Engring., Acad. Architecture for Health, Health Facility Inst., PB4Y Assn., U. Ill. Alumni Assn. Avocations: genealogy, entomology, travel. Office: HDR Architecture Inc 8550 W Bryn Mawr Ave Ste 900 Chicago IL 60631-3223 Office Phone: 773-380-7900. Business E-Mail: mark.balasi@hdrinc.com.

BALBACH, STANLEY BYRON, lawyer; b. Normal, Ill., Dec. 26, 1919; s. Nyle Jacob and Gertrude (Cory) B.; m. Sarah Troutt Witherspoon, May 22, 1944; children: Stanley Byron Jr., Nancy Ann Fehr, Barbara Haines, Edith. BS, U. Ill., 1940, LLD, 1942. Bar: Ill. 1942, Fla. 1980, U.S. Ct. Appeals (7th cir.) 1961, U.S. Supreme Ct. 1950. Ptnr. Couchman & Balbach, Hoopeston, Ill., 1945-48, Webber & Balbach, Urbana, 1948—78, Balbach & Fehr, Urbana, 1978—. Nat. chmn. Jr. Bar Conf., 1955. Author: Reverse Mortgages, 1997, The Lawyers Guide to Retirement: Serving a New Clientele in a Second Career in Real Estate, 1998. Capt. USAAF, 1942-45 (pilot). Mem. ABA (ho. of dels. 1956, lawyer title guaranty fund com., past mem. coun. law office practice and real property, probate and trust law sects.), LWV, Ill. State Bar Assn. (elder law com., Laureate of the Acad. Ill. Lawyers 2002), Am. Judicature Soc., Masons, Rotary, Phi Delta Phi, Alpha Kappa Lambda. Home: 1009 S Douglas Ave PO Box 217 Urbana IL 61803 Office: Balbach & Fehr Box 301 102 E Broadway Ave Urbana IL 61801-2705 Office Phone: 217-367-1011.

BALCERZAK, STANLEY PAUL, retired hematologist, oncologist, director, medical educator; b. Pitts., Apr. 27, 1930; BS, U. Pitts., 1953; MD, U. Md., 1955. Diplomate Am. Bd. Internal Medicine, Am. Bd. Hematology, Am. Bd. Oncology. Instr. medicine U Chgo., 1959-60, U. Pitts., 1962-64, asst. prof., 1964-67; assoc. prof. medicine Ohio State U., Columbus, 1967-71, prof., 1971-99, prof. emeritus, 1999—, dir. div. hematology and oncology, 1969-94, dep. dir. Ohio State U. Comprehensive Cancer Ctr., 1984-97, assoc. chmn. dept. medicine, 1984-98, dir. Hemophilia Ctr., 1975-79, 1981-99. Mem. clin. rev. com. Am. Cancer Soc., N.Y.C., 1976-82 Contbr. chpts. to books, numerous articles to profl. jours. Served to capt. U.S. Army, 1960-62 Recipient numerous grants Fellow ACP; mem. Central Soc. for Clin. Research (chmn. subsplty. council in hematology 1980-81, councillor 1980-83), Am. Soc. for Clin. Oncology, Am. Assn. for Cancer Research, Am. Soc. Hematology, Phi Beta Kappa, Alpha Omega Alpha Home: 3113 N 3 Bs And K Rd Sunbury OH 43074-9582 Office: Ohio State U Divsn Hematology Oncology 320 W 10th Ave Columbus OH 43210-1240 Home Phone: 740-524-7191; Office Phone: 614-293-8729. Business E-Mail: balcerzak.1@osu.edu.

BALDWIN, DEWITT CLAIR, JR., pediatrician, educator; b. Bangor, Maine, July 19, 1922; s. DeWitt Clair and Edna Frances (Aikin) B.; m. Michele Albre, Dec. 27, 1957; children: Lisa Anne, Mireille Diane. BA, Swarthmore Coll., 1943; postgrad. Div. Sch., Yale U., 1943-45, MD, 1949; ScD (hon.), Northeastern Ohio U. Coll. Medicine, 2003. Diplomate Am. Bd. Med. Examiners, Am. Bd. Pediatrics, Am. Bd. Family Practice. Intern, then resident in pediatrics U. Minn. Hosps., Mpls., 1949-51; rsch. fellow Yale Child Study Ctr., New Haven, 1951-52; instr., asst. prof. pediatrics U. Washington Sch. Medicine, Seattle, 1952-57; resident in psychiatry Met. State Hosp., Waltham, Mass., 1957-58; chief resident in psychiatry Mass. Meml. Hosps., Boston, 1958-59; fellow in child psychiatry Boston City Hosp., 1959-61; asst. prof. pediatrics Harvard Med. Sch., Boston, 1961-67; prof., chmn. behavioral scis. and community health U. Conn. Health Ctr., Farmington, 1967-71; prof. chmn. behavioral scis. U. Nev. Sch. Medicine, Reno, 1971-73, dir. health scis. program, 1971-81, prof. psychiatry and behavioral scis., 1971-83, asst. dean rural health, 1977-83, prof. emeritus psychiatry and behavioral scis., 1983—; pres. Earlham Coll. and Earlham Sch. Religion, Richmond, Ind., 1983-84, Connor Prairie Pioneer Settlement Mus., Noblesville, Ind., 1983-84; dir. office edn. rsch. AMA, Chgo., 1985-88, dir. divsn. med. edn., rsch., info., 1988-91, scholar-in-residence, 1991—2002, sr. assoc. Inst. Ethics, 1991—2002, scholar-in-residence Accreditation Coun. for Grad. Med. Edn., 2002—; adj. prof. psychiatry and behavioral scis. Northwestern U. Med. Sch., Chgo., 1986—; adj. prof. med. edn. U. Ill. Coll. Medicine, Chgo., 1988-93; pres. Med. Edn. and Rsch. Assocs., Inc., Chgo., 1992—. Trustee Friends World Coll., Huntington, N.Y., 1980-83; bd. dirs. Nat. League ursing, N.Y.C., 1981-83, Gt. Lakes Colls. Assn., 1983-84, Am. Rural Health Assn., 1985-87; mem. Nat. Bd. Med. Examiners, 1979-88, Nat. Adv. Coun. Nursing Tng., 1978-82; mem. coun. acad. socs. AAMC, Washington, 1987-94. Author: (with others) Behavioral Sciences and Medical Education, 1983, other books; author, editor: (with others) Interdisciplinary Health Care Teams in Teaching and Practice, 1981, Interdisciplinary Health Team Training, 1978; contbr. over 200 articles to scholarly publs. Recipient Rsch. Career Devel.

award USPHS, 1961-67, Louis Gorin award in rural health, 1991, John P. McGovern award Health Scis., 1997; Commonwealth Fund fellow, 1951-52, Milbank Fund fellow, 1968, Rural Health fellow WHO, 1976. Mem. Assn. Behavioral Scis. and Med. Edn. (pres. 1978-79, 90-91), Nev. Bd. Oriental Medicine (pres. 1976-83). Democrat. Mem. Soc. Of Friends. Home: 1550 N Lake Shore Dr Chicago IL 60610 Office: Ste 2000 515 State St Chicago IL 60610 Business E-Mail: dbaldwin@acgme.org.

BALDWIN, EDWIN STEEDMAN, lawyer; b. St. Louis, May 5, 1932; s. Richard and Almira (Steedman) B.; m. Margaret Kirkham, July 1, 1958; children: Margaret B. Dozler, Edwin S. Jr., Harold K. AB, Princeton U., 1954; LLM, Harvard U., 1957. Bar: Mo. 1957, U.S. Dist. Ct. (ea. dist.) Mo. 1957. Assoc. Teasdale, Kramer & Vaughan, St. Louis, 1957-64; ptnr. Armstrong Teasdale, LLP, St. Louis, 1965-97, of counsel, 1998—. Fellow Am. Coll. Trust and Estate Counsel, St. Louis Country Club, Noonday Club. Republican. Episcopalian. Avocations: golf, hunting, sailing. Office: Armstrong Teasdale LLP 1 Metropolitan Sq Ste 2600 Saint Louis MO 63102-2740 Office Phone: 314-342-8055. Business E-Mail: tbaldwin@armstrongteasdale.com.

BALDWIN, PATRICIA ANN, lawyer; b. Detroit, May 3, 1955; d. Frank Thomas and Margaret Elyne Mathews; m. Jeffrey Kenton Baldwin, Aug. 23, 1975; children: Matthew, Katherine, Timothy, Philip. BA summa cum laude, Ball State U., 1976; JD, Ind. U., 1979. Bar: Ind. 1979, U.S. Dist. Ct. (so. dist.) Ind. 1979. Ptnr. Baldwin & Baldwin, Danville, Ind., 1979-94; dep. pros. atty. Hendricks County, Danville, 1980-90, pros. atty., 1995—; dep. pros. atty. Boone County, Ind., 1990-94. Sec.-treas., dir. T.F.W., Inc., Danville, 1983—90. Active Girl Scouts U.S., 1964—2000; vol. Boy Scouts Am., 1986—; mem. Hendricks County Rep. Women, 1976—, pres., 2001—03; mem. parish coun. Mary Queen of Peace Cath. Ch., 1976—80, 1981—83; bd. dirs. Cath. Social Svcs., Archdiocese of Indpls., sec. bd. dirs., 1986—92; bd. dirs. Cummins Mental Health Ctr., 1982—86, Youth as Resources Hendricks County, 1995—2001. Mem.: Hendricks County Bar Assn., Ind. Pros. Attys. Assn., Nat. Dist. Attys. Assn., Danville Conservation Club. Office: One Courthouse Sq #105 Danville IN 46122 Office Phone: 317-745-9283.

BALDWIN, SHAUN MCPARLAND, lawyer; b. Chgo., Oct. 19, 1954; BS, No. Ill. U., 1976; JD with distinction, John Marshall Law Sch., 1980. Bar: Ill. 1980, U.S. Dist. Ct. (no. dist.) Ill. 1980, U.S. Ct. Appeals (7th cir.) 1981. Assoc. McKenna, Storer, Rowe, White & Farrug, Chgo., 1980-86, Tressler, Soderstrom, Maloney & Priess, LLP, Chgo., 1986—87, ptnr., 1987—. Mem. ABA, Ill. Bar Assn., Def. Rsch. Inst. (chair ins. law com. 1996-98), Ill. Assn. Def. Trial Counsel (bd. dirs. 1996, amicus com. chair 1992—98), Ill. Appellate Lawyers Assn. (bd. dirs. 1987-89), John Marshall Alumni Assn. (bd. dirs. 1982-86), Internat. Assn. Def. Trial Counsel (chair membership com. 1996-97, chair casualty ins. com. 1995-96), Profl. Liability Underwriting Soc. Office: Tressler Soderstrom Maloney & Priess LLP 233 S Wacker Dr Ste 2200 Chicago IL 60606-6399 Office Phone: 312-627-4014. Business E-Mail: sbaldwin@tsmp.com.

BALDWIN, TAMMY, congresswoman, lawyer; b. Madison, Wis., Feb. 11, 1962; life ptnr. Lauren Azar. AB in Govt. and Math., Smith Coll., Northampton, Mass., 1984; JD, U. Wis., Madison, 1989. Mem. City Coun., Madison, Wis., 1986; supr. Dane County Bd. Suprs., 1986-1994; atty. pvt. practice, 1989-92; mem. Wis. State Assembly from 78th Dist., 1993-99, US Congress from 2nd Wis. dist., 1999—, mem. energy and commerce com. Mem.: Nat. Women's Polit. Caucus, Wis. State Bar Assn., Internat. Network Lesbian and Gay Officials, ACLU, NOW. Democrat. First woman to serve in the US House of Representatives. from Wis.; first openly gay person to be elected to Congress as a non-incumbent. Office: US Ho Reps 1022 Longworth Ho Office Bldg Washington DC 20515 Office Phone: 202-225-2906.

BALDWIN, WILLIAM D.G., lawyer; b. Rockford, Ill., Apr. 1, 1967; BA, U. Wis.-Madison, 1989; JD, Northern Ky. U., 1997. Bar: Ohio 1997. Student articles editor Northern Ky. Law Review, 1996—97; worked in instl. trust areas Northern Trust Co., Chgo., Fifth Third Bank, Cin.; ptnr. Vorys, Sater, Seymour and Pease LLP, Cin. Bd. mem., treasurer Hamilton County Alcohol and Drug Addiction. Named one of Ohio's Rising Stars, Super Lawyers, 2006. Mem.: ABA, Cin. Bar Assn. Office: Vorys Sater Seymour and Pease LLP Atrium Two Ste 2000 221 E Fourth St PO Box 0236 Cincinnati OH 45201-0236 Office Phone: 513-723-8595. Office Fax: 513-852-7812.

BALES, KENT ROSLYN, language educator; b. Anthony, Kans., June 19, 1936; s. Roslyn Francis and Irene E. (Brinkman) B.; m. Maria Gyorei, Aug. 25, 1958; children— Thomas Imre, Elizabeth Irene BA, Yale U., 1958; MA, San Jose State U., 1963; PhD, U. Calif., Berkeley, 1967. Instr. Menlo Sch., Menlo Park, Calif., 1958-63; acting instr. U. Calif., Berkeley, 1967; asst. prof. English U. Minn., Mpls., 1967-71, assoc. prof. English, 1971-82, prof. English, 1982—, chmn. dept. English, 1983—88, 2000—03. Vis. fellow Lit. Studies Inst., Budapest, Hungary, 1973-74, 80-81, 88-89. Contbr. chpts. to books and articles to profl. jours. Fulbright lectr., Budapest, 1980, Fulbright Rsch. fellow, Budapest, 1988-89. Mem. MLA. Home: 2700 Irving Ave S Minneapolis MN 55408-1049 Office: Univ Minn Dept English 207 Church St SE Minneapolis MN 55455-0134 E-mail: bales@umn.edu.

BALGEMAN, RICHARD VERNON, radiology administrator, alcoholism counselor; b. Berwyn, Ill., Dec. 25, 1929; s. Vernon Ernest and Regina Marie (Fitzgerald) B.; m. Wauneta Frances Laird, Nov. 15, 1952; children: Marcia, Kathleen, Barbara, Daniel. Student, Chgo. Art Inst., 1944; radiology technician, Cook County Grad. Sch. of Med., 1951; BA in Health Svc., Governor State U., 1976, MA in Sci., 1978. Cert. technologist; ordained Deacon Roman Cath. Ch., 1997. Radiology adminstr. Manteno (Ill.) Mental Health Ctr., 1951-84; adminstrv. asst. bus. office Shapiro Devel. Ctr., Kankakee, Ill., 1984-88; with St. James Hosp., Chicago Heights, Ill., 1990-99. Inventor DuPont Cronex Tech. Aid, 1965. Trustee Village of Manteno, 1969-72, chmn. planning commn., 1985-93; pres. Village View TV Channel 4; vol. Rialto Theater, Joliet, Ill. With USNG, 1948-56. Gov.'s award Ill. Dept. Mental Health, Manteno, 1971; named Citizen of Yr. Manteno Hist. Soc., 1996. Mem. Am. Legion, Rotary. Roman Catholic. Avocations: camping, making miniature furniture, writing, art. Home: 555 Park St Manteno IL 60950-1045

BALISTRERI, WILLIAM FRANCIS, pediatric gastroenterologist; b. Geneva, NY, June 24, 1944; s. Francis William and Mary (Yannotti) B.; m. Rebecca Ann McLeod, May 31, 1969; children: Anthony, Jennifer, William Phillip. Student, St. Bonaventure U., 1962; BA, SUNY, Buffalo, 1966; MD, U. Buffalo, 1970. Diplomate Am. Bd. Pediat., Sub. Bd. Pediat. Gastroenterology. Intern Children's Hosp. Med. Ctr., Cin., 1970-71, resident, 1971-72, postdoctoral fellow, 1972-74; rsch. fellow Mayo Clinic, Rochester, Minn., 1974; pediat. instr. Sch. Medicine U. Cin., 1972-74; staff pediatrician U.S. Naval Hosp., Phila., 1974-76; asst. prof. pediat. U. Pa. Sch. Medicine, 1976-78; from assoc. prof. pediat. to prof. medicine U. Cin. Sch. Medicine, 1978-91, prof. pediat., 1983—; prof. medicine U. Cin., 1991—. Bd. dirs. Am. Bd. Pediat., 1991-97, chmn. sub-bd. of pediatric gastroenterology, 1991-93; mem. ednl. coun. Nat. Hepatology Detection and Treatment Prevention Program, 1993-98. Author, editor: Pediatric Hepatology, 1990, Pediatric Gastroenterology and Nutrition, 1990, Jour. Pediatrics, 1995—, Liver Disease in Children 2000, 2005. Lt. comdr. USN, 1974-76. Recipient Disting. Alumnus award U. Buffalo Sch. Medicine, 1993, Disting. Alumnus award, 2005. Mem. Am. Assn. for Study of Liver Disease (pres. 1999-2000), N.Am. Soc. for Pediat. Gastroenterology and Nutrition (editor-in-chief Western Hemisphere Jour. 1991-95, pres. 1985-86), Am. Gastroenterol. Assn. Roman Catholic. Avocations: skiing, hiking. Office: Children's Hosp Med Ctr 3333 Burnet Ave Cincinnati OH 45229-3026 Office Phone: 513-636-4594. Business E-Mail: william.balistreri@cchmc.org.

BALK, ROBERT A., medical educator; BA, U. Mo., Kansas City, 1976, MD, 1978. Resident internal medicine U. Mo., Kansas City, 1978—81; fellow pulmonary and critical care medicine U. Ark., Little Rock, 1981—83, instr. medicine, 1981—83, asst. prof. medicine, 1983—85; staff physician Little Rock VA Med. Ctr., 1983—85; asst. prof. medicine Rush-Presbyn.-St. Luke's Med. Ctr., Chgo., 1985—88, assoc. prof., 1988—95, prof. medicine, 1995—, asst. dir. sect. pulmonary medicine, 1985—90, med. dir. respiratory care svcs., 1985-93, med. dir. noninvasive respiratory care unit, 1985—87, co-dir. med. intensive care unit, 1986—88, dir. med. intensive care unit, 1988-95, assoc. dir. sect. pulmonary & crit. care medicine, 1993—97, assoc. dir. sect. critical care medicine, 1995—2002, dir. pulmonary & critical care medicine fellowship tng. program, 1994—, dir. pulmonary and critical care medicine, 2002—; J. Bailey Carter prof. med. ctr. Rush Med. Coll., Chgo., 2002. Contbr. articles to profl. jours. Recipient Dedicated Svc. & Superior Individual Effort in Patient Care Alice Sachs Meml. award, 1991, Alfred Soffer Rsch. award, Am. Coll. Chest Physicians, 1995, Take Wing award, U. Mo.-Kansas City Sch. Medicine, 1998. Office: Rush Univ Med Ctr 1653 W Congress Pkwy Chicago IL 60612-3833 E-mail: rbalk@rush.edu.

BALKE, VICTOR HERMAN, bishop emeritus; b. Meppen, Ill., Sept. 29, 1931; s. Bernard H. and Elizabeth A. (Knese) B. BA in Philosophy, St. Mary of Lake Sem., Mundelein, Ill., 1954, STB in Theology, 1956, MA in Religion, 1057, STL in Theology, 1958; MA in English, St. Louis U., 1964, PhD, 1973. Ordained priest Diocese of Springfield, Ill., 1958, asst. pastor, 1958—62; chaplain St. Joseph Home Aged, Springfield, 1962—63; procurator, instr. Diocesan Sem., Springfield, 1963—70, rector, instr., 1970—76; ordained bishop, 1976; bishop Diocese of Crookston, Minn., 1976—2007, bishop emeritus Minn., 2007—. Mem.: Lions, KC. Roman Catholic. Office: Diocese of Crookston 1200 Memorial Dr Crookston MN 56716 Office Phone: 218-281-4533. Office Fax: 218-281-3328.*

BALL, DAN H., lawyer; BA cum laude, Bradley U., 1974; JD Order of the Coif, U. Mo., 1978. Bar: Mo. 1978, Ill. 1979. Ptnr., exec. com. Bryan Cave LLP, St. Louis. Fellow: Am. Coll. Trial Lawyers. Office: Bryan Cave LLP One Metropolitan Sq 211 N Broadway, Ste 3600 Saint Louis MO 63102 Office Phone: 314-259-2200. Office Fax: 314-552-8200. E-mail: dhball@bryancave.com.

BALL, DEBORAH LOEWENBERG, dean, education educator; BA, Mich. State U., 1976, MA, 1982, postgrad., 1981—83, PhD, 1988. Elementary classroom teacher, 1975—88; mem. faculty Mich. State U., East Lansing, 1988—96; Arthur F. Thurnau prof. U. Mich. Sch. Edn., Ann Arbor, 2000—03, William H. Payne collegiate prof. math., 2003—, interim dean, 2005—. Lead author Stds. for Tchg. sect. Profl. Stds. for Tchg. Math., Nat. Coun. Tchrs. Math., 1989—91; mem. adv. bd. Investigations in umber, Data, Space, 1991—96; mem. Commn. on Behavioral and Social Sci. Edn. Nat. Rsch. Coun., NAS, 1996—99, mem. math. learning study, 1999—2000; chair math. study panel RAND Project: Improving the Quality of Educational Research and Devel., 1999—2000; mem. commn. on undergrad. experience U. Mich., 2000—01; co-chair tchr. edn. study Internat. Commn. on Math. Instrn., 2002—; bd. trustees Math. Scis. Rsch. Inst. U. Calif., Berkeley, 2003—. Contbr. articles to profl. jours.; mem. editl. bd.: Am. Ednl. Rsch. Jour., 1999—, Jour. Ednl. Rsch., 1990—93, Elem. Sch. Jour., 1991—. Recipient Raymond B. Cattell Early Career award for programmatic rsch., Am. Ednl. Rsch. Assn., 1997, Award for outstanding Scholarship on Tchr. Edn., Assn. Colls. and Schs. of Edn. in State Univs. and Land Grant Colls. and Affiliated Pvt. Univs., 1990. Office: U Mich 1110 Sch Edn Bldg 610 E University Ann Arbor MI 48109-1259

BALL, JOHN ROBERT, healthcare executive; b. Opelika, Ala., July 16, 1944; s. John Cooper Jr. and Ellen Beverly (Williams) B.; m. Cornelia Anne Phillips, Aug. 13, 1966 (div. 1983); children: Kristen Anne, John Robert; m. Pamela Preston Reynolds, Jan. 9, 1988 (div. 2006). AB, Emory U., 1966; JD, Duke U., 1971, MD, 1972. Rsch. assoc. Duke U. Sch. Medicine, Durham, NC, 1971—72, resident in medicine, 1972-74; asst. to dir. office asst. sec. for health USPHS, Rockville, Md., 1974-76; chief med. audit br. bur. quality assurance HEW, Rockville, 1976-77; sr. policy analyst Office Sci. and Tech. Policy Exec. Office of Pres., Washington, 1978-81; assoc. exec. v.p. ACP, Phila., 1981-86, exec. v.p., 1986-94, also master; sr. scholar Assn. Acad. Health Ctrs., Washington, 1994-95; exec. v.p., acting pres., CEO Pa. Hosp., Phila., 1995-96, pres., CEO, 1996-99; sr. v.p. The Lewin Group, Falls Church, Va., 2000; exec. v.p. Am. Soc. Clin. Pathology, Chgo., 2002—. Robert Wood Johnson clin. scholar George Washington U., Washington, 1977-79; bd. mgrs. Pa. Hosp., 1988-97; bd. dirs. Milbank Meml. Fund, Holy Cross Hosp. Assoc. editor Jour. Am. Geriatrics Soc., 1984-86; mem. editorial bd. Internat. Jour. Tech. Assessment in Health Care, 1986-89, European Jour. Internal Medicine, 1988-94, Duke U. Law Jour., 1969-71; contbr. articles to profl. jours. Sr. surgeon USPHS, 1974-77. John Gordon Stipe scholar, Nat. Merit scholar, Emory U., 1962. Mem. Inst. Medicine of NAS, N.C. Bar Assn., Am. Clin. and Climatol. Assn., Soc. Med. Adminstrs. Democrat. Home Phone: 312-245-2814; Office Phone: 312-541-4885. Personal E-mail: johnrball@hotmail.com.

BALL, KENNETH LEON, manufacturing company executive, organizational development consultant; b. NYC, Aug. 11, 1932; s. Oscar and Elvira (Klein) B.; m. Patricia Ann (Whitley); children: David B. and Dana K. BA, Antioch Coll., Yellow Springs, Ohio, 1954; PhD, Washington Univ., St. Louis, 1958. Lic. psychologist, Mo. Gen. mgr. Pacific Coast div. Orchard Corp. Am., St. Louis, 1960-62, indsl. rels. dir., 1963-64, v.p. indsl. rels., 1965-66, v.p., dir., 1967-72, exec. v.p., dir., 1972-75, pres., dir., 1976-88; pres. Orchard Decorative Products, div. Borden, Inc., St. Louis, 1988-92, Ken Ball Mgmt. Resources, St. Louis, 1993—. Adj. prof. Washington Univ., 1978—79. Contbg. author: Humanizing Organizational Behavior, 1976; Making Organizatios Humane and Productive, 1981; contbg. articles to publ. Trust Antioch U., 1980-85, 89-2000; dir. Met. Employment and Rehab. Svc., St. Louis, 1975-2001, chair, 1985-86; dir. St. Louis chpt. Young Audiences, 1990; Narcotic Svc. Coun., 1976; MERS/Goodwill, 2001—, Assn. for Corp. Growth, 2005—. Human Rels. Rsch. Found. fellow, 1955-58. Mem.: APA, Soc. Psychologists in Mgmt. (dir. 1989—, pres. 1992—93). Home: 14312 Quiet Meadow Ct E Chesterfield MO 63017 Office: Ken Ball Mgmt Resources 165 N Meramec Ave Ste 400 Clayton MO 63105-3772 Mailing: PO Box 6607 Chesterfield MO 63005 Home Phone: 314-514-2455; Office Phone: 314-725-0320. Personal E-mail: kenlball@aol.com.

BALL, PATRICIA ANN, physician; b. Lockport, NY, Mar. 30, 1941; d. John Joseph and Katherine Elizabeth Ball; m. Robert E. Lee, May 18, 1973 (div. 2004); children: Heather Lee, Samantha Lee. BS, U. Mich., 1963; MD, Wayne State U., 1969. Diplomate Am. Bd. Internal Medicine, Am. Bd. Hematology, Am. bd. Med. Oncology. Intern, resident Detroit Gen. Hosp., 1969-71; resident Jackson Meml. Hosp., Miami, Fla., 1971-72; fellow Henry Ford Hosp., Detroit, 1972-74; staff physician VA Hosp., Allen Park, Mich., 1974-77; pvt. practice in hematology and oncology Bloomfield Hills, Mich., 1977—. Faculty dept. medicine Wayne State U. Sch. Medicine, Detroit, 1974—. Mem.: AMA, ACP, Mich. Soc. Hematology and Oncology, Oakland County Med. Soc., Mich. Med. Soc., Detroit Inst. Arts, Founders Soc., Alpha Omega Alpha. Avocations: photography, skiing. Office: 44038 Woodward Ave Ste 101 Bloomfield Hills MI 48302-5036 Office Phone: 248-360-8244. E-mail: pball@dmc.org.

BALLAL, DILIP RAMCHANDRA, mechanical engineering educator; b. Nagpur, India, Jan. 16, 1946; came to U.S., 1979; s. Ramchandra Govind Ballal and Padma (Balwant) Zadkar; m. Shubhangi Sadashiv Ayachit, Dec. 17, 1975; children: Rahul, Deepti. BSME, Coll. Engring., Bhopal, India, 1967; PhD, Cranfield Inst. Tech., Eng., 1972, DSc in Engring. (hon.), 1983. Registered profl. engr., Ohio. Lectr. mech. engring. Cranfield Inst. Tech., 1972-79; sr. staff engr. GM Rsch. Labs., Warren, Mich., 1979-83; prof. mech. engring. U. Dayton (Ohio), 1983—. Cons. GMR Labs. and GE Aircraft, Warren, Cin., 1987—. Author: (with others) Combustion Measurements and Modern Development in Combustion, 1990, 91; contbr. about 130 articles on combustion, turbulence, heat transfer and pollution to profl. jours. Project leader Engrs. Club Dayton, 1986, 88, 90; judge, organizer "Odyssey of Mind" Sch. Contest, Dayton, 1985, 87, 88; vice chmn. edn. com. Miami Valley Sch., Dayton, 1988, 90. Named Outstanding Engr., Engrs. Club, Dayton, 1988. Fellow ASME (chmn. combustion and fuels com. 1995—, Best Rsch. award 1986, 92), AIAA (Energy Systems award 1993). Achievements include patents on Ignitor Plug for Jet Engine Combustor. Home: 950 Olde Sterling Way Dayton OH 45459-3100 Office: U Dayton KL 465 300 College Park Ave Dayton OH 45469-0001 Office Phone: 937-229-4001. E-mail: dilip.ballal@gmail.com.

BALLARD, BARBARA W., state legislator; m. Albert L. Ballard. B in Music Edn., Webster Coll., 1967; MS, Kans. State U., 1976, PhD, 1980. Rep. dist. 44 State of Kansas, 1993—; adminstr., dir. U. Kans., 1980—, asst. vice-chancellor, 1998—. Democrat. Home: 1532 Alvamar Dr Lawrence KS 66047-1605

BALLARD, CHARLIE, state legislator; Mem. Mo. Ho. of Reps., Jefferson City, 1994—. Republican.

BALLARD, GREGORY A., mayor, retired military officer; b. Indpls., Nov. 20, 1954; s. Duard and Mary Ballard; m. Winnie Ballard, 1983; children: Erica, Greg Jr. BS in Econs., Indiana U., 1978; MA in Milt. Sci., Marine Corps U., Quantico, Va., 1997. Advanced through ranks to lt. col. USMC, 1996, ret., 2001; N.Am. ops. mgr. Bayer Pharms., Indpls., 2001—04; owner Golden Lion Transport, 2003—05; leadership and bus. mgmt. cons. pvt. practice, 2003—07; instr. in econs., mktg., mgmt. Ind. Bus. Coll., 2006—07; mayor City of Indpls., 2008—. Founder Indpls. Writers Group. Author: The Ballard Rules: Small Unit Leadership, 2005; contbg. editor: Ind. Minority Bus. Mag., Ind. Parenting Mag. Tutor, adv. bd. Lilly Boys and Girls Club. Decorated Legion of Merit, Meritorious Svc. medal, Kuwait Liberation medal, Marine Corps Expeditionary medal, Humanitarian Svc. medal, Outstanding Vol. Svc. medal. Republican. Roman Catholic. Achievements include defeating the two-term incumbent Democratic mayor by a margin of 4% with a small campaign budget. Avocation: golf. Office: City-County Bldg 200 E Wash St Indianapolis IN 46204 Office Phone: 317-327-3601. Office Fax: 317-327-3980.*

BALLBACH, PHILIP THORNTON, political consultant, investor; b. Lansing, Mich., May 22, 1939; s. Nathan Anthony and Thelma Frances (Bowes) B. BA, Mich. State U., 1960; student, U. Mich., 1960-61; MA, Mich. State U., 1967. Social worker State of Mich., Corunna, 1961-64; legis. aide State Rep. H. James Starr, Lansing, Mich., 1964-67; exec. asst. State Atty. Gen.'s Dept., Lansing, Mich., 1967-81; county commr. Ingham County, Mason, Mich., 1980-93. Pub., Lansing This Weekend, 1963-64, The Gooseneck Tidings, 1977. Coord. Greater Lansing Assn. for Cmty. Edn., 1961-66; mem. Lansing Bd. Election Canvassers, 1965-69; dir. Cmty. Mental Health Bd., Lansing, 1977-99; treas. Zolton Ferency for Gov. Com., 1977-83; county liaison Eastside Neighborhood Orgn., Lansing, 1980-93; commr. Tri-County Regional Planning Com., Lansing, 1981-84; chairperson Ingham County Emergency Planning Com., Mason, Mich., 1988-93; campaign dir. Citizens for Pub. Recycling, Lansing, 1990; treas. People Achieving Legis. Power, 1992-95; campaign coord. Citizens for a Better Lansing, 1993-2003; bd. dirs. Peace Edn. Ctr., 1999—. Recipient Achievement award Nat. Assn. Counties, 1986, Dem. Party Ferency Activist Achievement award, 1998. Mem.: Cost Militarium Edn. Team (co-chair 2007—08). Democrat. Avocations: writing, history studies, skiing, softball. Home: 2723 E Lake Lansing Rd East Lansing MI 48823-9703

BALLINTINE, DANIEL JOHN, lawyer; b. 1971; BA in Econs. cum laude, Carleton Coll. (completed at Cambridge U., Eng.), 1993; JD cum laude, U. Minn., 1995. Bar: Minn. 1995, US Dist. Ct. (dist. Minn.) 1997. Shareholder, mem. Employment Law Dept. Larkin, Hoffman, Daly & Lindgren, Ltd., Mpls. Mem. Minn. Bd. Architecture and Engring., 2001—. Named a Rising Star, Minn. Super Lawyers mag., 2006. Mem.: ABA, Minn. State Bar Assn., Hennepin County Bar Assn. Office: Larkin Hoffman Daly & Lindgren Ltd 1500 Wells Fargo Plz 7900 Xerxes Ave S Minneapolis MN 55431 Office Phone: 952-896-3288. E-mail: dballintine@larkinhoffman.com.

BALLMAN, PATRICIA KLING, lawyer; b. Cin., May 1, 1946; d. John Joseph and Margaret Elizabeth (Stacy) Kling; children: Andrew J., Cara E. BS with honors, St. Louis U., 1967; JD with honors, Marquette U., 1977. Bar: Wis. 1977, U.S. Dist. Ct. (ea. and we. dist Wis.) 1980, U.S. Ct. Appeals (7th Cir.) 1983, U.S. Ct. Appeals (8th Cir.) 1986, U.S. Supreme Ct. 1986. Ptnr. Quarles & Brady, Milw., 1977—. Officer lawyer regulation Dist. II Com. Chair pers. com. United Way, 2000—02; past chair Shorewood Bd. of Rev.; mem. Gov.'s Task Force on Ethics Reform in Govt., 2002; past pres. The Benedict Ctr.; bd. dirs. Wis. Law Found. Master: Fairchild Inns of Ct.; mem.: ABA, Am. Acad. Matrimonial Lawyers (pres. Wis. chpt. 2002—04), Wis. Bar Assn. (pres. 2002—03), Milw. Bar Assn. (pres. 1995—96). Office: Quarles & Brady 411 E Wisconsin Ave #2040 Milwaukee WI 53202-4461 Office Phone: 414-277-5000. Business E-Mail: pkb@quarles.com.

BALLOU, JOHN DENNIS, state legislator; Grad., Shawnee Mission North H.S., Kans., 1975. Plasterer, 1979-83; owner Ballou Plastering Inc., 1984-95; mem. Kans. State Ho. of Reps. Dist. 43, 1995—; owner, ptnr. Kleier Plastering, Inc., 1997—.

BALOW, LARRY C., state representative; b. Apr. 29, 1943; Attended, tech. coll., 1962—63. Former tool-die maker, firefighter, small bus. owner; state assembly mem. Wis. State Assembly, Madison, 1998—, mem. transp. projects commn., mem. colls. and univs., corrections and the cts., fin. instns., and ins. coms. Mem. Eau Claire (Wis.) Transit Commn.; mem. Eau Claire City Coun., 1995—99. Mem.: Eau Claire and Chippewa Falls C. of C. Democrat.

BALSAM, THEODORE, physician; b. NYC, Apr. 11, 1931; s. Abraham and Esther (Golden) B.; m. Barbara Korn, Dec. 25, 1952; children: Hugh, Adrienne, Lisbeth. BA, NYU, 1952; MD, Chgo. Med. Sch., 1957; MPH, Johns Hopkins U., 1959. Diplomate Am. Bd. Internal Medicine. Intern Charity Hosp., New Orleans, 1957-58; fellow Johns Hopkins U., Balt., 1958-59; resident in medicine Bklyn. Hosp., 1959-61, fellow in gastroenterology, 1961-62; physician USPHS, SI, 1964-97; pvt. practice Founders Med. Group, Chgo., 1997—. Pres. med. staff Louis A. Weiss Meml. Hosp., Chgo., 1976-78, 93-95, dir. patient hosp. orgn., 1996—. Mem. Sch. Bd., Lincolnwood, Ill., 1970-72. Fellow Am. Coll. Gastroenterology; mem. AMA, Ill. State Med. Soc., Chgo. Med. Soc. Avocation: travel. Office: Weiss Meml Hosp 4640 N Marine Dr Chicago IL 60640-5719 Office Phone: 773-564-5355.

BALZEKAS, STANLEY, JR., museum director; b. Chgo., Oct. 8, 1924; s. Stanley and Emily B.; widowed; children— Stanley, III, Robert, Carole Rene. BS, DePaul U., Chgo., 1950, MA, 1951. Pres. Balzekas Motor Sales, Chgo., 1952—, Balzekas Mus. Lithuanian Culture, Chgo., 1966—. Hon. consul for Republic of Lithuania, Palm Beach, Fla. Trustee Lincoln Acad., Cath. Charities, Am.-Lithuanian Coun.; chmn. Sister Cities/Chgo.-Vilnius Friendship Com., Trade & Cultural Ctr.; mem. adv. bd. Chgo. Cultural Affairs. Served with U.S. Army, 1942-45, ETO. Decorated Bronze Star; decorated 3d degree order Grand Duke Gediminas, Pres. Lithuania; recipient Wigilia medal Polish Geneal. Soc. Am., medal DAR, Disting. Alumni award DePaul U., 1991, Zygimantas Augustas medal Vilnius, 2001, Order Lithuanian Numismatics medal, 2003. Mem. Am. Assn. Mus., Ethnic Cultural Preservation Coun. (pres. 1977—), Press Club (Chgo.), Literary Club (Chgo.), City Club (Chgo., ethnic chmn.), Exec. Club (Chgo.), Am. Legion Office: 4030 S Archer Ave Chicago IL 60632-1140 Office Phone: 773-582-6500. E-mail: president@lithuanianmuseum.org.

BAMBERGER, DAVID, opera company executive; b. Albany, NY, Oct. 14, 1940; s. Bernard J. and Ethel K. Bamberger; m. Carola Beral, June 8, 1965; 1 son, Steven B. Student, U. Paris, 1961; BA, Swarthmore Coll., 1962; postgrad., Yale U., 1963; DHL (hon.), Swarthmore Coll., 1994. Mem. directing staff N.Y.C. Opera, 1966-70; guest dir. Nat. Opera Chile, 1970, Cin. Opera, 1968, Augusta Opera (Ga.), 1970, Pitts. Opera, 1971, 76, 81, Columbus Opera (Ohio); gen. dir. Cleve. Opera, 1976—. Artistic dir. Toledo Opera Assn., 1983-85. Bd. dirs. Opera Am., Nat. Alliance Musical Theatre Prodrs. Author: Jewish history textbooks; contbr. articles to Opera News. Office: Cleveland Opera 1422 Euclid Ave Ste 1052 Cleveland OH 44115-2063

BAMBERGER, RICHARD H., lawyer; b. Cleve., Sept. 18, 1945; BA, Bowdoin Coll., 1967; JD, Case Western Res. U., 1972. Bar: Ohio 1972. Law clk. to Hon. William K. Thomas U.S. Dist. Ct. (no. dist.), Ohio, 1972-74; ptnr. Baker & Hostetler, Cleve. Adj. prof. law Case Western Res. U., 1996—. Mem. ABA (mem. employee benefits com.), Ohio State, Cleve. Bar Assn. Office: Baker & Hostetler LLP 3200 Nat City Ctr 1900 E 9th St Ste 3200 Cleveland OH 44114-3475

BAN, STEPHEN DENNIS, gas industry executive; b. Hammond, Ind., Dec. 16, 1940; s. Stephen and Mary Veronica (Holecsko) Ban; m. Margie Cahill, Aug. 17, 1963; children: Stephen, Mary Beth, Brian. BSME, Rose Hulman Inst. Tech., 1962; MS in Engring. Sci., Case Inst. Tech., 1964, PhD in Engring., 1967. Chief divsn. fluid and chem. processes Battelle Columbus (Ohio) Labs., 1970-72, chief divsn. emission sys., 1972-76, corp. coord. engring. scis. program, 1972-76; v.p. R & D Bituminous Materials, Inc., Terre Haute, Ind., 1976-81, Gas Rsch. Inst., Chgo., 1981—2000, sr. v.p. R & D ops., 1983-86, exec. v.p., COO, 1986-87, pres., CEO, 1987—2000; dir. Office Tech. Transfer Argonne Nat. Lab., 2002—. Mem. indsl. adv. bd. U. Ill., Chgo., 1983—93; mem. Coun. Energy Engring. Rsch., Washington, 1983—87; mem. energy rsch. adv. bd. U.S. Dept. Energy, Washington, 1987—90, mem. adv. com. renewable energy and energy efficiency joint ventures, 1992—95; mem. Natural Gas Coun., 1993—97; bd. dirs. Energen Corp., Birmingham, Ala., 1991—, UGI Corp., Phila., 1992—, Amerigas Corp., Phila., 2006—. Fellow, NDEA, 1962—65, NSF, 1965—67. Mem.: U.S. Energy Assn., Sigma Xi, Tau Beta Pi. Office: 9700 S Cass Ave Argonne IL 60439-4832 Office Phone: 630-252-8111. Business E-Mail: sban@anl.gov.

BANAS, C(HRISTINE) LESLIE, lawyer; b. Swindon, Wiltshire, Eng., Oct. 29, 1951; arrived in U.S., 1957; d. Stanley M. and Helena Ann (Boryn) Banas; m. Dale J. Buras, May 1, 1976; children: Eric Dale Buras, Andrea Leigh Buras. BA magna cum laude, U. Detroit, 1973; JD cum laude, Wayne State U., Detroit, 1975. Bar: Mich. 1976, US Supreme Ct. 1980. Atty. Hyman & Rice, Southfield, Mich., 1976-77, Hyman, Gurwin, Nachman, Friedman & Winkelman, Southfield, 1977-82, ptnr., 1982-87, Honigman Miller Schwartz and Cohn LLP, Bloomfield Hills, Mich., 1987—. Contbr. articles to profl. jours. Bd. trustees Parade Co., 2007—, Detroit Pub. TV, 2007—. Recipient Inner Cir. award, Best Lawyers in Am., Superlawyers. Mem.: ABA, Urban Land Inst., Fed. Bar Assn., State Bar Mich. (bd. dirs. real property law sect. coun., coun. chair elect, chair elect real property law sect.), The Parade Co. (bd. trustees), Detroit Athletic Club, Inforum Ctr. Leadership (past pres.). Roman Catholic. Avocations: gardening, photography, skiing. Office: Honigman Miller Schwartz and Cohn LLP Ste 100 38500 Woodward Ave Bloomfield Hills MI 48304-5048 Office Phone: 248-566-8406. Business E-Mail: lbanas@honigman.com.

BANASZYNSKI, CAROL JEAN, secondary school educator; b. Hawkins, Wis., Jan. 3, 1951; BS in Biology, U. Wis., LaCrosse, 1973; MS in Profl. Devel., U. Wis., Whitewater, 1987; MS in Ednl. Leadership, Cardinal Stritch U., 2002. Tchr. Deerfield Cmty. Schs., 1973—. Coach Youth T-ball/softball; co-chairperson Adopt-A-Highway; group leader 4-H Club; counselor Boy Scout Environtl. Merit Badge program Recipient Wis. H.S. Tchr. of Yr., 1997-98, Wis. Tchr. of Yr. 1998, Award of Excellence Wis. Assn. of Sch. Bds., 1997, Wis. Dept. of Instrn., 1997, Wis. Edn. Assn. Coun., 1997, Wis. Legis. Citation for Tchg. Excellence, 1997-98; named Educator of Yr. Nat. H.S. Assn., 1998, Outstanding Tchr. Radioshack/Tandy, 1999; Kohl fellowship, 1997, Monsanto fellowship, 2000. Mem. ASCD, Nat. Biology Tchrs. Assn., Nat. Sci. Tchrs. Assn., Wis. Secondary Sci. Tchrs. (state conf. presenter), BioNet, DEA (scholarship com. chairperson), Wis. Edn. Assn. Coun.

BANCHET, JEAN, chef; Head chef, owner Le Francais, Wheeling, Ill. Office: Le Francais 269 S Milwaukee Ave Wheeling IL 60090-5097

BANDES, SUSAN JANE, museum director, educator; b. NYC, Oct. 18, 1951; d. Ralph and Bessie (Gordon) Bandes. BA, NYU, 1971; MA, Bryn Mawr Coll., 1973, PhD, 1978; postgrad., Mus. Mgmt. Inst., Berkeley, Calif., 1990. Asst. prof. Sweet Briar Coll., Va., 1978-83; project dir. Am. Assn. Mus., Washington, 1983-84; program officer J. Paul Getty Trust Grant Program, LA, 1984-86; prof., dir. Kresge Art Mus. Mich. State U., East Lansing, 1986—. Author, editor: Caring for Collections, 1984, Affordable Dreams: The Goetsch-Winckler House and Frank Lloyd Wright, 1991; author: Abraham Rattner, The Tampa Museum of Art Collection, 1997, Pursuits and Pleasures: Baroque Paintings from the Detroit Institute of Arts, 2003; editor: The Prints of John S. de Martelly, 1903-1979; author, curator: Pursuits and Pleasures: Baroque Painting from the Detroit Institute of Arts, 2003. Recipient award Am. Philos. Soc., 1981, Publ. award AIA, 1990; Samuel H. Kress fellow, 1972-73, 75-76, Whiting fellow, 1976-77; Fulbright-Hayes grant, 1974-75. Mem. Nat. Inst. for Conservation (treas. 1986-90), Mich. Alliance for Conservation (treas. 1994-95, sec. 1996-97, treas. 1997-98, pres. 1998-2000), Mich. Mus. Assn. (bd. dirs. 1987-92), Mich. Coun. for Humanities (coun. 1988-92), Midwest Art History Soc. (bd. dirs. 1997-2000). Avocation: collecting oriental rugs. Office: Mich State U Kresge Art Mus East Lansing MI 48824 Home Phone: 517-347-3437; Office Phone: 517-353-9834. Business E-Mail: bandes@msu.edu.

BANDYOPADHYAY, BISWANATH PRASAD, manufacturing engineer, educator, consultant; b. Bankura, West Bengal, India, Aug. 24, 1945; came to U.S, 1985; s. Amarnath and Bibha (Mukherjee) B.; m. Irina T. Tunik, Aug. 21, 1989; children: Anjeli, Sharmila. BSc in Physics (hons.), Burdwan U., India, 1964; MSME (hons.), People's Friendship U., Moscow, 1969, PhD in Mech. Engring., 1979; postgrad., U. Wis., St. Augustine, 1984. Asst. engr. (design) Mining Machinery Corp., Durgapur, India, 1969-70; asst. engr. Ctrl. Workshop, Korba, India, 1970-72; rsch. scientist Mech. Engring. Rsch. and Devel. Orgn., Poona, India, 1972-75; asst. prof. Indian Inst. Tech., Bombay, 1980-82; lectr. dept mech. engring. U. West Indies, Trinidad, 1982-85; asst. prof. dept. mech. engring. U. N.D., Grand Forks, 1985-89, assoc. prof., 1989—. Vis. lectr. Govt. Polytechnic, Poona, India, 1971-75; vis. lectr. U. Nederland Antilles, Curacao, 1983-84; mem. faculty Concordia U., Ottawa, Can., 1982; postdoctoral fellow Mich. Tech. U., 1984; postdoctoral rsch. fellow Auburn U., Ala., 1985; rsch. cons. Argonne at. Lab., Chgo., 1989, Oak Ridge (Tenn.) Nat. Lab., 1991—; cons. Lucas Western, N.D., 1990; attended numerous confs. and workshops. Contbr. articles to profl. jours. including: Jour. of Materials, Processing Tech., Jour. Mfg. Systems, others. Fellow Japan Ministry Edn., Toyohash, Japan, 1992, Riken Rsch. Ctr., Tokyo, 1994. Mem. ASME, Soc. Mfg. Engrs. (sr.). Achievements include: collaboration with Japanese scientist in area of mirror surface grinding of structural ceramics. Office: U ND Dept Engring Univ Sta Grand Forks ND 58202-8359

BANERJEE, PRASHANT, industrial engineer, computer scientist, educator; b. Calcutta, West Bengal, India, Apr. 15, 1962; came to U.S., 1986; s. Prabhat K. and Bani Banerjee; m. Madhumita Banerjee, Dec. 11, 1987; children: Jay, Ann. BSME, Indian Inst. Tech., Kanpur, India, 1984; MS in Indsl. Engring., Purdue U., 1987, PhD, 1990. Indsl. engr. Tata Steel Co., Jamshedpur, India, 1984-85; asst. prof. U. Ill., Chgo., 1990-96, assoc. prof., 1996—. Cons. Caterpillar Inc., Peoria, Ill., 1992, Motorola Inc., 1994—97, Monsanto, Inc., 1996—; tech. adv. bd. mem. Motorola Labs, 2002; chief tech. officer Indsl. Virtual Reality, Inc., 2000—. Author: Automation and Control of Manufacturing Systems, 1991, Object-oriented Technology in Manufacturing, 1992, Virtual Manufacturing, 2001; contbr. articles to profl. jours. Grantee NSF rsch., 1992, 1995, 2000, Nat. Inst. Standards and Tech. rsch., 1995. Fellow: ASME; mem.: Inst. Indsl. Engrs. Avocations: sports, current events, religious discussions. Home: 708 Kirstin Ct Westmont IL 60559 Office: Univ Ill Engring Dept Chicago IL 60607-7022

BANIAK, SHEILA MARY, accountant, educator; b. Chgo., Feb. 26, 1953; d. DeLoy N. and Ann (Pasko) Slade; m. Mark A. Baniak, Oct. 7, 1972 (div. Feb. 1994); 1 child, Heather Ann. AA in Acctg., Oakton C.C., 1986; student, Roosevelt U., 1986—; MBA, North Park Coll., Chgo., 1995; Cert. in Human Resources, North Park U., Chgo., 2001; student, Argosy U., 2003—. Cert. enrolled agt. IRS; accredited tax adviser Accreditation Coun. Accountancy and Taxation. Owner, mgr. Baniak and Assocs., Chgo., 1984—; acct. Otto & Snyder, Park Ridge, 1984-87; spl. projects coord., supplemental instr. Oakton CC, Des Plaines, Ill., 1986—, acctg. computer instr., 1987—; acctg. and credit mgr. Fragomen, Delrey, Bernsen & Loewy P.C., 1996—2004, fin. and human resources mgr., 1999—2004; bus. and tax cons. Benjamin & Birkenstein, P.C., 2005—; contr. The Wexler Firm LLP, 2005—06; bus. mgr. Soliant Consulting, 2007—. Adm. mem. acctg. Oakton C.C., Des Plaines, 1986—, cons., mem. Edn. Found., 1986—; instr. Ray Coll. Design, 1987—, dir. evening sch., 1994, fin. aid officer, Chgo. and Woodfield, 1994; mem. rsch. bd. advisors Am. Biog. Inst., Inc., 1988; tchr. fin. mgmt., retail math., bus. math., bus. computers, strategic retail mgmt. and econs.; part-time coll. instr. commerce dept. Northwestern Bus. Coll., 1995—; asst. to interim fin. dir. Art Inst. Ill., 1995-96; adj. faculty City Colls. Chgo., 2004—, Internat. Acad. Design and Tech., 2004—; mem. adj. faculty bus. and mktg. Internat. Acad. Design and Tech.; adj. faculty in bus. and mktg. Internat. Acad. Design, Schaumburg, Ill., 2005 Author: A Small Business Collection Cycle Primer for Accountants, 1985, The Mathematics of Business, 1989, Teaching Intermediate Accounting and Computerized Accounting. Ill. CPA Soc. scholar, 1984, Roosevelt U. scholar, 1986, Nat. Assn. Accts. scholar, 1985. Mem. Nat. Assn. Accts. (dir. cmty. responsibility suburban Chgo. chpt. 1986—, spkr. 1988, dir. profl. devel. seminars 1988, dir. comm. 1989—), Accreditation Coun. Accountancy and Taxation (enrolled agt., accredited cert. tax specialist), Nat. Assn. Tax Practitioners, Nat. Assn. Enrolled Agts., Ill. Soc. Enrolled Agts. (pres.; pres. N.W. Chgo. chpt. 1992, chmn. edn. 1990—). Home: 5718 W Cullom Ave Chicago IL 60634-1718 Personal E-mail: smb2411@sbcglobal.net.

BANKER, GILBERT STEPHEN, industrial and physical pharmacy educator, academic administrator; b. Tuxedo Park, NY, Sept. 12, 1931; s. Gilbert Miller and Mary Edna (Gladstone) B.; m. Gwenivere May Hughes, Mar. 31, 1956; children: Stephen, Susan, David, William. BS in Pharmacy, Union Coll., Albany, NY, 1953; MS, Purdue U., 1955, PhD, 1957; DSc (hon.), Purdue Univ., 2003. Research found. fellow Purdue U., West Lafayette, Ind., 1955-57, asst. prof. pharmacy, 1957-61, assoc. prof., 1961-64, prof., 1964-67, head indsl. and phys. pharmacy dept., from 1967; dean, prof. pharmacy U. Minn., Mpls., 1985-92; dean emeritus, disting. prof. drug delivery U. Iowa, Iowa City, 1992. In coop. tng. program Upjohn Co., Kalamazoo, 1958. Editor: Modern Pharmaceutics, 1970, 90, 95, 2000, Pharmaceuticals and Pharmacy Practice, 1980, Pharmaceutical Dosage Forms: Dispense Systems, 1988, 2d edit., 1994; contbr. articles to profl. jours.; patentee in field. Recipient Outstanding Alumnus of Yr. award Albany Coll. Pharmacy-Union U., 1977, Disting. Alumni award Sch. Pharmacy and Pharmacal Scis. Purdue U., 1989. Fellow Acad. Pharm. Scis. (v.p. 1971-72), Am. Pharm. Assn. (Indsl. Pharmacy award 1971, ho. dels. 1977-80), Am. Assn. Advancement of Scis., Am. Assn. Pharm. Scis. (chair 1993-94); mem. Sigma Xi (pres. Purdue chpt. 1971-72), Rho Chi. Office: Univ of Iowa Coll of Pharmacy Iowa City IA 52242 Home Phone: 319-354-9012; Office Phone: 239-593-4260. E-mail: gilbert-banker@uiowa.edu, gilgwen@mchis.com.

BANKOFF, SEYMOUR GEORGE, chemical engineer, educator; b. NYC, Oct. 7, 1921; s. Jacob and Sarah (Rashkin) B.; m. Elaine K. Forgash; children: Joseph, Elizabeth, Laura, Jay. BS, Columbia U., 1940, MS, 1941; PhD in Chem. Engring., Purdue U., 1952. Research engr. Sinclair Refining Co., East Chicago, Ind., 1941-42; process engr. du Pont Manhattan project U. Chgo., Richland, Wash., Arlington, N.J., 1942-48; asst. prof. dept. chem. engring. Rose Poly. Inst., Terre Haute, Ind., 1948-52, assoc. prof., 1952-54, prof., chmn. dept. chem. engring., 1954-58; NSF sci. faculty fellow Calif. Inst. Tech., Pasadena, 1958-59; prof. chem. engring. Northwestern U., Evanston, Ill., 1959—, Walter P. Murphy prof. chem., mech. and nuclear engring., 1971-92; prof. emeritus, 1992—; chmn. energy engring. council Northwestern U., 1975-80, chmn. Ctr. for Multiphase Flow and Transport, 1988—. Vis. scientist Centre d'Etudes Nucléaires, Commissariat d'Energie Atomique, Grenoble, France, 1980; vis. prof. Imperial Coll. Sci. and Tech., London, 1985; cons. to U.S. Nuclear Regulatory Commn., 1974-87, Los Alamos Sci. Lab., 1974-89, Electric Power Research Inst., 1984-86, Westinghouse, 1984—, Savannah River Lab., duPont, 1987—, Korea Atomic Energy Research Inst., 1988; mem. adv. council Ams. for Energy Independence, Washington, 1978—; chmn. vis. com. Brookhaven Nat. Lab., 1984, engring. tech. div. Oak Ridge at. Lab., 1986; pres. SGB Assocs. Inc., 1986—. Mem. editl. adv. bd.: Internat. Jour. Multiphase Flow, 1975—, Nuc. Engring. and Design, 1984—; editor 6 vols. on heat transfer; contbr. 200 articles on rsch. in heat transfer and control theory to profl. jours. Recipient Max Jakob Meml. award AICE and ASME, 1987, Donald Q. Kern award AIChE, 1996, Outstanding Chem. Engr. award Purdue U., 1994; named Disting. Engring. Alumnus, 1971; Guggenheim fellow, 1966, Fulbright fellow, 1967, Internat. Ctr. Health and Mass Transfer, Yugoslavia. Fellow AICE (chmn. edn. com. 1968-71, chmn. heat transfer and energy conversion divsn. 1987, Robert E. Wilson Nuc. Chem. Engring. award 1994, Heat Transfer and Energy Conversion Divsn. award 1995), ASME; mem. Am. Nuclear Soc. (co-chmn. U.S. Sci. com., 9th Internat. Heat Transfer Conf., U.S. del. Internat. Heat Transfer Assembly), Nat. Acad. Engring. Achievements include co-invention of resistivity probe for void fraction measurement in gas-liquid flows; contbn. to theory of boiling heat transfer, vapor explosions, stratified condensing flows, stability of thin liquid films. Office: Northwestern Univ Chem Engring Dept Evanston IL 60208-0001

BANKS, DONNA JO, food products executive; b. Ft. McClellan, Ala., Sept. 6, 1956; d. Walter Dow and Joanne (Phelps) Cox; m. Bobby Dennis Banks, Dec. 27, 1983; children: Cynthia Marie, Elizabeth Anne, Sarah Diane. BS, U. Tenn., 1979, MS, 1980; PhD, Mich. State U., 1984. Assoc. statistician Kellogg Co., Battle Creek, Mich., 1983-84, mgr. product evaluation and stats., 1984-87, dir. cereal product devel., 1987-91, v.p. rsch. and devel., 1991-97, sr. v.p. rsch. and devel., 1997—99, sr. v.p. global innovation, 1999—2000, sr. v.p. rsch., quality and tech., 2000—04, sr. v.p., worldwide innovation and operations, 2004—. Bd. mem. Mich. Life Scis. Corridor. Bd. mem. Mich. State U. Found. Named Disting. Alumni, Mich. State U. Coll. Agr. and Natural Resources, 2000; named one of 25 Masters of Innovation, BusinessWeek, 2006; named to Acad. Women Achievers, YWCA N.Y.C., 1998. Mem.: Product Devel. Mgmt. Assn., Am. Assn. Cereal Chemists, Internat. Food Techs., Am. Statis. Assn., Sigma Xi. Democrat. Baptist. Avocations: racquetball, tennis, needlecrafts, sewing. Office: Kellogg Co 1 Kellogg Sq Battle Creek MI 49016-3599

BANKS, ROBERT J., bishop emeritus; b. Boston, Mass., Feb. 26, 1928; s. Robert Joseph and Rita Katherine (Sullivan) Banks. AB, St. John's Sem., Brighton, Mass., 1949; STL, Gregorian U., Rome, 1953; JCD, Lateran U., Rome, 1957. Ordained priest Archdiocese of Boston, 1952; prof. canon law St. John's Sem., Brighton, Mass., 1959-71, acad. dean, 1967-71, rector, 1971-81; vicar gen. Archdiocese of Boston, 1984; ordained bishop, 1985; aux. bishop Archdiocese of Boston, Boston, 1985—90; bishop Diocese of Green Bay, Wis., 1990—2003, bishop emeritus, 2003—. Roman Catholic. Office: Diocese of Green Bay PO Box 23825 1910 S Webster Ave Green Bay WI 54305-3825 Office Phone: 920-437-7531. E-mail: rbanks@gbdioc.org.*

BANNEN, JOHN THOMAS, lawyer; s. James J. and Ruth J. Bannen; m. Carol A. Swanson, Aug. 16, 1975; children: Ryan M., Kelly A., Erin C. BA summa cum laude, Coll. St. Thomas, 1973; JD, Marquette U., 1976; LLM in Taxation, DePaul U., 1989; BA in Spanish, U. Wis., 2003. Bar: Wis. 1976, U.S. Dist. Ct. (ea. and we. dists.) Wis. 1976, U.S. Tax Ct. 1979, U.S. Claims Ct. 1983, U.S. Supreme Ct. 1984. Shareholder Charne, Clancy & Taitelman, S.C., Milw., 1976-91; ptnr. Quarles & Brady, Milw., 1991—. Bd. dirs. Guardianship Svcs. Indigents, Milw., 1983—87; mem. adv. bd. Sch. Sisters Notre Dame, 1993—98, pres., 1995—98; mem. coun. Christ the King Parish, Wauwatosa, Wis., 1989—93, trustee, 1996—98. Fellow: Am. Coll. Trust and Estate Counsel (state law coord. Wis. 1990—95, chmn. com. employee benefits 2001—05, state chair Wis. 2007—); mem.: ABA, Wis. Bar Assn. (bd. dirs. probate sect.), Assn. Advanced Life Underwriters (assoc.). Avocations: reading, gardening, Spanish language, cooking. Office: Quarles and Brady LLP Ste 2040 411 E Wisconsin Ave Milwaukee WI 53202-4497 Office Phone: 414-277-5859. E-mail: jtb@quarles.com.

BANNISTER, GEOFFREY, academic administrator, geographer; b. Manchester, Eng., Sept. 19, 1945; came to U.S., 1973; s. Leslie and Doris (Shankland) B.; m. Margaret Janet Sheridan, Jan. 28, 1968; children: Katherine, Janet. BA, U. Otago, New Zealand, 1967, MA with honors, 1969; PhD, U. Toronto, Can., 1974. Asst. prof. Boston U., 1973-77, acting chmn. geography, 1977-78, dean liberal arts, grad. sch., 1978-87; exec. v.p. Butler U., Indpls., 1987-89, pres., 1989—. Cons. Urban Affairs Ministry of State, Can., 1973; legal cons. U.S. Dept. of State 1982-84; bd. dirs. Somerset Group, Ind. Nat. Bank. Co-author atlas Spatial Dynamics of Postwar County Economic Change, 1977; contbr. articles to profl. jours. Chmn. bd. trustees Cambridge (Mass.) Montessori Sch., 1979-80; mem. corp. Sea Edn. Assn., Woods Hole, Mass., 1979-87; bd. dirs. United Way of Cen. Ind., 1990—, chmn. 1992 Premeire Campaign, edn. chmn.; bd. dirs. Greater Indpls. Progress Com., 1988—; pres. Midwest Collegiate Cons; chmn. World Rowing Championship, 1994. Fellow U. Toronto, 1970-71, Can. Council, 1972. Mem. at. Labor/Higher Edn. Coun., Nat. Assn. Scholars, Indpls. Bus. Jour. Blue Ribbon Panel, Indpls. Commn. on African-Am. Males, C. of C., Econ. Club, English Speaking Union U.S. (Indpls. br.), Coun. Urban Coll. of Arts, Letter and Scis., Kiwanis, Phi Beta Kappa. Avocations: bicycling, golf, skiing. Home: 891 Bug Hill Rd Ashfield MA 01330-9742

BANNISTER, MICHAEL E., automotive executive; BBA, Memphis State Univ. Held a number of br. and regional mgmt. oper. positions Ford Credit North Am. Region, 1973; mgr. orth Atlantic Region Ford Motor Credit Co., Dearborn, Mich., 1991, mgr. Atlantic Region, 1991—93, v.p. mktg., 1993—95; exec. dir. European sales ops. Ford Motor Credit Co. Europe, 1995—97; chmn. Ford Fin. Europe, 1997—2003; pres., COO Ford Motor Credit Co., Dearborn, Mich., 2003—04; group v.p. Ford Motor Co., Dearborn, Mich., 2004—; chmn., CEO Ford Motor Credit Co., Dearborn, Mich., 2004—. Office: Ford Motor Credit Co One American Rd Mail Drop 7440 Dearborn MI 48126-2701

BANNON, JOHN A., lawyer; BA, U. Va., 1979; MBA, Marymount U., 1988; JD with honors, U. Chgo., 1991. Bar: Ill. 1991, US Dist. Ct. (no. dist. Ill.) 1991. Ptnr. Schiff Hardin, Chgo. Capt. USAF. Office: Schiff Hardin LLP 6600 Sears Tower Chicago IL 60606-6473 Office Phone: 312-258-5597. Office Fax: 312-258-5600. E-mail: jbannon@schiffhardin.com.

BANOFF, SHELDON IRWIN, lawyer; b. Chgo., July 10, 1949; BSBA in Acctg., U. Ill., 1971; JD, U. Chgo., 1974. Bar: Ill. 1974, U.S. Tax Ct. 1974. Ptnr. Katten Muchin Rosenman LLP, Chgo., 1974—. Chmn. tax conf. planning com. U. Chgo. Law Sch., 1993-94. Co-editor Jour. of Taxation, 1984—; contbr. articles to profl. jours. Mem. ABA, Chgo. Bar Assn. (fed. taxation com., mem. exec. coun. 1980—, chmn. large law firm com., 1999-2000), Am. Coll. Tax Counsel. Office: Katten Muchin Rosenman LLP 525 W Monroe St Chicago IL 60661-3693 Office Phone: 312-902-5200. Business E-Mail: sheldon.banoff@kattenlaw.com.

BANSTETTER, ROBERT J., lawyer; b. 1940; BS, St Louis U., 1963; JD, U. Ill., 1966. Bar: Mo. 1967, Ill. 1966. Atty. Labor Rels. Internat. Shoe, 1966-70; v.p., gen. coun. & sec. Gen. Am. Life Ins. Co., 1992—. Office: Gen Amer Life Ins 13045 Tesson Ferry Rd Saint Louis MO 63128-3407

BANTON, STEPHEN CHANDLER, lawyer; b. St. Louis; s. William Conwell and Ruth (Chandler) B. AB, Bowdoin Coll., 1969; JD, Washington U., St. Louis, 1973, MBA, 1974. Bar: Mo. 1973, U.S. Dist. Ct. (ea. and we. dists.) Mo. 1973. Asst. pros. atty. St. Louis County, 1973-75; sole practice Clayton, Mo., 1975-83; ptnr. Quinn, Ground & Banton, Manchester, Mo., 1983—. Pres. Coll. for Living, 1997-98. Exploring chmn. St. Louis coun. Midland Dist. Scouts, 1975-77; pres. Am. Youth Hostels Ozarks area, 1976-80; trustee St. Louis Art Mus., 1985-94; mem. Rockwood Sch. Bd., 1997—. Served with USMC. Recipient Leadership award Lafayette Community Assn., 1983, Service award The Meramec Palisades Community Assn., 1985, Service award Profl. Remodeling Assn., 1985, Service award St. Louis Symphony Orch., 1985. Mem. ABA, Mo. Bar Assn., St. Louis County Bar Assn., Bar Assn. Met. St. Louis, Assn. Trial Lawyers Am., St. Louis County League of C. of C. (pres. 1978), West Port C. of C. (bd. dirs. 1978-81, Service award 1983), Rotary (pres. Ballwin club 1997-98), Toastmasters (adminstrv. v.p.), Lions (pres. 1977), Kiwanis (pres. West County club 2001-02), Gideons (pres. Frontenac 1999-2002). Republican. Office: Quinn Ground & Banton 14611 Manchester Rd Ballwin MO 63011-3700 Home: PO Box 107 Ballwin MO 63022-0107 Home Phone: 636-386-1110; Office Phone: 636-394-7242. Business E-Mail: scbanton@qgb-lawfirm.com.

BANWART, SIDNEY C., human resources executive; Diploma in Chem. Engring., Iowa State U.; MBA, U. Ill. Various engring. and mgmt. positions including devel. engr. Caterpillar, Inc., Peoria, Ill., 1968—86, mgr. quality control and engring., mgr. tech. svcs. Mexico, 1986—89, quality control mgr., tech. svcs. mgr., motor grade product mgr. Aurora and Decatur, 1989—95, gen. mgr. large engine ctr. Lafayette, Ind., 1995—97, v.p., head tech. svcs. divisn., 1997—2000, head component products divsn., 1998—2000, chief info. officer, head systems and processes divisn., 2000—04, v.p. human svcs. divisn. Peoria, Ill., 2004—. Bd. dirs. Carter Machinery, Salem, Va., Weitz Co., Des Moines. Recipient Ill. 4-H Alumni award, 2004. Mem.: Ill. Manufacturer's Assn., Human Resources Policy Assn. Office: Caterpillar Inc 100 NE Adams St Peoria IL 61629 Office Phone: 309-675-1000. Office Fax: 309-675-1182.

BANWART, WAYNE LEE, agronomy, environmental science educator; b. West Bend, Iowa, Jan. 9, 1948; s. Albert R. and Betty R. (Zaugg) B.; m. Charlen Ann Schrock, Mar. 22, 1970; children: Krista, Kara, Neil. MS, Iowa State U., 1972, PhD, 1975. Asst. prof. U. Ill., Urbana, 1975-79, assoc. prof., 1979-84, prof., 1984-89, prof., assoc. head dept. agronomy, 1989-94, asst. dean, 1994—. Vis. scientist Constrn. Engring. Lab., Champaign, 1985-86; chmn. Nat. Atmospheric Deposition Program, 1986. Co-author: (textbook) Soils and Their Environment, 1992. Mem. patient satisfaction com. HMO, Champaign, 1987-93; pres. citizen's adv. com. Mahomet-Seymour Schs., 1981. Nat. Coll. Tchrs. of Agr. fellow, 1987. Fellow Am. Soc. Agronomy (George D. Scarseth award 1973), Soil Sci. Soc. Am.; mem. Internat. Soil Sci. Soc., Gamma Sigma Delta (pres.). Achievements include discovery that agricultural crops subject to acid rain will suffer little or no yield reduction or physiological damage; discovery that plant uptake and translocation of TNT is very limited while RDX is readily taken up and concentrated in plant tissues; that organic amendments offer promise for bioremediation of soils contaminated with these explosives. Home: 3201 Sandhill Ln Champaign IL 61822 Office: U Ill 1301 W Gregory Dr Urbana IL 61801-9015 E-mail: wanwart@uiuc.edu.

BAPTIST, ALLWYN J., healthcare consultant; b. India, July 10, 1943; came to U.S., 1971; s. Peter L.G. and Trescilla (Lobo) B.; m. Anita Lobo, Sept. 8, 1973; children: Alan, Andrew, Annabel, Arthur. BCS, U. Calcutta, India, 1962; cert. mgmt., U. Chgo., 1978. CPA, Ill; chartered acct., India. Divisional acct. Rallis India Ltd., Bombay, 1967-71; mgr. Chgo. Blue Cross, 1972-79; sr. mgr. Price Waterhouse, Chgo., 1979-84; v.p., dir. Truman Esmond and Assocs., Barrington, Ill., 1984-86; ptnr. Laventhol and Horwath, Chgo., 1986-90, BDO Seidman, Chgo., 1991-2000; pres. Baptist Cons. Inc., 2000—. Mem. adv. bd. St. Mary of Nazareth Hosp., 1989—, mem. gov. bd., 1992-94, 96-98, lifetime trustee. Contbr. articles to profl. jours. Mem. fin. com. St. James Ch., Arlington Heights, Ill., 1987; mem. AICPA Health Care Com., 1991-94. Mem. Healthcare Fin. Mgmt. Assn. (dir., sec. 1983-85, pres. 1988-89, recipient William J. Follmer award 1984, Reeves award 1989, Muncie Gold award 1992, founders medal of honor 1998), India Cath. Assn. Am. (treas. 1980, 87, pres. 1988). Avocations: travel, reading, tennis, golf. Office: Bapt Cons Inc 126 E Wing St Arlington Heights IL 60004

BAR, ROBERT S., endocrinologist, educator; b. Gainesville, Tex., Dec. 2, 1943; s. Samuel and Emma (Kaplan) B.; m. Laurel Ellen Burns, June 23, 1970; children: Katharine June, Matthew Tomas. BS, Tufts Univ., 1964; MS in Biochemistry, Ohio State U., 1970, MD, 1970. Medicine intern Pa. Hosp., Phila., 1970-71; medicine resident Ohio State Univ., Columbus, 1971-72; asst. prof., dept. medicine Univ. Iowa, Iowa City, 1977-82, assoc. prof., dept. medicine, 1982-86, prof., dept. medicine, 1986. Acting dir. divsn. of endocrinology and metabolism, U. Iowa, 1985-90; dir. diabetes-endocrinology rsch ctr., U. Iowa, 1986—, nat. rsch. svc. award in endocrinology, 1984—, endocrinology fellowship program, 1979—, divsn. of endocrinology and metabolism, 1990—; mem. ad hoc study sect. NIH, 1985, dir. diabetes-endocrinology rsch. ctr. 1986; mem. editorial bd. Jour. of Clin. Endocrinology and Metabolism, 1984-87; mem study sect. at. Veterans Adminstrn., 1984-87; v.p. rsch. Nat. Am. Diabetes Assn., 1987-88; mem. orgn. com. Endothelium and Diabetes Symposium, Melbourne, 1988; dir. VA/JDF Diabetes Rsch. Ctr., 1997; mem. study sect. numerous assns. and coms.; guest reviewer numerous jours. Editor Endocrinology, 1987-89, Advances in Endocrinology and Metabolism, 1989—. Mem. Am. Diabetes Assn., Am. Soc. for Clin. Investigation, Assn. Am. Physicians, Endocrine Soc., Ctrl. Soc. for Clin. Rsch., Sigma Xi.

BARANY, JAMES WALTER, industrial engineering educator; b. South Bend, Ind., Aug. 24, 1930; s. Emery Peter and Rose Anne Barany; m. Judith Ann Flanigan, Aug. 6, 1960 (div. 1982); 1 child, Cynthia Getty. BSME, Notre Dame U., 1953; MS in Indsl. Engring., Purdue U., 1958, PhD, 1961. Prodn. worker Studebaker Corp., 1949-52; prodn. liaison engr. Bendix Aviation Corp., 1955-56; mem. faculty Sch. Indsl. Engring. Purdue U., West Lafayette, Ind., 1958—, now prof., indsl. engring. Sch. Indsl. Engring. Cons. Taiwan Productivity Ctr., Western Electric, Gleason Gear Works, Am. Oil Co., Timken Co. With US Army, 1954—55. Recipient Best Counselor award Purdue U., 1978, Best Engring. Tchr. award, 1983, 89, Outstanding Indsl. Engring. Tchr. award, 1983, 87, 89, Outstanding Tchr. award Purdue U., 1989, Marion Scott Faculty Exemplary Character award Purdue U., 1993, 2000, NSF and Easter Seal Found. rsch. grantee, 1961, 63, 64, 65; Purdue Tchg. Acad. founding fellow, 1997, Indiana Gov.'s Sagamore of the Wabash award, 1998; named Purdue Book Great Tchrs., 1999. Mem. Inst. Indsl. Engring. (life, Fellows award 1982, Disting. Educator award 1989, Disting. Svc. award 1992, Cert. of Svc. Appreciation 1994, Work Measurement award 2000, Young Engr. Mentoring award 2001), Soc. Mfg. Engr., Am. Soc. Engring. Edn., Methods Time Measurement Rsch. Assn., Human Factors and Ergonomics Soc., Order of Engr., Sigma Xi, Alpha Pi Mu, Tau Beta Pi (Eminent Engr. award 1982). Home: 1120 Northwestern Ave W West Lafayette IN 47906-2503 Office: Purdue U IE GRIS 315 N Grant St West Lafayette IN 47907-2023 Home Phone: 765-743-3308; Office Phone: 765-494-5435. Business E-Mail: jwb@ecn.purdue.edu.

BARBATO, ANTHONY L., hospital administrator, medical educator; BA, U. Windsor; MD, Stritch Sch. Medicine, Loyola U. Chgo. Cert. bd. cert. Am. Bd. Internal Medicine, Am. Bd. Endocrinology and Metabolism. Asst. prof. Stritch Sch. Medicine, Loyola U., Maywood, Ill., 1976—81, assoc. prof., 1981—86, prof. medicine, 1986—; dean Stritch Sch. Medicine, Maywood, Ill., exec. dean, asst. chmn., medicine for post-grad. edn., program dir., internal medicine residency; exec. v.p., health affairs Loyola U. Health Sys., Maywood, Ill., provost, health affairs, chief admin. officer, health affairs, v.p., health affairs, pres., CEO, 1995—. Chmn. Assoc. Academic Health Ctrs., 2000; sr. health policy adv. com. Rep. Danny Davis. Office: 2160 S First Ave Maywood IL 60153

BARBER, ROGER L., grain marketing company executive; With Scoular Co., Omaha, 1987—2001, contr., dir. corp. acctg., CFO, 2001. Office: Scoular 2027 Dodge St Omaha E 68102

BARBOSA, MANUEL, judge; b. Mex., Oct. 28, 1947; m. Linda Kupfer, Oct. 26, 1974; 3 children. BA, Ill. Benedictine Coll., 1969; JD, John Marshall Law Sch., 1969. Bar: Ill. 1977, U.S. Dist. Ct. (no. dist.) Ill. 1993. Chair Ill. Human Rights Commn., 1990-98; judge U.S. Bankruptcy Ct., Rockford, Ill., 1998—. Bd. dirs. Grand Victoria Found., 1977, YMCA, 1985, Rotary, 1992. Recipient Social Svc. award Quad County Urban League, 1992. Mem. ABA, Ill. Bar Assn., Kane County Bar Assn., Winnebago County Bar Assn. Roman Catholic. Avocations: sports, guitar, history.

BARCIA, JAMES A., state senator, former congressman; b. Bay City, Mich., Feb. 25, 1952; Grad., Saginaw Valley State U., 1974. Staff asst. to U.S. Senator Philip Hart, 1971; cmty. svc. coord. Mich. Cmty. Blood Ctr., Bay City, 1974-75; mem. Ho. of Reps. from 101st Mich. Dist., 1977-82, mem. edn. com., 1977-82, chmn. pub. works com., 1979-82, majority whip, 1979-82; mem. Mich. Senate, 1983-92, U.S. Congress from 5th Mich. dist., 1993—2002; mem. sci. and transp. and infrastructure coms.; senator, State of Mich., 31st Dist., 2003—. Mem. UAW Local 688, 1970-71, Saginaw Valley Univ. Bd. Control, 1973-74. Recipient disting. svc. award Saginaw Valley State U. Alumni Assn., 1977, Golden Eagle award Am. Fedn. Police; named Fed. Legislator of Yr., Mich. Credit Union League, Legislator of Yr., Satari Club Internat.; elected to Bay City Ctrl. Hall of Fame, 1981. Mem. NRA, Bay Area C. of C., Mich. Assn. Osteopathic Physicians and Surgeons (hon. lay mem.), Bay City Jaycees (Disting. Svc. award 1982), United Conservation clubs, Elks, Bay City Lions. Democrat. Home: 3190 Hidden Rd Bay City MI 48706-1203 Office: PO Box 30036 Lansing MI 48909-7536 also: 301 E Genessee Ste 502 Saginaw MI 48607

BARCLAY, KATHLEEN S., automotive executive; b. Milw. B in Bus., Mich. State U., 1978; MBA, MIT, 1991. With GM, Detroit, 1978—81; retail mgr. Southland Corp., Reno, Chgo.; human resource compensation mgr. Allen-Bradley Co., Milw.; with GM, Warren, Mich., 1985—, mgr. salaried personnel corp. staffs, 1987—88; mgr. labor rels. Chevrolet-Pontiac-GM Can., 1988—91, mgr. exec. compensation, 1991; dir. compensation GM, 1992—95, dir. human resources vehicle sales svc., 1995, gen. dir. human resources mgmt. N.Am. ops., 1996—98, v.p. global human resources, 1998—. Bd. dirs. Cowdrick Group, Mich. Virtual Univ. Bd. govs. MIT; alumni bd. dirs. Mich. State U. Sloan fellow, MIT, 1991. Fellow: Nat. Acad. Human Resources (bd. dirs.); mem.: Detroit Women's Econ. Club. Office: GM Corp 300 Renaissance Ctr Detroit MI 48265-3000 Office Phone: 313-556-5000, 313-556-1988. Fax: 248-696-7300.

BARCLAY, MARTHA JANE, science educator, research scientist; b. Warren County, Ill., July 5, 1948; d. George Leonard and Edna Virginia Ault; children: Brad children: Austin. BS, U. Ill., 1970; MS, Ind. U., 1972; PhD, U. Tenn., 1979. Registered dietitian. Asst. prof. U. Iowa, Iowa City, 1979—86; prof. Western Ill. U., Macomb, 1986—. Rschr. Coun. Food and Agrl. Rsch., Champaign/Urbana, 1997—2003, McDonough County Extension Coun. Treas. McDonough County Teen Ct. Bd., Macomb, 2000—02. Named Hospitality Educator of Yr., Illinois Hotel and Lodging Assn., 2001-2002. Mem.: Ill. Assn. Family and Consumer Scis., Am. Assn. Family and Consumer Scis., Ill. Dietetic Assn., Am. Dietetic Assn., Midwest CHRIE (pres. 1990—91), Internat. CHRIE. Office: Western Ill U 1 University Cir Macomb IL 61455 Office Phone: 309-298-1775. Business E-Mail: MJ-Barclay@wiu.edu.

BARD, JOHN FRANKLIN, consumer products executive; b. Owatonna, Minn., Mar. 1, 1941; s. Franklin Spencer and Nina Carolyn (Geyer) B.; m. Barbara Ann Bowers, Aug. 1, 1964; children: Steven George, Kristin Elizabeth Taylor. BS in Bus., Northwestern U., 1963; MBA, U. Cin., 1972. Internat. contr. Procter & Gamble Co., Cin., 1963-78; group v.p. Clorox Co., Oakland, Calif., k1978-84, dir., 1979-84; exec. v.p., pres., chief oper. officer Tambrands Inc., Lake Success, N.Y., 1985-90, dir., 1986-89; sr. v.p., exec. v.p. Wm. Wrigley Jr. Co., Chgo., 1990—, dir., 1999—. Bd. dirs. Alameda County YMCA, Oakland, 1979-87, L.I. United Way, 1989-90, Greater N. Mich. Ave. Assn., Chgo., 1991—; dir., vice-chmn. Keep Am. Beautiful, Inc. Mem. Tax Found. (policy com.), 410 Club, Econ. Club Chgo., Fin. Execs. Inst., Sea Pines Country Club (S.C.), Office: Wm Wrigley Jr Co 410 N Michigan Ave Chicago IL 60611-4213

BARDEEN, WILLIAM ALLAN, research physicist; b. Washington, Pa., Sept. 15, 1941; s. John and F. Jane (Maxwell) B.; m. Marjorie Ann Gaylord; children: Charles Gaylord, Karen Gail. AB in Physics, Cornell U., 1962; PhD in Physics, U. Minn., 1968, DSc (hon.), 2002. Rsch. assoc. SUNY, Stony Brook, 1966-68; mem. Inst. for Advanced Study, Princeton, N.J., 1968-69; asst. prof. Stanford (Calif.) U., 1969-72, assoc. prof., 1972-75; scientist Fermilab, Batavia, Ill., 1975-93, head theoretical physics, 1987-93, scientist, 1994—; head theoretical physics SSC Lab., Dallas, 1993-94. Vis. scientist CERN, Geneva, Switzerland, 1971-72, Max Planck Inst. for Physics, Munich, 1977, 86. Author: Barden-Bardeen Genealogy, 1993; editor: Symp. on Anomalies, Geometry, Topology, 1985; mem. editl. bd. Phys. Rev., 1981-84, 92-94, Jour. Math. Physics, 1986-90, European Physics Jour. C, 1997-2000; contbr. numerous articles to profl. jours. Trustee Aspen Ctr. for Physics, 1987-91. Fellowship Alfred P. Sloan Found., 1971-74, John Simon Guggenheim Found., 1985-86; recipient sr. scientist award Alexander von Humboldt Found., 1977 Fellow Am. Phys. Soc. (exec. com. divsn. of particles and fields 1988-90, J. J. Sajurai prize for theoretical particle physics 1996); mem. Am. Acad. Arts and Scis., NAS. Avocations: genealogy, basketball. Office: Fermilab MS 106 PO Box 500 Batavia IL 60510-0500

BARDEN, LARRY A., lawyer; b. 1956; BS, Miami Univ., Ohio, 1978; JD magna cum laude, Washington and Lee Univ., 1982. With Sidley Austin LLP, Chgo., 1982—, ptnr., mergers and acquisitions, 1989—, mem. exec. com., 1999—. Former faculty Northwestern Univ. Garrett Inst. Trustee Hadley Sch. for Blind; rep. Greater Chgo. Food Depository. Fellow: Am. Bar Found.; mem.: ABA, Chgo. Bar Assn., Order of Coif. Office: Sidley Austin LLP One S Dearborn St Chicago IL 60603 Office Phone: 312-853-7785. Office Fax: 312-853-7036. Business E-Mail: lbarden@sidley.com.

BARDEN, ROLAND EUGENE, university administrator; b. Powers Lake, ND, Sept. 11, 1942; s. Harry S. and Sena (Furness) B.; m. Carolyn Jane, Nov. 25, 1967; children: Carl, Janine, Ann. BS, U. N.D., 1964; MS, U. Wis., 1966, PhD, 1969. Postdoctoral fellow Case Western Res. U., Cleve., 1969-71; prof. U. Wyo., Laramie, 1971-89, dept. head, 1980-83, assoc. dean, 1983-84, assoc. provost, 1984-89; v.p. acad. affairs Minn. State U., Moorhead, 1989-94, pres., 1994—. Cons., evaluator orth Ctrl. Assn. Schs. and Colls., Chgo., 1988-05; commr. Tri Coll. U., 1989-94, dir. 1994—. Contbr. articles to profl. jours. Recipient Rsch. Career Devel. award NIH, 1976-80. Mem. Am. Chem. Soc., Am. Soc. Biochem. Molecular Biology. Avocations: hiking, reading, fishing. Office: Minn State U Moorhead Office Of President Moorhead MN 56563-0001 Office Phone: 218-477-2243. Business E-Mail: barden@mnstate.edu.

BARDON, JEB, state representative; m. Kristie Bardon. Grad., Purdue U., 1995. Owner, oper. Subway Sandwiches and Salads; state rep. dist. 25 Ind. Ho. of Reps., Indpls., 1998—, chmn. fin. instns. com., vice chmn. ins., corps, and small bus. com., mem. tech., R & D com. Democrat. Office: Ind Ho of Reps 200 W Washington St Indianapolis IN 46204-2786

BARENBOIM, DANIEL, conductor, pianist, music director; b. Buenos Aires, Nov. 15, 1942; s. Enrique and Aida (Schuster) Barenboim; m. Jaqueline DuPre, June 15, 1967 (dec.); m. Elena Bashkirova, Nov. 28, 1988; 2 children. Student, Mozarteum, Salzburg, Austria, Accademia Chigiana, Siena, Italy; grad., Santa Cecilia Acad., Rome, 1956. Music dir. Chgo. Symphony Orch., 1991—2006; gen. music dir. Deutsche Staatsoper Berlin, 1992—. Debut with Israel Philharm. Orch., 1953, Royal Philharm. Orch., 1953, debut as pianist Carnegie Hall, N.Y.C., 1957, Berlin Philharm. Orch., 1963, N.Y. Philharm. Orch., 1964, 1st U.S. solo recital, N.Y.C., 1958, as pianist performed in N.Am., South Am., Europe, Soviet Union, Australia, New Zealand, Near East, condr., 1962—, conducted English Chamber Orch., London Symphony Orch., Israel Philharm. Orch., N.Y. Philharm. Orch., Phila. Symphony, Boston Symphony, Chgo. Symphony Orch., others, musical dir. Orch. de Paris, 1975—89, Staatsoper Berlin, 1992—, artistic advisor Israel Festival, 1971—74, over 100 recs. as pianist and condr., debut as pianist at age 7, Buenos Aires. Named to Legion of Honor, France, 1987; recipient Beethoven medal, 1958, Harriet Cohen Paderewski Centenary prize, 1963, Beethoven Soc. medal, 1982, Prix de la Tolérance, Protestant Acad. of Tutzing, 2002, Wolf Prize in arts, Wolf Found., Israel, 2004, Praemium Imperiale award, Japan Art Assn., 2007. Office: Unter den Linden 7 D-10117 Berlin Germany

BARFIELD, JON E., employment company executive; b. 1951; BA with honours, Princeton U., 1974; JD, Harvard U., 1977. Assoc. Sidley & Austin; pres. Barfield Mfg. Co., Bartech Group, Livonia, Mich., 1981, chmn., ceo, 1995—. Bd. dirs. Granite Broadcasting Corp., bd. dir. Nat. City Corp., Tecumseh Products Co., Dow Jones & Co., BMC Software, dir. Pantellos Grp. Ltd. Partnership, Inc. Dir. Blue Cross Blue Shield of Mich., Children's Ctr.& Cmty. Found. Southeastern Mich. Mem.: Nat. Tech. Svcs. Assn. (past pres.), Henry Ford Kettering U. and Detroit Renaissance. (bd. of trustees), Emeritus Princeton U. (charter trustee). Office: Baretech Group Inc 17199 N Laurel Park Dr Ste 224 Livonia MI 48152-7903 Office Phone: 734-953-5050. Office Fax: 734-953-5075.

BARGER, AMY J., astronomer, educator; BA in Physics, U. Wis., Madison, 1993; PhD in Astronomy, U. Cambridge King's Coll., 1997. Postdoctoral fellow Inst. Astronomy U. Hawaii; asst. prof. to assoc. prof. astronomy U. Wis., Madison, 2000—. Vis. adj. astronomer dept. physics and astronomy U. Hawaii. Contbr. articles to sci. jours. Named one of Brilliant 10, Popular Sci. mag., 2005; recipient Annie J. Cannon award, Am. Astron. Soc., 2001, Newton Lacy Pierce prize, 2002, Maria Goeppert-Mayer award, Am. Phys. Soc., 2007; Marshall fellow, 1993—2001, Hubble fellow, 1999—2001, Chandra fellow at large, 1999—2001, Sloan fellow, 2002, Packard Found. fellow sci. and engring., 2003. Office: U Wis Madison Dept Astronomy 6512 Sterling Hall 475 N Charter St Madison WI 53706 Office Phone: 608-263-7106. Office Fax: 608-263-6386. E-mail: barger@astro.wisc.edu.

BARGER, VERNON DUANE, physicist, educator; b. Curllsville, Pa., June 5, 1938; s. Joseph F. and Olive (McCall) Barger; m. M. Annetta McLeod, 1967; children: Victor A., Amy J., Andrew V. BS, Pa. State U., 1960, PhD, 1963. Rsch. assoc. U. Wis., Madison, 1963-65, from asst. prof. to assoc. prof., 1965—67, prof. physics, 1968—, J.H. Van Vleck prof., 1983—, dir. Inst. Elem. Particle Physics Rsch., 1984—, Hilldale prof., 1987-91, Vilas prof., 1991—. Vis. prof. U. Hawaii, 1970, 79, 82, U. Durham, 1983, 84; vis. scientist CERN, 1972, Rutherford Lab., 1972, SLAC, 1975, Kavli Inst. for Theoretical Physics, U. Calif., Santa Barbara, 2003. Co-author: (book) Phenomenological Theories of High Energy Scattering, Classical Mechanics, Classical Electricity and Magnetism, Collider Physics. Recipient Alumni Fellow award, Pa. State U., 1974; Guggenheim fellow, 1972, Fermilab Frontier fellow, 1999. Fellow: Am. Phys. Soc. Methodist. Achievements include research in elementary particle theory and phenomenology; classification of hadrons as Regge recurrences; analyses of neutrino scattering and oscillations; weak boson, Higgs boson and heavy quark production; electroweak models; supersymmetry and grand unification; collider physics; cosmology. Office: U Wis Dept Physics 1150 University Ave Madison WI 53706-1302

BARIFF, MARTIN LOUIS, information systems educator, consultant; b. Chgo., Jan. 26, 1944; s. George and Mae (Goldberg) B. BS in Acctg., U. Ill., 1966, MA in Acctg., 1967, PhD in Acctg., 1973. CPA, Chgo. Asst. prof. acctg. and decision scis. Wharton Sch., Phila., 1973-78; vis. asst. prof. acctg. U. Chgo., 1978-79; assoc. prof. acctg. and mgmt. info. decision systems Case Western Res. U., Cleve., 1979-83; assoc. prof. info. mgmt. Ill. Inst. Tech., Chgo., 1983—, dir. Ctr. for Rsch. on Impacts of Info. Systems, 1983—2003, acad. dir. MS e-commerce program, 2000—02, dir. EBus cert. program, 2002—, dir. program rsch. EBus and info. tech., 2003—05. Exec. v.p. EDP Auditors Found., 1979-80; program chmn. Internat. Conf. Info. Systems, Phila., 1980; co-founder, bd. dirs. sec. Info. Integrity Coalition, 2001--; cons. in field. Contbr. articles to profl. jours.; mem. editl. bd. Computers and Security, 1992—, Info. & Mgmt., 2006-07. Bd. dirs. Community Accts. Inc. of Phila., 1974-75. Mem. AICPA, Inst. Ops. Rsch. Mgmt. Sci. (Info. Sys. Coll. chair. 1978-80, eBusiness sect. treas. 2008-) Ill. CPA Soc., Am. Acctg. Assn. (chmn. acctg., behavior and orgns. sect. 1987-88), Assn. Computing Machinery (sec. spl. interest group on security, auditing and control 1981-85), Soc. Info. Mgmt. (treas. Chgo. chpt. 1988-90, 1995-96, 2007-), Internat. Engring. Consortium (bd. dirs. ednl. overseers 1991-96), Internat. Internal Auditors (rsch. chair Chgo. chpt. 2001-), Assn. Bus. Procedures Mgmt. Profls. (bd. dirs. Chgo. chpt. 2003-), Soc. for Judgment and Decision-making, BTM Inst. (BTM Global Rsch. Coun. 2002-). Jewish. Avocations: running, flying, photography. Office: Ill Inst Tech 565 W Adams St Ste 422 Chicago IL 60661-3613 Office Phone: 312-906-6522. Business E-Mail: bariff@stuart.iit.edu.

BARKAN, STEVEN M., law librarian, educator; children: Davida, Daniel. AMLS, U. Mich.; JD, Cleve. State U. Reference libr. U. So. Calif. Law Libr.; rsch. libr. Supreme Ct. of US; assoc. law libr. U. Tex. Sch. Law; dir. Law Libr., assoc. dean to interim dean Marquette U. Law Sch.; dir. Law Libr., tchr. tort law U. Wis. Law Sch. Founding editor Perspectives, 1992, contbr. Fundamentals of Legal Rsch.; contbr. articles to profl. jours. Recipient Excellence in Academic Law Librarianship Award, West Pub. Co., 1993. Avocations: movies, music, travel. Office: Law Libr Rm 6358 975 Bascom Mall Madison WI 53706-1399 Office Phone: 608-262-1151. E-mail: smbarkan@wisc.edu.

BARKER, HAROLD KENNETH, former university dean; b. Louisville, Apr. 14, 1922; s. J.M. and Fannie Mae (Elliott) B.; m. Elizabeth Johns, Mar. 11, 1948 (dec.); children: Leslie Ann, Glenn Lewis.; m. Beverly Williams, Feb. 28, 1984. AB, U. Louisville, 1948, MA, 1949; PhD, U. Mich., 1959. Instr. Gunfire Prep. Sch., Hanau, Germany, 1946; sch. psychologist, vis. tchr. Bay City (Mich.) Pub. Schs., 1949-52; also instr. Bay City Jr. Coll.; sch. psychologist Ypsilanti (Mich.) Pub. Schs., 1952-53; instr. Eastern Mich. U., 1954-58; asst. dir. Bur. Appointments and Occupational Info., U. Mich., 1954-59; assoc. exec. sec. Am. Assn. Colls. Tchr. Edn., Washington, 1959-66, dir., 1972—; dean Coll. Edn., U. Akron, 1966-85, asst. to pres., 1985-87, dean emeritus, 1987. Bd. dirs. World U., San Juan, P.R., 1966—, Joint Council Econ. Edn., 1979 Editor: AACTE Handbook of International Education Programs, 1963; contbr. articles to profl. jours. and periodicals. Chmn. bd. dirs. Edwin Shaw Hosp., 1989; trustee U. Akron Found., 1994—. Recipient award outstanding profl. svc. Am. Assn. Colls. Tchr. Edn., 1966; named Hon. Alumni U. Akron, 1992. Mem. Phi Delta Kappa (internat. commn. 1962-69) Home: 1811 Brookwood Dr Akron OH 44313-5061 Office: Dept Devel Martin Univ Ctr U Akron Akron OH 44325-2603

BARKER, JEFF, theater and speech educator; m. Karen Barker; 3 children. Student, Greenville Coll.; BA in Theater, Seattle Pacific U., 1976; MA in Theater Performance, No. Ill. U.; MFA in Directing, U. SD. Mem. faculty to prof. theatre and speech Northwestern Coll., Orange City, Iowa, 1988—, endowed prof., 2006—. Dir. Drama Ministries Ensemble. Co-creator: (musicals) And God Said; author: (plays) Unspoken for Time, 1996 (Meritorious Achievement award, 1995), Kin (Grand Prize New Voices Iowa Playwrights Competition, 2002), That Bamboozler, Scapin!, September Bears, Sioux Center Sudan, David and Goliath, When Scott Comes Home, Elisha, Code Blue, The Final Approach of Flight 232, Word Against Word. Co-recipient Gold Medallion award, Kennedy Ctr. Am. Coll. Theatre Festival, 2003; recipient US Prof. of Yr. award, Carnegie Found. for Advancement of Tchg. and Coun. for Advancement and Support of Edn., 2006. Office: Dept Theatre and Speech Northwestern Coll 101 7th St SW Orange City IA 51041 Office Phone: 712-707-7093. E-mail: barker@nwciowa.edu.

BARKER, NANCY LEPARD, university official; b. Owosso, Mich., Jan. 22, 1936; d. Cecil L. and Mary Elizabeth (Stuart) Lepard; m. J. Daniel Cline, June 6, 1960 (div. 1971); m. R. William Barker, Nov. 18, 1972; children: Mary Georgia Harker, Mark L. Cline, Richard E., Daniel P., Melissa B. Van Arsdel, John C. Cline MD, Helen Grace Garrett, Wiley D., James G. BSc, U. Mich., Ann Arbor, 1957; DHum (hon.), Northwood U., 2001. Spl. edn. instr. Univ. Hosp. U. Mich., Ann Arbor, 1958-61; v.p. Med. Educator, Chgo., 1967-69; asst. to chmn., dir. careers for women Northwood U., Midland, Mich., 1970-77, asst. prof., chmn. dept. fashion mktg. and merchandising, 1972-77, dir. arts programs and external affairs, 1972-77, v.p. univ. rels., 1978-2001, office of the pres., 2001—; dir. Alden B. Dow Creativity Ctr., 2007—. Bd. dirs. Alden B. Dow Creativity Ctr., Midland; cons., lectr. in field. Co-author: (children's books) Wendy Well Series, 1970-72; contbr. chpts. to books, articles to profl. jours. Advisor Mich. Child Study Assn., 1972—; chmn. Matrix: Midland Festival, 1978; bd. dirs. Nat. Coun. of Women, 1971—, pres., 1983-85, chmn. centennial com., 1988; mem. exec. bd. Mich. ACE Network for Women Leaders in Higher Edn., 2001—; bd. dirs. ArtServe, Mich., 2003—, Family and Children's Svcs., Internat. Coun. Women, Paris. Nominee, (3) Mich. Women's Hall of Fame; named 1st ann. Disting. Educator of Yr., Am. Coun. on Edn./MI Network, 2001; named one of Outstanding Young Women in U.S. and Mich., 1974; recipient Hon. award, Ukrainian Nat. Women's League, 1983, Disting. Woman award, Northwood U., 1970, Outstanding Young Woman award, Jr. C. of C., 1974, Athena award, 2007. Mem. Am. Heart Assn.Internat. Coun. Women (bd. dirs. Paris 1991—), The Fashion Group, Internat. Furnishings and Design Assn. (pres. Mich. chpt. 1974-77), Mich. Women's Studies Assn. (founding mem.), Arts Midland Coun. (pres. 2 terms, 25th Anniversary award), Internat. Women's Forum, Mich. Women's Forum, Contemporary Rev. Club, Midland County Lawyers' Wives, Zonta, Phi Beta Kappa, Phi Kappa Phi, Alpha Lambda Delta, Phi Lambda Theta, Phi Gamma Nu, Delta Delta Delta. Office: Northwood Univ 209 Revere Midland MI 48640-4255 Home Phone: 989-631-9864; Office Phone: 989-631-9864. E-mail: barkermid@aol.com.

BARKER, SARAH EVANS, judge; b. Mishawaka, Ind., June 10, 1943; d. James McCall and Sarah (Yarbrough) Evans; m. Kenneth R. Barker, Nov. 25, 1972; 3 children. BS, Ind. U., 1965, LLD (hon.), 1999; JD, Am. U., 1969; LLD (hon.), U. Indpls., 1984; D in Pub. Svc. (hon.), Butler U., 1987; LLD (hon.), Marian Coll., 1991; LHD, U. Evansville, 1993; LLD (hon.), Wabash Coll., 1999, Hanover Coll., 2001; D of Civil Law (hon.), 2003. Bar: Ind. 1969, U.S. Dist. Ct. (so. dist.) Ind., 1969, U.S. Ct. Appeals (7th cir.) 1973, U.S. Supreme Ct., 1978. Legal asst. to senator U.S. Senate, 1969-71; spl. counsel to minority, govt. ops. com. permanent investigations subcom., 1971-72; dir. rsch. scheduling and advance Senator Percy Re-election Campaign, 1972; asst. U.S. atty. So. Dist. Ind., 1972-76, 1st asst. U.S. atty., 1976-77, U.S. atty., 1981-84; judge U.S. Dist. Ct. (so. dist.) Ind., 1984—, chief judge, 1994—2000. Assoc., then ptnr. Bose, McKinney & Evans, Indpls., 1977-81; mem. long range planning com. Jud. Conf. U.S., 1991-96, exec. com., 1989-91, standing com. fed. rules of practice and procedure, 1987-91, dist. judge rep., 1988-91; mem. jud. coun. 7th cir. Ct. Appeals, 1988-2000, jud. fellows commn. U.S. Supreme Ct., 1993-98; jud. adv. com., sentencing commn., 1995-97, bd. advisors, Ind. U., Purdue U., Indpls., 1989—; mem. pres.'s cabinet Ind. U., 1995—; bd. visitors Ind. U. Sch. of Law, Bloomington, 1984—; bd. dirs. Clarian Health Ptnrs., 1996—, Christian Theol. Sem., 1999-2001; bd. dirs. Einstein Inst. for Sci., Health and the Cts., 2001—. Recipient Peck award Wabash Coll., 1989, Touchstone award Girls Club of Greater Indpls., 1989, Leach Centennial 1st Woman award Valparaiso Law Sch., 1993, Most Influential Women award Indpls. Bus. Jour., 1996, Paul Buchanan award of excellence Indpls. Bar Found., 1998, Thomas J. Hennessy award Ind. U., 1995, Disting. Citizen fellow Ind. U., 1999-2001; named Ind. Woman of Yr., Women in Comm., 1986, Ind. Univ. Disting. Alumni, 1996, Disting. Citizen fellow Ind. U., 1999-2001, Singing Hoosiers Disting. Alumni award Ind. U., 2000, Man for All Seasons award St. Thomas More Soc., 2000. Mem. ABA, Ind. Bar Assn., Indpls. Bar Assn. (Antoinette Dakin Leach award 1993), Fed. Judges Assn. (exec. com., bd. dirs. 2001—), Com. on Budget (judicial conf. 2001-), Einstein Inst. Sci., Health and Cts. (bd. dirs. 2001-), U.S. Judicial Conf. (spl. redaction rev. panel 2000-), Christian Theol. Sem. (bd. trustees 1999-), Lawyers Club, Kiwanis. Republican. Methodist. Office: US Dist Ct 210 US Courthouse 46 E Ohio St Indianapolis IN 46204-1903

BARKER, WILLIAM THOMAS, lawyer; b. Feb. 28, 1947; s. V. Wayne and Cordelia (Whitten) B.; m. June K. Robinson, Jan. 30, 1981. BS, MS, Mich. State U., 1969; JD, U. Calif., Berkeley, 1974. Bar: Calif. 1975, Ill. 1976. Assoc. programmer-analyst Control Data Corp., Sunnyvale, Calif., 1969-71; law clk. Pa. Supreme Ct., Erie, 1974-75; assoc. Sonnenschein Carlin Nath & Rosenthal, Chgo., 1975-82, ptnr., 1982—. Moderator Ill. Ins. Law Forum, Counsel Connect, 1994-98; co-moderator Nat. Ins. Law gen. forum, 1996-98; moderator Ins. Law Forum, Lexis One, 2001. Bd. editors: Def. Counsel Jour., 1987—; editor Bad Faith Law Report, 1999-2001, contbg. editor 1990-99; mem. editl. bd. Ins. Litigation Reporter, 1987—. editl. dir. and sr. contbg. editor, 2001—; editor Covered Events, 1995-96, editor emeritus, 1996—; ins. law publs. bd. Def. Rsch. Inst., 1992-97; contbr. articles to profl. jours. Fellow Am. Bar Found. (life); mem. ABA (chair-elect com. on appellate advocacy, tort and ins. practice sect. 1994-95, chair 1995-96, chair gen. comm. bd. 1996-97), Internat. Assn. Def. Counsel (Yancey Meml. award for best article 1995, chair spl. com. on Amicus Curie 1996-97, chair ad hoc com. on interstate practice 2000-03), Chgo. Coun. Lawyers (sec. 1987-88, bd. govs. 1989-91, chair com. profl. responsibility 1990-95), Chgo. Bar Assn. (chmn. com. constl. law 1984-85), Def. Rsch. Inst., Assn. Profl. Responsibility Lawyers (chair com. on internat. trade in legal svcs. 2002-03), Am. Law Inst. Home: 132 E Delaware Pl Apt 5806 Chicago IL 60611-4951 Office: Sonnenschein Nath Et Al 8000 Sears Tower 233 S Wacker Dr Ste 8000 Chicago IL 60606-6491 Home Phone: 312-943-3703; Office Phone: 312-876-8140. E-mail: wbarker@sonnenschein.com.

BARKLEY, ANDREW PAUL, economics professor; b. Manhattan, Kans., Feb. 5, 1962; s. Paul Weston and Lela Mel (Kelly) B.; m. Mary Ellen Cates, July 14, 1984; children: Katherine Ann, Charles Kelly. BA in Econs., Whitman Coll., 1984; MA in Econs., U. Chgo., 1986, PhD in Econs., 1988. Asst. prof. Kans. State U., Manhattan, 1988-93, assoc. prof., 1993—98, prof., 1998—. Coffman disting. tchg. scholar Kans. State U., 2003—; vis. prof. Quaid-I-Azam U., Islamabad, Pakistan, 1990, U. Ariz., Tucson, 1994—95, U. Cambridge, England, 2002; faculty advisor Pakistan Student Assn., Kans. State U., Agrl. Econs. Club, 1989—94. Assoc. editor Review of Agrl. Econs., 1993—96. Recipient Agrl. and Rural Transp. Rsch. Paper award, 1994; named CASE Kans. Prof. of Yr., 1993. Mem.: Western Agrl. Econs. Assn. (Outstanding Undergrad. Tchg. award 1994), Nat. Agrl. Coll. Tchrs. Assn. (Knight Outstanding Jour. Article award 1992, Ctrl. Region Outstanding Tchr. 1994, Tchr. fellow 1994), Am. Agrl. Econs. Assn. (nat. advisor student sect. 1993—95, Outstanding Undergrad. Tchg. award 1995). Avocations: running, reading, travel. Home: 925 Wildcat Rdg Manhattan KS 66502-2927 Office: Kans State U Dept Agrl Econs Waters Hall Manhattan KS 66506 Office Phone: 785-532-4426. Business E-Mail: barkley@ksu.edu.

BARKLEY, JAMES M., lawyer, real estate company executive; b. 1951; BS, Indiana U., 1974; JD, Indiana U. Sch. of Law, 1977. Staff atty. Melvin Simon & Associates, Inc., Indianapolis, Ind., 1978—84, asst. gen. counsel, 1984—92, gen. counsel, 1992; gen. counsel, sec. Simon Property Group, Inc., Indianapolis, Ind., 1993—. Mem. Am. Coll. of Real Estate Lawyers, 1991—. Bd. dirs. Indiana Chamber of Commerce. Mem.: Indiana State Bar Assn., Indianapolis Bar Assn. Office: Simon Property Group Inc 115 W Wash St Indianapolis IN 46204 Office Phone: 317-636-1600.

BARKMEIER, WAYNE W., dentist, researcher, educator; b. Friend, Nebr., Mar. 29, 1944; m. Carolyn A. Johnsen; children: Kimberly, Jennifer, Wayne Jr. Postgrad., U. ebr., Lincoln, 1962—65; DDS, U. Nebr. Med. Ctr. Coll. Dentistry, 1965—69; MS, U. Tex. Health Sci. Ctr., Houston, 1973—75. Asst. prof., oral surgery Creighton U., 1978—79; pvt. practice Omaha, 1978—82; asst. prof., operative dentistry Creighton U., 1979—82; rsch. dentist L.D. Caulk Divsn., Dentsply Internat., Milford, Del., 1982—85, intramural rsch. mgr., 1985; asst. dean rsch. and assoc. prof. operative dentistry, Sch. Dentistry Creighton U., 1985—87, dir., Ctr. Oral Health Rsch., 1986—95, assoc. dean rsch., Sch. Dentistry, 1991—94, prof., operative dentistry, Sch. Dentistry, 1991—2000, prof. gen. dentistry, Sch. Dentistry, 2000—, dean, Sch. Dentistry, 1994—2005, dean emeritus, 2006—. Cons. on dental materials Nat. Bd. Test Constrn. Com. for Joint Commn. on Nat. Dental Exams.; past mem. Am. Dental Assn. Coun. on Dental Rsch. Mem. editl. bd. Operative Dentistry, article rev. cons. Jour. Am. Dental Assn., Am. Jour. Dentistry, Dental Materials, Jour. Dentistry, Quintessence Internat., Jour. Dental Edn., Mil. Medicine; contbr. more than 140 articles to profl. jours. Active duty USAF, 1969—78, brig. gen. USAFR, 1991—94. Office Phone: 402-280-5262.

BARKSDALE, CLARENCE CAULFIELD, retired banker; b. St. Louis, June 4, 1932; s. Clarence M. and Elizabeth (Caulfield) B.; m. Emily Catlin Keyes, Apr. 4, 1959; children: John Keyes, Emily Shepley. AB, Brown U., 1954; postgrad., Washington U. Law Sch., St. Louis, 1957-58, Rutgers U., 1964, Columbia U. Grad. Sch. Bus., 1968; LLD (hon.), Maryville Coll., St. Louis, 1976, Westminster Coll., Fulton, Mo., 1982, St. Louis U., 1989. From asst. cashier to chmn. bd., CEO Centerre Bank NA (formerly 1st Nat. Bank), St. Louis, 1960—76, chmn. bd., chief exec. officer, 1976-88; vice chmn. Bank of Am. (formerly Boatmen's Bancshares, Inc.), St. Louis, 1988-89; vice chmn. bd. dirs. Washington U., St. Louis, 1989—2005. Bd. dirs. Mo. Bot. Gardens,

Alzheimers Assn., Grand Ctr. Inc., Washington U., Mus. Contemporary Art, St. Louis Boy Scouts. With M.I. US Army, 1954—57. Mem. St. Louis Club, St. Louis Country Club, Bogey Club of St. Louis, Harbor Point Golf Club, Little Harbor Club, Wequetosing Golf Club (Harbor Springs, Mich.), Ocean Club, Gulfstream Golf Club, Gulf Stream Bath and Tennis Club (Delray Beach, Fla.), Alpha Delta Phi. Office: Washington U 7425 Forsyth Blvd Saint Louis MO 63105-2161 Office Phone: 314-935-4389. Business E-Mail: cedgy@wustl.edu.

BARLETT, JAMES EDWARD, data processing executive; b. Akron, Ohio, Jan. 1, 1944; s. Willard Paul and Pauline (Candlish) B.; m. Sue Patterson, June 20, 1964; 1 child, Jamie Catherine BA, U. Akron, 1967, MBA, 1971. Systems analyst B.F. Goodrich, Akron, Ohio, 1962-69; ptnr. Touche Ross & Co., Detroit, 1971-79; 1st. v.p., then sr. v.p. Nat. Bank Detroit, 1979-84; exec. v.p. ops. NBD Bancorp and Nat. Bank Detroit; exec. v.p. worldwide ops. and syss. MasterCard Internat. Corp.; pres., CEO Galileo Internat., Rosemont, Ill., 1994—, chmn., 1997—. Bd. dirs. TeleTech Holdings, Inc., Korn/Ferry Internat., Computer Communications Am., Detroit, Cirrus System, Inc., also vice chmn. Trustee Sta. WTVS-TV, Detroit, 1984—, Detroit Country Day Sch., 1984—. Served to 1st lt. U.S. Army, 1967-69, Vietnam Decorated Bronze Star, Army Commendation medal Mem. Am. Bankers Assn., Mich. Bankers Assn., Detroit Athletic Club, Econ. Club, Bloomfield Hills Country Club, Detroit Club, Bloomfield Open Hunt Club. Republican. Episcopalian. Avocations: jogging; reading. Office: Galileo Internat 9700 W Higgins Rd Rosemont IL 60018

BARLIANT, RONALD, federal judge; b. Chgo., Aug. 25, 1945; s. Lois I. Barliant; children: Claire, Anne. BA in History, Roosevelt U., Chgo., 1966; postgrad., orthwestern U., Chgo., 1966-67; JD, Stanford U., 1969. Bar: Ill. 1969, U.S. Dist. Ct. (no. dist.) Ill., U.S. Ct. Appeals (7th cir.). VISTA vol., staff atty. Cook County Legal Assistance Found., Chgo., 1969-72; assoc. Miller, Shakman, Hamilton and Kurtzon, Chgo., 1972-76, ptnr., 1976-88; judge U.S. Bankruptcy Ct. (no. dist.) Ill., Chgo., 1988—2002; pvt. practice Chgo., 2002—. Adj. prof. debtor-creditor rels. John Marshall Law Sch., 1991-92; bd. dirs. Cook County Legal Assistance Found., 1975-82; gen. counsel Chgo. Coun. Lawyers, 1983-86. Mem. Fed. Bar Assn. (bd. dirs. 1992-94), Nat. Conf. Bankruptcy Judges (bd. govs. 1997—). Avocations: opera, theater, golf, cubs baseball.

BARLOW, JOHN F., automotive glass products company executive; BS in Bus. Mgmt., Fla. So. U. Pres., CEO Western Auto Stores divsn. Western Auto Supply Co.; pres, COO Safelite Glass Corp. and Safelite AutoGlass, 1991, pres., CEO, 1997.

BARMANN, LAWRENCE FRANCIS, historian, educator; b. Maryville, Mo., June 9, 1932; s. Francis Lawrence and Clary Weber (LaMar) B. BA, St. Louis U., 1956, Ph.L., 1957, S.T.L., 1964; MA, Fordham U., 1960; postgrad., Princeton, 1965-66; PhD, Cambridge U., Eng., 1970. Tchr. history St. Louis U. High Sch., 1957-59; asst. prof. history St. Louis U., 1970-73, asso. prof., 1973-78, prof., 1978—, asst. dir. Am. Studies Program, 1981-83, prof. Am. studies, 1981-01, dir. Am. Studies Program, 1983-88, chair dept. Am. studies, 1999—2000, prof. theol. studies, 1996-01, ret., 2001, prof. emeritus, 2002—. Author: Newman at St. Mary's, 1962, Baron Friedrich von Hügel and the Modernist Crisis in England, 1972, The Letters of Baron Friedrich von Hügel and Professor Norman Kemp Smith, 1982; editor Sanctity and Secularity, 1999; contbr. articles profl. jours. Recipient award Mellon Faculty Devel. Fund, 1987, 92, 94, Emerson Electric Outstanding Tchr. award, 1999; rsch. grantee Am. Philos. Soc. PHila., 1971, Beaumont Fund, 1977, 82; Danforth assoc., 1978—. Mem.: Cambridge Soc. (founding 1977), Am. Cath. Hist. Assn., Phi Beta Kappa. Home: 5435 Vicar Ct Saint Louis MO 63119

BARNABY, ALAN, retail executive; BS in Bus. Adminstrn. and Econs., Emporia State U., 1972. Asst. mgr. Home Depot, Inc., Fla., 1983, store mgr. Fla., 1984, regional mgr. South Fla., 1985-88, regional mgr. Atlanta region, 1988-90, dir. store system, 1990-92, labor mgmt., 1992-94, sr. v.p. store ops., 1994-99, pres. Ea. Great Lakes region Mich., 1999—. Office: The Home Depot Inc # 300 12100 Inkster Rd Redford MI 48239-2585

BARNARD, TOM, radio personality; b. Minn. Morning Show host 92 KQRS-FM, Mpls. Recipient Marconi Radio award for Large Market Personality of Yr., Nat. Assn. Broadcasters, 2006. Office: 92 KQRS 2000 SE Elm St Minneapolis MN 55414 Office Phone: 612-617-4000. Office Fax: 612-623-9292. E-mail: morningshow@92kqrs.com.

BARNER, SHARON R., lawyer; BS cum laude, Syracuse U., 1979; JD, U. Mich., 1982. Bar: OH, Ill. Ptnr. Foley & Lardner LLP, Chgo., mem. mng. com., chairperson intellectual property litig. practice group. Contbr. articles to profl. jours. Mem.: ABA, Fed. Bar Assn., Nat. Bar Assn., Ill. State Bar Assn., Grateful Hand Found. (bd. dirs.). Office: Foley & Lardner LLP 321 N Clark St Ste 2800 Chicago IL 60610-4764 Office Phone: 312-832-4569. Business E-Mail: sbarner@foley.com.

BARNES, A. JAMES, dean; b. Napoleon, Ohio, Aug. 30, 1942; s. Albert James and Mary Elizabeth (Morey) Barnes; m. Sarah Jane Hughes, June 19, 1976; children: Morey Elizabeth, Laura LeHardy, Catherine Farrell. BA with high honors, Mich. State U., 1964; JD cum laude, Harvard U., 1967. Asst. prof. bus. adminstrn. Ind. U., 1967—69; trial atty. Dept. Justice, 1969—70, asst. to dep. atty. gen., 1973; asst. to adminstr. EPA, 1970—73; campaign mgr. for Gov. Milliken of Mich., 1974; ptnr. Beveridge, Fairbanks & Diamond, Washington, 1975—81; gen. counsel Dept. Agr., 1981—83; adj. prof. Georgetown U. Sch. Bus. Adminstrn., Washington, 1978—80; gen. counsel to dep. adminstr. EPA, 1983—85, dep. adminstr., 1985—88; dean Sch. Pub. Environ. Adminstrn., prof. pub. and environ. affairs Ind. U., 1988—2000, prof. pub. and environ. affairs, 1988—, adj. prof. law, 2001—. Spl. counsel Beveridge, Fairbanks & Diamond, Washington, 1988—97; cons., mediator, expert witness Nat. Acad. Pub. Adminstrn., 1988—; adj. prof. law Ind. U., 2001—. Co-author: Essentials of Business Law, 1994, Law of Commercial Transactions and Business Associations, 1995, Bus. Law and the Regulatory Environment, 2000, Law for Bus., 2005, Bus. Law: The Ethical, E-Commerce and Internat. Environ., 12th edit., 2004. Del. Ind. Rep. Conv., 1968, Mich. Rep. Conv., 1974. Named Sagamore of Wabash, 2000; recipient Outstanding Tchg. award, Ind. U., 1969, Trustee Tchg. award, Ind. U., 2005. Fellow: Nat. Acad. Pub. Adminstrn.; mem.: Sagamore of Wabash, Vineyard Haven Yacht Club (Mass.), Edgartown (Mass.) Yacht Club, Met. Club (Washington). Office: Ind U SPEA 418 Bloomington IN 47405 Office Phone: 812-856-2188. Business E-Mail: barnesaj@indiana.edu.

BARNES, BRENDA C., food products executive; b. Nov. 11, 1953; m. Randall C. Barnes; 3 children. BA in econ., Augustana Coll., 1975, LHD (hon.), 1997; MBA, Loyola U., 1978. With PepsiCo, 1975—98, v.p. mktg. Frito-Lay, bus. mgr. Wilson Spring Sporting Goods; pres. Pepsi-Cola S., 1992; COO Pepsi-Cola N. Am., 1994—96, pres., CEO, 1996—98; interim pres., COO Starwood Hotels & Resorts Worldwide Inc., 1999—2000; COO Sara Lee Corp., Chgo., 2004—05, pres., 2004—05, chmn., CEO, 2005—. Adj. prof. Kellogg Grad. Sch. Mgmt., 2002, N. Central Coll., 2002; bd. dirs. Avon Products Inc., 1994—2004, The NY Times Co., 1998—2008, Sara Lee Corp., 2004—, Lucas Film, LTD, PepsiAmericas, Inc., Grocery Manufactures Assn. Chair bd. trustees Augustana Coll.; mem. steering com. Kellogg Ctr. for Exec. Women, Northwestern U. Named one of 100 Most Powerful Women, Forbes mag., 2005—07, 50 Women to Watch, Wall Street Journal, 2005, 50 Most Powerful Women in Bus., Fortune mag., 2006. Mem.: Grocery Mfr. Assn. (bd. dir.). Office: Sara Lee Corp 3 First Nat Plz Chicago IL 60602 Office Phone: 312-726-2600.*

BARNES, GALEN R., insurance company executive; b. Vevay, Ind. m. June Ann Ladd; two children. Degree in maths., Ind. U. Actuarial officer Nationwide Mut. Ins. Co., Columbus, Ohio, 1975-81, vice pres. actuary, 1981—83; pres., COO Colonial Ins. Co., Calif., 1983-87; v.p. personal and comml. ins. svcs. Nationwide Ins. Co., Columbus, Ohio, 1987-89, sr. v.p. nationwide personal and comml. ins. svcs., 1989-93; pres., COO Wausau Ins. Co., Columbus, 1993-96; pres. ationwide Ins. Enterprise, 1996-99; pres., COO Nationwide Ins., 1999—. Bd. dirs. Ohio Dominican Coll., Franklin County United Way, Arthur C. James Cancer Hosp. Fellow Casualty Actuarial Soc., Am. Acad. Actuaries, Nat. Urban League Bd. Office: Nationwide Mut Ins Co 1 Nationwide Plz Columbus OH 43215-2220

BARNES, HARPER HENDERSON, critic, editor, writer; b. Greensboro, NC, July 2, 1937; s. Bennett Harper and Cora Emmaline Barnes; m. Janice Stauffacher, May 10, 1961 (div. 1985); m. Roseann Marie Weiss, May 31, 1986. Critic, reporter St. Louis Post-Dispatch, 1965-70, editor, critic, 1973-97; editor The Phoenix, Boston, 1970-72, St. Louis mag., 1997-99; pvt. practice St. Louis, 1999—. Instr. Washington U., St. Louis, 1990, 94. Author: Blue Monday, 1991, Standing on a Volcano, 2001. With U.S. Army, 1959-62. Avocations: bicycling, fishing. Office Phone: 314-535-9393. Personal E-mail: hbarnesl@mindspring.com.

BARNES, JAMES BYRON, university president; b. Akron, Ohio, Apr. 4, 1942; s. Roy and Kathleen (Elrod) B.; m. Tommie Schade, Aug. 14, 1965. AB in Social Sci., Ind. Wesleyan U., 1965; MEd in History, Kent State U., 1969; Ed.S. in History and Social Sci., Vanderbilt U., 1972; EdD in Social Sci. Edn., U. Ga., 1976. Assoc. prof. Cen. (S.C.) Wesleyan Coll., 1970-76, Ind. Wesleyan U., Marion, 1976-81, dean of coll., 1981-84; asst. gen sec. Dept. Edn. and Ministry Wesleyan Ch., Marion, 1984-85; v.p. acad. affairs Houghton (N.Y.) Coll., 1985-87; pres. Ind. Wesleyan U., Marion, 1987—. Mem. Grant Co. Community Found., Marion, 1987—; mem. adv. bd. Salvation Army, 1989—. Grantee NEH, 1987. Mem. Rotary, Marion/Grant County C. of C. Mem. Wesleyan Ch. Office: Ind Wesleyan U 4201 S Washington St Rm 4990 Marion IN 46953-4990

BARNES, JAMES GARLAND, JR., lawyer; b. Ga., Mar. 3, 1940; s. James Garland Sr. and Carolyn L. (Stewart) B.; m. Lucy Curtis Ferguson, Nov. 1976; children: Susan Whitney, David Lawrence, Matthew Martin. BA, Yale U., 1961; LLB, U. Mich., 1966. Bar: Ill. 1967. With firm Baker & McKenzie, Chgo., 1966—, ptnr., 1973—. Co-author: The ABCs of the UCC Article 5: Letters of Credit. Mem. adv. com. Ill. Sec. of State's Corp. Acts, 1981-95; U.S. del. to UN Commn. on Internat. Trade Law, Internat. C. of C., 1994-2000. Mem. ABA (chmn. letter of credit subcom. 1991-96), Ill. Bar Assn. (chmn. corp. and security law sect. 1977-78), Chgo. Bar Assn. (chmn. corp. law com. 1982-83, chmn. profl. responsibility com. 1983-84), Legal Club Chgo. Office: Baker & McKenzie 1 Prudential Pla 130 E Randolph St Ste 3700 Chicago IL 60601-6342 E-mail: james.g.barnes@bakernet.com.

BARNES, JAMES JOHN, historian, educator; b. St. Paul, Nov. 16, 1931; s. Harry George and Bertha (Blaul) B.; m. Patience Rogers Plummer, July 9, 1955; children— Jennifer Chase, Geoffrey Prescott BA, Amherst Coll., 1954, New Coll., Oxford, 1956, MA, 1961; PhD, Harvard U., 1960; DHL, Coll. of Wooster, 1976, Amherst Coll., 1999. Instr. history Amherst Coll., 1959-62; asst. prof. history Wabash Coll., Crawfordsville, Ind., 1962-67, assoc. prof. history, 1967-76, prof. history, 1976—2006, prof. emeritus, 2006—, chmn. dept. history, Hadley prof., 1979-97. Author: Free Trade in Books: A Study of the London Book Trade since 1800, 1964, Authors, Publishers and Politicians: The Quest for an Anglo-American Copyright Agreement 1815-54, 1974, (with Patience P. Barnes) Hitler's Mein Kampf in Britain and America 1930-39, 1980, (with Patience P. Barnes) James Vincent Murphy: Translator and Interpreter of Fascist Europe, 1880-1946, 1987, (with Patience P. Barnes) Private and Confidential Letters from British Ministers in Washington to the Foreign Secretaries in London, 1849-67, 1993, (with Patience P. Barnes) Nazi Refugee turned Gestapo Spy: The Life of Hans Wesemann, 1895-1971, 2001, (with Patience P. Barnes) The American Civil War through British Eyes: Dispatches from British Diplomats, vol. 1: Nov. 1860-Apr. 1862, 2003, vol. 2: April 1862-February 1863, 2005, vol. 3: February 1863-December 1865, 2005; (with Patience P. Barnes) Nazis in Pre-War London 1930-1939: The Fate and Rule of German Party Members and British Sympathizers, 2005; contbr. articles to profl. jours. Mem. Rhodes Scholar Selection Com. for Ind., 1965-89, Crawfordsville Cmty. Action Coun., 1966-69, Crawfordsville Cmty. Day Care Com., 1966-67; mem. vestry St. John's Episcopal Ch., 1966-69; mem. Ind. Adv. Com. State Rehab. Svcs. for Blind, 1979-81; trustee Ind. Hist. Soc., 1982—. Recipient Disting. Alumni award St. Paul Acad. and Summit Sch., 1989; Rhodes scholar, 1954-56, Fulbright scholar, 1978; Woodrow Wilson fellow, 1956-57, Kent fellow, 1958, Great Lakes Colls. Assn. Teaching fellow, 1958, Great Lakes Colls. Assn. Teaching fellow, 1975; rsch. grantee Amherst Coll., 1960-61, Social Sci. Rsch. Coun., 1962, 70, Wabash Coll., 1962—, Am. Coun. Learned Socs., 1964-65, 80, Am. Philos. Soc., 1964, 68, 76, 91; named Hon. Alumnus, Wabash Coll., 1994. Mem. Am. Hist. Assn., Ouiatenon Literary Soc., Conf. Brit. Studies, Rsch. Soc. Victorian Periodicals, Am. Rhodes Scholars, Soc. Historians Am. Fgn. Rels., Ind. Hist. Soc., Montgomery County Hist. Soc., Midwest Victorian Studies Assn. (pres. 1989-91), Ind. Assn. Historians, N.E. Victorian Studies Assn., Soc. for History of Authorship, Reading and Pub., Am. Coun. of Blind, Royal Over-Seas League (London), United Oxford and Cambridge Club of London, Phi Beta Kappa. Home: 7 Locust Hl Crawfordsville IN 47933-3347 Office: Wabash Coll History Dept Crawfordsville IN 47933 Office Phone: 765-361-6319. Business E-Mail: barnesj@wabash.edu.

BARNES, JAMES MILTON, retired physics and astronomy professor; b. Ypsilanti, Mich., July 5, 1923; s. J. Milton and Elsie (Fischer) B.; m. Marjorie Ruth Petersen, Dec. 17, 1949. BS, Eastern Mich. U., 1948; MS, Mich. State U., 1950, PhD, 1955. Asst. prof. Ea. Mich. U., Ypsilanti, 1955—58, assoc. prof., 1958—61, prof., 1961—88, head, dept. physics and astronomy, 1961—74, prof. emeritus, 1988—. With AUS, 1942—46. Mem. A.A.A.S. (life), Nat. Sci. Tchrs. Assn. (life), Am. Assn. Physics Tchrs., Sigma Xi, Sigma Pi Sigma, Pi Mu Epsilon. Clubs: Ann Arbor (Mich.) Country. Home: 4872 N Whitman Cir Ann Arbor MI 48103-9774 Office: Eastern Mich U Physics Dept Ypsilanti MI 48197

BARNES, KAREN KAY, lawyer; b. June 22, 1950; d. Walter William and Vashti (Greenlee) Sessler; m. James Alan Barnes, Feb. 12, 1972; children: Timothy Matthew, Christopher Michael. BA, Valparaiso U., 1971; JD, DePaul U., 1978, LLM in Taxation, 1980. Bar: Ill. 1978, U.S. Dist. Ct. (no. dist.) Ill. 1978. Ptnr. McDermott, Will & Emory, Chgo., 1978-88; prin. William M. Mercer, Inc. and predecessor firm, Chgo., 1989-93; staff dir. legal dept. McDonald's Corp., Oak Brook, Ill., 1993-95, home office dir. legal dept., 1995-97, mng. counsel, 1998—. Instr. John Marshall Grad. Sch. Law, Chgo., 1986-87; mem. adv. bd. John Marshall Sch. Law, 1996-2004; bd. dirs. Flutes Unlimited; mem. adv. bd. dirs. Plan Sponsor Mag., 2000-; mem. defined contbn. adv. bd. Internat. Bus. Forum, Inc., 2004-. Contbr. case note to DePaul Law Rev., 1976, note and comment editor DePaul Law Rev., 1976-77, editor Taxation For Lawyers, 1986-88; mem. editl. adv. bd. Thompson Pub. Co. retirement plan comms., 2005—. Named Super Lawyer in Ill., 2008; named one of 50 Most Influential People in 401(k) Industry, 401(k) Wire, 2007. Mem. Am. Coll. Employee Benefit Counsel (bd. dirs. 2006-), Chgo. Bar Assn. (chair employee benefits com. 1991-92, co-chair symphony orch. 1999-2001), Midwest Pension Conf. (name changed to Midwest Benefits Coun.), WEB (pres. Chgo. chpt. 1986-88, v.p. nat. bd. 1988, pres. 1989-90, mem. adv. bd. 2001—), Profit Sharing Coun. Am. (legal and legis. com. 1994—, bd. dirs. 1997-2004, 06-, 2d vice chair 1997-98, 1st vice chair 1998-2000, chair 2000-02). Lutheran. Home: 586 Crescent Blvd # 402 Glen Ellyn IL 60137 Office: McDonald's Corp 2915 Jorie Blvd Oak Brook IL 60523 Business E-Mail: karen.barnes@us.mcd.com.

BARNES, KAY, former mayor; b. Mar. 30, 1938; BS in Secondary Edn., U. Kans.; MS in Secondary Edn. and Pub. Adminstrn., U. Mo., Kansas City. Staff mem. Westport area Cross-Lines Coop. Coun.; pres. Kay Waldo, Inc., human resources devel. co., Kansas City, Mo.; mayor City of Kansas City, Mo., 1999—2007; candidate for U.S. Congress, 2007. Condr. over 400 pub. seminars Nat. Seminars, Inc.; cons., keynote spkr. 14 reginal confs. through U.S., Am. Bus. Women's Assn.; former co-host, prodr. cable TV show Let's Talk; former instr. U. Mo., Kansas City, U. Kans., Ctrl. Mich. U. Author: About Time! A Woman's Guide to Time Management. Co-founder Ctrl. Exch.; vol. Cross-Lines Coop. Coun.; a founder women's resource svc. U. Mo., Kansas City; developer multicultural women's speaking panels through western U.S.; mem. Jackson County (Mo.) Legislature, from 1974; mem. Kansas City City Coun., from 1979; chmn. Tax Increment Financing Commn., 1993-97; pres. bd. dirs. Women's Employment Network; mem. or dir. numerous other orgns., including Women's Found. Greater Kansas City, Greater Kansas City Sports Commn.; mem. chancellor's adv. bd. of Women's Ctr., U. Mo., Kansas City; co-chair of the US Conf. of Mayors Small Business/Partner America Task Force, mem. of the Conference's Community Development and Housing Standing Com.; serves Nat. Adv. Coun. of Fannie Mae. Named One of 7 Outstanding Women in Kansas City, 1977. Mem. Greater Kansas City C. of C. (com.). Home: Kay for Congress PO Box 14194 Kansas City MO 64152 Office Fax: 816-513-3518. Business E-Mail: mayor@kcmo.org.

BARNES, MICHAEL PHILLIP, judge; b. Peoria, Ill., Dec. 2, 1947; s. Lee Benedict and Alice Gertrude (Gorman) Barnes; m. Alberta R. Barnes, Aug. 7, 1971; children: Timothy L., John P. BA in History, St. Ambrose Coll., Davenport, Iowa, 1970; JD, U. Notre Dame, 1973. Pvt. practice St. Joseph County, South Bend, Ind., 1973—78, dep. pros. atty., 1973—78, pros. atty., 1978—98; judge Ind. Ct. of Appeals, 2000—. Chmn. Ind. Pros. Attys. Coun., Indpls., 1982—83, Indpls., 1992—93, Ind. State Correction Adv. Com., 1989, Am. Pros. Rsch. Inst., Alexandria, Va., 1996—97; pres. St. Joseph County Bar Assn., South Bend, 1992—93, Nat. Dist. Attys. Assn., Alexandria, 1995—96; chmn. resource mgmt. com. Ind. Ct. Appeals, 2001—02, chmn. continuous improvement com., 2005. Bd. dirs. Am. Cancer Soc., 1981-83, Alcoholism Coun. of St. Joseph County, 1983, Corvilla Inc., 1984; adv. bd. Community Based Corrections Project, 1983, Ind. U. at South Bend Paralegal Studies Prog., 1985; co-chmn. Nat. Child Abuse Prevention Wk., 1982; steering com. Community Edn. Roundtable Prog., Ind. U., 1986; adv. bd. Dismas House, 1989-90. Named Citizen of the Yr., Nat. Assn. Social Workers, 1990, Pacesetter award, Ind. Coalition Against Domestic Violence, 1989, Spl. Advocate award, Ind. Victim Assistance network, 1989, Domestic Violence Coalition Inc. award for outstanding svc., 1989, Community Svc. award, Better Bus. Bur., 1988, DAR Law Enforcement medal, 1987, Gov.'s award for exemplary project, Pretrial Diversion Prog., 1987, Community Svc. award, many others. Mem. Ind. Prosecuting Attys. Coun. (pres. 1982-83, ethics com. 1985), Ind. Bar Assn. (ethics com. 1986), Nat. Dist. Attys. Assn. (bd. dirs. 1987, pres. 1995-96), Ind. Criminal Justice Inst. (bd. dirs. 1989), St. Joseph County Bar assn., Ind. Bar Assn., Ill. Bar Assn., Nat. Dist. Attys. Assn. (pres. 1995-96), Ind. Judges Assn. Home: Ste 1270 115 W Washington St Indianapolis IN 46204-3419 Business E-Mail: mbarnes@courts.state.in.us.

BARNES, PAUL MCCLUNG, lawyer; b. Phila., June 27, 1914; s. Andrew Wallace and Luella Hope (Andrew) B.; m. Elizabeth McClenahan, Dec. 28, 1940 (dec.); children: Andrew M., Margaret L. Lenart, James D., John R. (dec.); m. Vera Prokop/Keller, Feb. 24, 2005. BA, Monmouth Coll., Ill., 1936; JD, U. Chgo., 1939. Bar: Colo. bar 1939. Assoc. Bannister & Bannister, Denver, 1939-40, Foley & Lardner, Milw., 1940-47, ptnr., 1948-88, of counsel, 1988—. Dir. Wis. Public Service Corp., 1974-77, Kickhaefer Mfg. Co., 1965-85, Attys. Liability Assurance Soc., Ltd., 1979-87; sec. Sta-Rite Industries, Inc., 1965-73 Mem. adv. bd. Milw. Protestant Home, 1975-87. Served with USNR, 1942-45. Mem. ABA, Wis. Bar Assn., Order of Coif. Office: Foley & Lardner 777 E Wisconsin Ave Ste 3800 Milwaukee WI 53202-5367 Personal E-mail: pbarnes@webtv.net.

BARNES, RICHARD GEORGE, physicist, researcher; b. Milw., Dec. 19, 1922; s. George Richard and Irma (Ott) B.; m. Mildred A. Jachens, Sept. 9, 1950; children: Jeffrey R., David G., Christina E., Douglas A. BA, U. Wis., 1948; MA, Dartmouth Coll., 1949; PhD, Harvard U., 1952. Teaching fellow Harvard, 1950-52; asst. prof. U. Del., 1952-55, asso. prof., 1955-56, Iowa State U., 1956-60, prof., 1960-88, chmn. dept. physics, 1971-75, prof. emeritus, 1988—; sr. physicist Ames Lab., U.S. Dept. Energy, 1960-88; assoc. Ames lab. US Dept. Energy, 1988—; chief physics divsn. Ames lab. AEC, 1971-75. Vis. rsch. prof. Calif. Inst. Tech., 1962-63; guest profl. Tech. U. Darmstadt, Germany, 1975-76; vis. prof. Cornell U., 1982-83; program dir. solid state physics NSF, 1988-89, condensed matter physics NSF, 1995; chmn. Metal Hydrides Gordon Rsch. Conf., 1987. Served with USAAF, 1942-43; C.E. AUS, 1944-46 (Manhattan Project). Recipient U.S. Sr. Scientist award Alexander von Humboldt Found., 1975-76 Fellow Am. Phys. Soc. Office: Iowa State U Physics Dept Ames IA 50011-0001

BARNES, ROBERT F, agronomist; b. Estherville, Iowa, Feb. 6, 1933; s. Chester Arthur and Pearl Adella (Stoelting) B.; m. Bettye Jeanne Burrell, June 25, 1955; children: Bradley R., Rebecca L. Reinalda, Roberta K. Nixon, Brian L. AA, Estherville Jr. Coll., 1953; BS, Iowa State U., 1957; MS, Rutgers U., 1959; PhD, Purdue U., 1963. Rsch. agronomist USDA-Agrl. Rsch. Svc., West Lafayette, Ind., 1959-70, lab. dir. University Park, Pa., 1970-75, staff scientist nat. program staff Beltsville, Md., 1975-79, assoc. dep. adminstr. So. region New Orleans, 1979-84, dep. adminstr. So. region, 1984-86; exec. v.p. Am. Soc. Agronomy, Madison, Wis., 1986-99; exec. dir. Agronomic Sci. Found., exec. dir. emeritus, 1999—; also fellow Am. Soc. of Agronomy, Madison, Wis. Asst. prof. Purdue U., West Lafayette, 1963-66; assoc. prof., 1966-70; adj. prof. Pa. State U., University Park, 1966-70; adj. prof. agronomy U. Wis., Madison, 1986-99; pres. Internat. Grassland Congress, Lexington, Ky., 1981; cons. Agronomic Sci. Found., Am. Soc. Agronomy. Editor: Forages, 1973, 85, 95, 2003; contbr. articles to profl. jours. With U.S. Army, 1953-55, Germany. Recipient H.S. Stubbs Meml. Lecture award Tropical Grassland Soc., Brisbane, Australia, 1984, Henry A. Wallace award Iowa State U., 1991; Robert F Barnes Grad. Edn. Award for forage and grazing lands established in his name, 2004. Fellow AAAS, Crop Sci. Soc. Am. (pres. 1984-85); mem. Am. Forage and Grassland Coun. (medallion 1981, Disting. Grasslander award 2001), Grazing Lands Forum (pres. 1986-87), Forage and Grassland Found. (pres. 1993-97). Avocations: walking, reading. Personal E-mail: rbarnes0206@sbcglobal.net.

BARNES, ROSEMARY LOIS, minister; b. Grand Rapids, Mich., Sept. 17, 1946; d. Floyd Herman and Cora Agnes (Beukema) Herms; m. Louis Herbert Adams, Feb. 22, 1969 (div. Oct. 1976); 1 child, Louis Herbert Jr.; m. Robert Jearold Barnes, Oct. 8, 1976. BA, Calvin Coll., 1968; D of Practical Ministry, Wagner Leadership Inst., 2004. Ordained to ministry Home Ministry Fellowship, 1980; cert. social worker. Group worker Kent County Juvenile Ct., Grand Rapids, Mich., 1966-68; tchr. Sheldon Elem. Sch., Grand Rapids, 1968-69; social worker Kent Dept. Social Services, Grand Rapids, 1969-75, 75-84; tchr., mission worker Emmanuel House, San Diego, 1975; co-pastor, founder River of Life Ministries, Grand Rapids, 1980—; instr. Gt. Lakes Inst. Bible Studies, Grand Rapids, 1988; pres., exec. dir. Home Ministry Fellowship, Inc., 2006—. Tchr., founder River of Life Sch. Christian Leadership, Grand Rapids, 1981—; v.p. Aglow, Grand Rapids, 1982-83; sec., treas. Western Mich. Full Gospel Ministers Fellowship, Grand Rapids, 1984-85; mem. bd. chaplains Dunes Correctional Facility, Saugatuck, Mich., 1986-91; coord. 1988 Washington for Jesus March, One Nation Under God, Inc.; co-pastor Gun Lake River of Life, 1988; prof. Great Lakes Inst., 1988; county coord. Grand Rapids Full Gospel Ministers Fellowship, 1990-92; co-pastor Defiance, Ohio River of Life, 1992-93; founder St. Joseph Sch. Christian Leadership. Participant TV show Ask the Pastor, 1993—; dir., prodr. TV show River Reflections, 1994—; Mich. women's coord. Let The Redeemed of the Lord Say So, 1994; sponsor Grand Rapids cable TV Jewish Jewels, 1995—. Bd. dirs. Alcohol Incentive Ladder, Grand Rapids, 1979; overseer River City Outreach Ch., 1994-99; pres./exec. dir. Home Ministry Fellowship Inc., 2006—. Mem. Women in Leadership. Republican. Mem. Ind. Charismatic Ch. Avocation: playing the trumpet. Address: PO Box 140735 Grand Rapids MI 49514-0735 Office Phone: 616-540-1766. Personal E-mail: RBarnesROL@aol.com.

BARNES, THOMAS JOHN, lawyer; b. Grand Rapids, Mich., Apr. 1, 1943; s. James and Adeline (Molenda) B.; m. Lynn Marie Owens, Aug. 19, 1967; children: Nicolle, Cynthia. BA in Acctg., Mich. State U., 1965, BA in Polit. Sci., 1966; JD, Wayne State U., 1972. Bar: Mich. 1972, U.S. Dsit. Ct. (ea. and we. dists.) Mich. 1972, U.S. Ct. Appeals (6th cir.) 1974, U.S. Dist. Ct. (no. dist.) Ind. 1994, U.S. Ct. Appeals (7th cir.) 1995. Ptnr. Varnum, Riddering, Schmidt & Howlett, Grand Rapids, 1972—. Arbitrator Mich. Employment Rels. Commn.; spkr. in field. Editor-in-chief Wayne Law Rev.; contbr. articles to profl. jours. Named a Leading Mich. Lawyer, Chambers; named one of Best Lawyers in Am., Michs. 100 Super Lawyers. Fellow Coll. Labor and Employment Lawyers; mem. ABA (nat. labor rels. bd. practice and procedures com.), Mich. Bar Assn. (labor coun., sec., treas. 1987-88, chmn. 1989-90), Grand Rapids Bar Assn. (former chair labor sect.) Roman Catholic. Avocations: reading, horse racing, sports. Office: 333 Bridge St NW Grand Rapids MI 49504 Home Phone: 616-868-6825; Office Phone: 616-336-6621. Business E-Mail: tjbarnes@varnumlaw.com.

BARNES, VIRGIL EVERETT, II, physics professor; b. Galveston, Tex., Nov. 2, 1935; s. Virgil Everett and Mildred Louise (Adlof) B.; m. Barbara Ann Green, 1957 (dec. 1964); 1 son, Virgil Everett III; m. Linda Dwight Taylor, 1970; children— Christopher Richard Dwight, Charles Jeffrey, Daniel Woodbridge. AB magna cum laude with highest honors, Harvard U., 1957; PhD, Cambridge U., Eng., 1962. Rsch. assoc. Brookhaven Nat. Lab., Upton, NY, 1962-64, asst. physicist, 1964-66, assoc. physicist, 1966-69; mem. faculty Purdue U., 1969—, prof. physics, 1979—; asst. dean Purdue U. (Sch. Sci.), 1974-78. Cons. in field. Author papers on exptl. high energy particle physics. NSF predoctoral fellow

Gonville and Caius Coll., Cambridge U., 1959-62; Marshall scholar Cambridge U., 1957-59; recipient Perkin Elmer prize Harvard U., 1956, Top Ten winner U.S. Westinghouse Sci. Talent Search, 1953. Mem. AAAS, AAUP, Am. Phys. Soc., N.Y. Acad. Scis., Phi Beta Kappa, Sigma Xi. Office: Purdue U Dept Physics West Lafayette IN 47907

BARNES, W. MICHAEL, electronics executive; B in Indsl. Engring., M in Indsl. Engring., Tex. A&M U., PhD in Ops. Rsch., 1968. Expert cons. Asst. Postmaster Gen., Washington; corp. ops. rsch. staff Collins Radio Co. now Rockwell Internat., 1968-72; dir. fin. MOS/Components Divsn. Rockwell Internat., Newport Beach, Calif., 1972-73; contr. Rockwell's Collins Comm. Switching Sys. Divsn., 1973-74, Rockwell Electronic Sys. Group, Dallas, 1974-77; v.p., gen. mgr. Rockwell's Collins Comm. Switching Sys. Divsn., 1977-82; v.p. fin. Rockwell's Telecom. Group, 1982-85, v.p. mktg. and bus. devel., 1985-89; corp. v.p. bus. devel. and planning Rockwell Internat. Corp., 1989-91, sr. v.p. fin. and planning, CFO, 1991—2001. Vis. prof. computer scis. So. Meth. U.; instr. maintainability engring. U.S. Army Logistics Tng. Ctr., Red River Depot; bd. dir. Advanced Micro Devices, Archer Daniels Midland Co., A.O. Smith Corp. amed Disting. Alumni, Tex. A&M U. Coll. Engring., 1992 Mem. Coun. Fin. Execs. (chmn. conf. bd. 1996). Mailing: AMD Bd Directors 1 AMD Pl PO Box 3453 Sunnyvale CA 94088-3453

BARNETT, JAMES A., state legislator; m. Yvonne Barnett. Mem. Kans. State Senate, 2001—, vice chair pub. health and welfare com., mem. fed. and state affairs com., mem. fin. instns. and ins. com., mem. health care reform legis. oversight com. Home: 1400 Lincoln Emporia KS 66801 Office: Ste 202 1301 W 12th Emporia KS 55801 Fax: 316-342-6520. E-mail: jbarnett@cadvantage.com, barnett@senate.state.ks.us.

BARNETT, MARILYN, advertising executive; b. Detroit; d. Henry and Kate (Boesky) Schiff; children: Rhona, Ken. BA, Wayne State U. Founder, part-owner, pres. Mars Advt. Co., Southfield, Mich. Bd. dirs. Mich. Strategic Fund; apptd. to Mich. bi-lateral trade team with Germany. Named Outstanding Retail Woman of Yr., Outstanding Retail Mktg. Exec., Oakland U., Entrepreneur of Yr., Oakland Exec. of Yr.; named to Mich.'s Top 25 Women Bus. Owners List. Mem. AFTRA (dir.), SAG, Exec. Women Am., Am. Women in Radio & TV (Top Agy. Mgmt. award, Outstanding Woman of Yr.), Internat. Women Forum, Com. of 200, Women's Econ. Club (Ad Woman of Yr.), Adcraft. Office: Mars Advt 25200 Telegraph Rd Southfield MI 48034-7496 Office Phone: 248-936-2234. Business E-Mail: barnettm@marsusa.com.

BARNETT, MARK WILLIAM, former state attorney general; b. Sioux Falls, SD, Sept. 6, 1954; s. Thomas C. and Dorothy Ann (Lievrance) Barnett; m. Deborah Ann Barnett, July 14, 1979. BS in Govt., U. S.D., 1976, JD, 1978. Bar: S.D. Pvt. practice, Sioux Falls, 1978—80; asst. atty. gen. State of S.D., Pierre, 1980—83, spl. prosecutor, 1984—90; ptnr. Schmidt, Schroyer, Colwill and Barnett, Pierre, 1984—90; atty. gen. State of S.D., Pierre, 1991—2003. Mem. S.D. Bar Commn., 1986—92, S.D. Law Enforcement Tng. Commn., 1987, S.D. Corrections Commn., 1987. Bd. dirs. D.A.R.E. Mem.: State's Atty. Assn. (bd. dirs. 1987—90), Am. Judicature Soc. (nat. bd. dirs. 1984—88), S.D. Bar Assn. (pres. young lawyers' sect. 1985). Republican. Avocations: golf, weightlifting, snowmobiling.

BARNETT, REX, state legislator; Mem. from dist. 4 Mo. State Ho. of Reps., 1995—. Home: 708 W Lincoln St Maryville MO 64468-2748 Office: State Capitol House Post Office House Post Office Rm 116-a2 Jefferson City MO 65101-1556

BARNETT, THOMAS GLEN, manufacturing executive; b. Olney, Ill., Aug. 15, 1946; s. Burl and Florence Ann (Gant) B.; m. Diana Kay O'Dell, Jan. 27, 1968; children— Kevin Thomas, Kelli Lyn. BS in Acctg., Millikin U., Decatur, Ill., 1968. C.P.A., Mo., Ill. Staff acct. Arthur Young & Co. (C.P.A.'s), Chgo., 1968-70, sr. acct., 1970-73, audit mgr., 1973-75; dir. internal audit Chromalloy Am. Corp., St. Louis, 1975-76, asst. controller, 1976-78, v.p., controller, 1978-80, exec. v.p. fin., 1979-87; chief fin. officer Marsh Co., Belleville, Ill., 1987-92, pres., chief operating officer, 1992—99; pres., CEO Union Fin. Group, 1999—2002; pres. Barnett & Assocs., LLC, 2002—04; pres., COO Jims Formal Wear, 2004—. Bd. dir. Jr. Achievement Gateway East, Belleville, 1988-95, United Way Metro East, Belleville, 1988-95, Meml. Hosp., 1991—, Mem. Found., Inc., 1990-95. Mem. AICPA, Fin. Execs. Inst., Mo. Soc. C.P.A.s, St. Clair Country Club (pres. 1988-89). Republican. Presbyterian. Office: One Tuxedo Park Trenton IL 62293 Home Phone: 618-397-5878; Office Phone: 618-224-9211 ext. 3131. Business E-Mail: tombarnett@jimsfw.com.

BARNETT, WILLIAM ARNOLD, economics professor; b. Boston, Oct. 30, 1941; s. Marcus Jack and Elizabeth Leah (Forman) B.; m. Melinda Gentry, Sept. 1, 1991. BS, MIT, 1963; MBA, U. Calif., Berkeley, 1965; MS, Carnegie Mellon U., 1972, PhD, 1974. System devel. engr., Apollo Project, Rocketdyne div. Rockwell Internat. Corp., Canoga Park, Calif., 1963-67; research econometrician Bd. Govs., Fed. Reserve System, Washington, 1973-81; Stuart Centennial prof. econs. U. Tex., Austin, 1981-90; prof. econs. Washington U., St. Louis, 1990—; Oswald Disting. prof. macroeconomics U. of Kans., 2002—. Vis. prof. econs. U. Aix-Marseille, Aix-en-Provence, France, 1979, Duke U., Durham, N.C., 1987-88; organizer ann. symposia in econ. theory and econometrics; assoc. dir. Ctr. for Econ. Rsch., U. Tex., Austin, 1981-90. Author: Consumer Demand and Labor Supply, 1981; editor Jour. Econometrics, 1979-80, 85, Cambridge U. Press Monograph series, 1985—, Cambridge U. Press Jour. Macroeconomic Dynamics, 1997—; assoc. editor Jour. Bus. and Econ. Stats., 1982-97; contbr. over 75 articles to profl. jours. Contract selection panel mem. NIH, Washington, 1983; cons. World Bank, Washington, 1985. R.K. Mellon Found. fellow, 1971-73; rsch. grantee NSF, Washington, 1977-89, Hogg Found., Houston, 1983. Fellow ICC Inst. (sr., editor 1983—), Am. Statis. Assn. (assoc. editor 1982—, fellow 1989—, program chair 1992—), Jour. Econometrics (charter fellow 1989—); mem. Inst. Math. Stats., Econometric Soc. (contbr. to jour.), Am. Econ. Assn Home: 1904 Inverness Dr Lawrence KS 66047-1832 Office: U Kans Dept Econs Lawrence KS 66045

BARNEY, CAROL ROSS, architect; b. Chgo., Apr. 12, 1949; d. Chester Albert and Dorothy Valeria (Dusiewicz) Ross; m. Alan Fredrick Barney, Mar. 22, 1970; children: Ross Fredrick, Adam Shafer, John Ross. BArch, U. Ill., 1971. Registered architect, Ill. Assoc. architect Holabird & Root, Chgo., 1972-79; prin. architect Orput Assoc., Inc., Wilmette, Ill., 1979-81; prin. architect, pres. Ross Barney Arch., Chgo., 1981—, also bd. dirs. Studio prof. Ill. Inst. Tech., Chgo., 1993-94; asst. prof. U. Ill., Chgo., 1976-78. Prin. works include Glendale Heights Post Office, Ill., Little Village Acad. Pub. Sch., Fed. Bldg., Oklahoma City, Swenson Sci. Bldg., U. Md. Plan commr. Village of Wilmette, 1986-88, mem. Econ. Devel. Commn., 1988-90, chmn. Appearance Rev. Commn., 1990-2000; trustee Children's Home and Aid Soc. Ill., Chgo., 1986—; mem. adv. bd. Small Bus. Ctr. for Women, Chgo., 1985—. Recipient Fed. Design Achievement award, 1992; Francis J. Plym travelling fellow, 1983. Fellow AIA (bd. dirs. Chgo. chpt. 1978-80, v.p. 1981-82, Disting. Svc. award Chgo. chpt. 1978, Ill. Coun. 1978, Firm award 1995, Honor award 1991, 94, 99, 2002, Thomas Jefferson award for pub. architecture 2005); mem. Nat. Coun. Archtl. Registration Bds. (cert.), Chgo. Women in Architecture (founding pres. 1978-79), Chgo. Network, Cliff Dwellers Club (bd. dirs. 1995). Home: 601 Linden Ave Wilmette IL 60091-2819 Office: Ross Barney Architects 10 W Hubbard St Chicago IL 60610 Office Phone: 312-832-0600 ext. 221. Business E-Mail: crb@r-barc.com.

BARNEY, CHARLES RICHARD, retired transportation executive; b. Battle Creek, Mich., June 7, 1935; s. Charles Ross and Helena Ruth (Croose) Barney; m. Grace Leone ightingale, Aug. 16, 1958; children: Richard Nolan, Patricia Lynn. BA, Mich. State U., 1957; MBA, Wayne State U., 1961. Fin. analyst Ford Motor Co., Dearborn, Mich., 1958—65; gen. mgr. RentCo divsn. Fruehauf Corp., Detroit, 1965—72; pres. Evans Trailer Leasing, Des Plaines, Ill., 1973—77; v.p., gen. mgr. U.S. Rlwy. Equipment Co., Des Plaines, 1972—77; pres. Evans Railcar divsn. Evans Trans. Co., 1978—84; pres. W.H. Miner divsn. Miner Enterprises, Geneva, Ill., 1985—2000; ret., 2000. Mem. exec. com. Rlwy. Progress Inst., 1984—2000, chmn., 1990—. Served to 1st lt. inf. US Army, 1958. Mem.: Ry. Supply Assn. (bd. dirs. 1977—80), Wildcat Run Country Club (bd. dirs. 2003—). Congregationalist. Home: 404 Cardiff Rd Venice FL 34293-4305

BARNHILL, CHARLES JOSEPH, JR., lawyer; b. Indpls., May 22, 1943; s. Charles J. and Phyllis (Landis) Barnhill; m. Elizabeth Louise Hayek, Aug. 14, 1971; children: Eric Charles, Colin Landis. BS in Econs., U. Pa., 1965; JD, U. Mich., 1968. Bar: Ill. 1968, U.S. Dist. Ct. (no. dist.) Ill. 1968, U.S. Ct. Appeals (7th cir.) 1969, U.S. Supreme Ct. 1972. Assoc. Kirkland & Ellis, Chgo., 1968; Reginald Heber Smith fellow Chgo. Legal Aid, 1968-69; assoc. Katz & Friedman, Chgo., 1969-72; ptnr. Davis, Miner, Barnhill & Galland, P.C. (now Miner, Barnhill & Galland), Madison, Wis., 1972—. Spl. master Fed. Dist. Ct. (no. dist.) Ill. Asst. editor: Mich. Law Rev., 1968. Chmn. Wis. Ctr. Tobacco Rsch. and Intervention, 1996; bd. dirs. Combined Health Appeal, Legal Assistance Found., Chgo., 1972—74, Old Town Triangle Assn., Chgo., 1972—75. Fellow: Am. Coll. Trial Lawers; mem.: ABA (chmn. employment litig. litig. section 1975—78), Order of Coif, Barristers Soc., Chgo. Coun. Lawyers (bd. dirs. 1974—76), Greater Madison Area Tennis Assn. (pres.). Office: Miner Barnhill & Galland 44 E Mifflin St Ste 803 Madison WI 53703-2800 Office Phone: 608-255-5200. Business E-Mail: cbarnhill@lawmbg.com.

BARNHOLT, BRANDON K., retail executive; COO, exec. v.p. mktg. Clark USA Inc. (now Clark Retail Group Inc.); CEO, pres. Clark Retail Group, Inc., Glen Ellyn, Ill., 1999—2005, White Hen Pantry, Inc., 2005—. Office: White Hen Pantry Inc Ste 300 700 E Butterfield Rd Lombard IL 60148

BARNICK, HELEN, retired judicial clerk; b. Max, ND, Mar. 24, 1925; d. John K. and Stacy (Kankovsky) Barnick. BS in Music cum laude, Minot State Coll., 1954; postgrad., Am. Conservatory of Music, Chgo., 1975-76. With Epton, Bohling & Druth, Chgo., 1968-69; sec. Wildman, Harrold, Allen & Dixon, Chgo., 1969-75; part-time assignments for temporary agy. Chgo., 1975-77; sec. Friedman & Koven, Chgo., 1977-78; with Lawrence, Lawrence, Kamin & Saunders, Chgo., 1978-81; sec. Hinshaw, Culbertson et al., Chgo., 1982; sec. to magistrate judge U.S. Dist. Ct. (we. dist.) Wis., Madison, 1985-91; dep. clk., case adminstr. U.S. Bankruptcy Ct. (we. dist.) Wis., Madison, 1992-94; ret., 1994. Chancel choir 1st Bapt. Ch., Mpls., Fourth Presbyn. Ch., Chgo., Covenant Presbyn. Ch., Madison, Wis.; choir, dir. sr. high choir Moody Ch., Chgo.; dir. chancel choir 1st Bapt. Ch., Minot, ND; mem. Festival Choir, Madison; bd. dirs., sec.-treas. Peppertree at Tamarack Owners Assn., Inc., Wisconsin Dells. Mem.: Bus. and Profl. Women Assn., Christian Bus. and Profl. Women (chmn.), Madison Civics Club, Symphony Orch. League, Sigma Sigma Sigma. Home: 7364 Old Sauk Rd Madison WI 53717-1213

BARNWELL, FRANKLIN HERSHEL, zoology educator; b. Chattanooga, Oct. 4, 1937; s. Columbus Hershel and Esther Bernice (Ireland) B.; m. Adrienne Kay Knox, June 13, 1959; 1 child, Elizabeth Brooks. BA, Northwestern U., 1959, PhD, 1965. Instr. biol. sci. Northwestern U., Evanston, Ill., 1964, research assoc., 1965-67; asst. prof. U. Chgo., 1967-70; from asst. prof. to prof. zoology, ecology and behavioral biology U. Minn., Mpls., 1970—, head dept. ecology, evolution and behavior, 1986-93. Mem. adv. panel NASA, 1963-67, NSF, Washington, 1980; faculty Orgn. for Tropical Studies, San Jose, Costa Rica, 1966-85, bd. dirs.; at. Confs. on Underground Rsch., bd. dirs., treas., 1990-96; investigator rsch. R/V Alpha Helix, various locations, 1979, vis. scientist. Contbr. articles on zoology to profl. jours. NSF fellow, 1965; named Minn. Coll. Sci. Tchr. of Yr., Minn. Acad. Sci. and Minn. Sci. Tchrs. Assn., 1997, dist. tchg. prof. of ecology, U. Minn., 1997; recipient Disting. Alumnus award McCallie Sch., Chattanooga, Tenn., 2006. Fellow Linnean Soc. London, AAAS; mem. Soc. Intergrative and Comparative Biology, Soc. for Rsch. on Biol. Rhythms, Assocs. Orgn. for Tropical Studies, Crustacean Soc. (founding and sustaining mem., bd. dirs., sec. 1991-98), Phi Beta Kappa, Sigma Xi. Office: U Minn Dept Ecology Evol & Behav 1987 Upper Buford Cir Saint Paul MN 55108-1051 Business E-Mail: fhb@umn.edu.

BARON, JEFFREY, retired pharmacologist; b. Bklyn., July 10, 1942; s. Harry Leo and Terry (Goldstein) Baron; m. Judith Carol Rothberg, June 27, 1965; children: Stephanie Ann, Leslie Beth, Melissa Leigh. BS in Pharmacy, U. Conn., 1965; PhD in Pharmacology, U. Mich., 1969. Rsch. fellow in biochemistry U. Tex. Southwestern Med. Sch., Dallas, 1969-71, rsch. asst. prof. biochemistry and pharmacology, 1971-72; from asst. prof. pharmacology to prof. emeritus U. Iowa, Iowa City, 1972—2002, prof. emeritus, 2002—. Mem. chem. pathology study sect. NIH, Bethesda, Md., 1983—87, mem. environ. health scis. rev. com., at. Inst. Environ. Health Scis., Research Triangle Park, NC, 1990—94. Contbr. chapters to books, articles to profl. jours. Recipient Rsch. Career Devel. award, NIH, 1975—80. Mem.: Internat. Soc. Study Xenobiotics, Soc. Toxicology, Am. Assn. Cancer Rsch., Am. Soc. Biochem. and Molecular Biology, Am. Soc. Pharmacology and Exptl. Therapeutics. Jewish. Achievements include discovery of of the role of heme synthesis in regulating the induction of cytochrome P450 in liver; participation in the discovery of oxygenated cytochrome P450; research in immunohistochemical localization of cytochromes P450 and other xenobiotic-metabolizing enzymes in liver and extrahepatic tissues. Personal E-mail: jeffrey-baron@uiowa.edu.

BARON, JOSEPH MANDEL, hematologist; b. Oak Park, Ill., 1938; BS in BioChemistry, U. Chgo., 1958; MD, U. Chgo. Pritzker Sch. Medicine, 1962; MS in Pharmacology, U. Chgo., 1962. Diplomate Am. Bd. Internal Medicine, Am. Bd. Hematology, Am. Bd. Med. Oncology. Intern U. Chgo. Hosps., 1962—63, resident internal medicine, 1963—64, 1966—68, fellow hematology, 1967—68, assoc. prof. medicine, hematology and oncology, 1975—. Office: Univ Chgo MC 2115 5841 S Maryland Ave Chicago IL 60637 Office Phone: 773-702-6114.

BARONE, JAMES L., state legislator; b. Chgo., May 20, 1941; m. Donita Barone. BSBA, Pitts. State U., 1962. With Bell Sys.-S.W. Bell Telephone, 1962-91; mem. Kans. Senate from 13th dist., Topeka, 1996—; ranking minority mem. commerce com.; mem. fin. instns. and ins. com.; ranking minority mem. utilities com.; mem. joint com. on econ. devel.; mem. joint com. on pensions, investments and benefits com. Named to Order Ky. Cols. Mem. Pittsburg State Alumni Assn. (bd. dirs.), Pittsburg C. of C., Eagles, Rotary, KC. Democrat. Office: 300 SW 10th Ave Rm 504-n Topeka KS 66612-1504

BARR, DAVID JOHN, engineering educator; b. Evansville, Ind., Mar. 5, 1939; s. Ralph Emerson and Selma Louise (Sander) B.; m. Kay Arlene Porter, Jan. 23, 1965; 1 child, John Matthew. C.E., U. Cin., 1962; MSCE, Purdue U., 1964, PhD, 1968. Registered profl. engr., Ohio. Asst. prof. civil engring. U. Cin., 1968-72; prof. geol. engring. U. Mo., Rolla, 1972—, chmn. dept. geol. and petroleum engring., 1987-92, dir. Mo. Mining and Mineral Resources Rsch. Inst., 1980-87, asst. to vice chancellor for acad. computing, 1986-87. Cons. in field. Author: (with others) Remote Sensing for Resource Managemnt, 1983; contbr. Ency. Applied Geology, 1984. Bd. dirs., fireman Rolla Rural Fire Protection Assn., 1975-88. Recipient New Tech. award NASA, 1973-74; NASA rsch. fellow Manned Spacecraft Ctr., Houston, 1969, 70. Mem. NSPE, ASCE (chmn. aerospace div. 1977), Mo. Soc. Profl. Engrs. (Rolla chpt. pres. 1992-93), Am. Soc. Photogrammetry (pres. Rolla region 1975), Soc. Mining Engrs., Assn. Engring. Geologists, Am. Soc. for Engring. Edn., Nat. Assn. Mineral Inst. Dirs. (nat. chmn. 1987-88). Avocations: hunting, fishing. Office: U Mo-Rolla Dept Geol and Petroleum Engring 129 McNutt Rolla MO 65401-0249

BARR, EMILY L., broadcast executive; BA in Film Studies, Carleton Coll., 1980; MBA in Mktg., George Washington U., 1986. News editor KSTP-TV, St. Paul, Minn., 1980-81, news promotion specialist, 1981-82; writer, prodr. WJLA-TV, Washington, 1983-85; advtg. & promotion mgr. KHOU-TV, Houston, 1985-87, dir. creative svcs., 1987-88; dir. broadcast ops. WMAR-TV, Balt., 1988-93, acting gen. mgr., 1993, asst. gen. mgr., 1993-94; pres., gen. mgr. Sta. WTVD, Raleigh, N.C., 1994-97, Sta. WLS-TV, Chgo., 1997—. Grad. leadership program Greater Balt. Com., 1990; active NAPTE, 1988—, BPME, 1983-93, CBS Promotion Caucus, 1987-88. Vol. Mus. Broadcast Comms.; bd. dirs. United Cerebral Palsy-Chgo., Children's Meml. Hosp. Found.; commr. Chgo. State St. Commn. Recipient Dante award Joint Civic com. for Italian Americans, 1998. Mem. Ill. Broadcast Assn., Chgo./Midwest TV Acad., Chgo. C. of C. (bd. dirs.), Chgo. Cen. Area Com. (bd. dirs.). Office: 190 N State St Chicago IL 60601-3302

BARR, JAMES, III, telecommunications company executive; b. Oak Park, Ill., Mar. 2, 1940; s. James Jr. and Florence Marie (Erichsen) B.; m. Joan Benning, Aug. 12, 1961; children: James IV, Brett Christopher, Heather Kathryn, Stephanie Alexandra. BS in Engring., Iowa State U., 1962; MBA, U. Chgo., 1967. Engr. Ill. Bell Tel. Co., Chgo., 1962-66, staff mgr. for regulatory affairs, 1966-69; dist. mgr. for planning AT&T, NYC, 1969-72, dir. regulatory affairs, 1975-80, dir. product mgmt. Basking Ridge, N.J., 1980-85, sales v.p. NYC, 1985-90; gen. mktg. mgr. Bell Can., Ottawa, Ont., 1972-75; pres., CEO, TDS TELECOM, Madison, Wis., 1990—2007. Exec. vp., bd. dirs. NY Bd. Trade, 1985—90; bd. dirs. Tel. and Data Sys., Chgo., Ctr. for Telecom. Mgmt., LA, TDS Telecom, Madison, Wis. Mem. dean's adv. coun. Bus. Sch. U. Wis., 1997—; bd. dirs. United Way Dane County; bd. trustees Edgewood Coll., Md., Wis. Republican. Roman Catholic.

BARR, JOHN ROBERT, retired lawyer; b. Gary, Ind., Apr. 10, 1936; s. John Andrew and Louise (Stentz) Barr; m. Patricia A. Ferris, July 30, 1988; children: Mary Louise, John Mills, Jennifer Susan, Anne Elizabeth Ferris. BA, Grinnell Coll., 1957; LLB cum laude, Harvard U., 1960. Bar: Ill. 1960. Assoc. Sidley Austin LLP, Chgo., 1960—69, ptnr., 1970—99, sr. counsel, 2000—02; ret., 2002. Mem. Commn. Presdl. Scholars, Washington, 1975—77, Ill. Ho. of Reps., 1981—83, Ill. Electric Utility Property Assessment Task Force, 1998—99. Chmn. Ill. Student Assistance Commn., 1985—2005; trustee Steppenwolf Theatre Co., Chgo., 1992—, mem. exec. com., 2005—07; chmn. Rep. Ctrl. Com. Cook County, Chgo., 1978—85; mem. Rep. state ctrl. com. 9th Congl. Dist. Ill., 1986—93; chmn. Ill. Bd. Regents, 1971—77; mem. Ill. Bd. Higher Edn., 1971—77, 1986—2005; trustee Grinnell Coll., 1996—, mem. exec. com., 2004—07. Mem.: ABA (chmn. task force utility deregulation state and local tax com. 1996—2003), Ill. Tax Found. (dir., trustee 2007—), Ill. State Bar Assn. (chmn. state tax sect. coun. 1986—87, sec. com. on legislation 2006—), Nat. Assn. State Bar Tax Sects. (sec-treas. 1989—90, vice chmn. 1990—91, chmn. 1991—92), Civic Fedn. (bd. dirs. 1993—97), Taxpayers Fedn. Ill. (mem. exec. com. 1983—2007, treas. 1990—92, vice chmn. 1992—95, chmn. 1995—97), Chgo. Bar Assn. (chmn. com. state and mcpl. taxation 1974—75), Emil Verban Soc., Evanston (Ill.) Hist. Ctr. (trustee 2001—07, pres. 2006—07), Chgo. Club, Lawyer's Club Chgo., Phi Beta Kappa. Episcopalian. Home: 1144 Asbury Ave Evanston IL 60202-1137 Office: Sidley Austin LLP One S Dearborn St Chicago IL 60603 Office Phone: 312-853-7447. Business E-Mail: jrbarr@sidley.com. E-mail: barrbob@comcast.net.

BARRAZA, LUPE, retail executive; Dist. mcht. Brand Ctrl.; store mgr. Whittier Stores; with Sears, 1983—; v.p., in-store ops. Sears, Roebuck & Co. Chain and dept. store mgr. The Ed Hardy Team. Office: Sears Roebuck & Co 3333 Beverly Rd Hoffman Estates IL 60179 Office Phone: 847-286-2500. Office Fax: 847-286-7829.

BARRÉ, LAURA, finance company executive; b. 1973; With Smith Barney Unit Citigroup Inc., 1999; analyst Bank One Corp., 2000; CFO, private client svcs. J.P. Morgan Chase & Co., Chgo. Bd. dirs. Arts of Life, 2004—. Named one of 40 Under Foty, Crain's Bus. Chgo., 2005. Office: Bank One Private Client Svcs IL-0291 300 S Riverside Plz Chicago IL 60606

BARRETT, CATHERINE L., state representative; b. Cin., June 14, 1941; married; 3 children. BA in Bus. Adminstrn., Union Inst., Cin.; grad., Ctr. Policy Alternatives Flemming Fellows Inst.; fellow, Coun. State Govts. Bowhay Inst. Legis. Leadership Devel. Former mayor, Forest Park, Ohio; state rep. dist. 32 Ohio Ho. of Reps., Columbus, 1998—, ranking minority mem., human svcs. subcom., edn. mem., health, and ins. coms. Past councilwoman Forest Park City Coun. Recipient Ohio Hunger Heroine award, Ohio Assn. 2d Harvest; Harvard JFK Sch. Govt. Sr. Execs. in State and Local Govt. fellow, Eleanor Roosevelt Global Leadership Inst. fellow. Mem.: LWV, Negro Women Coun., Ohio, Ky. and Ind. Regional Coun. Govts., Forest Park Bus. Assn., Cin. Woman's Polit. Caucus, Cin. C. of C., Forest Park Women's Club, Delta Sigma Theta. Democrat. Office: 77 S High St 10th fl Columbus OH 63215-6111

BARRETT, FRANK JOSEPH, lawyer, insurance company executive; b. Greeley, Nebr., Mar. 2, 1932; s. Patrick J. and Irene L. (Printy) B.; m. Ruth Ann Nealon, Aug. 20, 1956; children: Patrick, Mary, Anne, Karen, Thomas. BS in Law, U. Nebr., 1957; LLB, Nebr. Coll. Law, 1959. Bar: Nebr. 1959, U.S. Supreme Ct. 1976, arbitrator. Asst. gen. counsel, asst. sec. Nebr. Nat. Life Co., 1957—61; dir. ins. State of Nebr., Lincoln, 1961—67; exec. v.p., sec., gen. counsel Ctrl. Nat. Ins. Group Omaha, 1967—75; exec. v.p., chief counsel Mut. Omaha (and Affiliates), 1975—81; pres., CEO Ctrl. Nat. Ins. Co. Omaha, 1981—89, Ins. Rsch. Svc. Co., Omaha, 1989—; of counsel Lamson, Dugan & Murray, Omaha, 1990—. Bd. dir. Am. Family Life Assurance Co. State organizational chmn. 3 Nebr. gubernatorial campaigns. Served in U.S. Army, 1953-55, Korea. Recipient service citation Am. Nat. Red Cross, 1964, 65 Mem. ABA, Am. Arbitration Assn., Fedn. Ins. Counsels, Nebr. Bar Assn., Omaha Bar Assn., Consumer Credit Ins. Assn. (past pres. and dir.), Nat. Assn. Ind. Insurers (gov., past chmn.), Nat. Assn. Ins. Commrs. (past pres.), Am. Legion, Irish-Am. Cultural Soc., KC., ARIAS-U.S. (cert. arbitrator, cert. umpire) Democrat. Roman Catholic. Home: 516 S 119th St Omaha NE 68154-3115 Office Phone: 402-397-7300. Office Fax: 402-397-8450. Business E-Mail: fbarrett@ldmlaw.com.

BARRETT, JANET TIDD, academic administrator; b. Crystal City, Mo., Nov. 29, 1939; d. Lewis Samuel and Mamie Lou (Hulvey) Tidd; m. David Clark Barrett, June 3, 1961; children: Barbara, Pam. Diploma in nursing, St. Lukes Hosp. Sch. Nursing, 1960; BSN with honors, Washington U., St. Louis, 1964, MSN, 1979; PhD, St. Louis U., 1987. Assoc. prof. Maryville Coll., St. Louis, 1979-89; acad. dean Barnes Coll., St. Louis, 1989-91; dir. BSN program Deaconess Coll. Nursing, St. Louis, 1991-2000, acad. dean, 2000—02; nursing cons., 2002—. Contbg. author to Beare and Meyers: Principles of Medical-Surgical Nursing; dancer with St. Louis Strutters, 2003-. St. Lukes Hosp. scholar; recipient Sister Agnita Claire Day Rsch. award St. Louis U.; named Ms. Mo. Sr. Am., 2005. Mem.: Mo. League Nursing, Nat. League Nursing, St. Luke's Alumni Assn., Pi Lambda Theta, Sigma Theta Tau. Personal E-mail: barretjan@hotmail.com, jtbarrett02@charter.net.

BARRETT, JOHN F., insurance company executive; BBA, U. Cin. Coll. Bus. Adminstrn., 1971. Pres., CEO Bank NY; with Western & Southern Life Ins. Co., Cin., 1987—, exec. v.p., CFO, 1987—89, pres., COO, 1989—94, pres., CEO, 1994—, chmn., 2002—; pres., CEO Western & Southern Fin. Group, Cin., 2000—, chmn., 2002—. Dir. Fifth Third Bancorp, The Andersons Inc. Associated with Am. Coun. Life Ins., Catholic Inner City Schools, Cin., Cin. Bus. Com., Downtown Cin., Nat. Underground R.R. Freedom Ctr., Young President's Orgn. Mem.: Am. Bus. Roundtable. Office: Western & So Life Ins Co 400 E 4th St Cincinnati OH 45202

BARRETT, MICHAEL RYAN, federal judge; b. Cin., Jan. 14, 1951; BA, U. Cin., 1974; JD, U. Cin. Coll. Law, 1977. Bar: Ohio 1977. Adminstrv. hearing officer State of Ohio, 1977—78; asst. pros. atty., chief asst. pros. atty. Hamilton County Prosecutor's Office, 1978—84; assoc., ptnr. Graydon, Head & Ritchey, 1984—94; ptnr. Barrett & Weber, LPA, 1995—2006; judge US Dist. Ct. (So. dist.) Ohio, 2006—. Office: Potter Stewart US Courthouse Rm 815 100 E 5th St Cincinnati OH 45202 Office Phone: 513-564-7660.

BARRETT, NANCY SMITH, academic administrator; b. Balt., Sept. 12, 1942; d. James Brady and Katherine (Pollard) Smith; children: Clark, Christopher. BA, Goucher Coll., 1963; MA, Harvard U., 1965, PhD, PhD, Harvard U., 1968. Dep. asst. dir. Congl. Budget Office, Washington, 1975-76; sr. staff Council of Econ. Advisors, Washington, 1977; prin. research assoc. The Urban Inst., Washington, 1977-79; dep. asst. sec. U.S. Dept. Labor, Washington, 1979-81; instr. Am. U., Washington, 1966-67, asst. prof. econs., 1967-70, assoc. prof., 1970-74, prof., 1974-89; dean Coll. of Bus. Adminstrn. Fairleigh Dickinson U., Teaneck, J, 1989-91; provost, v.p. acad. affairs Western Mich. U., Kalamazoo, 1991-96, U. Ala., Tuscaloosa, 1996—2003, Wayne State U., Detroit, 2003—. Author: Theory of Macroeconomic Policy, 1972, 2d rev. edit., 1975, Theory of Microeconomic Policy, 1974, (with G. Gerardi and T. Hart) Prices and Wages in U.S., 1974; contbr. articles on econs. to profl. jours. Woodrow Wilson fellow, 1963-64; Fulbright scholar, 1973. Mem.: Am. Econs. Assn., Phi Beta Kappa. Office: Wayne State Univ 4092 Faculty Adminstrn Bldg Detroit MI 48202 Home: 2033 Shorepointe Grosse Pointe Woods MI 48236 Office Phone: 313-577-2200. E-mail: nancy.barrett@wayne.edu.

BARRETT, ROGER WATSON, lawyer; b. Chgo., June 26, 1915; s. Oliver R. and Pauline S. B.; m. Nancy N. Braun, June 20, 1940; children— Victoria Barrett Bell, Holly, Oliver. AB, Princeton U., 1937; JD, Northwestern U., 1940. Bar: Ill. 1940. Mem. firm Poppenhusen, Johnson, Thompson & Raymond, Chgo., 1940-43; 45-50; charge documentary evidence Nuremberg Trial, 1944-45; regional counsel Econ. Stablzn. Agy., Chgo., 1951-52; ptnr. Mayer, Brown

& Platt, Chgo., 1952-91, of counsel, 1991—. Life trustee Mus. Contemporary Art, Chgo. With AUS, 1943-45. Mem. ABA, Ill. Bar Assn., Chgo. Bar Assn., Am. Coll. Trial Lawyers, Indian Hill Club (Winnetka), Old Elm Club, Commonwealth Club (Chgo.), Caxton Club (Chgo.). Home: 39887 Sweetwater Dr Palm Desert CA 92211-7027 Office: Mayer Brown Rowe Maw Llp 230 S La Salle St Ste 400 Chicago IL 60604-1407

BARRETT, THOMAS M., mayor, former congressman; b. Milw., Dec. 8, 1953; m. Kristine Barrett; children: Thomas John, Anne Elizabeth, Erin, Kate. BA in Economics, U. Wis., 1976, JD with honors, 1980. Atty. Smith & O'Neill, Milw., 1982-84; mem. Wis. State Assembly, 1984-89, Wis. State Senate from 5th Dist., 1989-92, U.S. Congress from 5th Wis. dist., Washington, 1993—2002; mem. energy and commerce com.; mayor City of Milwaukee, 2004—. Bd. dirs. Sojourner Truth House, Shalom High Sch., Transcenter Home for Youth. Recipient Circle of Friends award Milw. Advocates for Retarded Citizens, 1989, Health Leadership award State Med. Soc., Govt. Leadership award Rehab. for Wis.; named to Clean Sixteen list for environ. voting record by Wis. Environ. Decade, 1987, 89, 90. Mem. Wis. Bar Assn., Phi Beta Kappa. Democrat. Office: 200 E Wells St City Hall Rm 201 Milwaukee WI 53202

BARRETT, WILLIAM E., former congressman; b. Lexington, Nebr., Feb. 9, 1929; s. Harold O. and Helen Stuckey B.; m. Elsie L. Carlson, 1952; children: William C., Elizabeth A., David H., Jane M. AB, Hastings Coll., Nebr., 1951; grad., Nebr. Realtors Inst. Cert. real estate broker, Nebr. Admissions counselor Hastings Coll., 1952-54, asst. dir. admissions, 1954-56; ptnr. Barrett Agy., Lexington, 1956-59; pres. Barrett-Housel & Assocs., Inc., 1970-90; former pres. Dawson County Young Rep.; del. Rep. Co. Conv., from 1958; mem. Nebr. Rep. State Exec. Com., 1964-66; chmn., formerly mem. Rep. Nat. Com., state coord. Mobilization of Rep. Enterprise Programs, 1965-66; del. Rep. Nat. Conv., 1968; mem. Nebr. Legislature, 1979-90, speaker, 1987-90; mem. 102nd-106th Congresses from 3rd Nebr. Dist., 1991-2001. Work in campaigns for various rep. candidate, 1960; officer Barrett-Housel & Assocs., Inc., 1969—; dir. Farmers State Bank; chmn. Agr. subcom. on Gen. Farm Commodities, mem. forestry, resource conservation & rsch. coms.; mem. oversight & investigations, worker protections, agr., edn. and workplace coms.; mem. Econ. & Ednl. Opportunity Com. Trustee, co-founder Nebr. Real Estate Polit. Edn. Com.; elder First Presbyn. Ch., Lexington; moderator Presbytery of Platte, 1972-73, chmn. gen. coun., 1973, mem. staff nominating com. Synod of Lakes and Prairies, from 1973. With USN, 1951-52. Named Legislator of Yr. Nat. Rep. Legislators Assn., 1990. Mem. Nebr. Assn. Ins. Agts., Nat. Assn. Ins. Agts., Dawson Co. Bd. Realtors, Nebr. Assn. Realtors, Nat. Assn. Realtors, Nebr. Jaycees (named one of three outstanding young men of Nebr. 1962), Rotary (Lexington). Republican.

BARRON, HAROLD SHELDON, lawyer; b. Detroit, July 4, 1936; s. George Leslie and Rose (Weinstein) B.; m. Roberta Yellin, Nov. 17, 1963; children: Lawrence Ira, Jean Louise. AB, U. Mich., 1958, JD, 1961. Bar: N.Y. 1963, Mich. 1961, Ill. 1983, Pa. 1992. Pvt. practice, NYC, 1962-68; practice in Southfield, Mich., 1968-83, Chgo., 1983-93, Pa., 1991—2002; atty. Hughes Hubbard & Reed, 1962-68; corp. counsel Bendix Corp., 1968-69, sec., assoc. gen. counsel, 1969-72, sec., gen. counsel, 1972-83, v.p., 1974-83; ptnr. Arnstein, Gluck, Lehr, Barron & Milligan, Chgo., 1983-86, Seyfarth, Shaw, Fairweather & Geraldson, Chgo., 1986-91; v.p., gen. counsel Unisys Corp., Blue Bell, Pa., 1991-92, sr. v.p., gen. counsel, 1992-94, sr. v.p., gen. counsel, sec., 1994-99, sr. v.p., gen. counsel, 1999-2001, vice chmn., 2001—02; counsel McDermott, Will & Emery, 2002—04; gen. counsel Pro-Build Holdings, Inc., 2006—07. Mem. nat. adv. coun. and faculty Practising Law Inst., NYC; bd. dirs. Royal Maccabees Life Ins. Co., Southfield, 1983—94; chmn. bd. F.A. Tucker Group, Inc., 1991—95. Editor: The Business Lawyer. Com. visitors U. Mich. Law Sch.; trustee Children's Hosp. Mich., Detroit, 1976-84; mem. Census Adv. Com. on Privacy and Confidentiality, 1975-76; mem. governing bd., adv. coun. Purdue U. Info. Privacy Rsch. Ctr.; bd. dirs. Citizens Rsch. Coun. of Mich., 1982-83, Greater Phila. Econ. Devel. Coalition. Served with AUS, 1961-62. Mem. ABA (coun. bus. law sect., bus. law sect., chmn. 2002-03, standing com. on fed. judiciary 2003-06, editor The Bus. Lawyer, Latin Am. legal initiatives coun., chmn. com. of corp. gen. counsel, sect. bus. law coun., com. corp. law and taxation, internat. bus. law com., com. devels. in investment svcs., com. long-range issues affecting bus. law practice, com. on corp. laws, commn. on asbestos litigation), Am. Arbitration Assn., Am. Soc. Corp. Secs. (securities law com.), Internat. Inst. Conflict Prevention and Resolution (exec. com., nat. panel disting. neutrals), Am. Law Inst., Mich. Bar Assn., Assn. Bar City NY (com. corp. law depts.), Carlton Club, Chgo. Club, Bryn Mawr Country Club (Chgo.), The Reserve (Indian Wells, Calif.). Office: 980 N Michigan Ave Ste 1400 Chicago IL 60611 Home Phone: 312-337-5642; Office Phone: 312-214-3908. Business E-Mail: hal@barronadr.com.

BARRON, HOWARD ROBERT, lawyer; b. Chgo., Feb. 17, 1930; s. Irwin P. and Ada (Astrahan) B.; m. Marjorie Shapira, Aug. 12, 1953; children: Ellen Barron Feldman, Laurie A. PhB, U. Chgo., 1948; BA, Stanford U., 1950; LLB, Yale U., 1953. Bar: Ill. 1953. Assoc. Jenner & Block, Chgo., 1957-63, ptnr., 1964-97; assoc. Schiff Hardin, Chgo., 1953, of counsel, 1997—. Contbr. articles to profl. jours. and books. Mem., then pres. Lake County Sch. Dist. 107 (now Dist. 112) Bd. Edn., Highland Park, 1964-71; pres. Lake County Sch. Bd. Assn., 1970-71; mem. Lake County High Sch. Dist. 113 Bd. Edn., Highland Park, 1973-77; mem. Highland Park Zoning Bd. Appeals, 1984-89. Lt. (j.g.) USNR, 1953-57. Mem.: ABA (com. corp. counsel litigation sect. 1983—2002, co-chmn. subcom. labor and employment law), Yale Club (N.Y.C.), Met. Club, Internat. Bar Assn., Yale Law Sch. Assn. of Ill. (pres. 1962), Yale Law Sch. Assn. (v.p. 1978—81), Chgo. Bar Assn., Fed. Bar Assn., Ill. State Bar Assn. (chmn. antitrust sect. 1968—69, sr. counselor 2003), Standard Club. Democrat. Home: 1366 Sheridan Rd Highland Park IL 60035-3407 Office: Schiff Hardin LLP 6600 Sears Tower Chicago IL 60606 Home Phone: 847-433-1288; Office Phone: 312-258-5558. Personal E-mail: hrb1366@aol.com. Business E-Mail: hbarron@schiffhardin.com.

BARRON, JOHN, editor; BA in Journalism, Marquette U. Asst. editor Crain's Chgo. Bus., 1980—84; with Detroit Monthly, 1984—95, editor, 1991—94; positions including reporter, Sunday Showcase editor, dep. features editor, features editor Chgo. Sun-Times, 1995—2003, exec. mng. editor, 2003—05, editor-in-chief, 2005—06, gen. mgr., 2007—; exec. editor Sun-Times News Group, Chgo., 2006—07. Office: Chgo Sun Times 350 N Orleans Chicago IL 60654 Office Phone: 312-321-3000. Business E-Mail: jbarron@suntimes.com.

BARRY, ANNE M., public health officer; BA in Occupl. Therapy, Coll. St. Catherine; JD, William Mitchell Coll. Law; MPH, U. Minn. Dep. commr. health Minn. Dept. Health, Mpls., commr. health, 1995—99; dep. fin. commr. Minn., 1999—; acting commr. fin. Minn., 2002. Office: Dept Fin 400 Centennial Bldg 658 Cedar St Saint Paul MN 55155

BARRY, JAMES PATRICK, lawyer; b. Muscatine, Iowa, July 17, 1960; s. Richard Paul and Janet Lynn (Hahn) B.; m. Cheryl Jo Mewhirter, Sept. 22, 1990. BS, Drury Coll., 1983; JD, Wash. U., 1986. Bar: U.S. Dist. Ct. (no. and so. dists.) Iowa, U.S. Dist. Ct. (we. dist.) Mo. Assoc. Otto and Lorence Law Firm, Atlantic, 1986-90; asst. county atty. Cass County, Iowa, Atlantic, 1987-90, county atty., 1991—; ptnr. Otto, Lorence & Barry, Atlantic, 1990—. Bd. dirs. ARC, Cass County chpt., Atlantic, 1987-90, YMCA, Atlantic, 1989-90; pres. and sec. Am., Heart Assn., Atlantic, 1988-89, bd. dirs., 1988-90; adv. fund dir. chmn. United Way, Atlantic, 1988. Mem. ABA, Mo. Bar Assn., Iowa State Bar Assn., Southwest Iowa Bar Assn., Cass County Bar Assn. (treas. 1988-89, sec. 1989-90, v.p. 1990-91), Elks, Atlantic Golf and Country Club (bd. dirs. 1990-91). Republican. Methodist. Avocations: fishing, hunting, golf, jogging, water-skiing. Office: Otto Lorence & Barry 522 Chestnut St Atlantic IA 50022-1248

BARRY, JONATHAN B., chemicals and communications executive; Degree, U. Wis. Exec. v.p. WYG Corp.; pres. Gammex-RMI Corp.; pres., owner W.T. Rogers Co.; pres., chmn. Good Bugs, Inc.; pres., owner J.B. Barry Co., Tyrol Basin Ski Resort, Mt. Horeb, Wis. Mem. bd. regents U. Wis., Wis.; mem. Dane County Bd. Suprs.; exec. Dane County; pres. bd. Wis. Tech. Coll. Sys.; mem. Wis. State Assembly, Madison.

BARRY, NORMAN J., JR., lawyer; b. Chgo., Apr. 1, 1950; BA, U. Notre Dame, 1972, JD, 1975. Bar: Ill. 1975. Ptnr. Donohue, Brown, Mathewson, & Smyth, Chgo. Office: Donohue Brown Mathewson & Smyth 140 S Dearborn St Ste 700 Chicago IL 60603-5201

BARRY, RICHARD A., public relations executive; b. Chgo., Nov. 11, 1934; BS in Polit. Sci., Loyola U., 1956; cert. in publ. and graphics, U. Chgo., 1958. Asst. editor No. Ind. Pub. Svc. Co., Hammond, 1956-58; dir. pub. rels. Loyola U., Chgo., 1958-66; dir. devel. and pub. rels. St. Xavier Coll., Chgo., 1966-68; sr. v.p. Daniel J. Edelman, Inc., Chgo., 1968-70; exec. v.p. PCI, Chgo., 1970-72; pres. Pub. Comms., Inc., Chgo., 1972—. Office: Alpha Communications 1000 Lake St Ste C Oak Park IL 60301-1128

BARSANO, CHARLES PAUL, medical educator, dean; BS in Biology, Loyola U., Chgo., 1969; PhD in Pathology, U. Chgo., 1974, MD, 1975. Diplomate Am. Bd. Internal Medicine. Resident internal medicine Barnes Hosp./Washington U., St. Louis, 1975-77; fellow endocrinology U. Chgo. Sch. Medicine, 1977-79, rsch. assoc. endocrinology, 1979-80; asst. prof. medicine Northwestern U. and Lakeside VA Med. Ctr., 1980-85, U. Health Scis./Chgo. Med. Sch. and North Chgo. VA Med. Ctr., 1985-87, assoc. prof., 1987-92, prof. medicine, 1992-98, assoc. prof. pharmacology and molecular biology, 1992-94, prof. pharmacology and molecular biology, 1994-98, acting dean Med. Sch., 1998—99, sr. assoc. dean for clin. affairs, vice-chmn. dept. medicine, 1999—2001, interim dean, 2001—03; staff physician med. svc./endocrinology sect. North Chgo. VA Med. Ctr.; with clin. affairs Chgo. Med. Sch. Rosalind Franklin U. Medicine and Sci., 2005—. Mem. editl. bd. Thyroid, 1990-95; mem. adv. bd. Toxic Substance Mechanisms, 1993-99. Recipient Bausch and Lomb Nat. Sci. award, 1965, Individual Nat. Rsch. Svc. award, 1979-80. Mem. Internat. Coun. for Control of Iodine Deficiency Disorders, Assn. Am. Med. Colls. (group on ednl. affairs sect. on resident edn.), Am. Assn. Clin. Endocrinologists, Am. Thyroid Assn. (fiscal com. 1982-85, pub. health com. 1986-88, membership com. 1990-93, chmn. membership com. 1993, local organizing com. 1994, bylaws com. 1995—), Endocrine Soc., Chgo. Endocrine Club (pres. 1984-85), Sigma Xi, Alpha Omega Alpha. Office: Clin Affairs Chgo Med Sch Rosalind Franklin U Medicine and Sci North Chicago IL 60064 E-mail: charles.barsano@rosalindfranklin.edu, cbflyer@aol.com.

BART, SUSAN THERESE, lawyer; b. Chgo., June 6, 1961; BA, Grinnell Coll., 1982; JD, U. Mich., 1985. Bar: Ill. 1985, U.S. Ct. Appeals (7th cir.) 1985. Law clk. to Hon. Richard D. Cudahy, Fed. Ct. Appeals (7th cir.), 1985—86; with Hopkins & Sutter, 1986—94, ptnr., 1992—94, Sidley Austin LLP, 1994—. Articles editor U. Mich. Law Review, Ann Arbor, 1984-85. Author: Education Planning and Gifts to Minors, 2004; co-author: Illinois Estate Planning: Forms and Commentary, 1997 (Outstanding Achievement award Assn. for Continuing Legal Edn., 1998), rev., 2005. Mem. bd. dirs., exec. com. Ill. Inst. Continuing Legal Edn.; sec., bd. dirs. The Next Theatre; mem. bd. trustees Roosevelt U.; mem. bd. dirs. Domestic Violence Legal Clinic. Mem. Phi Beta Kappa, Order of the Coif. Avocations: classics, literature, theater. Office: Sidley Austin LLP One S Dearborn St Chicago IL 60603

BARTA, JAMES JOSEPH, retired federal judge; b. St. Louis, Nov. 5, 1940; BA, St. Mary's U., 1963; JD, St. Louis U., 1966. Bar: Mo. 1966, U.S. Supreme Ct. 1969. Spl. agt. FBI, Cleve., and NYC, 1966-70; chief trial atty. St. Louis Cir. Atty., 1970-76; assoc. Guilfoil, Symington & Petzall, St. Louis, 1976-77; asst. U.S. atty. (ea. dist.) Mo. US Dept. Justice, St. Louis, 1977-78; judge US Bankruptcy Ct. (ea. dist.) Mo., St. Louis, 1978—2006, chief judge, 1986-89, 95-99. Lectr. Greater St. Louis Police Acad., 1970-76; mem. U.S. Supreme Ct. Adv. Com. on Bankruptcy Rules, 1987-94, chmn. tech. subcom. 1990-94, style subcom., 1992-94; mem. tech. adv. com. St. Louis Coun. on Criminal Justice, 1972-74; dir. Organized Crime Task Force, St. Louis, 1972-74; project dir. St. Louis Crime Commn., 1975-77. Fellow Am. Coll. Bankruptcy (cir. chmn. 1990-94, bd. dirs. 1994-97, sec. bd. dirs. 1995-97); mem. ABA, Am. Bankruptcy Inst. (bd. dirs. 1989-94), Am. Judicature Soc., Mo. Bar Assn., St. Louis Bar Assn., St. Louis Bar Assn. CLE Inst. (at-large 1989-93), Former Spl. Agts. FBI.

BARTA, JAMES OMER, priest, psychology educator, church administrator; b. Fairfax, Iowa, Oct. 22, 1931; s. Omer J. and Bertha (Brecht) B. BA, Loras Coll., 1952; Sacrae Theologiae Licentiatus, Gregorian U., Rome, 1956; PhD, Fordham U., 1962. Ordained priest Roman Cath. Ch., 1955. Prof. psychology Loras Coll., Dubuque, Iowa, 1957-94, v.p. acad. affairs, 1977-87, pres., 1987-94; archbishop's vicar Cedar Rapids (Iowa) region, 1994-99; vicar Gen. Archdiocese of Dubuque, 1999—. Roman Catholic. Office: Archdiocesan Chancery 1229 Mount Loretta Ave Dubuque IA 52003-7826

BARTCH, FLOYD O., police chief; b. St. Joseph, Mo., Mar. 2, 1941; BA, MA, Ctrl. Miss. State U. Patrolman St. Joseph Police Dept., 1965-67, North Kansas City Police Dept., 1967-68; patrolman through ranks to asst. chief of police Kansas City (Mo.) Police Dept., 1968-95, chief of police, 1996—. Recipient Meritorious Svc. award Urban League, 1981, 94, Difference Maker award, 1996. Office: Kansas City Police Dept 1125 Locust St Kansas City MO 64106-2687

BARTELL, ERNEST, economist, educator, priest; b. Chgo., Jan. 22, 1932; PhB, U. Notre Dame, 1953; AM, U. Chgo., 1954; MA, Coll. Holy Cross, 1961; PhD, Princeton U., 1966; LLD (hon.), China Acad., Taipei, Taiwan, 1975, St. Joseph's Coll., 1983, King's Coll., 1984, Stonehill Coll., 1992. Ordained priest Roman Cath. Ch., 1961. Instr. econs. Princeton U., NJ, 1965—66; asst. prof. econs. U. Notre Dame, Ind., 1966—68, assoc. prof., 1968—71, chmn. dept. econs., 1968—71, dir. Ctr. Study of Man in Contemporary Soc., 1969—71, prof. econs., 1981—2003, prof. emeritus, 2003—; exec. dir. Helen Kellogg Inst. Internat. Studies, 1981—97, fellow, 1997—; pres. Stonehill Coll., North Easton, Mass., 1971—77; dir. Fund for Improvement Post Secondary Edn. U.S. Dept. Health, Edn. and Welfare, Washington, 1977—79; dir. Project 80 Assn. Cath. Colls. and Univs., Washington, 1979—80; coord. overseas mission Priests of Holy Cross, Ind. Province, 1980—84, assoc. dir. Holy Cross Mission Ctr., 1984—95; asst. to pastor St. Anthony Ch., Ft. Lauderdale, Fla., 1993—2003. Active Inst. East-West Securities Studies Working Group on Sources in Instability, 1989-90, Internat. Ctr. Devel. Policy Commn. on U.S.-Soviet Rels., 1988-89, Overseas Devel. Coun., 1988-2000, The Bretton Woods Com., 1992-2002; mem. policy planning commn. Nat. Inst. Ind. Colls. and Univs., 1982-85; bd. dirs. Ctr. for Health Promotion, Internat. Life Scis. Inst. Author; Costs and Benefits of Catholic Elementary and Secondary Schools, 1969; co-editor: Business and Democracy in Latin America, 1995, The Child in Latin America, 2000; contbr. articles to profl. jours. Bd. regents U. Portland, Oreg., 1984-2004; bd. dirs. Missionary Vehicle Assn. Am., 1981-88, Big Bros. and Big Sisters Am., 1978-80, Brockton Cmty. Housing Corp., 1974-77, The Brighter Day, 1974-77, Brockton Hosp., 1973-77, King's Coll., Wilkes-Barre, Pa., 1969-82; trustee Emmanuel Coll., 1977-78, trustee emeritus Stonehill Coll., 2002—; trustee U. Notre Dame, 1974-2002, bd. fellows, 1974-2002, trustee emeritus 2002-; bd. regents U. Portland 1984-2004; trustee Regis Coll., 2002—; adv. bd. Brockton Art Ctr., 1974-77; exec. com. Opera New Eng., 1977. Recipient Fenwick Alumni Recognition award, 1974; named to Fenwick Hall of Fame, 1990; faculty fellow Kellogg Inst., 1997—. Fellow Soc. Values in Higher Edn.; mem. Am. Econ. Assn., Am. Assn. Higher Edn., Nat. Cath. Ednl. Assn. (chmn. govtl. rels. com. 1976-77, vice chmn. exec. com. 1976-77, chmn. mgmt. and planning com. 1974-76), Assn. Soc. Econs., Latin Am. Studies Assn., Young Pres. Orgn. (sec. 1974-77), Delta Mu Delta (hon.). Home: 211 Corby Hall Notre Dame IN 46556-5680 Office: U Notre Dame Kellogg Inst 211 Hesburgh Ctr Notre Dame IN 46556-5677 Office Phone: 574-631-7816. Business E-Mail: ebartell@nd.edu.

BARTELL, JEFFREY BRUCE, lawyer; b. Madison, Wis., Jan. 29, 1943; s. Gerald Aaron and Joyce Meta (Jaeger) B.; m. Angela Gina Baldi, Aug. 31, 1968; children: Jessica, Carey, Chad, Nicholas, Dana. BS in Econs., U. Wis., 1965, JD cum laude, 1968. Bar: Wis. 1968, U.S. Dist. Ct. (we. dist.) 1968, U.S. Dist. Ct. (ea. dist.) 1969, U.S. Ct. Appeals (7th cir.) 1970, U.S. Supreme Ct. 1971. Asst. atty. gen. State of Wis., Madison, 1968-71; counsel Wis. Citizens Study Com. on Jud. Orgn., Madison, 1971-72; commr. securities State of Wis., Madison, 1972-79; pres. N.Am. Securities Administrators Assn., 1978-79; ptnr. Michael, Best & Friedrich, Madison, 1979-83; mng. ptnr. Quarles & Brady, Madison, 1983—99, ptnr., 2000—. Lectr. on securities regulation U. Wis. Law Sch., Madison, 1982, 86, 92; mem. adv. com. on tender offers SEC, 1983. Pres. Madison Repertory Theatre, 1978—80; trustee Wis. Meml. Union, Madison, 1984—, Madison Rotary Found., 2001—04; chmn. Madison Civic Ctr. Endowment Fund, 1988—91, Wis. Found. for Arts, 1990—, Wis. Meml. Union, Madison, 2003—; officer, bd. dirs. Forward Wis., Inc., 1984—2005; bd. dirs. Madison Civic Ctr. Found., 1985—95, Friends of WHA-TV, 1996—2000, Ten Chimneys Found., 1997—2003, Overture Devel. Corp., 1998—, Friends of Monona Ter., 1999—2002, Meriter Health Svcs., Inc., 2000—, Meriter Hosp., Inc., 2000—, Wis. Med. Soc. Found., 2001—05, Monona Terr. Cmty. and Conv. Ctr., 2004—, Wis. Artistic Endowment Found., 2004—05. Capt. JACG USAR, ret. Mem. ABA (gavel awards com. 1992—), State Bar Wis. (dir. bus. law sect. 1983-91, chmn. sect. 1990-91, mem. bus. corp. law com. 1989-96), Dane County Bar, Wis. Law Alumni Assn. (pres. 1989-91), Rotary (bd. dirs. Madison 1987-88). Avocations: skiing, biking, music, golf. Office: Quarles & Brady US Bank Plaza PO Box 2113 Madison WI 53701-2113 Home Phone: 608-233-6262; Office Phone: 608-283-2432. E-mail: jbartell@quarles.com.

BARTELL, LAWRENCE SIMS, chemist, educator; b. Ann Arbor, Mich., Feb. 23, 1923; s. Floyd Earl and Lawrence (Sims) B.; m. Joy Hilda Keer, Aug. 16, 1952; 1 son, Michael Keer. BS, U. Mich., 1944, MS, 1947, PhD, 1951. Research asst. Manhattan project U. Chgo., 1944-45; mem. faculty Iowa State U., 1953-65, prof. chemistry, 1959-65, U. Mich., 1965—, Philip J. Elving prof. chemistry, 1987-94, prof. emeritus, 1994—. Vis. prof. Moscow State U., 1972, U. Paris XI, Orsay, France, 1973, U. Tex., 1978, 86; cons. Gillette Co., Chgo., 1956-62, Mobil Oil Corp., Paulsboro, NJ, 1960-84; mem. commn. on electron diffraction Internat. Union Crystallography, 1966-75 Assoc. editor: Jour. Chem. Physics, 1963-66; mem. editorial bd.: Jour. Computational Chemistry, 1979-90, Chem. Physics Letters, 1981-84. Served with USNR, 1945. Recipient Disting. Faculty Achievement award U. Mich., 1981, Disting. Faculty award Mich. Assn. Governing Bds., 1982, Creativity award NSF, 1982, Metz-Stark award, 2004. Mem. Am. Chem. Soc. (petroleum rsch. fund adv. bd. 1970-73), Am. Phys. Soc. (chmn. divsn. chem. physics 1977-78), Am. Crystallographic Assn., AAAS, Phi Beta Kappa, Sigma Xi, Phi Kappa Phi, Phi Lambda Upsilon, Alpha Chi Sigma. Home: 381 Riverview Dr Ann Arbor MI 48104-1847 Home Phone: 734-663-6120; Office Phone: 734-764-7375. Business E-Mail: lbart@umich.edu.

BARTH, DAVID KECK, retired wholesale distribution executive, consultant; b. Springfield, Ill., Dec. 7, 1943; s. David Klenk and Edna Margaret (Keck) B.; m. Dian Oldemeyer, Nov. 21, 1970; children— David, Michael, John. BA cum laude, Knox Coll., Galesburg, Ill., 1965; MBA, U. Calif., Berkeley, 1971. With data processing div. IBM Corp., Chgo., 1966; with No. Trust Co., Chgo., 1971-72; mgr. treasury ops., then treas. fin. services group Borg-Warner Corp., Chgo., 1972-79; treas. W.W. Grainger, Inc., Skokie, Ill., 1979-83, v.p., 1984-90; pres. Barth Smith Co., 1991—2001. Mem. faculty Lake Forest Grad. Sch. Mgmt., Ill., 1994—2006; bd. dirs. Indsl. Distbn. Group Inc., Atlanta. Served to lt. USNR, 1966-69. Mem. Econ. Club Chgo., Beta Gamma Sigma, Phi Delta Theta. Lutheran. Personal E-mail: davidbarth@sbcglobal.net.

BARTH, JOHN M., retired manufacturing executive; With Johnson Controls, Inc., Milw., 1969—, exec. v.p., 1992—98, bd. dir., 1997—, pres., COO, 1998—2002, pres., CEO, 2002—04, chmn., pres., CEO, 2004—06, chmn., CEO, 2006—07, chmn., 2007.

BARTH, ROLF FREDERICK, pathologist, educator; b. NYC, Apr. 4, 1937; s. Rolf L. and Josephine Barth; m. Christine Ferguson, Oct. 30, 1965; children: Suzanna, Alison, Rolf, Christofer. AB, Cornell U., 1959; MD, Columbia U., 1964. Diplomate Am. Bd. Pathology. Surg. intern Columbia-Presbyn. Med. Ctr., NYC, 1964-65; postdoctoral fellow Karolinska Inst., Stockholm, 1965-66; rsch. assoc. Nat. Inst. Allergy and Infectious Diseases, NIH, Bethesda, Md., 1966-68; resident pathology br. Nat. Cancer Inst., 1966-68, Nat. Inst. Health, 1968-70; Prof. dept. pathology and oncology U. Kans. Med. Ctr., Kansas City, 1970-77; clin. prof. dept. pathology Med. Coll. Wis. and U. Wis., Madison, 1977-79; prof. dept. pathology Ohio State U., Columbus, 1979—. Contbr. articles to profl. jours. Sr. asst. surgeon USPHS, 1966-70, inactive Res., 1970-2007. Grantee NIH. Mem. Am. Assn. Immunologists, Am. Assn. Cancer Rsch., Internat. Soc. for eutron Capture Therapy, Sigma Xi, Phi Kappa Phi; fellow Am. Assn. Adv. Sci. Office: Ohio State U Dept Pathology 165 Hamilton Hall 1645 Neil Ave Columbus OH 43210-1218 Office Phone: 614-292-2177. Business E-Mail: rolf.barth@osumc.edu.

BARTH, VOLKER J., electronics executive; b. Darmstadt, Germany; BSEE, Engring. Coll. Russelsheim, Germany, 1969; M in Electronics and Controls Engring., U. Darmstadt, Germany, 1974. Apprentice electrician Adam Opel subs. GM, 1963—74, exptl. engr., 1963—81, group engring.-vehicle fuel economy/car evaluation/field test, 1981—84; mgr. Opel Liaison office GM Overseas Corp., Tokyo, 1984—86; mgr. operational planning Adam Opel sub. SM, Germany, 1986—87, purchasing mgr., 1987—89, purchasing exec. in charge of advance purchasing and global sourcing, 1989—90; dir. purchasing GM do Brasil, Sao Paulo, Brazil, 1991—92, dir. materials mgmt., 1992—93; exec. dir. Worldwide Purchasing-Metallic, 1993—94; exec. dir. Worldwide Purchasing Delphi Corp., Troy, Mich., 1994—96; pres. Delphi S.Am., 1996—98; v.p. Delphi Corp., 1998—; pres. Delphi Europe, Middle East and Africa, 2003—. Office: World Hdqrs Delphi Corp 5725 Delphi Dr Troy MI 48098-2815 also: Delphi Corp BP 60059 2-64 Ave de la Plaine de France F-95972 Roissy Charles de Gaulle Cedex France

BARTHOLOMAY, WILLIAM C., insurance brokerage company and professional sports team executive; b. Evanston, Ill., Aug. 11, 1928; s. Henry C. and Virginia (Graves) B.; m. Sara Taylor, 1950, (div. 1964); children: Virginia, William T., Jamie, Elizabeth, Sara; m. Gail Dillingham, May 1968 (div. Apr. 1980). Student, Oberlin Coll., 1946-49, Northwestern U., 1949-50; BA, Lake Forest Coll., 1955. Ptnr. Bartholomay & Clarkson, Chgo., 1951-63; v.p. Alexander & Alexander, Chgo., 1963-65; pres. Olson & Bartholomay, Chgo. and Atlanta, 1965-69; sr. v.p. Frank B. Hall & Co. Inc., NYC and Chgo., 1969-72, exec. v.p., 1972-73, pres., 1973-74, vice chmn., 1974-90; chmn. bd., dir. Atlanta Braves, 1966—2004, chmn. emeritus, chmn. exec. com., 2004—; pvt. practice Chgo., 1990—91; pres. Near orth Nat. Group, 1991—2003; vice chmn., chmn. exec. com. Turner Broadcasting Sys., Inc., Atlanta, 2001—; vice chmn. Willis Group Holdings (NYSE), Chgo., 2003—. Bd. dirs. Midway Games, Inc., Exec. Coun. Maj. League Baseball, Maj. League Baseball Players Pension Plan; dir. Internat. Steel, 2002—05; dir. emeritus WMS Industries, Inc., Chgo., 2005—. Commr. Chgo. Park Dist., 1980-2002, Chgo. Pub. Bldg. Commn., 1989-2003; bd. dirs. Chgo. Maternity Ctr., Lincoln Park Zool. Soc.; trustee Adler Planetarium, Mus. Sci. and Industry, Roosevelt U., Chgo., Ill. Inst. of Tech.; past trustee Lake Forest (Ill.) Coll., Ogelthorpe Coll., Atlanta, Marymount Manhattan Coll., NY With USNR, 1951-54. Mem. Chief Execs. Orgn., World Pres.'s Orgn., Chgo. Pres.'s Orgn., at. Assn. CLU, Chgo. Assn. CLU, Chgo. Club, Racquet Club, Saddle and Cycle Club, Econ. Club, Onwentsia Club, Shoreacres Club (Lake Forest), Brook Club, Links Club, Racquet & Tennis Club, Doubles Club (N.Y.C.), Piedmont Driving Club, Atlanta Country Club, Peachtree Golf Club, Commerce Club. Episcopalian. Home: 180 E Pearson St Chicago IL 60611-2130 Office: Willis Group Holdings 10 S LaSalle St Ste 3000 Chicago IL 60603 also: Atlanta Braves PO Box 4064 Atlanta GA 30302-4064 Business E-Mail: bartholomay_wi@willis.com.

BARTHOLOMEW, LLOYD GIBSON, physician; b. Whitehall, NY, Sept. 15, 1921; s. Emerson F. and Minnie (Swinton) B.; m. Elisabeth Thrall, Dec. 27, 1943; children: Suzanne, Lynne, Lloyd Gibson, Deborah, Douglass Thrall. AA, Green Mountain Jr. Coll., 1939; BA, Union Coll., Schenectady, 1941; MD, U. Vt., 1944; MS in Internal Medicine (fellow), U. Minn., 1952; LHD (hon.), Green Mountain Coll., 1984. Diplomate Am. Bd. Internal Medicine, subsplty. bd. gastroenterology. Intern Mary Hitchcock Meml. Hosp., Hanover, NH, 1944-45, resident, 1945-46, 48-49; asst. internal medicine Dartmouth, 1948-49; 1st asst. div. internal medicine Mayo Clinic, Rochester, Minn., 1949-52, asst. to staff div. internal medicine, 1952-53; practice medicine, specializing in gastroenterology Rochester, 1952—; instr. internal medicine Mayo Found., U. Minn., 1952-58, asst. prof., 1958-63, assoc. prof. internal medicine, 1963-67, prof. medicine, 1967—, Mayo Med. Sch., 1973—. Attending physician St. Mary's, Meth. hosps., Rochester, 1952; mem. adv. bd. to surgeons gen. of armed forces and asst. sec. def., 1978-86; mem. policy bd. Bush Found., 1978-87. Contbr. articles profl. publs. Trustee Green Mountain Coll. Poultney, Vt., 1991—, chmn. bd. trustees, 1997-2003, trustee emeritus, 2003—. Capt. M.C. AUS, 1946-47; col. M.C., 1960-86, ret. Recipient Woodbury prize in medicine, 1944, Carbee prize in obstetrics, 1994, disting. svc. award U. Vt. Coll. Medicine, 1977, Henry J. Plummer disting. clinician award Mayo Found. Internal Medicine, 1992, disting. svc. award Green Mtn. Coll. Alumni Assn., 1995; named to Green Mtn. Coll. Athletic Hall of Fame, 2006. Mem. AMA (sec. gastroenterology sect. 1962-68, vice chmn. gastroenterlogy sect. 1968-69, chmn. 1969-70, mem. council sci. assembly 1969, chmn. program planning com. 1971-75, chmn. council sci. assembly 1974-76, chmn. council continuing physician edn. 1976-77), Minn. Med. Assn. (del. ho. dels. 1964—, chmn. scholarship and loan com. 1967—, alt. del. to AMA 1974-77, 85—, del. to AMA 1978-83, Pres.'s award 1983, Disting. Service award 1987), So. Minn. Med. Assn. (pres. 1963-64), Zumbro Valley

Med. Soc. (sec.-treas. 1969-70, v.p. 1970-71, pres. 1971-72), Soc. Med. Cons. to Armed Forces (mem. governing council 1980-86, pres. 1984, del. to AMA 1984-92), Am. Gastroent. Assn. (com. on procedures 1970-72, presdl. commn. on future of assn. 1973-74, com. on constn. and by-laws 1980-85), Minn. Soc. Internal Medicine, Sigma Xi. Mailing: 211 2nd St NW Apt 1214 Rochester MN 55901-2897

BARTLETT, ALEX, lawyer; b. Warrensburg, Mo., Aug. 7, 1937; s. George Vest and May (Woolery) B.; m. Sue Gloyd, June 5, 1961 (div. June 1978); children: Ashley R., Nathan G.; m. Eleanor M. Veltrop, Oct. 27, 1978. BA, Cen. Mo. State U., 1959; LLB, U. Mo., 1961. Bar: Mo. 1962, U.S. Ct. Mil. Appeals 1963, U.S. Supreme Ct. 1965, U.S. Dist. Ct. (we. dist.) Mo. 1966, U.S. Ct. Appeals (8th cir.) 1968. From assoc. to ptnr. Hendren & Andrae, Jefferson City, Mo., 1965-79; mem. Bartlett, Venters, Pletz & Toppins, P.C., Jefferson City, 1980-87; pvt. practice Jefferson City, 1987-90; mem. Husch & Eppenberger, LLC, Jefferson City, 1990—. With Transit Casualty Co. Receivership, 1986-90, commr. claims, 1986-87, spl. claims counsel, 1987-89, dir. legal affairs dept., 1989-90; lectr. law U. Mo., Columbia, 1965-66. Contbr. editor Mo. Law Rev., 1960-61. Served to capt. JAGC, U.S. Army, 1962-65. Mem. ABA, FBA, Mo. Bar Assn. (chmn. young lawyers sect. 1972-73, ct. modernization com. 1972-74, jud. reform com. 1974-76, chmn. cts. and jud. com. 1978-79, legis. com. 1981-84, President's award 1976, Smithson award 1976), Cole County Bar Assn., Am. Coll. Trial Lawyers (chmn. Mo. 1994-96), Order of Coif. Democrat. Office: Husch and Eppenberger PO Box 1251 235 E High St Jefferson City MO 65102-3236 Office Phone: 573-635-9118. Business E-Mail: alex.bartlett@husch.com.

BARTLETT, PAUL DANA, JR., agribusiness executive; b. Kansas City, Mo., Sept. 16, 1919; s. Paul D. and Alice May (Hiestand) B.; m. Joan Jenkins, May 14, 1949; children— J. Alison Bartlett Jager, Marilyn Bartlett Hebenstreit, Paul Dana III, Frederick Jenkins. BA, Yale U., 1941. Chmn. Bartlett and Co., Kansas City, Mo., 1961-77; pres., chmn. bd. Bartlett and Co. (formerly Bartlett Agri Enterprises, Inc.), Kansas City, 1977—, chmn., dir. Bd. dir. United Mo. Bank, United Mo. Bancshares. Lt. USN, 1942-46 Office: Bartlett and Company 4800 Main St Ste 600 Kansas City MO 64112-2509 Office Phone: 816-753-6300.

BARTLETT, SHERIE, printing company executive; m. Tom Bartlett. CEO, pres. Data Source, Kansas City, Mo. Office: Data Source Inc 1400 Universal Ave Kansas City MO 64120-2140 Fax: 816-483-3284. E-mail: info@data-source.com.

BARTLIT, FRED HOLCOMB, JR., lawyer; b. Harvey, Ill., Aug. 1, 1932; s. Fred Holcomb and Agnes Marie (Rahn) Bartlit; m. Jana Cockrell, Feb. 28, 1987. BS in Engring., US Mil. Acad., 1954; JD, U. Ill., 1960. Bar: Ill. 1960, US Ct. Appeals 7th cir. 1962, US Ct. Appeals 6th cir. 1969, US Ct. Appeals 10th cir. 1970, US Supreme Ct. 1970, US Ct. Appeals 8th cir. 1971, US Ct. Appeals 3rd cir. 1973, US Ct. Appeals 5th cir. 1978. Assoc. Kirkland & Ellis, Chgo., 1960—64, ptnr., 1964—93, Bartlit Beck Herman Palenchar & Scott LLP, Chgo., Denver, 1993—. Lectr. in field; mem. faculty Nat. Inst. Trial Advocacy, 1975—. Served US Army, 1954—58. amed one of America's Top Trial Lawyers --Who They Are & Why They Win, Glasser LegalWorks, 1996, 100 Most Influential Lawyers, Nat. Law Mag., 1997, 2006. Fellow: Internat. Acad. Trial Lawyers, Am. Coll. Trial Lawyers; mem.: Chgo. Bar Assn., Ill. Bar Assn., Castle Pines Golf, Mid-Am., Glen View. Republican. Presbyterian. Office: Bartlit Beck Herman Palenchar & Scott LLP 1899 W Ynkoop St 8th Fl Denver CO 80202

BARTLO, SAM D., lawyer; b. Cleve., Oct. 5, 1919; BBA, Case Western Res. U., 1941; JD, Cleve.-Marshall Law Sch., 1950. Bar: Ohio, 1950, U.S. Supreme Ct., 1958. Mem. firm Buckingham, Doolittle & Burroughs, Akron, Ohio, 1971-90. Capt. U.S. Army, 1942-46. Fellow Am. Bar Found. (life), Ohio Bar Found. (life, pres. 1981-82, trustee 1976-81); mem. ABA (bd. govs. 1989-92, ho. of dels. 1977-94, state del. 1981-89, exec. com. 1990-92, chair ops. com. 1991-92, trustee FJE resource coun. 1992-94), Akron Bar Assn. (pres. 1967-68, exec. com. 1968-7), Ohio State Bar Assn. (coun. dels. 1970-86, pres. 1977-78, exec. com. 1973-79), Am. Judicature Soc., Nat. Conf. Bar Presidents (trustee 1979-82), Ohio Legal Ctr. Inst. (pres. 1979-81, trustee 1977-81). Office: Buckingham Doolittle Burroughs PO Box 1500 Akron OH 44309-1500

BARTON, JANICE SWEENY, chemistry professor; b. Trenton, NJ, Mar. 22, 1939; d. Laurence U. and Lillian Mae (Fletcher) S.; m. Keith M. Barton, Dec. 20, 1967. BS, Butler U., 1962; PhD, Fla. State U., 1970. Postdoctoral fellow Johns Hopkins U., Balt., 1970-72; asst. prof. chemistry East Tex. State U., Commerce, 1972-78, Tex. Woman's U., Denton, 1978-81; assoc. prof. Washburn U., Topeka, 1982-88, prof., 1988—, chair chemistry dept., 1992—. Mem. undergrad. faculty enhancement panel NSF, Washington, 1990; mem. NSF instr. lab. improvement panel, 1992, 96, 99; mem. NSF-AIRE site visit team, 2000; WUKBRIN (NIH grant) coord., 2001—. Contbr. articles to profl. jours. Active Household Hazardous Waste Collection, Topeka, 1991, Solid Waste Task Force, Shawnee County, Kans., 1990; mem. vol. com. YWCA, Topeka, 1984-87; bd. dir. Helping Hand Humane Soc., 2002—; grant coord. Kans. Biomedical Rsch Infrastructure Network, 2002—. Rsch. grantee Petroleum Rsch. Fund, Topeka, 1984-86, NIH, Topeka, 1985-88; instrument grantee NSF, Topeka, 1986, 95. Mem. Am. Chem. Soc. (sec. Dallas-Ft. Worth sect. 1981-82), Kans. Acad. Sci. (pres.-elect 1991, pres. 1992, treas. 1995—), Biophys. Soc., Sigma Xi (pres. TWU club 1980-81), Iota Sigma Pi (mem.-at-large coord. 1987-93). Home: 3401 SW Oak Pky Topeka KS 66614-3218 Office: Washburn U Dept Chemistry Topeka KS 66621 E-mail: janice.barton@washburn.edu.

BARTON, JOHN JOSEPH, obstetrician, gynecologist, administrator, educator, researcher; b. Rockford, Ill., Mar. 19, 1933; s. L. David and Helen M. (Fox) B.; m. Lois Maltby, 1959 (div. 1965); children: Mary Katherine, Karen Ann. BA in History, U. Ill., 1957; BS in Medicine, U. Ill., Chgo., 1959, MD, 1961; student Law, Loyola U., Chgo., 1966-69. Diplomate Am. Bd. Ob.-Gyn.; cert. Advanced Cardiac Life Support. Rotating intern Cook County Hosp., Chgo., 1961-62, resident in ob.-gyn., 1962-65; fellow gynecologic pathology Northwestern U., Chgo., 1963, clin. asst. ob.-gyn., 1963-64, clin. instr. ob.-gyn., 1964-65, assoc. in ob.-gyn., 1965-71; prof. ob.-gyn. Cook County Grad. Sch. of Medicine, Chgo., 1965—; dir. ob.-gyn. rsch. and edn. Cook County Hosp., Chgo., 1965-69; chmn. ob.-gyn. Ill. Masonic Med. Ctr., Chgo., 1970—2001; assoc. prof. ob.-gyn. U. Ill. Coll. Medicine, Chgo., 1971-83, prof., 1983-93, lectr. in ob.-gyn., 1993—; prof. ob.-gyn. Rush Med. Coll., Chgo., 1993—; chmn. emeritus ob-gyn Ill. Masonic Med. Ctr., 2002—. Clin. clerkship subcom. U. Ill. Coll. Medicine, 1974-90, acad. senate 1977-91, 85-87, perinatal steering com., 1977-92, admissions com. 1985-91, screening subcom. 1988-89; ad hoc com. on rules for governance, Rush Med. Coll., Chgo., 1993—, curriculum com. 1993, com. on student evaluation and promotions, 1994—, core ckerkship subcom. of curriculum com. 1995—; editl. bd. Jour. Obstetrics and Gynecology, Am. Jour. Obstetrics and Gynecology, Internat. Jour. Obstetrics and Gynecology Contbr. numerous articles to profl. jours., chpts. to books. including Laparoscopy in Gynecologic Practice, 1972, Guidelines for Perinatal Care, 1983, Antepartum HIV Screenings: A Comparison of Methodologies, 1990. Vol. cons. Ob.-Gyn. Claremore (Okla.) Indian Hosp., 1979-80, 86, Fort Defiance (Ariz.) Indian Hosp., 1981, Red Crescent Soc., Heliopolis, Cairo, Egypt, 1987; vol. surgeon Internat. Red Cross and Red Crescent Soc. Vols., West Beirut, Lebanon, 1982; mem. Ill. Gov.'s AIDS adv. coun.; advisor, expert witness Atty. Gen. State of Ill. on Standards of Practice in Ob.-Gyn.; mem. com. formation of outcome-oriented surveillance systems for Ill. Dept. of Pub. Health, adv. com. to Health Planning Com. for Chgo., perinatal adv. com. Ill. Dept. Health, steering com. Mayor Washington's Infant Mortality Reduction Initiative and others. Sgt. USMC, 1950-55, Korea. Fellow Am. Coll. Obstetricians and Gynecologists (adv. coun. 1977-81, adv. coun. dist. VI 1977-81, chmn. Ill. sect. 1977-78, com. on profl. liability 1989-92, Jr. Fellow Rsch. prize award 1991), Ctrl. Assn. Obstetricians nd Gynecologists (ctrl. travel club, sci. awards com. 1985-89. chmn. 1987-89, Ann. prize award 1988), Chgo. Gynecol. Soc. (exec. com. 1994—, pres. 1995-96), Am. Coll. Surgeons, Soc. Contemporary Medicine and Surgery, Am. Soc. Clin. Hypnosis, Chgo. Inst. Medicine, Royal Soc. Medicine (London); mem. Ill. Assn. Maternal and Child Health, Assn. Profs. Gynecology and Obstetrics, Am. Pub. Health Assn., Phi Kappa Phi, Nu Sigma Nu. Avocations: rancher quarter horses, exotic animals, hounds, harleys. Home: Bar T Ranch 20516 Bunker Hill Rd Marengo IL 60152-8003 Office: Ill Masonic Med Ctr 836 W Wellington Ave Chicago IL 60657-9224 Personal E-mail: barthand2@aol.com.

BARTON, ROBERT H., III, automotive executive; BS in Civil and Elec. Engring., Lehigh U.; postgrad., Carnegie Mellon U. With Alcoa, 1955—96, various mktg. mgmt. positions including industry mgr.-bldg. constrn., N.Y. dist. sales mgr., gen. mgr. Alcoa Export, Alcoa gen. mgr. mktg. sales and distbn. European region, pres. Alcoa Conductor Products Co.; pres. Alcoa Fujikura Ltd., Mexico; non-exec. chmn. J.L. French Holdings, 1996—99; CEO Meridian Automotive Sys. Inc., Dearborn, Mich., chmn., pres., CEO, chmn., 2002—. Mem. internat. supplier adv. coun. Ford Motor Co.; bd. dirs. U.S. Alumweld Co., Outlook Nashville, Japan-Tenn. Soc.; chmn. Tenn. Del. S.E. Govs. U.S.-Japan Orgn. Capt., flight examiner USAF. Mem.: ASCE, Soc. Automotive Engrs.

BARTON, THOMAS J., chemistry professor, researcher; b. Dallas, Nov. 5, 1940; s. Ralph and Florence (Whitfield) Barton; m. Elizabeth Burton, Oct. 1, 1966; children: Ralph, Brett. BS, Lamar U., 1962; PhD in Organic Chemistry (hon.), U. Fla., 1967. NIH postdoctoral fellow Ohio State U., 1967; mem. faculty Iowa State U., Ames, 1967—, prof. chemistry, 1978—, disting. prof., liberal arts and scis., 1984—, program dir. Ames Lab., 1986—88, dir. Ames Lab (US Dept. Energy), 1988—2007, dir. Inst. for Phys. Rsch. and Tech., 1998—. Assoc. prof. U. Montpellier, France; exch. scientist NAS, Former Soviet Union, 1975, NATO, France; mem. coun. on materials scis. Dept. Energy, 1992—97; lectr. Japan Society for the Promotion of Science. Contbr. rsch. papers to profl. publs., editl. bd. Organometallics. Recipient Fredric Stanley Kipping award in organosilicon chemistry, 1982, Gov.'s medal for sci. tchg., 1983, Excellence in Tchg. faculty achievement award, Burlington No. Found., 1988, Outstanding Sci. Accomplishment in Materials Chem. award, Dept. Energy, Materials Sci. Rsch. Competition, 1989, Lab. Dir. of Yr. for Tech. Transfer, Fed. Lab. Consortium, 2003. Fellow: Japan Soc. Promotion of Sci.; mem.: Am. Chem. Soc. (Midwest award 1995). Methodist. Home: 815 Onyx Cir Ames IA 50010-8429 Office: Iowa State Univ Dept Chemistry 1605 Gilman Hall Ames IA 50011-3111 Office Phone: 515-294-2770. E-mail: barton@ameslab.gov.

BARTREM, DUANE HARVEY, retired military officer, residential designer, consultant; b. Lansing, Mich., June 4, 1928; s. Harvey Theodore and Ruby Leola (Thomas) B.; m. Frances Lillie Bushee, Sept. 12, 1948 (dec. Jan.19, 2000); children: Lawrence Duane, Jeffrey Earl. BA in Bus. Adminstrn., Columbia Coll., Mo., 1976. Enlisted U.S. Army N.G., Lansing, 1948, commd. 2d lt., 1951, advanced through grades to col., 1951-76, comdr. battery, 1956-60; facilities engr. Mich. at. Guard, Lansing, 1960-69, chief engr., 1969-76, comdr. 119 FA Bn., 1971-75, comdr. 46th Brigade, 1975-76, comptr., 1976-83, ret., 1983; prin. residential design office Lansing, 1955-60, Grand Ledge, Mich., 1967—. Leader local and regional levels Boy Scouts of Am.; chmn. congregation Bretton Woods Covenant Ch., Mich., 1986—89, v.p. congregation, 1995—. With USNR, 1946—48. Decorated Army Commendation with 3 clusters, Meritorious Svc. medal with 2 clusters, Legion of Merit. Mem. Mil. Officers Assn. (life), Mil. Order Fgn. Wars (sr. vice comdr. gen., 2003-05, comdr. gen. 2005—07, past comdr. gen. 2007-), Assn. of the U.S. Army (life, mem. resolutions com. 1973, 74, chair resolutions com. 1975, area v.p. 1976—, mem. adv. bd. 1978—, chair by-laws com. 1978—, past state pres., past region pres. 1988-92, coun. of trustees 1992-96, Pres.'s medal 1998), Grand Lodge Rotary (pres. 1989-90, Paul Harris award 1992), Boy Scouts Am. (pres. 1973-79, exec. bd. 1970—; disting. Eagle Scout 1989, Silver Beaver award 1969, Silver Antelope 1983, God and Svc. award 1992, James E. West fellow, 1910 Soc., Ernest Thompson Seton Mem. 1999). Avocation: golf. Home Phone: 517-627-9072; Office Phone: 517-627-9072. Personal E-mail: dhbartrem@aol.com.

BARTZ, MERLIN E., state legislator; b. Mason City, Iowa, Mar. 16, 1961; BA in Polit. Sci. and Music cum laude, Luther Coll., 1983. Livestock and grain farmer and laborer; with Grafton Industries, David Mfg. Co.; mem. Iowa Ho. of Reps., 1991-92, Iowa Senate from 10th dist., 1992—. Mem. Worth County Hist. Soc.; dir. ch. choir. Mem. Worth County Pork Prodrs., Farm Bur., N. Iowa Pheasants Forever, Ducks Unltd., Rotary Internat. Republican. Home: 2081 410th St Grafton IA 50440-7510 E-mail: merlin_bartz@legis.state.ia.us.

BASAR, TAMER, electrical engineer, educator; b. Istanbul, Turkey, Jan. 19, 1946; arrived in U.S., 1969; s. Munir and Seniye (Pirilsu) Basar; m. Tangul Unerdem, Dec. 27, 1975; children: Gozen, Elif. BSEE, Robert Coll., Istanbul, 1969; MS, Yale U., 1970, MPhil, 1971, PhD, 1972. Rsch. fellow Harvard U., Cambridge, Mass., 1972-73; sr. rsch. scientist Marmara Rsch. Inst., Gebze, Kocaeli, Turkey, 1973-80; adj. assoc. prof. Bogazici U., Istanbul, 1974-80; assoc. prof. elec. engring. U. Ill., Urbana, 1980-83, prof., 1983—, disting. prof., 1998—. Co-author: (book) Dynamic Noncooperative Game Theory, 1982, 3d edit., 1999, H-Infinity Optimal Control and Related Minimax Design Problems, 1991, 2d edit., 1995; editor: Dynamic Games and Applications in Econs., 1986, Control Theory: Twenty-Five Seminal Papers (1932-1981), 2001; co-editor: Differential Games and Applications, 1989, Advances in Dynamic Games and Applications, 1994; editor-in-chief: Automatica, 2004—; contbr. articles to profl. jours.; editor: 2 jours. in control theory; assoc. editor: 1 jour. in games, 1 jour. in control. Recipient Young Scientist award in Applied Math., Turkish Nat. Rsch. Coun., 1976, award, Sedat Simavi Found., 1979, medal of sci., Turkey, 1993, Drucker award, U. Ill. Urbana-Champagne, Coll. Engring., 2004, Quazza medal, Internat. Fedn. Automatic Control, 2005. Fellow: IEEE (v.p. Control Sys. Soc. 1997—98, pres.-elect 1999, pres. 2000, Disting. Mem. award 1993, Best Paper award 1995, Bode Lecture Prize award); mem.: NAE, European Acad. Scis., Am. Math. Soc., Game Theory Soc., Internat. Soc. Dynamic Games (pres. 1990—94), Soc. Indsl. Applied Math. Home: 2810 Valley Brook Dr Champaign IL 61822-7621 Office: U Ill 1308 W Main St Urbana IL 61801-2307 Business E-Mail: basar1@uiuc.edu.

BASART, JOHN PHILIP, electrical engineering and remote sensing researcher; b. Des Moines, Feb. 26, 1938; s. Philip Edwin and Hildreth Pauline (Belden) B.; m. Luann Kay Stow, Mar. 2, 1960; children— Jill Eileen Urban, Ann Marie BS, Iowa State U., 1962, MS, 1963, PhD in Elec. Engring., 1967. Rsch. assoc. Nat. Radio Astronomy Obs., Charlottesville, Va., 1967-69; system scientist Very Large Array, Socorro, N.Mex., 1979-81; asst. prof. elec. engring. Iowa State U., Ames, 1969-73, assoc. prof., 1973-80, prof., 1980-2000, prof. emeritus, 2000—. Campus coord. Iowa Space Grant Consortium. Contbr. articles to profl. jours. With USAF, 1955—59. Recipient student award IRE, 1962 Mem. IEEE (sr. mem.), AIAA, Am. Geophys. Union, Am. Astron. Soc., Internat. Astron. Union, Internat. Soc. for Optical Engring., Sigma Xi, Eta Kappa Nu, Tau Beta Pi, Phi Kappa Phi. Achievements include research in radio astronomy, image processing, wave propagation, remote sensing. Office: Iowa State U 2271 Howe Hl Rm 2348 Ames IA 50011-0001 E-mail: jpbasart@iastate.edu.

BASCOM, C. PERRY, retired foundation administrator, lawyer; b. Boston, July 30, 1936; s. William Richardson and Jean Ames (Hall) B.; m. Sally Cissel Greenwood, July 18, 1995; children: Elisabeth Brooke, Heather Ames, Sarah Duff Greenwood, Amy Greenwood Dunaway. BA, Yale U., 1958; LLB, Harvard U., 1961. Assoc. Bryan Cave, St. Louis, 1962-72, ptnr., 1972-95; adminstr. Gateway Found., St. Louis, 1995—2001, ret., 2001. Judge St. Louis Night Housing Ct., 1970-72; lectr. on various topics, including Truth in Lending, Real Estate Settlement Procedures Act, techniques in comml. bank lending, devels. in Mo. banking law, electronic funds transfers. Sr. warden Trinity Ch., St. Louis, 1974-78. Served with USAR, 1961-68. Mem. Mo. Bar Assn. Home: 4235 Olive St Saint Louis MO 63108 Home Phone: 314-367-1512. Personal E-mail: scgcpb@earthlink.net.

BASDEN, CAMERON, dancer; b. Dallas; Student, Joffrey Ballet Sch., 1976-77. Dancer Dallas Ballet, 1975-76, Joffrey II Dancers, NYC, 1977-79, Joffrey Ballet, NYC, 1979—, asst. ballet mistress, 1990-93, ballet mistress NYC, Chgo., 1993—. Prof. dance Manhattanville Coll. Actor: (films) The Company, 2003. Office: Joffrey Ballet 70 E Lake St Fl 1300 Chicago IL 60601-5917

BASHOOK, PHILIP G., medical association executive, educator; b. Bklyn., Mar. 10, 1943; children: Jeremy, Amy, Jeffrey, Gregory, Richard. BS in Zoology, U. Calif., Santa Barbara, 1965; MSc in Biology, Calif. State U., Northridge, 1968; EdD, U. B.C., Can., 1971. From asst. to assoc. prof, Ctr. Ednl. Devel. Health Sci. Ctr. U. Ill., Chgo., 1971-74; assoc. dir. Michael Reese Hosp. and Med. Ctr., Chgo., 1975-80, dir., 1980-87; dir. Office Edn. Am. Psychiatric Assn., Washington, 1987-90; dir. evaluation and edn. Am. Bd. Med. Specialities, Evanston, Ill., 1991—. Adj. assoc. prof. dept. med. edn. U. Ill. Coll. Medicine, Chgo., 1975-87, 91—; adj. assoc. prof. dept. psychiatry and behavior scis. George Washington, 1988-91; adj. assoc. prof. Northwestern U. Med. Sch., 1999—; mem. accreditation rev. com. Accreditation Coun. Continuing Med. Edn., 1980-87, vice chmn., 1982-87, mem. monitoring com., 1996—, vice-chair, 1999—. Co-author: Construction and Use of Written Simulations, 1976; author 17 books; contbr. chpts. to books and articles to profl. jours. Bd. dirs. Pub. Sch. Dist. # 69 Cook County, Ill., 1980-87, bd. sec., 1985-87.

BASHWINER, STEVEN LACELLE, lawyer; b. Cin., Aug. 3, 1941; s. Carl Thomas and Ruth Marie (Burlis) B.; m. Arden J. Lang, Apr. 24, 1966 (div. 1978); children: Heather, David; m. Donna Lee Gerber, Sept. 13, 1981; children: Margaret, Matthew. AB, Holy Cross Coll., 1963; JD, U. Chgo., 1966. Bar: Ill. 1966, U.S. Dist. Ct. (no. dist.) Ill. 1967, U.S. Dist. Ct. (ea. dist.) Wis. 1988, U.S. Dist. Ct. (no. dist.) Calif. 1994, U.S. Dist. Ct. (ea. dist.) Mich. 2003, U.S. Ct. Appeals (7th cir.) 1968, U.S. Ct. Appeals (4th cir.) 1990, U.S. Supreme Ct. 1970. Assoc. Kirkland & Ellis, Chgo., 1966-72, ptnr., 1972-76, Friedman & Koven, Chgo., 1976-86, Katten Muchin Rosenman LLP, Chgo., 1986—. Bd. dirs. Constl. Rights Found., Chgo. Served to sgt. USAFR, 1966-72. Mem. ABA, 7th Cir. Bar Assn., Chgo. Bar Assn., Chgo. Inn of Ct. (pres. 2004-05), Lawyers Club Chgo. Home: 834 Green Bay Rd Highland Park IL 60035-4630 Office: Katten Muchin Rosenman LLP 525 W Monroe St Ste 1900 Chicago IL 60661-3693 Home Phone: 847-432-0671; Office Phone: 312-902-5330. Business E-Mail: steven.bashwiner@kattenlaw.com.

BASIL, BRAD L., technology education educator; Tchr. Mt. Logan Mid. Sch., Chillicothe, Ohio, asst. prin.; tchr. Smith Mid. Sch., Chillicothe, 1988—. Recipient Tchr. Excellence for Ohio award Internat. Tech. Edn. Assn., 1992. Office: Smith Middle Sch 345 Arch St Chillicothe OH 45601-1519 also: Mt Logan Middle Sch 841 E Main St Chillicothe OH 45601-3509

BASKA, JAMES LOUIS, wholesale grocery company executive; b. Kansas City, Kans., Apr. 3, 1927; s. John James and Stella Marie (Wilson) B.; m. Juanita Louise Carlson, Oct. 14, 1950; children: Steven James, Scott David. BSBA, U. Kans., 1949; JD, U. Mo., 1960. Bar: Kans. 1960. Pres., chief exec. officer Baska Laundry Co., Kansas City, 1951-62; ptnr. Rice & Baska, Kansas City, 1962-76; corporate sec., gen. counsel Assoc. Wholesale Grocers Inc., Kansas City, 1976-77, v.p., sec., gen. counsel, 1977-79, exec. v.p., chief fin. officer, sec., gen. counsel, 1979-84, pres., chief exec. officer, 1984-92; pres. emeritus, 1992. Mem. SDC com. Wakefern Food Corp., 1998-2005; bd. dirs. Raley's, Riverwood Homes, Inc. Served as staff sgt. U.S. Army, 1944-46. Mem. Nat. Grocers Assn. (bd. dirs. 1980-89, chmn. 1987-88), Food Mktg. Inst. (bd. dirs. 1988-93). Republican. Roman Catholic. Avocations: hunting, golf. Office: Assoc Wholesale Grocers Inc PO Box 2932 5000 Kansas Ave Kansas City KS 66106-1135

BASS, LEE MARSHALL, food products company executive; b. 1950; s. Perry R. Bass and Nancy Lee; m. Ramona Bass. BA/BS, Yale U., 1979; MBA, U. Pa. Wharton Sch. Bus. With Bass Enterprises Prodn. Co., Ft. Worth, 1970—; chmn. bd. Nat. Farms, Inc., Kansas City, Mo., 1992—, also bd. dirs.; pres. Lee M. Bass Inc., Ft. Worth. Named one of Forbes' Richest Americans, 1999—, World's Richest People, Forbes mag., 1999—. Office: Nat Farms Inc 4800 Main St Kansas City MO 64112-2510 also: Bass Bros Enterprises 201 Main St Fort Worth TX 76102-3105 also: Lee M Bass Inc 201 Main St Fort Worth TX 76102-3105 Office: Modern Art Museum 3200 Darnell St Fort Worth TX 76107-2872

BASS, PAUL, retired medical educator; b. Winnipeg, Man., Can., Aug. 12, 1928; arrived in U.S., 1958; s. Benjamin and Sarah Bass; m. Ruth Zipursky, May 31, 1953; children: Stuart, Susan. BS in Pharmacy, U. B.C., 1953, MA in Pharmacology, 1955; PhD in Pharmacology, McGill U., 1957. Rsch. asst. Ayerst, McKenna & Harrison, Canada, 1956; fellow in biochemistry McGill U., 1957—58; fellow in physiology Mayo Found., 1958—60; assoc. lab. dir. Parke, Davis & Co., 1960-70; prof. pharmacology Sch. Pharmacy and Sch. Medicine, U. Wis., Madison, 1970-2000, prof. emeritus, 2001—. Mem. editl. bd. Am. Jour. Physiology, 1976—79, 1981—92, Jour. Pharmacology and Exptl. Therapeutics, 1980—99; contbr. chapters to books, articles to profl. jours. Mem.: Am. Gastroent. Assn., Am. Soc. Pharmacology and Exptl. Therapeutics. Office: 777 Highland Ave Madison WI 53705-2222 Office Phone: 608-262-5753. E-mail: pbass@wisc.edu.

BASS, STEVEN CRAIG, computer science educator; b. Indpls., July 29, 1943; s. Leland Ellsworth and Isabelle Frances (Ross) B.; m. Sara Ann Hiday, Sept. 4, 1965 (div. Apr. 1988); children: Leland Kai, Marshall Lynn; m. Kevyn Anne Salsburg, Jan. 2, 1989. BSEE, Purdue U., 1966, MSEE, 1968, PhD in Elec. Engring., 1971. Prof. elec. engring. Purdue U., Lafayette, Ind., 1971-88; prof. elec. and computer engring. George Mason U., Fairfax, Va., 1988-91; prin. engr. Mitre Corp., McLean, Va., 1988-91; prof. computer sci. and engring., chmn. dept. U. Notre Dame, Notre Dame, Ind., 1991-2000; co-owner St. John Condos, LLC, otre Dame, Ind., 2007—. Cons. Magnovox Co., Ft. Wayne, Ind., 1971-73, Admiral Corp., Chgo., 1973-76, Kimball Internat., Jasper, Ind., 1978-84, Tektronix Corp., Wilsonville, Oreg., 1987-88. Contbr. over 25 articles to profl. jours., delievered over 35 papers at sci. confs. Rescue officer Stockwell (Ind.) Vol. Fire Dept., 1985-88. Recipient numerous grants from NSF, USAF, IBM, Mitre Corp., others. Fellow IEEE (v.p. circuits and sys. soc. 1981, 91-93, mem. audio engring. soc.); mem. Tau Beta Pi. Roman Catholic. Achievements include 3 U.S. and 6 fgn. patents in the field of digital signal processing. Office Phone: 340-779-4218. Personal E-mail: stevenbass@earthlink.net. Business E-Mail: bass@cse.nd.edu.

BASSETT, LESLIE RAYMOND, composer, educator; b. Hanford, Calif., Jan. 22, 1923; s. Archibald Leslie and Vera (Starr) B.; m. Anita Elizabeth Denniston, Aug. 21, 1949; children— Wendy Lynn (Mrs. Lee Bratton), Noel Leslie, Ralph (dec.). BA in Music, Fresno State Coll., 1947; M.Music in Composition, U. Mich., 1949, A.Mus.D., 1956; student, Ecole Normale de Musique, Paris, France, 1950-51. Tchr. music pub. schs., Fresno, 1951-52; mem. faculty U. Mich., 1952—, prof. music, 1965—, Albert A. Stanley disting univ. prof., 1977—, chmn. composition dept., 1970, Henry Russel lectr., 1984, emeritus, 1992. Guest composer Berkshire Music Center, Tanglewood, Mass., 1973 Served with AUS, 1942-46. Fulbright fellow, 1950-51; recipient Rome prize Am. Acad. in Rome, 1961-63; grantee Soc. Pub. Am. Music, 1960, Nat. Inst. Arts and Letters, 1964, Nat. Council Arts, 1966; Guggenheim fellow, 1973-74, 80-81; recipient Pulitzer prize in music for Variations for Orch., 1966; citation U. Mich. regents, 1966; Walter Naumburg Found. rec. award for Sextet, 1974; Disting. Alumnus award Calif. State U., Fresno, 1978; Disting. Artist award Mich. Council Arts, 1981; Citation of Merit, U. Mich. Sch. Music Alumni, 1980 Mem. Am. Composers Alliance, Mich. Soc. Fellows, Am. Acad. of Arts and Letters, Pi Kappa Lambda, Phi Kappa Phi, Phi Mu Alpha. Methodist.

BASSETT, TINA, communications executive; b. Detroit; m. Leland Kinsey Bassett; children: Joshua, Robert. Student, U. Mich., 1974, 76-78, 81, Wayne State U., 1979-80. Advt. dir. Greenfield's Restaurant, Mich. and Ohio, 1972-73; dir. advt. and pub. rels. Kresco, Inc., Detroit, 1973-74; pub's. rep. The Detroiter mag., 1974-75; pub. rels. dir. Detroit Bicentennial Commn., 1975-77; prin. Leland K. Bassett & Assocs., Detroit, 1976-86; intermediate job devel. specialist Detroit Coun. of the Arts, 1977; project dir. Detroit image campaign dept. pub. info. City of Detroit, 1975, spl. events dir., 1978, dep. dir. dept. pub. info., 1978-83, dir. dept. pub. info., 1983-86; pres., prin. Bassett & Bassett, Inc., Detroit, 1986—. Publicity chmn. Under the Stars IV, V, VI, VII, VIII, IX and X, Benefit Balls, Detroit Inst. Arts Founders Soc., 1983-88, Mich. Opera Theater, Opera Ball, 1987, Grand Prix Ball, 1989; bd. dirs., co-chair, prodr. Music Hall Ctr. for Performing Arts, pub. chmn., 1996, bd. dirs., 2007—; bd. dirs. Weizman Inst. Sci., 1996-97, Detroit Inst. Arts, 2006—; mem. Cinema Arts Coun., 1996—. Named Outstanding Woman in Agy. Top Mgmt., Detroit chpt. Am. Women in Radio and TV, 1989, one of Most Powerful Women in Mich., CORP Mag., 2002. Mem. AIA (hon., pub. dir. 1990-91, bd. dirs., Richard Upjohn fellowship 1991), Detroit Hist. Soc., Internat. Women's Forum, Music Hall Assn., Pub. Rels. Soc. Am. (Advt. Woman of Yr. 1989), Woman's Advt. Club Detroit. Home: 30751 Cedar Creek Dr Farmington Hills MI 48336-4989 Office: Bassett & Bassett Inc 1400 First National Bldg 660 Woodward Av Detroit MI 48226-3581 Office Phone: 313-965-3010. Office Fax: 313-965-3016.

BASSI, SUZANNE HOWARD, retired secondary school educator, volunteer; b. Santa Ana, Calif., Feb. 26, 1945; d. David Gould and Marian (Matthews) H.; m. Roger Joseph Bassi, Aug. 25, 1973; children: Carrie, Steven, Gregory. BA, Rosary Coll., River Forest, Ill., 1966; MA in Teaching, U. Ill., Champaign, 1973. Tchr. Resurrection HS, Chgo., 1966-67, Proviso Twp. HS, Hillside, Ill., 1967-76; home day care operator Palatine, Ill., 1980-84; mem. bd. Palatine Elem. Sch. Dist. # 15, 1987-95. Vice chmn. Ed-Red, Park Ridge, Ill., 1993, chmn., 1994-96;

legis. chmn. Ill. Assn. Sch. Bds., North Cook divsn., Lombard, Ill., 1994-96; Rep. candidate dist. 54 Ill. Gen. Assembly, 1996, state rep. dist. 54, 1998—. Named Those Who Excel, Ill. State Bd. Edn., 1992. Mem. LWV (former bd. dir., legis. chair), Rep. Women's Roundtable. Republican. Roman Catholic. Home: 1272 S Falcon Dr Palatine IL 60067

BASSIOUNY, HISHAM SALLAH, surgeon, educator; b. Cairo, Mar. 30, 1954; m. Sandra Bassiouny; children: Deenah, Faith-Iman. Mb. Bch. Diploma with honors, Cairo U., 1977. Diplomate Am. Bd. Surgery; lic. surgeon, Ill., Mich., Md. Intern Cairo U. Hosps., 1977-78; surg. externship Linz (Austria) Gen. Hosp., 1980-81; intern Md. Gen. Hosp., Balt., 1981-82; resident Henry Ford Hosp., Detroit, 1982-86, clin. vascular fellow, 1986-87; postdoctoral rsch. fellow, instr. surgery U. Chgo., 1987-89, asst. prof. surgery, 1989-96, assoc. prof. surgery, 1996—, dir. non-invasive vascular lab., 1988—, Weiss Meml. Hosp., 1989—, dir. Chgo Ctr. for Minimally Invasive Vascular Therapy, 1998—. Mem. staff U. Chgo. Med. Ctr., Little Co. Mary Hosp., Weiss Meml. Hosp., dir. non-invasive vascular lab. Contbr. chpts. to books and numerous articles to profl. jours. Recipient Louis Block award, 1989; grantee W.L. Gore, 1987-89, NIH, 1988—, Mellon Found., 1990, U. Chgo., 1992-93, Washington Sqare Found., 1992, Am. Heart Assn., 1995—. Fellow ACS; mem. AAAS, AAS, Am. Heart Assn. (sci. coun. 1992—, coun. atherosclerosis, coun. cardio-thoracic and vascular surgery), Am. Venous Forum, Midwestern Vascular Soc., North Am. Vascular Biology Orgn., Internat. Soc. Cardiovascular Surgery, Chgo. Surg. Soc., Peripheral Vascular Surg. Soc., Soc. Vascular Surgery. Office: U Chgo 5841 S Maryland Ave # Mc5028 Chicago IL 60637-1463

BASTIAN, GARY WARREN, judge; b. St. Paul, Nov. 07; s. Warren John and Virginia (Brower) Bastian; children: Alexander, Christopher. BS, Wis. State U., 1970; JD, William Mitchell Co., 1974. Bar: Minn. 1975. Rschr. Minn. Taxpayers Assn., 1970-73; dir. IR rsch. staff Minn. Senate, 1974-85; project dir. labor mgmt. com. Minn. Sch., 1985-87; pvt. practice, 1987-91; asst. commr. Dept. Labor and Industry, 1991, dep. commr., 1991-95, commr., 1995-97; judge 2d Jud. Dist. Ramsey County, 1997—; presiding judge spl. cts., 2006—. Mem. Maplewood City council, Minn., 1980-90. mayor 1990-97; bd. dirs. East Communities Family Ctr., 1986-90, Minn. League of Cities, 1988-92, Nat. Assn. Govt. Labor Officials, 1995-97, sec.-treas., 1996-97, Ramsey-Washington Counties Suburban Cable Commn., 1991-97, State Fund Mut. Ins. Co., 1995-97, Minn. Safety Coun., 1996-97; chmn. Minn. Workers' Compensation Adv. Coun., 1995-97. Mem. Criminal Def. Svcs. Bd., 1998—; bd. dirs. U. Wis.-River Falls Found., 1997-2006; mem. Ramsey County Violence Coord. Coun., 1999—; mem. Hmong Ctr. Peace, 2002—. Recipient award of merit Local 320, Pub. and Law Enforcement Teamsters Mpls., 1979. Mem. Assn. Met. Municipalities (bd. dirs. 1981-89, pres. 1987-88), Suburban C. of C. (bd. dirs. 1979-84. Roman Catholic. Office: Ramsey County Courthouse 15 W Kellogg Blvd #600 Saint Paul MN 55102 Office Phone: 651-266-5165. E-mail: gary.bastian@courts.state.mn.us.

BASTIAN, ROBERT W., otolaryngologist; BA magna cum laude, Greenville Coll., 1974; MD, Washington U. Sch. Medicine, 1978. Lic. Ill., cert. Nat. Bd. Med. Examiners, Am. Bd. Otolaryngology, Royal Coll. Physicians and Surgeons Can. (Otolaryngology). Fellow, laryngology, Paris, 1983, Lyon, France, 1983, Erlangen, Germany, 1983, Marburg, Germany, 1983; chief resident, otolaryngology Washington U. Hosp., 1982—83, resident, otolaryngology, 1979—82; resident, surgery Jewish Hosp. of St. Louis, Washington U., 1978—79; attending staff Foster G. McGaw Hosp., Loyola U. Med. Ctr., Maywood, Ill., 1987—2003; asst. prof., otolaryngology Washington U. Sch. Medicine, 1984—87, Loyola U. Sch. Medicine, 1987—91; consulting staff Hines VA Hosp., Loyola U. Med. Ctr., 1987—2003; assoc. prof., otolaryngology Loyola U. Sch. Medicine, 1991—2000, prof., otolaryngology, 2000—03; attending staff Good Samaritan Hosp., 2003—; pres., dir. Bastian Voice Inst., Downers Grove, Ill., 2003—. Med. advisor Nat. Spasmodic Dysphonia Assn., 1998—; bd. advisor Voice Care Network, 2000—, VASTA, 2000—; invited spkr. in field. Referee for several profl. publications; contbr. chapters to books, articles to profl. jours. Named one of Top Doctors in Chgo., Chgo. Mag.; named to America's Registry of Outstanding Professionals, 2002, America's Top Physicians, 2003. Mem.: Ill. Soc. Opthalmology & Otolaryngology (pres. 2002, mem.-at-large 1999—2000), Chgo. Laryngologic and Otologic Soc., Ill. Laryngologic and Otologic Soc., Am. Acad. Otolaryngology (Head and Neck Surgery Honor award 1995). Office: Bastian Voice Inst 3010 Highland Pkwy Ste 550 Downers Grove IL 60515 Office Phone: 630-724-1100. Office Fax: 630-724-0084.*

BATAILLON, JOSEPH FRANCIS, chief federal judge; b. Omaha, Oct. 3, 1949; s. Joseph Franklin and Norma Jean (Lock) B.; m. Pamela Dawn Nelson, Aug. 17, 1971; children: Aimee, Jared, Margery, Patrick, Kathryn. BA in Polit. Sci., Creighton U., 1971, JD, 1974. Bar: Nebr. 1974, US Dist. Nebr. 1974, US Ct. Appeals (8th cir.) 1982. Dep. pub. defender Pub. Defender's Office County of Douglas, Omaha, 1971-80; assoc., trial atty. Sodoro, Daly & Sodoro, Omaha, 1980—97; judge US Dist. Ct. (Nebr. dist.), Omaha, 1997—, chief judge, 2004—. Def. counsel USAR, Omaha, 1976-86; commr. Nebr. Jud. Resources Commn., Lincoln, Nebr., 1986—; lector U. ebr. Med. Ctr., Omaha, 1988—. Congl. chair Nebr. Dem. Party, Lincoln, 1993-95, mem. parish coun. St. Pius X Ch., Omaha, 1988—; commr. Nebr. Jud. Resources Commn., Lincoln, 1986. With 403rd Military Police USAR, 1976—78. Recipient chair's award Douglas County Dems., 1990. Mem. ABA, Nebr. Bar Assn. (del. Omaha chpt. 1981—), Omaha Bar Assn., Nebr. Assn. Trial Attys., Nebr. Criminal Def. Atty.'s Assn., Optimists (pres. 1984-85). Roman Catholic. Office: RL Hruska US Courthouse Ste 3259 111 S 18th Plz Omaha NE 68102-1322

BATCHELDER, ALICE M., federal judge; b. Wilmington, Del., Aug. 15, 1944; m. William G. Batchelder III; children: William G. IV, Elisabeth. BA, Ohio Wesleyan U., 1964; JD, Akron U., 1971; LLM, U. Va., 1988; LHD (hon.), Lake Erie Coll., 1993; LLD (hon.), U. Akron Sch. of Law, 2001. Tchr. Plain Local Sch. Dist., Franklin County, Ohio, 1965—66, Jones Jr. High Sch., 1966-67, Buckeye High Sch., Medina County, 1967-68; assoc. Williams & Batchelder, Medina, Ohio, 1971-83; judge US Bankruptcy Ct., Ohio, 1983-85, US Dist. Ct. (no. dist.) Ohio, Cleve., 1985-91, US Ct. of Appeals (6th cir.), Cleveland, 1991—. Mem. Com. on Bankruptcy Edn., Fed. Jud. Ctr., 1988—91, Jud. Conf. Adv. Com. on Bankruptcy Rules, 1993—96, Jud. Conf. on US Com. on Automation and Tech., 2000—03. Editor-in-chief Univ. Akron Law Rev., 1971. Recipient Outstanding Alumni award, U. Akron Sch. of Law, 1993, Hon. award, 1996, Women of Distinction award, Medina County YWCA, 1997. Mem. Fed. Judge's Assn., Fed. Bar Assn., Medina County Bar Assn.

BATEMAN, C. BARRY, airport terminal executive; Airport dir. Gen. Mitchell Internat. Airport, Milw. Office: Gen Mitchell Internat Airport 5300 S Howell Ave Milwaukee WI 53207-6156

BATEMAN, JOHN JAY, classics educator; b. Elmira, NY, Feb. 17, 1931; s. Joseph Earl and Etha M. (Edwards) B.; m. Patricia Ann Hageman, July 5, 1952; children: Kristine M., Kathleen A., John Eric. BA, U. Toronto, 1953; MA, Cornell U., 1954, PhD, 1958. Lectr. Univ. Coll., U. Toronto, 1956-57; lectr., then asst. prof. U. Ottawa, 1957-60; mem. faculty U. Ill., Urbana, 1960—, prof. classics and speech, 1968-93; prof. emeritus, 1993—; head dept. classics U. Ill., 1966-73, chmn., 1988-92, acting dir. Sch. Humanities, 1973-74. Author, editor books and articles. Mem.: Am. Philol. Assn. (sec.-treas. 1968—73), Renaissance Soc. Am.

BATEMAN, LEONARD ARTHUR, engineering executive; BSEE, U. Man., Can., 1942, MSc, 1948. Pres., CEO Bateman & Assocs., Winnipeg, Man., Can. Decorated Order of Man.; recipient Gold Medal award CCPE, 1994. Office: Bateman & Assocs 231 Brock St Winnipeg MB Canada R3N OY7

BATEMAN, SHARON LOUISE, public relations executive; b. St. Louis, Oct. 18, 1949; d. Frank Hamilton and Charlotte Elizabeth (Hogan) Bateman. Student, Drury Coll., 1967-69; BJ, U. Mo., 1971. Asst. dir. pub. rels. Cardinal Glennon Hosp. Children, St. Louis, 1971-76; staff asst. pub. rels. Ozark Air Lines, St. Louis, 1976-80; mgr. corp. rels. Kellwood Co., St. Louis, 1980-83; mgr. corp. comm. May Dept. Stores Co., St. Louis, 1983-86, dir. corp. comm., 1986-94, v.p. corp. comms., 2000—06; mgr. comm. Arthur Andersen, St. Louis, 1995-96; mgr. editl. and adminstrv. svcs. Falk Design Group, St. Louis, 1996—2000; oper. v.p. corp. comms. and corp. giving Macy's, Inc., Cin., 2006—. Bd. dirs. St. Michael's Houses, 1996—97, Gateway Greening, 1999—2001, The Wellness Cmty., 2004—06, Cin. Ballet, 2007—. Recipient Best Regional Airline Employee Publ. award, Editor's Assn. Am. Transp. Assn., 1978. Mem.: Pub. Rels. Soc. Am. (sec.St. Louis chpt. 1983, bd. dirs. 1988—90, v.p. 1991), Internat. Assn. Bus. Comms. (pres. St. Louis chpt. 1977). Office: Macy's Inc 7 W Seventh St Cincinnati OH 45202

BATES, ERIC RANDOLPH, physician; b. Ann Arbor, Mich., Apr. 10, 1950; s. Richard Chester and Signe (Hegge) B.; m. Nancy Joanne Fortino, Sept. 25, 1976; children: Andrew, Alexis, Evan. AB, Princeton U., 1972; MD, U. Mich., 1976. Diplomate Am. Bd. Internal Medicine with added qualifications in cardiovascular diseases and interventional cardiology. Resident, internal medicine U. Mich., Ann Arbor, 1976—79, fellow, cardiovascular disease, 1981, instr. in internal medicine, 1981-84, asst. prof. internal medicine, 1984-89, assoc. prof. internal medicine, 1989-95, prof. internal medicine, 1995—, dir. cardiac catheterization lab., 1994—. Fellow ACP, Am. Coll. Cardiology, Am. Coll. Chest Physicians, Am. Heart Assn. Office: U Mich Cardiovascular Ctr Rm 2A398 1500 E Medical Center Dr Floor 3 Ann Arbor MI 48109 Office Phone: 734-936-5840. Office Fax: 734-936-7026.*

BATES, WILLIAM HUBERT, lawyer; b. Lexington, Mo., Apr. 14, 1926; s. George Hubert and E. Norma (Comer) B.; m. Joy LoRue Godbehere, Oct. 20, 1956; children: William Brand, Joy Ann. BA, U. Mo., 1949; JD, U. Mich., 1952. Bar: Mo. 1952. With Lathrop & Gage L.C., Kansas City, Mo., 1952—, chmn., 1988-95. Mem., pres. bd. curators U. Mo. Multi-Campus U., 1983-89. Sgt. U.S. Army, 1943-46, ETO. Recipient Brotherhood award NCCJ, 1984; Disting. Alumni award U. Mo., 1989, Geyer award for pub. svc., 1991. Fellow Am. Bar Found. (state chmn. 1990-97); mem. ABA (ho. of dels. 1990-93), Mo. Bar Assn. (bd. dirs. 1982-91, v.p., pres. 1988-89), Kansas City Bar Assn. (pres. Found. 1985-87), Lawyers Assn. Kansas City (Charles Evans Whittaker award 1990), Mo. C. of C. (chmn., bd. dirs. 1983-85), Greater Kansas City C. of C. (bd. dirs., chmn. 1975-92), Van Guard Club, Mercury Club, Beta Theta Pi (Man of Yr. award Kansas City 1985, Oxford Cup 1996). Democrat. Methodist. Avocations: golf, swimming, music. Home: 310 W 49th St Apt 1002 Kansas City MO 64112-3400 Office: Lathrop & Gage L C 2345 Grand Blvd Ste 2600 Kansas City MO 64108-2617 Home Phone: 816-756-3898; Office Phone: 816-292-2000. Business E-Mail: bbates@lathropgage.com.

BATIUK, THOMAS MARTIN, cartoonist; b. Akron, Ohio, Mar. 14, 1947; s. Martin and Verna (Greskovics) B.; m. Catherine L. Wesemeyer, June 26, 1971; 1 child, Brian. B.F.A., Kent State U., Ohio, 1969, cert. edn., 1969. Tchr. art Eastern Heights Jr. High Sch., 1969-72; syndicated cartoonist, 1972—. Cartoonist: comic strip Funky Winkerbean, 1972—, John Darling, 1979—, Crankshaft, 1987—; collections include Funky Winkerbean, 1973, Funky Winkerbean, Play It Again Funky, 1975, Funky Winkerbean, Closed Out, 1977, Yearbook, 1979, You Know You've Got Trouble When Your Mascot is a Scpaegoat, 1984, Football Fields are for Band Practice, 1986, Sunday Concert, 1987, Henry C. Dinkle-Live at Carnegie Hall, 1988, A Pizza Pilgrim's Progress, 1990, Funky Winkerbean: Gone with the Woodwinds, 1992, Would the Ushers Please Lock the Doors, 1994, Crankshaft: I've Still Got It, 1995; co-author: And One Slice With Anchovies!, 1993, Crankshaft, 1992; forward: A PArent's Guide to Band and ORchestra, 1991, Attack of the Band Moms, 1996. Recipient 46th Annual Ohio Gov.'s award-Journalism, 1995. Mem. Nat. Cartoonists Soc., Newspaper Features Coun. Office: care Universal Press Syndicate 4520 Main St Ste 700 Kansas City MO 64111-1816

BATON, MARY ROSE GALLAGHER, medical technician, entertainer; d. Charles Francis James and Ruth Alice Snyder Richards O'Gallagher; children: Donald Edward, David Charles, Elizabeth Anne, Sandra Marie. BSc, U. Wis., 1955. Registered med. technologist Bd. Registry, Am. Soc. Clin. Pathologists. With City/Found. Hosp., Madison, Wis., 1955-58; cert. med. technologist practitioner Madison, Wis., 1956—; owner Mary Rose Gallagher Baton. Candidate for office Dane County Rep. Party. Wis. State scholar, 1951. Mem. Chi Omega. Home and Office: 1902 # 124 Londonderry Dr Madison WI 53704 Office Phone: 608-243-1342.

BATSAKIS, JOHN GEORGE, pathology educator; b. Petoskey, Mich., Aug. 14, 1929; s. George John and Stella (Vlahkis) B.; m. Mary Janet Savage, Dec. 28, 1957; children: Laura, Sharon, George. Student, Va. Mil. Inst., 1947, Albion Coll., Mich., 1948-50; MD, U. Mich., 1954. Diplomate Am. Bd. Pathology. Intern George Washington Univ. Hosp., Washington, 1954-55; resident in pathology U. Mich. Hosp., Ann Arbor, 1955-59; prof. pathology U. Mich., Ann Arbor, 1969-79; chmn. dept. pathology M.D. Anderson Hosp. U. Tex., Houston, 1981-96, chm. and prof. emeritus dept pathology, 1996—. Ruth Legett Jones prof. U. Tex., Austin, 1982-96; adj. prof. oral pathology U. Tex. Dental Br., Houston; cons. Armed Forces Inst. Pathology, 1972—, VA Hosp., Ann Arbor, 1968-79; Hayes Martin lectr. Am. Soc. for Head and Neck Surgery, 1994; Gunnar Holmgren lectr. Swedish Nat. Ear, Nose, Throat Meeting, 1994; William Christopherson lectr. U. Louisville Dept. of Pathology, 1995; external examiner U. Hong Kong Dental Sch., 1995—; Francis A. Sooy lectr. dept. otolaryngology, head and neck surgery U. Calif., San Francisco, 1997; 2d Matthews lectr. dept. pathology Emory U., 1997; spkr. in field. Author: Tumors of the Head and Neck, 2d edit., 1979; co-author: Surgical Pathology of the Head and Neck, 2000; editor: Clin. Lab. Ann., 1981—86; co-editor: Advances in Anatomic Pathology, 1994—98; editor-in-chief Advances in Anatomic Pathology, 1998—2000; co-editor: Oral Cancer, 2003, Comprehensive Management of Head and Neck Tumors, 1999; mem. editl. bd. 13 jours., 1974—; contbr. articles to profl. jours. Bd. trustees, v.p. Mike Hogg Found., Houston, 1991—; trustee George C. Marshall Found., Lexington, Va., 1995-00, emeritus trustee, 2000—. Capt. U.S. Army, 1959-61. Recipient William H. Rorer award Am. Coll. Gastroenterology, 1972, Disting. Alumnus award Albion Coll., 1987, Reviewer of the Decade award AMA Archives Orolaryngology Head Neck Surgery, 1990, Presdl. award Am. Soc. Head and Neck Surgery, 1991, Harlan Spjut award Houston Soc. Clin. Pathologists, 1992, Honor award Am. Laryngologic Assn., 1995; Spl. Honored Guest of Am. Soc. for Head and Neck Surgery, 1993. Fellow ACP, Am. Soc. Clin. Pathologists, Coll. Am. Pathologists (Disting. Svc. award 2002), Am. Acad. Otolaryngology (assoc., honor award 1994), Royal Soc. Medicine. Republican. Episcopalian. Home: 1701 Hermann Dr Unit 1401 Houston TX 77004-7373

BATTENBERG, J. T., III, automotive company executive; BS in Indsl. Engring., Kettering U.; MBA Columbia U.; grad. advanced mgmt. program, Harvard U. With GM, 1986, mng. dir. GM Continental divsn. Belgium, gen. mgr. overseas truck ops. Eng., v.p. Buick-Oldsmobile-Cadillac group, 1986, v.p., group exec. Buick-Oldsmobile-Cadillac, v.p., group exec. automotive components group, 1992, sr. v.p., pres. group, 1992-95, exec. v.p., 1995; pres., CEO, chmn. bd. Delphi Corp. (formerly ACG Worldwide), Troy, Mich., 1995—2005. Mem. GM's Pres. Coun.; nat. adv. bd. Chase Manhattan Corp.; bd. dir. Sara Lee Corp., 2002-. Bd. trustees Kettering U.; bd. overseers Columbia U. Bus. Sch.; exec. bd. Detroit area Coun. of Boy Scouts Am.; exec. bd. Oakland County Automation Alley; bd. dirs. For Inspiration and Recognition of Sci. and Tech.; mem. Coun. on Competitiveness; adv. bd. Covisint; mem. Bus. Roundtable and Bus. Coun. Named Internat. Bus. Coun. World Trader of the Yr. Detroit Regional Chamber, 1998. Mem. Soc. of Automotive Engrs., Soc. of Body Engrs., Engring. Soc. of Detroit, Exec. Leadership Coun., Automobile Nat. Heritage Area, Econ. Club of Detroit (mem. exec. com.). Office: Delphi Corp 5725 Delphi Dr Troy MI 48098-2815

BATTERSBY, JAMES LYONS, JR., language educator; b. Pawtucket, RI, Aug. 24, 1936; s. James Lyons and Hazel Irene (Deuel) B.; m. Lisa J. Kiser, Aug. 6, 1990; 1 child, Julie Ann. BS magna cum laude, U. Vt., Burlington, 1961; MA, Cornell U., Ithaca, NY, 1962, PhD, 1965. Asst. prof. U. Calif., Berkeley, 1965—70; assoc. prof. English Ohio State U., Columbus, 1970—82, prof., 1982—. Cons. Ohio State U. Press, U. Ky. Press, U. Calif. Press, Prentice-Hall, McGraw Hill, Fairleigh Dickinson U. Press, U. Mich. Press, U. Ala. Press. Author: Typical Folly: Evaluating Student Performance in Higher Education, 1973, Rational Praise and atural Lamentation: Johnson, Lycidas and Principles of Criticism, 1980, Elder Olson: An Annotated Bibliography, 1983, Paradigms Regained: Pluralism and the Practice of Criticism, 1991, Reason and the Nature of Texts, 1996, Unorthodox Views: Reflections on Reality, Truth, and Meaning in Current Social, Cultural, and Critical Discourse, 2002, 7 Poets, 2005; contbg. author: Domestick Privacies: Samuel Johnson and the Art of Biography, 1987, Fresh Reflections on Samuel Johnson: Essays in Criticism, 1987, Criticism, History and Intertextuality, 1988, Beyond Poststructuralism: The Speculations of Theory and the Experience of Reading, 1996; contbr. articles to profl. jours. With US Army, 1954—57. Woodrow Wilson fellow, 1961-62, 64-65, Samuel S. Fels fellow, 1964-65, U. Calif. Summer Faculty fellow, 1966, Humanities Research fellow, 1969; recipient Kidder Medal U. Vt., 1961. Mem. MLA, Am. Soc. 18th Century Studies, Midwest Soc. 18th Century Studies, Royal Oak Found., Phi Beta Kappa, Phi Kappa Phi, Kappa Delta Pi. Home: 472 Clinton Heights Ave Columbus OH 43202-1277 Personal E-mail: batterjay@msn.com.

BATTEY, RICHARD HOWARD, judge; b. Aberdeen, SD, Oct. 16, 1929; m. Shirley Ann Battey; children: David, Russell, Dianne. BA, U. S.D., 1950, JD, 1953. Bar: S.D. 1953. Atty. City of Redfield, S.D., 1956-63; state's atty. Spink County, S.D., 1959-65, 81-84; chief judge U.S. Dist. Ct. S.D., Rapid City, 1994—, sr. judge, 1999—. Practicing atty., Redfield, 1956-85; mem. criminal laaw com. Jud. Conf. U.S., 1993-99; adj. prof. U. S.D., 1973-75. Served with AUS, 1953-55. Mem. Dist. Judges Assn. 8th Cir. Ct. Appeals (past pres.). Office: US Dist Ct 318 Fed Bldg 515 9th St Rapid City SD 57701-2626

BATTINO, RUBIN, retired chemistry professor; b. NYC, June 22, 1931; s. Sadik and Anna (Decastro) B.; m. Charlotte Alice Ridinger, Jan. 30, 1960; children— David Rubin, Benjamin Sadik BA, CCNY, 1953; MA, Duke U., 1954, PhD, 1957; MS, Wright State U., 1978. Lic. profl. clin. counselor, Ohio. Research chemist Leeds & orthrup Co., Phila., 1956-57; asst. prof. Ill. Inst. Tech., Chgo., 1957-66; prof. Wright State U., Dayton, Ohio, 1966-95, ret., 1995, prof. emeritus, 1995—. Vis. prof. U. Vienna, Austria, Oxford U., Eng., Hebrew U. Jerusalem, Ben Gurion U., U. New Eng., Australia, U. Canterbury, N.Z., Okayama U. Sci., Japan, Rhodes U., U. Turku, Finland. Author: (with S.E. Wood) Thermodynamics-An Introduction, 1968; Oxygen and Ozone, 1981, Nitrogen and Air, 1982, (with S.E. Wood) The Thermodynamics of Chemical Systems, 1990, (with T.L. South) Ericksonian Approaches, A Comprehensive Manual, 1999, 2d edit., 2005, Guided Imagery and other Approaches to Healing, 2000, Coping: A Practical Guide for People Who Have Life-Challenging Diseases and Their Caregivers, 2001, Meaning: The Life of Viktor E. Frankl, 2002, Metaphoria: Metaphor and Guided Metaphor for Psychotherapy and Healing, 2002, Expectation. The Very Brief Therapy Book, 2006; mem. editl. bd. Solubility Data Series, Jour. Chem. and Engring. Data; contbr. tech. papers to profl. jours. Fulbright fellow, 1979; recipient Outstanding Tchr. award Wright State U., 1979, 93, Outstanding Engr. award Engring. and Sci. Found., Dayton, 1985, Bd. Trustees award Wright State U., 1985. Mem. AAAS, Am. Chem. Soc., Internat. Union Pure and Applied Chemistry (commn.), Sigma Xi, Phi Lambda Upsilon Democrat. Jewish. Office: Wright State U Chemistry Dept Dayton OH 45435 Personal E-mail: rubin.battino@wright.edu.

BATTLES, JOHN MARTIN, lawyer; b. Pitts., Pa., May 10, 1957; s. John and Rosemarie B.; m. Mary Ann Battles; children: John David, Katherine Rose. BA, U. Pitts., 1978; BA in Bus. Adminstrn., U. Cin., 1980, JD, 1990. Asst. corp. counsel Cincom Systems, Cin.; now corp. counsel Lexis-Nexis Group, divsn. Reed Elsevier Inc., Dayton, Ohio. Home: 7 Crescent Ct Fort Thomas KY 41075-2113 Office: Lexis Nexis Group Div Reed Elsevier Inc 9443 Springboro Pike Miamisburg OH 45342-4425

BATZLI, GEORGE OLIVER, ecology educator; b. Mpls., Sept. 23, 1936; s. Oscar H. and Bertha M. B.; m. Sandra Lou Scharf, Jan. 2, 1959; children— Jeffrey, Samuel. BS in Psychology, U. Minn., 1959; MA in Biology, San Francisco State U., 1965; PhD in Zoology (Ecology), U. Calif., Berkeley, 1969. Rsch. assoc. U. Calif., Davis, 1969-71, lectr. biology Santa Cruz, 1971; asst. prof. zoology U. Ill., Urbana, 1971-76, assoc. prof. ecology, 1976-80, prof. ecology, 1980—2004, prof. emeritus, 2004—, head dept. ecology, ethology and evolution, 1983-88, 95-97. Sr. scientist rsch. in arctic environs., 1976-78, mem. ecology program adv. panel NSF, 1984-87, 2003, long term ecol. rsch. adv. panel alpine tundra, 1988, arctic tundra, 1992, tall grass prairie, 1999; rsch. scientist DSIR, .Z., 1979; chmn. ecology program U. Ill., 1976-82. Contbr. articles on ecology to profl. jours.; spl. issue editor Arctic and Alpine Research, 1980, Oikos, 1983; mem. editorial bd. Ecology, Ecol. Monographs, 1981-84. Fellow NSF, 1962-63, NIH, 1967-69, 69-71, Zool. Inst. U. Oslo, Norway, 1982. Fellow AAAS; mem. Am. Inst. Biol. Scis., Am. Soc. Mammalogy (C. Hart Merriam award 2002), Ecol. Soc. Am. Office: U Ill Shelford Vivarium 606 E Healey St Champaign IL 61820-5502 Business E-Mail: g-batzli@life.uiuc.edu.

BAUDLER, CLEL, state representative; b. Adair County, Iowa, Apr. 4, 1939; m. Mary Carole Baudler; 4 children. Trooper Iowa State Patrol, 1968—; mem. Iowa Ho. Reps., DesMoines, 1999—, mem. various coms. including agr., agr. and natural resources, appropriations and natural resources, vice chair jud. Republican. Roman Catholic. Office: 2260 Hwy 25 Greenfield IA 50849

BAUER, ALAN R., internet company executive; Internet distbn. leader The Progressive Corp., Mayfield Village, OH. Office: The Progressive Corp 6300 Wilson Mills Rd Cleveland OH 44143-2109

BAUER, BURNETT PATRICK, state legislator; b. LaPorte, Ind., May 25, 1944; s. Burnett Calix and Helen (Cryan) B.; m. Karen Bella, 1980; children: Bartholomew, Meagan, Maureen. BA, U. Notre Dame, 1966; postgrad., Miami U., 1966-68; MS, Ind. U. Ind. state rep. Dist. 7, 1970-91, Dist. 6, 1991—; asst. minority leader, 1977, 83; ranking minority leader Ind. Ho. Reps., 1984-89, chmn., ways and means, 1989, ranking minority mem., state budget com., 1989, ho. spkr., 2002—. Tchr. Muessel Jr. H.S., South Bend, Ind., 1968-74, Madison Jr. H.S., 1974-75, Dickinson Jr. H.S., 1976-78, Washington H.S.; asst. to supt. South Bend Cmty. Sch. Corp. Recipient Legis. award EPA Region V, 1976. Mem. K.C., Am. Fedn. Tchrs., Ind. State Tchrs. Assn. Home: 1307 Sunnymede Ave South Bend IN 46615-1017

BAUER, CHRIS MICHAEL, banker; b. Milw., Sept. 2, 1948; s. Heinz Gerald and Maria (Weber) B.; m. Susan Marie Branton, June 28, 1969. BBA, U. Wis., 1970; MBA, Marquette U., 1976. Mgmt. trainee 1st Wis. Nat. Bank, Milw., 1970-72, spl. enterprise officer, 1972-74, asst. mgr., 1974-75; v.p. 1st Wis.-Racine, 1976-78; pres. 1st Wis.-Brookfield, 1978-84; 1st v.p. Firstar Corp. (formerly 1st Wis. Corp.), Milw., 1984-86, sr. v.p., 1986-89; pres., COO Firstar Bank Milw. (formerly 1st Wis. Nat. Bank), Milw., 1989-91, chmn., CEO, 1991-99, 1999—; chmn, CEO Business Banc Group Ltd.; also bd. dirs. Firstar Bank Milw. (formerly 1st Wis. at. Bank). Bd. dirs. Aurora Health Care Metro Region, Milw. Pub. Libr. Found., J.A. of Wisconsin, Inc., Next Door Found., Siebert Lutheran Found., The Auto Club Group Inc., AAA Wisconsin; mem. Greater Milw. Com. Mem. Milw. Country Club, Univ. Club, Westmoor Country Club. Lutheran. Office: Bus Banc Group Ltd 18500 W Corporate Dr Ste 170 Brookfield WI 53045-6309

BAUER, FRED D., lawyer; b. Cleve., Oct. 27, 1965; BA, BS magna cum laude, U. Pa., 1987; JD cum laude, Harvard U., 1990. Bar: Ohio 1990, U.S. Dist. Ct. Ohio (No. dist.) 1991. Assoc. Baker & Hostetler, 1990—92; assoc. corr. counsel Bearings, Inc., 1992—94; asst. gen. counsel, asst. sec. Applied Indsl. Technologies, Inc., Cleve., 1994—2002, v.p., gen. counsel, sec., 2002—. Mem.: Am. Corp. Counsel Assn., Am. Soc. Corp. Secretaries, Ohio State Bar Assn., Cleve. Bar Assn. Office: Applied Indsl Technologies Inc One Applied Plz Euclid Ave at E 36th St Cleveland OH 44115-5015 Office Phone: 216-426-4753. Office Fax: 216-426-4804. E-mail: fbauer@applied.com.

BAUER, FRED T., technology products executive; b. 1943; married. Degree in electrical engring. cum laude, Mich. State U. Founder Simicon Co., late 1960s-72; divsn. mgr., corp. officer, v.p. Robertshaw; founder Gentex Corp., Zeeland, Mich., 1974, chmn., CEO; bd. dirs. Photobit Corp. Former dir. Jr. Achievment in Holland/Zeeland; former adv. bd. dirs. Underwriters Labs. Industry Coun. Recipient Master Entrepreneur of Yr. award Ernst & Young, 1988. Office: Gentex Corp 600 N Centennial St Zeeland MI 49464-1318

BAUER, JOSEPH W., lawyer, chemicals executive; b. Toledo, July 22, 1953; BA, U. Toledo, 1975, JD, 1981. Bar: Ohio 1981. Atty. Jones, Day, Reavis & Pogue; various positions in legal dept. Lubrizol Corp., Wickliffe, Ohio, 1985—91, v.p., gen. counsel, 1992—. Office: Lubrizol Corp 29400 Lakeland Blvd Wickliffe OH 44092

BAUER, JULIE A., lawyer; b. Elmhurst, Ill., Mar. 26, 1960; BA with distinction, U. Va., 1982; JD magna cum laude, U. Ill., 1985. Bar: Ill. 1985, U.S. Dist. Ct. Ill. (no. dist.) 1987, U.S. Dist. Ct. Ill. (ctrl. dist.) 1993, U.S. Ct. Appeals (7th cir.) 1993, U.S. Dist. Ct. Ill. (so. dist.) 2003. Law clk. U.S. Dist. Ct. Ill. (no. dist.), 1985—87; assoc. to ptnr. Winston & Strawn LLP, Chgo., 1987—, co-chair hiring com., mem. diversity initiative, mem. audit com. Pres. Pro Bono Advocates, 1997—99; mem. bd. visitors U. Ill. Coll. Law, 2001—04. Fellow:

Am. Bar Found.; mem.: Alliance for Women (exec. com. mem. 1999—2007, co-vice chair 2001—02, co-chair 2002—03), Seventh Cir. Bar Assn. (mem. bd. govs. 2004—06, sec. 2006—), Chgo. Bar Assn. (bd. mgrs. 2004—06), Order of Coif. Office: Winston & Strawn LLP 35 W Wacker Dr Chicago IL 60601-9703 Office Phone: 312-558-5973. Office Fax: 312-558-5700. E-mail: jbauer@winston.com.

BAUER, OTTO FRANK, academic administrator, communications executive, educator; b. Elgin, Ill., Dec. 1, 1931; s. Otto Leland and Cora Dorothy (Berlin) B.; m. Jeanette L. Erickson, May 27, 1956; children: Steven Mark, Eric Paul. BS, Northwestern U., 1953, MA, 1955, PhD, 1959; D of Humanitarian Svcs. (hon.), Clarkson Coll., 1999. Instr., then asst. prof. English USAF Acad., Colo., 1959-61, dir. debate, 1959-61; instr. to prof. Bowling Green State U., Ohio, 1961-71, dir. grad. admissions and fellowships, 1965-69, asst. dean Grad. Sch., 1967-69, asst. v.p., 1970-71; ACE fellow U. Calif.-Berkeley, 1969-70; prof. communication U. Wis.-Parkside, Kenosha, 1971-79; vice chancellor U. Wis. -Parkside, Kenosha, 1971-76; acting chancellor U. Wis.-Parkside, 1974-75; vis. prof. communication, spl. asst. to chancellor U. Wis., Madison, 1976-77; vice chancellor for acad. affairs U. Nebr., Omaha, 1979-94, prof. communication, 1979—2000, vice chancellor emeritus, 1995. Mem. Commn. on Instns. Higher Edn., North Ctrl. Assn. Colls. and Schs., 1975-77, 84-88, cons., evaluator, 1976—; cons. in field. Author: Fundamentals of Debate, 1966, rev. edit., 1999, Lower Moments in Higher Education, 1997, Trust and Distrust, 2005; co-author: Guidebook for Student Speakers, 1966; editor: Introduction to Speech Communication, 1968. Bd. dirs. United Way Kenosha County, Wis., 1973-79, Kenosha County coun. Girl Scouts U.S., 1977-79; chmn. spkrs. bur. United Way Midlands, Omaha, 1983, mem. allocations coms., 1985-93, steering com., 1989-93; bd. dirs. Fontenelle Forest Assn., 1987-94, v.p., 1990-92; bd. dirs. Clarkson Coll., 1992-2000, vice-chair, 1995-97, chair, 1997-2000. Recipient Faculty Disting. Svc. award U. Wis., Parkside, 1978, Chancellor's medal U. Nebr., Omaha, 1994, Disting. Svc. award U. Nebr. Aviation Inst., Omaha, 1994, named in his honor, 2000; named Faculty Man of Yr., Bowling Green State U., 1967, Exec. of Yr., Nat. Secs. Assn., Omaha, 1980; Clarion DeWitt Hardy scholar, 1949-53; humanitarian svc. award named in his honor Clarkson Coll., 1999. Mem. Am. Coun. on Edn. (exec. com. coun. of fellows 1982-85), at. Comm. Assn., Rotary.

BAUER, WILLIAM JOSEPH, federal judge; b. Chgo., Sept. 15, 1926; s. William Francis and Lucille (Gleason) Bauer; m. Mary Nicol, Jan. 28, 1950; children: Patricia, Linda. AB, Elmhurst Coll., 1949, LLD, 1969; JD, DePaul U., 1952, LLD (hon.), 1993; LLD, John Marshall Law Sch., 1987; LLD (hon.), Roosevelt U., 1994. Bar: Ill. 1951. Ptnr. Erlenborn, Bauer & Hotte, Elmhurst, Ill., 1953—64; asst. state's atty. Du Page County, Ill., 1952—56; 1st asst. state's atty., 1956—58; state's atty., 1959—64; judge 18th Jud. Cir. Ct., 1964—70; US dist. atty. No. Ill. Chgo., 1970—71; judge US Dist. Ct. (no. dist.), Chgo., 1971—75, US Ct. Appeals (7th cir.), 1975—86, chief judge, 1986—93, sr. judge Chicago, 1994—. Instr. bus law. Elmhurst Coll., 1952—59; adj. prof. law DePaul U., 1978—91; former mem. Ill. Supreme Ct. Com. on Pattern Criminal Jury Instrns.; chmn. Fed. Criminal Jury Instrn. Com. 7th Cir.; mem. Am. Judicature Soc., Ill. Assn. of Cir. and Appellate Ct. Judges, Ill. States Attys. Assn., Nat. Dist. Attys. Assn. Trustee Elmhurst Coll., 1979—, DePaul U., 1984—, DuPage Meml. Hosp.; bd. advisors Mercy Hosp. With US Army, 1945—47. Mem.: FBA (former bd. dirs.), ABA, Chgo. Bar Assn., DuPage County Bar Assn. (past pres.), Ill. Bar Assn., Legal Club (Chgo.), Law Club, Union League Club. Roman Catholic. Office: US Ct Appeals 219 S Dearborn St Ste 2754 Chicago IL 60604

BAUGHER, PETER V., lawyer; b. Chgo., Oct. 2, 1948; s. William and Marilyn (Sill) Baugher; m. Robin Stickney, Nov. 25, 1978; children: Julia Allison, Britton William Herbert. AB, Princeton U., 1970; JD, Yale U., 1973. Bar: Ill. 1974, U.S. Dist. Ct. (no. dist.) Ill. 1974, U.S. Ct. Appeals (7th cir.) 1974, U.S. Supreme Ct. 1987. Law clk. to judge U.S. Ct. Appeals (7th cir.), Chgo., 1973-74; from assoc. to ptnr. Schiff Hardin & Waite, Chgo., 1974-85; ptnr. Adams, Fox, Adelstein & Rosen, Chgo., 1985-89, Schopf & Weiss, LLP, Chgo., 1989—. Trustee Sta. WTTW Channel 11, Chgo., 1976—81, Kendall Coll., Evanston, 1980—92, WBEZ, Chgo. Pub. Radio, 1992—98, Ill. Humanities Coun., 1997—2003; pres. Chgo. Internat. Dispute Resolution Assn., 1997—. Mem. adv. com. Rep. Nat. Conv., Detroit, 1980; bd. dirs. Protestants for the Common Good, 2001—; mem. adv. com. Northwestern U. Sch. Law Ctr. Internat. Human Rights; bd. dirs. Sabre Found.; pres. Chgo. Lincoln Inn of Ct., 1994—96. Mem.: ABA, Chgo. Coun. Global Affairs, Am. Law Inst., Chgo. Bar Assn. (chair internat. and fgn. law com., chair fed civil practice com.), Ripon Soc. (chmn. 1975—76), Am. Coun. Germany, Mich. Shores Club, Econ. Club Chgo., Univ. Club. Home: 1310 Sheridan Rd Wilmette IL 60091-1834 Office: Schopf & Weiss LLP One S Wacker Dr Chicago IL 60606 Office Phone: 312-701-9300. E-mail: baugher@sw.com.

BAUKOL, RONALD OLIVER, retired finance company executive; b. Chgo., Aug. 11, 1937; s. Oliver Peter and Clara Marie (Haugstad) B.; m. Gay Lynn Gollan, Aug. 29, 1959; children: David, Andrew, Kathlyn. BSChemE, Iowa State U., 1959; MSChemE, MIT, 1960. Engr., group leader Procter & Gamble, Cin., 1960-66; lab. supr. 3M Co., 1966-70; White House fellow Washington, 1970-71; dept. mgr. dental, new enterprises, diagnostic depts. Minn. Mining & Mfg. Co., St. Paul, 1972-82; v.p., gen. mgr. 3M/Riker Labs., 1982-86; mng. dir., CEO 3M U.K. PLC, 1986-89; mng. dir. 3M Ireland, 1988-89; group v.p. Pharms. and Dental Products Group, 3M Co., St. Paul, 1989-90, Med. Products Group, 1990-91; v.p. Asia Pacific, 1991-94, Asia Pacific Can. and L.Am., 1994-95, exec. v.p. internat. ops., 1996—2002; ret., 2002. Bd. dirs. The Toro Co.; mem. exec. bd. Internat. C.of C., 2001-. Chmn. bd. ARC St. Paul, 1979-81, dir. regional blood com., 1972-86; mem. alumni assn. bd. dirs. Iowa State U., 1974-76, gov. found., 1990—; trustee Minn. Med. Found., 1990-93, Children's Hosp., St. Paul, 1993-95; trustee U.S. Coun. Internat. Bus., 1994—, vice-chmn., 2000—; mem. adv. coun. U. St. Thomas Ctr. Health and Med. Affairs, Minn., 1990-97, internat. programs adv. coun. Carlson Sch. Mgmt., U. Minn., 1998—, Children's Hosps. and Clinics Fedn., Minn., 2003; bd. dirs. Children's Health Care, St. Paul, 1995-97. Named Outstanding Young Alumnus, Iowa State U., 1969. Mem. Brit. Inst. Mgmt. (companion 1988-89). Methodist. Avocation: tennis. Office: 30 Seventh St East Ste 3050 Saint Paul MN 55101 Home Phone: 651-653-0109; Office Phone: 651-221-0582. Personal E-mail: robaukol@hotmail.com.

BAUM, BERNARD HELMUT, sociologist, educator; b. Giessen, Germany, Apr. 18, 1926; arrived in U.S., 1933, naturalized, 1934; s. Theodor and Beatrice (Klee) Baum; m. Barbara B. Eisendrath, June 13, 1953; children: David Michael, Jonathan Klee, Victoria, Lisa Baum Kritz. PhB, U. Chgo., 1948, MA, 1953, PhD, 1959. Qualifications rating examiner, bd. adviser U.S. CSC, Chgo., 1952-54; instr. human relations, psychology Chgo. Police Officers' Coll. Edn. Program, 1955-59; dir. orgnl. analysis CNA Ins., Chgo., 1960-66; assoc. prof. mgmt. and sociology U. Ill., Chgo., 1966-69, assoc. dean Coll. Bus. Adminstrn., 1967-68, prof. mgmt. and sociology, 1969—2002, prof. mgmt. and sociology emeritus, 2002—, prof. health policy and adminstrn. Sch. Pub. Health, 1973—2002, prof. emeritus, 2002—, dir. health policy and adminstrn. Sch. Pub. Health, 1977-92. Lectr. Roosevelt U., 1955—66, U. Chgo., 1961—68, Northwestern U., 1968—70, U. Colo., 1971—76; mem. spkr.'s bur. Adult Edn. Coun. Greater Chgo., 1963—76; team leader joint evaluation mission UN devel. program WHO primary health care and health mgmt. devel. projects in South Pacific, 1985; vis. scholar Chiang Mai U., Thailand, 1988. Author: Decentralization of Authority in a Bureaucracy, 1961, As If People Mattered: Dignity in Organizations, 2005; co-author: Basics for Business, 1968; co-editor: Intervention: the Management Use of Organizational Research, 1975; contbr. articles to profl. jours. Bd. dirs. Selfhelp Home for Aged, Chgo. With AUS, 1944—46, brig. gen. Ill. Army .G., ret. Decorated Legion of Merit, Bronze Star; recipient Bus. Adminstrn. and Social Sci. Doctoral Dissertaion award, Ford Found., 1960. Mem.: APHA, AAAS, Acad. Mgmt., Am. Acad. Polit. and Social Sci., Am. Sociol. Assn., Sigma Xi. Office: U Ill Sch Pub Health M/C 923 Chicago IL 60680 Home: Apt 3B 2610 Central St Evanston IL 60201-1354 Home Phone: 847-864-7171; Office Phone: 312-996-5760. Business E-Mail: bhbaum@uic.edu.

BAUMAN, JOHN DUANE, lawyer; b. Kaskaskia, Ill., Aug. 22, 1930; s. Louis Wells and Veronica Genevieve (Schmerbauch) B.; m. Avis Crysella Moore, Sept. 15, 1956; children: Mark Duane, Thomas Jon, Jeffery Paul. BA, SE Mo. U., 1952; JD, Washington U., St. Louis, 1957. Bar: Mo. 1957, Ill. 1957. Assoc. Baker, Kagy & Wagner, East Saint Louis, Ill., 1957-62; ptnr. Wagner, Bertrand, Bauman & Schmieder, Belleville, Ill., 1962-86, Hinshaw & Culbertson, Chgo. and Belleville, 1986—. Gen. counsel Okaw Valley coun. Boy Scouts Am., 1980—90; adv. bd. Ill. Dept. Agr., 1999—. With US Army, 1952—54. Mem. ABA, Ill. Bar Assn., Internat. Assn. Ins. Counsel (state membership chmn.), Assn. of Def. Trial Counsel (pres. 1975-76), St. Clair County Bar Assn. (pres. 1972-73), Horsemen's Benevolent and Protective Assn. (v.p. 1989-98), Ill. Thoroughbred Breeders and Owners Found. (bd. dirs. 1999-2002, v.p. 1996-99, sec.-treas. 1999-2000, pres. 2000-07), Bradenton Country Club, St. Clair Country Club (pres. 1982-84), Paducah Country Club, Elks, Mo. Athletic Club (emeritus 1998). Roman Catholic. Avocations: horse racing, golf. Office: Hinshaw & Culbertson PO Box 509 521 W Main St Belleville IL 62220-1533 Office Phone: 618-277-2400. Personal E-mail: jb222555@aol.com.

BAUMAN, JOHN E., JR., chemistry professor; b. Kalamazoo, Jan. 18, 1933; s. John E. and Teresa A. (Wauchek) B.; m. Barbara Curry, June 6, 1964; children— John, Catherine, Amy BS, U. Mich., 1955, MS, 1960, PhD, 1962. Chemist Midwest Research Inst., Kansas City, Mo., 1955-58; research assoc. U. Mich., Ann Arbor, 1958-61; prof. chemistry U. Mo., Columbia, 1961-97, prof. emeritus, 1997—. Active Mo. Symphony Soc. Recipient Faculty Alumni award, 1969, Amoco Teaching award, 1975, Purple Chalk award, 1980, all U. Mo. Mem. Am. Chem. Soc. (nat. lectr.), Mo. Acad. Sci., U. Mo. Retirees Assn. (pres. 2000—), Kiwanis, Sigma Xi, Alpha Chi Sigma. Roman Catholic. Home: 3703 S Woods Edge Rd Columbia MO 65203-6607 Office: Univ Mo 125 Chemistry Building Columbia MO 65211-7600 Personal E-mail: jbauman@centurytel.net. Business E-Mail: baumanj@missouri.edu.

BAUMAN, SUSAN JOAN MAYER, mayor, lawyer, commissioner; b. NYC, Mar. 2, 1945; d. Curt H. J. and Carola (Rosenau) Mayer; m. Ellis A. Bauman, Dec. 29, 1968. BS, U. Wis., 1965, JD, MS, 1981; MS, U. Chgo., 1966. Bar: Wis. 1981, U.S. Dist. Ct. (we. dist.) Wis. 1981, U.S. Ct. Appeals (7th cir.) 1983, U.S. Dist. Ct. (ea. dist.) Wis. 1985. Tchr. Madison (Wis.) Pub. Sch., 1970-78; research asst. U. Wis. Law Sch., Madison, 1981; ptnr. Thomas, Parsons, Schaefer & Bauman, Madison, 1981-84; sole practice Madison, 1984-85; ptnr. Bauman & Massing. Madison, 1985-87; pvt. practice, Madison, 1987-97; mayor City of Madison, 1997—2003; mem. Wis. Employment Rels. Commn., 2003—. Alderman Madison Common Coun., 1985-97, coun. pres., 1989-90; commr. equal opportunities com. City of Madison, 1985-89; mem. Econ. Devel. Commn., 1986-87, chmn. human resources com., 1987-90, mem. affirmative action com., 1988-93; mem. Cmty. Action Commn., 1988-97, pres., 1991-96; mem. Pub. Health Commn., 1991-97, Monona Terr. Conv. and Cmty. Ctr. Bd., 1993-97; pres. South Madison Health and Family Ctr., Inc., 1993-97; bd. visitors U. Wis. Coll. Letters and Scis., Madison, 1997—2003; mem. exec. com. Wis. Alliance Cities, 1996-2003; mem. adv. bd. U.S. Conf. Mayors, 1999—2003; dir. Safe Cmtys. Coalition Madison County. Mem. Wis. Bar Assn., Dane County Bar Assn., Wis. Indsl. Rels. Alumni Assn. (pres. 1985-86), Madison Civics Club. Democrat. Avocations: knitting, reading, backpacking, cross country skiing. Home: 125 N Hamilton St 407 Madison WI 53703 Office: Wis Employment Rels Commn 18 S Thornton Ave Madison WI 53707-7870 Office Phone: 608-266-3297. Personal E-mail: sjmbauman@aol.com.

BAUMAN-BORK, MARCEIL, health services administrator; b. Sidney, Nebr., Sept. 15, 1957; BA, Midland Luth. Coll., Fremont, NE, 1979; MD, U. Nebr. Med. Ctr., Omaha, 1983. Bd. cert. Am. Bd. Psychiatry & Neurology. Resident Menninger Sch. Psychiatry & Mental Health, Topeka; dir. gen. residency program Menninger Clinic, Topeka; co-founder, psychiatrist Heritage Mental Health Clinic, Topeka, 2003—. Presenter in field. Mem.: Am. Acad. Child and Adolescent Psychology, Kans. Med. Soc., Am. Psychoanalytic Assn., Am. Psychiatric Assn. Office: Heritage Mental Health Clinic 2921 SW Wanamaker Dr Topeka KS 66614

BAUMANN, DANIEL E., publishing executive; b. Milw., Apr. 10, 1937; s. Herbert F. and Agnes V. (Byrne) B.; m. Karen R. Weinkauf, Apr. 29, 1961; children: James W., Jennifer R., Colin D. BJ, U. Wis., 1958, MA in Polit. Sci., 1962, Cert. in Russian Area Studies, 1962. Reporter South Milwaukee (Wis.) Voice Jour., 1958-59, East St. Louis (Ill.) Jour., 1959-60; pub. rels. rep. Credit Union Nat. Assn., Washington, 1962-64; reporter Paddock Publs., Inc., Arlington Heights, Ill., 1964-66, mng. editor, 1966-68, exec. editor, 1968-70, editor and pub. Paddock Circle newspapers, 1970-75, v.p., editor, 1975-83, sr. v.p., gen. mgr., editor, 1983-86, pres., editor, 1986-90, dir., 1986—, pres., COO, 1990—2002, chmn., pub., 2002—. Recipient William Alan White award U. Kans., 1976. Avocation: travel. Office: Paddock Publs Daily Herald 155 E Algonquin Rd Arlington Heights IL 60005-4617

BAUMANN, EDWARD ROBERT, environmental engineering educator; b. Rochester, NY, May 12, 1921; s. John Carl and Lillie Minnie (Roth) B.; m. Mary A. Massey, June 15, 1946; children: Betsy Louise, Philip Robert. BSCE, U. Mich., 1944; BS in San. Engring, U. Ill., 1945, MS, 1947, PhD, 1954; NSF faculty fellow, U. Durham, Eng., 1959-60. Research assoc. U. Ill., 1947-53; assoc. prof. civil engring. Iowa State U., 1953-56, prof., 1956-91, Anson Marston Disting. prof. engring., 1972-91, emeritus Disting. prof., 1991—. Cons. Water Quality Office of EPA, Culligan Internat., Lakeside Engring. Co., Bolton & Menk, many cities and industries. Author: Sewerage and Sewage Treatment, 1958; mem. editorial bd.: Internat. Jour. Air and Water Pollution, London, 1960-67; asst. editor: San. Engr. Newsletter of ASCE, 1962-74; contbr. articles to profl. jours. V.p., treas. Water Found., Inc., 1978-83; mem. Iowa Bd. Health, 1975-76, Iowa State U. Rsch. Found., 1975-78, 83-91. With C.E., AUS, 1944-46. Recipient George B. Gascoigne medal Water Pollution Control Fedn., 1962, 80, Publs. award, 1963, Purification divsn. award Am. Water Works Assn., 1965, Anson Marston medal Iowa Engring. Soc., 1966, Disting. Svc. award, 1968, Gold medal Filtration Soc. Eng., 1970, Bedell award, 1977, Rsch. award, 1978, Philip F. Morgan award Water Pollution Control Fedn., 1986; named Water Works Man of Yr., 1972, Disting. Alumni award U. Ill. Alumni Assn., 1992. Fellow ASCE (life), Iowa Acad. Scis. (disting. sci. 1990), Am. Filtration Separations Soc. (F.M. Tiller award 1994); mem. NSPE (nat. bd. dirs.), AAUP, Am. Water Works Assn. (hon., life, internat. bd. dirs. 1978-80), Assn. Environ. Engring. Profs. (pres. 1967-70, 86-87, Nalco award, Founders award 1991), Am. Soc. Engring. Edn., Am. Inst. Chem. Engrs., Am. Acad. Environ. Engring. (diplomate), Filtration Soc. (Eng., bd. dirs., tech. editor, vice chmn. 1993, chmn. 1994, Fluid/Particle Separation Jour.), Rotary, Sigma Xi, Phi Kappa Phi (Centennial medal 1997), Chi Epsilon. Home: 1627 Crestwood Cir Ames IA 50010-5520 Office Phone: 515-233-6100. Business E-Mail: rbaumann13@mchsi.com. E-mail: robertba@bolton-menk.com.

BAUMER, MARTHA ANN, minister; b. Cleve., Sept. 12, 1938; d. Harry William and Olga Erna (Zenk) B. BA, Lakeland Coll., 1960; MA, U. Wyo., 1963; MDiv, United Theol. Sem., 1973; D Ministry, Eden Theol. Sem., 1990. Parish minister Congl. United Ch. of Christ, Amery, Wis., 1973-79; organizing minister United Ch. of Santa Fe (N.Mex.), 1979-85; conf. minister Ill. South Conf. United Ch. of Christ, Highland, Ill., 1985-93; pastor Windsor (Wis.) United Ch. of Christ, 1993-99; vis. prof. pastoral studies Eden Theol. Sem., St. Louis, 1999—. Trustee pension bds. United Ch. of Christ, N.Y.C., 1983—, mem., chair exec. coun., 1977-83; del. World Coun. Chs., 1961, 83; trustee Eden Theol. Sem., St. Louis, 1990-99. Contbr. articles to profl. publs. Vice chair Pensions Boards United Church of Christ, 2004—05. Mem. Coun. of Conf. Ministers United Ch. of Christ (sec.-treas. 1989-93). Office: Eden Theol Sem 475 E Lockwood Ave Saint Louis MO 63119-3124 E-mail: mbaumer@eden.edu.

BAUMGARDNER, EDWARD, financial company executive; CEO, pres. Potters Fin. Corp., East Liverpool, Ohio, 1994—. Office: Potters Fin Corp 519 Broadway St East Liverpool OH 43920-3137 Fax: 330-385-3508.

BAUMGARDNER, MICHAEL H., marketing professional; BA, MS, Ohio State U., PhD in Social Psychology. Consumer sci. specialist FDA, Washington; with Burke, Inc., Cin., 1979—, pres. Lectr. quantitative methods and psychology, Ohio State U., Ohio Dominican Coll., Columbus; spkr. in field. Contbr. articles to profl. publs., including Jour. Personality and Social Psychology, Psychol. Rev., others. Office: Burke Inc 805 Central Ave Fl 5 Cincinnati OH 45202-5747

BAUMGARDT, BILLY RAY, professional society administrator, agriculturist; b. Lafayette, Ind., Jan. 17, 1933; s. Raymond P. and Mildred L. Baumgardt; m. D. Elaine Blain, June 8, 1952; children: Pamela K. Baumgardt Farley, Teresa Jo Baumgardt Adolfsen, Donald Ray. BS in Agr., Purdue U., 1955, MS, 1956; PhD, Rutgers U., 1959. From asst. to assoc. prof. U. Wis., Madison, 1959-67; prof. animal nutrition Pa. State U., University Park, 1967-70, head dept. dairy and animal sci., 1970-79, assoc. dir. agrl. expt. sta., 1979-80; dir. agrl. research, assoc. dean Purdue U., West Lafayette, Ind., 1980-98; exec. v.p. Am. Registry Profl. Animal Scientists, Savoy, Ill., 1998—2003; coord. DISCOVER conf. series Am. Dairy Sci. Assn., Savoy, 1998—2007. Contbr. chapters to books, articles to profl. sci. jours. Recipient Wilkinson award, Pa. State U., 1979. Fellow: AAAS, Am. Soc. Nutritional Sci., Am. Dairy Sci. Assn. (pres. 1984—85, utrition Rsch. award 1966, award of Honor 1993, Disting. Svc. award 2003); mem.: Nat. Agrl. Biotech. Coun. (chair 1993—94), Am. Soc. Animal Sci., Am. Soc. Nutrition, Rotary, Sigma Xi. Home and Office: 2741 N Salisbury St West Lafayette IN 47906-1431 E-mail: baumgardt@purdue.edu.

BAUMGART, JAMES RAYMOND, state legislator; b. Dec. 22, 1938; 1 child. BA, U. Wis., Stevens Point. State assemblyman dist. 26 State of Wis., 1990-99; mem. Wis. Senate from 9th dist., Madison, 1999—. Outdoor writer. Mem. Sheboygan County Izaak Walton League (pres.). Democrat. Address: 722 N 26th St Sheboygan WI 53081-3727

BAUMGARTNER, JOHN H., gas industry executive; b. 1936; married. With Clark Oil & Refining Corp., Milw., 1956-82, retail sales rep., 1960-65, dist. mgr., 1965-72, regional mgr., 1972-74, v.p. retail mktg., asst. gen. sales mgr., 1974-75, sr. v.p. mktg., 1975-78, exec. v.p., 1978-82; pres. J.H. Baumgartner Enterprises, Brookfield, Wis., 1982—; v.p., owner Robert Kidd & Assocs. Inc., 1990—. Served with USMC, 1954-56. Office Phone: 651-210-4018.

BAUMGARTNER, WILLIAM HANS, JR., lawyer; b. Chgo., July 24, 1955; s. William H. and Charlotte Burnette (Lange) B.; m. Andrea Jean Coath, Oct. 6, 1984. BA, U. Chgo., 1976; JD magna cum laude, Harvard U., 1979. Bar: Ill. 1979, US Dist. Ct. (no. dist. Ill.) 1979, US Dist. Ct. (ea. dist. Wis.) 1994, US Ct. Appeals (3rd cir.) 1996, US Ct. Appeals (6th cir.) 1988, US Ct. Appeals (7th cir.) 1992, US Ct. Appeals (8th cir.) 1998, US Ct. Appeals (11th cir.) 1994, US Ct. Appeals (fed. cir.) 1991. Assoc. Sidley & Austin, Chgo., 1979-86, ptnr., 1986—. Mem. ABA, Chgo. Bar Assn., Phi Beta Kappa. Office: Sidley Austin LLP 1 S Dearborn St Chicago IL 60603 Office Phone: 312-853-7250. E-mail: wbaumgar@sidley.com.

BAUMHART, RAYMOND CHARLES, religious organization administrator; b. Chgo., Dec. 22, 1923; s. Emil and Florence (Weidner) B. BS, Northwestern U., 1945; PhL, Loyola U., 1952, STL, 1958; MBA, Harvard U., 1953; DBA, Harvard, 1963; LLD (hon.), Ill. Coll., 1977; DHL (hon.), Scholl Coll. Podiatric Medicine, 1983, Rush U., Chgo., 1987, Northwestern U., 1993, Xavier U., Cin., 1994, Ill. Benedictine Coll., 1994; DHL (hon.), Loyola U., 2007. Joined Jesuit Order, 1946; ordained priest Roman Cath. Ch., 1957. Asst. prof. mgmt. Loyola U., Chgo., 1962-64, dean Sch. Bus. Adminstrn., 1964-66, exec. v.p., acting v.p. Med. Ctr., 1968-70, pres., 1970-93; cons. to Cardinal George, Cath. Archdiocese of Chgo., 2000—. Alfred Ring lectr. U. Fla., 1988; John and Mildred Wright lectr. Fairfield U., 1992; D. B. Reinhart lectr. Viterbo Coll., 2000; bd. dirs. Ceres Food Group, Inc. Author: An Honest Profit, 1968, (with Thomas Garrett) Cases in Business Ethics, 1968, (with Thomas McMahon) The Brewer-Wholesaler Relationship, 1969; corr. editor: America, 1965-70. Trustee St. Louis U., 1967-72, Boston Coll., 1968-71; bd. dirs. Coun. Better Bus. Burs., 1971-77, Cath. Health Alliance Met. Chgo., 1986-93; mem. U.S. Bishops and Pres.'s Com. on Higher Edn., 1980-84, Jobs for Met. Chgo., 1984-85, Chgo. Health Care Industry, 1990-94. Recipient Gutenberg award, Chgo. Bible Soc., 2006; decorated cavalier Order of Merit, Italy, 1971, commendatore, 1994; recipient Rale medallion Boston Coll., 1976, Daniel Lord S.J. award Loyola Acad., Wilmette, Ill., 1992, Mary Potter Humanitarian award Little Company of Mary Hosp., Ill., 1993, Sword of Loyola Loyola U., Chgo., 1993, Theodore Hesburgh award Assn. Cath. Colls. and Univs., 1995; John W. Hill fellow Harvard U., 1961-62, Cambridge Ctr. for Social Studies Rsch. fellow, 1966-68. Mem. Comml. Club, Mid-Am. Club, Tavern Club. Roman Catholic. Business E-Mail: rbaumhart@archchgo.org.

BAUNER, RUTH ELIZABETH, library director; b. Quincy, Ill. d. John Carl and M. Irene (Nutt) B. BS in Edn., Western Ill. U., 1950; MS, U. Ill., 1956; postgrad., So. Ill. U., 1974, PhD, 1978. Asst. res. libr. Western Ill. U., Macomb, 1950; tchr., libr. Sandwich (Ill.) Twp. High Sch., 1950-54; circulation dept. asst. U. Ill. Libr., Urbana, 1955; asst. edn. libr. So. Ill. U., Carbondale, 1956-63, acting edn. libr., 1963-64, edn. and psychology libr., 1965-93, assoc. prof. curriculum and instrn. dept., 1971-93; coord. freshman yr. experience program, vis. assoc. prof. Coll. of Liberal Arts, Carbondale, 1994-96. Dir. Grad. Residence Ctr. Librs., So. Ill. U., 1973-79; subject matter expert Learning Resources Svc. Interactive Video, Carbondale, 1990-91, also scriptwriter; faculty emeritus So. Ill. U., 2004—. Co-author: The Teacher's Library, 1966; contbr. articles to profl. jours. Pres. alumni constituency bd. Coll. Edn., Carbondale, 1988—89; mem. Carbondale Bd. Ethics, 1989—2001; tchr. I Can Read Program, 2001—03; mem. Carbondale Citizens Adv. Commn., 1999—2001; bd. dirs. So. Ill. U. chpt. UN, 1985—86, 1994—97; mem. faculty bd. So. Ill. Learning in Retirement, mem. steering com., 2005—07; mem. faculty bd. So. Ill. U. Emeritus Assn., v.p.; bd. dirs. Jackson County AARP, 1997—99, 2001—03, 2006—, So. Ill. U. Emeritus Faculty Assn., 2004—; mem. friends bd. Mcleod Playhouse, 2005—. Recipient Luck Has Nothing To Do With It award, Oryx Press, 1993. Mem.: AAUW (univ. rep. Carbondale br. 1988—89), ALA, Ill. Libr. Assn., Assn. Coll. and Rsch. Librs. (chmn. edn. and behavioral scis. sect. 1976—77, Most Active Mem. award 1968—93), AAUP (v.p. So. Ill. U. chpt. 1972—73), Delta Kappa Gamma, Phi Kappa Phi, Phi Delta Kappa (Women of Distinction award 1999). Office: 1206 W Freeman St Carbondale IL 62901-2351

BAXTER, RANDOLPH, judge; b. Columbia, Tenn., Aug. 15, 1946; s. Lenon Pillow and Willie Alexine (Hood) B.; m. Yvonne Marie Williams, Nov. 26, 1980; children: Mark, Melissa, Scott, Kimberly Lynn. BS, Tuskegee Inst., 1967; JD, U. Akron, 1974. Bar: Ohio 1976, U.S. Dist. Ct. (no. dist.) Ohio 1978, U.S. Ct. Appeals (6th cir.) 1978, U.S. Supreme Ct. 1980. Salary analyst B.F. Goodrich Co., Akron, 1971-73; courts planner Criminal Justice Commn., Akron, 1973-76; dep. dir., pub. service dept. City Akron, 1976-78; asst. U.S. atty. U.S. Dept. Justice, Cleve., 1978-85, chief appellate litigation, 1982-85; judge U.S. Bankruptcy Court (no. dist.) Ohio, 1985-96, judge bankruptcy appellate panel U.S. Ct. Appeals for 6th Cir., 1996—; instr. real estate law Kent State U., 1974-78; adj. prof. U. Akron Coll. Law; v.p., dir. Alpha Phi Alpha Homes, Inc., Akron, 1971-85. Bd. dirs. Western Res. Hist. Soc., 1988-92, Akron Auto Assn., 1990—, Salvation Army, Akron, 1993—, Emmanuel Christian Acad., 1994—. Served to capt. AUS, 1968-71, Vietnam. Named Man of Yr., Akron Jaycees, 1977; recipient Disting. Service award City Akron, 1978, Spl. Achievement award U.S. Dept. Justice, 1981, 82, Disting. Vets. award Fed. Exec. Bd. Cleve., 1982. Mem. ABA, Akron Barristers Club (pres. 1978-79), Fed. Bar Assn., Nat. Bar Assn., Akron Bar Assn., Nat. Conf. Bankruptcy Judges, Am. Bankruptcy Inst., Comml. Law League Am., Alpha Phi Alpha. Office: US Bankruptcy Ct Key Tower 127 Public Sq Ste 3205 Cleveland OH 44114-1216

BAXTER, TIMOTHY C., prosecutor; b. Prairie du Chien, Wis., Sept. 2, 1964; s. Gary Lee and Shirley Esther (Volenec) B.; m. Margaret J. Baxter, May 23, 1992. BS, U. Wis., River Falls, 1987; JD, William Mitchell Coll. Law, St. Paul, 1990. Bar: Wis. 1990. Dist. atty. Crawford County, Praire du Chien, 1991—. Mem. ABA, Wis. Bar Assn., Jaycees (Prairie du Chien chpt., sec. 1992, pres. 1994). Avocations: reading, woodworking. Office: Crawford County Dist Atty Office 220 N Beaumont Rd Prairie Du Chien WI 53821-1405

BAXTER, WARNER L., electric power industry executive; BS in Acctg., U. Mo. Cert. CPA. Sr. mgr. Price WaterhouseCooper, LLC, Acctg. Auditing Svcs. Dept., St. Louis, 1983—93, Price WaterhouseCooper, LLC, SEC Svcs. Dept., NYC; asst. contr. Union Electric, 1995—96, contr., 1996—97; v.p., contr. Ameren Corp. and Ameren Svcs. (following Union Electric and CIPSCO merger), 1997—2001; sr. v.p., fin. Ameren, St. Louis, 2001—03, exec. v.p., CFO, 2003—. Mem.: Mo. Soc. CPA's, Am. Inst. CPA's, Coll. of Bus., Dean's Adv. Bd., Chancellor's Coun., U. Mo. (v.p.), Mo. Energy Policy Coun., Wyman Ctr. (bd. of trustees). Office: Ameren 1901 Chouteau Saint Louis MO 63166-6149

BAYER, GARY RICHARD, advertising executive; b. St. Louis, Mar. 15, 1941; s. Kenneth Joseph and Ruth Margarite (Johnson) B.; m. Jeanette Marie Stis, July 13, 1963; children: Gregory Scott, Keith Russell, Kristen Holly. BA, Washington U., 1963. Copywriter Adult Edn. Council of Greater St. Louis, St. Louis, 1962, D'Arcy Advt. Co., St. Louis, 1963-67; from v.p. creative dir. to sr. v.p. exec. creative dir. D'Arcy MacManus & Masius, St. Louis, 1968-80; pres. Adcom. div.

Quaker Oats Co., Chgo., 1980-85; pres., chief ops. officer Backer & Spielvogel Chgo., Inc., Chgo., 1985-87; chmn., CEO, chief creative officer Bayer Bess Vanderwarker Advt., Chgo., 1987-96; exec. v.p. devel. True North Comm., Chgo., 1996—. Chmn. Vols. Am., Ill. Mem. Am. Assn. Advt. Agys. (gov.-at-large 1988-95, sec.-treas. bd. dirs. 1991-92, bd. dirs. 1993-95, vice chair Ill. bd. govs.), Chgo. Advt. Fedn. (pres. 1990-93), Am. Advt. Fedn. (Hall of Fame judge 1994-95), Univ. Club, Met. Club, Phi Beta Kappa, Omicron Delta Kappa. Republican. Avocations: music, writing, travel, tennis, certified scuba diver. Home: 1010 E Illinois Rd Lake Forest IL 60045-2410 Office: True North Comms 101 E Erie St Chicago IL 60611-2812

BAYH, EVAN (BIRCH EVAN BAYH III), senator, former governor; b. Terre Haute, Ind., Dec. 26, 1955; s. Birch Evans Jr. and Marvella (Hern) B.; m. Susan; two children. BS in Bus. Economics, Ind. U., 1978; JD, U. Va., 1981. Bar: DC 1982, Ind. 1983. Law clk. US Dist. Ct., 1982—83; atty. Hogan & Harston, 1982—83, Bingham, Summers, Welsh & Spilman, Indianapolis, 1985—86; sec. of state State of Ind., Indpls., 1987-89, gov., 1989-96; ptnr. Baker & Daniel Assocs., Indpls., 1997-98; US Senator from Ind., 1999—; mem. Select Com. on Intelligence, Armed Svcs. Com., Banking, Housing & Urban Affairs Com., Small Bus Com. & Spl. Com. on Aging; sr. advisor Chatwell Investments. Chmn. Democratic Leadership Coun., 2001—05; mem. com. armed svc. US Senate, com. banking, housing and urban affairs. Author: From Father to Son: A Private Life in the Public Eye, 2003. Recipient Carolyn Mosby Above and Beyond award, Indiana Black Exposition, 1995, Breaking the Glass Ceiling award, Women Executives in State Govt., 1996, Good Govt. award, Cato Inst., 1996, Henry M. Jackson award, Jewish Inst. Nat. Security Affairs, 2004, Friend of Zion award, The Jerusalem Fund, 2004. Democrat. Episcopalian. Office: US Senate 463 Russell Senate Office Bldg Washington DC 20510-0001 also: Market Tower Ste 1650 10 W Market St Indianapolis IN 46204-2934 Office Phone: 317-554-0750, 202-224-5623. Office Fax: 202-228-1377, 317-554-0760.

BAYLESS, CHARLES T., agricultural products executive; Wtih Archer Daniels Midland Co., Decatur, Ill., 1957—, exec. v.p., 1998—, spl. asst. to CEO, 1999—. Office: Archer Daniels Midland Co 4666 E Faries Pkwy Decatur IL 62526-5666

BAYLESS, RICK, chef; b. Oklahoma City, 1953; m. Deann Bayless. Host PBS TV series Cooking Mexican, 1978—79; owner, chef Frontera Grill, Chgo., 1987—, Topolombampo, Chgo., 1989—; host PBS series Mexico One Plate at a Time With Rick Bayless, 2000—. N. Cheffs Collaborative 2000; ptnr. Frontera Foods, 1995; chef's coun. Chefs for Humanity. Author: Authentic Mexican, 1987, Rick Bayless's Mexican Kitchen, 1996, Salsas That Cook, 1999; co-author (with daughter Lanie Bayless): Rick & Lanie's Excellent Kitchen Adventures, 2004; co-author: (with Deann Groen Bayless) Mexican Everyday, 2005; appeared on TV programs: Today, Good Morning Am., This Morning, Martha Stewart Living, Cooking Live, In Julia's Kitchen with Master Chefs, Great Chefs of Am., others; contbr. to numerous food and cooking publs.; contbg. editor: Saveur. Named Best New Chef of 1988, Food and Wine mag., Best Am. Chef: Midwest, James Beard Found., 1991; recipient Nat. Chef of Yr. award, 1995, Chef of Yr. award, Internat. Assn. Culinary Professionals, 1995, Humanitarian award, 2007, Humanitarian of Yr., James Beard Found., 1998, Outstanding Restaurant award for Frontera Grill, 2007. Office: Frontera Grill 445 N Clark St Chicago IL 60610

BAYLOR, DON EDWARD, former professional baseball manager, retired professional baseball player; b. Austin, Tex., June 28, 1949; s. George Edward and Lillian Joyce B.; m. Rebecca Giles, Dec. 12, 1987; 1 child by previous marriage, Don Edward. Student, Miami-Dade Jr. Coll., Miami, Fla., Blinn Jr. Coll., Brenham, Tex. Profl. baseball player Balt. Orioles, 1970-76, Oakland Athletics, 1976, 1988, California Angels, 1976-82, NY Yankees, 1983-86, Boston Red Sox, 1986-87, Minn. Twins, 1987; mgr. Colo. Rockies, Denver, 1992-98, Chgo. Cubs, 2000—02; hitting/batting coach Atlanta Braves, 1999; bench coach NY Mets, 2003—04; hitting coach Seattle Mariners, 2005. Set new career record for hit by pitches; hit safely in 12 consecutive Am. League Championship Series games. Author: (with Claire Smith) Don Baylor, Nothing But the Truth: A Baseball Life, 1989. Chmn. nat. sports Cystic Fibrosis Found. Recipient Designated Hitter of Yr. award, 1985, 86, Roberto Clemente award, 1985; named Am. League's Most Valuable Player, 1979, Sporting News Player of Yr., 1979; player All-Star Game, 1979; named Nat. League Mgr. of Yr. Sporting News, 1995, Baseball Writers Assn. Am., 1995. Achievements include being a holder of Am. League playoff record most RBI (10), 1982, Am. League single season record most times hit by pitch (35), 1986.

BAYLOR, RICHARD C., financial company executive; m. Maura Baylor; 3 children. BS in Indsl. Edn., Bowling Green State U. With State Savs. Bank, Columbus, Ohio, 1989-98; exec. v.p., COO Camco Fin. Corp., Cambridge, Ohio, 1998-2000, pres., COO, 2000—. Mem. Ohio Mortgage Bankers Assn. (v.p. residential lending 1997). Office: Camco Fin Corp 6901 Glenn Hwy Cambridge OH 43725-8685

BAYLY, GEORGE V., manufacturing executive; MBA. Chmn., pres. & CEO Olympic Packing Inc., Ivex Packaging, Lincolnshire, Ill., 1991—2002; principal Whitehall Investors LLC, 2002—. Bd. dir. Carvel Inc., Chicago Stock Exchange, Field Industries, Packaging Dynamics, Roark Capital, Chargeurs Inc., France, Huhtamaki, Finland, US Can Corp., 2003, GBC, Miami U. of Ohio, Shedd Aquarium, United Way.

BAYM, GORDON ALAN, physicist, researcher; b. NYC, July 1, 1935; s. Louis and Lillian B.; children— Nancy, Geoffrey, Michael, Carol. AB, Cornell U., 1956; A.M., Harvard U., 1957, PhD, 1960. Fellow Universitetets Institut for Teoretisk Fysik, Copenhagen, Denmark, 1960-62; lectr. U. Calif., Berkeley, 1962-63; prof. physics U. Ill., Urbana, 1963—. Vis. prof. U. Tokyo and U. Kyoto, 1968, Nordita, Copenhagen, 1970, 76, Niels Bohr Inst., Copenhagen, 1976, U. Nagoya, 1979; vis. scientist Academia Sinica, China, 1979; mem. adv. bd. Inst. Theoretical Physics, Santa Barbara, Calif., 1978-83; mem. subcom. theoretical physics, physics adv. com. NSF, 1980-81, mem. phys. adv. com., 1982-85; mem. nuclear sci. adv. com. Dept. of Energy/NSF, 1982-86, subcom. on theoretical physics; mem. adv. com. physics Los Alamos Nat. Lab., 1988; mem. nat. adv. com. Inst. Nuclear Theory. Author: Lectures on Quantum Mechanics, 1969, Neutron Stars, 1970, Neutron Stars and the Properties of Matter at High Density, 1977, (with L.P. Kadanoff) Quantum Statistical Mechanics, 1962, (with C.J. Pethick) Landau Fermi Liquid Theory: Concepts and Applications, 1991; assoc. editor Nuclear Physics; mem. editorial bd. Procs. Nat. Acad. Scis., 1986-92. Trustee Assoc. U. Inc., 1986-90. Recipient Alexander von Humboldt Found. Sr. U.S. Scientist award, 1983; fellow Am. Acad. Arts and Scis.; Alfred P. Sloan Found. research fellow, 1965-68; NSF postdoctoral fellow, 1960-62 Fellow AAAS, Am. Phys.Soc. (exec. com. div. history of physics 1986-88, 96-97, chair forum history of physics 1994-95, chair-elect 1995-96; mem. NAS (chair physics sect. 1995-98), Am. Astron. Soc., Internat. Astron. Union.

BAYM (STILLINGER), NINA, literature educator, researcher, writer; b. Princeton, NJ, June 14, 1936; d. Leo and Frances (Levinson) Zippin; m. Gordon Baym, June 1, 1958; children— Nancy, Geoffrey; m. Jack Stillinger, May 21, 1971 BA, Cornell U., 1957; MA, Harvard U., 1958, PhD, 1963. Asst. U. Calif.-Berkeley, 1962-63; instr. U. Ill., Urbana, 1963-67, asst. prof. English, 1967-69, assoc. prof., 1969-72, prof., 1972—, Jubilee prof. liberal arts and scis., 1989—, dir. Sch. Humanities Urbana, 1976-87, sr. Univ. scholar, 1985, assoc. Ctr. Advanced Study, 1989-90, permanent prof. Ctr. Advanced Study, 1997—2004, Swanlund Endowed chair, 1997—2004. Author: The Shape of Hawthorne's Career, 1976, Woman's Fiction: A Guide to Novels By and About Women in America, 1978, 2d rev. edit., 1993, Novels, Readers and Reviewers: Responses to Fiction in Antebellum America, 1984, The Scarlet Letter: A Reading, 1986, Feminism and American Literary History, 1992, American Women Writers and the Work of History, 1790-1860, 1995, American Women of Letters and the 19th Century Sciences, 2002; gen. editor: Norton Anthology of American Literature; sr. editor Am. Nat. Biography; also author essays, edits., revs.; mem. editl. bd. Am. Quar., New Eng. Quar., Legacy, A Jour. of 19th Century Am. Women Writers, Jour. Aesthetic Edn. Am. Lit., Tulsa Studies in Women's Lit., Am. Studies, Studies Am. Fiction, Am. Periodicals, Hemingway Rev., Resources for Am. Lit. Study, Am. Lit. History, Cambridge U.P. Studies in Am. Lit. and Culture; mem. editl. adv. bd. PMLA. Guggenheim fellow, 1975-76, AAUW hon. fellow, 1975-76, NEH fellow, 1982-83; rec pient Arnold O. Beckman award U. Ill., 1992-93, Hubbell Lifetime Achievement medal, Am. Let. Sect., 2000. Mem. MLA (exec. com. 19th century Am. Lit. divsn., chmn. 1984, chmn. Am. Lit. sect. 1984, Hubbell Lifetime Achievement medal 2000), Am. Studies Assn. (exec. com. 1982-84, nominating com. 1991-93), Am. Lit. Assn., Am. Antiquarian Soc., Mass. Hist. Soc., athaniel Hawthorne Soc. (adv. bd.), Western Lit. Assn., Mortar Bd., Phi Kappa Phi, Phi Beta Kappa. Office Phone: 217-333-2390. Business E-Mail: baymnina@uiuc.edu.

BAYNE, DAVID COWAN, priest, educator, lawyer; b. Detroit, Jan. 11, 1918; s. David Cowan and Myrtle (Murray) B. AB, U. Detroit, 1939; LLB, Georgetown U., 1947, LLM, 1948; MA, Loyola U., Chgo., 1946, STL, 1953; SJD (grad. fellow), Yale, 1949; LLD (hon.), Creighton U., 1980. Bar: Fed. and D.C. 1948, Mich. 1960, Mo. 1963. Joined Soc. of Jesus, 1941; ordained priest Roman Catholic Ch., 1952; asst. prof. law U. Detroit, 1954-60; acting dean U. Detroit (Law Sch.), 1955-59, dean, 1959-60; research assoc. Nat. Jesuit Research Orgn., Inst. Social Order, St. Louis, 1960-63; vis. lectr. St. Louis U. Law Sch., 1960-63, prof. law, 1963-67; vis. prof. Mich. Law Sch., 1967, Inst. fur Auslandisches und Internationales Wirtschaftrecht, Frankfurt, 1967; prof. U. Iowa Coll. Law, Iowa City, 1967-88, prof. emeritus, 1988—. Vis. prof. U. Koln, Germany, 1970, 74 Author: Conscience, Obligation and the Law, 1966, 2d edit., 1988; The Philosophy of Corporate Control, 1986; editor legal materials; contbr. articles to profl. jours. Achievements include research in corp. law. E-mail: dcbsj@netzero.net, dcbsj@buckeye-express.com.

BAYS, JAMES C., lawyer; b. Denton, Tex., July 23, 1949; BA magna cum laude, Dartmouth Coll., 1971; JD, U. Va., 1974. Bar: Ohio 1974. Assoc. Jones, Day, Reavis & Pogue, 1974—78; counsel TRW, Inc., 1978—81, sr. counsel, 1981—85, v.p., asst. gen. counsel, 1985—92; v.p., asst. gen. counsel GenCorp, Inc., 1993—96; sr. v.p., gen. counsel, chief legal officer Invensys plc, London, 1996—2001; v.p., gen. counsel Ferro Corp., Cleve., 2001—. Mem. editl. bd.: Va. Law Review, 1972—74. Mem.: ABA, Ohio State Bar Assn., Cleve. State Bar Assn. Office: Ferro Corp 1000 Lakeside Ave Cleveland OH 44114-7000 Office Phone: 216-875-6122. Office Fax: 216-875-7275. E-mail: baysj@ferro.com.

BAZANT, ZDENEK PAVEL, engineering educator; b. Prague, Czechoslovakia, Dec. 10, 1937; came to U.S., 1968, naturalized, 1976; s. Zdenek and Stepanka (Curikova) B.; m. Iva Marie Krasna, Sept. 27, 1967; children: Martin Zdenek, Eva Stephanie. Civil Engr., Tech. U., Prague, 1960; PhD in Mechanics, Czechoslovak Acad. Sci., 1963; postgrad. diploma in theoretical physics, Charles U., Prague, 1966; doctorate (hon.), Czech Tech. U., Prague, 1991, Karlsruhe U., Germany, 1998, U. Colo., 2000, Poly. Milan, 2001, Institut Nat. des Scis. Appliques, Lyon, 2004, Vienna U. Tech., 2005. Registered structural engr., Ill. Scientist, adj. prof. Bldg. Rsch. Inst., Tech. U., Prague, 1963-67; docent habilitation Tech. U., Prague, 1967; vis. rsch. engr. Centre d'Étude et de Recherche du Bâtiment et des Travaux Publics, Paris, 1967, U. Toronto, 1967—68, U. Calif., Berkeley, 1969; assoc. prof. civil engring. Northwestern U., Evanston, Ill., 1969-73, prof., 1973-90, Walter P. Murphy prof., 1990—, coord. structural engring. program, 1974-78, 92—; founding dir. Ctr. for Concrete and Geomaterials, 1981-86. Cons. Argonne Nat. Lab., many other orgns. Author: Creep of Concrete in Structural Analysis, 1966, Stability of Structures: Elastic, Inelastic, Fracture and Damage Theories, 1991, Concrete at High Temperatures, 1996, Fracture and Size Effect, 1997, Scaling of Structural Strength, 2002, Inelastic Analysis of Structures, 2002; editor 16 books; editor in chief Jour. Engring. Mechanics, 1989-94; regional editor Internat. Jour. Fracture, 1991—; assoc. editor Applied Mechanics Rev., 1987—, Cement and Concrete Research Internat. Jour, 1970—, Materials and Structures, 1979— Solid Mechanics Archives, 1980-91, Materials and Structures, 1981—; mem. editl. bds. of 16 hours.; contbr. (with others) over 350 articles to profl. jours.; patentee in field. Recipient Best Engring. Book of Yr. award Soc. Am. Pubs., 1992, Outstanding New Citizen award Chgo. Citizenship Coun., 1976, A. von Humboldt award, 1990, Šolín medal Czech Tech. U., Prague, 1998, Stodola gold medal Slovak Acad. Scis., 1999, Highly Cited Scientist award Internat. Sci. Index, 2001; grantee NSF, 1970—, Air Force Office Scientific Rsch., 1975—, Los Alamos Sci. Lab., 1978-80, European Power Rsch. Inst., 1980—, Office aval Rsch., 1990—, Dept. Energy, 1984—; Ford Found. fellow, 1967-68, Guggenheim fellow, 1978-79, Kajima Found. fellow U. Tokyo, 1987, NATO fellow, Paris, 1988, Japan Soc. Promotion of Sci. fellow U. Tokyo, 1995-96. Fellow ASME (Worcester Reed Warner medal 1997), Am. Acad. Mechanics, ASCE (chmn. com. properties of materials 1976-78, 82-84, editor in chief Jour. Engring. Mechanics 1988-94, Walter L. Huber rsch. prize 1976, T.Y. Lin Prestressed Concrete award 1977, Newmark medal 1996, Croes medal 1997, Lifetime Achievement Award, 2003, von Kármán medal 2005), Am. Concrete Inst. (chmn. fracture mechanics com. 1985-92), Internat. Assn. for Fracture Mechanics of Concrete Structures (pres. 1991-93), Internat. Union Testing and Rsch. Labs. Materials Structures (chmn. com. on creep, L'Hermite gold medal 1975), Soc. Engring. Sci. (pres. 1993, Prager medal 1996); mem. NAS, NAE, Italian Nat. acad dei Lincei Rome, Lombard Acad. Milan, Engring. Acad. Czech Republic (fgn. mem.), Austrian Acad. Scis., U.S. Nat. Com. on Theoretical and Applied Mechanics, Internat. Assn. Structural Mechanics Reactor Tech. (coord. concrete structures divsn.), ASTM (mem. concrete com., skiing com.), Prestressed Concrete Inst., Am. Ceramic Soc. (D.M. Roy award 2001), Internat. Assn. Soil Mech. Found. Engring., Internat. Assn. Bridge and Structural Engring., Soc. Exptl. Mechanics, Am. Soc. Engring. Edn., Bldg. Rsch. Inst. Spain (hon., Torroja Gold medal 1990), Czech Soc. Civil Engring. (hon.), Czech Soc. Mechanics (award of merit 1993), Structural Engrs. Assn. Ill. (Meritorious Paper award 1992). Home: 707 Roslyn Ter Evanston IL 60201-1721 Office: Northwestern Univ Dept Civil Engring Evanston IL 60208-0001

BEACHLEY, NORMAN HENRY, mechanical engineer, educator; b. Washington, Jan. 13, 1933; s. Albert Henry and Anna Garnet (Eiring) B.; m. Marion Ruth Iglehart, July 18, 1959; children: Brenda Ruth, Rebecca Sue, Barbara Joan. B.M.E., Cornell U., 1956, PhD, 1966. Mem. tech. staff Hughes Aircraft Co., Culver City, Calif., 1956-57; mem. tech. staff Space Tech. Labs., Redondo Beach, Calif., 1959-63; mem. faculty U. Wis., Madison, 1966—, prof. mech. engring., 1978-94, prof. emeritus, 1994—. Cons. numerous orgns., 1967— Co-author: Introduction to Dynamic System Analysis, 1978. Served with USAF, 1957-59. Sci. and Engring. Research Council Gt. Britain fellow, 1981-82 Fellow Soc. Automotive Engrs.; mem. ASME, Sigma Xi. Achievements include research in field of energy storage powerplants for motor vehicles, 1970—. Home: 2332 Fitchburg Rd Verona WI 53593-9278 Office: U Wis 1513 University Ave Madison WI 53706-1539 Business E-Mail: beachley@wisc.edu.

BEACHY, ROGER, biologist, plant pathologist, researcher; b. Plain City, Ohio, Oct. 4, 1944; divorced; children: Kathryn C., Kyle A. BA, Goshen Coll., 1966; PhD in Plant Pathology, Mich. State U., 1973. Rsch. assoc. Cornell U., Ithaca, N.Y., 1973-76, U.S. Plant, Soil & Nutrition Lab., Ithaca, N.Y., 1976-78; from asst. prof. to prof. dept. biology Washington U., St. Louis, 1976—; joined Scripps Rsch. Inst., La Jolla, 1999, mem., head divsn. plant biology, Scripps Family chair, cofounder, Internat. Lab. for Tropical Agrl. Biotechnology; founding pres. & dir. Donald Danforth Plant Sci. Ctr., St. Louis, 1999—. Plant Virology fellow NIH, 1973-76; named Scientist of Yr., R&D mag., 1999; recipient Wolf award for agr., Wolf Found., Israel, 2001. Fellow AAAS, Am. Soc. Microbiology; mem. Am. Phytopath Soc. (Ruth Allen award 1990), Am. Soc. Plant Physiologists, Am. Soc. Virologists, Am. Soc. Biol. Chemists, Internat. Soc. Plant Molecular Biology, NAS (Wolf prize agr. 2001). Achievements include research in control of synthesis of soybean seed proteins, plant viral messenger RNAs, effects of virus gene products on infected host cells, gentetic transformation of plants for virus resistance. Office: Wash U Ctr Plant Sci and Biotech Dept Biology Saint Louis MO 63130 also: Scripps Rsch Inst Dept Cell Biology La Jolla CA 92037

BEAK, PETER ANDREW, chemistry professor; b. Syracuse, NY, Jan. 12, 1936; s. Ralph E. and Belva (Edinger) B.; m. Sandra J. Burns, July 25, 1959; children: Bryan A., Stacia W. BA, Harvard U., 1957; PhD, Iowa State U., 1961. From instr. to prof. chemistry U. Ill., Urbana, 1961—, Roger Adams prof. chemistry, 1997—2003, Jubilee prof. liberal arts and sci., 1990—, James R. Eiszner chair chemistry, 2003, CAS prof. chemistry. Cons. Abbott Labs., North Chicago, Ill., 1964—, Monsanto Co., St. Louis, 1969-99, G.D. Searle Co., Ill., 1987-2001, Pharmacia, 2001-02, Pfizer, 2003—05. Contbr. articles to profl. jours. A.P. Sloan Found. fellow, 1967-69; Guggenheim fellow, 1968-69 Fellow AAAS (chmn. chemistry sect. 1999), Am. Acad. Arts and Scis.; mem. NAS, Am. Chem. Soc. (editl. and adv. bds., sec. and divsn. officer, A.C. Cope scholar 1993, Mosher award 1994, Gilman award 1997, Gassman award 2000). Home: 304 E Sherwin Ave Urbana IL 61802 Home Phone: 217-344-6856. Business E-Mail: beak@scs.uiuc.edu.

BEAL, GRAHAM WILLIAM JOHN, museum director; b. Stratford-on-Avon, Eng., Apr. 22, 1947; came to U.S., 1973; s. Cecil John Beal and Annie Gladys (Barton) Tunbridge; m. Nancy Jane Andrews, Apr. 21, 1973: children: Priscilla Jane, Julian William John. BA, Manchester U., Eng., 1969; MA, U. London, 1972. Acad. asst. to dir. Sheffield City (Eng.) Art Galleries, 1972-73; gallery dir. U. S.D., Vermillion, 1973-74, Washington U., St. Louis, 1974-77; chief curator Walker Art Ctr., Mpls., 1977-83; dir. Sainsbury Ctr. for Visual Arts, Norwich, Eng., 1983-84; chief curator San Francisco Mus. Modern Art, 1984-89; dir. Joslyn Art Mus., Omaha, 1989-96, Los Angeles County Mus. Art, 1996-99, Detroit Inst. Arts, 1999—. Mem. Fed. Adv. Com. on Internat. Exhbns., 1991-94. Author: (book, exhbn. catalog) Jim Dine: Five Themes, 1984; co-author: (book, exhbn. catalog) A Quiet Revolution, 1987, David Nash: Voyages and Vessels, 1994, Sainsbury Collection Catalogue, vol. I, 1997, Joslyn Air Museum: Fifty Favorities, 1994, Joslyn Art Museum: A Building History, 1998, American Beauty: American Paintings and Sculpture from the Detroit Institute of Arts, 2002; Co-Author: Treasure of the DIA, 2007; contbg. to Apollo Mag., London, 1989-91. Trustee Djerassi Found., Woodside, Calif., 1987-89. Mem.: Am. Assn. Museums (trustee 2002—05), Assn. Art Mus. Dirs. (trustee 2002—04), Detroit Athletic Club, Century Club. Avocations: history, cooking, music. Office: Detroit Inst Arts 5200 Woodward Ave Detroit MI 48202 Business E-Mail: gbeal@dia.org.

BEALE, SUSAN M., electric power industry executive; Degree, Mich. State U.; law degree, U. Mich. Law Sch. Atty. Consumer Power and So. Calif. Edison; with Detroit Edison, 1982-95; v.p., corp. sec. DTE Energy, 1995—. Mem.: Am. Soc. Corp. Secs., Am. Corp. Counsel Assn. Office: Detroit Edison Co 2002 2nd Ave Detroit MI 48226

BEALKE, LINN HEMINGWAY, banker; b. St. Louis, Nov. 14, 1944; s. Charles Francis and Miriam Frances (Hemingway) B.; m. Jean Long Wells, Sept. 6, 1969; children: David Q.W., Emily R., Linn H. BA, U. Ark., 1966; MBA, Washington U., 1969. Fin. analyst Edison Brothers Stores, St. Louis, 1969-74; sr. v.p. Commerce Bank of St. Louis, 1975-78; v.p. fin. and adminstrn. Curlee Clothing Co., Lexington, Ky., 1978-80; vice chmn. County Bank of St. Louis, 1980-84, Southwest Bank of St. Louis, 1984—2004. Bd. dirs. Zoltek Cos., Inc.; bd. dirs. Miss. Valley Bancshares, pres., 1984-2002. Treas. Forsyth Sch., St. Louis, 1980-87; pres. Edgewood Childrens Ctr., Webster Groves, Mo., 1986-88; dir. Mo. Colls. Fund, Jefferson City, Mo., 1990-93. Mem. Mo. Bankers Assn. (dir. 1988-90, 99-2002), Fin. Execs. Inst. (pres. St. Louis chpt. 1989-90, dir. 1991-94), Am. Bankers Assn. Leadership Conf. (del. 1990-92), Racquet Club (v.p. 1987-89), Bellerive Country Club, St. Louis Country Club, Old Baldy Club, John's Island Club. Office: SW Bank St Louis PO Box 790178 Saint Louis MO 63179-0178 Home: 305 Carlyle Lake Dr Saint Louis MO 63141-7545 Personal E-mail: linnbealke@yahoo.com.

BEALL, CYNTHIA, anthropologist, educator; b. Urbana, Ill., Aug. 21, 1949; d. John Wood and J. Alene (Beachler) Beall. BA in Biology, U. Pa., 1970; MA in Anthropology, Pa. State U., 1972, PhD in Anthropology, 1976. Asst. prof. Case Western Res. U., Cleve., 1976—82, assoc. prof. of anthropology, 1982—87, prof. anthropology, 1987—. Co-editor: Jour. of Cross-Cultural Gerontology, 1986—95; contbr. articles to profl. jours. Active Internat. Rsch. Exch. Program, 1990, 1991. Fellow Nat. Program for Advanced Study and Rsch. in China, NAS, 1986—87, 1997; Rsch. grantee, NSF, 1981, 1983, 1986—87, 1993—95, 1997, 2000, 2002, 2005, Am. Fedn. for Aging Rsch., 1983, 1986, Nat. Geog. Soc., 1983, 1986—87, 1993, 1995. Fellow: AAAS; mem.: NAS (coun. 2002—05), Internat. Coun. Sci. (exec. bd. 2005—), Assn. Anthropology and Gerontology, Soc. Study Human Biology, Human Biology Coun. (exec. com. 1989—92, pres. 1992—94), Am. Assn. Phys. Anthropology (exec. com. 1989—92), Am. Anthrop. Assn., Am. Philo. Soc. Achievements include research in human adaptation to high altitude. Office: Case Western Res U Dept Anthropology 238 Mather Meml Bldg Cleveland OH 44106-7125 Business E-Mail: cmb2@case.edu.

BEALS, ROBERT J., ceramics engineer; Dir Hall China Co. Recipient Albert Victor Bleininger award Am. Ceramic Soc., 1994. Office: Hall China Co 438 Smithfield St East Liverpool OH 43920-1723

BEALS, VAUGHN LE ROY, JR., retired motorcycle manufacturing executive; b. Cambridge, Mass., Jan. 2, 1928; s. Vaughn Le Roy and Pearl Uela (Wilmarth) B.; m. Eleanore May Woods, July 15, 1951; children: Susan Lynn, Laurie Jean. BS, M.I.T., 1948, MS, 1954. Research engr. Cornell Aero. Lab., Buffalo, 1948-52, MIT Aero Elastic and Structures Research Lab., 1952-55; dir. research and tech. N.Am. Aviation, Inc., Columbus, Ohio, 1955-65; exec. v.p. Cummins Engine Co., Columbus, Ind., 1965-70, also dir.; chmn. bd., chief exec. officer Formac Internat., Inc., Seattle, 1970-75; dep. group exec. Motorcycle Products Group, AMF Inc., Milw., 1975-77, v.p. and group exec. Stamford, Conn., 1977-81; chief exec. officer Harley-Davidson, Inc., Milw., 1981-89, chmn., 1981-96, chmn. emeritus, 1996—. Mem. Desert Mountain Club, Desert Forest Golf Club, Forest Highlands Golf Club. Home: PO Box 3260 Carefree AZ 85377-3260 Office: Harley-Davidson Inc Box 653 3700 W Juneau Ave Milwaukee WI 53208-2865

BEAM, CLARENCE ARLEN, federal judge; b. Stapleton, Nebr., Jan. 14, 1930; s. Clarence Wilson and Cecile Mary (Harvey) Beam; m. Betty Lou Fletcher, July 22, 1951; children: Randal, James, Thomas, Bradley, Gregory. BS, U. Nebr., 1951, JD, 1965. Feature writer Nebr. Farmer Mag., Lincoln, 1951; with sales dept. Steckley Seed Co., Mount Sterling, Ill., 1954—58, advt. mgr., 1958—63; from assoc. to ptnr. Chambers, Holland, Dudgeon & Knudsen, Berkheimer, Beam, et al, Lincoln, 1965—82; judge US Dist. Ct. Nebr., Omaha, 1982—87, chief judge, 1986—87; cir. judge US Ct. Appeals (8th cir.), 1987—. Mem. com. on lawyer discipline Nebr. Supreme Ct., 1974—82; mem. Conf. Commrs. on Uniform State Laws, 1979—, chmn. Nebr. sect., 1980—82; mem. jud. conf. com. on ct. and jud. security, 1989—93; chmn., 1992—93. Contbr. articles to profl. jours. Mem. Nebr. Rep. Ctrl. Com., 1970—78. Capt. US Army, 1951—53, Korea. Scholar Roscoe Pound scholar, U. Nebr., Lincoln, 1964; Regents scholar, 1947. Mem.: Nebr. State Bar Assn. Office: US Ct Appeals 8th Cir 435 Federal Bldg 100 Centennial Mall N Lincoln NE 68508-3859 Office Phone: 402-437-5420.

BEAN, JERRY JOE, lawyer; b. Lebanon, Ind., Apr. 19, 1954; s. Russell Lowell and Mary Ethel (Jett) B.; m. Cheryl Lynn Smith, May 29, 1976; 1 child, Angela. B.A., Wabash Coll., 1976; D. Jurisprudence, Ind. U., 1979; Bars: U.S. Dist. Ct. (so. and no. dists.) Ind. 1979, 81. Exec. dir. Legal Aid Corp., Lafayette, Ind., 1979-80; dep. prosecuting atty. IV-D, Tippecanoe County Prosecutors Office, Lafayette, 1980-81, county ct., 1981-83, felony intake, 1983-84, chief dep. prosecutor, 1984—. Mem. ABA, Assn. Trial Lawyers Am., Ind. State Bar Assn., Tippecanoe County Bar Assn. Republican. Methodist. Lodge: Arman, Fraternal Order of Police (hon.). Office: Tippecanoe County Prosecutor's Office Court House Lafayette IN 47901

BEAN, MELISSA, congresswoman; b. Chgo., Jan. 22, 1962; m. Alan Bean; children: Victoria, Michelle. AA in Bus., Oakton Cmty. Coll., 1982; BA in Polit. Sci., Roosevelt U., 2002. Dist. sales mgr. DJC Corp., 1982—85; br. mgr. MTI Systems Inc. Arrow Electronics, 1985—89; dist. mgr. UDS Motorola, 1989—91; area mgr. SynOptics Comm. Inc., 1991—94; v.p. sales Dataflex Corp., 1994—95; pres. Sales Resources Inc., 1995—2004; mem. US Congress from Ill. Dist. 8, 2005—; mem. Fin. Svcs. com., Small Bus. com. Mem. Palatine C. of C.; past pres. Deer Lake Homeowners Assn. Mem.: Nat. Assn Women Bus. Owners, Barrington Area Profl. Women. Democrat. Serbian Orthodox. Office: 512 Cannon House Office Bldg Washington DC 20005 Office Phone: 202-225-3711. Office Fax: 202-225-7830.

BEANE, MARJORIE NOTERMAN, academic administrator; b. Adams, Minn., Oct. 3, 1946; d. Matthias Hubert and Anna Helen (Boegeman) Noterman. BA, Marillac Coll., St. Louis, 1969; MEd, U. Ariz., 1979; PhD, Loyola U., Chgo., 1988. Tchr. St. Alphonsus Sch., Prospect Heights, Ill., 1969-73; tchr., asst. prin. St. Raphael Sch., Chgo., 1973-75; prin. St. Theresa Sch., Palatine, Ill., 1975-84; pres. Mallinckrodt Coll. of the North Shore, Wilmette, Ill., 1986-90; sr. v.p. for adminstn. Loyola U., Chgo., 1991—. Trustee Mallinckrodt Coll. of the North Shore, 1980-90; cons. Jospehinum High Sch., Chgo., 1976, St. Viator High Sch., Arlington Heights, Ill., 1986. Mem. History of Women Religious,

Fedn. Ind. Ill. Colls. and Univs. (exec. com. 1989), Wilmette C. of C., Sisters of Christian Charity (councilor 1980-88). Rotary. Roman Catholic. Avocations: sewing, bicycling, swimming, travel. Office: Loyola U 820 N Michigan Ave Fl 1 Chicago IL 60611-2196

BEARD, ERIC A., pharmaceutical executive; B.Comml. and Fin. Sci., Hautes Etudes Comerciales; MBA, U. Leuven, Belgium. Fin. planning mgr. Baxter World Trade Corp., 1975, corp. v.p., 1998—, v.p. renal divsn. Europe, 1990—92, pres. renal divsn. Japan and Europe, 1992—98.

BEARDSLEY, JOHN RAY, public relations firm executive; b. Mpls., Jan. 10, 1937; s. Ray Homer Beardsley and Dorothy Louise (Refsell) Ripley; m. Sharon Ruth Olson, Aug. 24, 1960; children— Elizabeth Ruth, Alison Leigh, Leslie Anne BA, Augustana Coll., 1961. News editor Sioux Falls (S.D.) Argus Leader, 1961-64; city editor Worthington (Minn.) Daily Globe, 1964; Corr. AP, Fargo, N.D. and Mpls., 1965-68; comms. mgr. Pillsbury Co., Mpls., 1968-69; pub. rels. mgr. Dayton Hudson Corp., Mpls., 1969-70; successively account exec., v.p., sr. v.p. Padilla and Speer, Inc., Mpls., 1970-83, CEO, 1983-86; chmn., CEO Padilla Speer Beardsley Inc., 1987—, nat. dir. at large, 1991-92, treas., 1993, pres.-elect, 1994, pres., 1995. Mem. Pub. Rels. Soc. Am. (pres. Minn. chpt. 1981), Nat. Investor Rels. Inst. (v.p., dir. Minn. chpt. 1981-84), Mpls. Athletic Club Home: 3904 Williston Rd Minnetonka MN 55345-2054 Office: Padilla Speer Beardsley Inc Ste 400 1101 W River Pkwy Minneapolis MN 55415-1241

BEARMON, LEE, lawyer; b. Mpls. BBA with high distinction, U. Minn., JD with honors. Bar: Minn. 1956. Sr. v.p., exec. cons., chief legal officer Carlson Cos., Inc, Mpls., 1979—2000; former ptnr. Levitt, Palmer & Bearmon; and Levitt, Palmer, Bowen, Bearmon and Rotman; of counsel Briggs & Morgan, Mpls., 2000—. Bd. dir. Beth El Synagogue, Talmud Torah Found. 1st lt. to capt. JAG USAF. Named a Disting. Alumnus, Univ. Minn. Law Sch., 1999, Super Lawyer, Minnesota Law & Politics, MplsSt.Paul Mag., Twin Cities Bus. Monthly. Mem.: Am.-Israel C. of C.

BEARY, JOHN FRANCIS, III, rheumatologist, pharmaceutical executive, medical researcher; b. Melrose, Iowa, 1946; s. John F. and Dorothy (McGrath) B.; m. Bianca E. Mason, 1972; children: John Daniel, Vanessa, Webster, Nina. BS summa cum laude, U. Notre Dame, Ind., 1969; MD, Harvard U., Cambridge, Mass., 1973; MBA, Georgetown U., Washington, DC, 1988. Diplomate Am Bd. Internal Medicine, Am. Bd. Rheumatology, Am. Bd. Clin. Pharmacology. Flight surgeon 89th Mil. Airlift Wing (Air Force One), 1974—77; Osler medicine resident Johns Hopkins Hosp., Balt., 1977—78; rsch. fellow Cornell Hosp. Spl. Surgery, NYC, 1978—80; from asst. prof. to clin. prof. Sch. Medicine Georgetown U., Washington, 1980—2005; prin. dept. asst. sec. health affairs Dept. Def., Washington, 1981—83, appropriations task force for USNS Mercy and USNS Comfort, 1982; assoc. dean strategic planning Georgetown U. Sch. Medicine, Washington, 1984—87; sr. v.p. regulatory and sci. affairs Pharm. Rsch. and Mfg. Assn., Washington, 1988—97; sr. med. dir. bone and arthritis rsch. Procter and Gamble Pharma, Cin., 1997—. Steering com. Internat. Conf. on Harmonization of Pharm. Stds., 1990-97; clin. prof. rheumatology and immunology U. Cin., 1997—; mem. OMERACT Rheumatology Rsch. Com., 1998-2003; sci. com. Arthritis Found., Ohio, 1998-. Editor: Manual of Rheumatology, 1981, 5th edit., 2005; mem. editl. bd. Jour. Pharm. Medicine, 1990—, Drug Devel. Rsch., 1992-2000. Bd. dirs. Scleroderma Found., Washington, 1982—92. Served to capt. USNR, 1984—99. Recipient Disting. Mil. Grad. award, 1969, Rsch. award NY Arthritis Found., 1979, Disting. Pub. Svc. medal Dept. Def., 1983, Albia H.S. Career Achievement award, 1992, Navy and Marine Corps Commendation medal, 1997, Georgetown Med. Vicennial medal, 2003, 6th Naval Beach Bn. Normandy award, 2004. Fellow: ACP, Am. Coll. Rheumatology; mem.: Am. Soc. for Bone and Mineral Rsch., Osteoarthritis Rsch. Soc., Am. Soc. Clin. Pharmacology and Therapeutics, Am. Geriat. Soc., Weller-Brown Assn., Mil. Officers Assn., Johns Hopkins Med. and Surg. Assn., US Naval Inst., Harvard Club, Notre Dame Monogram Club, Chevy Chase Club. Office: Procter & Gamble Pharma 8700 Mason Montgomery Rd Mason OH 45040-8006 Office Phone: 513-622-3245.

BEASLEY, JIM SANDERS See LEE, JACK

BEATTIE, TED ARTHUR, zoological gardens and aquarium administrator; b. Salem, Ohio, Jan. 13, 1945; s. Don Earl and Frances (Webster) B.; children: Lauralyn, Sean, Kimberly; m. Penelope Johnson, July 13, 1985. BA in Journalism, Ohio State U., 1971, MA in Pub. Rels., 1972. Advt./pub. rels. dir. Shaw-Barton Co., Coshocton, Ohio, 1972-78; mktg. dir. Cin. Zoo, 1978-81; assoc. dir. Brookfield Zoo, Chgo., 1981-87; exec. dir. Knoxville (Tenn.) Zool. Gardens, 1987-92; dir., CEO Ft. Worth Zool. Pk., 1992-94; pres., CEO John G. Shedd Aquarium, Chgo., 1994—. Cons. Zoo Plan Assn., Wichita, Kans., 1981-88; apptd. U.S. Commn. on Ocean Policy, 2001-03. Vice chmn. and chmn. United Way campaign, Coshocton, 1977-78; mem. Leadership Knoxville, 1988. With U.S. Army, 1967-69, Vietnam. Fellow: Am. Assn. Zool. Pks. and Aquariums (bd. dirs. 1989—91, 1994—2002); mem.: Am. Zoo & Aquarium Assn. (v.p. 1998—99, pres. 2000—01), Sawgrass Country Club, Onwentsia Club, Arts Club, Chgo. Econ. Club. Avocations: golf, boating. Home: 260 E Chestnut St Apt 2802 Chicago IL 60611 Office: John G Shedd Aqarium 1200 S Lake Shore Dr Chicago IL 60605-2402

BEATTY, JOYCE, state representative; b. Dayton, Ohio; married; 2 stepchildren. BA in Speech, Ctrl. State U.; MS in Counseling Psychology, Wright State U.; PhD, Pacific Western U. Mgmt. cons.; state rep. dist. 27 Ohio Ho. of Reps., Columbus, 1999—, mem. civil and comml. law, fin. and appropriations, health, and rules and reference coms., mem. agr. and devel. subcom., asst. minority leader. Named Linden Pride Grand Marshall, 2000. Mem.: NAACP, Am. Soc. Tng. and Devel., Columbus Urban League (chmn. bd. dirs.), Ohio Legis. Black Caucus, Dem. Women's Caucus, The Links, Inc. (nat. endowment chair), United Negro Coll. Fund, Delta Sigma Theta. Democrat. Office: 77 S High St 14th fl Columbus OH 43215-6111

BEATTY, OTTO, JR., former state legislator, lawyer; m. Joyce Beatty; children: Otto III, Laural. BA, Howard U.; JD with honors, Ohio State U. Bar: Ohio. Ptnr. Beatty & Roseboro, Columbus; mem. Ohio Ho. of Reps., Columbus, 1980-99. Mem. pub. utilities com., vice chmn. civil and comml. law com., mem. judiciary and criminal justice com., state govt. com., fin. instns. com., set-aside rev. bd., ct. reorgn. com., state penitentiary devel. commn.; pres. Otto Beatty Jr. LPA Co., Otto Beaty Jr. & Assocs., real estate developers. Recipient Cmty. Svc. award Ohio Minority Bus. Assn., Outstanding Svc. award Franklin County Children's Svcs., award Black C. of C., Ea. Union Missionary Bapt. Assn., Ohio Assn. Real Estate Brokers, Pioneer award Ohio Equal Opportunities Ctr., 1992. Mem. ABA, Ohio Bar Assn. (lectr., Leadership award 1992), Columbus Bar Assn., Franklin County Trial Lawyers Assn. (past pres.), Nat. Conf. Black Lawyers, Nat. Inst. Justice, Black Elected Dems. Ohio, Robert B. Elliott Law Club (past pres.), Home: 233 N High St Columbus OH 43215-2405

BEAUBIEN, ANNE KATHLEEN, librarian; b. Detroit, Sept. 15, 1947; d. Richard Parker and Edith Mildred Beaubien; m. Philip Conway Berry, Feb. 7, 2004. Student, Western Mich. U., 1965-67; BA, Mich. State U., 1969; MLS, U. Mich., 1970. Reference libr., bibliographic instr. U. Mich. Libr., Ann Arbor, 1971-80, dir. MITS, 1980-85, dir. coop. access svc., 1985—, head bus. and fin. office, 1995—2000, grants officer, 2000—. Author: Psychology Bibliography, 1980; co-author: Learning the Library, 1982; contbg. articles to profl. jour., editor, conf. proc., 1987. Mem. vestry St. Clare's Episcopal Ch., Ann Arbor, 1986—89, 2002—03; pres. Ann Arbor Ski Club, 1978—79. Recipient Woman of Yr. Award, Ann Arbor Bus. and Profl. Women's Club, 1982, Disting. Alumnus Award Sch. Info. and Libr. Studies, U. Mich., 1987. Mem. ALA (Virginia Boucher-OCLC Disting. Interlibrary Loan Libr. award, 2007), Assn. Coll. and Rsch. Librs. (pres. 1991-92). Avocations: skiing, bicycling, ballroom dancing. Office: U Mich Libr 106 Hatcher Grad Libr Ann Arbor MI 48109 Office Phone: 734-936-2322. Business E-Mail: beaubien@umich.edu.

BEAUCHAMP, ROY E., career officer; b. July 1, 1945; Commd. U.S. Army, advanced through grades to maj. gen., 1997; with U.S. Army Tank--Automotive and Armaments Command, Warren, Mich. Office: US Army Automotive TACOM/AMSTA-CG Warren MI 48397-5000

BEAVER, FRANK EUGENE, critic, historian; b. Cleve., NC, July 26, 1938; s. John Whitfield and Mary Louise (Shell) B.; m. Gail Frances Place, June 30, 1962; children: Julia Clare, John Francis, Johanna Louise. BA, U. N.C., 1960, MA, 1966; PhD, U. Mich., 1970. Instr. speech Memphis State U., 1965-66; instr. radio-TV-motion pictures U. N.C., Chapel Hill, 1966-68; asst. prof. speech comm. U. Mich., Ann Arbor, 1969-74, assoc. prof., 1974-79, assoc. prof. comm., 1979-84, dir. grad. program in telecom. arts and film, 1981—86, prof., chmn. dept. comm., 1987-91, Arthur F. Thurnau prof., 1989—. Advisor Muskegon (Mich.) Film Festival, 2001. Film critic radio Stas. WUOM, WVGR, WFUM, Ann Arbor, Grand Rapids, Mich., 1975-97; author: Bosley Crowther, 1974, On Film, 1983, Dictionary of Film Terms, 1983, 94 (Mandarin-Chinese translation 1993), 3d edit., 2006, Oliver Stone: Wakeup Cinema, 1994, 100 Years of American Film, 2001; writer, dir. documentary film Under One Roof, 1967; editor (book series) Framing Film, Peter Lang, Pub., N.Y., 1998—; commentator Mich. Today-News-e, 2004—. Advisor Ann Arbor Film Festival, 1975—; bd. dirs. Mich. Theater Found., Ann Arbor, 1977-79, 86, Ann Arbor Summer Festival, 2005—; alumni adv. bd. Lambda Chi Alpha, Ann Arbor, 1989-94. With M.I. Corps, U.S. Army, 1962-65, Vietnam. Recipient Playwriting award Carolina Playmakers, 1962, Major Hopwood writing awards for drama and essays U. Mich., 1969, Outstanding Tchg. award Amoco Found., Ann Arbor, 1985; fellow NEH, 1975. Mem.: Azazels Club, Phi Kappa Phi, Kappa Tau Alpha. Home: 1050 Wall St #2F Ann Arbor MI 48105 Office: U Mich Screen Arts and Cultures 6525 Haven Hall Ann Arbor MI 48109-1045 Business E-Mail: fbeaver@umich.edu.

BEBAN, GARY JOSEPH, real estate corporation officer; b. San Francisco, Aug. 5, 1946; s. Frank and Anna (Consani) B.; m. Kathleen Hanson, June 14, 1968; children: Paul, Mark. BA in History, UCLA, 1968. Real estate specialist, sales and mgr. positions CB Comml., Calif. and Ill., 1970-87, pres. L.A., Chgo., 1987-89; sr. exec., mng. dir. CB Richard Ellis, Chgo., 1984—. Mem. IDRC, 1986—, UCLA Assocs., 1980—; bd. trustee New Hampton Sch. Recipient Heisman Trophy award .Y. Downtown Athletic Club, 1967; NCAA Scholar Athlete, 1968, Football Hall of Fame, 1988. Mem. Urban Land Inst., Nat. Realty Commn., UCLA Ctr. Fion. and Real Estate. Office: Cb Richard Ellis Inc 311 S Wacker Dr Ste 400 Chicago IL 60606-6619

BECHER, WILLIAM DON, retired electrical engineer, educator, writer; b. Bolivar, Ohio, Nov. 26, 1929; s. William and Eva Vernette (Richardson) Becher; m. Helen Norma Hager, Aug. 31, 1950; children: Eric Alan, Patricia Lynn. BS in Radio Engring., Tri-State U., 1950; MSEE, U. Mich., 1961, PhD, 1968. Registered profl. engr., Mich., N.J. Project engr. Bogue Electric, Paterson, NJ, 1950-53; sr. devel. engr. Goodyear Aircraft Corp., Akron, Ohio, 1953-57; sr. systems engr. Beckman Instruments, Fullerton, Calif., 1957-58; engring. supr. Bendix Aerospace Systems, Ann Arbor, Mich., 1958-63; rsch. engr. U. Mich., Ann Arbor, 1963-68, adj. prof. elec. engring., 1978-79, 81-94, lectr. elec. engring. Dearborn, 1964-68, prof. elec. engring., 1968-78, chmn., 1971-76; engring. dept. mgr. Environ. Rsch. Inst. Mich., Ann Arbor, 1977-79, assoc. dir., 1981-87, tech. cons., 1988-90, engr. emeritus, 1990—; dean engring. Coll. Engring. N.J. Inst. Tech., Newark, 1979-81; cons. Widbec Engr, Ann Arbor, 1978—. Pres. Mich. Computers & Instrumentation, Inc., Ann Arbor, 1983—87; prof., chmn. elec. engring. Calif. State U., Fresno, 1988. Author: (book) Courses in Continuing Education for Electronics Engineers, 1975, 1976, Logical Design Using Integrated Circuits, 1977, An Ocean Between, 2000. With US Army, 1953—55. Fellow GE, 1962—63. Mem.: IEEE (life; sr. mem.), Order of Engrs., Am. Soc. Engring. Edn., Tau Beta Pi, Sigma Xi, Eta Kappa Nu. Achievements include patents in field. Home and Office: Widbec Engring 691 Spring Valley Rd Ann Arbor MI 48105-1060

BECHERER, HANS WALTER, retired agricultural equipment executive; b. Detroit, Apr. 19, 1935; s. Max and Mariele (Specht) B.; m. Michele Beigbeder, Nov. 28, 1959; children: Maxime (dec.), Vanessa. BA, Trinity Coll., Hartford, Conn., 1957; postgrad., Munich U., 1958; MBA, Harvard U., 1962. Exec. asst. office of chmn. Deere & Co., Moline, Ill., 1966-69; gen. mgr. John Deere Export, Mannheim, Germany, 1969-73; dir. export mktg. Deere & Co., Moline, 1973-77, v.p., 1977-83, sr. v.p., 1983-86, exec. v.p., 1986-87, pres., 1987-90, COO, 1987-89, CEO, 1989-2000, chmn., 1990-2000. Bd. dirs. Schering-Plough Corp., JP Morgan Chase; mem. industry sector adv. com. U.S. Dept. Commerce, 1975-81; mem. Bus. Roundtable, 1989—; mem. adv. com. Chase Manhattan Bank Internat., 1990-98; trustee Com. for Econ. Devel., 1990—. Trustee St. Katherine's/St. Mark's Sch., Bettendorf, Iowa, 1983—. 1st lt. USAF, 1958-60. Named to Nat. Bus. Hall of Fame, Jr. Achievement, 2004. Mem. Coun. on Fgn. Rels., Conf. Bd., Equipment Mfgs. Inst. (bd. dirs. 1987-90), Rock Island (Ill.) Arsenal Golf Club. Republican. Roman Catholic. Mailing: JP Morgan Chase Bd Directors 270 Park Ave New York NY 10017-2070

BECHTEL, STEPHEN E., mechanical engineer, educator; BS in Engring. summa cum laude, U. Mich., 1979; PhD in Engring., U. Calif., Berkeley, 1983. Prof. dept. mech. engring. Ohio State U., Columbus, 1983—. Reviewer design, mfg. and computer-integrated engring. divsn., fluid dynamics and hydraulics directorate, thermal transport and thermal processing directorate NSF, 1985—, USDA food characterization, process, product rsch. program; cons. Hoechst Celanese Corp., Los Alamos Nat. Lab., Battelle Meml. Inst., Corning, Inc., Proctor & Gamble. Referee Jour. Rheology, Jour. Applied Mechanics, Jour. Non-Newtonian Fluid Mechanics, others. James B. Angell scholar U. Mich., 1976-79. Fellow ASME (mem. fluid mechanics com., elasticity com., applied mechanics divsn. 1989—, rec. sec. gen. com. 1991-92, rec. sec. exec. com. 1992-93, textile engring. divsn. exec. com., 2002-, Henry Hess award 1990); mem. Am. Acad. Mechanics, Soc. Rheology, Tau Beta Pi. Achievements include research in modeling of industrial polymer processing and fiber manufacturing, viscoelastic fluid flows, free surface flows and instability mechanisms, fundamental modeling of thermal expansion, material characterization, transducer characterization in non-destructive evaluation.

BECK, ANATOLE, mathematician, educator; b. Bronx, NY, Mar. 19, 1930; s. Morris and Minnie (Rosenblum) B.; m. Evelyn Torton, Apr. 10, 1954 (div.); children— ina Rachel, Micah Daniel; m. Eve-Lynn Siegel, Nov. 30, 2003. BA, Bklyn. Coll., 1951; MS, Yale U., 1953, PhD, 1956. Instr. math. Williams Coll., Williamstown, Mass., 1955-56; Office Naval Rsch. rsch. assoc. Tulane U., New Orleans, 1956-57; traveling fellow Yale U., 1957—58; from asst. to assoc. prof. U. Wis., Madison, 1958—66, prof. math., 1966—; chair of math. London Sch. Econ./U. London, 1973—75. Vis. prof. Cornell U., 1960, Hebrew U., Jerusalem, 1964-65, U. Göttingen, Fed. Republic Germany, 1965, U. Warwick, 1968, Imperial Coll., U. London, 1969, U. Erlangen, Fed. Republic Germany, 1969, U. Md., 1971, Tech. U. Munich, Fed. Republic Germany, 1973, London Sch. Econs. and Univ. Coll., U. London, 1985, 91-92, 94-97, 99—; v.p. Wis. Fedn. Tchrs., 1975-83; co-founder Wis. U. Union, 1984, pres., 1988-91. Author: Continuous Flows in the Plane, 1974, (with M.N. Bleicher and D.W. Crowe) Excursions into Mathematics, 1969, 2d edit., 2000, The Knowledge Business, 1997; contbr. articles to profl. jours. Recipient Disting. Alumnus award, Bklyn. Coll., 1976. Mem. Am. Math. Soc. (council 1973-75), Math. Assn. Am., AAUP, Sigma Xi, Phi Beta Kappa, Pi Mu Epsilon. Office: U Wis 480 Lincoln Dr 721 Van Vleck Hall Madison WI 53706-1329 Business E-Mail: abeck@wisc.edu.

BECK, BARBARA J., employment services executive; BS with honors, U. Colo., Boulder, 1982. Area v.p., gen. mgr. US-West Sprint Corp., 1996—2000; ind. cons., 2000—02; exec. v.p. US and Can. ops. Manpower, Inc., Milw., 2002—05, exec. v.p., pres. Europe, Mid. East and Africa, 2006—. Bd. dirs. Ecolab Inc., 2008—. Bd. trustees Boys and Girls Clubs Greater Milw., co-chair fundraising campaign, 2003; chmn.-elect Big Bros. Big Sisters Metro Milw.; co-chair Women's Initiative United Way Greater Milw.; mem. adv. coun. U. Wis. Sch. of Bus., Milw. Named one of Women of Influence, Milw. Bus. Jour., 2003. Office: Manpower Inc 5301 N Ironwood Rd Milwaukee WI 53217 Office Phone: 414-961-1000.*

BECK, JAMES M., lawyer; b. Kansas City, Mo., 1943; BA, Northwestern U., 1965; JD, U. Mo., 1968. Bar: Mo. 1968. Ptnr., chair Nat. Health Law Practice Group Shook, Hardy & Bacon LLP, Kansas City, Mo. Mem.: Greater Kansas City Soc. of Healthcare Attys., Mo. Soc. of Healthcare Attys. (bd. dirs.), Am. Assn. of Homes for the Aging, Am. Acad. of Hospital Attys., Am. Hosp. Assn., Am. Health Lawyers Assn., Kansas City Met. Bar Assn., Mo. Bar. Office: Shook, Hardy & Bacon LLP 2555 Grand Blvd Kansas City MO 64108 Office Phone: 816-559-2280. Office Fax: 816-421-5547. E-mail: jbeck@shb.com.

BECK, JAMES V., mechanical engineering educator; b. Cambridge, Mass., May 18, 1930; BS in Mech. Engring., Tufts U., 1956; SM in Mech. Engring., MIT, 1957; PhD in Mech. Engring., Mich. State U., 1964. Prof. mech. engring. Mich. State U., East Lansing, 1964-98, dir. heat transfer property measurement, prof. emeritus; pres. Beck Engring. Cons. Co., Okemos, Mich. Do-organizer Joint Am.-Russian Workshop on Inverse Problems in Heat Transfer, 1992. Contbr. articles to profl. publs. Achievements include research on inverse problem solutions for selected composite materials, development of a user-friendly three-dimensional transfer heat conduction program and measurement of temperature fields of electronic components using infrared thermography, multidimensional thermal and sensing properties of high termerature structures consisting of composites and CVD diamond films. Office: Mich State U Dept Mech Engring 2328E Engring Bldg East Lansing MI 48824 E-mail: beck@egr.msu.edu, jvb@BeckEng.com.

BECK, JILL, academic administrator, dancer, educator; b. Worchester, Mass., Aug. 10, 1949; d. John Jacob and Helen Bernadette Lindberg; m. Robert Joel Beck, Apr. 21, 1973. BA, Clark U., 1970; MA, McGill. U., 1976; PhD, CUNY, 1985. Cert. tchr., profl. reconstructor in Labanotation. Dir. edn. Dance Notation Bur., 1980—83; sr. lectr. South Australian Coll. Advanced Edn., Adelaide, 1983—85; guest faculty U. Mich., 1985, U. Colo., 1986, Denison U., 1987; faculty Am. Dance Festival, Durham, NC, 1985, Juliard Sch., NYC, 1985, asst. dir. dance divsn., 1988—89; chmn. theatre and dance dept. CUNY, 1985—87, dir. grad. studies dept. dance, 1987, chmn. dept. dance, Southern Meth. U.; faculty, cons. Hartford Ballet, Conn., 1983; dean Sch. Arts U. Calif., Irvine, 1995—2003; pres. Lawrence U., Wis., 2004—. Dir. dance revivals Doris Humphrey Choreography, 1981—, Anna sokolow Choreography, 1982—; project dir. CUNY Rsch. Found., 1981—82, Fund for Improvement Post-Secondary Edn., Washington, 1982—85, NEH, 1983—85, Conn. Coun. on Humanities and Arts, 1989—90; mem. profl. adv. com. Dance Notation Bur., 1982—84, 1985—88; mem. Internat. Conf. Kinetogrpaphy Laban, 1982—; mem. exec. com. Internat. Movement Notators Alliance, 1984—85; co-chmn. Soc. Dance History Scholars Conf., NYC, 1985—86; dir. program in advanced studies Am. Dance Festival, 1986; stage dir. student programs Lincoln Ctr., 1987; cons. Universal Ballet Co. Korea, 1988—89; founder and dir. ArtsBridge Am., 1996, daVinci Ctr. Learning through Arts, 2001. Editor: Dance otation Jour., 1983—85; author: serveral monographs, dance textbook and instructional videotapes. Recipient Exhibit award, CUNY, 1982, Jack Linquist award, Clara Barton award, Learning for Life award. Democrat. Avocations: travel, art. Office: Off of Pres Lawrence Univ PO Box 599 Appleton WI 54912

BECK, LOIS GRANT, anthropologist, educator, author; b. Bogota, Colombia, Nov. 5, 1944; d. Martin Lawrence and Dorothy (Sweet) Grant; m. Henry Huang; 1 dau., Julia Huang. BA, Portland State U., 1967; MA, U. Chgo., 1969, PhD, 1977. Asst. prof. Amherst (Mass.) Coll., 1973-76, Univ. Utah, Salt Lake City, 1976-80; from asst. to assoc. prof. Washington U., St. Louis, 1980-92, prof., 1992—. Author: Qashqa'i of Iran, 1986, Nomad, 1991; co-editor Women in the Muslim World, 1978, Women in Iran from the Rise of Islam to 1800, 2003, Women in Iran from 1800 to the Islamic Republic, 2004. Grantee Social Sci. Rsch. Coun., 1990, EH, 1990-92, 98, Am. Philos. Soc., 1998. Mem. Mid. East Studies Assn. (bd. dirs. 1981-84), Internat. Soc. Iranian Studies (exec. sec. 1979-82, edit. bd. 1982-91, coun. 1996-98). Office: Washington U Dept Anthropology CB1114 1 Brookings Dr Saint Louis MO 63130-4899 Office Phone: 314-935-5252. Business E-Mail: lbeck@artsci.wustl.edu.

BECK, PAUL ALLEN, dean, political science professor; b. Logansport, Ind., Mar. 15, 1944; s. Frank Paul and Mary Elizabeth (Flanegin) B.; m. Maria Teresa Marcano, June 10, 1967; children: Daniel Lee, David Andrew. AB, Ind. U., 1966; MA, U. Mich., 1968, PhD, 1971. Asst. prof. U. Pitts., 1970-75, assoc. prof., 1976-79; prof. Fla. State U., Tallahassee, 1979-87, chmn. dept., 1981-87; prof. Ohio State U., Columbus, 1987—, chmn. dept., 1991—2004; dean Coll. Social and Behavioral Scis. Ohio State U., Columbus, 2004—. Co-author: Political Socialization Across the Generations, 1975, Individual Energy Conservation Behaviors, 1980, Electoral Change in Advanced Industrial Democracies, 1984, Party Politics in America, 10th edit., 2003. Chmn. coun. Inter-Univ. Consortium for Polit. and Social Research, 1982-83, mem., 1980-83; mem. NSF polit. sci. panel, 1988-89. Recipient Disting. Svc. award Ohio State U., 2000, Disting. Scholar award Ohio State U., 2004. Mem. Am. Polit. Sci. Assn. (exec. coun. 1981-82, 93-94, book rev. editor 1976-79, program chair 1994, chair strategic planning com. 1999-2000, Goodnow award 2005, Eldersveld award, 2007), Midwest Polit. Sci. Assn. (exec. coun. 1987-90, mem. editl. bd. 1988-90, program chair 1991, v.p. 1996-98), So. Polit. Sci. Assn. (mem. editl. bd. 1982-87), Phi Beta Kappa, Pi Sigma Alpha (exec. coun.), Phi Kappa Phi. Democrat. Home: 7003 Perry Dr Columbus OH 43085-2815 Office: Ohio State U Coll Social and Behavioral Scis Columbus OH 43210-1341 Home Phone: 614-436-3978. E-mail: beck.9@osu.edu.

BECK, PHILIP S., lawyer; b. Chgo., Apr. 30, 1951; BA with academic distinction, U. Wis., 1973; JD magna cum laude, Boston U., 1976. Bar: Ill. 1977. Clerk U.S. Ct. Appeals DC Cir., 1976-77; ptnr. Kirkland & Ellis, 1977—93; founding ptnr. Bartlit Beck Herman Palenchar & Scott LLP, Chgo., 1993—. Editor-in-chief Boston U. Law Review. Bd. visitors Boston U. Sch. Law; bd. dir. Northwestern U. Settlement House. Named one of Top 10 Litigators, Nat. Law Jour., 2003. Fellow: Am. Bar Found., Internat. Acad. Trial Lawyers, Am. Coll. of Trial Lawyers. Office: Bartlit Beck Herman et al Courthouse Pl 54 W Hubbard St Chicago IL 60610-4645 Office Phone: 312-494-4400. Office Fax: 312-494-4440. Business E-Mail: philip.beck@bartlit-beck.com.

BECK, ROBERT N., nuclear medicine educator; b. San Angelo, Tex., Mar. 26, 1928; married, 1958. AB, U. Chgo., 1954, BS, 1955. Chief scientist Argonne Cancer Rsch. Hosp., 1957-67, assoc. prof., 1967-76; prof. radiol. sci. U. Chgo., 1976; dir. Franklin McLean Inst., 1977-94, dir. Ctr. Imaging Sci., 1986-98; prof. emeritus U. Chgo., 1998—. Cons. Internat. Atomic Energy Agency, 1966-68; mem. Internat. Com. on Radiation Units, 1968—, Nat. Coun. on Radiation, Protection & Measurements, 1970—. Recipient Aebersold award FDR, 1991. Mem. IEEE (Med. Imaging Sci. award 1996), Soc. Nuclear Med., Am. Assn. Physicists in Medicine, Soc. Magnetic Resonance. Achievements include research in development of a theory of the process by which images can be formed of the distribution of radioactive material in a patient in order to diagnose his disease. Office: U Chgo MC 2026 5841 S Maryland Ave Chicago IL 60637-1463 Business E-Mail: r-beck@uchicago.edu.

BECK, VAUGHN PETER, lawyer; b. Eureka, SD, Nov. 13, 1966; s. Floyd and Gladys M. (Zimmerman) B.; m. Julie I. Meier, Jan. 2, 1993; children: Emily I., Philip F. BS, U. S.D., 1989, JD, 1992. Bar: S.D. 1992, U.S. Dist. Ct. S.D. 1993. Legal intern Governmental Rsch. Bureau, Vermillion, SD, 1990, S.D. Pub. Utilities, Pierre, SD, 1991, Freiberg, Rudolf & Peterson, Beresford, SD, 1992; staff atty. Pub. Defenders Office, Deadwood, SD, 1992; atty. Beck Law Office, Ipswich, SD, 1993—. Bd. dirs. Ipswich Devel. Corp., 1993—, Ipswich Comml. Club, 1993—; com. mem. Consumer Protection S.D., 1994—. Mem. Ipswich Vol. Fire Dept., 1993—; trustee, officer United Church of Christ, 1993—. Republican. Office: Beck Law Office P O Box 326 509 Bloemendaal Dr Ipswich SD 57451 Office Phone: 605-426-6319. Business E-Mail: becklaw@valleytel.net.

BECK, WILLIAM G., lawyer; b. Kansas City, Mo., Mar. 4, 1954; s. Raymond W. Beck and Wanda Williams; m. Cheryl A. Beck; children: Collin M., Sergei M., Valentina M., Kseniya M., Ekaterina K. BA in Econs., U. Mo., Kansas City, 1974, JD, 1978. Bar: Mo. 1978, U.S. Dist. Ct. (we. dist.) Mo. 1978, U.S. Ct. Appeals (5th cir.) 1988, U.S. Dist. Ct. (ea. dist.) Mich. 1991, U.S. Dist. Ct. (no. dist.) Ill. 1992, U.S. Ct. Appeals (6th cir.) 1992, U.S. Dist. Ct. (ea. dist.) Wis. 1997, U.S. Ct. Appeals (2d cir.) 1997, U.S. Ct. Appeals (10th cir.) 1997, U.S. Supreme Ct. 1997, U.S. Ct. Appeals (1st cir.) 1998, U.S. Ct. Appeals (7th cir.) 1999, U.S. Dist. Ct. Colo. 2000, U.S. Dist. Ct. Rhode Island 2002, U.S. Dist. Ct. Mass. 2002, U.S. Dist. Ct. Kans. 2005. Shareholder Field, Gentry, Benjamin & Robertson, P.C., Kansas City, 1978-89; ptnr. Lathrop & Norquist, Kansas City, 1989-95, Lathrop & Gage, L.C., Kansas City, 1996—. Commr. Human Rels. Commn., Jackson County, Mo., 1985-89; chmn. Citizens Assn., Kansas City, 1991-92, 95-96; mem. Pub. Improvement Adv. Com., Kansas City, 1991-2001, vice chmn., 1995-98, chmn. 1998-2001, fin. chmn. cmty. infrastructure com., 1996-1997; mem. Waste Minimization Com., Kansas City, 1990-91; bd. mem. Regional Transit Alliance, 2001-03. Named a Mo.-Kans. Super Lawyer; named one of Best Lawyers in Am., Chambers Leading Lawyers for Bus. Office: Lathrop & Gage LC 2345 Grand Blvd Ste 2800 Kansas City MO 64108-2684 Office Phone: 816-460-5811. Business E-Mail: bbeck@lathropgage.com.

BECKER, DAVID, artist, retired educator; b. Milw., Aug. 16, 1937; s. Walter Gustav and Fern Bertha (Raddatz) B.; m. Catherine Claytor, Aug. 27, 1960 (div. 1981); children: Sarah Lynne, Amelia Elisabeth; m. Patricia Ann Fennell, Nov. 13, 1988; 1 child, Sloane Fennell. Student, Layton Sch. Art, 1956-58; BS, U. Wis., Milw., 1961; MFA, U. Ill., 1965. Asst. prof. Wayne State U., Detroit, 1965-71, assoc. prof., 1971-80, prof., 1980-85; assoc. prof. U. Wis., Madison, 1985—87, prof., 1987—2006, prof. emeritus, 2006—. Vis. prof. U. Wis., Madison, 1985—87; vis. artist Utah State U., Logan, 1981; art lectr. in field; rep. by Ann Nathan Gallery, Chgo. Exhbns. include Mus. Fine Arts, Boston, 1965, 75, Butler Inst. Am. Art, Youngstown, Ohio, 1967, 68, 72, Lawrence Stevens Gallery, Detroit, 1968, Detroit Inst. Arts, 1971, 77, 86, 91, Richard Nash Gallery, Seattle, 1974, Franz Bader Gallery, Washington, 1974, 77, 80, Madison (Wis.) Art Ctr., 1975, 79, Libr. of Congress, Washington, 1975, Honolulu Acad. Arts, 1975, 83, ADI Gallery, San Francisco, 1975, London Arts Gallery, Detroit, 1976, Boston Ctr. Arts, 1976, 78, Museo de Arte Moderno, Cali, Colombia, 1976, 77, 81, Bawag Found., Vienna, Austria, 1976, Bklyn. Mus., 1976, 84, Met. Mus., Miami, Fla., 1977, 80, Habatat Galleries, Dearborn, Mich., 1977, Visual Arts Ctr. Alaska, Anchorage, 1978, 86, Cranbrook Acad. Art, Bloomfield Hills, Mich., 1980, Associated Am. Artists Gallery, Phila., 1980, Phila. Art Alliance/Phila. Print Club, 1980, Kalamazoo (Mich.) Inst. Arts, 1980, 86, Nat. Mus. Am. Art, Washington, 1982, DeCordova Mus., Lincoln, Mass., 1982, 86, USIA, 1983, Saginaw (Mich.) Mus. Art, 1984, Brockton (Mass.) Mus. Art, 1984, Mich. Gallery, Detroit, 1986, Neville-Sargent Gallery, Chgo., 1986, Intergrafic, East Berlin, 1984, 87, 9th Brit. Internat. Print Biennale, Bradford, 1986, Jane Haslem Gallery, Washington, 1987, 90, 92-93, John Szoke Graphics, N.Y.C., 1988, Silvermine Gallery, Stamford, Conn., 1988, Elvehjem Mus. Art, Madison, 1989, Boston Printmakers 42d and 43d Nat. Print Exhbn., 1993, Fitchburg (Mass.) Mus. Art, 1990, New Orleans Mus. Art, 1990, NAD, .Y.C., 1986-87, 90-94, Hoyt Inst. Fine Arts, New Castle, Pa., 1992, Sodarco Gallery, Montreal, 1993, Davidson Galleries, Seattle, 1993, Galleria Mesa, Mesa, Ariz., 1993, Intergrafia, Katowice, Poland, 1994, Sapporo Internat. Print Biennale, Japan, 1993, Maastricht Internat. Print Biennale, The etherlands, 1993, Outside Art Fair, N.Y.C., 2002, Art Chgo., 2002, 03, 04, 05, 06, 07; permanent collections include: Libr. of Congress, Washington, Art Inst. Chgo., Rose Art Mus., Waltham, Mass., Chazen Mus. Art, Madison, Wis., Butler Inst. Am. Art, Minot (N.D.) Art Assn., Silvermine Guild Arts, New Canaan, Conn., Honolulu Acad. Arts, NY Pub. Libr., Detroit Inst. Art, Museo de Arte Moderno, Bklyn. Mus., Met. Mus., Miami, Nat. Mus. Am. Art, Washington, Portland (Oreg.) Art Mus., Art Ctr., South Bend, Ind., USIA, Prague, Czech Republic, Ann Nathan Gallery, Chgo., others. 1st lt. U.S. Army, 1961-63. Creative Artist grantee Mich. Coun. Arts, 1982; NEA Visual Arts fellow, 1993-94. Fellow The MacDowell Colony; mem. NAD (nat. academician). Home: 2512 Lunde Ln Mount Horeb WI 53572-2440 E-mail: dhbecker@wisc.edu.

BECKER, DAVID M., lawyer; married. JD, U. Iowa, 1986. Bar: Iowa 1986, Mo. 1987, Kans. 1988. Gen. counsel Seaboard Corp., Shawnee Mission, Kans., 1994—98, 1998—, v.p., 2001—. Office: Seaboard Corp 9000 W 67th St Shawnee Mission KS 66201 Office Phone: 913-676-8925. E-mail: david_becker@seaboardcorp.com.

BECKER, DAVID MANDEL, law educator, author, consultant; b. Chgo., Dec. 31, 1935; m. Sandra Kaplan, June 30, 1957; children: Laura, Andrew, Scott. AB, Harvard Coll., 1957; JD, U. Chgo., 1960. Bar: Ill. 1960. Assoc. Becker and Savin, Chgo., 1960—62; instr. law U. Mich., Ann Arbor, 1962—63; from asst. prof. law to prof. Washington U., St. Louis, 1963—93, Joseph H. Zumbalen prof. law, 1993—, assoc. dean external rels., 1998—, Joseph H. Zumbalen emeritus prof. law, 2004—. Author: (with David Gibberman) Legal Checklists, 1968, and ann. supplements; Legal Checklists-Specially Selected Forms, 1977, and ann. supplements; Perpetuities and Estate Planning: Potential Problems and Effective Solutions, 1993; contbr. numerous articles to profl. jours. Recipient Founders Day award Washington U. Alumni Assn., 1973, Tchr. of Yr. award Washington U., 1980, 89, Disting. Tchr. award Washington U. Sch. Law Alumni, 1988, Deans medal Washington U., 2005. Office: Washington U Sch Law Campus Box 1120 Saint Louis MO 63130-4899 Home: 540 North and South Rd #204 Saint Louis MO 63130 Office Phone: 314-935-6492.

BECKER, GARY STANLEY, economist, educator; b. Pottsville, Pa., Dec. 2, 1930; s. Louis William and Anna (Siskind) Becker; m. Doria Slote, Sept. 19, 1954 (dec.); children: Judith Sarah, Catherine Jean; m. Guity Nashat, Oct. 31, 1979; children: Michael Claffey, Cyrus Claffey. AB summa cum laude, Princeton U., 1951, PhD (hon.), 1991; AM, U. Chgo., 1953, PhD, 1955; PhD (hon.), Hebrew U., Jerusalem, 1985, Knox Coll., 1985, U. Ill., Chgo., 1988, SUNY, 1990, U. Palermo, Buenos Aires, 1993, Columbia U., 1993, Warsaw Sch. Econs., 1995, U. Econs., Prague, Czech Republic, 1995, U. Miami, 1995, U. Rochester, 1995; PhD, Hofstra U., 1997, U. d'Aix-Marselles, 1999, U. Athens, 2002; PhD (hon.), Harvard U., 2003, Hitotsubashi., 2005. Asst. prof. U. Chgo., 1954—57; from asst. prof. to assoc. prof. Columbia U., NYC, 1957—60, prof. econs., 1960—68, Arthur Lehman prof. econs., 1968—70; prof. econs. U. Chgo., 1970—83, univ. prof. econs. and sociology, 1983—, chmn. dept. econs., 1984—85, prof. Grad Sch. Bus., 2002—. Ford Found. vis. prof. econs. U. Chgo., 1969—70; assoc. Econs. Rsch. Ctr. Nat. Opinion Rsch. Ctr., Chgo., 1980—; mem. domestic adv. bd. Hoover Instn., Stanford, Calif., 1973—91, sr. fellow, 1990—; mem. acad. adv. bd. Am. Enterprise Inst., 1987—91; rsch. policy advisor Ctr. for Econ. Analysis Human Behavior Nat. Bur. Econ. Rsch., 1972—78; mem. and sr. rsch. assoc. Monetary Policy, Min. Fin., Japan, 1988—; bd. dirs. Unext.com, 1999—2003; affiliate Lexecon Corp., 1990—2002, LEAF, Inc., 2003—07. Author: The Economics of Discrimination, 1957, 2d edit., 1971, Human Capital, 1964, 3d edit., 1993, (Japanese transl.) Human Capital, 1975, (Spanish transl.), 1984, (Chinese transl.), 1987, (Romanian transl.), 1997, Human Capital and the Personal Distribution of Income: An Analytical Approach, 1967, Economic Theory, 1971, (Japanese transl.), 1976, 2nd edit., 2007; author: (with Gilbert Ghez) The Allocation of Time and Goods Over the Life Cycle, 1975; author: The Economic Approach to Human Behavior, 1976, (German transl.), 1982, (Polish transl.), 1990, (Chinese transl.), 1993, (Romanian transl.), 1994, (Italian transl.), 1998, A Treatise on the Family, 1981, expanded edit., 1991, (Spanish transl.) A Treatise on the Family, 1987, (Chinese transl.), 1988, 2000, Accounting for Tastes, 1996, (Czech transl.), 1998, (Chinese transl.), 1999, (Italian transl.), 2000; author: (with Guity Nashat Becker) The Economics of Life, 1996, (Chinese transl.), 1997, with Guity Nashat Becker: The Economics of Life, 1998, (Spanish transl.), 2002; author: (in German) Family, Society and State, 1996; author: (in Italian) L'approccio Economico al Comportamento Umano, 1998; author: (with Kevin M. Murphy) Social Economics, 2000; co-author: Becker-Posner Blog, 2005; editor: Essays in Labor Economics in Honor of H. Gregg Lewis, 1976; co-editor (with William M. Landes): Essays in the Economics of Crime and Punishment, 1974; columnist: Bus. Week, 1985—2004; contbr. articles to profl. jours. Named to Hall of Honor, Nat. Inst. Child Health and Devel., 2003; recipient W.S. Woytinsky award, U. Mich., 1964, Profl. Achievement award, U. Chgo. Alumni Assn., 1968, Frank E. Seidman Disting. award in Polit. Economy, 1985, Merit award, NIH, 1986, John R. Commons award, Omicron Delta Epsilon, 1987, Nobel prize in Econ. Sci., 1992, Lord Found. award, 1995, Irene Taueber award, 1997, Nat. medal Sci., 2000, Phoenix award, U. Chgo., 2000, Am. Acad. Achievement award, 2001, Heartland prize, 2002, Hayek award, 2003, John eumann Lecture award, Rojk Coll., Corvinus U., Budapest, 2004, Italian Presidency medal, 2004, Arrow award, 2005, Provost's Tchg. award, U. Chgo., 2006, Presdl. Medal of Freedom, The White House, 2007. Fellow: Am. Econ. Assn. (Disting., v.p. 1974, pres. 1987, John Bates Clark medal 1967), Am. Acad. Arts and Scis., Nat. Assn. Bus. Economists, Econometic Soc., Am. Statis. Assn.; mem.: NAE, NAS, Nat. Assn. Bus. Economists, Econ. History Assn., Pontifical Acad. Scis., Western Econ. Assn. (v.p. 1995—96, pres. 1996—97), Mont Pelerin Soc. (exec. bd. dirs. 1985—96, v.p. 1989—90, pres. 1990—92), Internat. Union for Sci. Study Population, Am. Philos. Soc., Nat. Assn. Bus. Economists, Phi Beta Kappa. Office: U Chgo Dept Econs 1126 E 59th St Chicago IL 60637-1580 Office Phone: 773-702-8168. Business E-Mail: gbecker@uchicago.edu.

BECKER, JOANN ELIZABETH, retired insurance company executive; b. Chester, Pa., Oct. 29, 1948; d. James Thomas and Elizabeth Theresa (Barnett) Clark; m. David Norbert Becker, June 7, 1969. BA, Washington U., St. Louis, 1970, MA, 1971. CLU, ChFC, FLMI/M, CFA. Tchr. Kirkwood (Mo.) Sch. Dist., 1971-73; devel. and sr. devel. analyst Lincoln Nat. Life Ins. Co., Ft. Wayne, Ind., 1973-77, systems programming specialist, 1977-79, sr. project mgr., 1979-81, asst. v.p., 1981-85, 2d v.p., 1985-88, v.p., 1988-91; pres., CEO The Richard Leahy Corp., Ft. Wayne, 1991-93; pres. Lincoln Nat. Corp. Equity Sales Corp, Ft. Wayne, 1993-94; v.p. portfolio mgmt. group Lincoln Nat. Investment Mgmt. Co., Ft. Wayne, 1994-97, dir. investment mgmt., sr. v.p., 1997—2000, ret., 2000. Contbr. articles to profl. jours. Bd. dirs. Ind. Humanities Coun., Indpls., 1991-96, treas., exec. com., 1994-95, devel. com., 1995-96; bd. dirs. Auburn Cord Duesenberg Mus., Ind., 1995-2000, devel. and exec. com., 1997-2000; bd. dirs. Priest Lake Mus., 2005—; pres. Priest Lake Mus. Assn., 2006—. Named Women of Achievement, YWCA, Ft. Wayne, 1986, Sagamore of Wabash, Gov. State of Ind., 1990. Fellow Life Mgmt. Inst. Soc. Ft. Wayne (pres. 1983-84, honors designation 1980); mem. Life Ins. Mktg. Rsch. Assn. (Leadership Inst. fellow, exec. com. 1993-94, fin. svcs. com. 1993-94), Am. Mgmt. Assn., So. Ariz. Watercolor Guild (chair fundraising com. 2006—), Ft. Wayne C. of C. (chmn. audit-fin. com. 1989-2000).

BECKER, JOHN ALPHONSIS, retired bank executive; b. Kenosha, Wis., Jan. 26, 1942; s. Paul Joseph and Hedwig (Hammacke) B.; m. Bonny J. Anderson, July 4, 1963; children: Danial, Todd, Kathryn, Erik BS, Marquette U., 1963, MBA, 1965. Asst. v.p. 1st Wis. Nat. Bank of Milw., 1970-73, v.p., 1973-76, 1st v.p., 1976-79; pres. 1st Wis. Nat. Bank of Madison, 1979-86; exec. v.p. 1st Wis. Nat. Bank of Milw., 1986-87, pres., chief oper. officer, 1987-89, also chief exec. officer, 1988-89, chmn., chief exec. officer, 1989-91; pres. Firstar Corp., Milw., 1990-99; ret., 1999. Div. chmn. United Way, Madison, 1984; trustee Edgewood Coll., Madison, 1980—; mem. fin. com. Madison Republican Com. Served to 1st lt. U.S. Army, 1965-67. Mem. Wis. Bankers Assn. (exec. com.), Greater Madison C. of C. (chmn. bd. 1983). Clubs: Madison, Maple Bluff Country. Roman Catholic.

BECKER, MICHAEL ALLEN, internist, rheumatologist, educator; b. NYC, Oct. 3, 1940; s. David S. and Sylvia M. (Salomon) B.; m. Mary E. Baim; children: David, Jonathan, Abigail, Arielle, Daniel. BA, U. Pa., Phila., 1961, MD, 1965. Diplomate Am. Bd. Internal Medicine, Am. Bd. Rheumatology. Intern Barnes Hosp., Washington U., St. Louis, 1965-66, resident, 1969-70; asst. prof. U. Calif., San Diego, 1972-77, assoc. prof., 1977-80; prof. medicine U. Chgo. Pritzker Sch. Medicine, 1980—. Mem. biochemistry study sect. NIH, Bethesda, Md., 1991-95. Contbr. numerous rsch. articles to med. publs. Sr. asst. surgeon USPHS, 1966-69, Pres. Purine and Pyrimidine Soc. Fellow, John Simon Guggenheim Meml. Found. Master Am. Coll. Rheumatology; mem. Am. Soc. Clin. Investigation, Assn. Am. Physicians. Office: U Chgo Med Ctr MC0930 Chicago IL 60637 Home Phone: 312-640-8801; Office Phone: 773-702-6899. Business E-Mail: mbecker@medicine.bsd.uchicago.edu.

BECKER, RICH, state legislator; b. St. Louis, Apr. 16, 1931; m. Nancy Becker; 2 children. BA, Ottawa U., 1992. Ret. sales exec. Sta. KSHB-TV, Kansas City; mem. Kans. Senate, Topeka, 1996—, mem. fin. instns. and ins. com., mem. pub. health and welfare com., mem. fed. and state affairs com. Mem. Humane Soc. Greater Kansas City, past bd. dirs.; bd. dirs. Johnson County C.C.; mem. Lenexa Hist. Soc.; mem. del. Rep. Nat. Conv., 1992; mayor Lenexa, Kans., 1983-95, mem. Lenexa City Coun., 1979-83. Mem. Kans. Mayors Assn. (past pres.)

BECKER, SCOTT, lawyer; b. Chgo., 1964; BS in Fin. & Acctg., U. Ill., 1986; JD, Harvard U., 1989. CPA Ill.; bar: Ill. 1989, Wis. 2000. Ptnr. Ross & Hardies (merged with McGuireWoods in 2003), Chgo., 1996—2003, McGuireWoods LLP, Chgo., 2003—, co-chair health care dept., 2003—. Office: McGuireWoods LLP Ste 4100 77 W Wacker Dr Chicago IL 60601-1815 Office Phone: 312-920-6016. Office Fax: 312-920-6135. Business E-Mail: sbecker@mcguirewoods.com.

BECKER, THOMAS BAIN, lawyer; b. St. Charles, Mo., Sept. 3, 1944; s. John Bruere and Marie Louise (Denker) B.; m. Linda Ann Flynn, May 25, 1974; children: Thomas Bain Jr., Shannon Flynn. BSBA, Georgetown U., 1966; MBA, U. Mo., Columbia, 1968, JD, 1976. Bar: Mo. 1976. Acct. Kerber, Eck & Braeckel, St. Louis, 1966, Rothaus, Bartels & Earley, St. Louis, 1968; acctg. analyst U.S. Dept. Commerce, Washington, 1971-73; shareholder Stinson, Mag & Fizzell, Kansas City, 1976-98, Gilmore & Bell, P.C., Kansas City, 1998—. Bd. dirs., v.p., pres. Westport Citizens Action Coalition, Kansas City, 1987—; bd. dirs. Hist. Kansas City Found., 1981-89, Kansas City Union Sta., Inc., 1988-97; bd. commrs., vice chair Mo. Housing Devel. Commn., 1995-98; mem. task force Mayor's Odyssey 2000, Kansas City, 1993; bd. dirs., vice chmn. Citizens Assn. Kansas City, 1996—. Recipient Community Svc. award Westport Coop. Svcs., 1991. Mem. ABA, at. Assn. Bond Lawyers, Rockhill Tennis Club (pres., bd. govs., treas. 1999—). Democrat. Roman Catholic. Avocations: sports, politics, reading, travel. Home: 816 Gleed Ter Kansas City MO 64109-2617 Office: Gilmore & Bell PC 2405 Grand Blvd Ste 1100 Kansas City MO 64108-2521 Home Phone: 816-531-2176; Office Phone: 816-221-1000. Business E-Mail: tbecker@gilmorebell.com.

BECKER, VANETA G., state representative; b. Alton, Ill., Oct. 7, 1949; m. Andrew C. Guarino. Attended, U. Evansville. Rep. dist. 75 State of Ind., 1981-91, rep. dist. 78, 1991—, ranking minority leader, 1991—; mem. pub. health & cities & towns coms.; mem. asst. minority caucus State of Ind.; realtor Don Cox & Assoc. Mem. bd. dirs. Albion Fellows Bacon Ctr., Patchwork Cent. Recipient Legis. Excellence award United Mine Workers, 1989; named Legislator of the Yr. Ind. Primary Health Care Assn., 1990. Mem. Nat. Assn. Realtors, Ind. Primary Health Care Assn., Evansville Zool. Soc., A Network of Evansville Women, Leadership Evansville, Crisis Prevention Nursery. Republican. Methodist. Home: 420 E Buena Vista Rd Evansville IN 47711-2720 Office: Ind Ho of Reps State Capitol Indianapolis IN 46204

BECKERS, JACQUES MAURICE, astrophysicist; b. Arnhem, The Netherlands, Feb. 14, 1934; came to U.S., 1962; s. Wilhelmus B.H. and Maria H. (Hermans) B.; m. Gerda M. Van Vuurden, Mar. 24, 1959 (div. Aug. 1995); children: Christina M., Michael P. PhD, U. Utrecht, The Netherlands, 1959; Dsc (hon.), Lund U., 2004. Astrophysicist Sacramento Peak Obs., Sunspot, N.Mex., 1962-79; astrophysicist, dir. Multiple Mirror Telescope Obs., Tucson, 1979-84, Advanced Devel. program Nat. Optical Astronomy Observatories, Tucson, 1984-88; astrophysicist European So. Obs., Garching, Fed. Republic of Germany, 1988-93, VLT Program Scientist, 1991-93; dir. Nat. Solar Observatory, Tucson, 1993-98, astronomer, 1998—2001; sr. scientist U. Chgo., 2001—. Mem. Norwegian Acad. Scis. (fgn.), Royal Netherlands Acad. Scis. (corr.). Office: Dept Astronomy and Astrophysics U Chgo Chicago IL 60637 Home Phone: 312-932-9251; Office Phone: 773-702-8747. E-mail: jbeckers@rcn.com.

BECKETT, THEODORE CHARLES, lawyer; b. Boonville, Mo., May 6, 1929; s. Theodore Cooper and Gladys (Watson) B.; m. Daysie Margaret Cornwall, 1950; children: Elizabeth Gayle, Theodore Cornwall, Margaret Lynn, William Harrison, Anne Marie. BS, U. Mo., Columbia, 1950, JD, 1957. Bar: Mo. 1957. Of counsel Baker, Sterchi, Cowden & Rice, LLC; instr. polit. sci. U. Mo., Columbia, 1956-57; asst. atty. gen. State of Mo., 1961-64. Mem. City Plan Commn., Kansas City, 1976-80; bd. curators U. Mo., 1995-2001, pres. 1998. 1st lt. U.S. Army, 1950-53. Mem.: ABA, SAR, Kansas City Bar Assn., Mo. Bar Assn., Blue Hills Country Club (Kansas City, Mo.), Order of Coif, Sigma Nu, Phi Alpha Delta. Presbyterian. Office: 2400 Pershing Rd Ste 500 Kansas City MO 64108 Office Phone: 816-471-2121.

BECKETT, VICTORIA LING, physician; m. Peter G.S. Beckett, 1954 (dec. 1974); 1 child, Paul T. (dec.); m. Joseph C. Sharp, 1996. BA, Mt. Holyoke Coll., 1945; MD, U. Mich., 1949; MA, St. Mary's U., 1995. Intern Mpls. Gen. Hosp., 1949-50; fellow Mayo Grad. Sch., 1951-55; clin. instr. Wayne State U. Sch. Medicine, Detroit, 1956-67; staff cons. internal medicine oncology svc. Henry Ford Hosp., Detroit, 1957-60; rsch. physician Darling Meml. Ctr., Detroit, 1965-69; rsch. assoc. rheumatology Trinity Coll. Dublin U., 1970-72, postgrad. tutor, 1972-73, dir., 1973-76; cons. physician in rheumatology Federated Dublin Vol. Hosps., 1973-76; staff cons. rheumatology Mayo Clinic, 1976-90, emeritus staff, 1990—; asst. prof. medicine Mayo Med. Sch., 1976-90; med. dir. Rochester Health Care Ctr., Minn., 1985—90. Author: Living Medicine: Memoir Snap Shots, 2004. Fellow: ACP; mem.: Mayo Med. Alumni Assn., Am. Coll. Rheumatology (ret. mem.), Minn. State Med. Assn., Zumbro Valley Med. Soc., Phi Beta Kappa, Sigma Xi. Methodist. Avocation: teaching exercise class. Office Phone: 507-284-2691.

BECKHOLT, ALICE, clinical nurse specialist; b. NYC, Aug. 7, 1941; d. Julius and Mary (Katz) Kalkow; m. Richard H. Polakoff, Aug. 12, 1962 (div. 1984); children: Katherine, Michael, Matthew; m. Kenneth Eugene Beckholt, Feb. 3, 1990. BA, Syracuse U., 1962; ADN, El Centro Coll., 1977; BSN, U. Tex., Arlington, 1980; MS, Tex. Women's U., 1988. RN Tex., Ohio. Staff nurse, outpatient mgr. Irving (Tex.) Cmty. Hosp., 1977—86; staff nurse Meth. Hosp., Dallas, 1986—89, U. Tex. S.W. Med. Ctr., Dallas, 1989—90; pediat. home care nurse various agys., Columbus, Ohio, 1990—94; advanced practice nurse, pub. speaking, preceptor Columbus Health Dept., 1994—. Adj. faculty Ohio State U., 2007—. Sec., 2nd v.p., 1st v.p., pres. Am. Cancer Soc., 1971-76, bd. dirs. Irving, Tex., 1971-90, BSE instr., nurse's com., 1990-97, triple touch coord., 1991-97, BSE faculty, 1986-90; vol., auction subchair Sta. KERA-TV, Dallas, 1972-84; CPR instr. Am. Heart Assn., 1984-98; med. adv. Ohio Support HELP. Recipient Outstanding Svc. award Am. Cancer Soc. Columbus chpt., 1992-93; named Outstanding Vol., Am. Cancer Soc., Irving, Tex., 1973, 74, 76. Mem.: APHA, Ohio Assn. Advanced Practice Nurses, Ohio Pub. Health Assn., Sigma Theta Tau. Avocations: gourmet cooking, classical music, travel. Home: 1444 Bexton Loop Columbus OH 43209-2904 Office: Columbus Dept Health 240 S Parsons Ave Columbus OH 43215-4022

BECKLEY, ROBERT MARK, architect, educator; b. Cleve., Dec. 24, 1934; s. Mark Ezra and Marie Elizabeth (Kuhl) Beckley; m. Jean Dorothy Love, Feb. 26, 1956 (div. May 1988); children: Jeffery, Thomas, James; m. Jytte Dinesen, Oct. 24, 1990. BArch, U. Cin., 1959; MArch, Harvard U., 1961. From asst. to assoc. prof. U. Mich., Ann Arbor, 1963—69, dean, prof., 1987—97, prof., 1997—2002, prof., dean emeritus, 2002—; from assoc. prof. to prof. U. Wis., Milw., 1969—86. Exec. v.p. Genesee Inst., 2004—07; prin. Beckley-Myers, Architects, Milw., 1980—91. Prin. works include Theater Facilities, 1980—81 (award, 1983), Theater Dist., 1981—82 (award, 1984), Bellevue Downtown Park, 1985 (1st place award, 1985). Recipient Distinction award, Milw. Art Mus., 1986. Fellow: AIA (Mich. Pres.'s award 1994), Graham Found., Inst. Urban Design; mem.: Assn. Collegiate Schs. Architecture (bd. dirs. 1987—90, pres. 1988—89, mem. Nat. Archtl. Accreditation Bd. 1990—92). Office: U Mich Coll Arch 2000 Bonisteel Dr Ann Arbor MI 48109-2069 Home: 2200 Fuller Ct Apt 1115 Ann Arbor MI 48105-2307

BECKMAN, DAVID, lawyer; b. Burlington, Iowa, 1950; BSIE, Iowa State U., 1973; MBA, JD, U. Iowa, 1976. Bar: Iowa 1976; CPA, Iowa. Ptnr. Beckman and Hirsch, Burlington, Iowa. Mem. Iowa Supreme Ct. Commn. on Cts. in the 21st Century, team co-chair, mem. steering com. Fellow Iowa State Bar Found.; mem. ABA (chair lotus notse interest group 1994-98), AICPA, Iowa Soc. CPAs (bd. dirs., sec., exec. com. 1985-88, ethics com. 1988—, chair by laws com. 1987-89, continuing profl. edn. com. 1983-86), Iowa State Bar Assn. (bd. govs. 1990-96, pres. 1998-99), Des Moines County Bar Assn. (pres. 1994-95), Gamma Epsilon Sigma. Office: Beckman and Hirsch 314 N 4th St Burlington IA 52601-5314 E-mail: ddb@iowalaw.com.

BECKMAN, TRACY, state legislator; b. Jan. 7, 1945; m. Janel Beckman; five children. Senator Dist. 26, Minn. State Senate, 1986—; mgr., Owatonna Canning Co., 1996—; cons., 1996—. vice-chmn. Econ. Devel. & Housing com., edn. com.; mem. Agrl. & Rural Devel. Com., Crime Prevention Com., Edn. Com., Edn. Funding Divsn., Fin. Com. & Govt. Ops. & Reform Com.; chmn. Crime Prevention Fin. Divsn., Joing Claims Divsn. State senator Dist. 26 Minn. State Senate, 1986-99; mgr. Owatonna Canning Co.; cons., 1996-99; state exec. dir. Farm Svc. Agy. USDA, St. Paul, 1999—. Vice-chmn. Econ. Devel. & Housing com., edn. com.; mem. Agrl. & Rural Devel. Com., Crime Prevention Com., Edn., Com., Edn. Funding Divsn., Fin. Com. & Govt. Ops. & Reform Com.; chmn. Crime Prevention Fin. Divsn., Joing Claims Divsn. Office: USDA Farm Svc Agy 375 Jackson St Ste 400 Saint Paul MN 55101-1828 Home: 1181 Edgcumbe Rd Apt 305 Saint Paul MN 55105-2833

BECKMEYER, HENRY ERNEST, anesthesiologist, pain management specialist, educator; b. Cape Girardeau, Mo., Apr. 13, 1939; s. Henry Ernest Jr. and Margaret Gertrude (Link) B.; m. Deborah Beckmyer; children: Henry IV, James, Martha, Leigh, Hillary. BA, Mich. State U., 1961; DO, Des Moines U., 1965. Diplomate Am. Bd. Med. Examiners, Am. Acad. Pain Mgmt.; cert. Am. Osteo. Bd. Anesthesiology. Chief physician migrant worker program and op. head start Sheridan (Mich.) Community Hosp., 1967-69; resident in anesthesia Bi-County Community Hosp./DOH Corp., Detroit, 1969-71, chief resident, 1968-69; staff anesthesiologist Detroit Osteo. Hosp./BCCH, 1971-75; founding chmn. dept. anesthesia Humana Hosp. of the Palm Beaches, West Palm Beach, Fla., 1975-79; assoc. prof. Mich. State U., East Lansing, 1979-88, prof. anesthesia, 1988—, chmn. dept. osteo. medicine, 1985-96; chmn. dept. osteo. surg. specialities, 1996-97; chief staff Mich. State U. Health Facilities, 1988-90, chmn. med. staff exec. and steering coms., 1988-90; chmn. of anesthesia St. Lawrence Hosp., Lansing, Mich., 1984-90, adminstrv. dir. dept. anesthesia and pain mgmt., 1994-98. Chief of staff Sheridan Cmty. Hosp., 1968-69; adminstrv. coun. Mich. State U., 1988-97, acad. coun., 1992-96, faculty coun., 1992-96, U. hearing bd., 2000-02, bylaws com., 2000-04, clin. practice bd., bd. dirs. sports medicine, athletic coun., 2003-05, pres.'s adv. com. on disability issues, 2007-; internal mgmt. com. Mich. Ctr. for Rural Health; cons. Ministry Health, Belize, Calif., 1993-97; amb. Midwestern U. Consortium Internat. Activities, 1993; chmn. com. student performance, 2002-03, com. on acad. policy, 2000-05, admission com., 2000-06, chmn. admissions com., 2003-07, MOA-MSUCOM liaison com. chair 2005-; adv. com. on pain mgmt. State of Mich., 1999-01; program chmn. Am. Russian Med. Exch., 1993-97; bd. dirs. Belize Med. Partnership. Spkr. Sta. WKAR, Mich. State U.; bd. dirs. Boy Scouts Am., W. Bloomfield, Mich., 1973-74, Palm Beach Mental Health, 1977-79, Care Choices HMO, Lansing, 1987-88; mem. adv. com. pain and symptom mgmt. State of Mich., 1999-02; mem. athletic coun. Mich. State U., 2003-05, self study subcom. NCAA, 2004-05. Fellow Am. Coll. Osteo. Anesthesiologists; mem. AMA, Am. Osteo. Coll. Anesthesiology (chmn. commn. on colls. 1988-89), Soc. Critical Care Medicine, Internat. Anesthesiology Rsch. Soc., Am. Coll. Physician Execs., Am. Osteo. Assn. (spkr., mem. evaluators registry), Am. Acad. Pain Mgmt., Am. Arbitration Assn., Mich. State Med. Soc., Mich. Pain Soc., Mich. Peer Rev. Orgn., Mich. Osteo. Assn. (chmn. edn. com. 2002—), Ingham County Med. Soc. (edn. com.), Am. Soc. Regional Anesthesia, Soc. Security Disability Evaluation, Soc. Internat. Scholars, Phi Beta Delta. Office: Mich State U West Fee Hall East Lansing MI 48824 Office Phone: 517-353-8470. Business E-Mail: beckmey1@msu.edu.

BECKWITH, BARBARA JEAN, journalist; b. Chgo., Dec. 11, 1948; d. Charles Barnes (dec.) and Elizabeth Ann (Nolan) Beckwith. BA in Journalism, Marquette U., 1970. News editor Lake Geneva (Wis.) Regional News, 1972-74; asst. editor St. Anthony Messenger, Cin., 1974-82, mng. editor, 1982—. Mem. Cath. Conf. Comm. Com., 1990—92. Mem.: Internat. Cath. Union of the Press (1st v.p. 2005—), Cath. Union of the Press, Cath. Journalism Scholarship Fund (bd. dirs. 1993—, v.p. 1995—96, pres. 1996—99, 2001—), Nat. Cath. Assn. for Broadcasters and Communicators (bd. dirs. 1989—96, 1997—98), Fedn. Ch. Press Assns. of Internat. Cath. Union of the Press (3d v.p. 1989—92, pres. 1992—2004, 3d v.p. 2004—, 2d v.p. 2005—), Cath. Press Assn. (bd. dirs. 1986—96, v.p. 1988—90, pres. 1990—92, best interview 1982, best photo story 1985, St. Francis de Sales award for outstanding contbn. to Cath. journalism 1994, best poetry 1997). Office: St Anthony Messenger 28 W Liberty St Cincinnati OH 45202-6498 Office Phone: 513-241-5615 x 170.

BECKWITH, DAVID E., lawyer; b. Madison, Wis., Mar. 5, 1928; m. Natalie Biart, Nov. 19, 1948; children: Steven V.W., John B., David T. BS, U. Wis., 1950, LLB, 1952. From assoc. to ptnr. Foley & Lardner, Milw., 1952-98; ret., 1998. Bd. editors Fed. Litigation Guide Reporter, 1985—. Mem. bd. regents U. Wis., Madison, 1977-84, pres., 1982-84; dir., chmn. U. Wis. Madison Found. With USN, 1945-46. Fellow Am. Bar Found., Am. Coll. Trial Lawyers; mem. Order of Coif, Phi Beta Kappa. Unitarian Universalist. Avocations: golf, skiing, fishing. Office: Foley & Lardner Firstar Ctr 777 E Wisconsin Ave Ste 3800 Milwaukee WI 53202-5367

BECKWITH, LEWIS DANIEL, lawyer; b. Indpls., Jan. 30, 1948; s. William Frederick and Helen Lorena (Smith) B.; m. Marcia Ellen Ride, June 27, 1970; children: Laura, Gregory. BA, Wabash Coll., 1970; JD, Vanderbilt U., 1973. Bar: Ind. 1973, U.S. Dist. Ct. (so. dist.) Ind. 1973. Assoc. Baker & Daniels, Indpls., 1973-80, ptnr., 1981—. Articles editor Vanderbilt Law Rev., 1972-73. Bd. dirs. Luth. Disabilities Ministries, Inc., 2003—, Luth. Child and Family Svcs. of Ind./Ky., Inc., 2004—. Named to Ind. Superlawyers for Environ. Law, 2004. Mem. ABA (assoc. editor occupational safety & health law 2002), Ind. Bar

Assn., Indpls. Bar Assn., Ind. C. of C. (com. occupational safety and health law 1982—), Ind. Constrn. Assn. (com. occupational safety and health 1988—, safety and health counsel), Order of Coif, Eta Sigma Phi, Beta Theta Pi. Republican. Lutheran. Avocation: sports. Office: Baker & Daniels 300 N Meridian St Ste 2700 Indianapolis IN 46204-1782 Home Phone: 317-849-8464; Office Phone: 317-237-1406. Business E-Mail: lew.beckwith@bakerd.com.

BECKWITH, SANDRA SHANK, federal judge; b. Norfolk, Va., Dec. 4, 1943; BA, U. Cin., 1965, JD, 1968. Bar: Ohio 1969, Ind. 1976, Fla. 1979, U.S. Dist. Ct. (so. dist.) Ohio 1971, U.S. Dist. Ct. Ind. 1976, U.S. Supreme Ct. 1977. Pvt. practice, Harrison, Ohio, 1969—77, 1979—81; judge Hamilton County Mcpl. Ct., Cin., 1977—79, 1981—86, commr., 1989—91; judge Ct. Common Pleas, Hamilton County Divsn. Domestic Rels., 1987—89; assoc. Graydon, Head and Ritchey, 1989—91; judge U.S. Dist. Ct. (so. dist.) Ohio, 1992—2004, chief judge, 2004—. Mem. Ohio Chief Justice's Code of Profl. Responsibility Commn., 1984, Ohio Gov.'s Com. on Prison Crowding, 1984-90, State Fed. Com. on Death Penalty Habeas Corpus, 1995—; pres. 6th Cir. Dist. Judges Assn., 1998-99; chair So. Dist. Ohio Automation Com., 1997—. Mem. advisory bd. Tender Mercies. Mem. Fed. Judges Assn., Fed. Bar Assn. (exec. com.), Judicial Conf. of U.S. (mem. com. on defender svcs.) Office: Potter Stewart US Courthouse Ste 810 Cincinnati OH 45202 Office Phone: 513-564-7610. Business E-Mail: sandra_beckwith@ohsd.uscourts.gov.

BEDARD, PATRICK JOSEPH, editor, writer, consultant; b. Waterloo, Iowa, Aug. 20, 1941; s. Gerald Joseph and Pearl Leona (Brown) B. BS in Mech. Engring, Iowa State U., 1963; M.Automotive Engring., Chrysler Inst. Engring., 1965. Product engr. Chrysler Corp., Highland Park, Mich., 1963-67; tech. editor Car and Driver mag., YC, 1967-69, exec. editor, 1969-78, editor-at-large, 1978—. Race driver, cons. in field; freelance writer mags. and TV films. Author: Expert Driving, 1987. Mem. Soc. Automotive Engrs., U.S. Ultralight Assn., Aero Sports Connection, Sports Car Club Am., Pi Tau Sigma. Roman Catholic. Achievements include first driver to win profl. road race in N.Am. in Wankel-powered car, 1973; raced at Indpls. 500, 1983-84; 1st driver to go 200 miles per hour at Indpls. in Stockblock-powered car, 1984. Home: Rt 1 Box 779 Port Saint Joe FL 32456 Office: Car and Driver 2002 Hogback Rd Ann Arbor MI 48105-9795

BEDNAROWSKI, KEITH, construction, design and real estate executive; BS, Marquette U. Joined Opus Corp., Minnetonka, Minn., 1969, advanced through mgmt. and sr. mgmt. positions, pres., CEO; chmn., CEO Opus Corp. and Opus LLC, Minnetonka, 1999—.

BEEBY, THOMAS H., architect; BS in Arch., Cornell Univ.; M in Arch., Yale Univ. Architect C.F. Murphy, Chgo., 1965-71; ptnr., prin., dir. design Hammond, Beeby, Rubert, Ainge Inc., Chgo., 1971—; mem. faculty dept. architecture Ill. Inst. Tech., Chgo., 1973-80; dir. Sch. Architecture U. Ill.-Chgo., Chgo., 1980-85; dean, prof. archtl. design Yale U. Sch. Architecture, 1985-91. Adj. prof. Archtl., Yale U., 1992—; mem. adv. bd. dept. arch. Ill. Inst. Tech., 1993—, trustee, 1997—. Designs exhibited: Art Inst. Chgo., Mus. Contemporary Art, Chgo., Cooper-Hewitt Mus., N.Y.C., Walker Art Ctr., Mpls., Venice Biennale; contbr. articles to profl. jours. Recipient Progressive Architecture citation, 1976, 87, 89, Louis Sullivan award, 1989. Fellow AIA (mem. nat. com. on design, nat. honor award 1984, 87, 89, 91, 93); mem. Soc. Archtl. Historians (bd. dirs. 1996-2000), U.S. State, Office Fgn. Bldg., Archtl. adv. bd., 1989-93, Graham Found. (bd. dirs. 1992—). Office: Hammond Beeby Rupert Ainge Inc 440 N Wells St Ste 630 Chicago IL 60610-4546

BEECHEM, KATHLEEN, bank executive; m. Pete Beechem. BA in English, Thomas More Coll.; MA, Indiana Univ. Exec. v.p. US Bank, Cincinnati, Ohio. Co-chmn. Women's Leadership Initiative United Way, Cincinnati; pres. bd. Jobs for Cincinnati Grads. Bd. dir. Cincinnati Youth Collaborative; exec. com. YWCA. Named one of 50 Most Powerful Women, Fortune Mag., 2004. Office: US Bancorp 800 Nicollet Mall Minneapolis MN 55402

BEEDLES, WILLIAM LEROY, finance educator, consultant; b. Independence, Kans., Apr. 9, 1948; s. Roy William Beedles and Opal Irene (Connor) Hunter; m. Margaret Ann Vanderlip, Dec. 21, 1974; children: Margaret Micaela, Patricia Opal, Cyrus Dean. BS, Kans. State U., 1970, MS, 1971; PhD, U. Tex., 1975. Asst. prof. Ind. U., Bloomington, 1975-78; vis. prof. Monash U., Melbourne, Victoria, Australia, 1984, U. NSW, Sydney, Australia, 1985; assoc. prof. to prof., dir. Masters program U. Kans., Lawrence, 1978—. Vis. rsch. fellow Pub. Utilities Commn., Austin, Tex., 1981 Contbr. articles to profl. jours. Capt. U.S. Army, 1970-78 Mem. Am. Fin. Assn., Western Fin. Assn., So. Fin. Assn. (assoc. editor jour. 1979-84), Fin. Mgmt. Assn. Congregationalist. Avocation: racquetball. Office: U Kans Summerfield Hall Lawrence KS 66045-7585 E-mail: wbeedles@ku.edu.

BEEKMAN, MARVIN LEE, lawyer; b. 1969; BSEE, Dordt Coll., Sioux Ctr., Iowa, 1991; JD, Hamline U. Sch. Law, St. Paul, 1994. Bar: Minn. 1994. Assoc. small intellectual property law firm; dir. ops. engring. co.; atty. Schwegman, Lundberg, Woessner & Kluth, P.A., Mpls. Named a Rising Star, Minn. Super Lawyers mag., 2006. Mem.: Minn. Intellectual Property Law Assn., Am. Intellectual Property Law Assn. Office: Schwegman Lundber Woessner & Kluth PA 1600 TCF Tower 121 S 8th St Minneapolis MN 55402 Office Phone: 612-373-6960. E-mail: mbeekman@slwk.com.

BEEKMAN, PHILIP E., retail company executive; b. 1931; married. AB, Dartmouth Coll., 1953. Pres. Colgate Palmolive Internat. Inc., NYC, 1953-77, Joseph E. Seagram & Sons, NYC, 1977-86; chmn., chief exec. officer, dir. Hook-SupeRX Inc., Cin., 1986-95; chmn., pres. Owl Hollow Enterprises Inc., Indpls., 1995—. Dir. Kroger Co., 1978-87. Office: 6693 E Pleasant Run Parkway So Indianapolis IN 46219-3441

BEELER, VIRGIL L., lawyer; b. Inpls., June 6, 1931; s. Elmer L. and Margaret Gwendolyn (Turney) B.; m. Patricia McAtee Walker; children: Stephen L., Philip E. AB in Econs., Ind. U., 1953, JD, 1959. Bar: Ind. 1959, U.S. Dist. Ct. Ind., U.S. Ct. Appeals (7th cir.), U.S. Supreme Ct., U.S. Tax Ct. Assoc. Baker & Daniels, Indpls., 1959-65, ptnr., 1966-95, of counsel, 1995—. Contbr. articles to profl. jours. 1st lt. US Army, 1954—56. Fellow Am. Coll. Trial Lawyers, Ind. Bar Found.; mem. Indpls. Bar Assn., Ind. State Bar Assn., 7th Cir. Bar Assn., Order of Coif, Phi Beta Kappa. Office: Baker & Daniels 300 N Meridian St Ste 2700 Indianapolis IN 46204-1782

BEEM, JACK DARREL, retired lawyer; b. Chgo., Nov. 17, 1931; AB, U. Chgo., 1952, JD, 1955. Bar: Ill. 1955. Assoc. firm Wilson & McIlvaine, Chgo., 1958-63; ptnr. firm Baker & McKenzie, Chgo., 1963—2004; ret., 2004. Decorated Order of the Sacred Treasure gold rays with rosette Japan. Mem. ABA, Chgo. Bar Assn., Japan-Am. Soc. Chgo. (pres. 1988-92), Am. Fgn. Law Assn. (chmn. Chgo. br.), Am. Law Inst., Univ. Club of Chgo., Tokyo Club, Tokyo Am. Club, Sons Am. Revolution, Phi Beta Kappa, Alpha Delta Phi. Home: 175 E Delaware Pl Apt 8104 Chicago IL 60611-7746 Personal E-mail: abojdb@comcast.net.

BEER, BARRETT LYNN, historian; b. Goshen, Indiana, July 4, 1936; s. Peter J. and Mabel M. B.; m. Jill (Parker), 1965. BA, DePauw U., Greencastle, Ind., 1958; MA, U. Cin., 1959; PhD, Northwestern U., Evanston, Ill., 1965. Instr. history Kent State U., Ohio, 1962—65; asst. prof. U. N.Mex., Albuquerque, 1965—68; assoc. prof. Kent State U., Ohio, 1968—76, prof., 1976—2002, prof. emeritus, 2002—; asst. dean Coll. Arts and Sci. U. N. Mex., Albuquerque, 1966—68; Fulbright prof. U. Tromso, Norway, 1983. Author: Northumberland: The Political Career of John Dudley, Earl of Warwick and Duke of Northumberland, 1973, Rebellion and Riot: Popular Disorder in Eng. during the Reign of Edward VI, 1982, 2nd edit., 2005; (with others) Recent Historians of Great Britain, 1990, Tudor England Observed: The World of John Stow, 1998; editor: (with S.M. Jack) The Letters of William, Lord Paget of Beaudesert, 1547-1563, 1974, The Life and Raigne of King Edward the Sixth (John Hayward), 1993, contbr., Oxford Dictionary of Nat. Biography, 2004. Am. Philos. Soc. grantee, 1966; Am. Coun. Learned Soc. grantee, 1973; fellow Newberry Libr., 1991, Folger Shakespeare Libr., 1997. Fellow Royal Hist. Soc.; mem. Conf. on Brit. Studies, Phi Beta Kappa. Episcopalian. Home: 445 Dansel St Kent OH 44240-2626 Office: Kent State U Dept History Kent OH 44242-0001 Business E-Mail: bbeer@kent.edu.

BEER, WILLIAM L., appliance company executive; From market analyst asst. to corp. strategy rsch. dir. Maytag Corp., Newton, Iowa, 1974-91, v.p. mktg., 1991-96, v.p. strategic mktg., 1996, sr. v.p. product supply, 1997, pres. major appliance divsn., 1998—. Office: Maytag Corp 403 W 4th St N Newton IA 50208-3026

BEERING, STEVEN CLAUS, academic administrator, medical educator; b. Berlin, Aug. 20, 1932; arrived in U.S., 1948, naturalized, 1953; s. Steven and Alice (Friedrichs) Beering; m. Catherine Jane Pickering, Dec. 27, 1956; children: Peter, David, John. BS summa cum laude, U. Pitts., 1954, MD, 1958, ScD (hon.), 1998; DSc (hon.), Ind. Cen. U., 1983, U. Evansville, Ind., 1984, Ramapo Coll., 1986, Anderson Coll., 1987, Purdue U., 2000; ScD (hon.), Ind. U., 1988; LLD (hon.), Hanover Coll., 1986, Tex. Wesleyan, 2001. Intern Walter Reed Gen. Hosp., Washington, 1958—59; resident Wilford Hall Med. Center, San Antonio, 1959—62, chief internal medicine, edn. coordinator, 1967—69; prof. medicine Ind. U. Sch. Medicine, Indpls., 1969—, asst. dean, 1969—70, assoc. dean, dir. postgrad. edn., 1970—74, dir. statewide med. edn. system, 1970-83, dean, 1974—83; chief exec. officer Ind. U. Med. Center, Indpls., 1974—83; pres. Purdue U. and Purdue U. Rsch. Found., West Lafayette, Ind., 1983—2000, pres. emeritus, 2000—; dir. emeritus Purdue Rsch. Found., West Lafayette, 2006—. Prof. pharmacology and toxicology Purdue U.; bd. dirs. NISource, Inc.; chmn. Med. Edn. Bd. Ind., 1974—83, Liaison Com. Med. Edn., 1976—81, Ind. Commn. Med. Edn., 1978—83. Contbr. articles to sci. jours. Sec. Ind. Atty. Gen.'s Trust, 1974—83; regent Nat. Libr. Medicine, 1987—91; trustee U. Pitts., 2000—. Lt. col. M.C. USAF, 1957—69. Fellow: ACP, Royal Soc. Medicine; mem.: Nat. Sci. Bd. (chmn.), Ind. Acad., Nat. Acad. Sci. Inst. of Medicine, Assn. Am. Univs. (chair 1995—96), Coun. Med. Deans (chmn. 1980—81), Assn. Am. Med. Colls. (chmn. 1982—83), Endocrine Soc., Am. Diabetes Assn., Am. Fedn. Med. Rsch., Meridian Hills Club, Skyline Club, Phi Rho Sigma (U.S. v.p. 1976—85), Alpha Omega Alpha, Sigma Xi, Phi Beta Kappa. Presbyterian. Home: 10487 Windemere Dr Carmel IN 46032 Office: Purdue U Office Pres Emeritus Rm 218 Memorial Union West Lafayette IN 47906-3584 Office Phone: 765-496-7555. Personal E-mail: sbeering@indy.rr.com. Business E-Mail: scb@purdue.edu.

BEERMANN, ALLEN J., former state official; b. Sioux City, Iowa, Jan. 14, 1940; BA, Midland Lutheran Coll., Fremont, Nebr., 1962; JD, Creighton U., Omaha, 1965; LLD (hon.), Midland Luth. Coll., 1995. Bar: Nebr. 1965. Legal counsel, adminstrv. asst. to sec. state, Nebr., 1965-67; dep. sec. state Nebr., 1967-71; sec. of state, 1971-95. Mem. Fed. Election Commn. adv. panel. Bd. dirs. NebraskaLand Found.; exec. bd. Cornhusker coun. Boy Scouts Am.; state chair N.E. Commn. Employer Support for Guard and Res., 1997-2002. Lt. col. U.S. Army, ret. Recipient Disting. Svc. plaque Omaha Legal Aid Soc., 1964, Silver Beaver award Boy Scouts Am., 1979, Fgn. Svc. Medallion Rep. of China, 2001, Homeland Def. Ribbon, 2001; named Outstanding Young Man Lincoln Jaycees, 1975, Outstanding Young Man Nebr. Jaycees, 1975 Mem. ABA, Nat. Assn. Secs. State (pres. 1976-77), Nebr. Bar Assn. (exec. dir. 1995—), Nebr. Press Assn., Am. Legion (fed. election commn. adv. panel, Cert. Appreciation). Republican. Lutheran. Office: Nebr Press Assn 845 S St Lincoln NE 68508-1226 Home Phone: 412-488-7624; Office Phone: 402-476-2851. Business E-Mail: nebpress@nebpress.com.

BEERS, ANNE, protective services official; BA in Edn., Hamline U., 1975. Trooper trainee Minn. State Patrol, 1975-76, trooper East Metro dist. 2400, 1976-80, trooper 1, 1981-83, lt., 1984-88, capt., 1988-92, comdr. East Metro dist. 2400, 1993-95, maj., 1995-97, chief, 1997—. Named Woman of Yr. Women's Transp. Sem. of Minn., 1998. Mem. Minn. Chiefs of Police Assn., Internat. Assn. of Women Police, Internat. Assn. of Chiefs of Police, Law Enforcement Opportunities, Minn. Assn. of Women Police (Carolen Bailey Mentoring award 1992), Minn. Police and Peace Officers Assn. Office: Minn State Patrol 444 Cedar St Ste 130 Saint Paul MN 55101-2142

BEERS, V(ICTOR) GILBERT, publishing executive; b. Sidell, Ill., May 6, 1928; s. Ernest S. and Jean B.; m. Arlisle Felten, Aug. 26, 1950; children: Kathleen, Douglas, Ronald, Janice, Cynthia. AB, Wheaton Coll., 1950; M.R.E., No. Baptist Sem., 1953, M.Div., 1954, Th.M., 1955, Th.D., 1960; PhD, Northwestern U., 1963. Prof. No. Baptist Sem., Chgo., 1954-57; editor Sr. High Publs., David C. Cook Pub. Co., Elgin, Ill., 1957-59, exec. editor, 1959-61, editorial dir., 1961-67; pres. Books for Living Inc., Elgin, 1967—; editor Christianity Today, 1982-85, sr. editor, 1985-87; pres. Scripture Press Publs. Inc., Wheaton, Ill., 1990-96, Scripture Press Ministries, 1990—. V.p. ministry devel. Cook Cmty. Ministries, 1996—2000. Author: more than 150 books, including: Family Bible Libr., 10 vols., 1971, The Book of Life, 23 vols., 1980. Bd. dirs. Christian Camps Inc., N.Y., Wheaton (Ill.) Youth Symphony, 1961-63, pres. 1962-63; trustee Wheaton Coll., 1975-92, adv. life trustee, 1992—; trustee Scripture Press Ministries, 1973—. Office: Scripture Press Ministries 250 Pennsylvania Ave Glen Ellyn IL 60137-4327 E-mail: gil3319@aol.com.

BEESON, GERALD A., investment company executive; b. 1973; m. Jennifer Beeson; 4 children. BS in Acctg. & Fin., DePaul U., 1994; MBA, U. Chgo., 1999. CPA. Intern Citadel Investment Group LLC, Chgo., 1993—97, asst. contr., 1995—97, global contr., 1997, assoc. treasury, 1997, dir. fin. and acctg., 1997—2000, mng. dir., global controller, 2000—03, sr. mng. dir., CFO, 2003—08, COO, 2008—. Mem. bd. dirs. Depository Trust & Clearing Corp.; mem. Chgo. Bd. Trade, Chgo. Mercantile Exchange. Office: Citadel Investment Group LLC 131 S Dearborn St Chicago IL 60603 Home: 14005 Bunratty Dr Orland Park IL 60467*

BEGGS, CAROL EDWARD, state legislator; m. Betty Beggs. Retailer; mem. Kans. State Ho. of Reps. Dist. 71, 1995—.

BEGGS, DONALD LEE, academic administrator; b. Harrisburg, Ill., Sept. 16, 1941; s. C. J. and Mary (Fitzgerald) Beggs; m. Shirley Malone, Mar. 19, 1963; children: Brent A., Pamela A. BS in Edn., So. Ill. U., 1963, MS in Edn., 1964; PhD, U. Iowa, 1966. Prof. So. Ill. U., Carbondale, 1966—98, assoc. dean grad. sch., 1970—71, asst. dean edn., 1973—75, acting asst. v.p. acad. affairs, 1975—76, assoc. dean edn., 1975—81, dean Coll. Edn., 1981—96, chancellor, 1996—98; pres. Wichita (Kans.) State U., 1998—, prof., 1999—. Cons. Ill. State Bd. Edn., 1966—, Quincy (Ill.) Pub. Schs., 1974—79, Chgo. Pub. Schs., 1977—80, Nat. Inst. Edn., Washington, 1983. Author: Measurement and Evaluation in the Schools, Evaluation and Decision Making in the Schools, 1971, Research Design in the Behavioral Sciences, 1969, Nat. Standardized Tests, 1980. Active United Way Campaign, 1978, Carbondale Schs. PTA, 1972—83; bd. dirs. NCAA, 2001—. amed Outstanding Tchr. in Edn., Coll. Edn., 1969; grantee, Ill. State Bd. Edn., 1979, Ill. Supt. Pub. Instrn., 1968, U.S. Office Edn., 1969. Mem.: Rsch. and Evaluation Adv. Council Ill. Office Edn. (chmn. 1982—83), Ill. Pub. Sch. Deans of Edn. (chmn. 1982—83), Am. Edn. Rsch. Assn. (sec. div. D. 1976—79), Phi Delta Kappa (one of 75 Young Leaders 1981). Office: Wichita State Univ Office of Pres 1845 Fairmount St Wichita KS 67260-0001

BEGGS, PATRICIA KIRK, performing company executive; BA, Stephens Coll., 1970; MBA, U. Cin., 1984. Mktg. dir. Provident Bank, Cin.; with pub. rels. dept. Ctrl. Trust Co. (now PNC Bank), Cin.; dir. mktg. Cin. Opera, 1984-91, asst. mng. dir., 1991-97, mng. dir., 1997—. Office: Cin Opera Assn Music Hall 1241 Elm St Cincinnati OH 45210-2231

BEGLEITER, MARTIN DAVID, law educator, consultant; b. Middletown, Conn., Oct. 31, 1945; s. Walter and Anne Begleiter; m. Ronni Ann Frankel, Aug. 17, 1969; children: Wendy Cara, Hilary Ann. BA, U. Rochester, 1967; JD, Cornell U., 1970. Bar: NY 1970, US Dist. Ct. (ea. dist.) NY 1971, US Ct. Appeals (2d cir.) 1975. Assoc. Kelley Drye & Warren, NYC, 1970—77; assoc. prof. Law Sch., Drake U., Des Moines, 1977—80, prof., 1980—87, 1993—2005, Richard M. and Anita Calkins disting. prof. law, 1987—93, Ellis and Nelle Levitt Disting prof. law, 2005—. Author (with Scoles, Halbach and Roberts): Problems and Materials on Decedents' Estates and Trusts, 7th edit., 2006; contbr. articles to legal jours. Fellow Am. Coll. Trust and Estate Counsel (academic fellow 2005-); mem. ABA (com. on estate and gift taxes, taxation sect. 1980—, com. malpractice, real property, probate and trust law sect. 1999—, com. on tax legislation and regulations, lifetime transfers, real property, probate and trust law sect. 1980-02, study com. law reform 1996-02, chmn. task force on spl. use valuation 1988-93, advisor Nat. Conf. Commns. on Uniform State Laws 1988-93), Iowa Bar Assn. (adviser, resource person, probate, trust sect. 1983-89, 93—), Am. Law Inst. (adviser restatement 3d trusts 1994—). Jewish. Avocations: science fiction, golf. Office: Drake U Sch Law 2507 University Ave Des Moines IA 50311 Home Phone: 515-225-3807; Office Phone: 515-271-2062. Business E-Mail: martin.begleiter@drake.edu.

BEGLEY, CHRISTOPHER B., pharmaceutical executive; b. Chgo., Apr. 13, 1952; married; 3 children. BBA, Western Ill. U.; MBA, No. Ill. U. V.p. mktg. V. Mueller Divsn., Am. Hosp. Supply Corp.; various positions Abbott Labs., Abbott Park, Ill., 1986—90, divisional v.p., gen. mgr. hosp. products bus. sector, 1990—93, v.p. hosp. products bus. sector, 1993—96, v.p. MediSense, Inc., 1996—98, v.p. Abbott HealthSystems, 1998—99, sr. v.p. chem. and agrl. products, 1999—2000, pres. hospital products div., 2000—04; CEO Hospira Inc. (spin-off from Abbott Labs.), Lake Forest, Ill., 2004—; chmn., CEO Hospira Inc., Lake Forest, Ill., 2007—. Bd. dir. Children's Meml. Hosp., Chgo.; mem. Healthcare Leadership Council, AdvaMed; mem. civic com. Comml. Club Found. Mem.: Econ. Club Chgo., Executives Club Chgo. Office: Hospira Inc 275 North Field Dr Lake Forest IL 60045

BEHBEHANI, ABBAS M., clinical virologist, educator; b. Iran, July 27, 1925; came to U.S., 1946, naturalized, 1964; s. Ahmad M. and Roguia B. (Tasougi) B.; married; children— Ray, Allen, Bita BA, Ind. U., 1949; MS, U. Chgo., 1951; PhD, Southwestern Med. Sch., U. Tex., 1955. Asst. prof. Baylor U. Coll. Medicine, Houston, 1960-64; assoc. prof. pathology U. Kans. Sch. Medicine, Kansas City, 1967-72, prof., 1972-90, prof. emeritus, 1990—. Author three books, 5 chpts. in books, more than 70 articles. Fellow Am. Acad. Microbiology; mem. AAAS, Am. Soc. Microbiology, Soc. Exptl. Biology and Medicine Muslim. Achievements include current research on history of smallpox, history of yellow fever and Persian founders of Islamic medicine during middle ages. Office: U Kans Med Ctr Dept Pathology & Lab Med Kansas City KS 66160-0001 Home: 6445 Muirfield Dr Paducah KY 42001-9734 E-mail: kulgener@kumc.edu.

BEHN, JERRY, state legislator; b. Boone County, Iowa, 1955; m. Dennise. Student, United Cmty. Schs., Boone. Farmer; county supr.; mem. Iowa Senate from 40th dist., 1996—. Mem. Iowa Assn. Bus. and Industry, Iowa Farm Bur. Republican. Home: 1313 Quill Ave Boone IA 50036-7575 Office: State Capitol 40th Dist 3 9th And Grand Des Moines IA 50319-0001 E-mail: jerry_behn@legis.state.ia.us.

BEHNING, ROBERT W., state legislator; b. Indpls., Jan. 18, 1954; m. Rosalie Dix; children: Nathan, Grant. BS, Ind. U., 1976. Vice ward chmn. Wayne Twp., Ind.; vol. Crane for Congrl. campaign; precinct committeman Decatur; registered and polling coord. Decatur Twp., 1991; mem. Eagle Creek GOP, Wayne Twp. GOP; 2nd v.p. Decatur Twp. GOP; Ind. state rep. Dist. 91, 1992—; mem. com. and econ. devel., labor and employment, 1993—; govt. affairs com., 1993—; chmn. elections and approtionment com. Ind. Ho. Reps. With L.S. Ayres & Co., Indpls., 1971-73, Great A&P Tea Co., 1973-84; co-owner Plants, Posies and Accents, Inpls., 1977-81; owner Berkshire Florist, Indpls., 1981—; bd. dirs. Multi Svc. Ctr. Mem. Decatur Twp. Civic Coun.; past pres. Luth. Laymen's League No 6. Mem. at. Fedn. Ind. Bus., Teleflora Golden Dove Club, Allied Florist Assn. (past dir.). Republican. Home: 3315 S Tibbs Ave Indianapolis IN 46221-2270

BEHNKE, MICHELLE A., lawyer; b. 1961; BA, JD, U. Wis. Bar: Wis. 1988. Pvt. practice. Spkr. in field; mem. bd. attys. profl. responsibility, dist. 9 com., 1994—2002; mem. bd. visitors Wis. Law Alumni Assn., 1995—; treas. Equal Justice Coalition, 1997—98. Contbr. articles to profl. jours. Mem.: ABA, Legal Assn. Women, Dane County Bar Assn., State Bar Wis. (co-chair diversity outreach com. 1994—99, bd. dirs. practice mgmt. sect. 1998—2000, pres.-elect 2003—04, pres. 2004—05), Madison Breakfast Rotary Chpt., Rotary Internat. Office: Atty at Law Ste 1 222 N Midvale Blvd Madison WI 53705 Office Phone: 608-233-9024.

BEHNKE, WILLIAM ALFRED, retired landscape architect; b. Cleve., Jan. 7, 1924; s. Walter William and Constance Helen (Ireson) B.; m. Virginia E. Woolever, Sept. 18, 1948; children: Lee, Deborah, Mitchel, Mark. B.Landscape Architecture, Ohio State U., 1951. Designer Grier Riemer Assos., Cleve., 1951-55; prin. William A. Behnke, Cleve., 1955-57; asso. Charles L. Knight, Cleve., 1957-58; partner Behnke, Szynyog & Ness, Cleve., 1958-61, Behnke, Ness & Litten, Cleve., 1961-70; mng. partner William A. Behnke Assoc., Cleve., 1970-89; ret. Assoc. prof. Kent State U., 1973-74; pres. Ohio State Bd. Landscape Archtl. Examiners, 1973; vice-chmn. Ohio Bd. Unreclaimed Strip Mined Lands, 1973-74; bd. dirs. Landscape Architecture Found., 1981-85, pres., 1983; mem. adv. bd. Trust for Pub. Lands, 1988—. Mem. Ohio Arts Coun., 1983-84; pres. metro bd. Lake County YMCA, 1989-90; bd. dirs. Ohio Presbyn. Retirement Svcs., Breckenridge Village, 2002. Served with USNR, 1943-46. Named Distinguished Alumnus Ohio State U., 1978; inductee Willoughby-Eastlake Sch. Dist. Hall of Fame, 1999. Fellow Am. Soc. Landscape Architects (v.p. 1977-79, pres. 1980-81). Home: 37334 Harlow Dr Willoughby OH 44094-5758 Office: William Behnke Assocs Inc 700 St Clair Ave W # 416 Cleveland OH 44113-1230 E-mail: wbehnke@earthlink.net.

BEHRENDT, DAVID FROGNER, retired journalist; b. Stevens Point, Wis., May 25, 1935; s. Allen Charles and Vivian (Frogner) B.; m. Mary Ann Weber, Feb. 4, 1961 (dec. Sept 1998); children: Lynne, Liza, Sarah. BS, U. Wis., 1957, MS, 1960. Reporter Decatur (Ill.) Review, 1957-58; reporter Milw. Jour., 1960-70, copy editor, 1970-71, editorial writer, 1971-84, editorial page editor, 1984-95; Crossroads sect. editor Milw. Jour. Sentinel, 1995-98. Home: 1522 N Prospect Ave #1402 Milwaukee WI 53202

BEHRENDT, RICHARD LOUIS, academic administrator; BA in Secondary Edn., U. Pitts., 1964, MEd in Secondary Edn., 1965; PhD in Higher Edn., U. Mich., 1980. Tchr. Mt. Lebanon (Pa.) HS, 1963, Hempfield Area HS, Greensburg, Pa., 1965; departmental asst. U. Mich., Ann Arbor, 1965-66; dir. instnl. rsch. Washtenaw Community Coll., Ypsilanti, Mich., 1967; asst. to pres. Ind. State U., Terre Haute, 1967-68, dir. student rsch., 1968-69; dir. instnl. rsch. Hagerstown (Md.) Jr. Coll., 1969-74, dir. instl. rsch. and dir. personnel svcs., 1974-76, dean of supportive svcs., 1976-81; dean of coll. svcs. Clark County Community Coll., orth Las Vegas, Nev., 1982-84; pres. Lincoln Trail Coll., Robinson, Ill., 1984-86, Sauk Valley Community Coll., Dixon, Ill., 1986—2005. Instr. bus. and speech U. Pitts., 1964; assoc. prof. mgmt. Frostburg (Md.) State Coll., 1971-74; mem. master planning com. Clark County Sch. Dist.; chmn. Washington County (Md.) Bd. Edn. Open versus Traditional Schs. Study Commn.; mem. Employment and Tng. Coun., Clark County, Nev., Pvt. Industry Coun., Nev., steering com. Correctional Ctr. Location, Ill. Contbr. articles to profl. jours. Bd. dirs. Community Theatre of Terre Haute, Family Svc. Agy. of Washington County (Md.), Big Bros. of Washington County, Crawford County (Ill.) Opportunities; v.p. bd. Potomac Playmakers, Md.; gen. vice chmn. United Way of Sterling-Rock Falls, 1988-89, chmn., 1989-90. Mem. Am. Assn. Higher Edn., Coll. and Univ. Pers. Assn., Assn. Instl. Rsch., Nat. Coun. on Community Svcs. and Continuing Edn., Md. Community Coll. Rsch. Group, Md. Community Coll. and Bus. Pers. Officers Assn., Nev. Assn. for Community Edn., Ill. Coun. Pub. Community Colls., Ill. Pres.'s Coun. (chmn. profl. devel. com.), Coun. North Cen. Community Jr. Colls. (sec., treas. 1987-88, 2d v.p. 1988-89, pres. 1989-90), Jaycees (Sterling, Ill. chpt.), Rotary (bd. dirs., pres.), Greater Sterling Area C. of C. (bd. dirs., v.p., pres.), Phi Delta Kappa. Address: 1878 Alistar Ct The Villages FL 32162 E-mail: behrenr@svcc.edu.

BEHRMAN, EDWARD JOSEPH, biochemistry educator; b. NYC, Dec. 13, 1930; s. Morris Harry and Janet Cahn (Solomons) B.; m. Cynthia Fansler, Aug. 29, 1953; children: David Murray, Elizabeth Colden, Victoria Anne. BS, Yale, 1952; PhD, U. Calif., Berkeley, 1957. Research asso. biochemistry Cancer Research Inst., Boston, 1960-64; bd. tutors biochem. scis. Harvard, 1961-64; asst. prof. chemistry Brown U., Providence, 1964-65; from mem. faculty to prof. emeritus Ohio State U., Columbus, 1965—2006, prof. emeritus, 2006—. Rschr. in peroxydisulfate and nucleotide chemistry. Contbr. articles to profl. jours. USPHS fellow, 1955-56, 57-60; NSF grantee, 1966-73; NIH grantee, 1973-81 Mem. Am. Chem. Soc., Royal Soc. Chemistry, Phi Beta Kappa, Sigma Xi. Home: 6533 Hayden Run Rd Hilliard OH 43026-9642 Office: Ohio State U Dept Biochemistry Columbus OH 43210 Office Phone: 614-292-9485. Business E-Mail: behrman.1@osu.edu.

BEIER, CAROL ANN, state supreme court justice; b. Kansas City, Kans., Sept. 27, 1958; Student, Benedictine Coll., 1976-77, The Poynter Inst., 1979; BS, U. Kans., 1981, JD, 1982-85; ML in Judicial Process, U. Va. Sch. Law, 2004. Bar: Kans., 1985, DC, 1988; US Dist. Kans., 1985; US Ct. Appeals (10th cir.) 1986. With Balloun & Bodinson, Olathe, Kans., 1983; jud. clk. U.S. Ct. Appeals (10th cir.), Olathe, 1985-86; staff atty. Nat. Women's Law Ctr., Washington, 1986-87; assoc. Arent, Fox, Kintner, Plotkin & Kahn, Washington, 1987-88, Foulston & Siefkin, Wichita, Kans., 1988-93, ptnr., 1993—2000; judge Kansas Ct. of Appeals, 2000—03; justice Kans. Supreme Ct., 2003—. Dir. Kans. Defender Project, Lawrence, 1989-90, Kans. Appellate Clinic, Lawrence, 1989-90; vis. asst. prof. U. Kans. Sch. of Law, Lawrence, 1989-90, lectr. Wichita State U., 1994; fellow Georgetown Women's Law and Pub. Policy Program, Washington, 1986-87. Articles editor U. Kans. Law Rev., 1984-85. Pres. Wichita Women Atty.'s Assn., 1993-94; bd. dirs. Kans. Civil Liberties Union, Wichita, 1990-94. Recipient Bernard Kilgore award, Soc. Profl. Jours., U. Kans., 1980, Louise Mattox Atty. of Achievement award Wichita Women's Attys. Assn., 2003. Fellow Kans. Bar Found., ABA, Sam A. Crow Inn of Ct. (master 2003-07); mem. ABA, Kans. Bar Assn., DC Bar, Wichita Bar Assn., Women's Atty. Assn. Topeka, Order of the Coif. Office: Kansas Supreme Ct 301 W 10th Topeka KS 66612

BEIERWALTES, WILLIAM HOWARD, physiologist, educator; b. Ann Arbor, Mich., Oct. 6, 1947; s. William Henry and Mary-Martha B.; m. Patricia Sue Olson, July 11, 1982; children: William N., Peter L., Nora R. BA, Kalamazoo Coll., 1969; PhD, U. N.C., 1978. Instr. Mayo Med. Sch., Rochester, Minn., 1979-81; sr. staff scientist Henry Ford Hosp., Detroit, 1981—. Prof. Wayne State U. Sch. Medicine, Detroit, 2004—. Contbr. articles to profl. jours. With US Army, 1971—72. Mem. Am. Physiol. Soc., Am. Heart Assn. (fellow coun. on high blood pressure 1992, fellow coun. on high blood pressure rsch. 2001, honor roll coun. on kidney 1988, chair rsch. fellowship com. Mich. chpt. 1987-90, 92-94, established investigator 1983-88), Am. Soc. Nephrology, Inter-Am. Soc. Hypertension, Mich. Soc. Med. Rsch. (bd. dirs. 1988-94, pres. 1992-94), Nat. Kidney Found. Mich. (rsch. rev. com. 1984-85, 88, 2004-06). Presbyterian. Avocation: collecting antique toy soldiers. Home: 750 Lakepointe St Grosse Pointe Park MI 48230-1706 Office: Henry Ford Hosp 2799 W Grand Blvd Detroit MI 48202-2689 Office Phone: 313-916-7494. Business E-Mail: wbeierw1@hfhs.org.

BEIHL, FREDERICK, retired lawyer; b. St. Joseph, Mo., Jan. 26, 1932; s. Ernst F. and Evelyn E. (Kline) B.; m. Lillis Prater, Mar. 3, 1962. AB, U. Mo., 1953, LLB, 1955. Bar: Mo. 1955, U.S. Supreme Ct. 1968. With Shook Hardy & Bacon, Kansas City, 1955-99, ptnr., 1961-99, shareholder, 1992-99; ret., 1999. Chmn. bd. dirs. UMKC Conservatory of Music, Kansas City, 1988-91, Visiting Nurses Assn., Kansas City, 1977-79; pres. Heart of Am. Family and Children Svcs., Kansas City, 1982-84, Friends of Art Nelson Mus., Kansas City, 1979-81. Avocations: tennis, skiing, art collecting. Office: Shook Hardy & Bacon 2555 Grand Blvd Kansas City MO 64108-2613 Business E-Mail: fbeihl@shb.com.

BEILEIN, JOHN PATRICK, men's college basketball coach; b. Feb. 5, 1953; m. Kathleen Beilein; children: Seana, Patrick, Mark, Andrew. B in Hist., Wheeling Jesuit U., 1975; MEd, Niagara U., 1981; degree (hon.), Wheeling Jesuit U., 2005. Head coach Newfane Ctrl. HS, NY, 1975—78, Erie CC, Buffalo, 1978—82, Nazareth Coll., Rochester, NY, 1982—83, Le Moyne Coll., Syracuse, NY, 1983—92, Canisius Coll., Buffalo, 1992—97, U. Richmond, 1997—2002, W.Va. U., Morgantown, 2002—07, U. Mich., Ann Arbor, 2007—. Co-chair W.Va. U. United Way campaign. Recipient Furfari award for Coll. Coach of Yr., W.Va. Sports Writers Assn., 2005. Achievements include coaching NIT champions, 2007. Office: U Mich Mens Basketball Athletic Dept 1000 S State St Ann Arbor MI 48109-2201

BEINEKE, LOWELL WAYNE, mathematics professor; b. Decatur, Ind., Nov. 20, 1939; s. Elmer Henry and Lillie Agnes (Snell) B.; m. Judith Rowena Wooldridge, Dec. 23, 1967; children: Jennifer Elaine, Philip Lennox. BS, Purdue U., 1961; MA, U. Mich., 1962, PhD, 1965. Asst. prof. Purdue U., Ft. Wayne, Ind., 1965-68, assoc. prof., 1968-71, prof., 1971-86, Jack W. Schrey prof., 1986—. Tutor Oxford (Eng.) U., 1974, The Open U., Milton Keynes, England, 1974, 75; vis. lectr. Poly. North London, 1980—81; vis. scholar Wolfson Coll., Oxford U., 1993—94, 2000—01; mem. SCR Keble Coll., 2000—01. Co-author (co-editor): Selected Topics in Graph Theory, 3 vols., 1978, 1983, 1988, Applications of Graph Theory, 1979, Graph Connections, 1997, Topics in Algebraic Graph Theory, 2004; assoc. editor Jour. Graph Theory, 1977—80, mem. editl. bd., 1977—, Internat. Jour. Graph Theory, 1991—95; editor: The Coll. Math. Jour.; co-editor: Congressus Numerantium, Vols., 1963—64, 1988; contbr. numerous articles to profl. jours. Corp. mem. Bd. for Homeland Ministries, United Ch. of Christ, .Y., 1988-91, del. Gen. Synod, 1989, 91. Recipient Outstanding Tchr. award AMOCO Found., 1978, Friends of the Univ., 1992, Outstanding Rsch. award Ind. U.-Purdue U. Ft. Wayne, 1999; Fulbright Found. grantee London, 1980-81, rsch. grantee Office Naval Rsch., Washington, 1986-89; fellow Inst. Combinatorics and its Applications, 1990—. Mem. Math. Assn. Am. (chairperson Ind. Sect. 1987-88, bd. govs. 1990-93, 2004-, mem. exec. com., 2006-, Disting. Tchg. award Ind. Sect. 1997, Disting. Svc. award Ind. Sect. 1998), Am. Math. Soc., London Math. Soc., Common Cause, Amnesty Internat., Summit Book Club, Internat. Affairs Forum, Sigma Xi (club pres. 1984-86, chpt. pres. 1997-98), Phi Kappa Phi (chpt. pres. 1993), Pi Mu Epsilon. Democrat. United Ch. Of Christ. Achievements include characterization of line graphs and thickness of complete graphs; enumeration of multidimensional trees. Home: 4529 Bradwood Ter Fort Wayne IN 46815-6028 Office: Ind U-Purdue U Dept of Math Scis 2101 E Coliseum Blvd Fort Wayne IN 46805-1445 Home Phone: 260-471-7074; Office Phone: 260-481-6223. Business E-Mail: beineke@ipfw.edu.

BEINERT, HELMUT, biochemist; b. Lahr, Germany, Nov. 17, 1913; came to U.S., 1947; m. Elisabeth Meyhoefer, 1955; 4 children. Dr rer nat, U. Leipzig, 1943; DSc, U. Wis., Milw., 1987, U. Konstanz, Germany, 1994. Rsch. assoc. Kaiser Wilhelm Inst. Med. Rsch., Germany, 1943-45; biochemist Air Force Aeromed Ctr., Germany, 1946, USAF, Sch. Aviation Medicine, 1947-50; postdoctoral rschr. U. Wis., Inst. Enzyme Rsch., Madison, 1950, rsch. assoc., 1951-52, asst. prof. to prof. enzyme chemistry, 1952-84, chmn. section III, 1958-84, prof. biochemistry, 1967-84, emeritus prof. enzyme chemistry and biochemistry, 1984—. Prof. biochemistry, dist. scholar residence Med. Coll. Wis., 1985-94; permanent guest prof. U. Konstanz, Germany, 1967. Recipient Rsch. Career award NIH, 1963, Sr. Scientist award Alexander von Humboldt Found., 1981, Keilin medal Biochem. Soc. London, 1985, Krebs medal Fed. European Biochem. Soc., 1989, Warburg medal German Soc. Biochem. and Molecular Biology, 1994, Lipmann plaque Am. Soc. Biol. Chem. Molecular Biology, 1993. Fellow Am. Acad. Arts and Sci., Wis. Acad. Scis. Arts and Letters; mem. NAS, Internat. EPR Soc., Am. Chemical Soc., Am. Soc. Biol., Chemistry and Molecular Biology, Soc. Biol. Inorganic Chemistry. Office: Univ Wis Inst Enzyme Rsch 1710 University Ave Madison WI 53726-4087

BEITLER, J. PAUL, real estate developer; b. Dec. 7, 1945; married, 3 children. BA, Mich. State U., 1967. Lic. comml. pilot; lic. real estate broker, Ill. Mktg. rep. Florist Transworld Deliver, Detroit, 1971-73; leasing rep. Helmsley-Spear of Ill., Inc., Chgo., 1973-74; dir. mktg. Canal Randolph Corp., Chgo., 1974-75; sr. v.p., dir. Rubloff Inc., Chgo., 1975-82; pres., CEO Beitler Co. (formerly Miglin-Beitler, Inc.), Chgo., 1982—. Lectr. in field. Editorial adv. bd. Metro Chgo. Office Guide. Bd. dirs. Ill. Capital Devel. Bd., Ill. Aeronatucis Commn., Mus. of Contemporary Art, Chgo., Chgo. Cen. Area Com.; adv. bd. City of Chgo., Mayor's Fellows Program, J.L. Kellogg Grad. Sch. Mgmt., Northwestern U., Ctr. for Real Estate Rsch.; adv. com. Affirmative Action div. Chgo. Urban League; mem. Chgo. Devel. Coun.; internat. bd. dirs. Frederic Remington Art Mus., N.Y.C.; arch. com. Art Inst. of Chgo.; pres.'s coun. Mus. of Sci. and Industry. With U.S. Army, 1970. Decorated Bronze Star, Army Commendation medal. Recipient 1990 Beautiful People award Chgo. Urban League, 1990 Comml. Real Estate Developer of the Yr., Chgo. Sun Times, Real Estate Achiever of the Yr. in comml. property mgmt. category Metro-Chgo. Real Estate Mag., 1991; inducted Chgo. Real Estate Hall of Fame, 2001. Mem. Aircraft Owners and Pilots Assn., Nat. Assn. Indsl. and Office Pks., Nat. Realty Com., Chgo. Assn. Commerce and Industry, Econ. Club of Chgo., Glen View Club, The Mid-Day Club, Birchwood Country Club, The East Bank Club, The Arts Club of Chgo. Achievements include feature in Crain's Chgo. Bus. Mag., 2006.

BEJA, MORRIS, English literature educator; b. NYC, July 18, 1935; s. Joseph and Eleanor (Cohen) B.; children: Andrew Lloyd, Eleni Rachel; m. Ellen Carol Jones, 1990. BA, CCNY, 1957; MA, Columbia U., 1958; PhD, Cornell U., 1963. From instr. to prof. English Ohio State U., Columbus, 1961-2000, prof. emeritus, 2001—. Vis. prof. U. Thessaloniki, Greece, 1965-66, Univ. Coll. Dublin, 1972-73, Northwestern U., Evanston, Ill., 2007. Author: Epiphany in the Modern Novel, 1971, Film and Literature, 1979, Joyce the Artist Manqué and Indeterminacy, 1989, James Joyce: A Literary Life, 1992; editor: Virginia Woolf's Mrs. Dalloway, 1996, Joyce in the Hibernian Metropolis, 1996, Perspectives on Orson Welles, 1995, Samuel Beckett: Humanistic Perspectives, 1983, James Joyce Newestlatter, 1977—, James Joyce's Dubliners and Portrait of the Artist, 1973; editor: (with E.C. Jones) Twenty-First Joyce, 2004. Pres. Internat. James Joyce Found., 1982-90, sec. 1990—; dir. Internat. James Joyce Symposia, 1982, 86, 92, 2004. With USAR, 1958-63. Guggenheim fellow, 1972-73; Fulbright lectr., 1965-66, 72-73. Mem. MLA, Internat. Virginia Woolf Soc. (trustee 1976-84), Am. Conf. Irish Studies. Jewish. Avocations: photography, travel, bicycling. Home: 1135 Middleport Dr Columbus OH 43235-4060 Office: Ohio State U Dept of English 164 W 17th Ave Columbus OH 43210-1326 E-mail: beja.1@osu.edu.

BELANGER, WILLIAM V., JR., state legislator; b. Mpls., Oct. 18, 1928; m. Lois Jean Winistorfer, 1953; seven children., St. Thomas Coll., 1948-50. With Honeywell Def. Sys., 1951-90, ret., 1990; mem. Minn. Senate, St. Paul, 1980—. Mem. Commerce and Consumer Protection Com., Rules and Adminstrn. Com., Taxes and Tax Laws Com. Cpl. US Army, 1946—51. Office: 10716 Beard Ave S Bloomington MN 55431-3616 also: State Senate 113 State Office Bldg Saint Paul MN 55155-0001 Home Phone: 952-881-4119; Office Phone: 651-296-5975. Business E-Mail: sen.bill.belanger@senate.com.

BELATTI, RICHARD G., state legislator; m. Marilyn Belatti; four children. Student, Coll. St. Thomas, U. S.D., Creighton U., Mayo Grad. Sch. Senator S.D. State Senate Dist. 13, 1989-92, former vice chmn. health and human svc. com., former mem. taxation com., transp. com.; rep. S.D. State Ho. Reps. Dist. 8, 1995-98, mem. health and human svc. and judiciary coms. Rep. cand. for S.D. State Senate, 2000. Home: 940 N Division Ave Madison SD 57042-3703

BELAY, STEPHEN JOSEPH, lawyer; b. Joliet, Ill., May 30, 1958; s. Donald L. and Miriam A. (Madden) B.; m. Trudy L. Patterson, Nov. 7, 1987; children: Jacob, Katherine. BA, U. Iowa, 1980, JD, 1983. Bar: Iowa 1983, U.S. Dist. Ct. (no. dist.) Iowa 1985. Pvt. practice, Cedar Rapids, Iowa, 1983-88; asst. county atty. State of Iowa, Burlington, 1988-89, Decorah, 1989-92, 95—; assoc. Anderson, Wilmarth & Van Der Maaten, Decorah, 1993-96; ptnr. Anderson, Wilmarth, Van Der Maaten & Belay, Decorah, 1997—. Chair Winneshiek County Rep. Party, Decorah, 1992-94. Mem. ABA (chair juvenile justice com. young lawyers divsn. 1992-93), Iowa State Bar Assn. (chair juvenile law com. young lawyers divsn. 1992-94), Lions (bd. dirs. 1991-93). Roman Catholic. Avocations: fishing, bicycling, camping. Home: 903 Pine Ridge Ct Decorah IA 52101-1135 Office: Anderson Wilmarth Van Der Maaten & Belay PO Box 450 Decorah IA 52101-0450

BELCASTRO, PATRICK FRANK, pharmacist, researcher; b. Italy, June 3, 1920; came to U.S., 1927, naturalized, 1943; s. Samuel and Sarah (Mosca) B.; m. Hanna Vilhelmina Jensen, July 6, 1963; children— Helen Maria, Paul Anthony. BS, Duquesne U., 1942; MS (Am. Found. Pharm. Edn. fellow), Purdue U., 1951, PhD in Pharmacy and Pharm. Chemistry (Am. Found. for Pharm. Edn. fellow), 1953. Instr. pharmacy Duquesne U., 1946-49; asst. prof. pharmacy Ohio State U., 1953-54; prof. indsl. pharmacy Purdue U., 1954-90, prof. emeritus, 1990—. Author: Physical and Technical Pharmacy, 1963; contbg. editor: (with others) Pharm. Tech, 1977—; contbr. to: (with others) Jour. Pharm. Scis. Served with U.S. Army, 1942-46. Mem. Am. Pharm. Assn., Rho Chi, Phi Lambda Upsilon. Roman Catholic. Home: 327 Meridian St West Lafayette IN 47906-2603 Office: Purdue U Sch Pharmacy and Pharm Scis West Lafayette IN 47907 E-mail: pbelcas1@purdue.edu.

BELCHER, LOUIS DAVID, marketing professional, retired mayor; b. Battle Creek, Mich., June 25, 1939; s. Louis George and Josephine (Johnson) B.; children: Debora Louise, Sheri Lynn, Stacy Elizabeth; m. Jane Elisabeth Dillon, May 8, 1987. Student, Kellogg Community Coll., 1959; BS, Eastern Mich. U., 1962. With GM, Livonia, Mich., 1962; adminstr. U. Mich., Ann Arbor, 1962-63; with NCR, Lansing, Mich., 1963-69, Veda, Inc., Ann Arbor, 1969-72; owner, v.p., treas. First Ann Arbor Corp., 1972-83; owner, chief fin. officer Third Party Services, Inc. and Data Scan, Inc., Ann Arbor, Mich., 1983-84; pres., chief exec. officer Data Scan, Inc., Ann Arbor, 1984-86, Ann Arbor Rod & Gun Co., 1986-88; ptnr. Shipman, Corey, Belcher, Ann Arbor, 1984-86; sr. asst. to pres. and dir. tech. svcs. Environ. Rsch. Inst. Mich., Ann Arbor, 1988-93; owner, prin. L. D. Belcher and Assocs. Mgmt. Cons., Ann Arbor, 1993—; v.p. Cybernet Syss. Corp., Ann Arbor, 1996-97; pres., CEO, owner, dir. Innovative Rsch. Corp., Ann Arbor, 1999—2007. Bd. dirs. Geosat Com., Inc., Washington; corp. dir. M.W. Microwave, Inc., Ann Arbor, Environment Tech. Corp., Ann Arbor, Innovative Rsch. & Svcs., Inc.; adv. bd. dirs. Mich. Consol. Gas Co.; exec. com. Ann. Conf. Earth Observations and Decision Making -A National Partnership, Washington, 1988—, Ann. Internat. Symposium on Remote Sensing of Environment, 1990—, Thematic Conf. Geol. Remote Sensing, 1990, Ann. Thematic Conf. Coastal and Marine Environment, 1992—; co-founder, dir. Ann Arbor IT Zone, 1999. Mem. City Coun., Ann Arbor, 1974-78, mayor pro tem, Ann Arbor, 1976-78, mayor, 1978-85; mem. adv. coun. region 5 SBA, Detroit, 1982-86; pres., bd. dirs. U. Mich. Theatre, 1983-85, Marcel Marceau World Ctr. for Mime, Inc., Ann Arbor, 1986-89; bd. dirs. Mich. Theatre Found., Ann Arbor, 1986-92; mem. nat. Rep. campaign team, 1980. Served to capt. Air N.G., 1956-70. Recipient Outstanding Alumni awards Kellogg C.C., Outstanding Alumni awards Ea. Mich. U. Coll. Bus., Silver Elephant award Rep. Party, Commendation Adminstr. Vets. Affairs, Commendation Ann Arbor Vets. Hosp.; Bügermedaille, City of Tübingen, Fed. Republic Germany; elected Mayor's Hall of Fame, 1995. Mem. AIAA, Air Force Assn., U.S. Conf. Mayors (past pres.), Mich. Conf. Mayors (chmn.), Am. Soc. for Photogrammertry and Remote Sensing, Am. Inst. Aeronautics and Astronautics, Ann Arbor Club. Republican. Mem. Ch. of Christ. Home: 1352 Cobblestone Ct Ann Arbor MI 48108-9553 Personal E-mail: belcherld@yahoo.com.

BELCK, NANCY GARRISON, dean, educator; b. Montgomery, Ala., Aug. 1, 1943; d. Lester Moffett and Stella Mae (Whaley) Garrison; m. Jack Belck, May 27, 1976; 1 child, Scott Brian. BS, La. Tech. U., 1964; MS, U. Tenn., 1965; PhD, Mich. State U., 1972. Cert. tchr., La. State textile specialist coop. extension svc. U. Ga., Athens, 1965-67, chair, dir. Tucson, 1976-79; asst. prof./instr. Mich. State U., East Lansing, 1967-73; family econ. researcher USDA Agrl. Res. Svcs., Hyatsville, Md., 1973-75, nat. extension evaluation coord. Washington, 1978-79; dean, prof. Coll. Human Ecology U. Tenn., Knoxville, 1979-87; dean, prof. Coll. Edn. Cen. Mich. U., Mt. Pleasant, 1987—91, interim provost, v.p. acad. affairs, 1988-89; provost, vice chancellor academic affairs La. State U., 1991—93; chancellor So. Ill. U., Edwardsville, 1994—97, U. Neb., Omaha, 1997—. Author: Development of Egyptian Universities Linkages, 1985, Mid-Career Administrators, 1986, Textiles for Consumers, 1990. Mem. exec. com. Mich. Milescular Inst., Midland, strategic planning team Pub. Schs., Mt. Pleasant, 1989—; chair Women's Networking Group, Mt. Pleasant, 1990—. Mem. Am. Home Econs. Assn., Am. Assn. for Higher Edn., Am. Assn. for Colls. Tchr. Edn., Am. Home Econs. Assn., Rotary, Sigma Iota Epsilon, Omicron Nu, Phi Delta, Kappa, Omicron Delta Kappa, Phi Kappa Phi. Avocations: gardening, walking, travel, international food tasting. Office: U of Nebraska at Omaha Office of the Chancellor Omaha NE 68182

BELEW, ADRIAN, guitarist, singer, songwriter, producer; Lead singer, co-guitarist King Crimson; v-drummer Projekct Two; former pop band The Bears. Performed on record and on tour with numerous entertainers and bands including Frank Zappa, David Bowie, Talking Heads, Laurie Anderson, David Byrne, Herbie Hancock, Paul Simon, Nine Inch Nails, Crash Test Dummies, others; albums: (with King Crimson) Discipline, 1981, Beat, 1982, Three of a Perfect Pair, 1984, The Compact King Crimson, 1987, Vrooom, 1994, Thrak, 1995, Thrakattak, 1996, (solo) Lone Rhino, 1982, Twang Bar King, 1983, Desire Caught by the Tail, 1986, Mr. Music Head, 1989, Young Lions, 1990, Desire of the Rhino King, 1991, Inner Revolution, 1992, Here, 1993, The Acoustic Adrian Belew, 1994, The Guitar as Orchestra, 1995, Op Zop Too Wah, 1996, Belewprints, 1998, Project Two/Space Groove, 1998, Salad Days, 1999, Coming Attractions, 2000, (with The Bears) The Bears, 1987, Rise and Shine, 1988; writer: Fantasy (by Mariah Carey); appeared in films Baby Snakes, Home of the Brave, Return Engagement; prodr. Caifanes/BMG, Santa Sabina/BMG, Jars of Clay/Essential-Silvertone, Sara Hickman/Shanachie, Rick Altizer/KMG, Irresponsibles/ABP.

BELL, ALBERT JEROME, lawyer; b. Columbus, Ohio, Apr. 24, 1960; s. Albert Leo and Jean Marie (DeFino) B.; m. Carla Jean Hudak, June 7, 1986; 2 children, Brian Albert, Kristin Elizabeth. BA, Ohio State U., 1982; JD, Capital U., 1985. Bar: Ohio 1985. Writer Battelle Meml. Inst., Columbus, 1982-84; pvt. practice law Columbus, 1985-86; vice-chmn., chief adminstrv. officer Big Lots Inc., Columbus, 1987—2004; CEO Moochie & Co., 2005—. Mem. adv. bd. devel. comm. chair, Annual Fund St. Charles Prep. HS; co-chmn. St. Paul Bldg. Campaign. Mem. ABA, Ohio Bar Assn., Columbus Bar Assn., Assn. Trial Lawyers Am., Internat. Assn. Corp. Real Estate Execs., Ohio State U. Alumni Assn. Roman Catholic. Avocations: golf, skiing, exercising.

BELL, BAILLIS F., airport terminal executive; Budget analyst City of Wichita, Kans., 1970-75; dir. Wichita Airport Authority, Kans., 1975—. Office: Witchita Airport Authority 2173 Air Cargo Rd Wichita KS 67209-1958

BELL, BRADLEY J., water treatment company executive; b. 1952; BS, U. Ill., 1974; MBA, Harvard U., 1978. Fin. analyst G.E., 1974-76; mgr. treasury analysis Bendix Corp., 1978-80; treas. Bundy Corp., 1983-87, v.p., treas., 1987; treas. Whirlpool Corp., Benton Harbor, Mich., 1987—97, v.p., 1990—97; sr. v.p., CFO Rohm & Haas Co., 1997—2003; exec. v.p., CFO Nalco Co., Naperville, Ill., 2003—. Bd. dirs. Idex Corp., Compass Minerals Internat. Office: Nalco Co 1601 W Diehl Rd Naperville IL 60563-1198

BELL, CLARK WAYNE, business editor, educator; b. Casper, Wyo., Feb. 7, 1951; s. Homer James and Jeanette (Hoban) B.; m. Victoria Anne Boucher, Jan. 2, 1971 (divorced); 1 child, Heidi Elizabeth; m. Suzanne Cerny, Mar. 6, 1989; 1 child, Natalie Taylor. BS, Drake U., 1973; MA, Loyola U., Chgo., 1978. Copy editor Chgo. Daily News, 1973-74, reporter, 1974-79; bus. columnist Chgo. Sun-Times, Chgo., 1979-84; exec. bus. editor Dallas Times Herald, 1984-86; editor, assoc. pub. Modern Healthcare Mag., Chgo., 1986—. Lectr. Northwestern U., Evanston, Ill., 1980-83; cons. editor Sales & Mktg. Mgmt. mag., N.Y.C., 1982-84. Bd. dirs. Youth Comm., Chgo., 1981-84, Next Theatre Co., Evanston, 1982-84, Heartland Alliance, 1994—, Chgo. Health Outreach, 1995—, Health Insights, 1996-99. Sloan fellow Princeton U., 1975-76. Mem. United Ch. Christ. Office: Modern Healthcare Crain Comm 360 N Michigan Ave Chicago IL 60601-3806

BELL, C(LYDE) R(OBERTS) (BOB BELL), foundation administrator; b. Balt., Apr. 12, 1931; s. William and Rachel (Roberts) B.; m. Carol Ann Murphy, June 14, 1980 (dec. Aug. 1997); children: Diane, Nancy, Mary Lynn, Catherine, Robert, Brian, Douglas, Jeffrey, Lawrence, Laura; m. Jean Creighton Chapman, Feb. 13, 1999. BS with distinction, U.S. Naval Acad., 1953. Registered profl. nuclear engr. Commd. ensign USN, 1953, advanced through grades to vice adm., 1987, ret., 1988; pres. Greater Omaha C. of C., 1989—. Bd. dirs. Ctr. for Human Nutrition, Omaha, WELCOM, Omaha. Trustee Boy Scouts Am., Omaha, 1990—; bd. dirs. NCCJ, Omaha, 1991—. Mem. Omaha Country Club, Omaha Club (Man of Yr. 1991), Omaha Plaza Club, Omaha Press Club. Avocations: golf, reading, performing arts. Office: Greater Omaha C of C 1301 Harney St Omaha NE 68102-1832 E-mail: gocc@accessomaha.com.

BELL, DELORIS WILEY, physician; b. Solomon, Kans., Sept. 30, 1942; d. Harry A. and Mildren H. (Watt) Wiley; children: Leslie, John. BA, Kans. Wesleyan U., 1964; MD, U. Kans., 1968. Diplomate Am. Bd. Ophthalmology. Intern St. Luke's Hosp., Kansas City, Mo., 1968-69; resident U. Kans. Med. Ctr., Kansas City, 1969-72; practice medicine specializing in ophthalmology Overland Park, Kans., 1973—. Mem. AMA, Kans. Med. Soc. (pres. sect. ophthalmology 1985-86, spkr. house 1994-97), Am. Acad. Ophthalmology (councillor 1988-93, chmn. state govtl. affairs 1993-97, bd. trustees 2000-03), Kans. Soc. Ophthalmology (pres. 1985-86), Kansas City Soc. Ophthalmology and Otolaryngology (sec. 1984-86, pres.-elect 1988, pres. 1989). Avocations: photography, travel. Office: 7000 W 121st St Ste 100 Shawnee Mission KS 66209-2010 Office Phone: 913-498-2015. Personal E-mail: cd2cdb@gmail.com.

BELL, GRAEME I., biochemistry and molecular biology educator; BSc in Zoology, U. Calgary, 1968, MSc in Biology, 1971; PhD in Biochemistry, U. Calif., San Francisco, 1977. Sr. scientist Chiron Corp.; prof. dept. biochemistry and molecular biology U. Chgo. Contbr. articles to profl. jours. Recipient Outstanding Sci. Achievement award Am. Diabetes Assn., Rolf Luft award Swedish Med. Soc., Gerold and Kayla Grodsky Basic Rsch. Scientist award Juvenile Diabetes Found. Internat. Office: U Chgo Howard Hughes Inst 5841 S Maryland Ave Rm Ambn237 Chicago IL 60637-1463 E-mail: g-bell@uchicago.edu.

BELL, JAMES A., aerospace transportation executive; b. LA, 1949; m. Mary Bell. B in Acctg., Calif. State U., LA. Acct. Rockwell, 1972, various positions including corp. sr. internal auditor, mgr. acctg. and mgr. gen. and cost acctg., 1972—86, dir. acctg., Rocketdyne, 1986—92; dir. bus. mgmt., Space Sta. Electric Power Sys., Rocketdyne unit Rockwell (acquired by The Boeing Co.), Chgo., 1992—96; v.p. contracts and pricing Boeing Space and Comm. The Boeing Co., Chgo., 1996—2000, sr. v.p. fin., corp. contr., 2000—03, exec. v.p., CFO, 2004—, interim CEO, pres., 2005. Bd. dirs. New Leaders for New Schs., LA Urban League, Joffrey Ballet; past bd. dirs. Charles Drew U. Medicine and Sci. Mem.: World Bus. Chgo. (bd. dirs.). Office: The Boeing Co 100 N Riverside Plz Chicago IL 60606-2609

BELL, JEANETTE LOIS, former state legislator; b. Milw., Sept. 2, 1941; d. Harold Arthur and Luella Ruth (Block) Jeske; m. Chester Robert Bell Jr., 1962; children: Chester R. III, Colleen M., Edith L. BA, U. Wis., Milw., 1988. State assemblywoman dist. 22 State of Wis., 1982-92, state assemblywoman dist. 15, 1993-96; mayor City of West Allis, Wis., 1996—. Chairwoman ways and means com. Wis. State Assembly. Active child abuse prevention program. Recipient Clean 16 Environment award, Child Abuse Prevention award. Mem. LWV. Home: 1415 S 60th St West Allis WI 53214-5159

BELL, JOHN WILLIAM, lawyer; b. Chgo., May 3, 1946; s. John and Barbara Bell; m. Deborah Bell, Aug. 25, 1974; children: Jason, Alicia. Student, U. So. Calif., 1964-65; BA, Northwestern U., 1968; JD cum laude, Loyola U., Chgo., 1971. Bar: Ill. 1971. Assoc. Kirkland & Ellis, Chgo., 1972-75; ptnr. Johnson & Bell, Ltd. (formerly Johnson, Cusack & Bell, Ltd.), Chgo., 1975—. Mem. ABA (vice chmn. products, gen. liability and consumer law com. sect. tort and ins. practice 1986-87, 88—, com. on torts and ins. practice sect.), Ill. Bar Assn., Chgo. Bar Assn. (tort liability sect., aviation com. 1982—, chmn. med.-legal rels. com. 1994-95), Internat. Assn. Ins. Def. Counsel, Ill. Def. Coun. (faculty mem. trial acad. 1994), Soc. Trial Lawyers Am., Ill. Trial Lawyers Assn., Am. Coll. Trial Lawyers, Fed. Trial Bar.

BELL, KAREN A., dean; BA in Sociol., SUNY, Potsdam; MFA in Dance, Sarah Lawrence Coll. Prof. SUNY Potsdam, Elmira Coll., Wells Coll.; visiting asst. prof. Cornell U.; prof. Ohio State U., 1980—; chairperson Dept. Dance, Ohio State U., 1995—; assoc. dean Coll. Arts. Ohio State U., 1995—2001, interim dean, 2001—02, dean, 2002—. Individual Artist Fellowship, Ohio Arts Coun., Academic Leadership Fellow, Com. Instl. Cooperation, 1991—92. Mem.: Nat. Assn. Sch. Dance (commn. accreditation, evaluator), Am. Coll. Dance Festival Assn. (bd. dirs., northeast regional rep.). Office: Office of Dean OSU Coll Arts 152 Hopkins Hall 128 North Oval Mall Columbus OH 43210 Office Phone: 614-292-5171. Office Fax: 614-292-5218. E-mail: bell.1@osu.edu.

BELL, KEVIN J., zoological park administrator; b. NY, Aug. 14, 1952; s. Joseph L. and Muriel E. (Beck) B.; m. Catharine Kleiman, Sept. 8, 1991. BS in Biology, Syracuse U., 1974; MS Zoology, SUNY, Brockport, 1976. Rsch. asst. Nat. Audubon Soc., Ea. Egg Rock, Maine, 1975; curator of birds Lincoln Park Zoological Gardens, Chgo., 1975-92, dir., 1993—; pres., CEO Lincoln Park Zool. Soc., Chgo., 1995—. Leader Zoo Soc. Tours to Africa, India, Nepal and Thailand. Contbr. articles to jours. in field. Office: Lincoln Pk Zool Gardens 2001 N Clark St Chicago IL 60614-4712 also: PO Box 14903 Chicago IL 60614-0903

BELL, LAWRENCE T., lawyer; b. 1948; BBA, St. Bonaventure U., 1970; JD, William Mitchell Coll. Law, St. Paul, Minn., 1979. Bar: Minn. 1979. Joined Ecolab Inc., St. Paul, 1979, internat. v.p. -adminstrn., 1986—91, named gen. counsel, 1998, now sr. v.p., gen. counsel, sec. Mem. bd. Twin Cities Pub. TV, St. Paul Chamber Orch.; bd. dirs. VocalEssence, 2002—; bd. trustees William Mitchell Coll. Law, 2004—. Office: Ecolab Inc 370 Wabasha St N Saint Paul MN 55102

BELL, MARVIN HARTLEY, poet, language educator; b. NYC, Aug. 3, 1937; s. Saul and Belle (Spector) B.; m. Mary Mammosser, 1958 (div.); m. Dorothy Murphy; children: athan Saul, Jason Aaron. BA, Alfred U., 1958, LHD (hon.), 1986; MA, U. Chgo., 1961; MFA, U. Iowa, 1963. Mem. faculty, Writers' Workshop U. Iowa, Iowa City, 1965—2005, Flannery O'Connor prof. letters, 1986—2005, Iowa poet laureate, 2000—04. Vis. lectr. Goddard Coll., 1970; disting. vis. prof. U. Hawaii, 1981; vis. prof. U. Wash., 1982; faculty Pacific U., 2004—, Pacific Luth. U., 2004-05; Lila Wallace-Reader's Digest Writing fellow U. Redlands, 1991-92, 92-93; Woodrow Wilson vis. fellow St. Mary's Coll. of Calif., 1994-95, Nebr. Wesleyan U., 1996-97, Pacific U., 1996-97, Hampden-Sydney Coll., 1998-99, W.Va. Wesleyan Coll., 2000-2001, Birmingham So. U., 2000-2001, Ill. Coll., 2002-03, Bethany Coll., 2003-04, Morningside Coll., 2008—; penn state erie behrend coll. 2008-, judge Lamont Award-Acad. Am. Poets, 1989-91, Pushcart Prizes, 1991, 97, Western Book Awards-Western States Arts Fedn., 1991, Nat. Poetry Series, NEA, N.C. Arts Coun., Coordinating Coun. Lit. Mags., Discovery Contest-Poetry Ctr. of 92nd St Y, N.Y.C., Poetry Soc. Am., Hopwood Awards, Tulsa Arts Coun., Anhinga Poetry Prize-Fla. State U. Press, numerous others; disting. poet-in-residence Wichita State U., 2004, Prague Seminar, 2002, 04; disting. vis. prof. Portland State U., 2007. Author: (poems) Things We Dreamt We Died For, 1966, A Probable Volume of Dreams, 1969 (Lamont award Acad. Am. Poets 1969), The Escape into You, 1971, 94, Residue of Song, 1974, Stars Which See, Stars Which Do Not See, 1977 (Nat. Book award finalist 1977), 92, These Green-Going-To-Yellow, 1981, Drawn by Stones, by Earth, by Things That Have Been in the Fire, 1984, New and Selected Poems, 1987, Iris of Creation, 1990, The Book of the Dead Man, 1994, Ardor: The Book of the Dead Man, vol. 2, 1997, Wednesday: Selected Poems, 1998, Poetry for a Midsummer's Night, 1998, Nightworks: Poems 1962-2000, 2000, Ashes Poetica, 2002, Rampant, 2004, Shakespeare's Wages, 2004, Mars Being Red, 2007 (L.A. Times Book award Finalia, 2008); (essays) Old Snow Just Melting: Essays and Interviews, 1983; (anthology) A Marvin Bell Reader, 1994; co-author: Segues: A Correspondence in Poetry, 1983, Annie-Over, 1988, editor, pub. Statements, 1959-64; poetry editor The Iowa Rev., 1969-71, guest poetry editor, 1980, 2005; poetry editor The Pushcart Prize, vol. XXI, 1996-97, editor-at-large vol. series, 1994-96, series editor, poetry, 1997—; columnist The Am. Poetry Rev., 1975-78, 90-92; series editor New Poets, Short Books series Lost Horse Press, 2006—; contbr. and commd. poetry to numerous mags. and anthologies. Fellow Guggenheim Found., 1977, NEA, 1978, 84; Sr. Fulbright scholar to Yugoslavia, 1983, Sr. Fulbright scholar to Australia, 1986; recipient Bess Hokin award Poetry, 1969, Emily Clark Balch prize Va. Quar. Rev., 1970, Am. Poetry Rev. prize, 1982, Lit. award Am. Acad. Arts and Letters, 1994, Shestack prize Am. Poetry Rev., 2003; Poet Laureate of Iowa, 2000-04. Home: 1416 E College St Iowa City IA 52245

BELL, ROBERT, orchestra executive; Ops. & pers. mgr. Toledo Symphony Orch., mng. dir., pres., CEO, 1984—. Office: Toledo Symphony Orch 1838 Parkwood Ave Ste 310 Toledo OH 43624-2502

BELL, ROBERT HOLMES, federal judge; b. Lansing, Mich., Apr. 19, 1944; s. Preston C. and Eileen (Holmes) B.; m. Helen Mortensen, June 28, 1968; children: Robert Holmes Jr., Ruth Eileen, Jonathan Neil. BA, Wheaton Coll., 1966; JD, Wayne State U., 1969. Bar: Mich. 1970, U.S. Dist. Ct. (we. dist.) Mich. 1970. Asst. prosecutor Ingham County Prosecutor's Office, Lansing, Mich., 1969-72; state dist. judge Mich. State Cts., 1973-78, state cir. judge Mason, 1979-87; judge US Dist. Ct. (we. dist.) Mich., Grand Rapids, Mich., 1987-2001, chief judge, 2001—. Office: US Dist Ct 602 Fed Bldg 110 Michigan St NW Grand Rapids MI 49503-2363 E-mail: kim@miwd.uscourts.gov.

BELL, RONALD A., lawyer; b. Jamaica, 1967; BS in Aerospace and Mech. Engring., Polytechnic U., 1988; MS in Aerospace and Mech. Engring., U. Cin., 1991; JD, Ohio State U., 1994. Bar: Ohio 1994, US Dist. Ct. Southern Dist. Ohio, US Tax Ct.; cert. CFA 2001. Ptnr. Squire, Sanders & Dempsey L.L.P., Cin. Mem., Leadership Cin. Class XXVI Greater Cin. Chamber of Commerce. Mem., Human Resources Com. Nat. Underground Railroad Freedom Ctr. Named one of Ohio's Rising Stars, Super Lawyers, 2006. Office: Squire Sanders & Dempsey LLP 312 Walnut St Ste 3500 Cincinnati OH 45202-4036 Office Phone: 513-361-1200. Office Fax: 513-361-1201.

BELL, SAMUEL H., federal judge, educator; b. Rochester, NY, Dec. 31, 1925; s. Samuel H. and Marie C. (Williams) B.; m. Joyce Elaine Shaw, 1948 (dec.): children: Henry W., Steven D.; m. Jennie Lee McCall, 1983. BA, Coll. Wooster, 1947; JD, U. Akron, 1952. Pvt. practice, Cuyahoga Falls, Ohio, 1956-68; asst. pros. atty. Summit County, Ohio, 1956-58; judge Cuyahoga Falls Mcpl. Ct., Ohio, 1968-73, Ct. of Common Pleas, Akron, Ohio, 1973-77, Ohio Ct. Appeals, 9th Jud. Dist., Akron, 1977-82, U.S. Dist. Ct. (no. dist.) Ohio, Akron, 1982-2000, sr. status, 1996; sr. judge. Adj. prof. Coll. Wooster, 1998-2003, Bell disting. lectr. in law, 1998—; adj. prof., adv. bd. U. Akron Sch. Law, past trustee Dean's club; bd. dirs. Jos. R. Miller Found; co-owner Bell Lettres Ltd. Co-author: Federal Practice Guide 6th Cir., 1996. Recipient Disting. Alumni award U. Akron, 1988, St. Thomas More award, 1987. Fellow Akron Bar Found. (trustee 1989-94, pres. 1993-94); mem. Fed. Bar Assn., Akron Bar Assn., Akron U. Sch. Law Alumni Assn. (Disting. Alumni award 1983), Charles F. Scanlon Akron Inn Ct. (pres. 1990-92), Masons, Phi Alpha Delta. Republican. Presbyterian. Office: US Dist Ct 433 US Court House Fed Bldg 2 S Main St Akron OH 44308-5836

BELL, SANDRA ELIZABETH, corporate financial executive; b. Toronto, Ont., Can., Apr. 23, 1957; came to U.S., 1961; d. Alexander James Bell and Marion Ann (Scaysbrook) Robinson. BA in Econs., Ohio State U., 1979; MBA, Harvard U., 1983. Mgmt. trainee, systems analyst First Nat. Bank of Cin., 1979-81; asst. v.p. E.F. Hutton & Co., NYC, 1983-87; v.p. The Deerpath Group, Lake Forest, Ill., 1988-91; mng. dir. Deutsche Bank Securities Inc., NYC, 1991—2004; exec. v.p., CFO Fed. Home Loan Bank of Cin., 2004—. Mem. Phi Beta Kappa. Avocations: skiing, tennis, reading. Office: Fed Home Loan Bank 221 E 4th St Fl 10 Cincinnati OH 45202 Home Phone: 513-474-3443; Office Phone: 513-852-7524. E-mail: bellse@fhlbein.com.

BELL, STEPHEN SCOTT (STEVE BELL), journalist, educator; b. Oskaloosa, Iowa, Dec. 9, 1935; s. Howard Arthur and Florance (Scott) B.; m. Joyce Dillavou, June 16, 1957; children: Allison Kay, Hilary Ann. BA, Central Coll., Pella, Iowa, 1959, PhD (hon.), 1969; MS in Journalism, Northwestern U., 1963. Announcer Radio Sta. KBOE, Oskaloosa, 1955-59; reporter WOI-TV, Ames, Iowa, 1959-60; news writer WGN Radio-TV, Chgo., 1960-61; reporter, anchorman WOW-TV, Omaha, 1962-65; anchorman Radio Sta. WNEW, NYC, 1965-66; corr. ABC News, 1967-86, assignments include Vietnam War corr. Vietnam, 1970-71, polit. corr., 1968, 72, chief Asia corr., 1972-73, White House corr. Washington, 1974-75; news anchorman World News This Morning and Good Morning Am., 1975-86; news anchor KYW-TV, Phila., 1987-91, USA Network Updates, 1989-92; prof. telecomm. Ball State U., Muncie, Ind., 1992—2007, endowed chmn. emeritus in telecomm., 2007—. Recipient Emmy nominations, 1965, 73, Overseas Press Club award, 1969, Headliner award, 1975 Mem. AFTRA, Council Fgn. Relations. Presbyterian (elder). Office: Ball State U Dept Telecommunications Muncie IN 47306-0001

BELL, WILLIAM VERNON, utility executive; b. Council Bluffs, Iowa, July 30, 1919; s. William Henry and Lillian May (Roper) B.; m. Virginia Nelson, Nov. 15, 1942; children— Patricia Jane, Stephen William. BS in Chem. Engring., U. Iowa, 1942. Registered profl. engr., Ind. Sales dir. Met. Utilities Dist., Omaha, 1946-62; sales mgr. Ind. Gas Co. Inc., Indpls., 1962-64, v.p., 1964-74, sr. v.p. gas supply and consumer services, 1974-85; bus. counselor SCORE, Carmel, IN, 1991—. Bd. mem., OH Valley Gas Co., bd. mem., Meals on Wheels. Served to capt. C.E., U.S. Army, 1942-46. Named Energy Man of Yr.-Ind., Ind. State Dept. Commerce, 1981, Ind. State Energy Service Award, 1984. Mem. Nat. Soc. Profl. Engrs., Am. Gas Assn. (chmn. mktg. sect.), Blue Flame Gas Assn.-Nebr. (chmn.), Midwest Gas Assn. Clubs: Kiwanis. Episcopalian. Office: Indiana Gas Co Inc 1630 N Meridian St Indianapolis IN 46202-1402

BELLE, GERALD, pharmaceutical executive; BSBA Mktg., cum laude, Xavier U., Cin., 1968; MBA, Northwestern U., 1969. Mem. staff Merrell-Nat. Labs., Cin., 1969-77, mem. sales and mktg. staff U.S. and Philippines Manila, 1978-82; East Asia regional mgr. pharms. Dow Chem. Pacific Ltd., Hong Kong, 1982-83; product group dir. Merrell-Nat. Labs., Cin., 1983-85; dir. product planning and promotion Lakeside Pharms., Cin., 1985-87; dir. mktg. Merrell Dow Pharms. KK, Tokyo, 1987-90; v.p. mktg. and sales Marion Merrell Dow Europe AG, Zurich, Switzerland, 1990-95; pres. Hoechst Marion Roussel Can., Montreal, Que., 1995-97; pres., N.Am., CEO Hoechst Marion Roussel, Inc. Hoechst Marion Roussel, Kansas City, Mo., 1997—99; pres. Aventis, N. Am. Pharm. (from merger of Hoechst Marion Roussel and Rhône-Poulenc Rorer), 1999—2004; exec. chmn. Merial Ltd., Duluth, Ga., 2004—07. Bd. dirs. Nat. Pharm. Coun., Mid-Am. Coalition on Health Care. Mem. Civic Coun. Greater Kansas City. Office: Merial Ltd Bldg 500 3239 Satellite Blvd Duluth GA 30096 Office Phone: 678-638-3000.

BELLER, STEPHEN MARK, retired academic administrator; b. Chgo., Aug. 14, 1948; s. I.E. and De Vera (Jameson) B.; m. Luanne Evelyn Heyl, June 28, 1970; children: Clancy Dee, Corby Lu. BS, U. Ill., 1970; MS, Western Ill. U., 1972; PhD, Oregon State U., 1977. Asst. head ed. Awards of Rotary Found., Evanston, Ill., 1972-73; asst. dean of students SUNY, Geneseo, N.Y., 1977-81; dean of student svcs. Tenn. Wesleyan Coll., Athens, 1981-83, MacMurray Coll., Jacksonville, Ill., 1984-88, Capital U., Columbus, Ohio, 1988-99, v.p., dean of student svcs., 1999—2003, v.p. emeritus, 2003—. Mem.: Phi Delta Kappa, Phi Kappa Phi. Methodist. Avocations: railroading, photography. Home: 174 W Bristol Oak Cir The Woodlands TX 77382-1272 Business E-Mail: sbeller@capital.edu.

BELLET, PAUL SANDERS, pediatrician, educator; b. Phila., June 28, 1945; BA, Johns Hopkins U., 1967; MD, U. Rochester, 1971. Diplomate Am. Bd. Pediat. Intern in pediat. Cleve. Met. Gen. Hosp., 1971-72; resident in pediat. Case Western Res., Cleve., 1972-73, fellow in pediat. cardiology, 1973-75; pediatrician USAF/Maxwell AFB Regional Hosp., Montgomery, Ala., 1975-77; asst. prof. pediat. U. Ala., Tuscaloosa, 1977-81, assoc. prof. of pediat., 1981-83; assoc. prof. pediat. Children's Hosp. Med. Ctr./U. Cin. Coll. Medicine, Cin., 1983-94, prof. pediat., 1994—2004, prof. emeritus pediat., 2004—. Author: The Diagnostic Approach to Symptoms and Signs in Pediatrics, 2d edit., 2002. Fellow Am. Acad. Pediat.; mem. Ambulatory Pediat. Assn., Cin. Pediat. Soc. Office: Cin Children's Hosp Med Ctr 3333 Burnet Ave Cincinnati OH 45229-3039 Home Phone: 513-772-8627; Office Phone: 513-636-4506. Business E-Mail: paul.bellet@cchmc.org.

BELLING, MARK, radio personality; b. Fox Valley, Wis. Grad., U. Wis., LaCrosse. News and program dir. WTDY-AM, Madison, Wis.; news dir. Springfield, Ill., St. Joseph-Benton Harbor, Mich., Oshkosh, Wis.; radio host 1130 WISN, Milw., 1989—. Recipient Best Radio Editorial, Milw. Press Club, Best Investigative Reporting in Midwest, Radio-Television News Dirs. Assn. Office: WISN 759 N 19th St Milwaukee WI 52233

BELLOCK, PATRICIA RIGNEY, state legislator; b. Chgo., Oct. 14, 1946; d. John Dungan and Dorothy (Comiskey) Rigney; children: Colleen, Dorothy. BA, St. Norbert Coll., 1968. With customer rels. 3M Corp., Chgo., 1968-69; tchr. jr. h.s. Milw. and Fairbanks, Alaska, 1970-72; v.p. sports corps. Dor-Mor-Pat Corp., River Forest, Ill., 1976-84; mem. DuPage County Bd. from Dist. 3, Wheaton, Ill., 1992-98, Ill. Ho. of Reps., Springfield, 1999—. Asst. treas. DuPage County Forest Preserve Dist. Bd. dirs. U. Ill. Gerontology Rsch., 1988-91; mem. DuPage County Bd. Health, Wheaton, 1990—, Care and Counseling Ctr., Downers Grove, 1977—, pres., 1986-89; pres. Ill. Women Legislators, 2005-06. Recipient award Ill. Health Dept., 1992, Woman of Yr. award Serenity House, Addison, Ill.; named Champion of Free Enterprise, Ill. C. of C., 2002-05. Roman Catholic. Office: 6301 S Cass Ave Westmont IL 60559-3277 Home: 431 Canterbury Ct Hinsdale IL 60521-2825

BELLOWS, LAUREL GORDON, lawyer; m. Joel J. Bellows. BA, U. Pa., 1969; JD, Loyola U., Chgo., 1974. Bar: Ill. 1974, Fla. 1975, U.S. Dist. Ct. (no. dist.) Ill. 1975, U.S. Dist. Ct. (no. dist.) Ga. 1980, Calif. 1981, U.S. Dist. Ct. (cen. dist.) Calif. 1980. Ptnr. Bellows and Bellows, Chgo., 1975—. Editor Loyola U. Law Rev., 1973-74; co-author: Trial Techniques in Business and Commercial Cases, 1988-2000. Past pres. women's bd. Traveller's Aid Soc., Chgo.; past chmn. Chgo. etwork, 1992—; mentor Woman of Destiny program, 1990-91. Mem. ABA (bd. govs. 2001—, sec.-treas. 1991-92, past chmn. commn. on women 1993-95, mem. fed. jud. com. 1999—), Ill. Bar Assn., Chgo. Bar Assn. (bd. mgrs. 1983-85, sec. 1987-89, pres. 1991-92, chair, ho. dels., 2006-), Women's Bar Assn. Ill., Women's Bar Assn. Ill. Found. (bd. dirs. 1988—), Am. Arbitration Assn. (arbitrator 1976—, award 1990). Office: Bellows and Bellows PC 209 S LaSalle St Ste 800 Chicago IL 60604 Office Phone: 312-332-3340. Business E-Mail: lbellows@bellowspc.com.

BELLUSCHI, ANTHONY C., architect; b. Portland, Oreg., Aug. 2, 1941; s. Pietro and Helen (Hemila) B.; m. Helen Risom, June 25, 1966 (div. 1975); children: Pietro Antonio, Catharine Camilla; m. Martha Mull Page, July 17, 1992. BArch, R.I. Sch. Design, 1966. Lic. arch. 28 states including N.Y., Mass., R.I., Calif., .J., Oreg., Ill., Fla., Ga. Draftsman Ernest Kump Assocs., San Francisco, 1964; designer Zimmer-Gunsel-Frasca, Portland, 1965; assoc. Jung/Brannen Assocs., Boston, 1968-73; prin., treas. Belluschi/Daskalakis Inc., Boston, 1973-77; sr. v.p. Charles Kober Assocs., LA, 1977-84; mng. ptnr. Kober/Belluschi Assocs., Chgo., 1984-87; pres. Anthony Belluschi Assocs. Inc., 1984-87; founder Anthony Belluschi Archs., Ltd., Chgo., 1988-2000; pres. Belluschi-OWP&P Arch. Inc., Chgo., 2000—03; cons. architect Chgo., 2003—, Strategic Alliance, NYC, Chgo., 2005—; with Perkins Eastman Architects, NYC, Chgo., 2005—. Archtl. cons. U.S. Peace Corps, El Salvador, 1966-68; trustee R.I. Sch. Design, 1986—, vice chmn., 1995-2000, chair bd., 2000-04. Bd. adv. Inland Arch. Mag., 1992-95. Bd. dirs. Friends of the Park, Chgo., 1993—. Recipient First prize sculpture contest RKO & Redevel. Agy., Boston, 1973, award of merit Mass. Commn. Housing, 1975, Alumni of Yr. award RISD, 1982-83. Fellow AIA (award of excellence 1997); mem. Urban Land Inst. (award of excellence 1997), Internat. Coun. Shopping Ctrs. (design awards for Erieview Galleria, Clevel., Bridgewater Commons, N.J., 1989, Sportsgirl Office/Retail Hirise Bldg., Melbourne, Australia, 1991, Park Meadows Retail Resort, Denver, Univ. Retail Ctr., Tampa, Fla., 1996, The Falls, Miami, 1996, Northwood Cafe, Appleton, Wis., 1999), RISD Alumni Assn. (founder Chgo. chpt.). Avocations: travel, automobiles, hunting. Home: The Coach House 119 W Chestnut St Chicago IL 60610-3254

BELLVILLE, MARGARET (MAGGIE BELLVILLE), communications executive; B in Social Scis., SUNY, Binghamton; grad. advanced mgmt. program, Harvard U. With GTE Wireless/Contel Cellular, Inc., 1986—93; sr. v.p. Century Comm., LA, 1993—95; from v.p. ops. to exec. v.p. ops. Cox Comm., Inc., 1995—2001; pres., CEO Incanta, Atlanta, 2001—02; exec. v.p. ops. Charter Comm., Inc., St. Louis, 2002—03, exec. v.p., COO, 2003—04. Mem. exec. vom., bd. dirs. Calif. Cable TV Assn.; bd. dirs. Cable Positive, Women in Cable and Telecomm. Found.; advisor Nat. Cable and Telecomm. Assn. Task Force on Diversity. Named Woman of Yr., Women in Cable, Calif. chpt., Woman to Watch, Women in Cable, Atlanta chpt., Woman of Yr., Women in Cable nat.; named one of Top 10 Women in Bus. in Atlanta. Office: Charter Comm Inc 12405 Powerscourt Dr Saint Louis MO 63131

BELOT, MONTI L., III, federal judge; b. Kansas City, Mar. 4, 1943; m. Karen Ann Neeley. BA, U. Kansas, 1965, JD, 1968. Law clk. to Hon. Wesley E. Brown U.S. Dist. Ct., Kans., 1971-73; asst. U.S. atty. Topeka, Kans., 1973-76; atty. Weeks, Thomas & Lysaught, Kansas City, Kans., 1976-83, Hall, Levy, Lively, DeVore, Belot & Bell, Coffeyville, Kans., 1983-91; U.S. dist. judge Kans., 1991—. Spl. asst. to U.S. Atty., Topeka, 1976-78; mem. adv. com. Civil Justice Reform Act. Trustee Coffeyville Regional Med. Ctr., Kans. U. Alumni Assn. With USN, 1968-71. Mem. Kansas Bar Assn., Southeast Kansas Bar Assn., Montgomery County Bar Assn. (pres. 1991), Kansas Bd. Law Examiners, Assn. Defense Trial Attys., U.S. Dist. Ct. Kansas, Coffeyville Rotary Club, Sigma Chi. Office: 111 US Courthouse 401 N Market St Wichita KS 67202-2089

BELSKY, MARTIN HENRY, law educator, dean; b. May 29, 1944; s. Abraham and Fannie (Turnoff) Belsky; m. Kathleen Waits, Mar. 9, 1985; children: Allen Frederick, Marcia Elizabeth. BA cum laude, Temple U., 1965; JD cum laude, Columbia U., 1968; cert. of study, Hague Acad. Internat. Law, The Netherlands, 1968; diploma in Criminology, Cambridge U., England, 1969. Bar: Pa. 1969, Fla. 1983, N.Y. 1987, U.S. Dist. Ct. (ea. dist.) Pa. 1969, U.S. Ct. Appeals (3d cir.) 1970, U.S. Supreme Ct. 1973. Chief asst. dist. atty. Phila. Dist. Atty.'s Office, Pa., 1969—74; assoc. Blank, Rome, Klaus & Comisky, Phila., 1975; chief counsel U.S. Ho. of Reps., Washington, 1975—78; asst. adminstr. NOAA, Washington, 1979—82; dir. ctr. for govtl. responsibility, assoc. prof. law U. Fla. Holand Law Ctr., 1982—86; dean Albany Law Sch., 1986—91, dean emeritus, prof. law, 1991—95; dean U. Tulsa Coll. of Law, Okla., 1995—2004, dean emeritus, prof. law, 2004—07; dean U. Akron Sch. Law, 2007—. Chmn. Select Commn. on Disabilities, NY, Spl. Commn. on Fire Svcs.; bd. advs. Ctr. Oceans Law and Policy; mem. corrections task force Pa. Gov.'s Justice Commn., 1971—75; adv. task force on cts. Nat. Adv. Commn. on Criminal Justice Standards and Goals, 1972—74; mem. com. on proposed standard jury instrns. Pa. Supreme Ct., 1974—81; lectr. in law Temple U., 1971—75; mem. faculty Pa. Coll. Judiciary, 1975—77; adj. prof. law Georgetown U., 1977—81; dean-elect U. Akron Sch. Law, Ohio, 2007—. Author (with Steven H. Goldblatt): (non-fiction) Analysis and Commentary to the Pennsylvania Crimes Codes, 1973; author: Handbook for Trial Judges, 1976, Law and Theology, 2005, (non-fiction) Rehnquist Court: A Retrospective, 2002; editor (in chief): (jour.) Jour. Transnat. Law, Columbia Law Sch., 1968; contbr. articles to legal pubs. Chmn. N.Y. region, mem. D.C. bd. Anti-Defamation League, 1977—78, chmn. N.Y. region, mem. nat. leadership coun.; exec. v.p. Urban League Northeastern N.Y. and Tulsa Urgan League; state chair exec. com. Okla. Anti-Defamation League; mem. magnet schs. task force Tulsa Pub. Schs., 2000, mem. woods task force, 2003—04; mem. Okla. Ethics Commn., 2002—04; v.p. at. Jewish Coun. on Pub. Affairs; pres. Tulsa Met. Ministry, Jewish Fedn. Tulsa; bd. dirs. Coun. on Aging and Disability; pres. Jewish Fedn.; mem. exec. com Nat. Conf. for Cmty. and Justice. Fellow Intenat., Columbia U. Law Sch.; scholar Stone. Mem.: ABA (del. young lawyers sect. exec. bd. 1973—75), Fund for Modern Cts. (bd. dirs.), Am. Law Inst., Am. Arbitration Assn. (referee N.Y. State Commn. on Jud. Discipline), Am. Soc. Internat. Law, Nat. Dist. Attys. Assn., Am. Judicature Soc. (bd. dirs.), Fed. Bar Assn., Fla. Bar Assn., Pa. Bar Assn. (exec. com. young lawyers sect. 1973—75), Phila. Bar Assn. (chmn. young lawyers sect. 1974—75), Albany County Bar Assn., N.Y. State Bar Assn., United Jewish Fedn. Northeastern N.Y. (v.p., pres. elect), Cardozo Soc., B'nai B'rith (v.p. lodge 1973—75), Sword Soc., Hudson-Mohawk Assn. Coll. and Univs. (v.p.), Temple U. Liberal Arts Alumni Assn. (v.p. 1971—75). Office: C Blake McDowell Law Ctr Akron OH 44325-2901 Home Phone: 918-645-7837, 918-749-3888; Office Phone: 330-972-6361.*

BELTER, WESLEY R., state legislator; b. Fargo, ND, Apr. 18, 1945; s. Wesley R. and Rachel (Dimmer) B.; m. Judy Grauman; children: Michael, Matthew, Mark. BS, MS, .D. State U., 1970. Farmer; mem. N.D. Ho. of Reps. from 22d dist., 1985—. Mem. Fin. and Taxation Com. N.D. Ho. of Reps., chmn. Transp. Com. Mem. drug adv. bd. Leonard Sch. Major N.D. Air Nat. Guard. Mem. Am. Legion, N.D. Stockmen's Assn., Lions (pres.), Farm Bur. Republican. Address: 15287 47th St SE Leonard ND 58052-9763

BELTING, HANS, art historian, educator, writer; b. Andernach, Germany, 1935; PhD, U. Mainz, Germany, 1959; LittD (hon.), Courtauld Inst. U. London, 2003. Prof. art history U. Heidelberg, Germany, 1970—80, U. Munich, Germany, 1980—93; prof. art history and media theory Staatliche Hochschule Fur Gestaltung, Karlsruhe, Germany, 1993—2002, prof. emeritus, 2002—; European Chair College de France, 2002—03; Mary Jane Crowe Prof. Art History Northwestern U., Chgo., 2003—. Has held vis. appointments Harvard U., Columbia U.; Getty Vis. Prof., Buenos Aires, 2002. Co-author: Mosaics and Frescoes of St. Mary Pammakaristos (Fethiye Camii) at Istanbul, 1978, Patronage in Thirteenth-Century Constantinople: An Atelier of Late Byzantine Book Illumination and Calligraphy, 1978; author: The End of the History of Art?, 1987, Max Beckmann: Tradition as a Problem in Modern Art, 1990, Likeness and Presence: A History of the Image Before the Era of Art, 1993, The Germans and Their Art: A Troublesome Relationship, 1998, The Invisible Masterpiece: The Modern Myths of Art, 2001, Hieronymus Bosch: The Garden of Earthly Delights, 2002, Art History After Modernism, 2003, Image and Its Public in the Middle Ages: Form and Function of Early Paintings of the Passion, others. Recipient Disting. Lifetime Achievement Award for Writing on Art, Coll. Art Assn., 2004. Mem.: Academia Europaea, Heidelberger Akademie der Wissenschaften, Orden pour le merite fur Wissenschaften und Kunste, Germany, Inst. Advanced Study, Berlin, Am. Acad. Arts and Sciences, Medieval Acad. Am. Office: Northwestern U Dept Art History Kresge Centennial Hall 1880 Campus Dr Evanston IL 60208-2208

BELTON, Y. MARC, food products executive; B in Econ. and Environ. Studies, Dartmouth Coll., 1981; MBA in Mktg. and Fin., U. Pa., 1983. Various positions General Mills, 1983-91, v.p., 1991-99, pres. Snack Products div. Mpls., 1999—. Office: General Mills Inc PO Box 1113 One General Mills Blvd Minneapolis MN 55440-1113

BELYTSCHKO, TED, engineering educator; b. Proskurov, Ukraine, Jan. 13, 1943; arrived in US, 1950; s. Stephan and Maria B.; m. Gail (Eisenhart), Aug. 1967; children: Peter, Nicole, Justine. BS in Engring. Sci., Ill. Inst. Tech., 1965, PhD in Mechanics, 1968; PhD (hon.), U. Liege, 1997; Doctorate (hon.), Ecole Ctrl., Paris, 2004, U. Lyon, 2006. Asst. prof. structural mechanics U. Ill., Chgo., 1968—73, assoc. prof., 1973—76, prof., 1976—77; Walter P. Murphy prof. and McCormick Disting. prof. mech. engring. Northwestern U., Evanston, Ill., 1977—, chair mech. engring., 1998—2002. Editor (assoc.): (jour.) Computer Methods in Applied Mech. and Engring., 1977—, Jour. Applied Mechanics, 1979—85; editor: Nuc. Engring. and Design, 1980—88, Engring. with Computers, 1984—98, Internat. Jour. Numerical Methods in Engring., 1998—; hon. editor: Internat. Jour. Computational Methods. Chmn. U.S. Nat. Com. on Theoretical and Applied Mechanics, 2004—06. NDEA Fellow, 1965-68; recipient Thomas Jaeger prize Internat. Assn. Structural Mechanics in Reactor Tech., 1983; Japanese Soc. Mech. Engr. Computational Mechanics Award, 1993; Gold medal Internat. Conf. on Computational Engring. and Sci., 1996; Computational Mechanics Award, Internat. Assn. for Computational Mechanics, 1998; Gauss Newton medal, 2002. Fellow: ASME (chmn. applied mechanics divsn. 1991, Pi Tau Sigma Gold medal 1975, Timoshenko medal 2001), Am. Acad. Arts and Scis.; mem.: NAE, ASCE (chmn. engring. mechanics divsn. 1982, Walter Huber Rsch. Prize 1977, Structural Dynamics and Materials Award 1990, Theodore von Karman medal 1999), Am. Acad. Mechanics (pres. 2004), Shock and Vibration Inst. (Baron medal 1999), U.S. Assn. Computational Mechanics (pres. 1992—94, von Neumann medal 2001, Computational Structural Mechanics Award 1997). Office: Northwestern Univ Mech Engring Dept 2145 Sheridan Rd Evanston IL 60208-3111 Office Phone: 847-491-7270. Business E-Mail: tedbelytschko@northwestern.edu.

BELZ, MARK, lawyer; b. Marshalltown, Iowa, July 19, 1943; s. Max Victor and Jean (Franzenburg) B.; m. Linda Cole, July 24, 1965; children: Aaron Sanderson, Jane Evangelyn. BA, Covenant Coll., Lookout Mountain, Ga., 1965; JD, U. Iowa, Iowa City, 1970; MDiv, Covenant Theol. Sem., St. Louis, 1981. Bar: Iowa 1970, Mo. 1976. Ptnr. Rosenberger, Peterson, Conway & Belz, Muscatine, Iowa, 1970-72, Keyes & Crawford, Cedar Rapids, Iowa, 1972-78, Belz & Belz, St. Louis, 1983-87; prin. Belz & Beckemeier, P.C., St. Louis, 1987-94, Belz & Jones, P.C., Clayton, Mo., 1995—. Author: Suffer the Little Children, 1989. Bd. dirs. Westminster Acad., 1977-85, Covenant Coll., 1972-81, Cono Christian Sch., 1993—; moderator Presbyn. Ch. Am., Atlanta, 1991-92, mem. standing jud. com., 1989—. Named Alumnus of Yr., Covenant Coll., 1989. Republican. Home: 7777 Bonhomme Ave Ste 1605 Saint Louis MO 63105-1941

BELZ, RAYMOND T., manufacturing executive; b. Chgo., 1941; BS, St. Vincent Coll., 1962; MBA, Ind. U., 1964. Sr. mgmt. USG Corp., Chgo., 1964-94, v.p., controller, 1994-96, v.p. fin. ops. N.Am. Gypsum & Worldwide Ceilings, sr. v.p., controller, 1999—.

BELZER, IRVIN V., lawyer; b. Kansas City, Apr. 6, 1948; BA, Oberlin Coll., 1970; JD cum laude, U. Mo., Kansas City, 1976. Bar: Mo. 1976. Atty. Smith, Gill, Fisher & Butts, Kansas City; mng. ptnr., group co-leader comml. litig. Bryan Cave LLP, Kansas City. Mem. bd. editors: U. Mo. at Kansas City Law Rev., 1975-76; cases and statutes editor: The Urban Lawyer, 1975-76. Mem. ABA, Mo. Bar, Lawyers Assn. Kansas City, Comml. Law League Am., Order of Bench and Robe. Office: Bryan Cave LLP One Kansas City Pl 1200 Main St, Ste 3500 Kansas City MO 64105 Office Phone: 816-391-7677. E-mail: ivbelzer@bryancave.com.

BENDER, BOB, advertising executive; Grad., Columbus Coll. Art & Design. With Lord, Sullivan & Yoder Inc., Worthington, Ohio, 1965—, mem. exec. com., bd. dirs., 1984—, pres., CEO, 1997—. Work included in publs. N.Y. Illustrators Ann., Creativity Ann., Advt. Age, Print, Graphis, Comm. Arts. Recipient N.Y. Art Dir.'s Gold award, 3 Silver awards. Office: Lord Sullivan & Yoder Inc 250 Old Wilson Bridge Rd Worthington OH 43085

BENDER, BRIAN, consumer products executive; Sr. v.p., CFO Sibley's and May D&F Divsn.; corp. v.p. capital planning and analysis May Dept. Stores Co.; sr. v.p., contr. Younkers, Des Moines; sr. v.p., CFO Proffitt's, Jackson, Miss., Egghead.com, ShopKo Stores, Green Bay, Wis., 2000—. Office: Shopko Stores Inc 700 Pilgrim Way Green Bay WI 54304

BENDER, CARL MARTIN, physics professor, consultant; b. Bklyn., Jan. 18, 1943; s. Alfred and Rose (Suberman) B.; m. Jessica Dee Waldbaum, June 18, 1966; children— Michael Anthony, Daniel Eric AB summa cum laude with distinction, Cornell U., 1964; AM, Harvard U., 1965, PhD, 1969. Mem. Inst. for Advanced Study, Princeton, NJ, 1969-70; asst. prof. math. MIT, Cambridge, 1970-73, assoc. prof., 1973-77; prof. physics Washington U., St. Louis, 1977—; research assoc. Imperial Coll., London, 1974. Cons. Los Alamos Nat. Lab., 1979—; vis. prof. Imperial Coll., London, 1986-87, 95-96, 2003-04, 06-, Technion Israel Inst. Tech., Haifa, 1995; vis. prof. dept. math. Imperial Coll, London, 2006-. Author: Advanced Mathematical Methods for Scientists and Engineers, 1978; editor: Am. Inst. Physic series on math. and computational physics; mem. editl. bds. Jour Math. Physics, 1980-83, Advances in Applied Math., 1980-85, Jour. Physics A, 1999-2003; editor-in-chief, Jour. Physics A, 2004—; contbr. more than 230 articles to sci. jours. Trustee Ctr. for Theoretical Study of Phys. Sys., Clark Atlanta U. Recipient Burlington No. Found. Faculty Achievement award, 1985, Fellows award Acad. Sci. St. Louis, 2002; Telluride scholar, 1960-63, NSF fellow, 1964-69, Woodrow Wilson fellow, 1964-65, Sloan Found. fellow, 1973-77, Fulbright fellowship to U.K., 1995-96, Lady Davis fellowship to Israel, 1995, Rockefeller Found. grantee to visit Bellagio Study and Conf. Ctr., 1999; Guggenheim Fellow, 2003-04, fellow Engring. and Phys. Scis. Rsch. Coun., London, 2003-04; Ulam fellow Los Alamos Nat. Lab., 2006—. Fellow: Inst. of Physics (U.K.), St. Louis Acad. Sci., Am. Phys. Soc. (vice chmn. Danny Heineman prize selection com., chmn. Danny Heineman prize selection com.); mem.: Assn. Mems. Inst. Advanced Study (trustee), Phi Kappa Phi, Phi Beta Kappa. Home: 509 Warren Ave Saint Louis MO 63130-4155 Office: Washington U Dept Physics Saint Louis MO 63130 Home Phone: 314-726-2396; Office Phone: 314-935-6216. Business E-Mail: cmb@wustl.edu.

BENDER, HARVEY A., biology professor; b. Cleve., June 5, 1933; m. Eileen Adelle Teper, June 16, 1956; children: Leslie Carol, Samuel David, Philip Michael. AB in Chemistry, Case Western Res. U., 1954, student, 1954-55; MS, Northwestern U., 1957, PhD, 1959. Diplomate Am. Bd. Medical Genetics (founding). Post-doctoral fellow USPHS U. Calif., Berkeley, 1959-60; asst. prof. biology U. Notre Dame, Ind., 1960-64, assoc. prof. Ind., 1964-69, prof. Ind., 1969—. Adj. prof. law U. Notre Dame, 1974-; dir. No. Ind. Regional Genetics Ctr., Meml. Hosp. South Bend (Ind.), 1979-2000, Gt. Lakes Regional Genetics Group, 1991-, Cancer Genetics Ctr., St. Joseph Regional Med. Ctr., 2000—, Cancer Genetics & Risk Assessment Ctr., St. Joseph Med. Ctr., South Bend, Ind.; NSF In-Svc. Inst. prof., fall term 1962-63; vis. prof. human genetics, rsch. assoc. Yale U., 1973-74; vis. prof. zoology So. Ill. U., Carbondale, summer 1978; adj. prof. medical genetics Ind. U., 1979—; vis. prof. natural scis. Washington Coll., Chestertown, Md., 1984; cons. Ednl. Rsch. Coun. Am., 1967-69, Pres.'s Com. on Mental Retardation, 1973, N.J. Inst. Tech., 1975-76, Ind. State Bd. of Health, 1991—, mem. sickle cell commn., 1987—, chronic disease commn., 1989—; genetics cons. Ind. State Bd. Health, 1991-. Editorial reviewer various profl. jours. Bd. dirs. Internat. Rels. Coun., 1961-69, v.p., 1962-64, pres., 1964-65; bd. dirs. Coun. for Retarded of St. Joseph County, 1964-76, 1st v.p., 1967-76; chmn. human rights com. No. Ind. State Hosp., 1980—. Pre-doctoral fellow USPHS, 1957-59, Cross-disciplinary fellow Yale U., 1973-74, Carnegie fellow, 2001-, KANEB fellow U. Notre Dame, 2002—; grantee IH, 1961-67, DOE, 1961—, United Health Svc., 1963-73, NSF, 1978-81, HEW, HHS, others; Carnegie Found. scholar, 2001—; named Disting. Hoosier, Govt. of Ind. 2006. Fellow AAAS; mem. AAUP, Am. Assn. Mental Deficiency, Am. Inst. Biol. Scientists, Am. Soc. Human Genetics, Genetics Soc. Am., Ind. Acad. Sci., Radiation Rsch. Soc., Soc. Devel. Biology, Soc. for Values in Higher Edn., Sigma Xi (regional lectr. 1977—, mem. nat. com. on sci. and society 1978-89, chmn. 1981-89, mem. nat. com. awards, 1981-86, chmn. 1981-83, dir.-at-large 1980-86, bd. dirs. nat. exec. com. 1983-84, long range planning com. 1986—). Office: U Notre Dame Dept Biol Scis Notre Dame IN 46556 Office Phone: 574-631-7075. Business E-Mail: bender@nd.edu.

BENDER, JOHN R., retired state legislator; b. Pitts., Dec. 14, 1938; s. John R. and Ruth (Brown) B.; m. Cookie Bender, 1963 (dec. Dec. 12, 1993); children: Jay, Jennifer. BS, U. Pitts., 1960, MA, 1962, PhD in Higher Edn., 1969. Dir. residence halls, 1960-61, 63-65; admissions asst. Pa. State U., 1961-62, 65-70, counselor, 1993-2000; ret.; dir. student activities Lorain County C. C., 1970-87; mem. Ohio Ho. of Reps. Columbus, 1993—. Mem. Elyria (Ohio) City Coun., 1984-89, 91-92, Elyria Planning Commn., 1984, Health Svc. Agy., 1991-92; bd. dirs. Lorain Internat. Assn.; mem. Lorain County Sr. Citizens Bd. Named Treas. of Yr., Nat. Assn. Campus Activities, 1984, 87, Nat. Environ. award Izaak Walton League, 1988. Mem. Western Res. Civil War Round Table, Urban League, Lorain County C. of C., KC, Phi Delta Kappa (Pitt Hall of Fame award 1960), Omicron Delta Kappa, Sigma Chi. Democrat. Home: 2346 Roxbury Rd Avon OH 44011

BENEDICT, BARRY ARDEN, university administrator; b. Wauchula, Fla., Feb. 7, 1942; s. Clifford Allen and Caroline Mae (Watzke) B.; m. Sharon Gail Parker; children: Erin, Beau, Brooke, Mark. BCE, U. Fla., 1965, MS in Engring., 1967, PhD in Civil Engring., 1968. Rsch. assoc. U. Fla., Gainesville, 1968-69, prof., 1980-86; asst. prof. Vanderbilt U., Nashville, 1969-72, assoc. prof., program dir., 1972-75; assoc. prof. Tulane U., New Orleans, 1975-77, U. S.C., Columbia, 1978-80; prof., dept. head La. Tech. U., Ruston, 1986-88, dean., Jack Thigpen prof., 1988-98; v.p. acad. affairs Rose-Hulman Inst. Tech., Terre Haute, Ind., 1998—. Project dir. La. NSF-EPSCoR, 1989-94; cons. to numerous industries; dir. Inst. Micromanufacturing, 1997-98. Contbr. articles to profl. jours. and chpts. to books. Mem. NSPE (gov.-at-large profl. engrs. in edn. divsn.), La. Dept. Econ. Devel., La. Transp. Rsch. Ctr. (vice chair 1993-98). Methodist. Avocation: jogging.

BENEDICT, ELISE, moving company executive; div.; 1 child, Steve; m. Marvin Howard; children: Kris, Kim Howard Parks. Grad. in journalism and mktg./acctg. Dispatcher, commn. saleswoman, claims mgr., sales mgr. Univ. Moving & Storage Co., Farmington Hills, Mich., gen. mgr., v.p., pres., CEO, 1986—; co-owner Univ. Bus. Interiors, 1996—. Office: Univ Moving & Storage Co 23305 Commerce Dr Farmington Hills MI 48335-2727 Fax: 810-615-4715.

BENES, ANDREW CHARLES, retired professional baseball player; b. Evansville, Ind., Aug. 20, 1967; Student, U. Evansville. With San Diego Padres, 1988-95, Seattle Mariners, 1995, St. Louis Cardinals, 1996-98, Ariz. Diamondbacks, 1998-99; pitcher St. Louis Cardinals, 1999—2002. Mem. U.S. Olympic Baseball Team, 1988, at. League All-Star Team, 1993. Named Sporting News Rookie Pitcher of Yr., 1989. Office: St Louis Cardinals 250 Stadium Plz Saint Louis MO 63102-1722

BENFIELD, LINDA E., lawyer; b. Denver, Colo., Feb. 23, 1960; BA magna cum laude, Colo. U., 1981; JD with honors, U. Chgo., 1985. Bar: Wis. 1985, D.C., Colo. Ptnr. Foley & Lardner LLP, Milw., chairperson environ. regulation practice group. Mem.: State Bar Wis., Colo. Bar Assn., D.C. Bar, Milw. Ballet (chairperson bd. 2003—, gen. counsel & bd. mem. 1996—2003), Racine Lead Adv. Bd. (mem. 1993—96), United Performing Arts Fund (cabinet 2003), Wildspace Dance Co. (bd. pres. 2001—03, bd. mem. 1995—2003). Office: Foley & Lardner LLP 777 E Wisconsin Ave Milwaukee WI 53202-5306 Office Phone: 414-297-5825. Office Fax: 414-297-4900. Business E-Mail: lbenfield@foley.com.

BENFORD, HARRY BELL, naval architect; b. Schenectady, Aug. 7, 1917; s. Frank Albert and Georgia (Rattray) B.; m. Edith Elizabeth Smallman, Apr. 26, 1941; children— Howard Lee, Frank Alfred, Robert James. BSE. in Naval Architecture and Marine Engring, U. Mich., 1940. With Newport News Shipbldg. Co., Va., 1940-48; mem. faculty U. Mich., Ann Arbor, 1948-59, 60-83, prof. naval architecture, 1959-83, prof. emeritus, 1983—, chmn. dept. naval architecture and marine engring., 1967-72. Exec. dir. maritime rsch. adv. com. NRC, 1959-60 Author 4 books, 150 tech. papers. Fellow Soc. Naval Architects and Marine Engrs. (hon. mem., pres.'s award 1957, Linnard prize 1962, Taylor medal 1976), Royal Instn. Naval Architects; mem Tau Beta Pi, Phi Kappa Phi. Office: U Mich Dept Naval Architecture Ann Arbor MI 48109-2145 E-mail: harben@engin.umich.edu.

BENJAMIN, ANN WOMER, former state legislator, lawyer; m. David M. Benjamin; children: Katherine, Johanna. BA magna cum laude, Vandberbilt U., 1975; JD, Case Western Reserve U., 1978. Bar: Ohio. Counsel Arter & Hadden, Cleve., 1984—; mem. Ohio Ho. Reps., Columbus, 1995—2002; dir. Ohio Dept. Ins., Columbus, 2003—. Adj. prof. law Case Western Reserve U., Cleve. Producer: Aurora (Ohio) Comty. Theatre; contbr. articles to Estate Planning. Trustee, advocate Broadway Sch. Music and Arts; former chmn. Aurora (Ohio) Civil Svc. Commn. Mem. Ohio Bar Assn., Cleve. Bar Assn., Portage County Bar Assn., Phi Beta Kappa. Office: Ohio Dept Ins 2100 Stella Ct Columbus OH 43215-1067

BENJAMIN, BEZALEEL SOLOMON, structural engineer, educator; b. Anand, India, Feb. 21, 1938; came to U.S., 1971; s. Solomon and Penninah (Ellis) B.; m. Nora Jacob David, Feb. 25, 1962; children— Ashley Bezaleel, Jennifer Elana B.E. in Civil Engring., Bombay U., India, 1957; D.I.C., Imperial Coll., London, 1958; MS in Engring., London U., 1959, PhD, 1965. Design engr. M.N. Dastur & Co., Bombay, 1961-63; postdoctoral fellow U. Surrey, Eng., 1965-66; prin. lectr. Hatfield Poly., Eng., 1966-71; asst. prof. archtl. engring. U. Kans., Lawrence, 1971-72, assoc. prof., 1972-76, prof., 1976—. Vis. Fulbright prof. Technion, Haifa, Israel, 1987-88. Author: The Analysis of Braced Domes, 1963, Structural Design with Plastics, 1969, Structures for Architects, 1975, Building Construction for Architects and Engineers, 1978, Structural Evolution: An Illustrated History, 1990, Statics, Strengths and Structures for Architects, 1992; (children's book) Susan Altencroft, 1976; (novels) Rampaging Lovers, 1988, A Nazi Among Jews, 1990, Bene Israel Tales, 1991, The Jewish Amendment, 1992, David Rahabi, 1993. Jewish. Avocation: writing. Office: U Kans Sch Architecture Lawrence KS 66045-0001 Home Phone: 785-843-4080; Office Phone: 785-864-4383. Business E-Mail: sben@ku.edu.

BENJAMIN, JANICE YUKON, development executive; b. Kansas City, Mo., Aug. 12, 1951; d. Stanley and Frances (Weneck) Yukon; m. Bert Lyon Benjamin, June 14, 1975; children: Brett David, Blair Yukon. AS, Bradford Coll., 1971; BA, Newcomb Coll., 1973; MA, U. Mo., 1978. Tchr. secondary, dept. chmn. Shawnee Mission (Kans.) Sch. Dist., 1973-80; career counselor Career Mgmt. Ctr., Kansas City, 1980-82, pres., owner, 1982-97; v.p., chief devel. officer Menorah Med. Ctr. Found., 1997—2001; dir., v.p. devel. KU Endowment Assn. U. Kans. Hosp., 2001—. Ptnr. Career Mgmt. Press, Kansas City, 1983-97, The MBL Human Resources Cons. Group, 1989-91. Co-author: How to Be Happily Employed, 1983, 2d edit., 1995; contbr. articles to profl. jours. Bd. dirs. Cmty. Jr. League, Kansas City, 1988-89, v.p., 1989-90, pres.-elect, 1990-91, pres., 1991-92; bd. dirs. Menorah Med. Ctr., Overland Park, Kans., 1995-97, gen. chair grand hosp. opening, 1996; bd. dirs. Menorah Med. Ctr. Aux., 1984-97, auditor, 1990-92, v.p., 1994-96; bd. dirs. Health Partnership Clinic of Johnson County, 1997-2001, sec., 2000-01; bd. dirs. Women's Found. Greater Kansas City, 1991-96, chair bd. devel., 1993-95; bd. dirs. Kansas City Friends of Alvin Ailey, 1992-94, co-chair planning com.; bd. dirs. Ctrl. Exch., Kansas City, vice-chair comms., 2000-01, co-chair capital campaign, 1999-2000, bd. chair 2003-05; mem. adv. bd. women's coun. U. Mo. Kansas City, 1988-89; initiator, sponsor Kansas City Youth Vol. Svc. awards United Way, 1989-90, adv. com. Heart of Am. United Way, 1994-97; mem. Promise Project steering com. Kansas City Consensus, 1994-96; co-chmn. Youth Declaration; adv. com. Vol. Connection, 1998; bd. dirs. The New Reform Temple, 1999-2002; mem. Kans. Pub. Employee Rels. Bd., 2000-03; mem. adv. bd. Health Partnership Clinic, 2001-05, mem. med. adv. bd. First Nat. Bank, 2002-2006; mem. Women's Pub. Svc. Network, 2004—. Recipient Miss T.E.E.N. Encouraging Excellence award, 1990; named one of 25 Up and Comers award Jr. Achievement of Mid. Am., 1994, a woman to watch in 2002, Kansas City Star. Mem. Assn. Acad. Med. Ctr., Greater K.C. Coun. Philanthropy. Republican. Jewish. Office: U Kans Hosp HEO 1215 3901 Rainbow Blvd Kansas City KS 66160 Office Phone: 913-588-1435. Business E-Mail: jbenjamin@kuendowment.org.

BENJAMIN, LLOYD WILLIAM, III, academic administrator; b. Painesville, Ohio, Sept. 2, 1944; s. Lloyd William and Shirley M (Emmett) Benjamin; m. Wieke van der Weijden; children: Saskia Jansje, Lloyd William. BA, Emory U., 1966; PhD, U. N.C., 1973. Prof. art history East Carolina U., Little Rock, 1970-76; prof. U. Ark., Little Rock, 1976—95, dean fine arts, 1983-88, dean arts and humanities, 1988-95; v.p. acad. affairs Valdosta State U., 1995-2000; pres. Ind. State U., 2000—. Pres. ISU Found. Author: History Early Netherlandish Painting, 1977, Art of Designed Environments-Netherlands, 1983; co-author: Drawings from the Collection of Herbert and Dorothy Vogel, 1986; also articles. Mem. Arts and Humanities Commn., 1990-91; pres. Ark. Endowment for Humanities, 1986, Friends of KLRE/KUAR, 1990. Mem.: Am. Assn. State Colls. and Univs. (AASCU) (state rep.). Office: Office of Pres Ind State U 217 N Sixth St Terre Haute IN 47809 Office Phone: 812-237-4000. E-mail: president@indstate.edu.

BENNANE, MICHAEL J., former state legislator; b. Detroit, Jan. 27, 1945; s. John M. and Harriet (Fortner) B. BA, Wayne State U., 1970, JD, 1997. Mem. Mich. State Ho. of Reps., 1977-97; pres. Bennane and Assocs., Detroit, 1997—. Assoc. spkr. pro tem, 1985-88; tchr. Christ the King Sch., Detroit, 1968-69; tchr., footbal lcoach St. Agatha H.S., 1969-74; ins. estate planner N.Am. Life Assurance Co., 1975-76. Transp. coord. Kennedy for Pres., 1972; state press. coord. McGovern for Pres., 1972; field coord. Reuther for Cong., 1974; mem. Emerson Cmty Homwowners Orgn., 17th Dist. Dems., Northwest Cmty. Orgn. Recipient Coach of Yr. award, Detroit News, 1969. Home: 9355 W Outer Dr Detroit MI 48219-4059

BENNER, RICHARD EDWARD, JR., marketing consultant, volunteer, investor; b. Jersey City, Dec. 7, 1932; s. Richard E. and Dorothy (Linstead) B.; m. Virginia Hart; children: Linda, Richard III, Christopher. BS, Lehigh U., 1954; postgrad., NYU, 1959-63. Sales exec. IBM Corp, Norwalk, Conn., 1955-58; with Avon Products, Inc., YC, 1959-78, group v.p. mktg. and internat., 1972-78; divsn. exec. v.p. Sara Lee, Kansas City, Mo., 1979-86; mktg. cons. Kansas City, 1987—. Bd. dirs. Game Hill, Inc., Weston, Mo., exec. com., chmn., bd, dirs., cons. Exec. Svc. Corp., 1993—; LINC, Local Investment commn., 21st Century Initiative; mentor Helzberg Entrepreneurial Mentoring Program, 1998—. Bd. dirs., pres. Northland Homes Partnership for the Homeless, 1988-94; active Eccumedia, 1987-89; maj. corp. com. chmn. United Way, N.Y.C., 1976; Rep. committeeman, Bergan County, 1973; mem. SCORE, 1990—, vice chmn., 1991-92; vice chair cmty. rels. Exec. Svc. Corps, 1990—, chmn., 1993-97, dir., 1997—; trustee Shepherd Ctr. North, 2000—; Stephen minister Luth. Ch., 1998—. With inf. U.S. Army, 1955-56. amed Mentor of Yr. (Kansas City), Helzberg Entrepreneuriel Mentoring Program, 1995—. Mem. Direct Selling Assn. Edn. Found. (bd. dirs. 1982-84). Clubs: Beaverkill Trout (Livingston Manor, N.Y.) (bd. dirs. 1975-78); Old Pike Country (bd. dirs. 1987-90). Lodges: Rotary (bd. dirs., Polio Plus area coord., past pres.). Avocations: fly fishing, investing, gardening. Home and Office: 4404 NW Normandy Ln Kansas City MO 64116-1553

BENNET, RICHARD W., III, retail executive; With May Dept. Stores Co., 1976—, pres., Famous-Barr St. Louis, pres., CEO Kaufmann's Pitts., vice chmn. St. Louis, 2000—. Office: May Dept Stores Co 611 Olive St Saint Louis MO 63101

BENNETT, BRUCE W., retired construction executive, civil engineer; b. St. Joseph, Mo., Dec. 24, 1930; s. Bruce W. and Laura Louella (Clark) B.; m. Barbara Gail Haase, July 26, 1957; children: Stacy Suzanne, Bruce W. BS in Civil Engring., U. So. Calif., 1954. Project mgr. George A. Fuller & Co., Chgo., 1956-61; contract mgr. Huber, Hunt & Nichols, Indpls., 1961-70, v.p., 1970-82, exec. v.p., 1982-84, pres., 1984-95, ret., 1995. Pres. Hunt Corp., 1988-95, bd. dirs. Served to capt. USAF, 1954-57 Mem. Archimedes Circle, David Wilson Assocs., Newcomen Soc. Clubs: Indpls. Athletic, Skyline (Indpls.). Republican. Avocations: tennis, golf. Home: 437 Seville Ave Newport Beach CA 92661-1528

BENNETT, DICK, college basketball coach; b. Pitts., Apr. 20, 1943; m. Anne; children: Kathi, Amy, Tony. BS in phys. edn., Ripon Coll., 1965; MEd, UW-Stevens Point. Basketball coach West Bend (Wis.) HS, 1965-66; coach various Wis HS teams, 1966-76, UW-Stevens Point, 1976-85, UW-Green Bay, 1985-95, U. Wis., Madison, 1995—2000, Wash. St. U., Pullman, 2003—06. 1st team at U. Wis. (17-15) appeared in 1996 N.I.T.; 2d team (18-10) made 2d U. Wis. appearance in .C.A.A. tournament in 50 yrs., put together sch.'s 1st 6-game winning streak since 1951. Named WSUC Coach of Yr., 1982, 1985, NAIA Coach of Yr., 1984, AIA Area IV Coach of Yr., 1985, Mid-Continent Coach of Yr., 1990, 1992, NABC Dist. 11 Coach of Yr., 1992, 1994, Basketball Times Midwest Coach of Yr., 1994. Achievements include 21-yr. collegiate coaching record, 395-214 (.649). Office: Bohler Athletic Complex Wash State Univ Basketball PO Box 641602 Pullman WA 99164-1602

BENNETT, DOUGLAS CARLETON, academic administrator; b. Rochester, NY, June 25, 1946; s. Frank Clinton Jr. and Roberta Lincoln (Evans) B.; m. Dulany Young Ogden, June 20, 1981 (div. 1993); 1 child, Thomas Baldrige; m. Ellen Trout, 1997. BA magna cum laude, Haverford Coll., 1968; M of Philosophy, Yale U., 1971, PhD, 1976. Asst. prof. dept. polit. sci. Temple U., Phila., 1976-80, assoc. prof., 1980-88, prof., assoc. dean Coll. Arts and Scis., 1988-89; provost Reed Coll., Portland, Oreg., 1989-93; exec. dir. Portland Area Libr. Sys., 1993-94; v.p. Am. Coun. Learned Socs., NYC, 1994-97; pres. Earlham Coll., Richmond, Ind., 1997—. Author: Transnational Corporations v.s. the State, 1985; contbr. numerous articles and book revs. to polit. sci. jours. Mem. nat. community rels. com. Am. Friends Svc. Commn., Phila., 1982-86, mem. Latin Am. panel internat. div., 1985-89, clk. Latin Am. panel, 1988-89; bd. trustees Germantown Friends Sch., 1985-89, Friends Sem., N.Y.C., 1996-97; trustee Germantown monthly meeting Soc. of Friends Ch., 1984-89. Recipient Alumni award Haverford Coll., 1988; fellow Woodrow Wilson Internat. Ctr. for Scholars, 1980-81; fellowship grantee Am. Coun. Learned Socs./Social Sci. Rsch. Coun., 1976-77, Carnegie Endowment for Internat. Peace, 1976-77. Mem. Ctr. for Rsch. Librs. (bd. dirs. 1997—). Democrat. Avocations: reading, films. Office: Earlham Coll 801 National Rd W Richmond IN 47374-4021 E-mail: dougb@earlham.edu.

BENNETT, GEORGE H., JR., lawyer, healthcare company executive; b. 1952; BS, U. Miami, 1975; JD, Ohio State U., 1978. Bar: Ohio 1978. Assoc. Mortiz McClure Hughes & Kerscher, 1978-80, Baker & Hostetler, 1980-83; gen. counsel Cardinal Distbn. Inc., 1984-86, v.p., 1986-91, v.p., chief adminstrv. officer, 1991-94; exec. v.p., gen. counsel Cardinal Health Inc., Dublin, Ohio, 1994-99. Office: Cardinal Health Inc 7000 Cardinal Pl Dublin OH 43017-1092

BENNETT, GRACE, publishing executive; Adminstrv. mgr. Detroit Free Press. Office: Detroit Free Press 600 W Fort St Detroit MI 48226-2706

BENNETT, JAMES E., finance company executive; m. Leigh Bennett; three children. BS, Cornell U., 1965; JD, Harvard U., 1968. Various dir. positions McKinsey's Co., Cleve. and Pitts., 1982-93; sr. exec. v.p., strategic and operational svcs. Key Corp, Cleve., 1998—. Past chmn. Cleve./San Jose Ballet; past chmn. Vis. Com., Weatherhead Sch. Mgmt., Case Western Res. U.; bd. dirs. The Cleve. Found., Cleve. Initiative for Edn., United Way Svcs. in Cleve.; chmn. Greater Cleveland Media Devel. Corp.

BENNETT, JON, state legislator; Mem. Ho. of Reps., Jefferson City, 1995—; mem. transp., labor, mcpl. corp. and higher edn. coms.; mem. appropriations com. for end. and public safety; mem. Ho. of Reps., Jefferson City. Republican.

BENNETT, LOREN, state legislator; b. Jan. 17, 1951; Grad., Schoolcraft Coll. Clk. Canton Twp., Mich.; mem. Mich. Senate from 8th dist., Lansing, 1995—. Chmn. natural resources and environ. affairs com. Mich. State Senate, vice chair fin. svc. com., local, urban & state affairs com. Address: PO Box 30036 Lansing MI 48909-7536

BENNETT, MARK WARREN, federal judge, lawyer, educator; b. Milw., June 4, 1950; BA in Polit. Sci., Gustavus Adolphus Coll., 1972; JD, Drake U., 1975. Bar: Iowa 1975, U.S. Dist. Ct. (so. dist.) Iowa 1975, U.S. Dist. Ct. (no. dist.) Iowa 1978, U.S. Ct. Appeals (7th cir.) 1981, U.S. Supreme Ct. 1978. Ptnr. Babich, Bennett and Nickerson, Des Moines, 1975—; judge US Dist. Ct. (no. dist.) Iowa, Sioux City, 1994—, chief judge, 1999—. Vis. prof. polit. sci. and sociology U. S.D., Vermillion, 1975-76; asst. prof. law enforcement adminstrn. Western Ill. U., Macomb, 1976-77; adj. prof. law Drake U., Des Moines, 1981—; lectr. law U. Iowa, summers 1984-85; guest lectr. on civil rights, employment discrimination and constl. litigation, 1981—. Del. Dem. Nat. Conv., 1972; trustee Legal Aid Soc. Polk County, 1978-83, pres. 1980-81; bd. dirs. ACLU, 1987—. Named Civil Libertarian of Yr. Iowa Civil Liberties Union, 1986. Fellow Iowa Acad. Trial Lawyers; mem. Iowa Bar Assn. (com. legal aid 1985—, study com. women and minorities involvement in bar assn. and jud. system Iowa 1987—, com. labor law 1988-89), Polk County Bar Assn. (pro bono com. 1985—), Iowa Assn. Trial Lawyers (co-chmn. amicus curiae com. 1986—, co-chmn. constl. law com. 1987—). Avocations: making brass mobiles, gardening, golf. Office: US Dist Ct Fed Bldg 320 6th St Ste 311 PO Box 838 Sioux City IA 51102-0838 Business E-Mail: mark_bennett@iand.uscourts.gov.

BENNETT, PATRICIA ANN, radio executive; 1 child, Jessica. BA in Communications, Sangamon State U., 1978, MA in Communications, 1981. Vol. coord. Sta. WSSR-FM, Springfield, Ill., 1977-79; sta. mgr. Stas. WRRS, KMUW, Wichita, Kans., 1979-85; gen. mgr. Sta. KGOU, Norman, Okla., 1985-87; mgr. sta. grant programs Corp. for Pub. Broadcasting, Washington, 1987-89; dir., gen. mgr. Sta. KWMU-FM, St. Louis, 1989—. Bd. dirs. NPR, 1992-94, 95-97; participant NPR Pub. Radio Conf., 1979-90, Pub. Broadcasting Svc. Conf., 1987-89, Corp. for Pub. Broadcasting Conf., 1977-80, Rocky Mountain Pub. Radio Meetings, 1987-89, SECA Meetings, 1987-89; bd. dirs. Pub. Radio in Mid-Am. Conf., 1986-88; mem. gerontology faculty Wichita State U., 1983-84; promotion and pub. svc. announcer Sta. KPTS-TV, Wichita, 1979-80; judge coord. Ohio State Awards, 1986-87. Mem. adv. com. for handicapped svcs. Wichita State U., 1980-82. Mem. Pub. Telecommunication Fin. Mgmt. Assn. (bd. dirs. 1990—), Alpha Epsilon Rho (pres. 1979-84, advisor 1990). Office: Sta KWMU-FM U Mo-St Louis 8001 Natural Bridge Rd Saint Louis MO 63121-4401

BENNETT, ROBERT THOMAS, political organization administrator, lawyer, accountant; b. Columbus, Ohio, Feb. 8, 1939; s. Francis Edmund and Mary Catherine (Weiland) Bennett; m. Ruth Ann Dooley, May 30, 1959; children: Robert Thomas, Rose Marie. BS, Ohio State U., 1960; JD, Cleve. Marshall Law. Sch., 1967. Bar: Ohio 1967. CPA Ernst and Ernst, Cleve., 1963—63; with tax asessing dept. Cuyahoga County Auditor's Office, Ohio, 1963—70; mem. firm. Bartunek, Bennett, Garofoli and Hill, 1975—79; mem. firm Bennett & Klonowski, 1979—83, Bennett & Harbarger, 1983—88. Contbr. articles to profl. pubs. Vice chmn. Cuyahoga Rep. Orgn., 1974—88; chmn. Ohio Rep. Party, 1988—; mem. Rep. Nat. Com., 1988—; chair Midwestern State Chmn.'s Assn.; bd. dirs. U. Hosp. Cleve./Southwest Gen. Health Ctr. Mem.: ABA, Capital Hill Club Washington, Citizens League Club, Ohio Soc. CPA, Am. Inst. CPA, Am. Soc. Atty.-CPA. Republican. Roman Catholic. Office: Ohio Rep Party 211 S 5th St Columbus OH 43215-5203 Home: 10810 Edgewater Dr Cleveland OH 44102-6133*

BENNETT, ROBERT WILLIAM, law educator; b. Chgo., Mar. 30, 1941; s. Lewis and Henrietta (Schneider) Bennett; m. Harriet Trop, Aug. 19, 1979. BA, Harvard U., 1962, LLB, 1965. Bar: Ill. 1966. Legal asst. FCC commr. Nicholas Johnson, 1966-67; atty. Chgo. Legal Aid Bur., 1967-68; asso. firm Mayer, Brown & Platt, Chgo., 1968-69; faculty Northwestern U. Sch. Law, Chgo., 1969—, prof. law, 1974—, dean, 1985-95, Nathaniel L. Nathanson prof., 2002—. Author (with LaFrance, Schroeder and Boyd): Handbook on Law of the Poor, 1973; author: Talking it Through: Puzzles of American Democracy, 2003, Taming the Electoral College, 2006. Knox Meml. fellow, London Sch. Econs., 1965—66. Fellow: Am. Bar Found. (pres., bd. dirs.); mem.: ABA, Am. Law Inst., Chgo. Coun. Lawyers (pres. 1971—72). Home: 2130 N Racine Ave Chicago IL 60614-4002 Office: Northwestern U Sch Law 357 E Chicago Ave Chicago IL 60611-3059 Office Phone: 312-503-8430. Office Fax: 312-503-5950. Business E-Mail: r-bennett@law.northwestern.edu.

BENNETT, THOMAS, orchestra executive; Exec. dir. S.D. Symphony Orch., Sioux Falls, 1996—. Bd. mem. Am. Symphony Orchestra League. Office: SD Symphony Orchestra Ste 116 300 N Dakota Ave Sioux Falls SD 57104-6020 E-mail: tombennett@sdsymphony.org.

BENNING, JOSEPH RAYMOND, principal; b. Streator, Ill., May 23, 1956; s. Joseph Charles and Shirley Ann (Smith) B.; m. Katherine Marie Turner, Apr. 24, 1976; children: Jennifer Nichole, Joseph Donald. BA, Augustana Coll, 1978; MS in Edn., No. Ill. U., 1988. Cert. state supr., teaching, Ill. Tchr., coach Fulton (Ill.) High Sch., 1978—79; recreation dir. Fulton Recreation Corp., 1979; tchr., coach Streator (Ill.) High Sch., 1979—80, Woodland High Sch., Streator, 1980—83; program dir. Ill. State Bd. Edn., Ottawa, 1983—85; prin. St. Mary Grade Sch., Streator, 1985—89; assoc. supt. schs. Cath. Diocese Peoria, Ill., 1989—91, supt. schs. Ill., 1991—94; prin. St. Bede Acad., Peru, Ill., 1994—99, St. Columba Sch., Ottawa, Ill., 1999—2005, Sacred Heart Sch., Lombard, Ill., 2005—. Pres. Streator Youth Football League, 1984-90; adv. bd. Streator High Sch., 1985-89; prins. adv. bd. Cath. Diocese Peoria, 1987-89. Recipient CJ McDonald award Streator Youth Football League, 1989. Mem. ASCD, Nat. Cath. Edn. Assn., Nat. Assn. Secondary Sch. Prin., Nat. Assn. Elem. Sch. Prin., Ill. Elem. Sch. Assn., Cath. Conf. Ill., KC. Roman Catholic. Avocations: sports, music. Office: Sacred Heart Sch 322 W Maple Lombard IL 60148 Office Phone: 630-629-0536. Personal E-mail: benningjr@hotmail.com.

BENNINGTON, RONALD KENT, lawyer; b. Circleville, Ohio, July 16, 1936; s. Ralph P. and Delorice (Dudley) B.; m. Barbara Schumm, June 19, 1959; children; Scott C., Amy E. BA magna cum laude, Kenyon Coll., 1958; JD summa cum laude, Ohio State U., 1961. Assoc. Black, McCuskey, Souers & Arbaugh, Canton, Ohio, 1961-65, ptnr., 1965—. Sec. Hoover Worldwide Corp., 1969-86; bd. dirs. United Hard Chrome, Inc. Bd. trustees Plain Twp., Canton, 1972-78, Malone Coll., Canton, 1982—, chmn. 1984-86, Timken Mercy Med. Ctr., Canton; adv. com. Kenyon Coll., Gambier, Ohio; mem. Leadership Canton; bd. dirs. ARC, Canton; fundraising United Way Fund Drive; trust com. Hoover Found.; ambassador Ohio Found. Ind. Colls.; steering com. Pro Football Hall of Fame, 1985—; Big Ten football ofcl., 1984—; trustee The Hoover Found., Canton, Greater Canton C. of C.; bd. assocs. Union Coll., Alliance, Ohio. Fellow Am. Bar Found., Ohio State Bar Found.; mem. ABA, Ohio Bar Assn., Stark County Bar Assn., Greater Canton C. of C. (bd. trustees), Ea. Ohio Football Ofcls. Assn. (pres. 1986—), Stark County Law Libr. Assn. (pres.). Republican. Presbyterian. Home: 3528 Darlington Rd NW Canton OH 44708-1714 Office Phone: 330-458-4220.

BENSELER, DAVID P., foreign language educator; b. Balt., Jan. 10, 1940; s. Ernest Parr and Ellen Hood Escar (Turnbaugh) B.; m. Suzanne Shelton, May 25, 1985; children: James Declan, Derek Justin. BA, West Wash. U., 1964; MA, U. Oreg., 1966, PhD, 1971. From asst. prof. to assoc. prof. Wash. State U., 1969—77; prof., chair dept. German, Ohio State U., 1977—91; chair dept. modern langs. and lits. Case Western Res. U., 1991-98, Louis D. Beaumont U. prof. humanities, 1991-98, Emile B. de Sauzé prof. modern lang. and lit., 1998—2004, Emile B. de Sauzé prof. emeritus modern lang. and lit., 2004—. Disting. vis. prof. fgn. langs. U.S. Mil. Acad., West Point, N.Y., 1987-88, N.Mex. State U., Las Cruces, 1989; founding dir. German Studies program Case Western Reserve U. and Max Kade Ctr. for German Studies; mem. numerous coms. Case Western Res. U., U.S. Military Acad., U.S. Naval Acad., U. Akron, Ohio State U., Wash. State U., Ind. U., Emory U., U. Md., U. Cin., U. Wis., Pa. State U., U. Va., U. Mich., various others; lectr., panel mem., workshop convr, cons. in field. Compiler, editor: (with Suzanne S. Moore) Comprehensive Index to the Modern Language Journal, 1916-1996, MLJ Electronic Index, 1997—; author/editor more than 75 other books, bibliographies, jours.; contbr. chpts. to books and articles to profl. jours. With USN, 1957—63. Decorated Bundesverdienstkreuz I. Klasse (Germany); recipient Army Commendation medal for disting. civilian svc. U.S. Mil. Acad., 1988; Lilly Found. Faculty Renewal fellow Stanford U., 1975, Fulbright grad. fellow, 1967-68, NDEA fellow, U. Oreg., 1964-67; various other grants, fellowships, scholarships. Mem. MLA, AAUP, Am. Assn. Applied Linguistics, Am. Assn. Tchrs. of German, Am. Coun. on the Tchg. of Fgn. Langs., Am. Goethe Soc., Am. Soc. for 18th Century Studies, German Studies Assn., Lessing Soc., Soc. German-Am. Studies, Phi Sigma Iota, Sigma Kappa Phi, Delta Phi Alpha. Office Phone: 216-368-3071. Business E-Mail: dpb5@case.edu.

BENSINGER, PETER BENJAMIN, consulting firm executive; b. Chgo., Mar. 24, 1936; s. Benjamin Edward and Linda Elkus (Galston) B.; m. Judith S. Bensinger; children: Peter Benjamin, Jennifer Anne, Elizabeth Brooke, Virginia Brette. BA, Yale, 1958; degree (hon.), San Marcos U., Peru, 1978; LLD (hon.), Dan Kook U., Seoul, Republic of Korea, 1980. Various mktg. positions Brunswick Corp., Chgo., 1958-65, new products mgr., 1966-68; gen. sales mgr. Brunswick Internat., Europe, 1965-66, spl. products mgr., 1966-68; chmn. Ill. Youth Commn., 1969-70; dir. Ill. Dept. Corrections, Chgo., 1970-73; exec. dir. Chgo. Crime Commn., 1973; adminstr. Drug Enforcement Adminstrn., Washington, 1976-81; pres. Bensinger, DuPont & Assocs., Chicago, 1982—. Chmn. Ill. Criminal Justice Info. Authority, 1991—; cons. various orgns.; del. White House Conf. on Corrections, 1971, Drug Abuse, 1988, U.S. Del. to Interpol, 1978. Pres. Lincoln Park Zool. Soc., Chgo., 1962-63; governing life mem., also mem. men's council Chgo. Art Inst.; mem. Ill. Alcoholism Adv. Council, Ill. Law Enforcement Commn., Ill. Council on Diagnosis and Evaluation Criminal Defendants, Ill. Narcotics Adv. Council; adv. com. Center for Studies in Criminal Justice, So. Ill. U., Center for Studies in Criminal Justice, U. Chgo.; vice chmn. ad hoc adv. com. U.S. Dept. Justice Nat. Inst. Corrections; mem. exec. com. Am. Bar Assn. at. Commn. Corrections; chmn. Ill. Task Force on Corrections, 1969; mem. bd. Fed. Prison Industries, Inc., 1973-85; bd. dirs. Jewish Fedn. Met. Chgo., Council Community Services Met. Chgo., Ill. Commn. on Children, Children's Meml. Hosp., Chgo., 1988—; bd. dirs., mem. exec. council Anti-Defamation League; regional bd. dirs. NCCJ; trustee Phillips Exeter Acad.; chmn. nat. law enforcement explorers conf. Boy Scouts Am., 1981, U.S. del. to, Interpol, 1978. Recipient Young Leadership award Jewish Fedn.-Welfare Bds. Met. Chgo., 1969, award for excellence John Howard Assn., 1972, Disting. Svc. award Govt. of Peru, 1978, U.S. Dept. of Justice award, EEO award, 1979, Disting. Svc. medal USCG, 1981, John Phillips award Phillips Exeter Acad., 1990, Lincoln medal Lincoln Acad., 1998, Lifetime Achievement award, Assn. Former Fed. Narcotics Agents, 2006. Mem. Am. Correctional Assn. (bd. dirs.), Assn. State Correctional Adminstrs. (sec. 1971-72, pres. 1972-73), Internat. Assn. Chiefs of Police (mem. exec. com.), Nat. Sheriffs Assn. (life), Chgo. City Club (bd. dirs.), Arts Club, Comml. Club Chgo., Yale Club (N.Y.C.), Shoreacres Club (Lake Bluff), Casino Club (Chgo.). Office: 20 N Wacker Dr Chicago IL 60606-2806

BENSON, AL BOWEN, III, oncologist, educator; b. Buffalo, Dec. 23, 1950; BA, SUNY, 1972; MD, SUNY, Buffalo, 1976. Diplomate Am. Bd. Internal Medicine, cert. med. oncology Am. Bd. Internal Medicine, diplomate internal medicine 1979, med. oncology 1983. Intern U. Wis. Hosps., Madison, 1976—77, resident medicine, 1977—79; co-dir. medicine Nat. Pub. Health Svc., Ill., 1979—81; fellow oncology U. Wis. Hosps., Madison, 1981—84; attending physician Northwestern Meml. Hosp., Chgo., 1984—, Lakeside VA Med. Ctr., Chgo., 1984—. Prof. medicine U. Ill., 1979—81, Northwestern U., 1984—, assoc. dir. clin. investigations, 1995—. Office: Northwestern Univ 676 N St Clair Ste 850 Chicago IL 60611-2998

BENSON, DONALD ERICK, finance company executive; b. Mpls., June 1, 1930; s. Fritz and Annie (Nordstrom) B.; children: Linda K., Nancy A., Stephen D.; m. Roberta Mann, 1992 BBA in Acctg., U. Minn., 1955. CPA, Minn. From staff to partnership Arthur Andersen & Co., Mpls., 1955-68, MEI Corp., Mpls., 1968-86; pres. MEI Diversified Inc., Mpls., 1986-94; exec. v.p. Marquette Fin. Companies, Mpls., 1992—; also bd. dirs. Bd. dirs. Mair Holdings, Inc., Minn. Twins Baseball Club, Mass. Mut. Corp. Investors, Mass. Mut. Participation Investors, Cargo Holdings Internat., Inc., First Calif. Fin. Group, Inc.; dir. Swedish Coun. Am. and its Royal Round Table Chmn. Bethel U. Found., St. Paul; past chmn. Pk. Nicollet Med. Services, Mpls.; past pres. Boys and Girls Clubs, Mpls., Minn. Mem. AICPA, Minn. CPA Soc., Mpls. Club, Interlachen Country Club

BENSON, JACK DUANE, mechanical engineer, research scientist; b. Mich. BSME, U. Mich., 1963, MSME, 1964. Mech. engr. Rsch. and Design Ctr. GM, 1964-98; pres. AFE Cons. Svcs., Commerce Twp., Mich., 1998—. Recipient Soichiro Honda medal ASME, 1997. Fellow Soc. Automotive Engrs. Achievements include research in fuels and their effect on vehicle performance. Office: AFE Cons Svcs 5900 Ford Rd Commerce Township MI 48382-1025

BENSON, JIM, finance company executive; Chmn., pres., chief exec. MetLife affiliate New Eng. Fin.; pres. individual svc. MetLife; chmn., pres., CEO GenAm. Fin. Corp., 2002; interim CEO Nat. Assn. of Insurance and Financial Advisors, 2002—03.

BENSON, JOANNE E., retired lieutenant governor; b. Jan. 4, 1943; m. Robert Benson; 2 children. BS, St. Cloud State U. Mem. Minn. Senate, St. Paul, 1991-94; lt. gov. State of Minn., St. Paul, 1994-98; CEO, Minn. Bus. Acad., St. Paul, 1999—2005.

BENSON, JOHN ALEXANDER, JR., internist, educator; b. Manchester, Conn., July 23, 1921; s. John A. and Rachel (Patterson) B.; children: Peter M., John Alexander III, Susan Leigh, Jeremy P. BA, Wesleyan U., Middletown, Conn., 1943; MD, Harvard Med. Sch., Boston, 1946. Diplomate Am. Bd. Internal Medicine (mem. 1969-91, sec.-treas. 1972-75, pres. 1975-91, pres. emeritus 1991—), Subsplty. Bd. Gastroenterology (mem. 1961-66, chmn. 1965-66). Intern Univ. Hosps., Cleve., 1946-47; resident Peter Bent Brigham Hosp., Boston, 1949-51; fellow Mass. Gen. Hosp., Boston, 1951-53; rsch. asst. Mayo Clinic, Rochester, Minn., 1953-54; asst. in medicine Mass. Gen. Hosp., 1954-59; instr. medicine Harvard U., 1956-59; head divsn. gastroenterology U. Oreg. Med. Sch., Portland, 1959-75, prof. medicine, 1965-93; prof. emeritus Oreg. Health & Sci. U., Portland, 1993—, interim dean Sch. Medicine, 1991—93, dean emeritus, 1993—, asst. dir. Ctr. for Ethics in Health Care, 1992—2003; prof. internal medicine U. Nebr. Coll. Medicine, Omaha, 2003—. Cons. VA Hosps., Madigan Gen. Army Hosp., John A. Hartford Found. Editorial bd.: Am. Jour. Digestive Diseases, 1966-73, The Pharos, 2000—; contbr. articles to profl. jours. Mem. Oreg. Med. Ednl. Found., 1967-73, dir., 1967-73, pres., 1969-72; bd. dirs. N.W. Ctr. for Physician-Patient Comm., 1994-99, Am. Acad. on Physician and Patient, 1994-99, chmn., 1995-98, Found. Med. Excellence, 1996-2003, pres., 1998-2000; trustee Oreg. Health and Sci. U. Found., 1999-2003. With USNR, 1947-49. Mem. AAS, AMA, ACP (master), Am. Gastroenterol. Assn. (sec. 1970-73, v.p. 1975-76, pres.-elect. 1976-77, pres. 1977-78), Am. Clin. and Climatol. Assn. (v.p. 1997), Am. Soc. Internal Medicine, Western Assn. Physicians, North Pacific Soc. Internal Medicine, Am. Fedn. Clin. Rsch., Federated Coun. for Internal Medicine, Am. Assn. Study Liver Disease, Western Soc. Clin. Investigation, Soc. Health and Human Values, Assn. Health Svcs. Rsch., Inst. Medicine NAS, Phi Beta Kappa, Sigma Xi, Alpha Omega Alpha. Office: 983332 Nebr Med Ctr Omaha NE 68198-3332 Office Phone: 402-559-4887. Business E-Mail: jabenson@unmc.edu.

BENSON, JOSEPH FRED, journalist, legal historian; b. St. Louis, Dec. 14, 1953; s. Max and Addie Marie (Klein) B.; m. Sandra Ann Mears, Oct. 29, 2000. AA, St. Louis C.C., 1974; AB cum laude, St. Louis U., 1976, AM, 1977, JD, 1985. Received Semicha St. Louis Beis Din, 2007. Legal historian, archivist Cir. Ct. St. Louis County, Clayton, Mo., 1978-85; columnist St. Louis Daily Record and St. Louis Countian, 1987—2000, spl. corres., 1989—2000, editl. writer, 1990—2000, cons. in constl. law, 1995—2000; editl. writer St. Peters Courier, 1998—2000; jud. archivist Supreme Ct. Mo., Jefferson City, 2000—. Asst. law libr. St. Louis County Ct. House Law Libr., 1979-85; adj. instr. Am. history Harris-Stowe State Tchrs. Coll., St. Louis, 1987; adj. asst. prof. bus. law Lincoln U., Jefferson City, Mo., 2002—; rsch. cons. law firm David C. Godfrey, Clayton, 1981-2000, Zwibelman, Edelman & Walter, Clayton, 1989-95, Law Firm of Scott E. Walter, P.C., 1997-2000; friend of the ct. 21st cir. Cir. Ct. St. Louis County, Mo., 1993-94; instr. Am. history Van Buren (Mo.) R-1 Pub. Schs., 1994-95; instr. Am. history and Am. govt. East Carter County R-II Pub. Schs., Ellsinore, Mo., 1995, U. City (Mo.) HS, 1995-96; Hillel lectr. U. Mo., Columbia, 2004; cons. in field. Columnist: Law In History, 1987-2000; contbr. Wentzville Union (Mo.) Legal Newspaper, 1995-2000; contbr. articles to profl. jours. Judge St. Louis County Bd. Elections, Clayton, 1978-84, supr., 82-84; incorporator Hist. Soc. St. Louis County, 1978, exec. dir., asst. sec., 1979-87, comm. Bicentential U.S. Constn., 1983-91; sexton, prayer leader Shaare Zedek Synagogue, University City, Mo., 1998-2000; pres. Hebrew Cemetery Assn., Jefferson City, 2001—; Chavurah leader on Judaism and Jewish Law, mem. Book Pub. subcom. US Dist. Ct. Ea. Dist. of Mo. Hist. Soc., 2005—; rabbi-in-residence Temple Beth El, Jefferson City, Mo., 2007-. Sam. A. Kessler Meml. scholar, 1981, Project '87: Bicentennial scholar, 1985-91; faculty fellow St. Louis U., 1983, 84. Mem. Am. Soc. Legal History, Supreme Ct. Mo. Hist. Soc., U.S. Supreme Ct. Hist. Soc., B'nai B'rith, Phi Alpha Theta, Phi Theta Kappa. Jewish. Avocations: cooking, tennis, gardening, collecting rare books. Home: 726 Kevin Dr Jefferson City MO 65109 Office Phone: 573-751-8725. Business E-Mail: jbenson@courts.mo.us. E-mail: jfbenson1953@yahoo.com.

BENSON, KEITH A., retail executive; Pres. mall div. Sam Goody and Suncoast Motion Picture Co. Musicland Stores Corp., Minnetonka, Minn., vice-chmn., CFO, 1997—. Office: Musicland Stores 10400 Yellow Cir Dr Minnetonka MN 55343

BENSON, KEVIN E., transportation executive; b. South Africa, Feb. 23, 1947; married. Grad., Witwatersrand Univ., Johannesburg, South Africa. CA, 1971. With Coopers & Lybrand, South Africa; joined Trizec-Hahn Corp., 1977, CFO, 1983—86, pres., 1986—95, CEO, 1987—95; CFO Canadian Airlines Internat., 1995—96, pres., CEO, 1996—2000; pres. Jim Pattison Group, 2000—01; pres., CEO Ins. Corp. British Columbia, 2001—02, Laidlaw Inc., 2002—03, Laidlaw Internat., aperville, Ill., 2003—. Bd. dir. Manulife Financial, 1995—. Office: Laidlaw International Ste 400 55 Shuman Blvd Naperville IL 60563

BENTLEY, CHARLES RAYMOND, geophysics educator; b. Rochester, NY, Dec. 23, 1929; s. Raymond and Janet Cornelia (Everest) B.; m. Marybelle Goode, July 3, 1964 (dec. Oct. 13, 2004); children: Molly Clare, Raymond Alexander. BS, Yale U., 1950; PhD, Columbia U., 1959. Rsch. geophysicist Columbia U., 1952-56; Antarctic traverse leader and seismologist Arctic Inst. N.Am., 1956-59; project assoc. U. Wis., 1959-61, asst. prof., 1961-63, assoc. prof., 1963-68, prof. geophysics, 1968-98, A.P. Crary prof. geophysics, 1987-98, prof. emeritus, 1998—. Recipient Bellingshausen-Lazarev medal for Antarctic rsch. Acad. Scis. USSR, 1971; NSF sr. postdoctoral fellow, 1968-69; NAS-USSR Acad. Sci. exch. fellow, 1977, 90 Fellow AAAS, Am. Geophys. Union, Arctic Inst. N.Am., Am. Polar Soc. (hon., bd. dirs.); mem. AAUP, Soc. Exploration Geophysicists, Internat. Glaciological Soc. (Seligman Crystal award 1990), Am. Quarternary Assn., Oceanography Soc., Am. Geol. Inst., Geol. Soc. Am., Phi Beta Kappa, Sigma Xi. Achievements include research on Antarctic glaciology and geophysics, satellite studies of geomagnetic anomalies, magnetotelluric exploration of Earth structure, satellite radar and laser altimetry, ice coring and drilling services. Office Phone: 608-238-8873. Business E-Mail: bentley@geology.wisc.edu.

BENTLEY, JEFFREY, performing company executive; Grad., U. Wash. Ballet dancer, NYC; from asst. to producing dir. to adminstrv. dir. Seattle Repertory Theatre, 1973-81; exec. dir. Northlight Theatre Co., Evanston, Ill.; mng. dir. dance ctr. Columbia Coll., Chgo., 1983-85; exec. dir. Eugene Ballet Co., Oreg.; dir. DanceAspen Festival and Sch., Aspen, Colo.; exec. dir. Royal Winnipeg Ballet, 1993-96, State Ballet of Mo. (now Kansas City Ballet), Kansas City, Mo., 1998—. Panelist, site visitor NEA, Colo. Coun. Arts, Ill. Arts Coun.; cons. Western States Art Fedn., Santa Fe, Found. Ext. and Devel. Am. Profl. Theatre. EA fellow Wash. State Arts Commn. Office: Kansas City Ballet 1601 Broadway Kansas City MO 64108

BENTON, WILLIAM DUANE, federal judge; b. Springfield, Mo., Sept. 8, 1950; s. William Max and Patricia F. (Nicholson) B.; m. Sandra Snyder, Nov. 15, 1980; children: Megan Blair, William Grant. BA in Polit. Sci. summa cum laude, Northwestern U., 1972; JD, Yale U., 1975; MBA in Accounting, Memphis State U., 1979; student Inst. Jud. Adminstrn., NYU, 1992; LLD (hon.), Ctrl. Mo. State U., 1994; LLM, U. Va., 1995; LLD (hon.), Westminster Coll., 1999. Bar: Mo. 1975; CPA, Mo. Ensign USN, 1972; advanced through grades to capt., 1993; judge advocate USN, Memphis, 1975-79; chief of staff for Congressman Wendell Bailey, Washington, 1980-82; pvt. practice Jefferson City, Mo., 1983-89; dir. revenue Mo. Dept. of Revenue, Jefferson City, 1989-91; judge Mo. Supreme Ct., Jefferson City, 1991—2004, chief justice, 1997-99; judge US Ct. Appeals (8th cir.), Kansas City, Mo., 2004—. Adj. prof. Westminster Coll., 1998-, U. Mo.-Columbia Sch. Law, 1998-. Contbr. articles to profl. jours.; mng. editor Yale Law Jour., 1974-75 Chmn. Multistate Tax Commn. Washington, 1990-91; chmn. Mo. State Employees Retirement System, Jefferson City, 1989-93; regent Ctrl. Mo. State U., 1987-89; dir. Coun. for Drug Free Youth, Jefferson City, 1989-97; mem. Mo. Mil. Adv. Com., 1989-91; mem. Mo. Commn. Intergovernmental Coop., Jefferson City, 1989-91; trustee, deacon 1st Bapt. Ch., Jefferson City. Danforth fellow JFK Sch. Govt. Harvard U., 1990. Mem. AICPA (tax com. 1983—), Mo. Bar Assn. (tax com. 1975—), Mo. Soc. CPA's (tax com. 1983—), Navy League, Mil. Order of World Wars, Vietnam Vets of Am., VFW, Am. Legion, Phi Beta Kappa, Beta Gamma Sigma, Rotary. Baptist. Lt. USN, 1975-80. Capt. JAGC USNR, 1993-2002. Office: 10-20 US Courthouse 400 E 9th St Kansas City MO 64106-2605 Office Phone: 816-512-5815.

BENTZ, DALE MONROE, retired librarian; b. York County, Pa., Jan. 3, 1919; s. Solomon Earl and Mary Rebecca (Wonders) B.; m. Mary Gail Menius, June 13, 1942; children: Dale Flynn, Thomas Earl, Mary Carolyn. AB, Gettysburg Coll., 1939; BSL.S., U. N.C. Chapel Hill, 1940; MS, U. Ill., 1951. With Periodicals dept. U. N.C. Library, Chapel Hill, 1940-41, Serials Dept., Duke U. Library, Durham, N.C., 1941-42; asst. librarian E. Carolina Tchrs. Coll., Greenville, N.C., 1946-48; head processing dept. U. Tenn. Library, Knoxville, 1948-53; assoc. dir. libraries U. Iowa, Iowa City, 1953-70, univ. librarian, 1970-86, univ. librarian emeritus, 1986—. Editor U. Tenn. Library Lectures, 1952; contbr. articles to profl. jours. Pres. Iowa City Bd. Edn., 1962-63 Mem. Iowa Library Assn. (pres., 1959-60), ALA (pres. resources and tech. services div. 1975-76), AAUP, Assn. Coll. and Research Libraries, Beta Phi Mu (pres. 1966-67) Clubs: Triangle (pres. 1958-59), Univ. Athletic (sec. 1979-80). Lutheran. Home: 701 Oaknoll Dr # 430 Iowa City IA 52246-5168 Personal E-mail: dalembentz@hotmail.com.

BENVENISTE, LAWRENCE M., dean; 1 child, Jeffrey. BS in math., U. Calif., Irvine, 1972; PhD in math., U. Calif., Berkeley, 1975. Staff economist for bd. governors FRS, Washington; mem. faculty U. Rochester, U. Pa., Northwestern U.; assoc. prof. fin. Wallace E. Carroll Sch. Mgmt., Boston Coll.; US Bancorp prof. fin. Carlson Sch. Mgmt., U. Minn., Twin Cities, 1996—99, chair fin. dept., 1999—2000, assoc. dean faculty and rsch., 2000—01, interim dean, 2001, dean, prof. fin., 2001—05; dean Goizueta Bus. Sch., Emory U., Atlanta, 2005—, Asa Griggs Candler prof. fin. Bd. dirs. Rimage Corp., 2003—, Alliance Data Systems. Office: Emory U Goizueta Bus Sch 1300 Clifton Rd Atlanta GA 30322 Office Phone: 404-727-6377. Business E-Mail: carol_hagins@bus.emory.edu.

BEN-YOSEPH, MIRIAM, social sciences educator; m. Yoav Ben-Yoseph, Dec. 24, 1974. BA, MA, Hebrew U., Jerusalem; PhD in French Lit., Northwestern U. V.p. market rsch. and tng. Continental Bank; faculty mem. to assoc. prof. Sch. New Learning DePaul U., Chgo., 1991—. Recipient US Prof. of Yr. award, Carnegie Found. for Advancement of Tchg. and Coun. for Advancement and Support of Edn., 2006. Office: Sch New Learning DePaul U 25 E Jackson Chicago IL 60604 Office Phone: 312-362-6560. E-mail: mben@depaul.edu.

BEPKO, GERALD LEWIS, retired academic administrator, law educator; b. Chgo., Apr. 21, 1940; s. Lewis V. and Geraldine S. (Bernath) B.; m. Jean B. Cougnenc, Feb. 24, 1968; children: Gerald Lewis Jr., Arminda B. BS, No. Ill. U., DeKalb, 1962; JD, Chgo. Kent Coll. Law Ill. Inst. Tech., 1965; LLM, Yale U., New Haven, 1972; D of Juridicial Sci. (hon.), Chgo. Kent Coll. Law Ill. Inst. Tech., 2003; LLD (hon.), Ind. U., Bloomington, 2007. Bar: Ill. 1965, U.S. Supreme Ct. 1968, Ind. 1973. Assoc. Ehrlich, Bundesen, Friedman & Ross, Chgo., 1965; spl. agt. FBI, 1965-69; asst. prof. law Ill. Inst. Tech.-Chgo. Kent Coll. Law, 1969-71; prof. Ind. U., Indpls., 1972-86, assoc. dean acad. affairs, 1979-81, dean, 1981-86, v.p., long-range planning, 1986—2003, chancellor, 1986—2002, interim pres., 2002—03, chancellor emeritus, 2003—, trustees prof., 2003—. Vis. prof. Ind. U.-Bloomington, summers, 1976, 77, 78, 80, U. Ill., 1976—77, Ohio State U., 1978—79; cons. and reporter Fed. Jud. Ctr.; bd. dirs. First Ind. Bank/Corp., 1988—2007, Ind. Energy Inc. & Ind. Gas Co., Inc., 1989—97, Indpls. Life Ins. Co., One Am. Ins., M&I Ind. Regional Bd., 2008—; mem. Conf. Commrs. on Uniform State Laws, 1982, mem. permanent editl. bd. for the Uniform Comml. Code, 1993—2004; mem. Ind. Lobby Registration Commn., 1992—2004, vice chair, 1992—96, chair, 1996—2000; mem. Ind. Commn. Higher Edn., 2006—. Author: (with Boshkoff) Sum and Substance of Secured Transactions, 1981; contbr. articles on comml. law to profl. jours. Bd. dirs. Lumina Found. for Edn., Riley Children's Found., 1998—, chair. exec. com., 2004—; bd. trustees Citizen's Gas & Coke Utility, 2002—. Indpls. Chgo. Title and Trust Co. Found. scholar 1962-65; Ford Urban law fellow, 1971-72. Fellow Am. Bar Found., Ind. State Bar, Indpls. Bar Found.; mem. ABA, Ind. State Bar Assn., Indpls. Bar Assn., Country Club Indpls. Methodist. Office: Ind U Sch Law Indpls Inlow Hall 219 530 W New York St Indianapolis IN 46202-3225 Office Phone: 317-278-9240.

BERACHA, BARRY HARRIS, retired food products executive; b. Bronx, NY, Feb. 28, 1942; s. Nissim Macy and Celia Grace (Sides) B.; m. Barbara Marie Capobianco, Dec. 23, 1967; children: Brian, Bradley, Bonnie. BChE, Pratt Inst., 1963; MBA, U. Pa., 1965. Ops. researcher Celanese Corp., 1965-67; tech. economist Sun Oil Co., 1964-65; with Anheuser-Busch Cos., Inc., 1967-96, v.p. corp. planning, 1974-76, v.p., group exec., 1976-96; chmn., CEO Earthgrains Co., Clayton, Mo., 1996—2001; exec. v.p. Sara Lee Corp., Clayton, 2001—03; CEO Sara Lee Bakery Group, Clayton, 2001—03; ret., 2003; non-exec. chmn. Pepsi Bottling Group, Somers, NY, 2007—08.

BERAN, GEORGE WESLEY, veterinary microbiology educator; b. Riceville, Iowa, May 22, 1928; s. John and Elizabeth (Buresh) B.; m. Janice Ann Van Zomeren, Dec. 21, 1954; children: Bruce, Anne, George. DVM, Iowa State U., Ames, 1954; PhD, Kans. U., 1959; LHD, Silliman U., Philippines, 1973. Diplomate Am. Coll. Vet. Preventive Medicine, Am. Coll. Epidemiology. Epidemic intelligence officer USPHS, 1954-56; asst. prof. biology Silliman U., Dumaguete City, Philippines, 1960-63, chmn. dept. agr., 1962-71, assoc. prof. microbiology, 1963-67, prof. microbiology, 1967-73; prof. vet. microbiology and preventive medicine Iowa State U., Ames, 1973-93, disting. prof. vet. microbiology, immunology-preventive med., 1993—, dir. Packer Heritage Mus., 2000—. Rsch. del. USSR/Iowa State U. exch. program, Moscow, 1989-90, Latvia, 1993; rsch. cons., Taiwan, 1983, 96, 98, Hungary, 1988, 90, U. Yucatan, 1989-90, 97, 98, 2003, Ukraine, 1996, Japan, 1998; vis. lectr. Nat. Inst. Vet. Bioproducts and Pharms., Beijing, Faculty Vet. Medicine, Huazhong Agrl. U. Wuhan, Peoples Republic of China, 1988; mem. WHO Expert Panel on Zoonoses, 1980-99; expert panel on risk assessment WHO-FAO; Fulbright prof. Ahmadu Bello U., Zaria, Nigeria, 1980; subcom. on drug use in animals NRC, 1993-98, mem. nat. adv. com. on microbiol. criteria for foods, 1997-99; adv. com. Wellcome Trust, 1998-99; mem. Food Safety and Inspection Svc. Task Force for Veterinarians, 1999-2000; mem. HACCP Based Inspection Models Project, 1999-2000; dir. Packer Heritage Mus., Iowa State U., Ames, WHO Collaborating Ctr. in Food Safety, 1994-2006; cons. in field. Editor: Viral Zoonoses, Vol. I-II, 1981, Bacterial, Rickettsial, Chlamydial and Mycotic, 1984, Sulfonamides and Public Health, 1989, Bacterial, Rickettsial, Chlamydial and Mycotic, 1994, Veterinary Medical Education at Iowa State University, 2007; contbr. articles to profl. jours., chpts. to books. Active Ames Humane League, Ames chpt. Ptnrs. of Ams., UN Assn.; election supr. OSCE, Bosnia, 1998, Kosovo, 2000; mem. adv. com. Nat. Cath. Rural Life Ctr., 2001. Recipient James H. Steele award World Vet. Epidemiology Soc., 1979, Nat. Meritorious Svc. award Livestock Conservation Inst., 1989, Gold Head Cane award Am. Vet. Epidemiology Soc., 1993. Mem. AVMA (mem. coun. pub. health and regulatory vet. medicine, Internat. Svc. award 1996, Pub. Svc. award 1999), Am. Coll. Vet. Preventive Medicine (pres.), Conf. Pub. Health Veterinarians (pres.), Am. Assn. Food Hygiene Veterinarians (Outstanding Tchr. award 1978), Assn. Tchrs. Vet. Pub. Health and Preventive Medicine, Iowa Vet. Med. Assn. (chair pub. health com.), Iowa Pork Producers Assn. (pseudorables com.), Practical Farmers Iowa (Svc. to Agr. award, Sustainable Agr. Achievement award), US Animal Health Assn. (com. on pseudorables, pub. health, food safety, feed safety, chair com. on feral swine), Cardinal Key, Sigma Xi, Phi Beta Delta, Phi Kappa Phi (pres.), Gamma Sigma Delta (Svc. to Agr. Merit award 1995), Phi Zeta, Alpha Zeta, Phi Eta Sigma. Home: 304 24th St Ames IA 50010-4834 Office: Coll Vet Medicine Iowa State U Rm 2280 Ames IA 50011-0001 Office Phone: 515-294-7630. Business E-Mail: gberan@iastate.edu.

BERAN, JOHN R., banker; BS in Indsl. and Sys. Engring., U. Dayton, MS in Mgmt. Sci. Exec. v.p. BancSystems Assn.; chmn., CEO Green Machine Network Corp.; sr. v.p. Electronic Payment Services Group Soc. Corp.; pres., CEO Money Access Svc.; exec. v.p., chief info. officer Comerica Inc., Detroit, 1995—. Bd. dir. WTVS Channel 56, U. Dayton; adv. com. mem. U. Dayton Sch. Engring.; bd. dir. Mich. Virtual U.; steering com. The Clearing House; exec. com. Banking Industry Tech. Secretariat. Office: Comerica Tower 500 Woodward Ave Detroit MI 48226-3416

BERCEAU, TERESE L., state representative; b. Green Bay, Wis., Aug. 23, 1950; m. Stuart Levitau. BS, U. Wis., 1978, postgrad. Mag. editor Wis. Counties Assn., 1981—83; career placement specialist U. Wis.-LaFollett Inst., 1983—88; state assembly mem. Wis. State Assembly, Madison, 1998—, mem. colls. and univs., family law, law revision, and urban and local affairs coms. Supr. Dane County Bd., Wis., 1992—2000; commr. Cmty. Devel. Authority, Wis., 1982—92; various task forces and city coms. Mem.: Nat. Women's Polit. Caucus, 1000 Friends of Wis., NOW. Democrat. Roman Catholic. Office: State Capitol Rm 208N PO Box 8952 Madison WI 53708-8952

BERCIER, DENNIS, state legislator; m. 2 children. Undergrad., Turtle Mountain; BA, U. N.D. Mem. N.D. Senate from 9th dist., Bismark, 1999—. Mem. Standing: Judiciary, transp.; Interim: Budget Com. on Human Svcs, Judiciary. Mem. Turtle Mountain Pow-Wow Com.; bd. dirs. Turtle Mountain Pow-Wow Com., Turtle Mountain Heritage Ctr., Miss Indian Am.; dir. FIPSE Drug and Alcohol Prog. with U.S. Army, Vietnam. Recipient N.D. DOT Minority Businessman of the Year, Turtle Mountain Cmty. Svc. award. Life mem. VFW. Democrat. Office: Dist 9 PO Box 1209 Belcourt ND 58316-1209 E-mail: dbercier@state.nd.us.

BERDAN, ROBERT J., lawyer, insurance company executive; b. Waukesha, Wis., Aug. 31, 1946; BS with honors, U. Wis., Milw., 1968, MS with honors, 1969; JD cum laude, Marquette Univ., 1975. Bar: Wis. 1975, US Ct. Appeals (7th cir.) 1975. V.p., head compliance and best practices dept. Northwestern Mutual Life Ins., 1996—2000, v.p., gen. counsel, sec., 2000—. Mem.: ABA, Milw. Bar Assn., State Bar Wis., Alpha Sigma Mu. Office: Northwestern Mutual Life Ins Legal Dept 720 E Wisconsin Ave Milwaukee WI 53202

BERENBAUM, MAY ROBERTA, entomology educator; b. Trenton, NJ, July 22, 1953; BS, Yale U., 1975; PhD, Cornell U., 1980. Asst. prof. entomology U. Ill., Urbana-Champaign, 1980-85, assoc. prof. entomology, 1985-90, prof. entomology, 1990-95, head dept., 1992—, Swanlund prof. entomology, 1996—. Assoc. editor Am. Midland aturalist, 1982-85; mem. editl. bd. Jour. Chem. Ecology, Chemoecology, Proceedings of the Nat. Acad. Scis. USA. Recipient Presdl. Young Investigator award NSF, 1984, Founder's award Entomol. Soc. Am., 1994. Fellow AAAS, Am. Assn. Arts and Sciences, Encol. Soc. Am. (George Mercer award, Robert MacArthur award); mem. NAS, Am. Philos. Soc., Entomol. Soc. Am. (fellow 2002; Founder's award), Phytochem Soc. Am., Internat. Soc. Chem. Ecology, Sigma Xi. Achievements include research in chemical aspects of insect-plant interaction, evolutionary ecology of insects, phototoxicity of plant products, host-plant resistance. Office: U Ill Dept Entomology 286 Morrill Hall 505 S Goodwin Ave Urbana IL 61801-3707 E-mail: maybe@uiuc.edu.

BERENS, MARK HARRY, lawyer; b. St. Paul, Aug. 4, 1928; s. Harry C. and Gertrude M. (Scherkenbach) B.; m. Barbara Jean Steichen, Nov. 20, 1954; children: Paul J., Joseph F. (dec.), John M., Stephen M., Thomas M., Michael M., Lisa B. Moran, James M., Daniel M. BS in Commerce (Acctg.) magna cum laude, U. Notre Dame, 1950, JD magna cum laude, 1951; postgrad., U. Chgo., 1951-53. Bar: Ill. 1951, D.C. 1955, U.S. Supreme Ct. 1971; CPA, Ill. Assoc. Mayer, Brown and predecessors, Chgo., 1956-61, ptnr., 1961-96; chmn., CEO Attys.' Liability Assurance Soc., Inc., Chgo., 1987-95; ptnr. Altheimer & Gray, Chgo., 1996—2003; of counsel Bell, Boyd & Lloyd LLP, Chgo., 2003—. Nat. chmn. Nat. Assn. Law Rev. Editors, 1950-51; chmn. bd. dirs. Attys. Liability Assurance Soc. (Bermuda) Ltd., 1979-95, bd. dirs. Accts. Liability Assurance Co., 1986-2004 Editor-in-chief Notre Dame Law Rev., 1950-51; contbr. articles to profl. jours. 1st lt. JAGC U.S. Army, 1953-56. Mem. D.C. Bar Assn., Chgo. Bar Assn., Am. Law Inst., The Comml. Bar Assn. (London), Union League Club, Lawyers Club of Chgo., Met. Club, Sunset Ridge Country Club (Northbrook). Republican. Roman Catholic. Home: 1660 North Ln Northbrook IL 60062-4708 Office: Bell Boyd & Lloyd LLP 70 W Madison St Chicago IL 60602 Business E-Mail: mberens@bellboyd.com.

BERENS, WILLIAM JOSEPH, lawyer; b. New Ulm, Minn., Dec. 12, 1952; s. Robert J. and Lorraine M. (O'Brien) B.; m. Janet Christiansen, June 13, 1975; children: Margaret, Elizabeth, Catherine. BA, Coll. St. Thomas, 1975; JD, U. Minn., 1978. Bar: Minn. 1978. Assoc. Dorsey & Whitney, LLP, Mpls., 1978-83, ptnr., estate and trust svcs. group.; chmn., tax, estate planning group, 1984—. Adj. prof. William Mitchell Coll. of Law, St. Paul, 1981-84. Fellow: Am. Coll. Trust and Estate Counsel. Office: Dorsey & Whitney LLP 50 S 6th St Minneapolis MN 55402-1498 Office Phone: 612-340-2621. Office Fax: 612-340-2868. E-mail: berens.bill@dorsey.com.

BERENSON, RED (GORDON A. BERENSON), hockey coach, retired professional hockey player; b. Regina, Sask., Can., Dec. 8, 1939; m. Joy Berenson; children: Kelly, Sandy, Gordie, Rusty. BS, U. Mich., 1962, MBA, 1966. Left wing Montreal Canadiens, 1961—66, NY Rangers, 1966—67, St. Louis Blues, 1967—71, 1974—78, Detroit Red Wings, 1971—74; asst. coach St. Louis Blues, 1978—79, head coach, 1979—82; asst. coach Buffalo Sabres, 1982—84; head coach U. Mich. Hockey Team, Ann Arbor, 1984—. Player Summit Series, 1972. Named to Mich. Sports Hall of Fame, U. Mich. Athletic Hall of Honor, Dekers Club Hall of Fame, Saskatchewan Sports Hall of Fame, 2000; recipient Jack Adams Award, 1981, Lester Patrick Award, 2006. Office: U Mich 1000 S State St Ann Arbor MI 48109-2202 Office Phone: 734-647-1201. E-mail: redbaron@umich.edu.

BERENZWEIG, JACK CHARLES, lawyer; b. Bklyn., Sept. 29, 1942; s. Sidney A. and Anne R. (Dubowe) B.; m. Susan J. Berenzweig, Aug. 8, 1968; children: Mindy, Andrew. BEE, Cornell U., 1964; JD, Am. U., 1968. Bar: Va. 1968, Ill. 1969. Examiner U.S. Pat. Off., Washington, 1964-66; pat. adviser U.S. Naval Air Systems Command, Washington, 1966-68; ptnr. Brinks, Hofer, Gilson & Lione and predecessor firm, Chgo., 1968—. Editorial staff Am. U. Law Rev., 1966-68; contbr. articles to profl. jours. Mem. ABA, Chgo. Bar Assn., Ill. State Bar Assn., Bar Assn. 7th Fed. Cir., Va. State Bar, Internat. Trademark Assn. (bd. dirs. 1983-85), Brand Names Edn. Found. (bd. dirs. 1993-2000), Meadow Club (Rolling Meadows, Ill.), Miramar Club (Naples, Fla.), Delta Theta Phi. Home: 127 W Oak St Apt A Chicago IL 60610-5422 Office: Brinks Hofer Gilson & Lione Ltd Ste 3600 455 N Cityfront Plaza Dr Chicago IL 60611-5599 Office Phone: 312-321-4212. Business E-Mail: jcb@brinkshofer.com.

BERG, CHARLES A., state legislator; b. Oct. 15, 1927; m. Carol Berg; seven children. Ctrl. Sch. Agriculture. Mem. Minn. Senate from 13th dist., 1973-74, 81—; farmer, 1996—. Chmn. Gaming Regulation Com.; mem. Agrl. & Rural Devel., Environ. & Natural Resources Com., Rules & Adminstrn. Com. Office: RR 1 Box 29 Chokio MN 56221-9706 also: State Senate State Capital Building Saint Paul MN 55155-0001

BERG, JOHN A., banker; b. Lemmon, SD, Sept. 18, 1945; s. Carl A. and Helen L. (Fields) Berg; m. Nancy Blair, Mar. 23, 1974; children: Cinthia, Megan, Kristen. BS, U. ND, 1967; MBA, U. Mo., 1972; postgrad. Stonier Sch. Banking, Rutgers U., 1979. Teller, proof clk. First Mcts. & Farmers Bank, Cavalier, ND, 1962—65; internal auditor Red River Nat. Bank, Grand Forks, ND, 1965—68, installment loan officer, 1968; asst. cashier No. City Nat. Bank, Duluth, Minn., 1972—74; liaison credit officer First Bank Sys., Mpls., 1974—76; pres., CEO Wayzata Bank & Trust, 1976—; v.p., sec. Northstar Bankcorp, Wayzata, 1979—; chmn., dir. Wayzata Mortgage Co., 1983—. Bd. dirs. Minn. State Bank. Chmn., bd. dirs. Ridgedale YMCA, Minnetonka, Minn., 1983—84; bd. dirs. Wayzata Area Pub. Sch. Found., 1983—84. With US Army, 1968—71. Decorated Bronze Star. Mem.: Minn. Bankers Assn., Rotary, Wayzata Club, Wayzata C. of C. (chmn., dir. 1981—82). Republican. Presbyterian. Office: Wayzata Bank & Trust Company 900 Wayzata Blvd E Wayzata MN 55391-1863

BERG, RICK ALAN, state legislator, real estate investor; b. Maddock, ND, Aug. 16, 1959; s. Bert R. and Francie (Brink) B.; m. Tracy Jane Martin, Sept. 19, 1987. BS in Agrl. Econ., N.D. State U., 1981. Cert. comml. investment mem. Mem. N.D. Ho. of Reps., Fargo, 1985—2002, Rep. caucus chmn., 1990-92, spkr., 1992—2002, majority leader, 2002—, chmn. Industry, Bus. and Labor com.; owner, broker Goldmark Comml. Corp. Mem. Farmhouse Frat. (bd. dirs., pres. 1990-94). Lutheran. Home: 6437 13th St N Fargo ND 58102-6012

BERG, THOMAS KENNETH, lawyer; b. Willmar, Minn., Feb. 10, 1940; s. Kenneth Q. and Esther V. (Westlund) B.; m. Margit Kathryn Larson, July 31, 1965; children: Erik, Jeffrey. BA, U. Minn., 1962, JD, 1965. Bar: Minn. 1965, U.S. Dist. Ct. Minn. 1968, U.S. Ct. Appeals (8th cir.) 1974, U.S. Supreme Ct. 1980. Atty. Dept. avy, Washington, 1965-67; assoc. Carlsen, Greiner & Law, Mpls., 1967-79; state rep. Minn. Ho. of Reps., St. Paul, 1970-78; U.S. atty. Dept. of Justice, Mpls., 1979-81; ptnr. Popham, Haik, Schnobrich & Kaufman, Mpls., 1981-97, Hinshaw & Culbertson, Mpls., 1997—. Treas. Moe for Gov. com., 2002. Chair Gov.'s Re-election Com., St. Paul, 1984-86, Gov.'s Commn. for Drug Abuse, Mpls., 1989; U.S. Senate candidate for endorsement Dem. Farmer Labor Party, Mpls., 1994; bd. dirs. League Conservative Voters, 2005—; trustee Wolf Ridge Environ. Learning Ctr., 2003—. Recipient Outstanding Narcotics Prosecution award U.S. Drug Enforcement Adminstrn., 1981. Master: Am. Health Lawyers Assn. Office: Hinshaw & Culbertson 333 South 7th St Minneapolis MN 55402

BERG, WILLIAM JAMES, language educator, writer, translator; b. Dunkirk, NY, Oct. 26, 1942; s. Francis John and Adalyn Huldah (Goodwin) B.; m. Verity Anne Fry, July 2, 1966 (div. 1985); children— Jennifer Anne, Jessica Lyn; m. Laurey Kramer Martin, Feb. 1, 1986; stepchildren: Stirling Brooke Martin, Hunter Kirk Martin. Cert. pratique, Sorbonne, Paris, 1962-63; BA, Hamilton Coll., 1964; MA, Princeton U., 1966, PhD, 1969. NDEA inst. asst. Hamilton Coll., Clinton, Y, 1964; teaching asst. Princeton (N.J.) U., 1966; instr. French U. Wis., 1967-68, asst. prof., 1968-73, assoc. prof., 1973-79, prof., 1979—, assoc. chmn. French dept., 1974-75, 78-79, 79-80, 90-92, 99-2000, chmn. dept. French and Italian, 1982-85, 2002; dir. Acad. Yr. Abroad, Paris and NYC, 1973-74. Outside examiner Swarthmore Coll., 1978, No. Ill. U., 1985, 86; outside program evaluator U. Mich., 1979; tenure reviewer Swarthmore Coll., 1982, Tulane U., 1985, Marquette U., 1992, 2000, U. Calif., Riverside, 2002, U. Wis.-Milw., 2007, U. Ala., 2007; invited lectr. Rice U., 1985, U. Tenn., 1993; full prof. reviewer Georgetown U., 1984, Swarthmore Coll., 1992, U. Mich., 1994, Northwestern U., 1996, U. Colo., 1997, Va. Tech., 1999, U. Mich., 2001, NYU, 200,; U. Oklahoma, 2002, Dartmouth Coll., 2006; editl. bd. Summa Publs., Birmingham, Ala., 1983—; reviewer panel for travel and collections NEH, 1989. Author: (with P. Schofer and D. Rice) Poèmes, Pièces, Prose, 1973, (with G. Moskos and M. Grimaud) Saint/Oedipus. Psychocritical Approaches to Flaubert's Art, 1982; (with L. Martin) Images, 1989, The Visual Novel, 1992, (with L. Martin) Emile Zola Revisited, 1992, Gustave Flaubert, 1997, (with S. Magnan, Y. Ozzello and L. Martin-Berg) Paroles, 1999, 3d edit., 2005, Imagery and Ideology, 2007; author study guides on Twain's Huckleberry Finn, 1986, Tom Sawyer, 1987; (with L. Martin) Flaubert's Madame Bovary, 1989, Zola's Germinal, 1989, Maupassant's Short Stories, 1992; translator: (with P. Scott) Graphics and Graphic Information-Processing, 1981; Semiology of Graphics (design award Midwest Books Competition 1983), 1983-84; mem. editl. bd. Substance, 1971-79; contbr. articles to profl. jours. Travel grant Am. Philos. Soc., 1969, Rsch. grant U. Wis., 1969, 75, 81-82, 86, 87; Vilas assoc., 1991-93, honors fellow, 1994—; Halverson-Bascom professorship, 1995-2000; recipient U. Wis. Chancellor's award for excellence in tchg., 1995. Mem. MLA, Am. Coun. Tchrs. Fgn. Langs., Am. Assn. Tchrs. French, Phi Beta Kappa. Home: 5201 Pepin Pl Madison WI 53705-4724 Office: U Wis Dept French and Italian Madison WI 53706 Office Phone: 608-262-3941. Business E-Mail: wjberg@wisc.edu.

BERGER, JERRY ALLEN, museum director; b. Buffalo, Wyo., Oct. 8, 1943; BA in Psychology, U. Wyo., 1965, BA in Art, 1971, MA in Art History, 1972. Curator collections U. Wyo. Art Mus., Laramie, 1972-88, asst. dir., 1980-83, 87-88, acting dir., 1984-86; dir. Springfield (Mo.) Art Mus., 1988—. Office: Springfield Art Mus 1111 E Brookside Dr Springfield MO 65807-1829 Office Phone: 417-837-5700. Business E-Mail: jberger@ci.springfield.mo.us.

BERGER, JOHN TORREY, JR., lawyer; b. St. Louis, Apr. 14, 1938; s. John Torrey Sr. and Maud Alice (Beattie) B.; m. Helen Lee Thompson, Aug. 26, 1961; children: John Torrey III, Helen E. JD, Washington U., 1963. Bar: Mo. 1963. Assoc. Lewis, Rice & Fingersh, L.C., St. Louis, 1963-70, mem., 1971—2005, chmn. real estate sect., 2005—06, of counsel, 2006—. Bd. dirs. Carr Lane Mfg. Co., St. Louis, St. Louis Audubon Soc., Logos Sch., St. Louis. Elder, trustee Presbyn. Ch., St. Louis, 1970-75, 75—. Mem. ABA (corp. sect., real estate sect.), Mo. Bar Assn. (real estate sect., banking and securities com.), Bar Assn. Met. St. Louis, Internat. Conf. Shopping Ctrs., SAR, Phi Delta Phi. Avocations: fishing, birding, photography. Home: 1257 Takara Ct Saint Louis MO 63131-1013 Office: Lewis Rice & Fingersh 500 N Broadway Ste 2000 Saint Louis MO 63102-2147 Office Phone: 314-444-7600. Business E-Mail: jberger@lewisrice.com.

BERGER, MELVIN, allergist, immunologist; b. Phila., Mar. 7, 1950; MD, Case Western Res. U., 1976, PhD in Biochemistry, 1976. Intern, resident in pediatrics Children's Hosp. Med. Ctr., Boston, 1976-78; fellow allergy and immunology Nat. Inst. Allergy and Infectious Diseases, Bethesda, Md., 1978-81; pediatrician, chief immunology-allergy divsn. Rainbow Babies and Children's Hosp., Cleve., 1984—. Prof. pediats. and pathology Case Western Res. U. With USPHS, 1978—81, col. USAR, 1981—2004. Fellow Am. Acad. Pediatrics, Am. Acad. Allergy, Asthma & Immunology. Office: Rainbow Babies Hosp Div Pediatrics/Immunology Cleveland OH 44106 Office Phone: 216-844-3237. Business E-Mail: mxb12@po.cwru.edu.

BERGER, MILES LEE, land economist; b. Chgo., Aug. 9, 1930; s. Albert E. and Dorothy (Ginsberg) B.; m. Sally Eileen Diamond, Aug. 27, 1955; children: Albert E., Elizabeth Ann. Student, Brown U., 1948-50. Engaged in real estate and fin. svc. fields, 1950—; mng. chmn. bd. Berger Fin. Svcs. Corp., Chgo., 1950—. Chmn. bd. Mid-Am. Appraisal & Rsch. Corp., Chgo., 1959-80, also dir.; chmn. bd. Real Estate Svcs. Corp., 1969—; vice chmn. bd., trustee Heitman Fin. Ltd., 1970-98; chmn. bd. Mid Town Bank Chgo., 1974-2001; vice chmn. bd., prin. econ. cons. Columbia Nat. Bank, Chgo., 1965-96; bd. dirs. Franklin Corp., Evans Inc., Franklin Capital Corp., Innkeepers USA Trust, Universal Health Svcs., Inc., Medallion Bank; trustee Heitman Mortgage Investors, Innkeepers Am. Mem., chmn. Chgo. Plan Commn., 1980-84; cons. city Chgo. on Ill. Ctrl. Air Rights, 1967—; trustee Latin Sch. Chgo., 1967-73, treas., 1953-55, bd. dirs. Latin Sch. Found.; bd. govs. Met. Planning Coun.; bd. mgrs. James Jordan Boys Club. Mem. Am. Inst. Real Estate Appraisers, Soc. Real Estate Appraisers, Soc. Real Estate Counselors, Am. Right-of-Way Assn., Nat. Assn. Housing and Redevel. Ofcls., Nat. Tax Assn., Internat. Assn. Assessing Officers, Lambda Alpha. Jewish (trustee synagogue). Home: 737 N Michigan Ave Ste 1570 Chicago IL 60611-7017 Home Phone: 312-943-4575; Office Phone: 312-255-0600. Personal E-mail: mberger670@aol.com.

BERGER, NATHAN ALLEN, medical educator, academic administrator; b. Phila., July 8, 1940; s. Meyer and Lillian (Salko) B.; m. Sosamma John, June 23, 1968; children: Joshua S., Ravi B., Sarina H. AB, Temple U., 1962; MD, Hahneman U., 1966. Intern Michael Reese Med. Ctr., Chgo., 1967-68; rsch. assoc. NIH, Balt., 1968-71; assoc. prof. Washington U. Sch. Medicine, St. Louis, 1971-82; prof. medicine, biochemistry, and oncology Case Western Res. U., Cleve., 1983, Hannah-Payne prof. experimental medicine, 1983—95, dir. cancer ctr., 1985-95, interim dean, v.p. med. affairs, 1995-96, dean, v.p. med. affairs, 1996—2002, dir. Ctr. Sci., Health and Soc., 2002—, dir. Sci. Enrichment and Opportunity Program, 2003—; med. dir. Case Mini Med. Sch., 2005—. Bd. trustees Edison Biotech. Am. Cancer Soc., U. Hosp. Cleve., Henry Ford Health System, Montefiore, Ohio Biomed. Rsch. and Tech. Task Force. Contbr. articles to profl. jours.; mem. editl. bd. Jour. Clin. Investigation, Jour. Biol. Chemistry, Cancer Rsch.; others. Lt. comdr. USPHS, 1968—71. Fellow Washington U. Sch. Medicine, 1971-82; Leukemia Soc. Am. scholar; named to Am. Cancer Soc. Hall of Fame, Cleve. Med. Hall of Fame. Mem. Am. Soc. Hematology, Am. Soc. Biol. Chemists, Am. Soc. Clin. Oncology, Am. Soc. Cancer Rsch., Am. Soc. Clin. Investigation, Am. Assn. Physicians, Alpha Omega Alpha. Office: Case Western Res U 10900 Euclid Ave Cleveland OH 44106-4971 Office Phone: 216-368-4084, 216-368-2059. Business E-Mail: nab@case.edu.

BERGER, P(HILIP) JEFFREY, animal science educator, geneticist; b. Newark, June 28, 1943; s. Philip Graham and Jean Bar (Weller) B.; m. Frances Ann Williams, June 25, 1965; children— Sarah Katherine, Philip Calvin BS, Delaware Valley Coll., 1965; MS, Ohio State U., 1967, PhD, 1970. Research and teaching asst. Ohio State U., Columbus, 1965-70; mem. faculty Iowa State U., Ames, 1972—, prof. animal sci., 1982—. Cons. computer applications, animal prodn. div. FAO, Rome, 1979; vis. coop. scientist Bet Dagan, Israel, 1980; participant 1st Animal prodn. Conf., San Jose, Costa Rica, 1981; developer mixed model animal prediction programs, 1972—; participant tech. transfer project to develop genetic evaluation program for dairy cattle in tunisia, 1988, Sabbatical Wageningen Agrl. U., The Netherlands, 1994. Contbr. articles to profl. jours. Mem. Am. Dairy Sci. Assn., Am. Soc. Animal Sci., Sigma Xi, Delta Tau Alpha Republican. Methodist. Home: 2518 Kellogg Ave Ames IA 50010-4863 Office: Ia State U Dept Animal Sci 225 Kildee Hl Ames IA 50011-0001 Business E-Mail: pjberger@iastate.edu.

BERGER, ROBERT MICHAEL, lawyer; b. Chgo., Jan. 29, 1942; s. David B. and Sophia (Mizock) B.; m. Joan B. Israel, Aug. 16, 1964; children: Aliza, Benjamin, David. AB, U. Mich., 1963; JD, U. Chgo., 1966. Bar: Ill. 1966, U.S. Supreme Ct. 1975. Law clk. to cir, judge Henry J. Friendly U.S. Ct. Appeals, 2d Circuit, NYC, 1966-67; atty. Chgo. Legal Aid Bur. Law Reform Unit, 1967-68; mem. firm Mayer Brown, Chgo., 1968-72, ptnr., 1972-2001; exec. v.p., gen. counsel, sec. Capri Capital LP, 2001—04; sr. counsel Krasnow, Saunders & Cornblath, 2001—. Lectr. Northwestern U. Law Sch., 1973, adj. prof., 1997-2007; adj. prof. grad. program in real estate law John Marshall Law Sch., 1995-97; summer inst. faculty Nat. Inst. Law-Focused Edn., Chgo., 1969-74; hearing bd. Ill. Supreme Ct. Atty. Disciplinary Sys., 1973-79; mem. Ill. Sec. State Adv. Com. on Revised Uniform Ltd. Partnership Act, 1984-88, mem. spl. tax adv. commn. to Ill. Dept. Ins., 1972; legal counsel Consumer Fedn. Ill., 1967-71; regional consumer adv. coun. coun. FTC, 1969; bd. dirs., chmn. program com. Legal Assistance Found., Chgo., 1975-78; mem. Highland Park (Ill.) Zoning Bd. Appeals, 1984-86; chmn. blue ribbon com. Cook County Recorder, 1989-92; real estate adv. bd. Dai-Ichi Kangyo Bank, Chgo., 1988-93; lectr. in field. Comment editor: U. Chgo. Law Rev, 1965-66; author: Law and the Consumer, 1969, 74; reporter Revised Uniform Ltd. Partnership Act, 1984-88; adv. com. Restatement of the Law of Property 3d-Mortgages; contbr. articles to profl. jours., chpts. to books. Pres. Am.-Israel C. of C., 2003—05; trustee Am. Friends of Hebrew U.; mem. exec. com. Primo Ctr. for Women and Children, 2001—05; bd. dirs. Am. Friends of Hebrew U. Mem. ABA (chmn. subcom. on rev. uniform ltd. partnership act 1981-85, chmn. com. on partnerships and unincorporated bus. orgns. 1985-88), Am. Law Inst., Am. Coll. Real Estate Lawyers (bd. govs. 1995-98, nominating com., vice chmn. program com.), Chgo. Bar Assn. (bd. mgrs. 1970-72, chmn. com. on real estate fin. 1984-86, chmn. real property law com. 1987-88), Chgo. Coun. Lawyers (founder, bd. govs. 1969-71), Order of Coif, Phi Beta Kappa, Phi Kappa Phi. Office: Krasnow Saunders Cornblath LLP 500 N Dearborn St Chicago IL 60610 Office Phone: 312-832-7894. Business E-Mail: rberger@ksc-law.com.

BERGER, SANFORD JASON, retired lawyer, securities dealer, real estate broker; b. Cleve., June 29, 1926; s. Sam and Ida (Solomon) Berger; m. Bertine Mae Benjamin, Aug. 6, 1950 (div. Dec. 1977); children: Bradley Alan, Bonnie Jean; life ptnr. Marcia Saul, 1978. BA, Case Western Res. U., 1950, JD, 1952. Bar: Ohio 52, U.S. Supreme Ct. 79, U.S. Ct. Appeals 81. Field examiner Ohio Dept. Taxation, Cleve., 1952; pvt. practice law Cleve., 1952—. Real estate cons., Cleve., 1960—; investment cons., Cleve., 1970—; lectr. The Art of Conversation and Body Lang. Contbg. author Family Evaluation in Child Custody Litigation, 1982, Child Custody Litigation, 1986, The Parental Alienation Syndrome and the Differentiation Between Fabricated and Genuine Child Sex Abuse, 1987, Family Evaluation in Child Custody Mediation, Arbitration and Litigation, 1989; copyright 10 songs:. Candidate police judge, East Cleveland, 1955; mem. Bd. Edn., Beachwood, Ohio, 1963; judge ct. common pleas Cuyahoga County, Ohio, 1986; judge Ct. Appeals, 1988, 1990, 1992, 1994; mayor Beachwood, 1967. With USMC, 1944—45, PTO. Recipient Cert. Appreciation, Phi Alpha Delta, 1969, Healer award, U.S. Supreme Ct. Chief Justice Warren Burger, 1987, Outstanding Ohio Citizen award, Ohio Gen. Assembly, 1987. Mem.: B'nai B'rith (edidtor 1968—70). Republican. Jewish. Avocations: poetry, writing lyrics, legal writing, drag racing, scuba diving. Office Phone: 440-461-5777. E-mail: sanlllmar@aol.com.

BERGER, WAYNE C., retail executive; b. Nappanee, Ind. m. Judy Berger; 3 children. BA in Econs., Ind. U. Sr. systems programmer, East Coast Data Ctr. The May Dept. Stores Co., 1978, various programming and systems pos., 1978—84, regional v.p., East Coast Data Ctr., 1984—93, regional v.p., Great Lakes Data Ctr., 1993—2003, sr. v.p. info. tech. St. Louis, 2003—. Office: May Dept Stores Co 611 Olive St Saint Louis MO 63101

BERGERE, CARLETON MALLORY, contractor; b. Brookline, Mass., Apr. 4, 1919; s. Jason J. and Anna Lillian B.; m. Jean J. Pach, Oct. 1, 1950. Student, Burdett Bus. Coll., 1938, Babsons Sch. Bus., 1940. Self-employed contractor, Chgo., 1949-57; pres. Permanent Bldg. Supply Co., Inc., Chgo., 1957-62, Gt. No. Bldg. Products, Inc., Chgo., 1962-67, C.M. Bergere Co., Inc., Cgho., 1967-96, Carleton M. Bergere & Assocs., 1996—. Served with USN, 1944. Named Man of Yr., Profl. Remodelers Assn. Greater Chgo., 1978. Mem. Nat. Assn. Remodeling Industry (pres. Greater Chicagoland chpt., exec. dir., reg. v.p. 1991-95, Pres.'s award 1990, Profl. award 1992), Chgo. Assn. Commerce and Industry (indsl. devel. com.), Better Bus. Bur. Met. Chgo., Industry Trade Practice Com. on Home Improvment (chmn., bd. dirs. 1992—), Nat. Panel Consumer Arbitrators, Exec. Club (Chgo.). Address: 175 E Delaware Pl Chicago IL 60611-1756

BERGERON, CLIFTON GEORGE, engineer, educator; b. LA, Jan. 5, 1925; s. Lewis G. and Rose C. (Dengel) B.; m. Laura H. Kaario, June 9, 1950; children— Ann Leija, Louis Kaario. BS, U. Ill., 1950, MS, 1959, PhD, 1961. Sr. ceramic engr. A. O. Smith Corp., Milw., 1950-55; staff engr. Whirlpool Corp., St. Joseph, Mich., 1955-57; research asso. U. Ill., Champaign-Urbana, 1957-61, asst. prof., 1961-63, asso. prof., 1963-67, prof., 1967-78, head dept. ceramic engring., 1978-86, prof. emeritus, 1988—. Cons. A. O. Smith Corp., Whirlpool Corp., Ingraham Richardson, U.S. Steel Corp., Pfaudler Corp., Ferro Corp. Editor, Ann. Conf. on Glass Problems. Served in U.S. Army, 1943-46, ETO. Recipient Everitt award for tchg. excellence U. Ill., 1975; NSF grantee, 1961-82. Fellow: Am. Ceramic Soc. (Outstanding Educator award 1988); mem.: Am. Soc. for Engring. Edn., Am. Assn. for Advancement of Sci., Nat. Inst. Ceramic Engrs. (Friedberg lectr. 1986, Greaves-Walker award for Profl. Achievement 2005), Keramos, Sigma Xi. Achievements include research in crystallization kinetics in glass; high temperature reactions. Home: 208 W Michigan Ave Urbana IL 61801-4944 Office: 105 S Goodwin Ave Urbana IL 61801-2901

BERGERON, PIERRE H., lawyer; b. Knoxville, Tenn., 1974; BA, Centre Coll., 1996; JD, U. Va., 1999. Bar: Ohio 1999, Ky. 2005, US Supreme Ct., US Ct. of Appeals Second Cir., US Ct. of Appeals Fifth Cir., US Ct. of Appeals Sixth Cir., US Ct. of Appeals Ninth Cir., US Ct. of Appeals Eleventh Cir., US Dist. Ct. Eastern Dist. Ky., US Dist. Ct. Western Dist. Ky., US Dist. Ct. Southern Dist. Ohio. Clerk US Ct. of Appeals Sixth Cir.; adj. prof. Sixth Cir. appellate practice, U. Cin.; sr. assoc. Squire, Sanders & Dempsey L.L.P. Editor (editor, contbg. author): Sixth Circuit Practice Manual. Named one of Ohio's Rising Stars, Super Lawyers, 2006. Mem.: Phi Beta Kappa. Office: Squire Sanders & Dempsey LLP 312 Walnut St Ste 3500 Cincinnati OH 45202-4036 Office Phone: 513-361-1200. Office Fax: 513-361-1201.

BERGERSON, DAVID RAYMOND, lawyer; b. Mpls., Nov. 23, 1939; s. Raymond Kenneth and Katherine Cecille (Langworthy) Bergerson; m. Nancy Anne Heeter, Dec. 22, 1962; children: W. Thomas C., Kirsten Finch, David Raymond. BA, Yale U., 1961; JD, U. Minn., 1964. Bar: Minn. 1964. Assoc. Fredrikson Law Firm, Mpls., 1964-67; atty. Honeywell Inc., Mpls., 1967-74, asst. gen. counsel, 1974-82, v.p., asst. gen. counsel, 1983-84, v.p., gen. counsel, 1984-92; pvt. practice law Mpls., 1992-94; v.p., sec. Telcom Sys. Svcs., Inc., Plymouth, Minn., 1994-96, dir., cons., 1996-97; v.p. bd. dirs. Hogan Bergerson, Inc., Mpls., 1997—. Mem. city coun. Minnetonka Beach, Minn., 2001—07; bd. dirs. Pillsbury Neighborhood Svcs., Inc., Mpls., 1983—92. Republican. Avocations: scuba diving, bird-hunting. Office: Hogan Bergerson Inc 4610 IDS Ctr Minneapolis MN 55402 Home: 16215 Holdridge Rd W Wayzata MN 55391 Office Phone: 952-471-9664. Personal E-mail: dbergerson1@mchsi.com.

BERGGREN, RONALD BERNARD, surgeon, retired educator; b. SI, NY, June 13, 1931; s. Bernard and Florence (Schmidt) B.; m. Mary Beth Griffith, Nov. 25, 1954; children: Karen Berggren Murray, Eric Griffith. BA, Johns Hopkins U., 1953; MD, U. Pa., 1957. Diplomate Am. Bd. Surgery, Nat. Bd. Med. Examiners, Am. Bd. Plastic Surgery (bd. dirs. 1982-88, chmn. 1987-88). Asst. instr. surgery U. Pa., 1958-62, instr., 1962-65; gen. surg. resident Hosp. U. Pa., 1958-62, resident plastic surgery, 1963-64, chief resident plastic surgery, 1964-65; sr. resident surgery Phila. Gen. Hosp., 1962-63; asst. prof. surgery Ohio State U. Sch. Medicine, 1965-68, dir. div. plastic surgery, 1965-85, assoc. prof. surgery, 1968-73, prof. surgery, 1973-86, emeritus prof. surgery, 1986—; attending staff Ohio State U. Hosps., chief of staff, 1983-85, hon. staff, 1986—. Attending staff, dir. div. plastic surgery Children's Hosp., Columbus, Ohio,

1965-90; v.p. Plastic Surgery Ednl. Found., 1984-85, pres., 1986-87; sec. Plastic Surgery Tng. Program Dirs., 1981-83, chmn., 1983-85; mem. med. adv. bd. Ohio Bur. for Children with Med. Handicaps, 1974-2004, mem. emeritus, 2004. Trustee Mid Ohio Health Planning Fedn., 1979-82, 84, PSRO, 1980-84, Scioto Valley Health Systems Agy., 1985-87; del. Coun. Med. Splty. Socs., 1982-90, dir., 1988-90. Recipient Disting. Svc. award Plastic Surgery Edn. Foun., 1990. Fellow: ACS (gov. 1996—2001, chair gov.'s com. on ambulatory surg. care); mem.: AMA, Coun. Plastic Surgical Orgn. (convenor 1996—2000), Coun. Med. Specialty Socs. (dir. 1989—90, sec. 1991—92, pres.-elect 1993, pres. 1994), Accreditation Coun. for Grad. Med. Edn. (rev. com. for plastic surgery 1983—90, mem. exec. com. 1987—90, designate chmn. 1988, chmn. 1989, mem. exec. com. 1994, chmn. 1994, institutional rev. com. 1996—2004, chair 2002—04, John C. Gienapp award 2005), Am. Soc. Maxillofacial Surgery, Am. Soc. Aesthetic Plastic Surgery (parliamentarian 1992—93), Am. Trauma Soc., Am. Burn Assn., Assn. Acad. Surgery, Am. Assn. Surgery Trauma, N.Y. Acad. Scis., Plastic Surg. Rsch. Coun. (chair 1975—76), Franklin County Med. Soc. (pres.-elect 1982—83, pres. 1983—84), Am. Assn. Plastic Surgeons (treas. 1982—85, v.p. 1988—89, pres.-elect 1989—90, pres. 1990—91), Am. Cleft Palate Assn., Ohio Valley Plastic Surg. Soc., Am. Soc. Plastic and Reconstructive Surgeons (spl. hon. citation 1995, Trustees award for spl. achievement in plastic surgery 2000), Columbus Surg. Soc., Ctrl. Surg. Soc., Alpha Kappa Kappa, Phi Kappa Psi, Sigma Xi. Office: 9787 Windale Farms Cir Galena OH 43021-9609 Personal E-mail: rbergg@aol.com.

BERGHOLZ, DAVID, foundation administrator; b. Chgo., Jan. 2, 1938; s. Arthur C. and Sarah (Tarler) B.; 1 child from previous marriage, Jonathan; m. Eleanor Jean Mallet, Sept. 17, 1970; children: Louis Daniel, Max Arthur. Student, U. Chgo., 1955-57; AB in Anthropology, U. Pitts., 1962. Asst. dir. com. on human resources Office of Mayor, City of Pitts., 1966-67; asst. to exec. dir. Allegheny Council to Improve Our Neighborhoods-Housing, Inc., Pitts., 1967-72; asst. to pres. Mallet & Co., Inc., Carnegie, Pa., 1972-73; assoc. planning Comprehensive Health Planning Assn. of Western Pa., Pitts., 1973-75; assoc. dir. cancer ctr. planning project Allegheny Gen. Hosp., Pitts., 1976-77; asst. exec. dir. Allegheny Conf. on Community Devel., Pitts., 1977-88; pres. Pub. Edn. Fund, Pitts., 1983-88; exec. dir. George Gund Found., Cleve., 1989—. Adj. assoc. prof. cmty. devel. Carnegie Mellon U., Pitts., 1985-88; mem. adv. com. Health Policy Inst.; mem. steering com. Robert Wood Johnson Affordable Health Care Project. Recipient Recognition award Boys and Girls Club of Western Pa., 1984, Pitts. Bd. Edn. award, 1986. Mem. Coun. on Founds., Coun. on Basic Edn., Ind. Sector, Phi Delta Kappa (Lay Leader award 1985). Office: George Gund Found 1845 Guildhall Bldg 45 W Prospect Ave Cleveland OH 44115-1039

BERGLIN, LINDA, state legislator; b. Oakland, Calif., Oct. 19, 1944; d. Freeman and Norma (Lund) Waterman; m. Glenn Sampson; 1 child, Maria. BFA, Mpls. Coll. Art and Design. Mem. Minn. Ho. of Reps., St. Paul, 1972-80, Minn. Senate, St. Paul, 1980—. Chmn. Health and Human Svcs. Com.; mem. senate judiciary com., family svcs. com., tax and tax laws com., others; mem. various legis. commns. including Econ. Status of Women, Healthcare Oversight Commn.; U.S. rep. U.S.-Japan Legis. Exch. Program; seminar participant health care reform U.S.-Sweden, also Austria, 1981; studied health care reform Great Britain, 1992; rep. Nat. Coun. State Legislatures Women's Network Del., Korea, 1989. Bd. dirs. Freedom House, Better Jobs for Women, founding mem., Cornerhouse, Whittier Alliance, founding, St. Stephen's Guild Hall, Orgnl. Industrialization Ctrs., Children's Theater; mem. scattered site housing com. Powderhorn Cmty. Coun., Food and Land Resource Ctr., Joint Urban Mission Project, Phillips Neighborhood Improvement Assn., numerous others; trustee Inst. Arts. Recipient Pub. Citizen of Yr. award Nat. Assn. Social Workers, 1980, Nursing Home Residents Adv. Coun. award, 1983, NAACP Cert. Appreciation, 1984, Common Space Mutual Housing award, 1984, Award of Excellence Minn. Dept. Human Svcs., 1986, Leadership award Mpls. Conv. Ctr. Greater Mpls. C. of C., 1986, Children's Champion award Children's Defense Fund, 1987, March of Dimes award, 1988, Child Health Care citation Am. Acad. Pediatrics and Children's Defense Fund, 1988, Health Span Coalition award, 1989, Outstanding Achievement award Med. Alley, 1989, Minn. Psychol. Assn. award, 1990, Disting. Svc. award Minn. Assn. Edn. Young Children, 1991, Cert. of Merit Minn. Women's Consortium, 1992, Minn. Assn. Cmty. Mental Health Programs, Inc., 1993, others; named Outstanding Woman of Yr. YWCA, 1980, Legislator of Yr. ARC, 1989, Pub. Official of Yr. Minn. Homes for the Aging, 1991, many other honors. Mem. Dem.-Farmer-Labor Party. Office: Minn Senate 309 State Capitol 75 Constitution Ave Saint Paul MN 55155-1606

BERGMAN, BRADLEY ANTHONY, trust company executive; b. Portsmouth, Va., Sept. 23, 1953; s. Willis Anthony and Suzanne (Florey) B.; m. Elizabeth Robertson, June 17, 1983; children: Alexander Nicholas, Katherine Suzanne. BS, Ill. State U., 1974; JD, Washburn Law Sch., 1978. Bar: Kans. 1978, Mo. 1981, Okla. 1987. Exec. v.p. United Mo. City Bank, Kansas City, 1980-85; sr. v.p. Bank Okla. Trust, Oklahoma City, 1986-87; exec. v.p. Johnson County Bank, Prarie Village, Kans., 1988; pres., chief exec. officer Kans. Trust Co., Prarie Village, 1988—. Mem. Kans. Bar Assn., Mo. Bar Assn., Okla. Bar Assn., Estate Planning Soc., Hallbrook Country Club. Home: 11804 Fairway Ave Shawnee Mission KS 66211-3040

BERGMAN, BRUCE E., municipal official; m.; 2 children. BA, Simpson Coll., 1970; JD, U. Houston, 1972. Clk. to Hon. M.E. Rawlings Iowa Supreme Ct., 1973-74; assoc. Williams, Hart, Lavorato & Kirtley, West Des Moines, Iowa, 1974-78, ptnr., 1978-79, Davis, Baker & Bergman, Des Moines, 1980-85, Isaacson, Clarke & Bergman, P.C., Des Moines, 1985-89; asst. city atty. City of Des Moines Legal Dept., 1989-90, solicitor, 1990-91, chief solicitor, 1991-96, corp. counsel, 1996—. Mem.: ABA, Internat. Municipal Lawyers Assn. (regional v.p. 2003—), Iowa Mcpl. Attys. Assn. (bd. dir. 1996—99, 2002—06, sec., treas. 2003, v.p. 2004, pres. 2005), Polk County Bar Assn., Iowa State Bar Assn. Home: 4508 49th St Des Moines IA 50310-2970 Office: Office of the Corp Counsel City of Des Moines City Hall 400 E 1st St Des Moines IA 50309 Office Phone: 515-283-4130. E-mail: bebergman@dmgov.org.

BERGONIA, RAYMOND DAVID, venture capitalist; b. Spring Valley, Ill., May 21, 1951; s. Raymond A. and Elva M. (Bernadini) B.; m. Linda Goble, Dec. 31, 1988; children: Alexandra, Andrew, Caroline, Margot. BBA, U. Notre Dame, 1973; JD, Harvard U., 1976. Bar: Ill. 1976, U.S. Dist. Ct. (no. dist.) Ill. 1976, U.S. Tax Ct. 1977; C.P.A., Ill. Assoc. Winston & Strawn, Chgo., 1976-79; legal counsel, v.p. adminstrn. Heizer Corp., Chgo., 1979-86; v.p. corp. fin. Chgo. Corp., 1986-89; exec. v.p., prin. N.Am. Bus. Devel. Co. L.L.C., Chgo., 1989—. Bd. dirs. numerous pvt. cos. Recipient Elijah Watts Sells award Am. Inst. C.P.A.s, 1973 Mem. ABA, Chgo. Bar Assn. Home: 605 Essex Rd Kenilworth IL 60043-1129 Office: NAM Bus Devel Co LLC 135 S La Salle St Chicago IL 60603-4159 Office Phone: 312-332-4950. Business E-Mail: dbergonia@northamericanfund.com.

BERGSTEIN, JERRY MICHAEL, nephrologist; b. Cleve., June 26, 1939; s. Sol R. and Hilda (Nittscoff) B.; m. Renee M. Hillman, July 7, 1963; children: Stephanie, Michael, Jeffrey. BA, UCLA, 1961; MD, U. Minn., 1965. Diplomate Nat. Bd. Med. Examiners, Am. Bd. Pediat., Am. Bd. Pediat. Nephrology; lic. physician, Ind. Intern in pediat. U. Minn., Mpls., 1965-66, jr. pediat. resident, 1966-67, chief pediat. resident, 1969-70, postdoctoral fellow in pediat. nephrology, 1970-73; asst. prof., head pediat. nephrology UCLA, 1973-77; assoc. prof. Ind. U. Sch. Medicine, Indpls., 1977-82, head pediat. nephrology, 1977—, prof., 1982—. Mem. adv. bd. Nat. Kidney Found. Ind., 1980—; mem. adv. coun. Am. Heart Assn., 1988—. Mem. editl. bd. Child Nephrology and Urology, 1980-90, Pediat. ephrology, 1995—; contbr. chpts. to books. Lt. comdr. USN, 1967-69. Recipient Fellowship USPHS, Washington, 1970; grantee Thrasher Fund, 1980, Amgen, 1990. Mem. Am. Soc. Nephrology, Am. Soc. Pediat. Nephrology, Am. Soc. Investigative Pathology, Soc. Exptl. Biology and Medicine. Achievements include research on the role of the fibrinolytic inhibitor plasminogen activator inhibitor-1 in the pathogenesis and outcome of the hemolytic-uremic syndrome; development of anti-tubular basement membrane antibody disease; development of radiation nephritis in bone marrow transplant patients. Office: James Whitcomb Riley Hosp for Children 702 Barnhill Dr Indianapolis IN 46202-5128 Business E-Mail: jbergste@iupui.edu.

BERGSTEIN, MELVYN, information technology executive; BS econ., Wharton Sch. Univ. Pa. CPA. With Arthur Andersen, LLP, 1968—89, ptnr., 1977—89, mng. dir., 1985—89; sr. v.p. sys. integration CSC Consulting and Tech., 1989—91; exec. mgmt. roles Tech. Solutions Co., 1991—93; co-found., chmn. Diamond Technology Ptnrs. (now DiamondCluster Internat.), 1994—, CEO, 1994—2005. Bd. dir. New Era of Networks, Inc.; adv. bd. Cross Atlantic Technology Fund; bd. dirs. Simon Property Group. Bd. trustees Chgo. Symphony Orch., Ravinia Festival; bd. overseers U. Pa. Sch. Engring.; bd. dirs. Rehab. Inst. Chgo. Mem.: Chgo. Club, Standard Club, Econ. Club, Comml. Club, Executives' Club Chgo. (bd. dirs.). Office: DiamondCluster Internat John Hancock Ctr Ste 3000 875 N Michigan Ave Chicago IL 60611

BERGSTROM, STIG MAGNUS, geology educator; b. Skovde, Sweden, June 12, 1935; s. Axel Magnus and Karin Margareta (Engberg) B.; m. Disa Birgitta Kullgren Fil. lic., Lund U., Sweden, 1961, doctorate (hon.), 1987. Amanuensis Lund U., 1958-62, asst. lectr., 1962-68; asst. prof. geology Ohio State U., Columbus, 1968-70, assoc. prof., 1970-72, prof., 1972—2002; dir. Orton Geol. Mus., 1968—2002. Contbr. numerous articles to profl. jours. With Swedish Army, 1955—56. Recipient Assar Hadding prize 1995, Raymond C. Moore medal, 1999, Golden medal Faculty of Sci., Charles U., Czech Rep., 1999, Pander Soc. medal, 2001; Am.-Scandinavian Found. fellow, 1964; Fulbright scholar, 1960; grantee numerous orgns., 1958—. Fellow Geol. Soc. Am., Ohio Acad. Sci.; mem. Royal Physiographic Soc. Office: Ohio State U Orton Geol Mus 155 S Oval Mall Columbus OH 43210-1308

BERGY, DEAN H., health products executive; Grad., U. Mich., Harvard PMD Program. Sr. mgr. Ernst & Young LLP; contr. Stryker, Kalamazoo, 1994—96, v.p., fin. med. divsn., 1996—98, v.p., fin., 1998—2003, v.p., CFO and sec., 2003—. Office: Stryker 2725 Fairfield Rd Kalamazoo MI 49001

BERICK, JAMES HERSCHEL, lawyer; b. Cleve., Mar. 30, 1933; s. Morris and Rebecca Alice (Gerdy) B.; m. Christine Berick; children: Michael, Daniel, Robert, Joshua. AB, Columbia U., 1955; JD, Case Western Res. U., 1958. Assoc. Burke, Haber & Berick, Cleve., 1958-60, ptnr., 1960-86, mng. ptnr., 1968-83; chmn. Berick, Pearlman & Mills Co. L.P.A., 1986-99; ptnr. Squire, Sanders & Dempsey, LLP, 2000—02, ret. ptnr., 2003—. Bd. dirs. The Town and Country Trust, The Town and Country Funding Corp.; sec. Cleve. Browns Football Co. LLC; lectr. law Case Western Res. U., 1969—78; mem. dean's adv. coun. Case Western Res. U. Sch. Law, 1998—, mem. bd. visitors, Cleve. Clinic Lerner Coll. Medicine, 2005—. Founding and life trustee Rock and Roll Hall of Fame and Mus.; mem. Shaker Heights (Ohio) Bd. Edn., 1980-83; bd. visitors Columbia Coll., 1981-87, 90-96, emeritus, 2000—2004, member, 2004-; bd. dirs. Univ. Circle Inc., 1994—2004; trustee Arthritis Found. of N.E. Ohio, mem. med. and sci. com. Mem.: Soc. of Benchers, Ct. of Nisi Prius, Seagate Beach Club, Union Club (Cleve.), Shoreby Club, Order of Coif. Home: 1225 S Ocean Blvd #801 Delray Beach FL 33483 Office: Squire Sanders & Dempsey LLP 4900 Key Tower 127 Public Sq Cleveland OH 44114-1216 Office Phone: 216-479-8450. E-mail: jberick@ssd.com.

BERKE, AMY TURNER, health science association administrator; b. Cleve., Oct. 27, 1942; d. Elliott L. and Evelyn (Silverman) Glicksberg; m. Donald Alan Turner, Dec. 16, 1962 (div. 1979); children: Matthew, Kelli; m. Joseph Jerold Berke, June 21, 1981; children: Richard, Rachel, Jason. Student, Ohio State U., 1960-63; BS, Wayne State U., 1965, MA, 1966. Tchr. Waterford (Mich.) Sch. System, 1965-67; v.p. Apt. Referral Service, Oak Park, Mich., 1970-73; instr. Detroit Coll. Bus., Dearborn, Mich., 1975-79; exec. dir. Detroit Neurosurgical Found., 1979—. Past bd. dirs. Internat. Mus. Surg. Sci., Friends of Belle Isle; bd. dirs. Goodwill Industries Found.; sec. bd. dirs. Jewish Home for Aged; mem. Citizens Adv. Wayne County Youth; commr., vice chair Detroit Recreation Adv. Commn.; commr. Youth Sports and Recreation Commn. Mem. Coun. Mich. Founds., Wayne State U. Alumni Club, Ohio State U. Alumni Club, Coun. of Mich. Founds., Detroit Area Grantmakers. Avocations: reading, hiking, aerobics, travel. Office: Detroit Neurosurg Found 3333 E Jefferson Ave Detroit MI 48207

BERKLEY, EUGENE BERTRAM (BERT), envelope company executive; b. Kansas City, Mo., May 8, 1923; s. Eugene Bertram (Bert) Berkowitz and Caroline Newman (Newburger) B.; m. Joan Meinrath, Sept. 1, 1948; children: Janet Lynn Berkley Dubrava, William (Bill) Spencer Berkley, Jane Ellen Berkley Levitt. BA, Duke U., 1948; MBA, Harvard U., 1950. Pres., CEO Tension Envelope Corp., Kansas City, Mo., 1962-88, chmn. bd., 1967—. Chmn. Global Envelope Alliance, 2005—. Author: Giving Back: Connecting You, Business and Community. Mem. Mayor's Prayer Breakfast Com., 1964-84, Kitchen Cabinet, Kansas City, Mo. Sch. Dist., 1990-92; pres. Civic Coun. Greater Kansas City, 1967-68, charter mem., bd. dirs. 1982-83; pres. C. of C. Greater Kansas City, 1968-69; trustee exec. com. Midwest Rsch. Inst., 1969-72; chmn. Comprehensive Needs and Svc. Survey Com., 1971, Ctr. Bus. Innovation, 1987-89, Global Envelope Alliance, 2005-07; bd. dirs. Can. Cellulose Co., Vancouver, BC, 1973-80, Menorah Med. Ctr. Bd., 1980-94, Kansas City Area Health Planning Coun., Inc., 1982-83, Nat. Minority Supplier Devel. Coun., 1989-98, Ctr. Entrepreneurial Leadership, 1991-2002, Nat. Youth Info. Network, 1997-04, Centerpoint for Leaders, Washington, 2001-, Inst. Ednl. Leadership Inc., Washington, Ewing Marion Kauffman Found; mem. exec. com., met. chmn. Nat. Alliance Businessmen Met. Kansas City, 1973; mem. exec. com. Ctr. Mgmt. Assistance, 1980-83; human resources com. Heart Am. United Way, 1983; chmn. bd. dirs. Human Svcs. Testing and Retng. Coun., 1983-90, Minority Supplier Coun., 1986-88; trustee, chmn. U. Kansas City, 1983-85, vice chmn., 1981-83, North Campus Devel. Com., policy bd., charter mem. U. Assocs.; mem. adv. bd. Nat. Parks and Conservation Assn., 1986—, Nat. Coun. Econ. Edn., 1993-95, U. Kans. Natural History Mus., 1994-2000; chmn. adv. com., bd. dirs. Ctr. for Workforce Preparation, U.S. C. of C., 1989-91; active Bus. Roundtable Dept. Social Svcs. State of Mo., 1989-99; founder, LINC, 1992; chmn. local investment commn. LINC Mo. Dept. Social Svcs., 1992-95, exec. comm., 1992—; dir. family and cmty. trust State of Mo., 1999-. Decorated Bronze Star; recipient Brotherhood award NCCJ, 1968, numerous other awards, including Mr. Kansas City award C. of C. of Greater Kansas City, 1972, Disting. Svc. award Johnson County Friends of the Libr. (Johnson County, Kans.), 1982, Chancellor's medal U. Mo.-Kansas City, 1989, Disting. Svc. to State Govt. award Nat. Govs. Assn., 2000. Mem. Envelope Mfrs. Assn. (exec. com. 1960-63, 67-70, 76-79, vice chmn. exec. com. 1981-83, v.p. 1981-83, pres. 1983-85), Flexographic Tech. Assn. (bd. dirs. 1993-97), Oakwood Country Club, Homestead Country Club. Achievements include patents in field. Avocations: fly fishing, race walking, camping, white water rafting, backpacking. Office: Tension Envelope Corp 819 E 19th St Kansas City MO 64108-1781 Home Phone: 913-362-6638; Office Phone: 816-471-3800. E-mail: bertberkley@tension.com.

BERKMAN, MICHAEL G., lawyer; b. Poland, Apr. 4, 1917; came to U.S., 1921; s. Harry and Bertha (Jay) B.; m. Marjorie Edelstein, Nov. 28, 1941; children— Laurel, William BS, U. Chgo., 1937, PhD, 1941; JD, DePaul U., 1958; LLM in Intellectual Property, John Marshall Law Sch., 1962; spl. courses, Harvard U., 1943, MIT, 1943. Bar: U.S. Patent Office 1960. Research chemist Argonne Nat. Lab., 1946-51; assoc. dir., chief chemist Colburn Labs., Chgo., 1951-59; instr. chemistry Roosevelt U., Chgo., 1946-49; patent lawyer Mann, Brown & McWilliams, Chgo., 1959-63; ptnr. Kegan, Kegan & Berkman, Chgo., 1963-84, Trexler, Bushnell, Giangiorgi & Blackstone, Chgo., 1984-91; pvt. practice law Glenview, Ill., 1991—. Chem. cons.; expert witness in patent law. Contbr. articles to profl. jours. Served to 1st lt. Signal Corps, U.S. Army, 1942-46. Mem. Am. Chem. Soc., ABA, Patent Law Assn., Chgo., Sigma Xi. Home and Office: 939 Glenview Rd Glenview IL 60025-3172

BERKOFF, ADAM T., lawyer; b. Milw., June 5, 1969; BA with honors & distinction, Univ. Wis., Madison, 1991; JD, Marquette Univ., 1994. Bar: Wis. 1994, Ill. 1994. Ptnr., chmn. Condominium & Complex Mixed-Use Devel. practice group DLA Piper Rudnick Gray Cary, Chgo. Adj. prof. DePaul Univ. Real Estate Ctr. Editor (exec.): Marquette Law Rev. Mem.: Chgo. Bar Assn. (mem. condominium subcom.), State Bar Assn. Wis., Golden Key, Iron Cross Soc. Office: DLA Piper Rudnick Gray Cary Suite 1900 203 N LaSalle St Chicago IL 60601-1293 Office Phone: 312-368-7266. Office Fax: 312-630-5331. Business E-Mail: adam.berkoff@dlapiper.com.

BERKOFF, MARK ANDREW, lawyer; b. Boston, Aug. 8, 1961; s. Marshall Richard and Bebe R. B.; m. Susan Lynn; children: Alexander, Rachel. BA with honors, U. Wis., 1983; JD, U. Chgo., 1986. Bar: Ill. 1987, U.S. Dist. Ct. (no. dist. Ill., no. dist. Ind.), U.S. Ct. Appeals (7th cir.) 1990. Ptnr. DLA Piper US LLP, Chgo., 1986—2008, co-chmn. fin. restructuring and bankruptcy practice group, 2005—. Contbr. articles to profl. jours. Vol. Am. Cancer Soc., Chgo., 1993-96; mem., past chmn. Corp. Donations Com. Make-A-Wish Found. No. Ill.; gen counsel Bus Products Credit Assn. Mem. ABA, Chgo. Bar Assn., Turnaround Mgmt. Assn., Am. Bankruptcy Inst., Phi Beta Kappa, Phi Kappa Phi. Avocations: sports, coin collecting/numismatics. Office: DLA Piper 203 N LaSalle St Suite 1900 Chicago IL 60601-1293 Office Phone: 312-368-4000. Office Fax: 312-236-7516. Business E-Mail: mark.berkoff@dlapiper.com.

BERKOFF, MARSHALL RICHARD, lawyer; b. Milw., Apr. 10, 1937; s. Louis S. and Edith E. (Cohen) B.; m. Bebe R. Brandwein, June 19, 1960; children: Mark Andrew, Jonathan Hale, Adam Todd. BA, U. Wis., 1959; LLB, Harvard U., 1962. Bar: Wis. 1962, U.S. Dist. Ct. (we. and ea. dists.) Wis. 1962. Ptnr. Michael, Best & Friedrich, Milw., 1962—. Co-author: Employment Law Challenges of 1987, 1987, Labor Relations: The New Rules of the Game, 1984, The Legal Issues of Managing Difficult Employees, 1987; author/editor Currier and Ives "The New Best 50", 1991. Chmn. Charles Allis and Villa Terrace Art Mus., Milw., 1983-96; chmn. Milw. County War Meml. Corp., 1989-94, bd. dirs., 1983; chmn. bd. dirs. St. Michael Hosp., Milw., 1988-89; bd. dirs. Covenant Health Care, 1993-95. Mem. ABA (labor and employment sect., hosp. and health care law sect.), Wis. Bar Assn., (chmn. labor law sect. 1977-78), Milw. Bar Assn., Am. Hist. Print Collector Soc. (pres. 1987-90, bd. dirs. 2002—). Avocations: writing, lithographs, fishing. Office: Michael Best & Friedrich 100 E Wisconsin Ave Ste 3300 Milwaukee WI 53202-4108 Home Phone: 414-352-2942. E-mail: mrberkoff@michaelbest.com.

BERKOWITZ, LAWRENCE M., lawyer; b. Leavenworth, Kans., Nov. 29, 1941; s. Barney and Sarah (Kramer) B.; m. Ursula Lustenberger, Sept. 2, 1969; children: Lizbeth Berkowitz, Leslie Berkowitz. BA Polit. Sci., U. Mich., 1963, JD, 1966. Bar: Mo. 1966, N. Mex. 1997, US Dist Ct. (ea., we. dist. Mo., Kans., N. Mex.), US Ct. Appeals (8th, 10th DC cir.), US Supreme Ct. Law clerk Judge John W. Oliver, U.S. Dist. Ct., we. dist. Mo., Kansas City, Mo., 1966-68; assoc., ptnr. Stinson, Mag & Fizzell, P.C., Kansas City, Mo., 1968-97; ptnr., litig. & mediation practices Berkowitz Oliver Williams Shaw & Eisenbrandt LLP, Kansas City, Mo., 1997—. Mng. ptnr. Stinson, Mag & Fizzell, Kansas City, 1991-92. Bd. dirs. Nelson Gallery Bus. Coun., Kansas City, 1989—, Downtown coun., Kansas City, 1992-93; trustee Kansas City Art Inst., 1994—. Fellow Am. Coll. Trial Lawyers, Am. Bar Found., Mo. Bar Found.; mem. ABA, Am. Judicature Soc., Kansas City Met. Bar Assn., Lawyers Assn. Kansas City, Mo. Bar Assn., Soc. Profls. Dispute Resolution. Avocations: tennis, hiking, skiing, history, reading. Office: Berkowitz Oliver Williams Shaw & Eisenbrandt Ste 500 Two Emanuel Cleaver Blvd Kansas City MO 64112 Office Phone: 816-627-0211. Office Fax: 816-561-1888. Business E-Mail: lberkowitz@bowse-law.com.

BERKOWITZ, SEAN M., lawyer; b. May 27, 1967; BS summa cum laude, Tulane U., 1989; JD cum laude, Harvard U., 1992. Bar: Ill. Assoc. Katten Muchin Rosenman LLP, Chgo.; asst. U.S. atty. (no. dist.) Ill. criminal divsn. US Dept. Justice, Chgo., 1998—2003, mem. Enron Task Force, 2003—05, dir. Enron Task Force, 2005—06; ptnr. litigation dept. Latham & Watkins LLP, Chgo., 2006—. Part owner Double Door nightclub, Chgo. Named one of 40 Under Forty, Crain's Bus Chgo., 2005, Litigation's Rising Stars, The Am. Lawyer, 2007. Avocations: running, motorcycling. Office: Latham & Watkins LLP Sears Tower Suite 5800 Chicago IL 60606

BERKSON, STUART M, lawyer; b. 1955; BA summa cum laude, Univ. of Ill.; JD, Harvard Univ. CPA Ill., 1977; bar: Ill. 1980. Ed. Harvard Law Review; ptnr. McDermott Will & Emery LLP. Recipient Elijah Watt Sells Gold Medal, 1977. Office: McDermott Will & Emery LLP 227 West Monroe St Chicago IL 60606 Business E-Mail: sberkson@mwe.com.

BERLAND, ABEL EDWARD, lawyer, real estate agent; b. Cin., Aug. 27, 1915; s. Samuel and Anne (Brod) B.; m. Meredith E. Tausig, Aug. 31, 1940; children: Michael Gardner, Richard Bruce, James Robert. JD, DePaul U., 1938, LHD, 1975. Bar: Ill. 1938. Vice chmn. Rubloff, Inc., Chgo. Real estate cons. Contbr. articles on real estate to profl. scholarly and trade jours. Life trustee, mem. acad. affairs com. DePaul U.; chmn. Civic Fedn. Chgo., 1989-90; bd. dirs. Crime Commn. Chgo.; mem. adv. bd. Salvation Army; mem. Newberry Libr. pres.'s coun. Fellow Brandeis U., 1958—; recipient Nat. Community Service award Jewish Theol. Sem. Am. Mem. Am. Chgo. Bar Assns., Nat. Assn. Realtors, Realtors Nat. Mktg. Inst. (C.C.I.M.), Am. Soc. Real Estate Counselors (pres. 1970), Pvt. Libraries Assn., Manuscript Soc., Am. Arbitration Assn. (nat. panel arbitrators), Shakespeare Soc. Am., Lex Legio, Assn. Internat. de Bibliophile, The Realty Club of Chgo. (pres. 1988), Gamma Mu, Pi Kappa Delta, Lambda Alpha, Omega Tau Rau. Clubs: Book of California; Caxton, Mid-Day, Economic, Brandeis University (founder 1949, pres. 1954), Standard (Chgo.); Grolier (N.Y.C.); Roxburghe of San Francisco; Philobiblon (Phila.). Home: 251 Sylvan Rd Glencoe IL 60022-1225

BERLAND, DAVID I., psychiatrist, educator; b. St. Louis, Aug. 1, 1947; s. Harry I. and Mildred (Cornblath) B.; m. Elaine Prostak, May 22, 1977; children: Katharine J., Rachel P. BA, U. Pa., 1969; MD, U. Mo., 1973. Diplomate Am. Bd. Psychiatry and Neurology. Resident psychiatry Menninger Found., Topeka, Kans., 1973-78, staff child and adolescent psychiatrist, 1978-83; dir. div. child and adolescent psychiatry St. Louis U. Med. Sch., 1983-93; with dept. adolescent psychiatry St. Luke's Hosp., Chesterfield, Mo., 1993-97; pvt. practice St. Louis, 1997—. Contbr. articles to profl. jours. Fellow Am. Acad. of Child and Adolescent Psychiatry; mem. AMA (rotating seat relative value update com. 1996-99), Soc. of Profs. of Child and Adolescent Psychiatry,. Jewish. Office: 7700 Clayton Rd Ste 103 Saint Louis MO 63117 Office Phone: 314-644-6910.

BERLINE, JAMES H., advertising and public relations executive; b. Youngstown, Ohio, Aug. 6, 1946; s. James Howard and Eloise Blanche (Smith) Berline; children: Erin Michele, Jess Brandon, Quincy Blaine. BA in Econs., U. Mich., 1968; MS in Advt., U. Ill., 1971. V.p. Campbell-Ewald Co., Detroit, 1971-76; sr. v.p. Batten Barton Durstine & Osborn Inc., Troy, Mich., 1976-78, exec. v.p. Southfield, Mich., 1984-85; pres. Yaffe Berline Inc., Southfield, 1980-82; pres., CEO Berline Group, Birmingham, Mich., 1982—. Bd. dirs. Leadership Detroit Alumni; pres. MAGNET (Mktg. and Advt. Global Network). Program chmn. United Found., Detroit, 1984; mem. adv. bd. Jr. League; founder Winning Futures; trustee Detroit Sci. Ctr., 1985—, Juvenile Diabetes Found., 1994; chmn. comm. com. Leadership Detroit, 1993; bd. dirs. Make-A-Wish Found., chmn., 2001—03; trustee CATCH, mem. exec. com., chmn. bd. dirs.; bd. dirs. Operation Able, Minds, 2003—, Children's Leukemia Found. Mich., 2007—. Mem.: Young Pres. Orgn. (chair office commn. 1994, trustee, com. chmn. Ea. Mich. chpt.), World Pres. orgn., Detroit C. of C. (mktg. com. 1987—88), Greater Detroit Alliance Bus. (bd. dirs. 1984—86), Birmingham Athletic Club (pres.), U. Mich. Grad. M Club (bd. dirs. 1986), U. Mich. Club Detroit (past bd. govs.), Adcraft Club (bd. dirs. 1980—99, pres. 1988). Avocations: squash, travel, golf. Office: 70 E Long Lake Rd Bloomfield Hills MI 48304 Office Phone: 248-593-7402.

BERLOW, ROBERT ALAN, lawyer; b. Detroit, Feb. 11, 1947; s. Henry and Shirley (Solovich) B.; m. Elizabeth Ann Goldin, Sept. 20, 1972; children: Stuart, Lisa. BA, U. Mich., 1968; JD, Wayne State U., 1971. Bar: Mich. 1971, U.S. Supreme Ct. 1978. Asst. to dean, instr. law sch. Wayne State U., Detroit, 1971-72; mem. Radner, Radner, Shefman, Bayer and Berlow, P.C., Southfield, Mich., 1972-78; gen. counsel Perry Drug Stores, Inc., Pontiac, Mich., 1978-80, gen. counsel, sec., 1980-82, v.p., gen. counsel, sec., 1982-88, sr. v.p., gen. counsel, sec., 1988-93, sr. v.p., chief adminstrn. officer, gen. counsel, sec., 1993-94, exec. v.p., gen. counsel, sec., 1994-95; sr. mem. Dykema Gossett, PLLC, Bloomfield Hills, Mich., 1995—, also chmn. retail practice group. Pres. Agy. for Jewish Edn., Metro Detroit, 1993-95, v.p., 1987-93; bd. dirs. Jewish Cmty. Ctr. Met. Detroit, 1989-2003, v.p., 1992-93, treas., 1996-97, sec., 1997-98. Mem. ABA, Mich. Bar Assn. (chair comml. leasing and mgmt. of real estate com. of real property law sect. 1993-98, chmn. real property law sect. 2001-2002). Avocations: sports, photography. Office: Dykema Gossett PLLC 39577 N Woodward Ave Bloomfield Hills MI 48304-2837 E-mail: r.berlow@dykema.com.

BERMAN, ARTHUR LEONARD, retired state legislator; b. Chgo., May 4, 1935; s. Morris and Jean (Glast) B.; m. Barbara Dombeck; children: Adam, Marcy Padorr. BS in Commerce & Law, U. Ill., 1956; JD, Northwestern U., 1958. Bar: Ill. 1958. Atty. pvt. practice, Chgo.; ptnr. White, White & Berman, Chgo., 1958-74, Maragos, Richter, Berman, Russell & White, Chtd., 1974—81, Chatz, Berman, Maragos, Haber & Fagel, Chgo., 1981-82, Berman, Fagel, Haber, Maragos & Abrams, Chgo., 1982-86, Karlin & Fleisher, Chgo., 1986-99; cons. Chgo. Bd. Edn., 2000—05. Spl. atty. Bur. Liquidations, Ill. Dept. Ins., 1962-67; spl. asst. atty. gen. Ill., 1967-68; mem. Ill. Ho. of Reps., 1969-76, Ill. Senate, 1977-99; legis. policy advisor to Chgo. Bd. Edn., 2000-06. Pres. 50th

Ward Young Dems., 1956-60; v.p. Cook County Young Dems., 1956-60, 50th Ward Regular Dem. Orgn., 1955-99; active 48th Ward Regular Dem. Orgn., 1967-99; exec. bd. Dem. Party, Evanston, Ill., 1973-99; bd. govs. State of Israel Bonds. Mem. ABA, Ill. Bar Assn., Chgo. Bar Assn. (bd. mgrs. 1988-89), Nat. Assn. Jewish Legislators (pres. 1987-89), U. Ill. Alumni Assn., Phi Epsilon Pi, Tau Epsilon Rho. Office: 6007 N Sheridan Rd Chicago IL 60660-3039 Office Phone: 773-769-2787. Personal E-mail: senatorart2000@aol.com.

BERMAN, DEBBIE L., lawyer; b. 1966; AB in Economics, summa cum laude, Brandeis U., 1987; JD cum laude, Harvard Law Sch., 1990. Bar: Ill., US Ct. (No. Dist. Ill.), US Tax Ct. Ptnr., co-chmn. trade secrets and unfair competition practice Jenner & Block LLP. Mem. alum. admissions coun. Brandeis Univ., 1990—; comm. mem. EZRA Multi-Service Ctr., 1996—; mem. bd. dir. Jewish Cmty. Ctr. Chgo., 1998—2003, Jewish United Fund/ Jewish Fedn. Chgo., 2003—; v.p., mem. bd. trustees Temple Anshe Sholom, Chgo., 2001—. Named Ill. Super Lawyer in 1st Amendment and media, 2005, Super Lawyer in bus. litigation, 2006—07; named one of 40 Under Forty, Crain's Bus. Chgo., 2005, New Stars, New Worlds, Lawdragon mag., 2006; recipient Chambers USA award for media and entertainment, 2006, Davis, Gidwitz & Glasser award, Jewish Union Fund/Jewish Fedn. Met. Chgo., 2005; fellow, Leadership Greater Chgo., 2007. Mem.: Chgo. Bar Assn., Ill. Bar Assn., ABA, Intellectual Property Law Assn. Chgo., Am. Intellectual Property Law Assn., Brandeis Univ. Nat. Alum. Assn., Phi Beta Kappa. Office: Jenner & Block LLP 330 N Wabash Ave Chicago IL 60611 Office Phone: 312-923-2764. Office Fax: 312-840-7764. E-mail: dberman@jenner.com.

BERMAN, LAURA, journalist, writer; b. Detroit, Dec. 8, 1953; d. Seymour Donald and Rose (Mendelson) B. AB, U. Mich., 1975. Writer, reporter Detroit Free Press, 1976-86; columnist The Detroit News, 1986-93; freelance writer, 1994—; sr. writer The Detroit News, 1995-98; columnist Detroit News, 1998—. Spkr. in field, vis. prof. Univ. Mich., Dearborn, 2005 Mem. Soc. Profl. Journalists. Office: The Detroit News 999 Haynes St Ste 260 Birmingham MI 48009 E-mail: lberman@detnews.com.

BERMAN, LAURA, sex therapist; BA in anthropology, U. Vt., 1990; MA in health edn., NYU Sch. Edn., 1992; MSW, NYU, 1994, PhD in philosophy, 1997. Fellow in human sexual therapy NYU Med. Ctr., 1997; former co-dir. (with sister Jennifer) Women's Sexual Health Clinic, Boston U. Med. Ctr.; co-dir. (with sister Jennifer) Network Excellence Women's Sexual Health; clinical asst. prof. ob-gyn. and psychiatry Feinberg Sch. Medicine Northwestern U.; dir. Berman Ctr., Chgo., 2004—; co-host (with sister Jennifer) Berman & Berman: For Women Only, Discovery Health Channel, 2004—. Co-author (with sister Jennifer): For Women Only: A Revolutionary Guide to Overcoming Sexual Dysfunction and Reclaiming Your Sex Life, 2001, Secrets of the Sexually Satisfied Woman, 2005; actor: (TV series) Sexual Healing, 2006. Found. bd. mem. Soc. Sci. Study Sexuality (SSSS). Named one of 40 Under 40, Crains' Chicago Business, 2005; recipient Rising Star Yr., Nat. Assn. Women Bus. Owners, LA, 2002, Women Action award, Israel Cancer Rsch. Fund, 2002. Mem.: Am. Assn. Sex Educators, Counselors, and Therapists, Internat. Soc. Study Women's Sexual Health, Am. Assn. Social Workers. Office: Berman Ctr LLC 211 E Ontario Ste 800 Chicago IL 60611 Office Phone: 800-709-4709, 312-255-8088. Office Fax: 312-255-8007.

BERMAN, LYLE, recreational facility executive; m. Janis Berman; 4 children. BA, U. Minn., 1964. With Berman Bucksin, 1964-79, pres., CEO, 1979-87, Wilsons, 1987-96; co-founder Grand Casino, 1990-98; chmn., CEO Rainforest Cafe, Inc., 1994—, Lakes Gaming Inc., 1998—. Dir. G-III Apperal Group, Ltd., Innovative Gaming Corp. Am., New Horizon Kids Quest Inc., Pk. Pl. Entertainment Corp., Wilsons. Recipient Gt. Traditions award B'nai B'rith, 1995, Gaming Exec. award, 1996. Office: 130 Cheshire Ln Minnetonka MN 55305-1053

BERMAN, MITCHELL A., orchestra executive; Gen. mgr. Wichita (Kans.) Symphony Orch. Office: Wichita Symphony Orch 225 W Douglas Ste 207 Wichita KS 67202

BERNABEI, MARC P., lawyer; b. Spring Valley, Ill., Apr. 1, 1954; m. Linda S. Bernabei; children: Jason, Cara, Liza. BA, Lewis U.; JD, No. Ill. U. Police officer, Spring Valley, 1975-81; pvt. practice Bernabei Assocs., Spring Valley, 1981-84; state's atty. Bureau County, Princeton, Ill., 1984—. Recipient Kahla Lansing Meml. award Kahla Lansing Meml. Com., 1992. Home: PO Box 91 Spring Valley IL 61362-0091 Office: Bureau County State's Atty's Office 700 S Main St Princeton IL 61356-2037

BERNARDIN, THOMAS L., advertising executive; Grad., Hillsdale Coll. Acct. dir. McCann-Erickson, Detroit, McCann-Erickson Europe; sr. v.p., dir. internat. ops. Campbell-Mithum-Esty Advt., Southfield, Mich., 1988—90, exec. v.p., mgmt. dir., 1990—92, pres., 1992—94, Bozell/North (formerly Campbell-Mithum-Esty Advt.), 1994—97; exec. v.p., gen. mgr. Bozell, NYC, 1997, pres., CEO; pres., COO Lowe US, NYC, 2003, pres., CEO, 2003—04; CEO Leo Burnett USA, 2004—05; pres. Leo Burnett Worldwide, 2004—05, chmn., CEO, 2005—. Bd. dirs. Lake Forest Hosp., Chgo., 2006—. David Rockefeller fellow, 2002. Mem.: Am. Advt. Fedn. (mem. exec. com., chair corp. mems.), Found. Fighting Blindness (trustee). Office: Leo Burnett Worldwide Inc 35 W Wacker Dr Chicago IL 60601 Office Phone: 312-220-5959. Office Fax: 312-220-3299.

BERNARDINI, CHARLES, lawyer, alderman; BS, U. Ill., 1968, JD, 1972; LLM, John Marshall Law Sch. Legis. asst. to Spkr. Ill. Ho. of Reps., 1972-73; sr. counsel Am. Hosp. Supply Corp., 1974-81; alternate del. Dem. Nat. Conv., 1980; spl. prosecutor for election fraud Cook County, Ill., 1981-83; commr., 1986-92; mem. Gov.'s Election Reform Commn., 1985; del. Dems. Abroad Dem. Conv., 1992; alderman City of Chgo., 1993-99; ptnr. Dykema Gossett Law Firm, Chgo., 1999—. Instr. internat. law Loyoa U. Chgo., Rome campus, 1981; counsel Allstate Ins. Co., 1983-91. Mem. Chgo.-Milan Sister City Com., 1988—. Mem. Am. C. of C. in Italy (mng. dir.). Office: Dykema Gossett Law Firm 10 S Wacker Dr #2300 Chicago IL 60606-7453 E-mail: crb43@aol.com.

BERNATOWICZ, FRANK ALLEN, management consultant; b. Chgo., Nov. 3, 1954; s. Chester and Pauline (Maciula) B.; m. Kathleen Ann Carlson, Apr. 29, 1978; children: Amy Elizabeth, Laura Ann. BSEE, U. Ill., 1976; MBA in Fin., Loyola U., Chgo., 1981, postgrad. in acctg., 1982-84. Registered profl. engr., Ill.; CPA, Ill. Engr. Commonwealth Edison Co., Chgo., 1976—79, gen. engr., 1979—82, prin. engr., 1982—84; sr. cons. Brenner Group, Chgo., 1984—85; supr. Ernst & Young (formerly Ernst & Whinney), Chgo., 1985, mgr., 1985—86; sr. mgr. Ernst & Young, Chgo., 1986—88, ptnr., 1989—96; prin. J. Alix & Assoc., Chgo., 1996—99; ptnr. PricewaterhouseCoopers, Chgo., 1999—2001, BDO Seidman, Chgo., 2001—03; mng. prin. FAB Adv. Svcs., LLC, Chgo., 2003—06; mng. dir. Huron Consulting Group, Chgo., 2006—; mng. prin. FAB Group, Inc., 2007—. Spkr. in field. Mem. bd. regents Mercy Boys Home, 1990—. Mem. ABA (assoc.), AICPA, Am. Bankruptcy Inst., Ill. Soc. CPAs, Nat. Soc. Profl. Engrs., Turnaround Mgmt. Assn., Comml. Law League, Am. Bankruptcy Inst., Chgo. Soc. Clubs (Met.). Avocations: golf, racquetball, computers, investments. Home: 6543 Hillcrest Dr Burr Ridge IL 60527 Office: FAB Group Inc 6543 Hillarest Dr Burr Ridge IL 60527 Office Phone: 630-655-3474. Business E-Mail: fbernatowicz@comcast.net.

BERNAUER, DAVID W., retired retail executive; b. Wadena, Minn., Apr. 25, 1944; m. Mary V. Bernauer; 3 children. BS, N.D. State U., 1967, D (hon.) of Pharmacy, 2000. Pharmacist Walgreen Co., 1967-79, dist. mgr., 1979-87, regional v.p. we. ops., 1987-90, v.p., treas., 1990-92, v.p. pres. purchasing, chief info. officer, 1992-94, sr. v.p., chief info. officer, 1996-99, pres., COO, 1999—2002, pres., CEO, 2002—03, CEO, 2003—06, chmn., 2003—07. Bd. dirs. Students in Free Enterprise; bd. trustees Field Mus., Chgo.; co-chmn. N.D. State U. Coll. Pharm. Devel. Fund. Recipient Dist. Alumni award, N.D. State U., 1999. Mem.: Nat. Assoc. Chain Drug Stores (exec. com., bd. dirs., past treasurer, chmn. 2007—).

BERNDT, ELLEN GERMAN, lawyer; b. Schenectady, NY, 1953; BS, Denison U., 1975; JD, Capital U., 1984. Bar: Ohio 1984. Legal asst. Borden Chem. Inc., Columbus, Ohio, 1978-84, corp. atty., 1984-90, asst. sec., corp. atty., 1990-96; corp. sec., asst. gen. counsel Hexion Specialty Chem., Inc. (formerly known as Borden Chem. Inc.), 1996—. Mem.: Ctrl. Ohio Corp. Counsel Assn. (pres. 1997), Soc. Corp. Sec. and Goverance Profls., Assn. Corp. Coun. Office: Hexion Specialty Chemicals Inc 180 E Broad St Columbus OH 43215-3799

BERNER, ROBERT LEE, JR., lawyer; b. Chgo., Dec. 9, 1931; s. Robert Lee and Mary Louise (Kenney) B.; m. Sheila Marie Reynolds, Jan. 12,. 1957; children: Mary, Louise, Robert, Sheila, John. AB, U. Notre Dame, 1953; LL.B., Harvard U., 1956. Bar: Ill. 1956, NY 1989. With Petit, Olin, Overmyer & Fazio, Chgo., 1957—63, Baker & McKenzie, Chgo., 1963—; ptnr., 1964—2000; sr. counsel, 2000—. Mem. vis. com. Northwestern U. Law Sch., 1981-85; mem. legal adv. com. N.Y. Stock Exch., 1995-98. Mem. vis. com. U. Chgo. Div. Sch., 1972—, chmn., 2001—05; mem. legal aid com. Met. Family Svcs., Chgo., 1972—, chmn., 1991—93; mem. adv. bd. Cath. Charities, Chgo., 1971—, Loyola U., 1972—; mem. coun. Coll. Arts and Letters, U. Notre Dame, 2001—; trustee Cath. Theol. Union, Chgo., 1999—; bd. dirs. Link Unltd., Chgo., 1972—, pres., 1990—92; bd. dir. World Trade Ctr. of Chgo., 1989—. Mem. ABA (chmn. bus. law sect. 1987-88), Ill. State Bar Assn., Chgo. Bar Assn., Legal Club Chgo. (pres. 1974-75), Law Club Chgo. (pres. 1991-92). Home: 932 Euclid Ave Winnetka IL 60093-1418 Office Phone: 312-861-2890. Business E-Mail: robert.l.berner@bakernet.com.

BERNHARD, ROBERT JAMES, mechanical engineer, educator; b. Algona, Iowa, July 28, 1952; s. David Louis and Darlene Justine (Kohlhaas) B.; m. Deborah S. Kell; children: Jay David, Jacqueline Elizabeth, Jonathan Christian, Justin Brian. BS in Mech. Engring., Iowa State U., 1973, PhD, 1982; MS, U. Md., 1976. Engr. Westinghouse Electric, Inc., Balt., 1973-77; asst. prof. Iowa State U., Ames, 1977-82; asst. prof. dept. mech. engring. Purdue U., West Lafayette, Ind., 1982-87, assoc. prof., 1987-91, prof., 1991—. Dir. Ray W. Herrick Labs Purdue U., 1994—, Inst. for Safe, Quiet, and Durable Hwys, 1998—; cons. to GM, Electricite de France, Automated Analysis; prin. investigator many firms; lectr. CETIM, U. Wis., U. Mich. Assoc. editor: Noise Control Engring. Jour., 1984-85, 90—. Fellow ASME (co-editor procs. 1989), Acoustical Soc. Am.; mem. AIAA, Soc. Automotive Engrs., Inst. Noise Control Engrs. (bd. dirs. 1988-97, pres. 1994), Am. Soc. Engring. Educators. Office: Purdue U 1077 Ray W Herrick Labs Lafayette IN 47907

BERNHARDSON, IVY SCHUTZ, lawyer; b. Fargo, ND, Aug. 22, 1951; d. James Newell and Phyllis Harriet (Iverson) Schutz; m. Mark Elvin Bernhardson, Sept. 1, 1973; children: Andrew Schutz, Jenna Clare. BA, Gustavus Adalphus Coll., St. Peter, Minn., 1973; JD, U. Minn., Mpls., 1978. Bar: Minn. 1978, U.S. Dist. Ct. Minn. 1978. Staff atty. Gen. Mills, 1978—83, assoc. counsel, 1983—85, sr. assoc. counsel, 1985—95, v.p., 1988—2000, assoc. gen. counsel, sec., 1995—2000; ptnr. Leonard Street and Deinard, Mpls., 2000—04; chief legal officer Hazelden Found., Center City, Minn., 2004—. Trustee Gustavus Adolphus Coll., 1989-98, Fairview Southdale Hosp., 1993-2001, chair, 1999-2001, bd. pensions Evangelical Luth. Ch. in Am.; dir. Fairview Healthcare Svcs., 1996-2002, vice chair, 1999-2002; bd. dirs. The Bush Found., 1997—; mem. complex case panel Am. Arbitration Assn. Recipient Alumni Achievement award, Gustavus Adolphus Coll., 2001. Mem. ABA, Am. Soc. Corp. Secs., Minn. Bar Assn., Hennepin County Bar Assn. Lutheran. Office: Hazelden Foundation 15245 Pleasant Valley Rd Center City MN 56012-0011

BERNICK, CAROL LAVIN, consumer products company executive; 3 children. BA, Tulane U., 1974. Dir., v.p. Alberto-Culver Co., 1984, exec. v.p. worldwide mktg., 1990; pres. Alberto-Culver USA, 1994, Alberto-Culver N.Am., 1998, vice chmn., 1998; pres. Alberto Culver Consumer Products Worldwide, 2002, chmn. bd., 2004—. Founder Friends of Prentice; mem. women's bd. Boys and Girls Clubs, Chgo.; regent Lincoln Acad. Ill.; mem. exec. com. of adv. bd. Kellogg Sch., orthwestern U.; vice chmn. Tulane U. Bd.; bd. dirs. Northwestern Meml. Healthcare. Recipient Leadership in Bus. award YWCA Met. Chgo., 1992, award for philanthropy Harvard Club of Chgo., Disting. Alumni award Tulane U., 2003. Mem. World Pres. Orgn., Econ. Club Chgo., Exec. Club Chgo., Com. 200 Chgo. etwork. Office: Alberto-Culver Co 2525 Armitage Ave Melrose Park IL 60160-1163 Office Phone: 708-450-3000. Personal E-mail: cbernick@alberto.com.

BERNICK, DAVID M., lawyer; b. San Francisco, June 16, 1954; s. Herman Charles and Joan (Schutz) B.; m. Christine A. Clougherty, Aug. 13, 1983; 1 child, Evan Daniel. BA, U. Chgo., 1974, JD, 1978; MA, Yale U., 1975. Bar: Ill. 1978. Ptnr., mem. firm com. Kirkland & Ellis, Chgo., 1984—. Mem. Comml. Club, Mid-Am. Club, Phi Beta Kappa. Office: Kirkland & Ellis LLP 200 E Randolph Dr 54th Fl Chicago IL 60601-6636 Office Phone: 212-446-4806, 312-861-2248. Office Fax: 212-446-4900, 312-861-2200. E-mail: dbernick@kirkland.com.

BERNICK, HOWARD BARRY, manufacturing executive; b. Midland, Ont., Can., Apr. 10, 1952; came to U.S., 1974, naturalized, 1976; s. Henry and Esther (Starkman) B.; m. Carol Lavin, May 30, 1976; children: Craig, Peter, Elizabeth. BA, U. Toronto, Ont., 1973. Investment banker Wood Gundy Ltd., Toronto, 1973-74, First Boston Corp., Chgo., 1974-77; dir. of profit planning Alberto Culver Co., Melrose Park, Ill., 1977-79, v.p. corp. devel., 1979-81, group v.p., chief fin. officer, 1981-85, exec. v.p., 1985-88, pres., COO, 1988-94, also bd. dirs., pres., CEO, 1994—2006; pres. Bernick Holdings Inc., Chgo., 2006—. Bd. dirs. AAR Corp., Wm. Wrigley Jr. Co. Mem. Cosmetic, Toiletry & Fragrance Assn., Econ. Club Chgo. Office: Bernick Holdings Inc 401 N Michigan Ave Chicago IL 60611

BERNSTEIN, H. BRUCE, lawyer; b. Omaha, Dec. 9, 1943; s. David and Muriel (Krasne) B.; m. Janice Ostroff, Aug. 27, 1967; children: Daniel J., Jill M. AB, Cornell U., 1965; JD, Harvard U., 1968. Bar: Ill. 1968, Ill. Supreme Ct. 1968, US Dist. Ct. no. dist. Ill. 1969, ea. dist. Wis. 1997, US Ct. of Appeals 7th cir. 1981, 6th cir. 1995. Ptnr. secured transactions Sidley Austin LLP, Chgo., 1974—, mem. exec. com. Gen. counsel Comml. Fin. Assn. 1995-2001 Past bd. dirs. Jewish Family and Cmty. Svc. Agy. Mem. ABA, Ill. Bar Assn. (past chmn. Comml., Banking and Bankruptcy Law section), Chgo. Bar Assn. (past chmn. Uniform Comml. Code Com.), Am. Coll. Comml. Fin. Attorneys, Am. Coll. Bankruptcy, Nat. Bankruptcy Conf., Standard Club, Northmoor Country Club, Harvard Club. Avocation: golf. Office: Sidley Austin LLP Ste 2500 One S Dearborn St Chicago IL 60603 Office Phone: 312-853-7635. Office Fax: 312-853-7036. Business E-Mail: bbernstein@sidley.com.

BERNSTEIN, JAMES C., retired commissioner; b. Boston; m. Cheryl Bernstein. BS in polit. sci., Augsburg Coll., Mpls. V.p. and rsch. mgr. Colle & McVoy Inc.; similar positions Peterson Morris & MacLachlan, Miller Publishing and Winona Rsch.; commr. Minn. Dept. Commerce, 1998—2002. With USAF, 1969—73, with US Army, 1977—78. Republican. Avocations: book collecting, softball, touch football.

BERNSTEIN, JAY, pathologist, researcher, educator; b. NYC, May 14, 1927; s. Michael Kenneth and Frances (Kaufman) B.; m. Carol Irene Kritchman, Aug. 11, 1957; children: John Abel, Michael Kenneth. BA, Columbia U., 1948; MD, SUNY, Bklyn., 1952. Diplomate Am. Bd. Pathology. Asst. pathologist Children's Hosp. Mich., Detroit, 1956-58, assoc. pathologist, 1959, attending pathologist, 1960-62, cons. in lab. medicine, 1977—93, cons. emeritus, 1993—; attending pathologist Bronx Mcpl. Hosp. Ctr., NYC, 1962-68; asst. prof. pathology Albert Einstein Coll. Medicine, Bronx, N.Y., 1962-64, assoc. prof. pathology, 1964-68; chmn. dept. anatomic pathology William Beaumont Hosp., Royal Oak, Mich., 1969-90, dir. Rsch. Inst., 1983-98, assoc. med. dir., 1990-98, hon. consulting pathologist, 1999—; clin. prof. pathology Wayne State U. Sch. Medicine, Detroit, 1977—99. Chmn. sci. adv. bd. Nat. Kidney Found. Mich., 1986-88, nat. sci. adv. bd., 1976-82; sci. advisor Nat. Inst. Child Health, USPHS, 1976-81; profl. adv. bd. Nat. Tuberous Sclerosis Assn., 1990-93; clin. prof. health sci. Oakland U., Rochester, Mich., 1980-90; vis. prof. pathology Albert Einstein Coll. Medicine, Bronx, 1974-2001; com. on renal disease WHO; cons. pathologist Internat. Study of Kidney Diseases in Children, Lupus Study Group. Co-editor: Perspectives in Pediatric Pathology; past contbg. editor Jour. Pediatrics; past mem. editl. bd. Pediatric Nephrology; mem. editl. bd. Jour. Urologic Pathology; contbr. articles to profl. jours. With USN, 1945-46. Recipient Henry L. Barnett award Am. Acad. Pediats., 1997. Mem. AMA, Am. Soc. Investigative Pathology, Internat. Acad. Pathology (U.S.-Can. divsn.), Am. Soc. Clin. Pathologists, Soc. Pediatric Pathology (co-founder, past pres., Farber lectr. 1982, Spl. Disting. Colleague award 1987, 97), Am. Pediatric Soc., Am. Soc. Nephrology, Internat. Pediat. Nephrology Assn., Renal Pathology Soc. (past pres., Renal Pathology Founder award 1997), Am. Soc. Pediatric Nephrology (Founder's award 1999). Office Phone: 248-898-1256. E-mail: jaybernstein@earthlink.net.

BERNSTEIN, LEROY GEORGE, state legislator; m. Kathleen Bernstein; 4 children. Former pres., owner Valley Movers, Inc.; mem. N.D. Ho. of Reps. from 45th dist., 1989—; speaker N.D. Ho. of Reps., 2001—. Vice chmn. Transp. Com. N.D. Ho. of Reps., mem. Indsl. Appropriations Com, Govt. Ops., Bus. and Labor Com. Mem. DAV, KC, U.S. C. of C., Am. Legion, Eagles. Republican. Address: 3949 N 10th St Fargo ND 58102-1048

BERNSTEIN, MARK D., theater director; Grad., U. Pa. Gen. mgr. Phila. Drama Guild; instr. financial mgmt. Nonprofit Arts Inst., Drexel U.; instr. Nonprofit Mgmt. Ctr., Wash. U.; mng. dir. The Repertory Theatre of St. Louis. Mem. nat. negotiating com. League of Resident Theatres; mem. citizens adv. panel Mo. Regional Arts Commission. Mem. membership com. Greater Phila. Cultural Alliance. Office: Repertory Theatre St Louis PO Box 191730 Saint Louis MO 63119-7730

BERNSTEIN, MERTON CLAY, law educator, arbitrator; b. NYC, Mar. 26, 1923; s. Benjamin and Ruth (Frederica (Kleeblatt)) B.; m. Joan Barbara Brodshaug, Dec. 17, 1955; children: Johanna Karin, Inga Saterlie, Matthew Curtis, Rachel Libby. BA, Oberlin Coll., 1943; LL.B., Columbia U., 1948. Bar: N.Y. 1948, U.S. Supreme Ct. 1952. Assoc. Schlesinger & Schlesinger, 1948; atty. NLRB, 1949-50, 50-51, Office of Solicitor, U.S. Dept. Labor, 1950; counsel Nat. Enforcement Commn., 1951, U.S. Senate Subcom. on Labor, 1952; legis. asst. to U.S. Sen. Wayne L. Morse, 1953-56; counsel U.S. Senate Com. on R.R. Retirement, 1957-58; spl. counsel U.S. Senate Subcom. on Labor, 1958; assoc. prof. law U. Nebr., 1958-59; lectr., sr. fellow Yale U. Law Sch., 1960-65; prof. law Ohio State U., 1965-75; Walter D. Coles prof. law Washington U., St. Louis, 1975-96, Walter D. Coles prof. emeritus, 1997—; mem. adv. com. to Sec. of Treas. on Coordination of Social Security and pvt. pension plans, 1967-68. Prin. cons. Nat. Commn. on Social Security Reform, 1982-83; vis. prof. Columbia U. Law Sch., 1967-68, Leiden U., 1975-76; mem. adv. com. rsch. U.S. Social Security Adminstrn., 1967-68, chmn., 1969-70; cons. Adminstrv. Conf. of the U.S., 1989, Dept. Labor, 1966-67, Russell Sage Found., 1967-68, NSF, 1970-71, Ctr. for the Study of Contemporary Problems, 1968-71. Author: The Future of Private Pensions, 1964, Private Dispute Settlement, 1969, (with Joan B. Bernstein) Social Security: The System That Works, 1988; contbr. articles to profl. jours. Del White Ho. Conf. Aging, 1995; active Bethany (Conn.) Planning and Zoning Commn., 1962—65, Ohio Retirement Study Commn., 1967—68, City of St. Louis Bd. Health, 1993—2000, Brewster (Mass.) Bd. Health, 2001—05, chair, 2002—04; pres. bd. Met. Sch. Columbus, Ohio, 1974—75; co-chmn. transition team for St. Louis Mayor Freeman Bosley Jr., 1993; candidate for Dem. nom. US Senate, Mo., 1991—92; bd. dirs. St. Louis Theatre Project, 1981—84. With AUS, 1943—45. Fulbright fellow, 1975-76, Elizur Wright award, 1965. Mem. ABA (sec. sect. labor rels. law 1968-69), Internat. Assn. for Labor Law and Social Security (bd. dirs. U.S. chpt. 1973-83, 88-91), Indsl. Rels. Rsch. Assn., Nat. Acad. Social Ins. (founding mem., bd. dirs. 1986-91), Am. Arbitration Assn. (mem. adv. com. St. Louis region 1987-2000), Fulbright Alumni Assn. (bd. dirs. 1976-78). Democrat. Jewish. Office Phone: 508-896-8383. Business E-Mail: bernstein@wulaw.wustl.edu.

BERNSTEIN, RICHARD, lawyer; b. 1974; B, U. Mich.; degree in Law, Northwestern U. Atty. Law Offices of Sam Bernstein, Farmington Hills, Mich. Adj. prof., Polit. Sci. U. Mich., Ann Arbor; bd. governors Wayne State U.; adv. bd. mem. Mich. Paralyzed Veterans; bd. mem. Tech Town; adv. com. mem. Mich. Anti-Defamation League, Am. Israel Pub. Affairs Com., Mich. Cmty. Scholars Prog., U. Mich., Max M. Fisher Found. Adv. bd. mem. United Jewish Fedn. of Metro. Detroit. amed one of 40 Under 40, Crain's Detroit Bus., 2006; named to Athletes with Disabilities Hall of Fame, 1999. Mem.: Mich. Assn. for Deaf & Hard of Hearing. Avocation: running. Office: Law Offices of Same Berstein 31100 Northwestern Highway Farmington Hills MI 48334 Office Phone: 248-737-8400.

BERNSTEIN, ROBERT, advertising executive; m. Phyliss Bernstein; children: Steven, David, Susan. Grad., U. Okla., 1960. With Potts Woodbury Advt., 1962-64; founder Bernstein-Rein, Kansas City, Mo., 1964—, pres, CEO. Bd. dirs., chmn. Mark Twain Bank Kansas City. Active Youth Vol. Corps, Epilepsy Found., Heart Am. Shakespeare Festival, Met. Luth. Ministry, STOP Violence Coalition, Children's Pl., Children's Mercy Hosp., Genesis Sch., Ronald McDonald Houses, Variety Club Kansas City; pres. Starlight Theatre Assn.; bd. dirs. Kansas City Art Inst. Recipient Spirit of Kansas City award, 1991, Hy Vile Cmty. Svc. award, 1995, Advt. Profl. of Yr. award Am. Advt. Fedn., 1995, Manking award Cystic Fibrosis award, 1995. Mem. Am. Assn. Advt. Agys., Nat. Assn. Broadcasters. Office: Bernstein-Rein Advt Inc 4600 Madison Ave Ste 1500 Kansas City MO 64112-3016

BERNTHAL, DAVID GARY, judge; b. Danville, Ill., Apr. 18, 1950; s. Albert F. and Mary Lou (Ackelmire) B. B, U. Ill., 1972, JD, 1976. Bar: U.S. Dist. Ct. (cen. dist.) Ill. Assoc. Brittingham, Sadler & Meeker, Danville, 1976-78; ptnr. Brittingham, Sadler, Meeker & Bernthal, Danville, 1979-80, Meeker & Bernthal, Danville, 1980-84, Snyder Meeker & Bernthal, Danville, Ill., 1984-86; assoc. judge 5th Jud. Cir. Ct., Danville, 1986—. Bd. dirs. Vermilion County chpt. ARC, 1982-87, Lakeview Meml. Found., 1984-87, Danville Area Community Coll. Found., 1985-87; mem. Danville Zoning Com., 1982-86. Mem. Vermillion County Bar Assn., Assn. Trial Lawyers Am., Ill. Judges Assn., Jaycees (Dist. Svc. award 1984). Mem. Vermillion County Bar Assn., Assn. Trial Lawyers Am., Am. Judges Assn., Ill. Judges Assn., Jaycees (Dist. Svc. award 1984), Rotary (pres., bd. dirs. Danville club 1980-84). Republican. Avocations: golf, travel. Office: US Dist Ct 201 S Vine St Urbana IL 61802-3369

BERNTHAL, HAROLD GEORGE, health products executive, director; b. Frankenmuth, Mich., June 11, 1928; s. Wilfred Michael and Olga Bertha (Stern) B.; m. Margaret Hrebek, Jan. 25, 1958; children: Barbara Anne, Karen Elizabeth, James Willard. BS in Chemistry, Mich. State U., 1950. Pres. Am. Hosp. Supply Corp., Evanston, Ill., 1974-85; chmn. Cobern Inc., Lake Forest, Ill., 1986—. Life trustee Northwestern Meml. Hosp., Chgo.; hon. bd. dirs. Valparaiso (Ind.) U.; former chair Wheat Ridge Ministries; former governing mem. Chgo. Symphony Orch. Served with AUS, 1950-52. Recipient Lumen Christi medal Valparaiso U., 1988. Mem. Health Industries Assn. (past pres.), Health Industry Mfr.'s Assn. (past mem. exec. com.), Pharm. Mfrs. Assn. (past chmn. med. device com., Knollwood Club, Old Elm Club, The Reserve, Bigfoot Country Club.

BERNTSON, GARY GLEN, psychiatry, psychology and pediatrics educator; b. Mpls., June 16, 1945; s. Edward Mathias and Meryle Berntson; m. Susan Berntson, July 11, 2002. BA, U. Minn., 1968, PhD, 1971. Postdoctoral fellow Rockefeller U., NYC, 1971-73; asst. prof. dept. psychology Ohio State U., Columbus, 1973-77, assoc. prof., 1977-81, prof., 1981—, prof. dept. pediatrics, 1983—, prof. of psychiatry, 1988—. Affiliate scientist Yerkes Regional Primate Rsch. Ctr., Emory U., Atlanta, 1984-95; mem. initial rev. group ADAMHA, Washington, 1989-91, NIMH, Washington, 1991-93, NIH, 2004—; mem. fellowship rev. panel NSF, Washington, 1991-95. Contbr. over 150 articles to profl. jours., 20 chpts. to books; co-editor: Handbook of Psychophysiology. Fellow NSF, 1969, USPHS, 1972. Mem. Soc. for Neurosci., Soc. for Psychophysiol. Rsch.; fellow AAAS. Achievements include novel concepts of control of the autonomic nervous system and psychosomatic relations. Office: Ohio State U Dept Psychology 1835 Neil Ave Columbus OH 43210-1222 Office Phone: 614-292-1749.

BEROLZHEIMER, KARL, retired lawyer; b. Chgo., Mar. 31, 1932; s. Leon J. and Rae Gloss (Lowenthal) B.; m. Diane Glick, July 10, 1954; children: Alan, Eric, Paul, Lisa. BA, U. Ill., 1953; JD, Harvard U., 1958. Bar: Ill. 1958, U.S. Ct. Appeals (7th cir.) 1964, U.S. Ct. Appeals (9th cir.) 1969, U.S. Supreme Ct. 1976. Assoc. Ross & Hardies, Chgo., 1958—66, ptnr., 1966—76; v.p. legal Centel Corp., Chgo., 1976-77, v.p., gen. counsel, 1977-82, sr. v.p., gen. counsel, 1982-88, sr. v.p., gen. counsel, sec., 1988-93; of counsel Ross & Hardies, Chgo., 1993—2003, McGuire Woods LLP, 2003—07; ret., 2008. Nat. adv. bd. Ctr. for Informatics Law, John Marshall Law Sch., Chgo., 1988-93; mem. Corp. Counsel Ctr., Northwestern U. Law Sch., 1987-93, mem. emeritus, 1993—; mem. adv. bd. Litigation Risk Mgmt. Inst., 1989-95; bd. dirs. Milton Industries, Chgo., 1973-2005, Devon Bank, Chgo., 1985—; cons. Mt. Pulaski Tel. and Elec. Co., Lincoln, Ill., 1981-86; sec., gen. counsel Consol. Water Co., Chgo., 1968-72; mem. human rels. task force Chgo. Cmty. Trust, 1988-90. Bd. dirs. The Nat.

Conf. Commn. and Justice, Chgo., presiding co-chmn., 1987-90, mem. nat. exec. bd. dirs., 1988-98, chair investment com., 1991-94, nat. co-chair, 1992-95, pres., 1993-94, chair, 1995-98; exec. bd. Internat. Coun. Christians and Jews, 1996-2000, v.p., 1998-2000; bd. dirs. Evanston (Ill.) Mental Health, 1975-82, chair, 1978-80; dir. Evanston Cmty. Found., 1996-2003, vice chair, chair grants com., 1996-98, chair, 1999-2001, chair coun. advisors, 2003—, chair governance com., 2007-, mem. invest com. 2002-; bd. dirs. Beth Emet Found., 1997; trustee Northlight Theatre, Evanston, 1992-2004, vice-chair, 1993-99; mem. coun. The Communitarian Network, 1993-96; trustee Beth Emet Synagogue, Evanston, 1985-87, 89, 2004-07, sec., 1985-89, exec. com. 2006-07; chair Capital Campaign Plan com., 1994-97; discrimination priority com. United Way, 1990-97, vice-chair, 1993; mem. assembly Parliament of the World's Religions, 1993; mem. Ill. atty. gen.'s ad hoc com. for creation of justice commn., 1994; adv. com. Ill. Justice Commn., 1995-96; adv. bd. Nat. Underground R.R. Freedom Ctr., 1997—. 1st lt. US Army, 1953—55, Aberdeen, Md., Ft. Stewart, Ga., Sullivan Barracks, Germany. Fellow Am. Bar Found.; mem. ABA (chair telcom. com. bus. law sect. 1982-86, dispute resolution com. 1986-90, office com. 1991-95, mem. Coalition for Justice 1993-97, bd. editors Bus. Law Today 1995-97, co-chair conflicts of interest com. 1997-2001, past chair 2001-03). Chgo. Bar Assn. (devel. of law com. 1963-77, chair 1971-73), Chgo. Coun. Lawyers. Democrat. Office: McGuire Woods LLP Ste 4100 77 W Wacker Dr Chicago IL 60601-1815 Home: 522 Church St Apt 6D Evanston IL 60201 Office Phone: 312-750-8642. Personal E-mail: dkberolz@comcast.net.

BERRY, CHUCK (CHARLES EDWARD ANDERSON BERRY), musician, composer; b. St. Louis, Oct. 18, 1926; s. Henry William, Sr., and Martha Banks Berry; m. Themetta Suggs, Oct. 1948; 4 children: Darlen Ingrid, Melody Exes, Aloha Isa Lei, Charles Edward Anderson, Jr. Popular artist in rock and roll music, plays guitar, saxophone, piano; concert, TV appearances, 1955—; rec. artist Chess Records; appeared in film Go, Johnny Go, Rock, Rock, Rock, 1956, Jazz on a Summer's Day, 1960, Let the Good Times Roll, 1973; composer: Rock 'n' Roll Music; albums include: After School Sessions, 1958, One Dozen Berry's, 1958, Rockin' At The Hops, 1959-60, New Juke Box Hits, 1960, Chuck Berry, 1960, More Chuck Berry, 1960, On Stage, 1960, Twist, 1960, You Can Never Tell, 1964, Greatest Hits, 1964, 2 Great Guitars, 1964, Chuck Berry in London, 1965, Fresh Berrys, 1965, St. Louis to Liverpool, 1966, Golden Hits, 1967, At the Fillmore, 1967, Medley, 1967, In Memphis, 1967, Concerto in B Goods, 1969, Home Again, 1971, The London Sessions, 1972, Golden Decade, 1972, St. Louis to Frisco to Memphis, 1972, Let the Good Times Roll, 1973, Golden Decade, Vol. 2, 1973, Bio, 1973, Back in the U.S.A., 1973, Golden Decade, Vol. 5, 1974, I'm a Rocker, 1975, Chuck Berry 75, 1975, Motorvatin', 1976, Rockit, 1979, Chess Masters, 1983, The Chess Box, 1989, Missing Berries: Rarities, 1990, On the Blues Side, 1993, others; soundtrack Hail! Hail! Rock n' Roll, 1987; author: autobiography Chuck Berry, 1987. Recipient Grammy award for Lifetime Achievement, 1984; named to Rock and Rock Hall of Fame, 1986. Office: Berry Park 691 Buckner Rd Wentzville MO 63385-5442

BERRY, DAVID J., former financial services company executive; b. Columbus, Ohio, Apr. 14, 1944; s. Maurice Glenn Berry and Janice (Eshelman) Read; m. Janet Lynn Tewksbury, Mar. 24, 1977; children: Jeffrey James, Jennifer Jean, Jon Andrew, Amy Jo. Student, Miami U., Oxford, Ohio, 1963-64, Ohio State U., 1965-66. Registered prin. SEC. Ind. fin. svc. salesman, 1966-74; gen. agt. Sun Life Assurance Co. Can., Columbus, 1975-85; pres. Strategic Info. Svcs., Columbus, 1986-87; v.p. IDS Life Ins. Co., Mpls., 1990—; assoc. mgr. IDS Fin. Svcs. Inc., Columbus, 1988, region dir., 1989; v.p. IDS Life Ins. Co., Mpls., 1991-2000; ret., 2000. Chmn. Agy. Mgmt. Tng. Coun., Columbus, 1982-83. Bell ringer Salvation Army, Columbus, 1975-85; vol. instr. Learning Disabled Children, Columbus, 1980-83; pres. PTA, Worthington, Ohio, 1983. Fellow Life Underwriting Tng. Coun., Columbus, 1981. Mem. Nat. Assn. Securities Dealers, Gen. Agts. and Mgrs. Assn. (pres. 1979-82), Mpls. Life Underwriters Assn. Avocations: travel, sports, poetry. Office: IDS Life Ins Co IDS Tower # 10 Minneapolis MN 55402-2100

BERRY, DEBORAH, state representative; b. Sept. 1958; Mem. Iowa Ho. Reps., DesMoines, 2003—, mem. various coms. including edn., human resources and judiciary. Waterloo City councilwoman. Mem.: Commn. on the Status of African Ams. Democrat. Office: State Capitol East 12th and Grand Des Moines IA 50319 Home: 241 Madison St Waterloo IA 50703

BERRY, RICHARD STEPHEN, chemist; b. Denver, Apr. 9, 1931; s. Morris and Ethel (Alpert) B.; m. Carla Lamport Friedman, Sept. 4, 1955; children: Andrea, Denise, Eric. AB, Harvard U., 1952, AM, 1954, PhD, 1956. Instr. chemistry Harvard U., 1956-57, U. Mich., 1957-60; asst. prof. Yale U., 1960-64; assoc. prof. U. Chgo., 1964-67, prof., 1967—, James Franck Disting. Svc. prof., 1989—; Arthur D. Little prof. MIT, 1968; Phillips lectr. Haverford Coll., 1968; spl. advisor to dir. Argonne Nat. Lab., 2004—. Cons. Avco-Everett Rsch. Labs., 1964—83, Argonne Nat. Lab., 1976—, Oak Ridge Nat. Labs., 1978—81, Los Alamos Sci. Lab., 1975—2005, mem. adv. com. theory; vis. prof. U. Copenhagen, 1967, 79; mem. adv. panel for chemistry NSF, 1971—73; mem. rev. com. radiol. and environ. rsch. divsn. Argonne Nat. Lab., 1970—76; mem. evaluation panel measures for air quality Nat. Bur. Standards; mem. numerical data adv. bd. NRC, 1978—86, chmn., 1981—86, mem. com. strengthening linkages between math. and scis., 1997—99, mem. steering com. panel on environ. monitoring, mem. com. on atomic and molecular sci., 1984—89; com. on chem. scis NAS-NRC, 1977—79; mem. adv. panel on health of sci. and tech. enterprise, mem. adv. panel on nat. labs. Office Tech. Assessment; mem. adv. bd. Environ. Health Resource Ctr., Chgo., Inst. for Theoretical Physics, Santa Barbara, 1989—91; mem. vis. com. divsn. applied physics Harvard U., 1977—81; Hinshelwood lectr. Oxford (Eng.) U., 1980; mem. adv. panel dept. chemistry Princeton U., 1978—81; prof. associé U. Paris-Sud, 1979—80; Newton Abraham prof. Oxford U., 1986—87, Phi Beta Kappa lectr., 1989—90, Welch Symposium lectr., 1995; pres. Telluride Summer Rsch. Ctr., 1989—93; chair com. transnat. exch. sci. data Nat. Rsch. Coun., 1994—97; Frederick Kaufman lectr. U. Pitts., 1996; Sackler lectr. Tel Aviv (Israel) U., 1999; F.C. Bartell lectr. U. Mich., 1999. Author: Understanding Energy, 1988; co-author: TOSCA, The Total Social Cost of Fossil and Nuclear Power, 1979, Physical Chemistry, 1980, 2d edit., 2000, Thermodynamic Optimization of Finite Time Processes, 2000; assoc. editor: Jour. Chem. Physics, 1971-74, Accounts Chem. Rsch., 1975-90, Revs. Modern Physics, 1983-95, Phys. Rev. A, 1986-92, Phys. Rev. E, 1992-94, Phys. Chemistry Chem. Physics, 1999-2002; bd. dirs. Bull. Atomic Scientists, 1974-83; adv. editor: Resources and Energy, 1978-92; contbr. articles to profl. jours. Recipient Heyrovsky medal Czech Acad. Sci., 1997; Alfred P. Sloan fellow, 1962-66; Guggenheim fellow, 1972-73; MacArthur prize fellow, 1983; Alexander von Humboldt Stiftung prize fellow, 1993. Fellow AAAS (chmn. chemistry sect. 1993-94), Am. Phys. Soc. (coun. 1993-95, publs. oversight com. 1996-2000, panel on pub. affairs, 2001—, chmn. few-body sys. topical group 1994-95), Am. Acad. Arts and Scis. (v.p. 1987-90, 95-98), Japan Soc. for Promotion of Sci.; mem. NAS (home sec. 1999-2003, chair report rev. com. 2000-04), Am. Chem. Soc., Royal Danish Acad. Arts and Letters (fgn.), Sigma Xi (nat. lectr. 1976-77). Office: Univ Chgo Dept Chemistry 5735 S Ellis Ave Chicago IL 60637-1403 Office Phone: 773-702-7021. E-mail: berry@uchicago.edu.

BERRY, WILLIAM LEE, business administration educator; b. Indpls., Dec. 24, 1935; s. George Lee and Anna Marie (Hansert) B.; m. Carol M. Berry; children: Ann Kathleen, Lee Michael, Lynn Colleen, Kimberly Ann. BS, Purdue U., West Lafayette, Ind., 1957; MS, Va. Poly. Inst., Blacksburg, 1964; DBA, Harvard U., Cambridge, Mass., 1969. Mfg. trainee GE, various locations, 1957-60, supr. mfg. Salem, Va., 1960-64; from asst. prof. to assoc. prof. indsl. mgmt. Purdue U., West Lafayette, Ind., 1968-76; prof. prodn. mgmt. Ind. U., Bloomington, 1976-82; C. Maxwell Stanley prof. prodn. mgmt. U. Iowa, Iowa City, 1982-87, sr. assoc. dean Coll. Bus. Adminstrn., 1983-87, dir. Mfg. and Productivity Ctr., 1986-87; Belk prof. bus. adminstrn., chmn. ops. mgmt. area U. N.C., Chapel Hill, 1988-92; prof. bus. adminstrn. Ohio State U., Columbus, 1992—2007, Richard Ross chair in mgmt., dir. Ctr. Excellence in Mgmt., 1995—2006, prof. emeritus, 2007. Vis. prof. IMD, Lausanne, Switzerland, 1987-88; cons. in field. Co-author: Operations and Logistics Management, 1972, Production Planning, Scheduling and Inventory Control: Concepts, Techniques and Systems, 1974, Master Production Scheduling: Principles and Practice, 1979, Manufacturing Planning and Control for Supply Chain Management, 1984, 5th edit., 2005, ITEC: Manufacturing Planning and Control/Manufacturing Strategy Simulation, 1992, Production and Inventory Control Integrated, 1992; contbr. articles to profl. jours. 1st Enterprise fellow Kenan Inst., 1988-90. Fellow Decision Scis. Inst. (v.p. 1983-84, sec. 1985-86, pres.-elect 1987, pres. 1988); mem. Inst. Indsl. Engrs. (v.p. 1979-81, dir., Disting. Service award 1979), Ops. Mgmt. Assn. (v.p. 1981-85, pres.-elect 1985-86, pres. 1986-87, dir., Disting. Leadership award 1987), Am. Prodn. and Inventory Control Soc., Inst. Mgmt. Sci., Ops. Research Soc. Office: Fisher Coll of Bus Ohio State U Columbus OH 43210

BERRYMAN, DIANA (KAPNAS), radio personality; b. Gary, Ind., Oct. 10; m. Patrick Berryman; 1 stepchild, Shannon. Radio host, morning program announcer, ops. dir. Sta. WMBI, Chgo. Office: WMBI 820 N LaSalle Blvd Chicago IL 60610

BERRYMAN, JAMES, state legislator; b. Feb. 17, 1947; m. Susan; children: Steve, Eric, Julie. Student, Adrian Coll., 1965-69. State senator Mich. State Senate, Dist. 17, 1990-98. Asst. minority whip, 1993, majority floor leader, 1995—, mem. tech. & energy, fin. svc., agrl. & forestry coms., Mich. State Senate. Mem. Adrian (Mich.) City Planning Commn., 1978-81; mem. Adrian City Commn., 1979-85; mayor City of Adrian, 1985; mem. Govs. Health Occupations Coun., 1989—; Dem. cand. for Congress, 1998. Mem. Mich. Assn. Mayors (pres. 1987—). Address: 676 Stonecrest Adrian MI 49221-9564

BERRYMAN, ROBERT GLEN, accounting educator, consultant; b. Freeport, Ill., Nov. 22, 1928; s. Loyd Vernon and Gladys Leone (Hicks) B.; m. Ruth Madelyn Bjorngjeld, Aug. 25, 1955; children: Peter, David, Kathryn. BSBA, Northwestern U., 1950, MBA, 1951; PhD, U. Ill., 1958. CPA, Ill., Minn. Staff auditor Deloitte & Touche, Chgo., 1951-54, mgr. Mpls., 1969-70; instr. U. Ill., Champaign, 1954-58; asst. prof. acctg. U. Minn., Mpls., 1958-61, assoc. prof., 1961-65, prof., 1965-95, dir. grad. studies in acctg., 1980-83, chmn. dept. acctg., 1963-65, 70-73, 1990-95; exec. dir. fin. Cedar Riverside Assocs., Mpls., 1974-75. Cons. in field.; PhD thesis adv. U. Minn., Mpls., Minn. Mem. editl. bd. Issues in Acctg. Edn., 1995-98; contbr. articles to profl. publs. Adviser to audit com. Minn. State Colls. and Univs., 1997-2001 Recipient Horace T. Morse-Amoco All Univ. Tchg. award U. Minn., 1976, Outstanding Tchr. award Carlson Sch. Mgmt., U. Minn., Green Eyeshade award Minn. Acctg. Assn., Tchg. award U. Minn. Alumni Assn., Mpls., 1978, Leon Radde Outstanding Educator award Inst. Internal Auditors, 1988. Mem. AICPA (chmn. acctg. theory subcom. 1979-83, continuing profl. edn. exec. com. 1979-82, bd. examiners 1980-83, Disting. Achievement in Acctg. Edn. award 1999), Inst. Internal Auditors (bd. regents 1979-83, bd. govs. Twin City chpt. 1981-91, cert. internal auditor), Minn. Soc. CPA (bd. dirs. 1965-69, 78-83, first recipient and honoree R. Glen Berryman award 1976), Accountability Minn. (pres. and bd. dirs.), Am. Acctg. Assn. (Outstanding Acctg. Educator 1994, Auditing Educator 1992). Home: 1462 Brenner Ave Saint Paul MN 55113-1671 Office: Univ MN Carlson Sch of Mgmt 321 19th Ave S Minneapolis MN 55455-0438

BERS, DONALD MARTIN, physiology educator; b. NYC, Dec. 13, 1953; s. Harold Theodore and Penny (Wall) B.; m. Kathryn Eileen Hammond, July 17, 1976; children: Brian Alexander, Rebecca Ann. BA, U. Colo., 1974; PhD, UCLA, 1978. Postdoctoral research fellow UCLA, 1978-79, asst. research physiologist, 1980-82, adj. asst. prof., 1981-87; postdoctoral research fellow Edinburgh (Scotland) U., 1979-80; asst. prof. U. Calif., Riverside, 1982-86, assoc. prof., 1986-89, prof., 1989-92, divisional dean, dir. biomed. scis. program, 1991-92; prof., chmn. dept. physiology Loyola U., Chgo., 1992—. Author: Excitation-Contraction Coupling and Cardiac Contractile Force, 1991, 2001; assoc. editor News in Physiol. Sci.; mem. editl. bd. Am. Jour. Physiology, Circulation Rsch., Jour. Pharm. and Exptl. Therapeutics, Jour. Molecular Cell Cardiology; contbr. articles to profl. jours. Bd. dirs. Am. Heart Assn., Riverside, 1985-92, pres., 1989-91. Fellow Am. Heart Assn., L.A., 1978-80, Brit.-Am., Am. Heart Assn., 1980-81; recipient New Investigator Rsch. award NIH, 1982-85, Rsch. Career Devel. award NIH, 1985-90. Fellow: Internat. Soc. Heart Rsch. (mem. coun.), Am. Heart Assn.; mem.: AAAS, Biophys. Soc. (mem. coun., mem. exec. bd.), Am. Physiol. Soc., Soc. Gen. Physiology.

BERSCHEID, ELLEN S., psychology professor, writer, researcher; b. Colfax, Wis., Oct. 11, 1936; d. Sylvan L. and Alvilde (Running) Saumer; m. Dewey Mathias Berscheid, ov. 21, 1959. BA, U. Nev., 1959, MA, 1960; PhD, U. Minn., 1965. Market rsch. analyst Pillsbury Co., Mpls., 1960-62; asst. prof. psychology and mktg. U. Minn., Mpls., 1965-66, asst. prof. psychology, 1967-68, assoc. prof., 1969-71, prof., 1971-88, Regents' prof. psychology, 1988—. Mem. NRC Assembly Behavioral and Social Scis., 1973-77. Co-author: Interpersonal Attraction, 1969, 78, Equity: Theory and Research, 1978, Close Relationships, 1983, Psychology of Interpersonal Relationships, 2005, also numerous articles; mem. numerous editl. bds., past editorships. Recipient Disting. Scientist award Soc. Exptl. Social Psychology, 1993. Fellow APA (Donald T. Campbell award 1984, editor Contemporary Psychology Jour. 1985-91, Disting. Sci. Contbn. award 1997, Presdl. Citation 2003), Soc. Personality and Social Psychology (pres. 1985), Soc. for Psychol. Study Social Issues, Am. Acad. Arts and Scis.; mem. Internat. Soc. for the Study Personal Relationships (pres. 1990-92), Soc. Exptl. Social Psychology (exec. bd. 1971-74, 77-80, 85-89, Disting. Scientist award 1993). Lutheran. Avocation: interior design. Home: 329 Park Cir Menomonie WI 54751 Office: U Minn Dept Psychology N309 Elliott Hall Minneapolis MN 55455 Business E-Mail: bersc001@umn.edu.

BERTAGNOLLI, LESLIE A., lawyer; b. Bloomington, Ill., Nov. 11, 1948; BA, Ill. State U., 1970, MA, 1971; PhD, U. Ill., 1975, JD, 1979. Bar: Ill. 1979. Ptnr. Baker & McKenzie, Chgo. Office: Baker & McKenzie 130 E Randolph Dr Ste 3700 Chicago IL 60601-6342

BERTENTHAL, BENNETT IRA, dean, psychologist, educator; b. NYC, Mar. 22, 1949; m. Meryl Bertenthal; 2 children. BA in Psychology, Brandeis U., 1971; MA in Devel. Psychology, U. Denver, 1976, PhD, 1978. Postdoctoral fellow Brain Rsch. Inst. and dept. pediats. UCLA Sch. Medicine, 1978-79; asst. prof. dept. psychology U. Va., 1979-85, assoc. prof., 1985, prof., 1991—, dir. devel. tng. program, 1989-96; asst. dir. NSF, Arlington, Va., 1997-99; prof. Dept. Psychology U. Chgo., 1999—2006; dean Coll. of Arts and Scis. Ind. U., Bloomington, 2007—. Mem. human devel. and aging study sect, Nat. Inst. Child Health and Human Devel., 1987, 91-96, chair, 1994-96; extramural reviewer NSF, Nat. Inst. Neurol. Diseases & Communicative Disorders, NIMH; cons. NINCDS; mem. performance and safety monitoring com. NINCDS, 1981-88; program com. Internat. Conf. Infant Studies, 1984, 88, 96, Southeastern Conf. Human Devel., 1988; mem. MacArthur Network on Transition From Infancy to Childhood, 1987-92; mem. MacArthur Network Task Force-Devel. of Computer Workstas. for Psychol. Rsch., 1988-92. Assoc. editor Devel. Psychology, 1988-90, mem. editl. bd., 1988-90; mem. editl. bd. Jour. Exptl. Child Psychology, 1985-88, Child Devel., 1980-83; reviewer Psychophysiology, infant Behavior and Devel., Perception and Psychophysics, Devel. Psychology, Child Devel., SRCD Monographys, Internat. Jour. Behavioural Devel., Jour. Exptl. Psychology, Human Perception and Performance. Recipient Boyd R. McCandless Young Scientist award, 1985, rsch. career devel. awarrd NIH, 1985-90, Cattell Sabbatical award, 1990, MHTP postdoctoral fellowship, 1978-79; grantee U. Va. Rsch. Policy Coun., 1979-80, 87-90, 89—, NIMH, 1979-80, 85-90, 91—, NINCDS, 1980-81, NIH, 1982-84, 85-88, 89—, John D. and Catherine T. MacArthur Found., 1984-85, 89—, Va. Ctr. Innovative Tech., 1985-86, NATO, 1989—, United Cerebral Palsey Rsch. and Edn. Found., 1989-90, McDonnell-Pew Program Cognitive Neuroscis., 1991-93 Fellow APA (program com. 1987, 88, nominations com. divsn. 7 1988, mem.-at-large divsn. 7 exec. com. 1995-98, mem. com. on sci. awards, 1991-94, chair, 1994), Am. Psychol. Soc.; mem. AAAS, Soc. Rsch. in Child Devel. (co-chair program com. 1995-97), Assn. Rsch. in Vision and Ophthalmology, Internat. Soc. Infant Studies, Internat. Soc. Study Behavioural Devel., Internat. Soc. Study of Posture and Gait, Psychonomic Soc. Office: Dean's Office Kirkwood Hall 104 130 S Woodlawn Ave Bloomington IN 47405-7104

BERTHOUEX, PAUL MAC, civil and environmental engineer, educator; b. Oelwein, Iowa, Aug. 15, 1940; s. George Albert and LaVadia Fay (McBride) B.; m. Susan Jean Powell, Sept. 8, 1962; 1 child, Stephanie Fay. BSCE, U. Iowa, 1963, MSCE, 1964; PhD, U. Wis., 1969. Registered profl. engr., Iowa. Instr. U. Iowa, Iowa City, 1964-65; asst. prof. civil engring. U. Conn., Storrs, 1965-67; chief rsch. engr. GKW Cons., Mannheim, Fed. Republic of Germany, 1969-71; prof. civil engring. U. Wis., Madison, 1971-99, emeritus prof., 1999—. Author: Strategy of Pollution Control, 1978, Statistics for Environmental Engineers, 1994, 2d edit., 2002; contbr. numerous articles to profl. jours. Recipient Radebaugh Prize, CSWPCA, 1989, 91. Mem. ASCE (Rudolf Herring medal 1974, 92), Water Environment Fedn. (Eddy medal 1971), U. Iowa Disting. Engring. Alumni Acad. Office: U Wis 1415 Johnson Dr Madison WI 53706-1607

BERTOLET, RODNEY JAY, philosophy educator; b. Allentown, Pa., Mar. 22, 1949; s. Frank and Helen (Johnson) B. BA, Franklin & Marshall Coll., 1971; PhD, U. Wis., 1977. Asst. prof. philosophy Purdue U., West Lafayette, Ind., 1977-82, assoc. prof. philosophy, 1982-90, prof. philosophy, 1990—, dept. head, 1991—. Author: What Is Said, 1990. Mem. Am. Philos. Assn., Ind. Philos. Assn. (pres. 1983-84). Office: Purdue Univ Dept Philosophy 100 N University St West Lafayette IN 47907-2098 Office Phone: 765-494-4275. E-mail: bertolet@purdue.edu.

BERTRAND, JAMES A., electronics executive; BSME, Carleton U., Ottawa, Ont., Can., 1979; MBA (GM fellow), U. We. Ont., London, Ont., Can., 1983. Product engr. to various pos. in engring. and fin. GM, Osshawa, Ont., Canada, 1979—86; mgr. overseas fin. analysis to dir. bus. devel. and analysis GM Treas.'s Office, YC, 1986—89; dir. fin. analysis and planning GM Europe, Zurich, Switzerland, 1989—92; comptroller Adam Opel AG, Ruesselscheim, Germany, 1992—95; exec. dir. bus. devel.-small cars GM Internat. Ops., Beijing, 1995—97, mem. Asia-Pacific Vehicle Strategy Bd., 1995—97; exec. dir. ops. Delphi Corp., Troy, Mich., 1997—98, v.p. ops., 1998—2003, v.p., 2003—; pres. Delphi Safety and Interior Sys. and Automotive Holdings Group, Troy, Mich., 2003—. Office: World Hdqrs Delphi Corp 5725 Delphi Dr Troy MI 58098-2815 also: Delphi Safety & Interior Sys M/L 480-009-130 1401 Crooks Rd Troy MI 48084

BERWICK, PHILIP, law librarian, director, dean; BA, U. Pa., 1973; JD, U. Toledo, 1978; AMLS, U. Mich., 1979. Mem. libr. staff U. Toledo Coll. Law, Law Libr. Congress; dir. law libr. George Mason U. Sch. Law; assoc. dean info. resources Law Libr., lectr. law Wash. U. Sch. Law, St. Louis. Mem.: ABA, Mid-Am. Assn. Law Librs., Am. Assn. Law Librs. Office: Wash U Sch Law Anheuser-Busch Hall One Brookings Dr Saint Louis MO 63130 Office Phone: 314-935-6440. E-mail: berwick@wulaw.wustl.edu.

BE SANT, CRAIG, marketing executive; Pres. TMP Worldwide, Chgo.; dir. mktg. Monster.com, Indpls., 1998—; mgr. recruiting adv. Chgo. Tribune. Office: Chgo Tribune 435 N Michigan Ave Chicago IL 60611-4066

BESCH, HENRY ROLAND, JR., pharmacologist, educator; b. San Antonio, Sept. 12, 1942; s. Henry Roland and Monette Helen (Kasten) B.; m. Frankie R. Drejer; 1 child, Kurt Theodore. B.Sc. in Physiology, Ohio State U., 1964, PhD in Pharmacology (USPHS predoctoral trainee 1964-67), 1967; USPHS postdoctoral trainee, Baylor U. Coll. Medicine, Houston, 1968-70. Instr. ob-gyn. Ohio State U. Med. Sch., Columbus, 1967-68; asst. prof. Ind. U. Sch. Medicine, Indpls., 1971-73, assoc. prof., 1973-77, prof., 1977, chmn. pharmacology and toxicology, 1977—2002, Showalter prof., 1980—; dir. Ind. State Dept. Toxicology, Indpls., 1991-96, dir. emeritus, 1996—. Can. Med. Rsch. Coun. vis. prof., 1979, Swiss Fed. Tech. Inst. vis. prof., 1995; investigator fed. grants, mem. nat. panels and coms.; cons. in field. Contbr. numerous articles pharm. and med. jours.; mem. editorial bds. profl. jours. Fellow Brit. Med. Research Council, 1970-71; Grantee Showalter Trust, 1975— Fellow Am. Coll. Cardiology, Am. Coll. Forensic Examiners; mem. AAAS, Am. Assn. Clin. Chemistry, Am. Physiol. Soc., Am. Soc. Biochem. Molecular Biology, Am. Soc. Pharmacology and Exptl. Therpeutics, Assn. Med. Sch. Pharmacology Chairs (exec. com. 1985-96, pres. 1994-96), Biochem. Soc., Cardiac Muscle Soc., Internat. Soc. Heart Rsch. (exec. com. Am. sect. 1986-92), Nat. Acad. Clin. Biochemistry, N.Y. Acad. Scis., Sigma Xi. Office: Ind U Sch Medicine 635 Barnhill Dr Indianapolis IN 46202-5126 Office Phone: 317-274-1555. E-mail: besch@iupui.edu.

BESHARSE, JOSEPH CULP, cell biologist, researcher; b. Hickman, Ky., Jan. 21, 1944; s. Herschell and June Elizabeth (Bush) B.; m. Janie Iris Robinson, Aug. 21, 1966; children: Joseph Galen, Kari Elizabeth. BA, Hendrix Coll., 1966; MA, So. Ill. U., 1969, PhD, 1973. Asst. prof. Old Dominion U., Norfolk, Va., 1972-75; postdoctoral fellow Columbia U., NYC, 1975-77; asst. prof. Emory U. Sch. Medicine, Atlanta, 1977-80, assoc. prof., 1980-84, prof., 1984-89; prof., chmn. dept. anatomy & cell biology U. Kans. Sch. Medicine, Kansas City, 1989-97; prof., chmn. dept. cell biology, neurobiology and anatomy Med. Coll. Wis., Milw., 1997—. Mem. study sect. NIH, Bethesda, Md., 1981-86, 92-96. Mem. editl. bd. Exptl. Eye Rsch., 1985-98, editor retina sect., 1997-2000; mem. editl. bd. Investigative Ophthalmology, 1987-92, Visual Neurosci., 1990-92; contbr. more than 100 articles to sci. jours. Rsch. grantee NIH, 1976-2001; recipient Rsch. Career Devel. award, 1979-84, Alcon Rsch. award, 1993. Democrat. Achievements include advances in understanding the cell biology of photoreceptors in the retina, in the regulation of retinal metabolism and the 24-hour photoreceptor clock (i.e. Circadian clock). Office: Med Coll Wis Dept Cellular Biology and Anatomy Milwaukee WI 53226

BESS, RONALD W., advertising executive; b. Bloomington, Ill., July 9, 1946; s. Bloice Monroe and Mary (Trussel) B.; m. Teresa N. Shute, July 22, 1970; children: Daniel, Laura. BS in Mktg., U. Ill., Champaign, 1968, M, 1972. Account exec. Foote, Cone and Belding, Chgo., 1972-75; v.p. account dir. Needham, Harper and Steers, Chgo., 1975-81; sr. v.p. group account dir. DDB Needham, Chgo., 1981-87; pres. Bayer Bess Vanderwarker, Chgo., Foote, Cone & Belding, Chgo.; chmn., CEO diversified group Young Rubicam Inc., NYC, 2001—03, vice chmn, Integration and Bus. Dev., 2003; CEO Euro RSCG-Chgo, Canada, 2004—. Office: Euro RSCG 36 E Grand Ave Chicago IL 60611

BESSETTE, ANDY F., diversified financial services company executive; BS, U. Conn.; MS, U. RI. Mkg. acct. exec. Sheraton Corp., 1977—80; various positions in corp. real estate and corp. svcs. Travelers Ins., 1980—99, v.p. corp. real estate and svcs., 1999—2002; sr. v.p., chief adminstrv. officer St. Paul Co., Inc., 2002—. Office: St Paul Cos 385 Washington Saint Paul MN 55102

BEST, WILLIAM ROBERT, internist, educator, dean; b. Chgo., July 14, 1922; s. Gordon and Marian Burton (Shapland) B.; m. Ruth Johanna Stuchlik, Sept. 2, 1944; children: Barbara Ann Best Mulch, Patricia Marian Best Williams. BS, U. Ill., 1945; MD, U. Ill., Chgo., 1947, MS, 1951; postgrad. math. biology, U. Chgo., 1964-65. Diplomate Am. Bd. Internal Medicine, Am. Bd. Hematology. From intern to fellow in hematology then to resident U. Ill. Hosp., 1947-51; asst. prof., assoc. prof. medicine U. Ill. Coll. Medicine, Chgo., 1953-67, prof., assoc. dean, 1972-81; chief Midwest Rsch. Support Ctr., VA Hosp., Hines, Ill., 1967-72, chief staff, 1981-92, sr. health svcs. rschr., 1992—; prof. medicine, assoc. dean for VA affairs Loyola U. Stritch Sch. Medicine, Maywood, Ill., 1981-92; chief staff U. Ill. Hosp., Chgo., 1976-81. Contbr. numerous articles to sci. jours. 1st lt. US Army, 1951—53. Named Alumnus of Yr., U. Ill. Med. Alumni Assn., 1980. Fellow ACP; mem. AMA (br. pres. 1985), Am. Statis. Assn., AAAS. Episcopalian. Avocations: sailing, computing, radio-controlled model airplanes. Home: 1712 Waverly Cir Saint Charles IL 60174-5869 Office: Ctr for Mgmt Complex Chronic Care Edward Hines Jr VA Hosp Hines IL 60141 Personal E-mail: w.and.r.best@sbcglobal.net. Business E-Mail: william.best@va.gov.

BETTERMANN, HILDA, state legislator; b. Oct. 22, 1942; m. William; two children., U. Minn., St. Cloud U., Moorhead U., Hamline U. Rep. Dist. 10B Minn. State Ho. of Reps., 1991-98, asst. minority leader, 1993-98; instr. Alexandria Tech. Coll., 1982—. Mem. Commerce Com., Econ. Devel. Com., Labor Mgmt. Rels., Agrl. & Higher Edn. Fin. Divsn. Coms.; mem. Minn. Bd. Med. Practice, 1998—; bd. dirs. Douglas County Hosp. Mem. NEA, Minn. Edn. Assn., Am. Vocat. Assn., Minn. Vocat. Assn., Minn. Sec. Assn., Nat. Sec. Assn. Office: 8435 Sara Rd NW Brandon MN 56315-8351

BETTIGA, MICHAEL J., retail executive; Various positions including pharmacy mgr., sr. v.p. retail health svcs. ShopKo Stores, Inc., Green Bay, Wis., 1977-99, sr. v.p. store ops., 1999—. Office: ShopKo Stores Inc 700 Pilgrim Way Green Bay WI 54304-5276

BETTMAN, SUZANNE (SUE BETTMAN), lawyer; b. June 1964; BA, Northwestern U.; JD, U. Ill. Sr. v.p., gen. counsel R.R. Donnelley & Sons Co., Chgo., 2004—. Spkr. in field. Office: RR Donnelley & Sons Co 111 S Wacker Dr Chicago IL 60606 Home: 521 W Stratford Pl Apt 2 Chicago IL 60657 Office Phone: 312-326-8000. Office Fax: 312-326-8594.

BETTS, DOUGLAS D., automotive executive; b. 1963; BA in Mech. Engring., Georgia Inst. Tech., Atlanta, 1984. Quality engr., supr. Buick City Complex, Gen. Motors, 1986—87; quality mgr., engr., tire bldg. Michelin Tire Corp., 1987—95, prodn. mgr., preparation area, 1995—97; gen. mgr., quality engrng., supplier quality assurance, inspection ops. Toyota Motor Corp., Princeton, Ind., 1997—2004; v.p., mfg. quality Nissan North Am., 2004—06, sr. v.p., total customer satisfaction, 2006—07; v.p., chief customer officer Chrysler LLC, Auburn Hills, Mich., 2007—. Bd. mem. Jr. Achievement SW Ind. Office: Chrysler LLC 1000 Chrysler Dr Auburn Hills MI 48326*

BETTS, GENE M., telecommunications industry executive; BBA, MBA, U. Kans. CPA. Various positions in audit and tax depts. Arthur Young, 1975; ptnr. Arthur Young & Co.; asst. v.p. tax dept. Sprint Corp., Overland, Kans., 1987-88, v.p., 1988-90, sr. v.p. fin. svcs. and taxes, 1990-98, sr. v.p., treas., 1998—. Office: Sprint World Hdqrs 6200 Sprint Pkwy Overland Park KS 66251

BETTS, HENRY BROGNARD, physiatrist, educator, health facility administrator; b. New Rochelle, NY, May 25, 1928; s. Henry Brognard and Marguerite Meredith (Denise) B.; m. Monika Christine Paul, Apr. 25, 1970. AB, Princeton U., 1950; MD, U. Va., 1954; DSc (hon.), Hamilton Coll., 1992; D in Pub. Svc. (hon.), Ohio State U., 2001. Diplomate: Am. Bd. Phys. Medicine and Rehab. Intern Cin. Gen. Hosp., 1954-55; resident, teaching fellow NYU Med. Center Inst. Rehab. Medicine (Rusk Inst.), NYC, 1958-63; practice medicine, specializing in phys. medicine and rehab. Chgo., 1963—; staff physiatrist Rehab. Inst. Chgo., 1963-64, assoc. med. dir., 1964-65, med. dir., 1965-86, med. dir., CEO, 1986—94, pres., CEO, 1994-97, past med. dir., pres., CEO, 1997—; chmn. Rehab. Inst. Found., 1997—2004. Chmn. dept. phys. medicine and rehab. Northwestern U. Med. Sch., 1967-94, prof., 1967—, Magnuson prof., 1994-97, assoc. mem. Robert H. Lurie Cancer Ctr., 1993—; cons. Northwestern Meml. Hosp., Chgo.; mem. adv. bd. Commn. on Future Structure of Vets. Health Care, Dept. Vets. Affairs, 1990-92, Vets. Adv. Com. on Rehab., 1990-96; med. adv. com. Spl. Olympics Internat., 1991—. Contbr. articles to profl. jours. Bd. dirs. Very Spl. Arts, 1981—, The Hastings Ctr., Nat. Orgn. on Disabilities, Old Masters Soc., Art Inst. Chgo.; chmn. Physicians Against Land Mines, Access Living, Am. Assn. People with Disabilities, The Admiral, Chgo. Botanic Garden, Crossroads Ctr./Antigua, Legal Clinic for the Disabled, World Com. Disability, World Rehab. Fund, Pres. Com. Employment of People with Disabilities, VSArts, 2001. Recipient Disting. Svc. award Ill. Congress Orgns. Physically Handicapped, 1982, Disting. Svc. award Marine Scholarship Found., Chgo., 1993, Individual Leadership award Infinitec-United Cerebral Palsy, 1994, Disting. Pub. Svc. award Am. Acad. Phys. Medicine and Rehab., 1994, John W. Goldschmidt award Nat. Rehab. Hosp., Washington, 1996, James Brady award Ill. Head Injury Assn., 1989, Disting. Svc. award Nat. Orgn. on Disabilities, 1989, Milton Cohen Disting. Career award Nat. Assn. Rehab. Facilities, 1990, Henry H. Kessler Human Dignity award Kessler Inst. Rehab. Inc., 1992, The Scopus award Am. Friends of the Hebrew U., 1995, The August W. Christmann award City of Chgo. Mayor's Office for People with Disabilities and MOPD Adv. Council, 1995, Hon. diploma Archeworks, Chgo., 1997, Achievement award Rusk Inst., 1997, Disting. Mem. award Am. Acad. Phys. Medicine and Rehab., 1998, Disting. Svc. award Am. Hosp. Assn., 1998, Disting. Alumnus award Dept. Rehab. Medicine Rusk Inst., NYU Med. Sch., 1998, Paul J. Corcoran Disting. lectr. Harvard Med. Sch. PM&R Grad., 1999, 2002, Madonna Spirit award Madonna Rehab. Hosp., 1999, Order of Lincoln award Lincoln Acad. Ill., 2001, Henry Russe Citation Exemplary Compassion in Healthcare, 2001, Lifetime Achievement award Am. Spinal Injury Assn., 2001, Order of Lincoln award Lincoln Acad. Ill., 2001; named Physician of Yr., Ill. Gov.'s Com., 1964, Exec. of Yr., Ill. Assn. Rehab. Facilities, 1989—; commended by Ill. Gen. Assembly, 1967; cited for meritorious svc. Pres.'s Com. on Employment of Handicapped, 1965. Mem. Ill. Med. Soc., Assn. Acad. Physiatrists (pres. 1968-69, bd. dirs. 1990-95, Pub. Svc. award 1998), Am. Congress Rehab. Med. (med. adv. com., pres. 1976-77, Gold Key 1984), Mid-Am. Soc. Phys. Med. and Rehab. (pres. 1969), Brain Trauma Found. (bd. dirs. 1990-93). Home: 1727 N Orleans St Chicago IL 60614 Office: Rehabilitation Inst 345 E Superior St Chicago IL 60611-4805 Office Phone: 312-238-6017. E-mail: hbetts@ric.org.

BETZ, HANS DIETER, theology studies educator; b. Lemgo, Lippe, Germany, May 21, 1931; came to U.S., 1963, naturalized, 1973; s. Ludwig and Gertrude Betz; m. Christel Hella Wagner, Nov. 10, 1958; children: Martin, Ludwig, Arnold. Student, Kirchliche Hochschule, Bethel, Fed. Republic Germany, 1951—52, U. Mainz, Fed. Republic Germany, 1952—55, U. Mainz, 1956—58, Westminster Coll, Cambridge, Eng., 1955—56; Doctor Theologiae, U. Mainz, Fed. Republic Germany, 1957; Habilitation, U. Mainz, 1966. Pastor Evangelical Ch., Rhineland, Fed. Republic Germany, 1961-63; from asst. prof. to prof. Sch. Theology, Claremont Grad. Sch., Calif., 1963-78; prof. N.T. and early Christian lit. U. Chgo., 1978-2000, Shailer Mathews prof., 1989—; prof. emeritus; chmn. dept. N.T. and early Christian lit. U. Chgo., 1985-94. Rsch. fellow Inst. Advanced Study, Hebrew U., Jerusalem, 1999. Author, editor numerous books and articles in German and English, 1959— Recipient Humboldt Rsch. prize, 1986; Lady Davis fellow Hebrew U., Jerusalem, Israel, 1990, Sackler scholar Tel Aviv U., 1995, McCarthy scholar Pontifical Biblical Inst., Rome, 2004; NEH rsch. grantee, 1970-83, Am. Assn. Theol. Schs. grantee, 1977, 84. Mem. Soc. Bibl. Lit. (pres. 1997), Studiorum Novi Testamenti Societas (pres. 1999-2000), Chgo. Soc. Bibl. Rsch. (pres. 1983-84). Office: U Chgo 1025 E 58th St Chicago IL 60637-1509

BETZ, RONALD PHILIP, pharmacist; b. Chgo., Nov. 26, 1933; s. David Robert and Olga Marie (Martinson) B.; m. Rose Marie Marella, May 18, 1963; children: David Christian, Christopher Peter. BS, U. Ill., 1955; MPA, Roosevelt U., 1987. Asst. dir. pharmacy U. Ill., Chgo., 1959-62; dir. pharmacy Mt. Sinai Hosp., Chgo., 1962-2001; pres. Pharmacy Systems, Inc., 1982-89; teaching assoc. Coll. Pharmacy, U. Ill., Chgo., 1977-88. Adj. clin. asst. prof. pharmacy, U. Ill., 1988-2001; pres. Pharmacy Svc. and Systems, 1972-81; dir. Ill. Coop. Health Data Systems, 1976-80. Contbr. articles to profl. jours. Bd. dirs. Howard/Paulina Redevel. Corp., 1983-92. With U.S. Army, 1956-58. Mem.: No. Ill. Soc. Hosp. Pharmacists (pres. 1966), Ill. Acad. Preceptors in Pharmacy (pres. 1972), Ill. Pharm. Assn. (pres. 1975), Am. Soc. Health Sys. Pharmacists, Kappa Psi. Democrat. Lutheran. Home: 1021 Sussex Dr Northbrook IL 60062-3328 E-mail: rbetznb@aol.com.

BETZOLD, DONALD RICHARD, state legislator; b. Mpls., Aug. 27, 1950; s. Donald A. and Georgiana (Beauchamp) B.; m. Leesa Marie Simonson, Aug. 11, 1989; 1 child, Ben Anthony. BA, U. Minn., 1972; JD, Hamline U., 1979. Bar: Minn. 1979. Atty., Brooklyn Center, Minn., 1980—; mem. Minn. Senate, St. Paul, 1993—. Col. JAGC, USAR, ret. Mem. Minn. State Bar Assn. (chair bar media com. 1987-90). Roman Catholic. Avocation: photography. Home: 6150 Briardale Ct NE Fridley MN 55432-5210 Office: Minn State Senate 111 Capitol Saint Paul MN 55155-0001

BEUGEN, JOAN BETH, communications executive; b. Mar. 9, 1943; d. Leslie and Janet (Glick) Caplan; m. Sheldon Howard Beugen, July 16, 1967. BS in Speech, orthwestern U., 1965. Founder, prin., pres. The Creative Establishment, Inc., Chgo., NYC, San Francisco and L.A., 1969—87; founder, pres. Cresta Comm. Inc., Chgo., 1988—. Spkr. on entrepreneurship for women. Contbr. articles to profl. jours. Trustee Mt. Sinai Hosp. Med. Ctr.; del. White House Conf. on Small Bus., 1979; bd. dirs. Chgo. Network, Chgoland Enterprise Ctr., Girl Scouts Chgo. Named Entrepreneur of Yr., Women in Bus.; recipient YWCA Leadership award, 1985. Mem.: Overseas Edn. Fund Women in Bus. Com., Nat. Women's Forum, Com. of 200, Women in Film, Chgo. Film Coun., Chgo. Audio-Visual Prodrs. Assn., Midwest Soc. Profl. Cons., Chgo. Assn. Commerce and Industry, Ill. Women's Agenda, Nat. Assn. Women Bus. Owners (pres. Chgo. bhpt. 1979), Econ. Club Chgo. Office: The Cresta Group 1050 N State St Chicago IL 60610-7829

BEUKEMA, JOHN FREDERICK, lawyer; b. Alpena, Mich., Jan. 30, 1947; s. Christian F. and Margaret Elizabeth (Robertson) B.; m. Cynthia Ann Parke, May 25, 1974; children: Frederick Parke, David Christian. BA, Carleton Coll., 1968; JD, U. Minn., 1971. Bar: Minn. 1971, US Ct. Mil. Appeals 1974, US Dist. Ct. Minn. 1975, US Ct. Appeals (8th cir.) 1981, US Ct. Appeals (fed. cir.) 1984, US Supreme Ct. 1988, US Dist. Ct. (we. dist.) Wis. 1997, US Ct. Appeals (9th cir.) 1999. Assoc. Faegre & Benson, Mpls., 1971, 75-79, ptnr., 1980—. Vestryman Cathedral Ch. St. Mark, Mpls., 1983-86, 2002-05, junior warden, 2006-07, senior warden, 2007-; bd. dirs. Neighborhood Involvement Program, Mpls., 1986-90, pres., 1989-90; bd. dirs. Ronald McDonald House of Twin Cities, 1991-97, sec., 1995-97. Lt. JAGC, USNR, 1972-75. Mem. ABA, Minn. State Bar Assn., Hennepin County Bar Assn. Republican. Episcopalian. Business E-Mail: jbeukema@faegre.com.

BEUMER, RICHARD EUGENE, retired engineering executive; b. St. Louis, Feb. 26, 1938; s. Eugene Henry and C. Florence (Braun) Beumer; m. Judith Louise Rockett, June 25, 1960; children: Kathryn, Karen, Mark. BSEE, Valparaiso U., Ind., 1959. Registered profl. engr., Mo., Ill., Ariz., Md., Okla., Ohio, Ga., Va., Mich., D.C., Mass., N.Y., N.C. With Sverdrup Corp. Cos., 1959—; v.p. Sverdrup & Parcel and Assocs., St. Louis, 1974—78; sr. v.p., exec. v.p., dir. Sverdrup & Parcel Assocs., St. Louis, 1979—81; pres. Sverdrup & Parcel Assos., St. Louis, 1982—85; sr. v.p. Sverdrup Corp., 1986—88, exec. v.p., 1989—92, pres., 1993; pres., CEO Sverdup Corp., 1994—95; chmn., CEO Sverdrup Corp., 1996—99; vice chmn. Jacobs Engring. Group, Inc., 1999—2003; ret., 2003. Ret. vice-chmn. Thrivent Fin. for Luths.; bd. dirs. Valparaiso U. Chmn. St. Louis Regional Chamber and Growth Assn., 1998—99; divsn. chmn. United Way St. Louis, 1980; bd. dirs. Downtown St. Louis, Inc., 1982—91, Jr. Achievement, St. Louis Sci. Ctr.; past chmn. Luth. Med. Ctr., St. Louis; trustee, chmn. St. Louis Luth. High Schs. Recipient Disting. Alumni award, Valparaiso U., 1983. Mem.: NSPE, Mo. Soc. Profl. Engrs., Constrn. Industry Round Table (past chmn.), Design Profls. Coalition (past chmn.), Cons. Engrs. Coun. Mo. (pres. 1980), Am. Cons. Engrs. Coun. (nat. bd. dirs. 1979—82), St. Louis Elec. Bd. (pres. 1983), The Bogey Club, Old Warson Club, The Moles. Lutheran. Personal E-mail: rebeumer@att.net.

BEUTLER, CHRISTOPHER JOHN, state legislator; b. Omaha, Nov. 14, 1944; s. John E. and Dorothy M. (Lanning) B.; m. Patty Hershey, 1967; children: Alexa, Erica, Mikahla, Samuel. BA, Yale U., 1966; JD, U. Nebr., 1973. Tchr. Peace Corps, Turkey, 1966-67; rschr. Nebr. Crime Commn., 1972-73; assoc. Cline, Williams, Wright, Johnson & Oldfather, Lincoln, 1973-78; pvt. practice, 1978—; mem. Nebr. Legislature from 28th dist., Lincoln, 1978-86, 90—; chmn. judiciary com. Nebr. Legislature, Lincoln, 1983-84, mem. natural resources com., mem. rules com., com. on coms., edn. com.; owner Beutler Svc. Inc., Lincoln, 2000—. Named to Benson H.S. Hall of Fame, 1984. Mem. Nebr. Bar Assn., Lincoln Bar Assn., Nebr. Art Assn., Kiwanis (mem. exec. com. 1976), Beta Theta Phi. Office: State Capitol Rm 1124 Lincoln NE 68509-4604

BEUTLER, FREDERICK JOSEPH, information scientist; b. Berlin, Oct. 3, 1926; came to U.S., 1936, naturalized, 1943; s. Alfred David and Kaethe (Italiener) B.; m. Suzanne Armstrong, Jan. 5, 1969; children— Arthur David, Kathryn Ruth, Michael Ernest. SB, MIT, 1949, SM, 1951; PhD, Calif. Inst. Tech., 1957. Faculty U. Mich., Ann Arbor, 1957—, prof. info. and control engring., 1963-90, prof. emeritus, 1990—, chmn. computer info. and control engring., 1970-71, 77-90, chmn. grad. elect. engring. systems program, 1985-90. Vis. prof. Calif. Inst. Tech., 1967-68; vis. scholar U. Calif. at Berkeley, 1964-65 Editorial cons. Math. Rev., 1965-67, 75-88; contbr. articles to profl. jours. and books. Bd. dirs. Ann Arbor Civic Theatre, 1976-78, 91-94. With AUS, 1945-46. Rsch. grantee NSF, 1971-81, 92-94, Air Force Office Sci., 1970-80, NASA grantee, 1959-69. Fellow IEEE (life); mem. Soc. Indsl. and Applied Math. (coun. 1969-74, mng. editor Jour. Applied Math. 1970-75, editor 1984-90, editor Rev. 1967-70), Am. Math. Soc., U. Mich. Retirees Assn. (bd. dirs., sec.-treas. 1994—), Barton Boat Club, Racquet Club of Ann Arbor, Rotary Club of Ann Arbor. Office: Elec Engr and Comp Sci Bldg Univ Michigan Ann Arbor MI 48109-2122 Business E-Mail: fjb@umich.edu.

BEVERLINE, JERRY, state agency administrator; Dir. land mgmt. Ill. Dept. Conservation, Springfield, 1994—. Office: Ill Dept Conservation 600 N Grand Ave W Springfield IL 62706-0001 Fax: 217-524-5612.

BE VIER, WILLIAM A., retired religious studies educator; b. Springfield, Mo., July 31, 1927; s. Charles and Erma G. (Ritter) Be V.; m Jo Ann King, Aug. 11, 1949; children: Cynthia, Shirley. BA, Drury Coll., 1950; ThM, Dallas Theol. Sem., 1955, ThD, 1958; MA, So. Meth. U., 1960; EdD, ABD, Wayne State U., 1968. With Frisco Rlwy., 1943-45, 46-51, John E. Mitchell Co., Dallas, 1952-60; instr. Dallas Theol. Sem., 1958-59; prof. Detroit Bible Coll., 1960-74, registrar, 1962-66, dean, 1964-73, exec. v.p., 1967-74, acting pres., 1967-68; prof., dean edn., v.p. for acad. affairs Northwestern Coll., Roseville, Minn., 1974-81, prof., 1981-95, prof. emeritus, 1995—. Editor The Discerner. Bd. dirs. Religion Analysis Svc., Mpls., 1979-2004, pres., 1989-2004. With USMC, 1945-46, 50-51; ret. col. Army Res. Mem. Res. Officers Assn., Ind. Fund Chs. of Am. (nat. exec. com. 1991-94, v.p. 1993-94), Huguenot Hist. Soc., Bevier-Elting Family Assn., Phi Alpha Theta.

BEVINGTON, DAVID MARTIN, English literature educator; b. NYC, May 13, 1931; s. Merle Mowbray and Helen (Smith) B.; m. Margaret Bronson Brown, June 4, 1953; children: Stephen, Philip, Katharine, Sarah. BA, Harvard U., 1952, MA, 1957, PhD, 1959. Instr. English Harvard U., 1959-61; asst. prof. U. Va., 1961-65, asso. prof., 1965-66, prof., 1966-67; vis. prof. U. Chgo., 1967-68, prof., 1968—, Phyllis Fay Horton disting. svc. prof. in the humanities, 1985—. Vis. prof. YU Summer Sch., 1963, Harvard U. Summer Sch., 1967, U. Hawaii Summer Sch., 1970, Northwestern U., 1974 Author: From Mankind to Marlowe, 1962, Tudor Drama and Politics, 1968, Action is Eloquence, Shakespeare's Language of Gesture, 1984, Shakespeare, 2002 2d edit., 2005, This Wide and Universal Theater: Shakespeare in Performance Then and Now, 2007; editor: Medieval Drama, 1975, The Complete Works of Shakespeare, 5th edit., 2003, The Bantam Shakespeare, 1988, English Renaissance Drama: A Norton Anthology, 2002. Served with USN, 1952-55. Guggenheim fellow, 1964-65, 81-82; sr. fellow Southeastern Inst. Medieval and Renaissance Studies, summer 1975; sr. cons. and seminar leader Folger Inst. Renaissance and Eighteenth-Century Studies, 1976-77 Mem. MLA, AAUP, Renaissance Soc. Am., Shakespeare Assn. Am. (pres. 1976-77, 95-96), Am. Acad. Arts and Scis., Am. Philos. Soc., Brit. Acad. Office: U Chgo English Dept 1115 E 58th St Chicago IL 60637-5418 Office Phone: 773-702-9899. Business E-Mail: bevi@uchicago.edu.

BEYER, MARCUS PAUL, lawyer; b. 1975; BA cum laude, St. Olaf Coll., 1997; JD, William Mitchell Coll. Law, 2000. Bar: Minn. 2000, US Dist. Ct. (dist. Minn.). Law clk. to Hon. Michael J. Roith Anoka County Dist. Ct., Minn.; atty. Steffens & Rasmussen; ptnr. Gadtke & Beyer, L.L.C., Edina, Minn. Named a Rising Star, Minn. Super Lawyers mag., 2006. Mem.: Minn. State Bar Assn., Hennepin County Bar Assn. Office Phone: 952-345-8004. E-mail: marcus.beyer@gadtkelaw.com.

BEZNER, JODY, agricultural products company executive; m. Kay Bezner. BS, Tex. Tech. U. Vice chmn. bd. dirs. Farmland Industries, Kansas City, Mo., 1991—; pres., gen. mgr. Benzer Cattle & Grain, Texline, Tex., 1997—. Pres. Texline Ind. Sch. Dist. Bd., 1989—, Dalhart Consumers Fule Assn.; active 4-H. Mem. Dallam-Hartley C. of C. (past bd. dirs.), XIT Rodeo and Reunion Assn. Office: Farmland Industries Inc 3315 N Oak Trfy Kansas City MO 64116-2798

BHATTACHARYA, PALLAB KUMAR, electrical engineering educator, researcher; b. Calcutta, West Bengal, India, Dec. 6, 1949; came to U.S., 1978; s. Promode Ranjan and Sipra (Chatterjee) B.; m. Meena Mukerji, Aug. 11, 1975, children: Ramona, Monica. BSc with honors, U. Calcutta, 1968, B of Tech., 1970, M of Tech., 1971; M of Engring., U. Sheffield, Eng., 1976, PhD, 1978. Sr. rsch. asst. Radar and Communication Ctr., Kharagpur, India, 1972-73; asst. stores officer Hindustan Steel Ltd., Rourkela, India, 1973-75; asst., then assoc. prof. dept. elec. engring. Oreg. State U., Corvallis, 1978-83; assoc. prof. dept. elec. engring. and computer sci. U. Mich., Ann Arbor, 1984-87, prof., 1987—, dir. Solid State Electronics Lab., 1991—. Invited prof. Swiss Fed. Inst. Tech., Lausanne, 1981-82. Contbr. articles to profl. jours. Fellow IEEE; mem. Am. Phys. Soc. Avocations: photography, music. Office: U Mich Dept Elec Engring & Comp Sci 2228 EECS Bldg Ann Arbor MI 48109-2122

BHUSHAN, BHARAT, mechanical engineer; b. Jhinjhana, India, Sept. 30, 1949; came to U.S., 1970, naturalized, 1977; s. Narain Dass and Devi (Vati) B.; m. Sudha Bhushan, June 14, 1975; children: Ankur, Noopur. BE Mech. Engring. with honors, Birla Inst. Tech. and Sci., 1970; MSME, MIT, 1971; MS in Mechanics, U. Colo., 1973, PhD in Mech. Engring., 1976; MBA, Rensselaer Poly. Inst., 1980; DSc, U. Trondheim, Norway, 1990; D of Tech. Scis., Warsaw U. Tech., Poland, 1996; D honoris causa, Metal Polymer Rsch. Inst., Nat. Acad. Scis. at Gomel, Belarus, 2000. Mem. rsch. staff dept. mech. engring. MIT, Cambridge, 1971-72; rsch. asst., instr. dept. mech. engring. U. Colo., Boulder, 1973-76; phys. tribology program mgr. R&D divsn. Mech. Tech. Inc., Latham, NY, 1976-80; rsch. scientist, tech. svcs. divsn. SKF Industries, Inc., King of Prussia, Pa., 1980-81; devel. engr., mgr., gen. products divsn. lab. IBM Corp., Tucson, 1981—86; rsch. staff mem., mgr. head-disk interface Almaden Rsch. Ctr., IBM Rsch. Divsn., San Jose, Calif., 1986-91; Ohio eminent scholar, Howard D. Winbigler prof. mech. engring. Ohio State U., Columbus, 1991—, dir. Nanotribology lab. info. storage, 1991—. Expert investigator Automotive Specialists, Denver, 1973-76; vis. sr. scientist dept. machine design and materials tech., Royal Norwegian Coun. for Sci. and Indsl. Rsch., U. Trondheim, 1987, USSR Acad. Sci., Moscow, Gomel, Vilnuis, Leningrad, 1989; vis. scholar dept. mech. engring., chemistry and materials sci. and mineral engring. U. Calif., Berkeley, 1989; Sony sabbatical chair prof. Sony Corp. Rsch. Ctr., Fujitsuka, Japan, 1997; guest prof. dept. physics and engring. U. Cambridge, 1999; Inst. Fine Tech., Tech. U. Vienna, 1999; sr. academic visitor, Ecole Polytechnique Federale de Lausanne, Inst. de Physique de la Matiere Complexe, Switzerland, 2003; gust prof. Eidgennoessische Tech. Hochschule, Switzerland, 2005; invited prof. Lab. Physicque des Solides, U. Paris, France, 2006; rsch. student supr.; spkr. over 250 invited presentations, 60 keynote and plenary addresses, and internat. confs. worldwide. Author: Tribology and Mechanics of Magnetic Storage Devices, 1990, 2d edit. 1996, Mechanics and Reliability of Flexible Magnetic Media, 1992, 2d edit. 2000, Principles and Applications of Tribology, 1999, Introduction to Tribology, 2002; co-author (with B.K. Gupta) Handbook of Tribology: Materials, Coatings and Surface Treatments, 1991; mem. editl. bd. Jour. Friction and Wear of Belarus, Tribology Letters and Storage; assoc. editor Jour. Tribology, 1986-90; co-editor Proceedings on Tribology and Mechanics of Magnetic Storage Systems Symposia, 1984-90; editor Handbook of Micro/Natrotribiology, 1995, 2d edit., 1999, Modern Tribology Handbook, Vol. 1 Principles of Tribology, 2001, Vol. 2 Materials, Coatings and Industrial Applications, 2001, Springer Handbook of anotechnology, 2004; editor 25 books; co-editor-in-chief Microsystem Technologies: Micro-& Nanosystems and Information Storage and Processing Systems, 2002; editor-in-chief, founding editor ASME series Advances in Info. Storage Sys., 1991-93, World Scientific, 1994-99; editor-in-chief CRC Mechanics and Materials Sci. series, Jour. Info. Storage and Processing Sys., 1999-2001; contbr. over 70 handbook chpts., 600 tech. papers, 60 tech. reports, 4005 articles to profl. jours. in field. Recipient Alfred Noble prize ASCE, IEEE, ASME, AIME, Western Soc. Engrs., 1981, George Norlan award, U. Colo., 1983, Regents Disting. Svc. award, 1985, GPD Achievement award IBM Corp., 1983, Invention Achievement award, 1985, Rsch. Divsn. award for Outstanding Achievement, 1987, Outstanding Tech. Achievement award, 1990, Tech. Excellence award Am. Soc. Engrs. India, 1989, Cert. Appreciation award NASA, 1987, Lumley Rsch. award, Ohio State U., 1997, 2001, Alexander von Humboldt Rsch. prize for Sr. Scientists U. Ulm, 1998-99, U. Karlsruhe, 1998-99, Fulbright Sr. Scholar award Tech. U. Vienna, 1999, UN Sr. TOKTEN Expert award, Dehli, Bangalore, India, 1999, Max Planck Found. Rsch. award for Outstanding Fgn. Scientists Max Planck Inst. for Metals Rsch., Düsseldorf, Germany, 2002; Ford Found. fellow MIT, 1971; grantee USN, NASA, Dept. Energy, USAF, Franco-Am. Commn. for Ednl. Exch. Interfound. grantee Ecole Ctrl. Lyon, 1999. Fellow STLE, IEEE, ASME (cert. of recognition Design Engring. Conf., Henry Hess award 1980, Burt L. Newkirk award 1983, Gustus L. Larson Meml. award 1986, Tribology Divsn. Best Paper award 1989, Melville medal for Best Current Original Paper 1992, Bd. Govs. award for Valued Svcs. as Founding Chair of ISPS Divsn. 1997, Bd. Govs. award for Valued Svcs. as Chair of ISPS Divsn. 1998, Charles Russ Richards Meml. award 2000, Robert Henry Thurston Lect. award, 2004), NY Acad. Scis.; mem. NSPE, IEEE (sr.), ASEE, Soc. Tribologists and Lubrication Engrs., Am. Soc. Lubrication Engrs., Am. Acad. Mechanics, Internat. Humanists Soc., Tri-City India Assn., Internat. Acad. Engring. Russia (fgn.), Byelorussian Acad. of Engring. and Tech. (fgn.), Acad. of Triboengring. of Ukraine (fgn.), Soc. of Tribologists of Belarus (hon.), Soc. Tribologists and Lubnicetim Engr., Rotary, Sigma Xi, Tau Beta Pi, Pi Tau Sigma. Hindu. Achievements include 16 US and fgn. patents in field; pioneer in tribology and mechanics of magnetic storage devices; leading researcher in field of micro/nanotribology using single probe microscopy. Home: 10235 Widdington Close Powell OH 43065-9059 Office: Ohio State University 650 Ackerman Rd Columbus OH 43202-4500 Office Phone: 614-292-0651. Business E-Mail: bhushan.2@osu.edu.

BIALOSKY, DAVID L., lawyer, automotive executive; b. 1958; AB in Engring. Scis., Dartmouth Coll.; JD, Northwestern U. Bar: Calif., Mich., Ohio. Mech. engr. Std. Oil Co. Ohio; assoc. Thompson, Hine & Flory, Cleve.; joined TRW, 1989, counsel automotive sector, sr. counsel occupant restraints and controls group, 1989; sr. counsel TRW Info. Sys. and Svcs., Orange County, Calif., 1996—97; v.p., asst. gen. counsel TRW Automotive, v.p., gen. counsel Livonia, Mich., 2002—04, exec. v.p., gen. counsel, 2004—. Office: TRW Automotive 12025 Tech Center Dr Livonia MI 48150 Office Phone: 734-266-2600. Office Fax: 734-266-4594.

BIBART, RICHARD L., lawyer; b. Apr. 10, 1942; m. Lois Ann Rey, Sept. 8, 1963; children: Laurie, Jennifer, Kristen, Ted. BA in Econs., Harvard U., 1964; JD, U. Mich., 1966. Bar: Ohio 1967, U.S. Tax Ct. 1967, U.S. Dist. Ct. (so. dist.) Ohio 1969. Assoc. Porter, Wright, Morris & Arthur, Columbus, Ohio, 1967-72, ptnr., 1972-84; v.p. corp. planning Red Roof Inns., Inc., Hilliard, 1984-86; mgmt. co. pres. Red Roof Inns, Inc., Hilliard, 1986-89, pres., CEO, 1989-91; ptnr. Baker & Hostetler LLP, Columbus, 1991—. Mem. ABA, Ohio Bar Assn., Columbus Bar Assn., Columbus Country Club. Office: Baker & Hostetler LLP 65 E State St Ste 2100 Columbus OH 43215-4215

BIBB, PAUL E., JR., (BUCK BIBB), bank executive; b. June 8, 1947; B in Mktg., Fla. State U., Tallahassee. With Commonwealth Corp., Tallahassee, 1973, Commonwealth Mortgage Corp., Houston; positions up to exec. v.p. Bank United Mortgage/Commonwealth United Mortgage, 1990—97; with Nat. City Corp., 1997—, CEO Nat. City Mortgage, sr. v.p. Mem.: Mortgage Bankers Assn. Am. (mem. residential lending com.). Office: Nat City Corp Nat City Ctr 1900 E Ninth St Cleveland OH 44114-3484 Office Phone: 216-222-2000.*

BICHA, KAREL DENIS, historian, educator; b. LaCrosse, Wis., Jan. 7, 1937; s. Stephen John and Lauretta Katherine (Horan) B.; m. Roberta Gail Gobar; children: Paul Edwin, Anne Marie. BA, U. Wis., 1958; PhD, U. Minn., 1963. Asst. prof. Colo. State U., Ft. Collins, 1963-64, U. Man., Winnipeg, Can., 1964-66, U. Minn., Morris, 1966-67; assoc. prof. Carleton U., Ottawa, Ont., Can., 1967-69, Marquette U., Milw., 1969-77, prof., 1977—. Author: American Farmer and the Canadian West, 1968, Western Populism, 1976, Czechs in Oklahoma, 1980, C.C. Washburn and the Upper Mississippi Valley, 1995. Am. Philos. Soc. grantee, 1964, 68, Can. Council grantee, 1966-68, NEH grantee, 1978-80, Bradley Inst. for Democracy and Pub. Values grantee, 1991, 97. Mem. Orgn. Am. Historians, Immigration History Soc. Office: Marquette U PO Box 1881 Coughlin Hall Dept Of Histo Milwaukee WI 53201-1881

BICKNELL, O. GENE, financial executive; Chmn., CEO, founder NPC Internat. Office: NPC International Inc PO Box 643 Pittsburg KS 66762-0643

BIDDLE, BRUCE JESSE, social psychologist, educator; b. Ossining, NY, Dec. 30, 1928; s. William Wishart and Loureide Jeanette (Cobb) B.; m. Ellen Catherine Horgan; children: David Charles, William Jesse, Jennifer Loureide; m. Barbara Julianne Bank, June 19, 1976. AB in Math., Antioch Coll., Yellow Springs, Ohio, 1950; postgrad., U. N.C., 1950-51; PhD in Social Psychology, U. Mich., 1957. Asst. prof. sociology U. Ky., 1957-58; assoc. prof. edn. U. Kansas City, 1958-60; assoc. prof. psychology and sociology U. Mo., Columbia, 1960-66, prof., 1966-2000, prof. emeritus, 2000—, dir. Ctr. Rsch. in Social Behavior, 1966-96. Vis. assoc. prof. U. Queensland, Australia, 1965; vis. prof. Monash U., Australia, 1969, vis. fellow Australian Nat. U., 1977, 85, 93. Author: (with R.S. Adams) Realities of Teaching: Explorations with Videotape, 1970, (with M.J. Dunkin) The Study of Teaching, 1974, (with T.L. Good and J. Brophy) Teachers Make a Difference, 1975, Role Theory: Expectations, Identities and Behaviors, 1979, (with D.C. Berliner) The Manufactured Crisis: Myths, Fraud, and the Attack on America's Public Schools, 1995, (with L.J. Saha) The Untested Accusation: Principals, Research Knowledge, and Policy Making in Schools, 2002; editor: (with W.J. Ellena) contemporary Research on Teacher Effectiveness, 1964, (with E.J. Thomas) Role Theory: Concepts and Research, 1966, (with P.H. Rossi) The New Media: Their Impact on Education, 1966, (with D.S. Anderson) Knowledge for Policy: Improving Education Through Research, 1991, (with T.L. Good and I.F. Goodson) International Handbook of Teachers and Teaching, 1997, Social Class, Poverty, and Education, 2001. Served with U.S. Army, 1954-56. Fellow APA, Am. Psychol. Soc., Australian Psychol. Soc.; mem. Am. Ednl. Research Assn., Australian Assn. Rsch. Edn., Am. Sociol. Assn., Midwest Sociol. Soc. Home: 924 Yale Columbia MO 65203-1874 Office: U Mo Dept Psychology McAlester Hall Rm 210 Columbia MO 65211-0001 Business E-Mail: BiddleB@missouri.edu.

BIDELMAN, WILLIAM PENDRY, astronomer, educator; b. LA, Sept. 25, 1918; s. William Pendry and Dolores (De Remer) B.; m. Verna Pearl Shirk, June 19, 1940; children: Lana Louise Stone (dec. Mar. 2000), Linda Elizabeth McKinley, Billie Jean Little, Barbara Jo Talley. Student, U. N.D., 1936-37; SB, Harvard, 1940; PhD, U. Chgo., 1943. Physicist, Aberdeen Proving Ground, Md., 1943-45; instr., then asst. prof. astronomy Yerkes Obs., U. Chgo., 1945-53; asst. astronomer, then. assoc. astronomer Lick Obs., U. Calif., 1953-62; prof. U. Mich., 1962-69, U. Tex. at Austin, 1969-70, Case Western Res. U., Cleve., 1970-86, prof. emeritus, 1986—. Chmn. dept., dir. Warner and Swasey Obs., 1970-75; mem. adv. panel on astronomy NSF, 1959-62; mem. NRC adv. com. on astronomy Office aval Rsch., 1964-67. Contbr. articles to profl. jours. Mem. Am. Astron. Soc. (councilor 1959-62, participant vis. prof. program 1961-65), Astron. Soc. Pacific (editor Publs. 1956-61), Internat. Astron. Union (commns. 29, 45, pres. 1964-67), Phi Beta Kappa. Presbyterian. Achievements include discovery of lines of mercury, krypton and xenon in stellar spectra; discovery of phosphorus stars; co-discovery of barium stars; research in spectral classification, astronomical data and observational astrophysics. Home: 3171 Chelsea Dr Cleveland Heights OH 44118-1256 Office: Case Western Res U Dept Astronomy 10900 Euclid Ave Cleveland OH 44106-7215 Office Phone: 216-368-4003. Business E-Mail: wsobs@grendel.astr.cwru.edu.

BIDWELL, CHARLES EDWARD, sociologist, educator; b. Chgo., Jan. 24, 1932; s. Charles Leslie and Eugenia (Campbell) B.; m. Helen Claxton Lewis, Jan. 24, 1959; 1 son, Charles Lewis. AB, U. Chgo., 1950, AM, 1953, PhD, 1956. Lectr. on sociology Harvard U., 1959-61; asst. prof. edn. U. Chgo., 1961-65, assoc. prof., 1965-70, prof. edn. and sociology, 1970-85, Reavis prof. edn. and sociology, 1985-2001, Reavis prof. emeritus edn. and sociology, 2001—, chmn. dept. edn., 1978-88, chmn. dept. sociology, 1988-94, dir. Ogburn-Stouffer Ctr., 1988-94. Author books in field; contbr. numerous articles to profl. jours.; editor Sociology of Edn., 1969-72, Am. Jour. Sociology, 1973-78, Am. Jour. Edn., 1983-88. With U.S. Army, 1957-59. Guggenheim fellow, 1971-72, Waller award for career of disting. scholarship, Am. Social. Assn., 2007. Fellow AAAS; mem. Sociol. Rsch. Assn., Nat. Acad. Edn. (sec.), Phi Beta Kappa. Office: Dept Sociology 1126 East 59th St Chicago IL 60637 Office Phone: 773-702-0388. E-mail: c-bidwell@uchicago.edu.

BIEBEL, PAUL PHILIP, JR., lawyer; b. Chgo., Mar. 24, 1942; s. Paul Philip Sr. and Eleanor Mary (Sweeney) B.; divorced; children: Christine M., Brian E., Jennifer A., Susan E. AB, Marquette U., 1964; JD, Georgetown U., 1967. Bar: Ill. 1967, U.S. Dist. Ct. (no. dist.) Ill. 1967, U.S. Ct. Appeals (6th cir.) 1985, U.S. Supreme Ct. 1972. Asst. dean of men Loyola U., Chgo., 1967-69; asst. state's atty. Cook County State's Atty., Chgo., 1969-75, dep. state's atty., 1975-81; 1st asst. atty. gen. Ill. Atty. Gen., Chgo., 1981-85; pub. defender Cook County Pub. Defender, Chgo., 1986-88; ptnr. Winston & Strawn, Chgo., 1985-86, 88-94, Altheimer & Gray, Chgo., 1994-96; judge Cir. Ct. Cook County, Ill., 1996—. Contbr. articles to profl. publs. Mem. Fed. Bar Assn. (bd. dirs., pres. 1994-95), Cath. Lawyers Guild (bd. dirs., Cath. Lawyer of Yr. 1988), Ill. Judges Assn., Ill. Appellate Lawyers, 7th Cir. Bar Assn., Chgo. Bar Assn. (chmn. com. 1991-93), Georgetown Law Alumni Assn. (bd. dirs. 1991-96). Roman Catholic. Avocations: reading, golf. Home: 5415 N Forest Glen Ave Chicago IL 60630-1523 Office: Presiding Judge Criminal Divsn RM 101 2600 S California Ave Chicago IL 60608 Home Phone: 773-725-9211; Office Phone: 773-869-3160. Personal E-mail: jorich73@cs.com.

BIEDERMAN, JERRY H., lawyer; b. Chgo., July 2, 1946; BA, Stanford U., 1968; JD, U. Chgo., 1971. Bar: Ill. 1971. Mng. ptnr. Neal, Gerber & Eisenberg, Chgo. Mem. ABA (law practice mgmt. sec.) Chgo. Bar Assn. Office: Neal Gerber & Eisenberg 2 N La Salle St Ste 2200 Chicago IL 60602-3801

BIEDRON, THEODORE JOHN, publishing and advertising executive; b. Evergreen Park, Ill., Nov. 30, 1946; s. Theodore John and Ione Margaret B.; m. Gloria Anne DeAngelo, ov. 7, 1970; children: Jessica Ann, Lauren. BA in Polit. Sci., U. Ill., 1968. Recruitment advt. mgr. Chgo. Sun-Times, 1968-74; classified advt. mgr. Pioneer press, Wilmette, Ill., 1974-76, v.p. advt. and promotion, 1993-94, sr. v.p. sales and mktg., 1994-97, exec. v.p., 1997-2000. Pub. North Shore mag., 1997-2000; classified mgr., v.p. Lerner Newspapers, Chgo., 1976-79, assoc. pub., 1980-82, advt. dir., 1982-87; v.p., classified advt. mgr. Chgo. Sun-Times, 1987-92; pres. Chicagoland Pub. Co. divsn. Chgo. Tribune, 2000—. Pres. Northeastern Ill. U. Found., 1998-2002; trustee Northlight Theater, 1993-98. Home: 404 Jackson Ave Glencoe IL 60022-Office: Chicagoland Pub Co 2000 S York Rd Oak Brook IL 60523 Personal E-mail: tbiedron@gmail.com.

BIEGEL, DAVID ELI, social worker, educator; b. NYC, July 3, 1946; s. Jack and Estelle (Lentin) B.; m. Margaret S. Smoot, Jan. 31, 1976 (div.); 1 child, Geoffrey S.; m. Ronna Kaplan, Oct. 26, 2003. BA, CCNY, 1967; MSW, U. Md., 1970, PhD, 1982. Field coord. United Farm Workers, AFL-CIO, Balt., 1971; exec. dir. Junction, Inc., Westminster, Md., 1971—72; dir. office planning and program devel. Cath. Charities, Balt., 1973—76; ctr. assoc., dir. neighborhood and family svcs. project U. So. Calif., Washington Pub. Affairs Ctr., 1976—80; asst. prof. social work U. Pitts., 1980—85, assoc. prof., 1985—86; Henry L. Zucker prof. social work practice Mandel Sch. Applied Social Scis., Case Western Res. U., 1987—, prof. psychiatry and sociology, 1987—, co-dir. Ctr. for Practice Innovations, 1991—97, chair doctoral program, 1998—2001, 2005. Co-dir. Cuyahoga County Cmty. Mental Health Rsch. Inst., 1994—2002; pres. Inst. for the Advancement of Social Work Rsch., 1999—2002; dir. rsch. and evaluation Ohio Substance Abuse and Mental Illness Coord. Ctr. Excellence, 2000—05; co-dir. Ctr. Substance Abuse and Mental Illness, 2002—. Co-editor: Evidence-Based Practices Series, Innovations in Practice and Service Delivery with Vulnerable Populations Series, Family Caregiving Applications Series; editor Practice Concepts sect., The Gerontologist, 2002-04; co-author: Neighborhood etworks for Humane Mental Health Care, 1982, Community Support Systems and Mental Health: Practice, Policy and Research, 1982, Building Support Networks for the Elderly: Theory and Applications, 1984, Social Networks and Mental Health: An Annotated Bibliography, 1985, Social Support Networks: A Bibliography 1983-1987, 1989, Aging and Caregiving: Theory, Research and Policy, 1990, Family Preservation Programs: Research and Evaluation, 1991, Family Caregiving in Chronic Illness: Alzheimer's Dsiease, Cancer, Heart Disease, Mental Illness, and Stroke, 1991, Family Caregiving: A Lifespan Perspective, 1994, The Jewish Aged in the U.S. and Israel: Diversity, Programs and Services, 1994, Innovations in Practice and Service Delivery with Vulnerable Populations Across the Lifespan, 1999; contbr. articles to profl. jours., chpts. to books. Cons. Vol. VISTA, Raton, N.Mex., and Balt., 1967-70; active Big Bros. Am., Balt., 1974-77' pres. bd. trustees Bridgeway, Inc., 2004-07; sec. bd. trustees Cmty. Care Network, Inc., 2006-07—. N.Y. State Incentive scholar, 1963-64; VISTA Fellows Program fellow, 1968-70. Fellow Gerontol. Soc. Am.; mem. NASW, Acad. Cert. Social Workers, Soc. Social Work Rsch. Democrat. Jewish. Home Phone: 216-371-3108; Office Phone: 216-368-2308. Business E-Mail: david.biegel@case.edu.

BIEHL, MICHAEL MELVIN, lawyer, writer; b. Milw., Feb. 24, 1951; s. Michael Melvin Biehl and Frieda Margaret (Krieg) Davis. AB, Harvard U., 1973, JD, 1976. Bar: Wis. 1976, U.S. Dist. Ct. (ea. dist.) Wis. 1976. Assoc. Foley & Lardner, Milw., 1976-84, ptnr., 1984—. Adj. prof. law Marquette U. Law Sch., 2001—. Author: Medical Staff Legal Issues, 1990, Doctored Evidence, 2002, Lawyered to Death, 2003; editor: Physician Organizations and Medical Staff, 1996. Mem. Mt. Sinai Med. Ctr. Clin. Investigations Com., Hastings Ctr.; election monitor first multi-party elections in Rep. Ga., 1990; dir. Colorlines Found. for Arts and Culture, Inc., chmn., bd. dirs. Milw. Psychiat. Hosp. and Aurora Behavioral Health Svcs. Mem. ABA, Am. Health Lawyers Assn., Am. Coll. of Med. Quality, Am. Soc. Law and Medicine, Sarasota Conservation Found. Mem. Unitarian Ch. Achievements include having the Michael Biehl Park in Venice, Florida named in his honor. Office: Foley & Lardner 777 E Wisconsin Ave Ste 3800 Milwaukee WI 53202-5367 Home: 908 Scherer Way Osprey FL 34229-6867 Office Phone: 414-297-5648.

BIELEMA, BRET, university football coach; b. Prophetstown, Ill., Jan. 13, 1970; BA in Mktg., Iowa Univ., 1992. Asst. coach Univ. Iowa, 1993—2001; co-defensive coord. Kansas St., 2002—03; defensive coord. Univ. Wis., 2004—05, head coach, 2006—. Achievements include being youngest head football coach in Div. I, CAA, 2006. Office: Univ Wisconsin Dept Athletics Kellner Hall 1440 Monroe St Madison WI 53711

BIELIAUSKAS, VYTAUTAS JOSEPH, psychologist, educator; b. Plackojai, Lithuania, Nov. 1, 1920; came to U.S., 1949, naturalized, 1955; s. Antanas and Anele (Kasparaite) B.; m. Danute G. Sirvydaite, Mar. 12, 1947; children—Linas A., Diana B., Aldona O., Cornelius V. PhD in Psychology, U. Tuebingen, 1943; PsyD, Xavier U., 2005. Diplomate Clin. Psychology, Marital Family Therapy, Am. Bd. Profl. Psychology. Asst. prof. U. Munich, Germany, 1944-48; instr. King's Coll., Wilkes-Barre, Pa., 1949-50; mem. faculty Sch. Clin. and Applied Psychology, Coll. William and Mary, 1950-58, prof. psychology, 1953-58, head dept. psychology, 1951-57; assoc. prof. Xavier U., Cin., 1958-60, chmn. dept. psychology, 1959-78, prof., 1960-78, Riley prof. psychology, 1978-88, disting. prof. psychology emeritus, 1988—. Author: A Psychologist Looks at the Dealth Penalty, Social Justice Review, 1993 (7-8), 2002, Community Relations Training for Police Supervisors, 1969; CSSS for the H-T-P Drawings, 1981, Politics, Ethics and Morality, Social Justice Review, 1994 (3-4), 2003; contbr. articles to profl. jours. Pres., exec. officer Lithuanian World Cmty., 1988-92; exec. v.p. Lithuanian-Am. Cmty., Inc., 1994-2000; adviser on spl. programs Pres. of Republic of Lithuania, 1995-96. Lt. col. M.S.C., USAR, 1958-65. Recipient Ellis Island medal of honor, 1990. Fellow APA (pres. divsn. 13, 1986, Dist. Svc. award divsn. 36 1998); mem. Ohio Psychol. Assn. (pres. 1978-79, Disting. Svc. award 1980), Soc. Personality Assessment, Internat. Assn. for Study Med. Psychology and Religion (pres. 1972-75), Cin. Acad. Profl. Psychology, Psychologists Interested in Religious Issues (pres. 1971, exec. sec. 1973-75), Cath. Acad. Scis. in the U.S.A. (academician 1987—). Office: Xavier U Dept Psychology Cincinnati OH 45207 Office Phone: 513-745-3710. Personal E-mail: vbieliaus@aol.com. Business E-Mail: bieliaus@xavier.edu.

BIELINSKI, DONALD EDWARD, financial executive; b. Chgo., June 27, 1949; s. Edward and Helen (Smialek) B.; m. Laura Ann Bicego, Mar. 10, 1984; children: Natalie, Michael, Rebecca, David. BS in Acctg., U. Ill., Chgo., 1971; postgrad., Stanford U., 1987. CPA, Ill. Jr. div. acct. W.W. Grainger, Inc., Niles, Ill., 1972-73, acctg. supr., 1973-74, acctg. mgr., 1974-79, dir. acctg., 1979-81, asst. contr., 1981-83, div. contr., 1983-85, v.p., corp. contr. Skokie, Ill., 1985-89, v.p. fin., 1989-90, v.p., chief fin. officer, 1990-96, s.r. v.p., 1996—. Mem. Orchard Village Bd., Niles, 1982-92; bd. dirs. U. Ill., 1989-92. Fellow Fin. Execs. Inst., Econ. Club Chgo. Office: WW Grainger Inc 100 Grainger Pkwy Lake Forest IL 60045-5201

BIELKE, PATRICIA ANN, psychologist; b. Bay Shore, NY, May 11, 1949; d. Lawrence Curtis and Marcella Elizabeth (Maize) Widdoes; m. Stephen Roy Bielke, July 10, 1971; children: Eric, Christine. BA, Carleton Coll., 1971; PhD, U. Minn., 0979. Lic. psychologist, Wis.; cert. marriage and family therapist. Rsch. asst. Nat. Inst. Mental Health, Washington, 1972-74; sch. psychologist Roseville Pub. Schs., St. Paul, 1978-79; psychologist Southeastern Wis. Med. and Social Svcs., Milw., 1979-93; staff psychologist Elmbrook Meml. Hosp., 1986-2000; pvt. practice Brookfield, Wis., 1991-2000; sch. psychologist Cedarburg (Wis.) Pub. Schs., 1999—2002, New Berlin (Wis.) Pub. Schs., 2000—. Bd. dirs. LWV, Brookfield, 1984-88, Elmbrook Sch. Bd., 1989-99. Mem. Nat. Sch. Psychologist Assn., Wis. Sch. Psychol. Assn. Home: 17455 Bedford Dr Brookfield WI 53045-1301 Office: New Berlin School Dist 18695 W Cleveland Ave New Berlin WI 53146

BIEN, JOSEPH JULIUS, philosophy educator; b. Cin., May 22, 1936; s. Joseph Julius and Mary Elizabeth (Adams) B.; m. Françoise Neve, Apr. 8, 1965. BS, Xavier U., MA, 1958; DTC, U. Paris, 1968; postgrad., Laval Univ., 1958, Emory U., 1961-62, U. Edinburgh, 1962; D (hon.), Lucian Blaga U., 1999. Asst. prof. philosophy Univ. Tex., Austin, 1968-73; asso. prof. philosophy Univ. Mo., Columbia, 1973-79, prof. philosophy, 1979—, chmn. dept. philosophy, 1976-80, 81-83, 1993—99; vis. prof. Tex. A&M U., 1980, Dubrovnik Inst. Postgrad. Studies, Yugoslavia, 1983, 84, 85, 89, co-dir. Croatia, 1990—; Mid-Am. States Univs. Assn. hon. lectr. in philosophy, 1985-86. Rsch. assoc. Russian and Slavic Rsch. Ctr., 1989-91; vis. prof. Lucian Blaga U., 1996, Hubei U., 1997, Wichita State U., 1998, U. Western Cape, 2000, Lille 3 U, 2002. Author: History, Revolution and Human Natue: Marx's Philosophical Anthropology, 1984; transl.: (M. Merleau-Ponty) Adventures of the Dialectic, 1973; editor: Phenomenology and the Social Sciences, A Dialogue, 1978, Political and Social Essays by Paul Ricoeur, 1974, Leviathan, 1986, Contemporary Social Thought, 1989, Ethics and Politics, 1992, Philosophical Issues and Problems, 1998. Am. Council Learned Socs. grantee, 1973; Dubrovnik Inst. Postgrad. Studies grantee, 1984; recipient U. Mo. faculty alumni award, 1998. Mem. Soc. Social and Polit. Philosophy (pres. 1979-80, 86-87, 93-94, 97-98), Ctrl. States Philos. Assn. (pres. 1978-79), Ctrl. Slavic Conf. (sec.-tres. 1977, 84), Southwestern Philosophy Soc. (pres. 1997-98). Democrat. Home: 100 W Brandon Rd Columbia MO 65203-3508 Office: Univ Mo Dept Philosophy Columbia MO 65211-0001

BIENEN, HENRY SAMUEL, academic administrator, political scientist, educator; b. NYC, May 5, 1939; s. Mitchell Richard and Pearl (Witty) Bienen; m. Leigh Buchanan, Apr. 28, 1961; children: Laura, Claire, Leslie. BA with honors, Cornell U., 1960; MA, U. Chgo., 1961, PhD, 1966. Asst. prof. politics U. Chgo., 1965—66; asst. prof. politics & internat. affairs Princeton U., NJ, 1966—69, assoc. prof., 1969—72, prof., 1972—95, William Stewart Tod prof. politics and internat. affairs, 1981—85, James S. McDonnell Disting. Univ. prof., 1985, dir. Ctr. Internat. Studies, 1985—92, chair dept. politics, 1973—76, dir. African studies progrm, 1977—78, 1983—84, dir. rsch. Woodrow Wilson Sch. Pub. & Internat. Affairs, 1979—82, dean, 1992—94; pres. Northwestern U., Evanston, Ill., 1995—. Mem. exec. com. Inter-Univ. Seminar on Armed Forces and Soc., 1968—78, Chgo. Coun. Global Affairs; mem. sr. review panel CIA, 1982—88; nat. co. dir. Movement for A New Congress, 1970—71; mem. Inst. Advanced Study, 1984—85, Ctr. Advanced Study in the Behavioral Scis., 1976—77; vis. prof. Makerere Coll., Kampala, Uganda, 1963—65, U. Coll., Nairobi, Kenya, 1968—69, U. Ibadan, 1972—73; bd. dirs. The Bear Stearns Cos., Inc., 2004—08; mem. Coun. on Fgn. Rels., Matthews Internat. Capital Mgmt., LLC, Consortium on Financing Higher Edn., John G. Shedd Aquarium, Steppenwolf Theatre, Alain Locke Charter Sch., Com. on Roles of Acad. Health Ctrs. in the 21st Century at Nat. Acad.'s Inst. of Medicine; Acad. fellow Carnegie Corp. on Internat. Devel. Program; cons. in field. Editor: World Politics, 1970—74, 1978—, Voices of Power: World Leaders Speak, 1995—; author: Tanzania: Party Transformation and Economic Development, 1967, The Military Intervenes: Case Studies in Political Change, 1968, Violence and Social Change, 1968, The Military and Modernization, 1970, Kenya: The Politics of Participation and Control, 1974, Armies and Parties in Africa, 1978, The Politcal Economy of Income Distribution in Nigeria, 1981, Political Conflict and Economic Change in Nigeria, 1985, Arms and the African Military Influence in Africa's International Relations, 1985, Of Time and Power: Leadership Duration in the Modern World, 1991, Power, Economics, and Security: The U.S.-Japanese Relationship, 1992. Bd. dirs. The Bear Stearns Co., Inc., Rasmussen Coll.; bd. govs., chair nominating & governance com., mem. exec. com. Coun. Fgn. Rels.; bd. dirs., mem. exec. com. Chgo. Coun. Global Affairs; bd. trustees John G. Shedd Aquarium, Steppenwolf Theatre, Alain Locke Charter Sch.; bd. govs. exec. & nominating com. Argonne Nat. Lab.; bd. trustees The Scholarly Jour. Archives. Recipient Profl. Achievement award, U. Chgo., 2000, Acad. Leadership award, Carnegie Corp., 2005; grantee, Rockefeller Found., 1968—69, 1972—73; Seeger fellow, 1989. Mem.: Assn. Am. Univs. (mem. big tea network branding com., chmn.), Am. Acad., Am. Polit. Sci. Assn., Civil Com. Comm. Club. Office: Northwestern U Z-130 Crown 633 Clark St Evanston IL 60208-0001 Business E-Mail: nu-president@northwestern.edu.*

BIERBAUM, ROSINA M., federal agency administrator; BS in Biology, Boston Coll., 1974, BA in English, 1974; PhD in Ecology and Evolution, SUNY, Stony Brook, 1985. Congressional fellow, 1980; sr. assoc. environ. program Office of Tech. Assessment U.S. Congress, Washington, 1991-93, sr. policy analyst Sci. Tech. Policy Office, 1993-96, asst. dir. environ. Sci. Tech. Policy Office, 1996, acting assoc. dir. Sci. Tech. Policy Office, 1996-97, apptd. assoc. dir. environ. Office Sci. Tech. Policy for the Pres., 1998—2001; dean, prof. environ. and natural resource policy and mgmt. Sch. of Natural Resources & Environment, U. Mich., 2001—. U.S. scientific expert, Permanent Ct. of Arbitration of Disputes Relating to Natural Resources and/or the Environ., in Hague, on the Bd. on Atmospheric Scis. and Climate of the Nat. Rsch. Coun. of the Nat. Academies; mem. exec. com., Inst. for Social Rsch., U. Mich.; mem. oversite com., Environ. and Energy Study Inst.; mem. design com., "The State of Nation's Ecosystems", H. John Heinz III Ctr.; lectr. in field. Mem. adv. bd. Frontiers in Ecology & the Environment, Ecological Soc. Am., mem. editl. bd. Consequences, reviewer International Panel on Climate Change; contbr. articles to profl. jours. Co-chair Def. Strategic Environ. R&D Program. Mem. Nat. Sci. & Tech. Coun. (mem. com. on environ. and natural resources), Nat. Ocean Rsch. Leadership Coun., Am. Geophysical Union (Waldo E. Smith medal, 2000), Energy Found., NAS (bd. dir. Atmospheric Chemistry and Climate); bd. dir. Fedn. Am. Scientists; fellow AAAS, Am. Acad. Arts & Scis. Office: U Mich Sch of Natural Resources and Environment 440 Church St 2046a Dana Ann Arbor MI 48109-1041 Office Phone: 734-764-6453, 734-764-2550. Business E-Mail: rbierbau@umich.edu.

BIERIG, JACK R., lawyer, educator; b. Chgo., Apr. 10, 1947; s. Henry J. and Helga (Rothschild) B.; m. Barbara A. Winokur; children: Robert, Sarah. BA, Brandeis U., 1968; JD, Harvard U., 1972. Bar: Ill. 1972, US Dist. Ct. (no. dist.) Ill. 1972, US Ct. Appeals (1st-3d, 5th-11th and DC cirs.) 1974, US Supreme Ct. 1980. Ptnr. Sidley Austin, LLP, Chgo., 1972—; prof. Ill. Inst. Tech.-Chgo. Kent Coll. Law, 1974-95; lectr. law. U. Chgo. Law Sch. and Harris Sch. Pub. Policy, 2000—. Chmn. legal sect. Am. Soc. Assn. Execs., 1994-95. Contbr. articles to profl. jours. Pres. Neighborhood Justice Chgo., 1983-87; pres. Jewish Vocat. Svc., 1997-99. Mem. Ill. Assn. of Hosp. Attys. (pres. 1991), Chgo. Bar Assn. (bd. govs., 1982-84). Clubs: Standard (Chgo.). Jewish. Office Phone: 312-853-7614. Business E-Mail: jbierig@sidley.com.

BIERLEY, PAUL EDMUND, aeronautical engineer, musician, author, publisher; b. Portsmouth, Ohio, Feb. 3, 1926; s. William Frederick and Minnie Genieve (Atkin) B.; m. Pauline Jeanette Allison, Sept. 17, 1948; children: Lois Elaine Bierley Walker, John Emerson. B of Aero. Engring., Ohio State U., 1953, DMusic (hon.), 2001. Aero. engr. N.Am. Aviation, Columbus, Ohio, 1953-73; engr., data mgr. Ellanef Mfg. Corp., Columbus, 1973-88; tubist Columbus Symphony Orch., 1965-81, Detroit Concert Band, 1973-92. Lectr. in field. Author: John Philip Sousa, A Descriptive Catalog of His Works, 1973, John Philip Sousa, American Phenomenon, 1973, rev. edit., 1986 (Deems Taylor award 1986), 2d rev. edit., 2000, Office Fun!, 1976, Hallelujah Trombone!, 1982, The Music of Henry Fillmore and Will Huff, 1982, The Works of John Philip Sousa, 1984, Sousa Band Fraternal Society News Index, 1997, Did Sousa's Band Play in Your Town?; co-author: (with K. Suzuki) All About Sousa Marches, 2001, also numerous articles, radio and TV copy, concert programs and record jackets; asst. condr., Rockwell Internat. Concert Band, 1961-76; tubist World Symphony Orch., N.Y.C., 1971, Brass Band of Columbus, 1984-97, Village Brass, 1983—; editor: Integrity Press, Columbus, 1982—, The Heritage Ency. of Band Music, 1991, supplement, 1996, El Capitan (John Philip Sousa), 1994, Marching Along (John Philip Sousa), 1994. Trustee Robert Hoe Found., Poughkeepsie, N.Y., 1984—, dir. rsch. Integrity Rsch. Found., 1999—. Recipient Deems Taylor award ASCAP, 1986, God and Country award Salvation Army, 1995, Ohioana Libr. Assn. Citation, 1996; inductee Wall of Fame, Portsmouth, Ohi, 1994, Columbus Sr. Musicians Hall of Fame, 1997. Fellow Acad. Wind and Percussion Arts; mem. Am. Bandmasters Assn. (hon., Edwin Franko Goldman citation 1974), Am. Sch. Band Dirs. Assn. (assoc., A. Austin Harding award 1990), Am. Fedn. Musicians, Sonneck Soc. for Am. Music, Nat. Band Assn., Assn. Concert Bands, Internat. Tuba-Euphoniuum Assn., Windjammers Unltd., John Philip Sousa Found. (Sudler medal 1986, Sudler Order of Merit 2001), Ohio Hist. Soc., Am. Aviation Hist. Soc., Westerville Hist. Soc., Masons, Phi Beta Mu (Outstanding Contbr. to Bands award 1983). Methodist.

BIERMAN, JANE, wood products company executive; Pres., founder Lincoln Wood Products, Inc., 1947—. Office: 701 N State St Merrill WI 54452-1355

BIES, GAREY D., state representative; b. Manitowoc, Wis., Oct. 26, 1946; married; 4 children. AD, Northeastern Tech. Coll., 1982; attended ext. pub. mgr. program, U. Wis., Madison, 1991—98. Chief dep. sheriff, Kewaunee, Wis.; project dir. for Door/Kewaunee Drug Task Force; state assembly mem. Wis. State Assembly, Madison, 2000—, chair, corrections and the cts. com., vice-chair, hwy. safety and tourism coms., mem. natural resources and vets. and mil. affairs coms.; mem. Door County Motor Vehicle Accident Prevention Coalition. Mem. Northern Door Child Care Bd.; trustee St. Rosalia Cath. Ch. Served USN, 1964—69. Mem.: Help of Door County, KC, Am. Legion Post 527. Republican. Office: State Capitol Rm 125 W PO Box 8952 Madison WI 53708-8952

BIFULCO, FRANK, toy company executive; b. 1950; Degree, United States Military Academy; MS engring. sciences, Cornell U.; MA bus. mgmt., Central Michigan U. Sr. v.p., sales Procter & Gamble, chief mktg. officer, ICG Commerce; sr. v.p., mktg. Coca-Cola North Am., 1994—2000; sr. v.p., chief mktg. officer Timberland Co., 2001—03; pres., US Games Hasbro Inc., 2003—08; sr. v.p., chief mktg. officer Home Depot, Inc., 2008—. Mailing: Home Depot Corp Office 1400 W Dundee Rd Arlington Heights IL 60004*

BIGELOW, CHANDLER, III, publishing executive; b. 1969; s. Chandler and Caroline E. (Newell) Bigelow; m. Elizabeth Notz Hines, Jan. 6, 1996. BA, Trinity Coll; MBA, U. Wis. With Spyglass Inc.; with fin. devel. program Tribune Co., 1998—99, corp. fin. mgr., 1999—2000, dir. corp. fin., 2000—01, asst. treas., 2001—03, v.p., treas., 2003—08, CFO, 2008—. Office: Tribune Co 435 N Michigan Ave Chicago IL 60611 Office Phone: 312-222-9100.*

BIGELOW, DANIEL JAMES, aerospace executive; b. Harrisville, Pa., Mar. 26, 1935; s. Raymond James and Hilda Irene (Graham) Bigelow; m. Elizabeth Jane Allison, Sept. 10, 1955; 1 child, Allison Jane. BFA in Art Advt., Kent State U., Ohio, 1957; MA in Edn., La. Tech. U., 1974; MS in Polit. Sci., Auburn U., 1986; MS, Air U., 1987; postgrad., Ohio State U., 1989—, Kent State U. Commd. 2d lt. USAF, 1957, advanced through grades to col., 1979, ret., 1987; command pilot 167 combat missions Vietnam; air attaché to Soviet Union, 1983—85; dir. Soviet program Air War Coll. Air U., Ala., 1985—87; gen. mgr. aerospace divsn. Modern Techs. Corp., Dayton, Ohio, 1988—98, dir. programs corp. hdqrs., 1998—2001, dir. bus. svcs. corp. hdqrs., 2002—03; dir. investor rels. and corp. comm. MTC Tech., Inc., Dayton, 2003—. Designer artwork, writer text MTC Annual Reports, 2002—06; designer MTC Website, 2003—07. Author, editor: Soviet Studies, 1968—88; contbr. articles to profl. jours. Comdr. Army and Air Force ROTC Corps of Cadets, 1957, Kent State U. Decorated Legion of Merit with one oak leaf cluster, DFC, 14 Air medals, Def. Superior medal; named Disting. Mil. Grad., Air Force ROTC, 1957, Disting. alumni, East Liverpool (Ohio) HS Alumni Assn., 2004; recipient U.S. Am. Nat. award, CIA Dir. William J. Casey, 1985. Mem.: AIAA, Intelligence and Nat. Security Alliance, Am. Electronics Assn., Nat. Mus. US Army (founding sponsor), Wright "B" Flyer Assn., Strategic Air Command Assn., 3rd Mil. Airlift Squadron Assn., Kent State U. Alumni Assn., Nat. Investor Rels. Inst., Nat. Mil. Intelligence Assn., Nat. Def. Indsl. Assn., Electronic Engring. and Mfg. Group (bd. dirs. 2006—), Internat. Test and Evaluation Assn., Inst. Navigation, Miami Valley Mil. Affairs Assn., Def. Planning and Analysis Soc., Dayton Area Def. Contractors Assn. (pres. 1999—2000, bd. dirs.), Internat. Platform Assn., Am. Def. Preparedness Assn., Acad. Polit. Sci., Army Aviation Assn. Am., Inc., Intelligence & Nat. Security Alliance, Assn. U.S. Army, Mil. Officers Assn. Am., Dayton Area C. of C. (vice-chmn. mil. and fed. affairs com. 2003—04, chmn. 2004—), Dayton Art Inst., Air Rescue Assn. (historian 1998—, chmn. reunion and symposium 2003, nat. bd. dirs.), Air Force Assn. (v.p. state legis. affairs 2001—02), F-86 Sabre Pilots' Assn., B-52 Stratofortress Assn., Ret. Officers' Assn., Airlift/Tanker Assn., Armed Forces Comm. and Electronics Assn., Pararescue Assn., Pedro Helicopter Assn., Air Force Mus. Found., Mil. Officer Assn. Am., Assn. Former Intelligence Officers, Air Force Assn. Cmty. Ptnrs., DFC Soc., Nat. Aviation Hall of Fame, Waco Hist. Soc., Royal Air Force Club, Discussion Club Dayton (v.p. 1999—2000), Am. Legion, Assn. Old Crows, Order Daedalians (flight capt., pres. 2001—02), Order Quiet Birdmen, Anciente Order Quiet Birdmen, Shriners, Scottish Rite, Masons, Blue Key. Presbyterian. Avocations: art, photography, jogging. Home: 2537 Indian Wells Trl Xenia OH 45385-9373 Office Phone: 937-610-0275. Business E-Mail: daniel.bigelow@mtctechnologies.com.

BIGGERT, JUDITH BORG, congresswoman, lawyer; b. Chgo., Aug. 15, 1937; d. Alvin Andrew and Marjorie Virginia (Mailler) Borg; m. Rody Patterson Biggert, Sept. 21, 1963; children: Courtney Ray, Alison Mailler, Rody Patterson, Adrienne Taylor. BA, Stanford U., 1959; JD, Northwestern U., 1963. Bar: Ill. 1963. Law clk. to presiding justice US Ct. Appeals (7th cir.), Chgo., 1963-64; sole practice Hinsdale, Ill., 1964—99; mem. Ill. Gen. Assembly, 1993—98, asst. Rep. leader, 1995—98; mem. US Congress from 13th Ill. dist., 1999—, mem. fin. svcs. com., edn. and workforce com. stds. ofcl. conduct, chmn. sci. com. subcom. on energy, mem. bipartisan working group on youth violence. Mem. bd. editors Law Rev., Northwestern U. Sch. Law, 1961-63. Pres. Hinsdale Twp. HS Dist. 86 Bd. Edn., 1983-85; pres. Jr. League Chgo., 1976-78, treas., bd. mgrs., 1966—; chmn. Hinsdale Antiques Show, 1980; pres. Oak Sch. PTA, Hinsdale, 1976-78; pres.-treas. Chgo. jr. bd. Travelers Aid Soc., 1965-70; Sunday sch. tchr. Grace Episcopal Ch., Hinsdale, 1978-80, 82-85; chair, treas., 2d v.p. bd. dirs.

Vis. Nurses Assn. Chgo., 1978; bd. dirs. Salt Creek Ballet, 1990-98. Recipient Servian award Jr. aux. U. Chgo. Cancer Rsch. Foun., Woman Yr. in Govt., Politics, and Civic Affairs DuPage YWCA, 1995, Hero of the Taxpayer, Am. for Tax Reform. 2000, 02, award for pub. svc., Am. Chem. Soc., 2003, Excellence in Edn., Nat. Assn. Coll. Admission Counseling, 2002, Friend of Edn., Ill. & Nat. Edn. Assn., 2002, Outstanding Leadership to Homeless and Victims of Domestic Violence, Chgo., Pub. Sch., 2002, Disting. Achievement for Protecting and Expanding Opportunities for Children and Youth Who Are Homeless, Chgo. Coalition for the Homeless, 2002, Spirit of Enterprise award US C. of C.; named one of 100 Women Making a Difference; inductee to Hinsdale Ctrl. HS Hall Fame, 1997. Mem. ABA, Ill. Bar Assn., DuPage Bar Assn., Coalition Women Legislatures. Republican. Office: US Ho Reps 1317 Longworth Ho Off Bldg Washington DC 20515-1313 also: Dist Off Ste 305 6262 S Rte 83 Willowbrook IL 60527 Office Phone: 202-225-3515.

BIGGINS, ROBERT A., state legislator; b. Oak Park, Ill., Oct. 20, 1946; m. Judy Biggins; children: Jennifer, Kevin. BA, Northeastern Ill. U., 1969. Assessor Addison Twp., Ill., 1973-77; Ill. state rep. Dist. 78, 1992—. Mem. Gen. Svcs., Consumer Protection, Fin. Insts. and Revenue Coms.; tchr. Mannheim Jr. H.S., orthlake, Ill., 1969, Daniel Webster Elem. Sch., Chgo., 1970-73; property tax cons., Chgo., 1977-81; ptnr. Property Assessment Advisors, Inc., 1981—, exec. v.p. Bd. dirs. Suburban Bank Elmhurst, 1975—, chmn., 1983-84; chmn. Bank of Bellwood, 1981-85; mem. Elmhurst Gardens Homeowners Assn. (past pres.), Edison Sch. PTA (past pres.). Recipient award Internat. Assn. Assessing Officers, 1990. Mem. DuPage County Assessors Assn. (legis. liaison 1975-76, pres. 1976), Inst. Property Taxation (cert.). Address: 114 W Vallette St Elmhurst IL 60126-4451

BIGGS, ROBERT DALE, Near Eastern studies educator; b. Pasco, Wash., June 13, 1934; s. Robert Lee and Eleonora Christina (Jensen) B. BA in Edn, Eastern Wash. Coll. Edn., 1956; PhD, Johns Hopkins U., 1962. Rsch. assoc. Oriental Inst. U. Chgo., 1963—64, asst. prof. Assyriology, 1964-67, assoc. prof. Assyriology, 1967-72, prof. Assyriology, 1972—2004, prof. emeritus, 2004—. Author: SA.Zi.GA: Ancient Mesopotamian Potency Incantations, 1967, Inscriptions from Tell Abu Salabikh, 1974, Inscriptions from al-Hiba-Lagash: The First and Second Seasons, 1976; co-author: Cuneiform Texts from Nippur, 1969, Nippur II: The orth Temple and Sounding E, 1978; editor: Discoveries from Kurdish Looms, 1983; assoc. editor: Assyrian Dictionary, 1964-87; editor Jour. Near Ea. Studies, 1971-2007; mem. editl. bd. Assyrian Dictionary, 1995—. Fulbright scholar Univ. Toulouse, France, 1956-57; fellow Baghdad Sch., Am. Schs. Oriental Rsch., 1962-63, Am. Rsch. Inst. in Turkey, 1972, Danforth fellow, 1956-62. Mem. Am. Oriental Soc. (pres. Mid. Western br. 1978-79), Archaeol. Inst. Am. (pres. Chgo. soc. 1985-92), Brit. Sch. Archaeology Iraq. Office: U Chgo 1155 E 58th St Chicago IL 60637-1540 Office Phone: 773-702-9540. Business E-Mail: r-biggs@uchicago.edu.

BILAND, ALAN THOMAS, computer integrated manufacturing executive; b. Pontiac, Mich., Sept. 13, 1958; s. Alfred T. and Janice J. (Bortreger) B.; m. Martha R. Wegner, Sept. 15, 1979; children: Benjamin A., Elizabeth L. BA in Biology and Psychology, Kalamazoo Coll., 1980; MBA, U. Wis., 1990. Computer aided design/computer aided mfg. Ronningen Rsch., Vicksburg, Mich., 1980-83; sr. industry cons. Computervision, Bedford, Mass., 1981-83; mgr. CAD/CAM N.Am. J.I. Case Co., Racine, Wis., 1985-91; mgr. U.K. Info. Svcs. J.I. Case, Doncaster, England, 1991—98; v.p. & CIO Snap-On Inc., Kenosha, Wis., 1998—2001, v.p. & CIO and pres. diagnostics and info group, 2001—. Mem. Computer and Automated Systems Assn., Soc. Mfg. Engrs. Republican. Lutheran. Avocations: fishing, travel, studying german. Office: Snap-On Inc 10801 Corporate Dr Pleasant Prairie WI 53158-1603

BILCHIK, GARY B., lawyer; b. Cleve., Dec. 7, 1945; s. Hyman M. and Leah (Gitleson) B.; m. Janice Rossen, Dec. 26, 1971; children: Susan, Steven. BBA, Ohio U., 1967; JD cum laude, Ohio State U., 1971. Bar: Ohio 1971, Fla. 1981. Atty., ptnr. Benesch, Friedlander, Coplan & Aronoff LLP, Cleve., 1981—. V.p. Jewish Family Svc., Cleve.; treas. Council Gardens, Cleve. Recipient Danzig Leadership award Jewish Family Svc., 1992. Mem. ABA, Ohio State Bar Assn., Cleve. Bar Assn. Democrat. Home: 25415 Letchworth Rd Cleveland OH 44122-4187

BILELLO, JOHN CHARLES, engineering educator, director; b. Bklyn., Oct. 15, 1938; s. Charles and Catherine (Buonadonna) B.; m. Mary Josephine Gloria, Aug. 1, 1959; children: Andrew Charles, Peter Angelo, Matthew Jonathan. B.E., NYU, 1960, MS, 1962; PhD, U. Ill., 1965. Sr. rsch. engr. Gen. Telephone & Electronics Lab., Bayside, NY, 1965-67; mem. faculty SUNY, Stony Brook, 1967-87, asst. prof., 1967-71, assoc. prof., 1971-75, prof. engring., 1975-87, dean, 1977-81; dean Sch. Engring and Computer Sci., prof. mech. engring. Calif. State U., Fullerton, 1986-89; prof. materials sci. and engring., prof. applied physics U. Mich., Ann Arbor, 1989—2004, dir. Ctr. Nanomaterials Scis., 1995—, emeritus, 2005—; v.p. R&D Metaglass Coatings, LLC, Ann Arbor, 2005—. Vis. rsch. assoc., Calif. Inst. Tech., Pasadena, 2003, vis. prof. Poly. of Milan, 1973-74; vis. scholar King's Coll., London U., 1983; vis. fellow NATO exchange scholar Oxford U., 1986; project dir. synchroton topography project Univ. Consortium, 1981-86; NATO vis. fellow Oxford (Eng.) U., 1998—. NATO sr. faculty fellow Enrico Fermi Center, Milan, Italy, 1973 Fellow Am. Soc. for Metals; mem. AIME, Am. Phys. Soc., Materials Rsch. Soc. Office: U Mich Dept Material Sci Engring Ann Arbor MI 48109

BILEYDI, SUMER, advertising agency executive; b. Antalya, Turkey, Feb. 7, 1936; came to U.S., 1957; s. Abdurrahman M. and Neriman (Akman) B.; m. Lois E. Goode, Dec. 30, 1961; children: Can M., Sera N. BA, Mich. State U., 1961, MA, 1962. Mktg. cons. Export Promotion Ctr., Ankara, 1962; planner Gardner Advt. Agy., St. Louis, 1963-65; planning supr. Batten, Barton, Durstine & Osborn, NYC, 1965-69; assoc. dir. Ketchum, Macleod & Grove, Pitts., 1969-73; sr. ptnr., dir. Carmichael Lynch, Inc., Mpls., 1974-91, sr. ptnr., 1992-98; CEO, pres. Manajans Thompson AS, Istanbul, Turkey, 1999-2001, ret., 2001. Cons. Carmichael-Lynch, Mpls., 1999-2004; cons. Leading Ind. Advt. Agy. Network, 1987-89, chmn., pres., 1989-91; CEO, pres. Global Mktg. Comm. Cons., Naples, Fla. Contbr. articles to profl. jours. Mem. Am. Mktg. Assn., Advt. Rsch. Found. Home: 4718 Navassa Ln Naples FL 34119-9554 Office Phone: 239-594-5056. E-mail: lbileydi@aol.com.

BILLER, JOEL WILSON, lawyer, retired diplomat; b. Milw., Jan. 17, 1929; s. Saul Earl and Mildred (Wilson) B.; m. Geraldine Pollack, May 1, 1955; children— Sydney, Andrew, Charles. BA, U. Wis., 1950; JD, U. Mich., 1953; MA, Northwestern U., 1959. Bar: Wis. 1953. Atty., Milw., 1953-55; vice consul Am. consulate, Le Havre, France, 1956-58; econ. officer Am. Embassy, The Hague, Netherlands, 1959-62; internat. relations officer State Dept., Washington, 1962-66; econ. officer, asst. dir. AID mission, Quito, Ecuador, 1966-69; econ. counselor Am. embassy, Buenos Aires, 1969-71; dir. AID mission, Santiago, Chile, 1971-73; spl. asst. to undersec. state for econ. affairs Washington, 1973-74; spl. asst. to dep. sec. state, 1974; dep. asst. sec. state for comml. and spl. bilateral affairs, 1974-76; dep. asst. sec. state for transp., telecommunications and comml. affairs, after, 1976; sr. v.p. Manpower Inc., Milw., 1979-97, sr. v.p., gen. counsel, 1997-98, sr. v.p. internat. corp. affairs, 1999—; pres. Internat. Confedn. of Pvt. Employment Agys., 2004—. Mem. Am. Fgn. Service Assn. Office: Manpower Inc 5301 N Ironwood Rd PO Box 2053 Milwaukee WI 53201-2053

BILLER, JOSE, neurologist, educator; b. Montevideo, Uruguay, Jan. 18, 1948; B in Medicine, A.V. Acevedo Inst., Montevideo, Uruguay, 1965; MD, U. de la Republica, Montevideo, Uruguay, 1974. Diplomate Am. Bd. Neurology and Vascular Neurology. Intern Maciel Hosp., Montevideo, Uruguay, 1974—76, Columbus Hosp., Chgo., 1976-77; resident in neurology Henry Ford Hosp., Detroit, 1977-78, Loyola U. Hosp., Hines VA Hosp., Ill., 1978-80, chief resident neurology Ill., 1979—80; fellow cerebral vascular diseases Bowman Gray Sch. Med., Winston Salem, NC, 1980-81, instr. neurology, 1981; asst. prof. neurology Loyola U., Chgo., 1982-84, prof., assoc. chmn. dept. neurology Stritch Sch. Med., 2003—, dir. neurology residency training program, 2003—05, acting chmn. dept. neurology, 2004—05, prof., chmn. dept. neurology, 2005—; asst. prof. neurology U. Iowa Coll. Medicine, Iowa City, 1984-87, assoc. prof. neurology, 1987-90, prof. neurology, 1990-91; prof. Northwestern Sch. Medicine, Chgo., 1991-94; dir. stroke program, dir. acute stroke care unit Northwestern Meml. Hosp., Chgo., 1991-94; prof., chmn. dept. neurology Ind. U., 1994—2003. Prof. ad-hororem U. of the Republic Sch. Medicine, Uruguay, 1997—; cons. physician neurology svc. VA Hosp., Iowa City, 1984—91; staff physician Northwestern Meml. Hosp., Chgo., 1991—94; neurology cons. Rehab. Inst. Chgo., 1991—94; active med. staff Ind. U. Hosps., 1994—2003, Loyola U. Hosp., 2003—; cons. Roudebush VA Med. Ctr., 1994—2003. Mem. editl. bd. Stroke, Stroke-Clin. Update, eurol. Rsch., internat. bd. editors CNS Drugs; editor: Seminars in Cerebrovascular Diseases and Stroke, Jour. Stroke and Cerebrovascular Diseases; contbr. articles to profl. jours., chapters to books. Fellow: ACP, Am. Heart Assn., Am. Acad. Neurology; mem.: AMA, Am. Neurol. Assn., Inter-Am. Coll. Physicians and Surgeons, Uruguayan Internal Medicine Soc. (hon.), Argentinian Neurol. Assn. (hon.), Uruguayan Neurol. Soc. (hon.), Internat. Stroke Soc., Am. Soc. Neurology Investigation, N.Y. Acad. Sci. Office: Maguire Bldg 105/2700 2160 S First Ave Maywood IL 60153 Office Phone: 708-216-2438. Business E-Mail: jbiller@lumc.edu.

BILLIG, ETEL JEWEL, theater director, actress; b. NYC, Dec. 16, 1932; d. Anthony and Martha Rebecca (Klebansky) Papa; m. Steven S. Billig, Dec. 23, 1956 (dec. Aug. 1996); children: Curt Adam, Jonathan Roark. BS, NYU, 1953, MA, 1955; student, Herbert Berghof Studio, NYC, 1955-56. Cert. elem. and high sch. tchr. Actress Washington Square Players, NYC, 1950-55, Dukes Oak Theatre, Cooperstown, NY, 1955, Triple Cities Playhouse, Binghampton, NY, 1956, Candlelight Dinner Playhouse, Summit, Ill., 1970, 73, 77, 79, 90; mng. dir. Theatre 31, Park Forest, Ill., 1971-73; asst. mgr. Westroads Dinner Theatre, Omaha, 1973-76; mng. dir., actress Forum Theatre, 1973, 94; mng. dir., actress, producing dir. Ill. Theatre Ctr., Park Forest, 1976—; mng. dir., actress Goodman Theatre, Chgo., 1987, 95, Ct. Theatre, 1990, Wisdom Bridge Theatre, 1991; dir. drama Rich Ctrl. H.S., Olympia Fields, Ill., 1978-86. Del. League of Chgo. Theatres Russian Exchange to Soviet Union, 1989; actress Drury Lane, Oak Brook, Ill., 1989; mem. adj. faculty theatre program Prairie State Coll., 2004—; cons. and lectr. in field. Appeared in films including the Dollmaker, Running Scared, Straight Talk, Stolen Summer; (TV series) Hawaiian Heat, Missing Persons, Untouchables. V.p. Nat. Coun. Jewish Women, Park Forest, 1968-70; sec. Community Arts Coun., Park Forest, 1984-86; pres. Southland Regional Arts Coun., 1986-92. Recipient Risk Taking award NOW, 1982, Athena award Matteson Area C. of C., 1997, Abby Found. award, 1997; grantee Nebr. Arts Coun., 1975, Ill. Arts Coun., 1995, 96, 2000; named Best of Chgo. drama muse for children Chgo. Mag., 2004, Entertainer of Yr. Star Pub. Newspaper, 2006; named to Park Forest Hall of Fame, 2000. Mem. AFTRA, SAG, Actors' Equity Assn., League Chgo. Theatres, Ill. Arts Coun. Theatre Panel, Prodrs. Assn. Chgo. Area Theatre (sec. 1988-89), Bus. in the Arts Coun. of C. of C. (charter), Rotary (bd. dirs. Park Forest chpt. 1988-97, sec. 2000, hall of fame 2000). Avocations: travel, antiques. Office: Ill Theatre Ctr PO Box 397 Park Forest IL 60466-0397 Office Phone: 708-481-3510. E-mail: ilthctr@sbcglobal.net.

BILLIG, THOMAS CLIFFORD, publishing executive, marketing professional; b. Pitts., Aug. 20, 1930; s. Thomas Clifford and Melba Helen (Stocky) Billig; m. Helen Page Hine, May 14, 1951; children: Thomas Clifford, James Frederick. BSBA summa cum laude, Northwestern U., 1956. Ins. mgr., asst. dir. pers., asst. to chmn. Butler Bros. (now City Products Corp.), Chgo., 1954-59; market rsch. mgr. R.R. Donnelley & Sons, Chgo., 1959-61; pres., dir. Indsl. Fiber Glass Products Corp., Scottville and Ludington, Mich., 1962-69; cons. mass mktg. mgr. Mpls., 1969-71; v.p. Mail Mktg. Systems and Services, St. Paul and Bloomington, Minn., 1971-74; pres., chmn., chief exec. officer Billig & Assocs., Mpls. and Duluth, Minn., 1974—; pres. NIARS Corp., Duluth, 1974—85, 1995—2003, Fins and Feathers Pub. Co., Mpls., 1977-89; pres., dir. N. Coast Mktg. Corp., St. Paul, 1992—; chmn., CEO Sportsman's Mktg. Inc., Superior, Wis., Lake Elmo, Minn., 1998—. Author: Nat. Ins. Advt. Regulation Svc., 1972—; author, pub.: NAIC Model Laws, Regulations and Guidelines, 1976—83. With USNR, 1948—56. Recipient Samuel Dresner Plotkin award, Northwestern U., 1956. Mem.: Beta Gamma Sigma, Delta Mu Delta. Office: 1423 N 8th St Superior WI 54880-6664 also: 3394 Lake Elmo Ave N Box 852 Lake Elmo MN 55042-9799 E-mail: niarsi@aol.com.

BILLINGS, CHARLES EDGAR, physician; b. Boston, June 15, 1929; s. Charles Edgar and Elizabeth (Sanborn) B.; m. Lillian Elizabeth Wilson, Apr. 16, 1955; 1 dau., Lee Ellen Billings Kreinbihl. Student, Wesleyan U., 1947-49; MD, N.Y. U., 1953; M.Sc. (Link Found. fellow), Ohio State U., 1960. Diplomate: Am. Bd. Preventive Medicine. Instr. to prof. depts. preventive medicine and aviation Sch. Medicine Ohio State U., 1960-73, dir. div. environ. health Sch. Medicine, 1970-73, clin. prof. Sch. Medicine, 1973-83, prof. emeritus, 1983—; rsch. scientist indsl. and systems engring., 1992—. Med. officer NASA Ames Rsch. Ctr., Moffett Field, Calif., 1973-76; chief Aviation Safety Rsch. Office, 1976-80, asst. chief for rsch. Man-Vehicle Systems rsch. divsn., 1980-83, sr. scientist, 1983-91; chief scientist Ames Rsch. Ctr., 1991-92; cons. Beckett Aviation Corp., 1962-73; surgeon gen. U.S. Army, 1965-77, FAA, 1967-70, 75, 83; mem. ATO-AGARD Aerospace Med. Panel, 1980-86; assoc. advisor USAF Sci. Adv. Bd., 1978-90; mem. human factors adv. panel U.K. Civil Aviation Authority, 1999-2001; mem. aviation adv. bd. Ohio U., 2000-01. Author: Aviation Automation: The Search for a Human-Centered Approach, 1997; contbr. chpts. to books, numerous articles in field to med. jours. Served to maj. USAF, 1955-57. Recipient Air Traffic Svc. award FAA, 1969, Walter M. Boothby rsch. award, 1972, PATCO Air Safety award, 1979, Disting. Svc. award Flight Safety Found., 1979, John A. Tamisea award, 1980, Laura Taber Barbour Air Safety medal, 1981, Outstanding Leadership medal NASA, 1981, 90, Jeffries Aerospace Med. Rsch. medal AIAA, 1986, Lovelace award NASA Soc. Flight Surgeons, 1996, Forrest and Pamela Bird award Civil Aviation Med. Assn., 2001, Henry L. Taylor Founders award Aerospace Human Factors Assn, 2002; Ames Rsch. Ctr. fellow, 1989. Fellow AIAA (assoc.), Royal Aero. Soc., Aerospace Med. Assn. (pres. 1979-80); mem. AMA, Internat. Acad. Aviation and Space Medicine. Office: 210 Baker ISE Bldg 1971 Neil Ave Columbus OH 43210-1210 Personal E-mail: chasbill@ix.netcom.com.

BILLION, JACK (JOHN JOSEPH BILLION), political organization administrator, retired orthopedic surgeon, former state representative; b. Sioux Falls, SD, Mar. 4, 1939; s. Henry Alphonse and Evelyn Margaret (Heinz) B.; div.; children: Matthew, Suzanne, John, James, Jane; m. Deborah Wagner, Mar. 22, 1980; children: Timothy, Allyson. BA, Loras Coll., 1960; MD, Stritch-Loyola U., 1964. Diplomate Am. Bd. Orthopedic Surgery. Resident orthopedics St. Francis Hosp., Peoria, Ill., 1964-69; orthopedic surgeon Sioux Falls, 1971-96; state rep. State of S.D., 1992-96. Vice-chair SD Dem. Party, 1997-98, chair, 2006-; chair Minnehaha Dem. Party, 2005-06; Dem. candidate for Gov. of SD, 2006. Maj. USAF, 1969-71. Fellow Am. Acad. Orthopedic Surgeons. Democrat. Office: SD Dem Party PO Box 1485 Sioux Falls SD 57101 Office Phone: 605-271-5405.*

BILLUPS, CHAUNCEY, professional basketball player; b. Sept. 25, 1976; m. Piper Riley; 2 children. Student, U. Colo., 1997. Guard Boston Celtics, 1996-97, Toronto Raptors, 1997-98, Denver Nuggets, 1998-00, Minn. Timberwolves, Mpls., 2000—02, Detroit Pistons, 2002—07. Named NBA Finals MVP, 2004; named to Ea. Conf. All-Star Team, NBA, 2006, 2007, 2008. Achievements include being a member of NBA Championship Team, 2004. Avocation: music. Office: c/o Detroit PIstons Palace of Auburn Hills 2 Championship Dr Auburn Hills MI 48326*

BILLUPS, NORMAN FREDRICK, college dean, pharmacist, educator; b. Portland, Oreg., Oct. 15, 1934; s. John Alexander and Myrtle I. (Morris) B.; m. Shirley Mae Brooks, July 7, 1956; children: Tamra Mae, Timothy Fredrick. Student, Portland State U., 1952-55; BS in Pharmacy, Oreg. State U., 1958, MS in Pharmacy, 1961, PhD (Am. Found. Pharm. Edn. fellow), 1963. Instr. Oreg. State U., 1958-60, grad. asst., 1960-63; asso. prof. pharmacy U. Ky., 1963-73, prof., 1974-77; dean, prof. pharmacy Coll. Pharmacy, U. Toledo, 1977-00; pharmacist Ohio, Oreg., Ky., 1961—. Dir. internat. adv. com. Pharm@Sea. Author: American Drug Index, ann, 1977—. Lay leader, chmn. pastor-parish com. local Meth. Ch. Recipient Rsch. Achievement award Am. Soc. Hosp. Pharmacists, 1975, Outstanding Svc. award Ky. Pharm. Assn., 1977; NIH rsch. fellow, 1962-63; Dean Norman F. Billups Disting. Svc. award established by U. Toledo Pharmacy Alumni Assn., 1992. Mem. Am. Assn. Colls. Pharmacy (Lyman award 1971), Am. Pharm. Assn., Ohio Pharm. Assn. (bd.dirs., Beal award 2001), Ohio Soc. Health Care Pharmacists, Toledo Acad. Pharmacy (bd. dirs., Pharmacist of Yr. 1997), Coun. Ohio Colls. Pharmacy (chmn. bd. trustees, chmn. coun.), Ky. Col. Commn., Sigma Xi, Phi Kappa Phi (pres. U. Toledo chpt.), Rho Chi (chpt. advisor, nat. exec. com.). Phi Lambda Sigma (chpt. adv.), Kappa Psi (grand coun. dep., nat. officer, named Outstanding Alumnus), Lambda Kappa Sigma (hon. mem., nat. patron).

BILSTROM, JON WAYNE, lawyer; b. Chgo., Mar. 1946; m. Kathy Bilstrom. BS, U. Iowa, 1968, JD, 1974. Bar: Iowa 1974, Ill. 1974, Mo. 1991. Gen. counsel Exchange Nat. Bank, Chgo.; v.p., gen. counsel First Wis. Corp., Milw.; ptnr. Katten Muchin & Zavis, Chgo.; gen. counsel, sec. Merc. Bancorp Inc., St. Louis, 1990—99; pres., CEO The Bar Plan Mut. Ins. Co., St. Louis, 2001—02; exec. v.p. governance, regulatory rels., and legal affairs, sec. Comerica Inc., Detroit, 2003—. Served US Army. Office: Comerica Inc Comerica Tower at Detroit Ctr 500 Woodward Ave MC 3391 Detroit MI 48226

BINDENAGEL, JAMES DALE, university executive; b. Huron, SD, June 30, 1949; s. Gordon Dean and Patricia Jean (Williams) B.; m. Jean Kathleen Lundfelt, Dec. 26, 1971; children: Annamarie, Carl Jakob. BA, U. Ill, 1971, MPA, 1977. Officer U.S. Embassy U.S. Dept. State, Seoul, Republic of Korea, 1975—77; U.S. consul U.S. Consulate, Bremen, Germany, 1977-79; econ. officer Office Ctrl. European Affairs U.S. Dept. State, Washington, 1980-83; polit. officer Am. Embassy, Bonn, Germany, 1983-86; acting dir. Can. affairs U.S. Dept. State, 1988-89; dep. chief mission Am. Embassy, Berlin, 1989-90; divsn. chief developing countries and trade orgns. U.S. Dept. State Econ. and Bus. Affairs Bur., 1991; dir. Rockwell Internat., 1991-92; dir. Office Ctrl. European Affairs U.S. Dept. State, Washington, 1992-94; dep. chief mission Am. Embassy, Bonn, Germany, 1994-96, chargé d'affaires, acting amb., 1996—97; sr. coord. New Transatlantic Agenda German Marshall Fund, 1997-98; dir. Washington Conf. on Holocaust-era Assets; amb. spl. envoy for Holocaust issues, 1999—2002; spl. negotiator Conflict Diamonds, 2002—03; v.p. Chgo. Coun. on Fgn. Rels., 2003—05, De Paul U., 2005—. Trustee Remembrance, Responsibility and Future Fund, 1999-02, Arthur F. Burns Fellowship, German-Am. C. of C. Midwest, Catholic Theol. Union, Am. Jewish Comm., Berlin, Am. Inst. Contemporary German Studies, Humanitarian Aid Found., Internat. Human Rights Law Inst., Internat. Aviation Law Inst., Grant Park Conservancy. Capt. USAR, 1971-74. Decorated comdrs. cross Order of Merit Germany; recipient V.P. Nat. Performance award, 1998, Disting. Honor award, U.S. State Dept., 2000, Presdl. Meritorious Svc. award, 2002. Mem.: Coun. Fgn. Rels., Am. Coun. on Germany, Am. Polit. Sci. Assn. (Congl. fellow 1987—88), Pi Sigma Alpha. Roman Catholic. Avocations: tennis, hiking. Home: 3740 N Lake Shore Dr Apt 4B Chicago IL 60613-4201 Office Phone: 312-362-8100. Personal E-mail: jbindenagel@earthlink.net. Business E-Mail: jbindena@depaul.edu.

BINDER, CHARLES E., magistrate judge; b. Kalamazoo, Mich., Apr. 23, 1949; married; two children. BA, Western Mich. U., 1971; JD, Duke U., 1974. Law clk. to Hon. Wendell Miles, 1974-76; pvt. practice, 1976-84; magistrate judge U.S. Dist. Ct. (ea. dist.) Mich., Bay City, 1984—. Mem. Fed. Magistrate Judges Assn., State Bar Mich., Bay County Bar Assn. Office: US Dist Ct Ea Dist Mich 1000 Washington Ave Rm 323 Bay City MI 48708-5749 Fax: (517) 894-8819.

BINDLEY, WILLIAM EDWARD, pharmaceutical executive; b. Terre Haute, Ind., Oct. 6, 1940; s. William F. and Gertrude (Lynch) B.; children: William Franklin, Blair Scott, Sally Ann. BS, Purdue U., 1961; grad. wholesale mgmt. program, Stanford U., 1966. Asst. treas. Controls Co. Am., Melrose Park, Ill., 1962-65; vice-chmn. E.H. Bindley & Co., Terre Haute, 1965-68; pres., chmn. bd., CEO Bindley Western Industries, Inc., Indpls., 1968—2001; CEO Priority Healthcare, Lake Mary, Fla., 1994—97, pres., 1996, now chmn. Scholl scholarship guest lectr. Loyola U., Chgo., 1982; guest lectr. Young Pres. Orgn., Palm Springs, Calif. and Dallas, 1981, 82, 84, Ctr. for Entrepreneurs, Indpls., 1983, Purdue U., West Lafayette, Inc., De Pauw U., Greencastle, Ind., disting. lectr. Georgetown U., Washington, 1989—, mem. adv. bd.; bd. dirs. Key Bank NA, Cleve., Shoe Carnival, Inc.; former owner basketball team Ind. Pacers. State dir. Bus. for Reagan-Bush, Washington and Indpls., 1980; trustee Marian Coll., Indpls., Indpls. United Way, St. Vincent Hosp., Indpls.; bd. dirs. Indpls. Entrepreneurship Acad., Nat. Enterpreneurship Found., U.S. Ski Team, chmn. fin., exec. com. mem.; mem. adv. bd. Rose Hulman Inst. Tech.; mem. pres.'s coun. Purdue U., dean's adv. bd. Named Hon. Ky. Col., 1980, Sagamore of the Wabash, Gov. Orr, State of Ind., 1989, Entrepreneur of Yr., State of Ind., 1992. Mem. Young Pres. Orgn. (area dir., chmn. 1982, award 1983), Nat. Wholesale Druggists Assn. (dir. 1981-84, Svc. award 1984), Purdue U. Alumni Assn. (life), Woodstock Club, Meridian Hills Countryn Club. Republican. Roman Catholic. Avocations: skiing, golf, tennis, boating. Office: Priority Healthcare 250 Technology Pk Lake Mary FL 32746

BINFORD, GREGORY GLENN, lawyer; b. Canton, Ohio, Oct. 8, 1948; s. Edwin and Helen Marie B. BA, Case Western Res. U., 1970, JD, 1973. Bar: Ohio 1973. Ptnr. Guren, Merritt, Cleve., 1973-84, Benesch, Friedlander, Cleve., 1984—. Councilman, Bratenahl, Ohio. Mem. ABA, Nat. Health Lawyers Assn., Cleve. Bar Assn. (former chair health law sect.). Office: BP America Bldg 200 Public Sq Ste 2300 Cleveland OH 44114-2378 Office Phone: 216-363-4617. Business E-Mail: gbinford@bfca.com.

BING, DAVID, retired professional basketball player, metal products executive; b. Washington, Nov. 29, 1943; children: Cassaundra, Bridgett, Aleisha. BA in Econ., Syracuse U., 1966. With Detroit Pistons, 1966-74, Wash. Bullets, 1975-77, Boston Celtics, 1977-78; owner, chmn., CEO, The Bing Group, Detroit, 1980—. Named Rookie of Yr., 1967, Basketball Hall of Fame, 1989, Most Valuable Player, NBA All-Star Game, 1976, Nat. Small Bus. Person of Yr., 1984, Nat. Minority Supplier of Yr., 1984; recipient Schick Achievement award, 1990. Achievements include named to First Team NBA All Star, 1968, 71, Second Team, 1974, All Rookie Team, 1967; leading scorer in Syracuse U. history; All-Star 7 times. Office: The Bing Group 11500 Oakland St Detroit MI 48211-1073

BINGAY, JAMES S., bank executive; b. Seattle; m. Jean Bingay. BS in Econs., Brown U., 1965; MS in Fin., U. Pa., 1967. Regional exec. Citibank, Cleve., 1970-90; group exec. v.p. Key Corp, Cleve., 1990—. Trustee Cleve. Play House, Cleve. Coun. on World Affairs; bd. dirs. Nat. Corp. Theatre Fund, Cleve. Inst. of Music. Lt. USN, 1967-70. Office: Key Corp 127 Public Sq Cleveland OH 44114-1216

BINGHAM, CHRISTOPHER, statistics educator; b. NYC, Apr. 16, 1937; s. Alfred Mitchell and Sylvia (Knox) B.; m. Carolyn Higinbotham, Sept. 23, 1967 AB, Yale U., 1958, MA, 1960, PhD, 1964. Research fellow Conn. Agrl. Expt. Sta., New Haven, 1958-64; research assoc. in math. and biology Princeton U., NJ, 1964-66; asst. prof. stats. U. Chgo., 1967-72; assoc. prof. applied stats. U. Minn., Mpls., 1972-79, prof., 1979—. Contbr. articles to profl. jours. Fellow Am. Statis. Assn., Inst. Math. Stats.; mem. Royal Statis. Soc., Biometric Soc., Soc. Indsl. and Applied Math Home: 605 Winston Ct Mendota Heights MN 55118-1039 Office: U Minn Sch Stats 313 Ford Hall 224 Church St SE Minneapolis MN 55455-0493 E-mail: kb@umn.edu.

BINKLEY, DAVID A., human resources specialist; BS, Mich. State U. Regional mgr. human resources Whirlpool Corp., Benton Harbor, Mich., 1984—86, mgr. employee rels. parts distbn. ctr. LaPorte, Ind., 1986—89, dir. exec. devel. corp. human resources, 1989—92; dir. human resources Whirlpool Corp. Europe, Comerio, Italy, 1992—94; dir., human resources Whirlpool Corp. Asia, Singapore, 1994—95, v.p. human resources Greater China, 1995—96; corp. dir. mgmt. resources Whirlpool Corp., Benton Harbor, Mich., 1996—98, v.p. human resources N.Am. divsn., 1998—2001, corp. v.p. global human resources, 2001—04, sr. v.p. global human resources, 2004—. Office: Whirlpool Corp 2000 N M-63 Benton Harbor MI 49022-2692 Office Phone: 269-923-5000. Office Fax: 269-923-5443.

BINSFELD, CONNIE BERUBE, former state official; b. Munising, Mich., Apr. 18, 1924; d. Omer J. and Elsie (Constance) Berube; m. John E. Binsfeld, July 19, 1947; children: John T., Gregory, Susan, Paul, Michael. BS, Siena Heights Coll., 1945, DHL (hon.), 1977; LLD (hon.), No. Mich. U., 1998; DHL (hon.), Mich. State U., 1998, Thomas Cooley Sch. of Law, 1999; LLD (hon.), Saginaw Valley State U., 2000, Lake Superior State U., 2000; DHL (hon.), U. Notre Dame, 2000, Grand Valley State U., 2000, DHL (hon.). County commr. Leelanau County, Mich., 1970-74; mem. Mich. Ho. of Reps., 1974-82, asst. rep. leader, 1979-81; del. Nav. Conv., 1980, 88, 92; mem. Mich. Senate, 1982-90, asst. rep. leader, 1979, 81; lt. gov. State of Mich., 1990-98. Mem. adv. bd. Nat. Park Sys. Named Mich. Mother of Yr., Mich. Mothers Com., 1977; Northwestern Mich. Coll. fellow; named to Mich. Women's Hall of Fame, 1998. Mem. Nat. Coun. State Legislators, LWV, Siena Heights Coll. Alumnae Assn. Republican. Roman Catholic. E-mail: Connieltgov@mailstation.com.

BINSTOCK, ROBERT HENRY, public policy educator, writer; b. New Orleans, Dec. 6, 1935; s. Louis and Ruth (Atlas) B.; m. Martha Burns, July 27, 1979; 1 dau., Jennifer. AB, Harvard U., 1956, PhD, 1965. Lectr. Brandeis U., Waltham, Mass., 1963-65, asst. prof., 1965-69, assoc. prof., 1969-72, Stulberg Prof. law and politics, 1972-84, dir. Policy Ctr. Aging, 1979-84; prof. aging, health and soc. Case Western Res. U., Cleve., 1985—. Mem. com. on an Aging Soc. Nat. Acad. Scis., Washington, 1982-86. Author: America's Political System, 1972, 5th edit., 1991, America's Political System: Urban, State and Local, 1972, 3d edit., 1979, Feasible Planning for Social Change, 1966; editor: The Politics of the Powerless, 1971, Too Old for Health Care?, 1991, Dementia and Aging, 1992, International Perspectives on Aging: Population and Policy Changes, 1982, Handbook of Aging and the Social Sciences, 1976, 5th edit., 2001, 6th edit., 2006, The Future of Long Term Care, 1996, Home Care Advances: Essential Research and Policy Issues, 2000, The Lost Art of Caring: A Challenge to Health Professionals, Families, Communities and Society, 2001, The Fountain of Youth: Cultural, Scientific, and Ethical Perspectives on a Biomedical Goal, 2004, Aging Nation: The Economics and Politics of Growing Older in America, 2006. Bd. dirs. White House Task Force on Older Ams., 1967-68; chmn. adv. panel Office Tech. Assessment, U.S. Congress, 1982-84; tech. adviser, del. White House Conf. on Aging, 1971, 81; trustee Boston Biomed. Research Inst., 1971-84; mem. gov.'s adv. com. Dept. of Elder Affairs Mass., 1974-84; chair, adv. bd. Nat. Acad. on Aging, 1991-95. Recipient Haak-Lilliefors award Mich. State U., 1979, Arthur S. Flemming award Nat. Assn. State Units on Aging, 1988, Key award APHA, 1992, Am. Soc. Aging award, 1994, Hall of Fame award, Am. Soc. Aging, 2006; fellow Ford Found., 1959-69; Rsch. grant NIH, 1968-73. Fellow Gerontol. Soc. Am. (pres. 1976, Donald P. Kent award 1981, Brookdale Prize award 1983), Assn. Gerontol. in Higher Edn. (Tibbitts award, 2007); mem. APHA (chair gerontol. health sect. 1996-97, Lifetime Achievement award 2005). Office: Case Western Res Univ 2040 Adelbert Rd Cleveland OH 44106-4901

BIONDI, LAWRENCE, academic administrator, priest; b. Chgo., Dec. 15, 1938; s. Hugo and Albertina (Marchetti) B. BA, Loyola U., Chgo., 1962, Ph.L., 1964, M.Div., S.T.L., Loyola U., Chgo., 1971; MS, Georgetown U., 1966, PhD in Sociolinguistics, 1975. Ordained priest Roman Cath. Ch., 1970. Joined Soc. Jesus; asst. prof. sociolinguistics Loyola U., Chgo., 1974-79, assoc. prof., 1979-81, prof., 1982-87, dean Coll. Arts and Scis., 1980-87; pres. St. Louis U., 1987—. Mem. Joint Commn. on Accreditation of Health Care Orgs., 1998—. Author: The Italian-American Child: His Sociolinguistic Acculturation, 1975, Poland's Solidarity Movement, 1984; editor: Poland's Church-State Relations in the 1980s, 1980, Spain's Church-State Relations, 1982. Trustee Xavier U., 1981-87, Loyola Coll., Balt., 1988-94, Santa Clara U., 1988-98, Kenrick-Glennon Sem., 1988-94, St. Louis U., 1982—, Loyola U., Chgo., 1988-97; bd. dirs. Epilepsy Found. Am., 1985-95, Civic Progress, St. Louis, 1987—, Regional Commerce and Growth Assn., 1987—, Mo. Bot. Gardens, 1987—, St. Louis Zoo, 1994, St. Louis Symphony, 1994, Harry S. Truman Inst. for Nat. and Internat. Affairs, 1987—, Tenet Health Care Sys., 1998—, St. Louis Sci. Ctr., 2000—, Boys Hope Girls Hope, 1996—, St. Louis Art Mus., 1997—, Grand Ctr., St. Louis, 1987—. Mellon grantee, 1974, 75, 76, 82; Humanitarian of Yr., Arthritis Found., 1999; Leon R. Strauss Urban Pioneer award, 2001. Mem. Linguistic Soc. Am., MLA, Am. Anthrop. Assn.; Knight of Italian Order of Merit. Office: St Louis U 221 N Grand Blvd Saint Louis MO 63103-2006 Office Phone: 314-977-7777.

BIRCK, MICHAEL JOHN, telecommunications industry executive; b. Missoula, Mont., Jan. 25, 1938; s. Raymond Michael and Mildred (Johnson) B.; m. Katherine Royer, Sept. 3, 1960; children: Kevin, Joni Birck Stevenson, Christopher. BSEE, Purdue U., 1960, PhD in Engring. (hon.), 1991; MSEE, NYU, 1962. Mem. tech. staff Bell Tel. Labs., Murray Hill, N.J., 1960-66; dir. engring. Communication Apparatus Corp., Melrose Park, Ill., 1967-68, Wescom, Inc., Downers Grove, Ill., 1968-75; co-founder, chmn. Tellabs, Inc., Naperville, Ill., 1975—, CEO, 1975—2000, 2002—04. Mem. bd. dirs. Tellabs Inc., Naperville, Ill., ITW, Glenview, Ill., Molex Inc., Lisle, Ill. Patentee in field. Dir. Purdue Rsch. Found., West Lafayette, 1989—; trustee Benedictine Univ., 1988—, Purdue U., 1999-; bd. dirs. Hinsdale Hosp., 1995, Ill. Math and Sci. Acad. Fund, Aurora, Mus. Sci. and Industry, Chgo. Recipient High Tech Entrepreneur award Crain's Ill. Bus., Chgo., 1984, Outstanding Engring. Alumni award Purdue U., 1991, Outstanding Master Entrepreneur award Inc. Mag./Ernst & Young, 1995; named Outstanding Elec. Engring. Alumnus Purdue U., 1995, IEEE Ernst Weber Engring. Leadership Recognition award, 2001, 2003 Medal of Honor, Electronic Industries Alliance. Mem. Hinsdale Golf Club. Republican. Roman Catholic. Avocations: running, tennis, golf. Office: Tellabs Inc 1415 W Diehl Rd Naperville IL 60563

BIRD, FORREST M., retired medical inventor; b. Stoughton, Mass., June 9, 1921; MD, PhD, ScD. Technical air tng. officer Army Air Corps; founder Bird Corp., Bird Space Tech. Corp., Sandpoint, Idaho. Trustee emeritus Am. Respiratory Care Found. Inventor Bird Universal Medical Respirator for acute or chronic cardiopulmonary care, 1958, "Babybird" respirator, 1970. Inductee Nat. Inventors Hall of Fame, 1995. Avocation: collector & pilot of 18 vintage flying aircraft. Office: Bird Space Tech Corp PO Box 817 Sandpoint ID 83864-0817

BIRD, LARRY JOE, professional sports team executive, retired professional basketball player; b. West Baden, Ind., Dec. 7, 1956; s. Joe and Georgia B; m. Dinah Mattingly Oct. 1, 1989; children: Corrie, Connor. Student, Ind. U., 1974, Northwood Inst., West Baden, Ind., 1974; BS, Ind. State U., 1979. Player Boston Celtics, 1979—92, spl. asst. to exec. v.p., 1992—97; head coach Ind. Pacers, Indpls., 1997—2000, pres. basketball ops., 2003—. Mem. US Men's Basketball Team World Univ. Games (gold medal), Sophia, Bulgaria, 1977, Barcelona Olympic Games (gold medal), Spain, 1992. Author: (with Bob Ryan) Drive, 1989; actor (film) Blue Chips, 1994. Named Collegiate Player of Yr., AP, UPI and Nat. Assn. Coaches, 1979, NBA Rookie of Yr., 1980, NBA All-Star Game MVP, 1982, NBA Finals MVP, 1984, 86, NBA MVP, 1984, 85, 86; named to NBA All-Rookie team, 1980, NBA All-Star Team, 1980-88, 90-92, All-NBA 1st team, 1980-88, NBA All-Def. 2nd team, 1982-84, NBA All-NBA 2nd team, 1990, Basketball Hall of Fame, 1998; named one of 50 Greatest Players in NBA hist., 1996. Achievements include winning NBA Championships as a member of the Celtics, 1981, 84, 86. Office: Ind Pacers 125 S Pennsylvania St Indianapolis IN 46204

BIRD, ROBERT BYRON, chemical engineering educator, author; b. Bryan, Tex., Feb. 5, 1924; s. Byron and Ethel (Antrim) Bird. Student, U. Md., 1941—43; BS, U. Ill., 1947; PhD, U. Wis., 1950; postdoctoral fellow, U. Amsterdam, 1950—51; DEng (hon.), Lehigh U., 1972, Washington U., 1973, Tech. U. Delft, Holland, 1977, Colo. Sch. Mines, 1986; ScD (hon.), Clarkson U., 1980, The Technion, Israel, 1993, Tex. A&M U., 1999; D in engring. sci. (hon.), Eidgenössische Tech. Hochschule, Zürich, Switzerland, 1994; DrEngring (hon.), Kyoto U., Japan, 1996; DSc (hon.), Iowa State U., 2007. Asst. prof. chemistry Cornell U., 1952—53, Debye lectr., 1973, Julian C. Smith lectr., 1988; rsch. chemist DuPont Exptl. Sta., 1953; mem. faculty U. Wis., 1951—52, 1953—57, prof. chem. engring., 1957—92, C.F. Burgess distinguished prof. chem. engring., 1968—72, John D. MacArthur prof., 1982—92, Vilas research prof., 1972—92, chmn. dept., 1964—68, emeritus prof., 1992—; Burgers prof. Technische Univ. Delft, The Netherlands, 1994. Vis. prof. U. Calif., Berkeley, 1977, Univ. Catholique de Louvain, Belgium, 1994; D. L. Katz lectr. U. Mich., 1971; W. N. Lacey lectr. Calif. Inst. Tech., 1974; K. Wohl Meml. lectr. U. Del., 1977; W. K. Lewis lectr. MIT, 1982; R. H. Wilhelm lectr. Princeton U., 1991; G. N. Lewis lectr. U. Calif., Berkeley, 1993; Ascher Shapiro lectr. MIT, 1997; lectr. Lectures in Sci. Humble Oil Co., 1959, 61, 64, 66; lecture tour Am. Chem. Soc., 1958, 75, Canadian Inst. Chemistry, 1961, 65; cons. to industry, 1965—90; mem. adv. panel engring. sci. divsn. NSF, 1961—64. Author (with others): Molecular Theory of Gases and Liquids, 2d printing, 1964; author: Transport Phenomena, 64th printing, 2002, Spanish edit., 1965, Czech edit., 1966, Italian edit., 1970, Russian edit., 1974, Chinese edit., 1990, revised 2d English edit., 2007, Chinese translation, 2004, Portuguese edit., 2004, Spanish edit., 2006, Een Goed Begin: A Contemporary Dutch Reader, 1963, 2d edit., 1971, Comprehending Technical Japanese, 1975, Chinese edit., 1985, Dynamics of Polymeric Liquids, Vol. 1, Fluid Mechanics, Vol. 2, Kinetic Theory, 1977, 2d edit., 1987, Japanese transl. Vol. 1, 1999, Vol. 2, 2004, Reading Dutch: Fifteen Annotated Stories from the Low Countries, 1985, Basic Technical Japanese, 1990, Technical Japanese Supplements: Polymer Science and Engineering, 1995, 100 Years of Chemical Engineering at the University of Wisconsin, 2005, also numerous rsch. publs.; Am. editor (with others) Applied Sci. Rsch., 1969—86, 1989—98; mem. adv. bd.: Indsl. and Engring. Chemistry, 1970—72, mem. editl. bd.: Jour. Non-Newtonian Fluid Mechanics, 1975—; contbr. Served to 1st lt. AUS, 1943—46. Decorated Bronze Star, knight Order Orange Nassau Netherlands; recipient Curtis McGraw award, Am. Assn. Engring. Edn., 1959, Westinghouse award, 1960, Corcoran award, 1987, Centennial Medallion, 1993, Nat. Medal Sci., 1987; Fulbright fellow, Holland, 1950, Guggenheim fellow, 1958, Fulbright lectr., 1958, Japan, 1962—63, Sarajevo, Yugoslavia, 1972. Fellow: AIChE (William H. Walker award 1962, Profl. Progress award 1965, Warren K. Lewis award 1974, Founders award 1989, Inst. Lect. award 1992 1992), Am. Acad. Arts and Scis., Am. Phys. Soc.; mem.: NAE, NAS, Royal Flemish Acad. Belgium for Scis and Arts (fgn.), Royal Dutch Acad. Scis. (fgn.), Soc. Rheology, Soc. Chem. Engrs. Japan (hon.), Am. Chem. Soc. (chmn. Wis. sect. 1966, unrestricted rsch. grant Petroleum Rsch. Fund 1963), Am. Assn. Netherlandic Studies, Wis. Acad. Scis., Arts and Letters, Am. Acad. Mechanics, Arts and Letters, Sigma Tau, Omicron Delta Kappa, Phi Kappa Phi, Alpha Chi Sigma, Tau Beta Pi, Sigma Xi (v.p. Wis. sect. 1959—60), Phi Beta Kappa. Office: U Wis Dept Chem and Biol Engring 3004 Engring Hall 1415 Engineering Dr Madison WI 53706-1607 Business E-Mail: bird@engr.wisc.edu.

BIRDSALL, DOUG, airline company executive; Chmn., CEO, pres. Travelmatin Corp.; sr. v.p., mktg., planning Continental Airlines; planning systems Ea. Airlines; v.p., mktg. alliances, strategic planning Northwest Airlines Corp, sr. v.p., alliances, 1999—. Office: Northwest Airline Corp 5101 Northwest Dr Saint Paul MN 55111-3075

BIRESI, MARK A., retail executive; Gen. counsel Burger King, 1985—2000; v.p. store ops. Ltd. Brands, Inc., Columbus, Ohio, 2000—01, sr. v.p. store ops., 2001—. Office: Ltd Bands Inc Three Ltd Pkwy Columbus OH 43230

BIRK, PEG J., lawyer; BA, U. Houston, 1976; JD, William Mitchell Coll. Law, 1983. Bar: Minn. 1983. Sr. corp. counsel St. Paul Companies, 1990—97; city atty. St. Paul, 1997—99; gen. counsel AM. Internat. Group, Inc., 1999, Domestic Brokerage Group; sr. v.p., gen. counsel Federated Mutual Ins. Co., Owatonna, Minn., 1999—. Bd. dirs. McKnight Found., Internat. Alliance Exec. Women; U.S. delegate Asian Pacific Econ. Corp., 2002—; bd. trustees Hamline U.; dep. Minn. Bus. Partnership. Office: Federated Mutual Ins Co 121 E Park Sq Owatonna MN 55060 Office Phone: 507-455-6915. Office Fax: 507-455-5997. E-mail: pjbirk@fedins.com.

BIRKETT, JOSEPH E., lawyer; b. Chgo. m. Patti Hill; 2 children. BA Polit. Sci. and English with honors, North Ctrl. Coll., Naperville, Ill., 1977; JD, John Marshall Law Sch., 1981. Bar: Ill. 1981. Asst. state's atty. DuPage County Office of the State's Atty., 1981-85, chief of maj. crimes unit, 1985-86, dep. chief criminal divsn., 1986-91, chief criminal divsn., 1991-96, DuPage County State's Atty., 1996—. Adj. faculty Nat. Louis U., Wheaton, Ill.; lectr. in field. Vol. coach DuPage County Crime Commn. Boxing Club. Mem. Assn. Govt. Attys. in Capital Litigation (pres. 2001), DuPage County Bar Assn., Delta Theta Phi. Roman Catholic. Address: 505 N County Farm Rd Wheaton IL 60187-3907

BIRKHOLZ, RAYMOND JAMES, metal products manufacturing company executive; b. Chgo., Nov. 11, 1936; s. Raymond I. and Mary (Padian) B.; m. Judy Ann Richards, Apr. 23, 1966; children: Raymond J. Jr., Scott C., Matthew R. BSME, Purdue U., 1958; MBA, U. Chgo., 1963. Registered prof. engr., Ill. V.p. apparatus divsn. Gen. Cable Corp., Westminster, Colo., 1973-77; v.p. ops. metals divsn. Ogden Corp., Cleve., 1977-80, v.p. mfg. and engring. NYC, 1980-81, pres. indsl. products, 1981-84, v.p., 1984-86; pres., COO Amcast Indsl. Corp., Dayton, Ohio, 1986-90; CEO Hollander Industries Corp., Dayton, Ohio, 1993-94; pres., CEO Republic Storage Systems Co., Inc., Canton, Ohio, 1994—. Home: 2268 Brookelake Dr Atlanta GA 30338-7015 Office: Republic Storage Systems Co 1038 Belden Ave NE Canton OH 44705-1454

BIRNEY, WALTER LEROY, religious administrator; b. Garden City, Kans., Apr. 25, 1934; s. Claude David and Mildred Elizabeth (Ferris) B.; m. Iva Lou Mosher, June 18, 1954; children: Mickey, Scotty, Gary, Lorrie, Lindie. BA, Dallas Christian Coll., 1956. Min. First Christian Ch., Benjamin, Tex., 1954-57, Bellaire Christian Ch., San Antonio, 1957-58, Copeland (Kans.) Christian Ch., 1958-84; coord. Nat. Missionary Conv., Copeland, 1966—. Dean, promoter Ashland (Kans.) Christian Camp, 1961-84; promoter S.W. Sch. Missions, Copeland, 1973-84. Named Outstanding Alumnus Dallas Christian Coll., 1988, Named to Dallas Christian Coll. Basketball Hall of Fame, 2004. Mem. Christian Ch. Avocation: running. Office: Nat Missionary Conv PO Box 11 Copeland KS 67837-0011 Office Phone: 620-668-5259. E-mail: wbirne11@aol.com.

BIRNKRANT, SHERWIN MAURICE, lawyer; b. Pontiac, Mich., Dec. 20, 1927; BBA, U. Mich., 1949, MBA, 1951; JD with distinction, Wayne State U., 1954. Bar: Mich. 1955, U.S. Dist. Ct. (ea. dist.) Mich. 1960, U.S. Supreme Ct. 1960, U.S. Ct. Appeals (6th cir.) 1966. Mem. Oakland County Bd. Suprs., 1967-68, Birnkrant & Birnkrant P.C., Bloomfield Hills, Mich., 1995—; asst. atty. City of Pontiac, Mich., 1956-67, city atty., 1967-83; of counsel Schlussel, Lifton, Simon, Rands, Galvin & Jackier, Southfield, Mich., 1983-90, Sommers, Schwartz, Silver & Schwartz, Southfield, 1990-95. Mem.: ABA (Mich. chmn. pub. contract law sect. 1979—97, chmn. urban, state and local govt. law sect. 1987—88, ho. dels. 1990—93, alt. del. to ho. dels. 1993—96, vice chmn. coordinating com. model procurement code state and local 1974—), Mich. Assn. Mcpl. Attys. (pres. 1975, coun. pres. 1992—), Oakland County Bar Assn. (chmn. ethics and unauthorized practices com. 1961—62), State Bar Mich. (chmn. pub. corp. law sect. 1973—74, coun. adminstrv. law sect. 1975—76). Office: Birnkrant & Birnkrant PC 7 W Square Lake Rd Bloomfield Hills MI 48302

BISGARD, GERALD EDWIN, biosciences educator, researcher; b. Denver, Aug. 4, 1937; s. Harry Herman and Lucille Margaret (Matson) B.; m. Sharon Kay Cummings, Sept. 9, 1961; children— Jennifer, Kristine, Bradley BS, Colo. State U., 1959, D.V.M., 1962; MS, Purdue U., 1967; PhD, U. Wis., 1971. Instr., then asst. prof. Purdue U., West Lafayette, Ind., 1962-69; asst. prof., then assoc. prof. bioscis. U. Wis., Madison, 1971-77, prof., 1977-2001, emeritus prof., 2001—, dept. chmn. bioscis., 1980-97. Vis. prof. U. Calif.-San Francisco, 1977-78; mem. respiratory and applied physiol. study sect. NIH, 1988-92. Recipient Merit award NIH, 1987; named NIH fellow, 1969-71, Fogarty NIH Sr. Internat. fellow Oxford U., 1993; grantee NIH, 1973—. Mem. Am. Soc. Vet. Physiologists and Pharmacologists (pres. 1982-84), Am. Physiol. Soc., AVMA, Wis. Assn. Biomed. Res. Edn. (pres. 1998-2000). Avocations: sailing, skiing, gardening, hiking. Office: U Wis Sch Vet Medicine 2015 Linden Dr W Madison WI 53706-1100

BISHARA, SAMIR EDWARD, orthodontist; b. Cairo, Oct. 31, 1935; children: Dina Marie, Dorine Gabrielle, Cherine Noelle. B. Dental Surgery, Alexandria U., Egypt, 1957; diploma in orthodontics, 1967; MS, U. Iowa, 1970, cert. in orthodontics, 1970, D.D.S., 1972. Diplomate Am. Bd. Orthodontics (pres. Coll. Diplomates 1992). Practice gen. dentistry, Alexandria, 1957-68; specializing in orthodontics Iowa City, 1970—; fellow in clin. pedontics Guggenheim Dental Clinic, NYC, 1959-60; resident in oral surgery Moassat Hosp., Alexandria, 1960-61, mem. staff, 1961-68; asst. prof. dentistry U. Iowa, 1970-73, assoc. prof., 1973-76, prof., 1976—. Vis. prof. Alexandria U., 1974. Contbr. articles profl. jours., chpts. in books. Fellow Am. Coll. Dentists, Internat. Coll. Dentists; mem. ADA, AAAS, World Fedn. Orthodontists (hon.), Am. Assn. Orthodontics, Internat. Dental Fedn., Internat. Assn. Dental Research, Am. Cleft Palate Assn., Assn. Egyptian Am. Scholars, Egyptian Orthodontic Soc. (hon.), Columbian Orthodontic Soc. (hon.), Greek Orthodontic Soc. (hon.), Mexican Bd. Orthodontists (hon.), Brit. Orthodontic Conf. (hon.), Omicron Kappa Upsilon, Sigma Xi Home: 1014 Penkridge Dr Iowa City IA 52246-4930 Office: U Iowa Coll Dentistry Orthodontic Dept Iowa City IA 52242

BISHOP, CAROLYN BENKERT, public relations counselor; b. Monroe, Wis., Aug. 28, 1939; d. Arthur C. and Delphine (Heston) Benkert; m. Lloyd F. Bishop, June 15, 1963. BS, U. Wis., 1961; grad., Tobe-Coburn Sch., NYC, 1962. Merchandising editor Co-Ed Mag., NYC, 1962-63; advt. copywriter Woodward & Lothrop, Washington, 1963-65; home furnishings editor Co-Ed Mag., NYC, 1965-68; editor Budget Decorating Mag., NYC, 1968-69; home furnishings editor Family Cir. Mag., NYC, 1969-75; v.p., pub., editorial dir. Scholastic, Inc., NYC, 1975-80; owner Mesa Store Home Furnishings Co., Aspen, Colo., 1980-83; dir. pub. rels. Snowmass Resort Assn., Snowmass Village, Colo., 1983-86; pres. Bishop & Bishop Mktg. Comm., Aspen, 1986-93, Monroe, 1993-99; acct. supr. Hiebing Group, 1999—. Mem. media rels. com. Colo. Tourism Bd., Denver, 1987-90. Author: 25 Decorating Ideas Under $100, 1969; editor: Family Circle Special Home Decorating Guide, 1973. Bd. dirs. Aspen Camp Sch. for the Deaf, 1987-90. Recipient Dallas Market Editorial award Dallas Market Ctr., 1973, Dorothy Dawe award Chgo. Furniture Market, 1973, Guardian of Freedom award, Anti-Defamation League Appeal, 1974. Mem. Rocky Mountain Pub. Rels. Group (chmn. 1991-93), Pub. Rels. Soc. Am. (accredited, small firms co-chair counselors acad. 1992-93), Aspen Writers' Found. (bd. dirs. 1991-93), Tobe-Coburn Alumni Assn., U. Wis. Alumni Assn. Democrat. Office: The Hiebing Group 315 Wisconsin Ave Madison WI 53703-4102

BISHOP, CHARLES JOSEPH, retired manufacturing executive; b. Gary, Ind., June 22, 1941; s. Charles K. and Angela (Marich) Yelusich; m. Yvonne M. Stazinski, June 8, 1963; children: Stephen, Scott. BS, Purdue U., 1963; PhD, U. Wash., 1969. Mgr. advanced energy systems Boeing Co., Seattle, 1969-77; mgr. sys. devel. Solar Energy Rsch. Inst., Denver, 1977-81; sr. v.p. tech. A.O. Smith Corp., Milw., 1981—2006; ret. Mem. adv. bd. S.W. Wis. Rsch. Ctr., Milw., 1987; bd. dirs. Indsl. Rsch. Inst., 1989—92, v.p., 1993, pres., 1995—96. Contbr. articles to profl. jours. Treas. Cedarburg Cmty. Scholarship Com., Wis., 1985—91; mem. Gov.'s Coun. Sci. and Tech., 1992—94; mem. nat. coun. Alverno Coll.; mem. indsl. liaison coun. U. Wis., Milw., 1985—, U. Wis. Coll. Engring., Madison, 1990—95. Recipient Cert. of Recognition award, NASA, 1975. Mem.: Milw. Athletic Club. Republican. Roman Catholic. Avocations: fishing, travel, golf.

BISHOP, DAVID T., state legislator; b. Mar. 29; m. Bea Bishop; 5 children. JD, Cornell U.; MPA, Harvard U. Pvt. practice law, 1954-76; rep. Dist. 30B Minn. Ho. of reps., 1982—, mem. ethics and judiciary coms., chmn. ways and means com., mem. capitol investment com. Office: 453 State Office Bldg Saint Paul MN 55155-0001

BISHOP, GEORGE FRANKLIN, political scientist, educator; b. New Haven, July 26, 1942; s. George Elwood and Mary Bridget (Trant) B.; m. Pama Mitchell, July 15, 1995; 1 child, Kristina. BS in Psychology, Mich. State U., 1966; MS in Psychology, Mich. State U., East Lansing, 1969; PhD, Mich. State U., 1973. Instr. multidisciplinary social sci. program Mich. State U., East Lansing, 1972-73; asst. prof. dept. sociology and anthropology U. Notre Dame, Ind., 1973-75; dir. Greater Cin. Survey, 1981-95; rsch. assoc. behavioral sci. lab U. Cin., 1975-77, sr. rsch. assoc. Inst. for Policy Rsch., 1981-93, dir. behavioral scis. lab., 1994-95, assoc. prof. polit. sci., 1982-87, prof., 1987—, dir. grad. cert. program in pub. opinion and survey rsch., 1999—; dir. Internet Pub. Opinion Lab. Univ. Cin., 2000—. Assoc. dir. Ohio Poll, 1981-95; guest prof. Zentrum für Umfragen, Methoden und Analysen, Mannheim, Germany, 1985, 90, 92, Rudolf Wildenmann Guest Prof., Ctr. for Survey Rsch. and Methodology (ZUMA-GESIS), Mannheim, Germany, 2007; fellow Ctr. Study of Dem. Citizenship, Dept. Polit. Sci., U. Cin., 1992-99, fellow Inst. Data Scis., 1996-98; summer inst. faculty Survey Rsch. Ctr., Inst. Social Rsch., U. Mich., summer 1993; sr. cons. Burke Mktg. Rsch., Inc., Cin., 1996-98. Author: The Illusion of Public Opinion, 2005 (Outstanding Academic Title Choice Mag., 2005); sr. editor: Presdl. Debates: Media, Electoral and Policy Perspectives, 1978; sr. author various articles in pub. opinion and survey rsch.; mem. editl. bd. Pub. Opinion Quar., 1987-90, Free Inquiry, 1999-2005; mem. editl. adv. bd. Pub. Perspective, 2000—03. Bd. trustees Clifton Town Meetings, Cin., 2004—, chair pub. safety com., 2004—. With N.G. US Army, 1960—63. NSF grantee, 1977-84. Mem. AAUP (Maita Levine Svc. award 2002), Midwest Assn. Pub. Opinion Rsch. (pres. 1977-78, Mapor fellow Disting. Scholarship in pub. opinion rsch. 1994), Am. Assn. Pub. Opinion Rsch., Am. Polit. Sci. Assn., World Assn. Pub. Opinion Rsch. (treas. 1983-85). Avocation: genealogy. Home: 825 Dunore Rd Cincinnati OH 45220-1416 Office: U Cin Cincinnati OH 45221-0001

BISHOP, JEROME C., lawyer; BA, Georgetown U., 1994, JD, 2001. Bar: Ohio 2002, US Dist. Ct. Southern Dist. Ohio. Assoc. Katz, Teller, Brant & Hild, Cin. Named one of Ohio's Rising Stars, Super Lawyers, 2006. Avocations: running, golf. Office: Katz Teller Brant & Hild 255 E 5th St Ste 2400 Cincinnati OH 45202-4724 Office Phone: 513-721-4532. Office Fax: 513-762-0061.

BISHOP, MARK, radio personality; Radio host WLVQ, Columbus, Ohio, 1979—98, WMMS, Cleve., 1990—94, WHK, 1994—96, WMJI, 1994—96, WTVN, Columbus, 1994—96, WMJI, 1998—. Office: WMJI 6200 Oaktree Blvd 4th Fl Cleveland OH 44131

BISHOP, MICHAEL, lawyer, state senator; b. 1967; Studied, Universidad de Sevilla, 1988, Cambridge U., U. Paris Sorbonne, 1992; BA, U. Mich., 1989; JD, Detroit Coll. Law, 1993. Admitted to Bar: Mich. 1993, Washington DC. Atty Booth Patterson P.C.; clerk Oakland County Cir. Ct., 1989—92; real estate broker, pres., owner Freedom Realty Inc, Rochester, Mich., Pro Management Inc., Rochester, Mich.; sr. atty. Simon, Galasso & Frantz PLC, Troy, Mich.; mem. Mich. Legis., 1998—; asst. majority leader Mich. Senate, Lansing, 2002—. Mem. Mich. State Com., 1995—97; chmn. Senate Banking and Fin. Inst. Com. Named one of 40 Under 40, Crain's Detroit Bus., 2006. Mem.: State Bar of Mich., Mich. Assn. Realtors, Sports Lawyer Assn., ABA, Michigamua Honorary Soc. Office: Simon, Galasso & Frantz PLC 363 W Big Beaver Rd Ste 300 Troy MI 48084 Office Phone: 248-720-0290. Office Fax: 248-720-0291.

BISHOP, MICHAEL D., emergency physician; b. Anna, Ill., Feb. 10, 1945; m. Mary Susan Wilkens, Dec. 28, 1965; children: Amy Elizabeth, Amanda Marie. AB, GreenvilleColl., 1967; MD, U. Ill., 1971. Diplomate Am. Bd. Emergency Medicine (oral examiner 1980—, dir. 1988-96, mem. exec. com. 1990-95, mem. several bd. coms., sec.-treas. 1991-92, pres.-elect 1992-93, pres. 1993-94). Intern Meth. Hosp. Dallas, 1971-72; emergency physician Bloomington (Ind.) Hosp., 1972—, Morgan County Meml. Hosp., Martinsville, Ind., 1978—, Fayette Meml. Hosp., Connersville, Ind., 1989—, Jackson County Meml. Hosp., Seymour, Ind., 1989—; gen. dir. Immediate Care Ctrs. in Ind., various cities, 1981—; clin. assoc. prof. med. scis. Ind. U., Bloomington, 1980—; pres., CEO Unity Physician Group P.C., Bloomington, Ind., 1971—. Bd. trustee, Sunday sch. tchr. Ellettsville (Ind.) Christian Ch.; bd. dirs. Peoples State Bank, Ellettsville; bd. dirs., sec. Ellettsville Bancshares, Ellettsville Elem. Sch. Bldg. Corp. Fellow Am. Coll. Emergency Physicians (charter, pres. Ind. chpt. 1979-80, nat. councillor 1976-81, 83, mem. nat. multi-hosp./multi-state blue ribbon task force 1981, mem. nat. ins. com. 1976-77, mem. coun. long-range planning com. 1981-82, mem. coun. steering com. 1983-85, chmn. medicare task force 1984-86, chmn. task force on physician payment reform 1986-88, mem. govt. affairs com. 1983-88, 89-93, chmn. 1984-87, 89-93, mem. nat. emergency medicine polit. action com. bd. trustees 1984-88, 89-93, chmn. 1987, 89-93, mem. fin. com. 1987-93, James D. Mills Outstanding Contbn. to Emergency Medicine award 1990, mem. awards com. 1991-93, mem. reimbursement com. 1992—, dir. 1995—, lectr. in field), AHA (mem. Ind. affil. faculty, ACLS), Am. Coll. Physician Execs., Soc. Acad. Emergency Medicine, Christian Med. Dental Soc., Ind. State Med. Assn., Med. Group Mgmt. Assn., Owen Monroe County Med. Soc. Office: Unity Physician Group PC 1155 W 3rd St Bloomington IN 47404-5016

BISHOP, STEPHEN GRAY, physicist; b. York, Pa., Jan. 26, 1939; s. John Schwartz and Carrie (Gray) B.; m. Helene Barbara Evenson, July 6, 1963; children: Hans Stephen, Lars Michael. BA in Physics with honors, Gettysburg Coll., 1960; PhD in Physics, Brown U., 1965. Postdoctoral rsch. assoc. physics Brown U., 1965-66; AS-NRC postdoctoral rsch. assoc. Naval Rsch. Lab., Washington, 1966-68, rsch. physicist, supr., 1968-80, head semiconductor br., 1980-89; dir. Engring. Rsch. Ctr. Compound Semiconductor Electronics and Microelectronics Lab. U. Ill., Urbana-Champaign, 1989-2000, prof. elec. and computer engring., 1989—, dir. Ctr. Optoelectronics Sci. and Techs., 1994-98, assoc. v.p. for tech. and econ. devel., 2001—04. With Max Planck Inst. fur Festkorperforschung, Stuttgart, West Germany, 1973-74; mem. navy com. Amorphous Semiconductor Tech. Rev., 1974, navy inter-lab. com. on pers. adminstrn., 1985; rsch. scientist Royal Signals and Radar Establishment, Great Malvern, U.K., 1978-79; adj. prof. physics SUNY, Buffalo, 1984—, U. Utah, 1986—; mem. tech. rev. com. Joint Svcs. Electronics program, 1980-89, tech. adv. com. Ctr. for Compound Semiconductor Microelectronics, U. Ill., Urbana-Champaign; mem. ONR Univ. Rsch. Initiative Rev. Panel, 1986, external rev. panel Ctr. for Electronic and Electro-Optic Materials, SUNY, Buffalo, 1988; mem. NSF Site Visit Rev. Panel for materials rsch. lab., U. Ill., NSF panel on light wave technology, 1988, NSF panel on interface of optical devices and systems, 1989; vis. com. Sherman Fairchild Ctr. for Solid State Studies, Lehigh U., 1991—; mem. Nat. Adv. Com., URI-ARO Ctr. for High-Frequency Microelectronics, U. Mich., 1993; edit. bd. Semiconductor Sci. and Tech., Inst. of Physics, 1992. Editor: (with others) Optical Effects in Amorphous Semiconductors, 1984, Proceedings of the MRS Symposium on the Microscopic Identification of Electronic Defects in Semiconductors, 1985; author: (with others) Deep Centers in Semiconductors, 1985, Gallium Arsenide Technology, 1990; contbr. more than 200 articles to profl. jours. Patentee in field. Trustee Gettysburg Coll., 1992—. Recipient Disting. Alumni award Gettysburg Coll., 1990. Felow Am. Phys. Soc., AAAS, Optical Soc. Am.; mem. IEEE, Lasers and Electronics Soc., Materials Rsch. Soc., Phi Beta Kappa, Sigma Pi Sigma, Sigma Xi (Pure Sci. award 1977), Tau Beta Pi (UIUC Chapt., Eminent Engr. award 1993). Office: Coordinated Scis Lab 1308 W Main St Urbana IL 61801-2307 E-mail: sgbishop@uiuc.edu.

BISKUPIC, STEVEN M., prosecutor, lawyer; b. Mar. 1961; BA, JD, Marquette U. Asst. US atty. (ea. dist.) Wis. US Dept. Justice, 1989—2002, US atty. (ea. dist.) Wis., 2002—. Office: 530 Fed Bldg 517 E Wisconsin Ave Milwaukee WI 53202

BISPING, BRUCE HENRY, photojournalist; b. St. Louis, Apr. 27, 1953; s. Harry and Marian B.; m. Joan M. Berg, Sept. 29, 1984; children: Erin Elizabeth Giovanna, Trevor Thomas. B.J., U. Mo., Columbia, 1975. Freelance Tribune, Columbia, Mo., 1968—71; Summer intern Cleve. Press, 1974, The Virginian/Pilot-Ledger Star, orfolk, 1975; staff photojournalist Mpls. Tribune, 1975-82, Mpls. Star and Tribune, 1982—. Freelance photographer Black Star Pub. Co., N.Y.C., 1975—, Sporting News, St. Louis, Business Week, Time, U.S. News World Report, Newsweek, Am. Illustrated, N.Y. Times, Los Angeles Times, other nat. and local publs.; past mem. faculty Mo. Photojournalism Workshop. Mem. Nat. Press Photographers Assn. (assoc. dir. Region 5 1981-82, dir. Region 5 1983-86, rep. to exec. com. 1984, Nat. Newspaper Photographer of Year award 1976, Regional Newspaper Photographer of Year award 1977, citation for dedication to profession 1985), Twin Cities News Photographers Assn. (pres. 1979-80), Profl. Assn. Diving Instrs. (open water instr. rating), Oldsmobile Club of Am. (bd. dirs. Minn. Club, news editor), Minn. Oldsmobile Club. Avocations: photography, reading, movies, walking, travel. Office: Mpls Tribune 6020 View Ln Edina MN 55436-1827 Home Phone: 952-927-5753; Office Phone: 612-673-7205. E-mail: bruceb65@citilink.com.

BISSELL, JOHN HOWARD, marketing executive; b. Bklyn., July 8, 1935; s. Donald Henry and Lillian (Eckberg) B.; m. Joan Becker, Sept. 7, 1963; children: John Edward, Mary Katherine. BA in Polit. Sci., Yale U., 1956. Brand mgr. Procter and Gamble, Inc., Cin., 1960-71; v.p., new products mktg. Frito-Lay, Inc., Dallas, 1971-80; v.p. mktg. The Stroh Brewery Co., Detroit, 1980-85, sr. v.p., spl. products div., 1985-91; pres. Stroh Foods, Inc. subs. The Stroh Brewery Co., Detroit, 1985-91; mng. ptnr. cons. div. Gundersen Ptnrs., L.L.C., Bloomfield Hills, Mich., 1991—. Chmn. corp. funds campaign Sta. WTVS, Detroit, 1986. Served as 1st lt. USAF, 1957-59. Mem. Adcrafters, Birmingham Athletic Club, Yale Club (N.Y.C.). Republican. Presbyterian. Home: 504 Greenbrier Dr Silver Spring MD 20910-4228

BITNER, JOHN HOWARD, lawyer; b. Indpls., Feb. 27, 1940; s. Harry M. Jr. and Jeanne B. (Eshelman) B.; m. Vicki Ann D'Ianni, 1961; children: Kerry, Holly, Robin. AB in English and History, Northwestern U., 1961; JD cum laude, Columbia U., 1964. Bar: Ill. 1964. Assoc. Bell, Boyd & Lloyd LLC, Chgo., 1964-71, mem., 1972—, chair corp. and secs. dept., 1988-99, firm vice chmn., 1992—99. Contbr. articles to profl. jours.; editor Columbia Law Rev. Active St. Gregory Episcopal Sch. Bd.; bd. visitors Columbia Law Sch, tutor, GED students at Jobs for Youth Fellow Am. Bar Found.; mem. ABA, Ill. Bar Assn., Union League, Glen View Club, Lawyers Club, Delta Upsilon, Phi Delta Phi Episcopalian. Avocations: tennis, reading, chess, golf. Home: 2329 Lincolnwood Dr Evanston IL 60201-2048 Office: Bell Boyd & Lloyd LLC 70 W Madison St Chicago IL 60602 Fax: (312) 827-8048. E-mail: jbitner@bellboyd.com.

BITONDO, DOMENIC, engineering executive; b. Welland, Ont., Can., June 7, 1925; came to U.S., 1950, naturalized, 1956; s. Vito Leonard and Vita Maria (Gallipoli) B.; m. Delphine May Dicola, June 11, 1949; children— Michael, Annamarie, David, Marisa. BS, U. Toronto, 1947, MS, 1948, PhD, 1950. Aerodynamist, Aerophysics div. N.Am. Aviation Co., Downey, Calif., 1950-51; project engr. to chief of aerodynamics Aerophysics Devel. Corp., Santa Barbara, 1951-59; staff engr. Northrup Corp., Hawthorne, Calif., 1959-60; head test planning and analysis TRW Systems, Inc., El Segundo, Calif., 1960-61; dept. head aeromechanics dept. Systems Research and Planning div., founder, dir. Advanced Ballistic Reentry Systems Program (ABRES) Aerospace Corp., El Segundo, 1961-63; dir. engring. Aerospace Systems div. Bendix Corp., Ann Arbor, Mich., 1963-69; engring. mgr. Apollo lunar sci. expts., 1966; dir., gen. mgr. Bendix Research Labs., Southfield, Mich., 1969-79; exec. dir. research and devel. Bendix Corp., Southfield, Mich., 1979—81; pres. Bitondo Assocs. Inc., Ann Arbor, 1981—. Gordon N. Patterson lectr. U. Toronto, 1976; trustee Central Solar Energy and Research Corp., Detroit, 1978-80; dir. Continental Controls Corp., San Diego.; Def. Research Bd. Can. asst., 1948, NRC asst., 1947 Contbr. tech. articles to profl. jours. Mem. AIAA, NRC (mem. com. on mgmt. tech.), NAS (mem. task force to Indonesia in methodology of tech. planning), Mich. Energy Resource Rsch. Assn. (trustee 1978), Nat. Mgmt. Assn. (Gold Knight award), Indsl. Rsch. Inst. (emeritus). Office: 5 Manchester Ct Ann Arbor MI 48104-6562 Office Phone: 734-971-4637. Personal E-mail: deldombitondo@aol.com.

BITTENBENDER, CHARLES A., lawyer; b. Plainfield, NJ, 1949; married, 2 children. BA, Claremont McKenna Coll., Claremont, Calif., 1971; JD, Cleveland State U., 1979. Bar: Ohio 1980. Various positions Ohio Bell Telephone Co., Cleveland, Ohio; atty. Jones, Day, Reavis & Pogue, Cleveland, Ohio; dep. gen. counsel G. D. Searle & Co., Chicago, Ill.; v.p., sec., gen. counsel Nacco Industries, Inc., Mayfield Heights, Ohio, 1990—. Mem.: ABA. Office: Nacco Industries Inc 5875 Landerbrook Dr Mayfield Heights OH 44124

BIXBY, FRANK LYMAN, retired lawyer; b. New Richmond, Wis., May 25, 1928; s. Frank H. and Esther (Otteson) B.; m. Katharine Spence, July 7, 1951; children— Paul, Thomas, Edward, Janet. AB, Harvard U., 1950; LLB, U. Wis., 1953. Bar: Ill. 1953, Wis. 1953, Fla. 1974. Ptnr. firm Sidley Austin Brown & Wood LLP, Chgo., 1963—97, sr. counsel, 1998—2005; ret., 2005. Editor-in-chief Wis. Law Rev, 1952-53; mem. editorial bd. Chgo. Reporter, 1973-89. Trustee MacMurray Coll., Jacksonville, Ill., 1973-85; bd. dirs. Chgo. Urban League, 1962-2006, v.p., 1972-86, gen. counsel, 1972—, chmn. 1986-89; bd. dirs. Community Renewal Soc., 1973-86, Voices for Ill. Children, 1987-90; chmn. trustees Unitarian Ch., Evanston, Ill., 1962-63; bd. dirs. Spencer Found., 1967-2001, chmn. 1975-90; mem. dist. 202 bd. edn. Evanston Twp. High Sch., 1975-81, pres., 1977-79. Recipient Man of Year award Chgo. Urban League, 1974 Mem. ABA, Ill. Bar Assn., Chgo. Bar Assn., Chgo. Coun. Lawyers, Chgo. Coun. Fgn. Rels., Order of Coif, Harvard Club (pres. 1964-65), Mid-Day Club., Phi Beta Kappa. Home: 505 N Lake Shore Dr Apt 4607 Chicago IL 60611-3409 Office: Sidley Austin LLP 1 S Dearborn St Chicago IL 60603-2000 Office Phone: 312-853-7429. Business E-Mail: fbixby@sidley.com.

BIXBY, HAROLD GLENN, manufacturing executive, director; b. Lamotte, Mich., July 14, 1903; s. Charles Samuel and Laura (Schenk) B.; m. Pauline Elizabeth Summy, July 3, 1928; children: Mary Louise and Richard Glenn (twins). AB, U. Mich., 1927, LL.D. (hon.), 1972. Began in accounting dept. Ex-Cell-O Corp., Detroit, 1928, asst. sec., 1929, controller, 1933, sec., treas. and dir., 1937, became v.p., treas., dir., 1947, pres., gen. mgr., 1951-70, chmn. bd., chief exec. officer, 1970-72, chmn. bd., 1972—, chmn. exec. com., 1973-79. Bd. dirs., hon. trustee Kalamazoo Coll. Mem. Greater Detroit C. of C., Tau Kappa Epsilon. Clubs: Economic, Detroit Athletic, Detroit Golf.

BIXENSTINE, KIM FENTON, lawyer; b. Providence, Feb. 26, 1958; d. Barry Jay and Gail Louise (Traverse) Weinstein; m. Barton Aaron Bixenstine, June 25, 1983; children: Paul Jay, Nathan Alexis. BA, Middlebury Coll., 1979; JD, U. Chgo., 1982. Bar: Ohio 1982, U.S. Dist. Ct. (no. and so. dists.) Ohio 1983, U.S. Ct. Appeals (6th cir.) 1983. Law clk. to presiding judge U.S. Dist. Ct. (so. dist.) Ohio, Cin., 1982-83; assoc. Jones, Day, Reavis & Pogue, Cleve., 1983-90, ptnr., 1991-99; sr. counsel TRW Inc., Cleve., 1999—2001, v.p., chief litig. counsel, 2002—03; v.p., dep. gen. counsel Univ. Hosp. Health Sys., Cleve., 2003—. Sec. Planned Parenthood Greater Cleve., 1992—93, v.p., 1994—96, pres., 1996—98; chair corp. giving subcom. Cleve. Bar Found. Campaign, 2001—02; bd. dir. Planned Parenthood Greater Cleve., 1991—99; bd. dirs. Boys and Girls Club Cleve., 2001—03, chair pub. rels. com., 2002—03. Mem.: Am. Arbitration Assn. (chair comml. adv. coun. N.E. Ohio chpt. 2000—05), Cleve. Bar Assn. (commn. women in the law 1988—2001, bd. dir. 1993—96, minority outreach com. 1993—99, chair standing com. lawyer professionalism 1994—96, bd. liaison to jud. selection com. 1996, nominating com. 1997—99, chair nominating com. 1998—99, long range planning com. 2002—03, judicial selection com. 2005—), Ohio Women's Bar Assn. (chair legis. com. 1994—95, trustee 1995—97, judicial selection com. 2005—). Avocations: jogging, reading, yoga. Office: Univ Hosps Health Sys Mail Stop 9115 3605 Warrensville Ctr Rd Shaker Heights OH 44122 Home Phone: 216-397-9576; Office Phone: 216-767-8228. Business E-Mail: kim.bixenstine@uhhospitals.org.

BIXLER, R. JEFFREY, lawyer; b. 1945; BS, U. Dayton; JD, U. Toledo, 1972. V.p., gen. counsel, sec. Manor Care Inc., Toledo, 1991—. Mem.: ABA. Office: HCR Manor Care 333 N Summit St Toledo OH 43604 Office Phone: 419-252-5500.

BLACK, DALE R., hotel and gaming company executive; b. 1963; m. Sheila Dawn Hilliard, Dec. 26, 1981; 2 children. BS in Acctg., So. Ill. U., 1984. Crew leader Bonanza restaurant, Mt. Vernon, Ill., 1979—84; staff acct. Arthur Andersen, 1984—91; contr. Creative Data Svcs., 1991—93; v.p., contr. Argosy Gaming Co., Alton, Ill., 1993—98, sr. v.p., CFO, 1998—2005; exec. v.p., CFO Trump Entertainment Resorts, Inc., Atlantic City, 2005—07, Isle of Capri Casinos, Inc., St. Louis, 2007—. Office: Isle of Capri Casinos Inc 600 Emerson Rd Ste 300 Saint Louis MO 63141

BLACK, DENNIS H., state legislator; b. Randolph, Nebr., Dec. 18, 1939; m. Faun Stewart. BS, Utah State U., 1963, MS, 1965. Mem. Iowa Ho. of Reps., 1982-94, Iowa Senate from 29th dist., 1994—. Dir. Jasper County Conservation Bd.; bd. dirs. Iowa Sister State: Newton Cmty. Sch.; mem. Taiwan Com.; dist. commr. Jasper County Soil Conservation. Mem. Terrace Hill Soc. (bd. dirs.), Iowa Peace Inst. (bd. dirs.), Jasper County Farm Bur., Izaak Walton League. Democrat. Home: 5239 E 156th St S Grinnell IA 50112-7511 Office: State Capitol Dist 29 3 9th And Grand Des Moines IA 50319-0001 E-mail: dennis_black@legis.state.ia.us.

BLACK, LARRY DAVID, library director; b. Section, Ala., Mar. 3, 1949; s. Haskin Byron and Mima Jean (Holcomb) B.; m. Mary Frances Patterson, Aug. 29, 1971; 1 child, Amy Susan. BA in History & Polit. Sci., U. Ala., 1971, MLS, 1972; M in Pub. Adminstrn., Ohio State U., 1981. Asst. dir. Bedsole Library Mobile (Ala.) Coll., 1972-73; dir. Baldwin County Libr. System, Summerdale, Ala., 1973-76; dir. libr. svc. Troy State U., Bay Minette, Ala., 1976-77; dir. main libr. Columbus Met. Libr., Ohio, 1977-83, asst. exec. dir. Ohio, 1983-84, exec. dir. Ohio, 1984—. Mem. Ohio Libr. Assn., Am. Soc. Pub. Adminstrs. Clubs: Cen. Ohio Corvette (Columbus). Democrat. Avocations: woodworking, gardening, auto restoration. Office: Columbus Met Libr 96 S Grant Ave Columbus OH 43215-4702 Home: 508 Oak Ridge Ct E Daphne AL 36526-4524

BLACK, NATALIE A., lawyer; b. 1949; AB, Stanford U., 1972; JD, Marquette U., 1978. Bar: Wisc. Group pres., gen. coun. Kohler Co., Kohler, Wisc. Mem. ABA. Office: Kohler Co Legal Dept 444 Highland Dr Kohler WI 53044-1515 Fax: 920-459-1583.

BLACK, RONNIE DELANE, religious organization administrator, mayor; b. Poplar Bluff, Mo., Oct. 26, 1947; s. Clyde Olen and Leona Christine Black; m. Sandra Elaine Hulett, Aug. 27, 1966; 1 child, Stephanie. BA, Oakland City Coll., Ind., 1969; M Div, So. Bapt. Theol. Sem., 1972. Ordained to ministry Gen. Assn. of Gen. Bapts., 1967. Pastor Gen. Bapt. Ch., Fort Branch, Ind., 1972-78; stewardship dir. Gen. Bapt. Hdqrs., Poplar Bluff, Mo., 1978-97, exec. dir., 1997—; councilman City of Poplar Bluff, 1985-97, mayor, 1990-92, 95-96. Mem. Gen. Bapt. Ch. Office: Gen Bapts 100 Stinson Dr Poplar Bluff MO 63901-8736

BLACK, SPENCER, state legislator; b. NYC, May 25, 1950; married. BA, SUNY, Stony Brook, 1972; MS, U. Wis., 1980, MA, 1981. State assemblyman dist. 77 State of Wis., 1984—. Edn. curator Wis. State Hist. Soc. Democrat. Address: 5742 Elder Pl Madison WI 53705-2516

BLACK, STEPHEN L., lawyer; b. Cin., Dec. 3, 1948; AB magna cum laude, in economics, Harvard U., 1971, JD, 1974. Bar: Ohio 1974, U.S. Ct. Appeals (6th cir.). Law clerk to Hon. George Edwards U.S. Ct. Appeals (6th cir.), 1974-75; mayor City of Indian Hill, Ohio, 1995-99; ptnr. Graydon, Head & Ritchey, Cin., 1980—. Bd. trustee, pres. Children's Home Cin. Inc., Cin. Law Libr. Assn., Harvard Club Cin., 1988-89, Harvard Alumni Assn., 1989-92, Seven Hills Sch., 1992-2001, Village of Indian Hill (councilman, 1989-99, mayor 1995-99), Am. Lung Assn. SW Ohio, Summerbridge Cin. Inc., Cin. Nature Ctr., 1989-95. Recipient Goodall Disting. Alumni award, Seven Hills Sch., 2003. Mem. Ohio State Bar Assn., Cin. Bar Assn. Avocation: small aircrafts. Office: Graydon Head & Ritchey 511 Walnut St 1900 5th 3rd Ctr Cincinnati OH 45202-3157 Office Phone: 513-629-2723. Office Fax: 513-651-3836. Business E-Mail: sblack@graydon.com.

BLACK, WILLIAM B., state legislator; b. Danville, Ill., Nov. 11, 1941; m. Sharon Black; 2 children. BA, William Jewel Coll.; MA, Ea. Ill. U.; postgrad., Ill. State U. Ill. state rep. Dist. 105, 1986—. Spokesman Econ. Devel. Com., mem. Edn. Com., Transp. and Motor Vehicles Com., Urban Redevel. Com., Elem. and Secondary Com., Human Svc. Com.; educator and adminstr. Office: 634 State House Springfield IL 62706-0001 Address: 7 E Fairchild St Danville IL 61832-3115

BLACKBURN, HENRY WEBSTER, JR., retired epidemiologist; b. Miami, Fla., Mar. 22, 1925; s. Henry Webster and Mary Frances (Smith) B.; m. Nelly Paula Trocme, Jan. 10, 1951 (div. 1984); children: John Keith, Katherine Ann, Heidi Elizabeth; m. Stacy Richardson, Sept. 1, 1991. Student, Fla. So. Coll., Lakeland, 1942—43; BS, U. Miami, 1947; MD, Tulane U., 1948, DSc (hon.), 1999; MS, U. Minn., 1957; DSc (hon.), U. Kuopio, Finland, 1982. Intern Chgo. Wesley Meml. Hosp., 1948-49; resident in medicine Am. Hosp. Paris, 1949-50; med. officer in charge USPHS, Austria, Fed. Republic Germany, 1950-53; med. fellow U. Minn., Mpls., 1953-56; ret. Divsn. Epidemiology, 1996; med. dir. Mut. Svc. Ins. Co., St. Paul, 1956; asst. prof. physiol. hygiene U. Minn., 1958-61, assoc. prof., 1961-68, prof., 1968—, lectr. medicine, 1956—, dir. lab. physiol. hygiene Sch. Pub. Health, 1972—, prof. medicine, 1972—, chmn. divsn. epidemiology, 1983-90, Mayo prof. pub. health, 1990-96. Vis. prof. U. Geneva, 1970; mem. adv. coun. Nat. Heart, Lung and Blood Inst., 1989-93; mem. com. on diet and health NRC, 1986-89; Ancel Keys lectr., 1991; mem. food adv. com. FDA, 1995-2000; Mayo chair in pub. health, 1988. Author: Cardiovascular Survey Methods, 1968, On the Trail of Heart Attacks in Seven Countries, 1995, "P.K." Irreverent Memoirs of a Preacher's Kid, 1999, If It Isn't Fun.Memoir of a Different Sort of Medical Life, Vol. I, 2001, Vol. 2, 2004; mem. editl. bd. numerous jours.; contbr. articles to profl. jours. Lt. (j.g.) USNR, 1942-50, capt. USPHS inactive res. Recipient Thomas Francis award in epidemiology, 1975, Naylor Dana award in preventive medicine, 1976, Louis Bishop award in cardiology, 1979, Gold Heart award Am. Heart Assn., 1990, Rsch. Achievement award Am. Heart Assn., 1992. Fellow APHA, Am. Coll. Cardiology, Am. Epidemiol. Soc.; mem. AAAS (chmn. med. sect.), Belgian Royal Acad. Medicine, Am. Heart Assn. (dir. 1971-74), Internat. Soc. Cardiology (coun. epidemiology 1971-74, chmn. 1986-91), Internat. Epidemiol. Soc., Alpha Omega Alpha, Phi Kappa Phi, Delta Omega. Office: U Minn Divsn Epidemiology 1300 S 2d St Minneapolis MN 55454-1075 Office Phone: 612-626-9396. Business E-Mail: blackburn@epi.umn.edu.

BLACKBURN, JOHN D., insurance company executive; BA, W Ill. Univ.; MA, Univ. Ill., Springfield, 1979. CLU. Agent through sr. v.p. mktg. Country Ins. & Fin. Services, Bloomington, Ill., 1982—2001, CEO, 2001—. Chmn. Cotton States Ins., Holyoke Mutual Ins. Co., Middlesex Mutual Assurance Co., MSI Preferred Ins. Co. Office: Country Insurance 1701 N Towanda Ave Bloomington IL 61702

BLACKIE, SPENCER DAVID, physical therapist, administrator; b. Endicott, NY, Sept. 27, 1946; s. Norman and June (Spencer) B.; m. Bonnie Jean Randall Moulton, June 11, 1967 (div. Apr. 1985); children: Rhonda, Randy, Brenda; m. Sharon Joan Clingman, May 10, 1986; children: Kristen, Sean, Alex. BS, Loma Linda U., 1968; MA, U. So. Calif., 1973; MS, Boston U., 1980; NMD, So. Coll. Naturopathic Medicine, 2002; D of Phys. Therapy, U. St. Augustine, 2003. Cert. in manual therapy, clin. specialist in orthop. phys. therapy, quantum medicine; bd. cert. naturopathic physician; bd. cert in iridology. Clin. dir. Loma Linda (Calif.) U. Med. Ctr., 1972-74; dir. rehab. svcs. New Eng. Meml. Hosp., Stoneham, Mass., 1974-84, Mt. Carmel Hosp., Colville, Wash., 1984-92, Regina Med. Ctr., Hastings, Minn., 1992—. Mem. Pool Com., Hastings, 1994; chmn. Parks and Recreation Bd., Colville, 1991-92. Capt. U.S. Army, 1969-71. Cmty. Fitness grantee Perrier Mineral Waters, Stoneham, 1978; decorated U.S. Army commendation medal. Mem. Am. Naturopathic Med. Assn., Am. Phys. Therapy Assn., Am. Occupl. Therapy Assn., Am. Acad. Orthop. Manual Phys. Therapy, Am. Soc. Hand Therapists, Am. Acad. Quantum Medicine, Internat. Iridology Practitioners Assn., Minn. and Wis. Occupl. Therapy Assn., Hastings Area Rotary Club (pres. 2003-04). Seventh-Day Adventist. Avocations: bicycling, guitar, Karate, hiking. Office: Regina Med Ctr 1175 Nininger Rd Hastings MN 55033-1056 E-mail: blackied@reginamedical.org.

BLACKSHERE, MARGARET, labor union administrator; BS in Elem. Edn., So. Ill. Univ., Edwardsville, MS in Urban Edn. Former elem. sch. tchr., Ill.; former pres. Am. Fedn. Tchrs.; sec.-treas. Ill. AFL-CIO, 1993—2000, pres., 2000—. Del. Dem. Nat. Conv., 1980—92; mem. Dem. Nat. Com.; bd. dir. Irish Am. Labor Coalition, Unemployment Ins. Adv. Bd. Bd. dir. United Way, Ill.; Alliance for Retired Americans. Named one of 100 Most Influential Women, Crain's Chgo. Bus., 2004; named to Union Hall of Honor, Ill. Labor History Soc., 1995. Office: Ill AFL-CIO 55 W Wacker Dr Chicago IL 60601 Office Phone: 312-251-1414.

BLACKWELL, HELEN E., chemistry professor; b. 1972; BA, Oberlin Coll., 1994; PhD in Organic Chemistry, Calif. Inst. Tech., 1999. Postdoctoral rschr. Schreiber Lab. Harvard U., 1999—2002; asst. prof. dept. chemistry U. Wis., Madison, 2002—. Contbr. articles to profl. jours. Named one of Top 35 Innovators Under the Age of 35, MIT Tech. Rev., 2005; recipient Early Career award, NSF, 2004, PROGRESS/Dreyfus award, Am. Chem. Soc., 2004, Shaw Scientist award, Greater Milw. Found., 2004, Cottrell Scholar award, Rsch. Corp., 2005. Office: Dept Chemistry Rm 5211a U Wis Madison 1101 University Ave Madison WI 53706-1396 Office Phone: 608-262-1503. E-mail: blackwell@chem.wisc.edu.

BLACKWELL, JEAN STUART, manufacturing executive; b. Dublin, Ga., Sept. 13, 1954; d. Price Barron and Jean Stuart (Babb) B. BA in Econs., Coll. William and Mary, 1976; JD cum laude, U. Mich., 1979. Bar: Ind. 1979, U.S. Dist. Ct. (so. dist.) Ind. 1979, U.S. Ct. Appeals (7th cir.) 1983, U.S. Supreme Ct. 1983. Assoc. Bose, McKinney & Evans, Indpls., 1979-85, ptnr., 1985-91, 1995—97; exec. dir. lottery commn. State of Ind., Indpls., 1991-93, budget dir., 1993—95; v.p., gen. counsel Cummins Inc., Columbus, Ind., 1997, v.p. HR, 1997—2001, v.p. bus. services, 2001—03, v.p., CFO, chief of staff, 2003—05, exec. v.p., CFO, 2005—08, exec. v.p., corp. responsibility, 2008—; CEO Cummins Found., 2008—. Commr. Supreme Ct. Commn. on Legal Edn., Ind., 1989-92; chairperson State Ethics Commn., Ind., 1991-92; adj. prof. Butler U., Indpls., 1989-91. Bd. mem. Ind. Leadership Celebration, 1986-92, Heritage Pl., Bd., 1991-92; govs. audit team Health and Human Svcs., Ind., 1991; mem. Regional Ctr. Planning Task Force, Indpls., 1991-92. Named Sagamore of the Wabash, Ind. Gov., 1991. Mem. ABA (vice chair 1985-91), Nat. Assn. Women Lawyers (bd. mem. 1990-92), Am. Coll. Mortgage Attys., Ind. Bar Assn. (bd. govs. 1988-92), Stanley K. Lacy Alumni, Mortar Bd., Omicron Delta Kappa, Omicron Delta Epsilon. Democrat. Methodist. Avocations: soccer, biking, camping, golf. Mailing: Cummins Inc PO Box 3005 Columbus IN 47202-3005 Office: Cummins Inc 500 Jackson St Columbus IN 47201*

BLACKWELL, JOHN, science educator; b. Oughtibridge, Sheffield, Eng., Jan. 15, 1942; came to U.S., 1967; s. Leonard and Vera (Brook) B.; m. Susan Margaret Crawshaw, Aug. 5, 1965; children: Martin Jonathan, Helen Elizabeth. BSc in Chemistry, U. Leeds, Eng., 1963, PhD in Biophysics, 1967. Postdoctoral fellow SUNY-Syracuse Coll. Forestry, 1967-69; vis. asst. prof. Case Western Res. U., Cleve., 1969-70, asst. prof., 1970-74, assoc. prof., 1974-77, prof. macromolecular sci., 1977—, chmn. dept., 1985-95, F. Alex Nason prof., 1991-2000, Leonard Case Jr. prof., 2001—, assoc. dean rsch. and grad. studies Case Sch. Engring., 2005—07. Vis. prof. Kennedy Inst. Rheumatology, London, 1975, Centre National de Recherche Scientifique, Grenoble, France, 1977, U. Frieburg, Fed. Republic Germany, 1982; chmn. Gordon Conf. on Liquid Crystalline Polymers, 1992; cons. in field. Author: (with A.G. Walton) Biopolymers, 1973; mem. editorial bd. Macromolecules, 1989-92; adv. bd. Jour. Macromolecular Sci.-Physics, 1986—; internat. adv. bd. Acta Polymerica, 1992—; contbr. articles to profl. jours. Recipient award for disting. achievement Fiber Soc., 1981, Sr. Scientist award Alexander von Humboldt Found., Max Planck Inst. for Polymer Rsch., Mainz, Fed. Republic Germany, 1991, Rsch. Career Devel. award, 1973-77. Fellow Am. Phys. Soc. (exec. com. divsn. high polymer physics 1986-90, vice chmn. 1987-88, chmn. 1988-89); mem. Am. Chem. Soc. (chmn. cellulose divsn. 1999, Anselm Payen award 1999, divsn. councillor 2000-03), Am. Crystallography Soc. (chmn. fiber diffraction spl. interest group 1993-94), Biophys. Soc. (chmn. biopolymer subgroup 1975-76), Fiber Soc. Episcopalian. Home: 12614 Cedar Rd Cleveland Heights OH 44106-3220 Office: Case Western Res U Case Sch Engring Cleveland OH 44106-7220 Office Phone: 216-368-6370. Business E-Mail: john.blackwell@case.edu.

BLACKWELL, KEN (JOHN KENNETH BLACKWELL), former state official, former mayor; b. Feb. 28, 1948; m. Rosa Blackwell; children: Kimberly, Rahshann, Kristin. BS, Xavier U., Cin., 1970, MEd, 1971. Cert. govt. fin. mgr. Mem. city coun., City of Cin., 1977-89, vice mayor, 1977-78, 85-86, mayor, 1979-80; vice-chmn. Cin. Employees Retirement Sys. Fund., 1988; dep. undersec. U.S. Dept. HUD, 1989-90; mem. Nat. Commn. Econ. Growth and Tax Reform, 1995; participant Nat. Summit on Retirement Income Savings, 1998; ptnr. Bituminex Co., 1978-82; coord. urban affairs, Xavier U., 1971-74, asst. prof. edn., 1974-77, assoc. prof., 1977-91, dir. cmty. rels., 1975-79, assoc. v.p., 1979-91; assoc. prof. U. cin., 1993; chmn. bd. adv. trustees Govt. Investment Found., Inc., 1999; ambassador U.N. Human Rights Commn., 1992-93; adv. bd. John M. Ashbrook Ctr. Pub. Affairs Ashland U., 1997; Children's Ednl. Opportunity Am. Found., 1999; bd. dirs. Black Alliance for Edn. Options; pres. Nat. Electronic Commerce Coord. Coun., 2002; bd.dir. Nat. Coun. UN, Internat. League Human Rights, nat. Coun. Lawyer's Com. for Human Rights, Pub. Tech., Inc., Internat. City Mgmt. Assn./Ret. Corp., Internat. Rep. Inst.; mem. Fed. Election Commn. adv. panel, 1999; bd. trustees Am. Coun. Young Polit. Leaders, 1995' treas. State of Ohio, 1994-99; sec. State of Ohio, 1999-2006; mem. Coun. Fgn. Rels. Contbr. articles to profl. jours. Mem. The Jerusalem com., 1981, Harvard Policy Group on Network-Enabled Svcs. and Givt.; co-chmn. Hamilton County Reagan-Bush campaign, Ohi, 1984; mem. exec. com. at. Conf. Rep. Mayors; co-chmn. Blacks for Bush campaign, Ohio, 1988; mem. adv. coun. Ohio victims of Crime, 1989; bd. dirs. Internat. Rep. Inst., 1993, Campaign Finance Inst., Physicians for Human Rights, Congressional Human Rights Found.; nat. chmn. Steve Forbes for Pres. campaign, 1999; bd. dirs. Wilberforce U., 1989; chmn. Cin. Riverfront Classic and Jamboree, 2000-01; mem. exec. bd. Youth Voter Corps, 2001; mem. nat. bd. visitors Mazza Collection, U. Findlay, 1999; hon. co-chair Meml. to Our Lost Children, 1995; trustee Grant/Riverside Hosps., 1996, Wilmington Coll., 1996; v.p. Nat. Electronic Commerce Coordinating Coun., 2001, 02; mem. bd. advisors John M. Ashbrook Ctr. Pub. Affairs, Ashland U., 1997; exec. bd. Youth Voter Corps., 2001; fellow Nat. Acad. of Pub. Adminstrn.; mem. nat. adv. bd. Princeton Review, Youth for Christ, Jewish Inst. for NAt. Security Affairs; adv. coun. Employee Welfare and Pension Plan U.S. Dept. of Labor. Fellow Harvard U., 1987, The Aspen Inst., 1984, Salzburg Seminar, Austria, 1988, Heritage Found., 1992, The Ditchley Found., 1993; scholar Urban Morgan Inst. Human Rights, 1993; recipient Disting. Alumnus award Xavier U., 1992, Superior Honor award U.S. Dept. State, 1993, Peace of City award Cin. Jewish Cmty. Rels. Coun., 1994, Family of Yr. award Nat. Coun. Negro Women, 1994, Advocacy award U.S. Small Bus. Adminstrn., 1995, Martin Luther King Dream Keeper award, 1996, Veritas award Albertus Magnus Coll., 1998, Thomas A. Van Meter scholar award Ashbrook Ctr., 1997, Pub. Svc. award NAACP, 1996, John M. Ashbrook award American Conservative Union and Ashbrook Ctr. Pub. Affairs, 2004; named one of Top 25 Pub. Sector Leaders, Govt. Tech. Mag., 2002. Mem. Nat. Govt. Fin. Officers Assn. (excellence award 1999), Nat. Assn. State Treasurers, Nat. Assn. State Auditors, Comptrs. and Treasurers (exec. com. 1995-99, Pres. award, 1996), Nat. Taxpayers Union, Nat. Assn. of Secs. of State (v.p. midwest region 2001), Nat. Assn. Securities Profls., Internat. City Mgmt. Assn. (bd. dirs. 1999), Federalist Soc., Econ. club of Columbus, Sigma Pi Phi. Republican. Office Phone: 614-466-2655. Office Fax: 614-644-0649. Business E-Mail: blackwell@sos.state.oh.us.

BLACKWELL, THOMAS FRANCIS, lawyer; b. Detroit, Nov. 25, 1942; m. Sandra L. Kroczek; children: Robert T., Katherine M. BA, U. Notre Dame, Ind., 1964; JD, U. Mich., 1967. Bar: Mich and U.S. Dist. Ct. (we. and ea. dists.) Mich. 1968, U.S. Ct. Appeals (6th cir.) 1969. Assoc. Smith, Haughey, Rice & Roegge, Grand Rapids, Mich., 1967-71, ptnr., 1971—, treas., 1979-85, 89—, exec. com., 1985-89. Spl. asst. atty. gen. State of Mich., 1972-82. Fellow Mich. State Bar Found.; mem. ABA, State Bar Mich., Grand Rapids Bar Assn., FBA, Products Liability Adv. Coun., Mich. Def. Trial Attys., Peninsular, Kent Country Club. Office: Smith Haughey Rice & Roegge 250 Monroe Ave NW Ste 200 Grand Rapids MI 49503-2251 Office Phone: 616-774-8000. E-mail: tblackwell@shrr.com.

BLACKWELL, TODD V., human resources specialist; BA in Edn., NC State U. Various positions including team leader, ops. team leader, store team leader, dist. human resources mgr., dist. team leader, regional v.p., sr. v.p. Mervyn's (a former subsidiary of Target Corp.), 1986—2000; sr. v.p. human resources Target Corp., Mpls., 2000—03, exec. v.p. human resources, assets protection, COO AMC world-wide sourcing co., 2003—. Chmn. Associated. Merchandising Corp. Bd. dirs. Kids Fitness for Life. Mem.: Omega Psi Phi. Office: Target Corp 1000 Nicoillet Mall Minneapolis MN 55403 Office Phone: 612-304-6073. Office Fax: 612-696-3731.

BLAD, BLAINE L., agricultural meteorology educator, consultant; b. Cedar City, Utah, Apr. 2, 1939; s. Carl Hamblin and Loueda (Allan) B.; m. Virginia Jean Blackham, Feb. 14, 1964; children: Debra Jean, Sheryl Kay, Colleen, Kenneth L., Stephen L., Kirk L., Kerry Kim. BS, Brigham Young U., 1964; MS, U. Minn., 1968, PhD, 1970. NDEA fellow U. Minn., St. Paul, 1964-67, technician, 1966-70, rsch. asst., 1967-70; asst. prof. U. Nebr., Lincoln, 1970-76, assoc. prof., 1976-82, prof., 1982—, head dept. agrl. meteorology, 1987-97, dir. Sch. Natural Resource Scis., 1997-2000; assoc. dir. Gt. Plains Regional Ctr. for Global Environ. Change, 1992—. Cons. NASA, Houston, 1978-80, Standard Oil Co. Ohio, Cleve., 1983-86. Author: Microclimate: Biological Environment, 1983; sect. editor: International Crop Science, 1992; assoc. editor Agronomy Jour., 1981-87. Scoutmaster Cornhusker coun. Boy Scouts Am., 1976-94. Fellow Am. Soc. Agronomy (chair div. 1976-77); mem. Crop Sci. Soc. Am., Gamma Sigma Delta (chair membership com. 1992). Mem. Lds Ch. Avocations: sports, reading, camping, fishing, hunting. Office: U Nebr Sch Natural Resource Scis 243 LW Chase Hall Lincoln NE 68583-0728 Home: PO Box 376 Kanosh UT 84637-0376

BLADE, MARK J., state legislator; b. Terre Haute, Ind., Dec. 16, 1953; m. Vickie Blade; children: Marcus, Stephanie, Yolanda, Mark Jr. BS, Ind. State U., 1976. Cmty. devel. planner West Ctrl. Ind. Econ. Devel. Dist., 1976-80; asst. dir. for cmty. and econ. devel. Terre Haute (Ind.) Dept. Redevel., 1980-86; dir. purchasing and warehousing Vigo County Sch. Corp., 1986—; mem. Ind. Senate from 38th dist., Indpls., 1997—; mem. fin. com., mem. govt. and regulatory affairs com.; mem. planning and econ. devel. com., ranking mem.; mem. pub. policy com. Mem. Vigo County Coun., 1992—, pres. pro tempore, 1994, pres. 1995, 96, pres., 1997; sec. Vigo County Dem. Ctrl. Com., 1993-96, treas., 1997—; trustee Ind. State U., 1996; v.p., pres. Ind. State U. Alumni Coun., 1991-96; bd. dirs. Family Svc. Assn. Bd., 1992-96, 1st v.p., 1995, 96; mem. adv. bd. Cmty. Corrections, 1990-94, pres., 1994; bd. dirs. United Way of the Wabash Valley, 1985-90, v.p. for allocations, pres.; bd. dirs. Trees, Inc., 1993-96. Democrat. Avocations: reading, travel. Office: 200 W Washington St Indianapolis IN 46204-2728

BLAGG, JOE W., retail executive; Chmn. bd. TruServ Corp., Chgo. Office: TruServ Corp 8600 W Bryn Mawr Ave Chicago IL 60631-3505

BLAGOJEVICH, ROD R., governor, former congressman; b. Chgo., Dec. 10, 1956; s. Rade and Millie (Govedarica) Blagojevich; m. Patti Mell; children: Amy, Annie. BA in History, Northwestern U., 1979; JD, Pepperdine U., 1983. Pvt. practice law, Chgo., 1983—86; asst. state atty. Cook County, Ill., 1986—88; mem. Ill. Ho. of Reps., 1992—96, US Congress from 5th Ill. dist., 1997—2003, mem. govt. reform and armed svcs. coms.; gov. State of Ill., Springfield, 2003—. Democrat. Office: Office of the Governor 207 State House Springfield IL 62706 also: 100 W Randolph Ste 16-100 Chicago IL 60601 Office Fax: 217-524-4049.

BLAHNIK, JOHN G., electronics executive; BS, U. Wis.; MBA, U. Chgo. Various fin. pos. in product cost, capital appropriations and product programs GM, Detroit, 1978—81; mgr. overseas fin. analysis GM Treas.'s Office, NYC, 1981, mgr. capital analysis, fin. staff, 1982, mgr. corp. financing, 1982—84, dir. cash resources mgmt. and fgn. exch., 1984, dir. fgn. exch. and internat. cash mgmt., 1984; treas. GM do Brasil, Brazil, 1984—87, gen. asst. comptroller, 1987, comptroller, 1988; exec. dir. GM L.Am. Ops., 1991—94; pres. Banco GM, 1991—94; dir. fin., Lansing (Mich.) Automotive Divsn. GM, 1994; sr. v.p., CFO Delco Electronics Corp., Troy, Mich., 1995, exec. dir. fin., 1996—98, treas., 1998—, v.p., 1998—2004, v.p. treasury, mergers, acquisitions, 2004—. Office: World Hdqrs Delphi Corp 5725 Delphi Dr Troy MI 48098-2815

BLAHUT, RICHARD EDWARD, electrical and computer engineering educator; b. Orange, NJ, June 9, 1937; s. Edward John and Julia Anna (Chamer) B.; m. Barbara Ann Krachenfels, Aug. 30, 1958; children: Gregory, Kenneth, Janice, Jeffrey. BS in Elec. Engring., MIT, 1960; MS in Physics, Stevens Inst. Tech., Hoboken, NJ, 1964; PhD in Elec. Engring., Cornell U., 1972. Engr. Kearfott (GPI), Little Falls, NJ, 1960-64, IBM, Owego, NY, 1964-94; courtesy prof. elec. engring. Cornell U., 1974-94; Henry Magnuski prof. and dept. head elec. and computer engring. U. Ill., Urbana, 1994—, adj. prof. elec. engring., 1986-94. Sys. cons. Ioptics Corp., Bellevue, Wash., 1994-99. Author: Theory and Practice of Error Control Codes, 1983, Fast Algorithms for Digital Signal Processing, 1985, Principles and Practice of Information Theory, 1987, Digital Transmission of Information, 1990, Algebraic Codes for Data Transmission, 2003, Theory of Remote Image Formation, 2005, Algebraic Codes on Lines, Planes and Curves, 2008. IBM fellow, 1980. Fellow IEEE (pres. info. theory group 1982, editor Transactions on Info. theory, Alexander Graham Bell award 1998, Claude E. Shannon award 2005), NAE. Republican. Roman Catholic. Home: 1502 BridgePoint Ln Champaign IL 61822-9272 Office: U Ill Dept of Elect and Computer Engring Urbana IL 61801 E-mail: blahut@uiuc.edu.

BLAIN, CHARLOTTE MARIE, internist, educator; b. Meadeville, Pa., July 18, 1941; d. Frank Andrew and Valerie Marie (Serafin) Blain; m. John G. Hamby, June 12, 1971 (dec. May 1976); 1 child, Charles J. Hamby. Student, Coll. of St. Francis, 1958—60, DePaul U., 1960—61; MD, U. Ill., Chgo., 1965. CLU; diplomate Am. Bd. Family Practice, Am. Bd. Internal Medicine. Intern, resident U. Ill. Hosps., 1967—70; fellow in infectious diseases U. Ill., 1968—69; pvt. practice specializing in internal medicine and family practice Elmhurst, Ill., 1969—. Instr. U. Ill. Hosp., 1969—70; asst. prof. Loyola U., 1970—71; mem. staff Elmhurst Meml. Hosp., 1970—; clin. asst. prof. Chgo. Med. Sch., 1978—95, U. Ill. Med. Sch., 1995—, Rush Med. Coll., 1997—. Contbr. articles to profl. jours., chapters to books. Bd. dirs., v.p. Elmhurst Art Mus. Fellow: ACP, Am. Acad. Family Practice; mem.: AMA, DuPage Med. Soc., Am. Profl. Practice Assn., Am. Soc. Internal Medicine, Univ. Club (Chgo.). Roman Catholic. Avocations: Hapki Do (Black Belt), Tae-Kwan-Do (Black Belt), skiing. Home: 320 Cottage Hill Ave Elmhurst IL 60126-3302 Office: 135 Cottage Hill Ave Elmhurst IL 60126-3330 Office Phone: 630-832-6633. Business E-Mail: cblain@mybclinic.com.

BLAIR, BEN, real estate company executive; JD, Washburn U., 1965. Chmn. Coldwell Banker Griffith & Blair Realtors, Topeka. Mem. bd. regents Washburn U., Kirkville, Mo.; trustee Washburn Endowment Assn., 1993—, past chmn. endowment bd. Office: Coldwell Banker Griffith & Blair 2222 SW 29th St Topeka KS 66611

BLAIR, CARY, insurance company executive; b. Hartford City, Ind. BS, Butler U. Joined Westfield Cos., 1961, from mgmt. trainee to exec. v.p., 1961-83; chmn., CEO Westfield Cos., Westfield Mgmt. and Westfield Fin., Westfield Ctr., Ohio.

BLAIR, EDWARD MCCORMICK, investment banker; b. Chgo., July 18, 1915; s. William McCormick and Helen Haddock (Bowen) B.; m. Elizabeth Graham Iglehart, June 28, 1941; children: Edward McCormick, Francis Iglehart. Grad., Groton Sch., 1934; BA, Yale U., 1938; MBA, Harvard U., 1940. With William Blair & Co., Chgo., 1946—, ptnr., 1950-61, mng. ptnr., 1961-77, sr. ptnr., 1977—. Bd. dirs. George M. Pullman Ednl. Found.; life trustee Coll. of Atlantic, Bar Harbor, Maine; life trustee U. Chgo., Rush-Presbyn.-St. Luke's Med. Ctr., Chgo., Art Inst. Chgo. Lt. comdr. USNR, 1941-46. Home: PO Box 186 Sheridan Rd Lake Bluff IL 60044 Office: William Blair & Co 222 W Adams St Chicago IL 60606-5307

BLAIR, LEONARD PAUL, bishop; b. Detroit, Apr. 12, 1949; s. Leonard and Helen Blair. BA in History, Sacred Heart Sem. Coll., Detroit; STB, Pontifical Gregorian U., Rome, 1974; STL, No. Am. Coll., Rome, 1978; STD, Pontifical U. of St. Thomas Aquinas, Rome, 1997. Ordained priest Archdiocese of Detroit, 1976; sec. to Cardinal Edmund Szoka Prefecture for Econ. Affairs of Holy See, Vatican City State; pastor St. Paul Parish, Grosse Point Farms, Ohio, 1997—2003; ordained bishop, 1999; aux. bishop Archdiocese of Detroit, 1999—2003; bishop Diocese of Toledo, 2003—. Roman Catholic. Office: Diocese of Toledo PO Box 985 1933 Spielbusch Toledo OH 43697 Office Phone: 419-244-6711. Office Fax: 419-244-4791.*

BLAKE, ALLEN H., bank executive; b. Chgo., 1942; Student, Washington U., 1964, student, 1965. Joined First Bank, Inc., St. Louis, 1984—, sr. v.p., CFO, 1984—99, COO, 1998—2003, pres., 1999—, CFO, 2001—05, CEO St. Louis, 2003—. Office: First Banks Inc 135 N Meramec Ave Saint Louis MO 63105 Office Phone: 314-854-4600.

BLAKE, DARCIE KAY, radio news director, anchor; b. Worland, Wyo., Aug. 29, 1958; d. Jerry Haley and Helen Ileen (Kerbel) Bloom; m. Paul Henry Reifschneider, Aug. 30, 1980; children: Sara Jayne, Mathew James. BS in Journalism, U. N.D., 1979. Anchor, reporter Sta. KFYR Radio, Bismarck, N.D., 1979, Sta. WHB Radio, Kansas City, Mo., 1980-82; news dir. Sta. KUDL Radio/Sta. WHB Radio, Kansas City, 1982—. Bd. dirs. Harvestors-Food Bank, Kansas City, 1990, Girl Scouts U.S., Kansas City, 1990; vol. Arthritis Assn (citation 1989), United Minority Media Assn. (citation 1989). Mem. Kansas City Press Club (bd. dirs. 1984-85), Radio/TV News Dirs., Kansas City Media Profls., Kans. Assn. Broadcasters, Soc. Profl. Journalists. Episcopalian. Avocations: golf, tennis.

BLAKE, NORMAN PERKINS, JR., computer company executive; b. NYC, Nov. 8, 1941; s. Norman Perkins and Eleanor (Adams) Blake; m. Karen Cromwell, Sept. 12, 1965; children: Kellie, Kimberly, Adam. BA, Purdue U., 1966, MA, 1967. With GE, 1967—74, mgr. strategic planning ops., plastics bus. divsn. Pittsfield, Mass., 1976—78, mgr. bus. devel. consumer products and services sector, 1978—79, staff exec. Fairfield, Conn., 1979; v.p., gen. mgr. comml. and indsl. fin. divsn. GE Credit Corp., Stamford, Conn., 1979—81, exec. v.p. fin. ops., 1981—84; pres., chmn., CEO Heller Internat. Corp., Chgo., 1984—90; chmn., CEO Heller Fin., Inc., Chgo., 1984—90, Heller Overseas Corp., Chgo., 1984—90; chmn., CEO, pres. U.S. Fidelity & Guaranty Co., Balt., 1990—98; chmn., pres. Fidelity & Guaranty Ins. Underwriters., Balt., 1990—98; vice-chmn. St. Paul Cos., Marco Island, Fla., 1990—98; chmn., pres., CEO Promus Hotel Corp., Memphis, 1998—99; CEO, chmn., pres. Comdisco, Inc., Rosemont, Ill., 2001—. With Top, Inc., Troy, Mich., 1974—76, pres., 1976; bd. dirs. Owens/Corning Fiberglas. Office: Comdisco 5600 N River Rd Ste 800 Rosemont IL 60018-5166

BLAKE, WILLIAM HENRY, credit and public relations consultant; b. Jasonville, Ind., Feb. 18, 1913; s. Straude and Cora (Pope) B.; m. Helen Elizabeth Platt, Jan. 2, 1937 (dec. Feb. 1990); children: William Henry, Allen Howard. Student, Knox Coll., 1932-35; BS, U. Ill., 1936, MS, 1941, postgrad., 1946; student, NYU, 1950-51, Am. U., 1955-56, 1958; grad., Columbia U. Grad. Sch. Consumer Credit, 1956, Northeastern Inst., Yale U., 1957. Cert. assn. exec. Tchr. Champaign (Ill.) Pub. Schs., 1936-41; exec. sec. Ill. Soc. CPAs, Chgo., 1941-44; dean men, assoc. prof. bus. adminstrn. Catawba Coll., 1947-51; dir. rsch. Nat. Consumer Fin. Assn., Washington, 1954-59; exec. v.p. Internat. Consumer Credit Assn., St. Louis, 1959-78; pres. Consumer Trends Inc., Blake Enterprises Cons., 1978—. Cons. Decatur Consumer Credit Assn., 1979-88; adminstr. Soc. Cert. Consumer Credit Execs., 1961-78 Author: Good Things of Life on Credit, 1960, rev., 1975, How to Use Consumer Credit Wisely, 1963, rev., 1975, Home Study Courses in Credit and Collections, 1968, Human Relations, 1969, Communications, 1970, Retail Credit and Collections, rev., 1974, Adminstrative Office Management, 1972, Consumer Credit Management, 1974; pub.: Consumer Trends Newsletter, The Credit World mag. Mem. pres.'s adv. cabinet Southeastern U.; adviser Office Edn. Assn.; chmn. public relations com. Ill. Heart Assn., 1979-85; bd. dirs. Salvation Army, Decatur, 1979—; mem. fund raising com. Sch. Edn., U. Ill., 1979-84; chmn. bd. trustees Alta Deana div. University City, 1970-73, congressional liaison, 1959-78; trustee Internat. Consumer Credit Assn. Ins. Trust and Retirement Program, 1960-78; mem. Session Westminster Presbyn. Ch., Decatur, 1971-84, fin. con., 1981-84, 89-92. trustee. 1981-84; apptd. by mayor to Decatur Aging Adv. Commn., 1991-94. Served to lt. USNR, 1944-47; lt. comdr. 1951-54, ret. Named Man of Yr., Mo. Consumer Credit Assn., 1977; recipient Knox Coll. Scroll of Honor, Knox-Lombard 50 Yr. Club, Galesburg, 1991, Alumni Achievement award Knox Coll., 1994, Class Agt. award, 1995. Mem. Credit Grantors Assn. Can. (bd. dirs. 1959-72), U.S. C. of C. (mem. banking and currency com. 1968-71, mem. trade assn. com. 1964-67), Am. Soc. Assn. Execs. (bd. dirs. 1965-66), Pub. Rels. Soc. Am. (chpt. sec.-treas. 1979-85), Internat. Platform Assn., Washington Trade Assn. Execs., Am. Pub. Rels. Assn. (nat. treas. 1960-61, chpt. pres. 1958-59), U. Ill. Alumni Assn., Press Club St. Louis, Capitol Hill Club (Washington), Exchequer Club (Washington), Rotary (pres. Decatur chpt. 1985-86, Paul Harris fellow 1984, Svc. Above Self award 1996, Hon. Rotarian of Month, Feb. 2005, Rotary Disting. award 2005), Phi Sigma Kappa. Republican. Home: 1133 Pine St Saint Louis MO 63101-1900

BLAKEY, G. ROBERT (GEORGE ROBERT BLAKEY), law educator; b. Burlington, NC, Jan. 7, 1936; BA, U. Notre Dame, 1957, JD, 1960. Bar: NC 1960, DC 1960, Colo. 1986, admitted to practice: U.S. Supreme Ct. 1963. Participated in Atty. General's Honor Program US Dept. Justice, 1960, spl atty. Organized Crime and racketeering sect., 1960—64; asst. prof. U. Notre Dame Law Sch., Ind., 1964—67, prof. law, 1967—74, 1980—85, William J. and Dorothy O'Neill prof. law, 1985—; spl. cons. Pres. Commn. for Law Enforcement and Adminstrn. of Justice, 1966—67, U.S. Senate Judiciary Com., Title III on wiretapping and electronic surveillance, 1967—68, Nat. Commn. on Reform of the Fed. Penal Law, 1968; chief counsel U.S. Senate Judiciary Com., Subcommittee on Criminal Laws and Procedures, 1969—73; prof. law, Cornell U., Ithaca, NY, 1973—80; dir. Cornell Inst. on Organized Crime, Cornell Law Sch., 1973—80; presdl. mem. Nat. Commn. on the Review of Fed. and State Law Relating to Wiretapping and Electronic Surveillance, 1974—75; chief counsel Nat. Comn. on the Review of Policy Toward Gambling, 1974—76; chief counsel, staff dir. U.S. House Select Com. on Assassinations, 1977—78; spl. cons. U.S. Judiciary Com. White Collar Crime, 1985—86, U.S. House Judiciary Com., White Collar Crime and RICO reform, 1988. Assoc. editor Law Review; author: (novels) Develop. of Law of Gambling, 1978; contbr. articles to profl. jours. Recipient Legal award, Assn. Fed. Investigators, 1969, Award of Merit, Nat. Acad. Forensic Sciences, 1979, Appreciation award, FBI, 1985, Pub. Justice Achievement award, Trial Lawyers for Pub. Justice, 1995, Charles Crutchfield Profl. Excellence award, NDLS Black Law Students Assn., 1996. Mem.: Am. Law Inst., Order of the Coif, Nat. Commn. for Rev. of Fed. and State Law Relating to Wiretapping and Electronic Surveillance (mem. 1974—76), Nat. Commn. on Rev. of Policy toward Gambling (mem. 1974—76), Nat. Commn. on Reform of Fed. Penal Law (mem. 1968), Phi Beta Kappa. Office Phone: 574-631-5717. Office Fax: 574-631-4197. Business E-Mail: G.R.Blakey.1@nd.edu.

BLAKLEY, DERRICK, newscaster; b. Chgo. B Journalism, Northwestern U., 1975; M Comms., U. Ill., 1976. Reporter Chgo. Tribune Newspaper, 1976—78, Sta. WBNS-TV, Columbus, Ohio, 1978—80; midwest reporter CBS News, Chgo., 1980—83, European, African, and Middle Eastern reporter London, 1984—87, Bonn, Germany, 1984—87; gen. assignment reporter NBC 5, Chgo., 1987—, weekend morning newcast anchor, weekend evening anchor, 1998—. Recipient award, Ohio AP, local emmy award. Mem.: Chgo. Assn. Black Journalists, Nat. Assn. Black Journalists. Office: NBC 454 N Columbus Dr Chicago IL 60611

BLANC, CARYN, retail executive; Sr. v.p. distbr. and store adminstrn. Kohl's Corp., Menomonee Falls, Wis. Office: Kohl's Corp 1700 Ridgewood Drive Menomonee Falls WI 53051-7026

BLANCHARD, ERIC ALAN, lawyer; b. 1956; BBA, U. Mich., 1978; JD, Harvard U., 1981. Bar: Ill. 1981. Atty. Schiff, Hardin & Waite, 1981-86; corp. atty. Dean Foods Co., Franklin Park, Ill., 1986-88, gen. coun., sec., v.p., pres. dairy divsn., 1988—; pres. Dean foods, 1999—2002; sr. v.p., sec., gen. counsel Tennant Co., Mpls., 2002, United Stationers Inc., Deerfeild, 2006—. Office: United Stationers Inc 1 N Parkway Blvd Ste 100 Deerfield IL 60015-2559 Office Phone: 847-627-7000. Office Fax: 847-627-7001.

BLANCHARD, J. A., III, publishing executive; b. 1943; BA, Princeton U., 1965; MS, Sloan Sch., MIT, 1978. Chmn., CEO Harbridge Merchant Services, Inc., 1991—93; exec. v.p. Gen. Instrument Corp., 1994—95; pres., CEO Deluxe Corp., St. Paul, 1995—96, chmn., 1996—2000; chmn., CEO eFunds Corp., Scottsdale, Ariz., 2000—02; non-exec. chmn. ADC, Mpls., 2003—. Office: ADC Investor Rels PO Box 1101 Minneapolis MN 55440-1101

BLAND, MARY GROVES, state legislator; b. Kansas City, Mo., Jan. 24, 1936; Student, Ottawa U., Penn Valley Coll., Pioneer C.C., Weaver Sch. Real Estate. Mem. Mo. Ho. of Reps. from 43rd dist., Jefferson City, 1980-98; cmty. specialist Lan Clearance for Redevel., Kansas City, 1971-79; mem. Mo. Senate from 9th dist., Jefferson City, 1999—. Vice-chmn. human rights and resources com., chair labor and indsl. rels. com., mem. aging families and mental health com., civil and criminal jurisprudence com., elections, vet. affairs and corrections com., pub. health and welfare com., health rev. com., cert. of need program com., joint com. on wetlands; free-lance cmty. cons., 1979—; exec. bd. Freedom, Inc. Active Mayor's Neighborhood Coun. on Crime Prevention; mem. S.E. eighborhood Coalition, U.S. Commn. on Civil Rights; active Niles Home for Children. Office: Mo State Senate Rm 334 State Capitol Building Jefferson City MO 65101

BLANDER, MILTON, chemist; b. Bklyn., Nov. 1, 1927; s. Benjamin and Yetta (Schwartzman) B.; children: Benjamin, Alice, Kathryn, Daniel, Joshua. BS, CUNY, 1950; PhD, Yale U., 1953. Rsch. assoc. Cornell U., Ithaca, NY, 1953-55; chemist Oak Ridge (Tenn.) Nat. Lab., 1955-62; chemist, group leader Rockwell Internat. Sci. Ctr., Thousand Oaks, Calif., 1962-71; sr. chemist, group leader Argonne (Ill.) Nat. Lab., 1971-97; founder Quest Rsch., South Holland, Ill., 1995—. Recipient Materials Rsch. award U.S. Dept. Energy, 1984, Alexander von Humboldt award. Fellow AAAS, Meteoritical Soc.; mem. Metall. Soc., Am. Chem. Soc., Electrochem. Soc. (Max Bredig award 1987), Norwegian Acad. Tech. Scis. E-mail: mblander2@aol.com.

BLANDFORD, COLLEEN M., lawyer; b. Cin., Apr. 15, 1969; BA in Polit. Sci., U. Cin., 1990, BA in Journalism, 1990; JD, U. Cin. Coll. Law, 1993. Bar: Ohio 1993, US Dist. Ct. Southern Dist. Ohio 1994, Commonwealth of Ky. 1999, US Ct. of Appeals Sixth Cir. 1999, US Dist. Ct. Eastern Dist. Ky. 2000. Arbitrator Hamilton County Ct. of Common Pleas; atty. Kohnen & Patton LLP, Cin. Named one of Ohio's Rising Stars, Super Lawyers, 2006. Mem.: Phi Beta Kappa. Office: Kohnen & Patton LLP PNC Ctr Ste 800 201 E 5th St Cincinnati OH 45202 Office Phone: 513-381-0656. Office Fax: 513-381-5823.

BLANDFORD, DICK, electrical engineering and communications educator; Chmn. dept. elec. engring. and computer sci. U. Evansville, Ind., 1994—. Office: U Evansville Dept Elec Engring/Computers 1800 Lincoln Ave Evansville IN 47722-0001

BLANFORD, LAWRENCE J., appliance company executive; With Johns Manville Corp., PPG Industries, Procter & Gamble Co., until 1997; v.p. strategic mktg. Maytag Corp., ewton, Iowa, 1997-99, pres. Maytag Internat., 1999—. Office: Maytag Corp 403 W 4th St N Newton IA 50208-3026

BLANK, DON SARGENT, dentist; b. Franklin, Nebr., Nov. 25, 1935; s. Thomas Wayne and Lila Louise (Sargent) B.; m. Janice Marie Halverson, June 10, 1962; children: Jeffrey, Steven, Randal. DDS, U. Nebr., 1960. Pvt. practice, McCook, Nebr., 1962--. Mailing: 811 Norris Ave Mc Cook NE 69001 Office Phone: 308-345-6760. E-mail: dblank@nebraska.edu.

BLANK, REBECCA MARGARET, economist; b. Columbia, Mo., Sept. 19, 1955; d. Oscar Uel and Vernie (Backhaus) B.; m. Johannes Kuttner, 1994; 1 child, Emily. BS, U. Minn., 1976; PhD, MIT, 1983. Cons. Data Resources, Inc., Chgo., 1976-79; asst. prof. econs. Princeton U., 1983-89; assoc. prof. econs. Northwestern U., Chgo., 1989-94, prof. econs., 1994-99; sr. staff economist Coun. of Econ. Advisors, Washington, 1989-90, mem., 1998-99; dean, Henry Carter Adams prof. Gerald R. Ford Sch. Pub. Policy, U. Mich., Ann Arbor, 1999—; co-dir. Nat. Poverty Rsch. Ctr., U. Mich., 2002—. Author: It Takes A Nation: A New Agenda for Fighting Poverty, 1997, Is the Market Moral?, 2004, other books; contbr. articles to profl. jours. Vis. Professorships for Women grantee, 1988-89; Sloan Found. fellow, 1982-83; recipient Jr. Faculty Teaching award Princeton U., 1985, David Kershaw award Assn. Pub. Policy Analysis and Mgmt., 1993, Richard Lester award for best book on labor econs., 1997. Mem. Am. Acad. Arts and Scis., Nat. Bur. Econ. Rsch., Am. Econs. Assn., Assn. of Pub. Policy Analysis and Mgmt., Indsl. Rels. Rsch. Assn. United Ch. of Christ.

BLANKENSHIP, EDWARD G., architect; b. Martin, Tenn., June 22, 1943; BArch, Columbia U., 1966, MSc in Arch., 1967; MLitt in Arch., Cambridge U., Eng., 1971. Sr. v.p. Landrum & Brown, Inc. Office: 218 Park Crest Dr Newport Beach CA 92657 Office Phone: 949-252-5214.

BLANKENSHIP, ROBERT EUGENE, biochemistry educator; b. Auburn, Nebr., Aug. 25, 1948; s. George Robert and Jane (Kehoe) Leech; m. Elizabeth Marie Dorland, June 26, 1971; children: Larissa Dorland, Samuel Robert. BS, Wesleyan U., Nebr., 1970; PhD, U. Calif., Berkeley, 1975. Postdoctoral fellow Lawrence Berkeley Lab., Berkeley, 1975-76, U. Washington, Seattle, 1976-79; asst. prof. Amherst Coll., Mass., 1979-85; assoc. prof. Ariz. State U., Tempe, 1985-88, prof., 1988—2006, dir. Ctr. Study of Early Events in Photosynthesis, 1988-91, chair, dept. chem. and biochem., 2002—06; Lucille P. Markey Disting. Prof. Arts and Scis. in biology and chemistry Washington U., St. Louis, 2006—. Author: Molecular Mechanisms of Photosynthesis, 2002; editor Anoxygenic Photosynthetic Bacteria, 1995; editor-in-chief Photosynthesis Rsch., 1988-99; cons. editor Advances in Photosynthesis, 1991-98; mem. editl. bd. Biophys. Jour., 2000-03, Biochemistry, 2001—, Internat. Jour. Astrobiology, 2001—, Current Chem. Biology, 2006—; contbr. 240 articles to sci. jours. Recipient Alumni award Nebr. Wesleyan U., 1991, Disting. Rsch. award Ariz. State U., 1992, Mentoring award Ariz. State U., 1998. Fellow AAAS, Ariz. Arts, Scis. & Tech. Acad.; mem. Am. Chem. Soc., Am. Soc. Microbiology, Biophys. Soc., Union Concerned Scientists, Internat. Soc. Photosynthesis Rsch. (pres. 2001-04), Internat. Soc. for Study of Origin of Life. Democrat. Avocations: hiking, cooking, travel, fossil collecting. Home: 6924 Columbia Ave Saint Louis MO 63130 Office: Washington Univ Depts Biology and Chemistry Campus Box 1137 Saint Louis MO 63130 Business E-Mail: blankenship@wustl.edu.

BLANKFIELD, BRYAN J., lawyer, automotive executive, accountant; BS, Drake U.; JD, Northwestern U. CPA. In-house legal counsel and cons. Waste Management, Inc., 1990—2002, assoc. gen. counsel, asst. sec., 1995—2002, v.p., 1998—2002; exec. v.p., gen. counsel, sec. Oshkosh Truck Corp., Wis., 2002—. Also advisor to CEO, bd. dir., sr. mgmt. OshKosh Truck Co. Office: Oshkosh Truck Corp 2307 Oregon St PO Box 2566 Oshkosh WI 54903 Office Phone: 920-235-9151.

BLANTON, LEWIS M., federal judge; b. Cape Girardeau, Mo., Mar. 5, 1934; AB, St. Louis U., 1958, MA, 1962; JD, U. Mo., 1965. Bar: Mo. Atty. Thompson, Walther & Shewmaker, St. Louis, 1965-69, Blanton, Rice & Sickal, Sikeston, Mo., 1969-71, Robison & Blanton, Sikeston, 1971-78; assoc. judge Cir. Ct. of Scott County, Mo., 1979-91; magistrate judge U.S. Dist. Ct. (ea. dist.) Mo., Cape Girardeau, 1991—. Contbr. articles to profl. jours. Mem. ABA, Mo. Bar, Scott County Bar Assn., Cape Girardeau County Bar Assn., Bar Assn. Met. St. Louis, Fed. Magistrate Judges Assn. Office: 111 US Courthouse 339 Broadway St Cape Girardeau MO 63701-7330

BLANTON, W. C., lawyer; b. LaRue County, Ky., Apr. 13, 1946; s. Crawford and Lillian (Phelps) B. BS in Math., Mich. State U., 1968, BA in Social Sci., 1968; MEd, U. Vt., 1970; JD, U. Mich., 1975. Bar: Ind. 1975, Minn. 1998, Mo. 2002, Kans. 2006, U.S. Dist. Ct. (no. and so. dists.) Ind. 1975, U.S. Dist. Ct. Minn. 1996, U.S. Dist. Ct. (we. dist.) Wis. 1996, U.S. Dist. Ct. (we. and ea. dists.) Mo. 2002, U.S. Ct. Appeals (7th cir.) 1977, U.S. Ct. Appeals (8th cir.)

1996, U.S. Ct. Appeals (6th cir.) 1998, U.S. Ct. Appeals (10th cir.) 2005. Residence hall dir. U. Wis., Madison, 1970-72; assoc. Ice Miller Donadio & Ryan, Indpls., 1975-81, ptnr., 1982-94, Popham, Haik, Schnobrich & Kaufman, Ltd., 1995-97, Oppenheimer Wolff & Donnelly LLP, Mpls., 1997—2002, Blackwell Sanders, LLP, Kansas City, Mo., 2002—, head of environ. practice group. Mem. ABA. Democrat. Avocations: skiing, travel, bridge. Office: Husch Blackwell Sanders LLP Ste 1000 4801 Main St Kansas City MO 64112 E-mail: wblanton@blackwellsanders.com.

BLASDEL, CHARLES R., state representative; b. Akron, Ohio, Jan. 29, 1971; married; 1 child. AS in Acctg. Mgmt., Ohio Valley Bus. Coll., East Liverpool. Registered investment advisor; state rep. dist. 1 Ohio Ho. of Reps., Columbus, 2000—, chair, banking pensions and securities com., mem. health, ins., and ways and means coms. Commr. Columbiana County Planning Commn.; blue ribbon com., chair indsl. parks com. St. Clair Twp.; treas., adv. bd. Salvation Army. Mem.: ARC (pres.), Calcutta Area C. of C. (pres.), Friends of East Liverpool, Rotary Internat. Republican. Office: 77 S High St 11th fl Columbus OH 43215-6111

BLASKE, NATHAN H., lawyer; b. Louisville, July 1, 1978; BBA, U. Ky., 2000; JD, Salmon P. Chase Coll. of Law, 2003. Bar: Ohio 2003, US Dist. Ct. Southern Dist. Ohio 2003, Ky. 2004, Ind. 2004, US Dist. Ct. Northern Dist. Ind. 2004, US Dist. Ct. Southern Dist. Ind. 2004, US Dist. of Appeals Sixth Cir. 2004. Assoc. Wood & Lamping, L.L.P., Cin. Named one of Ohio's Rising Stars, Super Lawyers, 2006. Mem.: Ky. Bar Assn., Ind. State Bar Assn., Ohio State Bar Assn., Cin. Bar Assn., ABA. Office: Wood & Lamping LLC 600 Vine St Ste 2500 Cincinnati OH 45202-2491 Office Phone: 513-852-6000. Office Fax: 513-852-6087.

BLASZKIEWICZ, DAVID, investment company executive; b. 1968; Dir. fin. Detroit Renaissance, 1994, sec., treasurer; pres. Detroit Investment Fund. Mgmt. and loan com. Lower Woodland Housing Fund; works with Real Estate Assistance Fund, Woodward Corridor Devel. Fund; bd. mem. Detroit Cmty. Loan Fund, Wayne State U. Rsch. and Tech. Park, Mich. Magnet Loan Fund, Detroit Downtown Devel. Authority. Named one of 40 Under 40, Crain's Detroit Bus., 2006. Office: Detroit Investment Fund 600 Renaissance Ctr Ste 1710 Detroit MI 48243 Office Phone: 313-259-6368. Office Fax: 313-259-6393.

BLATT, HAROLD GELLER, lawyer; b. Detroit, Apr. 8, 1934; s. Henry H. and Berdye (Geller) B.; m. Elaine K. Greenberg, July 9, 1960; children— Lisa K., James G., Andrew . BS, Washington U., St. Louis, 1955, LL.B., 1960; LL.M., NYU, 1961. Bar: Mo. 1960. Ptnr. Bryan Cave, St. Louis, 1961—. Dir. Artex Internat., Highland, Ill. Trustee Webster U., St. Louis, 1982-97, Washington U. Med. Ctr., St. Louis, 1983-96, Barnes-Jewish, Inc., 1993—; chmn. Jewish Hosp., St. Louis, 1983-88. 1st lt. U.S. Army, 1955-57. Mem. ABA, Mo. Bar Assn., Noonday Club (St. Louis), St. Louis Club.

BLATTNER, ROBERT A., lawyer; b. Lima, Ohio, July 9, 1934; s. Simon James and Estelle Leila (Aarons) B.; m. Judith Reinfeld, Feb. 5, 1964 (div. July 1980); children: Wendy Lynn, Lauren Jill; m. Eileen Savransky, Dec. 18, 1983 BA, Northwestern U., 1956; LLB, Case Western Reserve U., 1959. Bar: Ohio 1959, Ill. 1965, U.S. Supreme Ct. 1984. Assoc. Hribar & Conway, Euclid, Ohio, 1960-62, Ulmer & Berne, Cleve., 1962-65; exec. dir. Ohio State Legal Svcs., Columbus, Ohio, 1965-67; gen. counsel, dir. real estate Sawyer Bus. Colls., Evanston, 1967-72; assoc. Guren Merritt Feibel Sogg & Cohen, Cleve., 1972-75, ptnr., 1975-84, Benesch, Friedlander, Coplan & Aronoff, Cleve., 1984-93; shareholder Kaufman & Cumberland Co., LPA, Cleve., 1994—2000; pvt. practice Chagrin Falls, Ohio, 2001—. Author: Consumer Affairs, 1973, The Construction Loan Process, 1979, Real Estate Financing, 1978, Acquisition, Development and Financing of a Commercial Complex-A Case Study, 1982; contbr. articles to profl. jours. Pres. Am. Jewish Com., Cleve., 1980-82, officer, 1976-80, chmn. adv. com., 1998—; v.p. Criminal Justice Coord. Com., Cleve., 1980-84, Cleve. Play House, bd. dirs., 1978—, pres., 1992-94, chmn., 1994-96, v.p., 1996—. Recipient Max Freedman Young Leadership award, Cleve., 1974. Mem. ABA, Ohio State Bar Assn., Cleve. Bar Assn. (chmn. real estate com. 1978-79, chmn. real estate law insts. 1979, 82, 87). Jewish. Avocations: tennis, golf, classical music, reading. Office: 30799 Pinetree Rd #415 Cleveland OH 44124-5903

BLATZ, KATHLEEN ANNE, former state supreme court justice; BA summa cum laude, U. Notre Dame, 1976; MSW, U. Minn., 1978, JD cum laude, 1984; LHD (hon.), Hamline U., 1999. Psychiat. social worker, 1979—81; mem. Minn. Ho. of Reps., St. Paul, 1979—93, chmn. crime and family law, fin. instns. and ins. coms., 1985—86; judge Dist. Ct., Henne Pin County, 1993—96; justice Minn. Supreme Ct., 1996—98, chief justice, 1998—2005. Asst. minority leader Minn. House of Reps., 1987—90, 1993; dir. employee assistance prog. Fairview Community Hospital, 1979—81; assoc. atty. Popham, Haik, Schnobrich & Kaufman, 1984—88; asst. county atty. Hennepin County Attorney's Office, 1992—93; mem. Health and Human Services Com., Rules and Legislative Administration Com., Judiciary, Gen. Legislation Veterans Affairs and Elections Com., Taxes Com.; chair Nat. Ctr. for State Cts. Rsch. Advisory Council; mem. Conference of Chief Justices; bd. dirs. Riversource Funds, 2006—. Trustee Fairview Southdale Hospital; former mem. Children's Defense Fund Advisory Council, Governor's Task Force on Fetal Alcohol Syndrome; former vice-chair Minn. Supreme Ct. Foster Care and Permanency Task Force; former bd. mem. Big Brothers Big Sisters of Greater Minneapolis. Recipient Women in State Govt. "A Minn. Treasure" award, 27th Annual Women & Bus. Conference Career Achiev. award, 1999, Minn. Women Lawyers Myra Bradwell award, 2002, Minn. Council of Child Caring Agencies Distring. Service award, 2004. Mem.: Minn. State Bar Assn.

BLEIBERG, EFRAIN, medical clinic executive; MD, Autonomous U. of Nuevo Leon. Diplomate Am. Bd. Psychiatry and Neurology. Staff psychiatrist Menninger Clinic, pres.; instr., tng. analyst Topeka Inst. for Psychoanalysis; faculty Karl Menninger Sch. Psychiatry and Mental Health Scis. Editl. bd. Bull. of the Menninger Clinic.; contbr. numerous articles to profl. publs. Named One of Nation's Top Mental Health Profls. Good Housekeeping mag. Fellow Am. Psychiat. Assn., Am. Acad. of Child and Adolescent Psychiatry; mem. Am. Psychoanlytic Assn. Address: Menningers PO Box 809045 Houston TX 77280 Fax: 785-271-9723.

BLEIFUSS, JOEL, journalist; Freelance journalist, Spain, 1986; features writer Fulton Sun, Mo.; dir., Peace Studies Program U. Mo., 1979—81; reporter, columnist & editor In These Times mag, 1986—. Office: In These Times 2040 Milwaukee Ave Chicago IL 60647 E-mail: jbleifuss@inthesetimes.com.

BLENKINSOPP, JOSEPH, biblical studies educator; b. Bishop Auckland, Durham, Eng., Apr. 3, 1927; came to U.S., 1968; s. Joseph William and Mary (Lyons) B.; m. Irene H. Blenkinsopp, Mar. 30, 1968 (div. 1991); children: David, Martin; m. Jean Porter, July 10, 1993. BA with honors in History, U. London, 1948; STL, Internat. Theologate, Turin, Italy, 1956; Licentiate in Sacred Scripture in Bibl. Studies, Bibl. Inst., Rome, 1958; DPhil in Bibl Studies, Oxford U., Eng., 1967. Lectr. Internat. Theologate, Romsey, Eng., 1958-62, Heythrop Coll., Oxford U., 1965; vis. asst. prof. Vanderbilt U., Nashville, 1968, Chgo. Theol. Sem., 1968-69; assoc. prof. Hartford (Conn.) Sem. Found., 1969-70; assoc. prof. bibl. studies U. Notre Dame, Ind., 1970-75, prof. Ind., 1975-85, John A. O'Brien prof. Ind., 1985—. Rector Ecumenical Inst., Tantur, Israel, 1978; coord. excavation Capernaum (Israel) Excavation, 1980-87. Author: Prophecy and Canon, 1977 (nat. religious book award 1977), History of Prophecy in Israel, 1983, 2d edit., 1996, Wisdom and Law in the Old Testament, 1983, 2d edit., 1995, The Pentateuch, 1992, Sage, Priest, Prophet: The Intellectual Tradition in Ancient Israel, 1995. Grantee NEH, Oxford U., 1982-83. Mem. Am. Acad. Religion, Soc. Bibl. Lit. (editl. bd. 1987-90), Cath. Bibl. Assn. (pres. 1990), Soc. O.T. Studies, Assn. Jewish Studies. Roman Catholic. Office: U otre Dame 181 Decio Hall Notre Dame IN 46556-5644

BLESSING, LOUIS W., JR., state legislator, lawyer; b. Cin., Oct. 9, 1948; s. Louis W. and Rita (Robers) B.; m. Linda Lameier, 1973; children: Billy, Alex. BBA, U. Cin., 1970; JD, No. Ky. U., 1976. Bar: Ohio. Practice law, Cin.; mem. Ohio Ho. of Reps., Columbus, 1983-97, Ohio Senate from 8th dist., 1997—. Common pleas referee Hamilton County, Cin., 1980-82. Trustee Colerain Twp., 1979-82. Named Legislator of Yr., Hamilton County Twp. Assn., 1983, Watchdog of Treasury, 1988, 90. Mem. Cin. Bar Assn., Hamilton County Trustees and Clks. Assn., Phi Kappa Theta. Republican. Home: 3153 Mcgill Ln Cincinnati OH 45251-3111

BLEUSTEIN, JEFFREY L., motorcycle company executive; b. 1939; BS in Mech. Engring., Cornell U.; MS in Engring. Mechanics, PhD in Engring. Mechanics, Columbia U. Assoc. prof. engring. & applied sciences. Yale U., 1966—71; mem., ctrl tech. staff AMF, Inc., 1971; with Harley-Davidson Inc., Milw., 1975—, pres., Trihawk, Inc., 1984—85, v.p. parts and accessories divsn., 1985—88, exec. v.p., 1990—93, pres., COO, 1993—97, pres., CEO, 1997—98, chmn., CEO, 1998—2005, chmn., 2005—. Mem. bd. dirs. Harley Davidson Inc., 1996—, Brunswick Corp., 1997—, The Kohler Corp., 2003—; mem. Pres. Coun. on 21st Century Workplace US Dept. Labor, 2002—03. Mem. bd. dirs. Greater Milw. Com., Milw. Jewish Fedn., Milw. Florentine Opera, Med. Coll Wis.; regent emeritus Milw. Sch. Engring. Office: Harley Davidson Inc 3700 W Juneau Ave Milwaukee WI 53208

BLEVEANS, JOHN, lawyer; b. Danville, Ill., Mar. 29, 1938; s. Edward Harold and Angelita (Robinson) B.; m. Luanna Harrison Burdick, Aug. 17, 1962; children: Lincoln Edward, Melanie Catherine. BA, Trinity U., 1960; LLB, U. Tex., 1965. Bar: Tex. 1965, D.C. 1967, U.S. Supreme Ct. 1969, Ill. 1971. Mem. gen. counsel's office Acacia Mut. Life Ins. Co., Washington, 1967-68; trial and appellate atty., civil rights div. U.S. Dept. Justice, Washington, 1966-67, 69-70; exec. dir. Washington Lawyers' Com., Civil Rights Under Law, 1970-71; chief counsel Lawyers' Com., Civil Rights Under Law, Cairo, Ill., 1971-72; assoc. Mayer, Brown & Platt, Chgo., 1972-74, ptnr., 1974-83, 91-92; sr. v.p., assoc., gen. counsel Continental Ill. Nat. Bank and Trust Co. of Chgo., 1983-89; dep. gen. counsel Continental Bank N.A., Chgo., 1989-91; ptnr. Mayer, Brown & Platt, Chgo., 1991-92; of counsel Arthur Andersen & Co., Chgo., 1992-95, Hong Kong, 1996-97, Sydney, Australia, 1995-96. Tour guide Tri State Travel, Galena, Ill., 2002—, bus driver; pres. Hanover Ambulance, Inc., 2000-03, treas. 2006-07. Alderman City of Evanston, Ill., 1981-89; chmn. Evanston Zoning Bd. Appeals, 1991-92; vol. Hanover Ambulance, 1999—. Capt. USNR ret. Mem. Tex. Bar Assn., D.C. Bar Assn., Nat. Ski Patrol, Law Club Chgo. Home: 8634 Fisher Rd Hanover IL 61041-9561 E-mail: jakeb@netexpress.net.

BLEVINS, DALE GLENN, agronomy educator; b. Ozark, Mo., Aug. 29, 1943; 1 child, Jeremy. BS in Chemistry, S.W. Mo. State U., 1965; MS in Soils, U. Mo., 1967; PhD in Plant Physiology, U. Ky., 1972. Postdoctoral fellow botany dept. Oreg. State U., Corvallis, Oreg., 1972-74; asst. prof. botany U. Md., College Park, 1974-78; assoc. prof. agronomy dept. U. Mo., Columbia, 1978-86, prof., 1986—. Mem. Am. Soc. Plant Physiology, Am. Soc. Agronomy, Crop Sci. Soc. Am. Office: Univ Mo Divsn Plant Scis 1-31 Agriculture Building Columbia MO 65211-7140

BLEZNICK, DONALD WILLIAM, Romance languages educator; b. NYC, Dec. 24, 1924; s. Louis and Gertrude (Kleinman) B.; m. Rozlyn Burakoff, June 15, 1952; children— Jordan, Susan. BA, CCNY, 1946; MA, U. Nacional de Mex., 1948; PhD, Columbia U., 1954. Instr. romance langs. Ohio State U., 1949-55; prof. Pa. State U., 1955-67, U. Cin., 1967—, head dept., 1967-72. Vis. prof. Hebrew U., Jerusalem, 1974. Bibliographer, MLA Internat. Bibliography, 1966-81; rev. editor Hispania, 1965-73, editor-in-chief, 1974-83, editor's adv. coun., 1984—, El Ensayo Espanol del Siglo Veinte, 1964, Historia del Ensayo Espanol, 1962, Duelo en el Paraiso (Goytisolo), 1967, Madrugada (Buero Vallejo), 1969, (with W.T. Pattison) Representative Spanish Authors, 1971, Quevedo, 1972, Variaciones interpretativas en torno a la nueva narrativa hispanoamericana, 1972, Directions of Literary Criticism in the Seventies, 1972, Sourcebook for Hispanic Literature and Language, 1974, 3d expanded edit., 1995, Homenaje a Luis Leal, 1978, Studies on Don Quixote and other Cervantine Works, 1984, Critical Edition of La Diana (Jorge de Montemayor), 1990, The Thought of Contemporary Spanish Essayists, 1993, Studies in Honor of Donald W. Bleznick, 1995; translator (from Spanish and Portuguese) Identity in Dispersion: Selected Memoirs from Latin American Jews, 2000, History of the University of Cincinnati Faculty Council on Jewish Affairs, 2004; founder, exec. editor Cin. Romance Rev., 1982-88; field editor: Twayne Spanish Literature Series, 1981—; contbr. articles to profl. jours., Ency. Americana. With US Army CIC, 1946-47. Decorated Knight's Cross Order Civil Merit (Spain); Am. Philos. Soc. rsch. grantee, 1964; Downer fellow CCNY, 1947-48; U. Cin. Taft rsch. and publ. grantee, 1972, 75, 78, 83, 88, 89, 92; named 1 of 15 outstanding scholars in Spanish lit. in Cuadernos Salmantinos de Filosofia, Salamanca, Spain, 1977; recipient Rieveschl award for excellence in rsch. U. Cin., 1980, award Hispania, U. So. Calif., 1983; fellow U. Cin. Grad. Sch., 1984. Mem. AAUP, Am. Assn. Tchrs. Spanish and Portuguese (exec. com. 1975—, award 1984, v.p. 1992, pres. 1993, Honored for Outstanding Career 1995, disting. svc. award 1997), MLA, Los Ensayistas (adv. bd. 1976—), Comediantes, Midwest Modern Lang. Assn., Conf. Editors of Learned Jours. (exec. com. 1978-79), Celestinesca, Cervantes Soc. Am., Phi Beta Kappa (pres. Delta chpt. of Ohio 1971-72, 86-87), Sigma Delta Pi (state dir. Ohio 1968-74, Order of Don Quijote 1970, v.p. Midwest 1975-83, Jose Martel award 1980, hon. pres. 1998-), Phi Sigma Iota, Kappa Delta Pi. Home: 2444 Madison Rd Apt 1806 Cincinnati OH 45208-1255 Office: U Cin Dept Romance Langs Cincinnati OH 45221-0001 E-mail: donald.bleznick@uc.edu.

BLICKENSDERFER, MATTHEW C., lawyer; b. Tuscola, Ill., July 16, 1970; BA, Northwestern U., 1992; JD, Harvard U., 1995. Bar: Ill. 1995, US Dist. Ct. Northern Dist. Ill. 1995, US Ct. of Appeals Sixth Cir. 1996, US Ct. of Appeals Seventh Cir. 1999, US Dist. Ct. Southern Dist. Ohio 2001, US Dist. Ct. Eastern Dist. Mich. 2002, US Supreme Ct. 2003. Law clerk US Ct. of Appeals Sixth Cir., 1996—97; adj. prof. U. Cin. Coll. Law, 2002—06; editor-in-chief Sixth Cir. Practice Manual, Third Edition, 2006; atty. Frost Brown Todd LLC, Cin. Named Cin. Leading Lawyer, Cincy Bus. mag., 2006; named one of Ohio's Rising Stars, Super Lawyers, 2005, 2006. Office: Frost Brown Todd LLC 2200 PNC Ctr 201 E 5th St Cincinnati OH 45202-4182 Office Phone: 513-651-6162. Office Fax: 513-651-6981.

BLINDER, SEYMOUR MICHAEL, chemistry and physics professor, researcher; b. NYC, Mar. 11, 1932; s. Morris and Ida (Styszynskaya) B.; m. Frances Ellen Bryant, July 8, 1978; children: Michael Ian, Stephen Earl, Matthew Bryant, Amy Rebecca, Sarah Jane. AB, Cornell U., 1953; MA, Harvard U., 1955, PhD, 1958. Sr. physicist Applied Physics Lab., Johns Hopkins U., 1958-61; asst. prof. chemistry Carnegie Inst. Tech., 1961-62; vis. prof. Harvard U., 1962-63; prof. chemistry and physics U. Mich., 1963—95, prof. emeritus, 1995—. Author: Advanced Physical Chemistry, 1969, Foundations of Quantum Dynamics, 1974, Introduction to Quantum Mechanics in Chemistry, Materials Science and Biology, 2004; Mem. bd. editors: Jour. Am. Chem. Soc., 1978-80; contbr. rsch. articles to profl. jours. Guggenheim fellow, 1965-66; NSF sr. postdoctoral fellow, 1970-71 Mem. AAAS, Am. Phys. Soc., Philos. Soc. Washington, Phi Beta Kappa. Home: 1240 Ferdon Rd Ann Arbor MI 48104-3635 Office: U Mich Dept Chemistry Ann Arbor MI 48109-1055 Business E-Mail: sblinder@umich.edu.

BLOCH, HENRY WOLLMAN, diversified financial services company executive; b. Kansas City, Mo., July 30, 1922; s. Leon Edwin and Hortense Bienenstok; m. Marion Ruth Helzberg, June 16, 1951; children: Robert, Thomas M., Mary Jo, Elizabeth Ann. BS, U. Mich., 1944; D of Bus. Adminstrn. (hon.), Avila Coll., Kansas City, Mo., 1977, U. Mo., Kansas City, 1989; LLD (hon.), N.H. Coll., 1983, William Jewell Coll., Liberty, Mo., 1990, Kansas City Art Inst., 1999. Ptnr. United Bus. Co., 1946-55; hon. chmn., past CEO H & R Block, Inc., Kansas City, 1955—, also dir. Bd. dirs. Commerce Bancshares, Inc., Kansas City, CompuServe, Inc., Valentine Radford Advt.; past chmn. Midwest Rsch. Inst. Past bd. dirs. Menorah Med. Ctr.; bd. dirs., past pres. Menorah Med. Ctr. Found.; former mem. pres.'s adv. coun. Kansas City Philharmonic Assn.; chmn., dir. H & R Block Found.; past pres. of trustees U. Kansas City, Nelson-Atkins Mus. Art, trustee, dir., past chmn. bus. coun.; past bd. dirs. Jewish Fedn. and Coun. Greater Kansas City; dir., past pres. Civic Coun. Greater Kansas City; gen. chmn. United Negro Colls. Fund, 1986; bd. dirs. St. Luke's Hosp. Found., Internat. Rels. Coun., Kansas City Cmty. Found.; former mem. bd. dirs. Coun. of Fellows of Nelson Gallery Found., Am. Jewish Com.; former mem. bd. govs. Kansas City Mus. History and Sci.; bd. dirs. Midwest Rsch. Inst., vice chmn.; bd. dirs. Kansas City Symphony, past dir.; bd. dirs. Greater Kansas City Community Found.; gen. chmn. Heart of Am. United Way Exec. Com., 1978; past met. chmn. Nat. Alliance Businessmen; former mem. bd. regents Rockhurst Coll.; former mem. bd. chancellor's assocs. U. Kans. at Lawrence; former mem. bd. dirs. Harry S. Truman Good Neighbor Award Found.; bd. dirs. Internat. Rels. Coun.; bd. dirs., v.p. Kansas City Area Health Planning Coun.; past pres. Found. for a Greater Kansas City; dir. Mid-Am. Coalition on Health Care, St; Luke's Found.; trustee Jr. Achievement of Mid-Am.; vice chmn. corp. fund Kennedy Ctr. 1st lt. USAAF, 1943-45. Decorated Air medal with 3 oak leaf clusters; named Mktg. Man of Yr. Sales and Mktg. Execs. Club, 1971, Chief Exec. Officer of Yr. for svc. industry Fin. World, 1976, Mainstreeter of Decade, 1988, Entrepreneur of Yr., 1986; recipient Disting. Exec. award Boy Scouts Am., 1977, Salesman of Yr. Kansas City Advt. Club, 1978, Civic Svc. award Hyman Brand Hebrew Acad., 1980, Golden Plate award Am. Acad. Achievement, 1980, Chancellor's medal U. Mo.-Kansas City, 1980, Pres.'s trophy Kansas City Jaycees, 1980, W.F. Yates medal for disting. svc. in civic affairs William Jewell Coll., 1981, bronze award for svc. industry Wall Street Transcript, 1981, Disting. Missourian award NCCJ, 1982, Lester A. Milgram Humanitarian award, 1983, Hall of Fame award Internat. Franchise Assn., 1983; named to Bus. Leader Hall of Fame Jr. Achievement, 1980; honoree Sales and Mktg. Execs. Internat. Acad. of Achievement, 1991. Mem. Greater Kansas City C. of C. (past pres.), C. of C. Greater Kansas City (Mr. Kansas City award 1978), Acad. Squires, Golden Key Nat. Honor Soc. (hon.), Oakwood Country Club, River Club, Carriage Club, Kansas City Country Club. Jewish. Office: H&R Block Inc 4400 Main St Kansas City MO 64111-1812

BLOCH, RALPH JAY, professional association executive, marketing consultant; b. NYC, Sept. 21, 1942; s. Alexander and Catherine (La Bue) B.; m. Patricia Ann Cassone, Aug. 18, 1963 (div.); 1 child, Marci Suzanne; m. Helen Lightstone, June 19, 1988. BS, UCLA, 1965. Sales rep. Lowell Wood Co., LA, 1967-68; mgr. Home Furniture, LA, 1968-72, co-owner, gen. mgr., 1972-78; pres. Concepts III, Inc., Greenville, S.C., 1978-79; from western exec. v.p. to mktg. v.p. Nat. Home Furnishings Assn., 1979-83; pres., owner The Access Group, Inc., Chgo., 1984-99, Ralph J. Bloch & Assocs., Inc., Chgo., 1999—. Mem. Chgo. Soc. Assn. Execs., Am. Soc. Assn. Execs. Avocations: backpacking, hiking, sailing, cooking. Office: Ralph J Bloch & Assocs Inc Apt 7A 1430 N Astor St Chicago IL 60610-5717

BLOCK, ALLAN JAMES, communications executive; b. Oct. 1, 1954; s. Paul Jr. and Marjorie (McNab) B. BA, U. Pa., 1977. Coord. electronic tech. planning Toledo Blade Co., 1981-83, dir. electronic planning, 1984-85; dir. mktg. Buckeye Cablevision Inc., Toledo, 1985-87; v.p. cablevision and TV Blade Communications, Inc., Toledo, 1987-88, exec. v.p., 1989; co-CEO Blade Comm., Inc., Toledo, 1989—; vice-chmn. bd. Block Comm., Inc. (formerly known as Blade Comm., Inc.), Toledo, 1990—2001, mng. dir., prin. exec. officer, 2002—04, chmn. bd., prin. exec. officer, 2005—. Bd. dirs. Toledo Blade Co., P.G. Pub. Co., Buckeye Cablevision Inc. Bd. dirs. C-SPAN, Med. Coll. Ohio, 1991-2000, Nat. Cable TV Coop., Inc., 2000-03, Am. Cable Assn., 2002—. Mem. Toledo Club, Met. Club (N.Y.C.), Penn Club (N.Y.C.), Downtown Assn. (N.Y.C.), Duquesne Club (Pitts.), Inverness Club. Home: 235 14th St Toledo OH 43624-1401 Office: 6450 Monroe St Sylvania OH 43560 Home Phone: 419-242-6739; Office Phone: 419-724-6035. Business E-Mail: ABlock@blockcommunications.com.

BLOCK, JANICE L., lawyer; BA magna cum laude, Princeton U.; MS in Journalism, Northwestern U.; JD, Columbia U. Ctrl. regional counsel Microsoft Corp., 1998—2002, cons., 2002—04; ptnr. Tech., Telecommunications and Media Group Greenberg Traurig, LLP, Chgo., 2004—05; sr. v.p., gen. counsel, sec. Career Edn. Corp., Hoffman Estates, Ill., 2005—. Office: Career Edn Corp Ste 600 2895 Greenspoint Parkway Hoffman Estates IL 60169

BLOCK, JOHN ROBINSON, newspaper publisher, editor-in-chief; b. Toledo, Oct. 1, 1954; s. Paul Jr. and Marjorie Jane (McNab) B.; m. Susan Lynn Jones, July 20, 2002; 1 child Caroline McNab Jones Block. BA, Yale U., 1977. Reporter AP, Miami, Fla., 1977-78, NYC, 1978-80; Washington corr. The Toledo Blade, 1980-82, European corr. London, 1982-83, Sunday editor, 1983-85, asst. mng. editor, 1985-87, exec. editor, 1987-89; co-pub., editor-in-chief The Blade, Toledo, 1989—2001; co-pub. Pitts. Post-Gazette, 1989—2001, editor-in-chief, 1993—, pub., 2001—, The Blade and Pitts Post-Gazette, 2001; v.p., bd. dirs. P.G. Pub. Co., Pitts. Vice chmn., bd. dirs. Block comms., Inc., Toledo. Chmn. City Mgr.'s Hist. Preservation Com., Toledo, 1983-85; chmn. airport com. Toledo-Lucas County Port Authority, 1994-97. Mem. Am. Soc. Newspaper Editors, Soc. Profl. Journalists, Internat. Press Inst., Nat. Press Club (Washington), Yale Club (NYC), Belmont Country Club (Perrysburg, Ohio), Grolier Club (NYC), Duquesne Club (Pitts.), Athletic Club (Columbus, Ohio), Rockwell Springs Trout Club (Castalia, Ohio), Golf Club (Pitts.). Avocations: flying, book collecting. Home: 725 Devonshire St Pittsburgh PA 15213-2905 Office: The Blade 541 N Superior St Toledo OH 43697-0921 also: Pitts Post-Gazette 34 Blvd Of The Allies Pittsburgh PA 15222-1204*

BLOCK, NEAL JAY, lawyer; b. Chgo., Oct. 4, 1942; s. William Emmanual and Dorothy (Harrison) Block; m. Frances Keer, Apr. 19, 1970; children: Jessica, Andrew. BS, U. Ill., 1964; JD, U. Chgo., 1967. Bar: Ill. 1967, U.S. Dist. Ct. (no. dist.) Ill. 1967, U.S. Ct. Appeals (3d and 6th cirs.) 1968, U.S. Claims Ct. 1990, U.S. Ct. Appeals (fed. cir.) 1991. Atty., advisor U.S. Tax Ct., Washington, 1967-69; assoc. Baker & McKenzie, Chgo., 1969-74, ptnr., 1974—, client credit dir., 1989—2002. Adj. prof. law Kent Law Sch., Ill. Inst. Tech., Chgo., 1986—90. Mem.: AICPA (honorable mention award 1964), ABA, Ill. Soc. CPAs (silver medal 1964, Leading Ill. Atty. 1997), Ill. State Bar Assn., Chgo. Bar Assn. (chmn. fed. tax com. 1983—84). Office: Baker & McKenzie 1 Prudential Pla 130 E Randolph St Ste 3500 Chicago IL 60601-6342 E-mail: neal.j.block@bakernet.com.

BLOCK, PHILIP DEE, III, retired investment company executive; b. Chgo., Feb. 14, 1937; married; 2 children. BS in Indsl. Adminstrn. with high honors, Yale U., 1958. Trainee and engr. Inland Steel Co., Chgo., 1958-60, raw materials coordinator, 1961-65, gen. mgr. purchases, 1966-72, gen. mgr. corp. planning, 1973-76, v.p. materials and services, 1977-79, v.p. purchases, 1980-85; sr. v.p. Capital Guardian Trust Co., Chgo., 1986—2004; ret., 2004. Trustee Chgo. Hist. Mus., Shedd Aquarium Soc.; alumni trustee Latin Sch. of Chgo., 2005—; bd. dirs. Children's Meml. Hosp. With USAFR, 1959—64. Home: 1430 N Lake Shore Dr Chicago IL 60610-6682

BLOCK, WILLIAM K., JR., media executive; b. New Haven, Nov. 28, 1944; s. William and Maxine (Horton) B.; m. Carol Pauline Zurheide, Aug. 1, 1970; children: Diana, ancy, Katherine. BA, Trinity Coll., Hartford, Conn., 1967; JD, Washington and Lee U., 1972. Staff mem. Red Bank (N.J.) Register and Toledo Blade, 1972-77; advtg. mgr. Red Bank (N.J.) Register, Shrewsbury, NJ, 1977-79, sales mgr., 1979-80, pub., 1980-82; dir. ops. Toledo Blade Co., 1983-84, v.p. ops., 1984-86, v.p., gen. mgr., 1986-87, pres., 1987—, co-pub., 1990—, Pitts. Post Gazette, 1990—; v.p. Block Com., Inc., Toledo, 1987-88, pres., 1989—2001, chmn., 2002—. V.p. Toledo Sesquicentennial Commn., 1986-87; pres. Inland Press Assn., 1998-99; bd. dirs. Toledo Symphony, St. Luke's Hosp., Ohio Hist. Soc.; pres. Read for Literacy, Inc., 1989-2001; campaign chmn. United Way of Greater Toledo, 2003. With U.S. Army, Vietnam, 1968-70. Mem. Toledo Country Club, Toledo Club. Avocations: reading, travel, fishing. Office: Block Communications Inc 541 N Superior St Toledo OH 43660-0001

BLOM, DAVE, healthcare industry executive; married; 3 children. BS, Ohio State U.; MS in healthcare adminstrn., The George Wash. U. Asst. adminstr. Holden (Mass.) Hosp.; adminstr. Joel Pomerene Meml. Hosp., Millersburg, Ohio; pres. and CEO Grant Med. Ctr.; exec. v.p. and COO OhioHealth; pres. Columbus OhioHealth, 1998—, OhioHealth, 1999—, CEO, 2002—. Office: Ohio Health Sleep Services 7634 Rivers Edge Dr Columbus OH 43235-1329

BLOMQUIST, DAVID WELS, journalist; b. Detroit, June 16, 1956; s. August Wels and Sally Lou (Ball) B. AB, U. Mich., 1976; AM, Harvard U., 1978. Tchg. fellow Harvard U., Cambridge, 1978-82, asst. sr. tutor, 1981-82; supervising sect. editor CBS Inc., NYC, 1982-84; staff writer The Record of Hackensack, N.J., 1984-86, state polit. corr. N.J., 1986-89, chief polit. writer N.J., 1990-92, chief Trenton bur. N.J., 1992-94; dir. The Record Poll, Hackensack, 1992-99, dir. online devel., 1998-99; dir. new media Detroit Free Press, 1999—2001, sr. editor tech. and rsch., 2002—. Author: Elections and the Mass Media, 1982; contbr. articles to profl. jours. Mem. Am. Polit. Sci. Assn. (edn. com. 1984-86), N.J. Legis. Corrs. Club (pres. 1992), Harvard Club of N.Y., Nat. Press Club Washington. Avocations: music, ballet. Office: Detroit Free Press 600 W Fort St Detroit MI 48226-2706 E-mail: blomquist@freepress.com.

BLOOM, JANE MAGINNIS, emergency physician; b. Ithaca, NY, June 22, 1924; d. Ernest Victor and Miriam Rebecca (Mansfield) M.; m. William Lee Bloom, Mar. 31, 1944; children: David Lee, Jan Christopher, Carolyn Wells, Eric Paul, Joseph William, Robert Carl, Mary Catherine, Thomas Mark, Patrick Martin (dec.), Arthur Emerson. BS, U. Mich., 1968, MD, 1974. Diplomate Am. Bd. Internal Medicine, cert. in emergency medicine 2004. Rotating intern Wayne County Gen. Hosp., Eloise, Mich., 1974—75; resident in internal medicine St. Mary's Hosp., Rochester, NY, 1975-77; emergency physician Emergency Physicians Med. Group, Ann Arbor, 1986—2003. Fellow: Am. Coll. Emergency Physicians (life); mem.: AMA, Mich. State Med. Soc., Am. Coll. Physicians, Am. Med. Womens Assn., Am. Assn. Women Emergency Physicians, Washtenaw County Med. Soc. Avocations: bird watching, planting trees, classical music, walking. Home and Office: 537 Elm St Ann Arbor MI 48104-2515 Office Phone: 734-761-2435. Personal E-mail: jbmdfacep@aol.com.

BLOOM, STEPHEN JOEL, distribution company executive; b. Chgo., Feb. 27, 1936; s. Max Samuel and Carolyn (Gumbiner) B.; m. Nancy Lee Gillan, Aug. 24, 1957; children: Anne, Bradley, Thomas, Carolyn. BBA, U. Mich., 1958. From salesman to gen. mgr. Cigarette Svc. Co., Countryside, Ill., 1957-65, pres., CEO, 1965—; exec. v.p., CEO S. Bloom, Inc., Countryside; v.p., then sr. v.p. Philip Morris USA, now ret. Bd. dirs. Amerimark Fin. Corp. Active Chgo. Crime Commn. Named Man of Yr. Chgo. Tobacco Table, 1972; named to Tobacco Industry Hall of Fame, 1985. Mem. Nat. Automatic Mdsg. Assn. (Minuteman award 1974), Nat. Assn. Tobacco Distbrs. (chmn. nat. legis. com. Young Exec. of Yr. award, dir. 1978), Ill. Assn. Tobacco Distbrs., Young Pres. Orgn., Chgo. Pres. Orgn., Morningside Rancho Mirage Club (pres. 1996-97), Rotary. Lodges: Rotary. Home: 3 Hamill Ln Clarendon Hills IL 60514-1462 Office: 120 Park Ave New York NY 10017

BLOOMER, WILLIAM DAVID, radiologist, oncologist, educator; b. Aug. 19, 1944; s. Ward LaVern and Vera Catherine (Rochefort) B.; m. Lauren S. Taslitz, Aug. 10, 1986; children: Whitney Dana, Brian Andrew, Gregory Stewart. AB, U. Pa., 1966; MD, Jefferson Med. Coll., Phila., 1970. Diplomate Am. Bd. Radiology, Am. Bd. uclear Medicine. Intern Univ. Hosps., Cleve., 1970-71; clin. fellow in radiation therapy Harvard U. Med. Sch., Boston, 1971-74, instr., 1974-76, asst. prof., 1976-80, assoc. prof., 1980-83; rsch. mem. Harvard MIT Divsn. Health Scis. and Tech., Boston, 1978-83; mem. sr. common room Lowell House Harvard Coll., Boston, 1983-87; dir. radiotherapy, radiotherapist-in-chief Mt. Sinai Hosp., NYC, 1983-87; prof., chmn. dept. radiation oncology U. Pitts. Sch. Medicine, 1987-92; dir. Joint Radiation Oncology Ctr., 1987-92; dir. radiation oncology Presbyn. U. Hosp., Magee-Women's Hosp., Shadyside Hosp., 1987-92; assoc. dir. Pitts. Cancer Inst., 1987-92; pres. U. Radiotherapy Assocs., Inc., 1989-92; sr. lectr. engring. in medicine Carnegie Mellon U., 1989-92; chmn. radiation medicine Evanston Northwestern Healthcare, 1992—. Prof. radiology Northwestern U. Med. Sch., 1992—, pres. Radiation Medicine Inst., 1992—; dir. radiation oncology svcs. Condell Med. Ctr., 2004—. Contbr. articles to profl. jours. Mem. AAAS, Am. Coll. Radiology, Am. Soc. Therapeutic Radiologists, Soc. Nuclear Medicine, Am. Assn. Cancer Rsch., Am. Soc. Clin. Oncology, Am. Coll. Radiation Oncology (Gold medal 1998). Office: Evanston Northwestern Healthcare 2650 Ridge Ave Evanston IL 60201-1718

BLOOMFIELD, CLARA DERBER, oncologist, educator, medical institute administrator; b. Flushing, L.I., NY, May 15, 1942; d. Milton and Zelda (Trenner) Derber; m. Victor A. Bloomfield, June 11, 1962 (div. 1983); m. Albert de la Chapelle, Jan. 1, 1984. Student, U. Wis., 1959-62; BA, San Diego State U., 1963; MD, U. Chgo., 1968. Diplomate Am. Bd. Internal Medicine, Nat. Bd. Med. Examiners. Intern in medicine U. Chgo. Hosps. and Clinics, 1968-69, resident internal medicine, 1969-70, U. Minn., Mpls., 1970-71, med. oncology fellow, 1971-73, chief resident in medicine, Jan.-June, 1972, instr., 1972-73, asst. prof. medicine, 1973-76, assoc. prof., 1976-80, prof. medicine div. oncology, 1980-89, dir. fellowship program med. concology, 1987—89, mem. univ. senate, 1986-89, mem. all univ. Commn. on Women, 1988-89; prof. medicine, chief div. oncology SUNY, Buffalo, 1989—97; head dept. medicine Roswell Pk. Cancer Inst., Buffalo, 1989—97; William G. Pace III prof. cancer research Ohio State U. Coll. Med. & Pub. Health, 1997—, dir., div. hematology & oncology, dept. Internal Medicine, 1997—. Mem. Kettering selection com. GM Cancer Rsch. Found., 1986-87; cons. Office Tech. Assessment, U.S. Congress, 1988; participant, chair various coms. Internat. Human Gene Mapping Workshops, Helsinki, Finland, 1985, France, 1987, Internat. Workshops Chromosomes in Leukemia, Lund, Sweden, 1980, Chgo., 1982, Tokyo, 1984, London, 1987, Buffalo, 1991; mem. nat. and sci. adv. bds. NIH, 1977—, mem. bd. sci. counselors divsn. cancer treatment, 1991—, organizer Internat. Hodgkins Disease Symposium, 1981; bd. dirs. cancer and leukemia group B, 1982—, mem. other coms., 1973— sponsored clin. trial groups, Nat. Cancer Inst., cons. S.W. oncology group; mem. nat. and sci. adv. bd. Don and Sybil Harrington Cancer Ctr., Amarillo, Tex., 1979—, Med. Coll. Pa., 1988—; bd. trustees Berlex Oncology Found., 1992—; vis. prof. dept. medicine W.Va. U., 1973, U. Ariz., Tucson, 1979, U. Fla., Gainesville, 1979, Emory U., Atlanta, 1980, U. Chgo., 1982, George Washington U., Washington, 1982, U. Tex., San Antonio, 1982, Brown U., Providence, 1982, Mayo Clinic, Rochester, Minn., 1982, U. Zurich, Switzerland, 1983, U. P.R., 1984, U. Witwatersand, S. Africa, 1984, Nihon U., Tokyo, 1984, Leukemia Soc. Mass., 1991; frequent invited speaker, guest lectr. symposia, workshops, continuing edn. courses, seminars, med. congresses, univs. in U.S., Europe, S. Am., Scandinavia, Eng., Japan, Republic of South Africa, New Zealand. Author: (with others) Recent Advances in Bone Marrow Transplantation, Vol. VII, 1983, New Prespectives in Human Lymphoma, 1984, Neoplastic Diseases of the Blood, 1985, Current Therapy in Hematology/Oncology 1984-85, 1985, Medical Genetics: Past, Present, Future, 1985, Directions in Oncology, Vol. 1, 1985, Medical Oncology, Basic Principles and Clinical Management of Cancer, 1985, Tumor Aneuploidy, 1985, Malignant Lymphomas and Hodgkins Disease: Experimental and Therapeutic Advances, 1985, Current Therapy in Internal Medicine, 1987, Genetic Maps, Vol. 4, 1987; contbr. over 250 articles, abstracts to profl. jours.; editor ann. Adult Leukemia series in Cancer Treatment and Rsch., 1979-85; cons. editor Leukemia and Lymphoma Yearbook of Cancer, 1980—; assoc. editor Cancer Rsch., 1981-88, editor, 91, Leukemia Rsch., 1984-87, Leukemia, 1987-89; mem. editorial bd. Jour. Clin. Oncology, 1983-88, Cancer Genetics and Cytogenetics, 1983-87, Directions in Oncology, 1984-86, Cancer Rsch. Bull., 1984-85, Med. and Pediatric Oncology, 1987—, Blood, 1988—, Annals of Medicine, 1989—, Seminars in Oncology, 1989—; editorial bd. Am. Jour. Hematology, 1985, assoc. editor, 1988—; reviewer 23 med. jours. Recipient Nat. Bd. award Med. Coll. Pa., 1981, Past State Pres.' Bus. and Profl. Women award U. Tex. System Cancer Ctr., M.D. Anderson Hosp. and Tumor Clinic, Houston, 1987, Joseph H. Burchenal Clinical Rsch. award, Am. Assn. Cancer Rsch., 2004; prin. or co-prin. investigator 8 grants, NIH, 1975—, also ACS, 1980-84, Minn. State Spl. Coleman Leukemia Rsch. Fund, 1981-89, Coleman Leukemia Rsch. Fund Endowment, 1981—, Baltzar W.A. von Platen Found., 1984-85, Genentech/Hoffman -LaRoche, 1988—. Mem. ACP, AAAS, Am. Assn. Cancer Rsch., Am. Soc. Hematology, Am. Soc. Clin. Oncology (bd. dirs. 1991—), Am. Fedn. Clin. Rsch., Cen. Soc. Clin. Rsch., N.Y. Acad. Scis., Inst. Medicine, Internat. Assn. Comparative Rsch. Leukemia and Related Diseases, Med. Soc. Finland (external mem.), Phi Beta Kappa, Alpha Omega Alpha, Sigma Delta Epsilon. Office: Comprehensive Cancer Ctr 320 W 10th Ave Columbus OH 43210

BLOSSER, HENRY GABRIEL, physicist; b. Harrisonburg, Va., Mar. 16, 1928; s. Emanuel and Leona (Branum) B.; m. Priscilla May Beard, June 30, 1951 (div. Oct. 1972); children: William Henry, Stephan Emanuel, Gabe Fawley, Mary Margaret; m. Mary Margaret Gray, Mar. 16, 1973 (dec. Jan. 1995); m. Amy June Conley, May 11, 1995 (div. Feb. 1997); m. Lois Pearlena Lynch, Oct. 17, 1998. BS, U. Va., 1951, MS, 1952, PhD, 1954. Physicist Oak Ridge (Tenn.) Nat. Lab., 1954-56, group leader, 1956-68; assoc. prof. physics Mich. State U., East Lansing, 1958-61, prof., 1961-90, Univ. Disting. prof., 1990—, dir. Cyclotron Lab., 1961-89. Cons. Harper Hosp., Detroit, 1983—, Ion Beam Applications, Belgium, 1996—, others; adj. prof. radiation oncology Wayne State U., Detroit, 1996—. Bd. dirs. Midwest Univs. Rsch. Assocs., 1960-63. With USNR, 1946-48. Predoctoral fellow NSF, 1953-54, sr. postdoctoral fellow, 1966-67; Guggenheim fellow, 1973-74. Fellow Am. Phys. Soc. (Bonner prize 1992); mem. Sigma Xi, Phi Beta Kappa, Kappa Alpha. Home: 2350 Emerald Forest Cir East Lansing MI 48823-7200 Office: Mich State U Nat Cyclotron East Lansing MI 48824-1321 Business E-Mail: blosser@nscl.msu.edu.

BLOUIN, FRANCIS XAVIER, JR., history professor; b. Belmont, Mass., July 29, 1946; s. Francis X. and Margaret (Cronin) B.; m. Joy Alexander; children: Benjamin, Tiffany. AB, U. Notre Dame, 1967; MA, U. Minn., 1969, PhD, 1978. Asst. dir. Bentley Library U. Mich., Ann Arbor, 1974-75, assoc. archivist Bentley Library, 1975-81, dir. Bentley Library, 1981—, asst. prof. history and library sci., 1979-83, assoc. prof., 1983-89, prof., 1989—. Author: The Boston Region., 1980, Vatican Archives: An Inventory and Guide to Historical Documentation of the Holy See, 1998; editor: Archival Implications Machine., 1980, Intellectual Life on Michigan Frontier, 1985, Archives Documentation and Institutions of Social Memory, 2006. Trustee Much. Student Found., 1986-91; dir. Am. Friends of Vatican Libr., 1981—, Coun. on Libr. and Info. Resources, 2001—. Fellow Soc. Am. Archivist (mem. governing council 1985-88); mem. Am. Hist. Assn., Hist. Soc. Mich. (trustee 1982-88, pres. 1987-88), Assn. Records Mgrs. and Adminstrs., Internat. Council on Archives. Office: U Mich Bentley Hist Libr 1150 Beal Ave Ann Arbor MI 48109-2113 E-mail: fblouin@umich.edu.

BLOUNT, MICHAEL EUGENE, lawyer; b. Camden, NJ, July 9, 1949; s. Floyd Eugene and Dorothy Alice (Geyer) Durham; m. Janice Lynn Brown, Aug. 22, 1969; children: Kirsten Marie, Gretchen Elizabeth. BA, U. Tex., 1971; JD, U. Houston, 1974. Bar: Tex. 1974, Ill. 1980, D.C. 1981, U.S. Ct. Appeals (D.C. cir.) 1978, U.S. Ct. Mil. Appeals 1975, U.S. Supreme Ct. 1977. Atty. advisor Office of Gen. Counsel SEC, Washington, 1977-78, legal asst. to chmn., 1978-79; assoc. Gardner, Carton & Douglas, Chgo., 1980-84; ptnr. Arnstein, Gluck, Lehr, Barron & Milligan, Chgo., 1984-86, Seyfarth Shaw LLP, Chgo., 1987—. Lt. JAGC USN, 1974—77. Mem.: ABA (fed. regulation of securities com.), Internat. Bar Assn., Chgo. Bar Assn., Order of Barons, Assn. SEC Alumni, Univ. Club (Chgo.), Phi Alpha Delta (chpt. treas. 1973). Home: 1711 Galloway Dr Inverness IL 60010-5737 Office: Seyfarth Shaw LLP 131 S Dearborn St Ste 2400 Chicago IL 60603-5577 Home Phone: 847-991-9830; Office Phone: 312-460-5962. E-mail: mblount@seyfarth.com.

BLUESTEIN, VENUS WELLER, retired psychologist, educator; b. Milw., July 16, 1933; d. Richard T. and Hazel (Beard) Weller; m. Marvin Bluestein, Mar. 7, 1954. BS, U. Cin., 1956, MEd, 1959, EdD, 1966. Diplomate Am. Bd. Profl. Psychology. Psychologist-in-tng. Longview State Hosp., Cin., 1956-58; sch. psychologist Cin. Pub. Schs., 1958-65; asst. prof. psychology U. Cin., 1965-70, assoc. prof., 1970-79, prof., 1979-93, prof. emerita, 1993—, dir. sch. psychology program, 1965-70, co-dir. sch. psychology program, 1970-75, dir. undergrad. studies, 1976-91, dir. undergrad. advising, 1991-93. Cons. child psychologist. Sec., U.S. exec. com. rsch. Children's Internat. Summer Villages, 1964—68; chmn. Ohio Interuniv. Coun. Sch. Psychology, 1967. Editor Ohio Psychologist, 1961-68, co-editor, 1972-79; contbr. articles to profl. publs. Vol. Hamilton County Parks, 1982—, vol. naturalist, 1995—; vol. educator Cin. Zoo, 1982— Recipient George B. Barbour award, 1985, 20 Yrs. of Svc. award Cin. Zoo, 2002, Hamilton County Parks Dist., 2002. Mem. AAUP, APA, Nat. Assn. School Psychologists, Ohio Psychol. Assn. (citation 1972, Disting. Svc. award 1968), Southwestern Ohio Sch. Psychol. Assn., Cin. Psychol. Assn. (sec. 1961-62), Sch. Psychologists Ohio, Forum for Death Edn. and Counseling, Kappa Delta Pi, Sigma Delta Pi, Psi Chi (award for outstanding mentor 1985, award for outstanding contbns. to undergrad. psychology students 1994), mem. Norwood City Schs. Alumni Assn. (Disting. Hall Of Fame, 2007). Avocations: horseback riding, photography. Office: U Cin Dept Psychology Ml 376 Cincinnati OH 45221-0001

BLUFORD, GUION STEWART, JR., engineering company executive; b. Phila., Nov. 22, 1942; s. Guion Stewart and Harriet Lolita (Brice) B.; m. Linda M. Tull, Apr. 7, 1964; children: Guion Stewart, James Trevor. BS in Aerospace Engring., Pa. State U., 1964; grad., Squadron Officers Sch., 1971; MS in Aerospace Engring., Air Force Inst. Tech., 1974, PhD in Aerospace Engring., 1978; MBA, U. Houston, 1987; DSc (hon.), Fla. A&M U., Tallahassee, 1983, Tex. So. U, Houston, Va. State U., Petersburg, Morgan State U., Balt., Stevens Inst. Tech., Hoboken, NJ, Tuskegee U., Ala., Bowie State Coll., Md., Thomas Jefferson U., Phila., Chgo. State U., Georgian Ct. Coll., Drexel U., Phila., Kent State U., Ohio, Ctrl. State U., Wilberforce, Ohio. Commd. 2d lt. U.S. Air Force, 1965, advanced through grades to col., 1993, F-4C fighter pilot 12 Tactical Fighter Wing Cam Ranh Bay, Vietnam, 1966-67, T-38 instr. pilot 3630 Flying Tng. Wing Sheppard AFB, Wichita Falls, Tex., 1967-72; chief aerodynamics and airframe br. Air Force Flight Dynamics Lab., Wright-Patterson AFB, Dayton, Ohio, 1975-78; NASA astronaut Johnson Space Ctr., Houston, 1978-93; ret., 1993; v.p., gen. mgr. div. engring. svcs. NYMA Inc., Greenbelt, Md., 1993-97; v.p., gen. mgr. aerospace sector Fed. Data Corp., Bethesda, Md., 1997—2000; v.p. microgravity R&D ops. Northrup Grumman Info. Tech., Herndon, Va., 2000—02; pres. The Aerospace Tech. Group, 2002—. Decorated Air medal with 9 oak leaf clusters, Def. Superior Svc. medal, Legion of Merit, Air Force Commendation medal, Air Force Meritorious Svc. medal; named Black Engr. of Yr., 1991; named to Internat. Space Hall of Fame, 1997; recipient Mervin E. Gross award Air Force Inst. Tech., 1974, Disting. Nat. Scientist award Nat. Soc. Black Engrs., 1979, Group Achievement award, NASA, 1980, 1981, 1989, 2003, Nat. Intelligence medal of achievement, 1993, Space Flight medal, 1983, 1985, 1991, 1992, Def. Meritorious Svc. medal, 1989, 1992, 1993, NASA Disting. Svc. medal, 1994, NASA Exceptional Svc. medal, 1992, Disting. Alumni award, Pa. State U. Alumni Assn., 1983, Pa. Disting. Svc. medal, 1984, Disting. Alumni award, Air Force Inst. Tech., 2002, Univ. Houston, 2003. Fellow: AIAA (bd. dirs.); mem.: ENSCO (bd. dirs.), US Space Found. (bd. dirs.), Aerospace Corp. (trustee), Nat. Rsch. Coun. Aeronautics and Space Engring. Bd., Omicron Delta Kappa, Tau Beta Pi. Christian Scientist. Office: The Aerospace Tech Group PO Box 549 North Olmsted OH 44070-0549 Office Phone: 440-808-0417. Personal E-mail: gsbluford@roadrunner.com.

BLUHM, NEIL GARY, real estate company executive; b. 1938; married. BS, U. Ill.; JD, Northwestern U. CPA Ill.; bar: Ill. Ptnr. firm Mayer, Brown & Platt, Chgo., 1962-70; pres. JMB Realty Corp., Chgo., from 1970; pres., trustee JMB Realty Trust, Chgo., 1972—. Bd. dir. Chgo. Cares Inc., Urban Shopping Ctrs. Inc., 1993—2000, Northwestern U., Alzheimer's Disease & Related Disorders Assn., Whitney Mus. Am. Art; bd. trustees Art Inst. Chgo. Named one of Forbes' Richest Americans, 2006. Mem.: Bar State Ill., Real Estate Roundtable, Standard Club, Chgo. Club. Office: Urban Shopping Ctrs Inc 132 E Delaware Ste Ste 6501 Chicago IL 60611 also: JMB Realty Corporation 900 N Michigan Ave Fl 19 Chicago IL 60611-1542

BLUM, ARTHUR, social worker, educator; b. Cleve., May 25, 1926; s. Rebecca (Pivowar) Blum; m. Lenore Sharrie Secord, Dec. 26, 1954; children: Alex, Joel. AB, Western Res. U., 1950, MS in Social Adminstrn., 1952, DSW, 1960. Group worker Cleve. Jewish Community Ctr., 1952, Cleve. Child Guidance Ctr., 1954-58; project dir. Case Western Res. U., Cleve., 1958-60, prof. social work, 1960—, Grace Longwell Coyle chair, 1987—; prof. Smith Coll., Northampton, Mass., 1961-63. Cons. Bellefaire Regional Treatment Ctr., Cleve., 1962-85, City of East Cleve., 1967-70, Jewish Welfare Fedn., Cleve., 1968-72, Fedn. Cmty. Plannning, Cleve., 1976-78, others; vis. prof. Tel Aviv U., 1971-72, 79-80. Editor: Healing Through Living, 1971, Aging and Care Giving, 1990, Innovations in Practice and Service Delivery, 1999; contbr. numerous articles to profl. jours. Sgt. U.S. Army, 1945-46, with Med. Svcs. Corp, 1952-54. Recipient Outstanding Alumnus award Case Western Res. U., 1968. Mem. AAUP, Nat. Assn. Social Workers, Coun. Social Work Edn., Assn. Group Workers. Democrat. Jewish. Avocations: camping, sailing, racquetball, gardening. Office: Case Western Res U Sch Applied Social Scis Univ Circle Cleveland OH 44106

BLUM, JON H., dermatologist; b. Detroit, Aug. 9, 1944; s. David and Hedwig B.; m. Rosie Jacobs, June 25, 1967; children: Michael, Steven, Suzanne. BS, Wayne State U., 1965, MD, 1969. Diplomate Am. Bd. Dermatology. Intern Beaumont Hosp., Royal Oak, Mich., 1969-70; med. resident Henry Ford Hosp., Detroit, 1970-71, dermatology resident, 1971-74; dermatologist Farmington Hills, Mich., 1974—. Staff physician, William Beaumont Hosp.; cons., Internat. Hair Route, Mississauga, Ontario, Can., 1980—; clin. asst. prof. dermatology, Wayne State U., Detroit, 1976—. Author: (with others) Electrolysis, 1984. Mem. Am. Acad. Dermatology, Mich. Dermatology Soc., Mich. State Med. Soc., Oakland County Med. Soc. Avocation: computers. Office: 32905 W 12 Mile Rd Ste 330 Farmington Hills MI 48334-3345

BLUMBERG, AVROM AARON, physical chemistry professor; b. Albany, NY, Mar. 3, 1928; s. Samuel and Lillian Ann (Smith) B.; m. Eleanor Leah Simon, Aug. 5, 1955 (dec. Sept. 1967); 1 child, David Martin; m. Judith Anne Kohlhagen, Mar. 9, 1969; children: Susan Margaret, Jonathan Samuel. BS in Chemistry, Rensselaer Poly. Inst., 1949; PhD in Phys. Chemistry, Yale U., 1953. Fellow glass sci. Mellon Inst., Pitts., 1953-59, fellow polymer sci., 1959-63; from asst. to assoc. prof. phys. chemistry DePaul U., Chgo., 1963-75, prof., 1975—, head div. natural scis. and math., 1966-82, chmn. dept. chemistry, 1986-92. Vis. lectr. chemistry dept. U. Pitts., 1957-58; cons. in field. Author: Form and Function, 1972; contbr. articles to profl. jours. Participant scientists and speakers program Mus. Sci. and Industry, Chgo., 1985—; Dem. precinct capt., Evanston, Ill., 1970-78. Mem. Am. Chem. Soc. (speakers program Chgo. sect. 1983—), Royal Soc. Chem. London, Arms Control Assn., Sigma Xi. Jewish. Avocations: music, reading, art, travel, cooking. Home: 1240 S State St Chicago IL 60605-2405 Office: DePaul U Dept Chemistry 2320 N Kenmore Ave Chicago IL 60614-3210 Office Phone: 773-325-7345. Business E-Mail: ablumber@depaul.edu.

BLUNT, MATT (MATTHEW ROY BLUNT), governor, former state official; b. Strafford, Missouri, Nov. 20, 1970; s. Roy Blunt; m. Melanie Blunt, Mar. 1997; 1 child, William Branch. BA in History, US Naval Acad., Annapolis, Md., 1993. Mem. Mo. Gen. Assembly, 1999—2001; sec. state State of Mo., Jefferson City, 2001—05, gov., 2005—. With USN, 1993—98, lt. comdr. USNR, 1998—, engring. officer, USS Jack Williams, navigator, adminstrv. officer, USS Peterson. Decorated achievement award USN, US Marine Corps, Humanitarian Svc. Medal. Mem.: Mo. Farm Bureau, Am. Legion, State Historical Soc. Mo. Republican. Baptist. Achievements include serving in Operation Support Democracy in Haiti and in southern England in support of Operation Enduring Freedom while in the USN. Office: Office of Gov Mo Capitol Bldg Rm 216 Jefferson City MO 65101 also: PO Box 720 Jefferson City MO 65102 Office Phone: 573-751-3222. Office Fax: 573-526-3291. Business E-Mail: mogov@mail.state.mo.us.

BLUNT, ROY D., congressman; b. Niangua, Mo., Jan. 10, 1950; s. Leroy and Neva (Letterman) B.; m. Roseann Blunt (div. 2003), children: Matthew Roy, Amy Roseann, Andrew Benjamin.; m. Abigail Perlman, 2003. BA in Hist., S.W. Bapt. U., Mo., 1970; MA in Hist. & Govt., S.W. Mo. State U., 1972. Tchr. Marshfield HS, Mo., 1970-73; instr. Drury Coll., Springfield, Mo., 1973-82; clk. Greene County, Mo., 1973-85; sec. of state State of Mo., 1985-93; pres. S.W. Bapt. U., 1993-96; mem. US Congress from 7th Mo. dist., 1997—, chief dep. majority whip, 1999—2002, majority whip, 2002—07, interim majority leader, 2005—06, minority whip, 2007—. Mem. Fed. Election Commn. Adv. Panel; del. Atlantic Treaty Assn. Conf., 1987; mem. Congl. Com. on Commerce, 1999—2004, Internat. Rels., 1997-98, 2004-, Ho. Reps. Steering Com., 1997-; del. Nat. Hist. Publs. and Records Commn., 1997—; mem. ho. appropriations com., 1999. Co-author: Mo. Election Procedures: A Layman's Guide, 1977, Jobs Without People: The Coming Crisis for Missouri's Workforce, 1989; Voting Rights Guide for the Handicapped Bd. dirs. Ctr. Democracy; mem. Mo. Mental Health Advocacy Coun., 1998-99; mem. exec. bd. Am. Coun. of Young Polit. Leaders, 1998-99; chmn. Mo. Housing Devel. Commn., Kans. City, 1981, Rep. State Conv., Springfield, 1980; chmn. Gov.'s Adv. Coun. on Literacy; co-chmn. Mo. Opportunity 2000 Commn., 1985-87; Rep. candidate for lt. gov. of Mo., 1980; active local ARC, Muscular Dystrophy Assn., others. Named One of 10 Outstanding Young Americans US Jaycees, 1986, Springfield's Outstanding Young Man Jaycees, 1980, Mo.'s Outstanding Young Civic Leader, 1981, Mo. Republican of Yr. 2002; Recipient Disting. Mem. of Congress award, Am. Wire Producers Assn., 2002, Health Leadership award Am. Assn. of Nurse Anesthetists, 2003, Arthur T. Marix Congl. Leadership award Mil. Officers Assn. Am., 2004, Cmty. Health Defender award Nat. Assn. Cmty. Health Ctrs. Inc., 2005. Mem. Nat. Assn. Secs. of State (chmn. voter registration and edn. com., sec., v.p. 1990), Am. Coun. Young Polit. Leaders, Kiwanis, Masons. Republican. Baptist. Office: US House Reps 217 Cannon Ho Office Bldg Washington DC 20515-2507 Office Phone: 202-225-6536, 202-225-5604. E-mail: blunt@mail.house.gov.

BLUST, LARRY D., lawyer; b. Bushnell, Ill., Feb. 16, 1943; BS with high honors, U. Ill., 1965, JD with high honors, 1968. Bar: Ill. 1968; CPA, Ill. Former mem. Jenner & Block, Chgo.; ptnr., bus. practice Barnes and Thornburg LLP, Chgo., 2001—. Mem. Ill. Bd. CPA Examiners, 1978-81. Contbr. articles to profl. jours. Mem. ABA (tax sect., partnerships com. 1975-80, 1982-85), Order of the Coif. Office: Barnes and Thornburg Ste 4400 One No Wacker Dr Chicago IL 60606-2833 Office Phone: 312-214-8320. Business E-Mail: larry.blust@letlaw.com.

BLYSTONE, JOHN B., manufacturing executive; Degree in Math and Econs., U. Pitts., car. With GE, 1978, with aircraft engine divsn.; v.p. J.I. Case divsn. Tenneco, Inc., 1988-91; v.p., gen. mgr. GE superabrasives GE, 1991; pres., CEO Nuovo Pignone, Florence, Italy, 1994, Europe Plus Pole of GE Power Sys., 1995; chmn., pres., CEO SPX, 1995—. Office: Spx Corporation 801 W Norton Ave Ste 310 Muskegon MI 49441-4155

BOAG, SIMON, automotive executive; b. Ont., Canada, Oct. 8, 1965; BSME, U. Toronto, Ont., Can., 1988; MS in Mgmt. Sci., Stanford U., Calif., 2000. Paint asst. mgr. CAMI Automotive Inc., 1988, pres., 2000; paint area mgr. Ford Oakville Assembly Paint, Ont., 1991, GM Buick City, 1994, assembly area mgr., 1996, prodn. mgr. Flint, Mich., 1997; plant mgr. GM Oshawa Car Assembly, Ont., 2002; pres., mng. dir. GM Argentina, Paraguay and Uruguay, 2003; v.p. assembly, stamping ops., mfg. Chrysler Group, 2005, exec. v.p. procurement, supply, 2007—; head prodn. planning Mercedes-Benz Passenger Cars, 2006; co-chair Envi Chrysler LLC, 2007—. Named one of Canada's Top 40 under 40, 2002; recipient Young Leadership Excellence award, Automotive Hall of Fame, 2000; Sloan Fellowship, Stanford U., 2000. Office: Chrysler LLC PO Box 21-8004 Auburn Hills MI 48321

BOAL, CARMINE, state official; b. Mt. Pleasant, Iowa, Feb. 1956; d. Edward and Wilma Roth; m. Steve Boal; children: Rob, Beth, Mike. A in Exec. Secretarial/Legal, Am. Inst. Bus., 1976; postgrad., Drake U., 1978. State rep., Iowa, 1999—. Mem. adminstrn. and rules com.; vice chair edn. com.; mem. judiciary com.; mem. local govt. com.; mem. ways and means com.; precinct chair, cen. com. mem. Rep. Party; del. county, dist., and state convs. V.p. Ankeny Sch. Bd., 1996; parent vol. Ankeny Schs.; Sunday sch. tchr. Republican. Office: State Capitol E 12th and Grand Des Moines IA 50319

BOARDMAN, ELIZABETH DRAKE, computer security professional; b. Columbus, Ohio, Oct. 14, 1955; d. Jack Martin and Marilyn Hawk Boardman; children: Melissa Grimsley, Stephanie Grimsley. BS Bus. Adminstrn., Ohio State U., 1977; BS in Computer sci., We. Ill. U., 2003; MS in Computer Engring. and Info. Assurance, Iowa State U., 2007. Officer (lt., unrestricted line) U.S. Navy, Various, 1977—85; sr. computer software analyst Analysis & Tech., North Stonington, Conn., 1985—88; database adminstr. We. Ill. U., Macomb, Ill., 2000—02; tchg. asst. computer sci. Iowa State U., Ames, 2003; info. security specialist Boeing, 2005—. Mem., bd. of dirs. Girl Scouts Shining Trail Coun., Burlington, Iowa, 1995—99; fin. com. Trinity United Meth. Ch., Keokuk, Iowa, 2000—02; blue & gold officer U.S. Naval Acad., Annapolis, Md., 1992—94; vol. Girl Scouts of U.S.A., various, 1990—99; life mem. Girl Scouts. Comdr. USNR, 1985—2006. Named Iowa Cmty. Hero Olympic Torch Bearer, Iowa Com. for Olympic Torch Run, 1996. Mem.: Western Ill. Alumni Assn., Mil. Officers Assn. Am., The Ohio State U. Alumni Assn., Naval Res. Assn., Phi Kappa Phi, Upsilon Pi Epsilon, Chi Omega. Avocations: volunteer work, computers, travel.

BOARDMAN, EUNICE, retired music educator; b. Cordova, Ill., Jan. 27, 1926; d. George Hollister and Anna Bryson (Feaster) Boardman. B. Mus. Edn., Cornell Coll., 1947; M. Mus. Edn., Columbia U., 1951; Ed.D., U. Ill., 1963; DFA (hon.), Cornell Coll., 1995. Tchr. music pub. schs., Iowa, 1947-55; prof. music edn. Wichita State U., Kans., 1955-72; vis. prof. mus. edn. Normal State U., Ill., 1972-74, Roosevelt U., Chgo., 1974-75; prof. mus. edn. U. Wis., Madison, 1975-89, dir. Sch. Music, 1980-89; prof. music, dir. grad. program in music edn. U. Ill., Urbana, 1989-98; ret. Author: Musical Growth in Elementary School, 1963, 6th rev. edit., 1996, Exploring Music, 1966, 3d rev. edit., 1975, The Music Book, 1980, 2d rev. edit., 1984, Holt Music, 1987; editor: Dimensions of Musical Thinking, 1989, Dimensions of Musical Thinking: A Different Kind of Music, 2002, Up the Mississippi: A Journey of the Blues, 2002. amed to MENC Hall of Fame, 2004. Mem. Soc. Music Tchr. Edn. (chmn. 1984-86), Music Educators Nat. Conf. Avocations: reading, antiques.

BOARDMAN, ROBERT A., retired lawyer; b. 1947; BA, Muskingum Coll., 1969; JD, Case Western Reserve U., 1972. Bar: Ohio 1972, Colo. 1976. Assoc. atty. Roetzel & Andress, 1972-75, atty., 1975-83; asst. gen. coun., sec. Manville

Corp., Denver, 1983-87, v.p., sec., 1988-90; sr. v.p., gen. coun. Navistar Internat. Corp., Chgo., 1990—2004, ret., 2004. Office: Navistar Internat Corp 4201 Winfield Rd Warrenville IL 60555 Business E-Mail: robert.boardman@nav-international.com.

BOAT, THOMAS FREDERICK, pediatrician, pulmonologist, researcher, educator; b. Pella, Iowa, Sept. 7, 1939; s. Bert Reuben and Anne Marie (Schoenbohm) B.; m. Barbara Mary Walling, June. 9, 1962; children: Sarah Elizabeth, Mary Barbara, Anne Christine. BA, Cen. Coll., Pella, 1961; MS, U. Iowa, 1965, MD, 1966. Diplomate Am. Bd. Pediat., Am. Bd. Pediat. Pulmonology. Resident in pediat. U. Minn., Mpls., 1966-68; clin. assoc. NIH, Bethesda, Md., 1968-70; fellow in pediat. pulmonology Case Western Res. U., Cleve., 1970-72, instr. pediat., 1972-73, asst. prof., 1973-76, assoc. prof., 1976-81, prof., 1981-82; prof., chmn. dept. pediat. U. N.C., Chapel Hill, 1982-93; chmn. dept. pediat. U. Cin. Sch. Medicine, 1993—; dir. Cin. Children's Hosp. Rsch. Found., 1993—. Prin. investigator Pediat. Pulmonary Specialized Ctr. Rsch., NIH, 1991-93; chmn. Am. Bd. Pediat., 1994. Mem. editl. bd. Lung Rsch. Jour. Bd. dirs. Ronald McDonald House, Chapel Hill, 1985-88, Cystic Fibrosis Found., chmn. rsch. devel. program, 1983—. Lt. comdr. USPHS, 1968-70. Fellow: Am. Acad. Pediat.; mem.: Assn. Accreditation Human Rsch. Programs (v.p. 2007—), Inst. of Medicine, Assn. Med. Sch. Dept. Chairs (pres.-elect 1994—97, pres. 1997—99), Am. Thoracic Soc. (chmn. pediat. assembly 1983—84), Am. Pediat. Soc. (pres. 2000—01). Office: Children's Hosp Med Ctr 3333 Burnet Ave SEC D6 Cincinnati OH 45229-3039 Office Phone: 513-636-4588. Business E-Mail: thomas.boat@cchmc.org.

BOATRIGHT, MATT, agricultural products supplier, state agency administrator, director; Prin., owner Preferred Premium Beef Inc., 1987—, Mapelwood Acres Farm, 1987—; mem. Mo. Ho. Reps., Jefferson City, Mo., 1994—2002, chief staff Senator Scott, 2003—04; dep. dir. agr. State Mo., Jefferson City, 2005—. Republican. Office: Capitol Office Rm 105-H Jefferson City MO 65102

BOBAK, MARK T., lawyer; b. 1959; JD cum laude, St. Louis U. Sch. Law, 1984. With Anheuser-Busch Cos., St. Louis, 1992—96, assoc. gen. counsel, 1996—2000, v.p., corp. human resources, 2000—04, group v.p., chief legal officer, 2004—. Office: Anheuser-Busch Cos One Busch Pl Saint Louis MO 63118 Office Phone: 314-577-2000.

BOBERG, WAYNE D., lawyer; b. Vincennes, Ind., Sept. 28, 1952; s. Richard W. and Merom D. (Duke) B.; m. Nancy E. Messel, Sept. 11, 1971. Student, Kans. State U., 1970-73; BS in Bus. with distinction, Ind. U., 1975, JD magna cum laude, 1978. Bar: Ill. 1978, U.S. Dist. Ct. (no. dist.) Ill. 1978. Assoc. to ptnr. Winston & Strawn, Chgo., 1978—. Bd. dirs. Nat. Entrepreneurs Found., Bloomington, Ind., 1982—; mem. bd. trustees Chgo. Symphony Orch. Mem. ABA, Chgo. Bar Assn., Chgo. Athletic Assn. Office: Winston & Strawn 35 W Wacker Dr Ste 4200 Chicago IL 60601-9703 Office Fax: 312-558-5700. E-mail: wboberg@winston.com.

BOBINS, NORMAN R., retired bank executive; b. Nov. 14, 1942; m. Virginia Bobins. BS, U. Wis., 1964; MBA, U. Chgo., 1967. Sr. v.p. Am. Nat. Bank & Trust Co., 1967—81; sr. exec. v.p., chief lending officer Exch. Nat. Bank Chgo., 1981—90; sr. exec. v.p. ABN AMRO Bank N.V., Netherlands; pres., CEO LaSalle Bank Corp., Chgo., 1990—2007, chmn., 2007, chmn. emeritus, 2007—. Vice chmn. Standard Fed. Bank, N.A., bd. dirs.; mem. bd. Ill. Bus. Roundtable, chmn. emeritus; mem. bd. trustees CenterPoint Properties Trust; bd. dirs. Metal Management, Inc., 2006—, AAR Corp., 2007—. Mem. Chgo. Bd. Edn., 1994—; bd. trustees Chgo. Cmty. Trust; exec. bd. Auditorium Theatre Coun., Chgo.; bd. dirs. Terra Found. Arts; bd. trustees Field Mus., Art Inst. Chgo., U. Chgo. Hospitals. Recipient Disting. Svc. award, Anti-Defamation League B'nai B'rith, 1982, Human Rights medallion, Am. Jewish Com., 1992, Wexler award, Nat. REIA Fall Conf., 1995, Keshet Rainbow award, 1997, CANDO Person of Yr. award, 1997, Reach for Excellence award, Midtown Ednl. Found., 1998, Bus. Leadership award, DePaul U., 1999, Profl. of Yr. award, Harold Washington Coll. Bus., 2000, Jane Addams Hull House medal, 2000, Southwest Organizing Project Anti-Predatory Lending award, 2001, Chmn.'s award, Boys & Girls Clubs, 2002, Disting. Corp. Alumnus award, U. Chgo. Grad. Sch. Bus., 2003, Lifetime Achievement award, Assn. Corp. Growth, 2003, Richard J. Daley medal, 2005, Bus. Statesman award, Harvard Bus. Sch. Club Chgo., 2005, Lifetime Achievement award, Urban Land Inst., 2007, Daniel H. Burnham award, Chicagoland C. of C., 2007. Mem.: Comml. Club Chgo. (civic. com.), Banker's Club of Chgo. (pres.), Anti-Defamation League of B'nai B'rith (bd. dirs., Disting. Svc. award 1982). Republican.

BOBRICK, EDWARD ALLEN, retired judge; b. 1935; BS, U. Ill., 1958; JD, DePaul U., 1964. Bar: Ill. 1964. Pvt. practice, Chgo., 1965; trial lawyer US Dept. Labor, Chgo., 1966—75, counsel occupl. safety and health, 1975—78; adminstrv. law judge US Occupl. Safety and Health Rev. Commn., Chgo., 1978—85, Social Security Adminstrn., Chgo., 1985—90; magistrate judge U.S. Dist. Ct. (no. dist.) Ill., Chgo., 1990—2004. Commd. ensign USN, 1958. Decorated Commendation medal; recipient Disting. Svc. Career award, US Dept. Labor, 1978. Mem.: Decalogue Soc. Lawyers, Fed. Bar Assn., Ill. Jewish Judges Assn., US Magistrate Judges Assn., Naval Order of the US, Naval Res. Assn., Pilots-Lawyers Bar Assn. Avocations: flying, running, bicycling, carpentry, home restoration. Office: US Dist Ct 1822 Dirksen Bldg 219 Dearborn St Ste 2050 Chicago IL 60604-1800

BOCCIERI, JOHN A., state representative; b. Youngstown, Ohio, Oct. 5, 1969; married; 1 child. BS in Econs., St. Bonaventure U.; MA in Pub. Adminstrn., Webster U., MA in Bus. State rep. dist. 61 Ohio Ho. of Reps., Columbus, 2000—, ranking minority mem., ethics and elections subcom., mem. agr. and natural resources, commerce and labor, homeland security engring. and archtl. design, and state govt. coms., asst. minority whip. Mem. mil. support ops. Joint Force (Kosovo and Bosnia) and Southern Watch (Iraq); staff officer for mil. presdl. support; base compliance for START II Treaty, Open Skies Treaty, Chem. Weapons Compliance Treaty, Little Rock AFB. Former intern, legis. aide Ohio Ho. of Reps. C-130 pilot Ohio Air NG. Mem.: South County Dems., Dems. of the 17th Congl. Dist., St. Paul the Apostle Ch., Youngstown State U. Alumni Assn., Mahoning County Farm Bur., NG Assn. Ohio, Mahoning County Vets. Meml., Alliance Area Dem. Club, Carroll County, KC, Am. Legion, Pi Gamma Mu. Democrat. Office: 77 S High St 14th Fl Columbus OH 44321-6111

BOCHERT, LINDA H., lawyer; b. East Orange, NJ, May 13, 1949; BA, U. Wis., 1971, MS, 1973, JD, 1974. Bar: Wis. 1974. Dir. environ. protection unit Wis. Atty. Gen. Office, 1978-80; exec. asst. to the secy. Wis. Dept. Natural Resources, 1980-91; ptnr. Michael, Best & Friedrich, Madison, Wis., 1991—. Mem. ABA, Wis. State Bar Assn. Office: Michael Best & Friedrich PO Box 1806 Firstar Plaza 1 S Pinckney St Madison WI 53701-1806 Office Phone: 608-283-2271. Business E-Mail: lhbochert@michaelbest.com.

BOCIAN, PETER, beverage service company executive; BA, Mich. State U., M in Acctg., 1982. Various mgmt. positions NCR Corp., Dayton, Ohio, 1983—2002, CFO, v.p. retail solutions divsn., 1999—2002, CFO retail and fin. group, 2002—03, v.p., fin., CFO, 2003—07; exec. v.p., CFO Starbucks Corp., Seattle, 2007—. Office: Starbucks Corp 2401 Utah Ave S Seattle WA 98134

BOCK, BROOKS FREDERICK, emergency physician; b. Orange, NJ, Sept. 19, 1943; MD, Wayne State U., 1969. Intern Detroit Gen. Hosp., 1969-70; resident in surgery Wayne State U., 1970-71, resident in urology, 1971-73, prof., chmn. Dept. Emergency Medicine, 1985—2005; pvt. practice; specialist-in-chief emergency medicine Detroit (Mich.) Med. Ctr., 1985—2005, pres. Harper-Huntzel Hosp., 2005—. Mem. Am. Bd. Emergency Medicine, 1995—2004, pres., 2002—03. Mem. AMA, Am. Coll. Emergency Physicians, Mich. State Med. Soc., Wayne County Med. Soc. Home: 5764 Bloomfield Glens West Bloomfield MI 48322-2501 Office: 3990 John R Detroit MI 48201-2445 Home Phone: 248-626-6603; Office Phone: 313-745-6211.

BOCK, PETER ERNEST, state legislator; b. Milw., Dec. 12, 1948; s. Peter R. and Thelma J. (Miron) B. BA, U. Wis., Milw., 1977. Former parcel delivery worker; state assemblyman dist. 7 Wis. State Assembly, 1987—. Chmn. environ. resources com. Wis. State Assembly, 1993—, mem. health, natural resources, labor and job tng., state affairs, urban and local affairs coms. Chmn. Milw. County Dem. Com., 1985-86. Home: 420 S Blount St Madison WI 53703-3511

BOCKSERMAN, ROBERT JULIAN, chemist; b. St. Louis, Dec. 20, 1929; s. Max Louis and Bertha Anna (Kremen) B.; m. Clarice K. Kreisman, June 9, 1957; children: Michael Jay, Joyce Ellen, Carol Beth. BSc, U. Mo., 1952, MSc, 1955; postgrad., Far East Intelligence Sch, Tokyo, 1954. Chemist Sealtest Corp., Peoria, Ill., 1955-56; prodn. mgr. Allan Drug Co., St. Louis, 1957-59; rsch. chemist Monsanto Co., St. Louis, 1960-65, purchasing agt. Sauget, Ill., 1966-67; founder, pres. Pharma-Tech Industries, Inc., Union, Mo., 1967-84; tech. dir. Overlock-Howe Consulting Group, St. Louis, 1984-85; founder, pres. Conatech Consulting Group, Creve Coeur, Mo., 1985—. Sec., mem. industry packaging adv. com. Sch. of Engring. U. Mo., Rolla, 1979—, adj. prof. dept. food sci./nutrition, Columbia, adj. prof. dept. engring. mgmt., Rolla, vis. lectr., Clayton, Northwestern U., Evanston, Ill.; vol. tutor Ladue Sch. Dist.; tutor Parkway Sch. Dist., St. Louis, Clayton (Mo.) Sch. Dist.; tech. cons. Creve Coeur Fire Protection Dist.; cons. HAZMAT Team St. Louis County; mentor U. Mo. Dept. Food Sci. and Nutrition; tech. cons. hazardous products EPA, CPSC; mem. safety panel Info. Resources, Inc. Tech. reviewer Jour. Inst. of Packaging Profls., Jour. Packaging Tech., Mo. Waste Control Scholarship Grants and Research, Medical Device and Diagnostic Industry Jour., Medical Plastics and Biomaterials Publication.; mem. editl. adv. bd. The Forensic Examiner, Processing Mag.; panelist (Help Desk column) Medical Device and Diagnostic Industry mag., The Forensic Examiner; contbg. author: Packaging Forensics -Package Failure in the Courts. Mem. Mo. Waste Control Coalition; mem. stormwater engring. com. City of Creve Coeur, Mo., also mem. recycling and environ. com.; tech. cons. Hazmat Team, St. Louis County, Mo.; mem. St. Louis Emergency Response Team; nat. mem. Libr. Congress, Mo. Hist. Soc. With U.S. Army, 1952-54, Korea. Grantee Small Bus. Innovation, Clear Seas Rsch. Found. Mem. ASTM, Am. Coll. Forensic Examiners, Cons. Packaging Engring. Coun., Inst. Packaging Profls. (cert. packaging profl.), Am. Technion Soc., Inst. Food Technologists Arrangements (St. Louis), Nat. Forensic Ctr., Teltech Resource Network, Am. Chem. Soc., Am. Plastics Coun., Mo. Acad. Scis., N.Y. Acad. Sci., Acad. Sci. St. Louis, Assn. Cons. Chemists and Chem. Engrs., Am. Nutraceutical Assn., Nat. Dir. Expert Witnessess, Rotary Internat., Wash. U. Century Club, Juvenile Diabetes Rsch. Found., Sigma Xi. Achievements include research on toxicological effects of additives from packaging materials upon foodstuffs, on biological and photo degradation of polymers, on technology of form/fill/seal packaging engineering, new sterilization technologies for medical devices and pharmaceuticals, barrier properties of polymer films, toxicology of chemical dusts and fumes, and food irradiation effects on humans, neurotoxicity of organic solvents. Home: 54 Morwood Ln Creve Coeur MO 63141-7621 Office: Conatech Cons Group 501 N Lindbergh Blvd Ste 105 Creve Coeur MO 63141-7844 Office Phone: 314-995-9767. Business E-Mail: rjbockserman@conatech.com.

BODDICKER, DAN, state official; b. Vinton, Iowa, Nov. 18, 1962; m. Carla Boddicker; children: Josh, Jacob, Cheyanne, Michael, Matthew. AAS, Kirkwood C.C., 1985. State rep., Iowa, 1993—; co-chair Cedar County Rep. Cen. Com., 1990—96; profl. musician, 1981—84; technician ENERTRAC, 1985—86; elec. engr. HWH Corp., 1986—. Child Support Recovery Adv. Com.; mem. Iowa Right to Life; bd. dirs. Dads Against the Divorce Industry, 2001—. Mem.: NRA, ALEC. Republican. Roman Catholic.

BODEM, BEVERLY A., state legislator; b. Wis., Feb. 22, 1940; m. Dennis Bodem; 3 children. Student, U. Wis. State rep. Mich. Ho. Reps., Dist. 106, 1991-98; constituent svcs. dir. Sen. Mike Goschka. Mem. tourism and recreation com., co-chair econ. devel. com., conservation, environ. and great lakes com. and pub. health com., chair task force tourism, mem. task force sr. policy, Mich. Ho. Reps. Bd. dirs. Boys and Girls Club of Alpena. Mem. Club Alpena, Lions.

BODENHAMER, DAVID JACKSON, historian, educator; b. Macon, Ga., May 4, 1947; s. David Jackson and Mary Elizabeth (Cox) B.; m. Penny Jo McClelland, Dec. 27, 1988. BA, Carson-Newman Coll., 1969; MA, U. Ala., 1970; PhD, Ind. U., 1976. Asst. prof., then assoc. prof. U. So. Miss., Hattiesburg, 1976-84, prof., asst. v.p. acad. affairs, 1985-88; dir. Polis Ctr. Ind. U., Indpls., 1989—. Head N.Am. team, exec. com. Electronic Cultural Atlas Initiative, 1997—. Author: Pursuit of Justice, 1986, Fair Trial, 1991; author, editor: Encyclopedia of Indianapolis, 1994; co-editor: Ambivalent Legacy, 1984, Bill of Rights in Modern America, 1992, History of Indiana Law, 2006, Our Rights, 2006; editor-in-chief Indiana Online: An Electronic Encyclopedia. Chmn. bd. dirs. South Miss. Community Action Agy., Hattiesburg, 1978-82; bd. dirs. Pine Belt Family YMCA, Hattiesburg, 1982-86; steering com. Regional Ctr. Plan, Indpls, 1989-92; mem. steering com. New Ind. State Mus. Task Force, 1998—, regional ctr. plan, 2002. With U.S. Army, 1970-72. Mem. Am. Soc. Legal History, Orgn. Am. Historians. Office: Polis Ctr Ste 100 1200 Waterway Blvd Indianapolis IN 46202-5140 Office Phone: 317-274-2455. E-mail: intu100@iupui.edu.

BODENSTEIN, IRA, lawyer; b. Atlantic City, Nov. 9, 1954; s. William and Beverly (Grossman) B.; m. Julia Elizabeth Smith, Mar. 9, 1991; children: Sarah Rose, George William, Jennie Kathryn. Student, Tel Aviv U., 1974-75; BA in Govt., Franklin & Marshall Coll., 1977; JD in Econs., U. Miami, 1980. Bar: Ill. 1980, U.S. Dist Ct. (no. dist.) Ill. 1980, U.S. Ct. Appeals (7th cir.) 1982, Fla. 1983. Assoc. James S. Gordon Ltd., Chgo., 1980-85, mem., 1985-89, Portes, Sharp, Herbst & Fox, Ltd., Chgo., 1990-91; shareholder Towbin & Zazove, Ltd., Chgo., 1991-93; ptnr. D'Ancona & Pflaum, Chgo., 1993-98; U.S. Trustee Region 11, Chgo., 1998—2006, Region 9, Cleve., 2001—02; mem. Shaw, Gussis, Fishman, Glantz, Wolfson & Towbin, LLC, Chgo., 2006—. Pres., bd. dirs., benefit chmn. Gus Giordano Jazz Dance, Chgo., 1990—; treas. Chgo. Pub. Art Group, 1995-99. Mem. ABA (bus. law sect., rep. young lawyers divsn. dist. 15, 1986-87, ann. meeting adv. com. 1990, spkr. spring meeting 1996, 97), Chgo. Bar Assn. (bd. dirs. young lawyers sect. 1985-87, chmn.-elect 1987-88, chmn. 1988-89, antitrust com., chmn. athletics com. 1984-85, bd. mgrs. 1990-92, chmn. pub. affairs and media rels. com., chmn. assn. meetings com., membership com. 1996, cert. of appreciation 1984-93, 96-97). Democrat. Jewish. Home: 2848 W Wilson Ave Chicago IL 60625-3743 Office: Shaw Gussis Fishman et al 321 N Clark St Ste 800 Chicago IL 60610 Office Phone: 312-666-2861. Office Fax: 312-275-0556. E-mail: ibodenstein@shawgussis.com.

BODIKER, RICHARD WILLIAM, SR., state legislator; b. Richmond, Ind., Aug. 17, 1936; m. Nancy Bodiker; 7 children. Student, Ball State U., Ind U. East. Mem. Richmond Common Coun., 1983-86; Ind. state rep. Dist. 56, 1986—; mem. commerce com., utility regulatory flexibility com.; interstate coop com. and econ. devel. and govt. affairs com.; mem. Ind. Ho. of Reps., Richmond Power and Light, 1983-86. With Dana Engine Products. Mem. Richmond Evening Optimist, Richmond/Wayne County C. of C., Cambridge City C. of C. Office: State House Rm 336 Indianapolis IN 46204-2728 Home: 4286 S C Ct Richmond IN 47374-6030

BODMER, ROLF A., medical educator; MS in Natural Scis., U. Basel, Switzerland, 1980, PhD in Biochemistry and Neurobiology, 1983. Postdoctoral fellow Friedrich Miescher-Institut, Basel, 1983-84, Albert Einstein Coll. Medicine, Bronx, N.Y., 1984; rsch. assoc. Dept. Physiology and Biochemistry U. Calif., San Francisco, 1984-90; asst. prof. biology U. Mich., Ann Arbor, 1990—. Contbr. over 20 rsch. articles to profl. jours. Grantee NIH, Am. Heart Assn., Muscular Dystrophy Assn. Achievements include research in cellular and molecular analysis of neural and mesodermal development; identification and characterization of genes involved in pattern formation and specifying cellular identities during neurogenesis and mesoderm/heart differentiation. Office: U Mich Dept Biology 3013 Natural Sci Bldg 1048 Ann Arbor MI 48109-1048

BOE, DAVID STEPHEN, musician, educator, dean; b. Duluth, Minn., Mar. 11, 1936; s. Egbert Thomas and Beatrice Ella (Steen) Boe; m. Sigrid North, July 23, 1961; children: Stephen, Eric. BA, St. Olaf Coll., Northfield, Minn., 1958; M.Mus., Syracuse U., 1960. Asst. prof. music U. Ga., 1961-62; mem. faculty Oberlin Coll. Conservatory Music, Ohio, 1962—, prof. organ and harpsichord, 1976—, dean, 1976-90; organ recitalist U.S. and Europe, 1962—. Mem. advanced placement music com. Coll. Entrance Exam. Bd., 1980—83; vis. prof. Fla. State U., 1991, U. Notre Dame, 1991—92. Trustee Westfield Ctr., 2000—06; chmn. scholarship com. Presser Found., 2002—; dir. music, organist First Luth. Ch., Lorain, Ohio, 1962—2002. Scholar Fulbright, Germany, 1960—61. Mem.: Nat. Assn. Schs. Music (trustee, sec. 1981—87), Phi Beta Kappa, Pi Kappa Lambda (nat. pres. 1986—90). Business E-Mail: david.boe@oberlin.edu.

BOE, GERARD PATRICK, health science association administrator, educator; b. Washington, Jan. 20, 1936; s. Harold David and Bernice Virginia (Lemon) Boe; m. Irene Margaret Dazevedo, Oct. 24, 1959 (div. Jan. 1988); children: Steven Alan, Christine Ann; m. Charlotte Greene Hudson, Dec. 30, 1989. BS in Biology, W.Va. Wesleyan Coll., 1958; MS in Clin. Pathology, Ohio State U., 1969; PhD in Edn. and Mgmt., Tex. A&M U., 1976. Commd. 2d lt. U.S. Army, 1963, advanced through grades to lt. col.; health care adminstr., 1963—81; ret., 1981; adminstrv. dir. Ga. Radiation Therapy Ctr., Augusta, 1981—83; pres. Profl. Mgmt. Cons., Augusta, 1983—89; exec. dir. Am. Med. Technologists, Park Ridge, Ill., 1989—. Faculty Webster U., So. Ill. U., 1980—. Contbr. articles to profl. jours. Recipient cert. of appreciation, ARC, 1976, Pres.'s award, Augusta chpt. Internat. Mgmt. Coun., 1989. Mem.: Am. Soc. Clin. Pathologists (cert.), Inst. Cert. Profl. Mgrs. (bd. regents 1990—), Clin. Lab. Mgmt. Assn., Nat. Clearing House for Licensure, Enforcement and Regulation, Soc. Armed Forces Med. Lab. Scientists (Pres.'s award 1982). Republican. Methodist. Avocations: coin collecting/numismatics, stamp collecting/philately, sports, racquetball. Office: Am Med Technologists 710 Higgins Rd Park Ridge IL 60068-5737

BOEHM, JAMES, state legislator; m. Pat Boehm. Mem. N.D. Ho. of Reps. from 31st dist., 1991—. Vice chmn. Edn. Com. N.D. Ho. of Reps., mem. Transp. Com. Mem. Sch. Bd. Mem. KC, Future Farmers Am. (hon. state farmer), Elks, Moose, Eagles. Republican. Address: 3477 34th St Mandan ND 58554-8113

BOEHM, PEGGY, state agency administrator; BA, Mount Holyoke Coll. Dir. Ind. Budget Agy., Indpls., 1997—2000; exec. dir. White River State Pk., Indpls., 2000—. Office: White River State Pk 801 W Washington St Indianapolis IN 46204

BOEHM, THEODORE REED, state supreme court justice; b. Evanston, Ill., Sept. 12, 1938; s. Hans George and Frances (Reed) B.; children from previous marriage: Elisabeth, Jennifer, Sarah, Macy; m. Margaret Stitt Harris, Jan. 27, 1985. AB summa cum laude, Brown U., 1960; JD magna cum laude, Harvard U., 1963. Bar: D.C. 1964, Ind. 1964, U.S. Supreme Ct. 1975. Law clk. to Chief Justice Warren, Justices Reed and Burton, U.S. Supreme Ct., Washington, 1963-64; assoc. Baker & Daniels, Indpls., 1965-70, ptnr., 1970-88, 95-96, mng. ptnr., 1980-87; gen. counsel major appliances GE, Louisville, 1988-89; v.p., gen. counsel GE Aircraft Engines, Cin., 1989-91; dep. gen. counsel Eli Lilly & Co., 1991-95; justice Ind. Supreme Ct., Indpls., 1996—. Pres. Ind. Sports Corp., 1980-88; chmn. organizing com. 1987 Pan Am. Games, Indpls.; chmn. Indpls. Cultural Devel. Commn., 2001—. Mem. ABA, Am. Law Inst., Ind. Bar Assn., Indpls. Bar Assn. Office: Ind Supreme Ct State House Rm 324 Indianapolis IN 46204-2728 Office Phone: 317-232-2547. E-mail: tboehm@courts.state.in.us.

BOEHNE, RICHARD, newspaper company executive; m. Lisa Graybeal; children: Luke, Jacob. BS, No. Ky. U., 1981. Bus. reporter, editor Cin. Post; mgr. corp. comms. E. W. Scripps Co., Cin., 1988-89, dir. corp. comms. and investor rels., 1989-99, v.p. corp. comms. and investor rels., 1999—. Mem. mgmt. com. YMCA Camp Ernst; trustee Bapt. Convalescent Ctrs. of No. Ky.; Sunday sch. tchr. Highland Hills Bapt. Ch., Highland Hills, Ohio. Mem. Nat. Investor Rels. Inst. Office: E W Scripps Co 312 Walnut St Ste 2800 Cincinnati OH 45202-4067

BOEHNEN, DANIEL A., lawyer; b. Mitchell, SD, Aug. 5, 1950; s. Lloyd and Mary Elizabeth (Buche) B.; m. Joan Bensing, May 22, 197 (dec. 2006); children: Christopher, Lindsey. BS in Chem. Engring. cum laude, Notre Dame U., 1973; JD, Cornell U., 1976. Bar: Ill, U.S. Dist. Ct. (no. dist.) Ill., U.S. Ct. Appeals (7th and fed. cirs.), U.S. Supreme Ct. Atty. Allegretti, Newitt, Witcoff & McAndrews Ltd., Chgo., 1976—, assoc., 1982—; ptnr. Allegretti & Witcoff, Ltd., Chgo., 1986—, bd. dirs., 1993—95; founder McDonnell Boehnen Hulbert & Berghoff, LLP, Chgo., 1996—. Named one of Top IP Lawyers in Ill., Crain's Chgo. Bus., Super Lawyers for IP Litigation, Chgo. Mag., The Best Lawyer's in Am., Best Lawyers Pubs., Best Patent Trial Lawyers in Am., Chambers USA. Fellow Am. Bar Found.; mem. ABA, AIPLA, Cornell Law Assn. Chg. (past chmn.), Fed. Cir. Bar Assn. (past bd. dirs.), Assn. Patent Law Firms (past pres., bd. dirs.), Leading Lawyers Network (Ill., founding mem.). Office: McDonnell Boehnen Hulbert & Berghoff LLP 300 S Wacker Dr Chicago IL 60606-6709 Home Phone: 847-498-0486. Business E-Mail: boehnen@mbhb.com.

BOEHNEN, DAVID LEO, food service executive, lawyer; b. Mitchell, SD, Dec. 3, 1946; s. Lloyd L. Boehnen and Mary Elizabeth (Buche) Roby; m. Shari A. Bauhs, Aug. 9, 1969; children: Lesley, Michelle, Heather. AB, U. Notre Dame, 1968; JD with honors, Cornell U., 1971. Bar: Minn. 1971. Assoc. Dorsey & Whitney, Mpls., 1971—76, ptnr., 1977—89; sr. v.p. law and external rels. Supervalu Inc., Mpls., 1991—97, exec. v.p., 1997—. Vis. prof. law Cornell U. Law Sch., Ithaca, Y, 1982. Bd. govs. U. St. Thomas Law Sch.; mem. adv. coun. on arts and letters U. Notre Dame, 1993—; mem. adv. coun. Cornell U. Law Sch., 1983—92, chmn. coun., 1986—90; bd. dirs. Guthrie Theatre. Mem.: Spring Hill Golf Club, Minikahda Club (Mpls.). Roman Cath. Office Phone: 612-828-4151. E-mail: david.boehnen@supervalu.com.

BOEHNER, JOHN ANDREW, congressman; b. Cin., Nov. 17, 1949; s. Earl Henry and Mary Ann (Hall) Boehner; m. Deborah Lane Gunlack, 1973; children: Lindsay Maria, Tricia Ann BS in Bus., Xavier U., Cin., 1977. Mgr. Merrell-Dow Pharms., Inc., 1972—76; staff to pres. Nucite Sales, Inc., 1976—90; mem. Ohio State Ho. Reps., 1984-90, US Congress from 8th Ohio dist., 1991—, majority leader, 2006—07, minority leader, 2007—, chmn. edn. and the workforce com., 2001—06. Trustee Union Twp., 1982-84 Active Ohio Farm Bur. Named Friend of the Farm Bur., Friend of the Farm Bur. Assn., 2002; recipient Watchdog of the Treasury award, 1992, Jefferson award, Citizens for a Sound Economy, 1998, Golden Bulldog award, Watchdogs of the Treasury, 1998, Guardian of Seniors Rights, 60-Plus Coalition, 1998, Adam Smith Fed. Official award, Bus. Industry Polit. Action Com., 2001, Ground Water Protector award, Nat. Ground Water Assn., 2003, Bryce Harlow award, Bryce Harlow Found., 2005. Mem. Am. Heart Assn., Am. Legion, Butler County Farm Bur., Ohio Farm Bur., KC, Lakota Hills Homeowners Assn., Cin. C. of C., Dayton C. of C., Middletown C. of C. Republican. Roman Catholic. Office: US House Reps 1011 Longworth House Office Bldg Washington DC 20515-3508 Office Phone: 202-225-6205. Office Fax: 202-225-0704.

BOELTER, PHILIP FLOYD, real estate company officer, construction executive; b. Independence, Iowa, Mar. 25, 1943; s. Floyd Joseph and Eileen R. (Wilson) B.; m. Linda Lee Franck, June 7, 1964; children: Carrie Lynn, John Philip. BS in Indsl. Engring., Iowa State U., 1965; JD, U. Iowa, 1968. Ptnr. Dorsey & Whitney, Mpls., 1968—2002; exec. v.p., chief oper. officer Kraus-Anderson Cos., Inc., Mpls., 2002—. Trustee Gustavus Adolphus Coll., 1996-2005; bd. dir. Jr. Achievement of the Upper Midwest, 2003-04. Mem. Mpls. Athletic Club (treas. 1992, sec. 1993, v.p. 1994, pres. 1995). Lutheran. Avocations: landscape gardening, skiing, golf, reading, volleyball. Office: Kraus-Anderson 525 S 8th St Minneapolis MN 55404 Home Phone: 952-941-5438; Office Phone: 612-335-2704. E-mail: phil.boelter@k-a-c.com.

BOER, RALF REINHARD, lawyer; b. Berlin, Oct. 31, 1948; came to U.S., 1965; s. Karl Wolfgang Boer and Ingeborg (Krause) Serafin; m. Kathleen Marie Steinmetz, Jan. 5, 1974; children: Jessica, Charles, Alexander. BA cum laude, U. Wis., Milw., 1971; JD magna cum laude, U. Wis., Madison, 1974. Bar: Wis. 1974, U.S. Dist. Ct. (ea. dist.) Wis. 1974. Ptnr. Foley & Lardner, Milw., 1974—, ptnr.-Berlin office, 1975—76, mng. ptnr., 1992—, chmn. of firm, CEO, chmn. mgmt. com. Bd. dirs. Fiskars, Helsinki, Finland, Dynea, Hayward, Wis., Plexus Corp., Neenah, Wis. Author: German Labor-Management Relations Act, 1976. Bd. dirs. Internat. Inst. Wis., Milw., 1985-89; bd. dirs., adv. coun. U. Wis.-Milw. Internat. Bus. Ctr., 1987—. Mem. ABA, Wis. Bar Assn., Milw. Bar Assn. Fluent in german. Office: Foley & Lardner LLP 777 E Wisconsin Ave Ste 3800 Milwaukee WI 53202-5367 Office Phone: 414-297-5609. Business E-Mail: rboer@foley.com.

BOERNER, RALPH E. J., forest soil ecologist, plant biology educator; b. Bklyn., Oct. 2, 1948; s. Kurt Heinz and Erika Annalisa (Tappe) B.; m. Elizabeth Ann Wrobel, May 29, 1982; 1 child, Annalisa Marie. BS in Biology, SUNY, Cortland, 1970; MS in Biology and Marine Sci., Adelphi U., 1972; MPh in Botany, Rutgers U., 1974, PhD, 1980. Grad. tchg. asst. Adelphi U., Garden City, N.Y., 1970-72; environ. sci. N.Y. Dept. Environ. Protection, Huntington, N.Y., 1972; grad. tchg. asst., rsch. fellow Rutgers U., New Brunswick, N.J., 1972-74, 78-80; asst. prof. Burlington County Coll., Pemberton, N.J., 1974-78, Ohio State

U., Columbus, 1980-86, assoc. prof., 1986-93, prof., 1993—, chair dept. evolution, ecology and Organismal Biology, 1990—. Vis. prof. U. de Concepcion, Chile, 1987; cons. Columbus-Franklin County Met. Parks Commn., 1982—, Ohio Dept. Natural Resources, 1983—, The Nature Conservancy, 1988—, Denison U., 1991; contbr. papers to various profl. meetings. Mem. editl. bd. Mycorrhiza; contbr. articles and revs. to profl. jours. Bd. trustees The Nature Conservancy, 1987-95, also chair sci./land protection com., mem. strategic planning com. Predoctoral fellow NSF, 1972; grantee Columbia Gas Corp., 1982-85, Ohio Dept. atural Resources, 1982-83, 85-86, 86-87, 88, 89-90, 91-92, 92-93, 93-94, Columbia-Franklin County Met. Parks Dist., 1984-89, NSF, 1986-89, 87-88, 89-90, 90-92, Tinker Found., 1987, USDA Forest Svc., 1993; recipient Alumni award for disting. tchg. Ohio State U., 1989, Oak Leaf award The Nature Conservancy, 1992. Fellow AAAS; mem. Am. Inst. Biol. Scis., Acad. Tchg., Ecol. Soc. Am. (mem. Buell Award com. 1981-86, chmn. 1982-85, mem. program com. 198-688, mem. awards com. 1983-86, chmn. local arrangements ann. meeting 1987, mem. profl. ethics com. 1994—), Internat. Assn. Ecology, Internat. Assn. Landscape Ecology, Natural Areas Assn., So. Appalachian Bot. Club, Soil Ecology Soc. Am., Torrey Bot. Club (mem. Hervey Award com. 1980), Sigma Xi.

BOERS, TERRY JOHN, sportswriter, radio and television personality; b. Harvey, Ill., Sept. 13, 1950; s. John and Ruth (Rubottom) B.; m. Carolyn Grace Imgruet, Feb. 20, 1971; children: John, Joseph, Cary, Chris. BJ, No. Ill. U., 1972. Sports editor Sun-Jour. Newspapers, Lansing, Ill., 1972-73; asst. sports editor Star Publs., Chicago Heights, Ill., 1973-78; sports copy editor Detroit Free Press, 1978-80, Chgo. Sun-Times, 1980-82, beat reporter, 1982-88, 90-92, columnist, 1988-90. Panelist program The Sportswriters, Sta. WGN-Radio, Chgo., 1988-92; panelist cable TV program Sportsfire, 1990-91, 94-97, co-host, 1990-91; co-host afternoon program Sta. WSCR, Chgo., 1992-99; co-host morning program Sta. WSCR, Chgo., 1999—; sports columnist Arlington Heights Daily Herald, 1994-98. Author articles for sports mags. Recipient 1st Pl. award for column Ill. AP Sports Editors, 1988, Peter Lisagor award, 1989. Office: Sta WSCR-AM 4949 W Belmont Ave Chicago IL 60641-4384

BOESE, GIL KARYLE, cultural organization administrator; b. Chgo., June 24, 1937; s. Carl H. and Winifred A. Boese; m. Lillian R. Boese; children: Ann Carroll, Peter Austin, Sara Elisabeth. BA, Carthage Coll., Ill., 1959; MS, No. Ill. U., 1965; PhD; NIMH trainee 1970, Johns Hopkins U., 1973. Instr. biology Thornton Community Coll., Harvey, Ill., 1965-67; asst. prof. biology Elmhurst (Ill.) Coll., 1967-69; dep. dir. Chgo. Zool. Park, Brookfield, Ill., 1971-80; dir. Milw. County Zool. Gardens, Milw., 1980-89; pres. Zool. Soc. Milw. County, Milw., 1989—, Found. for Wildlife Conservation, 1993—. Tech. cons. Belize Zoo and Tropical Edn. Ctr.; founder Birds without Borders Aves Sin Frontera internat. dir., mgr. Runaway Creek Nature Preescree, Belize program; dir. Miller Brewery Friends of the Field. Bd. dirs. Dian Fossey Gorilla Found., chmn. 1998-99, internat. coordinating com., pres., 1997—; bd. dirs. Lewa Conservancy Kenya; improvement assn. bd. dirs. Pewaukee Lake, Wis. Fellow Royal Geog. Soc., Am. Assn. Zool. Parks and Aquariums (bd. dirs.); mem. Hemmingway Soc., Adventurers Club. Office: Zool Soc Milw County 10005 W Bluemound Rd Milwaukee WI 53226-4346 E-mail: boese@zoosociety.org.

BOETTGER, NANCY J., state legislator; b. Chgo., May 1, 1943; m. H. David Boettger; 4 children. BS, Iowa State U., 1965; BA, Buena Vista Coll., 1982. Owner farm, 1965—; spl. edn. tchr., 1965-66; tchr. jr. H.S., 1982-86; dir. edn. Myrtoe Meml. Hosp., 1986-99; mem. Iowa Senate from 41st dist. (now 29th dist.), 1994—2004, asst. majority leader, 1996—2004. Mem. Midwest Legis. Coun., 1996-2000. Mem. First Bapt. Ch., People Who Care; former bd. dirs. Harlan Cmty. Libr.; former mem. dean's adv. bd. Iowa State U. Ext. Mem. PEO, Am. Legis. Exchange Coun., Midwest Coun. State Govts. (chair health and human svcs. 1997-99), Coun. State Govts. (mem. drug task force 1998), Iowa Coun. Internat. Understanding Bd., Shelby County Found. for Edn. (former exec. dir.), Farm Bur., Pork Prodrs. Republican. Home: 926 Ironwood Rd Harlan IA 51537-5308 Office: State Capitol Dist 41 3 9th And Grand Des Moines IA 50319-0001 E-mail: nancy_boettger@legis.state.ia.us.

BOFF, KENNETH RICHARD, engineering research psychologist; b. NYC, Aug. 17, 1947; s. Victor and Ann (Yunko) B.; m. Judith Marion Schoer, Aug. 2, 1969 (dec. Apr. 1997); children: Cory Asher, Kyra Melissa; m. Jacque Aelanda Coppler, Aug. 20, 1999. BA, CUNY, 1969, MA, 1972; MPhil, Columbia U., 1975, PhD, 1978. Research scientist Human Resources Lab., Wright Patterson AFB, Ohio, 1977-80; sr. scientist Armstrong Aerospace Med. Rsch. Lab. (now Airforce Rsch. Lab.), Wright Patterson AFB, Ohio, 1980—, dir. design tech., 1980-91, dir. human engring. div., 1991—97; chief scientist, human effectiveness directorate Air Force Rsch. Lab., 1997—2007; Edenfield Exec.-in-Residence Sch. Ind. & Sys. Engring. Georgia Inst. Tech., 2002—04; prin. scientist Tennebaum Inst. Ga. Inst. Tech., Atlanta, 2007—. Project custodian Internat. Air. Standard Coordination Com., Washington, 1984; chmn. com. Tri-Service Human Factors Tech. Adv. Group, Washington, 1984—; chair human factors com. NATO Adv. Group Aerospace R&D, Paris, 1992—; chair human sys. tech. panel Dept. Def., 1994-97; U.S. coord. NATO Rsch. and Tech. Orgn. Human Factors, 1997—. Editor: Handbook of Perception and Human Performance, 1986, Human Engineering Data Compendium, 1988, System Design: Behavioral Perspectives on designers, Tools and Organizations, 1987, Organizational Simulation, 2005; contbr. articles to profl. jours. Travel grantee Rank Prize Found., Cambridge, Eng., 1984; named Air Force Scientist of the Quarter, 1989; recipient Patent award for rap-com display tech., 1989, Human Factors Soc. award for best publ., 1989. Fellow Internat. Ergonomics Assn., Human Factors and Ergonomics Soc.; mem. IEEE (sr.), Human Factors Soc., Am. Psychol. Assn. (div. 21 engring. psychology). Avocations: computers, photography.

BOGAARD, JONATHAN HARVEY, lawyer; b. Humboldt, Iowa, Mar. 25, 1957; m. Milena B. Vujovich, Nov. 26, 1983; children: Joseph Daniel, Jonathan Thomas. BBA in Acctg., U. Iowa, 1978, MA in Acctg., 1981, JD, 1981. Bar: Ill. 1981, Iowa 1981, U.S. Dist. Ct. (no. dist.) Ill. 1981, U.S. Tax Ct. 1983, U.S. Ct. Appeals (7th cir.) 1999. Assoc. McDermott, Will & Emery, Chgo., 1981—86, ptnr., 1986—91, Vedder Price, Chgo., 1991—. Bd. dirs. North Suburban YMCA, Northbrook, Ill., 1997—2002. Office: Vedder Price 222 N LaSalle Ste 2600 Chicago IL 60601-1003 Office Phone: 312-609-7651. Business E-Mail: jbogaard@vedderprice.com.

BOGAS, KATHLEEN LAURA, lawyer; b. Detroit, Mar. 4, 1951; d. Edward Joseph and Eleanor Laura (Hughes) B.; m. Frank Kavanaugh Rhodes III, Jan. 2, 1982; children: Katherine Bogas, Frank Kavanaugh IV. AB U. Detroit, 1972, JD 1975. Bar: Mich. 1975. Assoc., Sachs, Nunn, Kates, Kadushin, O'Hare, Helveston & Waldman, P.C. (Sachs Waldman P.C.), Detroit, 1975-80, ptnr., 1981-2001, mng. dir., 1993, ptnr. Eisenberg & Bogas PC, 2002-Mng. editor Jour. Urban Law, 1974-75. Mem. ATLA, Mich. Trial Lawyers Assn. (exec. bd. 1981—, chmn. jud. qualifications com. 1981—, chmn. ct. rules com. 1983-84, treas. 1993-94, sec. 1994-95, v.p. 1995, pres.-elect 1996-97, pres. 1997-98), Am., State Bar of Mich. (jud. qualifications com. 1983-89, 2003—, negligence coun., 1984-93, chair 1992-93, advanced tech. task force 1987-93), Women Lawyers of Mich. (labor and employment coun. 2002—), Detroit Bar Assn., Oakland County Bar Assn., Mich. Civil Rights Commn. (hearing referee 1983—), Am. Arbitration Assn., U. Detroit Sch. of Law Alumni Assn. (bd. dirs. 1986-92), Met. Trial Lawyers Assn. (bd. dirs. 1987-91), Nat. Employment Lawyers Assn. (co-chair trial practice com. 1994, exec. bd., 1999-, v.p. 2004-05, 1st v.p. 2005-2006), Women's Econ. Club of Detroit. Democrat. Office: Eisenberg & Bogas Ste 145 33 Bloomfield Hills Pkwy Bloomfield Hills MI 48304 Office Phone: 248-258-6080. Office Fax: 248-285-9212. Business E-Mail: klb@ebpclaw.com.

BOGGS, CATHERINE J., lawyer; b. Denver, 1954; BA, U. Denver, 1976; MS, Mich. State U., 1977; JD, U. Denver, 1981. Bar: Colo. 1981, Oreg. 1991, Calif. 1993. Atty. Sherman & Howard, 1982—90, Stoel Rives, 1991—93, Baker & McKenzie, Chgo., 1993—. Trustee Rocky Mountain Mineral Law Found., 2001—. Mem.: ABA, Soc. Mining, Metallurgy and Exploration, Soc. Mining, Oreg. State Bar Assn., Colo. Bar Assn., Calif. State Bar Assn. Office: Baker & McKenzie One Prudential Plz 130 East Randolph Dr Chicago IL 60601 Office Phone: 312-861-8000.

BOGGS, ROBERT J., former state senator; m. Judie Sylak; children: Larissa, Kelly, Kristin. BS, Am. U., 1969; postgrad., Youngstown State U.; MPA, Kent State U. Mem. Ohio Ho. of Reps., Columbus, 1973-83, former chmn. edn. com. and edn. rev. com.; mem. Ohio Senate, 1983-96; commr. Ashtabula County, 1996—. Ranking minority mem. energy and natural resources com., mem. state and local govt. com., hwys. and transp. com., minority leader; mem. adj. faculty U. San Francisco, McLaren Coll. Bus. Co-chmn. Ohio Lake Erie Shore Area Redevel. Task Force; chmn. Ohio High Speed Rail Authority; mem. transp. and comm. com., mem. econ. devel. com. Nat. Conf. State Legislators. Recipient Disting. Svc. award Gt. Lakes Commn., Ohio Sea Grant Program, Ohio Environ. Coun., Western Res. Conservation Club, Ohio County Treas. Assn., Lake County Trustees and Clks. Assn., Elem. Adminstrs. Assn., Ohio Assn. Secondary Adminstrs. Mem. Ohio Trustees and Clks. Assn. (assoc.), Am. High Speed Rail Assn. (bd. dirs.), Farm Bur., Sierra Club, Omicron Delta Kappa. Democrat. Home: 2281 Morning Pt Rock Creek OH 44084-9654 Office: 25 W Jefferson St Jefferson OH 44047

BOGINA, AUGUST, JR., former state official; b. Girard, Kans., Sept. 13, 1927; s. August and Mary (Blazic) B.; m. Nancy L. Pock, 1988; children: Kathleen A., August III, Michael E., Mark A., Kathleen R., Korey A. BS Engring., Kans. State U., 1950. Registered profl. engr., Kans., Mo., Colo., Okla.; registered land surveyor Kans., Mo. Owner Bogina & Assocs., Lenexa, Kans., 1962-70; pres. Bogina Cons. Engrs., 1970-95; partner Bogina Petroleum Engineers, 1983-95; mem. Kans. Ho. of Reps., 1974-80, Kans. Senate, 1980-95; chair Kans. State Bd. Tax Appeals; ret., 1999. Precinct committeeman Kans. Republican party, 1970-74, chmn. city com., 1972-74. Served with U.S. Army, 1946-48. Mem. Nat. Soc. Profl. Engrs., Mo. Soc. Profl. Engrs., Kans. Engring. Soc., Kans. Soc. Land Surveyors, Mo. Registered Land Surveyors. Roman Catholic.

BOGUE, ALLAN GEORGE, historian, educator; b. London, Ont., Can., May 12, 1921; married; 3 children. BA, U. Western Ont., 1943, MA, 1946; PhD, Cornell U., 1951; LL.D., U. Western Ont., 1973; D.Fil (hon.), U. Uppsala, 1977. Lectr. econs. and history, asst. librarian U. Western Ont., 1949-52; from asst. prof. to prof. history U. Iowa, 1952-64, chmn. dept., 1959-63; prof. history U. Wis.-Madison, 1964-68, chmn. dept., 1972-73, Frederick Jackson Turner prof. history, 1968-91. Mem. hist. adv. com. Math. Soc. Sci. Bd., 1965-71; Scandinavian-Am. Found. Thord-Gray lectr., 1968; mem. Council Inter-Univ. Consortium Polit. Research, 1971-73, 89-91; vis. prof. history Harvard U., 1972; dir. Social Sci. Research Coun., 1973-76 Author: Money at Interest, 1955, From Prairie to Corn Belt, 1963, Frederick Jackson Turner: Strange Roads Going Down, 1998, The Earnest Men, 1981, Clio and the Bitch Goddess, Quantification in American Political History, 1983, The Congressman's Civil War, 1989, The Farm on the North Talbot Road, 2001; co-author, editor: The West of the American People, 1970; co-author, contbr.: The Dimensions of Quantitative Research in History, 1972; co-editor, contbr.: American Political Behavior: Historical Essays and Readings, 1974; co-editor: The University of Wisconsin: One Hundred and Twenty Five Years, 1975, The Jeffersonian Dream: Studies in the History of American Law Land Policy and Development, 1996, numerous articles and book reviews. Lt. Can. Army, 1943—45, capt. Can. Res. Army, 1951—52. Social Sci. Rsch. Coun. fellow, 1955, 66, Guggenheim fellow, 1970, H.E. Huntington Libr. fellow, 1991, 93, Sherman Fairchild Disting. fellow Calif. Inst. Tech., 1975, Ctr. for Advanced Study in the Behavioral Scis. fellow, 1985, NEH fellow, 1985. Fellow Agr. Hist. Soc. (pres. 1963-64); mem. Orgn. Am. Historians (pres. 1982-83), Am. Hist. Assn., Econ. Hist. Assn. (pres. 1981-82), Social Sci. Hist. Assn. (pres. 1977-78), Western Hist. Assn. (hon. life). Avocation: competitive Samoyed dog training. Office: 1914 Vilas Ave Madison WI 53711 Office Phone: 608-255-5643. Business E-Mail: agbogue@wisc.edu.

BOGUE, ANDREW WENDELL, federal judge; b. Yankton, SD, May 23, 1919; s. Andrew S. and Genevieve Bogue; m. Florence Elizabeth Williams, Aug. 5, 1945; children—Andrew Stevenson, Laurie Beth, Scott MacFarlane. BS, S.D. State U., 1941; LL.B., U. S.D., 1947. Bar: S.D. 1947. States atty. Turner County, S.D., 1952-67; judge 2d Jud. Cir., S.D., 1967-70, U.S. Dist. Ct. S.D., Rapid City, 1970—, chief judge, from 1980, sr. judge, 1985—. Mem. S.D. Bar Assn., Fed. Judges Assn. Episcopalian. Office: US Courthouse Fed Bldg Rm 244 515 9th St Rapid City SD 57701-2626

BOGUE, ERIC H., state legislator, lawyer; b. Oct. 4, 1964; Bar: S.D. Lawyer pvt. practice, Dupree, S.D.; mem. S.D. Ho. of Reps., Pierre, 1995-96, S.D. Senate from 28th dist., Pierre, 1999—. Mem. judiciary and tax coms., appropriations com., vice chair govt. ops. and audit com. S.D. Ho. of Reps. Republican. E-mail: boguelaw@gwtc.net.

BOGUT, ANDREW, professional basketball player; b. Melbourne, Australia, Nov. 28, 1984; s. Michael and Anne Bogut. Student, U. Utah, Salt Lake City, 2003—05. Forward-ctr. Milw. Bucks, 2005—. Ctr. Australian Nat. Team Olympic Games, Athens, Greece, 2004, Internat. Basketball Fedn. (FIBA) World Championships, 2006. Founder Andrew Bogut 4 Found. Named MVP, Internat. Basketball Fedn. Jr. World Championships, Greece, 2003, Player of Yr., Mountain West Conf., 2004, at. Player of Yr., Basketball Times, 2005, ESPN; named to All-Tournament Team, Great Alaska Shootout, 2004, First-Team All Dist. 13, Nat. Assn. Basketball Coaches, 2004, Mountain West Conf., 2004, All-Rookie First Team, NBA, 2006. Office: Milw Bucks 1001 N Fourth St Milwaukee WI 53203

BOH, IVAN, philosophy educator; b. Dolenji Lazi, Yugoslavia, Dec. 13, 1930; s. France and Marija (Mihelic) B.; m. Magda Kosnik, Aug. 30, 1957; children: Boris, Marko. BA, Ohio U., 1954; MA, Fordham U., 1956; PhD, U. Ottawa, Ont., Can., 1958. Instr. Clarke Coll., Dubuque, Iowa, 1957-59, asst. prof., 1959-62; vis. asst. prof. U. Iowa, 1962-63; Fulbright research fellow U. Munich, Germany, 1964-65; asso. prof. Mich. State U., 1966-69; prof. philosophy Ohio State U., Columbus, 1969-95, prof. emeritus, 1995—. Rsch. in Spanish librs., 1972-73; MUCIA exch. prof. Moscow State U., 1979-80; Fulbright sr. rsch. fellow U. Ljubljana (Yugoslavia), 1982-83; Irex and Fulbright sr. rsch. fellow U. Halle-Wittenberg, German Dem. Republic, and Jagiellonsky U. (Poland), 1986-87 Author: Epistemic Logic in the Later Middle Ages, 1993; contbr. articles to profl. jours. Recipient Evans Latin prize Ohio U., 1954. Mem. Am. Philos. Assn., Am. Catholic Philos. Assn., Medieval Acad. Am. Office: Ohio State U Dept Philosophy Columbus OH 43210 Home: 5132 Banbridge Ln Dublin OH 43016-4311

BOHLKE, ARDYCE, state legislator; b. Omaha, Nov. 2, 1943; m. Jan Bohlke, 1967; children: Jon Jr., Jason. BS, U. Nebr., 1965. Mem. from dist. 33 Nebr. State Senate, Lincoln, 1992—, mem. com. on coms., natural resources and rules coms., vice chair edn. com. Past pres. Hastings Bd. Edn., Hastings YWCA. Mem. LWV (past pres.), Bus. and Profl. Women, Rotary. Office: 7 Village Dr Hastings NE 68901-2436

BOHM, FRIEDRICH (FRIEDL) K. M., architectural firm executive; Degree in architecture, U. Vienna; M in City and Regional Planning, Ohio State U. With NBBJ, Columbus, Ohio, 1975—, mng. ptnr., 1987-97, pres., chmn., 1997—. Hon. consul to Austria; advisor internat. policy Prime Min. Austria; bd. dirs. Huntington Nat. Bank, M/I Homes. Recipient Disting. Alumnus award Ohio State U., numerous design awards and recognitions; named Entrepreneur of Yr., INC. mag., 1992; Fulbright scholar. Fellow AIA. Office: NBBJ 1555 Lake Shore Dr Columbus OH 43204-3825

BOHM, GEORG G. A., physicist; b. Brünn, Czechoslovakia, Oct. 7, 1935; came to U.S., 1966; s. Gustav Anton and Olga B.; m. Marga L. Girak; children: Astrid, Alexander. BSEE, U. Vienna, Austria, 1957, PhD in Physics, 1962, postgrad., 1962-64. Scientist Max-Planck Inst. Physikalische Chemie, Göttingen, Germany, 1972-75; group leader, mgr. Firestone Tire & Rubber Corp., Westbury, N.Y., 1967-72, asst. dir. rsch. lab. Akron, Ohio, 1973-93; dir. rsch. Bridgestone/Firestone, Akron, 1993—. Bd. dirs. Bridgestone Firestone Rsch. Inc.; vis. prof. IAEA, Vienna, 1964-66; adv. panel Nat. Acad. Sci., Washington, 1994-95; adv. bd. Ctr. Molecular & Microstructure Composite Case Western U./Akron U., 1990-94. Mem. editl. bd. Jour. Rubber Chemistry & Tech., 1982-85; contbr. articles to profl. jours.; patentee in field. Mem. Am. Chem. Soc. Avocations: chess, tennis, golf. Office: Bridgestone/Firestone Rsch 1200 Firestone Pkwy Akron OH 44317-0002

BOHM, HENRY VICTOR, physicist; b. Vienna, July 16, 1929; came to U.S., 1941, naturalized, 1946; s. Victor Charles and Gertrude (Rie) B.; m. Lucy Margaret Coons, Sept. 2, 1950 (dec. Oct. 2003); children: Victoria Rie, Jeffrey Ernst Thompson. AB, Harvard U., 1950; MS, U. Ill., 1951; PhD, Brown U., 1958. Jr. physicist GE, 1951, 53-54; teaching, research asst. Brown U., 1954-58, research assoc., summer 1958; staff mem. Arthur D. Little, Inc., Cambridge, Mass., 1958-59; asso. prof. physics dept. Wayne State U., Detroit, 1959-64, acting chmn. physics dept., 1962-63, prof., 1964-93, prof. emeritus Detroit, 1993—, v.p. for grad. studies and research, 1968-71, v.p. for spl. projects, 1971-72, provost, 1972-75, on leave, 1978-83, interim dean Coll. Liberal Arts, 1984-86; pres. Argonne Univs. Assn., 1978-83. Vis. prof. Cornell U., 1966-67, U. Lancaster, Eng., summer 1967, Purdue U., winter, 1977, Rensselaer Poly. Inst., winter 1992; cons.-examiner commn. on instns. higher edn. N. Central Assn. Colls. and Schs., 1971-80, mem. commn., 1974-78. Bd. dirs. Center for Research Libraries, Chgo, 1970-75, chmn., 1973; bd. overseers Lewis Coll., Ill. Inst. Tech., 1980-83. Ltjg. USNR, 1951—53. Fellow Am. Phys. Soc.

BOHN, ROBERT G., transportation company executive; Dir. ops. European automotive group Johnson Controls; v.p. ops. Oshkosh (Wis.) Truck Corp., 1992—94, pres., COO, 1994-97, pres., CEO, 1997—2000, chmn., pres., CEO, 2000—07, chmn., CEO, 2007—. Bd. dir. Graco Inc. Office: Oshkosh Truck Corp 2307 Oregon St Oshkosh WI 54902

BOHNHOFF, DAVID ROY, agricultural engineer, educator; b. Plymouth, Wis., June 10, 1956; s. Roy Arthur and Jean Audrey (Manneck) B.; m. Rhonda Kay Johanning, July 2, 1982; children: Benjamin, Christian, Aaron. BS in Agrl. Engring., U. Wis., Platteville, 1978; MS in Agrl. Engring., U. Wis., Madison, 1985, PhD in Agrl. Engring., 1988. Registered profl. engr., Wis. Design engr. Gehl Co., West Bend, Wis., 1979-80; dairy farmer Calmset Farms, Plymouth, Wis., 1981-82; rsch. asst. agrl. engring. dept. U. Wis., Madison, 1982-87, lectr. agrl. engring., 1987-88, asst. prof. agrl. engring., 1988-93, assoc. prof. agrl. engring., 1993-95; divsn. rsch. and product devel. mgr. Lester Bldg. Systems, Lester Prairie, Minn., 1995-96; assoc. prof. biological sys. engring. U. Wis., Madison, 1996-2000, prof. biological sys. engring., 2000—. Mem. Midwest Plan Svc., Ames, Iowa, 1988-95, chmn., 1993-94, mem. constrn. sect. com. 1993-95, chmn. task force, 1990, mem. design and constrn. com., 1988-94. Contbr. articles, reports to profl. jours. Youth soccer coach Regent Soccer Club, Madison, 1989-94, Madison 56ers Soccer Club, 1994-95, youth basketball coach YMCA, Madison, 1994; youth softball coach Madison Area Sch.-Cmty. Recreation League, Madison, 1994; Cub Scout den leader Boy Scouts Am., Madison, 1991-92; project leader 4-H Club, Madison, 1992-95, Glencoe Cmty. Recreational Soccer coach, 1996. Named Outstanding Recent Alumnus U. Wis.-Platteville, 1993, Young Engr. of Yr. ASAE Wis. Sect., 1994; named to Nat. Rural Builder Hall of Fame Rural Builder, 1996. Mem. Am. Soc. Agrl. Engring. (chmn. structures com. 1994-96, post and pole design com. 1991-97; mem. various coms., chmn. Wis. sect. 1991-92, program chair 1990-91, sec.-treas. 1989-90, 97-98, nominating com. 1988-89, career devel. com. 1998—, awards chair, 2000—, tech. reviewer trans. and Jour. Applied Engring. in Agr., Outstanding Paper award 1992, Superior Paper award 1997, Henry Giese Structures and Environ. award 2000), Nat. Frame Builders Assn. (mem. rsch. & edn. com., mem. editl. rev. com., Bernon C. Perkins award 1996, 2000), Alpha Gamma Rho (alumni sec. Beta Gamma chpt. 1980, pres. 1980-81), Alpha Zeta, Gamma Sigma Delta. Lutheran. Avocations: all sports, woodworking, playing cards. Home: 5931 Schroeder Rd Madison WI 53711-2573 Office: U Wis Biol Systems Engring 460 Henry Mall Madison WI 53706-1533

BOHO, DAN L., lawyer; b. Chgo., Sept. 18, 1952; s. Lawrence M. and Genevieve A. (Zurek) Boho; m. Sheri L. Krisco, Sept. 10, 1977; children: Courtney, Ashely. BA, Loyola U., Chgo., 1974, JD, 1977. Bar: Ill. 1977, US Dist. Ct. (no. dist.) Ill. 1977. Sr. ptnr., leader litig. group Hinshaw & Culbertson, Chgo., 1977—. Fellow: Am. Coll. Trial Lawyers; mem.: ABA, Chgo. Bar Assn. (chmn. professionalism com.), Chgo. Trial Lawyers Club (past pres.), Ill. Bar Assn. (past del. assembly), Advs. Soc., Ill. Def. Coun., Def. Rsch. Inst., Ill. Soc. Trial Lawyers (past bd. dirs.), Fedn. Ins. and Corp. Counsel (past chmn. comml. law sect.), BOMA Chgo., Japan Am. Soc. (past bd. dirs.), Polish Am. Assn. (past chmn. bd. dirs.), Heartland Alliance (past bd. dirs.), Phi Alpha Delta (past pres. Webster chpt.). Avocations: travel, tennis, skiing. Office: Hinshaw & Culbertson 222 N La Salle St Ste 300 Chicago IL 60601-1081 Office Phone: 312-704-3453. Office Fax: 312-704-3001. Business E-Mail: dboho@hinshawlaw.com.

BOHR, NICK, reporter; BS in Broadcast Journalism, Marquette U. With WXRO Radio, Beaver Dam, WYKY, Beaver Dam, WBEV, Beaver Dam, WISN-AM Radio, Beaver Dam; reporter WISN 12, Milwaukee, Wis., 1994—. Office: WISN PO Box 402 Milwaukee WI 53201-3331

BOIES, WILBER H., lawyer; b. Bloomington, Ill., Mar. 15, 1944; s. W. H. and Martha Jane (Hutchison) B.; m. Victoria Joan Steinitz, Sept. 17, 1966; children: Andrew Charles, Carolyn Ursula. AB, Brown U., 1965; JD, U. Chgo., 1968. Bar: Ill. 1968, U.S. Dist. Ct. (no. dist.) Ill. 1968, U.S. Dist. Ct. (ea. dist.) Wis. 1973, U.S. Ct. Appeals (7th cir.) 1974, U.S. Ct. Appeals (5th cir.) 1975, U.S. Ct. Appeals (3d cir.) 1977, U.S. Supreme Ct. 1978, U.S. Ct. Appeals (8th cir.) 1994, U.S. Ct. Appeals (9th cir.) 1995. Assoc. Altheimer & Gray, Chgo., 1968-71; ptnr. McDermott, Will & Emery, Chgo., 1971—. Contbr. articles to profl. jours. Active Internat Inst. for Conflict Prevention and Resolution, panel mem. Fellow Chgo. Bar Found.(life); mem. ABA, Am. Bar Found., Bar Assn. 7th Fed. Cir., Chgo. Bar Assn. (chmn. class litigation com. 1991-92), Chgo. Coun. Lawyers, Lawyers Club Chgo., Met. Club. Office: McDermott Will & Emery 227 W Monroe St Ste 4400 Chicago IL 60606-5096 Office Phone: 312-984-7686. E-mail: bboies@mwe.com.

BOLAND, JAMES C., sports association executive; Joined Ernst & Young LLP, 1976, vice chmn. ctrl. region, 1988-96; pres., CEO Cavs/Gund Arena Co., Cleve., 1998—2003, vice chmn., 2003—. Bd. dir. Goodyear Tire & Rubber Co., Sherwin-Williams Co., 1998—, Internat. Steel Group Inc., Invacare Corp. Trustee Bluecoats, Inc., Harvard Bus. Sch. Club, Cleve. Office: Cavs/Gund Arena Co 1 Center Ct Cleveland OH 44115

BOLAND, MICHAEL JOSEPH, state legislator; b. Davenport, Iowa, Aug. 20, 1942; s. Francis Charles and Opal (Waites) B.; m. Mary Rose Lavorato, 1967; children: Susan, Barbara Ann. BA, Upper Iowa U., Fayette, 1967; MSE, Henderson State U., Arkadelphia, 1972. Del. County and Iowa State Conv., 1970; East Moline chmn. and 36th legis. dist. chmn. Polit. Action Coms. for Edn., 1974-75; mem. Bicentennial Com.; del. Ill. State Dem. Conv., 1978; alt. del. Dem. Nat. Mid-Term Conf., 1978; del. Dem. Nat. Conv., 1980; mem. from dist. 71 Ill. Ho. of Reps., 1994—. Coord. West Ill. Coalition for Polit. Honesty's Legis. Cutback Amendment; mem. United Twp. H.S. Bd. Edn., 1984-85; v.p. Citizens Utility Bd., Ill.civ Nat. bd. dirs. UN Reform Campaign Com.; libr. bd. trustees, East Moline, Ill., 1975-79. Named one of 11 Who Made a Difference in Ill., Chgo. Tribune Sunday Mag. Mem. LWV (mem. govt. com. 1980-81), Ill. Coalition Polit. Honesty (bd. dirs. 1987), Consumers and Taxpayers Together (founding mem.). Address: 2041-J Stratton Bldg Springfield IL 62706-0001 also: 4416 River Dr Moline IL 61265-1734

BOLAND, RAYMOND JAMES, bishop emeritus; b. Tipperary, Ireland, Feb. 8, 1932; Student, Nat. U. Ireland and All Hallows Sem., Dublin. Ordained priest Archdiocese of Washington, 1957; ordained bishop, 1988; bishop Diocese of Birmingham, Ala., 1988—93, Diocese of Kansas City-St. Joseph, Mo., 1993—2005, bishop emeritus Mo., 2005—. Roman Catholic. Office: Diocese of Kansas City-St Joseph 300 East 36th St PO Box 419037 Kansas City MO 64141-6037 also: 2552 Gillham Rd Kansas City MO 64108 Office Phone: 816-756-1850. Office Fax: 816-456-2105. E-mail: bishopboland@diocesekcsj.org.*

BOLANDER, WILLIAM J., mechanical engineer; b. Rolla, Mich., 1960; m. Beth Bolander; 2 children. BA in Mechanical and Electrical Engring., 1983; MME, Purdue U., 1984. With Saturn; algorithm technical resource leader (automotive engr.) General Motors Powertrain, Pontiac, Mich., 1994. Recipient Jerome H. Lemelson prize for Excellence in Invention and Innovation MIT, 1995, 4 Boss Kettering awards. Achievements include patents for vehicle engine ignition timing system with adaptive knock retard, coast-sync-coast downshift control methods for clutch-to-clutch transmission shifting, valve position sensor diagnostic, throttle position sensor error recovery control method, vehicle ignition system having adaptive knock retard with starting temperature correction, method for adjusting engine output power to compensate forloading due to a variable capacity air conditioning compressor, fuel control system for engine during coolant failure. Office: General Motors Corp/GM Tech Ctr 30200 Mound Rd Warren MI 48092-2025

BOLCHAZY, LADISLAUS JOSEPH, publishing company executive; b. Michalovce, Slovakia, June 7, 1937; AA in Classics, Divine Word Coll. and Sem., Conesus, NY, 1960; BA in Philosophy, St. Joseph's Coll. and Sem., Yonkers, NY, 1963; MA in Classics, NYU, 1967; PhD in Classics, SUNY, Albany, 1973. Permanent cert. Latin tchr., .Y. Tchr. Latin and English, Sacred Heart High Sch., Yonkers, 1962-65; instr. Siena Coll., Loudonville, N.Y., 1966-67; asst. prof. La Salette Coll. and Sem., Altamont, N.Y., 1971-75; vis. asst. prof. Millersville (Pa.) State Coll., 1975-76, Loyola U., Chgo., 1976-77, adj. prof., 1979—; owner, mgr. U.S. Graphics, Chgo.-Scan Typographers, Inc., 1985—; pres. Bolchazy-Carducci Pubs., Inc., Wauconda, Ill., 1978—. Organizer seminar APA, 1975; condr. NEH summer inst. on Sophocles and Thucydides, Cornell U., 1976, on ancient history U. Mich., Ann Arbor, 1977; host Myth Is Truth, Sta. WLUC, Loyola U., 1977, Sta. WRRG, Triton Coll., 1978. Author: Hospitality in Early Rome, 1977, reprinted as Hospitality in Antiquity, 1994, A Concordance to the "Utopia" of St. Thomas More, 1978, The Coin-Inscriptions and Epigraphical Abbreviations of Imperial Rome, 1978, (with others) A Concordance to Ausonius, 1982; co-editor: The Ancient World, 1978—, The Classical Bulletin, 1988—; contbr. articles to profl. jours. Pres. Slovak-Am. Internat. Cultural Found., Inc., 1998. Teaching fellow SUNY, 1967-71; rsch. grantee Loyola U., 1977. Home: 698 Golf Ln Barrington IL 60010-7329 Office: Bolchazy Carducci Pub Inc 1000 Brown St Ste 101 Wauconda IL 60084-3120

BOLCOM, WILLIAM ELDEN, composer, educator, musician; b. Seattle, May 26, 1938; s. Robert Samuel and Virginia (Lauermann) B.; m. Fay Levine, Dec. 23, 1963 (div. 1967); m. Katherine Agee Ling, June 8, 1968 (div. 1969); m. Joan Clair Morris, Nov. 28, 1975. BA, U. Wash., 1958; MA, Mills Coll., 1961; postgrad., Paris Conservatoire de Musique, 1959-61, 64-65; D of Mus. Art, Stanford U., 1964; D of Music (hon.), San Francisco Conservatory, 1994, Albion Coll., 1995; studied with, Berthe Poncy Jacobson, 1949-58, John Verrall, 1951-58, Leland Smith, 1961-64, Darius Milhaud, 1957-61; George Rochberg, 1966. Acting asst. prof. music dept. U. Wash., Seattle, 1965-66; lectr., asst. prof. music Queens Coll., CUNY, Flushing, 1966-68; vis. critic music theater Drama Sch., Yale U., 1968-69; composer in residence Theater Arts Program, NYU, NYC, 1969-71; asst. prof. U. Mich. Sch. Music, Ann Arbor, 1973-77, assoc. prof., 1973-83, prof., 1983-94, Ross Lee Finney disting. prof. composition, 1994—, chmn. composition dept., 1998—2003; artist in residence Am. Acad. Rome, 2003; Ernest Bloch composer in residence U. Calif. Berkeley, 2005. Mem. jury Nat. Endowment for Arts, 1976-77, 84, 85. Composer: 6 symphonies, 1957, 64, 79, 86, 89, 97, String Quartets 1-8, 1950-65, String Quartet #9 (Novella), 1972, String Quartet #10, 1988, Décalage for cello and piano, 1961-62, Fantasy-Sonata for piano, 1960-62, Concertante for Flute, Oboe, Violin, and Orch, 1960, cabaret opera Dynamite Tonite, 1960-63, rev., 1966, Octet, 1962, Concerto-Serenade for Violin and Strings, 1964, 12 Etudes for Piano, 1959-66, Fives, Double Concerto for Violin, Piano and Strings, 1966, Morning and Evening Poems (Cantata), 1966, Session I for Chamber Ensemble, 1965, Session II for violin and viola, 1966, Session III for clarinet, violin, cello, piano, percussion, 1966, Session IV for chamber ensemble, 1967, Black Host for organ, percussion and taped sounds, 1967, Piano Rags, 1967-74, cabaret opera Greatshot, 1967-69, Praeludium for vibraphone and organ, 1969, Dark Music for timpani and cello, 1970, Duets for Quintet, 1970, Unpopular Songs, 1969-71, Hydraulis for organ, 1971, Commedia for chamber orch, 1971, Whisper Moon (chamber ensemble), 1971, Frescoes for two pianists, 1971, Seasons for solo guitar, 1974, Open House, song cycle on poems by Roethke, 1975, Piano Concerto, 1975-76, Piano Quartet, 1976, Revelation Studies for Carillon, 1976, Mysteries for Organ, 1976, score for stage works Puntila (Brecht), 1976, Man is Man (Brecht), 1977, Beggar's Opera (posthumous collaboration with Darius Milhaud), 1978, Violin Sonatas, 1956, 78, 92, 94, 12 Gospel Preludes for Organ, 1979, 81, 84, Humoresk for organ and orch., 1969, Brass Quintet, 1979, 24 Cabaret Songs, 1963-96, Aubade for Oboe and Piano, 1982, Songs of Innocence and of Experience (Blake), 1956-82 (Grammy awards for Best Classical Album, Best Choral Performance, Best Classical Contemporary Composition, and Best Prodr., 2005), Violin Concerto in D, 1983, Lilith (saxophone, piano), 1984, Abendmusik, 1977, Little Suite of Dances in E flat for clarinet and piano, 1984, Orphée-Sérénade, 1984, Fantasia Concertante for viola, cello and orch., 1985, Capriccio for Violoncello and Piano, 1985, orchestral dance suite Seattle Slew, 1986, 12 New Etudes for Piano, 1977-86 (recipient Pulitzer Prize, 1988), Spring Concertino for Oboe and Chamber Orch., 1986-87, Five Fold Five for woodwind quintet and piano, 1985-87, Clarinet Concerto, 1990, (musical) Casino Paradise (libretto Arnold Weinstein), 1986-90, Fairy Tales for viola, cello, bass, 1987-88, Sonata for Violoncello and Piano, 1989, (song cycle on Am. women poets) I Will Breathe a Mountain, 1989-90, The Mask (chorus and piano), 1990, Recuerdos for two pianos, 1991, opera McTeague (libretto A. Weinstein and R. Altman), 1990-92, Lyric Concerto for flute and orch., 1993, Trio for clarinet, violin and piano, 1993, Sonata for 2 pianos in one movement, 1993, Suite for play Broken Glass by Arthur Miller, 1994, Let Evening Come (soprano, viola, piano), 1994, A Whitman Triptych, (mezzo-soprano and orchestra), 1995, GAEA Concertos 1-3 for Left Hand and Orch., 1996, Second Piano Quartet, 1995, Briefly It Enters, 1996 (voice and piano), Fanfare for the Detroit Opera House, 1996 (brass), Cabaret Songs, Vol. 3&4 (voice and piano), 1996, Nine Bagatelles, 1996 (piano), Spring Trio, 1996 (piano trio), Turbulence-A Romance, 1996 (2 voices and piano), Sixth Sym., 1997, Collusions (piano written with Curtis Curtis-Smith), 1998, Illuminata (film score written with Arnold Black), 1998, A View From the Bridge (opera), 1998, The Digital Wonder Watch (voice and piano), 1999, The Miracle (male chorus, woodwind quintet, percussion), 1999, Bird Spirits (piano), 2000, Concerto Grosso for Saxophone Quartet and Orch., 1999-2000, From the Diary of Sally Hemings (medium voice and piano), 2000, Piano Quintet (string quartet and piano), 2000, Song (for band), 2001, Naumburg Cycle (baritone and piano), 2001, Borboryçm (organ), 2001; pianist in recs: (with Gerard Schwarz) Cornet Favorites, (with Clifford Jackson, baritone) An Evening with Henry Russell, (with mezzo-soprano Joan Morris) OtherSongs of Leiber and Stoller, (with Joan Morris and Max Morath) These Charming People, (with Joan Morris) The Girl on the MagazineCover, (with Joan Morris) Songs of Ira and George Gershwin, (with Joan Morris and Lucy Simon) The Rodgers and Hart Album, (with Joan Morris and Max Morath) More Rodgers and Hart, (with Joan Morris) Silver Linings (anthology of Jerome Kern), (with Joan Morris) Blue Skies (anthology of Irving Berlin), (with Joan Morris) Black Max (Bolcom cabaret songs with A. Weinstein poetry), (with Joan Morris) Lime Jello: An American Cabaret, (with Joan Morris) Night & Day (anthology of Cole Porter), (with Joan Morris) Let's Do It, (with Sergiu Luca) Works for Violin and Piano (by Bolcom), (with Joan Morris) After the Ball, Vaudeville, Songs of the Great Ladies of the Musical Stage, Wild About Eubie, (with Joan Morris and Clifford Jackson and chorus) Who Shall Rule This American Nation: Songs of Henry Clay Work, (with Joan Morris and Robert White) Orchids in the Moonlight and The Carioca (songs of Vincent Youmans), (with Joan Morris) Moonlight Bay-Songs As Is and Songs As Was; recs. Bolcom's 4th Symphony (Grammy nominee 1987), Violin Concerto, 5th Symphony, Fantasia Concertante (Am. Composers Orch.), 10th String Quartet (Stanford String Quartet), 1st and 3rd Symphonies, Seattle Slew Suite (Louisville Orch.), Orphée-Sérénade (Grammy nominee 1994), others; solo recordings include Heliotrope Bouquet, Pastimes and Piano Rags, Bolcom Plays His Own Rags, Piano Music of George Gershwin, Piano Music of Darius Milhaud, Bolcom: 12 Etudes, Euphonic Sounds (Scott Joplin anthology); author: (with Robert Kimball) Reminiscing with Sissle and Blake, 1973, Trouble in the Music World, 1988; editor book of essays: The Aesthetics of Survival by George Rochberg, 1982; contbr. to Grove's Dictionary, 6th edit; contbg. editor: Annals of Scholarship. Recipient Kurt Weill award, 1963, William and Noma Copley award, 1960, Marc Blitzstein Award for Excellence Am. Acad. Arts and Letters, 1965, NY State Coun. award, 1971, Nat. Endowment for Arts award, 1974, 1979, 1982-84, Koussevitzky Found. award, 1974, 1993, Henry Russel award, U. Mich., 1977, Henry Russel Lectureship, 1997, Mich. Arts Coun. award, 1986, Gov.'s Arts award, 1987, Pulitzer Prize in Music, 1988, Citation of Merit, U. Mich. Sch. Music Alumni Assn., 1989, Disting. Achievement award, U. Wash., 1993, Alumnus Summa Laude Dignatus award, 2003, Alfred I. Du Pont award, Del. Symphony Assn., 1994, Nat. Medal Arts, Nat. Endowment for Arts, 2006; named Composer of Yr., Am. Guild Organists, 1998, Outstanding Classical Composer, Detroit Music Awards, 2006, Composer of Yr., Musical Am., 2007; Guggenheim Found. fellow, 1964, 1968; Rockefeller Found. grantee, 1965, 1969, 1972. Mem. Am. Acad. Arts and Letters, Am. Music Ctr., Am. Composer Alliance, Am. Repertory Theatre (bd. dirs.), Charles Ives Soc. (bd. dirs.), Delta Omicron (nat. patron), Azazels. Home: 3080 Whitmore Lake Rd Ann Arbor MI 48105-9649 Office: U Mich Sch Music 2243 Moore Bldg Ann Arbor MI 48109 E-mail: wbolcom@umich.edu.*

BOLDING, JAY D., food products executive; B in Adminstrn., Kansas State U. CPA. With KPMG Peat Marwick; v.p., CFO, treas. Allen & O'Hara, 1995—97; v.p. bus. processes and fin. analysis ConAgra Foods, Inc., Omaha, 1997—99, sr. v.p., 1999—2000, sr. v.p., controller, 2000—. Office: ConAgra Foods Inc 1 ConAgra Dr Omaha NE 68102-5001

BOLDT, MICHAEL HERBERT, lawyer; b. Detroit, Oct. 11, 1950; s. Herbert M. and Mary Therese (Fitzgerald) B.; m. Margaret E. Clarke, May 25, 1974; children: Timothy (dec.), Matthew. Student, U. Detroit, 1968-70; BA, Wayne State U., 1972; JD, U. Mich., 1975. Bar: Ind. 1975, U.S. Dist. Ct. (so. dist.) Ind. 1975, U.S. Ct. Appeals (7th cir.) 1979, U.S. Supreme Ct. 1980, U.S. Ct. Appeals (D.C. cir.) 1983. Assoc. Ice Miller, Indpls., 1975-81, ptnr., 1982—. Contbr. articles to profl. jours. Bd. dirs. Brooke's Place for Grieving Young People, Inc. Mem. Ind. State Bar Assn., Indpls. Bar Assn., Highland Golf and Country Club (bd. dirs.). Office: Ice Miller LLP Ste 3100 1 American Sq Indianapolis IN 46282-0200 Office Phone: 317-236-2327. Business E-Mail: Michael.Boldt@icemiller.com.

BOLDT, OSCAR CHARLES, construction executive, director; b. Appleton, Wis., Apr. 20, 1924; s. Oscar John and Dorothy A. (Bartmann) B.; m. Patricia Hamar, July 9, 1949; children: Charles, Thomas, Margaret. BSCE, U. Wis., Madison, 1948; degree (hon.), Ripon Coll., Wis., 2001, Lawrence U., Appleton, Wis., 2003, U. Wis., Madison, 2006. Pres. O.J. Boldt Constrn. Co., Appleton, 1950-79, CEO, chmn. bd. dirs., 1979-84; chmn. bd. dirs. The Boldt Group Inc., Appleton, 1984—; sec. W.S. Patterson Co., 1963-89. Trustee Lawrence U., 1981—; emeritus bd. dirs. M&I Bank, LA, 2002 Chmn. bd. dirs. Cmty. Found. for Fox Valley Region, 1991-93; pres. Appleton YMCA, 1955-57, Appleton Meml. Hosp., 1975-76; bd. dirs. Theda Care (formerly United Health) Wis., 1990-99; co-chmn. fund drive Fox Cities United Way, 1994. 2d lt. USAAF, 1943-45. Named to Paper Industry Internat. Hall of Fame, 2000, Wis. Bus. Hall of Fame, 2003, Jr. Achievement Hall of Fame, 2003, Appleton H.S. Hall of Fame, 1999; recipient Disting. Svc. award, Appleton Jaycees, 1960, Disting. Engr. award, U. Wis., 1985, Walter Rugland Cmty. Svc. award, 1988, Master Entrepreneur award, Ernst and Young, 1991, Renaissance award, 1991, Regent's award, St. Olaf's Coll., 1993, Exec. of Yr. award, N.E. Wis.'s Sales and Mktg. Mag., 1994, Disting. Alumni award, U. Wis. Alumni Assn., 1999, Disting. Contractor award, ASCE, 2000, Wis. Assoc. Gen. Contractor Horizon award, 2003, Walter A. Nushert, Sr. Constructor award, 2005, Samuel C. Johnson Distinction in Corporate Leadership award, Wis. State Hist. Soc., 2007. Mem. Appleton Area C. of C. (pres. 1967), Appleton Rotary (pres. 1975-76, Vocat. Svc. award 1977, Paul Harris fellow, 1979), Riverview Country Club (pres. 1968-69). Republican. Presbyterian. Office: The Boldt Group Inc PO Box 373 2525 N Roemer Rd Appleton WI 54911-8623 Home: 2751 Fox Run Appleton WI 54914 Office Phone: 920-225-6100. Business E-Mail: oscar.boldt@boldt.com.

BOLE, GILES G., physician, researcher, medical educator; b. Battle Creek, Mich., July 28, 1928; s. Giles Gerald, Sr. and Kittie Belle B.; m. Elizabeth J. Dooley, May 11, 1985; children: David Giles, Elizabeth Ann. BS, U. Mich., Ann Arbor, 1949, MD, 1953. Diplomate Am. Bd. Internal Medicine. Resident in internal medicine U. Mich., Ann Arbor, 1953-56, fellow rheumatology Rackham arthritis research unit, 1958-61, asst. prof. internal medicine, 1961-64, assoc. prof. internal medicine, 1964-70, prof. internal medicine, 1970—; physician-in-charge Rackham Arthritis Research Unit, Ann Arbor, 1971-86, chief rheumatology div., 1976-86; assoc. dean clin. affairs, sr. assoc. dean Med. Sch. U. Mich., Ann Arbor, 1986-88, exec. assoc. dean Med. Sch., 1988-90, interim dean Med. Sch., 1990-91, dean Med. Sch., 1991-96, dean emeritus Med. Sch., 1996—. Dir. U. Mich. Arthritis Ctr., Ann Arbor, 1977-86; bd. govs. Am. Bd. Internal Medicine, 1979-83, chmn. rheumatology com., 1979-83. Capt. M.C., USAF, 1956-58. Recipient Borden Academic Achievement award U. Mich., 1953; Postdoctoral Research fellow Arthritis Found., 1961-63 Mem. Am. Fed. Clin. Rsch. (chmn. Midwest sect. 1967-68), Cen. Soc. Clin. Rsch. (pres. 1976-77), Am. Rheumatism Assn. (pres. 1980-81). Office: U Mich Med Sch M 7300 Med Sci I 4101 Med Sci Bldg 1 C-wing Ann Arbor MI 48109-0600

BOLER, JOHN M., manufacturing executive; b. Marion, Ohio, 1934; m. Mary Jo Lombardo. Grad. with bus. degree, John Carroll Univ., Cleve., Ohio, 1956; Degree (hon.), John Carroll Univ., 1996; LHD (hon.), St. Joseph Coll., Rensselaer, Ind., 2001; degree (hon.), Ursuline Coll., Pepper Pike, Ohio, 2001. With Clevite Corp. (acquired by Gould, Inc.); v.p. adminstrn. Gould, Inc.; founder Boler Co., Itasca, Ill., 1977, pres., CEO & chmn., 1977—. Bd. dir. Anchor Cross Soc.; chmn. Am. Cancer Soc. Found.; trustee John Carroll Univ.; assoc. trustee Bradley Univ.; former mem. adv. bd. Willis Corroon, Ill.; bd. trustee Rush Univ. Med. Ctr. Army Transportation Corps and active reserves. Achievements include (with wife) being involved with several philanthropic endeavors. Office: Boler Co 500 Park Blvd Ste 1010 Itasca IL 60143-1285

BOLGER, DAVID P., former insurance company executive; b. Aug. 23, 1957; BS in Acctg./Fin., Marquette U., 1979; MM in Fin., Northwestern U., 1980. Credit analyst Am. Nat. Bank & Trust Co., Chgo., 1980-82, comml. banking officer, 1982-89, sr. v.p., CFO, 1989-92, exec. v.p., 1992-93, exec. v.p., treas., 1993-94, pres., 1996-98; exec. dir. Banc One, Chgo., 1998—2001; exec. v.p. fin. & adminstrn. Aon Corp., Chgo., 2003—07, exec. v.p. fin. & adminstrn., CFO, 2003—07; COO Chgo. 2016 Olympics Com., 2007—. Dean's adv. coun., Coll. Bus. Adminstrn. Marquette U.; alumni adv. bd., J.L. Kellogg Grad. Sch. Mgmt. Northwestern U.; bd. dir. Mercy Hosp. & Med. Ctr., Impulse Theatre Co., Fist Non-Profit Ins. Co.; active United Way/Crusade of Mercy; bd. dir. Merit Sch. of Music, Lincoln Park Zoo. Mem.: Robert Morris Asscos., Chgo. Hist. Soc., Execs. Club Chgo.*

BOLIN, STEVEN ROBERT, veterinarian researcher; b. Tokyo, July 12, 1950; s. Robert Cornwall and Irene Fay (Temple) B.; m. Carole Ann Sawyer, May 23, 1981; children: Christopher, Matthew, Sarah, Kelsey. DVM, Purdue U., 1974, MS, 1979, PhD, 1982. Lic. veterinarian, Ind. Veterinarian pvt. practice, Ottawa, Ill., 1974-77; rsch. scientist Nat. Animal Disease Ctr., Ames, Iowa, 1982-84, lead scientist, 1984—, rsch. leader, 1992—. Contbr. over 80 sci. articles on viral disease of cattle and swine to profl. jours. and chpts. to books. Cubmaster Pack 196, Ames, 1994-96. Recipient Salmon award Nat. Assn. Fed. Veterinarians, 1987, Pestivirus Rsch. medal European Vet. Virology Soc., 1992. Mem. Am. Vet. Med. Assn., U.S. Animal Health Assn., Nat. Assn. Fed. Veterinarians, Conf. Rsch. Workers in Animal Disease. Achievements include rsch. accomplishments in the discovery of pathogenic mechanisms associated with mucosal disease of cattle; definition of factors of virulence for bovine viral diarrhea virus; definition of methods for identifying separate groups of bovine viral diarrhea virus. Office: USDA Nat Animal Disease Ctr Ames IA 50010-0070

BOLINDER, SCOTT W., publishing company executive; b. 1951; m. Jill Bolinder; children: Jamie, Jesse, Anna. BA in Literature, Wheaton Coll., 1973; MSW, U. Ill., 1975. Adv. sales Huebner Pub. Co., 1979-80; pub. dir. Campus Life Mag., 1980-81, exec. v.p., 1981-82; sr. v.p. Christianity Today Inc., Carol Stream, Ill., 1982-89; v.p., pub. Zondervan Pub. House, Grand Rapids, Mich., 1989—. Bd. dirs. Edn. Assistance Ltd.; active Thornapple Evang. Covenant Ch., Grand Rapids. Capt. US Army, 1975-79. Mem. Acad. Cert. Social Workers. Avocations: music, reading, tennis, biking, Moroccan cooking. Office: Zondervan Pub House 5300 Patterson Ave SE Grand Rapids MI 49512-9512

BOLKCOM, JOE L., state legislator; b. Bloomington, Minn., July 29, 1956; m. Karen Kubby. BA in Sociology, St. Ambrose U., 1983; MA in Pub. Affairs, U. Iowa, 1988. Dir. Sr. Edn., Inc., 1981-86, Sr. Advs., Inc., 1986-88; with Johnson County Health Dept., 1988-92; supr. Johnson County, 1993—; mem. Iowa Senate from 39th dist., 1998—. Mem. Iowa Ground Water Assn., Am. Fedn. Tchrs. (local 716), Iowa Civil Liberties Union. Democrat. Roman Catholic. Home: 728 2d Ave Iowa City IA 52245 Office: State Capitol Dist 39 3 9th And Grand Des Moines IA 50319-0001 E-mail: joe@joebolkcom.org.

BOLLENBACHER, HERBERT KENNETH, steel company official; b. Wilkinsburg, Pa., Apr. 16, 1933; s. Curtis W. and Ebba M. (Frendberg) B.; m. Nancy Jane Cercena, June 29, 1957; children: Mary E., Kenneth E. AB, U. Pitts., 1960, MEd, 1963. Cert. safety prof. Staff asst. tng. J & L Steel Co., Pitts., 1963-66; mgr. tng., devel. and accident prevention Textron Corp., Pitts., 1966-72; supr. safety Copperweld Steel Co., Warren, Ohio, 1972-75, mgr. safety, security, 1975-78, mgr. human resources conservation, 1978-94; exec. v.p. Charles Mgmt., Inc., 1994-2001; cons. 2001—; adj. faculty Pa. State U. mem. Eastminster Presbytery Com. on Ministry; bd. dirs. Trumbull County Prison Ministry. With U.S. Army, 1954-56. Mem. Am. Soc. Safety Engrs. (past pres. Ohio-Pa. chpt., Ohio Safety Profl. of Yr. 1983-84, 92-93), Ohio Soc. Safety Engrs. (state chaplain), Am. Iron and Steel Inst. (chmn. safety task force), Mfrs. Assn. Eastern Ohio and Western Pa. (safety chmn., Safety Profl. of Yr. award 1984, coord. Ohio seat belt coalition 1986, Gov.'s spl. recognition award), Gov.'s Traffic Safety Coun., 1989, Trumbull Camp Gideons Internat. (past pres.), Ohio Gideons (area coord., membership cabinet), Rotary (Paul Harris fellow, pres., benefactor, Ideal of Svc. in Workplace award), Boy Scouts Am. (western reserve coun., loss prevention com.) Girl Scouts (Lakes to River Coun., loss prevention com.) Presbyterian (elder). Contbr. articles to profl. jours. Avocations: softball; volleyball; reading.

BOLLS, IMOGENE LAMB, English language educator, poet; b. Manhattan, Kans., Sept. 25, 1938; d. Don Q. and Helen Letson (Keithley) Lamb; m. Nathan J. Bolls, Jr., Nov. 24, 1962; 1 child, Laurel Helen. BA, Kans. State U., 1960; MA, U. Utah, 1962. Instr. French Kans. State U., Manhattan, 1959-60; instr. English U. Utah, Salt Lake City, 1960-62; instr. to prof. Wittenberg U., Springfield, Ohio, 1963—. Poet-in-residence, dir. journalism program Wittenberg U.; tchg. poet Antioch Writers' Workshop Antioch Coll., summers, 1992—93; intensive seminar poet Antioch Writers' Workshop Antioch Coll., summer, 1994; poetry tchr. Ohio Poet-in-the-Schs. program, 1972—82; poetry instr. acad. camp; state and nat. poetry judge. Author: (poetry) Glass Walker, 1983, Earthbound, 1989, Advice for the Climb, 1999, works represented in anthologies; contbr. more than 600 poems to mags. Recipient Individual Artist award Ohio Arts Coun., 1982, 90, Poetry prize S.D. Rev., 1983, Poetry award Kans. Quarterly, 1985, Ohioana Poetry award Ohioana Libr. Assn., 1995; finalist Vassar Miller Prize in Poetry, 1994; grantee Ireland, 1986, France, 1990, Am. Southwest. Mem. Acad. Am. Poets (assoc.), Poetry Soc. Am., Women in Comm. Avocations: Native American cultures, hiking, photography, music, travel. Address: PO Box 2917 Taos NM 87571

BOLNICK, HOWARD JEFFREY, insurance company executive, educator, investor; b. Detroit, Oct. 27, 1945; s. Arnold J. and Rebecca (Schuff) B.; m. Kay Zimring, Nov. 29, 1970; children: Lori Ann, Lee Scott. AB with distinction, U. Mich., 1966; MBA, U. Chgo., 1970. Actuary CNA Ins. Cos., Chgo., 1967-76; prin. Coopers & Lybrand, Chgo., 1976-80; pres. bd. dirs. Celtic Life Ins. Co., Chgo., 1980—95; pres. Celtic Health Plans, Chgo., 1994—95; pres., CEO Radix Health Connection, 1997—2001; chmn., CEO InFocus Fin. Group, 2001—06. Adj. prof. Kellogg Grad. Sch., Northwestern U., 1996—; fellow Inst. for Health Svcs. Rsch. and Policy Studies, Northwestern U., 1996-2002. Contbr. articles to profl. and trade publs. Bd. dirs. Schwab Rehab. Ctr., Chgo., 1982-85, Mt. Sinai Med. Ctr., Chgo., 1985-87, Grant Hosp., Chgo., 1991-93, Fla. Small Employer Health Reins. Program, 1992-93; mem. Ill. Comprehensive Health Inst. Plan Bd., Chgo., 1987—, chmn. fin. com., 1989-2002. Fellow Soc. Actuaries (bd. dirs. 1990-92, 94-96, 97-2001, v.p. 1994-96, pres. elect 1997-98, pres. 1998-99); mem. Internat. Actuarial Assn. (chmn. health sect. 2003—), Am. Acad. Actuaries (bd. dirs. 1990-94, 97—, v.p. 1992-94), Health Ins. Assn. Am. (bd. dirs. 1988-90). Jewish. Avocations: scuba diving, travel. Personal E-mail: hbolnick@sbcglobal.net.

BOLTON, WILLIAM J., food products executive; b. 1946; Pres. Jewel Food Stores, Melrose Park, Ill., 1991-95; corp. COO markets Am. Food Stores, 1995; chmn., CEO Bruno's Inc., Birmingham, Ala., 1995-97; exec. vice-pres., pres., COO Retail Food Cos. SUPERVALU Inc., Eden Prairie, Minn., 1997—. Office: SUPERVALU Inc 11840 Valley View Rd Eden Prairie MN 55344-3691

BOMBA, STEVEN J., controls company executive; BS in Physics, U. Wis., MS in Physics, PhD in Physics, U. Wis. Positions with Collins Group Rockwell Internat., v.p. advanced mfg. techs. Milw., 1987-90; positions with Tex. Instuments, Mobil R & D; dir. corp. tech. devel. Allen-Bradley, 1978-85, v.p. corp. tech., 1985-87, Johnson Controls, Inc., Milw., 1990—. Office: Johnson Controls Inc 5757 N Green Bay Ave Milwaukee WI 53209-4408

BOMBARDIR, BRAD, professional hockey player; b. British Columbia, Can., May 5, 1972; Hockey player Minn. Wild, 2000—. Named All Star, Am. Hockey League, 1996; named to 56th selection, Entry Draft, 1990. Office: Minn Wild 317 Washington St Saint Paul MN 55102

BOMCHILL, FERN CHERYL, lawyer; b. Chgo., Feb. 25, 1948; BA, U. Mich., 1969; JD, U. Chgo., 1972. Bar: Ill. 1972, U.S. Dist. Ct. (no. dist.) Ill. 1972, U.S. Ct. Appeals (7th cir.) 1986, U.S. Dist. Ct. (ea. dist.) Mich. 1999. Ptnr. Mayer, Brown & Platt, Chgo. Mem. ABA, Fed. Bar Assn. (bd. dirs. Chgo. chpt.), Chgo. Coun. Lawyers, Law Club Chgo., Legal Club Chgo., The Menomonee Club for Boys and Girls (bd. dirs., pres. 1993-94). Office: Mayer Brown & Platt 190 S La Salle St Ste 3100 Chicago IL 60603-3441 Office Phone: 312-701-7331. Office Fax: 312-706-8608. Business E-Mail: fbomchill@mayerbrown.com.

BOMKE, LARRY K., state legislator; b. Springfield, Ill., June 6, 1950; m. Sally Jo; 2 children. Student, Lincoln Land C.C. Ptnr. Ins. Agy.; mem. Ill. Senate, Springfield, 1995—, mem. exec. appts. com., local govt. & elections com. Republican. Office: State Capitol 111 Capitol Bldg Springfield IL 62706-0001

BONA, JERRY LLOYD, mathematician, educator; b. Little Rock, Feb. 5, 1945; s. Louis Eugene and Mary Eva (Kane) B.; m. Pamela Anne Ross, Dec. 23, 1966 (div. Aug. 2005); children: Rachael Elizabeth, Jennifer Dani'el. BS in Applied Math. and Computer Sci., Washington U., St. Louis, 1966; PhD in Math., Harvard U., 1971; Doctorate (hon.), U. Bordeaux, 2006; distinction honorifica, Universidad Nacional de Trujillo, Peru. Rsch. fellow U. Essex, Colchester, England, 1970-72; L. E. Dickson instr. U. Chgo., 1972-73, from asst. prof. to assoc. prof. to prof., 1973-86; prof. Pa. State U., University Park, 1986-90, Raymond Shibley prof., 1990-95, acting chmn., 1990-91, chmn., 1991-95; CAM prof. math. and physics U. Tex., Austin, 1995—2002; prof. U. Ill., Chgo., 2002—, chmn. Rsch. fellow dept. math. Harvard U. 1970, 73; U.K. Sci. and Engring. Rsch. Coun. sr. vis. fellow Fluid Mechanics Rsch. Inst., U. Essex, 1973, 74, 75, 77, 78; vis. rsch. assoc. Brookhaven Nat. Lab., 1976, 77; NAS exch. visitor to Poland, 1977; vis. prof. Centro Brasileiro Pesquisas Fisicas, Rio de Janeiro, 1980, Math. Rsch. Ctr., 1980-81, U. Brasilia, 1982, Lab. Anvendt Matematisk Fysik, Danish Tech. Sch., 1982, Inst. Math. and its Applications, U. Minn., 1985, 88, 90, 91, 2001; rsch. prof. Applied Rsch. Lab., Pa. State U., 1986-95; prof. invité U. Paris-Sud, Ctr. d'Orsay, 1982, 86-87, 92, 2001, 03, l'Inst. at. Sci. Rsch.-Oceanology, U. Que., 1982-87, Ecole Normale Superieure de Cachan, 1990-91, dir. rsch. CNRS, 1995, U. Bordeaux, 1995, 2001, 03, 08; invited prof. Inst. Pure and Applied Math., Rio de Janeiro, 1991, 93, 99, 2000, 02, 07, Acad. Sinica, Beijing, 1991, 96, 99, Math. Scis. Rsch. Inst., Berkeley, Calif., 1994, U. de Paris Nord, Math. Lab. Villetaneuse, 1993, 95, 99, 2006, U. Oxford, 1995, UNICAMP Campinas, 1998, 2000, 01, 04, 05, 06, TATA Inst., Bangalore, 1999, 2001, 03-04, vis. adj. prof., 2005—; Inst. Sci. de la Mer, U. Que., vis. adj. prof., 1999-2004; invited prof. U. de Paris Val du Marne, 2008; coll. coun. U. Chgo., 1981-84; task force on undergrad. edn. Pa. State U., 1989-91, hon. degree recepient recommendation com., 1994-95; mem. adv. com. NSF Divsn. Math. Scis., 1990-93, chmn., 1990-92; sci. adv. com. basic rsch. math. scis. U.S. Army Rsch. Office, 1979-82, review com. divsn. math. and computer sci. Argonne Nat. Lab., 1984-90, chmn., 1985-89; rev. panel, site visit team NSF Sci. and Tech. Ctrs., 1988; mem. NATO postdoctoral fellowships rev. panel, 1991; mem. ABET evaluating team, 1992; chmn. proposal rev. panel Dept. Energy, 1993; co-dir. Math. Edn. Reform Network, 1993—2004; vis. com. dept. math. U. Ill., Chgo., 1993, MIT, 1993-97, CUNY Bklyn. Coll., 1994, U. NC, 1996, Howard U., 1999, Fla. State U., 2000, James Franc Inst. U. Chgo., 2000-07, U. Okla., 2004, U. Tenn., 2005, Purdue U., Ind. U. Indpls., 2005, Ryerson U., 2007; forum post secondary edn. Math. Scis. Edn. Bd., 1994-2004; chmn. nat. vis. com. NY Collab. for Excellence in Tchr. Prep. in Math., Sci., Tech., 1996-2000; spkr., lectr. in field. Mem. editl. bd. SIAM Jour. Math. Anal., 1979—2005, editor-in-chief, 1987-92, 35 others; contbr. articles to profl. jours. Grantee W. M. Keck Found., 1989, NSF, 1972—; NSF grad. fellow Harvard U., 1966-70; Woodrow Wilson fellow Harvard U., 1966-67. Fellow AAAS (nat. com. chair 1994-97, nat. elected office 2001-05); mem. Soc. for Indsl. and Applied Math. (com. mng. editors 1987-92, com. on coms. and appts. 1988-95, vis. lectr. 1992—, rep. to AAAS sect. com. on math. 1994-97, nat. com. chair 1987-92, Am. Math. Soc. (nat. com. chair 1989-96, 99-2005, com. to select Steele prize winner 1984-87, adv. com. on newsletter on collegiate math. edn. 1987-88, bd. judges for Nat. Sci. and Engring. Fair 1990-91, chmn. liaison com. AAAS 1990-92, com. on edn. 1992-96, chmn. subcom. grad. and postdoctoral edn. 1993-95, univ. lectr. series com. 1994—, chmn., 1999-2005, nomination com. 1995-97, chmn. nomination com. 1995-96, com. on coms., chmn.

1998-2002, math. surveys and monographs editl. com. 2003—), Math. Assn. Am. (com. on undergrad. program in math. 1987-91, subcom. on major in math. scis. 1989-90, subcom. on calculus reform and 1st 2 yrs. 1989-91, rep. to AAAS sect. com. on math. 1993-96, program of cons. 1994—2004), Tau Beta Pi. Achievements include setting up a fluid mechanics lab in math. depts.; helping to organize interdisciplinary programs in science, engineering, economics, finance, computer science and mathematics. Office: Univ Ill 851 S Morgan St MC 249 Chicago IL 60607 Home Phone: 312-946-1406; Office Phone: 312-413-2567. Business E-Mail: bona@math.uic.edu.

BONACORSI, ELLEN E., lawyer; BA, Stanford U., 1976; JD, Harvard U., 1979. Bar: Mo 1979, Ill 1981. Ptnr. Bryan Cave LLP, St. Louis. Mem.: Phi Beta Kappa. Office: Bryan Cave LLP One Metropolitan Square 211 N Broadway, Ste 3600 Saint Louis MO 63102 Office Phone: 314-259-2804. E-mail: eebonacorsi@bryancave.com.

BONACORSI, MARY CATHERINE, lawyer; b. Henderson, Ky., Apr. 24, 1949; d. Harry E. and Johanna M. (Kelly) Mack; m. Louis F. Bonacorsi, Apr. 23, 1971; children: Anna, Kathryn, Louis. BA in Math., Washington U., St. Louis, 1971; JD, Washington U., 1977. Bar: Mo. 1977, Ill. 1981, U.S. Dist. Ct. (ea. dist.) Mo., U.S. Dist. Ct. (so. dist.) Ill., U.S. Ct. Appeals (8th cir.), U.S. Supreme Ct. 1995. Ptnr. Thompson Coburn, St. Louis, 1977—. Chairperson fed. practice com. eastern dist., St. Louis, 1987—, eight cir. jud. conf. com., St. Louis, 1987—. Named one of Best Lawyers Am., 2006. Fellow Am. Bar Found.; mem. ABA, ATLA, Mo. Bar Assn., Met. St. Louis Bar Assn., Am. Bd. Trial Advocates (assoc.), Order of Coif. Office: Thompson Coburn LLP One US Bank Plz Saint Louis MO 63101 Office Phone: 314-552-6014. E-mail: mbonacorsi@thompsoncoburn.com.

BONAPARTE, WILLIAM, communications company executive; b. Chgo., Dec. 11, 1942; Degree in Elec. Engring., Milw. Sch. of Engring., 1976. PBX installation foreman Ill. Bell Telephones Co., Chgo., 1971-73, KCX foreman, 1973-75, equipment cable engr., 1975-76, mgr. personnel, supt. PBX installation, 1978-81, wire chief, mgr. bus. services, 1981—84; area mgr. then area staff mgr., Chgo. S. Services AT&T, 1984—86; CEO, pres. Bonaparte Connection, Inc., 1986—91, Bonaparte Corp., 1991—2005, chmn., CEO, 2005—. Office: Bonaparte Corp 1455 S Michigan Ave Chicago IL 60605

BONAVENTURA, LEO MARK, gynecologist, educator; b. Aug. 1, 1945; s. Angelo Peter and Wanda D. (Kelleher) B.; married; children: Leo Mark, Dena Anne, Angela Lorena, icole Palmira, Leah Michelle, Adam Xavier. MD, Ind. U., 1970. Diplomate Am. Bd. Obstetrics and Gynecology, Am. Bd. Reproductive Endocrinology and Infertility. Intern in surgery Cook County Hosp., Chgo., 1970—71; resident in ob-gyn. Ind. U. Hosps., 1973—76, fellow in reproductive endocrinology and infertility, 1976—78; asst. prof. ob-gyn. Ind. U., 1976—, asst. head sect. reproductive endocrinology and infertility, 1978—80, head sect., 1980—81. Contbr. articles to profl. jours. With USN attached to USMC, 1971—73. Mem.: Am. Fertility Soc., Can. Fertility Soc., Soc. Reproductive Surgeons., Soc. Reproductive Endocrinologists, Am. Coll. Obstetricians and Gynecologists, Cen. Assn. Ob-Gyn. Roman Catholic. Office Phone: 317-251-9048.

BOND, CHRISTOPHER SAMUEL (KIT BOND), senator, lawyer; b. St. Louis, Mar. 6, 1939; s. Arthur D. and Elizabeth (Green) B.; m. Linda Pell; 1 child, Samuel Reid. BA with honors, Princeton U., 1960; LLB, U. Va., 1963. Bar: Mo. 1963, U.S. Supreme Ct. 1967. Law clk. to presiding chief justice U.S. Ct. of Appeals (5th cir.), Atlanta, 1963-64; assoc. Covington & Burling, Washington, 1965-67; pvt. practice law Mexico, Mo., 1968; asst. atty. gen., chief counsel consumer protection div. State of Mo., 1969-70, gov., 1973-77, 81-85; auditor, 1971-73; ptnr. Gage & Tucker, Kansas City, 1985-87; US Senator from Mo., 1987—; chmn. small bus. com. 104th Congress. Mem. appropriations com., 1991—, chmn. subcom. on VA, HUD and ind. appropriations agys., 1991—, subcom. on def., 1993—, subcom. on fgn. ops., 1999—, subcom. on transp., 1995—; budget com., 1989—, environment and pub. works com., 1995—, subcom. on drinking water, fisheries and wildlife, 1995—; chmn. small bus. com., senate Rep. policy com.; pres. Gt. Plains Legal Found., Kansas City, Mo., 1977-80; chmn. Rep. Gov.'s Assn., Midwestern Gov.'s Conf., chmn. con. on econ. and community devel., 1981-83, chmn. con. on energy and environment, 1983-84. Republican. Presbyn. Office: US Senate 274 Russell Senate Bldg Washington DC 20510-0001 also: District Office Ste 204 1001 Cherry St Columbia MO 65201-7931 Office Phone: 202-224-5721, 573-442-8151. Office Fax: 202-224-8149, 573-442-8162. E-mail: kit_bond@bond.senate.gov.

BOND, RICHARD L., food products executive; BSBA, Elizabethtown Coll., 1969. Bd. dir. IBP, Inc., 1995—2001, pres., COO, 1997—2001; co-COO, Group President, Fresh Meats and Retail Tyson Foods Inc., 2001—03, pres., COO, 2003—06, pres., CEO, 2006—. Bd. dirs. Tyson Foods Inc., 2001—; vice-chmn. Am. Meat Inst. Office: c/o Tyson Foods Inc PO Box 2020 Springdale AR 72765

BOND, RICHARD LEE, lawyer, state senator; b. Kansas City, Kans., Sept. 18, 1935; s. Clarence Ivy and Florine (Hardison) B.; m. Sue S. Sedgwick, Aug. 23, 1958; children: Mark, Amy. BA, U. Kans., 1957, JD, 1960. City atty., Overland Park, Kans., 1960-62; adminstrv. asst. to Congressman Robert Ellsworth, Washington, 1961-66, Congressman Larry Winn, Washington, 1967-85, Congressman Jan Meyers, Washington, 1986; chmn. bd. dirs. Home State Bank, Kansas City, 1983-94; ptnr. Bennett, Lytle, Wetzler et al, Prairie Village, Kans., 1986-89; senator State of Kans., Topeka, 1985-2001, senate pres., 1997-2001. Vice chmn. Guaranty Bank and Bancshares, Kansas City, Kans., 1995-2002. Mem. Kans. Bd. Regents, 2002—. Named State Legislator of Yr. Governing Mag., 2002. Republican. Presbyterian. Avocations: gardening, tennis, hunting, fishing. Home: 9823 Nall Ave Shawnee Mission KS 66207-2915

BONDER, SETH, mechanical engineer; BS in Mech. Engring., U. Md.; PhD in Indsl. Engring., Ohio State U. Prof. dept. indsl. engring. U. Mich., dir. sys. rsch. lab.; founder, former CEO Vector Rsch. Inc., Ann Arbor, Mich. Capt. USAF. Recipient Patriotic Service Award, Sec. of Army, George E. Kimball Medal. Mem.: AE, Internat. Fedn. Operational Rsch. Socs. (v.p.), Military Ops. Rsch. Soc. (pres.), Ops. Rsch. Soc. Am. (pres.). Office: Vector Rsch PO Box 134001 Ann Arbor MI 48113-4001

BONDRA, PETER, professional hockey player; b. Luck, Ukraine, Feb. 7, 1968; m. Luba Bondra; children: Petra, David. Right wing Washington Capitals, 1990—2004, Ottawa Senators, 2004—05, Atlanta Thrashers, 2005—06, Chgo. Blackhawks, 2006—. Mem. Team Slovakia, World Cup of Hockey, 1996, Slovakian Olympic Hockey Team, Nagano, Japan, 1998, Torino, Italy, 2006; player NHL All-star game, 1993, 1996—99. Office: Chgo Blackhawk Hockey Team 1901 W Madison St Chicago IL 60612

BONFIELD, ARTHUR EARL, law educator; b. NYC, May 12, 1936; s. Louis and Rose (Lesser) B.; m. Doris (Harfenist), June 10, 1958 (dec. 1995); 1 child, Lauren; m. Eva Tsalikian, Apr. 8, 2000. BA, Bklyn. Coll., 1956; JD, Yale U., 1960, LLM, 1961, post grad. (sr. fellow), 1961-62; DHL (hon.), Cornell Coll., 1999. Bar: Conn. 1961, Iowa 1966. Asst. prof. U. Iowa Law Sch., 1962-65, assoc. prof., 1965-66, prof., 1966-69, Law Sch. Found. disting. prof., 1969-72, John Murray disting. prof., 1972—2003, Alan D. Vestal disting. chair, 2003—, assoc. dean for rsch. Law Libr., 1985—. Vis. prof. law U. Mich., 1970, U. Tenn, 1972, U. C, 1974, Hofstra U., 1977, Lewis and Clark U., 1984; gen. counsel spl. joint com. state adminstrv. procedure act Iowa Gen. Assembly, 1974-75; spl. counsel adminstrv. procedure exec. br. State of Iowa, 1975; chmn. com. constl. law Nat. Conf. Bar Examiners Multi-State Bar Exam, 1977-2003; reporter 1981 Model State Adminstrv. Procedure Act, Nat. Conf. Commrs. Uniform State Laws, 1979-81; cons. Ark. State Constl. Conv., 1980; chmn. Iowa Governor's Com. State Pub. Records Law, 1983; Iowa commr. Nat. Conf. Commrs. on Uniform State Laws, 1984-2000; chmn. Iowa Gov.'s Task Force on Uniform Adminstrv. Rules, 1985-92; chmn. Iowa Gov.'s Task Force Team on Regulatory Process, Rule Making, and Rules Rev., 1999-2000; gen counsel, Freedom of Info., Open Meetings and Pub. Records Study Com., Down Gen. Assembly, 2007-08. Prin. draftsman Iowa Civil Rights Act, 1965; Iowa Fair Housing Act, 1967; Iowa Adminstrv. Procedure Act, 1974; Iowa Open Meetings Act, 1978; Iowa Civil Rights Act, 1978; Amendments to Iowa Pub. Records Law, 1984; Amendments to Iowa Administrv. Procedure Act, 1998; author: State Administrv. Rule Making, 1986; State and Federal Administrv. Law, 1989; contbr. numerous articles to law jours. Recipient Outstanding Svc. to Civil Liberties Award, Iowa Civil Liberties Union, 1974, Hancher Finkbine Outstanding Faculty Mem. Award, U. Iowa, 1980, Faculty Excellence Award, Iowa Bd. Regents, 1995, Outstanding Law Sch. Tchg. Award, U. Iowa, 1996, 2006; Frederick Klocksiem fellow Aspen Inst. Humanistic Studies, 1978. Mem. ABA (chmn. divsn. state adminstrv. law 1976-80, coun. 1980-84, chmn. sect. 1987-88, sect. adminstrv. law and regulatory practice); Am. Law Inst. (life mem.); Iowa State Bar Assn. (chmn. com. adminstrv. law 1971-85, coun. sect. adminstr. law 1990-93, 94-97, 98-99, 2000-03, 05-08, reporter and mem., task force on state adminstrv. law reform 1994-96; Pres. Award Outstanding Svc. to Bar and Public 1996); Am. Coun. Learned Soc. (del. from Assn. Am. Law Sch. 1984-94). Avocation: collecting rare 16th-18th century English books. Home: 206 Mahaska Dr Iowa City IA 52246-1606 Office: U Iowa Sch Law Iowa City IA 52242 Business E-Mail: arthur-bonfield@uiowa.edu.

BONGIOVI, ROBERT P., career officer; BSc in Aerospace Engring., U. Notre Dame, 1969; MSc in Aerospace Engring., MIT, 1970. Commd. 2d. lt. USAF, 1970, advanced through grades to major gen., 1999; program mgr. Norton AFB, Calif., 1970-75; various assignments Wright-Patterson AFB, Ohio, 1975-82, 92-98; dir. requirements, 1998—; various assignments The Pentagon, Washington, 1983-87, 88-92, Indsl. Coll. Armed Forces, Washington, 1987-88. Decorated Legion of Merit with oak leaf cluster, Defense Meritorious Svc. medal with oak leaf cluster.

BONHAM, RUSSELL AUBREY, chemistry professor; b. San Jose, Calif., Dec. 10, 1931; s. Russell Aubrey and Margaret Florence (Wallace) B.; m. Miriam Anne Dye, Mar. 23, 1957; children: Frances, Margaret, Anne. BA, Whittier Coll., 1954; PhD, Iowa State U., 1958. Instr. Ind. U., Bloomington, 1958-60; postdoctoral fellow aval Rsch. Lab., 1960; asst. prof. math. U. Md., 1960; asst. prof. chemistry Ind. U., Bloomington, 1960-63, assoc. prof., 1963-65, prof. chemistry, 1965-95, prof. emeritus, 1996—; rsch. prof. chemistry Ill. Inst. Tech., Chgo., Ill., 1995—. Co-author: High Energy Electron Scattering, 1974; mem. editorial bd.: The Jour. of the Brazilian Chem. Soc., 1989-2000; contbr. over 175 articles and papers to profl. jours. Recipient Fulbright fellowship U. Tokyo, 1964-65, Guggenheim fellowship, 1964-65, Humboldt prize, 1977, 81. Fellow Am. Phys. Soc., AAAS; mem. Am. Phys. Soc., Am. Crystallographic Assn., Am. Chem. Soc., Sigma Xi. Achievements include research on electron impact cross section measurements of molecular species of interest to low pressure processing plasmas and X-Ray scattering from gases. Office: Ill Inst Tech Dept Biol Chem Phys Scis 3101 S Dearborn Chicago IL 60616

BONINI, JAMES, federal official; BA in Criminal Justice, Indiana U. of Pa., 1986; MPA, U. So. Calif., 1988. Administrv. asst. South Bay Mcpl. Ct. Los Angeles County, Calif., 1987—88, sr. adminstrv. asst. Calif., 1988—89, divsn. head budget and mgmt. svcs. Calif., 1989; chief dep. ct. adminstr. Ct. Common Pleas, Montgomery County, Pa., 1990—91, dist. ct. adminstr. Berks County, Pa., 1991—96; clk. of ct. U.S. Bankruptcy Ct. No. Dist. Ind., South Bend, 1996—2003, U.S. Dist. Ct. So. Dist. Ohio, Columbus, 2003—. Office: US Dist Ct Joseph P Kinneary US Courthouse Rm 260 85 Marconi Blvd Columbus OH 43215 Office Phone: 614-719-3030.

BONIOR, DAVID EDWARD, former congressman, educator; b. Detroit, June 6, 1945; s. Edward John and Irene (Gaverluk) B.; children: Julie, Andy BA, U. Iowa, 1967; MA in History, Chapman Coll., Calif., 1972. Mem. Mich. Ho. of Reps., 1973-77, U.S. Congress from 10th Mich. dist., 1977—2002; mem. com. on rules; Dem. whip, 1991—2002; prof. Wayne St. Univ., Coll. Urban, Labor & Met. Affs., Detroit, 2003—. Mem. VA, passport svs. and social security coms. U.S. Congress, 1999-2002. Author: The Vietnam Veteran: A History of Neglect, 1984 Served in USAF, 1968-72. Democrat. Roman Catholic. Office: Wayne St Univ 656 W Kirby St 3198 CULMA/FAB Detroit MI 48202

BONNER, BRIGID ANN, marketing professional; b. Mpls., Apr. 27, 1960; d. John Patrick and R. Jeanne (Crahan) B. BS in Journalism and Indsl. Adminstrn., Iowa State U., Ames, 1982; MBA, Harvard U., 1988. Mktg. statistician Fingerhut, Minnetonka, Minn., 1982-83; mktg. rep. IBM Corp., Mpls., 1983-88, exec. cons., 1988-90, mktg. mgr., 1990-92, sector mgr., 1992—. Mem. com. United Way of Minn., Mpls., 1989—. Mem. Harvard Bus. Sch. Club Minn. (bd. dirs. Mpls. chpt. 1989, pres. 1992—, mgmt. assistance program cons. 1990—). Republican. Roman Catholic. Avocations: travel, running, tennis, bicycling. Home: 25 Willow Woods Dr Excelsior MN 55331-8426 Office: IBM Corp 650 3rd Ave S Ste 500 Minneapolis MN 55402-4300

BONNER, DENNIS, state legislator; b. Springfield, Mo., Mar. 14, 1964; BA, U. Mo., 1992, MA, 1994, student. Mem. Mo. Ho. of Reps., Jefferson City. Mem. appropriations com., commerce com. (vice chmn), labor com., local govt. and related matters com., joint com. on pub. employee retirement (chmn.), joint com. on econ. devel., policy & planning. Founding bd. mem. Northwest Cmtys. Devel. Corp.; citizen adv. bd. Cmty. Svc. League. Mem. Jackson County Hist. Soc., Am. Legion. Democrat. Home: 606 NE La Costa St Lees Summit MO 64064-1330

BONOW, ROBERT OGDEN, cardiologist, educator; b. Camden, NJ, Mar. 11, 1947; m. Patricia Jeanne Hitchens, Sept. 12, 1982; children: Robert Hitchens, Samuel Crawford. BS in Chem. Engring. (magna cum laude), Lehigh U., Bethelehem, Pa., 1969; MD, U. Pa. Sch. Medicine, Phila., 1973. Diplomate in internal medicine and cardiovasc. disease Am. Bd. Internal Medicine. Intern in medicine Hosp. U. Pa., Phila., 1973-74, resident, 1974-76; clin. assoc. cardiology br. Nat. Heart, Lung and Blood Inst., Bethesda, Md., 1976-79, sr. investigator, attending physician cardiology br., 1979-92, chief nuclear cardiology sect., 1980-92, dep. chief, 1989-92; Goldberg disting. prof. medicine, Feinberg Sch. Medicine Northwestern U. Med. Sch., Chgo., 1992—; chief divsn. cardiology orthwestern Meml. Hosp., Chgo., 1992—; attending physician dept. medicine VA Lakeside Med. Ctr., Chgo., 1993—2003, Evanston Hosp., Ill., 1994—. Pfizer vis. prof. cardiovasc. medicine Yale U., 1992, U. Mass., 1998; AHA/ACC Task Force on Practice Guidelines Com. on Cardiac Radlonuclide Imaging, 1993-95; chair com. on mgmt. of patents with valvular heart disease, 1996—; vis. prof. various univs., 1982-99; mem. bd. extramural adivsors NHLBI, NIH, 2000—; mem. clin. rsch. roundtable Inst. of Medicine, Nat. Acad. Sci.; working group on methods/technologies Nat. Heart Attack Alert Program, 1994-; co-dir. Bluhm Cardiovascular Inst.; mem. Northwestern Med. Faculty Found.; invited presenter at sci. sessions, symposia and acad. med. ctrs. Mem. editl. bd. Am. Jour. Cardiology, 1983—, Jour. Am. Coll. Cardiology, 1983-87, 91-95, Circulation, 1986—, Cardiovascular Imaging, 1988—, Am. Jour. Cardiac Imaging, 1990-95, Internat. Jour. Cardiac Imaging, 1990-95, Jour. Heart Valve Disease, 1982-95, Jour. Nuclear Cardiology, 1993—, Jour. Nuclear Medicine, 1994-2000, Cardiologia, 1995—, Am. Heart Jour., 1998—; contbr. over 350 publs. in med. jours. and textbooks. Recipient NIH Director's award, 1986, USPHS Commendation medal, 1990, USPHS outstanding svc. medal, 1991; named to The Country's Best Doctor List, Good Housekeeping, America's Top Doctors, Best Doctors in America. Fellow ACP, Am. Coll. Cardiology (exhibits com. 1986-92, 1999-2000, program com. 1991-92, chair extramural edn. com., 1998—, trustee 1999-2004, Disting Fellowship award, 2000, Disting. Svc. award, 2006), Am. Heart Assn. (chmn. sci. session program com. 1998-2000, bd. dirs. 1999-2004, Coun. on Clin. Cardiology, 1999-2001, chmn. Clin. Sci. Com. 2001-2002, pres. 2002-03, bd. dir. greater midwest affiliate, 2000-2006, Nat. Leadership award, 2003, Disting. Achievement award 2005, Golden Heart award, 2007); mem. AAAS, Am. Bd. Internal Medicine (subsplty. bd. cardiovasc. disease 1996-2001), Am. Soc. Clin. Investigation, Assn. Am. Physicians, Am. Heart Assn. Met. Chgo. (bd. govs. 1992-98, rsch. coun. 1992-98, pres. 2001-02), Am. Soc. Nuclear Cardiology (bd. dirs. 1994-98, chmn. edn. com. 1994-2000, nominating com. 1994-96), Assn. Profs. Cardiology (nominating com. 1993—, councillor 1994—, sec., treas. 1996-99, v.p. 1999-2000, pres. 2000-01), Chgo. Cardiology Group (pres. 1994-96),, Am. Fedn. Clin. Rsch., Assn. Am. Physicians, Assn. Univ. Cardiologists, Ctrl. Soc. Clin. Rsch., Alpha Omega Alpha. Office: Northwestern U Med Sch Cardiology Divsn 201 E Huron St Galter 10-240 Chicago IL 60611 Office Phone: 312-695-1105. Office Fax: 312-695-1434.*

BONSIGNORE, MICHAEL ROBERT, former electronics and computer company executive; b. Plattsburg, NY, Apr. 3, 1941; m. Sheila Bonsignore. BA, US Naval Acad., 1963; postgrad., Tex. A&M U. Various mktg. and bus. devel. positions aerospace group Honeywell Inc., 1969—72, various mktg. and ops. mgmt. positions marine sys. divsn., 1972—81, gen. mgr. marine sys. divsn., 1981—82, pres. Honeywell Europe, 1982—87, exec. v.p. internat. divsn., 1987—90, exec. v.p., COO internat. and bldg. ctrl., 1990—93, bd. dirs., 1990, chmn., 1993—2000, CEO, 1999—; chmn. bd. Honeywell Inc. (merged with Allied Signal), 2000—02; mem. exec. adv. bd. Carlson Sch. of Mgmt., U. of Minnesota, 2002—. Bd. dirs. Honeywell Medtronic Inc., Alliance to Save Energy, New Perspective Fund Inc., U.S.-China Bus. Coun., Investment and Svc. policy Advt. Com. Office: Carlson Sch of Management 321 19th Ave S Rm 4-300 Minneapolis MN 55455

BOOK, THOMAS TODD, state representative; b. 1968; BA, Western Mich.U.; postgrad., Coll. William and Mary. Lawyer, Scioto County, Ohio; small bus. owner; state rep. dist. 89 Ohio Ho. of Reps., Columbus, 2002—, ranking minority m em. civil and comml. law com., mem. agr. and natural resources, banking pensions and securities, ins., and juvenile and family law coms. Democrat. Office: 77 S High St 10th fl Columbus OH 43215-6111

BOOKER, JOSEPH W., JR., warden; b. Bradford, Tenn., Sept. 25, 1954; m. Jackie Booker, Dec. 30, 1989; 5 children. Postgrad., Calif. Coast U. Capt. Fed. Correctional Instn., Tucson, Ariz., 1987-89, Met. Correctional Ctr., San Diego, 1989-91, assoc. warden Chgo., 1991-92, U.S. Penitentiary, Marion, Ill., 1992-95; warden Fed. Correctional Instn., Florence, S.C., 1995-97, U.S. Penitentiary, Bur. of Prisons, Dept. of Justice, Leavenworth, Kans. Bd. dirs. N.Am. Wardens Assn. Sgt. USMC, 1972-76. Mem. Law Enforcement Correctional Adminstrs., Strategic Threat Intelligent Network Group, Am. Correctional Assn. Methodist. Avocations: golf, basketball, fishing.

BOOKSTEIN, ABRAHAM, information science educator; b. NYC, Mar. 22, 1940; s. Alex and Doris (Cohen) B.; m. Marguerite Vickers, June 20, 1968. BS, CCNY, 1961; MS, U. Calif., Berkeley, 1966; PhD, Yeshiva U., 1969; MA, U. Chgo., 1970. Asst. prof. U. Chgo., 1971-75, assoc. prof. info. sci., 1975-82, prof. info. sci., 1982—. Vis. prof. Royal Inst. Tech., Stockholm, 1982, UCLA, 1985; vis. disting. scholar OCLC, Columbus, Ohio, 1988; bd. dirs. Religion Index, Evanston, Ill., 1984-96; adv. bd. Info. Sci. Rsch. Inst., U. Nev., 1995—. Bd. editors Info. Processing and Mgmt., Scientometrics, Information Retrieval, 1997—; editor Prospect for Change in Bibliographic Control, 1977, Operations Research: Implications for Librarians, 1970; contbr. articles to profl. jours. NSF grantee, 1981, 85, 93, U.S./Israel Binational Sci. Found. grantee, 1993-94; Fulbright fellow, India, 1992. Mem. IEEE Computer Soc., Am. Soc. Info. Scis. (Rsch. award 1991), Internat. Soc. Scientometrics and Informetrics (founding mem., chmn. conf. program com. 1995, keynote spkr., 1991, 97), Assn. Computing Machinery/SIGIR (gen. chmn. ann. internat. conf. 1991), Phi Beta Kappa. Avocations: personal computing, music, literature. Office: U Chgo/CILS 1010 E 59th St Chicago IL 60637-1512 Office Phone: 773 70c re68.

BOONE, MORELL DOUGLAS, information technology educator; b. Londonderry, Northern Ireland, Dec. 15, 1942; arrived in U.S., 1946; s. Paul J. and Margaret (Hill) B.; m. Carolyn June Gallagher, July 6, 1968; children— Ian Charles, Megan Elizabeth BS, Kutztown State Coll., Pa., 1964; MS, Syracuse U., 1968, PhD, 1980. Librarian Pennridge Schs., Perkasie, Pa., 1964-66; reference librarian Hobart and William Smith Colls., Geneva, NY, 1968-70; lectr. Syracuse U., NY, 1970-72; dean learning resources U. Bridgeport, Conn., 1973-80; dir. Ctr. of Ednl. Resources Eastern Mich. U., Ypsilanti, 1980—85, dean learning resources and techs., 1986—2001, prof. interdisciplinary tech., 2001—04, prof., dir. Sch. Tech. Studies, 2004—06, prof., dean College of Tech., 2006—. Presenter at profl. meetings; cons. for internat. ednl. devel. Iran, Swaziland, Yemen, others. Co-author: Training Student Library Assistants, 1991; mem. editl. bd. Libr. Hi Tech.; contbr. articles to profl. jours. Chmn. Community Cablecasting Commn., Ypsilanti, 1981-84, Ypsilanti Ednl. Found., 1988-94; pres. bd. dirs. Meals on Wheels, Ypsilanti, 1998—. Named to Pennridge H.S. Wall of Fame, 2001. Mem. ALA, EDUCAUSE, Soc. Coll. and Univ. Planning, Kiwanis. Democrat. Presbyterian (elder). Avocations: gardening, reading, travel. Home: 5774 Pineview Dr Ypsilanti MI 48197-8983 Office: Eastern Mich U 109 Sill Hall Ypsilanti MI 48197 Home Phone: 734-484-4384; Office Phone: 734-487-0354. Business E-Mail: mboone@emich.edu.

BOOTHBY, WILLIAM MUNGER, retired mathematics professor; b. Detroit, Apr. 1, 1918; s. Thomas Franklin and Florence (Munger) B.; m. Ruth Robin, June 8, 1947; children— Daniel, Thomas, Mark. AB, U. Mich., 1941, MA, 1942, PhD, 1949. Mem. faculty Northwestern U., Evanston, Ill., 1948-59; fellow Am.-Swiss Found. for Sci. Exchange, Swiss Fed. Inst. Tech., Zurich, 1950-51; assoc. prof. Washington U., St. Louis, 1959-62, prof. math., 1962-88, ret., 1988—. NSF sr. postdoctoral fellow Inst. for Advanced Study, Princeton, N.J., 1961-62, U. Geneva, Switzerland, 1965-66; professeur associe U. Strasbourg, France, 1971, 77 Author: Introduction to Differentiable Manifolds and Riemannian Geometry; co-editor: Symmetric Spaces; contbr. articles to profl. jours. Served with USAAF, 1942-46. Mem. Am., London math. Socs., Math. Assn. Am., Soc. Indsl. and Applied Math., Sigma Xi. Home: 6954 Cornell Ave Saint Louis MO 63130-3128 Office: Washington U Dept Math Saint Louis MO 63130-4899

BOOZELL, MARK ELDON, state official; b. Mason City, Iowa, Mar. 4, 1955; s. Eldon Dwayne Boozell and Betty Jean (Gordon) Kruger; m. Susan Elizabeth Abelt, Nov. 26, 1977; children: Kari Elizabeth, Lindsay Patricia. BA, Augustana Coll., 1977. Budget analyst rep. staff Ill. Ho. of Reps., Springfield, 1977-78, dep. dir. rep. staff, 1978-80; legis. liaison Ill. Dept. Transp., Springfield, 1980-83; dir. legis. affairs Ill. Sec. State, Springfield, 1983-95; chief of staff Office of Gov., State of Ill., Springfield, 1998-99; exec. v.p. Aon Corp., Chgo., 1999—. Named one of Outstanding Young Men Am., 1980. Republican. Lutheran. Home: 24706 Royal Lytham Dr Naperville IL 60564-8100 Office: State of Ill Office of Gov Capitol Bldg Rm 207 Springfield IL 62706-0001

BOPP, JAMES, JR., lawyer; b. Terre Haute, Ind., Feb. 8, 1948; s. James and Helen Marguerite (Hope) B.; m. Cheryl Hahn, Aug. 8, 1970 (div.); m. Christine Marie Stanton, July 3, 1982; children: Kathleen Grace, Lydia Grace, Marguerite Grace. BA, Ind. U., 1970; JD, U. Fla., 1973. Bar: Ind. 1973, U.S. Supreme Ct. 1977. Dep. atty. gen. State of Ind., Indpls., 1973-75; ptnr. Bopp & Fife, Indpls., 1975-79, Brames, Bopp, Abel & Oldham, Terre Haute, Ind., 1979-92, Bopp, Coleson & Bostrom, Terre Haute, 1992—. Dep. prosecutor Vigo County, Terre Haute, 1979-86; gen. counsel Nat. Right to Life Com., Washington, 1978—; pres. at. Legal Ctr. for Medically Dependent and Disabled, 1984—; gen. counsel James Madison Ctr. Free Speech, 1997—; instr. law Ind. U., 1977-78; mem. com. at. Conf. Commrs. Uniform State Laws, 2005—. Editor: Human Life and Health Care Ethics, 1985, Restoring the Right to Life: The Human Life Amendment, 1984; editor-in-chief Issues in Law and Medicine, 1985—. Mem. Pres.'s Com. Mental Retardation, 1984—87, mem. congl. biomed. ethics adv. com., 1987—89; mem. White House Conf. on Families, Washington, 1980, White House Conf. on Aging, Mpls., 1981, Free Speech & Election Law Practice Group The Federalist Soc., former co-chmn. election law subcom., 1996—2005; bd. govs. Rep. Nat. Lawyers Assn., 2002—; alt. del. Rep. Nat. Conv., 1992, 1996, del., mem. platform com., 2000, 2004; mem. Rep. Nat. Com., 2006—; state treas. Ind. Rep. State Party, 2005—06, gen. counsel, 2005—, nat. committeeman, 2006—; chmn. Vigo County Election Bd., 1991—93; del. Rep. State Conv., Indpls., 1980, 1982, 1984, 1986, 1990, 1992, 1994, 1996, 1998, 2000, 2002, 2004, 2006; chmn. Vigo County Rep. Ctrl. Com., 1993—97; mem. nat. com. UNESCO, 2004—06; bd. dirs. Leadership Terre Haute, 1986—89, Alliance for Growth and Progress, Terre Haute, 1993—97; chmn. bd. dirs. Hospice of Wabash Valley, Terre Haute, 1982—88. Mem. Ind. State Bar Assn., Terre Haute Rotary (bd. dir. 1984-86). Republican. Roman Catholic. Home: 1124 S Center St Terre Haute IN 47802-1116 Office: Bopp Coleson & Bostrom 1 S 6th St Terre Haute IN 47807-3510 Home Phone: 812-232-5465; Office Phone: 812-232-2434. Personal E-mail: jboppjr@aol.com.

BORCH, RICHARD FREDERIC, pharmacology and chemistry educator; b. Cleve., May 22, 1941; s. Fred J. and Martha (Kananen) B.; m. Anne Wright Wilson, Sept. 8, 1962; children: Karen, Eric. BS, Stanford U., 1962; MA, PhD, Columbia U., 1965; MD, U. Minn., 1975. NIH postdoctoral fellow Harvard U., Cambridge, Mass., 1965-66; prof. chemistry U. Minn., Mpls., 1966-82, med. resident, 1975-76; dean's prof. pharmacology, prof. chemistry U. Rochester, N.Y., 1982-96; dir. U. Rochester Cancer Ctr., 1992-96; now dept. head medicinal chemistry & molecular pharmacology Purdue U., Lafayette, Ind., dir. Cancer Ctr., Lilly disting. prof., 1992-96. Dir. U. Rochester Cancer Ctr., 1993—; mem. cancer rsch. manpower com. Nat. Cancer Inst., 1982-86, chmn. cancer rsch. manpower rev. com. 1984-86; cons. 3M Pharms., St. Paul, 1972—. Contbr. over 70 articles to profl. jours.; patentee in field. Recipient Coll. Chemistry Tchr. award Minn. sect. Am. Chem. Soc., 1982, Louis P. Hammett award Columbia U., 1965, James P. Wilmot Disting. Professorship, U. Rochester, 1983-86; Alfred

P. Sloan Found. fellow, 1970-72. Mem. AAAS, Am. Chem. Soc., Am. Assn. Cancer Resch., Am. Soc. Pharmacology and Exptl. Therapeutics. Office: Purdue U Cancer Ctr Hansen Life Scis Rsch Bldg S University St West Lafayette IN 47907-1524

BORCHERT, DONALD MARVIN, philosopher, educator; b. Edmonton, Alta., Can., May 23, 1934; s. Leo Ferdinand and Lillian Violet (Bucholz) B.; m. Mary Ellen Cockrell, Dec. 27, 1960; children: Carol Ellen, John Witherspoon. AB, U. Alta., Edmonton, 1955; BD, Princeton Theol. Sem., 1958, PhD, 1966; ThM, Ea. Bapt. Theol. Sem., 1959. Teaching fellow Princeton Theol. Sem., NJ, 1960-61; asst. prof. Juniata Coll., Huntingdon, Pa., 1966-67, Ohio U., Athens, 1967-71, assoc. prof., 1971-75, prof. philosophy, 1975—2006, assoc. dean Coll. Arts and Scis., 1980-86, chmn. dept. philosophy, 1987—2002; emeritus prof. philosophy, 2006—. Author: Being Human in a Technological Age, 1979, Introduction to Modern Philosophy, 1981, 7th edit., 2001, Exploring Ethics, 1986, Medical Ethics, 1992, Philosophy of Sex and Love, 1997; editor in chief: Encyclopedia of Philosophy Supplement, 1996, Compendium of Philosophy and Ethics, 1999, Encyclopedia of Philosophy, 10 vols., 2006; contbr. articles to profl. jours. Assoc. Danforth Found. Nat. Humanities Inst. fellow, 1976-77; NEH Implementation grantee, 1981. Mem. Ohio Philos. Assn. (v.p. 1983-85, pres. 1985-90), Ohio Humanities Council (vice chmn. 1981-83, chmn. 1983-85). Presbyterian. Home: 9 Coventry Ln Athens OH 45701-3717 Office: Ohio U Dept Philosophy Ellis Hall Athens OH 45701 Office Phone: 740-593-4588. E-mail: borchert@ohio.edu.

BORCOVER, ALFRED SEYMOUR, journalist; b. Bellaire, Ohio, May 1, 1931; s. Joseph and Kate (Florman) B.; m. Doris E. Wellner, Sept. 13, 1958 (div. 1966); m. Linda A. Gredig, Oct. 11, 1989. BSc in Journalism, Ohio State U., 1953; MSJ, Northwestern U., 1957. Writer Northwestern U., Evanston, Ill., 1957-58; reporter, copy editor Chgo. Tribune, 1959-63, asst. travel editor, 1963-73, assoc. travel editor, 1973-79, editor travel sect., 1979-81, travel editor, columnist, 1981-93; ret., 1994. Freelance travel columnist/writer, 1994—. Author: Dollarwise Guide to Chicago, 1967; contbg. editor Fodor's Chicago, 1985-88; contbr. to Around the World with the Experts, 1970, WGN Travel Show, 1986-93; travel columnist Prodigy On-line Svc., 1990-96. Served to 1st lt. USAF, 1953-55 Recipient spl. citation George Hedmon Awards, 1965, Outstanding Achievement in Travel Writing award N.Y. Travel Writers Assn., 1976, Econ. Impact Writing award Travel Industry Assn. Am., 1983, Lowell Thomas Writing award, 1986; Gold Medal Writing award Pacific Asia Travel Assn., 1987, Cen. States Consumerism Reporting award, 1987, Alumni Svc. award Northwestern U., 1991, Cen. States Best Fgn. Series award, Cen. States Henry E. Bradshaw Meml. Writing award, 1991, Ctrl. States Fgn. Series and U.S. Article awards, 1992, Earl R. Lind Consumer Edn. award Better Bus. Bur. of Chgo., 1993, Ctrl. States Commentary award, 2004, Ctrl. States Consumer Reporting award, 2005. Mem. Soc. Am. Travel Writers (pres. 1973-74), Chgo. Headline Club (pres. 1983-84), Medill Sch. Journalism Alumni Assn. (bd. dirs. 1984-89, pres. 1989-91), Northwestern U. Alumni Assn. (bd. dirs. 1986-90), Soc. Profl. Journalists. Democrat. Jewish. Avocations: tennis, music, photography. Home and Office: 1022 Michigan Ave Evanston IL 60202-1436 Personal E-mail: aborcover@aol.com.

BORDEN, ERNEST CARLETON, oncologist, educator; b. Norwalk, Conn., July 12, 1939; s. Joseph Carleton and Violet Ernette (Lanneau) B.; m. Louise Dise, June 24, 1967; children: Kristin Louise, Sandra Lanneau. AB, Harvard U., 1961; MD, Duke U., 1966. Diplomate Am. Bd. Internal Medicine, Am. Bd. Med. Oncology. Intern Duke U. Med. Ctr., 1966-67; asst. resident in internal medicine Hosp. of U. Pa., 1967-68; med. officer Viropathology Lab., Nat. Communicable Disease Ctr., USPHS/Atlanta, 1968—70; clin. instr. dept. medicine Emory U. Sch. Medicine, Grady Meml. Hosp., 1968-70; postdoctoral fellow oncology divsn. dept. medicine Johns Hopkins U. Sch. Medicine, Balt., 1970-73; asst. prof. divsn. clin. oncology and depts. human oncology and medicine Wis. Clin. Cancer Ctr., Univ. Hosps. and Sch. Medicine, U. Wis.-Madison, 1973-79, assoc. prof., 1979-83, assoc. dir., 1981-90, prof., 1983-90, Am. Cancer Soc. prof. clin. oncology, from 1984; prof. depts. medicine and microbiology Med. Coll. Wis., Milw., 1990-94; also dir. Med. Coll. Wis. Cancer Ctr.; prof. oncology, medicine, microbiology, pharmacology U. Md. Sch. Medicine, Balt., 1994-98; dir. U. Md. Cancer Ctr., 1994-98; dir. ctr. cancer drug discovery and devel. Cleve. Clinic Found., 1998—; prof. molecular medicine Cleve. Clinic Found. Sch. Medicine Case Western Res. U., 2004—. Chief divsn. clin. oncology William S. Middleton VA Hosp., 1977-81; cons. staff Madison Gen. Hosp., 1974-90; dep. dir. Taussig Cancer Inst. Cleve Clinic Found., 2008-Assoc. editor Jour. Interferon Rsch., 1980—, Jour. Biologic Response Modifiers, 1982-90; mem. editl. bd. Cancer Immunology and Immunotherapy, 1981-89, Investigational New Drugs, 1982—, Jour. Nat. Cancer Inst., 1987-91, Jour. Cancer Rsch., 1993-98, Jour. Bioactive and Compatible Polymers, Jour. Biol. Regulators and Homeostatic Agts., 1986, Clin. Cancer Rsch., 1998—; contbr. 300 articles to profl. jours. Recipient Disting. Svc. award Am. Cancer Soc., 1994. Fellow ACP; mem. AAAS, Am. Soc. Microbiology, Am. Assn. Cancer Rsch., Southwest Coop. Oncology Group, Am. Soc. Clin. Oncology, Am. Assn. Immunologists, Am. Fedn. Clin. Rsch., Soc. Biol. Therapy (pres. 1986-88), Internat. Soc. Interferon Rsch. (pres. 1987-89). Unitarian Universalist. Office Phone: 216-444-8183. Business E-Mail: bordene@ccf.org.

BORDO, GUY VICTOR, conductor; MusB, MusM, U. Mich.; studied with Gustav Meier, Tanglewood Music Ctr.; studied with Carl St. Clair, PhD in Orchestral Conducting; student of Victor Yampolsky, Northwestern U. Music dir., conductor Sheboygan Symphony Orch., Wis., 1992; musical dir. Richmond Symphony Orch., 1997—. Guest conductor Orch. Lithuania, St. Christopher Chamber Orch., Kansas Opera, Elmhurst Symphony (Ill.) Orch., Light Opera Works Chgo., Lexington Philharmonic and the Waterloo/Cedar Falls (Iowa) Symphony, 1997. Office: Richmond Symphony Orch PO Box 982 Richmond IN 47375 Business E-Mail: rso1@skyenet.net.

BOREN, CLARK HENRY, JR., general and vascular surgeon; b. Marinette, Wis., Nov. 23, 1947; s. Clark Henry and Maryon Lillian (Peterson) Boren; children: Jenna Marie, Matthew William, Nathan Clark. BMS, Northwestern U., 1971, MD with distinction, 1973. Diplomate Am. Bd. Surgery. Resident in gen. surgery U. Calif.-H.C. Moffitt Hosp., San Francisco, 1973-79; rsch. fellow in vascular surgery Ft. Miley VA Hosp., 1976-77; vascular fellow Med. Coll. Wis./Milwaukee County Med. Complex, Milw., 1979-80; mem. staff Fox Valley Surg. Assocs., Ltd., Appleton, Wis., 1980—, pres., 1997—. Chmn. bd. United Health Wis., 1995—99. Contbr. articles to profl. jours. Mem.: AMA, ACS, Am. Assn. Vascular Surgery, Wis. Surg. Soc., Midwest Vascular Soc., Peripheral Vascular Surgery Soc., Wis. State Med. Soc., Phi Kappa Psi, Phi Eta Sigma, Phi Beta Pi, Alpha Omega Alpha. Democrat. Home: 330 W River Rd Appleton WI 54915 Office: Fox Valley Surg Assocs 1818 N Meade St Appleton WI 54911-3454 Home Phone: 920-996-0189; Office Phone: 920-731-8131. Business E-Mail: clark.boren@thedacare.org.

BORGDORFF, PETER, church administrator; Exec. dir. of ministries Christian Ref. Ch. in N. Am., 1990. Office: Christian Ref Ch in N Am 2850 Kalamazoo Ave SE Grand Rapids MI 49560-0001

BORGENS, RICHARD, biologist; b. Little Rock, May 7, 1946; BS, N. Tex. State U., 1970, MS, 1973; PhD in Biology, Purdue U., 1977. Rsch. assoc. biology Purdue U., 1977-78, Yale U., 1978-80; assoc. staff scientist Jackson Lab., Bar Harbor, Maine, 1980-81; staff scientist Inst. Med. Rsch., 1981-98; fellow Nat. Paraplegia Found., 1978-80; Dir., prof. devel. anatomy Purdue U. Ctr. Paralysis Rsch., 1998—. Mem. Am. Soc. Zoologists, Soc. Devel. Biology. Office: Purdue Univ Dept Anatomy 1244 VCPR West Lafayette IN 47907-1244

BORGER, JOHN PHILIP, lawyer; b. Wilmington, Del., Apr. 19, 1951; s. Philip E. and Jane (Smyth) B.; m. Judith Marie Yates, May 24, 1974; children: Jennifer, Christopher, Nicholas. BA in Journalism with high honors, Mich. State U., 1973; JD, Yale Law Sch., 1976. Bar: Minn. 1976, U.S. Dist. Ct. Minn. 1976, U.S. Ct. Appeals (8th cir.) 1979, U.S. Supreme Ct. 1983, N.D. 1988, U.S. Dist. Ct. N.D. 1988, Wis. 1993. Editor-in-chief Mich. State News, East Lansing, 1972-73; assoc. Faegre & Benson, LLP, Mpls., 1976-83, ptnr., 1984—. Bd. dirs. Milkweed Edits., 1995-01; adj. prof. U. Minn. Sch. Journalism and Mass Comm., 1999. Contbr. articles to profl. jours. Named to State News Hall of Fame, Mich. State U., 2007; recipient Freedom of Info. award, Minn. Soc. Profl. Journalists, 2002, First Amendment Award, St. Cloud State U. Dept. Mass. Comms., 2001. Mem. ABA (chmn. media law and defamation torts com. torts and ins. practice sect. 1996-97), Minn. Bar Assn., State Bar Assn. N.D., Wis. Bar Assn., Hennepin County Bar Assn. Office: Faegre & Benson LLP 2200 Wells Fargo Ctr 90 S 7th St Ste 2200 Minneapolis MN 55402-3901 Office Phone: 612-766-7501. Business E-Mail: jborger@faegre.com.

BORGMAN, JAMES MARK, editorial cartoonist; b. Cin., Feb. 24, 1954; s. James Robert and Florence Marian (Maly) B.; m. Lynn Goodwin, Aug. 20, 1977 (dec. 1999). BA, Kenyon Coll., 1976. Editorial cartoonist Cin. Enquirer, 1976—, King Features Syndicate, 1980—; contbr. to Newsweek Broadcasting's Cartoon-A-Torial (animated editorial cartoon feature), 1978-81. Author: (collection of editorial cartoons) Smorgasborgman, 1982, The Great Communicator, 1985, The Mood of America, 1986, Jim Borgman's Cincinnati, 1992, Disturbing the Peace, 1995; co-creator comic strip Zits, 1997. Recipient Sigma Delta Chi award, 1978, 95, Thomas Nast prize, 1980, 2d prize for editorial cartooning Internat. Salon Cartoons of Montreal, 1981, Ohio's Gov.'s award, 1990, Pulitzer Prize for editorial cartooning, 1991, Nat. Headliner award, 1991, Reuben award for outstanding cartooning of yr., 1993. Mem. Nat. Cartoonists Soc. (Best Editorial Cartoonist award 1987, 88, 89, 94, Best Comic Strip award 1998, 99). Office: 312 Elm St Cincinnati OH 45202-2739

BORIN, GERALD W., zoological park administrator; CEO, dir. Columbus (Ohio) Zool. Park Assn., Inc., 1994—. Office: Columbus Zool Gardens PO Box 400 Powell OH 43065-0400

BORISY, GARY G., science administrator, researcher, molecular biology professor; b. Chgo., Aug. 18, 1942; s. Philip and Mae Borisy; children: Felice, Pippa, Alexis. BS, U. Chgo., 1962, PhD, 1966. Postdoctoral fellow NSF, Cambridge, Eng., 1966-67, NATO, Cambridge, 1967-68; asst. prof. U. Wis., Madison, 1968-72, assoc. prof., 1972-75, prof., 1975-80, Perlman-Bascom prof. life scis., 1980—2000, chmn. lab. molecular biology, 1981—2000; Leslie B. Arey prof. in cell, molecular & anatomical sci. Northwestern U. Feinberg Sch. of Medicine, 2000—06, assoc. v.p. rsch., 2003—06; dir., CEO Marine Biological Lab., Woods Hole, Mass., 2006—. Mem. numerous panels NIH and other govt. agys., ACS, HHMI; mem. Marine Biol. Lab. Editor Jour. Biol. Chemistry, 1978-80, Jour. Cell Biology, 1980-82, Internat. Rev. Cytology, 1971-91, Cell Motility and the Cytoskeleton, 1986-94, Jour. Cell Sci., 1988—; contbr. over 200 articles to profl. jours. Recipient Romnes award U. Wis., 1975-80, NIH Merit award, 1989, Zeiss award, 2005; grantee NIH, NSF, ACS. Fellow AAAS, Am. Acad. Arts. & Scis., 2004; mem. Am. Soc. Cell Biology, Am. Soc. Biochemistry and Molecular Biology, Sigma Xi. Office Phone: 508-289-7300. E-mail: gborisy@mbl.edu.

BORLING, JOHN LORIN, military officer; b. Chgo., Mar. 24, 1940; s. Edward Gustav and Vivian K. (Strietelmeir) Borling; m. Myrna Lee Holmstedt, June 22, 1963; children: Lauren, Megan. BS, U.S. Airforce Acad., 1963; grad., Armed Forces Staff Coll., 1975, Nat. War Coll., 1980, Harvard U., 1991. Commd. 2d lt. USAF, 1963, advanced through grades to maj. gen., 1989, prisoner of war Vietnam, 1966-73, fighter pilot, comdr., 1974-80, asst. dir. ops. HQ Pentagon Washington, 1981-82, comdr. 86th Combat Support Group Ramstein, Germany, 1982-83, comdr. 86th Fighter Group, 1983-84, exec. officer to COS NATO Mons, Belgium, 1984-86, dep. plans/analysis HQ/SAC Jt. Stategic Target Planning Staff Omaha, 1986-87, comdr. HQ 57th Air Divsn. Minot, ND, 1987-88, dep. ops. HQ SAC Omaha, 1988-91; dir. operational reg(s) HQ Pentagon, 1991-92; dep. chief of staff NATO, Norway, 1992-94, chief of staff, sr. U.S. mil. officer in Scandinavia, 1994-96; pres., CEO United Way, Chgo., 1997-98; dir. The 5th Media, Chgo., 1999—. Chmn. Performance Cons. Group, 2000—; pres., CEO SOS Am., 2000—; advisor AMSAM Biotechnologies Inc.; chmn., CEO, 100 Mission LLC, 2005—; mem. Armed Forces Policy Coun., Chgo., Coun. Fgn. Rels., Chgo., Chgo. Com.; mem. adv. com. Ill. Fatherhood Initiative, Chgo.; mentor Harris Sch., U. Chgo. Founder, charter mem. Ramstein Coun. Internat. Rels., 1983; v.p., bd. dirs. Opera Omaha, 1988—91; treas., bd. dirs. White Ho. Fellow Found., 1991—; adv. bd. Stanton Chase Internat., Maritime Trust Co.; bd. govs. Chgo. Mil. Acad.; bd. dirs. Nat. Jazz Mus., 2000; vice-chmn. Chgo. Meml. Day Parade Com., 2000; dir. Stars & Stripes Relief Fund, 2001; mem. adv. com. Kellog Sch., orthwestern U. Decorated Def. Distin. Svc. medal with oak leaf cluster, Air Force Disting. Svc. medal, Silver Star, Def. Superior Svc. medal, Legion of Merit with oak leaf cluster, DFC with oak leaf cluster, Bronze Star with V device and 2 oak leaf clusters, Air medal with 5 oak leaf clusters, Purple Heart with one cluster; named to Ill. Aviation Hall of Fame, 2004; recipient George Washington medal, Freedom Found., Valley Forge, Pa., 1975, Good Scout award, Boy Scouts Am., Chgo., 1974, Eagle Am. Hero award, Benedictine U., 2001, Patriot's award, City of Chgo., 2001; White Ho. fellow, 1974, Harvard U., 1998. Mem.: VFW, Air Force Assn., Assn. Grads. USAF Acad., Execs. Club Chgo., Comml. Club Chgo., Daedalians. Avocations: music, sports, reading. Office: SOS America Box 1543 Rockford IL 61110-1543 Office Phone: 405-447-2977. Business E-Mail: jlb@pcgok.com.

BORMAN, PAUL DAVID, judge; BA, U. Mich., 1959, JD, 1962; LLM, Yale U., 1964. Staff atty. U.S. Commn. on Civil Rights, 1962-63; asst. U.S. atty. U.S. Atty. Office, 1964-65; spl. counsel Mayor's Devel. Team, 1967-68; asst. prosecuting atty. Wayne County Prosecutor's Office, 1974-75; dist. judge U.S. Dist. Ct. (ea. dist.) Mich., Detroit, 1994—. Mem. ABA, Fed. Bar Assn., State Bar Mich., Oakland County Bar Assn. Office: US Courthouse 740 231 W Lafayette Blvd Detroit MI 48226-2700

BORN, JAMES E., art educator, sculptor; b. Toledo, Nov. 16, 1934; s. Elmer Arthur and Dorthy (Halstead) B.; m. Donna Jones; children: Karl, Anna Born Ross, Thomas, Christopher, Tanya. BA, Toledo U., 1959; MFA, U. Iowa, 1962. Grad. teaching asst. U. Iowa, Iowa City, 1964-65; asst. prof. Calif. State U., Arcata, 1962-65, Calif. Western U., San Diego, 1965-67, Calif. State U., Turlock, 1967-69; prof. art Ctrl. Mich. U., Mt. Pleasant, 1969—. Represented in permanent collections Outdoor Sculpture Exhibit, Southfield, Mich., 1991; exhibited in one-man show Gallery Abbott Kinney, Venice, Calif., 1992, Mich. Competition, Birmingham, Bloomfield Art Ctr., 1992, Commn. Trans World Airlines, LA Airport, Calif., San Diego Mus. Art, 1995, Mt. Clemens (Mich.) Art Mus., 1993-95, Saginaw Art Mus., 1993-94. Recipient honor award Battle Creek Art Mus., 1982, 1st award sculpture Ball State U., 1982, grand award S.W. Ark. Art Mus., 1982, 1st award sculpture Mt. Clemens Art Mus., 1989, sculpture award Saginaw Art Mus., 1992. Home: 2716 Greenfield Ave Los Angeles CA 90064-4032 Office: Ctrl Mich U Art Dept Mount Pleasant MI 48859-0001

BORN, SAMUEL ROYDON, II, retired lawyer, mediator; b. Atwood, Ill., Apr. 19, 1945; s. Samuel Roydon and Mary Elizabeth (Derr) B.; m. Brenda Alice Anderson, June 18, 1988; children: Samuel R. III, Holly Jean, Julie Chamberlain Sipe. Student, Northwestern U., 1963-64, Am. U., fall 1966; BA, Simpson Coll., 1967; JD, Ind. U., 1970. Bar: Ind. 1970, U.S. Dist. Ct. (so. dist.) Ind. 1970, U.S. Ct. Appeals (7th crct.) 1975, U.S. Dist. Ct. (no. dist.) Ind. 1990, U.S. Supreme Ct. 2003. Ptnr. Ice Miller, Indpls., 1970—2006; ret., 2006. Mem. safety com. Associated Gen. Contractors Ind., 1988—2006. Co-author: Safety and Health Guide for Indiana Business, 1999, 5th edit., 2004; mem. bd. editors: Ind. Law Jour., 1969—70; contbr. articles to profl. jours. Mem. bd. visitors Ind. U. Sch. Law, 1988-89, 95-98; chmn. ch. cmty. athletics First Bapt. Ch., Indpls., 1975-78, trustee, 1978-80. Fellow Am. Bar Found., Ind. Bar Found., Indpls. Bar Found.; mem. ABA (mem. nat. conf. bar pres. 1987-99, ho. of dels. 1988-98, labor and employment law sect., ADR sect.), Ind. State Bar Assn. (bd. govs. 1990-99, pres. 1997-98, labor law sect., ADR sect.), Indpls. Bar Assn. (bd. mgrs. 1987-95, pres. 1988, ADR sect.), U.S. C. of C. (occupl. safety and health adminstrv. coun. 1981-86, 2000—06), Ind. C. of C. (past chmn. occupl. safety health com.), Ind. Mfrs. Assn. (pers. labor rels. com. 1982-99), Highland Golf and Country Club, Crooked Stick Golf Club, Univ. Club, Indpls. Lawyers Club, Masons, Shriners, Kiwanis, Phi Eta Sigma, Sigma Alpha Epsilon Presbyterian. Avocations: golf, fly fishing, public speaking, driving. Home: 5202 Grandview Dr Indianapolis IN 46228-1938 Office Phone: 317-569-3000. Business E-Mail: cborn@mede8.com.

BORNSTEIN, GEORGE JAY, literary educator; b. St. Louis, Aug. 25, 1941; s. Harry and Celia (Price) B.; m. Jane Elizabeth York, June 22, 1982; children— Benjamin, Rebecca, Joshua. AB, Harvard U., 1963; PhD, Princeton U., 1966. Asst. prof. MIT, Cambridge, 1966-69, Rutgers U., 1969-70; assoc. prof. U. Mich., Ann Arbor, 1970-75, prof. English, 1975—, C.A. Patrides prof. lit., 1995—. Cons. various univ. presses, scholastic jours., funding agys., 1970—; mem. adv. bd. Yeats: An Annual, 1982-2003, South Atlantic Rev., 1985-88, Rev., 1991—2005, Text, 1993-2006, Paideuma, 2003—, Textual Cultures, 2006—. Author: Yeats and Shelley, 1970, Transformations of Romanticism, 1976, Postromantic Consciousness of Ezra Pound, 1977, Poetic Remaking, 1988, Material Modernism: The Politics of the Page, 2001; editor: Romantic and Modern, 1977, Ezra Pound Among the Poets, 1985, W.B. Yeats: The Early Poetry, vol. 1, 1987, vol. 2, 1994, W.B. Yeats: Letters to the New Island, 1990, Representing Modernist Texts, 1991, Palimpsest: Editorial Theory in the Humanities, 1993, W.B. Yeats: Under the Moon, the Unpublished Early Poetry, 1995, Contemporary German Editorial Theory, 1995, The Iconic Page in Manuscript, Print, and Digital Culture, 1998, W.B. Yeats: Early Essays, 2007. Cubmaster Wolverine council Boy Scouts Am., 1977-79. Recipient good teaching award Amoco Found., 1983, Warner Rice prize for rsch. in humanities, 1988, Rosenthal award for Yeats studies W.B. Yeats Soc., 2000; fellow Am. Coun. Learned Soc., 1972-73, NEH fellow, 1982-83, fellow Old Dominion Found., 1968, fellow Guggenheim Found., 1986-87. Mem. MLA (exec. com. Anglo-Irish 1976-80, exec. com. 20th Century English 1980-85, exec. com. Poetry 1987-92, exec. com. bibliography and textual studies 1993-98, exec. com. methods of rsch. 1998-2003), Soc. Textual Scholarship (program chair 1997, exec. com. 1998-, pres. 2006-07), Am. Conf. on Irish Studies (book prize judge 1991), Racquet Club, Princeton Club (N.Y.C.), Phi Beta Kappa. Home: 2020 Vinewood Blvd Ann Arbor MI 48104-3614 Office: U Mich Dept English Ann Arbor MI 48109-1003 Business E-Mail: georgeb@umich.edu.

BORNSTEIN, MORRIS, economist, educator; b. Detroit, Sept. 4, 1927; m. Reva Rice, Apr. 7, 1962; children— Susan, Jane. AB, U. Mich., 1947, A.M., 1948, PhD, 1952. Economist U.S. Govt., 1951-52, 55-58; mem. faculty U. Mich., Ann Arbor, 1958—, prof. econs., 1964—, dir. Center Russian and E. European Studies, 1966-69. Assoc. Harvard U. Russian Rsch. Ctr., 1962-63; vis. rsch. fellow Hoover Instn., Stanford, 1969-70; cons. in field, 1959—; mem. joint com. on Eastern Europe Am. Coun. Learned Socs.-Social Sci. Rsch. Coun., 1977-80. Author: Soviet National Accounts for 1955, 1961, The Soviet Economy, 1962, 4th edit., 1974, Comparative Economic Systems, 1965, 7th edit., 1994, Economia di Mercato ed Economia Pianificata, 1973, Sistemas economicos comparados, 1973, Plan and Market, 1975, Chinese transl., 1980, The Soviet Economy: Continuity and Change, 1981, East-West Relations and the Future of Eastern Europe, 1981, The Transfer of Western Technology to the USSR, 1985, French transl., 1985, contbr. articles to profl. jours.; mem. editorial bd. Jour. Comparative Econs., 1986-88, Problems of Economic Transition, 1987-97, Soviet Economy and Post Soviet Affairs, 1988-2003, Economic Policy in Transitional Economies, 1994—, Communist Economies and Econ. Transformation, 1997-98, Post-Soviet Geography and Econs., 1997-98, Post-Communist Economies, 1999—. With U.S. Army, 1953-55. Ford Found. faculty fellow, 1962-63, Sr. Fgn. Rsch. fellow French Ministry Rsch. and Tech., 1991. Mem. Am. Econ. Assn., Assn. Comparative Econ. Studies (exec. com. 1965-67, 73-75). Office: U Mich Dept Econs Ann Arbor MI 48109-1220

BOROWITZ, JOSEPH LEO, pharmacologist, educator; b. Columbus, Ohio, Dec. 19, 1932; s. Joseph Peter and Anna Louise (Grundei) B.; divorced, 1985; children: Jon Joseph, Peter Joseph, Lynn Anne. BS in Pharmacy, Ohio State U., 1955; MS in Pharmacology, Purdue U., 1957; PhD in Pharmacology (NIH fellow), Northwestern U., 1960. Chief biokinetics br. Sch. Aerospace Medicine, San Antonio, 1960—62; postdoctoral fellow dept. pharmacology Harvard U. Med. Sch., Boston, 1963—64; instr., then asst. prof. pharmacology Wake Forest U. Sch. Medicine, 1964—69; assoc. prof. pharmacology and toxicology Purdue U., 1969—74, prof., 1974—; sabbatical leave to Basel, Switzerland, 1984; vis. prof. sch. pharmacy U. P.R., 2001; sabbatical leave to Cambridge, England, 1976. Adj. prof. pharmacology Ind. Sch. Medicine, 1980—. Contbr. articles to profl. jours. Treas. Tippecanoe County (Ind.) Comprehensive Health Planning Coun., 1971-76. Capt. USAR, 1960. Recipient award for excellence in teaching Bowman Gray Sch. Medicine, 1969, Henry Heine award for excellence in teaching Purdue U. Coll. Pharmacy, 1983; named NIH postdoctoral fellow, 1962-64; grantee NSF, 1965-68, NIH, 1971-74, 86-89, 89-94, 94-98, 1999-2004, 2004—, U.S. Army Med. Rsch., 1989-96, 97-2000. Mem.: Rho Chi. Roman Catholic. Office: Purdue U Dept Med Chem and Molec Pharmacology West Lafayette IN 47907 Home Phone: 765-463-3001. E-mail: borowitz@pharmacy.purdue.edu.

BORRONI-BIRD, CHRISTOPHER E., transportation engineer; PhD in Chemistry, Cambridge U., 1991. Post-doctoral fellowship U. Tokyo; joined Chrysler Corp., 1992; tech. mgmt. Daimler-Chrysler; dir., design and vehicle tech. interface General Motors Rsch. Lab., Warren, Mich., 2000—, dir. Hy-Wire program, lead engr., dir., Sequel (hydrogen fuel cell car).

BORROR, DAVID S., lawyer; BA, Ohio State U.; JD, Ohio State U. Coll. Law. Pvt. practice Porter, Wright, Morris & Aurthur, Columbus, Ohio, 1982-87; bd. dirs. Dominion Homes, Inc., 1985—, v.p., 1985-88, gen. counsel, 1988-93, exec. v.p., 1988—. Office: Dominion Homes Warranty Services PO Box 5000 Dublin OH 43016-5555

BORROR, DOUGLAS G., construction company executive; b. Dayton, Ohio, 1955; m. Kim Borror; children: Danielle, Donald. BA in History, Ohio State U., 1977. Lic. Real Estate Broker. With Huntington Nat. Bank, Columbus, 1977-79, Borror Corp. (now Borror Realty Co. Inc.), Dublin, Ohio, 1979—; pres. Dominion Homes, Inc., Dublin, Ohio, 1987—99, CEO, 1992—; chmn. bd. Dominion Homes, Inc., Dublin, Ohio, 1999—. Bd. dir. Ohio Indemnity, Baninsurance Corp., 2004—, Columbia Gas of Ohio, Inc., Huntington Nat. Bank, Capital South Redevelopment Corp., Command Alkon Corp. Edn. chair Young President's Orgn., Columbus Chpt.; adv. bd. Goodwill Industries; bd. dir. Young President's Orgn., Internat., Wellington Sch., Recreation Unlimited; bd. trustee Ohio State U., 2004—; chmn. Columbus Riverfront Commons Corp.; bd. realtors Town of Columbus. Office: Dominion Homes Warranty Services PO Box 5000 Dublin OH 43016-5555

BORROR, RANDY L., state representative; b. Wells County, Ind. m. Kelly Borror; children: Jessica, Joshua, Sydney. BS in Pub. and Environ. Affairs, Ind. U. V.p. Bodenhafer, Mayer & Assocs., ISU/Stewart Brimner Group; No. Ind. regional dir. Assoc. Builders & Contractors of Ind.; pres. Liberty Constrn., Inc.; mem. Gaylor Group, Inc.; state rep. dist. 84 Ind. Ho. of Reps., Indpls., 2001—, mem. ways and means, and labor and employment coms. Fin. com., lasting legacy monuments Ft. Wayne Bicentennial; house constrn. chair Survive Alive; past Marion County phone bank coord. U.S. Sen. Richard Lugar; past project dir., fundraising Nat. Rep. Senatorial Com., U.S. Sen. Richard Lugar; past fin. chair Paul Helmke for Mayor Com.; mem. Rep. Hdqs. renovation project; bd. dirs. Big Brothers/BigSisters Northeast Inc., Three Rivers Ambulance Authority. Mem.: Assoc. Builders & Contractors of Ind. (pres.-elect, bd. dirs.), Nat. Assn. Home Builders (past dir. polit. affairs/fin.), Greater Ft. Wayne C. of C. (mem. legis. coun.), Delta Upsilon. Republican. Methodist. Office: Ind Ho of Reps 200 W Washington St Indianapolis IN 46204-2786

BORST, LAWRENCE MARION, state legislator; b. Champaign County, Ohio, July 16, 1927; s. Lawrence M. and Mary (Waldeck) B.; m. Eldoris Borst; children: Philip, Elizabeth, David. DVM, Ohio State U. Mem. Ind. Ho. of Reps., 1966-68; del. Rep. Nat. Conv., 1968—; mem. state tax and financing policy com.; mem. funds mgmt. oversight com.; mem. Ind. Senate from dist. 36; chmn. fin. taxation com. Ind. Senate Dist. 36, 1968—, ranking mem. pensions and labor com., ethics com. ins., fin. inst. and transp. coms., interstate coop coms.; chmn. Ind. budget com. Home: 681 Foxmere Ter Greenwood IN 46142-4812 Office: 4994 Hayes St Gary IN 46408-4354

BORST, PHILIP CRAIG, veterinarian, councilman; b. Columbus, Ohio, May 19, 1950; s. Lawrence M. and Eldoris B.; m. Jill Patrice Alexander, Sept. 12, 1980; children: Alex, Eric. BS, Purdue U., 1972, DVM, 1975. Vet. Shelby St. Animal Clinic, Indpls., 1975—. Bd. dirs. Ind. Sports Corp., Indpls. Mem. Indpls. City-County Coun., 1980—, pres.; del. Ind. State Rep. Convention, 1982; bd. dirs. Indpls. Conv. and Visitors Assn.; mem. bd. dirs. Indpls. Downtown, Inc.; mem. exec. com. 2000 NCAA Final Four. Named Best City-County Councilman Indpls. Mag., 1986; recipient Svc. to Mankind award Southside Indpl. Sertoma Club, 1987. Mem. Cen. Ind. Vet. Med. Assn. (pres. 1990), Purdue Vet. Med. Alumni Assn. (pres. 1988). Republican. Methodist. Avocations: golf, basketball, Purdue athletics. also: City-County Coun Office 200 E Washington St Ste 241 Indianapolis IN 46204-3310

BOSMA, BRIAN CHARLES, state legislator; b. Indpls., Oct. 31, 1957; s. Charles Edward and Margaret Hagge Bosma; m. Cheryl Lyn Hollingsworth, 1982. BSE, Purdue U., 1981; JD, Ind. U., 1984. Environ. engr. Ind. State Bd. Health, 1981-83; precinct committeeman Marian County Rep. Ctrl. Com., Ind., 1983-86; atty. Bingham, Summers, Welch & Spilman, Indpls., 1984-85, Kroger,

Gardis & Regas, 1986—; ward vice chmn. Marian County Rep. Ctrl. Com., Ind., 1987—; legis. and congrl. liaison Ind. State Dept. Edn., 1985-86; Ind. state rep. Dist. 50, 1986-91, Dist. 88, 1991—; ranking mem. com., mem. ways and means com. Ind. Ho. Reps., mem. elections and apportionment, environ. affairs and natural resources coms. Recipient Commencement Spkr. award Ind. U. Law Sch., 1984, Lacy Exec. Leadership award Indpls. C. of C., 1986; named Outstanding Freshman Legislator Ind. Broadcasters Assn. Mem. ABA, Ind. Bar Assn., Indpls. Bar Assn. (Pres. Spl. award 1984), Ind. Environ. Policy Commn., Assn. Retarded Citizens Trust (adv. bd.), Nat. Rep. Lawyers Assn., Lawrence C. of C., Beta Sigma Psi, Phi Delta Phi. Republican. Home: 8971 Bay Breeze Ln Indianapolis IN 46236-8568

BOSNICH, BRICE, chemistry professor; b. QLD, Australia, 1936; BS, U. Sydney, Australia, 1958; PhD, Australian NAt. U., 1962. Lectr. U. Coll., London, 1966-69; assoc. prof. U. Toronto, Can., 1970-75, prof., 1975-87, U. Chgo., 1987—. Contbr. articles to profl. jours. Office: U Chgo Dept Chem 5735 S Ellis Ave Chicago IL 60637-1403

BOSSMANN, LAURIE, controller, hardware company executive; m. Jeff Bossmann; two children. BS, No. Ill. U. CPA, Ill. With KPMG Peat Marwick; gen. acctg. mgr. Ace Hardware Corp., 1986-90, asst. contr., 1990-94, contr., 1994—, v.p., 1997—, v.p. mdse., 2000—. Mem. AICPA, Ill. CPA Soc. Office: 2200 Kensington Ct Oak Brook IL 60523-2103

BOST, MIKE, state legislator; Ill. state rep., 1995—. Office: 300 E Main St Carbondale IL 62901-3029

BOSTICK, RUSSELL M., information technology executive; b. Feb. 4, 1957; BA in Chemistry and Math., Wabash Coll.; MBA in Marketing, U. Chgo. Technology positions IBM, 1979—94, CNA Insurance, 1994—97; chief technology officer Corp. Software & Technology, Norwood, Mass., 1997—98, Chase Ins., 1998—2005; chief information officer Zurich Life US; exec. v.p., chief information officer Conseco, Inc., Carmel, Ind., 2005—. Chmn. bd. gov. IT Resources Ctr. Office: Conseco Inc 11825 N Pennsylvania St Carmel IN 46032 Office Phone: 317-817-2426.

BOSTWICK, JARRETT T., lawyer; b. Somerville, NJ, July 9, 1973; BA, George Washington U., 1995; JD, Gonzaga U. Sch. Law, 1998; LLM in Taxation, U. Wash. Sch. Law, 1999. Bar: Wash. 1998, Ill. 2004. Assoc. Treacy Law Grp., PLLC, Seattle; dir. wealth planning Nat. Fin. Ptnr. Wealth Design Ctr.; sr. mgr. personal fin. counseling grp. Ernst & Young, LLP; ptnr. wealth planning & philanthropy grp. Gardner, Carton & Douglas, Chgo.; atty. Handler, Thayer & Duggan, LLC, Chgo. amed one of Top 100 Attys., Worth mag., 2005. Office: Handler Thayer & Duggan LLC 191 N Wacker Dr 23rd Fl Chicago IL 60606-1633 Office Phone: 312-641-2100. Office Fax: 312-641-6866. E-mail: jbostwick@htdlaw.com.

BOSWELL, GINA R., cosmetics executive; b. Jan. 3, 1963; married; 2 children. BBA summa cum laude, Boston U., 1984; MA in Pub., Pvt. Mgmt., Yale U., 1989. CPA. Sr. assoc. Arthur Andersen, Boston, 1984—87; engagement mgr. Marakon Associates, Greenwich, Conn., 1989—93; with Estee Lauder Cos. Inc., 1992—95, v.p. investor rels., 1995—97, v.p. bus. devel., 1997—99; head, e-bus. to v.p. bus. devel. Ford Motor Co., 1999—2003; v.p. corp. strategy, bus. devel. Avon Products, Inc., 2003—05, sr. v.p., COO N. Am., 2005—08; pres. global brands Alberto-Culver Co., Melrose Park, Ill., 2008—. Bd. dirs. Applebee's Internat., 2005—, Manpower Inc., 2007—. Named one of America 's Top Women in Bus.-Game Changers, Pink mag. & Forté Found., 2007; grantee Henry Crown Fellowship, Aspen Inst., 2005. Office: Alberto-Culver Co 2525 Armitage Ave Melrose Park IL 60160 Office Phone: 212-282-5623.*

BOSWELL, LEONARD L., congressman; b. Harrison County, Mo., Jan. 10, 1934; s. Melvin and Margaret B.; m. Dody Boswell; 3 children. BA in Bus. Adminstrn., Graceland Coll., 1969. Commd. 2d lt. U.S. Army, 1956, advanced through grades to lt. col. Vietnam, Germany, Portugal, resigned, 1976; mem. Iowa Senate, 1984-96, pres., 1993-97; mem. U.S. Congress from 3d Iowa dist., 1997—; mem. transp. and infrastucture com., agr. com., select copm. on intelligence, 1999—. Grain and livestock farmer Decatur County, 1976—. Past pres., bd. dirs. local Coop. Elevator, Lamoni. Decorated DFC (2), Bronze Star (2). Mem. VFW, Am. Legion, Cattleman's Assn., Lamoni Lions Club. Democrat. Office: US Ho of Reps 1427 Longworth HOB Washington DC 20515-0001 Business E-Mail: Rep.Boswell.ia03@Mail.house.gov.

BOSWORTH, DOUGLAS LEROY, manufacturing executive, educator; b. Goldfield, Iowa, Oct. 15, 1939; s. Clifford Leroy and Clara (Lonning) Bosworth; m. Patricia Lee Knock, May 28, 1961; children: Douglas, Dawn. BS in Agrl. Engring, Iowa State U., 1962; MS in Agrl. Engring, U. Ill., 1964. With Deere & Co., Moline, Ill., 1959-94, divsn. engr. disk harrows, 1971-76, mgr. mfg. engring., 1976-80, works mgr., 1980-85, mgr. mfg., 1985-89, engring. test mgr., 1989-94; pres. WorkSpan, Inc., Mahomet, Ill., 1994—2001, Ill. Tech. Ctr., Savoy, Ill., 1995-97. Mem. Engring. Accreditation Commn., 1985—90; v.p. Skills, Inc.; mem. Assoc. Employers Bd., 1989—91; adj. engring. prof. U. Ill., Champaign-Urbana, 1995—. Active Am. Cancer Soc., Rock Island Unit; bd. dirs. United Med. Ctr., 1984—95; exec. com. Quad-City United Way, 1984—89. Mem.: Am. Soc. Agrl. Engrs. (chmn. Ill.-Wis. 1973—74, nat. bd. dirs. 1974—76, 1979—82, v.p. 1979—82, pres. elect 1991—92, pres. 1992—93, Engring. Achievement Young Designer award 1973), Rotary, Gamma Sigma Delta, Alpha Epsilon, Sigma Xi. Lutheran. Home and Office: WorkSpan Inc 1111 E Briarcliff Dr Mahomet IL 61853-9558 E-mail: dlbos@mchsi.com.

BOTEZ, DAN, physicist; b. Bucharest, Romania, May 22, 1948; arrived in US, 1976, naturalized; s. Emil and Ecaterina (Iacob) B.; m. Lynda Diane Arnold, Sept. 25, 1976; children: Anca, Adrian. BSEE with highest honors, U. Calif., Berkeley, 1971, MSEE, 1972, PhD, 1976; PhD (hon.), U. Politechnica, Bucharest, Romania, 1995. Fellow IBM Thomas J. Watson Rsch. Ctr., Yorktown Heights, NY, 1976-77; tech. staff RCA David Sarnoff Rsch. Ctr., Princeton, NJ, 1977-82, rsch. leader, 1982-84; dir. device devel. Lytel Inc., Somerville, NJ, 1984-86; chief scientist TRW Electro-Optic Rsch. Ctr., Redondo Beach, Calif., 1986, lab dir., 1986-87; sr. staff scientist TRW Rsch. Ctr., Redondo Beach, Calif., 1987-93, TRW tech. fellow, 1990-93; Philip Dunham Reed prof. elec. engring. U. Wis., Madison, 1993—; founder, bd. dirs. AlfaLight Inc., Madison, 2000—. Author: Electro-Optical Communications Dictionary, 1983, Diode-Laser Arrays, 1994; contbr. over 250 articles to profl. jours.; holder 44 U.S. patents. Named Outstanding Young Engr., IEEE Lasers and Electro-Optics Soc., San Jose, 1984, recipient Key to Future award, 1984. Fellow IEEE (chmn. tech. com. on semiconductor lasers 1989-90), Optical Soc. Am.; mem. Phi Beta Kappa. Independent. Eastern Orthodox. Avocations: tennis, travel, photography, skiing. Home: 200 N Prospect Ave Madison WI 53726-4027 Office: U Wis Dept Elec Engring 1415 Engineering Dr Madison WI 53706-1607 Home Phone: 608-231-3432; Office Phone: 608-265-4643. Business E-Mail: botez@engr.wisc.edu.

BOTSFORD, JON DOUGLAS, lawyer; b. Muskegon, Mich., Aug. 1, 1954; s. Lawrence Wayne and June Arleigh (Hanson) B; m. Joan Elizabeth Nims; children: Jackson, Tess, Matthew. BA, Mich. State U., 1976; JD, UCLA, 1979. Bar: Ill. 1979, U.S. Ct. Appeals (6th cir.) 1980, U.S. Dist. Ct. (no. dist.) Ill. 1981, Calif. 1982, Mich. 1982, U.S. Dist. Ct. (we. dist.) Mich. 1982, U.S. Supreme Ct 1984, U.S. Tax Ct. 1985. Law clk. to Hon. Albert Eagel U.S. Ct. Appeals, 6th Cir., 1979-80; atty. Jenner & Block, Chgo., 1980-82, Warner, Norcross & Judd, Grand Rapids, Mich., 1982-85, Steelcase Inc., Grand Rapids, 1985—87, sr. atty., 1987—92, asst. gen. counsel, 1992—97, gen. counsel, sec., 1997—98, v.p., gen. counsel, sec., 1998—99, sr. v.p., sec., chief legal officer, 1999—. Contbr. articles to profl. jours. Planning commr. Caledonia (Mich.) Township, 1997—99. Mem. ABA, Ill. State Bar Assn., State Bar Calif., State Bar Mich., Grand Rapids Bar Assn. Democrat. Office: Steelcase Inc 901 44th St SE Grand Rapids MI 49508-7575

BOTT, HAROLD SHELDON, accountant, management consultant; b. Chgo., Dec. 12, 1933; s. Harold S. and Mary (Moseley) B.; m. Audrey Anne Connor, May 15, 1964; children: Susan, Lynda. AB, Princeton U., 1955; MBA, Harvard U., 1959; postgrad., U. Chgo., 1960-62. Adminstrv. asst. to exec v.p. Champion Paper, Hamilton, Ohio, 1959-61; mgmt. cons. Arthur Andersen & Co., Chgo., 1961-65, mgr., 1965-71, ptnr., 1971-89. Mng. dir. mgmt. info. cons., ptnr. Andersen Cons., 1988-91; ptnr. Strategic Svcs. Ctr.; vice-chmn. The Assn. Mgmt. Cons., 1982-84; bd. dirs. Harvard Bus. Sch. Assocs.; faculty Grad. Sch. Bus., U. Chgo., 1994-2000; of counsel Omnitech Cons., 1994-2000; pres. H.S. Bott Co., 1994-2003. Officer, pres., dir. Urban Gateways, 1965—90; treas., dir. sch. bd., pres. Kenilworth Caucus, 1990; dir. The Cradle, 2000—03, Kenilworth United Fund, 1983—89; mem. pres.'s vis. com., trustee Chgo. Theol. Sem., 2002—; bd. dirs. Orch. of Ill., 1988—89, The Joseph Sears Found., 2000—04, co-pres., 2001—; commodore Kenilworth Sailing Club, 1987—88; bd. dirs. Alliance Français Chi, 1994, Alliance Francaile Chi, 2003, 2004. With USN, 1955—56. Mem. AICPA, Ill. Soc. CPA's, Kenilworth Club (treas., bd. dirs. 1975-79), Kenilworth Hist. Soc. (bd. dirs. 1995—), Indian Hill Club, Chgo. Club. Republican. Congregationalist. Home: 305 Kenilworth Ave Kenilworth IL 60043-1132 Business E-Mail: pete.bott@gsb.uchicago.edu.

BOTTI, ALDO E., lawyer; b. Bklyn., Dec. 27, 1936; s. Ettore and Filomena (DeLucio) B.; m. Sheila Higgins, Aug. 4, 1967; children: Michael, Joseph, Mark, Sarah, Elizabeth, John. BA, Rockhurst Coll., 1962; JD, St. Louis U., 1965. Bar: Ill. 1966, U.S. Dist. Ct. (no. and so. dists.) Ill. 1967, U.S. Supreme Ct. 1973, U.S. Ct. Appeals (7th cir.) 1979. Assoc. Frank Glazer & William O'Brien, Chgo., 1966-69; asst. state's atty. DuPage County, Wheaton, Ill., 1969-71, pub. defender, 1971-72; sr. ptnr. Botti, Marinaccio & DeLongis, Ltd., Oak Brook, Ill., 1972—. Atty. Village of Villa Park, 1985-88; gen. counsel Ill. State Crime Commn. Mem. Opera Theatre Ill., 1981-84; bd. dirs. Cmty. House, Hinsdale, Ill., 1988-91, mid-Am. chpt. ARC, 1991-94; chmn. bd. dirs. Hinsdale Cmty. Svcs., 1972-73; elected chmn. DuPage County, 1990-94; pres. Metro. Counties Coun., 1991-93. Served in U.S. Army, 1955-58. Mem. ABA, Ill. Bar Assn., Chgo. Bar Assn., DuPage County Bar Assn. (chmn. speakers bur. 1975-78, chmn. pub. relations 1973-75, gen. counsel 1988-89), Am. Judicature Soc., Assn. Trial Lawyers Am. Clubs: Butterfield Country (Oak Brook). Republican. Roman Catholic. Avocations: reading, painting. Office: Botti Marinaccio & DeLongis 720 Enterprise Dr Hinsdale IL 60523-1908

BOTTOM, DALE COYLE, marketing executive, director, management consultant; b. Columbus, Ind., June 25, 1932; s. James Robert and Sarah Lou (Coyle) B.; m. Frances Audrey Wilson, June 6, 1954 (div.); children: Jane Ellen, Steven Dale, Sharon Lynn, Carol Ann; m. Elaine McAuliffe, Aug. 20, 1988. BS, Ball State U., Muncie, Ind., 1954. Admissions counselor Stephens Coll., Columbia, Mo., 1958-61; exec. asst., then staff v.p. Inst. Fin. Edn., Chgo., 1961-67, pres., 1967-92; exec. v.p., chief fin. officer U.S. League Savs. Instns., 1985-89; chmn., dir. SAF-Systems & Forms Co.; sec.-gen. Internat. Union Fin. Instns., Chgo., 1989-95; cons. Resource Strategies Internat., Hinsdale, Ill., 1995—; assoc. v.p., dir. strategic svcs. Inland Real Estate Auctions, Inc. Bd. dirs. Savs. Instn. Ins. Group, Ltd., v.p., CFO; bd. dirs. Edgebrook Bank. Chmn. bd. Barrington (Ill.) United Meth. Ch., 1981; v.p. Chgo. Rotary One, 1967-80. Capt. USAF, 1955-67; comdr. USNR (ret.), 1967-78. Recipient Award of Distinction, Ball State U., 2003. Mem. SAR, Fin. Mgrs. Soc. (dir.), Savs. Instns. Mktg. Soc. Am., Navy League, Ind. Soc. Chgo., Tavern Club (v.p. 1993), Medinah Country Club, Hinsdale Golf Club, Sons of Am. Rev. Republican. Avocations: genealogy, travel, walking. Home and Office: 606 Burr Ridge Clb Burr Ridge IL 60527-5209 Personal E-mail: d.bottom@comcast.net.

BOTTOMS, ROBERT GARVIN, academic administrator; b. Birmingham, Ala., June 28, 1944; s. Dalton Garvin and Mary Inez (Cruce) Bottoms; m. Gwendolynn Jean Vickers, June 14, 1968; children: David Timothy, Leslie Clair. BA, Birmingham So. U., 1966; BD, Emory U., 1969; D of Ministry, Vanderbilt U., 1972. Chaplain Birmingham (Ala.) So. Coll., 1973—74, asst. to pres., 1974—75; asst. dean, asst. prof. church and ministry Vanderbilt U., Nashville, 1975—78; v.p. for univ. rels. DePauw U., Greencastle, Ind., 1978—79, exec. v.p. external rels., 1979—83, exec. v.p., 1983—86, acting pres., 1985, pres., 1986—. Cons. Arthur Vining Davis Found., Jacksonville, Fla., 1978—79, Luth. So. Sem., Columbia, SC, 1979—80; cons. theol. edn. The Lilly Endowment, Indpls., 1979—82; cons. Fund for Theol. Edn., NYC, 1981—82; chmn. audit com. Centel Cable TV Co., Oak Brook, Ill., 1987—89; Am. ctr. for internat. leadership organizer Edn. Policy Commn. U.S.-USSR Emerging Leaders Summit, Phila., 1988. Author: Lessons in Financial Development, 1982. Chmn. com. on ch. and coll. Episcopal Diocese Ind., 1979—84; bd. advisors Vanderbilt Div. Sch., 1980—93; bd. trustees Seabury-Western Theol. Sem., 2001—; bd. dirs. Joyce Found., 1994—2002, 2004—, G.M. Constrn. Inc., Indpls., 1998—2001, The Posse Found., 2001—, Women in Govt., Washington, 2001—03, Ctr. Leadership Devel., Indpls., 2003—. Recipient CASE V Chief Exec. Leadership award, 2000. Mem.: NCAA (coun. 1989—95, subcom. eligibility appeals), Ind. Colls. Ind. Found. (bd. dirs. 1987—2005, nominating com. 1990—97), Great Lakes Colls. Assn. (bd. dirs. 1987—, chair 1994—96), Ind. Colls. of Ind. (bd. dirs. 1987—, exec. com. 1991—), Am. Coun. Edn. (commn. on women in higher edn. 1990—91), Assn. Governing Bds. Univs. and Colls. (coun. pres. 1997—), Nat. Assn. Schs. and Colls. United Meth. Ch. (bd. dirs. 1987—91), Nat. Assn. Ind. Colls. and Univs. (task force increasing participation of minorities in ind. higher edn. 1989—95), Nat. Coun. Chs. (governing bd. 1985—91), Chgo. Club., Cosmos Club (Washington), Univ. Club of N.Y.C., Columbia Club (Indpls.). Avocation: boating. Home: 125 Wood St Greencastle IN 46135 Office: DePauw Univ Office of Pres 313 S Locust St Greencastle IN 46135-0037 Office Phone: 765-658-4800. Office Fax: 765-658-4224.

BOUBEKRI, MOHAMED, architecture educator; Diploma in Arch., U. Scis. and Tech. Oran, Algeria, 1983; MArch, U. Colo., Denver, 1985; PhD in Arch., Tex. A&M U., 1990. Lic. arch., Algeria, 1983. Jr. archtl. designer Kalik Arch., Mo., 1980—82, Electronic Transcations Assn. U., 1982—83; asst. prof. Concordia U., Montreal, Canada, 1990—93, U. Ill. Sch. Arch., Champaign-Urbana, 1993—99, assoc. prof., 1999—, chair practice and tech. faculty, 2002—. Mem.: Illuminating Engring. Soc. N.Am. (mem. daylighting com. 1995—). Office: Univ Ill Champaign Sch Arch 318 TH Buell Hall MC 621 611 E Lorado Taft Dr Champaign IL 61820

BOUCHARD, MICHAEL J., state legislator; b. Flint, Mich., Apr. 12, 1956; s, Donald A. and Doris (Sams) B.; m. Pamela Johnson, 1988; 1 child, Makayla Kathryn. BA, Mich. State U., 1979; grad., Mich. Law Enforcement Ctr. Police officer Bloomfield Twp. (Mich.), 1977-78; pub. safety officer Beverly Hills (Mich.), 1978-88; pres. TACT, Inc., 1986-91; pres, founder Beverly Hills Gourmet Yogurt & Ice Cream, 1989-91; state rep. Mich. Ho. Reps.; state senator Mich. State Senate, Dist. 13. Chair fin. svc., vice chair families, mental & health & human svcs., mem. tech. & energy, asst. majority leader, Mich. State Senate. Del. Mich. State Rep. Conv., 1984-91; coun. mem. Village of Beverly Hills, 1986-90, pres., 1989-90; treas. 18th Dist. Rep. Com., 1989-91; chmn. Oakland County Rep. Campaign Com., 1990; mem. Oakland County Young Reps.; bd. dirs. Birmingham/Bloomfield Cultural Com. Recipient Leadership award Am. Cancer Humanitarian Com., Outstanding Svc. award March of Dimes, Legis. of Yr. award Police Officers Assn. Mich., Humanitarian award Arab-Am. & Chaldean Coun., Birmingham Bro. Rice Disting. Alumnus award. Mem. Birmingham/Bloomfield C. of C. (bd. dirs.). Address: PO Box 30036 Lansing MI 48909-7536

BOUCHARD, THOMAS JOSEPH, JR., psychology professor, researcher; b. Manchester, NH, Oct. 3, 1937; s. Thomas and Florence (Charest) B.; m. Pauline Marina Proulx, Aug. 13, 1960; children: Elizabeth, Mark. BA, U. Calif., Berkeley, 1963, PhD, 1966. Asst. prof. U. Calif., Santa Barbara, 1966-69, U. Minn., Mpls., 1969-70, assoc. prof., 1970-73, prof., 1973—, chmn. dept. psychology, 1985-91. Dir. Minn. Ctr. Twin and Adoption Rsch., U. Minn., 1980—. Assoc. editor: jours. Jour. Applied Psychology, 1977—80, Behavior Genetics, 1982—86; contbr. articles jours. more than 175 articles to profl. jours. With USAF, 1955-58. Fellow AAAS, APA, Am. Psychol. Soc.; mem. Phi Beta Kappa, Sigma Xi. Office: U Minn Dept Psychology 75 E River Rd Minneapolis MN 55455-0280 Home: PO Box 880104 Steamboat Springs CO 80488 E-mail: bouch001@tc.umn.edu.

BOUCHER, BILL, state legislator; b. Central Falls, RI, Nov. 13, 1937; m. Dee Boucher; 3 children. Attended, Longview Cmty. Coll., U. Kans. Mo. State rep., Dist. 48 Mo. State Ho. of Rep., 1992—. Mem. Hickman Mills Sch. Bd., 1984—90; adv. bd. Kans. City Salvation Army; mem. South Kans. City Citizens Crusade Against Crime; adv. bd. Alliance for Safe Highways; founding mem. Big Brothers of Kans. City; mem. C. of C., Raytown, Grandview, South Kans. City. Served USAF, 1957—61. Recipient Pub. Svc. award, Mo. Assn. Social Welfare, 1994, Friend of Children award, Pediatric Nurses Assoc. and Practitioners, 1995, Exemplary Leadership award, Mo. Head Injury Adv. Coun., 1996, State Ofcl. of Yr., Nat. Industries for Blind, 1997, Legislator of Yr. award, Mo. Alliance Animal Legis., 1997, Pres. award, Mo. Rehabilitation Assn., 1997. Mem.: Southern Cmty. Coalition, Disabled Am. Veterans, Optimists Club, Lions Club Internat., Raytown Democratic Club, Am. Legion. Democrat. Catholic. Home: 11320 Sunnyslope Dr Kansas City MO 64134-3148 Office: Mo House of Representative 201 West Capitol Ave Rm 313-3 Jefferson City MO 65101 Office Phone: 573-751-7335. Office Fax: 573-526-1964. E-mail: bboucher@services.state.mo.us.

BOUCHER, MERLE, state legislator; m. Susan Boucher; 4 children. AA, N.D. State U.; BS, Mayville State U., ND. Mem. N.D. Ho. of Reps. from 9th dist., 1991—; farmer. Mem. Human Svcs. and Agr. Coms. N.D. Ho. of Reps. Mem. Rolette Cmty. Improvement Inc., Rolette Jobs Auth. Mem. N.D. Edn. Assns. Democrat. Office: D Ho of Reps State Capitol Bismarck ND 58505

BOUDREAU, LYNDA L., state agency administrator; m. Jim Boudreau. Rep. Minn. Ho. of Reps., 1994—2004, speaker pro tempore. Chair, health and human svc. policy com. Office: 559 State Office Bldg 100 Rev Martin Luther Ling Jr Blvd Saint Paul MN 55155 Office Phone: 651-201-5807. E-mail: lynda.boudreau@state.mn.us.

BOUDREAU, ROBERT JAMES, nuclear medicine physician, researcher; b. Lethbridge, Alta., Can., Dec. 27, 1950; came to U.S., 1983; s. George Joseph Boudreau and Eleanor Joyce (Dalzell) Hamilton; m. Francine Suzanne Archambault, Jan. 16, 1982. BSc with highest honors, U. Sask., Saskatoon, Can., 1972; PhD, U. B.C., Vancouver, Can., 1975; MD, Calgary U., Can., 1978. Diplomate Am. Bd. Nuclear Medicine. Resident in diagnostic radiology and nuclear medicine McGill U., Montreal, Que., Can., 1978-82; asst. prof. U. Minn., Mpls., 1983-87, assoc. prof., 1987-93, prof., 1993-99, prof. emeritus, 2000—, dir. grad. studies dept. radiology, 1987-91, dir. nuclear medicine divsn., 1987-2000. Author book chpts.; contbr. articles to profl. jours. Recipient Gold Key award Soc. Chem. Industry, 1972, Soc. Clin. Investigation Young Investigator award, 1978; Can. Heart Found. Med. Scientist fellow, 1976-78. Fellow Royal Coll. Physicians; mem. Soc. Chiefs of Acad. Nuclear Medicine Sects. (treas. 1989-93), Soc. Nuclear Medicine (edn. and tng. com. 1983-91, trustee 1994-95, bd. govs. ctrl. chpt. 1989—, treas. 1992-94, pres. 1994-95), Radiol. Soc. N.Am. Avocations: skiing, boating, travel, computers.

BOUDREAU, THOMAS M., lawyer, health products executive; b. St. Louis, 1951; BA cum laude, Maryville Coll., 1973; JD magna cum laude, St. Louis U., 1979. Bar: Mo. 1979, US Dist. Ct. (ea. dist. Mo.) 1979, US Tax Ct. 1980. Ptnr. Husch & Eppenberger, St. Louis, 1986—94; v.p., gen. counsel Express Scripts Inc., Md. Heights, Mo., 1994, sr. v.p., gen. counsel, sec., 1994—. Co-author: The Law of Lender Liability, 1990; asst. editor St. Louis U. Law Jour., 1978-79. Fellow: Am. Coll. Comml. Fin. Lawyers; mem.: ABA. Office: Express Scripts Inc 13900 Riverport Dr Maryland Heights MO 63043

BOULANGER, RODNEY EDMUND, energy company executive; b. Detroit, Apr. 4, 1940; m. Nancy Ann Ewigleben, Dec. 29, 1962; children: Brent, Karla, Melissa. BS, Ferris State Coll., Big Rapids, Mich., 1963; MBA, U. Detroit, 1967. Various fin. planning and econ. positions Am. Nat. Resources Co., 1963-78; v.p. system econs. and diversification Am. Natural Service Co., Detroit, 1978-80; v.p. fin. adminstrn ANG Coal Gasification Co., Detroit, 1980-82, v.p., fin. sec., 1983-84; treas., chief fin. officer Gt. Plains Gasification Assocs., Detroit, 1982-84; exec. v.p., chief fin. and adminstrv. officer ANR Pipeline Co., Detroit, 1984-86; pres., CEO ANG Coal Gasification Co., Bismarck, N.D., 1986-87, Midland Congeneration Venture, 1987-95; with CMS Generation Co., Dearborn, Mich., 1995—. Bd. dirs. Chem. Bank. Mem. Tournament Players Club, Detroit Athletic Club, Duck Lake County Club (Albion, Mich.), Caloosa Country Club (Fla.), Beta Gamma Sigma.

BOUMA, ROBERT EDWIN, lawyer; b. Ft. Dodge, Iowa, July 19, 1938; s. Jack and Gladys (Cooper) B.; m. Susan Lawson, Nov. 26, 1963; children: James, Whitley. BA, Coe Coll., 1960; JD, U. Iowa, 1962. Bar: Iowa 1962, N.Y. 1964, Ill. 1985. Asso. Cravath, Swaine & Moore, NYC, 1962-70; gen. counsel Xerox Data Systems Co., Los Angeles, 1970-73; sr. group counsel Xerox Corp., Rochester, N.Y., 1973-76; asso. gen. counsel Monsanto Co., St. Louis, 1976-78; sr. v.p., gen. counsel Household Internat., Prospect Heights, Ill., 1978-84; ptnr., chmn. firm trial dept. McDermott Will & Emery LLP, Chgo., 1984—. Trustee Coe Coll., Ill. Inst. Continuing Legal Edn. Served with USN, 1962-63, v.p. bd. dir. IA Law Sch. Found. Mem. ABA (co-chmn. com. on corp. counsel lit. sect.), Chgo. Bar Assn. Clubs: Mid-Day (Chgo.); Winter (Lake Forest, Ill.), Onwentsia (Lake Forest, Ill.); Legal of Chgo. Home: 901 Church Rd Lake Forest IL 60045-1457 Office: McDermott Will & Emery LLP 227 W Monroe St Ste 3100 Chicago IL 60606-5096 Office Fax: 312-984-7700, 312-984-7718. Business E-Mail: rbouma@mwe.com.

BOUNSALL, PHILLIP A., electronics company executive; Sr. mgr. Ernst & Young LLP; CFO Walker Info., Inc., 1994-96; exec. v.p., CFO, treas. Brightpoint, Inc., Indpls., 1996—. Office: Brightpoint 501 Airtech Pkwy Plainfield IN 46168-7408

BOUQUIN, BERTRAND, chef; b. Nevers, France, Apr. 26, 1970; m. Tanya Bouquin. Mem. staff restaurants in Lyons, Avignon, France and Switzerland; sous-chef Restaurant Bruneau, Brussels, 1995—97, Restaurant Daniel, NY, 1997—2000; chef Club XIX, Calif., 2000—01, Maisonette, Cin., 2021—. Office: Maisonette 4149 Walton Creek Rd Cincinnati OH 45227-3917

BOURDON, CATHLEEN JANE, professional society administrator; b. Sparta, Wis., July 13, 1948; d. Cletus John and Josephine Marie (Bourdon) Scheurich; children: Jill Krzyminski, Jeff Krzyminski. BA in Polit. Sci., U. Wis., 1973, MLS, 1974. Tchr. Peace Corps, Arba Minch, Ethiopia, 1969-72; asst. prof., dir. Alverno Coll. Libr., Milw., 1974-83; dep. exec. dir. Assn. Coll. and Rsch. Librs., Chgo., 1983-93; exec. dir. Ref. and User Svcs. Assn. divsn. ALA Assn. Specialized and Coop. Libr. Agys., Chgo., 1993—2007; assoc. exec. dir. ALA, 2007—. Mem. ALA (pres. Staff Assn. 1987-88). Avocations: movies, reading. Office: ALA 50 E Huron St Chicago IL 60611-5295 Office Phone: 312-280-3217. E-mail: cbourdon@ala.org.

BOURGUIGNON, ERIKA EICHHORN, anthropologist, educator; b. Vienna, Feb. 18, 1924; d. Leopold H. and Charlotte (Rosenbaum) Eichhorn; m. Paul H. Bourguignon, Sept. 29, 1950. BA, Queens Coll., 1945; grad. study, U. Conn., 1945; PhD, Northwestern U., 1951; DHL, CUNY, 2000. Field work Chippewa Indians, Wis., summer 1946; field work Haiti; anthropologist Northwestern U., 1947-48; instr. Ohio State U., 1949-56, asst. prof., 1956-60, assoc. prof., 1960-66, prof., 1966-90, acting chmn. dept. anthropology, 1971-72, chmn. dept., 1972-76, prof. emeritus, 1990—; dir. Cross-Cultural Study of Dissociational States, 1963-68. Bd. dirs. Human Relations Area Files, Inc., 1976-79 Author: Possession, 1976, rev. edit., 1991, Psychological Anthropology, 1979, Italian transl., 1983; editor, co-author: Religion, Altered States of Consciousness and Social Change, 1973, A World of Women, 1980; co-author: Diversity and Homogeneity in World Societies, 1973; adv. editor: Behavior Sci. Rsch., 1976-79; assoc. editor Jour. Psychoanalytic Anthropology, 1977-87; mem. editl. bd. Ethos, 1979-89, 97—2005, 2005—, Jour. Haitian Studies, 2000—, Anthropology of Consciousness, 2002—; editor: Margaret Mead: The Anthropologist in America—, Occasional Papers in Anthropology, No. 2, Ohio State U. Dept. Anthropology, 1986; (with Barbara Rigney) Exile: A Memoir of 1939 by Bronka Schneider, 1998; contbr. articles to profl. jours. Fellow Am. Anthrop. Assn.; mem. Ctrl. State Anthrop. Soc. (treas. 1953-56, exec. com. 1995-98), Ohio Acad Sci., World Psychiat. Assn. (transcultural psychiatry sect.), Am. Ethnol. Soc., Current Anthropology (assoc.), Soc. for Psychol. Anthropology (nominations com. 1981-82, bd. dirs. 1991-93, lifetime achievement award 1999), Soc. for the Anthropology of Religion, Phi Beta Kappa, Sigma Xi. E-mail: bourguignon.1@osu.edu.

BOURNE, JAMES E., lawyer; b. Charleston, W.Va., Jan. 13, 1940; BA, Ind. U., 1962, JD, 1965. Bar: Ind. 1965. Law clk. to Hon. William E. Steckler, U.S. Dist. Ct. (so. dist.) Ind., 1965—67; atty. Wyatt, Tarrant & Combs, LLP, New Albany, Ind. Mem. faculty Nat. Inst. for Trial Advocacy. Fellow: Am. Coll. Trial Lawyers; mem.: ABA, Ind. State Bar Assn. (pres.-elect 2001—02, pres. 2002—03), Leadership So. Ind., Def. Trial Counsel Ind., Def. Rsch. Inst. Office: Wyatt Tarrant Combs LLP Cmty Bank Bldg 101 W Spring St New Albany IN 47150-3440

BOURNE, PATRICK J., state legislator; b. Omaha, Apr. 11, 1964; m. Cindy Bourne, May 18, 1985 (dec.); 1 child, Jack. A, S.E. C.C., 1984; BSBA, U. Nebr., Omaha, 1994; JD, Creighton U., 1997. Bar: Nebr. Atty.; mem. Nebr. Legislature from 8th dist., Lincoln, 1998—. Mem. ABA, Nebr. State Bar Assn., Omaha Bar Assn. Home: 5121 Erskine St Omaha NE 68104-4352 Office: State Capitol Dist 8 PO Box 94604 Rm 1101 Lincoln NE 68509

BOUSQUETTE, JANINE M., retail executive; BA, U. Mich. With Procter & Gamble Co., 1982—94, asst. brand mgr. Comet cleaner, Lava soap, Coast soap, brand mgr. Biz bleach, brand mgr. Downy fabric softener, mktg. dir. Bounce fabric softener, mktg. dir. new products, sr. mktg. dir. Max Factor Internat.; v.p. mktg. flavors Pepsi-Cola Divsn., PepsiCo Inc., 1995—96, v.p. mktg. Pepsi trademark brands, 1997—99; exec. v.p., chief mktg. officer e-Toys Inc., Santa Monica, Calif., 1999—2001; cons., 2001—02; exec. v.p., chief customer and mktg. officer Sears, Roebuck & Co., Hoffman Estates, Ill., 2002—. Mem. Phi Beta Kappa. Office: Sears Roebuck & Co 3333 Beverly Rd Hoffman Estates IL 60179

BOUTIETTE, VICKIE LYNN, elementary school educator, reading specialist; b. Valley City, ND, Mar. 13, 1950; BS in Elem. Edn., Valley City State U., 1972; MS in Reading, Moorhead State U., 1997; postgrad., U. S.D., 1998—. 4th-5th grade tchr. Pillsbury Pub. Sch., 1973-74; 3rd grade tchr. West Fargo Pub. Schs., 1984-90, remedial reading tchr., elem. tchr., 1993-98, Reading Recovery tchr. leader, 1998—. Sunday sch. tchr., 1975—, ch. newsletter editor, 1993—; vol. U. Minn. Hosps. and Clinics, 1991-93. Recipient Nat. Educator Award Milken Family Found., 1998, Courage award N.D. Edn. Assn., 1994, Disting. Alumni award Minn. State U. Moorhead, 2002, Alumni Merit award Valley City State U., 2000; Christa McAuliffe fellowship, 2000; named N.D. Tchr. of Yr., 1998, West Fargo Tchr. of Yr. 1997-98. Mem. NEA, West Fargo Edn. Assn. (exec. bd. 1989-90, elem. chairperson 1988-89, pub. rels. chairperson 1988-90), N.D. Edn. Assn., Valley Reading Assn. (rec. sec. 1997—), N.D. Reading Assn., Phi Delta Kappa, Alpha Mu Gamma (pres. 1972). Home: 7103 64th Ave S Fargo ND 58104-5715 Office: Westside Elem Sch 945 7th Ave W West Fargo ND 58078-1429 Fax: 701-356-2119.

BOUTON, MARSHALL MELVIN, academic administrator; b. NYC, Aug. 8, 1942; s. Percy Marshall and Mary Fuller (Melvin) B.; m. Barbara Elizabeth Linn, Sept. 14, 1968; children: Christopher, Alexander. BA cum laude in History, Harvard Coll., 1964; MA in South Asian Studies, U. Pa., 1968; PhD in Polit. Sci., U. Chgo., 1980. Exec. sec., program dir. The Asia Soc., NYC, 1975-77; spl. asst. to amb. U.S. Embassy, New Delhi, 1977-80; dir. policy analysis, internat. security affairs Dept. Def., Near East, South Asia, Africa, 1980-81; dir. contemporary affairs The Asia Soc., NYC, 1981-87, v.p. pres. program planning external affairs, 1987-90, exec. v.p., 1990-2001; pres. Chgo. Coun. on Fgn. Rels., 2001—. Tng. project dir. Peace Corps, Sacramento, summer 1967, tng. coord., Estes Park, Colo., summer 1968; tng. assoc. in internat. devel. The Ford Found., New Delhi, 1968-69; lectr. divsn. of social scis. U. Chgo., 1973-75; vis. scholar So. Asian Inst. Columbia U., 1975-77; internat. adv. bd. Ctr. Advanced Study India, U. Pa. Internat. Inst. Strategic Studies, Chgo. Sister Cities; internat. program bd. world affairs Coun. Am.; mem. bd. Pacific Coun. Internat. Policy Comml. Club Club, Econ. Club. Chgo.; cons. World Bank, 1980-81. Author: Agrarian Radicalism in South India, 1985, India's Problem is not Politics, 1998, Foreign Affairs, May/June 1998; co-author: Korea at the Crossroads: Implications for American Strategy, 1987; editor, co-editor: India Briefing; contbr., editor numerous articles to profl. jours. NSF Dissertation Rsch. fellow, 1972-74, U.S. Agy. on Internat. Devel. grantee, 1974-77, Rockefeller Found. travel grantee, 1977. Mem.: Am. Polit. Sci. Assn., Assn. for Asian Studies, Coun. on Fgn. Rels., Mid-Am. Club, Met. Club Washington, Univ. Club of Chgo., Chgo. Club, Harvard Club. Office: Chgo Coun on Fgn Rels Ste 1100 332 S Michigan Ave Chicago IL 60604

BOUTWELL, ROSWELL KNIGHT, oncology educator; b. Madison, Wis., Nov. 24, 1917; s. Paul Winslow and Clara Gertrude (Brinkhoff) B.; m. Luella Mae Fairchild, Sept. 25, 1943; children— Paul F., Philip H., David K. BS in Chemistry, Beloit Coll., 1939; MS in Biochemistry, U. Wis., 1941, PhD, 1944; DSc, Beloit Coll., 1980. Instr. U. Wis., 1945-49, asst. prof., 1949-54, assoc. prof., 1954-67, prof. oncology med. ctr. Madison, 1967—. Vis. lectr. Inst. for Environ. Medicine, NYU, summer 1966; mem. cancer study group Wis. Regional Med. Program, 1967-70; mem. adv. com. on inst. research grants Am. Cancer Soc., 1967-74, chmn., 1972-74; mem. food protection com. NRC, 1971-75; mem. lung cancer segment Nat. Cancer Inst., 1971-75; mem. adv. com. on pathogenesis of cancer Am. Cancer Soc., 1960-63; mem. Nat. Cancer Adv. Bd., 1983-90; chief research Radiation Effects Research Found., Hiroshima, Japan, 1984-86; prof. emeritus, 1988—. Mem. editorial adv. bd. Cancer Research, 1959-64, assoc. editor, 1973-83; mem. editorial bd. Jpn. J. Cancer Res., 1985—; assoc. editor: Nutrition and Cancer, 1988—; mem. sci. adv. bd. Internat. Coun. for Coordinating Cancer Rsch., 1989-92, Dermigen, 1990—. Mem. Monona Grove Sch. Bd., 1952-54; bd. dirs. Madison Gen. Hosp. Found. Recipient Kenneth P. DuBois award Soc. Toxicology, 1998, medal of honor Am. Cancer Soc., 1998. Fellow AAAS, Am. Assn. Cancer Research (dir.), Am. Soc. Biol. Chemists (Clowes award). Office: U Wis Dept Oncology McArdle Lab 1400 University Ave Rm 1125 Madison WI 53706-1526 Office Phone: 608-262-5182. E-mail: rboutwell@msn.com.

BOWE, WILLIAM J(OHN), lawyer; b. Chgo., June 23, 1942; s. William John Sr. and Mary (Gwinn) B.; m. Catherine Louise Vanselow, 1979; children: Andrew M., Patrick D. BA, Yale U., 1964; JD, U. Chgo., 1967. Bar: Ill. 1967, Tenn. 1984. Assoc. Ross, Hardies, O'Keefe, Babcock, McDougall & Parsons, Chgo., 1967—68; assoc., then ptnr. Roan & Grossman, Chgo., 1971—78; v.p., gen. counsel, sec. The Bradford Exch. Ltd., Niles, Ill., 1979—83; asst. gen. counsel, v.p., gen. counsel United Press Internat. Inc., Nashville, 1984—85; v.p. to exec. v.p., gen. counsel, sec. Ency. Britannica, Inc., Chgo., 1986—; sec. William Benton Found., Chgo., 1987—96; pres. Merriam-Webster, Inc., Springfield, Mass., 1995—96, Ency. Britannica Edni. Corp., Chgo., 1995—99. Part-time faculty Summer Law Inst. Kenneth Wang Law Sch., Soochow U., Suzhou, China, 2005. Mem. bd. editors Intellectual Property Studies, Chinese Acad. Social Studies, Beijing, 1996-99; contbr. articles to legal jours. Mem. The Annenberg Washington Program Anti-Piracy Project, Washington, 1988—89; bd. dirs. Internat. Anticounterfeiting Coalition, Washington, 1993—96, chmn., 1994—96; gen. counsel Gov.'s Task Force on Sch. Fin., Chgo., 1975—76; trustee Hull Ho. Assn., Chgo., 1977—79; pres., bd. dirs. Clarence Darrow Cmty. Ctr., Chgo., 1975—84; mem. bd. overseers Ill. Inst. Tech.-Kent Coll. Law, 1982—86; mem. Gov.'s Task Force on Workforce Preparation, 1991—93, Gov.'s Work Group on Early Childhood Care and Edn., 1994—95, Gov.'s Edn. Summit, 2000—02. With US Army, 1968—71. Mem.: ABA, Software and Info. Industry Assn. (govt. affairs coun. 1999—), Software Publs. Assn. (govt. affairs com. 1997—99), Intellectual Property Assn. Chgo., Chgo. Bar Assn., Ill. Bar Assn., Ill. State C. of C. (bd. dirs. 1989—96, mem. edn. com. 1989—99), The Cliff Dwellers (bd. dirs. 2004—07, pres. 2006—07). Office: Ency Britannica Inc 331 N LaSalle St Chicago IL 60610-4707 Office Phone: 312-347-7084. E-mail: wbowe@eb.com.

BOWEN, BRENT, aviation educator; MBA, Oklahoma City U.; D in higher Edn. and Aviation, Okla. State U. Cert. airline transp. pilot FAA, flight instr. FAA, advanced-instrument ground inspector FAA, aviation safety counselor FAA, aerspace edn. counselor FAA. Disting. prof. aviation U. Nebr. Found., Omaha, 1992—; dir. Aviation Inst. U. Nebr., Omaha, dir. aviation and transp. policy and rsch., 2000—; grad. faculty fellow U. Nebr. Sys.-wide Grad. Coll. Industry cons., pilot, former fixed-based operator and air carrier operator; invited spkr., panelist NAS/Transp. Rsch. Bd.; apptd. mem. Nat. Rsch. Coun. Steering Group on Small Aircraft Transp. Sys. Contbr. articles to profl. publs. Recipient award, Am. Mktg. Assn., AIAA, FAA, Embry-Riddle Aero. U., W. Frank Barton Sch. Bus., Travel and Transp. Rsch. Assn. Mem.: Nebr. Acad. Scis., Aerospace State Assn. (gov.'s del.), Internat. Air Transp. Rsch. Group (procs. editor, network com. leader), World Aerospace Edn. Orgn. (past pres., award), Coun. on Aviation Accreditation (com. chair), Univ. Aviation Assn. (bd. dirs., award), Alpha Eta Rho. Achievements include research in development of national Airline Quality Rating; aviation applications of public productivity enhancement and marketing in areas of service quality evaluation, forecasting, and student recruitment in collegiate aviation programs. Office: U Nebr Allwine Hall 6001 Dodge St Omaha NE 68182-0508

BOWEN, GARY ROGER, architect; b. Page, Nebr., Apr. 24, 1942; s. Roger David and Eugenia (Luben) B.; m. Elizabeth Ann Humphrey, Aug. 4, 1962; children: Ann, Leslie. Student Wayne State Coll., 1958-59; B.Arch., U. Nebr., 1964, M. Arch., 1974. Registered architect, Nebr., Iowa; cert. Nat. Council Archtl. Registration Bds. With Howell, Killick, Partridge, Amis, London, 1963, F.W. Horn Assocs., Quincy, Ill., 1964-66, Leo A. Daly Co., Omaha, 1966-72; ptnr. Hartman Morford Bowen, Omaha, 1972-74; prin. Bahr Vermeer Haecker, Omaha, 1974—, pres., 1996-2004; vis. critic Coll. Architecture, U. Nebr.; vis. lectr. Coll. Architecture, Kansas State U.; dir. Landmarks Inc., Omaha. bd. dirs. Western Heritage Soc., Joslyn Castle Inst., Archtl. Found. Nebr., Omaha. Am. Collegiate Schs. of Architecture Fgn. Work Exchange scholar, 1963; recipient Housing Mag. Homes for Better Living Nat. Design award, 1981, 4 Ctrl. States Honor awards. Chmn. Omaha Pk. Bd.; Omaha Preservation Commn., 2003—; bd. dirs. Joslyn Castle Friends. Mem. AIA (nat. bd. dirs. 1994-96, Coll. of Fellows 1996, Richard Upjohn fellow 1996, regional rep. Coll. of Fellows 2004-06), Nebr. Soc. Architects (22 honor awards), Nebr. Coll. Architecture Alumni Assn. (bd. dirs.), Omaha Country Club. Republican. Methodist. Home: 6044 Country Club Oaks Pl Omaha NE 68152-2009 Office: Bahr Vermeer Haecker Arch 1425 Jones St Omaha NE 68102-3212 E-mail: gbowen@bvh.com.

BOWEN, GEORGE HAMILTON, JR., astrophysicist, educator; b. Tulsa, June 20, 1925; s. George H. and Dorothy (Huntington) B.; m. Marjorie Evelyn Brown, June 19, 1948; children— Paul Huntington, Margaret Irene, Carol Ann, Dorothy Elizabeth, Kevin Leigh. BS with honor, Calif. Inst. Tech., 1949, PhD, 1952. Asso. biologist Oak Ridge at. Lab., 1952-54; asst. prof. physics Ia. State Coll., 1954-57; asso. prof. physics Iowa State U., 1957-65, prof., 1965-92, emeritus prof. astrophysics, 1993—. Served with USNR, 1944-46. Recipient Iowa State U. Outstanding Tchr. award, 1970, Faculty citation Iowa State U. Alumni Assn., 1971 Mem. Am. Astron. Soc., Astron. Soc. Pacific, Am. Assn. Physics Tchrs. (chmn. Iowa sect. 1966-67), Internat. Astron. Union, Sigma Xi, Tau Beta Pi. Home: 1919 Burnett Ave Ames IA 50010-4970 Office: Iowa State U Dept Physics & Astronomy Ames IA 50011-3160

BOWEN, MICHAEL ANTHONY, lawyer, writer; b. Ft. Monroe, Va., July 16, 1951; s. Harold James and Judith Ann (Carter-Waller) B.; m. Sara Armbruster, Aug. 30, 1975; children: Rebecca Elizabeth, Christopher Andrew, John Armbruster, Marguerite Judith, James Harold. AB summa cum laude, Rockhurst Coll., 1973; JD cum laude, Harvard U., 1976. Bar: Wis. 1976, U.S. Dist. Ct. (ea. and we. dists.) Wis., U.S. Ct. Appeals (4th, 5th, 7th, 8th and 10th cirs.), Wis. Supreme Ct. Assoc. Foley & Lardner, Milw., 1976-84, ptnr., 1984—. Author: Can't Miss, 1987, Badger Game, 1989, Washington Deceased, 1990, Fielder's Choice, 1991, Faithfully Executed, 1992, Act of Faith, 1993, Corruptly Procured, 1994, Worst Case Scenario, 1996, Collateral Damage, 1999, The Fourth Glorious Mystery, 2000; co-author: The Wisconsin Fair Dealership Law 1988, contbr. articles to profl. journs. Recipient Best Lawyers in Am., America's Leading Lawyers for Bus., Chambers USA, Wis. Super Lawyers, Law & Politics Media Inc., 2006. Mem. ABA, Wis. Bar Assn., Milw. Bar Assn., St. Thomas More Lawyers' Soc. (pres. 1983), Milw. Young Lawyers' Assn. (pro bono legal services 1982). Roman Catholic. Avocations: photography, running, cross country skiing. Office: Foley & Lardner 777 E Wisconsin Ave Milwaukee WI 53202-5367 Office Phone: 414-297-5538. Office Fax: 414-297-4900. Business E-Mail: mbowen@foley.com.

BOWEN, STEPHEN STEWART, lawyer; b. Peoria, Ill., Aug. 23, 1946; s. Gerald Raymond and Frances Arlene (Stewart) Bowen; m. Joan Elizabeth Logan, June 18, 2005; children: David, Claire. BA cum laude, Wabash Coll., 1968; JD cum laude, U. Chgo., 1972. Bar: Ill. 1972, US Dist. Ct. (no. dist.) Ill. 1972, US Tax Ct. 1977. Assoc. Kirkland & Ellis, Chgo., 1972-78, ptnr., 1978-84, Latham & Watkins, Chgo., 1985—. Adj. prof. masters in taxation program DePaul U., Chgo., 1976—80; lectr. Practicing Law Inst., Chgo., LA, 1978—84, NYC, 1986—2007. Mem. vis. com. Div. Sch. U. Chgo., 1984—2005, mem. vis. com. Law. Sch., 1991—93; mem. planning com. U. Chgo. Tax Conf., 1985—, chair, 1995—98; trustee Wabash Coll., 1996—. Fellow: Am. Coll. Tax Counsel; mem.: ABA, Ill. State Bar Assn., Econ. Club Chgo., Met. Club (Chgo.), Phi Beta Kappa, Order of Coif. Office: Latham & Watkins Sears Tower Ste 5800 Chicago IL 60606-6306

BOWEN, WILLIAM JOSEPH, management consultant; b. NYC, May 13, 1934; s. Edward F. and Mary Alice (Drooney) B.; children: William J., Timothy M., Priscilla A., Robert B.; m. Betsy Bass, Oct. 31, 1983. BS, Fordham U., 1956; MBA, NYU, 1963. Trainee Smith, Barney, NYC, 1959-61; asst. v.p. Citicorp, NYC, 1961-67; v.p. Hayden, Stone, NYC, 1967-69; 1st v.p. Shearson Hammill, NYC, 1969-73; assoc. Heidrick & Struggles, 1973-77, ptnr., 1977—, mgr. Chgo., 1978-81, pres., CEO, 1981-83, vice chmn. NYC, Chgo., 1983—. Capt. USAF, 1956-59. Mem. Chgo. Club, Onwentsia Club, N.Y. Club, Marco Polo, Union League (N.Y.C.). Republican. Office: Heidrick & Struggles Inc Sears Tower 233 S Wacker Dr Ste 7000 Chicago IL 60606-6350

BOWER, GLEN LANDIS, judge, lawyer; b. Highland, Ill., Jan. 16, 1949; BA, So. Ill. U., 1971; JD (hon.), Ill. Inst. Tech., 1974. Bar: Ill. 1974, US Ct. Mil. Appeals 1975, US Ct. Appeals (7th cir.) 1976, US Dist Ct. (so. dist.) Ill. 1977, US Dist. Ct. (cen. dist.) Ill. 1992, US Supreme Ct. 1978, US Tax Ct. 1984, US Ct. Claims 1986, US Dist. Ct. (no. dist.) Ill. 1994, US Ct. Veterans Appeals 1995. Sole practice, Effingham, Ill., 1974-83; prosecutor Effingham County, Ill., 1976-79; mem. Ill. House of Reps., Springfield, 1979-83; asst. dir., gen. counsel Ill. Dept. Revenue, Springfield, Ill., 1983-90; Presdl. apptd. chmn. US R.R. Retirement Bd., 1990-97; asst. to Ill. Sec. of State, 1998-99; apptd. dir. revenue State of Ill., 1999—2003; sr. advisor US SBA, Washington, 2004—05; judge US Immigration Ct., Chgo., 2005—. Mil. aide to Gov. of Ill., 1999-2003; liaison mem. Adminstrv. Conf. of US, 1991-95; mem. Nat. Adv. Com. for Juvenile Justice and Delinquency Prevention, Washington, 1976-80, US Econ. Adv. Bd. of US Dept. Commerce, Washington, 1981-85, Ill. Gen. Assembly State Adv. Com. on Cir. Ct. Fin., Springfield, 1984; mem. Revenue Bd. Appeals, Chgo., 1985-87, chmn., 1986-87; mem. Com. of 50 on Ill. Constn., 1987-88; adv. com. on electronic tax adminstrn. IRS, 2000-2003, So. Ill. U. Pub. Policy Inst., 2000. Co-editor: Handbook on State Taxation, 1991; contbr. articles to profl. jour. Bd. dir. Dana-Thomas House Found., Springfield, Ill., 1989-90; trustee McKendree Coll., Lebanon, Ill., 1978-81; chmn. State of Ill. Organ and Tissue Donors Adv. Bd., 1993-98. Lt. col. USAFR, 1974—99, ret. Recipient Disting. Svc. award So. Ill. U., 1971, Recognition citation Am. Legion, 1980, Outstanding Svc. cert. to tchg. profession Ill. Edn. Assn., 1981, Disting. Svc. award Am. Vets., 1980, 82, Presdl. citation Navy League US, 1981, Constitution award Mus. of Our Nat. Heritage, 1988, Silver Good Citizenship medal Ill. Soc. SAR, 1990, Profl. Achievement award Ill. Inst. Tech., 1993, Friend of History award Ill. State Hist. Soc., 1994, Alumni Achievement award So. Ill. U., 1994, Disting. Alumnus award So. Ill. U. Coll. Liberal Arts, 2000, Outstanding Civilian Svc. Medal, Dept. Army, 2003; named Outstanding Freshman Legislator, Ill. Edn. Assn., 1980, Legislator of Yr., Ill. Assn. Rehab. Socs., 1981, 82. Fellow: Am. Bar Found. (life), Ill. Bar Found. (life); mem.: US Capitol Hist. Soc. (charter), Effingham County Mental Health Assn. (pub. affairs com. 1977—78), SBA Adv. Coun., Effingham Regional Hist. Soc. (bd. dir. 1973—77), Ill. State Hist. Soc. (v.p. 1979—81, Ralph C. Francis award 1967), Nat. Assn. Tax Adminstrs. (vice chmn. attys. sect. 1985—86, chmn. 1986—88, vice chmn. attys. sect. 1988—89), Effingham County Bar Assn. (sec. 1976—77, pres. 1983—84), Ill. State Bar Assn. (labor law sect. coun. 1976—77, sec. state taxation sect. coun. 1987—88, vice-chair 1988—89, chair 1989—90, sect. coun. on employee benefits 1991—98, sect. coun. on adminstrv. law 2000, Bd. Gov.'s award 1999), Fed. Tax Adminstrs. (bd. trustees 2001—03), Am. Coun. Young Polit. Leaders (life; One of 10 dels. to China 1988, del. to East Asia-Pacific internat. alumni summit Tokyo 2006), Sons of Am. Revolution, Field Mus. of Natural History, Smithsonian Assocs., Abraham Lincoln Assn., Res. Officers Assn. (life), The Nat. Sojourners (life), So. Ill. Univ. Alumni Assn. (life), Am. Legion (life), Effingham County Old Settlers Assn. (pres., bd. dir. 1983—86), Art Inst. of Chgo., So. Ill. U. Carbondale Found. (bd. dir. 1993—2002), Army and Navy Club Washington D.C., Kiwanis (pres. 1977—78), Shriners (life), Phi Alpha Delta (life). Methodist. Office: US Immigration Ct Ste 1900 55 E Monroe St Chicago IL 60603

BOWERS, BEGE KAYE, literature and communications educator, academic administrator; b. Nashville, Aug. 19, 1949; d. John and Yvonne Bowers. BA in English cum laude, Vanderbilt U., 1971; student, U. Mich., 1985; MACT, U. Tenn., 1973, PhD, 1984. Asst. loan officer Ctr. for Fin. Aid and Placement, Baylor U., Waco, Tex., 1975-76; editorial asst. Wassily Leontief, NYU, NYC, 1976-78; instr. bus. English Florence-Darlington Tech. Coll., Florence, SC, 1979-80; tchr. English and French St. John's High Sch., Darlington, SC, 1980-82; teaching asst. dept English U. Tenn., Knoxville, 1982-84; from asst. prof. English to prof. Youngstown (Ohio) State U., 1984—92, prof., 1992—, asst. to dean Coll. Arts and Scis., 1992-93, dir. profl. writing and editing, 1996-2000, assoc. to the dean Coll. Arts and Scis., 2001—02, asst. provost acad. programs and planning, 2002—05, interim provost, 2005, v.p. acad. affairs, 2005, assoc. provost acad. programs and planning, 2005—. Freelance editor MLA, NYC, 1978-80; cons. Project Arete, Youngstown and Mahoning County Pub. Schs., 1984-87, Youngstown Pub. Schs., 1986, 87-88, 90-91, Macmillan Pub. Co., 1986, Trumbull County Schs., Ohio, 1988, Akron Beacon Jour., 1994-95, Ohio Dept. Edn., 1998-2001, Ohio Bd. Regents, 2002—; chair Mahoning Area Consortium Tech. Prep. Governing Bd., 2002—. Co-editor: CEA Critic, 1998—2002, CEA Forum, 1988—2004; co-editor: (with Barbara Brothers) Reading and Writing Women's Lives: A Study of the Novel of Manners, 1991; co-editor: (with Chuck Nelson) Internships in Technical Communication, 1991; co-editor: (with Mark Allen) Annotated Chaucer Bibliography, 1986—96, 2002 (MLA award for disting. bibliography, 2004); mem. editl. bd. South Atlantic Rev., 1987—89; editor: more than 40 pamphlets, 7 children's books, and 1 videoscript. Alumni Found. Rsch. fellow U. Tenn., 1978, dissertation fellow U. Tenn., 1983, Davis editl. fellow U. Tenn., 1984; Grad. Rsch. Coun. grantee Youngstown State U. Mem.: MLA, Gould Soc. (pres. faculty com. 1991—93), No. Ohio Soc. for Tech. Comm., Soc. for Tech. Comm. (Jay R. Gould award for excellence in tchg. tech. comm. 1999, Disting. Chpt. Svc. award 2001, Assoc. fellow award 2002), Assn. Tchrs. Tech. Writing, New Chaucer Soc. (asst. bibliographer 1986—), Coll. English Assn. Ohio, Coll. English Assn. (exec. bd., Disting. Svc. award 1996, Lifetime Achievement award 2005), Phi Beta Kappa, Phi Kappa Phi (web mgr. 2005—, pres. 1991—92, sec. 1994—98, exec. bd. 1998—). Office: Youngstown State U Office of the Provost Youngstown OH 44555-0001 Office Phone: 330-941-1560. E-mail: bkbowers@ysu.edu.

BOWERS, CURTIS RAY, JR., chaplain; b. Lancaster, Pa., Feb. 6, 1933; s. Curtis Ray and Oleita (Geisler) B.; m. Doris Jean, June 18, 1955; children: Sharon, William, Stephen. BA, Asbury Coll., 1958; MDiv, Asbury Theol. Sem., 1960. Pastor Methodist Ch., Cynthiana, Ky., 1956-60, Ch. of the Nazarene, Cape May, N.J., 1960-61; chaplain U.S. Army, 1961-84; dir. chaplaincy ministries Ch. of the Nazarene, Kansas City, Mo., 1984-2000. Author: Forward Edge of the Battle Area: A Chaplain's Story. Col. U.S. Army, 1961-84. Decorated Silver Star; named Srs. Double Inter-Svc. Tennis Champion, 1982; named to 327th Infantry Regimental Hall of Fame, 1998; recipient Outstanding Chaplain of Yr. award, Ch. of the Nazarene, 2000. Mem. Ch. Of The Nazarene. Avocation: tennis. Home: 3523 Portland Ave Nampa ID 83686-7993 Home Phone: 208-442-1689. Personal E-mail: crbowers11@juno.com.

BOWERS, JOHN C., association executive; b. Plattsburg, Mo., Dec. 18, 1939; s. Raymond and Ruth Charlotte (Anderson) Bowers; children: John Bradford, Craig Andrew, Beth Anne. BS, S.W. Mo. State U., 1961. Mgr. Augusta C. of C., Kans., 1964—66; exec. v.p. Newton C. of C., Kans., 1966—70; pres., gen. mgr. Jefferson County C. of C., 1970—90; exec. mgr. Branson/Lakes Area C. of C., Mo., 1990—. 1st lt. US Army, 1962—64. Mem.: C. of C. of U.S., Am. C. of C. Execs. (com. chmn. 1973—74, cert. chamber exec. 1985), Mountain States Assn., Kans. Jaycees, Mo. C. of C. (pres. 1983—84, Outstanding State V.P. award 1966), Colo. C. of C. Execs. (pres. 1976—77). Republican. Office: Branson/Lakes Area C of C PO Box 220 Branson MO 65615-0220

BOWIE, E(DWARD) J(OHN) WALTER, hematologist, researcher; b. Church Stretton, Shropshire, Eng., Mar. 10, 1925; came to U.S., 1958; s. Edgar Ormond and Ann Brown (Lorrimer) B.; m. Gertrud Susi Ulrich, Dec. 22, 1948; children— Katherine Ann, Christopher John, John Walter, James Ulrich MA, Oxford U., Eng., 1950, BM, BCh, 1952, DM, 1981; MS, U. Minn., 1961. House physician Univ. Coll. Hosp., London, 1953; sr. house officer Bethlem Royal and Maudsley Hosps., London, 1953-54; pvt. practice medicine Treherne, Man., Canada, 1954; fellow in medicine Mayo Clinic, Rochester, Minn., 1958-60, cons. in internal medicine and hematology, 1961-90, head sect. hematology research, 1971-89; prof. medicine and lab. medicine Mayo Med. Sch., Rochester, Minn., 1974-90, prof. emeritus, 1990-96, ret., 1996. Invited spkr. Gordon Confs., 1973, 76, 78, Royal Soc., London, 1980; chmn. thrombosis coun. Internat. Soc. and Fedn. Cardiology, 1991; internat. dir. Thrombosis Vascular Tng. Ctrs. Co-author 6 books; assoc. editor Jour. Lab. and Clin. Medicine, 1976-80; contbr. chpts. to books, numerous articles to profl. jours. Recipient Judson Daland travel award Mayo Found., 1963, named Disting. Investigator, 1988, Disting. Alumnus Mayo Found., 1996. Fellow ACP, AMA, Royal Coll. Pathology; mem. AAAS, Am. Heart Assn. Internat. Soc. on Thrombosis and Haemostasis (v.p. 1980-81, Disting. Career award 1991), Am. Soc. Hematology, Internat. Com. on Thrombosis and Haemostasis (chmn. 1989-90), Ctrl. Soc. for Clin. Rsch., Am. Fedn. for Clin. Rsch., World Fedn. Haemophilia. Office: Emeritus Section Mayo Clinic Rochester MN 55905

BOWIE, NORMAN ERNEST, university official, educator; b. Biddeford, Maine, June 6, 1942; s. Lawrence Walker and Helen Elizabeth (Jacobsen) B.; m. Bonnie Jean Bankert, June 11, 1966 (div. 1980); children: Brian Paul, Peter Mark; m. Maureen Burns, Sept. 19, 1987. AB, Bates Coll., 1964; PhD, U. Rochester, 1968. Mem. faculty Lycoming Coll., Williamsport, Pa., 1968-69; asst. prof. philosophy Hamilton Coll., Clinton, NY, 1969-74, assoc. prof., 1974-75, U. Del., Newark, 1975-80, prof., 1980-89, dir. Ctr. for Study of Values, 1977-89; Elmer L. Andersen chair corp. responsibility U. Minn., Mpls., 1989—, chair dept. strategic mgmt. and orgn., 1992-95; fellow in ethics and professions Harvard U., 1996-97; Dixons prof. bus. ethics and social responsibility London Bus. Sch., 1999-2000. Lynette S. Autrey vis. prof. bus. ethics Rice U., spring 1986; vis. prof. Sch. Mgmt. U. Scranton, 1986-87, Sch. Bus. Adminstrn., Georgetown U., 1988-89; exec. v.p. seminars The Aspen Inst., 1998-99. Author: Towards a New Theory of Distributive Justice, 1971, Business Ethics, 1982, (with Ronald Duska) 2nd edit., 1990, University Business Partnerships: An Assessment, 1994, Business Ethics: A Kantian Perspective, 1999, Management Ethics, 2005; co-author: The Individual and the Political Order, 1977, 4th edit., 2007, (with Patrick E. Murphy, Gene R. Lazniak and Thomas A. Klein) Ethical Marketing, 2005; editor: Ethical Issues in Government, 1981, Ethical Theory in the Last Quarter of the Twentieth Century, 1983, Making Ethical Decisions, 1985, Equal Opportunity, 1988, Guide to Business Ethics, 2001; co-editor: Ethical Theory and Business, 1979, 8th edit., 2008, Ethics, Public Policy and Criminal Justice, 1982, The Tradition of Philosophy, 1986, Ethics and Agency Theory, 1992; co-editor Bus. and Profl. Ethics Jour., 1981-88; assoc. editor Bus. Ethics Quar., 2005-. Mem. N.Y. Coun. for Humanities, 1974-75. NDEA fellow, 1965-68 Mem. Acad. Mgmt., Am. Philos. Assn. (nat. exec. sec. 1972-77), Am. Soc. for Value Inquiry (pres. 1980-81), Soc. Bus. Ethics (pres. 1988), Phi Beta Kappa. Home: PO Box 508 Trappe MD 21673-0508 Office: Carlson Sch Mgmt 321 19th Ave S Minneapolis MN 55455-0438 Office Phone: 612-625-6807. Business E-Mail: nbowie@umn.edu.

BOWLES, BARBARA LANDERS, investment company executive; b. Nashville, Sept. 17, 1947; d. Corris Raemone Landers and Rebecca (Bonham) Jennings; m. Earl Stanley Bowles, ov. 27, 1971; 1 son, Terrence Earl. BA, Fisk U., 1968; MBA, U. Chgo., 1971. Chartered fin. analyst. From bank official to v.p. First Nat. Bank of Chgo., 1968-81; asst. v.p. Beatrice Cos., Chgo., 1981-84; v.p. investor rels. Kraft Inc., Chgo., 1984—89; pres., founder The Kenwood Group Inc., Chgo., 1989—2005; vice chair The Profit Investment Group, 2006—. Bd. dirs. Black & Decker Corp., Hyde Pk. Bank. Bd. dirs. Children's Meml. Hosp., Wis. Energy, and Dollar Gen. Corp. The Chgo. Urban League; coun. mem. Grad. Sch. Bus. U. Chgo. Scholar United Negro College Fund, 1989. Mem. NAACP (life), Assn. Investment Mgmt. and Rsch., Chgo. Fisk trustee (1998-). Mem. United Ch. of Christ. Avocations: tennis, bridge. Office Phone: 312-828-1600. E-mail: kenwoodg@aol.com.

BOWLES, EVELYN MARGARET, state legislator; b. Worden, Ill., Apr. 22, 1921; d. Ira Milton and Anna (Augustine) B. AA, Ill. State U., 1941; student, Greenville Coll., 1947, Southwest Photo Arts Inst., Dallas, 1945—46, Lewis & Clark C.C., 1984. Tchr. Livingston Elem. Sch., Edwardsville Elem. Sch., 1941—43, 1946—50; chief dep. County Clks. Office, Edwardsville, Ill., 1951-74; county clk. Madison County, Edwardsville, 1974—94; state senator Ill. Senate, Springfield, 1974—. Mem. Madison County Welfare Com., 1980—; meml. chmn. Cancer Soc., Edwardsville, Ill., 1980—; bd. dirs. Madison County Hospice, Granite City, sec., 1983-84; pres. adv. bd. Rape and Sexual Abuse Care Ctr., 1984-86; mem. voting systems som. Ill. Bd. Elections; pres. parish council

St. Mary's Ch., mem. lector soc. Served with USMC, 1943-45, USCG. Recipient Alice Paul award Metro-East NOW, 1979. Mem. Ill. Assn. Clks., Recorders, Election Officials and Treas., Ill. Assn. County Officials, Ill. Fedn. Bus. and Profl. Women (Outstanding Working Women of Ill. 1986), Collinsville Bus. and Profl. Women (Boss of Yr. 1976), Edwardsville Bus. Profl. Women (pres. 1957-58, Woman of Achievement award 1978), Metro-East Women's Assn., Am. Legion. Avocations: reading, yard work, fishing. Office: Senator Evelyn Bowles 307 Henry St Ste 210 Alton IL 62002-6326

BOWLING, JOHN C., academic administrator; Pres. Olivet Nazarene U., 1991—.

BOWLSBY, BOB, athletic director; b. Jan. 10, 1952; m. Candice Bowlsby; children: Lisa, Matt, Rachel, Kyle. BS, Moorhead State U., 1975; MS, U. Iowa, 1978. Asst. athletic dir. No. Iowa U., athletic dir., 1984-91, U. Iowa, Iowa City, 1991—2007, Stanford U., Calif., 2007—. Chair NCAA Divsn. I Mgmt. Coun., 1997-99; mem. NCAA Divsn. I Basketball com., 2000-03, chair, 2004-05. Chmn. Big Ten Championships and awards com.; chair NCAA Olympic Sports Liaison Com., CAA/USOC liaison com., Olympics com. mem; bd. dirs. Iowa Games. Mem. Nat. Assn. Collegiate Dir. of Athletics (exec. com.). Office: Stanford U Stanford CA 94305-6150 Office Phone: 319-335-9435. E-mail: robert-bowlsby@uiowa.edu.

BOWMAN, BARBARA TAYLOR, early childhood educator; b. Chgo., Oct. 30, 1928; d. Robert Rochon and Dorothy Vaugn (Jennings) Taylor; m. James E. Bowman, June 17, 1950, 1 child, Valerie Bowman Jarrett. BA, Sarah Lawrence Coll., 1950; MA, U. Chgo., 1952; DHL (hon.), Bankstreet Coll., 1988, Roosevelt U., 1998, Dominican U., 2002, Gov.'s State U., 2002, Wheelock Coll., 2005. Tchr. U. Chgo. Nursery Sch., 1950—52, Colo. Women's Coll. Nursery Sch., Denver, 1953—55; mem. sci. faculty Shiraz U. Nemazee Sch. Nursing, Shiraz, Iran, 1955—61; tchr. spl. edn. Chgo. Child Care Soc., 1965—67; mem. faculty Erikson Inst., Chgo., 1967—, dir. grad. studies, 1978—94, pres., 1994—2002, prof. early edn., 2002—; chief officer early childhood edn. Chgo. Pub. Schs., 2004—. Mem. early childhood com. Nat. Bd. Profl. Tchg. Stds., 1998-2002; cons. early childhood edn., parent edn.; chair com. on early childhood pedagogy NRC, 1998-99. Contbr. articles to profl. jours. Bd. dirs. Ill. Health Edn. Com., 1969—71, Inst. Psychoanalysis, 1970—73, Ill. Adv. Coun. Dept. Children and Family Svcs., 1974—79, Child Devel. Assoc. Consortium, 1979—81, Chgo. Bd. Edn. Desegregation Commn., 1981—84, Bus. People in Pub. Inst., 1980—, High Scope Ednl. Rsch. Found., 1986—93, Gt. Books Found., 1988—, Cmty.-Corp. Sch., 1988—90; mem. Family Resource Coalition, 1992—96, mem. nat. bd. profl. tchr. stds., 1996—2002. Mem. Ill. Assn. Edn. Young Children, Nat. Assn. Edn. Young Children (pres. 1980-82), Chgo. Assns. Edn. Young Children (pres. 1973-77), Black Child Devel. Assn., Am. Ednl. Rsch. Assn. Achievements include research in early education teaching and school improvement. Office: Erikson Inst 420 N Wabash Ave Chicago IL 60611-3568 E-mail: bbowman@erikson.edu.

BOWMAN, BILL, state legislator; b. Baker, Mont., May 26, 1946; m. Karen Bowman; 3 children. BS, Dickinson State U. Auctioneer, owner farm implement dealership, Bowman; mem. N.D. Senate from 39th dist., Bismark, 1991—. Mem. human svcs. com.; chmn. agr. com. N.D. State Senate. Recipient Bronze award Vigortone Premix Sales. Mem. N.D. Stockmen's Assn., N.D. Wheat Growers Assn., N.D. Implement Dealers Assn., Rotary. Republican. Home: RR 2 Box 227 Bowman D 58623-9802

BOWMAN, FRANK O., law educator; b. 1955; BA, Colo. Coll., 1976; JD, Harvard U., 1979. Bar: Colo. 1979. Trial atty. criminal divsn. U.S. Dept. Justice, Washington, 1979—82; spl counsel Yates & Crane, P.C., Durango, Colo., 1982—83; dep. dist. atty. Denver, 1983—86; pvt. practice Colo., 1986—87; assoc. Anderson, Campbell & Laugesen, P.C., Denver, 1987—89; dep. chief so. criminal divisn. Fla., 1989—95; spl. counsel U.S. Sentencing Commn., Washington, 1995—96; assoc. prof. law Ind. U., 1999—2002, M. Dale Palmer prof. law, 2002—. Vis. prof. Washington & Lee, 1994—95, Gonzaga, 1996—99; acad. advisor criminal law com. U.S. Jud. Conf., 1998—2001. Co-author: Federal Sentencing Guidelines Handbook; contbr. articles to profl. jours.; mem. editl. bd.: Federal Sentencing Reporter, Criminal Justice Review. Office: Ind Univ Sch Law Lawrence W Inlow Hall Rm 316 530 W NY St Indianapolis IN 46202-3225 Office Phone: 317-274-2862. Office Fax: 317-278-3326. E-mail: frbowman@iupui.edu.

BOWMAN, JAMES EDWARD, pathologist, educator; b. Washington, Feb. 5, 1923; s. James Edward and Dorothy (Peterson) B.; m. Barbara Taylor, June 17, 1950; 1 child, Valerie June. BS, Howard U., 1943, MD, 1946. Intern Freedmen's Hosp., Washington, 1946-47; resident pathology St. Lukes Hosp., Chgo., 1947-50; chmn. dept. pathology Provident Hosp., 1950-53, Shiraz (Iran) Med. Ctr. Nemazee Hosp., 1955-61; vis. prof., chmn. dept. pathology faculty of medicine U. Shiraz, 1959-61; dir. labs. U. Chgo., 1971-80, prof. dept. pathology, medicine, com. on genetics, biol. scis., collegiate div., 1972-93, dir., 1973-93, prof. emeritus, 1993—. Cons. pathology, div. hosp. and med. facilities HEW, USPHS, 1968; mem. Health and Hosps. Governing Commn., Cook County, 1969-72; mem. exec. com. hemalytic anemia study group NHLI, NIH, Bethesda, Md., 1973-75, Sabbatical fellow Ctr. for Advanced Study in Behavioral Scis., Stanford U., 1981-82, Ethical, Legal & Social Issues, Nat. Human Genome Program NIH/DOE. Contbr. to books and articles to profl. jours. Capt. M.C., AUS, 1953-55. Spl. rsch. fellow NIH Galton Lab., Univ. Coll., London, 1961-62. Mem. Coll. Am. Pathologists, Am. Soc. Clin. Pathologists, Am. Soc. Human Genetics, Cen. Soc. Clin. Rsch., Am. Soc. Hematology, Am. Assn. Phys. Anthropologists, Acad. Clin. Lab. Physicians and Scientists. Home: 4929 S Greenwood Ave Chicago IL 60615-2815 Office: U Chgo Dept Pathology 5841 S Maryland Ave Chicago IL 60637-1463 E-mail: jbowman@uchicago.edu.

BOWMAN, JOHN J., judge; b. Oak Park, Ill., Jan. 13, 1930; 5 children. BS, U. Ill., 1952; JD, John Marshall Law Sch., 1959. Pvt. practice law, 1959-72; state's atty. DuPage County, Ill., 1973—76, circuit judge Ill., 1976-90; presiding judge 2d dist. Ill. Ct. Appeals, Oak Brook Terrace, 1998—2000; justice 2d Dist. Appellate Ct., 1990—. With US Army, 1952—54, Japan. Mem.: Alpha Tau Omega.

BOWMAN, LEAH, fashion designer, consultant, photographer, educator; b. Chgo., Apr. 21, 1935; d. John George and Alexandra (Colovos) Murges; m. Veron George Broe, Aug. 31, 1954; 1 child, Michelle; m. John Ronald Bowman, Feb. 28, 1959 Diploma, Sch. of Art Inst., Chgo., 1962. Designer Korach Bros. Inc., Chgo., 1962-65; costume designer Hull House South Theatre, Chgo., 1966-67, Wellington Theatre, Chgo., 1966-67; from instr. to prof. emeritus Sch. of Art Inst., Chgo., 1967—2001, prof. emeritus, 2001—. Prodr. fashion performances and style exhbns.; vis. prof., cons. SNDT Women's U., Bombay, 1980, 85, 92, Ctrl. Acad. Arts and Design, Beijing, People's Republic of China, 1987; faculty sabbatical exhbn. Sch. of Art Inst., 1986, 93. Recipient Fulbright award, Coun. for Internat. Exchange for Scholars, India, 1980, Pres. award, Art Inst. Chgo., 1991, Honoror's award, Sch. of Art Inst., Chgo., 1998, Disting. Faculty award, Sch. Art Inst. Chgo., 2005. Office: Sch of Art Inst Chgo 37 S Wabash Ave Chicago IL 60603-3002

BOWMAN, LOUIS L., emergency physician; b. Toledo, Nov. 1, 1953; s. Louis J. and Jacquelyn (Perkins) B.; m. Deborah Lynn Hayden, Sept. 30, 1977; children: Heather, Kara, Jason, Benjamin, Michelle. BA in Chemistry, U. Toledo, 1976; DO, Kirksville Coll. Osteo. Med., 1980. Diplomate Am. Bd. Emergency Medicine. Intern Doctor's Hosp., Columbus, Ohio; emergency physician Scioto Emergency Physicians, Columbus, Ohio, 1981—95; med. dir. emergency medicine Columbus Cmty. Hosp., 1987-92; med. dir. Mid-Ohio Sports Car Course, Lexington, 1988—; med. dir., chmn. dept. medicine Med. Ctr. Hosp., Chillicothe, Ohio, 1995. Fellow Am. Coll. Emergency Physicians; Am. Osteo. Assn., Ohio Osteo. Assn., Columbus Acad. Osteo Medicine. Republican. Methodist. Avocations: golf, photography, travel, weightlifting. Office: Ambulatory Care Affiliates PO Box 292642 Columbus OH 43229-8642

BOWMAN, PASCO MIDDLETON, II, judge; b. Timberville, Va., Dec. 20, 1933; s. Pasco Middleton and Katherine (Lohr) Bowman; m. Ruth Elaine Bowman, July 12, 1958; children: Ann Katherine, Helen Middleton, Benjamin Garber; m. Katharine Risher Pitt, Aug. 19, 2006. BA, Bridgewater Coll., 1955; JD, NYU, 1958; LLM, U. Va., 1986; LLD (hon.), Bridgewater Coll., 1988. Bar: N.Y. 1958, Ga. 1965, Mo. 1980. Assoc. firm Cravath, Swaine & Moore, NYC, 1958—61, 1962—64; asst. prof. law U. Ga., 1964—65, assoc. prof., 1965—69, prof., 1969—70, Wake Forest U., 1970—78, dean, 1970—78; vis. prof. U. Va., 1978—79; prof., dean U. Mo., Kansas City, 1979—83; judge US Ct. Appeals (8th cir.), Kansas City, Mo., 1983—2003, chief judge, 1998—99, sr. judge, 2003—. Mng. editor: NYU Law Rev., 1957—58, reporter, chief draftsman: Georgia Corporation Code, 1965—68. Col. USAR, 1959—84. Fulbright scholar, London Sch. Econs. and Polit. Sci., 1961—62, Root-Tilden scholar, 1955—58. Mem.: Mo. Bar, NY Bar. Office: US Ct Appeals 8th Circuit 10-50 US Courthouse 400 E 9th St Kansas City MO 64106-2607 Office Phone: 816-512-5800.

BOWMAN, ROGER MANWARING, real estate company officer; b. Duluth, Minn., Dec. 3, 1916; s. Lawrence Fredrick and Gladys (Manwaring) B.; m. Judith Claypool, Apr. 10, 1942 (dec. 1993); Ann, David, Mary Bowman Johnson, Lawrence II. Student, U. Mich., 1934—36, Wayne State U., 1937. Pres. North Star Airways, Duluth, 1946-50, orth Star Engrng. Co., Duluth, 1946-50, Superior (Wis.) Aero, 1946-50, Lawrence F. Bowman Co., Duluth, 1950-70, Gen. Cleaning Corp., Duluth, 1954-92, Bowman Corp., Duluth, 1970-83, Bowman Properties, Duluth, 1983-92; chmn. Deltona Corp., Miami, Fla., 1985-89. Cons. Topeka Group, Duluth, 1985-89; bd. dirs. Parish Corp., Minn. Power, Norwest Bank; chmn. Bowman Properties, 1988-96, Gen. Cleaning Corp., 1985—; mng. gen. ptnr. 6 ltd. partnerships, 1990—. Chmn. St. Louis County Welfare, Duluth, 1964-69, chmn. Govs. Real Estate Adv. Commn., 1968-70; pres. Duluth Devel. Corp., 1960-68; trustee Ordean Found., 1968-92; bd. dirs. Duluth Bd. Realtors, 1958-62; pres. Duluth Bldg. Owners and Mgrs. Assn. Internat., 1963-65. Lt. col. USMCR, 1940-45. Recipient Silver Beaver award Boy Scouts Am., 1959, Mayor's Commendation City of Duluth, 1976. Mem. Duluth Steam Coop. (bd. dirs. 1970-86), Duluth Bldg. Owners and Mgrs. Internat., Duluth Bd. Realtors, Real Property Adminstrs., Kitchi Gammi Club (dir. 1974-78), Northland Country Club, Boca Raton Resort and Club, Delray Beach Yacht Club. Republican. Episcopalian. Avocation: cooking. Office: 575 Wells Fargo Ctr Duluth MN 55802 Home Phone: 561-276-2047. Personal E-mail: rbowman16@aol.com.

BOWMAN, RUSSELL, museum director; Former dir. Milw. Art Mus. Office: Milwaukee Art Museum 750 N Lincoln Memorial Dr Milwaukee WI 53202-4018

BOWMAN, WILLIAM SCOTT (SCOTTY BOWMAN), professional hockey coach; b. Montreal, Can., Sept. 18, 1933; s. John and Jane Thomson (Scott) B.; m. Suella Belle Chitty, Aug. 16, 1969; children: Alicia Jean, David Scott, Stanley Glen, Nancy Elizabeth and Robert Gordon (twins). Student, Sir George Williams Bus. Sch., 1954; LHD (hon.), Canisius Coll., Buffalo, 2003. Scout exec. Club de Hockey Canadien, Montreal, 1956-66, coach, 1971-79; coach, gen. mgr. St. Louis Blues Hockey Club, 1966-71; coach, gen. mgr., dir. hockey ops. Buffalo Sabres Hockey Club, 1979-86; TV analyst Hockey Night in Can., 1987-90; dir. player devel. Pitts. Penguins Hockey Club, 1990-91, interim head coach, 1991-92, head coach, 1992-93, Detroit Red Wings Hockey Club, 1993—2002, dir. player pers., 1993—2002, cons., 2002—. Mem. Hockey Hall of Fame Selection Com.; head coach Team Can., 1976. Recipient Jack Adams award, 1977, 96, Victor award for NHL Coach of Yr., 1993, 96, 2002, Stanley Cup Championship, 1973, 1976-79, 1992, 1997-98, 2002, Lester Patrick award 2001, award Can. Soc. N.Y., 2001, Wayne Gretzky award 2002; named NHL Exec. of Yr. Sporting News, 1979-80, NHL Coach of Yr. Sporting News, 1995-96, Hockey News, 1976-77, 93-97, NHL Exec. of the Yr. Hockey News, 1996-97, NHL Coach of Yr., 1967-68, Hockey News Coach of Yr., 1968, 76, 95-96, Exec. of Yr., 1997; inducted into Hockey Hall of Fame, 1991, Mich. Sports Hall of Fame, 1999, Buffalo Sports Hall of Fame, 2000, Can. Walk of Fame, 2003, Can.'s Sports Hall of Fame, 2004, Quebec Sports Hall of Fame, 2005; holder NHL career regular season records for wins (1,244) and winning percentage (.670); holder NHL career playoffs records for wins (223) and games (353); recipient Stanley Cup as head coach Montreal Canadiens, 1973, 76-79, Pitts. Penguins, 1992, Detroit Red Wings, 1997-98, 2002; only coach in NHL history to win Stanley Cup with 3 different teams. Office: Detroit Red Wings Joe Louis Arena 600 Civic Center Dr Detroit MI 48226-4419

BOYCE, DAVID EDWARD, transportation and regional science educator; b. Newark, Ohio, June 24, 1938; s. Francis Henry and Martha Ann (Neutzel) B.; m. Nani Kulish, 1992; children: Lynn, Susan, Michael, Anna, Gregory. BSCE, Northwestern U., 1961; M in City Planning, U. Pa., 1963, PhD in Regional Sci., 1965. Registered profl. engr., Ohio. Rsch. economist Battelle Meml. Inst., Columbus, Ohio, 1964-66; asst. prof. U. Pa., Phila., 1966-70, assoc. prof., 1970-74, prof., 1974-77; prof. transp. and regional sci. U. Ill., Urbana, 1977-88, Chgo., 1988—2003, prof. emeritus, 2003—. Sr. vis. fellow Brit. Sci. Rsch. Coun., Leeds, Eng., 1972-73; vis. prof. optimization U. Linkoping and Royal Inst. Tech., Sweden, 1983, 96. Co-author: Metropolitan Plan Making, 1970, Optimal Subset Selection, 1974, Regional Science, Retospect and Prospect, 1991, Modeling Dynamic Transportation Networks, 1996; co-editor Environment and Planning, 1979-88; assoc. editor Transp. Sci., 1978-94. Mem. Regional Sci. Assn. (sec. 1969-78, internat. conf. coord. 1978-86, pres. 1987), Informs (transp. sci. coun. 1978-80).

BOYCE, GREGORY H., energy executive; b. 1954; BS in Mining Engrng., U. Ariz., 1976; completed advanced mgmt. prog., Grad. Sch. Bus., Harvard U. Exec. asst. to vice chmn. Std. Oil of Ohio, 1983—84; dir. Govt. & Pub. Affairs Kennecott Corp., pres. Kennecott Minerals Co., 1993—94, pres., CEO Kennecott Energy Co., 1994—99; CEO energy Rio Tinto PLC, 2000—03; pres., COO Peabody Energy Corp., 2003—05, pres., CEO, 2006—07, chmn., CEO, 2007—. Bd. dir. Marathon Oil Corp., 2008—; mem. Coal Industry Adv. Bd. Internat. Energy Agy.; past bd. mem. Ctr. Energy & Econ. Devel., Western Regional Coun., Nat. Coal Coun., Mountain States Employers Coun., Wyo. Bus. Coun. Bd. dir. St. Louis Regional Chamber and Growth Assn.; mem. Civic Progress in St. Louis; mem. adv. coun. Dept. Mining & Geol. Engring., Univ. Ariz., Sch. Engring. & Applied Sci. Nat. Coun., Washington Univ., St. Louis. Mem.: Bus. Roundtable (bd. mem.), Nat. Mining Assn. (bd. mem.), Ctr. for Energy & Econ. Develop. (bd. mem.). Office: Peabody Energy Corp 701 Market St Saint Louis MO 63101-1826 Office Phone: 314-342-7574. Office Fax: 314-342-7720. E-mail: gboyce@peabodyenergy.com.*

BOYD, BARBARA, state legislator; m. Robert Boyd; 1 child, Janine. BS, St. Paul's Coll., 1965. Mem. Ohio Ho. of Reps., Columbus, 1992—. Named Officer of Yr. No. Ohio Police Benevolent Assn., 1989; recipient Black Women's History award, 1992. Mem. LWV, Delta Sigma Theta.

BOYD, BELVEL JAMES, newspaper editor; b. Winnemucca, Nev., May 15, 1946; s. James Connolly and Alice La Ferne (Elliott) B.; m. Carolyn Marie Friesen, Aug. 10, 1968 (div. July 1992); children: David, Christopher, Phillip; m. Jeanette St. John, Oct. 21, 2000. BS in Secondary Edn., Oreg. Coll. Edn., 1968; MA in Journalism, U. Mo., 1974; postgrad., Harvard U., 1979-80. Copy editor, reporter Idaho Statesman, Boise, 1974-76, state editor, 1976-77, editor editl. page, 1977-80; editl. writer Mpls. Tribune, 1980-82; dep. editor editl. page Star Tribune, Mpls., 1982—. Vestryman St. Mark's Cathedral, Mpls., 1983-90. Sgt. U.S. Army, 1968-72, Vietnam. Nieman fellow in journalism Harvard U., 1979-80. Mem. Nat. Conf. Editl. Writers. (chmn. for aff. com. 1997—). Home: 3305 46th Ave S Minneapolis MN 55406-2342 Office: Star Tribune 425 Portland Ave Minneapolis MN 55488-0002 E-mail: boyd@startribune.com.

BOYD, BYRON A., labor union administrator; b. Seattle; m. Susan Boyd; 2 children. Brakeman promoted to locomotive engr. Union Pacific R.R., 1971; asst. pres. U.T. Union, mem. Local 117 Vancouver, Wash., pres., 2001—. Office: 14600 Detroit Ave Cleveland OH 44107-4250

BOYD, DEBORAH ANN, pediatrician; b. Urbana, Ohio, Jan. 30, 1955; d. John A. Sr. and Juanita Jean (Routt) B. BA cum laude, Wittenberg U., 1977; MD, U. Cin., 1982. Diplomate Am. Bd. Pediatrics, Nat. Bd. Med. Examiners. Intern Children's Hosp. Med. Ctr., Cin., 1982—83, pediat. resident, 1982—85; pediatrician Nat. Health Svc. Corps, Springfield, Ohio, 1985—89, Cmty. Hosp. Health Care Ctr., Springfield, 1989—97; staff pediat. primary care ctr., clin. faculty Children's Hosp. Med. Ctr., Cin., 1998—. Mem. Continuing med. edn. com. Mercy Med. Ctr., Springfield, 1989—, infection control com., 1987—. Adv. com. Miami Valley Child Devl. Ctr., Springfield, 1985—, New Parents as Tchrs., 1986—. Mem. Assn. of Clinicians for the Underserved, Am. Acad. Pediats., Ambulatory Pediat. Assn. Democratic. Avocations: bicycling, photography, basketball, music, church activities. Home: 12132 S Pine Dr Apt 240 Cincinnati OH 45241-1743 Office: Dept Gen Com Pediatrics Children's Hosp Med Ctr 3333 Burnet Ave Fl 4 Cincinnati OH 45229-3026 Office Phone: 513-636-7594.

BOYD, JOSEPH DON, diversified financial services company executive; b. Muncie, Ind., Jan. 22, 1926; s. Joseph Corneluis and Waneta May (Barrett) B.; m. Cynthia Reiley, Dec. 28, 1957; children— Jane Elizabeth, Craig A., Michael J. AB (Rector scholar), DePauw U., 1948; MA, Northwestern U., 1950, Ed.D., 1955. Ednl. asst. First Meth. Ch., Anderson, Ind., 1948-49; residence hall counselor Northwestern U., Evanston, Ill., 1949-50, univ. examiner, instr. edn., guidance lab. asst., 1952-54, dean men, asst. prof. edn., 1955-61; exec. dir. Ill. Scholarship Commn., 1961-80; dir. instnl. relations and research Nat. Coll. Edn., Evanston, 1981-84; pres. Joseph D. Boyd & Assocs., Deerfield, Ill., 1984—. Residence hall dir., head tennis coach, asst. basketball coach Albion Coll., 1950-52 Mem. Nat. Assn. Adminstrs. State Scholarship Programs, Phi Delta Kappa, Delta Tau Delta, Phi Eta Sigma. Clubs: Rotarian. Methodist. Home: 1232 Warrington Rd Deerfield IL 60015-3145 Office: 600 Deerfield Rd Deerfield IL 60015-3229 Office Phone: 847-940-4145. Business E-Mail: jboyd@christumcdeerfield.org.

BOYD, ROZELLE, retired academic administrator; b. Indpls., Apr. 24, 1934; s. William Calvin Sr. and Ardelia Louise (Leavell) B. BA, Butler U., 1957; MA, Ind. U., 1965. Welfare dept. worker Marion County DPW, Indpls., 1956-57; tchr. Crispus Attucks High Sch., Indpls., 1957-68, adult edn. counselor, 1958-68; asst. dean U. Div., Ind. U., Bloomington, 1968-78, assoc. dean, 1978-82, dir., 1982-98; ret., 1998. Pres. Indpls. City County Coun.; Dem. nat. committeeman, Dem. Party; mem. coms. Nat. League of Cities. Mem. Alpha Phi Alpha. Presbyterian. Office: Office City-County Coun 241 City-County Bldg 200 E Washington St Indianapolis IN 46204-3307 Home Phone: 317-547-3282; Office Phone: 317-327-4240. Personal E-mail: rboyd18019@aol.com. Business E-Mail: rboyd@indygov.org.

BOYD, WILLARD LEE, academic administrator, educator, lawyer, museum director; b. St. Paul, Mar. 29, 1927; s. Willard Lee and Frances L. (Collins) Boyd; m. Susan Kuehn, Aug. 28, 1954; children: Elizabeth Kuehn, Willard Lee, Thomas Henry. BS in Law, U. Minn., 1949, LLB, 1951; LLM, U. Mich., 1952, SJD, 1962. Bar: Minn. 1951, Iowa 1958. Assoc. Dorsey & Whitney, Mpls., 1952—54; from instr. to prof. law U. Iowa, Iowa City, 1954—64, assoc. dean Law Sch., 1964, v.p. acad. affairs, 1964—69, pres., 1969—81, 2002—03, pres. emeritus, 1981—; pres. The Field Mus., Chgo., 1981—96, pres. emeritus, 1996—. Chmn. Nat. Mus. Scis. Bd., 1988—96; chair bd. dirs. Harry S Truman Libr. Inst., 1997—2001; past pres. Nat. Com. Accrediting; past mem. adv. bd. Met. Opera; past adv. bd. Ill. Humanities Coun., Ill. Arts Coun., Chgo. Cultural Affairs Bd., Nat. Arts Coun.; past pres. Ill. Arts Alliance; adv. com. edn. arts Getty Ctr.; adv. com. cultural property U.S. Dept. State, 2003—. Chmn. Am. Assn. Univs. Recipient Charles Frankel prize, Nat. Endowment for Humanities, 1989. Mem.: ABA (com. social labor and indsl. legislations 1963—65, chmn. 1965—66, coun. 1975—82, sect. legal edn. and admission to bar chmn. 1980—81, chmn. coun. of sect. on legal edn. and admission), Am. Law Inst., Am. Acad. Arts & Sci., Iowa Bar Assn. Home: 620 River St Iowa City IA 52246-2433 Office: Univ Iowa Law Sch Iowa City IA 52242-1113 Home Phone: 319-339-5948; Office Phone: 319-335-9004. Business E-Mail: willard-boyd@uiowa.edu.

BOYDA, NANCY, congresswoman; b. St. Louis, Aug. 2, 1955; m. Steve Boyda; 7 children. BS in Chem. & Edn., William Jewell Coll., 1977. Analytical chemist, field inspector EPA, 1978; mgmt. position Marion Laboratories; mem. US Congress from 2nd Kans. dist., 2007—, mem. agrl. com., armed svcs. com. Democrat. Methodist. Office: 1711 Longworth House Office Bldg Washington DC 20515 also: 510 SW 10th Ave Topeka KS 66612

BOYE, ROGER CARL, academic administrator, journalism educator; b. Lincoln, Nebr., Feb. 8, 1948; s. Arthur J. and Matilda J. (Danca) B. BA with distinction, U. ebr., 1970; MS in Journalism with highest distinction, Northwestern U., 1971. News editor The Quill, Chgo., 1971-73; instr. Medill Sch. Journalism, orthwestern U., Evanston, Ill., 1973-76; vis. prof. journalism Niagara U., Niagara Falls, NY, 1976-78; gen. mgr. The Quill, 1980-84, bus. mgr., 1984-86; asst. dean, asst. prof. Medill Sch. Journalism Northwestern U., 1986-92, asst. dean, assoc. prof., 1992—2004, assoc. prof., 2004—05, assoc. prof. emeritus, 2005—. Judge various journalism awards and contests, 1970s—; master comm. residential coll. Northwestern U., 1989—96, 2004—. Weekly columnist Chgo. Tribune, 1974-93; contbr. Ency. Britannica Book of the Yr. and the Compton Yearbook, 1982-99; contbg. editor The Numismatist, 2001--. Recipient Maurice M. Gould award Numismatic Lit. Guild, 1981, 92; named to Medill Sch. Journalism Hall of Achievement. Mem. Phi Beta Kappa, Kappa Tau Alpha. Office: orthwestern Univ Medill Sch Journalism 1845 Sheridan Rd Evanston IL 60208-0815 Office Phone: 847-491-2069. Business E-Mail: r-boye@northwestern.edu.

BOYEA, EARL ALFRED, JR., bishop; b. Pontiac, Mich., Apr. 10, 1951; s. Earl Alfred and Helen Marie (Connor) B. AB, Sacred Heart Seminary, 1973; STB, Gregorian U., Rome, 1976, STL, 1980; MA, Wayne State U., 1984; PhD, Cath. U., 1987. Deacon St. Benedict Parish, Waterford, Mich., 1977-78; ordained priest Archdiocese of Detroit, 1978; asst. pastor St. Michael Parish, Monroe, Mich., 1978-79, St. Timothy Parish, Trenton, Mich., 1980-84; asst. prof. Sacred Heart Maj. Sem., Detroit, 1987-90, assoc. prof., 1990-95, acad. dean, 1990—2000, prof., 1995—2000; rector, pres. Pontifical Coll. Josephinum, Columbus, Ohio, 2000—02; ordained bishop, 2002; aux. bishop Archdiocese of Detroit, 2002—08; bishop Diocese of Lansing, Mich., 2008—. Contbr. articles to profl. jours. Mem. Am. Cath. Hist. Assn., Cath. Bibl. Assn., Nat. Cath. Ednl. Assn., Am. Cath. Hist. Soc. Roman Catholic. Office: Diocese of Lansing 300 W Ottawa St Lansing MI 48933-1977*

BOYER, JOHN WILLIAM, history professor, dean; b. Chgo., Oct. 17, 1946; s. William Dana and Mary Frances (Corbley) B.; m. Barbara Alice Juskevich, Aug. 24, 1968; children: Dominic, Alexandra, Victoria. BA, Loyola U., 1968; MA, U. Chgo., 1969, PhD, 1975. From asst. prof. to assoc. prof. U. Chgo., 1975-85, prof., 1985—, Martin A. Ryerson Disting. Svc. prof., 1996—, acting dean divsn. social scis., 1992-93, dean of the coll., 1992—. Author: Political Radicalism in Late Imperial Vienna, 1981, Culture and Political Crisis in Vienna, 1995, Three Views of Continuity and Change at the University of Chicago, 1999; editor: Jour. of Modern History. Capt. USAR, 1968-80. Recipient Theodor Körner prize Theodor Körner Found., 1978, John Gilmary Shea prize Am. Cath. Hist. Assn., 1982, Ludwig Jedlicka Meml. prize Kuratorium des Ludwig-Jedlicka-Gedächtnispreises, 1996, Austrian Cross Hon. Sci. and Art, First Class, 2004, Karl von Vogelsang State History prize Republic of Austria, 2006; Alexander von Humboldt fellow, 1980-81. Mem. Austrian Acad. Scis. (corr.). Roman Catholic. Avocation: cooking. Home: 1428 E 57th St Chicago IL 60637-1838 Office: U Chgo 1126 E 59th St Chicago IL 60637-1580 also: U Chgo Press Jour Divsn 1427 E 60th St Chicago IL 60637 Office Phone: 773-702-8576. Business E-Mail: jwboyer@uchicago.edu.

BOYKIN, RICHARD RENARDA, lawyer, former legislative staff member; b. Jackson, Miss., Sept. 9, 1968; s. George Albert and Burnette (Knight) B. BA, Ctrl. State U., 1990; JD, U. Dayton, 1994. Bar: Ill. 1994. Tchg. asst. U. Dayton (Ohio), 1993-94, legal intern, 1994; legis. fellow office of Sen. Carol Moseley Brown (Ill.) U.S. Congress, Washington, 1994-95; contract atty. Attys. Per Diem, Washington, 1995-96, Aspen Sys. Corp., Washington, 1996-97; chief of staff to Rep. Danny K. Davis US Congress, Washington, 1997—2007; ptnr. Barnes & Thornburg LLP, Chgo., 2007—. Assoc. min. Met. Bapt. Ch., motivational spkr. Recipient: Martin Luther King Dream Classic award, Nat. Assn. Community Health Centers Svc. award, the John C. Stennis Leadership Award, ELI Disting. Leadership award, Litigation award, US Dept. Justice, Congl. Black Caucus Fellows award, Am. Jurisprudence award; Stennis fellow Sen. John C. Stennis Fellowship, 1999-00. Mem. ABA, Chgo. Bar Assn., Ill. State Soc. (bd. dirs.). Baptist. Avocations: reading, racquetball, basketball. Office: Barnes & Thornburg LLP One Wacker Dr Ste 4400 Chicago IL 60606 E-mail: richard.boykin@BTLaw.com.

BOYKINS, MICHAEL L., lawyer; b. Jan. 17, 1965; BS, U. Wis., 1987, JD, 1990. Ptnr., co-chmn. firm racial & ethnic diversity com. McDermott Will & Emery LLP. Fellow: Am. Coll. Investment Counsel; mem.: Chgo. Com.

Minorities in Large Law Firms (bd. dir.), Econ. Club Chgo., Wis. Bar Assn., Ill. Bar Assn. Office: McDermott Will & Emery LLP 227 W Monroe St Chicago IL 60606 Office Phone: 312-984-7599. Office Fax: 312-984-7700. Business E-Mail: mboykins@mwe.com.

BOYKO, CHRISTOPHER ALLAN, federal judge; b. Cleve., Oct. 10, 1954; s. Andrew and Eva Dorothy (Zepko) B.; m. Roberta Ann Gentile, May 29, 1981; children: Philip, Ashley. B in Polit. Sci. cum laude, Mt. Union Coll., 1976; JD, Cleve. Marshall Coll. Law, 1979. Bar: Ohio 1979, Fla. 1985, U.S. Dist. Ct. (no. dist.) Ohio 1979, H.S. Ct. Appeals (6th cir.) 1990, U.S. Tax Ct. 1986, U.S. Supreme Ct., 1988. Prin. Boyko & Boyko, Parma, Ohio, 1979—93, 1995; asst. prosecutor City of Parma, 1981-87, prosecutor, 1987—93, dir. of law, 1987-93; exec. v.p., gen. counsel copy Am., Inc., 1993-94; judge Parma Mcpl. Court, 1993, Ct. Common Pleas, Cuyahoga County, Ohio, 1996—2004, Judicial Corrections Bd., 1999—2004; chair Ct. Vet. Svc. Com., 2000—04, policy com., 2003—04; judge U.S. Dist. Ct. (No. dist.) Ohio, 2005—. Guardian ad litem Juvenile Ct., 1979-93; legal advisor spl. weapons and tactics divsn. City of Parma Police Dept., 1984-93; chief counsel S.W. Enforcement Bur., 1991-93; mem. faculty Ohio Jud. Coll., Nat. Jud. Coll., lectr. FBI Nat. Acad. jud. editor Law and Fact Com., 1999-2003. Active Citizens League of Greater Cleve., 1985-2004; former trustee Cops & Kids, Inc., Cleve. Bar Assn., 2000—, County Bar Assn.; mem. Parma Drug Task Force, 1987-1993; mem. adv. com. Parmadale Children's Svcs., 1991—; mem. St. Anthony's Sch. Commn. Mem.: Ohio State Bar Assoc. Pro Bono Program (chancellor of district), Nat. Inst. Trial Advocacy (steering com. 2003—), Mt. Union Coll. Alumni Assn., Am. Inns of Ct. Found. (John B. Manos Inn of Ct. 2004—07), Parma Bar Assn. (past pres., past trustee), Cleve. Bar Assn. (former past bd. trustees, lectr. in law), Ohio Bar Assn., Fla. Bar Assn., Elks. Byzantine Catholic. Avocations: martial arts, reading, fitness. Office: 801 W Superior Ave Cleveland OH 44113 Office Phone: 216-357-7151. Business E-Mail: christopher_boyko@ohnd.uscourts.gov.

BOYLAN, ARTHUR J., judge; Judge 8th jud. dist. Minn. Dist. Ct.; magistrate judge U.S. Dist. Ct., Minn., 1996—.

BOYLAN, JOHN LESTER, financial executive, accountant; b. Columbus, Ohio, Aug. 23, 1955; s. James Robert and Ruth Isabella (Capes) B.; m. Susan Marie Stakes, May 21, 1983; children: David, Laura. BBA, Ohio State U., 1977. CPA, Ohio. Staff acct. Deloitte, Haskins & Sells, Columbus, 1977-80, sr. acct., 1980-83, mgr., 1983-86; dir. fin. planning Lancaster Colony Corp., Columbus, 1986-90, asst. treas., 1987-90, treas., 1990—, CFO, 1997—, dir., 1998—. Mem. Ohio Mfrs. Assn. (dir., treas. 1992—). Office: Lancaster Colony Corp 37 W Broad St Ste 500 Columbus OH 43215-4177

BOYLE, ANN M., dean, dental educator; BA, Case Western Reserve U., 1971; DMD, Fairleigh Dickinson U., 1975, MA in Ednl. Psychology, 1984. Cert. gen. practice Hackensack Hosp., 1976; managament cert. Harvard U., 1999. Mem. faculty Coll. Dental Med. Fairleigh Dickinson U., 1976—90; chair restorative dept., 1988—90; chair restorative dept. to assoc. dean acad. affairs Sch. Dentistry Case Western Reserve U., Cleveland, 1991—94; assoc. dean Sch. Dental Med. So. Ill. U., 1995—2002, acting dean, 2002—03, dean, prof. restorative dentistry, 2003—. Extramural pvt. practice. Fellow: Pierre Fauchard Acad., Am. Coll. Dentists; mem.: ADA (mem. commn. on Dental Accreditation), Internat. Assn. Dental Rsch., Am. Assn. Dental Rsch., Am. Dental Edn. Assn., Acad. Operative Dentistry. Office: So Ill U Sch Dental Med 2800 College Ave Bldg 273/2300 Alton IL 62002

BOYLE, ANNE C., state commissioner; b. Omaha, Dec. 22, 1942; m. Mike Boyle; children: Maureen, Michael, James, Patrick, Margaret. Chmn., co-chmn. various polit. campaigns, Omaha, 1974-78; office coord. for U.S. Senator James Exon., 1979-81; corp. and polit. fundraiser, 1983-85, 88; campaign mgr. pub. rels. firm, Omaha, 1990-91; pres. Universal Rev. Svcs., Omaha, 1992—; mem. Nebr. Pub. Svc. Commn., Lincoln, 1996—. Active Clinton for Pres. Campaign, organizer fund raisers, host open house, Omaha, 1992; cons., lobbyist, 1994-95. Former nat. committeewoman Nebr. Young Dems.; chmn. Douglas County Dem. Ctrl. Com.; mem. jud. nominating com. for Douglas County Juvenile Ct.; chmn. inaugural ball invitation com. for gov. of Nebr., 1982; co-chmn. Midwestern Govs. Conf., 1984, Jefferson-Jackson Day Dinner, 1976, 82; del. Dem. Nat. Conv., 1988, 92, 96; mem. Nebr. Rev. com. for Fed. Appts. to U.S. Atty., U.S. Marshall and 8th Dist. Ct. Appeals Fed. Judgeship, 1993-95; mem. Nebr. Dem. Ctrl. Com.; mem. Fin. Com. to Reelect Gov. Ben Nelson; mem. Nebr. Interagy. Coun. on Homeless, President's Adv. Com. on Arts, 1995; Nebr. authorized rep. '96 Clinton-Gore Campaign; Bd. dirs. Bemis Ctr. for Contemporary Arts, Omaha; chmn. Nebr. Dem. Party, 1999-2001. Mem. Nat. Assn. Regulatory Utility Commrs. and Mid-Am. Regulatory Commrs. Democrat. Office: PO Box 94927 Lincoln NE 68509-4927

BOYLE, FRANK JAMES, state legislator; b. Phillips, Wis., Feb. 20, 1945; s. Frank and Mary Boyle; m. Kate Boyle; children: Annie, Patrick. BA, U. Wis., 1967. Former bldg. contractor and constrn. worker. Mgmt. commr. Douling Lake, Wis., 1976—; former county supr. Douglas County Bd.; state assemblyman dist. 73 State of Wis., 1986—; sec. Douglas County Dem. Com.; pres. Tri-Lake Civic Club; v.p. Summit Vol. Fire Dept. Mem. Am. Legion. Home: 4900 E Tri Lakes Rd Superior WI 54880-8637

BOYLE, KAMMER, financial planner, investment advisor, research analyst, options trader; b. New Orleans, June 17, 1946; d. Benjamin Franklin and Ethel Clair (Kammer) B.; m. Edward Turner Barfield, July 23, 1966 (div. 1975); children: Darren Barfield, Meloe Barfield. BS in Mgmt. magna cum laude, U. West Fla., 1976; PhD in Indsl./Organizational Psychology, U. Tenn., 1982. Lic. psychologist, Ohio, Tenn.; reg. securities rep. InterSecurities, Inc., Nat Assn. Securities Dealers. Pvt. practice mgmt. psychology, Knoxville, 1978-81; tchg. and rsch. asst. U. Tenn., Knoxville, 1977-81; mgmt. trainer U.S. State Dept., Washington, 1978; cons. PRADCO, Cleve., 1982-83; pres., cons. Mgmt. and Assessment Svcs., Inc., Cleve., 1983-90; pres. Kammer Investment Co., Cleve., 1989-96; fin. asst. advisor O'Donnell Securities Corp., Cleve., 1997-98; registered securities prin., investment advisor rep. and retirement specialist Wealth Charter Group, 1998—2004, asset mgr., options trader, rsch. analyst, 2005—. Mem. editl. rev. bd. Jour. of Managerial Issues, 1987; author and presenter ann. Conf. APA, 1980, Southeastern Psychol. Conf., 1979, ann. Conf. Soc. Indsl./Orgnl. Psychologists, 1987, ann. conf. Am. Soc. Tng. and Devel., 1988. Mem. Jr. League Am., Pensacola, Fla., 1970-75; treas. Bar Aux., Pensacola, 1971. Recipient Capital Gifts Stipend U. Tenn., 1976-80; Walter Bonham fellow, 1980-81. Mem. APA, Cleve. Psychol. Assn., Orgn. Devel. Inst., Acad. of Mgmt., Soc. Advancement Mgmt. (pres. 1974-75), Am. Soc. Tng. and Devel. (chpt. rep. career devel. 1984-86), Cleve. Psychol. Assn. (bd. dirs. 1987-88), Real Estate Investor's Assn. (Cleve., trustee/sec. 1992-94), Mensa. Office: Wealth Charter Group 1154 Castleton Rd Cleveland OH 44121

BOYLE, KEVIN GERARD, historian, educator, writer; b. Detroit, Oct. 7, 1960; s. Kevin C. and Anne Boyle; m. Victoria Lynn Getis, Jan. 4, 1992; children: Abigail Grace, Hannah Claire. BA, U. Detroit, 1982; PhD, U. Mich., 1990. Asst. prof. history U. Toledo, 1990—94; asst./assoc. prof. history U. Mass., Amherst, 1994—2002; assoc. prof. history Ohio State U., Columbus, 2002—. Author: The UAW and the Heyday of American Liberalism, 1945-1968, 1995, Arc of Justice: A Saga of Race, Civil Rights, and Murder in the Jazz Age, 2004 (Nat. Book Award for Nonfiction, 2004, Heartland prize, 2005); co-author: Muddy Boots and Ragged Aprons: Images of Working-Class Detroit, 1900-1930, 1997; editor: Organized Labor and American Politics, 1894-1994: The Labor-Liberal Alliance, 1998. Fellow, Rockefeller Found., 1990—91, Mary Ball Wash. Chair in Am. History, J. William Fulbright Found., 1997—98, Am. Coun. Learned Socs., 2001—02, EH, 2001—02, John Simon Guggenheim Found., 2001—02. Home: 173 N Stanwood Rd Bexley OH 43209 Office: Ohio State Univ Dept History Dulles Hall Columbus OH 43210 Office Phone: 614-292-7101.

BOYLE, PATRICIA JEAN, retired state supreme court justice; b. Detroit, Mar. 31, 1937; Student, U. Mich., 1955-57; BA, JD, Wayne State U., 1963. Bar: Mich. Practice law with Kenneth Davies, Detroit, 1963; law clk. to U.S. Dist. judge, 1963-64; asst. U.S. atty., Detroit, 1964-68; asst. pros. atty. Wayne County, dir. research, tng. and appeals Detroit, 1969-74; Recorders Ct. judge City of Detroit, 1976-78; U.S. dist. judge Eastern Dist. Mich., Detroit, 1978-83; assoc. justice Mich. Supreme Ct., Detroit, 1983-98, ret., 1999. Active Women's Rape Crisis Task Force, Vols. of Am. Named Feminist of Year Detroit chpt. NOW, 1978; recipient Outstanding Achievement award Pros. Attys. Assn. Mich., 1978, 98, Mich. Women's Hall of Fame award, 1986, Law Day award ABA, 1998, Champion of Justice award State Bar Mich., 1998. Mem. Women Lawyers Assn. Mich., Fed. Bar Assn., Mich. Bar Assn., Detroit Bar Assn., Wayne State U. Law Alumni Assn. (Disting. Alumni award 1979) Avocation: reading. Address: 10765 Oxbow Lake Shore Dr White Lake MI 48386

BOYLE, WILLIAM CHARLES, engineering educator; b. Mpls., Apr. 9, 1936; s. Robert and Daphne Boyle; m. Nancy Lee Hahn, Apr. 11, 1959; children: Elizabeth Lynn, Michele Jenette, Jane Lynette, Robert William. CE, U. Cin., 1959, MS in Sanitary Engring., 1960; PhD in Environ. Engring., Calif. Inst. Tech., 1963. Registered profl. engr., Wis., Ohio. With Milw. Sewerage Commn., 1955-56; civil engr. O. G. Loomis & Sons, Covington, Ky., 1956-59; asst. engr. Ohio River Valley Water Sanitation Commn., summer 1959; asst. prof. dept. engring. U. Wis., Madison, 1963-66, assoc. prof., 1966-70, prof. dept. civil and environ. engring., 1970-96, chmn. dept. civil and environ. engring., 1984-86, assoc. chair, 1988-96, emeritus prof., 1996—2006. Vis. prof. Rogaland Distriktshogskole, Stavanger, Norway, 1975-76; vis. prin. engr. Montgomery Engrs. Inc., Pasadena, Calif., 1988-89; cons. Procter & Gamble Co., Monsanto Co., S.B. Foot Tanning Co., Wis. Canners & Freezers Assn., Wis. Concrete Pipe Assn., Oscar Mayer & Co., Bartlett-Snow, Hide Svc. Corp., W.R. Grace & Co., Lake to Lake Dairies, Milw. Tallow, Wausau Paper Co., Packerland Packing Co., Ray-O-Vac, U.S. Army CERL, Owen Ayres & Assocs., Donohue Engrs., Davy Engrs., Carl C. Crane, Green Engring., RSE divsn. Ayres & Assocs., Schreiber Corp. Inc., Sanitaire, J.M. Montgomery, Engrs., Camp, Dresser, McKee, Phila. Mixing Sys., Polkowski, Boyle, & Assocs., Rust E&I Com.; peer rev. panel on environ. engring. EPA; accreditation visitor Accreditation Bd. for Engring. and Tech., 1990—. Contbr. chapters to books, articles to profl. jours. Sr. warden St. Andrews Episcopal Ch., Madison, 1972-74, treas., 1979-85. Recipient Engring. Disting. Alumnus award U. Cin., 1986, Founders award U.S.A. nat. com. Internat. Assn. Water Pollution Rsch. & Control, 1988, commendation EPA, 1989; Mills Found. scholar U. Cin., 1954-59; USPHS trainee, U. Cin., 1959-60; fellow Ford Found., Calif. Inst. Tech., 1960-61, USPHS, Calif. Inst. Tech., 1961-63 Mem. ASCE (life, advisor U. Wis. student chpt. 1968-71, chmn. student affairs com. 1970-72, chmn. profl. activities com. 1972-74, nat., control mem. tech. coun. on codes and standards-environ. standards 1999—, chmn. environ. stds. devel. coun. 1998-2001, chair oxygen transfer standards com., 1975-2002, history and heritage com., vice chair water infrastructure security enhancement stds., reviewer EED Jour., Rudolf Hering medal 1975, Engring. Achievement award Wis. chpt. 1986, Engr. of Yr. award Wis. sect. 1998), Water Environment Fedn. (life, rsch. com., joint task force-pretreatment of wastewater, tech. practice com.-energy in treatment plant design, chmn. program com., bd. control, 1996-98, jour. reviewer, chmn. tech. practice com. task force on aeration, Radebaugh award 1978, Eddy award com. 1992-98, Harrison Prescot Eddy Rsch. medal 1989, chmn. rsch. symposia, editl. bd. 2004-07, water environ. rsch. found. 2005-07, Gordon Maskew Fair medal for environ. engring. edn., 1992, Arthur Sydney Bedell award 2001, (2007 honorary mem.), Am. Water Works Assn. (life, chmn. task group on oxygen transfer), Am. Acad. Environ. Engrs. (diplomate, life, accreditation vis. Accreditation Bd. Engring and Tech., chmn. edn. com. 1993, trustee 1994-97, pres. 1999-2000, rep. bd. dir. ABET, 1994-2000, commr. Engr. Accreditation comm. 2001-05, Stanley E. Kappe award 2002), Am. Foundrymen's Soc. (com. on waste disposal, Outstanding Rsch. Paper award environ. cen. div. 1989), Sigma Xi, Theta Tau, Phi Eta Sigma, Chi Epsilon, Tau Beta Pi (advisor U. Wis. student chpt. 1994-96). Episcopalian. Avocations: photography, travel. Home: 105 Carillon Dr Madison WI 53705-4614 Office: Univ Wis 2256 Engineering Hall 1415 Engineering Dr Madison WI 53706-1607 E-mail: boyle@engr.wisc.edu.

BOYNTON, IRVIN PARKER, retired assistant principal; b. Chgo., Mar. 27, 1937; s. Ben Lynn and Elizabeth (Katterjohn) B.; m. Alyce Jane Coyle, Sept. 3, 1964; children: Gregory Allen, Cathy Lynn, Julie Marie, Michael Irvin, Jonathan David. BA, Ohio Wesleyan U., 1959; BS, U. Akron, 1964; MEd, Wayne State U., 1968; counseling endorsement, Siena Heights Coll., 1988. Cert. tchr., Ohio, Mich. Spl. edn. tchr., acting prin. Sagamore Hills Children's Psychiat. Hosp., Cleve., 1961-64; spl. edn. tchr. Fairlawn Ctr., Pontiac, Mich., 1964-68, Walled Lake (Mich.) High Sch., 1968-71; asst. prin. Oakland Tech. Ctr./Southwest Campus, Wixom, Mich., 1971-98; ret., 1998. Mem. spl. needs guideline com. Mich. Dept. Edn., Lansing, 1973-78; keynote speaker Utah Secondary Conf., Salt Lake City, 1978; evaluator North Cen. Accreditation Assn., Waterford, Mich., 1971-73; adv. com. State Tech.Instn. and Rehab. Ctr., Plainwell, Mich., 1978-85. Pres. Roger Campbell Ministries, Waterford, 1987—. Cited as exemplary spl. needs program U. Wis. Mem. ASCD, Am. Vocat. Assn., Mich. Occupational Edn. Assn., Mich. Occupational Spl. Needs Assn. (Outstanding Spl. Needs Educator), Nat. Assn. Vocat. Spl. Needs Personnel (Outstanding Spl. Needs Program 1975), Phi Delta Kappa. Republican. Home: 4901 Juniper Dr Commerce Township MI 48382-1545 Personal E-mail: irvinboynton@comcast.net.

BOYNTON, RICK, performing company executive; life ptnr. Criss Henderson, 1991. BS in Theatre, Northwestern U. Talent agent Harrise Davidson and Assoc., head feature film, TV and theatre dept.; casting dir., assoc. Jane Alderman Casting; artistic dir. Marriott Theatre, Lincolnshire; casting dir. Chgo. Shakespeare Theatre, Ill., 1997—2001, assoc. artistic dir. Ill., creative prodr. Ill., 2005—. Bd. dirs. Nat. Alliance Musical Theatre, co-chmn. Festival of New Musicals, NY, 2003—; lectr. Northwestern U. Actor: (plays) 1776 (Joseph Jefferson award), A Flea in Her Ear (Joseph Jefferson award); dir.: Forever Plaid. Recipient Trailblazer award, Bailiwick Repertory Theatre, 2004. Office: Chicago Shakespeare Theatre 800 East Grand Ave Chicago IL 60611

BOYNTON, SANDRA KEITH, illustrator, cartoonist, stationery products executive; b. Orange, NJ, Apr. 3, 1953; d. Robert Whitney and Jeanne Carolyn (Ragsdale) B.; m. James Patrick McEwan, Oct. 28, 1978; 1 dau., Caitlin Boynton McEwan. BA in English, Yale U., 1974, postgrad. Sch. Drama, 1976-77; postgrad., U. Calif.-Berkeley Drama Grad. Sch., 1974-75. Designer Recycled Paper Products, Inc., Chgo., 1974—, v.p., 1980—; illustrator greeting cards, 1975—. Illustrator/author: Hippos Go Berserk, 1977, If At First, 1979, Gopher Baroque, 1979, The Compleat Turkey, 1980, Chocolate: The Consuming Passion, 1982, Moo, Baa, La La La, 1982, The Going to Bed Book, 1982, But Not the Hippopotamus, 1982, Opposites, 1982, A is for Angry, 1983, Blue Hat, Green Hat, 1984, Doggies, 1984, Chloë and Maude, 1985, Christmastime, 1987, Oh My, Oh My, Oh Dinosaurs, 1993, One, Two Three, 1993, Barnyard Dance, 1993, Birthday Monsters, 1993, Pajama Time, 2000, Yay, You!: Moving Out, Moving Up, Moving On, 2001 (Publishers Weekly picture book bestseller, 2005), Philadelphia Chickens, 2002, Snuggle Puppy, 2003, Fuzzy, Fuzzy, Fuzzy!, 2003, Belly Button Book, 2005, (with Jamie MacEwan) Story of Grump and Pout, 1983, The Heart of Cool, 2001; Albums: Grunt: Pigorian Chant, 1999 (Amazon.com bestseller), (with Michael Ford): Rhinoceros Tap, 1996, Philadelphia Chickens, 2002. Mem. Soc. Of Friends. Known for creating famed birthday card greeting "Hippo Birdies Two Ewes.".

BOYSE, PETER DENT, academic administrator; b. Saginaw, Mich., Mar. 24, 1945; s. John Wesley and Ellen Elizabeth (Dent) B.; m. Barbra Ann Meehan, Sept. 2, 1972; children: Heather, Cassandra. BA, Albion Coll., 1967; MS, U. Mich., 1969, Oreg. State U., 1973, PhD, 1987. Nuclear scientist Westinghouse, Pitts., 1969-71; dir. student activities Calif. State U., Northridge, 1973-74, epic dir., 1974-76; dir. student devel. Linn-Benton Community Coll., Albany, Oreg., 1976-79, ctr. dir., 1979-82, asst. to pres., 1982-88; exec. v.p., COO Delta Coll., University Center, Mich., 1988—92, pres., 1993—. Facilitator Emerging Leaders Inst., Ann Arbor, Mich., 1990; chair Mich. C. of C. Assn., 2000-01. Contbr. articles to profl. jours. Chair Bd. League Innovation, 2003. Mem. Am. Assn. C. of C. (mem. bd. 2001-04). Avocations: reading, golf, travel. Office: Delta Coll 1961 Delta Dr University Center MI 48710-0001 Home: 6084 Old Hickory Dr Bay City MI 48706-9068

BOZEMAN, THEODORE D., religion educator; b. Gainesville, Fla., Jan. 27, 1942; s. Simuel Bozeman and Kathleen Ford; m. Hannelore Bozeman, July 29, 1973. BA, Eckerd Coll., 1964; BD, Union Theol. Sem., NYC, 1968; ThM, Union Sem., Richmond, Va., 1970; PhD, Duke U., 1974. Prof. U. Iowa, 1974—. Author: Protestants in an Age of Science, 1977, To Live Ancient Lives, 1988, The Precisionist Strain, 2004. NEH fellow, 1982, 95; recipient James Henley Thornwell award Presbyn. Hist. Assn., 1975. Mem. Am. Soc. Ch. History, Orgn. Am. Historians, So. Hist. Assn., Am. Hist. Assn. Office: U Iowa Dept Religious Studies Iowa City IA 52242 Business E-Mail: d-bozeman@uiowa.edu.

BOZZOLA, JOHN JOSEPH, botany educator, researcher; b. Herrinn, Ill., Oct. 22, 1946; PhD, So. Ill. U., 1977. Instr. Med. Coll. Pa., Phila., 1976-79, asst. prof. microbiology, 1979-83; dir. Electron Microscopy Ctr./So. Ill. U., Carbondale, 1983—, assoc. prof. botany dept., 1985-93, prof., 1993—. Contbr. rsch. articles on electron microscopy to profl. jours. Recipient Young Investigator award Nat. Inst. Dental Rsch., Washington, 1978. Mem. Microscopy Soc. Am., Am. Soc. Microbiology, Ill. State Acad. Sci., Sigma Xi, Phi Kappa Phi, Kappa Delta Pi. Avocations: photography, bicycling, gardening, painting, computers. Office: So Ill U Ctr for Electron Microscopy Carbondale IL 62901 E-mail: bozzola@siv.edu.

BRACE, C. LORING, anthropologist, educator; b. Hanover, NH, Dec. 19, 1930; s. Gerald Warner and Huldah (Laird) B.; m. Mary Louise Crozier, June 8, 1957; children: Charles L., Roger C., Hudson H. BA, Williams Coll., 1952; MA, Harvard U., 1958, PhD, 1962. Instr. U. Wis., Milw., 1960-61; asst. prof., then assoc. prof. U. Calif., Santa Barbara, 1961-67; assoc. prof. anthropology U. Mich., Ann Arbor, 1967-71, prof., 1971—, curator phys. anthropology Mus. Anthropology, 1967—. Author: Human Evolution, 1965, 2d edit., 1977, Stages of Human Evolution, 1967, 5th edit., 1995, Atlas of Human Evolution, 1971, 2d edit., 1979, Evolution in an Anthropological View, 2000, Race Is a Four-Letter Word: The Genesisi of the Concept, 2005. With U.S. Army, 1954-56. Fellow AAAS (chmn. sect. H); mem. Am. Ahthrop. Assn., Am. Assn. Phys. Anthropology, Dental Anthropology Assn. (pres. 1988-90), History of Sci. Soc. Home: 1020 Ferdon Rd Ann Arbor MI 48104-3631 Office: U Mich Mus Anthropology 1109 Geddes Ave Ann Arbor MI 48109-1079 Office Phone: 734-936-2951. E-mail: clbrace@umich.edu.

BRACE, FREDERIC F. (JAKE BRACE), air transportation executive; married; 3 children. B in Indsl. Engring., U. Mich.; MBA, U. Chgo. Various fin. mgmt. positions Am. Airlines, Dallas; mgr. oper. budgets United Airlines, Elk Grove Village, Ill., 1988, v.p., contr., 1991—93, v.p. corp. devel., 1993—94, v.p., contr., corp. devel., 1994—95, v.p. fin. analysis, contr., 1995—98, v.p. fin., 1998—99, sr. v.p. fin., treas., 1999—2001; sr. v.p., CFO UAL Corp. and United Airlines, Elk Grove Village, Ill., 2001—02, exec. v.p., CFO, 2002—. Chmn. bd. dirs. United Airlines Employees' Credit Union; bd. dirs. Equant, GetThere.com, Galileo. Trustee Mus. Sci. and Industry, Chgo. Office: UAL Corp 1200 E Algonquin Rd Elk Grove Village IL 60007

BRACKER, CHARLES E., plant pathologist, educator, researcher; b. Portchester, NY, Feb. 3, 1938; married, 1963; 2 children. BS, U. Calif., Davis, 1960, PhD in Plant Pathology, 1964. Rsch. asst. plant pathology U. Calif., Davis, 1960-64; from asst. prof. to assoc. prof., 1964-73; prof. botany and plant pathology dept. Purdue U., West Lafayette, Ind., 1973—, George B. Cummins Disting. prof. mycology. Annual lectr. Mycological Soc. Am., 1991. Recipient Ruth Allen award Am. Phytopathological Soc., 1983. Fellow AAAS; mem. Mycological Soc. Am. (disting. mycologist award 1993), Brit. Mycological Soc., Electronic Micros Soc., Am. Soc. Cell Biology. Achievements include research in fungal ultrastructure and development; developmental cytology; cell wall formation; endomembrane system and organelles; cell growth and reproduction; morphogensis cell ultrastructure. Office: Purdue University Rm 1155 Dept of Botany & Plant Pathology West Lafayette IN 47907

BRADBURY, DANIEL JOSEPH, library administrator; b. Kansas City, Kans., Dec. 7, 1945; m. Mary F. Callaghan, May 10, 1967 (div. 1987); children—Patricia, Tracy, Amanda, Anthony, Sean, m. Jobeth Baile Cannady, Nov. 23, 1988. BA in English, U. Mo., Kansas City, 1971; M.L.S., Emporia State U., 1972; LittD, Baker U., 1992. Assoc. dir. extension service Waco-McLennan Library, Tex., 1972-74; library dir. Rolling Hills Consol. Library, St. Joseph, Mo., 1974-77, Janesville Pub. Library, Wis., 1977-83; dir. leisure services City of Janesville, 1982-83; library dir. Kansas City Pub. Library, Mo., 1983—; interim exec. dir. Kansas City Sch. Dist., Mo., 1985. Faculty Baylor U., Waco, 1973-74; participant Gov.'s Conf. on Library and Info. Sci., Wis., 1979; mem. council Kansas City Metro Library Network, 1984—, pres., 1987, mem. coordinating bd. for higher edn. library adv. com., 1984—, chmn., 1986-87, pres. 1991—; bd. dirs. Greater Kansas City Coun. Philantrophy. Bd. dirs. Arrowhead Library System, Janesville, 1978-83, Mid-Town Troost Assn., Kansas City, St. John's Sch., Janesville, 1980-83, Pub. Sch. Retirement Fund, Kansas City, 1995—, treas., 1996—; bd. dirs. Jackson County Hist. Soc., 1998—, treas., 1999-2000, v.p.-elect, 2000—. amed Libr. of Yr. Libr. Jour., N.Y.C., 1991; recipient Disting. Grad. award Emporia State U., 1985, Cornerstone award Kansas City Econ. Devel. Corp., 1988, Achievement award U. Mo. Alumni Assn., 2000; Hon. Doctorate, Baker U., 1991. Mem. ALA (various offices 1972—), Am. Soc. Pub. Adminstrs. (bd. dirs. Kansas City chpt. 1994—), Mo. Libr. Assn. (legis. chmn. 1984-85), Libr. Adminstrn. and Mgmt. Assn. (sec. 1983-85), Wis. Libr. Assn. (pres. 1982). Lodges: Rotary. Roman Catholic. Home: 4545 Wornall Rd # 5 Kansas City MO 64111-3209

BRADEN, BERWYN BARTOW, lawyer; b. Pana, Ill., Jan. 10, 1928; s. George Clark and Florence Lucille (Bartow) B.; m. Betty J.; children— Scott, Mark, Mathew, Sue, Ralph, Ladd, Brad Student, Carthage Coll., 1946-48, U. Wis., 1948-49, JD, 1959. Bar: Wis. 1959, U.S. Supreme Ct. 1965. Ptnr. Genoar & Braden, Lake Geneva, Wis., 1959-63; individual practice law Lake Geneva, Wis., 1963-68, 72-74; ptnr. Braden & English, Lake Geneva, Wis., 1968-72, Braden & Olson, Lake Geneva, Wis., 1974—2002, Gagliardi Braden Olson and Capelli, Lake Geneva, 2002—06, Braden Olson Drapler, Lake Geneva, 2007—. City atty. City of Lake Geneva, 1962-64, 2006—; tchr. Law Sch., U. Wis., 1977 Bd. dirs. Lake Geneva YMCA. Mem. ABA, Walworth County Bar Assn. (pres. 1962-63), State Bar Wis. (chmn. conv. and entertainment com. 1979-81, chmn. adminstrn. Justice and Judiciary com., 1986-87, bench bar rels. com., 1987-90, mem. exec. com. Wis. Bicentennial Com. on Constn.), Wis. Acad. Trial Lawyers (sec. 1975, treas. 1976, dir. 1977-79) Office: 716 Wisconsin St Lake Geneva WI 53147-1826 also: PO Box 940 Lake Geneva WI 53147-0940 Home: 41 Golf Pkwy Madison WI 53704 Office Phone: 262-248-6636. Business E-Mail: BBraden@bodlaw.net.

BRADEN, JAMES DALE, former state legislator; b. Wakefield, Kans., Aug. 2, 1934; s. James Wesley and Olive (Reed) B.; m. Naomi Carlson, July 3, 1952 (div. Jan. 1983); children: Gregory, Michael, Ladd, Amy; m. Margie Clark Tidwell, Sept. 17, 1983; stepchildren: Richard, Lon, Dale. Grad. high sch., Wakefield. CLU, The Am. Coll. Meat cutter, Wakefield, 1952-64; ins. agt., securities broker Braden Fin. Svcs., Clay Ctr., Kans., 1964—; state rep. Kans. Ho. of Reps., Topeka, 1974-91, house majority leader, 1985-87, speaker of the house, 1987-91. Past chmn. econ. devel. com. Nat. Conf. State Legislatures, legis. coordinating council, calendar and printing com.; past chmn. assessment and taxation com.; mem. Council of State Govts. intergovtl. affairs com.; past chmn. taxation task force of Midwestern Conf. of Council State Govts.; chmn. Interstate Cooperation Commn.; former mem. State Fin. Council, Kans. Inc.; past chmn. Legis. Commn. on Kans. Econ. Devel.; past mem. Kans. Pub. Agenda Commn. Active St. Paul's Episcopal Ch., Clay Ctr.; mem. Rep. Party Exec. Com. Mem. NALU, Kans. Assn Ins. and Fin. Advisors (past pres.), Million Dollar Round Table (life), Rotary, Masons, Shriners, Elks. Episcopalian. Avocations: hunting, fishing, flying, sailing. Home: PO Box 58 Clay Center KS 67432-0058 Office: Braden Fin Svcs 1101 5th St # 58 Clay Center KS 67432-2021 Office Phone: 785-632-3601. E-mail: jbraden@eaglecom.net.

BRADING, CHARLES RICHARD, state representative; b. Lima, Ohio, Feb. 19, 1935; s. Richard H. Brading; m. Sandra Berry, June 26, 1963; children: William, Sarah, Amanda. BS in Pharmacy, Ohio No. U., 1957. From employee to owner Rhine and Brading Pharmacy, Wapakoneta, Ohio, 1958-92; state rep. State of Ohio, Columbus, 1991—. Bd. dirs. Wapakoneta Indsl. Devel. Inc.; mem. Wapakoneta City Coun., 1964-66, pres. 1974-75, 86-88; mayor of Wapakoneta, 1988-91. With U.S. Army, 1958-59, 61-62. Recipient Disting. Svc. award Wapakoneta Area Jaycee, 1965, Bowl of Hygeia award 1973, Retailer of Yr. 1978, Outstanding Achievement in Profession of Pharmacy award Merck, Sharp & Dohme 1991, Significant Contbn. to Profession of Pharmacy Beal award 1992, Alumni award Ohio No. U., 1993. Mem. Am. Pharm. Assn., Nat. Assn. Retail Druggists, Nat. Assn. Bds. of Pharmacy, Ohio State Pharm. Assn. (chmn. legis. com. 1971, chmn. bd. Pharmacy Replacement com. 1985), No. Ohio Pharm. Assn. (pres. 1969), Ohio State Bd. Pharmacy (apptd. 1976-84, pres. 1979-80), Wapakoneta C. of C., Auglaize County Hist. Soc., Elks, Eagles, Am. Legion, Masons, Shriners, Rotary Club (pres. 1971, Paul Harris fellow). Republican. Home: 1216 Oakridge Ct Wapakoneta OH 45895-9464

BRADLEY, ANN WALSH, state supreme court justice; b. Richland Center, Wis. married; 4 children. BA, Webster Coll., 1972; JD, U. Wis., 1976. Former high school tchr.; atty. priv. practice, 1976—85; judge Marathon County Circuit Ct., Wausau, Wis., 1985—95; justice Wis. Supreme Ct., Madison, Wis., 1995—. Former assoc. dean and faculty mem. Wis. Judicial Coll.; former chair Wis. Jud. Conference; lecturer ABA Asia Law Initiative; commr. Nat. Conference on Uniform Laws. Bd. of visitors U. Wis. Law Sch. Fellow: Am. Bar Found.; mem.: ABA, State Bar of Wis. (Bench Bar Com.), Am. Law Inst., Am. Judicature Soc. (Harley award 2004). Office: Wis Supreme Ct PO Box 1688 Madison WI 53701-1688

BRADLEY, BOB, professional soccer coach; b. Montclair, NJ, Mar. 3, 1958; B.History, Princeton U.; M.Sports Adminstrn., Ohio U. Head coach soccer Ohio U., Athens, 1980-81; asst. coach U. Va., 1982-83; head coach Princeton U., 1984-95; asst. coach D.C. United, 1995-97; head coach Chgo. Fire, 1997—, New York MetroStars, USA Soccer, 2006—. Named Major League Soccer's 1998 All Sport Coach of the Yr., NCAA Divsn. I Men's Coach of the Yr., 1993, winningest coach MLS history. Office: MetroStars Third Fl One Hammon Plz Secaucus NJ 07094

BRADLEY, FRAN, state legislator; b. June 13, 1942; m. Mary Knofczynski, Aug. 31, 1963; children: Al, Michele, Scott, Chris. BSME, S.D. State U.; postgrad., U. Minn. Engr., mgr. IBM; rep. Dist. 29B Minn. Ho. of Reps., 1994—. Mem.: Jaycees (pres. Minn. chpt. 1973—74, named Outstanding Young Minnesotian 1975). Office: 100 Rev Dr Martin Luther King Jr Blvd Saint Paul MN 55155

BRADLEY, JENNETTE B., former state official, lieutenant governor; b. Oct. 2, 1952; m. Michael C. Taylor. BA in Psychology, Wittenberg U. Lic. registered rep. Nat. Assn. Securitites Dealers. Exec. dir. Columbus Met. Housing Authority; sr. v.p. pub. fin. banker Kemper Securities; sr. v.p., pub. funds mgr. Huntington at. Bank; councilwoman Columbus (Ohio) City Coun., 1991—2002, chair parks and recreation com., chair utilities and energy generation coms., chair safety com., mem. safety and judiciary com., mem. adminstrn. com., mem. recreation and parks com., mem. health, housing and human svcs. com., mem. zoning com.; lt. gov. State of OH, 2003—05, treas., 2005—06; dir. OH Dept. Commerce, 2003—05. Mem. fin., adminstrn. and intergovernmental rels. steering and policy coms. Nat. League Cities. Grad. Leadership Columbus; trustee Wittenberg U.; bd. mem., former chair Joint Columbus and Franklin County Housing Adv. Bd. Recipient Woman of Achievement award, YWCA. Republican. Achievements include being the first African-American woman to be elected as Lt. Governor in Ohio and in the nation's history.

BRADLEY, RICHARD EDWIN, retired academic administrator; b. Omaha, Mar. 9, 1926; s. Louis J. and Betsy (Winterton) B.; m. Doris I. McGowan, June 8, 1946; children— Diane, Karen, David. Student, Creighton U., 1946-48; BSD., U. Nebr., 1950, D.D.S., 1952; MS, State U. Iowa, 1958. Instr. State U. Iowa, 1957-58; asst. prof. Creighton U., 1958-59; asst. prof., chmn. dept. periodontics U. Nebr., 1959-62, assoc. prof., 1962-65, prof., 1965-67; assoc. dean Coll. Dentistry, 1967-68, dean, 1968-80; pres., dean Baylor Coll. Dentistry, 1980-90, pres., dean emeritus, 1990—; clin. prof. Coll. Dentistry U. Nebr. Med. Coll., Lincoln, 1990—; cons. dental edn., 199-93. Mem. Commn. A. Coun. on Dental Edn., 1986-93; pres. Am. Assn. Dental Schs., 1977-78; mem. nat. adv. com. on health professions edn. Dept. Health and Human Resources, 1982-86; pres. Am. Fund for Dental Health, 1986-87; mem. bd. of vis. Temple Univ. Sch. of Dentistry, 2001—. Editor: The New Dentist, 1992-94; contbg. editor Orban's Textbook of Periodontics, 1963; contbr. Clark's Clin., 1980. Mem. bd. visitors Temple U. Sch. Dentistry, 2003-. With USNR, 1944—46. Established Dr. Richard and Doris Endowed Fund periodontics U. Nebr. Found., 2006. Fellow AAAS, Internat. Coll. Dentists; mem. ADA, Am. Acad. Peridontology Found. (bd. dirs., pres. 1994-96), Am. Coll. Dentists (regent 1992-96, v.p. 1997-98, pres. Found. 2001-02), Sigma Xi, Omicron Kappa Upsilon. Office: U Nebraska Coll Dentistry Lincoln NE 68583-0740

BRADLEY, THOMAS A., insurance company executive; With St. Paul Cos., Inc., St. Paul, sr. v.p. fin., CFO, 2001—04, Zurich North America, 2004—. Office: Zurich No America 550 W Washington Blvd Chicago IL 60661 Office Fax: (651) 310-8294.

BRADLEY, WALTER A., III, utilities company executive; Chief info. officer, v.p. Northwestern Corp., Sioux Falls, S.D. Office: Northwestern Corp 125 S Dakota Ave Sioux Falls SD 57104

BRADLEY, WALTER JAMES, emergency physician; b. Chgo., July 6, 1956; s. Walter James and Anna L. (Barbee) B. BS, Augsburg Coll., 1978; MD, U. Ill., 1984; MBA, U. South Fla., 1995. Diplomate Am. Bd. Emergency Medicine. Flight physician Flight for Life Milw. County Regional Med. Ctr., 1985-90; med. dir. PALS program Trinity Med. Ctr., Moline, Ill., 1990—. Edn. dir. Sinai-Samaritan Med. Ctr., 1988-90, EMS dir., 1987-90; paramedic base sta. physician Milw. County Regional Med. Ctr., 1985-90; pres. Emergency Medicine Mgmt. & Diagnostics, Trinity Med. Ctr., 1990—, dir. EMS svcs., 1990—, dir. regional trauma ctr., 1995—; state med. dir. Basic Traum Life Support, 1994—; pres., COO Trinity Ambulance, Inc.; pres., CEO Emergency Medicine Mgmt. and diagnostics, 1995—. Fellow Am. Coll. Emergency Physicians; mem. AMA, Am. Coll. Emergency Physicians, Am. Coll. Physician Execs., Nat. Assn. Managed Care Physicians, Nat. Assn. Emergency Med. Svcs. Physicians. Office: Trinity Med Ctr 2701 17th St Rock Island IL 61201-5351 E-mail: bradleyw@trinityqc.com.

BRADLEY, WILLIAM STEVEN, art museum director; b. Salina, Kans., Aug. 20, 1949; s. William Bernard and Jane Ray (Gebhart) B; m. Kathryn Mann, Mar. 18, 1972; children: Kate, Christina, Megan, Emma, Drew. BA, U. Colo., 1971; MA, Northwestern U., 1974, PhD, 1981. Instr. Wells Coll., Aurora, N.Y., 1979-81; curator, asst. prof. Tex. Tech. U. and Mus., Lubbock, Tex., 1982-85; chief curator San Antonio Mus. Art, 1985-86; dir. Alexandria (La.) Mus. Art, 1987-92, Davenport (Iowa) Mus. Art, 1992—2001; asst. prof. art dept. Mesa State Coll., Grand Junction, Colo., 2006—. Vis. lectr. Cornell U., Ithaca, N.Y., 1980-81; cons. Am. Assn. Mus., Washington, 1989—. Author: Emil Nolde, 1986; editor: (catalog) Elemore Morgan, 1992, Emery Clark, 1989; reviewer Inst. Mus. Svcs., 1985-90. V.p. La. Assn. Mus., Baton Rouge, 1988, 90. Home: 576 1/2 Garden Grove Ct Grand Jct CO 81501-6908 Office: Mesa State Coll Art Dept 1100 North Ave Grand Junction CO 81501 Home Phone: 970-257-1785; Office Phone: 970-248-1073. E-mail: Wm549@aol.com, sbradley@mesastate.edu.

BRADSHAW, BILLY DEAN, retired retail executive; b. Decatur, Ill., June 25, 1940; s. Lester H. and Gertrude (Davis) B.; children: Deborah, Amanda. Grad., Lakeview High Sch., Decatur, Ill., 1959. Retail div. supr. Schnepps Assocs., Decatur, 1964-74; store mgr. Firestone Tire & Rubber Co., Decatur, 1975—, ret., 2001. Coach Decatur's Boys Baseball, 1965-69. With USAF, 1960-64. Mem. Am. Motorcyclist Assn., Tennesse-Squire, Am. Legion. Avocations: boating, golf. Home: 24 Lake Grove Clb Decatur IL 62521-2321 E-mail: btennsqr@aol.com.

BRADSHAW, CONRAD ALLAN, retired lawyer; b. Campbell, Mo., Dec. 22, 1922; s. Clarence Andrew and Stella (Cashdollar) B.; m. Margaret Crassous Sanderson, Dec. 31, 1959; children: Dorothy A., Lucy E., Charlotte L. AB, U. Mich., 1943, JD, 1948. Bar: Mich. 1948. With Warner, Norcross & Judd, LLP, ret., 2005. Lt. USNR, 1943—46. Mem. ABA, State Bar Mich. (chmn. corp., fin. and bus. law sect. 1976), Grand Rapids Bar Assn. (pres. 1970) Office: 900 Fifth Third Ctr 111 Lyon St NW Grand Rapids MI 49503 Office Phone: 616-752-2344.

BRADSHAW, JEAN PAUL, II, lawyer; b. May 12, 1956; married; children: Andrew, Stephanie. BJ, JD, U. Mo., 1981. Bar: Mo. 1981, U.S. Dist. Ct. (we. dist.) Mo. 1982, U.S. Dist. Ct. (so. dist.) Ill. 1988, U.S. Ct. Appeals (8th cir.) 1986, U.S. Supreme Ct. 1987. Assoc. Neale, Newman, Bradshaw & Freeman, Springfield, Mo., 1981-87, ptnr., 1987-89; U.S. atty. we. dist. Mo. U.S. Dept. Justice, Kansas City, 1989-93; of counsel Lathrop & Gage, Kansas City, 1993-99, mem., 2000—, chair dept. health law, 2000—05. Named Spl. Asst. Atty. Gen. State of Mo., 1985-89; mem., chmn. elect U.S. Atty. Gen.'s adv. com., office mgmt. and budget subcom., sentencing guidelines subcom.; mem. com. infractions NCAA Divsn. II, 2005—. Chmn. Greene County Rep. cen. com., 1988-89; pres. Mo. Assn. Reps., 1986-87; bd. dirs. Greene County TARGET, 1984-89; mem. com. on resolutions, family and community issues and del. 1988 Rep. Nat. Conv.; mem. platform com. Mo. Reps., 1988; chmn. Greene County campaign McNary for Gov., 1984, co-chmn. congl. dist. Dole for Pres., 1988, regional chmn. Danforth for Senate, 1988, co-chmn. 7th congl. dist. Webster for Atty. Gen., 1988; county chmn. U. Mo.-Columbia Alumni Assn., 1985-87; bd. dirs. Springfield Profl. Baseball Assn., Inc.; past mem. Mo. Adv. Coun. for Comprehensive Psychiat. Svcs., former bd. dirs. Ozarks Coun. Boy Scouts Am.; pres. bd. trustees St. Paul's Episcopal Day Sch., 1997-2002. Named Outstanding Recent Grad. U. Mo.-Columbia Sch. Law, 1991. Mem. ABA, NCAA (divsn. II com. Infractions, 2005—), Mo. Bar Assn., Kansas City Met. Bar Assn., U. Mo.-Columbia Law Sch. Alumni Assn. (v.p. 1988-89, pres. 1990-91), Law Soc. U. Mo.-Columbia Law Sch. Office: 2345 Grand Blvd Ste 2800 Kansas City MO 64108-2612 Office Phone: 816-460-5507. Business E-Mail: jpbradshaw@lathropgage.com.

BRADTKE, PHILIP JOSEPH, architect; b. Chgo., Aug. 13, 1934; s. Felix Anthony and Frances Agnes (Mach) B.; m. Diane Gloria Westol, Oct. 19, 1963 (div. July 1987); children: Michael, Christine; m. Catherine Adler, Nov. 25, 1989. BArch cum laude, U. Notre Dame, 1957. Registered architect, Ill. Project architect Belli & Belli, Chgo., 1957-64; project mgr., v.p. A.M. Kinney Assoc., Inc., Evanston, Ill., 1964-80, v.p., pres., 1987-96; v.p., sr. assoc. Kober/Belluschi Assoc., Chgo., 1980-87; archtl. divsn. mgr., v.p. Patrick Engring. Inc., Glen Ellyn, Ill., 1996—. Lectr. U. Notre Dame, 1975. Commr. bldg. dept. Village of Glenview, Ill., 1980-83, commr. appearance commn., 1983—. Recipient Hon. Mention award Beaux Arts Inst. Design, 1955, 1st prize award Ch. Property and Adminstrn. Mag., 1956, 1st Mention award Indpls. Home Show Archtl. Competition, 1956, Hon. Mention award, 1959, Modernization Excellence award Bldgs. Mag., 1985. Mem. AIA (corp., housing com. 1968, chmn. honor awards com., 1973, treas., 1975-76), Notre Dame Club, Glenview Shoreline Tennis Team (capt. 1976—). Roman Catholic. Avocations: tennis, golf, basketball. Home: 1441 Canterbury Ln Glenview IL 60025-2252

BRADY, DANIEL R., state legislator; b. Oct. 7, 1953; m. one child. BA, OH U. Mem. Cleveland City Coun., 1986-96, Ohio Ho. of Reps., Columbus, 1995-98, Ohio Senate from 23rd dist., Columbus, 1999—. Democrat. Office: State House 23rd Dist Senate Bldg Columbus OH 43215

BRADY, EDMUND MATTHEW, JR., lawyer; b. Apr. 24, 1941; s. Edmund Matthew and Thelma (McDonald) B.; m. Marie Pierre Wayne, May 14, 1966; children: Edmund Matthew III, Meghan, Timothy. BSS, John Carroll U., 1963; JD, U. Detroit, 1966; postgrad., Wayne State U., 1966—69; DHL (hon.), U. Detroit, 1998. Bar: Mich. 1966, US Dist. Ct. (ea. dist.) Mich. 1966, US Ct. Appeals (6th cir.) 1973, US Supreme Ct. 1974. Sr. ptnr. Vandeveer & Garzia, 1973—90, Plunkett & Cooney, P.C., 1990—2003; ptnr. Garan Lucow Miller P.C., Detroit, 2003—04. Village clk. Grosse Pointe Shores, Mich., 1975-80; trustee St. John Hosp. and Med. Ctr., Detroit, 1992-2000, chmn., 1994-2000, Grosse Pointe Acad., Mich., 1977-83, adv. trustee, 1983-89; vice chmn. St. John Physicians Hosp. Orgn., 1994-95; supr. Grosse Pointe Twp., 1994-2000, trustee, 1989-2000; pres., dir. Grosse Pointe Hockey Assn., 1969-70; bd. dirs., chmn. maj. gifts divsn. 1st Fund, St. John Hosp. Guild; bd. dirs., pres. Friends of Bon Secours Hosp.; trustee, mem. exec. com., mem. fin. com. St. John Health Sys., 1998-2000. Recipient award of distinction U. Detroit Law Alumni, 1981, Michael Franck award State Bar of Mich. Rep. Assembly, 1998, Respected Advocate award Mich. Trial Lawyers Assn., 1998; named U. Detroit Mercy Law Sch. Alumnus of Yr., 2003. Fellow Am. Bar Found. (life), Mich. State Bar Found. (life); mem. ABA, Am. Coll. Trial Lawyers, Inter. Soc. Barristers, Am. Bd. Trial Advocates, Assn. Def. Trial Counsel (dir. 1975-80, pres. 1980-81), Mich. Def. Trial Counsel (dir. 1980-81), Def. Rsch. Inst. (Exceptional Performance citation 1981), Cath. Lawyers Soc., Soc. Irish-Am. Lawyers (founding dir. 1979-81), Detroit Bar Assn. (dir. 1986-91, sec.-treas. 1988, pres.-elect 1989-90, pres. 1990-91), State Bar Mich. (commr. 1991-98, treas. 1994, v.p. 1995, pres.-elect 1996, pres. 1997-98), Mich. Super Lawyers, Country Club of Detroit, Detroit Athletic Club, Delta Theta Phi. Republican. Roman Catholic. Personal E-mail: edmundbrady@comcast.net.

BRADY, JAMES S., lawyer; b. Grand Rapids, Mich., Sept. 17, 1944; s. George Joseph and Emily Mae (Sherman) B.; m. Catherine Ann Yared, Aug. 6, 1966; children: Monica Rose, Michael George, Paul Samuel. BS, Western Mich. U., 1966; JD, U. Notre Dame, 1969. Bar: Mich. 1969. Asso. Roach, Twohey, Maggini & Brady (and predecessors), 1969-77, partner, 1972-77; U.S. atty. Western Dist. Mich., Grand Rapids, 1977-81; mem. firm Miller, Johnson, Snell & Cummiskey, Grand Rapids, 1981—, chmn. litigation sect., 1992-99. Mem. teaching faculty Nat. Inst. Trial Advocacy, 1979-80, Inst. Continuing Legal Edn., 1980, trial skills U. Mich.; adj. prof. Cooley Law Sch., Lansing, Mich.; chmn. bd. trustees Western Mich. U. Pres. Grand Rapids Jaycees, 1975-76; legal counsel Mich. Jaycees, 1976-77; pres. Villa Elizabeth Adv. Bd., 1977-79; bd. dirs. Legal Aid and Defender Soc., 1970-77; mem. planning council Grand Rapids United Way, 1976-80, chmn. standing com., 1975-77; mem. adv. com. Kent County Sheriff's Dept., 1975-77; bd. dirs. Cath. Social Services; chmn. bd. Jr. Achievement. Recipient Disting. Service award Grand Rapids Jaycees, 1978 Mem. ABA, Fed. Bar Assn., Mich. Bar Assn., Grand Rapids Bar Assn. (dir. 1973-74, found. com., pres.), State Bar Mich. (criminal jurisprudence com., spl. com. law and media), Am. Trial Lawyers Assn. Clubs: Peninsular, Blythefield, Grand Rapids Press. Roman Catholic. Office: 800 Calder Plaza Bldg Grand Rapids MI 49503

BRADY, TERRENCE JOSEPH, mediator, arbitrator, retired judge; b. Chgo., Dec. 24, 1940; s. Harry J. and Othele R. Brady; m. Debra René, Dec. 6, 1969; children: Tara René, Dana Rose. BA cum laude, U. St. Thomas, St. Paul, 1963; JD, U. Ill., 1968. Bar: Ill. 1969, U.S. Dist. Ct. (no. dist.) Ill. 1970, U.S. Ct. Appeals (7th cir.) 1971. Pvt. practice, Crystal Lake, Ill., 1969-70, Waukegan, 1970-77; assoc. judge 19th Jud. Cir., 1977—2004, ret., 2004; mediator, arbitrator pvt. practice, 2004—. Lectr. Ann. Ill. Assoc. Judge Seminars, Statewide Ill. Traffic Conf., 1982, Lake County Bar Assn. Seminar, 1983, 88, others; invited participant Law and Econs. Seminar, U. Kans., 2000, Judicial Faculty Development, Ill. Judicial Conf., 2000; vis. jud. faculty Nat. Jud. Coll., U. Nev. Reno, 1997, condr. seminar civil mediation, 1999; materials author and lectr. in field, 1997; author, presenter, lectr. in field, 1998-; long range planning com. 19th Jud. Circuit, Lake County, Ill., 1999; alt. faculty mem., Chancery and Miscellaneous Remedies, 2000, Settlement Techniques, 2002; mem. delegation of Am. judges, Mexican Govt. Jud. Visitation Program, Mex.,2001. Author: Settle It, The Docket, 1998, The Six Steps of a Jury Trial, 1999, Civil Discovery-Rule 213-Keys to Compliance, 1999; author and lectr., SCR 213-2000 Update, The Docket, 2000; mem. editl. bd. The Docket; contbr. articles to profl. jours. With US Army, 1963—64, with US Army, 1968—69. Mem. ISBA (bench and bar sect. coun., adv. polls com., assembly mem. 2000-), LCBA (civil trial, med., legal coms.), Ill. Bar Assn. (com. on jud. adv. polls 1994—, vice-chair adv. polls 1998, task force on domestic violence 1998—, chair jud. adv. polls, 1999, sec. com. on jud. adv. polls 1997-99, bench and bar coms., jud. evaluating com.), Ill. Judges Assn. (bd. govs.), Ill. Bar Found., Lake County Bar Assn., Libertyville Racquet Club. Avocations: tennis, golf, writing, reading. Office Phone: 847-362-7885, 847-840-3044. Business E-Mail: tjbrady63@yahoo.com.

BRADY, WILLIAM E., state legislator; m. Nancy Brady; children: Katie, William, Duncan. Grad., Ill. Wesleyan U., 1983. Founder, pres., oper. officer Brady Weaver Realtors/Better Homes & Gardens, 1984—, Brady Property Mgmt., 1984—; co-founder, sec. Brady & Assocs. Constrn. & Devel., 1986—; pres. Decade 200 Mortgage Svcs., Inc., 1991—; mem. from 88th dist. Ill. Ho. of Reps. Bd. dirs. YMCA, 1990—; v.p. bd. dirs. Ctrl. Cath. H.S. Found., 1980-94; mem. Rep. Ctrl. Com., 1986—; active in polit. campaigns of Ed Madigan and Jim Edgar. Mem. Bloomington/Normal Assn. Realtors (bd. dirs. 1990—), Bloomington/Normal Homebuilders Assn., McLean County Young Reps. (bd. dirs. 1986—), McLean County C. ofC. (bd. dirs. 1987-90, sec. 1990-91). Office: 2203 Eastland Dr Ste 3 Bloomington IL 61704-7924 Home: 1202 Elmwood Rd Bloomington IL 61701-3319

BRADY, WILLIAM ROBERT, state senator; b. Parsons, Kans., May 25, 1956; s. William Frances and Mary (Hemmer) B.; m. Nancy Brady. AA, Labette Cmty. Coll., 1975; BA, Pitts. State U., 1977, MS, 1981. Former atty. Maloney, Hedman & Assocs.; mem. Kans. Ho. of Reps., Topeka, 1981-90, mem. edn. com., agenda chmn., house leader; mem. U.S. Senate from Kans., Washington, 1991-97. Owner, floral and greenhouse. Active Patrick's Parish Coun.; bd. dirs. Youth Coun. Shelter. Mem. Parsons C. of C., Lions, Rotary (citizenship scholar Parsons 1974). Democrat. Address: 1235 Stone Creek Dr Lawrence KS 66049-4788

BRAEUTIGAM, RONALD RAY, economics professor, educational association administrator; b. Tulsa, Apr. 30, 1947; s. Raymond Louis and Loys Ann (Johnson) B.; m. Janette Gail Carlyon, July 27, 1975; children: Eric Zachary, Justin Michael, Julie Ann. BS in Petroleum Engring., U. Tulsa, 1969; MSc in Engring.-Econ. Systems, Stanford U., 1971, PhD in Economics, 1976. Petroleum engr. Standard Oil Ind., Tulsa, 1966—70; staff economist Office of Telecomm. Policy, Exec. Office of Pres., Washington, 1972—73; from asst. to prof. econs. Northwestern U., Evanston, Ill., 1975—, dir. bus. instns. program, 1995—2004, Harvey Kapnick prof. Bus. Instns. dept. econs., 1990—, Charles Deering McCormick prof. tchg. excellence, 1997—2000, assoc. dean, 2004—06, assoc. provost, 2006—. Vis. prof. Calif. Inst. Tech., Pasadena, 1978-79, sr. rsch. fellow Internat. Inst. Mgmt., Berlin, 1982-83, 91. Co-author: The Regulation Game, 1978, Price Level Regulation for Diversified Public Utilities, 1989, Microeconomics: An Integrated Approach, 2002; assoc. editor Jour. Indsl. Econs., Cambridge, Mass., 1987-90; mem. editorial bd. MIT Press Series on Regulation, Cambridge, 1980-90, Jour. Econ. Lit., 1987-91, Rev. Indsl. Orgn., 1991—2004, Microeconomics, 2005. Coach Skokie (Ill.) Indians Little League, 1985-91, Evanston Youth Baseball Assn., 1991-96. Grantee, Dept. Transp., NSF, Ameritech, Sloan Found., Mellon Found. Mem. Am. Econ. Assn., Econometric Soc., Internat. Telecommunications Soc. (bd. dirs. 1990-97), European Econ. Assn., European Assn. for Rsch. in Indsl. Econs. (exec. com. 1992—, pres. 1997-99), Soc. Petroleum Engrs. Avocations: travel, music, languages. Home: 731 Monticello St Evanston IL 60201-1745 Office: Northwestern U Office of the Provost Evanston IL 60208-0001

BRAGG, MICHAEL B., engineering educator; BS in Aero. & Astronautical Engring., U. Ill., 1976, MS in Aero. & Astronautical Engring., 1977; PhD in Aero. & Astronautical Engring., Ohio State U., 1981. Prof. aerospace engring. U. Ill., Urbana. Invited lectr. First Bombardier Internat. Workshop, Montreal, 1991; cons. U.S. cos.; mem. FAA and other adv. panels. Contbr. numerous articles to profl. jours. Fellow AIAA (assoc., mem. 4 nat. tech. coms., Losey Atmospheric Scis. award 1998, chair applied aerodynamics tech. com., presenter); mem. Soc. Automotive Engrs. (past chmn. aircraft icing tech. com.). Achievements include research on reduction of maximum lift capability, increasing of drag leading to reduction of aircraft controllability due to ice accretion; unsteady aerodynamics. Office: U Ill 306 Talbot Lab 104 S Wright St Urbana IL 61801-2935 E-mail: mbragg@uiuc.edu.

BRAGG, RUSSELL J., food products executive; BS, Widener U., 1957. With Pillsbury, 1959—76, dir., 1976—80, v.p., 1980—83, group v.p., 1983—87; pres. Pillsbury Indsl. Foods, 1988—89; chmn., CEO Grand Met. Foodsvc. USA, 1989—92; with ConAgra Foods, Inc., Omaha, 1992—; pres. ConAgra Flour Milling Co., 1995—97, ConAgra Poultry Co., 1997—98; now sr. v.p. operational improvements ConAgra Foods, Inc., Omaha. Office: ConAgra Foods Inc 1 ConAgra Dr Omaha NE 68102-5001

BRAKE, CECIL CLIFFORD, retired diversified manufacturing executive; b. Ystrad, Mynach, Wales, Nov. 14, 1932; came to U.S., 1967; s. Leonard James and Ivy Gertrude (Berry) B.; m. Vera Morris, Aug. 14, 1954; children— Stephen John, Richard Colin, Vanessa Elaine Chartered engr.; B.Sc. in Engring., U. Wales, 1954; M.Sc., Cranfield Inst., Bedford, Eng., 1957; grad. A.M.P., Harvard U. Sch. Bus., 1985. Mgr. research and devel. Schrader Fluid Power, Wake Forest, NC, 1968-70, engring. mgr., 1970-75; mng. dir. Schrader U.K. Fluid Power, 1975-77; v.p., gen. mgr. Schrader Internat., 1977-78; group v.p. Schrader Bellows, Fluid Power, Akron, Ohio, 1978-82; exec. v.p. Scovill, Inc., Waterbury, Conn., 1982-86; pres. Yale Security, Inc. subs. Scovill, Inc.; group exec. Eagle Industries, Inc., Chgo., 1986—; retired, 1997. Chief oper. officer Mansfield (Ohio) Plumbing Products Inc., Hart and Cooley Inc., Holland, Mich., Caron Internat., Inc., Rochelle, Ill., Caron Internat., Inc., Rochelle, Ill., Chemineer Inc., Dayton, Ohio, Pulsafeeder Inc., Rochester, N.Y., Clevaflex Inc., Cleve., Equality Specialties Inc., N.Y.C., De Vilbiss Co., Toledo, Hill Refrigeration, Trenton, N.J., Air-Maze Corp., Bedford Heights, Ohio, Burns Aerospace Corp., Winston Salem, N.C., Atlantic Industries, Inc., Nutley, N.J., Stimsonite Products, Niles, Ill.; ptnr., owner Prince of Wales Inc.; bd. dirs. CFI Industries. Avocations: sailing, golf. Office: Eagle Industries Inc 2 N Riverside Plz Chicago IL 60606-2600 Home: 1461 Sabal Palm Dr Boca Raton FL 33432 also: 112 Melville Ave Fairfield CT 06825-2005 E-mail: cecilclifffb@aol.com.

BRALEY, BRUCE, congressman; b. Grinnell, IA, Oct. 30, 1957; m. Carolyn Kalb, 1983; children: Lisa, David, Paul. BA, Iowa State U., 1980; JD, U. Iowa, 1983. Atty. Dutton, Braun, Staack and Hellman, PLC; mem. US Congress from 1st Iowa dist., 2007—, mem. oversight & govtl. reform com., small bus. com., transp. & infrastructure com. Mem., Bd. Dirs. Iowa Legal Aid. Pres. Waterloo Dollars for Scholars prog., Big Brothers/Big Sisters of Northeast Iowa; mem., Platform Com. 2nd Congl. Dist. Dem. Party, 1998, Black Hawk County Dem. Party, 1998—2004, 1st Congl. Dist. Dem. Party, 2004; vol. Kerry Edwards Campaign, 2004; precinct coord. John Edwards for Pres. Campaign, 2004. Co-recipient Couple of Yr., Big Brothers/Big Sisters of Northeast Iowa; recipient Vol. Performance award, Cedar Valley Mayor, 1998. Mem.: Vis. Nurses Assn., Iowa Trial Lawyers Assn. Democrat. Presbyterian. Office: 1408 Longworth House Office Bldg Washington DC 20515 also: 501 Sycamore St Ste 623 Waterloo IA 50703

BRALY, ANGELA FICK, health insurance company executive, lawyer; b. July 2, 1961; married; 3 children. BBA, Tex. Tech. U., 1983; JD, So. Meth. U., 1985. Bar: Mo. 1985. Ptnr. Lewis Rice & Fingersh LC, St. Louis, 1987—99; interim gen. counsel RightCHOICE Managed Care Inc., St. Louis, 1997—98, exec. v.p., gen. counsel., corp. sec., 1999—2003; pres., CEO Blue Cross Blue Shield of Mo., St. Louis, 2003—05; exec. v.p., gen. counsel, chief pub. affairs officer WellPoint, Inc., Indpls., 2005—07; pres., CEO Wellpoint, Inc., Indpls., 2007—. Bd. dirs. Wellpoint, Inc., 2007—. Named one of The 25 Most Influential Women in Bus., St. Louis Bus. Jour., 2000, The Top 25 Women in Healthcare, Modern Healthcare mag., 2007, 100 Most Powerful Women, Forbes Mag., 2007. Mem.: ABA, Am. Health Lawyers Assn., State Bar Mo., Bar Assn. Met. St. Louis, St. Louis Health Lawyers Network. Office: WellPoint Inc 120 Monument Cir Indianapolis IN 46204 Office Phone: 317-488-6000.

BRAMNIK, ROBERT PAUL, lawyer; b. NYC, Nov. 17, 1949; s. Abe and Ruth (Richman) B.; m. Sheryl Ann Kalus, Aug. 12, 1973; children: Michael Lawrence, Andrew Martin. BA, CCNY, 1970; JD, Bklyn. Law Sch., 1973. Bar: N.Y. 1974, Ill. 1980, U.S. Dist. Ct. (so. and ea. dists.) N.Y. 1974, U.S. Dist. Ct. (no. dist.) Ill. 1980, U.S. Dist. Ct. (ctrl. dist.) Ill. 1982, U.S. Ct. Appeals (2d cir.) 1974, U.S. Ct. Appeals (4th cir.) 1987, U.S. Ct. Appeals (3d and 7th cirs.) 1992, U.S. Ct. Fed. Claims 1994, U.S. Supreme Ct. 1977. Sr. trial atty. NYSE, Inc., NYC, 1973-75; asst. gen. counsel E.F. Hutton & Co., Inc., NYC, 1975-77, Nat. Securities Clearing Corp., NYC, 1977-79; with Arvey, Hodes, Costello and Burman, Chgo., 1979-86, ptnr., 1982-86, Wood, Lucksinger & Epstein, Chgo., 1987-88, Altheimer & Gray, Chgo., 1988-97, Wildman, Harrold, Allen & Dixon, Chgo., 1997—2003, Duane Morris LLP, Chgo., NYC, 2003—. Lectr. Securities Industry Assn. Compliance and Legal div., N.Y.C., 1980-91, 95-2001. Vice chmn. Ill. Adv. Com. on Commodity Regulation, Chgo., 1985-89, chmn., 1989-95. Fellow: Ill. Bar Found.; mem.: ABA (com. on futures and derivatives regulation, com. on fed. regulation of securities), Nat. Futures Assn. (arbitrator 1991—, hearing com. 2001—), Nat. Assn. Sec. Dealers (arbitrator 1981—), Assn. of Bar of City of N.Y. Jewish. Office: Duane Morris LLP 227 W Monroe St Ste 3400 Chicago IL 60606 Office Phone: 312-499-0121. Business E-Mail: rpbramnik@duanemorris.com.

BRAMSON, JAMES B., dentist, dental association administrator; DDS, U. Iowa Coll. Dentistry, 1979. Pvt. practice, Mass.; exec. dir. Mass. Dental Soc., 1997—2001, ADA, Chgo., 2001—. Grantee Hillenbrand Fellowship. Mem.: Mass. Dental Soc., ADA (dir. Coun. on Dental Practice 1990—97, sec./treas. Endowment and Assistance Fund Inc. 1990—97, dir. Commn. on Relief Fund Activities). Office: ADA 211 E Chicago Ave Chicago IL 60611 also: ADA Ste 1200 1111 14thSt NW Washington DC 20005

BRANAGAN, JAMES JOSEPH, lawyer; b. Johnstown, Pa., Mar. 5, 1943; s. James Francis and Caroline Bertha (Schreier) B.; m. Barbara Jeanne Miller, June 19, 1965; children: Sean Patrick, Erin MacKay, David Michael. BA in English Lit. with honors magna cum laude (Woodrow Wilson fellow), Kenyon Coll.,

Gambier, Ohio, 1965; LLB cum laude, Columbia U., 1968. Bar: Ohio 1968. Assoc. Jones, Day, Reavis & Pogue, Cleve., 1968-72; with Leaseway Transp. Corp., Cleve., 1972-81, gen. counsel, 1975-80, sec., 1979-81, v.p. corp. affairs, 1980-81; also officer, dir. Leaseway Transp. Corp. (subsidiaries); v.p. Premier Indsl. Corp., Cleve., 1981-82; sr. counsel TRW Inc., 1982-88; pvt. practice Cleve., 1988—; treas., gen. counsel, sec. Biomec Inc., 1998—2003. Mem. ABA, Ohio Bar Assn., Cleve. Bar Assn., Phi Beta Kappa. Business E-Mail: bizlaw2@oh.rr.com.

BRANCEL, BEN, state agency administrator; m. Gail Brancel; children: Micheleen, Tod, Brandon. Degree, U. Wis., Platteville. Mem. State Assembly, 1986-97, assembly spkr., 1997; sec. Wis. Dept. Agr., Trade and Consumer Protection, 1997—. Mem. joint fin. com., gov.'s coun. on tourism, legis. coun., legis. audit com., joint com. on employment rels., state claims bd. Former mem. Portage Sch. Bd.; former chmn. Town of Douglas. Mem. Wis. Dairies Coop., Marquette County Farm Bur., Marquette Holstein Assn., World Dairy Authority. Office: PO Box 8911 Madison WI 53708-8911

BRANCH, JOSEPH C., lawyer; BA, Marquette U., 1967, JD magna cum laude, 1971. Bar: Wis. 1971. Ptnr. Foley & Lardner LLP, Milw., mem. ins. industry practice group. Editl. rev. bd. Jour. Ins. Regulation, 1985—; bd. dirs. Fedn. Regulatory Counsel. Co-author: Insurers Operating Under Assumed or Fictitious Names: When, How &.What?!, LLC Bandwagon: Insurers Beware. Mem.: Internat. Assn. Ins. Law, Defense Research Inst., Inc., Milw. Bar Assn., ABA (tort & ins. practice sect., com. lawyers profl. liability), State Bar Wis. (chmn. ins. com. 1980—86, bd. gov., exec. com.). Office: Foley & Lardner LLP 777 E Wisconsin Ave Milwaukee WI 53202-5306 Office Phone: 414-297-5837. Business E-Mail: jbranch@foley.com.

BRAND, GEORGE EDWARD, JR., retired lawyer; b. Detroit, Oct. 25, 1918; s. George Edward and Elsie Bertie (Jones) B.; m. Patricia Jean Gould, June 7, 1947; children— Martha Christine, Carol Elsie, George Edward. BA, Dartmouth Coll., 1941; postgrad., U. Minn., Harvard U., 1941; JD, U. Mich., 1948. Bar: Mich. 1948, U.S. Supreme Ct. 1958. Mem. firm George E. Brand, Detroit, 1948-63, Butzel, Long, Gust, Klein & Van Zile, P.C., Detroit, 1963—; ptnr., dir., pres. Butzel, Long, Gust, Klein & Van Zile, 1974-89; ret. Served with USNR, 1942-46. Recipient Individual citation as fighter dir. officer in Solomon Islands, 1943. Fellow Am. Bar Found., Am. Coll. Trial Lawyers; mem. ABA, Am. Judicature Soc., Detroit Bar Assn., VFW. Clubs: N.S.S.C. Home: 1233 Kensington Ave Grosse Pointe Park MI 48230-1101

BRAND, MYLES, sports association and former academic administrator; b. NYC, May 17, 1942; s. Irving Philip and Shirley (Berger) B.; m. Wendy Hoffman (div. 1976); 1 child: Joshua; m. Margaret Zeglin, 1978. BS, Rensselaer Poly. Inst., Troy, NY, 1964; PhD, U. Rochester, 1967; PhD (hon.), Rensselaer Poly. Inst., Troy, NY, 1991. Asst. prof. philos. U. Pitts., 1967—72; assoc. prof. to prof., dept. chmn. U. Ill., Chgo., 1972—81; prof., dept. head U. Ariz., Tucson, 1981—83, dir. cognitive sci. prog., 1982—85, dean social & behavioral scis. Tucson, 1983—86; provost, v.p. acad. affairs Ohio State U., Columbus, 1986—89; pres. U. Oreg., Eugene, 1989—94, Ind. U., Bloomington, 1994—2002, NCAA, Indpls., 2003—. Author: Intending and Acting, 1984; editor: The Nature of Human Action, 1970, The Nature of Causation, 1976, Action Theory, 1976. Bd. dirs. Ariz. Humanities Coun., 1984-85, Am. Coun. Edn., Washington, 1992-97. Named one of Most Influential People in the World of Sports, Bus. Week, 2007. Mem. Clarion Hosps. Assn. of Am. Phi, Assn. Am. Univs. (pres. 1999). Office: NCAA Travel Svc 111 Water St New Haven CT 06511-5759

BRAND, STEVE AARON, lawyer; b. St. Paul, Sept. 5, 1948; s. Allen A. and Shirley Mae (Mintz) B.; m. Gail Idele Greenspoon, Oct. 9, 1977. BA, U. Minn., 1970; JD, U. Chgo., 1973. Bar: Minn. 1973, U.S. Dist. Ct. Minn. 1974, U.S. Supreme Ct. 1977. Assoc. Briggs & Morgan, St. Paul, 1973-78, ptnr., 1978-91, Robins, Kaplan, Miller & Ciresi, LLP, 1991—. Pres. Jewish Vocat. Svc., 1981—84, Sholom Found., 1996—99; bd. dirs. Friends of the St. Paul Libr., 1997—2005; pres. Mt. Zion Hebrew Congregation, 1985—87. Mem. ABA, Minn. Bar Assn. (chmn. probate and trust law sect. 1984-85), Hebrew Union Coll.-Jewish Inst. Religion (bd. overseers 1987—, vice-chmn. 1996—), Am. Coll. Trust and Estate Counsel (Minn. chair 1991-96, regent 1998-2004), Ramsey County Bar Found. (pres. 1995-2000), Phi Beta Kappa, B'nai Brith. Democrat. Home: 1907 Hampshire Ave Saint Paul MN 55116-2401 Office: Robins Kaplan Miller & Ciresi LLP 2800 LaSalle Plz 800 Lasalle Ave Minneapolis MN 55402-2015 Home Phone: 651-698-8211; Office Phone: 612-349-8731. Business E-Mail: sabrand@rkmc.com.

BRANDES, JOANNE, lawyer; BA, U. Wis., Eau Claire; JD, Willamette U. Assoc. Herz, Levin, Teper, Chernof & Sumner, SC, 1978—81; with S.C. Johnson & Son, Inc., 1981—96; sr. v.p., gen. counsel S.C. Johnson Comml. Markets, Inc., 1997—2002; exec. v.p., chief adminstrv. officer, gen counsel JohnsonDiversey, Inc. (formerly Johnson Wax Profl.), Sturtevant, Wis., 2002—. Dir. JohnsonFamily Funds, Inc., Andersen Corp. Inc., Bright Horizons Family Solutions Inc., Watertown, Mass., 1998—. Regent emeritus U. Wis., Wis., 1996—; past mem. Gov.'s Commn. on Glass Ceiling; chmn. Wis. Child Care Coun.; past president Racine Area United Found. Named Working Mother of Yr., Working Mother mag., 1994; named to Eau Claire Alumni Hall of Honor, U. Wis., 1995, 2002; recipient Bus. Jour. Women of Influence award, 2002. Office: JohnsonDiversey, Inc 8310 16th St PO Box 902 Sturtevant WI 53177-0902

BRANDL, JOHN EDWARD, public affairs educator; b. Aug. 19, 1937; m. Rochelle Jankovich; children: Christopher, Mary Katherine, Amy. BA in Econs. with honors, St. John's U., Collegeville, Minn., 1959; MA in Econs., Harvard U., 1962, PhD in Econs., 1963. Lectr. econs. Boston Coll., 1961-62; systems analyst Office of Sec. Def., Washington, 1963-65; asst. prof. econs. St. John's U., Collegeville, 1965-67; asst. prof., rsch. assoc. Inst. for Rsch. on Poverty, dir. Systematic Analysis Program U. Wis., Madison, 1967-68; dep. asst. sec. HEW, Washington, 1968-69; from assoc. prof. to prof. pub. affairs U. Minn., Mpls., 1969—, dir. sch. pub. affairs, 1969-76, dean Hubert H. Humphrey Inst. Pub. Affairs, 1997—2002; rep. State of Minn., Mpls., 1977-78, 81-86, senator, 1987-90. Exec. bd. Ctr. for Policy Rsch. in Edn., 1986-96; vis. lectr. dept. econs. U. Philippines, 1968; vis. prof. pub. adminstrn. and pub. policy U. Sydney, Australia, 1973; teaching fellow dept. econs. Warsaw Sch. Econs., 1992-95. Author: Money and Good Intentions are Not Enough, 1998; (with A. aftalin) Twin Cities Regional Strategy, 1981; co-editor: Public Policy and Educating Handicapped Persons, 1982; mem. editl. bd. Urban Affairs Quarterly, 1971-74, Sage Profl. Papers Adminstrv. Scis., 1972-76, Jour. Policy Analysis and Mgmt., 1981—; cons. editor Improving College and University Teaching, 1979-82; contbr. articles to pprofl. jours. Bd. dirs. Tri-Cap Community Action Agy. Inc., Mpls., 1966-67; trustee Mpls. Soc. Fine Arts, 1983-86; pres. Twin Cities Citizens' League, 1993; nat. adv. coun. St. John's U., Minn., 1975-91; chmn. Twin Cities Met. Coun. Cable TV Adv. Com., 1972-73, mem. FCC Cable Adv. Coun., 1972-73, Minn. State Planning Adv. Com., 1971-73, Gov.'s Adv. Com. on Mgmt. and Personnel Devel., 1971-76, Gov.'s Coun. of Econ. Advisors, 1971-76; Mem. study group Nat. Assessment of Student Achievement., 1986, Nat. Tchrs. Coun. Edn. Testing Svc., 1986-92, Nat. Commn. Indsl. Innovation, 1984-86; bd. dirs. policy studies orgns., 1985-90; asst. majority leader Minn. Ho. of Rep., 1983-84, minority caucus steering com., 1985-86; bd. regents St. John's U., Minn, 1991-2000. Recipient Presdl. prize Am. Evaluation Assn., 1988, Disting. Svc. award Nat. Govs. Assn., 1996 Fordham Found. prize for excellence in edn., 2005. Fellow Nat. Acad. Pub. Adminstrn.; mem. NIMH (rsch. edn. adv. com. 1980-84), Assn. for Pub. Policy Analysis and Mgmt. (v.p. 1983-84, pres. 1986-87), Am. Soc. Pub. Adminstrn. (bd. dirs. Minn. chpt. 1975-76), Cath. Econ. Assn. (coun. dirs. 1968), Harvard Grad. Soc. (coun. 1988-91), Delta Epsilon Sigma.

BRANDMAIER, JEFF, diversified financial services company executive; MS in Info. Sys., Stockton State Coll.; MBA in Fin., Pace U. Mgmt. IBM; sr. mgr. KPMG Nolan, orton & Co.; chief info. officer The Money Store, 1995—2001; sr. v.p., chief info. officer H&R Block, Inc., Kans. City, Mo., 2001—. Avocation: amateur competitive equestrian. Office: H&R Block 4400 Main St Kansas City MO 64111

BRANDON, DAVID A., food service executive; b. 1952; m. Jan Brandon. AB, tchg. cert., U. Mich., 1974. With Procter & Gamble Distbg. Co., 1974-79, GFV Comm., Inc., 1979-83, COO, exec. v.p., dir., 1983-86; COO, exec. v.p., pres., dir. Valassis Inserts, Inc., Livonia, Mich., 1986—99; pres., CEO Valassis Communication, Inc., Livonia, Mich., 1989—99, chmn., 1997—98; chmn., CEO Domino's Pizza, Inc., Ann Arbor, Mich., 1999—. Bd. dirs. TJX Cos., Burger King Corp., 2003—, Kaydon Corp. Bd. regents U. Mich., 1999—2006; bd. dirs. Detroit Renaissance, Purple Rose Theatre Co. Office: Dominos Pizza Inc 30 Frank Lloyd Wright Dr PO Box 997 Ann Arbor MI 48106-0997 Business E-Mail: brandod@dominos.com. E-mail: dabran@umich.edu.

BRANDT, DEBORAH, English educator; BA in English with highest distinction, Rutgers U., 1974; MA in English, Ind. U., 1981, PhD in English, 1983. Assoc. instr.dept. English Ind. U., 1979-81; asst. prof. dept. English U. Wis., Madison, 1983-90, assoc. prof. English, dir. intermediat composition dept. English, 1990—. Rep. Madison campus working group writing instrn. and assessment Alliance Undergrad. Edn., 1988-92; reviewer Harcourt Brace Jovanovich, So. Ill. U. Press, U. Wis. Press, U. Pitts. Press. Author: Literacy as Involvement: The Acts of Writers, Readers, and Texts, 1990, Literacy in American Lives, 2001 (U. Louisville Grawemeyer award in Edn., 2003); co-editor: Written Comm., 1993— (David H. Russell award Disting Rsch. Tchr. Eng. 1993); asst. editor: Coll. English, 1981-83; assoc. editor: First Labor, 1980; poetry editor: Indiana Writers, 1979; contbr. numerous chpts. to books, articles to profl. jours. Literacy vol. project Jamaa, Madison Urban League, Wis. Recipient Louisville Grawemeyer award, 2003. Mem. Am. Fedn. Tchrs., Nat. Coun. Tchrs. English (exec. com. conf. on coll. composition and comm., Promising Researcher award 1984), Nat. Coun. Rsch. in English, Midwest Modern Lang. Assn. (Writing in Coll. sect. adv. com. 1986-89, sec., acting chair 1984-85). Office: U Wisconsin Dept English 6185 Helen C White Hall 600 N Park St Madison WI 53706

BRANDT, DONALD EDWARD, utilities company executive; b. St. Louis, July 22, 1954; s. Edward H. and Margaret E. (Hertling) b.; m. Jeanine M. Pulay, Nov. 1, 1986; 1 child, Matthew. BSBA, St. Louis U., 1975. CPA, Mo. Audit mgr. Price Waterhouse, St. Louis, 1975-83; sr. v.p. fin. and corp. svc. Union Electric Co., St. Louis, 1983—. Mem. Fin. Execs. Inst., Am. Inst. CPA's, Mo. Soc. CPA's. Clubs: Mo. Athletic (St. Louis). Roman Catholic. Office: Ameren Corporation 1901 Chouteau Ave Saint Louis MO 63103-3003

BRANDT, IRA KIVE, pediatrician, geneticist; m. Dorothy Godfrey; children: Elizabeth, Laura, William, Rena. AB, NYU, 1942; MD, Columbia U., 1945. Diplomate Am. Bd. Pediatrics, Am. Bd. Med. Genetics. Intern Morrisania City Hosp., NYC, 1945-46; resident Lincoln Hosp., NYC, 1948-50; fellow pediatrics Yale U., New Haven, 1955-57, asst. prof., 1957-61, assoc. prof., 1961-68; chmn. dept. pediatrics Children's Hosp., San Francisco, 1968-70; clin. prof. pediatrics U. Calif., San Francisco, 1970; prof. pediatrics and med. genetics Ind. U. Sch. Medicine, Indpls., 1970-89, prof. emeritus, 1989—. Served to capt. U.S. Army, 1946-47, 52 Mem. Am. Pediatric Soc., Am. Acad. Pediatrics, Soc. Pediatric Rsch., Soc. Inherited Metabolic Disorders, Am. Soc. Human Genetics, Am. Coll. Med. Genetics. Office: Ind U Sch Medicine Dept Pediatrics 702 Barnhill Dr # 0907 Indianapolis IN 46202-5128 Business E-Mail: ibrandt@iupui.edu.

BRANDT, JOHN REYNOLD, editor, journalist; b. Amarillo, Tex., Aug. 25, 1959; s. Reynold Francis Jr. and Patricia Levonne (Wallace) B.; m. Svetlana Stevovich, May 28, 1989; children: Emma Evangeline Stevovich Brandt, Aidan Reynold Stevovich Brandt. BA, Case Western Reserve U., Cleve., 1981. Sales rep. Merrell Dow Pharmaceuticals, Cleve., 1982-84, Miles Pharmaceuticals, Cleve., 1984-88, Tokos Perinatal Nursing Svcs., Cleve., 1988-89; sr. assoc. M. Zunt Assocs., Cleve., 1989-90; dir. mgmt. devel. CSA Health System, Cleve., 1990-91; assoc. editor Corp. Cleve. Mag., 1991-94; from exec. editor to pub. IndustryWeek Mag., Cleve., 1994—2000; chief editl. dir. Exec. Mag., 2000—03, pres., pub., 2001—03; pres. John R. Brandt, Inc., 2000—; CEO MPI Group, Inc., 2003—. V.p. Inst. Environ. Edn., Cleve., 1990-91. Bd. dirs. Work in N.E. Ohio Coun., 1997—; judge Workforce Excellence Awards of Nat. Assn. Mfrs., 1997-2000, Am. Bus. Media Neal awards, 2000. Recipient numerous awards in field from Am. Bus. Press, Assn. of Area Bus. Publs., The Press Club of Cleve., March of Dimes, Am. Soc. Bus. Press Editors. Mem. Press Club of Cleve. (dir. 1994-2001, v.p. 1996-98, pres. 1998-99). Office: 2835 Sedgewick Rd Cleveland OH 44120-1837 Office Phone: 216-991-8390. Personal E-mail: jbrandt@mpi-group.net.

BRANDT, WILLIAM ARTHUR, JR., consulting executive; b. Chgo., Sept. 5, 1949; s. William Arthur and Joan Virginia (Ashworth) B.; m. Patrice Bugelas, Jan. 19, 1980; children: Katherine Ashworth, William George, Joan Patrice, John Peter. BA with honors, St. Louis U., 1971; MA, U. Chgo., 1972, postgrad., 1972-74. Asst. to pres. Pyro Mining Co., Chgo., 1972-74; commentator Sta. WBBM-AM, Chgo., 1977; with Melaniphy & Assocs., Inc., Chgo., 1975-76; pres., CEO, cons. Devel. Specialists, Inc., Chgo., 1976—. Mem. adv. bd. Sociol. Abstracts, Inc., San Diego, 1979-83; chair, Ill. Fin. Authority 2008-. Contbr. articles to profl. jours. Bd. Trustees, Loyola U., Chgo.; Nat. Advisory Council, Inst. Govt. Studies, U. Calif. at Berkeley; bd. dirs, Bay Area Bankrupt Forum., Future Music, Inc.; Life trustee Fenwick H.S.; trustee Comml. Law League of Am., Internat. Coun. Shopping Ctrs., Nat. Assn. Bankruptcy Trustees, Ill. Sociol. Assn., Midwest Sociol. Soc., Urban Land Inst., Am. Bankruptcy Inst.; mem. Fla. del. to Dem. Nat. Conv., 1996, also mem. Dem. Party Platform Com., 2000. LaVerne Noyes scholar, 1971-74. Mem. Am. Bankruptcy Inst., Internat. Assoc. Restructuring, Insolvency and Bankrupty Profls.; Am. Sociol. Assn., Amelia Island Plantation Club, Union League Club Chgo., City Club of Miami, gov. mem. Chicago Symphony, Clinton/Gore '96 Natl. Finance Bd., mnging. trustee Democratic Natl. Comm., maj. trust mem. Democratic Senatorial Campaign Comm., Zoological Soc. Miami Metro Zoo (life), Mich. Shores Club. Democrat. Roman Catholic. Office: 26 Broadway New York NY 10004 also: 345 California St Ste 1150 San Francisco CA 94104 also: 70 West Madison St, Ste 2300 Chicago IL 60602 also: 333 South Grand Ave Ste 4070 Los Angeles CA 90071 also: Ill Fin Authority 180 N Stetson #2555 Chicago IL 60601 Office Phone: 312-263-4141. Office Fax: 312-651-1350, 312-651-1300.

BRANSFIELD, JOAN, principal; Prin. Sch. St. Mary, Lake Forest, Ill. Recipient Elem. Sch. Recognition award U.S. Dept Edn., 1989-90, Nat. Disting. Prin. award, 1998. Office: Sch of St Mary 185 E Illinois Rd Lake Forest IL 60045-1915

BRANSON, TIMOTHY E., lawyer; b. 1960; BA in Polit. Sci. and Econ. with honors, U. Wis., Madison, 1983; JD with distinction, U. Iowa, 1986. Bar: Minn. 1986. Assoc. Dorsey & Whitney LLP, Mpls., 1986—93, ptnr., trial group, co-chair, ERISA litig., 1994—. Adj. prof. Hamline Law Sch., 1993. Office: Dorsey & Whitney LLP Ste 1500 50 S Sixth St Minneapolis MN 55402-1498 Office Phone: 612-343-7920. Office Fax: 612-340-8856. Business E-Mail: branson.tim@dorsey.com.

BRANSTAD, TERRY EDWARD, healthcare facility executive, former governor; b. Leland, Iowa, Nov. 17, 1946; s. Edward Arnold and Rita (Garl) B.; m. Christine Ann Johnson, June 17, 1972; children: Eric, Allison, Marcus. BA, U. Iowa, 1969; JD, Drake U., 1974; LHD (hon.), U. Osteopathic Med. & Health Svc., Buena Vista Coll., Marycrest Coll.; LLD (hon.), Clarke Coll., Dubuque. Bar: Iowa. Sr. ptnr. firm Branstad-Schwarm, Lake Mills, Iowa, until 1982; farmer Lake Mills; mem. Iowa Ho. of Reps., 1973-78; lt. gov. State of Iowa, 1979-82, gov., 1983-99; chmn. Edn. Commn. of the US, 1997—98; founder Branstad & Assocs., West Des Moines, 1999; former ptnr. Kayfman, Patee, Branstad & Miller, Washington; former fin. advisor Robert W. Baird & Co.; chmn. Pres. Commn. for Excellence in Spl. Edn., 2001—03; pres., CEO Des Moines U. Osteopathic Med. Ctr., Des Moines, 2003—. Bd. dirs. Am. Legion of Iowa Found., Iowa Health Sys., Cementech, Featherlite, Liberty Bank, Living History Farms, Advanced Analytical Tech., Inc., vis. prof., U. Iowa. With US Army, 1969—71. Decorated Army commendation medal. Mem. Nat. Govs. Assn. (chmn., 1989), Rep. Govs. Assn. (task chair, 1997), Midwestern Govs. Assn., Midwest Gov. Conf. (chmn. 1986-87), Coun. State Govts. (chmn. 1991), Am. Inst. CPAs (pub. mem. 2003), Am. Legion, Farm Bur., U. Iowa Alumni Assn. (Disting. Alumni award, 1999), Alpha Gamma Rho, Lions, KC, Des Moines Rotary (hon.), Sons of Norway. Republican. Roman Catholic.*

BRASHEAR, KERMIT ALLEN, state legislator, lawyer; b. Crawford, Nebr., Mar. 16, 1944; s. Kermit A. and Marguerite (Pokorny) B.; m. Susan Wolf (div.); 1 child, Kermit A. III; m. Kathleen K. Wellman, Aug. 9, 1971; children: Kurth A., Kord A. BA, U. Nebr., 1966, JD, 1969. Bar: Nebr. 1969, Tex. 1994, Colo. 1996, U.S. Dist. Ct. Nebr. 1969, U.S. Ct. Appeals (8th cir.) 1976, U.S. Supreme Ct. 1976, U.S. Ct. Appeals (10th cir.) 1982, U.S. Tax Ct. 1987, U.S. Dist. Ct. (ea. dist.) Mich. 1987, U.S. Dist. Ct. Ariz. 1995. Ptnr. Nelson & Harding, Omaha, 1969-88, Heron, Burchette et al., Omaha, 1989, Brashear & Ginn, Omaha, 1990—; mem. ebr. Legislature from 4th dist., Lincoln, 1995—. Spl. asst. atty. gen. State of Nebr., 1977-90. Mem. Republican Nat. Com., 1983-85; chmn. Nebr. Republican Party, 1983-85; candidate Republican Gubernatorial Nomination, Nebr., 1986. Lutheran.

BRASHEARS, DONALD ROBERT, advertising agency executive; b. Mexico, Mo., May 23, 1947; s. Robert Vaughn and Gail Curtis (Dollins) B.; m. Deborah Jane Williams, Dec. 20, 1969; children: Michelle, Matthew, Joshua, Katherine, Emily. BA in Psychology, Ctrl. Meth. Coll., Fayette, Mo., 1969; BJ in Advt., U. Mo., 1971. Acct. exec. J.B. Neiser & Co., San Diego, 1971-76; v.p., acct. supr., mgmt. supr. Marsteller Inc., LA, 1976-79, group v.p. Chgo., 1979-86; sr. v.p. Cramer-Krasselt, Chgo., 1986-93, exec. v.p., gen. mgr., 1993—, bd. dirs. Milw., 1993—. Recipient Clio award, 1987, Effie award, 1994. Republican. Baptist. Avocations: golf, tennis, running. Office: Cramer-Krasselt 225 N Michigan Ave Ste 800 Chicago IL 60601-7690 E-mail: dbrashea@c-k.com.

BRASITUS, THOMAS ALBERT, gastroenterologist, educator; b. Bridgeport, Conn., Aug. 2, 1945; s. Albert Joseph and Mary Frances (Gazdowskas) B.; m. Christine Ann Legace, Aug. 19, 1967; children: Kristie, Thomas Jr. BA, U. Conn., 1963; MD, Jefferson Med. Sch., Phila., 1967. Asst. prof. Columbia U., NYC, 1977-83; assoc. prof. U. Chgo., 1983-86, prof., 1986—, Walter Lincoln Palmer disting. sci. prof. of medicine, 1987—. Dir. sect. of gastroenterology U. Chgo., 1985—. Contbr. numerous articles to profl. and sci. jours., 1973—. Bd. dirs. Gastrointestinal Rsch. Found., Chgo., 1985—. Maj. USAF, 1975-77. Recipient Merit award Nat. Cancer Inst./NIH, 1986—. Mem. Am. Assn. Physicians, Am. Soc. for Clin. Investigation, Am. Soc. for Biochemistry and Molecular Biology, Chgo. Soc. Gastrointestinal Endoscopy (pres. 1989-90), Chgo. Soc. Gastroenterology (pres. 1990-91). Avocations: sports, travel, bridge. Office: U Chgo Kirsner Ctr Study Digestive Diseases 5841 S Maryland Ave Chicago IL 60637-1463 Home: 21 Morley Rd Cooperstown NY 13326-6516

BRASS, ALAN W., healthcare executive; MS in Hosp. and Health Svc. Adminstrn., Ohio State U., 1973. Pres., CEO Pro Medica Health Sys., 1998—. Recipient Pub. Health Svc. Traineeship award, 1973. Fellow Am. Coll. Healthcare Execs. Office: 2121 Hughes Dr Toledo OH 43606-3845

BRATER, DONALD CRAIG, dean, educator; b. Oak Ridge, Tenn., 1945; m. Stephanie Brater; 1 child, Aimee. BA in chemistry, Duke U., 1967; MD in pharmacy, Duke U. Med. Sch., 1971. Intern Duke U., 1970—71; resident in medicine U. Calif., San Francisco, 1971—73, fellow in clin. pharmacology, 1973—76; mem. faculty Southwestern Med. Sch.; joined faculty Ind. U. Sch. Medicine, 1986, chmn. dept. medicine, John B. Hickam prof. medicine, prof. pharmacology and toxicology, 1990—2000, Walter J. Daly prof., 2000—, dean, 2000—. Pres. U.S. Pharmacopoeia; bd. mgrs. Inproteo, Indpls.; adj. faculty mem. Purdue U. Sch. Pharmacy; active with Indpls. U. Sch. Medicine program in Kenya. Recipient Duke Med. Alumni Award, 2000, Friends of Pharmacy Award, Purdue U. Sch. Pharmacy, 2003. Mem.: Assn. Profs. Medicine, Am. Soc. Clin. Pharmacology and Therapeutics, Assn. Am. Physicians, Am. Soc. Clin. Investigation. Office: Ind U Sch Medicine 1120 W South Dr Fesler Hall Indianapolis IN 46202-5114

BRATHWAITE, ORMOND DENNIS, chemistry professor; b. Parish Land, Barbados, Jan. 19, 1956; s. Dennis Berisford and Erin Eulene (Forde) B.; m. Maria Roslyn Alleyne, May 28, 1983; children: Marcus, Shayna. BS in Med. Tech., York Coll., 1982; MA in Biochemistry, CCNY, 1985; PhD in Biochemistry, CUNY, 1991. Phlebotomy technician, med. technologist intern Brookdale Hosp. Med. Ctr., Bklyn., 1981—84; adj. instr. CCNY, NYC, 1985—91; asst. rsch. scientist Borough Manhattan CC, NYC, 1991—94; asst. prof. chemistry and biology Cuyahoga CC, Highland Hills, Ohio, 1994—. Adj. instr. Bklyn. Coll., 1982-83; adj. prof. biology Kean Coll. NJ, Union, 1988-89; vis. scientist dept. cancer biology Cleve. Clinic Found., 1994-95. Recipient US Prof. of Yr. award, Carnegie Found. for Advancement of Tchg. and Coun. for Advancement and Support of Edn., 2006. Avocations: ping pong/table tennis, running, swimming, gardening, reading. Office: Cuyahoga CC 4250 Richmond Rd Highland Hills OH 44122-6104 Office Phone: 216-987-2401. E-mail: Ormond.Brathwaite@tri-c.edu.

BRAUCH, WILLIAM LELAND, lawyer; B, U. Wis., Milw., 1980; JD, U. Iowa, 1987. Asst. atty. gen. Consumer Protection Divsn., Des Moines, 1987-95, spl. asst. atty. gen., dir., 1995—. Pres. Beaver Dale Neighborhood Assn. Recipient Consumer Advocate award Nat. Assn. Consumer Advocates. Mem. ABA (vice-chmn. consumer protection commn.), Polk County Bar Assn. Office: Consumer Protection Divsn Hoover State Office Bldg Fl 2 Des Moines IA 50319-0001

BRAUER, KEITH E., medical products executive; b. Palatine, Ill. BS, Ind. U., 1970; MBA, U. Mich., 1973. Assoc. fin. analyst, internat. oper. Eli Lilly, 1974—76, staff fin. analyst, pharm. divsn., 1976—77, mktg. analyst, 1977—78, dir. corp. affairs, 1986—88, exec. dir. internat. fin., 1988, exec. dir., fin. and chief acctg. officer; bus. planning coord. Eli Lilly, Med. Devices, Diagnostics Divsn., 1978—81, admin.; contr. Elizabeth Arden, Inc. (formerly Lilly subs.), 1981—84; v.p., fin. treas. Physio-Control Corp., Lilly subs., Redmond, Wash., 1984—86; v.p., CFO Guidant Corp., Indpls., 1994—. Mem. adv. bd. U. Mich. Bus. Sch. Corp.; chmn. bd. dirs. and fin. com. Cmty. Hosp. Ind., Inc.; bd. trustee Ind. Mus. Art. Mem.: Fin. Exec. Inst., Beta Gamma Sigma.

BRAUN, BRUCE, lawyer; BA, Haverford Coll., 1985; JD, U. Va., 1989. Bar: Ill., US Dist. Ct., No. Dist. Ill. Law clk. to Honorable Joel M. Flaum, US Ct. Appeals, Seventh Circuit, 1989—90, to Honorable William H. Rehnquist, Chief Justice, US Supreme Ct., 1990—91; assoc., ptnr. Winston and Strawn LLP, 1991—. Lectr. Loyola U. Law Sch., 1992—98; adj. prof. appellate practice Northwestern U. Sch. Law, 2002—. Pres. CARPLS (Cook County Legal Aid Hotline). Office: Winston and Strawn LLP 35 W Wacker Dr Chicago IL 60601-9703 Office Phone: 312-558-5600.

BRAUN, JOSEPH J., lawyer; b. Cin., Aug. 6, 1973; BA, U. Ky., 1994; JD, U. Toledo, 1998. Bar: Ohio 1998, US Dist. Ct. Southern Dist. Ohio 2000. Prosecutor Mayor's Ct., Wyoming, Ohio; assoc. Strauss & Troy. Mem. Clermont County Mental Health Bd., 1998—99; trustee Clermont County Pub. Libr., 1999—. Named one of Ohio's Rising Stars, Super Lawyers, 2006. Mem.: Assn. Trial Lawyers Am., Ohio Trial Lawyers Assn., Cin. Bar Assn., Ohio State Bar Assn., ABA. Office: Strauss & Troy Federal Reserve Bldg 150 E 4th St Cincinnati OH 45202-4018 Office Phone: 513-621-2120. Office Fax: 513-241-8259.

BRAUN, ROBERT CLARE, retired association and advertising executive; b. Indpls., July 18, 1928; s. Ewald Elsworth and Lila (Inman) B. BS in journalism-advtg., Butler U., 1950; postgrad., Ind. Univ., 1957-66. Reporter Northside Topics Newspaper, Indpls., 1949; advt. mgr., 1950; asst. mgr. Clarence E. Crippen Painting Co., Indpls., 1951; corp. sec. Auto-Imports, Ltd., Indpls., 1952-53; pres. O.R. Brown Paper Co., Indpls., 1953-69; pres., chief exec. ofcr. Robert C. Braun Advt. Agy., 1959-70; with Zimmer Engraving Inc., Indpls, IN, 1964-69; former chmn. bd. O.R. Brown Paper, Inc. Advtg. cons. Rolls Royce Motor Cars, 1957-59, exec. dir., CEO Historic Landmarks Found., Ind., 1969-73, exec. v.p. Purchasing Mgmt. Assn., Indpls., 1974-85, Midwest Office Systems abd Equipment Show, 1974-85, Grand Valley Indsl. Show, 1974-85; Evansville Indsl. Show, 1982-85, Ind Bus. Opportunity Fair, 1985-88. Author: The Mr. Eli Lilly That I Knew, 1977. Editor: Historic Landmarks News, 1969-74; Hoosier Purchaser mag., 1974-85, I.R.M.S.D.C. News, 1985-88. Contbr. articles to profl. jours. Chmn. Citizens' Adv. Com. to Marion County Met. Planning Dept., 1963; pres. museum com. Indpls. Fire Dept., 1966-76; mem. adv. com. Historic Preservation Commn. Marion County, 1967-73; Midwestern artifacts cons. to curator of White House, Wash., 1971-73; mem. chmn. Mayor's Contract Compliance Adv. Bd., 1977-91; mem. Mayor's subcom. for Indpls. Stadium, 1981-83; adv. bd., exec. com. Indpls. Office Equal Opportunity 1982—; mem. Ind. Minority Bus. Opportunity Counc., 1985-88; mem. Met. Mus. Art, Indpls. Mus. of Art bd. dirs. Historic Landmarks Found. Ind., 1960-69; dir., sec. Ind. Arthritis and Rheumatism Found., 1960-67, pres., 1969, dir., 1970-90, hon. lifetime dir., 1992—, dir. Assoc. Patient Svcs., 1976-91, dir. emeritus, 1992; pres. Amanda Wasson Meml. Trust, 1961-72. Recipient Meritorious Svc. awd. St. Jude's Police League, 1961; citation for meritorious svc. Am. Legion Police Post 56, 1962; Tafflinger-Holiday Park appreciation awd., 1973; Nat. Vol. Svc. Citation, Arthritis Found., 1979; Margaret Egan Meml. awd. Ind. Arthritis Found., 1980; Indpls. Profl. Fire Fighters meritorious svc. awd., 1982. Mem. Marion County Hist. Soc. (dir. 1964—, pres. 1965-69, 74-76, 1st v.p. 1979), Am. Guild Organists (mem. Indpls. chpt., charter mem. Franklin Coll. br.), Indpls. Humane Soc., Ind. Mus. Soc. (treas., dir. 1967-74), Internat. Fire Buff Assocs., Indpls. Second Alarm Fire Buffs (sec.-treas. 1967, pres. 1969), Ind. Hist. Soc., Nat. Hist. Soc., Nat. Trust Historic Preservation, Smithsonian Assn., Friends of Cast Iron Architecture, Soc. Archtl. Historians, Am. Heritage Soc., N.A.P.M. Editors Grp. (nat. sec. 1979-81, nat. chmn./pres. 1981-84), Am. Assn. State and Local History, Decorative Arts Soc. Indpls., Ind. Soc. Assn. Execs., Nat. Assn. Purchasing Mgmt. (W.L. Beckham internat. pub. rels. awd. 1983), purchasing Mgmt. Assn. Indpls. (dir. 1974—), Victorian Soc. Am. (nat. sec. 1971-74), Lambda Chi Alpha, Alpha Delta Sigma, Sigma Delta Chi, Tau Kappa Alpha. Club: Indpls. Press, Rolls-Royce Owners. Home: 1415 W 52nd St Indianapolis IN 46228-2316 Personal E-mail: rbraun1@comcast.net.

BRAUN, WILLIAM JOSEPH, life insurance underwriter; b. Belleville, Ill., May 21, 1925; s. Walter Charles and Florence (Lauer) B.; m. Elizabeth Ann Braun, July 7, 1951; children: Brian William (dec.), Roger Edward, Christopher Burnes, Thomas Barrett, Maura Tracey. BS in Mktg, U. Ill., 1949; grad., Inst. Life Ins. Mktg., So. Methodist U., 1950. CLU; chartered fin. cons.; accredited estate planner Nat. Assn. Estate Planners. Life underwriter Mass. Mut. Life Ins. Co., Decatur, Ill., 1949—. Pres. Am. Soc. C.L.U.s, 1976-77; bd. dirs. Am. Coll. C.L.U.s, Bryn Mawr, Pa., 1975-78 Served with USNR, 1943-46. Decorated Navy Air medal; recipient Lifetime Achievement award Mass. Mut. Fin. Group, 2005. Life mem. Million Dollar Round Table; Nat. Assn. Life Underwriters, Nat. Assn. Estate Planning Couns. (pres. 1985-86), KC, Decatur Club, Country Club Decatur, Decatur Athletic Club. Roman Catholic. Home: 4606 E Powers Blvd Decatur IL 62521-2549 Office: Mass Mutual Decatur Club Bldg 158 W Prairie Decatur IL 62523-1230 Home Phone: 217-428-1635; Office Phone: 217-429-4351.

BRAUNSTEIN, MARY, energy consulting company executive; AD in Elec. Engring., U. Cin., 1966. Project mgr. elec. & gas metering, customer billing; with Elec. distbn. & Engring.; mgr. info. tech. Cadence Networks, Cin. Trainer, mentor Rehab. Program Data Processing, U. Cin. Recipient J.H. Randolph award, 1993. Mem. Assns. Systems Mgmt. (past pres.). Office: Cadence Networks 105 E 4th St Ste 250 Cincinnati OH 45202-4006

BRAVERMAN, HERBERT LESLIE, lawyer; b. Buffalo, Apr. 24, 1947; s. David and Miriam P. (Cohen) B.; m. Janet Marx, June 11, 1972; children: Becca Danielle, Benjamin Howard. BS in Econs., U. Pa., Phila., 1969; JD, Harvard U., Cambridge, Mass., 1972. Bar: Ohio 1972, US Dist. Ct. Ohio 1972, US Supreme Ct. 1975, US Ct. Appeals (6th cir.) 1980, US Ct. Claims 1980. Assoc. Hahn, Loeser, Freedheim, Dean & Wellman, Cleve., 1972-75; sole practice Cleve., 1975-87; ptnr. Porter, Wright, Morris & Arthur, Cleve., 1987—96, Walter & Haverfield LLP, Cleve., 1996—. Councilman Orange Village, Ohio, 1988—, pres., 1998-01. Capt. USAR, 1970—82. Fellow Am. Coll. Trust and Estate Counsel; mem. ABA, Ohio Bar Assn., Bar Assn. Greater Cleve. (former chmn. estate planning trust and probate sect.), Suburban East Bar Assn. (pres. 1978-80), Rotary (Cleveland Heights pres. 1980), B'nai Brith (local pres. 1978-84), Wharton Club Cleve. (pres. 1991-2007), Am. Jewish Congress (Ohio pres. 1992—). Avocations: golf, symphony, reading. Home: 3950 Orangewood Dr Cleveland OH 44122-7406 Office: Walter & Haverfield LLP Ste 3500 1301 E 9th St Cleveland OH 44114-1821 also: 2000 Auburn Dr Ste 200 Beachwood OH 44122 Office Phone: 216-928-2903. Personal E-mail: hlblaw@aol.com. Business E-Mail: hbraverman@walterhav.com.

BRAVO, KENNETH ALLAN, lawyer; b. Cleve., July 27, 1942; BS, Rutgers U., 1964; JD cum laude, Ohio State U., 1967. Bar: Ohio 1967, D.C. 1967. Trial atty. Criminal Divsn., U.S. Dept. Justice, 1967-69, spl. atty., 1969-79; ptnr. Benesch, Friedlander, Coplan & Aronoff, Cleve., 1979-94; of counsel Ulmer & Berne LLP, Cleve., 1994-96, ptnr., 1997—. Mem. ABA, Ohio Bar Found. (life), Ohio State Bar Assn. (coun. of dels. 1992—, bd. govs. 2001—04), Fed. Bar Assn. (bd. trustees No. dist. Ohio chpt. 2002—), Cleve. Bar Assn. (chmn. fed. ct. com. 1984-85, trustee 2001-02), Cuyahoga County Bar Assn. (chmn. fed. ct. com. 1980-82, chmn. cert. grievance com. 1986-88), Nat. Assn. Criminal Def. Lawyers, Lawyer-Pilots Bar Assn., Jud. Conf. 8th Dist. Ohio (life), Jud. Conf. 6th Cir. U.S. Ct. Appeals (life), Ohio State U. Law Alumni Soc. (pres.). Office: Ulmer & Berne LLP 1660 W 2nd St Ste 1100 Cleveland OH 44113-1454 Home Phone: 216-381-5910; Office Phone: 216-583-7102. Business E-Mail: kbravo@ulmer.com.

BRAXTON, EDWARD KENNETH, bishop; b. Chgo., June 28, 1944; s. Cullen L. and Evelyn Braxton. Studied, Quigley Preparatory Sem., Niles Coll. Sem.; MA, STL, St. Mary of the Lake Sem., Mundelein, Ill.; PhD in Religious Studies, Cath. U., Louvain, Belgium, 1975, STD in Systematic Theology, 1975; post-doctoral fellowship, U. Chgo. Div. Sch., 1975—76. Ordained priest Archdiocese of Chgo., 1970; assoc. pastor Holy Name Cathedral, Chgo., 1970—71, Sacred Heart Parish, Winnetka, Ill., 1971—73, St. Felicitas Parish, Chgo., 1975—76; William A. Coolidge Chair of Ecumenical Thought Harvard U., 1976—77; pastoral ministry St. Paul's Parish, Cambridge, Mass., 1976—77; vis. prof. U. Notre Dame, 1977—78; chancellor for theol. affairs to Bishop James A. Hickey, Cleveland, 1978—80; spl. asst. for theol. affairs to Archbishop James A. Hickey, Washington, 1980—83; scholar in residence N.Am. Coll., Rome, 1983; dir. Calvert House Cath. Student Ctr. U. Chgo., 1983—86; ofcl. theol. cons. to William H. Sadlier Inc., NYC, 1986—92; pastor St. Catherine of Siena Parish, Oak Park, Ill., 1992—95; ordained bishop, 1995; aux. bishop Archdiocese of St. Louis, 1995—2000; bishop Diocese of Lake Charles, La., 2000—05, Diocese of Belleville, Ill., 2005—. Contbr. numerous articles to journals including Harvard Theol. Rev., Theol. Studies, Louvain Studies, Irish Theol. Quarterly, New Cath. Encyclopedia, Origins, Commonweal, America, Nat. Cath. Reporter, and others. Mem. US Conf. Cath. Bishops. (chmn. com. on Am. Coll. Sem. at U. Louvain; mem. com. on liturgy, mem. com. on evangelization) Roman Catholic. Avocations: white-water rafting, travel, reading. Office: Diocese of Belleville Chancery Office 222 S Third St Belleville IL 62220 Office Phone: 618-277-8181. Office Fax: 618-277-0387.*

BRAY, DONALD LAWRENCE, religious organization executive, minister; b. Olwein, Iowa, Oct. 14, 1942; s. Arthur L. and Rachel C. (Archer) B.; m. Joy F. Failing, Aug. 15, 1964; children: Juli, Steven, Jeffrey. BA in Religion, Ind. Wesleyan U., 1964, DD (hon.), 1993; MA in Religion, Olivet Nazarene U., 1965. Ordained to ministry Wesleyan Ch., 1967. Pastor Mich. Dist. Wesleyan Ch., Grand Rapids, Mich., 1965-68; missionary Wesleyan World Missions, Indpls., 1968-77, dir. personnel, 1977-84, asst. gen. sec., 1984-88; dist. supt. Delta dist. Wesleyan Ch., Jackson, Miss., 1988-92; gen. dir. Wesleyan World Missions, Indpls., 1992—. Adj. prof. Wesley Bibl. Sem., Jackson, 1989-92. Author: (tng. manual) Christian Witness, 1985; contbr. articles to profl. jours. Trustee So. Wesleyan U., Central, S.C., 1989-99. Mem. Evang. Fellowship of Mission Agys. (bd. dirs. 1994—), U.S.-World Evang. Fellowship (bd. dirs.), Ind. Wesleyan U. Alumni Assn. (bd. dirs. 1984-86). Office: PO Box 50434 Indianapolis IN 46250-0434

BRAY, JOAN, state legislator; b. Lubbock, Tex., Sept. 16, 1945; m. Carl Hoagland; 2 children. BA, Southwestern U., 1967; MEd, U. Mass., 1971. Former tchr., journalist; former dist. dir. for Congresswoman Joan Kelly Horn; mem. dist. 84 Mo. Ho. of Reps., St. Louis, 1992—. Bd. dirs. Citizens for Modern Transit. Flemming fellow, 1995. Mem. PTO, Nat. Womens Polit. Caucus. Democrat. Home: 7120 Washington Ave Saint Louis MO 63130-4312

BRAY, RICHARD D., state legislator; b. Martinsville, Ind., Mar. 1, 1931; m. Maurine Bray; 3 children. AB, JD, Ind. U. Precinct committeeman; prosecuting atty. Morgan County, 1959-70; chmn. state wages adjustment bd., 1973-74; mem. Ind. Ho. of Reps from 47th dist., 1974-90; mem. county and twp. com. Ind. Ho. of Reps., mem. govt. affairs com., co-chmn. cts. com.; criminal and civil procedures com., elections com., elections com., agrl. and small bus. com.; ranking mem. judiciary com. Ind. Ho. Reps.; mem. Ind. Senate from dist. 37, 1992—; mem. corrections com. Ind. Senate dist. 37, 1992—. Pres. Sheriff Merit Bd., 1971-74. Mem. Masons, Scottish Rite, Shriners, Elks, Moose. Home: 289 E Morgan St Martinsville IN 46151-1546

BRAZELTON, WILLIAM THOMAS, chemical engineer, educator, dean; b. Danville, Ill., Jan. 22, 1921; s. Edwin Thomas and Gertrude Ann (Carson) B.; m. Marilyn Dorothy Brown, Sept. 23, 1943; children— William Thomas, Nancy Ann. Student, Ill. Inst. Tech., 1939-41; BS in Chem. Engring, Northwestern U., 1943, MS, 1948, PhD, 1952. Chem. engr. Central Process Corp., 1942-43; instr. chem. engring. Northwestern U., 1947-51, asst. prof., 1951-53, asso. prof., 1953-63, prof., 1963-91, prof. emeritus, 1991—, chmn. dept., 1955-56, asst. dean Technol. Inst., 1960-61, assoc. dean, 1961-94, acting asst. dean, 1994-96, ret., 1996. Engring. and ednl. cons., 1949— Mem. Prospect Heights (Ill.) Bd. Edn., 1957-61; bd. dirs., exec. com. Chgo. Area Pre-Coll. Program. Recipient Vincent Bendix Minorities in Engring. award ASEE, 1986. Mem. Am. Inst. Chem. Engrs. (chmn. Chgo. sect. 1966-67), Am. Chem. Soc., Am. Soc. Engring. Edn. (chmn. Ill.-Ind. sect. 1963-64, 73-74, Vincent Bendix Minorities in Engring. award, 1986), Soc. for History of Tech., Soc. for Indsl. Archeology, Sigma Xi, Tau Beta Pi, Phi Lambda Epsilon, Alpha Chi Sigma, Triangle. Home: 10 E Willow Rd Prospect Heights IL 60070-1332 Office: Northwestern U Technol Institute Evanston IL 60208-0001 Business E-Mail: wtb@northwestern.edu.

BREAUX, BILLIE J., state legislator; b. June 23, 1936; BS, W.Va. State U.; MS, Ind. U. Tchr. Indpl. Pub. Sch.; mem. Ind. Senate from 34th dist., 1990—; mem. legis. appropriations and elections; mem. natural resources, pensions and labor coms.; mem. corrections, cime and civil program com.; mem. health and environ. affairs com. and pub. policy com. Ind. State Senate Dist. 34. Mem. Indpls. Edn. Assn. (past pres.), Friends of Urban League (pres.), Indpls. Urban League, State Tchrs. Assn. Office: State House 200 W Washington St Indianapolis IN 46204-2728

BRECHT, ROBERT P., bank executive; Mgr. comml. loan dept. Peoples Savs. Bank, 1986-88, sr. v.p., then exec. v.p., 1988; exec. v.p. Firstbancorp. Ohio, Akron, exec. v.p. corp. retail; pres., CEO FirstMerit Peoples Bank, Ashtabula, Ohio. Office: 3 Cascade Plz Ste 7 Akron OH 44308-1124

BRECKENRIDGE, JOANNE, political organization administrator; Attended, Ctrl. Meth. Coll., Fla. U. Mem. Nat. Fedn. Rep. Women, 1975—, mem.-at-large, 1996-97, regent, 4th v.p., dir. region 6, 1988-99, 3d v.p. dir. region 3, 2000-01, regent, 1984-2002. Pres. Mo. Fedn. Rep. Women; club pres. St. Louis Rep. Women Com. Spkr. in field. Co-chair fundraisers for U.S. Congress, State Senate and House candidates; active Bush Campaign, 1996, Dole/Kemp Advance Team, 1996; alternate del. Rep. Nat. Conv., 1976, 84, 92; Mo. Rep. chmn. of youth for Reagan, 1980; pres. Mo. Fedn. Rep. Women, 1992-96, Rep. Women's Club South, 2000; mem. Rep. Com., Concord Twp., 2004—; active Kirkwood Bapt. Ch., mem. mission team to St. Lucia. Joanne Breckenridge Legis. Day scholarships named in her honor by Mo. Fedn. Rep. Women. Office: 5838 Five Oaks Pkwy Saint Louis MO 63128-1403 Fax: 314-416-1954.

BRECKON, DONALD JOHN, academic administrator; b. Port Huron, Mich., June 11, 1939; s. Robert Joseph and Margaret Elizabeth (Wade) B.; m. Sandra Kay Biehn, Sept. 4, 1959; children: Lori E., LeeAnne M., Lisa C., Lynanne U. AA, St. Clair County C.C., 1959; BS, Central Mich. U., 1962, MA, 1963; postgrad., U. Wis., 1965-66, Western Mich. U., 1968; MPH, U. Mich., 1968; PhD, Mich. State U., 1977; D of Pub. Svc. (hon.), Ctrl. Mich. U., 2001. Instr. hrealth edn. Central Mich. U., Mt. Pleasant, 1963-68, asst. prof., 1968-72, assoc. prof., 1972-81, prof. health edn., 1978-81, asst. dean health, phys. edn. and recreation, 1981-82, assoc. dean edn., health and human svcs., 1982-86, dean grad. studies/assoc. provost for rsch., 1986-87; pres. Park Coll./Park U., Parkville, Mo., 1987—2001. Author: Hospital Health Education: A Guide to Program Development, 1982, Community Health Education: Setting, Roles and Skills, 1985, 3d rev. edit., 1994, Microcomputer Applications to Health Education and Health Science, 1986, Matters of Life and Death, 1987, Managing Health Promotion Programs: Leadership Skills for the 21st Century, 1997; contbr. articles to profl. jours. Bd. dirs. St. Lores Northland Hosp. Recipient Central Mich. U. Tchg. Effectiveness awrd, 1975, Disting. Svc. award Mich. Alcoholism and Addiction Assn., 1977, Disting. Alumni award St. Clair County, 1988, Centennial award Ctrl. Mich. U., 1992, Northlander of Yr. award Kans. City Northland regional C. of C.; Mich. Dept. Edn. scholar, 1971, Yale U. Drug Dependence Inst. scholar, 1973, Midwest Inst. Alcohol Studies, Mich. Dept. Pub. Health scholar, 1974; Am. Coun. on Edn. Leadership dEvel. program fellow, 1979. Mem. Mich. Pub. Health Assn. (pres. 1976-77), Am. Pub. Health Assn., Soc. Pub. Health Edn. (pres. 1978-79), Am. Hosp. Assn. (coun. govs.). Home: 7320 NW Katie Cir Kansas City MO 64152-1988 Office: Park Coll Office of Pres Parkville MO 64152

BREE, MARLIN DUANE, publisher, author; b. Norfolk, Nebr., May 16, 1933; s. George F. and Luile Bree; m. Loris Bree; 1 child, William Marlin. BA, cert. in journalism, U. Nebr., 1955. Mng. editor Davidson Pub. Co., 1958-61; editor Greater Mpls. mag., 1962-63; pub. rels. specialist Blue Shield, 1964-67; editor Sunday Mag., Star and Tribune, Mpls., 1968-72; columnist Corp. Report, Mpls., 1973-77; publs. cons., 1978-83; co-founder, ptnr., editorial dir. Marlor Press, Inc., St. Paul, 1983-91, co-owner, pub., 1992—. Chmn. Midwest Book Awards, St. Paul, 1992; judge Boating Writers Internat. Writing Contest, 2005-07. Author: In the Teeth of the Northeaster: A Solo Voyage on Lake Superior, 1988, Call of the North Wind: Voyages and Adventures on Lake Superior, 1996, Wake of the Green Storm: A Survivor's Tale, 2001, Broken Seas: True Tales of Extraordinary Seafaring Adventures, 2005; co-author: Alone Against the Atlantic, 1981, Kid's Travel Fun Book, 2007. Dir. comm. Mpls. Bicentennial Celebration, 1976. With US Army, 1955—57. Named Pub. of Yr., Midwest Ind. Pubs. Assn., 1994; recipient Golden Web award, 2003-04, Writing award Boating Writers Internat., 2003, 07, Grand Prize, Boating Writers Internat., 2004. Mem.: St. Paul Sail and Power Squadron (hon.). Avocation: sailing. Office: Marlor Press Inc 4304 Brigadoon Dr Saint Paul MN 55126-3100 Business E-Mail: marlin.marlor@minn.net.

BREECE, ROBERT WILLIAM, JR., lawyer, investment company executive; b. Blackwell, Okla., Feb. 5, 1942; s. Robert William Breece Sr. and Helen Elaine (Maddox) Breece Robinson; m. Elaine Marie Keller, Sept. 7, 1968; children: Bryan, Justin, Lauren BSBA, Northwestern U., 1964; JD, U. Okla., 1967; LLM, Washington U., St. Louis, 1970. Bar: Oklahoma 1967, Mo. 1970. Pvt. practice, St. Louis, 1968—. Pres., chmn. bd. dirs. Crown Capital Corp., St. Louis. Mem. ABA, Internat. Bar Assn., Mo. Bar Assn., Forest Hills Country Club (pres. 1978), St. Louis Club, Club at Mediterra, Assocs. for Corp. Growth, Commanderie de Bordfaux, Phi Alpha Delta, Beta Theta Pi. Personal E-mail: rwbreece@comcast.net.

BREHL, JAMES WILLIAM, lawyer; BS in Engring., U. Notre Dame, 1956; JD, U. Mich., 1959. Bar: Minn. and various fed. cts. Lawyer Maun & Simon, St. Paul, 1963-2000; law practice and mediation/arbitration Nuetral Svcs., 2000—; of counsel Martin & Squires, St. Paul, 2006—. Contbr. articles to law jours. Mem. Minn. Bar Assn. (exec. com. 1996-97), Ramsey County Bar Assn. (exec. coun. 1977-80, 87-90, pres. 1993-94). Office Phone: 651-767-3745. Personal E-mail: jdbrehl@aol.com.

BREHM, SHARON STEPHENS, psychology professor, former academic administrator; b. Roanoke, Va., Apr. 18, 1945; d. John Wallis and Jane Chappel (Phenix) Stephens; m. Jack W. Brehm, Oct. 25, 1968 (div. Dec. 1979) BA, Duke U., 1967, PhD, 1973; MA, Harvard U., 1968. Clin. psychology intern U. Wash. Med. Ctr., Seattle, 1973-74; asst. prof. Va. Poly. Inst. and State U., Blacksburg, 1974-75, U. Kans., Lawrence, 1975-78, assoc. prof., 1978-83, prof. psychology, 1983-90, assoc. dean Coll. Liberal Arts and Scis., 1987-90; prof. psychology, dean Harpur Coll. of Arts and Scis. SUNY, Binghamton, 1990-96; prof. psychology and interpersonal comm., provost Ohio U., Athens, 1996—2001; v.p. acad. affairs Ind. U., 2001—03, sr. advisor to pres., 2004—05; chancellor Ind. U. Bloomington, 2001—03, prof. dept. psychology, 2001—. Vis. prof. U. Mannheim, 1978, Istituto di Psicologia, Rome, 1989; Fulbright sr. rsch. scholar Ecole des Hautes Etudes en Sciences Sociales, Paris, 1981-82; Soc. for Personality and Social Psychology rep. APA's Coun. of Reps., 1995-2000; chair governing bd. Ohio Learning etwork, 1996-99 Author: The Application of Social Psychology to Clinical Practice, 1976, (with others) Psychological Reactance: A Theory of Freedom and Control, 1981, Intimate Relationships, 1985, 2d edit., 1992, (with others) Social Psychology, 1990, 4th edit., 1999, also numerous articles, and chpts. Mem. APA (fin. com. 1999-2001, 2002-04, pres. elect, 2005-). Office: Ind U 1101 E 10th St Bloomington IN 47405-7000 Personal E-mail: sbrehm@indiana.edu.

BREILLATT, JULIAN PAUL, JR., biochemist, biomedical engineer; b. Pensacola, Fla., Mar. 2, 1938; s. Julian Paul and Ruth (Walser) B.; m. Gaye Sorensen, Apr. 9, 1962; children: Elise, Adrienne, Alain, Andre. BA in Biochem., U. Calif., Berkeley, 1959; PhD in Biochem., U. Utah, 1967. Rsch. assoc. Oak Ridge (Tenn.) Nat. Lab., 1967-69, rsch. scientist, 1967-74, acting dir. molecular anatomy program, 1974-77; rsch. supr. E I DuPont, Wilmington, Del., 1977-78, sr. rsch. chemist, 1978-85; Baxter rsch. scientist Baxter Healthcare Corp., Round Lake, Ill., 1986-90, rsch. dir., 1990-94, sr. rsch. dir., 1994—. Contbr. articles to scientific jours.; patentee in field. Active Boy Scouts Am., 1949—. Recipient IR-100 Indsl. Rsch. award, 1977. Mem. Lds Ch. Office: Baxter Healthcare Corp Baxter Tech Pk Round Lake IL 60073-0490

BREIMAYER, JOSEPH FREDERICK, patent lawyer; b. Belding, Mich., May 4, 1942; s. Ronald and Crystal Helen (Reeves) B.; m. Margaret Anne Murphy, Aug. 26, 1967; children: Kathleen A., Deborah L., Elizabeth L. BEE, U. Detroit, 1965; JD, George Washington U., 1969. Bar: D.C. 1970, N.Y. 1973, Minn. 1975. Cooperative engr. Honeywell Inc, Mpls., 1962-65; patent examiner U.S. Patent and Trademark Office, Washington, 1965-70; patent atty. Eastman Kodak Co., Rochester, NY, 1970-73; sr. patent counsel Medtronic Inc., Mpls., 1973-90; assoc. Fredrikson & Byron, Mpls., 1990-93. Pres. Good Shepherd Home and Sch. Assn., 1984; precinct chmn. Dem. Farmer Labor Party, 1980-82. Mem. Minn. Intellectual Property Law Assn. (treas. 1986). Avocations: boating, skiing, travel. Home: 4700 Circle Down Golden Valley MN 55416-1101 Home Phone: 763-374-9684; Office Phone: 763-528-2831. Personal E-mail: jfbpatent@aol.com.

BREISACH, ERNST A., historian, educator; b. Schwanberg, Austria, Oct. 8, 1923; came to US, 1953; s. Otto and Maria (Eder) B.; m. Herma E. Pirker, Aug. 2, 1945; children: Nora Sylvia, Eric Ernst. PhD in History, U. Vienna, Austria, 1946; D in Econs., Wirtschafts U., 1950. Prof. Realgymnasium Vienna XIV, Austria, 1946-52; assoc. prof. Olivet Coll., Mich., 1953-57; prof. Western Mich. U., Kalamazoo, 1957-96. Author: Introduction to Modern Existentialism, 1962, Caterina Sforza: A Renaissance Virago, 1967, Renaissance Europe, 1300-1517, 1973, Historiography: Ancient, Medieval, and Modern, 1983, 2d edit., 1994, 3rd edit., 2007, American Progressive History, 1993, On the Future of History: The Postmodernist Challenge and Its Aftermath, 2003; editor: Classical Rhetoric and Medieval Historiography, 1985. Nat. Found. for Humanities fellow, 1989-90. Mem. Am. Hist. Assn. Home: 1700 Bronson Way Apt 145 Kalamazoo MI 49009-9108 Office: Western Mich U Dept History Kalamazoo MI 49008 Personal E-mail: ebreisach@sbcglobal.net.

BREITENBECK, JOSEPH M., retired bishop; b. Detroit, Aug. 3, 1914; s. Matthew J. and Mary A. (Quinlan) B. Student, U. Detroit, 1932-35; BA, Sacred Heart Sem., Detroit, 1938; postgrad., Gregorian U., Rome, Italy, 1938-40; S.T.L., Catholic U., Washington; J.C.L., Lateran U., Rome, 1949. Ordained priest Roman Catholic Ch., 1942; asst. at St. Margaret Mary Parish, Detroit, 1942-44; sec. to Cardinal Mooney, 1944-58, Cardinal Dearden, 1959; pastor Assumption Grotto, 1959-67; consecrated bishop, 1965; ordained titular bishop of Tepelta and aux. bishop of Detroit, 1965-69; bishop of Grand Rapids, Mich., 1969-90. Episcopal adviser Nat. Cath. Laymens Retreat Conf. Mem. Nat. Conf. Cath. Bishops (com. chmn.) Home and Office: Chancery Office 660 Burton St SE Grand Rapids MI 49507-3202

BREMER, CELESTE F., judge; b. San Francisco, 1953; BA, St. Ambrose Coll., 1974; JD, Univ. of Iowa Coll. of Law, 1977; EdD, Drake U., 2002. Asst. county atty. Scott County, 1977-79; asst. atty. gen. Area Prosecutors Div., Iowa, 1979; with Carlin, Liebbe, Pitton & Bremer, 1979-81, Rabin, Liebbe, Shinkle & Bremer, 1981-82; with legal dept. Deere and Co., 1982-84; corp. counsel Economy Forms Corp., 1985-89; magistrate judge U.S. Dist. Ct. (Iowa so. dist.), 8th cir., Des Moines, 1984—; ed. D. Drake U. Sch. of Edn., 2002. Instr. Drake Univ. Coll. of Law, 1985—88, 2005—06. Mem. ABA, Fed. Magistrate Judge Assn., Nat. Assn. Women Judges, Am. Judicature Soc., Iowa State Bar Assn. (bd. govs., 1987-90), Iowa Judges Assn., Iowa Supreme Ct. Coun. on Jud. Selection (chmn. 1986-90), Iowa Orgn Women Attys., Polk County Bar Assn., Polk County Women Attys. Office: US Courthouse Ste 435 123 E Walnut St Des Moines IA 50309-2036 Office Phone: 515-284-6200.

BREMER, JOHN M., lawyer; b. 1947; BA, Fordham U., 1969; JD, Duke U., 1974. Bar: Wis. 1974. From atty. law dept. to sr. exec. v.p. Northwestern Mut. Life Ins., Milw., 1974—2002, COO, 2002—. Office: Northwestern Mutual Life Ins Co 720 E Wisconsin Ave Milwaukee WI 53202-4703

BRENDTRO, LARRY KAY, psychologist; b. Sioux Falls, SD, July 26, 1940; s. A. Kenneth and Bernice (Matz) B.; m. Janna Agena, July 14, 1973; children: Daniel Kenneth, Steven Lincoln, Nola Kristine. BA, Augustana Coll., 1961; MS, S.D. State U., 1962; PhD, U. Mich., 1965. Prin. Crippled Children's Hosp. and Sch., Sioux Falls, 1962-63; psychology intern Hawthorn Ctr., Northville, Mich., 1964-65; instr. U. Mich., 1965; asst. prof. U. Ill., Urbana, 1966-67; pres., CEO Starr Commonwealth, Albion, Mich., 1967-81; prof. Augustana Coll., Sioux Falls, S.D., 1981-99; founder Reclaiming Youth Internat., Lennox, SD, 1997—. Mem. U.S. Coordinating Coun. on Juvenile Justice and Delinquency Prevention, 1997—. Co-author: The Other 23 Hours, 1969, Positive Peer Culture, 1974, 1985, Re-educating Troubled Youth, 1983, Reclaiming Youth at Risk, 1990, 2002; co-editor: Reclaiming Children and Youth, 1992—, Reclaiming Our Prodigal Sons and Daughters, 2000, Troubled Children and Youth, 2004, No Disposable Kids, 2005, Kids Who Outwit Adults, 2005, The Resilence Revolution, 2006. Lutheran. Home and Office: Reclaiming Youth Internat PO Box 57 Lennox SD 57039-0057 Office Phone: 605-647-2532. E-mail: courage@reclaiming.com.

BRENNAN, CHARLES MARTIN, III, construction company executive; b. New Haven, Jan. 30, 1942; s. Charles Martin Jr. and Margaret Mary (Gleeson) B.; m. Mary Day Ely, June 22, 1966; children: Elizabeth Brennan Lekberg, Cynthia Brennan Annibali. BA, Yale U., 1964; MBA, Columbia U., 1969. Gen. mgr. New Haven Malleable Iron co., 1966-68; fin. analyst Scovill Mfg. co., 1969-71; treas. Cerro Corp., NYC, 1971-74, Gould Inc., Chgo., 1974-76; mng. dir. Imperial Trans Europe N.V. (46 percent subs. of Gould Inc.), London, 1976-79; v.p. Latin Am. Gould, Inc., Sao Paulo, Brazil, 1979-80, sr. v.p., chief. fin. officer Chgo., 1980-88, also bd. dirs.; chmn., chief exec. officer MYR Group Inc., Rolling Meadows, Ill., 1988—. Bd. dirs. ROHN Industries, Inc., Control Devices Inc., Northwestern Meml. Hosp., Mettawa Open Lands Assn., Lake County Rep. Fedn.; trustee Village of Mettawa, Ill. Mem. Chgo. Club, Comml. Club Chgo., Econ. Club Chgo. Republican. Episcopalian. Avocations: skiing, golf, fly fishing, shooting. Office: The MYR Group Inc 1701 Golf Rd Ste 1012 Rolling Meadows IL 60008-4227

BRENNAN, JAMES JOSEPH, lawyer, bank executive; b. Chgo., July 14, 1950; s. John Michael and Rosemary (Rickard) Brennan; m. Donna Jean Blessing, June 2, 1973; children: Michael James, Laura Jessica. BS, Purdue U., 1972; JD, Indiana U., 1975. Bar: Ind. 1975, U.S. Dist. Ct. (so. dist.) Ind. 1975, U.S. Tax Ct. 1975, U.S. Ct. Appeals (6th cir.) 1976 U. S. Ct. Appeals (4th cir.) 1977, Ill., 1978, U.S. Dist. Ct. (no. dist.) Ill. 1978, U.S. Ct. Appeals (7th cir.) 1978, U.S. Supreme Ct. 1981. Law clk. to judge U.S. Dist. Ct. (ea. dist.), Tenn., 1975-77; ptnr. Pope, Ballard, Shepard & Fowle, Ltd., Chgo., 1977-87, Hopkins & Sutter, Chgo., 1987-91; ptnr., co-chmn. fin. svcs. group Barack, Ferrazzano, Kirschbaum & Perlman, Chgo., 1991-99; exec. v.p. corp. affairs, gen. counsel BankFinancial Corp., 2000—. Chmn. legal affairs com. Ill. Bankers Assn., Chgo., 1986, chmn. bank counsel sect., 1987; lectr. programs for bankers, bank examiners, accts. and bank counsel; participant drafting of various Ill. banking laws; adj. prof. grad. sch. bank law Ill. Inst. Tech. Kent Coll. Law, 1992-2000. Articles editor Ind. Law Rev., 1974—75; editor: Ill. Bankers Assn. Law Watch, 1988—94; contbr. articles to profl. jours. 1st recipient Disting. Bank Counsel award, Ill. Bankers Assn., 1989. Mem. Riverside Golf Club (bd. dirs. 1992-2000, sec.-treas. 1995-98), Western Golf Assn. (bd. dirs. 1998—, Evans Scholars (Purdue chpt. 1968-72, pres. 1970-71). Business E-Mail: jbrennan@bankfinancial.com.

BRENNAN, JOSEPH, lawyer; m. Molly Tschida Brennan; 2 children. Grad., Vanderbilt U.; JD, Ind. U. Ind. contractor Miller, Faucher, Chertow, Cafferty & Wexler, Chgo.; dep. purchasing agent, dir. contracts, asst. corp. counsel City of Chgo.; corp. counsel BlueMeteor Inc., 1999—2001; gen. counsel, sec. T-Systems .Am. Inc., 2001—05; v.p. external affairs, gen. counsel The Field Mus. of Natural History, 2005—. Office: The Field Mus of Natural History 1400 S Lake Shore Dr Chicago IL 60605-2496 Office Phone: 312-922-9410.

BRENNAN, MAUREEN, lawyer; b. Morristown, NJ, Aug. 7, 1949; BA magna cum laude, Bryn Mawr Coll., 1971; JD cum laude, Boston Coll., 1977. Bar: Pa. 1977, U.S. Dist. Ct. (ea. dist.) Pa. 1978, Ohio 1989. Atty. U.S. EPA, Washington, 1977-80; asst. dist. atty. Phila. Trial and Appellate Divs., 1980-84; in-house environ. counsel TRW Inc., 1985-87; assoc. Baker & Hostetler LLP, Cleve., 1987-91, ptnr., 1991—. Adj. prof. Case Western Res. U., Cleve., 1990-92, 00-06. Active Cleve. Tree Commn., 1991-96, co-chair, 1993-95; trustee Clean-Land Ohio, 1990-2000; rep. Canal Heritage Corridor Com., 2000—; mem. Cuyahoga County Greenspace Working Group, 1999-2002; bd. dirs. Crown Point Ecology Ctr., 2001--. Recipient Bronze Medal for Achievement, U.S. EPA, 1980. Mem. ABA (natural resources and environ. sect., standing com. environ law 1996-98), Pa. Bar Assn. (environ. law com.), Ohio State Bar Assn. (environ. law com.), Cleve. Bar Assn. (environ. law sect., chair wetlands com. 1991-92, sect. chair 1996-97, mem. steering com. adv. OEPA on Brownfield regulations 1995-97). Office: Baker & Hostetler LLP 3200 Nat City Ctr 1900 E 9th St Ste 3200 Cleveland OH 44114-3475 Office Phone: 216-861-7957. Business E-Mail: mbrennan@bakerlaw.com.

BRENNAN, NOELLE C., lawyer; JD, DePaul U., 1995. Assoc. Katten Muchin & Zavis; trial atty., supervisory atty. Equal Employment Opportunity Commn.; ptnr. Brennan & Monte Ltd. Adj. prof. employment discrimination; ct. apptr. monitor overseeing hiring practices and compliance with ct. orders City of Chgo. Named one of 40 Under 40, Crain's Chgo. Bus., 2005. Office: Brennan & Monte Ltd Ste 1530 20 South Clark St Chicago IL 60603 Office Phone: 312-422-0001. Office Fax: 312-422-0008. E-mail: nbrennan@brennan-monte.com.

BRENNAN, PATRICIA FLATLEY, nursing and systems engineering educator; b. July 21, 1953; BSN, U. Del., 1975; MSN, U. Pa., 1979; MS in Indsl. Engring., U. Wis., 1984, PhD in Indsl. Engring., 1986. RN, Ohio. Staff nurse surg. ICU Lankenau Hosp., Phila., 1975-76; clin. nurse mgr./practitioner Friends Hosp., Phila., 1976-80; asst. prof. psychiat. nursing Marquette U., Milw., 1980-83; lectr. quantitative analysis U. Wis., Madison, 1984; asst. prof. nursing and systems engring. Frances Payne Bolton Sch. Nursing, Case Inst. Tech., Case Western Res. U., Cleve., 1986-89, assoc. prof., 1989-92; Lillian Moehlman-Bascom prof. nursing U. Wis., Madison, prof., indsl. engring. Mem. health care study sect. Nat. Ctr. Health Svcs. Rsch., 1989—; participant Coun. Nurse Researchers, 1981—, at. Conf. on Nursing Minimum Data Set, Milw., 1985, Nursing Use of Decision Support Workshop, Killarney, Ireland, 1988; guest lectr. Coll. Nursing, U. Wis., 1986, 89; mem. vis. faculty Campus for the Professions, U. Md., 1987, 89, 91, 92, U. Wis., 1989, U. Calgary, Alta., Can., 1989; presenter numerous profl. and ednl. orgns., 1981—. Mem. editorial bd. Computers in Nursing, 1988—; reviewer publs. Symposium on Computer Applications in Med. Care, 1982—, Rsch. in Nursing and Health, 1985—, Tech. MEDINFO86, 1985; contbr. articles to profl. publs. Mem. adv. bd. Sch. Nursing, U. Md., 1986—; active data consortium AIDS Commn. Cleve., 1989; vol. Am. Cancer Soc., 1983-86. Rsch. grantee Marquette U., 1981, Regner Fund, 1982, USPHS, 1982-86, Cleve. Found., 1987, NIH, 1987—, Mellon Found., 1987, Nat. Ctr. Nursing Rsch. 1988-91, Nat. Inst. on Aging, 1989—. Fellow Am. Acad. Nursing; mem. ANA, AACCN (mem. info. systems task force 1986-87), Ohio Nurses Assn. (mem. rsch. assembly, mem. GCNA), Am. Inst. Decision Scis. (mem. membership com., reviewer ann. meetings), Inst. Indsl. Engrs. (chpt. devel. chairperson 1987—), Inst. Medicine, The Mgmt. Sci. Inst.-Ops. Rsch. Soc. Am., Sigma Xi, Sigma Theta Tau. Office: U Wis-Madison K6/346 Clin Sci Ctr 600 Highland Ave Madison WI 53792 also: 372 Mechanical Engineering 1513 University Ave Madison WI 53706 Office Phone: 608-263-5251. Office Fax: 608-262-8454. E-mail: pbrennan@engr.wisc.edu.

BRENNAN, ROBERT LAWRENCE, educational director, psychometrician; b. Hartford, Conn., May 31, 1944; BA, Salem State Coll., 1967; M of Art in Tchg., Harvard U., 1968, EdD, 1970. Rsch. assoc., lectr. Grad. Sch. Edn., Harvard U., Cambridge, Mass., 1970-71; asst. prof. edn. SUNY, Stony Brook, 1971-76; sr. rsch. psychologist Am. Coll. Testing Program, Iowa City, 1976-79, dir. measurement rsch. dept., 1979-84, asst. v.p. for measurement rsch., 1984-92, disting. rsch. scientist, 1990-94. Dir. Iowa Testing Programs, 1994-2002; adj. faculty Sch. Edn. U. Iowa, 1979-94, E.F. Lindquist prof. edn. measurement, 1994—, dir. ctr. for advanced studies in measurement and assessment, 2002—. Author: Elements of Generalizability Theory, 1983, Test Equating Methods and Practices, 1995, Generalizability Theory, 2001, Test Equating, Scaling and Linking Methods and Practices, 2004; editor: Methodology Used in Scaling the Act Assessment and P-ACT, 1989, Cognitively Diagnostic Assessment, 1995, Educational Measurement, 4th edit., 2007; assoc. editor Applied Psychological Measurement, 1982—, Jour. Ednl. Measurement, 1978-83, 96—; contbr. articles to profl. jours. Harvard U. prize fellow, 1967. Fellow: APA; mem.: Iowa Acad. Edn. (pres. 1996—99), Psychometric Soc., Nat. Coun. Measurement Edn. (bd. dirs. 1987—90, v.p. 1995, pres. 1997—98, Tech. Contbn. award 1997, Career Contbn. award 2000), Am. Statis. Assn., Midwestern Ednl. Rsch. Assn. (pres. 1987—88), Am. Ednl. Rsch. Assn. (v.p. 1994—96, Divsn. D award 1980, E.F. Lindquist Career Contbn. award 2004). Home: 1925 Liberty Ln Coralville IA 52241-1071 Office: Univ Iowa 210D Lindquist Ctr Iowa City IA 52242-1533 Office Phone: 313-335-5405. Business E-Mail: robert-brennan@uiowa.edu.

BRENNAN, ROBERT WALTER, association executive; s. Walter R. and Grace A. (Mason) B.; m. Mary J. Engler, June 15, 1962; children: Barbara, Susan (twins). BS Edn., U. Wis., 1957. Tchr., coach Waukesha HS, Wis., 1959-63; asst. track coach U. Wis.-Madison, 1963-69; head track coach, 1969-71; exec. asst. to mayor City of Madison, 1972-73; pres. Greater Madison C. of C., Madison, 1973-2004; cons. U. Wis.-Madison Chancellor's Office, Corp. Rels., 2004—. Mem. adv. council U. Wis.-Madison Sch. Edn., 1984—; mem. Madison Urban League, 1971—; bd. dirs. Cherokee Park, Inc., Wis. Nordic Sports Found.; dir. Wis. C. of C. Execs., 1974-76, Very Slp. Arts-Wis., 1983-2000, World Dairy Ctr. Authority, 1993-95, Wis. Exec. Residence Found., 1993-, Wis. Sesquicentennial Commn., 1998, U. Wis.-Madison Bus. Sch. Weinart Applied Ventures Program, 1997-; chmn. bd. dirs. Wis. Innovation Network, 1987-; sec., treas. Wis. Tech. Coun., 2000-. Second lt. US Army. Named Madison's Favorite Son, 1971; recipient Pen & Mic Club award, 1971, Know Your Madisonian award, 1975, Religious Heritage of Am. award, 1978, Nat. award Family Found. of Am., 1980. Mem. Wis. Alumni Assn. (nat. bd. dirs. 1981-2000, pres. 1985-86, chmn. bd. 1986-87), "W" Club (life, cert. of merit), Downtown Rotary Club (dir. 1974-76), Phi Epsilon Kappa, Theta Delta Chi (life). Home: 5514 Comanche Way Madison WI 53704-1026 Office: Greater Madison C of C 615 E Washington Ave Madison WI 53703-2952 Home Phone: 608-249-1848; Office Phone: 608-263-1394. Personal E-mail: rwbrennan@charter.net. Business E-Mail: rwbrennan@bascom.wisc.edu.

BRENNAN, SCOTT M., lawyer, political organization administrator; b. Des Moines, Iowa, 1962; m. Elizabeth Brennan; children: Alexandra, Joseph. BA, Grinnell Coll., 1985; JD, U. Iowa, 1993. Bar: Iowa 1994. Aide to US Senator Tom Harkin, Washington; sr. shareholder Litigation Divsn. Davis, Brown, Koehn, Shors & Roberts, PC, Des Moines, former pres. bd. dirs. Bd. dirs. Link Assocs.; chair Iowa Dem. Party, 2006—. Chair Polk County Compensation Bd. Named one of 40 community leaders under the age of 40, Des Moines Business Record, 2001. Mem.: 21st Century Forum (bd. dirs., pres.), Polk County Bar (pres.-elect). Democrat. Office: Davis, Brown, Koehn, Shors & Roberts, PC 666 Walnut St, Ste 2500 Des Moines IA 50309 also: Iowa Dem Party 5661 Fleur Dr Des Moines IA 50321 Office Phone: 515-288-2500. Office Fax: 515-243-0654.*

BRENNAN, WILLIAM P. (BILL BRENNAN), computer company executive; B in Econs., U. Ill. Various positions IBM Corp., 1979—93; ind. bus. cons., 1993—2003; v.p. sales and product ops. Forsythe Technology, Inc., Skokie, Ill., 2003—05, pres., 2005—. Bd. dirs. Forsythe Solutions Group, Inc., Forsythe Techology, Inc. Mem.: Soc. Info. Mgmt. Office: Forsythe Technology Inc 7770 Frontage Rd Skokie IL 60077 Office Phone: 847-213-7000.

BRENNECKE, ALLEN EUGENE, lawyer; b. Marshalltown, Iowa, Jan. 8, 1937; s. Arthur Lynn and Julia Alice (Allen) B; m. Billie Jean Johnstone, June 12, 1958; children: Scott, Stephen, Beth, Gregory, Kristen BBA, U. Iowa, 1959, JD, 1961. Bar: Iowa 1961. Law clk. U.S. Dist. Judge, Des Moines, 1961—62; assoc. Mote, Wilson & Welp, Marshalltown, Iowa, 1962—66; ptnr. Harrison, Brennecke, Moore, Smaha & McKibben, Marshalltown, 1966—2000; of counsel Moore, McKibben, Goodman, Lorenz & Ellefson, LLP, Marshalltown, 2000—. Contbr. articles to profl. jours. Bd. dirs. Marshalltown YMCA, 1966-71; bd. trustees Iowa Law Sch. Found., 1973-86, United Meth. Ch., Marshalltown, 1978-81, 87-89; fin. chmn. Rep. party 4th Congl. Dist., Iowa, 1970-73, Marshall County Rep. Party, Iowa, 1967-70. Fellow ABA (chmn. ho. of dels. 1984-86, bd. govs. 1982-86), Nat. Jud. Coll. (bd. dirs. 1982-88), Am. Coll. Trusts and Estates Counsel, Am. Coll. Tax Counsel, Am. Bar Found., Iowa Bar Assn. (pres. 1990-91, award of merit 1987); mem. Masons, Shriners, Promise Keepers. Republican. Methodist. Avocations: golf, travel, sports. Office: Moore McKibben Goodman Lorenz & Ellefson LLP 302 Masonic Temple Marshalltown IA 50158 Office Phone: 641-752-4271. Personal E-mail: blackbear703@marshallnet.com. Business E-Mail: attorneys@marshalltownlaw.com.

BRENNEMAN, HUGH WARREN, JR., judge; b. Lansing, Mich., July 4, 1945; s. Hugh Warren and Irma June Brenneman; m. Catherine Brenneman; 2 children. BA, Alma Coll., 1967; JD, U. Mich., 1970. Bar: Mich. 1970, D.C. 1975, U.S. Dist. Ct. (we. dist.) Mich. 1974, U.S. Dist. Ct. Md. 1973, U.S. Ct. Mil. Appeals 1971, U.S. Ct. Appeals (6th cir.) 1976, U.S. Ct. Appeals (D.C. cir.) 1981, U.S. Supreme Ct. 1980. Law clk. Mich. 30th Jud. Cir., Lansing, 1970-71; asst. U.S. atty. Dept. Justice, Grand Rapids, Mich., 1974-77; assoc. Bergstrom, Slykhouse & Shaw PC, Grand Rapids, 1977—80; magistrate judge US Dist. Ct. (we. dist.) Mich., Grand Rapids, 1980—. Instr. Western Mich. U., Grand Valley State U., 1989-92. Active Gerald R. Ford coun. Boy Scouts Am., 1984—, v.p., 1988—92, pres., 2006—; mem. Grand Rapids Hist. Commn., 1991—97, pres., 1995—97; dir. Cmty. Reconciliation Ctr., 1991; past bd. dirs. Welcome Homes for the Blind; pres. Rotary Charities Found., Grand Rapids, 2006—. Capt. JAGC US Army, 1971—74. Recipient Disting. Alumnus award Alma Coll., 1998. Fellow Mich. State Bar Found.; mem. FBA (pres. Western Mich. chpt. 1979-80, nat. del. 1980-84), U.S. Dist. Ct. Hist. Soc. (pres. 2002-04), State Bar Mich. (rep. assembly 1984-90), D.C. Bar Assn., Grand Rapids Bar Assn. (chmn. U.S. Constn. Bicentennial com., co-chmn. Law Day 1991), Fed. Magistrate Judges Assn., Am. Inns of Ct. (master of bench Grand Rapids chpt., pres.), Phi Delta Phi, Omicron Delta Kappa, Rotary (past pres., Paul Harris fellow), Econ. Club of Grand Rapids (past bd. dirs.). Congregationalist. Office: US Dist Ct West Mich 110 Michigan St NW Rm 580 Grand Rapids MI 49503-2313 Office Phone: 616-456-2568.

BRENNER, ELIZABETH (BETSY BRENNER), publishing executive; b. Bellevue, Wash. m. Steven Ostrofsky. BJ, MBA, Northwestern U. City news reporter The Chgo. Tribune, 1977, bus. news reporter, columnist, 1978; with mktg. dept. NY Times; with retail advt. and circulation posts Miami Herald, Rocky Mountain News, Denver, sr. v.p. sales and mktg., 1994—96; pub. Bremerton Sun, Wash., 1996—98, The News Tribune, Tacoma, 1998—2004; pres. & pub. Milw. Jour. Sentinel, 2004—; v.p. Journal Comm. Inc., 2004—06, exec. v.p., 2006—; COO Journal Comm. Inc. Pub. Businesses, 2006—. Bd. dirs. Econ. Devel. Bd, Tacoma, Mus. Glass, Greater Tacoma Cmty. Found., exec. coun.; mem. Tacoma adv. coun. U. Wash.; co-chmn. campaign Olympic Coll. Libr. Kitsap County; bd. dirs. United Way of Greater Milw., Boys & Girls Club, Greater Milw. Com. Named to Hall of Achievement, Northwestern U. Medill Sch. Journalism, 2006. Mem.: Audit Bur. Circulations (Liason com.), ewspaper Assn. Am. (Mktg. com.). Office: Milwaukee Journal Sentinel PO Box 371 Milwaukee WI 53201 Office Phone: 414-224-2954. E-mail: betsy.brenner@mail.tribnet.com, bbrenner@journalsentinel.com.*

BRENNER, MARK LEE, academic administrator, physiologist, educator; b. Boston, June 19, 1942; s. Harry D. and Beatrice (Price) B.; m. Ruth Abramson, Aug. 30, 1964; children: Jonathan, Tamara. BS, U. Mass., 1964, MS, 1965; PhD, Mich. State U., 1970. From asst. prof. to prof. horticultural scis. U. Minn., St. Paul, 1970—98, assoc. dean Grad. Sch., 1989-94; assoc. v.p. rsch., 1992-94; v.p. rsch. and dean Grad. Sch., 1994-98; vice chancellor rsch. and grad. edn. Ind. U.-Purdue U., Indpls., 1998—; assoc. v.p. rsch. Ind. U., Bloomington, Ind., 1998—. Cons. Abbott Labs., Chgo., 1988-89, Monsanto Corp., St. Louis, 1982-86, 88; bd. dir. Coun. Govt. Rels., ETS-GRE; v.p. bd. dirs. Assn. Accreditation Human Rsch. Protection Programs, Inc.; mem. Coun. Rsch. Policy and Grad. Edn., 1999—. Contbr. articles to profl. jours. Fellow Am. Soc. Horticultural Scis. (Outstanding Grad. Educator award 1993); mem. Am. Soc. Plant Physiologists (exec. com. 1986-89), Internat. Plant Growth Substance Assn. (sec.-treas. 1988-91), Minn. Chromatography Forum (pres. 1980-81, Palmer award 1986). Home: 8070 Lynch Ln Indianapolis IN 46250-4222 Office: Office of Vice Chancellor Rsch and Grad Edn Admin Bldg 122 355 N Lansing St Rm 122 Indianapolis IN 46202-2596 Business E-Mail: mbrenner@iupui.edu.

BRENT, HELEN TERESSA, school nurse; b. Grand Rapids, Mich., Oct. 4, 1946; d. William Henry and Anita Broyles Burress; m. Robert Lee Brent, June 10, 1967. AS, Grand Rapids C.C., 1966; diploma, Butterworth Hosp. Sch. Nursing, 1968; BSN summa cum laude, U. Mich., 1981; MPA, Western Mich. U., 1992. RN, Mich. Staff nurse Butterworth Hosp., Grand Rapids, Mich., 1968-69, head nurse psychiat. unit, 1969-72; DON Forest View Psychiat. Hosp., Grand Rapids, Mich., 1972-75; asst. DON, staff devel. coord. Kent Oaks Psychiat. Unit Kent Community Hosp., Grand Rapids, Mich., 1975-80; DON Kent Community Hosp. Complex, Grand Rapids, Mich., 1980-94; psychiat. nurse Pine Rest Christian Mental Health Svcs., Grand Rapids, 1994—; health planner Kent County Pub. Health Dept., Grand Rapids, 1996-97; sch. nurse Grand Rapids Pub. Schs., 1997—. Adj. faculty nursing divsn. Grand Rapids C.C., 1999—. Mem. adv. coun. Mich. Family Planning Mich. Dept. Cmty. Health, 1991-99, Family Outreach Ctr., Grand Rapids, 1980-95; mem. hospice care study panel United Way Kent County, 1984; vol. nursing health svcs. Kent County chpt. ARC, Grand Rapids, 1974—; vol. mediator West Mich. Dispute Resolution Ctr., 1995—. Recipient Outstanding Svc. award Family Outreach Ctr. Kent County Cmty. Mental Health, 1988, Helen Barnes award for outstanding vol. contbns. in nursing svcs. Kent County chpt. ARC, 1994, Eugene Browning Med. Svc. award Giants Orgn., Grand Rapids C.C., 1995. Mem. Vis. Nurses Assn. West Mich.(bd. dirs. 1991-2000), Nat. Black Nurses Assn. (local chpt. 1999—), Harambe Black Nurses Assn. Grand Rapids. Democrat. Avocations: travel, reading. Home: 3834 Old Elm Dr SE Kentwood MI 49512-9523 Office: Grand Rapids Pub Schs KEC Mayfield 225 Mayfield Ave NE Grand Rapids MI 49503-3768 E-mail: hbrent5558@webtv.net, BrentH@grps.k12.mi.us.

BRENTLINGER, PAUL SMITH, venture capital executive; b. Dayton, Ohio, Apr. 3, 1927; s. Arthur and Welthy Otello (Smith) B.; m. Marilyn E. Hunt, June 23, 1951; children: Paula, David, Sara. BA, U. Mich., 1950, MBA, 1951. With Harris Corp., Melbourne, Fla., 1951-84, v.p. corp. devel., 1969-75, v.p. fin., 1975-82, sr. v.p. fin., 1982-84; ptnr. Morgenthaler Ventures, Cleve., 1984—. Former chmn., bd. dirs. Hypres, Inc., Elmsford, NY; former chmn., bd. trustees Cleve. Inst. Art, 1992—98. Mem. Union Club, Phi Beta Kappa. Home: 2755 Eaton Rd Cleveland OH 44122-1800 Office: Morgenthaler 50 Public Sq Ste 2700 Cleveland OH 44113-2236

BRESKE, ROGER M., state legislator; b. Nov. 8, 1938; Grad. high sch. Former tavern owner; mem. Wis. Senate from 12th dist., Madison, 1990—. Mem. Tavern League Wis. (former pres.), Nat. Lic. Beverage Assn. (v.p.). Home: 8800 State Highway 29 Eland WI 54427-9409 Office: PO Box 7882 Madison WI 53707-7882

BRESTEL, MARY BETH, librarian; b. Cin., Feb. 5, 1952; d. John Wesley and Laura Alice (Knoop) Seay; m. Michael Charles Brestel, Aug. 3, 1974; 1 child, Rebecca Michelle. BS, U. Cin., 1974; MLS, U. Ky., 1984. Libr. asst. history and lit. dept. Pub. Libr. Cin. and Hamilton County, 1974-78, children's asst. Pleasant Ridge br., 1978-81, children's asst. Westwood br., 1981-84, reference libr. sci. and tech. dept., 1984-90, 1st asst. sci. and tech. dept., 1990-92, mgr. dept., 1992—. Mem. Ohio Libr. Coun., Columbus, 2001—. Mem. United Methodist Ch. Office: Pub Libr Cin and Hamilton County Sci and Tech Dept 800 Vine St Cincinnati OH 45202-2071 Home Phone: 513-481-0185; Office Phone: 513-369-6938. Business E-Mail: marybeth.brestel@cincinnatilibrary.org.

BRETHERTON, FRANCIS P., atmospheric and oceanic sciences educator; Prof. atmospheric and oceanic scis., dir. Space Sci. and Engring. Ctr., U. Wis., Madison, Wis., 1988-94, prof. atmospheric and oceanic scis., 1994—. Recipient Cleveland Abbe Award for Distinguished Service to Atmospheric Sciences, Am. Meteorological Assn., 1994 Office: U Wis Space Sci & Engring Ctr 1225 W Dayton St Madison WI 53706-1612

BRETT, GEORGE HOWARD, baseball executive, former professional baseball player; b. Glen Dale, W.Va., May 15, 1953; s. Jack Francis and Ethel (Hansen) B. Student, Longview C.C., Mo., El Camino Coll., Torrance, Calif. Former third baseman Kansas City (Mo.) Royals Profl. Baseball Team, v.p. baseball ops. Player Am. League All-Star Game, 1976—88. Named Am. League batting champion, 1976, 80, 90, Am. League Most Valuable Player, 1980; player Am. League All-Star Game, 1976-88; Inductee Baseball Hall of Fame, Cooperstown, N.Y., 1999. Address: care Kansas City Royals attn: vp ops PO Box 419969 Kansas City MO 64141-6969

BRETZ, WILLIAM FRANKLIN, retired elementary and secondary education educator; b. Urbana, Ill., May 30, 1937; s. William Franklin and Lois Evelyn (Scheffler) B. AA, Springfield Coll., Ill., 1957; BA, Ill. Coll., 1959; MA, Georgetown U., 1972. Cert. tchr., Ill. Chief page Ill. Senate, Springfield, 1957-63; tchr. history Lanphier High Sch., Springfield, 1964-78, Benjamin Franklin Sch., Springfield, 1979—, chmn. social sci. dept., 1989-94; ret., 1994. Staff mem. U.S. Ho. of Reps., Washington, 1975; site interpreter Lincoln's Tomb, Springfield, 1988—. Mem. Animal Protective League, Springfield. Scholar, Georgetown U., 1959—60. Mem. NEA, Ill. Edn. Assn., Springfield Edn. Assn., Ctr. for French Colonial Studies in Ill., Nat. Trust for Hist. Preservation, U.S. Capitol Hist. Soc. Home: 2325 S Park Ave Springfield IL 62704-4354

BREU, GEORGE, accountant; b. Milw., May 8, 1954; s. George and Grace (Rossmaier) B.; m. Nancy Lee Roblee, June 6, 1987; children: Michael G., Lisa A. BBA in Acctg. cum laude, U. Wis., Milw., 1976. CPA Wis. Audit staff Reilly, Penner & Benton, Milw., 1976-78; tax mgr. Radke, Schlesner & Wernecke, S.C., Milw., 1978-88; contr. Megal Devel. and Constrn. Corp., Milw., 1988-2000; pres. George Breu CPA, S.C., Brookfield, Wis., 2000—. Treas. Elmbrook Hist. Soc., Brookfield, Wis., 1981—83. Mem. Am. Inst. CPA's (tax divsn.), Wis. Inst. CPA's, Germany Philatelic Soc. (treas. Milw. chpt. 1978—), U. Wis. Milw. Philatelic Soc. (founder, treas. 1972-81), Milw. Philatelic Soc. Inc. (corp. registered agt. 1986-2005), U. Wis. Milw. Alumni Assn., Beta Gamma Sigma, Phi Eta Sigma. Republican. Roman Catholic. Avocations: stamp collecting/philately, reading history, travel. Home: 15840 Fieldbrook Dr Brookfield WI 53005-1419 Office: George Breu CPA SC 15840 Fieldbrook Dr Brookfield WI 53005-1419 Office Phone: 262-781-6135. Personal E-mail: gbreu@aol.com.

BREWER, ERIC, professional hockey player; b. Vernon, BC, Can., Apr. 17, 1979; Defenseman NY Islanders, 1998—, Edmonton Oilers, 2000—05, St. Louis Blues, 2005—, capt., 2008—. Mem. Team Can., World Championships, 2001, 2003—04; mem Team Can., Olympic Games, Salt Lake City, 2002; mem. Team Can., World Cup of Hockey, 2004. Named to NHL All-Star Game, 2003. Achievements include being a member of gold medal Canadian Hockey team, Salt Lake City Olympic Games, 2002; being a member of World Cup Champion Team Canada, 2004. Office: St Louis Blues Hockey Club Scottrade Ctr 1401 Clark Ave Saint Louis MO 63103*

BREWER, MARILYNN B., psychology professor; PhD social psychology, Northwestern U., 1968. Dir. Inst. Social Sci. Research, UCLA; prof. psychology UCLA, Ohio State U., 1993. Editor Personality & Social Psychology Rev. Jour. Recipient Kurt Lewin Award, SPSSI, 1995, Donald T. Campbell Award for Distinguished Research Social Psychology, 1992. Fellow: Am. Acad. Arts & Sci.; mem.: Soc. Psychol. Study Social Issues (pres. 1984—85), Soc. Personality & Social Psychology (pres. 1990—91), Am. Psychol. Soc. (pres. 1993—95). Office: Dept Psychology Ohio State U 1885 Neil Ave Columbus OH 43210-1222 Office Phone: 614-292-9640. E-mail: Brewer.64@osu.edu.

BREWER, MARK COURTLAND, political organization administrator, lawyer; b. Hammond, Ind., Apr. 1, 1955; s. Harold Russell and Carol Joan (Odell) B. AB with honors, Harvard U., 1977; JD, Stanford U., 1981. Bar: U.S. Dist. Ct. (ea. and we. dist.) Mich. 1983, U.S. Ct. Appeals (6th cir.) 1983. Law clk. U.S. Ct. Appeals (5th cir.), Austin, 1981-82; law clk. to justice Mich. Supreme Ct., Lansing, 1982-83; assoc. Sachs, Waldman, O'Hare, P.C., Detroit, 1983-89; mem. Sachs, Waldman & O'Hare, Detroit, 1989-95. Pres. Stanford Pub. Interest Law Found. Palo Alto, Calif., 1980-81; bd. dirs. Mich. Protection and Adv. Svc., Lansing, Mich. Contbr. articles on AIDS discrimination, drug testing, and employee privacy to profl. pubs. Mem. Macomb County Dem. Com., Mich., 1982—, 12th Congl. Dist. Dem. Com. Macomb County, 1983-93, 10th Congl. Dist. Dem. Com. Macomb County, 1993—2003; chmn. Mich. Dem. Party, 1995-; vice chair Dem. Nat. Com. Mem. ATLA, ABA, FBA (pres. ea. dist. Mich., bd. dirs. 1999-2000), State Bar Mich. (Outstanding Young Lawyer 1988), Mich. Trial Lawyers Assn., Assn. State Dem. Chairs (pres.), Sierra Club. Democrat. Lutheran. Office: Mich Democratic Party 606 Townsend St Lansing MI 48933-2313 Office Phone: 517-371-5410.*

BREWER, PAUL HUIE, advertising executive, artist, portrait painter; b. Jan. 24, 1934; s. Ralph Wright and Margot (Riviere) Brewer; m. Anita Hines, May 16, 1953 (div. 1971); children: Anita Joy(dec.), Launa Riviere; m. Carole Lynn Kuhrt, July 8, 1972; children: Nicole Renee, Brett Kuhrt. BA, La. Coll., Pineville, 1956; degree in advt. design, Famous Artists Schs., Westport, Conn., 1959. Artist Ralph Brewer's Studio and Engraving Co., Alexandria, 1952—54; art dir. Sta. KALB-TV, Alexandria, 1954—56; designer New Orleans Pub. Svc. Co., 1956; artist King Studio, Chgo., 1957; asst. art dir. Continental Casualty Co., Chgo., 1957—58; designer, art dir. Field Enterprises divsn. Chgo. Sun-Times, then dir. design; art dir. State Farm Ins. Cos., Bloomington, Ill., 1973, dir. art and design, 1973—77; prodn. mgr., exec. art dir. U.S. Savs. and Loan League, Chgo., 1977—, corp. v.p., 1983—. Cons. Johns Byrne Co., 1991, Darwill, 1992—93; instr. Wilmette (Ill.) Park Dist., 1997—, Glencoe (Ill.) Park Dist., 1997—, Winnetka (Ill.) Park Dist., 1997—, Deerpath (Ill.) Art League, 2003—, Suburban Fine Arts Ctr., 2003—. One-man shows include La. Coll., 1963, Chgo. Pub. Libr., Chgo. Press Club, Who Am I?, 1973, Represented in permanent collections Union League Club, Chgo., Ill. Bell Telephone Co., Standard Rate & Data, Krantzen Studio, Red Buttons, Lee Bolivier, Edward P. Morgan, others, Jack Benny, Danny Kaye, Danny Thomas, Pablo Picasso, Mrs. Marshall Field IV, Phil Silvers, David Susskind, Leonard Bernstein, Chuck Connors, Merve Griffin, Bob Newhart, Mike Singletary, Carol Kuhrt, others, New in the City, Count a Lonely Cadence, Who Am I?. Advt. dir. Artists Guild Bull., 1965; chmn. Artist Guild Chgo. Watercolor Show, 1967; bd. dirs. Artists Guild Chgo. Credit Union, House of Wray Corp. Ill., North Shore Art League, Lake County Art Commn., Deerpath Art League; elder Presbyn. Ch. Recipient award, Am. Newspaper Guild, Artists Guild Chgo., Famous Artists Sch., Graphic Arts Coun. Chgo., Hartford Illustrationaward, 1968, Chgo. III award, 1970, Nat. award, Louisville Rotogravure Assn., 1975, 3 SIMSA nat. awards, 1977, 2 SIMSA nat. awards, 1979, award, Union League Chgo., award of excellence, Hopper Paper Co., 1978, 1979, 2 Addy awards, State of Iowa, 1980, Nat. Merchandising award, P.O.P.I.A., 1980, 2 nat. awards, Fin. Insts. Mktg. Assn., 1984, award, Internat. Paper Co., 1984, Fima award, 1989, 1990, award, Chgo. Fin. Advertisers, 1990, awards of excellence in painting for In View exhbn., Highland Park, Ill., 2004—06. Mem.: La. Coll. Alumni Assn., North Shore Art League, Chgo. Soc. Typographic Arts, Chgo. Soc. Communicating Arts (bd. dirs.), Deerpath Art League, Am. Soc. Portrait Artists, Famous Artists Sch. Alumni Assn., Artists Guild Chgo., Am. Watercolor Soc. (assoc.). Home: 1160 S Green Bay Rd Lake Forest IL 60045-4065 also: 3630 Lee St Alexandria LA 71302-3929 also: 1400 S Shore Dr Delavan WI 53115-3627 Office Phone: 847-295-4119. Personal E-mail: paulbrewerart@aol.com.

BREWER, ROBERT ALLEN, physician; b. Inpls., Jan. 29, 1927; s. Robert Dewayne and Viola Mae (Grant) Brewer; m. Mildred Noreen Barnett, Jan. 1, 1950 (dec. May 1997); children: Robert A. Jr., Raymond, Richard, Brian, Andrew. AA, St. Petersburg Jr. Coll., Fla., 1949; AB, Ind. U., 1952; MD, Ind U., Inpls., 1955. Emergency dept. staff physician Mound Park Hosp., St. Petersburg, Fla., 1960; staff physician Pinellas Hosp., Largo, Fla., 1961-68; pvt. practice Logansport, Ind., 1969—. Mem. Cass County Rep. Com., Logansport, Ind.; candidate for city coun., 1995. Capt. US Army, 1957—59. Mem.: AMA, Cass County Med. Assn., Ind. Med. Assn., Am. Acad. Family Practitioners (bd. cert. diplomate). Republican. Avocations: stamp collecting/philately, coin collecting/numismatics. Office: PO Box 119 803 E Broadway Logansport IN 46947-0119 Home: 3415 W 296th St Kirklin IN 46050

BREWSTER, GREGORY BUSH, telecommunications educator; b. Richmond, Ind., Sept. 6, 1959; s. Robert Riggs and Nancy Huff (Terrell) B.; m. Gerianne Smith, Aug. 1, 1981. BA in Math. magna cum laude, Carleton Coll., 1981; MS in Computer Sci., U. Wis., 1983, PhD in Computer Sci., 1994. Mem. tech. staff AT&T Bell Labs., aperville, Ill., 1987-90; assoc. dir. grad. telecom. DePaul U., Chgo., 1990-94, dir. grad. telecom., asst. prof., 1995—2000, assoc. prof., 2000—, assoc. dean, 2002—. Mem. IEEE, ACM, Spl. Interest Group on

Comm. and Performance, Sigma Xi, Phi Beta Kappa. Avocations: music, piano, dogs. Office: DePaul Univ Sch of Computer Sci 243 S Wabash Ave Chicago IL 60604-2302 Office Phone: 312-362-6587. Office Fax: 312-362-6116. E-mail: brewster@cti.depaul.edu.

BREWSTER, JAMES HENRY, retired chemistry professor; b. Ft. Collins, Colo., Aug. 21, 1922; s. Oswald Cammann and Elizabeth (Booraem) B.; m. Christine Barbara Germain, Jan. 23, 1954; children— Christine Carolyn, Mary Elizabeth, Barbara Anne. AB, Cornell U., 1942; PhD, U. Ill., 1948. Chemist Atlantic Refining Co., Phila., 1942-43; postdoctoral fellow U. Chgo., 1948-49; instr. Purdue U., 1949-50, asst. prof., 1950-55, assoc. prof., 1955-60, prof., 1960-91, prof. emeritus, 1991—. With Am. Field Service, 1943-45. Fellow AAAS; mem. Am. Chem. Soc., Chem. Soc. (London), Royal Soc. Chemistry, Phi Beta Kappa, Sigma Xi, Phi Lambda Upsilon. Achievements include research in bond molecular orbitals, relation optical rotation and constitution, and origins of life. Home: 334 Hollowood Dr West Lafayette IN 47906-2146 Office: Purdue U Dept Chemistry Lafayette IN 47907 E-mail: jbrewst2@Purdue.edu.

BREYER, K. JON, lawyer; b. NYC, July 24, 1974; BA, Lehigh U., 1996; JD, William Mitchell Coll. Law, 2000. Bar: Minn. 2000, US Dist. Ct. (dist. Minn.). Law clk. Minn. Ct. Appeals, Hennepin County Dist. Ct., 2000—01; assoc. Fruth, Jamison and Elsass, P.A., Mpls. Named a Rising Star, Minn. Super Lawyers mag., 2006. Mem.: Douglas Amdahl Inns of Ct., ABA, Fed. Bar Assn. (mem. Minn. chpt.), Minn. State Bar Assn., Hennepin County Bar Assn. Office: Fruth Jamison & Elsass PA 3902 IDS Ctr 80 S 8th St Minneapolis MN 55402 Office Phone: 612-344-9700. E-mail: jbreyer@fruthlaw.com.

BRIAND, MICHAEL, chef; Mem. staff various pastry shops, Brittany, Paris and Bern, Switzerland; chef Froggy's French Cafe, Highwood, Ill.; exec. chef Little Dix Resort, Virgin Gorda; pastry chef Ambria, Chgo., 1994—, Mon Ami Gabi. Office: Ambria 2300 N Lincoln Park W Chicago IL 60614

BRICCETTI, JOAN THERESE, theater manager, arts management consultant; b. Mt. Kisco, NY, Sept. 29, 1948; d. Thomas Bernard and Joan (Filardi) B. AB in Am. History, Bryn Mawr Coll., 1970. Adminstrv. asst., program guide editor Sta. WIAN-FM, Indpls., 1970-72; adminstrv. asst. T. Briccetti, condr., Indpls., 1970-72; dir. pub. rels. The Richmond (Va.) Symphony, 1972-73, mgr., 1973-80, St. Louis Symphony Orch., 1980-84, gen. mgr., 1984-86, chief oper. officer, 1986-92; ind. cons. for arts Arts & Edn., 1993—; mng. dir. Metro Theater Co., St. Louis, 1996—. Cons., panelist Arts Couns. Ohio, Va., Ky. Active orch. and planning sects., music programs Nat. Endowment fot the Arts, 1974-78, chmn. orch. panel, 1975-78, cons., evaluator, panelist, 1974—, mem. first challenge grant rev. panel, 1977, co-chmn. recording panel, 1983-84; mem. grant rev. panel Va. Commn. for the Arts, 1976-78; adv. bd. Eastern Music Festival, 1977-83, Richmond Friends Opera, 1979-80; adv. coun. Va. Alliance for Arts Edn., 1978, Federated Arts Coun. Richmond, 1979-80; steering com. BRAVO Arts, 1978-79 (gov.'s award); cons. Tenn. Arts Commn., 1979-80; bd. dirs. Theatre IV, Richmond, 1974-80, Am. Music Ctr, N.Y.C., 1980-84, St. Louis Forum, 1983—, New City Sch., St. Louis, 1987—, Metro Theatre Co., 1994—; mem. challenge grant evaluation panel Ky. Arts Commn., 1983; participant Leadership St. Louis, 1983-84, bd. dirs., 1987-89; commr. subdistrict Mo. History Mus., 1987—, sec., 1993; speaker, panelist, cons. numerous arts orgns. Mem. Am. Symphony Orch. League (chmn. orch. library info. svc. adv. com., recruiter, mem. final interview com., advisor mgmt. fellowship program), Regional Orch. Mgrs. Assn. (v.p. 1976, policy com. 1977-79), Women's Forum Mo. Office: Metro Theatre Co 8308 Olive Blvd Saint Louis MO 63132-2814 Office Phone: 314-997-6777. Office Fax: 314-997-1811.

BRICE, ROGER THOMAS, lawyer; b. Chgo., May 7, 1948; s. William H. and Mary Loretta (Ryan) B.; m. Carol Coleman, Aug. 15, 1970; children: Caitlin, Coleman, Emily. AB, DePaul U., 1970; JD, U. Chgo., 1973. Bar: Ill. 1973, Iowa 1973, U.S. Ct. Appeals (10th, 4th, 6th and 7th cirs.) 1975, U.S. Dist. Ct. (no. and ctrl. dists.) Ill. 1977, 1995, U.S. Trial Bar (no. dist.) 1982, U.S. Supreme Ct. 1978. Staff atty. Office of Gen. Counsel NLRB, Washington, 1974-76; assoc. Kirkland & Ellis, Chgo., 1976-79, Reuben & Proctor, Chgo., 1979-80, ptnr., 1980-86, Isham, Lincoln & Beale, Chgo., 1986-88, Sonnenschein, Nath & Rosenthal LLP, Chgo., 1988—. Legal counsel, bd. dirs. Boys and Girls Clubs Chgo., 1991—. Fellow Coll. Labor and Employment Lawyers. Roman Catholic. Home: 3727 N Harding Ave Chicago IL 60618-4026 Office: Sonnenschein Nath & Rosenthal LLP 233 S Wacker Dr Ste 7800 Chicago IL 60606-6409 Home Phone: 773-463-5048; Office Phone: 312-876-3112. E-mail: rbrice@sonnenschein.com.

BRICHFORD, MAYNARD JAY, archivist; b. Madison, Ohio, Aug. 6, 1926; s. Merton Jay and Evelyn Louise (Graves) B.; m. Jane Adair Hamilton, Sept. 15, 1951; children— Charles Hamilton, Ann Adair Brichford Martin, Matthew Jay, Sarah Lourena. BA, Hiram Coll., Ohio, 1950; MS, U. Wis., Madison, 1951. Asst. archivist State Hist. Soc. Wis., 1952-56; methods and procedures analyst Ill. State Archives, 1956-59; records and space mgmt. supr. Dept. Adminstrn. State of Wis., Madison, 1959-63; archivist U. Ill., Urbana, 1963-95, asso. prof., 1963-70, prof., 1970—. Contbr. articles to profl. jours. Mem. gen. commn. on archives and history United Meth. Ch., 1988-96; bd. chmn. U. Ill. YMCA, 1987-89. With U.S. Navy, 1944-46. Council on Library Resources grantee, 1966-69, 70-71; at. Endowment for the Humanities grantee, 1976-79; Fulbright grantee, 1985; Am. Phil. Soc. grantee, 1992. Fellow Soc. Am. Archivists (pres. 1979-80); mem. Ill. Archives Adv. Bd. (chmn. 1979-84) Republican. Methodist. Home: 409 Eliot Dr Urbana IL 61801-6725 Office: 106A Arch Rsch Ctr 1707 S Orchard St Urbana IL 61801-3607 Business E-Mail: brichfor@uiuc.edu. E-mail: brich2@prairienet.org.

BRICKEY, KATHLEEN FITZGERALD, law educator; b. Austin, Tex., Sept. 16, 1944; d. Robert Bernard and Ina Marie (Daw) Fitzgerald; m. James Nelson Brickey, Aug. 22, 1969. BA, U. Ky., 1965, JD, 1968. Criminal law specialist/cons. Ky. Crime Commn., Frankfort, Cin., 1968-71; exec. dir. Ky. Judicial Conf. and Coun., Frankfort, 1971-72; adj. prof. law U. Ky., Lexington, 1972; asst. to assoc. prof. law U. Louisville, 1972-76; assoc. prof. to prof. law Washington U., St. Louis, 1976-89, George Alexander Madill prof. law, 1989-93, James Carr prof. of criminal jurisprudence, 1993—, Israel Treiman faculty fellow, 2001—02. Cons. U.S. Sentencing Commn., 1988, 91; witness U.S. Senate Com. on Judiciary, Washington, 1986. Author: Kentucky Criminal Law, 1974, Corporate Criminal Liability, 1984, 2d edit., 1992-94, Corporate and White Collar Crime, 1990, 4th edit., 2006; contbr. articles to profl. jours. Mem. Am. Law Inst., Soc. for Reform of Criminal Law, Assn. Am. Law Schs. (sect. on criminal justice chair 1989, exec. com. 1985-91, 94-95). Office: Washington U Sch Law Campus 1120 Saint Louis MO 63130 E-mail: brickey@wulaw.wustl.edu.

BRICKEY, SUZANNE M., editor; b. Grand Rapids, Mich., Apr. 4, 1951; d. Robert Michael and Elizabeth (Rogers) Stankey; m. Homer Brickey, Jr. BA, Ohio U., Athens, 1973; B.J., U. Mo., Columbia, 1977. Editor Living Today, The Blade, Toledo, 1980-82, Toledo Mag., The Blade, 1982-92; asst. editor Features, Toledo, 1992—. Mem. Toledo Press Club, Toledo Rowing Club. Home: 2510 Kenwood Blvd Toledo OH 43606-3601 Office: The Blade 541 N Superior St Toledo OH 43660-0001 E-mail: suebrickey@theblade.com.

BRICKLER, JOHN WEISE, lawyer; b. Dayton, Ohio, Dec. 29, 1944; s. John Benjamin and Shirley Hilda (Weise) B.; m. Marilyn Louise Kuhlmann, July 2, 1966; children: John, James, Peter, Andrew, Matthew. AB, Washington U., St. Louis, 1966; JD, Washington U., 1968. Bar: Mo. 1968, US Supreme Ct. 1972, US Dist. Ct. (ea. dist.) Mo. 1974, US Ct. Appeals (8th cir.) 1974. Assoc. Peper, Martin, Jensen, Maichel and Hetlage, St. Louis, 1973-77, ptnr., 1978-98, Blackwell Sanders Peper Martin LLP, St. Louis, 1998—2003, Spencer Fane Britt & Browne LLP, 2003—. Chmn. Concordia Pub. House, St. Louis, 1998-2001, Green Park Lutheran Sch., St. Louis, 2006-. Bd. dirs. Luth. Family and Children's Svcs. Mo., St. Louis, 1988-93, vice chmn., 1988-89, Green Pk. Luth. Sch., 2003—, chmn., 2006—. Capt. JAGC, U.S. Army, 1969-73. Mem. ABA, Nat. Assn. Bond Lawyers, Bar Assn. Met. St. Louis. Office: Spencer Fane Britt & Browne LLP 1 N Brentwood Blvd Ste 1000 Saint Louis MO 63105-3925 Office Phone: 314-333-3930. Business E-Mail: jbrickler@spencerfane.com.

BRICKMAN, KENNETH ALAN, state agency administrator; b. Hannibal, Mo., Sept. 10, 1940; s. Roy Frederick and Nita Wilma (Swearingen) B.; m. Mildred Darlene Myers, Aug. 10, 1963; children: Heather Katherine, Erik Alan. BS in Bus. and Econs., Culver-Stockton Coll., Canton, Mo., 1963; JD, U. Mo., 1970. Bar: Ill. 1970, Mo. 1970, US Supreme Ct. 1975. Ptnr. firm Scholz, Staff & Brickman, Quincy, Ill., 1970-78; pres. real estate brokerage Landmark of Quincy, Inc./Better Homes & Gardens, 1978-79; counsel, chief counsel Ill. Dept. Commerce and Cmty. Affairs, Springfield, 1980—85; gen. counsel, dep. dir. Ill. State Lottery, Springfield, 1986-91; sec.-treas., exec. v.p. La. Lottery Corp., Baton Rouge, 1991-95; exec. v.p. Iowa Lottery, Des Moines, 1995—. Served as capt. USAF, 1963-67. Mem. Culver Stockton Coll. Alumni Assn. (pres. 1979). Office: Iowa Lottery 2323 Grand Ave Des Moines IA 50312-5307

BRICKSON, RICHARD ALAN, lawyer; b. Madison, Wis., Feb. 10, 1948; s. William Louis and Nancy May (Gay) B.; m. Marilyn Joan Serenco, June 20, 1971; children: Jennifer Lynne, Katherine Anne, Evan Leigh. BA, Wabash Coll., Crawfordsville, Ind., 1970; JD, Georgetown U., Washington, DC, 1973. Bar: Mo. 1973. Staff atty. The May Dept. Stores Co., St. Louis, 1973-77, assoc. gen. counsel, 1977-79, asst. gen. counsel, 1979-81, counsel, 1981-82, counsel, sec., 1982-88, sr. counsel, sec., 1988—2005; divsnl. v.p. law Macy's Inc., 2006—. Office: Macy's Inc 611 Olive St Saint Louis MO 63101-1721

BRIDE, NANCY J., lawyer; b. Oct. 7, 1970; BA, Bowdoin Coll., 1992; JD, Notre Dame Law Sch., 1997. Bar: Ohio, US Dist. Ct. Southern Dist. Ohio, US Ct. of Appeals, Sixth Cir. Team in tng. mentor Leukemia & Lymphoma Soc.; vol. The Point, Wills for Heroes Prog.; mentor Cin. Youth Collaborative; orgnaizer Am. Breast Cancer Soc.; hostess Bacchanalian Soc. Wine Tasting Fundraiser. Named one of Ohio's Rising Stars, Super Lawyers, 2006. Mem.: Cin. Bar Assn. (Ct. Common Pleas Com.), Ohio State Bar Assn., ABA, Notre Dame Club of Cin. Office: Greenebaum Doll & McDonald PLLC 2800 Chemed Ctr 255 E 5th St Cincinnati OH 45202-4728 Office Phone: 513-455-7600. Office Fax: 513-455-8500.

BRIDENBAUGH, PHILLIP OWEN, anesthesiologist; b. Sioux City, Iowa, Dec. 17, 1932; s. Lloyd Donald and Harriet (Anderson) B.; m. Kathleen Conway, June 22, 1957 (div. Apr. 1980); children: Sue, Tom, Dan; m. Diann Hurd, Mar. 7, 1981; children: Rob, Jeff. BA, U. Nebr., 1954; MD, U. Nebr., Omaha, 1960. Diplomate Am. Bd. Anesthesiology. Staff anesthesiologist Mason Clinic, Seattle, 1965-70, dir. dept. anesthesia, 1970-77; prof., chmn. dept. anesthesiology U. Cin. Med. Ctr., 1977—2003. Pres. UAA, Inc., Cin., 1977—. Co-editor: Neural Blockade, 1980, 2d edit., 1988, 3d edit., 1997: sect. editor Anesthesia and Analgesia, 1989-95; sr. editor Regional Anesthesia, 1989-97. Trustee Wood Libr. Mus. Anesthesiology, 1992-94; chmn. World Fedn. Socs. Anesthesiology Founds., 2004—. 1st lt. U.S. Army, 1954-56. Mem. Assn. Univ. Anesthetists, Soc. Acad. Anesthesia Chmn. (pres. 1988-90), Am. Soc. Anesthesiology (bd. dirs., v.p. sci. affairs 1992-94, 1st v.p. 1994-95, pres. elect 1995-96, pres. 1996-97, immediate past pres. 1997-98), Am. Soc. Regional Anesthesia (pres. 1990-91), Ohio Soc. Anesthesiologists (pres. 1991-92). Office: U Cin Dept Anesthesia 231 Albert Sabin Way Cincinnati OH 45267-0001 E-mail: bridenpo@uc.edu.

BRIDGELAND, JAMES RALPH, JR., lawyer; b. Cleve., Feb. 16, 1929; s. James Ralph and Alice Laura (Huth) B.; m. Margaret Louise Bates, March 24, 1950; children: Deborah, Cynthia, Rebekah, Alicia, John. BA magna cum laude, U. Akron, 1951; MA, Harvard U., 1955, JD, 1957. Bar: Ohio 1957. Mem. internat. staff Goodyear Tire & Rubber Co., Akron, Ohio, 1953-56; ptnr. Taft, Stettinius & Hollister, Cin., 1957—; dir., mem. exec. com. Firstar Corp. and Star Bank Cin.; dir. SHV N.Am., Inc., The David J. Joseph Co., Robert A. Cline Co., Art Stamping, Inc., Seinau-Fisher Studios, Inc.; instr., lectr. in lit. U. Cin. Pres., trustee Cin. Symphony Orch.; sec., trustee Louise Taft Semple Found.; trustee Cin. Opera Co., Hillside Trust, Jobs for Cin. Grads., Cin. Inst. Fine Arts; past bd. dirs. Legal Aid Soc.; mayor, mem. coun. City of Indian Hill, Ohio, 1985-91; pres. Indian Hill Sch. Bd., 1971-77. 1st lt. USAF, 1951-53, Korea. Mem. ABA, Ohio Bar Assn., Cin. Bar Assn., Am. Arbitration Assn., Harvard Law Sch. Assn. (past pres. Cin. chpt.), Harvard Alumni Assn. (nat. v.p. 1978-85). Harvard Club (pres. 1983-84), Queen City Club, Commonwealth Club (treas. 1984-86), Queen City Optimist Club, Recess Club, Assn. Literary Scholars and Critics, Cin. Optimist Club, Cin. Literary Club. Republican. Episcopalian. Home: 8175 Brill Rd Cincinnati OH 45243-3937

BRIDGES, JACK EDGAR, electronics engineer; b. Denver, Jan. 6, 1925; s. Byron Edgar and Edith Katherine (Kimmel) B.; m. Martha Jane Ernest, Dec. 22, 1951; children: Victoria Ann, Amelia Joan, Cynthia Sue. BSEE, U. Colo., 1945, MSEE, 1947. Instr. elec. engr. Iowa State Coll., Ames, 1947-48; antenna engr. Andrew Corp., Chgo., 1948-49; rsch. engr. Zenith Radio Corp., Chgo., 1949-55; head of color TV rsch. Magnavox, Ft. Wayne, Ind., 1955-56; chief electronics engr. Warwick Mfg., Niles, Ill., 1956-61; sr. sci. adv. IIT Rsch. Inst., Chgo., 1961-92; chmn. Interstitial, Park Ridge, Ill., 1993—. Patentee in field; contbr. articles to profl. jours. With USN, 1943-46. Recipient Browder J. Thompson prize Inst. Radio Engrs., 1956, Disting. Engring. Alumnus award U. Colo., 1983. Fellow IEEE (life, cert. of achievement Group on EMC, 1976, Prize Paper award Power Engring. Soc., 1980); mem. Eta Kappa Nu, Tau Beta Pi, Sigma Xi. Home and Office: 1937 Fenton Ln Park Ridge IL 60068-1503

BRIDGES, ROGER DEAN, historian; b. Marshalltown, Iowa, Feb. 10, 1937; s. Floyd F. and Beatrice Andrea (Pipher) B.; m. Karen Maureen Buckley, June 4, 1960; children: Patrick Sean, Kristin Joy, Jennifer Lynn. BA, Iowa State Tchrs. Coll., 1959; MA, State Coll. of Iowa, 1962; PhD, U. Ill., 1970; LHD, Lincoln Coll., Ill., 1987, Tiffin U., 1994. Tchr., libr. Keokuk (Iowa) Pub. Schs., 1959—62; instr. in history Bradley U., Peoria, Ill., 1967; asst. prof. history U. S.D., Vermillion, 1968—69; asst. editor Papers of Ulysses Grant, Carbondale, Ill., 1969—70; dir. rsch. Ill. State Hist. Libr., Springfield, 1970—76, head libr., 1976—85; dir. Ill. State Hist. Libr./Ill. Hist. Preservation Agy., Springfield, 1985—87; dir., editor Lincoln legal papers project, asst. state historian Ill. Hist. Preservation Agy, Springfield, 1987—88; exec. dir. Rutherford B. Hayes Presdl. Ctr., Fremont, Ohio, 1988—2003, exec. dir. emeritus, 2004—. Instructional asst. prof. Ill. State U., Normal, 1974—84, Normal, 2005—06, asst. prof., 2005—07, adj. prof. history, 2006—; adj. prof. Sangamon State U., Springfield, 1985—88, Bowling Green State U., Ohio, 1989—2003. Author, editor: Illinois: Its History and Legacy, 1984; asst. editor: Papers of Ulysses S. Grant, vol. 4, 1972. Bd. dir. Springfield Urban League, 1976-82, Gt. Am. People Show, New Salem, Ill., 1978-85, McLean County Hist. Soc., 2005-; bd. dir. and pres. Conv. and Visitors Bur. Sandusky County, Fremont, 1988-99; bd. dir., sec. and v.p. Birchard Pub. Libr. Sandusky County, 1988-2003, 1996-99; active Abraham Lincoln Bicentennial Commn. McLean County, Ill., 2006—. Nat. Hist. Publs. Commn. fellow, 1969-70; recipient Disting. Svc. awrd Springfield Urban League, 1977. Mem. Am. Hist. Assn., So. Hist. Assn., Abraham Lincoln Assn. (bd. dirs. 1985-, pres. 2004-06), Orgn. Am. Historians, Soc. for Historians of Gilded Age and Progressive Era (sec./treas. 1989-2003, mem. coun. 2004-06, sec. 2006—, Dist. Svc. award 2007), Ill. State Hist. Soc. (bd. dirs. 2003-06, bd. adv. 2006—07, Disting. Svc. award 1988), Ohio Acad. History (exec. coun. 1996-98), trustee Ohioana Library Assn., 1998-2003), McLean County Hist. Soc. (bd. dirs. 2005—), C. of C. Sandusky County (bd. dirs. 1999-2002), David Davis Mansion Found. (bd. dirs. 2003-). Democrat. Baptist. Home: 2804 Mockingbird Ln Bloomington IL 61704 Home Phone: 309-664-5476; Office Phone: 309-664-5476. Personal E-mail: rdbridges@insightbb.com. Business E-Mail: rdbridg@ilstu.edu.

BRIDGEWATER, BERNARD ADOLPHUS, JR., retired retail executive; b. Tulsa, Mar. 13, 1934; s. Bernard Adolphus and Mary Alethea (Burton) Bridgewater; m. Barbara Paton, July 2, 1960; children: Barrie, Elizabeth, Bonnie. AB, Westminster Coll., Fulton, Mo., 1955; LLB, U. Okla., 1958; MBA, Harvard, 1964. Bar: Okla. 1958, U.S. Ct. Claims 1958, U.S. Supreme Ct. 1958. Asst. county atty., Tulsa, 1962; assoc. McKinsey & Co., mgmt. cons. Chgo., 1964-68, prin., 1968-72, dir., 1972-73, 75; assoc. dir. nat. security and internat. affairs Office Mgmt. and Budget, Exec. Office Pres., Washington, 1973-74; exec. v.p. Baxter Travenol Labs., Inc., Chgo. and Deerfield, Ill., 1975-79, dir., 1975-85; pres. Brown Group, Inc., Clayton, Mo., 1979-87, 90-99, CEO, 1982-99, chmn., 1985-99, also dir.; now ret.; cons. TIAA-CREF, NYC. Adv. dir. Schroder Venture Ptnrs. LLC, NYC. Author (with others): Better Management of Business Giving, 1965. Trustee Rush-Presbyn. St. Luke's Med. Ctr., 1974—84, Washington U., St. Louis, 1983—94, 1995—2003, 2004—, Barnes Hosp., St. Louis, 1987—90; bd. visitors Harvard U. Bus. Sch., 1987—93. Served to lt. USNR, 1958—62. Recipient Rayonier Found. award, Harvard U., 1963; George F. Baker scholar, 1964. Mem.: Indian Hill Country Club, Log Cabin Club, St. Louis Country Club, Phi Alpha Delta, Omicron Delta Kappa, Beta Theta Pi. Office: 9909 Clanton Rd Ste 216 Saint Louis MO 63124 Office Phone: 314-991-9990.

BRIDGMAN, G(EORGE) ROSS, lawyer; b. New Haven, Dec. 27, 1947; s. George Ross Bridgman and Betty Jean (Soderquist) Burrows; m. Patricia Hess; children: Taylor Wilson, Katharine June, Elizabeth Honey. BA cum laude, Yale U., 1970; JD, Northwestern U., 1973. Bar: Ohio 1973, U.S. Dist. Ct. (so. dist.) Ohio 1974, U.S. Dist. Ct. (no. dist.) Ohio 1976, U.S. Ct. Appeals (6th cir.) 1984, U.S. Supreme Ct. 1990. Assoc. Vorys, Sater, Seymour & Paese, Columbus, Ohio, 1973-80, ptnr., 1980—. Mem. editorial bd. Northwestern U. Law Rev., Chgo., 1972-73. Trustee Columbus Jr. Theatre of the Arts, 1976-80, pres., 1978-80; trustee, v.p. London (Ohio) Pub. Libr., 1979-84; bd. dirs. Ctrl. Ohio Regional Coun. on Alcoholism, Columbus, 1987-89; trustee Kidscope, Columbus, 1988-89, Recovery Alliance, Columbus, 1989-97, Ohio Parents for Drug-Free Youth, 1991-99; mem. exec. bd. Simon Kenton coun. Boy Scouts Am., 1996—; mem. Columbus Symphony Chorus, 1999—; bd. dirs. Ohio Drug Assistance Program, 2005—, Ohio Lawyers Assistance Program, 2005. Fellow: Coll. Labor and Employment Lawyers; mem.: ABA, Nat. Assn. Coll. and Univ. Attys., Ohio Bar Assn., Columbus Bar Assn., Columbus Country Club, Capital Club. Republican. Episcopalian. Office: Vorys Sater Seymour & Pease PO Box 1008 52 E Gay St Columbus OH 43215-3161 E-mail: grbridgman@vssp.com.

BRIDGMAN, THOMAS FRANCIS, retired lawyer; b. Chgo., Dec. 30, 1933; s. Thomas Joseph and Angeline (Gorman) B.; m. Patricia A. McCormick, May 16, 1959; children: Thomas, Kathleen Ann, Ann Marie, Jane T., Molly. BS cum laude, John Carroll U., 1955; JD cum laude, Loyola U., Chgo., 1958. Bar: Ill. 1958, U.S. Dist. Ct. 1959. Assoc. McCarthy & Levin, Chgo., 1958, Baker & McKenzie, Chgo., 1958—96, ptnr., 1962—96. Trustee John Carroll U., 1982-88. Fellow Am. Coll. Trial Lawyers, Am. Bd. Trial Advs. (adv.), Internat. Acad. Trial Lawyers (past pres.), Union League Club, Beverly Country Club (Chgo., pres. 1983). Democrat. Roman Catholic. Home: 9400 S Pleasant Ave Chicago IL 60620-5646 Office: Baker & McKenzie 1 Prudential Plaza 130 E Randolph St Ste 3700 Chicago IL 60601-6342

BRIGGS, ROBERT W., lawyer; m. Joanne Briggs. BA, Duke U., 1963; JD, Ohio State U. Coll. of Law, 1966. Bar: Ohio 1966, NY 1984, U.S. Dist. Ct., No. Dist. of Ohio, U.S. Tax Ct. Atty. Herndon & Bartlo, 1970—71, Buckingham, Doolittle & Burroughs, Ohio, 1971—85, bd. of managers Ohio, 1985—2000, pres., CEO Ohio, 1990—2000, chmn. emeritus Ohio, 2001—. Chair Fund for Our Economic Future. Trustee John S. and James L. Knight Found., 2002—, vice chair, 2005—, mem., grants review com., mem., investment com., mem., pension plan investment com.; trustee Cleve. Orch., Catholic Diocese of Cleve. Found., N.E. Ohio Tech. Coalition; trustee, bd. chair Nat. Inventors Hall of Fame; co-trustee, exec. dir. GAR Found. Recipient Disting. Svc. award, Akron Community Found., Hope award, N.E. Ohio Chapter of Multiple Sclerosis Soc. Mem.: Akron Bar Assn., Ohio State Bar Assn., NY State Bar Assn., ABA. Office: Buckingham, Doolittle & Burroughs 50 S Main St PO Box 1500 Akron OH 44309

BRIGHI, ROBERT J., principal; Prin. Arthur W. Erskine Elem. Sch., Cedar Rapids, Iowa. Recipient Elem. Sch. Recognition award U.S. Dept. Edn., 1989-90. Office: Arthur W Erskine Elem Sch 600 36th St SE Cedar Rapids IA 52403-4314

BRIGHT, MYRON H., federal judge; b. Eveleth, Minn., Mar. 5, 1919; s. Morris and Lena A. Bright; m. Frances Louise Reisler, Dec. 26, 1947; children: Dinah Ann, Joshua Robert. AA, Eveleth Junior Coll, 1939; BSL, U. Minn., 1941, JD, 1947. Bar: N.D. 1947, Minn. 1947. Assoc. Wattam, Vogel, Vogel & Bright, Fargo, ND, 1947—49, ptnr., 1949—68; judge US Ct. Appeals (8th cir.), Fargo, 1968—85, sr. judge, 1985—; disting. prof. law St. Louis U., 1985—88, emeritus prof. of law, 1989—95. Lectr. Thomas Jefferson Sch. of Law, 2003—. Capt. USAF, 1942—46. Recipient Francis Rawle award, ALI-ABA, 1996, Lifetime Achievement award, U. N.D. Law Sch., 1998, Herbert Harley award, AJS, 2000. Mem.: ABA, Fed. Judges Assn., Cass County Bar Assn., Bar Assn. Met. St. Louis, US Jud. Conf. (com. on adminstrn. of probation sys. 1977—83, adv. com. on appellate rules 1987—90, com. on internat. jud. rels. 1996—2003), N.D. Bar Assn. Office: US Ct Appeals 8th Cir 655 1st Ave N Ste 340 Fargo ND 58102-4952 also: Thomas F Eagleton US Courthouse 111 S 10th St Rm 26 325 Saint Louis MO 63102

BRIGHTFELT, ROBERT, diagnostic company executive; BS with distinction, MS with distinction, U. Nebr.; MBA, U. Ga. Various positions in healthcare and diagnostics DuPont Diagnostics, Dade Behring, Deerfield, Ill., group pres. for Chemistry products divsn., pres. Global Products. E-mail: brightrw@dadebehring.com.

BRIGHTON, GERALD DAVID, retired finance educator; b. Weldon, Ill., May 14, 1920; s. William Henry and Geneva (Ennis) B.; m. Lois Helen Robbins, June 7, 1949; children: Anne, William, Joan, John, Jeffrey. BS, U. Ill., 1941, MS, 1947, PhD, 1953. CPA Ill. Instr. accountancy U. Ill., Urbana, 1947-53, prof., 1954-83, Ernst & Whinney Disting. prof., 1983-88, prof. emeritus, 1988—, dir. undergrad. acctg. program, 1978-86; staff acct. Touche, Niven, Bailey & Smart, Chgo., 1953-54. Cons. G.D. Brighton, C.P.A., Urbana, 1954—; vis. prof. U. Tex.-Austin, 1973; program specialist Dept. HUD, Washington, 1979; vice chmn. U. Ill. Athletic Assn., Urbana, 1982-86 Contbr. articles to profl. jours. Alderman City of Urbana, 1967-69; officer, bd. dirs. U. Ill. YMCA, Champaign, 1959-81, 89-95, trustee, 2002—; bd. dirs. Wesley Found., U. Ill., 1986—; treas. John Gwinn for Congress, Urbana, 1982-83, Green Meadows coun. Girl Scouts U.S., 1981-83. Served to maj. U.S. Army, 1941-46. AACSB Faculty fellow, 1978-79; recipient Bronze Tablet for high honors U. Ill., 1941 Mem. AICPA (hon.), Ill. Soc. CPAs (disting.), Am. Acctg. Assn., Assn. Govt. Accts., Govtl. Fin. Officers Assn., Nat. Tax Assn., Tax Inst. Am. Democrat. Methodist. Home: 501 Evergreen Ct Urbana IL 61801-5928 Office: U Ill 1206 S 6th St Champaign IL 61820-6978 Personal E-mail: gbrighton@sbcglobal.net.

BRILL, LESLEY, literature and film studies educator; b. Chgo., Sept. 3, 1943; s. Walter Henry and Fay (Trolander) B.; m. Megan Parry, Jan. 18, 1970; children: Benjamin, Calista. BA, U. Chgo., 1965; MA, SUNY, Binghamton, 1967; PhD, Rutgers U., 1971. Asst. prof. English U. Colo., Boulder, 1970-80, assoc. prof., 1981-89, chmn. dept. English, 1981-85, grad. dir., 1985-87; prof. English dept. Wayne State U., Detroit, 1989—, prof. and chmn. dept. English, 1989-94. Vis. lectr. U. Kent, Canterbury, Eng., 1978-79; vis. prof. U. Paul Valery, Montpellier, France, 1984, U. de Nantes, France, 1995. Author: The Hitchcock Romance: Love and Irony in Hitchcock's Films, 1988, John Huston's Filmmaking, 1997, Crowds, Power and Transformation in Cinema, 2006; contbr. articles on lit. and film to profl. jours. Rockefeller Found. fellow, 1977-78. Mem. Soc. Cinema Studies. Office: Wayne State U Dept English Detroit MI 48202 E-mail: aa4525@wayne.edu.

BRIMIJOIN, WILLIAM STEPHEN, pharmacologist, neuroscientist, educator, researcher; b. Passaic, NJ, July 1, 1942; s. William Owen and Georgiana (Macklin) Brimijoin; m. Margaret Murray Ross, June 22, 1964 (div. Nov. 2002); children: Megan Rebekkah Brimijoin-Vaules, William Owen, Alexander Ross. AB in Psychology, Harvard Coll., 1964; PhD in Pharmacology, Harvard U., 1969. Asst. prof Mayo Med. Sch., Rochester, Minn., 1972-76, assoc. prof., 1976-80, prof. pharmacology, 1980—, Winston and Iris Clement prof., 1989—; chair dept. molecular pharmacology Mayo Clinic, Rochester, Minn., 1993—2003. Cons. Mayo Clinic Rochester Minn., 1971-72, voting staff 1972—; vis. scientist Karolinska Inst. Stockholm, Sweden, 1978-79, U. Würzburg, Germany, 1987-88, Chinese Acad. Scis. Shanghai br., 1999-2004; assoc. dir., dean Mayo Grad. Sch., Rochester, 1983-87; mem. behavioral and neurosci. study sect. NIH, 1989-93, sci. adv. panel U.S. EPA, 1993-2005, sci. adv. bd. internat. conf. on cholinesterase; mem. Gulf War Grants Rev. Bd. Dept. Def., 1997-99. Mem. editl. bd. Muscle and Nerve Jour., 1980-88, Diabetes Jour., 1985-93; author: Over the River and Through the Woods, 2004; contbr. to numerous profl. jours.; patentee in field. With USPHS, 1969-71. Recipient Career Devel. award NIH, 1975, Javits Neuroscience Investigator award NINDS, 1987, Sr. Disting. U.S. Scientist award Humboldt Found., 1987-88, Mayo Disting. Investigator award Mayo Clinic, 1993. Mem. Soc. Neuroscience (social issues com. 1987), Internat. Soc. Neurochemistry, Am. Soc. Neurochemistry (program com. 1993-94), Am. Soc. Pharmacology and Exptl. Therapeutics. Avocations: languages, creative writing. Office: Mayo Clinic Dept of Pharmacology 200 1st St SW Rochester MN 55905-0002 Business E-Mail: brimijoi@mayo.edu.

BRIN, DAVID, writer, astronomer; b. Glendale, Calif., Oct. 6, 1950; s. Herbert Henry and Selma (Stone) B; m. Cheryl Ann Brigham; 3 children. BS in Astronomy, Calif. Inst. Tech., 1973; MS in Elec. Engring., U. Calif.-San Diego, 1977, PhD in Space Sci., 1981. Electronics engr. Hughes Aircraft Co., Carlsbad, Calif., 1973-77; profl. novelist Bantam Books, NYC, 1980—; postdoctoral fellow Calif. State Inst., LaJolla, Calif., 1982—85. Instr. physics, astronomy, writing San Diego State U., San Diego CC, 1982—85. Author: (novels) Sundiver, 1980, Startide Rising (Nebula award 1983, Hugo award 1983, Locus award), 1983, The Practice Effect (Balrog award), 1984, (with Gregory Benford) Heart of the Comet, 1986, Earth, 1990 (nominee Hugo award, 1994); (novellas and novellettes) The Tides of Kithrup, 1981, The Loom of Thessaly, 1981, The Postman (runner-up Hugo award 1983), 1982, Cyclops (nominee Hugo award 1985), 1984, Glory Season, 1993, Brightness Reef, 1996 (nominee Hugo award), Infinity's Shore, 1996, The Transparent Society, 1998 (Obeler Freedom of Speech award), (series) Startride Rising (Nebula award), 1983, Sundiver, 1985, The Uplift War, 1987 (Hugo and LOCUS awards for best novel, nominee Nebula award), Heaven's Reach, 1998, Foundation's Triumph, 1999, Forgiveness, 2001, Kiln People, 2002, Contacting Aliens: The Illustrated Guide to David Brins Uplift Universe, 2002; (collections) The River of Time, 1986, Otherness, 1994, Tomorrow Happens, 2003, (stories for anthologies) War of the Worlds: Global Dispatches, 1996; contbr. short stories, sci. fact articles, and sci. papers to profl. publs. Nominated for John W. Campbell award for best new author of 1982 Mem. Am. Assn. Aeronautics and Astronautics, Sci. Fiction Writers Am. (sec. 1982-84) Avocations: backpacking, music, eclecticism. Office: care Phantasia Press 5536 Crispin Way Rd West Bloomfield MI 48323-3405

BRINK, DAVID RYRIE, lawyer; b. Mpls., July 28, 1919; s. Raymond Woodard and Carol Sybil (Ryrie) B.; m. Irma Lorentz Brink; children: Anne Carol, Mary Claire, David Owen, Sarah Jane. BA with honors, U. Minn., 1940, BSL with honors, 1941, JD with honors, 1947; LLD, Capital U., 1981, Suffolk U., 1981, Mitchell Coll. Law, 1982. Bar: Minn. 1947, U.S. Dist. Ct. Minn. 1947, U.S. Tax Ct. 1967, U.S. Supreme Ct. 1980, U.S. Ct. Appeals (D.C. Cir.) 1982. Assoc. firm Dorsey & Whitney, Mpls., 1947-53, ptnr., 1953-89, head Washington office, 1982-84, ret. ptnr. Trustee Lawyers Com. Civil Rights Under Law, 1978—; bd. dirs. Nat. Legal Aid and Defender Assn., 1978-80; U.S. panelist for Dispute Resolution under Free Trade Agreement with Can.; bd. visitors U. Minn. Law Sch., 1978-81; chmn. trust and estates dept. Dorsey & Whitney, 1956-82 Mem. editl. bd. U. Minn. Law Rev, 1941-42; contbr. articles to profl. jours. Bd. govs. Am. Coll. Trust and Estate Counsel Found., 1987-95. Served to lt. comdr. USNR, 1943-46. Recipient Outstanding Achievement award U. Minn., 1982 Fellow Coll. Law Practice Mgmt. (hon.), Am. Coll. Trust and Estate Counsel (regent, exec. com.); mem. ABA (gov. 1974-77, 80-83, pres. 1981-82), Ctrl. and Ea. European Legal Initiative, Com. on Law and Nat. Security, Com. on Substance Abuse, Adv. Com. to Commn. on Lawyers Assistance Programs 2000-2003, Com. on Specialization, chmn. 1977-80, Fund Pub. Edn. ABA (pres. 1981-82), Am. Bar Found. (state chmn. 1977-80, gov. 1980-83), Am. Bar Retirement Assn. (pres. 1976-77), Am. Judicature Soc. (bd. dir. 1988—), Nat. Conf. Bar Pres., Inst. Jud. Adminstrn., Am. Arbitration Assn. (trustee 1981—), Can.-U.S. Law Inst. (adv. bd. 1987—), Minn. Bar Assn. (pres. 1978-79), Internat. Mgmt. and Devel. Inst., Hennepin County Bar Assn. (pres. 1967-68), Street Law (nat. adv. bd. 1982-85, chmn. 1983-84), Lawyers Concerned Lawyers (bd. dir. 2003—), N.W. Athletic Club, Sr. Tennis Players Club, Inc. Office: Dorsey & Whitney # 50 S 6th St Minneapolis MN 55402

BRINK, MARION FRANCIS, trade association administrator; b. Golden Eagle, Ill., Nov. 20, 1932; s. Anton Frank and Agnes Gertrude B. BS, U. Ill., 1955, MS, 1958; PhD, U. Mo., 1961. Rsch. biologist U.S. Naval Radiol. Def. Lab., San Francisco, 1961-62; assoc. dir. div. nutrition rsch. Nat. Dairy Council, Chgo., 1962-65, dir. div. nutrition rsch., 1965-70, pres., 1970-85; exec. v.p. ops. United Dairy Industry Assn., Rosemont, 1985-88, chief exec. officer, 1988-91. Vice chmn. human nutrition adv. com. USDA, 1980-81. Contbr. articles to profl. jours. Recipient citation of merit U. Mo. Alumni Assn. Mem. Am. Soc. for Nutritional Scis., Am. Soc. Clin. Nutrition, Am. Dietetic Assn., Dairy Shrine Club, Soc. for Nutrition Edn., Chgo. Nutrition Assn., Alpha Tau Alpha, Gamma Sigma Delta. Home: 444 Highcrest Dr Wilmette IL 60091-2358

BRINKMAN, DALE THOMAS, lawyer; b. Columbus, Ohio, Dec. 10, 1952; s. Harry H. and Jean May (Sandel) B.; m. Martha Louise Johnson, Aug. 3, 1974; 3 children: Marin Veronica, Lauren Elizabeth, Kelsey Renee. BA, U. Notre Dame, 1974; JD, Ohio State U., 1977. Bar: Ohio 1977, U.S. Dist. Ct. (so. dist.) Ohio 1979. Assoc. Schwartz, Shapiro, Kelm & Warren, Columbus, 1977-82; asst. tax counsel Am. Elect. Power, Columbus, 1982; gen. counsel Worthington Industries, Inc., Columbus, 1982-99, v.p. adminstrn., gen. counsel, sec., 1999—, corp. sec., 2000—. Author: Ohio State U. Law Jour.,1975-76, editor, 1976-77. Trustee, officer Friends of Dahlberg Ctr., Columbus, 1980-86; dir., officer Assn. for Developmentally Disabled, Columbus, 1986-94. Mem. ABA, Ohio State Bar Assn., Columbus Bar Assn. Republican. Roman Catholic. Office: Worthington Industries 200 W Old Wilson Bridge Rd Worthington OH 43085-2247 E-mail: dtbrinkm@worthingtonindustries.com.

BRINKMAN, JOHN ANTHONY, historian, educator; b. Chgo., July 4, 1934; s. Adam John and Alice (Davies) B.; m. Monique E. Geschier, Mar. 24, 1970; 1 son, Charles E. AB, Loyola U., Chgo., 1956, MA, 1958; PhD, U. Chgo., 1962. Rsch. assoc. Oriental Inst., U. Chgo., 1963, dir. inst., 1972-81, asst. prof. Assyriology and ancient history, 1964-66, assoc. prof., 1966—70, prof., 1970—84, Charles H. Swift disting. svc. prof., 1984—2001, chmn. dept., 1969—72, Charles H. Swift disting. svc. prof. emeritus, 2001—. Ann. prof. Am. Schs. Oriental Rsch., Baghdad, 1968-69; chmn. Baghdad Schs. Com., 1970-85, chmn. exec. com., 1973-75, trustee, 1975-90; chmn. vis. com. dept. Near Ea. langs. and civilizations Harvard U., 1995-2001. Author: Political History of Post-Kassite Babylonia, 1968, Materials and Studies for Kassite History, Vol. I, 1976; Prelude to Empire, 1984; editorial bd. Chgo. Assyrian Dictionary, 1977—, State Archives Assyria, 1985—; editor in charge Babylonian sect. Royal Inscriptions of Mesopotamia, 1979-91; contbr. numerous articles to profl. jours. Fellow Am. Research Inst., in Turkey, 1971; sr. fellow Nat. Endowment Humanities, 1973-74; Guggenheim fellow, 1984-85, Emeritus fellow, Mellon Found., 2005-07. Fellow Am. Acad. Arts and Scis.; mem. Am. Oriental Soc. (pres. Middle West chpt. 1971-72), Am. Schs. of Oriental Rsch., Brit. Sch. Archaeology in Iraq, Deutsche Orient Gesellschaft, Brit. Inst. Archaeology at Ankara. Roman Catholic. Home: 1321 E 56th St Apt 4 Chicago IL 60637-1762 Office: U Chgo 1155 E 58th St Chicago IL 60637-1569 Office Phone: 773-702-9545.

BRINKMAN, TOM, JR., state representative; b. Cin., Dec. 6, 1957; married; 6 children. BA, George Washington U. Printer; state rep. dist. 34 Ohio Ho. of Reps., Columbus, 2000—, vice chair, ways and means com., mem. commerce and labor, judiciary, and mcpl. govt. and urban revitalization coms. Mem.: Coalition Opposed to Additional Spending and Taxes. Republican. Office: 77 S High St 11th fl Columbus OH 43215-6111

BRINKMEYER, SCOTT S., lawyer; b. Chgo., Sept. 27, 1949; BA, DePauw U., 1971; JD, St. Louis U., 1975. Bar: Mich. 1975, cert.: Am. Arbitration Assn. Nat. Panel (civil neutral arbitrator) 2004, US Dist. Ct., Western Dist. Mich. (mediator) 2005. Atty. Mika, Meyers, Beckett & Jones, PLC, Grand Rapids, Mich. Jud. law clk. Mo. Ct. appeals, 1974. Assoc. editor St. Louis U. Law Jour., 1974. Pres. Grand Rapids Rotary Dist. 290, 1997—98. Fellow: Mich. State Bar Found., Am. Bar Found.; mem.: ABA (Ho. Del. 2003—04), Grand Rapids Bar Assn., Def. Rsch. Inst., Mich. Def. Trial Counsel, State Bar Mich. (rep. assembly 1992—2004, bd. commrs. 1995—2004, exec. com. 1996—98, chair 2003—04, pres. 2003—04, sects. on environ. law, litigation, negligence law, dispute resolution, exec. com. 1999—2004). Office: Mika Meyers Beckett and Jones 900 Monroe Ave NW Grand Rapids MI 49503-1423

BRINZO, JOHN S., mining executive; b. 1942; married. BS, Kent State U., 1964; MBA, Case Western Res. U., 1968. Fin. & mgmt. positions Cleveland-Cliffs, Inc., Cleve., 1969—83, v.p., controller, 1983—87, sr. v.p. fin., 1987—89, exec. v.p. fin., 1989—97, exec. v.p. fin. & planning, 1997, pres., CEO, 1997—2000, chmn., CEO, 2000—03, chmn., pres., CEO, 2003—05, chmn., CEO, 2005—06, chmn., 2006—07. Chmn. Nat. Mining Assn.; mem. Am. Iron & Steel Inst.; bd. dir. Brink's Co. Trustee Great Lakes Sci. Ctr., Kent State Found.

BRISBANE, ARTHUR SEWARD, newspaper publisher; b. NYC, Sept. 30, 1950; s. Seward Scatcherd and Doris Mae (Fauser) B.; m. Jo Ellen Hull, Oct. 16, 1982; children: Allison Faith, Madeline Mariah, Laura Calista. AB, Harvard Coll., 1973. Child care worker McLean Hosp., Belmont, Mass., 1973-74; freelance musician, 1974-76; reporter Glen Cove (N.Y.) Guardian, 1976-77, Kansas City (Mo.) Star & Times, 1977-79, columnist, 1979-84; reporter Washington Post, 1984-87, asst. city editor, 1987-89; columnist Kansas City Star, 1990-92, editor, v.p., 1992-97, pub., pres., 1997—2004; sr. v.p. Knight Ridder, Inc., 2005—06. Author: Arthur Brisbane's Kansas City, 1982. Avocations: tennis, reading.

BRISCOE, JOHN W., lawyer; BA, Westminster Coll., 1963; JD, U. Mo., 1966. Bar: Mo. Ptnr. Briscoe, Rodenbaugh & Brannon, Hannibal, Mo.; prosecuting atty. Ralls County, Mo. Pres. Mo. Bar, bd. govs., 1990—. Pres. bd. dirs. Barkley Cemetery Assn.; active Boy Scout Am. Troop 106 Com.; bd. dirs. Hannibal C. of C.; active Truman State U. Parents Coun., 1995—97; apptd. bd. govs. Truman State U., 1997—; active Trinity Episcopal Ch. Mem.: Hannibal Elks Club, New London Lions Club. Office: Briscoe Rodenbaugh & Brannon PO Box 446 423 S Main St New London MO 63459

BRISCOE, MARY BECK, federal judge; b. Council Grove, Kans., Apr. 4, 1947; m. Charles Arthur Briscoe. BA, U. Kans., 1969, JD, 1973; LLM, U. Va., 1990. Rsch. asst. Harold L. Haun, Esq., 1973; atty.-examiner fin. divsn. ICC, 1973—74; asst. U.S. atty. for Wichita and Topeka, Kans. Dept. Justice, 1974—84; judge Kans. Ct. Appeals, 1984—95, chief judge, 1990—95; judge US Ct. Appeals (10th cir.), Topeka, 1995—. Named to Women's Hall of Fame, Univ. Kans., 2001; recipient Univ. Kans. Law Soc. Disting. Alumnus award, 2000. Fellow: Kans. Bar Found., Am. Bar Found.; mem.: ABA, Women Attys. Assn. Topeka, Kans. Bar Assn. (Outstanding Svc. award 1992), Topeka Bar Assn., Nat. Assn. Women Judges, Am. Judicature Soc., U. Kans. Law Soc., Kans. Hist. Soc., Washburn Law Sch. Assn. (hon.). Office: US Ct Appeals 10th Cir 645 Massachusetts Ste 400 Lawrence KS 66044-2235 also: US Ct Appeals 10th Cir Byron White US Courthouse 1823 Stout St Denver CO 80257

BRISTO, MARCA, human services administrator; b. Albany, NY, June 23, 1953; d. Earl C. and Dorothy (Moore) B.; m. J. Robert Kettlewell, Oct. 15, 1988; children: Samuel Clayton Kettlewell, Madeline Elizabeth Kettlewell. BA in Sociology, Beloit Coll., 1974; BSN, Rush Coll. Nursing, Chgo., 1976. Cert. nursing. RN Rush Presbyn. St. Luke's Med. Ctr., Chgo., 1976-77, Northwestern Meml. Hosp., Chgo., 1977, family planning nurse specialist, 1978-79; exec. dir., co-founder Access Living Met. Chgo., 1979-84, pres., CEO, 1984—. Chair Nat. Coun. Disability, Washington, 1994-2002, Ill. Pub. Action Coun., 1989-94, U.S. delegate U.N. world summit on urban living and shelter, 1996, bd. dirs. Disability Funders Network, 2002-. Mem. Pres.'s Com. on Employment of People with Disabilities; mem. Pres.'s Task Force on Employment of Adults with Disabilities; bd. dirs. Rehab. Inst. Chgo.; mem. Leadership Greater Chgo.; mem. The Chgo. Network. Avocations: cooking, travel. Office: Access Living of Metropolitan Chicago 614 W Roosevelt Rd Chicago IL 61614

BRISTOL, NORMAN, lawyer, arbitrator, retired food products executive; b. Bronx, NY, June 14, 1924; s. Lawrence and Bell (Allchin) B.; m. Doreen Kingan, Mar. 28, 1952 (dec. June 2001); children: Charles L., Norman, Alexander, Barnaby; m. Sally Hume, May 28, 2004. Grad., Phillips Exeter Acad., 1941; AB, Yale, 1944; LLB, Columbia Law Sch., 1949. Bar: N.Y. bar 1950, Mich. bar 1954. Atty. Root, Ballantine, Harlan, Bushby & Palmer, NYC, 1949-53; with Kellogg Co., Battle Creek, Mich., 1954-78, asst. gen. counsel, 1958-64, sec., 1960-78, gen. counsel, 1964-78, sr. v.p., 1968-75, dir., 1972-78, exec. v.p., 1975-78; atty. Howard & Howard, Kalamazoo, 1979-93. Mem. Gull Lake Comty. Schs. Bd. Edn., 1963-70, pres., 1965-67; trustee Kalamazoo Symphony Soc., Inc., 1983-94, pres., 1990-91; bd. dirs. Southwest Mich. Land Conservancy, Inc., 1996-2001. Lt. (j.g.) USNR, 1943-46. Mem. State Bar Mich., Kalamazoo Bar Assn. Home and Office: 2962 Sylvan Dr Hickory Corners MI 49060-9319

BRITT, KENT A., lawyer; b. Indpls., Nov. 27, 1970; BS, Ind. U., 1994; JD, U. Cin., 1997. Bar: Ohio 1997, US Dist. Ct. Southern Dist. Ohio 1997. Assoc. Vorys, Sater, Seymour and Pease LLP, Cin. Mem. Greater Cin. Chamber of Commerce Bus. Retention Com. Named one of Ohio's Rising Stars, Super Lawyers, 2006. Mem.: FBA, ABA (mem., Litig. Sect. 1997—), Ohio State Bar Assn., Cin. Bar Assn., Phi Alpha Delta. Office: Vorys Sater Seymour and Pease LLP Ste 2000 Atrium Two PO Box 0236 221 E Fourth St Cincinnati OH 45201-0236 Office Phone: 513-723-4488. Office Fax: 513-852-7818.

BRITTON, CLAROLD LAWRENCE, lawyer, consultant; b. Soldier, Iowa, Nov. 1, 1932; s. Arnold Olaf and Florence Ruth (Gardner) B.; m. Joyce Helene Hamlett, Feb. 1, 1958; children: Laura, Eric, Val, Martha. BS in Engring., U. Mich., Ann Arbor, 1958, JD, 1961, postgrad. Bar: Ill. 1961, U.S. Dist. Ct. (no. dist.) Ill. 1962, U.S. Ct. Appeals (7th cir.) 1963, U.S. Supreme Ct. 1970, Mich. 1989. Assoc. Jenner & Block, Chgo., 1961-70, ptnr., 1970-88; pres. Britton Info. Sys., Inc., 1991—2006, Britton Data Sys. Inc., 2006—. Lectr. DePaul U., 1988. Author: Computerized Trial Notebook, 1991, Trial By Notebook, 2002; asst. editor Mich. Law Rev., 1960. Comdr. USNR, 1952-57. Fellow Am. Coll. Trial Lawyers; mem. ABA (litigation sect., antitrust com., past regional chmn. discovery com. 1961), Ill. State Bar Assn. (chmn. Allerton House Conf. 1984, 86, 88, chmn. rule 23 com. 1985-87, chmn. civil practice and procedure coun. 1987-88, antitrust com.), Chgo. Bar Assn. (past chmn. fed. civil procedure com., mem. judiciary and computer law coms., civil practice com.), 7th Cir. Bar Assn., Def. Rsch. Inst. (com. on aerospace 1984), Mich. Bar Assn., Ill. Assn. Trial Lawyers, Order of Coif, Law Club (Chgo.), Racine Yacht Club (Wis.), Macatawa Yacht Club (Mich.), Masons, Alpha Phi Mu, Tau Beta Pi. Republican. Lutheran. Office: 8463 Pawnee Trail Pinckney MI 48169 Home Phone: 810-231-4894; Office Phone: 810-231-3572. Personal E-mail: cbritton@brittonis.com. Business E-Mail: Britton@ic.net.

BRITTON, SAM, state legislator; m. to Kaye Britton; 1 child, Samuel. BS, U. Cin. Real estate agt. Britton and Assocs., Cin.; treas. Avondale Redevelop. Corp., Cin.; mem. Ohio Ho. of Reps., Columbus. Mem. adv. bd. Cin. Comty. Devel. Mem. NAACP (life), Madisonville Comty. Coun. (past pres.), Cin. Area Bd. Realtors, Ohio Assn. Realtors (trustee), Black Male Coalition, Kappa Alpha Psi Office: Ohio Ho of Reps Ohio State Bldg Columbus OH 43215

BRIZZOLARA, CHARLES ANTHONY, lawyer, director; b. Chgo., Nov. 20, 1929; s. Ralph D. and Florence H. (Hurley) B.; m. Audree Doyle, Aug. 24, 1968. BA, Lake Forest Coll., Ill., 1951; JD, Ill. Inst. Tech., 1957. Bar: Ill. 1959. Practiced law, Chgo., 1959-67; with Walter E. Heller & Co., also Walter E. Heller Internat. Corp. (later Amerifin Corp.), Chgo., 1967-85; v.p., sec., gen. counsel Walter E. Heller & Co., also Walter E. Heller Internat. Corp., 1974-85, sr. v.p., 1980-85; v.p. Chgo. Bears Football Club, Inc., 1975-88; mem. firm Chadwell & Kayser Ltd., 1985-90; ptnr. Michael Best & Friedrich, LLC, Chgo., 1990—2002; of counsel Berger, Newmark and Fenchel P.C., Chgo., 2003—04, Kane, Carbonara & Mendoza, Chgo., 2004—06, Fioretti, Lower & Carbonara, Chgo., 2007—. Bd. dirs. Abacus Real Estate Fin. Co., Walter E. Heller & Co. S.E., Heller Factoring (Hong Kong) Ltd., Factoring Serfin, S.A., Chandler Leasing Corp., 1975-80; lectr. seminars Am. Mgmt. Assn. Editor: Chgo.-Kent Law Rev, 1956. Bd. dirs. Cath. Charities Archdiocese of Chgo., 1978-99, sec., 1991-94; bd. dirs. Ill. Inst. Tech. Chgo. Kent Alumni Assn., 1980-89. Served with AUS, 1952-54. Mem. Internat. Bar Assn., Ill. Bar Assn. Roman Catholic. Home: Apt 20G 253 E Delaware Pl Chicago IL 60611-1758 Office: 222 S Riverside Plaza Chicago IL 60606

BRO, RUTH HILL, lawyer; b. Brookings, SD, July 9, 1962; BA, Northwestern U., 1984; JD, U. Chgo., 1994. Atty. McBride Baker & Coles (now Holland & Knight), 1994—99, Baker & McKenzie LLP, Chgo., 1999—2001, ptnr., 2001—. Editor: The E-Bus. Legal Arsenal: Practitioner Agreements and Checklists, 2004; co-author: Online Law, 1996, 6th edit., 2000; mem. editl. bd.: SciTech Lawyer, ABA, 2004—, Internet Law & Strategy, Am. Lawyer Media, 2005—, exec. editor, chair bd. dir.: Privacy & Data Protection Legal Reporter, Am. Lawyer Media, 2005—06; contbr. articles to profl. jours. Mem.: ABA (founder e-privacy law com., chair-elect sci. and tech. law sect., mem. info. security com.), Ill. Bar Assn., Chgo. Bar Assn. (computer law com.). Office: Baker & McKenzie LLP One Prudential Plz 130 East Randolph Dr Chicago IL 60601 Home Phone: 630-734-3950; Office Phone: 312-861-7985. Business E-Mail: bro@bakernet.com.

BROAD, MATTHEW, lawyer; m. Cathy Broad; children: Ben, Sarah. BA bus. econ., U. Calif. Santa Barbara, 1981; JD, Hastings College of Law, 1984. Counsel-leg. dept. Boise Cascade Corp., Boise, Ill., 1984—89, assoc. gen. counsel, 1989—2004; corp. sec. OfficeMax Inc. (formerly Boise Cascade Corp.), 1989—, exec. v.p., gen. counsel, 2004—. Office: OfficeMax Inc 263 Shuman Blvd Naperville IL 60563

BROADIE, THOMAS ALLEN, surgeon, educator; b. St. Paul, June 26, 1941; s. Thomas Edward and Laura Marjorie (Allen) B.; m. Victoria Taylor, July 20, 1968; children: Frances, Thomas. AB, Princeton U., 1963; MD, Northwestern U., 1967; PhD, U. Minn., 1977. Diplomate Am. Bd. Surgery. Intern, resident Johns Hopkins Hosp., 1967-69; resident U. Minn., 1969-75; from asst. prof. to prof. surgery Ind. U., Indpls., 1978-92, prof., 1992—. Mem. at large Com. on Trauma, Chgo., 1990-97; chmn. Ind. State Com. on Trauma, Indpls., 1991-97. Fellow ACS (pres. Ind. chpt. 1989-90, gov. at large 1992-97); mem. Soc. Univ. Surgeons, Midwest Surg. Assn. (pres. 1995-96), Ctrl. Surg. Assn., Am. Assn. Surgery Trauma, Western Surg. Assn., Am. Assn. Endocrine Surgeons, Am. Thyroid Assn. Office: Wishard Meml Hosp Dept Surgery 1001 W 10th St Indianapolis IN 46202-2859

BROCK, KATHY, newscaster; married; 2 children. Degree in Journalism, Wash. State U. Anchor and reporter KWSU-TV, Pullman, Wash., KEPR-TV, Pasco, KCBI-YV, Boise, Idaho; weekend anchor and reporter KUTV-TV, Salt Lake City, 1984, anchor noon and 6pm news, 1985—90; co-anchor News This Morning and reporter WLS-TV, Chgo., 1990—93, co-anchor 6pm news, 1993—, co-anchor 10pm news, 2003—. TV Journalist (documentaries) Mali, West Africa, 1989 (Edward R. Murrow award, 1989, IRIS award, 1989). Office: WLS-TV 190 N State St Chicago IL 60601

BROCK, THOMAS DALE, retired microbiology professor; b. Cleve., Sept. 10, 1926; s. Thomas Carter and Helen Sophia (Ringwald) B.; m. Mary Louise Louden, Sept. 13, 1952 (div. Feb. 1971); m. Katherine Serat Middleton, Feb. 20, 1971; children: Emily Katherine, Brian Thomas. BS, Ohio State U., 1949, MS, 1950, PhD, 1952. Research microbiologist Upjohn Co., Kalamazoo, 1952-57; asst. prof. Western Res. U., Cleve., 1957-59, Ind. U., Bloomington, 1960-61, assoc. prof., 1962-64, prof., 1964-71; E.B. Fred prof. natural scis. U. Wis., Madison, 1971-90, prof. emeritus, 1990—, chmn. dept. bacteriology, 1979-82; pres. Sci. Tech. Pubs., Madison, 1990-94, Savanna Oak Found., 2000—. Found. for Microbiology lectr., 1971-72, 78-79 Author: Milestones in Microbiology, 1961, Principles of Microbial Ecology, 1966, Thermophilic Microorganisms, 1978, Biology of Microorganism, 7th edit., 1994, Basic Microbiology with Applications, 3d edit., 1986, A Eutrophic Lake, 1985, Thermophiles: General, Molecular and Applied Microbiology, 1986, Robert Koch: A Life in Medicine and Bacteriology, 1988, The Emergence of Bacterial Genetics, 1990, Shorewood Hills: An Illustrated History, 1999. Recipient Rsch. Career Devel. award NIH, 1962-68, Waksman award Soc. Indsl. Microbiology, 2003, Aldo Leopold award in Restoration Ecology, 2006, Invader Crusader award State of Wis., 2007. Fellow AAAS; mem. Am. Soc. for Microbiology (hon. mem., chmn. gen. div. 1970-71, Fisher award 1984, Carski award 1988) Home and Office: 1227 Dartmouth Rd Madison WI 53705-2213

BROCK, WILLIAM ALLEN, III, economist, educator; b. Phila., Oct. 23, 1941; s. William and Margaret Brock; m. Joan Brock, Aug. 31, 1962; 1 child, Caroline. AB in Math. with honors, U. Mo., 1965; PhD, U. Calif., Berkeley, 1969. Asst. prof. econs. U. Rochester, NY, 1969-71; assoc. prof. U. Chgo., 1972-75, prof., 1975-81; from assoc. prof. to full prof. Cornell U., 1974-77; Romnes prof. econs. U. Wis., Madison, 1981—, F.P. Ramsey prof. econs., 1984—, W.F. Vilas rsch. prof., 1990—. Vis. assoc. prof. U. Rochester, 1973; cons. U.S. Dept. Justice, SBA, EPA, FTC. Assoc. editor: Jour. Econ. Theory, Internat. Econ. Rev., 1972—99; contbr. articles to profl. jours.; co-author (with A. Malliaris): (book) Differential Equations, Stability and Chaos in Dynamic Economics, 1989; co-author: (with D. Hsieh, B. LeBaron) Nonlinear Dynamics, Chaos and Instability: Statistical Theory and Economic Evidence, 1991. Recipient Roger F. Murray 3d Pl. prize, Inst. Quantitative Rsch. Fin., 1989; NSF grantee, 1970—2003, Sherman Fairchild Disting. scholar, Calif. Inst. Tech., 1978, Guggenheim fellow, 1987—88. Fellow: Am. Econs. Assn. (disting.), Econometric Soc.; mem.: AAAS, NAS. Office: U Wis Dept Econs 1180 Observatory Dr Madison WI 53706-1320

BROCKA, BRUCE, editor, educator, application developer; b. Davenport, Iowa, Nov. 1, 1959; s. Donald H. and Daisy Ann (Robertson) B.; m. M. Suzanne St. Ledger, Mar. 17, 1984; children: Melinda Athena, Bennett Paul. BS, St. Ambrose U., 1981; MS, U. Iowa, 1984. Instr. Army Mgmt. Engring. Coll., Rock Island, Ill., 1984-90; exec. editor, assoc. pub. Exec. Scis. Inst., Davenport, 1986—. Editor: Quality Control and Applied Statistics, 1987—, Operations Research/Management Science, 1987—, Automation in Quality Assurance, 1988, Biostatistica, 1990—, Quality Management, 1992; contbr. articles on sci. tech. to profl. jours. Ptnr. Summit Lane Properties. Republican. Avocation: historic preservation. Home and Office: 1005 Mississippi Ave Davenport IA 52803-3938

BROCKMANN, WILLIAM FRANK, retired health facility administrator; b. South Bend, Ind., Nov. 14, 1942; s. Ervin William and Elizabeth Marie (Casaday) B.; m. Ellen Meier, June 10, 1967; children: William Edward, Rebecca Jayne. BS in Mgmt., Ind. U., 1966; MHA, St. Louis U., 1968. Administrv. asst. St. Anthony Hosp., Okla. City, 1968; asst. hosp. adminstr. Caylor-Nickel Med. Ctr., Bluffton, Ind., 1972-77, hosp. adminstr., 1977-86, pres., 1986-89, CEO, 1989—2000, mem. exec. com., 1985—2000; pres. River Ter. Estates Retirement Cmty., Bluffton, Ind., 2000—; CEO Bluffton Regional Med. Ctr., 2000—02; ret., 2002. Bd. dirs. Old First Nat. Bank. Gen. campaign mgr. Wells County United Way, 1973; past pres. Bluffton United Meth. Ch., Wells County Found.; pres., bd. dirs. Wells County Coun. on Aging; spkr. in field. Capt. M.S.C. US Army, 1969—71, vietnam vet. Life fellow Am. Coll. Healthcare Execs. (Regents award 2001); mem. Ind. Hosp. Assn. (chmn. bd. 1990-91, Disting. Svc. award 2001), Am. Hosp. Assn. (ho. dels. 1991-93), Ind. Chi Phi Alumni Assn. (pres. 2002-06), Chi Phi (Alumnus of Yr. award). Republican. Methodist. Achievements include leading a successful merger of Wells Cmty. Hosp. and Caylor-Nickel Med. Ctr. into Bluffton Regional Med. Ctr. in 2000. Avocations: scuba diving, pool, reading, golf, travel. Home: 1127 Ridgewood Ln Bluffton IN 46714-3827

BROCKWAY, LEE J., architect; b. Mecosta, Mich., Aug. 13, 1932; s. Byron Maxwell and Mildred Loro (Wolfe) B.; m. Mary Haglind, Aug. 4, 1956; children: David, Michael, Anne McDonough, Bill. BArch, U. Notre Dame, 1955. Archtl. intern Haughey, Black and Williams, Architects, Battle Creek, Mich., 1959-61; chief architect Charles W. Cole & Son, Engrs. and Architects, South Bend, Ind., 1961-65; ptnr. The Shaver Partnership, Architects and Engrs., Michigan City, Ind., 1965-73; owner, architect Brockway Assocs., Architects, Michigan City, 1974-76; prin., corp. dir. Fanning/Howey Assoc., Inc., Michigan City, Ind., 1976-98, prin. emeritus, 1998—. Pres. Ind. Soc. Architects, 1990. Recipient Outstanding Svc. award Ind. soc. Architects, 1987, 89, Mich. City C. of C., 1978. Mem. AIA (corp. mem., mem. nat. com. on architecture for edn. 1978—, chmn. 1988), Coun. for Archtl. Rsch., Nat. Coalition Edn. Facilities (chmn. 1991-92), Coun. Edn. Facility Planners (bd. dirs. 1986-92, pres. 1990-91). Home: 2922 Belle Plaine Trl Michigan City IN 46360-1777 Office: Fanning Howey Assoc Inc PO Box 584 Michigan City IN 46361-0584

BROD, STANFORD, graphics designer, educator; b. Cin., Sept. 29, 1932; s. Morris and Rebecca (Mitman) B.; m. McCrystle Wood; children: Deborah, Daniel, Michael. BS in Design, U. Cin., 1955. Graphic designer Rhoades Studio, Cin., 1955-62; tchr. exptl. typography Art Acad. Cin., 1960-75; graphic designer Lipson, Alport & Glass Assocs., Inc. and predecessor firm Lipson Jacob, Assocs. Inc., Cin., 1962-94, Wood/Brod Design, Cin., 1994—; prof. graphic design U. Cin., 1962—. Tchr. illustration and packaging Art Acad. Cin., 1991-92, 94, 96-98, 2001-05, 07, tchr. corp. identity, 1992-97, 2002-05, 06, tchr. advt. design, corp. design, 1994-97, tchr. visual comms., 1997-98, exhbn. design, 1999, 2002, 2007. Exhibited in group shows at Mus. Modern Art, N.Y.C., 1966, Urban Walls, Cin., 1972, City Banners, Sao Paulo, Brazil, 1975, ITC Ctr., N.Y.C., 1981, Tel

Aviv Mus., 1982, Internat. Art Exhbn., Dusseldorf, Germany, 1982, Calligraphia U.S.A./USSR, 1990-96, UN, 1994; one-man shows include Skirball Mus. Hebrew Union Coll., Cin., 1989. Recipient Communications Arts awards, 1959, 64, 66, 70, 73, 76, Creativity on Paper awards, 1960-67, Internat. Typographic awards, 1965, 70, N.Y. Type Dirs. Club award, 1968, Typographic Composition Assn. awards, 1970-76. Office: 3662 Grandin Rd Cincinnati OH 45226-1117 Personal E-mail: stan_brod@excite.com.

BRODELL, ROBERT THOMAS, internal medicine educator; b. Rochester, NY, Nov. 24, 1953; s. Harold Louis and Alma Jean (Moreland) B.; m. Linda P. Brodell, July 2, 1977; children: Lindsey Ann, Julie Lynn, David William, Erin Elizabeth, Nathan Thomas. BA, Washington and Jefferson Coll., 1975; MD, U. Rochester, 1979. Bd. cert. in dermatology and dermatopathology. Asst. prof. dermatology Washington U., St. Louis, 1984-85; asst. prof. internal medicine Northeastern Ohio U. Coll. Medicine, Rootstown, Ohio, 1986-90, 1990-94, prof. internal medicine, 1994—, master tchr., 1997—. Asst. clin. prof. dermatology Case Western Res. U., Cleve., 1986-94, assoc. clin. prof., 1994—; chmn. Midwest Congress Derm. Socs., Dayton, Ohio, 1995—. Trustee Ohio divsn. Am. Cancer Soc., Columbus, 1992—; bd. dirs. Warren (Ohio) Sports Hall of Fame, 1996. Named Cleve. Cavaliers Profl. Basketball Team Fan of Year, 1997. Fellow Am. Acad. Dermatology, Am. Soc. Dermatopathology; mem. AMA, Ohio State Med. Assn., Wilderness Med. Assn., Ohio Dermatol. Assn. (trustee 1994—), Am. Cancer Soc. (v.p. Ohio divsn. 1999-2000, pres. Ohio divsn. 2000—), Masons (Master Old Erie # 3), Phi Beta Kappa, Alpha Omega Alpha. Home: 2660 E Market St Warren OH 44483-6204 Office: ortheastern Ohio Univ Coll Med PO Box 95 4209 State Route 44 Rootstown OH 44272-9698 E-mail: rtb@neoucom.edu.

BRODEN, THOMAS FRANCIS, III, French language educator; b. South Bend, Ind., Nov. 19, 1951; s. Thomas F. and Joanne Marjorie (Green) B.; m. Marcia C. Stephenson, Oct. 14, 1989. AB, U. Notre Dame, Ind., 1973; AM, Ind. U., 1976, PhD, 1986; postgrad., Coll. France, Paris, 1979-80. Asst. d'anglais Lycee Henri IV and Inst. Nat. Telecomm., Paris, 1979-80, Lycee St.-Louis and Inst. Nat. Agronomique, Paris, 1981-82; lectr. French U. Notre Dame, Ind., 1984-87; vis. asst. prof. Tulane U., New Orleans, 1987-88; asst. prof. French U. Nebr., Lincoln, 1988-91, Purdue U., West Lafayette, Ind., 1991-97, assoc. prof. French, 1997—, chmn. French sect., 1999—2001. Editor Newsletter for Paris-Greimassian Semiotics, 1990-92, 97, La Mode en 1830, 2000. Decorated chevalier Ordre Palmes Academiques; Notre Dame scholar, 1969-73; Rotary fellow, 1973-74, French Govt. fellow, 1981-82, Purdue Ctr. for Humanistic Studies fellow, 2006, Camargo Found. fellow, 2007; grantee NEH, 1990; named Coll. Tchr. of Yr., Ind., 2005. Mem. MLA, Am. Assn. Tchrs. French, (Tchr. of Yr. for Ind. 2005), Ind. Fgn. Lang. Tchrs. Assn. (Coll. Tchr. of Yr. 2005), Semiotic Soc. Am. (exec. bd. 1992-94), Toronto Semiotic Cir., Can. Semiotic Assn., Assn. Internat. de Semiotique Visuelle. Avocations: jogging, biking, gardening. Office: Purdue U Fgn Langs Stanley Coulter Hall West Lafayette IN 47907 Office Phone: 765-494-3828. Business E-Mail: broden@purdue.edu.

BRODERICK, B. MICHAEL, JR., state legislator, banker; Banker, Canton, S.D.; mem. S.D. Ho. of Reps., Pierre, S.D. Mem. agr., nat. resources and transp. coms. S.D. Ho. of Reps.

BRODERICK, DENNIS JOHN, lawyer, retail executive; b. Pitts., Dec. 7, 1948; m. Marian Kinney. BA, U. Notre Dame, 1970; JD, Georgetown U., 1976. Bar: Ohio 1976. Assoc. Hahn, Loeser, Freidheim, Dean & Wellman, Cleve., 1976-81; staff atty. Firestone Tire & Rubber Co., Akron, Ohio, 1982—84, sr. atty., 1984—85, asst. gen. counsel, 1985—87; v.p., dep. gen. counsel for regions Macy's Inc. (formerly Federated Dept. Stores, Inc.), Cin., 1987-88; v.p., gen. counsel Macy's Inc., Cin., 1988-90, sr. v.p., gen. counsel, 1990—, sec., 1993—. Served USN, 1970—73. Mem.: Black Lawyers' Assn. of Cin., Cin. Bar Assn., Am. Corp. Counsel Assn. (dir N.E. Ohio Chpt. 1986). Avocations: motorcycling, motorboating, horseback riding, golf. Office: Macy's Inc 7 W 7th St Cincinnati OH 45202-2424

BRODEUR, ARMAND EDWARD, pediatric radiologist; b. Penacook, NH, Jan. 8, 1922; s. Felix and Patronyne Antoinette (Lavoie) B.; m. Gloria Marie Thompson, June 4, 1947; children: Armand Paul, Garrett Michael, Mark Stephen, Mariette Therese, Michelle Bernadette, Paul Francis. AB, St. Anselm Coll., 1945; MD, St. Louis U., 1947, M.Rd., 1952; LLD (hon.), St Anselm Coll., 1974. Intern St. Louis U. Hosps., 1947-48, resident in pediat., 1948-49; resident in radiology St. Louis U. Hosps. and St. Louis U. Grad. Sch., 1949-52; asst. dean. St. Louis Sch. Medicine, 1947, assoc. dean, 1950—52; instr. St. Louis U. Sch. Medicine, 1952-60, sr. instr., 1960-62, asst. prof., 1962-65, assoc. prof., 1965-70, prof. radiology, 1970—, chmn. dept. radiology, 1975-78, vice chmn. dept., 1978-88, prof. pediat., 1979—, prof. juvenile law, 1979—; pvt. practice specializing in pediat. radiology St. Louis, 1954-56; radiologist-in-chief Cardinal Glennon Meml. Hosp. for Children, St. Louis, 1956-88, Shriners Hosp. for Children, 1988—; assoc. v.p., bd. govs. Cardinal Glennon Children's Hosp., St. Louis. Lectr. and cons. in field; med. dir. radiography Sanford Brown Coll., 1996—. Radio show host Doctor to Doctor, Sta. KMOX-CBS, St. Louis; host weekly To Your Health; health reporter Sta. KMOV-TV, also Sta. WFUN-FM, Sta. KSIV-AM; TV host Sta. WCVB Channel 5, Boston; author: Radiologic Diagnosis in Infants and Children, 1965, Radiology of the Pediatric Elbow, 1980, Radiologic Pathology for Allied Health Professions, 1980, Child Maltreatment, 1993, also monographs; contbr. articles to profl. jours., numerous tchg. tapes. Bd. dirs. ARC, TB Soc., March of Dimes, 15 others. With U.S. Army, 1942-46, with USPHS, 1952-54. Decorated Knight Equestrian Order Holy Sepulchre Jerusalem; recipient Mo. Health Care Communicator of Yr. award, 1991, Welby award Nat. Acad. Radio and TV Health Communicators, Health-care Leadership award Met. Hosp. St. Louis, 1994, numerous civic awards; Armand Brodeur Day proclaimed by City of St. Louis; named St. Paul Man of Yr., 1991; ann. lecture named in his honor dept. radiology St. Louis U. Sch. Medicine, 1998; named one of very few Top Radiologists in Am., 2002-03. Fellow Am. Coll. Radiology, Am. Acad. Pediat.; mem. AMA (Bronze medal, Golden Apple), Soc. Pediat. Radiology, Radio. Soc. N.Am., Nat. Assn. Med. Communicators (charter, co-founder, pres. 1987-88), Nat. Assn. Physician Broadcasters (founder, pres., Lifetime Achievement award), Sigma Xi, Alpha Omega Alpha, Alpha Sigma Nu, Phi Beta Kappa, Rho Kappa Sigma. Roman Catholic. Home: 6 Huntleigh Trails Ln Saint Louis MO 63131-4801 Office: 2001 S Lindbergh Blvd Saint Louis MO 63131-3579

BRODHEAD, WILLIAM MCNULTY, lawyer, retired congressman; b. Cleve., Sept. 12, 1941; s. William McNulty and Agnes Marie (Franz) B.; m. Kathleen Garlock, Jan. 16, 1965; children: Michael, Paul. AB, Wayne State U., 1965; JD, U. Mich., 1967. Bar: Mich. 1968, D.C. 1983. Tchr., Detroit, 1964-65; atty. City of Detroit, 1969-70; mem. Mich. Ho. Reps., 1971-74, 94th-97th Congresses from 17th Dist., mem. com. on ways and means, 1977-82, mem. budget com., 1979-80; chmn. Democratic Study Group, 1981-82; ptnr. firm Plunkett & Cooney P.C., Detroit, 1982—. Trustee The Skillman Found., Mich.'s Children; chair Focus: Hope-Covenant House of Mich.; dir. Citizens Rsch. Coun. of Mich. Home: 5096 Mirror Lake Ct West Bloomfield MI 48323-1534 Office: Law Offices of William Brodhead 31700 Middlebelt Rd Ste 150 Farmington Hills MI 48334 Office Phone: 248-539-7720. E-mail: wbrodhead@wbrodhead.com.

BRODKEY, ROBERT STANLEY, chemical engineering educator; b. LA, Sept. 14, 1928; s. Harold R. and Clara (Goldman) B.; m. Martha Mahr, Dec. 22, 1958 (div. Nov. 1971); 1 son, Philip Arthur; m. Carolyn Patch, Dec. 6, 1975. AA in Chemistry, San Francisco City Coll., 1948; BS with highest honors, U. Calif.-Berkeley, 1950, MS in Chem. Engring, 1950; PhD in Chem. Engring. (Gulf Oil fellow), U. Wis., 1952. Rsch. chem. engr. Esso Rsch. & Engring. Co., Linden, NJ, 1952-56, Esso Std. Oil Co., Bayway, NJ, 1956-57; asst. prof. chem. engring. Ohio State U., Columbus, 1957-60, assoc. prof., 1960-64, prof., 1964-92, prof. emeritus, 1992—. Cons. on turbulent motion, mixing kinetics, rheology, 2-phase flow, fluid dynamics, image processing and analysis; expository lectr. GAMM Conf., 1975; vis. prof. Japan Soc. Promotion Sci., 1978; Clyde chair engring. U. Utah, fall 1994. Author: Transport Phenomena, A Unified Approach, 1988, reprint edit., 2004, The Phenomena of Fluid Motions, 1967, reprint edit., 1995, 2004; editor: Turbulence in Mixing Operations, 1975; contbr. articles to profl. jours. Recipient Outstanding Paper of Yr. award Can. Jour. Chem. Engring., 1970; NATO sr. fellow in sci. Max Planck Institut für Strömungsforschung, Göttingen, Fed. Republic Germany, 1972; Alexander Von Humboldt Found. sr. U.S. scientist award, 1975, 83; sr. rsch. award Coll. Engring. Ohio State U., 1983, 86; Disting. Sr. Rsch. award Am. Soc. Engring. Edn., 1985; Chem. Engr. lectureship award Am. Soc. Engring. Edn., 1986; North Am. Mixing Forum award, 1994. Fellow AAAS, AIChE, Am. Phys. Soc., Am. Inst. Chemists, Am. Acad. Mechanics; mem. Am. Chem. Soc., Soc. Engring. Sci., Soc. Rheology, Sigma Xi, Phi Lambda Upsilon, Alpha Gamma Sigma, Phi Beta Delta. Achievements include patents in field. Office: Ohio St Univ 140 W 19th Ave Columbus OH 43210-1110 Home Phone: 614-262-3967; Office Phone: 614-292-2609. Business E-Mail: brodkey.1@osu.edu.

BRODSKY, WILLIAM J., investment company executive; b. NYC, 1944; AB, Syracuse U., 1965, JD, 1968. Bar: N.Y. 1969, Ill. 1985. Atty. Model, Roland & Co., 1968-74; with Am. Stock Exch., 1974-82, exec. v.p. ops., 1979-82; exec. v.p., COO Chgo. Merc. Exch., 1982-85, pres., CEO, 1985-97; chmn., CEO Chgo. Bd. Options Exch., 1997—. Mem. internat. adv. com. Fed. Res. Bank N.Y.; mem. adv. coun. J.L. Kellogg Grad. Sch. Mgmt.; bd. dirs. Peoples Energy Corp. Bd. trustees orthwestern Meml. Healthcare, chair investment com.; trustee Syracuse U. Recipient inclusion, Jr. Achievement Chgo. Bus. Hall of Fame, 2001, Lifetime Achievement award, Anti-Defamation League, 2003. Mem. N.Y. State Bar Assn., Swiss Futures and Options Assn. (bd. dirs.), Econ. Club Chgo., Comml. Club Chgo.; chair, Northwestern Memorial Hosp. Investment Com.; Coun. on Foreign Relations in New York City Achievements include: selection for inclusion into Derivatives Hall of Fame, 2000, Jr. Achievement Chgo. Bus. Hall of Fame, 2001. Office: Chgo Bd Options Exch LaSalle at Van Buren Chicago IL 60605-7413 Office Phone: 312-786-5600.

BRODY, HOWARD, medical educator; b. Chgo., 1949; MD, Mich. State U., 1976. Diplomate Am. Bd. Family Practice. Resident in family practice U. Va., Charlottesville, 1977—80; prof. dept. family practice Coll. Human Medicine Mich. State U., East Lansing; hosp. appt. Sparrow Hosp. Mem.: STFM, NAS (mem. Inst. Medicine), AAFP. Office: Mich State U Dept Family Practice B-100 Clinical Ctr East Lansing MI 48824-1313 Home Phone: 517-694-2396; Office Phone: 517-353-3544 ext. 427. Business E-Mail: brody@msu.edu.

BRODY, LAWRENCE, lawyer, educator; b. St. Louis, Aug. 12, 1942; s. Max and Jeannette (Cohen) B.; m. Janice Dobinsky, Dec. 25, 1967; 1 child, Michael Allen. BS in Econs., U. Pa., 1964; JD, Washington U., St. Louis, 1967; LLM in Tax, NYU, 1968. Bar: Mo. Assoc. atty. Husch, Eppenberger, Donohue, Elson & Cornfeld, St. Louis, 1968-74, ptnr., 1974-86, Bryan Cave, LLP, St. Louis, 1986—, group leader Pvt. Client. Adj. prof. Washington U. Sch. Law, 1968—. Author: Missouri Estate Planning, 1988; author, editor Life Insurance Counsellor Series, 1990, 91. Fellow Am. Coll. of Trust and Estate Counsel, Am. Coll. Tax Counsel; mem. Adv. Bd. of Tax Mgmt. Office: Bryan Cave LLP One Metropolitan Square 211 N Broadway Ste 3600 Saint Louis MO 63102-2733 Office Phone: 314-259-2652. E-mail: lbrody@bryancave.com.

BROECKER, SHERRY, state legislator; b. Feb. 14, 1951; m. Jerry Broecker; 3 children. Student, U. Minn. Self-employed custom picture framer; rep. Dist. 53B Minn. Ho. of Reps., 1994—. Home: 1355 7th Ave SE Forest Lake MN 55025-2053

BROEKER, JOHN MILTON, lawyer; b. Berwyn, Ill., May 27, 1940; s. Milton Monroe and Marjorie Grace (Wilson) B.; m. Linda J. Broeker, Dec. 9, 1983; children: Sara Elizabeth, Ross Goddard; stepchildren: Terrance Mercil Jr., Johnny Mercil, Veronica Mercil. BA, Grinnell Coll., 1962; JD cum laude, U. Minn., 1965. Bar: Minn. 1965, Wis. 1968, U.S. Ct. Appeals (8th cir.) 1966, U.S. Dist. Ct. Minn. 1967,. U.S. Tax Ct. 1969, U.S. Ct. Appeals (5th cir.) 1971, U.S. Dist. Ct. (we. dist.) Wis. 1982, U.S. Supreme Ct. 1984. Law clk. to presiding judge U.S. Ct. Appeals (8th cir.), 1965-66; ptnr. Gray, Plant, Mooty, Mooty & Bennett, Mpls., 1966-71, Broeker, Geer, Fletcher & LaFond and predecessor firms, Mpls., 1971-91; v.p., gen. counsel NordicTrack, Inc., Mpls., 1991-94; founder Broeker Enterprises, 1992—; pres. Legal Mgmt. Strategies, Inc., Mpls., 1994—; of counsel Popham, Haik, Schnobrich & Kaufman, Ltd., Mpls., 1995-96, Halleland, Lewis, Nilan, Sipkins & Johnson, Mpls., 1996-97; pvt. practice, 1997—. Instr. U Minn. Law Sch., 1967-72; lectr. convs. and seminars, 1969—; lectr. U. Minn. Ctr. for Long Term Care Edn., 1972-77, Gt. Lakes Health Congress, 1972, Sister Kenney Inst., 1972. Contbr. articles to legal jours. Bd. dirs. Minn. Environ. Scis. Found., Inc., 1971-73; bd. dirs. Project Environ. Found., 1977-83, chmn., 1980-82; mem. alumni bd. Grinnell Coll., 1968-71; chmn. MInnetonka Environ. Quality and Natural Resources Commn., 1971-72; trustee The Writers Project, Inc., 1999-2001. Recipient Outstanding Alumni award Grinnell Coll., 1973. Mem. ABA (forum com. on health law 1978-91), Minn. Bar Assn. (chmn. environ. law com. 1970-72), State Bar Wis., Hennepin County Bar Assn. (chmn. environ. law com. 1976-77, legis. com. 1972-76, health law com. 1977-79), Am. Soc. Hosp. Attys., Minn. Soc. Hosp. Attys., Am. Health Care Assn. (legal coordinating com. 1970-75, labor com. 1973-74), Nat. Health Lawyers Assn., Minn. Thoroughbred Assn. (bd. dirs. 1991-92), Minn. Quarterhorse Racing Assn. (bd. dirs. 1994—2003, pres. 1997-99), Sierra Club (nat. dir. 1974-76, chmn. chpt. 1971-72, regional v.p. 1973-74). Home: 11402 Burr Ridge Ln Eden Prairie MN 55347-4717 Office: 8120 Penn Ave S Ste 151Q Bloomington MN 55431-1326 Office Phone: 952-886-0435. Business E-Mail: jbroeker@msn.com.

BROGAN, LISA S., lawyer; b. Chgo., Apr. 23, 1963; BA, Northwestern U., 1984, JD, 1987. Bar: Ill. 1987, U.S. Dist. Ct. (no. dist.) Ill. 1988, U.S. Ct. Appeals (fed. cir.) 1989, U.S. Ct. Appeals (7th cir.) 1994. Atty. Baker & McKenzie, Chgo., 1987—. Mem.: ABA, Ill. State Bar Assn., Chgo. (Ill.) Bar Assn. Office: Baker & McKenzie One Prudential Plz 130 East Randolph Dr Chicago IL 60601

BROMBACHER, BRUCE E., mathematics educator; b. Bucyrus, Ohio, July 3, 1948; s. Willard W. and Aurelia R. (Beisheim) B.; m. Marcia L. Mertz, June 9, 1973; children: Ryan E., Erin E. BS, Heidelberg Coll., 1970; MS, Ohio State U., 1975. Tchr. Upper Arlington (Ohio) Schs., 1976—. Sgt. U.S. Army, 1970-72, Vietnam. Named at. Tchr. Yr., 1982. Mem. NEA, Ohio Edn. Assn., Upper Arlington Edn. Assn., Nat. Coun. Tchrs. Math., Ohio Coun. Tchrs. Math., Ohio Mid. Sch. Assn., Sch. Sci. and Math. Assn., Columbus and Suburban Coun. Tchrs. of Math., Math. Assn. Am., Nat. State Tchrs. of Yr., Nat. Mid. Sch. Assn., Phi Delta Kappa, Kappa Delta Phi. Methodist. Home: 291 Electric Ave Westerville OH 43081-2676

BROMLEY, RICHARD, lawyer; b. Rosetown, Sask., Feb. 8, 1944; s. Arthur Amos and Elsie Anna Freda (Frerichs) B.; m. Marilyn Kay Bill, Aug. 12, 1966; children: Douglas Arthur, Shannon Kimberly, Lindsay Erin. BA, U. Iowa, 1966, JD, 1968. Bar: Iowa 1968, Ill. 1969, US Tax Ct., US Ct. Claims, US Ct. Appeals (5th, 7th, 8th, 10th, fed. cirs.), US Supreme Ct. Ptnr. Foley & Lardner LLP, Chgo. Lectr. Law Sch., DePaul U., Chgo., 1984-89; adj. prof. Kent. Coll. Law, Ill. Inst. Tech., Chgo., 1987-89; sr. v.p., bd. dirs. Ins. Tax Conf. Editor: Iowa Law Rev., 1967-68; bd. advisors Ins. Tax Law Rev., 1989—. Vice chmn., bd. dirs. Chgo. Crime Commn., 1993-2007; sec., bd. dirs. Lookingglass Theatre. Mem. ABA (chmn. com. on taxation of ins. cos.), Fed. Bar Assn. (ins. co. tax com.), Chgo. Bar Assn. (exec. coun. fed. tax com.), Legal Club Chgo., Union League Club, Waushara Country Club (Wautoma, Wis.), Order of Coif. Lutheran. Office: Foley & Lardner LLP 321 N Clark St Ste 2800 Chicago IL 60610-4764 Office Phone: 312-832-4517. Business E-Mail: rbromley@foley.com.

BROMM, CURT, state legislator; b. Oakland, Nebr., Mar. 19, 1945; m. Vicki Nodlinski, 1968; children: Jason, Jenefer, John, Jina, Jaron. Student, U. Nebr. Past county atty. Saunders County; mem. Nebr. Legislature from 23rd dist., Lincoln, 1992—; mem. bus. and labor com. Nebr. Legislature, Lincoln, mem. natural resources and urban affairs com., vice chmn. rules com., speaker of the legislature, 2002—. Chmn. bd. dirs. Saunders County Sch. Reorgn. Bd.; mem., pres. Wahoo Pub. Sch. Bd. Mem. Nebr. State Bar Assn. Home: 1448 N Pine St Wahoo NE 68066-1449 Office: Nebraska Unicameral Legislature State Capitol PO Box 94604 Lincoln NE 68509-4604

BRONSON, DAVID LEIGH, physician, educator; b. Bath, Maine, Mar. 24, 1947; s. Frank Edgar Bronson and Edna Louise (Sullivan) Belanger; m. Susan Kylei McEvoy, May 27, 1973 (div. Dec. 1988); children: Chad Devin, Carly Anne, Jaclyn Ruth, Jonathan David; m. Kathleen Susan Franco, Jan. 30, 1993; children: Roberto Anthony Franco, John Carlos Franco. BA, U. Maine, 1969; MD, U. Vt., 1973. Diplomate Am. Bd. Internal Medicine, Am. Bd. Geriatrics. Med. resident U. Wis., Madison, 1973-74, U. Vt., Burlington, 1974-76, asst. prof. medicine, 1977-83, assoc. prof. medicine, 1983-92, vice chmn. dept. medicine, 1990-92; chmn. dept. internal medicine Cleve. Clinic Found., 1992-96, chmn. regional med. practice, 1995—; assoc. prof. internal medicine Ohio State U., Columbus, 1992—; clin. prof. medicine Pa. State U., Hershey, 1995—. Pres. med. staff, trustee Med. Ctr. Hosp. Vt., Burlington, 1989-90; trustee Univ. Health Ctr., Burlington, 1987-92. Contbr. numerous articles to profl. jours. Fellow ACP; mem. Am. Coll. Physician Execs., Am. Mgmt. Assn., Med. Group Mgmt. Assn., Am. Fedn. for Clin. Rsch., Soc. Gen. Internal Medicine. Office: Cleve Clinic Found 9500 Euclid Ave # S13 Cleveland OH 44195-0001

BRONSON, MICHAEL J., lawyer; b. Cin., May 14, 1976; BA in Polit. Sci., Denison U., 1998; JD, Vanderbilt U. Law Sch., 2001. Bar: Ohio 2001. Clerk Chief Judge, US Dist. Ct. Eastern Dist. NC; assoc. Vorys, Sater, Seymour and Pease LLP, Cin. Mng. editor Vanderbilt Law Review. Named one of Ohio's Rising Stars, Super Lawyers, 2006. Office: Vorys Sater Seymour and Pease LLP Ste 2000 Atrium Two PO Box 0236 221 E Fourth St Cincinnati OH 45201-0236 Office Phone: 513-723-4492. Office Fax: 513-852-7807.

BROOKE, JOHN L., history professor; b. Mass., May 19, 1953; m. Sara C. Balderston, July 31, 1979. BA in History and Anthropology, Cornell U., 1976; MA in History, U. Pa., 1977, PhD in History, 1982. Vis. asst. prof. Amherst (Mass.) Coll., 1982-83; asst. prof. to prof. Tufts U., Medford, Mass., 1983-2001; dept. chair, 1996-97; prof. Ohio State U., Columbus, 2001—. Author: The Heart of the Commonwealth: Society and Political Culture in Worcester County, Massachusetts, 1713-1861, 1989, The Refiner's Fire: The Making of Mormon Cosmology, 1644-1844, 1994; contbr. articles to scholarly jours. Recipient award at. Soc. Daus. Colonial Wars, 1989, E. Harold Hugo Meml. Book prize Old Sturbridge Village Rsch. Libr. Soc., 1989, Merle Curti award for intellectual history, 1991, book prize for Am. history Nat. Hist. Soc., 1991, Bancroft prize Columbia U., 1995, ann. book prize Soc. for Historians of Early Am. Republic, 1995, ann. book award New Eng. Hist. Assn., 1995; S.F. Haven fellow Am. Antiquarian Soc., 1982, faculty rsch. fellow Tufts U., 1983, 88, Charles Warren fellow Harvard U., 1986-87, jr. fellow NEH, 1986-87, sr. fellow Commonwealth Ctr., 1990-91, fellow Am. Coun. Learned Socs., 1990-91, NEH fellow 1997-98, Guggenheim fellow, 1997-98. Mem. AAUP, Am. Antiq. Soc., Am. Hist. Assn., Orgn. Am. Historians, Mass. Hist. Soc. Democrat. Home: 1097 Wyandotte Rd Columbus OH 43212-3245

BROOKS, BENJAMIN RIX, neurologist, educator; b. Cambridge, Mass., Dec. 1, 1942; s. Frederic Manning and Miriam Adelaide (Rix) B.; m. Susan Jane Whitmore, May 31, 1970; children: Nathaniel Phillips, Alexander Whitmore, Joshua Cushing. AB cum laude, Harvard U., 1965, MD magna cum laude, 1970. Diplomate Am. Bd. Psychiatry and Neurology, Am. Bd. Internal Medicine. Intern, asst. resident Harvard Med. Svc., Boston City Hosp., 1970-72; resident in neurology Mass. Gen. Hosp., Boston, 1972-74; clin. assoc. med. neurology br. Nat. Inst. Neurolog. Diseases and Stroke, Bethesda, Md., 1974-76; rsch. fellow neurovirology div. Johns Hopkins Med. Sch., Balt., 1976-78, asst. prof. neurology dept., 1978-82; assoc. prof. neurology and med. microbiology U. Wis. Med. Sch., Madison, 1982-87, prof., 1987—; staff neurologist William S. Middleton Meml. VA Hosp., Madison, 1982-84, chief neurology svc., 1984—. Examiner Am. Bd. Psychiatry and Neurology, Evanston, Ill., 1980—; chmn. neuropharmacologic drugs adv. com. FDA, Rockville, Md., 1982-85; vis. prof. various schs., U.S., Eng., Fed. Republic Germany, Japan, Spain. Editor: Amyotrophic Lateral Sclerosis, 1987, Brain Rsch. Bull., 1980-90; contbr. papers, revs., abstracts to profl. publs., chpts. to books. Mem. ushers com. Grace Episcopal Ch., Madison, 1983—; mem. talented and gifted evaluation com. Madison Sch. Bd., 1986; mem. com. on VA manpower of the Inst. of Medicine of the Nat. Acad. Scis. Lt. comdr. USPHS, 1974-76. Recipient Nat. Rsch. award Nat. Inst. Neurolog. and Communicative Disorders and Stroke, 1976-78, Tchr.-Investigator Devel. award, 1978-82. Mem. Am. Acad. Neurology (chair govt. svcs. sect. 1995—, mem. animal rsch. com. 1990-95), Am. Neurolog. Assn., Wis. Neurolog. Soc. (sec.-treas. 1985-87, v.p. 1988, pres.-elect 1989, pres. 1990), Soc. for Neurosci., .Am. ALS Care Registry (adv. com.), Soc. Exptl. Neuropathology, Am. Soc. Microbiology, Internat. Soc. Neuroimmunology, Assn. VA Neurologists (pres. 1994-96, councilor 1996—), Soc. In Vitro Biology, Tissue Culture Assn., World Fedn. Neurology Rsch. Group on Motor Neuron Diseases (steering com.). Republican. Avocations: running, sailing, swimming, bicycling, hiking. Office: Wm S Middleton Meml VA Hosp 2500 Overlook Ter Madison WI 53705-2254

BROOKS, ERNIE L., lawyer; b. Dayton, Ohio, Dec. 8, 1942; BSEE, Gen. Motors Inst., 1967; MSEE, Purdue U., 1967; JD summa cum laude, Georgetown U. and Wayne State U., 1972. Bar: Mich. 1972, registered: US Patent and Trademark office. Pres. Brooks Kushman, P.C., Southfield, Mich. Note and comment editor: Wayne Law Rev., 1971—72. Named one of Top 10 Trial Lawyers in Am., Nat. Law Jour., 2006. Mem.: ABA, Mich. Intellectual Property Law Assn., Ill. State Bar Assn. Office: Brooks Kushman PC 1000 Town Ctr 22nd Fl Southfield MI 48075 Office Phone: 248-358-4400. Office Fax: 248-358-3351. E-mail: ebrooks@brookskushman.com.

BROOKS, KENNETH N., forestry educator; m. Pamela Naylor; children: Marianne, Robin, Cherie, Nicole. BS in Range Sci., Utah State U., 1966; MS in Watershed Mgmt., U. Ariz., 1969, PhD in Watershed Mgmt., 1970. Hydrologist North Pacific Divsn. Corps of Engrs., Portland, Oreg., 1971-73, Tng. and Methods br. Hydrologic Engring. Ctr., Davis, Calif., 1973-75; asst. prof. dept. forest resources U. Minn., St. Paul, 1975-79, assoc. prof., 1979-85, prof., 1985—, dir. grad. studies in natural resources sci. and mgmt., 1987—; fellow Environment and Policy Inst. East-West Ctr., Honolulu, 1983—84. Cons. nat. and internat. agencies and firms including Food and Agrl. Orgn. of UN, U.S. Agy. for Internat. Devel., World Bank; condr. workshops in field; Fulbright lectr., Taiwan, 1997-98. Co-author: Guidelines for Economic Appraisal of Watershed Management Projects, 1987, Integrated Watershed Mgmt., 2007, Hydrology and the Management of Watersheds, 1991, 3d edit. 2003, Challenges in Upland Conservation: Asia and the Pacific, 1993, Dryland Forestry, 1995; contbr. articles to profl. jours. Am. Inst. Hydrology (chmn. bd. registration 1995-2003, sec. 1992), Soc. Am. Foresters (chmn. water resources working group 1991-93), Am. Water Resources Assn. (dir. West North Ctrl. dist. 1987-90), Western Snow Conf., Internat. Soc. Tropical Foresters, Xi Sigma Pi, Sigma Xi, Phi Kappa Phi. Business E-Mail: kbrooks@umn.edu.

BROOKS, MARION, newscaster; BA in English, Spelman Coll. Weekend anchor Sta. WABG-TV, Greenville, Miss., anchor weekday 6 pm and 11 pm newscasts; gen. assignment reporter, morning anchor Sta. WJKS-TV, Jacksonville, Fla., 1991—93; gen. assignment reporter Sta. KTVI-TV, St. Louis, 1993—96, weekend anchor; anchor noon newscast, reporter 5 pm and 6 pm newscasts Sta. WSB-TV, Atlanta, 1996—98; co-anchor 5 pm and 10 pm weekend newscasts Sta. WMAQ-TV, Chgo., 1998—, co-anchor 4:30 pm and 5 pm weekday newscasts, healthwatch reporter. Mem.: Nat. Assn. Black Journalists. Office: NBC 454 N Columbus Dr Chicago IL 60611

BROOKS, PETER, radio director; m. Lynette Brooks; children: Megan, Kirsten. Mgr. Family Life Radio stas., Albuquerque, Mason; with Family Life Comms. WUGN, Midland, Mich., 1977—, gen. mgr. Avocations: community theater, racquetball. Mailing: 510 E Isabella Rd Midland MI 48640

BROOKS, PHILLIP, advertising executive; b. 1955; With Affiliate of Excellence Co., Mpls., 1976—, now pres.; with Excellence Co., Mpls., pres., CEO. Office: The Excellence Co 600 Lakeview Point Dr Saint Paul MN 55112-3494

BROOKS, RANDY, research company executive; BS, U. Maryland, 1973; MBA, U. Cin., 1975. Pres., founder Directions Rsch., 1988—. Speaker at industry events, ARF, AMA, AMA Tutorial Conf., CASRO, MRA; bd. mem. U. Ga. MMR program; bd. mem. MRA-CBOK com. Office: Directions Rsch Inc 401 E Court St Ste 200 Cincinnati OH 45202-1379

BROOKS, RICHARD DICKINSON, lawyer; b. Daytona Beach, Fla., Sept. 17, 1944; m. Betty Jane Huba, Aug. 28, 1971; children: Hillary Ann, Richard Jason. BA, Marietta Coll., Ohio, 1967; JD, Case Western Res. U., 1972. Bar: Ohio 1972, U.S. Dist. Ct. (so. dist.) Ohio 1975, U.S. Ct. Appeals (6th cir.) 1993. Atty. Bridgewater Robe Brooks & Keifer, Athens, Ohio, 1972-87, Arter & Hadden, Columbus, Ohio, 1987—2003, Bailey Cavalieri LLC, Columbus, 2003—. Coach Upper Arlington Cub Scout Baseball, Columbus, 1989-90; pres. A.T.C.O. Inc. Sheltered Workshop, Athens, 1986; bd. dirs. Athens C. of C., 1984-87. Sgt. U.S. Army, 1968-70, Vietnam. Fellow Am. Bar Found., Ohio Bar Found. (pres. 1988); mem. ABA, Ohio Bar Assn. (exec. com. 1979-83),

Columbus Bar Assn. (environ. law com.), Athens County Bar Assn. (pres. 1978-79), Ohio CLE Inst. (bd. dirs. 1989-90), Ohio State Legal Svcs. Assn. (bd. dirs. 1982—). Avocations: basketball, tennis, fishing, furniture restoration. Office: Bailey Cavalieri LLC 10 W Broad St Ste 2100 Columbus OH 43215-3422 Office Phone: 614-229-3285. E-mail: richard.brooks@baileycavalieri.com.

BROOKS, RICHARD L., professional football coach; b. Forest, Calif., Aug. 20, 1941; BA in Phys. Edn., Oreg. State U., 1963, MA in Edn., 1964. Asst. freshman coach Oreg. State U., 1963, defensive line coach, 1965-69, 73, head coach, 1977-94; asst. coach Norte Del Rio H.S., 1964; linebackers coach UCLA, 1970, 76; defensive backs/spl. teams coach San Francisco 49'ers, 1974-75; head coach St. Louis Rams, 1995—. Named Coll. Football Coach of Yr., The Sporting News, 1994. Achievements: coached team to victory Independence Bowl, 1989, coached team to 1st place Pacific 10 Conf., 1994. Office: St Louis Rams Matthews Dickey Boys Club Saint Louis MO 63115-1276

BROOKS, ROGER, state legislator; Rep. S.D. State Ho. Reps. Dist. 10, until 2000, mem. agr. and natural resources and edn. coms.; ret. Computer cons.

BROOKS, ROGER KAY, insurance company executive; b. Clarion, Iowa, Apr. 30, 1937; s. Edgar Sherman and Hazel (Whipple) B.; m. Marcia Rae Ramsay, Nov. 19, 1955 (div. Sept. 1989); children: Michael, Jeffrey, David; m. Saulene Richer, Mar. 17, 1990. BA in Math., magna cum laude, U. Iowa, 1959. Actuarial asst. Central Life Assurance Co., Des Moines, 1959—64, asst. sec., 1964-68, v.p., 1968-70, exec. v.p., 1970-72, pres., COO, 1972—94; CEO AmerUs (merger of Central Life and American Mutual), 1994—, chmn. emeritus, 2006—. Mem. Des Moines Devel. Com. Named to Iowa Bus. Hall of Fame, Iowa Ins. Hall of Fame; recipient Alexis de Toqueville Soc. award, United Way, Ctrl. Iowa, 2004. Fellow Soc. Actuaries; mem. Greater Des Moines C. of C. (past chmn.), Actuaries Club of Des Moines (past pres.), Phi Beta Kappa. Presbyterian (elder). Club: Des Moines (past pres.). Office: AmerUs Group PO Box 1555 Des Moines IA 50306-1555 Business E-Mail: rbrooks@doextra.com.

BROOKS, SUSAN W., prosecutor; Grad., Miami U.; JD, Ind. U., 1985. Ptnr. McClure, McClure & Kammen, 1985—97; dep. mayor City of Indpls., 1998—99; of counsel Ice Miller Law Firm, Indpls., 2000—01; US atty. (so. dist.) Ind. US Dept. Justice, 2001—. Mem. Atty. Gens. Adv. Com., 2002—03, 2005—, vice chair, 2006—. Chair United Way's Violence and Safety Impact Coun.; protocol chair World Police & Fire Games, Indpls., 2001; nominating com. Hoosier Capitol Girl Scouts Coun.; adv. bd. Marion County Commn. on Youth; mem. Ind. Fed. Cmty. Defender Bd.; bd. mem. Jr. League of Indpls., Little Red Door Cancer Agy., Marion County Commn. on Youth, Network of Women in Bus., Greater Indpls. Progress Com. Named Influential Woman of Indpls, Indpls. Bus. Jour., 1999, Who's Who in Law, 2002; named to 40 under 40 list; recipient Alumnae of Year, Ind. U. Sch. Law, 2006. Office: US Attys Office 10 W Market St Ste 2100 Indianapolis IN 46204 Office Phone: 317-226-6333.

BROOME, MARION, dean; BSN, Med. Coll. Georgia, 1973; MN in Family Health Nursing, U. S.C., 1977; PhD in Child and Family Devel., U. Georgia, 1984; post-doctoral studies, U. Ala., 1986—88. Nursing sci. study section NIH, 1997—2001; assoc. dean, prof. rsch. U. Ala., 1999—2004; cons. Ind. U. Sch. Nursing, 2004—, dean, 2004—. Pres. Soc. Pediatric Nurses; bd. dirs. Assn. Care of Children's Health, Midwest Nursing Rsch. Soc. Office: Ind U Sch Nursing Office Ednl Svcs 1111 Middle Dr NU 117 Indianapolis IN 46202-5107

BROPHY, JERE EDWARD, education educator, researcher; b. Chgo., June 11, 1940; m. Arlene Sept. 21, 1963; children: Cheryl, Joseph. BS in Psychology, Loyola U., Chgo., 1962; MA in Human Devel., U. Chgo., 1965, PhD in Human Devel., 1967; Doctorate (hon.), U. Liege, 2004. Rsch. assoc., asst. prof. U. Chgo., 1967-68; from asst. to assoc. prof. U. Tex., Austin, 1968-76; staff devel. coord. S.W. Ednl. Devel. Lab., Austin, 1970-72; prof. Mich. State U., East Lansing, 1976-92, co-dir. Inst. for Rsch. on Tchg., 1981-93, univ. disting. prof., 1993—. Co-author: Teacher-Student Relationships: Causes and Consequences, 1974; editor (book series) Advances in Research on Teaching, 1989—. Fellow Ctr. for Advanced Study in the Behavioral Scis., 1994. Fellow: APA, Internat. Acad. Edn., Am. Psychol. Soc.; mem.: Nat. Soc. for the Study of Edn., Nat. Coun. for the Social Studies, Nat. Acad. Edn., Am. Ednl. Rsch. Assn. (Palmer O. Johnson award 1983, Presdl. citation 1995). Office: Mich State U 213B Erickson Hall East Lansing MI 48824-1034

BROPHY, JERE HALL, manufacturing executive; b. Schenectady, Mar. 11, 1934; s. Gerald Robert and Helen Dorothy (Hall) B.; m. Joyce Elaine Wright, Aug. 18, 1956; children: Jennifer, Carolyn, Jere. BS in Chem. Engring, U. Mich., 1956, BS in Metall. Engring, 1956, MS, 1957, PhD, 1958. Asst. prof. Mass. Inst. Tech., 1958-63; sect. supr. nickel alloys sect. Paul D. Merica Research Lab., Inco, Inc., Suffern, NY, 1963-67, research mgr. non-ferrous group, 1967-72, asst. mgr., 1972-73, mgr., 1973-77; dir. research and devel. and dir. Paul D. Merica Research Lab., Inco, Inc. (Inco Research and Devel. Center), 1978-80; dir. advanced tech. initiation INCO Ltd., NYC, 1980-82; v.p., dir. Materials and Mfg. Tech. Ctr. TRW Inc., Cleve., 1982-86, v.p. mfg. and materials devel. automotive sect., 1986-88; v.p. technology Brush Wellman Inc., Cleve., 1988-96; cons., 1996—. Author: (with J. Wolff) Thermodynamics of Structure; Contbr. (with J. Wolff) tech. articles to profl. jours. Fellow Am. Soc. Metals, AAAS; mem. Am. Inst. Mining and Metall. Engrs. (dir. IMD div. 1973-76), Am. Mgmt. Assn. (research and devel. council 1975-87). Clubs: Edgewater Yacht. Episcopalian. Home and Office: 31905 Jackson Rd Chagrin Falls OH 44022-1707

BROSNAHAN, ROGER PAUL, retired lawyer; b. Kansas City, Mo., Aug. 9, 1935; s. Earl and Helen (Mottin) Brosnahan; m. Jill Farley, Aug. 2, 1958; children: Paul, Connor, Helen, Farley, Tracy, Hugh, Lee. BS, St. Louis U., 1956; LLB, Mich. U., 1959. Bar: Mo. 1959, Minn. 1959, U.S. Supreme Ct. 1971, U.S. Dist. Ct. Appeals (8th cir.) 1975, U.S. Dist. Ct. Appeals (6th cir.) 1984, U.S. Dist. Ct. Appeals (10th cir.) 1999. Ptnr. Streater, Murphy, Brosnahan & Langford, Winona, Minn., 1959-78, Kutak, Rock & Huie, Mpls., 1979-82, Robins, Kaplan, Miller & Ciresi, Mpls., 1982-93, Brosnahan, Joseph & Suggs P.A., Mpls., 1993-99; prin. Law Offices of Roger P. Brosnahan, Winona, 1999—2005. Mem.: ABA (state del. 1976—88), Nat. Conf. Bar Pres. (pres. 1980—81), Minn. Bar Assn. (pres. 1974—75), Minn. Trial Lawyers Assn. Democrat. Roman Catholic. Office: Roger P Brosnahan Inc 116 Center St Winona MN 55987 Office Phone: 507-457-3000. Fax: 507-457-3001. E-mail: rpbros@mwt.net.

BROSZ, DON, retired state legislator; b. Alpena, SD, Sept. 17, 1931; Salesperson Procter & Gamble Dist. Co., 1962-82, sales and unit mgr., 1982-90; mem. S.D. Ho. of Reps., Pierre, 1995-97, S.D. Senate, Pierre, 1998—, mem. agr. and taxation coms., 1998—2003, mem. agr. com., chair edn. com. and taxation com. Mem. edn. and judiciary coms. S.D. Ho. of Reps. Bd. visitors S.D. U. Med. Sch.; mem. adv. bd. Sr. Companions for Eastern S.D.

BROTMAN, BARBARA LOUISE, journalist, writer; b. NYC, Feb. 23, 1956; d. Oscar J. and Ruth (Branchor) Brotman; m. Chuck Berman, Aug. 28, 1983; children: Robin, Nina. BA, Queens Coll., 1978. Writer, columnist Chgo. Tribune, 1978—. Recipient Ill. Newspapers Column Writing award, UPI, 1984, Peter Lisagor award, Sigma Delta Chi, 1984; John S. Knight fellow for profl. journalism, 2004. Avocation: broomball. Office: Chgo Tribune Co 435 N Michigan Ave Chicago IL 60611-4066

BROUDER, GERALD T., academic administrator; Interim chancellor, provost Columbia (Mo.) Coll., 1992-95, pres., 1995—. Office: Columbia Coll 1001 Rogers St Columbia MO 65216-0001

BROUS, THOMAS RICHARD, lawyer; b. Fulton, Mo., Jan. 7, 1943; s. Richard Pendleton and Augusta (Gilpin) B.; m. Patricia Catlin, Sept. 12, 1964; (dec. Sept. 1999); children: Anna Catlin Brous, Joel Pendleton Brous; m. Mary Lou McClelland Kroh, Sept. 8, 2001. BSBA, Northwestern U., 1965; JD cum laude, U. Mich., 1968. Bar: Mo. 1968, U.S. Dist. Ct. (we. dist.) Mo. 1968, U.S. Ct. Mil. Appeals 1968, U.S. Supreme Ct. 1971. Assoc. Watson & Marshall L.C., Kans. City, Mo., 1968-78, ptnr., 1978-96, mng. ptrn., 1992-94; shareholder Stinson, Mag & Fizzell, P.C., Kans. City, Mo., 1996—2002; ptnr. Stinson Morrison Hecker LLP, Kans. City, 2002—. Adj. faculty U. Kans. Sch. of Law, 2006—; mem. steering com. U. Mo. Kansas City Law Sch. Employee Benefits Inst., 1990—2001, chmn. 1992-93; with Ctrl. Mtn. Tax Exempt and Govtl. Entities Coun. IRS, 1997-2005. Author: Chapter 26, III Missouri Business Organizations, 1998, Chapter 10, Missouri Specialized Business Entities, 2006; asst. editor Mich. Law Rev., 1966-68. Mem. vestry St. Andrews Episcopal Ch., Kansas City, 1974-77, Grace & Holy Trinity Cathedral, 1994—, chancellor, 1998—; trustee Kansas City Repertory Theatre, Inc., 1990—, pres., 1995-98; v.p., treas. Barstow Sch., Kansas City, 1982-86; dir. Met. Orgn. to Counter Sexual Abuse, Kansas City, 1992-95; vis. com. Divinity Sch. U. Chgo., 2006-. Capt. US Army, 1968—72. Mem. ABA, Univ. Club (pres. 1988-89), Greater Kansas City Soc. Hosp. Attys., Kansas City Met. Bar Assn., Heart of Am. Employee Benefit Conf., The Mo. Bar Assn. (vice-chair employee benefits com. 1997-2000), Mo. Soc. Hosp. Attys., Delta Upsilon, Beta Gamma Sigma. Episcopalian. Avocations: reading, hiking, gardening. Office: Stinson Morrison Hecker LLP 1201 Walnut Ste 2800 Kansas City MO 64106 Office Phone: 816-691-3368. Personal E-mail: tbrous@stinson.com.

BROWMAN, DAVID L(UDVIG), archaeologist; b. Dec. 9, 1941; s. Ludvig G. and Audra (Arnold) B.; m. M. Jane Fox, Apr. 24, 1965; children: Lisa, Tina, Becky. BA, U. Mont., 1963; MA, U. Wash., 1966; PhD, Harvard U., 1970. Hwy. archaeologist Wash. State Hwy. Dept., Olympia, 1964-66; field dir. Yale U., New Haven, 1968-69; tutor Harvard U., 1969-70; mem. faculty Washington U., St. Louis, 1970—, prof. archeology, 1984—, chmn., 1986—. Dir. Cons. Survey Archeology, St. Louis, 1976—, Inst. Study of Plants, Food and Man, Kirkwood, Mo. 1979-84: cons. St. Louis Dept. Parks and Recreation, 1978—. Editor/author: Advances in Andean Archaeology, 1978, Economic Organization of Prehispanic Peru, 1984, Risk Management and Arid Land Use Strategies in the Andes, 1986, New Perspectives on Americanist Archaeology, 2002; editor: Cultural Continuity in Mesoamerica, 1979, Early Native Americans, 1980. Charter mem. Confluence St. Louis, 1983; mem. Gov.'s Adv. Coun. Hist. Preservation, 1982-89, sec. 1989-91. NSF fellow, 1967, grantee, 1974-75, 85—. Fellow AAAS; mem. Soc. Profl. Archaeologists (sec.-treas. 1981-83, grievance coord. 1997-98), AAUP (chpt. pres. 1980-82), Registry Profl. Archaeologists (grievance coord. 1998-99), Mo. Assn. Profl. Archaeologists (v.p. 1981-82), Mo. Archaeology Soc. (trustee 1977—), Sigma Xi (chpt. pres. 1985-). Roman Catholic. Avocations: hiking, gardening. Office: Washington U Campus Box 1114 Saint Louis MO 63130-4899 Office Phone: 314-935-5231. Business E-Mail: dlbrowma@wustl.edu.

BROWN, ALAN CRAWFORD, lawyer; b. Rockford, Ill., May 12, 1956; s. Gerald Crawford and Jane Ella (Herzberger) B.; m. Dawn Lestrud, Apr. 16, 1998; children: Parker Crawford, Sydney Danielle, Sarah Kate, Drew Kristen, Connor Austin. BA magna cum laude, Miami U., Oxford, Ohio, 1978; JD with honors, U. Chgo., 1981. Bar: Ill. 1981, U.S. Dist. Ct. (no. dist.) Ill. 1981, U.S. Tax Ct. 1986. Assoc. Kirkland & Ellis, Chgo., 1981-87; sr. assoc. Coffield Ungaretti Harris & Slavin, Chgo., 1987-89; ptnr. McDermott, Will & Emery, Chgo., 1989—2001, Neal, Gerber & Eisenberg, Chgo., 2001—. Deacon Northminster Presbyn. Ch., Evanston, Ill., 1989-92; apiarist Chgo. Botanic Garden, Glencoe, Ill., 1988-97. Mem. Order of Coif, Phi Beta Kappa. Office: Neal Gerber & Eisenberg Ste 2200 Two North LaSalle St Chicago IL 60602-3801 Office Phone: 312-269-8066. E-mail: acbrownesq@aol.com, abrown@ngelaw.com.

BROWN, ARNOLD LANEHART, JR., pathologist, educator, dean; b. Wooster, Ohio, Jan. 26, 1926; s. Arnold Lanehart and Wilda (Woods) B.; m. Betty Jane Simpson, Oct. 2, 1949; children— Arnold III, Anthony, Allen, Fletcher, Lisa. Student, U. Richmond, 1943—45; MD, Med. Coll. Va., 1949. Diplomate Am. Bd. Pathology. Intern Presbyn.-St. Luke's Hosp., Chgo., 1949-50, resident, 1950-51, 53-56, asst. attending pathologist, 1957-59; practice medicine specializing in pathology Rochester, Minn., 1959-78; cons. exptl. pathology, anatomy Mayo Clinic, Rochester, 1959-78, also prof., chmn. dept., 1968-78; prof. pathology U. Wis., Madison, 1978—, dean Med. Sch., 1978-91. Mem. nat. cancer adv. coun. NIH, 1971-74, HEW, 1972-74; chmn. clearing house on environ. carcinogens Nat. Cancer Inst., 1976-80, chmn. com. to study carcinogenicity of cyclamate, 1975-76; mem. Nat. Com. on Heart Disease, Cancer and Stroke, 1975-79; mem. com. on safe drinking water NRC, 1976-77; mem. award assembly Gen. Motors Cancer Rsch. Found., 1978-83, vice chmn., 1982-83; co-chmn. panel on geochemistry of fibrous materials related to health risks Nat. Acad. Scis.-NRC, 1978-80; chair working group Internat. Agy. for Rsch. on Cancer, Lyon, France, 1979, 83, 87. Contbr. articles to profl. jours. Bd. sci. counselors Nat. Inst. Environ. Health Scis., NIH Nat. Toxicology Program, 1992—. With USNR, 1943-45, 51-53. at. Heart Inst. postdoctoral fellow, 1956-59 Mem. Am. Soc. Exptl. Pathology, Internat. Acad. Pathology, Assn. Am. Med. Colls. (chmn. coun. deans 1984-85). Home: 211 2Nd St NW Apt 1503 Rochester MN 55901-2896 Home Phone: 507-529-8878. Personal E-mail: arnoldbro@msn.com.

BROWN, ARNOLD M., state legislator; b. Sherman, SD, Mar. 5, 1931; Mem. S.D. Ho. Reps. Dist. 7, Pierre, 1993-96; mem. health and human svc. and transp. coms. S.D. Ho. Reps.; mem. S.D. Senate from 7th dist., Pierre, 1997—, spkr., 2002—. Home: 1718 Teton Pass Brookings SD 57006-3626

BROWN, B. ANDREW, lawyer; b. Charleston, W.Va., Mar. 10, 1957; BA in History, Stanford U., 1979; MPA, Harvard U., 1981; JD, Duke U., 1986, MA in Philosophy, 1986. Bar: Minn. 1989. Legis. aide Sen. Gary Hart, Washington, 1981-82; atty. Donovan, Leisure, Newton & Irvine, Washington, 1986-88, Willkie, Farr & Gallagher, Washington, 1989, Dorsey & Whitney, Mpls., 1990—, ptnr., 1995—, head regulatory group, co-chmn. environ., natural resources, energy practice group. Office Phone: 612-340-5612. Office Fax: 612-340-8800. Business E-Mail: brown.andrew@dorsey.com.

BROWN, BOYD ALEX, physicist, researcher; b. Columbus, Ohio, Sept. 25, 1948; s. Frank L. and E. Catherine (Chenoweth) B.; m. Mary J. Hohenstein, July 21, 1984; children: Elizabeth Lorraine, Mark Alexander. BA in Physics, Ohio State U., 1970; MS in Physics, SUNY, Stony Brook, 1971, PhD in Physics, 1974. Research fellow Japan Soc. for the Promotion of Sci., Tokyo, 1974-75; research assoc. Mich. State U., East Lansing, 1975-78; research officer Oxford U., Eng., 1978-82; assoc. prof. physics Mich. State U., East Lansing, 1982-90, prof. physics, 1990—. Contbr. more than 400 articles to physics jours. Recipient Humboldt sr. rsch. fellow, 1991—, Dist. Faculty award, 2004 Fellow Am. Phys. Soc.; mem. The Am. Phys. Soc., Sigma Pi Sigma. Avocations: music, books. Office: Mich State U Cyclotron Lab East Lansing MI 48824

BROWN, CHARLES ERIC, health facility administrator, biochemist; b. Nov. 23, 1946; s. Charles E. and Dorothy R. (Riddle) B.; m. Kathy Louise Houck, July 24, 1971; 1 child, Eric Nathaniel. BA in Chemistry, SUNY, Buffalo, 1968; PhD in Biochemistry, Northwestern U., 1973. Instr., fellow depts. chemistry, biochemistry, molec. biol. Northwestern U., Evanston, Ill., 1973-75; rsch. fellow Roche Inst. Molecular Biology, Nutley, N.J., 1975-77; from asst. prof. biochemistry to assoc. prof. Med. Coll. Wis., Milw., 1977-88; analytical bus. devel. coord. BP Rsch., 1988-92; analytical rsch. mgr. BP Chems. Ltd., 1992-94; dir. Rsch. Resources Ctr. U. Ill., Chgo., 1994—. Adj. prof. chemistry U. Ill., Chgo., 1994—, adj. prof. mech. engring., 1998—; cons. Nicolet Instrument Corp., Metriflow, Inc., 1984-88. Contbr. articles in field to profl. jours., chpts. to books; developer biomedical and petrochemical equipment and techniques; patentee in field. Recipient Tech. Merit award Johnson Wax, 1987; NIH predoctoral fellow, 1968-72; Cottrell Rsch. grantee, 1979-82, Arthritis Found. grantee, 1984, Retirement Rsch. Found. grantee, 1987-88. Fellow Royal Soc. Chemistry; mem. AAAS, Internat. Soc. Magnetic Resonance, Soc. Neurosci., Am. Chem. Soc., Am. Soc. Pharmacology and Exptl. Therapeutics, Am. Soc. for Mass Spectrometry, Microscopy Soc. Am., Materials Rsch. Soc., Sigma Xi, Phi Lambda Upsilon. Office: Rsch Resources Ctr U Ill 901 S Wolcott Ave # E102 Msb Chicago IL 60612-7307 E-mail: charlieb@uic.edu.

BROWN, CHARLIE, state representative; b. Williston, SC, Mar. 8, 1938; m. Angela Baker; 1 child, Charlisa. BS, Cheyney U.; MPA, Ind. U. Founder Mayor Hatcher's Youth Found., Gary, Ind.; CEO Gary (Ind.) Cmty. Mental Health Ctr.; risk mgr. City of Gary; state rep. dist. 3 Ind. House of Reps., 1982—, chmn. pub. health com., local govt. com., environ. affairs com., ins. and corp. com., family and children com., ranking minority mem. pub. health com. Bd. dirs. Lake County Hosp. Bldg. Authority; cons. mgmt. and health; mem. Med. Ctr. of Gary, Nat. Civil Rights Mus. and Hall Fame & Benson & Taylor Ensemble Co. Mayor Hatcher's Youth Found., Gary. Mem. Gary Frontiers Svc. Club, Black Minority Health Adv. Coun., Nat. Black Caucus State Legislators, Interagency Coun. on Black and Minority Health. Democrat. Home: 9439 Lake Shore Dr Gary IN 46403-1609

BROWN, COLLEEN, broadcast executive; BA bus admin and pol sci, U Dubuque, Iowa; MBA, U Colo. Gen. mgr. Sta. KPNX-TV, Phoenix, till 1998; v.p. broadcast Lee Enterprises, 1998-99, pres. Davenport, Iowa, 1999—2000; sr v.p. bus dev Belo Corp, Dallas, 2000—. Mem. March of Dimes. Mem. Young Press Assn. Office: AH Belo Corp 400 S Record St PO Box 655237 Dallas TX 75265-5237

BROWN, CRAIG J., printing company executive; BA, MBA, Bowling Green State U. Various positions Std. Register Co., Dayton, Ohio, 1975-94, v.p. fin., treas., CFO, 1994-98, sr. v.p. adminstrn., treas., CFO, 1998—. Office: Std Register Co 600 Albany St Dayton OH 45408

BROWN, DAVID MITCHELL, pediatrician, educator, dean; b. Chgo., Nov. 11, 1935; m. Sandra Miriam Brown BS, U. Ill., Urban, 1956; MD, U. Ill., Chgo., 1960. Intern U. Ill. Research-Edn. Hosp., Chgo., 1960-61; resident in pediatrics U. Minn., Mpls., 1961-63, fellow in endocrinology and metabolism, 1963-65; attending staff pediatric eoncrinology USAF Hosp., San Antonio, 1965-67; asst. prof. pediatrics, lab. medicine and pathology U. Minn., Mpls., 1967-70, assoc. prof., 1970-73, dir. clin. labs., 1970-84, prof. pediatrics, lab. medicine and pathology, 1974—, dean. Med. Sch., 1984-93, dir. Gen. clin. Rsch. Ctr., med. dir. clin. trials unit, 1997—2002. Mem. adv. com. on rsch. on women's health NIH, 1995-99; co-chair orgainzing com. 7th Internat. Symposium on Basement Membranes, 1995; mem. planning com. NIH 3d Internat. Symposium on Kidney Disease of Diabetes Mellitus, 1991. With USAF, 1965-67. Recipient USPHS Research Career Devel. award, 1968-73 Mem. AAAS, Acad. Clin. Lab. Physicians and Scientists, Am. Diabetes Assn., Am. Pediatric Soc., Am. Physiol. Soc., Am. Soc. Clin. Pathology, Am. Soc. Nephrology, Am. Soc. Pediatric Nephrology, Central Soc. for Clin. Research, Endocrine Soc., Internat. Soc. Nephrology, Lawson Wilkins Soc. Pediatric Endocrinology, Mpls. Pediatris Soc., Orthopaedic Research Soc., Soc. Pediatric Nephrology, Soc. Pediatric Research, Am. Assn. Pathologists, Am. Soc. Bone and Mineral Research, Internat. Acad. Pathology, Assn. Am. Med. Colls. (chmn. council acad. Socs.), Am. Assn. Pathologists, Am. Soc. Cell Biology, Minn. Soc. Clin. Pathology, Alpha Omega Alpha. Home: 2571 Abbey Hill Dr Hopkins MN 55305-2332 Office: PO Box 404 516 Delaware St SE Minneapolis MN 55455-0356

BROWN, DONALD JAMES, JR., lawyer; b. Chgo., Apr. 21, 1948; s. Donald James Sr. and Marian Constance (Scimeca) B.; m. Donna Bowen, Jan. 15, 1972; children: Megan, Maura. AB, John Carroll U., 1970; JD, Loyola U., Chgo., 1973. Bar: Ill. 1973, U.S. Dist. Ct. (no. dist.) Ill. 1973, U.S. Tax Ct. 1982. Asst. to state's atty. Cook County, Ill., 1973-75; assoc. Baker & McKenzie, Chgo., 1975-82, ptnr., 1982-95, Donohue, Brown, Mathewson & Smyth, Chgo., 1995—. Office: Donohue Brown et al 140 S Dearborn St Chicago IL 60603-5202 E-mail: donald.brown@dbmslaw.com.

BROWN, EDNA, state representative; b. Toledo, Ohio, Apr. 7, 1940; widowed; 4 children. With CHP 1184, 1992, 2002; state rep. Ohio Ho. of Reps., Columbus, 1994—, minority leader, 1999—2001, ranking minority mem. human svcs. and aging com., mem. criminal justice, econ. devel. and tech., and ins. coms.; mayor Toledo, 2001. Councilwoman Toledo City Coun., 1994—. Mem.: Am. Fedn. State, County, Mcpl. Employees, NAACP, Dem. Women's Club. Democrat. Methodist. Office: 77 S High St 10th fl Columbus OH 43215-6111

BROWN, EDWIN WILSON, JR., preventive medicine physician, educator; b. Youngstown, Ohio, Mar. 6, 1926; s. Edwin Wilson and Doris (McClellan) B.; m. Patricia Ann Currier, Aug. 9, 1952; children: Edwin Wilson, John Currier, Wende Patricia. Student, Carnegie Inst. Tech., 1943, Amherst Coll., 1943—44, Houghton Coll., 1946—47; MD, Harvard U., 1953, MPH (Nat. Found. fellow), 1957. Rsch. fellow U. Buffalo, 1953-54; intern E.J. Meyer Meml. Hosp., Buffalo, 1954-55; resident pub. health Va. Dept. Health, 1955-56; tchr. medicine specializing in preventive medicine Boston, 1958-61, Hyderabad, India, 1961-63; assoc. med. dir. People-to-People Health Found., Washington, 1965-66; assoc. prof. medicine Ind. U.-Purdue U., Indpls., 1966-85, dir. divsn. internat. affairs, 1966-74, assoc. dean student svcs., dir. internat. svcs., 1979-85; pres. Internat. Med. Assistance, Inc., Indpls., 1986—. Med. dir. Ind. Dept. Correction, 1974-76; sr. med. edn. advisor King Faisal U., Dammam, Saudi Arabia, 1977-78; field dir. Harvard Epidemiol. Project, Egedesminde, Greenland, 1956-57; asst. prof. preventive medicine Sch. Medicine Tufts U., 1958-61; dep. chief staff Boston Dispensary, 1961; vis. prof. preventive medicine Osmania Med. Coll., Hyderabad, India, 1961-63; asst. dir. divsn. internat. med. edn., dir. AAMC-AID project internat. med. edn. Assn. Am. Med. Colls., Evanston, 1963-65; exec. sec. Study Group on Childhood Accidents, Boston, 1959-61; rsch. assoc. Sch. Pub. Health, Harvard U., 1959-60; dir. Curtis Pub. Co., Inc.; cons. Boston City Health Dept., 1959-60, WHO, 1973-74; chmn. bd. dirs. Med. Assistance Programs, Inc. Contbr. articles to profl. jours. Bd. dirs. Paul Carlson Found., Campus Teams, Iran Found., CARE/MEDICO, Internat. Students Inc. Served with AUS, 1944-46, ETO. Recipient Pub. Svc. award Vets. Day Coun. Indpls., 1996, Patriarch of Antioch's award Knight Comdr. of Order of St. Mark, 1998. Fellow Am. Pub. Health Assn.; mem. Assn. Tchrs. Preventive Medicine, Indian Assn. Advancement Med. Edn., Mass. Med. Soc., Internat. Policy Forum (bd. govs.), Nat. Policy Coun., Rotary Internat., Sigma Xi. Home and Office: 8153 Oakland Rd Indianapolis IN 46240-2747 Home Phone: 317-257-7454; Office Phone: 317-257-7455. Personal E-mail: Ed@TheBrowns.com, ewhindy@aol.com.

BROWN, ERIC A., food products executive; Group v.p. prepared foods Hormel Foods Corp., Austin, Minn., 1999—. Office: Hormel Foods Corp One Hormel Pl Austin MN 55912-3680

BROWN, FREDERICK LEE, health facility administrator; b. Clarksburg, W.Va., Oct. 22, 1940; s. Claude Raymond and Anne Elizabeth (Kiddy) B.; m. Shirley Fiille Brown; children: Gregory Lee, Michael Owen-Price, Kyle Stephen, Kathryn Alexis. BA in Psychology, Northwestern U., Evanston, Ill., 1962; MBA in Health Care Adminstrn., George Washington U., Washington, 1966; LHD (hon.), U. Mo., 1995. Vocat. counselor Cook County Dept. Pub. Aid, Chgo., 1962-64; from adminstrv. resident to v.p. ops. Meth. Hosp. Ind., Inc., Indpls., 1965—72, v.p. ops., 1972-74; exec. v.p., COO Meml. Hosp. DuPage County, Elmhurst, Ill., 1974-82, Meml. Health Svcs., Elmhurst, 1980-82; pres., CEO CH Health Techs., Inc., St. Louis, 1983-93, Christian Health Svcs., St. Louis, 1986-93, CH Allied Svcs., Inc., St. Louis, 1988-93, BJC Health Sys., St. Louis, 1993—98, vice-chmn., 1999—2000; pres., CEO Christian Hosp. NE-NW, 1982—88, No. Ariz. Healthcare, Flagstaff, 2003—04. Adj. instr. Washington U. Sch. Medicine, St. Louis, 1982—2001; mem. chancellor's coun. U. Mo., 1990—94; mem. exec. com. HealthLink, Inc., 1986—92; pres., CEO Village North, Inc., 1986—93; chmn. shareholder comm. com. Am. Healthcare Systems, Inc., 1985—86, vice chmn., 1992; bd. dirs. Commerce Bank St. Louis, Am. Excess Inc. Ltd.; mem. corp. assembly Blue Cross Blue Shield Mo., 1991—95; vis. scholar, exec. in residence The George Washington U., 2001—02. Contbr. articles to profl. jours. Co-chmn. hosp. divsn. United Way Greater St. Louis, 1983, chmn., 1984, chmn. health svcs. divsn., 1985—86, vice chmn. region, 1988, bd. dirs., 1986—2001, exec. com., 1991—, chmn. audit com., 1992—2001; active Kammergild Chamber Orch., 1984—88, v.p., 1985—88, bd. dirs., 1987—91; active Mo. Heart Inst., 1988—92, Alton Meml. Hosp., 1987—91, bd. dirs., 1987—91; mem. exec. bd. St. Louis Area coun. Boy Scouts Am., 1989—2000, activities coun. chmn., 1993—95; chmn. Friends of Scouting Campaign, 1991—92; mem. medicaid budget task force Mo. Dept. Social Svcs., 1990; mem. emergency rm. svcs. task force St. Louis Regional Med. Ctr., 1985; mem. corp. assembly Blue Cross Blue Shield of Mo., 1991; bd. dirs. Sold on St. Louis, 1991—93, St. Louis Reg. Commerce & Growth Assn., 1993—98; bd. trustees Webster Hills Math. Ch., 1990—92, communion steward, 1987. Fellow Am. Coll. Healthcare Execs. (chmn. credentials com. 1978, chmn. task force governance and constituencies 1986-88; mem. Gold Medal award com. 1985, com. on ethics 1989-91, chmn. awards and testimonials com., 1992-93, bd. regents 1991-93, gov. dist. V, 1993-98); mem. Am. Acad. Med. Adminstrs. (life, state dir. 1988—, Health Care Exec. of Yr. 1990, Statesman in Healthcare, 1992), Hosp. Pres.'s Assn., Advt. Club Greater St. Louis, Am. Hosp. Assn. (coun. on mgmt. 1987, alt. del. for healthcare systems 1988-90, del. to ho. of dels. for health care systems 1991, fin. com. chair 1995, chair-elect 1998, chmn. 1999), APHA, George Washington U. Alumni Assn. for Health Svcs. Adminstrn. (preceptor 1975-93, Alumnus of Yr. award 1981, Frederick Gibbs award, 1993), Hosp. Assn. Met. St. Louis (bd. dirs. 1984-94, chmn. bd. 1988-89, sec. 1985-86, treas. 1987, chmn. coun. on pub. affairs and comm. 1985, vice chmn. 1987, various coms.), Greater St. Louis Health Care Alliance (co-chair 1992-96), Mo. Hosp. Assn. (mem. coun. on rsch. and policy devel. 1983-88, chmn. coun. on multi-instnl. hosps. 1986-88, mem. dist. coun. pres.'s 1986-89, bd. dirs.

1988-92, chmn. bd. trustees 1990), Ctrl. Ea. Profl. Rev. Orgn. (bd. dirs. 1982-85, various coms.), St. Louis Met. Med. Soc. (lay advisor 1990-92), Healthcare Execs. Study Soc., Internat. Health Policy and Mgmt. Inst. (bd. dirs. 1988—), Am. Protestant Health Assn. (bd. dirs. 1988-93, chmn. 1992-93), Pinnacle Peak Country Club, Forest Highlands Country Club. Republican. Home: 8409 E La Junta Rd Scottsdale AZ 85255-2859 Office Phone: 928-607-3069. Personal E-mail: fredlbrown@cox.net.

BROWN, GENE W., steel company executive; b. Warsaw, Ind., Feb. 16, 1936; s. Dean L. and Ilean (Clase) B.; m. Beverly A. Sink, Feb. 25, 1956; children: Lisa Jo, Scott Eugene. BSME, Purdue U., 1960; MBA, Northwestern U., 1967. Engr. Ill. Tool Works, Chgo., 1957-67; gen. mgr. Chgo. Gasket Co., 1967-69; ops. mgr. Maremont Corp., Harvey, Ill., 1969-74; gen. mgr. Marmon Group, Chgo., 1974-77; pres. Whittar Steel Strip, Detroit, 1977-88, Lisco Inc., Detroit, 1979—. also: 677 N 175 W Valparaiso IN 46385-8542 Office: Lisco Inc 277 Melton Rd Chesterton IN 46304-9746 Office Phone: 219-405-7295.

BROWN, GLENN F., transportation executive, department chairman; Pres. Contract Freighters, Inc., Joplin, Mo., 1986—. Office: Contract Freighters Inc 4701 E 32nd St Joplin MO 64804-3482 Fax: 417 782-3723.

BROWN, GRANT CLAUDE, retired state legislator; m. Linda Landes. Farmer, rancher, 1959—; state rep. dist. 36, 1991-98. Chmn. constrn. rev. com., 1993—; vice chmn. joint constrn. rev. com.; mem. fin. and taxation com. N.D. Ho. Reps. Sec. Ch. Trust Fund. Recipient Outstanding Young Men Am. award, 1970. Mem. County Farm Bur. (pres.), Stockmen's Legion, Masons (past master), Elks. Republican. Home: PO Box 175 Dunn Center ND 58626

BROWN, GREGORY K., lawyer; b. Warren, Ohio, Dec. 9, 1951; s. George K. and Dorothy H. (Gaynor) B.; m. Joy M. Feinberg, Apr. 10, 1976. BS in Bus. & Econs., U. Ky., 1973; JD, U. Ill., 1976. Bar: Ill. 1976. Assoc. atty. McDermott, Will & Emery, Chgo., 1976-80, Mayer, Brown & Platt, Chgo., 1980-84; ptnr. Keck, Mahin & Cate, Chgo., 1984-93, Oppenheimer Wolff & Donnelly, Chgo., 1994-97, Seyfarth, Shaw, Fairweather & Geraldson, Chgo., 1997-2000, Gardner, Carton & Douglas, Chgo., 2000—06, Katten Muchin Rosenman LLP, 2006—. Contbg. author: The Handbook of Employee Ownership Plans, 2005, Employee Stock Ownership Plans, 2005. amed One of the Top Benefits Lawyers Nat. Law Jour., 1998. Mem.: ABA (chair employee stock ownership plan com., tax law sect. Nat. Ctr. Employee Ownership, Employee Stock Ownership Plan Assn. chair legis. and regulatory adv. c 1997—99), Internat. Pension and Employee Benefit Lawyers Assn., Chgo. Bar Assn. (chmn. employee benefits com. 1988—89). Avocations: basketball, bicycling, golf, opera, theater. Office: Katten Muchin Rosenman 525 W Monroe St Chicago IL 60661-3693 Home Phone: 773-549-0559; Office Phone: 312-902-5404. Business E-Mail: gregory.brown@kattenlaw.com.

BROWN, GREGORY Q., communications executive; b. Aug. 14, 1960; BA in Economics, Rutgers U., 1982. Various sales and marketing positions AT&T, 1983—87; joined Ameritech, 1987; pres. Ameritech New Media Inc., 1994—96, Ameritech Custom Bus. Svcs.; chmn., CEO Micromuse Inc., San Francisco, 1999—2003; exec. v.p., pres., CEO comml., govt. & indsl. solutions sector Motorola, Inc., Schaumburg, Ill., 2003—05, exec. v.p., pres. networks & enterprise, 2005—07, pres., COO, 2007, pres., CEO, 2008—. Bd. dir. R.R. Donnelley & Sons Co., 2001—03, Micromuse, Inc., Nat. Merit Scholarship Corp., Chgo. Coun. Fgn. Rels., Motorola, Inc., 2007—; mem. Pres. Nat. Security Telecom. Advisory Com., 2004; mem. Coll. Engring Advisory Coun. U. Notre Dame. Mem. bd. overseers Rutgers U. Office: Motorola Inc 1303 E Algonquin Rd Schaumburg IL 60196

BROWN, HERBERT RUSSELL, lawyer, writer; b. Columbus, Ohio, Sept. 27, 1931; s. Thomas Newton and Irene (Hankinson) B.; m. Beverly Ann Jenkins, Dec. 2, 1967; children: David Herbert, Andrew Jenkins. BA, Denison U., 1953; JD, U. Mich., 1956. Assoc. Vorys, Sater, Seymour and Pease, Columbus, Ohio, 1956, 60-64, ptnr., 1965-82; treas. Sunday Creek Coal Co., Columbus, 1970-86; assoc. justice Ohio Supreme Ct., Columbus, 1987-93. Mem. Ohio Ethics Commn., 2002-04, Ohio Public Defender Commn., 2004-; examiner Ohio Bar, 1967-72, Multi-State Bar, 1971-76, Dist. Ct. Bar, 1968-71; commr. Fed. Lands, Columbus, 1967-68, Lake Lands, Columbus, 1981; bd. dirs. Thurber House, 1992-94, Sunday Creek Coal Co.; adj. prof. Ohio State U. Coll. Law, 1997-2000; panelist Am. Arbitration Assn., 1993—. Author: (novels) Presumption of Guilt, 1991, Shadows of Doubt, 1994, (plays) You're My Boy, 1999, Peace with Honor, 2000, Power of God, 2002, The Duchess, 2007; mem. editl. bd. U. Mich. Law Rev., 1955-56. Trustee Columbus Bar Found., 1993—2003, pres., 2001—02; candidate Ohio State Legis.; deacon, mem. governing bd. 1st Cmty. Ch., 1966—80; bd. dirs. Ctrl. Cmty. House Columbus, 1967—75. Capt. JAGC US Army, 1956—57. Recipient Disting. Alumni citation, Denison U., 2003. Fellow Am. Coll. Trial Lawyers; mem. Ohio Bar Assn., Columbus Bar Assn. Democrat.

BROWN, JACK WYMAN, architect; b. Detroit, Oct. 17, 1922; s. Ernest E. and Mary Morse (Jones) B.; m. Joan M. Graham, Oct. 4, 1971; 1 dau., Elizabeth. BS, U. Mich., 1945. Designer Odell, Hewlett & Luckenbach, Inc., Birmingham, Mich., 1952-57; pres. Brown Assocs. Architects, Inc., Bloomfield Hills, Mich., 1957—; part-time instr. design Lawrence Inst. Tech., 1959. Mem. Mayor Detroit Task Force, 1969-70. Served with USNR, 1943-46. Co-recipient 1st prize nat. competition design Nat. Cowboy Hall Fame, 1967; recipient Institutions mag. award, 1980 Mem. AIA (chmn. working coms.), Am. Soc. Ch. Architecture (dir. 1960-64, 72—), Mich. Soc. Architects (design award St. Regis Ch. 1969, Fox Hills Elem. Sch. 1970, Andor Office Bldg. 1972, CAM Design award 1992). Home: 5980 Braemoor Rd Bloomfield Hills MI 48301-1419 Office: Brown Teefey Assocs Archs PC 4190 Telegraph Rd Bloomfield Hills MI 48302-2079 E-mail: jandjbrown@aol.com.

BROWN, JAMES WARD, mathematician, educator, author; b. Phila., Jan. 15, 1934; s. George Harold and Julia Elizabeth (Ward) B.; m. Jacqueline Read, Sept. 3, 1957; children: Scott Cameron, Gordon Elliot. AB, Harvard U., 1955; AM, U. Mich., 1958, PhD (Inst. Sci and Tech. predoctoral fellow), 1964. Asst. prof. math. U. Mich., Dearborn, 1964-66, assoc. prof., 1968-71, prof., 1971—, acting chmn. dept., 1974, 85. Asst. prof. Oberlin Coll., 1966-68; editorial cons. Math. Rev., 1970-85; dir. NSF Grant, 1969 Author: (with R.V. Churchill) Complex Variables and Applications, 7th edit., 2004, Internat. Student edit., 1996, Japanese edit., 2004, Spanish edit., 2004, Chinese edit., 2005, Korean edit., 2004, Greek edit., 1993, Fourier Series and Boundary Value Problems, 6th edit., 2003, internat. student edit., 1993, Japanese edit., 1980; contbr. articles to U.S. and fgn. sci. jours. Recipient Disting. Faculty award U. Mich.-Dearborn, 1976, Disting. Faculty award Mich. Assn. Governing Bds. Colls. and Univs., 1983 Mem. Am. Math. Soc., Research Club of U. Mich., Sigma Xi. Home: 1710 Morton Ave Ann Arbor MI 48104-4522 Office: 4901 Evergreen Rd Dearborn MI 48128-1491

BROWN, JARED, theater director, educator, writer; BFA, Ithaca Coll., 1960; MA Theatre, San Francisco State Coll., 1962; PhD Theatre, U. Minn., 1967. Instr. creative writing St. Paul Pub. Sch. System, 1962-63; teaching asst. U. Minn., 1963-64, instr. Communication Dept., 1964-65; from asst. prof. to prof. dept. theatre Western Ill. U., 1965-89, acad. dir. Semester in London, 1979-80; dir. Sch. Theatre Arts, Prof. Theatre Arts Ill. Wesleyan U., 1989—2002; adj. prof. Ill. State U., 2003—. Aided devel. (policies, curriculum), Theatre Dept. Western Ill. U., 1971; panel discussant Western Ill. U., 1973, 1974; chmn. panel Ill. Theatre Assn. Convention, 1976; panel discussant Assn. Theatre in Higher Edn. Convention, 1987; disting. faculty lectr. Western Ill. U., 1986, dir. grad. program dept. theatre, 1975-89, chmn. directing, theatre history and playwriting programs, dept. theatre, 1972-89; mem. panel judges to award NEH Summer Stipends, Ill., 1990; mem. panel to award NEH Fellowship Grants, 2004; judge Am. Coll. Theatre Festival, 1973-74, 89-90; mem. various theatre coms. Ill. Wesleyan U.; mem. various coms. Univ., Coll. Fine Arts, Dept. Theatre Western Ill. U.; spkr., presenter in field. Author: The Fabulous Lunts, A Biography of Alfred Lunt and Lynn Fontanne, 1986, (Barnard Hewitt award 1987), Zero Mostel: A Biography, 1989, The Theatre in America During the Revolution, 1995, Alan J. Pakula: His Films and His Life, 2005 (Writers Notes Book award), Moss Hart, A Prince of the Theatre, 2006, also 15 plays; dir. 100 plays including The Merchant of Venice, Hedda Gabler, Henry IV, La Ronde, Death of a Salesman, Cat on a Hot Tin Roof, A Streetcar Named Desire, Who's Afraid of Virginia Woolf, You Can't Take It With You, Brighton Beach Memoirs, Inherit the Wind, Peter Pan, Bye Bye Birdie, Guys and Dolls, Kiss Me Kate, 110 In The Shade, Annie, Funny Girl, Broadway Bound, Tartuffe, Antigone, She Loves Me, Noises Off, Doubt, Sight Unseen, Bedroom Farce, Once in a Lifetime; appeared in My Fair Lady, Western Ill. U., 1978, On The Twentieth Century, 1986, Russian Dressing, 2005, Morning's at Seven, 2007, various radio and TV programs; contbr. chpts. to texts, 20 scholarly articles to profl. jours. Recipient stipend NEH, 1988, DuPont award for tchg. excellence, 1997; named Best Dir., The Pantagraph, 1991, 92, 94, 96; grantee Ill. Arts Coun., 1980, 81, 87, Western Ill. U., 1983-85, 86-87, 89, Cultural Arts Devel. Fund, 1980-89, Ill. Wesleyan U., 1990, Artistic/Scholarly Devel. grantee, 1999, 2002. Mem. Nat. Collegiate Players, Phi Kappa Phi, Theta Alpha Phi. Home: 18 Chatsford Ct Bloomington IL 61704-6220 Office: Sch Theatre Arts Ill Wesleyan U Bloomington IL 61702 Office Phone: 309-664-0708. E-mail: jbrown@iwu.edu.

BROWN, JEANETTE GRASSELLI, retired director; b. Cleve., Aug. 4, 1928; d. Nicholas W. and Veronica Gecsy; m. Glenn R. Brown, Aug. 1, 1987. BS summa cum laude, Ohio U., 1950, DSc (hon.), 1978; MS, Western Res. U., 1958, DSc (hon.), 1995, Clarkson U., 1986; D Engring. (hon.), Mich. Tech. U., 1989; DSc (hon.), Wilson Coll., 1994, Notre Dame Coll., 1995, Kenyon Coll., 1995, Mt. Union Coll., 1996, Cleveland State U., 2000, Kent State U., 2000, Ursuline Coll., 2001; DSc, Youngstown State U., 2003; DSc (hon.), U. Pecs, Hungary, 2002. Project leader, assoc. Infrared Spectroscopist, Cleve., 1950-78; mgr. analytical sci. lab. Standard Oil (name changed to BP Am., Inc. 1985), Cleve., 1978-83, dir. technol. support dept., 1983-85, dir. corp. rsch. and analytical scis., 1985-88; disting. vis. prof., dir. rsch. enhancement Ohio U., Athens, 1989-95; ret., 1995. Bd. dirs. AGA Gas, Inc., USX Corp., McDonald Investments, BDM Internat., BF Goodrich Co., Nicolet Instrument Corp.; mem. bd. on chem. sci. and tech. NRC, 1986-91; chmn. U.S. Nat. Com. to Internat. Union of Pure and Applied Chemistry, 1992-94; mem. joint high level adv. panel U.S.-Japan Sci. and Tech., 1994-2001, Ohio Bd. Regents, 1995—, chmn., 2000-2002; vis. com. Nat. Inst. Stds. and Tech., 1988-91. Author, editor 8 books; editor: Vibrational Spectroscopy; contbr. numerous articles on molecular spectroscopy to profl. jours.; patentee naphthalene extraction process. Bd. dirs. N.E. Ohio Sci. and Engring. Fair, Cleve., Martha Holden Jennings Found., Cleve. Clinic Found., Sci. Svc. Inc.; chair bd. dirs. Cleve. Scholarship Programs, Inc., 1994-2000; trustee Holden Arboretum, Cleve., 1988—, Edison Biotech Ctr., Cleve., 1988-95, Cleve. Playhouse, 1990-96, Garden Ctr. Greater Cleve., 1990-93, Mus. Arts Assn., 1991—, Gt. Lakes Sci. Ctr., 1991—, Rainbow Babies and Children's Hosp., 1992-95, Nat. Inventors' Hall of Fame, 1993-2006, Ohio U., 1985-94, chmn. 1991-92; chair steering com. Mellen Ctr. Cleve. Clinic, 1996—, Cleve. Orchestra, 2000-; chair bd. dirs. ideastream, PBS, NPR, Ideastream Pub. TV and Radio, 2003-06; chair bd. dirs. Great Lakes Sci. Ctr., 2006. Recipient Disting. Svc. award Cleve. Tech. Soc. Coun., 1985, Great Am. award, 2004; named Woman of Yr. YWCA, 1980; named to Ohio Women's Hall of Fame State of Ohio, 1989, Ohio Sci. & Tech. Hall of Fame, 1991, Humanitarian award Nat. Conf. Cmty. Justice, 2000, Medal of Honor, Ellis Island, 2002. Mem. Am. Chem. Soc. (chair analytical divsn. 1990-91, Garvan medal 1986, Analytical Chem. award 1993, Encouraging Women into Careers in Sci. award 1999), Soc. for Applied Spectroscopy (pres. 1970, Disting. Svc. award 1983), Coblentz Soc. (bd. govs. 1968-71, William Wright award 1980), Royal Soc. Chemistry (Theophilus Redwood lectr. 1994), Phi Beta Kappa, Iota Sigma Pi (pres. fluorine chpt. 1957-60, nat. hon. mem. 1987). Republican. Roman Catholic. Avocations: swimming, dance, music. Home: 150 Greentree Rd Chagrin Falls OH 44022-2424

BROWN, JOBETH GOODE, food products executive, lawyer; b. Oakdale, La., Sept. 15, 1950; d. Samuel C. Goode and Elizabeth E. (Twiner) Baker; m. H. William Brown, Aug. 4, 1973; 1 child, Kevin William. BA, Newcomb Coll. Tulane U., 1972; JD, Wash. U., 1979. Assoc. Coburn, Croft & Putzell, St. Louis, 1979-80; staff atty. Anheuser-Busch Cos. Inc., St. Louis, 1980-81, exec. asst. to v.p. sec., 1982-83, asst. sec., 1983-89, sec., v.p., 1989—. Trustee Anheuser-Busch Found., St. Louis, 1989—, Girls, Inc., St. Louis; bd. dirs. Jr. Achievement Miss Valley, Inc., Met. Assn. Philanthropy. Mem.: ABA, Am. Soc. Corp. Secs. (pres. 1992), Bar Assn. Met. St. Louis, Mo. Bar Assn., Mo. Women's Forum, Algonquin Golf Club, Order of Coif. Republican. Office: Anheuser-Busch Cos Inc One Busch Pl 202-6 Saint Louis MO 63118-1852

BROWN, JOEL S., evolutionary ecologist, educator; PhD, U Ariz. Head, Ctr. for Rsch. on Urban Ecology U. Ill. Chgo., prof. biology. Contbr. articles to profl. jours. Office: Univ Ill Chgo Dept Biol Sciences SES 3352 M/C 066 845 W TaylorSt Chicago IL 60607-7060 Office Phone: 312-996-4289. Office Fax: 312-413-2435. Business E-Mail: squirrel@uic.edu.

BROWN, JOHN WILFORD, health products executive; b. Paris, Tenn., Sept. 15, 1934; s. Albert T. and Treva (Moody) Brown; m. Rosemary Kopel, June 7, 1957; children: Sarah Beth, Janine. BSChemE, Auburn U., 1957. Process engr. Ormet Corp., Hannibal, Ohio, 1958-62; sr. engr. Thiokol Chem. Corp., Marshall, Tex., 1962-65; with Squibb Corp., Princeton, NJ, 1965-72, asst. to pres., 1970-72; pres. Edward Weck & Co. divsn. Squibb Corp., NYC, 1972-77; chmn. bd. dirs. Stryker Corp., Kalamazoo, 1979—, pres., CEO, 1979—2003. Named one of 400 Richest Ams., Forbes mag., 2006. Mem. Am. Chem. Soc., Health Industries Mfg. Assn. (bd. dirs.). Democrat. Mem. Ch. of Christ. Mailing: Stryker Corp 2725 Fairfield Rd Portage MI 49002

BROWN, KIRK, secretary of transportation; b. Harriburg, Ill., 1946; BCE, Vanderbilt U. Registered profl. engr., Ill. Deputy dir. planning, programming Ill. Dept. Transp., Springfield, dir. planning, programming, 1985-91, sec., 1991—. Mem. Nat. Soc. Profl. Engrs. (Ill. chpt.). Office: Illinois Dept Transportation Office of Public Affairs 2300 S Dirksen Pkwy Springfield IL 62764-0001

BROWN, LAURENCE DAVID, retired bishop; b. Fargo, ND, Feb. 16, 1926; s. John Nicolai and Ada Amelia (Johnson) B.; m. Virginia Ann Allen, Sept. 6, 1950; children: Patricia Ann, Julia Louise, Claudia Ruth. BS, U. Minn., 1946; BA, Concordia Coll., 1948; M of Theology, Luther Theol. Sem., 1951. Ordained to ministry Evang. Luth. Ch., 1951. Pastor Our Savior's Luth. Ch., New Ulm, Minn., 1951-55; nat. assoc. youth dir. Evang. Luth. Ch., Mpls., 1955-60; nat. youth dir. Am. Luth. Ch., Mpls., 1960-68; instn. dir. Tchr. Tng., U. Minn., Mpls., 1968-69; exec. dir. Freedom from Hunger Found., Washington, 1969-73; sr. pastor St. Paul Luth. Ch., Waverly, Iowa, 1973-79; bishop Iowa Dist. Am. Luth. Ch., Des Moines, 1979-89, N.E. Iowa Synod, Evang. Luth. Ch. in Am., Waverly, 1989-92; prof. religion Wartburg Coll., Waverly, Iowa, 1992-93; interim sr. pastor Ctrl. Luth. Ch., Mpls., 1994-95, Calvary Luth. Ch., Mpls., 1996-97; ret. Bd. regents Luther Coll., Decorah, Iowa, 1989-92, Wartburg Coll., 1988-92, Wartburg Theol. Sem., Dubuque, Iowa, 1988-91, Self-Help, Inc., 1989-94. Author: Take Care: A Guide for Responsible Living, 1983; contbr. articles to profl. jours. Lt. USN, 1943-46. Lutheran. Avocation: reading. Home: 7500 York Ave S 916 Edina MN 55435

BROWN, MARK E., manufacturing executive; b. Peosta, Iowa; BA, U. Iowa. Acct. Whirlpool Corp., Marion, Ohio, 1973, mgr. Columbia plant SC, 1988, contr. North Am. Appliance Group, 1991—93, v.p., procurement North Am. Appliance Group, 1993—95, gen. mgr. mktg. North Am. Appliance Group, 1995—96, contr. Whirlpool Asia, 1996—97, corp. v.p, contr., 1997—99, exec. v.p., CFO, 1999—2002, sr. v.p. global strategic sourcing, 2002—. Office: Whirlpool Corp 2000 N M-63 Benton Harbor MI 49022

BROWN, MATTHEW S., lawyer; b. Chgo., Jan. 29, 1955; BA magna cum laude, Conn. Coll.; JD, Georgetown U., 1978. Bar: Ill. 1978. Ptnr. Katten Muchin Rosenman LLP, Chgo. Mem.: ABA, Chgo. Bar Assn. Office: Katten Muchin Rosenman 525 W Monroe St Chicago IL 60661 Office Phone: 312-902-5207. Office Fax: 312-577-8726. E-mail: matthew.brown@kattenlaw.com.

BROWN, MELVIN F., finance company executive; b. Carlinville, Ill., June 4, 1935; s. Ben and Selma (Frommel) B.; m. Jacqueline Sue Hirsch, Sept. 2, 1962 (dec.); children: Benjamin Andrew, Mark Steven; m. Pamela Turken, Sept. 12, 1992. AB, Washington U., 1957, JD, 1961. Bar: Mo. 1961. Pvt. practice, St. Louis, 1961-62; asst. to gen. counsel Union Elec. Co., St. Louis, 1962-65; sec., atty. ITT Aetna Corp., St. Louis, 1965-72, v.p., gen. counsel, 1972; also dir.; corp. sec., gen. counsel ITT Fin. Corp., 1974-77, exec. v.p., 1977-95; pres. ITT Comml. Fin. Corp., 1977-95, St. Louis, 1977-95; pres., CEO Deutsche Fin. Svcs., 1995-96, vice chmn., 1997-98. Bd. dirs. Falcon Products, Foundors Bancshares. Mem. Mo. Commn. Dem. Party Constn. By-Laws and Party Structure, 1969-70, Mo. Dem. Platform Com., 1966, 68; mem. bd. adjustment City of Clayton, Mo., 1974—; chmn. St. Louis chpt. Am. Jewish Com., 1968—; mem. nat. coun. Washington U. Sch. Law; bd. trustees Mo. Hist. Soc.; trustee Whitaker Charitable Found.; trustee Maryville U., St. Louis Symphony Soc.; pres. Gateway chpt. Leukemia Soc.; mem. Rsch. Hon. col. Mo. Gov.'s Staff. Capt. AUS, 1957-64. Mem. Bar Assn. Met. St. Louis (pres. young lawyers sect. 1965-66), Mo. Bar Assn. Office: Deutsche Fin Svcs 655 Maryville Centre Dr Saint Louis MO 63141-5815

BROWN, MIKE, professional basketball coach; b. Mar. 5, 1970; s. Paul and Katie Brown; m. Carolyn Brown; children: Elijah, Cameron. Student, Mesa CC; grad. in Bus., U. San Diego, 1992. Video coord. to scout Denver Nuggets, 1992—97; asst. coach Washington Wizards, 1997—99, scout, 1999—2000; asst. coach San Antonio Spurs, 2000—03; assoc. head coach Ind. Pacers, 2003—05; head coach Cleve. Cavaliers, 2005—. Office: Cleve Cavaliers Quicken Loans One Center Ct Cleveland OH 44115-4001

BROWN, MORTON B., biostatistics educator; b. Montreal, Que., Can., Dec. 15, 1941; s. Israel I. and Leah (Shaikovitch) B.; m. Raya Sobol, Oct. 16, 1969; children— Danit, Alon B.Sc., McGill U., 1962; MA, Princeton U., 1964, PhD, 1965. Asst. research statistician UCLA, 1965-68, assoc. research statistician, 1975-77; vis. lectr. Tel Aviv U., 1968-69, sr. lectr., 1969-75, assoc. prof. stats., 1975-81; prof. biostatistics U. Mich., Ann Arbor, 1981—, chmn. dept., 1984-87; interim dir. biometrics core Ctr. for Clin. Investigation and Therapeutics, 1998—. Editor: BMDP Statistical Software, 1977 Fellow Royal Statis. Soc.; mem. Internat. Statis. Inst., Am. Statis. Assn., Biometric Soc., Inst. Math. Stats. Office: U Mich Dept Biostats Ann Arbor MI 48109-2029

BROWN, NANCY FIELD, editor; b. Troy, NY, Feb. 20, 1951; d. Robert Grant and Barbara Katherine (Field) B. BS in Journalism, Mich. State U., East Lansing, 1974. Asst. editor Mich. Am. Legion, Lansing, 1974-76, State Bar of Mich., Lansing, 1976-78, editor, 1976—, sr. dir. pubs., 1995-98, asst. exec. dir. publs., 1998—. Mem. Nat. Assn. Bar Execs. (cons. pubs. com. Chgo. chpt. 1989—), Mich. State U. Alumni Assn., Nat. Assn. Desktop Pubs., Am. Soc. Assn. Execs. Presbyterian. Avocations: reading, writing, photography, travel. Office: State Bar of Mich 306 Townsend St Lansing MI 48933-2012

BROWN, NEIL W., bank executive; Audit ptnr. KPMG LLP; exec. v.p., treas., CFO TCF Fin. Corp., 1998—2005, pres., CFO, 2005—. Chmn. bd. dirs. Vail Place. Office: TCF Financial 200 Lake Street East Wayzata MN 55391-1693

BROWN, OLEN RAY, microbiologist, biomedical researcher, educator; b. Hastings, Okla., Aug. 18, 1935; s. Willis Edward and Rosa Nell (Fulton) B.; m. Pollyana June King, Aug. 30, 1958; children: Barbara Kathryn, Diana Carol, David Gregory. BS in Lab. Tech., Okla. U., 1958, MS in Bacteriology, 1960, PhD in Microbiology, 1964. Diplomate Am. Bd. Toxicology. Instr. Sch. Medicine, U. Mo., Columbia, 1964-65, asst. prof., 1965-70, assoc. prof., 1970-77, prof. dept. molecular microbiology and immunology, 1981-96, rsch. prof., 1996—2001; joint appointments, prof. depts. microbiology and biomed. scis. Coll. Vet. Medicine, U. Mo., 1977-96, prof. biomed. scis., 1987-96. Guest lectr. Ross U., St. Kitts, W.I., 1984, 88; asst. dir. Dalton Rsch. Ctr., U. Mo., 1974-78, Dalton rsch. investigator grad. sch., 1968—; grant peer reviewer for program projects SCOR and Superfund grants NIH, 1979, Nat. Inst. Environ. Health Scis., Dept. Commerce, EPA, 1986, 90-99, Am. Inst. Biol. Scis. for Dept. Def., USAMRMC, Fund for Improvement of Secondary Edn., 2002; cons. drug abuse policy office White House, 1982, Immunol. Vaccines, Inc., Columbia, 1984—, Lab. Support, Inc., Chgo., 1988-89, Ea. Rsch. Group, Lexington, Mass., 1991—, Teltech, Mpls., 1992—, Scis. Internat., Inc., Alexandria, Va.; judge top 100 products for 1996, 99, Rsch. and Devel. Mag. Author: Laboratory Manual for Veterinary Microbiology, 1973, The Art and Science of Expert Witnessing, 2002; co-author: elem. and advanced lab. manuals for med. microbiology, 2 vols., 1978, 79; contbr. Progress in Clinical Research, Vol. 21, 1978, 79, Oxygen, 5th Internat. Hyperbaric Conf., Vols. I, II, 1974, 79, numerous articles to profl. jours.; book and film critic AAAS, Washington, 1986—; item preparer Am. Coll. Test, Med. Coll. Admissions Test, 1981—; mem. editorial staff Biomed. Letters, 1981—; responder Sci. and Math. Helpline for Mus. Sci. Discovery, Harrisburg, Pa., 1996—, reviewer profl. jours. Track and field ofcl. U. Mo. and Big Eight Conf., Columbia, 1979-86. Investigative rsch. grantee Office Naval Rsch., Dept. Def., 1968-81, NIH, 1976-88, NIEHS, 1981-94, 95—, USAID, 1983-86, Nat. Inst. Dental Health Scis., 1989-92. Fellow Am. Inst. Chemists (cert. chemistry and chem engring., profl. program bd. 1989-90, sd com. chemistry and environ. concerns); mem. Top One Percent Soc., Soc. Toxicology, Internat. Soc. Study Xenobiotics, Am. Chem. Soc., Am. Heart Assn., Internat. Soc. Exposure Analysts, Nat. Space Soc., Oxygen Soc., Columbia Track Club (sec.-treas. 1979-82). Avocations: long-distance running, painting. Office: U Mo Dalton Rsch Ctr Columbia MO 65211-0001 Office Phone: 573-449-7444. E-mail: browno@missouri.edu.

BROWN, PAM, state legislator; b. San Antonio, Tex., Sept. 12, 1952; m. F. Steve Brown; 1 child, Paul D. BA, U. Nebr., Lincoln. Mem. Nebr. Legislature from 6th dist., Lincoln, 1995—. Mem. Nebr. human genetics tech. commn. Bd. dirs. United Way of the Midlands, Westside Schs. Found. Office: State Capitol Rm 1012 Lincoln NE 68509

BROWN, PAUL, former publishing executive; MA, Cambridge U., 1976. With Butterworth Group Reed Elsevier, U.K., South Africa, N.Am., 1976—94; v.p., gen. mgr. legal info. svcs. Lexis-Nexis, Dayton, Ohio, 1994—96, COO legal info. svcs., 1996—99; pres., CEO Matthew Bender Pub., NYC, 1999—2000.

BROWN, PETER C., movie theater company executive; b. 1959; Founder, chmn. Entertainment Properties Trust, 1997—2003; CFO AMC Entertainment Inc., Kansas City, Mo., co-chmn., 1998—99, chmn., CEO, pres. Mo., 1999—. Bd. dir. Nat. Assn. Theatre Owners, Nat. CineMedia, Midway Games Inc. Office: AMC Entertainment Inc 920 Main St Kansas City MO 64105 Office Phone: 816-221-4000.

BROWN, PETER W., lawyer; b. St. Louis, June 28, 1944; s. Willis Andrew and Alice Louise (Heckel) B.; m. Lynne K. Lochmoeller, Nov.27, 1970; children: Jeff, Emily. BA, Westminster Coll., 1966; JD, Washington U., 1969; LLM in Taxation, U. Mo., Kansas City, 1977. Bar: Mo. 1969, Kans. 1982, US Dist Ct. (we. dist. Mo.) 1990, US Tax Ct. 1979. Estate tax atty. IRS, St. Louis, 1969-72, mgr. estate tax and gift tax grp. Kansas City, 1973-75; ptnr. Brown, Koralchik & Fingersh, Overland Park, Kans., 1975-85, Husch & Eppenberger, Kansas City, Mo., 1986—2006, Lathrop & Gage, Kansas City, 2006—. Bd. dirs. Briarcliff Devel. Co., Inc., Garney Cos., Inc., Major Brands, Inc. Dir. Estate Planning Symposium, Kansas City; mem. tax. and legal com. Jewish Cmty. Found., Kansas City; mem. steering and project oversight coms. Kauffman Ctr. Performing Arts Ctr. Named one of Top 100 Attys., Worth mag., 2006. Fellow Am. Coll. Trust and Estate Coun. (mem. bus. planning and charitable gift coms.); mem. ABA, Kans. Bar Assn., Mo. Bar Assn., Estate Planning Soc. Kansas City, Lawyers Assn. Greater Kansas City. Presbyterian. Avocations: tennis, golf, water activities, reading. Office: Lathrop & Gage 2345 Grand Blvd Ste 2800 Kansas City MO 64108 Office Phone: 816-460-5403. Office Fax: 816-292-2001. E-mail: pbrown@lathropgage.com.

BROWN, PHILIP ALBERT, lawyer; b. Gettysburg, Pa., June 12, 1949; s. Clyde Raynor and Jean (McCullough) B.; m. Donna Leslie Lohr, May 25, 1985; 1 child, Andrew Raynor. BA in History, George Washington U., 1971; JD, U. Mich., 1974. Bar: Ohio 1974. Assoc. Vorys, Sater, Seymour & Pease, Columbus, Ohio, 1974-81, ptnr., 1981—. Arbitrator Nat. Assn. Security Dealers: mem. Ohio civil legal needs assessment implementation com. Ohio Supreme Ct., 1991-94. Trustee Legal Aid Soc. Columbus, 1985-91, pres. 1989-90; trustee Ohio State Legal Svcs. Assn., 1994—; mem. Nat. Coun. for Arts and Scis. of George Washington U. Fellow Columbus Bar Found.; mem. Phi Beta Kappa. Avocation: fishing. Office: Vorys Sater Seymour & Pease 52 E Gay St Columbus OH 43215-3161

BROWN, RICHARD ELLSWORTH, state legislator; Gen. agt. Luth. Brotherhood, Sioux Falls, S.D.; mem. S.D. Ho. of Reps., Pierre. Chmn. edn. com., S.D. Ho. of Reps., mem. state affairs com.

BROWN, RICHARD HOLBROOK, library director, historian, researcher; b. Boston, Sept. 25, 1927; s. Joseph Richard and Sylvia (Cook) Brown. BA, Yale U., 1949, MA, 1952, PhD, 1955. Instr. history U. Mass., Amherst, 1955—59, asst. prof., 1959—62; assoc. prof. No. Ill. U., De Kalb, 1962—64; dir. Amherst

Project, Amherst and Chgo., 1964—72; dir. rsch. and edn. Newberry Libr., Chgo., 1972—83, acad. v.p., 1983—94, sr. rsch. fellow, 1994—. Vis. prof. history and edn. Northwestern U., Evanston, Ill., 1971—84; cons. NEH, 1977—; bd. dirs. Chgo. Metro History Fair, 1977—, pres., 1984—91; cons. Ctr. Study So. Culture, U. Miss., 1979—; mem. Ill. Humanities Coun., 1980—86, chmn., 1982—83. Author: The Hero and the People, 1964, The Missouri Compromise: Political Statesmanship or Unwise Evasion?, 1964; gen. editor: Amherst Project Units in American History, 25 vols., 1964—75. Recipient George Washington Eggleston prize, Yale U., 1955; Andrew Mellon Postdoctoral fellow, U. Pitts., 1960—61. Mem.: Orgn. Am. Historians, Social Sci. Edn. Consortium (pres. 1975—77), Am. Antiquarian Soc. Democrat. Roman Catholic. Office: The Newberry Libr 60 W Walton St Chicago IL 60610-3380 Home Phone: 313-787-1113; Office Phone: 312-255-3594. Business E-Mail: brownr@newberry.org.

BROWN, ROBERT GROVER, engineering educator; b. Shenandoah, Iowa, Apr. 25, 1926; s. Grover Whitney and Irene (Frink) B. BS, Iowa State Coll., 1948, MS, 1951, PhD, 1956. Instr. Iowa State Coll., Ames, 1948-51, 53-55, asst. prof., 1955-56, assoc. prof., 1956-59, prof., 1959-76, Disting. prof., 1976-88, Disting. prof. emeritus, 1988—; research engr. N. Am. Aviation, Downey, Calif., 1951-53. Cons. various aerospace engring. firms., 1956— Author: (with R.A. Sharpe, W.L. Hughes) Lines, Waves and Antennas, 1961, (with J.W. Nilsson) Linear Systems Analysis, 1962, (with Patrick Y.C. Hwang) Introduction to Random Signals and Applied Kalman Filtering with MATLAB Exercises and Solutions, 3d edit., 1997. Fellow IEEE, Inst. Navigation (Burka award 1978, 84, Weems award 1994). Home: 16E Venetian Dr Clear Lake IA 50428-1005

BROWN, RONALD DELANO, endocrinologist; b. Grosse Pointe, Mich., Dec. 28, 1936; s. Carroll Bradley and Alice Ruth (Chapper) B.; m. Marylee Ethel Lucas, July 27, 1957; children: Linda Diane, Kent William, Mark Steven. BS with distinction, U. Mich., 1959, MD with distinction, 1963. Diplomate Am. Bd. Internal Medicine, subspecialty in endocrinology and metabolism; lic. physician Mich. Intern Detroit Gen. Hosp., 1963-64; asst. resident in medicine U. Calif. Med. Ctr., San Francisco, 1966-68; chief resident in medicine San Francisco Gen. Hosp., 1968-69; fellow in endocrinology Vanderbilt U., Nashville, 1969-71, instr. medicine, 1969-71, asst. prof. medicine, 1971-73; assoc. prof. medicine Baylor Coll. Medicine, Houston, 1973-74, Mayo Med. Sch., Rochester, Minn., 1975-80; prof. medicine Health Scis. Ctr., U. Okla., Oklahoma city, 1980-93; clin. staff St. Joseph's Mercy Hosp., Clintown Twp., Mich., 1993—. Dir. U. Okla. Hypertension Ctr., 1986-93; chief clin. hypertension Health Scis. Ctr., U. Okla., 1980-93; chief hypertension VA Hosp., Oklahoma City, 1980-86; dir. multidisciplinary hypertension rsch. tng. program (NIH), Mayo Clinic, Rochester, 1977-80; chief endocrinology Ben Taub Hosp., Houston, 1973-74, assoc. dir. clin. rsch. ctr., 1973-74; coord. Tenn. Mid-South Regional Hyper-Control Program, Vanderbilt U., 1971-73; lectr. in field. Editl. bd. Jour. Clin. Endocrinology and Metabolism, 1987-91; reviewer for Life Scis., Annals of Internal Medicine, Jour. Lab. Clin. Medicine, Am. Jour. Medicine, Endocrinology, Mayo Clinic Proceedings, Steroids; contbr. 58 articles to profl. jours. Capt. USAF, 1964-66. Fellow ACP. Am. Coll. Endocrinologists; mem. Am. Soc. Hypertension, Am. Assn. Clin. Endocrinologists, Phi Kappa Phi, Phi Lambda Upsilon, Alpha Omega Alpha. Office: Ronald D Brown MD 7237 1st St Marine City MI 48039-2801

BROWN, ROWLAND CHAUNCEY WIDRIG, library and information scientist, consultant; b. Detroit, Oct. 11, 1923; s. Rowland Chauncey and Rhea (Widrig) B.; m. Kathleen Heather Sayre, May 18, 1946; children: Stephanie Anne Kugelman, Geoffrey Rowland Sayre (dec.), Kathleen Heather. BA cum laude, Harvard U., 1947, JD, 1950; sr. in mgmt. Sloan Sch., MIT, 1969; D. Humane Letters (hon.), Ohio Dominican Coll., 1999; D. in cmty. devel., Franklin U., 2005. Bar: D.C. 1951. Counsel Econ. Sablzn. Agy., 1950-52; staff counsel SBA, 1954; counsel Machinery and Allied Products Inst., Washington, 1955-59; with Dorr Oliver, Stamford, Conn., 1959-70, pres., 1968-70; pres., chief exec. officer Buckeye Internat., Inc., Columbus, Ohio, 1970-80; chief exec. officer Online Computer Libr. Ctr., Columbus, 1980-89; with R. Brown & Assocs., Columbus. Adv. bd. tchg. and learning Ohio State U. Sr. internat. cons. Coun. for Ethics Econs. inter-profl. panel on tech. and ethics; hon. trustee Columbus Cmty. Cable Access; bd. dirs., visitor's bd. Ohio Dominican Coll.; trustee Coun. for Pub. Deliberation, Civic Life Inst. Decorated Air medal (3), Purple Heart, Korean Republic citation. Mem. Am. Soc. Info. Sci., Am. Assn. for Higher Edn., N.Y. Harvard Club, Columbus Club, Columbus Rotary. Home: 1806 Maxfield Dr Columbus OH 43212 Office Phone: 614-448-3753. E-mail: rcwbrow@columbus.rr.com.

BROWN, SANDRA LEE, art association administrator, consultant, artist; b. Chgo., July 9, 1943; d. Arthur Willard and Erma Emily (Lange) Boettcher; m. Ronald Gregory Brown, June 21, 1983; 1 child, Jon Michael. BA in Art and Edn., N.E. Ill. U., 1966; postgrad., No. Ill. U. Cert. K-9 tchr., Ill. Travel agt. Weiss Travel Bur., Chgo., 1959-66; tchr. Chgo. Sch. Sys., 1966-68, Schaumburg (Ill.) Sch. Dist. 54, 1968-94, creator coord. peer mentoring program for 1st-yr. tchrs., 1992-96; cons. Yardstick Ednl. Svcs., Monroe, Wis., 1994—2003; exec. dir. Monroe Arts Ctr., 1996—2001, Monroe Area Coun. for the Arts, Madisonville, Tenn., 2002—03; arts mgmt. cons. Helping Hands, Non-Profit Consulting, Knoxville, Tenn., 2003—, Tenn. Arts Commn. Arts cons.; mem. adv. bd. Peer Coaching and Mentoring Network, Chgo. suburban region, 1992-94; peer cons. Schaumburg Sch. Dist. 54, 1988-94. Exhibited in solo and group exhibitions, Court House Gallery, Woodstock, Ill., Millburn (Ill.) Gallery, Gallerie Stefanie, Chgo., Monroe Arts Ctr., Athens Art Ctr., Athens, Tenn., Chumley/Orr Gallery, Cleve., Tenn. Campaign chmn. for mayoral candidate, Grayslake, Ill., 1989; campaign chmn. for trustee Citizens for Responsible Govt., Grayslake, 1991. Mem. Lakes Region Watercolor Guild, Delta Kappa Gamma (chmn. women in arts Gamma chpt. Ill. 1992-94, Alpha Mu chpt. 1995-97), Cmty. Arts League (Athens, Tenn.). Avocations: gardening, musician for barn dances, pre-war Appalachian, blues and cajun music, research collecting 78 rpm records. Home and Office: Helping Hands Non-Profit Consulting PO Box 1456 Athens TN 37371

BROWN, SHERROD CAMPBELL, senator, former congressman, former state official; b. Mansfield, Ohio, Nov. 9, 1952; s. Charles G. and Emily (Campbell) Brown; m. Connie Schultz; children: Emily, Elizabeth; 2 stepchildren. BA in Russian Studies, Yale U., 1974; MEd, Ohio State U., 1979, MPA, 1981. Mem. Ohio State Ho. Reps., Columbus, 1975-82; sec. state State of Ohio, Columbus, 1983-91; mem. US Congress from 13th Ohio dist., 1993—2007, mem. energy and commerce com., ranking minority mem. health subcommittee, mem. internat. rels. com., founding mem. India Caucus, founding mem. Taiwan Caucus; US Senator from Ohio, 2007—; mem. agrl., nutrition, & forestry com., banking, housing & urban affairs com., health, edn., labor, & pensions com., vets affairs com. Instr. polit. sci. Ohio State U., Mansfield, 1979-80, faculty assoc. Mershon Ctr., 1991-93. Author: Congress from the Inside: Observations from the Majority and the Minority, 1999, Myths of Free Trade, 2004. Recipient Eagle Scout Am. 1966, Friend of Edn. award, 1978, Disting. Pub. Health Legislator of Yr. award, APHA, 2002. Mem. Nat. Assn. Secs. State Democrat. Lutheran. Office: US Senate 2332 Rayburn House Office Bldg Washington DC 20515

BROWN, STEPHEN S., telecommunications industry executive; B in Bus. Mktg., Tex. Tech. U.; M in Mgmt. Info. Sys., Naval Post Grad. Sch. Dir. sys. integration GE Aerospace; dir. enterprise integration and telecom. Pillsbury; CIO Imation; v.p., CIO Micron Electronics; sr. v.p., CIO Carlson Cos., Minnetonka, Minn., 2000—. With USMC. Office Phone: 763-212-1330.

BROWN, THEODORE LAWRENCE, chemistry professor; b. Green Bay, Wis., Oct. 15, 1928; s. Lawrence A. and Martha E. (Kedinger) B.; m. Audrey Catherine Brockman, Jan. 6, 1951; children: Mary Margaret, Karen Anne, Jennifer Gerarda, Philip Matthew (dec.), Andrew Lawrence. BS in Chemistry, Ill. Inst. Tech., 1950; PhD, Mich. State U., 1956. Mem. faculty U. Ill., Urbana, 1956—, prof. chemistry, 1965-93, prof. chemistry emeritus, 1993—, vice chancellor for rsch., dean Grad. Coll., 1980-86, dir. Beckman Inst. for Advanced Sci. and Tech., 1987-93. Vis. scientist Internat. Meteorol. Inst., Stockholm, 1972; Boomer lectr. U. Alta., Edmonton, Can., 1975; Firth vis. prof. U. Sheffield, Eng., 1977; mem. bd. govs. Argonne Nat. Lab., 1982-88, Mercy Hosp., Urbana, 1985-89, Chem. Abstracts Svc., 1991-96, Arnold and Mabel Beckman Found., 1994—, Am. Chem. Soc. Pub., 1996-2001; adv. bd. Spatial Learning and Intelligence Ctr., 2006-. Author: (with R.S. Drago) Experiments in General Chemistry, 3d edit., 1970, General Chemistry, 2d edit., 1968, Energy and the Environment, 1971, (with H.E. LeMay and B.E. Bursten) Chemistry: The Central Science, 1977, 10th edit., 2006, Making Truth: Metaphor in Science, 2003; assoc. editor Inorganic Chemistry, 1969-78; contbr. articles to profl. publs. Mem. Govt.-Univ.-Industry Roundtable Coun., 1989-94; bd. dirs. Champaign County Opportunities Industrialization Ctr., 1970-79, chmn. bd. dirs., 1975-78. With USN, 1950-53. Sloan rsch. fellow, 1962-66, NSF sr. postdoctoral fellow, 1964-65, Guggenheim fellow, 1979. Fellow AAAS, Am. Acad. Arts and Scis.; mem. Am. Chem. Soc. (award in inorganic chemistry 1972, award for disting. svc. in advancement of inorganic chemistry 1993), Philosophy of Sci. Assn., Cognitive Sci. Soc., Soc. for Social Studies of Sci., Sigma Xi, Alpha Chi Sigma. Avocations: films, literature, running. Home: Apt 203 10751 Crooked River Rd Bonita Springs FL 34135-1727 also: W Bay Blvd Suite 904 N Estero FL 33928 E-mail: tlbrown1@earthlink.net.

BROWN, THOMAS D., pharmaceutical executive; Divsnl. v.p. diagnostic comml. opers. Abbott Labs., Abbott Park, Ill., 1993, v.p. diagnostic comml. opers., 1993-98, sr. v.p. diagnostic opers., 1998—, corp. officer, 1993. Office: Abbott Labs 100 Abbott Park Rd Abbott Park IL 60064-3502

BROWN, THOMAS K., automotive executive; B in Econ. and Fin., Am. Internat. Coll. Former exec. dir. corp. purchasing and transp. QMS Inc.; former v.p. supply mgmt. United Tech. Automotive; dir. purchasing global strategic planning and process leadership Ford Motor Co., Dearborn, Mich., 1999—2000, exec. dir. mfg. procurement ops., 2001—02, v.p. global purchasing, 2002—04, sr. v.p., global purchasing, 2004—. Office: Ford Motor Co 1 American Rd Dearborn MI 48126

BROWN, TIMOTHY N., state legislator; b. Bloomington, Ill., May 29, 1956; BA, Ill. Wesleyan U.; MD, U. Ill. Resident Indpls. Meth. Hosp., 1982—85; physician Crawfordsville (Ind.) Family Care, 1985—; rep. Dist. 41 Ind. Ho. of Reps., Indpls., 1994—, asst. Rep. floor leader, mem. appointments and claims, pub. health, and tech. R & D coms. Asst. clin. prof. medicine Ind. U. Mem. Ind. State Med. Assn. Methodist. Office: PO Box 861 Crawfordsville IN 47933-0861 also: Ind Ho of Reps 200 W Washington St Indianapolis IN 46204-2786

BROWN, TREVOR, dean; Dean journalism Ind. U., Bloomington. Office: Ind U Sch Journalism Ernie Pyle Hall Rm 200 940 E 7th St Bloomington IN 47405-7108

BROWN, WESLEY ERNEST, federal judge; b. Hutchinson, Kans., June 22, 1907; s. Morrison H. H. and Julia (Wesley) B.; m. Mary A. Miller, Nov. 30, 1934 (dec.); children: Wesley Miller, Loy B. Wiley; m. Thadene N. Moore (dec.) Student, Kans. U., 1925-28; LLB, Kansas City Law Sch., 1933. Bar: Kans. 1933, Mo. 1933. Pvt. practice, Hutchinson, 1933-58; county atty. Reno County, Kans., 1935-39; referee in bankruptcy U.S. Dist. Ct. Kans., 1958-62, judge, 1962-79, sr. judge, 1979—. Apptd. Temporary Emergency Ct. of Appeals of U.S., 1980-93; dir. Nat. Assn. Referees in Bankruptcy, 1959-62; mem. bankruptcy divsn. Jud. Conf., 1963-70; mem. Jud. Conf., U.S., 1976-79. With USN, 1944-46. Mem. ABA, Kans. Bar Assn. (exec. council 1950-62, pres. 1964-65), Reno County Bar Assn. (pres. 1947), Wichita Bar Assn., S.W. Bar Kan., Delta Theta Phi. Office: US Dist Ct 414 US Courthouse 401 N Market St Wichita KS 67202-2089

BROWN, WILLIAM MILTON, retired electrical engineering educator, emeritus chief scientist; b. Wheeling, W.Va., Feb. 14, 1932; s. John David and Marjorie Jennie (Walter) B.; m. Norma Jean Hulett, Aug. 24, 1963; children: Cherryl Lynn, Mark William, Jennifer Christine. BS in Elec. Engring, W.Va. U., 1952; MS, Johns Hopkins U., 1955, D.Engring., 1957. Registered profl. engr. Asst. instr. physics, W.Va. U., 1950-52; engr. Air Arm div. Westinghouse Electric Corp., Balt., 1952-54; project supr. countermeasures group radiation lab. Johns Hopkins U., Balt., 1954-57; also part-time lectr.; mem. tech. staff Inst. Def. Analysis, Weapons Systems Evaluation Group, The Pentagon, 1957-58; mem. faculty U. Mich., Ann Arbor, 1958—73, prof. elec. engring., 1963-73, adj. prof., 1975—92, head radar and optics lab., 1960-68; pres., founder Environ. Research Inst. Mich., 1972-94; founder, chmn. Mich. Devel. Corp., Ann Arbor, 1992-94; head dept. elec. and computer engring. Air Force Inst. of Tech., Wright-Patterson AFB, Ohio, 1995—2000; chief scientist, sensors directorate Air Force Rsch. Lab, 2000—05, chief scientist emeritus, 2005. Cons. in field; mem. USAF Scientific Adv. Bd., 1982-87, U.S. Army Sci. Bd., 1981-85. Author: Analysis of Time-Invariant Systems, 1963; co-author: Random Processes, Communications and Radar, 1969; assoc. editor: IEEE Trans. Aerospace and Electronic Systems, 1965-74; editor-in-chief, 1974-88; Contbr. articles to profl. jours. Recipient First in Coll. prize W.Va. U., 1952, High Tech. Entrepreneur of Yr. award Mich., 1991, Dawd award Mil. Sprinsing Symposium, 2005; named to Laureate Electronics, Aviation Weekly, 2003. Fellow IEEE; mem. Nat. Acad. Engring., IEEE Aerospace and Electronic Sys. Soc. (Pioneer award 2003). Home and Office: 2642 Cortina Ln Vail CO 81657 Personal E-mail: brownwm314@msn.com.

BROWN, ZAK, marketing executive; b. LA, Nov. 7, 1972; m. Tracy Brown. Former GT2 Championship Series Race Car Driver, 1997—2000; currently pres., CEO Just Marketing, Inc. Office: Just Marketing 10960 Bennett Parkway Zionsville IN 46077

BROWNBACK, SAM DALE, senator, lawyer; b. Parker, Kans., June 12, 1956; m. Mary S. Stauffer; children: Abby, Andy, Liz, Mark, Jenna. BS in Agrl. Economics, with honors, Kan. State U., 1979; JD, U. Kans., 1982. Bar: Kans. 1982. Farm broadcaster KKSU; instr. law Kans. State U.; city atty. Ogden & Leonardville, Kans.; sec. agr. State of Kans., Topeka, 1986—93; mem. US Congress from 2nd Kans. dist., Washington, 1994-96; US Senator from Kans., 1996—. Mem. commn. security and coop. in Europe US Senate, com. appropriations, com. judiciary, congressional-exec. commn. China. Co-author: (with Jim Nelson Black) From Power to Purpose: A Remarkable Journey of Faith and Compassion, 2007 Pres. Kans. Prayer Breakfast; developer Family Impact Statement; vice chmn. Riley County Rep. Com. Recipient Hon. Am. Farmer degree, FFA; named Outstanding Young Person, Osaka, Japan Jaycees, Kansan of Distinction, 1988, Award for Manufacturing Excellence Nat. Assn. Manufacturers, 2001, Oncology Nursing Soc. Honor award, 2002, US Oncology Medal of Honor, 2002, William Wilberforce award Prison Fellowship, 2003, Pro Deo et Patria medal Christendom Coll., Va., 2005. Mem.: Nat. Future Farmers Am. (v.p. 1977), Am. Judicature Soc., Am. Agrl. Law Assn., Riely County Bar Assn., Kans. Bar Assn., ABA. Republican. Roman Catholic. Office: US Senate 303 Hart Senate Office Bldg Washington DC 20510-0001 also: District Office 612 S Kansas Ave Topeka KS 66603 Office Phone: 202-224-6521, 785-233-2503. Office Fax: 785-233-2616, 202-228-1265. E-mail: sam_brownback@brownback.senate.gov.

BROWNE, DONALD ROGER, speech communication educator; b. Detroit, Mar. 13, 1934; s. A. and L. Browne; m. Mary Jo Rowell, Aug. 23, 1958; children: Mary Kathleen, Stuart Roger, Steven Rowell. BA, U. Mich., 1955, MA, 1958, PhD, 1961. Corr. Voice of Am., fgn. service officer U.S. Info. Agy., Tunis, Tunisia and Conakry, Guinea, 1960-63; asst. prof. broadcasting Boston U., 1963-65; asst. prof. speech Purdue U., West Lafayette, Ind., 1965-66; assoc. prof. U. Minn., Mpls., 1966-70, prof., 1970—, dept. chair, 1989-93, 96-99. Fulbright lectr., Beirut, 1973-74; vis. lectr. Lund U., Sweden, spring 1993. Author: International Radio Broadcasting, 1982, Comparing Broadcast Systems, 1989 (BEA/NAB Electronic Media Book of Yr. award 1989, Outstanding Acad. Book in Comm. Category, Choice, 1990), Television/Radio News & Minorities, 1994, Electronic Media and Indigenous Peoples, 1996, Electronic Media and Industrialized Nations, 1999, Ethnic Minorities, Electronic Media and the Public Sphere, 2004. Mem.Civic Orch. Mpls., 1966—. Served with U.S. Army, 1955-57. NATO fellow, Brussels, 1980. Mem. Broadcast Edn. Assn., Assn. for Edn. in Journalism and Mass Comm., Civic Orch. Mpls. Episcopalian. Avocation: playing trombone. Office: Univ of Minn 224 Church St SE Ford Hall Minneapolis MN 55455

BROWNE, RAY BROADUS, popular culture educator; b. Millport, Ala., Jan. 15, 1922; s. Garfield and Annie Nola (Trull) Browne; m. Olwyn Orde, Aug. 21, 1952 (dec.); children: Glenn, Kevin; m. Alice Pat Matthews, Aug. 25, 1965; 1 child, Alicia. AB, U. Ala., 1943; A.M., Columbia U., 1947; PhD, UCLA, 1956. Instr. U. ebr., Lincoln, 1947-50; instr. U. Md., College Park, 1956-60; asst. prof., assoc. prof. Purdue U., Lafayette, Ind., 1960-67; prof. popular culture Bowling Green (Ohio) State U., 1967—, Univ. disting. prof., 1975—. Author, editor: Melville's Drive to Humanism, 1971, Popular Culture and the Expanding Consciousness, 1973, The Constitution and Popular Culture, 1975, Dominant Symbols in Popular Culture, 1990, The Many Tongues of Literacy, 1992, Continuities in Popular Cultures, 1993, The Cultures of Celebrations, 1994, Popular Culture Studies in the Future, 1996, Lincoln-Lore: Lincoln in Contemporary Popular Culture, 1996, Pioneers in Popular Culture Studies, 1998, The Defining Guide to United States Popular Culture, 2000, The Detective as Historian, 2000, vol. II, 2007, Preview, 2001, Mission Underway: The History of the Popular Culture Association/American Culture Association and Popular Culture Movement, 2002, Popular Culture of the Civil War and Reconstruction, 2003, Murder on the Reservation: American Indian Crime Fiction, 2004, Popular Culture Studies Across the Curriculum, 2005, Profiles of Popular Culture, 2005, The Detective as Historian: History and Art in Historical Crime Fiction, vol. II, 2007, creator, editor: Jour. Popular Culture, 1967—82, Jour. Am. Culture, 1977—82, Values and Popular Culture, 2008. With US Army, 1942—46. Mem.: Am. Culture Assn. (sec.-treas. 1977—), Popular Culture Assn. (treas. 1970—, founder, sec. 1970—2002). Democrat. Avocation: scholarly research. Home: 210 N Grove St Bowling Green OH 43402-2335 Office: Bowling Green U Bowling Green OH 43403-0001 Office Phone: 419-372-7861. Business E-Mail: rbrowne@bgsu.edu.

BROWNING, DON SPENCER, religious educator; b. Trenton, Mo., Jan. 13, 1934; s. Robert Watson and Nelle Juanita Browning; m. Carol LaVeta Browning, Sept. 28, 1958; children: Elizabeth Dell, Christopher Robert. AB, Ctrl. Meth. Coll., Fayette, Mo., 1956; DDiv, Ctr. Meth. Coll., Fayette, Mo., 1984; BD, U. Chgo., 1959, PhD, 1964; DDiv, Christian Theol. Sem., Indpls., 1990; DDiv (hon.), U. Glasgow, Scotland, 1998. Asst. prof. Phillips U., Enid, Okla., 1963-65; instr. Div. Sch. U. Chgo., 1965-66, asst. prof., 1966-69, assoc. prof., 1969-77, prof., 1977-79, Alexander Campbell prof. ethics and social sci., 1979—. Cadbury lectr. U. Birmingham, England, 1998; Woodruff prof. Emory U., 2001—03. Author: Atonement and Psychotherapy, 1966, Generative Man: Society and Good Man in Philip Rieff, Norman Brown, Erich Fromm and Erik Erikson, 1973, The Moral Context of Pastoral Care, 1976, Pluralism and Personality: William James and Some Contemporary Cultures of Psychology, 1980, Religious Ethics and Pastoral Care, 1983, Religious Thought and the Modern Psychologies, 1987, 2d edit., 2004, A Fundamental Practical Theology, 1991; co-author: From Culture Wars to Common Ground: Religion and the American Family Debate, 1997, 2d edit., 2000, Reweaving the Social Tapestry: Toward a Public Philosophy and Policy of Families, 2001, Marriage and Modernization, 2003; sr. advisor (PBS documentary) Marriage--Just a Piece of Paper?; co-editor: Sex, Marriage and Family in the World Religions, 2006, Equality and the Family, 2006, American Religions and the Family, 2007, Christian Ethics and the Moral Psychologies, 2007. Recipient Oskar Pfister award Am. Psychiat. Assn., 1999; Guggenheim fellow, 1975-76, fellow Inst. Religion in Age of Sci., 2003; Lilly Endowment grantee, 1991-97, 1997, for Religion, Culture and Family Project, 1991-2003. Home: 5513 S Kenwood Ave Chicago IL 60637-1713 Office: Univ of Chicago Divinity Sch Chicago IL 60637 Business E-Mail: dsbrowni@uchicago.edu.

BROWNLEE, KARIN S., state legislator; m. Doug Brownlee; 4 children. BS in Microbiology, Kans. State U. Co-owner Patrons Mortgage Co.; mem. Kans. Senate, Topeka, 1996—, mem. commerce com., mem. fin. instns. and ins. com., 1996—, mem. utilities com., mem. claims against the state com., mem. arts and cultural resources com. Mem. steering com. Leadership Olathe, 1994—; mem. QPA issues com. Olathe Sch. Dist., 1993; mem. adv. com. Mahaffie Farmsted; women's ministry leader Olathe Bible Ch.; del. Rep. Nat. Conv., 1996; vice chair Johnston Rep. Party, 1994-96; chair Olathe Rep. Party, 1992-94. Mem. Olathe Area C. of C. Republican. Office: 300 SW 10th Ave Rm 143-n Topeka KS 66612-1504

BROWNLEE, ROBERT HAMMEL, lawyer; b. Chester, Ill., Dec. 15, 1951; s. Robert Mathis and Geneva (Hammel) B.; m. Sue F., June 17, 1978. BS, So. Ill. U., Carbondale, 1973; JD, Vanderbilt U., Nashville, 1976. Bar: Mo. 1976, Ill. 1977, U.S. Dist. Ct. (ea. and we. dists.) Mo. 1976, U.S. Dist. Ct. (so. and cen. dists.) Ill. 1977, U.S. Ct. Appeals (8th cir.) 1979, Ky. 1999, U.S. Supreme Ct. 1999. Assoc. Thompson & Mitchell, St. Louis, 1976-82; ptnr. Thompson Coburn, St. Louis, 1982—. Mng. editor Vanderbilt Law Review, Nashville, 1975-76; mem. Bar Assn. of Met. St. Louis, 1976—, Ill. State Bar Assn., Springfield, Ill., 1977—, Am. Bankruptcy Inst., 1988—, Ky. Bar, 1999—. Co-author: Rights of Secured Creditors in Bankruptcy, 1987, Lender Liability in Missouri, 1988, Protection of Secured Interests in Bankruptcy, 1989, Litigation in Bankruptcy Proceedings, 1994, Interlocutory Appeal Issues Before the Bankruptcy Reform Commission, 1996; Author: Bankruptcy Impact on Commercial Leases, Advanced Missouri Real Estate Law, 1997, updated, 1999, 2001, Impact of the Bankruptcy Review Commission's Report on Creditor Issues, 1997, Vendor Protection in Maritime Bankruptcy Reorganizations, 2003, The Sarbanes-Oxley Act of 2002: Potential Impacts on Future Administration of Large Chapter II Cases, 2003, rev. edit., 2006. Mem. Friends of the St. Louis Zoo., 1986—, St. Louis Bot. Garden Sponsors, 1987—; builder of the community United Way of Greater St. Louis, 1988—. Fellow Am. Coll. Bankruptcy Lawyers (8th cir. coun. 2005—); mem. ABA (litigation sec. 1976—, co-chair jury instrn. subcom. of bankruptcy and insolvency com. 1994-99, bus. sec. 1976—, vice-chair claims trading subcom. bus. bankruptcy com. 1998-2001, chmn. subcom. adminstrn., U.S. trustee and jurisdiction and venue 2002-05, co-chmn. planning subcom. 2006—), Mo. Athletic Club, Mo. Bankers Assn. (chmn. legal adv. bd. 1997-98). Avocations: fishing, american art pottery, antiques, gardening. Office: Thompson Coburn LLP 1 US Bank Plz Ste 2600 Saint Louis MO 63101-1643 Office Phone: 314-552-6017. Business E-Mail: rbrownlee@thompsoncoburn.com.

BROWNRIGG, JOHN CLINTON, lawyer; b. Detroit, Aug. 7, 1948; s. John Arthur and Sheila Pauline (Taffe) B.; m. Rosemary F. Brownrigg; children: Brian M., Jennifer A., Katharine T. BA, Rockhurst Coll., 1970; JD cum laude, Creighton U., 1974. Bar: Nebr. 1974, U.S. Dist. Ct. Nebr. 1974, U.S. Tax Ct. 1977, U.S. Ct. Appeals (8th cir.) 1990. Ptnr. Eisenstatt, Higgins, Kinnamon, Okun & Brownrigg, P.C., Omaha, 1974-80, Erickson & Sederstrom, P.C., Omaha, 1980—. Lectr. law trial practice Creighton U. Sch. Law, Omaha, 1978-83; dir. Legal Aid Soc., Inc., Omaha, 1982-88, pres., 1987-88, devel. coun., 1989—; dir. Nebr. Continuing Legal Edn., Inc., 1991-93. Chmn. law sect. Archbishop's Capital Campaign, Omaha, 1991; dir. Combined Health Agys. Drive, 2001-03. Sgt. USAR, 1970-76. Fellow Nebr. State Bar Found. (dir. 1991-93); mem. Nebr. State Bar Assn. (pres. 1992-93), Nebr. Assn. Trial Attys., Omaha Bar Assn. (pres. 1990-91). Avocations: golf, bicycling, hiking. Office: Erickson & Sederstrom PC Ste 100 10330 Regency Parkway Dr Omaha NE 68114-3761

BROXMEYER, HAL EDWARD, medical educator; b. Bklyn., Nov. 27, 1944; s. David and Anna (Gurman) B.; m. C. Beth Biller, 1969; children: Eric Jay, Jeffrey Daniel. BS, Bklyn. Coll., 1966; MS, L.I. U., 1969; PhD, NYU, 1973. Postdoctoral student Queens U., Kingston, Ont., Canada, 1973-75; assoc. rschr., rsch. assoc. Meml. Sloan Kettering Cancer Ctr., NYC, 1975-78, assoc., 1978-83, assoc. mem., 1983; asst. prof. Cornell U. Grad. Sch., NYC, 1980-83; assoc. prof. Ind. U. Sch. Medicine, Indpls., 1983-86, prof. medicine, microbiology and immunology, 1986—; sci. dir. Walther Oncology Ctr., Indpls., 1988—, chmn. microbiology and immunology, 1997—, Disting. prof., 2004—. Mem. hematology II study sect. NIH, Bethesda, Md., 1981—86, 1995—2000, chair, 1997—2000; adv. com. NHLBI, NIH, Bethesda, 1991—94; chmn. bd. sci. counselors Nat. Space Biomed. Rsch. Inst., 1997—2006, mem. coun., 1999—2006; bd. dirs. Nat. Disease Rsch. Interchange, 1998—, chmn., 2007—; co-chmn. sec. hematopoiesis Faculty of 1000 Medicine. Assoc. editor Exptl. Hematology, 1981—90, Jour. Immunology, 1987—92, Stem Cells, 1996—97, Brit. Jour. Haematology, 1998—, editor Jour. Leukocyte Biology, 1995—, sr. editor Stem Cells and Devel. (formerly Jour. Hematotherapy and Stem Cell Rsch.), 2000—, mem. editl. bd. Blood, 1983—87, Biotech. Therapeutics, 1988—95, Internat. Jour. Hematology, 1991—, Jour. Lab. Clin. Medicine, 1992—2006, Jour. Exptl. Medicine, 1992—, Annals Hematology, 1993—, Cell Transplantation, 1994—, Critical Rev. Oncology/Hematology, 1995—, Stem Cells, 1998—, Jour. Blood and Marrow Transplantations, 1998—, Cytokines, Cellular and Molecular Therapy, 1998—, Current Trends Immunology, 2004—, Internat. Jour. Biol. Scis., 2006—; contbr. over 630 articles to profl. jours. Ednl. com. Leukemia Soc. Am., Indpls., 1983—86; nat. career devel. study sect. Leukemia and Lymphoma Soc., NY, 1991—95, 2000—04. Recipient Founder's Day award NYU, 1973, Merit award Nat. Cancer Inst.; Leukemia Soc. Am. award, 1987-95, Spl. Fellow award, 1976-78, Scholar award, 1978-83, Gold medal City of Paris, 1993, World of Difference award Ind. Health Industry Forum, 1997, Landsteiner award Am. Assn. Blood Banks, 2002, Health Care Heroes award Indpls. Bus. Jour., 2002, Prestigious External Recognition award

Ind. U. Purdue U. Indpls., 2003, Disting. Alumni award L.I. U., Bklyn. Ctr., 2005, Dr. Joseph T. Taylor Excellence in Diversity award Ind. U. Purdue U. Indpls., 2006, Dirk van Bekkum award Autologous Blood and Bone Marrow Soc., 2006, E. Donnall Thomas prize Am. Soc. Hematol, 2007. Mem.: AAAS, Am. Soc. Blood and Marrow Transplantation, Am. Fedn. Clin. Rsch., Am. Soc. Hematology (coun. 2000—05, v.p. 2008., E. Donnall Thomas prize 2007), Internat. Soc. Stem Cell Rsch., Internat. Soc. Exptl. Hematology (pres. 1990—91), Am. Assn. Immunologists, Am. Assn. Cancer Rsch., Soc. Leukocyte Biology, NY Acad. Scis. Achievements include 13 patents in field. Avocation: competitive Olympic-style weightlifting. Home: 1210 Chessington Rd Indianapolis IN 46260-1630 Office: Ind U Sch Medicine 950 W Walnut St Rm 302 Indianapolis IN 46202-5181 Office Phone: 317-274-7510. Office Fax: 317-274-7592. Business E-Mail: hbroxmey@iupui.edu.

BRUBAKER, ROBERT LORING, lawyer; b. Louisville, May 22, 1947; s. Robert Lee and Betty (Brock) B.; m Jeannette Marie Montgomery, Dec. 21, 1968; children: Benjamin Brock, Anne Montgomery. BA, Earlham Coll., 1969; JD, U. Chgo., 1972. Bar: Ohio 1972, U.S. Dist. Ct. (so. dist.) Ohio 1973, U.S. Ct. Appeals (6th cir.) 1975, U.S. Supreme Ct. 1978, U.S. Ct. Appeals (D.C. cir.) 1979, U.S. Ct. Appeals (3d, 4th and 7th cirs.) 1995. Asst. atty. gen. Atty. Gen.'s Office State of Ohio, Columbus, 1972-76; assoc. Porter Wright Morris & Arthur, Columbus, 1976-78, ptnr., 1979—. Editor: Ohio Environmental Law Handbook, 1990, 5th edit., 2004, Deposition Strategy, Law and Forms: Environmental Law. Fellow Am. Bar Found.; mem. ABA (natural resources, energy and environ. law sect., pub. utility sect., chmn. environ. law com., standing com. on environ. law), Ohio Bar Assn. (environ. law com.), Air and Waste Mgmt. Assn. (chmn. S.W. Ohio chpt. 1990-91, chmn. East Ctrl. sect. 1991-92), Columbus Bar Assn. (environ. law com.), Nat. Coal Coun., The Breathing Assn. (bd. dirs.) Home: 2661 Wexford Rd Columbus OH 43221-3217 Office: Porter Wright Morris & Arthur 41 S High St Ste 2800 Columbus OH 43215-6194 Home Phone: 614-488-5530; Office Phone: 614-227-2033. Business E-Mail: rbrubaker@porterwright.com.

BRUCE, ISAAC ISIDORE, professional football player; b. Ft. Lauderdale, Florida, Nov. 10, 1972; Postgrad in phys. edn., Memphis State, 1992. Wide receiver L.A. Rams, 1994—95, St. Louis Rams, 1995—2006; winner Super Bowl 35, 2000. Bd. dirs. Childhaven; donator children orgn., homeless. Recipient Daniel F. Reeves Memorial award, 1996, Carroll Rosenbloom award, 1994. Achievements include first Rams receiver to earn consecutive Pro Bowl invitations; ranked fifth in FL's all-time single season reception list; first player in history to record three consecutive games with at least 170 receiving yards.

BRUCE, PETER WAYNE, lawyer, insurance company executive; b. Rome, NY, July 12, 1945; s. G. Wayne and Helen A. (Hibling) B.; m. Joan M. McCabe, Sept. 20, 1969; children: Allison, Steven. BA, U. Wis., 1967; JD, U. Chgo., 1970; postgrad., Harvard Bus. Sch., 1986. Bar: Wis. 1970. Atty. Northwestern Mut. Life Ins. Co., Milw., 1970-74, asst. gen. counsel, 1974-80, gen. counsel, sec., 1980—, v.p., 1983-87, sr. v.p., gen. counsel, sec., 1987-90, sr. v.p. ins. ops., 1990-95, exec. v.p. ins. ops. & adminstrn., chief compliance officer, 1995-98, exec. v.p. accumulation products and long term care, 1998-2000, sr. exec. v.p. ins. ops. and long term care, 2000, sr. exec. v.p., 2000—. Bd. dirs. Northwestern Mut. Life Ins. Co., Milw., Northwestern Long-Term Care Ins. Co., Alverno Coll. Badger Meter Found., Growth Design Corp. Former chmn. Alverno Coll., Curative Rehab. Ctr., former mem. Shorewood Civic Improvement Found.; chair Milw. Archdiocese Resource Devel. Coun.; bd. dirs., chair Curative Found.; mem. Milw. Archdiocese Cath. Cmty. Found.; mem. Village of Shorewood (Wis.); mem. Village Shorewood Cmty. Devel. Assn., Wis. Equal Justice Fund; former mem. Planning and Devel. Commn. Mem. Wis. Bar Assn., Milw. Bar Assn., Am. Law Inst. Office: Northwestern Mut Life Ins Co 720 E Wisconsin Ave Milwaukee WI 53202-4703

BRUCE, TERRY LEE, congressman; b. Olney, Ill., Mar. 25, 1944; m. Charlotte Roberts; children: Emily Anne, Ellen Catherine JD, U. Ill., 1969. Mem. farm labor staff Dept. Labor, Washington; then mem. staff Congressman George Shipley and Ill. Senator Philip Benefiel legis. intern, 1969-70; mem. Ill. Senate, Springfield, 1970-85, asst. majority leader, 1975-85; mem. from Ill. Dist. 11 US Ho. of Reps, Washington, 1985—93; majority whip-at-large, 1990. Democrat. Office: 419 Condon Ter SE Washington DC 20032-3711 Mailing: PO Box 206 Olney IL 62450

BRUCKEN, ROBERT MATTHEW, lawyer; b. Akron, Ohio, Sept. 15, 1934; s. Harold M. and Eunice B. (Boesel) B.; m. Lois R. Gilbert, June 30, 1960; children: Nancy, Elizabeth, Rowland, Gilbert. AB, Marietta Coll., 1956; JD, U. Mich., 1959. Bar: Ohio 1960. Assoc. Baker & Hostetler, Cleve., 1960-69, ptnr., 1970—2004. Trustee Marietta Coll., 1983—, Lakeside Chautaugua Found., 2007-; treas. Leader Shape, Inc., 1990—. Served with AUS, 1959-60. Mem. Ohio State Bar Assn. (chmn. probate and trust law sect. 1981-83), Cleve. Bar Assn. (chmn. probate ct. com. 1973-75), Am. Coll. Trust and Estate Counsel, Phi Beta Kappa. United Ch. Of Christ. Office: 3200 National City Ctr 1900 E Ninth St Cleveland OH 44114 Office Phone: 216-861-7552. Business E-Mail: rbrucken@bakerlaw.com.

BRUCKNER, MARTHA, academic administrator; B, M, U. Nebr., Omaha; Doctorate, U. Nebr., Lincoln. Assoc. supt. for ednl. svcs. Millard (Nebr.) Pub. Schs.; tchr. h.s,. asst. prin., prin. pub. schs.; assoc. prof., chairperson ednl. adminstrn. U. Nebr., Omaha. Contbr. articles to profl. jours. Recipient award, Nebr. Coun. Sch. Adminstrs., Nebr. Schoolmasters Orgn. Mem.: ASCD (pres. 2005—06, bd. dirs., budget liaison, organizer student chpt. U. Nebr., Omaha). Office: Don Stroh Adminstrn Ctr 5606 S 147th St Omaha NE 68137 Home Phone: 402-339-1823; Office Phone: 402-895-8301. E-mail: mmbruckner@mpsomaha.org.

BRUEGMANN, ROBERT, architectural historian, educator; b. Chgo., May 21, 1948; s. Karl A. and Margaret (Cartwright) B. BA, Principia Coll., Elsah, Ill., 1970; PhD, U. Pa., 1976. Historian Hist. Am. Bldgs. Survey, Nat. Park Svc., various locations, 1973-78; lectr. Phila. C.C., 1975-76, Phila. Coll. Art, 1976-77; asst. prof. archtl. history U. Ill., Chgo., 1977-83, assoc. prof., 1983-93, prof. art history, architecture, urban planning, 1993—, chmn. art history, 2001—06. Author: Benicia: Portrait of an Early California Town, 1980, Holabird & Root: An Illustrated Catalog of Works, 1991 (Wittenborn award 1991), The Architects and the City: Holabird and Roche 1880-1918, 1997 (Spiro Kostof award Soc. Archtl. Historians 1998), Sprawl: A Compact History, 2005; contbr. articles to profl. jours. Bd. dirs. Graham Found., Chgo., 1998—2004, 2006—. Fellow NEH, 1983-84, Temple Hoyne Buell Ctr., Columbia U., 1989, Inst. Humanities at U. Ill., Chgo., 1992. Mem. Soc. Archtl. Historians, Chgo. Archtl. Found., Chgo. Archtl. Club (bd. dirs. 1989-92). Office: U Ill Art History Dept M/C 201 935 W Harrison St 206 Chicago IL 60607-3532 Office Phone: 312-413-2469. Business E-Mail: bbrueg@uic.edu.

BRUENING, RICHARD P(ATRICK), lawyer; b. Kansas City, Mo., Mar. 17, 1939; s. Arthur Louis, Jr. and Lorraine Elizebeth (Gamble) B.; m. Jane Marie Egender, Aug. 25, 1962; children: Christiana G., Paul R., Erin E. AB, Rockhurst Coll., 1960; JD, U. Mo. at Kansas City, 1963. Bar: Mo. 1963. Since practiced in, Kansas City; law clk. U.S. Dist. Judge R.M., Duncan, 1963-65; assoc. firm Houts, James, McCanse & Larison, 1965-68; gen. atty. Kansas City So. Ry. Co., 1969; asst. gen. counsel Kansas City So. Industries, Inc., 1970-76, gen. counsel, 1976-82, v.p., gen. counsel, 1982—, sr. v.p., gen. counsel Transp. Group, 1992—. Bd. dirs. Kansas City So. Ry. Co.; mem. Mo. Press-Bar Commn., 1981-85, Mo. Rail Improvement Authority, 1984-86, chmn., 1984-85; mem. bd. commrs. Port Authority Kansas City, 1995-98; mem. Mo. Total Transp. Commn., 1997—. Bd. dirs. Friends of Zoo, Inc., 1987-98, Heart of Am. Shakespeare Festival, 1995—, Brain Injury Assn., 1999—; bd. dirs. Performing Arts Found./Folly Theatre, 1983-90, sec., 1984-90; mem. exec. com., trustee Conservatory Music, U. Mo., Kansas City. Mem. ABA, Mo. Bar Assn., Kansas City Bar Assn., Lawyers Assn. Kansas City, Nat. Assn. R.R. Trial Counsel (exec. com.), Practising Law Inst., Kansas City Country Club, Kansas City Club, River Club, Phi Delta Phi, Omicron Delta Kappa. Roman Catholic. Home: 5049 Wornall Rd #8AB Kansas City MO 64112

BRUESCHKE, ERICH EDWARD, physician, researcher, educator; b. nr. Eagle Butte, SD, July 17, 1933; s. Erich Herman and Eva Johanna (Joens) B.; m. Frances Marie Bryan, Mar. 25, 1967; children: Erich Raymond, Jason Douglas, Tina Marie, Patricia Frances, Susan Eva. BS in Elec. Engring, S.D. Sch. Mines and Tech., 1956; postgrad., U. So. Calif., 1960-61; MD, Temple U., 1965. Diplomate Am. Bd. Family Practice, also cert. in geriatrics. Intern Germantown Dispensary and Hosp., Phila., 1965-66; mem. tech. staff Hughes Research and Devel. Labs., Culver City, Calif., 1956-61; practiced gen. medicine Fullerton, Calif., 1968-69; dir. research Ill. Inst. Tech. Research Inst., Chgo., 1970-76; research asst. prof. Temple U. Sch. Medicine, 1965-69; mem. staff Mercy Hosp. and Med. Center, Chgo., 1970-76; vis. prof. Rush Med. Coll., Chgo., 1974-76, prof., chmn. dept. family practice, 1976—95, program dir. Rush. Christ family practice residency, 1978-93, vice dean, 1992—93, acting dean, 1993-94, dean, 1994-2000, v.p. univ. affairs, 2000—02; trustee Anchor HMO, 1976-81, v.p. med. and acad. affairs, 1981—2000; trustee Synergon Health Systems, 1993-98; vice chmn., bd. dirs. Rush Presbyn. St. Lukes Health Assocs., disting. prof. medicine, 2002—, Rush Med. Coll. of Rush U., 2002—. Bd. dirs. Comprehensive Health Planning Met. Chgo., 1971—74, Fedn. of Ind. Ill. Colls. and Univs., West Suburban Higher Edn. Consortium; adv. com. Edn. to Careers, Health and Medicine/Chg. Bd. Edn.; med. dir. Chgo. Bd. of Health West Side Hypertension Ctr., 1974—78; sr. attending Presbyn.-St. Luke's Hosp., Chgo., 1976—2003; vis. attending Rush U. Hosp., Chgo., 2003—. Editor-in-chief Disease-a-Month, 1998-2003; assoc. editor Primary Cardiology, 1979-85; cons. editor for family practice Hosp. Medicine, 1986-2003; med. editor World Book/Rush Presbyn. St. Lukes/Med. Ency., 1987-2003; contbr. articles to profl. jours. Served with M.C., USAF, 1966-68. Named Physician Tchr. of Yr. Ill. Acad. Family Physicians, 1988, alumni of yr. Temple U. Sch. Medicine, 1996. Master Mason; fellow Am. Acad. Family Physicians, Inst. of Medicine of Chgo.; mem. IEEE (chmn. Chgo. sect. Engring. in Medicine and Biology group 1974-75), Internat. Soc. for Artificial Internal Organs, Am. Fertility Soc., Am. Occupational Med. Assn. (recipient Physician's recognition award 1969, 72, 75), Am. Wireless Assn., Chgo. Med. Soc., Am. Heart Assn., Am. Wireless Assn., Assn. for Advancement Med. Instrumentation, N.Y. Acad. Scis., Sigma Xi, Phi Rho Sigma, Eta Kappa Nu, Alpha Omega Alpha, Am. Rocket Soc., Inst. of Radio Engrs., Am. Med. Assn. Home: 319 N Lincoln St Hinsdale IL 60521-3442

BRUININKS, ROBERT H., academic administrator, psychologist, educator; b. Mich. m. Susan Andrea Hagstrum; children: Robert, Brian, Brett. BS in Spl. Edn., Music and Social Sci., Western Mich. U., 1964; MA, Vanderbilt U., 1965, PhD in Edn., 1968. Joined as asst. prof. ednl. psychology U. Minn., 1968, Emma M. Birkmaier prof. ednl. leadership Mpls., 1991—94, dean Coll. Edn. and Human Devel., 1991—97, exec. v.p., provost, 1997—2002, pres., 2002—, prof. ednl. psychology. Dir. Devel. Disabilities Office Govs. Coun. on Developmental Disabilities, State Planning Agy., Minn., 1974—76; mem. J. William Fulbright Fgn. Scholarship Bd., 2003—. Contbr. chapters to books, articles to profl. jours. Trustee Com. for Econ. Devel. Named Minnesotan of Yr., Minn. Monthly Mag., 2004; recipient Disting. Alumni award, Mich. U. Alumni Assn., 2004; nat. leadership fellow, Kellogg Found., 1981—84. Fellow: APA, Am. Psychol. Soc., Am. Assn. on Mental Retardation (pres. 1990—91, Edn. award 1996); mem.: Nat. Assn. State Univs. and Land-Grant Colls. (bd. dirs.). Office: Univ Minn 202 Morrill Hall 100 Church St SE Minneapolis MN 55455 Office Phone: 612-626-1616. Business E-Mail: upres@umn.edu.

BRUMBACK, CHARLES TIEDTKE, retired newspaper executive; b. Toledo, Sept. 27, 1928; s. John Sanford and Frances Henrietta (Tiedtke) B.; m. Mary Louise Howe, July 7, 1951; children: Charles Tiedtke Jr., Anne Meyer, Wesley W., Ellen Allen. BA in Econs., Princeton U., 1950; postgrad., U. Toledo, 1953-54. CPA, Ohio, Fla. With Arthur Young & Co., CPAs, 1950—57; bus. mgr., v.p., treas., pres., CEO Sentinel Star Co. subs. Tribune Co., Orlando, Fla., 1957-81; pres., CEO Chgo. Tribune subs. Tribune Co., 1981-88, pres., COO, 1988-90, CEO, 1990-95; chmn. Tribune Co., 1993-95. Trustee Culver Ednl. Found. 1st lt. U.S. Army, 1951-53. Decorated Bronze star. Mem. Fla. Press Assn. (treas. 1969-76, pres. 1980, bd. dirs.), Am. Newspaper Pubs. Assn. (bd. dirs., treas. 1991-92), ewspaper Assn. Am. (bd. dirs., sec., 1992-93, vice chmn. 1993-94, chmn. 1994-95), Comml. Club Chgo., Chgo. Club. Home Fax: 941-362-7370.

BRUMFIELD, JIM, news executive; Bur. chief Detroit Met. Network News, 1997—. Office: 5032 Rochester Rd Ste 200 Troy MI 48085-3454

BRUMMEL, MARK JOSEPH, religious organization administrator; b. Chgo., Oct. 28, 1933; s. Anthony William and Mary (Helmreich) B. BA, Cath. U. Am., 1956, STL, 1961, MSLS, 1964. Joined Order of Claretians, Roman Cath. Ch., 1952; ordained priest Order of Caretians, Roman Cath. Ch., 1960; librarian, tchr. St. Jude Sem., Momence, Ill., 1961-70; asso. editor U.S. Cath. mag., Chgo., 1971-72; editor U.S. Cath. Mag., 1970—2002; dir. St. Jude League, Chgo., 1970—2002, 2005—. Treas. Eastern Province Claretians, 1998—, also bd. dirs.; bd. dirs. Chgo. Family Health Ctr.; adminstr. Our Lady of Guadalupe Ch., 2006-07. Editor Today mag., 1970-71; contbr. article to publ. Chmn. bd. Eighth Day Ctr. for Justice, Chgo., 1988-92; bd. dirs. Assn. of Chgo. Priests, 1994-96; mem. Ill. Cath. Conf., 1993-96. Mem. Cath. Press Assn. (St. Francis De Sales award 1996), Associated Ch. Press (v.p. 1985-87). Avocation: photography. Home: 3200 E 91st St Chicago IL 60617 Office: Claretian Missionaries 205 W Monroe St Fl 7 Chicago IL 60606-5033 Home Phone: 773-768-0793; Office Phone: 312-236-7782. Business E-Mail: brummelm@claretians.org.

BRUNER, PHILIP LANE, arbitrator; b. Chgo., Sept. 26, 1939; s. Henry Pfeiffer and Mary Marjorie (Williamson) B.; m. Ellen Carole Germann, Mar. 21, 1964; children: Philip Richard, Stephen Reed, Carolyn Anne. AB, Princeton U., 1961; JD, U. Mich., 1964; MBA, Syracuse U., 1967. Bar: Wis. 1964, Minn. 1968. Mem. Briggs and Morgan P.A., Mpls., St. Paul, 1967-83; founding shareholder Hart and Bruner P.A., Mpls., 1983-90; ptnr. Faegre & Benson, Mpls., 1991—2007, head constrn. law group, 1991—2001. Dir. Global Engr. Constrn. Group, Jams Inc.; adj. prof. William Mitchell Coll. Law, St. Paul, 1970—76, 2006—07, U. Minn. Law Sch., Mpls., 2003—07; chmn. Supreme Ct. Minn. Bd. CLE, Mpls., 1994—98. Co-author: Bruner and O'Conner on Construction Law, 7 vols., 2002; contbr. articles to profl. jours. Mem. Bd. Edn., Mahtomedi Ind. Sch. Dist. 832, 1978-86; bd. dirs. Mahtomedi Area Ednl. Found., 1988-94, 2002—, pres., 1988-91, 2002—07; bd. dirs. Minn. Ch. Found., 1975—, pres., 1989-97; chmn. constrn. industry adv. bd. West Group, 1991—. Served to capt. USAF, 1964-67. Decorated Air Force Commendation Medal; recipient Disting. Service award St. Paul Jaycees, 1974; named One of Ten Outstanding Young Minnesotans, Minn. Jaycees, 1975. Fellow Am. Coll. Constrn. Lawyers (founding mem., pres. 2006—07), ACCL Princeton Symposium(chair, 2006);,Nat. Contract Mgmt. Assn., Am. Bar Found.; mem. ABA (chmn. internat. constrn. divsn. forum com. on constrn. industry 1989-91, chmn. fidelity and surety law com. 1994-95, regional chmn. pub. contract law sect. 1990-96, recipient Forum com Cornerstone award, 2005), Internat. Bar Assn., Inter-Pacific Bar Assn. (vice chmn. internat. constrn. com. 1995-97), Minn. Bar Assn. (vice chmn. litigation sect. 1979-81), Wis. Bar Assn., Hennepin Bar Assn., Am. Arbitration Assn. (nat. panel arbitrators), Mpls. Club. Presbyterian. Home: 8432 80th St N Stillwater MN 55082-9331 Office: Jams 71 S Wacker Dr Suite 3090 Chicago IL 60606 Office Phone: 612-766-7412. E-mail: pbruner@faegre.com, Philipbruner@hotmail.com.

BRUNER, STEPHEN C., lawyer; b. Chgo., Nov. 11, 1941; s. Henry Pfeiffer and Mary Marjorie (Williamson) B.; m. Elizabeth Erskine Osborn, Apr. 7, 1973; children: Elizabeth, David. BA summa cum laude, Yale U., 1963; JD cum laude, Harvard U., 1967. Bar: Ill. 1967, U.S. Dist. Ct. (no. dist.) Ill. 1971, U.S. Ct. Appeals (7th cir.) 1983, U.S. Supreme Ct. 1988. Assoc. Winston & Strawn, Chgo., 1971-76, ptnr., 1976-82, capital ptnr., 1982-01. Lectr. Northwestern U. Sch. of Law, 1983-84; cons. Commn. on Govt. Procurement, 1972; mem. Landmarks Commn., Oak Park, Ill., 1978-81; bd. govs. Oak Park-River Forest Community Chest, 1985-90; elected mem. Bd. Edn. Oak Park and River Forest High Sch., 1993-01. Served to lt. USN, 1968-71. Recipient Navy Achievement medal; Corning Found. travelling fellow, 1963-64. Mem. ABA (litigation and pub. contracts sects.), Chgo. Bar Assn., Am. Arbitration (panel of arbitrators), Chgo. Coun. on Fgn. Rels., Econ. Club, Univ. Club, Yale Club, Harvard Club (Chgo.). Office: Winston & Strawn 35 W Wacker Dr Chicago IL 60601-1695

BRUNGARDT, PETE, state legislator; m. Rosie Brungardt. Mem. Kans. State Senate, 2001—, vice chair fed. and state affairs com., mem. commerce com., mem. corrections and juvenile justice oversight com., mem. fin. instns. and ins. com., mem. pub. health and welfare com. Home: 522 Fairdale Rd Salina KS 67401 Office: 436 S Ohio St Salina KS 67401 E-mail: peterose@midusa.net, brungardt@senate.state.ks.us.

BRUNING, JAMES LEON, academic administrator, educator; b. Bruning, Nebr., Apr. 1, 1938; s. Leon G. and Delma Dorothy (Middendorf) Bruning; m. E. Marlene Schaff, Aug. 24, 1958; children: Michael, Stephen, Kathleen. BA, Doane Coll., 1959; MA, U. Iowa, 1961, PhD, 1962. Chmn. dept psychology Ohio U., Athens, 1972-76, acting dean arts and scis., 1976-77, assoc. dean, 1977-78, vice provost, 1978-81, provost, 1981-93, acting pres., 1991, trustee prof., 1993—, v.p. regional higher edn., 1998—99, dir. Enterprise project, 2002—03. Planning cons. NCHEMS, Boulder, Colo., 1979—80; provost Shawnee (Ohio) State U., 1996. Author: (book) Computational Handbook of Statistics, 1997, Research in Psychology, 1970; contbr. articles to profl. jours. Chair task force Ohio Bd. Regents, 1994—95. Grantee, Esso, 1963—64, NIMH, 1963—66, EPDA, 1974—75, OBOR, 1989—91. Mem.: APA (vis. scientist), AAAS, Midwestern Psychol. Assn., Sigma Xi. Democrat. Lutheran. Home: 6148 Melnor Dr Athens OH 45701-3577 Office: Ohio U Psychology Dept Athens OH 45701 Business E-Mail: bruningj@ohio.edu.

BRUNING, JON CUMBERLAND, state attorney general; b. Lincoln, Nebr., Apr. 30, 1969; s. Roger Howard and Mary Genevieve (Cumberland) Bruning; m. Deonne Leigh Niemack, July 8, 1995, two children, Lauren Caroline, Jon Cumberland Jr. BA with high distinction, U. Nebr., 1990, JD with distinction, 1994. Bar: Nebr. 1994, US Dist. Ct. Nebr. 1994, US Ct. Appeals (8th cir.) 1994. Pvt. practice, Papillion, Nebr., 1993-97; mem. Nebr. Legislature from 3rd dist., Lincoln, 1997—2002; atty. gen. State of Nebr., 2003—. Mem., Gretna United Methodist Ch., Nebr. State Bar Assn., Phi Beta Kappa. Republican. Methodist. Home: 17501 Riviera Dr Omaha E 68136-1951 Office: Office of Atty Gen State Capitol PO Box 98920 Lincoln NE 68509-8920 Office Phone: 402-471-2682.

BRUNKHORST, ROBERT JOHN, computer programmer, analyst; b. Waverly, Iowa, Dec. 5, 1965; s. John Blaine and Edna C. (Atkins) B.; m. Kris Nielsen, Sept. 12, 1992; 1 child, Karalynn Kristine. BS in Computer Sci., Loras Coll., 1989. Computer programmer Century Cos. Am., Waverly, 1990—, computer analyst. Press intern Sen. Charles Grassley, Washington, fall 1986. State rep. State of Iowa, 1992—; organizer Solid Waste Adv. Com., Waverly, 1990—; active Boy Scouts Am., N.E. Iowa, 1982—. Mem. Jaycees, Farm Bur. Home: 413 10th St NE Waverly IA 50677-2739

BRUNNER, GORDON F(RANCIS), household products company executive; b. Des Plaines, Ill., Nov. 6, 1938; s. Frank Anthony and Alfreida Elizabeth (Eslinger) B.; m. Nadine Marie Slosar, Aug. 10, 1963; children: Christine Marie Conselyea, Pamela Ann, Meggan Therese. BChemE, U. Wis., 1961; MBA, Xavier U., Cin., 1965. With Procter & Gamble Co., 1961—, mgr. product coordination European Ops., Brussels, 1977-81, mgr. research and devel. European Ops., 1981-83, mgr. research and devel. U.S. Cin., 1983-85, v.p. R&D U.S., 1985-87, sr. v.p. R&D U.S., 1987—, also bd. dirs. Mem. exec. com. Campaign for Chemistry, Am. Chem. Soc., 1990. Patentee in field. Corp. chmn. United Way, 1990-91; mem. adv. coun. Citizens Against Substance Abuse, 1990; trustee The Christ Hosp., Cin. Mus. Natural History, Xavier U., Ohio U., com. econ. devel.; mem. Govt.-Univ.-Industry Rsch. Roundtable; nat. adv. com. Coll. Engring., U. Mich.; mem. Mgmt. Policy Coun., Conf. Bd. Internat. Coun. Mgmt. Innovation & Tech.; mem. tour equipment adv. com. PGA; chmn. Cin. Campaign for U. Wis.; mem. selection com. Evals Scholarship; sci. adv. bd. Bowling Green State U.; Cin. chmn. Habitat for Humanity; Cin. chmn. BIO/START; mem. Ohio Sci. and Tech. Coun.; mem. Evans Scholarship selection com. Western Golf Assn. Recipient Exec. Achievement award Xavier U., 1991, Disting. Svc. award U. Wis., 1992; Evans scholar Western Golf Assn., 1956. Mem. Am. Oil Chemists Soc., Engring. Soc. Cin., Cin. Coun. on World Affairs, Am. Chem. Soc., Mgmt. Policy Coun., Evans Scholar Alumni Assn., Comml. Club, Queen City Club, Hyde Park Country Club Cin., Crystal Downs Country Club (Frankfort, Mich.). Roman Catholic. Avocations: golf, tennis, woodworking, gardening. Home: 7300 Sanderson Pl Cincinnati OH 45243-4045 Office: Procter & Gamble Co 1 Procter And Gamble Plz Cincinnati OH 45202-3393

BRUNNER, JENNIFER LEE, state official, lawyer; b. Springfield, Ohio, Feb. 5, 1957; d. Samuel Lawrence and Barbara Lee (Swan) Junk; m. Rick Louis Brunner, May 27, 1978; children: J. Katherine, Laura J., Johnathon P. BA cum laude in Sociology, Miami U., Oxford, Ohio, 1978; JD, Capital U., Columbus, Ohio, 1983. Bar: Ohio 1983, US Dist. Ct. (so. and no. dists. Ohio) 1983, US Ct. Appeals (6th cir.) 1983. Com. sec., legis. aide Ohio State Senate, Columbus, 1979-81; legis. counsel, dep. dir. Staff of Sec. State Sherrod Brown, Columbus, Ohio, 1983-87; assoc. Walter, Haverfield, Buescher and Chockley, Columbus, 1987-89; of counsel J. Richard Lumpe, 1989; prin. The Brunner Firm Co., L.P.A., Columbus; judge Ct. Common Pleas Franklin County, 2000—05; sec. state State of Ohio, Columbus, 2007—. Legal, past bd. dirs. Downtown Playschool, Columbus, 1985-87. Contbr. articles to profl. jours.; pub., editor: Polit. Action Quar., 1990—91. Active statewide campaign re-election Sherrod Brown Sec. State, Columbus, 1985; mem. Federated Dem. Women of Ohio, 1985; treas. Westerville City Schs. Levy campaign; treas. Judge Jon Marshall campaign; mem. Ohio Student Loan Commn.; mem. Franklin County Bd. Elections, 1997; bd. mem. Mental Health Assn. Franklin County A.R. McMicken scholar Miami U., 1977; recipient Extra Mile award Nat. Alliance for the Mentally Ill, 2002. Mem. ABA, Ohio Bar Assn., Columbus Bar Assn., Columbus Area Women's Polit. Caucus, Bus. and Profl. Women's Club (Young Career Woman of Yr. 1985), YWCA, Univ. Club, Order of Curia, Omicron Delta Kappa. Avocations: interior design, art, music. Office: Office Sec State Borden Bldg 180 E Broad St Columbus OH 43215

BRUNNER, KIM M., insurance company executive, lawyer; b. 1949; BA, Augustana Coll.; JD, Univ. Ariz. Chief counsel Ill. Ins. Dept.; atty. Nationwide Ins. Co.; with State Farm Ins. Cos., Bloomington, Ill., 1987—, assoc. gen. counsel, 1991-93, v.p.-counsel, 1993-97, sr. v.p., then exec. v.p., sec., gen. counsel, 1997—. Co-chmn. Civil Justice Reform Group; mem. bd. overseers RAND Inst. for Civil Justice. Office: State Farm Ins Cos 1 State Farm Plz Bloomington IL 61710-0001 Office Phone: 309-766-2311.

BRUNNER, VERNON ANTHONY, marketing executive; b. Chgo., Aug. 9, 1940; s. Frank Anthony and Alfrieda (Eslinger) B.; divorced; children: Jack Daniel, Amanda Josephine; m. Sharon Ann Walschon, July 1, 1972; 1 child, Suzanne Marie. BS in Pharmacy, U. Wis., 1963. Registered pharmacist. Mgr. store Walgreen Co., Chgo., 1963-71, dist. mgr. Deerfield, Ill., 1971-75, dir. merchandising, 1975-77, dir. mktg., 1977-78, v.p. mktg., 1978-82, sr. v.p. mktg., 1982-90, exec. v.p. mktg., 1990—. Bd. dirs. Walgreen. Mem. Evans Scholar Alumni Assn. Roman Catholic. Office: Walgreen Co 200 Wilmot Rd Deerfield IL 60015-4616

BRUNNGRABER, ERIC HENRY, banker; b. Madison, Wis., Feb. 12, 1957; s. Eric G. and Lois M. (Ihde) B.; m. Ann M. Roberson, May 30, 1987. BSBA in Fin., U. Mo., 1979; MBA in Fin., St. Louis U., 1982; diploma, U. Del., 1991. Asst. to chmn. Cass Bank & Trust Co., St. Louis, 1979-82, mgr. spl. projects, 1982-84, asst. v.p. comml. lending, 1986-88, v.p., treas., 1989-92, exec. v.p., 1993—; mgmt. cons. Cass Bus. Cons., St. Louis, 1984-86; v.p., sec. & CFO Cass Comml. Corp., Bridgeton, Mo. Mem. Robert Morris Assocs. Office: Cass Comml Corp 13001 Hollenberg Dr Bridgeton MO 63044

BRUNO, GARY ROBERT, lawyer; b. Green Bay, Wis., Oct. 7, 1951; s. Robert John and Mary Lois (Eparvier) B.; m. Terry Lynn Ott, Oct. 22, 1977. BBA in Fin. and Regional Planning, U. Wis., Green Bay, 1973; JD, John Marshall Law Sch., 1977. Bar: Wis. 1977, U.S. Dist. Ct. Wis. 1978. Sole practice, Green Bay and Shawano, Wis., 1977-78; prosecutor Code of Fed. Regulation Ct., Keshena, Wis., 1978; asst. dist. atty. Menominee and Shawano Counties, Shawano, 1978-82, dist. atty., corp. counsel, adminstr. child support agy., 1982—. Mem. exec. com. Fed. Law Enforcement Coordinating Com. Ea. Dist. Wis., Milw., 1985—. V.p. Big Bros./Big Sisters, Shawano, 1981-83, bd. dirs. 1980—; bd. dirs. Alcohol and Drug Ctr. Shawano, 1979-82; mem. exec. bd. Reps., Shawano, 1985—. Mem. ABA, Wis. Bar Assn., Shawano County Bar Assn. (sec., treas. 1982, v.p. 1983, pres. 1984), Nat. Dist. Atty. Assn., Wis. Dist. Atty. Assn. Clubs: Shawano. Lodges: Optimists (2d v.p. Shawano 1985—, bd. dirs. 1979-85, optimist of yr. award 1984). Avocations: community service, scuba diving, hunting. Home: 1413 E Lieg St Shawano WI 54166-3613 Office: Dist Atty Office 311 N Main St Shawano WI 54166-2100

BRUNS, BILLY LEE, electrical engineer, consultant; b. St. Louis, Nov. 21, 1925; s. Henry Lee and Violet Jean (Williams) Bruns; m. Lillian Colleen Mobley, Sept. 6, 1947; children: Holly Renee, Kerry Alan, Barry Lee, Terrence

William. BA, Washington U., St. Louis, 1949; postgrad., Sch. Engring., St. Louis, 1959-62; EE, ICS, Scranton, Pa., 1954. Registered profl. engr., Mo., Ill., Wash., Fla., La., Wis., Minn., N.Y., N.C., Iowa, Pa., Miss., Ind., Ala., Ga., Va., R.I., Wyo. Supt., engr., estimator Schneider Electric Co., St. Louis, 1950-54, Ledbetter Electric Co., St. Louis, 1954-57; tchr. indsl. electricity St. Louis Bd. Edn., 1957-71; pres. B.L. Bruns & assocs. Cons. Engrs. Inc., St. Louis, 1963-72; v.p., chief engr. Hosp. Bldg. & Equipment Co., St. Louis, 1972-76; pres., prin. B.L. Bruns & Assocs. Cons. Engrs., St. Louis, 1976—. Tchr. elec. engring. U. Mo. St. Louis extension, 1975-76. Tech. editor The National Electrical Code and Blueprint Reading, Am. Tech. Soc., 1959-65. Mem. Mo. Adv. Coun. on Vocat. Edn., 1969-76, chmn., 1975-76; leader Explorer post Boy Scouts Am., 1950-57. Served with AUS, 1944-46, PTO, Okinawa. Decorated Purple Heart. Mem. NSPE, ASHRAE, Mo. Soc. Profl. Engrs., Profl. Engrs. in Pvt. Practice, Illuminating Engrs. Soc., Am. Mgmt. Assn., Nat. Fire Protection Assn. (health care divsn., archtl./engr. divsn.), Masons. Baptist. Home: 1243 Hobson Dr Ferguson MO 63135-1422 Personal E-mail: bandcbruns@aol.com.

BRUNSVOLD, JOEL DEAN, state legislator, educator; b. Mason City, Iowa, Feb. 26, 1942; s. Burnell Raymond and Esther Agusta (Geilendeld) B.; m. Barbara Louise Bashaw, Feb. 22, 1964; children: Timothy, Theodore. BA, Augustana Coll., 1964; student, Black Hawk Coll./We. Ill. U., 1969-71. Tchr. Sherrard (Ill.) Cmty. Unit # 200, 1969-83; mem. Ho. of Reps., Rock Island, Ill., 1982—. Trustee, Milan, Ill., 1973-77, mayor, 1977-83. Mem. NEA, Ill. Edn. Assn., C. of C., Ducks Unlimited, Pheasants Forever, Phi Omega Phi. Democrat. Lutheran. Avocation: hunting. Home: 12810 25th Street Ct Milan IL 61264-4984

BRUSHABER, GEORGE KARL, academic administrator, minister; b. Milw., Dec. 15, 1938; s. Ralph E. and Marie C. (Meister) B.; m. N. Darleen Dugar, Jan. 27, 1962; children: Deanna Lyn Dalberg, Donald Paul. BA, Wheaton Coll., 1959, MA, 1962; MDiv, Gordon-Conwell Theol. Sem., 1963; PhD, Boston U., 1967. Ordained to ministry Bapt. Gen. Conf., 1966. Prof. philosophy, chair dept. Gordon Coll., Wenham, Mass., 1963-72; dir. admissions and registration Gordon-Conwell Theol. Sem., 1970-72; v.p., acad. dean Westmont Coll., Santa Barbara, Calif., 1972-75; v.p., dean of coll. Bethel. Coll., St. Paul, 1975-82; pres. Bethel U., St. Paul and San Diego, 1982—. Staley Found. lectr. Anderson U., Sioux Falls Coll.; sec. for higher edn. Bapt. Gen. Conf., Arlington Heights, Ill., 1982—; cons., evaluator Minn. Humanities Commn., St. Paul. Editor Gordon Rev., 1965-70; pub., founding editor Christian Scholar's Rev., 1970-79; exec. editor Christianity Today, 1985-90, chmn. sr. editors, 1990-2000; contbr. articles to religious jours. Bd. dirs. Youth Leadership, Mpls., 1982-2004, Fairview Elders' Enterprises Found., 1989-96, Scripture Press Ministries Found., 1994-2005; adv. bd. Mpls./St. Paul Salvation Army, 1992--; chair bd. Scripture Press Ministries, 1994-2005; adv. coun. Evang. Environ. Network, 1994—; mem. Commn. on Minorities in Higher Edn. Am. Coun. Edn., 1995-99. Mem. Nat. Assn. Evangs. (trustee 1982—), Minn. Pvt. Coll. Coun. (bd. dirs. 1982—), Minn. Consortium Theol. Sems. (bd. dirs. 1982—), Cook Comm. Internat. (bd. dirs. 1998-2007), Coun. Ind. Colls. (bd. dirs. 1984-89), Am. Philos. Assn., Evang. Theol. Soc., Am. Assn. Higher Edn., Swedish Coun. Am. (bd. dirs. 2000—), Am. Assn. of Pres. of Indenp. Coll. and Univ. (bd. dirs.), Soc. Christian Philosophers, Christian Environ. Assn. (bd. dirs.), Christian Coll. Consortium (bd. dirs.), Fellowship Evang. Sem. Pres., Cook Comm. Ministries (vice chmn. bd. dirs. 1999-2007), North Oaks Country Club. Home and Office: Bethel Univ 3900 Bethel Dr Saint Paul MN 55112-6902

BRUSKEWITZ, FABIAN WENDELIN, bishop; b. Milw., Sept. 6, 1935; s. Wendelin and Frances Bruskewitz. STD, Gregorian U., Rome, 1969. Ordained priest Archdiocese of Milw., 1960; pastor Saint Bernard Parish, Wauwatosa, Wis.; bishop Diocese of Lincoln, Nebr., 1992—, ordained bishop, 1992. Author: (book) Bishop Fabian Bruskewitz: A Shepherd Speaks, 1997. Named a Prelate of Honor, 1980. Roman Catholic. Office: Chancery Office PO Box 80328 Lincoln NE 68501-0328*

BRUSTAD, ORIN DANIEL, lawyer; b. Chgo., Nov. 11, 1941; s. Marvin D. and Sylvia Evelyn (Peterson) B.; m. Ilona M. Fox, July 16, 1966; children: Caroline E., Katherine L., Mark D. BA in History, Yale U., 1963, MA, 1964; JD, Harvard U., 1968. Bar: Mich. 1968, U.S. Dist. Ct. (so. dist.) Mich. 1968. Assoc. Miller, Canfield, Paddock and Stone, Detroit, 1968-74, sr. ptnr., 1975—, chmn. employee benefits practice group, 1989-96, dep. chmn. tax dept., 1989-93. Bd. dirs. Electrocon Internat., Inc., Ann Arbor, Mich. Mem. editl. adv. bd. Benefits Law Jour.; contbr. articles to profl. jours. Fellow Am. Coun. Employee Benefits Counsel (charter); mem. ABA, Mich. Bar Assn., Detroit Bar Assn., Mich. Employee Benefits Conf. Avocations: sailing, skiing, reading, piano. Home: 1422 Macgregor Ln Ann Arbor MI 48105-2836 Office: Miller Canfield Paddock & Stone 150 W Jefferson Ave Fl 25th Detroit MI 48226-4432 Home Phone: 734-994-4406; Office Phone: 313-496-7605. E-mail: odbrusta@aol.com, brustad@millercanfield.com.

BRUVOLD, KATHLEEN PARKER, retired lawyer; BS in Math., U. Denver, 1965; MS in Math., Purdue U., 1967; JD, U. Cin., 1978. Bar: Ohio 1978, U.S. Dist. Ct. (so. dist.) Ohio 1978, U.S. Dist. Ct. (ea. dist.) Ky. 1979. Mathematician bur. rsch. and engring. U.S. Post Office, 1967; instr. math. Purdue U., West Lafayette, Ind., 1967-68, asst. to dir., tng. coord., programmer Administrv. Data Processing Ctr., 1968-71; instr. math. Ind. U., Kokomo, 1969-70; pvt. practice Cin., 1978-80; asst. dir. Legal Adv. Svcs. U. Cin., 1980-89, assoc. gen. counsel, 1989—2002; asst. atty. gen. State of Ohio, 1983—2002; ret., 2002. Chair Ohio pub. records com. Inter-univ. Coun. Legal Advisors, 1980-84; presenter various confs. and symposiums. Active com. group svcs. allocation United Way and Community Chest; v.p. Clifton Recreation Ctr. Adv. Coun., 1983-84; vice chair Cin. Bilingual Acad. PTA, 1989-90. U. Denver scholar, Jewel Tea Co. scholar; at. Merit finalist. Mem. ABA, Nat. Assn. Coll. and Univ. Attys. (bd. dirs., co-chair taxation sect., com. ann. meeting arrangements, program com., publs. com., bd. ops. com., JCUL editl. bd. nominations com., honors and award com., intellectual property sect., com. continuing legal edn. 1992-2002), Ohio Bar Assn., Cin. Bar Assn. (com. taxation, program chmn. 1985-86, sec. 1986-87, com. computer law). Home: 536 Evanswood Pl Cincinnati OH 45220-1527

BRUYN, KIMBERLY ANN, public relations executive, consultant; b. Grand Rapids, Mich., Jan. 25, 1955; BA in English, Calvin Coll., Grand Rapids, 1977; MS in Journalism, U. Kans., 1979. Advt. copywriter, acct. exec. Mendenhall, Jones & Leistra Advt., Grand Rapids, 1979-81; advt. copywriter Johnson & Dean Advt., Grand Rapids, 1981-82; pub. rels. analyst Amway Corp., Ada, Mich., 1982-84, sr. pub. rels. analyst, 1984-85, sr. pub. rels. specialist, 1986-87, pub. rels. supr., 1987-88, pub. rels. mgr., chief corp. spokesperson, 1988-93, sr. mgr. pub. rels., chief corp. spokesperson, 1993-98; v.p. comms. The Windquest Group, Grand Rapids, 1998-2000; exec. dir. Straightline Pub. Rels., 2000—01; sr. cons. The Grey Stone Group, Grand Rapids, Mich., 2001—. Mem. pub. rels. and mktg. com. Grand Rapids Symphony Orch., 1992; mem. planning com. Spl. Olympics Festival of Trees, Grand Rapids, 1990-92, Gerald R. Ford Presdl. Mus. 10th Anniversary Celebration, Grand Rapids, 1992; bd. dirs. Celebration on the Grand, 1989-96, co-chair, 1993, 94; co-chair pub. rels. Heart Ball, Am. Heart Assn., 1996-2001; chair pub. rels. Van Andel Arena Grand Opening, 1996, Presdl. Tribute to Gerald R. Ford, 1997. Mem. PRSA (Spectrum award 1990-98), Direct Selling Assn. (chair comm. com. 1997-98). Office: Greystone Group Inc 678 Front NW Ste 159 Grand Rapids MI 49504 E-mail: kimb@greystonegp.com.

BRYAN, DAVID, radio personality; b. Brinnell, Iowa, Feb. 8, 1952; 2 children. Student, North West Mo. State U. Radio host WDAF, Westwood, Kans., 1981—. Avocation: exercise. Office: WDAF 4935 Belinder Rd Westwood KS 66205

BRYAN, JOHN HENRY, food and consumer products company executive; b. West Point, Miss., 1936; BA in Econs. and Bus. Adminstrn., Rhodes Coll., Memphis, 1958. Joined Bryan Foods, 1960; with Sara Lee Corp. (formerly known as Consol. Food Corp.), Chgo., 1960—; from exec. v.p. to pres. Sara Lee Corp. (formerly known as Consol Food Corp.), Chgo., 1974, CEO, 1975—2000, chmn. bd., 1976—2000, also bd. dirs.; consultant Sara Lee Corp., Chgo., 2001—. Bd. dirs. GM Corp., 1993—, BP p.l.c., Goldman Sachs Group, Inc. Chmn. bus. adv. coun. Chgo. Urban League; bd. govs. Nat. Women's Econ. Alliance, Chgo.; trustee, vice chmn., exec. com. U. Chgo., Rush-Presbyn.-St. Luke's Med. Ctr.; trustee Com. Econ. Devel.; trustee, treas. Art Inst., Chgo.; chmn. Catalyst, Chgo. com. Chgo. Coun. on Fgn. Rels.; mem. trustee's coun. Nat. Gallery Art, Washington; mem. Pres.'s com. on the arts and humanities; bd. dirs. Bus. Com. for Arts. Decorated Legion of Honor France, Order of Orange Nassau The Netherlands, Order of Lincoln medallion; named Man of Yr., Harvard Bus. Sch. Club Chgo., Exec. Yr., Crain's Chgo. Bus., 1992; named to Jr. Achievement Chgo. Bus. Hall of Fame, 1992, Miss. Hall of Fame, 1992; recipient Nat. Humanitarian award, NCCJ, William H. Albers award, Food Mktg. Inst. Mem.: Bus. Roundtable, Bus. Coun., Grocery Mfrs. Assn. (sr.; past chmn. bd.). Office: Sara Lee Corp 3 1st Nat Plz 70 W Madison St Ste 4500 Chicago IL 60602-4260

BRYAN, LAWRENCE DOW, retired college president, consultant; b. Barberton, Ohio, Jan. 30, 1945; s. W. Richard and Celia A. (Evans) B.; m. Marjorie Napier, June 15, 1968; children: Mark Evans, Alexa Marie. BA, Muskingum Coll., 1967; MDiv., Garrett Theol. Sem., 1970; PhD, Northwestern U., 1973. Tchg. asst. Nat. Coll. Edn., Evanston, Ill., 1969-71; biog. rsch. fellow Garrett Theol. Sem., Evanston, 1972-73; asst. prof. religious studies, chaplain McKendree Coll., Lebanon, Ill., 1973-77, asst. v.p. acad. affairs, 1977-78, dean, 1978-79, assoc. prof., 1978-79; prof. philosophy and religion, v.p., dean Franklin (Ind.) Coll., 1979-90; pres. Kalamazoo Coll., 1990-96, MacMurray Coll., Jacksonville, Ill., 1997—2007. Trustee Parkstone Group of Funds, 1994-98. Mem. Forum for Kalamazoo County, 1990-94, Kalamazoo Symphony Orch. Bd., 1990-96; pres. Heyl Found., Kalamazoo, 1990-96; bd. dirs. Bronson Hosp., 1991-96; trustee Interlochen Ctr. for Arts, 1994-97; pres. Jacksonville Main St. Bd. Dirs. Mem. Internat. Bonhoeffer Soc., Fed. Ind. Ill. Colls. and Univs., Rotary, Phi Sigma Tau, Delta Sigma Rho-Tau Kappa Alpha, Alpha Psi Omega, Theta Alpha Phi. Methodist.

BRYAN, NORMAN E., dentist; b. South Bend, Ind., Jan. 20, 1947; s. Norman E. and Frances (Kuhn) B.; m. Constance C. Cook, Feb. 23, 1974 (div. Apr. 1985); m. Linda Markley, Dec. 31, 1986; 1 child, Noelle. AB, Ind. U., 1969; DDS, Ind. U. Purdue U., Indpls., 1973. Expert TMJ, head ache, sleep disorders, Elkhart, Ind., 1973—. Specialist Temporomandibular Joint Disfunction. Author: Canine Endodontics, 1982. Mem. ADA, Ind. Dental Assn., Elkhart Dental Assn. (pres. 1976-77, 84-86), Am. Acad. Craniofacial Pain, Acad. Dental Sleep Medicine, Lakes Cruising Club (Chgo.). Republican. Avocations: sailing, photography, painting. Office: 505 Vistula St Elkhart IN 46516-2809 Home Phone: 574-264-0980; Office Phone: 574-293-2003.

BRYAN, WAYNE, producer; Producing dir. Music Theatre of Wichita, Kans. Office: Music Theatre of Wichita 225 W Douglas Ave Ste 202 Wichita KS 67202-3100

BRYANT, BARBARA EVERITT, academic administrator, researcher, retired marketing professional, federal agency administrator; b. Ann Arbor, Mich., Apr. 5, 1926; d. William Littell and Dorothy (Wallace) Everitt; m. John H. Bryant, Aug. 14, 1948; children: Linda Bryant Valentine, Randal E., Lois. AB, Cornell U., 1947; MA, Mich. State U., 1967, PhD, 1970; HonD, U. Ill., 1993. Editor art Chem. Engring. mag. McGraw-Hill Pub. Co., NYC, 1947-48; editl. rsch. asst. U. Ill., Urbana, 1948-49, free-lance editor, writer, 1950-61; with continuing edn. adminstrn. dept. Oakland Univ., Rochester, Mich., 1961-66; grad. rsch. asst. Mich. State U., East Lansing, 1966-70; sr. analyst to v.p. Market Opinion Rsch., Detroit, 1970-77, sr. v.p., 1977-89; dir. Bur. of the Census, U.S. Dept. Commerce, 1989-93; rsch. scientist Ross Sch Bus., U. Mich., 1993—. Author: High School Students Look at Their World, 1970, American Women Today & Tomorrow, 1977, Moving Power and Money: The Politics of Census Taking, 1995; contbr. articles to profl. jours. Mem. U.S. Census Adv. Com., Washington, 1980—86, Mich. Job Devel. Authority, Lansing, 1980—85; state editor LWV of Mich., 1959—61; bd. dirs. Roper Ctr. for Pub. Opinion Rsch., 1993—2007; mem. nat. adv. com. Inst. for Social Rsch., U. Mich., 1993—. Fellow: Am. Statis. Assn.; mem.: Am. Assn. Pub. Opinion Rsch., Am. Mktg. Assn. (pres. Detroit 1976—77, midwestern v.p. 1978—80, v.p. mktg. rsch. 1982—84, found. trustee 1993—2001), Rotary, Cosmos Club. Republican. Presbyterian. Avocation: swimming. Home: 1505 Sheridan Dr Ann Arbor MI 48104-4051 Office: Ross Sch of Business U Mich Ann Arbor MI 48109-1234 Office Phone: 734-763-9062. Business E-Mail: bryantb@umich.edu.

BRYANT, DAVID J., lawyer; b. Fostoria, Ohio, Dec. 17, 1961; BS, U. Ill., 1984; JD, Northwestern U., 1987. Bar: Ill. 1987. Ptnr. comml. real estate law Katten Muchin Zavis Rosenman, Chgo. Mem.: ABA, Pension Real Estate Assn., Nat. Assn. Real Estate Investment Trusts, Chgo. Bar Assn. Office: Katten Muchin Zavis Rosenman 525 W Monroe St, Ste 1600 Chicago IL 60661 Office Phone: 312-902-5380. Office Fax: 312-577-8665. E-mail: david.bryant@kmzr.com.

BRYANT, DONALD L., JR., insurance and benefits company executive; b. Mt. Vernon, Ill., June 30, 1942; s. Donald Loyd and Eileen (Gallaway) B.; m. Barbara Frances Murphy, July 9, 1981; children: Derek Lawrence, Christina Murphy, Justin Donald. BA, Denison U., Granville, Ohio, 1964; JD, Washington U., St. Louis, 1967. CLU, Chartered fin. cons. Chmn., chief exec. officer Donald L. Bryant Assocs., St. Louis, 1968-75, Bryant Group, Inc., St. Louis, 1975—. Owner family vineyard, Napa Valley, Calif. Pres. Herbert Hoover Boys Club, St. Louis, 1987—; active Arts and Edn. Coun. Greater St. Louis, 1983—, Dance St. Louis, 1988—, Opera Theatre St. Louis, 1985—, Boy Scouts Am., 1972—, St. Louis Art Mus., 1990; bd. trustees Mus. Modern Art. Named Outstanding Alumni, Sch. of Law Washington U., 1990; named one of Top 200 Collectors, ARTnews Mag., 2004. Mem. Million Dollar Round Table (life), The Internat. Forum, Assn. Advanced Life Underwriters, St. Louis Assn. Life Underwriters, Estate Planning Coun. St. Louis, Mo. Bar Assn., ABA, Bellerive Country Club (St. Louis) (golf champ 1976), Vintage Club (Indian Wells, Calif.), Winged Foot (Mamaroneck, N.Y.), Castle Pines (Castlerock, Calif.), Meadowood (Napa Valley, Calif.), Sunningdale Golf. Republican. Presbyterian. Avocations: wine, golf, collecting abstract expressionism, especially de Kooning, contemporary art. Office: Bryant Group Inc 701 Market St Ste 1200 Saint Louis MO 63101-1884 Office Fax: 314-231-4859.

BRYANT, JOHN, utilities executive; Economist Unilever; corp. planner Brit. Oxygen Co.; mgr. worldwide ops. ind. oil svc. and mfg. co.; with Brit. Sugar Corp, 1989; mgr. ind. power bus. Midlands Electricity plc, 1991; v.p. Cinergy Corp., Cin., 1998—; pres. Cinergy Global Resources, Cin., 1998—. Office: Cinergy Corp 139 E 4th St Cincinnati OH 45202

BRYANT, JOHN A., food products executive; b. Brisbane, QLD, Australia, Nov. 6, 1965; m. Alison Bryant; 6 children. B Commerce, Australian Nat. U.; MBA, U. Pa. Various leadership positions Deloitte & Touche, Marakon and A.T. Kearney; with Kellogg Australia and Kellogg Europe, 1998; v.p. strategy devel./bus. understanding Kellogg N.Am.; v.p. fin. planning cereal Kellogg Co., 1998—2000, v.p. trade mktg., mem. sales leadership team Kellogg USA, 2000; sr. v.p., CFO Kellogg USA, 2000—02; sr. v.p. Kellogg Co., 2002, exec. v.p., 2002—, CFO, 2002—04, 2005—07; pres. Kellogg Internat., 2004—07; CFO, pres. Kellogg North Am., 2007—. Recipient Palmer Grad. scholarship, Wharton Sch., U. Pa. Mem.: Securities Inst. Australia (assoc.), Inst. Chartered Accts. Australia (assoc.). Office: Kellogg Co PO Box 3599 1 Kellogg Sq Battle Creek MI 49016-3599

BRYANT, KEITH LYNN, JR., history professor; b. Oklahoma City, Nov. 6, 1937; s. Keith Lynn and Elsie L. (Furman) B.; m. Margaret A. Burum, Aug. 14, 1962; children: Jennifer Lynne, Craig Warne. BS, U. Okla., 1959, MEd, 1961; PhD, U. Mo., 1965. From asst. prof. to prof., assoc. dean U. Wis., Milw., 1965-76; prof. Coll. Liberal Arts Tex. A&M U., College Station, 1976-88, head dept. history Coll. Liberal Arts, 1976-80, dean, 1980-84; prof. history U. Akron, Ohio, 1988-2000, head dept. Ohio, 1988-95, prof. emeritus Ohio, 2000—. Cons. So. Ry., NEH. Author: Alfalfa Bill Murray, 1968, Arthur E. Stilwell, Promoter with a Hunch, 1971, History of the Atchison, Topeka and Santa Fe Railway, 1974, William Merritt Chase: A Genteel Bohemian, 1991, Culture in the American Southwest, 2001; co-author: A History of American Business, 1983; bd. editors Western Hist. Quar., 1984-87, Southwestern Hist. Quar., 1980-87; editor Railroads in the Age of Regulation, 1900-1980, 1988. Various offices local Rep. Party, Okla., Tex.; chmn. Bush for Pres., Brazos County, 1979-80. Served to 1st lt. U.S. Army, 1959-60. Recipient William H. Kiekhofer award U. Wis., 1968, George W. and Constance M. Hilton book award Ry. and Locomotive Hist. Soc., 1990, David P. Morgan Article award Ry. and Locomotive Hist. Soc., 1998; grantee Am. Philos. Soc., 1968, NEH, 1984. Mem. So. Hist. Assn. (chmn. Frank Owsley book award com. 1988), Western History Assn., Tex. Hist. Assn., Lexington Group, S.W. Conf. Humanities Consortium (pres. 1982-83). Home: PO Box 5366 Bryan TX 77805-5366

BRYANT, L. EDWARD, lawyer; b. Olney, Ill., Dec. 2, 1941; BS, Northwestern Univ., 1963, JD, 1967. Bar: Ill. 1967. Ptnr. Gardner Carton & Douglas LLP, Chgo., 1967—, founder health law dept., 1979, mem. mgmt. com., 1980—89, chmn. practice council, 1995—97. Instr. Kellogg Grad. Sch. Bus. Northwestern Univ., Health Law Inst. Loyola Univ. Chgo. Mem. legal adv. com. Catholic Health Assn. Mem.: ABA, Am. Health Lawyers Assn., Ill. Assn. Healthcare Attys. (co-founder 1976, pres. 1979), Chgo. Bar Assn. Office: Gardner Carton & Douglas Ste 3700 191 N Wacker Dr Chicago IL 60606-1698 Office Phone: 312-569-1259. Office Fax: 312-569-3259. Business E-Mail: ebryant@gcd.com.

BRYCHTOVA, JAROSLAVA, sculptor; b. Semily, Czechoslovakia, 1924; m. Stanislav Libensky (dec. Feb. 2002). Student, Acad. Applied Arts, Prague, Czechoslovakia, 1945—51, Acad. Fine Arts, Prague, 1947—50. Designer Zeleznobrodské sklo, Zelezny Brod, Czech Republic, 1950—84. Guest lectr. Pilchuck Summer Sch., Stanwood, Wash., Ctr. Creative Studies, Detroit, others; presenter in field. also: Heller Gallery 420 W 14th St New York NY 10014-1064 Office Phone: 212-414-4014.

BRYENTON, GARY LYNN, lawyer; b. Litchfield, Ohio, Oct. 21, 1939; s. Harlan R. and Amber (Chidsey) B.; m. Barbara A. Brown, March 29, 1960; children: Elisabeth Ann, Susan Michelle. AB, Heidelberg Coll., 1961; JD, Western Res. U., 1965. Bar: Ohio 1965, U.S. Ct. Appeals (6th cir.) 1965, U.S. Dist. Ct. (no. dist.) Ohio, U.S. Supreme Ct. 1970. Assoc. Baker & Hostetler, Cleve., 1965-72, ptnr., 1972—, mng. ptnr., 1989—. Bd. dirs. Great Lakes Theater Festival, Nat. Conf. Christians and Jews, Greater Cleve. Roundtable, Heidelberg Coll.; chmn. Cleve. Indians Major League Baseball Club, Rock and Roll Hall of Fame and Mus. Mem. Ohio State Bar Assn., Valley Forge Assn., Soc. Benchers, Nisi Prius, Heidelberg Coll. Pres. Club. Princeton U. Parents Club, Stanford U. Parents Club, Club at Soc. Ctr. (chmn.), Westwood Country Club, Union Club, Audubon Country Club, Order of Coif. Home: 4370 Valley Forge Dr Fairview Park OH 44126-2825 Office: Baker & Hostetler 3200 National City Ctr Cleveland OH 44114-3485

BRYFONSKI, DEDRIA ANNE, publishing executive; b. Utica, NY, Aug. 21, 1947; d. Lewis Francis and Catherine Marie (Stevens) B.; m. Alexander Burgess Cruden, May 24, 1975 BA, Nazareth Coll., Rochester, NY, 1969; MA, Fordham U., 1970. Editorial asst. Dial Press, NYC, 1970-71; editor Walker & Co., NYC, 1971-73; from editor to v.p., assoc. editl. dir. Gale Rsch. Co., Detroit, 1974—84, from sr. v.p., editl. dir. to pres., CEO, 1984—98; pres. Gale Pub. Gale Group, Farmington Hills, Mich., 1999—2002; exec. v.p. Thomson Gale, Farmington Hills, 2003—06; pres. Rethorica, Grosse Pointe, Mich., 2007—. Author: The New England Beach Book, 1974; editor: Contemporary Literary Criticism, Vols. 7-14, 1977-80, Twentieth Century Literary Criticism, vols. 1-2, 1977-78, Contemporary Issues Criticism, vol. 1, 1982, Contemporary Authors Autobiography Series, vol. 1, 1984 Bd. dirs. Friends of Detroit Pub. Libr., 1980-89, pres., 1984-86; bd. dirs. Friends of Librs. U.S.A., 1995-2003. Mem. ALA, Assn. Am. Pubs. (chmn. libraries com. 1983-85, exec. council gen. pub. div. 1985-87, co-chmn. joint com. resources and tech. services div. 1983-85), Am. Friends of Vatican Libr. (bd. dirs. 2005—). Home and Office: 546 Lincoln Rd Grosse Pointe MI 48230-1218 E-mail: rethorica@comcast.net.

BRZEZINSKI, ROB, professional sports team executive; m. Leah Brzezinski. BS in Edn., Nova Southeastern U., 1992, JD, 1995. Bar: Fla. Staff counsel Miami Dolphins, 1993—98; dir. football adminstrn. Minn. Vikings, 1999—2000, v.p. football adminstrn. Office: Minn Vikings 9520 Vikings Dr Eden Prairie MN 55344

BUBENZER, GARY DEAN, agricultural engineering educator, researcher; b. Bicknell, Ind., Aug. 21, 1940; s. Ernest and Nelda (Telligman) B.; m. Sandra Lee Capehart, June 10, 1962; children— Nathan Edward, Brian Peter A.S., Vincennes U., 1960; BS, Purdue U., 1962, MS, 1964; PhD, U. Ill., 1970. Registered profl. engr., Wis. Instr. agrl. engring. U. Ill., Urbana, 1964-69; asst. prof. U. Wis., Madison, 1969-74, assoc. prof., 1974-79, prof., 1979—, chmn. dept. agrl. engring., 1983-88; guest scholar Kyoto U., Japan, 1981. Contbr. articles to profl. jours. Named Outstanding Instr., Coll. Agr. and Life Sci., U. Wis., 1983; recipient faculty-alumni citation Vincennes U., 1984 Fellow Am. Soc. Agrl. Engrs. (chmn. soil and water div. 1983-84, engr. of the yr. Wis. sect. 1988, Hancor Honor award 1998). United Methodist. Home: N8690 Poplar Grove Rd New Glarus WI 53574-9728 E-mail: gdbubenz@facstaff.wisc.edu, bubenzer@chorus.net.

BUBRICK, MELVIN PHILLIP, surgeon; b. Chgo., June 2, 1944; m. Barbara Lynn Jacobs, Jan. 26, 1969; children: Jerome Bradley, Ellen Jeanne, Dena Beth. BA with honors, U. Ill., 1964, MD, 1968. Diplomate Am. Bd. Surgery, Am. Bd. Colon and Rectal Surgery; lic. Minn. Intern in surgery Univ. Hosps., Madison, Wis., 1968-69; resident in gen. surgery Hennepin County Gen. Hosp., Mpls., 1969-74; postdoctoral fellow colon and rectal surgery U. Minn. Health Scis. Ctr., Mpls., 1974-75; clin. instr. div. colon and rectal surgery U. Minn., Mpls., 1975-77, clin. asst. prof., 1977-78, clin. asst. prof. dept. surgery, 1978-80, asst. prof., 1980-87, assoc. prof., 1987—; chief surgery, program dir. surg. residency Hennepin County Med. Ctr., 1988-94; pres. Hennepin Facility Assocs., 1995—2000, chmn. bd. dirs., 1991—2001. V.p. Mpls. Med. Rsch. Found., 1991-2000; chmn. bd. dirs. Hennepin Faculty Assocs., 1991-2000, CEO, 1991-2001. Author: (with others) Conn's Therapy, 1985, The Pancreas. Principles of Medical and Surgical Practice, 1985, Applied Therapeutics: The clinical use of drugs, 4th rev. edit., 1988; contbr. over 90 articles to Minn. Med. jour., Am. Surg. jour., Diseases of Colon and Rectum, Surgery, others. Bd. dirs. Mpls. Med. Rsch. Found., Inc., 1981-89. Mem. AMA, ACS, Am. Assn. Surgery of Trauma, Am. Soc. Colon and Rectal Surgeons (co-chair Self Assessment Exam. Com. 1984-85), Am. Soc. Microbiology, Assn. Program Dirs. of Surgery, Cen. Surg. Assn., Collegium Internat. Chirurgiae Digestivae, Soc. Surgery of Alimentary Tract, Minn. Assn. Pub. Teaching Hosps., Minn. Surg. Soc., Minn. Med. Assn., Mpls. Surg. Soc., Hennepin County Med. Soc. (mem. and chair various coms. 1975—, Hennepin faculty assoc. 1983—). Achievements include research in assessment of bursting strength and healing of intestinal anastomoses, predictive value of surface oximetry in assessing healing in irradiated bowel, use of antibiotic microspheres for infected vascular grafts and peritonitis, clinical and anatomic assessment of first rib-clavicular decompression on subclavian catheters and pacemaker leads, influence of nutritional deficits in intestinal anastomotic strength, iron chelation with a Deferoxamine (DFO) conjugate in hemorrhagic shock. Personal E-mail: mbubrick@comcast.net.

BUBULA, JOHN, chef; Chef de cuisine Morton's of Chgo., Boston; chef Boston Harbor Hotel, Boston Four Seasons; owner, chef Thyme, Chgo. Office: Thyme 464 N Halsted Chicago IL 60622

BUCHANAN, BRUCE, publishing executive; Editor, pub. Olanthe Daily News, Kans., 1990—95, Hutchinson News, Kans., 1996—; mem. mgmt. staff Harris Enterprises Inc., Hutchinson, Kans., 1995—, v.p., COO, 1997—2006, pres., CEO, 2006—. Office: Harris Enterprises Corp 1 N Main St Hutchinson KS 67501 Office Phone: 620-694-5830.

BUCHANAN, MARGARET E., publishing executive; m. Greg Buchanan; 2 children. BA, MBA, U. Cin. Various mgmt. positions Rockford Register Star, Ill.; pres. & pub. Elmira Star-Gazette, NY, 1996—99, Idaho Statesman, Boise, 1999—2003, Cin. Enquirer, 2003—. Bd. trustees U. Cin., 2006—. Mem. Cin. Bus. Com., Comml. Club., Cin., Women's Leadership Collaborative, Cin., Northern Ky. Vision 2015 Leadership Team; bd. dirs. Marvin Lewis Cmty. Fund, Fine Arts Fund, Cin. Ctr. City Devel. Corp. Named one of Career Women of Achievement, Cin. YMCA, 2006. Office: Cin Enquirer 312 Elm St Cincinnati OH 45202

BUCHELE, WESLEY FISHER, retired agricultural engineering educator; b. Cedar Vale, Kans., Mar. 18, 1920; s. Charles John and Bessie (Fisher) B.; m. Mary Jagger, June 12, 1945 (dec. 2000); children: Rod, Marybeth, Sheron, Steven BS, Kans. State U., 1943; MS, U. Ark., 1951; PhD, Iowa State U., 1954. Registered profl. engr., Iowa, Calif. Jr. engr. John Deere Tractor Works, Waterloo, Iowa, 1946—48; asst. prof. U. Ark., Fayetteville, 1948—51; agrl. engr. USDA, Ames, Iowa, 1954—56; assoc. prof. Mich. State U., East Lansing, 1956—63; prof. Iowa State U., Ames, 1963—89, prof. emeritus, 1989—; ret., 1989. Vis. prof. U. Ghana, Legon, 1968-69, Beijing Agrl. Engring. U., 1983-84; vis. scientist Commonwealth Sci. and Indsl. Rsch. Orgn., Australia, Internat. Inst., Tropical Agr., Ibadan, Nigeria, 1979-80, Internat. Rice Rsch. Inst., Manila,

1991-92; cons. engr. Detroit Arsenal, Ordnance Corps, Waterways Exptl. Sta., Corps of Engrs., US Steel Corp., GM, Detroit, 1974-76; bd. dirs. Farm Safety 4 Just Kids, Earlham, Iowa, Self-Help, Inc., Waverly, Iowa, JAC Tractor Co Author 18 books; inventor 23 patents Mem. Ames Energy Com., 1974-75; advisor Living History Farm, Urbandale, Iowa, 1965—, bd. govs., 1984—. Maj. U.S. Army, 1943-46, PTO; maj. Ordnance Corps, USAR, 1946-69, ret Named Eminent Engr., Iowa Engring. Soc., 1989; recipient Outstanding Engring. award, U. Ark., 2005, Disting. Alumni 7th Coll. Engring., 2005. Fellow Am. Soc. Agrl. Engrs. (bd. dirs. 1978-80, McCormick-Case award 1988, Henry A. Wallace award for significant contbn. to agr. 2003, Outstanding Engring. Alumni award 2005), Nat. Inst. Agrl. Engrs.; mem. AAAS, Soc. Automotive Engrs., Am. Soc. Agronomy (com. 1961-65), Steel Ring, Internat. Assn. Mechanization of Field Experiments (v.p. 1964-93), Internat. Platform Assn., Osborne Club, Toastmasters Avocations: photography, travel, golf, inventing, writing. Home and Office: 239 Parkridge Cir Ames IA 50014-3645 Office Phone: 515-292-2933. Personal E-mail: wbuchele@msn.com.

BUCHENROTH, STEPHEN RICHARD, lawyer; b. Bellefontaine, Ohio, Feb. 8, 1948; s. Richard G. and Patricia (Muller) B.; m. Vicki Anderson, June 6, 1974; children: Matthew Brian, Sarah Elizabeth. BA, Wittenburg U., Springfield, Ohio, 1970; JD, U. Chgo., 1974. Bar: Ohio 1974, U.S. Dist. Ct. (so. and no. dists.) Ohio 1974, U.S. Ct. Appeals (6th cir.) 1974. Ptnr. Vorys, Sater, Seymour & Pease, Columbus, Ohio, 1974—. Author: Ohio Mortgage Foreclosures, 1986, Ohio Franchising Law, 1990, also chpts. in books. Trustee, v.p. Godman Guild Assn., Columbus, 1977-83; trustee, sec. Neighborhood Homes, Inc., Columbus, 1977-85; bd. rev. Worthington Pers., 1981—; pres. Worthington Alliance for Quality Edn., 1989-91; bd. adv. paralegal program Capitol U. Law Sch., 1991-2004; pres. chmn. bd. trustees Worthington Edn. Found., 1997-98; mem. Ohio Supreme Ct. Commn. on CLE, 1994-2000, chmn., 1999; bd. advisors C.H.A.D.D. of Ctrl. Ohio, 1993-97; trustee Wittenberg U., 2000—, vice chmn 2005—; bd. trustees Ohio Legal Assistance Found., 2006—. Recipient Cmty. Svc. award, Legal Assts. Ctrl. Ohio, 1987. Mem.: ABA (forum com. franchising), Am. Coll. Real Estate Lawyers, Columbus Bar Assn. (pres. 1992—93, bd. govs., Bar Svc. medal 2000), Ohio State Bar Assn. (bd. govs. real property sect. 1994—, chmn. real property sect. 2003—05, real property splty. bd. 2003—, coun. dels., chmn. legal assts. com., chmn.). Republican. Lutheran. Home: 2342 Collins Dr Columbus OH 43085-2810 Office: Vorys Sater Seymore & Pease 52 E Gay St PO Box 1008 Columbus OH 43215-3161 Home Phone: 614-436-0098; Office Phone: 614-464-6366. Business E-Mail: srbuchenroth@vssp.com.

BUCHSIEB, WALTER CHARLES, orthodontist, director; b. Columbus, Ohio, Aug. 30, 1929; s. Walter William and Emma Marie (Held) b.; m. Betty Lou Risch, June 19, 1955; children: Walter Charles II, Christine Ann. BA, Ohio State U., 1951, DDS, 1955, MS, 1960. Pvt. practice dentistry specializing in orthodontics, Dayton, Ohio, 1959-93. Cons. orthodontist Miami Valley Hosp., Children's Med. Ctr., Dayton; orthodontic cons. Columbus Children's Hosp.; assoc. prof. dept. orthodontics Ohio State U. Coll. Dentistry, 1984—2004, clinic dir., 1993—98, mem. dean's adv. com.; mem. fin. and program com. United Health Found., 1971—73; com. chmn. Vigl Williams endowed chair orthodontocs Ohio State U. Bd. dirs. Hearing and Speech Ctr., 1968-82, 2d v.p., 1976-78, pres., 1978-79; orthodontic advisor State of Ohio Dept. Health, Bur. Crippled Children's Svcs., 1983-84; elder Luth. ch., 1965-68, v.p. 1974. Capt. AUS, 1955-58. Fellow Am. Coll. Dentists (pres. Ohio sect. 1988); mem. ADA (alt. del. 1968, del. 1991, coun. on ann. sessions and internat. rels. 1984-88), Am. Assn. Dental Schs., Am. Cleft Palate Assn., Am. Assn. Dental Schs., Internat. Assn. Dental Rsch., Ohio Dental Assn. (sec. coun. legis. 1969-78, v.p. 1978-79, pres.-elect 1979-80, pres. 1980-81, polit. action com. 1987-95, Coun. on constn. and By-Laws 1988-92, Achievement award 1989), Dayton Dental Soc. (pres. 1970-71), Am. Bd. Orthodontics, Gt. Lakes Assn. Orthodontists (sec.-treas. 1972-75, pres. 1977-78, Disting. Svc. award 2005), Internat. Coll. Dentists, Am. Assn. Orthodontists (chmn. coun. legis. 1976, speaker of house 1982-85, ad hoc com. to revise by-laws, coun. on govtl. affairs 1988-96, recipient James E. Brophy Dist. Svc. award 1992, Disting. Svc. award, 2005, bd. mem. polit. action com.), Pierre Fauchard Acad. (chmn. cen. Ohio), Coll. Diplomats Am. Bd. Orthodontics (pres. 1990-91), Ohio State U. Alumni Assn. (advs. group), Delta Upsilon (pres. Ohio State U. alumni chpt. 1997-99, alumni advisor 2000—), Psi Omega, Masons, Rotary (pres. 1973-74, Paul Harris fellow). Republican. Lutheran. Home: 1212 Harrison Pond Dr New Albany OH 43054-9553 Office: Ohio State U Orthodontics Dept 305 W 12th Ave Columbus OH 43210-1267 Business E-Mail: walt1520@aol.com.

BUCHWALD, HENRY, surgeon, educator, researcher; b. Vienna, June 21, 1932; arrived in U.S., 1939, naturalized; s. Andor and Renee (Franzos) B.; m. Emilie D. Bix, June 6, 1954; children: Jane Nicole, Amy Elizabeth, Claire Gretchen, Dana Alexandra. BA summa cum laude, Columbia U., 1954, MD, 1957; MS in Biochemistry, PhD in Surgery, U. Minn., 1967. Diplomate Am. Bd. Surgery. Intern Columbia/Presbyn. Med. Ctr., NYC, 1957-58; resident fellow in surgery U. Minn., Mpls., 1960-67; asst. prof. surgery U. Minn. Med. Sch., Mpls., 1967-70, assoc. prof., 1970-77, prof. surgery, prof. biomed. engring., 1977—, dir. grad. surg. tng., resident tng. program, in-tng. exam., chmn. credentials com.; chair Owen and Sarah Davidson Wangensteen Chair in Exptl. Surgery, 2001—. Pres. Minn. Inventors Hall of Fame, 1989-92, chmn. bd. dirs. 1992-94; vis. prof., lectr. McLaren Gen. Hosp., Flint., Mich., 1979, Buffalo Surg. Soc., Mpls., 1980, G.P. Wratten Surg. Symposium, Washington, 1980, Frontiers of Medicine Series, Chgo., 1980, Minn. Endocrine Club, Mpls., 1980, Symposium on Surgery, Tokyo, 1980, Northwestern Med. Assn., Sun Valley, Idaho, 1981, Mayo Clinic, Rochester, Minn., 1981, BSG/Glaxo Internat. Tchg. Day, Norwich, Eng., 1982, Mass. Gen. Hosp., Boston, 1983, SUNY, Stony Brook, 1984, DC Gen. Hosp., Washington, 1984, LA Surg. Soc., 1987, Sch. Dentistry, Dept. Continuing Edn., U. Minn., 1988, others; Alfred Strauss vis. lectr., Chgo., 1989; dir. postgrad. course Bariatric Surgery Primer, ACS; spkr., presenter, cons. in field. Author: (with others) Hepatic, Biliary and Pancreatic Surgery, 1980, Lipoproteins and Coronary Atherosclerosis, 1982, Atherosclerosis: Clinical Evaluation and Therapy, 1982, Nutrition and Heart Disease, 1982, Advances in Vascular Surgery, 1983, Advances in Surgery, 1984, others; contbr. Gibbon's Surgery of the Chest, 4th edit., 1983, Hardy's Textbook of Surgery, 1983, Implantable Pumps: ASAIO Primers in Artificial Organs, 1987, editor, author (textbook) Surgical Management of Obesity, 2006, (book) Pioneer of Gastrointestional Surgery, 2006; contbr. over 300 articles to profl. jours., trans.; mem. editorial bd. Chirurgia Generale, Jour. Clin. Surgery, Infu-Systems Internat., Diabetes, Nutrition and Metabolism, Obesity Surgery Jour. Am. Soc. Artificial Int. Orgn., Jour. Bacteriol. Surgery, Online Jour. Current Clin. Trials, also guest editor other jours. Capt. SAC, USAF, 1958-60. Recipient Inventor of Yr. award Minn. Inventors Hall of Fame, 1988, 90, Clin. Scholar award U. Minn., 1991, Diehl award U. Minn.; recipient numerous rsch. grants univs., Nat. Heart and Lung Inst., Nat. Cancer Inst., Nat. Inst. Arthritis, Metabolism and Digestive Diseases, NIH, med. founds., pharm. cos., corps., 1956—. Fellow ACS (gov. 1999—, Samuel D. Gross award 1969), Am. Surg. Assn., Soc. Univ. Surgeons, Ctrl. Surg. Assn. (program com. 1982-85, chmn. 1984-85, treas. 1992-94, pres. 1997-98), Assn. Acad. Surgery (Disting. Svc. award 1976), Epidemiology Coun. and Cardiovasc. Coun. Am. Heart Assn. (established investigator), Am. Coll. Cardiology, Soc. Surgery Alimentary Tract, Soc. Clin. Trials (program com. 1984-85); mem. AAAS, Minn. Surg. Assn. (First Clin. Rsch. award 1965), Mpls. Surg. Assn., Minn. Heart Assn., Am. Assn. History Medicine, Am. Soc. Artificial Internal Organs (program com. 1984-87, sect. editor Trans.), Internat. Study Group Diabetes Treatment with Implantable Insulin Delivery Devices (sec.-gen. 1984-88, chmn. 1989-94), St. Paul Surg. Soc. (hon.), Am. Coll. utrition (mem. editorial bd.), Am. Soc. Bariatric Soc. (pres. 1998-99), Internat. Soc. Obesity Surgery (pres. 2003-04), Owen H. Wangeensteen Soc. (pres. 2007), Paleopathology Club, Alpha Omega Alpha. Avocations: running, riding, tennis, reading, chess. Office: 420 Delaware St SE Minneapolis MN 55455 Office Phone: 612-625-8413. Business E-Mail: buchw001@umn.edu.

BUCHY, JIM, food products executive; b. Greenville, Ohio, Sept. 24, 1940; s. George Jacob and Amba (Armbruster) B.; m. Sharon Lynn Steinvall, 1965; children: Kathryn, John. BS, Wittenberg U., 1962. Pres. Charles G. Buchy Packing Co., Greenville, 1977—; mem. Ohio Ho. of Reps., Columbus, 1983—2000. Mem. Greenville Bd. Edn., 1980-82; dist. del. Rep. Nat. Conf.; mem. Darke County (Ohio) Rep. Exec. Com.; chmn. Darke Econ. Found., 1977-82; bd. dirs. Greenville Indsl. Park; past pres. Darke County Rep. Men's Club. Mem. Darke County C. of C., Rotary, Phi Mu Delta. Home: North Broadway PO Box 899 Greenville OH 45331-0899

BUCK, JAMES RUSSELL, state legislator; m. Judith Ann Buck. BA, BS, MBA, Ind. Wesleyan Coll. Mem. Ind. State Ho. of Reps. Dist. 38, mem. commerce & econ. devel., ins., corp. & small bus. coms., mem. roads and transp. com., vice-chmn. labor and employment com. Mem. Nat. Assn. Realtors, Ind. Assn. Realtors, Kokomo Bd. Realtors. Home: 4407 Mckibben Dr Kokomo IN 46902-4719

BUCK, WILLIS R., JR., lawyer; b. 1952; BA, Williams Coll., 1973, Oxford Univ., 1975; MPhil, Yale Univ., 1979; JD, Univ. Chgo., 1984. Bar: Ill. 1985. Law clk. Judge Milton I. Shadur, US Dist Ct. no. dist. Ill., 1984—85; atty. Sidley Austin LLP, Chgo., 1985—90, London, 1990—93, ptnr., fin. & securitization Chgo., 1993—. Office: Sidley Austin LLP One S Dearborn St Chicago IL 60603 Office Phone: 312-853-7819. Office Fax: 312-853-7036. Business E-Mail: wbuck@sidley.com.

BUCKINGHAM, ELIZABETH C., lawyer; b. 1964; AB magna cum laude, Smith Coll., 1985; JD, Harvard Univ., 1988. Bar: DC 1988, Minn. 1994. Ptnr., co-head, trademark and litig. group Dorsey & Whitney LLP, Mpls. Articles editor Harvard Jour. on Legis., 1987—88, lectr., writer in field. Mem.: Minn. Intellectual Property Lawyers Assn., Internat. Trademark Assn., Midwest Intellectual Property Inst., WomenVenture (bd. dir. 2000—), Phi Beta Kappa. Office: Dorsey & Whitney LLP Ste 1500 50 S Sixth St Minneapolis MN 55402-1498 Office Phone: 612-343-2178. Office Fax: 612-340-8856. Business E-Mail: buckingham.elizabeth@dorsey.com.

BUCKLER, ROBERT J., energy distribution company executive; Sr. v.p. energy mktg. & distbn. Detroit Edison, 1974-97; pres. energy distbn. DTE Energy Corp., Detroit, 1998—. Office: DTE Energy Co 2000 2d Ave Detroit MI 48226-1279

BUCKLEY, GEORGE W., manufacturing executive; b. Sheffield, Eng., Feb. 23, 1947; divorced; 5 children; m. Carol Buckley; 2 children. BSc in elec. and electronic engring., Univ. Huddersfield, Eng., 1972, PhD, 1975, U. Southhampton, 1975; DSc (hon.), Univ. Huddersfield, Eng. Rsch. officer UK Ctrl. Electricity Generating Bd., 1975; gen. mgr. dist. heating Detroit Edison Co., 1976—86; pres. generator div. GEC Turbine Generators Ltd., Stafford, England, 1986—88; dir., pres. ctrl. services unit Brit. Railways, 1988—93; pres. elec. motors divsn. Emerson Elec. Co., 1993—97; pres. Mercury Marine unit Brunswick Corp., Fond du Lac, Wis., 1997, corp. sr. v.p., 1999, corp. exec. v.p., 2000, pres., COO, 2000, chmn., CEO Lake Forest, Ill., 2000—05; chmn., CEO, pres. 3M Corp., 2005—. Bd. dir. Tyco Internat. Ltd, 2002—, Ingersoll-Rand Co., Thule AB. Office: 3M Co 3M Ctr Saint Paul MN 55144-1000

BUCKLEY, JOSEPH PAUL, III, computer technician; b. Chgo., July 6, 1949; s. Joseph Paul and Helen (Lavelle) B.; m. Patricia Nemeth, June 17, 1972; children: Megan, Michael, Patrick, Thomas. BA, Loyola U., Chgo., 1971; MS in Detection of Deception, Reid Coll. Detection of Deception, Chgo., 1973. Lic., Ill. Detection of deception examiner John E. Reid & Assocs., Inc., Chgo., 1971—, chief polygraph examiner, 1978-80, dir. Chgo. office, 1980-82, pres. corp. Chgo., Milw., 1982—. Chmn. Ill. Detection of Deception Examiner Com., 1978-82; mem. adv. com. Office of Tech. Assessment, 1983 Co-author: Criminal Interrogation and Confessions, 1st edit., 1962, 4th edit., 2001, The Investigator Anthology, 1999, Essentials of the Reid Technique, 2004; contbr. articles to profl. jours. Mem. Am. Polygraph Assn. (v.p. 1979-80, chmn. pub. rels. com. 1979-80, 84-95, awards), Ill. Polygraph Soc. (v.p. 1981, pres. 1982-83), Am. Acad. Forensic Scis., Am. Mgmt. Assn., Am. Soc. Indsl. Security (investigations com. 1983-89), Spl. Agts. Assn., Internat. Pers. Mgmt. Assn., Internat. Assn. Chiefs Policy, Chgo. Crime Commn. Home Phone: 815-455-3261. E-mail: jbuckley@reid.com.

BUCKLEY, PAMELA KAY, educational association administrator; BA in English, U. Evansville, 1964; MAT, U. Louisville, 1970; EdD in Curriculum and Instrn., U. Houston, 1977. Various ednl. positions, 1964—78; prog. staff devel. coord. U. Houston Tchr. Corps Project, 1978—80, assoc. project dir., 1981; assoc. rsch. scientist Far West Lab. Ednl. R & D, San Francisco, 1980; tng. mgr. tng. divsn. City of Houston Civil Svc. Dept., 1981—83; sr. instr. manpower devel. divsn. The Gulf Bank, Kuwait, 1984—85; faculty developer staff instructional devel. dept. Houston Cmty. Coll. Sys., 1985—88; co-dir. Commonwealth Ctr. Edn. Tchrs. James Madison U., Harrisonburg, 1988—92, assoc. prof. Coll. Edn. and Psych., 1988—92; sr. tng. specialist tng. divsn. Kuwait Inst. Sci. Rsch.; dir. Eisenhower Math/Sci. Consortium, 1992; positions up to v.p. tech. assistance and tng. Appalachia Ednl. Lab.; exec. dir., CEO Hands On Sci. Outreach; dir. mktg. govt. divsn. Gallup Orgn.; prog. dir. RTI Internat.; exec. dir. Kappa Delta Pi, Indpls., 2006—. Contbr. articles and revs. to profl. jours. Mem. ASTD, ASCD, Am. Ednl. Rsch. Assn., Assn. Tchr. Educators, Phi Delta Kappa. Office: Kappa Delta Pi Internat Honor Soc Edn 3707 Woodview Trace Indianapolis IN 46268-1158 Office Phone: 317-871-4900 ext. 222. E-mail: buckleyp@kdp.org.

BUCKLO, ELAINE EDWARDS, United States district court judge; b. Boston, Oct. 1, 1944; married. AB, St. Louis U., 1966; JD, Northwestern U., 1972. Bar: Calif. 1973, U.S. Dist. Ct. (no. dist.) Calif. 1973, Ill. 1974, U.S. Dist. ct. (no. dist.) Ill. 1974, U.S. Ct. Appeals (7th cir.) 1983. Law clk. U.S. Ct. Appeals (7th cir.), Chgo.; pvt. practice, 1973-85; U.S. magistrate judge U.S. Dist. Ct. (no. dist.) Ill., Chgo., 1985-94, judge, 1994—. Spkr. in field. Contbr. articles to profl. jours. Mem. jud. conf. com. on adminstrn. Magistrate Judge Sys., 1998-2004; mem. vis. com. No. Ill. U. Sch. Law, 1994—; mem. orthwestern U. Law Bd., 1996-99. Mem. ABA (standing com. law and literacy 1995-98, assoc. editor Litigation), FBA (v.p. 1990-92, pres. Chgo. chpt. 1992-93), Women's Bar Assn. Ill. (bd. dirs. 1994-96), Chgo. Coun. Lawyers (pres. 1977-78). Office: US Dist Ct No Dist Everett McKinley Dirksen Bldg 219 S Dearborn St Ste 1446 Chicago IL 60604-1794

BUCKSBAUM, JOHN, real estate company executive; BA in Econs., U. Denver. Pres. Gen. Growth Calif.; CEO, bd. dir. Gen. Growth Properties, Inc., 1999—. Chmn., mem. exec. com. Internat. Council Shopping Centers; trustee Nat. Assn. REITs, Urban Land Inst.; mem. Nat. Realty Roundtable; mem. adv. bd. Univ. Calif. Real Estate Ctr.; chmn. Zell/Lurie Real Estate Ctr., Wharton Sch. Bd. mem. U.S. Ski & Snowboard Team Found., USA Cycling Found., World T.E.A.M. Sports; trustee Univ. Chgo. Hospitals. Mem.: Young Presidents Org. Office: Gen Growth Properties inc 110 N Wacker Dr Chicago IL 60606-1511

BUCKSBAUM, MATTHEW, real estate investment trust company executive; b. Marshalltown, Iowa, Feb. 20, 1926; s. Louis and Ida (Gerwin) B.; m. Carolyn Swartz, Aug. 3, 1952; children: Ann B. Friedman, John. BA in Econ. cum laude, U. Iowa, 1949. Owner, operator Regional Supermarket Chain, Marshalltown, 1949-54; owner, developer Pvt. Real Estate, Iowa, 1954-64; chmn. emeritus Gen. Growth Properties, Chgo., 1964—. Trustee, past chmn. Aspen (Colo.) Music Festival and Sch.; bd. dirs. Chgo. Symphony Orch., Lyric Opera Chgo. Sgt. USAF, 1944-46, PTO. Named one of Forbes' Richest Americans, 2005—, World's Richest People, Forbes mag., 2006—. Mem.: Nat. Assn. Real Estate Investment Trusts, Urban Land Inst., Internat. Coun. Shopping Ctrs. (past chmn.), Order of Artus, Phi Beta Kappa. Jewish. Office: General Growth Properties Inc 110 N Wacker Dr Chicago IL 60606-1511 Office Phone: 312-960-5123. Office Fax: 312-960-5463.

BUCKWALTER, JOSEPH ADDISON, orthopedic surgeon, educator; b. Ottumwa, Iowa, June 21, 1947; s. Joseph Addison and Carole Ann (Kelly) B.; m. Kathleen Coen, May 31, 1975; children: Jody, Andrea, Abigail. BS with high distinction, U. Iowa, 1969, MS, 1972, MD, 1974. Diplomate Am. Bd. Orthopaedic Surgery (recert., oral examiner 1988—, dir. 1990—, mem. examinations com. 1992—, chmn. examinations com. 1992-93, chmn. cert. renewal com. 1992—); lic. surgeon Iowa. Intern in internal medicine U. Iowa, Iowa City, 1974-75, resident in orthopaedics, 1975-77, 78-79, Nat. Rsch. Svc. Award rsch. fellow, 1977-78, from asst. prof. to assoc. prof. orthopaedic surgery, 1979-85, prof. orthopaedic surgery, 1985—. Mem. R&D devel. com. VA Med. Ctr. Com., 1985-88; mem. orthopaedic tumor therapy group U. Iowa Cancer Ctr., 1981—, cancer edn. subcom., 1982-90; mem. grants and fellowships adv. com. Iowa City Vets. Med. Ctr., 1983-86, chief orthopaedic surgery, 1987-91; mem. Arthritis Found. Rsch. Com., 1985-86; mem. panel NIH Consensus Devel. Confs., Bethesda, Md., 1984, 88; mem. rheumatology rsch. adv. bd. Syntex Corp., 1987-94; mem. adv. bd. WHO Multinational Collaborative Study on Predictors of Osteoarthritis, 1992; mem. sci. adv. com. Specialised Ctr. Rsch. on Osteoarthritis Rush-Presbyn.-St. Luke's Med. Ctr., Chgo., 1993—; mem. Nat. Arthritis and Musculoskeletal and Skin Diseases Adv. Coun., NIH, 1993—; disting. lectr. Hosp. Spl. Surgery, N.Y.C., 1982, Coll. Physicians and Surgeons-N.Y. Orthopaedic Hosp., 1988, U. N.Mex., 1989; guest lectr. Wilford Hall Med. Ctr., San Antonio, 1983, vis. prof., 1984; vis. prof. U. Miami, Fla., 1986, Cath. Med. Colls., Seoul, Republic of Korea, 1989, U. Pitts., 1993, Ohio State U., Columbus, 1994; vis. orthopaedic prof. U. So. Calif., L.A., 1990; Am. Orthopaedic Assn. 1991 Internat. vis. prof. Nuffield Orthopaedic Ctr., Oxford (Eng.) U., 1991, vis. prof. orthopaedics, 1991; vis. prof. orthopaedics, U. N.C., 1991; OREF Hark lectr. and vis. prof. U. Wash., Seattle, 1992; Watson Jones lectr. Royal Coll. Surgeons (Gt. Britain), 1992; A.M. Rechtman lectr. Phila. Orthopaedic Soc., 1993; Predl. guest spkr. 1993 Japanese Orthopaedic Assn. Rsch. Meeting, Matsumoto, Japan, 1993; Kelly Rsch. Award vis. prof. Mayo Clinic, Rochester, Minn., 1993; participant numerous workshops and confs. Cons. reviewer: Jour. Bone and Joint Surgery, 1979—, cons. editor for rsch., 1989—; bd. assoc. editors: Jour. Orthopaedic Rsch., 1982-85, mem. editl. adv. bd., 1985-88, co-editor-in-chief, 1993—; mem. editl. adv. bd. Orthopaedics, 1986-90; reviewer: The Lancet, 1993—; contbr. articles to profl. jours. Student rsch. fellow U. Iowa Coll. Medicine, 1970. Fellow Am. Inst. Med. and Biol. Engring. (founding), Am. Acad. Orthopaedic Surgeons (mem. com. basic scis. 1983-85, chmn. com. evaulation 1985-90, mem. at large, bd. dirs. 1988-89, mem. steering com. for devel. Musculoskeletal Conditions in U.S. 1990-92, chmn. coun. for rsch. and sci. affairs 1990-93, 94—, sec. 1993-94); mem. AAAS, Inst. Medicine, Internat. Soc. Limb Salvage, Brit. Orthopaedic Assn. (companion mem.), Orthopaedic Rsch. Soc. (sec.-treas. 1985-88, bd. dirs. 1985-91, pres. 1989-90), Am. Orthopaedic Assn. (exch. fellowship com. 1989-90, chmn. internat. vis. prof. com. 1993—), Am. Orthopaedic Soc. for Sports Medicine (chmn. rsch. awards com. 1988-90, rsch. com. 1989-91), Internat. Skeletal Soc., Iowa Orthopaedic Soc., Johnson County Med. Soc., Musculoskeletal Tumor Soc., 20th Century Orthopaedic Assn., Girdlestone Orthopaedic Soc., Phi Beta Kappa, Alpha Omega Alpha. Office: U Iowa Hosps Dept Orthopaedics 200 Hawkins Dr Iowa City IA 52242-1009 Office Phone: 319-356-2595.

BUCKWALTER, KATHLEEN C., academic administrator, educator; BSN, U. Iowa; MA in Psychiatric/Mental Health Nursing, U. Ill., Chgo., PhD in Nursing. Assoc. dir. Gerontological Nursing Interventions Rsch. Ctr., dir. Ctr. on Aging U. Iowa, Found. disting. Prof., assoc. provost health scis., 1997—. Contbr. over 200 articles to profl. jours., 75 chpts. to books; editor: Nursing Diagnosis and Intervention for the Elderly (Maas, M., Buckwalter, K.C., Hardy, M.A.), 1991, Geriatric Mental Health: Current and Future Challenges, 1992, others. Mem.: IOM. Office: U Iowa Coll Nursing 101 Nursing Bldg 234 CMAB Iowa City IA 52242

BUDA, JAMES B., lawyer, manufacturing executive; b. South Bend, Ind., Mar. 9, 1947; BA, Ball State U., 1969; JD, U. Notre Dame, 1973. Bar: Ind. 1973, Ill. 1987, U.S. Ct. Appeals (7th cir.) 1987, U.S. Supreme Ct. 1987. Atty., legal dept. and other positions Caterpillar, Inc., 1987—96, assoc. gen. counsel, 1996—99, assoc. gen. counsel, legal services divsn. UK, 1999—2001, v.p., legal services divsn., gen. counsel, sec. Peoria, Ill., 2001—. Mem. Civil Justice Reform Group. Mem.: ATLA, ABA, Gen. Counsel Roundtable, Corp. Exec. Bd., CLO Roundtable, Assn. Gen. Counsels, Am. Soc. Corp. Secs., Internat. Assn. Def. Counsel, Fedn. Corp. and Ins. Counsel, Def. Rsch. Inst., Am. Corp. Counsel Assn., Ind. State Bar Assn., Ill. State Bar Assn. Office: Caterpillar Inc Legal Dept 100 E Adams St Peoria IL 61629-7310 Office Phone: 309-675-4428. Business E-Mail: budajb@cat.com.

BUDAK, MARY KAY, state legislator; b. Phila. m. Michael S. Budak, 1953; children: Kathy Budak Norred, Michael S. III, Patricia A. Budak Jones. Student, Temple U., 1950-51, Purdue U., 1968-80. Owner, mgr. Budak Memls. Inc., 1960-81; sec. to campaign coord. Michigan City Mayor Campaign, Ind., 1966-79; mem. Ind. Ho. of Reps., 1980—, mem. various coms., ranking majority mem. judiciary com., former ranking Rep. mem. family and children com., asst. Rep. whip. Pres. Miss Ind. Scholar Pageant, 1970-74, former mem. exec. bd.; mem. exec. bd. Michiana Sheltered Workshop, 1981-86, Parents & Friends of Handicapped; asst. Rep. WAIP; bd. dirs. Stepping Stone for Spousal Abuse. Named Outstanding Woman in Politics, 1982, Outstanding Legislator, Fraternal Order Police and State Employees, 1983. Mem. LWV, LaPorte County Grange, LaPorte GOP Women's Club (v.p. 1979-81), Bus. & Profl. Women's Club, LaPorte Rep. Women's Club, LaPorte Homemakers Ext. Club, VFW Aux., Rotary. Roman Catholic. Home: 5144 N Pawnee Trl La Porte IN 46350-7565 Office: State House State Capital Indianapolis IN 46204

BUECHLER, BRADLEY BRUCE, plastics company executive, accountant; b. St. Louis, Dec. 5, 1948; s. Phillip Earl and Mildred M. (Braun) B.; m. Stephanie A. Walker, June 20, 1969; children: Sheila, Lisa, Brian. BSBA, U. Mo., St. Louis, 1971. CPA, Mo. Audit mgr. Arthur Andersen & Co., St. Louis, 1971-81; corp. controller Spartech Corp., St. Louis, 1981-83, exec. v.p., COO, 1984-87, pres., COO, 1987-91, pres., CEO, 1991—, chmn., 1999—. Bd. regents St. Louis U., 1994—; mem. corp. bd. St. Joseph Inst. for the Deaf, 1995—; bd. dirs. Boy Scouts Am., 1998, 2005. With Mo. Army N.G., 1969-75; mem. corp. bd. Portage Plastics Corp, 2000—, Mem. AICPA, Soc. Plastics Industry (chmn. sheet prodrs. divsn., bd. dirs. 1993-95, mem. exec. com. color and additive compounders divsn.). Methodist. Avocations: golf, baseball. Office: Spartech Corp 120 S Central Ave Ste 1700 Clayton MO 63105-1735

BUEHRER, STEPHEN, state senator; b. Toledo, Ohio, Jan. 1, 1967; married; 3 children. BS in Edn., Bowling Green State U., 1989; JD, Capital U., 1997. Atty.; mem. Ohio Ho. of Reps., Columbus, 1998—2006, mem. criminal justice com., chair state govt. com., asst. majority fl. leader, 2001—04; mem. Ohio Senate, Columbus, 2007—. Mem.: United Conservatives of Ohio, Coun. State Govt. (chmn. midwest-Can. rels. com.), Am. Legis. Exch. (state co-chair, Nat. Legislator of Yr. 2002), Ohio Twp. Assn., Fulton County Bar Assn., Ohio Bar Assn., Bowhay Legis. Leadership Inst., Ohio Right to Life, C. of C., Nat. Assn. Sports Legislators, Ohio Farm Bur., Fulton County Hist. Soc., Ducks Unlimited, Pheasants Forever. Republican. Office: First Flr Statehouse Rm #125 Columbus OH 43215 Business E-Mail: sd01@mailr.sen.state.oh.us.

BUEHRLE, MARK (ALAN), professional baseball player; b. St. Charles, Mo., Mar. 23, 1979; Attended, Jefferson Coll., Hillsboro, Mo. Pitcher Chgo. White Sox, 2000—. amed to Am. League All-Star Team, 2002, 2005, 2006. Achievements include leading the American League in innings pitched during the 2004 and 2005 seasons. Office: Chgo White Sox 333 W 35th St Chicago IL 60616*

BUETOW, DENNIS EDWARD, physiologist, educator; b. Chgo., June 20, 1932; s. Earl Frank and Helen Anna (Roeske) Buetow; m. Mary Kathleen Carney, Oct. 29, 1960; children: Katherine, Thomas(dec.), Michael, Ellen. BA, UCLA, 1954, MS, 1957, PhD, 1959. Biologist NIH, Bethesda, Md., 1959-65; biochemist Balt. City Hosps., 1959-65; assoc. prof. physiology U. Ill., Urbana, 1965-70, prof., 1970—2000, head dept. physiology and biophysics, 1983-88, prof. emeritus, 2000—. Cons. in field. Contbr. articles to profl. jours. Grantee, NIH, NSF, Life Ins. Med. Rsch. Fund, Am. Heart Assn., USDA. Fellow: AAAS, Gerontol. Soc.; mem.: Am. Soc. Plant Biology, Am. Fedn. Aging Rsch., Soc. Protozoologists, Am. Physiol. Soc., Am. Soc. Cell Biology. Home: 2 Eton Ct Champaign IL 61820-7602 Office: Univ Ill 524 Burrill Hall Urbana IL 61801 Business E-Mail: d-buetow@uiuc.edu.

BUFALINO, VINCENT JOHN, cardiologist, medical administrator; b. May 29, 1952; m. Joan Bufalino; 2 children. Grad. magna cum laude, Loyola U.; MD, Loyola U. Stritch Sch. Medicine, 1977. Cert. internal medicine, cardiovasc. disease. Intern and resident, internal medicine and cardiology Loyola Stritch Sch. Medicine; fellow to chief fellow, cardiovascular disease Loyola U. Foster McGaw Hosp.; pres., CEO Midwest Heart Specialists, chmn. bd., Midwest Heart Found.; med. dir., cardiologist Edward Heart Hosp., Naperville, Ill. Mem. practicing physicians adv. coun. HHS, 2006—. Recipient Man of Yr. Michelangelo award, Italo-Am. at. Union, 1998, Leonardo DiVinci award for Excellence, Order Sons of Italy in America, 2004. Mem.: Am. Heart Assn. (past pres. greater midwest affiliate, nat. bd. dirs., chmn. advocacy coord. com., chair, reimbursement access and coverage task force, expert panel mem., disease mgmt., mem. steering com., Get With the Guidelines, Physician of Yr. award 1997, Coeur d'or (Heart of Gold) award 2001, Chmn.'s award for Excellence in Vol. Leadership 2005, Am. Heartsaver Long-Haul award 2002), DuPage County Med. Soc. (bd. dirs.). Office: Midwest Heart Specialists Edward Heart Hosp 4th Fl 801 S Washington St Naperville IL 60566*

BUFE, NOEL CARL, program director; b. Wyandotte, Mich., Dec. 25, 1933; s. Carl Frederick and Alcha D. (Brumfield) B.; m. Nancy Carolyn Sinclair, Mar.

23, 1957; children: Kevin, Lynn, Bruce, Carol. BS, Mich. State U., 1956, MS in Criminal Justice, 1971, PhD, 1974. Exec. trainee and security investigation J.L. Hudson Co., Detroit, 1956-57, office mgr., 1960-62; rsch. investigator Wayne State U., Detroit, 1962; adminstrv. asst. to sec. bd. police commrs. Met. Police Dept., St. Louis, 1964; mgmt. cons. hwy. safety divsn. Internat. Assn. Chiefs of Police, Washington, 1964-66; exec. sec. Mich. Law Enforcement Officers Tng. Coun., Lansing, 1966-67; exec. dir. office hwy. safety planning Mich. Govs.' Hwy. Safety Rep., 1967-74; dep. adminstr. Nat. Hwy. Traffic Safety Adminstrn., 1974-75; adminstr. office criminal justice programs Mich. Dept. Mgmt. and Budget, Lansing, 1975-78; dir. traffic inst. Northwestern U., Evanston, Ill., 1978-99; chmn. nat. safety Itasca, Ill., 1999—. Bd. mem. com. for strategic transp. rsch. study Nat. Rsch. Coun. Transp. Rsch. Bd., 1989-91; chairperson, vice chairperson injury rsch. grant rev. com. Ctr. for Disease Control, 1986-91; chairperson police equipment tech. adv. com. U.S. Dept. Justice, 1987; bd. dirs. Nat. Commn. Against Drunk Driving, 1986; presdl. appointee Nat. Hwy. Safety Adv. Com. U.S. Dept. Transp., 1986; mem. Pres.-elect Ronald Reagan's Task Force on Adminstrn. Justice, 1980; mem. traffic safety adv. coun. Ill. Sec. State. Contbr. articles to profl. jours. Chairperson bd. elders Community Christian Ch., Lincolnshire, Ill., 1983-85; pres. Okemos (Mich.) Sch. Bd., 1975-78; chairperson Okemos Community Recreation Program, 1971-74. Inducted into Football Hall of Fame Roosevelt High Sch., 1992, Disting. Grads. Hall of Fame, 1993, Wyandotte, Mich. Sports Hall of Fame, 1995. Mem. Nat. Safety Coun. (bd. dirs., v.p. for traffic safety, exec. com. 1987, 88, chairperson traffic divsn. 1984-87, chair fin. com., 1995-96, vice chmn. bd., 1996—), Mich. State U. Sch. Criminal Justice Alumni Assn. (pres. 1984-86), Il. Assn. Chiefs of Police, Univ. Club, Nat. Sheriffs Assn. (hwy. safety com.), Internat. Assn. Chiefs of Police (vice chairperson enforcement equipment adv. com. 1975-76, chairperson weapons subcom. 1977, chairperson phys. security 1979, hwy. safety com. 1974-78), Mich. State U. S. Club (life.). Avocations: golf, boating, cross country skiing, professional and college sports. Office: Northwestern U Traffic Inst 1121 Spring Lake Dr Itasca IL 60143-3200 Home: 4385 Turfway Trl Harbor Springs MI 49740-8853

BUFFETT, WARREN EDWARD, entrepreneur, investment company executive; b. Omaha, Aug. 30, 1930; s. Howard Homan and Leila (Stahl) B.; m. Susan Thompson, Apr. 19, 1952 (dec. July 29, 2004); children: Susan A., Howard, Peter; m. Astrid Manks, Aug. 30, 2006. Student, U. Pa., 1947-49; BS, U. Nebr., 1950; MS, Columbia, 1951. Investment salesman Buffett-Falk & Co., Omaha, 1951-54; security analyst Graham-Newman Corp., NYC, 1954-56; gen. partner Buffett Partnership, Ltd., Omaha, 1956-69; chmn. & CEO Berkshire Hathaway Inc., Omaha, 1970—. Chmn. bd. Berkshire Hathaway, Inc., Nat. Indemnity Co.; bd. dirs. The Coca-Cola Co., 1989-, The Washington Post Co., 1974-86, 96-. Life trustee Grinnell Coll., 1968—, Urban Institute. Named one of Forbes Richest Americans, 2006, Forbes World's Richest People, 2001, 2002, 2003, 2004, 2005, 2006, 2007, 2008, The World's Most Influential People, TIME mag., 2007, 25 Most Powerful People in Bus., Fortune Mag., 2007. Mem.: Am Acad Arts & Scis. Ranked number two on the World's Richest People list by Forbes magazine in 2001, 2002, 2003, 2004, 2005, 2006, 2007, ranked number one, 2008. Office: Berkshire Hathaway Inc 1440 Kiewit Plz Omaha NE 68131*

BUGGE, LAWRENCE JOHN, lawyer, educator; b. Milw., June 1, 1936; s. Lawrence Anthony and Anita (Westenberg) B.; m. Mary Daly, Nov. 28, 1959 (div.); m. Elaine Andersen, Jan. 29, 1977; children: Kristin, Laura, Jill, David, Carol. AB, Marquette U., 1958; JD, Harvard U., 1963. Bar: Wis. 1963. Assoc. Foley and Lardner, Milw., Madison, Wis., 1963-70, ptnr., 1970-96, of counsel, 1996—. Pres. Nat. Conf. Commrs. on Uniform State Laws, 1989-91; adj. prof. law U. Wis. Law Sch., Madison, 1997—. Mem. Wis. Bar Assn. (pres. 1980-81), Mil. Bar Assn. (pres. 1974-75), Milw. Young Lawyers Assn. (pres. 1969-70). Home: 313 Walnut Grove Dr Madison WI 53717-1228 Office: Foley & Lardner PO Box 1497 150 E Gilman St Madison WI 53701-1497 Personal E-mail: lbugge@charter.net.

BUGHER, ROBERT DEAN, professional society administrator; b. Lafayette, Ind., Oct. 17, 1925; s. Walter Earl and Lillie Victoria (Feldner) B.; m. Patricia Jean McConnell, Sept. 7, 1945; children: Vickie Leigh, Robert James. Student, Millsaps Coll., 1943, Miami U., Oxford, Ohio, 1944; BS in Civil Engring, Purdue U., 1948; MPA, U. Mich., 1951. Staff engr. Mich. Mcpl. League, 1948-53; mgr. Mcpl. Purchasing Svc., 1951-53; sec.-treas. Mich. Mcpl. Utilities Assn., 1951-53; asst. dir. Am. Pub. Works Assn., 1953-58, exec. dir., 1958-89, exec. dir. emeritus, 1990—. Lectr. Internat. Seminar on Ekistics, Athens, Greece, 1970; chmn. nat. adv. coun. Keep Am. Beautiful, Inc., 1974-75; chmn. Nat. Conf. on Solid Waste Disposal Sites, Washington, 1971; advisor pub. mgmt. program Northwestern U., 1977-82; bd. dirs. Pub. Adminstrn. Svc., Chgo., 1958-73; trustee Nat. Acad. Code Adminstrs.; chmn. Coun. Internat. Urban Liaison, 1982-84; trustee Nat. Tng. and Devel. Svc., Am. Consortium for Internat. Pub. Adminstrn.; adv. com. internat. divsn. GAO, 1979-80. Editor: pub. works sect. Municipal Yearbook Internat. City Mgmt. Assn., 1953-58, People Making Public Works History-A Century of Progress 1894-1994, 1998; cons. editor pub. works sect., Mcpl. Pub. Works Adminstrn., 1957; chmn. adv. bd. Internat. Ctr. Acad. State and Local Govts., 1985-87. Served to 1st lt. USMCR, 1943-45. Mem. ASCE (life), Am. Pub. Works Assn. (hon.), Internat. Pub. Works Fedn. (treas. 1985-89, sec.-gen. 1990), Am. Soc. Assn. Execs., Am. Soc. Pub. Adminstrn., Internat. Union Local Authorities (pres. U.S. sect. 1977-79, v.p. 1968-70, 75-77), Internat. Solid Wastes and Pub. Cleansing Assn. (v.p. 1968-70), Internat. Fedn. Mcpl. Engrs. (treas. 1976-79), Pub. Works Hist. Soc. (hon., treas. 1975-89), Sigma Alpha Epsilon. Baptist. Home: 7501 E Thompson Peak Pkwy Unit 124 Scottsdale AZ 85255 Office: 2345 Grand Blvd Ste 700 Kansas City MO 64108-2625 Business E-Mail: rdbugher@cox.net.

BUGIELSKI, ROBERT JOSEPH, state legislator; b. Chgo., June 5, 1947; s. Edward Leon and Lottie Regina (Ptak) B.; m. Dona Rosalie Obrzut, Aug. 2, 1980. BS in Bus. Edn., Chgo. State U., 1971. Tchr. Weber High Sch., Chgo., 1971-83; asst. athletic dir., 1973-78; dir. devel. Weber High Sch., Chgo., 1974-83, adminstrv. bd. dirs., 1975-83; rep. Ill. Gen. Assembly, Chgo., 1987—. Named Legislator of Yr. Am. Legis. Exch. Coun., 1991. Democrat. Roman Catholic. Office: 6839 W Belmont Ave Chicago IL 60634-4646

BUHR, FLORENCE D., county official; b. Strahan, Iowa, Apr. 7, 1933; d. Earnest G. and May (Brott) Wederquist; m. Glenn E. Buhr, 1955; children: Barbara, Lori Lynn, David. BA, U. No. Iowa, 1954. Precinct chair Polk County Dem. Ctrl. Com., Iowa, 1974-79; clerk, sec. Iowa Ho. Reps., 1974-79, 81-82; rep. dist. 85 State of Iowa, 1983-90, asst. majority leader Ho. Reps., 1985-90; state senator Iowa State Senate, 1991-95, asst. majority leader, 1992-95; Polk County supr. Des Moines, 1995—. Chairwoman Polk County Bd. Suprs., 1997. Democrat. Presbyterian. Home and Office: 4127 30th St Des Moines IA 50310-5946

BUHRMASTER, ROBERT C., manufacturing executive; b. 1947; B in Mech. Engring., Rensselaer Poly. Inst.; MBA, Dartmouth Coll. With Corning Inc., Corning, N.Y.; exec. v.p. Jostens, Inc., Mpls., 1992-93, pres., COO, 1993, CEO, 1994, chmn. bd. dirs., 1998—. Bd. dirs. Toro Corp., Nat. Alliance of Bus. Pres. Viking coun. Boy Scouts. Am.; past bd. dirs. Exec. Coun. Fgn. Diplomats, Marietta Corp. Mem. U.S. Advanced Ceramics Assn. (founding mem.). Office: Jostens 3601 Minnesota Dr STE 400 Bloomington MN 55435-6008 Office Fax: 952-897-4116.

BUHROW, WILLIAM CARL, religious organization administrator; b. Cleve., Jan. 18, 1934; s. Philip John and Edith Rose (Leutz) B.; m. Carole Corinne Craven, Feb. 14, 1959; children: William Carl Jr., David Paul, Peter John, Carole Lynn. Diploma, Phila. Coll. Bible, 1954; BA, Wheaton Coll., Ill., 1956, MA, 1959. Ordained to ministry Gen. Assn. Regular Bapt. Chs., 1958. Asst. pastor (Hydewood Park Bapt. Ch.), N. Plainfield, NJ, 1959-63; with Continental Fed. Savs. & Loan Assn., Cleve., 1963-81, sr. v.p., 1971-75, pres., chief exec. officer, dir., 1975-81; chmn. bd. Security Savs. Mortgage Corp., Citizens Service Corp., New Market Corp., CFS Service Corp., 1975-81; trustee Credit Bur. Cleve., 1975-81, Bldg. Expositions, Inc., 1974-84; registered rep. IDS/Am. Express, Cleve., 1982-83; gen. credit mgr. Forest City Enterprises, Inc., Cleve., 1983-85; pres. Forest City Ins. Agy., Inc., Cleve., 1983-85; asst. v.p. Mellon Fin. Services Corp., Cleve., 1985-87; exec. adminstr. The Gospel Ho. Ch. and Evangelistic Ctr., Walton Hills, Ohio, 1988—. Trustee Bapt. Bible Coll. and Theol. Sem., Clarks Summit, Pa., 1977-90; vice chmn. bd. deacons Cedar Hill Bapt. Ch., Cleveland Heights, Ohio, 1981-87; trustee, sec. and treas. Gospel House Prison Ministry Found., 1992—. Mem. Christian Bus. Men's Com. Internat., Nat. Assn. Ch. Bus. Adminstrn. Baptist. Home: 1044 Linden Ln Lyndhurst OH 44124-1051 Office: 14707 Alexander Rd Cleveland OH 44146-4924

BUJOLD, TYRONE PATRICK, lawyer; b. Duluth, Minn., Dec. 4, 1937; s. Dewey J. and Lucille C. (Donahue) B.; m. Delia H. Goulet, Sept. 17, 1960; children: Christopher Andrew, Anne Elizabeth, Lara Suzanne. BS, Marquette U., 1959; JD, U. Minn., 1962. Bar: Minn. 1962, U.S. Dist. Ct. Minn. 1963, U.S. Ct. Appeals (8th cir.) 1964, Wis. 1983, U.S. Dist. Ct. (we. dist.) Wis. 1985, N.D. 1987. Assoc. Furuseth & Bujold, International Falls, Minn., 1962-63, Sullivan, MacMillan, Hanft & Hastings, Duluth, 1963-68, ptnr., 1968-85, Robins, Kaplan, Miller & Ciresi, Mpls., 1985—. Mem. faculty CLE program, Minn., 1965—, Inst. CLE, Ann Arbor, Mich., 1975—, Nat. Inst. Trial Advocacy, 1983—. Mem. Commn. Fair Housing and Employment Practices, Duluth, 1970-78, City Charter Commn., Duluth, 1983-85, Plymouth, Minn., 1991—. Mem. Am. Coll. Trial Lawyers, Internat. Soc. Barristers, Am. Bd. Trial Advocates. Roman Catholic. Avocations: reading, theater, guitar, swimming.

BUKOVAC, MARTIN JOHN, horticulturist, educator; b. Johnston City, Ill., Nov. 12, 1929; s. John and Sadie (Fak) B.; m. Judith Ann Kelley, Sept. 5, 1956; 1 dau., Janice Louise. BS with honors, Mich. State U., 1951, MS, 1954, PhD, 1957; D honoris causa, U. Bonn, Germany, 1995. Asst. prof. horticulture Mich. State U., East Lansing, 1957-61, assoc. prof., 1961-63, prof., 1963; NSF sr. postdoctoral fellow Oxford U., U. Bristol, Eng., 1965-66; univ. disting. prof., 1992—. Vis. lectr. Japan Atomic Energy Rsch. Inst., 1958; adviser IAEA, Vienna, 1961; NAS exch. lectr. Coun. Acads., Yugoslavia, 1971; vis. scholar Va. Poly. Inst., Blacksburg, 1973; guest lectr. Polish Acad. Scis., 1974; disting. vis. prof. N.Mex. State U., 1976; vis. prof. Japan Soc. Promotion Sci., Osaka Prefecture U., 1977; guest lectr. Serbian Sci. Coun., Fruit Rsch. Inst., Cacak, Yugoslavia, 1979; John A. Hannah Disting. lectr. Mich. State Hort. Soc., 1980; vis. prof. U. Guelph, Ont., Can., 1982, Ohio State U., 1982, U. Zagreb, Yugoslavia, 1983, Ohio State U., 1990; collaborator Agrl. Rsch. Svc. USDA, 1982-2003; guest rschr. Hort. Rsch. Inst., Budapest, Hungary, 1983, Inst. Obstbau und Gemusebau U. Bonn, Fed. Republic Germany, 1986; Batjer Meml. lectr. Wash. State Hort. Soc., 1985; mem. agrl. rsch. adv. com. Eli Lilly Co., Indpls., 1971-88; cons. Dept. Agr.; disting. lectr. Dept. Sci. and Tech. Peoples Republic China, 1984; commencement spkr. Mich. State U., 1986; mem. internat. adv. bd. divsn. life scis. Ctr. for Nuclear Studies, Atomic Energy Commn., Grenoble, France, 1993-2000; Monselise Meml. lectr. Hebrew U., 1994; Agrl. Rsch. Svc. B.Y. Morrison Meml. lectr., 1994, Kermit Olson Meml. lectr. Univ. Minn., 1997; pres. Martin J. Bukovac Inc., 1996-2001; Donald L. Reichard Meml. lectr., Ohio State U., 1999; sci. exch. lectr. Nara (Japan) Inst. Sci. and Tech., 2000. Mem. exec. adv. bd. Ency. of Agrl. Scis., 1991-96; mem. editl. adv. bd. Ctr. for Agr. and Bioscis. Internat., 1989-2003; internat. editl. bd. Horticultural Sci., Budapest; mem. editl. bd. Ency. of Agrl. Sci., 1991-96. Pres. Okemos Music Patrons, Mich., 1973-74; bd. dirs. Mich. State U. Press, 1983-92. 1st lt. U.S. Army, 1951-53. Recipient citation meritorious rsch. Am. Hort. Soc., 1970, Disting. Faculty award Mich. State U., 1971, Disting. Svc. award Mich. Hort. Soc., 1974, Disting. Faculty award Mich. Assn. Governing Bds., 1986, Hatch Meml. Medallion award USDA, 1987, Industry Man of Yr. award Nat. Cherry Festival, 1987, Alexander von Humboldt Rsch. prize, 1995, Am. Soc. Agrl. Engring. Outstanding Paper award, 1995, Gold Veitch Meml. medal Royal Hort. Soc., 2003, Spiridon Brusina medal Croatian Soc. for Natural Scis., 2004; Bukovac Disting. Lectr. established in his honor Mich. State Hort. Soc., 1995. Fellow AAAS, Am. Soc. Hort. Sci. (hon. life, pres. 1974-75, Joseph Harvey Gourley award 1969, 76, Marion Meadows award 1975, citation of appreciation 1975, Carroll R. Miller award 1980, Outstanding Rschr. award 1988, M.A. Blake award for disting. grad. tchg. 1975, Hall of Fame inductee 2001); mem. NAS, Am. Chem. Soc., Am. Soc. Plant Biologists (Dennis R. Hoagland award 1988), Bot. Soc. Am., Scandinavian Soc. Plant Physiologists, Japanese Soc. Plant Physiologists, Internat. Soc. Hort. Sci., Soc. Exptl. Biology, Croatian Soc. Plant Physiologists (hon.), Mich. State U. Faculty Club, Sigma Xi (pres. 1978-79 rsch. award Kedzie chpt.), Phi Kappa Phi, Gamma Sigma Delta. Home: 4428 Seneca Dr Okemos MI 48864-2946 Office: Mich State U Dept Horticulture East Lansing MI 48824 Business E-Mail: bukovacm@msu.edu.

BUKTA, POLLY, state representative; b. Greenville, Pa., Apr. 3, 1937; m. Michael Bukta. BS, Mercyhurst Coll., 1962; postgrad., U. No. Iowa, 1967. Elem. tchr., Clinton, Iowa, 1967—2000; ret., 2000—; mem. Iowa Ho. Reps., Des-Moines, 1997—, mem. various coms. adminstrn. and rules, edn. and transp., asst. minority leader, 2001—02, 2003—04, 2005—. Mem.: NEA, NACCP, AAUW, Clinton Area C. of C., Clinton Edn. Assn., Iowa State Tchrs. Assn., Clinton Womens Club, Delta Kappa Gamma. Democrat. Office: State Capitol East 12th and Grand Des Moines IA 50319 also: 604 S 32nd St Clinton IA 52732 Office Phone: 515-281-7331. Personal E-mail: pollyb03@msn.com.

BULGER, BRIAN WEGG, lawyer; b. Chgo., May 27, 1951; s. John Burton and Mary Jane (Wegg) B.; m. Laura Ellen McErlean, Sept. 12, 1981; children: Burton, Kevin. AB cum laude, Georgetown U., 1972, JD, 1977. Bar: Ill. 1977, U.S. Dist. Ct. (no. dist.) Ill. 1977, U.S. Ct. Appeals (4th, 7th and 8th cirs.) 1977, U.S. Supreme Ct. 1980. From assoc. to ptnr. Pope Ballard Shepard & Fowle, Chgo., 1977-87; ptnr., dept. head Katten Muchin & Zavis, Chgo., 1987-94; founding ptnr. Meckler, Bulger & Tilson, Chgo., 1994—. Adj. prof. U. Wis. Mgmt. Inst., Milw., 1980-2000, U. Chgo. Grad. Sch. Bus., 2000— Contbr. articles to profl. jours. Mem. ABA (former chair pub. employer labor rels. com. sect. on urban state and govt. law), Ill. State Bar Assn., Georgetown Law Alumni (bd. dirs. 1984-93). Roman Catholic. Avocations: baseball, reading, boating, skeet shooting. Office: Meckler Bulger Tilson Ste 1800 123 N Wacker Dr Chicago IL 60606

BULLARD, GEORGE, newspaper editor; b. Middlesboro, Ky., Feb. 8, 1945; s. George Kibert and Frances Rose (Costanzo) B.; m. Donna DeVoe, Nov. 29, 1980 (div. May 1989); m. Susan Burzynski, Mar. 21, 1992. BA in Journalism, Mich. State U., 1971. Editor-in-chief Mich. State News, East Lansing, 1970-71; reporter The Detroit News, 1971-86, dep. city editor, 1986-87, city editor, 1987-95, asst. mng. editor/religion writer, 1995-98. Contbr. articles to newspapers and mags., 1975-86. Mem. Leadership Detroit, 1988-89. Sgt. U.S. Army, 1963-66, Korea. Fellow Religious Pub. Rels. Coun. Avocations: flying private plane, amateur radio, skiing. Office: Detroit News 615 W Lafayette Blvd Detroit MI 48226-3197

BULLARD, JAMES B., bank executive; b. Forest Lk., Minn., 1961; m. Jane Callahan; 2 children. BS in Quantitative Methods, Info. Sys., & Economics, St. Cloud State U., Minn., 1984; PhD in Econs., Ind. U., Bloomington, 1990. Economist Fed. Res. Bank St. Louis, 1990, policy advisor, briefing coord., Fed. Open Market Com., macroeconomics sect. chief, dep. dir. rsch. for monetary analysis, v.p., rsch. economist, pres., CEO, 2008—. Instr. Southern Ill. U., Edwardsville, 1992, 99, 2002, U. Mo., St. Louis, 1994, 97, 2000, 03, Wash. U., St. Louis, 1994, 98, 2000—; visitor Santa Fe Inst., 1995, Bank of Eng., London, 1996. Co-editor: Jour. Econ. Dynamics and Control; contbr. articles to profl. jours. Mem.: Econometric Soc., Soc. Econ. Dynamics, Soc. Promotion Econ. Theory, Am. Econ. Assn. Office: St Louis Fed PO Box 442 Saint Louis MO 63166-0442 Office Phone: 314-444-8444.

BULLARD, WILLIS CLARE, JR., lawyer; b. Detroit, July 12, 1943; s. Willis C. and Virginia Katherine (Gilmore) B.; children: Willis C. III, Melissa Ann, Kaila Michelle. AB, U. Mich., 1965; JD, Detroit Coll. Law, 1971. Bar: Mich. 1971. Practice of law, Detroit, 1971-77, Troy, Mich., 1977-80, Milford, Mich., 1983—; supr. Highland Twp., Mich., 1980-82; mem. Mich. Ho. of Reps., 1983-96, Mich. Senate from 15th dist., Lansing, 1996—2002; mem. from 2d dist. County Commn., 2003—, chmn. bd., 2005—. Asst. Rep. caucus chmn., 1983-84, asst. Rep. floor leader, 1985-88, chmn. House Rep. campaign, 1987-90; chmn. House taxation com., 1993-96; chmn. task force Midwestern Legis. Conf. Coun. State Govts., 1985-86; mediator cir. and dist. cts., 1988—. Bd. dirs. Dunham Lake Property Owners Assn., 1975-78, treas., 1975-76, pres., 1976-78; mem. Dunham Lake Civic Com., 1982-87; trustee Highland Twp., 1978-80, mem. zoning bd. appeals, 1979. Named Legislator of Yr. Mich. Twp. Assn., 1984, Nat. Rep. Legislator of Yr., 2000. Mem. Oakland County Bar Assn., State Bar Mich., Oakland County Assn. Twp. Suprs. (sec.-treas. 1981), Michigamua. Clubs: U. Mich. of Greater Detroit, Highland Republican, Highland Men's (sec. 1979, pres. 1980). Republican. Home: 1849 Lakeview Dr Highland MI 48357-4817 Office Phone: 248-684-1444.

BULLOCK, JOSEPH DANIEL, pediatrician, educator; b. Cin., Jan. 23, 1942; s. Joseph Craven and Emilie (Woide) B.; m. Martha Foss, June 20, 1964; children: Jennifer Zane, Sarah Harrison. BA, Wittenberg U., 1963; MD, Ohio State U., 1967, degree in pediatrics, 1969; degree in immunology, allergy, U. Calif., San Francisco, 1971. Diplomate Am. Bd. Pediat., Am. Bd. Allergy and Immunology. Clin. prof. pediatrics Ohio State U., Columbus, 1971—; pres. Midwest Allergy Assocs., Inc., Worthington, Ohio, 1971—. Contbr. articles to profl. jours. Active fund raising Wittenberg U., Springfield, Ohio, 1980-83, Columbus Sch. for Girls, 1977-86. Served to capt. USAF, 1967-71. Recipient Mead Johnson award, 1965. Fellow Am. Acad. Pediatrics, Am. Acad. Allergy, Am. Coll. Allergists (Bd. Regents 1979-82, Clemens von Pirquet award 1968, 69, 70, 71), Am. Thoracic Soc., Interasma, Ohio Soc. Allergy and Immunology (pres. 1985-87). Clubs: Columbus Country; The Golf (New Albany, Ohio); Indian Creek Country (Miami Beach, Fla.), The Surf (Surfside, Fla.). Republican. Lutheran. Home: 189 N Parkview Ave Columbus OH 43209-1435 Office: 8080 Ravines Edge Ct Columbus OH 43235-5424 Office Phone: 614-846-5944.

BULLOCK, STEVEN CARL, lawyer; b. Anderson, Ind., Jan. 19, 1949; s. Carl Pearson and Dorothy Mae (Colle) B.; m. Debra Bullock; children: Bradford, Christine, Justin, Evan. BA, Purdue U., 1971; JD, Detroit Coll., 1985. Bar: Mich. 1985, U.S. Dist. Ct. (ea. dist.) 1985, Ct. of Appeals (6th cir.) 1993, U.S. Supreme Ct. 1993. Pvt. pracitce, Inkster, Mich., 1985—. With USAF, 1971-75. Mem. Mich. Bar Assn. (criminal law sect.), Detroit Bar Assn., Detroit Founders Soc., Recorder's Ct. Bar Assn., Suburban Bar Assn., Nat. Assn. Criminal Def. Attys., Criminal Def. Lawyers of Mich., Wayne County Criminal Def. Bar Assn. Avocations: golf, travel. Office: 2228 Inkster Rd Inkster MI 48141-1811 Office Phone: 313-562-6500. E-mail: lawone123@aol.com.

BULLOCK, WILLIAM HENRY, bishop emeritus; b. Maple Lake, Minn., Apr. 13, 1927; s. Loren W. and Anne C. (Raiche) B. BA in Philosophy, U. Notre Dame, 1948, MA in Liturgy and Religious Edn., 1962; EdS in Edn. and Adminstrn., St. Thomas U., St. Paul, 1969, LHD (hon.), 2005; HHD (hon.), St. Ambrose U., Davenport, Iowa, 1989. Ordained priest Archdiocese of St. Paul and Mpls., 1952, aux. bishop, 1980-87; ordained bishop, 1980; assoc. pastor Ch. of St. Stephens, Mpls., 1952-55, Ch. of Our Lady of Grace, Edina, Minn., 1955-56, Ch. of Incarnation, Mpls., 1956-57; instr. St. Thomas Acad., St. Paul, 1957—71, headmaster Mendota Heights, Minn., 1967—71; pastor Ch. of St. John the Baptist, Excelsior, Minn., 1971-80; bishop Diocese of Des Moines, 1987—93, Diocese of Madison, Wis., 1993—2003, bishop emeritus, 2003—. V.p. Wis. Cath. Conf.; mem. Cath. Relief Svcs. Bd. Trustee St. Francis Sem. Mem. KC (4th degree), US Bishops-Region II, at. Conf. Cath. Bishops (mem. com. evangelization), Knights of Holy Sepulchre, Cath. Relief Svcs. (exec. com., Africa com., com. overseas programs and ops.) Knights of Holy Sepulchre. Roman Catholic. Office: Diocese of Madison Cath Pastoral Ctr PO Box 44983 Madison WI 53744-4983*

BULLY-CUMMINGS, ELLA M., police chief; b. Japan; d. Daniel Lee Bully; m. William Cummings. BA with hons. in Pub. Adminstrn., Madonna State U., 1993; JD cum laude, Mich. State U., 1998. Bar: Mich. 1998. From police officer to chief police Detroit (Mich.) Police Dept., 1977—2003, chief police, 2003—; assoc. Miller, Canfield, Paddockand Stone, PLC, 1999—2000, Foley & Lardner, 2000—02. Mem.: Mich. Assn. Chiefs Police, Nat. Orgn. Black Law Enforcement Execs., Internat. Assn. Chiefs Police, Wolverine Bar Assn., Nat. Bar Assn. Office: Detroit Police Dept 1300 Beaubien Detroit MI 48226

BULRISS, MARK, chemicals executive; BSCE, Clarkson U., 1973. Process engr. Procter & Gamble, 1973-77; gen. mgr. GE Plastics, 1977-93; pres. laminates divsn. AlliedSignal Inc., 1993-95, pres. electronics materials divsn., 1995-96, pres. polymers divsn., 1996-98; pres., CEO Great Lakes Chem., Indpls., 1998—, chmn. bd. dirs., 2000—. Office: Great Lakes Chemical Corp 199 Benson Rd Waterbury CT 06749-0001

BUMP, BEVIN B., lawyer; b. Chadron, Nebr., Sept. 7, 1926; Attended, Chadron State Coll.; BS, JD, Univ. Nebr., 1952. Bar: Nebr. 1952, US Dist. Ct. Nebr. Dist. 1952. City atty., Chadron, Nebr., 1953—2006; dep. county atty. Dawes County, Nebr., 1955—59, county atty. Nebr., 1959—70; atty. Bump & Bump, Chadron, ebr., 1952—. Fellow: Am. Coll. Trust & Estate Counsel; mem.: Am. Bar Found., Nebr. Bar Found., Am. Judicature Soc., Nebr. Assn. Trail Attys., Nebr. County Atty. Assn. (pres. 1966), Nebr. State Bar Assn. (pres. 1990—91), W Nebr. Bar Assn. (pres. 1978—79), ABA (bd. gov. 2004—). Office: Bump & Bump PO Box 1140 Chadron NE 69337-1140 Office Phone: 308-432-4411.

BUNCH, HOWARD MCRAVEN, engineering educator, researcher; b. Texarkana, Tex., Aug. 20, 1926; s. Howard Phillips and Truby Electra (Lowrance) B.; m. Frances Findlater, Dec. 19, 1953; children: James Allday, John Findlater, Howard Carscaden, Helen Clare. BA, U. Tex., 1949, MBA, 1958. Cert. mgmt. acct., mfg. engr., tech. observer. V.p. Bunch Riesen Co., San Angelo, Tex., 1949-56; sec.-treas. United Butone Co., San Angelo, Tex., 1956-57; sr. engr. S.W. Rsch. Inst., San Antonio, 1957-63, head indsl. econs. Houston, 1963-68; v.p. Olson Labs., Dearborn, Mich., 1968-73; cons. Ann Arbor, Mich., 1973-76; rsch. scientist U. Mich., Ann Arbor, 1976—99, Navsea prof., 1981—99, emeritus prof., 1999—. Hon. prof. (life) Zhenziang (China) Shipbuilding Inst., 1987, vis. prof., 1983; vis. lectr. MIT, 1984—. Author: Ship Production, 1988; contbr. articles to profl. jours. Fellow Soc. Naval Archs. and Marine Engrs. (William H. Webb medal 1993). Office: U Michigan Dept Naval Arch 2600 Draper Dr Ann Arbor MI 48109-2145

BUNCHER, CHARLES RALPH, epidemiologist, educator, biostatistician; b. Dover, NJ, Jan. 18, 1938; BS, MIT, 1960; MS, Harvard U., 1964, ScD, 1967. Statistician Atomic Bomb Casualty Comsn., NAS, 1967-70; chief biostatistician Merrell-Nat. Labs., 1970-73, asst. prof. stats., 1970-73; prof. and dir. divsn. epidemiology and biostats. Med. Coll., U. Cin., 1973-96, prof. biostats. and epidemiology, 1973—, dir. grad. edn., 2001—. Editor: Pharmaceutical Industry, 2006. Fellow Am. Stats. Assn., Am. Coll. Epidemiology; mem. APHA, Soc. Epidemiol. Rsch., Soc. Med. Decision Making, Soc. Clin. Trials, Tau Beta Pi, Delta Omega. Achievements include design of experiments; clinical trials; screening; risk analysis; statistical research; pharmaceutical research; biostatistical analysis; pharmaceutical statistics; diagnosis; treatment; research in ALS epidemiology; cancer epidemiology; environmental epidemiology; occupational epidemiology. Office: U Cincinnati Div of Epidemiology & Biostatistics PO Box 670183 Cincinnati OH 45267-0183 Office Phone: 513-558-1410. Business E-Mail: charles.buncher@uc.edu.

BUNDY, BILL, radio personality; b. Menomonie, Wis. Grad. broadcasting, Brown Inst., Mpls.; postgrad., U. Wis. With CNN, CBS; radio host, news anchor Sta. WCCO Radio, Mpls. Office: WCCO 625 2nd Ave S Minneapolis MN 55402

BUNDY, DAVID DALE, librarian, educator; b. Longview, Wash., Sept. 27, 1948; s. Cedric Dale and Florence (Prichard) B.; m. Consuelo Ann Briones, Dec. 19, 1969 (div. 1982); children: Keith Dale, Cheryl Ann; m. Melody Lynn Garlock, June 14, 1986; children: Rachel Lynn, Lydia Marie, Joel David. BA, Seattle Pacific U., 1969; MDiv, ThM, Asbury Theol. Sem., Wilmore, Ky., 1973; Licentiate, Cath. U. Louvain, Louvain-la-Neuve, Belgium, 1978. Dean Inst. Univ. Ministry Louvain, 1977-81; rsch. asst. Cath. U. Louvain, 1978-85; assoc. prof. Christian Origins, collection devel. libr. Asbury Theol. Sem., Wilmore, 1985-91; libr., assoc. prof. ch. history Christian Theol. Sem., Indpls., 1991—. Dir. Wesleyan Holiness Studies Ctr., Wilmore, 1990-91. Author: Keswick, 1985; editor: Pietist and Wesleyan Studies; contbr. articles to profl. jours. Grantee Fondation Universitaire, Belgium, 1977-84, Pew Charitable Trusts, 1988, Wesleyan/Holiness Studies Ctr., 1992, NEH, 1989—. Mem. N.Am. Patristic Soc., Symposium Syriacum (internat. dir. 1988—), Am. Acad. Religion, Assn. Christian Arabic Studies (editor Mid. Ea. Christian Studies), Wesleyan Theol. Soc. Democrat. Mem. United Meth. Ch. Office: Christian Theol Sem 1000 W 42d St PO Box 88267 Indianapolis IN 46208-0267 Home: 1009 N Pasadena Ave Azusa CA 91702-2119

BUNGE, CHARLES ALBERT, library science educator; b. Kimball, Nebr., Mar. 18, 1936; s. Louis Herman and Leona Hazel (Cromwell) B.; m. Joanne C. VonStoeser, Aug. 20, 1960; children: Lorraine A., Jeffrey C. Stephen L. AB, U. Mo., 1959; MSLS, U. Ill., 1960, PhD, 1967. Reference libr. Daniel Boone Regional Libr., Columbia, Mo., 1960-62; Ball State Tchrs. Coll., Muncie, Ind., 1962-64; rsch. assoc. Libr. Rsch. Ctr., U. Ill., 1964-67; mem. faculty Sch. Libr.

and Info. Studies U. Wis., Madison, 1967—97, prof. emeritus, 1997—. Author: Professional Education and Reference Efficiency, 1967; columnist: Wilson Library Bull, 1972-81. Mem. ALA (pres. ref. and adult svcs. divsn. 1987-88, chair com. on accreditation 1990-92, Mudge award 1983, mem. coun. 1993-96, Beta Phi Mu award 1997), Assn. Libr. and Info. Sci. Edn. (pres. 1980-81, Prof. Contribution award 1997), Wis. Libr. Assn. (pres. 1972-73, Libr. of Yr. 1983), Phi Beta Kappa, Beta Phi Mu. Home: 509 Orchard Dr Madison WI 53711-1316

BUNKOWSKE, EUGENE WALTER, religious studies educator; b. Wecota, SD, July 3, 1935; s. Walter Adolph and Ottille Sophie (Richter) B.; m. Bernice Bock; children: Barbara, ancy, Walter, Joel. AA, Concordia Acad. and Jr. Coll., St. Paul, 1955; BA, Concordia Seminary, 1958, BD, MDiv, 1960; MA in Linguistics, UCLA, 1964, C Phil in Linguistics, 1968, PhD in Linguistics, 1976; LittD, Concordia Coll., 1983; DD, Christ Coll., 1991; DLitt, Concordia U., St. Paul, 1997. Missionary Luth. Ch.-Mo. Synod, Africa, 1960-82, congl. pastor, pioneer ch. planter, 1960-74, chmn. Nung Udoe dist., 1960-61, builder chs., schs., hosp., 1960-67, medical worker Ogoja Province, 1961-66, justice of peace Ogoja Province, 1962-74, chmn. Ogoja dist., 1964-69, chmn. Evang. Luth. Mission in Nigeria, 1965-67, analyzer Yala lang., orthography devel. & Bible translator, 1967-71, counselor to Yala Paramount Chief, 1969-74, fourth v.p., 1989-92, 95-98, third v.p., 1992-95; dir. mission Concordia Theol. Seminary, Ft. Wayne, Ind., 1982-88, mission prof., 1982—2002, mission chair prof., 1986—2002, grad. prof. mission, 1990—2002, chmn. dept. pastoral ministries, 1985-88, chmn. mission dept., 1988—90, supr. D Missiology program, chmn. Mission and Comm. Congress, 1984—; Fiechtner chair prof. Oswald Hoffmann Sch. Christian Outreach Concordia U., St. Paul, 2002—. Ling. cons. and adminstr. Luth. Bible Translators, Liberia, Sierra Leone, 1970-74; dir. Vacation Inst. for Tng. in Applied Linguistics and Bible Translation, U. Liberia, Monrovia, 1971-74; cons. United Bible Socs., 1974-80, regional translations coord., 1980-82; cons. Near West Side Cleve. Cluster, St. Paul Internat. Mission Bd. Author: Orede, 1973, Woka yi Ijona, 1974, Topics in Yala Grammar, 1976, God's Mission in Action, 1986, The Body of Christ in Mission, 1987, God's Communicators in Mission, 1988, Receptor Oriented Gospel Communication, 1989, The State of Gospel Communication Today, 1990, Church Growth: A Biblical Perspective, 1991, The Role of the Laity in Gospel Communications, 1992, The Christian Family: Nurture and Outreach, 1993, Multicultural Outreach: Bridging Cultures -Theirs and Ours, 1995, Struggling with Change: Reaching the Lost in Changing Times, 1999, The Lutherans in Mission, 2000; translator Yala Bible, 1967-74; contbr. articles to religious and profl. publs., chpts. to books. Mem. God's Word to Nations Bible Soc. (bd. dirs., trans. and tech. cons.), World Mission Prayer League (bd. dirs.), All Nations Mission (bd. dirs., cons.), Luth. Soc. for Missiology (founding organizer). Republican. Lutheran. Avocations: travel, reading, hiking. Office Phone: 651-603-6252. Business E-Mail: bunkowske@csp.edu.

BUNN, RONALD FREEZE, retired lawyer, academic administrator, political scientist; b. Jonesboro, Ark., Aug. 11, 1929; s. S. Neal and Velma (Freeze) B.; m. Rita E. Hess, Mar. 29, 1955; children: Robin Gail, Katharine Sue, Lisabeth Joann. BA, Rhodes Coll., 1951, LLD (hon.), 1973; MA, Duke U., 1953, PhD, 1956; postgrad., U. Cologne, Fed. Republic Germany, 1954-55; JD, U. Mo., 1989. Bar: Harorrd Inst. Ednl. Mgmt., 1983, Mo. 1990. Instr. U. Tex., Austin, 1956-59, asst. prof., 1960-64; asso. prof. La. State U., Baton Rouge, 1964-67, U Houston, 1967-69; prof., dean U Houston (Grad. Sch.), 1969-74, interim dean arts and scis., 1972-74, asso. dean faculties, 1974-75, acting v.p., dean faculties, 1975-76; v.p. acad. affairs State U. N.Y. at Buffalo, 1976-80; provost U. Mo., Columbia, 1980-86, prof. polit. sci., 1986—2000, prof. emeritus, 2000—; ptnr. Shurtleff, Froeschner and Bunn, Columbia, 1992—2007; adj. prof. law U. Mo., Columbia, 2001. Vis. lectr. Ind. U., 1962; cons. Coun. Grad. Schs., 1970-77. Author: (with others) Politics and Civil Liberties in Europe, 1967, German Politics and the Spiegel Affair: A Case Study of the Bonn System, 1968; contbr.: Employers Assns. and Industrial Relations, 1984; News and Notes editor: Jour. Politics, 1968-70; contbr. articles profl. jours. Bd. dirs. S.W. Center for Urban Research, Houston, chmn. bd., 1975-76. Fulbright predoctoral scholar, 1954-55, Fulbright rsch. scholar, 1963; NATO sr. fellow in sci., 1973, Paul Harris fellow, Rotary Found. Mem. Mo. Bar Assn. (labor law com.), Admitted US Dist. Ct., US 8th Cir. Ct, So. Polit. Sci. Assn. (past mem. exec. coun.), Nat. Employment Lawyers Assn., Southwestern Polit. Sci. Assn. (past v.p.), Am. Coun. on Germany, Phi Beta Kappa (pres. Mo. Alpha chpt. 1986-88), Omicron Delta Kappa, Rotary, Tiwanis, Sigma Alpha Epsilon, Pi Sigma Alpha. also: 25 N 9th St Columbia MO 65201-4845

BUNN, WILLIAM BERNICE, III, occupational health and environmental medicine executive, epidemiologist, lawyer; b. Raleigh, NC, June 28, 1952; s. William Bernice Jr. and Clara Eva (Ray) B.; m. Shirley Welch, July 31, 1982; children: Ashley Howell, Elizabeth Jordan. AB, Duke U., 1974, MD, JD, 1979; MPH, U. N.C., 1983. Diplomate Am. Bd. Internal and Occupational Medicine. Intern, then resident in internal medicine Duke U. Med. Ctr., 1981-83, fellow in occupational medicine dept. community medicine, 1983; asst. prof. Sch. of Medicine Duke U., Durham, N.C., 1984-86, dir. rsch. in occupational medicine Sch. of Medicine, 1985-86; dir. occupational health and environmental affairs Bristol Myers Co., Wallingford, Conn., 1986-87, sr. dir. occupational health and environ. affairs, 1987-88; asst. clin. prof. Yale U., New Haven, 1986—; clin. asst. prof. U. Colo., Boulder, 1989; assoc. clin. prof. U. Cin., 1989—; corp. med. dir. Manville Sales Corp., Denver, 1988, v.p., corp. med. dir., 1988-89, sr. dir. for health safety and environ., v.p., 1989-92; dir. internat. med. affairs Mobil Corp., Princeton, N.J., 1992—; med. dir., dir. health, workers compensation, health benefits & safety Navistar Internat. Corp., Chgo., v.p. health safety and productivity, 1998—, v.p. health safety security and productivity, 2003—; prof. Northwestern U. Sch. Medicine; assoc. prof. U. Ill. Sch. Medicine. Cons. author, co-editor Dellacorte Publs., N.Y.C., 1984-87; sci. adv. bd. U.S. EPA, Washington, 1991—; chmn. radiation epidemiology com. AS, Washington, 1991-95; assoc. prof. clin. preventive medicine Northwestern Sch. Medicine; bd. sci. counselors Nat. Inst. Occupl. Safety and Health. Author: (with others) Effects of Exposure to Toxic Gases, 1986; author, editor: Poisoning, 1986, Occupational Problems in Clinical Practice; editor: Occupational and Environmental Medicine; editor, author: Issues in International Occupational and Environmental Medicine, 1997, International Occupational and Environmental Medicine, 1998. Bd. dirs. Colo. Safety Assn., Denver, 1988-90, Gaylord Hosp., Wallingford, 1987-88, Meriden-Wallingford Hosp., 1986-88, Chem. Industry Inst. Toxicology, 1989-91, Am. Coll. Occupational and Environ. Medicine, 1993—. NIOSH scholar, 1980; NIH fellow, 1982-83, Nat. Inst. Occupational Safety and Health fellow, 1983-84. Fellow Am. Occupl. Medicine Assn. (co-chmn. acad. affairs com. and publs. com. 1985-90, nat. affairs com. 1985-86, chmn. pubs. com. 1990, bd. dirs. 1993—, chair internat. coun. 1994, sec. 1995, mem. exec. com. 1995), Am. Coll. Occupl. and Environ. Medicine; mem. ACP, AMA, APHA, Occupl. Medicine Assn. Conn. (sec., pres.-elect 1986-88), Internat. Coll. Occupl. Health, Phi Beta Kappa, Phi Eta Sigma. Office: 455 Cityfront Plaza Dr Chicago IL 60611-5503 also: Yale U Dept Epidemiology & Pub Health New Haven CT 06520 also: U Colo Sch Pharmacy Dept Toxicology Boulder CO 80309-0001 also: U Cin Dept Occupational Med Cincinnati OH 45267-0001

BUNNELL, LINDA HUNT, academic administrator; d. Byron and Bobbye Bunnell. BA in English and Comm., Baylor U., 1964; MA in English Lang. and Lit., U. Colo., 1967, PhD in English Lit., 1970. Asst. prof. English U. Calif., Riverside, 1970-77, asst. dean coll. humanities, 1972—77; from asst. dean to dean academics Calif. State U. Sys., 1977-87; vice chancellor acad. affairs Minn. State U. Sys., St. Paul, 1987-93; chancellor U. Colo., Colorado Springs, 1993—2001; sr. v.p. higher edn. Coll. Bd., 2001—02; CEO Bunnell Assocs., Colo. Springs, Colo., 2002—04; chancellor U. Wis., Stevens Point, 2004—. Active Minn. Women's Econ. Round Table, 1989-93; mem. exec. com. Nat. Coun. for Accreditation Tchr. Edn., 1996-99; bd. dirs. Aspirus Health Care, 2005-. Mem. St. Paul chpt. ARC; mem. cmty. bd. Norwest Bank, Colorado Springs, 1997—, mem. El Pomar awards for Excellence com., 1997—; mem. leadership commn. Am. Coun. Edn., 1997-2000; mem. subcom. ROTC; mem. edn. com. U.S. Army, 1998-2001. Recipient Disting. Alumni award Baylor U., 1995; named leader of yr., Colo. Springs Econ. Devel. Coun., 2001; Woodrow Wilson dissertation fellow, Univ. Colo. Avocations: gardening, baseball, cooking, sable burmese cats. Office: U Wis Stevens Point 2100 Main St Stevens Point WI 54481-3897 Office Phone: 715-346-2123. Business E-Mail: lbunnell@uwsp.edu.

BUOEN, ROGER, newspaper editor; Nat. news editor Star Tribune. Office: Star Tribune 425 Portland Ave Minneapolis MN 55488-0002

BURACK, ELMER HOWARD, management educator; b. Chgo., Oct. 21, 1927; s. Charles and Rose (Taerbaum) B.; m. Ruth Goldsmith, Mar. 18, 1930; children— Charles Michael, Robert Jay, Alan Jeffrey BS, U. Ill., 1950; MS, Ill. Inst. Tech., 1956; PhD, Northwestern U., 1964. Prodn. supt. Richardson Co., Melrose Park, Ill., 1953-55; prodn. control mgr. Fed. Tool Corp., Lincolnwood, Ill., 1955-59; mgmt. cons. Booz, Allen & Hamilton, Chgo, 1959-60; mem. faculty Ill. Inst. Tech., Chgo, 1960-78, prof. mgmt., 1978; prof. mgmt., chair U. Ill.-Chgo., 1978—, head dept., dir. doctoral studies CBA, 1990-96, prof. mgmt. emeritus, 1997. Pres. Ill. Mgmt. Tng. Inst., 1975-77; mem. Ill. Gov. Adv. Coun. Employment and Tng., 1976-83, vice chmn., 1980-83; mem. NSF mission to Russia, 1979. Author: Manpower Planning, 1972, Personnel Management, 1982, Growing-Careers for Women, 1980, Introduction to Management, 1983, Career planning and Management, 1983, Planning for Human Resources, 1983, Creative Human Resource Planning, 1988, Career Management, 1990, Corporate Resurgence and the New Employment Relationships, 1993, Human Resource Planning, 4th edit., 2001, Retiring Retirement, 2002; contbr. articles to profl. jours. With USAAF, 1945-47 Research grantee Dept. Labor, 1965-68; recipient Alumni award for disting. svc. Coll. Bus. U. Ill., Chgo., 1996. Mem. Nat. Acad. Mgmt. (chmn. pers./human resource divsn. 1974-75, health divsn. 1978-79), Human Resource Mgmt. Assn. Chgo. (pres. 1974-75), Soc. Human Resource Mgmt., Pers. Accreditation Inst. (bd. dirs. 1978-89), Midwest Human Resource Planners Group (founding mem., bd. dirs. 1984-95), B'nai B'rith. Office: U Ill MC243 601 S Morgan St Rm 718 Chicago IL 60607-7100

BURATTI, DENNIS P., lawyer; b. Madison, Wis., 1949; JD, U. Wis., 1973. Bar: Wis. 1973, Minn. 1973. Gen. counsel Ryan Cos., Mpls. Office: Ryan Companies Ste 300 50 S 10th St Minneapolis MN 55403

BURBACH, MIKE, editor; BA in Journalism and German, U. ND, 1982. With Grand Forks Herald, ND; news editor AgWeek Mag., Grand Forks; mng. editor Aberdeen Am. ews, SD, 1990—92; editor Minot Daily News, ND, 1992—95; asst. bus. editor Detroit Free Press, 1995—97; v.p., exec. editor Columbus Ledger-Enquirer, Ga., 1997—2004; mng. editor Akron Beacon Jour., Ohio, 2004—. Office: Akron Beacon Journal 44 E Exchange St PO Box 640 Akron OH 44309-0640

BURBANK, GARY, radio personality; b. July 29, 1941; Radio host 700 WLW, Cin.

BURCH, STEPHEN KENNETH, finance company executive, real estate investor; b. Fairmont, W.Va., Feb. 1, 1945; s. Kenneth Edward and Gloria Lorraine (Wilson) B.; m. Juliana Yuan Yuan, June 17, 1972 (div. Feb. 1985); children: Emily, Adrien. AB in Econs., Washington U., St. Louis, 1969. V.p. TSI Mgmt., Los Angeles, 1970-71; pres. Investors Choice Cattle Co., Los Angeles, 1972-76; v.p. Clayton Brokerage Co., St. Louis, 1976-84; pres. Yuan Med. Lab., St. Louis, 1976-78; v.p. Restaurant Assocs., St. Louis, 1982-83, Am. Capital Equities, St. Louis, 1984-89; pres. Burch Properties, Inc., St. Louis, 1984—; owner Clayton-Hanley, Inc., St. Louis, 1987-88; pres., owner Clayton Securities Services, Inc., St. Louis, 1988—2005; CEO Huntleigh Securities Corp., 2000—06, also bd. dirs. Mng. ptnr. 600 S. Ptnrs., St. Louis, 1976-87, Midvale Ptnrs., St. Louis, 1979—; mng. mem. Del Coronado Investment Co., LLC, 1997—, sec., treas. Equity Concepts, Inc., St. Louis, 1992-. Bd. dirs. AMC Cancer Rsch. Ctr., 1989-91. Mem. Sigma Phi Epsilon (pres. alumni bd. 1981-87). Avocations: wine, movies. Office: Equity Concepts Inc Bonhomme Ave 24th Fl Saint Louis MO 63105 Personal E-mail: burchproperties@hotmail.com.

BURCH, THADDEUS JOSEPH, JR., physics professor, priest; b. Balt., June 4, 1930; s. Thaddeus and Francis Fidelis (Greenwell) B. AB, Bellarmine Coll., 1954; MA, Fordham U., 1956, MS, 1966, PhD, 1968; STB, Woodstock Coll., 1960, STL, 1962. Ordained priest, Roman Cath. Ch., 1961. Joined S.J. Roman Cath. Ch., 1948; asst. prof. St. Joseph's Coll., Phila., 1969-72, Fordham U., NYC, 1972-74; vis. assoc. prof. U. Conn., Storrs, 1974-76; assoc. prof. Marquette U., Milw., 1976-80, prof., 1980—, chmn. dept. physics, 1977-86, acting dean grad. sch., 1985-87, dean grad. sch., 1987—2003, dir. spl. projects, 2003—, acting vice provost rsch. and dean Grad. Sch., 2005, dir. spl. projects, 2005—. Univ. del. Argonne (Ill.) Univs. Assn., 1977-82; instl. rev. bd. Med. Coll. Wis., 2000— Contbr. articles on physics to profl. jours. Mem. Am. Phys. Soc., Am. Assn. Physics Tchrs., Sigma Xi Home: 230 Jefferson St Leonardtown MD 20650-4800 Office: 1404 W Wisconsin Milwaukee WI 53233 Business E-Mail: thaddeus.burch@marquette.edu.

BURCHAM, EVA HELEN (PAT), retired electronics technician; b. Bloomfield, Ind., Apr. 11, 1941; d. Paul Harold and Hazel Helen (Buzan) B. Grad., Blackstone Sch. of Law, 1988, Paralegal Inst., Phoenix, 1991; grad. paralegal, So. Career Inst., Boca Raton, Fla., 1991; grad. in Forensics, PCDI, 2007. With Naval Weapons Support Ctr./Crane Div. Naval Surface Warfare, Crane, Ind., 1967-76, 78-80; electronics technician Naval Weapons Support Ctr., Crane, Ind., 1980-97; ret., 1980. With U.S. Army, 1976-77, with Res. 1977-81. Named to Am. Women's Hall of Fame. Mem. NAFE (exec. bd. chair), NOW, Am. Soc. Naval Engrs., Soc. Logistics Engrs., Am. Legion, Federally Employed Women, Fed. Women's Program, Profl. Women's Network (pres. 1993, bd. dirs.), Blacks in Govt., Nat. Paralegal Assn. (registered paralegal), Nat. Fedn. Paralegal Assn., Inc., Toastmasters (gov.). Roman Catholic. Home: 200 W Washington St Loogootee IN 47553-2324 Personal E-mail: pat_burcham@yahoo.com.

BURCHINOW, NARAN U., lawyer; b. Newark, 1953; m. Eileen Conlon; children: Alexandra, Emily, Stephanie, Victoria. Grad., Princeton U., 1975, Boston U., 1978. Pvt. practice Csaplar & Bok, Boston, Fine & Ambrogne, Chgo.; sr. atty. Continental Bank N.A., Chgo., 1987—91; ops. counsel, gen. counsel Deutsche Fin. Svcs. (formerly ITT Comml. Fin. Corp.), St. Louis, 1991—2004; gen. counsel The Andersons, Inc., 2004—. Office: The Andersons Inc 480 W Dussel Dr Maumee OH 43537 Office Phone: 419-893-5050. Office Fax: 419-891-6670.

BURDI, ALPHONSE ROCCO, anatomist; b. Chgo., Aug. 28, 1935; s. Alphonse Rocco and Anna (Basilo) B.; m. Sandra Shaw, Mar. 22, 1968; children— Elizabeth Anne, Sarah Lynne. BS, No. Ill. U., DeKalb, 1957; MS, U. Ill., 1959, U. Mich., 1961, PhD, 1963; Doctorate (hon.), U. Athens, Greece, 2000. Predoctoral fellow physiology U. Ill., 1957-59; NSF summer fellow U. Mich., 1960, NIH trainee, 1960-61, NIH predoctoral research fellow, 1962, mem. faculty, 1962—, prof. emeritus cell and devel. biology, 2003—. Rsch. scientist emeritus Ctr. Human Growth and Devel., 2003; dir. integrated pre-med.-med. program U. Mich. Mem. editorial bd.: Cleft Palate Jour. 1972-88, Am. Jour. Phys. Anthropology, 1971-75, C.C. Thomas Am. Lectr. Series in Anatomy, 1971-88, Jour. Dental Research, 1977-87. Grantee NIH. Mem. Internat. Assn. Dental Research, Am. Assn. Dental Research, Am. Cleft Palate Assn., Teratology Soc., Am. Assn. Anatomists, Am. Assn. Phys. Anthropology, Sigma Xi. Home: 2600 Page Ct Ann Arbor MI 48104-6249 Office: U Mich Dept Cell & Devel Biology Basic Science Research Bldg Ann Arbor MI 48109-0616 Office Phone: 734-764-4358. Business E-Mail: alburdi@umich.edu.

BURDISS, JAMES E., paper company executive; b. May 15, 1951; BS, So. Ill. U.; MBA, U. Va. With Ernst & Young LLP, 1995—97; prin. Computer Scis. Corp., 1997—2001; sr. dir. enterprise transformation project Smurfit-Stone Container Corp., Chgo., 2001—02, v.p., chief info. officer, 2002—. Office: Smurfit Stone Container 150 N Michigan Ave Chicago IL 60601

BURG, RANDALL K., federal judge; b. Mpls., Apr. 11, 1951; BA, U. Minn., 1973, JD, 1976. Part-time magistrate judge U.S. Dist. Ct. Minn., Bemidji, 1990—.

BURGDOERFER, STUART, retail executive; m. Laney Burgdoerfer; 2 children. BS, Ind. U.; MBA Mgmt. Strategy, Northwestern U. Mgr. CSC Index, Deloitte and Touche; sr. dir. fin., dir. strategic and fin. planning Pizza Hut/Tricon Global Restaurants, 1992—98; v.p. fin. planning Limited Brands, Inc., Columbus, Ohio, 1998; CFO White Barn Candle Co., Ltd. Brands, 1999—2000; v.p. to sr. v.p. fin., controller Limited Brands., Inc., Columbus, Ohio, 2000—04; sr. v.p. fin. Home Depot, 2004—06; exec. v.p. fin. Limited Brands, Inc., Columbus, Ohio, 2006—07; exec. v.p., CFO Limited Brands., Inc., Columbus, Ohio, 2007—. Office: Limited Brands Inc 3 Limited Pkwy Columbus OH 43230

BURGESS, JAMES EDWARD, publishing executive; b. LaCrosse, Wis., Apr. 5, 1936; s. William Thomas and Margaret (Forseth) B.; m. Catherine Eleanor, Dec. 20, 1958; children: Karen E. Burgess Hardy, J. Peter, Sydney Ann, R. Curtis Student, Wayland Acad.; BS, U. Wis. Pub. Ind. Record, Helena, Mont., 1969-71, Tribune, LaCrosse, Wis., 1971-74; v.p. newspapers Lee Enterprises, Davenport, Iowa, 1974-81, exec. v.p., 1981-84, dir., 1974-85, Madison (Wis.) Newspapers, Inc., 1975-93, pres., 1984-93; pub. Wis. State Jour., Madison, 1984-94. Chmn. Edgewood Coll., Madison, 1984—; founder Future Madison, Inc.; chmn. SAVE Commn.; chair bd. dirs. Madison Cmty. Found., U. Wis. Med. Found.; v.p. Madison Mus. Modern Art. Mem. Wis. Newspaper Assn. (past pres.), Inland Daily Press Assn. (pres., chmn. 1982-84), Wis. Assn. Lakes (bd. dirs., pres., chair). Home: 125 N Hamilton St Madison WI 53703

BURGESS, JAMES HARLAND, physics professor, researcher; b. Portland, Oreg., May 11, 1929; m. Dorothy R. Crosby, June 10, 1951; children: Karen, Donald, Joanne. BS, Wash. State U., 1949, MS, 1951; PhD, Washington U., St. Louis, 1955. Sr. engr. Sylvania Electric Products, Mountain View, Calif., 1955-56; research assoc. Stanford U., Palo Alto, Calif., 1956-57, asst. prof. physics, 1958-62; assoc. prof. Washington U., St. Louis, 1962-73, prof., 1973-98, prof. emeritus, 1998—. Cons. in field, 1956-66. Mem. Am. Phys. Soc., Am. Assn. Physics Tchrs., Phi Beta Kappa, Sigma Xi Office: Washington U Physics Dept 1 Brookings Dr Saint Louis MO 63130-4899 Business E-Mail: jhb@wuphys.wustl.edu.

BURGESS, RICHARD RAY, oncologist, molecular biologist, biotechnologist, educator, researcher, consultant; b. Mt. Vernon, Wash., Sept. 8, 1942; s. Robert Carl and Irene Marjorie (Wegner) B.; m. Ann Baker, June 17, 1967; children— Kristin, Andreas BS in Chemistry, Calif. Inst. Tech., 1964; PhD in Biochemistry and Molecular Biology, Harvard U., 1969. Helen Hay Whitney fellow Inst. Molecular Biology, Geneva, 1969-71; asst. prof. oncology McArdle Lab. Cancer Research U. Wis., Madison, 1971-77, assoc. prof., 1977-82, prof., 1982—, dir. Biotech. Ctr., 1984-96, James D. Watson Prof. Oncology, 2001—. Cons. in field; mem. SF study sect. in biochemistry, 1979-84; chmn. bd. Consortium for Plant Biotech. Rsch., Inc., 1992-96. Series editor U. Wis. Biotech. Ctr. Resource Manuals; editor-in chief Jour. Protein Expression and Purification, 1990—; contbr. articles to profl. jours. Bd. dirs. Coun. Biotech. Ctrs., 1991-93; mem. Gov.'s Coun. on Biotech. Grantee NSF, 1978-80, 85-90, NIH, 1980—, Nat. Cancer Inst., 1971—; Guggenheim fellow, 1983-84; recipient medal Waksman Inst., 1999. Fellow Am. Acad. Microbiology; mem. Am. Soc. Biochemistry and Molecular Biology, Am. Chem. Soc. (Pfizer award 1982), Am. Assn. Cancer Research, Am. Soc. Microbiology, Protein Soc. Home: 10 Knollwood Ct Madison WI 53713-3479 Office: U Wis McArdle Lab Cancer Rsch 1400 University Ave Madison WI 53706-1526 Office Phone: 608-263-2635. Business E-Mail: burgess@oncology.wisc.edu.

BURGHART, JAMES HENRY, electrical engineer, educator; b. Erie, Pa., July 18, 1938; s. Chester Albert and Mary Virginia (Burke) B.; m. Judith Ann Hoff, July 8, 1961; children— Jill Kathryn, Mark Alan. BS in Elec. Engring, Case Inst. Tech., 1960, MS (U.S. Steel Found. fellow 1961-63), 1962, PhD, 1965. Asst. prof., then assoc. prof. elec. engring. SUNY, Buffalo, 1969-75; prof. elec. engring. Cleve. State U., 1975—2005, chmn. dept., 1975-85, 89-97; ret. Served as officer USAF, 1965-68. Mem. IEEE (chmn. Cleve. sect. 1980-81, sec. region 2 1989-96, profl. activities coord. region 2 1997-2000, Ohio area chair region 2 2001—2002, awards and recognition chair, 2003, admission and advancement com. 2006-08), Sigma Xi, Eta Kappa Nu. Home: 5501 Strathaven Dr Cleveland OH 44143-1970 Office: 1983 E 24th St Cleveland OH 44115-2403 Address: 2121 Euclid Ave Cleveland OH 44115 E-mail: j.burghart@ieee.org.

BURHOE, BRIAN WALTER, automotive executive; b. Worcester, Mass., Apr. 9, 1941; s. Walter De Forest and Dorothy Merrium Burhoe; m. Lynda Clayton, May 28, 1960 (div. May 1972); children: Mark S., Ty C., Scott M.; m. Joan Elaine Bredenberg, Oct. 21, 1989. Arts Baccalaureate, Clark U., Worcester, 1963, MA in History, Internat. Rels., 1971; cert. advanced mgmt. program, Northwestern U., 1985. Tchr. Orleans Sch. Sys., Mass., 1965-67; mgr. labor rels. Ill. Ctrl. RR, Chgo., 1967-74, exec. asst., 1974-77; dir. human resources Midas Internat. Corp., Chgo., 1977-79, v.p. human resources, 1979-89, sr. v.p. human resources, 1989—97; pres. The Old Bookseller, Inc., 1997—. Mem.: Ill. Safety Coun. (chmn. 1992—94). Avocation: collecting out of print books. Home and Office: 325 ebraska St Frankfort IL 60423

BURICK, LAWRENCE T., lawyer; b. Dayton, Ohio, May 15, 1943; s. Lee and Doris (Brenner) B.; m. Cynthia Joy Rosen, Aug. 31, 1969; children: Carrie R., Samuel J. BA, Miami U., 1965; JD, Northwestern U., 1968. Bar: Ohio 1968. Assoc. Smith & Schnacke, Dayton, 1969-78, ptnr., 1978-89, Thompson Hine LLP, Dayton, 1989—. Chmn. Dayton Jewish Ctr., Ohio, 1982—83, Jewish Cmty. Rels. Coun., 1980—81; pres. Jewish Fedn. Greater Dayton, Ohio, 1989—93, bd. dirs., 1977—2003; chmn. United Jewish Campaign, 1997—99; bd. dirs. Jewish Edn. in Svc. to N.Am., 1994—99, v.p., 1997—99; mem. Dayton region Nat. Conf. Cmty. and Justice, 1997—, v.p., 1999—2002, chair, 2002—04; bd. dirs. Beth Abraham Synagogue, 1997—2003. Recipient Wasserman Leadership award, Jewish Fedn. Greater Dayton, 1978. Mem. Ohio State Bar Assn., Dayton Bar Assn., Am. Bankruptcy Law Forum, Am. Bankruptcy Inst. Office: Thompson Hine LLP PO Box 8801 2000 Courthouse Plz NE Dayton OH 45401-8801 E-mail: larry.burick@thompsonhine.com.

BURISH, THOMAS GERARD, academic administrator, psychology professor; b. Peshtigo, Wis., May 4, 1950; s. Bennie Charles and Donna Mae (Willkom) B.; m. Pamela Jean Zebrasky, June 19, 1976; children: Mark Joseph, Brent Christopher. AB summa cum laude, U. Notre Dame, 1972; MA, U. Kans., 1975, PhD, 1976. Lic. psychologist, Tenn. Asst. prof. psychology Vanderbilt U., Nashville, 1976-80, assoc. prof., 1980-86, prof., 1986—2002, dir. clin. tng., 1980-84, chair dept. psychology, 1984-86, assoc. provost, 1986—92, provost, 1992—2002; pres. Washington and Lee U., Lexington, Va., 2002—05; provost U. Notre Dame, 2005—, prof. psychology, 2005—. Mem. cancer rsch. manpower rev. com. Nat. Cancer Inst., 1991-96; mem. breast cancer rsch. panel US Army Med. Rsch., 1995-2001. Co-editor: Coping with Chronic Disease, 1983, Cancer, Nutrition and Eating Behavior, 1985; co-author: Behavior Therapy, 1987, Health Psychology, 1991. Chmn. St. Mary's Sch. Bd., Nashville, 1982-83; participant Leadership Nashville, 1989-90; chair, bd. dir. Am. Cancer Soc., 2004-05. Fellow Am. Psychol. Assn., Am. Psychol. Soc.; mem. Acad. Behavioral Medicine Rsch., Phi Beta Kappa. Roman Catholic. Office: U Notre Dame 300 Main Bldg otre Dame IN 46556 Office Phone: 574-631-6631.

BURK, ROBERT S., lawyer; b. Mpls., Jan. 13, 1937; s. Harvey and Mayme (Cottle) B.; m. Eunice L. Silverman, Mar. 22, 1959; children: Bryan, Pam, Matt. BBA in Indsl. Rels., U. Minn., 1959; LLB, William Mitchell Coll. Law, 1965. Bar: Minn. 1966; qualified neutral under Rule 114 of the Minn. Gen. Rules of Practice, 1995—. Labor rels. cons. St. Paul Employers Assn., 1959-66; labor rels. mgr. Koch Refining Co., St. Paul, 1966-72, mgr. indsl. rels., 1972-75, mgr. indsl. rels., environ. affairs, 1975-77; sr. atty. Popham, Haik, Schnobrich & Kaufman, Ltd., Mpls., 1977-95, pres., CEO, 1986-90; ptnr. Burk & Seaton, P.A., Edina, Minn., 1995-2001, Burk & Landrum, P.A., Edina, 2001—07. Chair bd. trustees William Mitchell Coll. Law, St. Paul, 1994-96, sec. 1991, trustee emeritus, 2006—. Recipient Hon. Ronald E. Hachey Outstanding Alumnus award William Mitchell Coll. Law Alumni Assn., 1993, Disting. Svc. award William Mitchell Coll. Law, 2004. E-mail: rburk@burklandrum.com.

BURKE, ANNE M., state supreme court justice; b. Chgo., Feb. 3, 1944; m. Edward M. Burke; children: Jennifer, Edward, Emmett(dec.), Sarah; 1 foster child. BA in Edn., DePaul U., 1976; JD, IIT/Chgo.-Kent Coll. Law, 1983. Bar: Fed. Ct. No. Dist. Ill. 1983, U.S. Ct. Appeals (7th cir.) 1985, cert.: Trial Bar Fed. Dist. Ct. 1987. Phys. edn. tchr. Chgo. Park Dist.; pvt. practice, 1983—94; judge Ill. Ct. Claims, 1987—94; spl. counsel to Gov. Child Welfare Services State of Ill., 1994—95; judge Ill. Appellate Ct. (1st dist.), Chgo., 1995—96, 1996—2006; justice Ill. Supreme Ct., Chgo., 2006—. Founder of the Chgo. Special Olympics. Grantee, Kennedy Found. Avocations: dance, antiques. Office: Ill Supreme Ct 160 N LaSalle St Chicago IL 60601 Office Phone: 312-793-5470.

BURKE, BRIAN B., former state legislator, lobbyist; b. Milw., Apr. 19, 1958; s. Thomas Joseph and Mary White (Higgins) B.; m. Patricia J. Coorough, Aug. 7, 1982; children: Colleen Marie, Kathleen Clare, Erin Elizabeth. BA magna cum laude, Marquette U., 1978; JD, Georgetown U., 1981; grad., FBI Citizen's Acad., Milw., 1999. Bar: Wis. 1981, U.S. Dist. Ct. (ea. and we. dists.) Wis. 1981,

U.S. Ct. Appeals (7th cir.) 1983, U.S. Supreme Ct. 1984. Asst. dist. atty. Milwaukee County, Milw., 1981-84; alderman Milw. Common Coun., 1984-88; mem. Wis. Senate, Madison, 1988—2003; lobbyist Arjo Wiggins Appleton, Washington, 2004—. Mem. editl. bd. Georgetown Internat Law Jour.; contbr. articles to profl. jours. Trustee Milw. Pub. Libr., 1984-88, Pabst Theatre Bd., Milw., 1984-88, Milw. County Federated Libr. Sys., 1997—; commr. Milw. Met. Sewerage Dist., 1990—, Milw. Redevel. Authority, 1985-88, Wis. Ctr. Dist. Bd., 1996—, Hist. Preservation Commn., Milw., 1987-88; exec. bd. Wis. Pub. Utility Inst., 1993—; mem. State Capitol and Exec. Residence Bd., 1996—, Wis. Trust for Hist. Preservation, 1992—; mem. Dem. Leadership Coun., Nat. Conf. State Legis. Environ. Com.; mem. Wis. Environ. Edn. Bd., 1995—; mem. U. Wis. Hosps. and Clinics Authority, 1996—. Named Legislator of Yr. Wis. Urban Transit Assn., 1997, Vietnam Vets. Am., 1997-2000, Wis.'s Environ. Decade Clean 16 award, 1989-00, Bridge Builder's award Nature Conservancy, 1994, Profl. Firefighters Wis., 2001; recipient Cesar Chavez Humanitarian award Hispanic Leadership Coun., 1994, Friend of Wis. Jewish Cmty. award Wis. Jewish Conf., 1994, Friend of Hispanic Cmty. award United Cmty. Ctr., 1994, Hon. Riverkeeper award Friends of the Menomonee River, 1996, Disting. Svc. award Wis. Alliance of Cities, 1992-98, Atty. Gen.'s award for outstanding leadership on law enforcement issues, 1999, Clean Energy Leadership award, 1999, Voices of Courage in Public Policy award Wisc. Coalition Against Sexual Assault, 2000, Comdr.'s award for pub. svc Dept. of Army, 1999, Ptnrs. for Survival award Equal Justice Coalition of State Bar of Wis., 2000, Gaylord Nelson award 1000 Friends of Wis., 2000, Promise to the Earth Award, Greening Milw., 2001, Svc. to Marquette award Marquette Alumni, 2001, Lifetime Achievement award Wis. Environ. Decade, 2002; named to Washington H.S. Hall of Fame, 2001. Mem. Washington Heights Neighborhood Assn., State Hist. Soc., Hispanic C. of C., Greater Mitchell Street Assn., Shamrock Club of Wis., Phi Beta Kappa. Democrat. Roman Catholic. Avocation: tennis.

BURKE, CAROL A., lawyer; b. 1951; children: Stephen, Louisa. BA, Smith Coll., 1973; JD, George Wash. U., 1976. Bar: DC 1976, Okla. 1977, Calif. 1977, Ill. 1983. Atty. Baker & McKenzie, Rome, Econ. Crime Project, Chgo.; spl. counsel, assoc. gen. counsel legal dept. Chgo. Bd. of Trade, sr. v.p., gen. counsel, 1994—95, exec. v.p., chief of staff, gen. counsel, 1995—. Mem.: ABA (former co-chmn. contracts markets subcom.).

BURKE, DANIEL J., state legislator; b. Chgo., Dec. 17, 1951; Student, Loyola U., Berlitz Sch. Lang., DePaul U. Dep. city clk., Chgo, 1979—; Ill. state rep. Dist. 23, 1991—. Mem Edn. Appropriations, Election Law, Elem. & Secondary Edn., Labor and Commerce, Transp. & Vehicles Coms., Ill. Ho. of Reps. Mem. Internat. Mcpl. Clks. Assn. (legis. co-chmn.), Gov. Fin. Officers Assn. Address: 2650 W 51st St Chicago IL 60632-1560

BURKE, DERMOT, choreographer; m. Karen Russo; children: Daniel, Kevin, Margaret Kathleen. Ballet master, resident choreographer, artistic dir. Am. Repertory Ballet Co., 1979-92; exec. dir. Dayton (Ohio) Ballet, 1992—. Choreographer Pacific Northwest Ballet, Am. Repertory Ballet, Dayton Ballet. Office: Dayton Ballet 140 N Main St Dayton OH 45402-1750

BURKE, EDWARD MICHAEL, alderman; b. Chgo., Dec. 29, 1943; s. Joseph and Ann (Dolan) B.; m. Anne Marie McGlone, 1968; children: Jennifer, Edward, Emmett, Sarah. BA, DePaul U., 1965, JD, 1968. Atty. Klafter & Burke; underwriter Lloyd's of London, 1980—; alderman Chgo. City Coun., 1969—. Mem. com. on budget and govt. ops., vice chair rules and ethics com., mem. energy, environ. protection and pub. utilities com., police and fire com., zoning com.; former chmn. Dem. com. and alderman 14th ward, Chgo. Mem. Chgo. and Cook County Criminal Justice Commn., 1975; counsel Ill. Mcpl. Problems Commn., 1975; mem. Econ. Devel. Commn.; mem. Chgo. Plan Commn.; bd. dirs. Navy Pier Devel. Authority, USO; mem. Ill. Com. for Employer Support of the Guard and Res., One Hundred Club of Cook County, Military Order of World Wars, Southwest Realty Bd., Back of the Yards Businessman's Assn., SW Parish Neighborhood Fedn., Chgo. Lawn C. of C.; chmn. Police and Firemen's Death Benefit Fund; hon. mem. Chgo. Conv. and Tourism Bd. 1st lt. U.S. Army Res. Recipient Order of the Holy Family Evangelical Catholic Diocese of the Northwest, 1999, Public Svc. awrd Mex. Am. C. of C., 1999, Leadership award Kelly H.S. Cmty. Coun., 1999, Brighton Park Neighborhood Coun. Svc. award, 1999, Support for Bosnian Peace Keepers Appreciation award NATO, 1999, Catholic Lawyer of Yr. award Catholic Lawyers Guild of Chgo., 1998, Achievement in Gov. award Aspira, 1998, Rerum Novarum award St. Joseph Seminary Archdiocese of Chgo., 1998, Man of Yr. award Ill.-Ireland C. of C., 1995, Advocate of Yr. award AHA, Father Terme award for Outstanding Civic Leadership Cenacle Retreat House, 1992, Loyalty Day award VFWUS, 1992, Legislative Svc. award, Chgo. Lung Assn, 1991, Statesman of Yr. award Internat. Union of Operating Engrs. Local 150, 1991, Recognition award Soc. Human Resource Professionals, 1991, Pax et Bonum award, St. Peter's Catholic Ch., 1991, Brotherhood award for Outstanding Civic Svc. Nat. Conf. of Christians and Jews, 1991, Appreciation award Am. Cancer Soc., 1991, Disting. Citizen award Mt. Carmel H.S., 1991, Chgo. Father of Yr. award Chgo. Father's Day Com., 1990, Irishman of Yr. award, Chgo. Limerick Assn., 1990, Gratitude award Chgo. Firefighters Union Local No. 2, 1989, Ill. Enterprise Zone award Ill. Dept. of Commerce and Cmty. Affairs, 1989, Man of Yr. award Men of Tolentine, 1985, Ill. Assn. of Retarded Citizens award, 1981, Man of Yr. award Chgo. Police Capts. Assn., 1975. Mem. ABA, Ill. Bar Assn., Chgo. Bar Assn., Moose, K of C (4th degree, Leo XIII coun.), Celtic Lawyers' Assn. Am., Order of Holy Sepulchre, Irish Fellowship Club (chmn. bd. dirs.), Am. Legion (Frank Leahy Post 1974), Sovereign Military Order of Malta, Ill. Com. for Employer Support of the Guard and Reserve. Roman Catholic. Office: 2650 W 51st St Chicago IL 60632-1560

BURKE, JAMES DONALD, museum administrator; b. Salem, Oreg., Feb. 22, 1939; s. Donald J. and Ellin (Adams) B.; m. Diane E. Davies, May 17, 1980 BA, Brown U., 1961; MA, U. Pa., 1966; PhD, Harvard U., 1972. Curator Yale U. Art Gallery, New Haven, 1972-78; asst. dir. St. Louis Art Mus., 1978-80, dir., chief exec. officer, 1980-99, dir. emeritus, 1999—. Cons., panel mem. IRS, Washington, 1980—; scholar-in-residence Washington U., St. Louis, 1999—, Mercantile Libr., U. Mo., St. Louis, 1999—. Author: Jan Both, 1974, Charles Meyron, 1974; contbr. articles to profl. jours.; organizer in field. Pres. St. Louis Art Mus. Found., 1985—99, Gateway Found., 1986—. Fulbright fellow, 1968-69 Mem. Coll. Art Assn., Print Council Am., Am. Assn. Mus., Assn. Art Mus. Dirs. Office: Saint Louis Art Mus One Fine Arts Dr Forest Park Saint Louis MO 63110

BURKE, KATHLEEN B., lawyer; b. Bklyn., Sept. 2, 1948; BA, St. John's U., 1969, JD, 1973. Bar: Ohio 1973. Ptnr. Jones Day, Cleve. Bd. dirs. Notre Dame Coll. Ohio, chair, 2002—06; bd. dirs. Ctr. Families and Children. Mem. Leadership Cleve.; pres. Cleve. Skating Club, 2000-02., 2000—02; trustee Ohio Legal Assistance Found., 2007—, bd. dirs. Named a Woman of Achievement, Cleve. YWCA, 2004; recipient Ohio Bar medal, 2002. Fellow: Ohio State Bar Found. (pres. 2000); mem.: ABA (state del. 2002—, litigation sect. and ho. of dels.), Ohio State Bar Assn. (pres. 1993—94), Am. Law Inst. Office: Jones Day North Point 901 Lakeside Ave E Cleveland OH 44114-1190 Office Phone: 216-586-3939. Business E-Mail: kbburke@jonesday.com.

BURKE, KENNETH ANDREW, advertising executive; b. Sept. 9, 1941; s. Frank Flory and Margret Anne (Tomè) B.; m. Karen Lee Burley, July 1, 1968; children: Allison Leigh Hart, Aric Jason. BSBA in Mktg., Bowling Green State U., Ohio, 1965. Mem. Green Bay Packers Nat. Football League, Sask. Roughriders, Can. Football League; acct. exec. lang, Fisher, Stashower, Cleve., 1967-69; v.p., acct. supr. Tracy-Locke, Dallas, 1969-72; v.p. Grey Advt., NYC, 1972-76, Griswold Eshleman, Cleve., 1976-79; sr. v.p., gen. mgr. Simpson Mktg., Columbus, Ohio, 1979-81; pres., CEO, chmn. Martcom Inc., Columbus, Ohio, 1981-91; chmn. ret. Ad Factory, Inc., Advt. and Mktg., Ad Factory Outlets, Columbus, Ohio, 1991-98; exec. v.p. Berkshire Product Inc., Tampa, Fla., 1983-89. Bd. dirs. Ad Factory, Newport Mktg. Svcs. Author: (children's stories) Bordini and the Black Knight, 1975. Mem. adv. bd. columbus chpt. Am. Cancer Soc., 1980-88. Recipient USN Achievement award Am. Legion USN Meml. Found., 1975. Mem. NRA, Am. Mktg. Assn., Columbus Advt. Fedn., NFL Alumni Assn., Columbus Numis. Soc., Am. Numis. Assn, Columbus NFL Alumni, Cleve. Advt. Club (Merit award 1968), Columbus C. of C., Upper Arlington C. of C., Theta Chi. Republican. Roman Catholic. Home: 1753 Bedford Rd Columbus OH 43212-2004 Office: Ad Factory Corp Offices 22 Gay Street Columbus OH 43215

BURKE, LEO, dean, director; BA in Sociology, U. Notre Dame, 1970; MS in Polit. Sci., Orgnl. Devel., Aurora U.; MA in Polit. Sci., Orgnl. Devel., Ind. U. Dir. strategy Motorola U., Schaumburg, Ill., dir., dean coll. leadership and transcultural studies; assoc. dean, dir. exec. edn. U. Notre Dame-Mendoza Coll. Bus., 2001—. Achievements include establishing and implementing the annual and long-term plans cited as one of the world's most successful and comprehensive corporate universities. Office: U Notre Dame 126 Mendoza Coll Bus Notre Dame IN 46556-5646 Office Phone: 574-631-5285. Office Fax: 574-631-6783. E-mail: Leo.Burke.77@nd.edu.

BURKE, PAUL E., JR., government agency administrator, consultant; b. Kansas City, Mo., Jan. 4, 1934; s. Paul E. and Virgnia (Moling) B.; m. Debbie Weihe; children: Anne Elizabeth, Kelly Patricia, A. Catherine, Jennifer Marie. BSBA, U. Kans., 1956. Mem. Kans. Ho. of Reps., 1972-74, Kans. Senate, 1975-97, majority leader, 1985-89, pres., 1992—96; pres., chairman/CEO Issues Mgmt. Group, Inc., Lawrence, Kans., 1996—. Chmn. Legis. Coordinating Coun., 1995; pres.-elect at. Conf. State Legislatures, 1990-91, pres., 1992; pres. Nat. Conf. State Legislatures Found., 1994; mem. Fed. Adv. Commn. Intergovtl. Rels., 1993-96. Councilman City of Prairie Village, Kans., 1959-63; mem. Kans. Turnpike Authority, 1965-69, chmn., 1969; mem. adv. bd. Sect. Corrections, 1973-78; mem. Gov.'s Mil. Adv. Coordinating Coun., 2002--. Capt. USAF, 1956-59; Capt. USNR, 1963-88. Mem. Kans. Assn. Commerce and Industry, Masons, Shriners, Rotary. Republican. Episcopalian. Address: 2009 Camelback Dr Lawrence KS 66047

BURKE, RACHEL E., lawyer; b. Newcastle Upon Tyne, Eng., Aug. 31, 1971; BS, Miami U., 1993; JD, Coll. of William & Mary, 1996. Bar: Ohio 1996, US Dist. Ct. Southern Dist. Ohio 1997, US Dist. Ct. Northern Dist. Ohio 2006. Of counsel Porter Wright Morris & Arthur LLP, Cin. Trustee Cin. Fire Mus. Named one of Ohio's Rising Stars, Super Lawyers, 2006. Mem.: Order of Coif, ABA, Ohio State Bar Assn., Cin. Bar Assn. Office: Porter Wright Morris & Arthur LLP 250 E Fifth St Ste 2200 Cincinnati OH 45202-5118 Office Phone: 513-369-4236. Office Fax: 513-421-0991.

BURKE, RAYMOND LEO, archbishop; b. Richland Center, Wis., June 30, 1948; s. Thomas F. and Marie Burke. Grad., Holy Cross Seminary, La Crosse, Wis., 1968; BA, Catholic Univ. of Am., 1970, MA, 1971; STB, Pontifical Gregorian Univ., Rome, 1974, MA, 1975, licentiate in canon law, 1982, diploma in Latin Letters, 1983, JCL, 1984; D (hon.), Ave Maria Univ., 2005. Ordained priest Diocese of La Crosse, Wis., 1975; assoc. rector Cathedral of St. Joseph the Workman, La Crosse, Wis., 1975—84; instructor of religion Aquinas High Sch., La Crosse, Wis., 1977—84; moderator of Curia and vice-chancellor Diocese of La Crosse, 1984, adjunct judicial vicar, 1985; visiting prof. of Canonical Jurisprudence Pontifical Gregorian U., Rome, 1985—94; ordained bishop, 1995; bishop Diocese of La Crosse, Wis., 1995—2003; archbishop Archdiocese of St. Louis, Mo., 2004—. Bd. dirs. Nat. Catholic Rural Life Conference, 1995, bd. pres., 1996—2001; mem. Canonical Affairs Com. Nat. Conference of Catholic Bishops, 1997—99; mem. Commn. on Religious Life and Mission US Conference of Catholic Bishops, 2001—03; nat. dir. Marian Catechist Apostolate, 2000—; pres. bd. directors Shrine of Our Lady of Guadalupe, La Crosse, Wis., 2001—; spiritual dir. Real Presence Assn., 2002—; mem. Vatican's Congregation for Clergy, 2003—; bd. trustee Catholic Univ. of Am., 2006—; judge Supr. Tribunal of the Apostolic Signatura, 2006—. Named Knight Comdr. with Star, Equestrian Order of the Holy Sepulchre, 1997. Mem.: Canon Law Soc. Am. (Role of Law award 2000), Canon Law Soc. of Great Britain & Ireland, Canadian Can Law Soc., Canon Law Soc. of Australia & New Zealand, Fellowship of Cath. Scholars. Roman Catholic. Office: Archdiocese of St Louis 4445 Lindell Blvd Saint Louis MO 63108*

BURKE, STEVEN FRANCIS, organization executive; b. St. Paul, May 23, 1952; s. Paul Stanley and Irene Marie (Wagner) B.; m. Kathleen Mary Frost, Mar. 23, 1974; children: Susan, Kathleen, Elizabeth, Michael, Thomas. BS, U. Minn., 1974; owner pres. mgmt. program, Harvard U., 1991. V.p. N.Am. Outdoor Group Inc., Minnetonka, Minn., 1978-84, exec. v.p., 1984-88, pres., 1988-90, pres., CEO, 1990—99; pres. N.Am. World Travel Inc., Minnetonka, Minn., 1989-91, also bd. dirs., 1989-91. Mgr. Bur Oak Properties LLC; bd. dirs. Larson and Burke Inc., Hopkins, Minn., Comml. Banl Chaska, Minn. Mem. pastoral coun. St. Hubert Cath. Ch., Chanhassen, Minn., 1984-85; pres. Wildlife Forever Inc., Hopkins, 1987—; bd. dirs. Holy Family Cath. H.S., Victoria, 1999—. Capt. USMC, 1974-78. Mem. RA, N.Am. Hunting Club (pres. 1978—), N.Am. Fishing Club (pres. 1988—). Avocations: hunting, fishing, golf, scuba diving, flying. Office: Comml Bank Chaska 609 N Walnut St Chaska MN 55318-2075

BURKE, THOMAS A., manufacturing executive; b. Sioux Falls, SD; BS in Engring., Purdue U., 1979. Engring., mgmt. positions Ford Motor Co., 1980; v.p., N.Am., Asian ops. Visteon Corp., Van Buren Twp., Mich., v.p., European and S.Am. ops., 2001—02, v.p., N.Am. ops., 2002—05; exec. v.p. Modine Mfg. Co., Racine, Wis., 2005—06, exec. v.p., COO, 2006—08, pres., CEO, 2008—. Bd. dirs. Racine County United Way. Mem.: Soc. Mech. Engrs., Soc. Automotive Engrs. Office: Modine Mfg Co 1500 DeKoven Ave Racine WI 53403-2552 Office Phone: 262-636-1200. Office Fax: 262-636-1424.

BURKE, THOMAS JOSEPH, JR., lawyer; b. Oct. 23, 1941; s. Thomas Joseph and Violet (Green) B.; m. Sharon Lynne Forke, Aug. 29, 1964; children: Lisa Lynne, Heather Ann. BA, Elmhurst Coll., 1963; JD, Chgo.-Kent Coll. Law, 1966. Bar: Ill. 1966, U.S. Dist. Ct. (no. dist.) Ill. 1967, U.S. Ct. Appeals (7th cir.) 1972, U.S. Supreme Ct. 1972, U.S. Ct. Appeals (11th cir.) 1994, U.S. Ct. Appeals (6th cir.) 1995. Assoc. Lord, Bissell & Brook, Chgo., 1966-74, ptnr., 1974—2003; of counsel Hall, Prangle & Schoonveld, LLC, 2004—. Fellow: Am. Coll. Trial Lawyers; mem.: Assn. Advancement Automotive Medicine, Soc. Automotive Engrs., Product Liability Adv. Coun., Ill. Assn. Def. Trial Counsel, Def. Rsch. Inst., Soc. Trial Lawyers, Chgo. Bar Assn., Mid-Day Club, Phi Delta Phi, Pi Kappa Delta. Republican. Roman Catholic. Office: Hall Prangle & Schoonveld LLC 200 S Wacker Dr Ste 3300 Chicago IL 60606 Office Phone: 312-267-6229. Business E-Mail: tburke@hpslaw.com.

BURKE, THOMAS RICHARD, community college administrator; b. St. Louis, Oct. 2, 1944; s. Lloyd Richard and Frances Elizabeth (Yelton) B.; m. Sara Lou Janes, July 3, 1969; 1 child, Kimberly Ayre. BA, U. Miss., 1970, MA, 1972, PhD, 1981. Instr. Mountain Empire C.C., Big Stone Gap, Va., 1972-74, asst. prof., 1974-77, assoc. prof. history, 1977-80, acting pres., 1977, dean instrn., 1976-80; v.p. Three Rivers C.C., Poplar Bluff, Mo., 1980-86; pres. Independence C.C., 1986—, Kansas City (Kans.) C.C. Chmn. City of Poplar Bluff Hist. Commn. Served with USAF, 1965-69. Edn. Professions Devel. Act fellow, 1970-72. Mem. Am. Assn. Cmty. and Jr. Colls. (chmn. 1984-85), Kans. Assn. C.C. (chmn.), S.E. Kans. Consortium Colls. and Univs., Mo. Hist. Assn., Phi Delta Kappa, Masons, Shriners. Methodist. Office: Kansas City CC Office of Pres 7250 State Ave Kansas City KS 66112-3003

BURKETT, RANDY JAMES, lighting designer; b. DuBois, Pa., Nov. 12, 1955; s. Lloyd John and Helen Louise (North) B.; m. Carol Jeanne Collins, Aug. 22, 1981; 1 child, Meredith. B in Archtl. Engring., Pa. State U., 1978. Application engr. Johns-Manville, Denver, 1978-80; lighting designer HOK, St. Louis, 1980-82, assoc., 1982-85, v.p., 1986-88; pres. Randy Burkett Lighting Design, Inc., St. Louis, 1988—. Contbr. articles to profl. jours. Recipient Internat. Illumination Design Award of Excellence, 1987, 89, 93, 96, Edison award, 1993. Mem. Illuminating Engring. Soc., Internat. Assn. Lighting Designers (pres. 1996--97). Home: 5334 Chapelford Ln Saint Louis MO 63119-5017 Office: Randy Burkett Lighting Design 609 E Lockwood Ave Ste 201 Saint Louis MO 63119-3287

BURKHARDT, EDWARD ARNOLD, rail transportation executive; b. NYC, July 23, 1938; s. Edward Arnold Burkhardt Sr. and Kathryn C. Dow; m. Sandra Kay Schwaegel, June 9, 1967; 1 child, Cynthia Kay. BS Indsl. Adminstrn., Yale U., 1960. Various operating positions Wabash R.R., St. Louis, 1960-64, Norfolk and Western Rlwy., St. Louis, 1964-67; asst. to gen. mgr. Chgo. Northwestern Railway Co., 1967-68, gen. supt. transp., 1968-70, asst. v.p. transp., 1970-76, v.p. mktg., 1976-79, v.p. transp., 1979-87; bd. dirs., chmn., pres., CEO Wis. Ctrl. Transp. Corp., Chgo., 1987-99; chmn. Tranz Rail Ltd., 1993-99; bd. dirs., pres. Algoma Ctrl. Rlwy. Inc., 1995-99; bd. dirs., chmn., CEO English, Welsh and Scottish Ry. Ltd., 1995-99; bd. dirs., chmn. Australian Transport Network, 1997-99; pres./CEO Rail World, Inc., 1999—; pres. RailPolska, 1999—. Chmn. Baltic Rail Svc., 2000—, Estonian Ry. Ltd., 2001—07, Navirail Ltd., Estonia, 2007—, Montreal, Maine & Atlantic Ry. Ltd., 2003—; bd. dirs. Valeant Pharms. Internat., Aliso Viejo, Calif., 2001—07, Poly Medica Corp., Wakefield, Mass., 2001—07. Trustee Village of Kenilworth, Ill., 1984—93; bd. dirs. John W. Barringer R.R. Libr., St. Louis, Wheeling & Lake Erie Rlwy. Co., Lake Superior Mus. Transp., Duluth, Minn. Named Hon. consul New Zealand, Chgo. Mem.: Am. Assn. R.R. Supts., Union League Club, Western Ry. Club. Republican. Episcopalian. Office: Rail World Inc Ste 500N 8600 W Bryn Mawr Ave Chicago IL 60631-3579 Business E-Mail: eaburkhardt@railworld-inc.com.

BURKHART, CRAIG GARRETT, dermatologist, researcher; b. Toledo, Apr. 15, 1951; s. Garrett Giles and Mary Katherine (Egarius) Burkhart; m. Anna Kristina Jutila, Apr. 12, 1975; children: Kristina Maria, Craig Nathaniel, Heidi Rebecca. BA, U. Pa., 1972; MD, Med. Coll. Ohio, 1975; MPH, U. Toledo, Ohio, 1983. Diplomate Am. Bd. Dermatology. Intern, resident, fellow U. Mich. Hosps., 1976-79; pvt. practice dermatologist, 1979—; pres. Gar-Nat Lab., Inc., 1997—. Clin. prof. medicine Med. U. Ohio; clin. asst. prof. dermatology Ohio U. Coll. Osteo. Medicine. Editor: Jour. Dermatology and Allergy, 1980—; mem. editl. bd. Jour. Current Adolescent Medicine, 1980—, mem. editl. adv. bd. Ohio State Med. Jour., 1982—, Cortlandt Forum, 1999—; contbr. chpts. to books, articles to profl. jours. Mem. Toledo Zoo, Toledo Mus. Art. F. M. Douglass Found. Rsch. grantee, 1998, 2000, 2001. Mem.: AMA, Ohio Dermatologic Found. (bd. dirs. 2005—, v.p. 2006—), Toledo Acad. Medicine (bd. dirs. 2002—, v.p. 2005—), Mich. Dermatologic Assn., Ohio State Med. Assn., Ohio Dermatologic Assn. (bd. dirs. 2002—, pres. 2005—), Acad. Dermatology, U. Toledo Alumni Assn. (bd. dirs. 2006—), Med. U. Ohio Alumni Assn. (bd. dirs. 2000—03), Phi Beta Kappa (pres. N.W. Ohio 1984—86). Achievements include patents in field. Home: 4556 Crossfields Rd Toledo OH 43623-2628 Office: 5600 Monroe St Ste 106B Sylvania OH 43560-2728 Office Phone: 419-885-3403. Personal E-mail: cgbakb@aol.com.

BURKHART, WILLIAM R., lawyer; b. May 30, 1965; m. Theresa A. Burkhart. B in polit. sci., U. Fla.; JD, Harvard U., 1990. Bar: Pa. 1990. Atty. Reed Smith Shaw & McClay LLP, Pitts.; joined The Timken Co., Canton, Ohio, 1994, atty., corp. atty., legal counsel for Europe, Africa, and West Asia Colmar, France, dir. affiliations and acquistions Canton, Ohio, 1998—2000, sr. v.p., gen. counsel, 2000—. Mem. law coun. Manufacturers Alliance. Bd. dirs. Ohio C. of C.; mem. Vision Coun. Program Adv. Subcom. Ctrl. Stark County United Way, Ohio. Office: The Timken Co 1835 Dueber Ave SW Canton OH 44706-2798

BURKHOLDER, DONALD LYMAN, mathematician, educator; b. Octavia, Nebr., Jan. 19, 1927; s. Elmer and Susie (Rothrock) B.; m. Jean Annette Fox, June 17, 1950; children: Kathleen, Peter, William. BA, Earlham Coll., 1950; MS, U. Wis., 1953; PhD, U. N.C., 1955. Asst. prof. math. U. Ill., Urbana, 1955-60, assoc. prof., 1960-64, prof., 1964-98, prof. Ctr. for Advanced Study, 1978-98, prof. emeritus, 1998—. Sabbatical leaves U. Calif., Berkeley, 1961-62, Westfield Coll., U. London, 1969-70; vis. prof. Rutgers U., 1972-73; researcher Stanford U., 1961, Hebrew U., 1969, Mittag-Leffler Inst., Sweden, 1971, 82, U. Paris, 1975, Institut des Hautes Etudes Scientifiques, 1986, U. Edinburgh, 1986, Tel Aviv U., 1989, U. New South Wales, 1991; Mordell lectr. Cambridge U., 1986; Zygmund lectr. U. Chgo., 1988; trustee Math. Scis. Rsch. Inst., 1981-84; bd. govs. Inst. Math. and Its Applications, 1983-85, chmn., 1985. Editor: Annals Math. Statistics, 1964-67. Fellow Inst. Math. Statistics (Wald lectr. 1971, pres. 1975-76); mem. NAS, Am. Math. Soc. (mem. editorial bd. Trans. 1983-85), London Math. Soc., Am. Acad. Arts and Scis. Achievements include research in probability theory and its applications to other branches of analysis. Home: 506 W Oregon St Urbana IL 61801-4044 Business E-Mail: donburk@math.uiuc.edu.

BURKHOLDER, WENDELL EUGENE, retired entomology educator, researcher; b. Octavia, Nebr., June 24, 1928; s. Elmer and Susie Burkholder; m. Leona Rose Flory, Aug. 18, 1951; children: Paul Charles, Anne Carolyn, Joseph Kern, Stephen James. AB, McPherson Coll., 1950; M.Sc., U. Nebr., 1956; PhD, U. Wis., 1967. Rsch. entomologist U.S. Dept. Agr., 1956-96; asst. prof. U. Wis.-Madison, 1967-70, asso. prof., 1970-75, prof. entomology, 1975-96; prof. emeritus, 1996—. Lectr. in field. Mem. editorial bd.: Jour. Chem. Ecology, 1980-96, Jour. Stored Products Rsch., 1992-98; contbr. chpts. to books and articles to profl. jours. Served with U.S. Army, 1951-53. NSF grantee, 1972-75, 79; Rockefeller Found. grantee, 1974-77; Nat. Inst. Occupational Safety and Health grantee, 1977-79 Mem. AAAS, Entomol. Soc. Am., Wis. Entomol. Soc., Wis. Acad. Sci. Arts, and Letters, Internat. Soc. Chem. Ecology, Sigma Xi. Achievements include patents in field. Home: 1726 Chadbourne Ave Madison WI 53726-4108 Office: U Wis Entomology Dept 237 Russell Lab Madison WI 53706-1598

BURKS, KEITH W., pharmaceutical executive; Exec. v.p. Bindley Western Industries, Inc., Indpls., 1993-2001; pres. Bindley Western a Cardinal Health Co., Indpls., 2001; ptnr. Bindley Capital Partners, Indianapolis. Office: Bindley Capital Partners Ste 500 8909 Purdue Rd Indianapolis IN 46268

BURLEIGH, WILLIAM ROBERT, media executive; b. Evansville, Ind., Sept. 6, 1935; s. Joseph Charles and Emma Bertha (Wittgen) B.; m. Catherine Anne Husted, Nov. 28, 1964; children: David William, Catherine Anne, Margaret Walden. BS, Marquette U., Milw., 1957; LLD (hon.), U. So. Ind., 1979. From reporter to editor, pres. Evansville Press, 1951-77; editor Cin. Post, 1977-83; v.p., gen. editl. mgr. Scripps-Howard Newspapers, Cin., 1984-86, sr. v.p. newspapers and publs., 1986-90, exec. v.p., 1990-94, pres., COO, 1994-96, pres., CEO, 1996-99; chmn., CEO E.W. Scripps Co., Cin., 1999-2000, chmn., 2000—. With AUS, 1957-58. Mem. Queen City Club, Cin. Lit. Club, Cin. Country Club, Cin. Comml. Club, Alpha Sigma Nu. Roman Catholic. Office: E W Scripps 312 Walnut St Cincinnati OH 45202-4024

BURMASTER, ELIZABETH, school system administrator; b. Balt., July 26, 1954; m. John Burmaster; 3 children. B in Music Edn., U. Wis., Madison, 1976, M in Ednl. Adminstrn., 1984. Vocal music and creative dramatics dir. Longfellow Elem. and Sennett Middle Sch., Madison, Wis., 1976—78; choral and drama dir. East HS, Madison, 1978—85; asst. prin. Marquette Middle Sch., Madison, 1985—88; fine arts coord. Madison Sch. Dist., 1988—90; prin. Hawthorne Elem., Madison, 1990—92, Madison West HS, 1992—2001; state supt. pub. instrn. State of Wis., Madison, 2001—. Mem. Govs. Econ. Growth Coun., Coun. Chief State Sch. Officers, chair task force on early childhood learning, bd. dirs.; bd. mem., past chair Nat. Ctr. for Learning and Citizenship. Nat. bd. sdvisor Pre-K ow; mem. bd. regents U. Wis.; mem. Edn. Commn. of the States, Wis. Tech. Coll. Sys. Bd., Ednl. Comms. Bd., Very Spl. Arts Wis., Gov.'s Work-Based Learning Bd.; bd. dirs. TEACH Wis. Mem.: Coun. of Chief State Sch. Officers (pres.), SAI-Music Assn., Tempo Internat., Assn. Wis. Sch. Adminstrs. Mailing: Dept Pub Instruction 125 S Webster St PO Box 7841 Madison WI 53707-7841

BURMEISTER, PAUL FREDERICK, farmer; b. Great Bend, Kans., June 11, 1938; s. Ferdinand Frederick Adam and Gertrude Nellie (Hanson) B. BA in Chemistry and Agr., Ft. Hays State U., 1960; postgrad., U. Kans., 1961. Farmer, Claflin, Kans., 1952-61, 64—. Farmer coop. Kans. Agrl. Experiment Sta., Ft. Hays Br. Sta., Hays, Kans., 1970, Kans. Rural Ctr., Whiting, 1991-92; panel mem. Kans. Sustainable Agr. Conf., Great Bend and Salina, 1991-92; mem. Kans. Natural Resource Coun., Topeka, 1975—, Nat. Resources Def. Coun., NYC, 1975—; participant U. Akron Nat. Energy Forum, 1976, Nat. Low-Level Radioactive Waste Mgmt. Strategy Rev. Workshop, Washington, 1981, Office Radiation Programs, EPA, Denver, 1978; guest spkr., Rapid City, S.D., 1993; mem. farmer adv. com. Sunshine Farm Project, The Land Inst., Salina, 1995-2001. Contbr. articles to environ. and agrl. jours. Vol. Am. Peace Corps, Ludhiana, India, 1961-63; local organizer campaign Union of Concerned Scientists, Cambridge, Mass.; lobbyist on environ. protection and conservation issues, Topeka, 1976-80; mem. Renew Am., Washington, 1980—; mem. The Menninger Found., Topeka, 1989—, Environ. Action, 1982—; lay mem. ad hoc task force on ecology Christian lifestyle United Ch. of Christ, 1977-78, commn. on outreach Kans.-Okla. conf., 1988-96, 98-99, network environ. and econ. responsibility; del. to 23rd Gen. Synod meeting of United Ch. of Christ, Kansas City, Mo., 2001; mem. Kans.-Okla. Conf. Coun. United Ch. Christ, 1999-2003; participant Kans. Citizens Forum Com. for Humanities, Topeka, 1987; bd. trustees Clara Barton Hosp. Found., Hoisington, Kans., 2005-. With USNG, 1963—69. Recipient Bankers award Banks of Barton County, Kans. and U.S. Soil Conservation Svc., 1990. Mem. Nat. Wildlife Fedn. (life), Nat. Coun. Returned Peace Corps Vols., Nat. Arbor Day Found., World Wildlife Fund (charter), Am. Wind Energy Assn., Am. Solar Energy Soc. (life), Heartland Renewable Energy Soc., Midwest Renewable Energy Assn., 1998—, Kans. Assn. Wheat Growers, Kans. Farmers Union (life), Kans. Organic Prodrs., Inc.,

Friends of the Earth, Cousteau Soc. (founding yr. mem.), Kans. State Hist. Soc. (life), Kans. Wildlife Fedn., Sierra Club (life), Native Forest Coun., Ducks Unltd. Inc., Environ. Def., Wilderness Soc., Friends of India, Rainforest Alliance, Nat. Parks Conservation Assn., Nature Conservancy, Tau Kappa Epsilon (sec. 1958-59, scholar 1959), Phi Eta Sigma (historian 1958-59), Phi Kappa Phi, Delta Epsilon. Avocations: photography, hiking, exploring. Address: 1332 NE 180th Rd Claflin KS 67525-9219 Home Phone: 620-587-3919; Office Phone: 620-587-3919.

BURNETT, JEAN B., biochemist; b. Flint, Mich., Feb. 19, 1924; d. Chester M. and Katheryn (Krasser) Bullard; B.S., Mich. State U., 1944, M.S., 1945, Ph.D. (Council fellow), 1952; m. James R. Burnett, June 8, 1947. Research assoc. dept. zoology Mich. State U., East Lansing, 1954-59, dept. biochemistry, 1959-61, acting dir. research biochem. genetics, dept. biochemistry, 1961-62, assoc. prof., asst. chmn. dept. biomechanics, 1973-82, prof. dept. anatomy, 1982-84, prof. dept. zoology, Coll. Natural Sci. and Coll. Osteo. Medicine, 1984—; assoc. biochemist Mass. Gen. Hosp., Boston, 1964-73; prin. research assoc. dermatology Harvard, 1962-73, faculty medicine, 1964-73, also spl. lectr., cons., tutor Med. Sch.; vis. prof. dept. biology U. Ariz., 1979-80. USPHS, NIH grantee, 1965-68; Gen. Research Support grantee Mass. Gen. Hosp., 1968-72; Ford Found. travel grantee, 1973; Am. Cancer Soc. grantee, 1971-73; Internat. Pigment Cell Conf. travel grantee, 1980; recipient Med. Found. award, 1970. Mem. AAAS, Am. Chem. Soc., Am. Inst. Biol. Sci., Genetics Soc. Am., Soc. Investigative Dermatology, N.Y. Acad. Scis., Sigma Xi (Research award 1971), Pi Kappa Delta, Kappa Delta Pi, Pi Mu Epsilon, Sigma Delta Epsilon. Home: PO Box 805 Okemos MI 48805-0805

BURNETT, RALPH GEORGE, lawyer; b. Milw., Apr. 13, 1956; s. Ralph G. and Joan T. Burnett; m. Eileen M. Gallagher, May 31, 1980; children: Christopher, Jessica, Thomas, Sarah, Andrew. BA, Marquette U., 1978; JD, U. Wis., 1981. Bar: Wis. 1981, U.S. Dist. Ct. (ea. and we. dists.) Wis. 1981, U.S. Ct. Appeals (7th cir.) 1981, U.S. Dist. Ct. (we. dist.) Mich. 1997, U.S. Ct. Appeals (6th cir.) 1997. Law clk. to Hon. Judge Harlington Wood U.S. Ct. Appeals 7th Cir., Chgo., 1981-82; lawyer Smith & O'Neil, Milw., 1983-84, Trowbridge, Planert & Schaefer, Green Bay, Wis., 1985-86, Liebmann, Conway, Olejniczak & Jerry, S.C., Green Bay, Wis., 1986—. Officer Robert J. Parins Inn of Ct., Green Bay, 1997—. Co-author: Wisconsin Trial Practice, 1999. Mem. allocations com. United Way N.E. Wis., Green Bay, 1988-91; bd. mem. paralegal program N.E. Wis. Tech. Coll., Green Bay, 1993-2000; bd. mem. parish coun. St. Mary's Ch., De Pere, 1997-2003; bd. mem. Cerebral Palsy, Green Bay, 1989-92; bd. mem. steering com. Notre Dame Sch., De Pere, 1998. Fellow Am. Coll. Trial Advocates, Am. Coll. Trial Lawyers, Am. Bar Found., Wisc. Bar Found.; mem. ABA, State Bar Wis. (bd. dirs., chmn. litigation sect. 1996-99, pres-elect 2003, pres. 2003-04), Wis. Acad. Trial Lawyers (bd. dirs. 1995-2000; amicus committer, constitutional challenge com., exec. com., regional dir. N.E. Wis. chpt., pres.-elect 2002-03). Avocations: woodworking, athletics. Office: Liebmann Conway Olejniczak & Jerry SC 231 S Adams St PO Box 23200 Green Bay WI 54305 Business E-Mail: RGB@lcojlaw.law.

BURNETT, ROBERT A., retired publisher; b. Joplin, Mo., June 4, 1927; s. Lee Worth and Gladys (Plummer) B.; m. Gloria M. Cowden, Dec. 25, 1948; children: Robert A., Stephen, Gregory, Douglas, David, Penelope. AB, U. Mo., 1948. Salesman Cowden Motor Co., Guthrie Center, Iowa; then Equitable Life Assurance Soc., Joplin, Mo.; retired chmn., CEO Meredith Corp.; ret., 1991. Bd. dirs. Hartford Fin. Svcs., ITT Industries. Served with AUS, 1945-46. Congregationalist. Home: 2942 Sioux Ct Des Moines IA 50321-1446

BURNITZ, JEROMY, professional baseball player; b. Westminster, Calif., Apr. 15, 1969; Baseball player N.Y. Mets, 1993-94, Cleve. Indians, 1995-96, Milw. Brewers, 1996—2001, LA Dodgers, 2002, NY Mets, 2003, Colo. Rockies, 2004, Chgo. Cubs, 2005. Office: Chgo Cubs Wrigley Field 1060 W Addison Chicago IL 60613

BURNS, C(HARLES) PATRICK, hematologist, oncologist; b. Kansas City, Mo., Oct. 8, 1937; s. Charles Edgar and Ruth (Eastham) B.; m. Janet Sue Walsh, June 15, 1968; children: Charles Geoffrey, Scott Patrick. BA, U. Kans., 1959, MD, 1963. Diplomate Am. Bd. Internal Medicine, subsplty. bds. hematology, med. oncology. Intern Cleve. Met. Gen. Hosp., 1963-64; asst. resident in internal medicine Univ. Hosps., Cleve., 1966-68, sr. resident in hematology, 1968-69; instr. medicine Case Western Res. U., Cleve., 1970-71; asst. chief hematology Cleve. VA Hosp., 1970-71; asst. prof. medicine U. Iowa Hosps., Iowa City, 1971-75, assoc. prof. medicine, 1975-80, prof., 1980—2006, prof. emeritus, 2006—, dir. sect. med. oncology, co-dir. divsn. hematatol./oncology, 1980-85, dir. div. hematology, oncology, blood marrow transplantation, 1985-99. Vis. scientist Imperial Cancer Rsch. Fund Labs., London, 1982-83; cons. U.S. VA Hosp.; mem. study sect. on exptl. therapeutics NIH, Cancer Ctr. Support Rev. Commn. Nat. Cancer Inst., NIH, NIH Cancer Clin. Investigation Rev. Com., Com. H Nat. Cancer Inst., VA Med. Rsch. Svc. Career Devel. Com.; mem. external adv. com. U. Oreg. Cancer Ctr., 1994-2000; mem. oncology group external adv. com., ACS, 2004-; cons. Irish Rsch. Bd., Dublin, 2000— Mem. bd. assoc. editors Cancer Rsch., 1988-2000, rsch. and publs. on hematologic malignancies, tumor lipid biochemistry, leukemia and oncology, role of oxidation in cancer treatment. Vol. Medicine Clinic, Hilton Head, SC. Served to capt. USMC, 1964—66. Am. Cancer Soc. fellow in hematology-oncology, 1968-69, USPHS fellow in medicine, 1969-70; USPHS career awardee, 1978; Outstanding Paper Presentation, Am. Oil Chemists Soc., 1992. Fellow ACP; mem. AAAS, Am. Bd. Internal Medicine (subsplty. bd. hematology test writing com. 1992-98, com. on recent advances in hematology, 2002—, chair 2006—), Am. Soc. Hematology, Am. Assn. Cancer Rsch., Internat. Soc. Hematology, Ctrl. Soc. Clin. Rsch., Am. Soc. Clin. Oncology, Soc. Exptl. Biology and Medicine, Oxygen Soc., Royal Soc. Medicine, Am. Fedn. Clin. Rsch., Internat. Soc. for the Study of Fatty Acids and Lipids, Phi Beta Pi, Lambda Chi Alpha, Alpha Omega Alpha. Home: 2046 Rochester Ct Iowa City IA 52245-3246 Office: U Iowa Univ Hosps Dept Medicine Iowa City IA 52242 Office Phone: 319-356-2038. Business E-Mail: c-burns@uiowa.edu.

BURNS, DANIEL T., corporate lawyer; BA, Brown U., 1973; JD, Vanderbilt U., 1976. Bar: Ill. 1976, Fla. 1977. Gen. atty. Roper Corp., 1976-80; atty. Cotter & Co., Chgo., 1980-88, gen. counsel, 1988-90, v.p., 1990—. Address: Cotter & Co 8600 W Bryn Mawr Ave Chicago IL 60631-3579

BURNS, DIANN, newscaster; m. Marc Watts; 1 child. BA in Politics and Mass Comm., Cleve. State U., Ohio; MA, Columbia U. Grad. Sch. of Journalism, NYC. Gen. assignment reporter Cleve. Plain Dealer; sports editor, photographer and reporter Cleve. Call and Post; field prodr. and reporter Ind. Network News of .Y.; reporter to weekend anchor WLS-TV, Chgo., 1985—94, co-anchor 5pm and 10pm news, 1994—2003; co-anchor 5pm, 6pm and 10pm news WBBM-TV, Chgo., 2003—. Spokesperson Pediatric AIDS Chgo.; hon. co-chair Ricky Byrdsong Mem. Race Against Hate. Office: WBBM-TV 630 N McClurg Ct Chicago IL 60601

BURNS, SISTER ELIZABETH MARY, retired hospital administrator; b. Estherville, Iowa, Mar. 3, 1927; d. Bernard Aloysius and Viola Caroline (Brennan) B. Diploma in Nursing, St. Joseph Mercy Sch. Nursing, Sioux City, Iowa, 1952; BS in Nursing Edn, Mercy Coll., Detroit, 1957; M.Sc. in Nursing, Wayne State U., 1958; Ed.D., Columbia U., 1969. Joined Sisters of Mercy, Roman Cath. Ch., 1946; nursing supr. Mercy Med. Ctr., Dubuque, Iowa, 1952-55; supr. orthopedics and urology St. Joseph Mercy Hosp., Sioux City, 1955-56; dir. Sch. Nursing, 1958-63; chmn. dept. nursing Mercy Coll. of Detroit, 1963-73; dir. health svcs. Sisters of Mercy, 1973-77; pres., CEO Marian Health Ctr., Sioux City, 1977-87; sabbatical leave, 1988; ret., 2006. Coord. life planning Sisters of Mercy, 1989-90, mem. province adminstrv. team, 1990-98; cons. Trinity Health, 2001—. Bd. dirs. Mercy Sch. Nursing of Detroit, 1968-77, Mercy H.S., Farmington Hills, Mich., 2000-05; mem. exec. com. Greater Detroit Area Hosp. Coun., 1973-77; trustee St. Mary Coll., Omaha, 1981-82, Briar Cliff Coll., Sioux City, 1981-87, Battle Creek Health Sys., 1998-2000, 02-04, Mercy Med. Ctr., Sioux City, Iowa, 2001-05; chmn. Mercy Health Adv. Coun., 1978-80. Mem. Western Iowa League for ursing (pres. 1960-62), Nat. League for Nursing, Sisters of Mercy Shared Svcs. Coordinating Com., Cath. Hosp. Assn. (trustee 1977-80), Sisters of Mercy Health Corp. (trustee 1988-90, governance coord. 1998-2001), Mercy Health Svcs. (chair bd. 1990-95, membership bd. 1995-98, historian 1998-2004). Address: 28554 Eleven Mile Farmington MI 48336-1507 Business E-Mail: eburns@mercydetroit.org.

BURNS, ELIZABETH MURPHY, media executive; b. Superior, Wis., Dec. 4, 1945; d. Morgan and Elizabeth (Beck) Murphy; m. Richard Ramsey Burns, June 24, 1984. Student, U. Ariz., 1963-67. Promotion and programming sec. Sta. KGUN-TV, Tucson, 1967-68; programming and traffic sec. Sta. KFMB-TV, San Diego, 1968-69; owner, operator Sta. KKAR, Pomona, Calif., 1970-73; co-owner, pres. Evening Telegram Co. (parent co. Murphy Stas.); pres. Morgan Murphy Stas., Madison, Wis., 1976—. Bd. dirs. Nat. Guardian Life Ins. Co., Republic Bank, Nat. Assn. Broadcasters, various media stas. and corps. Mem. Wis. Broadcasters Assn., Madison Club, Northland Country Club (Duluth), Boulders Country Club (Carefree, Ariz.), Bishop's Bay Country Club, Silverleaf Golf Club (Scottsdale, Ariz.). Roman Catholic. Avocations: golf, travel. Home: 180 Paine Farm Rd Duluth MN 55804-2609 Office: Sta WISC-TV 7025 Raymond Rd Madison WI 53719-5053 Personal E-mail: emb@embtv.com.

BURNS, JAMES B., prosecutor; b. Quincy, Ill., Sept. 21, 1945; married; 3 children. BA in History, Northwestern U., 1967, JD, 1971. Former profl. basketball player Chgo. Bulls, Dallas Chaparrals; asst. U.S. atty., then dep. chief and chief criminal litigation divsn. U.S. Dept. Justice, Chgo., 1971-78; assoc. Isham, Lincoln & Beale, Chgo., 1978-80, ptnr., 1980-88, Keck, Mahin & Cate, Chgo., 1988-93; U.S. atty. for no. dist. Ill. U.S. Dept. Justice, Chgo., 1993-97; pvt. practice Sibley & Austin, Chgo., 1997-00; inspector general State of Illinois, Springfield, 2000—, State of Illinois, Chgo. Bd. trustees orthwestern U., Evanston, Ill., 1981-83; Dem. candidate for lt. gov. State of Ill., 1990. Office: Office Sec of State Ste 5-400 100 W Randolph Chicago IL 60601

BURNS, LARRY WAYNE, marshall; b. May 5, 1949; m. Donna Swords, Aug. 20, 1975; 2 children. AA, Okaloosa Walton C.C., Valparaiso, Fla., 1972; BS in Criminology, Fla. State U., 1974. With Scranton Office, Mid. Dist. Pa., 1975-77; with hdqrs. office Columbia, 1977-78; dep. marshal in charge U.S. Marshal Svc., Florence, S.C., 1978-82, supr. no. dist. Ga. Atlanta, 1982-85; chief dep. U.S. marshal Office of U.S. Marshal for No. Dist. Ind., South Bend, 1985—. Mem. Masons, Phi Theta Kappa.

BURNS, MICHAEL J., former automotive parts company executive; b. Monticello, Ind., Mar. 1, 1952; B of Mech. Engring., Kettering U., 1975; MBA, U. Pa., 1979. Ops. mgr. Delco electronics GM Corp., Singapore, 1981—85, from treas. office staff to dir. overseas fin. analysis NY, 1985—87, from head hybrid electronics ops. to v.p. vehicle sys. bus. unit Delco electronics Singapore, 1988—93, v.p. Delphi Harrison thermal sys. Lockport, NY, 1994—95, v.p., gen. mgr. Delphi Delco electronics sys., 1996—98, group v.p., pres. Europe divsn. Zurich, Switzerland, 1998—2004; chmn. pres., CEO Dana Corp., Toledo, 2004—08. Supervisory bd. Adam Opel AG; bd. dirs. Saab Automobile AB; key exec. Wharton Sch.-U. Pa. Mem.: European Automobile Mfrs. Assn. (bd. dirs.), Soc. Automotive Engrs., Swiss-Am. C. of C. (bd. dirs.).*

BURNS, PETER C., science and engineering educator; b. Fredericton, New Brunswick, Can., Oct. 17, 1966; came to U.S., 1995; s. Carman George Burns and Ruth Joyce Linden; m. Tammy E. Chesley, 1992; children: Kelson O., Sarah V. BSc with honors, U. New Brunswick, Can., 1988; MSc in Geology, U. Western Ont., Can., 1990; PhD in Geology, U. Man., Can., 1994. Rsch. fellow U. Cambridge, England, 1994-95; post doctoral fellow U. N.Mex., 1995-96; vis. asst. prof. U. Ill., Urbana-Champaign, 1996-97; from asst. prof. to assoc. prof., dir. grad. studies U. Notre Dame, 1997-99, assoc. prof., 1999—2002, prof., 2002—, Massman chair dept. civil engring. and geol. sci., 2002—. Contbr. articles to profl. jours. Recipient Donath medal Geol. Soc. Am., 1999, award Mineral. Soc. Am., 2001. Fellow: Mineral. Soc. Am. (life MSA award 2001); mem.: Am. Chem. Soc., Mineral. Assn. Can. (councillor 1997—2005, Young Scientist medal 1998, Hawley medal 1997). Achievements include research in mineralogy and crystallography, mineralogy of nuclear waste disposal, environmental mineralogy, mineral crystal structures and crystal chemistry, mineral structure energetics, mineral paragenesis. Office: U Notre Dame 160 Fitzpatrick Engring Notre Dame IN 46556 E-mail: pburns@nd.edu.

BURNS, RICHARD RAMSEY, lawyer; b. Duluth, Minn., May 3, 1946; s. Herbert Morgan and Janet (Strobel) B.; children: Jennifer, Brian; m. Elizabeth Murphy, June 15, 1984 BA distinction, U. Mich., 1968, JD magna cum laude, 1971. Bar: Calif. 1972, U.S. Dist. Ct. (no. dist.) Calif. 1972, U.S. Ct. Appeals (9th cir.) 1972, Minn. 1976, U.S. Dist. Ct. Minn. 1976, Wis. 1983, U.S. Tax. Ct. 1983. Assoc. Orrick, Herrington, Rowley & Sutcliffe, San Francisco, 1971—76; ptnr. Hanft, Fride, P.A., Duluth, 1976—. V.p. bus. devel. and gen. counsel Morgan Murphy Media, Madison, Wis., 1982—. Chmn. Duluth-Superior Area Cmty. Found., 1988-90; chair United Way Greater Duluth, Inc., 1998-99; bd. dirs. Northland Coll., Ashland, Wis. Fellow Am. Coll. Trust and Estate Counsel (state chair); mem. Calif. Bar Assn., Wis. Bar Assn., Minn. Bar Assn. (past. exec. com., past chmn. probate and trust coun.), 11th Dist. Bar Assn. (past pres., past chmn. ethics com.), Arrowhead Estate Planning Coun. (pres. 1980), Northland Country Club (pres. 1982), Boulders Club, Silverleaf Golf Club and Spa, Kitchi Gammi Club. Republican. Avocations: travel, golf, reading, fishing. Home: 180 Paine Farm Rd Duluth MN 55804-2609 Office: Hanft Fride PA 1000 First Bank Pl 130 W Superior St Ste 1000 Duluth MN 55802-2056 Home Phone: 218-525-3995; Office Phone: 218-722-4766. Business E-Mail: rrb@hanftlaw.com.

BURNS, ROBERT ARTHUR, lawyer; b. Independence, Iowa, 1944; BS, Iowa State U., 1966; JD, U. Iowa, 1972. Bar: Minn. 1972, Iowa 1972. Ptnr. Dorsey & Whitney L.L.P., Mpls., 1978—. Office: Dorsey & Whitney LLP Ste 1500 50 S Sixth St Minneapolis MN 55402-1498 E-mail: burns.bob@dorsey.com.

BURNS, ROBERT PATRICK, law educator; b. NYC, Mar. 23, 1947; s. Frances William and Helen (Moskol) B.; m. Mary Elizabeth Griffin, June 7, 1975; children: Matthew, Elizabeth. AB, Fordham U., 1969; JD, U. Chgo., 1974, PhD, 1982. Bar: Ill. 1974, U.S. Dist. Ct. (no. dist.) Ill. 1974, U.S. Ct. Appeals (7th cir.) 1977, U.S. Supreme Ct. 1978. Litigation atty. Legal Assistance Found., Chgo., 1974-79, dir. atty. training, 1979; gen. counsel Ill. Legis. Commn., Springfield, 1979-80; prof. law Northwestern U., Chgo., 1980—. Tchr. Nat. Inst. Trial Advocacy, South Bend, Ind., 1981—. Author: A Theory of the Trial, 1999, Problems and Materials in Evidence and Trial Advocacy, 2001, exercises and Problems in Professional Responsibility, 2001, Evidence in Context, 2001; contbr. articles to profl. jours. Bd. dirs. Evanston Dems., Ill., 1984. Kent fellow Danforth Found., 1974, NSF fellow, 1970. Mem. ABA, Soc. for Values in Higher Edn. Roman Catholic. Office: Northwestern U Sch Law 357 E Chicago Ave Chicago IL 60611-3059 E-mail: r-burns@law.northwestern.edu.

BURNS, STEPHANIE A., chemicals executive; PhD in Organic Chemistry, Iowa State U.; post-doctoral student, U. Languedoc-Rousillon, France. Rschr. Dow Corning, Midland, Mich., 1983—87, prod. devel. mgr., electronics industry, 1987—94, dir. women's health, 1994—97, sci., tech. dir., Europe Brussels, 1997—99, industry dir. life scis., Europe to European elec. industry dir., 1999—2000, exec. v.p. Midland, Mich., 2000—03, pres., 2003—, COO, 2003—04, CEO, 2004—, chmn., 2006—. Bd. dirs. Dow Corning, 2000—, Manpower Inc., Chem. Bank Midland area, Mich. Molecular Inst. Adv. bd. Chem. & Engring. News. Bd. trustees Midland Cmty. Ctr. Named Mich. Woman Exec. of Yr., 2003; named one of 100 Most Powerful Women, Forbes Mag., 2005—07; recipient Vanguard award, Chem. Edn. Found., 2006. Mem.: Soc. Chem. Industry (mem. exec. com.), Am. Chem. Coun. (bd. dirs.), Am. Chem. Soc. Office: Dow Corning PO Box 994 Midland MI 48686-0994 Office Phone: 989-496-7881. Office Fax: 989-496-6731.

BURNS, TERRENCE MICHAEL, lawyer; s. Jerome Joseph Burns and Eileen Beatrice (Collins) Neary; m. Therese Burns, Mar. 24, 1979; 4 children. BA, Loyola U., Chgo., 1975; JD, DePaul U., 1978. Bar: Ill. 1978, U.S. Dist. Ct. (no. dist.) Ill. 1978, U.S. Ct. Appeals (7th cir.) 1979, U.S. Supreme Ct. 1985, U.S. Dist. Ct. (no. dist.) Ind. 1989. Asst. state's atty. Cook County, Chgo., 1979-85; ptnr. Dykema Gossett Rooks Pitts, Chgo., 1985—. Mem. inquiry bd. Ill. Supreme Ct. Atty. Registration and Disciplinary Commn., Chgo., 1986-90, chair hearing bd., 1990—; mem. coun. regents Loyola U., Chgo., 2002—. Mem. ABA (ann. meeting adv. com.), Chgo. Bar Assn. (treas. 1997-99, 2d v.p. 1999-2000, 1st v.p. 2000-01, pres. 2001-2002, bd. mgrs. 1995-97, chair fin. com. 1997-99, criminal law com. 1979-83, jud. candidate evaluation com. 1981-86, 87-95, chmn. investigation divsn. evaluation com. 1991-92, chmn. hearing divsn. evaluation com. 1992-93, gen. chmn. 1993-95, ct. liaison com. 1993-95, tort reform subcom. 1997), Chgo. Bar Found. (bd. dirs. 1999-2000). Roman Catholic. Office: Dykema Gossett Rooks Pitts 10 S Wacker Dr Ste 2300 Chicago IL 60606-7407

BURNS, THAGRUS ASHER, manufacturing company executive, former life insurance company executive; b. Columbia City, Ind., Feb. 19, 1917; s. Harlow A. and Hazlette (Wise) B.; m. Dorothy Kimble, May 1, 1942; children: Steven L., Gerald A. AB, Wabash Coll., 1939. With Lincoln Nat. Life Ins. Co., Ft. Wayne, Ind., 1939-80, treas., 1967-80, Lincoln Nat. Life Co., 1967-80, Lincoln Nat. Corp., 1968-80; pres. Burns Mfg. Inc., Ft. Wayne, 1980—. Treas., dir. Lincoln Nat. Life Found. Served to lt. USNR, 1942-45. Mem. Financial Execs. Inst., Phi Beta Kappa. Achievements include inventor automatic feeder for typewriter, inserting machine and clipping catcher for hedge trimmer. Home and Office: 2525 Abbey Dr Apt 3 Fort Wayne IN 46835-3127

BURR, BROOKS MILO, zoology educator; b. Toledo, Aug. 15, 1949; s. Lawrence E. and Beverly Joy (Herald) B.; m. Patti Ann Grubb, Mar. 5, 1977 (div. July 1987); 1 child, Jordan Brooks; m. Ingrid M. Hansen, May 25, 1999. BA, Greenville Coll., 1971; MS, U. Ill., 1974, PhD, 1977. Cert. scuba diver Nat. Assn. Underwater Instrs. Lab. instr. dept. biology Greenville (Ill.) Coll., 1971-72; rsch. asst. Ill. Natural History Survey, Champaign, 1972-77, affiliate scientist Ctr. for Biodiversity Urbana, 1989—; from asst. prof. to prof. dept. zoology So. Ill. U., Carbondale, 1977—. Adv. panel US Fish and Wildlife Svc., 1990—; adj. prof. dept. biology U. N.Mex., Albuquerque, 1991—; adj. prof. dept. ecology, ethology and evolution U. Ill., 1993—. Co-author: A Distributional Atlas of Kentucky Fishes, 1986, A Field Guide to Fishes, North America North of Mexico, 1991 (selected as one of Outstanding Acad. Books of 1992, Choice Mag.); contbr. articles to profl. jours. Recipient Paper of Yr. award Ohio Jour. Sci., 1986, Coll. Sci. Rsch. award, So. Ill. Univ., 2001; Phi Kappa Phi Outstanding scholar So. Ill. U., 2002. Mem. AAAS, Am. Soc. Ichthyologists and Herpetologists (sec., mem. exec. com. 1990-94, pres.-elect 2000, pres. 2001—), Soc. Systematic Zoology, Biol. Soc. Washington, Assn. Systematic Collections, Sigma Xi (Leo M. Kaplan award 1990), Phi Kappa Phi (Scholar of Yr. 2002). Achievements include the discovery and description of 10 species of fish new to science from North American fresh waters. Home: 203 S Wedgewood Ln Carbondale IL 62901-2147 Office: So Ill Univ Dept Zoology Carbondale IL 62901-6501 Home Phone: 618-559-0243; Office Phone: 618-453-4112. Business E-Mail: burr@zoology.siu.edu.

BURR, DAVID BENTLEY, anatomy educator; b. Findlay, Ohio, June 28, 1951; s. Willard Bentley and Dorothy Eleanor (Beiler) B.; m. Lisa Marie Pedigo; children: Kathryn Lise, Michael David, Erik Johan. BA, Beloit Coll., Wis., 1973; MA, U. Colo., 1974, PhD, 1977. Instr. anatomy U. Kans. Med. Ctr., Kansas City, 1977-78, asst. prof. anatomy, 1978-80; asst. prof. anatomy and orthop. surgery W.Va. U., Morgantown, 1980-83, assoc. prof., 1983-86, prof., 1986-90; chmn. dept. anatomy and cell biology, prof. anatomy, bioengring. and orthopedic surgery Ind. U., Indpls., 1990—. Mem. adv. bd. dirs. Primate Found. Am., Tempe, Ariz., 1978—; cons. County Med. Examiner, Morgantown, 1983-89; mem. Adv. Group for the Treatment Human Remains, USDA, Monongahela Nat. Forest Svc., 1989; cons. ASA, 1990-91, Am. Inst. Biol. Sci., NAS, 1990—, U.S. Congress Office Tech. Assessment, 1990; mem. biochemistry study sect. Arthritis found., 1992-95; spl. grants rev. com. NIH, 1996-2000. Author: Structure, Function & Adaptation of Compact Bone, 1989, Skeletal Tissue Mechanics, 1998, Musculoskeletal Fatigue and Stress Fracture, 2001, Bridging the Gap Between Dental and Orthopaedic Implants, 2002; mem. editl. bd. Bone, 1993-2003, Jour. Bone and Mineral Metabolism, 1994-, Jour. Biomech., 1999-, Calcif. Tiss. Int., 2000-; assoc. editor Bone, 2004—, Jour. Musculoskeletal Neuronal Interactions, 2004—, Exptl. Biol. Medicine, 2006—; contbr. articles to profl. jours. Pres. First Ward Sch. PTA, Morgantown, 1987—88; sec. Cub Scout Pack Com., 1989; chmn. troop com. Boy Scouts Am., 1993—95; linesman Morgantown Soccer League, 1988; sec. Classic Ragtime Soc., 1997—98; clk. witness and svc. First Friends Meeting, 1999—2001; mem. adminstrv. bd. Epworth United Meth. Ch., Indpls., 1992—93. Rsch. grantee NIH, 1988—, Orthopedic Rsch. and Edn. Found., 1985-86. Mem.: Internat. Soc. for Musculoskeletal and Neuronal Interactions (bd. dirs. 1999—2000, 2002—), Assn. Anatomy, Cell Biology and Neurobiology Chairpersons (pres. 2001—02), Am. Anatomy Assn. (exec. com. 1998—2001, chmn. jour. trust fund com. 2002—04, sec.-treas. 2004—05, pres. 2007—), Orthop. Rsch. Soc. (chmn. membership com. 2002—03, program chair 2005—06, pres.-elect 2007—), Internat. Soc. Bone Mineral Rsch., Am. Soc. Bone Mineral Rsch. Avocations: piano, softball, racquetball, stamps, reading. Office: Ind U Sch Medicine Dept Anat & Cell Biology 635 Barnhill Dr Indianapolis IN 46202-5126 Office Phone: 317-274-7496. Business E-Mail: dburr@iupui.edu.

BURR, TRACY L., food products executive; BS, U. Utah; M in Accountancy, Utah State U. CPA Tex., Calif., Utah. N.Am. corp. contr. Albert Fisher N.Am.; ptnr. Ernst & Young LLP, Deloitte & Touche; exec. v.p., CFO Schwan Food, Marshall, Minn., 2002—. Office: Schwan Food 115 W College Dr Marshall MN 56258

BURRELL, GARY, retired manufacturing executive; BS, Wichita State U.; MS, Rensselaer Polytechnic Inst. Dir., v.p. engring Lowrance Electronics, King Radio Corp., Allied Signal; co-founder Garmin Corp., 1989, co-chmn., 1989—2004, chmn. emeritus, 2004—. Named one of Forbes' Richest Americans, 2006. Office: Garmin Internat Inc 1200 E 151st St Olathe KS 66062

BURRELL, THOMAS J., marketing communication executive; m. Joli Burrell. Founder, chmn., CEO Burrell Comm., Chgo., 1971—2004, chmn. emeritus, 2004—. Office: Burell Communications 233 N Michigan Ave #29 Chicago IL 60601-5519

BURRIS, JOHN EDWARD, academic administrator, biologist, educator; b. Feb. 1, 1949; s. Robert Harza and Katherine (Brusse) Burris; m. Sally Ann Sandermann, Dec. 21, 1974; children: Jennifer, Margaret, Mary. AB, Harvard U., 1971; postgrad., U. Wis., 1971—72; PhD, U. Calif., San Diego, 1976. Asst. prof. biology Pa. State U., University Park, 1976—83, assoc. prof. biology, 1983—85; dir. bd. biology NRC/NAS, Washington, 1984—89; exec. dir. Commn. Life Scis., 1988—92; dir., CEO Marine Biology Lab, Woods Hole, Mass., 1992—2000; pres. Beloit College, Beloit, Wis., 2000—. Adj. assoc. prof. biology Pa. State U., University Park, 1985—89, adj. prof., 1989—2001; chmn. adv. com. student sci. enrichment program Burroughs Wellcome Fund, 1995—2002; life and microgravity scis. and applications adv. com. NASA, 1997—2001; trustee Krasnow Inst., 1999—2002. Bd. dirs. Radiation Effects Rsch. Found., Grass Found., 2001—07, Naples Stazione Zoologica, Consiglio Sci. Mem.: AAAS (bd. dirs. 2002—06), Am. Inst. Biol. Sci. (pres. elect 1995, pres. 1996), Phi Beta Kappa. Office: 700 College St Beloit WI 53511 Home Phone: 608-363-2299; Office Phone: 608-363-2201. Business E-Mail: burrisj@beloit.edu.

BURRIS, JOSEPH STEPHEN, agronomy educator; b. Cleve., Apr. 18, 1942; s. Charles Richard and Catherine T. (Pravica) B.; m. Joan Peterson; children: Jeffery S., John C., Jennifer K., Jason R. BS, Iowa State U., 1964; MS, Va. Poly. Inst., 1965, PhD, 1967. Research asst., Nat. Def. fellow Va. Poly. Inst., Blacksburg, 1964-67, dir. tobacco analysis lab., 1967; asst. prof. Iowa State U., Ames, 1968-72, assoc. prof., 1972-76, prof. agronomy and seed sci., 1976-99, prof. emeritus, 1999—; pres. Burris Cons., Ames, 1999—. Internat. cons. on seed prodn. FAO/UN Devel. Program, World Bank. Contbr. articles to profl. publs. Pres. PTA, Ames, 1980-81. Mem. Am. Soc. Agronomy, Crop Sci. Soc. Am. (Seed Sci. award 1998), Assn. Ofcl. Seed Analysts Methodist. Office: Burris Cons 1707 Burnett Ave Ames IA 50010-5338

BURRITT, DAVID B., manufacturing executive; b. 1955; BS in Acctg., Bradley Univ., 1977; MBA, Univ. Ill., 1990; completed Exec. Program, Stanford Univ., 1998, Aspen Inst., 2005. CPA, Cert. Mgmt. Acct. Inventory, budget acct., foundry ops. to gen. office fin. reporting Caterpillar, Peoria, Ill., 1978—90, mgr., bus. measurements, 1990—94; bus., mgr. Cat Belgium SA; gen. mgr., strategic, bus. svcs. Europe, Africa, Middle East, Switzerland; corp. controller Caterpillar Inc., Peoria, Ill., 2002—04, v.p., CFO, 2004—. Mem.: Fin. Execs. Internat., Inst. Mgmt. Acct., AICPA, Phi Kappa Phi (life). Office: Caterpillar Inc 100 NE Adams St Peoria IL 61629 Office Fax: 309-675-1000.

BURROUGHS, CHARLES EDWARD, lawyer; b. Milw., June 9, 1939; s. Edward Albert and Ann Monica (Bussman) B.; m. Kathleen Walton, Jan. 30, 1965; children— James, Michael, Lauri, Stephanie. B.S., U. Wis.-Madison, 1962, LL.B., 1965; LL.M., George Washington U., 1968. Bar: Wis. 1965, U.S. Dist. Ct. (ea. and we. dists.) Wis. 1965, U.S. Ct. Clms. 1967, U.S. Ct. Mil. Apls. 1967, U.S. Ct. Apls. (7th cir.) 1969, U.S. Supreme Ct. 1968. Assoc., Porter & Porter, Milw., 1969-71, Purtell, Purcell, Wilmot & Burroughs, 1971-86; ptnr.

VonBriesen & Purtell, 1986-91, Hinshaw & Culbertson, Milw. Served to capt. U.S. Army, 1965-69. Mem. ABA, AHLA, HFMA, State Bar Wis. (pres. health law sect.). Roman Catholic. Club: Milw. Athletic. Home: 10937 N Hedgewood Ln Mequon WI 53092-4907

BURROUGHS, HAROLD R., lawyer; BA cum laude, Middlebury Coll., 1982; JD cum laude, U. Mich., 1990. Bar: Mo 1990. Ptnr., group dep. Banking, Bus. and Pub. Fin. Bryan Cave LLP, St. Louis. Office: Bryan Cave LLP One Metropolitan Square 211 N Broadway, Ste 3600 Saint Louis MO 63102 Office Phone: 314-259-2706. E-mail: hrburroughs@bryancave.com.

BURROUGHS, MARGARET TAYLOR GOSS, artist, former museum director; b. St. Rose, La., Nov. 1, 1917; d. Alexander and Octavia (Pierre) Taylor; m. Bernard Goss, 1937; 1 child, Gayle; m. Charles Burroughs, 1949; 1 adopted child, Paul. BA in Edn, Art Inst. Chgo., 1946, MA, 1948; LHD (hon.), Lewis U., 1972; DHL (hon.), Chgo. State U., 1983. Tchr. art Chgo. Public Schs., 1944-68; prof. humanities Kennedy King Coll., Chgo., 1969-79; exec. dir., founder DuSable Mus. African Am. History, Chgo., 1961-84, dir. emeritus, 1984—; group shows include: LA County Mus., 1976, Corcoran Gallery, 1980; mem. Chgo. Council Fine Arts, 1976-80, Nat. Commn. Negro History and Culture, 1981—; founder Nat. Conf. Artists, 1959. Fellow NEH, 1968. Office: DuSable Museum 740 E 56th Pl Chicago IL 60637-1495 Office Phone: 312-374-4737.

BURROWS, BRIAN WILLIAM, retired research and development company executive; b. Burnie, TAS, Australia, Nov. 15, 1939; came to US, 1966; s. William Henry and Jean Elizabeth (Ling) B.; 1 child, Karin; m. Penny Nathan Kahan, 1998. BSc, U. Tasmania, 1960, BSc with honors, 1962; PhD, Southampton U., 1966. Staff scientist Tyco Labs., Inc., Waltham, Mass., 1966-68; lectr. Macquarie U., Sydney, Australia, 1969-71; chef de sect. Battelle-Geneva, Switzerland, 1971-75; group leader Inco, Ltd., Mississauga, Ont., Canada, 1976-77; program mgr., lab. dir. Gould, Inc., Rolling Meadows, Ill., 1977-86; v.p. rsch. and tech. USG Corp., Chgo., 1986—2005, ret., 2005. Contbr. articles to tech. jours.; patentee in field. Fellow: AAAS; mem.: Union League Club. Home: 927 Longmeadow Ct Barrington IL 60010-9391

BURSON, CHARLES W., lawyer, retired agricultural products executive; b. Memphis, Aug. 28, 1944; s. Leo R. and Josephine (Wainman) Burson; m. Marion Cornell, 1971; children: Clare, Kate. BA, U. Mich., 1966; MA, Cambridge U., England, 1968; JD, Harvard U., 1970. Assoc. Burson & Burson and Burson & Walkup, Memphis; ptnr. Wildman, Harrold, Allen, Dixon, & McDonnell, Memphis, 1981-88; atty. gen. State of Tenn., Nashville, 1988—96; legal counsel to v.p. The White House, Washington, 1993-99, asst. to pres., chief of staff & counselor to v.p., 1999—2001; exec. v.p., sec., gen. counsel Monsanto Co., St. Louis, 2001—06, spl. asst. & counsel to CEO, 2006; of counsel Bryan Cave LLP, St. Louis, 2007—. Del. Tenn. Constl. Conv., 1977, (chmn. State Spending Limitation Com.). Mem. at. Assn. Attys. Gen. 1988-97 (pres. 1994-95, chair FTC working group, mem. exec. com. securities group, chair consumer protection com. 1990-91, vice chair securities working group, Wyman award 1994), Tenn. Bd. Law Examiners, 1982-88 (pres. 1987-88). Jewish. Office: Bryan Cave LLP One Metropolitan Sq 211 N Broadway Sq Ste 3600 Saint Louis MO 63102 E-mail: charles.burson@bryancave.com.

BURSTEIN, RICHARD JOEL, lawyer; b. Detroit, Feb. 9, 1945; s. Harry Seymour and Florence (Rosen) B.; m. Gayle Lee Handmaker, Dec. 21, 1969; children: Stephanie Faith, Melissa Amy. Grad., U. Mich., 1966; JD, Wayne State U., 1969. Bar: Mich. 1969, U.S. Ct. Appeals (ea. dist.) Mich. 1969. Ptnr. Smith Miro Hirsch & Brody, Detroit, 1969-81, Honigman Miller Schwartz & Cohn, Detroit, 1981—. Bd. dirs. Sandy Corp., Troy, Mich.; bd. dirs. Met. Affairs Corp., Detroit; co-chmn. Artrain. Mem. Am. Coll. Real Estate Lawyers. Office: Honigman Miller Schwartz & Cohn Ste 100 38500 Woodward Ave Bloomfield Hills MI 48304-5048

BURTON, CHARLES VICTOR, neurosurgeon; b. NYC, Jan. 2, 1935; s. Norman Howard and Ruth Esther (Putziger) B.; m. Joy Burton; children— Matthew, Timothy, Andrew, Dawn, Stacy, Chad. Student, Johns Hopkins U., Balt., 1952-56; MD, N.Y. Med. Coll., 1960. Diplomate Am. Bd. Neurol. Surgery, Nat. Bd. Med. Examiners, Am. Bd. Forensic Medicine, Am Bd. Spinal Surgery. Intern surgery Yale U. Med. Ctr., 1961—62; asst. resident neurol. surgery Johns Hopkins Hosp., Balt., 1962—66, chief resident, 1966—67; assoc. chief surgery, chief neurosurgery USPHS Hosp., Seattle, 1967—69; vis. research affiliate Primate Ctr., U. Wash., 1967—69; asst. prof. neurosurgery Temple U. Health Scis. Ctr., Phila., 1970—73, assoc. prof., 1973—74, neurol. research coordinator, 1970—74; dir. dept. neuroaugmentive surgery Sister Kenny Inst., Mpls., 1974—81, med. dir. Low Back Clinic, 1978—81; med. dir. Inst. Low Back & Neck Care, Mpls., 1981—2004, Ctr. Restorative Spine Surgery, St. Paul, 2004—, Pounceforte Techs. Ltd., 2006—. Biomed. Instrumentations Internat., Ltd., 1988-92; co-chmn. Joint eurosurg. Com. on Devices and Drugs, 1973-77; chmn. adv. panel on neurologic devices FDA, 1974-77, Internat. Standards Orgn., 1974-76; mem. U.S. Biomed. Instrumentation Del. to Soviet Union, 1974; co-chmn. Am. Bd. Spine Surgery. Editor Neuroorthopedics jour., 1987-1998, editor The Burton Report; editor-in-chief www.burtonreport.com, 2000, 04, 06. Rsch. fellow, Nat. Polio Found., 1956, HEW, 1958, neurosurg. fellow, Johns Hopkins Hosp., 1960—61, 1962—67, 1969—70. Fellow ACS (exec. com. Minn. chpt. 1989-92); mem. Congress Neurol. Surgeons (chmn. com. materials and devices 1972-79), Am. Assn. eurol. Surgeons, Minn. Neurosurg. Soc., AAAS, ASTM (chmn. com. materials 1973-78), Internat. Soc. Study of Lumbar Spine (exec. com. 1986-89), N.Am. Spine Soc. (exec. com. 1987-91, chmn. com. on profl. conduct 1991-92, dir. coun. mem. affairs 1992-94, bd. dirs. 1990-94), Am. Nat. Standards Inst. (med. device tech. adv. bd. 1973-78), Am. Bd. Spine Surgery (bd. dirs. 1997—, vice chair 2002—, chair ethics com. 1998—), Philadelphia County Med. Soc. (med.-legal com. 1970-74), Minn. Med. Assn. (Gold medal award, subcom. on med. testimony 1978—), Hennepin County Med. Soc. (med.-legal com. 1975—), Mpls. Acad. Medicine, Cor et Manus Soc., Profl. Assn. Diving Instrs. (underwater photography splty. diver), Am. Back Soc., Twin Cities Spine Soc. (pres. 1994-95), Back Pain Assn. Am. (hon. chmn. 1995—), Am. Bd. Spine Surgery (bd. dirs. 1997, chmn. ethics com., v.p. 2002—, chmn. med.-legal com., co-chmn. 2002—), Assn. Ethics Spine Surgery (bd. dirs. 2007—), Johns Hopkins U. Alumni Assn. (pres. Minn. chpt. 1988-92), Yale Surg. Soc., Alpha Epsilon Delta. Achievements include patents for surgical devices, operating room fiberoptic headlights, clinical therapy systems and techniques. Home: The Lowry 901 350 St Peter St Ste 901 Saint Paul MN 55102 Office: Ctr Restorative Spine Surgery Ste 220 Gallery Tower Office Bldg 514 St Peter St Saint Paul MN 55102 Office Phone: 651-287-8781. Business E-Mail: cburton@restorativespinesurgery.com. E-mail: burtrep@ens.net.

BURTON, CHERYL, newscaster; b. Chgo. BS in Psychology and Biology, U. Ill., Champaign. Host Minority Bus. Report WGN-TV, Chgo., 1989; reporter WMBD-TV, Peoria, Ill., 1990; weekend anchor KWCH-TV, Wichita, Kans., 1990—92, host Viewpoint, 1990—92; weekend co-anchor and reporter WLS-TV, Chgo., 1992—2003, co-anchor and contbg. anchor 5 pm news, 2003—. Vol. Boys and Girls Club of Am., Rush-Presbyn./St. Luke's Fashion Show; motivational spkr. Chgo. Pub. Sch.; bd. mem. City Yr., Chgo. Recipient Kizzy Image and Achievement award, 1998, Phenomenal Woman award, Expo Today's Black Woman, 1997, Emmy award, 2002. Mem.: Nat. Assn. of Black Journalists, Chgo. Assn. of Black Journalists (now named Russ Ewing award 1996, 2003), Life with Lupus Guild, Delta Sigma Theta. Office: WLS-TV 190 N State St Chicago IL 60601

BURTON, DAN L., congressman; b. Indpls., June 21, 1938; m. Barbara Jean Logan, 1959; children: Kelly, Danielle Lee, Danny Lee II. Mem. Ind. Ho. Reps., Indpls., 1967-68, 77-80, Ind. State Senate, 1969-70, 81-82; owner ins. and real estate firm, 1968—; mem. U.S. Congress from 5th Ind. dist. (formerly 6th), 1983—. Mem. internat. rels. com.; chmn. govt. reform and oversight com. Pres. Vols. of Am.; pres. Ind. Christian Benevolent Assn., Com. for Constl. Govt., Family Support Ctr. Served with U.S. Army, 1957-58. Republican. Office: US Ho Reps 2185 Rayburn Ho Office Bldg Washington DC 20515-1405

BURTON, DONALD JOSEPH, chemistry professor; b. Balt., July 16, 1934; s. Lawrence Andrew and Dorothy Wilhelmina (Koehler) B.; m. Margaret Anna Billing, June 21, 1958; children— Andrew, Jennifer, David, Julie, Elizabeth. BS, Loyola Coll., Balt., 1956; PhD, Cornell U., 1961; postgrad., Purdue U., 1961-62. Asst. prof. chemistry dept. U. Iowa, Iowa City, 1962-67, assoc. prof., 1967-70, prof., 1970—, Roy Carver/Ralph Shriner prof. chemistry, 1989—. Recipient Gov.'s Sci. Medal for Sci. Achievement, 1988; Japanese Soc. for Promotion Sci. fellow, 1979 Mem. Am. Chem. Soc. (chmn. fluorine divsn. 1978, award for creative work in fluorine chemistry 1984, Midwest Chemistry award 1990, ACS divsn. Fluorine Chemistry Disting. Svc. award 2003), Chem. Soc. London, Sigma Xi, Alpha Chi Sigma. Home: 105 Notting Hill Ln Iowa City IA 52245-9217 Office: U Iowa Dept Chemistry Iowa City IA 52242 Office Phone: 319-335-1363. Business E-Mail: donald-burton@uiowa.edu.

BURTON, GARY L., state legislator; b. Knoxville, Iowa, Aug. 26, 1945; m. Jennifer Grant; children: Dianne, Todd, Lance, Melinda, Tye, Nathan. BS, Ea. N.Mex. U., 1968. Former mem. Joplin (Mo.) City Coun.; Mo. State rep. Dist. 128, 1988—; ins. agt. Mem. energy and environ. com., budget com., appropriations/edn. and transp. coms., ins. com., mines and mining com., state parks com., recreation and natural resources com. Mo. Ho. Reps.; former mem. Joplin Exec. Call Program, econ. devel. market, area solid waste, chamber govt. affairs and Joplin mote tax coms. Mem. Elks, Joplin C. of C., Mo. Life Underwriters, Mo. Spl. Olympics (state treas.). Home: 1101 S Willard Ave Apt D Joplin MO 64801-3780

BURTON, RAYMOND CHARLES, JR., retired transportation company executive; b. Phila., Aug. 29, 1938; s. Raymond Charles and Phyllis (Clifford) B.; m. Madeline Ann Starmann, Feb. 13, 1999; children: Carolyn Starmann, Raymond Starmann. BA, Cornell U., 1960; MBA, U. Pa., 1963. Various operating positions Santa Fe Ry. Co., 1963-68, asst. controller, 1968-69; asst. treas. Santa Fe Industries, Chgo., 1969-74; asst. v.p. planning, treas. Burlington No., Inc., 1974-79, v.p. and treas. St. Paul and Seattle, 1979-82; v.p. planning Internat. Harvester Co., Chgo., 1982; chmn., pres., CEO, TTX Co., Chgo., 1982-2000; pres., CEO, Railbox Co., Railgon Co., Chgo., 1982-2000; ret., 2000. 1st lt. U.S. Army, 1960-61. Mem.: Met. Club. Republican. Presbyterian.

BURTON, WOODY, state legislator; b. Indpls., June 11, 1945; m. Volly Burton; children: Woody Lee, Jeff, April Stirling. Student, Ind. U. Real estate broker, mgr., carpenter Better Homes & Gardens; mem. Ind. State Ho. of Reps. Dist. 58, 1988—, mem. elections and apportionment com., mem. ins., corp. and small bus., roads and transp. coms., mem. ways and means com., chmn. fin. com. Mem. Johnson County Coun., 1980-84, County Planning Commn., 1983, County Coun. on Aging, 1983-85. Mem. Nat. Assn. Realtors, Ind. Assn. Realtors, Met. Indpls. Bd. Realtors, Ind. Auctioneers Assn., Greenwood Masonic Lodge, Scottish Rite, Murat Shrine.

BURZYNSKI, JAMES BRADLEY, state legislator; b. Christopher, Ill., July 13, 1955; m. Judy Burzynski; 2 children. AA, Rend Lake CC; BA, Ill. Wesleyan Coll. Tchr. Pinckneyville Mid. Schs.; farm bur. mgr. Clark, Clinton counties; govtl. affairs dir. DeKalb County Farm Bur.; chmn. DeKalb County Rep. Com.; mem. Ill. State Ho. Reps., 1990—93, Ill. State Senate Dist. 35, 1993—. Chair licenced activities com.; mem. state govt. ops. com.; mem. exec. edn. and higher edn. appropriations com.; senate rep. caucus chmn., 2003—. Adv. bd. DeKalb Salvation Army. Mem.: C. of C. Rockford, C. of C. Belvidere, C. of C. Rochelle, C. of C. Dekalb, Midwest Higher Edn. Commn., C. of C. Sycamore, Sycamore Kiwanis. Address: 505 Dekalb Ave Sycamore IL 60178-1719 Office Phone: 815-895-6318. E-mail: info@senatorbrad.com.

BURZYNSKI, SUSAN MARIE, newspaper editor; b. Jackson, Mich., Jan. 1, 1953; d. Leon Walter and Claudia (Kulpinski) B.; m. James W. Bush, May 22, 1976 (div. 1989); children: Lisa M., Kevin J.; m. George K. Bullard, Jr., Mar. 21, 1992. AA, Jackson C.C., 1972; BA, Mich. State, 1974. Reporter Saratogian, Saratoga Springs, N.Y., 1974, Gongwer News Svc., Lansing, Mich., 1975, The State Jour., Lansing, 1975-79; Metro editor Port Huron (Mich.) Times Herald, 1979-82, mng. editor, 1982-86; asst. city editor Detroit News, 1986-87, Sunday news editor, 1987, news editor, 1988-91, asst. mng. editor/news, 1991-96, asst. mng. editor, recruiting and tng., 1996-98, asst. mng. editor, adminstr., 1998-2000, assoc. editor, 2000—04, mng. editor, 2004—. Roman Catholic. Avocations: swimming, tennis, bicycling, knitting. Office: Detroit News 615 W Lafayette Blvd Detroit MI 48226-3197 Office Phone: 313-222-2772. Business E-Mail: sburzynski@detnews.com.

BUS, JAMES STANLEY, toxicologist; b. Kalamazoo, June 27, 1949; s. Charles J. and Sena (Wolthuis) B.; m. Gerda W. Hekman, Apr. 20, 1974; children: Sara E., Timothy J., Brian M. BS in Medicinal Chemistry, U. Mich., 1971; PhD in Pharmacology, Mich. State U., 1975. Diplomate Am. Bd. Toxicology (v.p., pres. 1985-87). NIH predoctoral trainee Dept. Pharmacology, Mich. State U., East Lansing, 1971-75; asst. prof. environ. health U. Cin., 1975-76; scientist I (biochem. toxicologist) Chem. Industry Inst. Toxicology, Research Triangle Park, NC, 1977-84, scientist II (biochem. toxicologist), 1984-86; assoc. dir. pathology/toxicology, dir. drug metabolism rsch. The Upjohn Co., Kalamazoo, 1986-89; toxicology rsch. lab. Dow Chem. Co., Midland, Mich., 1989-91, project mgr., 1992-93, rsch. mgr., tech. dir., 1994—2001, dir. external tech., 2001—. Adj. assoc. prof. curriculum in toxicology U. N.C., Chapel Hill, 1984-88; adj. prof. pharmacology/toxicology Mich. State U., East Lansing, 1987—; safety assessment bd. advisors Merck, Sharp & Dohme Lab., West Point, Pa., 1985-86; mem. bd. sci. counselors EPA, 1996-2003, mem. sci. adv. bd., 2003-; mem. sci. adv. bd. NTP, 1997-2001, NCTR (FDA), 2006-. Co-editor: Patty's Industrial Hygiene and Toxicology, Vol. 3B, 1995; assoc. editor Toxicology and Applied Pharmacology, 1989-92, speciality editor, 2003—; editl. bd. Reproductive Toxicology, 1986-96; contbr. articles to profl. jours. Trustee Covenant Coll., Lookout Mountain,. Ga., 1984-87. Recipient Robert A. Scala award, Environ. Occupl. Health Sci. Inst., Rutgers U., 1999, Disting. Alumni award, Mich. State U. Dept. Pharmacol. Toxicology, 2001. Fellow Acad. Toxicology Scis.; mem. Soc. Toxicology (pres. 1996-97, Achievement award 1987), Am. Soc. for Pharmacology and Exptl. Therapeutics, Teratology Soc., Am. Conf. Govt. Indsl. Hygiene (mem. chem. substances threshold limit value com. 1993-2002), Nat. Acad. Scis. (emerging issues and data on environ. contaminants com. 2002—2007, bd. on environ. scis. and toxicology 2005-). Republican. Achievements include research dealing with mechanisms of chemical toxicity, including oxidant and glutathione mediated toxicities. Office: Dow Chemical Co Toxicology Rsch Lab 1803 Bldg Midland MI 48674-0001 Office Phone: 989-636-4557. Business E-Mail: jbus@dow.com.

BUSCH, ANNIE, library director; b. Joplin, Mo., Jan. 6, 1947; d. George Lee and Margaret Eleanor (Williams) Chancellor; 1 child, William Andrew Keller. BA, Mo. U., 1969, MA, 1976; D in Pub. Affairs (hon.), Mo. State U., 2007. Br. mgr. St. Charles City Coun. Libr., Mo., 1977-84, Springfield/Greene County Libr., Mo., 1985-89, exec. dir., 1989—. Exec. bd. Mo. Libr. Network Corp., St. Louis, 1991-96; bd. dirs. Jordan Valley Innovation Ctr. Adv. bd. Springfield Pub. Sch. Found., 1992—94, St. John's Health Sys., Boys and Girls Town, Good Cmty. Task Force, 1999—2002; pres. Ozarks Regional Info. On-Line etwork, Springfield, 1993—98; mem. Gov.'s Commn. on Informational Tech., Cmty. Task Force, Springfield, 1993—98, Cmty. Partnership of the Ozarks, 1998; exec. bd. Mo. Rsch. and Edn. Network, pres., 1996—97; task force Mo. Goals 2000, Mo. Census 2000 Complete Count Com., 1999—2000; coord. com. Springfield Vision 20/20; chair Sec. of State Adv. Coun., 2001—05; adv. com. S.W. Mo. State U. Coll. Humanities and Pub. Affairs; bd. dirs. Ozarks Pub. TV, 1994—2000, Every Kid Counts, Wilson's Creek Nat. Battlefield Found., Mayors Commn. for Children, 2005—; bd. trustees Forest Inst. Profl. Psychology. Mem.: Mo. Libr. Assn. (exec. bd. 1990—94, pres. 1993—94), Springfield Area C. of C. (bd. dirs.), Springfield Rotary (pres. 1998—99). Office: Springfield-Greene Cty Libr PO Box 760 Springfield MO 65801-0760 Home Phone: 417-887-8485; Office Phone: 417-847-8120 ext 5. E-mail: annie@mail.sgcl.org.

BUSCH, ARTHUR ALLEN, lawyer; b. Flint, Mich., July 25, 1954; s. William Allen and Anna Elizabeth (York) B.; m. Bernadette Marie-Therese Regnier, Aug. 28, 1982. BA, Mich. State U., 1976, MLIR, 1977; JD, T.M. Cooley Law Sch., 1982. Bar: Mich. 1982, U.S. Dist. Ct. (ea. dist.) Mich. 1984. Supr. pers. Nat. Gypsum Co., Gibsonburg, Ohio, 1977-78; instr. Mich. State U., East Lansing, 1980-82; pvt. practice Flint, 1982-92; instr. C.S. Mott C.C., Flint, 1978—. Counsel Flint City Coun., 1982-84; cons. labor atty. City of Flint, 1984; prosecutor Genesee County, 1993—. Commr. Genesee County, 1986-92, mem. planning com., pks. and recreation; active Valley Area Agy. on Aging. Mem. Mich. Bar Assn., Genesee County Bar Assn. Democrat. Baptist.

BUSCH, AUGUST ADOLPHUS, III, retired brewery company executive; b. St. Louis, June 16, 1937; s. August Anheuser and Elizabeth (Overton) Busch; m. Susan Marie Hornibrook, Aug. 17, 1963 (div. 1969); children: August Adolphus IV, Susan Marie II; m. Virginia L. Wiley, Dec. 28, 1974; children: Steven August, Virginia Marie. Student, U. Ariz., 1957—58, Siebel Inst. Tech., 1960—61. With Anheuser-Busch, Inc., St. Louis, 1957—2002, pres., 1974—75, CEO, 1975—2002, chmn., 1977—2006. Bd. dirs. Southwestern Bell Tel. Co., 1980—83, AT&T Inc. (formerly SBC Comm. Inc.), 1983—, Emerson Electric Co., Grupo Modelo SA de CV; chmn., Corporate Governance and Nominating Com. AT&T Inc., San Antonio, mem., Corp. Devel. Com., mem., Exec. Com. Exec. bd. St. Louis Boy Scouts Am.; bd. dirs. United Way Greater St. Louis. Mem.: Log Cabin Club, St. Louis Country Club.

BUSCH, AUGUST ADOLPHUS, IV, brewery company executive; b. June 15, 1964; s. August Adolphus Busch III and Susan Marie (Hornibrook). BS in Fin., St. Louis U., MS in Bus. Adminstrn.; Brewmaster's degree, Internat. Brewing Inst., Berlin; Ph.D in Bus. Adminstrn. (hon.), Webster U., 2006. Line foreman Anheuser-Busch, Inc., St. Louis, exec. asst. to brewing v.p., with mktg. dept., 1989, brand dir., 1991, v.p. brand mgmt., 1994, v.p. mktg., 1996—2000, v.p. mktg. and wholesale ops., 2000—02, pres., 2002—, CEO, 2006—, mgmt. com., bd. dirs.; group v.p. mktg. and wholesale ops. Anheuser-Busch Cos., Inc., St. Louis, 2000—06, strategy com. mem., pres., CEO, 2006—. Chmn. Beer Inst.; bd. mem. FedEx Corp., Memphis, 2003—. Bd. mem. Muscular Dystrophy Assn., Loyola Inst., St. Louis, The BackStoppers; mem. adv. bd. Am. Paralysis Assn., Gen. Henry Hugh Shelton Leadership Initiative, NC State U.; bd. fellows Claremont U. Ctr. and Grad. Sch.; bd. govs. Cardinal Glennon Hosp., St. Louis; gen. co-chmn. St. Louis Am. Found. Awards program. Named Corp. Mktg. Exec. of Yr., Delaney Report, 1999, Lew Wasserman Spirit of Democracy Man of Yr., 2003, Advertiser of Yr., 48th Cannes Internat. Advt. Festival, 2001; named to Am. Advt. Fedn. Hall of Achievement, 2000; recipient Intrepid Salute award, Gerald S. Snyder Heart award, Larry King Cardiac Found. Office: Anheuser Busch Cos Inc One Busch Pl Saint Louis MO 63118

BUSCH, JOHN ARTHUR, lawyer, business executive; b. Indpls., Mar. 23, 1951; s. John L. and Betty (Thomas) B.; m. Barbara Ann Holt, June 23, 1973; children: Abigail, Elizabeth, Amanda, Rachel. BA, Wabash Coll., 1973; JD, Duke U., 1976. Bar: Wis. 1976, U.S. Dist. Ct. (ea. we. dists.) Wis., U.S. Ct. Appeals (5th and 7th cirs.) 1976. Assoc. Michael, Best & Friedrich, Milw., 1976-83, ptnr., 1983—; chmn. litigation dept. Michael Best & Friedrich, 1990—95, mgmt. com., 1995—2001, mng. ptnr. Milw. office, 2003—04; CEO Lorman Edn. Svcs., Eau Claire, 2006—. Mem. ad hoc com. on alternative dispute resolution Milw. Cir. Ct., ad hoc com. on multidisciplinary practices State Bar, mem. bd. govs., 2001-03. Treas. North Shore Rep. Club, Milw., 1984-85, vice chmn., 1985-86, chmn., 1987-89; del. Rep. State Conv., Milw., 1986; mem. local rules adv. com. Ea. dist., Wis.; mem. com. Fed. Bench Bar; bd. dir. New Am. Policy Inst., 2005—; bd. trustees Mich. Maritime Mus., bd. dir., 2005—. Master: Am. Inns of Ct.; mem.: ABA, Wis. Bar Assn., Milw. Bar Assn. Home: 1025 E Lyon St Milwaukee WI 53202 Office: Michael Best & Friedrich 100 E Wisconsin Ave Ste 3300 Milwaukee WI 53202-4108 Office Phone: 414-225-4977. Business E-Mail: jabusch@michaelbest.com.

BUSCH, ROBERT HENRY, geneticist, researcher; b. Jefferson, Iowa, Oct. 22, 1937; s. Henry and Lena Margaret (Osterman) B.; m. Mavis Ann Bushman, Nov. 23, 1958; children: Shari Lynne, Todd William. BSc, Iowa State U., 1959, MSc, 1963; PhD, Purdue U., 1967. Asst. prof. N.D. State U., Fargo, 1967-72, assoc. prof., 1973-77, prof., 1977-78; rsch. geneticist USDA-ARS/U. Minn., St. Paul, 1978—. Cons. Nat. Hail Ins. Coun., Ill. and Colo., 1969-75, Internat. Atomic Energy Agy., UN. Developer 9 wheat varieties; contbr. chpts. to books, articles to profl. jours. Recipient Dedicated Svc. award Polk County Crop Improvement Assn., East Grand Forks, Minn., 1984; named Premier Seedsman Minn. Crop Improvement Assn., St. Paul, 1985. Fellow Crop Sci. Soc. Am. (editor 1976-78, com. chair 1988-90, bd. dirs. 1989-90), Am. Soc. Agronomy (Achievement award, Midwest Sr. Sci. 1998). Methodist. Avocations: sailing, fishing. Home: 2485 Galtier Cir Saint Paul MN 55113-3609 Office: U Minn Dept Agronomy Saint Paul MN 55108

BUSCHBACH, THOMAS CHARLES, geologist, consultant; b. Cicero, Ill., May 12, 1923; s. Thomas Dominick and Vivian (Smiley) B.; m. Mildred Merle Fletcher, Nov. 26, 1947; children— Thomas Richard, Susan Kay, Deborah Lynn BS, U. Ill., 1950, MS, 1951, PhD, 1959. Geologist, structural geology, stratigraphy, underground storage of natural gas Ill. Geol. Survey, 1951-78; coordinator New Madrid Seismotectonic Study, U.S. Nuclear Regulatory Commn., 1976-85; research prof. geology St. Louis U., 1978-85; geologic cons. Champaign, Ill., 1985—. Served to lt. comdr. USNR, 1942-47 Fellow Geol. Soc. Am. Home: 604 Park Lane Dr Champaign IL 61820-7631 Office: PO Box 1608 Champaign IL 61824-1608 Office Phone: 217-356-3667. E-mail: tcbusch@aol.com.

BUSCHMANN, SIEGFRIED, retired manufacturing executive; b. Essen, Germany, July 12, 1937; s. Walter and Frieda Maria (von. Stamm) B.; m. Rita Renate Moch, May 7, 1965; children: Verena, Mark. Diploma, Wilhelms U. Various exec. positions Thyssen AG, Duesseldorf, Germany, 1964-82; pres. Thyssen Holding Corp., Troy, Mich., 1982-99; chmn. ThyssenKrupp USA, Inc., 1999—2006; ret., 2006; sr. v.p. The Budd Co., Troy, 1982-83, sr. v.p., CFO, 1983-86, vice chmn., CFO, 1986-89, chmn., CEO, 1989—2001, chmn. bd., 2001—02. Chmn. exec. bd. Thyssen Budd Automotive GmbH, Essen, Germany, 1997—99; v.chmn., exec. bd. Thyssen Krupp Automotive AG, Bochum, Germany, 1999—2001, mem. supervisory bd., 2001—05. Avocation: golf. Office: Thyssenkrupp USA Inc PO Box 5084 3155 W Big Beaver Rd Troy MI 48007-5084

BUSDICKER, GORDON GENE, retired lawyer; b. Winona, Minn., Oct. 12, 1933; s. Harry John and Edna Mae (Rogers) B.; m. Noreen Decker; children— Karla E., Pamela J., Alison G., Neal A. BA, Hamline U., St. Paul, 1955; JD, Harvard U., 1958. Bar: Minn. Atty. Aluminum Co. of Am., Pitts., 1958-61; assoc. Faegre & Benson, Mpls., 1961-67, ptnr., 1967-99, ret., 1999. Trustee Hamline U., St. Paul, 1973—. Mem. ABA, Minn. Bar Assn., Interlachen Golf Club. Republican. Congregationalist. Avocations: boating, genealogy. Home: 3833 Abbott Ave S Minneapolis MN 55410-1036 Office Phone: 612-925-2091. Personal E-mail: busdick1@gmail.com.

BUSELMEIER, BERNARD JOSEPH, insurance company executive; b. Detroit, Feb. 10, 1956; s. Bernard August and Rita Mathilda (Cook) Buselmier; m. Carolyn Diane Karamon, Mar. 22, 2003; 1 child, Andrew Joseph. BBA in Acctg., U. Detroit, 1980, MBA, 1990. Various fin. positions ins. group Auto Club Mich., Dearborn, Mich., 1974-81; various fin. positions Motors Ins. Corp., Detroit, 1981-89, treas., 1989-98, v.p., treas., 1993-98; exec. v.p., CFO, Integon Corp., Winston-Salem, N.C., 1998-99; CFO GMAC Ins. Personal Lines, St. Louis, 1999—. Office: GMAC Ins Personal Lines 13736 Riverfort Dr Ste 700 Maryland Heights MO 63043

BUSEY, ROXANE C., lawyer; b. Chgo., June 15, 1949; BA cum laude, Miami U., 1970; MAT, Northwestern U., 1971, JD, 1975. Bar: Ill. 1975. Ptnr. Baker & McKenzie LLP, Chgo. Bd. mem. Holy Family Ministries, 2005—. Mem. ABA (chair antitrust sect. 2001-02, chmn. task force antitrust modernization 2004-07; chair health com., antitrust sect. 1989-92, antitrust sect. coun. 1992-95, officer 1995-03), Ill. State Bar Assn. (chair antitrust coun. 1984-85), Chgo. Bar Assn. (chair antitrust sect. 1990-91). Office: Baker & McKenzie LLP 1 Prudential Plz 130 E Randolph Dr Ste 3500 Chicago IL 60601 Office Phone: 312-861-8281. Office Fax: 312-698-2038. Business E-Mail: roxane.c.busey@bakernet.com.

BUSHNELL, WILLIAM RODGERS, agricultural research scientist; b. Wooster, Ohio, Aug. 19, 1931; s. John and Dyllone (Hempstead) B.; m. Ann Holcomb, Sep. 20, 1952; children: Thomas H., John A., Mary D. AB, U. Chgo., 1951; BS, Ohio State U., 1953, MS, 1955; PhD, U. Wis., 1960. Plant physiologist agrl. rsch. svc. U.S. Dept. Agr., St. Paul, 1960—. Adj. prof. U. Minn., St. Paul, 1973—. Contbr. numerous rsch. articles in plant sci. jours.; editor books in field. Named U.S. Sr. Scientist Alexander Von Humboldt Found., Germany, 1984. Fellow Am. Phytopathological Soc. Avocations: vineyard, folk music. Office: USDA Cereal Disease Lab 1551 Lindig St Saint Paul MN 55108-1050

BUSS, DANIEL FRANK, environmental scientist; b. Milw., Jan. 13, 1943; s. Lynn Charles and Pearl Elizabeth (Ward) B.; m. Ann Makal, Jan. 22, 1977; children: Jessica, Jonathan. BS, Carroll Coll., 1965; MS in Biology, U. Wis., 1972, MS in Environ. Engring., 1977, P.D.D. in Environ. Engring., 1985. Registered profl. engr., Wis. Dir. limnological studies Aqua-Tech, Inc., Waukesha, Wis., 1969-72; project mgr. environ. studies Point Beach Nuclear Plant, Two

Creeks, Wis., 1972-76; assoc., dir. aquatic studies environ. sci. div. Camp Dresser & McKee, Inc., Milw., 1977—, dir. indsl. service, 1978-90, office mgr., coord. for environ. assesments Milw., 1990—; mgr. Buss Environ. Cons. LLC, Milw. Lectr. nuc. power and environ., environ. auditing; mgr. hazardous waste superfund projects, dredge disposal planning projects; asbestos insp., mgmt. planner EPA, 1988, nat. accounts mgr. performance environ. site assessments property trans.; instr. environ. site assessments according to domestic and internat. stds. with consideration of bus. environ. risk for real property; crew leader, project task mgr. Hurricane Katrina Asbestos Bldg. Inspections, St. Bernard Parish, La., 2006. Author: An Environmental Study of the Ecological Effects on Lake Michigan of the Thermal Discharge from the Point Beach Nuclear Plant, 1976, Environmental Auditing--A Systematic Approach, 1984; contbr. articles to profl. jours, chpts. to books Mem. ASCE (chmn. site constrn. and remediation implementation manual task com.),Am. Nuclear Soc. (sec.-treas. Wis. sect., program mgr. waste disposal studies, program mgr. for remedial programs involving jet fuel and deicer contamination at Gen. Mitchell Internat. Airport), Midwest Soc. Electron Microscopists, Internat. Soc. Theoretical and Applied Limnology and Oceanography, Internat. Assn. Gt. Lakes Rsch., Am. Indsl. Hygiene Soc., Nat. Assn. Environ. Profls., Fed. Water Pollution Control Adminstrn., Cons. Engrs. Coun. (chmn. liaison com. Ill. and Chgo. Bar Assn., mem. com. for devel. site investigation manual ASCE, sec. ASCE com. to develop remedial design, feasibility study manual), Am. Assn. Environ. Engrs. (diplomate 1990, cert. hazardous materials mgr. 1988, hazard control mgr. 1988), Program mgr. design, construction mgmt., oper. UV/Oxidation system (used for treating herbicide contaminated ground water in Wisconsin), Am. Acad. Environ. Engrs. (Wis. state rep.), Glendale Wis. Econ. Devel. Com. and Bus. Coun., Sigma Xi. Achievements include research in environmental baseline studies and permitting of a public bulk terminal port in New Orleans. Home: 5543 N Shasta Dr Milwaukee WI 53209-4924 Office Phone: 414-559-8808. E-mail: danbuss@wi.rr.com.

BUSS, DARYL, veterinarian, dean; b. Rock Rapids, Iowa, Sept. 20, 1945; s. Herman Arend and Etta Esther (Klaasen) B.; m. Sharon Grace Haken, June 21, 1968; 1 child, Jennifer. BS, U. Minn., 1966, DVM, 1968; MS, U. Wis.-Madison, 1974, PhD, 1975. Intern Am. med. Ctr., NYC, 1968-69; assoc. vet. Hillcrest Animal Hosp., White Bear Lake, Minn., 1969-70; instr. Coll. of Vet. Medicine, U. Minn., St. Paul, 1970-71, Sch. of Vet. Medicine, U. Pa., Phila., 1971-72; rsch. fellow U. Wis., Madison, 1972-75; postdoctoral fellow Max Planck Inst. for Physiol. and Clin. Rsch., Bad Nauheim, Germany, 1975-76; assoc. prof. Coll. of Vet. Medicine, U. Fla., Gainesville, 1976-79, prof., chair dept. physiol. scis., 1979-94; dean, prof. cardiovascular physiology Sch. of Vet. Medicine, U. Wis., Madison, 1994—. Mem. Morris Animal Found. rsch. adv. bd., 1984-87; ad hoc mem. NIH, Dept. Health and Human Svcs. Internat. and Coop Projects Study Sect., 1993; vis. prof. Max Planck Inst. for Physiol. and Clin. Rsch., 1988-89. Contbr. articles to profl. jours. Grantee NIH, Am. Heart Assn. (Fla. affiliate), Merck Rsch. Found., others. Mem. Am. Vet. Med. Assn., Wis. Vet. Med. Assn. (exec. bd. 1994—), Am. Physiol. Soc., Am. Heart Assn. (mem. coun. on basic scis.), Internat. Soc. for Heart Rsch., Phi Kappa Phi, Sigma Xi, Phi Zeta. Avocations: history, photography, antiques, cooking. Office: Sch Vet Medicine U Wis Office 2170A 2015 Linden Dr W Madison WI 53706-1100 Office Phone: 608-263-6716. Business E-Mail: bussd@svm.vetmed.wisc.edu.

BUSSE, KEITH E., manufacturing executive; BA in Bus., U. Saint Francis; MBA, In. U, 1978. Division controller to v.p. Nucor Corp., 1972—93; founder Steel Dynamics, Fort Wayne, Ind., 1993, pres., CEO, 1993—2007, chmn., CEO, 2007—. Named Entrepreneur of the Yr., Ernst & Young, 1997; named one of the top 10 entrepreneurs in the U.S., Business Week, 1997, the best 5 Undiscovered CEO's, Investor Magazine, 1999; recipient Distinguished Alumnus Award, Indiana University, 1991. Office: c/o Steel Dynamics 6714 Pointe Inverness Way Fort Wayne IN 46804

BUSSMAN, DONALD HERBERT, lawyer; b. Lakewood, Ohio, July 15, 1925; s. Herbert L. and Hilda L. (Henrichs) B. PhB, U. of Chgo., 1947, JD, 1951. Bar: Ill. 1951. Atty. Swift & Co., Chgo., 1950-84; pvt. practice Chgo., 1985—. With U.S. Army, 1944-46. Mem. ABA, Chgo. Bar Assn., Am. Assn. of Individual Investors. Office: 860 N Dewitt Pl Ste 2101 Chicago IL 60611-5780 Home Phone: 312-649-9066.

BUTCHVAROV, PANAYOT KRUSTEV, philosophy educator; b. Sofia, Bulgaria, Apr. 2, 1933; s. Krustyu Panayotov and Vanya (Tsaneva) B.; m. Sue Graham, Sept. 28, 1954; children: Vanya, Christopher. BA, Robert Coll., Istanbul, 1952; MA, U. Va., 1954, PhD, 1955. Instr. philosophy U. Balt., 1955-56; asst. prof. U. S.C., 1956-59; asso. prof. Syracuse U., 1959-66, prof., 1966-68; vis. prof. U. Iowa, 1967-68, prof., 1968—, chmn. dept. philosophy, 1970-77; univ. found. disting. prof., 1995—. Vis. prof. U. Miami, Coral Gables, Fla., 1979-80; Simon lectr. U. Toronto, 1984; guest prof. Akad. für Philosophie, Liechtenstein, 1997. Author: Resemblance and Identity, 1966, The Concept of Knowledge, 1970, Being Qua Being, 1979, Skepticism in Ethics, 1989, Skepticism About the External World, 1998; editor: Jour. Philosophical Rsch., 1993—; mem. editl. bd.: Midwest Studies in Philosophy, Philos. Monographs; contbr. numerous articles and revs. to profl. jours. Mem. Am. Philos. Assn. (program com. 1971, chmn. 1975, nominating com. 1978, chmn. 1993-94, pres. ctrl. div. 1992-93), Ctrl. States Philos. Assn. (v.p. 1987-88, pres. 1988-89), Phi Beta Kappa.

BUTLER, JAMES E., automotive executive; CFO Venture Ind., Fraser, Mich. Office: Venture PO Box 278 Fraser MI 48026-0278 Office Fax: (810) 296-8863.

BUTLER, JOHN MUSGRAVE, financial consultant; b. Bklyn., Dec. 6, 1928; s. John Joseph and Sabina Catherine (Musgrave) Butler; m. Ann Elizabeth Kelly, July 9, 1955; children: Maureen, John, Ellen, Suzanne. BA cum laude, St. John's U., 1950; MBA, NYU, 1951. CPA N.Y., Ill. Sr. acct. Lybrand, Ross Bros. & Montgomery (CPAs), NYC, 1953-59; sr. auditor ITT Corp., NYC, 1959-62; asst. to contr. Dictaphone Corp., Bridgeport, Conn., 1962-63, contr. Bridgeport, Rye, NY, 1964—68; v.p. acctg. Chgo. & North Western Ry. Co., 1968-69, v.p. fin. and acctg., 1969-72, Chgo. and North Western Transp. Co., 1972-79, sr. v.p. fin. and acctg., 1979-89, dir., 1976-89, trustee, 1978-82, acting sr. v.p. fin. and acctg., 1994; sr. v.p. fin. and acctg., dir. CNW Corp., 1985-89; cons. in fin. and acctg. for bus., 1989—2005; instr. fin. DePaul U., Chgo., 1989—2001. Dir. Cath. Med. Mission Bd., NYC, 1998—2000. With USCGR, 1951—53. Roman Catholic.

BUTLER, JOHN WILLIAM, JR., lawyer; b. Detroit, Feb. 18, 1956; s. John William Sr. and Lucille Elmira (Miller) B. AB magna cum laude, Princeton U., 1977; JD, U. Mich., 1980. Bar: Mich. 1980, US Dist. Ct. (ea. and we. dists. Mich.) 1981, US Ct. Appeals (6th cir.), Ill. 1992. Assoc. Honigman, Miller, Schwartz & Cohn, Detroit, 1980-81; ptnr. Butzel, Keidan, Simon, Myers & Graham, Detroit, 1981-90; ptnr., co-leader corp. restructuring Skadden, Arps, Slate, Meagher & Flom, LLP, Chgo., 1990—. Chmn. bd. govs. Comml. Fin. Assn. Edn. Found.; co-chmn. INSOL 2005 World Congress; dir. Am. Bd. Certification, 1993—2003; group of Thirty-Six INSOL Internat., 1995—; chmn. Am. Bd. Certification, 1997. Contbr. chapters to books. Bd. govs. Hugh O'Brian Youth Leadership, 1998—; mem. exec. adv. coun. Children Affected by AIDS, 2003—; co-chair Renaissance American/BeardGroup Corp. Reorganizations Conf., 1999—, Healthcare Transactions Conf., 2000—. Named leader in the corp. restructuring and insolvency field, Chamber's Global, Chambers USA; named one of Top Dozen Restructuring Lawyers in Am., Turnarounds & Workouts, Top Ten Worldwide Restructuring Lawyers, Global Counsel, 2002, "Dealmakers of Yr.", The Am. Lawyer, 2004; named to Client Svc. All Star Team, BTI Consulting Group, 2004; recipient Chmn.'s award, Turnaround Mgmt. Assn., 2001. Fellow Am. Coll. Bankruptcy, 1997, Internat. Solvency Inst., 2002; mem. ABA, Am. Bankruptcy Inst.(dir. 1992-98), Comml. Law League Am., Fed. Bar Assn., Mich. Bar Assn., Oakland County Bar Assn., Detroit Bar Assn., Turnaround Mgmt. Assn. (dir. 1991-99 & 2001-, chmn. 1996-97, chmn. award 2001, chmn. anniversary convs., 10th (1998) and 15th (2003)); assoc. gen. counsel, Comml. Fin. Assn., 1998-2002. Republican. Presbyterian. Avocation: officiate HS and Coll. football teams. Office: Skadden Arps Slate Meagher & Flom 333 W Wacker Dr Chicago IL 60606 Office Phone: 312-407-0730. Office Fax: 312-407-8501. E-mail: jbutler@skadden.com.

BUTLER, KEVIN M., electronics executive; B in Psychology, U. Notre Dame, 1977, M in Psychology, 1979. Various pos., including prodn. supr., plant pers. mgr., sr. adminstr. classified employee complensation, mgr. exec. compensation GM Chevrolet Motor Divsn., 1976—89; dir. human resources GM Hydramatic divsn., Ypsilanti, Mich., 1989—91; dir. GM Health Care Plans, 1991—95; gen. dir. GM Health Care initiative staff, 1995—97; gen. dir. human resources Delphi Corp., Troy, Mich., 1997—2000, v.p. human resource mgmt., 2000—, mem. strategy bd., exec. champion pers. team. Exec. com. Midwest Bus. Group on Health. Adv. bd. Ind. U., Kokomo, Xavier U. Health Adminstrn.; bd. dirs. Am. Soc. Employers. Office: World Hdqrs Delphi Corp 5725 Delphi Dr Troy MI 48098-2815 Office Phone: 248-813-2000. Office Fax: 248-813-2670.

BUTLER, LOUIS BENNETT, JR., state supreme court justice; b. Chgo., Feb. 15, 1952; s. Louis Bennett and Gwendolyn (Prescott) Butler; m. Irene Marianne Hecht, Aug. 30, 1981; children: Jessica Marianne, Erika Nicole. BA, Lawrence U., 1973; JD, U. Wis., Madison, 1977. Bar: Ill. 1978, Wis. 1979, US Dist. Ct. (no. dist.) Ill. 1978, US Dist. Ct. (ea. dist.) Wis. 1979, US Ct. Appeals (7th cir.) 1979, US Supreme Ct. 1983. Tng. asst. legal writing U. Wis. Law Sch., Madison, 1974—76; patient right adv. Bur. Mental Health, 1976, hearing examiner, 1975—77; legal intern Prisoner's Legal Assistance, Chgo., 1977—78; atty. Independence Bank, 1978—79; appellate atty. Office State Pub. Defender, Milw., 1979—92; judge Milw. Mcpl. Ct., 1992—2002, Milw. County Cir. Ct., 2002—04; justice Wis. Supreme Ct., 2004—. Adj. prof. Marquette U., 1991—92; mem. faculty Nat. Jud. Coll., Reno, 2001—04; bd. dirs. criminal law sect. State Bar Wis., mem. individual rights and responsibilities sect. Active South Shore Cmty. Orgn., Chgo., 1978; pres. adv. bd. Adaptive Behavior Ctr., Chgo. Reed Mental Health Ctr., 1978. Mem.: NAACP, Wis. Black Lawyer's Assn. (treas. 1984—85, bd. dirs. 1984—, pres. 1985—86), Ill. State Bar Assn., Wis. Bar Assn. Democrat. Roman Catholic. Office: Wisc Supreme Ct PO Box 1688 Madison WI 53701-1688 Home Phone: 414-963-9649; Office Phone: 608-266-1884. Business E-Mail: louis.butler@wiscourts.gov.

BUTLER, MARGARET KAMPSCHAEFER, retired computer scientist; b. Evansville, Ind., Mar. 7, 1924; d. Otto Louis and Lou Etta (Rehsteiner) Kampschaefer; m. James W. Butler, Sept. 30, 1951; 1 child, Jay. AB, Ind. U., 1944; postgrad., U.S. Dept. Agr. Grad. Sch., 1945, U. Chgo., 1949, U. Minn., 1950. Statistician U.S. Bur. Labor Statistics, Washington, 1945-46, U.S. Air Forces in Europe, Erlangen and Wiesbaden, Germany, 1946-48, U.S. Bur. Labor Statistics, St. Paul, 1949-51; mathematician Argonne (Ill.) Nat. Lab., 1948-49, 51-80, sr. computer scientist, 1980-92; dir. Argonne Code Ctr. and Nat. Energy Software Ctr. Dept. Energy Computer Program Exch., 1960-91; spl. term appointee Argonne Nat. Lab., 1993—2006. Cons. AMF Corp., 1956—57, OECD, 1964, Poole Bros., 1967. Author: Careers for Women in Nuclear Science and Technology, 1992; editor Computer Physics Communications, 1969-80; contbr. (chpt.) The Application of Digital Computers to Problems in Reactor Physics, 1968, Advances in Nuclear Sci. and Technology, 1976; contbr. articles to profl. jours. Treas. Timberlake Civic Assn., 1958; rep. mem. nomination com. Hinsdale Caucus, Ill., 1961-62; coord. 6th dist. ERA, 1973-80; elected del. Rep. Nat. Conv., 1980; bd. mgr. DuPage dist. YWCA Met. Chgo., 1987-90; computer and info. sys. adv. bd. Coll. DuPage, 1987-95; industry adv. bd. computer sci. dept. Bradley U., 1988-91; vice chair Ill. Women's Polit. Caucus, 1987-90; chair voters svc. LWV, Burr-Ridge-Willowbrook, 1991-93; vol. Morton Arboretum, 1996-2005, Friends of Indian Prairie Pub. Libr., 2000-02, LaGrange Park Friends Libr., 2002—; bd. dirs. Plymouth Place Residents Coun., 2003-05, recording sec., 2006—; treas. Plymouth Landing Gift Shoppe, 2004—, spl. fin. and program coms., 2005-06. Recipient cert. of leadership Met. YWCA, Chgo., 1985, Merit award Chgo. Assn. Technol. Socs., 1988; named to Fed. 100, 1991; named Outstanding Woman Leader of DuPage County Sci., Tech. and Health Care, 1992. Fellow Am. Nuclear Soc. (mem. publs. com. 1965-71, bd. dirs. 1976-79, exec. com. 1977-78, chmn. bylaws and rules com., 1979-82, profl. women in ANS com. 1991-93, reviewer for publs., spl. award math. and computer divsn. 1992); mem. Assn. Computing Machinery (exec. com., sec. Chgo. chpt. 1963-65, publs. chmn. nat. conf. 1968, reviewer for publs.), Assn. Women in Sci. (pres. Chgo. area chpt. 1982, nat. exec. bd. 1985-87), Nat. Computer Conf. (chmn. Pioneer Day com. 1985, tech. program chmn. 1987). Independent. Home: 107 Brewster Lane La Grange Park IL 60526-6003

BUTLER, MERLIN GENE, physician, medical geneticist, educator; b. Atkinson, Nebr., Aug. 2, 1952; s. Garold Melvin and Berdena June (Sandall) B.; m. Ranae Ilene Kisker, Oct. 2, 1976; children: Michelle Ranae, Brian Gene. BA with very high distinction, Chadron State Coll., 1974, BS with very high distinction, 1975; MD, U. Nebr., Omaha, 1978; MS, U. Nebr., Lincoln, 1980; PhD, Ind. U., Indpls., 1984. Supervising physician Med. Info. Svcs., Omaha, 1978-80; rsch. assoc. dept. biology U. Notre Dame, South Bend, Ind., 1983-84; med. dir. North Ctrl. Ind. Regional Genetics Ctr., South Bend, 1983-84; dir. cytogenetics Meml. Hosp., South Bend, 1983-84; NIH postdoctoral fellow dept. med. genetics Sch. Medicine Ind. U., Indpls., 1980-83, adj. asst. prof. dept. med. genetics Sch. Medicine, 1984; asst. prof. dept. pediatrics Sch. Medicine Vanderbilt U., Nashville, 1984-90, dir. regional genetics program Sch. Medicine, 1984-98, dir. Cytogenetics Lab. dept. pediatrics Sch. Medicine, 1989-98, assoc. prof. dept. pediatrics, 1990-98, assoc. prof. dept. pathology, 1991-98, investigator John F. Kennedy Ctr. Rsch. on Edn. and Human Devel., Peabody Coll., 1987-98; assoc. dir. Inst. Behavior and Genetics; assoc. prof. dept. orthopedics Vanderbilt U., 1994-98. Adj. assoc. prof. dept. pediatrics Meharry Med. Coll., Nashville, 1988-98; genetics cons. Baptist Hosp., Nashville, 1985-98, Westside Hosp., Nashville, 1985-98, Nashville Gen. Hosp., 1985-98, chief, section of Med. Genetics and Molecular Medicine, Children's Mercy Hosp., Kansas City, Mo., 1998—, William R. Brown prof., chmn., 1998—, prof. dept. pediats., U. Mo.-Kansas City Sch. Medicine; mem. epidemiology genetic diseases subcom. Ind. State Bd. Health, 1983-84; faculty interviewer Vanderbilt U., 1987; peer reviewer Am. Jour. Human Genetics, Am. Jour. Med. Genetics, Clin. Genetics, Am. Jour. Diseases of Children, Dysmorphology and Clin. Genetics, Am. Jour. Mental Retardation, Jour. Pediatrics, So. Med. Jour., Human Mutations, Cancer Genetics and Cytogenetics, Pediatrics, Genomics, Prader-Willi Perspectives; mem. ad-hoc grant review com. NIH, 1990—, craniofacial assessment team Vanderbilt U., 1992-98; lectr., presenter in field. Author: Fragile X Syndrome: A Major Cause of X-Linked Mental Retardation, 1988, 1989; author: (with others) Genetics for the Medically Oriented, 1983, Novak's Textbook of Gynecology, 11th edit., 1988, Birth Defects Encyclopedia, 1990, Prader-Willi Syndrome and Other Chromosome 15q Deletion Disorders, 1992, Human Genetics: New Perspectives, 1994, 1992 International Fragile X Conference Proceedings, 1992, Prader-Willi and Angelman Syndromes Examples of Genetic Imprinting in Man, 1994, Prader-Willi Syndrome: A Guide for Parents and Physicians, 1995, Prader-Willi Syndrome: Clinical and Genetic Findings, 2000' editor: Genetics of Developmental Disabilities, 2005, Management of Prader-Willi Syndrome, 2005, Guide to America's Top Physicians, 2005; mem. editl. bd. Prader-Willi Perspectives, 1992—; contbr. numerous articles to profl. jours. including ature and New England Jour. Medicine. Grant reviewer March of Dimes Birth Defects Found., 1985—. Recipient Disting. Svc. award Chadron State Coll., 1986, Teaching award Osler Inst., 1989; grantee Univ. Rsch. Coun., 1985, 92-93, Tenn. Dept. Mental Health and Mental Retardation, 1986-91, Clin. Nutrition Rsch. Unit, 1986-88, Joseph P. Kennedy, Jr. Found., 1988, Clin. Rsch. Ctr. Meharry Med. Coll., 1989-98, Dept. Pathology, 1992-93, Orthopedic Rsch. Edn. Found., 1993-95, NIH, 1995—; Cancer Rsch. grantee Ind. U. Med. Ctr., 1980, Biomed. Rsch. Support grantee, 1985, 88, 89—, Clin. Rsch. grantee March of Dimes Birth Defects Found., 1987, 88, 90-92, Lyle V. Andrews Meml. scholar, 1974. Fellow Am. Coll. Med. Genetics (founder, diplomate, lab. practice subcom. 1993); mem. AMA (Physician Recognition award 1984, 87, 00), AAAS, Am. Bd. Med. Genetics (cert. clin. genetics and clin. cytogenetics), Am. Genetics Assn., Am. Soc. Human Genetics (cytogenetics resource com. 1992-97), Am. Fedn. Clin. Rsch., Coll. Am. Pathologists (cytogenetics resource com. 1992-97, molecular pathology resource com. 1993-97), So. Med. Assn., Davidson County Pediatric Soc., Metro. Med. Soc., Prader-Willi Syndrome Assn. (med. rsch. task force 1985—, diagnostic task force 1991—, sci. adv. bd. 1991—, chair 2000—), N.Y. Acad. Scis., Sigma Xi, Phi Chi. Avocations: gardening, camping, fishing, collecting sports memorabilia. Home: 6410 Hillside St Shawnee KS 66218-9070 Office: Children's Mercy Hosp 2401 Gillham Rd Kansas City MO 64108-4698 E-mail: mgbutler@cmh.edu.

BUTLER, RICHARD D., state treasurer; b. Rapid City, SD, Mar. 2, 1946; m. Karen Henry, Nov. 29, 1968; children: Adrian, Paul, Adriana, Cornelia. BA, U. S.D. Owner comml. ins. agy.; flour miller; treas. State of S.D., 1995—. Mem. State Bd. Fin., S.D. Pub. Deposit Protection Commn.; ex-officio mem. S.D. Investment Coun. Mem. Assn. Operative Millers. Anglican Catholic. Democrat. Office: Office of State Treas 500 E Capitol Ave Ste 212 Pierre SD 57501-5070 Fax: 605-773-3115. E-mail: dickb@st-treas.state.sd.us.

BUTT, EDWARD THOMAS, JR., lawyer; b. Chgo., Oct. 27, 1947; s. Edward T. and Helen Kathryn (Guy) B.; m. Leslie Laidlaw Hilton, Oct. 20, 1972; children: Julie Guy, Andrew McNaughton. BA, Lawrence U., 1968; JD, U. Mich., 1971. Bar: Ill. 1971, U.S. Dist. Ct. (no. dist.) Ill. 1971, Wis. 1975, U.S. Dist. Ct. (ea. dist.) Wis. 1978, U.S. Ct. Appeals (7th cir.) 1978, U.S. Ct. Claims 1982, U.S. Ct. Appeals (6th cir.) 1986, U.S. Ct. Appeals (6th cir.) 1987, Mich. 1997. Assoc. Wildman, Harrold, Allen & Dixon, Chgo., 1971-75, 76-78, ptnr., 1979-94, Lund & Butt, S.C., Minocqua, Wis., 1975-76; of counsel Swanson, Martin & Bell, Chgo. and Lisle, Ill., 1994—. Bd. dirs. Constl. Rights Found., Chgo. Mem. ABA, State Bar Wis., State Bar Mich., Def. Rsch. Inst., Crystal Lake Yacht Club, Crystal Downs Country Club. Avocations: distance running, sailing, golf. Home: Michabou Shores 1006 Tiba Rd Frankfort MI 49635-9216 Office: Swanson Martin & Bell 2525 Cabot Dr Ste 204 Lisle IL 60532

BUTT, P. LAWRENCE, lawyer; b. Indpls., 1941; BBA, U. Cinn., 1964; JD, Ind. U., 1968. Bar: 1968. With Marsh Supermarkets, Inc., Indpls., 1977—, v.p., counsel, sec., 1992—97, sr. v.p., counsel, sec., 1997—. Bd. dirs. Marsh Supermarkets, Inc. Office: Marsh Supermarkets Inc 9800 Crosspoint Blvd Indianapolis IN 46256-3350 Office Phone: 317-594-2100. Office Fax: 317-594-2704.

BUTTERBRODT, JOHN ERVIN, real estate company officer; b. Beaver Dam, Wis., Feb. 14, 1929; s. Ervin E. and Josephine M. (O'Mare) B.; m. June Rose Bohalter, Sept. 27, 1952; children— Claire, Daniel, Larry. U. Agriculture short course, 1946-47. Cert. tchr. real estate, rental weatherization inspector, real estate appraiser, sr. profl. appraiser; internat. cert. farm appraiser; cert. gen., lic. appraiser, Wis. Vice-pres. Pure Milk Assn., 1967-69; pres. Asso. Milk Producers, Inc. Chgo., 1969-75, State Brand Creameries, Madison, Wis., 1970—, Wis. Real Estate Co., Wis. Real Estate of Burnett Inc., 1978—, Sunset Hills Golf & Supper Club Inc., 1979—; chmn. bd. Realty World-Wis. Real Estate, Inc., 1985—; treas. Real Estate Cons., 1983—. Dir. Town Mut. Ins. Co., Central Milk Sales, Central Milk Producers Coop. Pres. Sch. Bd., 1968; bd. dirs. Nat. Milk Producers Fedn., Central Am. Coop. Fedn., World Dairy Expo. Recipient Am. Farmer degree Future Farmers of Am., 1949, hon. degree, 1973; Outstanding Wis. Farmer award, 1965; Outstanding Wis. 4-H Alumni award, 1973; named Realtor of Yr., 1979 Mem.: United Dairy Industry Assn. Republican. Office: 1708 N Spring St Beaver Dam WI 53916-1106 Office Phone: 920-887-1733. Business E-Mail: johnb@wisreal.com.

BUTTERFIELD, JAMES T., small business owner; b. Galion, Ohio, July 9, 1951; s. Carlos and Ethel Louise (Miller) B.; m. Mary Anne Shaffo, May 17, 1986; children: Jacob Alan, Emily Lauren. Cert. plumbing insp., 1986, backflow insp., 1981, cert. pipe welder, 1992, refrigerant handling technician, 1994, EPA, 1994, automatic sprinkler installer, 1997, gas line installer Dept. Trans., 2001, brazing, Ohio, 2005, nat. testing cert. med. gas. installer, 2005; lic. low pressure steam operator, 1976, plumbing contractor, Ohio, 1995, hydronics contractor, Ohio, NC, 2001, elec. contractor, Ohio, 2001, heating, ventilating, air conditioning contractor, Ohio, 2001. Apprentice Don Barnett Plumbing, Galion, Ohio, 1968-69, Rinehart Plumbing and Heating, Galion, Ohio, 1969-71; owner Butterfield Plumbing and Heating, Galion, Ohio, 1972—2004, Galion Sheet Metal, Ohio, 1982—2004; plumbing and piping foreman Pete Miller Inc., Marion, Ohio, 2004—. Mem. Am. Soc. Sanitary Engrs., Ohio Assn. Plumbing Insps. Home: 375 W Atwood St Galion OH 44833-2553 Office: Butterfield Plumbing and Heating PO Box 33 Galion OH 44833-0033 E-mail: bfield751@msn.com.

BUTTIGIEG, JOSEPH J., bank executive; BBA, U. Notre Dame, 1968; JD, Mich. State U. Coll. Law, 1975. Various to sr. v.p. Manufacturer's Bank, Detroit, 1972-89, exec. v.p., 1989-91; exec. v.p. global corp. banking Comerica, Inc., Detroit, 1995-99, vice-chmn. bus. bank, 1999—. Office: Comerica Inc MC 6401 PO Box 650282 Dallas TX 75265-0282 Office Phone: 214-462-4471.

BUTTREY, DONALD WAYNE, lawyer; b. Terre Haute, Ind., Feb. 6, 1935; s. William Edgar and Nellie (Vaughn) B.; children: Greg, Alan, Jason; m. Karen Lake, Mar. 23, 1985. BS, Ind. State U., 1956; JD, Ind. U., 1961. Bar: Ind. 1961, U.S. Dist. Ct. 1961, U.S. Ct. Appeals (7th cir.) 1972, U.S. Tax Ct. 1972, U.S. Supreme Ct. 1972. Law clk. to chief judge Steckler, US Dist. Ct. So. Dist. Ind., 1961-63; mem. McHale, Cook & Welch, P.C., Indpls., 1963—2006, pres., 1986-93, chmn., 1993—2001; of counsel Wooden & McLaughlin, LLP, 2001—. Chmn. Ctrl. Region IRS-Bar Liaison Com., 1984; jud. nominating com. Marion County Mcpl. Ct., 1993-96; mem. Estate Planning Coun. Indpls., 1990—. Note editor Ind. Law Jour., 1960-61. Trustee Ind. State U., 1992-2000, v.p. bd., 1997-2000; bd. dirs. Ind. State U. Found., 1991—. With AUS, 1956-58, Korea. Fellow Am. Coll. Tax Counsel, Am. Bar Found., Ind. State Bar Found., Indpls. Bar Found. (pres. 1993-96, Buchanan award 1999); mem. ABA (taxation, real property, probate and trust sect., liaison IRS-Bar Liaison com., taxation sect. 1995-96), Ind. State Bar Assn. (bd. govs. 1994-96, taxation, real property, probate and trust sect., chmn. taxation sect. 1982-83), Indpls. Bar Assn. (pres. 1990, mem. probate, taxation sects.), Highland Golf and Country Club, Columbia Club, Univ. Club (bd. dirs. 1997-2000). Presbyterian. Home Phone: 317-846-9290; Office Phone: 317-639-6151 ext. 309. Business E-Mail: dbuttrey@woodmaclaw.com.

BUTZBAUGH, ALFRED M., lawyer; b. Benton Harbor, Mich., July 25, 1940; AB, U. Mich., 1963, JD, 1966; MBA, U. Chgo., 1983. Bar: Mich. 1967, Tex. 1991. Ptnr. Butzbaugh & Dewane, St. Jospeh, Mich. Mem. ABA, State Bar Mich. (rep. assembly 1973-79, commr. 1992—, treas. 1996-97), State Bar Tex., Berrien County Bar Assn. (pres. 1982-83). Office: Butzbaugh & Dewane PLC Law and Title Bldg 811 Ship St Saint Joseph MI 49085-1171 E-mail: Al.bdlaw@parrett.net.

BUXTON, WINSLOW HURLBERT, paper company executive; Degree in Chem. Engring., U. Washington, 1961. Pres. Niagara of Wis. Paper Corp., 1986-89; with Pentair Inc., St. Paul, 1986—, v.p. paper group, 1989-90, pres., COO, dir., 1990-92, chmn., pres., 1993-99, chmn., CEO, 1999-2000, chmn., 2000—. Office: Pentair Inc 5500 Wayzata Blvd Ste 800 Minneapolis MN 55416-1261

BUYER, STEVEN EARLE, congressman, lawyer; b. Rensselaer, Ind., Nov. 26, 1958; m. Joni Geyer; children: Colleen, Ryan. BS in Bus. Adminstrn., The Citadel, 1980; JD, Valparaiso U., 1984. Officer Med. Svc. Corps U.S. Army, 1980, spl. asst. to U.S. Atty. Va., 1984-87; dep. atty. gen. Ind., 1987-88; atty., 1988—92; legal counsel 22nd Theater Army, Saudi Arabia, 1990-91; legal advisor U.S Armed Forces/Western Enemy Prisoner of War Camps/War Crimes Interrogations, Saudi Arabia, 1991; mem. U.S. Congress from 4th Ind. Dist., 1993—. Mem. com. on energy & commerce, U.S. Ho. of Reps.; mem. health, Energy and Air quality, environment & hazardous materials subcoms.; mem. com. on vet.'s affairs, chmn. subcom. oversights & investigations. Natl. Gaurd and Reserve Components Caucus Decorated Bronze Star. Republican. Office: US Ho Reps 2230 Rayburn Ho Office Bldg Washington DC 20515-1405

BYAL, NANCY LOUISE, food editor; b. Plainfield, NJ, Mar. 12, 1944; d. Albert William and Anna Marie (Goering) Zeiner; m. Wayne Ole Byal, May 2, 1967; 1 child, Jason David. BS, Iowa State U., 1965. Cert. home economist; cert. culinary profl. Product counselor Gen. Mills, Inc., Mpls., 1965-67; assoc. food editor Better Homes & Gardens Books Meredith Corp., Des Moines, 1968-72, assoc. food editor Better Homes & Gardens, 1972-74, sr. food editor, 1974-83, sr. dept. head Food and Nutrition, 1983-86, exec. food editor Better Homes and Gardens, 1986—. Chair, com. mem. Iowa State U. Coll. Family and Consumer Scis. Adv. Com., Ames; chmn., exec. mem. Julia Child Cookbook Awards Com. Editor, author: Better Home and Gardens Fondue Cook Book, 1970, Better Home and Gardens Salad Book, 1969. Named Home Economist in Bus. of Yr., Iowa Home Economists in Bus., 1992. Mem. Internat. Assn. Culinary Profls., Am. Inst. Food and Wine (mem. tast and health com.), Am. Assn. Family and Consumer Scis., Luth. Women's Missionary League. Avocations: gardening, crafting, reading. Office: Meredith Corp 1716 Locust St Des Moines IA 50309-3023

BYARS, DENNIS M., state legislator; b. Beatrice, Nebr., Aug. 23, 1940; m. Janet A. Busboom, Apr. 10, 1981; children: Mark, Jonathan. Student, U. Nebr., Doane Coll. Former small bus. owner; mem. Nebr. Legislature from 30th dist., Lincoln, 1988-94, 98—. Dir. cmty. support, govt. rels. Martin Luther Home Found.; mem. Beatrice Sch. Bd., 1970-72; chmn. Gage County Bd. Suprs., 1976-83; former chmn. Nat. Conf. State Legislatures Task Force on Devel. Disabilities; mem. Gov.'s Planning Coun. on Devel. Disabilities; faculty mem. pres. com. Mental Retardation Nat. Collaborative Acad.; pres. Beatrice Retail

Coun.; chmn. Gage County Indsl. Devel. Bd.; bd. dirs. Gage County United Way, Gage County Red Cross; mem. capital campaign adv. com. YMCA Found.; mem. adv. bd. Nebr. Dept. Social Svcs.; bd. trustees Pershing Coll. With Nebr. Army NG. Recipient Pub. Svc. award City of Beatrice, Meritorious Svc. Recognition, Gage County, Outstanding Leadership award Nat. Conf. State Legislatures; named Legislator of Yr., Nebr. Hosp. Assn., Nebr. County Ofcl. of Yr., Pub. Ofcl. of Yr., Assn. Retarded Citizens. Mem. U. Nebr.--Lincoln Alumni Assn. (life mem.), Beatrice C. of C. (Good Neighbor award), Beatrice Sertoma Club, Beatrice Cmty. Hosp. Centurian Club, Rotary (hon. mem.) Home: 823 N 8th St Beatrice NE 68310-2344 Office: State Capitol Dist 30 PO Box 94604 Rm 1208 Lincoln NE 68509

BYARS, LEISA, marketing professional, music company executive; b. Warren, Ohio, 1967; m. Delfon McSpadden. BA in Econs. and Govt., Oberlin Coll.; MA in Pub. Policy, U. Mich.; MBA in Mktg. and Fin., U. Pa. From mem. staff to group mgr. Innovative Mktg. Solutions Group Ford Motor Co., Dearborn, Mich., 1995—2000, group mgr. Innovative Mktg. Solutions Group, 2000, mgr., global media, agency, events and alliances; v.p. mktg. EMI Christian Music Group EMI, Tenn., 2005—. Recipient Outstanding Women in Mktg. and Comms. award, Ebony Mag., 2001. Office: EMI CMG PO Box 5010 Brentwood TN 37024-5010

BYE, KERMIT EDWARD, federal judge, lawyer; b. Hatton, ND, Jan. 13, 1937; s. Kermit Berthrand and Margaret B. (Brekke) Bye; m. Carol Beth Soliah, Aug. 23, 1958; children: Laura Lee, William Edward, Bethany Ann. BS, U. N.D., 1959, JD, 1962. Bar: ND 1962, US Dist. Ct. ND 1962, US Ct. Appeals (8th cir.) 1969, US Supreme Ct. 1974, Minn. 1981. Dep. securities commr. State of ND, 1962—64, spl. asst. atty. gen., 1964—66; asst. U.S. atty. US Atty.'s Office, Dist. ND, 1966—68; ptnr. Vogel Brantner Kelly Knutson Weir & Bye, Fargo, ND, 1968—2000; judge US Ct. Appeals (8th cir.), Fargo, 2000—. Mem. adv. com. appellate rules U.S. Jud. Conf., 2005—. Mem. editl. bd.: N.D. Law Rev., 1961—62. Chmn. Red River Human Svcs. Found., 1980—83; S.E. Mental Health and Retardation Ctr., Inc. Fellow: Am. Bar Found.; mem.: ABA (state del. 1986—95, bd. govs. 1999—2001, state del. 2002—), Minn. Bar Assn., Cass County Bar Assn., N.D. State Bar Assn. (pres. 1983—84). Lutheran. Office: 655 1st Ave N Ste 330 Fargo ND 58102 Business E-Mail: zhanna@ce8.uscourts.gov.

BYERLY, REX R., state legislator; m. Linda Byerly; 1 child. BS, Nat. Coll., Rapid City, Mich. Computer cons.; state rep. dist. 1, 1991—. Mem. appropriations com.; chmn. human resources com. N.D. Ho. Reps. Mem. CAP. Mem. Exptl. Aviation Assn., Williston Basin Racing Assn., Moose. Republican. Home: PO Box 968 Williston ND 58802-0968

BYERS, GEORGE WILLIAM, retired entomology educator; b. Washington, May 16, 1923; s. George and Helen (Kessler) B.; m. Martha Esther Sparks, Feb. 25, 1945 (div. 1953); children: George William, Carolyn Sylvia; m. Gloria B. Wong, Dec. 16, 1955; children: Bruce Alan, Brian William, Douglas Eric. BS, Purdue U., 1947; MS, U. Mich., 1948, PhD, 1952. Asst. prof. dept. entomology U. Kans., Lawrence, 1956-60, curator Snow Entomol. Mus., 1956-83, dir., sr. curator, 1983-88, assoc. prof., 1960-65, prof. entomology, 1965-88, prof. dept. systematics and ecology, 1969-88, chmn. dept. entomology, 1969-72, 84-87, ret., 1988. Vis. prof. Mountain Lake Biol. Sta. U. Va., alt. summers, 1961-92, U. Minn. biol. sta., 1970. Author: several book chpts.; contbr. articles to profl. jours. With U.S. Army, 1942-46, 53-56, WWII and Korea; lt. col. M.S.C., USAR, ret. Rackham fellow U. Mich., 1952-53; NSF grantee, 1958-87, 97-99. Mem. Entomol. Soc. Am. (editl. bd. Annals 1967-72, chmn. 1971-72), Entomol. Soc. Can., Ctrl. States Entomol. Soc. (pres. 1958-59), Entomol. Soc. Washington, Soc. Systematic Biology (editor Syst. Zool. jour. 1963-66), Phi Beta Kappa, Phi Kappa Phi, Sigma Xi. Avocations: invertebrate paleontology, photography, ornithology. Home: 909 Holiday Dr Lawrence KS 66049-3006 Office: U Kans Entomology Divsn Natural History Mus Lawrence KS 66049-2811 Office Phone: 785-864-4538. Business E-Mail: ksem@ku.edu.

BYERS-PEVITTS, BEVERLEY, college administrator, educator; b. Ohio County, Ky., Aug. 15, 1939; d. Stanley Beveridge and Vera Elizabeth (Amos) Byers; m. Robert Richard Pevitts, June 12, 1966; 1 child, Robert Stanley. BA, Ky. Wesleyan Coll., 1961; MA, So. Ill. U., 1967, PhD, 1980. Dir. theatre and faculty Dept. English, Speech, Drama Young Harris (Ga.) Coll., 1966-69; dir. theatre and asst. prof. speech and theatre arts Western Carolina U., Cullowhee, NC, 1969-71; coord. supplementary progr., asst. prof. Eng. and drama Pfeiffer Coll., Misenheimer, NC, 1972-74; dir. and prof. speech and theatre Ky. Wesleyan U., Owensboro, 1974-86; chair theatre arts U. Nev., Las Vegas, 1986-89, prof. and dir. grad. studies in theatre arts, 1986-90; dean coll. of humanities and fine arts, prof. U. No. Iowa, Cedar Falls, 1990-95; v.p. acad. affairs Tex. Woman's U., Denton, 1995—2001; pres. Park U., Parkville, Mo., 2001—. Lectr. in field; conductor workshops in field. Editor: Theatre Topics, 1990-93; contbr. articles to profl. jours.; author: (plays) Reflections in a Window, 1982, rev., 1983, Beauty and the Beast, 1982, Time and the Rock, 1981, Family Haven, 1979, Take Courage, Stand Beside Us, 1977, A Strange and Beautiful Light, 1976-77; co-author: Epilogue to Glory, 1966. Bd. dirs. Waterloo/Cedar Falls Symphony Orch., 1990-94, Iowa Citizens for the Arts, 1991-94; coord. spl. drama programs WeCan, Inc., Las Vegas, 1986; tchr. Elderhostel Program; program coord. NOW. NEH Seminar grantee U. Wis.-Milw., 1983, NYU, 1977; recipient Outstanding Alumni award Ky. Wesleyan Coll., 1983; named Disting. Woman Am. Theatre Assn., 1977; grantee Ford Found., Exxon Corp.; elected to Nat. Theatre Conf., 1992—. Mem. Assn. for Theatre in Higher Edn. (founding pres. 1986-87, bd. govs. 1986-89), Assn. for Communication Adminstrn. (exec. com. 1988-91), Univ. and Coll. Theatre Assn. of Am. Theatre Assn. (pres. 1985-86), League Profl. Theatre Women N.Y., Internat. Coun. of Fine Arts Deans, Coun. of Colls. of Arts and Scis., Order of Oak and Ivy, Alpha Psi Omega. Avocations: gourmet cooking, travel, collecting antiques. Office: Park Univ 8700 NW River Park Dr Kansas City MO 64152 E-mail: president@mail.park.edu.

BYNOE, PETER CHARLES BERNARD, investment banker, lawyer; b. Boston, Mar. 20, 1951; s. Victor Cameron Sr. and Ethel May (Stewart) B.; m. Linda Jean Walker, Nov. 20, 1987. BA, Harvard U., 1972, JD, MBA, Harvard U., 1976. Bar: Ill. 1982; cert. real estate broker, Ill. Exec. v.p. James H. Lowry & Assocs., Chgo., 1977-82; chmn., CEO Telemat Ltd., Chgo., 1982—; exec. dir. Ill. Sports Facilities Authority, Chgo., 1988-92; mng. gen. ptnr. Denver Nuggets, 1989-92; ptnr., Land Use & Devel., Project Finance practices DLA Piper US LLP, Chgo., 1995—; mng. dir., co-chmn. corp. fin. Loop Capital LLC, Chgo., 2008—. Bd. dirs. Uniroyal Tech. Corp., Jacor Comms., Ind., Blue Chip Broadcasting, Covanta Holding Corp., 2004-Chmn. Chgo. Landmarks Commn., 1985-87; vice chmn., chmn. exec. com. Goodman Theater; dir. Chgo. Econ. Club, 1993-2000, Ill. Sports Facilities Authority, 1993-2005; trustee Rush-Presbyn. St. Luke's Med. Ctr.; bd. overseers Harvard U., 1993-2002; mem. Chgo. Art Inst.; dir. The CORE Ctr. Named one of Am.'s Top Black Lawyers, Black Enterprise mag., 2003; named to Diversity 2005 Most Influential List, Fortune Mag., 2005. Mem.: Lawyers Club of Chgo., Chgo. Planning and Devel. Commn. (chmn. 1997—2004), Chgo. Coun. Foreign Relations (dir. 1995—2000), Econ. Club (dir. 1993—2000), East Bank Club. Democrat. Achievements include being the first African American owner of a National Basketball Association team. Avocations: squash, tennis, racquetball, skiing, travel, golf. Office: DLA Piper US LLP Suite 1900 203 N La Salle St Chicago IL 60601-1293 also: Loop Capital Markets 200 W Jackson Blvd Ste 1600 Chicago IL 60606 Office Phone: 312-368-4090. Office Fax: 312-630-7333. E-mail: peter.bynoe@dlapiper.com.*

BYOM, JOHN E., food company executive; b. Dec. 15, 1953; B of Acctg., Luther Coll. Internal auditor, credit analyst Maytag Corp., Newton, Iowa; controller, acting gen. mgr. Internat. Multifoods Corp., Monnetonka, Minn., 1979, pres., 1999—2000, sr. v.p., chief fin. officer, 2000—. Mem.: Inst. Mgmt. Accts. Office: International Multifoods 1 Strawberry Ln Orrville OH 44667-1241

BYRD, JAMES EVERETT, lawyer; b. Cin., Aug. 1, 1958; BS, U. Dayton, Ohio, 1980, JD cum laude, 1984. Law clk. U.S. Dist Ct. (so. dist.), Ohio, 1983; assoc. Smith & Schnacke, Dayton, 1984-89; v.p., gen. counsel Internat. Cargo Svcs., Virginia Beach, Va., 1989-91; assoc. Beale, Balfour et al., Richmond, Va., 1991-92; corp. counsel Huffy Corp., Dayton, 1992-94; ind. corp. legal cons., 1994-95; sr. dir., assoc. gen. counsel Lexis Nexis divsn. Reed Elsevier, Inc., Dayton, 1995—. Pres. Condominium Owners Assn., Dayton, 1995-99. Mem. ABA, Ohio Bar Assn., Va. Bar Assn. Office: Lexis Nexis 9443 Springboro Pike Miamisburg OH 45342-4425 E-mail: james.e.byrd@lexisnexis.com.

BYRD, LORELEE, state treasurer; b. Bassett, Nebr., Apr. 14, 1956; m. Scott Byrd, 1976 (div.); children: Amy, Ryan. Auditor Mut. Protective Ins. and Mut. Ins.; aide to state and fed. lawmakers; unclaimed property admin., 1995; dep. state treas. Nebr., 1995—2001; state treas. Nebr., 2001—. Past mem. Rep. State Ctrl. Com., Douglas County Rep. Ctrl. Com.; past pres. Metro Right to Life; past mem. bd. dirs. Nebr. Right to Life; aide to Senator Sharon Beck Omaha; aide to Owen Elmer Indianola; aide to U.S. rep. Doug Bereuter Nebr. Office: PO Box 94788 Lincoln NE 68509-4788 E-mail: lbyrd@treasurer.org.

BYRD, VINCENT C., food products company executive; With J. M. Smucker Co., Orrville, Ohio, 1977—, treas., v.p. procurement and tech. svcs., 1988-95, v.p., gen. mgr. consumer market, 1995—. Office: J M Smucker Co 1 Strawberry Ln Orrville OH 44667-1241

BYRD-BENNETT, BARBARA, school system administrator; m. Bruce Bennett; 1 child, Nailah Bennett. BA in English, L.I. U.; M in English Lit., NYU; MEd, Pace U.; Doctorate (hon.), John Carroll U., Notre Dame Coll. Elem. sch. tchr., Manhattan and Bronx, NY, 1965—75; adj. assoc. prof. Coll. of New Rochelle, 1975—91; spl. asst. to Manhattan Supt. for Curriculum, 1982—84; priin. PS 36, Manhattan, NY, 1984—92; adj. assoc. prof. CCNY, 1989—93; dep. exed. dir. for instrn. and profl. devel. N.Y.C. Schs., 1992—94; supt. Chancellor's Dist., N.Y.C. Sch. Sys., 1996—98; CEO Cleve. Mcpl. Sch. Dist., 1998—. Apptd. to edn. com. States Nat. Ctr. for Ednl. Accountability; apptd. to vis. com. Mandel Sch. Applied Scis. Recipient Cleve. Bus. Woman of Yr., 2001. Mem.: Urban Supts. Assn. Am. (v.p.), Internat. Women's Forum. Office: Cleve Mcpl Sch Dist 1380 E Sixth St Cleveland OH 44114

BYRNE, C. WILLIAM, JR., athletics program director; b. Boston; m. Marilyn Kent; children: Bill, Greg. BBA, Idaho State U, 1967, MBA, 1971. Dir. alumni rels. Idaho State, 1971—76; exec. dir. Lobo Club, U. N.Mex., Albuquerque, 1976-79; asst. athletic dir. San Diego State U., 1980-82; assoc. dir., adminstr. Duck Athletic Fund, U. Oreg., Eugene, 1983-84, dir. athletic dept., 1984-92; dir. athletics U. Nebr., Lincoln, 1992—2002, Tex. A&M U., Coll. Sta., 2003—. Bd. dir. Nat. Football Found.; chair Big 12 Bd. Athletic Dirs. Named Ctrl. Region NACDA/Continental Athletic Dir. Yr., Hall of Champions dedicated in his honor, Autzen Stadium, 1993, Nat. Fundraiser Yr., Nat. Athletic Fundraisers Assn.; recipient Carl Maddox Sports Mgmt. award, US Sports Acad., 2007. Mem. at. Assn. Collegiate Dirs. of Athletics (exec. com., pres., John L. Toner award 2002), U.S. Collegiate Sports Coun. (v.p., bd. dirs.), All-Am. Football Found. (v.p.), Football Assn. (bd. dirs.), NCAA (spl. events com., mktg. com., cert. com.), Nat. Football Found. (bd. dirs.), Big 12 Bd. of Athletic Dirs. (chair). Office: Tex A&M Univ Athletics Dept PO Box 30017 College Station TX 77842-3017

BYRNES, BRUCE L., consumer products company executive; b. Columbus, Ohio, Mar. 29, 1948; BA in Philosophy of Religion, Princeton U., 1970. Brand asst. Procter & Gamble Co., Cin., 1970—71, sales trainee, 1971—72, asst. brand mgr., 1972—74, brand mgr., 1974—78, assoc. advt. mgr. paper products divsn., 1978—82, advt. mgr. coffee divsn., 1982—84, advt. mgr. packaged soap and detergent divsn., 1984—86, mgr. packaged soap and detergent divsn., 1986—87, v.p. packaged soap and detergent divsn., 1987—90, v.p. No. Europe, 1990—91, pres., paper and beverage products, Procter & Gamble Europe, group v.p., 1991—95, pres., paper products-U.S., Procter & Gamble N.Am., group v.p., 1995—96, pres., health care products-U.S., Procter & Gamble N.Am., group v.p., 1996—97, pres., health care products-N.Am., Procter & Gamble N.Am., group v.p., 1997—99, pres., global health care and corp. new ventures, 1999—2000, pres., global beauty care and global health care, 2000—02, vice chmn. & pres. global beauty, global feminine and global health care, 2002—04, vice chmn. household products, 2002—, vice chmn. baby care, family care and pet health & nutrition businesses, 2006—07, vice chmn. glob. brand bldg., 2007—. Bd. dir. Cin. Bell Inc., 2003—. Mem. steering coun. Success by 6, 2002—; bd. trustee Cin. Art Mus., 1996—; maj. firms chair 1999 Fine Arts Fund Campaign, 1998—99. Office: Procter & Gamble Co 1 Procter & Gamble Plz Cincinnati OH 45202

BYRNES, CHRISTOPHER IAN, engineering educator; b. NYC, June 28, 1949; s. Richard Francis and Jeanne (Orchard) Byrnes; children: Kathleen, Alison, Christopher; m. Gwendolyn Renee Byrnes, Feb. 14, 2005. BS in math., Manhattan Coll., 1971; MS in math., U. Mass., 1973, PhD in math., 1975; D of Tech. (hon.), Royal Inst. Tech., Stockholm, 1998. Registered profl. engr., Mo. Instr. U. Utah, Salt Lake City, 1975-78; asst. prof. Harvard U., Cambridge, Mass., 1978-81, assoc. prof., 1981-85; rsch. prof. Ariz. State U., Tempe, 1985-89; prof. Washington U., St. Louis, 1989—, Edward H. and Florence G. Skinner prof., 1998—, chmn. dept. systems sci. and math., 1989—91, dean Sch. Engring. and Applied Sci., 1991—2006. Adj. prof. Royal Inst. Tech., Stockholm, 1985—90; cons. Sci. Sys., Inc., Cambridge, 1980—84, Sys. Engring., Inc., Greenbelt, Md., 1986; sci. advisor Sherwood Davis & Geck, 1996—98, Cernium Inc., 2002—, Midwest Bank Ctr., 2002—07; mem. NRC; bd. dirs., chmn. nominating and governance com. Belden Inc., 1995—2006; chmn. bd. dir. Ctr. Emerging Techs., 1993—2003, chmn. emeritus; pres., bd. dir. WUTA, Inc., 1991—2004; mem. bus. bd. adv. Newberry Group Inc., 2002—. Editor: (book series) Progress in Systems Control, 1988, Foundations of Systems and Control, 1998—2001; Nonlinear Synthesis, 1991, 13 other books; contbr. numerous articles to profl. jours., book revs. Recipient Best Paper award, IFAC, 1993. Fellow: IEEE (George Axelby award 1991, 2003, Hendrik W. Bode Lecture prize 2008), Acad. Sci. St. Louis, Japan Soc. for Promotion Sci.; mem.: AIAA, AAAS, Regional Chamber for Growth Assn. (vice chmn. tech., chmn. Tech. Gateway Alliance 2000—03), Royal Swedish Acad. Engring. Sci. (fgn.), Am. Math. Soc., Soc. Indsl. Applied Math. (program com. 1986—89, Reid prize 2005), Tau Beta Pi, Sigma Xi. Avocations: cooking, fishing, travel. Office: Washington U Dept Elec and Sys Engring 1 Brookings Dr Saint Louis MO 63130-4899 Office Phone: 314-935-6067. Business E-Mail: chrisbyrnes@wustl.edu.

BYRUM, DIANNE, state legislator, small business owner; b. Mar. 18, 1954; d. Cecil Dershem and Mary D.; m. James E. Byrum; children: Barbara Anne, James Richard. AA, Lansing Cmty. Coll.; BS cum laude, Mich. State U. Rep. dist. 68 Mich. Ho. of Reps. from 68th dist., Lansing, 1991-94; mem. Mich. Senate from 25th dist., Lansing, 1995—; owner Blackhawk Hardware, Leslie, Mich., 1983—, Panther Hardware, Stockbridge, Mich., 1991—. Minority vice chair agr. and forestry, health policy and sr. citizens; mem. tech. and energy com., capitol com.; chair dem. caucus. Recipient Disting. Citizen award Ingham County Soil Conservation Dist., 1991, Disting. Alumnus award Lansing Cmty. Coll., 1993. Mem. Mich. Retail Hardware Assn., Lansing Regional C. of C., South Lansing Bus. Assn., South Lansing-Everett Kiwanis. Democrat. Office: Mich State Senate 125 W Allegan PO Box 30036 Lansing MI 48909-7536 E-mail: sendbyrum@senate.state.mi.us.

CABELA, RICHARD N., retail executive; b. Nebr. m. Mary A. Cabela; 9 children. Student, Regis Coll., 1956—58. Founder Cabela's Inc., 1961, chmn., dir., 1965—. Exec. com. Direct Marketing Ednl. Found. Regent Regis Univ., 1994—, bd. trustees. Recipient Small Businessman of the Yr. award, 1970, Nebr. Hall of Fame award, 1994, Alumni Achievement award, Regis Univ., 2003. Roman Catholic. Office: Cabela's One Cabela Dr Sidney NE 69160 Office Phone: 308-254-5505. Office Fax: 308-254-4800.

CABEZAS, HERIBERTO, chemical engineer, researcher; b. La Esperanza, Las Villas, Cuba; arrived in U.S., 1967, naturalized, 1974; s. Heriberto and Ana Rosa C.; m. Isaura Vazquez. BSChemE magna cum laude, NJ Inst. Tech., Newark, 1980; MSChemE, U. Fla., 1981, PhD in Chem. Engring., 1985. Asst. prof. chem. engring. U. Ariz., 1985-93; leader simulation and design team, sustainable tech. divsn. EPA Nat. Risk Mgmt. Rsch. Lab., Cin., 1994-2000; chief sustainable environ. br. sustainable tech. div. EPA Nat. Risk Mmgt. Rsch. Lab., Cin., 2000—. Cons. Nat. Inst. Stds. and Tech., Gaithersburg, Md., 1986-93, rschr. biotech. divsn., 1993-94; adj. prof. dept. civil and environ. engring. U Cinn., 2007-. Contbr. numerous articles to profl. jours., chapters to books. Chair environ. divsn. Am. Inst. Chem. Engrs., 1996; external adv. bd. Inst. Environ. Sci. and Policy U. Ill., Chgo., 2003—. With USN, 1971—75. Recipient Disting. Alumni Achievement award, NJ Inst. Tech. Alumni Assn. Mem. AIChE, AAAS, AAEE, Tau Beta Pi, Omega Chi Epsilon. Roman Catholic. Achievements include development of Paris II solvent design software, waste reduction WAR algorithm for chemical process design, Regional Sustainable Systems Management Methodology. Office: US EPA 26 W Martin Luther King Dr Cincinnati OH 45268-0001 Business E-Mail: cabezas.heriberto@epa.gov.

CABRERA, MIGUEL (JOSE MIGUEL CABRERA), professional baseball player; b. Maracay, Venezuela, Apr. 18, 1983; s. Miguel and Gregoria Cabrera; m. Rosangel Cabrera; 1 child, Rosangel. Third baseman Fla. Marlins, 2003—07, Detroit Tigers, 2008—. Named to Nat. League All-Star Team, Maj. League Baseball, 2004—07; recipient Silver Slugger award, 2005—06. Achievements include being the second youngest Marlin in franchise history at 20 years and 63 days old; being a member of the World Series Champion Florida Marlins, 2003. Mailing: c/o Detroit Tigers Comerica Pk 2100 Woodward Ave Detroit MI 48201*

CABRERA, ORLANDO (LUIS), professional baseball player; b. Cartagena, Colombia, Nov. 2, 1974; s. Jolbert and Josefina Cabrera; m. Eliana Cabrera. Shortstop Montreal Expos, 1997—2004, Boston Red Sox, 2004, LA Angels of Anaheim, 2005—07, Chgo. White Sox, 2008—. Recipient Gold Glove award, 2001, 2007. Achievements include being a member of the World Series Champion Boston Red Sox, 2004; ranking number one in fielding percentage (.938) and third in batting and RBI's among all American League shortstops in the 2007 season. Office: c/o Chgo White Sox US Cellular Field 333 W 35th St Chicago IL 60616 Office Phone: 714-940-2000.*

CACCHIONE, PATRICK JOSEPH, health association executive; b. Syracuse, NY, Mar. 19, 1959; s. Nicholas Phillip and Ruth Helen (Liadka) C.; m. Pamela Carol Zurkowski, Oct. 8, 1988. BA, Hobart Coll., 1981; MPA, Am. U., 1983. Rsch. asst. Brookings Instn., Washington, 1982-83; field organizer Mondale for Pres. Campaign, Washington, 1983-84; legis. asst. Office of Congressman Tom Luken, Washington, 1985-86; cons. Am. Express Co., Washington, 1986, Francis, McGinnis and Rees Assocs., Washington, 1986; legis. asst. Law Office of Raymond D. Cotton, Washington, 1987-88; dir. legis. affairs Nat. Assn. Med. Equipment Suppliers, Alexandria, Va., 1988-90; v.p. govt. affairs Daus. of Charity Nat. Health System, St. Louis, 1991-98; v.p. advocacy/comm. Carondelet Health System, St. Louis, 1998—. Cons. Carondelet Health System, St. Louis, 1992—; candidate U.S. House Rep., First Dist. Mo., 1993—. Contbr. articles to profl. publs. Vol. Harriet Woods for Senate, St. Louis, 1986, Guardian Angels Settlement, St. Louis, 1991-92, Jack Garvey for Cir. Atty., St. Louis, 1992; campaign mgr. Dianne Smith for County Coun., Silver Spring, Md., 1990; bd. dirs. Compton Heights Civic Assn., St. Louis, 1992. Mem. St. Louis Ambassadors, Women in Govt. Rels., Democratic Club, Healthcare Fin. Mgrs. Assn., Network. Democrat. Roman Catholic. Avocations: golf, reading, movies, antiques, travel. Office: Cardondelet Health System 13801 Riverport Dr Maryland Heights MO 63043-4828 Home: 3419 Hawthorne Blvd Saint Louis MO 63104-1622

CACIOPPO, JOHN TERRANCE, psychologist, educator, researcher; b. Marshall, Tex., June 12, 1951; s. Cyrus Joseph and Mary Katherine (Kazimour) Cacioppo; m. Barbara Lee Andersen, May 17, 1981 (div. 1998); children: Christina Elizabeth, Anthony Cyrus; m. Wendi L. Gardner, Sept. 8, 2001. BS in Econs., U. Mo., Columbia, 1973; MA in Psychology, Ohio State U., 1975, PhD in Psychology, 1977. Asst. prof. psychology U. Notre Dame, Ind., 1977-79, U. Iowa, Iowa City, 1979-81, assoc. prof., 1981-85, prof. psychology, 1985-89, Ohio State U., 1989-98, Univ. chaired prof. psychology, 1998-99; Tiffany-Margaret Blake disting. svc. prof. U. Chgo., 1999—. Vis. faculty Yale U., 1986, U. Hawaii, 1990, U. Chgo., 1998—99; tng. grant dir. NIMH Social Psychology, 1993—98; co-dir. Inst. for Mind and Biology, 1999—2004, dir. social psychology program, 1999—2005; dir. Ctr. Cognitive and Social Neurosci. U. Chgo., 2004—. Editor: Psychophysiology, 1994—97; contbr. articles to profl. jours. Active John D. and Catherine T. MacArthur Found. Network on Mid-Body Integrations, 1995-98; bd. dirs. Ohio State U. Rsch. Found., 1993-98 Recipient Early Career Contbn. award Psychophysiology, 1981, Troland Rsch. award NAS, 1989, Disting. Sci. Contbr. Psychophysiol., Soc. Psychophysiol. Rsch., 2000; NSF grantee, 1979—, Campbell award Soc. Personality and Social Psychology, 2000. Fellow: APA (past pres. 2 divsns., Disting. Sci. Contbn. award 2002), Acad. Behavioral Medicine Rsch., Am. Psychol. Soc. (keynote spkr. ann. meeting 2002, bd. & dir. 2002—, pres. 2007—); mem.: AAAS, Assn. for Psychol. Sci. (pres.-elect), Am. Acad. Arts and Scis., Soc. Exptl. Psychologists, Soc. Exptl. Social Psychology, Soc. Personality and Social Psychology (pres. 1995), Soc. Psychophysiol. Rsch. (bd. dirs. 1985—88, officer 1991—94, pres. 1992—93, bd. dirs. 1998—2000), Sigma Xi (nat. lectr. 1996—98). Office Phone: 773-702-1962.

CADOGAN, WILLIAM J., telecommunications company executive; b. 1948; With AT&T, 1971-86, Intelsat, 1986-87, ADC Telecomm. Inc., Mpls., 1987—, pres., COO, 1990—, CEO, 1991—, chmn., 1994—. Office: ADC Telecomm Inc PO Box 1101 Minneapolis MN 55440

CADY, MARK S., state supreme court justice; b. Rapid City, SD, July 12, 1953; married; 2 children. Undergrad. degree, Drake U., JD, 1978. Law clk. 2d Jud. Dist. Ct., 1978-79; asst. Webster County atty.; with law firm Ft. Dodge; dist. assoc. judge, 1983—86; dist. ct. judge, 1986—94; judge Iowa Ct. Appeals, 1994—98, chief judge, 1997—98; justice Iowa Supreme Ct., 1998—. Author: (book) Curbing Litigation Abuse and Misuse: A Judicial Response. Chmn. Supreme Ct. Task Force on Ct.'s and Cmty.'s Response to Domestic Abuse. Mem.: Webster County Bar Assn., Iowa State Bar Assn. Office: Iowa Supreme Ct 1111 E Ct Ave Des Moines IA 50319 E-mail: MarkS.Cady@jb.state.ia.us.

CAFARO, ANTHONY M., real estate developer, retail executive; Prin., owner The Cafaro Co., Youngstown, Ohio, 1995—. Office: The Cafaro Co PO Box 2186 2445 Belmont Ave Youngstown OH 44504-0186 Fax: 330-743-2902.

CAFFERTY, PASTORA SAN JUAN, education educator; b. Cienfuegos, Las Villas, Cuba, July 29, 1940; arrived in US, 1947; d. Jose Antonio and Hortensia (Horruitiner) San Juan; m. Michael Cafferty, Apr. 13, 1971 (dec. 1973); m. Henry P. Russe, Aug. 18, 1988 (dec. 1991). BA, St. Bernard Coll., 1967; MA, George Washington U., 1969, PhD, 1971; DHC, Columbia Coll., 1987. Instr. George Washington U., Washington, 1967-69; asst. to sec. U.S. Dept. Transp., Washington, 1969-70, U.S. HUD, Washington, 1970-71; asst. prof. U. Chgo., 1971-76, assoc. prof., 1976-83, prof., 1983—2005, prof. emeritas, 2005—. Bd. dirs. Waste Mgmt. Inc., Houston, Harris Fin. Corp., Chgo., Integrys, Chgo. Author: The Politics of Language: The Dilemma of Bilingual Education for Puerto Ricans, 1981, Backs Against The Wall, 1983, The Dilemma of American Immigration, 1983, Hispanics in the U.S.A., 1985, 2d edit., 1992, Hispanics: An Agenda for 21st Century, 1999, 2d edit., 2002. Bd. dirs. Lyric Opera Assn., Chgo., 1990—, Rush Univ. Med. Ctr., 1993— White House fellow U.S. Govt., 1969-70. Mem. Chgo. Yacht Club. Democrat. Roman Catholic. Office: U Chgo 969 E 60th St Chicago IL 60637-2677 Business E-Mail: p-cafferty@uchicago.edu.

CAHILL, DAVID G., materials scientist, engineer, educator; b. Feb. 15, 1962; BS in Engring. Physics, Ohio State U., 1984; PhD in Exptl. Condensed Matter Physics, Cornell U., 1989. Grad. rsch. asst. Cornell U., Ithaca, N.Y., 1984-89; postdoct. rsch. assoc. IBM Watson Rsch. Ctr., 1984-89; asst. prof. dept. materials sci. and engring. U. Ill., Urbana-Champaign, 1989-91, assoc. prof. dept. materials sci. and engring., 1997—. Coord. materials sci. and engring. component Jr. Engr. Technical Soc., minority intro. to engring. program, 1992-95; workshop co-chair heat trasport in amorphous solids 7th Internat. Conf. Phonon Scattering in Condensed Matter, Ithaca, N.Y., 1992; mem. pre-proposal rev. panel Optical Sci. Engring. Initiative NSF, 1996, Career award rev. panel DMR Electronic Materials, 1997, nanotechnology proposal review panel, 1998; mem. scientific adv. com. Dynamic Crystal Surfaces and Interfaces, 1996; co-organizer March meeting nanometer-scale morphology of surfaces and interfaces divsn. of material physics Am. Phys. Soc., Kansas City, 1997, sessions on thermo-phys. properties of thin films 13th Symposium on Thermophys. Properties, 1997; lead organizer Evolution of Surface and Thin Film Microstructure Mateials Rsch. Soc., Boston, 1997; cons. INRAD, Northvale, N.J., 1991, Hoechst Celanese, Summit, N.J., 1993, United Technologies, East Hartford, Conn., 1993-96, Pratt & Whitney, West Palm Beach, Fla., 1994-96, HiPatent, Chgo., 1996-98, Read-Rite, Fremont, Calif., 1998, Sumitomo Metal Industries, Kyoto, Japan, 1998; presenter in field. Contbr. numerous articles to profl. jours., chpts. to books. Advisor electronic materials group materials tech. workshop for high sch. tchrs. NSF, 1995. Grad. fellow NSF, 1984-87; recipient Charles Luck award

Internat. Thermal Conductivity Conf., 1989. Fellow Am. Vacuum Soc. (Peter Mark meml. award 1998, mem. exec. bd. nanometer-scale sci. and tech. divsn. 1995-97). Office: U Il Dept Material Sci & Engring 1101 W Springfield Ave Urbana IL 61801-3005 Fax: 217-244-1631. E-mail: d-cahill@vive.edu.

CAHILL, PATRICIA DEAL, radio station executive; b. St. Louis, Oct. 9, 1947; d. Richard Joseph and Dorothy (Deal) C.; m. children: Lindsay Cahill, Jessica Cahill Crump. BA, U. Kans., 1969, MA, 1971. Continuity dir. Sta. KANU-FM, Lawrence, Kans., 1970, audio reader dir., 1970-73; reporter Sta. KCUR-FM, Kansas City, Mo., 1973-75; news dir. Sta. KMUW-FM, Wichita, Kans., 1975, gen. mgr., 1976-87, Sta. KCUR-FM, Kansas City, 1987—. Asst. prof. communications studies U. Mo. Kansas City, 1987—; dir. Nat. Pub. Radio, 1982-88, exec. com., 1983-88, chair tech. and distbn., 1985-88. Chmn. Wichita Free U., 1979-81; v.p. Planned Parenthood Kans., 1986-87; bd. dirs. Kansas City Cultural Alliance. Recipient Matrix award Wichita chpt. Women in Commn., 1986, Alumni Honor citation U. Kans., 1993. Mem. Pub. Radio Mid. Am. (pres. 1979-80, 89-93), Radio Rsch. Consortium (bd. dirs. 1981—), Kans. Pub. Radio Assn. (bd. dirs. 1980-87). Office: Sta KCUR 4825 Troost Ave Ste 202 Kansas City MO 64110-2030

CAIN, ALBERT CLIFFORD, psychologist, educator; b. Chgo., July 19, 1933; s. Edward Arthur and Fae Anita (Shafton) C.; m. Barbara Strean, Nov. 15, 1959; children: Steven, Kenneth. BA, U. Mich., 1954, PhD, 1962. From asst. prof. to assoc. prof. dept. psychology and psychiatry U. Mich., Ann Arbor, Mich., 1962-69, prof. dept. psychology, 1969—, chmn. dept. psychology, 1981-91; chief psychologist Child. Psychiat. Hosp., Ann Arbor, Mich., 1964-69. Mem. rev. com. Ctr. Studies of Suicide Prevention NIMH, 1969—72; dir. U. Mich. Child Bereavement Project. Editor: Survivors of Suicide, 1972; contbr. articles to profl. jour. Recipient Shneidman award Am. Assn. Suicidology, 1973. Fellow APA, Am. Orthopsychiatric Assn. (bd. dir. 1978-81, editor jour. 1983-88); mem. Phi Beta Kappa. Home: 1927 Hampton Ct Ann Arbor MI 48103-4521 Office: U Mich Dept Psychology 2251 East Hall 530 Church St Ann Arbor MI 48109-1109

CAIN, J. MATTHEW, prosecutor; b. Cleve., Oct. 3, 1943; m. Karen, 1965 J. Telliard; 4 children. BSBA, Ohio State U., 1966; postgrad., Golden Gate Coll., 1968-70; JD cum laude, Ohio State U., 1966. Bar: Ohio 1972, U.S. Supreme Ct. 1979, U.S. Dist. Ct. (no. dist.) Ohio 1981, U.S. Ct. Appeals (6th cir.) 1983. Employee rels. & ins. Diamond Shamrock Corp., 1966-73; asst. county prosecutor Cuyahoga County, Ohio, 1973-80; asst. U.S. atty. Cleve., 1980—; chief criminal divsn. Office of U.S. Atty. (no. dist.) Ohio, 1987—. With USN, 1960-63. Office: US Attorneys Office 801 W Superior Ave Ste 400 Cleveland OH 44113-1052

CAIN, MADELINE ANN, mayor; b. Cleve., Nov. 21, 1949; d. Edward Vincent and Mary Rita (Quinn) C. BA, Ursuline Coll., 1973; MPA, Cleve. State U., 1985. Tchr. St. Augustine Acad., Lakewood, Ohio, 1973-75; clk. coun. legis. aide Lakewood City Coun., 1981-85; legis. liaison Cuyahoga County Bd. Commrs., Cleve., 1985-88; mem. Ohio Ho. of Reps., Columbus, 1989-95; mayor City of Lakewood, Lakewood, Ohio, 1995—. Mem. Cudell Neighborhood Improvement Corp., West Blvd. eighborhood Assn.; trustee Malachi House. Mem. Lakewood Bus. and Profl. Women, Lakewood C. of C., City Club. Democrat. Roman Catholic. Office: Lakewood City Hall 12650 Detroit Ave Lakewood OH 44107-2891

CAIN, R. WAYNE, sales, finance and leasing company executive; b. 1937; BA, Wayne State U., 1959; LLB, N.Y.U., 1962. Lawyer Cleary, Gottlieb, Steen & Hamilton, 1962-63; with Chrysler Corp., Chrysler Fin. Corp., 1965-81; asst. treas. Navistar Internat. Corp., 1981-85; v.p., treas. Navistar Fin. Corp., 1985—2001, sr. v.p. fin., 2001—; v.p., treas. Harco Leasing Co., Inc. Del. With USAF, 1963-65. Office: Navistar Fin Corp 2850 W Golf Rd Rolling Meadows IL 60008-4050

CAIN, TIM J., lawyer; b. Angola, Ind., July 12, 1958; s. Nancy J. (Nichols) C.; m. Debra J. VanWagner, Feb. 28, 1976; children: Christine M., Stephanie L., Katherine S., Jennifer A. BA in Polit. Sci. with honors, Ind. U., 1980; JD, Valparaiso U., 1984; MBA, Ind. Wesleyan U., 1991; LLM in Internat. Bus. and Trade with honors, John Marshall Law Sch., 2001. Bar: Ind. 1984, U.S. Dist. Ct. (no. and so. dists.) Ind. 1984, U.S. Supreme Ct., 2002. Assoc. Hartz & Eberhard, LaGrange, Ind., 1984-85; pub. defender LaGrange Cir. Ct., 1985-86; sr. assoc. Eberhard & Assocs., LaGrange, 1985-86; chief dep. to Pros. Atty.'s Office, LaGrange, 1986-87; ptnr. Eberhard & Cain, LaGrange, 1986-89; pvt. practice LaGrange, 1989-95; pros. atty. La Grange (Ind.) County, 1991—2002; ptnr. Williams and Cain, Ft. Wayne, Ind., 2002—07; gen. counsel KZRV, L.P., Shipshewana, Ind., 2008—. Asst. atty. La Grange County, La Grange; atty. Town of Shipshewana, Ind., 1984-93. Coach Orland (Ind.) Little League, 1977-79, Prairie Hts. Baseball, LaGrange, 1986-90; pres. Prairie Hts. H.S. Dollars for Scholars, LaGrange, 1989; active LaGrange County Coun. on Aging, 1989-91, Prairie Hts. At-Risk Students Com., 1989—, LaGrange County 4-H Fair Assn., 1993-97. Mem.Ind. Bar Assn., LaGrange County Bar Assn. (sec.-treas. 1986-87, v.p. 1987-89, pres. 1990-93). Clubs: Exchange (pres. 1988-89). Republican. Home: 360 S 900 E Lagrange IN 46761-9529 Office: PO Box 895 Angola IN 46703 Office Phone: 260-668-6251, 260-768-4016 404. Business E-Mail: tcain@kz-rv.com.

CAINE, STANLEY PAUL, college administrator; b. Huron, SD, Feb. 11, 1940; s. Louis Vernon and Elizabeth (Holland) C.; m. Karen Anne Mickelson, July 11, 1964; children: Rebecca, Kathryn, David. BA, Macalester Coll., 1962; MS, U. Wis., 1964, PhD, 1967; LLD, Hanover Coll., 2000; LittD, MacMurray Coll., 2003. Asst. prof. history Lindenwood Coll., St. Charles, Mo., 1967-71; from asst. to assoc. prof. history DePauw U., Greencastle, Ind., 1971-77; prof. history, v.p. for acad. affairs Hanover (Ind.) Coll., 1977-89; pres. Adrian (Mich.) Coll., 1989—. Bd. dirs. NCAA Coun., 1995-96, vice chair mgmt. coun. divsn. III, 1997-99, pres.'s coun., 1999-2002; cons., evaluator North Ctrl. Assn., 1984—. Author: The Myth of a Political Reform, 1970; contbr. to book The Progressive Era, 1974; co-editor: Political Reform in Wisconsin, 1973. Bd. dirs. Nat. Assn. Schs., Colls. and Univs. of United Meth. Ch., 1994-97, 2000—, pres., 2002-03; mem. Lenawee Tomorrow, Adrian, 1989—. Recipient D.C. Everest prize Wis. State Hist. Soc., 1968; Woodrow Wilson fellow, 1962-63, Nat. Presbyn. fellow Presbyn. Ch. U.S., 1963-65 Mem. Orgn. Am. Historians, Nat. Assn. Ind. Colls. Univs. (bd. dirs. 1997-2000), Rotary. Methodist. Avocations: sports, reading. Office: Adrian Coll Office of Pres 110 S Madison St Adrian MI 49221-2518 Home Phone: 517-263-1648. Business E-Mail: scaine@adrian.edu.

CAIRNS, JAMES DONALD, lawyer; b. Chelsea, Mass., Aug. 7, 1931; s. Stewart Scott and Kathleen (Hand) C.; m. Alice Crout Cairns, June 18, 1988; children from previous marriage: Douglas S., Timothy H., Pamela S., Heather M. AB, Harvard U., 1952; JD, Ohio State U., 1958. Bar: Fla. 1974, Ohio 1958, US Dist. Ct. (no. dist.) Ohio 1975, US Tax Ct. 1963, Supreme Ct., 2000. Ptnr. Squire, Sanders & Dempsey, Cleve., 1958-95, Spieth, Bell, McCurdy & Newell, Cleve., 1995—. Served to lt. (j.g.) USNR, 1952-55. Mem. ABA, Am. Coll. Trust and Estate Counsel, Fla. Bar Assn., Ohio State Bar Assn., Bar Assn. Greater Cleve., Union Club, Edgewater Yacht Club, Shoreby Club. Democrat. Episcopalian. Office: Spieth Bell McCurdy Newell 2000 Huntington Bldg 925 Euclid Ave Cleveland OH 44115-1408 Home Phone: 216-451-6488; Office Phone: 216-696-4700. Personal E-mail: dcairns@att.net. Business E-Mail: dcairns@spiethbell.com.

CAIRNS, JAMES ROBERT, mechanical engineering educator; b. Indpls., Feb. 4, 1930; s. John Joseph and Agatha Bertha (Krebs) C.; m. Catherine I. DiCicco, Feb. 6, 1954; children: James Robert, Steven J., Michael P., Daniel F., Timothy E., Robert B. BS in Mech. Engring, U. Detroit, 1954; MS in Enging, U. Mich., 1959, PhD, 1963. Registered profl. engr., Mich. cert. energy mgr. Instr. U. Detroit, 1954-57, U. Mich., Ann Arbor, 1957-63, asst. prof. Dearborn, 1963-65, asso. prof., 1965-68, prof. mech. engring., 1968—, chmn. engring. div., 1964-73, acting dean, 1973-75, dean, 1975-81. Cons. and expert witness in product liability litigation. Contbr. articles to profl. jours. Ford Faculty fellow, 1960-63 Mem. ASME, ASHRAE, Assn. Energy Engrs., Am. Soc. Engring. Edn., Common Cause, Tau Beta Pi, Pi Tau Sigma. Roman Catholic. Home: 836 Dover Dr Dearborn Heights MI 48127-4144 Office: 4901 Evergreen Rd Dearborn MI 48128-2406 Personal E-mail: bobcairns@comcast.net. Business E-Mail: bcairns@umich.edu.

CAISMAN, SAUL, lawyer; BS in Commerce, DePaul U., JD. CPA Ill. Ptnr. internat. corp. svc. KPMG LLP, Chgo., mid-west area risk mgmt. ptnr.-tax. Treas. & dir. US Marketing Scholars Fund; v.p., treas. & dir. British-Am. C. of C. Midwest; bd. dir. Inst. Internat. Edn. Named a leading individual, Internat. Tax Rev. mag., 2004; named one of leading tax advisors in US, 1997—2001, Euromoney mag., 1998—99, Mondaq Survey, 2000. Mem.: Internat. Fiscal Assn. (exec. com. midwest branch). Office: KKMG LLP 303 E Wacker Dr Chicago IL 60601-5255 Office Phone: 312-665-5289. E-mail: scaisman@kpmg.com.

CALAHAN, DONALD ALBERT, electrical engineering educator; b. Cin., Feb. 23, 1935; s. Joseph Dexter and Loretta Margaret (Reichling) C.; m. Martha Meyer, Aug. 22, 1959; children: Donald Theodore, Patricia Susan, Mary Susan, Judith Lynn. BS, U. Notre Dame, 1957; MS, U. Ill., 1958, PhD, 1960. Asst. prof. elec. engring. U. Ill., 1961-65; prof. elec. engring. U. Ky., 1965-66; prof. computer engring. U. Mich., Ann Arbor, 1966—. Indsl. cons. in high speed computation, 1976— Author: Modern Network Synthesis, 1964, Computer-Aided Network Design, 1967, rev. edit., 1972, Introduction to Modern Circuit Analysis, 1974. Served to 1st lt. U.S. Army, 1961-62. Fellow IEEE. Roman Catholic. Home: 3139 Lexington Dr Ann Arbor MI 48105-1461 Office: U Mich Dept Elec Engring & Computer Sci Ann Arbor MI 48109

CALAMOS, JOHN PETER, SR., brokerage house executive; b. Aug. 28, 1940; s. Peter and Mary (Kyriakopoulos) Calamos; m. Jackie Calamos, Aug. 15, 1962; children: John Peter Jr. and Laura Lynn. BS in Econs., Ill. Inst. Tech., 1963, MBA in Fin., 1965. Registered rep. DuPont Walston Co., Chgo., 1971-74, Loeb Rhoades Co., Chgo., 1974, Bache & Co., Chgo., 1974-75, Hornblower-Weeks Co., Chgo., 1975-76; sr. v.p. Woodlard & Co., Chgo., 1976-77; pres., mng. dir. Calamos Asset Mgmt., Inc., Oak Brook, Ill., 1977—, CEO. Pres. Calamos Convertible Income Fund, Oak Brook, 1985—. Author: Investing in a Convertible Securities: A Guide to Their Risks and Rewards, 1988; contbr. articles to profl. jours. Served as maj. USAF, 1965-70, Vietnam. Named one of 400 Richest Ams., Forbes mag., 2006. Mem. Internat. Assn. Fin. Planners, Chgo. Assn. Commerce and Industry, Assn. Investment Mgmt. Sales Execs., Inst. Investment Mgmt. Cons., Investment Mgmt. Cons. Assn. Clubs: Sky Haven (Aurora, Ill.) (pres.). Avocations: airplanes, tennis. Office: Calamos Asset Mgmt Inc 1111 E Warrenville Rd Naperville IL 60563-1405

CALCATERRA, EDWARD LEE, construction company executive; b. St. Louis, Mar. 26, 1930; s. Frank John and Rose Theresa (Ruggeri) C.; m. Patricia Jean Marlow, July 4, 1953; children— Christine, Curtis, David, Richard, Tracy BSC.E., U. Mo., Rollo, 1952. Registered profl. engr., Mo. Estimator J.S. Alberici Constrn. Co., St. Louis, 1955-57, mgr. project, 1957-63, v.p. ops., 1963-71, sr. v.p., 1971-76, exec. v.p., 1976-91, pres., 1991-96; exec. dir. J.S. Albenci Constrn. Co., St. Louis, 1996—. Bd. dirs. Cardinal Ritter Inst., St. Louis, 1980-83; bd. regents Rockhurst Coll., Kansas City, Mo., 1983—. Served with U.S. Army, 1953-55 Mem. Assoc. Gen. Contractors St. Louis (pres. 1980) Roman Catholic.

CALDWELL, CHARLES M., federal judge; b. 1954; BS, Evansville U., 1976; JD, Northwestern U., 1979. Asst. U.S. trustee U.S. Dist. Ct. (so. dist.) Ohio, 1988-93; staff atty. bankruptcy divsn. Adminstrv. Office U.S. Cts., Washington, 1986-88; bankruptcy judge U.S. Bankruptcy Ct., Columbus, 1993—. Office: US Bankruptcy Ct 170 N High St Columbus OH 43215-2403 Office Phone: 614-469-6638. E-mail: charles_caldwell@ohsb.uscourts.gov.

CALICO, ROBERT A., dean; BS in Aerospace Engring., U.Cin., 1966, MS in Aerospace Engring., 1968, PhD in Aerospace Engring., 1971. Aerospace design engr. Advanced Sys. Br. LTV Aerospace, Dallas, 1966—68; instr. dept. aerospace engring. U. Cin., 1969—72; from asst. prof. to prof. Air Force Inst. Tech., Wright AFB, Dayton, Ohio, 1972—, dean Grad. Sch. Engring., 1990—. Named Disting. Alumni, U. Cin. Coll. Engring., Disting. Engr., Engring. and Sci. Found. Dayton. Fellow: AIAA (assoc.); mem.: Engring and Sci. Found. (bd. trustees), Am. Soc. Engring. Edn., Sigma Xi, Sigma Gamma Tau, Tau Beta Pi. Office: USAF Inst Tech Office of Pub Affairs Wright Patterson AFB Dayton OH 45433-7765

CALINESCU, ADRIANA GABRIELA, curator, art historian; b. Bucharest, Romania, Dec. 30, 1941; came to U.S., 1973; d. Nicolae and Tamara Gane; m. Matei Alexe Calinescu, Apr. 29, 1963; children: Irena, Matthew. BA, Cen. Lyceé, Bucharest, 1959; MA in English, U. Bucharest, 1964; MLS, Ind. U., 1976, MA in Art History, 1983. Asst. prof. Inst. Theater and Cinema, Bucharest, 1967-73; rsch. assoc. Ind. U. Art Mus., Bloomington, 1979-83, Thomas T. Solley curator ancient art, assoc. scholar, 1992—. Vis. assoc. mem. Am. Sch. Classical Studies, Athens, Greece, 1984. Author: The Art of Ancient Jewelry, 1994, Egypt After Alexander, 2005; author, co-editor: Ancient Art from the V. G. Simkhovitch Collection, 1988; editor: Ancient Jewelry and Archaeology, 1996. NEA fellow, 1984; grantee Salzburg Seminar, 1970, NEA, 1987, 93, Kress Found., 1991, Internat. Rsch. and Exchanges Bd., 1991. Mem. Am. Inst. Archaeology, Classical Art Soc., Beta Phi Mu. Office: Ind U Art Mus E 7th St Bloomington IN 47405 Office Phone: 812-855-1033.

CALISE, WILLIAM JOSEPH, JR., lawyer; b. NYC, May 22, 1938; s. William Joseph and Adeline (Rota) C.; m. Kathryn A. Verner; children: Kimberly Elizabeth, Andrea Elizabeth. BA, Bucknell U., 1960; MBA, JD, Columbia U., 1963. Bar: N.Y. 1963, D.C. 1981. Assoc., then ptnr. Chadbourne & Parke, NYC, 1967—94; sr. v.p., gen. counsel, sec. Rockwell Automation, Inc. (formerly Rockwell Internat.), Milw., 1994—2004. Bd. dirs. Henry St. Settlement, N.Y.C., 1977-94, Jr. Achievement Inc., 1999-2004; mem. Allendale (N.J.) Sch. Bd., 1977-80. Capt. U.S. Army, 1964-66. Mem. Assn. Bar N.Y.C., Assn. Gen. Counsel. Roman Catholic. Office Phone: 805-564-1888. Personal E-mail: casacalise@cox.net.

CALKINS, HUGH, foundation executive; b. Newton, Mass., Feb. 20, 1924; s. Grosvenor and Patty (Phillips) C.; m. Ann Clark, June 14, 1955; children: Peter, Andrew, Margaret, Elizabeth. AB, LLB, Harvard U., 1949, D (hon.) in Law, 1985. Bar: Ohio 1950. Law clk. to presiding judge U.S. Ct. Appeals (2d cir.), YC, 1949-50; law clk. to justice Felix Frankfurter U.S. Supreme Ct., Washington, 1950-51; from assoc. to ptnr. Jones, Day, Reavis & Pogue, Cleve., 1951-90; tchr. elem. schs. Cleve. City Sch. Dist., 1991-94. Contbr. articles on fed. income tax to profl. jours. Mem. Cleve. Bd. Edn., 1965-69; assoc. dir. Pres.'s Commn. on Nat. Goals, Washington, 1960; mem., pres., fellow Harvard U., 1968-85; mem. task forces Cleve. Summit on Edn., 1990-94; chair, treas., trustee Initiatives in Urban Edn., 1991—. Capt. USAF, 1943-46. Mem. ABA (chmn. tax sect. 1985-86), Am. Law Inst. (coun.), City Club, Cleve. Skating Club, Rowfant Club, Phi Beta Kappa. Democrat. Unitarian Universalist. Home and Office: 3345 N Park Blvd Cleveland OH 44118 Home Phone: 216-321-5339; Office Phone: 216-397-9749. Personal E-mail: calk2@adelphia.net.

CALKINS, RICHARD W., former college president; b. June 3, 1939; BA in Music, Albion Coll., 1960; MA in Edn., Mich. State U., 1966, MA, 1971, postgrad., 1972—; Doctorate (hon.), Ferris State U., 1992. Vocal music tchr. Ridgeview Jr. High Sch., 1961-64, Creston High Sch., 1964-68, asst. dir. pers., 1968-71, gen. assoc. supt., 1971-74, asst. supt. pers. and community svcs., 1974-75; pres. Grand Rapids (Mich.) C.C., 1975-98; ret., 1998. Cons. in field. Bd. dirs. religious activities Epworth Assembly, Ludington, Mich., 1960-82; mins. music Eastminster Presbyn. ch., Grand Rapids, 1964-93; v.p. planning, mem. exec. com. Downtown Mgmt. Bd., 1985-91; pres. Grand Rapids C.C. Found., 1978—; bd. dirs. Mich. Info. Tech. Network, 1988—; mem. Mid Am. Training Group, 1989—, Downtown Planning Com., 1991, Nat. Modernization Forum, 1990-91, Nat. Coalition Advance Tech. Ctrs., 1990—, Alliance for Mfg. Productivity, 1990—, IBM CIM Higher Edn., 1990—; bd. dirs., mem. pub. policy and pers. coms. YMCA, 1989-92; chair edn. div. United Way Kent County, chair major accounts, 1992; founding bd. dirs. Noorthoek Acad., 1989—; bd. dirs. edn. and summer facility coms. Grand Rapids Symphony, 1989— Mem. Indsl. Tech. Inst., Am. Assn. Community and Colls., Assn. C.C. Trustees, Assn. Tchr. Educators, Mich. Assn. Sch. Adminstrs., Mich. Assn. Pub. Adult Continuing Educators, Mich. Assn. Tchr. Educators, Mich. C.C. Assn. (chair polit. action com. 1983—, exec. com. 1987-90, v.p. 1987-88, past pres. 1989-90, treas. 1990-91), C.C. Assn. for Tech. Transfer, Grand Rapids Dunkers Club, Peninsular Club Grand Rapids, Phi Delta Kappa. Office: Grand Rapids Community Coll 143 Bostwick Ave NE Grand Rapids MI 49503-3201 Home: 1010 Lakeridge Ct Colleyville TX 76034-2825

CALKINS, STEPHEN, lawyer, educator; b. Balt., Mar. 20, 1950; s. Evan and Virginia (Brady) C.; m. Joan Wadsworth, Oct. 18, 1981; children: Timothy, Geoffrey, Virginia. BA, Yale U., 1972; JD, Harvard U., 1975. Bar: N.Y. 1976, D.C. 1977, U.S. Dist. Ct. D.C. 1979. Law clk. to FTC commr. S. Nye, Washington, 1975-76; assoc. Covington & Burling, Washington, 1976-83; assoc. law prof. Wayne State U., Detroit, 1983-88, prof., 1988—, dir. grad. studies, 2004—07, assoc. v.p., 2008—; gen. counsel FTC, Washington, 1995-97; of counsel Covington & Burling, Washington, 1997—, program dir. conf. bd. antitrust conf., 2001—07. Vis. assoc. prof. law U. Mich., Ann Arbor, 1985, U. Pa., Phila., 1987; vis. prof. law U. Utrecht, Netherlands, 1989; chair career devel. Wayne State U., 1990-91. Author: (with Gellhorn and Kovacic) Antitrust Law and Economics in a Nutshell, 5th edit., 2004, (with Rogers, Patterson and Anderson) Antitrust Law: Policy and Practice, 4th edit., 2008; editor: Antitrust Law Developments, 1984, 86, 88; editor legal book revs. The Antitrust Bull., 1986—; articles editor Antitrust, 1991-95. Co-chair Class of 1972 Yale Alumni Fund, 2004-07, chair 2007-; class agent Harvard Law Sch. Found., 2007-; counsel Ind. Commn. on Admissions Practices in Cranbrook Sch., Detroit, 1984-85; mem. Northville Zoning Bd. Appeals, 1987-95; rep.-at-large Assn. Yale Alumni Assembly, 1989-92; bd. dirs. Yale Alumni Assn. of Mich., 2002-; elder First Presbyn. Ch. Northville, 1989-92. Rsch. fellow Wayne State U., 1984; USAID grantee, 1999-2004; recipient FTC award disting. svc., 1997, Donald H. Gordon Tchg. award, 2006. Fellow: Am. Bar Found., Am. Antitrust Inst. (sr.); mem.: ABA (counsel to com. on FTC 1988—89, coun. antitrust sect. 1988—91, 1997—2000, coun. adminstrv. law sect. 1999—2002, coun. antitrust sect. 2006—, Antitrust sect. 50th anniversary pub. award 2002), Am. Assn. Law Schs. (sec. antitrust sect. 1987—91, chair-elect 1991—93, chair 1993—95), Am. Law Inst., Anthony Wayne Soc., Northville Swim Club, Detroit Yale Club, Detroit Harvard Club. Presbyterian. Avocations: reading, skiing, rollerblading. Home: 317 W Dunlap St Northville MI 48167-1404 Office: Wayne State U 4092 Faculty Adminstrn Bldg 656 W Kinly Detroit MI 48202 Office Phone: 313-577-2257. Business E-Mail: calkins@wayne.edu.

CALLAHAN, J(OHN) WILLIAM (BILL CALLAHAN), judge; b. Rockville Centre, NY, Feb. 8, 1947; s. Peter Felix and Catherine L. C. BA, Mich. State U., 1971, JD cum laude, 1974. Atty. Bank of Commonwealth, Detroit, 1974-76; assoc. Hoops & Hudson, P.C., Detroit, 1976-79, Tyler & Canham, P.C., Detroit, 1979-80, Stark & Reagan, P.C., Troy, Mich., 1980-81; pvt. practice Farmington Hills, Mich., 1981-86; mem. Plunkett & Cooney, P.C., Detroit, 1986-96; judge Wayne County Cir. Ct., Detroit, 1996—. Bd. dirs. Vietnam Vets. Am. Chpt. 9, Detroit, 1981-85. With USMC, 1967-69, Vietnam. Mem. Detroit Bar Assn. Office: 1813 City-County Bldg Detroit MI 48226

CALLAHAN, MICHAEL R., lawyer; b. NYC, Apr. 11, 1953; BA, No. Ill. U.; JD, DePaul U., 1979. Bar: Ill. 1979. Law clerk to Justice Daniel P. Ward Ill. Supreme Ct., 1979—81; ptnr. head Health Care Practice group Katten Muchin Zavis Rosenman, Chgo. Adj. prof. DePaul Coll., Masters in Health Law Prog. Mem.: ABA, Am. Health Lawyers Assn., Ill. Assn. of Hosp. Attys., Chgo. Bar Assn. Office: Katten Muchin Zavis Rosenman 525 W Monroe St Chicago IL 60661 Office Phone: 312-902-5634. Office Fax: 312-577-8945. Business E-Mail: michael.callahan@kattenlaw.com.

CALLAHAN, PATRICK, communication media executive; Bur. chief UP Internat., Pierre, SD, 1999—; state bur. chief Dakota News Network. Office: DNN 214 W Pleasant Dr Pierre SD 57501

CALLAHAN, RICHARD G., prosecutor; b. St. Louis, Apr. 22, 1947; s. George G. and Doris M. (Ohmer) C.; children: Maureen, Jerry, Mary Kay, Tim, Mike. AB, Georgetown U., Washington, 1968, JD, 1972. Asst. prosecutor St. Louis Cir. Attys. Office, 1972-78, Cole County, Jefferson City, Mo., 1979-86, pros. atty., 1987—. Office: 311 E High St # 3 Jefferson City MO 65101-3250

CALLAHAN, WILLIAM E., JR., federal judge; b. Evanston, Ill., Sept. 15, 1948; BA, Marquette U., 1970, JD, 1973. Atty. Goldberg, Previant and Uelman, 1973-75; asst. U.S. atty. Eastern Dist. Wis., 1975-82, 1st asst. U.S. atty., 1982-84; atty. Davis & Kuelthau, S.C., 1984-95; magistrate judge U.S. Dist. Ct. (ea. dist.) Wis., Milw., 1995—. Office: 247 US Courthouse 517 E Wisconsin Ave Milwaukee WI 53202-4500

CALLAHAN, WILLIAM PATRICK, bishop; b. Chgo., June 17, 1950; s. William and Ellen Callahan. B in Radio and TV Comm., Loyola U., Chgo., 1973; MDiv, U. Toronto, 1976. Professed Order of Friars Minor Conventual, 1970, ordained priest, 1977; assoc. pastor St. Josaphat Parish, 1977—78; dir. vocations for Conventual Franciscans Archdiocese of Milw., 1978—84; assoc. pastor Holy Family Parish, Peoria, Ill., 1984—87, pastor, 1987—94; rector St. Josaphat Parish, 1994—2005; spiritual dir. Pontifical N.Am. Coll., Rome, 2005—07; ordained bishop, 2007; aux. bishop Archdiocese of Milw., 2007—. Roman Catholic. Office: Archdiocese of Milw 3501 S Lake Dr Milwaukee WI 53207 Office Phone: 414-769-3300. Office Fax: 414-769-3408.*

CALLANDER, KAY EILEEN PAISLEY, business owner, retired education educator, writer; b. Coshocton, Ohio, Oct. 15, 1938; d. Dalton Olas and Dorothy Pauline (Davis) Paisley; m. Don Larry Callander, Nov. 18, 1977. BSE, Muskingum Coll., New Concord, Ohio, 1960; MA in Speech Edn., Ohio State U., Columbus, 1964, postgrad., 1964-84. Cert. elem., gifted, drama, theater tchr., Ohio. Tchr. Columbus Pub. Schs., Ohio, 1960-70, 80-88, drama specialist Ohio, 1970-80, classroom, gifted/talented tchr. Ohio, 1986-90, ret. Ohio, 1990; sole prop. The Ali Group, Kay Kards, 1992—. Coord. Artists-in-the Schs., 1977-88; ednl. cons. Innovation Alliance Youth Adv. Coun., 1992—; cons., presenter in field. Producer-dir., Shady Lane Music Festival, 1980-88; dir. tchr. (nat. distbr. video) The Trial of Gold E. Locks, 1983-84; rep., media pub. relations liason Sch. News., 1983-88; author, creator Trivia Game About Black Americans; presenter for workshop by Human Svc. Group and Creative Edn. Coop., Columbus, Ohio, 1989. Benefactor, Columbus Jazz Arts Group; v.p., bd. dirs. Neoteric Dance and Theater Co., Columbus, 1985-87; tchr., participant Future Stars sculpture exhibit, Ft. Hayes Ctr., Columbus Pub. Schs., 1988; tchr. advisor Columbus Coun. PTAs, 1983-86, co-chmn. reflections com., 1984-87; mem. Columbus Mus. Art, Citizens for Humane Action, Inc.; upt.'s adv. coun. Columbus Pub. Schs., 1967-68; presenter Young Author Seminar, Ohio Dept. Edn., 1988, Illustrating Methods for Young Authors' Books, 1986-87; cons. and workshop leader seminar/workshop Tchg. About the Constitution in Elem. Schs., Franklin County Ednl. Coun., 1988; sponsor Minority Youth Recognition Awards, 1994. Named Educator of Yr., Shady Lane PTA, 1982, Columbus Coun. PTAs, 1989, winner Colour Columbus Landscape Design Competition, 1990; Sch. Excellence grantee Columbus Pub. Schs.; Commendation Columbus Bd. Edn. and Ohio Ho. of Reps. for Child Assault Prevention project, 1986-87; first place winner statewide photo contest Ohio Vet. Assn., 1991; recipient Muskingum Coll. Alumni Disting. Svc. award, 1995. Mem. ASCD, AAUW, Assn. for Childhood Edn. Internat., Ohio Coun. for Social Studies, Franklin County Ret. Tchrs. Assn., Nat. Mus. Women in the Arts, Ohio State U. Alumni Assn., US Army Officers Club, Navy League, Liturgical Art Guild Ohio, Columbus Jazz Arts Group, Columbus Mus. Art, Nat. Coun. for Social Studies, Columbus Art League, Columbus Maennerchor (Damen sect.). Republican. Avocations: painting, photography, swimming, golf, playing piano and organ. Home: 9131 Indian Mound Rd Pickerington OH 43147 Personal E-mail: paiscallander@embarqmail.com.

CALLAWAY, KAREN A(LICE), journalist; b. Daytona Beach, Fla., Sept. 5, 1946; d. Robert Clayton III and Alice Johnston (Webb) Callaway. BS in Journalism, Northwestern U., 1968. Copy editor Detroit Free Press, 1968-69; asst. woman's editor, features copy editor, news copy editor, asst. makeup editor Chgo. Am. and Chgo. Today, 1969-74; asst. makeup editor Chgo. Tribune, 1974-76, asst. news editor, 1976-81, assoc. news editor spl. sect., 1981-2000, assoc. news editor vertical publs., 1993-2000, asst. news editor spl. sect., 2000—. Adviser Jr. Achievement Tribune sponsored co., Chgo., 1976—77; editor Infant Mortality sect., 1989; vis. prof. student chpt. Soc. Profl. Journalists, Northwestern U., 1989. Chmn. Class of 1968 20th reunion Northwestern U., Evanston, Ill., 1989, seminar day com., 1989—90, chmn., 1991; alumni bd. Medill Sch. Journalism, Evanston, Ill., 1991—99; vol. Northwestern U. Settlement Assn., Chgo. Mem.: Soc. Profl. Journalists, Chgo. Headline Club, Kappa Delta. Methodist. Avocations: swimming, cooking, travel. Office: Chicago Tribune 435 N Michigan Ave Ste 500 Chicago IL 60611-4041 Office Phone: 312-222-3515.

CALLEN, JAMES DONALD, plasma physicist, nuclear engineer; b. Wichita, Kans., Jan. 31, 1941; s. Donald Dewitt and Bonnie Jean (Walton) C.; m. Judith Carolyn Chinn, Aug. 26, 1961; children: Jeffrey Scott, Sandra Jean. BS in Nuclear Engring., Kans. State U., 1962, MS in Nuclear Engring., 1964; PhD in Nuclear Engring., MIT, 1968. Postdoctoral fellow Inst. for Advanced Study, Princeton, NJ, 1968-69; asst. prof. aeros. and astronautics MIT, Cambridge, 1969-72; mem. rsch. staff fusion energy divsn. Oak Ridge (Tenn.) Nat. Lab., 1972-74, group leader, 1974-75, head plasma theory sect., 1975-79; prof. nuc. engring. and physics U. Wis., Madison, 1979-86, D.W. Kerst prof. engring. physics and physics, 1986—. Mem. editor. bd. Nuc. Fusion Jour., 1978-97; assoc. editor divsn. plasma physics Phys. Rev. Letters Jour., 1980-85; contbr. over 165 articles to profl. jours. Recipient Dept. of Energy Disting. Assoc. award, 1988, Disting. Career award Fusion Power Assocs., 2002; named to Coll. Engring. Hall of Fame, Kans. State U., 1991; Fulbright fellow Tech. Hogesch., Eindhoven, etherlands, 1962-63; Guggenheim fellow, 1986. Fellow Am. Phys. Soc. (chmn. divsn. plasma physics 1986), Am. Nuc. Soc.; mem. NAE, AAAS. Office: U Wis 1500 Engineering Dr Madison WI 53706-1609 Business E-Mail: callen@engr.wisc.edu.

CALLENDER, JAMES SUTTON, JR., lawyer, state legislator; b. Mayfield, Ky., Jan. 9, 1965; s. James Sutton Sr. and Patricia Rhea (Dycus) C.; m. Andrea Lynn Schembre, June 11, 1990; children: Ashley Rhea, James Sutton III. BA in History, Cleve. State U., 1989; JD, Cleve. Marshall Law Sch., 1992. Bar: Ohio 1992. Assoc. Robert H. Myers, Jr. & Assocs., Painesville, Ohio, 1992-94; ptnr. James S. Callender Jr., Painesville, 1994-97, Eastlake, 1997—; rep. State of Ohio, 1996—. Chmn., pres. Retinitis Pigmentosa Found., Cleve., 1990-93; chmn. Willowick (Ohio) Recreation Bd., 1992-94; vice chmn. bd. trustees Lake County (Ohio) Hist. Soc., 1994—; mem. exec. com. and ctrl. com. Lake County Republican Party. Mem. ABA, Ohio State Bar Assn., Lake County Bar Assn. (grievance com.), Masons. Methodist. Office: 35475 Vine St Ste 200 Eastlake OH 44095-3147 Home: 9920 Ashwood Trl Mentor OH 44060-7202

CALLINAN, TOM, editor-in-chief; b. 1948; m. Maureen Callinan; 3 children. Corr. St. Cloud Daily Times, Minn., 1975; various positions Little Falls Daily Transcript, 1977—83; from asst. city editor to mng. editor Argus Leader, Sioux Falls, Minn., 1983—86; editor Lansing State Jour., 1986—91; exec. editor Fort Myers News-Press, 1991—94; editor Dem. and Chronicle and Times-Union, Rochester, NY, 1994—2000, v.p. news, 1994—2000; editor The Ariz. Republic, Phoenix, 2000—02; editor & v.p. Cin. Enquirer, 2002—. Named Gannett's Editor of Yr., 1997; recipient six Gannett Pres.'s Rings in News. Office: Cincinnati Enquirer 312 Elm St Fl 18 Cincinnati OH 45202-2724 Office Phone: 513-768-8551. E-mail: tcallinan@enquirer.com.

CALLOW, WILLIAM GRANT, retired judge; b. Waukesha, Wis., Apr. 9, 1921; s. Curtis Grant and Mildred G. C.; m. Jean A. Zilavy, Apr. 15, 1950; children: William G., Christine S., Katherine H. PhB in Econs, U. Wis., 1943, JD, 1948. Bar: Wis.; cert. for Fla. mediation. Asst. city atty. City of Waukesha, 1948—52, city atty., 1952—60; county judge Waukesha, 1961—77; justice Supreme Ct. Wis., Madison, 1978—82; ret., 1992. Asst. prof. U. Minn., 1951-52; mem. faculty Wis. Jud. Coll., 1968-75; Wis. commr. Nat. Conf. Commrs. on Uniform State Laws, 1967—; arbitrator Wis. Employment Rel. Commn.; arbitrator-mediator bus. disputes; arbitration and mediation nat. and internat. res. judge, 1992—. With USMC, 1943-45; with USAF, 1951-52, Korea. Recipient Outstanding Alumnus award U. Wis. 1973 Fellow Am. Bar Found.; mem. ABA, Dane County Bar Assn., Waukesha County Bar Assn. Episcopalian. Personal E-mail: justicehi@aol.com.

CALLSEN, CHRISTIAN EDWARD, health products executive; b. 1938; married. AB, Miami U., 1959; MBA, Harvard U., 1966. With Cole Nat. Corp., Cleve., 1966-87, various mgmt. and v.p. positions, 1966-87, exec. v.p., 1983-87; pres. Hyatt Legal Svcs., Cleve., 1987-90, Profl. Vet. Hosps., Detroit, 1991, Profl. Med. Mgmt., Cleve., 1992—2000, Applied Med. Tech., Cleve., 1993-96; chmn., CEO Allen Med. Sys., Cleve., 1995-99; pres. Polymer Concepts, Inc., 1999; chmn. TAGA Med. Techs., Inc., 2000—05. Lt. USN, 1959-64. Office: 7561 Tyler Blvd Ste 8 Mentor OH 44060-4867 Home: 21 Clinton St Hudson OH 44236 Office Phone: 440-953-9605. Personal E-mail: cec235@aol.com.

CALVERT, CHARLES, state representative; b. Cleve., Apr. 13, 1939; married; 3 children. BA in Fin. and Acctg., Baldwin Wallace Coll.; postgrad., Cleve. State U. Ret. CFO NASA Glenn Rsch. Ctr.; state rep. dist. 69 Ohio Ho. of Reps., Columbus, 1998—, chair, fin. and appropriations com., mem. rules and reference com. Former foster parent; past pres. 4 local sch. bds. Served US Army. Named Outstanding Legislator, United Conservatives of Ohio, 2000; recipient Watchdog of the Treasury award, 2000. Mem.: SPCA, Twp. Assn., Medina County AARP, Farm Bur., Our Lady Help of Christians Parish, Friends of the Park Dist., Medina-Summit Land Conservancy, numerous local Cs. of C., Medina County Rep. Party. Republican. Office: 77 S High St 13th fl Columbus OH 43215-6111

CAMAROTTO, DAVID EARLE, lawyer; BA, St. John's U., 1997; JD, William Mitchell Coll. Law, 2000. Bar: Minn. 2001, US Dist. Ct. (dist. Minn.). Jud. law clk. to Hon. John J. Sommerville Hennepin County, Minn.; atty. Johnson & Lindberg, Mpls., Bassford Remele, P.A., Mpls. Named a Rising Star, Minn. Super Lawyers mag., 2006. Mem.: Minn. Def. Lawyers Assn., Hennepin County Bar Assn., Minn. State Bar Assn. Office: Bassford Remele PA 33 S 6th St Ste 3800 Minneapolis MN 55402-3707 Office Phone: 612-376-1618. E-mail: davidc@bassford.com.

CAMBERN, ANDREA, newscaster, reporter; m. Brett Cambern. Student, Ariz. State U. With Sta. KTSP-TV, Phoenix, Sta. KVOA-TV, Tucson; owner pub. rels. firm; anchor, reporter Sta. WBNS-TV, Columbus, Ohio, 1991—. Named Female Anchor of Yr., Nat. Assn. Television Journalists; recipient Emmy awards (4). Office: WBNS-TV 770 Twin Rivers Dr Columbus OH 43215

CAMDEN, CARL T., human resources company executive; b. Wilmington, Del., 1954; BA in Psychology/Speech, Southwest Baptist Coll., 1975; MA in Clin. Psychology/Speech Comm., Central Mo. State U., 1977; DCom., Ohio State U., 1980. Assoc. prof. communications Cleve. State U.; co-founder, co-owner North Coast Behavioral Rsch. Group; co-pres. Wyse Advt.; sr. v.p., dir. corp. mktg. KeyCorp.; sr. v.p. corp. mktg. Kelly Svcs. Inc., Troy, Mich., 1995—97, exec. v.p. mktg. & strategy, 1997—98, exec. v.p., field ops. sales & mktg., 1998—2001, exec. v.p., COO, 2001, COO, 2001—06, pres., 2001—, CEO, 2006—. Mem. labor adv. bd. Fed. Reserve Bank Chgo.; mem. ERISA adv. council, 2000—02. Mem. bd. vis. Fuqua Sch. Bus., Duke Univ., Sch. Nursing, Oakland Univ. Recipient William J. Heartwell award, NASWA, 2004. Office: Kelly Svcs Inc 999 W Big Beaver Rd Troy MI 48084-4782*

CAMERON, JOHN M., nuclear scientist, educator, administator; b. Aug. 9, 1940; BSc, Queens U., Ireland, 1962; MSc, UCLA, 1965, PhD, 1967. Tech. asst. U.K. Atomic Energy Authority, Eng., 1962-63; asst. prof. UCLA, 1967-68; rsch. assoc. U. Wash., Seattle, 1968-70; asst. prof. to prof. U. Alta., 1970-87; dir. Cyclotron Facility, prof. dept. physics Ind. U., Bloomington, 1987—. Asst. dir. initial ops. TRIUMF, Vancouver, 1973-74; vis scientist U. Paris, SIN Switzerland, 1977-78; staff scientist Nat. Saturne Lab., France, 1981-82; dir. Nuclear Rsch. Ctr., U. Alta., 1985-87. Fellow Am. Phys. Soc. Office: IN Univ Bloomington Cyclotron Facility 2401 Milo Sampson Ln Bloomington IN 47408-1368 Office Phone: 812-855-3316.

CAMERON, OLIVER GENE, psychiatrist, educator, psychobiology researcher; b. Evanston, Ill., Aug. 28, 1946; s. Gene Oliver and Elizabeth Marie (Burns) C.; m. Susan Linda Friedman, June 22, 1972; children— Leah Victoria, Peter Sean. B.A., U. otre Dame, 1968; Ph.D., U. Chgo., 1972, M.D., 1974. Diplomate Am. Bd. psychiatry and Neurology. Med. intern U. Mich., Ann Arbor, 1974-75, psychiatry resident, 1975-78, psychiatry fellow, 1978-79, asst. prof. psychiatry, 1979-86, assoc. prof., 1986-92, prof., 1992—; dir. anxiety disorders program, dept. psychiatry, 1984-85, dir. adult psychiatry outpatient program, dept. psychiatry, 1985-90, Combined Mood & Anxiety Program, 1994—. Contbr. articles to profl. jours. Mem. Am. Psychiatric Assn., Am. Psychosomatic Soc., AAAS, Sigma Xi. Avocations: photography; travel; golf. Home: 1215 Southwood Ct Ann Arbor MI 48103-9735 Office: U Mich 1500 E Medical Center Dr Ann Arbor MI 48109-0005

CAMERON, PATRICIA, advertising executive; Exec. v.p. Campbell Mithun Esty, Mpls. Office: Campbell Mithun Esty 222 S 9th St Minneapolis MN 55402-3803

CAMINKER, EVAN H., dean, law educator; BA summa cum laude, UCLA; JD, Yale Law Sch. Faculty mem. UCLA, 1991—99; prof. U. Mich. Sch. Law, Ann Arbor, 1999—, assoc. dean, 2001—03, dean, 2003—. Clerk for Justice William J. Brennan U.S. Supreme Court; for Judge William A. Norris Ninth Cir. Ct. of Appeals; atty. Ctr. for Law in Pub. Interest, Los Angeles, Wilmer, Cutler & Pickering, Washington, DC; dep. asst. atty. gen. Office of Legal Coun., U.S. Dept. Justice, 2000—01. Sr. editor Yale Law Jour.; contbr. articles to law jours. Recipient Benjamin Scharps Prize, Disting. Profs. Award for Civil Liberties Edn., ACLU; Coker Fellow. Office: U Mich Law Sch 324 Hutchins Hall 625 S State St Ann Arbor MI 48109-1215 Office Phone: 734-764-0514. Office Fax: 734-763-1055. Business E-Mail: caminker@umich.edu.

CAMP, DAVID LEE, congressman, lawyer; b. Midland, Mich., July 9, 1953; m. Nancy Keil, Sept. 10, 1994; children: Andrew, David, Lauren. BA magna cum laude, Albion Coll., Mich., 1975; JD, U. San Diego, 1978. Bar: Mich., Calif., DC, admitted to practice: US Supreme Ct., US Dist. Ct. (Ea. Dist.) Mich., US Dist. Ct. (So. Dist.) Calif. With Riecker, Van Dam, Looby & Barker, 1978-90; spl. asst. atty. gen. Mich., 1980-84; adminstrv. asst. to Congressman Bill Schuette, 1985-87; state rep. 102nd Dist. Mich., 1989-91; mem. U.S. Congress from 10th (now 4th) Mich. dist., 1991—, mem. ways and means com., asst. minority whip, mem. select com. on homeland security. Chmn. Spkrs. Correction Day Com. Mem.: Midland County Bar Assn., ABA. Republican. Office: US Congress 137 Cannon Bldg Washington DC 20515-2204 also: District Office 135 Ashman Dr Midland MI 48640 Office Phone: 202-225-3561, 989-631-2552. Office Fax: 202-225-9679, 989-631-6271.

CAMPBELL, ALEX, mobile marketing executive; b. 1976; BS in Econs., U. Pa. Wharton Sch. Co-head paging co., Chgo., 1998; co-founder, CEO Vibes Media, Chgo., 1998—. Named one of Top 40 Under 40, Crain's Chgo. Bus., 2006. Mem.: Mobile Mktg. Assn. (mem. mobile strategies and best practices com.). Office: Vibes Media 205 W Wacker Dr 23rd Fl Chicago IL 60606

CAMPBELL, ANDREW, manufacturing executive; V.p. fin., CFO Duplex Products, Inc., 1994—95, pres., bd. dirs., 1995—96; sr. v.p. fin., CFO Safety Kleen Corp., 1997—98; exec. v.p. fin. and adminstrn., CFO Dominick's Supermarkets, Inc., 1998; acting CFO Foamex Internat., Inc., 1999; v.p., CFO Pactiv Corp., Lake Forest, Ill., 1999—2001, sr. v.p., CFO, 2001—. Office: Pactiv Corp 1900 W Field Ct Lake Forest IL 60045

CAMPBELL, BRUCE CRICHTON, hospital administrator; b. Balt., July 21, 1947; s. James Allen and Elda Shaffer (Crichton) C.; m. Linda Page Cottrell, June 28, 1969; children: Molly Shaffer, Andrew Crichton. BA, Lake Forest Coll., 1969; MHA, Washington U., St. Louis, 1973; DPH, U. Ill., 1979; MA, Northwestern U., Evanston, Ill., 2007. Adminstrv. asst. Passavant Meml. Hosp., Chgo., 1970-71; adminstrv. resident Albany (N.Y.) Med. Center Hosp., 1972-73; adminstrv. asst. Rush-Presbyn.-St. Luke's Med. Center, Chgo., 1973-75, asst. adminstr., 1975-77, asst. v.p., 1977-79, v.p. adminstrv. affairs, 1979-83; chmn. dept. health systems mgmt. Rush U., Chgo., 1977-81, dean Coll. Health Scis., 1981-83; exec. dir. U. Chgo. Hosps. and Clinics, 1983-85; lectr. Grad. Sch. Bus., U. Chgo., 1983-85; pres. Campbell Assocs., Chgo., 1985-92; exec. v.p. Ill. Masonic Med. Ctr., Chgo., 1993, pres., 1993-2000, Advocate Luth. Gen. Hosp., Park Ridge, Ill., 2000—. W.K. Kellogg Found. fellow, 1977; Leadership Greater Chgo. fellow, 1984-85 Fellow Am. Coll. Healthcare Execs.; mem. Young Adminstrs. Chgo. (pres. 1977), Assn. Univ. Programs in Health Adminstrn., Am. Hosp. Assn., Ill. Hosp. Assn., Chgo. Hosp. Council. Office: Advocate Luth Gen Hosp 1775 Dempster St Park Ridge IL 60668

CAMPBELL, BRUCE IRVING, lawyer; b. Mason City, Iowa, July 7, 1947; s. E. Riley Jr. and Donna May (Andresen) C.; children: Anne, John; m. Beverly J. Evans. BA, Upper Iowa U., 1969; JD, Harvard U., 1973. Bar: Iowa 1973, U.S. Dist. Ct. (so. dist.) Iowa 1973, U.S. Dist. Ct. (no. dist.) Iowa 1974, U.S. Tax Ct. 1976, U.S. Ct. Appeals (8th cir.) 1977, U.S. Ct. Claims 1982. Shareholder Davis, Brown, Koehn, Shors & Roberts, P.C., Des Moines, 1973—. Adj. prof. law Drake U., Des Moines, 1974-90. Trustee Upper Iowa U., Fayette, 1978—, chair bd. trustees, 1992—2002; sec., dir. Iowa Natural Heritage Found., 2001—. Mem. ABA, Iowa State Bar Assn., Polk County Bar Assn. Republican. Home: 62 Meadowbrook Cir Cumming IA 50061-1014 Office: Davis Brown Koehn Shors & Roberts PC 666 Walnut St Ste 2500 Des Moines IA 50309-3904 Home Phone: 515-285-6480. E-mail: bruce.campbell@lawiowa.com.

CAMPBELL, COLIN, obstetrician, gynecologist, dean; b. Washington, June 24, 1927; s. Colin and Margaret (Kingsland) Masters C.; m. Catherine Marian Hayden, Aug. 20, 1952; children: Catherine, Janet, Philip. AB, Stanford U., 1949; MD, CM, McGill U., 1953; EdM, Temple U., 1967; DHL, U. Akron, 1991. Diplomate Am. Bd. Ob-Gyn. Intern George Washington Hosp., Washington, 1953-54; asst. resident in pathology U.S. VA Hosp., Coral Gables, Fla., 1954; gen. practice resident Dade County Hosp., Kendall, Fla., 1955; gen. practice medicine Perrine, Fla., 1955-57; asst. resident, resident in ob-gyn. Hosp. for the Women of Md., Balt., 1957-60; practice medicine specializing in ob-gyn. Balt., 1960-61; instr. ob-gyn. Temple U., Phila., 1961-64; asst. prof. ob-gyn. U. Mich., Ann Arbor, 1964-67, assoc. prof., 1967-71, prof., 1971-78, asst. dean Med. Sch., 1972-76, assoc. dean, 1976-78; prof. ob-gyn., dean U. Ala. Sch. Primary Med. Care, Huntsville, 1978-83; prof. ob-gyn., pres., dean Northeastern Ohio Univs. Coll. Medicine, Rootstown, 1983-92, pres., dean emeritus, 1992—. Contbr. numerous articles to profl. jours. Fellow ACOG. Home: 4741 Mint Dr Memphis TN 38117-4010 Office: Northeastern Ohio Us Coll Medicine 4209 State Route 44 Rootstown OH 44272-9698

CAMPBELL, DOROTHY MAY, management consultant; d. George S. May. V.p. George S. May Intl Co Del, Park Ridge, Ill., 1962—; also bd. dirs. Office: George S May Intl Co Del 303 S Northwest Hwy Park Ridge IL 60068-4232

CAMPBELL, DUGALD K., automotive company executive; b. St. Thomas, Ont., Can., 1946; BA, U. West Ont., 1970. Pres., CEO Tower Automotive, Inc., Mpls. Office: Tower Automotive 4508 IDS Ctr Minneapolis MN 55402

CAMPBELL, EDWARD JOSEPH, retired machinery company executive; b. Boston, Feb. 21, 1928; s. Edward and Mary (Doherty) C.; divorced; children: Gary, Kevin, Diane. BSME, orthwestern U., 1952, MBA, 1959. With Am. Brakeshoe Co., 1952-58, Whirlpool Corp., 1958-65; gen. mgr. Joy Mfg. Co., 1965-67; exec. v.p. J.I. Case Co. subs. Tenneco, Inc., 1968-78; pres., chief exec. officer Newport News Shipbuilding & Dry Dock Co. subs. Tenneco, Inc., Va., 1979-91; pres. J.I. Case Co. subs. Tenneco Inc., Racine, Wis., 1992-94. Bd. dir. Global Marine, Zurn Industries, Titan Internat., ABS Group; chmn. Campbell Enterprises. Mem. bd. and adv. coun. Webb Inst., Northwestern U., William & Mary Coll., U. Wis. Vet. Medicine Sch., Hampden & Sydney Coll.; chmn. Navy League US Found., elected ato AE 1986 (Nat. Acad. of Engrng., With USNR, 1946-48. Home: 1 Deepwood Dr Unit A1 Racine WI 53402-2868 Office: PO Box 8 Racine WI 53401-0008

CAMPBELL, F(ENTON) GREGORY, academic administrator, historian; b. Columbia, Tenn., Dec. 16, 1939; s. Fenton G. and Ruth (Hayes) C.; m. Barbara D. Kuhn, Aug. 29, 1970; children: Fenton H., Matthew W., Charles H. AB, Baylor U., 1960; postgrad., Philipps U., Marburg/Lahn, Germany, 1960-61; MA, Emory U., 1962; postgrad., Charles U., Prague, Czechoslovakia, 1965-66; PhD, Yale U., 1967; postgrad., Harvard U., 1981. Rsch. staff historian Yale U., New Haven, 1966-68, spl. asst. to acting pres., 1977-78; asst. prof. history U. Wis., Milw., 1968-69; asst. prof. European history U. Chgo., 1969-76, spl. asst. to pres., 1978-87, sec. bd. trustees, 1979-87, sr. lectr., 1985-87; pres., prof. history Carthage Coll., Kenosha, Wis., 1987—. Fellow Woodrow Wilson Internat. Ctr. Scholars, Smithsonian Instn., Washington, 1976-77; participant Japan Study Program for Internat. Execs., 1987; bd. dir. Thrivent Mut. Funds, Johnson Family Mut. Funds., Prairie Sch., United Health Systems, Wis. Author: Confrontation in Central Europe, 1975; joint editor Akten zur deutschen auswartigen Politik, 1918-1945, 1966-96; contbr. articles and revs. to profl. jours. Fulbright grantee, 1960-61, 73-74; Woodrow Wilson fellow, 1961-62; U.S.A.-Czechoslovakia Exch. fellow, 1965-66, 73-74, 85. Mem. Mid-Day Club (Chgo.), Coun. on Fgn. Rels. (NYC), Phi Beta Kappa, Omicron Delta Kappa. Office: Carthage Coll Kenosha WI 53140-1360 Home Phone: 262-551-8087; Office Phone: 262-551-5858. Business E-Mail: poc@carthage.edu.

CAMPBELL, HARRY, communications executive; BA in East Asian History and Econs., Vanderbilt U.; MBA, Ind. U. Various sr. mktg. pos. Procter & Gamble Co.; various leadership pos., including asst. v.p.-emerging markets for Consumer Svcs. Group Sprint Corp.; exec. v.p., co-owner Mktg. Assocs. Internat. (MAI), 1997—2001; pres., CEO uclick.com, 1997—2001; v.p.-sales and mktg. Sprint's Mass Markets Orgn. (MMO), 2001—02, pres. Overland Park, Kans., 2002—. Office: 6360 Sprint Pkwy Overland Park KS 66251

CAMPBELL, JANE LOUISE, former mayor; b. May 19, 1953; d. Paul and Joan (Brown) C.; m. Hunter Morrison, Dec. 8, 1984; children: Jessica Elizabeth, Catherine Joanna. BA in History, U. Mich., 1974; MS in Urban Studies, Cleve. State U., 1980. Mem. State of Ohio Ho. of Reps. 11th dist., Columbus, 1984—92, majority whip, 1992—2000; mayor City of Cleve., 2001—05. Apptd. mem. Nat. Com. on Welfare Reform; mem. Cuyahoga County Plan Commn., Fin. and Appropriations Com., Ways and Means Com., Aging and Housing Com.; active Nat. Coun. State Legislators, vice-chair Human Svcs. Com., Children, Families and Youth Com., past pres. Women's Network, mem. Federal Budget and Taxation Com.; chair Abused, Neglected Children Oversight Com.; vice-chair Select Com. on Child Abuse and Juvenile Justice, 1989; mem. gov. task force on Adolescent Sexuality and Pregnancy, 1986, com. to Study Ohio's Sch. Found. Program Distribution of State Funds to Sch. Dists., 1991; exec. dir. Friends of Shaker Square, 1982-84; nat. field dir. ERAmerica, 1979-82; founding dir. Womenspace, 1975-79. Elder Heights Christian Ch. Recipient Legislative Leadership award Ohio Psychological Assn., 1986, Legislative award Ohio Hunger Task Force, 1987, Recognition award Ohio Primary Care Assn., 1987, Dean's Disting. Alumni award Cleve. State Univ., 1987, Hall of Fame award Nat. Senior Citizens, 1988, State Public Official of the Year award Ohio Chpt. Nat. Assn. of Social Workers, 1988, Found. award Ohio Chpt. ACLU, 1988, Legislative award Ohio Assn. of Counseling and Devel., 1989, Ohio Assn. of County Bds. of Mental Retardation/Developmental Disabilities award, 1989, Cancer Fighter award Ireland Cancer Ctr., 1990, Legislative award Ohio Human Svcs. Dirs. Assn., 1990, Hosephine Irwin award Womenspace, 1991, Spcl. Recognition award Providence House, 1991, Citizen award Ohio Assn. for the Edn. of Young Children, 1991, Legislator of the Year award Greater Cleve. Nurses Assn., 1991, Legislative award Nat. Assn. of Sch. Psychologists, 1992, Outstanding Svc. award Public Children's Svcs. Assn., 1992., numerous others. Democrat. Office: Cleveland City Hall 601 Lakeside Ave Rm 202 Cleveland OH 44114 Office Phone: 216-664-3990. Business E-Mail: mayorcampbell@city.cleveland.oh.us.

CAMPBELL, JOHN CREIGHTON, political science educator; b. NYC, June 12, 1941; s. Charles Edward and Ruth (Creighton) C.; m. Ruth Zimring, Sept. 21, 1962; children: David Riggs, Robert Charles, Judy Fredericka. BA, Columbia Coll., 1965; Cert. East Asian Inst., Columbia U., 1973, PhD in Polit. Sci., 1973; postgrad., Interuniv. Ctr. Japanese Lang., Tokyo, 1965-66. Staff assoc. Social Sci. Rsch. Coun., NYC, 1970-73; asst. prof. polit. sci. U. Mich., Ann Arbor, 1973-80, assoc. prof., 1980-91, prof., 1991—, dir. Ctr. Japanese Studies and East Asia Nat. Resource Ctr., 1982-87, dir. East Asia Bus. Program, 1984-88, 90—, dir. Japan Tech. Mgmt. Program, 1991-93, co-dir., 1993—. Fellow Woodrow Wilson Internat. Ctr. for Scholars, Washington, 1980-81; vis. prof. law Keio U., Tokyo, 1989-90, vis. prof. medicine, 1997-99; sec., treas. Assn. for Asian Studies, 1994-2000; vis. prof., acting dir. Kyoto Ctr. Japanese Studies; vis. prof. Doshisha U., Kyowo, 2001; chmn. governing bd. Kyoto Ctr. for Japanese Studies, 2001—. Author: Contemporary Japanese Budget Politics, 1977, How Policies Change: The Japanese Government and the Aging Society, 1992; (with Naoki Ikegami) The Art of Balance in Health Policy, 1997; editor: (with Naoki Ikegami) Containing Health Care Costs in Japan, 1996, Long-Term Care for Frail Older People: Reaching for the Ideal System, 1999; contbr. articles to profl. jours., chpts. to books. With U.S. Army, 1959-62, Japan. Ford Found. travel and study fellow, 1972, Fulbright-Hayes fellow U.S. Dept. State, Japan, 1976-77, 89-90, Japan Found. fellow, 1980, Abe fellow, 1997-98; recipient Masayoshi Ohira Meml. prize, 1993. Mem. Assn. Asian Studies (bd. dirs. 1994-2000, chair Bibliography of Asian Studies adv. com. 2000-01, Disting. Lectr. 1994), Am. Polit. Sci. Assn., Internat. House of Japan. Democrat. Avocations: reading, music. Home: # 1212 800 Victors Way Ann Arbor MI 48108-1767 also: 505 S State St Ann Arbor MI 48109-1045 E-mail: jccamp@umich.edu.

CAMPBELL, JON R., diversified financial services company executive; b. Byron, Minn., Feb. 14, 1955; m. Susan Campbell. BSB, U. Minn., 1977. With Norwest Corp., 1977—98, regional credit trainee Omaha, 1977—79; from comml. banking officer to sr. level positions Norwest Bank, St. Paul, 1979—86; v.p., chief credit officer Twin Cities Cmty. Banking, 1986—87; sr. regional credit officer Minn. Cmty. Banking, 1987—88; regional mgr. Twin Cities Cmty. Banking, 1988—90; regional pres. for Ill. & Ind. Norwest Corp., 1990—93; pres. Norwest Bank, Ariz., 1993—98; (Norwest Corp. merged with Wells Fargo & Co., 1998); regional pres. Wells Fargo & Co., Phoenix, 1998—2000, Mpls., 2000—02, regional pres. Great Lakes region, 2002—; pres., CEO Wells Fargo Bank, Minn., 2002—. Exec. com. Minn. Bus. Partnership. Chmn. adv. bd. Grow Minn.!; bd. dirs. Greater Twin Cities United Way, Capital City Partnership, Minn. Orchestral Assn.; bd. trustees Mpls. Found.; bd. overseers Carlson Sch. Mgmt., U. Minn. Office: Wells Fargo & Co 90 S 7th St Minneapolis MN 55479

CAMPBELL, JOSEPH LEONARD, trade association executive; b. Independence, Mo., 1938; BS in Acctg., U. Kans., 1960, MS in Acctg., 1963. CPA, Mo. Audit mgr. Arthur Young & Co., Kansas City, Mo., 1962-75; v.p., sec., treas. Assoc. Wholesale Grocers, Kansas City, Kans., 1975—. Active Boy Scouts Am., Overland Park, Kans., 1983-93. Mem. AICPA. Office: Associated Wholesale Grocers Inc PO Box 2932 Kansas City KS 66110-2932

CAMPBELL, KARLYN KOHRS, speech educator; b. Blomkest, Minn., Apr. 16, 1937; d. Meinhard and Dorothy (Siegers) Kohrs; m. Paul Newell Campbell, Sept. 16, 1967 (dec. Mar. 1999). BA, Macalester Coll., 1958; MA, U. Minn., 1959, PhD, 1968; LHD (hon.), Mich. State U., 2004. Asst. prof. SUNY, Brockport, 1959-63; with The Brit. Coll., Palermo, Italy, 1964; asst. prof. Calif. State U., LA, 1966-71; assoc. prof. SUNY, Binghamton, 1971-72, CUNY, 1973-74; prof. comms. studies U. Kans., Lawrence, 1974-86, dir. women's studies, 1983-86; prof. comms. studies U. Minn., Mpls., 1986—, dept. chair, 1993—96, 1999—2005. Inaugural Gladys Borchers lectr. U. Wis., Madison, 1974; vis. prof Dokkyo U., Tokyo, 2005-. Author: Critiques of Contemporary Rhetoric, 1972, rev. edit., 1997, Form and Genre, 1978, The Rhetorical Act, 1982, rev. edit. 2002, The Interplay of Influence, 1983, rev. edit., 2005, Man Cannot Speak for Her, 2 Vols., 1989, Deeds Done in Words, 1990, editor: Women Public Speakers in the United States, 1800-1925: A Bio-Critical Sourcebook, 1993, Quar. Jour. Speech, 2001-04; co-editor: Guilford Revisioning Rhetoric series, 1995-2000; mem. editl. bd. Comm. Monographs, 1977-80, Quar. Jour. Speech, 1981-86, 92-94, editor, 2001—, Critical Studies in Mass Comm., 1993-99, Rhetoric and Pub. Affairs, 1997-2000, Philosophy and Rhetoric, 1988-93; contbr. articles to profl. jours. Recipient Woolbert Rsch. award, 1987, Winans-Wichelns Book award, 1990, Ehninger Rsch. award, 1991, Elizabeth Andersch award, U. Ohio, 2004; Tozer scholar Macalester Coll., 1958, Tozer fellow, 1959; fellow Shorenstein Barone Ctr., JFK Sch. of Govt., Harvard, 1992; Disting. Woman scholar U. Minn., 2002. Mem. at. Comm. Assn. (disting. scholar award 1992, Francine Merritt award for significant contbns. to the lives of women in comm. 1996 Women's Caucus), Ctrl. States Speech Comm. Assn., Rhetoric Soc. Am., Phi Beta Kappa, Pi Phi Epsilon. Office: U Minn Dept Comm Studies 225 Ford Hall 224 Church SE Minneapolis MN 55455 Home Phone: 612-333-2306. Business E-Mail: campb003@umn.edu.

CAMPBELL, KEVIN PETER, physiology and biophysics educator; b. Bklyn., Jan. 19, 1952; s. Miller Jerome and Anna L. (Telesco) C.; m. Anna A. Derragon, Jan. 5, 1974; children: Colleen, Kerry, David. BS in Physics, Manhattan Coll., 1973; MS, U. Rochester, 1976, PhD, 1979. Grad. fellow U. Rochester, NY, 1973-77, teaching asst. NY, 1976-78; Elon Huntington Hooker fellow dept. radiation biology and biophysics, U. Rochester (N.Y.), 1977-78; Med. Rsch. Coun. postdoctoral fellow U. Toronto, Ont., Canada, 1978-81; asst. prof. dept. physiology and biophysics U. Iowa, Iowa City, 1981-85, assoc. prof., 1985-88, prof., 1988—, Found. Disting. prof., 1989—, Howard Hughes Med. Inst. investigator, 1989—. Mem. editorial bd. Jour. Biol. Chemistry, Circulation Rsch., Cell Calcium; reviewer for Nature, Jour. Clin. Investigation, Jour. Cell

Biology, Proc. NAS, Archives Biochem. and Biophysics, Molecular Pharmacology, Biophys. Jour.; contbr. numerous articles and abstracts to profl. jours. Patentee immunogen conjugates and use; co-patentee in field. Grantee NIH, NSF, NATO, Muscular Dystrophy Assn., 1981—; recipient Amgen award Am. Society Biochemistry and Molecular Biology, 1994, Internat. Albert Fleckenstein award, G. Conte prize, Elsevier Sci. award. Mem. AAAS, Biophys. Soc. (officer 1988—), N.Y. Acad. Scis., Soc. Gen. Physiologists, Am. Physiology Soc., Am. Soc. Cell Biology, Am. Soc. Biochem. Chemists, Am. Heart Assn. (established investigator, coun. high blood pressure rsch., cell transport and metabolism rsch. study com. 1989—), Inst. Medicine, NAS, Sigma Xi (Bendix award), Phi Beta Kappa; fellow Am. Acad. Arts and Sciences Roman Catholic. Office: U Iowa HHMI 400 Eckstein Med Rsch Ctr Iowa City IA 52242

CAMPBELL, PATRICK D., manufacturing executive; b. Douglas, Mich., July 15, 1952; BS in Mgmt., Walsh Coll., 1975; MS in Mgmt., Saginaw Valley State Coll., 1980. Trainee Gen. Motors, Saginaw, Mich., 1976—82, various fin. positions, 1982—86, dir., capital and program analysis Zurich, Switzerland, 1986—87, comptroller, Adam Opel AG Tech. Devel. Ctr. Rüsselsheim, Germany, 1987—89, with Cadillac Motor Divsn., GM Elec. Vehicles, 1989—94, CFO, internat. opers., 1994—99, v.p., fin., GM Europe, 1994—95, exec. dir., investor relations and worldwide benchmarking analysis, 2000—01, v.p., fin., 2001—02; sr. v.p., CFO 3M Co., St. Paul, 2002—. Office: 3M Co 3M Ctr Saint Paul MN 55144 Office Phone: 651-736-0042. Office Fax: 651-733-9973.

CAMPBELL, TERRY M., food products executive; BSc in Fin., St. Joseph's Coll. Asst. treas. Burger King Corp.; v.p., asst. treas. Harcourt, Brace, Jovanovich; pres. Pheonix Resources, Inc.; exec. v.p., CFO Farmland Industries, Inc., Kansas City, Mo., until 2000; CFO HNTB Companies, Kansas City, Mo. Mem. Nat. Assn. Corp. Treas., Coop. Finance Assn. (bd. dirs.), Heartland Wheat Growers Inc. (bd. dirs.). Office: HNTB Companies 715 Kirk Dr Kansas City MO 64105

CAMPBELL, WILLIAM EDWARD, mental hospital administrator; b. Kansas City, Kans., June 30, 1927; s. William Warren and Mary (Bickerman) C.; m. Joan Josselyn Larimer, July 26, 1952; children: William Gregory, Stephen James, Douglas Edward. Student, U. Nebr., 1944-45, MS, 1975; student, U. Mich., 1945, Drake U., 1948; BA, U. Iowa, 1949, MA, 1950; PhD in Psychology, U. Nebr., Lincoln, 1980. Psychologist Dept. Pub. Instrn., State of Iowa, 1951-52; hosp. adminstr. Mental Health Inst., Cherokee, Iowa, 1952-68; dir. planning and rsch. Dept. Social Svcs., State of Iowa, 1968-69; supt. Glenwood Rescource Ctr. (formerly Glenwood State Hosp. Sch.), Iowa, 1969—, Clarinda Mental Health Inst., Iowa, 1979—, founder and first warden, Clarinda Correctional Facility; assoc. prof. mental health adminstrn. Northwestern U., Chgo., 1982—; pres. River Bluffs Cmty. Mental Health Ctr., 1971—, also bd. dirs. Dir. Shared Mental Health Svcs., Clarinda/Glenwood; founder, chmn. Regional Drug Abuse Adv. Coun.; adj. prof. Sch. Pub. Health U. Minn., also preceptor grad. students in mental health adminstrn.; vis. faculty Avepane U., Caracas, Venezuela; adj. prof. Coll. Medicine and Health Adminstrn. Tulane U.; mem. vis. staff dept. psychiatry U. ebr. Med. Ctr.-Creighton U. St. Joseph Med. Ctr.; apptd. State of Iowa Dept. Human Svcs. Exec. Mgmt. Team, 1997; doctoral advisor U. Neb., 2000—. Author works in field. UN spl. cons. to Venzuela for UNESCO; bd. dir. Polk County Mental Health; v.p., bd. dir. Mercy Hosp., Coun. Bluffs, Iowa; state pres. United Cerebral Palsy; charter mem., bd. dir. Pub. Broadcasting Sta. KIWR, Council Bluffs, Iowa, Glenwood-Mills County Econ. Devel. Found., Inc., 1985—; charter mem., bd. dir. Mills County Econ. Devel., 1987, Glenwood Resource Ctr., 1993—; bd. dir. On-With-Life, adminstr., 2005-; bd. dir., mem. human rels. and fin. coms. On-With-Life Found., bd. dir. Glenwood C. of C.; charter mem., organizer Loess Hills Alliance, 1998—, mem. land protection, econ. devel. and long range planning coms., 1999—; mem. Glenwood City Tree Bd.;vol. at hosps., also in mental health and substance abuse, and long term care orgns. Served with AUS, 1944-46; col. Res. Decorated Army Commendation medal; recipient Meritorious Service medal U.S. Army, 1982. Fellow Assn. Mental Health Adminstrs. (nat. com. chmn. 1970); mem. Assn. Med. Adminstrs., Am. Hosp. Assn. (nat. governing bd. psychiat. services sect., charter panelist nat. adv. panel on mental health services, mem. governing body psychiat. services sect.), Iowa Hosp. Assn., Health Planning Council of Midlands, Assn. Univ. Programs in Health Adminstrn. (mem. nat. task force on edn. of mental health adminstrs. 1969—), Am. Assn. on Mental Deficiency (chmn. adminstrn. sect. Region 8), Nat. Rehab. Assn., Assn. Retarded Children, Mental Health Assn., Phi Beta Kappa. Home: 307 Louise Ave Glenwood IA 51534

CAMPBELL, WILLIAM J., JR., lawyer; b. Nov. 5, 1948; BA, U. Chgo., 1970; JD, U. Mich., 1973. Bar: Ill. 1973, U.S. Dist. Ct. (no. dist.) Ill. 1973, U.S. Ct. Appeals (7th cir.) Calif. 1974, U.S. Dist. Ct. (ctrl. dist.) Calif. 1974, U.S. Ct. Mil. Appeals 1976, U.S. Supreme Ct. 1978, U.S. Dist. Ct. (ctrl. dist.) Ill. 1979, U.S. Ct. Appeals (2nd, 5th and 9th cirs.) 1980, U.S. Dist. Ct. (no. dist.) Calif. 1983. Ptnr. Rudnick & Wolfe, Chgo.; ptnr., comml. litig. DLA Piper Rudnick Gray Cary, Chgo. Lt. USN, 1973-76; JAGC, USNR, 1970-82. Office: DLA Piper Rudnick Gray Cary 203 N La Salle St Ste 1900 Chicago IL 60601-1210 Office Phone: 312-368-7050. Office Fax: 312-236-7516. Business E-Mail: william.campbell@piperrudnick.com.

CAMPER, JOHN JACOB, writer, academic administrator; b. Toledo, Sept. 8, 1943; m. Cleraine Uguccioni, Mar. 27, 1971 (div. May 1981); 1 child, Sarah; m. Mary C. Galligan, Jan. 9, 1988; 1 child, Joseph. BA, Kenyon Coll., 1964. Reporter Detroit News, 1965-68; reporter, critic Chgo. Daily News, 1968-78; editorial writer Chgo. Sun-Times, 1979-84; dept. head external relations Regional Transp. Authority, Chgo., 1984-85; media coord. Chgo. World's Fair Authority, 1985; reporter Chgo. Tribune, 1985-90; assoc. chancellor for pub. affairs U. Ill., Chgo., 1990-97; dep. press sec., speech writer Mayor of Chgo., 1997—2007; v.p. Chgo. Pub. Rels. Forum, 1995-97, pres., 1997-98. Bd. dirs. Family Svc. Mental Health Ctr. of Oak Park and River Forest, 1990-97. Recipient Peter Lisagor award Chgo. Headline Club, 1983, UPI award, Chgo., 1983, Stick-O-Type, Chgo. Newspaper Guild, 1983, Nat. Assn. Black Journalists award, 1987. Home: 1846 W Newport Ave Chicago IL 60657-1024 Office: 502 City Hall 121 N Lasalle St Chicago IL 60602-1202 E-mail: jcamper@cityofchicago.org.

CAMPI, JOHN PAUL, automotive executive; b. Somerville, NJ, June 27, 1944; s. Anthony Edward and Winifred Virginia (Kay) C.; m. Cathy Sue Corkey, June 5, 1963 (div. June 1977); children: Christina Belli, Elizabeth, John.; m. Gail Rita Sapanaro, Oct. 18, 1980. BS in Acctg., Ind. U., 1966; MBA, Case Western Res. U., 1988. Divsn. controller and various Federal Mogul Corp., Southfield, Mich., 1966-74; divsn. controller Abbott Labs., Faultless Rubber, Ashland, Ohio, 1974-76; controller Carborundum Corp.-E.M.D., Niagra Falls, N.Y., 1976-78; group controller Allen Group, Cleve., 1978-79; asst. corp. controller Parkin Hannifin Corp., Cleve., 1979-88; sr. mgr. Price Waterhouse, Cleve., 1988-90; v.p. fin. J.I. Case Constrn. Group, Racine, Wis., 1990-91; founder, pres. Genesis Consulting Group, Inc., Racine, 1991—2002; v.p., chief procurement officer for global sourcing & logistics E.I. du Pont de Nemours & Co., 2002—03; sr. v.p. global sourcing & supply chain The Home Depot, Inc., 2003—07; exec. v.p. for procurement Chrysler LLC, 2008—. Activity acctg. chmn. Cleve. Assn. Mfrs., 1988-89. Contbr. articles to profl. jours. Bd. trustees Case Western Reserve U. Mem. Fin. Execs. Inst., Inst. Mgmt. Accountants, Cleve. Assn. Mfrs. (activity acctg. chmn. 1988-89, acad. rels. com. I.M.A. 1990—). Republican. Episcopalian. Avocations: golf, travel, racquet ball, books, writing. Office: Chrysler LLC 1000 Chrysler Dr Auburn Hills MI 48326*

CAMSTER, BARON OF See WIEMANN, MARION JR.

CANDLER, JAMES NALL, JR., lawyer; b. Detroit, Jan. 25, 1943; s. James Nall and Lorna Augusta (Blood) C.; m. Jean Ward McKinnon, Mar. 8, 1974; children: Christine, Elizabeth, Anne. AB, Princeton U., 1965; JD, U. Mich., 1970. Bar: Mich. 1970. Assoc. Dickinson Wright PLLC, Detroit, 1970-77, ptnr., 1977—. Adj. prof. real estate planning U. Detroit Sch. of Law, 1975-80. Bd. dirs. Detroit Inst. Ophthalmology, 1983—, chmn., 1994—. Lt. USNR, 1965-67. Mem. Internat. Assn. Attys. and Execs. in Corp. Real Estate, State Bar Mich. (chmn. real property law sect. 1998-99), Am. Coll. of Real Estate Lawyers, Grosse Pointe Club (chmn. 1987-89), Country Club of Detroit. Republican. Avocations: sailing, golf, platform tennis. Home: 211 Country Club Dr Grosse Pointe Farms MI 48236-2901 Office: 500 Woodward Ave Ste 4000 Detroit MI 48226-3425 Office Phone: 313-223-3513. E-mail: jcandler@dickinson-wright.com.

CANEPA, JOHN CHARLES, banking consultant; b. Newburyport, Mass., Aug. 26, 1930; s. John Jere and Agnes R. (Barbour) C.; m. Marie Olney, Sept. 13, 1953; children: Claudia, John J., Peter C., Milissa L. AB, Harvard U., 1953; MBA, NYU, 1960. With Chase Manhattan Bank, NYC, 1957-63; sr. v.p. Provident Bank, Cin., 1963-70; past pres., chmn. bd., CEO Old Kent Fin. Corp., Grand Rapids, Mich., 1970-95; past pres., past chief exec. officer Old Kent Bank & Trust Co., Grand Rapids, 1970-95; consulting prin. Crowe Chizek, Grand Rapids, Mich., 1995—. Served with USN, 1953-57. Office: Crowe Chizek 400 Riverfront Plaza Grand Rapids MI 49503 E-mail: jcanepa@crowechizek.com.

CANFIELD, ROBERT CLEO, lawyer; b. St. Joseph, Mo., Sept. 10, 1938; s. Robert Charles Canfield and Nadine (Ressler) Thomas; m. Patricia Joan Harms, June 8, 1958; children: Tamara, Robert, Michael. AB, DePauw U., 1960; LLB, U. Mich., 1963. Bar: Mo. 1963, U.S. Dist. Ct. (we. dist.) Mo. 1964. Assoc. Watson, Ess, Marshall & Enggas, Kansas City, Mo., 1963-72, ptnr., 1972-92; sr. v.p., gen. counsel, sec. DST Sys., inc., Kansas City, 1992—. Mem. exec. bd. Boy Scouts Am., Kansas City, 1982—. Mem. ABA, Mo. Bar Assn., Kansas City Club. Republican. Methodist. Home: 9722 Sagamore Rd Shawnee Mission KS 66206-2314 Office: DST Systems Inc 333 W 11th St Kansas City MO 64105-1634

CANNING, JOHN RAFTON, urologist; b. Evanston, Ill., Dec. 5, 1927; s. Claude E. and Martha C. Canning; m. Elizabeth Learned, Sept. 11, 1948; 1 dau., Sarah Blee; m. Jacqueline Maartense, Apr. 3, 1970; children— John R., Richard, Roberta. BA, Lake Forest Coll., Ill., 1951; MD, Northwestern U., 1955, MS, 1956. Diplomate: Am. Bd. Surgery, Am. Bd. Urology. Intern St. Luke's Hosp., Chgo., 1955; resident in gen. surgery VA Hosp., Hines, Ill., 1956-60, resident in urology, 1966-68; chest fellow Presbyn.-St. Luke's Hosp., Chgo., 1963; asst. chief vascular surg. sect. VA Hosp., Hines, 1960-66, asst. chief urology surg. sect., 1968, chief urology, 1969—86; asst. prof. urology Loyola U. Stritch Sch. Medicine, Maywood, Ill., 1969-82, prof. urology, 1982—, chmn. dept., 1979-86; attending urologist Cook County Bur. Health, 1995—. Fellow A.C.S.; mem. AMA, Ill. Urol. Soc. (exec. com.), Chgo. Urol. Soc. (pres. exec. com.), Chgo. Med. Soc., Soc. Univ. Urologists. Clubs: Chgo. Yacht. Office: Loyola U Stritch Sch Medicine Dept Urology Maywood IL 60153

CANNON, DAVID JOSEPH, lawyer; b. Milw., Aug. 6, 1933; s. George W. and Florence (Dean) c.; m. Carol Nevins, Mar. 10, 1962; children: Charles, Courtney. BS, Marquette U., 1955, JD, 1960. Bar; Wis. 1960, U.S. Dist. Ct. (ea. dist.) Wis. 1960, U.S. Ct. Appeals (7th cir.) 1969, U.S. Ct. Appeals (8th cir.) 1976, U.S. Dist. Ct. (we. dist.) Wis. 1976, U.S. Ct. Appeals (5th cir.) 1978, U.S. Ct. Appeals (4th cir.) 1997. Atty. Cannon & Cannon, Milw., 1960-66; asst. dist. atty. Milw. County Dist. Atty., 1966-68, dist. atty., 1968; U.S. atty. Dept. Justice Ea. Dist. Wis., Milw., 1969-73; ptnr. Michael, Best & Friedrich, Milw., 1973—. Office: Michael Best & Friedrich 100 E Wisconsin Ave Ste 3300 Milwaukee WI 53202-4108 Home: 13600 Park Cir N Elm Grove WI 53122-2557 Home Phone: 262-786-4565; Office Phone: 414-225-4978.

CANNON, PATRICK D., federal offical, broadcaster; married; five children. Comm. specialist Mich. Dept. Labor, Bur. Workers' Disability; staff rsch. specialist; dir. Senate Ctrl. Office, Audio Comm. Divsn.; exec. dir. Mich. Commn. Disability Concern, Lansing, 1988-97, Mich. Commn. Blind, Lansing, 1997—. Bd. dirs. Capital Area Transp. Authority; mem. Pres.'s Com. Employment People with Disabilites; apptd. U.S. access Bd., 1995; presentor in field. Mem. Pres.'s com. Employment of People with Disabilities, Gov.'s com. People with Disabilities, Access Bd., 1995—, Advanced Am. with Disabilities Act Tng. Network, Capital Area Ctr. Indep. Living, All Peoples' Theater, Riverwalk Theater; bd. trustees BoarsHead Theater, Capitol Area Transp. Authority; co-chair Gov.'s State Am. with Disabilites Act Implementation Task Force; chair Mich. Am. with Disabilities Act Steering Com.; trainer Windmills; active People's Theatre, Easter Seal Soc., St. Vincent Home. Mem. Nat. Rehab. Assn. Avocations: baseball, movies, theater, hotdogs, sunshine. Office: Mich Commn Blind PO Box 30652 Lansing MI 48909-8152

CANNON, PATRICK FRANCIS, public relations executive; b. Braddock, Pa., Mar. 2, 1938; s. Peter J. and Kathleen (Donnelly) C.; children by previous marriage: Patrick F. Jr., Elizabeth Kathleen; m. Jeanette Krema, Nov. 22, 1986. BA, Northwestern U., 1969. Ops. mgr. Compact Industries, Albert Lea, Minn., 1968-72; pub. info. dir. Dept. Pub. Works, Chgo., 1970-72; acct. exec. Humes & Assocs., Chgo., 1972-77; freelance journalist, cons. Oak Park, Ill., 1977-79; mgr. pub. rels. and prodn. Lions Clubs Internat., Oak Brook, Ill., 1979-2001; pvt. comms. cons., writer, 2001—. Author: Hometown Architect--The Complete Buildings of Frank Lloyd Wright in Oak Park and River Forest, Illinois, 2006, Prairie Metropolis-Chicago and the Birth of a New American Home, 2008; editor: Water in Rural America, 1973, Wastewater in Rural America, 1974, We Serve: A History of the Lions Clubs, 1991; exec. prodr., writer (pub. TV documentaries) With Very Little.Blindness Prevention in Developing Countries, 1991, The Search for Light, 1993, A Dangerous Time for Kids, 1997; contbr. articles to profl. jours. and mags. Exec. dir. Civic Arts Coun. Oak Park, 1977-79; vol. svc. com. Frank Lloyd Wright Preservation Trust, 1988-94, pub. programs com., 1995-96, chmn. Wright Plus Housewalk, 1996, tour com., 2004—. Named PR All Star 1996, Inside PR Mag.; recipient awards Publicity Club of Chgo., PRSA, Internat. Assn. of Bus. Comms., U.S. Film and Video Festival, others. Mem. Lions (pres. 1983-84). Roman Catholic. Avocations: history, horse racing. Home and Office: 243 Iowa St Oak Park IL 60302-2347 Office Phone: 708-383-0579. E-mail: patnette@comcast.net.

CANO, JUVENTINO, manufacturing company executive; b. Estapillo, Mex., 1956; cam to U.s., 1974; m. Hermila Cano; 3 children. Grad., Benito Juarez H.S., Tecoman, Mex. Pres., CEO Cano Container Corp., Aurora, Ill., 1986—. Mem. adv. bd. Merchants Bank, Aurora, Joseph Corp., Aurora. Mem. Aurora Sch. Bus. Partnership; bd. dirs. Aurora Econ. Devel. Commn., Mercy Svc. Found., Waubonsee C.C. Found.; mem. exec. bd. Aurora Cmty. Mobilization Adv. Bd. Recipient Mfg. Firm of Yr. award, 1993, Hispanic 500 award Hispanic bus. Mag., 1994. Mem. USHCC (bd. dirs. Region IV 1997, Region IV Hispanic Businessman of Yr. 1995), Aurora Hispanic C. of C. (pres. bd. dirs.), Greater Aurora C. of C. (bd. dirs.), Urban League (bd. dirs.). Office: Cano Container Corp 2300 Raddant Rd Ste A Aurora IL 60504-9101 Fax: 630-585-7501.

CANTIE, JOSEPH S., automotive executive; BS in Bus. Adminstrn. and Acctg., SUNY, Buffalo, 1985. CPA. Acct. KPMG Peat Marwick, 1985—95; mgr. fin. and bus. analysis Lucas Varity (U.K.), 1995, v.p., corp. contr., 1998—99; v.p. investor rels. TRW, Inc., 1999—2001, v.p. fin., 2001—02; v.p., CFO TRW Automotive, Livonia, Mich., 2002—04, exec. v.p., CFO, 2004—. Adj. prof. acctg. SUNY, Buffalo, 1993—95. Mem.: AICPA. Office: TRW Automotive 12025 Tech Center Dr Livonia MI 48150

CANTOR, BERNARD JACK, lawyer; b. NYC, Aug. 18, 1927; s. Alexander J. and Tillie (Henzeloff) Cantor; m. Judith L. Levin, Mar. 25, 1951; children: Glenn H., Cliff A., James E., Ellen B., Mark E. BME, Cornell U., 1949; JD, George Washington U., 1952. Bar: DC 1952, U.S. Patent Office 1952, Mich. 1952, registered: U.S. (patent atty.), Can. Examiner U.S. Patent Office, Washington, 1949-52; pvt. practice Detroit, 1952-88; ptnr. firm Harness, Dickey & Pierce, Troy, Mich., 1988—. Lectr. in field. Contbr. articles to profl. jours. Mem. nat. bd. govs. Am. Jewish Com.; mem. exec. coun. Detroit area Boy Scouts Am., 1972—. With US Army, 1944—46. Recipient Ellsworth award patent law, George Washington U., 1952, Shofar award, Boy Scouts Am., 1975, Silver Beaver award, 1975, Disting. Eagle award, 1985. Fellow: Mich. State Bar Found.; mem.: ABA, Am. Technion Soc. (nat. bd. regents), Cornell Engring. Soc., Am. Arbitration Assn. (arbitrator), Am. Intellectual Property Law Assn., Mich. Patent Law Assn., Oakland Bar Assn., Detroit Bar Assn., Mich. Bar Assn. (dir. econs. sect., arbitrator State of Mich. grievance com.), Beta Sigma Rho, Phi Delta Phi, Pi Tau Sigma. Home: 5685 Forman Dr Bloomfield Hills MI 48301-1154 Office: Harness Dickey & Pierce 5445 Corporate Dr Troy MI 48098-2683 Home Phone: 248-626-5259; Office Phone: 248-641-1600. Personal E-mail: bjcantor@aol.com. Business E-Mail: cantor@hdp.com.

CANTOR, GEORGE NATHAN, journalist; b. Detroit, June 14, 1941; s. Harold and Evelyn (Grossman) C.; m. Sheryl Joyce Bershad, Dec. 7, 1975; children: Jaime, Courtney. BA, Wayne State U., 1962. Reporter, editor Detroit Free Press, 1963-77; columnist Detroit News, 1977—; commentator WWJ-Radio, Detroit, 1981-90, WXYZ-TV, Detroit, 1982-90; editl. page writer Detroit News. Author: The Great Lakes Guidebook, 3 vols., 1978-80. Bd. dirs. Greater Detroit Area Hosp. Council, 1983. Recipient Malcolm Bingay Wayne State U., 1962; recipient Paul Tobenaw Meml. Columbia U., 1980, Disting. Achievement UPI, 1982 Mem. Phi Beta Kappa Jewish. Office: Detroit News 615 W Lafayette Blvd Detroit MI 48226-3197

CANTRELL, DUANE L., retail executive; Degree in Econs., Kans. State U., 1978; postgrad., U. Va. From merchandiser to exec. v.p. ops., sr. v.p. retail ops., sr. v.p. merchandise distbn. and planning Payless ShoeSource, Inc., Topeka, 1978—99; exec. v.p. retail ops. Payless ShoeSource, 1999—2002, pres., dir., 2002—. Trustee Kansas State U. Found.; chmn. adv. bd. Coll. Bus. Adminstrn. Kans. State U., mem. Mike Ahearn adv. bd. Office: Payless ShoeSource Inc 3231 SE 6th Ave Topeka KS 66607-2207

CANTY, DAWN M., lawyer; b. Chgo., June 21, 1964; AB, U. Chgo., 1986; JD, U. Mich., 1989. Bar: Ill. 1989. Ptnr. Katten Muchin Zavis Rosenman, Chgo. Mem.: ABA, Am. Bar Assn., Trial Bar of No. Dist. of Ill. Office: Katten Muchin Zavis Rosenman 525 W Monroe St Chicago IL 60661 Office Phone: 312-902-5253. Office Fax: 312-577-8607. E-mail: dawn.canty@kmzr.com.

CAPE, JAMES ODIES E., fashion designer; b. Detroit, Nov. 18, 1947; s. Odies E. and Juanita K. (Brandon) C. Student, Henry Ford C.C., 1973-75, Am. Acad. Dramatic Arts, YC, 1975-76, Pace U., 1977-78. Trapeze artist Mills Bros. Circus, 1962; skater Ice Capades, 1971-72; creator, dir., instr. skating program City of Southfield, Mich., 1972, 73; haute couture designer James E. Cape & Assocs., Dearborn, Mich., 1986—. Mem. Marji Kunz scholarship award com. Wayne State U., Detroit. Film reviewer Times-Herald Newspapers, 1989-90; clothing designs pub. in various mags. and newspapers; creations for TV and stage including the Emmys, The Am. Music Awards, Dick Clark-ABC Prodns., Showtime Spl. Aretha, Trump Castle, Atlantic City, The Chgo. Theater, Kennedy Ctr., Washington, Radio City Music Hall; co-prodr. Eartha Kitt, A Night in Paris; spl. commd. designs various celebrities; spl. publicity creations for Detroit Inst. Arts, Am. Lung Assn.; producer, host TV show "Town Talk." Recipient Pre-silver, bronze medals U.S. Figure Skating Assn., 1969, Citation award City of Dearborn, 1994, Wayne County (Mich.) Resolution award, 1993, Spl. Tribute award State of Mich. Ho. of Reps., 1994, Page award Herald Newspapers, 1999-2000. Mem. AFTRA, Actors Equity, Soc. for Cinephiles. Home: James E Cape & Assocs 500 N Rosevere Dearborn MI 48128 Office Phone: 313-561-4575. E-mail: JamesECape@aol.com.

CAPEN, CHARLES CHABERT, veterinary pathology educator; b. Tacoma, Sept. 3, 1936; s. Charles (Kenneth) and Ruth (Chabert) C.; m. Sharron Lee Martin, June 27, 1968. DVM, Wash. State U., Pullman, 1960; MS, Ohio State U., Columbus, 1961, PhD, 1965. Diplomate Am. Coll. Veterinary Pathologists. Instr. dept. vet. pathology Ohio State U., Columbus, 1962—65, asst. prof. dept. vet. pathology, 1965—67, assoc. prof., 1967—70, prof., 1970—, prof. endocrinology Coll. Medicine, 1972—, chmn. dept. vet. pathobiology, 1981—94, chmn., 1982—94, interim chmn. dept. bioscis., 1994—97, chmn., 1997—2002, disting. univ. prof., 2001—. Israel Doniach Meml. lectr. Brit. Endocrine Soc. meeting, Manchester, 1989; plenary lectr. Italian Soc. Endocrinology Congress, Pisa, 1995. Editor: (series) Animal Models of Human Disease, 1979—96; mem. editl. bd.: Lab. Investigation, 1988—2006; Vet. Pathology, 1986—87; Am. Jour. Pathology, 1984—88; Exptl. and Toxicologic Pathology, 1990—2005; Food and Chem. Toxicology, 1993—2000; Drug and Chem. Toxicology, 1994—97; Toxicology and Ecotoxicology News, 1993—2006; Handbook on Rat Tumor Pathology WHO/IARC, 1991—96. Mem. Opera Columbus, 1982—, Columbus Symphony Assn., 1972—. Named Disting. U. Prof., Ohio State U., 2001; recipient Disting. scholar award, 1993, Dean's Tchg. Excellence award for grad. edn., Coll. Vet. Medicine, 1993, Disting. Vet. Alumnus award, Wash. State U., 1997, Career Achievement award in canine rsch., Am. Vet. Med. Found., 1997. Fellow: Am. Assn. Advancement of Sci.; mem.: AVMA (Nat. Borden rsch. award 1975, small animal rsch. award 1984, Gaines rsch. award 1987, excellence in canine rsch. award 1995, George Scott Meml. award of Toxicology Forum 1997), Am. Assn. Clin. Chemistry (Outstanding Contbns. Animal Clin. Chemistry award 2004), Soc. Toxicol. Pathologists (pres. 1997—98, Career Achievement award 2006), U.S. Can. Acad. Pathology (coun. 1989—92), Inst. Medicine/NAS, Am. Coll. Vet. Pathologists (coun. 1975—81, pres. 1978—79, diplomate, disting. mem.). Avocations: travel, wildlife and nature photography. Office: The Ohio State U Dept Vet Bioscis 1925 Coffey Rd Columbus OH 43210-1005 Office Phone: 614-247-6206. Business E-Mail: capen.2@osu.edu.

CAPERS, CYNTHIA FLYNN, dean, nursing educator; Diploma, Freedman's Hosp., Washington, 1965; BSN, U. Md., 1968; MSN, U. Pa., 1981, PhD in Culture and Nursing, 1986. Assoc. prof., course coord. Thomas Jefferson U., Phila., 1989-93; dir. undergrad. programs, assoc. prof. LaSalle U. Sch. Nursing, Phila., 1993-96, interim dean, assoc. prof., 1996-97; dean, prof. U. Akron Coll. of Nursing, 1997—. M. Elizabeth Carnegie vis. prof. in nursing rsch. Howard U., 1998; recipient Outstanding Achievement, Leadership and Svc. Med. Soc. of Ea. Pa., 1997, Disting. Nurse award Pa. Nurses Assn., 1995, Nurse Excellence award Pa. Nurses Assn., 1991; named Woman of Yr. YWCA of Germantown, 1992. Contbr. articles to profl. jours. Bd. trustees Am. Heart Assn., 1998-2000, Coming Together Project, Akron, 1998—, The Akron Cmty. Found., 1999—, Summa Health Sys. Hosp. Bd., 2000—; adv. bd. LaSalle U. Neighborhood Nursing Ctr., 1997-98, Coll. of Health, Edn., and Human Resources U. Scranton, 1992-96, Govs. Sch. of Health Care Professions in Pa., 1990-97; vice chmn. Pa. State Bd. of Nursing, 1991, chmn., 1992, 93; bd. mgrs. The Phila. Found., 1993-97. Office: U Akron Coll Nursing Mary E Gladwin Hl Akron OH 44325-0001 Fax: 330-972-5737.

CAPLAN, ALLAN HART, lawyer; BA, U. Manitoba, 1966; JD, William Mitchell Coll. Law, 1974. Bar: Minn. 1974, Wis. 1988, Fed. Ct. Former asst. atty., Hennepin County; former pub. defender; ptnr. Caplan Law Firm P.A., Minn., 1983—. Spkr. in field. Named Minn. Super Lawyer Criminal Def., Mpls.-St. Paul Mag., Minn. Law and Politics. Mem.: NACDL (life), Minn. State Bar Assn., Hennepin County Bar Assn. Office: Caplan Law Firm PA 525 Lumber Exchange Bldg 10 S 5th St Minneapolis MN 55402 Office Phone: 612-341-4570. Office Fax: 612-341-0507. E-mail: acaplan@caplanlaw.com.

CAPLAN, ARNOLD I., biology professor; b. Chgo., Jan. 5, 1942; s. David and Lillian (Diskin) C.; m. Bonita Wright, July 4, 1965; children: Aaron M., Rachel L. BS, Ill. Inst. Tech., 1963; PhD, Johns Hopkins U., 1966. Asst. prof. Case Western Res. U., Cleve., 1969-75, assoc. prof., 1975-81, prof. devel. genetics, anatomy, 1981-88, dir. cell molecule basis aging tng. program, 1981—, dir. skeletal rsch. ctr., 1986—, prof. biophysics, physiology, 1989—. Vis. prof. U. Calif., San Francisco, 1973, Inst. de Chimie Biologique, Strasbourg, France, 1976-77; Erna and Jakob Michael vis. prof. Weizmann Inst. Sci., Rehovot, Israel, 1984-85. Contbr. articles to profl. jours. Recipient Career Devel. award NIH, 1971-76; Am. Cancer Soc. fellow, 1967-69; Josiah Macy Faculty scholar Case Western Res. U., 1976-77. Mem. Am. Assn. Orthopaedics Surgery (Elizabeth Winston Lanier Kappa Delta award 1990), Orthopaedics Rsch. Soc., Soc. Devel. Biology, AAAS, Am. Soc. Cell Biology. Office: Case Western Res U Dept Biology 2080 Adelbert Rd Cleveland OH 44106-2623

CAPONIGRO, JEFFREY RALPH, public relations counselor; b. Kankakee, Ill., Aug. 13, 1957; s. Ralph A. and Barbara Jean C. (Paul) Caponigro; m. Stephanie L. Caponigro, Oct. 28, 2006. BA, Ctrl. Mich. U., 1979. Sports reporter Observer and Eccentric newspaper, Rochester, Mich., 1974-75, Mt. Pleasant (Mich.) Times, 1975-77, Midland (Mich.) Daily News, 1977-79; acct. exec. Desmond & Assocs., Oak Park, Mich., 1979-80; v.p. Anthony M. Franco, Inc., Detroit, 1980-84; chmn., pres., CEO Shandwick USA (formerly Casey Comm. Mgmt., Inc.), Southfield, 1984—95; founder & CEO Caponigro Public Relations Inc., Detroit, 1995—. Contbr. author: Best Sports Stories, 1978, The Crisis Counselor, 2000. Mem. Pub. Rels. Soc. Am. Office: #1750 4000 Town Ctr Southfield MI 48075-1411 also: 101E Kennedy Blud St 4100 Tampa FL 33607

CAPORALE, D. NICK, lawyer; b. Omaha, Sept. 13, 1928; s. Michele and Lucia Caporale; m. Margaret Nilson; children: Laura Diane Stevenson, Leland Alan. BA, U. ebr.-Omaha, 1949, MSc, 1954; JD with distinction, U. Nebr.-Lincoln, 1957. Bar: Nebr. 1957, U.S. Dist. Ct. Nebr. 1957, U.S. Ct. Appeals 8th cir. 1958, U.S. Supreme Ct. 1970. Judge Nebr. Dist. Ct., Omaha, 1979—82, Nebr. Supreme Ct., Lincoln, 1982—98; of counsel Baird Holm LLP, 1998—. Lectr. U. Nebr., Lincoln, 1982—84, 2000—03. Pres. Omaha Community Playhouse, 1976. Served to 1st lt. US Army, 1952—54, Korea. Decorated Bronze Star; recipient Alumni Achievement U. Nebr.-Omaha, 1978; Disting.

Alumni Award, U. Nebr. Coll. Law, 2004. Fellow Am. Coll. Trial Lawyers, Internat. Soc. Barristers; mem. Order of Coif. Office: Baird Holm LLP 1500 Woodmen Tower Omaha NE 68102 Office Phone: 402-344-0500. Business E-Mail: dncaporale@bairdholm.com.

CAPP, DAVID A., prosecutor; JD, Valparaiso U., 1977. Criminal divsn. chief US Atty.'s Office, Dyer, 1988-91; 1st asst. atty. US Dept. Justice, Dyer, US atty. (no. dist.) Ind., 1999—2001, acting US atty (no. dist.) Ind., 2007—. Office: US Attys Office 5400 Federal Plz #1500 Hammond IN 46320-1843

CAPPARELLI, RALPH C., state legislator; b. Chgo., Apr. 12, 1924; s. Ralph and Mary (Drammis) C.; m. Cordelia Capparelli; children: Ralph, Valerie. BS, No. Ill. U. 1st v.p. 41st Ward Dem. Orgn., Chgo., 1965—; Ill. state rep. Dist. 13, 1971—. Asst. majority whip, ex officio mem. Com. Intergovt. Coop. Com., exec. mem. Fin. Inst. Com. and Transp. and Motor Vehicles Com., Ill. Ho. of Reps.; supr. recreation Chgo. Pk. Dist., 1953-67; advisor Columbia Bank, Chgo., 1967—; sec.-treas. Jefferson Travel, 1968—; former tchr. Decorated Battle Star. Mem. Nat. Recreation Soc., Ill. Recreation Soc., Lions, K.C. (4th degree), Eagles, Am. Legion, Sigma Nu. Home: 7446 N Harlem Ave Chicago IL 60631-4404

CAPPEL, HARRY W., lawyer; b. Salem, Oreg., May 25, 1970; BA in Polit. Sci., U. Cin., 1993; JD, U. Cin. Coll. Law, 1996. Bar: Ohio 1996, Ky. 2002, Ind. 2003. Ptnr. Graydon Head & Ritchey LLP, Cin. Vol. St. Lawrence Sch.; mentor U. Cin.; vol. coach Dearborn County YMCA. Named one of Ohio's Rising Stars, Super Lawyers, 2005, 2006. Mem.: Elder Bus. Professionals Assn., Ind. State Bar Assn., Ky. Bar Assn., Ohio State Bar Assn., Cin. Bar Assn. Office: Graydon Head & Ritchey LLP 1900 Fifth Third Ctr Cincinnati OH 45202 Office Phone: 513-629-2709. Office Fax: 513-651-3836.

CAPPO, JOSEPH C., journalist, writer; b. Chgo., Feb. 24, 1936; s. Joseph V. and Frances (Maggio) Cacioppo; m. Mary Anne Cappo, May 7, 1967; children: Elizabeth, John. BA, DePaul U., 1957. Reporter Hollister Publs., Wilmette, Ill., 1961-62, Chgo. Daily News, 1962-68, bus. columnist, 1968-78; columnist Crain's Chgo. Bus., 1978—, pub., 1979-89, editor at large, 2003—; v.p. Crain Comm., Inc., 1981-89, sr. v.p. group pub., 1989-95, sr. v.p. internat., 1996—2003; pres. Crain Comms. of Mex., 2001—02. Pub. Advt. Age, 1989—92, publishing dir., 1992—99; dir. Assn. Area Bus. Publs., 1982—88, pres., 1985—86. Author: Future Scope: Success Strategies for the 1990's and Beyond, 1990, The Future of Advertising: New Clients, New Media, New Consumers in the Post Television Age, 2003. Bd. dirs. Off the Street Club, Chgo., 1981—, Chgo. Advt. Fedn., 1987-93, Mus. Broadcast Comm., 1984-90, Ill. Coun. on Econ. Edn., 1990-95. With U.S. Army, 1959-61. Recipient award Ill. Press Assn., 1962, (with other Daily News staffers) Nat. Headliner award, 1966, Disting. Alumni award DePaul U., 1975, Page One award Chgo. Newspaper Guild, 1978, Peter Lisagor award Sigma Delta Chi, 1978, Outstanding Achievement award in comm., Justinian Soc. Lawyers, 1979, Champion award YWCA of Met. Chgo., 1984, Media Svc. award Chgo. Lung Assn., 1990, Dante award Joint Civic Com. Italian-Ams., 2003. Mem.: Bus. and Econ. Writers (bd. govs. 1984—89), Econ. Club (Chgo.), Internat. Advt. Assn. (world bd. 1994—, sr. v.p. 1996—98, world pres. 1998—2000), Delta Mu Delta (hon.). Roman Catholic. Office: Crain Communications Inc 360 N Michigan Ave Chicago IL 60601-3806

CARANO, KENNETH A., state representative; b. Youngstown, Ohio, Mar. 4, 1944; married; 3 children. Grad., Youngstown State U. Ret. tchr. Austintown (Ohio) H.S.; state rep. dist. 38 Ohio Ho. of Reps., Columbus, 2000—, ranking minority mem., rules and reference com., mem. edn. and ways and means coms., mem. fed. grant rev. and edn. oversight subcom. Mem. Mahoning County Chem. Dependency Exec. Bd.; Job s for Our Valley com.; bd. trustees Austintown Twp.; committeeman Austintown Dem. Precinct. Named to Coaches Hall of Fame, Ohio H.S. Speech League. Mem.: NEA, Nat. Coun. Tchrs. of English, NFL, OHSSL, Austintown Edn. Assn., Northeast Ohio Edn. Assn., Ohio Edn. Assn. (Outstanding Local Treas.), Austiintown Fitch H.S.-PTA Alumni, Mahoning County Trustees Assn., Ohio Trustees Assn., St. Marion's Ch., Carovillesi Mutual Aid Soc. (4th of July com.), Youngstown State U. Alumni Assn., Austintown Optimist Club, South County Dem. Club, Austintown Dem. Club, Eagles. Democrat. Office: 77 S High St 10th Columbus OH 43215-6111

CARBONARI, BRUCE A., consumer products company executive; b. Dec. 25, 1955; BS in Fin. & Acctg., Boston Coll., 1977, MA in Mgmt. Sciences; MS, Rensselaer Poly. Inst., 1984. With Price Waterhouse & Co., NYC, 1977-81; various managerial positions Moen, Inc., North Olmsted, Ohio, 1981-84, asst. contr., 1984-85, corp. contr., CFO, 1985-90, pres., COO, 1990; pres., CEO Fortune Brands Home & Hardware, Deerfield, Ill., 2001—05, chmn., CEO, 2005—07; pres., COO Fortune Brands, Inc., Deerfield, Ill., 2007, pres., CEO, 2008—. Bd. dirs. Fortune Brands, Inc., 2007—; vice chmn. Joint Ctr. for Housing Studies, Harvard U. Office: Fortune Brands Inc 520 Lake Cook Rd Ste 400 Deerfield IL 60015-5633*

CARBONE, ANTHONY J., chemicals executive; m. Patricia; children: Christopher, Carolyn. BS in Mech. Engring., Yale U.; MBA, Ctrl. Mich. U. Various tech. svc. and devel. positions Dow Chem. Co., Midland, Mich., 1962-67, sect. head, 1967-69, group mgr. TS&D, 1969-70, product sales mgr. laminated and coated products, 1970-72, mktg. mgr. laminated and coated products, 1972-74, group v.p. Dow Plastics, Chems., Plastic bus. group, 1993-95; also bd. dirs., mem. exec. com.; mktg. dir. Dow Lat. Am., Coral Gables, Fla., 1974-76; bus. mgr. STYROFOAM brand functional products adn sys. dept. Dow U.S.A., Midland, 1976-80, dir. mktg. functional products and sys., 1980-83, gen. mgr. coatings and resins dept., 1983-87, gen. mgr. separation sys. dept., 1983-86, v.p. Dow Plastics, 1987-91; group v.p. Dow Plastics Dow N.Am., 1991-93; exec. v.p. Dow Chem. Co., Midland, 1996—2000, vice chmn., 2000—. Bd. dir. Rockwell Collins. Mem. adv. coun. Heritage Found. Mem. Am. Plastics Coun.(mem. bd., exec. com.), Am. Chem. Soc., Soc. Plastic Industries. Office: The Dow Chem Co 2030 Dow Ctr Midland MI 48674

CARDELLA, TOM, sales executive; Founder, pres. Access Direct Telemktg. Svcs. Inc., Cedar Rapids, Iowa, 1995—. Recipient Entreneur of Yr., Ernst & Young, 1998, INC 500 award, INC 500 Mag., 2000. Office: Access Direct Telemarketing 4515 20th Ave SW Ste C Cedar Rapids IA 52404-1224

CARDOZO, RICHARD NUNEZ, marketing professional, educator, entrepreneur; b. Mpls., Feb. 13, 1936; s. William Nunez and Miriam (Honig) C.; m. Arlene Rossen, June 29, 1959; children: Miriam, Rachel (dec.), Rebecca. AB, Carleton Coll., 1956; MBA, Harvard U., 1959; PhD, U. Minn., 1964. Asst. prof. bus. adminstrn. Harvard U., 1964-67; assoc. prof. mktg. U. Minn., 1967-71, prof., 1971—2000, Curtis L. Carlson chair in entrepreneurial studies, 1987-2000, prof. entrepreneurial studies, strategic mgmt., 2000—02, prof. emeritus, 2002—; dir. Ctr. for Exptl. Studies in Bus., 1969-73, chmn. dept. mktg., 1975-78; dir. Case Devel. Ctr., 1980-2000, Entrepreneurial Studies Ctr., 1987-2000. Dir. Nat. Presto Industries, Brownstone Distbg., Valspar Corp., 1976-96, Best Buy Co., 1985-92; Fulbright lectr. Hebrew U., Jerusalem, 1980; vis. prof. bus. adminstrn. Harvard U., Grad. Sch. Bus., 1982-83; adj. prof. U. Miami, 2003—; cons. in field; mem. editl. bd. Jour. Mktg., 1976-93, Jour. Mktg. Rsch., 1976-82, Jour. Bus. Venturing, 1987-2002. Author: Product Policy: Cases and Concepts, 1979; co-author: (with others) Problems in Marketing, 4th edit, 1968, New Product Forecasting, 1981, Business Financing, 1999; contbr. articles to profl. jours. Dir. Kids, Inc., 1971—76. Fellow, Ford Found., Kaiser, 1961—63; Fulbright fellow, London Sch. Econ., 1956—57. Mem. Am. Mktg. Assn. (entrepreneurship rsch. award 2006), AAAS, Product Devel. and Mgmt. Assn., Acad. Mgmt. Home: 202A Sunrise Dr Key Biscayne FL 33149 Personal E-mail: dickcardozo@aol.com.

CAREY, CHARLES P., mercantile exchange executive; b. Chgo., 1954; MBA, We. Ill. U. Mem. MidAmerica Commodity Exchange, 1976—78, Chgo. Bd. Trade, 1978—2007, exch. dir., 1990—96, full-mem. dir. exch., 1996, first vice chmn., 1999—2001, chmn., 2003—07; vice chmn. CME Group Inc., 2007—. Served on numerous exec. and spl. fin. committees. Office: CME Group Inc 20 S Wacker Dr Chicago IL 60606

CAREY, CHRISTOPHER L., financial company executive; Sr. v.p., contr. holding co., CFO Corestates Bank; CFO Provident Fin. Group Inc., Cin., 1999—. Office: Provident Fin Group Inc 1 E 4th St Cincinnati OH 45202-3717

CAREY, JOHN ALLEN, mayor; b. Wellston, Ohio, Apr. 18, 1959; s. John A. and Sylia Lucille (Scites) C. BA in Polit. Sci., Ohio U., 1981. Dist. rep. Congressman Clarence Miller, Lancaster, Ohio, 1981-88; mayor City of Wellston, 1988—. Mem. Jackson-Vinton Econ. Devel. Bd., 1988—; mem., sec. Jackson County Community Improvement Bd., 1988—; mem. Jackson-Vinton Jail Com., 1992; mem. exec. com. Pub. Works Integrating Com., Portsmouth, Ohio, 1991. Candidate State Rep., 92nd Dist. Ohio, 1990; regional chmn. DeWine for U.S. Senate, Ohio, 1992. Named Newsmaker of Yr. Wellston Sentry, 1988, Man of Yr. Wellston C. of C., 1989; recipient Friendship award Wellston Masonic Temple, 1989. Republican. Methodist. Avocation: collecting political badges. Office: City of Wellston 203 E Broadway St Wellston OH 45692-1521

CAREY, JOHN LEO, lawyer; b. Morris, Ill., Oct. 1, 1920; s. John Leo and Loretta (Conley) C.; m. Rhea M. White, July 15, 1950; children: John Leo III, Daniel Hobart, Deborah M. BS, St. Ambrose Coll., Davenport, Ia., 1941; JD, Georgetown U., 1947, LLM, 1949. Bar: Ind. 1954, DC 1947, Ill. 1947. Legis. asst. Senator Scott W. Lucas, 1945-47; spl. atty. IRS, Washington, 1947-54; since practiced in South Bend; ptnr. Barnes & Thornburg, 1954—, now of counsel; law prof. taxation Notre Dame Law Sch., 1968-90. Trustee LaLumire Prep. Sch., Laporte, Ind. Served with USAAF, WW II; to lt. col. USAF, Korean War. Decorated D.F.C., Air medal. Mem. ABA (bd. govs. 1986-89, treas. 1990-93), Ind. Bar Assn. (pres. 1976-77), St. Joseph County Bar Assn., Signal Point Country Club, Quail Valley City Club. Office: 600 1st Source Bank Ctr 100 N Michigan St South Bend IN 46601-1630 Home: 940 St Annes Ln Vero Beach FL 32967

CAREY, PAUL RICHARD, biophysicist; b. Dartford, Kent, Eng., June 17, 1945; arrived in Can., 1969; s. Charles Richard and Winifred Margaret (Knight) C.; m. Julia Smith, Sept. 4, 1966 (div. May 1991); children: Emma, Sarah, Matthew; m. Marianne Pusztai, Mar. 7, 1992. BS in Chemistry with honors, U. Sussex, Eng., 1966, PhD, 1969. Postdoctoral fellow Nat. Rsch. Coun., Ottawa, Ont., Canada, 1969-71, rsch. officer, 1971-94; mgr. Ctr. for Protein Structure Design, head protein lab. Inst. for Bio. Scis., Ottawa, Ont., Canada, 1987-93; prof. dept. biochemistry Case Western Res. U., 1995—, dir. Cleve. Ctr. Structural Biology, 2000—. Adj. prof. Dept. Biochemistry, U. Ottawa, 1987-94, prof., 1994; prof. dept. biochemistry Case Western Reserve U. Author: Biochemical Applications of Raman and Resonance Raman Spectroscopies, 1982; contbr. over 220 articles to profl. jours.; patentee in field. Fellow Chem. Inst. Can.; mem. Am. Chem. Soc., Can. Protein Engring. Network (Adminstrv. body 1990-93), Internat. Network Protein Engring. Ctrs. Achievements include first demonstration of resonance Raman spectroscopy providing vibrational spectrum of a substrate or drug in active site of an enzyme; generation of first quantitative relationship between active site bond lengths and reactivity by combining resonance Raman spectroscopy, enzyme kinetics and x-ray crystallography; using a Raman micoscope to follow chemical reactions in protein and RNA crystals; elucidation of mechanism of sunlight degradation of biological insecticide from B. thuringiensis; research on use of lasers in fingerprint detection. Office: Case Western Res U Dept Biochemistry Cleveland OH 44106-4935 Business E-Mail: paul.carey@case.edu.

CAREY, RON, political organization administrator; Grad., Northwestern Coll., Minn., 1981. Mem. exec. com. Minn. Rep. Party, 1991—97, sec.-treas., 1997—2005, chmn., 2005—; dir. retail sales Intuit, Inc., 1991—2006. Del. Rep. Nat. Conv., 1992, 96; state co-chair Phil Gramm for Pres.; chmn. Minn. Autism Ctr. Republican. Office: Minn Rep Party 525 Park St Ste 250 Saint Paul MN 55103*

CARLIN, DENNIS J., lawyer; b. Chgo., Aug. 23, 1941; s. Herbert E. and Lillian (Schneider) C.; children: Gregory A., H. David, Stuart B. BBA, U. Wis., 1963; JD, DePaul U., 1967; LLM in Taxation, Georgetown U., 1971. Bar: Ill. 1967; CPA. Auditor Checkers, Simon & Rosner, Chgo., 1963-67; assoc. tax ct. litigation divsn. IRS, Washington, 1967-71; ptnr. Frankel, McKay, Orlikoff, Denten & Kostner, Chgo., 1971-77, Horwood & Carlin, Chgo., 1977-82, Drinker Biddle Gardner Carton (formerly Gardner, Carton & Douglas), Chgo., 1982—; vice-chmn. Gardner, Carton & Douglas, Chgo., 1998—2003. Contbr. articles to profl. jours. Mem. atty. divsn. Jewish United Fund; bd. dirs., exec. com., chmn. Coun. Jewish Elderly. Mem. ABA, Am. Coll. Tax Counsel, Chgo. Bar Assn. (former chmn. fed. tax com.), Nat. Strategy Forum, NYU Inst. Fed. Taxation, DePaul U. Alumni Coun., Am. Israeli C. of C., Twin Orchard Country Club. Avocations: golf, skiing, reading, music, theater. Office: Biddle Drinker Gardner Carton 191 N Wacker Dr Ste 3400 Chicago IL 60606-1698 Office Phone: 312-569-1245. Business E-Mail: dennis.carlin@dbr.com.

CARLIN, DONALD WALTER, retired food products executive, consultant; b. Gary, Ind., Aug. 27, 1934; s. Walter Joseph and Mabel (Ebert) C.; m. Kathleen Susan McCone, Jan. 21, 1961; children: Michael Scott, Karen Mary, Mark Steven. BS in Engring, U. Notre Dame, 1956; LLB, U. Mich., 1959; grad., Advanced Mgmt. Program, Harvard U., 1978. Bar: Ind. 1959, Ill. 1960. Assoc. to ptnr. Soans, Anderson Luedeka & Fitch, Chgo., 1960-72; sr. atty. Kraft Inc., Glenview, Ill., 1972-73, v.p., asst. gen. counsel, 1974-79, sr. v.p., gen. counsel, 1979-81, sr. v.p., gen. counsel, sec., 1981-86, v.p., assoc. gen. counsel, 1986-89; v.p., dep. gen. counsel Kraft Gen. Foods, Northfield, Ill., 1989-92. Bd. visitors Sch. Medicine, U. Calif., Davis, 1990—; bd. dirs. Monterra Homeowners Assn., v.p. bd. dirs. 2004, pres. 2005-07. Mem. ABA (hon.; com. corp. law depts. sect. bus. law), Assn. Gen. Counsel (emeritus), Westmoreland Country Club (bd. dirs. 1989-94, pres. 1993-94), Notre Dame Club (Chgo.), Ironwood Country Club (pres. 2000-03, bd. dirs. 2000-03). Home and Office: 333 Regentwood Rd orthfield IL 60093-2762 also: 72-930 Carriage Tr Palm Desert CA 92260

CARLIN, SYDNEY, state representative; b. Wichita, Kans., Nov. 20, 1944; m. John Carlin; 4 children. BS in Social Sci. City commr. City of Manhattan, Kans., 1993—96, mayor, 1996—97; state rep. Dist. 66, Kans., 2003—. Democrat. Roman Catholic. Office: 521-S State Capitol 300 SW 10th Ave Topeka KS 66612 Office Phone: 785-296-7651. Business E-Mail: carlin@house.state.ks.us.

CARLINI, PAT, newscaster; married; 3 children. Grad., Ohio State U. With Sta. WVAH-TV, W.Va.; anchor, reporter Sta. WCHS-TV, Charleston; with the Bob and Tom Show morning team Q-95 Radio, 1988—; anchor Sta. WTHR-TV, Indpls., 1988—. Office: WTHR-TV 1000 N Meridian St Indianapolis IN 46204

CARLISLE, RICK (RICHARD PRESTON CARLISLE), former professional basketball coach, retired professional basketball player; b. Ogdensburg, NY, Oct. 27, 1959; m. Donna Carlisle; 1 child, Abigail Claire. Student, U. Maine; BA in Psych., U. Va., 1984. Profl. basketball player Boston Celtics, 1984—87, NY Knicks, 1987—88, NJ Nets, 1989, asst. coach, 1989—94, Portland Trail Blazers, 1994—97, Ind. Pacers, 1997—2000; head coach Detroit Pistons, 2001—03, Ind. Pacers, 2003—07, exec. v.p. basketball ops., 2006—07. Named Coach of Yr., NBA, 2002. Achievements include teams that have ranked no lower than 16th in the league in scoring and have ranked in the top-10 during four of those seasons; won NBA Championship as a member of the Boston Celtics, 1986. Avocations: golf, piano.

CARLISLE, RONALD DWIGHT, nursery owner; b. Bismarck, ND, Oct. 28, 1940; m. Neva Carlisle, May 18, 1968. BS, Black Hills State Coll., 1966. Policy issue mgr. Provident Life Ins. Co., Bismarck, N.D., 1966-83; workers compensation commr. Bismarck, 1983-85; delivery driver Premium Beverage, Bismarck, 1985-86; owner trees N M Ore, Bismarck, 1986—; mem. N.D. Legislature. Chair Dist. 52-Dist. 30, Bismarck; del. Rep. State Conv., 1976, 78, 80, 82, 84, 86, 88, 90, 92, 94, 96, 98, 2000, 2002. With USN, 1958-62. Recipient Guardian of Small Bus. award NFIB, 1991. Mem. Am. Vets. (life), N.D. Nursery Assn., Elks, NRA. Address: PO Box 222 Bismarck ND 58502-0222

CARLOCK, MAHLON WALDO, financial planner, consultant, retired school system administrator; b. Plymouth, Ind., Sept. 17, 1926; s. Thorstine Clifford and Katheryn G. (Gephart) C.; m. Betty L. Dobbs, Aug. 27, 1954; children: Mahlon W. II, Rhena M., Shawn R. BS, Ind. U., 1951, MS, 1956. Tchr. jr. high Martinsville Schs. Corp., Brooklyn, Ind., 1952-53; tchr. high sch. Indpls. Pub. Schs., 1953-63, asst. to dean of boys, 1963-73, asst. dean of boys, 1973-75, bus. mgr., 1976-87; fin. cons. Indpls., 1987-93; property builder, owner Ind. Sgt. U.S. Army, 1945-47. Mem. NEA (life), Indpls. Edn. Assn. (rep. 1958-63). Republican. Baptist. Avocation: investing in real estate. Home and Office: 9705 E Michigan St Indianapolis IN 46229-2564

CARLOTTI, RONALD JOHN, food scientist; b. Martins Ferry, Ohio, Sept. 20, 1942; s. John Peter and Mary Rose (Pilla) C.; m. Eileen Theresa Dorsey, May 17, 1969; children: Lori Ann, Christina Maria, Jennifer Ann, Theresa Maria. Student, Wheeling Jesuit U., W.Va., 1960—63; BS, Ohio State U., 1964; MS, W.Va. U., 1966, PhD, 1970; MM, Aquinas Coll., 1996. Postdoctoral fellow dept. biochemistry U. Iowa, Iowa City, 1971—72, asst. rsch. scientist dept. pediats., 1973—74; corp. nutritionist Kellogg Co., Battle Creek, Mich., 1974—77; mgr. nutrition/basic rsch. Frito Lay divsn. Pepsico, Dallas, 1977—82, prin. scientist new products Frito Lay divsn., 1982—85; sr. rsch. scientist Amway Corp., Ada, Mich., 1985—89; dir. food sci. and tech. Country Home Bakers, Grand Rapids, Mich., 1990—93; pres. Carlotti and Assocs., Grand Rapids, 1994; pres., CEO Natura Inc., Lansing, Mich., 1995—2001; regulatory affairs and devel. specialist Ranir Corp., Grand Rapids, 2002—05. Tech. rep. Snack Food Assn., Crystal City, Va., 1978-82, Grocery Mfrs. Am., Washington, 1975-77; nutritionist Am. Frozen Food Assn., Washington, 1990-93; vis. asst. prof. chemistry Grand Valley State U., Allendale, Mich., 2002; adj. faculty Davenport U., 2004—, Baker Coll., Muskegon, Mich. 2005—, Allen Pk., Mich., 2006—. Contbr. articles to profl. jours. Pres. Mary Immaculate Sch. Bd., Dallas, 1981-83. Recipient Lovable Spud award, Nat. Potato Promotion Bd., Denver, 1981. Mem. Am. Chem. Soc., Am. Assn. Cereal Chemists, Inst. Food Tech. Roman Catholic. Achievements include start-up of new biotechnology-based food and chemical ingredients company, development of patented taste-appealing shelf-stable blend of fruit juice and milk, development of patented antioxidant system protecting food, pharmaceuticals and plastics against air and/or photo-oxidation, development of nutritionally improved (low fat/low calorie) prototype of Tostitos Baked tortilla chips, of high potency dry dog food, of nutritionally improved fruit pies for diabetics, of specially formulated pumpkin pie which will not allow for the growth of pathogenic bacteria innoculated after baking in testing required to verify that the product can be stored at ambient temperature for up to five days; initiation of tech. and regulatory functions for corporate products. Home: 6921 Maplecrest Dr SE Grand Rapids MI 49546-9208

CARLSON, ARNE HELGE, former governor; b. NYC, Sept. 24, 1934; s. Helge William and Kerstin (Magnusson) C.; children by previous marriage: Arne H. Jr., Anne Davis; m. Susan Shepard, July 12, 1985; 1 child, Jessica Shepard. BA, Williams Coll., 1957; postgrad., U. Minn., 1957-58. Mem. advt. staff Control Data, Bloomington, Minn., 1962-64; councilman Mpls. City Council, 1965-67; ind. businessman Mpls., 1968-69; legislator Minn. Ho. Reps., St. Paul, 1970-78; state auditor State of Minn., St. Paul, 1978-90, gov., 1991-99; chmn. bd. RiverSource Funds, Mpls., 1999—2006, bd. mem., 2006—. Bd. dirs. Minn. Land Exch. Bd., St. Paul, FloMet LLC, Rideau Recog Solutions; trustee Minn. State Bd. Investment, St. Paul, 1979-99. Bd. dirs. Exec. Coun., St. Paul, KidsFirst Scholarship Fund Minn., 1999-2002, Fairview Lakes Regional Health Care, 2002-04; sec. Minn. Housing Fin. Agy., St. Paul, 1979-91; past pres. Pub. Employees Retirement Assn., St. Paul, 1985-88; adv. bd. mem. Nat. Heritage Acad., 2001-; mem. Nat. Gov.'s Assn., Midwest Gov.'s Assn., Great Lakes Govs.; mem. Nat. Ednl. Goals Panel of Nat. Gov.'s Assn. Bush Found. Leadership fellow, 1971; recipient Children's Champion award Minn. Children's Def. Fund, Nat. Audubon Soc. award, Small Bus. Guardian award Nat. Fedn. Ind. Businesses, 1994, Great Blue Heron award N.Am. Waterfront Mgmt. Plan/U.S. Fish & Wildlife Svc., 1995; named Rep. of Yr. Nat. Ripon Soc., 1993; finalist Outstanding Mutual Fund Trustee of Yr., 2004, 06. Republican. Avocations: reading, squash, sports. Office: RiverSource Funds 901 Marquette Ave Ste 2810 Minneapolis MN 55402-3268 Home: 145 Holly Ln N Minneapolis MN 55447 Home Phone: 763-249-0310; Office Phone: 612-330-9284.

CARLSON, BRUCE MARTIN, anatomist; b. Gary, Ind., July 11, 1938; s. Martin E. and Esther (Granquist) C.; m. Jean Ann Hyslop, Aug. 18, 1968; children: Martin, James. BA, Gustavus Adolphus Coll., 1959; MS, Cornell U., 1961; MD, PhD, U. Minn., 1986. Exchange scientist Inst. of Devel. Biology, Moscow, 1965-66; Fulbright fellow Hubrecht (Netherlands) Inst., 1973-74; Joshiah Macy scholar U. Helsinki, Finland, 1981-82; exchange scientist Inst. of Physiology, Prague, Czechoslovakia, 1971; asst. prof. of anatomy to prof. U. Mich., Ann Arbor, 1966—2006, prof. biology, 1979—2006, prof. emeritus, 2006—, chmn. dept. anatomy and cell biology, 1988-2000, rsch. scientist Inst. Gerontology, 1989—2006, dir. Inst. Gerontology, 2000—04. Fellow Fetzer Inst., Kalamazoo, Mich., 1990-96, trustee, 1998—; mem. study sects. NIH, 1986-90, Nat. Bd. Med. Examiners, 1994-96; NIH Fogerty fellow, U. Otago, Dunedin, New Zealand, 1999-00. Author: The Regeneration of Minced Muscles, 1972, Patten's Foundations of Embryology, 1974, 4th edit., 1981, 5th edit., 1988, 6th edit., 1996, Regeneration (in Russian), 1986, Human Embryology and Developmental Biology, 1994, 3d edit., 2004, Principles of Regenerative Biology, 2007, Beneath the Surface, 2007; editor: From Message to Mind, 1988, Regeneration and Transplantation, 1990, others. Recipient Disting. Alumni award Gustavus Adolphus Coll., 1979, Newcomb-Cleveland prize AAAS, 1972, 650th Anniversary medal, Charles U., Prague, silver medal Russian Acad. Nat. Scis., 2004, Henry Gray award Am. Assn. Anatomists, 2004. Fellow: Russian Acad. Natural Scis., Am. Assn. Anatomists; mem.: Gerontol. Soc. Am., Internat. Soc. Devel. Biology, Soc. Devel. Biologists, Assn. of Anatomy, Cell Biology and Neurobiology Chairpersons (pres. 1995), Am. Soc. Ichthyologists and Herpetologists, Am. Soc. Zoologists (divsn. chmn. 1987—89), Am. Assn. Clin. Anatomists, Am. Assn. Anatomists (nominating com. 1991, exec. com. 1994, pres. 1997—99). Lutheran. Achievements include invention of techniques of free muscle transplantation. Home: 3838 Curlew Ln Ann Arbor MI 48103-9404 Office: U Mich Inst of Gerontology Ann Arbor MI 48109 Business E-Mail: brcarl@umich.edu.

CARLSON, CHRIS, lumber company executive; Pres. Carlson Co., Madison, Wis., 1994—. Office: The Carlson Co 2305 Daniels St Madison WI 53718-6705 Fax: 608-222-9087.

CARLSON, E. DEAN, state official; Sec. Dept. Transp., Topeka.

CARLSON, EDWARD C., anatomy educator, cell biologist, department chairman; b. Iron Mountain, Mich., Feb. 22, 1942; s. Clarence H. and Rachel O. (Olsen) C.; m. Pam R. Carlson, 1995; children: Scott Edward, Susan Rebecca. BA, Bethel Coll., 1964; PhD, U. N.D., 1970. Spl. instr. dept. biology Bethel Coll., St. Paul, 1964-66; instr. anatomy U. Ariz., Tucson, 1970-72, asst. prof., 1972-77; assoc. prof. human anatomy U. Calif., Davis, 1977-81, prof., 1981—; chmn. dept. anatomy and cell biology U. N.D., Grand Forks, 1981—. Rsch. anatomist Calif. Primate Rsch. Ctr., Davis, 1982-85; co-dir. N.D. Diabetes Ocular Rsch. Ctr., Grand Forks, 1988—. Contbr. articles to profl. jours. Rsch. grantee Juvenile Diabetes Found., Am. Heart Assn., NIH, EPSCOR, NSF. Mem. Am. Assn. Anatomists, Am. Soc. for Investigative Pathology, Am. Soc. Cell Biology, Microcirculatory Soc. Avocations: running, fishing. Office: U ND Dept Anatomy & Cell Biol Grand Forks ND 58202 Home Phone: 701-272-8360; Office Phone: 701-777-2101. Business E-Mail: ecarlson@medicine.nodak.edu.

CARLSON, JAMES R., food products executive; Asst. counsel Sara Lee Corp., 1973; sr. v.p., CFO Sara Lee Bakery; exec. v.p., COO PYA/Monarch, 1991-93; pres. PYA/Monarch, 1993; v.p. Sara Lee Corp., 1993-97, sr. v.p. corp. strategy, 1997—. Office: Sara Lee Corp Three 1st National Plz Chicago IL 60602-2600

CARLSON, JANET LYNN, chemistry professor; b. Mpls., Aug. 31, 1952; d. Donald S. and Katheryn F. (Kubo) Maeda; m. James G. Carlson, June 26, 1976. BA, Hamline U., 1974; PhD, Stanford U., 1978. Asst. prof. Macalester Coll., St. Paul, 1978-87, assoc. prof., 1987—. Contbr. articles to profl. jours.

CARLSON, JEFFREY, lawyer; b. Valley City, ND, Sept. 24, 1954; BA magna cum laude, Concordia Coll., 1976; JD cum laude, U. Minn., 1979. Bar: Minn. 1979, U.S. Dist. Ct. Minn. Regional counsel Supervalu, Inc., Eden Prairie, Minn. Mem. Hennepin County Bar Assn., Minn. State Bar Assn. Office: Supervalu Inc 11840 Valley View Rd Eden Prairie MN 55344-3643

CARLSON, JENNIE PEASLACK, bank executive; b. Ft. Thomas, Ky., June 11, 1960; d. Roland A. and Shirley (Willen) Peaslack; m. Charles I. Michaels, Aug. 13, 1983 (div. May 1989); m. Richard A. Carlson, May 2, 1992. BA in English, Centre Coll., 1982; JD, Vanderbilt U., 1985. Bar: Ohio 1985, Minn. 2002. Atty. Taft, Stettinius & Hollister, Cin., 1985-91; sr. v.p., dep. gen. counsel Star Banc Corp., Cin., 1991—95; gen. counsel Star Bank Corp., Firstar Corp, 1995—2001; dep. gen. counsel U.S. Bancorp, 2001, exec. v.p., human resources Mpls., 2002—. Office: US Bancorp US Bancorp Ctr 800 Nicollet Mall Minneapolis MN 55402 Office Phone: 612-303-7699. E-mail: jennie.carlson@usbank.com.

CARLSON, LEROY THEODORE, JR., telecommunications industry executive; b. 1946; AB, Harvard U., 1968, MBA, 1971. Fin. analyst, mgr. fin. analysis and planning, mgr. acctg. Singer Corp., 1971-74; v.p. Telephone and Data Systems, Inc., 1974-78, exec. v.p., 1978-81, pres., 1981-86, pres., CEO, 1981—; chmn. bd. Am. Paging Sys., Inc., 1998. Chmn. bd. Am. Paging, Inc., TDS Telecomm., U.S. Cellular Corp., Am. Portable Telecom. Mem. U.S. Telephone Assn. (bd. dirs.), Nat. Rural Telecom. Assn. (bd. dirs.). Office: Telephone & Data Sys Inc 30 N La Salle St Ste 4000 Chicago IL 60602-2587

CARLSON, LYNDON RICHARD SELVIG, state legislator, secondary school educator; b. Mpls., Apr. 18, 1940; s. Lyndon C. and Shirley (Gittens) C.; m. Carole Moss, Dec. 7, 1968; children: Tonya, Lyndon Jr., Philip. BS, Minn. State U., Mankato, 1964. Mem. Minn. Ho. of Reps., St. Paul, 1972—. Recipient Pub. Svc. award Met. State U., 1983, Carroll award Minn. Vocat. Assn., 1990, Disting. Svc. award U. Minn. Extension Svc., 1990. Mem. Minn. Fedn. Tchrs. Office: Minn Ho of Reps 283 State Office Bldg Saint Paul MN 55155-0001

CARLSON, MICHAEL, chef; b. 1975; Chef Trio, Chgo., Spiaggia, Chgo.; sous chef Lovitt, Chgo.; co-owner, chef Schwa, Chgo., 2005—. Recipient Am. Best New Chef award, Food and Wine Mag., 2006. Office: Schwa in c/o Michael Carlson 1466 N Ashland Ave Chicago IL 60622 Office Phone: 773-252-1466.

CARLSON, ROBERT JAMES, bishop; b. Mpls., June 30, 1944; s. Robert James and Jeanne Catherine (Dorgan) C. BA, St. Paul Sem., 1964, MDiv, 1976; JCL, Catholic U. Am., 1979. Ordained priest Archdiocese of St. Paul and Mpls., 1970, vice chancellor, Vocation Office, 1976—79, dir., Vocation Office, 1977, chancellor, 1979—83, aux. bishop, 1983—94; asst. St. Raphael Ch., Crystal, 1970—72; assoc. St. Margaret Mary Ch., Golden Valley, 1972—73, administr., 1973—76; pastor St. Leonard of Port Maurice, Mpls., 1982—84; coadjutor bishop Diocese of Sioux Falls, SD, 1994—95, bishop, 1995—2004, Diocese of Saginaw, Mich., 2005—. Author: Going All Out: An Invitation to Belong, 1985. Pres. Nat. Found. Cath. Youth Ministry, Washington, 1989—97; bd. govs. N.Am. Coll. Rome, 1997—2001; active Sioux Falls Humane Soc., 2003—05; Episcopal moderator Nat. Cath. Com. on Scouting, 1993—97, USA/Can. Coun. Serra Internat., 1996—2001; bd. dirs. St. Paul Sem., 1984—2000; bd. trustees Sacred Heart Sem., Detroit, 2005—; bd. dirs. Mt. Angel Sem., Portland, Oreg., 1995—2001, St. John V. Coll. Sem., U. St. Thomas, St. Paul, 1997—2001, Hennich-Glennon Sem., St. Louis, 1998—2001. Decorated Papal Knight, Knight Comdr. with star Holy Sepulchre of Jerusalem; recipient Friendship award, Knights and Ladies of St. Peter Claver, 1990, St. De LaSalle Meml. award, Cretin H.S. Alumni Assn., 1990, Humanitarian of Yr. award, SD Right to Life, 1998, Dist. Svc. award, Serra Internat., 2002, Cosmopolitan Club Sioux Falls, 2002, Our Lady of Guadalupe medal, Inst. for Priestly Formation, 2003, Hon. Canon, Ch. of Holy Sepulchre, Jerusalem, 2003, Pat Mackan award, Network Inclusive Cath. Educators, 2006. Mem.: US Conf. Cath. Bishops (chair ad hoc com. cath. charismatic renewal 2005—, chair life and ministry com. 2006—), Canon Law Soc. Am. Roman Catholic. Avocation: hunting. Office: Diocese of Saginaw 5800 Weiss St Saginaw MI 48603 Office Fax: 517-797-6670. Business E-Mail: rcarlson@dioceseofsaginaw.org.

CARLSON, STEPHEN CURTIS, lawyer; b. Mpls., Mar. 22, 1951; s. Curtis Harvey and Edna Mae (Pfunder) C.; m. Patricia Jane Brown, Aug. 21, 1976; children: Elizabeth Buckley, Susan Pfunder, Julie Desloge. AB magna cum laude, Princeton U., 1973; JD, Yale U., 1976. Bar: Minn. 1977, Ill. 1977, U.S. Dist. Ct. Minn. 1977, U.S. Dist. Ct. (no. dist.) Ill. 1977, U.S. Dist. Ct. (cen. dist.) Ill. 1991, U.S. Dist. Ct. (we. dist.) Mich. 2002, U.S. Ct. Appeals (7th and 8th cirs.) 1977, U.S. Ct. Appeals (6th cir.) 1987, U.S. Ct. Appeals (9th cir.) 1989, U.S. Ct. Appeals (1st cir.) 2004. Law clk. to presiding justice Minn. Supreme Ct., St. Paul, 1976-77; assoc. Sidley Austin LLP, Chgo., 1977—83, ptnr., 1983—. Rep. precinct capt. 1st Ward 11th Precinct, Chgo., 1985-91. Mem. ABA, Ill. Bar Assn., Chgo. Bar Assn., Am. Inns of Ct., Legal Club (sec.-treas. 1997-99, v.p. 1999), 7th Cir. Bar Assn., Nordic Law Club (v.p. 1987-90, pres. 1990-91), Def. Rsch. Inst., Princeton Club, Lawyers Club Chgo. (v.p. 2000-01, pres. 2001-02), Yale Law Sch. Assn. (exec. com. 2004—), Dearborn Park Prairie Single Family Homes Assn. (sec. 1997-2003, pres. 2003—), Dearborn Park Unit One Townhomes Condominium Assn. (pres. 1987-88), Yale Club, Mid-Day Club, Civil War Roundtable, Phi Beta Kappa. Presbyterian. Avocations: theater, opera, symphony. Home: 1323 S Federal St Chicago IL 60605-2716 Home Phone: 312-663-0356; Office Phone: 312-853-7717. Business E-Mail: scarlson@sidley.com.

CARLSON, TERRANCE L., lawyer, aerospace transportation executive; b. Superior, Wis., Jan. 21, 1953; s. Einar August and Carol (McAuley) C.; m. Jeanette Michele Leehr, Mar. 13, 1987; children: Aurora Brita Leehr, Henry Einar, Stephen Michael. BS in Bus. with high distinction, U. Minn., 1975; JD cum laude, U. Mich., 1978. Bar: Calif. 1978, U.S. Dist. Ct. (cen. dist.) Calif. 1978. With Gibson, Dunn & Crutcher, 1978-94, London, 1981-87, ptnr.-in-charge Hong Kong, 1987-89; v.p., gen counsel Allied Signal Aerospace, Torrance, CA, 1994; dep. gen. counsel AlliedSignal (now Honeywell Internat.); sr. v.p. bus. devel., gen. counsel, sec. PerkinElmer Inc., 1999—2001; sr. v.p., gen. counsel, corp. sec. Medtronic Inc., Mpls., 2001—. Adj. prof. London Law Ctr. U. Notre Dame, 1983-87, Pepperdine U., London, 1984; exec. dir. Annual Multi-Species Invitational (Since 1973). Contbr. articles to legal publs. Mem. Soc. English and Am. Lawyers (com. 1985-87), Royal Auto. Club, Am. Club. Avocations: fishing, guitar. Office: Allied Signal Aerospace 2525 W 190th St Torrance CA 90504-6002 also: Medtronic Inc 710 Medtronic Pky NE Minneapolis MN 55432-5604

CARLSON, THOMAS DAVID, lawyer; b. Mpls., Aug. 17, 1944; s. David W. and Grace M. (Laser) Carlson; m. Jane A. Gleeson; children: Amy A., Ryan T., Madeline Jane. BA, Colgate U., 1966; JD cum laude, U. Minn., 1969. Bar: Minn. 1969, U.S. Dist. Ct. Minn. 1969, U.S. Supreme Ct. 1973. Law clk. to Hon. Earl R. Larson U.S. Dist. Ct. (fed. dist.) Minn., Mpls., 1969-70; assoc. Best & Flanagan, Mpls., 1970-74, ptnr., 1974-91, Lindquist & Vennum, Mpls., 1991—. Trustee Groves Acad.; asst. varsity hockey coach Edina HS. Fellow: Am. Coll. Trust and Estate Counsel; mem.: ABA, Hennepin County Bar Assn., Minn. State Bar Assn., Colgate U. Alumni Assn. (trustee), Spring Hill Golf Club (bd. dirs.), Colgate Silver Puck Club (trustee), Minikahda Club, Mpls. Club. Office: Lindquist & Vennum 4200 IDS Ctr Minneapolis MN 55402

CARLSON, THOMAS JOSEPH, real estate developer, lawyer; b. St. Paul, Jan. 12, 1953; s. Delbert George and Shirley Lorraine (Willardson) C.; m. Chandler Elizabeth Campbell, July 15, 1973; 1 child, Thomas Chandler. BA, George Washington U., 1975; JD, U. Mo., Kansas City, 1979. Reporter Springfield (Mo.) News-Leader, 1975-76; editor Buffalo (Mo.) Reflex, 1976-77; assoc. Woolsey Fisher, Springfield, 1980-83; pvt. practice law Springfield, 1983-86; ptnr. Carlson & Clark, 1986-93, Carmichael, Carlson, Gardner & Clark, Springfield, 1993-94; mayor City of Springfield, 1987-93, 2001—; U.S. Bankruptcy trustee Springfield, 1982-98; pvt. practice, 1994-98. CEO, Resorts Mgmt., Inc., 1995—; bd. dirs. ITEC Attractions, Inc., Great So. Bancorp; lectr. in field. Contbr. articles to profl. jours. Mem. Ozark Trail coun. Boy Scouts Am.; mem. Springfield City Coun., Mo., 1983—87, 1997—2001, Airport Bd. Springfield, 1994—97; chmn. Springfield-Branson Leadership Com., Springfield, 1993—; bd. dir. Mo. Cmty. Devel. Corp. Iniative, Mo. Commn. on Intergovtl. Cooperation; mem. bd. govs. Mo. State U., 2003—05; adv. coun. Fannie Mae Southwestern Regional Housing and Cmty. Devel.; Bd. mem. Mo. Health and Ednl. Facilities Authority, 2005—. Mem.: Mo. Mcpl. League (bd. mem. 2003—), Nat. League of Cities (bd. mem. 2005—), Mo. Bar Assn. (Disting. Young Lawyer award 1989). Presbyterian. Office: 205 W Walnut Ste 200 Springfield MO 65806-2115

CARLSON, WALTER CARL, lawyer; b. Chgo., Sept. 14, 1953; s. LeRoy T. and Margaret (Deffenbaugh) C.; m. Debora M. DeHoyos, June 20, 1981; children: Amanda, Greta, Linnea. BA magna cum laude, Yale U., 1975; JD magna cum laude, Harvard U., 1978. Bar: Ill. 1978, US Dist. Ct. (no. dist.) Ill. 1980, (ea. dist.) Wis. 1992, US Supreme Ct. 1991. Law clk. to presiding justice U.S. Dist. Ct. No. Dist., Chgo., 1978-80; ptnr. securities litig. Sidley Austin LLP, Chgo., 1986—, mem. exec. com., 2002—. Bd. dirs. Telephone and Data Sys., Inc., Chgo. (non-exec. chmn.), mem. and former chmn. audit com. 1989-2001, chmn., 2002-; bd. dirs. U.S. Cellular Corp., 1989—, chmn. audit com. 1989-2001; bd. dirs. Aerial Comm., Inc., 1996-2000. Mem. Dist. 65 Sch. Bd., Evanston, Ill., 1993-2001, pres., 1997-2001. Mem. ABA, US Supreme Ct. Hist. Soc., Am. Judicature Soc., Seventh Cir. Bar Assn., Chgo. Hist. Soc., Chgo. United. Office: Sidley Austin LLP One South Dearborn Chicago IL 60603 Home Phone: 847-864-6869; Office Phone: 312-853-7734. Business E-Mail: wcarlson@sidley.com.

CARLSSON, BO AXEL VILHELM, economics professor; b. Ulricehamn, Sweden, July 22, 1942; arrived in U.S., 1984; s. Carl Axel Valentin and Dagmar Elisabet (Karlsson) C.; m. Glenda Joyce Bishop, Dec. 28, 1965; children: Eric, Mark, Amy. BA, Harvard U., 1968; MA, Stanford U., 1970, PhD, 1972; Docent, Uppsala U., Sweden, 1980. Sr. rsch. assoc. Indsl. Inst. Econ. and Social Rsch., Stockholm, 1972-84, dep. dir., 1977-81; Umstattd prof. indsl. econs. Case Western Res. U., Cleve., 1984-2000, de Windt prof. indsl. econs., 2000—07, chmn. dept. econs., 1984-87, assoc. dean rsch. and grad. programs Weatherhead Sch. Mgmt., 1996—2001, dir. PhD programs and rsch., 2001—05, faculty dir., exec. doctor mgmt. program, 2005—, Carlton prof. Economics, 2007—. Vis. scholar MIT, 1982; cons. World Bank, Washington, 1983-87, Swedish Fedn. Industries, Stockholm, 1984-89; min. of fin. Stockholm, 1993-94, Econ. Commn. for L.Am., 1996; project dir. Sweden's Tech. Sys., Stockholm, 1987—; mem. Indsl. and Sci. Coun., Nat. Bd. Tech. Devel., 1987-98; chair sci. adv. bd. Danish Rsch. Unit for Indsl. Dynamics, 1996—; mem. internat. evaluation panel Acad. of Finland, 2004. Author: Technology and Industrial Structure, 1979, Industrial Subsidies, 1980, Swedish Industry Facing the 80s, 1981; editor: Industrial Dynamics, 1989, Technological Systems and Economic Performance, 1995, Technological Systems and Industrial Dynamics, 1997, Technological Systems in the Bio Industries: An International Study, 2002. Mem. Swedish cultural orgns. Mem. Europe Assn. Rsch. Indsl. Econs. (pres. 1983-85, exec. com.), Am. Econ. Assn., Ea. Econ. Assn. (bd. dirs. 1989-92), Internat. J.A. Schumpeter Soc. (prize selection com. 1988-90, 94-96, 2002-04), Assn. Christian Economists. Methodist. Home: 2708 Rochester Rd Cleveland OH 44122-2167 Office: Case Western Res Univ Weatherhead Sch Mgmt Dept Econs Cleveland OH 44106-7235 Home Phone: 216-464-1774; Office Phone: 216-368-4112. Business E-Mail: Bo.Carlsson@case.edu.

CARLSTROM, JOHN E., astronomy educator; b. Hyde Park, NY, Feb. 24, 1957; AB in Physics, Vassar Coll., 1981; PhD in Physics, U. Calif., Berkeley, 1981. Subramanyan Chandrasekhar Disting. Svc. prof. dept. Astronomy and Astrophysics, dept. physics Enrico Fermi Inst., U. Chgo., 2001—. Dir. Ctr. for Astrophysical Rsch. in Antarctica. Packard fellow, David and Lucille Packard Found., 1994, John D. and Catherine T. MacArthur Found. fellow, 1998, James S. McDonnell Centennial fellow, 1999; recipient NASA medal for Exceptional Scientific Achievement, 1997, Beatrice M. Tinsley prize, Am. Astron. Soc., 2006. Mem.: Am. Acad. Arts and Sciences. Office: U Chgo Dept Astronomy and Astrophys 5640 S Ellis Ave LASR Box 21-LASR 109 Chicago IL 60637 Office Phone: 773-834-0269. Office Fax: 773-834-1891. Business E-Mail: jc@hyde.uchicago.edu.

CARLTON, DENNIS WILLIAM, economics professor; b. Boston, Feb. 15, 1951; s. Jay and Mildred C.; m. Jane R. Berkowitz, 1971; children: Deborah, Rebecca, Daniel. BA summa cum laude, Harvard U., 1972; MS in Ops. Research, MIT, 1974, PhD in Econs., 1975. Instr. econs. MIT, Cambridge, Mass., 1975-76; asst. prof. econs. U. Chgo., 1976-79, assoc. prof., 1979-80; prof. U. Chgo. Law Sch., 1980-84, U. Chgo. Grad. Sch. Bus., 1984—; with Lexecon, Chgo., 1977—2006; dep. assty. atty. gen., 2006—. Author: Market Behavior Under Uncertainty, 1984 (Outstanding Dissertation award 1984), (with J. Perloff) Modern Industrial Organization, 2005; co-editor Jour. Law and Econs., 1980—. Recipient P.W.S. Andrews prize Jour. Indsl. Econs., 1979. Mem. Am. Econ. Assn., Econometric Soc., Phi Beta Kappa. Jewish. Office: Univ Chgo Grad Sch Business 5807 S Woodlawn Chicago IL 60637-1511

CARLTON, TERRY SCOTT, retired chemist, educator; b. Peoria, Ill., Jan. 29, 1939; s. Daniel Cushman and Mabel (Smith) C.; m. Claudine Fields, 1960; children: Brian, David. BS, Duke U., 1960; PhD (NSF grad. fellow 1960-63), U. Calif., Berkeley, 1963. Mem. faculty Oberlin (Ohio) Coll., 1963—, prof. chemistry, 1976-2001, prof. emeritus, 2001—, chmn. dept., 1980-83. Vis. prof. chemistry U. N.C., Chapel Hill, 1976. Co-author: Composition, Reaction and Equilibrium, 1970. Home: 143 Kendal Dr Oberlin OH 44074-1906 Office: Oberlin Coll Dept Chemistry and Biochemistry Oberlin OH 44074-1097 E-mail: terry.carlton@oberlin.edu.

CARMAN, KAM, announcer; b. Phoenix; m. David Kramer; children: Kellan Charles Kramer, Jacquelyn Casey Kramer 1 stepchild, Courtlandt Kramer. Grad., No. Ariz. U. News/weather anchor KNAZ-TV, Flagstaff, Ariz.; on-camer, meteorologist Weather Channel, Atlanta; meteorologist Jim Harper and The Breakfast Club, WNIC-FM Radio, Detroit; weathercaster WJBK-TV, Detroit, co-anchor New Morning, 2000—01, morning weathercaster, 2001—02, co-anchor News Morning 5am, 2002—, co-anchor News at Noon. Office: WJBK Fox 2 PO Box 2000 Southfield MI 48037-2000

CARMEN, IRA HARRIS, political scientist, educator; b. Boston, Dec. 3, 1934; s. Jacob and Lida (Rosenman) Carmen; m. Sandra Vineberg, Sept. 6, 1958 (div. June 1999); children: Gail Deborah, Amy Rebecca; m. Lawrence Lowell Putnam, Mar. 16, 2000. BA, U. N.H., 1957; MA, U. Mich., 1959, PhD, 1964. Asst. prof. Ball State U., 1963-66; assoc. prof. Coe Coll., 1966-68; prof. polit. sci. U. Ill., 1968—. Mem. Inst. Genomic Biology U. Ill., 2004—; mem. recombinant DNA adv. com. IH, 1990—94; vis. lectr. Tamkang U., Taiwan, 1991; organizer numerous internat. meetings. Author: Movies, Censorship, and the Law, 1966, Power and Balance, 1978, Cloning and the Constitution, 1986, Politics in the Laboratory: The Constitution of Human Genomics, 2004; contbr. articles to profl. jours. Sr. advisor Bush-Quayle Nat. Jewish Campaign Com., 1988; mem. Pres. George Bush's Inaugural Educators Adv. Com., 1989; guest del. Rep. Nat. Conv., 1992; mem. Rep. Nat. Com., Rep. Jewish Coalition, Straight Talk Am. Grantee, NSF, 2007; vis. scholar, Yale Law Sch., 1981. Mem.: AAAS, Assn. Politics and Life Scis. (chmn. coun. 2000—03), Human Genome Orgn., Phi Beta Kappa. Office: U Ill Dept Polit Sci Urbana IL 61801 Home Phone: 217-373-5814; Office Phone: 217-333-3880. Business E-Mail: icarmen@uiuc.edu.

CARMICHAEL, JIM, state representative; married; 5 children. Student mgmt. tng., Walsh Coll. Ret. mgr. East Ohio Gas Co.; state rep. dist. 3 Ohio Ho. of Reps., Columbus, 2000—, chair, state govt. com., mem. agr. and natural resources, energy and environment, and pub. utilities coms., mem. ethics and elections subcom. Past mem., chmn. Wayne County (Ohio) Bd. Elections. Republican. Office: 77 S High St 11th fl Columbus OH 43215-6111

CARMICHAEL, LLOYD JOSEPH, lawyer; BA, S.W. Mo. State U., 1969; JD, U. Ark., 1974. Atty. Carmichael, Gardner and Clark, Springfield, Mo., 1992. Former chmn. Mo. State Dem. Party.

CARNAHAN, BRICE, chemical engineer, educator; b. New Philadelphia, Ohio, Oct. 13, 1933; s. Paul Tracy and Amelia Christina (Gray) C. BS, Case Western Res. U., 1955, MS, 1957; PhD, U. Mich., 1965. Lectr. in engring. biostats. U. Mich., Ann Arbor, 1959-64, asst. prof. chem. engring. and biostatics, 1965-68, assoc. prof., 1968-70, prof. chem. engring., 1970—. Vis. lect. Imperial Coll., London, England, 1971-72; vis. prof. U. Pa., 1970, U. Calif.-San Diego, 1986-87; mem., chmn. Curriculum Aids for Chem. Engring. Edn. com. Nat. Acad. Engring., 1974-75 Author: (with H.A. Luther and J.O. Wilkes) Applied Numerical Methods, 1969, (with J.O. Wilkes) Digital Computing and Numerical Methods, 1973; Editorial bd.: Jour. Computers and Fluids, 1971—, Computers and Chemical Engineering, 1974—. Mem. communications com. Mich. Council for Arts, 1977—. Recipient Chem. Engr. of Yr. award Detroit Engring. Soc., 1987, 3M award Am. Soc. for Engring. Edn., 1990. Fellow AIChE (Computers in Chem. Engring. award 1981, chmn. CAST div. 1981); mem. AAAS, Assn. for Computing Machinery, Soc. for Computer Simulation, Sigma Xi, Sigma Nu. Office Phone: 734-764-3366. Business E-Mail: carnahan@umich.edu.

CARNAHAN, ELLEN, venture capitalist; BBA magna cum laude, Univ. Notre Dame; MBA with highest honors, Univ. Chgo. CPA Ill. With Price Waterhouse & Co.; mgr., fin. planning & analysis Trailer Train Co.; v.p. mktg. & planning SPSS Inc.; with William Blair Capital Ptnrs. LLC, Chgo., 1988—, now mng. dir., head tech. investing. Bd. dir. CPRi, Inc., Vericept, Chgo. Software Assn., WPS Resources Corp., 2003—. Bd. dir. Chgo. Communities in the Schools, Chgo. Network. amed one of 100 Most Influential Women, Crain's Chicago Business, 2004; recipient Luminary award, Girl Scouts of Chgo., 2003. Mem.: Ill. Venture Capital. Assn. (bd. dir., Fellowship award 2003), Women Corp. Directors, Ill. Info. Tech. Assn. (bd. dir.), Chgo. Software Assn. Office: Wm Blair Capital Ptnrs 222 W Adams St Chicago IL 60606 Office Phone: 312-364-8250. Office Fax: 312-236-5728.

CARNAHAN, JOHN ANDERSON, retired lawyer; b. Cleve., May 8, 1930; s. Samuel Edwin and Penelope (Moulton) C.; m. Katherine A. Halter, June 14, 1958; children: Peter M., Allison E., Kristin A. BA, Duke U., 1953, JD, 1955. Bar: Ohio 1955. Pvt. practice, Columbus, Ohio, 1955-78; ptnr. Arter & Hadden, Columbus, 1978-99; in-house counsel The XLO Group, Cleve., 2000—04; ret. Lectr. Ohio Legal Ctr. Inst., 1969, 73-74. Editor Duke Law Jour., 1954-55; chmn. bd. editors Ohio Lawyer, 1986-91; contbr. articles to profl. jours. Chmn. UN Day, Columbus, 1960; pres. Capital City Young Republican Club, 1960; bd. dirs. Columbus Cancer Clinic, pres., 1978-81; bd. dirs. Columbus chpt. ARC, 1979-87; mem. governing bd. Hannah Neil Mission, Inc., 1974-78; chmn. Duke Alumni Admissions Adv. Com., 1965-79. Named one of Outstanding Young Men of Columbus, 1965. Fellow Am. Bar Found. (life, chmn. Ohio fellows 1988-95), Columbus Bar Found. (life); mem ABA (ho. of dels. 1984-95), Ohio State Bar Found. (trustee 1986-90), Nat. Conf. Bar Pres., Ohio State Bar Assn. (coun. of dels. 1965-67, exec. com. 1977-81, 82-85, pres.-elect 1982-83, pres. 1983-84, Ritter award for outstanding contbns. adminstrn. justice 1987), Columbus Bar Assn. (bd. govs. 1970-72, sec.-treas. 1974-75, pres. 1976-77, Professionalism award 1996), Kit Kat Club (past pres.), Crichton Club. Presbyterian. Home and Office: 767 S 5th St Columbus OH 43206-2145 Office Phone: 614-648-9442. Personal E-mail: jac5830@aol.com.

CARNAHAN, ROBIN, state official; b. Mo., Aug. 4, 1961; d. Mel and Jean Carnahan. BA in Economics with honors, William Jewell Coll., Liberty, Mo., 1983; JD, U. Va. Sch. Law, 1986. Atty., corp. & bus. law Thompson & Mitchell, St. Louis; spl. asst. to chmn. Export-Import Bank of US; sec. state State of Mo., Jefferson City, 2004—. Mem. Nat. Dem. Inst. Democrat. Baptist. Office: Office Sec State 600 W Main PO Box 1767 Jefferson City MO 65101 Office Phone: 573-751-4936. Fax: 573-751-2490. Business E-Mail: sosmain@sos.mo.gov.

CARNAHAN, RUSS (JOHN RUSSELL CARNAHAN), congressman, lawyer; b. Rolla, Mo., July 10, 1958; m. Debra Carnahan; children: Austin, Andrew. Student, U. Mo., Rolla, 1976—77, Richmond Coll., London, 1978; BS in Pub. Adminstrn., U. Mo., Columbia, 1979; JD, U. Mo. Sch. Law, Columbia, 1983. Atty. BJC Healthcare, 1995—; mem. Mo. State Ho. Reps., 2000—04, US Congress from 3rd Mo. dist., 2005—. Mem. transp. & infrastructure com., fgn. affairs com. and sci. & tech. com. US Congress, vice chmn. subcommittee on internat. orgns., human rights and oversight, sr. majority whip. Mem. Compton Heights Neighborhood Assn., Landmarks Assn. St. Louis, State Hist. Soc. Mo., St. Louis Regional Commerce and Growth Assn., Pub. Policy Com.; mem. Friends Tower Grove Pk. Mo. Bot. Gardens and DeMenil Mansion; mem. govt. rels. com. United Way Greater St. Louis; chmn. Miss. River Pky. Commn. Recipient Lewis & Clark Statesman award, St. Louis Regional C. of C., 2002, Legis. award, St. Louis Bus. Jour., 2002. Mem.: Bar Assn. Mo. (Legis. award 2002), Bar Assn. Met. St. Louis. Democrat. Office: US House Reps 1710 Longworth House Office Bldg Washington DC 20515 Office Phone: 202-225-2671, 202-225-7452.

CARNES, JAMES EDWARD, state legislator; b. Wheeling, W.Va., Feb. 19, 1942; s. Edward A. and Avis E. (Hoop) C.; m. Nancy Ann Taylor, 1962; children: Jeffrey, Karen. Student, Bethany Coll., Coll. of Commerce, Wheeling, W. Va. Book keeper C. V. & W. Coal Co., 1962-69; office mgr. Cravat Coal Co., Holloway, Ohio, 1969—; owner, mgr. Carnes Mobile Home and Appliances, Barnesville, Ohio; sec.-treas. McCants Ins. Agy., Newcomerstown, Ohio; mem. Ohio Senate from 20th dist., Columbus, 1994—. Former chmn. legis. com. Ohio State Senate, Columbus; mem. Bd. Electors, State of Ohio, 1970-82, Ohio Commn. on Aging; regional chmn. Ohio State Manpower Coun. Pres. Rep. Club, 1970; mem., chmn. Belmont County Ctrl. and Exec. Coms., 1970-82. Finalist in 1959, 60, Prince of Peace Contests, Ohio; named hon. Lt. Gov. State of Ohio. Mem. Belmont County Hist. Soc., Flushing (Ohio) Rotary Club. Office: 47403 Puskarich Rd Saint Clairsville OH 43950-9458

CARNEY, BRIAN P., retail executive; V.p., contr. Revco D.S., Inc. (acquired by CVS Corp.), 1992-96, sr. v.p. fin., 1996-97; exec. v.p., CFO Jo-Ann Stores, Inc., Hudson, Ohio, 1997—. Office: Jo-Ann Stores Inc 5555 Darrow Rd Hudson OH 44236

CARNEY, JOHN F., III, academic administrator; m. Patricia Carney; children: Anna, Catherine. BA in Civil Engring., Merrimack Coll., 1963; MA, Northwestern U., 1963, PhD, 1966. Rsch. scientist Northwestern U., 1966; asst. prof. U. Conn., 1966—69, assoc. prof., 1969—74, prof., 1974—81; prof., head Auburn U., 1981—83; prof. civil engring. Vanderbilt U., 1983—96, assoc. dean for grad. affairs, 1993—96, assoc. dean for rsch. and grad. affairs, 1993—96; provost, v.p. for acad. affairs Worcester Poly. Inst., Mass., 1996—2005; chancellor U. Mo., Rolla, 2005—. Editor: Effectiveness of Highway Safety Improvements, 1986; contbr. articles to profl. jours. Fellow: Am. Soc. of Civil Engrs.; mem.: ASCE, Soc. Automotive Engrs. Office: U Mo 206 Parker Hall 1870 Miner Circle Rolla MO 65409-0910 Office Phone: 573-341-4416. E-mail: jfc3@umr.edu.

CARNEY, JOSEPH BUCKINGHAM, lawyer; b. Greensburg, Ind., July 8, 1928; s. Edward O. and Grace Rebecca (Buckingham) C.; m. Constance J. Caylor, July 8, 1950; children: Elizabeth, Joseph Buckingham Jr., Julia, Sarah. AB, DePauw U., 1950; LLB, Harvard U., 1953. Bar: D.C. 1953, Ind. 1953, U.S. Dist. Ct. (so. dist.) Ind. 1953, U.S. Supreme Ct. 1957, U.S. Ct. Appeals (7th cir.) 1961; ind. cert. mediator. Assoc. Hogg, Peters & Leonard, Ft. Wayne, Ind., 1953-54, Baker & Daniels, Indpls., 1957-62, ptnr., 1962—95, mem. mgmt. com., 1993-94, sec., 1994, of counsel, 1996—. Mem. lawyers com. Nat. Ctr. State Cts., Williamsburg, Va., 1985—; assoc. Environ. Law Inst., Washington. Co-chmn. bd. dirs. Parkinson Awareness Assn. Ctrl. Ind., Inc.; past pres. Interfaith Homes, Inc., Indpls.; past chmn., elder Northwood Christian Ch., Indpls. 1st lt. U.S. Army, 1954-57. Recipient Disting. Alumni award DePauw U., 1984. Mem. ABA, Ind. Bar Assn., Indpls. Bar Assn., Am. Judicature Soc., 7th Cir. Bar Assn. (pres. 1983-84), Univ. Club, Columbia Club, Contemporary, Lawyers Club Indpls. (past pres.), Phi Eta Sigma, Phi Gamma Delta (bd. dirs. 1974-78, sec. 1976-78, pres. 1980-82), Phi Gamma Delta Ednl. Found. (bd. dirs. 1994-2005, pres. 1996-98). Avocations: scuba diving, travel, photography. Office: Baker & Daniels 300 N Meridian St Ste 2700 Indianapolis IN 46204-1782 Home Phone: 317-848-5199; Office Phone: 317-237-0300.

CARNEY, TANA, real estate company executive; BA, Goucher Coll.; MA, Case Western Reserve U. Former public info. specialist Cuyahoga County Treasurer's Office, staff assoc., adminstrn. of justice com.; asst. property mgr. Landmark Mgmt., Ltd. Advisory trustee West Side Ecumenical Ministry; trustee Goucher Coll., Cleve. Found., 2001—; bd. mem. Cuyahoga County Library Found. Office: Landmark Mgmt 530 Euclid Ave 37 Cleveland OH 44115

CARNEY, THOMAS DALY, lawyer; b. Detroit, Mar. 28, 1947; s. Willam C. and Mary L. (Daly) Carney; m. Anne C. Filson; children: Thomas, David, Kristen. BA, U. Mich., 1969, JD, 1972. Bar: Mich. 1972. Assoc. Cross, Wrock, Miller & Vieson, Detroit, 1973—77, mem. firm., 1977—79; corp. counsel Hoover Universal, Inc., Ann Arbor, 1979—81, sec., gen. counsel, 1981—83, v.p., sec. gen. counsel, 1983—86; counsel Dickinson, Wright, Moon, Van Dusen & Freeman, Detroit, 1986—87, ptnr., 1988—94; named v.p., gen. counsel, sec. Borders Group Inc., Ann Arbor, 1994, now sr. v.p., gen. counsel., sec. Mem.: ABA, Assn. Corp. Counsel, Am. Soc. Corp. Secs., Mich. Bar. Assn., Barton Hills Country Club. Office: Borders Group Inc 100 Phoenix Dr Ann Arbor MI 48108

CARO, WILLIAM ALLAN, physician, educator; b. Chgo., Aug. 16, 1934; s. Marcus Rayner and Adeline Beatrice (Cohen) Caro; m. Ruth Fruchtlander, June 15, 1959 (dec.); children: Mark Stephen, David Edward; m. Joan Peters, Oct. 18, 1997. Student, U. Mich., 1952-55; BS in Medicine, U. Ill., 1957, MD, 1959. Intern Cook County Hosp., Chgo., 1959-60; resident in internal medicine U. Ill. Rsch. and Ednl. Hosps., 1960-61; resident in dermatology Hosp. U. Pa., 1961-62, 64-66; Earl D. Osborne fellow dermal pathology Armed Forces Inst. Pathology, Washington, 1966-67; asst. in medicine U. Ill. Coll. Medicine, 1960-61; asst. instr. U. Pa. Med. Sch., 1961-62, 64-66; from asst. prof. to assoc. prof. dermatology Northwestern U. Med. Sch., 1967—81, prof., 1981—; pvt. practice specializing in dermatology Chgo., 1967—. Chief dermatology sect. MacDonald Army Hosp., Ft. Eustis, Va., 1962—64; attending physician Chgo.

Wesley Meml. Hosp., 1969—72, Northwestern Meml. Hosp., 1972—, mem. med. exec. com., 1977—79; cons. Rehab. Inst. Chgo., Mcpl. Tb Sanitarium Chgo., 1968—74. Mem. editl. bd. Cutis, 1975—; assoc. editor: Year Book Pathology and Clin. Pathology, 1977—80. Mem. medicine adv. bd. U. Ill. Coll. Medicine, 1988—; trustee orthwestern Meml. Hosp. Chgo., 1986—87, bd. dirs., 1988—91, Northwestern Meml. Corp., 1987—2000, mem. exec. com., 1988—91. Served as capt. M.C. USAR, 1962—64. Mem.: AMA, Am. Bd. Dermatology (diplomate 1966, bd. dirs. 1981—91, v.p. 1989—90, pres. 1990—91), Dermatology Found. (Clark W. Finnerud award 2002), Pacific Dermatol. Assn., Internat. Soc. Dermatology, Am. Soc. Dermatopathology (pres.-elect 1995—96, bd. dirs. 1995—2000, pres. 1996—97), Am. Dermatol. Assn. (bd. dirs. 1993—98, v.p. 2004—05), Chgo. Dermatol. Soc. (editor trans. 1971—73, pres. 1983—84, Founders award 1992), Am. Acad. Dermatology (Gold award sci. exhibit 1970), U. Ill. Med. Alumni Assn. (exec. bd. 1977—80), Phi Kappa Phi, Alpha Omega Alpha. Office: 676 N Saint Clair St Ste 1840 Chicago IL 60611-2927

CAROLAN, DOUGLAS, wholesale company executive; BS, Western Mich. U., 1964. Store mgr. to dir. mktg. div. Nat. Tea Co., 1962-83; sr. v.p. Associated Wholesale Grocers, Inc., Kansas City, Kans., 1983-86, chief ops. officer, exec. v.p., sec., 1986—, CEO, pres., 1998—2000. Bd. dirs. UMB Bank, Food Mktg. Inst. Bd. dirs. Kans. City area food bank Harvesters.

CAROLLO, RUSSELL, journalist; b. New Orleans; B in History, Southeastern La. U., 1980; B in Journalism, La. State U., 1982; Journalism fellow, U. Mich., 1989-90. General assignment reporter The Spokesman-Rev., Spokane, Wash., 1986-90; spl. projects and computer assisted reporter Dayton (Ohio) Daily News, 1990-93; mil. and projects reporter The News Tribune, Tacoma, Wa., 1993-94; spl. projects reporter Dayton Daily News, 1994—. Reported refugee crisis in Goma, Zaire, 1994; reported Am. troop deployment in Bosnia, 1995-96; journalism fellowship to report in Japan, 1997. Reporter: (series) Flawed and Sometimes Deadly, 1997, Military Secrets, 1995, Prisoners on Payroll, 1994, Lives on the Line, 1992, A Trust Betrayed, 1988, Cashdance, 1984. Winner 1998 Pulitzer prize for nat. reporting; Pulitzer prize finalist, 1996, 92; U. Mich. Journalism fellow, 1989-90, Internat. Ctr. for Journalists fellow, Japan, 1997; recipient Investigative Reporters and Editors awards, 1992, 95, 96 (Gold medal), Harvard U. Goldsmith award, 1996, White House Corr. Assn. Edgar A. Poe award, 1995, Soc. Profl. Journalists Nat. Award for Investigative Reporting, 1995, John Hancock award, 1992, Polk award, 1998, Nat. Headliner Best of Show award, 1998. Office: Dayton Daily News Cox Newspapers Inc 45 S Ludlow St Dayton OH 45402-1858

CARP, LARRY, lawyer; b. St. Louis, Jan. 26, 1926; s. Avery and Ruth C. Student, U. Mo., Columbia, 1944; cert., Sorbonne U., Paris, 1946; BA, Washington U., St. Louis, 1947; postgrad., Grad. Inst. Internat. Studies, Geneva, 1949; JD, Washington U., St. Louis, 1951. Bar: Mo. 1951, U.S. Dist. Ct. (ea. dist.) Mo. 1951. Mem. U.S. Dept. of State, Washington, 1951-53; mem. staff Senator Paul H. Douglas (Dem. Ill.), Washington, 1953-54; assoc. Fordyce, Mayne, Hartman, Renard, and Stribling, St. Louis, 1954-63; sole practice St. Louis, 1963-68; ptnr. Carp & Morris, St. Louis, 1968-90, Carp, Sexauer and Carr, St. Louis, 1990-94, Carp and Sexauer, St. Louis, 1994—. Assoc. counsel, acting chief counsel US Senate Subcom. on Constitutional Rights, Washington, 1956; life mem. bd. trustees Acad. Sci., St. Louis, 1984—; mem. St. Louis Regional US Export Expansion Coun., 1964-74; mem. Mo. Commn. on Human Rights, 1966-78, vice chmn., 1977-78; bd. dirs. Pastoral Counselling Inst. for Greater St. Louis, 1964-91, St. Louis Ctr. for Internat. Rels., 1998-2006; mem. adv. bd. George Engelmann Math. and Science Inst., 1992-96; legal advisor Image, Inc., St. Louis, 1998-2003. Co-author: (musicals) Pocahontas, The Pied Piper, Androcles; author: (musicals) For the Love of Adam, The Red Ribbon, Famous Last Words, GOD KNOWS!; contbr. articles on immigration law to newspapers and profl. jours. Mem. Common Cause, 1966-78, chmn. Mo. chpt., 1973-75; bd. dirs. Internat. Inst. of Metro St. Louis, 1980-86, English Speaking Union, St. Louis, 1985—, Mo. Prison Arts Program, 1999-2003; US presdl. appointee as sr. adviser and US pub. del. to UN 55th Gen. Assembly, 2000-2001. With US Army, 1944-46, ETO. Decorated (2) Battle Stars; Rotary Internat. fellow Grad. Inst. Internat. Studies, Geneva, 1948-49; award Outstanding Svc. Recognition of Spl. Needs Hispanic Community IMAGE, St. Louis, 1984; named to Best Lawyers in Am. in immigration law, 1994-. Fellow Am. Acad. Matrimonial Lawyers; mem. ABA (immigration law coord. com., 1986-89, chmn. immigration law com. gen. practice sect. 1981-86), Mo. Bar Assn., Bar Assn. Met. St. Louis (chmn. internat. law and trade com. 1973-79, chmn. immigration law com. 1989-92), Am. Immigration Lawyers Assn., UNA-USA Assn. (bd. dirs. St. Louis chpt. 1999-2003), Phi Delta Phi. Office: Carp and Sexauer 225 S Meramec Ave Ste 325 Saint Louis MO 63105-3511 Office Phone: 314-863-4300. Office Fax: 314-727-0308. E-mail: carpandsexauer@msn.com.

CARPENTER, CHRIS, professional baseball player; b. Exeter, NH, Apr. 27, 1975; m. Alyson Carpenter; 1 child, Sam. Pitcher Toronto Blue Jays, 1997—2002, St. Louis Cardinals, 2002—. Named Nat. League All-Star Starting Pitcher, 2005, NL Pitcher Yr., Players Choice awards, 2006; recipient NL Cy Young award, MLB, 2005. Office: St Louis Cardinals 250 Stadium Plz Saint Louis MO 63102-1722 Home: Bedford NH

CARPENTER, DAVID WILLIAM, lawyer; b. Chgo., Aug. 26, 1950; s. William Warren and Dorothy Susan (Jacobs) C.; m. Jane Ellen French, Aug. 18, 1973 (div. Jan. 2001); children: Johanna Lindsay, Julie Rachel; m. Orit Karni, Mar. 26, 2004. BA cum laude, Yale U., 1972; JD magna cum laude, Boston U., 1975. Bar: Mass. 1975, Ill. 1979, DC 1980, US Ct. Appeals (1st cir.) 1977, US Dist. Ct. (no. dist.) Ill. 1979, DC 1995, US Ct. Appeals 3rd. cir. 1981, DC cir. 1982, 7th cir. 1982, 10th cir. 1985, 8th cir. 1986, 9th cir. and 11th ciruits 1987, 2nd, 5th and 6th circuits, 1990, 4th cir. 2000, US Supreme Ct. 1981. Law clk. to presiding justice US Ct. Appeals (1st cir.), Portland, Maine, 1975-77, US Supreme Ct., Washington, 1977-78; assoc. Sidley & Austin (now Sidley Austin LLP), Chgo., 1978-82; ptnr. Sidley Austin LLP, Chgo., 1982—, and mem. exec. com., 1994—. Lectr. Ill. Inst. Tech., Chgo., 1980—82. Bd. dirs., sec. Chgo. Coun. for Young Profls., 1985-90; bd. dirs., exec. com. Brennan Ctr. for Justice, NYC, 1995-2004; bd. dirs. Lyric Opera Chgo., 1999—. Democrat. Mem. United Ch. Christ. Office: Sidley Austin LLP One S Dearborn St Chicago IL 60603 Office Phone: 312-853-7237. Business E-Mail: dcarpenter@sidley.com.

CARPENTER, DOROTHY FULTON, retired state legislator; b. Ismay, Mont., Mar. 13, 1933; d. Daniel A. and Mary Ann (George) Fulton; m. Thomas W. Carpenter, June 12, 1955; children: Mary Ione, James Thomas. BA, Grinnell Coll., 1955. Elem. tchr., Houston and Iowa City, 1955-58; mem. Iowa Ho. of Reps., 1980-94, asst. minority fl. leader, 1982-88, chair ethics and state govt. coms., 1992-94; ret., 1994. Bd. dirs. Planned Parenthood Fedn. of Am., 1977—80; pres. Planned Parenthood of Iowa, 1970; mem. West Des Moines Human Rights Commn., 1999—2004; fin. chair Episcopal Diocese, Iowa, 1979—80. Recipient Grinnell Coll. Alumni award, 1980; named Citizen of Yr., West Des Moines C. of C., 1999.

CARPENTER, JOHN MARLAND, engineer, physicist; b. Williamsport, Pa., June 20, 1935; s. John Hiram and Ruth Edith (Johnson) Carpenter; m. Rhonda DeCardy, 1991; children: John Marland Jr., Kathryn Ann, Susan Marie, Janet Elaine. BS in Engring. Sci, Pa. State U., 1957; MS in Nuclear Engring, U. Mich., 1958, PhD, 1963. Fellow Oak Ridge Inst. Nuclear Studies, 1957-60; postdoctoral fellow Inst. Sci. and Tech., U. Mich., 1963-64, mem. faculty univ., 1964-75, prof. nuclear engring., 1973-75; vis. scientist nuclear tech. br. Phillips Petroleum Co., 1965; solid state sci. div. Argonne (Ill.) Nat. Lab., 1971-72, 73; physics div. Los Alamos Sci. Lab., 1973; sr. physicist solid state sci. div., mgr. intense pulsed neutron source project Argonne Nat. Lab., 1975-77, program dir., 1977-78, tech. dir., 1978—. Mem. U.S. del. to USSR on fundamental properties of matter, 1977; co-founder Internat. Collaboration on Advanced Neurton Sources, 1977; vis. scientist Japanese Lab. for High Energy Physics, 1982, 93; mem. indsl. and profl. adv. coun. Coll. Engring., Pa. State U., 1984—87; mem. nat. steering com. Advanced Neutron Source, 1986—95, mem. exec. com.; mem. grad. faculty Iowa State U., 1988—93; mem. internat. sci. coun. AUSTRON, Austria, 1993—; mem. external rev. com. Accelerator Prodn. Tritium Project Los Alamos Nat. Lab., N.Mex., 1995—98; mem. internat. adv. com.Scientific Coun. on Condensed Matter Investigations with Neutrons Russian Ministry of Sci. and Tech., 1996—; sr. tech. advisor exptl. facilities divsn. SNS Oak Ridge Nat. Lab., 1999—; vis. scientist Rutherford Appleton Lab., 1997—; mem. steering com. spallation neutron source Oak Ridge Nat. Lab., 1996—98, sci. adv. com. for spallation neutron source, 1996—2001. Author: (with Motoharu Kimura) Living with Nuclei, 1993, editor; patentee nuclear instrumentation, neutron scattering, time dependent neutron thermalization, pulsed spallation neutron sources, neutron scattering instrumentation, structure and dynamcs of amorphous solids. Presdl. appointee vis. com. dept. nuclear engring. MIT, 1989-95. Recipient Disting. Svc. award, U. Mich. Dept. Nuc. Engring., 1967, L.J. Hamilton Disting. Alumnus award, 1977, Disting. Performance award for work at Argonne Nat. Lab., U. Chgo., 1982, Ilja M. Frank prize, Joint Inst. Nuc. Rsch., 1998, merit award, Dept. Nuc. Engring. and Radiol. Scis., U. Mich. Alumni Soc., 2001. Fellow Condensed Matter Physics Divsn, Am. Phys. Soc.; mem. Am. Nuclear Soc. (sect. chmn. 1974-75), Neutron Scattering Soc. Am. (mem. subcom. on pulsed spallation sources 1993—, mem. pulsed source steering com.). Office: Argonne Nat Lab Intense Pulsed Neutron Source Argonne IL 60439 E-mail: jmcarpenter@anl.gov.

CARPENTER, KENNETH RUSSELL, international trading executive; b. Chgo., May 22, 1955; s. Kenneth and Margaret (Lucas) C.; 1 child, Matthew. AS in Aviation, Prairie State Coll., Chicago Heights, Ill., 1979. Respiratory therapist, Harvey, Ill., 1980-83; dir., owner, ptnr. Pulmonary Therapy Inc., Harvey, 1983—; v.p. Home Air Joliet Ltd., Harvey, 1984—; dir., owner Air Systems Internat. Export/Import Med. Equipment, Chicago Heights, 1981—, Air Systems, Ft. Lauderdale, 1991—, Home Ortho Ltd., Harvey, 1985—; pres., CEO Profl. Yacht Svcs., Inc., Chicago Heights, 1987-94; owner CLZ Exporting Inc., Chicago Heights, 1993-95; owner, CEO, Profl. Yacht Svcs., Chicago Heights, 1997—, Info. Plus Inc., Chicago Heights, 1997—. Acquisition and mgmt. of investment real estate KRLC, 1991—; dir. pub. rels. Lansing (Ill.) Med. Group, 1990; dir. pulmonary rehab. Cardio-Pulmonary Assocs., Munster, Ind., 1990—, CLZ Exporting, 1992—; maj. importer/exporter of durable med. oxygen equipment worldwide, KRLC Mktg., 1996—; founder Wilderness Trading Group, 2002. Pilot CAP, 1979-86. With USN, 1973-77. Mem. Am. Assn. Respiratory Therapy (cert.), Nat. Assn. Med. Equipment Suppliers, Ill. Assn. of Med. Equipment Suppliers, Am. Biog. Inst., Steger C. of C., Ill. C. of C. Avocations: flying, boating, computer programming. Home and Office: 23030 Miller Rd Steger IL 60475-5932 Office Phone: 708-757-6343.

CARPENTER, MICHAEL H., lawyer; b. Huntington, W.Va., Mar. 3, 1953; BA, Ohio State U., 1974, JD, 1977. Bar: Ohio 1977. Former ptnr. Jones, Day, Reavis & Pogue, Columbus, Ohio; ptnr. Carpenter & Lipps LLP, Columbus, 1994—. Mem. Order of Coif, Phi Beta Kappa. Office: Carpenter & Lipps LLP 280 Plaza Ste 1300 280 N High St Columbus OH 43215 Office Phone: 614-365-4100. Business E-Mail: carpenter@carpenterlipps.com.

CARPENTER, NOBLE OLDS, retired bank executive; b. Cleve., May 8, 1929; s. John W. and Maribel (Olds) C.; m. Ann Lindemann, Oct. 13, 1956 (dec. Aug. 1987); children: John L., Noble Olds, Robert W.; m. Sharon D. D'Atri, Aug. 11, 1990. AB cum laude, Princeton, 1951. Cert. comml. lender. Comml. Lending div. Am. Bankers Assn. Vice pres. Central Nat. Bank, Cleve., 1951-65; chmn., pres., chief exec. officer, dir. Central Trust Co. of Northeastern Ohio, N.A., Canton, 1965-91; dir. Bank One, Akron, Ohio, 1991-97. Mem. Internat. Exec. Svc. Corps.; dir. Mountain Lake Tree & Land Co., Ltd. Dep. sheriff Stark County; bd. dirs. Aultman Hosp. Devel. Found., Blue Coats, Inc., Greater Canton Partnership; trustee State Troopers of Ohio. Named outstanding Young Man of Year Jr. C. of C., 1965 Mem. Cleve. Pres. Orgn., Brookside Country Club. Home: 2503 Charing Cross NW Canton OH 44708-3221 E-mail: NC29@aol.com.

CARPENTER, SHARON QUIGLEY, municipal official; Tchr. history St. Louis Pub Schs.; elected recorder of deeds City of St. Louis, 1980—. Mem. Mo. Reapportionment Comn. Dem. Committeewoman 23rd ward St. Louis, 1964—; chair Dem. Ctrl. Com. St. Louis; founding mem, 1st chair, bd. dirs. Maria Droste Residence, St. Louis; mem. Mo. Commn. on Intergovernmental Rels, 1996—, adv. bd. Cath. Youth Coun., St. Louis., 1997—. Mem. Recorders' Assn. Mo. (past pres.). Office: City of St Louis Office Recorder of Deeds Market & Tucker Aves Rm 126 Saint Louis MO 63103

CARPENTER, SUSAN KAREN, defender; b. New Orleans, May 6, 1951; d. Donald Jack and Elise Ann (Diehl) C. BA magna cum laude with honors in English, Smith Coll., 1973; JD, Ind. U., 1976. Bar: Ind. 1976. Dep. pub. defender of Ind. State of Ind., Indpls., 1976-81, pub. defender of Ind., 1981—; chief pub. defender Wayne County, Richmond, Ind., 1981. Bd. dirs. Ind. Pub. Defender Coun., Indpls., 1981—; Ind. Lawyers Comm., Indpls., 1984-89; trustee Ind. Criminal Justice Inst., Indpls., 1983—. Mem. Criminal Code Study Commn., Indpls., 1981—, Supreme Ct. Records Mgmt. Com., Indpls., 1983—, Ind. Pub. Defender Commn., 1989—, Ind. Supreme Ct. Commn. on Race and Gender Fairness, 2000—. Mem. Ind. State Bar Assn. (criminal justice sect.), Nat. Legal Aid and Defender Assn., Nat. Assn. Defense Lawyers, Phi Beta Kappa. Office Phone: 317-232-2475. Business E-Mail: scarpenter@iquest.net.

CARPENTER, TIMOTHY W., state legislator; b. Milw., Feb. 24, 1960; BA, U. Wis., Milw., 1982. Former delivery svc. courier; rep. for dist. 20 Wis. Ho. of Reps., 1984-92, rep. for dist. 9, 1992—; chmn. health com. Wis. State Assembly. Mem. 4th Congl. Dist. Dem. Com., former chmn. Mem. Wilson Park Advancement Assn. Democrat. Home: 2957 S 38th St Milwaukee WI 53215-3519

CARPENTER, WILL DOCKERY, chemicals executive; b. Moorhead, Miss., July 13, 1930; s. Horace Aubrey and Celeste (Brian) C.; m. Hellen E. Dodd, Mar. 26, 1960; children: Celeste, Bill. BS in Agronomy, Miss. State U., 1952; MS in Plant Physiology, Purdue U., 1956, PhD in Plant Physiology, 1958, DSc (hon.), 1999; grad. exec. program in bus. adminstrn., Columbia U., 1980; DSc (hon.), Miss. State U., 2005. Research biochemist Monsanto Co., St. Louis, 1958-60, agrl. research chemist, 1960-61, staff agrl. devel., 1961-65; mgr. market devel. Monsanto Agrl. Div., St. Louis, 1965-71; dir. product devel. Monsanto Agrl. Products Co., St. Louis, 1971-77, dir. environ. ops., 1977-80, dir. environ. mgmt./environ. policy staff, 1980-84, gen. mgr. tech., 1984-86; v.p. technology Monsanto Agrl. Co., St. Louis, 1986-90, v.p., gen. mgr. new products, 1990-92; chmn., bd. dirs. Agridyne Techs. Inc. Served to capt. U.S. Army, 1952-54, Korea. Fellow Weed Sci. Soc. Am. (treas. 1975, pres. 1980); mem. Indsl. Biotech. Assn. (bd. dirs. 1986—), Chem. Mfrs. Assn. (chmn. environ. mgmt. com. 1982-84, chmn. chem. warfare disarmament com. Washington 1985—), North Cen. Weed Control Conf. (pres. 1977, hon. mem. 1982). Office: 456 Conway Meadows Dr Chesterfield MO 63017-9625 E-mail: wdchdc@aol.com.

CARR, BONNIE JEAN, professional ice skater; b. Chgo., Sept. 29, 1947; d. Nicholas and Agnes Marie (Moran) Musashe; m. James Bradley Carr, Dec. 8, 1984; children: Brittany Jean, James Bradley II, Brooke Anderson. BS, Northwestern U., 1969; JD (hon.), Loyola U., Chgo., 1978. Skater Adventures on Ice, Mpls., 1961; prin. skater Jamboree on Ice, Chgo., 1961-68; society editor The Free Press, Colorado Springs, Colo., 1969; prin. skater, publicist on tour, asst. lighting dir., tour ednl. tutor Holiday on Ice Internat., 1970-74; skating dir. William McFetridge Sports Ctr., Chgo., 1975-86; choreographer, prin. skater Ice Time, USA, Mundelein, Ill., 1975—. Skating coach St. Bronislava Athletic Club, Chgo., 1967-69; publicity dir. Amateur Skating Assn. Ill., Chgo., 1968; founder, dir. skating programs for blind, hearing impaired and mentally handicapped, Chgo., 1975-85; phys. fitness advisor Exec. Health Seminars, Chgo., 1979; founder, dir. skating programs Fred Hutchinson Cancer Rsch. Ctr., Seattle, 1985-86; guest spkr. Am. Cancer Soc., Columbia, S.C., 1973; conditioning coach Riverside Wellness and Fitness Ctr., Richmond, Va., 1989-91, Southampton Rec. Assn., Richmond, 1991-94; figure & speed skating coach Va. Spl. Olympics, 1991—. Recipient Key to City, Mobile, Ala., 1973, Svc. Recognition award Spl. Olympics, Chgo., 1984. Mem. Am. Guild Variety Artists, Am. Coun. on Exercise (cert. 1990-96). Baptist. Avocations: writing, public speaking, choreography. Home and Office: Ice Time USA 7478 Mt Chestnut Rd Roanoke VA 24018-7748 Personal E-mail: bonniejcarr@verizon.net.

CARR, GARY THOMAS, lawyer; b. El Reno, Okla., July 25, 1946; s. Thomas Clay and Bobbye Jean (Page) C.; m. Ann Elizabeth Smith, Jan. 5, 1985. AB, Washington U., St. Louis, 1968, BSCE, 1972, JD, 1975. Bar: Mo. 1975, U.S. Dist. Ct. (ea. and we. dists.) Mo. 1975, U.S. Ct. Appeals (8th cir.) 1977, U.S. Ct. Appeals (fed. cir.) 1980, U.S. Ct. Appeals (5th cir.) 1991, U.S. Ct. Fed. Claims, 2004. Jr. ptnr. Bryan, Cave, McPheeters & McRoberts, St. Louis, 1975-83, ptnr., 1984-99. Lectr. law Washington U., 1978-82, adj. prof., 1982-85; sec., dir. Bruton-Stroube Studios, Inc., 1978—. Trustee Parkview Subdiv. Assn., St. Louis, 1982-90, 2003—. 1st lt. U.S. Army, 1968-71, Vietnam. Mem. ABA, Mo. Bar Assn., St. Louis Bar Assn., Order of Coif. Avocations: woodworking, hunting, fishing, automobiles. Office: PO Box 300129 Saint Louis MO 63130-0430 Home Phone: 314-725-3726; Office Phone: 314-725-6464. E-mail: gtc10485@aol.com.

CARR, GEORGE FRANCIS, JR., retired lawyer; b. Bklyn., Feb. 11, 1939; s. George Francis and Edith Frances (Schaible) C.; m. Patricia Louise Shiels, Jan. 30, 1965; children: Frances Virginia, Anne McKenzie, Margaret Edith. BA, Georgetown U., 1961; LLB, Harvard U., 1964. Bar: Ohio 1964, U.S. Dist. Ct. Ohio 1964. Assoc. Kyte, Conlan, Wulsin & Vogeler, Cin., 1964-70, ptnr., 1970-78, Frost & Jacobs, Cin., 1978-82; sec., counsel Baldwin-United Corp., Cin., 1982-84, v.p., spl. counsel, 1984-85; sole practice Cin., 1985-86; ptnr. Douglas, Carr and Pettit, Milford, Ohio, 1987-88; staff v.p., assoc. gen. counsel Penn Cen. Corp., Cin., 1988-92, Gen. Cable Corp., Highland Heights, Ky., 1992-95, ret., 1995. Treas. Cave Hill Farm Property Owners Assn., Cin., 1998—, Heritage Club Co., Cin., 2003—. Bd. dirs. Ctr. for Comprehensive Alcoholism Treatment, Cin., 1975-87, pres., 1980-83; bd. dirs. NCCJ, Cin., 1975-82. With US Army, 1965—67. Avocations: real estate construction and development, geology, hiking, physical fitness. Home: 7150 Ragland Rd # 4 Cincinnati OH 45244-3148

CARR, JAMES GRAY, federal judge; b. Boston, Nov. 14, 1940; s. Edmund Albert and Anna Frances C.; m. Eileen Margaret Glynn, Dec. 17, 1966; children: Maureen M., Megan A., Darrah E., Caitlin E. AB, Kenyon Coll., 1962; LLB, Harvard U., 1966. Bar: Ill. 1966, Ohio 1972, US Dist. Ct. (no. dist.) Ill. 1966, US Dist. Ct. (no. dist.) Ohio 1970, US Supreme Ct. 1980. Assoc. Gardner & Carton, et al., Chgo., 1966-68; staff atty. Cook County Legal Asst. Found., Evanston, Ill., 1968-70; prof. U. Toledo Law Sch., 1970-79; magistrate judge US Dist. Ct. (no. dist.) Ohio, Toledo, 1979-94, judge, 1994—, chief judge, 2005—; judge Fgn. Intelligence Surveillance Ct., 2002—. Adj. prof. law Chgo. Kent Law Sch., 1969, Loyola U., Chgo., 1970; reporter, juvenile rules com. Ohio Supreme Ct., Columbus, 1971-72; reporter, mem. nat. wiretap com. US Congress, Washington, 1976-77. Contbr. articles to profl. law jours. Founder, bd. dirs. Child Abuse Ctr., Toledo, 1970-84; active Lucas County Mental Health Bd., Toledo, 1984-89, Lucas County Children Svcs. Bd., Toledo, 1989-94. Fulbright fellow, 1977-78. Mem. ABA (reporter, elec. survey stds. 1979-80, mem. task force on tech. and law enforcement 1995-99), mem. task force on jury initiatives 1995-98), Toledo Bar Assn. (bd. dirs.), Phi Beta Kappa. Roman Catholic. Office: US Dist Ct 203 US Courthouse 1716 Spielbusch Ave Toledo OH 43624-1363 Office Phone: 419-259-6420. E-mail: james_g_carr@ohnd.uscourts.gov.

CARR, JEFFREY W., lawyer, manufacturing executive; BA in Govt. and Fgn. Affairs, U. Va.; JD with honors, Georgetown U. Law Ctr. Founder, mgr. Internat. Adv. Svcs. Group, Ltd.; law clk. Judge Schwartz, U.S. Dist. Ct., Del.; atty., internat. trade Willkie Farr & Gallagher, Washington; atty. Wald Harkrader & Ross, Washington; internat. counsel FMC Technologies, Phila., 1993—97, assoc. gen. counsel, energy & airport sys. bus. groups, 1997—2001, v.p., gen. counsel Chgo., 2001—. Office: FMC Technologies 200 E Randolph Dr Chicago IL 60601 Office Phone: 312-861-6000.

CARR, LLOYD H., retired college football coach; b. Hawkins County, Tenn., July 30, 1945; m. Laurie McCartney; children: Melissa, Brett, Jason, Ryan, Emily, Jarrett. Student, U. Mo.; BS in Edn., Northern Mich. U., 1968, MEd, 1970. Asst. coach Nativity High, Detroit, 1968—69, Belleville HS, Mich., 1970—73, Eastern Mich. U., 1976—77, U. Ill., 1978—79; head coach John Glenn HS, Westland, Mich., 1973—75; defensive secondary coach U. Mich., 1980—87, defensive coord., 1987—94, asst. coach, 1990—94, head football coach, 1995—2008; ret., 2007. Mem. bd. NCAA Rules Com. Founder U. Mich. Women's Football Acad.; co-founder Coach Carr Cancer Fund, 1998—; chmn. WJR/Special Olympics Golf Outing, Mich.; co-chmn. United Way Campaign, Washtenaw County, 2002. Named Regional Class A Coach of Yr., 1975; named to Cath. League Hall of Fame, 1997, Northern Mich. U. Hall of Fame, 1997, Jewish Sports Hall of Fame, 2004; recipient Paul "Bear" Bryant award, Nat. Sportscasters & Sportswriters Assn., 1997. Mem.: Am. Football Coaches Assn. (mem. bd. trustees). Achievements include leading the University of Michigan Wolverine's to five Big Ten titles, 1997, 1998, 2000, 2003 and 2004.

CARR, PETER WILLIAM, chemistry professor; b. Bklyn., Aug. 16, 1944; s. Peter V. and Kathleen T. Carr; m. Leah Phillips, 1966; children: Sean, Erin, Kelly. BS in Chemistry, Polytech Inst. Bklyn., 1965; PhD in Analytical Chemistry, Pa. State U., 1969. Rsch. asst., assoc. Brookhaven Nat. Lab., 1965, 66; postdoctoral assoc. Stanford U. Med. Sch., 1968; faculty mem. U. Ga., 1969-77; prof. chemistry U. Minn., 1977—. Cons. Leeds and Northrup, Hewlett Packard, 3M Co., Cabot Inc.; pres. ZirChrom Separations, Inc., 1995-2002, Agilent Technologies; pres. Symposium Analytical Chemistry in Environment, 1976. Mem. edit. adv. bd. Analytical Chemistry, Talanta, Jour. Chromatography, LC/GC, Chromatographia, Separation Sci. and Tech.; contbr. over 350 articles to profl. jours. Recipient L.S. Palmer award Minn. Chromatography Forum, 1984, Benedetti-Pichler award Am. Microchem. Soc., 1990, award in Fields Analytical Chemistry Ea. Analytical Symposium, 1993, S. Nogare award Del. Valley Chromatography Forum, 1996, award in chromatography ISCO, 1997, award in separation sci. Ea. Analytical Symposium, 2000, Pitts. Conference award in analytical chemistry, 2004. Mem. Am. Chem. Soc. (chmn. subdivsn. chromatography and separation sci. of Analytical Chemistry divsn. 1988-89, Chromatography award 1997), Minn. Chromatography Forum. Office: U Minn Dept Chemistry 207 Pleasant St SE Minneapolis MN 55455-0431 Office Phone: 612-624-0253.

CARR, STEPHEN HOWARD, materials engineer, educator; b. Dayton, Ohio, Sept. 29, 1942; s. William Howard and Mary Elizabeth (Clement) C.; m. Virginia W. McMillan, June 24, 1967; children: Rosamond Elizabeth, Louisa Ruth. BS, U. Cin., 1965; MS, Case Western Res. U., 1967, PhD, 1970. Coop. engr. Inland divsn. GM, Dayton, 1960-65; asst. prof. materials sci. and engring. and chem. engring. Northwestern U., Evanston, Ill., 1970-73, assoc. prof., 1973-78, prof., 1978—, dir. Materials Rsch. Ctr., 1984-90, asst. dean engring., 1991-93, assoc. dean engring., 1993—. Cons. in field. Contbr. articles to profl. jours. Recipient Outstanding Alumni Achievement award U. Cin. Coll. Engring., 1993. Fellow Am. Soc. for Metals Internat., Am. Phys. Soc.; mem. AIChE, Soc. Automotive Engrs. (Ralph R. Teetor award 1980), Plastics Inst. Am. (Ednl. Svc. award 1975), Am. Chem. Soc., Soc. Plastics Engrs., Materials Rsch. Soc. Achievements include patents in plastics and textiles fields. Home: 2704 Harrison St Evanston IL 60201-1216 Office: Northwestern U 2145 Sheridan Rd Evanston IL 60208-0834 Business E-Mail: s-carr@northwestern.edu.

CARR, STEVE, public relations executive; V.p. pub. rels. Cramer-Krasselt, Chgo., 1995-96, sr. v.p. pub. rels., 1996—. Office: Cramer-Krasselt 225 N Michigan Ave Chicago IL 60601-7601 Fax: 312-938-3157.

CARR, WALTER STANLEY, lawyer; b. Chgo., May 5, 1945; s. Robert Adams and Margaret (Wiley) C.; m. Mary Baine, Sept. 20, 1969. BS, U. Pa., 1967; JD, U. Chgo., 1970. Bar: Ill. 1970. From assoc. to ptnr. McDermott, Will & Emery, Chgo., 1970-86; v.p. Miami Corp., Chgo., 1987—. Pres. Hull House Assn., Chgo., 1989; bd. dirs. Planned Parenthood Assn. Chgo. Area, 1980—. Mem. ABA, Ill. Bar Assn., Chgo. Bar Assn., Chgo. Estate Planning Council. Clubs: Univ. (Chgo.). Home: 507 W Briar Pl Chicago IL 60657-4633 Office: Miami Corp 410 N Michigan Ave Ste 590 Chicago IL 60611-4252

CARR, WILEY NELSON, hospital administrator; b. Dayton, Ohio, Dec. 29, 1940; s. Russell Earl and Anna Lee (Stroud) C.; m. Grace Elizabeth Brown, June 4, 1960 (div.); children: Wiley Nelson, Alison Mary Ann, G. Elizabeth, Joshua William, Joy Kathleen; m. Sharon L. Kersey, Aug. 22, 1997. Student, Miami U., Oxford, Ohio, 1959-62; BSJ, Ohio U., 1963, MS, 1964; MBA, Xavier U., Cin., 1974. Lic. nursing home adminstr., Ky. Dir. pub. rels. Western Coll. for Women, Oxford, 1964-67, dir. devel., 1967-70; dir. devel. and community rels. St. Elizabeth Med. Ctr., Covington, Ky., 1970-74, asst. adminstr., 1974-83, v.p., chief operating officer Edgewood, Ky., 1983-90; pres., CEO, Porter Meml. Hosp., Valparaiso, Ind., 1990—. Bd. dirs. BetterCare, Inc., Cin.; sec. Tri-State Healthcare Laundry, Edgewood, 1989-90. Pres. Tri-State Community Cancer Orgn., Cin., 1988—; bd. dirs. United Way Porter County, Community Devel. Corp., Valparaiso, N.W. Ind. Forum, YMCA Valparaiso. Fellow Am. Coll. Healthcare Execs.; mem. Ind. Hosp. Assn. Republican. Methodist. Avocations: golf, hiking, swimming. Office: Porter Memorial Hospital 814 Laporte Ave Valparaiso IN 46383-5898 Home: 7503 Turner Ridge Rd Crestwood KY 40014-8973

CARRAWAY, MELVIN J., protective services official; m. Karen Carraway; children: Rachel, Maya. BMus, Heidelberg Coll., 1975; grad., FBI Nat. Acad., 1984. Comdr. enforcement divsn. Ind. State Police, supt., 1997—. Exec. dir. Ind. State Emergency Mgmt. Agy./Dept. of Fire and Bldg. Svcs. With U.S. Army. Office: Ind State Police 100 N Senate Ave Indianapolis IN 46204-2273

CARREN, JEFFREY P., lawyer; b. Chgo., Oct. 8, 1946; AB with high honors, U. Ill., 1968; JD, Northwestern U., 1972. Bar: Ill. 1973, U.S. Dist. Ct. (no. dist.) Ill. 1973, U.S. Ct. Appeals (7th cir.) 1976, U.S. Supreme Ct. 1980. Formerly ptnr. Winston & Strawn, Chgo.; ptnr. Laner, Muchin, Dombrow, Becker, Levin & Tominberg Ltd., Chgo., 1994—. Editor notes and comments Northwestern U. Law Rev., 1971-72/ Edmund James scholar. Mem. ABA (tax and bus. sects.), Ill. State Bar Assn. (employee benefits sect.), Chgo. Bar Assn. (employee benefits com), Am. Arbitration Assn. (panel arbitrators), Phi Eta Sigma. Office: Laner Muchin et al 515 N State St Chicago IL 60610-4324 Office Phone: 312-467-9800. E-mail: jcarren@lanermuchin.com.

CARRICK, KATHLEEN MICHELE, law librarian; b. Cleve., June 11, 1950; d. Michael James and Genevieve (Wenger) C. BA, Duquesne U., Pitts., 1972; MLS, U. Pitts., 1973; JD, Cleve.-Marshall U., 1977. Bar: Ohio 1977, U.S. Ct. Internat. Trade 1983. Rsch. asst. The Plain Dealer, Cleve., 1973-75; head reference SUNY, Buffalo, 1977-78, assoc. dir., 1978-80, dir., asst. prof., 1980-83; dir., assoc. prof. law Case Western Res. U., Cleve., 1983—. Cons. Mead Data Central, Dayton, Ohio, 1987-91. Author: Lexis: A Research Manual, 1989, From Litchfield to Lexis: A Bibliography of American Legal Education, 2004; contbr. articles to profl. jours. Fellow Am. Bar Found.; mem. ABA, Am. Law Inst., Am. Assn. Law Librs., Assn. Am. Law Schs., Scribes. Home: 1317 Burlington Rd Cleveland OH 44118-1212 Office: Case Western Res U 11075 East Blvd Cleveland OH 44106-5409 Office Phone: 216-368-6357. Business E-Mail: kxc4@case.edu.

CARRICO, VIRGIL NORMAN, physician; b. Cumberland, Md., Aug. 28, 1940; s. Virgil Norman and Lucille E. Carrico; m. Nina Lois Lemper, Aug. 17, 1963; children: Pamela Beth Carrico-Miller, Sandra Kelly (dec.). BA, Wabash Coll., 1962; MD, Ind. U., 1966. Diplomate Am. Bd. Family Practice. Intern Marion County Gen. Hosp., Indpls., 1966-67; resident in family practice Akron (Ohio) City Hosp., 1970-72, chief resident in family practice, 1972, assoc. dir. family practice residency, 1972; chief family practice Bryan Cmty. Hosp., chief of staff, 1977-78, preceptor Bryan Area Health Edn. Ctr.; past preceptor cmty. medicine Med. Coll. Ohio, Toledo, clin. asst. prof. family medicine, clin. prof. family medicine; past preceptor preventive medicine and family practice Ohio State U.; med. dir. Bryan Area Health Edn. Ctr. Past pres., bd. dirs. Bryan Med. Group, Inc. Contbr. articles to profl. jours. Trustee YWCA, Bryan, Ohio, v.p., 1990-92; bd. dirs. United Fund, pres., 1990-92; bd. dirs. Jr. Achievement, 1981-83, Bryan Area Found. Capt. USAF, 1967-70. Fellow Am. Acad. Family Physicians (bylaw coms. 1989, 90, 91, 92, nat. chmn. 1993, chmn. patient care svcs. commn. 1988-89, chmn. mem. svcs. commn. 1989-90); mem. Soc. Tchrs. Family Medicine, Ohio Acad. Family Medicine, Am. Acad. Family Medicine, Williams County Med. Soc. (rpes. 1976-79, sec.-treas., v.p. 1980-83), Ohio Acad. Family Physicians (del. to ho. of dels. 1972-85; pres. Fulton County chpt. 1973-85, chmn. resident affairs subcom., nominating com., student awards, fin. com., ref. com. of the ho. of dels.; treas. 1985-87, v.p. 1987-89, bd. dirs. 1983-92, pres.-elect 1990-91), Rotary Internat. Avocations: golf, travel, reading. Office: Bryan Med Group 442 W High St Bryan OH 43506-1681 Office Phone: 419-636-4517. Personal E-mail: bmg@bright.net.

CARRINGTON, MICHAEL DAVIS, criminal justice and security consultant; b. South Bend, Ind., Mar. 9, 1938; s. Herman Lakin and Margaret (Davis) C.; m. Lynn Ogden, Feb. 8, 1958; children: Michael O. (dec.), Jill A., Elizabeth A., Gretchen L. BA, Ind. U., 1970; MALS, Valparaiso U., 1971. Parole officer State of Ind., South Bend, 1970-71; chief probation officer St. Joseph County, South Bend, 1971-74; dir. pub. safety City of South Bend, 1974-76, mayor's asst., 1976-80; adj. assoc. prof., dir. safety, security, police Ind. U., South Bend, 1979-94; presdl. appointment as U.S. Marshal Northern Dist. of Ind., South Bend, Ind., 1994—2002; ret. U.S. Marshal's Svc., 2002—. Cons. in pvt. security Pan Am. Games, Indpls., 1987; cons. on Bur. Motor Vehicles security study Gov. of Ind., 2003-04; security advance agt. Olympic Torch Relay, Ind., 1984, Hands Across Am., Ind., 1986; mem. alcoholic beverage bd. St. Joseph County, South Bend, 2007—. Mem. Ind. Parole Bd., 2004—05. Named Ky. Col., 1984, Hon. Big Bro. of Yr., 1974; recipient Sagamore of the Wabash award, 1984, 2002, 2004, Disting. Alumnus award, Coll. Arts and Scis., Ind. U., South Bend, 2002. Mem.: Assn. of Threat Assessment Profls. Presbyterian. Avocations: travel, reading, walking, working. Office: Box 96 South Bend IN 46624 Home Phone: 574-272-5857; Office Phone: 574-210-8575. E-mail: carringtonconsulting@comcast.net.

CARROLL, BARRY JOSEPH, manufacturing and real estate executive; b. Highland Park, Ill., Jan. 22, 1944; s. Wallace Edward and Lelia (Holden) C.; m. Barbara Ann Pehrson, July 16, 1965; children: Megan, Sean, Deirdre, Colleen, Oona. Student, Boston Coll., 1961-63; AB, Shimer Coll., 1966; MBA, Harvard U., 1969. Lic. real estate broker, Ill. Account rep. Amerad Advt. Service, Chgo., summers 1966, 67; staff analyst Jamesbury Valve Co., Worcester, Mass., 1968; asst. to pres. Am. Gage & Machine Co., Elgin, Ill., 1969; pres. J.C. Deagan Co., Chgo., 1969-77; v.p. Internat. Metals & Machines, Des Plaines, 1977-92, bd. dir.; v.p. Katy Industries, Elgin, 1984-94, bd. dir.; pres. Katy Comm., Inc. (WIVS-AM, WXRD-FM, WAIT AM/FM), 1986-92, Sta. W45AJ-TV, Rockford, Ill., 1989-92. V.p., bd. dir. Pehrson-Long Assocs., Real Estate Mgmt., Am. Machine & Sci. Inc., CRL Inc., Carroll Internat. Corp. (chmn. 1992), GFS Holdings Co.; bd. dir. XPS Mktg. Inc. Author: (monograph) Talking with Business, 1986; author of appendix/editor: What I Do Best: The Biography of Wallace Edward Carroll, 1992; editor/author: Private Means/Public Ends, 1987; author: Lake Forest, A Very Special Place, 1996; producer, dir. indsl. films, including In There Punching, 1965, The Story of Mallet Instruments, 1975, Digging Lake County, 1999; dir./host (cable TV series) Area Arts, 2000—. Spl. asst. U.S. Sec. Edn., Washington, 1983-84; Presdl. Exch. exec., Washington, 1983-84; bd. govs. United Rep. Fund, Chgo., 1986-92; mem. Nat. Inst. Edn. Commn. Edn. and Tech., U.S. Dept. Edn., 1984-85; trustee Shimer Coll., 1970—, chmn. bd. trustees, 1975-78; trustee Barat Coll., Lake Forest, 1983—2001, life trustee, 1999—; trustee St. Xavier U., Chgo., 1988-94, Lake County Regional Sch. Bd., 1993—; trustee Am. Ireland Fund, 1982-2001, sec., 1991-99; bd. dirs. Lake Forest Symphony, 1970—, Pageant of Peace/Nat. Christmas Tree, 1987-2000, Lake Forest Symphony Sch. of Music., 1991—, Roosevelt U., Chgo., 1996-2005, U. Ill. Eye Rsch. Inst., 1996—; bd. dirs. Chgo. Crime Commn., 1993—, treas., 1994-98; mem., chmn. Lake Forest Cultural Arts Commn., 1997—; chair adv. bd. Inst. Metro. Affairs Roosevelt U., 1998—; trustee Auditorium Theatre Roosevelt U., 2003—, chmn. fin. com., 2003—; mem. pres.'s coun. U. Ill., 1996—. Shimer fellow Shimer Coll., Mt. Carroll, Ill., 1972, Shimer Hero award Shimer Coll., Waukegan, Ill., 1980, Dr. Letters, 1995. Mem. Woods Hole Oceanographic Inst. Assn., Ill. Mfrs. Assn. (bd. dir. 1989-2005, treas. 1991-95), Am. Inst. Aeronautics and Astronautics, Assn. for Mfg. Tech. (bd. dir. chmn. pub. affairs com. 1988-93), Elawa Farm Commn.(dir.), Lake Forest, Lake Forest Onwentsia Club, Chgo. Club, Washington Met. Club, East Chop Beach Tennis and Yacht Clubs, Edgartown Yacht Club, West Palm Beach Bath and Tennis Club, Soc. Colonial Wars in the State of Ill. (treas. 1988-94, gov. 1998-2000), Nat. Soc. Colonial Wars (dep. gov. gen. 2002—05) Soc. Cin. Avocations: flying, sailing, scuba diving, photography. Office: Wildwood LLC 60 N Stonegate Lake Forest IL 60045 Business E-Mail: bcarroll@carrollintl.com.

CARROLL, DANNY, state representative; b. Colorado Springs, Colo., Aug. 19, 1953; m. Joy Carroll; children: Curtis, Danae, Joni. BS, Milligan Coll., 1975. Broker Ramsey-Weeks Real Estate, 1987—99; co-owner Carroll's Pumpkin Farm, 1991—; mem. Iowa Ho. Reps., DesMoines, 1995—, mem. edn. com., mem. human resources com., mem. local govt. com., mem. rules and adminstrn. com., mem. adminstrv. rules rev., 1996—, asst. majority leader. Bd. dirs. Iowa Telecom, mgr. cmty. rels. Mem. Powshiek County Bd. Suprs., 1984—94; active Poweshiek Area Devel. Coun., 1988—, Poweshiek County Farm Bur. Mem.; N.Am. Farmers Dist. Mktg. Assn., Iowa Fruit and Vegetable Growers, Grinnell Kiwanis Club (past pres.), Kiwanis. Republican. Office: State Capitol East 12th and Grand Des Moines IA 50319 also: 244 400th Ave Grinnell IA 50112

CARROLL, DONNA M., academic administrator; MA, U. Cin., 1977, PhD in Edn., 1981. Program dir. U. Cin.; dean of students Fairleigh Dickenson U., Madison, NJ, Mt. Vernon Coll., Washington, v.p. devel.; sec. Fordham U., 1991—94, exec. sec. Bd. Trustees, 1991—94; pres. Dominican U., River Forest, Ill., 1994—. Recipient Chief Exec. Leadership award, Coun. Advancement and Support of Edn., 2004. Office: Dominican U 7900 W Division River Forest IL 60305

CARROLL, FRANK JAMES, lawyer, educator; b. Albuquerque, Feb. 10, 1947; s. Francis J. and Dorothy (Bloom) C.; m. Marilyn Blume, Aug. 9, 1969; children: Christine, Kathleen, Emily. BS in Acctg., St. Louis U., 1969; JD, U. Ill., 1973. Bar: Iowa 1973, U.S. Dist. Ct. Iowa, U.S. Tax Ct., U.S. Ct. Appeals (8th cir.); CPA, Mo., Iowa. Acct. Arthur Young & Co., St. Louis, 1969-70; shareholder Davis, Brown, Koehn, Shors & Roberts, P.C., Des Moines, 1973—. Lectr. law Drake U. Law Sch., Des Moines, 1976-86, lectr. Sch. Bus., 1988-92; bd. dirs. Iowa Agr. Devel. Authority, Iowa State Bar Assn.; adj. prof. Drake U. Law Sch., 2007—. Mem. commr.'s adv. group Internal Revenue Svc., Washington, 1989; mem. U. Mo. Kansas City Sch. Law, 1995. Mem. ABA, Iowa Bar Assn. (chmn. bus. law sect. 1995-98, chmn. corp. counsel sect. 2001-2003, bd. govs. 2003-07), Polk County Bar Assn. (bd. dirs. 2003-07), Des Moines C. of C., Wakonda Club, Des Moines Variety Club (bd. dirs. 1998), Beta Gamma Sigma. Home: 5725 Harwood Dr Des Moines IA 50312-1203 Office: Davis Brown Koehn Shors Roberts PC 666 Walnut St Ste 2500 Des Moines IA 50309-3904 Office Phone: 515-288-2500. Business E-Mail: frankcarroll@lawiowa.com.

CARROLL, HOWARD WILLIAM, state legislator; b. July 28, 1942; s. Barney M. and Lyla (Price) C.; m. Eda Stagman, Dec. 1, 1973; children: Jacqueline, Barbara. BBA, Roosevelt U., 1964; postgrad., Loyola U., 1964-65; JD, DePaul U., 1967. Bar: Ill. 1967. Staff atty. Chgo. Transit Authority, 1967-71; pvt. practice, 1971—; ptnr. Carroll & Sain, Chgo., 1974—; mem. Ill. Senate, Springfield, 1973-99, asst. minority leader, 1993-99, chmn. appropriations com., 1977-93. Mem. Legis. Info. System Commn., Ill. Comprehensive Health Ins. Bd.; vice chmn. State Employees Suggestion Award Bd.; mem. fed. budget and taxation com. State-Fed. Assembly; mem. Assembly Com. on State's Legis. Fiscal Affairs and Oversight; prof. complemental faculty Rush U. Coll. Health Scis., Chgo.; lectr. in field. Mem. Ill. Ho. of Reps., 1971-72; chmn. fin. com. Chgo. and Cook County Dem. Crtl. Com., 1982-84, treas., 1984-2000; committeeman 50th Ward Dem. Orgn., 1980-2000; mem. platform com. Ill. Dem. Com., 1974—; former mem. youth adv. bd. Dem. Nat. Com.; del. nat. and Ill. Dem. convs.; v.p. Young Dem. Clubs Am., 1971-73, also former gen. counsel; mem. exec. bd. Atlantic Alliance Young Polit. Leaders, 1970-73; active numerous civic orgns.; mem. exec. com., vice chmn. Jewish United Fund, 1977-2006; trustee Michael Reese Health Trust, 2006-; vice chmn. bd. trustees Weiss Meml. Hosp. Found.; officer Jewish Cmty. Rels. Coun.; former chair govt. affairs Jewish Fedn. Met. Chgo., now vice chmn.; founder Howard W. Carroll Found.; vice chmn. Jewish Found. Met. Chgo., Jewish United Found, Northshore Ctr. Performing Arts Found. Recipient numerous awards, including cert. of appreciation Decalogue Soc. Lawyers, 1972, Hemophilia Found. Ill., 1988, City Colls. Chgo., 1992, Disting. Svc. award State of Israel Bonds, 1974, Self-Help Assn., 1986, citation for meritorious svc. DAV, 1986, Legislator of Yr. award Child Care Assn. Ill., 1988, Ill. Coun. on Long Term Care, 1988, Outstanding Legislator award Am. Acad. Ophtholmology, 1989, Legis. Advocacy award Ill. Coun. for Gifted, 1991, Founders medal Montay Coll., 1992, Peace Advocate award Ill. Coalition Against Domestic Violence, 1998, Spl. award Comprehensive Health Ins. Plan, Chgo., 1998, award Northshore Ctr. Performing Arts, 1999, Spl. Svc. award Anti Defamation League, 2001, Ytshak Rabin Inaugural Visionary award State of Israel, 2003; named Ill. Health Care Outstanding Legislator of Yr., 1995. Mem. Chgo. Bar Assn. (Disting. Lawyer and Legislator award 1974), Zionist Orgn. Chgo., Masons (32d degree), B'nai B'rith (bd. dirs. West Rogers Park). Office: 7250 N Cicero Ave Lincolnwood IL 60712 Home: 31 Indian Hill Rd Winnetka IL 60093-3940 Office Phone: 847-568-7000. Business E-Mail: senhwc@carrollandsain.com.

CARROLL, JAMES J., lawyer; b. Chgo., Jan. 10, 1948; BS magna cum laude, DePaul U., 1969, JD summa cum laude, 1972. Bar: Ill. 1972, U.S. Tax Ct. 1980, U.S. Supreme Ct. 1981. Of counsel Sidley & Austin, Chgo., 1995-99, ptnr., 1978-95; dir., pres. Wrigley Mgmt. Inc., Chgo., 1995-99; trust counsel Northern Trust Co., 1999—. Lectr. Ill. Inst. for Continuing Legal Edn. Editor-in-chief DePaul Law Rev., 1971-72. Sec. Lakewood Estates Homeowners Assn.; bd. dirs. David and Ruth Barnow Found., 1979, Wrigley Family Found., 1993-99; active Ill. Atty. Gen.'s Charitable Adv. Coun. With USAR, 1970-76. Mem. Ill. State Bar Assn. (chmn. children's rights subcom. 1972-73), Chgo. Bar Assn. (probate practice com. 1977-88, lectr.), Death and Tax Soc., Law Club Chgo., Legal Club Chgo., Phi Eta Sigma, Beta Alpha Psi. Office: Northern Trust Co 181 W Madison St M 9 Chicago IL 60675-0001 E-mail: jjc@notes.ntrs.com.

CARROLL, ROBERT WAYNE, mathematics professor; b. Chgo., May 10, 1930; s. Walter Scott and Dorothy (Le Monnier) C.; m. Berenice Jacobs, Sept. 7, 1957 (div. June 1974); children: David Leon, Malcolm Scott; m. Alice von Neumann, Sept. 1974 (div. Mar. 1977); m. Joan Miller, Jan. 1979 (dec. Apr. 2001), m. Denise Bredt, May 2003. BS, U. Wis., 1952; PhD, U. Md., 1959. Aero. research scientist NASA, Cleve., 1952-54; NSF postdoctoral fellow, 1959-60; asst. prof. Rutgers U., 1960-63, assoc. prof., 1963-64; assoc. prof. math. U. Ill., Urbana, 1964-67, prof., 1967-97, prof. emeritus, 1997—. Author: Abstract Methods in Partial Differential Equations, 1969, Transmutation and Operator Differential Equations, 1979, Transmutation, Scattering Theory and Special Functions, 1982, Transmutation Theory and Applications, 1985, Mathematical Physics, 1988, Topics in Soliton Theory, 1991, Quantum Theory, Deformation and Integrability, 2000, Calculus Revisited, 2002, Fluctuations, Information, Gravity, and the Quantam Potential, 2006, 07; co-author: Singular and Degenerate Cachy Problems, 1976; assoc. editor Jour. Applicable Analysis, 1970—; contbr. over 200 articles to profl. jours. Served with U.S. Army, 1954-57. Mem. Am. Math. Soc., Am. Phys. Soc. Avocations: foreign languages, cello. Home: 1314 Brighton Dr Urbana IL 61801-6417 Office: Univ Ill Math Dept Urbana IL 61801 Business E-Mail: rcarroll@math.uiuc.edu.

CARROLL, THOMAS JOHN, retired advertising executive; b. St. Paul, Aug. 15, 1929; s. William H. and Neva (Saller) C.; m. Eleanor Rose Schmid, Aug. 27, 1955; children: David G., Thomas John, Ann Catherine, Robert G., Paul William. BA, St. Mary's Coll., Winona, Minn., 1952; cert., Grad. Sch. Mgmt., UCLA, 1977. Pharm. salesman A.H. Robins, Davenport, Iowa, 1955-70; advt. salesman Modern Medicine mag., Chgo., 1970-72; advt. exec. D'Arcy, McManus & Massius, St. Paul, 1972-73; dir. mktg. communications AMA, Chgo., 1973-92; cons. Carroll Media Svcs., LaGrange Park, Ill., 1992—. Editor Synergy mag., 1975-92, The Voice Quar., 1996—. Dir. pub. rels. St. Francis Xavier Sch. Bd., La Grange, Ill., 1977-79, Organist St. Francis Xavier Ch., La Grange, 1964-91; bd. trustee La Grange Park Libr. Dist., 1994—, v.p.; adminstrv. assoc. St. Francis Xavier Ch., La Grange, 1996—. Mem. Phar. Advt. Coun., Midwest Healthcare Mktg. Assn. (bd. dirs.), Med. Mktg. Assn., Am. Guild Organists, Chgo. Area Theatre Orgn. Enthusiasts, La Grange Field Club, La Grange Tennis Assn. (past pres.), St. Francis Xavier Men's Club. Republican. Roman Catholic. Home and Office: 2419 Enterprise Dr Westchester IL 60154

CARROLL, WILLIAM J., municipal official; b. Aug. 24, 1944; BS in Acctg., Univ. Toledo, 1969; grad. Adv. Mgmt. Program, Harvard Bus. Sch., 1994. Gen. mgr., after market prodn. divsn. Hayes-Dana, 1987—89, v.p., after market prodn. divsn., 1989—93, pres., 1993—95, Dana Distribution Svc. Group, 1995—96, pres., diversified products and distribution, 1996—97, pres., automotive sys. group, 1997—2004, pres., COO, 2004; dir., econ., cmty. devel. City of Toledo, Ohio, 2004—. Office: City of Toledo Ste 1710 One Government Ctr Toledo OH 43604 Office Phone: 419-245-1286.

CARROLL, WILLIAM KENNETH, lawyer, educator, psychologist, theologian; b. Oak Park, Ill., May 8, 1927; s. Ralph Thomas and Edith (Fay) C.; m. Frances Louise Forgue; children: Michele, Brian. BS in Edn., Quincy Coll., Ill., 1950, BA in Philosophy, 1950; MA, Duquesne U., 1964; STL, Cath. U., 1965; PhD, U. Strasbourg, France, 1968; JD, Northwestern U., 1972. Bar: Ill. 1972, U.S. Dist. Ct. (no. dist.) Ill 1972, U.S. Ct. Appeals (7th cir.) 1973; lic. clin. psychologist, Ill. Asst. editor Franciscan Press, Chgo., 1955-60; asst. prof. psychology and religion Carlow Coll., Pitts., 1962-65, Loyola U., Chgo., 1968-70; staff atty. Fed. Defender Program, Chgo., 1972-75; prof. law John Marshall Law Sch., Chgo., 1975—. Bd. dirs. Am. Inst. Adlerian Studies; law reporter ABA Criminal Justice Mental Health Stds. Project, 1981-83; cons. legal issues Am. Psych. Assn.; standing com. on mental health law, Ill. Author: (with Kosnik et al.) Human Sexuality, 1977; Eyewitness Testimony, Strategies and Tactics, 1984, 2d edit., 2003; contbg. author: By Reason of Insanity, 1983, Law for Illinois Psychologists, 1985, Law and Mental Health Professionals, 2002. Bd. dirs. Chgo. Sch. Profl. Psychology, 1978-82; bd. adv. Ill. Sch. Profl. Psychology, 1985. Recipient Am. Juris award, 1970; U. Chgo. scholar, 1968-69. Fellow Inst. Social and Behavioral Pathology (chmn. 1987—); mem. ABA, AAUP, APA (Outstanding Contbn. to Psychology award 1998, com. on legal issues 1995—), Ill. Psychol. Assn., Cath. Theol. Soc. Am. Avocation: flying. Office: John Marshall Law Sch 315 S Plymouth Ct Chicago IL 60604-3968 Business E-Mail: 7carroll@jmls.edu.

CARRUTHERS, PHILIP CHARLES, lawyer, prosecutor, former state legislator; b. London, Dec. 8, 1953; s. J. Alex and Marie Carruthers. BA, U. Minn., 1975, JD, 1979. Bar: Minn. 1979, U.S. Dist. Ct. Minn. 1979, U.S. Ct. Appeals (8th cir.) 1979. Assoc. Nichols & Kruger, and predecessor firm, 1979-81; ptnr. Nichols, Starks, Carruthers and Kaster, Mpls., 1982-84, Luther, Ballenthin & Carruthers, Mpls., 1985—92, Carruthers & Tallen, Mpls., 1992—93; pvt. practice Mpls., 1994—2000; pros. atty. City of Deephaven, Minn., 1979-2000, City of Woodland, Minn., 1980-2000; mem. Minn. Ho. of Reps., St. Paul, 1987-2000, majority leader, 1993-96, spkr. of house, 1997-98; dir. prosecution divsn. Ramsey County Attys. Office, St. Paul, 2000—. Co-author: The Drinking Driver in Minnesota: Criminal and Civil Issues, 1982; note and comment editor Minn. Law Rev., 1978-79. Mem. Met. Coun. of Twin Cities Area, St. Paul, 1983-87. Mem. Minn. Trial Lawyers Assn. (bd. govs. 1982-86), Minn. State Bar Assn., Hennepin County Bar Assn. Democratic Farmer-Labor Party. Roman Catholic. Home: 6018 Halifax Pl Brooklyn Center MN 55429-2440 Office: 315 Government Ctr W 50 W Kellogg Blvd Saint Paul MN 55102-1657 Office Phone: 651-266-3263. E-mail: Phil.Carruthers@Co.Ramsey.mn.us.

CARSON, ANDRÉ D., congressman, marketing specialist; b. Indpls., Oct. 16, 1974; m. Mariama Shaheed; 1 child, Salimah. BA in Criminal Justice Mgmt., Concordia U.; MA in Bus. Mgmt., Ind. Wesleyan U. Local bd. officer, investigator Ind. State Excise Police; mktg. specialist Cripe Architects & Engrs.; committeeperson Center Twp. of Marion County, Ind.; mem. Indpls. City-County Coun. from 15th dist., 2007—08, US Congress from 7th Ind. dist., 2008—. Mem. IndyParks Kennedy/King Park Adv. Bd.; bd. mem. Citizens Neighborhood Coalition. Named one of The Power 150, Ebony mag., 2008. Democrat. Muslim. Office: US Congress 2455 Rayburn Ho Office Bldg Washington DC 20515 also: One N Capitol Ave Ste 200 Indianapolis IN 46204*

CARSON, ROGER, radio personality; 1 child, Katie. Radio host Lake 93, The Lakd of The Ozarks, 1979—81, KMOX, St. Louis, 1981—82, WHB, Kansas City, 1982—89, local sta., 1989—93, KUDL, Westwood, Kans. Office: KUDL 4935 Belinder Westwood KS 66205

CARSON, SAMUEL GOODMAN, retired bank executive; b. Glens Falls, NY, Oct. 6, 1913; s. Russell M.L. and Mary (Goodman) C.; m. Alice Williams, Oct. 14, 1939; children: Russell L., Frances Elizabeth (Mrs. Thomas E. Brady Jr.), Mary Goodman (Mrs. John A. Fedderke), Kathryn Williams (Mrs. Robert Richards), Samuel Goodman. BA magna cum laude, Dartmouth Coll., 1934. With Aetna Life Ins. Co., 1934-68; with Toledo Trust Co., 1967-84, exec. v.p., 1968, pres., 1969-84, chief exec. officer, 1970-84, chmn., 1976-84; chmn., dir. Toledo Trustcorp, Inc., 1976-84, ret., 1984. Dir. Kiemle-Hankins Co., Plastic Technologies, Inc., Carson Assocs., Inc. Mem. Ottawa Hills Bd. Edn., 1954-64; pres. United Appeal Greater Toledo Area, 1969, campaign chmn., 1964; Bd. dirs., trustee Toledo chpt. ARC, 1950—, chmn., 1959-61; trustee Toledo Hosp., 1960—, v.p., 1963-65, pres., 1966-69; bd. dirs. Community Chest Greater Toledo, 1962-65, pres., 1965; pres. Boys' Club Toledo, 1961-64, trustee, 1957—; trustee Toledo Mus. Art, 1967—, sec.-treas., 1969, v.p., 1973-78, pres., 1978-80. Recipient Service to Mankind award Sertoma Club Toledo, 1965, Man and Boy award Boys' Clubs Am., 1966, Pacemaker of Yr. award U. Toledo Coll. Bus. Adminstrn. Alumni Assn., 1969 Mem. Toledo Area C. of C. (trustee 1961-62, 73-76, pres. 1974-75), Phi Beta Kappa, Phi Gamma Delta. Clubs: Rotarian, Toledo Country, Toledo. Lodges: Rotary. Republican. Congregationalist. Office: 425 Madison Ave Toledo OH 43604-1229

CARSON, VAN, lawyer; BA, Mt. Union Coll., 1963; LLB, Duke U., 1966. Bar: Ohio 1966, registered: Supreme Ct. Ohio 1966, US Ct. Appeals (6th cir.) 1976, US Supreme Ct. 1981, US Ct. Appeals (7th cir.) 1993, US Ct. Appeals (DC cir.) 1993, US Dist. Ct., DC 1996. Ptnr. Squire, Sanders & Dempsey LLP, Cleve., chmn., Environ., Health & Safety Practice Group. Exec. com. mem. & vice chmn. of bd. dir. Ohio C. of C. Mem.: Ohio State Bar Assn. (environ. law com.), Cleve. Bar Assn. (environ. law com.), ABA (Litig. Sect.), Order of Coif. Office: Squire Sanders & Dempsey LLP 4900 Key Tower 127 Public Sq Cleveland OH 44114-1304 Office Phone: 216-479-8559. Office Fax: 216-479-8780. Business E-Mail: vcarson@ssd.com.

CARTER, ADAM, radio personality; b. South St. Paul, Minn. BA Comms., St. Peter and Bustavus Adolphus Coll., 1998. News dir., morning show host Sta. KZAT-FM, Tama and Toledo, Ohio; morning anchor Stas. WAXX-FM and WAYY-AM, Eau Claire, Wis., 1999—2001; news anchor Sta. WCCO Radio, Mpls., 2001—. Recipient award, AP, Wis. Broadcasters Assn. Office: WCCO 625 2nd Ave S Minneapolis MN 55402

CARTER, CURTIS LLOYD, museum director, aesthetics and philosophy educator, author; b. Moulton, Iowa, Oct. 1, 1935; s. Lloyd Joseph and Helen Edna (Wood) C.; m. Jean Elaine Watson, June 12, 1960; 1 child, Curtis Lloyd, Jr. BA, Taylor U., 1960; MDiv., Boston U., 1963, PhD., 1971. Instr. Marquette U., Milw., 1969-71, asst. prof., 1971-84, prof., 1984—, chmn. com. fine arts, 1975-84; dir. Haggerty Mus. Art, Marquette U., 1984—; chmn. Nat. Bicentennial Dance Conf., Cambridge, Mass., 1976; panelist, referee NEH Individual Research Project, Washington, 1983, Media Panel, Washington, 1984; chmn., speaker World Congress Aesthetics, Montreal, Can., 1984, Joyce and Vico Conf., Venice, Italy, 1985; advisor Bay View High Sch., Milw., 1982—. Gen. editor and essayist: (Art Mus. Catalogue) Selected Works, 1984. Contbr. articles and essays to profl. jours. and publs. Founding pres., bd. dirs. ARTREACH Milw., 1975—; v.p., bd. dirs. Charles Allis Art Mus., Milw., 1979—; bd. dirs. Music From Almost Yesterday, Milw., 1978—, Wis. Heritages, Inc., Milw., 1979—, Goals for Greater Milw. 2000, 1982—, Studio Watts Artist's Housing Project, Los Angeles, 1982—, Milw. Ctr. Photography, 1982—. Grantee Wis. Arts Bd., 1979, NEA, 1979, 80, 81, Inst. Mus. Services, 1982, 84, Mellon Found., 1982, Wis. Humanities, 1984, J. Paul Getty Trust, 1985. Mem. Am. Assn. Museums, Am. Philos. Assn., Am. Soc. for Aesthetics (nat. conf. chmn. 1980), Am. Dance Guild (chmn. nat. bicentennial dance conf. 1976, mem. nat. exec. com.), Hegel Soc. Am., Semiotics Soc. Am., Coll. Art Assn., Am. Assn. U. Adminstrs., Nat. Dance Critics Assn., Internat. Metaphysical Soc. (chmn.-speaker World Cong. Philosophy, Montreal, Can. 1983), Milw. Area Mus. Assocs. Avocation: travel. Home: 2609 E Menlo Blvd Milwaukee WI 53211-2649 Office: Haggerty Museum Art Marquette U 13th Clybourn Milwaukee WI 53233

CARTER, JAMES HARVEY, retired state supreme court justice; b. Waverly, Iowa, Jan. 18, 1935; s. Harvey J. and Althea (Dominick) C.; m. Jeanne E. Carter, Aug. 1965; children: Carol, James. BA, U. Iowa, 1956, JD, 1960. Law clk. to judge U.S. Dist. Ct, 1960-62; assoc. Shuttleworth & Ingersoll, Cedar Rapids, Iowa, 1962-73; judge 6th Jud. Dist., 1973-76, Iowa Ct. Appeals, 1976-82; justice Iowa Supreme Ct., Des Moines, 1982—2006, sr. justice, 2006—. Office: Iowa Supreme Ct Judicial Branch Bldg 1111 E Ct Ave Des Moines IA 50319 Home Phone: 319-366-0027; Office Phone: 319-398-3920 500. Business E-Mail: james.carter@jb.state.ia.us.

CARTER, MELINDA, municipal official; b. Springfield, Ohio; BA in English lit., Ohio U., 1986; JD, Capital U., 1989. Assoc. Beatty and Roseboro, Columbus, Ohio; spl. counsel Ohio Atty. Gen. Columbus; exec. dir. New Salem Cmty. Reinvestment Corp., Columbus; exec. asst. to the dir. Equal Bus. Opportunity Commn., City of Columbus, exec. dir., 1996—. Mem. New Salem Missionary Bapt. Ch. Mem. Ohio U. Alumni Assn., Nat. Coalition 100 Black Women, Network Black Women for Justice, Alpha Kappa Alpha. Office: Equal Bus Opportunity Commn City of Columbus 109 N Front St Fl 4 Columbus OH 43215-2806

CARTER, PAMELA LYNN, former state attorney general; b. South Haven, Mich., Aug. 20, 1949; d. Roscoe Hollis and Dorothy Elizabeth (Hadley) Fanning; m. Michael Anthony Carter, Aug. 26, 1971; children: Michael Anthony Jr., Marcya Alicia. BA cum laude, U. Detroit, 1971; MSW, U. Mich., 1973; JD, Ind. U., 1984. Bar: Ind. 1984, U.S. Dist. Ct. (no. dist.) Ind. 1984, U.S. Dist. Ct. (so. dist.) Ind. 1984. Rsch. analyst, treatment dir. U. Mich. Sch. Pub. Health and

UAW, Detroit, 1973—75; exec. dir. Mental Health Ctr. for Women and Children, Detroit, 1975—77; consumer litigation atty. UAW-Gen. Motors Legal Svcs., Indpls., 1983—87; securities atty. Sec. of State, Indpls., 1987—89; Gov.'s exec. asst. for health and human svcs. Gov.'s Office, Indpls., 1989—91, dep. chief of staff to Gov., 1991—92; with Baker & Daniels, 1992—93; atty. gen. State of Ind., Indpls., 1993—96; ptnr. Johnson & Smith, 1996—97; v.p., gen. mgr. Europe, Mid. East & Africa Cummins Engine Co., Inc., Columbus, Ind., 1998—. Author (numerous poems). Active Jr. League, Indpls., Dem. Precinct, Indpls., Cath. Social Svcs., Indpls. Named Breakthrough Woman of the Year, 1989; named one of Outstanding Young Woman of America, 1977; recipient Outstanding Svc. award, Ind. Perinatal Assn., 1991, Cmty. Svc. Coun. Ctrl. Ind., 1991, Non-profl. Healthcare award, Family Health Conf. Bd. Dirs., 1991, award for excellence, Women of the Rainbow, 1991. Mem.: Ind. Bar Assn., Nat. Bar Assn., Coalition of 100 Black Women. Democrat. Avocations: gardening, hiking, travel, reading. Office: VP, Global Sales & Marketing Cummins Engine Co Inc 500 Jackson St Columbus IN 47201

CARTER, ROY ERNEST, JR., retired journalist, educator; b. Ulysses, Kans., Apr. 7, 1922; s. Roy Ernest and Inez (Anderson) C.; m. Ruby Maxine Rice, Mar. 28, 1948; children: Phyllis Diane, Patricia Inez, Susan Dolores. BA, Ft. Hays State U., 1948; MA, U. Minn., 1951; PhD, Stanford U., 1954; Prof. h.c., U. Chile, 1982. Reporter, editor, editorial writer various newspapers, 1942-48, 51; high sch. tchr. Hutchinson, Kans., 1948-50; assoc. prof., chmn. dept. journalism Ohio Wesleyan U., 1951-52; acting assoc. prof. journalism Stanford U., 1952-54; research prof. journalism, mem. Inst. Research in Social Sci. of U. N.C., 1954-58; prof. journalism, sociology and internat. relations U. Minn., 1958-90, prof. emeritus, 1990—, prof. ind. and distance learning. Lectr., Quito, Ecuador, 1961, Chile, Argentina, Uruguay, 1991; vis. prof. U. Chile, 1962-63, 82, U. Concepción, Chile, 1964, 66-68, 91, U. Costa Rica, 1971, 84, U. Pernambuco, Brazil, 1972, U. P.R., 1978-79, 86, Cath. U. Uruguay, 1987, U. del Salvador, Buenos Aires, 1989, Fla. Internat. U., 1992-96, U. Md., 1996-98; cons. to mktg., pub. opinion rsch. firms, internat. orgns. Author: North Carolina Press-Medical Study, 1957, (with R.O. Nafziger, D.M. White et al.) Introduction to Mass Communication Research, 1963; Assoc. editor of: Journalism, Quarterly, 1958-63; Contbr. articles to sci. jours. Recipient Kellogg Found. grant Stanford, 1952-53, sr. Fulbright-Hays award Chile, 1962-63, sr. Fulbright-Hays award Costa Rica, 1971, sr. Fulbright award Argentina, 1989, Social Sci. Research Council grants, 1962, 68; Rotary fellow, Uruguay, 1987 Fellow Am. Sociol. Assn.; mem. Assn. Edn. Journalism, World Assn. Pub. Opinion Research, Sigma Delta Chi, Phi Kappa Phi. Episcopalian. Achievements include research in Costa Rica, 1975, 91, El Salvador and Chile, 1976, P.R., 1979, Uruguay, 1982-89, 93—, Colombia, 1993, Peru, 1994. Office: U of Minn Journalism Sch 206 Church St SE Minneapolis MN 55455-0488

CARTER, STEVE, state attorney general; b. Lafayette, Ind., 1954; m. Marilyn Carter; 3 children. BA in Econs., Harvard U., 1976; JD, Ind. U., 1983, MBA. Chief city-county atty. Indpls.-Marion County; chief of staff Former Mayor Stephen Goldsmith Ind.; legis. counsel Ind. State Senate; chief of staff, agrl. asst. Ind. Lt. Gov. John Mutz; atty. gen. State of Ind., 2001—. Mem.: Nat. Assn. Attys. Gen. (pres., mem. Exec. Working Grp., Internal Rels. Com., Exec. Com., Fin. Com., bd. dirs., Mission Found. 2006—07). Republican. Office: Office Atty Gen Ind Govt Ctr S 5th Fl 402 W Washington St Indianapolis IN 46204

CARTER, VALERIE, food products executive; d. John and Katherine Daniels. BA in Bus. Adminstrn., Lincoln U., 1978; Masters Degree, Cardinal Stritch Coll., 1982. Mgmt. trainee Firstar Bank (formerly First Wis. Nat. Bank), 1978; auditor MGIC Investment Corp., 1981; co-founder V&J Foods, 1984, CEO. Recipient Sacajawea award for creativity, 1997; named Entrepreneur of Yr., Ernst & Young and Merrill Lynch, 1994. Mem. Milw. World Festival Inc. (pres. bd.). Office: 6933 W Brown Deer Rd Milwaukee WI 53223-2103

CARTER, WILLIAM H., chemicals executive; Ptnr. Price Waterhouse LLP, 1975—95; exec. v.p., CFO Borden Chemical Inc., Columbus, Ohio, 1995—2005; interim pres., CEO BCP Mgmt. (sub. of Borden), 2000; exec. v.p., CFO Hexion Specialty Chemicals (merger of Borden & RRP LLC), Columbus, Ohio, 2005—. Office: Hexion Specialty Chemicals 180 E Broad StFl 30 Columbus OH 43215

CARTIER, BRIAN EVANS, consumer products company executive; b. Providence, Apr. 12, 1950; s. Clarence Joseph and Mary Anna (Evans) C. BA, RI Coll., 1972; MEd, Springfield Coll., Mass., 1973. Exec. dir. Arthritis Found. Conn., Hartford, 1976-78, dep. exec. dir. N.Y. chpt. NYC, 1979; exec. dir. Found. for Chiropractic Edn. and Rsch., Arlington, Va., 1979-90, Nat. Ct. Reporters Assn., 1990-98; CEO Nat. Assn. Coll. Stores, Oberlin, Ohio, 1998—. Mem. Am. Mgmt. Assn. (cert. assn. exec.), Am. Soc. Assn. Execs., US C. of C. Republican. Roman Catholic. Office: NACS 500 E Lorain St Oberlin OH 44074-1238

CARTWRIGHT, CAROL ANN, retired academic administrator; b. Sioux City, Iowa, June 19, 1941; d. Carl Anton and Kathryn Marie (Weishapple) Becker; m. G. Phillip Cartwright, June 11, 1966; children: Catherine E., Stephen R., Susan D. BS in Early Childhood Edn., U. Wis., Whitewater, 1962; MEd in Spl. Edn., U. Pitts., 1965, PhD in Spl. Edn., Ednl. Rsch., 1968. From instr. to assoc. prof. Coll. Edn. Pa. State U., University Park, 1968-72, from assoc. prof. to prof., 1972-79, dean acad. affairs, 1981-84, dean undergrad. program, vice provost, 1984-88; vice chancellor acad. affairs U. Calif., Davis, 1988-91, prof. human devel., 1988-91; pres. Kent State U., Ohio, 1991—2006. Bd. dirs. First Energy Corp. (formerly Ohio Edison), Akron, 1992—, KeyCorp., Cleve., PolyOne Corp., The Davey Tree Expert Co., Kent; exec. bd. Nat. Coun. for Accreditation Tchr. Edn., 2002—05; chair NCAA Exec. Com., 2002-05; mem. N.E. Ohio Coun. Higher Edn., 1991-2006, Knight Commn. Intercollegiate Athletics, 2000-. Editorial bd. Topics in Early Childhood Special Education, 1982-88, Exceptional Education Quarterly, 1982-88. Pres., bd. dirs. Child Devel. Coun. of Center County, Title XX Day Care Contractor, 1977-80; bd. dirs. Center County United Way, State College, Pa., 1984-88, Urban League of Greater Cleve., 1997—; bd. mem. Davis (Calif.) Art Ctr., 1988-91, Davis Sci. Ctr., 1989-91; bd. dirs. Ohio divsn. Am. Cancer Soc., 1993-2000, nat. bd. dirs., 1993—; mem. nat. bd. First Ladies Libr.; bd. trustees Woodrow Wilson Internat. Ctr. for Scholars, 1999—; bd. dirs. Ctr. for Rsch. Librs., 2002—. Named to Ohio Women's Hall of Fame; recipient Disting. Alumni award, U. Wis.-Whitewater, U. Pittsburgh Sch. Edn., Clairol Mentor award, Women of Achievement award, YWCA of Greater Cleve., Franklin Delano Roosevelt award for Excellence, March of Dimes. Mem. AAUW, Am. Coun. Edn. (Commn. on Women in Higher Edn., 2003-), Am. Ednl. Rsch. Assn., Am. Assn. for Higher Edn., Nat. Assn. State Univs. and Land-Grant Colls., Coun. for Exceptional Children, the Greater Akron Chamber, Cleve. Tomorrow. Roman Catholic. Avocations: walking, reading, travel. Home: 1703 Woodway Rd Kent OH 44240-5917 E-mail: ccartwri@kent.edu.

CARTWRIGHT, JAMES WILLIAM (BILL CARTWRIGHT), professional basketball coach, retired professional basketball player; b. Lodi, Calif., July 30, 1957; m. Sheri Cartwright; children: Justin, Jason, James, Kristin. Student, U. San Francisco, MA in Orgnl. Devel. and Human Resources. Basketball player N.Y. Knicks, 1979—88, Chgo. Bulls, 1988—94, Seattle Supersonics, 1994—95, NBA World Championships; asst. coach Chgo. Bulls, 1996—2001, head coach, 2001—03; asst. coach New Jersey Nets, 2004—. Named One time NBA All-Star, 1980, 3 time All Am. Player of Yr., WCC's 50 Greatest Student-Athletes of All-Time; named to NBA Ea. Conf. All-Star Team, 1980; recipient NBA All-Rookie Team honors, 3 time West Coast Conf. Player of Yr. Achievements include Dons all-time leading scorer; helped the Bulls win 55 victories in each of his final five seasons in Chicago including the first back-to-back 60+ win seasons in Bulls history, 1990-92. Office: New Jersey Nets Continental Airlines Arena 50 Rte 120 East Rutherford NJ 07073

CARUS, ANDRE WOLFGANG, educational publishing firm executive; b. LaSalle, Ill., June 24, 1953; s. Milton Blouke and Marianne (Sondermann) C. MA, St. Andrews U., Scotland, 1977; PhD, Cambridge U., Eng., 1981; MBA, U. Chgo., 1990. Editor Ernst Klett Verlag, Stuttgart, Fed. Republic Germany, 1979-81; instr., asst. to dir. curriculum lab. sch. U. Bielefeld (Fed. Republic Germany), 1981-82; project dir. reading Open Ct. Pub. Co., Peru, Ill., 1983-85, dir. reading, 1985-86, v.p., gen. mgr., 1986-88, pres., 1988-90; pres., chief operating officer Carus Pub. Co., Chgo., 1990—, bd. dirs., chmn. Mem. Am. Ednl. Rsch. Assn., Nat. Coun. for the Social Studies, Nat. Coun. Tchrs. of Math., Assn. for Supervision and Curriculum Devel., Am. Econ. Assn., Univ. Club Chgo., Union League Club Chgo. Office: Open Court Pub Co 315 5th St Peru IL 61354-2859

CARUS, MILTON BLOUKE, children's periodicals publisher; b. Chgo., June 15, 1927; s. Edward H. and Dorothy (Blouke) C.; m. Marianne Sondermann, Mar. 3, 1951; children: Andre, Christine, Inga. BS in Elec. Engring, Calif. Inst. Tech., 1949; postgrad. in Chemistry, U. Freiburg, Germany, 1949-51; postgrad., Sorbonne U., Paris, 1951. Devel. engr. Carus Chem. Co., Inc., LaSalle, Ill., 1951—55, asst. gen. mgr., 1955—61, exec. v.p., 1961—64, chmn., CEO, 1964—90, Carus Corp., Peru, 1990—; editor Open Ct. Pub. Co., 1962—67, pub., pres., 1967—88, pub., 1988—89, sr. cons., 1989—; pub. Cricket mag., 1973—89; sr. cons. Cricket mag. group, 1989—2000, chmn., 2000—. Treas. Bookbird Internat. Bd. Books Young People, 1994-1996. Chmn. Ill. Valley Cmty. Coll. Com., 1965-67; pres. Internat. Baccalaureat N.Am. Inc., 1977, chmn., 1980-89; mem. IBO Coun., Geneva, 1977-94; co-trustee Hegeler Inst., 1968-89, chmn., 1989-; mem. employment and tng. com. U.S. Chamber, 1981-85; mem. Nat. Coun. on Ednl. Rsch. Nat. Inst. Edn., Dept. Edn., 1982-85, vice chmn., 1983-85; trustee Parliament of World's Religious, 1988—; mem. Ill. Gov.'s Task Force on Sch.-to-Work, 1994-96. Mem. Ill. Valley Indsl. Assn. (pres. 1970—), Chem. Mfrs. Assn. (dir. 1977-80), Ill. Mfrs. Assn. (dir. 1972-77, 1988-99, chmn. edn. com. 1988—), LaSalle County Hist. Soc. (dir. 1979-85), Phila Soc., Ill. State C. of C. (edn. com. 1973-75). Avocations: reading, travel, music, gardening, languages. Office: Carus Corp Hdqrs 315 5th St Peru IL 61354-2859 Office Phone: 815-224-6674. Business E-Mail: mbcarus@caruschem.com.

CARUSO, FRED, plastics manufacturing company executive; Formerly CEO, pres. Comml. Fin. Svcs., Inc., Tulsa, Okla.; treas. Transilwrap Co., Inc., Franklin Park, Ill. Office: Transilwrap Co Inc 9201 Belmont Ave Franklin Park IL 60131

CASAD, ROBERT CLAIR, legal educator; b. Council Grove, Kans., Dec. 8, 1929; s. Clair L. and Eula Imogene (Compton) C.; m. Sally Ann McKeighan, Aug. 20, 1955; children: Benjamin Nathan, Joseph Story, Robert Clair, Madeleine Imogene. AB, U. Kans., 1950, MA, 1952; JD with honors, U. Mich., 1957; SJD, Harvard U., 1979. Bar: Kans. 1957, Minn. 1958, U.S. Dist. Ct. Kans. 1957; U.S. Ct. Appeals (10th cir.) 1985. Instr. law U. Mich., Ann Arbor, 1957-58; assoc. firm Streater & Murphy, Winona, Minn., 1958-59; asst. prof. law U. Kans., Lawrence, 1959-62, assoc. prof., 1962-64, prof., 1964-81, John H. and John M. Kane prof. law, 1981-97; John H. and John M. Kane prof. law emeritus, 1997. Vis. prof. UCLA, 1969—70, U. Ill., 1973—74, U. Calif., Hastings, 1979—80, U. Colo., 1982, U. Vienna, 1986, U. Mich., 1986, U. Valladolid, 1988, Chuo U., 1992, U. Salamanca, 1995, Emory U., 2001—02. Author: Jurisdiction and Forum Selection, 1988, 2nd edit., 1999, Jurisdiction in Civil Actions, 1983, 2d edit., 1991, (with Richman) 3d edit., 1998, Expropriation Procedures in Central America and Panama, 1975, (with others) Kansas Appellate Practice, 1978, Civil Judgment Recognition and the Integration of Multiple State Associations, 1982, Res Judicata in a Nutshell, 1976; (with Fink and Simon) Civil Procedure: Cases and Materials, 2d edit., 1989, (with Gard) Kansas Code of Civil Procedure Annotated, 4th edit., 2003, (with Clermont) Res Judicata: A Handbook on its Theory, Doctrine and Practice, 2001; Kans. Civil Jury Instruction Handbook, 2007; contbr. numerous articles to legal jours. Mem. civil code adv. com. Kans. Jud. Coun. 1st lt. USAF, 1952-53. Recipient Coblentz prize Sch. Law, U. Mich., 1957, Rice prize U. Kans. Law Sch., 1976, 83, 84, 88, 89, medal Dana Fund for Internat. and Comparative Legal Studies, 1981, Balfour Jeffrey Rsch. prize U. Kans., 1984; Ford fellow, 1965-66, fellow in law Harvard U., 1965-66, OAS fellow, 1976, NEH fellow, summer 1978; grantee Dana Fund for Internat. and Comparative Legal Studies. Mem. Am. Law Inst., ABA, Kans. Bar Assn., Order of Coif. Democrat. Home: 1130 Emery Rd Lawrence KS 66044-2515 Personal E-mail: casad@sunflower.com. Business E-Mail: casad@ku.edu.

CASALE, THOMAS BRUCE, medical educator; b. Chgo., Apr. 21, 1951; m. Jean M. Casale; 1 son, Jeffrey G. BS cum laude, U. Ill., 1973; MD, Chgo. Med. Sch., 1977. Diplomate Am. Bd. Internal Medicine, Am. Bd. Allergy and Immunology. Resident in internal medicine Baylor Coll. Medicine, Houston, 1977-80; med. staff fellow lab. clin. investigation NIAID, NIH, Bethesda, Md., 1980-84; from asst. prof. to prof. internal medicine U. Iowa, Iowa City, 1984-94, prof. internal medicine, 1994-96; dir. Nebr. Med. Rsch. Inst., 1996-99; adj. prof. pediatrics Coll. Medicine U. Nebr., 1996—; clin. prof. medicine Creighton U., Omaha, 1997-99, prof., assoc. chair dept. medicine, dir. clin. rsch., 1999—, chief allergy/immunology, 2001—. Chief med. staff fellow lab. clin. investigation, NIAID, NIH, Bethesda, 1982-83; attending physician VA Med. Ctr., Iowa City, 1984-96, staff physician, 1986-96, clin. investigator, 1991-96; asst. dir. tchg. allergy/immunology divsn. dept. internal medicine U. Iowa, Iowa City, 1989-92, acting dir., 1992, dir., 1993-96, faculty interdisciplinary immunology grad. degree program U. Iowa, 1993-96; bd. dirs. Am. Bd. Allergy and Immunology, Am. Acad. Allergy, Asthma and Immunology; reviewer over 15 profl. and sci. jours. Contbr. over 200 articles to profl. publs.; mem. editl. bd. Jour. Allergy Clin. Immunology, 1988-93, clin. asthma revs., 1996-99, Allergy & Clinical Immunology Internat., 1997-2002, Jour. World Allergy Org., 2003—; editor Respiratory Digest, 1999—, Ann. Allergy, Asthma & Immunology, 1999—. Mem. asthma technical adv. group Am. Lung Assn., 1989-96. Lt. commdr. USPHS, 1980-83, USPHS Res., 1983—. Recipient Dr. John J. Sheinin Rsch. award Chgo. Med. Sch., 1977, Clin. Investigator VA, 1991-96, Am. Soc. Clin. Investigation, 1992; grantee NIH, 1986-91, 87-90, 92-93, 93-94, VA Merit Rev., 1986-89, 89-92, 92-96, Environ. Health Sci. Core Ctr., 1990-96, Novartis Pharms., 1997—, Sepracor, Inc., 1997, Immune Tolerance etwork, 2003—, others. Fellow ACP, Am. Acad. Allergy Immunology (cutaneous allergy com. 1985-90, postgrad. edn. com. 1988-91, chmn. 1989-90, program com. dermatologic diseases sect. 1988-93, sec. 1989-90, vice chmn. 1990-91, chmn. 1991-92, prof. edn. coun. 1998—, chair 1998—, sec. 1993-95, vice chair 1995—, chmn. bronchoalveolar lavage com. 1991-95, 98—, others), Am. Coll. Allergy Immunology (profl. allergy/immunology edn. com. 1989-94)); mem. Am. Acad. Allergy Asthma Immunology (bd. dirs. 2001—, sec., treas. 2004—, pres.-elect 2006-07, pres. 2007-08, past pres. 2008-), Am. Fedn. Clin. Rsch., Am. Thoracic Soc. (sec. allergy immunology and inflammation scientific assembly 1990-91, chair-elect 1991-93, chair program com. 1992-93, chair 1993-95, long-range planning and policy com. sci. assembly on allergy immunology and inflammation 1991-96, sci. conf. com. 1991-93, bd. dirs. 1993-95, chair asthma adv. com. 1995-99), Am. Bd. Allergy and Immunology (bd. dirs. 1999—, co-chmn. 2003-04, chmn. 2005-), Iowa Soc. Allergy Immunology (pres. 1987-89), Am. Assn. Immunologists, Midwest Sect. Am. Fedn. Clin. Rsch., Ctrl. Soc. Clin. Rsch., Am. Soc. Clin. Invest., Am. Lung Assn. (mem. rsch. coordinating com. 1996-99), European Respiratory Soc. Office: Creighton U Dept Medicine 601 N 30th St Ste 5850 Omaha NE 68131-2137 Office Fax: 402-280-4115. Business E-Mail: tbcasale@creighton.edu.

CASCORBI, HELMUT FREIMUND, anesthesiologist, educator; b. Berlin, July 13, 1933; came to U.S., 1958; s. Gisbert and Isa (Ruckert) C.; m. Ann M. Morgan, Aug. 7, 1965; children: Alicia Maria, Kathryn Ann. MD, U. Munich, W. Ger., 1957; PhD, U. Md., 1962. Prof., chmn. dept. anesthesiology Case Western Res. U., Cleve., 1980-2000. Mem. Am. Soc. Anesthesiologists, AMA, Assn. Univ. Anesthetists, Am. Soc. Pharmacology and Exptl. Therapeutics Home: 2844 Fairmount Blvd Cleveland OH 44118-4059 Office: Univ Hosps Cleve 11100 Euclid Ave Cleveland OH 44106-1736 E-mail: helmut.cascorbi@uhhs.com.

CASE, DONNI MARIE, investment company executive, consultant; b. Chgo., Feb. 20, 1948; d. Donald Milton and Felecia Virginia Schuette; m. Lawrence Lee Hewitt, Apr. 20, 1996. BA in Econs., U. Ill., 1970. Pres. Fin. Rels. Bd., Chgo., 1972—2005. Bd. dirs. Inst. Bus. and Profl. Ethics Depaul U. Mem.: Kaplan U., Grad. Sch. Bus., Chicago Network (bd. mem.). Home: 2417 N Geneva Ter Chicago IL 60614-5914 E-mail: donni.case@comcast.net.

CASE, GREGORY C., insurance company executive; b. 1962; m. Mamie Case. BA summa cum laude, Kans. State U., 1985; MBA, Harvard U., 1989. With Fed. Reserve Bank Kansas City; investment banker Piper, Jaffray and Hopwood; ptnr., head fin. svc. & global ins. practices McKinsey & Co., 1988—2005; pres., CEO Aon Corp., Chgo., 2005—. Bd. dir. Discover Fin. Services, 2007—. Mem.: Economic Club of Chgo., Fin. Services Roundtable, Internat. Ins. Society, Inc. Office: Aon Corporation 200 E Randolph St Chicago IL 60601*

CASE, KAREN ANN, lawyer; b. Milw., Apr. 7, 1944; d. Alfred F. and Hilda M. (Tomich) Case. BS, Marquette U., 1963, JD, 1966; LLM, NYU, 1973. Bar: Wis. 1966, U.S. Ct. Claims 1973, U.S. Tax Ct. 1973. Ptnr. Meldman, Case & Weine, Milw., 1973-85, Meldman, Case & Weine divsn. Mulcahy & Wherry, S.C., 1985-87; Sec. of Revenue State of Wis., 1987-88; ptnr. Case & Drinka, S.C., Milw., 1989-91, Case, Drinka & Diel, S.C., Milw., 1991-97, CoVac, 1997—. Lectr. U. Wis., Milw., 1974-78; guest lectr. Marquette U. Law Sch., 1975-78; dir. WBBC, 1998—. Contbr. articles to legal jours. Mem. gov.'s Commn. on Taliesin, 1988, gov.'s Econ. Adv. Commn., 1989-91, pres.'s coun. Alverno Coll., 1988-94, nat. coun., 1998-2000; bd. dirs. WBCC, 1998—. Fellow Wis. Bar Found. (dir. 1977-90, treas. 1980-90); mem. ABA, Milw. Assn. Women Lawyers (founding mem., bd. dirs. 1975-78, 81-82), Milw. Bar Assn. (bd. dirs. 1985-87, law office mgmt. chair 1992-93), State Bar Wis. (bd. govs. 1981-85, 87-90, dir. taxation sect. 1981-87, vice chmn. 1986-87, 90-91, chmn. 1991-92), Am. Acad. Matrimonial Lawyers (bd. dirs. 1988-90), Nat. Assn. Women Lawyers (Wis. del. 1982-83), Milw. Rose Soc. (pres. 1981, dir. 1981-83), Friends of Boerner Bot. Gardens (founding mem., pres. 1984-90), Profl. Dimensions Club (dir. 1985-87), Tempo Club (sec. 1984-85). Office: CoVac 9803 W Meadow Park Dr Hales Corners WI 53130-2261 Home Phone: 941-387-4352; Office Phone: 414-425-5672.

CASE-SCHMIDT, MARY E., pathologist, educator; b. Jefferson City, Mo., Feb. 27, 1943; BA, U. Mo., 1965; MD, St. Louis U. Sch. Medicine, 1969. Resident in pathology St. Louis U. Sch. Medicine, St. Louis, 1969—71, asst. in pathology, 1969—73; postdoctoral fellow Nat. Inst. Neurol. Disease and Stroke, St. Louis, 1971—72; resident in neuropathology St. Louis U. Sch. Medicine, 1972—73, instr. in pathology, 1973—75; vis. asst. prof. neuropathology U. Mo., Sch. Medicine, Columbia, Mo., 1975—77; asst. prof. pathology St. Louis U. Sch. Medicine, 1975—81; cons. neuropathology St. Luke's Hosp., East and West, 1973—77; asst. med. examiner St. Louis County, 1975—88, City of St. Louis, 1977—80; assoc. prof. pathology St. Louis U. Sch. Medicine, 1981—99; dep. chief med. examiner City of St. Louis, 1980—85; cons. neuropathology St. John's Mercy Hosp., St. Louis, 1973—88; spl. projects, divsn. forensic and environ. pathology St. Louis U. Sch. Medicine, 1985—; chief med. examiner St. Charles County, 1986—, St. Louis County, 1988—, Jefferson County, 1992—, Franklin County, 1993—; prof. pathology St. Louis U. Health Scis. Ctr., 1999—, co-dir., divsn. forensic pathology, 1996—. Dean's adv. bd. St. Louis U., 2000—; bd. dirs. Greater St. Louis Region Critical Incident Stress Mgmt. Team, 1995—; mem. Nat. Medicolegal Rev. Panel for Devel. Guidelines for Death Invest. for Nat. Inst. Justice, 1996—. Recipient Spl. Leadership award for Professions, Meto. St. Louis YWCA, 1990, Norman Westbrook "Hall of Fame" award, Mo. Police Juvenile Officers Assn., 1992, Recognition award "Teen Drinking and Driving", St. Louis Metro. Med. Soc., 2001, Spl. Recognition award, St. Charles Crime Stoppers, 2002. Fellow: Am. Acad. Forensic Sci. (ethics com. 2001—), Am. Soc. Clin. Pathology, Coll. Am. Pathologists; mem.: AMA, Nat. Assn. Med. Examiner (bd. dir. 2000—, exec. com. 2001—), Am. Assn. Neuropathologists, Internat. Acad. Pathology, St. Louis Path. Soc., St. Louis Metro. Med. Soc., Am. Profl. Soc. on Abuse of Children, Mo. State Med. Assn., Mo. Network of Cert. Pathologists for Child Death Autopsies (chmn. 1996—), Am. Journal Forensic Medicine and Pathology. Office: St Louis U Sch Medicine Dept Pathology 1402 S Grand Saint Louis MO 63104-1004

CASEY, JOHN ALEXANDER, lawyer; b. Wisconsin Rapids, Wis., Apr. 7, 1945; s. Samuel Alexander and Ardean A. AB, Stanford U., 1967; JD, U. Mich., 1970. Ptnr. Quarles & Brady, Milw., 1970—. Office: Quarles & Brady 411 E Wisconsin Ave Ste 2040 Milwaukee WI 53202-4497 Office Phone: 414-277-5383. Business E-Mail: jac@quarles.com.

CASEY, KENNETH LYMAN, neurologist; b. Ogden, Utah, Apr. 16, 1935; s. Kenneth Lafayette and Lyzena (Payne) C.; m. Jean Louise Madsen, June 21, 1958; children— Tena Jeanette, Kenneth Lyman, Teresa Louise. BA, Whitman Coll., Walla Walla, Wash., 1957; MD with honors, U. Wash., Seattle, 1961. Diplomate Am. Bd. Neurology and Psychiatry. Intern in medicine Cornell U. Med. Center-N.Y. Hosp., 1961-62; USPHS officer lab. neurophysiology NIMH, 1962-64; fellow in psychology McGill U., Montreal, Que., Canada, 1964-66; mem. faculty U. Mich. Med. Sch., Ann Arbor, 1966—, prof. neurology and physiology, 1978—2005, prof. emeritus neurology, prof. emeritus molecular and integrative physiology, 2005—; resident in neurology U. Mich Hosp., 1971-74; chief neurology svc. VA Med. Center, Ann Arbor, 1979—2002, cons. in neurology, 2002—. Sci. adv. com. Santa Fe Neurol. Inst., 1984—. Assoc. editor Clin. Jour. Pain, 1984—, Pain, 1991—; editor-in-chief Am. Pain Soc. Jour. Pain Forum, 1991-99; contbr. articles to profl. jours., chpts. to books. Grantee, NIH, 1966—; Spl. fellow, 1964—66, Bristol-Myers rsch. grantee, 1988—93. Fellow: Am. Acad. Neurology; mem.: Internat. Assn. Study Pain (hon. life mem.), Wayne County Med. Soc. (Rhoades lectr. and medalist 2002), Am. Pain Soc. (pres. 1984—85, F.W.L. Kerr Basic Sci. Rsch. award and lecture 1998, named hon. life mem. 2005), Soc. Neurosci., Am. Neurol. Assn., Am. Acad. Neurology, Am. Physiol. Soc., Alpha Omega Alpha (J.J. Bonica disting. lectr. and award 1991), Sigma Xi, Phi Beta Kappa. Unitarian Universalist. Achievements include named lectureship established in his honor by Pfizer Co. in 2002. Home: 2775 Heatherway St Ann Arbor MI 48104-2852 Office: VA Med Ctr Neurology Svc 2215 Fuller Rd Ann Arbor MI 48105-2300 Business E-Mail: kencasey@umich.edu.

CASILLAS, FRANK C., former state agency administrator; Assst. U.S. sec. labor Ronald Reagan, Washington; dir. financial institional dept. Financial Institutions Dept., Chgo., 1994—. Office: Financial Institutions Dept 100 W Randolph St Ste 15-700 Chicago IL 60601-3234

CASKEY, HAROLD LEROY, state legislator; b. Hume, Mo., Jan. 3, 1938; s. James Alfred and Edith Irnen (Anderson) C.; m. Kay Head, 1974; 1 child, Kyle James. AB, Ctrl. Mo. State U., 1960; JD, U. Mo., Columbia, 1963. Pros. atty. Bates County, 1967-72; city atty. Butler, Mo., 1973-76; pvt. practice; mem. from dist. 31 Mo. Senate, 1977—, chmn. ethics com., civil and criminal jurisprudence com., vice chmn. judiciary com. Asst. prof. NE Mo. State U., 1975-76. Mem. Mo. Bar Assn., Am. Judicature Soc., Fellowship Christian Politicians, Am. Criminal Justice Educators, Order Coif, Acacia, Phi Alpha Delta, Kappa Mu Epsilon, Alpha Phi Sigma. Democrat. Baptist. Office: Rm 320 State Capitol Building Jefferson City MO 65101-1556 also: PO Box 45 Butler MO 64730-0045

CASON, MARILYNN JEAN, academic administrator, lawyer; b. Denver, May 18, 1943; d. Eugene Martin and Evelyn Lucille (Clark) C.; married. BA in Polit. Sci., Stanford U., 1965; JD, U. Mich., 1969; MBA, Roosevelt U., 1977. Bar: Colo. 1969, Ill. 1973. Assoc. Dawson, Nagel, Sherman & Howard, Denver, 1969-73; atty. Kraft, Inc., Glenview, Ill., 1973-75; corp. counsel Johnson Products Co., Inc., Chgo., 1975-86, v.p., 1977-86, mng. dir. Lagos, Nigeria, 1980-83, v.p. internat. Chgo., 1986-88; v.p., gen. counsel DeVry, Inc., Chgo., 1989-96, sr. v.p. gen. counsel, corp. sec., 1996—. Trustee Arthritis Found., Atlanta, 1993—96, Chgo. Symphony Orch., 1997—2003; bd. dirs. Ill. chpt. Arthritis Found., Chgo., 1979—, chmn., 1991—93; bd. dirs. Internat. House, Chgo., 1986—92, Interfaith House, Chgo., 1996—2002, Ill. Humanities Coun., Chgo., 1987—96, chmn., 1993—96; bd. dirs. Lit. for All of Us, 1997—, chmn., 2002—. Mem. ABA, at. Bar Assn., Cook County Bar Assn. (pres. cmty. law project 1986-88), Stanford Club (Chgo., pres. 1985-87). Office: DeVry Inc 1 Tower Ln Ste 1000 Oakbrook Terrace IL 60181-4663 Home: 2333 Central St Apt 405 Evanston IL 60201-1475 Office Phone: 630-574-1901. Business E-Mail: mcason@devry.com.

CASPAR, JOHN M., manufacturing executive; BS, Drexel Inst. Tech.; MBA, Okla. State U. Exec. v.p. internat., CFO Mitek, Inc., St. Louis, 1987-94; v.p., CFO Petrolite Corp., St. Louis; fin. cons.; sr. v.p. fin., CFO DT Industries, Inc., Springfield, Mo., 2001—. Office: Dt Industries Inc 313 Mound St Dayton OH 45402-8370

CASPER, RICHARD HENRY, lawyer; b. Chgo., Nov. 4, 1950; s. Edson Lee and Dorothy Ellen (Klemp) C.; m. Betty Gene Ward, Aug. 26, 1972; children: Terrance, Laura, Russell, Jeremy. AB, Bowdoin Coll., 1972; JD, Northwestern U., 1975. Bar: Wis. 1975, U.S. Dist. Ct. (ea. dist.) Wis. 1975. Assoc. Foley & Lardner LLP, Milw., 1975-82, ptnr., 1982—. Pres. Milw. Chamber Orchestra, 1988—90; bd. dirs. Florentine Opera Co., 1998—. Recipient Order of Coif,

1975; scholar James Bowdoin, Bowdoin Coll., 1972. Mem.: Milw. Bar Assn., Mem. Wis. Bar Assn. Office: Foley & Lardner LLP 777 E Wisconsin Ave Milwaukee WI 53202-5367 Office Phone: 414-297-5612. Business E-Mail: rcasper@foley.com.

CASS, EDWARD ROBERTS (PETER CASS), hotel and travel marketing professional; b. La Porte, Ind., Nov. 21, 1941; s. Edward Smith and Shirley (Mazur) C.; m. Marilyn Brooks, Apr. 1, 1967; children: Edward Brooks Cass, Alexander Brooks Cass. AB in History, Hamilton Coll., 1964; MBA in Mktg./Fin., Syracuse U., 1970. Dir. mktg., gen. sales mgr. Mohawk Airlines Inc., NYC, 1964-72; sr. v.p., gen. mgr. The Travel Industry Assn. Am., Washington, 1972-78; gen. mgr., COO Tri-Met, Oreg. and Wash., 1978-81; v.p. unregulated activities Pacific Telecom, subsidiary of Pacificorp, Vancouver, Wash., 1982-83; pres., founder Transax Data Corp., Falls Church, Va., 1983-85; pres., CEO Transax Data divsn. of Jour. of Commerce Knight-Ridder Inc., Bridgewater, N.J., 1985-94, Preferred Hotels & Resorts Worldwide, Chgo., 1994—. Office: IndeCorp Corp 311 S Wacker Dr Ste 1900 Chicago IL 60606-6676 Home: 3746 N Yacht Ter Beverly Hills FL 34465-4462

CASSELL, SAMUEL JAMES, professional basketball player; b. Balt., Nov. 18, 1969; Grad., Dunbar H.S., Balt., San Jacinto Coll., 1993. Basketball player Houston Rockets, 1994-96, Pheonix Suns, 1996, Dallas Mavericks, 1996-97, NJ Nets, East Rutherford, 1997-99, Milw. Bucks, 1998—2005, LA Clippers, 2005—08, Boston Celtics, 2008—. Mem. Houston Rockets NBA championship teams, 1994, 95; won Fleer ShootAround, 1996 All-Star Weekend, San Antonio, Tex. Office: Boston Celtics 226 Causeway St 4th Fl Boston MA 02114

CASSENS WEISS, DEBRA SUE, professional association administrator, publishing executive; b. Chgo., Nov. 2, 1956; d. Kenneth Henry and Geraldine Cassens; m. Dean J. Moss, Aug. 9, 1981 (div. 1996); m. David Weiss, Aug. 23, 2003. BA in English, U. Ill., 1978; JD, DePaul U., 1983. Bar: Ill. Newscaster WMRO, WAUR Radio, Aurora, Ill., 1979-81; reporter, editor City News Bur., Chgo., 1984-85; consumer news rschr. WMAQ-TV News, Chgo., 1985-86; reporter ABA Jour., Chgo., 1986—, asst. mng. editor to mng. editor, sr. writer. Office: ABA Jour 321 N Clark St Chicago IL 60610 Home: Apt 408 500 E Saint Charles Rd Lombard IL 60148 E-mail: weissd@staff.abanet.org.

CASSIDY, JOHN HAROLD, lawyer; b. St. Louis, June 18, 1925; s. John Harold and Jennie (Phillips) C.; m. Marjorie Blair, Nov. 26, 1947; children: Patricia, John, Brian. AB, Washington U., 1949, JD, 1951. Bar: Mo. 1951, U.S. Dist. Ct. (ea. dist.) Mo. 1951, U.S. Ct. Appeals (8th crct.) 1951, U.S. Supreme Ct. 1955. Atty. U.S. Govt., St. Louis, 1951-56; pvt. practice St. Louis, 1956-59; atty. Crown Zellerbach Corp., San Francisco, 1959-61, Ralston Purina Co., St. Louis, 1961-89, v.p., 1975-85, v.p., sec., sr. counsel, 1985-89. Served with U.S. Mcht. Marine, 1943-45. Mem.: ABA, Am. Soc. Corp. Secs., St. Louis Bar Assn., Mo. Bar Assn. Republican.

CASSINELLI, JOSEPH PATRICK, astronomy educator; b. Cin., Aug. 23, 1940; s. Herbert John and Louise Margaret (Schlottman) C.; m. Mary LeFever; children: Joseph Michael, Carolyn Marie, Mary Kathleen. BS in Physics, Xavier U., 1962; MS in Physics, U. Ariz., 1965; PhD in Astronomy, U. Wash., 1970. Research asst. Kitt Peak at. Obs., Tucson, 1963-65; research engr. Boeing Co., Seattle, 1965-66; postdoctoral research assoc. Joint Inst. for Lab. Astrophysics, Boulder, Colo., 1970-72; postdoctoral fellow U. Wis., Madison, 1972-73, asst. prof., 1973-77, assoc. prof., 1977-81, prof., 1981—2005, emeritus prof., 2005—, chmn. astronomy dept., 1986-89. Vis. scientist Space Astronomy Lab., Utrecht, the Netherlands, 1975-76, Space Telescope Sci. Inst., 1991, High Altitude Obs., 1998; Donders chair U. Utrecht, 1985; sr. vis. fellow dept. physics and astronomy U. Glasgow, Scotland, 1998, 2000. Co-author: Introduction to Stellar Winds, 1999. Langley Abbot research fellow Harvard Smithsonian Ctr. for Astrophysics, 1981; Fulbright research fellow Sonnenborgh Obs., 1986. Mem. Am. Astron. Soc., Internat. Astron. Union. Roman Catholic. Home: 1520 Chandler St Madison WI 53711-2210 Office: U Wis Astronomy Dept 475 N Charter St Madison WI 53706-1582 Business E-Mail: cassinelli@astro.wisc.edu.

CASTELE, THEODORE JOHN, radiologist; b. New Castle, Pa., Feb. 1, 1928; s. Theodore Robert and Anne Mercedes (McNavish) C.; m. Jean Marie Willse, Oct. 20, 1951; children: Robert, Ann Marie, Richard, Mary Kathryn, Thomas, Daniel, John. BS, Case Western Res. U., 1951, MD, 1957. Diplomate Am. Bd. Radiology, 1962. Intern then resident U. Hosps. Cleve., 1957-61, fellow, 1961-62; dir. of radiology Luth. Med. Ctr., Cleve., 1968-75, 77-89, chief of staff, 1975-81; pres. Med. Ctr. Radiologists, Inc., Cleve., 1978-95; v.p. med. and copr. devel. Health Cleve. Inc., 1989-91; chmn. Lakeshore Radiology Inc., Cleve., 1991-96, emeritus chmn., 1996—. Med. editor sta. WEWS-TV-ABC, Cleve., 1975-99; chmn. bd. Med. Cons. Imaging Co., Cleve., 1981-97; asst. clin. prof. radiology Case Western Res. U., chmn. dean's tech. coun. Sch. Medicine, 1996—, chmn. vis. com. Cleve. Health Scis. Libr., chmn. campaign for future of acad. medicine, 1998—. Exec. editor Prime mag., 2000—. Chmn. Southwestern dist. Greater Cleve. coun. Boy Scouts Am., 1969, 73; mem. bd. med. cons. Cleve. Police Dept., pres., 1988-90; trustee Comty. Dialysis Ctr., chmn. 1997-99, chmn. emeritus, 2000—; active Luth. Med. Ctr. Found., chmn. bd. trustees, 1969-75, pres., 1988-90; trustee Case Western Res. U., Blue Cross/Blue Shield Ohio, Greater Cleve. Hosp. Assn., Fairview Health, Luth. Med. Ctr., 1975-80, Fairview Hosp. Found.; bd. trustees Fairview Luth. Hosp. Found., 1999—, No. Ohio Lung Assn.; chmn. Health Mus. Cleve., 1996—, Humility of Mary Healthcare Sys., 1995-98; dir. Coun. Pub. Reps. for NIH, 1999-2001. With USN, 1946-47. Recipient Order of Merit award Boy Scouts Am., 1971, Silver Beaver award, 1972, Nat. Disting. Eagle Scout award, 1984, Frances Payne Bolton Sch. of Nursing Disting. Svc. award, 1990, Outstanding Philanthropist award Nat. Soc. of Fundraising Execs., 1991, Alumnus of the Yr. award Dept. Radiology of Case Western Res. U., 1996, LMC Found. Women's Bd. award, 1996, Luth. Hosp. award Fairview Health Sys. Bd., 1996, Midwest Nursing Rsch. Soc. Media award, 1998, Lamplighter Humanitarian award 2001; named Knight of the Equestrian, Order of the Holy Sepulchre of Jerusalem, 1993—; recipient Magis award St. Ignatius H.S.; named to Med. Hall of Fame, Case Western Res. U., Cleve. Mag., 1999, o. Ohio Italian-Am. Found., 1999. Fellow Am. Coll. Radiology; mem. AMA (Physician Spkr. Gold award 1978, 80, Silver 1979, Bronze 1978, Benjamin Rush award 1989, Golden Achievement award Golden Age Ctrs., 1996, chmn. Ohio del. 1987-96), Ohio State Med. Assn. (5th dist. councilor 1977-79, Spl. award 1979, Disting. Svc. award 1997), Cleve. Radiol. Soc. (pres. 1969-70), Cleve. Med. Libr. Assn. (pres. 1996, 97-98), Case Western Res. U. Med. Alumni Assn. (pres. 1971-72, 91-92, Disting. Svc. award 1987, Spl. Trustees award 1997, Univ. medal 1998), Cleve. Acad. Medicine (pres. 1974-75, Disting. Mem. award 1990, Disting. Svc. award 1984, Spl. Honor award and portrait 1998), Ohio State Radiol. Soc. (Silver award 1990). Home: 18869 Canyon Rd Cleveland OH 44126-1703 Office: Case Western Reserve Univ Sch Medicine Cleveland OH 44106

CASTELLINA, DANIEL J., financial executive; Degree in Acctg., U. Notre Dame; MBA, Xavier U. CPA, Ohio. With Deloitte & Touche; asst. treas. E.W. Scripps Co., Cin., 1971-75, treas.-sec., 1975-79, v.p., contr., 1979-85, sr. v.p. fin. and adminstrn., 1986—. Trustee Greater Cin. for Econ. Edn., Gradison Growth Trust. Officer U.S. Army, 1962-64. Mem. AICPA, Fin. Execs. Inst., Internat. Newspaper Fin. Execs., Ohio Soc. CPAs.

CASTELLINO, FRANCIS JOSEPH, university dean; b. Pittston, Pa., Mar. 7, 1943; s. Joseph Samuel and Evelyn Bonita C.; m. Mary Margaret Fabiny, June 5, 1965; children— Kimberly Ann, Michael Joseph, Anthony Francis. BS, U. Scranton, 1964; MS, U. Iowa, 1966, PhD in Biochemistry, 1968; LLD, U. Scranton, 1983; DSc (hon.), U. Waterloo, Ont., Can., 1994. Postdoctoral fellow Duke U., Durham, N.C., 1968-70; mem. faculty dept. chemistry & biochemistry U. Notre Dame, Ind., 1970—, prof., 1977—; dean U. Notre Dame (Coll. Sci.), 1979—2002. Contbr. articles to profl. jours. NIH fellow, 395201968-70 Fellow N.Y. Acad. Scis., AAAS; mem. Am. Heart Assn., Am. Chem. Soc., Am. Soc. Biol. Chemistry. Roman Catholic. Office: Univ Notre Damei Dept Chemistry & Biochemistry 256 Nieuwland Sci Hall otre Dame IN 46556-5670

CASTILLO, RUBEN, federal judge; b. Chgo., 1954; BA, Loyola U., 1976; JD, Northwestern U., 1979. Bar: Ill. 1979. Assoc. Jenner & Block, Chgo., 1979—84; asst. US atty. (No. dist.) Ill. US Dept. Justice, 1984—88; regional counsel Mexican Am. Legal Def. & Edn. Fund, Chgo., 1988—91; ptnr. Kirkland & Ellis, Chgo., 1991-93; judge US Dist. Ct. (no. dist.) Ill., 1994—. Adj. prof. Northwestern U., 1988—; vice chair, US Sentencing Commn., 1999-. Mem. ABA, Latin Am. Bar Assn., Chgo. Bar Found., Chgo. Coun. Lawyers (v.p. 1991-93). Office: U S Courthouse 2378 Dirksen Bldg 219 S Dearborn St Chicago IL 60604-1702

CASTLE, HOWARD BLAINE, retired religious organization administrator; b. Toledo, July 15, 1935; s. Russell Wesley and Letha Belle (Hobbs) C.; m. Patricia Ann Haverty, Aug. 12, 1957; 1 child Kevin Blaine. AB, Marion Coll., 1958; postgrad., Valparaiso U., 1960. Pastor The Wesleyan Ch., Valparaiso, Ind., 1958-60, Toronto, Ohio, 1963-69; assoc. pastor Northridge Wesleyan Ch., Dayton, Ohio, 1960-63; exec. dir. gen. dept. youth Wesleyan Ch. Hdqrs., Marion, Ind., 1968-72, dir. field ministries gen. dept. Sunday schs., 1972-74, exec. dir. curriculum, 1980-81; mng. editor WIN Mag., Marion, Ind., 1969-72; asst. gen. sec. Gen. Dept. of Local Ch. Edn., Marion, Ind., 1974-80; gen. dir. estate planning Wesleyan Ch. Internat Ctr., Indpls., 1982—2002, ret., 2002. Editor Ohio dist. The Wesleyan Ch., Columbus, 1961-69; gen. conf. del. The Wesleyan Ch., Anderson, Ind., 1968, Greensboro, N.C., 2000. Writer: Curriculum-Religious Adult Student/Teacher, 1982—, Light from the Word, 1982—. Mem. Christian Holiness Partnership, Christian Stewardship Assn., Christian Mgmt. Assn. Mem. Wesleyan Ch. Avocations: music, reading. Personal E-mail: castlehb@aol.com.

CASTON, J(ESSE) DOUGLAS, retired medical educator; b. Ellenboro, NC, June 16, 1932; s. Lemuel Joseph and Myrtice Elizabeth (Vassey) C.; m. Mary Ann Keeter, June 1, 1958; children: John Andrew, Elizabeth Anne, Mary Susan. AB, Lenoir Rhyne Coll., 1954; MA, U. N.C., 1958; PhD, Brown U., 1961. Fellow Carnegie Instn., Washington, Balt., 1961-62; asst. prof. anatomy Case Western Res. U., Cleve., 1962-71, assoc. prof., 1971-76, prof., 1976-98, co-dir. Devel. Biology Ctr., 1971-77, prof. emeritus, 1999—. Cons. Diamond Shamrock Corp., Cleve., 1975-77; coordinator Core Acad. Program, Sch. Medicine, 1985-94. Patentee folate assay, methotrexate assay; contbr. numerous articles to sci. jours., 1962—. With AUS, 1954—56. Fellow H.W. Wilson, 1956; grantee USPHS, 1963—, Cancer Soc., 1963— Mem. Am. Chem. Soc., AAAS, Am. Soc. Zoologists and Developmental Biologists, Biophys. Soc., Soc. Cell Biology, Am. Assn. Anatomists Episcopalian.

CASTORINO, SUE, communications executive; b. Columbus, Ohio, May 5, 1953; m. Randy Minkoff, Oct. 23, 1983. BS in Speech, Northwestern U., Evanston, Ill., 1975. Producer, community affairs Sta. WBBM-TV, Chgo., 1975; news anchor, reporter Sta. WBBM, Chgo., 1981—86; news reporter Sta. WHTH-AM/FM, Newark, Ohio, 1975; news anchor, reporter Sta. WERE, Cleve., 1975—78, Sta. WWWE, Cleve., 1978—81; founder, pres. Sue Castorino: The Speaking Specialists, Chgo., 1986—. Pvt. voice coach; active internat. exec. comm. tng. in media, crisis and issue mgmt.; presenter, lectr. in field. Author: North Shore Mag., 1987—92; active voice-over and on-camera talent, 1986—. Recipient Golden Gavel award, Chgo. Soc. Assn. Execs., 1991, various news reporting awards, AP, UPI, Chgo., 1981—86. Avocations: sports, films, piano. Office: The Speaking Specialists Ste 2602 435 N Michigan Ave Fl 2602 Chicago IL 60611-4001 Office Phone: 312-527-2252.

CASTRO, JAN GARDEN, writer, art educator, consultant; b. St. Louis, June 8, 1945; d. Harold and Estelle (Fischer) Garden; 1 child, Jomo Jemal. Student, Cornell U., Ithaca, NY, 1963—65; BA, U. Wis., 1967; pub. cert., Radcliffe Coll., 1967; MA in Tchg., Washington U., St. Louis, 1974, MA, 1994. Life cert. tchr. secondary English, speech, drama and social studies, Mo. Tchr., writer, St. Louis, 1970—80; dir. Big River Assn., St. Louis, 1975-85; adj. prof. humanities Lindenwood Coll., 1980—2005, Touro Coll., NYC, 2006—. Co-founder, dir. Duff's Poetry Series, St. Louis, 1975-81; founder, dir. River Styx P.M. Series, St. Louis, 1981-83; arts cons. Harris-Stowe State Coll., 1986-87; vis. scholar Am. Acad. in Rome, summer 2000. Contbg. author: rev. books San Francisco Rev. Books, 1982—85, Am. Book Rev., 1990—93, Mo. Rev., 1991, New Letters, 1993, 1996, Tampa Rev., 1994—2000, The Nation, Am. Poetry Rev., Sculpture Mag., 1997—; author: (poetry) Mandala of the Five Senses, 1975, The Art and Life of Georgia O'Keeffe, 1985, 1995, Memories and Memoirs.Contemporary Missouri Authors, 2000, (poetry) The Last Frontier, 2001—, Sonia DeLaunay: La Moderne, 2002—, (online pub.) Notebooks of My Other Selves, 2007 (finalist Fulton award); contbg. editor: (jours.) Sculpture Mag. (13 cover stories) Seeking St. Louis, Voices from a River City, 1670—2000; editor: River Styx mag., 1975—86; co-editor: (essays) Margaret Atwood: Vision and Forms, 1988; co-prodr.(TV host, co-prodr.): (shows) The Writers Cir., Double Helix, 1987—89. Mem. University City Arts and Letters Commn., Mo., 1983-84. NEH fellow UCLA, 1988, Johns Hopkins U., 1991, Camargo Found. fellow (Cassis, France), 1996; recipient Arts and Letters award St. Louis Mag., 1985, Editor's award and editor during G.E. Younger Writers award to River Styx Mag., Coord. Coun. for Lit. Mags., 1986, Arts award Mandrake Soc. Charity Ball, 1988, Leadership award YWCA St. Louis, 1988. Mem. MLA, CAA, PEN Am. Ctr., at. Coalition Ind. Scholars (bd. 2006), Margaret Atwood Soc. (founder), Art Table. Home: PO Box 486 New York NY 10159-0486 Personal E-mail: jancastro1@gmail.com.

CATALANO, GERALD, accountant; b. Chgo., Jan. 17, 1949; s. Frank and Virginia (Kreiman) C.; m. Mary L. Billings, July 4, 1970; children: James, Maria, Gina. BSBA, Roosevelt U., 1971. CPA, Ill. Jr. acct. Drebin, Lindquist and Gervasio, Chgo., 1971, Leaf, Dahl and Co., Ltd., Chgo., 1971-77, prin., 1978-80, ptnr., 1980-82; prin. Gerald Catalano, CPA, Chgo., 1982-83; ptnr. Barbakoff, Catalano & Assocs., Chgo., 1983-87; pres. Barbakoff, Catalano & Caboor Ltd., Chgo., 1993—. V.p. Tri-City Oil, Inc., Addison, Ill., 1983-93; treas. Uncle Andy's, Inc., 1991-94; corp. officer Bionic Auto Parts, Inc.; bd. dirs. EDT, Inc., treas., 1993—; ptnr. PetCatMusic Publ., 1996—; owner IEP Record Group, 1996—, dir. United Community Lisle, IL, 2001-. Pres. Young Dems., Roosevelt U., 1967-71; trustee U. Ill. Russo Scholarship Fund, 1989—; dir. Elmhurst Jaycees, 1976. Mem. AICPA, ASCAP (assoc.), NARAS (assoc.), Ill. CPA Soc., Theosophical Soc. Roman Catholic. Office: 1 S 376 Summit Ave Oakbrook Terrace IL 60181 E-mail: jerryc@catboor.com.

CATALDO, C. A., hotel executive; b. Chgo., Oct. 23, 1933; Student, Loyola U.; grad. bus. mgmt. program, Harvard U., 1973. Founder Hostmark Hospitality Group, 1974—, chmn., CEO Schaumburg, 1994—. Past chmn., bd. dirs. Chgo. Convention and Tourism Bur. Active City of Hope Med. Ctr., Maryville Acad., Boy Scouts Am. Recipient Awards Nat. Restuarant Assn., award Holiday Inn's Top 10 Restaurant Mgrs., 1968, Innkeeper of Yr. award Holiday Inn, Spirit of Life award, Lifetime Achievement award Roosevelt U. Manfred Seinfeld Sch. in Hospitality Mgmt., 1998; med. rsch. fellowship established in his name City of Hope, 1982. Mem. Greater Chgo. Hotel/Motel Assn., Am. Hotel/Motel Assn. (bd. dirs.), Ill. Hotel and Motel Assn. (bd. dirs.). Office: Hostmark Hospitality Group 11 Plaza Dr Schaumburg IL 60173

CATALDO, ROBERT J., hotel executive; b. Chgo., Sept. 1, 1941; Pres., COO Hostmark Hospitality Group, 1996—. Office: Hostmark Hospitality Group 11 Plaza Dr Schaumburg IL 60173

CATALLO, HEATHER, newscaster; b. Mich. Graduate, S.I. Newhouse Sch. of Pub. Comm., Syracuse, NY. Reporter WTVH-TV, Syracuse, NY; police beat reporter KREM-TV, Spokane, Wash.; investigative reporter WXYZ-TV, Detroit, 1999—, anchor Sunday morning and noon shows, 1999—. Recipient Hearst Nat. TV award Excellence, 1998. Office: WXYZ-TV 20777 W Ten Mile Rd Southfield MI 48037

CATCHINGS, TAMIKA DEVONNE, professional basketball player; b. Stratford, NJ, July 21, 1979; d. Harvey Catchings and Wanda Cathings. Grad., U. Tenn., 2001, M in Sports Studies, 2005. Player Ind. Fever, 2001—. Mem. USA Basketball Women's Sr. Nat. Team, 2004; pres. WNBA Players Assn. Host Catch the Fever basketball camp, 2002, 2003, Catch the Fitness clinic, 2003. Named Naismith Player of Yr., 2000, AP Player of Yr., 2000, US Basketball Writers Assn. Player of Yr., 2000, Kodak/Women's Basketball Coaches Assn. Player of Yr., 2000, Coll. Women's Basketball Player of Yr., ESPY Awards, 2001, WNBA Rookie of Yr., 2002, WNBA Defensive Player of Yr., 2005, 2006; named to WNBA Ea. Conf. All-Star Team, 2002—07, All-WNBA First Team, 2002, 2003, 2006, WNBA All-Defensive First Team, 2005, 2007; recipient Reynolds Soc. Achievement Award, Mass. Eye and Ear Infirmary, Off-Season WNBA Cmty. Assist award, 2002, 2003. Achievements include winning a Gold medal as a member of the US Women's Basketball FIBA Jr. World Championship Team, 1997; winner, Gold medal, US Women's Basketball FIBA World Championship Team, 2002, US Women's Olympic Team, Athens, 2004. Office: Ind Fever Conseco Fieldhouse 125 S Pennsylvania St Indianapolis IN 46204

CATES, GARY, state representative; b. Petersburg, Va., Dec. 27, 1955; married; 2 children. BS in Civil Engring., Va. U. Tech.; MBA, U. Dayton. State rep. dist. 55 Ohio Ho. of Reps., Columbus, 1995—, chair ethics and elections subcom., vice chair rules and reference com., mem. ins. and state govt. coms., speaker pro tempore. Trustee, pres. Union Twp., Ohio, 1992—93, v.p. Ohio, 1991, Ohio, 1994—95. Named one of Outstanding Young Men of Am., U.S. Jaycees, 1983, 1985; recipient Watchdog of the Treasury award (2), United Conservatives of Ohio, Guardian of Small Bus., Nat. Fedn. Ind. Bus. Mem.: Ohi Twp. Assn., Butler County Twp Assn., OKI Regional Coun. Govts., St. Maximillian Kolbe Parish, Mid-Miami Valley C. of C., Southeast Butler County Twp. C. of C., Sr. Citizens, Inc. (bd. trustees), Optimist Club, Lakota/West Chester Kiwanis Club. Republican. Office: 77 S High St 14th fl Columbus OH 43215-6111

CATHCART, RICHARD J., technology company executive; BA in Engring. Scis., U.S. Air Force Acad. V.p., gne. mgr. worldwide bldg. control divsn. Honeywell, v.p. bus. devel.; exec. v.p. corp. devel. Pentair Inc., St. Paul, exec. v.p., pres. water and fluid techs. group, COO water group, 2000—05, vice-chmn., 2005—07. Office: Pentair Inc 5500 Wayzata Blvd Ste 800 Minneapolis MN 55416-1261

CATHEY, CHRISTOPHER D., lawyer; b. Nov. 2, 1973; BA, U. Fla., 1994; JD, U. Cin., 1999. Bar: Ohio 1999, Fla. 2003, Ky. 2003, US Ct. of Appeals Sixth Cir., US Dist. Ct. Southern Dist. Ohio. Assoc. Ulmer & Berne LLP, Cin. Named one of Ohio's Rising Stars, Super Lawyers, 2006. Fellow: Cin. Acad. of Leadership for Lawyers; mem.: Ohio State Bar Assn. (Banking, Comml., Bankruptcy Com.), ABA (Litig., Bus. Sections). Office: Ulmer & Berne LLP 600 Vine St Ste 2800 Cincinnati OH 45202 Office Phone: 513-698-5000. Office Fax: 513-698-5001.

CATIZONE, CARMEN A., health science association administrator, secretary; BS, U. Ill., 1983, MS, 1987. Exec. dir., sec. Nat. Assn. of Bds. of Pharmacy, Mount Prospect, Ill. Named Alumnus of Yr., Univ. Ill. Coll. Pharmacy, 1997. Office: Nat Assn of Bds of Pharmacy 1600 Feehanville Dr Mount Prospect IL 60056-6014 Office Phone: 847-391-4502. Fax: 847-698-0124. E-mail: exec-office@nabp.net.

CATTANACH, ROBERT EDWARD, JR., lawyer; b. Thorp, Wis., Jan. 14, 1949; s. Robert Edmund Sr. and Irene Louise (Papierniak) C.; m. Terry Theirl, June 9, 1972; children: Philip, Sarah, Katherine. BS, U.S. Naval Acad., 1972; JD, U. Wis., 1975. Bar: Wis. 1975, U.S. Supreme Ct. 1980, Minn. 1983, U.S. Dist. Ct. (8th cir.) 1989. Spl. counsel to Sec. of Navy, Washington, 1976-78; trial atty. U.S. Dept. of Justice, Washington, 1978-80; ptnr., chair litigation dept. Oppenheimer Wolff & Donnelly, St. Paul, 1983-94; ptnr., co-chmn., telecom. Dorsey & Whitney LLP, Mpls., 1994—. Articles editor U. Wis. Law Rev., 1974-75. Mem. St. Paul Heritage Preservation Commn., 1993-98. Mem. ABA, Wis. Bar Assn. (pres. non-resident divsn. 1990-92), Minn. Bar Assn., Fellow, Am. Bar Found. Avocations: cross-country skiing, bicycling. Office: Dorsey & Whitney LLP 50 S 6th St Ste 1500 Minneapolis MN 55402-1553 Office Phone: 612-340-2873. Office Fax: 612-340-8800. Business E-Mail: cattanach.robert@dorsey.com.

CATTANEO, MICHAEL S., heating and cooling company executive; b. Detroit, May 30, 1948; s. Alex and Bernadine (Krause) C.; m. Nancy Lucille Horsch, Sept. 6, 1969; children: Michael Alex, Jason Ryan. Cert., Lawrence Inst. Tech., 1970, Macomb Coll., 1977. Service tech. Reliable Heating and Cooling, Detroit, 1965-69; service supr. Artic Air Inc., Detroit, 1969-77; supt. Kropf Service Inc., Detroit, 1977-78; owner Greater Detroit Heating and Cooling, Inc., 1978—, J.B. Air Conditioning Inc., 1978—. Mech., tech. educator, Career Prep. Ctr., Warren, Mich., 1982-83; tech advisor Macomb Prosecutor's Office div. consumer fraud, Mt. Clemens, Mich., 1985—; pres. Catt Enterprises Real Estate and Investments; mng. ptnr. B.P.C. Group Investments LLC; v.p. Reit Air Mgmt. Inc.v.p. Catt Air Ballancing Inc. Named Republican of Yr., Mich., 2000, Republican Businessman of Yr., 2002. Mem. Italian Cultural Ctr. (Warren), Ams. Italian Origin, Mich. Italian C. of C. Republican. Roman Catholic. Avocations: fishing, hunting, competitive shooting, golf, auto racing. Office: Greater Detroit Heating and Cooling Inc 31485 Groesbeck Ste B Fraser MI 48026-1961 E-mail: catt8484@aol.com.

CAULEY, PATRICK C., lawyer; BS, JD, U. Mich. CPA. Ptnr. Bodman, Longley & Dahling, LLP, Detroit; asst. gen. counsel Hayes Lemmerz Internat., Inc., Northville, Mich., 1999—2004, v.p., gen. counsel, sec., 2004—. Office: Hayes Lemmerz Internat 15300 Centennial Dr Northville MI 48167 Office Phone: 734-737-5000.

CAVALLINO, ROBERT P., radiologist; b. NYC, Nov. 12, 1934; MD, Tufts U., 1959. Cert. radiology 1968. Intern Tripler Gen. Hosp., Honolulu, 1959—60; resident NY Hosp., Cornell Med. Ctr., NY, 1964—67; prof. Rush Med. Coll.; chmn. radiology Ill Masonic Med Ctr., Chgo., 1983—. Office: Ill Masonic Med Ctr Dept Radiology 836 W Wellington Ave Chicago IL 60657

CAVANAGH, MICHAEL FRANCIS, state supreme court justice; b. Detroit, Oct. 21, 1940; s. Sylvester J. and Mary Irene (Timmins) C.; m. Patricia E. Ferriss, Apr. 30, 1966; children: Jane Elizabeth, Michael F., Megan Kathleen BA, U. Detroit, 1962, JD, 1966. Bar: Mich. 1966. Law clk. to judge Ct. Appeals, Detroit, 1966-67; atty. City of Lansing, Mich., 1967-69; ptnr. Farhat, Story, et al., Lansing, Mich., 1969-73; judge 54-A Dist. Ct., Lansing, 1973-75, Mich. Ct. Appeals, Lansing, 1975-82; justice Mich. Supreme Ct., Lansing, 1983—, chief justice, 1991—95. Supervising justice Sentencing Guidelines Com., Lansing, 1983-94, Mich. Jud. Inst., Lansing, 1986-94, 2001—; bd. dirs. Thomas M. Cooley Law Sch., 1979-88; chair Mich. Justice Project, 1994-95, Nat. Inter-branch Conf., Mpls., 1994-95; supreme ct. liaison Mich. Indian Tribal Cts., Mich. State Cts. Bd. dirs. Am. Heart Assn. Mich., 1982—, chmn. bd. Am. Heart Assn. Mich., Lathrup Village, 1984-85; bd. dirs. YMCA, Lansing, 1978. Mem. ABA, Fed. Bar Assn., Ingham County Bar Assn., Inst. Jud. Adminstrn., Soc. of Irish/Am. Lawyers (pres. 1987-88). Democrat. Roman Catholic. Avocations: jogging, racquetball, fishing. Office: Mich Supreme Ct PO Box 30052 925 W Ottawa St Lansing MI 48933-1067 Office Phone: 517-373-8683.

CAVANAUGH, JAMES W., lawyer; b. Ft. Dodge, Iowa, 1948; m. Annie Cavanaugh; children: Bridget, James, Matthew, Kevin, Michael, Mark. BA, U. Notre Dame, 1971; JD, St. Louis U., 1974; MA, Georgetown U., 1978. Bar: Iowa 1972, Ga. 1974, Minn. 1982. With Hormel Foods Corp., Austin, Minn., 1982—, sr. v.p. external affairs, corp. sec., 2001—, sr. v.p., gen. counsel, 2005—. With USAF, Vietnam. Mem.: ABA, State Bar of Ga, Minn. State Bar Assn., Iowa State Bar Assn. Avocations: bicycling, skiing, basketball. Office: Hormel Foods Corp 1 Hormel Pl Austin MN 55912 Office Phone: 507-437-5901.

CAVANAUGH, STEVEN M., healthcare company executive; BA magna cum laude, U. Toledo; MA in Fin., U. Mich. Joined Manor Care, Inc., Toledo, 1993, gen. mgr. inpatient and outpatient rehab. ops., v.p., dir. corp. devel., 1999—2006, CFO, 2006—. Mem. Bus. Adv. Coun., U. Toledo. Office: Manor Care Inc 333 N Summit St Toledo OH 43604 Office Phone: 419-252-5554.

CAVNER, NADIA, investment company executive; BS, Tex. Wesleyan U.; MBA, Tex. Christian U. Sr. v.p., sr. fin. cons. US Bancorp Investments, Springfield, Mo.; exec. v.p., head brokerage div. Signature Bank, Springfield, Mo., 2005—, head Nadia Cavner Group; bd. mem. City Bancorp Inc. Mem. Mo. Health and Edn. Facilities Authority. Mem.: Am. Bible Soc. (fin. com.), Springfield Cmty. Found. (fin. com. adv. bd.). Office: Signature Bank PO Box 4023 Springfield MO 65808-4023

CAWOOD, JAMES M., III, lawyer; b. Ft. Thomas, Ky., Apr. 28, 1972; BA, U. Ky., 1995; JD, Salmon P. Chase Coll. Law, 1999. Bar: Ky. 1999, US Dist. Ct. Eastern Dist. Ky. 2000, US Dist. Ct. Western Dist. Ky. 2001, Ohio 2004. Atty. def. firm, Ky.; ptnr. Freund, Freeze & Arnold, Cin. Named one of Ohio's Rising Stars, Super Lawyers, 2006. Mem.: ABA, Northern Ky. Bar Assn., Ky. Bar Assn., Ohio State Bar Assn., Cin. Bar Assn., Ky. Acad. Trial Lawyers, Salmon P. Chase Inn of Ct., Def. Inst. Rsch., Ohio Assn. Civil Trial Attorneys. Office: Freund Freeze & Arnold Ste 1400 Fourth and Walnut Ctr 105 E Fourth St Cincinnati OH 45202-4035 Office Phone: 513-665-3500. Office Fax: 513-665-3503.

CECERE, ANDREW, bank executive; b. 1960; m. Kathy M. Cecere; 1 child. B, U. St. Thomas, 1982; MBA, U. Minn., 1991. Sr. v.p. fin. U.S. Bancorp, Mpls., 1992—96, sr. v.p. acquisition integration and process mgmt., 1996-99, sr. v.p. ops. and adminstrn. wholesale banking, 1999, vice chmn. comml. svcs., 1999—2001, CFO, 2000—01, vice-chmn. wealth mgmt., 2001—07, vice-chmn., CFO, 2007—. Bd. dir. Fair Isaac Corp., DeCare Internat. Bd. dir. Greater Twin Cities United Way, Capital City Partnership; mem. bd. overseers Carlson Sch. Mgmt., U. Minn. Office: US Bancorp US Bancorp Ctr 800 Nicollet Mall Minneapolis MN 55402

CECERE, DOMENICO, homebuilding company executive; b. June 10, 1949; BA in Fin. and Acctg., U. Okla. V.p. fin. indsl. controls Honeywell, Inc., v.p. fin. home and bldg. controlling bus., v.p. fin. European bus. Brussels; v.p., contr. Owens Corning, Toledo, 1993-95, pres. roofing sys. bus., 1995-98, sr. v.p., CFO, 1998-2000, exec. v.p., COO, 2000-01; cons. Gryphon Investors; sr. v.p., CFO KB Home, LA, 2002—. Office: 7th Fl 10990 Wilshire Blvd Los Angeles CA 90024

CEDERBERG, JAMES, retired physics professor; b. Oberlin, Kans., Mar. 16, 1939; s. J. Walter and Edith E. (Glad) C.; m. Judith Ness, June 10, 1967; children: Anna Sook, Rachel Eun. BA, U. Kans., 1959; MA, Harvard U., 1960, PhD, 1963. Lectr., rsch. assoc. Harvard U., Cambridge, Mass., 1963-64; from asst. prof. to prof. St. Olaf Coll., Northfield, Minn., 1964—80, prof., 1980—92, Grace A. Whittier prof. sci., 1992—2005; prof. emeritus, 2006—. Councilor Coun. on Undergrad. Rsch., 1985-91, 92-95, pres. physics coun., 1985-88; summer rsch. assoc. U. Mich., 1967, Harvard U., 1980; fellow Duke U., 1969-70, Harvard U., 1976-77; vis. prof. U. Washington, 1991-92, U. Canterbury, Christchurch, New Zealand, 1998-99. Recipient Distinguished Svc. Citation awd., Am. Assn. Physics Tchrs., 1993; fellow NSF, Woodrow Wilson; grantee NSF, RUI Fellow: Am. Phys. Soc. (Undergraduate Rsch. prize 2002); mem.: Am. Assn. Physics Tchrs., Sigma Xi, Pi Mu Epsilon, Sigma Pi Sigma, Phi Beta Kappa. Lutheran. Office: St Olaf Coll 1520 Saint Olaf Ave Northfield MN 55057-1098 Office Fax: 507-646-3968. Business E-Mail: ceder@stolaf.edu.

CEKO, THERESA C., lawyer, educator; BA, U. Chgo., 1981; JD, DePaul U., 1984. Clin. prof. Loyola U., Chgo., 1987—, dir. Cmty. Law Ctr., 1999—. Contbr. articles to Ill. Ct. publ. Office: Loyola U Chgo Sch of Law 25 E Pearson Ste 1400 Chicago IL 60611 Office Phone: 312-915-7836. Business E-Mail: tceko@luc.edu.

CELESIA, GASTONE GUGLIELMO, neurologist; b. Genoa, Italy, Nov. 22, 1933; came to U.S., 1959, naturalized, 1970; s. Raffaele Amadeo and Ottavia (Tortrino) C.; m. Linda Irene Pike, Aug. 1, 1964; children: Gloria, Laura. MD, U. Genoa, 1959; MS, McGill U., Montreal, 1965. Diplomate Am. Bd. Psychiatry and Neurology in Neurology, Am. Bd. Psychiatry and Neurology in Clin. Neurophysiology. Intern Madison Gen. Hosp., Wis., 1960; fellow neurophysiology U. Wis., Madison, 1960-62, asst. prof. neurology, 1966-69, assoc. prof., 1970-73, prof., 1974-79, 1979-83; resident in neurology Montreal Neurol. Inst./McGill U., Montreal, Que., Canada, 1962-66; chief neurology svc. VA Hosp., Madison, 1979-83; prof. neurology Loyola U., Chgo., 1983—99, chmn. dept. neurology, 1983-99, prof. neurology, 2000—03; cons. Exec. Svc. Chgo., 2003—. Cons. Exec. Svc. Core of Chgo. Editor in chief: Electroenceph. Clin. Neurophysiol., 1988-99; contbr. articles to profl. jours. Fellow Am. Acad. Neurology; mem. AMA, Am. Acad. Clin. Neurophysiology (pres. 1993-95), Am. Neurol. Assn., Wis. Neurol. Soc. Wis. Med. Alumni Assn., Wis. Neurol. Soc. (pres. 1975-76), Soc. Neurosci., Am. Epilepsy Soc., AAAS, Am. Soc. Office: 25 E Washington St Ste 1500 Chicago IL 60602-1804 Personal E-mail: g.celesia@comcast.net.

CENTANNI, ROSS J., engineering executive; b. 1946; BS, La. State UNiv.; MBA, La. State Univ. With B.F. Goodrich Co., Hooker Chem. divsn. Occidental Petroleum; mgr. corp. planning Cooper Industries, Quincy, Ill., 1981, dir. mktg. Gardner-Denver Indsl. Machinery divsn., 1985-90, v.p., gen. mgr. Gardner-Denver Indsl. Machinery divsn., 1990-93; pres., CEO Gardner Denver, Inc., Quincy, 1993—, chmn. bd., 1998—. Bd. dir. Esterline Technologies, Denman Services, Petroleum Equip. Suppliers Assn.; mem. exec. com. Internat. Compressed Air & Allied Machinery Com. Office: 1800 Gardner Expy Quincy IL 62305-9364 Office Fax: 217-228-8247.

CENTOFANTI, DEENA, announcer; m. Keith Stironek; 1 child, Casey Stironek. BS in Mass Comm., Miami U., Oxford, Ohio. Anchor WSYZ-TV, Ohio; prodr. WBNS-TV, Ohio; anchor/reporter WTOV-TV, Ohio; anchor WWHO-TV, Columbus, Ohio, 1994—97; co-anchor morning news WJBK-TV, Detroit, 1997, co-anchor Fox 2 News Weekend, 1997—, health reporter. Recipient Emmy award, 1999, award for gen. excellence in reporting, Mich. AP. Office: WJBK Fox 2 Po Box 2000 Southfield MI 48037-2000

CEPERLEY, DAVID MATTHEW, physics professor; BS in Physics and Maths., U. Mich., 1971; PhD in Physics, Cornell U., 1976. Postdoct. fellow Lab. Physique Theorique, Orsay, France, 1976-77, Rutgers U., NJ, 1977-78; staff scientist Nat Resource for Computation in Chemistry Lawrence Berkeley Lab., 1978-81; staff scientist Lawrence Livermore Nat. Lab., 1981-87; assoc. prof. physics U. Ill., 1987-91, prof. physics Champaign-Urbana, 1991—. Staff scientist Nat. Ctr. for Supercomputing Applications, 1987—, assoc. dir. applications, 1997-98; on sabbatical U. Trento, Italy, 1985-86 IRRMA Ecole Poly. Lausanne, Switzerland, 1993; coord. workshop Inst. Theoretical Physics U. Calif., Santa Barbara, 1994; rschr. Beckman Inst. Advanced Sci. and Tech, Frederick Seitz Materials Research Laboratory; co-organizer numerous workshops Contbr. numerous articles to profl. jours. Grad. fellow NSF, 1971-74, Joliot-Curie fellow, 1976-77; recipient Eugene Feenberg meml. award for many-body physics, 1994. Fellow Am. Phys. Soc. (Aneesur Rahman prize for computational physics 1998); mem. AAAS, Am. Acad. Arts & Scis., NAS Achievements include development and contributions to fermion quantum Monte Carlo methods, contributions to understanding of physical or formal understanding of quantum many-body systems, mainly his calculation of the energy of electron gas; pioneer in the development and application of Path Integral Monte Carlo methods for quantum systems at finite temperatures. Office: 4141 Beckman Inst 405 N Mathews Urbana IL 61801-2325 Fax: (217) 244-2909.

CERNUGEL, WILLIAM JOHN, consumer products company executive, distributor; b. Joliet, Ill., Nov. 19, 1942; m. Laurie M. Kusnik, Apr. 22, 1967; children: Debra, James, David. BS, No. Ill. U., 1964. CPA, Ill. Sr. supr. KPMG LLP, Chgo., 1964-70; asst. corp. contr. Alberto-Culver Co., Melrose Park, Ill., 1970-71, corp. contr., 1972—74, v.p., contr., 1974-82, v.p. fin., 1982-93, sr. v.p. fin., 1993-2000, sr. v.p., CFO, 2000—. Mem. bd. govs., treas. Gottlieb Meml. Hosp., Melrose Park; assoc. mem. bd. advisors Coll. Bus., No. Ill. U. Mem. AICPA, Am. Mgmt. Assn. (fin. coun.), Inst. Mgmt. Accts., Ill. Soc. CPAs, Fin. Exec. Internat., Lions. Home: 8111 Lake Ridge Dr Burr Ridge IL 60527-5977 Office: Alberto-Culver Co 2525 Armitage Ave Melrose Park IL 60160-1163

CERNY, WILLIAM F., state legislator; m. Patricia Cerny. Rep. S.D. State Ho. of Reps. Dist. 29, S.D. State Ho. of Reps. Dist. 25, 1993—, minority whip, mem. appropriations com. Farmer. Home: RR 1 Box 2 Burke SD 57523-9501

CERONE, DAVID, academic administrator; m. Linda Sharon Cerone. Dir. and mem. summer faculty Meadowmount Sch. Music; prof. violin Oberlin Conservatory, 1962—71; chmn. string dept. and Kulas prof. Cleve. Inst. Music, 1971—81, pres., 1985—, Mary Elizabeth Callahan pres. chair; mem. violin faculty Curtis Inst. Music, 1975—85, head violin dept., 1981—85. Founder Cleve. Chamber Music Seminar, 1974; co-founder and dir. ENCORE Sch. Strings; bd. advisors Artistic Svcs.; juror various violin competitions; bd. dirs. Univ. Cir., Inc., Avery Fisher Artist Program. Cleve. Orch. debut, 1987, former mem. Cleve. Chamber Players; musician: (violin and chamber ensemble) Donald Erb's View of Space and Time, 1987, Canterbury Trio, 1984—89. Mem. Leadership Cleve. Class of 1989. Named Person of Yr., Am. Italian Heritage, 1994; recipient No. Ohio Live Award of Achievement, 1986. Mem.: Suzuki Assn. (aux. dir. internat. bd.). Office: Cleve Inst Music 11021 East Blvd Cleveland OH 44106-1705 Office Phone: 216-791-5000. E-mail: ceroned@cs.com.

CERRA, FRANK BERNARD, dean; b. Oneonta, NY, Feb. 13, 1943; m. Kathie Krieger; children: Josh, Christa, Nicole. BA in Biology, SUNY, Binghamton, 1965; MD, Northwestern U., 1969. Diplomate Nat. Bd. Med. Examiners, Am. Bd. Surgery. Intern, resident in surgery Buffalo Gen. Hosp., 1969—74; staff surgeon U. Minn. Hosp. Clinic, Mpls.; prof. U. Minn. Med. Sch., 1981—, dean, prof. surgery Mpls., 1995—96, sr. v.p. health scis., 1996—. Clin. asst. instr. surgery SUNY, Buffalo, 1969—75, asst. prof., 1975—80, assoc. prof. surgery and biophysics, 1980; interim head surgery U. Minn., 1994—95, dean med. sch., 1995—96, provost acad. health ctr., 1996—; rsch. asst. pharmacology Upstate Med. Ctr., 1963—64; rsch. asst. transplantation Northwestern U., 1967—69; rsch. assoc. immunology and cardiovasc. rsch. labs. Buffalo Gen. Hosp., 1972—73, SUNY, Buffalo, 1974—75; dir. surg. critical care, dir. nutrition support svcs. U. Minn. Hosp. and Clinic; vis. lectr. in exptl. surgery Harvard U., 1991; vis. prof. Rush Presbyn.-St. Lukes Med. Ctr., 1991. Editor: Perspective in Critical Care, 1988—91, Critical Care Outlook, 1988—90, Critical Care Medicine, 1990—; mem. editl. bd.: Drug Intelligence & Clin. Pharmacy Panel on Critical Care, 1982—87, Nutrition, 1982—, Critical Care Medicine, 1983—, Circulatory Shock, 1987—93, Jour. Parenteral and Enternal Nutrition, 1987—93, Am. Jour. Surgery, 1987—, Shock, 1993—, Current Opinion in Gen. Surgery, 1992—, Jour. Critical Care Nutrition, —; contbr. articles to profl. jours. Mem. acute care com. Found. for Health Care Evaluation, 1983—86; adv. group Minn. Emerging Infections Program, 1995—. Recipient Owen Wangensteen award, 1987, Therapeutic Frontiers Rsch. award, Am. Coll. Clin. Pharmacy, 1990, Disting. Investigator award, Am. Coll. Critical Care Medicine, 1993; Clark Found. fellow, 1965—69, Kellogg Nutrition fellow, 1987—89, Surg. Infection Soc. Rsch. fellow, 1988—90, Soc. Critical Care Medicine Lilly Rsch. fellow, 1990—93, Svc. award fellow, NIH, 1994—96, United Health Found. Rsch. Tng. grantee, 1972—73. Fellow: ACS (chmn. pre-postoperative care com. 1985—87), Coll. Critical Care Medicine, Am. Coll. Nutrition; mem.: AAAS, AMA, Hennepin County Med. Soc., Am. Soc. Home Care Physicians, Am. Soc. for Artificial Internal Organs (membership com. 1994—95), Internat. Assn. for the Surgery Trauma and Surg. Intensive Care, Soc. Internat. Surgery, Shock Soc., Surg. Biology Club, St. Paul Surg. Soc., Assn. for Surg. Edn., Am. Assn. for the Surgery Trauma, Ctrl. Surg. Assn., Soc. Univ. Surgeons (exec. coun. 1984—85), Assn. Internat. Anesthesistes-Reanimateurs D'Expression, Assn. for Acad. Surgery, Soc. Critical Care Medicine (treas. 1990, pres. 1991—92), Am. Soc. Parenteral and Enteral Nutrition (bd. govs. 1987—88), Soc. for Surgery the Alimentary Tract, Soc. Parenteral Alimentation. Achievements include patents pending for for the prevention of catabolism, nutrition support of immune function. Office: 420 Delaware St SE # 501 Minneapolis MN 55455-0374 also: U Minn Health & Scis Ctr 410 Ch RC 426 Church St SE Minneapolis MN 55455 Fax: 612-625-5000.

CESARIO, ROBERT CHARLES, marketing executive; b. Chgo., Apr. 6, 1941; s. Valentino A. and Mary Ethel (Kenny) C.; m. Susan Kay DePoutee; children: Jeffrey, Bradley. BS in Gen. Edn., Northwestern U., 1975; postgrad., DePaul U., 1975. Mgr. fin. ops. Midas Internat. Corp., Chgo., 1968-73; dir. staff ops. Am. Hosp. Supply Corp., McGaw Park, Ill., 1973-76; v.p. Car X Svc. Sys. Inc., Chgo., 1976-78, v.p. oil svcs., 1983-84; v.p. Chicken Unltd. Enterprises Inc., Chgo., 1978-83; pres. Growth Strategies, Inc., 1984-87; pres., CEO Lube Pro's Internat., Inc., 1987—2004; CEO Franchise Strategies, Inc., Chgo., 2005—. With USMC, 1960-62. Office: Franchise Strategies Inc 360 East Randolph St Ste 2103 Chicago IL 60601

CHABOT, STEVEN JOSEPH, congressman, lawyer; b. Cin., Jan. 22, 1953; s. Gerard Joseph and Doris Leona (Tilly) Chabot; m. Donna Daly, June 22; children: Erica, Randy. BA in Hist., Coll. William & Mary, Williamsburg, Va., 1975; JD, Salmon P. Chase Coll. Law, Highland Heights, Ky., 1978. Bar: Ohio; cert. tchr., Ohio. Tchr. St. Joseph Sch., Cin., 1975-76; atty. pvt. practice, Cin., 1978-95; mem. City Coun., Cin., 1985-90, Hamilton County Commn., Ohio, 1990-94, US Congress from 1st Ohio dist., 1995—, mem. judiciary com., mem. fgn. affairs com., ranking mem. small bus. com. Republican. Roman Catholic. Avocations: reading, spending time with family. Office: US House Reps 129 Cannon House Office Bldg Washington DC 20515-3501 Office Phone: 202-225-2216. Office Fax: 202-225-3012.

CHADEN, LEE A., apparel and former food products executive; BS in Indsl. Engring., Purdue U.; MBA, U. Calif., Berkeley. Brand mgr. Procter & Gamble, 1966—70; sr. product mgr. Playtex Apparel, Inc., 1970—74, pres., Playtex Can., 1974—76, area v.p., internat. divsn., 1976—77, v.p., gen. mgr., family products divsn., 1977—79; ptnr. Mktg. Corp. of Am., 1979—81; prin. Gen. Consumer Elecs., 1981—83; CEO Interac Corp., 1983—85; gen. ptnr. Marketcorp Ventures, 1985—91; pres., U.S. and Westfar divsns. of Playtex Sara Lee Corp., 1991—94, pres., CEO, Sara Lee Intimates, 1994—95, v.p., 1995—98, sr. v.p., 1998—99, CEO, Sara Lee Branded Apparel, 1999—2001, sr. v.p., human resources, 2001—03, exec. v.p., 2003—06, CEO, branded apparel unit, 2004—06, exec. chmn. branded apparel, 2006; exec. chmn. Hanesbrands Inc., Winston Salem, NC, 2006—07, non-exec. chmn., 2007—. Office: Hanesbrands Inc 1000 E Hanes Mill Rd Winston Salem NC 27105

CHADICK, GARY ROBERT, lawyer; b. Manhasset, NY, June 19, 1961; s. Howard and Norma (Cohen) C.; m. Lori J. Branson, Sept. 22, 1990, children: Jonathan, Jennifer BA cum laude, Union Coll., Schenectady, 1983; JD, George Washington U., 1986. Bar: Calif. 1987, U.S. Dist. Ct. (cen. dist.) Calif. 1987, D.C. 1988, U.S. Ct. Appeals (fed. cir.) 1988, Iowa, 2002. Research and writing asst. George Washington U., Washington, 1984-85; summer assoc. Epstein, Becker, Borsody and Green, Washington, 1985; assoc. McKenna & Cuneo, LA, 1986-92; asst. gen. counsel, group counsel & divsn. counsel Litton Industries, Woodland Hills, 1992—2001; sr. v.p., gen. counsel, sec. Rockwell Collins, Inc., Cedar Rapids, 2002—. Lectr. SBA, Washington, 1985, Nat. Contracts Mgmt. Assn., Orange County chpt., L.A., 1987, Pepperdine Law Sch., 1988; in-house lectr. Terminations and Claims, 1990-91. Fed. Publs. Truth in Negotiation Act, San Jose, Calif., 1990; co-author: Cost Acctg. Standards: New Developments, 1989. Active Big Bros.-Big Sisters Program, Schenectady, 1982, United Way contbr. Mem. ABA (bus.law sec.), Nat. Contracts Mgmt. Assn., Am. Soc. Corp. Sec., Am. Corp. Counsel Assn., Nat. Assn.Stockplan Profls., Aerospace Industries Assn. (chmn. legal com. 1999-2000) Avocations: soccer referee, golf. Office: Rockwell Collins Inc 400 Collins Rd NE Cedar Rapids IA 52498

CHADWICK, ERIC HUGH, lawyer; b. 1968; BS, Iowa State U., 1991; JD with honors, William Mitchell Coll. Law, 1994. Bar: Minn. 1994, US Dist. Ct. (dist. Minn.), US Ct. Appeals (8th cir.), US Ct. Appeals (Fed. cir.). Law clk. to Hon. Peder B. Hong Minn. 1st Jud. Dist.; atty. trial dept. Dorsey & Whitney, L.L.P., 1996; ptnr. Patterson, Thuente, Skaar & Christensen, P.A., Mpls., 1997—. Editor: William Mitchell Law Rev. Named a Rising Star, Minn. Super Lawyers mag., 2006. Office: Patterson Thuente Skaar & Christensen PA 4800 IDS Ctr 80 S 8th St Minneapolis MN 55402 Office Phone: 612-349-5778. E-mail: chadwick@ptslaw.com.

CHADWICK, GREGORY D., endodontist; DMD, UNC Chapel Hill Sch. Dentistry, 1973, MS in endodontics, 1976. Pvt. practice, Charlotte, NC; adj. faculty UNC Sch. Dentistry, Charlotte. Fellow: Pierre Fouchard Acad., Acad. of Dentistry Internat., Am. Coll. of Dentists; mem.: ADA (pres. 2001—02). Office: 130 Providence Rd Charlotte NC 28207

CHAFEL, JUDITH ANN, education educator; b. Rochester, NY, Apr. 8, 1945; d. James Arthur and Florence Joan (Santangelo) Chafel. AB, Vassar Coll., 1967; MSEd, Wheelock Coll, 1971; PhD, U. Ill., 1979. Cert. elem. tchr., Mass., N.J., N.Y. Tchr. Spruce St. Sch., Lakewood, NJ, 1972-74, Sodus (N.Y.) Primary Sch., 1974-76; grad. research and teaching asst. U. Ill., Urbana, 1976-79; vis. asst. prof. U. Tex., Austin, 1979-80; asst. prof. dept. curriculum and instrn. Ind. U., Bloomington, 1980-86, assoc. prof., 1986—2001, prof., 2001—; mem. profl. staff U.S. Ho. Reps., Washington, 1989-90. Adj. assoc. prof. philanthropic studies Ctr. on Philanthropy, 1991-2001; reviewer Hist. Publs. and Records Commn., Nat. Archives, Washington, 1979, Little, Brown and Co., Boston, 1982-84, Office for Ednl. Rsch. and Improvement, US Dept. Edn., 1991, 93. Mem. editl. adv. bd. Early Child Devel. and Care, 1985—, Youth and Soc., 1995-2005, Jour. of Poverty: Innovations on Social, Political and Economic Inequalities, 1998—; cons. editor Early Childhood Rsch. Quar., 1988-91, 92-95, 2005—; contbr. editor Am. Jour. of Orthopsychiatry, 2000—; reviewer, book editor; contbr. articles to profl. jours.; contbr. chapts. to books. Proffitt Endowment grantee, Ind. U., 1982, 88, 1998, Ctr. on Philanthropy grantee, 1991, Spencer Found. grantee, 1985, 98; Congl. Sci. fellow Soc. Rsch. in Child Devel., 1989. Mem. Soc. Rsch. in Child Devel. (program com. 1986, 92), Am. Ednl. Rsch. Assn. (program com. various yrs., nominations com. 1986, 88, chair 1993-95, mem.-at-large spl. interest group on early edn. and child devel. 1991-93), Nat. Assn. Edn. Young Children, Assn. Childhood Edn. Internat. (pub. com. 1982-84, bull. and pamphlets rev. editor jour. 1982-84, rsch. com. 1984-88), Nat. Soc. for the Study of Edn.

CHAFFEE, PAUL CHARLES, newspaper editor, publisher; b. Racine, Wis., Aug. 10, 1947; s. Raymond Russell and Ellen Mary (Tiles) C.; m. Bonnie Louise Burmeister, Aug. 9, 1969. BA in Journalism, U. Minn., 1969. Reporter Grand Rapids (Mich.) Press, 1969-79, asst. met. editor, 1979-81; met. editor Saginaw (Mich.) News, 1981-88, editor, 1988—, pub., 2006—. Founding mem. adv. bd. dept. journalism Ctrl. Mich. U., Mt. Pleasant, 1987—, pres. bd. publs., 2004—; past mem. Hispanic adv. bd. dept. journalism Mich. State U.; past pres. bd. dirs. Mich. AP Editl. Assn.; past bd. dirs. Mid Am. Press Inst.; dirs. adv. bd. Susu Coll. Bus. Mgmt. Bd. dirs. Salvation Army, Saginaw, 1986—, St. Charles Cmty. Schs. Found., Mich., 1994—, Westlund Child Guidance Clinic, 1995-99, Saginaw Bay Symphony, 1996—, Saginaw Cmty. Found.; steering bd. Leadership Saginaw; adv. bd. Saginaw County Jr. League; past steering com. Bridge Ctr. Racial Harmony; bd. fellows Saginaw Valley State U. Mem.: Nat. Assn. Hispanic Journalists, Soc. Profl. Journalists, Am. Soc. Newspaper Editors, Saginaw Country Club. Avocation: gardening. Office: Saginaw News 203 S Washington Ave Saginaw MI 48607-1283

CHAFFIN, DON BRIAN, industrial engineering educator, research director; b. Sandusky, Ohio, Apr. 17, 1939; m. 1966; 3 children. B of Indsl. Engring., Gen. Motors Inst., 1962; MS in Indsl. Engring., U. Toledo, 1964; PhD in Engring., U. Mich., 1967. Registered profl. engr., Ohio; cert. prof. ergonomist. Quality ctrl. engr. New Departure Divsn. GM Corp., Ohio, 1960-62, inspection foreman Ohio, 1962-63; project engr. Micrometrical Divsn. Bendix Corp., Mich., 1963-64; asst. prof. phys. medicine U. Kans., 1967-68, asst. prof. indsl. engring., 1968-70, assoc. prof. indsl. engring., 1970-77; prof. indsl. and ops. engring. U. Mich., Ann Arbor, 1977-93, dir. Ctr. for Ergonomics, 1980-97, Disting. Univ. prof. and Johnson prof. indsl. engring. and biomed. engring., 1993—. Fellow AAAS, Human Factors Soc. (Paul Fitts award 1992), Am. Indsl. Hygiene Assn. (Edward Baier award 1994), Ergonomics Soc., Am. Inst. Med. and Biol. Engring.; mem. NSPE, NAE, Am. Inst. Indsl. Engrs. (Baker Disting. Rschr. award 1991), Am. Soc. Biomechanics (Borrelli award), Sigma Xi. Achievements include research on effects and applications of electromyography for measuring human performance, concepts of biomechanics for injury prevention in skeletal-muscle system; expanding the teaching of physiological, neurological and anatomical concepts related to the simulation of human motions and exertions in the design of operated systems in manufacturing and service organizations, and in vehicle operation and maintenance. Office: U Mich Ctr Ergonomics 1656 IOE Bldg Ann Arbor MI 48109-2117

CHAFFIN, GARY ROGER, business executive; b. Satanta, Kans., June 6, 1937; s. Owen Charles and Leona Irene (Dale) C.; m. Charlotte Daisy Hawley, Aug. 17, 1958; children: Darcy Lea, Charla Cai, Darren Roger, Charles Dale. BA, U. Kans., 1960. Loan officer Limerick Fin., Lawrence, Kans., 1959-60; asst. mgr. Chaffin Grocery, Moscow, Kans., 1960-62; store mgr. Chaffin Inc. Gibson Discount Ctrs., 1962-68; gen. mgr. Chaffin,Inc., Dodge City, Kans., 1968-85; pres. Chaffin, Inc., Dodge City, Kans., 1985—, Great S.W. BanCorp, 1978-97, Chaffin Acquisition Co., Inc., 1999—2003. Bd. dirs., sec. Dodge City C.C. Found., 1996-98; bd. dirs., v.p. Dodge City Area Cmty. Found. Republican. Methodist. Avocations: golf, travel. Office: Chaffin Gibsons PO Box 520 Dodge City KS 67801-0520 also: Chaffin Inc 1313 Minneola Rd Dodge City KS 67801

CHAIT, JON FREDERICK, human resources specialist, lawyer; b. Bakersfield, Calif., Aug. 9, 1950; s. Michael and Irene (Goddard) C.; m. Mary Lardner, Feb. 13, 1988; children: Jamie E., Meredith L. BA magna cum laude, UCLA, 1972, JD, 1975. Bar: Wis. 1975. Assoc. Foley & Lardner, Milw., 1975-79, Godfrey & Kahn, S.C., Milw., 1979-82, ptnr., 1982-89; exec. v.p., CFO, bd. dirs. Manpower Inc., Milw., 1989-98, mng. dir. internat. ops., 1995-98; chmn., CEO Magenta.com, 1998-2000, Spring Group PLC, London, 2000—. Bd. dirs. Marshall & Ilsley Corp., Milw., M&I Data Svcs., Milw., Krueger Internat., Inc., Green Bay, Wis. Mem. ABA, Am. Soc. Corp. Secs., Univ. Club, Milw. Country Club, Milw. Club, Phi Beta Kappa.

CHAKRABARTI, SUBRATA KUMAR, marine research engineer; b. Calcutta, India, Feb. 3, 1941; came to U.S., 1964, naturalized, 1981; s. Asutosh and Shefali C.; m. Prakriti Bhaduri, July 23, 1967; children: Sumita, Prabal. BSME, Jadavpur U., 1963; MSME, U. Colo., 1965, PhD, 1968. Registered profl. engr., Ill. Asst. engr. Kuljian Corp., Calcutta, 1963—64, Simon Carves Ltd., Calcutta, 1964; instr. engring. U. Colo., Boulder, 1965—66; hydrodynamicist CB&I Tech. Svcs. Co. (formerly Chgo. Bridge and Iron Co.), Plainfield, Ill., 1968—70; head analytical group CB&I Tech. Svcs. Co., 1970—79, dir. marine rsch., 1979—95, dir. structural devel., 1995—96; pres. Offshore Structure Analysis, Inc., Plainfield, 1996—; prof. CME/MIE U. Ill., Chgo., 2005—. Vis. prof. U.S. Naval Acad., Annapolis, Md., 1986, 88, Indian Inst. Tech., Madras, 1996; presenter in field. Author: Hydrodynamics of Offshore Structures, 1987, Nonlinear Methods in Offshore Engineering, 1990, Offshore Structure Modeling, 1994, Theory and Practice of Hydrodynamics and Vibration, 2002; editor: Fluid Structure Interaction in Offshore Engineering, 1994, Fluid Structure Interaction, 2001, Fluid Structure Interaction II, 2003, Fluid Structure Interaction III, 2005; tech. editor Applied Ocean Rsch., 1998—, Numerical Modelling in Fluid-Structure Interactions, 2005;: Fluid Structure Interaction IV, 2007; tech. editor: Handbook of Offshore Engineering, 2005; mem. editl. bd. Applied Ocean Rsch., Marine Structures, Topics in Engring., Advances in Fluid Mechanics series, assoc. editor Energy Resources Tech., 1983—86; contbr. articles to profl. jours., chapters to books. Recipient Gold medal Jadavpur U., 1963, Eminent Scientist medal Wessex Inst., 2005, Disting. Engring. Alumni award U. Colo., 2006; named Outstanding New Citizen, 1981; U. Colo. fellow, 1968. Fellow AAAS, ASCE (publ. com. waterway divsn., James R. Croes Gold medal 1974, Freeman scholar 1979), ASME (exec. com., editor jour. offshore mechanics and arctic engring. divsn. 1986-96, chmn. divsn., 1987-88, awards com. 1983-2004, tech. session devloper, chmn. 1983—, chmn. tech. program com. 1988-89, tech. program chair, 2004, Ralph James award 1984, co-editor proc. internat. symposium, Offshore Mechanics and Arctic Engring. achievement award 1990, Ten Paper award 1991, Disting. Svcs. award 1998, Lifetime Achievement award 2005), NAS (com., design group, marine structures group 1989-91, chmn. 1992-95), Nat. Acad. Engring., Sigma Xi. Achievements include patents in field. Office: Offshore Structure Analysis Inc 13613 Capista Dr Plainfield IL 60544-7966 Office Phone: 815-436-4863. Personal E-mail: chakrab@aol.com. Business E-Mail: chakrab@uic.edu.

CHAKRABARTY, ANANDA MOHAN, microbiologist; b. Sainthia, India, Apr. 4, 1938; arrived in U.S., 1965; s. Satya Dos and Sasthi Bala (Mukherjee) Chakrabarty; m. Krishna Chakraverty, May 26, 1965; children: Kaberi, Asit. BSc, St. Xavier's Coll., 1958; MSc, U. Calcutta, India, 1960, PhD, 1965. Sr. rsch. officer U. Calcutta, 1964-65; rsch. assoc. biochemistry U. Ill., Urbana, 1965-71, prof. dept. microbiology Med. Ctr., 1979-89, disting. prof., 1989—; mem. staff GE R&D Ctr., Schenectady, NY, 1971-79. Editor: (book) Genetic Engineering, 1977, Biodegradation and Detoxification of Environmental Pollutants, 1982. Named Scientist of Yr., Indsl. Rsch. Mag., 1975; recipient Inventor of the Yr. award, Patent Lawyers' Assn., 1982, Pub. Affairs award, Am. Chem. Soc., 1984, Disting. Scientist award, EPA, 1985, Merit award, NIH, 1986, Pasteur award, 1991, Proctor & Gamble award, 1995; scholar, U. Ill., 1989. Mem.: Am. Soc. Biol. Chemists, Am. Soc. Microbiology. Home: 206 E Julia Dr Villa Park IL 60181-3340 Office: U Ill Med Ctr Dept Microbiology M/C 790 835 S Wolcott Ave Chicago IL 60612-7340 Home Phone: 630-834-4388; Office Phone: 312-996-4586. Business E-Mail: pseudomo@uic.edu.

CHAKRABARTY, DIPESH, history professor; PhD, Australian Nat. U., 1984. Prof. history dept. U. Chgo., prof. S. Asian languages & civilizations. Author: Habitations of Modernity: Essays in Wake of Subaltern Studies, 2002, Provincializing Europe: Postcolonial Thought & Historical Difference, 2000, Rethinking Working-Class History: Bengal, 1890-1940, 1989. Fellow: Am. Acad. Arts & Sci.; mem.: Am. Historical Rev. (editl. com.), Public Culture (editl. com.), Postcolonial Studies Jour. (founding editor), Critical Inquiry, Subaltern Studies Series (founding mem., co-editor). Office: University of Chicago 1130 E 59th St Chicago IL 60637 Office Fax: 773-834-3254, 773-702-8642.

CHALEFF, CARL THOMAS, investment company executive; b. Indpls., Nov. 21, 1945; s. Boris Carl and Betty J. (Miller) C.; m. Carolyn F. Heath, Apr. 26, 1970 (div. Apr. 1985); children: Fritz. Eric; m. Darlene Finkel, Dec. 13, 1987. BS in Econs., Purdue U., 1969; MBA in Fin., Xavier U., 1976. Asst. v.p. Am. Can Corp., YC, 1969-70, sales mgr. Cin., 1970-73; account exec. Merrill Lynch, Cin., 1973-76; v.p. Oppenheimer, Chgo., 1976-81; assoc. dir. Bear Stearns & Co., Chgo., 1981-88; ptnr., mng. dir. CIBC Oppenheimer, 1988—2004; pres. Polaris Capital Ptnrs., 2004—. Former pres. bd. dirs. Nat. Kidney Found. Ill.; exec. coun. U. Chgo. Childrens Hosp., Boy Scouts Am., 1992-94; former pres. bd. dirs. AIDS Care, 1992-98, bd. dir. Adler Planetarium & Mus., Chgo., 1998-2005; treas., bd. dir., Jobs for Youth; bd. dirs. Nat. Kidney Found. Mem. Chgo. Bond Club, Am. Arbitration Assn., Nat. Bd. Arbitrators, East Bank Club, Rainbows (bd. dirs. 1984-96), Met. Club, Chgo. Mercantile Exch. Club, Chgo. Yacht Club, Ctr. for Excellence in Edn. (bd. dirs. 1990-92), Chgo. Filmmakers (bd. dirs. 1986-98). Avocations: sailing, skiing, tennis. Home: 55 W Goethe St Chicago IL 60610-7406 Office Phone: 312-327-5280. Business E-Mail: chaleff@polarischicago.com.

CHAMBERS, CHARLES MACKAY, academic administrator, lawyer, consultant; b. Hampton, Va., June 22, 1941; s. Charles McKay and Ruth Ellanora (Wallach) C.; m. Barbara Mae Fromm, June 9, 1962; children: Charles M., Catherine M., Christina M., Carleton M. BS, U. Ala., 1962, MS, 1963, PhD, 1964; JD, George Washington U., 1976; DSc (hon.), Lawrence Tech. U., Southfield, Mich., 2006. Bar: Va. 1977, DC 1978, US Patent and Trademark Office, 1978, US Supreme Ct. 1980, US Dist. Ct. DC 1985, US Ct. Appeals (DC cir.) 1987, US Dist. Ct. (ea. dist.) Va. 1988, US Ct. Appeals DC, 1987, US Ct. Appeals (4th cir.) 1990, Mich. 1994; cert. comml. pilot, multiengine, land and instrument. Aerospace engr. NASA, Huntsville, Ala., 1962-63; rsch., teaching asst. U. Ala. Rsch. Inst., Huntsville, Ala., 1963-64; research fellow NASA, Cambridge, Mass., 1964-65; assoc. prof. U. Ala., Tuscaloosa, 1965-69; mng. dir. Univ. Assocs., Washington, 1969-72; prof., assoc. dean George Washington U., Washington, 1972-77; v.p., gen. counsel Council on Postsecondary Accreditation, Washington, 1977-83; exec. dir. Am. Inst. Biol. Sci., Washington, 1983-87; pres. Am. Found. Biol. Scis., Washington, 1987-93, Lawrence Tech. U., 1993—2006, chancellor, 2006—. Cons., evaluator, accreditation rev. coun. commn. on instns. of higher edn. Noth Ctrl. Assn. Colls. and Schs., Chgo.; bd. dirs. Automation Alley, Mich. Sci. and Math. Alliance, Mich. Small Aircraft Transp. Sys. Author: (with others) Understanding Accreditation, 1983; pub. BioScience; contbr. chpts. to books. Mem. Diocesan Adv. Coun., Arlington, Va., 1978-84, Fairfax County Dem. Com., Va., 1979-95; judge No. Va. Sci. Fair, 1976—; trustee, sec. Southeastern U., Washington, 1983-87; trustee BIOSIS, Inc., Phila. and London, 1991-93; mem. Oakland County Workforce Devel. Bd., Mich., 1996—; bd. dirs. Automation Alley, 1999—, Detroit area coun. Boy Scouts Am., 2003-. Recipient Citizenship award Am. Legion, 1959, Olive Branch award Editors and Writers Com., NYC, 1986, Horace H. Rackham award Engring. Soc. Detroit, 2004; fellow NSF, 1964. Fellow AAAS; mem. ABA, AAUP, Am. Assn. Univ. Adminstrs. (pres. 1984-85), Engring. and Sci. Devel. Found. (bd. dirs., pres. 1996-2000, fellow Engring. Soc. 1997), Am. Coun. Edn. (bus. and higher edn. forum), Soc. Automotive Engrs., Nat. Soc. Black Engrs. (hon.), The Engring. Soc. Detroit (bd. dirs. 1999—), Assn. Ind. Colls. and Univs. Mich., Mich. Small Aircraft Transp. Program, Detroit Regional C. of C. (bd. dirs.), Circumnavigators Club, Detroit Econ. Club (bd. dirs.), Detroit Athletic Club, Cosmos Club, Capitol Hill Club, Phi Beta Kappa, Sigma Xi, Tau Beta Pi. Roman Catholic. Avocations: flying, history, sailing. Office: Lawrence Tech U 21000 W 10 Mile Rd Ste M351 Southfield MI 48075-1058 Personal E-mail: mail@charleschambers.com.

CHAMBERS, DONALD ARTHUR, biochemistry and molecular medicine educator; b. NYC, Sept. 24, 1936; AB, Columbia U., 1959, PhD, 1972. Rsch. biochemist dept. surgery Harvard Med. Sch./Mass. Gen. Hosp., Boston, 1961-66; rsch. fellow in hematology dept. surgery Harvard Med. Sch./Beth Israel Hosp., Boston, 1967-68; faculty fellow in chem. biology Columbia U., NYC, 1969-71; asst. rsch. biochemist Ctr. for Med. Genetics dept. medicine U. Calif. Med. Ctr., San Francisco, 1972-74, lectr. in biochemistry and biophysics, 1972-74, asst. prof. molecular biology and biochemistry, 1974-75; asst. prof. biol. chemistry and dermatology U. Mich., Ann Arbor, 1975-79, assoc. prof. biol. chemistry, 1979; prof. molecular biology U. Ill., Chgo., 1979—, prof. biol. chemistry, 1980—, rsch. prof. dermatology, 1981—, prof. biol. psychiatry, 1996. Assoc. mem. Dental Rsch. Inst. U. Mich., 1978-79, adj. rsch. investigator Dept. Biol. Chemistry, 1979—; dir. Ctr. for Molecular Biology of Oral Disease, U. Ill., Chgo., 1979—, interim head dept. biochemistry, 1985, head dept. biochemistry, 1986—; vis. scholar Green Coll., Oxford U., 1989-93, hon. vis. fellow, 1993—; sr. rsch. assoc. Wellcome Unit History of Medicine, Oxford. 2000--; fellow Honors Coll., 1985—. Phi Kappa Phi lectr., 1991, Sigma Xi lectr., 2001; nat. action com. Am. Assn. Dental Rsch., 1981—; study sect. rev. NIH, 1983-86, 92, 98—. Mem. editl. bd.: Perspectives in Biology and Medicine. Recipient James Howard McGregor prize Columbia U., 1971; named Inventor of Yr., U. Ill., 1990; fellow in hematology NIH, 1967-68, fellow in chem. biology, 1969-71; Rsch. grantee NIH, Am. Cancer Soc., Office of Naval Rsch.,1986—, Helene Curtis, Inc., 1988—, Tng. grantee NIH-NIGMS, 1975-79, NIH-NIAMDD, 1976-79, 77-80, NIH-NIDR-NIAMDD, 1980—, NIH-NCI, 1982-88, NIH-NIDCR, 2003-, NIH-NIAID, 2003-. Mem. AAAS, Am. Assn. Med. Colls., Am. Assn. Immunology, Am. Chem. Soc., Am. Fedn. Clin. Rsch., Am. Soc. Biol. Chemistry, Am. Soc. Cell Biology, Am. Soc. Microbiology, Internat. Assn. Dental Rsch. (com. on rsch. progress 1982-85, chmn. 1984-85, chmn. grad. tng. forum com. exptl. pathology sect. 1983), Assn. Dept. Chmn. Biol. Chemistry, Chgo. Assn. Immunologists, N.Y. Acad. Scis. (organizer meeting The Double Helix, 40 Yrs. 1993), Royal Soc. Medicine, Soc. Investigative Dermatology, Oxford Med. Alumni Assn. (N.Am. rep. 2000—), Green Coll. Oxford Soc. (N.Am. rep. 2000—), Athenaeum Club London, Phi Kappa Phi, Sigma Xi (NIDCR 1998, spl. emphisii panel), Sigma Xi (pres.-elect 2000, pres. 2001), Oxford Med. Alumni (N.Am Sec. 2001-). Achievements include patents (U.S., Can.) for method of determining periodontal disease, (with other) method of quantifying aspartate amino transferase in periodontal disease; research in role of cyclic nucleotides, prostaglandins, hormones and other regulatory factors in the regulation of cell function, proliferation and differentiation, in molecular medicine in neural-immune interactions, the regulatory mechanisms of host-microbial interactions, in the history and devel. of concepts in the bio-med. scis. Office: U Ill Coll Med Dept Biochemistry 1819 W Polk St # C 536 Chicago IL 60612-7331 also: Ctr Molecular Biol Oral Diseases 801 S Paulina St # C 860 Chicago IL 60612-7210 Office Phone: 312-996-1294. Business E-Mail: donc@uic.edu.

CHAMBERS, ERNEST, state legislator; b. July 10, 1937; Mem. Nebr. Legislature from 11th dist., Lincoln, 1970—; mem. agr., bus. and labor coms. Nebr. Legislature, Lincoln, vice chmn. judiciary com., exec. bd. Address: Nebr Legislature Rm 1107 PO Box 94604 Lincoln NE 68509-4604

CHAMBERS, ROYD, state official; b. Des Moines, Iowa, June 1961; State rep., Iowa, 2003—. Vice chair edn. com.; mem. appropriations com.; mem. pub. safety com.; mem. transp. com.; mem. agrl. and natural resources com. Mem. Mus. Bd. Sheldon. Republican. Office: State Capitol E 12th and Grand Des Moines IA 50319

CHAMPAGNE, RONALD OSCAR, medical association administrator; b. Woonsocket, RI, Jan. 2, 1942; s. George Albert and Simone (Brodeur) C.; m. Ruth Inez DesRuisseux, Nov. 25, 1970 BA, Duquesne U., 1964; MA, Cath. U. Am., 1966, Fordham U., 1970, PhD, 1973. Instr. math. Sacred Heart U., Bridgeport, Conn., 1966-69; asst. prof. math. Manhattanville Coll., Purchase, N.Y., 1969-75, dir. advanced studies program, 1973-75; prof. math., v.p., dean of faculty Salem Coll., W.Va., 1975-82; prof. math., pres., trustee St. Xavier U., Chgo., 1982-94, pres. emeritus, 1994—; prof. philosophy, v.p. for devel. Roosevelt U., Chgo., 1996—2001; sr. v.p. devel. Alzheimer's Assn., 2001—. Author: LP Spaces of Complex Valued Functions, 1966; A Formalization of the Dialectical Development of Intelligence, 1974 Mem. Mat. Assn. Am., Philosophy of Sci. Assn., Carlton Club, Econs. Club Chgo., Exec. Club Chgo. Roman Catholic. Office: Alzheimers Assn 225 N Mich Ave Fl 17 Chicago IL 60601-7633

CHAMPION, NORMA JEAN, communications educator, state legislator; b. Oklahoma City, Jan. 21, 1933; d. Aubra Dell and Beuleah Beatrice (Flanagan) Black; m. Richard Gordon Champion, Oct. 3, 1953 (dec.); children: Jeffrey Bruce, Ashley Brooke. BA in Religious Edn., Cen. Bible Coll., Springfield, Mo., 1971; MA in Comm., Mo. State U., 1978; PhD in Tech., U. Okla., 1986. Producer, hostess The Children's Hour, Sta. KYTV-TV, NBC, Springfield, 1957-86; asst. prof. Cen. Bible Coll., 1968-84; prof. broadcasting Evangel U., Springfield, 1978—; mem. Springfield City Coun., 1987-92, Mo. Ho. of Reps., Jefferson City, 1993—2002, Mo. Senate, 2003—, chair aging and health com., appropriations, edn. Adj. faculty Assemblies of God Theol. Sem., Springfield, 1987—, pres. coun.; bd. dirs. Global U.; mem. Commn. on Higher Edn., Assemblies of God, 1998—; spkr. Internat. Pentecostal Press Assn. World Conf., Singapore, 1989. Mem. bd. Mo. Access to Higher Edn. Trust, 2003-, pain mgmt. bd., 2004-, Boys & Girls Town of Mo.; adv. coun. pain mgmt.; judge Springfield (Mo.) City Schs. Recipient commendation resolution Mo. Ho. of Reps., 1988; numerous awards for The Children's Hour; Aunt Norma Day named in her honor City of Springfield, 1976; named 20 Most Influential Women in Ozarks, Springfield Bus. Jour., 2005. Mem. Nat. Broadcast Edn. Assn., Mo. Broadcast Edn. Assn., Nat. League Cities, Mo. Mcpl. League (human resource com. 1989, intergovtl. rels. com. 1990), Nat. Assn. Telecom. Officers and Advisors, PTA (life). Republican. Mem. Assemblies of God Ch. Avocations: gardening, reading, yoga. Home: 3609 S Broadway Ave Springfield MO 65807-4505 Office: Evangel Univ 1111 N Glenstone Ave Springfield MO 65802-2125 Office Phone: 573-751-2583. Business E-Mail: normachampion@senate.mo.gov.

CHAMPLEY, MICHAEL E., electric power industry executive; b. 1949; With Detroit Edison, 1977-92; v.p. mktg. and sales DTE Energy Co., Detroit, 1992-97, sr. v.p., 1997—. Office: DTE Energy Co 2000 2nd Ave Detroit MI 48226-1203

CHAMPLIN, STEVEN KIRK, lawyer; b. Omaha, July 6, 1944; m. Marjorie Eckenberg, Mar. 15, 1969; children: Anne, Paul, Jane. BA, Vanderbilt U., 1966; JD cum laude, U. Minn., 1969. Bar: Minn. 1969, U.S. Dist. Ct. Minn., U.S. Ct. Appeals (8th cir.). Pub. defender Hennepin County, Mpls., 1972-73; assoc. Dorsey & Whitney, Mpls., 1969-70, 71-72, 73-75, ptnr., comml. litig., 1976—, and co-chmn., construction & design law. Capt. U.S. Army, 1970-71. Mem. USTA. Office: Dorsey & Whitney LLP 50 S 6th St Ste 1500 Minneapolis MN 55402-1553 Office Phone: 612-340-2913. Office Fax: 612-340-2868. Business E-Mail: champlin.steve@dorsey.com.

CHANDLER, CHARLES Q., IV, energy executive; BA bus. adm., Kansas State Univ., 1975; MBA, Northwestern Univ., 1976. Pres., dir. INTRUST Fin. Corp.; chmn., CEO INTRUST Bank; chmn. bd. dir. Westar Energy. Bd. dir. Slavation Army, Wesley Medical Ctr., Kansas Soc. Crippled Children. Office: Westar Energy PO Box 889 Topeka KS 66601-0889 Office Phone: 785-575-6300.

CHANDLER, CHRISTOPHER MARK (CHRIS CHANDLER), professional football player; b. Everett, Wash., Oct. 12, 1965; Degree in econ., Wash. State U., 1988. Quarterback Indpls. Colts, 1988—89, Tampa Bay Buccaneers, 1990—91, Phoenix Cardinals, 1991—93, L.A. Rams, 1994, Houston Oilers, 1995—96, Atlanta Falcons, 1997—2001, Chicago Bears, 2002—04, St. Louis Rams, 2004—; mem. Pro Bowl team, 1997. Office: c/o St Louis Rams 1 Rams Way Earth City MO 63045

CHANDLER, KATHLEEN LEONE, mayor, educator, state representative; b. Detroit, Sept. 19, 1932; d. Telford Reginald and Beatrice Leone (Smith) McRae; m. Charles Clarence Chandler, July 12, 1958; children: Susan Chandler Kambrick, Elizabeth Chandler Marks, Jennifer Chandler Dolan. BA, Mich. State U., 1956, MA, 1957; MPA, Kent State U., 1990. Tchr. Macomb County, Mt. Clemens, Mich., 1952-54, Irving (Tex.) Pub. Schs., 1959-60, Marquette (Mich.) Pub. Schs., 1960-62; reading cons., dir. reading clinic Livonia (Mich.) Pub. Schs., 1957-59; grad. asst. Mich. State U., East Lansing, 1957-61; mem. coun. City of Kent, Ohio, 1980-89, mayor Ohio, 1990—96; commr. Portage County, Portage, Ohio, 1997—2002; mem. Ohio Ho. of Reps., 2003—. Instr. Kent State U., 1984-92; mem. legis. policy com. Ohio Mcpl. League; mentor conflict resolution Urban Ctr., Cleve. State U., 1991; mem. cts./govt. issues resolution program Ohio Com. on Dispute Resolution and Conflicts Mgmt.; mem. univ. liaison com. Kent City; mem. Tri County Infrastructure Study Com.; mem. legis. effectiveness and govt. com. CSL. Bd. dirs. Portage County Literacy Coalition; charter mem. Leadership Portage County; mem. Kent Environ. Coun., Kent Vision 2000, exec. com., steering com.; mem. City of Kent Human Justice Com., League of Cities, Ohio Task Force on Regional Competitiveness and Coop., Akron Area Infrastructure Alliance, Ohio Statewide Intercity Rail Coalition; mem. leadership acad. adv. bd. Cleve. State U., Northeast Ohio Mayor's Think Tank, 1996, mem. County and Township Gov., mem. subcom., Growth and Land Use, Econ. Devel and Tech., Mcpl. Gov. and Urban Affairs, Vet. Affairs, select com. Quality Edn. for Ohio's Sch. Children, Competetive Edge For Job Creation and Retention. Mem. LWV, NAACP, Ohio Coll. Coun. of Internat. Reading Assn., Kent C. of C. (hon.), Univ. Women Kent State U., Mayors Assn. Ohio, Ohio Mcpl. League, Phi Beta Delta, Phi Kappa Phi, Phi Beta Delta Internat. Scholars. Democrat. Avocations: reading, travel. Home: 428 Dansel St Kent OH 44240-2627 Office: Riffle Center 77 South High St Columbus OH 43215-6111 Office Phone: 614-466-2004. Business E-Mail: district68@ohr.state.oh.us.

CHANDLER, KENT, JR., lawyer; b. Chgo., Jan. 10, 1920; s. Kent and Grace Emeret (Tuttle) C.; m. Frances Robertson, June 19, 1948; children: Gail, Robertson Kent. BA, Yale U., 1942; JD, U. Mich., 1949. Bar: Ill. 1949, U.S. Dist. Ct. (no. dist.) Ill. 1949, U.S. Ct. Appeals (7th cir.) 1955, U.S. Ct. Claims 1958. Assoc. Wilson & McIlvaine, Chgo., 1949-56, ptnr., 1957-94, spl. counsel to firm, 1994-98; of counsel Bell Jones & Quinlisk, Chgo., 1998—2007, Jones & Quinlisk LLC, Chgo., 2007—. Bd. dirs. Internat. Crane Found. Mem. zoning bd. appeals City of Lake Forest, Ill., 1953-63, chmn., 1963-67, mem. plan commn., 1955-69, chmn., 1969-70, pres. bd. local improvements, 1970-73, mayor, 1970-73, mem. bd. fire and police commn., 1975-82, chmn., 1982-84. Served to maj. USMCR, 1941-46. Mem. ABA, Ill. State Bar Assn., Chgo. Bar Assn., Lake County Bar Assn., Lawyers Club Chgo. (pres. 1985-86), Univ. Club, Onwentsia Club (Lake Forest), Old Elm Club (Highland Park, Ill.). Republican. Presbyterian. Office: 205 N Michigan Ave Ste 2500 Chicago IL 60601 Office Phone: 312-606-8797.

CHANDLER, KEVIN, former state legislator; b. Mar. 31, 1960; m. Kathleen Chandler; 1 child. BA, U. Minn.; JD, Cath. U. Am. State senator Dist. 55 Minn. State Senate, 1993-97; atty., 1996—. Home: 5339 W Bald Eagle Blvd White Bear Lake MN 55110-6410

CHANDLER, MELANIE LYNN, surgical technologist, paralegal; b. Hammond, Ind., Oct. 11, 1967; d. Michael Edward and Mary Josephine Simkins; children: Courtney, Brian, Lindsey. Student paralegal studies, Calumet Coll. St. Joseph, 2001. Cert. surgical technologist. Cert. nurses aide Resthaven Christian Svs., South Holland, Ill., 1996—98; gastrointestinal lab technician Adv. Trinity Hosp., Chicago, Ill., 1998—2000, cert. surg. technologist, 1997—; paralegal Barry Sherman & Assocs., Hammond, Ind., 2002—. Latex allergy liason Adv. Trinity Hosp., Chgo., 1999—. Mem.: Calumet Coll. Paralegal Club (sec., treas. 2002). Office: Barry Sherman & Assocs 6920 Hohman Ave Hammond IN 46320 Personal E-mail: melaniechandler@aol.com.

CHANDLER, RICHARD GATES, lawyer; b. Stockton, Calif., July 6, 1952; s. Kensal Roberts and Barbara (Gates) Chandler; m. Heidi Pankoke, Oct. 22, 1994. BA, Lawrence U., 1974; JD, U. Chgo., 1977. Bar: Wis. 1977. Assoc. Minahan & Peterson SC, Milw., 1979—84; legis. counsel to State Rep. Tommy G. Thompson, Wis. Assembly, Madison, 1985—86; legis. asst. Congressman Robert W. Kasten, Jr., Washington, 1977—78; budget dir. State of Wis., 1987—2001; sec. Dept. Revenue, Madison, Wis., 2001—03; public policy cons. Chandler Cons. LLC, Madison, 2003—. Mem.: Phi Beta Kappa. Republican. Methodist. Home: 810 Ottawa Trail Madison WI 53711-2941 Office Phone: 608-628-0433.

CHANDRASEKARAN, BALAKRISHNAN, computer scientist, educator; b. Lalgudi, Tamil Nadu, India, June 20, 1942; came to U.S., 1963; s. Srinivasan and Nagamani Balakrishnan; m. Sandra Mamrak, Oct. 21, 1978; 1 child, Mallika. B in Engring., Madras U., Karaikudi, India, 1963; PhD, U. Pa., 1967. Devel. engr. Smith Kline Instruments, Phila., 1964-65; rsch. specialist Philco-Ford Corp., Blue Bell, Pa., 1967-69; asst. prof. computer and info. sci. Ohio State U., Columbus, 1969-71, assoc. prof., 1971-77, prof., 1977-95; sr. rsch. scientist, 1995—; dir. Lab. for Artificial Intelligence Rsch., Columbus, 1983—. Co-chmn. Symposium on Potentials and Limitations of Mech. Intelligence, Anaheim, Calif., 1971; chmn. Norbert Wiener Symposium, Boston, 1974; sci. dir. Summer Sch. on Computer Program Testing, SOGESTA, Urbino, Italy, 1981; vis. scientist Lawrence Livermore Nat. Lab., Livermore, Calif., summer 1981, cons. fall 1981; vis. scientist MIT Computer Sci. Lab., 1983; dir. NIH Artificial Intelligence in Medicine Workshop, 1984; organizer panel discussion on artificial intelligence and engring. ASME, 1985; vis. scholar Stanford U., 1990-91; keynote spkr. World Congress on Expert Sys., Mexico City, 1998, Internat. Conf. on Diagrammic Reasoning, Callaway Gardens, Ga., 2002; tech. area leader US Army Rsch. Labs. Tech. Alliance on Decision Architectures, 2001—. Editor: Diagrammatic Reasoning, 1995; co-editor Computer Program Testing, 1981; editor ACM Sigart Spl. Issue on Structure, Function, and Behavior, 1985; assoc. editor Artificial Intelligence in Engring., 1986—; mem. bd. editors Internat. Jour. Pattern Recognition & Artificial Intelligence, Med. Expert Systems, Artificial Intelligence in Engring.; assoc. editor Internat. Jour. Human-Computer Interactions, 1996—. Recipient Outstanding Paper award Pattern Recognition Soc., 1976; Moore fellow U. Pa., 1964-67. Fellow IEEE (editor-in-chief Expert Jour. 1990-94), Am. Assn. for Artificial Intelligence (chmn. workshops on diagrammatic reasoning 1992), Assn. for Computing Machinery; mem. Sys. Man and Cybernetics Soc. IEEE (v.p. 1974-75, pattern recognition com. 1969-72, assoc. editor Trans. 1973—, guest editor spl. issue on distributed program solving 1981). Democrat. Avocation: travel. Home: 2053 Iuka Ave Columbus OH 43201-1415 Office: Ohio State U Dept Computer and Info Sci 2015 Neil Ave Columbus OH 43210-1210 Office Phone: 614-292-0923. Business E-Mail: chandra@cse.ohio-state.edu.

CHANEY, WILLIAM ALBERT, retired history professor; b. Arcadia, Calif., Dec. 23, 1922; s. Horace Pierce and Esther (Bowen) Chaney. AB, U. Calif., Berkeley, 1943, PhD, 1961. Mem. faculty Lawrence U., Appleton, Wis., 1952-99, George McKendree Steele prof. western culture, 1966-99, Steele prof. emeritus, 1999—, chmn. dept. history, 1968-71, 95-96. Vis. prof. Mich. State U., 1958. Author: The Cult of Kingship in Anglo-Saxon England: The Transformation from Paganism to Christianity, 1970, reprinted, 1999; contbr. articles to profl. jours. and encys. Grantee, Am. Coun. Learned Socs., 1966—67; Jr. fellow, Harvard Soc. Fellows, 1949—52. Fellow: Royal Soc. Arts; mem.: AAUP, MLA, Archeol. Inst. Am., Conf. Brit. Studies, Am. Soc. Ch. History, Medieval Acad. Am., Am. Hist. Assn. Episcopalian. Home: 215 E Kimball St Appleton WI 54911-5720 Office: Lawrence Univ Dept History Appleton WI 54912 Office Phone: 920-832-6676.

CHANG, R. P. H., materials science educator; b. Chung King, Peoples Republic China, Dec. 22, 1941; s. Joseph K. Cho; m. Bennie Chang; children: Vivian, Samuel. BS in Physics, MIT, 1965; PhD in Plasma Physics, Princeton U., 1970. Postdoctoral fellowship Princeton Plasma Physics Lab., 1970-71; mem. tech. staff AT&T Bell Labs., Murray Hill, N.J., 1971-86; prof. Material Sci. & Engring. Northwestern U., 1986—. Dir. Materials Rsch. Ctr., 1989—. 7 original inventions 1977—; author over 170 sci. publs.; co-author chpts. in Plasma Diagnostics and Material Sci. & Engring.; co-editor: Plasma Synthesis & Etching of Electronic Materials, 1985. Fellow Am. Vacuum Soc.; mem. Am. Physics Soc., Materials Rsch. Soc. (pres. 1989), Internat. Union of Materials Rsch. Socs. (pres. 1991-92). Office: Northwestern U Dept Materials Sci Engring 2225 N Campus Dr Evanston IL 60208-0876

CHANG, Y. AUSTIN, materials engineer, educator; m. P. Jean Ho, Sept. 15, 1956; children: Vincent D., Lawrence D., Theodore D. BS in Chem. Engring, U. Calif., Berkeley, 1954; PhD in Metallurgy, U. Calif., 1963; MS in Chem. Engring, U. Wash., 1955. Chem. engr. Stauffer Chem. Co., Richmond, Calif., 1956-59; postdoctoral fellow U. Calif.-Berkeley, 1963; metall. engr. Aerojet-Gen. Corp., Sacramento, 1963-67; assoc. prof. U. Wis.-Milw., 1967-70, prof., 1970-80, chmn. materials dept., 1971-78, assoc. dean research Grad. Sch., 1978-80; prof. dept. materials sci. and engring. U. Wis., Madison, 1980—, chmn. dept., 1982-91, Wis. Disting. prof., 1988—. Mem. summer faculty Sandia Labs., Livermore, Calif., 1971; vis. prof. Tohuku U., Sendai, Japan, fall 1987, MIT, Cambridge, fall 1991; NRC Disting. lectr. in material sci. Nat. Cheng Kung U., Tainan, Taiwan, 1987-88; adj. prof. U. Sci. Tech., Beijing, 1987—, hon. prof., 1995-96, adv. bd., 1996—; hon. prof. Ctrl. South U. Technology, Changsha, Hunan, 1996—, S.E. U., Nanjing, 1997, N.E. U., Shenyang, 1998; Winchell Lectr., Purdue U., 1999; summer faculty Quantum Structure Resh. Initiative, Hewlett-Packard Laboratories, Palo Alto, 1999; Belton Lectr. CSIRO, Clayton, Victoria, Australia, 2000. Co-author four books on phase equilibria and thermodynamic properties; co-editor four books; contbr. 300 scholarly articles in metall. and materials field to profl. jours. Mem. bd. Goodwill Residential Cmty., Inc., Milw., 1978-80; mem. Wis. Gov.'s Asian Am. Adv. Coun., 1980-82, at. Acad. Engring., 1996. Recipient Outstanding Instr. award U. Wis., Milw., 1972, Byron Bird award U. Wis., Madison, 1984, Alloy Phase Diagram Internat. Comm. Best Paper award, 1999; named hon. prof. Southeast U. Nanjing, 1997, Northeast U., Shenyang, 1998. Fellow Am. Soc. Metals Internat. (Fellow award 1978, trustee 1981-84, Hall of Fame award Milw. chpt. 1986, Albert Easton White Disting. Tchr. award 1994, Albert Sauveun Achievement award 1996), Minerals, Metals and Materials Soc. (v.p., 1999, pres. 2000, William Hume-Rothery award 1989, Educator award 1990, Extraction and Processing lectr. award 1993, Mathewson award 1996, John Bardeen award 2000); mem. NSPE, NAE, Orgn. Chinese Ams. (chpt. pres. 1979-81), Nat. Assn. Corrosion Engrs., Electrochem. Soc., Materials Rsch. Soc., Am. Phys. Soc., Chinese Acad. Scis. (fgn. academician, 2000), Sigma Xi, Tau Beta Pi, Phi Tau Phi, Alpha Sigma Mu (pres. 1984-85, hon. life). Office: U Wis 1509 University Ave Madison WI 53706-1538

CHANG, YOON IL, nuclear engineer; b. Seoul, Korea, Apr. 12, 1942; came to U.S., 1965; s. Paul Kun and In Sil (Hahn) C.; m. Ok Ja Kim, Dec. 19, 1966; children: Alice, Dennis, Eugene. BS in Nuclear Engring., Seoul Nat. U., 1964; ME, Tex. A & M U., 1967; PhD, U. Mich., 1971; MBA, U. Chgo., 1983. Mgr. spl. projects uclear Assurance Corp., Atlanta, 1971-74; asst. nuclear engr. Argonne (Ill.) Nat. Lab., 1974-76, group leader, 1976-77, sect. head, 1977-78, assoc. divsn. dir., 1978-84, gen. mgr. IFR program, 1984-94, dep. assoc. lab. dir. for engring. rsch., 1994—98, assoc. lab. dir. for engring. rsch., 1998—2002, interim lab. dir., 1999—2001, assoc. lab. dir. at large, 2002—06, disting. fellow, 2006—. Recipient E. O. Lawrence award U.S. Dept. Energy, 1994. Fellow Am. Nuclear Soc. (Walker Cisler award 1997—). Home: 2020 Palmer Dr Naperville IL 60564-5664 Office: Argonne Nat Lab 9700 Cass Ave Argonne IL 60439-4803 Home Phone: 630-305-8792; Office Phone: 630-252-4856. E-mail: ychang@anl.gov.

CHAO, BEI TSE, mechanical engineering educator; b. Soochow, China, Dec. 18, 1918; arrived in U.S., 1948, naturalized, 1962; s. Tse Yu and Yin T. (Yao) C.; m. May Kiang, Feb. 7, 1948; children: Clara, Fred Roberto. BS in Elec. Engring. with highest honor, Nat. Chiao-Tung U., China, 1939; PhD (Boxer Indemnity scholar), Victoria U., Manchester, Eng., 1947. Asst. engr. tool and gage div. Central Machine Works, Kunming, China, 1939-41, asso. engr., 1941-43, mgr. tool and gage div., 1943-45; research asst. U. Ill., Urbana, 1948-50, asst. prof. dept. mech. engring., 1951-53, assoc. prof., 1953-55, prof., 1955-87, prof. emeritus, 1987—, head thermal sci. div., 1971-75, head dept. mech. and indsl. engring., 1975-87; assoc. mem. U. Ill. (Center for Advanced Study), 1963-64. Cons. to industry and govtl. agys., 1950-94; vis. Russell S. Springer prof. mech. engring. U. Calif., Berkeley, 1973; mem. reviewing staff Zentralblatt für Mathematik, Berlin, 1970-82; mem. U.S. Engring. Edn. Del. to Visit People's Republic of China, 1978; mem. adv. screening com. in engring. Fulbright-Hays Awards Program, 1979-81, chmn., 1980, 81; mem. com. U.S. Army basic sci. rsch. NRC, 1980-83; Prince disting. lectr. Ariz. State U., 1984; bd. dirs. Aircraft Gear Corp., 1989-94. Author: Advanced Heat Transfer, 1969; tech. editor Jour. Heat Transfer, 1975-81; mem. adv. editl. bd. Numerical Heat Transfer, 1977-95; mem. hon. edit. bd. Internat. Jour. Heat and Mass Transfer, 1987-97, Internat. Comm. in Heat and Mass Transfer, 1987-97; contbr. numerous articles on mech. engring. to profl. jours. Recipient Outstanding Tchr. award, Ill. Mech. Engring. Alumni, 1978, Max Jakob Meml. award, ASME/Am. Inst. Chem. Engrs., 1983, Tau Beta Pi Daniel C. Drucker eminent faculty award, 1985; Univ. scholar, 1985. Fellow AAAS, ASME (hon.; Blackall award 1957, Heat Transfer award 1971, William T. Ennor Mfg. Tech. award 1992), Am. Soc. Engring. Edn. (Outstanding Tchr. award 1975, Western Electric Fund award 1973, Ralph Coats Roe award 1975, Benjamin Garver Lamme award 1984, Centennial Medallion 1993); mem. Nat. Acad. Engring., Academia Sinica, Chiao-Tung U. Alumni Assn. (pres. Midwest sect. 1975-76), Tau Beta Pi, Pi Tau Sigma (hon.). Home: 101 W Windsor Rd Apt 6103 Urbana IL 61802-6663 Office: Univ Ill 264 Mech Engring Bldg 1206 W Green St Urbana IL 61801-2906 Personal E-mail: btmchao@hotmail.com.

CHAO, MARSHALL, chemist; b. Changsha, Hunan, China, Nov. 20, 1924; came to U.S., 1955; s. Heng-ti and Hwei-yng C.; m. Patricia Hu, July 20, 1968; 1 dau., Anita A. BS, Nat. Central U., Nanking, China, 1947; MS, U. Ill., 1958, PhD, 1961. Tech. asst. Taiwan Fertilizer Co., Taipei, 1949-55; research chemist Dow Chem. Co., Midland, Mich., 1960-72, research specialist, 1973-80; research leader Dow chem. Co., Midland, Mich., 1980-86; sr. assoc. Omni Tech Internat., Ltd., Midland, 1986—. Author: Taiwan Fertilizers, 1951; editor newsletter Midland Chinese Christian Fellowship, 1987-94; contbr. articles to profl. jours.; patentee in field. Mem. Ch. Council Grace Bapt. Ch., Taipei, 1951-55; deacon 1st Baptist Ch., Midland, 1974-76. Univ. fellow U. Ill., 1957-60 Fellow Am. Inst. Chemists; mem. Am. Chem. Soc., Electrochem. Soc. (sect. chmn. 1973-74, 83-84, councilor 1974-76, 85—, vice chmn. 1964-65), Soc. Electronanalytical chemistry (charter), N.Y. Acad. Scis., Mensa, Sigma Xi, Phi Lambda Upsilon Clubs: Midland Chinese (chmn. 1975-76), Tittabawassee Toastmasters (sec.-treas. 1976-77). Home: 1206 Evamar Dr Midland MI 48640-7213 Office: Omni Tech Internat Ltd 2715 Ashman St Midland MI 48640-4449 E-mail: mschao@aol.com.

CHAPDELAINE, ROLAND JOSEPH, academic administrator; b. Springfield, Mass., Aug. 23, 1946; s. Roland George and Therese Rose (LaRose) C.; m. Pamela Jeanne Mearns, Aug. 24, 1968; children: Eric Roland, Denise Elizabeth. BA, Providence Coll., 1968; MS, Ball State U., 1969, EdD, 1976. Instr. biology Ball State U., Muncie, Ind., 1969-72; assoc. prof. Howard Community Coll., Columbia, Md., 1972-78, div. chmn., 1975-80, coordinator faculty devel., 1978-80, acting dean students, 1982-83, dean instrn., 1980-86; v.p. acad. affairs Mohave Community Coll., Kingman, Ariz., 1986—. Co-chmn. adv. com. Columbia Assn. Urban Lake Water Quality Project, 1976-86; advisor Solar Energy Ednl. Project State of Md., 1977; cons. various community colls., Md., Pa., N.J., 1974—; lectr. Md. Acad. Scis., Balt., 1976-80; mem. Project Cooperation Task Force on Value added Instrn., 1988—. Contbr. articles to profl. jours. Vice-chmn. AYRA Youth Baseball, Howard County, Md., 1982; bd. dirs. St. John's Parish, Howard County, 1980-84; co-chmn. Citizens Adv. Com. Critical Areas Planning, Howard County, 1976-77; edn. coordinator Middle Patuxent Environ. Assn., Howard County, 1974-78; appointed State Commn. for Study of Future of Md. Community Coll., 1985-86; bd. dirs. Industry Edn. Alliance Council, Howard County, 1984-86, Hist. Savage Mill Mus., 1985-86; mem. Cholesterol Edn. Task Force, 1988—; selected participant Rising Star League for Innovation Leadership Inst., 1988; mem. Ariz. Task Force on Awarding Credit, 1988-89. Recipient Cert. Appreciation, Md. Dept. Vocat. Edn., 1982, Spl. Achievement award Howard Community Coll., 1986; grantee NSF, 1981, FIPSE, 1984, 85. Mem. Ariz. Acad. Adminstrs. (exec. com. 1988-89), Nat. Council Staff Program and Orgnl. Devel. (regional dir. 1984-85, Cert. Appreciation 1985), Nat. Council Instructional Adminstrs. (regional dir. 1980-85, dir. nat. issues 1985-86, sec. 1986, v.p., pres. elect 1987-88, pres. 1988—, co-chair Project Cooperation, 1988-89), Council Md. Deans (pres. 1983-84), Nat. Council for Staff, Program and Orgnl. Devel. (regional dir.), Md. Consortium of Biol. Scientists (steering com. 1973-80), Howard County C. of C. (leadership tng. program 1986); Ariz. Media Assn. (adminstr. of Yr. 1987). Lodges: Rotary (sec. Kingman Rt.66, 1988—, program chair 1987-88, mem. exec. leadership inst. 1988—), Elks (Kingman Lodge 468, chaplain 1988-89). Democrat. Roman Catholic. Home: 3705 Martingale Dr Kingman AZ 86401-2926 Office: Rock Valley College 3301 N Mulford Rd Rockford IL 61114-5699

CHAPLIN, DAVID DUNBAR, medical research specialist, educator; b. London, Aug. 28, 1952; came to U.S., 1952; s. Hugh Jr. and Alice Elizabeth (Dougherty) C.; m. Jane Ellen Bryant; children: Vernon H., Rosalind K., Daniel B. AB, Harvard U., 1973; MD, PhD, Washington U., St. Louis, 1980. Intern, then resident Parkland Meml. Hosp., Dallas, 1980-82; post-doctoral fellow dept. genetics Harvard U. Med. Sch., Boston, 1982-84; asst. prof. medicine Washington U. Sch. Medicine, St. Louis, 1984-91, prof. medicine, 1995—; assoc. investigator Howard Hughes Med. Inst., St. Louis, 1984—. Assoc. editor: The New Biologist, 1990-92, Diabetes, 1992-96; contbr. articles to profl. jours. Mem. grants com. Arthritis Found., Atlanta, 1989-92, NIAID AITR, 1998—. Scholar Harvard U., 1972, 73; Jane Coffin Childs Fund for Med. Rsch. fellow, 1982-84. Mem. Am. Soc. Clin. Investigation, Am. Fedn. Clin. Rsch., Am. Assn. Immunologists, Am. Soc. Human Genetics, Assn., Assn. Am. Physicians, Alpha Omega Alpha. Democrat. Roman Catholic. Office: Howard Hughes Med Inst 10050 Clin Scis Res Bldg 660 S Euclid Ave # 8022 Saint Louis MO 63110-1010 E-mail: cahplin@im.wustl.edu.

CHAPLIN, HUGH, JR., preventive medicine physician, educator; b. NYC, Feb. 4, 1923; m. Alice Dougherty, June 16, 1945; 4 children; m. Lee Nelken Robins, Aug. 5, 1998. AB, Princeton U., 1943; MD, Columbia U., 1947. Diplomate Am. Bd. Internal Medicine, Nat. Bd. Med. Examiners. Intern Mass. Gen. Hosp., Boston, 1947-48, resident, 1948-50; fellow in hematology Brit. Postgrad. Med. Sch., London, 1951-53; physician in charge Clin. Center Blood Bank, NIH, Bethesda, Md., 1953-55; Commonwealth Fund fellow Wright Fleming Inst. Microbiology, London, 1962-63, Josiah Macy Faculty scholar, 1975-76. Instr. in medicine Washington U. Sch. Medicine, St. Louis, 1955-56, asst. prof. medicine and preventive medicine, 1956-62, asso. dean, chmn. admissions com., 1957-62, asso. prof., 1963-65, prof., 1965, William B. Kountz prof. preventive medicine, 1965-83; dir. IWJ Inst. of Rehab., St. Louis, 1964-72; prof. pathology, dir. Barnes Hosp. Blood Bank, St. Louis, 1983-91; emeritus prof. pathology and medicine, 1991—; mem. Am. Standards Com. for Blood Transfusion Equipment; mem. subcom. on transfusion problems NRC, 1959-62, mem. com. on blood and transfusion problems, 1963-67; chmn. ad hoc blood program research com. ARC, 1967-73, bd. govs., 1978-84 Assoc. editor Transfusion, 1960-98; contbg. editor Vox Sanguinis, 1960-79. Served with USNR, 1942-45. Mem. Am. Fedn. Clin. Research, Central Soc. Clin. Research, Am. Soc. Clin. Investigation, Assn. Am. Physicians, Am., Internat. socs. hematology, Brit. Med. Research Soc., Brit. Royal Soc. Medicine, Am. Assn. Blood Banks (sci. program com. 1959-60, Emily Cooley award 1968, Morton Grove-Rasmussen award 1985), Phi Beta Kappa, Alpha Omega Alpha, Sigma Xi. Office: Washington U Sch Medicine Box 8118 4949 Barnes Hospital Plz Saint Louis MO 63110-1003 E-mail: hughchapln@yahoo.com.

CHAPMAN, ALGER BALDWIN, financial services company executive, lawyer; b. Portland, Maine, Sept. 28, 1931; s. Alger Baldwin, Sr. and Elizabeth (Ives) Chapman; m. Beatrice Bishop, Oct. 30, 1983; children: Alger III, Samuel P., Andrew I., Henry H. BA, Williams Coll., 1953; JD, Columbia U., 1956. Bar: N.Y. 1957. Pres. Shearson, Hammill & Co., 1970-74; co-chmn. Shearson & Co., 1974-81; vice chmn. Am. Express Bank, 1982—86; chmn., CEO Chgo. Bd. Options Exch., 1986-97; vice chmn. ABN Amro, Inc., 1997—2001; chmn. ABN Amro Fin. Svcs, 1998—2004; dir. The Cambridge Group, Chgo., 2005—. Bd. dirs. HDO; chmn. Prime Ins.; adv. comm. chmn. Actuarial Holdings. Mem.: Econ. Club, Country Club Little Rock, Glenview Club, Comml. Club, Met. Club (NYC), Racquet Club Chgo., Chgo. Club. Avocations: golf, reading. Home: 33 Hickory Hills Cir Little Rock AR 72212 Office: 227 W Monroe St Ste 3200 Chicago IL 60606 Office Phone: 312-961-9914.

CHAPMAN, DARRIAN, sportscaster; children from previous marriage: Marrisa, Jordan. Student, U. Mass. Sports dir. Sta. WGR Newsradio 55, Buffalo; broadcast analyst Buffalo Bisons Baseball Club, Buffalo; with NBC4, Washington, 1995—, sports segment prodr., weekend morning sports anchor, sports reporter, subs. host for The George Michael Sports Machine; weekend sports anchor, sports reporter NBC 5, Chgo., 2000, lead sports anchor for evening and nightly news broadcasts; host NBC5's Sports Sunday at 10:30 pm, Chgo. Avocations: baseball, classical music, biking, cooking. Office: NBC 454 N Columbus Dr Chicago IL 60611

CHAPMAN, JOSEPH ALAN, academic administrator; b. Salem, Oreg., Apr. 28, 1942; s. Archie and Andyth Loraine (Fallin) C.; m. Gale Willner, Oct. 30, 1978; children: Valerie, Jennifer. BS, Oreg. State U., 1965, MS, 1967, PhD, 1970. Wildlife biologist US Fish and Wildlife Svc., 1965—67; faculty rsch. asst. U. Md., Frostburg, 1969-70, rsch. asst. prof., 1970-74; assoc. prof., head Appalachian Environ. Lab., Frostburg, 1974-78, prof., head, 1978-83; prof., head fisheries and wildlife dept. Utah State U., Logan, 1983-89, prof., dean natural resources, 1989—96; sr. v.p. and provost Mont. State U., Bozeman, 1996—99; pres. ND State U., 1999—. Adj. prof. wildlife S. Garrett C.C., McHenry, Md., 1973-83; adj. prof. biology Frostburg State Coll., 1975-83; vis. prof. animal ecology U. de Los Andes, Merida, Venezuala, 1981-82; dep. chmn. Internat. Union for Conservation of Nature and Natural Resources/Species Survival Commn., Lagomorph Group, Gland, Switzerland, 1978-81, chmn., 1982-91, mem. emeritus, 1991. Editor: Wild Animals of North America, 1979, Worldwide Furbearer Conference Proceedings, 1981, Wild Mammals of North America, 1982, Rabbits, Hare, and Pikas, 1990; contbr.: Wild Animals of North America, 1979. Recipient Outstanding Book award S.E. sect. The Wildlife Soc., 1982, The Wildlife Soc., 1984, President's award Nat. Assn. Student Personnel Adminstr., 2005, Greater North Dakotan award, ND C. of C., 2006. Fellow Inst. for Biology London, Explorers Club N.Y.; mem. Am. Soc. Mammalogists (life). Office: Office of President ND State Univ Old Main 102 PO Box 5167 Fargo ND 58105

CHAPMAN, LOREN J., psychology professor; b. Muncie, Ind., Jan. 5, 1927; s. Herbert L. and Lurana Gertrude (Treff) C.; m. Jean Marilyn Paulsen, June 6, 1953; children: Nancy, Laurence. AB cum laude, Harvard U., Cambridge, Mass., 1948; MS, Northwestern U., Evanston, Ill., 1952, PhD, 1954. USPHS postdoctorate research fellow U. Chgo., 1954-56, instr., asst. prof., 1956-59; assoc. prof. U. Ky., Lexington, 1959-62; from assoc. prof. to prof. Southern Ill. U., Carbondale, 1962-67; prof. U. Wis., Madison, 1966-93, NIMH rsch. scientist, 1988-93; prof. emeritus, 1994—. Author: Disordered Thought in Schizophrenia, 1973; contbr. articles to profl. jours. Recipient Disting. Scientist award Soc. for Sci. Clin. Psychology, 1992; NIMH research grantee, 1952-97. Fellow AAAS, APA (Disting. Sci. award for application of psychology 1999); mem. Am. Psychopathol. Assn., Soc. Rsch. Psychopathology (pres. 1989, Joseph Zubin award 1992), Am. Psychol. Soc. (William James fellow 1995). Home: 129 Richland Ln Madison WI 53705-4834 Office: Univ Wis Dept Psychology 1202 W Johnson St Madison WI 53706-1611 Office Phone: 608-238-8426. Business E-Mail: lorenchapman@mindspring.com.

CHAPMAN, STEPHEN JAMES, columnist; b. Brady, Tex., Feb. 25, 1954; s. Thurman James and Betty Dee (Sell) C.; m. Fern Brenda Schumer, Sept. 10, 1983, (div.); 3 children AB cum laude, Harvard Coll., 1976; student, U. Chgo. Sch. Bus., 1982-84. Assoc. editor The New Republic, Washington, 1978-81; editorial writer, columnist The Chicago Tribune, 1981—. Office: Chgo Tribune 435 N Michigan Ave Chicago IL 60611-4041 Business E-Mail: schapman@tribune.com.

CHAPPELEAR, STEPHEN ERIC, lawyer; b. Columbus, Ohio, Dec. 25, 1952; s. Thornton White and Phyllis Evelyn (Williams) C.; m. Sharon Sue Starr, June 8, 1974; children: Katherine Sue, Christopher Charles. BA, Ohio State U., 1974, JD, 1977. Bar: Ohio 1977, U.S. Dist. Ct. (so. dist.) Ohio, U.S. Dist. Ct. (no. dist.) Ohio, U.S. Dist. Ct. (ea. dist.) Wis., U.S. Tax Ct., U.S. Ct. Appeals (6th cir.). Assoc. Emens, Hurd, Kegler & Ritter, Columbus, 1977—82, prin., 1983—2001, Kegler Brown Hill & Ritter, Columbus; ptnr. Hahn, Loeser & Parks, Columbus, 2001—. Mem. exec. coun. Nat. Conf. Bar Pres., 1997-2000; pres. Met. Bar Caucus, 2001-02. Author: The Complete Book of Jury Verdicts II, Franklin County, Ohio, 1985-91, The Complete Book of Franklin County Jury Verdicts, 1990, So What's Your Case Realy Worth?: A Decade of Jury Trial Verdicts, 1995; editor jour. Bar Briefs, 1986-88; contbr. articles to profl. jour. Fellow Am. Bar Found. (co-chair), Ohio State Bar Found. (trustee), Columbus Bar Found.; mem. ABA (ho. dels., litig. sect., chmn. real estate litig. com., trial and ins. practice sect. ethics and professionalism com.) Ohio State Bar Assn. (bd. gov., coun. dels., former chair fed. cts. and practice com., litig. sect., bd. gov., pres. 2002-03), Columbus Bar Assn. (bd. govs., pres. 1995-96), Am. Inns of Ct. (Franklin chpt. pres. 1994-95, 2005-06), Million Dollar Adv. Forum, ew Albany Country Club. Avocations: sports, movies, theater, writing. Office: Hahn Loeser & Parks 65 E State St Ste 1400 Columbus OH 43215-4213 Office Phone: 614-233-5148. Office Fax: 614-233-5149.

CHARFOOS, LAWRENCE SELIG, lawyer; b. Detroit, Dec. 7, 1935; s. Samuel and Charlotte (Salkin) C.; m. Jane Emerson. Student, U. Mich., 1953-56; LLB, Wayne State U., 1959. Bar: Mich. 1959, Ill. 1965. Pvt. practice, Detroit, 1960-63; pres., ptnr. Charfoos & Christensen PC, Detroit, 1967—; theatrical producer, legitimate theater mgr. Chgo., 1963-67. Cons. med.-legal problems Mich. Med. Soc., Mich. Hosp. Coun., ATLA; US cts. com. State Bar Mich. Author: The Medical Malpractice Case: A Complete Handbook, 1974, Daughters at Risk, 1981, Personal Injury Practice, Technique and Technology, 1986; contbr. articles to profl. jours. Trustee Lawrence S. Charfoos Found. Elected to Inner Circle of Advocates, 1973, named one of Best Lawyers in Am., 2006. Mem. ABA, Mich. Bar Assn. (com. U.S. cts. 1999-2003), Detroit Bar Assn. (past dir.), Am. Bd. Profl. Liability Attys. (founder, past pres.), Internat. Acad. Trial Lawyers. Office: 5510 Woodward Ave Detroit MI 48202-3804 Office Phone: 313-875-8080. Business E-Mail: lcharfoos@c2law.com.

CHARLA, LEONARD FRANCIS, lawyer, publishing executive; b. New Rochelle, NY, May 4, 1940; s. Leonard A. and Mary L. Charla; m. Kathleen Gerace, Feb. 3, 1968 (div. Dec. 1988); children: Larisa, Christopher; m. Elizabeth A. Du Mouchelle, Aug. 27, 1993. BA, Iona Coll., New Rochelle, NY, 1962; JD, Cath. U., Washington, DC, 1965; LLM, George Wash. U., Washington, DC, 1971. Bar: DC 1967, NJ 1970, Mich. 1971. Tech. writer IRS, Washington, 1966-67; atty. adv. ICC, 1967, atty., 1968-69; mgmt. intern HEW, 1967-68; atty. Bowes & Millner, Transp. Cons., Newark, 1969-71; atty. legal staff GM, Detroit, 1971-85, sr. counsel, 1985-87, asst. gen. counsel, 1987-89; sr. v.p. Clean Sites Inc., Alexandria, Va., 1989-90; atty. Butzel Long, Detroit, 1990—2005; pres. Countinghouse Press, Inc., Bloomfield, Mich., 1997—. Mem. faculty Coll. Creative Studies, Detroit, 1978—89, adj. asst. prof., 1988—89; faculty art U. Mich., 1980, 1984—89, adj. asst. prof., 1988—89; disting. vis. prof. U. Detroit Mercy Law Sch., 2004; instr. Henry Ford Cmty. Coll., Dearborn, Mich., 2004—; pres. 38 Huguenot Corp., 2000—. Author: Never Cooked Before/Gotta Cook Now!, 1999; pub.: A Letter from Marty (Mary O'Herron), 2004, The Freya Project (Phil Rosette), 2004, The Better Bottom Line, 2005. Bd. dirs. Gt. Lakes Performing Artists Assocs., 1983—85, Mich. Assn. Cmty. Arts Agys., 1983—89, 1992—93, vice chair, 1986—88, chair, 1988—89; active Info. Network Superfund Settlements, 1988—2004; bd. dirs. Friends Modern Art, Detroit Inst. Arts, 1996—2003, v.p., 1998—2003; bd. dirs. Art Ctr. Mt. Clemens, Mich., 1997—2005, chair facilities com., v.p. Mich., 2001—04; bd. govs. Cath. U. Am. Alumni, 1982—2002, v.p., 1993—98, Cranbrook Writers Guild, Birmingham, Mich., 2005—07; bd. regents Cath. U. Am., 1992—2002, Birmingham Bloomfield Art Assn., 1987—88, 1994—95; sec. Green Pine Acres Condo Assn., 2005—. Mem.: ABA, State Bar Assn. (mem. arts com. entertainment and sports sect. 1979—, chmn. 1980—81, mem. coun. 1992—2004). Office: Countinghouse Press 6632 Telegraph Rd 311 Bloomfield Hills MI 48301 Home Phone: 248-642-7191; Office Phone: 248-642-7191. Office Fax: 248-642-7192. Personal E-mail: nuhuguenot@aol.com, lcharla@comcast.net.

CHARLES, ALLAN G., obstetrician, educator; b. NYC, Nov. 15, 1928; s. Harry G. and Alice (Grotzky) C.; m. Phyllis V. J. Vail, June 28, 1957; children: Della Marie, Aaron Joseph, David Jonathan. AB cum laude, NYU, 1948, MD, 1952. Diplomate: Am. Bd. Ob-gyn. Intern Phila. Gen. Hosp., 1952-53; resident in ob-gyn. Mt. Sinai Hosp., NYC, 1955-57, Michael Reese Hosp., Chgo., 1957-60, clin. asst., 1960-61, assoc. attending physician, 1961-69, attending physician, 1969—; co-dir. Michael Reese Hosp. (Rh-Investigative Clinic), 1963—, vice-chmn. dept. ob-gyn., 1971, pres. staff, 1978, bd. dirs., 1981-84; chief ob-gyn. Michael Reese Hosp., 1990-99; chmn. rsch. and edn. found. Michael Reese Hosp. Med. Staff, 1996-2000; pvt. practice specializing in office gynecology Chgo., 1960—. Courtesy staff Chgo. Lying-In-Hosp.; clin. asst. prof. ob-gyn. U. Ill. Coll. Medicine, Chgo., 1960-64, Chgo. Med. Sch., 1964-72; clin. prof. Pritzker Sch. Medicine, U. Chgo., 1972-84; attending physician Northwestern Meml. Hosp., 1984-90; prof. clin. ob-gyn. Northwestern U., 1983; clin. prof. ob-gyn. U. Ill. Coll. Medicine, 1991. Author: Rh Iso Immunization and Erythroblastosis Fetalis, 1969; Contbr. articles to profl. jours. Fellow Am. Coll. Obstetricians and Gynecologists, Internat. Coll. Surgeons (chmn. Am. sect. ob-gyn. 1979-83, sec., asst. treas. Am. sect.), Ctrl. Assn. Obstetricians and Gynecologists; mem. AMA, Ill., Chgo. med. socs., Chgo. Gynecol. Soc. (v.p. 1980—, sec. 1988-90, pres.-elect, 1992, pres. 1993-94). Achievements include developing substitute for uterine tube, Rh-sensitization. Home: 1150 N Lake Shore Dr Apt 22GH Chicago IL 60611 Office: 55 E Washington St Fl 37 Chicago IL 60602-2103 Office Phone: 312-263-5517. Personal E-mail: charles0920@sbcglobal.net.

CHARLES, GERARD, performing company executive, choreographer; b. Folkstone, Eng. m. Catherine Yoshimura; 1 child, Max. Student, Royal Ballet Sch. Ballet master BalletMet, Les Grands Ballets Canadiens; profl. dancer Ballet Internat., London, Milw. Ballet; assoc. artistic dir. BalletMet Columbus, artistic dir., 2001—. Choreographer, tchr., restager of works internationally in field. Choreographer The Sleeping Beauty, Coppelia; artistic dir.: Cinderella. Choreographic fellow, Nat. Endowment for Arts. Office: BalletMet Columbus 322 Mount Vernon Ave Columbus OH 43215 E-mail: gcharles@balletmet.org.

CHARLESWORTH, BRIAN, biologist, genetics and evolution educator; b. Brighton, Sussex, Eng., Apr. 29, 1945; came to U.S., 1985; s. Francis Gustave and Mary (Ryan) C.; m. Deborah Maltby, Aug. 19, 1967; 1 child, Jane. BA, Cambridge U., Eng., 1966, PhD, 1969. Postdoctoral fellow U. Chgo., 1969-71, prof. biology, 1985-88, prof. ecology and evolution, 1988-92, chmn. dept., 1986-91, G.W. Beadle Disting. Svc. prof., 1992-97; lectr. in genetics U. Liverpool (Eng.), 1971-74; lectr. in biology U. Sussex, Brighton, Eng., 1974-82, reader in biology, 1982-85; rsch. prof. Royal Soc. Univ. Edinburgh, Edinburgh, 1997—. Author: Evolution in Age-Structured Populations, 1980. Fellow Royal Soc. London, Am. Acad. Arts and Scis.; mem. Genetical Soc. Britain, Am. Soc. Naturalists, Genetics Soc. Am., Soc. Study of Evolution. Avocations: reading, classical music. Home: 39 Minto St Chicago IL 60637-1825 Office: U Edinburg Dept Ecology and Evolution 1101 E 57th St Dept And Chicago IL 60637-1503

CHARNAS, LAWRENCE, neurologist; MD, U. Pa. Diplomate Am. Bd. Med. Genetics, Am. Bd. Neurology. With Harvey Inst. for Human Genetics, Balt. Office: Divsn Ped eurology Box 486 Mayo 420 Delaware St SE Minneapolis MN 55455-0374 Fax: 410-828-2919. E-mail: charnas@gbmc.org.

CHARNAS, MICHAEL (MANNIE), investment company executive; b. Cleve., Sept. 24, 1947; s. Max and Eleanor (Gross) Charnas; m. Mimi F. Stein, June 10, 1990; 1 child from previous marriage, Matthew. BBA, Ohio State U., 1969, MBA in Fin., 1971. Page Ohio Ho. of Reps., 1969; mem. Ohio Staters, Inc., 1969; fin. analyst Addressograph-Multigraph, Inc., Cleve., 1971-73; asst. to pres., dir. planning and budget 1st Nat. Supermarkets, Inc. (Pick-N-Pay), Cleve., 1975-78, asst. to pres., v.p. planning and budgets, 1978-79, sr. v.p. fin., adminstr., 1979-81, sr. v.p., CFO, adminstrv. officer Hartford, Conn., 1981-86; founder Charnas Mktg. and Investment Co., 1986—; pres., owner Indsl. Pallet and Packaging Co., Beachwood, Ohio, 1986-94; regional v.p. Pallet Pallet, Inc. (formerly Indsl. Pallet and Packaging Co.), Toronto, 1995-97; co-owner Samm Properties and Samm Mgmt. Svcs., Ltd., 1998—2007; owner, operator Self Storage Facilities, Ohio, Fla.; owner, CEO Pallet Distbrs., Inc., 1999—2001; v.p., owner PMC Investment Group, 2003—. Co-owner Fat Burrito, Inc., a Qdoba Mexican Grill Restaurants franchise; franchisee Qdoba Mexican Grill Restaurants, Ill., Iowa. Recipient Weatherhead 100 award, Weatherhead Sch. Bus. Case Western Res. U., 2006. Jewish. Avocations: tennis, reading, collecting modern classic cars. Office: 3659 Green Rd Ste 105 Cleveland OH 44122 Office Phone: 216-378-3306. E-mail: bizwiz924@cs.com.

CHARO, ROBIN ALTA, law educator; b. Bklyn., June 6, 1958; d. Jon and Ethel (Munach) C. AB in Biology (cum laude), Harvard-Radcliffe Coll., 1979; JD, Columbia U. Sch. Law, 1982. Bar: N.Y. 1983. Asst. dir. Legis. Drafting Rsch. Fund, Columbia U., NYC, 1982—83, assoc. dir., 1983—85; lectr. Columbia Law Sch., NYC, 1983-85; Fulbright Jr. lectr. in Am. Law, assoc. prof. U. Paris, Pantheon-Sorbonne, 1985-86; legal analyst, biol. applications program Congl. Office of Tech. Assessment, Washington, 1986-88; AAAS Diplomacy fellow, policy develop. divsn. of office of population U.S. Agy. for Internat. Devel., Washington, 1988-89; asst. prof., law & bioethics, dept. med. history & bioethics U. Wis. Law Sch., U. Wis. Med. Sch., Madison, 1989—95; assoc. prof. law U. Wis. Law Sch., Madison, 1995—98, Warren P. Knowles prof. law & bioethics, 1998—2003, Elisabeth S. Wilson prof., 2003—. Cons. N.J. Bioethics Comm., Draft Legsi. on Living Wills, 1988, Congl. Office of Tech. Assessment, 1988-92, U.S. AID, Office of Population 1988-91, Can. Law Reform Commn., Ottawa, Can., 1989-90, Comm. on Uniform Laws, Draft Legislation on Surrogacy, 1989, NIH office Protection from Rsch. Risks; mem. NIH Human Embryo Rsch. Panel, 1993-94, Presdl. at. Bioethics Adv. Comm., 1996-2001, ethics standard working group, Calif. Inst. for Regenerative Medicine, 2005-; vis. lectr. and professorships Fachbereich Rechtswissenschaft, Justus-Liebig-Univ., Giessen, Germany, 1992, Centre de Droit de la Famille, Université de Lyon, France, 1992, Escuela Latinoamericana de la Bioetica, La Plata, Argentina, 1992, Instituto Superior de la Medicina, Santiago, Cuba, 1996, Nova Law Sch., Ft. Lauderdale, Fla., 2001, Facultad Latinoamericana de Ciencias Sociales, Buenos Aires, Argentina, 2003, U. Va. Law Sch., Charlottesville, Virginia), 2004, vis. prof. law, U. Calif. Berkeley Law Sch., 2006-; mem. bioethics adv. bd., Howard Hughes Med. Inst., 2004-, Internat. Soc. for Stem Cell Rsch., 2004-; mem. adv. bd., project on reproductive genetics, Ctr. for Genetics and Pub. Policy, John Hopkins U., 2004-; current mem. com. to review the FDA and U.S. nat. system for assurance of drug safety. Contbr. articles to profl. jours.; mem. editl. bd. Cloning: Science and Policy, 98-, Monash Bioethics Review, 99-, Am. Jour. Bioethics, 2000-01, Public Library of Science, 2003-; policy review editor Journal of Law, Medicine, Healthcare, and Ethics, 1993-. Active U. Wis. Human Subjects Com., Madison, U. Wis. Hosp. Ethics Com., Madison, Abortion Strategy Group, Madison; cons. Rural South Cen. Wis. Perinatal Substance Abuse Project, 1989-; mem. Univ. Bioethics Adv. Com., U. Wis., 1998-, mem. stem cell rsch. program, 2003-; bd. dir. Alan Guttmacher Inst., 1991-96, 98-2000, 2002-,Found. for Genetic Medicine, 1997-Nat. Med. Com. Planned Parenthood Fedn. Am., 2004-; mem. scientific adv. bd. CuresNow, 2002-, Juvenile Diabetes Rsch. Found., WiCell, 2002-, Wis. Stem Cell Rsch. Program, 2004-. Fulbright grantee, 1985-86. Fellow AAAS, Wis. Acad. Sciences, Arts and Letters, Inst. Soc., Ethics & Life Sciences; mem. Internat. Bioethics Assn., Am. Soc. Law and Medicine, NAS(cons.; mem. bd, on life sciences, 2001-, mem.comm. on preventing destructive applications of biotechnology, 2002-03), Inst. Medicine (cons.; mem. com. on smallpox vaccination program implementation, 2002-05, mem. comm. on HIVNET 012 HIV Perinatal Transmission Trials, 2004-, mem. assess the drug safety system in the US, 2005-; (in conjunction with NRC) BLS liasion, comm. on embryonic stem cell rsch guidelines, 2004-, mem. adv. com. human embryonic stem cell rsch., 2006-), Soc. for the Advancement of Women's Health, 1998-2000, Am. Assn. Bioethics (bd. dir.), Open Soc. Inst. Program on Reproductive Health & Rights, 1999-. Democrat. Jewish. Avocations: travel, folk and salsa music, foreign languages, poker, reading, rollercoaster riding, home renovation. Office: U Wis Law Sch Law Bldg 975 Bascom Mall Rm 5211C Madison WI 53706-1399 Office Phone: 608-262-5015. Office Fax: 608-262-5485. Business E-Mail: racharo@wisc.edu.

CHARRON, JOSEPH LEO, bishop emeritus; b. Redfield, SD, Dec. 30, 1939; BA, MA, U. Dayton; STL, Lateran U. Ordained priest Soc. of Precious Blood, 1965; asst. theology prof. St. John's U., Collegeville, Minn., 1970—76; asst. gen. sec. US Catholic Conf., 1976—79; assoc. gen. sec. Nat. Conf. Cath. Bishops, 1976—79; Kansas City Provincial dir. CPPS, 1979—87; aux. bishop Archdiocese of St. Paul and Mpls., 1990—93; ordained bishop, 1990; bishop Diocese of Des Moines, 1994—2007, bishop emeritus, 2007—. Admin. comm. Nat. Conf. Cath. Bishops/U.S. Cath. Conf. Mem.: Cath. Theol. Soc. Am., Soc. Precious Blood. Roman Catholic. Office: Diocese of Des Moines 601 Grand Ave PO Box 1816 Des Moines IA 50309 Office Phone: 515-237-5039. Office Fax: 515-237-5071. E-mail: bishop@dmdiocese.org.*

CHARROW, JOEL, pediatrician, geneticist, educator, director; b. NYC, May 24, 1951; s. Saul David and Doris Elaine (Yates) C.; m. Martha K. McClintock, Oct. 23, 1982; children: Benjamin Whitmore, Julia Rachel. BS in Chemistry and Psychology, Antioch Coll., 1972; MD, Mt. Sinai Sch. Medicine, 1976. Diplomate Nat. Bd. Med. Examiners, Am. Bd. Pediatrics; diplomate in clin. genetics and biocehem. genetics. Am. Bd. Med. Genetics. Pediatric intern Children's Meml. Hosp./Northwestern U. Med. Sch., Chgo., 1976-77, resident in pediatrics, 1977-79, fellow in clin. and biochem. genetics, 1979-81; attending physician Children's Meml. Hosp., Chgo., 1981; from asst. prof. to assoc. prof. pediatrics Northwestern U. Med. Ctr., Chgo., 1981-94, prof. pediatrics, 2002—; dir. Genetics Lab., head sect. clin. genetics Children's Meml. Hosp., Chgo., 1991—, head, divsn. genetics, birth defects, metabolism, 2006—. Mem. adv. bd. Fabry Disease Registry, 2001—. Contbr. chpts. to books, more than 50 articles to profl. jours. Regional coord. Internat. Collaborative Gaucher Group, 1994—; mem. health profl. adv. com. March of Dimes, Chgo., 1986-2004; mem. sci. adv. com. Nat. Tay-Sachs and Allied Diseases Assn., 1984—; mem. State of Ill. Genetic and Metabolic Diseases Adv. Com., 1989-97; mem. Genetics Task Force of Ill., 1982—, v.p., 1990-91, pres., 1991-93. Recipient Bela Schick Pediatric Soc. award Mt. Sinai Sch. Medicine, 1976. Fellow Am. Coll. Med. Genetics (founding), Am. Acad. Pediatrics; mem. Midwest Soc. for Pediatric Rsch., Soc. for Inherited Metabolic Disorders, Bone Dysplasia Soc., Internat. Neurofibromatosis Assn., Alpha Omega Alpha. Office: Children's Meml Hosp Sect Clin Genetics 2300 N Childrens Plz Chicago IL 60614-3394 Office Phone: 773-880-4462.

CHASE, ALYSSA ANN, editor; b. New Orleans, Dec. 23, 1965; d. John Churchill and Alexandra Andra (de Monsabert) C.; m. Robert Brian Rebein, July 1, 1995; children: Alexandra Maria Rebein, Rowen Jakob Rebein. BA in Lit. in English, U. Kans., 1988; BA in Studio Art magna cum laude, SUNY, Buffalo, 1994. Asst. editor Dial Books for Young Readers, NYC, 1989-90; assoc. editor Holiday House, Inc., NYC, 1990-92, Buffalo (N.Y.) Spree Mag., Buffalo, N.Y., 1992-95; copy editor, writer The Riverfront Times and St. Louis Mag., St. Louis, Mo., 1995-97; mng. editor St. Louis Mag., 1997-98; editor RCI Premier Mag., Indpls., 1998—. Freelance copy writer, proofreader, copy editor and/or rschr. Harper Collins Children's Books, N.Y.C., 1990-92, Morrow Jr. Books, N.Y.C., 1990-92, Tambourine Books, N.Y.C., 1990-92, Lothrop, Lee & Shepherd Books, N.Y.C., 1990-92, Dorling Kindersley, Inc., N.Y.C., 1990-92, The Humanist: Prometheus Books, 1993, Printing Prep, Buffalo, 1994, Georgette Hasiotis, Buffalo, 1994, August Tavern Creek Developers, St. Louis, 1996; tchg. artist, docent coord., tour guide The Arts in Edn. Inst. of Western N.Y., Cheektowaga, N.Y., 1995. Mem. Phi Beta Kappa. Avocations: painting, creative writing, travel, gardening, running. Home: 306 N Ridgeview Dr Indianapolis IN 46219-6127

CHASE, CLINTON IRVIN, psychologist, educator; b. Aug. 14, 1927; m. Patricia Cronenberger; 1 child. BS in Psychology with honors, U. Idaho, 1950, MS in Adminstrn., 1951; PhD in Ednl. Psychology, U. Calif.-Berkeley, 1958. Asst. to dean students Wash. State U., 1951-52; sch. psychologist Piedmont Pub. Schs., Calif., 1957-58; asst. prof. ednl. psychology Idaho State U., 1958-61, Miami U., Oxford, 1961-62, Ind. U., Bloomington, 1962-64, assoc. prof., 1964-68, prof., 1968-95; prof. emeritus Indiana U., Bloomington, 1995—; assoc. dir. Bur. Evaluative Studies and Testing Ind. U., Bloomington, 1962-70, dir., 1970-89, chmn. dept. ednl. psychology, 1970-74; dir. Ind. Testing and Evaluation Svc., Bloomington, 1976-87, Ind. Ctr. for Evaluation, 1988-94; owner, mgr. Ind. Testing and Evaluation Svc., 1990—. Author: (with H. Glenn Ludlow) Readings in Educational and Psychological Measurement, 1966, Elementary Statistical Procedures, 1967, 3d edit., 1984, Measurement for Educational Evaluation, 1974, 2d edit., 1978; (with L.C. Jacobs) Developing and Using Tests Effectively, 1992, Contemporary Assessment for Educators, 1999; mem. editl. bd. Jour. Edn. Measurement, 1985-97; contbr. more than 120 articles to profl. jours. Served with USN, 1945-46; to capt. USAF, 1952-55. Named Ky. Col., 1998. Fellow Am. Psychol. Assn. (divsn. 15), Am. Ednl. Rsch. Assn., Nat. Coun. on Measurement in Edn., Phi Beta Kappa, Kappa Delta Pi E-mail: chase@indiana.edu.

CHATO, JOHN CLARK, mechanical and bioengineering educator; b. Budapest, Hungary, Dec. 28, 1929; s. Joseph Alexander and Elsie (Wasserman) C.; m. Elizabeth Janet Owens, Aug. 1954; children: Christine B., David J., Susan E. ME, U. Cin., 1954; MS, U. Ill., 1955; PhD, MIT, 1960. Co-op student, trainee Frigidaire div. GMC, Dayton, Ohio, 1950—54; grad. fellow U. Ill., Urbana, 1954—55; grad. fellow, inst. MIT, Cambridge, 1955—58, asst. prof., 1958—64; assoc. prof. U. Ill., Urbana, 1964—69, prof., 1969—96, prof. emeritus, 1996—, chmn. exec. com. bioengring. faculty, 1972—78, 1982—83, 1984—85, asst. dean of engring., 1997—98. Cons. Industry and Govt., 1958—; dir., founder Biomed. Engring. Systems Team, Urbana, Ill, 1974-78; assoc. editor Jour. Biomech. Engring., 1976-82. Patentee in field; contbr. articles to profl. jours., chpts. to books on heat transfer, bio-heat transfer, refrigeration, air conditioning, cryogenics, and thermal systems. Com. mem. troop 6 Boy Scouts Am., Urbana, 1984—86; com. mem. Urbana Plan Commn., 1973—78; mem. adv. com. Urbana Park Dist., 1981—84; 2nd v.p. Champaign County Izaak Walton League, 1986, 1st v.p., 1987, pres., 1988—92, bd. dirs., state dir., 1992—; mem. Urbana Postal Customer Adv. Coun., 2002—; trustee 1st Presbyn. Ch., Urbana, 1976—78, 1999—2001, elder, 1982—85, 2004—07; bd. dirs. Univ. YMCA, Champaign, Ill., 1976—78, 1987—90, Champaign-Urbana Mass Transit Dist., 2005—. Recipient Tobin award Champaign County Izaak Walton League, 1992, Cmty. Svc. award Urbana Park Dist., 1996, Russell Scott Meml. award, Cryogenic Engring. Conf., 1979; named Disting. Engring. Alumnus, U. Cin., 1972, U. Ill., 2005; NSF fellow 1961, Fogarty Sr. Internat. fellow 1978-79; Japan Soc. Promotion of Sci. fellow, 1997. Fellow: ASHRAE (treas. East Ctrl. Ill. chpt. 1984, sec. 1985, 1987, 1st v.p. 1988, pres. 1989), ASME (exec. com. bioengring. divsn. 1992—96, sec. 1993—94, chmn. 1994—95, Charles Russ Richards Meml. award 1978, H.R. Lissner award 1992, Dedicated Svc. award 2000), Am. Inst. Med. and Biol. Engrs.; mem.: IEEE (sr.), Am. Soc. Engring. Edn., Internat. Inst. Refrigeration (assoc.), Audubon Soc. Champaign County (bd. dirs. 1988—89, v.p. 1990, treas. 1991—93, v.p. 1995—96, treas. 1998—99, pres. 2000—02, bd. dirs. 2002, pres. 2005—06, Audubon Presdl. Recognition award 2007), Exch. Club Urbana (bd. dirs. 1989—91, 1995—96, pres.-elect 1996—97, pres. 1997—98, dist. dir. 2001—05). Presbyterian. Achievements include research in fields of heat transfer, bio-heat transfer, refrigeration, air conditioning, cryogenics, and thermal systems. Avocations: tennis, photography, birdwatching, hiking, kayaking. Office: U Ill Dept Mech Sci and Enging 1206 W Green St Urbana IL 61801-2906 Business E-Mail: jbchato@uiuc.edu.

CHATTERJEE, JAYANTA, architecture and planning educator; b. Calcutta, India, Mar. 19, 1936; arrived in US, 1959; s. Hari C. and Asha (Mukherjee) Chatterjee; m. Janet Ley Smith, Aug. 31, 1968; children: Eric, Brinda. BArch, Indian Inst. Tech., 1958; AA, Arch. Assn. Sch. Arch., 1959; M in Regional Planning, U. NC, 1962; MArch in Urban Design, Harvard U., 1965. Asst. prof. U. of Cin., 1967-72, assoc. prof., 1972-77, assoc. dean, 1975-77, prof., 1977—, dir. sch. planning, 1977-82, acting dean, 1982-83, dean, 1982-2001, prof. arch. and planning, 2001—. Regional designer Met. Area Planning Commn., Boston, 1965—67; urban scholar Cities Recovery Program, Cleve., 1981—82. Co-author: The Partnership Planning, 1982, Rebuilding American Cities, 1983, Breaking the Boundaries, 1989; co-editor/founder: Jour. Planning, Education and Research, 1981-84. Mem. Ohio Eminent Scholar Rev. Panel, 1985, Urban Design Rev. Bd., Cin., 1988—; chmn. design review bd. U. Cin., 1987—; mem. historic conservation bd. City of Cin., 2004—; bd. dirs. Arts Consortium, Cin., 1983—87, Contemporary Arts Ctr., Cin., 1983—, Hillside Trust, Cin., 1983—84, Bethesda Hosp., Inc., Cin., 1982—95, Total Living Concept, Inc., Cin., 1976—88, Ctr. Mediation of Disputes, Cin., 1989—92, The Emery Ctr., Cin., 1988—90, Better Housing League, Cin., 1989—92, Archtl. Found., Cin., 1990—, pres., 2003—05; bd. dirs. Season Found. for Good Govt., 2003—, pres., 2004—06. Recipient Apple award Archtl. Fedn. Cin., 1996, Disting. Alumnus award U. N.C., 1996, Disting. Svc. award Assn. Coll. Schs. of Planning, 1991. Fellow Am. Inst. Cert. Planners (editl. bd. AICP Casebook 1991-93, tech. adv. bd. 1993-96); mem. AIA (assoc.; Thomas Jefferson award pub. arch. 2000), Am. Planning Assn. (pres. Ohio chpt. 1970-72, editorial adv. bd. Jour. APA), Ptnrs. of Ams. (Ohio-Parana), Assn. Collegiate Schs. of Planning (pres. 1983-85, Jay Chatterjee award 1998), Internat. Coun. Fine Arts Deans, Cin. Post/Corbett Found. (Lifetime achievement award in Arts 1999). Office: U Cin Coll of Design Architecture Art and Planning PO Box 210016 Cincinnati OH 45221-0016 Office Phone: 513-556-1204. Office Fax: 513-556-3288. Business E-Mail: jay.chatterjee@uc.edu.

CHATTERTON, ROBERT TREAT, JR., reproductive endocrinology educator; b. Catskill, NY, Aug. 9, 1935; s. Robert Treat and Irene (Spoor) Chatterton; m. Patricia A. Holland, June 24, 1956 (div. 1965); children: Ruth Ellen, William Matthew, James Daniel; m. Astrida J. Vanags, June 4, 1966 (div. 1977); 1 child, Derek Scott; m. Carol J. Lewis, May 24, 1985. BS, Cornell U., 1958, PhD, 1963; MS, U. Conn., 1959. Postdoctoral fellow Med. Sch. Harvard U., 1963-65; rsch. assoc. div. oncology Inst. Steroid Rsch. Montefiore Hosp. and Med. Ctr., NYC, 1965-70; asst. prof. Coll. Medicine U. Ill., 1970-72, assoc. prof. Coll. Medicine, 1972-79; prof. Med. Sch. Northwestern U., Chgo., 1979—. Mem. sci. adv. com. AID, chairperson Instnl. Rev. Bd. Northwestern U., 1982—83, mem. intellectual properties com., 1987—95, chairperson radiation safety com., 2000—02; dir. Immunoassay Facility, R. H. Lurie Cancer Ctr. Northwestern U. Med. Sch., 1997—; dir. clin. labs., dept. ob-gyn. Northwestern Med. Facutly Found., 1996—99, dir. shared clin. labs., 1999—. Contbr. articles to profl. jours. Grantee, NIH, 1972—90, 1995—2006, NSF, 1975, 1995—98, AID, 1971—86, Army Office Rsch., 1987—94. Mem.: AAAS, Am. Assn. Clin. Rsch., Am. Assn. Cancer Rsch., Chgo. Assn. Reproductive Endocrinologists (pres. 1987—88), Soc. Study Reproduction, Soc. Gynecologic Investigation, Endocrine Soc., Am. Chem. Soc., N.Y. Acad. Scis., Phi Kappa Phi, Sigma Xi. Presbyterian. Achievements include patents for method of totally suppressing ovarian follicular devel. and method of ovulation detection. Home: 6001 N Knox Ave Chicago IL 60646-5821 Office: Northwestern U Olson 8408 710 N Fairbanks Ct Chicago IL 60611-3015 Home Phone: 773-777-1311; Office Phone: 312-503-5272. Business E-Mail: chat@northwestern.edu.

CHAUDHARY, SATVEER, state senator; b. June 12, 1969; BA, St. Olaf Coll., 1991; JD, U. Minn., 1995. Mem. Minn. Ho. Reps., 1996-2000, Minn. State Senate, 2000—, vice chair finance com., mem. capital investement, mem. judiciary environ. natural resources, transp., and state govt. budget divsn.; owner Chaudhary Cons. Law clk., intern Hennepin County Atty.'s Office, Minn.; aide Minn. Atty. Gen. Hubert H. Humphrey III. Co-chair Anoka County Legis. Delegation; hon. adv. coun. Asian-Pacific Endowment for Cmty. Devel.; mem. Coalition of Labor Union Women, Minn. Outdoor Heritage Alliance; hon. chair Minn. Cricket Assn.; mem. Minn. Welcome Com. for The Dalai Lama, U. Minn. Indsl. Rels. Adv. Coun., Twin Cities Internat. Citizen Award Com.; Fridley Human Resources Commn.; vol. Mounds View Festival in the Park; mem. New Brighton Hist. Soc., New Brighton Sportsmen's Club, Minn. Pheasants Forever Soc.; state affirmative action officer Minn. DFL Party; co-founder, chair Minn. Asian-Indian Dem. Assn.; bd. dirs. World Trade Ctr., St. Paul, A Blanket of Hope. Named Legislator of the Yr., Coll. Dems. of Minn., 1999; recipient Cert. of Commendation, Legal Aid Soc. of Minn., Cert. of Appreciation, DFL Party, 1995, Achievement award, Indian Assn. Minn. Mem.: New Brighton Eagles, Bass Anglers Soc. Am., Columbia Hts. Lions. Dfl. First Asian Indian sen. in Am. history and first Asian-Am. mem. of Minn. legis. Office: Minn Senate 75 Rev Dr Martin Luther King Jr Blvd Saint Paul MN 55155 E-mail: sen.satveer.chaudhary@senate.mn.

CHAVERS, BLANCHE MARIE, pediatrician, educator, researcher; b. Clarksdale, Miss., Aug. 2, 1949; d. Andrew and Mildred Louise C.; m. Gubare Mpambara, May 21, 1982; 1 child, Kaita. BS in Zoology, U. Wash., 1971, MD, 1975. Diplomate Am. Bd. Pediats. Intern U. Wash., Seattle, 1975-76, resident in pediatrics, 1976-78; instr. U. Minn., Mpls., 1982, asst. prof. pediatrics, 1983-90, assoc. prof. pediatrics, 1990-99, prof. pediatrics, 1999—. Attending physician dept. pediatrics, U. Minn. Sch. Medicine, Mpls., 1982. Co-editor: Am. Jour. Kidney Diseases, 2001—; contbr. articles to profl. jours. Recipient Clin. Investigator award NIH, 1982; Pediatric Nephrology fellow U. Minn., 1978-81. Mem. Am. Soc. Nephrology, Am. Soc. Pediatric Nephrology, Internat. Soc. ephrology, Internat. Soc. Pediatric Nephrology, Am. Soc. Transplantation, Internat. Pediatric Transplant Assn. Democrat. Methodist. Avocations: tennis, reading, collecting African artifacts, art. Office: Univ Minn MMC 491 420 Delaware St SE Minneapolis MN 55455-0348

CHEAP, RICHARD A., lawyer, bank executive; b. 1951; BA, John Carroll U.; JD, Northwestern U.; M in Taxation, Georgetown U. Bar: 1977. Atty. Porter, Wright, Morris & Arthur, Columbus, Ohio, 1981—87, ptnr., 1987—98; exec. v.p., gen. counsel, sec. Huntington Nat. Bank, 1998—; gen. counsel, sec. Huntington Bancshares, Inc., 1998—, v.p., dir. sec., 2001—. Mem.: ABA. Office: Huntington Bancshares Inc 41 S High St Huntington Ctr Columbus OH 43287

CHECCHI, ALFRED A., air transportation executive, financial consultant; b. 1948; BA, Amherst Coll., 1970; MBA, Harvard Univ., 1974. V.p. Marriott Corp., 1975-82; prin. Bass Bros., 1982-86; pres. Alfred Checchi Assocs., Inc., 1986—; co-chmn., bd. dirs. Wings Holdings Inc., 1997—; bd. dirs. Northwest Airlines, Inc., St. Paul, 1997—, co-chmn., 1998; candidate gov. Calif., 1991—97; pres. Washington Strategic Ptnrs., 2002—07. Exec. and adv. bd. mem. J.E. Robert Cos., 2002—06; exec. adv. bd. mem. Elizabeth Glaser Pediat. AIDS Founds. Office Phone: 310-721-6083.

CHECKETTS, DAVE (DAVID WAYNE CHECKETTS), professional sports team executive; b. Salt Lake City, Sept. 16, 1955; s. Clyde Alvin and Edith (Jones) C.; m. Deb Leishman, June 2, 1977; children: Spencer, Katie, Nathaniel, Andrew, Benjamin, Elizabeth. BS, U. Utah, 1979; MBA, Brigham Young U., 1981. Mgmt. cons. Bain and Co., Boston, 1980-83; exec. v.p. Utah Jazz, NBA, Salt Lake City, 1983-84, pres., 1984-87, pres., gen. mgr., 1987-88, gen. mgr., 1988-89; v.p. devel. NBA, NYC, 1990—91; pres. NY Knickerbockers, NBA, 1991—94; pres., CEO Madison Sq. Gardens, 1994—2001; founder, chmn. Sports Capital Ptnrs. (SCP), 2001—; chmn. SportsWest Comm., 2002—; prin. owner, operator Real Salt Lake (MLS franchise), Salt Lake City, 2004—; prin. owner. gov. St. Louis Blues, 2006—. Bd. dirs. JetBlue Airways Corp., 2000—, Citadel Broadcasting Corp., 2002—, McLeodUSA Inc., 2004—. Trustee Salt Lake Visitor and Conv. Bur., 1986. Mem. LDS Ch. Lodge: Rotary. Avocations: basketball, golf, water sports, photography. Office: St Louis Blues Hockey Club Scottrade Ctr 1401 Clark Ave Saint Louis MO 63103*

CHEE, CHENG-KHEE, artist, educator; b. Xienyou, Fujian, China, Jan. 14, 1934; arrived in came to U.S., 1962, naturalized, 1980; s. Ya-Jie and Xien-chun (Zheng) C.; m. Sing-Bee Ong, Aug. 28, 1965; children: Yi-Hung, Yi-Min, Wan-Ying, Yen-Ying. BA, Nanyang U., Singapore, 1960; MA, U. Minn., 1964. Asst. libr. anyang U., 1961-62; tchg. asst. U. Minn., Mpls., 1963-64, libr. Duluth, 1965-68, instr., 1968-80, asst. prof., 1981-88, assoc. prof., 1988—. One-man shows include Zhejiang Acad. Fine Arts, 1984, 87, Tweed Mus. Art, U. Minn., 1982-83, 91-92, Shanghai U. Acad. Fine Arts, China, 1987, Tianjin Acad. Fine Arts, China, 1988, Phipps Ctr. for Arts, Wis., 1991, Cannon Rotunda U.S. Ho. Office Bldg., Washington, 1993, Singapore Nat. Art Mus., 1997, Minn. Mus. Am. Art, 1997, Bloomington Ctr. for Arts, Minn., 2003; exhibited in group shows Am. Watercolor Soc. Ann., Nat. Acad. and Salmagundi Club, N.Y.C., 1975, 78, 79, 81, 91, 94-95, 98, 2001, 03, Foothills Art Ctr., Golden, Colo., 1976, 78, 80, 84, 90, 92-93, Allied Artists Am., Nat. Arts Club, N.Y.C., 1980, 82, 91-97, 99-2001, 03, Cmty. Arts Ctr., Old Forge, N.Y., 1982-83, 86, 89, 91-92, 95-98, 2000, 02-04, Nat. Watercolor Soc. Ann. Exhbn., 1983-85, 92, 96, 2002-03, Knickerbocker Artists USA Ann. Exhbn., 1980-81, 89-93, Sumi-e Soc. Am. Ann. Exhbn., 1979-84, 86, Mitchell Mus., Ill., 1983, Mpls. Inst. Arts, 1978, Nat. Taiwan Art Edn. Inst. Watercolor Exhbn. Artist of Taiwan, U.S. and Australia, 1994; author portfolio Cheng-Khee Chee Watercolors, 1984, 87, 91, 94, 96, (book) The Watercolor World of Cheng-Khee Chee, 1997; author exhbn. catalog, 1973-82, Retrospective Exhbn., 1982, China Exhbn. Tour, 1987, Singapore Nat. Art Mus. Exhbn., 1997, Bloomington Art Ctr., Minn., 2003; contbr. to books: Watercolor Energies, 1983, Learn Watercolor, The Edgar Whitney Way, 1994, Splash 3: Ideas and Inspirations, 1994, The Best of Watercolor, 1995, Splash 4: The Splendor of Light, 1996; illustrator: (children's books) Old Turtle, 1992 (AABBY award, Internat. Reading Assn. award 1993), Splash 5: The Glory of Color, 1998, The Best of Watercolor, Vol. 3, 1999, Swing Around the Sun, 2003, Noel, 2005. Recipient Gold medal of honor Allied Artists of Am. exhibit, 1980, Knickerbocker Artists Exhbn., 1989, Silver medal of honor Am. Watercolor Soc. Exhbn., 1991, High Winds medal Am. Watercolor Soc. Exhbn., 1994, Grand award Akron Soc. Artists Grant Nat. Exhbn., 1994, Colo. Centennial award Rocky Mountain Nat. Watermedia Exhbn., 1976, Grumbacher Gold medal Midwest Watercolor Soc. Exhbn., 1984, 85, 98, Gold award Ga. Watercolor Soc. Exhbn., 1985, 98, Gold medal and Purchase prize Knickerbocker Artists 43rd Ann. Grand Nat. Open Juried Exhbn., 1993, Chancellor's Disting. Svc. award U. Minn., 1994, Silver award Calif. Watercolor Assn., 1998; named Best in Show Sumi-e Soc. Am., 1984, 86, New Orleans Art Assn. 11th Nat. Art Exhbn., 1986, Western Colo. Watercolor Soc. Ann. Nat. Exhbn., 1993, Red River Watercolor Soc. 1st Nat. Art Exhbn., 1994, La. Watercolor Soc. 26th Ann. Internat. Exhbn., 1996, Duluth Arts and Cultural Cmty. Enrichment award, 2004; Duluth's Cultural Amb. to the World, Mayor Doty, 1994, Arts and Culture Cmty. Enrichment award Duluth Depot Found., 2004. Mem. Am. Watercolor Soc. (Dolphin fellow), Nat. Watercolor Soc., Rocky Mountain Nat. Watermedia Soc., Allied Artists Am., Knickerbocker Artists USA, Transparent Watercolor Soc. Am. (Master Watercolorist), Watercolor USA Honor Soc., Sumi-e Soc. Am., others. Home: 1508 Vermilion Rd Duluth MN 55812-1526 Office Phone: 218-724-2554. Home Fax: 218-724-6153.

CHEELY, DANIEL JOSEPH, lawyer; b. Melrose Park, Ill., Oct. 24, 1949; s. Walter Hubbard and Edith Arlene (Orlandino) C.; m. Patricia Elizabeth Dorsey, May 14, 1977; children: Mary Elizabeth, Daniel, Katherine, Laura, Anne-Marie, Thomas, Susan, Michael, William. AB, Princeton U., 1971; JD, Harvard U., 1974. Bar: Ill. 1974, U.S. Dist. Ct (no. dist.) Ill. 1975, U.S. Ct. Appeals (7th cir.) 1975. Ptnr. Baker & McKenzie, Chgo., 1974-81, ptnr. litigation, 1981-85, capital ptnr. litigation, 1985-94; ptnr. Mauck, Bellande & Cheely, Chgo., 1994-2000, Bellande, Cheely & O'Flaherty, Chgo., 2000—05, Cheely, O'Flaherty & Ayres, Chgo., 2005—. Liaison counsel Asbestos Claims Facility, Chgo., 1985-88, bus. devel. com., 1987-90, Chgo. assoc. train com., 1988-91, chmn. Chgo. assoc. evaluation; liaison coun. Com. for Claims Resolution, 1988-89; cons. Midwest Theol. Forum, 2003—. Advisor Midtown Sports and Cultural Ctr., Chgo., 1974—; mem. River Forest Regular Reps., Ill., 1980-88, Ill. Rep. Assembly, Chgo., 1984—; pres. Cath. Evidence Forum, 1984—; pres. Ch. History Forum, 1994—; dir. Cath. Citizens of Ill., 1997—; bd. dirs. Cath. Lawyers Guild, 2000—; cons. Midwest Theological Forum, 2003-. Mem. ABA (vice chmn. environ. law sect. 1989-97), Ill. Bar Assn., Appellate Lawyers Soc. Ill., Chgo. Bar Assn., Trial Lawyers Club. Chgo., Serra Club (v.p. Chgo. chpt. 1988-89, 92-94, 96—, treas. 1989-92), United Rep. Fund, Phi Beta Kappa. Roman Catholic. Avocations: history, christian apologetics, travel. Office: Cheely O'Flaherty & Ayres 19 S La Salle St Ste 1203 Chicago IL 60603-1406 Office Phone: 312-853-8714. Personal E-mail: dcheely@aol.com. Business E-Mail: dcheely@lawchicago.net.

CHEFITZ, JOEL GERALD, lawyer; b. Boston, Aug. 27, 1951; s. Melvin L and Bernice L (Kahn) Chefitz; m. Sharon P Garfinkel, 1972; children: Sandra Beth, Meira Sarah, Michael Hanan. AB cum laude, Boston U., 1972, JD magna cum laude, 1976. Bar: Ill 1976, US Dist Ct (no Dist) Ill 1977, US Ct Appeals (3d cir) 1981, US Supreme Ct 1983, US Ct Appeals (7th cir) 1984, US Ct Appeals (9th cir) 1993, US Ct Appeals (2d cir) 1994, US Ct Appeals (5th cir) 1996, US Ct Appeals (4th cir) 1998, US Ct Appeals (fed cir) 2000, US Ct Appeals (DC cir) 2001. Law clk. to presiding justice U.S. Dist. Ct. Mass., Boston, 1976-77; assoc. Kirkland & Ellis, Chgo., 1977-82, ptnr., 1982-86, Katten Muchin & Zavis, Chgo., 1986—2002, Howrey Simon Arnold & White, Chgo., 2002—. Editor: (jour) Boston Univ Law Rev, 1975—76; contbr. articles to profl jours. Bd. dirs. Legal Assistance Found. Met. Chgo., Gastrointestinal Rsch. Found. Scholar Am Jurisprudence, Boston Univ, 1973—76, CJS, 1975, Bigelow, 1976. Mem.: ABA, 7th Cir Asn, Chicago Bar Asn, East Bank Club. Office Phone: 312-595-1522. E-mail: chefitzj@howrey.com.

CHELBERG, BRUCE STANLEY, holding company executive; b. Chgo., Aug. 14, 1934; s. Stanlye Andrew and Josephine Marie (Mohn) C.; children: Stephen E., david M., Kimberly Anne. BS in Commerce, U. Ill., 1956; LLB, 1958. Bar: Ill. 1958. Atty. Trans Union Corp., Chgo., 1958-64; asst. gen. counsel, 1964-68; pres. Getz Corp., San Francisco, 1968-71; v.p. Trans Union Corp., Chgo., 1971-78; pres., COO, 1978-81; sr. v.p. Whitman Corp. (formerly IC Industries, Inc.), Chgo., 1982-85, exec. v.p., 1985-92, chmn., CEO, 1992, also bd. dirs. Bd. dirs. First Midwest Bank corp., Northfield Labs, Snap-On-Tools, Inc. Bd. dirs. Arlington Heights Pub. Sch. Dist. 25, Ill., 1974-83, higher edn. State Ill., 1988-1999. Mem. Ill. State Bar Assn., Chgo., Met. (Chgo.), World Trade (San Francisco).

CHELETTE, TAMARA LYNNE, biomedical engineer; b. Morgantown, W.Va., July 11, 1962; d. Charles Caruthers and Nancy Ruth (Williams) Cook; m. Murry René Chelette, June 1, 1985; children: Murry René Jr., Andrew John. BS in Engring., Boston U., 1984; PhD of Biomed. Scis., Wright State U., 1994. Registered profl. engr., Ohio. Intern clin. engring. Mass. Eye and Ear Infirmary, Boston, 1983-84; biomed. engr. VA, Little Rock, 1984-86, Dayton, Ohio, 1986-87; biomed. sys. engr. Krug Internat., Dayton, 1987-89; biomed. engr. human effectiveness directorate Air Force Rsch. Lab., Wright-Patterson AFB, Ohio, 1989—. Adj. prof. Wright State U., Dayton, 1994—. Patentee in field; contbr. articles to profl. jours. Treas. Wright-Patt Young Heroes Assn., Dayton, 1992—. Recipient Outstanding Achievement award Soc. Women Engrs., 1982, Arthur Flemming award, Washington JayCees, 1995, Dayton English and Sci. Found. outstanding engr. of Miami Valley award, 2000. Fellow Aerospace Human Factors Assn.; mem. IEEE (Fritz Russ award in biomedical engring. 2000) Aerospace Med. Assn. (assoc. fellow, Innovative Rsch. award 1994, pres. life scis. br. 1996, Eric Liljencrantz award 1997, Paul Bert award 1998), Engring. in Medicine and Biology Soc., SAFE Assn. (v.p. Wright Bros. chpt. 1994-95, pres. 1998-99). Avocation: gardening. Office: Air Force Rsch Lab Bldg 824 Rm 206 2800 Q St Wright Patterson AFB OH 45433-7008

CHELIOS, CHRIS (CHRISTOS K. CHELIOS), professional hockey player; b. Chgo., Jan. 25, 1962; Student, U. Wis. Defenseman Montreal Canadiens, Que., 1981—90, Chgo. Blackhawks, 1990—99, Detroit Red Wings, 1999—. Mem. Team USA, World Cup of Hockey, 1996, 2004, USA Olympic Hockey Team, Nagano, 1998, Salt Lake City, 2002; player NHL All-Star Game, 1985, 1990—94, 1996—98, 2000, 02. Founder Cheli's Children's Found., 1992. Named All Star Tournament Team, NCAA, 1983; named to All-Rookie Team, HL, 1985, First All-Star Team, 1989, 1993, 1995, 1996, 2002, Second All-Star Team, 1991, 1997; recipient James Norris Meml. Trophy, 1989, 1993, 1996, Bud Light Plus/Minus Award, 2002, Mark Messier Leader of Yr. Award, 2007. Achievements include being a member of Stanley Cup Champion Montreal Canadiens, 1986, Detroit Red Wings, 2002; being a member of silver medal winning USA Hockey Team, Salt Lake City Olympics, 2002; served as Captain to Team USA, Salt Lake City Olympic Games, 2002, World Cup of Hockey, 2004. Office: Detroit Red Wings 600 Civic Center Dr Detroit MI 48226-4419

CHELLE, ROBERT FREDERICK, electric power industry executive, educator; b. New Brunswick, NJ, July 18, 1948; s. Robert and Frances (Brown) C.; m. Karen Ann Cederburg, Aug. 7, 1971; children: Robert, Pamela. BA, Bethany Coll., 1970; MBA, U. Dayton, 1972. Asst. contr. Tait Mfg. Co., Dayton, Ohio, 1972-73; pres. High Voltage Maintenance Corp., Dayton, 1973-99; dir. Crotty Ctr. for Entrepreneurial Leadership, U. Dayton, 1999—. Bd. dirs. The Siebenthaler Co., Dayton; adv. bd. U. Dayton Sch. Bus., 1994—. Contbr. articles to profl. jours. Chmn. Dayton C. of C., 1993, County Corp., Dayton, 1995. Recipient Cert. Appreciation Montgomery County Commn., Dayton, 1984-85, Up and Comer award for engring. City of Dayton, 1988. Mem. Nat. Elect. Testing Assn., Ohio Bar Assn. (mem. profl. ethics com. 2001—), Rotary (pres. 1984-85). Presbyterian. Avocations: yachting, fishing.

CHEMA, THOMAS V., government official, lawyer, academic administrator; b. East Liverpool, Ohio, Oct. 31, 1946; s. Stephen T. and Dorothy Grace (McCormack) C.; m. Barbara Burke Orr, Aug. 15, 1970; children: Christine, Stephen. AB, U. Notre Dame, 1968; JD, Harvard U., 1971. Bar: Ohio 1971, U.S. Supreme Ct. 1977. Assoc. Arter and Hadden, Cleve., 1971-79, ptnr. 1979-85, 1989-2003; of counsel Tucker, Ellis and West, 2003--; co-founder, pres. Gateway Cons. Group, Inc., 1994-; pres.Hiram Coll., Ohio, 2003--; exec. dir. Ohio Lottery Commn., Cleve., 1983-85, Gateway Econ. Devel. Corp. Greater Cleveland, 1990-95; chmn. Pub. Utilities Commn. Ohio, Columbus, 1985-89; chmn. Ohio Bldg. Authority, 1990-96. Candidate for Ohio Senate, 1980; campaign mgr., Senator Howard M. Metzenbaum, 1976; co-chmn. task force on violent crime, Cleve., 1981-83; trustee Hiram Coll., 1994—2003, Cleve. Works, Inc., 1995-98, Cleve. City Club, 1993-96, Sisters of Charity of St. Augustine Health Sys., 1994—, Hist. Gateway eighborhood, Inc., 1995—; dir. Transtechnology, Inc., Fairport Funds. Mem. ABA (adv. coun.), Nat. Assn. Regulatory Utility Commrs., Nat. Assn. State Lotteries (bd. dirs.), Greater Cleve. Bar Assn., Ohio State Bar Assn., Cleve. Legal Aid Soc., Ohio Legal Assistance Found. (chmn. 1996-99), Electric Power Rsch. Inst., Sr. Citizens Resources Inc. (trustee), Hospice Coun. No. Ohio (sec., trustee, legal counsel), Citizens League, NAACP, League Women Voters, Am. Soc. Pub. Adminstrs. Trustee, St. Ignatius High Sch., Prospect Vision, Inc., Downtown Devel. Coords. Cleve. Found. Arch. Democrat. Roman Catholic. Club: City (Cleve., trustee 1993—). Avocation: skiing. Home: 18580 Parkland Dr Cleveland OH 44122-3469 Office: Office of President Hiram College Hiram OH 44234 Home Phone: 330-569-5120; Office Phone: 330-569-6112. Business E-Mail: chematv@hiram.edu.

CHEMBERLIN, PEG, minister, religious organization administrator; b. York, Nebr., Sept. 27, 1949; d. Charles Norman and Donna May (Chemberlin) Bean. BA with distinction, U. Wis., Parkside, 1973; grad., United Theol. Sem. Twin Cities, 1982. Ordained deacon Moravian Ch. Am., 1982, consecrated presbyter Moravian Ch. Am., 1986. Formerly dir. campus ministries, tchr., youth min.; also outreach min., parish intern pastor; exec. dir. Minn. Coun. Chs., 1995—. Former pres., former program chmn. Nat. Assn. Ecumenical and Interfaith Staff, 1992, 97; hon. campaign chair Minn. Food Share, 2003. Recipient Women of Excellence award Minn. Gov., 1994, NOVA Peace and Justice award, 1985; Angel of Reconciliation award, 2003. Mem.: Nat. Coun. of Ch. (mem. governing bd. 2003—07). Office: Minn Coun Chs 122 W Franklin Ave Minneapolis MN 55404-2447

CHEMERS, ROBERT MARC, lawyer; b. Chgo., July 24, 1951; s. Donald and Florence (Weinberg) C.; m. Lenore Ziemann, Aug. 16, 1975; children: Brandon J., Derek M. BA, U. So. Calif., 1973; JD, Ind. U.-Indpls., 1976. Bar: Ind. 1976, Ill. 1976, U.S. Dist. Ct. (so. dist.) Ind. 1976, U.S. Dist. Ct. (no. and so. dists.) Ill. 1977, U.S. Ct. Appeals 7th cir.) 1977, U.S. Ct. Appeals (5th cir.) 1985. Assoc. Pretzel & Stouffer, Chgo., 1976-79, officer, 1979-81, dir., 1981—. Author: IICLE -Civil Practice, 1978, rev. edit. 1982, 87; IICLE Settlements, 1984. Mem. ABA, Ill. State Bar Assn., Chgo. Bar Assn., Def. Rsch. Inst., Ill. Def. Counsel, Appellate Lawyers Assn. Office: Pretzel & Stouffer One S Wacker Dr Chicago IL 60606 Business E-Mail: rchemers@pretzel-staouffer.com.

CHEN, DAVID, spinal cord injury physician; b. Mpls., Minn., Dec. 16, 1960; BA summa cum laude in Fin., Univ. Ill., 1983; MD, U. Ill. Coll. Medincine, 1987. Cert. physical medicine and rehab. Intern Northwestern U. Med. Sch., Chgo., 1987—88, resident, 1988—91; dir., spinal cord injury program Rehab. Inst. of Chgo., 1994—, med. dir., spinal cord injury, 1996—. Named one of 40 Under 40, Crain's Bus. mag., 1997; recipient Bronze Tablet award, U. Ill., 1979—83, Alumni Recognition award, Naperville (Ill.) Central High Sch., 1999. Mem.: Am. Spinal Injury Assn., Midwest Reg. Spinal Cord Injury Care System (dir. data acquisition unit 1993—), Khi Kappa Phi, Alpha Lambda Delta, Phi Beta Kappa. Office: Rehab Inst Chgo 345 E Superior St Chicago IL 60611 Business E-Mail: d-chen@northwestern.edu.

CHEN, DI, electronics executive, optical engineer, consultant; b. Chekiang, China, Mar. 15, 1929; came to U.S., 1954, naturalized, 1972; s. Hsun Yu and chien (Wang) C.; m. Lynn C. Wang, June 14, 1958; children: Andrew A.J., Daniel T.Y. BS, Nat. Taiwan U., 1953; MS, U. Minn., 1956; PhD, Stanford U., 1959. Asst. prof. U. Minn., Mpls., 1959-62; rsch. fellow Honeywell Co., Bloomington, Minn., 1962-80; tech. dir. Optical Peripherals Lab., Colorado Springs, Colo., 1980-84; co-founder, exec. v.p. tech. Optotech, Inc., 1984-89; pres. Chen and Assocs. Cons., 1989—. V.p. tech. and engring. Literal Corp., Colorado Springs, 1990-91; chmn., then co-chmn., advisor, sr. advisor Optical Data Storage, 1983-98. Topical editor Applied Optics Jour., 1991-97; contbr. articles to profl. jours, chpts. to ref. books; patentee in field. Founder, chair bd. dirs. Chinese Am. Assn. Minn., 1965—79. Recipient Honeywell Sweatt Scientists and Engrs. award, 1972. Fellow IEEE (life, chmn. IEEE-MAG Twin Cities chpt. 1974); mem. SPIE, Optical Soc. Am., Sigma Xi, Eta Kappa Nu. Office Phone: 952-472-1036. E-mail: dichen2127@frontiernet.net.

CHEN, KUN-MU, electrical engineering educator; b. Taiwan, China, Feb. 3, 1933; came to U.S., 1957, naturalized, 1969; s. Tsa-Mao and Che (Wu) C.; m. Shun-Shun Chen, Feb. 22, 1962; children: Margaret, Katherine, Kenneth, George. BS, Nat. Taiwan U., 1955; MS, Harvard, 1958, PhD, 1960. Research assoc. U. Mich., 1960-64; vis. prof. Chao-Tung U., Taiwan, 1962; asso. prof. elec. engring. Mich. State U., 1964-67, prof., 1967-95, Richard M. Hong Endowed prof. elec. engring., 1995—99, dir. elec. engring. grad. program, 1967-70, Richard M. Hong prof. emeritus, 1999—. Vis. prof. Tohoku U., Japan, 1989, Nat. Taiwan U., 1989, 2007. Author articles on electromagnetic radiation, plasma physics, electromagnetic bioeffects. Recipient Disting. Faculty award Mich. State U., 1976, Outstanding Achievement award in sci. and engring. Taiwanese Am. Found., 1984; Withrow Disting. scholar Coll. Engring., Mich. State U., 1993; C.T. Loo fellow, 1957; Gordon McKay fellow Harvard U., 1958-60. Fellow IEEE, AAAS; mem. Internat. Union Radio Sci. (commn. A, B and C), AAUP, Sigma Xi, Phi Kappa Phi, Tau Beta Pi. Home: 7585 Mona Ln San Diego CA 92130 Office: Mich State U Dept Elec Engring East Lansing MI 48824 Business E-Mail: chen@msu.edu.

CHEN, MICHAEL MING, mechanical engineering educator; b. Hankow, China, Mar. 10, 1933; came to U.S., 1953, naturalized, 1965; s. Kwang Tzu and Hwei Chuing (Deng) C.; m. Ruth Hsu, Oct. 15, 1961; children: Brigitte (dec.), Derek, Melinda. BS, U. Ill., 1955; SM, MIT, 1957, PhD, 1961. Sr. staff scientist research and devel. Avco Corp., Wilmington, Mass., 1960-63; asst. prof. engring. and applied sci. Yale U., 1963-69; asso. prof. mech. engring. N.Y. U., 1969-73; prof. mech. engring. and bioengring., dept. mech. and indsl. engring. U. Ill., Urbana-Champaign, 1973-91; prof. mech. engring. and applied mechanics U. Mich., Ann Arbor, 1991—. Dir. thermal systems program NSF, 1991-93; cons. A.D. Little Co., NIH, Argonne Nat. Lab., Bell Labs. Asso. editor: Applied Mechanics Rev.; contbr. to profl. publs. Fellow ASME (Heat Transfer Meml. award 1990); mem. AIChE, Minerals, Metals and Materials Soc., Am. Phys. Soc., Sigma Xi, Phi Kappa Phi, Tau Beta Pi, Pi Tau Sigma. Office: U Mich Dept Mech Engring 2350 Hayward St Ann Arbor MI 48109-2125

CHEN, SHOEI-SHENG, retired mechanical engineer; b. Taiwan, Jan. 26, 1940; s. Yung-cheng and A-shu Chen; m. Ruth C. Lee, June 28, 1969; children: Lyrice, Lisa, Steve. BS, Nat. Taiwan U., 1963; MS, Princeton U., 1966, MA, 1967, PhD, 1968. Rsch. asst. Princeton U., 1965—68; asst. mech. engr. Argonne Nat. Lab., Ill., 1968—71, mech. engr., 1971—80, sr. mech. engr., 1980—2001; ret., 2001. Cons. to Internat. Atomic Energy Agy. to assist developing countries in R & D of nuc. reator sys. components, 1977, 79, 80, 94; cons. NASA, NRC, Rockwell Internat., others. Author: Flow-Induced Vibration of Circular Cylinderical Structures, 1987; mem. internat. adv. editl. bd. Acta Mechanica Solida; adv. bd. JSME Internat. Jour.; assoc. editor Applied Mechs. Rev., Jour. of Pressure Vessels Tech.; contbr. articles to profl. jours. Recipient Disting. Performance award U. Chgo., 1986, ASME pressure vessel and piping medal, 2001. Fellow ASME (chmn. tech. subcom. on fluid and structure interactions pressure vessels and piping divsn. 1987-90, honors chmn. 1990-94, exec. com. 1990-96, organizer symposia, tech. program chmn. 1994, conf. chair ASME/JSME pressure vessels and piping conf. 1995, pressure vessels and piping divsn., chmn. 1995-96, senate pres. 1997-98, honors and awards chair of materials and structures tech. group 1996-99), Instn. Diagnostic Engrs.; mem. Am. Acad. Mechanics, Acoustical Soc. Am., Sigma Xi. Personal E-mail: ss@sschen.com. E-mail: sschen88@gmail.com.

CHENEVICH, WILLIAM L., bank executive; Grad., City Coll. N.Y.; master's, CUNY. Chief indsl. engr. space programs Grumman Aerospace; with Carte Blanche Corp. Citicorp, LA; pres., COO Security Pacific Automation Co., Inc.; exec. v.p., dir. info. svcs. Home Savings of Am.; group exec. v.p., head sys. group and software devel. Visa Internat., San Francisco; vice chmn., dir. info. svcs. and ops. Firstar Corp., Milw., 1999—. Office: Firstar Corp 777 E Wisconsin Ave Milwaukee WI 53202-5300

CHENEY, DUANE, state representative; b. NYC, July 27, 1948; m. Elaine Cheney; 2 children. BSE, SUNY, Cortland, 1970, MSE, 1975. Phys. edn. instr. McGraw Ctrl. Sch., 1970—79; uni-serv dir. Ind. State Tchrs. Assn., 1979—98; state rep. dist. 10 Ind. Ho. of Reps., Indpls., 1998—, vice chair, human affairs com., mem. appointments and claims, edn., and ways and means coms. Mem.: Prevent Child Abuse Porter County, Calumet Project, Am. Assn. Ret. Persons, Portage Exch. Club, Sons of Am. Legion Post 260. Democrat. Roman Catholic. Office: Ind Ho of Reps 200 W Washington St Indianapolis IN 47204-2786

CHENEY, JEFFREY PAUL, manufacturing executive; b. Laona, Wis., Feb. 28, 1956; s. Joseph C. and Gordie Lee (Bodoh) C.; m. Rhoda L. Mueller, Feb. 14, 1981; children: Lisa Marie, Mathew Steven. BS in Bus., U. Wis., Green Bay, 1979; MBA, Marquette U., 1986. CPA. Fin. analyst Kohler (Wis.) Co., 1979-81, sr. planning analyst, 1981-82, mgr., planning, 1982-83, mgr., corp. planning, 1984-86, controller, 1986-90, treas., 1990—; sr. v.p. fin., CFO Kohler, 1999—. Treas., Kohler Found. Trust, 1990, Kohler Preservation Trust, 1991. Republican. Office: Kohler Co 444 Highland Dr Kohler WI 53044

CHENEY, PAUL D., physiologist, educator; b. Jamestown, NY, Oct. 10, 1947; married; 2 children. BS, SUNY, Fredonia, 1969; PhD, SUNY, Syracuse, 1975. Fellow in physiology U. Wash. Sch. Medicine, Seattle, 1974-77; rsch. asst. prof. dept. physiology and biophysics U. Wash., 1977-78; asst. prof. physiology U. Kans. Med. Ctr., Kansas City, 1978-88, prof. physiology, 1988—. Mem. Soc. Neurosci, Sigma Xi. Office: U Kansas Med Ctr R L Smith Rsch Ctr 3901 Rainbow Blvd Kansas City KS 66160-0004

CHENG, HERBERT SU-YUEN, mechanical engineering educator; b. Shanghai, Jan. 15, 1929; came to U.S., 1949; s. Chung-Mei and Jing-Ming (Xu) C.; m. Lily D. Hsiung, Apr. 11, 1953; children: Elaine, Elise, Edward, Earl. BSME, U. Mich., 1962; MSME, Ill. Inst. Tech., 1956; PhD, U. Pa., 1961. Jr. mech. engr. Internat. Harvester Co., Chgo., 1952-53; project engr. Machine Engring. co., Chgo., 1953-56; instr. Ill. Inst. Tech., Chgo., 1956-57, U. Pa., Phila., 1957-61; asst. prof. Syracuse (N.Y.) U., 1961-62; rsch. engr. Mech. Tech. Inc., Latham, N.Y., 1962-68; assoc. prof. Northwestern U., Evanston, Ill., 1968-74, prof., 1974—, Walter P. Murphy prof., 1987—2002, dir. Ctr. for Engring. Tribology, 1984—88, 1992—96, prof. emeritus, 2002—. V.p. Gear Rsch. Inst., Naperville, Ill., 1985-90; cons. GM, Chrysler Corp., Deere Co., Nissan, E.T.C., 1970-2002. Contbr. articles to profl. jours. Deacon South Presbyn. Ch., Syracuse, 1961-62, 1st Presbyn. Ch. Schenectady, N.Y., 1962-68. Named a hon. prof. Nat. Zhejiang (People's Republic of China) U., 1985. Fellow ASME (hon., Mayo D. Hersey award 1990, D.F. Wilcock award 1999), Soc. Tribologists & Lubrication Engrs. (hon., Nat. award 1987, CAP Alfred Hunt award 1997); mem. NAE, Inst. Mech. Engrs. (U.K., Tribology gold medal 1992), Am. Gear Mfrs. Assn. (acad. mem.). Avocations: peking opera, tennis. Office: Northwestern U Dept Mech Engring 2145 Sheridan Rd Evanston IL 60208-0834

CHENG, STEPHEN ZHENG DI, chemistry professor, polymer engineer; b. Shanghai, Aug. 3, 1949; came to U.S., 1981, naturalization, 1992; s. Luzhong and Jingzhi (Zhang) C.; m. Susan Lian Zhi Xue, June 28, 1978; 1 child, Wendy D.W. BS in Math., East China Normal U., 1977; MS in Polymer Engring., China Textile U., 1981; PhD in Polymer Chemistry, Rensselaer Poly. Inst., 1985. Postdoctoral and rsch. assoc. Rensselaer Poly. Inst., Troy, N.Y., 1985-87; asst. prof. polymer sci. U. Akron, Ohio, 1987-91, assoc. prof. polymer sci. Ohio, 1991-95, prof. polymer sci., trustee Ohio, 1995—. Faculty rsch. assoc. Maurice Morton Inst. of Polymer Sci., U. Akron, 1987—, faculty rsch. assoc. Inst. Polymer Engring., 1988—; vis. prof. sci, U. of Tokyo, 1994; vis. prof. polymer sci. and engring. Sichun Union U., China, 1994—; fgn. mem. acad. steering com. Nat. Polymer Physics Open Lab., Chinese Acad. Sci., 1994—, guest prof. polymer sci. Guangzhou Inst. Chemistry, 1994—, guest prof. polymer sci. Changchun Inst. Applied Chemistry, 1995—; guest prof. polymer materials and engring. Zhengzhou U., China, 1994—; guest prof. polymer sci. and engring. Peking U., 1996—, Zhejiang U., 1996—; guest prof. U. Sci. and Tech. of China, 1996—; mem. orgn. com. The First Conf. Worldwide Young Chinese Chemists, Beijing, 1995; adv. prof. polymer sci. Chinese Textile U., 1995—, Fudan U., 1996—, Hebei U. of Tech., 1996—; cons., spkr. in field; project dir. thin film optics Sci. and Tech. Ctr. for Advanced Liquid Crystalline Optical Materials, NSF, 1994—, assoc. dir. Ctr. for Molecular and Microstructure of Composites, 1996—; hon. mem. acad. steering com. Nat. Key Lab. of Chem. Fiber Structure Modification, China Textile U., 1995—; internat. lectr. in field. Editor: Jour. Macromolecular Sci. Part B, Physics, 1995—; adv. bd. Polymer Internat. Jour., 1990—, Marcromolecules, 1996—, Trends in Polymer Sci., 1992—; editl. bd. Jour. Macromolecular Sci., Rev. of Macromolecular Chemistry and Physics, 1992—, Thermochemica Acta, 1992—, Macromolecular Chemistry and Physics, 1994—, Macromolecular Rapid Communications, 1994—, Jour. Polymer Rsch., 1995—, Internat. Jour. Analysis and Characterization, 1995—; vol. editor: Liquid-Crystalline Polymer Systems: Technological Advances, 1996, Handbook of Thermal Analysis and Calorimetry, Vol. 3, 1997; contbr. chpts. to books and more than 180 articles to profl. jours.; patentee in field. Bd. trustees Akron Internat. Inst., 1995—. Grantee in field; recipient Presdl. Young Investigator award NSF and White House, 1991, Appreciation cert. U. Akron Bd. Trustees, 1992, 94, John H. Dillon Medal, Am. Phys. Soc., 1995, Outstanding Rschr. award U. Akron, 1997; named Disting. corp. Inventor, Am. Soc. Patent Holders, Inventure Place and Home of the Nat. Inventors Hall of Fame, 1995. Fellow Am. Phys. Soc., N.Am. Thermal Analysis Soc. (exec. coun. 1991-93, 94-96, awards vice chmn. 1991-92, awards chmn. 1992-93, meeting vice chmn. 1994, meeting chmn. 1995, others); mem. Am. Chem. Soc. (Akron Sect. award 1994), Soc. Plastics Engrs. (awards com. 1991-94), Materials Rsch. Soc., Soc. Advancement Material and Process Engring., Internat. Confedn. for Thermal Analysis (edn. com. 1996—), Material Rsch. Soc., Internat. Liquid Crystal Soc. Achievements include research on solid state of polymeric materials including phase transition thermodynamics, kinetics, molecular motion, crystal structure and morphology, liquid crystal polymers, surface and interface structures, high-performance polymer fibers, films for microelectronic and optical applications, high temperature composites, computer simulation of molecular dynamics and modeling. Office: U Akron Morton Inst Polymer Sci Akron OH 44325-0001

CHERNEY, JAMES ALAN, lawyer; b. Boston, Mar. 19, 1948; s. Alvin George and Janice (Elaine) Cherney; m. Linda Bienenfeld. BA, Tufts U., 1969; JD, Columbia U., 1973. Bar: Ill. 1973, U.S. Supreme Ct. 1977, U.S. Ct. Appeals (7th cir.) 1979, U.S. Ct. Appeals (3d cir.) 1982, U.S. Ct. Appeals (10th cir.) 1984, U.S. Ct. Appeals (8th and 9th cirs.) 1987. Assoc. Kirkland & Ellis, Chgo., 1973-76, Hedlund, Hunter & Lynch, Chgo., 1976-79, ptnr., 1979-82, Latham & Watkins, Chgo., 1982—. Bd. of ComtyHealth, comty-based health care provider West Side Chgo., bd. and Past pres. Temple Sholom Chgo. and Saddle & Cycle Club Chgo. Mem. Antitrust Law and Litig. Law Sect. ABA, Chgo. Bar Assn. Office: Latham & Watkins LLP Ste 5800 Sears Tower 233 S Wacker Dr Chicago IL 60606-6306 Office Phone: 312-876-7715. Office Fax: 312-993-9767. Business E-Mail: james.cherney@lw.com.

CHERRY, DANIEL RONALD, lawyer; b. Mpls., Dec. 31, 1948; s. Clifford D. and Ruby E. (Norman) C.; m. Dianne Brown, Jan. 24, 1971 (dec.); children: Matthew A., Kathryn E.; m. Q. Rhea Walker, Oct. 25, 1998. SB, MIT, 1970; JD cum laude, Harvard U., 1976. Bar: Ohio 1976, U.S. Dist. Ct. (no. dist.) Ohio 1976, U.S. Patent and Trademark Office 1978, U.S. Ct. Appeals (6th and Fed. cirs.) 1982, Ill. 1987, U.S. Dist. Ct. (no. dist.) Ill. 1987. Assoc. Squire, Sanders & Dempsey, Cleve., 1976-85, ptnr., 1985-87; ptnr., prin. Welsh & Katz, Ltd., Chgo., 1987—2007; ptnr., Duane Morris, 2007—. Co-author: Patent Practice, 1997. With USCG, 1970-73. Mem. ABA, Ohio State Bar Assn., Ill. State Bar Assn., Chgo. Bar Assn., Am. Intellectual Property Law Assn., Intellectual Property Law Assn. Chgo., Licensing Execs. Soc. Office: Duane Morris 227 W Monroe St Ste 3400 Chicago IL 60606 Home: 2001 Schiller Ave Wilmette IL 60091 Business E-Mail: drcherry@duanemorris.com.

CHERRY, JOHN D., JR., lieutenant governor, former state senator; b. Sulphur Springs, Tex., May 5, 1951; s, John D. Sr. and Margaret L. (Roark) C.; m. Pamela M. Faris, 1979; children: Meghan M., John D. BA, U. Mich., 1973, MA, 1984. Chmn. 7th Cong. Dist. Dem. Com., Mich., 1973-75; adminstrv. asst. Mich. State Sen. Gary Corbin, 1975-81; Mich. polit. dir. Am. Fedn. State, County & Munic Employees AFL-CIO, 1981-82; mem. Mich. Ho. Reps. from 79th dist., Lansing, 1983-86, Mich. State Senate from 28th dist. (formerly 29th dist.), Lansing, 1987—2002, minority leader, mem. legis. coun.; lt. gov. State of Mich., Lansing, 2003—. Mem. Genesee County Dem. Exec. Bd., 1983-2002; mem. Mich. Jobs Comm. Bd., 1996-2000; del. Dem. Nat. Conv., 1996, 2000, 04; treas. Nat. Lt. Govs. Assn., 2004-05; vice chair Great Lakes Commn., 2005-. Named Conservationist of Yr., Mich. United Conservation Club, 2005. Democrat. Mailing: Office Lt Governor PO Box 30013 Lansing MI 48909 Office Phone: 517-373-6800. Office Fax: 517-241-3956.

CHERRY, PETER BALLARD, electrical products corporation executive; b. Evanston, Ill., May 25, 1947; s. Walter Lorain and Virginia Ames (Ballard) C.; m. Crissy Hazard, Sept. 6, 1969; children: Serena Ames, Spencer Ballard. BA, Yale U., 1969; MBA, Stanford U., 1972. Analyst Cherry Elec. Products Corp., Waukegan, Ill., 1972-74, data processing and systems mgr., 1974, treas., 1974-77; v.p. fin. and bus. devel. Cherry Elec. Products Corps., Waukegan, Ill., 1977-80; exec. v.p. Cherry Elec. Products Corp., Waukegan, Ill., 1980-82, pres., chief oper. officer, 1982-86; pres., chief exec. officer Cherry Corp., Waukegan, 1986-92, chmn., pres., 1992—. Trustee Lake Forest Coll., Ill., 1982-90; trustee Lake Forest Hosp., 1982—, chmn., 1989-92. Mem.Onwentsia Club. Office: Cherry Corp 10411 Corporate Dr Pleasant Prairie WI 53158

CHERRY, ROBERT W., state representative; b. Shelbyville, Ind., Oct. 22, 1947; divorced; 3 children. BS, Purdue U. Farmer; pub. sch. tchr., 1970—72; with Ind. Dept. Edn., 1972—74, Farm Credit Ctr., 1976—88; dir. local govt. rels. Ind. Farm Bur., 1988—; state rep. dist. 53 Ind. Ho. of Reps., Indpls., 1998—, mem. fin. instns. and local govt. coms., asst. Rep. caucus chmn. Mem. bd. Ind. Appeals, 1970—72; mem. Hancock County Planning Commn., 1972—82, Greenfield Bd. Zoning Appeals, 1975—88; at large mem. Hancock County Coun., 1992—98; past chmn. Agrl. Adv. Coun.; appt. by gov. Ind. State Bd. Tax Commrs. Mem.: Farm Bur., Greater Greenfield C. of C., Murat Shrine, Masons, Kiwanis, Elks. Republican. Office: Ind Ho of Reps 200 W Washington St Indianapolis IN 46204-2786

CHERYAN, MUNIR, agricultural and biochemical engineering educator; b. Cochin, Kerala, India, May 7, 1946; came to U.S., 1968; B. Tech. with honor, Indian Inst. Tech., Kharagpur, 1968; MS, U. Wis., 1970, PhD, 1974. From asst. prof. to assoc. prof. food and biochemical engring. U. Ill., Urbana, 1976-85, prof. food and biochemical engring., 1985—. Cons. UN Devel. Program, 1985—. Author: Ultrafiltration Handbook, 1986, Ultrafiltration and Microfiltration Handbook, 1988; mem. editl. bd. Jour. Food Engring., 1985, Jour. Food Process Engring., 1985—, Internat. Dairy Jour., 1989—, Membrane Tech. Newsletter, 1997—; patentee for protein hydrolysis. Recipient Gardners award Assn. Food Scientists and Technologists, India, 1988, A.D.M. award Am. Oil Chemists Soc., 1984, Rsch. Team award Am. Soybean Assn., 1991, Rsch. and Commercialization award Nat. Corn Growers Assn., 1993, Archer-Daniels-Midland award, Am. Oil Chem. Soc. Mem. Am. Inst. Chemical Engrs., Inst. Food Technologists, Am. Chemical Soc., N.Am. Membrane Soc. Office: U Ill Agrl Bioprocess Lab 1302 W Pennsylvania Ave Urbana IL 61801

CHESLEY, STANLEY MORRIS, lawyer; b. Cin., Mar. 26, 1936; s. Frank and Rachel (Kinsburg) C.; children: Richard A., Lauren B. BA, U. Cin., 1958, LLB, 1960. Bar: Ohio 1960, Ky. 1978, W.Va. 1981, Tex. 1981, Nev. 1981. Ptnr. Waite, Schneider, Bayless & Chesley Co., Cin., 1960—. Contbr. articles to profl. jours. Past chmn. bd. commrs. on grievances and discipline Supreme Ct. Ohio; past pres. Jewish Fedn. Cin.; nat. vice chair, bd. govs., United Jewish Coms.; exec. bd., nat. bd. govs. Am. Jewish Com.; nat. bd. govs. Hebrew Uninon Coll.; exec. com. U.S. Holocaust Meml. Mus. Mem. bd. of dirs. Am. Jewish Joint Distbn ABA, ATLA, FBA, Am. Judicature Soc., Melvin M. Belli Soc., Ohio Bar Assn., Ky. Bar Assn., W.Va. Bar Assn., Tex. Bar Assn., Nev. Bar Assn., Cin. Bar Assn. Office: Waite Schneider Bayless & Chesley 1513 4th and Vine Tower Cincinnati OH 45202 Office Phone: 513-621-0267. Personal E-mail: wsbclaw@aol.com.

CHESSER, MICHAEL J., gas and electric power industry executive; BS, Ga. Tech. Univ.; MBA, Loyola Coll., Balt. With Balt. Gas & Electric; pres., COO Atlantic Energy Inc., 1994—98; pres., CEO Itron Inc., Spokane, Wash., 1999—2000, GPU Energy, Morristown, NJ, 2000—02; chmn., CEO United Water Resources, Harrington Park, J, 2002—03, Great Plains Energy, Kansas City, Mo., 2003—. Bd. mem. Edison Elec. Inst., Elec. Power Rsch. Inst. Trustee Univ. Mo., Kansas City, Midwest Rsch. Inst.; bd. mem. Heart of Am. United Way, Partnership for Children; mem. leadership bd. Mid-Am. Regional Council; mem. Civic Council Greater Kansas City, Kans. Bus. Edn. Partnership. Office: Great Plains Energy 1201 Walnut St Kansas City MO 64106 Mailing: Great Plains Energy PO Box 418679 Kansas City MO 64141-9679

CHESTER, JOHN JONAS, lawyer, educator; b. Columbus, Ohio, July 13, 1920; s. John J. and Harriet Bonnadine (Rice) C.; m. Cynthia Johnson, Apr. 18, 1959; children: John, James, Joel, Cecily. AB cum laude, Amherst Coll., Mass., 1942; JD, Yale U., New Haven, Conn., 1948. Bar: Ohio 1948. Ptnr. Chester & Chester, Columbus, 1948-57, Chester & Rose, Columbus, 1958-70, Chester Willcox and Saxbe and predecessor firm, Columbus, 1971—. Spl. counsel Pres. of US, 1974. adj. prof. Ohio State U. Coll. Law. Past bd. dirs. Grant Riverside Meth. Hosps.; past chmn. Doctor's Hosp.; past chmn., bd. dirs. Ohio Health, 2001—; past trustee Doctor's Hosp., Columbus Sch. for Girls, Columbus Acad., Shepherd Hill Hosp., Ohio Hist. Found., Ohio Hist. Soc.; active Ohio Gen. Assembly, 1953-58; dir. emeritus Ohio Health, 2005—; dir. Navy Meml. Found., 2006—. Lt. USNR, 1942-46. Mem. ABA, Ohio State Bar Assn., Columbus Bar Assn., Am. Coll. Trial Lawyers, Columbus Club, Columbus Athletic Club, Rocky Fork Hunt and Country Club. Republican. Episcopalian. Home: 4906 Riverside Dr Columbus OH 43220-2876 Office: Chester Willcox & Saxbe 65 E State St Ste 1000 Columbus OH 43215-3442 Office Phone: 614-221-4000. Business E-Mail: jackchester@cwslaw.com.

CHIARA, MARGARET MARY, former prosecutor, lawyer; b. 1943; BA, Fordham U.; MA in Edn. Adminstrn., Pace U.; JD, Rutgers U., 1979. Assoc. French and Lawrence, Cassopolis, Mich., 1979—82; prosecuting atty. Cass County Prosecutor's Office, 1982—96; adminstr. Trial Ct. Assessment Commn., 1997—98; policy and planning dir. Office of Chief Justice of Mich. Supreme Ct., 1999—2001; US atty. (we. dist.) Mich. US Dept. Justice, 2001—07.

CHICO, GERY J., lawyer, school system administrator; BA, U. Ill., 1979; JD, Loyola U., Chgo., 1985. Dep. chief of staff Mayor Richard Daley, Chgo., 1991-92; gen. counsel Chgo. Devel. Coun.; chief of staff Mayor Richard Daley, Chgo., 1992-96; ptnr., head govt. and mcpl. fin. group Altheimer & Gray, Chgo.; pub. bldg. commr. City of Chgo.; pres. Sch. Reform Bd. Trustees, Chgo. Active numerous civic groups. Active numerous profl. assns., including Mex.-Am. C. of C. (past pres.). Office: Sch Reform Bd Trustees Chicago Bd Edn 125 S Clark St Chicago IL 60603-5200

CHICOINE, DAVID LYLE, academic administrator; b. Elk Point, SD, June 17, 1947; s. Roland and Evelyn (Lyle) C.; m. Marcia Kay Elgie, Mar. 8, 1969; children: Jason, Joshua. BS, S.D. State U., 1969; MS, U. Del., 1971; MA, Western U., 1978; PhD, U. Ill., 1979. Area extension adv. Coop. Extension Service, Urbana, Ill., 1971-77; prof. Inst. Govt. and Pub. Affairs U. Ill., Urbana-Champaign, 1984—2007, asst. prof. dept. agr. econs., 1979-84, assoc. prof., 1984-87, prof., head Dept. Agrl. Econs., 1988—95, dean Coll. Agrl., Consumer and Environ. Sci., 1995—2001, v.p. tech. and econ. devel., 2001—06, interim v.p. academic affairs, 2006; pres. SD State U., Brookings, 2007—07. Mem. Bd. Govs. for Argonne Nat. Lab., U. Chgo., 2003—06. Co-author: Government Structure and Local Public Finance, 1985; co-editor: Financing Rural Infrastructure, 1987, Financing Economic Development, 1987; contbr. more than 100 articles to profl. jours. Recipient Legis. leadership award, Ill. Farm Bur., 1981, research awards/grants several founds. and govt. agys., 1982-88. Mem. Am. Agriculture Econs. Assn., Am. Econs. Assn., Midwest Econs. Assn., Nat. Tax Assn. Home: 929 Harvey Dunn St Brookings SD 57006

CHICOINE, ROLAND ALVIN, farmer, former state legislator; b. Rural Elk Point, SD, Dec. 10, 1922; s. Elmire Joseph and Louise Marie (Ryan) C.; m. Evelyn Marie Lyle, June 18, 1945; children: Jeffrey R., David L., Marcia M. Quinn, Daniel B., Timothy K., Brian Elmire, Ellen Little, Nicole Louise Klein. Owner, farmer, Elk Point, 1942-90; state rep. S.D. State Legislature, 1980—86, 1993—2000, state senator, 1987—92. Mem. Elk Point Local Dist. Sch. Bd., 1971-80; bd. dirs. Union County Farmers Home Adminstrn.; 4-H leader (40 yrs.) Sioux Livestock 4-H Club, state past pres. Named Family of Yr., S.D. State U., 1989, Eminent Farmer of Yr., S.D. State U., 1998. Mem. County Crop Improvement Assn. (past chmn. bd. dirs.), County Livestock Improvement Assn. (past chmn. bd. dirs.), S.D. State Irrigators Assn. (past state chmn. and organizer), S.D. Water Congress (past bd. dirs.), Union County Livestock Assn. (resolutions com. 1980—), Fed. Land Bank Assn. (Sioux Falls area chmn., bd. dirs. 1970-84, Omaha 4 state adv. bd. 1976-80), S.C. State 4-H Leaders Assn. (state chmn.), Eminent Farmers Assn. (pres. 2001-02) Lions(pres. Elk Point chpt. 2002). Democrat. Roman Catholic. Avocation: golf. Address: 32648 480th Ave Elk Point SD 57025-6833

CHIEGER, KATHRYN JEAN, consumer products company executive; b. Detroit, July 13, 1948; BA, Purdue U., 1970; MA, U. Mich., 1974; MBA, U. Denver, 1983. Libr. U. Mich., Ann Arbor, 1970-74; staff aide U.S. Sen. Gary Hart, Denver, 1974-79; dir. fin. rels. Petro-Lewis Corp., Denver, 1979-86; dir. investor rels. Kraft Inc., Glenview, Ill., 1987-89; v.p. corp. affairs Gaylor Container Corp., Deerfield, Ill., 1989-96; v.p. corp. and investor rels. Brunswick Corp., Lake Forest, Ill., 1996—. Mem. Nat. Investor Rels. Inst. (chpt. bd. dirs. 1979-84, v.p. mem. 1982-83, pres. 1983-84, nat. bd. dirs. 1984-88), Investor Rels. Assn., Chgo. Coun. Fgn. Rels., Sr. Investor Rels. Roundtable. Office: Brunswick Corp 1 N Field Ct Lake Forest IL 60045-4811 Office Phone: 847-735-4612. Business E-Mail: kathryn.chieger@brunswick.com.

CHILCOTE, GARY M., museum director, reporter; b. St. Joseph, Mo., Nov. 2, 1934; s. Merrill and Mary Thelma C.; m. Mary Carolyn Abmeyer, April 2, 1958; children: Douglas A., Carolyn D. BA, Northwest Mo. State U., Maryville, 1956. News-press spl. corr. St. Joseph News-Press/Gazette, 1954—2002; mus. dir. Patee House Mus. and Jesse James Home, St. Joseph, 1963—. Vocat. tchr. Hillyard Tech. Sch., St. Joseph, 1964-91. Author, editor Pony Express Mail, 1972—; featured on History Channel, Discovery Channel, Good Morning Am. and others. Staff sgt. Mo. Air Guard, 1957-63. Recipient Cmty. Heritage award, Mo. Humanities Coun., 2007. Mem. Nat. Pony Express Assn. (nat. dir., nat. v.p. 1990—), Pony Express Hist. Assn. (bd. dirs., co-founder 1963), James-Younger Gang (nat. pres. 1997—, 98-99). Republican. Office: Patee House Mus/Jesse James Ho Mus 1202 Penn St Saint Joseph MO 64503-2560 Office Phone: 816-232-8206. Business E-Mail: patee@ponyexpress.net.

CHILCOTE, LEE A., lawyer; b. Cleve., May 5, 1942; BA, Dartmouth Coll., 1964; BE, Thayer Sch. Engring., 1965; JD, U. Calif., San Francisco, 1972. Bar: Ohio 1972. Ptnr. Chilcote Law Firm, Cleve. Bd. dirs., The Chilcote Co., sec., 1972—. Trustee Hough Housing Corp. 1972-88, Neighborhood progress Inc. 2005-, Cuyahega Valley Nat. Pk.; bd. dirs. Cleve. Warehouse Dist. Local Devel. Corp., 1986—. Mem. ABA (real property and corp. sects.), Am. Coll. Real Estate

Lawyers, Cleve. Bar Assn., Order of Coif, Thurston Soc. Office: The Chilcote Law Firm The Cedar Grandview Bldg 12434 Cedar Rd Ste No 3 Cleveland Heights OH 44106 Office Phone: 216-795-4117. Business E-Mail: lee.chilcote@chilcotelaw.com.

CHILDERS, L. DOYLE, state legislator; b. Ironton, Mo., Nov. 25, 1944; s. Lawrence Arlin and Jewel Nicks C. AS, Sch. Ozarks, 1964, BS, 1972; postgrad., Southwestern Mo. State U. Active U.S. Peace Corps., Cen. Am., 1965-69; sci. chmn. Reeds Spring RIV Sch. System, 1972-82; Mo. State rep. Dist. 29, 1983-96, Mo. state sen., 1996—. Active Reeds Spring Comm. Betterment Assn. Mem. Lions, Delta Kappa Phi. Home: PO Box 127 Reeds Spring MO 65737-0127 Office: MO House of Rep Rm 102BB 201 West Capitol Avenue Jefferson City MO 65101

CHILDERS, MARY ANN, newscaster; m. Jay Levine. BS in Speech, Northwestern U., Evanston, Ill. Assoc. prodr. Phil Donahue Show, Chgo.; with WAVE-TV, Louisville, WTHR-TV, Indpls.; anchor, med. editor and reporter WLS-TV, Chgo., 1980—94, WBBM-TV, Chgo., 1994—, co-anchor 11am and 4pm and med. editor. Hon. bd. mem. Y-Me, Nat. Kidney Found. of Ill., Nat. Spinal Cord Injury Assn.; mem. Chgo. Cancer Rsch. Found.; mem. nat. adv. coun. Northwestern U. Sch. of Speech; mem. Chgo. Network. Recipient 3 Emmy awards. Office: WBBM-TV 630 McClurg Ct Chicago IL 60601

CHILDRESS, BRAD, professional football coach; b. Aurora, Ill., June 27, 1956; m. Dru-Ann Childress; children: Kyle, Andrew, Christopher, Cara. Graduate, Ea. Ill. U. Wide receivers coach Illinois U., 1978—84; quarterbacks coach Indianapolis Colts, 1985; offensive coord. No. Ariz. U., 1986—89, Utah U., 1990—92; quarterback coach, offensive coord. Univ. Wisconsin, 1992—98; quarterback coach Phila. Eagles, 1999—2001, offensive coord., 2002—06; head coach Minn. Vikings, 2006—. Office: Minnesota Vikings 9520 Viking Dr Eden Prairie MN 55344

CHILDS, ERIN C., lawyer; b. Chgo., 1977; BA, St. Louis U., 1998; JD, U. Cin., 2002. Bar: Ohio 2002, US Dist. Ct. Southern Dist. Ohio 2002, US Ct. of Appeals Sixth Cir. 2004. Assoc. Thompson Hine LLP, Cin. Ct. apptd. special adv. ProKids. Named one of Ohio's Rising Stars, Super Lawyers, 2006. Mem.: Ohio State Assn., ABA, Cin. Bar Assn. (sec., Young Lawyers Divsn.). Office: Thompson Hine LLP 312 Walnut St 14th Fl Cincinnati OH 45202-4089 Office Phone: 513-352-6756. Office Fax: 513-241-4771.

CHILES, STEPHEN MICHAEL, retired lawyer; b. July 15, 1942; s. Daniel Duncan and Helen Virginia (Hayes) C.; m. Deborah E. Nash, June 13, 1964; children: Stephen, Abigail. BA, Davidson Coll., 1964; JD, Duke U., 1967. Bar: N.Y. 1970, Pa. 1978, Wis. 1981, Ill. 1986, U.S. Dist. Ct. (ea. dist.) Pa. 1978, U.S. Tax Ct. 1978, U.S. Supreme Ct. 1978. Officer trust dept. Irving Trust Co., NYC, 1970-75, v.p., 1975-77; assoc. atty. Stassen Kostos & Mason, Phila., 1978-79, mem., shareholder, 1979-85; ptnr. McDermott, Will & Emery LLP, Chgo., 1986—2004, of counsel, 2005—06. Contbr. articles to profl. jours. Served to capt. U.S. Army, 1967-69. Decorated Bronze Star, Army Commendation medal. Mem.: State Bar Wis., Landings Club, (Savannah, Ga.). Republican. Episcopalian. Personal E-mail: smchiles@comcast.net.

CHIN, CHENG, physicist, educator; BS in Physics, Nat. Taiwan U., 1993; PhD in Physics, Stanford U., Calif., 2001. Postdoctoral fellow physics dept. Stanford U., 2001—03; vis. prof. U. Innsbruck Inst. Exptl. Physics, Austria, 2003, vis. scientist, 2003—05; vis. prof. Swiss Fed. Inst. Tech. (ETH), Zurich, 2005; asst. prof. dept. physics and James Franck Inst. U. Chgo., 2005—. Contbr. articles to sci. jours. Recipient Young Rschr. award, Overseas Chinese Physics Assn., 2006; Alfred P. Sloan fellow, 2006—, Packard fellow, 2006—. Office: Dept Physics U Chgo 929 E 57th St Chicago IL 60637 Office Phone: 773-702-7192. Office Fax: 773-834-5250. E-mail: cchin@uchicago.edu.

CHIN, NEE OO WONG, reproductive endocrinologist; b. Hong Kong, Nov. 27, 1955; came to U.S., 1958; s. Bing Leong and Din Sui (Gee) C.; m. Shelly Loraine Crumrine, June 25, 1977; children: Jason Lei, Taryn Mae. BA, U. Cin., 1977; MD, Ohio State U., 1981. Diplomate Am. Bd. Ob-Gyn. Resident Duke U. Med. Ctr., Durham, .C., 1981-84, chief resident, 1984-85; fellow Ohio State U. Coll. Medicine, Columbus, Ohio, 1985-87; teaching staff Good Samaritan Hosp., Cin., 1987—; clin. asst. prof. U. Cin. Med. Ctr., 1987—; dir. assisted reproductive techs. The Christ Hosp., Cin., 1992—. Mem. High Sch. for the Health Profl. subcom., Cin., 1989—. Author: (with others) Current Therapy in Obstetrics, 1988; contbr. articles to profl. jours. Named to Honorable Order of Ky. Cols., Gov. Martha Collins of Ky., 1987. Fellow Am. Coll. Ob-Gyn.; mem. AAAS, Am. Fertility Soc., Soc. Assisted Reproductive Tech., Soc. for Immunology Repro., Cin. Ob-Gyn. Soc. (med. malpractice com. 1989—), Acad. Medicine Cin. Avocations: tennis, Karate. Office: 2814 Mack Rd Fairfield OH 45014 Home Phone: 513-771-9533; Office Phone: 513-326-4300. Personal E-mail: neeoowchinmd@aol.com.

CHING, WAI YIM, physics professor, researcher; b. Shaoshing, China, Oct. 18, 1945; came to U.S., 1969; s. Di-Son and Hung-Wong (Sung) C.; m. Mon Yin Lung, Dec. 27, 1975; children: Tianyu, Kunyu. BSc, U. Hong Kong, 1969; MS, La. State U., 1971, PhD, 1974. Rsch. assoc., lectr. U. Wis., Madison, 1974-78; asst. prof. U. Mo., Kansas City, 1978-81, assoc. prof., 1981-84, prof. physics, 1984-88, curators' prof., 1988—, chmn. physics dept., 1990-98. Cons. Argonne (Ill.) at. Lab., 1978-82, vis. scientist, 1985-86; vis. prof. U. Sci. and Tech., Hefei, China, 1983; guest scientist Max-Planck Inst. für Metallforschung, Stuttgart, Germany, 1997. Contbr. articles to profl. jours. Recipient N.T. Veatch award for disting. rsch., 1985, 2004; Trustee fellow U. Mo., Kansas City, 1984, 90. Fellow: Am. Ceramic Soc.; mem.: AAAS, Materials Rsch. Soc., Am. Vacuum Soc., Am. Phys. Soc., Sigma Xi. Achievements include the study of theoretical condensed matter physics and materials sciences; electronic, magnetic, optical, dynamical structural and superconducting properties of ordered and disordered solids. Home: 2809 W 119th St Leawood KS 66209-1104 Office: U Mo Dept Physics Robert H Flarsheim Hall 5100 Rockhill Rd Kansas City MO 64110-2481 Home Phone: 913-491-6766. Business E-Mail: chingw@umkc.edu.

CHINN, REX ARLYN, chemist; b. Bosworth, Mo., Apr. 5, 1935; s. Loren Herbert and Lima (Stanton) C.; m. Wanda June Williams, May 31, 1959 (dec.); children: Timothy Michael, Sharon Rose Chinn-Heritch, Jonathan Daniel; m. Victoria Loraine Hunter. BS in Chemistry, S.W. Mo. State Coll., 1961; grad., Cleve. Inst. Electronics. Lic. Bapt. minister. Rsch. asst. U. Mo. Med. Ctr., Columbia, 1961-65, William S. Merrell Co., Cin., 1965-67; lab. supr. U.S. Indsl. Chem. Co., Rsch. div., Cin., 1967-72; mgr. quality assurance Cloudsley Co., Cin., 1972-74; dir. tech. affairs Woodson Tenent Labs., Memphis, 1974-77; quality engr. Nat. Ind. for the Blind, Earth City, Mo., 1977-96; owner/mgr. The Master's Image, Maryland Hts., Mo., 1987—. Freelance field prodns. KNLC, Channel 24, St. Louis, 1987—; freelance audo rec. for ACTS Inc., 1996-2000; dir. video ops. Mission Gate Prison Ministry, 2000-2001; video cons.; environ. control sys. cons. Contbr. articles to profl. jours; producer: More Than a Fighting Chance, 1989. Founder, dir. Christian Alliance of Video Ministries, 2002—. With US Army, 1954—56. Mem. Media Comms. Assn. Republican. Avocations: art, photography, electronics, motorcycling, guitar. Home and Office: The Masters Image 12079 Ameling Rd Maryland Heights MO 63043-4148 Office Phone: 314-434-1409. E-mail: themastersimage@sbcglobal.net.

CHIPMAN, JOHN SOMERSET, retired economist, educator; b. Montreal, Que., Can., June 28, 1926; s. Warwick Fielding and Mary Somerset (Aikins) C.; m. Margaret Ann Ellefson, June 24, 1960; children: Thomas Noel, Timothy Warwick. Student, U. Chile, Santiago, 1943—44; BA, McGill U., Montreal, 1947, MA, 1948; PhD, Johns Hopkins U., 1951; postdoctoral, U. Chgo., 1950—51; Doctor rerum politicarum honoris causa, U. Konstanz, Germany, 1991, U. Würzburg, 1998; D in Social and Econ. Scis., U. Graz, Austria, 2001. Asst. prof. econs. Harvard U., Cambridge, Mass., 1951—55; assoc. prof. econs. U. Minn., Mpls., 1955—60, prof., 1961—81, Regents' prof., 1981—2007. Fellow Ctr. for Advanced Study in Behavioral Scis., Stanford, Calif., 1972-73; Guggenheim fellow, 1980-81; vis. prof. econs. various univs.; permanent guest prof. U. Konstanz, 1985-91; bd. dirs. Leuthold Funds, Inc., 1995-. Author: The Theory of Intersectoral Money Flows and Income Formation, 1951; editor: (with others) Preferences, Utility, and Demand, 1971, Preferences, Uncertainty and Optimality, 1990, (with C.P. Kindleberger) Flexible Exchange Rates and the Balance of Payments, 1980; co-editor Jour. Internat. Econs., 1971-76, editor, 1977-87; assoc. editor Econometrica, 1956-60, Can. Jour. Stats., 1980-82; adv. bd. Jour. Multivariate Analysis, 1988-92. Recipient Humboldt Rsch. award for Sr. U.S. Scientists, 1992, 2003. Fellow AAAS, Econometric Soc. (coun. 1971-76, 81-83), Am. Statis. Assn., Am. Acad. Arts and Scis., Am. Econ. Assn. (disting.); mem. NAS (nat. assoc. 2004, chair sect. econ. scis. 1997-2000, James Murray Luck award 1981), Internat. Statis. Inst., Am. Philos. Soc., Inst. Math. Stats., Can Econ. Assn., Royal Econ. Soc., History of Econs. Soc. Home: 2121 W 49th St Minneapolis MN 55419-5229 Office: U Minn Dept Econs 1035 Heller Hall 217 19th Ave S Minneapolis MN 55455-0400 Office Phone: 612-625-2816. Business E-Mail: jchipman@umn.edu.

CHIPPARONI, GUY, communications company executive; married; two children. BS in Journalism, Ill. State U., 1981. Sr. mng. dir. of pub. affairs Hill & Knowlton, Chgo., 1992-97; pres., pub. affairs KemperLesnik Comms., Chgo., 1997—. Apptd. to bd. Met. Pier and Exposition Authority to oversee Navy Pier and McCormick Place, Chgo., 1998. Office: KemperLesnik Comms Ste 1500 455 N Cityfront Plaza Dr Chicago IL 60611-5313 Fax: 312-755-0274.

CHISHOLM, JACKY CLARK, singer, evangelist; b. Detroit; d. Mattie Moss Clark; m. Glynn Chisholm; children: Angel, Michael, Aaron. Mem. The Clark Sisters, 1970—. Co-founder, adminstr. Clark Conservatory Music, Detroit, 1979. Singer: (albums) Expectancy, 2005, (with The Clark Sisters) Bringing It Back Home, 1971, Sincerely, 1983, Heart & Soul, 1985, Is My Living In Vain?, 1985, Conqueror, 1989, Christmas, 1990, Count It All Joy, 1990, He Gave Me Nothing, 1990, Unworthy, 1990, You Brought the Sunshine, 1990, Miracle, 1994, Live: One Last Time, 2007 (Best Traditional Gospel Album, Grammy Awards, 2008), (songs) Blessed & Highly Favored, 2007 (Best Gospel Performance & Best Gospel Song, Grammy Awards, 2008). Active in Red Cross; spokesperson Am. Diabetes Assn.; active in Greater Emmanuel Institutional Church of God in Christ, Detroit; dir. youth choir New St. Paul Tabernacle Church of God in Christ, Detroit; pres. nat. your choir Church of God in Christ, Inc.*

CHISHOLM, MALCOLM HAROLD, chemistry professor; b. Bombay, Oct. 15, 1945; arrived in U.S., 1972; s. Angus and Gweneth Robey Chisholm; m. Cynthia Ann Truax, May 1, 1982; children: Calun R.I., Selby Scott, Derek Adrian. BS in Chemistry, Queen Mary Coll., London, 1966, PhD in Chemistry, 1969; DSc (hon.), London U., 1981. Postdoctoral fellow U. Western Ont., London, 1969-72; asst. prof. Princeton U., NJ, 1972-78; assoc. prof. chemistry Ind. U., Bloomington, 1978-80, prof., 1980-85, disting. prof. chemistry, 1985-99; disting. univ. prof. Ohio State U., Columbus, 2000—. Vis. prof. Cambridge U., 1986, 94, Humboldt U., 1986—; cons. in field. Editor: Polyhedron, Chem. Comm., Dalton Transactions; mem. editl. bd. Inorganic Chemistry, Organometallics, Inorganic Chimica Acta, Inorganic Syn. Inc., Jour. Cluster Sci., Chem. European Jour., Can. Jour. Chemistry, Chem. Record; contbr. articles to profl. jours. Recipient Basolo medal, Northwestern U., 2004, Bailar medal, U. Ill., 2006. Fellow: NAS, AAAS, Am. Chem. Soc. (Akron sect. award 1982, Buck Whitney award 1987, Inorganic Chemistry award 1989, Disting. Svc. award 1999, Basolo medal 2004, Bailar medal 2006), Royal Soc. Chemistry (Corday Morgan medal 1981, award for Transition Metal Chemistry, Centenary Lectr. and medal, Mond Lectr. and medal), Duetche Accademie Leopoldina, Am. Acad. Arts and Scis., Royal Soc. London (Davy medal). Home: 100 Kenyon Brook Dr Worthington OH 43085-3629 also: 38 Norwich St Cambridge CB2 1NE England Office: Ohio State U Dept Chemistry 100 W 18th Ave Columbus OH 43210-1185 Office Phone: 614-292-7216. Business E-Mail: chisholm.4@osu.edu.

CHITWOOD, JULIUS RICHARD, retired librarian; b. Magazine, Ark., June 1, 1921; s. Hoyt Mozart and Florence (Umfrid) C.; m. Aileen Newsom, Aug. 6, 1944. AB cum laude, Ouachita Bapt. Coll., Ark., 1942; M.Mus., Ind. U., 1948; MA, U. Chgo., 1954. Music supr. Edinburgh (Ind.) Pub. Schs., 1946-47; music and audiovisual librarian Roosevelt Coll., Chgo., 1948-51; humanities librarian Drake U., 1951-53; spl. cataloger Chgo. Tchrs. Coll., 1953; asst. circulation librarian Indpls. Pub. Library, 1954-57, coordinator adult services, 1957-61; dir. Rockford (Ill.) Pub. Library, 1961-79, No. Ill. Library System, Rockford, 1966-76; ret., 1979. Chmn. subcom. library system devel. Ill. Library Adv. Com., 1965—; adv. com. U. Ill. Grad. Sch. Library Sci., 1964-68; cons. in field, participant workshops Pres. Rockford Regional Academic Center, 1974-76; Mem. history com. Ill. Sesquicentennial Commn.; mem. Mayor Rockford Com. for UN, 1962-70; sect. chmn. Rockford United Fund, 1966-70; exec. Rockford Civic Orch. Assn., 1962-70. Served to maj., inf. AUS, 1942-45, ETO. Recipient Ill. Librarian of Year award, 1974 Mem. ALA (chmn. subcom. revision standards of materials, pub. library div. 1965-66, pres. bldg. and equipment sect. library adminstrn. div. 1967-68, chmn. staff devel. com. personnel adminstrn. sect., library adminstrv. div. 1964-68, pres. library adminstrn. div. 1969-70), Ill. Library Assn. (v.p. 1964-65, pres. 1965-66). Unitarian Universalist. Home: 3662 E Covenanter Dr Bloomington IN 47401-4681

CHIVETTA, ANTHONY JOSEPH, architect; b. St. Louis, Dec. 7, 1932; s. Anthony Joseph and Antoinette (Piazza) C.; m. Dolores Krekeler; children: Anthony Joseph III, Victoria, Christopher. BArch, Washington U., St. Louis, 1955. V.p. Hastings & Chivetta Architects, Inc., St. Louis, 1961-95, chmn., 1995—. Mem. alumni bd. Washington U. Sch. Architecture, St. Louis, 1987-88. Bd. dirs. Chaminade Coll. Prep., St. Louis, 1975-78, St. Joseph's Inst. for the Deaf, St. Louis, 1993—. Mem. AIA. Clubs: St. Louis. Office: Hastings & Chivetta Architects Inc 700 Corporate Park Dr Ste 400 Saint Louis MO 63105-4209

CHIZEWER, DAVID J., lawyer; b. Chgo., Apr. 4, 1966; BA magna cum laude in Econs., Pomona Coll., 1988; JD, U. Chgo., 1991. Bar: Ill. 1991. Prin. Goldberg, Kohn, Bell, Black, Rosenbloom & Moritz, Chgo. Named one of The Nation's Top Litigators, Nat. Law Jour., 2007; recipient Child Adv. award, Am. Assn. Pediat., 2005, Excellence in Pro Bono award, US Dist. Ct. (no. dist. Ill.), 2006; Leadership Fellow, Leadership Greater Chgo. Prog. Mem.: Def. Rsch. Inst., Chgo. Bar Assn., ABA, Phi Beta Kappa. Office: Goldberg Kohn Suite 3700 55 E Monroe St Chicago IL 60603-5802 Office Phone: 312-201-3938. Office Fax: 312-863-7438. Business E-Mail: david.chizewer@goldbergkohn.com.

CHLEBOWSKI, JOHN FRANCIS, JR., leasing company executive; b. Wilmington, Del, Aug. 19, 1945; s. John Francis and Helen Ann (Cholewa) C.; m. Mary L. Ahern, Sept., 1997; children: J. Christopher, Lauren R. BS, U. Del., Newark, 1967; MBA, Pa. State U., State College, 1971. Fin. analyst Jones & Laughlin Steel, Pitts., 1971-74; mgr. fin. analysis W.R. Grace & Co., NYC, 1974-75, mgr. fin. planning Dallas, 1975-77; v.p. planning Polumbus Co., Denver, 1977-78; asst. treas. W.R. Grace & Co., NYC, 1978-83; v.p. fin. planning GATX Corp., Chgo., 1983-84, v.p. fin., 1984-86, v.p. fin., chief fin. officer, 1986-94; pres. GATX Terminals Corp., Chgo., 1994—97, pres., CEO, 1998, Lakeshore Op. Ptnr. LLC, Chgo. Bd. dir. Laidlaw Internat., Inc., NRG Energy, Inc., PRP-GP, LLC, Heartland Alliance, pres. bd. dirs., 1992-93. Leadership Greater Chgo. fellow, 1984-85 Mem.: The Racquet Club, Anglers Club, Beta Gamma Sigma. Roman Catholic.

CHO, WONHWA, biomedical researcher; b. Seoul, Korea, Apr. 27, 1958; BS in Chemistry, Seoul Nat. U., 1980, MS in Chemistry, 1982; PhD in Chemistry, U. Chgo., 1988. Postdoctoral fellow Calif. Inst. Tech., Pasadena, 1988-90; assoc. prof. chemistry U. Ill., Chgo., 1990-96, assoc. prof., 1996—; arthritis investigator, 1992-95; investigator Am. Heart Assn., 1999—. Mem. Am. Soc. Biochemistry & Molecular Biology, Am. Chem. Soc. Office: U Ill Chgo Dept Chemistry 845 W Taylor St Chicago IL 60607-7056

CHOCOLA, CHRIS (JOSEPH CHRISTOPHER CHOCOLA), former congressman, lawyer; b. Jackson, Mich., Feb. 24, 1962; m. Sarah Chocola; children: Caroline, Colin. BLS, Hillsdale Coll., 1984; JD magna cum laude, Thomas Cooley Law Sch., 1988. Mgmt. trainee Soc. Nat. Bank, Cleve., 1984, fgn. exch. trader; credit mgr. Chocola Cleaning Materials; corp. counsel CTB Internat. Corp., Milford, Ind., 1988—94, CEO, 1994—99, chmn. bd. dirs., 1999—2002; mem. US Congress from 2nd Ind. dist., 2003—07, asst. majority whip, 2003—04, mem. ways and means com., agrl. com., small bus. com.; transp. & infrastructure com. Mem. coun. advisors South Bend Ctr. for the Homeless; bd. dirs. Oaklawn Psychiat. Ctr. Mem.: Rotary Club. Republican. Presbyterian.

CHOKEY, JAMES A., lawyer; b. Pitts., Sept. 2, 1943; AB, U. Pitts., 1965; JD, Duquesne U., 1969. Bar: Pa. 1969, U.S. Dist. Ct. (we. dist.) Pa., Wis. 1973. Atty. Westinghouse Electric Corp., 1972-73; v.p., gen. counsel, sec. Joy Mfg., 1973-87, RTE Corp., 1987-88, A.O. Smith Corp., 1989-91; v.p., gen. counsel Cooper Industries Inc., Houston, 1991—; v.p. corp. affairs, gen. counsel Beloit (Wis.) Corp.; exec. v.p., sec. and gen. counsel Joy Global (Harnischfeger Industries Inc.), Milw., 1997—. Mem. ABA, Am. Corp. Counsel Assn. (pres. we. Pa. chpt. 1985-86). Office: Joy Global PO Box 554 Milwaukee WI 53201-0554 E-mail: jchokey@HII.com.

CHOLDIN, MARIANNA TAX, librarian, educator; b. Chgo., Feb. 26, 1942; d. Sol and Gertrude (Katz) Tax; m. Harvey Myron Choldin, Aug. 28, 1962; children: Kate and Mary (twins). BA, U. Chgo., 1962, MA, 1967, PhD, 1979. Slavic bibliographer Mich. State U., East Lansing, 1967—69; Slavic bibliographer, instr. U. Ill., Urbana, 1969—73, Slavic bibliographer, asst. prof., 1973—76, Slavic bibliographer, assoc. prof., 1976—84, head Slavic and East European Libr., 1982—89, head, prof., 1984—2002, dir. Russian and East European Ctr., 1987—89, C. Walter and Gerda B. Mortenson Disting. prof., 1989—2002, dir. Mortenson Ctr. for Internat. Libr. Programs, 1991—2002, prof. emerita, 2003—. Author: Fence Around the Empire: Russian Censorship, 1985; editor: Red Pencil: Artists, Scholars and Censors in the USSR, 1989, Books, Libraries and Information in Slavic and East European Studies, 1986. Chair Soros Found. Network Libr. Program Bd., 1997—2000; pres. Rudomino Libr. Coun., 2005—; mem. Russian-American Joint Working Group on Library Corp., 2007. Recipient Pushkin gold medal for contbns. to culture, Russian Presdl. Coun. on Culture, 2000. Mem. ALA (John Ames Humphry/OCLC/Forest Press award 2005, Internat. Librarianship award 2005), Am. Assn. for Advancement of Slavic Studies (pres. 1995), Phi Beta Kappa. Jewish. Home: 888 S Michigan Ave #403 Chicago IL 60605 Personal E-mail: mcholdin@ameritech.net.

CHOLE, RICHARD ARTHUR, otolaryngologist, department chairman; b. Madison, Wis., Oct. 12, 1944; s. Arthur Steven and Wendy Elveyn (Danielczyk) C.; m. Cynthia Beiseker, Dec. 27, 1969; children: Joseph Michael, Timothy Thomas, Katharine, Melinda. Student, U. Calif., Berkeley, 1962-65; MD, U. So. Calif., 1969; PhD in Otolaryngology, U. Minn., 1977. Diplomate Am. Bd. Otolaryngology. Rotating intern U. So. Calif. Med. Ctr., 1969-70; med. fellow dept. surgery Sch. Medicine U. Minn., 1972-73, med. fellow dept. otolaryngology Sch. Medicine, 1973-77; asst. prof. dept. otolaryngology-head and neck surgery Sch. Medicine U. Calif., Davis, 1977-81, assoc. prof., 1981-84, prof., 1984-98, acting chmn. dept., 1985, chmn., 1985—98; chmn. dept. otolaryngology Washington U., St. Louis, 1998—. Mem. sci. rev. com. Deafness Rsch. Found., 1986—; mem. communicative disorders rev. com. Nat. Inst. Deafness and Communication Disorders, 1989—94; staff cons. Dept. Air Force, David Grant USAF Med. Ctr., Travis AFB, Calif., 1981—98; keynote spkr. 92d Japan Oto-Rhino-Laryngol. Soc. Meeting, Fukuoka City, Japan, 1990—; faculty mem. 4th Internat. Cholesteatoma Conf., Niigata City, Japan, 1992; bd. dirs. Am. Bd. Otolaryngology, 2000—; adv. coun. at. Deafness and Other Communication Disorders, 2001—; lectr. in field; bd. sci. counselors NIDCD, NIH, 2004—; bd. dirs. Barnes Jewish Hosp., 2005—; mem. residence rev. com. ACGME, 2002—05. Mem. editorial bd. Laryngoscope, 1985-87; mem. exec. editorial bd. Otolaryngology-Head and Neck Surgery, 1990—; contbr. numerous articles to profl. jours., book chpts., revs.; patentee in field. Mem. profl. edn. com. Am. Cancer Soc., 1977-78, Sacramento Noise Control Hearing Bd., 1977—, Greater Sacramento Profl. Standards Rev. Orgn., 1978-79; deacon 1st Bapt. Ch., Davis, 1979-82, elder, 1983-88. Recipient 1st pl. award Am. Acad. Ophthalmology and Otolaryngology, 1977, care recognition awards U. Calif., Davis, 1988-91; rsch. grantee NIH, Nat. Inst. Aging, Nat. Inst. Neurol. and Communicative Disorders and Stroke, Nat. Inst. on Deafness and Other Communication Disorders, Deafness Rsch. Found., Am. Otol. Soc., U. Calif., 1978-91. Mem. Collegeum Otorhinolaryngologicum Amicitiae Sacrum (U.S. group), Am. Acad. Otolaryngology-Head and Neck Surgery (Honors award 1984, com. on rsch. 1987—, rsch. coordinating coun. 1987—, continuing edn. com. 1991—), Am. Otol. Soc. (trustee rsch. fund 1986—, sec.-treas. 1989—, pres. 2001—), Assn. for Rsch. in Otolaryngology (pres. 1999-2000, award of merit com. 1988—), Am. Laryngol., Rhinol. and Otol. Soc., Am. Soc. for Bone and Mineral Rsch., Assn. Acad. Depts. Otolaryngology-Head and Neck Surgery (coun. 1986—), Calif. Med. Assn. (sci. adv. panel, sect. on otolaryngology-head and neck surgery 1986-98), Sacramento Soc. Otolaryngology and Maxillofacial Surgery, Soc. Univ. Otolaryngologists-Head and Neck Surgeons. Achievements include research in in experimental cholesteatoma, experimental otosclerosis, the aging auditory system, osteoclast cell biology. Office: Washington U Sch Med CB8115 660 S Euclid Ave # 8115 Saint Louis MO 63110-1010 E-mail: choler@msnotes.wustl.edu.

CHOOKASZIAN, DENNIS HAIG, retired financial executive; b. Chgo., Sept. 19, 1943; s. Haig Harold and Annabelle (Kalkanian) C.; m. Karen Margaret Genteman, Mar. 18, 1967; children: Jeffrey, Michael, Kerry. BS in Chem. Engring., Northwestern U., 1965; MBA in Fin., U. Chgo., 1967; MS in Econs., London Sch. of Econs., 1968. CPA, Ill.; cert. mgmt. cons. Mgmt. cons. Touche Ross & Co., Chgo., 1968-75; CFO, CNA Fin. Corp., Chgo., 1975-90; pres., COO CNA, Chgo., 1990-92; chmn., CEO, CNA Ins., Chgo., from 1992, now bd. dirs. Bd. dirs. Loews Corp., Mercury Fin. Pres. Found. for Health Enhancement; bd. dirs. Nat. Boy Scouts Am., orthwestern Meml. Hosp., Nat. Merit Scholarship Corp.; mem. adv. coun. U. Chgo. Grad. Sch. of Bus.; mem. adv. bd. Northwestern U. Kellogg Grad. Sch. of Bus., Inroads; trustee Northwestern U., 1996—. Mem. AICPAs, Ill. Soc. CPAs, Westmoreland Country Club (Wilmette), East Bank Club (Chgo.), The Econ. Club of Chgo., The Execs. Club of Chgo. (dirs.' table), Am. Inst. Assn., Am. Coun. of Life Ins., Ins. Svcs. Office, Beta Gamma Sigma. Republican. Avocations: skiing, tennis, triathlons, golf. Home: 1100 Michigan Ave Wilmette IL 60091-1976 Office: CNA Cna Plz Chicago IL 60685-0001

CHOPLIN, JOHN M., II, lawyer; b. Cedar Rapids, Iowa, Nov. 10, 1945; s. John M. and Joyce G. (Mickelsen) C.; m. Linda H. Kutchen, Feb. 14, 1969; children: Julie, John, James. BA, Drake U., 1967; JD, U. Mich., 1974. Bar: Ind. 1974, U.S. Dist. Ct. (so. dist.) Ind. 1974, U.S. Ct. Appeals (7th cir.) 1976, U.S. Supreme Ct. 1977, U.S. Ct. Appeals (6th cir.) 1983, U.S. Dist. Ct. (no. dist.) Ind. 1991. Assoc. Wilson, Tabor & Holland, Indpls., 1974—80; ptnr. Norris, Choplin & Schroeder LLP, Indpls., 1980—. Committeeman precinct Carmel Reps., Ind., 1982-84. Served to capt. USAF, 1969-73. Mem. ABA, Ind. Bar Assn., Indpls. Bar Assn., Lawyers-Pilots Bar Assn., Ind. Trial Lawyers Assn., Am. Assn. for Justice, Phi Beta Kappa, Omicron Delta Kappa. Baptist. Avocations: water sports, tennis, flying. Home: 8553 Twin Pointe Cir Indianapolis IN 46236-8903 Office: Norris Choplin & Schroeder 101 W Ohio St Ste 900 Indianapolis IN 46204-4213 Office Phone: 317-269-9330.

CHORENGEL, BERND, international hotel corporation executive; b. Itzehoe/Holstein, Germany, 1944; Student, Columbia U., Cornell U. With Hilton Hotels, Bangkok, Manila, Hong Kong; exec. asst. mgr. food and beverage Hyatt Regency Hong Kong, 1969—70, resident mgr. then mgr., 1970—73; gen. mgr. Hyatt Singapore, 1973—79; v.p. S.E. Asia Hyatt Internat. Corp., 1979—82, sr. v.p. Europe, Africa and the Middle East, 1982, exec. v.p., COO, 1982—84, pres. Chgo., 1984—, also bd. dirs.; gen. mgr. Hyatt Carlton Tower, London, 1982. Bd. dirs. Hyatt Hotel Corp.; founding mem. Singapore Conv. Bur.; former dir. Singapore Indsl. Tng. Bd., former chmn. hotel and restaurant trade adv. com. Active Chgo.-Hamburg Sister Cities Program. Recipient Corp. Hotelier of the World award, 1990.

CHOU, CLIFFORD CHI FONG, research engineering executive; b. Taipei, Taiwan, Dec. 19, 1940; came to U.S., 1966, naturalized, 1978; s. Ching piao and Yueh li (Huang) C.; m. Chu hwei Lee, Mar. 23, 1968; children: Kelvin Lin yu, Renee Lincy. PhD, Mich. State U., 1972. Rsch. asst. Mich. State U., East Lansing, 1967-70, Wayne State U., Detroit, 1970-72, rsch. assoc., 1972-76; rsch. engr. Ford Motor Co., Dearborn, 1976-81, sr. rsch. engr., 1981-82, prin. rsch. engr. assoc., 1982-89, prin. staff engr., 1989-93, sr. engring. specialist, 1993-95, staff tech. specialist, 1995—2003, tech. leader, 2003—07; ret., 2007. Adj. prof. Mich. Technol. U., 1997-2002, 2003—2007, Wayne State U., 2007—; lectr. to China under UN Devel. Program, 1987, 93, 95, lectr. to Taiwan under Automotive Rsch. and Test Ctr., 1991, 97, 98, 2005; organizer Safety Test Methodology, SAE session chair, 1997-2008, SAE fellow nom. com., 2004-07, IBEC session chair 1999, 2000, 2004; coord. Detroit Automobile Tech. Conf., 1993, session chair, 1997; mem. safety and environ. systems planning com. IBEC '98, 1997-2000, 01-03; indsl. acad. adv. to PhD Coms., U. Mich., 1995-98, Mich. Tchrs. U., 1997-2000, Wayne State U., 2006—2007; tchr. in field; co-organizer 6th U.S. Nat. Conf. on Computational Mechs., crashworthiness session, Dearborn, 2001; mem. safety tech. com. China SAE, 2002—, mem. nomination com., 2004-07. US regional editor Internat. Jour. Vehicle Safety,

2005-; contbr. chpts. to books, articles to profl. jours. Recipient Safety Engring. Excellence award Nat. Hwy. Traffic Safety Adminstrn., 1980, Best Paper award IBEC, 2002; grantee Soc. Automotive Engrs. Fellow: ASME, Soc. Automotive Engrs. (Forest R. McFarland award 2000, 2006, Arch T. Colwell Merit award 2008); mem.: AIAA, Detroit Chinese Am. Assn., Mich. Chinese Acad. Profl. Assn. (bd. dirs. 1992—93, pres. 1993—94, advisor 1994—, seminar spkr. 2000), Ford Chinese Club (pres. 1991—92), Sigma Xi. Achievements include 13 patents. Avocations: travel, karaoke, ballroom dancing. Home: 28970 Forest Hill Dr Farmington Hills MI 48331-2439 Office: Wayne State U Bioengring Ctr 818 W Hancock Detroit MI 48201 Home Phone: 248-489-5926; Office Phone: 313-577-0703. Business E-Mail: chou@rrb.eng.wayne.edu.

CHOW, JOAN K., food products executive; b. 1960; BA in Linguistics, Cornell U., Ithaca, NY; MBA, U. Pa. Wharton Sch. Bus. Various mgmt. positions Johnson & Johnson Products Inc., 1986—91, Info. Resources Inc., 1991—98; various mgmt. positions through sr. v.p., chief mktg. officer Sears Roebuck & Co., 1998—2007; exec. v.p., chief mktg. officer ConAgra Foods, Inc., Omaha, 2007—. Office: ConAgra Foods Inc 1 ConAgra Dr Omaha NE 68102-5001 Office Phone: 402-595-4000.

CHOW, POO, wood technologist; b. Shanghai, Apr. 27, 1934; arrived in U.S., 1960, naturalized, 1971; m. Ai-Yu Kuo, July 17, 1965; children: Eugenia, Andrew E. MS in Forest Products, La. State U., 1961; PhD in Wood Sci. and Tech., Forestry, Mich. State U., 1969. Lab. dir. Pope and Talbot, Inc., Oakridge, Oreg., 1962-67; asst. prof. wood sci. U. Ill., Urbana, 1969-74, assoc. prof., 1974-80, prof., 1980—2006, prof. emeritus, 2006—. Sr. Fulbright scholar, Fed. Republic Germany; cons. to industry; external examiner U. Ibadan, Nigeria; expert witness. Contbr. numerous articles to profl. jours.; patentee in field. Mem. ASTM, Forest Products Soc., Soc. Wood Sci. and Tech., Am. Railway Engrs. and Maintenance-of-Way Assn., Internat. Rsch. on Wood Preservation Group, German Wood Technology Soc., RR Tie Assn., Am. Wood Preservatives Assn. Office: Univ Ill 1102 S Goodwin Ave Urbana IL 61801-4730

CHOWNING, ALAN B., state representative; m. Patty Marshall; children: LeQuita, Nicole. AS in Aerospace Tech., Vincennes U., 1970. Lic. pilot, cert. flight instr. FAA. V.p. Sullivan Aviation Inc.; state rep. dist. 45 Ind. Ho. of Reps., Indpls., 2002—, vice chmn., rds. and transp. com., mem. agr., natural resources and rural devel., commerce and econ. devel., and local govt. coms. Mem. Sullivan County Cmty. Econ. and Employment Devel. Corp., Sullivan County Redevel. Commn.; supr. Soil and Water Conservation Dist.; county commr. Sullivan County, Ind., 1993—2000; bd. dirs. Local Farm Bur. Coop. Mem.: Ind. Farm Bur., Aircraft Owners and Pilots Assn. Democrat. Office: Ind Ho of Reps 200 W Washington St Indianapolis IN 46204-2786

CHRISMAN, BRUCE LOWELL, physicist, administrator; b. Stillwater, Okla., Mar. 16, 1943; s. Everett Lowell and Lavinia Evelyn (Roether) C.; m. Barbara JoAnn Karnuth, May 17, 1975; children: Brenden Lowell, Brady Kenneth. SB, MIT, 1964; MS, U. Ill., 1965, PhD, 1971; MBA, U. Chgo., 1975; MA (hon.), Yale U., 1983. With Fermi at. Accelerator Lab., Batavia, Ill., 1970-88, physicist, 1970-75, exec. asst., 1975-79, bus. mgr., 1979-83, assoc. dir. adminstrn., 1984-88, 91—; v.p. adminstrn. Yale U., New Haven, 1983-84; assoc. dir. adminstrn. Superconducting Super Collider, Dallas, 1988-89; dir. adminstrn. Wildman, Harrold, Allan & Dixon, Chgo., 1989-91. Bd. dirs. Sch. Dist. 41, Glen Ellyn, Ill., 1986-95; bd. overseers Ill. Inst. Tech. Rice Campus, 1997—. Mem. Sigma Xi (pres. 1981-83). Home: 701 Forest Ave Glen Ellyn IL 60137-3905 Office: Fermi Nat Accelerator Lab PO Box 500 Batavia IL 60510-0500 Office Phone: 630-840-2359. E-mail: BruceChrisman@Mac.com.

CHRISMER, RICH, state legislator; b. Apr. 9, 1946; m. Mary Margaret Parson, 1972; children: Richard, Anna, Laura, Mark. AA, St. Louis C.C., Florissant Valley. Mo. State rep. Dist. 16; svc. technician. Bd. dirs. Pro-Life Citizen Mo. Mem. K.C. (4th degree). Home: 1200 Braddock Pl Apt 714 Alexandria VA 22314-1667

CHRISTENSEN, A(LBERT) KENT, anatomy educator; b. Washington, Dec. 3, 1927; s. Albert Sherman and Lois (Bowen) C.; m. Elizabeth Anne Reynolds Sears, Aug. 26, 1952; children: Anne, Kathleen Martha, Albert David, Jennifer, John Sears. AB, Brigham Young U., 1953; PhD, Harvard U., 1958. Postdoctoral fellow Cornell Med. Coll., 1958-59, Harvard Med. Sch., Boston, 1959-60, instr. dept. anatomy, 1960-61; asst. prof. dept. anatomy Stanford Sch. Medicine, Palo Alto, Calif., 1961-68, assoc. prof., 1968-71; prof., chmn. dept. anatomy Temple U. Sch. Medicine, Phila., 1971-78; prof. anatomy and cell biology U. Mich. Med. Sch., Ann Arbor, 1978-99, chmn. dept. anatomy and cell biology, 1978-82, prof. emeritus, 1999—. Contbr. articles to profl. jours. With USMC, 1946-47. Mem. AAAS, Am. Soc. Cell Biology, Am. Assn. Anatomists (pres. 1984-85), Microscopy Soc. Am. Office: U Mich Med Sch Dept Cell & Devel Biology Med Sci II Bldg Ann Arbor MI 48109-0616 E-mail: akc@mich.edu.

CHRISTENSEN, DAVID ALLEN, retired manufacturing executive; b. 1935; BS, S.D. State U., 1957. With John Morrell & Co., 1960-62, Raven Industries Inc., Sioux Falls, S.D., 1962—, product mgr., 1964-71, pres., chief exec. officer, 1971-2000; ret., 2000. Served with AUS, 1957-60. Office: Raven Industries Inc PO Box 5107 Sioux Falls SD 57117-5107

CHRISTENSEN, DOUGLAS D., school system administrator; BA in Biology and Edn., Midland Luth. Coll., Fremont, Nebr., 1965; MA Edn. Adminstrn. and Curriculum Develop., U. ebr.-Lincoln, 1970, PhD, 1978. Tchr. Holdrege Sr. H.S., Nebr., 1965-70; h.s. prin. Bloomfield Cmty. Schs., Nebr., 1970-74, supt. of schs. Nebr., 1974-76; county supt. of schs. Knox County Ctr., Nebr., 1975-76; supt. of schs. Colby Pub. Schs. Unified Sch. Dist. #315, Nebr., 1978-85, North Platte Pub. Schs., ebr., 1985-90; assoc. commr. of edn. Nebr. Dept. of Edn., Lincoln, 1990-92, dep. commr. of edn., 1992-94, commr. edn., 1994—. Adj. prof., Emporia State U., Empora, Kans, 1986-, for curriculum and instruction and ednl. adminstrn., U. Nebr.-Lincoln, 1990-;presenter, cons. in field. Contbr. articles to profl. jours. Chair North Platte Area Econ. Devel. Task Force, 1986-90, Coun. for Inter-Agy. Cooperation, 1986-90; liturgist First Luth. Ch., 1986-90, chair fin. com., 1988-90; bd. dirs. Mid-Nebr. Cmty. Found., 1989-90, Mari Sandoz Soc., 1990-, Universal Srv. Adminstrv. Co.; mem. Nebr. Commn. for the Protection of Children, 1994—; advanced planning com. Southwood Luth. Ch., 1994-; bd. trustee Nebr. State Coll.; mem. adv. coun. Natice Am. Edn.; mem. steering com., Edn. Commn. of the States Recipient Spirit of PTA award Nebr. PTA, 1997-98, Cornerstone award Future Farmers Am., 1998, Walter Turner award Am. Assn. Ednl. Svc. Agys., 1998, David Hutchinson award U. Nebr., 1998, Burnham Yates award Nebr. Coun. Econ. Edn., 1999, U. Nebr.-Lincoln Teachers Coll. Alumni Assn. award Excellence, 2002, Disting. Svc. award, Nebr. Coun. Sch. Administrators, 2004; named Pub. Ofcl. of Yr. Governing Mag., 2003 Mem. ASCD (pres. Kans. affiliate 1984-85), Am. Assn. of Sch. Adminstrs. (Nebr. Supt. of Yr. 1990), Coun. Chief State Sch. Officers (v.p., bd. dirs. 1997—), Nebr. Coun. of Sch. Adminstrs., Rotary Internat. (pres. 1981-82), Nebr. Ctr. for Ednl. Excellence (chair 1985-90, bd. dirs. 1989-90), Midland Luth. Coll. Alumni Assn. (pres. 1992-93), Nebr. Info. Tech. Commn., Nebr. Ednl. Telecommunications Comn., Mari Sandoz Soc. Office: Commrs Office Dept of Edn PO Box 94987 Lincoln NE 68509-4987 also: 301 Centennial Mall S 6th Fl Lincoln NE 68509

CHRISTENSEN, GARY M., building materials company executive; Various sr. mgmt. positions GE, Trane Corp.; joined Pella Corp., Iowa, 1990, now pres., CEO Iowa, also bd. dirs. Iowa.

CHRISTENSEN, MARVIN NELSON, venture capitalist; b. W. Branch, Iowa, July 15, 1927; s. Peter Ancher and Martha Henrietta (Neilsen) C.; m. Mary Lou Miller, Dec. 17, 1949 (dec. June 1999); children: Stephen R., Barbara; m. Virginia Thompson, 2001. BS, U. Iowa, 1950. Pvt. practice ins. and real estate, Iowa City, 1955-69; asst. to pres. Gen. Growth Cos., Des Moines, 1970-72; acquisitions dir. Life Investors of Iowa, Cedar Rapids, 1972-80; chmn., CEO Bus. Comml. Realty, Denver, 1980—, Colo. Internat. Devel., Colorado Springs, 1984—; chmn. Byers (Colo.) State Bank, 1987-89, Farmer's State Bank, Waubun, Minn., 1988-96. Founder, adminstr. Waubun Area Devel. Enterprises, 1988—. Columnist: View from My Window (monthly newspaper); contbr. many articles to nat. pubs. Lt. (j.g.) USNR, 1944-46. Mem. Am. Bankers Assn., Minn. Bankers Assn., Masons, Elks, Eagles, VFW. Avocations: writing, cabinet making, fishing. Home: RR 2 Waubun MN 56589-9802 also: 246 E Bain Dr Tidewater OR 97390

CHRISTENSEN, NIKOLAS IVAN, geophysicist, educator; b. Madison, Wis., Apr. 11, 1937; s. Ivan Rudolph and Alice Evelyn (Ethen) C.; m. Karen Mary Luberg, June 18, 1960; children— Kirk Nathan, Signe Kay. BS, U. Wis., 1959, MS, 1961, PhD, 1963. Rsch. fellow in geophysics Harvard U., Cambridge, Mass., 1963-64; asst. prof. geol. scis. U. So. Calif., 1964-66; prof. U. Wash., Seattle, 1966-83, Purdue U., Lafayette, Ind., 1983-97; Weeks disting. prof. U. Wis., Madison, 1997—2004, emeritus prof., 2004—; hon. prof. U. BC, Vancouver, Canada, 2007. Mem. Pacific adv. panel Joint Oceanographic Instns. for Deep Earth Sampling, Seattle, 1973-75, mem. igneous and metamorphic petrology panel, 1973-75, mem. ocean crust panel, 1974-77; mem. adv. panel on oceanography NSF, 1976-78, mem. adv. panel on earth scis. 1994-97; mem. adv. panel on continental lithosphere NRC, 1979-83; mem. adv. panel Internat. Assn. Geodesy, 1980-88. Contbg. author: Geodynamics of Iceland and the North Atlantic Area, 1974; Contbr. numerous articles to profl. jours. NSF grantee, 1968—. Fellow Geol. Soc. Am. (chmn. geophysics divsn. 1984-86, assoc. editor Geology 1985-89, George P. Woollard award 1996), Am. Geophys. Union (assoc. editor Jour. Geophys. Rsch. 1998-2001). Achievements include research on nature of Earth's interior. Home: 11310 Marine Ln Anacortes WA 98221 Office: Dept Geology and Geophys U Wisc Madison WI 53706

CHRISTENSEN, GORDON A., law educator; b. Salt Lake City, June 22, 1932; s. Gordon B. and Ruth Arzella (Anderson) C.; m. Katherine Joy deMik, Nov. 2, 1951 (div. 1977); children: Gordon Scott, Marjorie Lynne, Ruth Ann, Nanette; m. Fabienne Fadeley, Sept. 16, 1979. BS in Law, U. Utah, 1955, JD, 1956; SJD, George Washington U., 1961. Bar: Utah 1956, U.S. Supreme Ct. 1971, DC 1978. Law clk. to chief justice Utah Supreme Ct., 1956-57; assoc. firm Christenson & Callister, Salt Lake City, 1956-58; atty. Dept. of Army, N.G. Bur., Washington, 1957-58; atty., acting asst. legal adviser Office of Legal Adviser, U.S. Dept. State, Washington, 1958-62; asst. gen. counsel for sci. and tech. U.S. Dept. Commerce, 1962-67, spl. asst. to undersec. of commerce, 1967, counsel to commerce tech. adv. bd., 1962-67, chmn. task force on telecom. missions and orgn., 1967, counsel to panel on engring. and commodity stds., tech. adv. bd., 1963-65; assoc. prof. law U. Okla., Norman, 1967-70, exec. asst. to pres., 1967-70; univ. dean for ednl. devel., ctrl. adminstrn. SUNY, Albany, 1970-71; prof. law Am. U. Law Sch., Washington, 1971-79, dean, 1971-77; on leave, 1977-79; Charles H. Stockton prof. internat. law U.S. Naval War Coll., Newport, RI, 1977-79; dean, Nippert prof. law U. Cin. Coll. Law, 1979-85, univ. prof. law, 1985—98, prof. emeritus, dean emeritus, 1998—. Assoc. professorial lectr. in internat. affairs George Washington U., 1961-67; vis. scholar Harvard U. Law Sch., 1977-78, Yale Law Sch., 1985-86, Law Sch. U. Maine, Portland, 1997; Wallace S. Fujiyama vis. disting. prof. law Univ. Hawaii Law Sch., 1997; participant summer confs. on internat. law Cornell Law Sch., Ithaca, NY, 1962, 64; cons. in internat. law U.S. Naval War Coll., Newport, 1969; faculty mem., reporter seminars for experienced fed. dist. judges Fed. Jud. Ctr., Washington, 1972-77. Author: (with Richard B. Lillich) International Claims: Their Preparation and Presentation, 1962, The Future of the University, 1969; contbr. articles to legal jours. Cons. Ctr. for Policy Alternatives MIT, Cambridge, 1970-81; mem. intergovtl. com. on Internat. Policy on Weather Modification, 1967; v.p. Procedural Aspects of Internat. Law Inst., NYC, 1962-2001, trustee, 1962-, Glenn Weaver Found. Law Psychiatry, Cinn., 2006-. With intelligence sect. USAF, 1951—52, Japan. Fellow Grad. Sch. U. Cin. Mem. Am. Soc. Internat. Law (mem. panel on state responsibility), Utah Bar Assn., Cin. Bar Assn., Order of Coif, Lit. Club (Cin.), Cosmos Club (Washington), Phi Delta Phi, Kappa Sigma. Home and Office: 3465 Principio Ave Cincinnati OH 45208-4242 Personal E-mail: christga@msn.com.

CHRISTENSON, GREGG ANDREW, bank executive; b. Kalamazoo, June 11, 1958; s. Elmer J. and Marie E. (Durrstein) C.; m. Karen Peterson. BA, Mich. State U., 1980. CPA. Auditor Price Waterhouse, NYC, 1980-82; with Bankers Trust Co., NYC, 1982-92, v.p., 1987-92; sr. v.p. Huntington Nat. Bank, Columbus, Ohio, 1992-2000, Troy, Mich., 2000—. Bd. dirs. Holy Family Regional Sch., Mich. Bankers Assn., Mich. Interfaith Trust Fund, Venture, Inc., Oakland Livingston Human Svcs. Agy. Mem. Mich. State Alumni Assn., Mich. Bankers Assn. (bd. dirs.). Republican. Roman Catholic. Office Phone: 248-269-2034. Business E-Mail: gregg.christenson@huntington.com.

CHRISTENSON, JAMES E., lawyer; Sr. v.p., gen. counsel., sec. Herman Miller, Inc., Zeeland, Mich., 1989—, and v.p., Latin Am. Office: Herman Miller, Inc PO Box 302 Zeeland MI 49464-1366 Office Phone: 616-654-5234.

CHRISTENSON, LE ROY HOWARD, missions mobilizer; b. Rochester, NY, Oct. 28, 1948; s. Howard Le Roy and Sigrid (Anderson) Christenson; m. Pamala Jean Mattson, Jan. 26, 1974; children: Nathan Lee, David Wayne. BS, Valparaiso U., 1970; MS, Purdue U., 1972; MA in Religion, Trinity Evangelical Divinity Sch., Chgo., 2006. CLU. Corp. actuary Western Life Ins. Co., St. Paul, 1972-84; v.p., reins. actuary Am. United Life Ins. Co., Indpls., 1984—99, exec. v.p., 1999—2000; pvt. practice cons. Fishers, Ind., 2001—02; Great Lakes assoc. dir. Advancing Chs. in Missions Commitment (ACMC), 2002—06; with Pioneers, 2007—. Fin. cons. Mgmt. Assistance Program, Mpls., 1982. Bd. mem. Interserve, 1996—2004; mission conf. chmn. Faith Missionary Ch., Indpls., 1987—89, elder, 1991—93, 1999—2002, 2006—, elder chmn., 1993, 2000—02, mission com. chmn., 1995—2000, 2006—07, vice chmn., 2003—06, sr. pastor search team, 2003—04; bd. dirs. Lake Wapogasset Bible Camp, Mpls., 1982—83, Christian Businessman's Com., Indpls., 1985—88, Interserve, 1996—2004, chmn. nominating com., 1999—2004, mem. exec. com., 1999—2001; age group leader Pioneer Club, Indpls., 1983, 1987. Fellow: Soc. Actuaries (chmn. audit working group reins. sect. 1985—88, vice chmn. reins. sect. 1988—89, 1995—96, chmn. 1989—90, 1996—97, sec.-treas. reins. sect. 1994—95); mem.: Indpls. Actuarial Club (pres. 1987—88), Tri-State Actuarial Club (Indpls. rep. 1984—90, chmn. 1989—90), Am. Acad. Actuaries. Avocations: bible study, bicycling, motorcycling, hiking. Office: ACMC PO Box 841 Fishers IN 46038-0841 Personal E-mail: LeeChristenson@sbcglobal.net.

CHRISTENSON, LINDA, state legislator; m. Duane Christenson; 4 children. BA, MS, Minot State U. English tchr.; mem. N.D. Ho. of Reps. from 18th dist., Bismarck, 1994-98; mem. judicary, govt. and vet. affairs coms. N.D. Ho. of Reps., Bismarck; mem. N.D. Senate from 18th dist., Bismarck, 2000—. Bd. dirs. Firehall Cmty. Theater, United Health Svc. Named Martin Luther King Educator of Yr., N.D., 1991. Mem. Grand Forks Edn. Assn. Address: 3424 Cherry St Apt A5 Grand Forks ND 58201-7692

CHRISTIAN, EDWARD KIEREN, broadcasting station executive; b. Detroit, June 26, 1944; s. William Edward and Dorothy Miriam (Kieren) C.; m. Judith Dallaire, Nov. 25, 1966; children: Eric, Dana. BA, Wayne State U., 1966, postgrad.; MA, Cen. Mich. U., 1980. Mgr. John C. Butler Co., Detroit, 1968-69; nat. sales mgr. WCAR Radio, Detroit, WSUN Radio, St. Petersburg, Fla., 1969-70; v.p., gen. mgr., ptnr. WCER Radio, Charlotte, Mich., 1970-74; pres. Josephson Internat. Broadcast, 1975-86; pres., CEO Saga Comm., Inc., Detroit, 1986—. Pres., CEO, bd. dirs. Stas. WSNY-FM, WODB-FM, WJZA, WJZK, Columbus, Ohio, Sta. WNOR-FM, Norfolk, Va., Sta. WAFX, Norfolk, WJOI AM Norfolk, Stas. WKLH-FM, WHQG-FM, WJYI-AM, WFMR-FM, WJMR-FM Milw., Stas. KRNT, KSTZ-FM, KIOA-AM/FM, KAZR FM, KLTI FM, KPSZ AM, Des Moines, Sta. WLRW-FM and WIXY-FM, WCFF FM/WXTT, Champaign, Ill., Stas. WYMG-FM, WQQL-FM, WDBR-FM, WABZ FM, WTAX-AM, Springfield, Ill., Stas. WGAN-AM/WMGX, WZAN-AM/WYNZ-FM, WPOR/FM, WBAE-AM, WVAE, Portland, Maine, Sta. WFEA-AM/WZID-FM, WQLL-FM, Manchester, N.H., Sta. WAQY-FM, WHNP-AM, Springfield, Mass., WHMP-AM, WLZX-FM, WSRI, Northampton, Mass., WHMQ-AM, WHAI-AM, WPVQ, Greenfield, Mass., KOAM TV, KFJX TV, Joplin, Mo., WNAX-AM/FM, Yankton, SD, KGMI, KISM-FM, Bellingham, Wash., KBAI-AM, KAFE FM, Bellingham, Wash., Victoria Tex., KUNU TV, KXTS TV, KAVU TV, KVCT TV, KMOL TV, Victoria, WXVT TV, Greenville, Miss., KICD AM-FM, KLLT, Spencer, Iowa, WKFN, WJQI, WZZP-FM, WCVQ-FM, WVVR-FM, Clarkesville, Tenn., KDXY-FM, KDEZ-FM, KJBX-FM, Jonesboro A.K., WKNE-FM, WKBK-AM, WSNI-FM, WUQL-FM, WINQ-FM, Keene, N.H., WKVT-AM/FM, WRSY, Brattleboro, Vt., WHCU AM, WNYY AM, WQNY FM, WYXL/WIII, Ithaca, NY, WINA AM, WVAX-AM, WWWV FM, WQMZ FM, WCNR, Charlottesville, Va., Mich. Radio Network, Ill. Radio Network, others; Mich. Farm Radio Network, Minn. Radio News Network; Bd. dirs., Nat. Assn. Broadcasters, Broadcast Found., chmn. Arbitron Radio Adv. Coun., 1978-79; bd. dirs. All Industry Music Licensing Com.; adj. prof. Ctrl. Mich. U. Bd. dirs. Am. Auto Immune Related Disease Found., 1995—; bd. mem. St. John Hosp.; consul Republic of Iceland for Mich., Ohio and Ind., 1996—. Mem. Alpha Epsilon Rho (nat. adv. coun. 1980—). Home: 21 Newberry Pl Grosse Pointe Farms MI 48236-3749 also: 3310 Sabal Cove Dr Longboat Key FL 34228-4154 Office: Saga Communications Inc 73 Kercheval Ave Grosse Pointe Farms MI 48236-3603 E-mail: echristian@sagacommunications.com.

CHRISTIAN, JOE CLARK, medical genetics researcher, educator; b. Marshall, Okla., Sept. 12, 1934; s. Roy John and Katherine Elizabeth (Beeby) C.; m. Shirley Ann Yancey, June 5, 1960; children: Roy Clark, Charles David. BS, Okla. State U., 1956; MS, U. Ky., 1959, PhD, 1960, MD, 1964. Cert. clin. geneticist, Am. Bd. Med. Genetics. Resident internal medicine Vanderbilt U., Nashville, 1964-66; asst. prof. med. genetics Ind. U., Indpls., 1966-69, assoc. prof., 1969-74, prof., 1974-99, assoc. dean basic scis. and regional ctrs., 1996-98, prof. emeritus, assoc. dean emeritus, 1999—. Served with USAR, 1953-60. Mem.: AMA, Am. Soc. Human Genetics. Democrat. Methodist. Avocations: bicycling, farming. Office: Ind U Dept Med/Molecular Genetics 975 W Walnut St Dept Med Indianapolis IN 46202-5181 E-mail: jcristi@iupui.edu.

CHRISTIAN, JOHN EDWARD, health science association administrator, educator; b. Indpls., July 12, 1917; s. George Edward and Okel Kandus (Waltz) C.; m. Catherine Ellen Spooner, July 23, 1948; 1 dau., Linda Kay. BS, Purdue U., 1939, PhD, 1944. Control chemist Upjohn Co., 1939-40; faculty Purdue U., Lafayette, Ind., 1940—, prof. pharm. chemistry, 1950-59, head dept. radiol. control, 1956-59, prof. bionucleonics, head dept., 1959-82; chmn. adminstrv. com. Trace Level Research Inst., 1960-88; dir. Inst. for Environmental Health, 1965-88; head Sch. Health Scis., 1979-82, Hovde Disting. prof., 1979-88, Hovde Disting. prof. bionucleonics and health scis. emeritus, 1988—. Vis. prof. radiation therapy Ind. U. Sch. Medicine, 1970-88; Harvey Washington Meml. lectr. Purdue U., 1955; Edward-Kremers Meml. lectr. U. Wis., 1956; vis. lectr. U. Tex., 1959, Taylor U. Am. Sci. Lecture Series, Upton, Ind., 1960; Julius A. Koch Meml. lectr. U. Pitts., 1961 Assoc. editor Radiochem. Letters. Mem. revision com. U.S. Pharmacopeia, 1950-60, mem. adv. panel on radioactive drugs, 1960-70; adv. com. isotope distbn. AEC, 1952-58, mem. med. adv. com., 1967-75; mem. radiation and chem. def. sect. Ind. Dept. Civil Def., 1954—; vice chmn. Radiation Control Adv. Commn., Ind., 1958—; mem. exec. com. Ind. Comprehensive Health Planning Council, 1972-76; mem. adv. com. radiopharms. FDA, 1970-75; mem. Ind. Gov.'s Pesticide Council, 1970-73; Alumni research councilor Purdue Research Found., 1964-88; mem. Ind. Environmental Mgmt. Bd., 1972-87, Nat. Energy Policy Task Force, Dept. Energy, 1981-83; mem. Bd. Grants Am. Found. for Pharm. Edn., 1989—. Recipient award Chilean Iodine Ednl. Bur., 1956, Julius Sturmer award Phila. Coll. Pharmacy and Sci., 1958, Leather medal Purdue U., 1971, Hovde Faculty Purdue U. fellow, 1988. Fellow AAAS (past sec. and chmn. pharm. sci. sect., mem. council), Ind. Acad. Sci.; mem. AMA (spl. affiliate), AAUP, Am. Inst. Architecture (bd. dirs. 1998—, Gibson award 1999), Am. Assn. Colls. Pharmacy (past mem. exec. com., chmn. conf. tchrs., chmn. conf. grad. study and grad. tchrs., chmn. com. study grad. edn. in pharmacy), Am. Chem. Soc. (past chmn. Purdue sect.), Am. Pharm. Assn. (Ebert medal 1957, Justin L. Powers Research Achievement award 1963, past chmn. sci. sect.), Acad. Pharm. Sci. (past v.p.), Ind. Pharm. Assn., Am. Pub. Health Assn., Am. Nuclear Soc., Am. Soc. Bacteriology, Health Phys. Soc., Historic Landmarks Found. of Ind. (bd. dirs., exec. com. 1997—), Frank Lloyd Wright Bldg. Conservancy (Wright Spirit award 1997), Sigma Xi (past pres. Purdue chpt., research award Purdue chpt. 1950), Rho Chi, Phi Lambda Upsilon, Sigma Pi Sigma., Eta Sigma Gamma, Gamma Sigma Delta. Home: 1301 Woodland Ave West Lafayette IN 47906-2371 Office: Purdue U Sch Health Scis Civil Engring Bldg West Lafayette IN 47907

CHRISTIAN, JOHN M., lawyer; b. Wichita, Kans., Sept. 15, 1948; AB with honors, Princeton U., 1970; JD with honors, U. Mich., 1973. Bar: Ill. 1974. Mem. Cahill, Christian & Kunkle, Ltd., Chgo. Adj. prof. law IIT/Chgo.-Kent Coll. Law. Mem. ABA, Chgo. Bar Assn. (mem. spl. task force ins. 1985-86, spl. com. lawyers profl. liability ins. 1987-88, chmn. tort litigation com. 1986-87).

CHRISTIAN, RICHARD CARLTON, dean, former advertising agency executive; b. Dayton, Ohio, Nov. 29, 1924; s. Raymond A. and Louise (Gamber) C.; m. Audrey Bongartz, Sept. 10, 1949; children: Ann Christian Carra, Richard Carlton Jr. BS in Bus. Adminstrn, Miami U., Oxford, Ohio, 1948; MBA, Northwestern U., 1949; LLD (hon.), at.-Louis U., 1986; postgrad., Denison U., The Citadel, Biarritz Am. U. Mktg. analyst Rockwell Mfg. Co., Pitts., 1949-50; exec. v.p. Marsteller Inc., Chgo., 1951-60, pres., 1960-75; bd. dirs., exec. com. Young and Rubicam, Inc., 1979-84; chmn. bd. Marsteller Inc., 1975-84, chmn. emeritus, 1984—; assoc. dean Kellogg Grad. Sch. Mgmt. Northwestern U., 1984-91, assoc. dean Medill Sch. Journalism, 1991-99. Dir., chmn. Bus. Publs. Audit Circulation, Inc., 1969-75; spkr. in field. Trustee Northwestern U., 1970-74, Nat.-Louis U., Evanston, Ill., 1970-92, James Webb Young Fund for Edn., U. Ill., 1962-95; pres. at. Advt. Rev. Coun., 1976-77; bd. adv. coun. mem. Miami U.; mem. adv. coun. J.L. Kellogg Grad. Sch. Mgmt., Northwestern U.; v.p., dir. Mus. Broadcast Comm.; dir. Can. U.S. Ednl. Exch. (Fulbright Found.), 1988-92. With inf. AUS, 1942-46, ETO. Decorated Purple Heart, 1945; recipient Ohio Gov.'s award 1977, Alumni medal, Alumni, Merit and Svc. awards Northwestern U.; named to the Advt. Hall of Fame, 1991. Mem. Am. Mktg. assn., Indsl. Mktg. Assn. (founder, chmn. 1951), Bus. Profl. Advt. Assn. (life mem. Chgo., pres. Chgo. 1954-55, nat. v.p. 1955-58, G. D. Crain award 1977), U. Ill. Found., orthwestern U. Bus. Sch. Alumni Assn. (founder, pres.), Am. Assn. Advt. Agys. (dir., chmn. 1976-77), Am. Acad. Advt. (1st disting. svc. award 1978), orthwestern U. Alumni Assn. (nat. pres. 1968-70), Mid-Am. Club, Comml. Club, Econ. Club Chgo., Kenilworth Club, Westmoreland Country Club, Alpha Delta Sigma, Beta Gamma Sigma, Delta Sigma Pi, Phi Gamma Delta. Baptist. Home: 2 Arbor Ln Apt 412 Evanston IL 60201

CHRISTIANS, CLIFFORD GLENN, communications educator; b. Hull, Iowa, Dec. 22, 1939; s. Arnold and Verbena Janette (Geerdes) Christians; m. Priscilla Jean Kreun, June 13, 1961; children: Glenn Clifford, Ted Arnold, Paul Raymond. AB, Calvin Coll., 1961; ThM, Fuller Theol. Sem., 1965; MA, U. So. Calif., 1966; PhD, U. Ill., 1974. Dir. comm. Christian Ref. Home Ministries, Grand Rapids, Mich., 1966—70; rsch. asst. prof. comm. U. Ill., Urbana, 1974—80, rsch. assoc. prof. comm., 1980—87, rsch. prof. comm., 1987—, Charles H. Sandage Disting. prof., 2005—. Rsch. fellow Calvin Ctr. for Christian Scholarship, Grand Rapids, 1983-84; vis. scholar in ethics Princeton (N.J.) U., spring, 1979; inst. fellow U. Chgo., 1986-87, vis. scholar, 2006; Pew Evangel. scholar in ethics Oxford U., spring, 1995; dir. Inst. Rsch. Comms., Urbana, 1987—2001. Co-author: Jacques Ellul: Interpretive Essays, 1981, Good News: Social Ethics and The Press, 1993, Media Ethics: Cases and Moral Reasoning, 1998, Communication Ethics and Universal Values, 1997, Moral Engagement in Public Life: Theorists fro Contemporary Ethics, 2002; editor: Critical Studies in Mass Communication, 1992-95. Bd. dirs. Empty Tomb, Inc., Champaign, Ill., 1986—; elder Christian Ref. Ch., Champaign, 1974-82; bd. dirs. Univ. YMCA, Champaign, 1974-77, Judah Christian Sch., Champaign, 1984-90. Rsch. fellow, Program for Cultural Values and Ethics, 1990. Mem. Soc. for Philosophy and Tech., Assn. for Edn. in Journalism and Mass Comm. (chair qualitative studies divsn. 1980-81), Internat. Assn. Mass Comm. Rsch. (program co-chair 1991-94), Ellul Studies Forum, Nat. Comm. Assn. Democrat. Avocations: fishing, travel, reading. Home: U Ill Inst Comm Rsch 1002 W William St Champaign IL 61821 Office: U Ill Comm Dept 810 S Wright St Urbana IL 61801 Office Phone: 217-333-1549. Business E-Mail: cchrstns@uiuc.edu.

CHRISTIANSEN, JAY DAVID, lawyer; b. Slayton, Minn., Mar. 22, 1952; s. Holger K. and Dagny (Fjelstad) C.; children: Tyler, Carrie, Jayne. BA, Luther Coll., 1974; JD, Vanderbilt U., 1977. Ptnr. Faegre & Benson, Mpls., 1977—. Mem. ABA (chmn. 1997-99, health law sect., mem. ho. dels. 1999-2002), Order of Coif. Office: Faegre & Benson 90 S 7th St Minneapolis MN 55402-3901 E-mail: jchristi@faegre.com.

CHRISTIANSEN, KEITH ALLAN, lawyer; b. Madison, Wis., Dec. 14, 1943; s. Herman Louis and Faith Louise (Haase) C.; m. Sheila Irene Stangel, Apr. 11, 1966; children: Douglas, Jeffrey. BS, U. Wis., 1965, JD, 1968. Bar: Wis. 1968, Fla. 1973, U.S. Dist. Ct. (ea. dist.) Wis. 1968. Assoc. Foley & Lardner LLP, Milw., 1968-74, ptnr., 1975—. Co-author: Marital Property Law in Wisconsin, 1984, 3d edit., 2004. Active Potawatomi coun. Boy Scouts Am. 1975—, past pres.; v.p. Area 3 Ctrl. Region Boy Scouts. Am., 1992—. Fellow Am. Coll. Trust and Estate Counsel; mem. Mid-winter Estate Planning Clinic, Estate Counselors Forum. Republican. Office: Foley & Lardner LLP 777 E Wisconsin Ave Ste 3800 Milwaukee WI 53202-5306 Office Phone: 414-297-5746. E-mail: kchristiansen@foley.com.

CHRISTIANSEN, RAYMOND STEPHAN, librarian, educator; b. Oak Park, Ill., Feb. 15, 1950; s. Raymond Julius and Anne Mary (Fusek) Christiansen; m. Phyllis Anne Dombkowski, Nov. 25, 1972; 1 child, Mark David. BA, Elmhurst Coll., 1971; MEd, No. Ill. U., 1974. Lic. lay min. Episcopal Ch., 1990. Dept. dir. Elmhurst Coll., Ill., 1971—73; asst. law libr. media svcs. Lewis U., Glen Ellyn, Ill., 1974—77; asst. prof. edn. Aurora U., Ill., 1977—90, assoc. prof., 1990—2003, emeritus prof., 2003—; media cons., 1977—; media libr. Aurora U., 1977—82, instnl. developer, 1982—89, dir. media svcs., 1985—2003, dir. ednl. facilities and tech. planning, 2003—04; dir. libr. Kaneville Pub. Libr., Ill., 2005—. Media cons., 1977—. Author: (video series) Rothblatt on Criminal Advocacy, 1975, (book) Index to SCOPE the UN Magazine, 1977. Mem.: Phi Eta Sigma, Alpha Psi Omega. Home: 424 S Gladstone Ave Aurora IL 60506-5370 Office: Kaneville Pub Libr Dir 2 S 101 Harter Rd PO Box 29 Kaneville IL 60144 Office Phone: 630-557-2441. Business E-Mail: kanepublib@aol.com.

CHRISTIANSEN, RICHARD DEAN, retired newspaper editor; b. Berwyn, Ill., Aug. 1, 1931; s. William Edward and Louise Christine (Dethlefs) C. BA, Carleton Coll., Northfield, Minn., 1953; postgrad., Harvard U., 1954; LHD (hon.), DePaul U., 1988. Reporter, critic, editor Chgo. Daily News, 1957-73, 74-78; editor Chicagoan mag., 1973-74; critic-at-large Chgo. Tribune, 1978-83, entertainment editor, 1983-91, chief critic, sr. writer, 1991—2002; ret., 2002. Author: A Theater of Our Own: A History and a Memoir of 1,001 Nights in Chicago, 2004. Served to cpl. U.S. Army, 1954-56. Recipient award Chgo. Newspaper Guild, 1969, 74, Joseph Jefferson award, 1996, Chgo. Area Emmy award, 1967, Excellence in the Arts award DePaul U., 1998, Peter Lisagor award for criticism, 2002, Lifetime Achievement award Chgo. Headline Club, Soc. Profl. Journalists, 2005, Ill. State Hist. Soc. award, 2005; named to Chgo. Journalism Hall of Fame, 1998. Mem. Am. Theatre Critics Assn., Chgo. Acad. TV Arts and Scis., Soc. Midland Authors, Headline Club Chgo. (Peter Lisagor award 2002), Arts Club Chgo. (dir.), Phi Beta Kappa (Living Treasure award, 2003), Sigma Delta Chi. Republican. Lutheran. Personal E-mail: rchris5568@aol.com.

CHRISTIANSEN, RICHARD LOUIS, orthodontist, educator, dean; b. Denison, Iowa, Apr. 1, 1935; s. John Cornelius and Rosa Katherine C.; m. Nancy Marie Norman, June 24, 1956; children: Mark Richard, David Norman, Laura Marie. DDS, U. Iowa, 1959; MSD, Ind. U., Indpls., 1964; PhD, U. Minn., 1970; PhD (hon.), Nippon Dental U., Tokyo, 2000. Prin. investigator Nat. Inst. Dental Research NIH, Bethesda, Md., 1970-73, chief craniofacial anomalies program br., 1973-81, dir. extramural at. Inst. Dental Research, 1981-82; prof. dept. orthodontics U. Mich., Ann Arbor, 1982—, dean, Sch. Dentistry and dir. W.K. Kellogg Found. Inst., 1982—2001, prof., dean emeritus, 2001—. Organizer state-of-the -art workshops in field of craniofacial anomalies and other aspects of oral health; founder Internat. Union Schs. Oral Health, 1985; organizer oral health conf. in Poland, 1989, Jordan, 1995. Contbr. chpts. to books and articles to profl. jours. Chmn. Region III United Way, U. Mich., Ann Arbor, 1984; chmn., v.p. Trinity Luth. Ch., Rockville, Md., 1975; v.p. and chmn. planning task force Trinity Luth. Ch., Ann Arbor, chmn. bd. Sequoia Sr. Housing; vice chmn., bd. dirs. Luth. Soc. Svcs. Mich., 1997—; with USPHS, 1959-82, mem. dental prof. adv. com., 2005. Recipient Commendation medal USPHS, 1980, Cert. of Recognition NIH, 1982, others; named Dental Alumnus of Yr., U. Iowa, 2005, Southeast Mich. Philanthropy award, 2006. Fellow Internat. Coll. Dentists, Am. Coll. Dentists, Pierre Fauchard Acad.; mem. Am. Assn. Orthodontists, Am. Assn. Dental Sch., ADA (rsch. coun.), Mich. Dental Assn., Am. Assn. Dental Rsch. (dir. craniofacial biology group 1975-79, v.p. 1979-80, pres. 1981-82), Omicron Kappa Upsilon (com. mem.). Achievements include research in craniofacial research and international oral health. Avocations: reading, jogging, tennis, sailing. Business E-Mail: vista@umich.edu.

CHRISTIANSON, DARCEY K., broadcast engineer; b. Albert Lea, Minn., Sept. 13, 1958; s. Darrell D. and Darla L. (Jensen) C.; m. Renae A. Rue. Student, Austin Vocat. Tech., Minn., 1979. Asst. chief engr. Sta. KWOA-AM-FM, Worthington, Minn., 1979-80; chief engr. Stas. KATE/KCPI-FM, Albert Lea, 1980—. Contract engr. Sta. KJLY-FM, Blue Earth, Minn., 1986-88. Mem. Nat. Assn. Radio and Telecommunications Engrs. Republican. Avocations: softball, fishing. Office: Stas KATE/KCPI-FM 305 S 1st Ave Albert Lea MN 56007-1777

CHRISTIANSON, JAMES D., real estate developer; b. Bismarck, ND, Aug. 18, 1952; s. Adolph M. and Elizabeth M. C.; m. Deborah Jaeger, Oct. 10, 1987. Student, Bismarck Jr. Coll., 1970, 1971-72, U. N.D., 1971. Lic. pvt. pilot; lic. realtor. Gen. mgr. and supr. Nutrition Search, Bismarck, 1974-76; gen. mgr. Home Still, Inc., Bismarck, 1976-78; v.p. Good Heart Assocs., Bismarck, 1978-82; pres. N. W. Devel. Group, Bismarck, 1982—, First Realty Bismark Inc., 1990-93, N.W. Realty Group, Bismarck, 1994—. Chmn. bd. Basin State Bank, Stanford, Mont., 1986-94; mem., vice chair Ctr. City Partnership, 1994—; mng. prin. N.W. Lodging Group, LLC. Supr. editor: Nutrition Almanac, 1975. Mem. Bismarck Centennial Com., 1986-89, Bismarck Parking Authority, 1996—; bd. trustees Bismarck State Coll., 1999—.; chmn., pres. Bismarck Hist. Soc., 2005—. Recipient Outstanding Citizen award Mayor and City Commn., Bismarck, 1982. Mem. Downtown Bus. and Profl. Assn. (bd. dirs. 1989—, pres. 1991). Avocations: travel, reading, computers, golf. Office: N W Devel Group Inc PO Box 1097 Bismarck ND 58502-1097

CHRISTIANSON, STANLEY DAVID, finance company executive; b. Chgo., Dec. 8, 1931; s. Stanley Olai and Emma Josephine (Johnson) D.; m. Elin J. Ballantyne, July 25, 1959; children: Erica Joanna, David Ballantyne. BS, U. Ill., 1954; MBA, U. Chgo., 1960. Auditor Price Waterhouse & Co., Chgo., 1956-58; asst. to controller Miehle-Goss-Dexter, Inc., Chgo., 1960-67, v.p. adminstrn. Goss Div., 1967-69; dir. mgmt. systems MGD Graphics Systems-N.Am. Rockwell (formerly Miehle-Goss-Dexter), Chgo., 1969-70; v.p. fin. Duchossois/Thrall Group (formerly Thrall Car Mfg. Co.), Chicago Heights, Elmhurst, Ill., 1970-83; vice chmn., bd. dirs. Thrall Enterprises, Inc., Chgo., 1983—. Bd. dirs. Midwestern U., 1992-98, chmn., 1997-98. Bd. govs. Internat. House, U. Chgo., 1988-2000, chmn. 1997-2000; trustee Cmty. Theatre Guild, Valparaiso, Ind., 2001-, chmn., 2005-06; mem. Hobart (Ind.) Plan Commn., 1986-92, pres., 1988-92. Capt. U.S. Army, 1954-56. Home: 141 Beverly Blvd Hobart IN 46342-4346 Office: Thrall Enterprises Inc 180 N Stetson Ste 3020 Chicago IL 60601-6223

CHRISTIE, JAMES R., technology company executive; BS in Applied Chemistry, Heriot-Watt U., Edinburgh, Scotland; diploma in bus. adminstrn., U. Edinburgh, PhD in Chem. Engring. With Atlantic Richfield Co., Occidental Petroleum Corp.; chmn., CEO applied chems. divsn. Hickson Internat., 1987-93; pres. Valenite Milacron Inc., Cin., 1993-97, corp. officer, v.p. Valenite and Widia, 1997-2000, group v.p. metalworking techs., 2000—. Office: Milacron Inc 2090 Florence Ave Cincinnati OH 45206-2455

CHRISTMAN, RICHARD M., manufacturing executive; BS in Mech. Engring., Rose Hulman Inst. Tech.; MBA in Mktg. and Fin., U. Mich. Various sales and mktg. positions Case Corp., Racine, Wis., 1975, sr. v.p. European sales and mktg., sr. v.p. N.Am. sales and mktg., v.p. product mgmt., strategic planning, 1995—. Office: Case Corp 700 State St Racine WI 53404-3392

CHRISTMANN, RANDEL DARVIN, state legislator; b. Hazen, ND, June 16, 1960; B in Bus. Adminstrn., N.D. State U., 1982. Truck driver, rancher, Hazen, N.D.; mem. N.D. Senate from 33rd dist., Bismark, 2000—. Mem. fin. and taxation com. N.D. State Senate, vice-chmn. natural resources com., vice chmn. interim N.D./S.D. Commn. Mem. NRA, Farm Bur. N.D., Stockmen's Assn. Office: 401 3rd Ave NE Hazen ND 58545-4424

CHRISTNER, THEODORE CARROLL, architect; b. Quincy, Ill., Oct. 3, 1932; s. Thornton Carroll and Mable Irene (Trogdon) C.; m. Jo Hartmann, 1957 (div. 1980); children: Eric, Kitsy, Caellen, Erin; m. Claudia Trautman, Oct. 4, 1986; 1 child: Adrienne. BArch, Culver-Stockton Coll., 1952, Washington U., St. Louis, 1957. Registered architect, Mo. Staff architect Fischer, Frichtel Design and Constrn., St. Louis, 1961-62; assoc. Gale and Cannon, St. Louis, 1962-63; pres. The Christner Partnership, Inc., St. Louis, 1963-95; chmn. bd. dirs. Christner, Inc., 1995—. Bd. dirs. Ecumencial Housing Prodn. Corp., mem exec. com. Bd. dirs., v.p. Ecumenical Housing Corp., St. Louis, 1988—; bd. dirs. Mt. St. Rose Hosp., 1967-75; chmn. bd. St. Joseph's Hosp. Hospice, 1988—; mem. Commn. for Future Washington U., 1988; mem. nat. coun. Wash. U. Sch. Architecture, 1988—. Mem. AIA (dir. 1986), Am. Arbitration Assn. Avocations: golf, tennis, skiing, flying. Home: 6319 San Bonita Ave Saint Louis MO 63105-3115 Office: Christner Inc 7711 Bonhomme Ave Clayton MO 63105-1908

CHRISTOFFEL, KATHERINE KAUFER, pediatrician, epidemiologist, educator; b. NYC, June 28, 1948; d. George and Sonya (Firstenberg) Kaufer; children: Kevin, Kimberly. BA, Radcliffe Coll., 1969; MD, Tufts U., 1973; MPH, Northwestern U., 1981. Diplomate Am. Bd. Pediat., Nat. Bd. Med. Examiners. Intern Columbus (Ohio) Children' Hosp., 1972-73; resident then fellow Children's Meml. Hosp., Chgo., 1973-76; asst. prof. Sch. Medicine U. Chgo., 1976-79; asst. prof., then assoc. prof. Northwestern U. Med. Sch., Chgo., 1979-91, prof., 1991—; dir. Nutrition Evaluation Clinic Children's Meml. Hosp., Chgo., 1982-2000; med. dir. violent injury prevention ctr. Children's Meml. Med. Ctr., Chgo., 1993—2000, interim dir. Mary Ann and J. Milburn Smith Child Health Rsch. Program, 2000—03, interim co-dir. Children's Meml. Inst. for Edn. and Rsch., 2001—03, med. and rsch. dir. Consortium to Lower Obesity in Chgo. Children, 2003—, dir. Ctr. on Obesity Mgmt. and Prevention, 2004—. Dir. then assoc. dir. Pediatric Practice Rsch. Group, Chgo., 1984-97; dir. statis. scis. and epidemiology program Children's Meml. Inst. for Edn. and Rsch., 1994-2000; chmn. steering com. HELP Network, Chgo., 1993-99, pres. bd. dirs., 1999—2006. Contbr. numerous articles to med. jours. Named one of 10 Most Powerful Women in Medicine in Chgo., Chgo. Sun Times, 2004; recipient M. Fay Spencer Disting. Woman Physician Scientist award, Nat. Bd. Hahnemann Med. Sch., 1997. Fellow Am. Acad. Pediat. (spokesperson on firearms 1985—, injury com. 1985-93, coun. on pediatric rsch. 1996-2000, chair adolescent violence task force 1994, 1st Injury Control award 1992); mem. APHA (Disting. Career award 1991), Am. Coll. Epidemiology, Soc. for Pediatric Rsch., Am. Pediat. Soc., Ambulatory Pediatric Assn. (bd. dirs. 2000-2003, Rsch. award 2000). Avocations: hiking, walking, creative writing, photography. Office: Childrens Meml Hosp 2300 N Childrens Plz #157 Chicago IL 60614-3394

CHRISTOFORIDIS, A. JOHN, radiologist, educator; b. Greece, Dec. 24, 1924; s. John P. and Ada A. C.; m. Ann Dimitriadis, Nov. 11, 1961; children: John, Gregory, Alex, Jimmy. MD summa cum laude, Nat. U. Athens, Greece, 1949; M.M.Sc., Ohio State U., 1957; PhD, Aristotelian U., Greece, 1969. Instr. to prof. Ohio State U., Columbus, 1956-74, clin. prof., 1974—; chmn. dept. radiology Aristotelian U., Salonika, Greece, 1971; prof., chmn. dept. radiology Med. Coll. Ohio, Toledo, until 1982; prof., chmn. dept. Ohio State U., Columbus, 1982—. Researcher in chest and gastrointestinal radiology; cons. Greek Ministry Health, Batelle Meml. Inst., Columbus. Contbr. to textbook Atlas of Axial Sagittal and Coronal Anatomy with Computed Tomography and Magnetic Resonance; author: Radiology for Medical Students, 4th edit., 1988, Diagnostic Radiology-Thorax, 1989; contbr. articles to profl. jours., chpts. to books. Served to lt. M.C. Greek Army, 1950-52. Recipient Silver award Ohio Med. Assn., 1969, awards Heart Assn., 1960, awards Batelle Meml. Inst., 1965, awards Astra Co., 1967, awards Lung Assn., 1970-71; named Hon. Citizen City of Thessalonike, 1973; Ohio Geriatrics Med. grantee, 1980; NSF grantee, 1980 Fellow Am. Coll. Chest Physicians, Am. Coll. Radiology; mem. AAA, AMA, AAUP, Ohio Radiol. Soc., Assn. Univ. Radiologists, Radiol. Soc. N. Am., Soc. Chmn. Acad. Radiology Depts., Fleishner Soc. (charter), Am. Hellenic Ednl. Progressive Assn., Greek-Am. Progressive Assn., Acad. of Athens (corr. mem.). Greek Orthodox. Office: Ohio State U 410 W 10th Ave Columbus OH 43210-1240

CHRISTOPHER, DAVID L., bank executive; Chmn., CEO Wayne Bancorp, Inc., 1989—. Office: 112 W Liberty St Wooster OH 44691-4802

CHRISTOPHER, DORIS K., consumer products company executive; m. Jay Christopher, 1967; children: Julie, Kelley. BS in Home Econs., U. Ill., 1967. Cert. in family and consumer svcs. H.S. home econs. tchr.; with U. Ill. Coop. Extension Svc.; founder, chmn. The Pampered Chef Ltd. (acquired by Berkshire Hathaway, 2002), Addison, Ill., 1980—. Appeared on various TV programs including Oprah Winfrey Show, NBC Weekend Today, CNBC, CNN. Author: Come to the Table: A Celebration of Family Life, 1999, The Pampered Chef: The Story of One of America's Most Beloved Companies, 2005. Recipient Torch award Marketplace Ethics, Better Bus. Bureau, Chgo. & No. Ill., 1998. Mem.: Direct Selling Assn. (bd. dirs. 1992—, past chairperson), Am. Assn. Family and Consumer Scis., America's Second Harvest, Com. of 200. Office: The Pampered Chef 1 Pampered Chef Lane Addison IL 60101-5630 Office Fax: 630-261-8522.

CHRISTOPHER, JOHN E., lawyer; b. Charlottesville, Va., May 18, 1967; BA, U. Ky., 1990; JD, Salmon P. Chase Coll. Law, 1993; LLM in Taxation, U. Fla., 1994. Bar: Ky. 1994, US Tax Ct. 1994, Ohio 1995. Ptnr. Dinsmore & Shohl LLP, Cin. Named one of Ohio's Rising Stars, Super Lawyers, 2006. Mem.: Cin. Bar Assn., Ohio State Bar Assn., Ky. Bar Assn., ABA. Office: Dinsmore & Shohl LLP 255 E Fifth St Ste 1900 Cincinnati OH 45202-4700 Office Phone: 513-977-8481. Office Fax: 513-977-8141.

CHRISTOPHER, SHARON A. BROWN, bishop; b. Corpus Christi, Tex., July 24, 1944; d. Fred L. and Mavis Lorraine (Krueger) Brown; m. Charles Edmond Logsdon Christopher, June 17, 1973. BA, Southwestern U., Georgetown, Tex., 1966; MDiv, Perkins Sch. Theology, 1969; DD, Southwestern U., 1990; DST, McMurray Coll., 1996. Ordained to ministry United Meth. Ch., 1970; elected bishop 1988. Dir. Christian Edn. First United Meth. Ch., Appleton, Wis., 1969-70, assoc. pastor, 1970-72; pastor Butler United Meth. Ch., Butler, Wis., 1972-76, Calvary United Meth. Ch., Germantown, Wis., 1972-76, Aldersgate United Meth. Ch., Milw., 1976-80; dist. supt. Ea. Dist. Wis. Conf. United Meth. Ch., 1980-85; asst. to bishop Wis. Conf. Wis. Conf. United Meth. Ch., Sun Prairie, Wis., 1986-88; bishop North Cen. jurisdiction United Meth. Ch., Minn., 1988-96, bishop Ill. area Ill. area, 1996—, resident bishop Ill. area Springfield, 1996—. Contbr. articles and papers to religious publs. Bd. dirs. Nat. Coun. Chs. of Christ, 1988—, United Meth. Ch. Bd. of Ch. & Soc., 1988-92, bd. discipleship, 1992—; trustee Hamline U., St. Paul, 1988-96; gen. and jurisdictional conf. del., 1976, 80, 84, 88; mem. N. Cen. Jurisdiction Com. on Episcopacy, 1984-88, Com. on Investigation, 1980-88, Gen. Bd. Global Ministries, 1980-88, chmn. Mission Pers. Resources Program Dept., 1984-88. Named one of Eighty for the Eighties, Milw. Jour., 1980.

CHRISTOPHERSON, AL, farm association executive; m. Diane Christopherson; children: Todd, Scott. BS in Agrl. Econs., U. Minn. Owner, operator diversidifed crop and livestock farm, Pennock, Minn.; v.p. Minn. Farm Bur. Fedn., 1978—88, pres., 1988—. Bd. dirs. Midwestern region Am. Farm Bur. Mem., chmn. bd. Agrl. Utilization and Rsch. Inst.; chmn. River Resource Alliance; bd. advisors and govs. Ctr. for Internat. Food and Agrl. Policy, U. Minn., Minn. Office: PO Box 64370 Saint Paul MN 55164

CHRISTOPHERSON, MYRVIN FREDERICK, college president; b. Milltown, Wis., July 21, 1939; s. Fred J. and Inger J. (Haug) C.; m. Anne Christine Marking, June 10, 1967; children: Kirsten (Clark), Berit (Achenbach), Bjorn Christopherson, Nisse Christopherson. BA, Dana Coll., 1961; MS, Purdue U., 1963, PhD, 1965; DD (hon.), Wartburg Theol. Sem., 1998. Teaching asst., instr. Purdue U., West Lafayette, Ind., 1961-65; asst. prof. speech U. Wis., Madison, 1965-69, assoc. prof. communication Stevens Point, 1969-76, prof. communication, 1976-86, assoc. dean. fine arts and communication, 1970-86; pres. Dana Coll., Blair, Nebr., 1986—2005, pres. emeritus, 2005—; pres. Dana Coll. Found. Inc., 2006—. Cons. Wis. Telephone, Milw., 1968-78, AT&T, N.Y.C., 1969-71, 1st Fin. Corp., Stevens Point, 1980-86; commr. Nebr. Coordinating Commn. for Post Sec. Edn., 1989-91; mem. N.E. jud. nominating commn. Ct. Appeals No. 3 Steering Com.; mem. adv. bd. Thrivent Fin. For Lutherans, 2002-05. Author: Speaker's Trainer's Guide, 1970, The Company Speaker, 1979; editor: Jour. of the Wis. Communication Assn., 1978—80. Mem. adv. bd. The Lutheran, 1987—94, chmn., 1992—94; bd. dirs. Blair Cmty. Found., 1999—, Planned Giving Svcs., Nebr., chmn., 1992—94; ann. fund appeal chmn. Meml. Cmty. Hosp., 1994; trustee Palmer Chirpractic U., 1998—2004; mem. coun. pres. Evangel. Luth. Ch. in Am., 1999—, vice chmn., 1999—2000, chmn., 2000—, memls. com. churchwide assembly, 2001; mem. pastoral call com. First Luth. Ch., 1995, mem. ch. coun., 1999; mem. Nebr. Ednl. Fin. Authority, 1991—, chmn., 1992—99, 2001, 2004—06, vice chmn., 2002—03; fellow Found. Ind. Higher Edn., DC. Decorated Knight 1st Class Order of Dannebrog, 2005; Gt. Plains Athletic Conf. All-Academic award named Christopherson award, A.T. Weaver Outstanding Comm. Tchr., 1979; recipient Cmty. Svc. award Blair Area Chamber, 2004, Acad. award, Great Plains Athletic Conf., 2005, NE Govs. Outstanding Pub. Svc. award, 2006; inducted into Wall of Honor, Unity High Sch., Polk County, Wis.; fellow Palmer Coll. Chiropractic, Palmer Coll. Chiropractic-West. Fellow: Found. for Ind. Higher Edn. (sec. 2003—05, bd. dirs. 2005); mem.: Coun. of Pres., Luth. Edn. Conf. N.Am. (vice chmn. 1994—95, chmn. 1995—96), Nebr. Ind. Coll. Found. (exec. com. 1990—92, vice chmn. 1992—93, chmn. 1994—95), Nebr. Bus. Higher Edn. Forum, Nat. Assn. Intercoll. Athletics (coun. of pres. 1999—2005), North Ctrl. Assn. Colls. and Schs. (cons.-evaluator 1997—2005, accreditation rev. coun. 2001—, team chair 2002—05), Nebr. Ednl. TV Coun. for higher Edn., Assn. Ind. Colls. Nebr. (chmn. 1992—93), Nat. Assn. Ind. Colls. and Univs. (bd. dirs. 1997—99, 2003—05, chmn.Great Plains athletic conf. coun. pres. 2004—05), Danish Brotherhood Blair (hon mem. Nebr. lodge). Avocations: travel, reading, writing, antiques. Business E-Mail: mchristo@dana.edu.

CHROMIZKY, WILLIAM RUDOLPH, accountant; b. Chgo., Jan. 21, 1955; s. Rudolph Joseph and Helen M. Chromizky; m. Laura Lee Lamoureux, Oct. 24, 1992. BS, No. Ill. U., 1977; M of Mgmt., Northwestern U., 1987. CPA, Ill. Sr. auditor Arthur Andersen & Co., Chgo., 1977-83; supr. internal audit AM Internat., Chgo., 1983-84, mgr. fin. reporting, 1984-85, dir. acctg., 1985; mgr. bus. analysis Premark Internat., Inc., Deerfield, Ill., 1985-87, dir. fin. reporting, 1987-2000; v.p. external reporting Aon Corp., Chgo., 2001—. Vol. CPAs for the Pub Interest, Chgo., 1990-92; mem. fin. com. Brother Rice H.S., 1995—, bd. dirs., 1999—. Mem.: AICPA, Fin. Execs. Inst. Avocations: skiing, tennis, bowling. Office: Aon Corp 200 E Randolph St Chicago IL 60601 Home Phone: 630-985-5421; Office Phone: 312-381-3489. Business E-Mail: william_chromizky@asc.aon.com.

CHRONISTER, ROCHELLE BEACH, former state legislator; b. Neodesha, Kans., Aug. 27, 1939; m. Bert Chronister, 1961; children: Pam, Phillip. AB, U. Kans. State rep. dist. 13 Kans. Ho. of Reps., until 1999; former asst. majority leader; sec. for social and rehab. svcs. Kans. Cabinet, 1995-99. Chmn. Kans. Rep. Party, 1989—. amed Woman of Yr., Neodesha C. of C. Mem. AMA (aux.), Bus. and Profl. Women. Methodist. Home: RR 2 Box 321 A Neodesha KS 66757-9562

CHRYSLER, RICHARD R., former congressman; b. St. Paul, Apr. 29, 1942; m. Katie; children: Richard R., Phil, Christie Ann. With Chevrolet divsn. Gen. Motors Corp., 1960-64, Hurst Performance, Inc., Brighton, Mich., 1966-76; founder, chmn. Cars & Concepts, Inc., Brighton, 1976-86, RCI; U.S. congressman Mich. 8th Dist., 1995-96; pres. JPE, Inc., 1998-99; vice chmn. ASCET, Inc., 1999; pres. Ideal Steel, Hamburg, Mich., 1999—. Bd. dirs. Mich. Nat. Bank. Patentee skylite T-roof.

CHU, JOHNSON CHIN SHENG, retired physician; b. Peiping, China, Sept. 25, 1918; arrived in U.S., 1948, naturalized, 1957; s. Harry S.P. and Florence (Young) Chu; m. Sylvia Cheng, June 11, 1949; children: Stephen, Timothy. MD, St. John's U., 1945. Intern Univ. Hosp., Shanghai, 1944-45; resident, research fellow NYU Hosp., 1948-50; resident physician in charge State Hosp. and Med. Ctr., Weston, W.Va., 1951-56; chief services, clin. dir. State Hosp., Logansport, Ind., 1957-84, ret., 1998. Active mem. Meml. Hosp., Logansport, Ind., 1968—. Contbr. articles to profl. jours. Fellow: Am. Coll. Chest Physicians, Am. Psychiat. Assn.; mem.: AAAS, AMA, Cass County Med. Soc., Ind. Med. Assn. Achievements include research in cardiology and pharmacology. Office: Southeastern Med Ctr Walton IN 46994

CHUGH, YOGINDER PAUL, mining engineering educator; came to U.S., 1965, naturalized, 1975; s. Atma Ram and Dharam (Devi) C.; m. Evangeline Negron, July 18, 1970; children: Anjeli K., Shirmilee M., Pauline E. BS, Banaras Hindu U., 1961; MS, Pa. State U., 1968, PhD, 1970. Cert. 1st class mine mgr., India. Instr. Banaras Hindu U., India, 1961-64; asst. mgr. Andrew Yule Coal Co., India, 1961-64; research asst. Pa. State U., University Park, 1965-70; rsch. assoc. Henry Krumb Sch. Mines Columbia U., NYC, 1971, research assoc., 1971; research engr. Ill. Inst. Tech. Research Inst., Chgo., 1971-74; planning engr. Amax Coal Co., Indpls., 1974-76; assoc. prof. Dept. Mining Engring. So. Ill. U., Carbondale, 1977-81, prof. Dept. Mining Engring., 1981—. Acting chmn., Dept. Mining Engring., So. Ill. U., 1981-82, chmn., 1984—; dir. Coal Combustion Residues Mgmt. Program; chmn. PhD. com., 1983-86, active numerous other univ. coms; cons. to nat. and internat. coal cos., state and fed. mining and mineral agys.; dir. Coal Combustion Residues Mgmt. Program, 1990—; bd. dirs. Accreditation Bd. for Engring. and Tech., 1989-92. Author: (with K.V.K. Prasad) Workshop on Design of Coal Pillars in Room-and-Pillar Mining, Workshop on Design of Mine Openings in Room-and-Pillar Mining, 1984; editor (with others) Proceedings of the First Conference on Ground Control Problems in the Illinois Coal Basin, 1980, Proceedings First International Conference on Ground Control in Longwall Mining and Mining Subsidence, 1982, Proceedings of the Polish-American Conference on Ground Control in Room-and-Pillar Mining, 1983; editor Ground Control Room and Pillar Mining, 1983 (Soc. Mining Engrs. award 1983), Longwall Mining Subsidence, 1983 (Soc. Mining Engrs. award 1984), Proceedings of the Second Conference on Ground Control Problems in the Illinois Coal Basin, 1985, Proceedings of the Third and Fourth Conference on Ground Control Problems in the Midwestern U.S., 1990, 92; contbr. over 50 articles to profl. jours., also many research reports; inventor roof truss, 1990. V.p. India Assn., Indpls., 1975. Recipient numerous research grants state and fed. agys., pvt. coal cos.; named Disting. Alumnus Banaras Hindu U., 1985, Outstanding Alumnus Achievement award Pa. State U., 1996. Mem. AIME (active rock mechanics unit com. 1978-82, various pubs. coms.1979-85, geomechanics com. 1984-85), ASTM, ASCE, Internat. Soc. Rock Mechanics (coordinator 1986—), Internat. Bur. Strata Mechanics, Ill. Mining Inst. (bd. dirs.), Ind. Mining Inst., Soc. Geologists and Mining Engrs. (faculty advisor 1977-78, 80-84), Soc. Exptl. Stress Analysis, Am. Soc. Higher Edn., Sigma Xi. Lodges: Rotary. Avocations: tennis, boating, badminton, computers. Office: So Ill U-Carbondale Mining & Mineral Resources Rsch Inst Coal Extraction Rsch Ctr Carbondale IL 62901

CHUNG, DO SUP, agricultural engineering educator; b. Inchon, Korea, Mar. 20, 1935; married, 1961; 2 children. BS, Purdue U., 1958; MS, Kans. State U., 1960, PhD in Chem. Engring., Food Sci., 1966. From instr. to assoc. prof. agrl. engring. Kans. State U., Manhattan, 1965-80, prof. agrl. engring., 1980—. Mem. agrl. rsch. svc. divsn. USDA, 1967-70. Fellow Am. Soc. Agrl. Engrs.; mem. AICE, Am. Assn. Cereal Chemists (Stanley Watson award, 2003), Inst. Food Tech. Achievements include research in adsorption, desorption and absorption of water by cereal products, heat transfer in grain investigations, physical properties of grains and handling of grain for minimizing damage investigations. Office: Kansas State Univ Agricultural Engineering Dept Seaton Hall Rm 148 Manhattan KS 66506

CHUNG, PAUL MYUNGHA, mechanical engineer, educator; b. Seoul, Dec. 1, 1929; came to U.S., 1947, naturalized, 1956; s. Robert N. and Kyungsook (Kim) C.; m. E. Jean Judy, Mar. 8, 1952; children: Maurice W., Tamara P. BSME, U. Ky., 1952, MS, 1954; PhD, U. Minn., 1957. Asst. prof. mech. engring. U. Minn., 1957-58; aero. research scientist Ames Research Center, NASA, Calif., 1958-61; head fluid physics dept. Aerospace Corp., San Bernardino, Calif., 1961-66; prof. mech. engring. U. Ill., Chgo., 1966-95, head dept. energy engring., 1974-79, dean engring., 1979-94, prof., dean emeritus, 1995—. Mem. tech. adv. com. Ill. Inst. Environ. Quality, 1975-77; corp. mem. Underwriters Lab., 1983-95; cons. to industry, 1966—. Author: Electric Probes in Stationary and Flowing Plasmas, 1975, Russian edit., 1978, numerous papers in field; contbr. chpt. to Advances in Heat Transfer, 1965, Dynamics of Ionized Gasses, 1973. Bd. govs. YMCA, Redlands, Calif., 1965—67. Fellow AIAA (nat. tech. com. on plasmadynamics 1972-74, com. on propellants and combustion 1976-80); mem. AIChE (nat. com. on internat. activities 1992-94), Am. Soc. Engring. Edn. (exec. bd. engring. dean's coun. 1983-84), Sigma Xi, Tau Beta Pi, Pi Tau Sigma, Phi Kappa Phi. Home: 2003 E Lillian Ln Arlington Heights IL 60004-4215 Office: Univ Ill Off of Dean Chicago IL 60680 E-mail: jjpc2003@earthlink.net.

CHUNG, YIP-WAH, engineering educator; b. Hong Kong, Nov. 8, 1950; came to U.S., 1973, naturalized, 1983. BS in Physics and Math., U. Hong Kong, 1971, MPhil in Physics, 1973; PhD in Physics, U. Calif., Berkeley, 1977. Asst. prof. Northwestern U., Evanston, Ill., 1977-82, assoc. prof. material sci. and engring., 1982-85, prof., 1986—, dept. chair, 1992—. Mem. editl. bd. Tribology Letters; assoc. editor ASME Jour. Tribology, 1997—; publ. several articles in profl. jours. Active Cmty. Rels. Commn., Wilmette, Ill., Rsch. Grants Coun., Hong Kong; trustee Village of Wilmette, 1997-2001. Lee Pui Hing Meml. scholar, 1970; Earl C. Anthony scholar, 1974; recipient Ralph A. Teetor award, 1990, Tribology divsn. award ASME, 1991; Innovative Rsch. award, ASME, 2002. Fellow Japan

Soc. for Promotion of Sci., ASM Internat.; mem. ASEE, Am. Phys. Soc., Metal. Soc., Am. Vacuum Soc. (chair Ill. chpt. 1991-94, bd. dirs. 1998-2000), Soc. Tribologists and Lubrication Engrs., ASM Internat. Office: Northwestern Univ Dept Mat Sci & Engring 2220 Campus Dr Evanston IL 60208-3108

CHUPP, TIMOTHY EDWARD, physicist, educator, academic administrator; b. Berkeley, Calif., Nov. 30, 1954; AB, Princeton U., 1977; PhD in Physics, U. Wash., 1983. Instr., asst. prof. physics Princeton U., 1983-85; from asst. prof. to assoc. prof. physics Harvard U., 1985-91; assoc. prof U. Mich., Ann Arbor, 1991-94, prof. physics, 1994—. Fellow Alfred P. Sloan Found., 1987. Recipient Presdl. Young Investor award NSF, 1987. Fellow Am. Phys. Soc. (I.I. Rabi prize 1993). Achievements include research in low energy particle physics particularly by study of symmetries accessible with polarization; weak interactions: CP violation and time reversal violation; fundamentals of quantum mechanics; structure of nucleons; biomedical and technological applications of lasers and optical pumping. Office: U Mich Dept Physics Ann Arbor MI 48109

CHURAY, DANIEL J., lawyer; b. Sewickley, Pa., Aug. 23, 1962; m. Lynn Churay; children: Ryan, Addison, John. BA in Economics, U. Tex., Austin, 1985; JD, U. Houston Law Ctr., 1989. Bar: Tex. 1989. Atty. Fulbright & Jaworski LLP, Houston, 1989—95; dep. gen. counsel, asst. sec. Baker Hughes Inc., 1995—2000, acting gen. counsel, corp. sec., 2000; sr. counsel Fulbright & Jaworski LLP, Houston, 2000—02; sr. v.p., gen. counsel, sec. YRC Worldwide Inc., Kans., 2002—. Mem.: ABA, Tex. Bus. Law Found., Tex. State Bar Assn., Am. Corp. Counsel Assn. Office: YRC Worldwide Inc 10990 Roe Ave Overland Park KS 66211

CHURCH, DOUGLAS D., lawyer; b. Indpls., Jan. 22, 1944; AB in Govt. and Economics, Ind. U., 1966; JD, Ind. U., 1970. Bar: Ind. 1970. Law clk. to Hon. George B. Hoffman Jr. Ind. Ct. Appeals, 1968—70; assoc. Church Church Hittle & Antrim, Noblesville, Ind., 1970—71, ptnr., 1971—87, mng. ptnr., 1987—2005, sr. ptnr., 2005—. Town atty. Town of Fishers, 1980—; city atty. City of Noblesville, 1988—96. Named Man of Yr., Greater Indianapolis YMCA Hamilton County Br., 1997; recipient Irv Merritt award, Greater Ind. Masters Swim Assn., 1989, Josiah K. Durfee award, Noblesville Preservation Alliance, 2000. Mem.: Ind. Bar Found., Ind. Mcpl. Lawyers Assn. (pres. 1999—2000), Am. Bd. Trial Advocates, Ind. Trial Lawyers Assn., ABA (Gold Key award 1970), Ind. State Bar Assn. (bd. gov. 1980—81, chmn. young lawyers sect. 1981—82, local govt. law sect. 1981—82, bd. gov. 1998—2000, v.p. 2005—06, pres.-elect 2006—07, pres. 2007—08, Citation of Merit 1982, Cinch Strap award 2000, 2004), Hamilton County Bar Assn. (pres. 1980—81, Frank Campbell Svc. award 1997). Office: Church Church Hittle & Antrim PO Box 10 Noblesville IN 46061-0010

CHURCHILL, ROBERT WILSON, state legislator, lawyer; b. Waukegan, Ill., Apr. 10, 1947; s. George Oliver and Helga C. (Carlson) Churchill; children: Abigail Lee, Julia Aubrey, Christine Lizbeth. BA, Northwestern U., Evanston, Ill., 1969; JD, U. Iowa, 1972. Pres., sr. ptnr. Churchill, Quinn, Richtman & Hamilton Ltd., Grayslake, Ill., 1972—; trustee Lake Villa Twp., Ill., 1981-83; mem. Ill. Ho. Reps., 1983-99, 2003—07; minority whip Ill. Gen. Assembly, 1987-89, asst. minority leader, 1989-91, dep. minority leader, 1991-94, 97-99; majority leader, 1995-97; chmn. Rep. Ctrl. Com. Lake County, Ill., 1990-94. Co-chmn. Ill. Econ. and Fiscal Commn., Springfield, 1991-95, Space Needs Commn., 1997-99; mem. Ill. Prisoner Review Bd., 1999-2001; chief counsel, dir. legis. Ill. Ho. Reps., 2001-02. Del. Rep. Nat. Conv., 1980, 1992, 1996, 2004, alt. del., 1984. Mem. ABA, Lake County Bar Assn., Lake Villa Lions. Republican.

CHURCHILL, STEVEN WAYNE, former state legislator, marketing professional; b. Akron, Ohio, May 8, 1963; s. Wayne Stevenson and Carol Sue (Gurney) C. BA, Iowa State U., 1985. Fin. asst. The Governor Branstad Com., Des Moines, 1986, fin. dir., 1988-90; mktg. mgr. Iowa Dept. Econ. Devel., Des Moines, 1987; devel. officer Simpson Coll., Indianola, Iowa, 1990-93; fundraising cons. The Churchill Group, Johnston, Iowa, 1993-97; v.p. mktg. Mid-Am. Group, West Des Moines, Iowa, 1997—. State Rep., Johnston, Iowa, 1993-99; commr. Iowa Civil Rights Commn., Des Moines, 1991-92; deacon Plymouth Congl. Ch., 1988-91, 96-99; admissions amb. Iowa State U., 1990-92; mem. Greater Des Moines Leadership Inst., 1998-99; chmn. Chef's Auction Dinner, March of Dimes, 1999; bd. dirs. Salisbury House Found., 2004—. Recipient Comdr.'s Award for Pub. Svc., Dept. of the Army, 1991; named one of 10 Outstanding Young Iowans, Iowa Jaycees, 1995, one of Forty under 40 Ctrl. Iowans for Profl. Accomplishments and Cmty. Involvement Des Moines Bus. Record, 2000. Mem. Bull Moose Club (pres. 1990-91), Rotary of Des Moines (pres. 1991-92, team leader group study exch. to The Netherlands 2000), Sigma Alpha Epsilon (pres. 1989-90, Order of the Lion 1990, 96, 99, Merit Key award 2000, chmn. Robert D. Ray scholarship golf benefit 2002), vol. mentor Big Brothers, Big Sisters. Avocations: history, travel, stand-up comedy. Home: 6140 Nottingham Johnston IA 50131-8713 Office: Mid-Am Group 4700 Westown Pkwy Ste 303 West Des Moines IA 50266-6718 Office Phone: 515-224-3646. E-mail: swc@midamericagroup.com.

CHURCHWELL, EDWARD BRUCE, astronomer, educator; b. Sylva, NC, July 9, 1940; s. Doris L. Churchwell; m. Dorothy S. Churchwell, June 24, 1964; children: Steven T., Beth M. BS, Earlham Coll., 1963; PhD, Ind. U., 1970. NASA fellow Ind. U., Bloomington, 1963; postdoctoral fellow Nat. Radio Astronomy Obs., Charlottesville, Va., 1970; Heinrich Hertz postdoctoral fellow Max Planck Inst. Radioastronomie, Bonn, Germany, 1970-72, staff scientist, 1972-77; asst. prof. U. Wis., Madison, 1977-79, assoc. prof., 1979-83, prof., 1983—, Alfred E. Whitford prof. astronomy, 2002—. Fellow NASA, 1985, Fulbright Rsch., 1988—89. Mem.: Internat. Astron. Union, Am. Astron. Soc. Office: U Wis Washburn Observatory 475 N Charter St Madison WI 53706-1582 E-mail: churchwell@astro.wisc.edu.

CHVALA, CHARLES JOSEPH, state legislator; b. Merrill, Wis., Dec. 5, 1954; s. John Patrick and Mary Ann (Severt) C.; children: Ted, Jessica. BA, JD, U. Wis., 1978. Bar: Wis. Atty. DeWitt, Sundby, Huggett & Schumacher, 1979-81, Smith, Chvala & Merg, 1981-83, Boushea, Newton & Seagall, 1983-92; lobbyist Citizen's Utility Bd., 1981-82; mem. Wis. State Assembly, 1983-85, Wis. Senate from 16th dist., Madison, 1985—; majority leader Wis. Senate, 1995—; pvt. practice Madison, Wis., 1996—. Mem. Citizens Utility Bd., Wis. Environ. Decade, Wis. Farmers Union; bd. dirs. World Dairy Ctr. Authority Nat. Merit scholar. Mem. State Bar Wis., Dane County Bar Assn. Democrat. Office: State Senate State Capitol Rm 211 S PO Box 7882 Madison WI 53707-7882

CIALKOWSKI, DAVID MICHAEL, lawyer; b. South Holland, Ill., Feb. 22, 1973; BA cum laude, U. Ill., 1995; JD, U. Ill. Coll. Law, 1998. Bar: Ill. 1998, Minn. 2000. Assoc. Zimmerman Reed, P.L.L.P., Mpls., 2001—. Contbr. articles to profl. pubs. Named a Rising Star, Minn. Super Lawyers mag., 2006. Mem.: ABA, Minn. State Bar Assn., Hennepin County Bar Assn., Phi Beta Kappa. Office: Zimmerman Reed PLLP 651 Nicollet Mall Ste 501 Minneapolis MN 55402 Office Phone: 612-341-0440. E-mail: dmc@zimmreed.com.

CIANCIO, RONLAD J., lawyer; AB, U. Notre Dame, 1963; JD, Northwestern U., 1966, MBA, 1988. Assoc. Vescelus, Leetz, Perry, 1966—71; sr. atty. Miles Labs., Inc., 1971—77; gen. counsel EMI Med. Inc., 1977—81; sr. atty. GATX Corp., Chgo., 1981—84, asst. gen. counsel, 1984—2000, v.p. corp. counsel, 2000, v.p., gen. counsel, sec., 2000—04, sr. v.p., gen. counsel, sec., 2004—. Office: GATX Corp 500 W Monroe St 42nd Fl Chicago IL 60661

CIANI, ALFRED JOSEPH, dean; b. NYC, June 29, 1946; s. Joseph Alfred and Aurora Smiles (VanOver) C.; m. Sharon Skolkey, Aug. 16, 1968 (div. 1979); children: Mieke Jo, Gabriel Wolf; m. Lesley Lockwood, Aug. 9, 1980; children: Joseph Alfred, Clinton Lockwood. BA, U. Albany, 1969; MA, Coll. of St. Rose, 1972; EdD, Ind. U., 1974. Tchr. Greater Amsterdam Schs., NY, 1969—72; rsch. asst. Ind. U., Bloomington, 1972—73, assoc. instr., 1973—74; vis. prof. U. Wis., Milw., 1980; asst. prof. U. Cin., 1974—79, assoc. prof., 1979—2002, assoc. dean, info. officer, 1988—2003, prof. emeritus, 2003—. Pres. Ohio Internat. Reading Assn., Columbus, 1981-82; outside cons. State of Miss., Jackson, 1982-84, State of Ky., 1996-99, State of W.Va., 1972-74, 97-98, City of N.Y. Pub. Schs.; cons., U. Oreg. Profl. Devel., Eugene, 1979-80, Nashville Schs., 1982-83, State of W.Va., N.Y.C. Pub. Schs.; mem. Dean's Cabinet; mem. Urban Schs. Task Force. Author: Motivating Reluctant Readers, 1981; editor: (book series) Reading in Content Areas, 1979-81; rev. editor: Rsch. in Mid. Level Edn., 1995—. Sch. bd. Newport Ctrl. Cath. HS, 2003—07. Grantee Ford Found., 1990, IBM, 1990. Mem. AAUP, Internat. Reading Assn., Am. Ednl. Rsch. Assn. (nat. coms.), Assn. Tchr. Educators (nat. coms.), Nat. Coun. Tchrs. English (nat. coms.),, Nat. Mid. Sch. Assn. (nat. coms.), Nat. Reading Coun., Phi Delta Kappa, Kappa Delta Pi (counselor). Democrat. Roman Catholic. Avocations: reading, walking. Office: U Cin Mail Location 02 Cincinnati OH 45221-0001 E-mail: alfred.ciani@uc.edu.

CIARAMITARO, NICK, prosecutor; b. Detroit, Dec. 17, 1951; s. Sam and Catherine (Sorentino) C.; m. Peggy Houlihan. BA cum laude, U. Detroit, 1974; JD, Wayne State U., 1979. City clk. City of Roseville (Mich.), 1977-78; law clk. Mich. Atty. Gen. Frank Kelley & Atty. Michael P. Long, 1977; state rep. Mich. Ho. Reps., Dist. 27, 1979-98; asst. prosecutor Macomb County, Mt. Clemens, Mich., 1991—. Mem. appropriations com., Mich. Ho. Reps., 1991-98. Chmn. Macomb County Young Dem., Mich., 1972, vice chmn., 1972-73, officer-at-large, 1972-74; dir. registration Macomb Voters Registrar Com., 1972; alt. del. Dem. State Ctrl. Com., 1971-72; vice chmn. Mich. Young Dem., 1973-75; exec. bd. 12th Congl. Dist. Dem. Com., 1972; assoc. field staff reporter Mich. State Dem. Party, 1973-76; staff mem. U.S. Rep. James O'Hara, 1973-77; del. Dem. Nat. Mid-Term Conf., 1974; mem. exec. bd. Macomb County Dem. Comm., 1974—; mem. Friends Roseville Libr., Roseville Bicentennial Com., treas., 1976—; officer-at-large Mich. Dem. Party, 1997—. Mem. Lions, Jaycees, Alpha Sigma Nu. Office: Prosecutors Office Macomb County Bt Bldg 40 N Main St Fl 6 Mount Clemens MI 48043-5658

CICCARELLI, JOHN A., manufacturing executive; b. Boston, 1939; Grad., Northeastern U., 1963. Pres., CEO, bd. dirs. Dayton (Ohio) Superior Corp. Office: Dayton Superior Corp Ste 130 7777 Washington Village Dr Dayton OH 45459

CICCHINO, SAMUEL, deputy marshal; b. Newark, June 15, 1944; m. Zabel Kazanjian, Sept. 6, 1965; 3 children. AS in Police Sci., Brookdale C.C., Lynchcross, NJ, 1981. Enlisted USMC, 1961, advanced through ranks to sgt., 1971; dep. U.S. Marshal, Trenton, N.J., 1971-81, supervisory dept. Cin., 1981-83, Miami, Fla., 1983-84, chief dep. LA, 1984-88, marshal Cen. Dist. Calif., 1988-90, chief dep. LA, 1990-92, chief dep. So. Dist. Ohio Columbus, 1992—, acting marshal Western Dist. Louisville, 1997-98. Master sgt. USMCR, 1971—. Decorated Purple Heart, Vietnamese Cross of Gallantry; recipient Disting. Svc. Plaque, Nat. Mgmt. Negotiating Team, 1985, Letter of Appreciation, Pres. Ronald Reagan, 1990, award Atty. Gen.'s Commn. on Pornography, 1986, Calif. Atty. Gen. Van De Camp, 1990, Gov. Dukmajian of Calif., 1990, Disting. Achievement award Fed. Bar Assn., 1992. Mem. NRA, Fraternal Order Police. Mil. Order Purple Heart, Spl. Agts. Assn., Rep. Presdl. Trust. Baptist. Avocations: collecting coins, pistol and rifle shooting, archery. Office: Office of US Marshal So Dist Ohio 85 Marconi Blvd Rm 460 Columbus OH 43215-2835

CICERO, FRANK, JR., lawyer; b. Nov. 30, 1935; s. Frank and Mary Cicero; m. Janice Pickett, July 11, 1959; children: Erica, Caroline. AB with hons., Wheaton Coll., 1957; M in Pub. Affairs, Woodrow Wilson Sch. of Pub. & Internat. Affairs, 1962; JD, U. Chgo., 1965. Bar: Ill., U.S. Supreme Ct. 1965, various U.S. Ct. of Appeals and Dist. Cts. Polit. sci. instr. Wheaton Coll., Ill., 1957—58; assoc. Kirkland & Ellis, LLP, Chgo., 1965—70, ptnr., 1970—. Mem. vis. com. U. Chgo. Law Sch., 1971—74, 1996—99, 2003—, lectr., 1989—90, 1991—92; del. 6th Ill. Constl. Conv., 1969—70; mem. Jud. Conf. Civil Rules Adv. Com., 2003—06. Bd. editors: law rev. U. Chgo. Law Rev.; contbr. articles to profl. jours. Recipient Joseph Henry Beale prize, U. Chgo., 1963, Outstanding Young Man award, Evanston Jaycees, 1970. Fellow: Am. Coll. Trial Lawyers; mem.: ABA, Bar Assn. 7th Fed. Cir., Ill. State Bar Assn., Internat. Bar Assn., Saddle and Cycle Club (bd. govs. 1984), Mid-Am. Club (gov. 1981—84), Ventana Canyon Golf Club, Glen View Club, Chgo. Club. Office: Kirkland & Ellis LLP 200 E Randolph Dr Ste 6000 Chicago IL 60601-6636 Office Phone: 312-861-2216.

CICIRELLI, VICTOR GEORGE, psychologist; b. Miami, Fla., Oct. 1, 1926; s. Felix and Rene (DeMaria) C.; m. Jean Alice Solveson, Aug. 9, 1953; children: Ann Victoria, Michael Felix, Gregory Sheldon. BS, Notre Dame U., 1947; MA, U. Ill., Urbana, 1950; M.Ed., U. Miami, 1956; PhD (Univ. fellow), U. Mich., 1964; PhD, Mich. State U., 1971. Asst. prof. ednl. psychology U. Mich., 1963-65; dir. student teaching for elem., secondary and M.A.T. programs U. Pa., 1965-67; assoc. prof. early childhood edn. Ohio U., 1967-68; dir. research Nat. Evaluation of Head Start Westinghouse Learning Corp. at Ohio U., 1968-69; Office Edn. postdoctoral fellow U. Wis. Inst. Cognitive Learning, 1969-70; prof. human devel. Purdue U., 1970-73, prof. devel./aging psychology, 1974—, dir. devel. psychology program, 1977-78, 80-81, 82-83, 92-93, 96, 99-2001. Vis. sci. fellow Max Planck Inst. for Human Devel. and Edn., Berlin, 1991; fellow Ctr. for Health Policy Rsch., J. Hillis Miller Health Sci. Ctr., Sch. Medicine, U. Fla., Gainesville, 1991; Petersen vis. scholar in gerontology and family studies Oreg. State U., 2004-05; rsch. adv. bd. Calif. Commn. for Tchr. Preparation and Licensing, 1973-78; scholar NSF Inst., Ohio U., 1956, Am. U., 1958, U. Fla., 1960; cons. in field. Author: Helping Elderly Parents: Role of Adult Children, 1981, Family Caregiving: Autonomous and Paternalistic Decision Making, 1992, Sibling Relationships Across the Life Span, 1995, Older Adults' Views on Death, 2002; mem. editl. bd.: Jour. Marriage and the Family, 1990—; contbr. articles to profl. publs. Bd. dirs. Nat. Com. on Prevention of Elder Abuse, 1988-91; mem. adv. com. Ind. Geriatric Edn. Ctr., U. Ind., 1991. Grantee OEO, 1968-69, 71-73, U.S. Office Edn., 1971-73; Nat. Inst. Edn., 1973-74, NIH, 1973-74, Office Child Devel., 1973-74, Nat. Ret. Tchrs. Assn./Am. Assn. Ret. Persons Andrus Found., 1978-82, 90-92, 95, Retirement Rsch. Found., 1984-85, 87-89; fellow Andrew Norman Inst. Advanced Study, Andrus Gerontology Ctr., U. So. Calif., 1984, Gerontology Soc., 1983-84. Fellow APA, Gerontol. Soc.; mem. Internat. Soc. Study Behavioral Deve., Am. Psychol. Soc., Am. Assn. Aging, Nat. Coun. on Family Rels., Soc. for Chaos Theory, Phi Kappa Phi. Roman Catholic. Home: 1221 N Salisbury St West Lafayette IN 47906-2415 Office: Purdue U Dept Psychol Sci West Lafayette IN 47907 Office Phone: 765-494-6925. Business E-Mail: victor@psych.purdue.edu.

CIERPIOT, CONNIE, former state legislator; b. Kansas City, June 6, 1953; m. Charles Michael Cierpiot; 2 children. Mem. from dist. 52 Mo. Ho. of Reps., Jefferson City, 1994—2002. Mem.: bd. Truman Neurological Center, bd. Jackson County United Way, Concerned Women for Amer., Santa Fe Trails Women's Republican Club, Jackson County Republican Comm. Republican.

CIEZADLO, JANINA A., art critic, educator; MFA in Printmaking, Ind. U., Bloomington, MA in Comparative Lit. Adj. prof., dept. liberal edn. Columbia Coll.; adj. asst. prof., dept. art and design U. Ill. at Chgo. Published (reviews, scholarly monographs, articles, poetry, exhibited art work), art critic Chgo. Reader, Afterimage, Jour. of Media Arts and Cultural Criticism. Mem.: Chgo. Art Critics Assn. Address: 7200 West Oak 4NE River Forest IL 60305 Office: U Ill at Chgo 106 Jefferson Hall MC036 Chicago IL 60612 Office Phone: 312-996-3337. Business E-Mail: janina@uic.edu.

CIFELLI, JOHN LOUIS, lawyer; b. Chicago Heights, Ill., Aug. 19, 1923; s. Antonio and Domenica (Liberatore) C.; m. Irene Romandine, Jan. 4, 1948; children— Carla, David, John L., Bruce, Thomas, Carol. Student, Bowdoin Coll., 1943, Norwick Mil. Acad., 1943, Mt. Piliar Acad., 1943, U. Ill. Extension Ctr., 1946—47; LLB, DePaul U., 1950, JD (hon.), 1975. Bar: Ill. 1950, U.S. Supreme Ct. 1960. Ptnr. Piacenti, Cifelli & Sims, Chicago Heights, 1950—78; 1978pres. John L. Cifelli & Assocs., Chicago Heights, 1978—85; sr. ptnr. Cifelli Baczynski & Scrementi Ltd. (now Cifelli & Scrementi), Chicago Heights, 1985—; spl. counsel City of Chicago Heights, 1961—72; village atty. Village of Richton Park, Ill., 1962—77, Village of Ford Heights, Ill., 1984—89. Counsel Maj. League Umpires Assn., 1973-78, Ill. High Sch. Baseball Coaches Assn., 1975-89. Sec. Bd. Fire and Police, Chicago Heights, 1959-65; co-founder Small Fry Internat. Basketball, 1969, pres., 1969—; coach, baseball coordinator Chicago Heights Park Dist., 1970-75; coach Babe Ruth League Baseball, 1972, 74, 75, asst. Ill. dir., 1973; dir. Ill. tournament, 1973. Served to 2d lt. USAAF, 1942-45, ETO. Mem. ABA, Ill. Bar Assn., Ill. Trial Lawyers Assn., Asns. Trial Lawyers Am., Justinian Soc. Lawyers, Isaac Walton League, Italo Am. Vets. Group, VFW (judge adv. 1951-72), Cath. War Vets. (judge adv. 1951-70), Am. Legion. Clubs: Chicago Heights Country (bd. dirs. 1972-76), Mt. Carmel; Pike Lake Fishing (Wis.). Lodges: Moose, Amaseno. Republican. Avocations: hunting, fishing, golf. Home: 879 Amico Dr Chicago Heights IL 60411 Office: Cifelli & Scrementi Ste 212 1010 Dixie Hwy Chicago Heights IL 60411-3555 Office Phone: 708-754-6200. Business E-Mail: cifellilawfirm@msn.com.

CIOFFI, MICHAEL LAWRENCE, lawyer; b. Cin., Feb. 2, 1953; s. Patrick Anthony and Patricia (Schroeder) C.; children: Michael A., David P., Gina M. BA magna cum laude, U. otre Dame, 1975; JD, U. Cin., 1979. Bar: Ohio 1979, U.S. Dist. Ct. (so. dist.) Ohio 1980, U.S. Dist. Ct. (no. dist.) Ohio 1983, U.S. Ct. Appeals (6th cir.) 1985. Asst. atty. gen. Ohio Atty. Gen., Columbus, 1979-81; from assoc. to ptnr. Frost & Jacobs, Cin., 1981-87; staff v.p., asst. gen. counsel Penn Cen. Corp., Cin., 1988-93; v.p., asst. gen. counsel Am. Fin. Group, Cin., 1993-2000; ptnr. Blank Rome LLP, Cin., 2000—. Adj. prof. law U. Cin. Coll. Law, 1983—. Author: Ohio Pretrial Litigation, 1991, rev. ed., 2007; co-author: Sixth Circuit Federal Practice Manual, 1993, 3d edit., 2006. Bd. dirs. Charter Com. of Greater Cin., 1985—88. Recipient Goldman Prize for Tchg. Excellence U. Cin. Coll. Law, 1995, Nicholas Longworth Disting. Alumni award, 1996, Adj. Faculty Tchg. Excellence award, 2000. Mem. ABA, Fed. Bar Assn. (mem. exec. com., pres.1994), Ohio Bar Assn., Cin. Bar Assn. Avocations: tennis, travel. Office: Blank Rome LLP 201 E 5th St Cincinnati OH 45202

CIPLIJAUSKAITE, BIRUTE, humanities educator; b. Kaunas, Lithuania, Apr. 11, 1929; came to U.S., 1957; d. Juozas and Elena (Stelmokaite) C. BA, Lycée Lithuanien Tubingen, 1947; MA, U. Montreal, 1956; PhD, Bryn Mawr Coll., 1960. Permanent mem. Inst. Rsch. in Humanities U. Wis., Madison, 1974, asst. prof., 1961-65, assoc. prof., 1965-68, prof., 1968-73, John Bascom prof., 1973—. Author: Solitude and Spanish Contemporary Poetry, 1962, Poetry and the Poet, 1966, Baroja, a style, 1972, Plenitude as Commitment: The Poetry of Jorge Guillén, 1973, The Generation of 1898 and History, 1981, The Unsatisfied Woman: Adultery in Realist Novel, 1984, Contemporary Women's Novel (1970-85), 1988, Literary Sketches, 1992, Of Signs and Significations. I: Games of the Avant-Garde, 1999, Carmen Martín Gaite, 2000, Guilleniana, 2002, Construction of the Feminine I in Literature, 2004; editor: (Luis de Góngora), Complete Sonnets, 1969, 75, 79, 81, 85, 99, critical edit., 1989, facsimile edit., 2007, Jorge Guillén, 1975, (with C. Maurer) The Will to Humanism. Homage to Juan Marichal, 1990, Novísimos, postnovísimos, clásicos: Poetry of the 80s in Spain, 1991; translator: (Juan Ramón Jiménez), Platero and I, 1982, (María Victoria Atencia), Trances of the Holy Virgin, 1989, Voices Within Silence: Contemporary Lithuanian Poetry, 1991, Birute Pukeleviciute, Lament, 1994, (with Nicole Laurent-Catrice) Twenty Lithuanian Poets of Today, 1997, (Vidmante Jasukaityte), The Miraculous Grass Along the Fence, 2002, (J. Degutytė and B. Pukelevičiute) Between the Sun and Dispossession, 2002, (Mercè Rodoreda) The Girl of the Doves, 2002, (Nijole Miliauskaitė) Forbidden Room, 2003, (with Emilio Coco) That Rustle of Nordic Herbs. Anthology of Lithuanian Contemporary Poetry, 2006, others. Guggenheim fellow, 1968 Mem. Assn. For Advancement Baltic Studies (v.p. 1981), Asociación Internacional de Hispanistas, Order Alfonso X elSabio (named commdr. Spain, 2003) Office: U Wis Inst Rsch in Humanities 1225 Linden Dr Madison WI 53706-1209

CIRELLI, MARY M., state representative; b. Uniontown, Pa., July 4, 1939; married; 2 children. Grad., Canton (Ohio) City Sch. LPN Program; attended, Malone Coll. LPN; state rep. dist. 52 Ohio Ho. of Reps., Columbus, 2000—, ranking minority mem., vets. affairs subcom., mem. county and twp. govt., energy and environment, health, and human svcs. and aging coms., mem. regulatory reform subcom. Mem. Mayor's task force on pay equity, Canton, Ohio. Mem.: Red Cross Gray Ladies, Canton Friendship Ctr., Canton Preservation Soc. (bd. dirs.), Stark County Hunger Task Force, Canton McKinley Alumni, Dem. Womens Club. Democrat. Office: 77 S High St 10th fl Columbus OH 43215-6111

CIRESI, MICHAEL VINCENT, lawyer; b. St. Paul, Apr. 18, 1946; s. Samuel Vincent and Selena Marie (Bloom) Ciresi; m. Ann Ciresi; children: Caroline, Dominic, Adam. BBA, U. St. Thomas, 1968; JD, U. Minn., 1971; LLD (hon.), Southwestern U., 2001. Bar: Minn. 1971, U.S. Dist. Ct. Minn. 1974, U.S. Ct. Appeals (8th cir.) 1971, U.S. Supreme Ct. 1981, U.S. Ct. Appeals (2d cir.) 1986, U.S. Ct. Appeals (9th cir.) 1987, U.S. Ct. Appeals (10th cir.) 1990, NY 1995, Fed. Cir. 1998, U.S. Ct. Appeals (5th cir.) 1999. Assoc. Robins, Kaplan, Miller & Ciresi, Mpls., 1971—78, ptnr., 1978—, exec. bd., 1983—, chmn. exec. bd., 1995—2006. Trustee U. St. Thomas, Saint Thomas Acad. Performing Arts; bd. dirs. Minn. Early Learning Found.; candidate U.S. Senate, 2000; bd. govs. U. St. Thomas Sch. Law; bd. dirs. Inst. Jud. Adminstrn. Sch. Law NYU; bd. dirs. Lawyers' Com. Civil Rights Under Law, Regions Hosp. Found., Pub. Radio Internat. Named Product Liability Lawyer of Yr., Australian Nat. Consumer Law Assn., 1989, Trial Lawyer of Yr., Trial Lawyers for Pub. Justice Found., 1998; named one of Ten of the Nation's Top Trial Lawyers, Nat. Law Jour., 1989, 1993, 100 Most Influential Lawyers, 1997, 2000, 2006; recipient Lifetime Achievement Award, Minn. Trial Lawyers, 1998, Disting. Alumnus Award, U. St. Thomas, 1999, Outstanding Achievement Award, U. Minn., 1999, Ellis Island Medal of Honor, Nat. Ethnic Coalition of Orgns. Found., 2002. Mem.: ATLA, ABA, Am. Coll. Trial Lawyers, Internat. Acad. Trial Lawyers, Trial Lawyers for Pub. Justice, Inner Cir. of Advocates, Internat. Bar Assn., Am. Bd. Trial Advocates, Ramsey County Bar Assn., Hennepin County Bar Assn., Minn. State Bar Assn. Roman Catholic. Avocations: sports, U.S. history. Home: 1247 Culligan Ln Saint Paul MN 55118-4151 Office: Robins Kaplan Miller & Ciresi 2800 Lasalle Plz Minneapolis MN 55402 Office Phone: 612-349-8533. Business E-Mail: mvciresi@rkmc.com.

CISCHKE, SUSAN MARY, automotive executive; b. Detroit, 1954; BS, Oakland U., 1979; MS in Mech. Engring. and Mgmt., U. Mich., Dearborn. Engr. DaimlerChrysler Corp. (formerly Chrysler Corp.), 1976, gen. mgr. sci. labs. and proving grounds, 1994—96, v.p. vehicle certification, compliance and safety affairs, 1996—99, sr. v.p. regulatory Affairs and passenger car ops., 1999—2001; v.p. environ. and safety engring., chief safety officer Ford Motor Co., Dearborn, Mich., 2001—07, sr. v.p. sustainability, environ. and safety engring., 2007—. Bd. mem. Chgo. Climate Exchange, Henry Ford Health Sys. Found., Detroit Sci. Ctr.; Ford Motor Co. liaison World Bus. Coun. for Sustainable Devel.; mem. nat. adv. com. U. Mich. Coll. Engring. Bd. dirs. Inforu, Ctr. for Leadership; chair Women's Initiative United Way of S.E. Mich. Named one of Most Influential Women, Crain's Detroit Bus. Mem.: Women's Econ. Club (mem. leadership bd.), Engring. Soc. Detroit (Horace H. Rackham Award 1997), Soc. Women Engineers (Upward Mobility Award 2000), Soc. Automotive Engrs. Office: Ford Motor Co 1 American Rd Dearborn MI 48126

CISSELL, JAMES CHARLES, lawyer; b. Cleve., May 29, 1940; s. Robert Francis and Helen Cecelia (Freeman) C; children: Denise, Helene-Marie, Suzanne, James. Student, Sophia U., Tokyo, 1961; AB, Xavier U., 1962; postgrad., Ohio State U., 1963—64; JD, U. Cin., 1966; D. Tech. Letters, Cin. Tech. Coll., 1979. Bar: Ohio 1966, U.S. Dist. Ct. (so. dist.) Ohio 1967, U.S. Ct. Appeals (6th cir.) 1978, U.S. Supreme Ct. 1980, U.S. Dist. Ct. (ea. dist.) Ky. 1981. Pvt. practice law, 1966—78, 1982—2003; asst. atty. gen. State of Ohio, 1971-74; first v.p. Cin. Bd. Park Commrs., 1973-74; vice mayor City of Cin., 1976-77; U.S. atty. So. Dist. Ohio, Cin., 1978-82. Adj. instr. law No. Ky. U., 1982-86; pres. Nat. Assn. Former U.S. attys., 2001-02; mem. Legis. Task Force to Study Eminent Domain and It's Use and Application in the State of Ohio, 2006—. Author: Oil and Gas Law in Ohio, 1964, Federal Criminal Trials, 6th edit., 2003; editor: Proving Federal Crimes. Gen. chmn. amateur pub. links championship U.S. Golf Assn., 1987; mem. coun. City of Cin., 1974-78, 85-87, 89-92; clk of cts., Hamilton County, 1992-2003; judge Hamilton County Probate Ct., 2003-; commr. Recreation Bd. Cin., 1974, Planning Bd. Cin., 1977; pres. Ohio Clk. of Cts. Assn., 1998; mem. Ohio Bicentennial Commn., 1998-2003; mem. Ohio Cts. Futures Commn., 1998-2000; mem. Ohio Supreme Ct. Adv. Com. on Tech. and the Cts., 2000—, privacy of access subcom. of Supreme Ct. adv. com. on tech. of the Cts. Recipient Econ. Opportunity award, Dr. Martin Luther King Jr. Holiday Commn., 2002; fellow, Ford Found., 1973—74. Mem. Ohio Bar Assn., Cin. Bar Assn., Fed. Bar Assn., Former U.S. Attys. Assn. (pres. 2002-03), Greater Cin. Golf Assn. (pres. 2003-). Avocations: golf, table tennis. Office: William Howard Taft Law Ctr 230 E 9th St 10th Fl Cincinnati OH 45202 Office Phone: 513-946-3535. Business E-Mail: jcissell@probatect.org.

CLACK, FLOYD, former state legislator; b. Houston, Dec. 21, 1940; m. Brenda J. Jones; children: Michael, Mia. BS, Tex. So. U., 1965; MA, Ea. Mich. U., 1972. State rep. Mich. Ho. Reps., Dist. 80, 1983-94, Mich. Ho. Reps., Dist. 48, 1995-97. Vice chmn. Dem. black caucus, majority whip, mem. standing com. labor, standing com. coll. & univs., standing com. constrn. rev. & women's rights, chmn. standing com. corrections, ad hoc spl. com. alternatives fo rhigh risk students, 2d vice chmn. majority caucus, mahority vice chmn., standing com. civic rights, mem. standing com. mental health, standing com. corp. & fin., standing com. ins., criminal justice com., ad hoc spl. com. studying Mich. fin. inst., Mich. Ho. Reps. Mem. exec. bd. Genesee County Dem. Com., Mich.; co-chmn. Mayor's Hail Task Force; del. Dem. Nat. Conv.; chmn. Genesee County Jackson for Pres. Caucus, Jesse Jackson for Pres. com., Flint, 1988; founder Floyd Clack Cmty Project; chmn. Mott Found. Tribute Com. & Floyd J. McCree Tribute Com.; mem. New Paths, Inc. Adv. Coun.; bd. dirs. Eastside Teen Ctr.; bd. trustees Don Haley Scholar; founder, bd. dirs. Youth Leadership Ins., Flint. Recipient Svc. award Concerned Pastors Assn., 1982, Greater Flint Afro-Am. Hall of Fame, Toll Fel., 1987, David McMahon award Mech. Edn. Assn., 150% Achiever Lansing Stae Jour. Mem. NEA, Am. Corrections Assn., Mich. Corrections Assn., United Tchrs. Flint (chmn. human rels. com.), John W. Stevenson Lodge No. 56, Lions (charter, past v.p., Man of Yr. 1982), Met. C. of C., Urban League, Kappa Alpha Psi. Home: 3120 Helber St Flint MI 48504-2921

CLAEYS, JEROME JOSEPH, III, investment company executive; b. South Bend, Ind., Oct. 23, 1942; s. Jerry F. and Evadna (Shoemaker) Claeys; m. Barbara Lauman, May 4, 1974; children: Elizabeth Anne, Matthew Jerome, Andrew Francis, Katherine Ellen. BS, Georgetown U., 1965; MBA, U. Notre Dame, 1969. First v.p. White Weld & Co., YC, 1969—76; exec. v.p. JMB Realty Corp., Chgo., 1977—89; chmn. JMB Instl. Realty Corp. (JMB Instl. Realty Corp. merged with Heitman Fin.), Chgo., 1990—94; co-chmn. Heitman Capital Mgmt., 1995; chmn, CEO Heitman Financial LLC, 1999—2002, chmn., 2002—. With US Army, 1965—67. Decorated Bronze Star with oak leaf cluster. Mem.: PREA, Real Estate Roundtable. Roman Cath. Office: Heitman Financial 191 N Wacker Dr Ste 2500 Chicago IL 60606 Office Phone: 312-541-6740. Business E-Mail: jerry.claeys@heitman.com.

CLANCY, PATRICIA, state representative; b. Cin., Aug. 10, 1952; BS, U. Cin. State rep. dist. 29 Ohio Ho. of Reps., Columbus, 1996—2004, mem. fin. and appropriations, rules and reference, and state govt. coms., mem. agr. and devel., and ethics and elections subcoms., majority fl. leader; state senator Ohio Senate Dist. 8, Columbus, 2005—, mem. fin. and fin. instns. com., mem. health, human svcs. and aging com., mem. hwys. and transp. com., mem. ins., commerce and labor com., vice chair judiciary and criminal justice com. Mem. Hamilton County Solid Waste Dist. Task Force, Colerain Ave. Task Force; past pres., trustee Colerain Twp. Mem.: Hamilton County Twp. Assn. (sec.-treas.), Colerain Twp. Hist. Soc., Colerain Twp. Rep. Club (sec.), Hamilton County Rep. Club. Republican. Office: Ohio Senate Statehouse Rm 143 Columbus OH 43215

CLAPP, KENT W., insurance company executive; b. Montpelier, Ohio; BS in Acctg., Tri-State Univ., Angola, Ind.; graduate Advanced Mgmt. Program, Harvard Sch. Bus.Adminstrn., 1989. CPA 1972. Corp. controller Blue Cross, NW Ohio (merged into Medical Mutual), 1976—89; sr. v.p. Medical Mutual of Ohio, Cleve., 1989—92, COO, 1992—97, pres., 1992—, CEO, 1997—, chmn., 1997—. Graduate Leadership Cleve., 1992; bd. dir. Harvard Bus. Club, Cleve., United Way Greater Cleve. Named Bus. Exec. Yr., Sales & Mktg. Execs, Cleveland, 2002; named an honoree at NE Ohio Multiple Sclerosis Soc. Dinner of Champions, 2002; recipient Franklin Delano Roosevelt Humanitarian award, March of Dimes, 2000. Office: Medical Mutual Ohio 2060 E Ninth St Cleveland OH 44115 Office Phone: 216-687-6514. Office Fax: 216-687-7632.

CLAPPER, LYLE NIELSEN, magazine publisher; b. Evanston, Ill., Apr. 24, 1941; s. John Marion and Edna (Nielsen) C.; m. Lynn Dewey, Sept. 1, 1962 (div. June 1978); children: John Scott, Susan Louise; m. Marie Petersen, Jan. 1, 1980; children: Jeffrey Leland, Anne Reinke. Student, Cornell U., 1959-60; BS in Quantative Econs., U. Ill., 1964. Chief exec. officer Clapper Communications (pubs. Crafts 'N Things mag., Pack-O-Fun mag., Decorative Arts Painting mag., Cross Stitcher Mag., Bridal Crafts mag.), Des Plaines, Ill., 1960—. Dir. AirLifeLine Midwest, 1995-2000. Avocations: teaching flying, photography, computer programming.

CLAPPER, MARIE ANNE, magazine publisher; b. Chgo., Nov. 21, 1942; d. Chester William and Hazel Alice (Gilso) Reinke; m. William Neil Petersen, Aug. 17, 1963 (div. 1975); children: Elaine Myrtice Petersen, Edward William Petersen; m. Lyle N. Clapper, Jan. 1, 1980; children: Jeffrey Leland, Anne Reinke stepchildren: John Scott, Susan Louise Clapper Kashmier. Student, Augustana Coll., Rock Island, Ill., 1960-63; EdB, Northeastern U., 1964. Writer Pack-o-Fun mag., Park Ridge, Ill., 1976-77, editor Des Plaines, Ill., 1977-78, pub., 1990—; asst. to pub., circulation dir. Crafts 'n Things mag., Des Plaines, Ill., 1978-82, pub., 1982—, Decorative Arts Painting mag., Des Plaines, 1990—, The Cross Stitcher mag., Des Plaines, 1991—, 101 Bridal Ideas mag., Des Plaines, 1991—; pub., pres. Clapper pub., 2005—. Host TV show The Crafts 'n Things Show, 1984-86, Crafting for the 90s, 1990-94; author: EveryDay Matters, 1996. Mem. TEC, Mag. Pubs. Am. (bd. dirs.), Hobby Industry Am. (bd. dirs., treas. 1998-99). Office: Crafts 'n Things 2400 E Devon Ave Ste 375 Des Plaines IL 60018-4618

CLAREY, JOHN ROBERT, executive recruiter, consultant; b. Waterloo, Iowa, June 5, 1942; s. Robert J. and Norma (Knox) Clarey; m. Kathleen Ann Kingsley, June 5, 1965; children: Sharon Diane, Suzanne Marie. BSBA, Iowa State U., 1965; MBA, U. Pa., 1972. Fin. analyst Ford Motor Co., Dearborn, Mich., 1972-74; cons. Price Waterhouse, Chgo., 1974-75, mgr., 1975-76; assoc. Heidrick & Struggles, Chgo., 1976-81, v.p., ptnr., 1981-82; pres. Clarey, Andrews & Klein, Inc., orthbrook, Ill., 1982—. Served to lt. USN, 1965—70, Vietnam. Mem.: Assn. Exec. Search Cons., Lifeline Pilots, Sunset Ridge Country Club (Northbrook), Mid-Am. Club (Chgo.), Stick and Rudder. Republican. Roman Catholic. Avocations: flying, microcomputers, tennis. Home: 1347 Hillside Rd Northbrook IL 60062-4612 Office: Clarey Andrews & Klein Inc 1200 Shermer Rd Ste 108 Northbrook IL 60062-4563 Personal E-mail: jackclarey@ameritech.net. Business E-Mail: jack@clarey-a-klein.com.

CLARK, BEVERLY ANN, retired lawyer; b. Davenport, Iowa, Dec. 9, 1944; d. F. Henry and Arlene F. (Meyer) C.; m. Richard Floss; children: Amy and Barry (twins); stepchildren: Heather, Gretchan. Student, Mich. State U., 1963—65; BA, Calif. State U., Fullerton, 1967; MSW, U. Iowa, 1975, JD, 1980; grad., Iowa Massage Inst., 1999. Bar: Iowa 1980; lic. social worker, Iowa; nat. cert. lic. massage therapist. Probation officer County of San Bernardino, San Bernardino, Calif., 1968, County of Riverside, Riverside, Calif., 1968-69; social worker Skiff Hosp., Newton, Iowa, 1971-73, State of Iowa, Mitchellville, 1973-74, planner Des Moines, 1976-77, law clk., 1980-81; corp. counsel Pioneer Hi-Bred Internat., Inc., Des Moines, 1981-2000; atty. Jasper County Legal Aid, 2002—03; pvt. practice, 2000—06; ret., 2006. Instr. Des Moines Area C.C., Ankeny, Iowa, 1974—75, 2000—; adj. prof. Drake Law Sch., 1993—96, Buena Vista U., 2002—; pub. Sweet Annie Press; past owner Annie's Place, The B&B Connection Gift Catalog. Editor: Proceedings: Bicentennial Symposium on New Directions in Juvenile Justice, 1975; author monthly column Wellfem-In-Law; contbr. articles to prof. jours. Founder Mother of Twins Club, Newton, 1971; co-chmn. Juvenile Justice Symposium, Des Moines, 1974-75; mem. Juvenile Justice Com., Des Moines, 1974-75; mem. Nat. Offender Based State Corrections Info. Sys. Com., Iowa rep., 1976-78; incorporator, dir. Iowa Dance Theatre, Des Moines, 1981; mem. Pesticide User's Adv. Com., Fort Collins, Colo., 1981-88; co-developer Iowa Migrant Ombudsmen Project, Pioneer, Inc. and Proteus, Inc. Recipient Disting. Alumni award U. Iowa, 1990, Nat. award Ctr. for Pub. Resources. Mem.: DAR, ABA (termination-at-will subcom. 1982—2000, subcom. on devel. individual rights in work place), Iowa Bar Assn. E-mail: clarklaw@pcpartner.net.

CLARK, CHARLES M., JR., medical school administrator; b. Greensburg, Ind., Mar. 12, 1938; s. Charles Malcolm and Mary Louise (Christian) C.; m. Julia Berg Freeman, Jan 27, 1963 (div. 1982); children: Margaret Louise, Brian Alexander; m. Eleanor DeArman Kinney, June 25, 1983; 1 child, Janet Marie Clark. BA, Ind. U., 1960, MD, 1963. From asst. prof. to prof. medicine Ind. U., Indpls., 1969—, from asst. prof. to prof. pharmacology, 1970—; assoc. chief staff rsch. and devel. VA Hosp., Indpls., 1988—2002; dir. Diabetes Rsch. and Tng. Ctr., Indpls., 1977—2002; co-dir. Regenstrief Inst., Indpls., 1993-97; assoc. dean Ind. U. Sch. Medicine, Indpls., 2002—. Chmn. Safety and Quality com. DCCT, 1982-93, Nat. Diabetes adv. bd., 1987-88; chair Nat. Diabetes Edn. Program, 1995-2002; vis. prof. Facultad de Ciencias Medicas, U. Nacional de la Plata, Argentina, 1999-2000. Editor Diabetes Care, 1996-2001; contbr. numerous articles to profl. jours. Lt comdr. USPHS, 1967-69. Fulbright scholar, 2004—05. Mem. ACP, Am. Soc. Clin. Investigation, Internat. Diabetes Fedn., Am. Diabetes Assn. (Banting award 1989, J.K. Lilly award 2003). Office: 714 N Senate Ave EF 200 Indianapolis IN 46202 Home Phone: 317-466-7858; Office Phone: 317-274-0104. E-mail: chclark@iupui.edu.

CLARK, CLIFFORD EDWARD, JR., history professor; b. BayShore, NY, July 13, 1941; s. Clifford Edward and Helen C.; m. Grace Williams, Aug. 20, 1966; children: Cynthia Williams, Christopher Allen, Susan McGrath. BA, Yale U., 1963; MA, Harvard U., 1964, PhD in Am. Civilization, 1968. History tutor Harvard U., Cambridge, Mass., 1966-67; instr. Amherst (Mass.) Coll., 1968-69, asst. prof., 1969-70; from asst. to assoc. prof. Carleton Coll., Northfield, Minn., 1970-80, prof. history, 1980—, M.A. and A.D. Hulings prof. Am. studies, 1982—, dir. summer acad. programs, 1984—2002, chmn. history dept., 1986-89. Cons. Minn. Humanities Commn., Mpls., 1976—, Minn. Hist. Soc., Mpls., 1982—; Northfield Sch. Bd., 1978-87; editl. cons. Winterthur Portfolio, Del., 1983-92. Author: Henry Ward Beecher, Spokesman for a Middle-Class America, 1978, The American Family Home, 1800-1960, 1986; (with others) The Enduring Tradition, 6th edit. 2006; editor: Minnesota in a Century of Change: The State and Its People Since 1900, 1989 Mem. Northfield Heritage Preservation Commn., 1986—. Fellow Woodrow Wilson Found., 1964, 67; Demonstration grantee NEH, 1978, sr. fellow NEH, 1980; recipient Younger Humanist Summer Stipend, NEH, 1973. Mem. Am. Studies Assn., Am. Hist. Assn., Orgn. Am. Historians, Northfield Hist. Soc. Episcopalian. Avocations: woodworking, squash. Home: 718 4th St E Northfield MN 55057-2316 Office: Carleton Coll Dept History One N College St Northfield MN 55057 Office Phone: 507-646-4208. Business E-Mail: cclark@carleton.edu.

CLARK, DAVID W., retail executive; m. Kay Clark; 3 children. Grad., U. Cin., 1974. Pers. mgr. Lazarus, 1978—79, regional pers. mgr., 1979—81; employee rels. mgr. Rockwell Internat., Columbus, Ohio, 1981—82, Federated Dept. Stores, Cin., 1982—85, v.p., employee rels. Chgo., 1985—88; sr. v.p. of human resources and corp. tng. Lazarus, 1988—95; v.p., exec. and organizational develop., diversity mgmt. and tng. Federated Dept. Stores, 1995—2002, sr. v.p., human resources, 2002—. Office: Federated Dept Stores 7 W 7th St Cincinnati OH 45202

CLARK, DWIGHT EDWARD, sports team executive, former professional football player; b. Kinston, NC, Jan. 8, 1957; BA, Clemson U., 1979. Wide receiver San Francisco 49ers, NFL, 1979—87, exec. v.p., dir. football ops., 1995—98, played in Super Bowl, 1981, 1984; v.p., dir of football ops. Cleve. Browns, 1998—. Mem. NFL All-Star Team, 1981, 82. Office: c/o Cleveland Browns 76 Lou Groza Blvd Berea OH 44017-1238

CLARK, ELOISE ELIZABETH, biologist, educator; b. Grundy, Va., Jan. 20, 1931; d. J. Francis Emmett and Ava Clayton (Harris) C. BA, Mary Washington Coll., 1951; PhD Zoology, U. N.C., 1958; DSc, King Coll., 1976; postdoctoral rsch., Washington U., St. Louis, 1957—58, U. Calif. Berkeley, 1958—59. Rsch. asst., then instr. U. N.C., 1952—55; from instr. to asst. prof. Columbia U., 1959—65, assoc. prof. biol. sci., 1966—69; with NSF, Washington, 1969—71, head molecular biology, 1971—73, divsn. dir. biol. and med. scis., 1973—75, dep. asst. dir. biol., behavioral and social scis., 1975—76, asst. dir. biol., behavioral and social scis., 1976-83; prof. biol. sci. to trustee prof. emeritus Bowling Green State U., Ohio, 1983—2002, trustee prof. emeritus, 2002—. Instr. Marine Biol. Lab., Woods Hole, Mass., 1958—62; v.p. acad. affairs Bowling Green State U., Ohio, 1983—96. Contbr. articles to profl. jours. and congl. hearings. Mem. alumnae bd. Mary Washington Coll., U. Va., 1967—70; bd. regents Nat. Libr. Medicine, 1973—83; mem. policy group competitive grants program U.S. Dept. Agr.; mem. White House Interdepartmental Task Force on Women, 1978—80, Task Force for Conf. on Families, 1980, Com. on Health and Medicine, 1976—80; vice chmn. Com. on Food and Renewable Resources, 1977—80; mem. selective excellence task force Ohio Bd. Regents, 1984—85; mem. Ohio Adv. Coun., Coll. Prep. Edn., 1983—84, Ohio Inter-Univ. Coun. for Provosts, 1983—96, chmn., 1984—85, 1995—96; nat. adv. rsch. resources coun. NIH, 1987—89; mem. informal sci. edn. panel NSF, 1986—88, adv. com., social, behavioral and econ. scis., 1997—2000; program adv. coun. sci., tech. and pub. policy Harvard U., 1988—90, mem. editl. bd. Forum, 1997—2001; mem. governing bd. OhioLink, 1990—96, vice chair, 1992, chair, 1993—94. Named Disting. Alumnus Mary Washington Coll., 1975; Wilson scholar, 1956; E.C. Drew scholar, 1956; USPHS postdoctoral fellow, 1957-59; recipient Disting. Svc. award NSF, 1978 Mem. AAAS (coun. 1969-71, bd. dirs. 1978-82, pres.-elect, 1992, pres., 1993, chmn. bd. 1994), Soc. Gen. Physiology (sec. 1965-67, coun. 1969-71), Biophys. Soc. (coun. 1975-76), Am. Soc. Cell Biology (coun. 1972-75), Marine Biol. Lab. (trustee 1993), Nat. Assn. State Univs. and Land Grant Colls. (higher edn. and tech. com. 1988-93, com. info. tech. 1994-96), Consortium Social Sci. Assn. (bd. dirs. 1993-96), Ohio Coun. Rsch. and Econ. Devel., Assn. Women Sci. (bd. dirs. 1998-2001), Phi Beta Kappa (com. qualifications 1985-2006, chair 1998-2004, senate 1996-2006, exec. com. 1997-2003), Sigma Xi, Omicron Delta Kappa Home: 1222 Brownwood Dr Bowling Green OH 43402-3503 also: 451 Crowfields Dr Asheville NC Office Phone: 419-372-9390. E-mail: eclark@bgsu.edu.

CLARK, FRANK M., utilities executive; B in Bus. Adminstrn., DePaul Univ., JD, LLD (hon.), 2004; DHL (hon.), Governors State Univ., 2005. Mgmt. positions ComEd, Chgo., 1966—2000, exec. v.p., 2000—01, pres., 2001—05; exec. v.p., chief of staff Exelon Corp. (holding co. of ComEd), 2004—05; chmn., CEO ComEd, Chgo., 2005—. Bd. dir. Harris Fin. Corp., Waste Mgmt. Inc., 2002—, Aetna Inc., 2006—. Chmn. Metro. Family Services; trustee Adler Planetarium & Astronomy Mus., DePaul Univ., Chgo. Symphony Orch., Univ. Chgo. Hosp. & Health Sys.; bd. mem. Abraham Lincoln Presdl. Libr. Found., Governors State Univ. Found., Big Shoulders Fund, Ill. Council Econ. Edn., Ill. Mfr. Assn. Named one of 50 Most Powerful Black Executives in Am., Forbes mag.; recipient Nat. Humanitarian award, Nat. Conf. for Cmty. & Justice, Rerun Novarum award, Loyola Univ., HistoryMakers award, 2002. Mem.: Chgo. Bar Assn. Office: ComEd 37th Flr 10 S Dearborn St Chicago IL 60690

CLARK, GARY R., newspaper editor; b. Cleve., June 27, 1946; s. Dale Francis and Mary Louise (Rozeski) C.; m. Caryn Elaine Helm, Dec. 18, 1976; children: Jessica Lynn, Brian Michael. BA, Ohio State U., 1973, MA, 1978. Reporter Chronicle-Telegram, Elyria, Ohio, 1973-77, The Plain Dealer, Cleve., 1978-88, state editor, 1988-89, nat. editor, 1989, city editor 1989-90, mng. editor, 1990—2000; city editor The Columbus Dispatch, 2000—02; mng. editor for news The Denver Post, 2003—. Tchg. assoc. Ohio State U., Columbus, 1977-78; juror, Pulitzer Prize, 1996. Sgt. USMC, 1966-69, Vietnam. Recipient Best of Show award, Ohio Soc. Profl. Journalists, 1999. Mem. AP Mng. Editors, Am. Soc. Newspaper Editors, Investigative Reporters and Editors, Cleve. City Club. Office: Mng Ed Denver Post 1560 Broadway Denver CO 80202

CLARK, J. MURRAY (MURRAY CLARK), political organization administrator, lawyer; m. Janet Clark; children: James, Holly, Katherine, Anne. BA, Kenyon Coll., 1979; JD, Ind. U., Indianapolis, 1982. Bar: Ind. 1982, admitted: US Dist. Ct., No. Dist. Ind., US Dist. Ct., So. Dist. Ind. Senator Ind. State Senate, Dist. 29, 1994—2005, mem. econ. devel. & tech. com., mem. ins. & fin. inst. com., mem. govt. affairs subcommittee; rep. precinct committeeman & ward chmn. Ind.; atty. Clark, Quinn, Moses & Clark; ptnr. Baker & Daniels LLP, 2005—; chmn. Ind. Rep. Party, 2007—. Chief sgt. of arms State Rep. Conv., 1992, del., 94, 96, Rep. Nat. Conv., 1996—; chmn. Washington Twp. Adv. Bd., 1992—94; counsel, chmn. Marion County Election Bd.; treas. Marion County Rep. Ctrl. Com., 2000—04. Mem. bd. dirs. Marion County Sheriff's Motorcycle Drill Team, St. Elizabeth's Home, Children's Bur. Found., Hundred Club; mem. bd. trustees Brebeuf Prep. Sch., Indianapolis Found.; coach Washington Twp. Youth Soccer League, First Baptist Ch. Little League; mem. Carmel-Clay C. of C., police Action League, Police Athletic League, Nora-Northside Cmty. Coun. Named an Ind. Super Lawyer, 2008; named one of Best Lawyers in Am., 2008; recipient 40 Under 40 award, Indianapolis Bus. Jour., 1997, Adoption Legis. award, Ind. Life Coalition, 1999, Legis. award, Ind. Liberty Fedn., 2000, Ind. Conf. Legis. Leadership award, Am. Assn. U. Professors, 2001, Fred B. McCashland Disting. Alumnus award, Brefeuf Jesuit Prep. Sch., 2001, Guardian of Small Bus., Nat. Fedn. Ind. Bus., 2001, Small Bus. Champion award, Ind. C. of C., 2004. Mem.: Lawyers Club Indianapolis, Ind. Bar Assn. (Land Use and Zoning Sect. award 1995), Indianapolis Bar Assn. (chmn.), Pie, Eagle Creek & Wayne Twp. Rep Clubs, Washington Twp. Rep. Club (v.p.), Am. Bus. Club. Republican. Office: Ind Rep Party 47 S Meridian St 2nd Fl Indianapolis IN 46204 also: Baker & Daniels LLP 300 N Meridian St Ste 2700 Indianapolis IN 46204 Office Phone: 317-635-7561, 317-237-1433. Office Fax: 317-237-1000. Business E-Mail: murray.clark@bakerd.com, mclark@indgop.org.*

CLARK, JAMES ALLEN, lawyer, educator; b. Canton, Ill., Nov. 13, 1948; s. Howard R. and Helen (McElwain) C. BS in Edn., Miami U., Oxford, Ohio, 1971, BA in Polit. Sci., 1971; MS in Urban Studies, Cleve. State U., 1974; JD, Case Western Res. U., 1977. Bar: U.S. Dist. Ct. (no. dist.) Ohio 1977, U.S. Ct. Appeals (6th cir.) 1978, U.S. Dist. Ct. (no. dist.) Ill. 1979, U.S. Ct. Appeals (7th cir.) 1980, U.S. Supreme Ct. 1981, U.S. Ct. Appeals (D.C. cir.) 1985, U.S. Dist. Ct. (ea. dist.) Wis. 1986, U.S. Ct. Appeals (8th cir.) 1994. Law clk. U.S. Dist. Ct., Cleve., 1977-79; assoc. Schiff Hardin & Waite, Chgo., 1979-85, ptnr., 1985--; prof. De Paul U. Law Sch., Chgo., 1985—. Mem. Order of the Coif. Office: Schiff Hardin & Waite 7200 Sears Tower Chicago IL 60606 Business E-Mail: jclark@schiffhardin.com.

CLARK, JAMES E., lawyer; b. Washington, Sept. 2, 1948; AB, Brown U., 1970; JD, U. Chgo., 1976. Bar: Ill. 1976. Ptnr. comml. law Sidley Austin Brown & Wood LLP (formerly Sidley & Austin), Chgo. Mem. faculty Practicing Law Inst., 1989. Lt. USN, 1970-72. Mem. ABA (chmn., subcom. acquisition fin. commercial fin. svcs. com. Bus law sect. 1990—94), Chgo. Bar Assn., Ill. State Bar Assn., Fellow Am. Coll. Comml. Fin. Lawyers, Phi Beta Kappa. Office: Sidley Austin Brown & Wood LLP Bank One Plz 10 S Dearborn St Chicago IL 60603 Office Phone: 312-853-7776. Office Fax: 312-853-7036. Business E-Mail: jclark@sidley.com.

CLARK, JAMES MURRAY, lawyer, former state legislator; b. Indpls., Nov. 3, 1957; m. Janet Campbell. BA, Kenyon Coll., 1979; JD, Ind. U., 1982. Mem. Clark, Quinn, Moses & Clark LLP, 1982—2005; mem. from dist. 29 Ind. Senate, Indpls., 1994—2005, mem. govt. and regulatory affairs, mem. health and environ. affairs com., mem. fin. inst. com., judiciary coms.; ptnr. Baker & Daniels LLP, Indpls., 2005—. Office: Baker & Daniels LLP 300 N Meridian St Ste 2700 Indianapolis IN 46204

CLARK, JAMES NORMAN, insurance executive; b. Decatur, Ill., Jan. 30, 1932; s. John W. and Pearl (Allen) C.; m. Marlene F. Geason, Oct. 10, 1953; children— Paul R., Donald A., Robert S., Christine A. Tax and acctg. mgr. Caterpillar Tractor Co., 1957-66; mgr. tax dept. Towmotor Corp., 1966-68; with Western & So. Life Ins. Co., Cin., 1968—, exec. v.p., 1980—, also bd. dirs. Dir. Columbus (Ohio) Life Ins. Co. Former trustee Good Samaritan Hosp. Found. Capt. USAF, 1954-57. Mem. Life Office Mgmt. Assn. (prin. rep.), Fin. Exec. Inst. (former nat. chmn.), Tax Execs. Inst. Office: Western & So Life Ins Co 400 Broadway St Cincinnati OH 45202-3312

CLARK, JAMES RICHARD, lawyer; b. Madison, Wis., Mar. 30, 1946; s. James F. and Gloria J. Clark; m. Martha C. Conrad, Mar. 18, 1950; children: Lindsey Kelley, Chad. BA, Ripon Coll., 1968; JD, U. Wis., 1971. Bar: Wis. 1971, U.S. Dist. Ct. (we. and ea. dists.) Wis. 1972, U.S. Ct. Appeals (7th cir.) 1973, U.S. Dist. Ct. (no. dist.) Ill. 1974, U.S. Supreme Ct. 1976. Assoc. Foley & Lardner, Milw., 1971-78, ptnr., 1978—. Editor-in-chief Wis. Law Rev., 1971. Trustee Ripon Coll., 1985—. 1st lt. U.S. Army, 1971. Mem. ABA, Am. Coll. Trial Lawyers, Am. Bd. Trial Advs., Def. Rsch. Inst., 7th Cir. Bar Assn., Wis. Bar Assn., Ripon Coll. Alumni Assn. (past pres.), Tripoli Country Club, Order of Coif, Phi Beta Kappa. Home: 9719 N Dalewood Ln Mequon WI 53092-6210 Office: Foley & Lardner Firstar Ctr 777 E Wisc Ave Milwaukee WI 53202 Office Phone: 414-297-5543. Business E-Mail: jclark@foley.com.

CLARK, JUDY, newscaster; m. Tom Clark; 2 children. Grad., U. Wis., Eau Claire. Reporter, anchor WAXX-WAYY; noon anchor NewsCenter 13 WEAU-TV, Eau Claire, Wis., 1992—98, anchor at five and ten, 1998—. Avocations: reading, fishing, gardening. Office: WEAU-TV PO Box 47 Eau Claire WI 54702

CLARK, KAREN, state legislator; BS, Coll. St. Teresa, Winona, Minn.; MPA, Harvard U. Mem. Minn. Ho. of Reps., 1981—, mem. jobs and econ. devel. com., commerce com. Recipient Martin Luther King, Jr. award, 1987, Minn. Alliance Progressive Leadership award, 1991, Leadership award Nat. Gay & Lesbian Task Force. Office: Minn State House Office Bldg 100 Constitution Ave Saint Paul MN 55155-1232

CLARK, LYNN G., botanist, educator; BS in Botany & Horticulture, Mich. State Univ., 1979; PhD in Botany, Iowa State Univ., 1986. Temporary asst. prof., dept. botany Iowa State U., 1986—87, asst. to assoc. prof., dept. botany, 1987—2000, dir., Ada Hayden Herbarium, dept. Botany, 1989—, prof., dept. botany, 2000—, interim chair, dept. botany, 2001. Contbr. articles to profl. jours. Achievements include with colleagues discovering a new species of North American bamboo. Office: Dept Ecology Evolution & Organismal Biology Iowa State Univ 345 Bessey Hall Ames IA 50011-1020 Office Phone: 515-294-8218. Office Fax: 515-294-1337. Business E-Mail: lgclark@iastate.edu.

CLARK, MURRAY See CLARK, J.

CLARK, NOREEN MORRISON, behavioral science educator, researcher; b. Glasgow, Scotland, Jan. 12, 1943; arrived in US, 1948; d. Angus Watt and Anne (Murphy) Morrison; m. George Robert Pitt, Dec. 3, 1982; 1 child, Alexander Robert. BS, U. Utah, 1965; MA, Columbia U., 1972, MPhil, 1975, PhD, 1976. Rsch. coord. World Edn. Inc., NYC, 1972-73; asst. prof. Sch. Pub. Health Columbia U., NYC, 1973-80, assoc. prof., 1980-81, Sch. Pub. Health U. Mich., Ann Arbor, 1981-85, prof., chmn. dept. health behavior and health edn., 1985-95; prof. pediat. and com. diseases, Marshall H. Becker prof. pub. health U. Mich. Med. Sch., Ann Arbor, 1995—2005, dean, 1995—2005, dir. ctr. mng. chronic disease, 2005—, Myron E. Wegman Disting. Univ. prof., 2006—. Adj. prof. health adminstrn. Sch. Pub. Health Columbia U., 1988—; prin. investigator NIH, 1977—; adv. com. pulmonary diseases Nat. Heart, Lung & Blood Inst., Rockville, Md., 1983-87, adv. com. for prevention, edn. and control, 1987-91, coord. com. Nat. Asthma Edn. Program, 1991—; assoc. Synergos Inst., NYC, 1987-99; nat. adv. environ. health scis. coun. NIH, 1999-2002; task force on preventive cmty. svc. CDC, 2002-05 Co-author: Evaluation of Health Promotion, 1984; editor Health Edn. and Behavior, 1985-97; assoc. editor Ann. Rev. of Pub. Health, 2002-05; mem. editl. bd. Women in Health, Advances in Health Edn. and Promotion, Home Health Care Services Quar.; contbr. articles to profl. jours. Bd. dirs., adv. Aaron Diamond Found., 1989-96, Family Care Internat., NYC, 1987—, Internat. Asthma Coun., 1996-2000, Am. Lung Assn., NYC, 1988—, World Edn., Inc., 1998-. Mem. Soc. Pub. Health Edn. (pres. 1985-86, Disting. Fellow award 1987), APHA (chair health edn. sect. 1982-83, Derryberry award in behavioral sci. 1985, Disting. Career award 1994), Am. Thoracic Soc. (Health Edn. Rsch. award Nat. Asthma Edn. Program 1992, Healthtrac Found. Health Edn. award, 1997), Internat. Union Health Edn., Soc. Behavioral Medicine, Coun. Fgn. Rels., Inst. Medicine of AS, Pi Sigma Alpha. Office: U Mich Sch Pub Health 109 Observatory St Ann Arbor MI 48109-2029 Office Phone: 734-763-1457.

CLARK, R. KERRY (KERRY CLARK), health products executive; b. Ottawa, Ont., Can., Apr. 29, 1952; B in Commerce, Queen's U., 1974. Brand asst. P&G Can. Procter & Gamble, 1974—75, asst. brand mgr. P&G Can., 1975—76, brand mgr. P&G Can., 1976—80, assoc. advt. mgr. P&G Can., 1980—84, assoc. advt. mgr. P&G Far East (Japan), 1984—85, advt. mgr. P&G Far East (Japan), 1985—87, gen. mgr. hard surface cleaners Cin., 1987—91, v.p., gen. mgr. laundry products Procter & Gamble USA, 1991—95, pres. laundry and cleaning products-U.S., Procter & Gamble N.Am., group v.p., 1995—97, pres. laundry and cleaning products-N.Am., Procter & Gamble N.Am., group v.p., 1997—98, exec. v.p. The Procter & Gamble Co., pres. Asia, Procter & Gamble Asia, 1998—99, pres.-Asia, 1999, pres. global feminine protection and Asia, 1999—2000, pres. global market devel. orgn., 2000—01, pres. global market devel. and bus. ops., 2001—02, vice chmn. bd. dirs., 2002—06, pres. global market devel. and bus. ops., 2002, vice chmn., pres. global health, baby and family care, 2004—06; pres., CEO, bd. dir. Cardinal Health Inc., Dublin, Ohio, 2006—07, chmn., CEO, 2007—. Mem. mgmt. bd. GS1; bd. dirs. EAN Internat.; past mem. Am. C. of C. in Japan; past vice chairperson The Soap and Detergent Assn., NY; bd. dirs. Textron Inc. Chmn. bd. dirs. Cin. Zoo and Bot. Gardens; mem. Leadership Cin., Class XIX; past mem. Greater Cin. United Way Cabinet; chmn. Alexis de Tocqueville Soc., 2005. Mem.: Bacchus Soc. Am., Indian Hill Club, Queen City Club, Kenwood Country Club, The Commonwealth Club. Office: Cardinal Health Inc 7000 Cardinal Pl Dublin OH 43017

CLARK, ROBERT ARTHUR, mathematician, educator; b. Melrose, Mass., May 3, 1923; s. Arthur Henry and Persis (Kidder) C.; m. Jane Burr Crofut Kinder, June 25, 1966. Student, Colo. Coll., 1940-42; BA, Duke, 1944; MA, MIT, 1946, PhD, 1949. Instr., research asso. MIT, 1946-50, vis. asst. prof., 1956-57; faculty Case Inst. Tech. (now Case Western Res. U.), Cleve., 1950—, prof. math., 1964-85, prof. emeritus, 1985—, acting head dept. math., 1960-61, assoc. chmn. dept. math., 1974-79, 82-84, exec. officer, 1981-82. Vis. mem. U.S. Army Math. Research Center, Madison, Wis., 1961-62 Mem. AAAS, Am. Math. Soc., Math. Assn. Am., Soc. Indsl. and Applied Math., Phi Beta Kappa, Sigma Xi. Achievements include spl. research asymptotic integration theory of differential equations and theory thin elastic shells. Home: 7469 Sherman Rd Gates Mills OH 44040-9769 Office: Case Western Res Univ Dept Math Cleveland OH 44106

CLARK, ROBERT KING, communications educator, consultant, actor, model; b. Springfield, Mass., Apr. 12, 1934; s. Harry Robert and Alice (McClure) C.; m. Suzanne Chapin, Apr. 9, 1966; children— Jennifer, Jeffrey, Anne Elizabeth BA, U. Wyo., 1956; MA, U. Tenn., 1960; PhD, Ohio State U., 1971. Instr. journalism U. Tenn., Knoxville, 1958; instr. speech Westminster Coll., New Wilmington, Pa., 1959-61; faculty Bowling Green State U., Ohio, 1963—, prof. radio-TV film, 1980-84, prof. emeritus, 1985—; gen. mgr. Sta. WBGU-FM, 1976-85. Cons. in field; lectr. in field; seminar leader in field; yoga instr./therapist. Contbr. articles to profl. jours. Presbyterian. Office: 1064 Village Dr Bowling Green OH 43402-1231 Personal E-mail: rkclark@wcnet.org.

CLARK, STEPHEN ROBERT, lawyer; b. Chgo., July 1, 1966; m. Laura Sliney. BA, U. Notre Dame, 1988; JD, St. Louis U., 1991. Bar: Mo. 1991, Ill. 1992, US Dist. Ct. (ea. dist.) Mo. 1991, US Dist. Ct. (cen. dist.) Ill. 1993, US Claims Ct, 1993, US Dist. Ct. (ea. dist.) Wis., 1998, US Dist. Ct. (we. dist.) Mo, 1999, US Dist. Ct. (so. dist.) Ill., 2003, US Dist. Ct. (no. dist.) Ill., 2003, US Dist. Ct. (so. dist.) Ind., 2004, US Dist. Ct. (dist. Kans.), 2005, US Ct. Appeals (8th cir.), 2003, US Ct. Appeals (5th cir.), 2003, US Ct. Appeals (10th cir.), 2004. Assoc. Greensfelder, Hemker & Gale, P.C., St. Louis, 1991—98, officer, 1998—99; ptnr. Polsinelli Shalton Welte Suelthaus PC, St. Louis, 1999—2006, Blackwell Sanders Peper Martin LLP, St. Louis, 2007—. Co-author: Death Penalty Resource Book of the US Ct. of Appeals for the 8th Circuit, 1991. Mem., econ. devel. campaign St. Louis Regional Chamber and Growth Assn.; pres., father's club Villa Duchesne/Oak Hill Sch. Devel. Com., 2005—06; mem., devel. bd. St. Patrick Ctr., 1992—97; mem., parish coun. Ch. of Annunziata, 2003—, chair, fin. com., 2005—; mem., adv. bd. Entrepreneurship Inst.; vol., lawyers prog. Legal Services Eastern Mo. Mem. ABA, Bar Assn. Met. St. Louis, Ill. State Bar Assn., Mo. Bar Assn., Psi Chi. Office: Blackwell Sanders Peper Martin LLP 720 Olive St Ste 2400 Saint Louis MO 63101 Office Phone: 314-345-6482. Office Fax: 314-345-6060.

CLARK, TONY, state commissioner; Student, Mich. State U., 1990-91; BS in Polit. Sci., N.D. State U., 1994, BS in History Edn., 1996; MPA, U. N.D., 2002. Mem. Dist. 44 N.D. Ho. of Reps., 1994-97; adminstrv. officer N.D. Tax Dept., 1997-99; commr. N.D. Dept. Labor, 1999-2000, N.D. Pub. Svc., 2001—, 2001—. Adult leader Boy Scouts Am. Named Eagle Scout Boy Scouts Am. Mem. Phi Kappa Phi. Office: 600 E Boulevard Ave Bismarck ND 58505-0480

CLARK, WESLEY M., manufacturing executive; b. 1952; BA magna cum laude in Philosophy, U. Calif., LA, Calif., 1974; MBA, Stanford U. With Cummins Engine Co.; mem. sr. mgmt. team Granite Rock, 1984—91; from mgr. to pres., COO W.W. Grainger, Inc., Lake Forest, Ill., 1992—2001, pres., 2001—04, COO, 2001—04. Bd. dir. W.W. Grainger, Inc. Bd. dir. Mex. Fine Arts Ctr. Mus.; bd. trustees The Lincoln Found. Bus. Excellence, Am. Second Harvest Nat. Food Bank Network, Preserve to Enjoy. Mem.: Econ. Club Chgo., Exec.'s Club Chgo.

CLARK, WILLIAM ALFRED, federal judge; b. Dayton, Ohio, Aug. 27, 1928; s. Webb Rufus and Dora Lee (Weddle) C.; m. Catherine C. Clark, Apr. 5, 1952; children: Mary Clark Youra, Jennifer Clark Kinder, Cynthia S., Andrea G. AB, U. Mich., 1950, JD, 1952. Bar: Ohio 1952, Mich. 1953. Pvt. practice, Dayton, 1954—57; assoc. Frank J. Svoboda, Dayton, 1957—73; ptnr. Legler, Lang & Kuhns, Dayton, 1973-82, Pickrel, Schaeffer & Ebeling, Dayton, 1982-85; judge so. dist. Ohio U.S. Bankruptcy Ct., Dayton, 1985-99, chief judge, 1993-99; apptd. recalled bankruptcy judge, 1999—. Judge Montgomery County Ct., Dayton, 1958-62; trial counsel in eminent domain Asst. Atty. Gen. Ohio, Dayton, 1963-70; tchr. bus. law Dayton chpt. Cert. Property and Casualty Underwriters, 1963-83; arbitrator Montgomery County Common Pleas Ct., Am. Arbitration Assn., Better Bus. Bur. Contbr. to Ohio Practice and Procedure Handbook, 1962. Lt. USAF, 1952-54. Named Alumnus of Yr., U. Mich. Club, Dayton, 1965. Mem. ABA, Ohio State Bar Assn. (chmn. eminent domain 1979-82), Dayton Bar Assn. (treas. 1964-65), Nat. Conf. Bankruptcy Judges, Lawyers Club. Republican. Avocations: tennis, other sports, reading, travel. Office: US Bankruptcy Ct Federal Bldg 120 W 3rd St Dayton OH 45402-1872

CLARK-COLE, DORINDA GRACE, singer, evangelist; b. Detroit, Oct. 19, 1957; d. Mattie Moss Clark; m. Greg Cole. DD (hon.), Mt. Carmel Theological Sem., Fresno, Calif., 2004. Mem. The Clark Sisters, 1970—. Founder, CEO Lifeline Prodns., 1999; founder Singers & Musicians Conf., 1999; adminstr. Clark Conservatory Music, Detroit. Singer: (albums) Dorinda Clark-Cole, 2002 (Soul Train Lady of Soul award for Best Female Gospel Artist), The Rose of Gospel, 2005, (with Clark Sisters) Bringing it Back Home, 1971, Sincerely, 1983, Heart and Soul, 1985, Is My Living in Vain?, 1985, Conqueror, 1989, Christmas, 1990, Count it All Joy, 1990, He Gave Me Nothing, 1990, Unworthy, 1990, You Brought the Sunshine, 1990, Miracle, 1994, Live: One Last Time, 2007 (Best Traditional Gospel Album, Grammy Awards, 2008), (songs) Blessed & Highly Favored, 2007 (Best Gospel Song & Best Gospel Performance, Grammy Awards, 2008). V.p. Internat. Music Dept. Church of God in Christ; adminstr. Greater Emmanuel Institutional Church of God in Christ, Detroit. Church Of God In Christ. Office: care Harvestime Ministries Ste 204 19161 Schaefer Hwy Detroit MI 48235 Office Phone: 866-744-7664. Office Fax: 313-862-8464.*

CLARKE, CHARLES FENTON, lawyer; b. Hillsboro, Ohio, July 25, 1916; s. Charles F. and Margaret (Patton) C.; m. Virginia Schoppenhorst, Apr. 3, 1945 (dec. July 1989); children: Elizabeth, Margaret, Jane, Charles Fenton, IV; m. Lesley Wells, Nov. 13, 1998. AB summa cum laude, Washington and Lee U., 1938; LLB, U. Mich., 1940; LLD (hon.), Cleve. State U., 1971. Bar: Mich. 1940, Ohio 1946. Pvt. practice, Detroit, 1942, Cleve., 1946—; ptnr. firm Squire, Sanders & Dempsey, 1957—, adminstr. litigation dept., 1979-85. Trustee Cleve. Legal Aid Soc., 1959-67; pres. Nat. Assn. R.R. Trial Counsel, 1966-68; life mem. 6th Circuit Jud. Conf.; chmn. legis. com. Cleve. Welfare Fedn., 1961-68; master bencher Manos Inn of Ct., 1991—; bd. dirs. Wheeling and Lake Erie R.R. Co. Pres. alumni bd. dirs. Washington and Lee U., 1970-72; pres. bd. dirs. Free Med. Clinic Greater Cleve., 1970-86; trustee Cleve. Citizens League, 1956-62, Cleve. chpt. ACLU, 1986-93; bd. dirs. citizens adv. bd. Cuyahoga County (Ohio) Juvenile Ct., 1970-73; bd. dirs. George Jr. Republic, Greenville, Pa., 1970-73, Bowman Tech. Sch., Cleve., 1970-91; vice chmn. Cleve. Crime Commn., 1973-75; exec. com. Cuyahoga County Rep. Orgn., 1950—; councilman Bay Village, Ohio, 1948-53; pres., trustee Cleve. Hearing and Speech Ctr., 1957-62, Laurel Sch., 1962-72, Fedn. Cmty. Progress, 1984-90; mem. planning commn. Cleveland Heights, 1994-2003. Fellow Am. Coll. Trial Lawyers; mem. Greater Cleve. Bar Assn. (trustee 1983-86), Cleve. Civil War Round Table (pres. 1968), Cleve. Zool. Soc. (dir. 1970), Phi Beta Kappa. Clubs: Skating, Union (Cleve.); Tavern, Rowfant. Presbyterian. Home: 2262 Tudor Dr Cleveland Heights OH 44106-3210 Office: Squire Sanders & Dempsey 4900 Key Tower 127 Public Sq Cleveland OH 44114-1304 Office Phone: 216-479-8551, 216-479-8500. Business E-Mail: cclarke@ssd.com.

CLARKE, CORNELIUS WILDER, religious organization administrator, minister; b. White Plains, NY, May 11, 1935; s. Cornelius Wilder and Margaret (Sutherland) C. BS, Nyack Coll., 1957; B of Div., Gordon Divinity Sch., 1960; MDiv, Gordon Conwell Theol. Sem., 1978. Ordained minister 1964. Pastor Missionary Alliance Ch., Bennington, Vt., 1960-65, Rock Hill Alliance Ch., Boston, 1965-73; sr. pastor Cranford (N.J.) Alliance Ch., 1973-76; dir. personnel Christian & Missionary Alliance, Nyack, N.Y., 1976-78; sr. pastor Simpson Meml. Ch., Nyack, N.Y., 1978-89; dist. supt. New Eng. Dist. of Christian & Missionary Alliance, South Easton, Mass., 1989-97; pastor Hillside Chapel, Beaver Creek, Ohio, 1998—. Trustee Nyack Coll., 1989-95. Avocations: golf, sailing, backpacking, fishing, travel. Office: Hillside Chapel 3515 Shakertown Rd Beavercreek OH 45430-1423 E-mail: nclarke@hillsidecma.org.

CLARKE, KENNETH STEVENS, insurance company executive; b. South Bend, Ind., Aug. 18, 1931; s. Walter Robert and Mattie Marie (Boley) C.; m. Vivian Elizabeth Long, July 5, 1958; children— Patrick Stevens, Mary Elizabeth, Margaret Christine, Daniel Whitman. MS, U. Ill., 1957, PhD, 1963. Program cons. Chgo. Heart Assn., 1957-59; supr. recreation and athletics U. Ill. div. rehab.-edn., 1959-63; cons. health and fitness AMA, Chgo., 1963-68; coordinator continuing edn. Am. Acad. Orthopedic Surgeons, 1968-70; prof. health scis. Mankato (Minn.) State U., 1970-73; prof., chmn. health edn. Pa. State U., 1973-77; dean Coll. Applied Life Studies U. Ill., Urbana, 1977-81; asst. sec. gen. U.S. Olympic Com., Colorado Springs, Colo., 1981-89; sr. v.p. risk analysis SLE Worldwide, Inc., Ft. Wayne, Ind., 1989—. Cons. athletic injury prevention; founder Nat. Athletic Injury/Illness Reporting System; active Pa. Emergency Med. Svcs. Coun., 1974-77; chmn. NCAA Med. Aspects of Sports, 1974-79; v.p. Nat. Safety Coun., 1987-89. Editor: Standard Nomenclature of Athletic Injuries, 1966, (with J.C. Hughston) Bibliography of Sports Medicine, 1970, Fundamentals of Athletic Training, 1971, Drugs and the Coach, 1972, 2d edit., 1976; contbr. profl. articles to ednl. and med. jours. Served with CIC U.S. Army, 1953-55. Recipient Spl. citation Nat. Fedn. State High Sch. Assns., Achievement award U.S. Baseball Fedn., Disting. Service to Safety award Nat. Safety Council; named to Nat. Wheelchair Athletic Assn. Hall of Fame; named Safety Profl. of Yr., Hoosier Safety Coun. Fellow Am. Coll. Sports Medicine (past chair ethics com.); mem. AAHPER, Am. Acad. Phys. Edn., Assn. for Advancement Health Edn., Am. Orthopedic Soc. for Sports Medicine (hon.), U. Ill. Alumni Assn. (Merit award), Rotary Internat. Roman Catholic. Home: 27751 Calle Rabano Sun City CA 92585-3949 Office: 1712 Magnavox Way Fort Wayne IN 46804-1538 E-mail: Kenneth_clarke@asg.aon.com.

CLARKE, MILTON CHARLES, lawyer; b. Chgo., Jan. 31, 1929; s. Gordon Robert and Senoria Josephine (Carlisa) C.; m. Dorothy Jane Brodie, Feb. 19, 1955; children: Laura, Virginia, Senoria K. BS, Northwestern U., 1950, JD, 1953. Bar: Ill. 1953, Mo. 1956, U.S. Dist. Ct. (we. dist.) Mo. 1961, U.S. Ct. Appeals (8th cir.) 1961. Assoc. Swanson, Midgley, Gangwere, Clarke & Kitchin, Kansas City, Mo., 1955-61, ptnr., 1961-91; of counsel Olsen & Talpers, P.C., Kansas City, 1994—. Served with U.S. Army, 1953-55. Mem. Rotary. Office: Olsen and Talpers PC 1950 Ten Main Ctr 920 Main St Kansas City MO 64105-2011 Office Phone: 816-421-2050. Personal E-mail: miltonclarke@hotmail.com.

CLARKE, PETER D., lawyer; b. Worcester, Mass. BBA with highest distinction, U. Mich., 1972; JD magna cum laude, Ind. U., 1975. Bar: Ill. 1975, DC. Gen. counsel OGE Energy Corp., 1997—; ptnr. Jones Day, Chgo. Mem.: ABA, Order of the Coif. Office: Jones Day 77 W Wacker Chicago IL 60601-1692 Office Phone: 312-269-1519. Office Fax: 312-782-8585. E-mail: pdclarke@jonesday.com.

CLARKE, RICHARD LEWIS, health science association administrator; b. Indpls., Sept. 9, 1948; s. John Richard and Opal (Emmons) C.; m. Linda DeMattia, Aug. 12, 1972; children: John, Laura, R. Bradley. BS, Bradley U., 1971; MBA, U. Miami, 1972. Bus. mgr. Jackson Meml. Hosp., Miami, 1973-76; controller Palmetto Gen. Hosp., Hialeah, Fla., 1976-80; sr. v.p. fin. Swedish Med. Ctr., Englewood, Colo., 1980-86; pres. Healthcare Fin. Mgmt. Assn., Westchester, Ill., 1986—. Bd. dirs., treas. Colo. Hosp. Assn. Trust, Denver. Fellow Healthcare Fin. Mgmt. Assn.; mem. Am. Soc. Assn. Execs., Econ. Club of Chgo. Avocations: sailboat racing, skiing. Office: Healthcare Fin Mgmt Assn 2 Westbrook Corp Ctr Ste 700 Westchester IL 60154

CLARKE, ROY, physicist, researcher; b. Bury, Lancashire, England, 1947; BSc in Physics, U. London, PhD, 1973. Rsch. assoc. Cavendish Lab., Cambridge, U.K., 1973-78; James Franck fellow U. Chgo., 1978-79; prof. U. Mich., Ann Arbor, 1979-86; dir. applied physics program, 1986—2002. Co-founder k-Space Assocs. Inc. Editor: Synchrotron Radiation in Materials Research, 1989. Fellow Am. Phys. Soc. Achievements include development of novel methods for real-time x-ray and electron diffraction studies; patents for quasiperiodic optical coatings and epitaxial spin-valve devices. Office: U Mich Randall Lab Ann Arbor MI 48109-1040

CLARK-SHEARD, KAREN VALENCIA, gospel singer, evangelist; b. Detroit; d. Mattie Moss and Elbert Clark; m. John Drew Sheard, June 16, 1984; children: Kierra Sheard, John Drew Sheard II. Mem. The Clark Sisters, 1970—. Singer: (albums) Finally Karen, 1997 (4 Stellar awards), 2nd Chance, 2002, The Heavens Are Telling, 2003, It's ot Over, 2006, (with The Clark Sisters) Bringing It Back Home, 1971, Sincerely, 1983, Heart & Soul, 1985, Is My Living In Vain?, 1985, Conqueror, 1989, Christmas, 1990, Count It All Joy, 1990, He Gave Me Nothing, 1990;: (albums) Unworthy, 1990, You Brought the Sunshine, 1990, Miracle, 1994, Live: One Last Time, 2007; songwriter Blessed & Highly Favored, 2007 (Grammy award, Best Gospel Song, 2008). Church Of God In Christ. Office: 19190 Schaefer Hwy Detroit MI 48235 Office Phone: 313-864-7170. Office Fax: 313-864-7409.*

CLARY, BRADLEY G., lawyer, educator; b. Richmond, Va., Sept. 7, 1950; s. Sidney G. and Jean B. Clary; m. Mary-Louise Hunt, July 31, 1982; children: Benjamin, Samuel. BA magna cum laude, Carleton Coll., 1972; JD cum laude, U. Minn., 1975. Bar: Minn. 1975, US Dist. Ct. Minn. 1975, US Ct. Appeals (10th cir.) 1977, US Ct. Appeals (8th cir.) 1979, US Ct. Appeals (6th cir.) 1980, US Ct. Appeals (7th cir.) 1981, US Supreme Ct. 1986, US Ct. Appeals (4th cir.) 1989, US Ct. Appeals (9th cir.) 1991. Assoc. Oppenheimer Wolff & Donnelly, St. Paul, 1975-81, ptnr., 1982-2000; from legal writing dir. Law Sch. to clin. prof. U. Minn., 1999—, Vaughan G. Papke clin. prof. law, 2004—06, dir. applied legal instrn., 2004—. Adj. prof. Law Sch. U. Minn., Mpls., 1985-99; adj. instr. William Mitchell Coll. Law, St. Paul, 1995-96, 98, adj. prof., 1997, 99. Author: Primer on the Analysis and Presentation of Legal Argument, 1992; co-author: Advocacy on Appeal, 2001, 2d edit., 2004, Successful First Depositions, 2001, 2d edit., 2006, Successful Legal Analysis and Writing: The Fundamentals, 2003, 2d edit., 2006. Vestryman St. John Evangelist Ch., St. Paul, 1978-81, 98-00, pledge drive co-chmn., 1989-90, sr. warden, 2000-2002; mem. alumni bd. Breck Sch., Mpls., 1981-85, 89-96, exec. com., 1991-96, dir. emeritus, 1996—; mem. adv. bd. Glass Theatre Co., West St. Paul, Minn., 1982-87; mem. antitrust adv. panel dept. health State of Minn., 1992-93. Mem. ABA (adv. group antitrust sect. 1987-89, corp. counseling com.), Minn. Bar Assn. (program chmn. antitrust sect. 1986-87, treas. 1987-88, vice-chmn. 1989-90, co-chmn. 1990-92, governing coun. appellate practice sect. 2001-03, 2003-06), Phi Beta Kappa Avocations: tennis, sailing. Office: U Minn Law Sch 229 19th Ave S Rm 444 Minneapolis MN 55455-0400

CLARY, ROSALIE BRANDON STANTON, timber farm executive, civic worker; b. Evanston, Ill., Aug. 3, 1928; d. Frederick Charles Hite-Smith and Rose Cecile (Liebich) Stanton; m. Virgil Vincent Clary, Oct. 17, 1959; children: Rosalie Marian Hawley, Frederick Stanton, Virgil Vincent, Katheleen Clary Gorman. BS, Northwestern U., 1950, MA, 1954. Tchr. Chgo. Pub. Schs., 1951-61; faculty Loyola U., Chgo., 1963; v.p. Stanton Enterprises, Inc., Adams County, Miss., 1971-89; timber farmer, trustee Adams County, Miss., 1975—. Author Family History Record, geneaology record book, Kenilworth, Ill., 1977—. Lectr. Girl Scouts U.S., Winnetka, Ill., 1969-71, 78-86, Cub Scouts, 1972-77; badge counselor Boy Scouts Am., 1978-87; election judge Rep. Com., 1977—; vol. Winnetka Libr. Geneaology Projects Com., 1995—. Mem. Nat. Soc. DAR (Ill. rec. sec. 1979-81, nat. vice chmn. program com. 1980-83, state vice regent 1986-88, state regent 1989-91, rec. sec. gen. 1992-95, state parliamentarian 1999—), Am. Forestry Assn., Forest Farmers Assn., North Suburban Geneal. Soc. (governing bd. 1979-86, 99—, pres. 1997-99), WInnetka Hist. Soc. (governing bd. 1978-90, 95—), Internat. Platform Assn., Delta Gamma (mem. nat. cabinet 1985-89). Roman Catholic. Office: PO Box 401 Kenilworth IL 60043-0401 Home: 711 Oak St Apt 305 Winnetka IL 60093-2546

CLASSON, ROLF ALLAN, pharmaceutical company executive; b. Nassjo, Sweden, Aug. 20, 1945; s. Allan K.E. and May Britt (Lagerquist) C.; m. Birgitta Larsson, Feb. 3, 1968; children: Peter, Karin, Erik. M in Bus. Econs., Gothenburg U., 1969. Personnel mgr. Pharmacia, Uppsala, Sweden, 1969-74; mgmt. cons. Asbjorn Habberstad, Stockholm, 1974-77; mktg. mgr. Pharmacia, Uppsala, 1977-80; div. gen. mgr. Tarkett, Ronneby, 1980; pres. Pharmacia Infusion, Uppsala, 1981-84, Pharmacia Devel. Co. Inc., Piscataway, NJ, 1984-90; pres., chief oper. officer Pharmacia Biosystems AB, 1990—91; exec. v.p. Bayer Corp., 1995—2002, exec. v.p., worldwide mktg., sales & services, group diagnostics, 1991—92, pres., group diagnostics, 1995—2002, sr. v.p., sales & services, group diagnostics, 1992—95, chmn. exec. comm., health care div., 2002—04; vice-chmn. Hillenbrand Industries, Batesville, Ind., 2004—05, interim pres., CEO, 2005—06, chmn., 2006—. Mem. supv. bd. Bayer HealthCare AG; bd. dir. Enzon Pharmaceuticals, ISTA Pharmaceuticals, Millipore Corp., Auxilium Pharmaceuticals. Office: Hillenbrand Industries Mail Code K71 1069 State Route 46 E Batesville IN 47006-8835

CLATWORTHY, CATHERINE LYNN, educational trainer, graphics designer; b. Chatham, Ont., Can., June 10, 1963; d. John Ferguson Clatworthy and Patricia Anne (Maynard) Clatworthy. A.O.C.A., Ont. Coll. Art and Design, Toronto, 1985. Graphic designer Burton Kramer Assocs., Toronto, 1985—87; co-owner/mgr. The Allery, Toronto, 1987—98; tng. ctr. instr. Larson-Juhl Co., Atlanta, 1998—2003; v.p., mktg. mgr. Dakota Framing Specialties, Inc., Watertown, SD, 2000—02; propr., cons. LilyCrest, Huron, SD, 2002. Com./facilitator Color Mktg. Group, Alexandria, Va., 2000—; mem. Visual Arts Ont., Toronto, 1985—; educator/lectr. Profl. Picture Framers Assn., Jackson, Mich., 1996—; mem. Can. Conservation Inst., Ottawa, 1998—, Am. Inst. Conservation, Washington, 2002—. Author: The Art of Colour & Design for the Art and Framing Industry, 1999; contbr. mags., newspapers, and interviews in field. Mem.: Visual Arts Ont., Profl. Picture Framers Assn., Color Mktg. Group. Avocations: art, antiques, travel, photography, cooking. Home: 712 W 5th St Yankton SD 57078-3805 E-mail: lilycrest@hur.midco.net.

CLAUSEN, ROBERT A., chemicals executive; BSBA, U. Mo. With Inernat. Harvester Co., 1968; various mgmt. positions Monsanto's Comml. Products Co., dir. results mgmt., 1977—79; controller Monsanto Polymer Products Co., 1979—83; bur. dir. Rubber Chems., 1983—85, asst. treas., 1985—87; dir. fin. Monsanto Europe-Africa, 1987—91, Monsanto L.Am., 1991—92; v.p. asset mgmt. Monsanto, 1992—94; pres. Monsanto Bus. Svcs., 1994—97; vice chmn., CEO, chief adminstrv. officer Solutia Inc., 1997—. Mem. CFO's exec. com. The Conf. Bd.; mem. adv. bd. St. Louis U. Boeing Inst. Internat. Bus.; bd. trustees Maryville U.; mem. adv. bd. Orgn. Cons. Svcs. Mem.: Fin. Execs. Inst., Am. Chem. Soc. Office: Solutia Inc PO Box 66760 Saint Louis MO 63166-6760 also: Solutia Inc 575 Maryville Ctr Dr Saint Louis MO 63141

CLAUSING, ALICE, state legislator; b. June 7, 1944; BA, U. Wis., Oshkosh. Property mgr.; mem. from dist. 10 Wis. State Senate, Madison, 1992—, mem. child abuse and neglect prevention bd., mem. Minn.-Wis. boundary area com., mem. Miss. River Pkwy. com. Mem. Wis. Assn. of Lakes, John Muir Sierra Club. Office: 1314 Wilson Ave Menomonie WI 54751-2927

CLAUSING, ARTHUR MARVIN, mechanical engineering educator; b. Palatine, Ill., Aug. 17, 1936; s. Arthur Fred and Emma Marie (Opfer) C.; m. Willa Louise Spence, Dec. 19, 1964; children— Erin, Kimberly BS in Mech. Engring., Valparaiso U., 1958; MS in Mech. Engring., U. Ill., 1960, PhD in Mech. Engring., 1963. Research asst. U. Ill., Urbana, 1962-63, asst. prof., 1963-68, assoc. prof., 1968-84, asst. dean coll. engring., 1982-83, 98—, prof. mech. engring., 1984-98, assoc. head. dept. mech. and indsl. engring., 1987-98, prof. emeritus mech. and indsl. engring., 1998—; cons. Solar Energy Research Inst., 1984-86, M.A.N. Neve Technologie, Munich, Fed. Republic Germany, 1980-87, Ill. Power Co., 1979-81. Author: Numerical Methods in Heat Transfer, 1969; editor Am. Soc. Mech. Engrs. Jour. of Solar Energy Engring., 1984-88; contbr. articles to profl. jours. Recipient Instructional award U. Ill., 1967; Standard Oil award for devel. of heat transfer lab., 1968; Fulbright scholar, 1983; Valparaiso U. Disting. Alumnus award, 1985; ASME fellow, 1997. Mem. ASME, ASHRAE, Am. Soc. Engring. Edn., Internat. Solar Energy Soc. Lutheran. Avocations: running; bicycling; photography; music. Home: 3626 SE Insley Ct Portland OR 97202-4352

CLAVER, ROBERT EARL, television producer, director; b. Chgo., May 22, 1928; s. Louis E. and Sara M. (Sosna) C.; 1 child, Nancy Beth. BS in Journalism, U. Ill., 1950. Prodr.-writer: first 1000 Captain Kangaroo shows (Sylvania award, Peabody award); prodr., dir.: (TV shows) Here Comes the Brides, 1968-70, The Interns, 1970-71, Partridge Family, 1970-74, Gloria, CBS-TV, 1982-83, Small Wonder, 1985, New Love American Style, 1985, New Leave It to Beaver, 1986-87, Charles in Charge, 1987, Out of This World, 1987-91, numerous other series; dir.: (TV shows) Welcome Back Kotter, ABC-TV, 1977-78, All's Fair, CBS-TV, Housecalls, CBS-TV, 1979-80, Mork and Mindy, ABC-TV, 1981-82. With U.S. Army, 1951-53. Mem. Dirs. Guild Am.

CLAWSON, CURTIS J., manufacturing executive; MBA, Harvard U. Various positions Allied Signal, Arvin Industries; pres. Beverage Cans Am. Bus. Unit Am. Nat. Can Group Inc., 1998—99, pres., COO Chgo., 1999—2000; chmn., pres., CEO Hayes Lemmerz Internat., Northville, Mich., 2001—. Office: Hayes Lemmerz Internat 15300 Centennial Dr Northville MI 48167

CLAY, CLARENCE SAMUEL, acoustical oceanographer; b. Kansas City, Mo., Nov. 2, 1923; s. Clarence Samuel and Mary Else (Hall) C.; m. Andre Jane Edwards, Mar. 27, 1945; children: Arnold, Jo, David, Michael. BS, Kans. State U., 1947, MS, 1948; PhD in Physics, U. Wis., 1951. Asst. prof. U. Wyo., Laramie, 1950-51; physicist Carter Oil Co., Tulsa, 1951-55; rsch. scientist Columbia U., Dobbs Ferry, N.Y., 1955-67; prof. dept. geol. geophysics U. Wis., Madison, 1967-89, emeritus prof., 1989—. Author: Elementary Exploration Seismology, 1990, (with I. Tolstoy) Ocean Acoustics, 1966, (with H. Medwin) Acoustical Oceanography, 1977, Fundamentals of Acoustical Oceanography, 1997; (with I. Tolstoy) Ocean Acoustics, 1987. Fellow Acoustical Soc. Am. (Silver medal in Acoustical Oceanography, 1993); mem. Sigma Xi. Home: 5109 St Cyr Rd Middleton WI 53562 Office: U Wis Weeks Hall 1215 W Dayton St Madison WI 53706-1600

CLAY, ERIC L., federal judge; b. Durham, NC, Jan. 18, 1948; BA, U. N.C., 1969; JD, Yale U., 1972. Bar: Mich. 1972, US Dist. Ct. (ea. dist.) Mich. 1972, US Supreme Ct. 1977, US Ct. Appeals (6th cir.) 1978, US Dist. Ct. (we. dist.) Mich. 1987, US Ct. Appeals (DC cir.) 1994. Law clk. to Judge Damon J. Keith US Dist. Ct. (ea. dist.) Mich., 1972—73; atty., shareholder, dir. Lewis, White & Clay, P.C., Detroit, 1973—97; judge US Ct. Appeals (6th cir.), Detroit, 1997—. Hearing panelist Atty. Discipline Bd., State of Mich., 1985—97. Fellow John Hay Whitney, Yale U. Mem.: ABA, Wolverine Bar Assn., Detroit Bar Assn., at. Assn. Railroad Trial Counsel, Nat. Bar Assn., US Sixth Jud. Conf. (life), Phi Beta Kappa. Office: Potter Stewart US Cthse 100 E 5th St Cincinnati OH 45202-3988

CLAY, WILLIAM LACY, former congressman; b. St. Louis, Mo., Apr. 30, 1931; s. Irving C. and Luella (Hyatt) C.; m. Carol A. Johnson, Oct. 10, 1953; children: Vicki, Lacy, Michelle. BS in Polit. Sci, St. Louis U., 1953. Real estate broker, from 1964; mgr. life ins. co., 1959-61; alderman 26th Ward, St. Louis, 1959-64; bus. rep. state, county and municipal employees union, 1961-64; edn. coord. Steamfitters local 562, 1966-67; mem. U.S. Congress from 1st. Mo. dist., Washington, 1969-2001; former ranking minority mem. edn. and the workforce. Served with AUS, 1953-55. Mem. NAACP (past exec. bd. mem. St. Louis), CORE, St. Louis Jr. C. of C. Democrat.

CLAY, WILLIAM LACY, JR., congressman; b. St. Louis, July 27, 1956; s. William L. and Carol Ann (Johnson) C.; m. Ivie Lewellen, Jan. 24, 1992; 2 children. BS in Govt. and Politics, U. Md., Coll. Pk., 1983; student, Harvard U. John F. Kennedy Sch. Govt.; LLD (hon.), Lincoln U., Harris-Stowe State U. Cert. paralegal; lic. real estate salesman, Mo. Mem. Mo. State House of Reps., Jefferson City, 1983—91, Mo. State Senate, 1991—2001, US Congress from 1st Mo. dist., 2001—, mem. fin. svcs. com. and govt. reform com., chmn. subcommittee on info. policy, the census and the nat. archives; mem. Congl. Black Caucus. Chmn. Mo. Jesse Jackson 1988 Presdl. Campaign; Jackson del. to 1988 Dem. Nat. Conv.; committeeman to Dem. Nat. Com.; bd. dirs. William L. Clay Scholarship and Rsch. Fund., Congl. Black Caucus Found. Recipient Most Influential Black Americans, Ebony mag., 2006. Mem. Ams. Dem. Action (Outstanding Legis. Mo. chpt. 1985, 86). Democrat. Roman Catholic. Office: US House of Reps 434 Cannon House Office Bldg Washington DC 20515 Office Phone: 202-225-2406.

CLAYBORNE, JAMES F., JR., state legislator; b. St. Louis, Mo., Dec. 29, 1963; Sen. from dist. 37 Ill. State Senate, 1995—. Office: First Ill Bank Bldg 327 Missouri Ave # 422 East Saint Louis IL 62201-3088

CLAYBURGH, RICHARD SCOTT, state tax commissioner; m. Jane Clayburgh; 2 children. BA, Concordia Coll., Moorhead, Minn., 1982; MBA, U. N.D., 1990, JD, 1994. Bar: N.D. 1994, Minn. 1994. Atty.; state rep. dist. 17, 1989-96; atty. Warcup & Clayburgh, Grand Forks, 1994-96; state tax commr. State of N.D., Bismarck, 1997—2005; pres. ND Bankers Assn. Sec. N.D. State Bd. Equalization; pub. mem. Nat. Bd. for Cert. of Orthopaedic Technologists. Past bd. dirs. Spl. Olympics, past chmn. State Summer Games. Mem. Fedn. Tax Adminstrs. (trustee), Minn. Bar Assn., N.D. Bar Assn. (info. and svc. com.), Nat. Fedn. Ind. Bus., N.D. Industrial Devel. Assn., Sons of Norway, Bismarck-Mandan C. of C., Rotary, Elks. Republican. Home: 4300 Overland Rd Bismarck ND 58503-8830

CLAYPOOL, DAVID L., lawyer; b. Springfield, Ill., 1946; BA in History, Ill. Coll., 1968; JD with high distinction, U. Iowa, 1975. Bar: Iowa 1975. Ptnr., pub. fin. practice and ptnr.-in-charge Dorsey & Whitney, LLP, Des Moines. Editor notes and comments Iowa Law Review, 1974-75. Capt. U.S. Army, 1968-72 Mem. Iowa State Bar Assn., Pol County Bar Assn., Nat. Assn. Bond Lawyers, Iowa Mcpl. Attys. Assn., Order of Coif. Office: Dorsey & Whitney LLP 801 Grand Ave Ste 3900 Des Moines IA 50309-2790 Home Phone: 515-440-0773; Office Phone: 515-283-1000. Business E-Mail: claypool.david@dorsey.com.

CLAYTON, JOHN ANTHONY, radio broadcast executive; b. St. Louis, Dec. 3, 1958; s. James Dale and Sharon Lee (Sack) C.; m. Lynn Marie Staley, Oct. 24, 1992. BA in Bus. Adminstrn., U. Mo., 1981, BA in German and Radio TV, Film, 1981. Radio announcer KHMO, Hannibal, MO, 1981-82; prodn. dir. KSIV, St. Louis, 1982-83; news dir. KPCQ-FM, Powell/Cody, Wyo., 1983-84; ops. mgr./interim gen. mgr. KVOK-KJJZ-FM, Kodiak, Alaska, 1984-85; asst. program dir. KFUO-FM Classic 99, St. Louis, 1985—. Author critical rev. St. Louis Guitar Soc. Newsletter, 1990—. Bd. mem. Alaska Visitors Assn., Kodiak br., 1984-85; bd. mem. Guitar Found. Am., St. Louis Consortium, 1996. Avocations: guitar study, golf, fishing, woodworking, wine. Office: Classic 99 KFUO-FM 85 Founders Ln Saint Louis MO 63105-3059

CLAYTON, ROBERT MORRISON, III, commissioner; b. Hannibal, Mo., Aug. 20, 1969; s. Robert M. II and Frances (Price) Clayton; m. Erin Clayton; children: Olivia, Paige. BA, So. Meth. U., 1991; JD, U. Mo., Kansas City, 1994. Ptnr. Clayton & Curl LLC, Hannibal, 1994—2003; mem. Mo. Ho. of Reps. from 10th dist., 1995—2002; mem. exec. com. So. Legisl. Conf. and Coun. State Govts.; commr. Mo. Pub. Svc. Commn., Mo., 2003—. Bd. dir., chmn. com. internat. relations Nat. Assn. Regulatory Utility Commrs. (NARUC). Sr. articles editor: The Urban Lawyer, 1993. Mem. Hist. Bethel German Colony, Hannibal Arts Coun.; sec. Mo. Universal Svc. Fund Bd.; bd. mem. Mark Twain Home Found., Aves. Domestic Violence Shelter, N.E. Sheltered Workshop, Affordable Cmty. Edn. Bd., Kids In Motion Adv. Bd.; mem. ARUC Telecom. Com.; chmn. Mo. Universal Svc. Bd.; mem. Fed. Comm. Bar Assn. and the Pub. Utility; mem. Comm. and Transp. Law Sect. Am. Bar Assn. Recipient U. Mo. Kans. City Law Found. Decade award. Mem.: Delta Theta Phi, Jaycees, Hannibal C. of C., Kansas City Met. Bar Assn. (Pres.'s award), Mo. Bar Assn. (Pres.'s award). Democrat. Office: Mo Public Service Commn Governor Office Bldg 200 Madison St Jefferson City MO 65101 Office Phone: 573-751-4221. Office Fax: 573-526-7341. Business E-Mail: Robert.clayton@psc.mo.gov.

CLEAR, JOHN MICHAEL, lawyer; b. St. Louis, Dec. 16, 1948; s. Raymond H. and Marian (Clark) Clear; m. Isabel Marie Bone, May 10, 1980; 1 child, Thomas Henry. BA summa cum laude, Washington U., St. Louis, 1971; JD with honors, U. Chgo., 1974. Bar: Mo. 1974, D.C. 1975, U.S. Ct. Appeals (5th and D.C. cirs.) 1975, U.S. Supreme Ct. 1977, U.S. Ct. Appeals (3d cir.) 1978, U.S. Ct. Appeals (8th cir.) 1980, U.S. Ct. Appeals (9th cir.) 1990, U.S. Dist. Ct. (so. dist.) Ill. 1995, U.S. Ct. Appeals (7th cir.) 1997. Law clk. to judge U.S. Ct. Appeals (5th cir.), Atlanta, 1974-75; assoc. Covington & Burling, Washington, 1975-80; jr. ptnr. Bryan, Cave, McPheeters & McRoberts, St. Louis, 1980-81, ptnr., 1982—. Mem. ABA, Mo. Bar Assn., D.C. Bar Assn., St. Louis Met. Bar Assn., Am. Law Inst., Order of Coif., Racquet Club, Noonday Club, Fox Run Golf Club, Phi Beta Kappa. Office: Bryan Cave LLP One Metropolitan Sq Saint Louis MO 63102-2750 Office Phone: 314-259-2283. Business E-Mail: jmclear@bryancave.com.

CLEARY, MICHAEL J., educational administrator; Exec. dir. Nat. Assn. Collegiate Dirs. Athletics. Office: NACDA PO Box 16428 Cleveland OH 44116-0428

CLEARY, PAMELA ANN, symphony executive; b. Omaha, Jan. 24, 1947; d. Carson Poe Jr. and Helen D. (Nelson) Dole; m. David O. Gilson, June 18, 1965 (div. 1977); children: Kevin D., Kyle, Kreg; m. John P. Cleary, Sept. 13, 1980; children: Shawn, Robert, Kevin M., Daniel, Charles, Colleen. BSBA, U. Nebr., 1977. Acct., bus. mgr. Northwestern Steel & Supply, Omaha, 1977-84; sr. dir. fin. and adminstrn. Omaha Symphony Assn., Omaha, 1984-93, exec. dir., 1992—. Mem. DAR, Oak Hills Country Club. Republican. Roman Catholic. Home: 5706 Oak Hills Dr Omaha NE 68137-3316 Office: Omaha Symphony Assn 1605 Howard St Omaha NE 68102-2705

CLEASBY, JOHN LEROY, civil engineer, educator; b. Madison, Wis., Mar. 1, 1928; s. Clarence Allen and Othelia Amanda (Swanson) C.; m. Donna Jean Haugh, Sept. 2, 1950; children: Teresa, Richard, Lynne. BS, U. Wis., 1950, MS, 1951; PhD, Iowa State U., 1960. Diplomate: Am. Acad. Environ. Engrs.; registered profl. engr., Iowa. Inspection engr. Standard Oil Co. Ind., Whiting, 1951—52; project engr. Consoer Townsend & Assocs., Chgo., 1952—54; from instr. to prof. Iowa State U., Ames, 1954—83, disting. prof., 1983—94, disting. prof. emeritus, 1994—. Vis. prof. Univ. Coll. London, 1975-76; cons. World Bank, Washington, Pan Am. Health Orgn., WHO, U. Sao Paulo Co-author: Water Supply Engineering, 1962; contbr. articles to profl. jours. Served with USN, 1945-46. Recipient Outstanding Tchr. award, Iowa State U., 1977, David R. Boylan Eminent Faculty award for rsch., 1989. Mem. ASCE (sec. Environ. Engring. divsn. 1969-73, pres. Iowa sect. 1966, Hering medal 1968, 70, 83, Norman medal 1980), NAE (life.), Am. Water Works Assn. (trustee Water Quality divsn. 1981-87, chmn. 1985, chmn. Iowa sect. 1982, hon., Publs. awards 1962, 80, Divsn. Best Paper awards 1970, 92, 95, Rsch. award 1982, Abel Wolman award 1997), Kiwanis. Am. Baptist. Office: Iowa State U 487 Town Engring Ames IA 50011-0001 Home Phone: 515-233-3412; Office Phone: 515-233-3412. Business E-Mail: cleasby@iastate.edu.

CLEAVER, EMANUEL, II, congressman, former mayor, minister; b. Waxahachie, Tex., Oct. 26, 1944; s. Lucky and Marie (McKnight) Cleaver; m. Dianne Donaldson, June 1970; children: Evan Donaldson, Emanuel III and Emiel Davenport (twins), Marissa Dianne. BS in Sociology, Prairie View A&M U., Tex., 1968; MDiv, St. Paul Sch. Theology, Kansas City, Mo., 1974; DD (hon.), Baker U., 1988. Ordained to ministry United Meth. Ch. Sr. pastor St. James United Meth. Ch., Kans. City, Mo., 1969—; coun. mem. Kans. City, Mo., 1979—91, mayor pro-tem, 1987-91, mayor, 1991—99; spl. adv. to Andrew Cuomo US Sec. of Housing and Urban Devel., 1999—2000; host Under the Clock KCUR-FM pub. radio, Kans. City, Mo., 2000—04; mem. US Congress from 5th Mo. dist., 2005—, mem. fin. svcs. com. Lectr. to chs., schs., civic and social orgns. nationwide. Chmn. Kans. City Coun. Plans and Zoning Com., 1984-87, Policy and Rules Com., 1987-91; mid-cen. regional v.p. So. Christian Leadership Conf. (Drum Major for Justice award 1991); founder, co-chair Kans. City Harmony In A World of Difference. Recipient William Yates Disting. Svc. Medallion William Jewel Coll., 1987, Pub. Svc. award Am.-Jewish Com., 1991, Junteenth Man of Yr. award Black Archives of Mid-Am. Inc., 1991, Disting. Citizen award Greater Kans. City Urban Affairs Coun., 1991, Cmty. Svc./Leadership award Webster U., 1991, Disting. Svc. award Park Coll., 1991, Friend of Youth award Boys & Girls Clubs, 1991, Outstanding Contbns. to Black Cmty. award Concerned Citizens Black Clergy of Atlanta, 1991, Rainbow award, 1992, 100 Most Influential Kansas Citizens award Kans. City Globe, 1991, 92, 93, Bridge Builders award Kans. City Globem 1992, Harold L. Holiday Sr. Civil Rights award NAACP, 1992, Disting. Grad. award St. Paul Sch. Theology, 1993, Kans. City Anti-Apartheid award, 1993, James C. Kirkpatrick Excellence for Govt. award, 1993, Disting. Citizen of Midwest award NCCJ, 1993, Gov. award for local elected ofcl. of yr. State of Mo., 1994; named one of Most Influential Black Americans, Ebony mag., 2006. Mem. NAACP, Greater Kans. City C. of C. (Centurions Leadership award 1987), Alpha Phi Alpha. Democrat. Office: US House Reps 1641 Longworth House Office Bldg Washington DC 20515-2505 Office Phone: 202-225-4535.

CLEGG, CHRISTOPHER R., lawyer; BA, U. Calif., Berkeley; MA in Internat. Studies, John Hopkins U.; LLB, Georgetown U. Pvt. practice, Cleve., Seattle; sr. corp. counsel Goodrich Aerospace; v.p. BFGoodrich Performance Materials; sr. v.p., gen. counsel, sec. Noveon Inc., 2001—04, Commonwealth Industries, 2004, Aleris Internat., Inc., Beachwood, Ohio, 2004—. Mem.: Am. Soc. Corp. Secretaries, Am. Corp. Counsel Assn. Office: Aleris Internat, Inc 25825 Science Park Dr Beachwood OH 44122

CLEGG, KAREN KOHLER, lawyer; b. Junction City, Kans., Jan. 7, 1949; d. John Emil and Delores Maxine (Letkeman) Kohler; m. Stephen J. Clegg Jr., Mar. 28, 1970. BS, Emporia State U., 1970; JD, U. Kans., 1975; MBA, Rockhurst Coll., 1989. Bar: Kans. 1975, U.S. Dist. Ct. Kans. 1975, Mo. 1977, U.S. Dist. Ct. (we. dist.) Mo. 1977. Asst. atty. gen. State of Kans., Topeka, 1975-77; atty. The Bendix Corp., Kansas City, Mo., 1977-81, sr. atty., 1981-84; counsel Allied Corp. (now Allied Signal, Inc.), Kansas City, 1984-90, v.p. adminstrn., 1990—93, v.p. field svcs. Columbus, Md., 1994—95, v.p. ops. Kansas City, 1995—2001; pres. Honeywell Fed. Mfg. and Technologies Honeywell Internat., 2001—02, v.p. def. and space programs, Honeywell Aerospace; ret. Mem. council human resources mgmt. adv. bd. Commerce Clearing House, Chgo., 1985-88. Sec. Assn. Greater Devel. Coll. Blvd., Shawnee Mission, Kans., 1986-87; bd. dirs. adv. council Avila Coll. Bus., Kansas City, 1984—, Dimension's Unltd., Kansas City, 1985-86. Mem. ABA, Mo. Bar Assn., Am. Soc. Personnel Adminstrn. (v.p., bd. dirs. EEO 1985, profl. services 1986-87), Greater Kansas City C. of C. (centurian leadership program). Avocations: music, theater, art, reading, travel. Office: Honeywell 2000 E 95th St Kansas City MO 64131-3030 Home: 6909 Burnt Sienna Cir Naples FL 34109-7828

CLELAND, ROBERT HARDY, federal judge; b. 1947; BA, Mich. State U., 1969; JD, U. N.C., 1972. Pvt. practice, Port Huron, Mich., 1972-75; chief trial atty. County Prosecuting Atty's. Office, Port Huron, 1975-80; prosecuting atty. St. Clair County, 1981-90; judge U.S. Dist. Ct. (ea. dist.) Mich., Detroit, 1990—. Positions with Port Huron Hosp., 1989-91, United Way of St. Clair County, 1988-90, Civic Theater of Port Huron, Blue Water YMCA, First Congl. Ch. of Port Huron, MADD, St. Clair Rep. Party. Mem. ABA, Mich. Bar Assn., St. Clair County Bar Assn., Prosecuting Atty's. Assn. Mich. (pres. 1988-89). Office: US Dist Ct Theodore Levin US Courthous 231 W Lafayette Blvd Rm 707 Detroit MI 48226-2775

CLELAND, W(ILLIAM) WALLACE, biochemistry educator; b. Balt., Jan. 6, 1930; s. Ralph E. and Elizabeth P. (Shoyer) C.; m. Joan K. Hookanson, June 18, 1967 (div. Mar. 1999); children: Elsa Eleanor, Erica Elizabeth. AB summa cum laude, Oberlin Coll., 1950; MS, U. Wis., 1953, PhD, 1955. Postdoctoral fellow U. Chgo., 1957-59; asst. prof. U. Wis., Madison, 1959-62, assoc. prof., 1962-66, prof., 1966—, M.J. Johnson prof. biochemistry, 1978—, Steenbock prof. chem. sci., 1982—2002. Contbr. articles to profl. biochem. and chem. jours. Served with U.S. Army, 1957-59. Grantee NIH, 1960—, NSF, 1960-94; recipient Stein and Moore award Protein Soc., 1999. Mem. NAS, Am. Acad. Arts and Scis., Am. Soc. Biochemistry and Molecular Biology (Merck award 1990), Am. Chem. Soc. (Alfred R. Bader Bioinorganic or Bioorganic Chem. award 1993, Repligen award 1995). Achievements include development of dithiothreitol (Cleland's Reagent) as reducing agent for thiol groups; development of application of kinetic methods for determining enzyme mechanism. Office: Enzyme Inst 1710 University Ave Madison WI 53726-4087 Home Phone: 608-244-3938; Office Phone: 608-262-1373. E-mail: cleland@biochem.wisc.edu.

CLEM, ALAN LELAND, retired political scientist, educator; b. Lincoln, Nebr., Mar. 4, 1929; s. Remey Leland and Bernice (Thompson) Clem; m. Mary Louise Burke, Oct. 24, 1953; children: Andrew, Christopher, Constance, John, Daniel. BA, U. Nebr., 1950; MA, Am. U., Washington, DC, 1957, PhD, 1960. Copywriter, rsch. dir. Ayres Advt. Agy., Lincoln, 1950-52; press sec. to Congressman Carl Curtis of Nebr., 1953-54; press sec. to Congressman R. D. Harrison of Nebr., 1955-58; info. specialist Fgn. Agrl. Svc., Dept. Agr., 1959-60; from asst. prof. to assoc. prof. polit. sci. U. SD, Vermillion, 1960—64, prof., 1965—; assoc. dir. Govtl. Rsch. Bur., 1962-76, chmn. dept. polit. sci., 1976-78; ptnr. Opinion Survey Assocs., 1964-88, ret., 1996. State analyst Comparative State Elections Project, U. N.C., 1968—73; dir. Mt. Rushmore Presdl. Inst., 1970—71; mem. adv. com. state and local govt. stats. US Census Bur., 1970—74. Author: (book) Prairie State Politics: Popular Democracy in South Dakota, 1967, The Making of Congressmen: Seven Campaigns of 1974, 1976, American Electoral Politics: Strategies for Renewal, 1981, Law Enforcement: The South Dakota Experience, 1982, The Government We Deserve, 1985, 5th edit., 1995, Congress: Powers, Processes and Politics, 1989, Government by the People? South Dakota Politics in the Last Third of the 20th Century, 2002; editor: Contemporary Approaches to State Constitutional Revision, 1969; contbr. articles to profl. jours. Active Vermillion City Coun., 1965—69; sr. warden St. Paul's Episcopal Ch., Vermillion, 1971—73, treas., 1996—2006. Recipient Alumni Achievement award, U. Nebr. Coll. Arts and Scis., 1998; Nat. Conv. faculty fellow, 1964. Mem.: Am. Polit. Sci. Assn., Midwest Polit. Sci. Assn. (mem. exec. coun. 1970—72, mem. editl. bd. Am. Jour. Polit. Sci. 1971—72), Mensa, Vermillion Golf Assn. (pres. 1986—87), Alpha Tau Omega, Phi Beta Kappa, Sigma Delta Chi, Pi Sigma Alpha (mem. nat. coun. 1986—89), Phi Alpha Theta. Republican. Home: 608 Colonial Ct Vermillion SD 57069

CLEM, JOHN RICHARD, physicist, educator; b. Waukegan, Ill., Apr. 24, 1938; s. Gilbert D. and Berenda May (Moyer) Clem; m. Judith Ann Paulsen, Aug. 27, 1960; children: Paul Gilbert, Jean Ann. BS, U. Ill., 1960, MS, 1962, PhD, 1965. Rsch. assoc. U. Md., College Park, 1965-66; vis. rsch. fellow Tech. U., Munich, 1966-67; from asst. prof. to assoc. prof. physics Iowa State U., Ames, 1967—75, prof., 1975—, disting. prof. in liberal arts and scis., 1989, now disting. prof. emeritus, physics, chmn. dept. physics, 1982-85. Vis. staff mem. Los Alamos Nat. Lab., 1971—83, cons., 1997—2001, Argonne Nat. Lab., Ill., 1971—76, Brookhaven Nat. Lab., Upton, NY, 1980—81, Oak Ridge (Tenn.) Nat. Lab., 1981, Allied-Signal, Torrance, Calif., 1990—92, Am. Superconductor Corp., Westborough, Mass., 1996—97, Pirelli Cable Corp., Lexington, SC, 1996—97; guest prof. U. Tuebingen, Germany, 1978; cons. IBM Watson Rsch. Ctr., Yorktown Heights, NY, 1982—85, vis. scientist, 1985—86, Electric Power Rsch. Inst., Palo Alto, Calif., 1992—93; vis. prof. applied physics Stanford U., 1992—93. Editor: Virtual Jour. Applications Superconductivity; sci. editor: newsletter High-Tc Update, 1987—2003; contbr. articles to profl. jours. Recipient award for sustained outstanding rsch. in solid state physics, U.S. Dept. Energy; Fulbright Sr. Rsch. fellow, 1974—75, NATO grantee, 1979—82. Fellow: London Inst. Physics, Am. Phys. Soc. (chair divsn. condensed matter physics 1994—95); mem.: AAUP, Iowa Acad. Sci., Sigma Xi, Phi Kappa Phi, Tau Beta Pi. Democrat. Presbyterian. Achievements include patents in field. Avocation: singing. Office: Iowa State Univ 17 Physics Ames IA 50011-3160 Home Phone: 515-292-4758. Business E-Mail: clem@ameslab.gov.

CLEMENCE, ROGER DAVIDSON, landscape architect, educator; b. Worcester, Mass., Jan. 20, 1936; s. Luther Davidson and Dorothy (Kay) C.; m. Margaret Ann Weinandy, Aug. 19, 1961; children: Peter, Benjamin, Ellsabeth. AB, Amherst Coll., 1957; MArch, U. Pa., 1960, M in Landscape Architecture, 1962. Registered landscape architect, Minn. Instr., asst. prof. Coll. Architecture and Design U. Mich., Ann Arbor, 1962-66; assoc. prof. Sch. Architecture and Landscape Architecture U. Minn., Mpls., 1966-73, dir. Urban Edn. Ctr., Sch. Architecture and Landscape Architecture, 1970-77, interim head Sch. Architecture and Landscape Architecture, 1984, mem. urban studies faculty Coll. Liberal Arts, 1973—97, mem. Am. studies faculty Coll. Liberal Arts, 1986—97, dir. grad. studies in architecture Sch. Architecture and Landscape Architecture, 1978-85, prof. dept. architecture, 1973, assoc. dean Coll. of Architecture and Landscape Architecture, 1989-95, acting dean, spring 1993, interim dean, 1995-96. Landscape arch., planner, Mpls., 1963; collegiate program leader Minn. Ext. Svc., 1993-97, prof. emeritus, summer 1997—. Co-creator 10-part TV series The Meanings of Place, 1986. Mem. Minn. Com. on Urban Environment, 1979-88, Designer Selection Bd., 1980-85, chmn., 1983-84; mem. Mpls. Fed. Cts. Master Plan Com., 1991-92. Recipient Morse-Alumni Disting. Tchg. award, 1974, Pub. Svc. award Minn. Soc. Landscape Architects, 1982, Lob Pine award, 1996, CALA Disting. Svc. award, 1995; T.P. Chandler fellow U. Pa. Grad. Sch. Fine Arts, 1960-62; HWS Cleveland Vis. scholar U. Minn., 2000-06. Fellow Am. Soc. Landscape Architects; mem. AIA (prof. affiliate Minn. chapt. 1979), MASLA, Tau Sigma Delta. Democrat. Mem. Unitarian Universalist Assn. Avocations: photography, writing, golf, reading, gardening. Office: U Minn CALA 89 Church St SE Minneapolis MN 55455-0109

CLEMENS, RICHARD GLENN, lawyer; b. Chgo., Oct. 8, 1940; s. James Ralston and Jeanette Louise (Moellering) C.; m. Judith B. Clemens, Aug. 19, 1967; 1 child, Kathleen. BA, U. Va., 1962, JD, 1965. Bar: Ill. 1965. Assoc. Sidley Austin LLP, Chgo., 1965—66, Washington, 1968—71, Brussels, 1972—73, ptnr. Chgo., 1973—2005, sr. counsel, 2005—07. Capt. US Army, 1966-68. Mem. ABA, Chgo. Bar Assn., Lawyers Club Chgo. Office: Sidley Austin LLP 1 S Dearborn St Chicago IL 60603 Office Phone: 312-853-7642. Business E-Mail: rclemens@sidley.com.

CLEMENT, HENRY JOSEPH, JR., diversified building products executive; b. New Orleans, May 14, 1942; s. Henry Joseph Sr. and Margaret (Dowd) C.; m. Kathleen Erin Shean; children: Colleen and Collette (twins). BS, Loyola U., 1973. Sales rep. GE, New Orleans, 1972-77, mgr. product planning Louisville, Ky., 1977-79, mgr. internat. market Tyler, Tex., 1979-83; v.p. internat. sales Phillips Industries, Inc., Dayton, Ohio, 1983-84, pres. internat. div., 1984-88; pres. internat. group Tomkins Industries, Dayton, 1988-94; pres. Crescent Group, Inc., Dublin, Ohio, 1994—. Vice chmn., bd. dirs. Shaanxi-Hytec, Ltd., Xian, Chila, 1988-89. Loan exec. United Way, New Orleans, 1974, Tyler, 1979. Mem. Miami Valley (Ohio) Internat. Trade Assn. (trustee), Blue Key (Cross Key Svc. award 1973). Republican. Roman Catholic. Home: 4666 Chatham Ct Dublin OH 43017-8607 E-mail: cresgroup@cs.com.

CLEMENTS, DONALD M., utilities executive; With Am. Electric Power Co. Inc., Columbus, Ohio, 1994-98, pres. comms., resources, 1998—. Pres. Am. Electric Power Resourced Svc. Co., 1998—. Office: Am Electric Power Co Inc 1 Riverside Plz Columbus OH 43215-2355

CLEMMER, DAVID E., chemistry professor, researcher; b. 1965; BS, Adams State Coll., 1987; PhD in Chemistry, U. Utah, 1992. Postdoctoral fellow Himeji Inst. of Tech., Japan, 1992—93; postdoctoral rsch. assoc. Northwestern U., 1993—95; prof. chemistry Indiana U., 1995—, Robert & Marjorie Mann chair chemistry. Mem. U.S. Defense Sci. Study Group. Author: (over 80 scientific articles including) Gas-phase DNA: Oligothymidine Ion Conformers, 1997, Magic Number Clusters of Serine In The Gas Phase, 2001, Coupling Ion mobility Separations, Collisional Activation Techniques, and Multiple Stages of MS For Analysis of Complex Peptide Mixtures, 2002. Named one of Brilliant 10, Polular Sci. mag., 2002; recipient Early Career award, Nat. Sci. Found., 1996, Finnegan award, Am. Soc. for Mass Spectrometry, 1997, Alfred P. Sloan Rsch. Fellowship, 1998—2000, TR-100 Rsch. Innovation award, MIT Tech. Review Mag., 1999, Arthur F. Findeis award, Am. Chemical Soc., 1999, Eli Lilly Analytical Chemistry award, 2000, Pittcon Achievement award, 2002. Office: Indiana U Chemistry Dept 800 E Kirkwood Ave Bloomington IN 47405-7102

CLEMONS, JOHN ROBERT, lawyer; b. Oak Park, Ill., June 9, 1948; BA, U. Iowa, 1970; JD, DePaul U., 1975. Asst. village mgr. Village of Riverside, Ill., 1970-72; co-dir. dist. 208 Youth Ctr., Riverside, 1970-73; area dir. S.W. area Cook County OEO, 1972-73; clk., legal rschr. Klein, Thorpe & Jenkins, attys., Chgo., 1974-75; asst. state atty.'s Jackson County, Murphysboro, Ill., 1975-80, state's atty., 1980-88; adj. prof., lectr. So. Ill. U., Carbondale, 1978—; ptnr. So. Ill. Law Ctr.,LLC, Carbondale, 1991—; pres. Mt. Joy Enterprises, Inc. Home: 375 Mount Joy Rd Murphysboro IL 62966-4464 Office: 813 W Main St Carbondale IL 62901-2537 Office Phone: 618-529-4000. Business E-Mail: silc@ll.net.

CLEVELAND, ASHLEY, musician; b. Knoxville, Tenn., Feb. 2, 1957; m. Kenny Greenberg. Singer: (albums) Big Town, 1991 (1991's 10 Most Overlooked Albums, Billboard), Bus Named Desire, 1993 (1994's 10 Most Overlooked Albums, Billboard), Lesson of Love, 1996 (Grammy award for Best Rock Gospel Album, 1996, Nashville Music award for Best Contemporary Christian Album, 1996, Grammy award for Best Rock Gospel Album, 1996), You Are There, 1998 (Grammy award for Best Rock Gospel Album, 1999), Second Skin, 2002, Men & Angels Say, 2005, Before the Daylight's Shot, 2006 (Grammy award for Best Rock Gospel Album, 2008), (with various artists) Songs from the Loft, 1994 (Dove award for Praise & Worship Album of Yr., 1994), (with Rich Mullins & A Ragamuffin Band) The Jesus Record, 1999 (Dove award for Pop Album of Yr., 1999); appearances (TV series) Austin City Limits, Saturday Night Live, TNN Country News, American Music Shop, 1991, CCM-TV, 1993, Gospel Music Assn. Dove Awards, 1994, 1996, 1998, The Road, 1994, Prime Time Country, 1996, Peace In The Valley, CeCe's Place, Stone Country: A Tribute To The Rolling Stones, 1997, Profiles in Praise, 1999. Spokesperson Songs of Hope & Recovery for Everyone (SHARE). Office: care Pam Kistler Street Level Artists Agy 107 E Ctr St Warsaw IN 46580 Office Phone: 574-269-3413.*

CLEVELAND, CLYDE, retired city official; b. Detroit, May 22, 1935; m. Mary; 1 child. Student, Wayne State U. Pub. aid worker City of Detroit, 1958, 60-64; supervisor cmty. svc. Mayor's Com. Human Resources Devel., Detroit, 1965-68; cmty. planner Inner City Bus. Improvement Forum, 1968-71; city councilman City of Detroit, 1974—2001; ret., 2001. Del. Dem. Nat. Conv., 1980; former vice chair Mich. State Dem. Party; co-campaign mgr. Jesse Jackson Victory in Mich., 1988; vice chair Southeastern Mich. Coun. Govts.; cmty. orgn. specialist New Detroit, Inc., 1971-73. Served in U.S. Army, Korea. Mem. NAACP, Elks, People's Cmty. & Civic League, Assn. Study Negro Life & History, Booker T. Washington Bus. Assn., Shriners, Masons. Baptist. Home Phone: 313-894-2658; Office Phone: 313-575-7046.

CLEVERT, CHARLES NELSON, JR., federal judge; b. Richmond, Va., Oct. 11, 1947; s. Charles Nelson and Ruby Clevert. BA, Davis and Elkins Coll., 1969; JD, Georgetown U., 1972. Bar: Wis. 1972, US Dist. Ct. (ea. dist.)/Wis. 1974, US Ct. Appeals (7th cir.) 1975. Adminstrv. aide DC Dept. Corrections, 1970—71; law clk. Law Enforcement Assistance Adminstrn., Washington, 1972; asst. dist. atty. Milw. County, Milw., 1972—75; asst. atty. US ea. dist. Dept. Justice, Milw., 1975—77; spl. asst. atty. No. Dist., Chgo., 1977; chief judge, ea. dist. US Bankruptcy Ct., Milw., 1977—; lectr. law sch. U. Wis., 1987—89. Judge Nat. Moot Ct. Competition; judge trial practice Marquette U. Mem.: Thomas E. Fairchild Am. Inn Ct. (pres.), 7th Cir. Bar Assn., Wis. Assn. of Minority Atty., Milw. Bar Assn., Nat. Bar Assn. (jud. council), Nat. Conf. Bankruptcy Judges (pres. 1989—90, chair endowment edn.), Am. Bankruptcy Inst. (bd. dir.), Am. Judicature Soc. (bd. dir.), ABA (mem. exec. bd. nat. conf. fed. trial judges), US Cts. Fellow Am. Coll. Bankruptcy (mem. judges adv. com. Adminstrv. Office), Jud. Conf. of the US and Bankruptcy (mem. budget com.), Milw. Council on Alcoholism and Drug Dependence (bd. dir. 1982—94), African Meth. Episc. Ch., Local Edn. Agy., Inc., Milw. Forum, Milw. Club Frontiers Internat. (v.p. 1981), Alpha Sigma Phi, Alpha Phi Alpha. Ame. Office: Rm 208 US Courthouse 517 E Wisconsin Ave Milwaukee WI 53202-4500

CLIFFORD, CAROLYN, news correspondent, reporter; b. Detroit; married; 3 children. Grad., Mich. State U. Anchor 10 pm news WLFL-TV, Raleigh, NC; anchor 10 pm newscast WPGH-TV, Pitts.; co-anchor Action News This Morning and Noon WXYZ-TV, Southfield, Mich., 1998—. Spkr. in field. Recipient Heroes award for media, Karmanos Cancer Inst., 1999, Emmy award for best news anchor, 2003. Office: WXYZ-TV 20777 W Ten Mile Rd Southfield MI 48037 Home Phone: 248-615-9170; Office Phone: 248-827-7777. E-mail: wxyzcarolyn@yahoo.com.

CLIFFORD, ROBERT A., lawyer; b. Evergreen Park, Ill., Mar. 24, 1951; s. George Leonard and Shirley Marie (Meyer) C.; m. Joan Elizabeth Makowski, July 29, 1973; children: Erin Elizabeth, Tracy Ann. BS in Commerce, DePaul U., 1973, JD, 1976. Bar: Ill. 1976, US Dist. Ct. (no. dist. Ill.) 1976, US Supreme Ct. 1981, US Dist. Ct. (ea. dist. Wis.) 1993, US Dist. Ct. (ctrl. dist. Ill.) 1993, US Ct. Appeals (7th cir.) 1996. Assoc. Philip A. Corboy & Assocs., Chgo., 1974-82, Corboy & Demetrio, Chgo., 1982-84; ptnr. Clifford & Henely, Chgo., 1984-85; prin. ptnr. Clifford Law Offices, Chgo., 1985—; cons. and lectr. in law; mediation panelist Endispute of Chgo., 1982—; mem. bd. overseers Rand Inst. Civil Justice 1998-. Contbr. articles to profl. jours. Mem. adv. coun., DePaul U. Coll. Law, 1987—; bd. trustees DePaul U., 1987—; mem. bd. advs. Mercy Hosp. & Med. Ctr. 1988-; mem. adv. bd. Geroulis Ednl. Found. 1990-. Named one of Top Ten Litigators, Nat. Law Jour., 1993, Top Ten Lawyers in Ill., Nat. Law Jour., 1999, Top Ten Most Influential Lawyers in Ill., Am. Rsch. Corp., 2000, 30

Toughest Lawyers, Chgo. Mag., 2002, Top 5 Most Respected and Feared Plaintiff Attys., Corp. Legal Times, 2004. Fellow Chgo. Bar Found; master Chgo. Inn of Ct. (pres. 1994-95); mem. ABA (chair litig. sect. 2001-02, chair Task Force Terrorism & Law 2001-02), Fed. Bar Assn., Ill. State Bar Assn., Chgo. Bar Assn. (bd. mgrs. 1992-94, ABA del. 2003-05), Kane County Bar Assn., Lake County Bar Assn., N.W. Suburban Bar Assn., Am. Law Inst., Inner Cir. Advocates, Nat. Jud. Coll., Am. Inn of Ct., Am. Judicature Soc., Ill. Com. for Jud. Independence, Am. Soc. Law and Medicine, Am. Inst. Aeronautics and Astronautics, Assn. Trial Lawyers of Am. (mem. membership com. 1989-), Ill. Attys. for Criminal Justice, Ill. Inst. Continuing Legal Edn., Soc. Trial Lawyers of Am., Ill. Trial Lawyers Assn. (mem. exec. com. 1986-, pres. 1990), Trial Lawyers Club Chgo., Ill. State and Chgo. Soc. of Phys. Medicine and Rehab., Exec. Club Chgo., DePaul U. Alumni Assn. (past pres.). Roman Catholic. Clubs: Butler Nat. Golf (Oak Brook, Ill.); Inverness Golf (Ill.); Dairymen's Country (Boulder Junction, Wis.). Office: Clifford Law Offices 120 N LaSalle St 31st Fl Chicago IL 60602 Office Phone: 312-899-9090. Office Fax: 312-251-1160. E-mail: rclifford@cliffordlaw.com.

CLIFTON, DOUGLAS C., retired newspaper editor; b. Bklyn., July 14, 1943; s. Norman Stanton and Anne Frances (Montesano) C.; m. Margaret E. Clifton, Dec. 18, 1965; children: Amy Elizabeth Clifton Gallup, Clay Norman. BA in Polit. Sci., Dowling Coll., 1965. Positions including reporter, city editor, dep. mng. editor Miami Herald, 1970-87; news editor Washington bur. Knight Ridder, 1987-89; mng. editor Charlotte Observer, NC, 1989-91; sr. v.p., exec. editor Miami Herald, 1991-99; editor Plain Dealer, 1999—2007. Lt. U.S. Army, 1966-69, Vietnam. Named Editor of Yr., Editor & Pub. Mag., 2003; recipient Spl. Recognition award, AP Soc. Ohio, 2007. Mem.: Am. Soc. Newspaper Editors (freedom of info. com. 2003—). E-mail: dclifton@plaind.com.

CLIFTON, JAMES ALBERT, physician, educator; b. Fayetteville, NC, Sept. 18, 1923; s. James Albert Jr. and Flora M. (McNair) Clifton; m. Katherine Rathe, June 25, 1949; children: Susan M.(dec.), Katherine Y., Caroline M. BA, Vanderbilt U., 1944, MD, 1947. Diplomate Am. Bd. Internal Medicine (mem. 1972-81, mem. subsplty. bd. gastroenterology 1968-75, chmn. 1972-75, mem. exec. com. 1978-81, chmn. 1980-81). Intern U. Hosps., Iowa City, 1947—48, resident dept. medicine, 1948—51; staff dept. medicine Thayer VA Hosp., Nashville, 1952—53; asst. clin. medicine Vanderbilt Hosp., Nashville, 1952—53; cons. physician VA Hosp., Iowa City, 1965—93; assoc. medicine dept. internal medicine Coll. Medicine, U. Iowa, 1953—54, chief divsn. gastroenterology, 1953—71, asst. prof. medicine, 1954-58, assoc. prof., 1958—63, prof., 1963—91, prof. emeritus, 1991—, traveling fellow, 1964, vis. prof. dept. physiology, 1964, vice chmn. dept. medicine, 1967—70, chmn. dept. medicine Coll. Medicine, 1970—76, Roy J. Carver prof. medicine, 1974—91, Roy J. Carver prof. emeritus, 1991—, dir. James A. Clifton Ctr. Digestive Diseases, 1985—90, interim dean, 1991—93. Investigator Mt. Desert Isle Biol. Lab., Salisbury Cove, Maine, 1964; vis. faculty mem. Mayo Found. and Mayo Clinic, 1966; vis. prof. dept. medicine U. N.C. Chapel Hill, 1970; cons. gastroenterology and nutrition tng. grants com. at. Inst. Arthritis and Metabolic Diseases, NIH, 1964—68, chmn., 1965—68; mem. Nat. Adv. Arthritis and Metabolic Diseases Coun., 1970—73; mem. gastroenterology tng. com. VA, Washington, 1967—71, chmn. tng. grants com., 1971—73; mem. med. adv. bd. Digestive Disease Found., 1969—73; vis. prof. gastroenterology U. London (St. Marks Hosp.), 1984—85; mem. sci. adv. com. Ludwig Inst. Cancer Rsch., Zurich, 1984—95. Internat. editl. bd. Italian Jour. Gastroenterology, 1970—90, Gastroenterology, 1964—68. Recipient Disting. Alumnus of Yr. award, Vanderbilt U. Sch. Medicine, 1984, Disting. Alumnus of Yr. Achievement award, U. Iowa Coll. Medicine, 2000, Disting. Mentoring award, 2002, Disting. Alumni award, U. Iowa Alumni Assn., 2004; fellow, NIH, USPHS, 1955—56, Evans Meml. Hosp., Mass. Meml. Hosps., also Boston U. Sch. Medicine, 1955—56; Phi Connell scholar, Vanderbilt U., 1943—44. Fellow: ACP (bd. regents 1972—79, pres. 1977—78, Alfred Stengel award 1984, Laureate award 1989); mem.: AAUP, AAAS, AMA (liaison com. grad. med. edn. 1976—77), Internat. Soc. Internal Medicine (exec. com. 1978—80), Assn. Profs. Medicine (councillor 1972—73, sec.-treas. 1973—75), Assn. Am. Med. Colls., Am. Physiol. Soc., Soc. Exptl. Biology and Medicine, Assn. Am. Physicians, Am. Clin. and Climatol. Assn. (v.p. 1984), Am. Fedn. Clin. Rsch., Am. Soc. Internal Medicine (Internist of Yr. award Iowa chpt. 1986), Am. Assn. Study Liver Disease, Am. Heart Assn., Am. Gastroent. Assn. (pres. 1970—71), Inst. Medicine NAS, U. Iowa Assn. Emeritus Faculty (pres. 1999—2000), U. Iowa Retirees Assn. (pres. 1999—2000). Home: 39 Audubon Pl Iowa City IA 52245-3437 Office: U Iowa Hosp and Clinics 4 JCP Hawkins Dr Iowa City IA 52242 Home Phone: 319-351-1561; Office Phone: 319-356-1771. Personal E-mail: zybumjim@mchsi.com. Business E-Mail: james-clifton@uiowa.edu.

CLIFTON, JAMES K., market research company executive; m. Susan Clifton; children: Nicole, Jonathan, Jackie. DHL (hon.), Medgar Evers Coll., Jackson State Univ.; DComm (hon.), Bellevue Univ. Chmn., CEO Gallup Org., Washington, 1988—. Chmn. Thurgood Marshall Scholarship Fund. Office: Gallup Organization 901 F St NW Washington DC 20004

CLIFTON, THOMAS E., academic administrator, minister; m. Audrey Vought; children: Sandra, Jill Clifton Mallard. Student, Duke Divinity Sch.; M in Divinity, Crozer Theol. Sem., Rochester, NY; MS in Personnel Counseling, Wright State U., Dayton; D in Ministry, Princeton Theol. Sem. Pastor First Bapt. Ch., Perry, Ohio, 1967-70, Sidney, Ohio, 1970-73; assoc. pastor Binkley Bapt. Ch., Chapel Hill, N.C., 1973-77; pastor First Bapt. Ch., Lafayette, Ind., 1977-85, Penifield, .Y., 1985-93; pres. Ctrl. Bapt. Theol. Seminary, Kansas City, Kans., 1993—2003. Writer: Bapt. Leader, Capitol Report; (curriculum) Judson Press. Office: Ctrl Bapt Theol Sem 741 N 31st St Kansas City KS 66102-3964

CLIFTON-SMITH, RHONDA DARLEEN, art educator, art center administrator; b. Dyersburg, Tenn., Mar. 19, 1954; d. Charles Burton Clifton and Mary Opal (Carter) Harris; m. Michael Frederick Smith, Feb. 14, 1980 (dec. Sept. 1981). BS in Art Edn., Columbus Coll., 1977; MA in Hist. Administrn., Eastern Ill. U., 1986. Asst. cataloging libr. Lawton (Okla.) Pub. Libr., 1978-79; registrar Mus. of the Great Plains, Lawton, 1979-82; curator Boot Hill Mus., Dodge City, Kans., 1982-94; exec. dir. Carnegie Ctr. for Arts, Dodge City, 1994—; drawing and painting instr. Dodge City H.S. Author: (booklet) Dodge City: The Early Years, 1985; co-author: (booklet) Cattle and Wheat: Agricultural Growth in 19th Century Dodge City, 1985. Mem. Am. Assn. Mus., Am. Assn. State & Local History (c-chair mem. com. 1990-92), Kan. Mus. Assn. (treas. 1989—, area rep. 1982-85), Mt. Plains Mus. Assn., Soroptimists Internat. Avocations: painting, theater, drawing. Office: Carnegie Ctr for Arts 701 2d Ave Dodge City KS 67801 E-mail: carnegie@dodgecity.net.

CLINE, THOMAS WILLIAM, real estate leasing company executive, management consultant; b. Flint, Mich., Oct. 17, 1932; s. Leo D. and Helen (Wolohan) C.; m. Joanne Greiner, July 18, 1959; children: Robert Arthur, Thomas John, Mary Elizabeth. BS, U. Detroit, 1954, JD, 1956. Bar: Mich. 1957. Gen. atty. Wickes Corp., Saginaw, Mich., 1958-61, sec., gen. counsel, 1961-69, sr. v.p., gen. counsel, 1969-71, sr. v.p., sec., 1971-80, dir., 1964-70, 74-80; sr. v.p., group officer, dir. Wickes Cos. Inc., Saginaw, 1980-83; pres. Cline Mgmt. Co., Saginaw, 1983—; pres., COO Signature Corp., Chgo., 1984-85; exec. v.p., COO Seitner Bros. Inc., Saginaw, 1986—2004. Bd. dirs. Mid-Am. Life Assurance Co., Mich. Nat. Bank, Saginaw, Can. West Fin. Svcs.(U.S.) Inc., Aristar Inc. Chmn. fin. com. Diocese of Saginaw, 1970-72; chmn. Saginaw Cath. Schs. Study Com., 1969, Nat. assn. Boys Clubs Am.; bd. dirs. San Diego Symphony Assn., 1975-78, Econ. devel. Corp. San Deigo County, 1975-78, also vice-chmn., Saginaw Japanese Cultural Ctr. and Tea House; vice chmn. Boys Clubs San Diego, 1975-77; trustee Saginaw Gen. Hosp. Assn., 1971-72, 73-75; trustee, fin. chmn. Saginaw Coop. Hosp. Inc., 1972; trustee, v.p. United Way of Saginaw County; bd. fellows Saginaw Valley Coll., 1973-75, chmn. bus. fund dr., 1978; mem. adv. bd. Delta Coll., U. San Diego, 1975-78, San Diego State U. Bus. Sch., 1975-78, Saginaw Art Mus., 1986-94; mem. instnl. rev. bd. Saginaw Valley State U., 2002-07; mem. fin. com. Diocese San Diego, 1975-78; bd. dirs. Mich. State C. of C., 1973-75, Saginaw Symphony Assn. 1984-88, also v.p.; chmn. Saginaw Met. Area Nat. Alliance of Bus., 1979-80; bd. dirs. San Diego C. of C., 1976-77; ann. programs fund stategic advisor Rotary Found., 2001-03; pres. Big Creek Fishing Lodge, 2000-03; bd. dirs. Saginaw Hall of Fame, 2005—, Saginaw Valley State U. Humanities Series. With U.S. Army, 1956-58. Recipient Svc. Above Self award, 1999. Mem. Mich. Bar Assn., Mich. Mfrs. Assn. (bd. dirs. 1980-88), U.S. C. of C. (adv. com.), Saginaw Club (bd. dirs., v.p. 1991), Serra Club Saginaw County (pres., bd. dirs.), Rotary (pres. Saginaw 1990-91, dist. gov. 1994-95, chair dist. found.1996-2000, del. coun. on legis. 1998, nat. advisor to Rotary Found. 2001-03), Blue Key Soc., Delta Sigma Pi, Beta Alpha Psi, Delta Theta Pi. Home and Office: 4640 Ashland Dr Saginaw MI 48603-4605

CLIPPERT, CHARLES FREDERICK, lawyer; b. Detroit, May 21, 1931; s. Harrison Frank and Ethelyn (Reuss) C.; m. Lynne Davison, June 6, 1959; children: Martha G. Shannon, Charles Frederick III, Thomas Harrison. BA, U. Mich., 1953, LLB, 1959. Bar: Mich. 1959. Assoc. Dickinson, Wright, Moon, Van Dusen & Freeman, Bloomfield Hills, Mich., 1959-67, ptnr., 1967-97, mem. exec. com., 1986-89; mem. Dickinson Wright PLLC, Bloomfield Hills, Mich., 1998-2000, cons. mem., 2001—. Commr. City of Birmingham, Mich., 1964-70, mayor, 1969-70; gov. Cranbrook Schs., Bloomfield Hills, 1978-99; trustee Cranbrook Ednl. Community, Bloomfield Hills, 1980-98, sec., 1989-93. Lt. (j.g.) USNR, 1953-56; mem. endowment com. The Consortium of Endowed Episcopal Parishes, 1998-2003. Fellow Am. Bar Found., Mich. Bar Found.; mem. ABA, State Bar Mich. (real property law coun. 1980-85, mem. select com. on professionalism 1992-99, mem. alternate dispute resolution coun. 1999-2006), Oakland County Bar Assn. (bd. dirs. 1985-91, pres. 1990-91), Orchard Lake Country Club (gov. 1986-92, pres. 1991-92), Am. Arbitration Assn. (panel of neutral arbitrators 1997—), Pi Sigma Alpha. Office: Dickinson Wright PLLC Ste 2000 38525 Woodward Ave Bloomfield Hills MI 48304-2971 Mailing: PO Box 509 Bloomfield Hills MI 48303-0509 Office Phone: 248-433-7212. Business E-Mail: cclippert@dickinsonwright.com.

CLONINGER, CLAUDE ROBERT, psychiatrist, epidemiologist, educator, researcher; b. Beaumont, Tex., Apr. 4, 1944; s. Morris Sheppard and Marie Concetta (Mazzagatti) Cloninger; m. Sharon Lee Rogan, July 11, 1969; children: Bryan Joseph, Kevin Michael. BA, U. Tex., 1966; MD, Washington U., St. Louis, 1970; MD, PhD (hon.), U. Umea, Sweden, 1983. Diplomate Am. Bd. Psychology and Neurology. Instr. psychiatry Washington U., St. Louis, 1973—74, asst. prof., 1974—78, assoc. prof., 1978—81, prof., 1981—, prof. genetics, 1978—, prof. psychology, 1989—, Wallace Renard prof. psychiatry, 1991—, head dept. psychiatry, 1989—94, dir. ctr. psychobiology personality, 1994—. Psychiatrist-in-chief Barnes and Renard Hosps., St. Louis, 1989—94; vis. prof. U. Hawaii, Honolulu, 1978—79, U. Umea, Sweden, 1980; chmn. NIMH Psychopathology Rev. Com., Washington, 1980—84; cons. WHO, Geneva, 1981—, Am. Psychiat. Assn., Washington, 1978—, Nat. Inst. on Alcohol Abuse and Alcoholism, 1984—99, Inst. Medicine, 1986; chmn. genetics initiative schizophrenia NIMH, 1989—97; mental health commr. State of Mo., 1990—95; taskforce mem. psychiatry for person World Psychiatric Assn., 2006—. Author: Feeling Good: The Science of Well-Being, 2004, others; editor: Jour. Behavior Genetics, 1980—86, Am. Jour. Human Genetics, 1980—83; assoc. editor Genetic Epidemiology, 1983—92, Human Heredity, 1989—, mem. editl. bd. Arch. Gen. Psychiatry, Comprehensive Psychiatry, Neuropsychopharmacology, Jour. Comprehensive Psychiatry, Jour. Psychiat. Rsch., Jour. Med. Genetics; contbr. articles to profl. jours. Recipient Rsch. Scientist award, NIMH, 1975, 1980, 1985, Strecker award, Inst. Pa. Hosp., 1988, James B. Isaacson award, ISBRA, 1992, Lifetime Achievement award, Am. Soc. Addiction Medicine, 2000, Finnish Psychiatry Assn. Annual medal, Lifetime Achievement award, Internat. Soc. Psychiat. Genetics, 2003. Fellow: AAAS, Am. Psychopathol. Assn. (treas. 1984—89, v.p. 1990, pres. 1991—93, sec. 1994—96, Samuel Hamilton award 1993), Am. Psychiat. Assn. (Adolph Meyer award 1993); mem.: Rsch. Soc. Alcoholism (bd. dirs. 1987—90), Inst. Medicine of NAS, Behavior Genetics Assn. (editl. bd. 1980—), Am. Soc. Human Genetics (editl. bd. 1980—83). Avocations: gardening, reading, travel. Home: 12950 Huntbridge Forest Dr Saint Louis MO 63131 Office: Wash Univ Dept Psychiatry Campus Box 8134 660 S Euclid Saint Louis MO 63110-1002 Home Phone: 314-863-1338; Office Phone: 314-362-7005. Business E-Mail: clon@tci.wustl.edu.

CLOONAN, JAMES BRIAN, investment company executive; b. Chgo., Jan. 28, 1931; s. Bernard V. and Lauretta D. (Maloney) C.; m. Edythe Adrianne Ratner, Mar. 26, 1970; children: Michele, Christine, Mia; stepchildren: Carrie Madorin, Harry Madorin. Prof. Sch. Bus. Loyola U., Chgo., 1966-71; pres. Quantitative Decision Sys., Inc., Chgo., 1972-73; chmn. bd. Heinold Securities, Inc., Chgo., 1974-77; prof. grad. sch. bus. DePaul U., Chgo., 1978-82; chmn. Investment Info. Svcs., 1981-86; pres. Mktg. Sys. Internat. Inc., 1985-87, Analytics Sys. Inc., 1987—. Bd. dirs., chmn. Mktg. Svcs. Internat., Inc. Author: Estimates of the Impact of Sign and Billboard Removal Under the Highway Beautification Act of 1965, 1966, Stock Options-The Application of Decision Theory to Basic and Advanced Strategies, 1973, An Introduction to Decision Making for the Individual Investor, 1980, Expanding Your Investment Horizons, 1983, A Lifetime Strategy for Investing in Common Stocks, 1988, Maximum Return Minimum Risk, 2003. Mem.: Am. Assn. Individual Investors (pres. 1979—92, chmn. 1992—), Am. Mktg. Assn. Home: 1242 N Lake Shore Dr Chicago IL 60610-2361 Office: Am Assn Individual Investors 625 N Michigan Ave Chicago IL 60611-3110 Office Phone: 312-280-0170. E-mail: jbcaaii@aol.com.

CLOSEN, MICHAEL LEE, retired law educator; b. Peoria, Ill., Jan. 25, 1949; s. Stanley and Dorothy Closen. BS, MS, Bradley U., 1971; JD, U. Ill., 1974. Bar: Ill. 1974. Instr. U. Ill., Champaign, 1974; jud. clk. Ill. Appellate Ct., Springfield, 1974-76, 77-78; asst. states atty. Cook County, Chgo., 1978; prof. law John Marshall Law Sch., Chgo., 1976—2003; notary pub. State of Fla., 2004—, State of Ill., 1990—2003. Reporter Ill. Jud. Conf., Chgo., 1981—2002; arbitrator Am. Arbitration Assn., Chgo., 1981—2003; lectr. Ill. Inst. Continuing Legal Edn., Chgo., 1981—2002, BRI, 1985—; vis. prof. No. Ill. U., 1985—86, adj. prof., 1990, St. Thomas U., 1991, Loyola U., Chgo., 1999—2002; vis. prof. U. Ark., 1993, 96; arbitrator Cook County Cir. Ct. Mandatory Arbitration Program, 1990—2002, Will County Cir. Ct. Mandatory Arbitration Program, 1996—2002; dir. Ctr. for Legal Edn., Ltd., 1995—96. Author: (casebook) Agency and Partnership Law, 1984, Agency and Partnership Law, 3d edit., 2000; author: (with others) Contracts, 1984, Contracts, 3d edit., 1992, AIDS Cases and Materials, 1989, AIDS Cases and Materials, 3d edit., 2002, Notary Law and Practice, 1997, Contract Law and Practice, 1998; co-author: (book) The Shopping Bag: Portable Art, 1986, AIDS Law in a Nutshell, 2d edit., 1996, Legal Aspects of AIDS, 1991; contbr. articles to profl. jours. Named One of Outstanding Young Men in Am., 1981; recipient Svc. award, Am. Arbitration Assn., 1984—85, 5-Yr. Cmty. Achievement award, Ill. Politics Mag., 1998. Mem.: at. Notary Assn. (cons. 2004—, Achievement award 1998).

CLOSIUS, PHILLIP J., dean, law educator; BA, U. Notre Dame; JD, Columbia U. Atty. Kelley Drye & Warren, New York, NY; faculty mem. U. Toledo Sch. Law, 1979—, dean, prof. law, 1999—. Contbr. articles to law jours.; pub. in fields of Sports Law, Constl. Law and Law and Lit. Mem.: ABA, Toledo Bar Assn., Ohio State Bar Assn., Assn. Am. Law Sch. Office: U Toledo Sch Law 2801 W Bancroft Toledo OH 43606 Office Phone: 419-530-2379. Office Fax: 419-530-4526. E-mail: Phillip.Closius@utoledo.edu.

CLOYD, G. GIL, information technology executive; Joined Proctor & Gamble Co., 1970—; v.p. Proctor and Gamble Distributing Co., Cin.; global v.p. for consumer products, v.p. corporate R&D in Asia; chief technology officer Proctor and Gamble Co., 2000—. Named Technology Leader of Yr., Industry Week, 2004. Office: Proctor and Gamble 1 Proctor & Gamble Plz Cincinnati OH 45202 Office Phone: 513-983-1100. Office Fax: 513-562-4500.

COAR, DAVID H., federal judge; b. Birmingham, Ala., Aug. 11, 1943; s. Robert and Lorayne C.; children: Chinyelu, Kamau, Jamila. BA, Syracuse U., 1964; JD, Loyola U., 1969; LLM, Harvard U., 1970. Bar: Ill. 1969, Ala. 1971. Atty.-extern NAACP Legal Def. and Edn. Fund, Inc., NYC, 1970-71, Crawford & Cooper, Mobile, Ala., 1971-72, Adams, Baker & Clemon, Birmingham, 1972-74; prof. DePaul U. Law Sch., Chgo., 1974-79, 82-86; U.S. trustee U.S. Justice Dept., Chgo., 1979-82; bankruptcy judge U.S. Bankruptcy Ct., Chgo., 1986-94; dist. ct. judge U.S. Dist. Ct., Chgo., 1994—. Bd. dirs. Boys and Girls Club, Chgo. Mem. ABA, Am. Coll. Bankruptcy, Law Club, Legal Club Chgo., Chgo. Inns of Ct. Office: US Dist Ct 219 S Dearborn St Ste 1478 Chicago IL 60604-1705

COASE, RONALD HARRY, economist, educator; b. Willesden, Eng., Dec. 29, 1910; arrived in U.S., 1951; s. Henry Joseph and Rosalie (Giles) Coase; m. Marian Ruth Hartung, Aug. 7, 1937. B of Commerce, London Sch. Econs., 1932; DSc in Econs., U. London, 1951; D Rer. Pol. (hon.), Cologne U., Germany, 1988; D of Social Sci. (hon.), Yale U., 1989; LLD (hon.), Washington U., St. Louis, 1991, U. Dundee, Scotland, 1992; DSc (hon.), U. Buckingham, Eng., 1995; DHL (hon.), Beloit Coll., 1996; PhD (hon.), U. Paris, 1996; DHum (hon.), Clemson U., 2003. Sir Ernest Cassel Travelling scholar, 1931—32; asst. lectr. Dundee Sch. Econs., 1932—34, U. Liverpool, England, 1934—35; from asst. lectr. to lectr. to reader London Sch. Econs., 1935—51; prof. U. Buffalo, 1951—58, U. Va., Charlottesville, 1958—64, U. Chgo., 1964—, now Clifton R. Musser prof. emeritus, sr. fellow in law and econs. Law Sch. Statistician, then chief statistician Ctrl. Statis. Office, Offices War Cabinet, England, 1941—46. Author: British Broadcasting, A Study in Monopoly, 1950, The Firm, the Market and the Law, 1988, Essays on Economics and Economists, 1994; editor: Jour. Law and Econs., 1964—82. Mem. hon. com. Eurosci. Named Rockefeller fellow, 1948; recipient Nobel prize in econs., 1991, Innovations award, The Economist, 2003; fellow Ctr. for Advanced Study Behavioral Scis., 1958—59; Sr. Rsch. fellow, Hoover Instn., Stanford U., 1977, hon. fellow, London Sch. Econs. Fellow: European Acad., Am. Econ. Assn. (disting.), Brit. Acad. (corr.), Am. Acad. Arts and Scis.; mem.: Internat. Soc. for New Instnl. Econs. (founding pres. 1997), Mont Pelerin Soc., Royal Econ. Soc. Office: U Chgo Laird Bell Law Quadrangle 1111 E 60th St Chicago IL 60637-2776 Home: The Hallmark 2960 N Lake Shore Dr Chicago IL 60657 Home Phone: 773-755-0409; Office Phone: 773-702-7342.

COATS, JAMES O., state legislator; m. Alice Coats. BS, N.D. State U. Tchr.; ret.; state rep. dist. 34, 1991-99; ret. Mem. industry, bus. and labor, polit. subdvsns. coms. N.D. Ho. Reps. Recipient Golden Rule award, 1991. Mem. VFW, Am. Legion (dept. comdr.), Mandan Golden Age Club (pres.), Elks, Eagles, Amvets. Democrat. Home: 391 E Brandon Dr Bismarck ND 58503-0440

COBERLY, LEANN, internist; b. July 1, 1963; MD, Univ. Cin., 1989. Resident Duke Univ. Med. Ctr., asst. chief resident; with Univ. Cin., 1992—, dir. student edn. for internal medicine, co-chairperson, R-1 Selection Com.; practices Hoxworth Faculty Practice, Ohio, Jewish Hosp. Cholesterol Ctr., Ohio. Office: Hoxworth Faculty Practice Hoxworth Ctr 2nd Fl 3130 Highland Ave Cincinnati OH 45219 Office Phone: 513-584-4503. Office Fax: 513-584-0462.

COBEY, RALPH, industrialist; b. Sycamore, Ohio, Aug. 15, 1909; m. Hortense Kohn, Feb. 28, 1944; children: Minnie, Susanne. ME, Carnegie Inst. Tech., 1932; DSc (hon.), Findlay Coll., 1958. Pres. Perfection Steel Body Co., Galion, Ohio, 1945-70, Perfection-Cobey. Co., Galion, Ohio, 1949-70, Eagle Crusher Co., 1954-90, chmn. bd., 1990—; pres. Philips-Davies Co., 1965-70, Cobey Co., 1946-70, Diamond Iron Works, 1972-90, Austin-Western Crusher Co., 1974-90, Scoopmobile Co., 1978-90, Madsen Co., 1979-90, World Wide Investment Co., 1950—. Aide in preparation of prodn. and design of Army tanks OPM, 1939-42. Mem. contbg. com. NCCJ, 1951-55, now area chmn. spl. gifts com.; founder, pres. Harry Cobey Found.; area chmn. U.S. Savs. Bonds; mem. pres.'s adv. coun. for devel. Ashland Coll., Ohio, mem. Ohio Gov.'s Citizens' Task Force on Environ. Protection, 1971-72, Pres.'s Tax Com., 1962-66; pioneer chaplain svcs. in indsl. plants; mem. Ohio Expns. Commn., 1964, Radio Free Europe Com.; chmn. Cmty. Heart Fund Campaign, 1971-72; pres., spl. gifts chmn. Crawford County Heart Fund, 1972-78; mem. Ohio fin. bd. Heart Fund, 1973—; mem. Ohio Rep. Fin. Com.; mounted dep. sheriff, Morrow County (Ohio), 1974-84; bd. dirs., chmn. long range planning com. Johnny Appleseed Area coun. Boy Scouts of Am.; hon. life mem. Galion Cmty. Ctr.; trustee Galion City Hosp. Found. Bd.; mem. pres.'s coun. Ohio State U.; chmn., founder Minnie Cobey Meml. Libr.; founder, chmn. bd. trustees Louis Bromfield Malabar Farm Found.; bd. dirs. Morrow County United Appeals; State of Ohio amb. of natural resources; numerous other civic activities. Capt. USAAF, 1942-46, 51, Korea. Baden-Powel World fellow King Carl Gustaf of Sweden, 1992; recipient Disting. Citizen of Yr. award Heart of Ohio Coun., Boy Scouts Am., 1995, Lifetime Commitment to Humanitarianism award from Rep. Joan Lawrence, Ohio Ho. Reps., 1996, award Louis Bromfield Soc., 2001, resolution from Ohio Dist. 5 Agy. on Aging, Cert. of Appreciation USDA, 2003; inductee Ohio State Fair Hall of Fame, 1992, Ohio Agrl. Hall of Fame, 1999, Ohio Natural Resources Hall of Fame, 2001, Ohio Sr. Citizens Hall of Fame, 2002, N. Ctrl. Ohio Entrepreneural Hall of Fame, 2003; Ralph Cobey Day in City of Galion, 1995, City of Bucyrus, 1999. Mem. AM, Nat. Assn. 4-H Clubs, Future Farmers Am., U.S. C. of C. (mem. taxation, fgn. affairs, labor rels. coms.), Masons (32 degree, awarded 75 yr. pin 2007), Shriners (sec.-treas.). Home: 4270 State Route 309 Galion OH 44833-9618 Office: Eagle Crusher Co Inc PO Box 537 Galion OH 44833-0537

COCHRAN, DALE M., former state agency administrator; b. Ft. Dodge, Iowa, Nov. 20, 1928; s. Melvin and Gladys C.; m. Jeannene Hirsch, 1952; children: Deborah, Cynthia, Tamara. BS, Iowa State U., 1950. Rep. Iowa State Rep. Dist. 14, 1965-86; spkr. of house Iowa Ho. of Reps., 1975-78, exec. com. mem. nat. conf. state legis. and coun. state govt.; sec. agrl. Iowa, 1987—2003; owner of farm. Pres. Midwestern Assn. State Depts. Agrl. and Mid-Am. Int. Agrl. Trade Coun. Farm editor: Ft. Dodge Messenger. Recipient Altig award Nat. Fedn. Blind, Sweepstakes award Friends of Agrl. Mem. Iowa Assn. Soil (hon. life), Iowa Soybean Assn. (bd. dirs. 1969-75), Lions, Pi Kappa Phi, Gamma Sigma Delta.

COCHRAN, JOHN R., bank executive; b. Council Bluffs, IA, 1943; m. Bette Chochran; 3 children. BA econ. and fin., U. Iowa; Stonier Grad. Sch. of Banking, Rutgers U., NJ. Teller Hawkeye State Bank, Iowa City, 1966-67; with Norwest Bancorporation, Minneapolis, MN, 1967-95; pres. and CEO 5th Norwestern Bank, Minneapolis, 1976-79, various Norwest Banks, 1979-84; regional pres. Norwest Corp., NE, 1984-86; pres. and CEO Norwest Bank, Omaha, 1986-95, FirstMerit Corp., Akron, OH, 1996—, now chmn. CEO. Office: FirstMerit Corp 7th Fl 3 Cascade Plz Ste 7 Akron OH 44308-1124

COCHRAN, WILLIAM C., state legislator; b. New Albany, Ind., Aug. 25, 1934; m. Judith Ann Bocard; children: Sherry Lee, Rex Charles, Richard Paul. Student, Ind. U. Realtor Brooks Realtors; rep. Dist. 72 Ind. Ho. of Reps., 1974—, vice chmn. interstate coop. com., mem. from dist. 72, mem. judiciary com., ways and means com. Clk. Cir. Ct., Floyd County, 1967-74; vol. March of Dimes. Recipient Outstanding Cmty. Svc. award, 1970. Mem. VFW, FOB, Manzanita Tribe Redmen, Elks, Masons. Home: 4330 Green Valley Rd New Albany IN 47150-4258

CODY, THOMAS GERALD, retail executive, lawyer; b. NYC, Nov. 4, 1941; s. Thomas J. Cody and Esther Mary Courtney; m. Mary Ellen Palmer, Nov. 26, 1966; children: Thomas Jr., Mark, Amy, Anne. BA in Philosophy, Maryknoll Coll., 1963; JD, St. John's U., 1967; LLD (hon.), Cen. State U., Wilberforce, Ohio, 1985. Bar: .Y. 1967. Assoc. Simpson Thacher & Bartlett, N.Y., 1967-72; asst. prof. law sch. St. John's U., N.Y., 1972-76; sr. v.p., gen. counsel, sec. Pan Am. Airways, N.Y., 1976-82; sr. v.p. law and pub. affairs Macy's Inc. (formerly Federated Dept. Stores Inc.), Cin., 1982-88; exec. v.p. legal & human resources Macy's Inc., Cin., 1988—2003, vice chmn. legal, human resources and external affairs, 2003—. Trustee Xavier U., Cin., Children's Hosp. Med. Ctr., Cin; bd. dirs. Cin. USA Regional Chamber Mem. ABA, Bankers Club, Queen City Club, Hyde Park Country Club, Commonwealth Club of Cin. Roman Catholic. Office: Macy's Inc 7 W 7th St Cincinnati OH 45202-2424 Office Phone: 513-579-7768.

COE, FREDRIC L., internist, educator, researcher; b. Chgo, Dec. 25, 1936; s. Lester J. and Lillian (Chaitlen) C.; m. Eleanor Joyce Brodny, May 5, 1965; children: Brian, Laura. AB, U. Chgo., 1955, MS, 1957, MD, 1961. Diplomate Am. Bd. Internal Medicine. Intern Michael Reese Hosp., Chgo., 1961-62, resident, 1962-65, U. Tex. S.W. Med. Sch., 1967-69; chmn. nephrology Michael Reese Hosp., 1972-82; prof. medicine U. Chgo., 1977—, prof. physiology, 1979—; chmn. nephrology A.M. Billings Hosp., Chgo., 1982—; founder, pres. Litholink Corp., 1995—. Author: Nephrolithiasis, 1978, 2d edit. (with J. Parks), 1987, (with B. Brenner and F.C. Rector) Renal Physiology, 1986, Clinical Nephrology; editor: Renal Therapeutics, 1978, Nephrolithiasis, 1980, Hypercalciuric States, 1983, (with M. Favus) Disorders of Bone and Mineral Metabolism, 1993, 2d edit., 2001; editor-in-chief Yearbook of Nephrology, 1991-96; editor: (with others) Kidney Stones: Medical and Surgical Management, 1996. Served to capt. USAF, 1961-67. Recipient Belding Scribner medal for lifetime achievement in clin. rsch. Am. Soc. Nephrology, 2000; Univ. of Chgo. Distingguished Svc. Award, 2001; grantee NIH, 1977-. Fellow ACP; mem. Am. Soc. Clin. Investigation, Am. Physiol. Soc., Assn. Am. Physicians Jewish. Achievements include first evidence for hyperuricosuria as cause of calcium renal stones; discovery of nephro calcin a protein inhibitor of crystal growth; first demonstration that human idiopathic hypercalciuria is hereditary. First evidence that apatile plaque begins inthe basement membranes of the renal thin limbs of

Henle's loop. Home: 5490 S Shore Dr Chicago IL 60615-5984 Office: U Chgo Med Ctr 5841 S Maryland Ave Chicago IL 60637-1463 Office Phone: 773-702-1475. Business E-Mail: f-coe@uchicago.edu.

COELING, HARRIET VAN ESS, nursing educator, editor; b. Grand Rapids, Mich., Dec. 3, 1943; d. Louis and Helen Angeline (DeGraff) Van Ess; m. Kenneth J. Coeling, June 27, 1970; children: Valerie Coeling Nandor, Beverly Coeling Corder. BSN, U. Mich., 1966, MS, 1968; PhD, Bowling Green State U., 1987. RN, Ohio; clin. nurse specialist. Head nurse, clin. specialist Presbyn. Univ. Hosp., Pitts., 1968-70; instr. U. Pitts. Sch. Nursing, 1970-72; staff devel. instr. Braddock (Pa.) Hosp., 1976-78, Med. Coll. Ohio, Toledo, 1978-83; asst. prof. U. Mich. Sch. Nursing, Ann Arbor, 1987-88, Kent (Ohio) State U. Coll. Nursing, 1988-93, asoc. prof., 1994—2004, prof., 2004—. Editor, Online Jour. Issues in Nursing, ANA/Kent State U., 1998—; contbr. articles to profl. jours. Vol. St. Malachi Healthcare Clinic, Cleve., 1993-98. Tchr. and Nonsvc. fellow Bowling Green State U., 1983-87; Nursing Practice award, ANA. Mem. Nat. Assn. Clin. Specialists, Ohio Assn. Advanced Practice Nurses, Ohio Nurses Assn. (chair human rights com. 1998—2002), Greater Cleve. Nurses Assn., Midwest Nursing Rsch. Assn., Christian Assn. Psychol. Studies, Sigma Theta Tau (Excellence in Use of Tehc. award 1997). Christian. Avocations: travel, swimming. Office: Kent State U 1743 Settlers Reserve Westlake OH 44145 Business E-Mail: hcoeling@kent.edu.

COFFARO, STEVEN C., lawyer; b. Cin., July 31, 1970; BA, Miami U., 1992; JD, U. Cin. Coll. Law, 1995. Bar: Ohio 1995, US Dist. Ct. Southern Dist. Ohio 1995, Ky. 1996, Ind. 1997, US Dist. Ct. Northern Dist. Ind. 1997, US Dist. Ct. Southern Dist. Ind. 1997, US Dist. Ct. Western Dist. Ky. 1998, US Dist. Eastern Dist. Ky. 1998, US Ct. of Appeals Sixth Cir. 2002, US Dist. Ct. Northern Dist. Ohio 2005, US Ct. of Appeals Second Cir. 2005. Ptnr. Keating Muething & Klekamp PLL, Cin. Involved with St. Xavier High Sch. Named Leading Lawyer, Cincy Bus. Mag., 2005, 2006; named one of Ohio's Rising Stars, Super Lawyers, 2006. Mem.: St. Francis Xavier Soc., Ohio State Bar Assn., Ky. Bar Assn., Ind. State Bar Assn., Cin. Bar Assn., ABA, Order of Coif. Office: Keating Muething & Klekamp PLL One E Fourth St Ste 1400 Cincinnati OH 45202 Office Phone: 513-579-6400. Office Fax: 513-579-6457. E-mail: scoffaro@kmklaw.com.

COFFEY, JOHN LOUIS, federal appellate judge; b. Milw., Apr. 15, 1922; s. William Leo and Elizabeth Ann (Walsh) Coffey; m. Marion Kunzelmann, Feb. 3, 1951; children: Peter, Elizabeth Mary Coffey-Robbins. BA, Marquette U., 1943, JD, 1948; MBA (hon.), Spencerian Coll., 1964, D (hon.) in Bus., 1973. Bar: Wis. 1948, US Dist. Ct. 1948, US Supreme Ct. 1980. Asst. city atty. City of Milw., 1949—54; judge Civil Ct., Milw. County, 1954—60, Milw. County Mcpl. Ct., 1960—62; judge criminal divsn. Cir. Ct., Milw. County, 1962—72, sr. judge criminal divsn., 1972—75, chief presiding judge criminal divsn., 1976, judge civil divsn., 1976—78; justice Wis. Supreme Ct., Madison, 1978—82; judge US Ct. Appeals (7th cir.), Chgo., 1982—2004, sr. judge, 2004—. Mem. Wis. Bd. Criminal Ct. Judges, 1960—78, Wis. Bd. Circuit Ct. Judges, 1962—78. Mem. adv. bd. St. Mary's Hosp., 1964—70; mem. Milw. County coun. Boy Scouts Am., 1970—78; chmn. vol. svcs. adv. com. Milw. County Dept. Pub. Welfare, 1970—72; chmn. St. Eugene's Sch. Bd., 1967—70; pres. St. Eugene's Ch. Coun., 1974; bd. dirs., mem. exec. bd. Milw.-Waukesha chpt. ARC; chmn. adv. bd. St. Joseph's Home for Children, 1958—65. With USNR, 1943—46. Named Outstanding Young Man of Yr., Milw. Jr. C. of C., 1951, 1 of 5 Outstanding Young Men of Yr., Jr. C. of C., Wis. State, 1957; recipient Outstanding Law Alumnus of Yr. award, Marquette U., 1980, Merit award, Marquette U. Alumni Assn., 1985, Alumni Merit award, Marquette U. HS, 2001. Fellow: Am. Bar Found.; mem.: State Bar Assn. Wis., Ill. State Bar Assn., 7th Cir. Bar Assn., Marquette U. Law Alumni Assn. (Disting. Profl. Achievement Merit award 1985), Marquette U. M Club (former dir.), Nat. Lawyers Club, Am. Legion (Disting. Svc. award 1973), Alpha Sigma Nu (Marquette U. chpt.), Phi Alpha Delta (hon.). Roman Catholic.

COFFEY, SUSANNA JEAN, artist, educator; b. New London, Conn. d. Edwin Raymond and Magel C. (Willingham) C. BFA magna cum laude, U. Conn., 1977; MFA, Yale U., 1982. Tchg. asst. Yale U., 1982—; F.H. Sellers prof. painting Art Inst. Chgo., Oxbow, Mich., 1985—. Vis. artist various schs., 1983—; adj. assoc. prof. U. Ill., 1983; vis. critic Royal Coll. Art, London, 1995, Vt. Studio Ctr., 1994; panel mem. Harvard Ctr. Religious Studies, 2001. Illustrator: The H Hymn to Demeter, 1989, Monovassia (Eleni Fourtouni), 1979; one-woman shows include The Cultural Ctr. of the Chgo. Pub. Libr., 1986, Weatherspoon Gallery, Greensboro, N.C., 1993, Alpha Gallery, 1995, 2001, 04, Galeria Alejandro Sales, Barcelona, 1995, Tibor De Nagy Gallery, 1996-97, 2001, 2003, others; represented in permanent collections Northwestern U., Evanston, Ill., Art Inst. Chgo., Mpls. Mus. Art, Bryn Mawr (Pa.) Coll., Boston Mus. Fine Arts, Weatherspoon Gallery, and pvt. collections. Individual Artists grant Conn. Commn. on the Arts, 1980, Chgo. Artists Abroad grant, 1990, Ill./Arts Coun. grant, 1985, 92, Studio Program grant Marie Walsh Sharpe Found., 1992, Nat. Endowment for the Arts grant, 1993; Guggenheim fellow, 1996; recipient Louis Comfort Tiffany Found. award, 1993, Acad. award in art Am. Acad. of Arts and Letters, 1995; named to Nat. Acad. Design, 2001. Office: Sch of the Art Inst of Chgo 37 S Wabash Ave Chicago IL 60603-3002

COFFMAN, JAMES RICHARD, academic administrator, veterinarian, educator; b. Lyndon, Kans., July 19, 1938; s. Harry Thomas and Eleanor Louise (Lowe) C.; m. Sharon Sue eill, June 10, 1960; children: David Neill, Michael James, Scott Thomas. BS, Kans. State U., 1960, DVM, 1962, MS, 1969. Pvt. practice equine vet., Wichita, Kans., 1962-65, Oklahoma City, 1969-71; inst. vet. medicine Kans. State U., Manhattan, 1965-69, prof., head dept. surgery and medicine, vet. medicine, 1981-84, prof. vet. medicine, dean, 1984-87, provost, 1987—2004; assoc. prof. vet. medicine and surgery U. Mo., Columbia, 1971-75, prof., 1975-81, dir. Equine Ctr., 1973-78; prof., head dept. surgery and medicine Sch. Vet. Medicine Kans. State U., Manhattan, 1981-84, prof., dean, 1984-87, provost, 1987—2004, provost emeritus vet. clin. sci., 2004—. Chair Nat. rsch. Coun., Bd. on Agr. subcom., 1999. Author: Equine Chemistry and Pathophysiology, 1981; equine editor Compendium on Continuing Edn. 1980-83, mem. editorial bd., 1980-85; editor in chief Equine Sportsmedicine, 1981-85; mem. editorial bd. Jour. Equine Medicine and Surgery, 1979-80; adv. bd. Equine Vet. Jour., 1980—; contbr. numerous articles to profl. jours. Bd. dirs. St. Mary Hosp., Manhattan, 1989—. Recipient Disting. Tchr. award Norden Labs., 1969. Mem. Am. Coll. Vet. Internal Medicine (diplomate, pres. 1978-79, chmn. bd. regents 1979-80), Am. Assn. Equine Practitioners (dir. at large 1982-83, v.p. 1984, pres. 1986-87), Am. Vet. Med. Assn. (trustee profl. liability ins. trust 1978-85, chmn. 1980-82), Nat. Acads. Practice Vet. Medicine (exec. bd. 1985-87, founding com. mem. 1985-97), Kans. Vet. Med. Assn., Nat. Assn. State Univs. and Land Grant Colls. (coun. chief acad. officers 1997-2004, exec. coun. on acad. affairs), Rotary (bd. dirs. 1989-90), Phi Kappa Phi, Gamma Sigma Delta, Phi Zeta. Avocation: painting. Home: 200 Waterbridge Rd Manhattan KS 66503-2512 Business E-Mail: sncjre@kanas.net.

COFFMAN, TERRENCE J., retired academic administrator; b. 1945; m. Wallis Coffman. Student, Corcoran Coll. Art and Design, Lacoste Sch. Arts. Dean then pres. Md. Coll. Art and Design, Silver Spring, 1973—83; pres. Milw. Inst. Art & Design, 1983—2003; ret., 2003. Instr. Smithsonian Instn., Washington; artist-in-residence Milw. Inst. Art & Design. Author: A Walk Through the Wheatfields: The Missing Journals of Vincent van Gogh. Recipient Milw.'s Frank Kirkpatrick award, 2001. Avocation: playing acoustic guitar. Office: Milw Inst Art & Design 273 E Erie St Milwaukee WI 53202-6003

COFIELD, ROBERT HAHN, orthopedic surgeon, educator; b. Cin., Oct. 24, 1943; s. Robert Hedrick and Virginia (Hahn) C.; m. Pamela Joyce Haarbauer, Aug. 12, 1967; children: Robert, Stacey, Virginia. BA, Washington and Lee U., 1965; MD, U. Ky., 1969; MS, Mayo Grad. Sch. Medicine, 1976. Diplomate Am. Bd. Orthopedic Surgery. Intern Charity Hosp./Tulane U., New Orleans, 1970; cons. Mayo Clinic, Rochester, Minn., 1975—; from instr. to assoc. prof. Mayo Med. Sch., Rochester, 1975-88, prof., 1988—; vice chmn. dept. orthopedics Mayo Clinic, Rochester, 1992-97, Frank R. and Shari Caywood prof. orthopedic surgery, 1993, chmn. dept. orthopedics, 1997—2005; assoc. dean Mayo Grad. Sch., Rochester, 1992-94, dean, 1994-98; pres. Am. Bd. Orthopaedic Surgery, Chapel Hill, 1999-2000. Editor-in-chief Jour. Shoulder and Elbow Surgery, 1990-96; contbr. chpts. to books, more than 200 articles to profl. jours.; co-inventor humeral resect. guide; co-designer Cofield total shoulder sys. Lt. comdr. USNR. Mem. AMA, Am. Acad. Orthopedic Surgery, Am. Bd. Orthopedic Surgery (dir. 114—), Am. Orthopedic Assn., Am. Shoulder and Elbow Surgeons (founding sec.-treas. 1982-87, pres. 1988-89). Republican. Presbyterian. Office: Mayo Clinic 200 1st Ave NW Rochester MN 55901-3004 Office Phone: 507-284-2995.

COGGS, G. SPENCER, state legislator; b. Milw., Aug. 6, 1949; s. Calvin Jr. and Erma (Bryant) C.; m. Gershia Christina Brown, 1971; children: Mariama, Kijana. AA, Milw. Area Tech. Coll., 1975; BS, U. Wis., Milw., 1976. Former health officer, postal worker, printer City of Milw.; mem. from dist. 16 Wis. State Assembly, Madison, 1982-92, 93—, chmn. spkr.'s task force on gang violence, mem. com. on urban and local affairs, com. on rules, mem. com. on children and human svcs., com. on colls./univs., mem. coms. on employment and tng.; mem. com. on criminal justice and pub. safety; vice chmn. majority caucus, 1985, 87, 89. Mem. Wis. State Job Tng. Coord. Coun., Job Tng. Partnership Act, 1983—. Mem. Milw. Truancy Com.; mem. N.W. Corridor Rapid Transit Adv. Com., Sherman Park Rapid Transit Adv. Com.; bd. dirs. Isaac Coggs Cmty. Health Ctr. Mem. NAACP, Urban League (bd. dirs., health and social svc. com.), Wis. Pub. Health Assn., Nat. Conf. State Legislators (mem. transp. and comms. com.). Home: 3732 N 40th St Milwaukee WI 53216-3027 Office: State Capitol Rm 214 N PO Box 8952 Madison WI 53708

COHAN, LEON SUMNER, lawyer, retired electric company executive; b. Detroit, June 24, 1929; s. Maurice and Lillian (Rosenfeld) C.; m. Heidi Ruth Seelmann, Jan. 22, 1956; children: Nicole, Timothy David, Jonathan Daniel. BA, Wayne State U., 1949, JD, 1952. Bar: Mich. 1953. Pvt. practice, Detroit, 1954-58; asst. atty. gen. State of Mich., Lansing, 1958-61, dep. atty. gen., 1961-72; v.p. legal affairs Detroit Edison Co., 1973-75, v.p., 1975-79, sr. v.p., gen. counsel, 1979-93; counsel Barris, Sott, Denn & Driker, Detroit, 1993—. Bd. dirs. Oakland Commerce Bank. Trustee Mich. Cancer Found.; bd. dirs. Concerned Citizens for Arts in Mich., U. Mich. Musical Soc.; mem. arts commn. Detroit Inst. Arts; mem. Race Rels. Coun. Met. Detroit. With U.S. Army, 1952-54. Recipient Disting. Alumni award Wayne State U. Law Sch., 1972, Disting. Svc. award Bd. Govs., Wayne State U., 1973, Judge Ira W. Jayne award NAACP, 1987, Israel Histadrut Menorah award, 1987, Knights of Charity award Pontifical Inst. for Fgn. Missions, 1989, Fellowship award Am. Arabic and Jewish Friends of Met. Detroit, Judge Learned Hand Human Rels. award, 1991, Gov.'s Arts award for Civic Leadership in the Arts, Michiganian of Yr. award Detroit News, 1993. Mem. ABA, Detroit Bar Assn., State Bar Mich. (Champion of Justice award 1993), Mich. Gen. Counsel Assn., Detroit Club. Democrat. Jewish. Home: 17 Eastbury Ct Ann Arbor MI 48105-1402 Office: Barris Sott Denn & Driker 15th Fl 211 W Fort St Lbby 15 Detroit MI 48226-3244 Business E-Mail: lscohan@comcast.com.

COHEN, ALAN H., retail executive; b. Indpls., Mar. 5, 1947; m. Linda Cohen; children: Nathan, Lauren. BS, Ind. U., 1969, JD, 1973. Atty., 1976—80; chmn., CEO The Finish Line, Inc., Indpls., 1976—, pres., 1976—2003. Mem. bd. vis. Ind. U. Law Sch.; mem. dean's adv. coun. Kelley Sch. Bus.; bd. dirs. Ctrl. Ind. Corp. Partnership. Nat. trustee Boy's and Girl's Clubs Am.; bd. dirs. Ind. C. of C. Named Entrepreneur of Yr., Inc. mag., 1991, Ernst & Young, 1991; recipient Spirit of Philanthropy award, Ind. U., 2002, Purdue U., 2002. Office: The Finish Line Inc 3308 N Mitthoeffer Rd Indianapolis IN 46235 Office Phone: 317-899-1022.

COHEN, ALLAN RICHARD, broadcast executive; b. Bklyn., Dec. 27, 1947; s. Ike and Fae C.; m. Roberta Segal, July 12, 1970; children: Evan, Stacie. BS, Hofstra U., 1970; MM, Poly. Inst. Bklyn., 1976. Electronics engr. Sperry Systems Mgmt. Div., Great Neck, NY, 1970-74; with CBS/Viacom, 1974—; dir. planning and adminstrn. WCBS-TV, 1977-79; v.p. personnel CBS Broadcast Group, 1979-80; v.p., gen. mgr. Sta. KMOX-TV, St. Louis, 1980-86, Sta. KMOV-TV, St. Louis, 1986—. Lectr. in comm. and journalism Washington U., St. Louis; mem. affiliates adv. bd. CBS. Restaurant critic, travel editor St. Louis Bus. Jour. Vice chmn. bd. dirs. St. Louis Symphony; bd. dirs. Paraquad, Jewish Hosp., United Way, Variety Club; mem. adv. bd. Nat. Coun. Jewish Women, St. Louis. Recipient Flair awards, Emmy awards. Mem. NATAS (v.p. St. Louis chpt. 1987-88, pres. 1989-91), Mo. Broadcasters Assn. (bd. dirs.), Ill. Broadcasters Assn., Nat. Assn. Broadcasters, St. Louis Jr. League (adv. bd.), Westwood Club, St. Louis Variety Club (bd. dirs.).

COHEN, BURTON DAVID, food service executive, lawyer; b. Chgo., Feb. 12, 1940; s. Allan and Gussy (Katz) C.; m. Linda Rochelle Kaine, Jan. 19, 1969; children: David, Jordana. BS in Bus. and Econs., Ill. Inst. Tech., 1960; JD, Northwestern U., 1963. Staff atty. McDonald's Corp., Oak Brook, Ill., 1964-69, asst. sec., 1969-70, asst. gen. counsel, 1970-76, asst. v.p., 1976-78, dep. dir. legal dept., 1978-80, v.p. franchising, asst. gen. counsel, asst. sec., 1980-89, sr. v.p., chief franchising officer, 1989-98; mng. ptnr. Burton D. Cohen & Assoc. LLC. Adv. dir., 1992-93, McDonald's Corp., 1992—; adv. bd. La. State U. Franchise U.; dir. Goodwill Enterprises Devel. Corp.; franchise mediator CPR Inst. for Dispute Resolution; adj. prof. Kellogg Grad Sch. Mgmt., orthwestern U.; bd. dirs. Dwyer Group, Cotlete; cons. Exec. Svc. Corps. Chgo.; sr. cons. Ifranchise Group; lectr., cons. in field. Author: Franchising: Second Generation Problems, 1969. With AUS, 1963-64. Mem. ABA, Ill. Bar Assn., Chgo. Bar Assn., Internat. Franchise Assn. (lectr.), Assn. Nat. Advertisers, Chgo. Coun. Fgn. Rels., Execs. Club (Chgo.), Tau Epsilon Phi, Phi Delta Phi. Office: 300 Cedar Ave Highland Park IL 60035

COHEN, CHARLES EMIL, art historian, educator; b. NYC, July 11, 1942; s. Philip and Hannah (Abramson) Cohen; m. Sondra Eileen Cohen, Sept. 27, 1964; children: Joshua K., Jonathan E. BA, Columbia U., 1963; MFA, Princeton U., 1965; PhD, Harvard U., 1971. Tutor Harvard U., Cambridge, Mass., 1967-68, head teaching fellow, 1969-70; asst. prof. art U. Chgo., 1970-75, assoc. prof., 1975-80, chmn. art dept., 1985—89, Resident Master Pierce Hall, Mary L. Block prof. art, 1980—, chmn. com. visual arts. Curator of drawings Pordenone 500th Anniversary, 1984; resident master Pierce Hall U. Chgo. Author: I Disegni di Pomponio Amalteo, 1975, Drawings of Giovanni Antonio da Pordenone, 1980, Art of Giovanni Antiorio da Pordenone: Between Dialect & Lang.; contbr. articles to profl. jours. Fellow Guggenheim Found., 1983, Am. Coun. Learned Socs., 1980, Gladys Krieble Delmas Found., 1989, NEH, summer 1983; Univ. fellow NEH, 1989-90. Mem.: Renaissance Soc. Am., U. Chgo. Renaissance Seminar, Midwest Art History Soc., Coll. Art Assn. Am. Jewish. Office: U Chgo Dept Art 5540 S Greenwood Ave Chicago IL 60637-1506 Office Phone: 773-702-5880. E-mail: cac5@uchicago.edu.

COHEN, CHRISTOPHER B., lawyer; b. Washington, July 10, 1942; m. Judith Calder; 2 children. BA, U. Mich., 1964, JD, 1967. Bar: Ill. 1968, Wis. 1986, D.C. 1972, U.S. Dist. Ct. D.C. 1969, U.S. Dist Ct. (no. dist.) Ill. 1968, U.S. Ct. Mil. Appeals 1977, U.S. Supreme Ct. 1974; lic. real estate broker, 1986. Clerk, lawyer Legal Aid Bur.-United Charities of Chgo., 1967-68; adminstrv. asst. to pres. Cook County Bd. Commrs., 1969-71; hearing officer Liquor Commn. Cook County, Chgo., 1970-71; alderman 46th ward Chgo. City Coun., 1971-77; atty. Schwartzberg, Barnett & Cohen, Chgo., 1973-77; midwest regional dir. U.S. Dept. HHS, Chgo., 1977-81; atty. Hinshaw, Culbertson, Moelmann, Hoban & Fuller, Chgo., 1981-82, Cassiday, Shade & Gloor, Chgo., 1982-85; ptnr. Holleb & Coff, Chgo., 1985-98; of counsel Buyer & Rubin, Chgo., 1998—2005; prin. Cohen Law Firm, Chgo., 1998—. Lectr. Northwestern U., 1973, 04, DePaul U., Chgo., 1981, U. Ill., Chgo., 1981, 82; adult edn. tchr. Francis Parker Sch., Chgo., 1979, 80, 81; bd. dirs. State of Ill. Hosp. Licensing Bd., 1987-97; bd. dirs. State of Ill. Med. Ctr. Commn., 1985-90; mem. fed. regional coun. 1977-81; nursing home adv. coun. Office of Ill. Atty. Gen., 1988-94; Dem. candidate U.S. Ho. Reps., 10th Congressional Dist. Ill., 1999; Wis. State Pub. Defender, 2005—; rep. adminstrv. appeals divsn. Ill. Sec. State, 2002—; adminstrv. law judge Ill. Dept. Employment Security, 2003-05, bd. rev., 2005-07; adminstrv. law judge, Cook County Sheriff's Police, 2007-. Contbr. articles to profl. jours. and nat. newspapers. Field organizer Humphrey for Pres., Chgo., 1968; asst. to Ill. field dir. Jimmy Carter for Pres., Chgo., 1976; active spl. projects, polit. unit Clinton/Gore Campaign, Little Rock, 1992; mem. govt. affairs com. Jewish Fedn. Met. Chgo., 1988—; mem. U. Mich. Law Sch. Alumni Fund, 1967—, Glenview Concert Band, 2001-02; fin. exec. bd. New Trier Township Dem. Orgn., 1993-98; bd. dirs. UNICEF Chgo., 1996-97. Mem. ABA (adminstrv. law and regulatory practice sect. 1990-95), Ill. State Bar Assn. (founding mem., chair health care sect. coun. 1986-87, mem. legis. com. 1988-90, assembly 1991-97, local govt. sect.), Chgo. Bar Assn. (vice chair urban affairs com. 1991, chair health law com. 1983, mem. real estate tax com.), D.C. Bar Assn., State Bar Wis. Office Phone: 847-867-8500. Business E-Mail: chris@chriscohen.com.

COHEN, EDWARD, state official; Commr. Dept. Correction, Indpls. Office: IGCS Rm E334 302 W Washington St Indianapolis IN 46204-4701

COHEN, EDWARD PHILIP, microbiology and immunology educator; b. Glen Ridge, NJ, Sept. 28, 1932; s. Harry and Rae (Berke) C.; m. Toba Joy Gold, Mar. 24, 1963; children— Mark L., Lauren L., Jennifer L., Jonathan M. Tuition scholarship student, U. Miami (Fla.), 1950-53; MD, Washington U., St. Louis, 1957. Diplomate: Am. Bd. Allergy and Immunology, Nat. Bd. Med. Examiners. Intern. U. Chgo. Hosps., 1957-58; research asso. Nat. Inst. Allergy and Infectious Diseases, NIH, 1958-60; resident in medicine U. Colo. Med. Center, 1960-61, instr. dept. medicine, 1962-74; instr., then asst. prof. microbiology U. Colo., 1963-65; asso. prof. Inst. Microbiology, Rutgers U., 1965-67; asso. prof. microbiology and medicine Rutgers Med. Sch., 1967-68; asso. prof. La Rabida-U. Chgo. Inst. and dept. medicine U. Chgo. Sch. Medicine, 1968-69, asso. prof. depts. medicine and microbiology, 1969-77, prof. microbiology, 1977-79, asst. dean, 1971-73; prof. microbiology and immunology, dean Sch. Basic Med. Scis., Coll. Medicine U. Ill., 1979-82, also prof. Ctr. Edn. and Research in Genetics, 1979-82, dir. Office of Research and Devel., 1982-84, prof. dept. microbiology and immunology, 1985—, research prof. dept. medicine, 1986—; dir. MD/PhD program U. Ill. Coll. Medicine, 1993—. Editor: Immune RNA, 1976, Medicine in Transition: The Centennial of the University of Illinois College of Medicine, 1981; co-editor: Membranes, Receptors and the Immune Response, 1980; contbr. over 200 articles and revs. to profl. jours. Sci. adv. bd. Leukemia Research Found., 1978-83; chmn. Biotech. Contact Group City of Chgo., 1982-83. Served with USPHS, 1958-60. Spl. postdoctoral fellow USPHS, 1961-63; Research Career Devel. grantee, 1963-65 Mem. Am. Assn. Immunologists, Am. Soc. Cell Biology, Am. Acad. Allergy, Acad. Medicine N.J., Am. Soc. Microbiology, Central Soc. Clin. Research, Chgo. Assn. Immunologists (pres. 1974-75), Chgo. Soc. Allergy, Inst. Medicine Chgo., Reticuloendothelial Soc. Home: 4737 S Kimbark Ave Chicago IL 60615-1901 Office: 835 S Wolcott Ave Chicago IL 60612-7340

COHEN, FREDERICK H., lawyer; b. Chgo., Feb. 28, 1965; BA in Fin., U. Ill., 1987; JD with honors, U. Chgo., 1990. Bar: Ill. 1990, US Dist. Ct. (no. dist. Ill.) 1991, US Ct. Appeals (7th cir.) 1991, US Supreme Ct. 2001. Prin. Goldberg, Kohn, Bell, Black, Rosenbloom & Moritz, Chgo. Adj. prof. Kent Coll. Law. Named Lawyer of Yr. for Taxpayers Against Fraud, 2007, Lawyer of Yr., Trial Lawyers for Pub. Justice, 2007; named one of The Nation's Top Litigators, Nat. Law Jour., 2007; recipient Equal Justice award, Sargent Shriver Nat. Ctr. Poverty Law, 2004, Child Health Adv. of Yr. award, Acad. Pediat., 2005, Excellence in Pro Bono award, US Dist. Ct. (no. dist. Ill.), 2006. Office: Goldberg Kohn Ste 3300 55 E Monroe St Chicago IL 60603-5802 Office Phone: 312-201-3929. Office Fax: 312-863-7429. E-mail: frederick.cohen@goldbergkohn.com.

COHEN, IRA, legislative staff member; b. Chgo., Sept. 6, 1947; With Rep. Danny K. Davis, Washington, 1979—, issues and comm. dir., 1996—. Office: Office of Rep Danny K Davis 3333 W Arthington St Ste 130 Chicago IL 60624-4102

COHEN, JEROME, psychology educator, electrophysiologist; b. Pitts., May 27, 1925; s. Abraham Wolfe and Dorothy (Middleman) C.; m. Florence A. Chanock, Oct. 28, 1945; children— Marcus, Mara, Aaron. AA, Princeton U., 1943; BA, U. Pitts., 1947; MA, Cornell U., 1949; PhD, U. Pitts., 1951. Instr. U. Pitts., 1950-51; asst. prof., assoc. prof. Antioch Coll., Yellow Springs, Ohio, 1951-57; prof. psychiatry and behavioral sci. and neurology Northwestern U. Med. Sch., Chgo., 1957-93, prof. emeritus, 1993—. Dir. Electroencephalography Lab. Presbyn.-St. Lukes Hosp., Chgo., 1967-72, Cook County Hosp., Chgo., 1973-99; vis. scientist Neurol. Inst., U. London, 1963-64; vis. prof. Hebrew U., 1972-73, Stanford U., winter 1984. Lt. (j.g.) USNR, 1943-46. Commonwealth Fund fellow, 1963-64 Mem. Am. EEG Soc., Am. Psychol. Assn., Psychophysiol. Research Soc., Internat. Brain Research Soc., AAUP, AAAS, Am. Soc. for Applied Psychophysiology and Biofeedback, Sigma Xi.

COHEN, MALCOLM STUART, economist; b. Mpls., Jan. 17, 1942; s. Jack Alvin and Lorraine Ethel (Hill) Cohen; m. Judith Ann Arenson, Sept. 25, 1965; children: Laura, Randall, Ilona. BA in Econs. summa cum laude, U. Minn., 1963; PhD in Econs., MIT, 1967. Labor economist U.S. Bur. Labor Stats., Washington, 1967-68; lectr. U. Md., College Park, 1968; asst. to v.p. state rels. and planning U. Mich., Ann Arbor, 1968-70, various tchr. positions, 1968-85, co-rsch. dir. Inst. Labor and Indsl. Rels., 1973-80, dir. Inst. Labor and Indsl. Rels., 1980-93; cons. Corp. Pub. Broadcasting, 1994-97; lectr. indsl. rels. ctr. U. Minn., 1994-96; pres. Employment Rsch. Corp., Ann Arbor, 1997—. Project dir. various projects, Washington, 1968—92; expert witness discrimination and econ. loss various clients, 1982—; cons. Mich. Senate Fiscal Agy., Lansing, 1988, U.S. Dept. Labor, 1995—2001, EEOC, 1996—. Co-author: A Micro Model of Labor Supply, 1970, Global Skill Shortages, 2002; author: Labor Shortages: As Am. Approaches the 21st Century, 1995; contbr. articles to profl. jour. Mem.: Internat. Indsl. Rels. Assn., Labor and Employment Rels. Assn., Nat. Assn. Forensic Economists. Avocations: jogging, genealogy. Office: Employment Rsch Corp Ste 250 3820 Packard Rd Ann Arbor MI 48108-3348 Office Phone: 734-477-9040. Business E-Mail: malco@umich.edu. E-mail: mc@employmentresearch.com.

COHEN, MARLENE LOIS, pharmacologist; b. New Haven, May 5, 1945; d. Abraham David and Jeanette (Bader) C.; m. Jerome H. Fleisch, Aug. 8, 1976; children: Abby F. Fleisch, Sheryl B. Fleisch. BS, U. Conn., 1968; PhD, U. Calif., San Francisco, 1973. Registered pharmacist, Calif., Conn. Postdoctoral fellow Roche Inst. of Molecular Biology, Nutley, NJ, 1973-75; sr. pharmacologist Eli Lilly & Co., Indpls., 1975-80, rsch. scientist, 1980-85, sr. rsch. scientist, 1985-89, rsch. advisor, 1989-94, disting. rsch. fellow, 1994—2002; co-founder Creative Pharmacol. Solutions LLC, Carmel, Ind., 2002—. Adj. asst. prof. dept. pharmacology and toxicology Ind. U. Sch. Medicine, Indpls., 1976-82, adj. assoc. prof., 1982-86, adj. prof., 1987—; rsch. asst. Pfizer Labs., Groton, Conn., 1967; cons. Drug Dependence Inst., Yale U., New Haven, 1974. Mem. editl. bd. Jour. Clin. and Exptl. Hypertension, 1978—99, Procs. of the Soc. for Exptl. Biology and Medicine, 1979-84, Life Sci., 1984—, Jour. Pharmacology and Exptl. Therapeutics, 1987-2006, Current Drugs: Serotonin 1992-2000, Current Topics in Pharmacology, 1994-2000; mem. Molecular Interventions Adv. Bd., 1999-2005; ad hoc reviewer for profl. jours.; author: (with others) Principles of Medicinal Chemistry, 1974, 3d edit., 1989, New Antihypertensive Drugs, 1976, The Serotonin Receptors, 1988, The Peripheral Actions of 5-Hydroxytryptamine, 1989, Central and Peripheral 5-HT3 Receptors, 1992; contbr. articles to profl. jours. Recipient Disting. Alumni award, U. Conn. Sch. Pharmacy, 2002. Mem. Soc. for Exptl. Biology and Medicine, Am. Soc. for Pharmacology and Exptl. Therapeutics (chair subcom. on women in pharmacology 1984-89, chairperson nominating com. 1984, com. on profl. affairs 1984-89, membership com. 1989-92, bd. publs. trustees 1989—95, pres. 2001), Serotonin Club (councilor 1987-90, nomenclature com. 1988—2000), Alpha Lambda Delta, Phi Kappa Phi, Rho Chi. Office: Creative Pharmacol Solutions LLC 10532 Coppergate Ste 101 Carmel IN 46032 Office Phone: 317-571-9878. Personal E-mail: marlenelcohen@aol.com.

COHEN, MARYJO R., manufacturing executive; BS in Bus. Adminstrn., U. Mich., 1973, JD, 1976. Bar: Mich. 1976. Assoc. resident counsel Nat. Presto Industries, 1976-82, asst. to treas., 1982-83, treas., 1983-86, v.p., 1986-89, pres., 1989—, CEO, 1995—, COO, CFO. V.p. subsidiaries and divsns. Canton Sales & Storage Co., Century Leasing & Liquidating, Inc., Jackson Sales and Storage Co., Nat. Def. Corp., Nat. Holding Investment Co., Presto Export Ltd., Presto Mfg. Co., Presto Products Mfg. Co. Office: Nat Presto Industries 3925 N Hastings Way Eau Claire WI 54703

COHEN, MELANIE ROVNER, lawyer; b. Chgo., Aug. 9, 1944; d. Millard Jack and Sheila (Fox) Rovner; m. Arthur Wieber Cohen, Feb. 17, 1968; children: Mitchell Jay, Stephanie Tomasky, Jennifer Sue, Jason Canel. AB, Brandeis U., 1965; JD, DePaul U., 1977. Bar: Ill. 1977, U.S. Dist. Ct. (no. dist.) Ill., US Ct. Appeals (7th cir.), US Supreme Ct. 1998. Law clk. to Justice F.J. Hertz U.S. Bankruptcy Ct., 1976-77; ptnr. Antonow & Fink, Chgo., 1977-89, Altheimer & Gray, Chgo., 1989—2003, Quarles & Brady, Chgo., 2003—08; mediator/arbitrator ADR Sys. Mem. Supreme Ct. Ill. Atty. Registration and Disciplinary Commn. Inquiry Bd., 1982-86, Hearing Bd., 1986-94; instr. secured and consumer transactions creditor-debtor law DePaul U., Chgo., 1980-90, 1994-96; instr. real estate and bankruptcy law John Marshall Law Sch. LLM program, Chgo., 1996-98, 2004-06; bd. dir. Bankruptcy Arbitration and Mediation Svcs. Contbr. articles to profl. jours. Panelist, spkr., bd. dir., v.p. Brandeis U.

Nat. Alumni Assn., 1981-90; life mem. Brandeis Nat. Women's Com., 1975—, pres. Chgo. chpt., 1975-82; mem. Glencoe (Ill.) Caucus, 1977-80; chair lawyers com. Ravinia Festival, 1990-91, chmn. sustaining com., 1991, mem. annual fund, 1991—. Fellow, Brandeis U. Fellow: Am. Coll. Bankruptcy; mem.: ABA (co-chair com. on enforcement of creditors' rights and bankruptcy), Leading Lawyer's Network, Internat. Women's Insolvency and Restructuring Confederation, Internat. Fedn. Insolvency Profls., Internat. Insolvency Inst., Turnaround Mgmt. Assn. (pres. Chgo./midwest chpt. 1990—92, internat. bd. dirs. 1990—2004, mem. mgmt. com. 1995—2003, pres. internat. bd. dirs. 1999—2000, chmn. internat. bd. dirs. 2000—01, Leading Lawyer 2004—), Comml. Fin. Assn. Edn. Found. (bd. govs.), Ill. Trial Lawyers Assn., Comml. Law League, Chgo. Bar Assn. (chmn. bankruptcy reorgn. com. 1983—85, Super Lawyer 2005—), Ill. State Bar Assn. Home: 167 Park Ave Glencoe IL 60022-1351 Office: Quarles & Brady 500 W Madison Ave Ste 3700 Chicago IL 60661 Office Phone: 312-715-5050, 847-242-9075. Personal E-mail: melaniecohen@comcast.net. Business E-Mail: mcohen@quarles.com.

COHEN, MELVIN SAMUEL, manufacturing executive; b. Mpls., Jan. 16, 1918; s. Henry and Mary (Witebsky); m. Eileen Phillips; children: Amy, Maryjo. BS, U. Minn., 1939, JD, 1941. Bar: Minn. 1941, U.S. Supreme Ct. 1944. Pvt. practice, Mpls., until 1942; with legal div., rationing sect. Office Price Adminstrn., Washington, 1942-43; pub. counsel Civil Aero. Bd., Washington, 1943-44; with Nat. Presto Industries, Inc., Eau Claire, Wis., 1944—, treas., 1950-51, v.p. adminstrn., treas., 1951-54, exec. v.p., 1954-60, pres., 1960-75, chmn. bd., 1975—. Chmn. bd. dirs., pres., dir. Nat. Holding Investment Co., Jackson (Miss.) Sales & Storage Co., Presto Mfg. Co., chmn. bd., pres., dir., Nat. Presto Industries Export Corp., Eau Claire, Presto Internat. Ltd., Hong Kong; pres., dir. Presto Products Mfg. Co., Canton Sales and Storage Co.; v.p., dir. Nat. Pipeline Co., Cleve. Nat. Automatic Pipeline Ops., Inc., Escanaba, Mich.; bd. dirs. 1st Nat. Bank, Eau Claire; mem. industry adv. com. for aluminum industry and internat. combustion engine industry during Korean War for Nat. Prodn. Authority. Editor Minn. Law Rev., 1939-41. Office: Nat Presto Industries Inc 3925 N Hastings Way Eau Claire WI 54703-0485

COHEN, MORTON A., venture capitalist; b. Montreal, Can., Apr. 13, 1935; s. Lillian (Bloom) C.; m. Rosalie Cohen, June 5, 1960; children: Carl, Joanne, Margaret. AB, Concordia U., Montreal, 1957; MBA, U. Pa., 1959. Salesman, analyst Merrill Lynch, Montreal, 1960-65, Baker Weeks, Montreal, 1965-70, Kippen & Co., Montreal, 1970-72; pres. Yorkton Securities, Montreal, 1972-77, MAC Mgmt. Assocs., Montreal, 1977-80, Bel-Fran Investments, Toronto, Ont., Can., 1980-82; chmn., chief exec. officer Clarion Capital Corp., Cleve., 1982—, First City Technology Ventures, Cleve., 1982—. Bd. dirs. Monitek, Hayward, Calif., Environ. Protection Sys., Inc., Atlanta, Abaxis, Inc., Sunnyvale, Calif., Small's Oilfield Svcs. Corp., Big Springs, Tex., Zemex Corp. Mem. Fin. Analysts Soc. Avocations: tennis, golf. Office: Cohesant Technologies Inc 5845 W 82nd St Ste 102 Indianapolis IN 46278

COHEN, NORTON JACOB, lawyer; b. Detroit, Nov. 5, 1935; s. Norman and Molly Rose (Natinsky) Cohen; m. Lorelei Freda Schuman, June 16, 1957 (dec. Jan. 1996); children: Debrah Anne, Sander Ivan. Student, U. Mich., 1953-55, U. Detroit, 1955-56; JD, Wayne State U., 1959. Bar: Mich. 1959, Tex. 1962, U.S. Dist. Ct. (ea. dist.) Mich. 1963, U.S. Ct. Appeals (6th cir.) 1966, U.S. Supreme Ct. 1970. Law clk. to presiding justice Mich. Supreme Ct., Lansing, 1959; assoc. Zwerdling, Miller, Klimist & Maurer, Detroit, 1963—68; legal dir. ACLU of Mich., Detroit, 1968—69; sr. dir. Miller, Cohen, Martens, Ice & Geary, P.C., Southfield, Mich., 1971—97, Miller Cohen, P.L.C., Detroit, 1997—. Mem. exec. bd. Met. Detroit ACLU, 1969—93, chmn., 1972—74; vice chair Equal Justice Coun., Detroit, 1970—74; spl. counsel workers compensation Mich. AFL-CIO, 1983—86; mem. dir.'s adv. coun. Workers Compensation Bur. Mich. Dept. Labor, 1986—99; chmn. Southfield Dem. Party, Mich., 1965—67; co-chair Robert F. Kennedy for Pres., Oakland County, Mich., 1968; mem. B'nai B'rith, Am. Jewish Com. Served to capt. JAGC US Army, 1960—63. Decorated Army Commendation medal; named to Mich. Worker's Compensation Hall of Fame, 2000; recipient Spirit of Detroit award, Detroit Common Coun., 1982. Fellow: Coll. Workers' Compensation Lawyers; mem.: ABA (labor co-chair workers compensation com. sect. labor & employment law 1989—96, 2005—), Fed. Bar Assn. Jewish. Office: Miller Cohen PLC 600 W Lafayette Blvd Fl 4 Detroit MI 48226-3125 Home Phone: 248-626-9133; Office Phone: 313-964-4454. Business E-Mail: yourlawyers@millercohen.com.

COHEN, RAYMOND, retired mechanical engineer, educator; b. St. Louis, Nov. 30, 1923; s. Benjamin and Leah (Lewis) C.; m. Katherine Elise Silverman, Feb. 1, 1948 (dec. May 1985); children: Richard Samuel, Deborah Elise, Barbara Beth; m. Lila Lakin Cagen, Nov. 30, 1986. BS, Purdue U., 1947, MS, 1950, PhD, 1955. Profl. engr., Ind., 1955. Instr. mech. engring. Purdue U., 1948-55, asst. prof., 1955-58, assoc. prof., 1958-60, prof., 1960-98, asst. dir. Ray W. Herrick Labs., 1970-71, dir., 1971-93, acting head Sch. Mech. Engring., 1988-89, Herrick prof. engring., 1994-99, Herrick prof. emeritus engring., 1999—. Cons. to industry. Departmental editor: Ency. Brit., 1957-62; editorial bd. Jour. Sound and Vibration, 1971-87; editor Internat. Jour. of Heating, Ventilating, Air Conditioning and Refrigerating Rsch., 1994-98. Served as sgt. inf. AUS, 1943-46. Recipient Kamerlingh Onnes gold medal, 1995; NATO sr. fellow in sci., 1971 Fellow ASME, ASHRAE; mem. NSPE, Am. Soc. Engring. Edn., Soc. Exptl. Mechanics, Internat. Inst. Refrigeration (chmn. U.S. nat. com. 1992-95, U.S. del. 1992-99, Merit medal 2003), Acoustical Soc. Am., Inst. Noise Control Engring. (pres. 1990), Sigma Xi, Pi Tau Sigma, Tau Beta Pi. Home: 2501 Spyglass Dr Valparaiso IN 46383 Office: Purdue U Ray W Herrick Labs 140 S Intramural Dr West Lafayette IN 47907-2031 Personal E-mail: rcohen81@comcast.net.

COHEN, RICHARD J., state legislator; b. Oct. 5, 1949; BA, Northwestern U.; JD, William Mitchell Coll. Law. Mem. Minn. Ho. of Reps., St. Paul, 1977-78, 1983-86, Minn. Senate from 64th dist., St. Paul, 1986—; atty., 1996—. Chmn. State Govt. Divsn. Fin. Com.; mem. Crime Prevention com., Ethics & Campaign Reform & Judiciary coms. Office: 517 Capitol Bldg 75 Constitution Ave Saint Paul MN 55155-1601 also: State Senate State Capital Building Saint Paul MN 55155-0001

COHEN, RONALD S., accountant; b. Lafayette, Ind., July 13, 1937; s. William and Stella (Fleischman) C.; m. Nancy Ann Plotkin, May 29, 1960; children: Philip, Douglas. BS in Acctg., Ind. U., 1958. CPA Ind. Staff acct. Crowe, Chizek & Co., South Bend, Ind., 1958—65, ptnr., 1965—2003, mng. ptnr., 1982—94, chmn. bd. dirs., 1994—2000. Chmn. Horwath Internat., 1999—; mem. dean's adv. coun. Ind. U. Sch. Bus., 1996—. Commr. Housing Authority of South Bend, 1976-85, also vice-chmn.; pres. Jewish Fedn., 1979-82; bd. dirs. United Way of South Bend, 1987-90. Served to lt. USAR, 1958-66. Mem. AICPA (bd. dirs. 1990-97, vice-chmn. 1994, chmn. 1995), Ind. Soc. CPAs, Ind. U. Sch. Bus. Alumni Assn. (bd. dirs. 1992-95). Democrat. Jewish. Office: Crowe Chizek & Co PO Box 7 330 E Jefferson Blvd South Bend IN 46601-2366 Office Phone: 574-236-8677. E-mail: rcohen@crowechizek.com.

COHEN, SANFORD NED, pediatrician, educator, academic administrator; b. NYC, June 12, 1935; s. George M. and Fannie Leah (Epstein) Cohen; m. Judith Luskind, June 22, 1958 (div. 1984); m. Sandra Hoffman, June 13, 1992. AB, Johns Hopkins U., Balt., 1956, MD, 1960. Diplomate Am. Bd. Pediatrics. Intern in pediat. Johns Hopkins Hosp., 1960-61, resident, 1961-63; from instr. to assoc. prof. NYU Sch. Medicine, NYC, 1965-74; chmn., prof. pediat. Wayne State U. Sch. Medicine, Detroit, 1974-81, prof. pediat., 1991-98, prof. emeritus, 1998—, dir. Child Rsch. Ctr., 1975—81, assoc. dean, 1981-86, dir. Devel. Disability Inst., 1983—86, sr. v.p. acad. affairs, provost, 1986-91. Pediatrician-in-chief Children's Hosp. Mich., Detroit, 1974—81; adj. faculty U. Mich. Sch. Pub. Health, Ann Arbor, 1980—90; chair steering com. NIH Network Pediat. Pharmacology Rsch. Units, 1994—98, mem. adv. com., 1999—2002; reviewer Inst. Medicine Nat. Acad. Sci.; mem. profl. adv. coun. Children's Med. Rsch. Inst., Oklahoma City, 1999—; vol. cons. Lee Meml. Health Sys., Ft. Myers, Fla., 2000—; mem. adv. bd. Children's Hosp. S.W. Fla., 2003—; chmn. adv. com. to dean Fla. Gulf Coast U., 2006—. Editor: Progress in Drug Therapy in Children, 1981; contbr. articles to profl. jours. Mem. bd. health, Leonia, NJ, 1972—74; mem. Bd. Police Commrs., Detroit, 1995—99, chmn., 1997—98; co-pres. Temple Judea, 2004—. John and Mary R. Markle scholar acad. medicine, 1968—74. Mem.: Soc. Pediat. Rsch. (v.p. 1980—81), Sr. and Ret. Physicians Assn. (pres. 2001—06), Midwest Soc. Pediat. Rsch. (pres. 1979—80), Am. Pediat. Soc. Avocations: reading, golf. Office: Children's Hosp Mich 3901 Beaubien St Detroit MI 48201-2119 Office Phone: 313-745-5214. Business E-Mail: scohen@med.wayne.edu.

COHEN, TED, philosopher, educator; b. Danville, Ill., Dec. 13, 1939; s. Sam and Shirley E. Cohen; m. Julie Simon, Apr. 18, 1940 (div. 1992); children: Shoshannah, Amos; m. Ann Rutherfurd Collier Austin, 1994. AB, U. Chgo., 1962; MA, Harvard U., 1965, PhD, 1972. Prof. philosophy U. Chgo., 1967—, chmn. dept. philosophy, 1974-79. Author: Jokes, 1999, Korean transl., 2002, Dutch transl., 2005; editor: Essays in Kant's Aesthetics, 1982, Pursuits of Reason, 1993; contbr. articles to profl. jours. Bd. dirs. Ctr. Rehab. and Tng. Disabled, B'nai Brith Hillel Found. of U. Chgo., KAM Isaiah Israel Congregation, Chgo., 1980—, mem. faculty religious sch.; chmn. com. gen. studies humanities U. Chgo., 1991—. Named William R. Kenan Jr. Disting. Prof. Humanities, Coll. William and Mary, 1986—87; grantee, Am. Coun. Learned Socs., 1980, 1985. Mem.: Am. Philos. Assn. (v.p. 2005, pres.-elect 2005), Am. Soc. Aesthetics (pres. 1997—), Phi Beta Kappa (vis. scholar 2000—01). Avocation: baseball theory and practice. Office: U Chgo Dept Philosophy 1050 E 59th St Chicago IL 60637-1559 Home: 5816 S Blackstone Ave Chicago IL 60637 Home Phone: 773-288-4694; Office Phone: 773-702-8506. Business E-Mail: tedcohen@midway.uchicago.edu.

COHLER, BERTRAM JOSEPH, psychologist, educator; b. Chgo., Dec. 3, 1938; s. Jonas Robert and Betty (Cahn) C.; m. Anne Meyers, June 11, 1962 (dec. Dec. 1989); children: Jonathan Richard, James Joseph. BA, U. Chgo., 1961; PhD, Harvard U., 1967; cert. in adult analysis, Inst. Psychoanalysis, 1989. Diplomate Am. Bd. Psychoanalysis, Am. Bd. Examiners in Profl. Psychology. Lectr. social relations Harvard U., Cambridge, Mass., 1967-69; assoc. dir. Sonia Shankman Orthogenic Sch., 1969-72, 94-96; dir. Orthogenic Sch. U. Chgo., 1969-72, 94—; asst. prof. U. Chgo., 1969—75, assoc. prof., 1975—81, William Rainey Harper dept. chair, 1977—, prof. depts. psychology, edn. and psychiatry, 1981—. Co-dir. Univ. Ctr. Health anf Aging Soc., 1987—; sci. and profl. staff dept. psychiatry Michael Reese Hosp., Chgo., 1980-90; cons. The Tresholds, Chgo., 1972-81, Inst. Psychoanalysis, Chgo., 1972—, Ill. State Psychiat. Inst., Chgo., 1977-82; pres. bd. Ctr. Religion and Psychotherapy, Chgo. Author (with H. Grunebaum et al.): Mentally Ill Mothers and Their Children, 1975, 1982, Mothers, Grandmothers and Daughters, 1981; author: (with others) Parenthood as an Adult Experience, 1983, The Invulnerable Child, 1987, Handbook of Clinical Research on Adolescence, 1993; author: (with R. Galatzer-Levy) The Essential Other, 1993; author: The Course of Gay and Lesbian Lives, 2000; author: (with R. Galatzer-Levy) The Psychoanalytic Study of Lives Over Time, 1999; author: (with others) Rethinking Psychoanalysis and the Homosexualities, 2002; author: Writing Desire, 2007. Bd. dirs. Horizons Cmty. Svcs., Chgo.; mem. initial rev. group in aging NIMH, Washington, 1982—86, Mental Health Spl. Projects, 1988—2003. Recipient Quantrell prize for disting. tchg. U. Chgo., 1975, 99, Lily Gondor award Postgrad. Ctr. for Mental Health, 2000, Henry A. Murray award APA and Soc. for Personology, 2006; fellow Inst. Medicine, 1975. Fellow Gerontol. Soc., Soc. Projective Techniques Am. Orthopsychiat. Assn. (bd. dirs. 1981-84, pres. elect 1991, pres. 1992), Am. Psychol. Assn. (chmn. profl. affairs com. divsn. 39 1981-83, editor Psychoanalytic Psychology 1987-97, Fund for Sci. reserved Science Advisor, 2007-, pres. sect. II 1992); mem. Am. Sociol. Assn., Am. Anthrop. Assn., Am. Assn. Psychiat. Svcs. to Children (Alexander Gralnick award), Soc. Rsch. in Child Devel., Chgo. Assn. Psychoanalytic Psychology (pres. 1983-84), Am. Psychoanalytic Assn. Home: 5408 S Blackstone Ave Chicago IL 60615-5407 Office: U Chgo 5730 S Woodlawn Ave Chicago IL 60637-1603 Office Phone: 773-702-3574. Business E-Mail: bert@midway.uchicago.edu.

COHN, AVERN LEVIN, district judge; b. Detroit, July 23, 1924; s. Irwin I. and Sadie (Levin) C.; m. Joyce Hochman, Dec. 30, 1954 (dec. Dec. 1989); m. Lois Pincus Cohn, June 1992; children: Sheldon, Leslie Cohn Magy, Thomas. Student, John Tarleton Agrl. Coll., 1943, Stanford U., 1944; JD, U. Mich., 1949. Bar: Mich. 1949. Practiced in, Detroit, 1949-79; mem. firm Honigman Miller Schwartz & Cohn, Detroit, 1961-79; sr. judge U.S. Dist. Ct., 1979—. Mem. Mich. Civil Rights Commn., 1972-75, chmn., 1974-75; Mem. Detroit Bd. Police Commrs., 1975-79, chmn., 1979; bd. govs. Jewish Welfare Fedn., Detroit, 1972—. Served with AUS, 1943-46. Mem. ABA, Mich. Bar Assn., Am. Law Inst. Office Phone: 313-234-5160. E-mail: avern_cohn@mied.uscourts.gov.

COHN, EDWARD L., commissioner corrections department; BA in History, Polit. Sci., Culver-Stockton Coll., 1961; MA in Forensic Studies, Ind. U., 1977. From parole agent to commr. Gary (Ind.) Dept. Correction, 1965-1996; commr. Ind. Dept. Correction, Indpls., 1996—. Active Special Olympics Ind., Law Enforcement Torch Run, Optimist Club Plainfield (past pres.), Lake County Assn. Crime, Delinquency (past pres.), Govs. Council Impaired, Dangerous Driving, Advisory Resource Council Culver-Stockton Coll. Mem. A.S.C.A. (juvenile issues com., technol. com.), Nat. Inst. Justice Am. Correctional Assn. (Ind. chpt., past pres.), Criminal Justice Inst. (bd. trustees), Assn. State Correctional Adminstrs., Correctional Accreditation Mgrs. Assn., Law Enforcement Tech. Advisory Council, Fraternal Order Police. Office: Indiana Dept of Correction E334 Ind Govt Ctr South 302 W Washington St Indianapolis IN 46204-4701

COHN, GERALD B., federal judge; b. 1939; BA, Ill. Coll., 1961; JD, U. Chgo., 1964. Magistrate judge Ill. So. Dist., East St. Louis, 1981—. Served with U.S. Army, 1965-67, Res., 1967-71. Office: US Courthouse 750 Missouri Ave East Saint Louis IL 62201-2954 E-mail: gcohn@aol.com.

COHOON, DENNIS, state representative; b. DesMoines, Mar. 29, 1953; Student, Southeastern C.C., 1974; BA, Iowa Wesleyan Coll., 1977; postgrad., U. Iowa. Spl. edn. tchr. Burlington Cmty. H.S.; mem. Iowa Ho. Reps., DesMoines, 1987—, ranking mem. capitals appropriations com., mem. various coms. including econ. devel., edn., transp. Active DesMoines County Dist. Ctrl. Com., Oak St. Bapt. Ch. With U.S. Army Nat. Guard. Mem.: Burlington Edn. Assn., Geode Edn. Assn., Iowa State Edn. Assn. Democrat. Office: State Capitol East 12th and Grand Des Moines IA 50319 also: 816 Randall Ln Burlington IA 52601

COLANDER, PATRICIA MARIE, newspaper editor; b. Chgo., Oct. 25, 1952; d. Charles L. Colander and Mary Elizabeth Connors; m. Paul Michael Ansell, Aug. 18, 1980 (div. Jan. 1993); children: Charles Thomas, Ida Kay Ansell; m. Jeffery A. Kumorek, Dec. 12, 1997. BJ, U. Ill., 1973. Staff writer Chgo. Tribune, 1973-77, Chgo. Reader, 1977-81; adj. prof. Medill Sch. Journalism Northwestern U., 1982-87; editor Copley Newspapers, Chgo. suburbs, No. Ill., 1987-92; asst. mng. editor The Times, 1992-93, pub. Ill. edits., 1993-96, mng. editor Munster, Ind., 1996—. Exec. devel. program Am. Press Inst., Reston, Va., 1994. Author: Thin Air: The Life and Mysterious Disappearance of Helen Brach, 1982, Hugh Hefner's First Funeral and Other True Tales of Love and Death in Chicago, 1985. Recipient awards AP, 1987, 88, 89, Suburban Newspapers Am., 1988. Mem. Inland Press Assn. (award 1991), Hoosier State Press, Tavern Club Chgo. Office: The Times 601 45th Ave Munster IN 46321-2819

COLANGELO, CARMON, artist, printmaker, educator; b. Toronto, Oct. 29, 1957; came to U.S., 1981; s. Patrick and Coreen (Ciciretto) C.; m. Susan Jane Berry, Oct. 6, 1984; children: Jessica Lynn, Ashley Coreen, Chelsea Michelle. BFA in printmaking & painting, U. Windsor, Ontario, Can., 1981; MFA in printmaking, La. State U., 1983. Instr. La. State U., Baton Rouge, 1984; asst. prof. art W.Va. U., Morgantown, 1984—88, grad. coord., 1986—99, assoc. prof., 1988—94, dir. grad. studies in art, 1989—2006, assoc. chair div. art, 1993, chair, prof. art, 1993—97; dir., prof. art Lamar Dodd Sch. Art, U. Ga., Athens, 1997—2006; disting. rsch. prof. U. Ga., Athens, 2003—06; dean, Sam Fox Sch. Design and Visual Arts Washington U., St. Louis, 2006—, Desmond Lee prof. collaboration in arts, 2006—. Founding dir. Ideas for Creative Exploration, U. Ga. Exhibited prints in shows U.S.-Korea Internat., 1989, Boston Printmakers 42d, 1990, Silvermine Internat., 1992, New World Contemporary Prints, Balt., 1993; solo exhbns.: Re-tracings, John and Jane Allcott Gallery, U. Chapel Hill, NC, 2001, Street Gallery, Liverpool Contemporary Biennial, Eng., Fountain of Age, Sandler-Hudson Gallery, Atlanta, 2002, Phantasmasoria, Scuola Internat. di Grafica, Venice, Italy, 2003, Laura Mesaros Gallery, W.Va., 2004, Phantasmasoria, Maseo de Pueblos, Guanajuato, Mex., 2004, Bruno David Gallery, St. Louis, 2006, 07; represented in collections Nat. Mus. Am. Art, Wash. DC, Whitney Mus. of Am. Art, Fla. State Art Mus., Musco Nat. del Grabado, Buenos Aires, Kennedy Mus. Art, Butler Mus. Am. Art, Fogg Art Mus., Bibliotechue Internat. Recipient Clemson Nat. award, 1993, 65th Nat. SAGA Purchase award, NY, 1993; featured in Printmaking: A Primary Form of Expression, 1992, Sr. Rsch. Fine Arts grant, U. Ga., 1998; named Disting. Rsch. prof., U. Ga., 2003, Deem Disting. lectr. W.Va. U., 2004. Mem. Boston Printmakers, L.A. Printmaking Soc., Phila. Print Club, Mo. Print Consortium, Coll. Art Assn, Coll. Art Assn. (bd. mem.), Nat. Coll. Art Adminstrs., Ga. Mus. Art (bd. mem.), So. Graphics Coun. (bd. mem., 1995-1997), Art Papers (bd. mem, 1998). Avocation: sports. Office: Wash Univ St Louis Campus Box 1213 One Brookings Dr Saint Louis MO 63160-4899 Office Phone: 314-935-9300. Business E-Mail: colangelo@wustl.edu.

COLBERT, VIRGIS W., food products executive; b. Jackson, Miss., Oct. 13, 1939; m. Angela Colbert; three children. BS in Indsl. Mgmt., Ctrl. Mich. U. Mfg. gen. supt. Chrysler Corp.; asst. to plant mgr. Miller Brewing Co., Reidsville, NC, 1979-80, prodn. mgr. Ft. Worth, 1980-81, profn. mgr. Milw., 1981, plant mgr., 1981-87, asst. dir. can mfg., 1987-88, dir. can. mfg., 1988, dir. container and support mfg., 1988-89, v.p. materials mfg., 1989-90, v.p. plant ops., 1990-93, sr. v.p. ops., 1993-95, sr. v.p. worldwide ops., 1995-97, exec. v.p., 1997—, also bd. dirs. and exec. com. Bd. dirs. Manitowoc Co., The Stanley Works, Sara Lee Corp., Merrill Lynch Co. Past chmn. bd. Thurgood Marshall Scholarship Fund; past chmn. bd. trustees Fisk U., Nashville; bd. dirs. Bradley Sports and Entertainment Corp. Ctr., Greater Milw. Open; exec. adv. com. Nat. Urban League's Black Exec. Exch. Program. Recipient various awards Jarvis Christian Coll., Tyler, Tex., So. U., New Orleans, N.C. AT&T, Greensboro, Clark Coll., Atlanta, Grambling (La.) State Coll., Fla. Meml. Coll., Miami, U. .C., Greensboro, Young Program of Nat. Alliance Bus., Svc. award Nat. Urban Leage, Trumpet award Turner Broadcasting Sys., 1996, Exec. Leadership Coun. Achievement award, 1998; named Harlem YMCA Black Achiever, Milw. YMCA Black Achiever, Phi Beta Sigma Fraternity Black Achiever, one of 50 Top Black Execs. in Corp. Am., Ebony Mag., 1992, one of 24 To Watch in '94, Ebony Mag., 1994, one of 12 Most Powerful Blacks in Corp. Am., Ebony Mag., 1998, one of Am.'s 40 Most Powerful Black Execs., Black Enterprise Mag., 1993, One of 50 Top Black Execs. in Corp. Am., Black Enterprise Mag., 2000, Beverage Exec. of Yr., Beverage Industry Mag., 2001, One of 50 Most Powerful Balck Execs. in Am., Fortune Mag., 2002, One of 75 Most Powerful African Ams. in Corp. Am., Black Enterprise Mag., 2005; inductee Scott H.S. Hall of Fame, Toledo, 1987. Mem. NAACP (life, Svc. award), 100 Black Men of Am. (hon.), Omega Psi Phi. Office: Miller Brewing Co 3939 W Highland Blvd Milwaukee WI 53201 Office Phone: 414-931-3823.

COLBY, JOY HAKANSON, critic; b. Detroit; d. Alva Hilliard and Eleanor (Radtke) Hakanson; m. Raymond L. Colby, Apr. 11, 1953; children: Sarah, Katherine, Lisa. Student, Detroit Soc. Arts and Crafts, 1945; BFA, Wayne State U., 1946; DFA (hon.), Coll. for Creative Studies, 1998. Art critic Detroit News, 1947—; originator exhibit Arts and Crafts in Detroit, 1906-1976; with Detroit Inst. Arts, 1976. Author: (book) Art and A City, 1956; contbr. articles to art periodicals. Mem. visual arts adv. panel Mich. Coun. Arts, 1974—79; mayor's appointment Detroit Coun. for the Arts, 1974; mem. Bloomfield Hills Arts Coun., 1974. Recipient Alumni award, Wayne State U., 1967, Art Achievement award, 1983, Headliner award, 1984, award arts reporting, Detroit Press Club, 1984, Art Leadership award, Coll. for Creative Studies, 1989. Office: 615 W Lafayette Blvd Detroit MI 48226-3124 Home Phone: 248-642-4542; Office Phone: 313-222-2276. Business E-Mail: jcolby@detnews.com.

COLE, DAVID EDWARD, automotive executive, educator; b. Detroit, July 20, 1937; s. Edward Nicholas and Esther Helen (Engman) C.; m. Carol Hutchins, July 9, 1965; children: Scott David, Christopher Carl. BS in Mech. Engring. and Math., U. Mich., 1960, MS in Mech. Engring., 1961, PhD, 1966. Engr. GM, Detroit, 1960—65; prof. U. Mich., Ann Arbor, 1967—, dir. Office for Study of Automotive Transp., 1978—2000; entrepreneur 6 cos., 1975—95; pres. Ctr. Auto Rsch. and Mgmt., ptnr. The Altarum Inst. Mich, 2000—03; chmn. Ctr. for Automotve Rsch. (ind. not for profit), 2003—. Bd. dirs. MSX Internat., Detroit, Saturn Electronics, Aurburn Hills, Mich., Plastech, Dearborn, R.L. Polk, Southfield, Mich., Campfire Interactive, Ann Arbor, Mich., Mich. Econ. Devel. Corp., Lansing, Mich. Ctr. Automotive Rsch., Ann Arbor, Strategic Econ. Investment & Commercialization Orgn., Denso Corp., Charitable Found., Mich. Renewable Fuels Commn., U. Mich. Energy Rsch. Coun.; mem. energy engring. bd. NRC, 1989-94; select panel U.S.-Can. Free trade Pact, 1988-91; co-chair Detroit Rennaisance Mobility Com. Author: Elementary Vehicle Dynamics, 1972; contbr. articles to profl. jours. Bd. trustees Hope Coll., 1994—2006; mem. Mich. Renewable Fuels Commn.; former bd. dirs. Automotive Hall of Fame, Dearborn. Fellow Soc. Automotive Engrs. (dir. 1980-83, 85-88, Teetor award 1969), Engring. Soc. Detroit (Horace H. Rackham medal 2000); mem. Chevalier of the Nat. Order of Merit from France, 1999, Soc. Mktg. Execs. (Mktg. Educator of Yr. 1998, Rene Dubos Environ. award 1998), Nat. Auto Dealers Assn. Found. (Freedom of Mobility award 1993), Swedens Royal Order of the Polar Star. Republican. Presbyterian. Avocations: hunting, fishing, boating, running, golf. Office: Ctr Auto Rsch 1000 Victors Way Ste 200 Ann Arbor MI 48108 Home Phone: 734-665-7990. E-mail: dcole@cargrop.org.

COLE, ELSA KIRCHER, lawyer; b. Dec. 5, 1949; d. Paul and Hester Marie (Pellegrom) Kircher; m. Roland J. Cole, Aug. 16, 1975; children: Isabel Ashley, Madeline Aldis. AB in History with distinction, Stanford U., 1971; JD, Boston U., 1974. Bar: Wash. 1974, U.S. Supreme Ct. 1980, Mich. 1989, Kans. 1997, Ind. 1999. Asst. atty gen., rep. dept. motor vehicles State of Wash., Seattle, 1974-75, asst. atty. gen., rep. dept. social and health svcs., 1975-76, asst. atty. gen., rep. U. Wash., 1976-89; gen. counsel U. Mich., Ann Arbor, 1989-97, NCAA, Indpls., 1997—. Presenter ednl. issues various confs. and workshops. Contbr. articles to profl. jours. Fellow: Nat. Assn. Coll. and Univs. Attys. (mem. nominations com., mem. site selection com. 1987—88, co-chair student affairs sect. 1987—88, program 1988—89, mem. fin. com., articles com., by-laws com. 1988—89, co-chair student affairs sect. 1988—89, bd. dirs. 1988—91, program 1989—90, chair profl. devel. com. 1990—91, program 1991—92, honors and awards, ethics com. 1991—92, program 1992—93, bd. ops. 1992—93, mem. nominations com., mem. site selection com. 1995—96, CLE com. 1995—96, program 1995—96, CLE com. 1996—97, pub. com. 1996—97, CLE com. 2000—02, honors and awards com. 2002—03, named NACUA fellow 1998); mem.: Nat. Sports Law Inst. (bd. advisors 2001—), Sports Lawyers Assn. (bd. dirs. 2001—), Indpls. Bar Assn. (sports and entertainment sect. bd. dirs. 2001—), Seattle-King County Bar Assn., Wash. Women Lawyers (pres. Seattle-King County chpt. 1986, state chair candidate endorsement com. 1987, v.p. membership, state bd. dirs. 1987—88, state chair candidate endorsement com. 1988), Wash. State Bar Assn. (chair law sch. liaison com. 1988—89). Office: Ncaa Travel Serivce 111 Water St New Haven CT 06511-5759 E-mail: ecole@ncaa.org.

COLE, KENNETH DUANE, architect; b. Ft. Wayne, Ind., Jan. 23, 1932; s. Wolford J. and Helen Francis (McDowell) Cole; m. Carolyn Lou Meyer, Apr. 25, 1953; children: David Brent, Denelle Hope, Diana Faith, Dawn Love. Student, Ft. Wayne Art Inst., 1950-51; BS in Architecture, U. Cin., 1957. Draftsman/intern Humbrecht Assocs., Ft. Wayne, 1957-58; ptnr., arch. Cole-Matott, Archs./Planners, Ft. Wayne, 1959-94, Cole & Cole Archs., Ft. Wayne, 1995—. Mem. adv. bd. Gen. Svcs. Adminstrn., Region 5, 1976, 78. Prin. works include Weisser Pk. Jr. HS, 1963, Brandt Hall, 1965, Bonsib Bldg., 1967, Lindley Elem. Sch., 1969, Young Elem. Sch., 1972, Study Elem. Sch., 1975, Old City Hall Renovation, 1978, Peoples Trust Bank Adminstrv. Svcs. Ctr., 1979, Cole Residence (Design award, 1988), Ossian Office Old 1st Nat. Bank, 1988, Perimeter Security Wall, Ind. State Prison. Bd. dirs. Ft. Wayne Art Inst., 1969—74, Izaak Walton League Am., Ft. Wayne, 1970—76, Arch, Inc., Ft. Wayne, 1975—77, Downtown Ft. Wayne Assn., 1977—82, Hist. Soc. Ft. Wayne and Allen County, 1982—88. Mem.: AIA (bd. dirs. o. INd. 1971—74, pres. 1974), Am. Arbitration Assn. (panel arbitrators 1980—96), Ft. Wayne Soc. Archs. (pres. 1970—71), Ind. Soc. Archs. (bd. dirs. 1973—76, sec. 1976, citation for remodeling Bonsib Bldg. 1978), Ft. Wayne C. of C. Lutheran. Home: 11602 Stellhorn Rd New Haven IN 46774-9775 Office: Cole And Cole Architects 10930 Stellhorn Rd New Haven IN 46774-9775 E-mail: kennethcole@grinsfelderarchitects.com.

COLE, KENNETH W., automotive executive; Grad., U. Tex., Austin; JD, U. Houston. Reg. dir. pub. govt. affairs Amoco Corp.; joined as v.p. pub. affairs Allied Corp., 1981; joined Washington office Allied Signal Inc., 1983, staff v.p. Washington office, 1985, v.p. govt. relations, 1988; v.p. govt. rels. GM Corp., 2001—, v.p. global public policy and govt. rels., 2007—, mem. automotive strategy bd., 2007—. Mem.: Nat. Assn. Bus. Polit. Action (past pres.), Business-Govt. Rels. Coun. (past pres.), Congl. Inst. (bd. dirs.), European Inst. (bd. dirs.),

Coun. Pub. Affairs Execs. (bd. dirs.), Pub. Affairs Coun. (bd. dirs.), Nat. Fgn. Trade Coun. (bd. dirs.), U.S. Capital Hist. Soc. (bd. dirs.), Wolf Trap Found. (bd. dirs.). Office: GM Corp 1660 L St NW Washington DC 20036 also: 300 Renaissance Ctr PO Box 300 Detroit MI 48265-3000

COLE, MONROE, neurologist, educator; b. NYC, Mar. 21, 1933; s. Harry and Sylvia (Firman) C.; m. Merritt Ellen Frindel, June 15, 1958; children: Elizabeth Anne, Victoria, Scott Frindel, Pamela Catherine. AB cum laude, Amherst Coll., 1953; MD magna cum laude, Georgetown U., 1957. Diplomate Am. Bd. Psychiatry and Neurology. Intern in medicine Seton Hall Coll. Medicine, Jersey City, 1957-58, asst. resident in medicine, 1958-59; asst. resident in neurology Mass. Gen. Hosp., Boston, 1959-60, rsch. fellow in neuropathology, 1960-61, rsch. fellow in neurology, 1961-62; teaching fellow in neurology Harvard U., Cambridge, Mass., 1959-60, 61-62, teaching fellow in neuropathology, 1960-61; clin. instr. in neurology Georgetown U., Washington, 1962-65; asst. prof. neurology, assoc. in anatomy Bowman Gray Sch. Medicine, Wake Forest U., Winston-Salem, N.C., 1965-69, assoc. prof., assoc. in anatomy, 1969-70; assoc. prof. neurology Case Western Res. U., Cleve., 1970, clin. assoc. prof., 1972—, assoc. prof., 1989-93, prof., 1993—2000; chief neurology Highland View Hosp., Cleve., 1970-72; neurologist U. Hosps. Cleve.; prof. emeritus Case Western Res. U., Cleve., 2000—. Contbr. chpts. and articles to med. publs. Served to capt. U.S. Army, 1962-65 Fellow ACP, Am. Acad. Neurology, AHA Stroke Coun.; mem. N.Y. Acad. Scis., Acad. of Aphasia, Assn. for Rsch. in Nervous and Mental Disease, Am. Assn. Neuropathologists (assoc.), Am. Neurol. Assn., Alpha Omega Alpha Office: Univ Hosps Cleve Dept Neurology 11100 Euclid Ave Cleveland OH 44106-1736 E-mail: mcole@nacs.net.

COLE, RANSEY GUY, JR., federal judge; b. Birmingham, Ala., May 23, 1951; s. Ransey Guy and Sarah Nell (Coker) Cole; m. Kathleine Kelley, Nov. 26, 1983; children: Justin Robert Jefferson, Jordan Paul, Alexandra Sarah. BA, Tufts U., 1972; JD, Yale U., 1975. Bar: Ohio 1975, D.C. 1982. Assoc. Vorys, Sater, Seymour and Pease, Columbus, Ohio, 1975—78, ptnr., 1980—86, 1993—95; trial atty. US Dept. Justice, Washington, 1978—80; judge US Bankruptcy Ct., Columbus, 1987—93, US Ct. Appeals (6th cir.), Cinn., 1995—. Bd. trustee March of Dimes, Ohio, 1985—88, YMCA, 1984—88, Neighborhood House, 1985—88, Columbus Area Internat. Prog., 1986—94, Children's Hospital, 1990—. Mem.: ABA, Columbus Bar Assn., Nat. Bar Assn. Office: US Courthouse 85 Marconi Blvd Rm 127 Columbus OH 43215-2823

COLE, THEODORE JOHN, osteopathic and naturopathic physician; b. Covington, Ky., May 30, 1953; s. John N. and Florence R. (Bruener) C.; m. Ellen Cole; children: Joren, Emily, Kevin, Aidan, Ronan. BA, Centre Coll., Danville, Ky., 1975; MA, Western Ky. U., 1978; DO, Ohio U., 1986. Diplomate Am. Osteo. Bd. Gen. Practice, Nat. Bd. Osteo. Examiners, Am. Naturopathic Med. Assn. Psychologist Comprehensive Mental Health Svcs., St. Petersburg, Fla., 1978-82; intern Detroit Osteo. Hosp., 1986-87; resident Doctors Hosp., Columbus, Ohio, 1987-88; pvt. practice, West Chester, Ohio, 1989—. Preceptor Ohio U. Coll. Osteo. Medicine, Athens, 1990—, U. Cin. Med. Sch., 1990—; dir. So. Ohio Coll. Nursing. Coach, Soccer Assn. for Youth, West Chester, 1989, 90, Liberty Sports Orgn., West Chester, 1990. Mem. Am. Osteo. Assn., Am. Assn. Osteopathy, Am. Coll. Gen. Practitioners, Am. Acad. Environ. Medicine, Am. Acad. Advancement of Medicine, Occidental Inst. Rsch. Found. Avocations: collecting art, hunting, camping, farming, tai chi. Office: The Cole Ctr for Healing/Cin Hyperbarics Ste 228 11974 Lebanon Rd Cincinnati OH 45241-1700 Home Phone: 513-373-0738; Office Phone: 513-563-4321. E-mail: tedcole@medscape.com.

COLE, THOMAS AMOR, lawyer; b. Phila., Nov. 2, 1948; s. George Lough and Elizabeth (Bush) C.; m. Carol L. Owen, Dec. 27, 1969 (div. 1979); children: Kirsten E., Lauren E.; m. Constance J. Ward, Nov. 17, 1979; children: Lindsay W., Emily C. BA with honors, Johns Hopkins U., 1972; JD with honors, U. Chgo., 1975. Bar: Ill. 1975, U.S. Dist. Ct. (no. dist.) Ill. 1975. Assoc. Sidley & Austin, Chgo., 1975-81; v.p. law Northwest Industries, Chgo., 1982-85; ptnr. Sidley & Austin, Chgo., 1981—, mgmt. com., 1988—, chair exec. com., 1998—2001, Sidley Austin Brown & Wood LLP, Chgo., 2001—06, Sidley Austin LLP, Chgo., 2006—. Adj. prof., U. Chgo. Law Sch.; chmn. exec. com. Northwestern U. Sch. Law, Garrett Corp., Securities Law Inst.; co-chair Tulane Corp. Law Inst.; bd. dirs. U. Chgo., Northwestern Meml. Hosp., Chgo. Coun. Global Affairs U. Chgo. Mem. ABA, Chgo. Bar Assn., Am. Law Inst., Chgo. Club, Econ. Club, Comml. Club, Law Club of Chgo., Order of Coif, Phi Beta Kappa. Democrat. Mem. Soc. Friends. Office: Sidley Austin LLP 1 S Dearborn St Chicago IL 60603-2000 Office Phone: 312-853-7473. Office Fax: 312-853-7036. Business E-Mail: tcole@sidley.com.

COLE, TOM, retail executive; b. St. Louis; Grad., Kent St. U. Various positions with Federated Dept. Stores, 1972—80; v.p., contr. Federated Dept. Stores, I. Magnin divsn., Calif., 1980—83; sr. v.p. fin. and adminstrn Federated Merchandising Group, 1983—87; sr. v.p. of fin. svcs. Lazarus Dept. Stores, 1987—88; pres., COO Federated Merchandising Group, 1988—95; pres. Federated Logistics, 1995; vice chair Federated Dept. Stores, 2003—. Mem.: Voluntary Interindustry Commerce Standards (bd. mem. 1995—, chmn. 2003—). Office: Federated Dept Stores 7 W 7th St Cincinnati OH 45202

COLEMAN, JOHN JOSEPH, III, surgery educator; b. Boston, Nov. 15, 1947; Grad., Harvard U., 1969, MD, 1973. Intern Emory U. Affiliated Hosp., Atlanta, 1973-74, resident in gen. surgery, 1974-78, resident in plastic surgery, 1978-80; fellow in surg. oncology U. Md., Balt., 1980; prof. surgery Ind. U., Indpls., 1980—86; chief plastic surgery Ind. U. Med. Ctr., Indpls., 1980—86, James E. Bennett prof. of plastic surgery & Wadley R. Glenn chair in surgery, 1986—91, prof. of surgery & chmn. plastic surgery, 1991—. Mem.: Am. Head and Neck Soc., Am. Bd. of Plastic Surgery (chmn. 2002—03). Office: U Plastic Surg Assocs 235 Emerson Hall 565 Barnhill Dr Indianapolis IN 46202-5112

COLEMAN, MARY SUE, academic administrator; b. Richmond, Ky, Oct. 2, 1943; m. Kenneth Coleman; 1 child, Jonathan. BA, Grinnell Coll., 1965; PhD, U. N.C., 1969; DSc (hon.), Dartmouth Coll., 2005, U. Notre Dame, 2007. NIH postdoctoral fellow U. N.C., Chapel Hill, 1969—70, U. Ky., 1971—72, instr., rsch. assoc. depts. biochemistry and medicine, 1972—75, asst. prof. dept. biochemistry, 1975—80, assoc. prof. dept. biochemistry, 1980—85, prof. dept. biochemistry, 1985—90; prof. dept. biochemistry and biophysics U. N.C., Chapel Hill, 1990—93; provost, v.p. for academic affairs, prof. biochemistry U. N.Mex., 1993—95; pres., prof. biochemistry, prof. biol. scis. U. Iowa, Iowa City, 1995—2002; pres. U. Mich., Ann Arbor, 2002—. NSF summer trainee Grinnell Coll., 1962; acting dir. basir rsch. U. Ky. Cancer Ctr., 1980—83; scientific cons. Abbott Labs., 1981—85, Collaborative Rsch., 1983—88; assoc. dir. rsch. L.P. Markey Cancer Ctr. U. Ky., 1983—90, dir. grad. studies biochem., 1984—87, trustee, 1987—90; assoc. provost, dean rsch. U. N.C., 1990—92; scientific cons. Life Techs., Inc., 1992; vice chancellor grad students and rsch. U. N.C., 1992—93; pres. Iowa Health Sys., 1995—2002; mem. Big Ten Coun. Pres.'s, 1995—2002; chair undergrad. edn. com. Am. Assn. Univs., 1997—; bd. trustees Univs. Rsch. Assn., 1998—; mem. task force on tchrs. edn. Am. Coun. Edn., 1998—; mem. Gov.'s Strategic Planning Coun., 1998—2000, Ind. Am. Pres.'s Coun., 1999—, Bus.-Higher Edn. Froum, 1999—; mem. rsch. accountability task force Am. Assn. Univs., 2000—; mem. stds. success adv. bd. Am. Assn. Univs. and he Pew Charitable Trusts, 2000—; co-chair Inst. Medicine Com. on Consequences of Uninsurance, 2000—; mem. Knight Commn., 2000—01; mem. exec. com. Am. Assn. Univs., 2001—; mem. bd. dirs. Johnson & Johnson, 2003—; bd. dirs. Meredith Corp., Am. Coun. Edn.; presenter in field. Mem. editl. bd.: Jour. Biol. Chemistry, 1989—93; contbr. articles to profl. jours. Trustee Crinnell Coll., 1996—; mem. bd. govs. Warren G. Magnuson Clin. Ctr., NIH, 1996—2000, State of Iowa Gov.'s ACCESS Edn. Commn., 1997; bd. dirs. United Way, Albuquerque, 1995; trustee John S. and James L. Knight Found., 2005—. Fellow postdoctiral fellow, Clayton Found. Biochem. Inst., U. Tex., 1970—71. Fellow: AAAS, Am. Acad. Arts and Scis.; mem.: Nat. Coll. Athletic Assn. (bd. dirs. 2002—), Nat. Assn. State Univs. ans Land Grant Colls. Coun. Cchief Acad. Officers (exec. com. 1993—95), Am. Soc. Biochem. and Molecular Biology, Am. Assn. Cancer Rsch.

COLEMAN, MICHAEL BENNETT, mayor; b. Indpls., Nov. 18, 1954; s. John and Joan Coleman; m. Frankie L. Coleman; children: Kimberly, Justin, John-David. BA in polit. sci., U. Cin., 1977; JD, U. Dayton, 1980. Pvt. practice; mayor City of Columbus, Ohio, 2000—. Mem. city coun. City of Columbus, 1992—99, pres., 1997—99. Mem. Columbus Convention Ctr. Citizens Adv. Group, 1986; bd. mem. Columbus Youth Corps, Inc., Rosemont Ctr., Veterans Meml. Convention Ctr., Black Family Adoption, Ctrl. Ohio Transit Authority. Recipient Cmty. Svc. Award, Columbus Bar Assn., Citizen's Leadership Award. Mem.: ABA (mem. Minority Coun. Demonstration Program 1990—), Nat. Conf. Black Lawyers, Ohio State Bar Assn. (mem. coun. of delegates 1990—), Robert B. Elliot Law Club (v.p. 1989). Office: Mayors Office 90 W Broad St Rm 247 2nd Fl Columbus OH 43215-9014 Office Phone: 614-645-7671. Office Fax: 614-645-5818. Business E-Mail: mac@columbus.gov.

COLEMAN, NORMAN, JR., senator, former mayor; b. Bklyn., Aug. 17, 1949; m. Laurie Casserly; children: Jacob, Sarah. BA in Political Sci., Hofstra U., 1971; JD, U. Iowa, 1976. Bar: Minn. Criminal prosecutor, civil litig. supr., chief lobbyist Minn. Atty. Gen.'s Office, 1976—86, asst. atty. gen., chief prosecutor & solicitor. gen., 1986—92; mayor City of St. Paul, 1994—2002; US Senator from Minn., 2003—. Active in creation of Minn. Drug Abuse Resistance Edn. program, also The Partnership for a Drug Free Minn.; adj. prof., William Mitchell Coll. Law, 1983-92; mem. com. agr., nutrition and forestry, US Senate, com. fgn. affairs, com. homeland security and govtl. affairs, com. small bus. and entrepreneuership. Humphrey fellow U. Minn.; Award Pub. Svc Woodrow Wilson Internat. Ctr. for Scholars, Award Excellence in Pub.-Pvt. Partnerships US Conf. Mayors, 2001, Mondale award Japan-Am. Soc. of Minn., 2001, Urban Innovator award Ctr. for Civic Innovation, The Manhattan Inst., 2001, Award Leadership in Inter-American Understanding Hudson Inst. Ctr. Latin Am. Studies, 2005. Republican. Jewish. Office: US Senate 320 Hart Senate Office Building Washington DC 20510 also: District Office Ste 100N 2550 University Ave West Saint Paul MN 55114-1098 Office Phone: 202-224-5641, 651-645-0323. Office Fax: 202-224-1152, 651-645-3110.

COLEMAN, PAUL DARE, physics and electrical engineering educator; b. Stoystown, Pa., June 4, 1918; s. Clyde R. and Catharine (Livengood) C.; m. Betty L. Carter, June 20, 1942; children— Susan Dare, Peter Carter. AB, Susquehanna U., 1940; MS, Pa. State U., 1942; PhD, MIT, 1951, DSc (hon.), 1978. Asst. physics Susquehanna U., 1938-40, Pa. State U., 1940-42; physicist USAF-WADC, Wright Field, Ohio, 1942-46, Cambridge Air Research Center, also; grad. research assoc. Mass. Inst. Tech., 1946-51; prof. elec. engring., dir. electro-physics lab. U. Ill. at Urbana, 1951—. Recipient meritorious civilian award, USAAF, 1946, Disting. Alumni award, Susquehanna U., 1980. Fellow AAAS, IEEE, MTT (Disting. Educator award 1994, Centennial medal 1984), Optical Soc. Am., Am. Phys. Soc.; mem. Sigma Xi, Pi Mu Delta, Pi Mu Epsilon, Eta Kappa Nu. Achievements include research on millimeter waves, submillimeter waves, relativistic electronics, far infrared molecular lasers, beam wave guides and detectors, chem. lasers, nonlinear optics, solid state electronics; inventor of the magnetic wiggler, the key component of the free electron laser. Home: 710 Park Lane Dr Champaign IL 61820-7633 Office: Univ Ill 133 Everitt Lab 1406 W Green St Urbana IL 61801-2918

COLEMAN, ROBERT LEE, retired lawyer; b. Kansas City, Mo., June 14, 1929; s. William Houston and Edna Fay (Smith) C. B of Music Edn., Drake U., 1951; LLB, U. Mo., 1959. Bar: Mo. 1959, Fla. 1973. Law clk. to judge U.S. Dist. Ct. (we. dist.) Mo., Kansas City, 1959-60; assoc. Watson, Ess, Marshall & Enggas, Kansas City, 1960-66; asst. gen. counsel Gas Svc. Co., Kansas City, 1966-74; v.p., corp. counsel H & R Block, Inc., Kansas City, 1974-94; ret., 1994. With U.S. Army, 1955-57. Mem.: ABA.

COLES, GRAHAM, conductor, composer; b. London, May 7, 1948; arrived in Canada, 1951; s. Walter Harold and Phyllis Irene Gwendoline (Conn) C. MusB, U. Toronto, 1972, MusM, 1974, EdB, 1991. Music dir. Kitchener-Waterloo (Ont.) Chamber Orch., 1985—; rental agt. Berandol Music Ltd. Examiner emeritus coll. of examiners Royal Conservatory of Music, Toronto. Composer numerous instrumental and vocal compositions. Mem. Can. League Composers, Can. Music Ctr. (assoc. composer), Assn. Can. Orchs. Home: 86 Weber St E Kitchener ON Canada N2H 1C7 Office Phone: 519-744-3828. E-mail: kwchamberorchestra@on.aibn.com.

COLESCOTT, WARRINGTON WICKHAM, artist, printmaker, educator; b. Oakland, Calif., Mar. 7, 1921; s. Warrington W. and Lydia (Hutton) C.; m. Frances Myers, Mar. 15, 1971; children by previous marriage: Louis Moore, Julian Hutton, Lydia Alice. AB, U. Calif., Berkeley, 1942, MA, 1947; postgrad., Acad. de la Grand Chaumiere, Paris, France, 1950-53, Slade Sch. Art, U. London (Eng.), 1957. Mem. faculty U. Wis., Madison, 1949-86, prof. art, 1957-86, Leo Steppat chair, prof., 1979-85, Leo Steppat chair (emeritus prof.), 1986—. Printmaker emeritus So. Graphics Coun., 1991; academician Nat. Acad. One-man shows include Perimeter Gallery, Chgo., 1985, 87-88, 91, 93, 95, 99, 2002, 05, Elvehjem Mus., Madison, Wis., 1989, Peltz Gallery, Milw., 2001, 04, 06, Quedlinburg, Germany, 2006; exhibited in group shows at Nelson-Atkins Mus., Kansas City, 1990, New Orleans Mus. Art, 2003, Milw. Art Mus. Retrospective, 2005, Ark. State U., Jonesboro, 2005 (Purchase award); represented in permanent collections Mus. Modern Art, Victoria and Albert Mus., London, Bibliotechque Nat., Paris, Met. Mus., Chgo. Art Inst., Bklyn. Mus., Phila. Mus. Art, Milw. Art Mus., Elvehjem Art Mus., Whitney Mus. Am. Art, Corcoran Gallery Art, Fogg Art Mus. Harvard U., Nat. Acad., NY; co-author (with Arthur Hove) Progressive Printmakers, 1999; etchings commd. Milw. Art Mus., NY Print Club, 2002, Corcoran Gallery Art, Washington, 2005 Fulbright fellow, 1957, Guggenheim fellow, 1965, Nat. Endowment Arts Printmaking fellow, 1975, Artist fellow, 1979, 83-84, 93-94; recipient Print award NAD, 1991-92, 95, 97, NSAL Award of Excellence, 1993, 99, award Internat. Triennial of Print, Cracow, Poland, 1997, award Boston Printmakers, 2003, Lifetime Achievement in Printmaking award So. Graphics Coun., 2006, Andrew Carnegie prize Printing, 2006. Fellow Wis. Acad. Sci. Arts and Letters. Office: 8788 County Hwy A Hollandale WI 53544-9801

COLETTA, JOHN, chef; Chef Four Seasons, NYC, Waldorf-Astoria, NYC, Atlanta Hilton Hotel; exec. chef Fairmont Hotel, Chgo.; chef Entre Nous, Primavera; exec. chef Sheraton Chgo. Hotel, 1991, Caesar's Palace, Las Vegas, Nev., Caliterra, Chgo.; regional exec. chef Whydham Hotels & Resorts, Itasca, Ill. Mem. Visiting Masters from the World of Food Program Epcot Internat. Food and Wine Festival, 1997. Named one of 15 America's Rising Star Chefs; recipient gold megal, Culinary Olympics, 1984. Office: Caliterra 633 N Saint Clair St Chicago IL 60611

COLGATE, J. EDWARD, mechanical engineering educator; b. Sept. 30, 1962; SB, MIT, 1983, SM, 1986, PhD in mech. engring., 1988. Asst. prof. Northwestern U., Evanston, Ill., 1988—94, assoc. prof., 1994—2002, prof. dept. mech. engring., 2002—; co-founder, dir., tech. adv. Stanley Cobotics Inc., pres., 1999—2000. Co-editor: Advances in Robotics, Mechatronics & Haptic Interfaces, 1993; editor (assoc.): IEEE Transactions on Robotics & Automation, 1998—, Jour. of Dynamic Systems, Measurement & Control, 1995—98; editor: (U.S.) Robotics & Computer Integrated Mfg., 1995—99; contbr. chapters to books, articles to profl. jours. Recipient Henry Hess award ASME, 1995. Mem.: ASEE, IEEE, ASME. Office: Northwestern U Dept Mech Engring 2145 Sheridan Rd Dept Mech Evanston IL 60208-0834

COLKER, DAVID A., former stock exchange executive; Grad., U. Va., 1979; JD, U.Va., 1982. Gen. counsel Nat. Stock Exch. (formerly Cin. Stock Exch.), 1984—90, exec. v.p., 1991—95, COO, 1995—98, pres., COO, 1998—2001, pres., CEO, 2001—06.

COLLADAY, ROBERT S., trust company executive, consultant; b. Flint, Mich., Sept. 24, 1940; s. Robert Harold and Mary Elizabeth (Strong) C.; m. Joan M. Hartsock; children: David, Jill, James, Christopher. BA, Alma Coll., 1962; postgrad., Nat. Trust Sch., Northwestern U., 1967. Asst. trust officer Comerica Bank-Detroit, 1968-71, trust officer, 1971-74, v.p., 1974-80, 1st v.p., 1980-83, sr. v.p., 1983-91, Comerica Inc., 1984-91; pres., prin. cons. Trust Consulting Svcs., Inc., Bloomfield Hills, Mich., 1991—. Cons. to bd. dirs. Southeast Mich. Trustee, chmn. investment com. Alma Coll., Mich. Republican. Presbyterian. Avocations: fishing, photography. Home: 22241 Village Pines Dr Franklin MI 48025-3568 Office: Trust Consulting Svcs Inc PO Box 1131 Bloomfield Hills MI 48303-1131 Office Phone: 248-644-6115.

COLLEN, JOHN, lawyer, educator; b. Chgo., Dec. 26, 1954; children: Joshua, Benjamin, Sarah, Joel. AB summa cum laude, Dartmouth Coll., 1977; JD, Georgetown U., 1980. Bar: Ill. 1980, U.S. Dist. Ct. (no. dist.) Ill. 1980, Trial 1982, U.S. Ct. Appeals (7th cir.) 1984, U.S. Supreme Ct. 1990. Ptnr. Quarles & Brady LLP, Chgo., 2007—. Mem. editl. adv. bd. Jour. Bankruptcy Law and Practice; adj. prof. law St. John's U. Author: Buying and Selling Real Estate in Bankruptcy, 1997; contbr. articles to profl. jours.; lectr. in field. Fellow Am. Coll. Bankruptcy; mem. ABA, Chgo. Bar Assn., Am. Bankruptcy Inst. (chmn. emeritus com. real estate bankruptcy), Phi Beta Kappa. Avocations: water sports, magic. Office: Quarles & Brady LLP Citigroup Ctr 500 W Madison St Ste 3700 Chicago IL 60661 Business E-Mail: jcollen@quarles.com.

COLLENS, LEWIS MORTON, retired academic administrator, law educator; b. Chgo., Feb. 10, 1938; m. Marge Collens; 1 child, Steven. BS, U. Ill., Urbana, 1960, MA, 1963; JD, U. Chgo., 1966. Bar: Ill. 1966. Assoc. Ross, Hardies, Chgo., 1966-67; spl. asst. to gen. counsel EEOC, Washington, 1967-68; asst. prof. Ill. Inst. Tech., Chgo. Kent Coll. Law, 1970-72, assoc. prof., 1972-74, prof., 1975—90; dean Coll. Law, Ill. Inst. Tech., 1974-90, pres., 1990—2007. Bd. dirs. Amsted Industries, Inc., Dean Foods Co., Inc.; trustee Latin Sch. Chgo. Dir. Ill. Coalition; bd. dirs. Alion Sci. and Tech. Mem. ABA, Ill. Bar Assn., Chgo. Bar Assn., Am. Law Inst., Mayors Coun. Tech. Advs., Econ. Club of Chgo. Office Phone: 312-567-5198. Office Fax: 312-567-3004. E-mail: collens@iit.edu.

COLLETT, LAWRENCE, diversified financial service company executive; b. 1943; With Cass Bank & Trust Co., 1963-83; chmn., pres., CEO Cass Comml. Corp., St. Louis, 1983—. Office: Cass Comml Corp 13001 Hollenberg Dr Bridgeton MO 63044

COLLEY, KAREN J., medical educator, researcher; b. Nov. 3, 1958; BS in Chemistry, Duke U., 1981; PhD in Molecular Biology, Washington U., St. Louis, 1987. Postdoctoral fellow dept. biol. chemistry UCLA, 1987—91; postdoctoral fellow NIH, 1990; asst. prof. dept. biochemistry U. Ill., Chgo., 1991—97, assoc. prof., 1997—. Mem. med. adv. bd. Leukemia Rsch. Found., 1994—, reviewer study sect., 1994—; outside reviewer NSF Grants, 1995—, VA Rsch. Grants, 1995—; mem. pathiobiochemistry study sect. NIH, 1998—. Reviewer: Jour. Biol. Chemistry, Jour. Cell Biology, Molecular and Chem. Neuropathology, Jour. Cell Sci., Devel. Biology; contbr. articles to profl. jours.; patentee in field. Recipient Established Investigator award, Am. Heart Assn., 1996; fellow (sr.), Am. Cancer Soc., 1991; grantee, 1992, U. Ill., 1992, 1996, Leukemia Rsch. Found., Inc., 1993. Mem.: AAAS, Soc. Glycobiology, Am. Soc. Biochemistry and Molecular Biology, Am. Soc. Cell Biology, Sigma Xi. Office: U Ill Dept Biochemistry and Molecular Biology 1819 W Polk St Chicago IL 60612-7331

COLLIE, JOHN, JR., insurance agent; b. Gary, Ind., Apr. 23, 1934; s. John and Christina Dempster (Wardrop) Collie; m. Jessie Fearn Shaw, Aug. 1, 1964; children: Cynthia Elizabeth Lunsford, Douglas A. H., Jennifer F. Weaver. AB in Econs., Ind. U., 1957. Assoc. risk mgmt., cert. sr. adv. Operator Collie Optical Lab., Gary, 1957-62; owner, operator Collie Ins. Agy., Gary, 1962—. Pres. Collie Realty and Investment, Ins. and Fin. Adv.; lectr. High Frontier, dist. chmn. 1st dist. com. secure; mem. employer support Guard & Res., Dept. Def.; affiliated broker Poe and Assocs., Valparaiso, Ind.; instr. Command and Gen. Staff Coll., 1973—77. Lt. col. USAR, 1957—86. Mem.: Nat. Fedn. Ind. Bus. (guardian, state adv. bd., N.W. Ind. adv. bd.), Leadership Coun. Am., Res. Officers Assn. (sec., pres. N.W. Ind. chpt., v.p. Ind. chpt.), Mil. Officer Assn. Am., Shriners, Masons (Gary Lodge 677, F and AM past master, treas., 32 degree), Phi Kappa Psi. Republican. Methodist. Office: Poe and Assocs 3190 Willow A Creek Rd Portage IN 46368 Business E-Mail: jcjr33@yahoo.com.

COLLIER, BARRY S., coach; m. Annette Collier, 1975; children: Casey, Brady, Clay. BS, Butler, 1973; MS, Ind. State U., 1977. Asst. coach Rose Hulman Inst., Seattle Ctrl. C.C., U. Idaho, U. Oreg., Stanford U.; head coach men's basketball Butler U., U. Nebr., Lincoln. Office: U Nebr 106 Devaney Sports Ctr Lincoln NE 68588

COLLIER, JAMES WARREN, retired lawyer; b. Dallas, July 31, 1940; s. J.W. and Mary Gertrude (Roberts) C.; m. Judith Lane, Dec. 27, 1964; children: Anne Elizabeth, Jennifer Susan. BA, U. Mich., 1962, JD, 1965. Bar: N.Y. 1966, Mich. 1968. Assoc. Simpson Thacher & Bartlett, NYC, 1965-66; tax atty. office gen. counsel Ford Motor Co., 1966-67; assoc. Dykema Gossett, Detroit, 1967-73, ptnr., 1973—2005, ret., 2005. Mem. Mich. Bar Assn., Econ. Club Detroit, Lochmoor Club. Office: Dykema Gossett 400 Renaissance Ctr # 3500 Detroit MI 48243-1603 E-mail: jcollier@dykema.com.

COLLIER, KEN O., editor; b. Mpls., Oct. 7, 1952; BA, Carleton Coll., 1976; MSc, UCLA, Santa Barbara, 1978. Instr. geology Carleton Coll., Northfield, Minn., 1980; owner Custom Furniture, Mpls., 1980-87; assoc. editor The Family Handyman Mag., Mpls., 1987-91; exec. editor Custom Furniture, Mpls., 1995—; sr. editor New Bus. Devel., Mpls., 1991-95; chief editor Am. Woodworker Mag./Home Svc. Publ., Eagan, Minn., 1998—. Office: Home Svcs Publ 2915 Commers Dr Ste 700 Eagan MN 55121-2398

COLLIER, THOM, state representative; b. 1964; married; 2 children. Completed courses, Dale Carnegie, Zig Ziglar, and Success Motivation Inst. Small bus. owner; state rep. dist. 90 Ohio Ho. of Reps., Columbus, 1999—, chair, econ. devel. and tech. com., mem. county and twp. govt., criminal justice, and ways and means coms. Parish coun., ch. deacon St. Vincent, St. Luke and Messiah Ch., h.s. religious edn. tchr., youth leader; bd. dirs. Christian Star Acad. Mem.: Toastmasters, Internat., Internat. Mgmt. Conf., Nat. Spkrs. Assn., Appalachia Svc. Project, Knox County Right to Life, Big Brothers/Big Sisters Knox County (award), Jr. Achievement North Ctrl. Ohio (Disting. Svc. award), Knox Pregnancy Svcs., Ohio Spkrs. Forum, Nat. Exch. Club (local club and Ohio-W.Va. dist. pres., nat. bd. dirs.). Republican. Office: 77 S High St 11th fl Columbus OH 43215-6111

COLLIN, THOMAS JAMES, lawyer; b. Windom, Minn., Jan. 6, 1949; s. Everett Earl and Genevieve May (Wilson) C.; m. Victoria Gatov, Oct. 11, 1985; children: Arielle, Elise, Sarah. BA, U. Minn., 1970; AM, Harvard U., 1972; JD, Georgetown U., 1974. Bar: Ohio 1975, U.S. Dist. Ct. (no. and so. dists.) Ohio 1975, U.S. Ct. Appeals (10th cir.) 1977, U.S. Supreme Ct. 1980, U.S. Ct. Appeals (6th cir.) 1981, U.S. Ct. Appeals (8th cir.) 1982, U.S. Ct. Appeals (7th cir.) 1997, U.S. Ct. Appeals (11th cir.) 1999. Law clk. to Judge Myron Bright U.S. Ct. Appeals, 8th Cir., St. Louis, 1974-75; assoc. Thompson, Hine LLP, Cleve., 1975-82, ptnr., 1982—. Author: Ohio Business Competition Law, 1994, (with others) Criminal Antitrust Litigation Manual, 1983; editor: Punitive Damages and Business Torts: A Practitioner's Handbook, 1998, Antitrust Law and Economics of Product Distribution, 2006; contbr. articles to profl. jours. Active Citizens League, Cleve., bd. trustees, 1994-99, v.p., 1995-97, pres. 1997-99; bd. trustees Citizens League Rsch. Inst., Cleve., 1999-2002. Mem. ABA (chair bus. torts and unfair competition com. antitrust sect. 1995-98, chair annual mtg. com. 2001-02, chmn. distbn. and franchising com. 2002-05), Ohio State Bar Assn. (bd. govs. antitrust sect. 1988-98). Republican. Avocations: book collecting, music. Home: 7879 Oakhurst Dr Cleveland OH 44141-1123 Office: Thompson Hine LLP 127 Public Sq Cleveland OH 44114-1216

COLLINS, ARTHUR D., JR., medical products executive; b. Lakewood, Ohio, Dec. 10, 1947; BS, Miami U., Oxford, Ohio, 1969; MBA, U. Pa., 1973. With Abbott Laboratories, 1978—84, div. v.p., 1984—89, corp. v.p. diagnostic products, 1989—92; pres. Medtronic Internat., 1992—94; exec. v.p. Medtronic Inc., Mpls., 1992—94, COO, 1994—96, pres., COO, 1996—2001, pres., CEO, 2001—02, chmn., CEO, 2002—07, chmn., 2007—. Bd. dir. U.S. Bancorp, Cargill Inc.; chmn. Advanced Med. Tech. Ind. Assn. Mem. bd. overseers Wharton Sch., Univ. Pa. Office: Medtronic Inc 710 Medtronic Pkwy Minneapolis MN 55432-5604

COLLINS, CARDISS, retired congresswoman; b. St. Louis, Sept. 24, 1931; m. George W. Collins (dec.); 1 child, Kevin. Student, Northwestern U.; LLD (hon.), John Marshall Law Sch., 1969, Winston-Salem State U., 1980, Spelman Coll., 1981, BarberScotia Coll., 1986; DHL (hon.), Rosary Coll., 1996; DrPsychology (hon.), Forest Inst. Profl. Psychology, 1993. Barber Scotia Coll.; mem. 93d-104th Congresses from 7th Ill. Dist., 1973-97; ret., 1997. Ranking minority mem. govt. reform & oversight com.; former chair. govt. activity and transp. subcom.; former chair commerce, consumer protection and competition subcom.; former majority whip-at-large; former asst. regional whip; former chair Congl. Black Caucus, sec.; dir. emeritus, former chair Congl. Black Caucus Found.; former chair Mems. Congress for Peace through Law; chairwoman Nielsen Media Rsch. Taskforce TV Measurement. Recipient award Roosevelt U., Loyola U., Scroll of Merit Nat. Med. Assn.; named to Hall of Fame Women's

Sports Found. Mem. NAACP, Nat. Coun. Negro Women (past v.p.), Chgo. Urban League, Black Women's Agenda, The Chgo. Network, The Links, Dem. Nat. Com., Alpha Kappa Alpha. Democrat. Baptist. Home: 1110 Roundhouse Ln Alexandria VA 22314-5934

COLLINS, DANIEL W., accountant, educator; b. Marshalltown, Iowa, Sept. 1, 1946; s. Donald E. and Lorine R. (Metge) C.; children: Melissa, Theresa BBA with honors, U. Iowa, Iowa City, 1968, PhD, 1973. Asst. prof. acctg. Mich. State U., East Lansing, 1973-76, assoc. prof., 1976-77; vis. assoc. prof. U. Iowa, Iowa City, 1977-78, assoc. prof., 1978-81, prof., 1981-83, Murray chaired prof. acctg., 1983-88, Henry B. Tippie prof. of acctg., 1989—; vis. IBM prof. bus. Fuqua Sch. Bus., Duke U., 1988-89, chmn. dept. acctg., 1995—2003; vis. full prof. Kellogg Sch. Mgmt., Northwestern U., 2005. Mem. Fin. Acctg. Stds. Adv. Coun., acad. adv. bd. Deloitte & Touche; mem. Arthur Andersen doctoral dissertation awards com., 1996-99; bd. dirs. Ira B. McGladrey Inst., U.S. Bank, Iowa City, Christian Ret. Svcs., Iowa City. Assoc. editor Acctg. Rev., 1980-86; mem. editl. bd. Jour. Acctg. and Econs., 1978-2006, Jour. Acctg. Rsch., 2001-06; contbr. articles to profl. jours. 2d lt. US Army, 1972. Recipient All Univ. Tchr. scholar award Mich. State U., 1976, Gilbert Maynard Excellence in Tchg. award U. Iowa, 1985, Collegiate Tchg. award, 1998; Univ. Faculty scholar U. Iowa, 1980-82, Faculty Excellence award Iowa Bd. Regents, 2000, Outstanding Acctg. Alumnus award, U. Iowa, 2003. Mem. Am. Acctg. Assn. (disting. vis. faculty mem. Doctoral Consortium 1980, 89, dir. Doctoral Consortium 1987, program dir. ann. conv. 1988, dir. publs. 1989-91, exec. com. 1989-91, Outstanding Acctg. Educator award 2001), Acctg. Rschrs. Internat. Avocations: jogging, gardening. Office: U Iowa Coll Bus W262 PBAB Iowa City IA 52242-1000 Home: 2301 Muddy Creek Ln Coralville IA 52241

COLLINS, DUANE E., manufacturing executive; BSME, U. Wis.; postgrad., Harvard U. Sales engr. Parker Hannifin Corp., Cleve., 1961, gen. sales mgr., ops. mgr. hose products divsn., gen. mgr., 1973-76, v.p. ops. fluid connectors group, 1976-80, pres. fluid connectors group, 1980-83, corp. v.p., 1983-87, pres. internat., 1987-88, corp. exec. v.p., pres. internat., 1988-92, vice chmn., 1992-93, CEO, 1993—2001, chmn., 2001—04. Bd. dirs. Parker Hannifin Corp., Sherwin-Williams Co., MeadWestvaco, MTD Holdings. Office: Parker Hannifin Corp 6035 Parkland Blvd Cleveland OH 44124-4141

COLLINS, JACQUELINE Y, state senator; b. McComb, Miss., Dec. 10; Grad. journalism, Northwestern Univ.; MA, Harvard's John F. Kennedy Sch. of Gov.; MA Human Svc. Admin., Spertus Coll.; MA Theol. Studies, Harvard Divinity Sch., 2003. State Senator 11 Senate, Dist. 16Ill., 2003—; min. of Comm. St. Sabina Cath. Ch., Chgo.; journalist in print, radio and TV; press sec. Congressman Gus Savage. Mem. Appropriations I, Environ. and Energy, Revenue (VC), Revenue Subcommittee on Spl. Issues. Recipient Emmy Award -nominated news editor, CBS-TV/ Chgo.; Legislative fellow with US Senator Hillary Rodham Clinton. Democrat. Catholic. Office: Capitol Bldg M-118 Springfield IL 62706 also: 1155 W 79th St Chicago IL 60620

COLLINS, JEFFREY G., lawyer, former prosecutor; b. Detroit, Mar. 16, 1959; m. Lois Collins; 2 children. BA in Psychology, Northwestern U., 1981; JD, Howard U. Sch. Law, 1984. Pvt. practice, 1984—94; appointed judge Detroit Recorder's Ct., 1994—96; cir. judge Wayne County Cir. Ct., 1997—98; judge Mich. Supreme Ct., 1998—2000, Mich. Ct. Appeals, 2000—01; U.S. atty. (ea. dist.) Mich. US Dept. Justice, 2001—04; atty., ptnr. litigation dept. Foley & Lardner LLP, 2004—. Mentor Man to Man program Paul Robeson Acad.; mem. Plymouth United Ch. of Christ, Detroit. Mem.: Mich. Assn. for Leadership Devel. (founder, dir. Wayne County chpt.).

COLLINS, JOSEPH P., lawyer; b. Chgo., Apr. 9, 1950; AB magna cum laude, Coll. Holy Cross, 1972; JD, NYU, 1975. Bar: Ill. 1975, US Dist. Ct., no. dist. Ill. 1977, US Ct. Appeals, 5th cir. 1978. Atty. Schiff Hardin & Waite, Chgo., 1975—94; ptnr. futures securities & derivatives practice Mayer Brown Rowe & Maw, Chgo. & YC, 1994—. Faculty mem. IIT Kent Coll. Law; mem. Ill. Sec. State Commodities Law Adv. Com. Cir. sec. NYU Sch. Law Root-Tilden Scholarship prog. Root-Tilden Scholar. Mem.: ABA (chmn. annual meeting 1994, mem. exec. council, com. on regulation of futures), Assn. Bar City of NY (chmn. futures commn. merchant subcom.), Chgo. Bar Assn. (past chmn. futures law com.). Office: Mayer Brown Rowe & Maw 1675 Broadway New York NY 10019-5820 also: Mayer Brown Rowe Maw LLP 71 S Wacker Dr Ste 3200 Chicago IL 60606 Office Phone: 312-701-8353, 212-506-2657. Office Fax: 312-706-9101, 212-849-5657. Business E-Mail: jcollins@mayerbrownrowe.com.

COLLINS, KATHLEEN, academic administrator, art educator; b. Chgo., BA in psychology, minor in fine arts, Stanford U.; MFA in photography. Chmn. applied photography dept. Sch. Photographic Arts & Sci., Rochester Inst. Tech., coord. summer workshops; dean Sch. Art & Design, NY State Coll. Ceramics, Alfred U., prof.; pres. Kans. City Art Inst., 1996—. Represented in permanent collections, Art Inst. Chgo., Cleve. Art Mus., Centro Cultural/Arte Contemporaneo, Mex. City, Mex., Chrysler Mus., Norfolk Va. Office: Office of President Kansas City Art Inst 4415 Warwick Blvd Kansas City MO 64111

COLLINS, KEVIN HEATH, lawyer; b. Cedar Rapids, Iowa, May 7, 1955; s. Thomas Martin and Joanne (Heath) C.; m. Sally A. Stephenson, June 11, 1985. BA, Creighton U., 1978; JD, U. Iowa, 1980. Bar: Iowa 1981, Hawaii 1982, U.S. Dist. Ct. (no. and so. dist.) Iowa 1981, U.S. Dist. Ct. Hawaii, 1982, U.S. Ct. Appeals (8th cir.) 1981, U.S. Ct. Appeals (9th cir.) 1982, U.S. Supreme Ct. 1984. Sr. v.p. Shuttleworth & Ingersoll, P.C., Cedar Rapids, 1980-82, 84—; assoc. Dinman & Yokoyama, P.C., Honolulu, 1982-84. Exec. com. United Way of East Cen. Iowa, Cedar Rapids, 1986-87, Retired Sr. Vol. Program, Cedar Rapids, 1986-89. Fellow Iowa Acad. Trial Lawyers, Assn. Am. Bd. Trial Advocates, Fedn. of Insurance & Corp. Counsel; mem. ABA, Am. Arbitration Assn. (panel mem.), Iowa State Bar Assn. (co-chair com. on delivery of legal svcs. to the elderly 1989-90, mem. law practice mgmt. sect. 1991-98, bd. govs. 1998-2001, v.p. 2001-02, pres.-elect 2002-03, pres. 2003-04), Hawaii State Bar Assn. Office: Shuttleworth Ingersoll PLC PO Box 2107 Cedar Rapids IA 52406-2107

COLLINS, LARRY WAYNE, computer technician, small business owner; b. Plainville, Ind., Mar. 23, 1941; s. Virgil Raymond and Eva Pauline (Hedden) C.; m. Donna Kay Miller, July 25, 1961 (div. Apr. 1983); children: Rex Aaron, Jill Renee; m. Mary Ellen McConn, Dec. 15, 1983; 1 child, Ann Marie. AS, Vincennes U., 1961; BS, U. Indpls., 1968, MBA, 1981. Computer programmer State of Ind., Indpls., 1963-64, systems analyst, 1964-65, asst. ops. mgr., 1965-66; mgr. systems and programming Community Hosp. of Indpls., 1966-67, dir. data processing, 1967-77, v.p. hosp. systems, 1977-84; v.p., mgr. Bethesda N. Hosp., Cin., 1984-85, group v.p., 1985-86; sr. v.p. Bethesda Oak Hosp., Cin., 1986-91; sr. v.p., chief info. officer Bethesda Hosp., Inc., Cin., 1991-95; ptnr. RHI, Inc., Maineville, Ohio, 1995-98; prin. Collins Cons., Maineville, 1998—. Bd. dirs. Tri-State Community Cancer Orgn., 1986-92, chmn., 1989-92; chmn. bd. dirs. Hospice of Cin., Inc., 1987-91; bd. dirs. Interfaith Hospitality Network Warren County, 2000—. Mem. Ind. Cen. U. Alumni Assn. (bd. dirs. 1984-88), Am. Coll. Healthcare Execs., Tri-State Health Adminstrs. Forum, Am. Mgmt. Assn., Am. Acad. Med. Adminstrs. (bd. dirs. 1993-98, chmn. elect 1996, chmn. 1997), Kiwanis (bd. dirs. Montgomery chpt. 1984-87). Methodist. Avocations: golf, photography. Home and Office: 7667 Hopkins Rd Ste 101 Maineville OH 45039-8682 E-mail: lwc7667@aol.com.

COLLINS, MARTHA, English language educator, writer; b. Omaha, Nov. 25, 1940; d. William E. and Katheryn (Essick) C.; m. Theodore M. Space, Apr. 1991. AB, Stanford U., 1962; MA, U. Iowa, 1965, PhD, 1971. Asst. prof. NE Mo. U., Kirksville, 1965-66; from instr. to prof. English U. Mass., Boston, 1966—2002, co-dir. creative writing, 1979—2000; Pauline Delaney prof., co-dir. creative writing Oberlin Coll., Ohio, 1997—2007. Author (poetry): The Catastrophe of Rainbows, 1985, The Arrangement of Space, 1991, A History of Small Life on a Windy Planet, 1993, Some Things Words Can Do, 1998, Blue Front, 2006; translator: The Women Carry River Water, 1997 (winner, American Literary Translators Assn. award, 1998), Green Rice, 2005. Fellow Bunting Inst., 1982-83, Ingram Merrill Found., 1988, NEA, 1990; grantee Witter Bynner/Santa Fe Art Inst., 2001, Lannan Found. Residency, 2003; recipient Pushcart prize, 1985, 96, 98, Di Castagnola award, 1990, Anisfield-Wolf award, 2007, Ohioana award, 2007. Mem. Poetry Soc. Am., Assoc. Writing Programs. Democrat.

COLLINS, MICHAEL J., medical company executive; BS in Econs., Northwestern U., 1974, MS in Adminstrn., 1976. Various bus. mgmt. positions drug and cosmetic chems. divsn. Mallinckrodt, 1976-81, bus. dir. drug and cosmetic chems. divsn., 1981-84, asst. gen. mgr. drug and cosmetic chems. divsn., 1985-86, gen. mgr., 1986-88, v.p., gen. mgr., 1988-89, sr. v.p., gen. mgr., 1990-91, group v.p. analgesics and pharm. specialties group, 1992, group v.p. pharm. specialties, 1992-95, pres. pharm. specialties divsn., 1995-98, pres. pharms. group, 1998—. Home: PO Box 5840 Saint Louis MO 63134-0840

COLLINS, MICHELLE L., venture capitalist; b. 1960; BS in Econ., Yale Univ., 1982; MBA, Harvard Univ., 1986. With corp. fin. dept. William Blair & Co., 1986—91, ptnr., 1991—98; co-founder, mng. dir. Svoboda Collins LLC, Chgo., 1998—. Bd. dir. Coldwater Creek, Inc., CDW Corp., 1996—, Molex, Lisle, Ill., 2003—. Bd. dir. Chgo. Sinfonietta, Erikson Inst.; bd. trustees Field Mus. Named one of 100 Most Influential Women, Crain's Chicago Business, 2004. Mem.: Harvard Bus. Sch. Club, Chgo., Comml. Club Chgo. Office: Svoboda Collins LLC Ste 1500 One N Franklin St Chicago IL 60606 Office Phone: 312-267-8750. Office Fax: 312-267-6025. Business E-Mail: mlc@svoco.com.

COLLISON, JIM, publishing executive; b. Blue Earth, Minn., May 24, 1933; s. Elliott Eugene and Rosa Theresa (Whitcomb) C.; m. Valerie Ann Thul, Oct. 28, 1954; children: Judith, Michelle, Daniel, Michael, Rebecca, David. BA, St. John's Univ., 1955. Sports editor Blue Earth Post and Faribault County Register, 1953; staff writer St. Cloud Daily Times, Minn., 1953-55, Waterloo Courier, Iowa, 1955-57, Mason City Globe Gazette, Iowa, 1958-63; bus. and edn. cons. Jim Collison Assoc., Mason City, Iowa, 1963-77; exec. dir. Employers of Am., Mason City, Iowa, 1978-81, pres., 1981—; pres., pub. Sunburst Publ., Mason City, Iowa, 1990—. Co-founder Employers of Am., 1978; chmn. bd. ISBE Ins. Alliance, Mason City, 1986—, Select Advantage, Inc., ISBE Bus. Ins. Assn., ISBE Employer Benefits Assn.; pres. Am. Corp. Advisors, Inc.; workshop presenter. Author: Skill Building in Advanced Reading, 1968, Mental Power in Reading, 1970, Complete Employee Handbook Made Easy, 1994, 97, 2001, The Employer Protection Workshop, 1996, No-How Coaching, 2001, Complete Suggestion Program Make Easy, 2001; pub., sr. editor (e-newletter) HRmadeEasy, Empowered Work; creator IdeaTracker software, 2003, Suggestion ProSoftware, 2006. Asst. min. Orchard (Iowa) Congreg. Ch., 1985—; designer Adult Literacy and Employment Reading Training Program. Democrat. Avocations: flower gardening, hiking. Home: 310 Meadow Ln Mason City IA 50401-1717 Office: Employers of Am PO Box 1874 Mason City IA 50402-1874

COLLOTON, STEVEN M., federal judge; b. Iowa City, Iowa, Jan. 9, 1963; AB, Princeton U., 1985; JD, Yale Law Sch., 1988. Law clk to Hon. Laurence H. Silberman US Ct. Appeals, DC cir., Washington, 1988—89; law clk. to Hon. William H. Rehnquist US Supreme Ct., Washington, 1989—90; special asst. to Asst. Atty. Gen. Dept. Justice Office Legal Counsel, 1990—91; asst. U.S. Atty. No. Dist. Iowa, 1991—99; assoc. counsel Office Ind. Counsel Kenneth W. Starr, 1995—96; ptnr. Belin Lamson McCormick Zumbach Flynn, Des Moines, 1999—2001; U.S. Atty. So. Dist. Iowa, 2001—03; judge US Ct. Appeals (8th cir.), Des Moines, 2003—. Office: US Courthouse Annex 110 E Court Ave Ste 461 Des Moines IA 50309-2053

COLOM, VILMA, alderman; b. San Juan, June 7, 1954; d. Andres and Niza (Miranda) C.; divorced; 1 child, Omar Otero. BA, Northeastern U., 1978; MA, U. Ill., 1980. Mem. U.S. Sen. Task Force, Washington, 1983-90; chmn. Nat. Puerto Rican Forum, NYC, 1986-89; pres. Colom Internat. & Assocs., 1986-88; bilingual educator Richard Yate Pub. Sch., 1993-95; alderman, committeeman 35th ward City of Chgo., 1995—. With nat. Hispanic affairs Allstate Ins., 1983-90. Asst. dir. U. Ill., Chgo., 1990-93; mem. adv. bd. LeadershipAm., 1994—; bd. dirs. Nat. Network Latino Women, 1995—; chmn. Chgo. office Nat. Puerto Rican Forum, .Y.C., 1986-89, mem. adv. bd. nat. hqrs.; mem. aux. bd. Golden Apple Found., fundraising chmn., 1995—; mem. corp. nat. bd. Nat. Svc. Jobs for Progress. Recipient Signature award Leadership Am., 1994, Hispanic State Law Enforcement award, 1996, Law Enforcement award Hispanic Inst., 1996, Internat. award Logan Sq. Lions Club, 1996; named Hispanic of Yr., 1996. Mem. Nat. Women's C. of C., Omega Sigma Alpha. Democrat. Office: 2540 N Ridgeway Ave #1 Chicago IL 60647-1118

COLON, PEDRO A., state representative; b. Ponce, PR, Apr. 7, 1968; married; 1 child. BA, Marquette U., 1991; JD, U. Wis., 1994. Atty.; state assembly mem. Wis. State Assembly, Madison, 1998—, mem. corrections and the cts., criminal justice, health, ways and means, and workforce devel. coms. Mem.: Nat. Assn. Latino Elected Ofcls., Wis. Hispanic Lawyers Assn., Modjeska Theatre Group, Inc. Democrat. Office: State Capitol Rm 5N PO Box 8952 Madison WI 53708-8952

COLONNA, ROCCO J., state legislator; m. Shirley J. Colonna; children: Tina Marie Colonna Rini, Lavaine Anne Colonna Cates, Danny V.M. BA, U.S. Armed Forces Inst.; postgrad., Internat. Data Processing Inst., Cuyahoga C.C., Baldwin Wallace Coll. Mem. Ohio Ho. of Reps., Columbus, 1975-98. Chmn. econ. devel. and small bus. com., labor-mgmt. com., mem. rules com., ways and means com., devel. financing adv. bd., select com. for tech., linked deposit adv. com., rep. to speaker on econ. devel. policy bd., mem. turnpike oversight com., motor vehicle inspection and maintenance program and policy planning com. Former mem. Brook Park (Ohio) Planning Commn., Brook Park Zoning and Bldg. Bd. Appeals; mem. Brook Park City Coun., 1970-74; mem. Ohio Gov.'s Tripartite Labor and Mgmt. Adv. Commn. Recipient Outstanding Leadership award Ohio C. of C., 1986, Legislator of Yr. award food industry com. Ohio Coun. Retail Mchts., 1980, AMVETS, 1990. Mem. Ohio Aerospace Inst., Am. Legion, Holy Name Soc., Eagles. Democrat. Home: 6477 Wolf Rd Brookpark OH 44142-3873

COLVIN, SHERRILL WILLIAM, lawyer; b. Jeffersonville, Ind., Sept. 13, 1938; s. Hewitt L. and Mary (Sutton) C.; m. Sarah Albin, Aug. 12, 1962; children: John, Betsy. AB, Wabash Coll., 1960; JD, Ind. U., 1965. Bar: Ind. 1965, US Supreme Ct. 1968. Ptnr. Haller & Colvin PC, Fort Wayne, Ind., 1965—. Mem. disciplinary commn. Ind. Supreme Ct., 1986-96, chair 1995-96, Ind. jud. and nom. commn., 2006-08; mem. faculty Nat. Inst. Trial Advocacy. Fellow Am. Coll. Trial Lawyers; mem. Ind. State Bar Assn. (pres. 2003-2004), Ind. Trial Lawyers Assn. (pres. 1991-92). Methodist. Office: Haller & Colvin 444 E Main St Fort Wayne IN 46802-1910 Office Phone: 219-426-0444. Business E-Mail: scolvin@hallercolvin.com.

COLVIN, THOMAS STUART, agricultural engineer, farmer; b. Columbia, Mo., July 17, 1947; s. Charles Darwin and Miriam Elizabeth (Kimball) C.; m. Sonya Marie Peterson, Sept. 11, 1982; children: Christopher, Kristel. BS, Iowa State U., 1970, MS, 1974, PhD, 1977. Registered profl. engr., Iowa. Farmer, Hawkeye and Cambridge, Iowa, 1970—; rsch. assoc. Iowa State U., Ames, 1972-77; agrl. engr. USDA/Agrl. Rsch. Svc., Ames, 1977—2005. Cons. WillowCreek Cons., Manning, Iowa, 1978-85. Sgt. USAF, 1970-72, Vietnam. Recipient Air Force Commendation medal USAF, 1971. Mem. Am. Soc. Agrl. Biol. Engrs. (power machinery stds. com. St. Joseph, Mich. 1989—, Iowa sec., Young Engr. of Yr. 1986, Engr. of Yr. 2004), Soil and Water Conservation Soc., Iowa Acad. Sci. (chair agrl. scis. sect. 1991-92), Sigma Xi, Alpha Epsilon (pres. 1978), Gamma Sigma Delta, Phi Mu Alpha. Achievements include design and development of first computer program to help farmers manage tillage and residue cover for erosion control. Office: Oxford Farms 55670 290th St Cambridge IA 50046-8617

COLWILL, JACK MARSHALL, physician, educator; b. Cleve., June 15, 1932; s. Clifford V. and Olive A. (Marshall) Colwill; m. Winifred Stedman, 1954; children: James F., Elizabeth Ann, Carolyn. BA, Oberlin Coll., 1953; MD (George Whipple scholar), U. Rochester, 1957. Diplomate Am. Bd. Med. Examiners, Am. Bd. Internal Medicine, Am. Bd. Family Practice. Intern Barnes Hosp., Washington U. Sch. Medicine, St. Louis, 1957—58; resident in medicine U. Washington Affiliated Hosps., Seattle, 1958—60; chief resident U. Hosp., 1960—61; instr. medicine, dir. med. outpatient dept. U. Rochester Sch. Medicine and Dentistry, 1961—62, sr. instr. medicine, dir. med. outpatient dept., 1962—64; asst. dean, asst. prof. medicine, asst. prof. cmty. health and med. practice U. Mo. Sch. Medicine, Columbia, 1964—67, assoc. dean, asst. prof., 1967—69, assoc. dean for acad. affairs, asst. prof., 1969—70, assoc. dean, assoc. prof., 1970—76, interim chmn. dept. family and cmty. medicine, 1976—77, prof., 1976—97, prof. emeritus, 1999—, chmn. dept., 1977—97, interim dean, 2000. Cons. Bur. Health Manpower, NIH, 1969—75, Office Divsn. Dir. USPHS, 1977—; mem. Coun. on Grad. Med. Edn. Health Resources and Svcs. Adminstrn., 1990—96. Contbr. articles to profl. jours. Chair commn. on Gulf War and Health Inst. of Medicine, NAS, 1999—2003; dir. Robert Wood Johnson Found. Generalist Physician Initiative, 1991—2000; bd. dirs. Am. Bd. Family Medicine, 1998—2003. Mem.: AMA, Inst. Medicine NAS, Am. Acad. Family Physicians (commn. on govtl. legis. affairs 1984—87), Soc. Tchrs. Family Medicine (bd. dirs. 1978—82, 1983—87, pres.-elect 1987—88, pres. 1988—89), Assn. Med. Am. Colls. (chmn. Midwest-Gt. Plains Group on Student Affairs 1971—73, nat. vice chmn. group 1973—74, chmn. working group on non-cognitive assessment 1974—77, adv. to com. on admissions assessment 1974—77), Alpha Omega Alpha. Office: U Mo-Columbia Sch Medicine Dept Family And Medicine Columbia MO 65212-0001 Office Phone: 573-882-2165.

COMBS, ERIC A., social studies educator; m. Elizabeth Ann Haver; 1 child, Olivia. Grad., Air Force Senior NCO Acad.; MEd, Univ. Dayton; Masters student in Ednl. Leadership, Antioch-McGregor Univ. Social studies tchr. Fairborn (Ohio) H.S. Served to sr. master sgt. (ret.) USAF. Decorated Meritorious Svc. Medal (three devices), Air Force Commendation Medal (three devices), Air Force Achievement Medal (one device), Air Force and Navy Marksman awards, Outstanding Airman of Yr. Ribbon; named Ohio Tchr. of Yr., 2007. Office: Fairborn High Sch 900 East Dayton-Yellow Springs Rd Fairborn OH 45324 Business E-Mail: ecombs@fairborn.k12.oh.us.

COMBS, ERIC K., lawyer; b. West Union, Ohio, Aug. 10, 1971; BA, Miami U., 1993; JD, U. Madison-Wis., 1996. Bar: Ohio 1996. Ptnr., Litig. Dept. Taft, Stettinius & Hollister LLP, Cin. Trustee West End Health Ctr., 1998—2003, mem., Adv. Bd.; assoc. mem., Allocation Com. Fine Arts Fund; tutor Taft Elem. Sch.; deacon Knox Presbyn. Ch. Named one of Ohio's Rising Stars, Super Lawyers, 2006. Mem.: Cin. Acad. of Leadership for Lawyers, Cin. Bar Assn. (bd. trustee), Order of Coif, Phi Beta Kappa. Office: Taft, Stettinius & Hollister LLP 425 Walnut St Ste 1800 Cincinnati OH 45202-3957 Office Phone: 513-381-2838. Office Fax: 513-381-0205.

COMBS, ROBERT KIMBAL, museum director; b. Oklahoma City, Mar. 5, 1955; s. Harold Lee and Joanna Jane (Barton) Combs; m. Lynn Marie Robison, June 9, 1979 (div. 1984); 1 child, Caitlyn. BA in History, San Francisco State U., 1978; cert. in museology, U. Calif., Berkeley, 1979; MA in Museology, John F. Kennedy U., 1980. Curator San Mateo (Calif.) County Mus., 1978-79; intern Smithsonian Instn., Washington, 1979; San Francisco Fine Arts Mus., 1979-81; curator Presidio Army Mus., San Francisco, 1981-83; dir. U.S. Army Engr. Mus., Ft. Leonard Wood, Mo., 1983—2001; prof. history Columbia Coll., Ft. Leonard Wood, 1984—2001; dir. 2d Inf. Div. Mus., Republic of Korea, 2001—04. Cons. Nat. Park Svc., San Francisco, 1978; dir. mus. educators forum, 1983-85; historian 2d Inf. Divsn., 1994-96, 2001-04; guest lectr. Kookmin U., Seoul, 1995. Editor: Fort Leonard Wood, 1941, 1991; contbr. articles and monographs to mags. and newspapers; appeared in numerous TV documentaries and programs. Bd. dirs. South Ctrl. Mo. Arts Coun., Rolla, 1991. Mem. Am. Assn. Mus., Am. Assn. State and Local History, Internat. Commn. on Mus., Commn. on Mil. Mus. in Am., Rolls Royce Owners Club. Avocations: travel, archaeology, theater. Address: care Caitlyn Rodriguez PO Box 401 Rolla MO 65401

COMELLA, PHILLIP L., lawyer; b. 1955; BA cum laude, Beloit Coll., 1978; JD with honors, George Washington U., 1983. Bar: Ill. 1983, US Ct. Appeals DC cir., US Dist. Ct. (no. dist.) Ill. Ptnr. Seyfarth Shaw LLP, Chgo., chmn., Environ. Safety & Toxic Tort Practice Group. Spkr. in field; contbr. articles to profl. jour. Mem.: Ill. State Bar Assn., ABA. Office: Seyfarth Shaw LLP 55 East Monroe St Ste 4200 Chicago IL 60603 Office Phone: 312-269-8501. Office Fax: 312-269-8869. Business E-Mail: pcomella@seyfarth.com.

COMEROTA, ANTHONY JAMES, vascular surgeon, biomedical researcher; b. Newark, Aug. 4, 1948; s. Louis Anthony and Eleanor Dorothy (Dombroski) C.; m. Elsa Benavides, Aug. 18, 1973; children: Anthony James, Maya Christine, Mark Anthony. BA, Millikin U., 1970; MD, Temple U., 1974. Diplomate Am. Bd. Surgery. Surg. resident Temple U. Hosp., Phila., 1974-78; vascular surgery fellow Good Samaritan Hosp., Cin., 1979-81; from asst. prof. to prof. surgery Temple U. Hosp, Temple U. Sch. Medicine, Phila., 1981-88, prof. surgery, chief vascular surgery, 1988—2002; dir. Ctr. for Vascular Diseases Temple U. Hosp., Temple U. Sch. Medicine, Phila., 1995—2002; dir., chief vascular surgery Jobst Vascular Ctr., Toledo; clin. prof. U. Mich., Ann Arbor, 2002—. Editor: Thrombolytic Therapy for Peripheral Vascular Disease, 1995; co-editor: Prevention of Venous Thromboembolism, 1994. Fellow ACS, Royal Australian Coll. Surgeons; mem. Am. Surg. Assn., Soc. Vascular Surgery, Peripheral Vascular Soc. (pres. 1988-89), Am. Venous Forum (pres. 2000-01), Phila. Acad. Surgery (pres. 1996-97), Temple U. Sch. Medicine Alumni Assn. (pres. 1993-95), Alpha Omega Alpha. Office: Jobst Vascular Ctr 2109 Hughes Dr # 400 Toledo OH 43606 Office Phone: 419-291-2088. Business E-Mail: acomerota@jvc.org.

COMISAR, MICHAEL E., restaurant manager; Mng. ptnr. Maisonette Restaurant, Cin. Office: Maisonette 4149 Walton Creek Rd Cincinnati OH 45227-3917

COMISKEY, MICHAEL PETER, lawyer; b. Oak Park, Ill., Oct. 13, 1948; s. John B. and Jeanne M. (Platt) C.; m. Barbara A. Twardowski, Apr. 24, 1981; children: Julianne, Bridget, Eleanor, Michael Patrick. BA, U. Notre Dame, 1970; JD magna cum laude (hon.), Harvard U., 1975. Bar: Ill. 1975, US Dist. Ct. (no. dist.) Ill. 1975, US Dist. Ct. (ctrl. dist.) Ill., US Court of Appeals (6th, 7th & 8th cirs), Supreme Ct. of Ill. Ptnr. Locke Lord Bissell & Liddell LLP, Chgo., 1983—. Spkr. in field. Contbr. articles to profl. jour. Mem. Notre Dame Alumni Assn., Notre Dame Club of Chgo.; bd of trustees Fenwick H.S. Mem.: Phi Beta Kappa, ABA (antitrust law, profl. responsibility and ins. practice sect.), Chgo Bar Assn. Office: Locke Lord Bissell & Liddell LLP 111 S Wacker Dr Chicago IL 60606 Office Phone: 312-443-0427. Office Fax: 312-896-6427. Business E-Mail: mcomiskey@lockelord.com.

COMISKEY, NANCY, newspaper editor; Mng. editor features The Indpls. News; dep. mng. editor features and readership The Star & The News, Indpls., 1998—. Office: The Indpls News PO Box 145 Indianapolis IN 46206-0145

COMPTON, CLYDE D., lawyer; BA in Polit. Sci., DePauw Univ.; JD, Ind. Univ. Sch. of Law, Bloomington. Bar: US Supreme Ct. Atty. Portage City Coun. and Portage Twp. Trustee, Hodges & Davis PC, Merrillville, Ind. Bd. dir. (past pres.) Vis. Nurse Assn.; bd. dir. Salvation Army, Goodwill Industries; mem. (past pres.), Ind. Univ. Law Sch. Alumni Assn.; master Calumet Am. Inn of Ct. Mem.: Am. Trial Lawyers Assn., Ind. Bar Found. (dir., treas., sec., pres.), Lake County Bar Assn., Am. Bar Assn., Indiana State Bar Assn. (pres.-elect 2004, bd. mgrs., mem., Ho. of Del., treas.). Presbyn. Office: Hodges & Davis PC 8700 Broadway Merrillville IN 46410 Office Phone: 219-641-8700. Office Fax: 219-641-8710. Business E-Mail: ccompton@hodgesdavis.com.

COMPTON, RALPH THEODORE, JR., electrical engineering educator; b. St. Louis, July 26, 1935; s. Ralph Theodore and Ethel (Evans) C.; m. Lorraine Fielding, Nov. 9, 1957; children: Diane Marie, Ralph Theodore III, Richard Thomas. S.B., MIT, 1958; M.Sc., Ohio State U., 1961, PhD, 1964. Jr. engr. DECO Electronics, Leesburg, Va., 1958-59; sr. engr. Battelle Meml. Inst., Columbus, Ohio, 1959-62; asst. supr. Antenna Lab., Columbus, 1962-65; asst. prof. Case Inst. Tech., Cleve., 1965-67; guest prof. Tech. Hochschule, Munich, 1967-68; assoc. prof. Ohio State U., Columbus, 1968-78, prof. elec. engring., 1978-91; pres. Compton Rsch., Inc., Columbus, 1992—. Cons. to various orgns., U.S., Europe, Israel, 1969—. Author: Adaptive Antennas-Concepts and Performance, 1988; contbr. chpts. to books, articles to profl. jours. Fellow Battelle Meml. Inst., 1961; NSF fellow, 1967; recipient Outstanding Paper awards Ohio State Electro-Sci. Lab., 1978, 80, 82, M. Barry Carlton award IEEE Aerospace and Electric Systems Soc., 1983, Sr. Research award Ohio State U. Engring. Coll., 1983 Fellow IEEE (assoc. editor Jour. Trans. on Antennas Propagation 1970); mem. Antenna and Propagation Soc. (chmn. Columbus chpt. 1971-72), Sigma Xi (sec.-treas. Case Inst. Tech. chpt. 1965-67), Pi Mu Epsilon Home and Office: 477 Poe Ave Worthington OH 43085-3036 Office Phone: 614-885-0907. Business E-Mail: compton@ieee.org.

COMPTON, WILLIAM F., retired air transportation executive; b. Apr. 1947; m. Dreana Compton. A in Aerospace, Miami-Dade Coll. Flight instr., 1966; pilot TWA, 1968; exec. v.p. ops. Trans World Airlines, Inc., St. Louis, 1996—97, pres., COO, 1997—99, pres., CEO, 1999—2001, TWA LLC (subsidiary Am. Airlines), 2001; ret. Chmn. TWA br. Air Lines Pilots Assn., 1991-95, mem. exec.

bd.; dir., gen. mgr., exec. v.p. Opa Locka Flight Ctr.; pilot Iran Air and Nigeria Airways; chief pilot Make Believe Farm/Arabian Horse World mag.; guest lectr. Stanford U. Grad. Sch. Bus./Law Sch., Midwest Acad. Mgmt.

CONANT, HOWARD ROSSET, steel company executive; b. Chgo., Sept. 30, 1924; s. Louis J. and Fredericka (Rosset) Cohn; m. Doris S. Kaplan, Dec. 14, 1947; children: Alison Sue, Howard R., Meredith Ann. BS, U. Pa., 1947. Pres., dir. Interstate Steel Co., Des Plaines, Ill., 1947-71, chmn. bd., 1971-90; pres., dir. Elliott Paint & Varnish Co., Chgo., 1961-76. Dir. The Valspar Corp., 1977-91; chmn. bd. dirs. White Products Corp., 1965-67. Discussion leader Center Study of Continuing Edn., 1955-62; dir. Com. for Sane Nuclear Policy, 1964-69; mem. Bus. Execs. Move for Vietnam Peace, 1965-73. Served with AUS, 1943-46, PTO. Mem. World Pres.' Orgn., Ridge and Valley Tennis Club, Carlton Club, East Bank Club. Home: 736 Greenacres Ln Glenview IL 60025-3204 Office: 445 N Wells St Ste 403 Chicago IL 60610-4534

CONARD, NORMAN DALE, secondary school educator; BS, Azusa Pacific U.; MA in Edn., Pepperdine U., 1976; MS in History, Pittsburg State U., 1990. Tchr. social studies Mara HS, LA, 1976—81, LAB HS, LA, 1981—85; tchr. social studies, creative art Uniontown HS, Kans., 1987—. Named to Nat. Tchrs. Hall of Fame, 2007; recipient Kans. State Tchr. of Yr., 1992, 100 Most Influential Educators in Am., Northern Life, 2000, Social Studies Outstanding Educator, Kans. Coun. for the Social Studies, 2001, Kans. City Save a Child Award, 2001, Civil Rights Award, NEA, Gov.'s Award for Excellence in Edn., 2004, Kansas History Date Tchr. of Yr., 2007. Office: Uniontown High Sch 601 E 5th St Uniontown KS 66779-0070

CONATON, MICHAEL JOSEPH, diversified financial services company executive; b. Detroit, Aug. 3, 1933; s. John Martin and Margaret Alice (Cleary) C.; m. Nancy D. Kelley, June 13; children: Catherine, Macaira (dec.), Michael, Margaret, Elizabeth. BS, Xavier U., 1955. Public accountant Stanley A. Hitter, C.P.A., Cin., 1956-58; controller The Moloney Co., Albia, Iowa, 1958-61; v.p. fin. The Midland Co., Cin., 1961-80, sr. v.p., chief fin. officer, 1980-83, exec. v.p., chief fin. officer, 1983-88, pres., chief operating officer, 1988—, also dir., vice-chmn., 1998—. Interim pres. Xavier U., 1990-91. City councilman, Albia, 1959-61; trustee, chmn. bd. Xavier U., 1972. Served to lt. USMC, 1955-56. Mem. Fin. Execs. Inst., New Ohio Inst. (chmn.), Cin. Soc. Fin. Analysts, Athenaeum of Ohio (trustee), Met. Club (chmn. bd.). Home: 736 Elsinboro Dr Cincinnati OH 45226-1706 Office: The Midland Company PO Box 1256 Cincinnati OH 45201-1256 Home Phone: 513-871-3276; Office Phone: 513-947-5211.

CONAWAY, CHARLES C., former retail company executive; b. Saginaw, Mich., June 9, 1960; s. Corinne Conaway; m. Lisa deBeaubien; 2 children. BS in acctg., Mich. State U., 1982; MBA in fin., U. Mich., 1984. Co-founder, exec. v.p., COO Reliable Drug Stores, Inc., Indpls., 1989-92; sr. v.p. pharmacy CVS Corp., Woonsocket, RI, 1992-95, exec. v.p., CFO, 1995-99, pres., COO, 1999-2000; chmn., CEO Kmart Corp., Troy, Mich., 2000—02.

CONCANNON, JAMES M., lawyer, educator, dean; b. Columbus, Ga., Oct. 2, 1947; s. James M. Jr. and Mary Jane Concannon; m. Melissa P. Masoner, June 9, 1988. BS, U. Kans., 1968, JD, 1971. Law clk. Kans. Ins. Commn., Topeka, 1971; rsch. atty. Kans. Supreme Ct., Topeka, 1971-73; asst. prof. law Washburn U., Topeka, 1973-75, assoc. prof. law, 1976-81, prof., 1981—2006, disting. prof., 2006—, dean, 1988-2001. Vis. prof. law Washington U., St. Louis, 1979; active Kans. Commn. on Pub. Understanding of Law, 1983-89, Task Force on Law Enforcement Consolidation, Topeka, 1991-92; mem. Nat. Conf. Commrs. on Uniform State Laws, 1998—, Pattern Instrns. for Kans.-Civil and Criminal Com., Kans. Jud. Coun., 2001—; mem. Kans. Commn. on Jud. Performance, 2006—. Co-author: Kans. Appellate Practice Manual, 1978, Kansas Statutes of Limitations, 1988; sr. contbn. editor: Evidence in America-Federal Rules in the States, 1987. Coord. Citizens to Keep Politics Out Of Our Courts, Topeka, 1984; mem. bd. dirs. Kans. Legal Svcs. for Prisoners, 2003—; co-reporter Citizens Justice Initiative, 1997-99; chmn. legal com. Concerned Citizens Topeka, 1995-99; bd. dirs. Mut. Funds Waddell and Reed, Inc., 1997—. Master: Topeka Am. Inn of Ct. (pres. 2001—02); fellow: Kans. Bar Found., Am. Bar Found. (state chair 2002—05); mem.: Assn. Am. Law Schs. (com. on bar admission, lawyer performance 1994—97), Kans. Bar Assn. (CLE com. 1976—2001, Outstanding Svc. award 1982, 2003), Washburn Law Sch. Alumni Assn. (life), Order of Coif. Office: Washburn U Law Sch 1700 SW College Ave Topeka KS 66621-0001

CONDRON, DANIEL RALPH, academic administrator, metaphysics educator; b. Chillicothe, Mo., Jan. 30, 1953; s. Ralph Wesley and Rosa Irene (Garber) C.; m. Barbara Gail O'Guinn, Feb. 29, 1992; 1 child, Hezekiah Daniel. BS, U. Mo., 1975, MS, 1978; DDiv, Coll. Metaphysics, Springfield, Mo., 1982, D in Metaphysics, 1985. Cert. counselor; ordained to ministry Interfaith Ch. of Metaphysics. Dir. Sch. Metaphysics, Des Moines, 1980, Kansas City, Mo., 1981, regional dir. Colo., 1982-85, Chgo. and Detroit, 1985-90, pres. bd. nat. hdqs. Windyville, Mo., 1988—; chancellor, prof. Coll. Metaphysics, Windyville, Mo., 1990—97, chmn bd., 1997—. Tchg. asst. U. Mo., Columbia, 1977; sales and mgmt. cons. Am. Media, Des Moines, 1980-83; spkr. in field. Author: Dreams of the Soul, 1991, Permanent Healing, 1992, Universal Language of Mind, 1994, Understanding Your Dreams, 1994, Seven Secret Keys to Prosperity and Abundance, 1996, Superconscious Meditation, 1997, The Four Stages of Growth, 2001, Atlantis: The History of the World, Vol. 1, 2002, Tao Te Ching, Interpreted and Explained, 2003, The Purpose of Life, 2004, The Secret Code of Revelation, 2006, The Emptiness Sutra, 2007; pub. jour. Thresholds Quar., 1988-; internat. radio and TV guest including BBC, Radio Hong Kong, Voice of Am., 1979—. Mem. Sch. Metaphysics Assocs. (pres.), Nat. Space Soc., Planetary Soc., Alpha Gamma Rho, Alpha Zeta. Achievements include implementer and designer of organic and bio-dynamic farming and agriculture at the 1500 acre College of Metaphysics campus, landscape designer and creator of energetic campus using sacred geometry, including octahedrons, cosehedrons and dodecahedrons placed along ley lines for 1500 acre college of metaphysics campus, discoverer and developer of the Universal language of mind as it applies to dreams, to the Bible and other holy works; discoverer of specific attitudes that cause specific disease and disorders in the body. Home: 163 Moon Valley Rd Windyville MO 65783 Office: Sch Metaphysics Nat Headquarters Windyville MO 65783

CONGALTON, SUSAN TICHENOR, lawyer; b. Mt. Vernon, NY, July 12, 1946; d. Arthur George and M. Marjorie Tichenor; m. Christopher William Congalton, May 29, 1971. BA summa cum laude, Loretto Heights Coll., 1968; JD, Georgetown U., 1971. Bar: NY 1972, Ill. 1986, Colo. 1990. Assoc. Reavis & McGrath (now Fulbright & Jaworski), YC, 1971-78, ptnr., 1978-85; v.p., gen. counsel, sec. Carson Pirie Scott & Co., Chgo., 1985-87, sr. v.p. fin. and law, 1987-89; mng. dir. Lupine LLC (formerly known as Lupine Ptnrs.), Chgo., 1989—; chmn., CEO Calif. Amforge Corp., 2002—. Bd. dirs. Harris Fin. Corp., Harris Bankcorp, Inc.; chmn. Cmty. Reinvestment Act Com., 1990-97, chmn. audit com., 1997—; chmn. bd., CEO, Calif. Amforge Corp., 2002—. Mem. editorial staff Georgetown U. Law Jour., 1969-70, editor, 1970-71. Bd. overseers Ill. Inst. Tech., Chgo., Chgo. Kent Coll. Law, 1985-89; bus. adv. coun. Bus. Sch., U. Ill., Chgo., 1987-90; planning com. Ann. Corp. Counsel Inst., 1986-89; bd. dirs. Ill. Inst. Continuing Legal Edn., 1992-95; mem. Chgo. Workforce Bd., 1995-98; chmn. Strategic Planning Task force, 1995-96, chmn. Performance Rev. Com., 1996-98. Mem. ABA, Nat. Assn. Corp. Dirs. (bd. dirs. Chgo. chpt. 2001—), Econ. Club Chgo., Chgo. Club (bd. dirs. 1996—2004, treas. 1999-02, sec. 2002—04). Office: Lupine LLC 1520 Kensington Rd Ste 112 Oak Brook IL 60523-2140

CONGER, WILLIAM FRAME, artist, educator; b. Dixon, Ill., May 29, 1937; s. Robert Allen and Catherine Florence (Kelly) C.; m. Kathleen Marie Onderak, May 23, 1964; children: Sarah Elizabeth, Clarisa Lynn. Student, Art Inst. Chgo., 1954, 56-57, 60, 62; BFA, U. N.Mex., 1960; MFA, U. Chgo., 1966. Asst. prof. Rock Valley Coll., Rockford, 1966-71; vis. lectr. Beloit Coll., 1969; prof., chmn. dept. art DePaul U., Chgo., 1971-85; vis. artist U. Chgo., 1976, 83, Cornell U., 1980; Sch. Art Inst. Chgo., 1985, Univ. Iowa; adj. prof. So. Ill. U., 1984; chmn. dept. art theory and practice Northwestern U., Evanston, Ill., 1985-99, prof., 1985—2006, prof. emeritus, 2006-; numerous lectures. One man shows Burpee Mus., Rockford, Ill., 1971, Douglas Kenyon Gallery, Chgo., 1974, 75, Krannert Ctr. for Arts, Urbana, Ill., 1976, Zaks Gallery, Chgo., 1978, 80, 83, Roy Boyd Gallery, Chgo., 1985, 87, 90, 92, 94, 96, 97, 98, 99, 2000, 01, 02, 04, 07, Janus Gallery, Santa Fe, 1992, Tarbel Mus., Ill., 1993, Univ. Club Chgo., 1998, Jonson Mus., Albuquerque, 1998, Walters Art Ctr., Tulsa, 2000, 01, Tadu Contemporary Santa Fe, 2003, 04, 05, Metropolitan Capitol Bank, Chgo., 2006; group shows include Art Inst. Chgo., 1963, 71, 73, 78, 80, 84-85, Mus. Contemporary Art, Chgo., 1976, 96-97, Krannert Mus., Urbana, 1976, Ill. State Mus., 1978, 88-89, E.B. Crocker Gallery, Sacramento, 1977, Phoenix Mus., 1977, Mitchell Mus., 1980, Notre Dame U., 1981, Sonoma State U., 1983, Cowles Mus., 1983, Arts Club Chgo., 1983-97, Sheldon Meml. Gallery, U. Nebr., 1984, Anchorage Fine Arts Mus., 1985, Ark Art Ctr., 1985, Block Mus., Northwestern U., 1986, 90, 96-97, 2005, 06, Smart Mus., 1996, Printworks Gallery, Chgo., 2001, 03, 05, EastSide Editions, San Francisco, 2006-07; represented in permanent collections Art Inst. Chgo., Mus. Contemporary Art, Chgo., Smart Mus., U. Chgo., Ill. State Mus., Chgo., No. Ill. U., DePaul U., Jonson Mus., U. N.Mex., Block Mus., City of Chgo. Public Art Collection, Bucknell U., Wellesley Coll., Brauer Mus., India, Wichita Art Mus., Kans., others; also pvt. collections U.S. and worldwide; numerous catalogs, revs. and commentary in Arts mag., Art Forum, Art in Am., Ciamese, Art News, Art Criticism, Art & Antiques; others; author essays in Whitewalls, Chicago/Art/Write, Psychoanalytic Perspectives on Art, Psychoanalytic Studies of Biography, Critical Inquiry, other jours., papers and career materials in archives of Am. art, Smithsonian Instn., DC. Bd. dirs. Ox Bow Art Sch., 1982-86; adv. bd. Renaissance Soc., 1988-99; bd. trustees St. Benedict H.S., Chgo., 1994—2000; vis. com., DePaul U. Art Mus., 2004-; referee NEH, 1989; interviewee TV and radio programs including Am. Art Forum. Recipient Bartels award Art Inst. Chgo., 1971; Clusmann award, 1973; Friedman awards U. Chgo., 1965, 66. Mem. Coll. Art Assn. Am., Sons of Am. Revolution, Soc. Mayflower Descendants, Aldren Kindred of Am., Arts Club Chgo., Phi Sigma Tau. Office: Northwestern U Dept Art Theory & Practice Rm 244 Kresge Hall Evanston IL 60201 Home: 3500 N Lake Shore Dr 15A Chicago IL 60657-1815 Studio: 3711 N Ravenswood Chicago IL 60613 Office Phone: 773-296-4595. Personal E-mail: w-conger@sbcglobal.net. Business E-Mail: w-conger@northwestern.edu.

CONIDI, DANIEL JOSEPH, private investigation agency executive; b. Chgo., Mar. 11, 1957; s. Joseph Frank and Gloria (Zimmerman) C. BS, SUNY, Albany, 1983; MA, Chgo. State U., 1987. Lic. pvt. detective Ill. Pres. Daniel J. Conidi-Assocs., Chgo., 1981—; cons. Office Cook County Sheriff, Chgo., 1983-90. Lectr. in field. Author: Professional Investigative Methods, 1984, Private Investigators Training Manual, 1986. Recipient cert. of appreciation Boys Town, 1982; named Ky. col. State of Ky., 1987. Mem. SAR (life), NRA (life).Cert. Fraud Examiners Assn. (cert). World Assn. Detectives, Internat. Police Congress, Coun. Internat. Investigators, Nat. Assn. Investigations and Security, Fraternal Order Police, Navy League (life), Univ. Club, Masons, Shriners, Am. Mensa (life), Experimental Aircraft Assn. (life), Am. Radio Relay League (life). Presbyterian. Avocations: flying, writing, amateur radio. Home: 500 Ashland Ave River Forest IL 60305-1825 Office: 734 N La Salle Dr Ste 1082 Chicago IL 60610-3530 Office Phone: 708-366-9900. Personal E-mail: dconidi@ameritech.net.

CONKLIN, MARA LORAINE, public relations executive; b. Vallejo, Calif., July 28, 1962; d. Kenneth J. and Laura T. (Siegrist) Cichosz; m. Rex D. Conklin, Sept. 6, 1986; children: Elisabeth, Emily, Margaret. BA, Marquette U., 1984. Nat. news editl. staff Nat. Safety Coun., Chgo., 1984-85; corp. comm. specialist Household Internat., Prospect Hgts., Ill., 1985-86; acct. supr. Posner McGrath Ltd., Lincolnshire, Ill., 1986-90, v.p., 1990-92, sr. v.p., 1992-94, exec. v.p., 1994-97, pres., 1997-98, Clarus Comms. Ltd., Libertyville, Ill., 1998—. Recipient Spectra award Internat. Assn. Bus. Communicators, 1992, 94, Silver Trumpet award Publicity Club Chgo., 1993. Mem. Marquette Club Chgo. (chair alumni com. 1986-94, pres. 1994-96). Office: Clarus Comms Ltd 620 Mullady Pkwy Libertyville IL 60048-3729

CONKLIN, THOMAS WILLIAM, lawyer; b. Chgo., Mar. 1, 1938; s. Clarence Robert and Ellen Pauline (Gleason) C.; children: Thomas William, Sarah Adrienne. BA, Yale U., 1960; JD, U. Chgo., 1963. Bar: Ill. 1964, Mich. 1997. Ptnr. Upton, Conklin & Leahy, Chgo., 1969-72, Conklin, Leahy & Eisenberg, Chgo., 1972-79, Conklin & Adler, Ltd., Chgo., 1979-87, Conklin & Roadhouse, Chgo., 1988-95; Rivkin, Radler & Kremer, Chgo., 1995-97; ptnr. Conklin, Murphy, Conklin & Snyder, Chgo., 1997—2004, Conklin & Snyder LLC, Chgo., 2004—05, Conklin & Conklin LLC, Chgo., 2005—. Contbr. numerous articles to legal jours. With USAF, 1963-64. Mem. ABA, Fed. Bar Assn., Am. Arbitration Assn., Internat. Assn. Ins. Counsel, Chgo. Bar Assn., Maritime Law Assn., Mich. Bar Assn., Chgo. Bar Assn., Union League Club Chgo, The Park Club of Kalamazoo. Home: PO Box 189 Bangor MI 49013-0189 Office: Conklin & Conklin LLC 53 W Jackson Blvd Ste 1150 Chicago IL 60604-3790

CONLEY, EUGENE ALLEN, retired insurance company executive; b. Nebraska City, Nebr., Oct. 3, 1925; s. Melville Evans and Margaret (Allen) C.; m. Erma Grace Fuller, June 27, 1948; children: Tom, Roger, John, Carol Sue. BS, U. Nebr., 1949; DSc (hon.), U. Nebr. Med. Ctr.; LLD (hon.), Nebr. Wesleyan U. C.L.U. Agt. Am. Mut. Life Ins. Co., Omaha, 1948-54, supr., supt. agts., v.p., dir. agts., dir. Des Moines, 1954-72; exec. v.p., dir. Guarantee Mut. Life Co., Omaha, 1972-76, pres., 1976-89, chmn. bd., 1989-90; retired, 1990. Bd. dirs. Omaha Zool. Soc.; trustee, past chmn. Nebr. Ind. Coll. Found.; bd. trustees U. Nebr. Found., Lincoln; civilian aide to sec. Army; mem. pres.'s adv. coun. Creighton U.; past chmn. bd. govs. Nebr. Wesleyan U.; co-chmn. fund drive United Way Midlands, 1976-77, pres., 1979-80; past crusade chmn. Am. Cancer Soc.; co-chmn. NCCJ; chmn. bd. Bishop Clarkson Coll., 1990; chmn. Omaha Community Found., 1991. Served with USNR, 1943-46. Recipient Americanism citation B'Nai B'rith, 1982, Builder award U. Nebr.; named Citizen of Yr. United Way, 1983 Mem. at. Assn. Life Underwriters, Coll. Life Underwriters, Omaha C. of C. (chmn. dir.), Phi Kappa Psi. Clubs: Omaha, Omaha Country, Plaza, Masons, Shriners. Office: Guarantee Centre 8801 Indian Hills Dr Omaha NE 68114-4059 Home: PO Box 150 Carmel CA 93921-0150

CONLIN, ROXANNE BARTON, lawyer; b. Huron, SD, June 30, 1944; d. Marion William and Alyce Muraine (Madden) Barton; m. James Clyde Conlin, Mar. 21, 1964; children: Jacalyn Rae, James Barton, Deborah Ann, Douglas Benton BA, Drake U., 1964, JD, 1966, MPA, 1979; LLD (hon.), U. Dubuque, 1975. Bar: Iowa 1966. Assoc. Davis, Huebner, Johnson & Burt, Des Moines, 1966-67; dep. indsl. commr. State of Iowa, 1967-68, asst. atty. gen., 1969-76; U.S. atty. So. Dist. Iowa, 1977-81; ptnr. Conlin, P.C., Des Moines, 1983—. Adj. prof. law U. Iowa, 1977-79; chmn. Iowa Women's Polit. Caucus, 1973-75, del. nat. steering com., 1973-77; cons. U.S. Commn. on Internat. Women's Year, 1976-77; gen. counsel NOW Legal Def. and Edn. Fund, 1985-88, pres., 1986-88; lectr. in field. Co-editor: AAJ Litigating Tort Cases, 6 vols., 2003; contbr. articles to profl. jours. Nat. committeewoman Iowa Young Dems.; pres. Polk County Young Dems., 1965-66; del. Iowa Presdl. Conv., 1972; Dem. candidate for gov. of Iowa, 1982; bd. dirs. Riverhills Day Care Ctr., YWCA; chmn. Drake U. Law Sch. Endowment Trust, 1985-86; bd. counselors Drake U., 1982-86; pres. founder Civil Justice Found., 1986-88; pres. Roscoe Pound Found., 1994-97; chair Iowa Dem. Party, 1998-99; chair Edwards For Pres. Iowa, 2004, 2008. Named scholarship in her honor, Kansas City Women Lawyers; named one of Top Ten Litigators, at. Law Jour, 1989, 100 Most Influential Attys., 1991, 50 Most Powerful Women Attys., Nat. Law Jour., 1998, 10 Most Influential Women Attys., 2002; recipient award, Iowa ACLU, 1974, Alumnus of Yr. award, Drake U. Law Sch., 1989, Ann. award, Young Women's Resource Ctr., 1989, Verne Lawyer Outstanding Mem. award, Iowa Trial Lawyers Assn., 1994, Rosalie Wahl award, Minn. Women Lawyers, 1998, Marie Lambert award, 2000, Mary Louise Smith award, YWCA, 2001, Lifetime Achievement award, Des Moines Human Rights Commn., 2003, Ruth Bader Ginsberg award, 2004, Iowa Juneteenth award, State of Iowa, 2005, Feminist Activist award, Bus. Record and Drake U., 2006, Pub. Justice award, ITLA, 2007; scholar Reader's Digest scholar, 1963—64, Fishcher Found., 1965—66. Mem.: AAJ (chmn. consumer and victims coalition com. 1985—87, chmn. edn. dept 1987—88, parliamentarian 1988—89, sec. 1989—90, v.p. 1990—91, pres.-elect 1991—92, pres. 1992—93, Lifetime Achievement award 2003, Champion of Justice award 2006, Leonard Ring Champion of Justice award 2006), ABA, NOW, Nat. Ctr. State Ct. Lawyers Com. (com. mem. 2003—), Nat. Inst. Trial Advocacy (bd. trustees 2003—06), Trial Lawyers Care (bd. dirs.), Inner Circle of Advocates, Higher Edn. Commn. Iowa (co-chmn. 1988—90), Iowa Acad. Trial Lawyers, Internat. Acad. Trial Lawyers, Assn. Trial Lawyers Iowa (bd. dirs.), Iowa Bar Assn., Chi Omega, Alpha Lambda Delta, Phi Beta Kappa. Office: Griffin Bldg 319 7th St Ste 600 Des Moines IA 50309-3826 Office Phone: 515-283-1111. Business E-Mail: rconlin@roxanneconlinlaw.com.

CONLIN, THOMAS, conductor; b. Arlington, Va., Jan. 29, 1944; BMus, Peabody Conservatory Music, 1966, MMus, 1967; studied with Leonard Bernstein, Erich Leinsdorf, Sir Adrian Boult. Artistic dir. Chamber Opera Soc., Balt., 1966-72; assoc. condr. N.C. Symphony Orch., 1972-74; music dir. Queens (N.Y.) Orchestral Soc., 1974-76; condr. Amarillo (Tex.) Symphony Orch., 1976-84, W.Va. Symphony Orch., 1983-2001, condr. laureate, 2001—; prin. condr. Toledo Opera, 2002—. Asst. prof. mus. CUNY, 1974-76. Recording: Naxos and Bridge. Recipient Grammy award for Contemporary Classical Composition, 2001, Indie award nomination for Best Orch. Rec., 2002. Mem. Am. Symphony Orch. League, Nat. Opera Assn., Condrs. Guild, Opera America. Studio: 8440 Augusta Ln Holland OH 43528 Office Phone: 419-867-6977. E-mail: theconmusic@aol.com.

CONLON, HARRY B., JR., banking company executive; b. Green Bay, Wis., May 15, 1935; s. Harry B. and Alice (O'Neil) C.; m. Margaret Sullivan. BS in Bus., U. Notre Dame, 1957; JD, U. Wis., 1963. With Continental Ill. Nat. Bank, Chgo., 1963-65; v.p. Kellogg-Citizens Nat. Bank, Green Bay, 1965-75, also bd. dirs.; chmn., chief exec. officer Associated Banc-Corp., Green Bay, 1975—. Served to lt. USNR, 1957-63. Mem. Wis. Bankers Assn. (bd. dirs. exec. counsel 1984-87), Bankers Round Table, Am. Bankers Coun.

CONLON, JAMES CHARLES, former state legislator; m. Janice D. Winters; 7 children. BS, U. Notre Dame; MEd, Pa. State U. Tchr.; rep. Dist. 19 Ind. Ho. of Reps., 1990-97, mem. cities and towns, edn. coms., mem. local govt. and natural resources coms., mem. urban affairs com., dep. spkr. pro tem. Mem. Crown Point (Ind.) City Coun., 1980-90; bd. mem. works and Pub. Safety, Crown Point, 1985-90, mem. planning com., 1987-90. Home: 341 Maple Ln Crown Point IN 46307-4544

CONLON, SUZANNE B., federal judge; b. 1939; AB, Mundelein Coll., 1963; JD, Loyola U., Chgo., 1968; postgrad., U. London, 1971. Law clk. to judge U.S. Dist. Ct. (no. dist.) Ill., 1968-71; assoc. Pattishall, McAuliffe & Hostetter, 1972-73, Schiff Hardin & Waite, 1973-75; asst. U.S. atty. U.S. Dist. Ct. (no. dist.) Ill., 1976-77, 82-86, U.S. Dist. Ct. (cen. dist.) Calif., 1978-82; exec. dir. U.S. Sentencing Commn., 1986-88; spl. counsel to assoc. atty. gen., 1988; judge U.S. Dist. Ct. (no. dist.) Ill., 1988—. Asst. prof. law De Paul U., Chgo., 1972-73, lectr., 1973-75; adj. prof. Northwestern U. Sch. Law, 1991-95; vice chmn. Chgo. Bar Assn. Internat. Inst., 1993—; vis. com. U. Chgo. Harris Grad. Sch. Pub. Policy, 1997—; bd. mem. DePaul U. Coll. Law, Internat. Human Rights Law Inst. Bd. mem. Ill. St. Andrew Soc. Mem. ABA, FBA, Am. Judicature Soc., Internat. Bar Assn. Judges Forum, Lawyers Club Chgo. (pres. 1996-97). Office: US Dist Ct No Dist Everett McKinley Dirksen Bldg 219 S Dearborn St Ste 2356 Chicago IL 60604-1878

CONLON, WILLIAM F., lawyer; b. Chgo., Jan. 14, 1945; AB, Ind. U., 1967; JD, U. Ill., 1970. Bar Ill. 1970, Iowa 1970, U.S. Supreme Ct. 1975. Asst. U.S. Atty. U.S. Attys. Office (no. dist.) Ill., 1974-79, chief civil divsn., 1977-79; ptnr. corp. criminal def. and internal investigations Sidley Austin Brown & Wood, Chgo., gen. counsel and mem. exec. com. Chmn. Ill. State Bd. Ethics, 1986-88, active, 1982-88, Jud. Inquiry Bd., 1992—97; adj. prof. law Northwestern U., 1991—. Pres. Glencoe (Ill.) Sch. Bd., 1987-88, active, 1981-89. 1st lt. US Army, 1970-72. Fellow Am. Coll. Trial Lawyers. Office: Sidley Austin Brown & Wood LLP Bank One Plz 10 S Dearborn St Chicago IL 60603 Office Phone: 312-853-7384. Office Fax: 312-853-7036. Business E-Mail: wconlon@sidley.com.

CONMY, PATRICK A., federal judge; b. 1934; BA, Harvard U., 1955; JD, Georgetown U., 1959. Bar: Va. 1959, N.D. 1959. Ptnr. Lundberg, Conmy et al, Bismarck, N.D., 1959-85; mem. Bismarck City Commn., 1968-76; state rep. N.D. House Reps., Bismarck, 1976-85; judge U.S. Dist. Ct. N.D., Bismarck, 1985—. Office: US Dist Ct Fed Bldg 220 E Rosser Ave Rm 411 PO Box 1578 Bismarck ND 58502-1578

CONN, GORDON BRAINARD, JR., lawyer; b. St. Louis, Dec. 20, 1944; BA, Macalester Coll., 1967; JD, U. Mich., 1970. Bar: Minn. 1970, U.S. Supreme Ct. 1986; cert. in bus. bankruptcy law Am. Bd. Certification. Law clk. to Chief Justice Minn. Supreme Ct., St. Paul, 1970-71; ptnr. Faegre & Benson, Mpls., 1971-99, Kalina, Wills, Gisvold & Clark, P.L.L.P., Mpls., 1999—. Mem. ABA, Am. Bankruptcy Inst., Minn. State Bar Assn., Comml. Law League Am., Nat. Assn. Bankruptcy Trustees. Office: # 560 6160 Summit Dr N Minneapolis MN 55430-2100 Office Phone: 612-789-9000. Business E-Mail: conn@kwge-law.com.

CONNEALY, MATT J., state legislator; b. Oakland, Nebr., Dec. 11, 1951; m. Judith Scherer Connealy, May 25, 1974; children: Maggie, Mick. Student, Coll. St. Thomas, St. Paul, U. Nebr., 1970-73. Farmer; mem. Nebr. Legislature from 16th dist., Lincoln, 1998—. Former mem. Lyons-Decatur N.E. Sch. Bd., Gov.'s Agr. Adv. Com., Nebr. Ethanol Authority and Devel. Bd., Archdiocesan Pastoral Coun., Archdiocese Omaha, Biomass to Energy Adv. Group, U.S. Dept. Energy, We. Area Power Adminstrn., Am. Corn Growers Bd., Elm Creek Task Force, Burt County Farm Crisis Com.; mem. coun. exec. com. and market devel. com. U.S. Feed Grains Coun.; mem. ctrl. com. and exec. com. agr. rep. Nebr. Dem. Party; mem. utilization and mktg. bd. Nebr. Corn Devel.; bd. dirs. Burt County Pub. Power; treas. Nebr. Farmers Union; mem. parish coun., instr. youth edn. Holy Family Cath. Ch. Home: 2999 Old Highway 118 Decatur NE 68020-2046 Office: State Capitol Dist 16 PO Box 94604 Rm 1101 Lincoln NE 68509

CONNELLY, DEIRDRE P., pharmaceutical executive; b. San Juan; BA in Econs. and Mktg., Lycoming Coll., Williamsport, Pa., 1983; grad. Advanced Mgmt. Program, Harvard U., 2000. Sales rep. Eli Lilly & Co., 1983—84, mktg. assoc. San Juan, 1984—89, sales supr. Phila., 1989—90, product mgr. diabetes San Juan, 1990—91, nat. sales mgr., 1991—92, mktg. & sales dir., 1992—93, mktg. & sales dir. Caribbean, 1993—95, gen mgr. Eli Lilly PR SA, 1995—97, regional sales dir., exec. dir. global mktg. Evista Indpls., 1997—2001, leader women's health bus. Lilly USA, 2001—03, exec. dir. human resources Lilly USA, 2003, v.p. human resources, 2004, sr. v.p. human resources, 2004—05, pres. Lilly USA, 2005—. Bd. dir. Macy's, Inc., 2007—. Named one of 50 Most Powerful Women in Bus., Fortune mag., 2006. Office: Eli Lilly & Co Lilly Corp Ctr Indianapolis IN 46285 Office Phone: 317-276-2000.

CONNELLY, JOHN JAMES, retired oil company technical specialist; b. Lima, Ohio, Aug. 14, 1935; s. Robert Vincent and Helen Josephine (Hay) C.; m. Aug. 22, 1959 (dec. Aug. 1991); children: Thomas, Kathleen, Joseph, Patrick; m. Virginia Connelly, July, 1993. BSChemE, Ohio State U., 1958; MBA with honors, Baldwin Wallace U., 1975. Registered profl. engr., Ohio. Engr. Std. Oil of Ohio, Lima, 1958-63; rsch. assoc. Battelle Meml. Inst., Columbus, Ohio, 1963-65; tech. specialist Owens Corning Fiberglas, Granville, Ohio, 1965-67; sr. engr. Std. Oil of Ohio, Lima, 1967-71, tech. program analyst Cleve., 1971-74, linear program specialist, 1974-78, fed. affairs analyst, 1978-81; project leader Std. of Ohio/Brit. Petroleum Am., Cleve., 1981-92; tech. specialist BP Am., Cleve., 1992-95; ret., 1995; part time tech. specialist Paramount Tech. Svcs., 1995—. Instr. Ohio State U., Lima, 1961-63. Advisor Jr. Achievement, Lima, 1960-62; treas. Harding Mid. Sch. PTA, Lakewood, Ohio, 1975-77, Music Parents Assn., Lakewood, 1978-80, Sch. Bd. Candidate Treas., Lakewood, 1981; mem. Vols. for Internat. Tech. Assistance, 1988—; vol. mediator Conflict Resolution Ctr., 2000—. Roman Catholic. Avocations: reading, biking, needlecrafts. Home: 2114 Hathaway Ct Avon OH 44011 Personal E-mail: jconnelly001@centurytel.net.

CONNETT, JIM, radio director; b. Effingham, Ill. BA in Comms., So. Ill. U., Edwardsville. Program dir. Classic 99, St. Louis. Office: Classic 99 85 Founders Ln Saint Louis MO 63105

CONNOLLY, C. LAWRENCE, lawyer; BA, U. Notre Dame, 1969; JD, Harvard U., 1972. Bar: Ill. 1972. V.p., gen. counsel Hewitt Assocs., LLC, Lincolnshire, Ill. Contbr. articles to numerous profl. jours.

CONNOLLY, GERALD EDWARD, lawyer; b. Boston, Oct. 13, 1943; s. Thomas E. and Grace J. (Fitzgerald) C.; m. Elizabeth Heidi Eckert, Jan. 6, 1968; children: Matthew F., Dennis F., David D., Edward F. BS, Coll. of Holy Cross, 1965; JD, U. Va., 1972. Bar: Wis. 1972, U.S. Tax Ct. 1973. From assoc. to ptnr. Whyte & Hirschboeck S.C., Milw., 1972-78; ptnr. Minahan & Peterson S.C., Milw., 1978-91, Quarles & Brady, 1991—. Bd. dirs., sec. Reinhart Real Estate

Group, Inc., Reinhart Retail Group; sec. Hometown Inc.; bd. dirs. Hatco Corp., Milw., Adaptive Engring. Lab., Inc., Diversatek, Inc., Medovations Inc., Sunlite Plastics, Inc., Milw.; sec. Radisson LaCrosse Hotel, Water Blasting Inc. Trustee Emory T. Clark Family Charitable Found., D.B. Reinhart Family Found.; mem. Circle of Care Children's Hosp. Wis.; vice chmn., bd. dirs. Children's Hosp. Wis. Found. Lt. USN, 1966-69. Mem.: ABA, Kiawah Island Club, North Shore Country Club, Order of Coif. Home: 10134 N Range Line Rd # 27W Mequon WI 53092-5435 Office: Quarles & Brady LLP 411 E Wisconsin Ave Ste 2040 Milwaukee WI 53202-4497 Office Phone: 414-277-5373. Business E-Mail: gec@quarles.com.

CONNOLLY, MIKE W., state legislator; b. Dubuque, Iowa, Oct. 31, 1945; m. Martha Fessler. BA, Loras Coll., 1967, MA, 1976. Tchr. Dubuque Sr. H.S., sch. adminstr.; mem. Iowa Ho. of Reps., Iowa Senate from 18th dist., 1988—. Mem. Greater Dubuque Devel. Corp. Mem. St. Joseph's Ch., Duuque County Dem. Party, Regional Coord. Coun. With U.S. Army Res. Mem. Dubuque Edn. Assn., Four Mounds Assn., Loras Club. Office: State Capitol Dist 18 3 9th And Grand Des Moines IA 50319-0001 Home: 2600 Renaissance Dr Apt 3 Dubuque IA 52001-3087 E-mail: mike_connolly@legis.state.ia.us.

CONNOLLY, WILLIAM M., state supreme court justice; b. 1938; Undergrad., Creighton U., 1956—59, JD, 1963. Dep. atty. Adams County, 1964—66, atty., 1967—72; pvt. law practice Hastings, 1972—91; former judge Nebr. Ct. of Appeals, Lincoln, 1992—94; assoc. justice Nebr. Supreme Ct., Lincoln, justice, 1994—. Mem.: Nebr. State Bar Assn. Office: Nebr Supreme Ct Room 2210 State Capital Bldg Lincoln NE 68509

CONNOR, CAROL J., library director; BA in Hist., Molloy Coll., 1964; MA in Hist., Georgetown U., 1970; MLS, Drexel U., 1972. Various adminstrv. positions in ednl. fields, various US Cities, 1964—72; spl. asst. tech. processes divsn. Lincoln City Librs., Nebr., 1972—73, coord. tech. processes divsn., 1973—76, asst. dir., 1976—78, dir., 1978—. Mem. Mayor's Com. for Internat. Friendship, Lincoln, 1973—; adv. com. U. Nebr., search for dean of librs., 1984-85; del. to cmty. retreat, Star Venture, 1986, edn. task force, 1987-88, vocat. edn. task force, 1988-89, downtown child care task force, 1988-89; mem. cmty. adv. com. Lincoln Pub. Schs. Search for English Cons., 1991, Search for Media Dir., 1992; mem. Nebr. Ctr. for Book Bd., 1990-95, Nebr. Libr. Commn. state adv. coun. 1985-86, Nebr. Lit. Festival Com., 1990-92; bd. dirs. Postsecondary Ednl. Librs. and Resource Ctrs. of Nebr. 1981-84, chair 1982; mem. edn. com. Am. Cancer Soc., Lancaster County, Nebr., 1989-91, Family Svcs. Bd., 1991—, vice chair chair elect 1992, chair, 1994; leadership Lincoln VI 1990-91; mem. Lincoln Cancer Ctr. adv. bd., 1988-94, vice chair 1991-94. Mem. ALA, (bylaws com., membership com., LITA/LAMA conf. com. 1996-97), Mountain Plains Libr. Assn. (chair continuing edn. com. 1984-85; membership devel. com. 1986-87, vice chair and chair of pub. libr. sect. 1975-77, v.p./ pres. elect 1996-97, pres. 1997-98), Nebr. Libr. Assn. (chair intellectual freedom com. 1975-76, state rep. to Mountain Plains Libr. Assn., 1984-86, vice chair and chair of pub. libr. sect. 1987-89), Urban Librs. Coun. (leadership progs. 1994-95), Capitol Bus. and Profl. Women (v.p. 1983), Downtown Lincoln Assn. (mktg. com. 1988-89). Office: Lincoln City Librs 136 S 14th St Lincoln NE 68508-1899 Office Phone: 402-441-8500. E-mail: library@lincolnlibraries.org.

CONNOR, CHRISTOPHER M., manufacturing executive; b. Pensacola, Fla., Mar. 24, 1956; m. Sara Connor; 3 children. BS, Ohio State U., 1978. Dir. advt. Sherwin-Williams' Paint Stores Group, 1983—85, pres., gen. mgr. western divsn., 1985—92, sr. v.p. mktg. group, 1992—94, pres., gen. mgr. diversified brands divsn., 1994—97, pres., 1997—99; vice chmn., CEO Sherwin-Williams Co., 1999—2000, chmn., CEO, 2000—. Bd. dir. Diebold Inc., Nat. City Corp. Chmn. bd. trustees Keep Am. Beautiful, Univ. Hosp. Health Sys., Cleve.; mem. Dean's adv. council Fisher Coll. Bus, Ohio State Univ.; bd. mem. Rock & Roll Hall of Fame & Mus, Cleve. Growth Assn., Catholic Diocese Cleve. Found., Music Arts Assn., Cleve. Orch., Walsh Jesuit H.S. Office: Sherwin-Williams Co 101 Prospect Ave NW Cleveland OH 44115-1075

CONNOR, KEVIN M., lawyer; b. 1962; BA, Vanderbilt U.; JD, U. Kans. Bar: 1988. Shareholder Seigfreid, Bingham, Levy, Selzer, and Gee, 1994, ptnr., 1995—2002; sr. v.p. legal AMC Entertainment, Kans. City, Mo., 2002—03, sr. v.p., gen. counsel, sec., 2003—. Office: AMC Entertainment Inc 920 Main St Kansas City MO 64105-2017 Office Phone: 816-221-4000. Office Fax: 816-480-4700.

CONNOR, LAURENCE DAVIS, retired lawyer; b. Columbus, Ohio, May 14, 1938; s. Laurence R. and Gladys C. (Davis) Connor; m. Clare Elizabeth Hartwick, Aug. 8, 1964; children: Jeffrey H., Lynne D. Scoville. BA, Miami U., Oxford, Ohio, 1960; JD, U. Mich., 1965. Bar: Mich. 1966, U.S. Dist. Ct. (ea. dist.) Mich. 1966, U.S. Ct. Appeals (6th cir.) 1973, U.S. Supreme Ct. 1979. Assoc. Dykema Gossett, Detroit, 1965-73, ptnr., 1973—2002, mem. exec. com., 1984-90, dir. litigation sect., 1987-91, ret., 2002. Pres. Vis. Nurse Assn. Met. Detroit, 1980—81, Vis. Nurse Corp., Detroit, 1986—88; mem. coun. sect. alternative dispute resolution State Bar Mich., 1992—, chairperson, 1996—97; asst. clin. prof. law U. Mich., 2002—05. Mem.: ABA, Oaks Club, Yondotega Club, Detroit Athletic Club, Country Club Detroit. Office Phone: 313-568-6573. Business E-Mail: lconnor@dykema.com.

CONNORS, JOHN, state representative; b. DesMoines, Dec. 2, 1922; m. Marjorie Leonard. Student, DesMoines C.C., Harvard U. Ret. capt. DesMoines Fire Dept., 1950—77; mem. Iowa Ho. Reps., DesMoines, 1973—, ranking mem. appropriations com., mem. adminstrn. and regulation com., mem. labor and indsl. rels. com., mem. local govt. com., mem. state govt. com., spkr. pro tempore, 1983—92, asst. minority leader, 1992—95. Labor arbitrator. First chmn. City-Wide Ctrl. Adv. Bd.; active DesMoines Friendship and Sister City Commn.; pres. Iowa Golden Gloves; past pres. Muscular Dystrophy Assn., Polk County Soc. for Crippled Children and Adults; active Capitol Hill Christian Ch.; trustee DesMoines Gen. Hosp.; former bd. mem. Logan Priority Bd. With USNR, WWII. Mem.: Nat. Golden Gloves Assn., Masons. Democrat. Office: 1316 E 22nd St Des Moines IA 50317

CONNORS, KENNETH ANTONIO, retired pharmacy educator; b. Torrington, Conn., Feb. 19, 1932; s. Peter Francis and Adeline (Gioia) C.; m. Patricia R. Smart, Dec. 30, 1972. BS, U. Conn., 1954; MS, U. Wis., 1957, PhD, 1959. Rsch. assoc. dept. chemistry Ill. Inst. Tech., Chgo., 1959-60, Northwestern U., Evanston, Ill., 1960-61; asst. prof. U. Wis. Sch. Pharmacy, Madison, 1962-65, assoc. prof., 1965-72, prof., 1972-97, prof. emeritus, 1997—, acting dean, 1991-93. Author: A Textbook of Pharmaceutical Analysis, 3d edit., 1982, Reaction Mechanisms in Organic Analytical Chemistry, 1973, Chemical Stability of Pharmaceuticals, 2d edit., 1986, Binding Constants, 1987, Chemical Kinetics, 1990, Thermodynamics of Pharmaceutical Systems, 2002. Served with U.S. Army, 1961. Fellow AAAS, Acad. Pharm. Scis., Am. Assn. Pharm. Scis.; mem. Am. Chem. Soc. Office: U Wis Sch Pharmacy 777 Highland Ave Madison WI 53705-2222

CONRAD, GEOFFREY WENTWORTH, archaeologist, educator; b. Boston, Dec. 24, 1947; s. Albert Austin and Ruth Wentworth (Cadieux) C.; m. Karen Ann Hildebrant, June 12, 1971; children: Matthew, Peter, Marc. AB, Harvard U., 1969, PhD, 1974. Curatorial asst. Smithsonian Inst., Washington, 1974-75; asst. prof. and asst. curator Harvard U., Cambridge, Mass., 1976-81, assoc. prof. and assoc. curator, 1981-83; dir. William Hammond Mathers Mus. Ind. U., Bloomington, 1983—, assoc. prof. anthropology, 1983-91, prof., 1991—, chair, 1991-95, assoc. dean faculties, 2003—05, spl. advisor for arts and humanities, office v.p. for rsch., 2004—06, assoc. vice provost for rsch., 2007—. Cons. Nat. Geog. Soc., Washington, 1982-83. Co-author: Religion and Empire, 1984, The Andean Heritage, 1982; co-editor: Ideology and Precolumbian Civilizations, 1992; contbr. articles to profl. jours.; mem. editl. bd. Jour. of Field Archaeology, 1986-96. Bd. dirs. Monroe County Hist. Soc., Bloomington, 1989-92. Grantee NSF, 1978, 85, Ind. Humanities Coun., 1983, 86, 88, 95, 2006, Wenner-Gren Found., 1987, Inst. Mus. and Libr. Svcs., 2000, 04, Howard Heinz Endowment, 2004. Fellow AAAS; mem. Archaeol. Inst. Am. (pres. Ctrl. Ind. chpt. 1989-91, acad. trustee 1994-97), Soc. Am. Archaeology, Assn. for Field Archaeology, Am. Assn. Mus., Internat. Assn. for Caribbean Archaeology, Assn. Midwest Mus., Assn. Coll. and Univ. Mus. and Galleries (Midwest rep. 1990-91) Home: 3130 Saint James Ct Bloomington IN 47401-7105 Office: Mathers Mus Ind U 601 E 8th St Bloomington IN 47408-3812 also: Ind U Dept Anthropology Student Bldg Bloomington IN 47405 Address: Ind U Office VP Rsch Franklin Hall 116-Y Bloomington IN 47405 Home Phone: 812-334-7681; Office Phone: 812-865-5340, 812-855-6066. Business E-Mail: conrad@indiana.edu.

CONRAD, KENT (GAYLORD KENT CONRAD), senator; b. Bismarck, ND, Mar. 12, 1948; m. Lucy Calautti, Feb. 1987; 1 child, Jessamyn Abigail. Student, U. Mo., 1967; BA in Govt. and Polit. Sci., Stanford U., 1972; MBA, George Washington U., 1975. Asst. to tax commr. State of N.D. Tax Dept., Bismarck, 1974-80, dir. mgmt. planning and personnel, 1980, tax commr., 1981-87; US Senator from ND Washington, 1987—. Com. Indian affairs US Senate, com. fin., com. budget, com. agr., nutrition and forestry. Recipient Award of Appreciation, ND Dry Pea and Lentil Assn., Nat. Health Leadership award, Am. Assn. Nurse Anesthetists, 1994, Hero Rural Edn. award, Nat. Rural Edn. Assn., 2002, Outstanding Support for Rural Edn. award, ND Coun. Edn. Leaders, 2002, Congressional Spl. Recognition award, Nat. Sch. Boards Assn., 2003, Cmty Health Defender award, Nat. Assn. Cmty. Health Centers, 2005, John M. Agrey award, Upper Great Plains Transp. Inst., ND State U., 2005. Democrat. Unitarian. Office: US Senate 530 Hart Senate Office Bldg Washington DC 20510-0001 also: US Federal Bldg Rm 104 102 North 4th St Grand Forks ND 58203 Office Phone: 202-224-2043, 701-775-9601. Office Fax: 202-224-7776, 701-746-1990.

CONRAD, WILLIAM MERRILL, architect; b. Sapulpa, Okla., Sept. 5, 1926; s. William Samuel and Lillian Lorraine (Strain) C.; m. Esther Marian Lenz, Nov. 8, 1952. BS in Architecture, U. Kans., 1950, BSBA, 1951. Lic. architect. Prin., architect William M. Conrad, F.A.I.A., Kansas City, Mo., 1956—; asst. prof., Sch. of Architecture and Urban Design U. Kans., Lawrence, 1956-59. Mem. adv. com. U. Kans. Sch. of Architecture and Urban Design, 1974-86; vis. Fulbright prof., U. Helsinki, 1958-59. Mem. Kans. City-St. Joseph Bldg. Commn., 1970-82; leader People to People Internat. Peace Mission Overseas Tours, 1994--. Recipient Patriotic Svc. award Dept. Army, 1974, 84, Nat. Friend of Park and Recreation award Nat. Assn. Park and Recreation Ofcls., 1982, Urban Design award Mcpl. Art Com., Kansas City, 1976, Disting. Alumnus award U. Kans. Sch. Arch. and Urban Design, 1993, Achievement award PTP Philippines, 1999, PTP Taiwan, 1999. Mem. AIA (treas. nat. conv. 1979, Kansas City chpt. pres. 1968, past sec., other offices, mem. numerous coms., Fellow, 1986, Cmty. Svc. award 1990, numerous other awards), SAR (Good Citizenship award 1997), Mo. Coun. Architects (past dir. and treas.), People to People Internat. (pres. Greater Kansas City chpt. 1972-74, chmn. Gt. Plains regional coun. 1974-77, chmn. bd. dirs., trustee 1985-89, internat. pres. 1988-91, Disting. Mem. award 1986, Eisenhower Lifetime Achievement award 1996), Optimists (past pres. Honor Club), Masons, Shriners (pres. 1990), Sertoma Kans. dist. gov. 1984-86, pres. Honor Club 1982-84, Sertoman of Yr. 1987, Outstanding Regional Sec. award 1995), Christian the Fourth Guild (hon. Denmark, 2000), Tau Beta Pi (life), Tau Sigma Delta. Methodist. Home: 6120 W 69th St Overland Park KS 66204-1411

CONRAN, JOSEPH PALMER, lawyer; b. St. Louis, Oct. 4, 1945; s. Palmer and Theresa (Bussmann) C.; m. Daria D. Conran, June 8, 1968; children: Andrew, Lizabeth, Theresa. BA, St. Louis U., 1967, JD with honors, 1970. Bar: Mo. 1970, U.S. Ct. Mil. Appeals 1971, U.S. Ct. Appeals (8th cir.) 1974. Assoc. Husch and Eppenberger, St. Louis, 1974-78, ptnr., 1978—, chmn. litigation dept., 1980-95, chmn. mgmt. com., 1995—. Mem. faculty Trial Practice Inst. Capt., JAGC, USAF, 1970-74. Mem. Bar Assn. Met. St. Louis (Merit award 1976, 77), Mo. Bar Assn. (bd. govs. 1987-92), Mo. Athletic Club (pres. 1986-87), Norwood Hills Country Club, St. Louis Club. Roman Catholic. Home: 53 Hawthorne Est Saint Louis MO 63131-3035 Office: Husch Eppenberger 190 Carondelet Plz Ste 600 Saint Louis MO 63105-3433 Office Phone: 314-480-1900. Business E-Mail: joe.conran@husch.com.

CONROY, JOE, former state legislator; m. Mary Ann Macksood; children: Kevin, Kelly, Tim, Christine, Colleen. State senator Mich. State Senate, Dist. 25, 1985-94, Mich. State Senate, Dist. 29, 1995-98. Mem. appropriations com., higher edn. & tech. com., Mich. State Senate; mem. human svc. com. & health com. at. Conf. State Legis. Home: 11487 Bay Shore Dr Fenton MI 48430-8828

CONROY, JOHN J., JR., lawyer; 7 children. BA summa cum laude, U. Notre Dame, 1975; grad., U. Strasbourg, U. Catholique de L'Ouest; JD, Northwestern U., 1979. Bar: Ill. 1979, U.S. Dist. Ct. (No. dist. Ill.) 1981. Law clk. Ill. Supreme Ct.; with Baker & McKenzie, Chgo., 1980—, ptnr., 1987—, N.Am. mng. ptnr., 1998—2004, chmn. exec. com., 2004—, chmn. global banking and fin. steering com., chmn. N.Am. regional coun. Fellow, Rotary Found. Mem.: ABA, Ill. State Bar Assn., Chgo. Bar Assn. Office: Baker & McKenzie One Prudential Plaza Ste 2500 Chicago IL 60601 Office Phone: 312-861-8171. E-mail: john.j.conroy@bakernet.com.

CONRY, THOMAS FRANCIS, mechanical engineering educator; b. West Hempstead, NY, Mar. 7, 1942; s. Thomas and Bridget Anne (Walsh) C.; m. Sharon Ann Silverwood, June 10, 1967; children: Christine Elizabeth, Carolyn Danielle, Anne Marie. BS, Pa. State U., 1963; MS, U. Wis., Madison, 1967, PhD, 1970. Registered profl. engr., Wis., Ill. Engr. Gen. Motors Corp., Milw., 1963-66, sr. research engr. Indpls., 1969-71; asst. prof. gen. engring. U. Ill., Coll. Engring., Urbana, 1971-75, assoc. prof. gen. and mech. engring., 1975-81, prof. gen. and mech. engring., 1981—2006, co-dir. mng. engring. program, 1986-89, head dept. gen. engring., 1987-98, founding coord. program in tech. and mgmt., 1995—98, prof. emeritus indsl. and enterprise sys. engring., 2006—. Sr. visitor U. Cambridge, Eng., 1978; cons. Zurn Industries, 1974-83, Ruhl Forensic, 2006-; staff cons. Sargent & Lundy, Engrs., 1977, 79; cons.-evaluator commn. on instns. of higher edn. North Ctl. Assn., 1983—; cons. indsl. firm on machine dynamics, optimization and tribology. NSF trainee, 1968-69; NASA/ASEE summer faculty fellow, 1974-75. Contbr. articles to profl. jours. Mem. Bd. Edn. St. Matthews Parish Roman Catholic Ch., Champaign, 1981-84. Recipient Edmond E. Bisson award, Soc. Tribologists and Lubrication Engrs., 2007. Fellow ASME (chmn. design engring. divsn. 1979-80, tech. editor Jour. Vibration, Acoustics, Stress and Reliability in Design, 1984-89, mem. bd. on comm. 1989-93, 96-00, mem. com. on fin. and investment 1999-04); mem. Am. Soc. Engring. Edn., Rotary, Sigma Xi, Lambda Chi Alpha, Phi Kappa Phi. Home: 3301 Lakeshore Dr Champaign IL 61822-5205 Office: 104 S Mathews Ave Urbana IL 61801-2925 Business E-Mail: tconry@uiuc.edu.

CONSTANT, ANITA AURELIA, publisher; b. Youngstown, Ohio, Jan. 5, 1945; d. Sandu Nicholas and Erie Marie (Tecau) C. BA, Ind. U., 1967; postgrad., Northwestern U., Evanston, Ill., 1991. Sales rep. Economy Fin. Inc., St. Louis, 1967-69; recruiter Case Western U. Hosp., Cleve., 1969-70; sales rep. Internat. Playtex Inc., Chgo., 1970-71, John Wiley & Sons, Inc., Chgo., 1971-77; sr. product mgr. CBS Pub. Inc., The Dryden Press, Chog., 1977-80; exec. editor Dearborn Fin. Pub., Inc., Chgo., 1980-81, v.p., 1981-89, sr. v.p., prin., 1989-97; cons. to pub. industry, 1997-98; prin. Ea. European investment venture EURO-TEC, 1997-99; sr. v.p., editor-in-chief Southwestern Coll. Pub. divsn. ITP Inc., 1988-94; sr. v.p. new bus. devel. South-Western/Thomson Learning, 2000—; v.p. devel. and contract mgmt. Riverside Pub. Divsn. Houghton Mifflin, 1995—. Bd. dirs. Romanian Heritage Ctr., Detroit, 1988—, Orthodox Brotherhood of Am., Detroit, 1985—. Mem.: Nat. Assn. Women Bus. Owners, Chgo. Book Clinic (bd. dirs. 1987—88, v.p. 1988—90, pres. 1990—91, past pres. 1991—92, Mary Alexander award 1995), Internat. Assn. Fin. Planners, Real Estate Educators Assn., Chgo. Women in Pub. Eastern Orthodox. Avocations: property development and renovation, hiking, bicycling. Office: 425 Springlake Dr Itasca IL 60143

CONSTANTINE, KATHERINE A., lawyer; b. 1955; BS in Fgn. Svc. magna cum laude, Georgetown U., 1977, JD, 1980. Bar: Minn. 1980. Assoc., gen. litig. Nichols, Kruger, Starks and Carruthers, 1980—83; assoc. Fabyanske Svoboda & Westra PA, 1983—85, Dorsey & Whitney LLP, Mpls., 1986—88, ptnr., banking comml. dept., 1989—, and co-chair, bus. restructuring and bankruptcy. Assoc. editor Georgetown's The Tax Lawyer, 1979—80. Named a Leading Atty. in bankruptcy law, Minn. Bus. Guidebook to Law and Leading Attorneys, 1994—96, Guide to Leading Am. Attorneys, 1998, Minn. Super Lawyer, 2000—03. Mem.: ABA, Am. Bankruptcy Inst., Minn. Women Lawyers, Hennepin Co. Bar Assn., Minn. State Bar Assn., Phi Beta Kappa. Office: Dorsey & Whitney LLP Ste 1500 50 S Sixth St Minneapolis MN 55402-1498 Office Phone: 612-340-8792. Office Fax: 612-340-2868. Business E-Mail: constantine.katherine@dorsey.com.

CONTE, LOU, choreographer, director; b. DuQuoin, Ill., Apr. 17, 1942; s. John and Floy Mae (Saunders) C. Student, Ellis DuBoulay Sch. Ballet, Chgo., 1961-68, So. Ill. U., 1960-62, Am. Ballet Theatre Sch., NYC, 1964-66. Lectr. Choreographer: Milw. Melody Top, 1966, (musicals) Mame, 1972, Boss, 1973; dir.: Lou Conte Dance Studio, Chgo., 1974—; artistic dir.: Hubbard St. Dance Co., Chgo., 1977-2000. Recipient Ruth Page Artistic Achievement award Chgo. Dance Coalition, 1986, Sidney R. Yates Arts Advocacy award, 1995, Chicagoan of Yr. award Chgo. Mag., 1999, laureate Lincoln Acad. Ill., 2002. Mem. AFTRA, Actors Equity Assn. Office: Lou Conte Dance Studio 1147 W Jackson Blvd Chicago IL 60607-2905

CONTE, RICHARD R., homebuilding and mortgage banking company executive; b. New Eagle, Pa., Apr. 26, 1947; s. Ralph and Dorothy (Toth)) C.; m. Laura Ann Fritz, July 29, 1972; children: Jerrod, Richard. BA, Columbia U., 1969; MBA, U. Pitts., 1975. Mgmt. trainee Western Pa. Nat. Bank, Pitts., 1969-71; loan officer Export-Import Bank of U.S., Washington, 1971-72; banking officer, export fin. Western Pa. Nat. Bank, Pitts., 1972-75; asst. v.p. internat. Equibank, Pitts., 1975-77, v.p. internat., 1977-79, v.p. corr. banking, 1979-80, v.p., mgr. multinat., 1980-81; treas. Ryan Homes Inc., Pitts., 1981-86; v.p., treas. NVR L.P., McLean, Va., 1986-89, v.p. fin., treas., 1989-90; chmn. Westinghouse Saus. Corp., Pitts., 1990-92; chmn. bd., CEO Rymac Mortgage Investment Corp., Steubenville, Ohio, 1988—. Chmn. pres. Ryan Mortgage Acceptance Corps. I, II, III, IV & V, Pitts., 1985—; pres., bd. dirs. Rymac Mortgage Investment Corp.; bd. dirs. Tri-Sach, Pitts., 1980-81; mem. Dist. Export Counsel, Pitts., 1978-81. Coach, adminstr. Ingomar (Pa.) Athletic Assn., 1987—. Mem.: Varsity (N.Y.C.). Avocations: golf, jogging, reading.

CONTI, LEE ANN, lawyer; b. Astoria, Oreg. BA with honors, So. Ill. U., 1970; JD summa cum laude, De Paul U., 1976. Bar: Ill. 1976, U.S. Dist. Ct. (no. dist.) Ill. 1976. Ptnr. Mayer, Brown & Platt, Chgo., 1983-94; assoc. gen. counsel Citizens Comm. Co., Stamford, 1994—2002. Contbr. articles to profl. jours. Mem. Bd. Edn. Cmty. Consol. Sch. Dist. 89, Du Page County, 1987-93. Recipient Am. Jurisprudence awards in Torts, Remedies. Mem. ABA, Am. Corp. Counsel Assn., Ill. State Bar Assn., Du Page County Bar Assn., Chgo. Bar Assn., Phi Kappa Phi, Pi Sigma Alpha, Phi Lambda Pi. Office: 635 S Park Blvd Glen Ellyn IL 60137-6977

CONTI, PAUL LOUIS, management consulting company executive; b. Utica, NY, Sept. 3, 1945; s. Louis Joseph and Dorothy Mae (Kellogg) C.; m. Lee Ann Scheuerman, Apr. 18, 1970; children: Meghan Elizabeth, Dawn Michelle. BA, So. Ill. U., 1972, MBA, 1974. Sr. cons. Lester B. Knight & Assocs., Chgo., 1974-76; dir. pers. Applied Info. Devel., Oak Brook, Ill., 1976-80; v.p. Comsi, Inc., Oak Brook, 1980-82; CEO Prestige Mgmt. Sys., Inc., Glen Ellyn, Ill., 1982-86; v.p. human resources Rand McNally & Co., Skokie, Ill., 1986-87; assoc. dir. Ernst & Young (formerly Ernst & Whinney), Chgo., 1987-93; regional v.p. Alexandria Alexander, Inc., Chgo., 1993-97; COO, sr. v.p. AON Corp., 1997-99; sr. v.p. Apropos Tech., Inc., Oak Brook, Ill., 1999—; pres., chief assets officer Vericlaim, Inc., Chgo., 1999—. Bd. dirs. So. Ill. U. Coll. Bus. Adminstrn. Lobbyist Invest in the Future, Invest in Edn., State of Ill., 1988; bd. dirs., exec. com. So. Ill. U.-Carbondale Found., 1991—, pres., 1994-97. Named to So. Ill. U. COBA Hall of Fame, 1988; named Cmty. Ambassador So. Ill. U., 1980. Mem. Soc. Human Resource Profls., Soc. Human Resources Mgmt., Human Resources Mgmt. Assn. of Chgo., Employment Mgmt. Assn., Pontikes Ctr. for Mgmt. Info. (bd. dirs. 1989—), So. Ill. U. Alumni Assn. (pres. 1986-88, bd. dirs. 1986—, exec. com. 1991—), Ideal Club (pres. 1986-88), McCullom Lake Club. Republican. Roman Catholic. Avocations: hunting waterfowl and upland game, golf, various participative sports, coaching women's fast pitch softball. Home: 635 S Park Blvd Glen Ellyn IL 60137-6977 Office Phone: 630-245-7005. Business E-Mail: pconti@vericlaiminc.com. E-mail: contip@msn.com.

CONTRENI, JOHN JOSEPH, JR., humanities educator; b. Savannah, Ga., Aug. 31, 1944; s. John Joseph Sr. and Elfriede Johanna (Hille) C.; m. Margarita Lee Partridge, July 3, 1986; children: Judith, Rachel, Daniel, Maureen, Jennifer Rogers, Paul Rogers. BA, St. Vincent Coll., 1966, HHD (hon.), 1996; PhD, Mich. State U., 1971. From asst. prof. to prof. history Purdue U., West Lafayette, Ind., 1971—, head dept. history, 1985-97, asst. dean Sch. Humanities, Social Sci. and Edn., 1981-85, interim head dept. fgn. langs. and lits., 1983—85, interim dean, Grad. Sch., 2002—04, dean, Grad. Sch., 2004—06, dean, Coll. Liberal Arts, 2006—. Pres. Midwest Medieval Conf., 1980-81. Author: The Cathedral School of Laon from 850 to 930: Its Manuscripts and Masters, 1978, (John Nicholas Brown prize 1982), Codex Laudunensis 468: A Ninth-Century Guide to Virgil, Sedulius, and the Liberal Arts, 1984; co-author: Glossae Divinae Historiae: The Biblical Glosses of John Scottus Eriugena, 1997: translator: Education and Culture in the Barbarian West, Sixth Through Eighth Centuries (Pierre Riché), 1976, Carolingian Learning, Masters, and Manuscripts, 1992; co-editor: Religion, Culture, and Society in the Early Middle Ages: Studies in Honor of Richard E. Sullivan, 1987, French Historical Studies, 1991-2000, Word, Image, Number: Communication in the Middle Ages, 2002; mem. editl. bd. Internat. History Rev., 2001-03; contbr. articles to profl. jours. and chpts. to books. Pres., bd. trustees Brookston-Prairie Twp. Pub. Libr., 1995-01. Grantee Am. Philos. Soc., 1973, 76, 82, 86, NEH, 1973, 86, Am. Coun. Learned Socs., 1975, 77-79, 83, 89, Purdue U., 1973, 75-76, 81, 83, 89, 99. Mem. Soc. for Promotion Eriugenian Studies, Medieval Acad. of Am. (councillor 1987-90, grantee 1973, fellow, 2003), Grad. Record Exam. Bd., Test English as a Fgn. Lang. Bd., Phi Beta Kappa. Home: 504 W 5th St Brookston IN 47923-8100 Office: Coll Liberal Arts Beering Hall 100 N Univ St West Lafayette IN 47907-2098 E-mail: contreni@purdue.edu.

CONVERSE, JAMES CLARENCE, agricultural engineering educator; b. Brainerd, Minn., Apr. 2, 1942; s. James L. and Doris E. (Beck) C.; m. Marjorie A. Swanson, Aug. 6, 1965; children— James, Julie, Mark, Katherine AA, Brainerd Jr. Coll, 1962; BS in Agrl. Engring., N.D. State U., 1964, MS in Agrl. Engring., 1966; PhD in Agrl. Engring., U. Ill., 1970. Asst. prof. agrl. engring. U. Wis., Madison, 1970-75, assoc. prof., 1975-80, prof., 1980—, chmn. dept., 1988-96. Fellow Am. Soc. Agrl. Engring. (Gunlogson countryside engring. award 1984). Roman Catholic. Avocation: soccer. Office: U Wis Dept Agrl Engring 460 Henry Mall Madison WI 53706-1533

CONVIS, GARY L., automotive parts company executive; b. Mich., Sept. 22, 1942; m. Debbie Convis. Degree in Math., Mich. State U., 1965. Joined Buick Motor Divsn. GM Corp., 1964; joined Ford Motor Co., 1966; plant gen. mgr. New United Motor Mfg., Inc., 1984, v.p. mfg., 1987, sr. v.p., 1994, exec. v.p., 1997, Toyota Motor Mfg., Ky., Inc., 2000—01, pres., 2001—06, chmn., 2006—07; exec. v.p. Toyota Motor Engring. & Mfg. N.Am., Inc., 2006—07; CEO Dana Holding Corp., Toledo, 2008—. Bd. dirs. Dana Holding Corp., 2008—, Cooper-Standard Holdings Inc., Cooper-Standard Automotive Inc. Bd. dirs. Japan/America Soc. Ky. Avocations: golf, boating, motorcycling. Office: Dana Holding Corp 4500 Dorr St Toledo OH 43615*

CONVISER, RICHARD JAMES, lawyer, educator, publications company executive; b. Chgo., Apr. 4, 1938; s. Jack and Florence Conviser; 1 child, Ryan Elizabeth BA, U. Calif.-Berkeley, 1959, JD, 1962; Dr. Jur, U. Cologne, Fed. Republic Germany, 1964. Bar: Calif. 1962, Ill. 1965. Assoc. Baker & McKenzie, Chgo., 1965-67; dep. European dir. European Office of Ill., Brussels, Belgium, 1968-69; prof. law DePaul U., Chgo., 1969-73, Chgo.-Kent Coll. Law, Ill. Inst. Tech., 1973—; sr. v.p. Harcourt Brace Pubs., NYC, from 1980; chmn., chief exec. officer Harcourt Profl. Edn. Group, Chgo., 1967—. Founder, dir. BAR/BRI Bar Rev., Chgo.; founder, dir. Conviser & Duffy CPA Rev., Chgo.; bd. dirs. Harcourt Profl. Edn., Exchange Nat. Bank, Chgo., Conviser-Duffy CPA Rev. Author: The Modern Philanthrophic Foundation: A Comparative Legal Analysis, 1965, The Law of Agency and Partnership, 1993; mng. editl. dir. Gilbert Law Summaries, L.A., 1978—. Mem. North Dearborn Pk. Assn.; trustee Emory U. Sch. Law, Atlanta, Libr. Internat. Rels., Inst. Internat. Edn. Fellow Col. W. Dinkelspiel Found., 1960-62, Newhouse Found., 1960-62; Ford Found. internat. law fellow, 1962-64 Mem. ABA, Calif. Bar Assn., Ill. Bar Assn., Chgo. Bar Assn. Clubs: Racquet of Chgo., Saddle and Cycle (Chgo.). Office: Harcourt Profl Edn Group 111 W Jackson Blvd Fl 7 Chicago IL 60604-3502

CONWAY, JAMES JOSEPH, radiologist, educator; b. Chgo., July 1, 1933; s. Frank and Mary (Tuohy) Conway; m. Dolores Mazer, June 30, 1956; children: Laurie, John, Cheryl. BS, DePaul U., 1959; MD, Northwestern U., 1963. Asst. instr. U. Pa., 1964—68; assoc. in radiology McGaw Med. Ctr. Northwestern U., Chgo., 1968—71, asst. prof. to assoc. prof. radiology, 1974—80; attendant radiology Children's Meml. Hosp., Chgo., 1968—98, prof. radiology, 1980—.

Contbr. articles over 110 to profl. jours. With US Army, 1953—55. Recipient Gold medal, Chgo. Radiol. Soc., 1993, Scroll of Appreciation award, Radiol. Soc. N.Am., 1983. Fellow: Am. Coll. Radiology, Am. Coll. Nuc. Physicians, P.R. Soc. Nuc. Medicine (hon.); mem.: Soc. Nuclear Medicine (pres. 1994—95). Avocation: collector of Chicago memorabilia. Office: Childrens Meml Hosp 2300 N Childrens Plz Chicago IL 60614-3394 Personal E-mail: nukedr@comcast.net.

CONWAY, JOHN K., lawyer; Gen. counsel Kemper Ins. Co., Long Grove, Ill. Office: Lumbermens Mutual Casualty Co 1 Kemper Dr Long Grove IL 60049-0001

CONWAY, LYNN, computer scientist, electrical engineer, educator; b. Mt. Vernon, NY, Jan. 2, 1938; BS, Columbia U., 1962, MSEE, 1963; D (hon.), Trinity Coll., 1997. Rsch. staff IBM Corp., Yorktown Heights, NY, 1964-68; sr. staff engr. Memorex Corp., Santa Clara, Calif., 1969-73; rsch. staff Xerox Corp., Palo Alto, Calif., 1973-78, rsch. fellow, mgr. VLSI systems area, 1978-82, rsch. fellow, mgr. knowledge systems area, 1982-83; asst. dir. for strategic computing Def. Advanced Research Projects Agy., Arlington, Va., 1983-85; prof. elec. engring. and computer sci., assoc. dean U. Mich. Coll. Engring., Ann Arbor, Mich., 1985—98, prof. emerita elec. engring. and computer sci., 1999—. Vis. assoc. prof. elec. engring. and computer sci. MIT, Cambridge, Mass., 1978-79; sci. adv. bd. USAF, 1987-90. Co-author: textbook Introduction to VLSI Systems, 1980; contbr. articles to profl. jours.; patentee in field. Mem. coun. Govt.-Univ.-Industry Rsch. Roundtable, 1993-98; mem. corp. Charles Stark Draper Lab., 1993—; mem. bd. visitors USAF Acad., 1996-2000, presdl. appt.; mem. Air Force Sci. and Tech. Bd., Nat. Acads., 2000—. Recipient Ann. Achievement award Electronics mag., 1981, Harold Pender award U. Pa., 1984, Wetherill Medal Franklin Inst., 1985, Sec. of Def. Meritorious Civilian Svc. award, 1985; named to Electronic Design Hall of Fame, 2002. Fellow IEEE; mem. AE, AAAS (named Engr. of Yr. 2005), Soc. Women Engrs. (Ann. Achievement award 1990), Assn. Computing Machinery. Avocations: canoeing, natural landscaping, travel. Office: U Mich 3640 CSE Bldg Ann Arbor MI 48109 Business E-Mail: conway@umich.edu.

CONWAY, MICHAEL MAURICE, lawyer; b. St. Joseph, Mo., Mar. 11, 1946; s. Michael Maurice and Genevieve (Hepburn) C.; m. Kathleen Stevens; children: Michael, Cara, Mary. BS in Journalism, Northwestern U., 1968; JD, Yale U., 1973. Bar: Ill. 1973, U.S. Dist. Ct. (no. dist.) Ill. 1973, U.S. Tax Ct. 1975, U.S. Ct. Claims 1976, U.S. Ct. Appeals (7th cir.) 1976, U.S. Ct. Appeals (1st cir.) 1979, U.S. Supreme Ct. 1980, U.S. Ct. Appeals (5th and 11th cirs.) 1981, U.S. Ct. Appeals (fed. cir. 1982). Ptnr. Hopkins & Sutter now Foley & Lardner, Chgo., 1979—, chmn. Chgo. litigation dept. Counsel U.S. Ho. Reps. com. on judiciary impeachment inquiry Richard M. Nixon, 1974. Chmn. Ill. Lawyers Com. Clinton/Gore, Chgo., 1992; alt. del. Dem. Nat. Conv., 1992, del., 1996. Mem. Am. Coll. Trial Lawyers. Roman Catholic. Avocation: baseball. Office: Foley & Lardner LLP 321 N Clark St Chicago IL 60610 Office Phone: 312-832-4351. Business E-Mail: mconway@foley.com.

CONYERS, JOHN, JR., congressman; b. Detroit, May 16, 1929; s. John and Lucille (Simpson) C.; m. Monia Estes; children: John Jr., Carl Edward. BA, Wayne State U., 1957, JD, 1958; LLD, Wilberforce U., 1969. Bar: Mich. 1959. Legis. asst. to Congressman John Dingell, 1959-61; sr. ptnr. firm Conyers, Bell & Townsend, 1959-61; referee Mich. Workmen's Compensation Dept., 1961-64; mem. U.S. Congress from 14th Mich. dist., 1964—; former chmn. Govt. Ops. Com., former chmn. subcom. on legis. and nat. security; ranking mem. Judiciary Com. Past dir. edn. Local 900, United Auto Workers; mem. adv. council Mich. Liberties Union; gen. counsel Detroit Trade Union Leadership Council; vice chmn. nat. bd. Ams. for Democratic Action; vice chmn. adv. council ACLU; an organizer Mems. Congress for Peace through Law; bd. dirs. numerous other orgns. including African-Am. Inst., Commn. Racial Justice, Detroit Inst. Arts, Nat. Alliance Against Racist and Polit. Repression, Nat. League Cities. Sponsor, contbg. author: Am. Militarism, 1970, War Crimes and the American Conscience, 1970, Anatomy of an Undeclared War, 1972; contbr. articles to profl. jours. Trustee Martin Luther King Jr. Ctr. for Non-Violent Social Change. Served to 2d lt. U.S. Army, 1950-54, Korea. Recipient Rosa Parks award SCLC; named one of Most Influential Black Americans, Ebony mag., 2006 Mem. NAACP (exec. bd. Detroit), Kappa Alpha Psi. Democrat. Baptist. Office: 2426 Rayburn Bldg Washington DC 20515-2214 also: District Office 669 Federal Building 231 W Lafayette Detroit MI 48226 Office Phone: 202-225-5126. E-mail: johnconyersjr@gmail.com.

COOK, DEBORAH L., federal judge, former state supreme court justice; b. Pitts., Feb. 8, 1952; BA in English, U. Akron, 1974, JD, 1978, LLD (hon.), 1996. Ptnr. Roderick & Linton, Akron, 1976-91; judge 9th dist. Ohio Ct. Appeals, 1991-94; justice Ohio Supreme Ct., 1995—2003; judge US Ct. Appeals, (6th cir.), Cincinnati, Ohio, 2003—. Bd. trustees Summit County United Way, Vol. Ctr., Stan Hywet Hall and Gardens, Akron Sch. Law, Coll. Scholars, Inc.; bd. dirs. Women's Network; vol. Mobile Meals, Safe Landing Shelter. Named Woman of Yr., Women's Network, 1991. Fellow Am. Bar Found.; mem. Omicron Delta Kappa, Delta Gamma (pres., Nat. Shield award). Office: 532 Potter Stewart US Courthouse 100 E Fifth St Cincinnati OH 45202-3988

COOK, DORIS MARIE, retired accountant, educator; b. Fayetteville, Ark., June 11, 1924; d. Ira and Mettie Jewel (Dorman) Cook. BSBA, U. Ark., Fayetteville, 1946, MS, 1949; PhD, U. Tex., Austin, 1968. CPA Okla., Ark. Jr. acct. Haskins & Sells, Tulsa, 1946-47; instr. acctg. U. Ark., Fayetteville, 1947-52, asst. prof., 1952-62, assoc. prof., 1962-69, prof., 1969-88, Univ. prof. and Nolan E. Williams lectr. in acctg., 1988-97, emeritus disting. prof., 1997—. Mem. Ark. State Bd. Pub. Accountancy, 1987-92, treas., 1989-91, vice chmn. 1991-92; mem. Nat. Assn. State Bds. of Accountancy, 1987-92; appointed Nolan E. Williams lectureship in acctg., 1988-97; Doris M. Cook chair in acctg. U. Ark., Fayetteville, 2000. Mem. editl. bd. Ark. Bus. Rev., Jour. Managerial Issues; contbr. articles to profl. jours. Recipient Bus. Faculty of Month award Alpha Kappa Psi, 1997, Outstanding Faculty award Ark. Tchg. Acad., 1997, Charles and Nadine Baum Outstanding Tchr. award, 1997, Outstanding Leadership and Svc. award for Women's History Month, 1999, AAUW, others. Mem. AICPA, Ark. Bus. Assn. (editor newsletter 1982-85), Am. Acctg. Assn. (chmn. nat. membership 1982-83, Arthur Carter scholarship com. 1984-85, membership Ark. 1985-87), Am. Women's Soc. CPAs., Ark. Soc. CPAs (life, v.p. 1975-76, pres. N.W. Ark. chpt. 1980-81, sec. Student Loan Found. 1981-84, treas. 1984-92, pres. 1992-97, chmn. pub. rels. 1984-88, 93-95, Outstanding Acctg. Educator award 1991, Outstanding Com. Svc. award 1995, Student Loan Found. Bd. award 2001, 21 Yrs. Outstanding Svc. award 2001), Acad. Acctg. Historians (life, trustee 1985-87, rev. bd. of Working Papers Series 1984-92, sec. 1992-95, pres.-elect 1995, pres. 1996), Ark. Fedn. Bus. and Profl. Women's Clubs (treas. 1979-80), Fayetteville Bus. and Profl. Women's Clubs (pres. 1973-74, 75-76, Woman of Yr. award 1977) Mortar Bd., Beta Gamma Sigma, Beta Alpha Psi (editor nat. newsletter 1973-77, nat. pres. 1977-78, Outstanding Alumni in Edn. Iota chpt. 1999, Outstanding Svc. award Iota chpt. 1997), Phi Gamma Nu, Alpha Lambda Delta, Delta Kappa Gamma (sec. 1976-78, pres. 1978-80, treas. 1989-2000), Phi Kappa Phi. Home: 1655 Amy Ave Glendale Heights IL 60139

COOK, DWIGHT C., state legislator; b. Moorhead, Minn., Dec. 14, 1951; m. Shirley; 3 children., N. D. State U. Owner Cook Indsl. Sales; mem. N. D. Senate from 34th dist., Bismark, 1997—. Chmn. Morton County Housing Authority; mem. Kiwanis, Am. Legion. Republican. Lutheran. Office: Dist 34 1408 17th St SE Mandan D 58554-4895 E-mail: dcook@state.nd.us.

COOK, GARY L., state legislator; m. Cheryl Cook. Grad., Ind. Law Enforcement Acad. Police officer/patrolman Plymouth (Ind.) Police Dept.; rep. Dist. 17 Ind. Ho. of Reps., 1990—, mem. county and twp. govt. affairs, environ. affairs com., mem. pub. safety, rds. and transp. coms., chmn. interstate coop. com., rds. transp. com., ranking minority mem. Mem. Marshall County Right to Life, Plymouth Arts Commn. Mem. FOB, Lions. Home: 418 Crimson Ln Plymouth IN 46563-7806

COOK, HARRY EDGAR, engineering educator; b. Americus, Ga., Feb. 14, 1939; m. 1961; 2 children. BS, Case Inst. Tech., 1960; MS, Northwestern U., 1962, PhD in Materials Sci., 1966. Sr. rsch. scientist Ford Motor Co., Detroit, 1967-69, sr. engr., 1969-70, prin. engr. chassis, engine, 1970-71, supr., 1971-72, sr. rsch. scientist metallurgy, 1977-78, mgr. materials engring., 1978-79, body component engr., 1979-81, mgr. body component engring. and metallurgy dept., 1981-85; from assoc. prof. to prof. metallurgy and mech. engring. U. Ill., Champaign-Urbana, 1972-77; dir. auto rsch. Chrysler Motors, Detroit, 1985-90; J. Gauthier prof. dept. mech. and indsl. engring. U. Ill., Champaign-Urbana, 1990-98, head dept. gen. engring., 1998—. Recipient Robert Lansing Hardy medal Am. Inst. Mining and Metall. Engrs. Fellow Am. Soc. Metals, Am. Soc. Automitive Engrs. (Teetor award 1977); mem. Nat. Acad. Engring. Achievements include research contributing to knowledge of phase transformation and friction materials; studies in competitiveness and leadtime. Office: U Ill Dept Gen Engring Transp Bldg 104 S Mathews Ave Rm 117 Urbana IL 61801-2925

COOK, JACK MCPHERSON, hospital administrator; b. Liberty, NC, Jan. 7, 1945; married BA, U. N.C., 1967; M Health Adminstrn., Duke U., 1969. Adminstrv. res. Durham (N.C.) County Gen. Hosp., 1968, Duke U. Med. Ctr., Durham, 1968-69; asst. adminstr. Cabarrus Meml. Hosp., Concord, N.H., 1969-74; v.p. profl. svcs. Meml. Med. Ctr., Springfield, Ill., 1974-76, pres., 1976-83, Christ Hosp., Cincinnati, Ohio, 1984-95; pres., ceo Health Alliance of Greater Cincinnati, Cincinnati, Ohio, 1995—2000. Contbr. articles to profl. jours. Fellow, Amer. Coll. of Healthcare Execs., 1981, recertified, 1992; Healthcare Execs. Study Soc., 1989-; pres., 1997; chair. Ohio Hosp. Assoc., 1997; Strategic Planning Com., Greater Cincinnati Hosp. Council Trustee, 1983-; chair., 1987; Trustee, Work & Rehab. Ctrs of Greater Cincinnati, 1993-95; Board of Advisors, Univ. of Cinn. Coll. of Bus. Admin., 1988-; Board of Dirs., Provident Ban Corp., 1992-; mem. Metro. Hosp. Governing Council of Amer. Hosp. Assoc., 1992-95; House of Delegates and Regional Policy Board, 1997; Board of dirs., Voluntary Hosp. of Amer., 1988-92; Physician Advisory Comm., 1988-89; chair., Shareholder Evaluation Comm., 1989-92; VHA Central Exec. Comm., 1986-92; Founder and first pres., Healthspan, 1991-1993. Home: 650 Reisling Knls Cincinnati OH 45226-1735

COOK, JULIAN ABELE, JR., federal judge; b. Washington, June 22, 1930; s. Julian Abele and Ruth Elizabeth (McNeill) C.; m. Carol Annette Dibble, Dec. 22, 1957; children: Julian Abele III, Peter Dibble, Susan Annette. BA, Pa. State U., 1952; JD, Georgetown U., 1957, LLD (hon.), 1992; LLM, U. Va., 1988; LLD (hon.), U. Detroit, 1996, Wayne State U., 1997. Bar: Mich. 1957. Law clk. to judge, Pontiac, Mich., 1957-58; pvt. practice Detroit, 1958-78; judge U.S. Dist. Ct. (ea. dist.) Mich., Detroit, 1978, chief judge, 1989-96, sr. judge, 1996—. Spl. asst. atty. gen. State of Mich., 1968-78; adj. prof. U. Detroit Sch. Law, 1971-74; gen. counsel pub. TV Sta. WTVS, 1973-78; labor arbitrator Am. Arbitration Assn. and Mich. Employment Rels. Commn., 1975-78; mem. Mich. State Bd. Ethics, 1977-78; instr. trial advocacy workshop Harvard U., 1988—, trial advocacy program U.S. Dept. Justice, 1989-90; com. on fin. disclosure Jud. Conf. U.S., 1988-93, chmn., 1990-93; screening panel NYU Root-Tilden-Snow Scholarship Program, 1991, 96—; mem. U.S. Sentencing Commn. Judicial Adv. Group, 1996-98; mem. nat. bd. trustees Am. Inn Ct., 1996—; mem. adv. com. Nat. Publs., 1994-96, chmn. nat. nominations and election com., 1994-95; pres. chpt. XI, Master of Bench, 1984-95. Contbr. articles to profl. jours. Exec. bd. dirs. Child and Family Svcs. Mich., 1968-89, past pres., 1975-76; bd. dirs. Am. Heart Assn. Mich., 1968-89, Hutzel Hosp., 1984-95; chmn. Mich. Civil Rights Commn., 1968-71; co-chair exec. com. Walter P. Reuther Libr. Labor and Urban Affairs, Wayne State U.; mem. bd. visitors Georgetown U. Law Ctr., 1992—. With Signal Corps, U.S. Army, 1952-54. Recipient Merit citation Pontiac Area Urban League, 1971, Pathfinders award Oakland U., 1977, Svc. award Todd-Phillips Home, Inc., 1978, Disting. Alumnus award Pa. State U., 1987, Georgetown U., 1989, Focus and Impact award Oakland U., 1985; resolution Mich. Ho. of Reps., 1971, Outstanding Community Svc. award Va. Park Community Investment Assocs., 1992, 1st Ann. Trailblazers award D. Augustus Straker Bar Assn., 1993, Renowned Jurist award Friends of African Art, 1993, Brotherhood award Jewish War Vets. U.S., 1994, Paul R. Dean award Georgetown U. Law Sch., 1997; named Boss of Yr., Oakland County Legal Secs. Assn., 1974, one of Mich. Most Respected Judges, Mich. Law Weekly, 1990-91; named one of the Best Judges, Detroit Monthly, 1991; named Disting. Citizen of Yr., NAACP Oakland County, Mich., 1970. Fellow Am. Bar Found., Mich. Bar Found. (vice-chmn. 1992-93, chmn. 1993—); mem. NAACP (mem. state constl. revision and legal redress com. 1963, Disting. Citizen of Yr. 1970, Presdl. award North Oakland County, Mich. chpt. 1987), ABA, Fed. Bar Assn. (fed.-state ct. seminar lectr. Detroit chpt. 1981—), Mich. Bar Assn. (chmn. constl. law com. 1969, vice-chmn. civil liberties com. 1970, co-chmn. profl. devel. task force 1984-87, U.S. cts. com. 1988-95, com. on professionalism 1991—, Champion of Justice 1994), Mich. Tribunal Assn. (bd. dirs. 3rd cir. 1992-98), Detroit Bar Assn. (Bench-Bar award 1987), Oakland County Bar Assn. (chmn. continuing legal edn. com. 1968-69, jud. liaison Dist. Ct. com. 1977, unauthorized practice law com. 1977), Wolverine Bar Assn. (Bench-Bar award 1987, D. Augustus Straker award 1988), Mich. Assn. Black Judges, Am. Inn of Ct. (founder Met. Detroit chpt., pres., master of bench, chmn. 6th cir. com. on standard jury instructions 1986—), Am. Law Inst., Union Black Episcopalians (Detroit chpt., Absalom Jones award 1988), Justice Frank Murphy Honor Soc.

COOK, RICHARD BORRESON, architect; b. Harvard, Ill., May 23, 1937; s. Ernest Keller and Clara Matilda (Borreson) C.; m. Shirley Jean Antrup,; children: Alan Blair, Elizabeth Ann, Rebecca Alica. BArch, U. Ill., 1962. Registered architect, Calif., Fla., Ill., Ind., Mich., Mo., N.D., N.Y., Ohio, Wis. Intern architect Skidmore, Owings & Merrill, Chgo., 1962-64, Ulrich Franzen & Assocs., NYC, 1964-65; assoc. I.W. Colburn & Assocs., Chgo., 1965-70, Metz, Train, Olson & Youngren, Chgo., 1970-78; pres. Orput Assocs., Wilmette, Ill., 1978-81, Stowell Cook Frolichstein, Chgo., 1981—, Green Cook Ltd., Chgo., 1981. Bd. dirs., pres. Chgo. Archtl. Assistance Ctr., 1983; chmn. handicapped subcom. Mayor's Commn. Bldg. Code Amendments, Chgo., chmn. constrn. industry affairs com.; speaker, presenter papers in field. Prin. projects with Stowell Cook Frolichstein and Cook, Hiltscher Assoc. include Countryside Mall, Fla., Orange Park Mall, Fla., Trinity Evangel. Div. Sch., Rolfing Libr. addition and renovation, Deerfield, Ill, renovation main br. U.S. Postal Svc., Chgo., City Colls. of Chgo., Main St. Sq. Shopping Ctr., Downers Grove, Ill., Chgo. Bd. Edn.; with Orput Assocs. Kenosha (Wis.) County Pub. Safety Bldg., Burnham Terr. Apts. for Elderly, Rockford, Ill., addition and renovation Garrett-Evangel. Sem. Libr., addition Elmhurst (Ill.) Pub. Libr., addition Lake Forest (Ill.) Sch. Mgmt., apt. bldg. renovation Gt. Lakes (Ill.) Naval Sta., Hickory Hills (Ill.) Mcpl. Bldg.; with Metz Train, Olson & Youngren, Inc. office and computer ctr. Lumbermen's Mut. Casualty Co., Long Grove, Ill., Safeguards Analytical Lab. Bldg. Argonne (Ill.) Nat. Lab., Cancer Virus Rsch. Lab. U. Chgo., pub. bldg. commn. John Hope Middle Sch., Chgo.; with I.W. Colburn & Assocs. Geophys. Sci. Bldg. U. Chgo, Cathedral Christ the King, Kalamazoo, dormitory complex and dining facilities Bryn Mawr Coll, Pa., lab. and office bldg. Standard "T" Chem. Co., Lisle, Ill., Temple Jeremiah, Northbrook, Ill. Mem. Evanston Planning Commn., 1997, chmn., 2002. Fellow AIA (dir. Ill. region 1988-89, chmn. T6B documents com., chmn. 1987 nat. conv., chmn. membership svcs. task force, mem. goals and grassroots '82 com.); mem. Ill. Council AIA (bd. dirs., pres., co-chmn. Midwest Regional Conf., mem. fin. and nominating coms.), Chgo. chpt. AIA (sec., v.p., 1st v.p., pres., mem. 1992 World's Fair Rev. Com., chmn. nominating com., mem. Logan Sq. Design Ctr.), Am. Arbitration Assn., Chgo. chpt. AIA Found. (pres.). Democrat. Congregationalist. Avocations: sculpting, photography. Home: 1330 Wesley Ave Evanston IL 60201-4141 Office: Stowell Cook & Frolichstein 33 W Grand Ave Chicago IL 60610-4306

COOK, STANTON R., media company executive; b. Chgo., July 3, 1925; s. Rufus Merrill and Thelma Marie (Borgerson) C.; m. Barbara Wilson, Sept. 23, 1950 (dec. Nov. 1994). BS in Mech. Engring., Northwestern U., 1949. With Shell Oil Co., 1949-51, Chgo. Tribune Co., 1951-81, v.p., 1967-70, exec. v.p. and gen. mgr., 1970-72, pres., 1972-74, pub., 1973-90, CEO, 1974-76, chmn., 1974-81; dir. Tribune Co., 1972-96, v.p., 1972-74, pres., 1974-88, chmn., 1989-92, CEO, 1974-90; chmn. Chgo. Nat. League Ball Club, Inc., 1990-94. Bd. dirs. AP, 1975-84, 2d vice chmn., 1979-84; bd. dirs. Newspaper Adv. Bur., 1973-92, Am. ewspaper Pubs. Assn., 1974-82; dep. chmn., bd. dirs. Fed. Res. Bank Chgo., 1980-83, chmn., 1984-85; bd. dirs. Robert R. McCormick Tribune Found., 1990-2001. Trustee Robert R. McCormick Trust, 1972-90, Savs. and Profit Sharing Fund of Sears Employees, 1991-94, U. Chgo., 1973-87, Mus. Sci. and Industry, Chgo., 1973—, Field Mus. Natural History, Chgo., 1973—, Gen. Douglas MacArthur Found., 1979—, Northwestern U., 1987—, Shedd Aquarium Soc., 1987—, Am. Newspaper Pubs. Assn. Found., 1973-82. Mem. Newspaper Assn. Am. (bd. govs. 1992), Chgo. Coun. Fgn. Rels. (bd. dirs. 1973-93), Comml. Club (past pres.), Econ. Club (life, past pres.), Glen Lake Assn. (pres. 2001-04). Home: 224 Raleigh Rd Kenilworth IL 60043-1209

COOK, STEVEN M., lawyer, construction executive; With Sears, Roebuck and Co., 1996—2006; v.p., dep. gen. counsel, corp. sec. Sears Holdings Corp.; v.p., gen. counsel, sec. Pulte Homes, Inc., Bloomfield Hills, Mich., 2006—. Office: Pulte Homes Inc 100 Bloomfield Hills Pky Bloomfield Hills MI 48304

COOK, SUSAN J., human resources specialist, manufacturing executive; BA, U. Colo.; MBA, Loyola U., 1977. Various positions in human resources including personnel mgr. IBM Corp.; v.p human resources Tandem Computers, Inc., Eaton Corp., Cleve., 1995—. Bd. dirs. Human Resources Policy Assn., CCL Industries, Inc. Office: Eaton Corp Eaton Ctr 1111 Superior Ave Cleveland OH 44114-2584 Office Phone: 216-523-5000. Office Fax: 216-523-4787.

COOK, WILLIAM M., manufacturing executive; b. Aug. 1954; BSBA, MBA, Va. Tech. Univ. Sr. v.p., comml. & indsl. Donaldson Co., Mpls., 1996—2000, sr. v.p. internat., CFO, 2001—04, pres., CEO, 2004—05, chmn., pres., CEO, 2005—. Office: Donaldson Co 1400 W 94th St Minneapolis MN 55431

COOKE, MICHAEL, editor-in-chief, publishing executive; b. England; m. Barbara Cooke; 3 children. BA, Auckland U., 1969. Joined Toronto Star, 1974, copy editor, city editor; co-mng. editor Montreal Gazette; mng. editor Edmonton Jour., 1992—95; editor-in-chief The Vancouver Province, 1995—2000, The Fin. Post, Canada, 1998; founding editor The Nat. Post, 1998; editor-in-chief Chgo. Sun-Times, 2000—05, 2006—. NY Daily News, NYC, 2005; v.p. editl. Sun-Times Media Group, Chgo., 2006—. Office: Chicago Sun Times 350 N Orleans St Ste 1270 Chicago IL 60654-2148 Office Phone: 312-321-3000. Office Fax: 312-321-3084. E-mail: mcooke@suntimes.com.*

COOKMAN, CLAUDE, journalist, educator; AB in Classical Greek with hons., Wheaton Coll., 1965; MS in Journalism, Columbia U., 1971; MFA in Art History, Princeton U., 1989, PhD in History of Photog., 1994. Reporter Anderson Herald, Ind., 1965, 1968—70; picture editor Assoc. Press, NYC, 1971—73; copy editor Herald-Jour., Syracuse, NY, 1973—74; picture editor Louisville Times, Louisville, 1974—81; graphics editor Miami Herald, 1981—84; copy editor Courier-Jour., Louisville, 1984—86; asst. instr. dept. art and archaeology Princeton U., 1988—89; assoc. prof. journalism Ind. U., Bloomington, 1990—. Adj. instr. Western Ky. U., Bowling Green, 1979, Bowling Green, 80; vis. lectr. U. Iowa, 1981; adj. instr. Barry U., Miami, 1984. Contbr. articles to profl. publs. Co-recipient Pulitzer prize, 1976; fellow Gretchen Kemp Tchg. fellow, Ind. U., 1993. Mem.: Soc. Photographic Edn., Nat. Press Photographers Assn. (Robin F. Garland Educator award 1999), Soc. News Design, Assn. Edn. Journalism Mass Comm. Office: Sch Jour Ind Univ Ernie Pyle Hall 209 940 E 7th St Bloomington IN 47405-7108

COOKS, R(OBERT) GRAHAM, chemist, educator; b. Benoni, South Africa, July 2, 1941; came to U.S., 1968; s. Audrey Owen Eva Mitchie; m. Maria-Luisa Raduan Ripoll, Aug. 19, 1967; children: Owen, Barry, Jude. BSc, U. Natal, 1961, PhD, 1965, Cambridge U., 1967. Asst. prof. Kansas State U., Manhattan, 1968-71; from assoc. dir. to disting. prof. Purdue U., Lafayette, Ind., 1971—. Author: Metastable Ions, 1973; contbr. articles to profl. jours.; patentee in field. Recipient ACS award in analytical chemistry Am. Chem. Soc., 1997. Mem. Am. Soc. Mass Spectrometry (pres. 1984-86), Internat. Mass Spectrometry Soc. (pres. 1997-2000). Home: 177 Prophet Dr West Lafayette IN 47906-1235 Office: Purdue U Dept Chemistry West Lafayette IN 47907 Business E-Mail: cooks@purdue.edu.

COOLEY, CHARLES P., chemicals executive; married; 3 children. BA in Philosophy, Yale Coll.; MBA, Dartmouth Coll. With nat. banking div. Mfrs. Hanover Trust Co., YC; various positions Atlantic Richfield; controller and v.p. fin. and adminstrn. ARCO Products Co.; asst. treas. corp. fin. Atlantic Richfield Co., LA; v.p., treas., CFO The Lubrizol Corp., Wickliffe, Ohio, 1998—. Office: The Lubrizol Corp 29400 Lakeland Blvd Wickliffe OH 44092

COOLEY, WILLIAM EDWARD, research scientist, consultant; b. St. Louis, Mar. 7, 1930; s. Charles Frederic and Lillian Marie (Williams) C.; m. Marion Grace Sherman, June 5, 1952; children: Charles, Marilyn, Harold, Noele. AB, Cen. Coll., 1951; PhD, U. Ill., 1954. Rsch. chemist Procter & Gamble Co., Cin., 1954-61, product devel. chemist, 1961-65, product devel. group leader, 1965-75, product devel. regulatory sect. mgr., 1975-90, regulatory affairs sect. mgr., 1990-91; worldwide regulatory coordination sect. mgr., 1991-94; pres. Cooley Cons., Inc., 1994—. Contbr. articles to profl. jours. Mem. Am. Assn. Dental Rsch., Internat. Assn. Dental Rsch., Drug Info. Assn., Assn. Food Drug Ofcls., Regulatory Affairs Profl. Soc. (bd. editors 1990), Consumer Healthcare Products Assn. (bd. dirs. 1987-91), Food and Drug Law Inst. Republican. Achievements include patents in field. Avocations: music, motorcycling, railroading, flying, astronomy. Home and Office: Cooley Cons Inc 531 Chisholm Trail Wyoming OH 45215-2517 Home Phone: 513-522-2491; Office Phone: 513-522-3797.

COOLLEY, RONALD B., lawyer; b. Manchester, NH, Feb. 15, 1946; s. Mace A. and Ruth A. C. BS, Iowa State U., 1969; MBA, JD, U. Iowa, 1972. Bar: Ill. 1974, Tex. 1987. Assoc. Mason, Kolehmainen, Chgo., 1973-87, Arnold, White & Durkee, Chgo., 1987—. Contbr. articles to profl. jours. Recipient Gerald Rose award John Marshall Law Sch., 1985, Rossman award, Patent and Trademark Office Soc., 1985. Mem. ABA (bd. dirs. 1988-90), Patent Law Assn. Chgo. (pres.1988-89).

COOMBE, V. ANDERSON, retired valve manufacturing company executive; b. Cin., Mar. 5, 1926; s. Harry Elijah and Mary (Anderson) C.; m. Eva Jane Romaine, Sept. 26, 1957; children— James, Michael, Peter. B.E., Yale, 1948. Asst. to pres. Wm. Powell Co., Cin., 1953-57, v.p., 1957-63, exec. v.p., 1963-69, pres., treas., 1969-91, chmn. bd., 1991—. Mem.: Cin. Country Club, Queen City Club (Cin.), Camargo Club (Cin.). Home: 6 Corbin Dr Cincinnati OH 45208-3302 Office: 2503 Spring Grove Ave Cincinnati OH 45214-1729

COONEY, KEVIN L., lawyer; b. 1969; BS in Chem. Engring., Purdue U., 1992; JD, Washington U., 1997. Bar: Ind. 1997, US Dist. Ct. Southern Dist. Ind. 1997, US Dist. Ct. Northern Dist. Ind. 1997, Ohio 1998. Mem. Shared Harvest Foodbank; trustee Liberty Twp. Parks Com., Purdue Club of Cin.; pres., trustee Friends of Liberty Twp. Parks & Recreation. Named one of Ohio's Rising Stars, Super Lawyers, 2006. Mem.: Greater Mutual Funds Assn., ABA, Ohio State Bar Assn., Ind. State Bar Assn., Cin. Bar Assn. Office: Frost Brown Todd LLC 2200 PNC Ctr 201 E Fifth St Cincinnati OH 45202-4182 Office Phone: 513-651-6800. Office Fax: 513-651-6981.

COONEY, PATRICK RONALD, bishop; b. Detroit, Mar. 10, 1934; s. Michael and Elizabeth (Dowdall) C. BA, Sacred Heart Sem., 1956; STB, Gregorian U., Rome, 1958, STL, 1960; MA, Notre Dame U., 1973. Ordained priest Archdiocese of Detroit, 1934, asst. chancellor, 1962—69, dir. dept. worship, 1969—83; assoc. pastor St. Catherine Ch., 1960—62; rector Blessed Sacrament Cathedral, 1977—83; aux. bishop Archdiocese of Detroit, 1982—83; ordained bishop, 1983; bishop Diocese of Gaylord, Mich., 1989—. Roman Catholic. Office: Diocese of Gaylord Pastoral Ctr 611 W North St Gaylord MI 49735-8349 Office Phone: 989-732-5147. Office Fax: 989-705-3589.*

COONS, JAMES WILLIAM, economist; b. Glen Ellyn, Ill., Oct. 8, 1957; s. Richard and Barbara (Hirt) C.; m. Margaret Ellen Sims, May 21, 1983; children: Sarah Ann, Katherine Elizabeth, Charles William. BA in Econs. and Math., DePauw U., 1979; MA in Econs., Ohio U., 1980. Staff economist Am. Electric Power, Columbus, Ohio, 1980-84; sr. economist Borden, Inc., Columbus, 1984-85; chief economist Huntington Nat. Bank, Columbus, 1985—. Mem. Fed. Res. Bank of Cleve. Econ. Roundtable, 1987—; dir. Cen. Ohio Coun. Econ. Edn., 1990—. Mem. Ohio Gov.'s Econ. Adv. Coun., Columbus, 1986—. Recipient grad. assistantship Ohio U., 1979-80. Mem. Nat. Assn. Bus. Economists, Am. Economy Assn., Capital Club, Beta Theta Pi. Avocations: golf, running, reading. Office: Huntington Ctr Columbus OH 43287-0001

COOPER, ARNOLD COOK, management educator, researcher; b. Chgo., Mar. 9, 1933; s. Millard and Sarah Ellen C.; m. Jean Phillips Lord, Sept. 12, 1959; children: Katherine Lord, David Andrew BS in Chem. Engring., Purdue U., 1955, MS in Mgmt., 1957, PhD (hon.), 2005; D in Bus. Adminstrn., Harvard U., 1962. Engr. Proctor & Gamble, Cin., 1957-58; asst. prof. Harvard U., Cambridge, Mass., 1961-63; assoc. prof. Purdue U., West Lafayette, Ind., 1963-70, prof., 1970-84, Weil prof. mgmt., 1984—2005, emeritus, 2005—. Vis. assoc. prof. Stanford Univ., Palo Alto, Calif., 1967-68; vis. prof. Manchester Bus. Sch., Eng., 1972, IMEDE Mgmt. Devel. Inst., Lausanne, Switzerland, 1977-78, U. Pa., 1995; past dir. Grad. Profl. Programs, chmn. Mgmt. Policy Com., Purdue U., West Lafayette; mem. Ind. Employment Devel. Commn., 1982-89, Fed. Adv. Com. on Indsl. Innovation, 1978-79 Author: The Founding of Technologically Based Firms, 1971; co-author: Small Business Management,

1966, Technical Entrepreneurship: A Symposium, 1972, The Entrepreneurial Function, 1977, New Business in America, 1990, Entrepreneurial Strategies, 2006; contbr. numerous articles to profl. jours. and bus. publs.; mem. editorial bd. Stategic Mgmt. Jour., 1979-2006, Jour. of Bus. Venturing, 1985-2005, Acad. of Mgmt. Jour., 1978-84, Jour. High Tech. Mktg., 1986-87. 2nd lt. U.S. Army, 1956 Recipient Honeywell Master Tchr. award, 1990, Murphy Tchg. award, Disting. Scholar award, Internat. Coun. on Small Bus., 1987, Ten Year Author award, Babson Entrepreneurship Conf., 1990, Internat. award for Entrepreneurship and Small Bus. Rsch., 1997, John S. Day Disting. Alumni Acad. Svc. award, 2001. Mem. Acad. Mgmt. (chmn. bus. policy and strategy divsn. 1978-79, Outstanding Paper award Entrepreneurship Divsn. 1991, 92, Coleman Entrepreneurship Mentor award, 1993, Richard D. Irwin outstanding educator award, 1999, Internat. Coun. Small Bus., Strategic Mgmt. Soc. (bd. govs. 1984-86), Soc. of Fellows. Home: 616 Ridgewood Dr West Lafayette IN 47906-2367 Office: Purdue Univ Krannert Sch of Mgmt 1310 Krannert West Lafayette IN 47907-1310 Business E-Mail: coopera@mgmt.purdue.edu.

COOPER, CHARLES GILBERT, cosmetics executive; b. Chgo., Apr. 4, 1928; s. Benjamin and Gertrude Cooper; m. Miriam Meyer, Feb. 11, 1951 (dec. Oct. 17, 1983); children: Debra, Ruth, Janet, Benjamin; m. Nancy Cooper BS in Journalism, U. Ill., 1949. With sales promotion dept. Maidenform Co., NYC, 1949-51; with circulation promotion dept. Esquire mag., Chgo., 1951-52; with Helene Curtis Industries Inc., Chgo., 1953-96, pres. salon div., 1971-75, pres. consumer products div., 1975-82, corp. exec. v.p., 1982-85, exec. v.p., COO, 1985-93, sr. v.p., 1993-96; sr. ptnr. GCG Ptnrs. Adj. prof. Loyola U. With AUS, 1952-53. Office: 200 S Wacker Dr Ste 4000 Chicago IL 60606

COOPER, CHARLES GORDON, retired insurance company executive; b. Providence, May 31, 1927; s. Irving and Helen Christina (Skog) C.; m. Barbara Caroline Termohlen, June 17, 1950; 1 dau., Marie Suzanne. BA, Ohio Wesleyan U., 1949. C.L.U. Group rep. Washington Nat. Ins. Co., 1949-53, asst. mgr., 1953-58, mgr., 1958-63, dir. assn. field services, 1963-65, asst. sec., 1965-67, 3d v.p., 1967-72, 2d v.p., 1972-77, v.p., 1977-79, sr. v.p., 1979-83, exec. v.p. Evanston, Ill., 1983-85, dir., mem. exec. com., 1979-85; sr. v.p.-mktg. Washington Nat. Corp., parent co. Washington Nat. Ins. Co., Evanston, 1983-85, cons., 1985—; pres. Charles G. Cooper & Assocs., Inc., 1985—95. Dir. Washington Nat. Trust Co., 1974-85, chmn. exec. com., 1979-85; chmn., dir. Washington Nat. Fin. Services, Inc., 1979-85; pres., dir. Washington Nat. Equity Co., 1973-85, chmn. bd., 1983-85 Bd. dirs. North Shore Assn. for Retarded, Evanston, 1983—. Served with USNR, 1945-46, PTO. Mem. Am. Coll. Life Underwriters, Chartered Life Underwriters, Nat. Assn. Life Underwriters, Chgo. Life Underwriters Assn., Nat. Assn. Health Underwriters, Chgo. Health Underwriters Clubs: Ivanhoe (Ill.). Lodges: Masons, Shriners. Republican. E-mail: coop1151@comcast.net.

COOPER, CORINNE, communications consultant, lawyer; b. Albuquerque, July 12, 1952; d. David D. and Martha Lucille (Rosenblum) Cooper. BA magna cum laude, U. Ariz., 1975, JD summa cum laude, 1978. Bar: Ariz. 1978, US Dist. Ct. Ariz. 1978, Mo. 1985. Assoc. Streich, Lang, Weeks & Cardon, Phoenix, 1978—82; asst. prof. U. Mo., Kansas City, 1982—86, assoc. prof., 1986—94, prof., 1994—2000, prof. emerita, 2000—; pres. Profl. Presence, Comm. Cons., Tucson, 2001—. Vis. prof. U. Wis., Madison, 1985, Madison, 91, U. Pa., Phila., 1988, U. Ariz., 1993, U. Colo., 1994. Author (with Bruce Meyerson): A Drafter's Guide to Alternative Dispute Resolution, 1991; author: How to Build a Law Firm Brand, 2005; editor: The Portable UCC, 1993, 3d edit., 2001, 4th edit., 2004, Getting Graphic I, 1993, II, 1994, The New Article 9, 1999, 2d edit., 2000; editor in chief: Bus. Law Today, 1995—97; mem. editl. bd. ABA Jour., 1999—2005; author, editor: Attorney Liability in Bankruptcy, 2006; contbr. articles to profl. jours., chapters to books. Legal counsel Mo. for Hart campaign, 1984; dir. issues Goddard for Gov. campaign, 1990. Mem.: ABA (mem. editl. bd. Bus. Law Today 1991—97, mem. unifrom comml. code com., chmn. bus. sect. membership com. 1992—94, mem. coun. bus. sect. 1992—96, sect. bus. law pubs. 1998—2002, mem. standing com. strategic comm. 2001—03, coun. gen. practice sect. 2003—05), Mo. Bar Assn. (mem. comml. law com.), Ariz. Bar Assn., Am. Assn. Law Schs. (mem. comml. law 1982—2000), Am. Law Inst., Phi Beta Kappa, Order of Coif, Phi Kappa Phi. Democrat. Jewish. Office: Profl Presence 4558 N 1st Ave Tucson AZ 85718 Business E-Mail: c2@professionalpresence.com.

COOPER, EDWARD HAYES, lawyer, educator; b. Highland Park, Mich., Oct. 13, 1941; s. Frank Edward and Margaret Ellen (Hayes) C.; m. Nancy Carol Wybo, June 29, 1963; children: Lisa, Chandra. AB, Dartmouth Coll., 1961; LL.B., Harvard U., 1964. Bar: Mich. 1965. Law clk. Hon. Clifford O'Sullivan, U.S. Ct. of Appeals, 1964-65; practice law, Detroit, 1965-67; adj. prof. Wayne State U. Law Sch., 1965-67; assoc. prof. U. Minn. Law Sch., 1967-72; prof. law U. Mich. Law Sch., Ann Arbor, 1972-88, assoc. dean for acad. affairs, 1981-94, Thomas M. Cooley prof. of law, 1988—. Advisor Am. Law Inst. Restatement of the Law, 2d Judgments, 1976-80, Complex Litigation Project, Restatement of the Law, 3d Torts-Apportionment, Fed. Jud. Code Project, Transnational Procedure Project, Internat. Jurisdiction Judgment, Internat. Intellectual Property, Aggregation; reporter fed. state jurisdiction com. Jud. Conf. US, 1985-91; mem. civil rules adv. com., 1991-92, reporter, 1992—; reporter Uniform Transfer of Litigation Act, 1989-91. Author: (with C.A. Wright and A.R. Miller) Federal Practice and Procedure: Jurisdiction, Vols. 13-19, 1975-81, 2d edit., 1984-2002, 3d edit., 1999—; contbr. articles to law revs. Mem. ABA, Mich. Bar Assn., Am. Law Inst. (council). Office: U Mich 330 Hutchins Law Sch Ann Arbor MI 48109-1215 Home Phone: 734-663-7098; Office Phone: 734-764-4347. Business E-Mail: coopere@umich.edu.

COOPER, HAL DEAN, lawyer; b. Marshall County, Iowa, Dec. 8, 1934; s. Truman Braton and Golda Frances (Chadwick) C.; m. Constance Bellinger Simms, Dec. 31, 1960; children: Shannon, Charles, Ellen. Student, Neb. U., 1952-54; BS in Mech. Engring., Iowa State U., 1957; JD with honors, George Washington U., 1963. Bar: Iowa 1963, Ohio 1963, U.S. Supreme Ct. 1971. Assoc., ptnr. Fay & Fay, Cleve., 1962-67; ptnr. Meyer, Tilberry & Body, Cleve., 1967-69, Yount, Tarolli, Weinshenker & Cooper, Cleve, 1969-72; trial judge U.S. Ct. Claims, Washington, 1972-75; ptnr. Jones, Day, Reavis & Pogue, Cleve., 1975-95, chmn. intellectual property sect., 1976—94; owner Halco Enterprises, Ltd., Austinburg, Ohio, 1995—; pvt. arbitrator, mediator, 1996—. Bd. trustees Ashtubula County Dist. Lib., 2004—, pres., 2005—08. With AUS, 1957—59. Mem.: Ashtabula County Bar Assn., Cleve. Intellectual Property Law Assn., Rotary, Clifton Club, Rowfant Club. Episcopalian. Avocation: bookbinding. Home Phone: 440-275-1333. Personal E-mail: halcon@windstream.net.

COOPER, ILENE LINDA, magazine editor, author; b. Chgo., Mar. 10, 1948; d. Morris and Lillian (Friedman) C.; m. Robert Seid, May 28, 1972 (div. 1995). BJ, U. Mo., 1969; MLS, Rosary Coll., 1973. Head of children's svcs. Winnetka (Ill.) Libr. Dist., 1974-80; editor children's books Booklist Mag., ALA, Chgo., 1981—. Author: Susan B. Anthony, 1983, Choosing Sides, 1990 (Internat. Reading Assn.-Children's Book Coun. choice 1990), Mean Streak, 1991, Jewish Holidays All Year Round, 2002, Sam I Am, 2004, (series) Frances in the Fourth Grade, 1991, The Dead Sea Scrolls, 1997, numerous others. Mem. Soc. Midland Authors, Soc. Children's Book Writers, Children's Reading Roundtable. Jewish. Office: Booklist Mag 50 E Huron St Chicago IL 60611-5295

COOPER, JAMES ALBERT, JR., electrical engineering educator; b. Columbus, Miss., Feb. 5, 1946; s. James Albert and Juanita (Perkins) C.; m. Barbara Crowder, Aug. 3, 1968; children: David Alan, Katherine Liann. BSEE, Miss. State U., 1968; MSEE, Stanford U., 1969; PhD, Purdue U., 1973. Mem. tech. staff Sandia Labs., Albuquerque, 1968-69; grad. rsch. asst. Sch. Elec. Engring. Purdue U., West Lafayette, Ind., 1970-72, prof., 1983—, dir. Purdue Optoelectronics Rsch. Ctr., 1986-89, Charles William Harrison prof., 2002—; mem. tech. staff Bell Labs., Murray Hill, NJ, 1973-83; co-dir. Birck Nanotech. Ctr., 2001—. Contbr. numerous articles to jours., chpts. to books; patentee in field. Fellow IEEE (assoc. editor Trans. on Electron Devices 1983-86). Republican. Mem. United Methodist Ch. Achievements include 13 patents in field; co-origination of the Time-of-Flight measurement technique for the study of high-field transport of electrons along semiconductor/insulator interfaces; design of Bell System's first microprocessor chip; co-development of first silicon carbide nonvolatile memory chips, first silicon carbide monolithic integrated circuits and first SiC DMOS power transistors. Office: Purdue U Birck Nantotech Ctr 1205 W State St West Lafayette IN 47907-2057

COOPER, JOHN MILTON, JR., history educator, author; b. Washington, Mar. 16, 1940; s. John Milton and Mary Louise (Porter) C.; m. Judith Karin Widerkrantz, June 9, 1962; children: John Milton III, Elizabeth Karin Doyle. AB summa cum laude, Princeton U., 1961; MA, Columbia U., 1962, PhD, 1968. Instr. history Wellesley (Mass.) Coll., 1965-67, asst. prof., 1967-70; asst. prof. history U. Wis., Madison, 1970-71, assoc. prof., 1971-76, prof., 1976-87, William Francis Allen prof. history, 1987-99, E. Gofdon Fox prof. Am. instns., 1999—, chmn. dept., 1988-91. Fulbright prof. Coun. Internat. Exch. Scholars, Moscow, 1987. Author: Vanity of Power, 1969, Walter Hines Page, 1977, Warrior and Priest, 1983, Pivotal Decades, 1990, Breaking the Heart of the World: Woodrow Wilson and the Fight for the League of Nations, 2001; editor: Causes and Consequences of World War I, 1971, The Wilson Era, 1991. Woodrow Wilson Found. fellow, 1961, NEH fellow, 1969, 91, Guggenheim Found. fellow, 1979. Mem.: Ctr. for Nat. Policy, State Hist. Soc. Wis. (bd. curators), Woodrow Wilson Birthplace Found. (hon. pres.), Coun. Fgn. Rels., So. Hist. Assn., Orgn. Am. Historians, Am. Hist. Assn., Rotary, Phi Beta Kappa. Democrat. Congregationalist. E-mail: jmcooper@facstaff.wisc.edu.

COOPER, KEN ERROL, retired management educator; b. Bryan, Ohio, Mar. 10, 1939; s. George Wayne and Agnes Anibel (Fisher) C.; m. Karen Cremean, June 17, 1961; children: Kristin, Andrew. BS, Bowling Green State U., 1961; MBA, Miami U., Oxford, Ohio, 1962; PhD, U. Minn., 1984. Chartered fin. cons. Instr. Miami U., 1962-63; lectr. U. Minn., 1965-67, 84-86; group v.p. Land O'Lakes, Inc., Mpls., 1967-82; v.p. fin. and adminstrn. Hamline U., 1982-84; dean Coll. Bus., Ohio No. U., Ada, 1986-90, prof., 1990-2000; prof., post chair for ethics and professions Am. Coll., Bryn Mawr, Pa., 1994-95, ret., 1995; lectr. Ohio No. U., 2003—; now lectr. in philosophy. Vis. prof. (on leave) Coll. of St. Thomas, St. Paul, 1981-82; vis. prof. mgmt. U. San Diego, 2001-02, U. Evansville, 2002-03, Appalachian State U. 2006, We. New Eng. Coll., 2006—, Ashland U., 2007—. Trustee Westmar Coll., 1980-86; bd. dirs., sec.-treas. Acad. Mgmt., 1989-95; mem. Iowa Supreme Ct. Adv. Coun., 1972-75, North Ctrl. Devel. Found.

COOPER, REGINALD RUDYARD, orthopedic surgeon, educator; b. Elkins, W.Va., Jan. 6, 1932; s. Eston H. and Kathryn (Wyatt) C.; m. Jacqueline Smith, Aug. 22, 1954; children: Pamela Ann, Douglas Mark, Christopher Scott, Jeffrey Michael. BA with honors, W.Va. U., 1952, BS, 1953; MD, Med. Coll. Va., 1955; MS, U. Iowa, 1960. Diplomate Am. Bd. Orthopedic Surgeons (examiner 1968-70). Orthopedic surgeon U.S. Naval Hosp., Pensacola, Fla., 1960-62; assoc. in orthopedics U. Iowa Coll. Medicine, Iowa City, 1962-65, asst. prof. orthopedics, 1965-68, assoc. prof. orthopedics, 1968-71, prof. orthopedics, 1971—, chmn. orthopedics, 1973-99, prof. emeritus orthopaedics, 2003—. Rsch. fellow orthopedic surgery Johns Hopkins Hosp., Balt., 1964-65; exch. fellow to Britain for Am. Orthopedic Assn., 1969. Trustee Jour. Bone and Joint Surgeons, 1989-94, chmn. 1993-94. Trustee Nat. Easter Seals Rsch. Found., 1977-81, chmn., 1979-81. Served to lt. comdr. USN, 1960—62. Mem. Iowa, Johnson County Med. Socs., Orthopedic Rsch. Soc. (sec.-treas. 1970-73, pres. 1974-75), Am. Acad. Orthopedic Surgeons (Kappa Delta award for outstanding rsch. in orthopedics 1971), Can. Orthopedic Assn., Am. Orthopedic Assn., N.Y. Acad. Sci., Assn. Bone and Joint Surgeons, AMA, Am. Rheumatism Assn., Am. Acad. Cerebral Palsy, Am. Acad. Orthopedic Surgeons (chmn. exams. com. 1978-82, sec. 1982, 2d v.p. 1985-86, 1st v.p. 1986-87, pres. 1987-88, ortho residency rev. com. 1989-95, chmn. 1993-95). Avocations: travel, photography, anthropology, history. Home: 201 Ridgeview Ave Iowa City IA 52246-1625 Office: U Iowa Hosps & Clinics 450 Newton Rd Iowa City IA 52242

COOPER, RICHARD ALAN, health policy consultant; b. Milw., Sept. 23, 1936; s. Peter and Annabelle (Schlomovitz) C.; m. Jaclyn Koppel, June 22, 1958 (dec.); children: Stephanie, Jonathan BS, U. Wis., 1958; MD, Washington U., St. Louis, 1961. Intern Harvard U. med. svcs. Boston City Hosp., 1961-63, resident in medicine, 1965-66, fellow in hematology Thorndike Meml. Lab., 1966-69; asst. prof. medicine Harvard U. Med. Sch., 1969-71; chief hematology divsn. Thorndike Meml. Lab. and Harvard Med. Svcs., Boston City Hosp., 1969-71; prof. medicine, dir. Cancer Ctr., chief hematology-oncology sect. U. Pa., Phila., 1971-85; prof. medicine, exec. v.p., dean Med. Coll. Wis., Milw., 1985-94, dir. health policy inst., 1992—2005; prof. medicine, sr. fellow Leonard Davis Inst. Health Econs., U. Pa., Phila., 2005—. Mem. editl. bd. Blood, 1979-84, Lipid Research, 1983-84. Served with USPHS, 1963-65. NIH grantee. Mem. Am. Soc. Hematology, Am. Fedn. Clin. Rsch., Am. Soc. Clin. Investigation, Assn. Am. Physicians, Am. Clin. Climatol. Assn., Phi Beta Kappa., Alpha Omega Alpha. Office: 3641 Locust Walk Philadelphia PA 19104-6218 Office Phone: 215-746-3173. Business E-Mail: cooperra@wharton.upenn.edu.

COOPER, RICHARD LEE, agronomist, educator; b. Rensselaer, Ind., Feb. 28, 1932; married, 1952; 4 children. BS, Purdue U., 1957; MS, Mich. State U., 1958, PhD in Plant Breeding and Genetics, 1962. Rsch. assoc. soybean breeding and genetics dept. agronomy and plant genetics U. Minn., 1961-67; from assoc. prof. to prof. agronomy U. Ill., Urbana-Champaign, 1969-77, rsch. leader USDA-ARS Regional Soybean Lab., 1967-76; USDA-ARS rsch. agronomist, prof. plant breeding Ohio Agrl. R & D Ctr. Ohio State U., Wooster, 1977—. Mem. adv. coun. Potash & Phosphate Inst., 1981-83; ARS fellow Agrl. Rsch. Assignment, Brisbane, Australia, 1990-91. Sr. Fulbright scholar, Australia, 1990-91; recipient Agronomic Rsch. award Am. Soc. Agronomy, 1997. Fellow Am. Soc. Agronomy (Agronomy Achievement award 1993, Agronomic Rsch. award 1997), Crop Science Soc. Am.; mem. Am. Soybean Assn. (Soybean Rsch. recognition award 1981, Meritorious Svc. award 1987). Achievements include research in solid seeding of soybeans with increases of 10-30% in yield; development of semidwarf soybean cultivars; maximum yield research in soybeans; breeding methodology (early generation testing); development of abiotic stress tolerant cultivars; subirrigation/drainage research. Office: Ohio Agrl R & D Ctr Dept Horticulture and Crop Science Wooster OH 44691

COOPER, ROGER, secondary school educator, former state legislator; b. Nov. 8, 1944; m. Margie. BA, Rockford Coll.; postgrad., Mankato State U. State rep. Minn. Ho. Reps., Dist. 15B, 1986-97; tchr. Bold High Sch., Olivia, Minn. Vice chmn. econ. devel. com., mem. govt. oper. com., vice chmn. health & human svc. com., mem. gen. legis., bet affairs & elec. agrl., hyman svcs. fin. divsn. & local govt. & met. affairs com., Minn. Ho. Reps. Home: 940 S 4th St Bird Island MN 55310-1170

COOPER, THOM R., transportation executive; Chmn. Jack Cooper Transport Co., Inc., Kansas City, 1938—. Office: Jack Cooper Transport Co Inc 2345 Grand Blvd Ste 400 Kansas City MO 64108-2625

COOPER, WILLIAM ALLEN, bank executive; b. Detroit, July 3, 1943; BS in Acctg., Wayne State U., 1967. CPA, Mich. With Touche, Ross & Co., Detroit, 1967-71; chm. Minn. Rep Party. Sr. v.p. Mich. Nat. Bank of Detroit, 1971-72; sr. v.p. Mich. Nat. Corp., 1971-78; exec. v.p. Huntington Nat. Bank, Columbus, Ohio, 1978-83, pres., 1983-84; pres., Am. Savs. & Loan Assn. of Fla., Miami, 1984-85, also dir.; chmn. bd., chief exec. officer TCF Bank, FSB, Mpls., 1985—; chmn., TCF Fin. Corp., Mpls., from 1987, now chmn. bd., past chief exec. officer, bd. dirs. Mem. AICPA. Office: TCF Bank Office of Chmn Bd 801 Marquette Ave Minneapolis MN 55402-3475 also: Minn Rep Party 480 Ceder Street Ste 560 Castle Rock MN 55010

COPELAND, DOUGLAS ALLEN, lawyer; b. St. Louis, Mar. 22, 1956; s. William H. and Margaret J. (Wilson) C.; m. Amy Elizabeth Miles, May 18, 1985; children: Gregory Miles, Margaret Jane. BA, U. Mo., 1977; JD, St. Louis U., 1980. Bar: Mo. 1980, Ill. 1981, U.S. Dist. Ct. (ea. dist.) Mo. 1981, U.S. Ct. Appeals (8th cir.) 1987, U.S. Supreme Ct. 1988. Assoc. Brackman, Copeland, Oetting, Copeland, Walther & Schmidt, St. Louis, 1980-84, ptnr., 1985-86, Copeland, Gartner, Thompson & Jeep, St. Louis, 1987-88, Copeland, Gartner & Thompson, St. Louis, 1988-92, Copeland, Gartner, Thompson & Farris, St. Louis, 1993, Copeland Thompson Farris PC, St. Louis. Mem. ABA, NSBA (coun. sch. attys.), Mo. Bar Assn. (young lawyers sect., chmn. 1990-91, coun. mem. 1982-92, coun. sch. attys., pres.-elect 2004, pres. 2005), St. Louis County Bar Assn. (pres. 1988-89, exec. com. 1983-90, Outstanding Young Lawyer 1987), Bar Assn. of Met. St. Louis, Estate Planning Coun. of St. Louis, Nat. Health Lawyers Assn. Republican. Baptist. Avocations: tennis, softball, hunting. Office: Copeland Thompson Farris PC Ste 1220 231 S Bemiston Ave Saint Louis MO 63105

COPELAND, EDWARD JEROME, lawyer; b. Chgo., Oct. 29, 1933; s. Harvey and Lilyan (Rubin) C.; m. Ruth Caminer, Sept. 2, 1962; children: Ellyn, Bradley. BA, Carleton Coll., 1955; JD, Northwestern U., 1958. Bar: Ill. 1959, N.Y. 1981. Mem. Ill. Ho. of Reps., Springfield, 1967-71; ptnr. Foss, Schuman, Drake & Barnard, Chgo., 1971-86, Wood, Lucksinger & Epstein, Chgo., 1986-88, Shefsky & Froelich, Ltd., Chgo., 1988-89, Schuyler, Roche & Zwirner, Chgo., 1989—. Chmn. Bank of orth Shore, Northbrook, Ill., 1976-81. Mem. Ill. Bd. Edn., 1975-83, chmn., 1981-83. Mem. ABA, Ill. Bar Assn., Chgo. Bar Assn. Republican. Office: One Prudential Plaza Ste 3800 Schuyler Roche & Zwirner 130 E Randolph St Chicago IL 60601-6312 Office Phone: 312-565-8327. Business E-Mail: ecopeland@srzlaw.com.

COPELAND, HENRY JEFFERSON, JR., former college president; b. Griffin, Ga., June 13, 1936; s. Henry Jefferson and Emory (Drake) C.; m. Laura Harper, Dec. 21, 1958; children: Henry Drake, Eleanor Harper. BA, Baylor U., 1958; PhD, Cornell U., 1966. Instr. Cornell U., Ithaca, NY, 1965-66; asst. prof. history Coll. Wooster, Ohio, 1966-69, assoc. dean, 1969-74, dean, 1974-77, pres., 1977-95, prof. history, 1995-98. Woodrow Wilson fellow, 1960 Presbyterian.

COPPER, JAMES ROBERT, manufacturing executive; b. St. Louis, Aug. 19, 1939; s. Charles Alva and Cora Imogene (Shifley) Copper; m. Patricia Leeper, Aug. 12, 1961; children: Susan, Robin, Julie. AB, Culver-Stockton Coll., 1961; MS, U. Tenn.-Knoxville, 1969. Tchr. Mo. Mil. Acad., Mexico, 1961-63; mgr. applications analysis Nuclear div. Union Carbide, Oak Ridge, Tenn., 1963-69; mgr. corp. mgmt. scis. Coca-Cola Co., Atlanta, 1969-76; v.p. strategic planning and analysis Pillsbury Co., Mpls., 1976-80; v.p. strategic planning IC Industries, Inc., Chgo., 1980-86, sr. v.p. corp. planning and devel., 1986-88; pres., COO Pet, Inc., St. Louis, 1988, pres., CEO, 1989—. Mem. Civic Progress; bd. dirs. YMCA Greater St. Louis, St. Louis area counc. Boy Scouts Am., United Way St. Louis, Boatmen's Nat. Bank of St. Louis, Christmas in St. Louis, St. Louis Variety Club, Culver-Stockton Coll. Mem. Mo. Athletic Club, St. Louis Club, Old Warson Country Club. Home: 5777 Gene Sarazen Dr Braselton GA 30517-4057

COPPERSMITH, SUSAN NAN, physicist; b. Johnstown, Pa., Mar. 18, 1957; d. Wallace Louis and Bernice Barbara (Evans) C.; m. Robert Daniel Blank, Dec. 20, 1981. BS in Physics, MIT, 1978; student, Cambridge U., 1978—79; MS in Physics, Cornell U., 1981, PhD in Physics, 1983. Rsch. assoc. Brookhaven Nat. Labs., 1983-85; postdoctoral mem. tech. staff AT&T Bell Labs., Murray Hill, NJ, 1985-86, mem. tech. staff, 1987—90, disting. mem. tech. staff, 1990—95; prof. physics U. Chgo., 1995—2001, U. Wis., Madison, 2001—, chair, physics dept., 2005—. Vis. lectr. Princeton U., 1986—87; mem. Aspen Ctr. Physics, 1991—2006, trustee, 1993—96, 2000—06; mem. interface program adv. com. Burroughs Wellcome Fund, 2001—06; mem. math. and phys. sci. adv. com. NSF, 2004—06. Assoc. editor: Revs. Modern Physics, 2002—05, mem. editl. bd.: Jour. Physics A, 2007—; contbr. articles to profl. jours. Recipient Vis. Professorship for women, NSF, 1986—87, Kellett Mid-Career award, U. Wis., 2007. Fellow AAAS (mem. nominating com. physics sect., 2003-06), Am. Phys. Soc. (chair nominating com., 2002, chair divsn. condensed matter physics, 2005), Am. Acad. Arts and Scis. Office: U Wis Dept Physics 1150 Univ Ave Madison WI 53706 Office Phone: 608-263-3279. Business E-Mail: snc@physics.wisc.edu.

COPPOCK, BRUCE, orchestra executive; m. Linda Marder. Cellist Boston Symphony Orch.; ops. & orch. mgr. St. Louis Symphony Orch., exec. dir., 1992-97; dep. dir. Carnegie Hall, NYC, 1997-98; v.p. Am. Symphony Orch. League, Washington, 1998-99; dir. Orch. Leadership Acad., Washington, 1998-99; pres., mng. dir. St. Paul Chamber Orch., 1999—. Mem. Boston Chamber Music Soc. (founder). Office: St Paul Chamber Orch 408 Saint Peter St Flr 3 Saint Paul MN 55102-1130

COQUILLETTE, WILLIAM HOLLIS, lawyer; b. Boston, Oct. 7, 1949; s. Robert McTavish and Dagmar (Bistrup) C.; m. Mary Katherine Templeton, June 19, 1971 (div. Oct. 1984); 1 child, Carolyn Patricia; m. Janet Marie Weiland, Dec. 8, 1984; children: Benjamin Weiland, Madeline Marie, Elizabeth Charlotte. BA, Yale U., 1971, Oxford U., 1973; JD, Harvard U., 1975. Bar: Ohio 1976, Mass. 1976. Law clk. to presiding justice Mass. Supreme Ct., Boston, 1975-76; assoc. Jones Day, Cleve., 1976-83, ptnr., 1984—. Trustee, pres. Cleve. Foodbank. Mem. Kirtland Club, Yale Club (NYC), Yale Alumni Assn. Cleve. (trustee, pres.), Assn. Marshall Scholars, Union Club Cleve. (trustee, sec.), Skating Club, Rowfant Club (trustee, pres.), NY Yacht Club. Office: Jones Day 901 Lakeside Ave E Cleveland OH 44114-1190 Office Phone: 216-586-7137. Business E-Mail: whcoquillette@jonesday.com.

CORAN, ARNOLD GERALD, pediatrician, surgeon; b. Boston, Apr. 16, 1938; s. Charles and Ann (Cohen) C.; m. Susan Myra Williams, Nov. 17, 1960; children: Michael, David, Randi Beth. AB, Harvard U., 1959, MD, 1963. Diplomate Am. Bd. Surgery, Am. Bd. Thoracic Surgery, Am. Bd. Pediat. Surgery. Intern in surgery Peter Bent Brigham Hosp., Boston, 1963-64, resident in general and thoracic surgery, 1964-69; resident in pediatric surgery Children's Hosp., Boston, 1966-68; chief pediat. surgery, assoc. prof. surgery U. So. Calif. Med. Sch., LA, 1972-74; chief pediat. surgery, prof. surgery U. Mich., Ann Arbor, 1974—2007; surgeon in chief C.S. Mott Childrens Hosp., Ann Arbor, 1981—2005. Contbr. articles to profl. jours. Lt. comdr. USN, 1970-72. Mem.: World Fedn. Pediat. Surgery (pres. 2005—07), Am. Pediat. Surg. Assn. (pres. 2001—02). Avocations: skiing, travel. Home: 505 E Huron St Apt 802 Ann Arbor MI 48104-1553 Office: CS Mott Childrens Hosp Rm F3970 Ann Arbor MI 48109-0245 Office Phone: 734-764-6482. Business E-Mail: acoran@umich.edu.

CORBATO, CHARLES EDWARD, geology educator, academic administrator; b. LA, July 12, 1932; s. Hermenegildo and Charlotte Carella (Jensen) C.; m. Patricia Jeanne Ferg, May 18, 1957; children: Steven, Barbara, Susan. BA, UCLA, 1954, PhD, 1960. Instr. geology U. Calif., Riverside, 1959, Los Angeles, 1959-60, asst. prof., 1960-66; assoc. prof. Ohio State U., Columbus, 1966-69, prof., 1969-92, chmn. dept. geology and mineralogy, 1972-80, assoc. provost office of acad. affairs, 1987-92, prof., assoc. provost emeritus, 1992—. Geophysicist U.S. Geol. Survey, 1966-74; dir. State Postsecondary Rev. Entity, Ohio Bd. Regents, 1994-95, dir. info. svcs., 1995-99. Fellow: Geol. Soc. Am.; mem.: Am. Geophys. Union, Delta Tau Delta. Home: 2400 Buckley Rd Columbus OH 43220-4616 Office: Ohio State U 125 S Oval Mall Columbus OH 43210-1308 Personal E-mail: ccorbato@columbus.rr.com.

CORBIN, DAVID R., state legislator; b. July 20, 1944; m. Betty Corbin. Mem. Kans. Ho. of Reps., Topeka, 1990-92; mem. from dist. 16 Kans. Senate, Topeka, 1993—. Chmn. energy and natural resources com., agrl. com.; mem. assessment and taxation coms.; farmer and commodity broker; market analyst Kans. Agrl. Network, 1983—. Mem. Farm Bur., Livestock Assn., Nat. Assn. Farmbroadcasters, El Dorado and Augusta C. of C., Lions, Kiwanis. Republican. Home: 5079 SW Fulton Rd Towanda KS 67144-9097

CORBIN, ROBERT L., state legislator; b. Appleton, Wis., Dec. 8, 1922; s. Lyle Dalton and Minnie (Yokers) C.; m. Edith Peters, 1948; children: Carol, Lynn Corbin. BA, Otterbein Coll. Buyer Rike Kumler, 1940-53; exec. pres. Foodcraft Mgmt. Corp., 1953-64, pres., 1964-79; mem. Oho Ho. of Reps. Columbus, 1977-2000, asst. majority floor leader, 1996. Named Restaurateur of Yr., Miami Valley Restaurant Assn., 1963. Mem. Ohio Restaurant Assn. (past pres.), Walnut Grove C. of C., Otterbein Coll. Alumni Assn. (past pres.), Dayton Agonis Club (past pres.), Pi Kappa Phi. Methodist. Home: 6388 Pebble Ct Dayton OH 45459-1917

CORBY, FRANCIS MICHAEL, JR., business executive; b. Chgo., Feb. 2, 1944; s. Francis M. and Jean (Wolf) C.; m. Diane S. Orselli, Aug. 5, 1972; children: Francis Michael III, Brian A., Christopher S. BA, St. Mary of the Lake, 1966; MBA, Columbia U., 1969. With Chrysler Corp., 1969-80; treasury mgr. Chrysler Peru S.A., Lima, 1973-74; fin. dir. Chrysler Wholesale Ltd., London, 1974-76; mng. dir. Chrysler Comml. S.A. de C.V., Mexico City, 1976-77; v.p., treas. Chrysler Fin. Corp., Troy, Mich., 1977-80; treas. Joy Mfg. Co., Pitts., 1980-83, contr., 1983-86, v.p., 1984-86; sr. v.p. fin., CFO Harnischfeger Industries, Inc., Milw., 1986-94, exec. v.p. fin. and adminstrn., 1994-99; exec. v.p. Frederick & Co., 2000-2001; exec. v.p., CFO Guide Corp., Pendleton, Ind., 2001—04; sr. v.p., CFO GST Autoleather Inc., Hagerstown, Md., 2004—05; exec. v.p., CFO, Exide Techs., Alpharetta, Ga., 2005—. Bd. dirs. Magnasphere Corp. Mem.: Country Club of Naples. Office: 13000 Deerfield Pkwy Bldg 200 Alpharetta GA 30004 Business E-Mail: fran.corby@exide.com.

CORCORAN, PHILIP E., wholesale distribution executive; b. 1954; Grad., St. Mary's, Winona, MN, 1976. CEO, co-founder, chmn. Comark, Inc., Bloomingdale, Ill., 1977—2002; vice chmn. Insight Enterprises Inc., Tempe, Ariz., 2002—. Chmn. bd. dir. Computing Tech. Industry Assn. (CompTIA). Named to Industry Hall of Fame, 2003. Office: Insight Enterprises Inc 1305 W Auto Dr Tempe AZ 85284

CORDERO, FRANCISCO JAVIER, professional baseball player; b. Santo Domingo, Dominican Republic, May 11, 1975; Pitcher Detroit Tigers, 1999, Tex. Rangers, 2000—06, Milw. Brewers, 2006—07, Cin. Reds, 2008—. Named to Am. League All-Star Team, 2004, Nat. League All-Star Team, 2007. Avocations: dominoes, billiards. Mailing: c/o Cin Reds Great American Ball Park 100 Main St Cincinnati OH 45202*

CORDES, EUGENE HAROLD, retired pharmacy and chemistry educator; b. York, Nebr., Apr. 7, 1936; s. Elmer Henry and Ruby Mae (Hofeldt) C.; m. Shirley Ann Morton, Nov. 9, 1957; children: Jennifer Eve, Matthew Henry James. BS, Calif. Inst. Tech., 1958; PhD, Brandeis U., 1962. Instr. chemistry Ind. U., Bloomington, 1962-64, asst. prof., 1964-66, assoc. prof., 1966-68, prof., 1968-79, chmn., 1972-78; exec. dir. biochemistry Merck, Sharp and Dohme Research Labs., Rahway, NJ, 1979-84, v.p. biochemistry, 1984-87; v.p. R & D Eastman Pharms., Malvern, Pa., 1987-88; pres. Sterling Winthrop Pharms. Rsch. divsn. Sterling Winthrop Inc., Collegeville, Pa., 1988-94; prof. U. Mich., Ann Arbor, 1995—2002; chmn. bd. dirs. Vitae Pharma (formerly Concurrent Pharms.), 2002—06. Author: (with Henry Mahler) Biological Chemistry, 1966, 2d. edit., 1971, Basic Biological Chemistry, 1969, (with Riley Schaeffer) Chemistry, 1973; also articles. Recipient NIH Career Devel. award, 1966; Alfred P. Sloan Found. fellow, 1968. Mem.: AAAS, Am. Soc. Biol. Chemists. Home: 3603 Saint Davids Rd Newtown Square PA 19073-1410 Personal E-mail: cordeseh@aol.com.

CÓRDOVA, FRANCE ANNE-DOMINIC, academic administrator, astrophysicist; b. Paris, Aug. 5, 1947; came to U.S., 1953; d. Frederick Ben Jr. and Joan Francis (McGuinness) C.; m. Christian John Foster, Jan. 4, 1985; children: Anne-Catherine Cordova Foster, Stephen Cordova Foster. BA in English with distinction, Stanford U., 1969; PhD in Physics, Calif. Inst. Tech., 1979; PhD (hon.), Loyola Marymount U., 1997. Staff scientist earth and space sci. div. Los Alamos Nat. Lab., 1979-89, dep. group leader space astronomy and astrophysics group, 1989; prof., head dept. astronomy and astrophysics Pa. State U., University Park, 1989—96; chief scientist NASA, Washington, 1993-96; vice chancellor for rsch., prof. physics U. Calif., Santa Barbara, 1996—2002, chancellor, disting. prof. physics and astronomy Riverside, 2002—07; pres. Purdue U., West Lafayette, Ind., 2007—. Mem. Nat. Com. on Medal of Sci., 1991-94; adv. com. for astron. scis. NSF, 1990-93, external adv. com. Particle Astrophysics Ctr., 1989-93; bd. dirs. Assn. Univs. for Rsch. in Astronomy, 1989-93; mem. Space Telescope Inst. Coun., 1990-93; mem. com. space astronomy and astrophysics Space Sci. Bd., 1987-90, internat. users com. Roentgen X-ray Obs., 1985-90, extreme ultraviolet explorer guest observer working group NASA, 1988-93, com. Space Sci. and Applications Group, NASA, 1991-93; mem. Hubble Telescope Adv. Camera Team, 1993; chair Hubble Fellow Selection Com., 1992; bd. dirs. SAIC Inc., 2008-Guest editor Mademoiselle mag., 1969; editor: Multiwavelength Astrophysics, 1988, The Spectroscopic Survey Telescope, 1990; contbr. articles to profl. jours. including Astrophysics Jour., Nature, Astrophysics and Space Scis., Advanced Space Rsch., Astron. Astrophysics, Mon. Nat. Royal Astron. Soc., chpts. to books. Named One of Am.'s 100 Brightest Scientists under 40, Sci. Digest, 1984; grantee NASA, 1979; recipient Distinguished Svc. medal, NASA, Kilby Laureate, 2000. Mem. Internat. Astron. Union (US nat. com. 1990-93), Am. Astron. Soc. (v.p. 1993-96, chair high energy astrophysics divsn. 1990, vice chair 1989). Achievements include research in analysis of ultra-soft x-ray emission from active galactic nuclei; observations and modeling of the winds from accretion disks; studies of the interstellar medium using ultraviolet spectroscopy of nearby hot binary stars; observations and modeling of extended x-ray emitting regions in close binary systems; understanding the accretion geometry of magnetic binaries with accreting white dwarfs; coordinating radio and x-ray observations of x-ray binaries in an effort to find a unified model for correlated behavior; search for evidence of galactic magnetic monopoles by identifying a class of ultrasoft x-ray emitters; studying the multispectial emission from neutron stars; making observations of x-ray emitting pulsars and their associated supernova remnants in the radio and infrared; conceiving space instruments and data systems for imaging detectors (co-principal investigator for optical/UV Telescope launched 1999 on ESA's X-Ray Multi-Mirror mission); making multifrequency observations of high-energy sources. Office: Purdue U Office of Pres Hovde Hall 610 Purdue Mall West Lafayette IN 47907*

CORE, ANTHONY E., state representative; b. Bellefontaine, Ohio, Dec. 16, 1964; married; 3 children. BS in Agr., Ohio State U., JD. Atty.; state rep. dist. 83 Ohio Ho. of Reps., Columbus, 1999—, chair, agr. and devel. subcom., mem. civil and comml. law, fin. and appropriations, and ways and means coms. Mem.: ABA, Logan County Bar Assn., Ohio State U. Alumni Band, Ohio Farm Bur., Kiwanis, Elks. Republican. Presbyterian. Office: 77 S High St 11th fl Columbus OH 43215-6111

COREY, JUDITH ANN, retired elementary school educator; b. Peoria, Ill., Dec. 1, 1937; d. Lyle William and Eileen A. (Zigrang) Springston; m. Thomas W. Corey, Aug. 12, 1961; children: John William, Jeffrey Michael, Gregory Lyle, Mark Andrew. BA in Bus., English, Marycrest Coll., 1960; MA in Counseling, Bradley U., 1972. Lic. tchr. K-12, Ill.; lic. clin. profl. counselor. Tchr. Riverview Sch., Spring Bay, Ill., 1960-61, Lincoln Sch., East Peoria, Ill., 1963-64; counselor Bradley U., Peoria, 1972-73; clin. psychologist intern Zeller Zone Ctr., Peoria, 1973; dean students Morton (Ill.) High Sch., 1974-85; tchr. Jefferson Sch., Morton, 1985—2002; ret., 2002. Contbr. poem to Worlds Greatest Contemporary Poems, 1981 (Hon. Mention). Campaign work Grace Bunn Lievens Ill. Rep., 89th Dist. Ill., Morton, 1994; mem. exec. bd. Ill. State Deans' Assn., 1980-84, historian, 1980-82, membership com., 1982-84. Named to Outstanding Young Women in Am., 1973. Mem. NEA, Ill. Edn. Assn., Morton Edn. Assn. (newsletter editor 1987-90, mem. exec. com. and maj. negotiator, 1987-2000, v.p. 1993-95), Assn. Play Therapy, Phi Kappa Phi (life), Kappa Gamma Pi, Pi Lambda Theta. Roman Catholic. Avocations: reading, writing, photography, music, nature.

COREY, KENNETH EDWARD, urban planning and geography educator, researcher; b. Cin., Nov. 11, 1938; s. Kenneth and Helen Ann (Beckman) C.; m. Marie Joann Fye, Aug. 26, 1961; children: Jeffrey Allen, Jennifer Marie. BA with honors, U. Cin., 1961, MA, 1962, M of Cmty. Planning, 1964, PhD, 1969. Instr. U. Cin., 1962-65, asst. prof. cmty. planning, 1965-69, assoc. prof., 1969-74, prof., 1974-79, head grad. comty. planning and geography, 1969-78; assoc. prof. cmty. planning and geography U. R.I., 1966-67; prof. geography, planning, chmn. dept. geography, dir. urban studies U. Md., 1979-89; prof. geography and urban and regional planning Mich. State U., East Lansing, 1989—, dean Coll. Social Sci., 1989—99, sr. rsch. advisor to v.p. for rsch. and grad. studies, 1999—2004. Vis. prof. geography Un Wales, Aberystwyth, 1974-75, Peking U., 1986; chmn. Cin. Model Cities Bd., 1974; Fulbright rsch. scholar Inst. S.E. Asian Studies, Singapore, 1986, Fulbright group study abroad, Sri Lanka, 1983; trustee Met. Washington Housing Planning Assn., 1980-82. Author: The Local Community, 1968, Undergraduate Geography Students, 1973, The Planning of Change, 3d edit., 1976, Information Tectonics, 2000, Urban and Regional Planning Technology, 2006. Bd. dirs. Potomac River Basin Consortium, Washington, 1982-85. Recipient Svc. award Cmty. Chest and Coun. Cin., 1979; recipient Svc. award Planning Divsn., 1979, Svc. award Coalition of Neighborhoods, Cin., 1979, 83, medal of city Mayor of Seoul, South Korea, 1980. Fellow Royal Geog. Soc.; mem. Am. Inst. Cert. Planners, Am. Planning Assn., Assn. Am. Geographers (award spl. group on planning and regional devel. 1985), Assn. Asian Studies, Asia Soc., World Future Soc. Democrat.

CORKINS, BOB, school system administrator; b. Jan. 25, 1961; m. Nancy Corkins; 2 children. BA, U. No. Iowa, 1983; JD, U. Kans., 1989. Exec. dir. Flint Hills Ctr., Wichita, Kans., 1998—2001, Kans. Legis. Edn. and Rsch., 2001—, Freestate Ctr. for Liberty Studies, 2001—; edn. commr. Kans. Dept. Edn., 2005—06. Office Phone: 785-296-3202. Office Fax: 785-296-7933. E-mail: bcorkins@ksde.org.

CORLETT, ED, automotive executive; CFO Meridian Automotive Sys., Dearborn, Mich. Office: Meridian Automotive Systems 550 Town Center Dr Dearborn MI 48126 Office Fax: (313) 356-4184.

CORLEY, WILLIAM EDWARD, hospital administrator; b. Pitts., Sept. 2, 1942; s. Robert Ray and Helen (Wise) C.; m. Angela Irvine Blose, Mar. 22, 1969; children: Laura, Matt BA in Bus. and Econs., Coll. of William and Mary, 1964; MHA in Hosp. Adminstrn., Duke U., Durham, 1966. Adminstrv. asst. Duke U., Durham, N.C., 1965-66; mgmt. cons. Booz, Allen & Hamilton, Chicago, 1968-71; assoc. hosp. dir. U. Ky., Lexington, 1971-75; hosp. dir. Milton S. Hershey Med. Ctr. of Pa. State U., Hershey, 1975-78; pres. Akron Gen. Med. Ctr., Ohio, 1978-84; pres., CEO Cmty. Health Network, 1984—. Bd. dirs. Vol. Hosps. Am. Tri-State, Indpls., Indpls. C. of C., Nat. City Bank, Indpls., Ind. Pro Health; tri-state chmn.; chmn. United Hosp. Svcs., Indpls., 1986-88; lectr. Ind. U.-Purdue U. at Indpls., 1984-98; high sch. basketball referee. Co-author: Ray E. Brown-A Manager's Manager: Lectures, Messages, Memoirs, 1990; contbr. articles to profl. jours. Chmn. United Hosp. Svc., 1986-88, Vol. Hosp. Am. Tri-State, 1989-91; bd. dirs. United Way. Named Sagamore of the Wabash, Gov. of Ind. Presbyterian. Avocations: photography, basketball, coaching, running. Home: 13570 N Gray Rd Carmel IN 46033-9708 Office: Cmty Health Network 1500 N Ritter Ave Indianapolis IN 46219-3095

CORLEY, WILLIAM GENE, engineering research executive; b. Shelbyville, Ill., Dec. 19, 1935; s. Clarence William and Mary Winifred (Douthit) C.; m. Jenny Lynd Wertheim, Aug. 9, 1959; children: Anne Lynd, Robert William, Scott Elson. BS in Civil Engring., U. Ill., Urbana-Champaign, 1958, MS in Structural Engring., 1960, PhD in Structural Engring., 1961. Lic. profl. engr., Ill.; registered profl. engr., Ariz., Va., Wash., Miss., Fla., La., Pa., Ala., Tenn., Tex., Utah, Md., Mich., Mass., Minn., Nebr., Mo., SD, SC, Kans., Ohio, NJ, NY, NC, Vt., W.Va.; registered civil engr., Calif., Hawaii; lic. structural engr., Ill.; chartered structural engr., UK. Devel. engr. Portland Cement Assn., Skokie, Ill., 1964-66, mgr. structural devel. sect., 1966-74, dir. engring. devel. divsn., 1974-86; sr. v.p. Constrn. Tech. Labs., Inc. (formerly Portland Cement Assn.), Skokie, 1986—. Adv. panels NSF.; prin. investigator, Bldg. Performance Study Okla. City Bombing; team leader, WTC Bldg. Performance Study. Contbr. articles to profl. jours. Pres. caucus Glenview Sch. Bd., Ill., 1971-72; elder United Presbyn. Ch., 1975-79; sec. bd. dirs. Assn. House, Chgo., 1976, treas., 1977, pres., 1978-79; chmn. bd. dirs. North Cook dist. ARC, bd. dirs. Mid-Am. chpt., chmn. North Region Coun., 1988-92; mem. Gov.'s Earthquake Preparedness Task Force, Ill. Recipient Wason medal, 1970, Martin Korn award Prestressed Concrete Inst., 1978, Authur J. Boase award Reinforced Concrete Rsch. Coun., 1986, Nat. Engring. award Am. Assn. Engring. Socs., 2007; named Tchr. of Yr., U. Ill., Chgo., Ill., 2004. Fellow: NSPE (Pres.'s award 2003), Inst. Structural Engrs.; mem.: NAE (award 2000), ASCE (hon. T.Y. Lin award 1979, lifetime achievement award 1994, Pres.'s award 2003, Lifetime Achievement in Design-OPAL award 2006, Chgo. Civil Engr. of Yr.), Nat. Coun. Examiners for Engrs. and Surveying, Am. Assn. Engring. Socs. (Nat. Engring. award 2006), Nat. Coun. Structural Engrs. Assns. (pres. 2007—08, Best Paper award 1999, Disting. Svc. award 1999), Post-Tensioning Inst., Nat. Coun. Examiners Engring. and Surveying (v.p., bd. dirs. 2002—04, pres. 2007—08, Disting. Svc. award 2000), Am. Concrete Inst. (hon.; bd. dirs. 1994—97, Bloem award 1978, Reese Structural Rsch. award 1986, Henry C. Turner award 1988, Ferguson lectr. 1991, Henry Crown award 1997, Lindau award 1999, Alfred E. Lindau award 2000), Structural Engrs. Assn. Ill. (pres. 1986—87, meritorious publ. award 1993, 1997, John Parmer award 1997, meritorious publ. award 2003), Internat. Assn. Bridge and Structural Engring., Earthquake Engring. Rsch. Inst. (chpt. sec., treas. 1980—82, chmn. 1984—86), Reunion Internat. des Laboratoires d'Essais et Rsch. sur Materiaux Constrn., U. Ill. Alumni Assn. (Chgo. Illini of Yr. 2004), Bldg. Seismic Safety Coun. (vice-chmn. 1983—85, sec. 1985—87), Chgo. Com. High-Rise Bldgs. (vice-chmn. 1978—82, chmn. 1982—84). Presbyterian. Office: Constrn Tech Labs Inc 5400 Old Orchard Rd Skokie IL 60077-1030 Office Phone: 847-972-3060. Office Fax: 847-965-6541. Business E-Mail: gcorley@ctlgroup.com.

CORLIN, RICHARD F., gastroenterologist; b. Newark; m. Catherine Corlin. Grad., Rutgers U.; MD, Hahnemann Med. Coll. Pvt. practice, Santa Monic, Calif. Mem. adv. com. Dir. of the NIH; asst. clin. prof. UCLA Sch. of Medicine. Lt. comdr. USPHS, 1968-70. Fellow ACP; mem. AMA (spkr. ho. of dels. 1997, mem., then chair coun. on long range planning and devel., chair commn. on svcs. to young physicians, chair study com. on hosp. med. staff, mem., chair reference coms., ad hoc com. on physician manpower 1987-88, spokesperson, Spkrs. Bur. award 1980, 81), Am. Gastroenterology Assn., Am. Soc. of Internal Medicine, So. Calif. Soc. of Gastrointestinal Endoscopy (past pres.), Calif. Med. Assn. (pres. 1992-93, vice spkr. and spkr. ho. of dels., bd. trustees), L.A. County Med. Assn. (pres. 1978-79). Office: AMA 515 N State St Chicago IL 60610-4325

CORNE, TODD, lawyer; b. Evansville, Ind., Aug. 5, 1966; s. George Butch and Patricia Sue Corne; m. Michelle Holweger. BS in Polit. Sci., U. Evansville, 1988; JD, Ind. U., 1991. Prosecutor Warrick County, Ind., 1995—. Mem. Ind. Prosecuting Atty. Death Penalty Com., Warrick County Bar Assn., Warrick County Domestic Violence Task Force. Republican. Avocations: hiking, reading. Office: Warrick County Prosecutor 1 County Sq Ste 180 Boonville IN 47601-1817 E-mail: wcpo@evansville.net.

CORNELIUS, KENNETH CREMER, JR., finance executive; b. Plainwell, Mich., Sept. 7, 1944; s. Kenneth Cremer and Hollie Jane (Tupper) C.; m. Mary Patricia Hagen, Aug. 19, 1967; children: Kari, Jay, Lee Ann. BA, Carleton Coll., 1966; MBA, U. Mich., 1967. Mgr. acctg. divsn. Maremont Corp., Nashville, 1972-74, mgr. regional acctg. divsn., 1974-75, divsn. contr., 1975-79, corp. contr., 1979-89, v.p., CFO Chgo., 1980-89, M-C Industries, Ann Arbor, Mich., 1989-92, Prestolite Electric Inc., Ann Arbor, 1992—. Capt. USAF, 1968-72. Mem. Phi Beta Kappa. Office: Prestolite 2311 Green Rd Ann Arbor MI 48105-1593 Home: 5889 Lafayette Ln Ann Arbor MI 48103-9139

CORNELL, EDWARD L., consumer products company executive; Exec. v.p. non-retail stores and internat. devel. Office Max, Inc., Shaker Heights, Ohio, 1997—. Office: Office Max Inc 3605 Warrensville Center Rd Shaker Heights OH 44122-5248

CORNELL, HARRY M., JR., furnishings company executive; b. 1928; married Grad., U. Mo., 1950. With Leggett & Platt, Inc., 1950—, salesman, 1950-53, gen. mgr., 1953-55, v.p., 1955-60, pres., chief exec. officer, from 1960, now chmn., chief exec. officer Carthage, Mo. Office: Leggett & Platt Inc PO Box 757 1 Leggett Rd Carthage MO 64836-9649

CORNELL, HELEN W., manufacturing executive; b. 1959; V.p. compressor ops., sec. Gardner Denver, Inc., Quincy, Ill. Office: 1800 Gardner Expy Quincy IL 62305-9364 Fax: 217-228-8247.

CORNELL, ROB, hotel executive; Sr. v.p. Preferred Hotels and Resorts Worldwide, Chgo., 1994—. Office: Preferred Hotels & Resorts Worldwide 311 S Wacker Dr Ste 1900 Chicago IL 60606-6676

CORNELL, WILLIAM DANIEL, mechanical engineer; b. Valley Falls, Kans., Apr. 17, 1919; s. Noah P. and Mabel (Hennessy) C.; m. Barbara L. Ferguson, Aug. 30, 1942; children: Alice Margaret, Randolph William. BS in Mech. Engring., U. Ill., 1942. Registered profl. engr., NY. Rsch. engr. Linde Air Products Co., Buffalo, 1942-48, cons. to Manhattan Dist. project, 1944-46; project engr. devel. of automatic bowling machine Am. Machine and Foundry, Buffalo, 1948-55; cons. Gen. Electric Co., Hanford, Wash., 1949-50; project engr. devel. of automatic bowling machine Brunswick Corp., Muskegon, Mich., 1955-59, mgr. advanced engring., 1959-72; mgr. advanced concepts and tech. Sherwood Med. Industries divsn. Am. Home Products Corp., St. Louis, 1972-85; mem. faculty Coll. Engring., U. Buffalo, 1946-47; cons. Cornell Engring., St. Louis, 1985—; mem. faculty Coll. Engring. Washington U., St. Louis, 1993-94. Patentee automatic golf and bowling game apparatus, med. instruments; developed new method of measuring hemoglobin, new method of counting platelets in whole blood Recipient avy E award, 1945, Manhattan Project Recognition award, 1945, Merit award Maritime Commn., 1945. Republican. Presbyterian. Achievements include development of compensating i.v. flow controller; a self-powered rotary motion sensor; improved IV fluied flow controller. Home and Office: 907 Camargo Dr Ballwin MO 63011-1506

CORNELL, WILLIAM HARVEY, clergyman; b. Pitts., May 27, 1934; s. Floyd Anderson and Audrey Fern (Wasson) C.; m. Betty Jean Yates, July 24, 1954; children: Deborah Jean, William Mark, Darla Ruth. AA, Central Wesleyan Coll., SC, 1953; AB in Religion, Ind. Wesleyan U., 1956. Ordained to ministry Wesleyan Meth. Ch., 1958. Clergyman Wilgus Wesleyan Meth. Ch., Gypsy, Pa., 1956-59, Wolf Summit (W.Va.) Wesleyan Meth. Ch., 1959-63, Canal Wesleyan Meth. Ch., Utica, Pa., 1968-73, Greenville (Pa.) Wesleyan Meth. Ch., 1973-76, Salem (Ohio) Wesleyan Meth. Ch., 1976-78, Sagamore (Pa.) Wesleyan Meth. Ch., 1963-68, 78-95, Niles (Ohio) Wesleyan Meth. Ch., 1995-2000, ret., 2000—. Mem. mission bd. Allegheny Wesleyan Meth. Connection, 1965—2003, sec., 1973-98, editor ann. jour., 1973-98, mem. adv. bd., 1978-98; sec. N.W. Indian Bible Sch., Alberton, Mont., 1969—. Republican. Avocations: hunting, travel. Home and Office: PO Box 115 7695 Rte 85 Beyer PA 16211

CORNFELD, DAVE LOUIS, lawyer; b. St. Louis, Dec. 24, 1921; s. Abraham and Rebecca (David) C.; m. Martha Herrmann, May 30, 1943; children: Richard Steven, James Allen, Lawrence Joseph. AB, Washington U., St. Louis, 1942, LLB, 1943. Bar: Mo. 1943. Practice law, St. Louis; ptnr. Husch & Eppenberger, 1954—2001, of counsel, 2001—. Adj. prof. Washington U., 1966-87. Co-author: Missouri Estate Planning, Will Drafting and Estate Administration, 2 vol., 1988, supplement, 2006; editor Law Quar. 1943. Bd. dirs. Jewish Fedn., St. Louis, 1977-80, 83-88, Jewish Ctr. for Aged, 1981-88; mem. adv. com. U. Miami Inst. Estate Planning, 1979—. Served with AUS, 1945-46. Disting. Alumnus award Washington U. Sch. Law, 2006. Mem. ABA (past chmn. com. taxation income estates and trusts, vice chmn. sect. taxation 1977-80, editor-in-chief Tax Lawyer 1977-80, sr. assoc. editor Probate and Property), St. Louis Bar Assn. (past chmn. taxation com), Am. Law Inst., Am. Coll. Trust and Estate Counsel (regent 1984-90), Am. Coll. Tax Counsel (regent 1980-88), Order of Coif. Jewish (trustee temple 1967-91). Club: Masons. Home: 834 Oakbrook Ln Saint Louis MO 63132-4812 Office: Husch & Eppenberger LLC 190 Carondelet Plz Ste 600 Saint Louis MO 63105-3441 Office Phone: 314-480-1616. E-mail: dcornfeld@charter.net, dave.cornfeld@husch.com.

CORNFELD, RICHARD STEVEN, lawyer; b. St. Louis, Aug. 21, 1950; s. Dave Louis and Martha (Herrmann) C.; m. Marcia Jackoway, Aug., 1, 1982; children: Lisa Sydney, Sarah Reva. AB, U. Mich., 1972; JD, Northwestern U., Chgo., 1975. Bar: Ill. 1975, U.S. Dist. Ct. (no. dist.) Ill. 1975, U.S. Dist. Ct. D.C. 1977, D.C. 1977, Mo. 1981. Assoc. Schwartz & Freeman, Chgo., 1975; law clk. to Hon. John F. Grady U.S. Dist. Ct. (no. dist.) Ill., Chgo., 1976; assoc. Bergson, Borkland, Margolis & Adler, Washington, 1976-80, Coburn, Croft & Putzell, St. Louis, 1980-83; ptnr. Thompson Coburn LLP and predecessor firms, St. Louis, 1983—, co-chair toxic tort practice group. Adj. prof. St. Louis U. Sch. Law, 2007—; pres. United Hebrew Congregation. Contbr. articles to profl. jours. Mem. ABA, Bar Assn. of Met. St. Louis, Mo. Bar, D.C Bar, Order of the Coif. Home: 21 Ladue Estates Dr Creve Coeur MO 63141-8321 Office: Thompson Coburn LLP One US Bank Plaza Saint Louis MO 63101-1693 Office Phone: 314-552-6023. Business E-Mail: rcornfeld@thompsoncoburn.com.

CORNING, JOY COLE, retired state official; b. Bridgewater, Iowa, Sept. 7, 1932; d. Perry Aaron and Ethel Marie (Sullivan) Cole; m. Burton Eugene Corning, June 19, 1955; children: Carol, Claudia, Ann. BA, U. No. Iowa, 1954; degree (hon.), Allen Coll. Nursing. Cert. elem. tchr., Iowa. Tchr. elem. sch. Greenfield (Iowa) Sch. Dist., 1951-53, Waterloo (Iowa) Cmty. Sch. Dist., 1954-55; mem. Iowa Senate, Des Moines, 1984-90, asst. Rep. leader, 1989-90; lt. gov. State of Iowa, Des Moines, 1991-99. Past chmn. Nat. Conf. Lt. Govs. Bd. dirs. Inst. for Character Devel.; mem. policy bd. Performing Arts Ctr., U. No. Iowa, also trustee UNI Found.; bd. dirs. Nat. Conf. Cmty. and Justice, Des Moines Symphony, Planned Parenthood of Greater Iowa. Named Citizen of Yr., Cedar Falls C. of C., 1984; recipient ITAG Disting. Svc. to Iowa's Gifted and Talented Students award, 1991, Pub. Svc. award Iowa Home Econs. Assn., 1994, Friend of Math. award Iowa Coun. Tchrs. of Math., 1995, Iowa State Edn. Assn. Human Rights award, 1996, Govs. Affirmative Action award, Spl. Recognition award Nat. Foster Parent Assoc., Des Moines Human Rights Commn. award, Pub. Svc. award Coalition for Family and Children's Svcs in Iowa, Friends of Iowa Civil Rights, Inc. award, Martin Luther King Jr. Lifetime Svc. award, 1999, Svc. award Des Moines Area Religious Coun., 2002, NCCJ Brotherhood-Sisterhood award, 2003, Senator Barry Goldwater award Planned Parenthood Fedn. Am., 2003; recognized for Extraordinary Advocacy for Children of Iowa chpt. Nat. Com. for Child Abuse, award for leadership Early Care and Edn. Congress, Alumni Achievement award U. No. Iowa; named among YWCA Women of Achievement, 2000, Woman of Influence, Bus. Record, 2003; Nat. Conf. for Cmty. and Justice honoree, 2003; named to Iowa Women's Hall Fame, 2004. Mem. AAUW, LWV, PEO, Nat. Assn. for Gifted Children (mem. adv. bd. 1991-99), Rotary Club, Delta Kappa Gamma, Alpha Delta Kappa. Republican. Mem. United Ch. Of Christ. Home: 2880 Grand Ave No 406 Des Moines IA 50312

CORNISH, KENT M., broadcast executive; b. Topeka, Kans., Nov. 29, 1954; BS in Journalism, U. Kans., 1976. V.p., gen. mgr. KTKA TV, Topeka, 1991—. Address: KTKA TV PO Box 4949 Topeka KS 66604-0949

CORRADINI, MICHAEL L., engineering educator; BSME, Marquette U., 1975; MS, MIT, 1976, PhD, 1978. With tech. staff Sandia Nat. Labs.; with faculty U. Wis., Madison, 1981—, Wis. disting. prof., assoc. dean for acad. affairs. Cons. adv. com. on reactor safeguards NRC. Named Presdl. Young Investigator in Reactor Safety, 1984. Fellow Am. Nuclear Soc.; mem. NAE. Office: U Wis 2630 Engineering Hall 1415 Engineering Dr Madison WI 53706 E-mail: corradini@engr.wisc.edu.

CORRIGAN, MAURA DENISE, state supreme court justice; b. Cleve., June 14, 1948; d. Peter James and Mae Ardell (McCrone) Corrigan; m. Joseph Dante Grano, July 11, 1976 (dec.). BA with hon., Marygrove Coll., 1969; JD with hon., U. Detroit, 1973; LLD (hon.), No. Mich. U., 1999, Mich. State U., 2003; JD (hon.), Mercy Law Sch., 2002, Ea. Mich. U., 2004, Schoolcraft Coll., 2005. Bar: Mich. 1974. Jud. clk. Mich. Ct. Appeals, Detroit, 1973—74; asst. prosecutor Wayne County, Detroit, 1974—79, asst. U.S. atty., 1979—89, chief appellate divsn., 1979—86, chief asst. U.S. Atty., 1986—89; ptnr. Plunkett & Cooney PC, Detroit, 1989—92; judge Mich. Ct. Appeals, 1992—98, chief judge, 1997—98; justice Mich. Supreme Ct., Detroit, 1999—, chief justice, 2001—04; mem. Family Support Coun. MIch. Vice chmn. Mich. Com. to formulate Rules of Criminal Procedure, Mich. Supreme Ct., 1982-89; mem. Mich. Law Revision Commn., 1991-98; mem. com. on standard jury instrns., State Bar Mich., 1978-82; lectr. Mich. Jud. Inst., Sixth cir. Jud. Workshop, Inst. CLE, ABA-Cin. Bar Litigation Sects., Dept. Justice Advocacy Inst.; v.p. Conf. Chief Justices, 2003-04; bd. dirs. Vista Maria. Co-author: book on civil procedure; contbr. chpt. to book, articles to legal revs. Vice chmn. Project Transition, Detroit, 1976-92; mem. citizens Adv. Coun. Lafayette Clinic, Detroit, 1979-87; bd. dirs. Detroit Wayne County Criminal Advocacy Program, 1983-86; pres., bd. dirs. Rep. Women's Bus. and Profl. Forum, 1991; mem. Pew Commn. on Children in Foster Care, 2003-05. Named disting. Alumna, Marygrove Coll., 2003, U. Detroit Mercy Law Sch., 2004, Detroit News Michiganian of Yr., 2005, Vista Maria Child Advocate of Yr., 2005, Angel in Adoption, Congl. Coalition on Adoption, 2005, Jurist of Yr., Police Officers Assn. Mich., 2006, Outstanding Judge, Spectrum Human Svcs., 2006; recipient award of merit, Detroit Commn. on Human Rels., 1974, Dir.'s award, Dept. Justice, 1985, Outstanding Practitioner of Criminal Law award, Fed. Bar Assn., 1989, award, Mich. Women's Commn., 1998, Grano award, 2001, Disting. Svc. award, HHS, 2002, disting. Alumna, St. Joseph Acad., 2004. Mem. Mich. Bar Assn., Detroit Bar Assn., Fed. Bar Assn. (pres. Detroit chpt. 1990-91), Inc. Soc. Irish Am. Lawyers (pres. 1991-92, Achievement award 2001), Federalist Soc. Office: Mich Supreme Ct 8-500 3034 W Grand Blvd Detroit MI 48202 Office Phone: 313-972-3232.

CORRIGAN, WILLIAM M., lawyer; b. St. Louis, Dec. 3, 1958; BBA, U. Notre Dame, 1981; JD, U. Mo., Columbia, 1985. Bar: Mo. 1985, Ill. 1986. Contbr. articles to profl. jours. Mem.: ABA, St. Louis County Bar Assn. (Outstanding Young Lawyer award 1992), Bar Assn. Met. St. Louis, Ill. State Bar Assn., Mo. Bar (chair Young Lawyers sect. 1992—93, bd. govs. 1995—, pres.-elect 2003, Pres.'s award 1993). Office: Armstrong Teasdale LLP One Metropolitan Sq Ste 2600 Saint Louis MO 63102-2740

CORS, JEANNE MARIE, lawyer; b. Bowling Green, Ohio, Jan. 7, 1968; BA in French, Marquette U., 1989, BA in German, 1989, BA in Polit. Sci., 1989; MA in Polit. Sci., U. Mich.; JD, Georgetown U. Law Ctr., 1999. Bar: Ohio 1999. Legis. asst. Senator Herb Kohl; assoc. Taft, Stettinius & Hollister LLP, Cin., mem., Women's Resource Grp. Named one of Ohio's Rising Stars, Super Lawyers, 2005, 2006; named to Leading Lawyers list, Cincy Bus. Mag., 2006. Mem.: Ohio State Bar Assn. (mem., Bd. Governors, Antitrust Sect.). Office: Taft Stettinius & Hollister LLP 425 Walnut St Ste 1800 Cincinnati OH 45202-3957 Office Phone: 513-381-2838. Office Fax: 513-381-0205.

CORSIGLIA, ROBERT JOSEPH, retired electrical construction company executive; b. Chgo., Jan. 22, 1935; s. John Robert and Marie Virgina Corsiglia; m. Patricia Ann Ryan, Jan. 26, 1960 (div. Jan. 1984); children: Nancee, Thomas, Karen; m. Emilie Clementz, Sept. 10, 1989. BSEE, Ill. Inst. Tech., Chgo., 1963. Registered profl. engr., Ill., Ind., Calif., Tex., Fla. CEO, pres. Hyre Electric Co. Ind., Highland, 1970-90, JWP/Hyre Electric Co. Ind., Highland, 1990—2004; CEO Midwestern region JWP Mech./Elec. Svcs. Inc., Oak Brook, Ill., 1991-93; chmn. C & H Engring. Co., Inc., Highland, 1984-90; sec.-treas. Adventures in Travel, Highland, 1984-95; ret., 2004. Bd. dirs. Bank One, Highland. Bd. dirs. No. Ind. Arts Assn., Munster, 1989-93, v.p. devel., 1990; bd. dirs. N.W. Ind. United Way, Highland, 1985, Chgo. Engring. Found., 1991-97; bd. dirs. IIT Alumni Bd., Chgo., 1985, v.p. adminstrn., 1986; mem. IIT Pres.' Coun., 1985—; mem. Legacy Found. Inc. Lake County, Griffith, Ind., 1993—; mem. exec. bd. Boy Scouts of Am. Calumet Coun., 1993—; pres. Nat. Elec. Contractors Assn., 1975, 76, 77. Served with U.S. Army, 1964-70. Mem. Internat. Brotherhood of Elec. Workers (hon.), Chgo. Pres. Orgn., Young Pres. Orgn., World Pres. Orgn., Union League Club. Republican. Roman Catholic. Avocations: collecting, golf. Home: 8701 Northcote Ave Munster IN 46321-2726 Home Phone: 219-923-6077; Office Phone: 219-923-6100. Personal E-mail: rjcorsig@sbcglobal.net.

CORSON, KEITH DANIEL, manufacturing executive; b. South Bend, Ind., Oct. 27, 1935; Student, Wichita State U., 1958-59. Mgmt. trainee Sears Roebuck & Co., Wichita, Kans., 1959-60; product mgr. Taylor Products div. Tecumseh Products, Inc., Elkhart, Ind., 1960-64; pres., chief ops. officer, coachmen Coachmen Industries, Middlebury, Ind., 1964-82; chief exec. officer Robertson's Dept. Stores, South Bend, 1982-83; pres., chief exec. officer Koszegi Products, Inc., South Bend, 1983-90; pres., chief oper. officer Coachman Industries, Elkhart, Ind., 1990—. Office: Coachman Industries Inc PO Box 3300 Elkhart IN 46515-3300

CORSON, THOMAS HAROLD, retired manufacturing executive; b. Elkhart, Ind., Oct. 15, 1927; s. Carl W. and Charlotte (Keyser) C.; m. Dorthy Claire Scheide, July 11, 1948; children: Benjamin Thomas, Claire Elaine. Student, Purdue U., 1945-46, Rennsselaer Poly. Inst., 1946-47, So. Meth. U., 1948-49. Chmn. bd. dirs. Coachmen Industries, Inc., Elkhart, 1965-97, chmn. emeritus, dir., 1997—2005, ret., 2005. Bd. dirs. R.C.R. Sci. Inc., Goshen, Ind., Micrology Labs., Inc., Goshen, Elkhart County Econ. Devel. Corp., Elkhart, Ind.; chmn., sec. Greenfield Corp., Middlebury. Adv. coun. U. Notre Dame; past trustee Ball State U.; dir., past trustee, past vice chmn. Interlochen Arts Acad. and Nat. Music Camp., Mich. With US Naval Air Force, 1945-47. Mem. Ind. Mfrs. Assn. (past dir.), Elkhart C. of C. (past bd. dirs.), Ind. C. of C. (past bd. dirs.), Ind. Hist. Soc. (past dir.), Royal Poinciana Golf Club, Elcona Club (past bd. dirs.), 33 Degrees, Mason, Shriners. Methodist. Home (Summer): PO Box 340 Middlebury IN 46540-0340

CORTESE, DENIS A., healthcare executive, medical educator; b. Phila., Feb. 27, 1944; MD, Temple U., 1970. Cert. Nat. Bd. Med. Examiners, diplomate Am. Bd. Internal Medicine, in pulmonary disease Am. Bd. Internal Medicine, cert. Am. Bd. Laser Surgery. Intern Mayo Clinic, Rochester, Minn., 1970—71; resident in internal medicine Mayo Grad. Sch. Medicine, Mayo Clinic, Rochester, 1970—72, resident in thoracic medicine, 1972—74; fellow in thoracic diseases and bronchoscopy Mayo Clinic, 1976, pulmonary medicine specialist, 1976; prof. medicine Mayo Med. Sch.; pres., CEO Mayo Clinic, Rochester, 2003—. Mem. Ctr. Corp. Innovation. Bd. trustees Healthcare Leadership Coun.; mem. Harvard/Kennedy Sch. Healthcare Policy Group; bd. govs. Mayo Clinic, Rochester, 1987—92, trustee, 1990—94, 1997—, chair bd. govs. Jacksonville, 1999—2002; bd. dirs. St. Luke's Hosp., Jacksonville, 1999—2002, chair exec. com., 2002. Fellow: Royal Coll. Physicians London; mem.: Inst. Medicine. Office: Mayo Clinic 200 1st St SW Rochester MN 55905 Office Phone: 507-284-2663.*

CORTS, JOHN RONALD, minister, religious organization executive; b. Hammond, Ind., Jan. 26, 1936; s. Charles Harold and Hazel (Vernon) Corts; m. Jo-Ann Ketchum, 1956; 1 child, Alicia Beth. BA, Trinity Coll., Clearwater, Fla., 1956. Ordained to ministry Gospel Tabernacle Ch., 1957. Pastor Christian Fellowship Ch., Tampa, Fla., 1957-58; registrar Trinity Coll., Clearwater, 1957; pastor First Evang. Bapt. Ch., St. Petersburg, Fla., 1958-62; exec. dir. Youth for Christ, Tampa, 1962-64; crusade assoc. Billy graham Assn., 1964-80; pastor Idlewild Bapt. Ch., Tampa, 1980-83; pres., COO Billy Graham Evangelistic Assn., Mpls., 1983—. Avocations: sports, drama, journalism. Office: Billy Graham Evangelistic Assn 1300 Harmon Pl Minneapolis MN 55403-1925

CORVINO, BETH BYSTER, lawyer; b. Dec. 8, 1956; m. John Corvino. BA, Ind. U.; JD with honors, DePaul U. Assoc. Katten Muchin Zavis Rosenman, 1982—83; various positions Am. Hosp. Supply Corp., Staley Continental Inc., 1983—89; asst. gen. counsel Whitman Corp., 1989—92; with Gen. Instrument Corp., 1992—98; v.p., gen. counsel, corp. sec. Chas. Levy LLC, 1998—2004; exec. v.p., gen. counsel, corp. sec. Laidlaw Internat. Inc., 2004—. Office: Laidlaw Internat Inc 55 Shuman Blvd Ste 400 Naperville IL 60563 Office Fax: 630-848-3167. Business E-Mail: bcorvino@laidlaw.com.

CORWELL, ANN ELIZABETH, public relations executive; b. Battle Creek, Mich. d. James Albert Corwell and Marion Elizabeth (Petersen) Shertzer. BA, Mich. State U., 1971, MBA, 1981; cert. fin., Wharton Sch., 1986. Sr. publicist City of Dearborn, Mich., 1972-76; sr. assoc. GM, Detroit, 1976-77, media coord. NYC, 1977, mgr. cmty. rels. Pontiac, Mich., 1977-81, mgr. internal comm., 1981-82; dir. pub. rels. Pillsbury Co., Mpls., 1982-85, Avon Products Inc., NYC, 1985-87; exec. v.p. MECA Internat., Flat Rock, Mich., 1987-95; v.p. coll. rels. William Tyndale Coll., Farmington Hills, Mich., 1995—. Dir. Mich. State U. Nat. Alumni Bd. Mem. Pub. Rels. Soc. Am., Women In Comm., Oakland County C. of C. (dir. 1988-91), Dearborn C. of C. (dir. 1989-91). E-mail: acorwell@williamtyndale.edu.

CORWIN, SHERMAN PHILLIP, lawyer; b. Chgo., June 29, 1917; s. Louis C. and Becky (Goodman) Cohen; m. Betty C. Corwin (dec. Jan. 1998); children: Susan M. Rothberg, Laurie L. Grad. valedictorian, Wilson Jr. Coll., 1937; BA, U. Chgo., 1939, JD cum laude, 1941. Bar: Ill. 1941, Mich. 1946, Colo. 1946. Assoc. Lederer, Livingston Kahn & Adsit, Chgo., 1941-43, Sonnenschein Nath & Rosenthal, Chgo., 1946-60, ptnr., 1960—, head estate planning and probate group, 1970-88. Editor: Estate Planning Handbook for Lawyers, 6th edit., 1976, 7th edit., 1980. Bd. dirs., officer North Suburban Synagogue Beth El, Highland Park, Ill., 1959-80; bd. dirs. Congregation Moriah, Deerfield, Ill., 1980-84; chmn. profl. adv. com. (estate planning) Jewish Fedn. Met. Chgo., 1985-87. Served to 1st lt. U.S. Army, 1944-46. Fellow Am. Coll. Trust and Estate Counsel; mem. Chgo. Bar Assn. (chmn. trust law com. 1970, chmn. Am. citizenship com. 1955), Chgo. Estate Planning Coun. (pres. 1983), Nu Sigma Kappa (past pres. local chpt.), Nu Beta Epsilon (past pres. local chpt.). Home: 400 E Ohio St Apt 2104 Chicago IL 60611-4615 Office: Sonnenschein Nath Et Al 8000 Sears Tower 233 S Wacker Dr Ste 8000 Chicago IL 60606-6491 Office Phone: 312-876-8031.

COSBEY, ROGER B., federal magistrate judge; b. 1950; BA, Western Mich. U., 1972; JD, U. Toledo, 1975. Bar: Ind. 1975. With Heckner & Assocs., Ligonier, Ind., 1975-81; judge Superior Ct., Noble County, Ind., 1982-90; magistrate judge U.S. Dist. Ct. (no. dist.) Ind., Ft. Wayne, 1990—. Presenter in field. Contbr. articles to profl. jours. Maj. JAGC, USAR, 1972-92. Fellow Allen County Bar Assn.; mem. Ind. State Bar Assn., Allen County Bar Assn., Fed. Magistrate Judges Assn., Am. Judicature Soc., Benjamin Harrison Am. Inns of Ct. (pres. Fort Wayne Ind. chpt. 1995-96), Supreme Ct. Historical Soc. Office: 1130 Adair Federal Bldg 1300 S Harrison St Fort Wayne IN 46802-3495

COSGRIFF, JAMES ARTHUR, physician; b. Lamberton, Minn., Mar. 18, 1924; s. James Arthur and Elsie Ann (Forster) C. BS summa cum laude, Coll. St. Thomas, 1944; MD, U. Minn., 1946. Intern St. Mary's Hosp., Duluth, Minn.; pvt. practice Olivia, Minn., 1949—. With USN, 1947-49. Fellow Am. Acad. Family Physicians; mem. Minn. Acad. Family Physicians (pres. 1963, Merit award 1964), Alpha Omega Alpha. Roman Catholic. Avocations: travel, photography, reading, music. Home: 802 E Park Ave Olivia MN 56277-1361 Office: Olivia Clinic 619 E Lincoln Ave Olivia MN 56277-1349 Office Phone: 320-523-2131.

COSGROVE, DELOS M. (TOBY COSGROVE), health facility administrator, surgeon; b. Watertown, NY, July 28, 1940; s. Delos M. and Margaret C.; m. Anita Desiderio, May 8, 1976; children: icole Ashley, Britt Lindsey. BA, Williams Coll., Williamstown, Mass., 1962; MD, U. Va., 1966. Diplomate Am. Bd. Surgery, Am. Bd. Thoracic Surgery. Intern Strong Meml. Hosp., Rochester, NY, 1966-67, resident in surgery, 1967-68, Mass. Gen. Hosp., Boston, 1970-72, sr. resident in cardiac surgery, 1973-74; registrar in cardiac surgery Brook Gen. Hosp., London, 1972-73; chief resident Boston Children's Hosp., 1974; assoc. staff dept. thoracic and cardiovascular surgery The Cleve. Clinic, 1975-76, profl. staff, 1976—, chmn. dept. thoracic and cardiovascular surgery, 1990—, CEO, 2004—, chmn., bd. governors, 2004—. Bd. trustees Healthcare Leadership Coun. Contbr. articles to profl. jours. Mem. Am. Assn. Thoracic Surgery (pres. 2000), Internat. Soc. Cardiovascular Surgery, Am. Coll. Cardiology, Am. Coll. Chest Physicians, ACS, Am. Heart Assn., AMA, Am. Surg. Assn., Cleve. Surg. Soc., Ohio State Med. Assn., Ohio Thoracic Soc., Cleve. Acad. Medicine, Soc. Thoracic Surgeons, Soc. for Thoracic Surg. Edn. (chmn. membership com. 1985-87), Peruvian Coll. Angiology (hon.), Chilean Soc. Cardiology (hon.), Dominican Republic Soc. Cardiology (hon.), Argentine Coll. Cardiology (hon., mem. editorial bd. The Annals of Thoracic Surgery). Avocation: sailing. Office: Cleve Clinic Surgery 9500 Euclid Ave Cleveland OH 44195-0001

COSIER, RICHARD A., dean, finance educator; b. Jackson, Mich., May 18, 1947; s. Roy A. and Wilma M. (Braund) C.; m. Rae L. Pettelle, June 14, 1969 (div. Feb. 1985); children: Jeffrey R., Nathan R.; m. Lynn M. Hays, Aug. 30, 1986; children: Courtney M., Kelsey L. BS, Mich. State U., 1969; MBA, Loyola U., 1972; PhD, U. Iowa, 1976. From asst. to assoc. prof. mgmt. Ind. U., Bloomington, 1976-86, prof. mgmt., 1986-92, chairperson, prof. mgmt., 1983-90, assoc. dean for acads., prof. mgmt., 1990-92; dean, Fred E. Brown chair U. Okla., Norman, 1993-99; Leeds prof. mgmt. Purdue U., 1999—, dean Krannert Grad. Sch. Mgmt. and Sch. Mgmt., 1999—, dir. Burton D. Morgan Ctr. Entrepreneurship, 2002—05; with faculty U. Notre Dame. Bd. dirs. Kite Realty Group Trust, Roll Coater, Inc., AACSB Internat.; cons. in field. Contbr. over 75 articles and book chpts. to profl. jours.; co-author mgmt. textbook; contbr. book chpts.; inventor patented packaging technique. Active with United Way Am.; mem. exec. com. Greater Lafayette Comty. Devel. Corp., 2001; chmn. United Way campaign Purdue U., 2003—. Fellow Richard D. Irwin. Mem.: Acad. Mgmt. Republican. Office: Krannert Sch Mgmt Rm 122 Purdue U West Lafayette IN 47907-1310 Office Phone: 765-494-4366. E-mail: rcosier@purdue.edu.

COSMOPOULOS, MICHAEL, archaeologist, educator; BA summa cum laude, U. Athens, 1981; DEUG, U. Sorbonne-Paris, 1983; diploma in Underwater Archaeology, Coun. Europe, 1984; MA, Wash. U., St. Louis, 1986, PhD, 1989. Prof. classics, dir. Centre for Hellenic Civilization U. Manitoba, Canada; Hellenic Govt. -Karakas Found. Prof. Greek Studies U. Mo., St. Louis, 2001—. Founder, pres. Pan-Macedonian Assn. of Manitoba, 1993; mem. mng. com. Am. Sch. of Classical Studies, Anthens. Mem.: Archaeological Inst. Can., Classical Assn. Manitoba, Archaeological Inst. Am. (acad. trustee, Excellence in Undergraduate Tchg. Award 2004), Archaeological Soc. Athens (life). Office: U Mo -St Louis 507 Clark Hall, UM 8001 Natural Bridge Rd Saint Louis MO 63121 E-mail: CosmopoulosM@msx.umsl.edu.

COSS, JOHN EDWARD, retired archivist; b. Spring Valley, Ill., Apr. 2, 1947; s. Edward Francis and Doris (Leonard) C.; m. Sherry Lee Ushman, June 4, 1973 (div. May 1979); 1 child, Stephen John; m. Brenda Lynn Gibson, May 30, 1981; 1 stepchild, Anthony Robert. AA, Ill. Valley C.C., 1967; BA, Northwest Mo. State U., 1970. Sr. archivist Ill. State Archives, Springfield, 1971—2002; ret., 2002. Mem. Ill. Fedn. Archivists, Archival Technicians & Photographers, Springfield Trades & Labor Coun. (del.). Methodist. Avocations: music, reading, golf. Home: 10470 E State Route 54 Buffalo IL 62515-7148 Personal E-mail: jcoss@springnet1.com.

COSS, ROCKY ALAN, lawyer; b. Dayton, Ohio, Apr. 6, 1951; s. Vernon F. and Necia Lea (Shaw) C.; m. Cheryl Sue Kelch, Sept. 9, 1972; children—: Tracey, Derek. B.A., Ohio State, 1973, J.D., 1976. Bar: Ohio, 1976, U.S. Supreme Ct., 1979, U.S. Dist. Ct. (so. dist.) Ohio 1982, U.S. Ct. Appeals (6th cir.) 1983. Sole practice, Hillsboro, Ohio, 1976-81; ptnr. Coss & Greer, Hillsboro, 1982—; pros. atty. Highland County, Ohio, 1977—. Mem. Steering com. City of Hillsboro, 1980-85; county chmn. Highland County Fund Drive; pres. Highland County Soc. Crippled Children and Adults, 1985-86; mem. enrollment com. Highland County Boy Scouts Am., 1977-78. Fellow Ohio State Bar Found.; mem. Ohio State Bar Assn., Highland County Bar Assn. (pres. 1982), Ohio Pros. Atty's. Assn. (v.p.), Nat. Dist. Atty's. Assn., ABA, Ohio Council Sch. Bd. Attys., Nat. Council Sch. Bd. Attys., Hillsboro Jaycees (v.p. 1978-83). Democrat. Methodist. Lodges: Rotary (pres. 1983-84), Masons, Elks. Home: PO Box 258 Hillsboro OH 45133-0258 Office: 14612 E Main St Hillsboro OH 45133

COSTA, ERMINIO, pharmacologist, cell biologist, educator; b. Cagliari, Italy, Mar. 9, 1924; s. Oreste and Gigina (Murgia) Costa; divorced; children: Max, Robert Henry, Michael John; m. Ingeborg Hanbauer, July 13, 1973. MD, U. Cagliari, 1947, PhD in Pharmacology, 1953; PhD in Biol. Sci. (hon.), U. Cagliari, Italy, 1986; DSc (hon.), Georgetown U., 1992; MD (hon.), U. Tampere, Finland, 1992. Asst. prof., assoc. prof. U. Cagliari, 1948—54, prof. pharmacology, 1954—56; physician II, med. rsch. assn. Thudichum Psychology Rsch., Galesburg, Ill., 1956—60; vis. scientist NIH, Bethesda, Md., 1960—61; dep. chief lab. chem. pharmacology Nat. Heart Inst., Bethesda, 1961—63, head sect. clin. pharmacology, 1963—65; assoc. prof. pharmacology Columbia U., NYC, 1965—68; chief lab. preclin. pharmacology St. Elizabeth's Hosp., Washington, 1968—85; dir. Fidia-Georgetown Inst. for the Neuroscis. Georgetown U., Washington, 1985—94, 1996—; McDonnel vis. prof. neurology Washington U. Sch. Medicine, St. Louis, 1994—; sci. dir., prof. biochemistry in psychiatry U. Ill. at Chgo. Psychiat. Inst., 1996—. Editor Neuropharmacology, 1967, Advanced Biochem. Psychopharmacology, 1968, contbr. 915 articles to profl. jours. Recipient Bennet award and Gold medal, Soc. Biol. Psychiatry, 1990, Gold medal Fed. II Univ., Naples, 1990, Premio Fiuggi award, Fiuggi Rsch. Found., 1988. Mem.: NAS, Am. Soc. Biol. Chemistry and Molecular Biology, Am. Soc. Physiology, Am. Soc. Pharmacology and Exptl. Therapeutics, Academia Nazionale Lincei, Peripatetic Club, Cosmos Club. Office: Psychiatric Ins Univ of Illinois at Chicago 1601 W Taylor St Chicago IL 60612-4310

COSTELLO, JERRY F., JR., congressman, former county official; b. Sept. 25, 1949; m. Georgia Jean Cockrum; children: Jerry, Gina, John. AA, Bayeville Area Coll., 1971; BA, Maryville Coll. of Sacred Heart, 1973. County bd. chmn. St. Clair County, Ill.; dir. ct. svcs. and probation 20th Jud. Cir. Campaign; chmn. Heart Assn., Belleville, Ill., 1983; vice chmn. Ill. div. United Way, 1984, chmn., 1985; mem. U.S. Congress from 21st (now 12th) Ill. Dist., 1988—; former mem. budget com.; mem. transp., infrastructure and sci. coms. Bd. dirs. Ill. Ctr. for Autism; active St. Clair County Big Bros./Big Sisters, Belleville Women's Crisis Ctr., Children's Ctr. for Behavioral Devel.; helped establish St. Clair County chpt. Vets. Outreach Info. Ctr.; mem. East St. Louis Econ. Opportunity Commn., Ill.; vice chmn. Southwestern Ill. Bus. Devel. Fin. Corp., 1985—; bd. dirs. So. Ill. Leadershp Council; pres. Urban Counties Council of Ill. Recipient cert. of Appreciation, Bus. and Profl. Women's Assn., 1985; honored Citizens League for Adequate Social Services; 1985 AAHMES Court #84, Daus. ISIS Ann. Humanitarian award, Gene Hughes award Ill. Ct. Services and Probation Assn. Democrat. Office: US Ho of Reps 2454 Rayburn House Off Bldg Washington DC 20515-1312

COSTELLO, JOHN WILLIAM, lawyer; b. Chgo., Apr. 16, 1947; s. William John and June Ester (O'Neill) C.; m. Maureen Grace Matthews, June 13, 1970; children— Colleen, William, Erin, Owen. BA, John Carroll U., 1969; JD, DePaul U., 1972. Bar: U.S. Dist. Ct. (no. dist.) Ill. 1982. Assoc. Arvey, Hodes, Costello & Burman, Chgo., 1972-76; ptnr., 1976-90, ptnr. Wildman, Harrold Allen & Dixon, 1990—. Co-author: (manual) The Bankruptcy Reform Act of 1978, 1981. Served to capt. U.S. Army, 1972-73. Mem. ABA (bus. bankruptcy com., jurisdiction and venue and secured creditors subcoms.), Ill. State Bar Assn. (former vice chmn., chmn. comml. banking and bankrupcy law sect. 1979-81), Am. Bankruptcy Inst., Turnaround Mgmt. Assn. (former bd. dirs. Midwest sect.). Democrat. Roman Catholic. Office: Wildman Harrold Aller & Dixon 225 W Wacker Dr Chicago IL 60606-1224 Office Phone: 312-201-2971.

COSTELLO, THOMAS, JR., lawyer, computer company executive; BA cum laude, Ohio U.; JD cum laude, Thomas M. Cooley Law Sch. Sr. v.p. human resources, gen. counsel, sec. Compuware Corp., 1995—. Asst. coach, asst. gen. mgr. Windsor Compuware Spitfires, Ontario Hockey League; fac. mem. Wayne State U. Mem.: State Bar Mich. (chairperson Computer Law Sec.), Generation of Promise Prog. (past pres., mem. bd. trustees, Bridge Builder Award 2004), Detroit Golf Club. Avocation: ASCAR. Office: Compuware Corp One Campus Martius Detroit MI 48226

COSTIGAN, EDWARD JOHN, retired investment banker; b. St. Louis, Oct. 31, 1914; s. Edward J. and Elizabeth Keane; m. Sara Louise Guth, Mar. 30, 1940 (dec. Nov. 6, 1988); children: Sally, Edward, John, James(dec.), Betsy, Robert, David, Louise; m. Mildred F. Fabick, Dec. 27, 1995. AB, St. Louis U., 1935; MBA, Stanford U., 1937. Analyst, v.p. Whitaker & Co., St. Louis, 1937-43; ptnr. Edward D. Jones & Co., 1943-72; sr. v.p. Stifel Nicolaus & Co. Inc., St. Louis, 1972-74, pres., 1974-79, vice chmn., 1979-83, emeritus, 1983. Gov. Nat. Assn. Securities Dealers, 1967-70, Investment Bankers Assn., 1968-69, Midwest Stock Exch., Chgo., 1962-64; bd. dirs. 12 cos. Trustee Cath. Cemeteries Arch Diocese St. Louis, 1956—. Mem. St. Louis Soc. Fin. Analysts (pres. 1956), Harvard Club St. Louis (pres. 1955), Bellerive Country Club, Mo. Athletic Club, Old Warson Country Club, Noonday Club. Republican. Roman Catholic. Office: 501 N Broadway Fl 8 Saint Louis MO 63102-2102

COTHORN, JOHN ARTHUR, lawyer; b. Des Moines, Dec. 12, 1939; s. John L. and Marguerite (Esters) C.; m. Connie Cason, Aug. 6, 1996; children: Jeffrey, Judith. BS in Math., U. Mich., 1961, BS in Aero. Engring., 1961, JD, 1980. Bar: Mich. 1981, U.S. Dist. Ct. (ea. dist.) Mich. 1981, U.S. Ct. Appeals (6th cir.) 1981, U.S. Dist. Ct. (we. dist.) Mich. 1986, U.S. Supreme Ct. Exec. U.S Govt., 1965-78; asst. prosecutor Washtenaw County, Ann Arbor, Mich., 1981-82; ptnr. Kitch, Saurbier, Drutchas, Wagner & Kenney P.C., Detroit, 1982-94, Meganck & Cothorn P.C., Detroit, 1994-97, Meganck, Cothorn & Stanczyk P.C., Detroit, 1997-98, Cothorn & Stanczyk, P.C., Detroit, 1998-2000, Cothorn & Braceful, Detroit, 2000—02, Cothorn & Assocs., P.C., Detroit, 2002—04, Cothorn & Mackley, P.C., 2004—. Served to capt. U.S. Army, 1961-65. Mem. ABA, Nat. Bar Assn. (numerous fed. and state coms.), Soc. Automotive Engrs., Assn. Def. Trial Counsel, Phi Alpha Delta. Republican. Avocations: bridge, golf. Office: 535 Griswold St Ste 530 Detroit MI 48226-3696 Office Phone: 313-964-7600. Business E-Mail: jcothorn@cothoronmackley.com.

COTTER, DANIEL A., diversified financial services company executive; b. Duluth, Minn., Dec. 26, 1934; BA, Marquette U., 1957; MBA, Northwestern U., 1960. With Truserv Corp., Chgo., 1959-99, chmn., CEO; retired, 1999. Office: Truserv Corp 8600 W Bryn Mawr Ave Chicago IL 60631-3579

COTTER, PATRICK LINNAE, lawyer; b. Rochester, Minn., Aug. 20, 1974; BA cum laude, Coll. St. Thomas, 1997; JD, William Mitchell Coll. Law, 2002. Bar: Minn. 2002, US Dist. Ct. (dist. Minn.) 2003. Pros. atty. Burnsville & Eagan; atty. Cotter Law Office, P.L.L.C., Mendota Heights, Minn., 2005—. Named a Rising Star, Minn. Super Lawyers mag., 2006; recipient Pub. Svc. award, Minn. Justice Found. Mem.: Minn. Assn. Criminal Def. Lawyers, Minn. Trial Lawyers Assn., Assn. Trial Lawyers of Am., Minn. State Bar Assn., Ramsey County Bar Assn., Dakota County Bar Assn., Vol. Lawyers Network, Delta Theta Phi. Office: Cotter Law Office PLLC 750 S Plz Dr Ste 218 Mendota Heights MN 55120 Office Phone: 651-686-5347. E-mail: pcotterlaw@gmail.com.

COTTON, LARRY, ranching executive; Pres. Cotton & Assocs., Howell, Mich. Office: Cotton and Assocs 131 Robin Ct Howell MI 48843-8776

COTTON, W(ILLIAM) PHILIP, JR., architect; b. Columbia, Mo., July 11, 1932; s. William Philip and Frances Barbara (Harrington) C. AB, Princeton U., 1954; MArch, Harvard U., 1960. Registered architect, Mo., Ill. Pvt. practice architecture, St. Louis, 1964—. Author: 100 Historic Buildings in St. Louis County, 1970. Treas. New Music Circle, St. Louis, 1968-96, Pub. Revenue Edn. Coun., St. Louis, 1977—; v.p. Music Diversions Soc., St. Louis, 1993—2005; pres. Collegium Vocale, 1999—. Recipient St. Louis AIA/CPC Urban Design Merit award, 2002, Pres.'s award, Landmarks Assn. St. Louis. Fellow AIA (Ctrl. States Spl. Honor award 1981, Rozier award for Hist. Preservation 1991); mem. Valley Sailing Club (commodore 1985). Roman Catholic. Home: 5145 Lindell Blvd Saint Louis MO 63108-1221 Office: W Philip Cotton Jr Architect 1221 Locust St Ste 1410 Saint Louis MO 63103-2364

COTTRELL, DAVID ALTON, school system administrator; b. Lima, Ohio, Sept. 8, 1941; s. Hiram David and Clara Marie (Williams) C.; m. Barbara Jean Campbell, Dec. 28, 1963; children: Richard, Deanna, Lynda. AA, Graceland Coll., 1961; BS in Edn., Bowling Green State U., 1964; MA, Kent State U., 1967; EdD, U. Akron, 1970. Cert. supt., Ohio. Social studies tchr. Fairview High Sch., Fairview Park, Ohio, 1964-68; curriculum rsch. specialist Geauga County Schs., Chardon, Ohio, 1968-70; asst. supt. Girard (Ohio) City Schs., 1970-75; supt. Northwood (Ohio) Local Schs., 1975-82, Franklin County Ednl. Svc. Ctr., 1982-87, 1987—. Mem. Berea Cable TV Commn., 1987—; chair suburban schs. Greater Cleve. United Way, 1989. Mem. Am. Assn. Sch. Adminstrn., Buckeye Assn. Sch. Adminstrs. (chair profl. rights and responsibility com.), Mid-Am. Assn. Sch. Adminstrs. Avocations: sailing, jogging, golf, tennis. Office: Franklin County Ednl Svc Ctr Edn Dept 1717 Alum Creek Dr Columbus OH 43207-1708

COTTRELL, FRANK STEWART, former lawyer, manufacturing executive; b. Boulder, Colo., July 11, 1942; s. Frank Stewart Sr. and Dorris Mary (Payne) C.; m. Janet Anne Goode, Jan. 8, 1966; children: Kristin, Jeffrey, Steven. AB, Knox Coll., 1964; JD, U. Chgo., 1967. Bar: Ill. 1967. Atty. Deere & Co., Moline, Ill., 1967-77, internat. atty., 1977-80, sr. atty., 1980-82, asst. gen. counsel, 1982-87, assoc. gen. counsel, corp. sec., 1987-91, gen. counsel, sec., 1991-93, v.p., gen. counsel, sec., 1993-98, sr. v.p., gen. counsel, sec., 1998—99. Mem. adv. bd. Butterworth Trust; trustee Knox Coll. Mem. ABA, Ill. Bar Assn., Assn. Gen. Counsel.

COUCH, DANIEL MICHAEL, healthcare executive; b. Chgo., July 1, 1937; s. Arthur Daniel and Helen Margret (Kreamer) C.; m. Marilee Hermon, Sept. 12, 1958; children: Laura Ann, Mark Allen, Kristina Lynn, Michelle Louise, Daniel Michael Jr. BS in Bus., Ind. U., 1958; MBA, Butler U., 1977. Field examiner Ind. State Bd. Accounts, Indpls., 1959-61; controller Community Hosp., Anderson, Ind., 1961-67; field rep. Am. Hosp. Assn., Chgo., 1967-68; treas./controller Health & Hosp. Corp. of Marion County, Indpls., 1968-71; assoc. adminstr. Winona Meml. Hosp., Indpls., 1971-78; pres. Huntington (Ind.) Meml. Hosp., 1978-80; dep. exec. dir. Truman Med. Ctr., Kansas City, Mo., 1980-99; CFO Health Care Found. Greater Kansas City, 2005—. Bd. dirs. Nat. Pub. Health and Hosp. Inst., Washington, 1987-90, chmn., 1989. Bd. dirs. mem. exec. com. Labor-Mgmt. Coun., Kansas City, Mo., 1982—2006, co-chmn, 1991—97; bd. dirs. Greater Kansas City Mental Health Found., 1984—93, pres., 1992—93; bd. dirs. Kansas City Care Ctr., 1990—, treas., 1999—; bd. dirs. Resource Devel. Inst., Kansas City, 1998—2005, pres., 2002—04; bd. dirs. Vis. Nurse Home Care Svcs., Kansas City, 1991—98, chmn., 1993—98; bd. dirs. A Rising Tide-The Greater Kansas City Healthcare Found., 2003—05. 1st lt. USAR, 1958—67. Fellow Am. Coll. Healthcare Execs. (life fellow, nominating com. 1995-99); mem. Am. Hosp. Assn. (ho. of dels. and Regional Policy Bd. 7 1989-92, governing coun. sect. met. hosps. 1990-93, chmn. 1993), Nat. Assn. Pub. Hosps. (bd. dirs. 1981-99, chmn. 1989), Kansas City Area Hosp. Assn. (bd. dirs. 1990-96), Greater Kansas City C. of C. (various coms. 1985-99), Healthcare Fin. Mgmt. Assn. (advanced), Kansas City Care Network (bd. dirs. 1995-99, pres. 1995-99), Family Health Ptnrs. (bd. dirs. 1995-99), Found. Fin. Officers Group, Masons, Rotary. Episcopalian. Avocations: golf, bowling, reading. Office Phone: 816-241-7006. E-mail: dcouch@healthcare4kc.org.

COUGHLAN, GARY PATRICK, pharmaceutical executive; b. Fresno, Calif., Feb. 14, 1944; s. Edward Patrick and Elizabeth Claire (Ryan) C.; m. Mary Cary Kelley, Dec. 21, 1967; children: Christopher, Sarah, Laura, Claire, Moira. BA, St. Mary's Coll., 1966; MA in Econs., UCLA, 1967; MBA, Wayne State U., 1971. Sr. fin. analyst Burroughs Corp., Detroit, 1969-72; with Dart Industries, LA, 1972-81, group v.p. field services, 1978-81, v.p. ops. services, 1981, Dart & Kraft Inc., Northbrook, Ill., 1981-82, v.p. fin., contr., 1984-85, sr. v.p. fin. affairs,

1985-86, sr. v.p., CFO, 1986; v.p. fin. retail food group Kraft Inc., Glenview, Ill., 1982-84, sr. v.p., CFO, 1986-88; sr. v.p. fin. Kraft Gen. Foods, Glenview, 1989-90; sr. v.p. fin., CFO Abbott Labs., Abbott Park, Ill., 1990-2001, ret., 2001. Instr. prof. fin. ext. program UCLA, 1974—80; bd. dirs. Arthur J. Gallagher, Itasca, Ill., VISA Inc., San Francisco, Chgo. Hort. Soc., Glencoe, Ill.; mem. adv. coun. Coun. Fgn. Rels., Chgo. Com. Mem. Fin. Execs. Inst. Republican. Roman Catholic. Home: 1135 Central Rd Glenview IL 60025-4432 Office: Ste 306 1200 Central Ave Wilmette IL 60091 Office Phone: 847-920-1677. Personal E-mail: gcoughlan@earthlink.com.

COUGHLAN, KENNETH L., lawyer; b. Chgo., July 8, 1940; BA, U. Notre Dame, 1962; JD, Northwestern U., Chgo., 1966. Bar: Ill. 1967. Trust officer Am. Nat. Bank & Trust Co., Chgo., 1969-72; sec. bd., sr. v.p., gen. counsel, cashier Ctrl. Nat. Bank., Chgo., 1972-82; sec., gen. counsel Ctrl. Nat. Chgo. Corp., 1976-82; sr. v.p., gen. counsel Exch. Nat. Bank, Chgo., 1982-83; gen. counsel Exch. Internat. Corp., Chgo., 1982-83; chmn. bd., pres. Union Realty Mortgage Co., Inc., Chgo., 1981-83; shareholder DeHaan & Richter P.C., 1983—2000; mem. Kelly, Olson, Michod, DeHaan & Richter, L.L.C. Capt. U.S. Army, 1966-68. Fellow Ill. Bar Found.; mem. ABA, Ill. State Bar Assn. (chmn. sect. on comml., banking and bankruptcy law 1981-82), Chgo. Bar Assn. (chmn. fin. instns. com. 1980-81, chmn. comml. fin. com. 1979-80), Lawyers Club (Chgo.).

COUGHLIN, KEVIN, state senator; BA, MPA, Bowling Green State U. State rep. Ohio Ho. of Reps., Columbus, 1997—2000; sen., 27th dist. Ohio State Senate, Columbus, 2000—, chair, state and local govt. and vets. affairs com., mem. fin. and fin. instns., health human svcs. and aging, ins., and commerce and labor coms. Vice chair Coun. State Govts. Midwestern Legis. Conf.; bd. overseers Blossom Music Ctr.; adv. bd. Akron Civic Theatre. Named Legis. of Yr., Ohio Soc. Prof. Engrs.; recipient Leadership award, Ohio Restaurant Assn., Guardian of Small Bus. award, Nat. Fedn. Ind. Businessmen of Ohio; Am. Marshall fellow, German Marshall Fund of U.S. Mem.: Fraternal Order of Police Assocs. Office: Senate Bldg Rm # 137, 1st fl Columbus OH 43215

COULMAN, GEORGE ALBERT, chemical engineer, educator; b. Detroit, June 29, 1930; s. William John Thompson and Mary (Dega) C.; m. Annette Marie Felder, Sept. 1, 1956; children: Karl, Paula. BS, Case Inst. Tech., 1952, PhD (Ford Found. fellow), 1962; MS, U. Mich., 1958. Process devel. engr. Dow Corning Corp., Midland, Mich., 1954-57; mgr. devel. Am. Metal Products Co., Ann Arbor, Mich., 1958-60; asst. prof. chem. engring. U. Waterloo (Ont., Can.), 1961-64; mem. faculty Mich. State U., East Lansing, 1964-76, prof. chem. engring., 1974-76, Cleve. State U., 1976—, chmn. dept., 1976-85, interim dean engring., 1988-89, dean Coll. of Engring., 1989-96, prof. emeritus, 1996—. Cons. in field. Author numerous papers in field. Served with AUS, 1952-54. Named Engr. of Yr., Nat. Engrs. Week Com., 1995. Mem. AICE, Am. Soc. Engring. Edn., Cleve. Engring. Soc. (bd. govs., 1st v.p.), Ohio Soc. Profl. Engrs. (outstanding engring. educator 1992), Cleve. Tech. Soc. Coun. (Disting. Svc. award 1992). Office: 1963 E 24th St Cleveland OH 44115-2403

COULSON, CHARLES ERNEST, lawyer; b. Belleville, Ill., Oct. 29, 1944; s. Charles Henry and Genevieve (Bell) C.; B.A., Kent State U., 1970; J.D. U. Akron, 1974. Bar: Ohio 1974, U.S. Dist. Ct. (no. dist.) Ohio 1976. Asst. prosecutor Lake County Prosecutor's Office, Painesville, Ohio, 1975-77, chief asst. prosecutor, 1977-79; ptnr. Coulson and Perez, Mentor, Ohio, 1979-82, Davies, Rosplock, Coulson, Perez, Deeb, and Harrell, Willoughby, Ohio, 1982—; law dir. City of Kirtland, Ohio, 1980—; parttime instr. bus. and real estate law Lakeland Community Coll., Mentor, 1979—. Served to 1st lt. U.S. Army, 1968-70, Vietnam. Mem. Assn. Trial Lawyers Am., Ohio Acad. Trial Lawyers, Ohio State Bar Assn., Lake County Bar Assn. Office: Davies Rosplock Coulson Perez Deeb and Harrell 4230 State Route 306 Willoughby OH 44094-9274

COULSON, ELIZABETH ANNE, physical therapist, educator, state representative; b. Hastings, Nebr., Sept. 8, 1954; d. Alexander and Marilyn (Marvel) Shafernich; m. William Coulson, Feb. 14, 1986. Student, Wellesley Coll., 1972-73; BS in Edn., U. Kans., 1976; cert. in phys. therapy, Northwestern U., Chgo., 1977; MBA, Keller Grad. Sch. Mgmt., 1985; postgrad., U. Ill., 1991. Lic. phys. therapist, Ill. Assoc. prof. dept. phys. therapy Chgo. Med. Sch., North Chicago, Ill., chmn. dept. phys. therapy, 1993-96. Contbr. articles to profl. jours. Trustee Northfield Twp., Ill., 1993-97; Ill. state rep. 17th dist., 1997—. Mem. APHA, Am. Phys. Therapy Assn. (Ill. del. 1986-93, chief del. 1991-93), Ill. Phys. Therapy Assn. (chmn. jud. com. 1989-91). Home: 1701 Sequoia Tr Glenview IL 60025-2022 Office Phone: 847-724-3233.

COULTER, CHARLES ROY, lawyer; b. Webster City, Iowa, June 10, 1940; s. Harold L. Coulter and Eloise (Wheeler) Harrison; m. Elizabeth Bean, Dec. 16, 1961; 1 child, Anne Elizabeth. BA in Journalism, U. Iowa, 1962, JD, 1965. Bar: Iowa 1965. Assoc. Stanley, Bloom, Mealy & Lande, Muscatine, Iowa, 1965-68; v.p. Stanley, Lande & Hunter, Muscatine, 1969—, also bd. dirs. County fin. chmn. Leach for Congress, 1980-96. Fellow Coll. of Law Practice Mgmt. (dir. 1994-2004, pres. 2001-04), Am. Bar Found., Iowa State Bar Found., Am. Coll. Trust and Estate Counsel; mem. ABA (mem. coun. law practice mgmt. sect. 1984-88, sec. 1988-89, vice chair 1989-90, chair 1991-92, chair coord. commn. legal tech. 1994-97, mem. standing com. on tech. and info. sys. 1997-98), Iowa Bar Assn., Muscatine County Bar Assn., Coralville Cmty. Fund (old brick bd. dirs.), Thirty-Three Club (pres. 1981), Rotary, Order of Coif. Episcopalian. Avocation: tennis. Office: Stanley Lande & Hunter 2201 E Grantview Dr Ste 200 Coralville IA 52241 Office Phone: 319-248-9000. Business E-Mail: chuckcoulter@slhlaw.com.

COUNSELL, PAUL S., retired advertising executive; Former CEO, Cramer-Krasselt Co., Milw.; now semi-ret., also counselor, Milw. Office: Cramer-Krasselt Co 733 N Van Buren St 4th Fl Milwaukee WI 53202-4799

COUNTRYMAN, DAYTON WENDELL, lawyer; b. Sioux City, Iowa, Mar. 31, 1918; s. Cleve and Susie (Schaeffer) Countryman; m. Ruth Hazen, Feb. 2, 1941 (dec.); children: Karen, Joan, James, Kay. BS, Iowa State Coll., 1940; LLB, State U. Iowa, 1948, JD, 1969. Bar: Iowa 1948. Practiced in, Nevada; ptnr. Hadley & Countryman, Nevada, Iowa, 1949-64; mem. Countryman & Zaffarano P.C., 1984-87, Dayton Countryman Law Offices, P.C., 1987—; county atty. Story County, Iowa, 1950-54; atty. gen. State of Iowa, 1954-56. Candidate for U.S. Senate, 1956, 1960, 68. Air Force Res. pilot USAAF, 1941—46. Mem. ABA, Iowa Bar Assn., Story County Bar Assn., VFW, Am. Legion, Iowa State U. Alumni Assn. (pres. 1970-71), Iowa 2B Jud. Dist. Assn., Masons, Lions (pres. 1975-76). Methodist. Office: PO Box 28 Nevada IA 50201-0028 Office Phone: 515-382-2605.

COURANT, PAUL NOAH, university librarian, economist, educator; b. Ithaca, NY, Jan. 5, 1948; s. Ernest David and Sara (Paul) Courant; m. Katherine Olive Johnson, Sept. 21, 1969 (dissolved 1984); children: Ernest Mendel, Noah Albert; m. Marta Anne Manildi, Jan. 30, 1988; 1 child, Samuel Robinson Manildi. BA, Swarthmore Coll., 1968; MA, Princeton U., 1972, PhD, 1973. Jr. economist Coun. Econ. Advisers, Washington, 1969—70, sr. economist, 1979—80; asst. prof. econs., pub. policy U. Mich., Ann Arbor, 1973—78, assoc. prof., 1978—84, prof. econs. and pub. policy, 1984—, dir. Inst. Pub. Policy Studies, 1983—87, 1989—90, chmn. econs. dept., 1995—97, assoc. provost, 1997—2001, provost, exec. v.p. acad. affairs, 2002—05, Harold T. Shapiro collegiate prof. pub. policy Gerald R. Ford Sch. of Pub. Policy, Arthur F. Thurnau prof. econs., prof. info., univ. libr., dean Univ. Librs., 2007—. Mem. task force long-term econ. growth State of Mich., 1983—84; cons. Mich. Dept. Commerce, Lansing, 1984—85, Congl. Budget Office, Washington, 1988—89; bd. dirs. Mich. Future. Author: (book) America's Great Consumption Binge, 1986; co-author: Economics, 12th edit., 1999; contbr. articles to profl. jours. Bd. dirs. Ctr. Watershed and Cmty. Health, Eugene, Oreg., 1997—. Grantee, NSF, 1976—77, 1979—81, 1994—97, Rockefeller Found., 1985—87, Nat. Cancer Inst., 1992—95. Mem.: Nat. Tax Assn., Assn. Pub. Policy Analysis and Mgmt. (mem. policy coun. 1994—98), Am. Econ. Assn. Avocations: sailing, skiing, tennis, hiking, clarinet. Office: U Mich 818 Hatcher Grad Libr S Ann Arbor MI 48109-3091 Office Phone: 734-764-9356. E-mail: pnc@umich.edu.

COURTNEY, DAVID W., chemical company executive; Exec. v.p., dir. mktg. Chemcentral, Bedford Park, Ill., exec. v.p., COO, 1997-98, CEO, 1998—. Office: Chemcentral 7050 W 71st St Bedford Park IL 60638-5902

COURTNEY, EUGENE WHITMAL, computer company executive; b. East St. Louis, Ill., Jan. 3, 1936; s. Eugene and Goldie Genell (Mitchell) C.; m. Barbara Ann Beckwith, Aug. 1, 1959; children: Kevin Eugene, Kyle Patrick. BSEE, Princeton U. with honors, 1957. Exec. v.p., gen. mgr., dir. Digital Sci. Corp., San Diego, 1970-75, pres., CEO, 1975-79; dir. Digital Sci./Europe, 1975-79; v.p. corp. devel. Topaz, Inc., San Diego, 1979, Nat. Computer Sys., Mpls., 1980-81, v.p., gen. mgr. scanning divsn., 1981-83, group v.p., 1983-88; exec. v.p., COO, dir. HEI Inc., Victoria, Minn., 1988-90, pres., CEO, 1990-99; dir., 1989-2000; prin. and dir. Triangle Industries, Inc., 1988—; pres., CEO RSI Sys., Edina, Minn., 1999-2001; prin. E.W. Courtney & Assocs., 2001—. Dir., chmn. Datakey, Inc., Mpls., 1995-2005; mem. Minn. Software Tech. Com., 1985-86; dir. Waters Instruments, Inc., Mpls., 2003—. Contbr. articles to profl. jours. Trustee, v.p. engring. San Diego Hall of Sci., 1974-79; mem. State of Calif. gov.'s task force on edn. and industry, 1977-78; mem. Rancho Santa Fe (Calif.) Park and Recreation Bd., 1978; mem. tech. adv. bd. Minn. Dept. Corrections, Shakopee, 1985-86. Am. Electronics Assn. (nat. bd. dirs., chmn. San Diego coun. 1976-79, chmn. Minn. coun. 1993-96), Princeton Club (N.Y.C.). Avocation: print collecting. Home: 509 Holly Ave Saint Paul MN 55102 also: Courtaparteen Kinsdale County Cork Ireland

COURTNEY, THOMAS, state senator; b. Sept. 1947; m. Donna Courtney; children: Dawn, Shawna, Brian. With Case/New Holland; state senator dist. 44 Iowa Senate, 2003—; mem. agr. com.; mem. bus. and labor rels. com.; mem. rules and adminstrn. com.; mem. state govt. com.; ranking mem. govt. oversight com. Former pres. Burlington Sch. Bd. With USAF. Mem.: UAW. Democrat. Office: State Capitol East 12th and Grand Des Moines IA 50319

COUSINS, STEVEN, lawyer; b. St. Louis, Mo., Feb. 15, 1954; BA, Yale U., 1977; JD, U. Pa., 1980. Bar: Mo. 1981. Ptnr. Armstrong Teasdale LLP, St. Louis. Mem. bd. editors Am. Bankruptcy Law Jour., 1997—2000. Co-author: Basic Bankruptcy in Missouri, 1989. Bd. trustees St. Louis Art Mus.; co-chair Inner-City HS Summer Internship Program, St. Louis Pub. Schs. Found.; gen. counsel/exec. com. St. Louis Regional Chamber & Growth Assn.; vice chmn. bd. trustees St. Louis Children's Hosp.; mem. property and facilities com. BJC Health Sys. Named one of Am. Top Black Lawyers, Black Enterprise Mag., 2003. Fellow: Am. Coll. Bankruptcy; mem.: ABA, Bar Assn. Met. St. Louis, Mo. Bar, Am. Bankruptcy Inst., The Pvt. Bank. Office: Armstrong Teasdale LLP One Metropolitan Sq Ste 2600 Saint Louis MO 63102-2740 Business E-Mail: scousins@armstrongteasdale.com.

COUSINS, WILLIAM, JR., retired judge; b. Swiftown, Miss., Oct. 6, 1927; s. William and Drusilla (Harris) C.; m. Hiroko Ogawa, May 12, 1953 (dec.); children: Cheryl Akiko, Noel William, Yul Vincent, Gail Yoshiko. BA, U. Ill., 1948; LLB, Harvard U., 1951. Bar: Ill. 1953, U.S. Dist. Ct. (no. dist.) Ill. 1961, U.S. Supreme Ct. 1975. Title examiner Chgo. Title & Trust Co., 1953-57; asst. state's atty. Cook County, Ill., 1957-61; sole practice Chgo., 1961-67; judge Circuit Ct. Cook County, Chgo., 1976-92; justice Ill. Appellate Ct., 1992—2002. Chair exec. com. 1st Dist. Appellate Ct., 1997-98; lectr. DePaul Law Sch., Chgo.; bd. dirs. Nat. Ctr. State Cts., 1996-2002; faculty advisor Nat. Jud. Coll., 1987; mem. exec. com. Ill. Jud. Conf., 1983-2002, former chmn. exec. com.; liaison assoc. judge coordinating com.; former chmn. Ill. Jud. Coun. Bd. dirs. Ind. Voters Ill., 1964-67, Ams. for Dem. Action, 1968, Operation PUSH, 1971-76, Nat. Ctr. for State Cts.; mem. Chgo. City Coun., 1967-76; del. Dem. Nat. Conv., 1972; asst. moderator United Ch. of Christ, N.Y.C., 1981; mem. disaster nvestigation panels. Served with U.S. Army, 1951-53. Decorated Army Commendation medal; named Judge of Yr., John Marshall Law Sch., Chgo., 1980; recipient Thurgood Marshall award Ill. Jud. Coun., 1992, Earl Burris Dickerson award Chgo. Bar Assn., 1998, C. Francis Stradford award, 2001. Mem. ABA, Nat. Bar Assn. (jud. coun., Raymond Pace Alexander award 1999, Hall of Fame 1994), Ill. Bar Assn. 1Access to Justice award 2002), Cook County Bar Assn. (former bd. dirs., Edward N. Wright award 1968, William R. Ming award 1974, Hall of Fame 1997), Alpha Kappa Alpha (Monarch award for Statesmanship 1995), Kappa Alpha Psi, Sigma Pi Phi, Delta Sigma Rho. Home: 1745 E 83rd Pl Chicago IL 60617-1714 Office Phone: 773-520-0910. E-mail: wmcousins1@sbcglobal.net.

COVALT, ROBERT BYRON, chemicals executive; b. Chgo., Nov. 8, 1931; s. Byron L. and Thelma A. (Adams) C.; m. Virginia, Aug. 17, 1952; children: Karen Elizabeth Clark, David Byron. BSChemE, Purdue U., 1953, DEng (hon.), 1992; MBA, U. Chgo., 1967. Devel. engr. B.F. Goodrich Chem. Co., Avon Lake, Ohio, 1953-54; with Morton Chem. div. Morton Thiokol, Inc., 1956—, v.p. engring. and mfg. Chgo., 1973-78, group v.p., 1978-79, pres., 1979-87; pres. specialty chems. group, group v.p. Morton Thiokol, Inc., 1987-89; pres. splty. chems. group, group v.p. Morton Internat. Inc., 1989-90, exec. v.p., 1990-94; chmn., pres. and CEO Sovereign Specialty Chems., Inc., 1994—2002, dir., 1994—2004; pres. RBC Assocs., Inc., Chgo., 2004—. Bd. dirs. CFC Internat. Served as 1st lt. USAF, 1954-56. Recipient Disting. Engring. Alumnus award Purdue U. Mem. AIChE, Am. Chem. Soc. Office: RBC Associates Inc 10 S Riverside Plz Ste 1800 Chicago IL 60606

COVEY, STEVEN K., lawyer; b. Chgo., Aug. 5, 1951; Bachelors, U. Ill., 1973; JD, DePaul U., 1977. Corp. sec. Navistar Internat. Corp., Warrenville, Ill., 1990—2000, dep. gen. counsel, 2004, sr. v.p., gen. counsel, 2004—; v.p. gen. counsel Navistar Fin. Corp., Warrenville, Ill., 2000—04. Office: Navistar Internat Corp 4201 Winfield Rd Warrenville IL 60555

COVINGTON, ANN K., lawyer, former state supreme court justice; b. Fairmont, W.Va., Mar. 5, 1942; d. James R. and Elizabeth Ann (Hornor) Kettering; m. James E. Waddell, Aug. 17, 1963 (div. Aug. 1976); children: Mary Elizabeth Waddell, Paul Kettering Waddell; m. Joe E. Covington, May 14, 1977. BA, Duke U., 1963; JD, U. Mo., 1977. Bar: Mo. 1977, U.S. Dist. Ct. (we. dist.) Mo. 1977. Asst. atty. gen. State of Mo., Jefferson City, 1977-79; ptnr. Covington & Maier, Columbia, Mo., 1979-81, Butcher, Cline, Mallory & Covington, Columbia, Mo., 1981-87; justice Mo. Ct. Appeals (we. dist.), Kansas City, 1987-89, Mo. Supreme Ct., 1989—2001, chief justice, 1993-95; ptnr. Bryan Cave, St. Louis, 2001—. Bd. dirs. Mid Mo. Legal Services Corp., Columbia, 1983-87; chmn. Juvenile Justice Adv. Bd., Columbia, 1984-87. Bd. dirs. Ellis Fischel State Cancer Hosp., Columbia, 1982-83, Nat. Ctr. for State Cts., 1998—; chmn. Columbia Indsl. Revenue Bond Authority, 1984-87; trustee United Meth. Ch., Columbia, 1983-86, Am. Law Inst., 1998—. Recipient Citation of Merit, U. Mo. Law Sch., 1993, Faculty-Alumni award U. Mo., 1993; Coun. of State Govt. Toll fellow, 1988. Fellow Am. Bar Found.; mem. ABA (jud. adminstrv. divsn., mem. adv. com. on Evidence Rules, U.S. Cts.), Mo. Bar Assn., Boone County Bar Assn. (sec. 1981-82), Am. Law Inst., Acad. Mo. Squires, Order of Coif (hon.), Mortar Bd. (hon.), Phi Alpha Delta, Kappa Kappa Gamma. Office: Bryan Cave One Metropolitan Sq 211 N Broadway Ste 3600 Saint Louis MO 63102-2750

COVINGTON, GEORGE MORSE, lawyer; b. Lake Forest, Ill., Oct. 4, 1942; s. William Slaughter and Elizabeth (Morse) C.; m. Shelagh Tait Hickey, Dec.28, 1966 (div. May 1995); children: Karen Morse, Jean Tait, Sarah Ingersoll Covington; m. Barbara Schilling Trentham, Dec. 19, 1998. AB, Yale U., 1964; JD, U. Chgo., 1967. Assoc. Gardner, Carton & Douglas, Chgo., 1970-75, ptnr., 1976-95; atty. pvt. practice, Lake Forest, Ill., 1995—. Lectr. in field. Contbr. articles to profl. jours. Active Grant Hosp. of Chgo., 1974-95, chmn. of bd. 1990-95; bd. dirs. Grant Healthcare Found., 1995—, chmn. 1999—2001; trustee Chgo. Acad. Sci., 1974-85, pres., 1980-82; trustee, chmn. Ill. chpt. Nature Conservancy, Chgo., 1974-88; bd. dirs. Latin Sch Chgo., 1979-80, Open Lands Project, Chgo., 1972-86, Chgo. Farmers, 1994-96; bd. dirs., sec. Lake Forest Open Lands Assn., 1984—; bd. dirs., sec., treas. Les Cheneaux Found., 1978—; bd. dirs. Student Conservation Assn., 1996-2005, vice chmn., 1999-2002, chmn., 2002-04; bd. dirs. Little Traverse Conservancy, 1998-2007; mem. Bd. Fire and Police Commrs., Village of Lake Bluff, Ill., 1991-2005. With U.S. Army, 1967-69. Mem. ABA, Ill. Bar Assn., Lake County Bar Assn., Chgo. Bar Assn., Univ. Club (bd. dirs. 1985-88), Commonwealth Club, Lawyers Club, Shoreacres (Lake Bluff, Ill.), Les Cheneaux Club (Cedarville, Mich.), Lambda Alpha. Office: 500 N Western Ave Ste 204 Lake Forest IL 60045-1955 Personal E-mail: gcovington@sbcglobal.net.

COWARD, NICHOLAS F., lawyer; BA, Union Coll.; JD, George Mason U., 1981. Bar: DC 1982. Mng. ptnr. Baker & McKenzie, Washington, DC, ptnr., exec. com. mem. Mem.: ABA. Office: Baker & McKenzie LLP One Prudential Plaza Ste 2500 Chicago IL 60601 Office Phone: 202-452-7021. E-mail: nicholas.f.coward@bakernet.com.

COWEN, ROY CHADWELL, JR., language educator; b. Kansas City, Mo., Aug. 2, 1930; s. Roy Chadwell and Mildred Frances (Schuetz) Cowen; m. Hildegard Bredemeier, Oct. 6, 1956 (dec.); 1 child, Ernst Werner (dec.). BA, Yale U., 1952; PhD, U. Gottingen, Federal Republic of Germany, 1960. Instr. U. Mich., Ann Arbor, 1960-64, asst. prof., 1964-67, assoc. prof., 1967-71, prof., 1971—, chmn. dept. Germanic langs., 1979-85. Author: (book) Christian Dietrich Grabbe, 1972, Naturalismus Kommentar zu einer Epoche, 1973, Hauptmann Kommentar zum dramatischen Werk, 1981, Poetischer Realismus: Kommentar zu einer Epoche, 1985, Das deutsche Drama im 19. Jahrhundert, 1988, Christian Dietrich Grabbe-Dramatiker ungeloester Widersprueche, 1998. With USN, 1952—56. Decorated Sr. Officer's Cross Federal Republic of Germany; recipient Williams Tchg. award, U. Mich., 1967; fellow Sr., NEH, 1972—73. Mem.: MLA, Internationale Vereinigung fur Germanistik. Democrat. Methodist. Home: 2874 Baylis Dr Ann Arbor MI 48108-1764 Office: U Mich Dept Germanic Langs/Lits Ann Arbor MI 48109 Business E-Mail: rcowen@umich.edu.

COWEN, STEPHEN, editor-in-chief; Attended, U. Chgo., 2005. Editor-in-chief U. Chgo. Law Jour. John M. Olin Fellow, 2004—05. Office: U Chgo Law Journal 1111 East 60th St Chicago IL 60637 E-mail: cowen@uchicago.edu.

COWGER, GARY L., automotive executive; b. Kansas City, Kans., 1947; m. Kay Cowger; 2 children. BS in Industrial Engring., General Motors Inst., 1970; MS in Mngmnt., MIT, 1978. Plant superintendent General Motors Corp., Kansas City, variety of engring. & mfr. positions, 1965—79, general superintendent Oldsmobile Division Lansing, Mich., 1979—80, production manager GM Assembly Division St. Louis, 1981—82, plant manager GM Assembly Division Wentzville, Mo., 1982—85, complex manager Lordstown Assembly facilities, 1985—87, mfr. mgr. Cadillac Motor div., 1987—90, exec. dir. adv. mfr. engring. GM Tech. Ctr. Warren, Mich., 1990—92, exec.-in-charge NAO Mfr. Ctr., 1993, pres. & mng. dir. Mexico div., 1994—98, v.p., 1994—; v.p. mfr. General Motors Europe, 1998; chmn. & mng. dir. Adam Opel AG, 1998; v.p. & group exec. Labor Relations, N.A. Internal Comm. General Motors Corp., 1998—2001, v.p. mfr. & labor relations, 2001, pres. General Motors N. Am., 2001—05. Co-chmn. fin. com. Mo. Gov.'s Com. on Sci. Tech. Vice chmn. bd. mgrs. St. Charles YMCA. bd. dirs. Mo. C. of C.; exec. com. St. Louis Regional Commerce and Growth Assn.; Gov.'s Hawthorn Found.; bd. dirs. Career Productivity Inst. of Lindenwood Coll., Mo. Incu Tech. Found.; adv. bd. dirs. St. Charles County Council of Chambers; pub. mem. Blue Cross Corp. Assembly; bd. trustees Lindenwood Coll.; pres.'s council St. Louis U. Office: Buick Oldsmobile Cadillac Group PO Box 444 Wentzville MO 63385-0444

COWLES, JOHN, JR., publishing executive, women's sports promoter, philanthropist; b. Des Moines, May 27, 1929; s. John and Elizabeth (Bates) C.; m. Jane Sage Fuller, Aug. 23, 1952; children: Tessa Sage Flores, John, Jane Sage, Charles Fuller. Grad., Phillips Exeter Acad., 1947; AB, Harvard U., 1951; LittD (hon.), Simpson Coll., 1965. With Cowles Media Co. (formerly Mpls. Star and Tribune Co.), 1953-83, v.p., 1957-68, editor, 1961-69, pres. or chmn., 1968—83, dir., 1956-84; pres. Harper's Mag., Inc., 1965-68, chmn. bd., 1968-72; dir. Harper & Row, Pubs., Inc., NYC, 1965-81, chmn., 1968-79. Dir. Des Moines Register & Tribune Co., 1960-84, Farmers & Mechanics Savs. Bank, Mpls., 1960-65, Cowles Comms., Inc., NYC, 1960-65, Equitable Life Ins. Co. Iowa, Des Moines, 1964-66, 1st Bank Systems, Inc., Mpls., 1964-68, A.P., NYC, 1966-75, Midwest Radio-TV, Inc., Mpls., 1967-76; fitness instr. Sweatshop Fitness Ctr., St. Paul, 1989-93; guest artist Bill T. Jones/Arnie Zane & Co., 1990-92; vice chmn. Women's Pro. Softball League LLC, Denver, 1994-02, chmn. Nat. Pro Fastpitch LLC, 2002-04; ptnr. St. Anthony Films LLC, 1998-04, "Herman USA", 2001; investor Block E Hotel Capital LLC, 2000—. Mem. adv. bd. on Pulitzer Prizes, Columbia U., 1970-83; campaign chmn. Mpls. United Fund, 1967; bd. dirs. Guthrie Theatre Found., 1960-71, pres., 1960-63, chmn., 1964-65, arch. selection com., 2000-01, endowment campaign steering com., 1987-91; trustee Phillips Exeter Acad., 1960-65; bd. dirs. Walker Art Ctr., 1960-69, 87-92, Minn. Civil Liberties Union, 1956-61, Urban Coalition Mpls., 1968-70, Mpls. Found., 1970-75, German Marshall Fund U.S., 1975-78; bd. dirs. Am. Newspaper Pubs. Assn., 1975-77; mem. govt. affairs com., 1976-79; mem. Woodhill Country Club, 1954-84, Century Assn., 1967-92, Coun. on Foreign Rels., 1969-92, Minn. Bus. Partnership, 1977-83, Minn. Project Corp. Responsibility, 1977-83, Trilateral Commn., 1978-82. Served to 2d lt. US Army, 1951-53. Hill fellow Humphrey Inst. U. Minn., 2005-06; named one of Ten Outstanding Men of Yr. U.S. Jr. C. of C., 1964, 200 Rising Leaders in Am. Time Mag., 1974; recipient John Phillips award Exeter, 1977, US Bank Sally Ordway Irvine award, St. Paul, 2000, Regents award U. Minn., 2004. Mem. Greater Mpls. C. of C. (dir. 1978-81, chmn. stadium site task force 1977-82), Mpls. Club, Mill Reef Club (Antigua), A.D. Club at Harvard, Signet Assn. at Harvard (pres. 1950-51). Home: 700 S 2nd St Loft 91 Minneapolis MN 55401 Office: 155 Fifth Ave S Ste 1000 Minneapolis MN 55401-2550 Office Phone: 612-359-9449.

COWLES, JOHN JAY, III, investment company executive, entrepreneur; b. Mpls., Nov. 1, 1953; s. John Jr. and Jane Sage (Fuller) C.; m. Elizabeth Page Knudsen, Sept. 8, 1984; children: Lucia, Colin, Maxwell. BA in Govt. cum laude, Harvard Coll., 1981; MBA, Harvard Bus. Sch., 1983. Pres., CEO Classic Printers, Prescott, Ariz., 1975-79, chmn., 1979-96; cons. Office Cable Comm. Boston City Hall, 1980-81; dir. planning Cowles Media Co., Mpls., 1985-88, vice chmn. bd. dirs., 1991-93, chmn. bd. dirs., 1993-98; dir. fin. analysis United Satellite Comm., Inc., NYC, 1983-85; v.p. Sentinel Pub. (divsn. Cowles Media Co.), Denver, 1988-91, Book Ventures, Inc., Mpls., 1992-93; pres., CEO Women's Pro Softball, Mpls., 1993-95; chmn. bd. Nat. Pro Fastpitch, Mpls., 1993—; mng. dir. Lawrence Creek, LLC, pvt. investment co., 2004—. Bd. dirs. St. Paul Riverfront Corp., chmn., 1998-2002, Open Book, Mpls., chmn., 1998-2002; vice chmn. St. Paul Found., 2004-, Unity Ave. Found. Bd. dirs. Minn. Ctr. Book Arts, Mpls., 1991-98, chmn. bd. dirs., 1995-98, acting exec. dir., 1995-97; bd. dirs. Prescott Coll., 1976-82, Mpls. Found., 1987-88, Guthrie Theater, Mpls., 1993-98. Mem. Mpls. Club. Office: Ste 804 123 N 3d St Minneapolis MN 55401 Office Phone: 612-359-9449. E-mail: jay@unityave.com.

COWLES, ROBERT L., state legislator; b. July 31, 1950; BS, U. Wis., Green Bay, 1975. Mem. from dist. 75 Wis. State Assembly, Madison, 1983-87; mem. from dist. 2 Wis. Senate, Madison, 1987—. Mem. Gov.'s Coun. on Recycling and Environ. Edn. Bd.; mem. joint com. on fin. Wis. House Reps. Office: 300 W Saint Joseph St Green Bay WI 54301-2328

COWLEY, ALLEN WILSON, JR., physiologist; b. Harrisburg, Pa., Jan. 21, 1940; m. Theresa Ann Malinoski BA, Trinity Coll., Hartford, Conn., 1961; MS, Hahnemann Med. Coll., Phila., 1965, PhD, 1968. Instr. physiology and biophysics U. Miss. Med. Ctr., Jackson, 1968-69, asst. prof. physiology and biophysics, 1969-72, assoc. prof. physiology and biophysics, 1973-75, prof. physiology and biophysics, 1975-80; prof. physiology, chmn. physiology dept. Med. Coll. Wis., Milw., 1980—; chmn. dept. physiology Marquette U., Milw., 1990—. Lectr. and invited spkr. in field; organizer various confs. Mem. editl. bd. Clin. and Exptl. Hypertension, 1977—, Am. Jour. Physiology: Circulation Sect., 1979-83, Hypertension, 1980-91, 93—, Am. Jour. Physiology: Regulatory, Integrative and Comparative Physiology, 1984-88, Internat. Jour. Cardiology, 1985—, Am. Jour. Physiology: Heart and Circulatory Physiology, 1987-89, Clin. Exptl. Pharmacology Physiology, 1993-96, Jour. Hypertension, 1993-96, Physiol. Revs., 1997—, News in Physiol. Scis., 1997—, assoc. editor 1988-91; guest editor Hypertension, Ann. Supplement Procs. Coun. for High Blood Pressure Rsch., 1981-84; contbr. 30 chpts. to books and symposia, over 180 articles to profl. jours. and conf. procs. Recipient numerous NIH rsch. grants, 1971—; recipient Established Investigatorship award Am. Heart Asnsn., 1973-78, Alumnus of Yr. award Hahnemann Med. Coll., 1975, MERIT award NIH, 1996. Fellow Am. Heart Assn. Coun. High Blood Pressure Rsch. (chmn. publs. com. 1982-84, mem. various coms., Disting. Achievement award 1996, Novartis award 1997), Am. Heart Assn. Coun. on Circulation (various coms.), Am. Physiol. Soc. Cardiovasc. Sect.; mem. Am. Physiol. Soc. (various coms., pres.-elect 1996-97, pres. 1997—, Ernest H. Starling Disting. lectureship 1996, Wiggers award 1997), Internat. Soc. Hypertension, Am. Soc. Nephrology, Microcirculation Soc., Assn. Chairmen Depts. Physiology (various offices and coms., pres. 1990), Hungarian Physiol. Soc. (hon.), Brazilian Acad. Sci. (hon.), Sigma Xi. Office: Med Coll Wisconsin Dept Physiology 8701 W Watertown Plank Rd Milwaukee WI 53226-3548

COWLISHAW, MARY LOU, government educator; b. Rockford, Ill., Feb. 20, 1932; d. Donald George and Mildred Corinne (Hayes) Miller; m. Wayne Arnold Cowlishaw, July 24, 1954; children: Beth Cowlishaw McDaniel, John, Paula Cowlishaw Rader. BS in Journalism, U. Ill., 1954; DHL, North Ctrl. Coll., 1999; DHL (hon.), Benedictine U., 2000. Mem. editorial staff Naperville (Ill.) Sun newspaper, 1977-83; mem. Ill. Ho. of Reps., Springfield, 1983—2003, chmn. elem. and secondary edn. com., 1995—97, vice-chmn. pub. utilities com., 1995—2003, mem. joint Ho.-Senate edn. reform oversight com., 1985—97; assoc. Ctr. for Govtl. Studies No. Ill. U., 2003—; adj. prof. North Ctrl. Coll., Naperville, Ill., 2003—. Mem. Ill. Task Force on Sch. Fin., 1990-96; vice chmn. Ho. Rep. Campaign Com., 1990—; co-chair Ho. Rep. Policy Com., 1991-2003; chmn. edn. com. Nat. Conf. State Legislatures, 1993-97; mem. Joint Com. Adminstrv. Rules, 1992-2003; commr. Edn. Commn. of the States, 1995-2002; chair, Ill. Women's Agenda Task Force, 1994—; mem. Nat. Edn. Goals Panel, 1996—, bd. govs. Lincoln Series for Excellence in Pub. Svc., 1996—. Author: This Band's Been Here Quite a Spell, 1983; columnist Ill. Press Assn., 2003—. Mem. Naperville Dist. 203 Bd. Edn., 1972-83; co-chmn. Ill. Citizens Coun. on Sch. Problems, Springfield, 1985-2003. Recipient 1st pl. award Ill. Press Assn., 1981, commendation aperville Jaycees, 1986, Golden Apple award Ill. Assn. Sch. Bds., 1988, 90, 92, 94, Outstanding Women Leaders of DuPage County award West Suburban YWCA, 1990, Activator award Ill. Farm Bur., 1996, 98, Bd. of Dirs. award Little Friends, Inc., 1998, Honor award Ill. Math. and Sci. Acad., 2002, Pub. Svc. award West Suburban Higher Edn. Consortium, 2002; named Best Legislator, Ill. Citizens for Better Care, 1985, Woman of Yr., Naperville AAUW, 1987, Best Legislator, Ill. Assn. Fire Chiefs, 1994, Outstanding Edn. Adv. Indian Prairie Sch. Dist. 204, 1994, Legislator of Yr., Ill. Assn. Pk. Dists., 1995; commr. Edn. Commn. of the States, 1994-2002; Mary Lou Cowlishaw Elem. Sch. named in her honor, 1997, Legislator of Yr., Ill. Assn. Mus., 1998. Mem. Am. Legis. Exch. Coun., Conf. Women Legislators, Nat. Fedn. Rep. Women, DAR, Naperville Rep. Women's Club (pres. 1994—). Methodist. Avocation: the violin. Home: 924 Merrimac Cir Naperville IL 60540-7107 Office: North Central Coll 30 N Brainard St Naperville IL 60540-4690

COWSIK, RAMANATH, physics professor; b. Nagpur, Madhya, India, Aug. 29, 1940; came to U.S., 1970; s. Ramakrishna K. and Saraswati C. (Ayyar) C.; m. Shyamala Balasubrahmanian, Aug. 20, 1979 (div. Feb. 1989); 1 child, Siddhartha. BS, Mysore U., Bangalore, India, 1958; MS in Physics, Karnatak U., India, 1960; PhD, Bombay U., 1968. Jr. rsch. assoc. Tata Inst. Fundamental Rsch., Bombay, 1961—, reader, 1975—, assoc. prof., 1977—, prof., 1984—, disting. prof.; asst. prof. U. Calif., Berkeley, 1970-73; vis. scientist Max-Planck Inst. Extension Physik, Munich, 1973-74; dir. Indian Inst. for Astrophysics, Bangalore, dir. emeritus, Vainu Bappu disting. prof.; prof. physics, dir. McDonnell Ctr. for Space Scis. Washington U., St. Louis. Vis. prof. Washington U., St. Louis, 1987-2001. Contbr. articles to jour. Physics Rev., Astrophys. Jour. Recipient Sarabhai award Hari om Scc./Phys. Rsch. Lab., 1981, Group Achievement award NASA, 1986. Fellow Indian Acad. Scis., Indian Nat. Sci. Acad. (Bhatnagar award 1984); mem. Am. Phys. Soc. (life), Internat. Astron. Union (life), NAS (fgn. assoc.). Achievements include development of the theory that weakly interacting particle relicts from the big bang are the constituents of dark matter and set the upper bound on the sum of their masses, in particular of neutrinos; recognized the cosmological significance of the hard x-ray background; derived the leaky box and nested leaky box models for cosmic rays; research in high energy astrophysics of nonthermal emissions from quasars and supernova remnants and in astroparticle physics and experimental gravitation; measurement of the double beta decay life-time of the tellurium-128 nucleus as 7.7x10 24 years the longest, implying the Majorana mass of the neutrino to be less than 1 eV. Office: Washington U Dept Physics Campus Box 1105 One Brookings Dr Saint Louis MO 63130-4899

COX, ALLAN JAMES, management consultant; b. Berwyn, Ill., June 13, 1937; s. Brack C. and Ruby D. C.; m. Jeanne Begalke, 1961 (div. 1966); 1 child, Heather; m. Bonnie Lynne Welden, 1966 (div. 1990); 1 child, Laura; m. Cheryl Patric, 1991. BA, No. Ill. U., 1961, MA, 1962; postgrad., McCormick Theol. Sem., Chgo., 1962-63, postgrad., 1973—75, Alfred Adler Inst. of Chgo., 1965-67, postgrad., 1975, Gestalt Inst. of Chgo., 1994-96. Instr. Wheaton (Ill.) Coll., 1963-65; assoc. Case and Co., Inc., Chgo., 1965-66, Spencer Stuart & Assos., Inc., Chgo., 1966-68; v.p. Westcott Assos., Inc., Chgo., 1968-69; founder, pres. Allan Cox & Assocs., Inc., 1969—; chmn. Berryman Comm. Co., Chgo., 1994-98; chmn. of the bd. Amateur Baseball, Inc., Chgo., 1992-96, CEO, 1996-98; chmn., CEO Assn. for Internat. Youth Sports, Inc., Chgo., 1998-99. Adj. staff Ctr. for Creative Leadership, Greensboro, NC, 1985-90; mem. vis. com. U. Chgo. Div. Sch., 1996-2005; mem. San Diego Regional Econ. Devel. Corp Author: Confessions of a Corporate Headhunter, 1973, Work, Love and Friendship, 1974, The Cox Report on the American Corporation, 1982, The Making of the Achiever, 1985, The Achiever's Profile, 1988, Straight Talk for Monday Morning, 1990, Redefining Corporate Soul: Linking Purpose and People, 1996, Your Inner CEO, 2007; columnist LA Times Syndicate, 1986-90; contbr. articles to profl. jours. Chmn. bd. Ctr. for Ethics and Corp. Policy, 1987-92; Elder Fourth Presbyn. Ch. of Chgo. Mem.: N.Am. Soc. Adlerian Psychology, Corp. Dirs. Forum, at. Assn. Corp. Dirs., Chgo. Club, Alpha Kappa Delta. Presbyterian. Office: 45 East Bellevue Pl Chicago IL 60611-1133 Office Phone: 312-337-8010. Business E-Mail: allan@allancox.com.

COX, CHARLES C., economist; b. Missoula, Mont., May 8, 1945; m. Monica Lewis, 1984. BA magna cum laude, U. Wash., 1967; AM, U. Chgo., 1970, PhD, 1975. Asst. prof. econs. Ohio State U., Columbus, 1972-80; nat. fellow Hoover Instn., 1977-78; asst. prof. mgmt. Tex. A&M U., College Station, 1980-82; chief economist SEC, Washington, 1982-83, commr., 1983-89, acting chmn., 1987; prin., sr. v.p. Lexecon, Inc., Chgo., 1989—. Nat. fellow Hoover Institution, 1977-78. Mem. Am. Econ. Assn., United Shareholders Assn. (chmn. 1990-93), Mt. Pelerin Soc., Phi Beta Kappa. Office: Lexecon Inc 332 S Michigan Ave Ste 1300 Chicago IL 60604-4397

COX, DAVID JACKSON, biochemistry professor; b. NYC, Dec. 22, 1934; s. Reavis and Rachel (Dunaway) C.; m. Joan M. Narbeth, Sept. 6, 1958 (dec. Oct. 8, 1982); children: Andrew Reavis, Matthew Bruce, Thomas Jackson; m. Tamara L. Compton, Nov. 26, 1983. BA, Wesleyan U., 1956; PhD, U. Pa., 1960. Instr. biochemistry U. Wash., 1960-63; asst. prof. chemistry U. Tex., 1963-67, assoc. prof., 1967-73; prof., head dept. biochemistry Kans. State U., 1973-89; prof. chemistry Ind. U./Purdue U., Ft. Wayne, 1989-2000, prof. emeritus, 2000—. Vis. prof. U. Va., 1970-71; dean arts scis. Ind. U./Purdue U., Ft. Wayne, 1989-96. NSF predoctoral fellow, 1956-59; NSF sr. postdoctoral fellow, 1970-71 Mem. Am. Soc. Biochemistry, Molecular Biology Soc., Am. Chem. Soc., Phi Beta Kappa, Sigma Xi. Democrat. Presbyterian. Home: 309 Crown Ln Bellingham WA 98229-5929 Personal E-mail: comcox@yahoo.com.

COX, JAMES ALLAN, chemistry professor; b. Chisholm, Minn., Sept. 19, 1941; s. Robert Earl and Mary Jean (Berdey) C.; m. Kersti Suik, Aug. 21, 1965; children: Kaila Ann, Alison Jean. AA, Hibbing State Coll., 1961; BChem, U. Minn., 1963; PhD, U. Ill., 1967. Lectr., rsch. assoc. U. Wis., Madison, 1967-69; faculty, prof. chemistry So. Ill. U., Carbondale, 1969-86; prof., chair chemistry Miami U., Oxford, Ohio, 1987-94, prof. chemistry, 1994—. Cons. NIH, Washington, 1988—; environ. chem. cons. various industries, 1980—. Author book chpts. on coal chemistry; contbr. more than 150 articles to environ., chem., and electrochemistry jours. Scholar, Miami U., 2005. Mem.: Soc. Electroanalytical Chemists, Electrochemistry Soc., Am. Chem. Soc. (ACS) (named Cin. Chemist Yr. 2002), Internat. Soc. Electrochemistry. Achievements include discovery of catalysts for oxidation of environmental pollutants and various biological compounds including insulin and various amino acids. Office: Miami U Chemistry-Hughes Hall Oxford OH 45056

COX, JEROME ROCKHOLD, JR., electrical engineer; b. Washington, May 24, 1925; s. Jerome R. and Jane (Mills) Cox; m. Barbara Jane Lueders, Sept. 2, 1951; children: Nancy Jane Cox Battersby, Jerome Mills, Randall Allen. SB, MIT, 1947, SM, 1949, ScD, 1954. Faculty Washington U., St. Louis, 1955—61, prof. elec. engring., 1961—2000, dir. Biomed. Computer Lab., 1964—75, prof. biomed. engring. in physiology and biophysics, Sch. Medicine, 1965—2000, chmn. computer labs., 1967—83, program dir. tng. program tech. in health care, 1970—78, chmn. dept. computer sci., 1975—91, prof. biomedicine, Inst. for Biomed. Computing, 1983—2000, Harold and Adelaide Welge prof. computer sci., 1989—98, dir. Applied Rsch. Lab., 1991—95, sr. prof., 1999—; v.p. Growth Networks, 1999—2000. Co-chmn. computers in cardiology conf., 1974—88; cardiology adv. com. Nat. Heart and Lung Inst., 1975—78; epidemiology biostatistics and bioengring. cluster Pres.'s Biomed. Rsch. Panel, 1975—76; chmn. divsn. computer rsch. and tech. rev. com. NIH, 1983—96, PROPHET adv. com., 1983—88; adv. com. Harvard-MIT Health Scis. and Tech., Boston, 1988—92; nat. neural circuitry database com. Inst. of Medicine, NAS, 1989—91; mem. Nat. Adv. Coun. Human Genome Rsch., 1990—95; adv. com. John Hopkins Biomed Engr, 2000—. Mem. editl. bd.: Computers and Biomed. Rsch., 1967—2000, Applied Mathematics Letters, 1987—96. Bd. dirs. Ctrl. Inst. Deaf, 1993—, Mass Sensors, Inc., 2000—. With US Army, 1943—44. Fellow: IEEE (mem. editl. bd. Trans. Biomed. Enring. 1969—71), St. Louis Acad. Sci. (bd. dirs. 1997—99), Am. Coll. Med. Informatics, Acoustical Soc. Am.; mem.: Inst. Medicine, Tau Beta Pi, Eta Kappa Nu, Sigma Xi. Achievements include patents for air traffic control; computerized tomography; medical display technology; network traffic pacing; design of. Office: Washington U Dept Computer Sci Campus Box 1045 One Brookings Dr Saint Louis MO 63130-4899 E-mail: jrc@cse.wustl.edu.

COX, MIKE (MICHAEL A. COX), state attorney general; b. 1961; s. John and Rita Cox; m. Laura M. Cox; 4 children. BA with distinction in Polit. Sci., U. Mich., 1986, JD, 1989. Asst. pros. atty. Office Pros. Atty. Oakland County, Pontiac, Mich., 1989—90; asst. pros. atty. spl. crimes sect. Office Pros. Atty. Wayne County, Detroit, 1990—2001, dep. chief homicide unit, 2001—03; atty. gen. State of Mich., Lansing, 2003—. With USMC, 1980—83. Mem.: Inc. Soc. Irish/Am. Lawyers, State Bar Mich. (criminal law sect.), Pros. Attys. Assn. Mich. (instr. Basic Sch.). Republican. Office: G Mennen Williams Bldg 7th Fl PO Box 30212 525 W Ottawa St Lansing MI 48909-0212 Office Phone: 517-373-1110.

COX, MITCHEL NEAL, editor; b. Portsmouth, Ohio, Sept. 8, 1956; s. Walter Eugene and Mary Agnes (Orlett) Cox; m. Lisa Renee LaLonde, Sept. 8, 1979 (dec. May 2001); children: Harmony, Leigh Ann, Katie. BS in Journalism, Ohio State U., 1985. Mng. editor The Puller, Columbus, Ohio, 1984-87; editor Bicycles Today, Columbus, 1985-87, Fur-Fish-Game, Columbus, 1987—. Mem. Outdoor Writers Assn. Am. Office: Fur-Fish-Game 2878 E Main St Columbus OH 43209-2698 Office Phone: 614-231-9585. E-mail: mitchcox@furfishgame.com.

COX, SEAN F., federal judge; b. Detroit, Sept. 24, 1957; B. Gen. Studies, U. Mich., 1979; JD, Detroit Coll. Law, 1983. Bar: Mich. 1983. Law clk. James Flynn, PC, 1983; assoc. Kitch, Saurbier, Drutchas, Wagner & Kenney, 1984—89, Bloom & Kavanaugh, 1989—90; ptnr. Cummings, McClorey, Davis & Acho, PC, 1990—96; judge 3rd Mich. Jud. Cir. Ct., 1996—2006, US Dist. Ct. (Ea. dist.) Mich., Detroit, 2006—. Office: US Dist Ct 5th Fl 231 W Lafayette Detroit MI 48226 Office Phone: 313-234-2650.

COX-HAYLEY, DEON MELAYNE, geriatrics services professional; b. Trenton, NJ, 1960; MD, U. Health Scis., Coll. Osteopathic Medicine, 1986. Cert. internal medicine 1990, geriatric medicine 1992, internal medicine 2000, geriatric medicine 2002. Intern Riverside Hosp., Wichita, Kans., 1986—87; resident U. Kans. Sch. Medicine, Wichita, 1987—90; fellowship U. Chgo. Hosps., Chgo., 1990—92; assoc. prof., medicine U. Chgo. Pritzker Sch. Med., Dept. Medicine, Divsn. Biological Scis.; med. dir. Windermere Sr. Health Ctr., Chgo. Office: 5841 S Md Ave MC 6098 Chicago IL 60637 Address: Windermere Sr Health Ctr and Dental Assoc 5549 S Cornell Ave Chicago IL 60615

COYLE, DOROTHY, government agency administrator; Grad., Marquette U., Milw., Northwestern U. Kellogg Sch. Mgmt., 2001. Dir. Chgo. Office of Tourism, 1999—. Bd. dirs. Visit Ill. Named one of Top 40 Under 40, Crain's Chgo. Bus., 2006. Office: Chgo Office of Tourism Chgo Cultural Ctr 78 E Washington St 4th Fl Chicago IL 60602-4801 E-mail: dcoyle@cityofchicago.org.

COYLE, MICHAEL J., medical administrator; Pres. Daig divsn. St. Jude Med. Inc. Office: 14901 Deveau Pl Minnetonka MN 55345-2126

COYNE, PATRICK IVAN, physiological ecologist; b. Wichita, Kans., Feb. 26, 1944; s. Ivan Lefranz and Ellen Lucille (Brown) C.; m. Mary Ann White, Aug. 22, 1964; children: Shane Barrett, Shannon Renee. BS, Kans. State U., 1966; PhD, Utah State U., 1970. R & D coord. U.S. Army Cold Regions Rsch. and Engring. Lab., Hanover, NH, 1970-72; asst. prof. forestry U. Alaska, Fairbanks, 1973-74; plant physiologist, environ. scientist Lawrence Livermore (Calif.) Nat. Lab., 1975-79, cons., 1980—; rsch. plant physiologist USDA/ Agrl. Rsch. Svc., Woodward, Okla., 1979-85; prof., head Agrl. Rsch. Ctr. Kans. State U., Hays, 1985-94, prof., head Western Kans. Agrl. Rsch. Ctrs., 1994—2006, prof. Agrl. Rsch. Ctr., 2006—. Mem. adv. coun. Kans. Geol. Survey, Lawrence, 1986-91. Contbr. 33 articles to profl. jours. Capt., U.S. Army, 1970-72. Mem. Am. Soc. Agronomy, Soil Sci. Soc. Am., Crop Sci. Soc. Am., Soc. Range Mgmt., Hays Area C. of C. (bd. dirs. 1988-90). Republican. Mennonite Brethren Ch. Home and Office: Kans State U Agrl Rsch Ctr 1232 240th Ave Hays KS 67601-9228

COZAD, JOHN CONDON, lawyer; b. Portland, Maine, Dec. 18, 1944; s. Francis E. and Arlyn Odell (Condon) C.; m. Linda Hickerson, Feb. 18, 1978. BA in Polit. Sci., Westminster Coll., Fulton, Mo., 1966; JD, U. Mo.-Columbia, 1972. Bar: Mo. 1972. Assoc. & ptnr. Field, Gentry, Benjamin, & Robertson, Kansas City, Mo., 1972-83; ptnr. Morrison & Hecker, Kansas City, Mo., 1983—; chmn. Mo. Rep State Party, 1995-99. Chmn. Mo. Hwy. and Transp. Commn., 1985-91; mem. desegregation monitoring com. U.S. Dist. Ct. (we. dist.) Mo., 1989-91; bd. curators U. Mo. Sys., 1991-96; bd. trustees U. Kansas City, 1991—; mem. Rep. at. Com., 1995-99. Lt. USNR, 1967-69, Vietnam. Decorated Bronze Star. Navy Commendation medals, Presdl. Unit Citation. Mem. Mo. Bar Assn., Kansas City Bar Assn., Carriage Club. Republican. Mem. Christian Ch. (Disciples Of Christ). Avocations: politics, pheasant hunting, reading. Home: RR 2 Box 140 Platte City MO 64079-9805

COZAD, RACHAEL BLACKBURN, museum director; m. Kanon Cozad. Exec. dir. Iris and B. Gerald Cantor Found., LA, 1994—2001; dir. Kemper Mus. Contemporary Art, Kansas City, Mo., 2001—. Office: Kemper Mus Contemporary Art 4420 Warwick Blvd Kansas City MO 64111-1821 Office Phone: 816-753-5784. Business E-Mail: rbcozad@kemperart.org.

CRABB, BARBARA BRANDRIFF, federal judge; b. Green Bay, Wis., Mar. 17, 1939; d. Charles Edward and Mary (Forrest) Brandriff; m. Theodore E. Crabb, Jr., Aug. 29, 1959; children: Julia Forrest, Philip Elliott. AB, U. Wis., 1960, JD, 1962. Bar: Wis. 1963. Assoc. Roberts, Boardman, Suhr and Curry, Madison, Wis., 1962-64; legal rschr. Sch. Law, U. Wis., 1968-70, Am. Bar Assn., Madison, 1970-71; US magistrate US Dist Ct. (we. dist.) Wis., Madison, 1971-79; judge U.S. Dist. Ct. (we. dist.) Wis., Madison, 1979—, chief judge, 1980-96, 2002—. Mem. Gov. Wis. Task Force Prison Reform, 1971-73 Membership chmn., v.p. Milw. LWV, 1966-68; mem. Milw. Jr. League, 1967-68. Mem. ABA, Nat. Assn. Women Judges, State Bar Wis., Dane County Bar Assn., U. Wis. Law Alumni Assn. Office: US Dist Ct PO Box 591 120 N Henry St Madison WI 53701-0591

CRABTREE, GEORGE, physicist; BS with distinction, Northwestern U., 1967; MS, U. Wash., 1968; PhD, U. Ill., 1974. Asst. physicist Argonne Nat. Lab., Solid State Sci. Divsn., 1974—79; physicist Argonne Nat. Lab., Materials Sci. and Tech. Divsn., 1979—85; assoc. divsn. dir. Argonne Nat. Lab., Materials Sci. Divsn., 1993—2001, sr. physicist, 1985—. Vis. prof. U. of Oreg., Dept. of Physics, 1977; rsch. scientist Ctr. de Rsch. sur lest Tres Basses Temperatures, 1986; group leader Argonne Nt. Lab., Superconductivity and Magnetism Materials Sci. Divsn., 1988—; adj. prof. No. Ill. U., 1989—. Divsn. assoc. editor Phys. Rev. Letters, 1998—; editor: Physica-C Superconductivity, 1987—; co-editor: Novel Materials and Techniques in Condensed Matter, 1982. Recipient awards for disting. performance at Argonne Nat. Lab., Dept. of Energy, U. of Chgo., 1982, awards for outstanding sci. accomplishments in solid state physics, 1982, 1985, Materials Sci. award for outstanding rsch. in solid state physics with implications for dept. of energy related energy tech., U.S. Dept. of Energy, 1995, R&D 100 award, 1996, Materials Sci. award for outstanding rsch. in solid state physics, U.S. Dept. of Energy, 1997, Fed. Lab. Consortium award for tech. transfer, magnetic flux imaging sys. Fellow: Am. Physical Soc. (past chair, exec. com.); mem.: Nat. Sci. Found. (theme leader 1991—2000), 6th Internat. Conf. on Materials and Mechanisms of Superconductivity and High Temperature Superconductors (mem.program com. 2000), Internat. Workshop on Vortex Dynamics (mem. org. and program com. 2001), Fla. State U., Nat. High Field Magnet Lab. (chair, external adv. com. 1998), Scholastic Honor Soc., Phi Eta Sigma, Engring. Honor Soc., Tau Beta Pi. Office: Argonne National Laboratory Materials Sci Bldg 223 Rm S238 9700 S Cass Ave Argonne IL 60439

CRACCHIOLO, JAMES M., diversified financial services company executive; BS, MBA, NYU. CPA. With Am. Express, 1982—2005; pres. Am. Express Travel Related Svcs. Internat., 1998—2003; group pres. Am. Express Global Fin. Svcs., 2000—05; chmn. Am. Express Bank Ltd., 2000—05; pres., CEO Am. Express Financial, 2000—05; chmn., CEO Am. Express Fin. Advisors, 2001—05, Ameriprise Fin. Inc., Mpls., 2005—. Bd. dirs. Tech Data Corp., 1999—. Mem. bd. adv. March of Dimes. Office: Ameriprise Financial Inc 243 Ameriprise Fin Ctr Minneapolis MN 55474

CRAFT, EDMUND COLEMAN, retired manufacturing executive; b. Plainfield, NJ, Dec. 23, 1939; s. Edmund Coleman and Ruth Irene (Morrell) C.; m. Gail Christensen; children: Edmund Coleman III, Elisabeth Gordon, William Todd. BS, Lycoming Coll., 1963; postgrad., Syracuse U., 1963-64; grad. exec. program, U. Minn., 1984. With Borg-Warner Corp., Detroit, adminstrv. asst. to chmn. Chgo., 1969-70; with Borg-Warner Ltd., Letchworth, Hertfordshire, Eng., 1970-75; v.p. hydraulics div. Borg-Warner, Wooster, Ohio, 1975-79; dir. hydraulics div. Donaldson Co. Inc., Mpls., 1979-83, v.p., 1983-2000; sr. advisor Global Aftermarket, 2000-2001; ret., 2001. Bd. dirs. Jr. Achievement of Upper Midwest Inc., 1993-2000, mem. exec. com., 1994-2000; divsn. chmn. United Way, Wooster, 1974. Mem. Automotive Filter Mfrs. Coun. (vice chmn. 1985-89, chmn. 1989-91, bd. dirs. 1991-2000), Dataw Island Club, Dataw Island Yacht Club. Republican. Presbyterian. Avocations: golf, boating. E-mail: craft@islc.net.

CRAFT, GERARD FORD, chef; m. Susan Craft; 1 child, Ellie. Chef Bistro Toujours; with Chateau Marmont, LA, Metropolitan, Salt Lake City; owner, exec. chef Niche, St. Louis, 2005—, Veruca Bakeshop & Café, St. Louis. Named Chef of Yr., Sauce mag., 2007; named one of America's Best New Chefs, Food & Wine Mag., 2008; named to 30 Under 30, St. Louis Bus. Jour., 2007. Office: Niche 1831 Sidney St Saint Louis MO 63104*

CRAHAN, JACK BERTSCH, retired manufacturing executive; b. Peoria, Ill., Aug. 24, 1923; s. John F. and Ann B. (Bertsch) C.; m. Peggy Furey, Sept. 9, 1944; children: Patrick Michael, Colleen Mary, Kevin Furey. BS, U. Minn., 1948. With Flexsteel Industries, Inc., Dubuque, Iowa, 1948—50, plant mgr., 1950-54, gen. mgr., v.p., 1955-70, exec. v.p., 1970-84, pres., 1985-89, vice-chmn., COO, 1989-90, chmn., CEO, 1990-99; ret., 1999. Trustee United Steel Workers Am. Pension Fund, 1960—99; dir. Pres.'s Coun. for Phys. Fitness in Industry, 1970—74, Dubuque Bank & Trust, 1970—94; bd. dirs. Dubuque Racing Assn., 1987—2000. Bd. regents Loras Coll., 1967-80; bd. dirs. Xavier Hosp., 1969-78, Boys Club Am., 1981-99. Served with USNR, 1942-43, with USMC, 1943-46, 53-54. Decorated DFC, Air medals (3). Mem. Am. Furniture Assn. (bd. dirs. 1967-74). Republican. Roman Catholic. Home: 1195 Arrowhead Dr Dubuque IA 52003-8594 Office: Flexsteel Industries Inc Brunswick Indsl Block PO Box 847 Dubuque IA 52004-0847 Office Phone: 563-556-7730. Business E-Mail: jzemann@flexsteel.com.

CRAIG, CLIFFORD LINDLEY, orthopaedic pediatric surgery educator; b. Detroit, Mar. 25, 1944; s. Paul Forrest and Dorothy Madeline (Denhart) C.; m. Laura Ann Hackley, June 20, 1976; children: Paul Edward, Julia Marie. BS, Tufts U., 1965; MD, U. Mich., 1969. Diplomat Am. Bd. Orthopaedic Surgery. Asst. prof. orthopaedic surgery Tufts U. Sch. Medicine, Boston, 1979-94, assoc. prof. orthopaedic surgery, 1994-99; clin. assoc. prof. orthopedic surgery U. Mich. Med. Sch., Ann Arbor, 1999—. Fellow Am. Coll. Surgery; mem. AMA, Am. Acad. Orthopaedic Surgery, Am. Acad. Pediatrics, Am. Acad. Cerebral Palsy, Am. Assn. Clin. Anatomy, Pediatric Orthopaedic Soc. of N.Am. Office: Univ Mich Med Ctr Taubman Center 2912 PO Box 328 Ann Arbor MI 48106-0328 E-mail: clcraig@umich.edu.

CRAIG, JAMES LYNN, physician, health services administrator; b. Columbia, Tenn., Aug. 7, 1933; s. Clifford Paul and Maple (Harris) Craig; m. Suzanne Anderson, July 20, 1957; children: James Lynn, Margaret; m. Roberta Annette Craig, May 17, 1980. Student, Mid. Tenn. State U., 1953; MD, U. Tenn., 1956; MPH, U. Pitts., 1963. Diplomate Am. Bd. Preventive Medicine. Intern U. Tenn. Meml. Hosp., Knoxville, 1957; resident in occupl. medicine U. Pitts., 1962-64, TVA, Chattanooga, 1964-65, physician, 1966-69, chief med. officer, 1969-74; corp. med. dir. Gen. Mills Corp., Mpls., 1974-76, v.p. corp. med. dir., 1976-80, v.p., dir. health and human svcs., 1980-98; adj. clin. prof. U. Minn., Mpls., 1979—, chmn. cmty. adv. com. Ctr. for Environ. and Health Policy, 1994-97, mem. adv. coun. health in scis., 1992-95, chmn. adv. bd. Ctr. for Environ. and Health Policy, 1994-97; pres. Family and Preventive Health Svcs., Inc., Mpls., 1998—. Clin. instr. U. Tenn., Memphis, 1970—74, Meharry Med. Sch., Nashville, 1972—74; mem. adv. bd. to dir. Ctr. Disease Control and Prevention, 1996—99; nat. adv. bd. Internat. Health and Media Awards, 1996—2006. Contbr. articles to profl. jours. Bd. dirs. Mpls. Blood Bank, 1976—88, Minn. Safety Coun., 1981—90, Minn. Heart Assn., Mpls., 1976—87, Children's Heart Fund, 1976—88, Meth. Hosp. Found., 1979—87, Park Nicolett Med. Found., 1987—93, Altcare, 1983—95, Meth. Hosp. Health Assn., 1987—93, Minn. Wellness Coun., 1986—91, Health Sys. Minn. Assocs., 1993—94, Health Sys. Minn. Inst. Rsch. and Edn., 1996—2000, chmn., 1997—2000, Park Nicollet Inst., 2000—01; trustee Minn. Med. Found., 2001—, Crossroads Coll., Rochester, 2007—; bd. dirs. Minn. Bible Coll., Rochester, 1978—83. Named Legacy Laureate, U. Pitts., 2000; recipient Cmty. Svc. award, Park Nicolett Med. Ctr., 1995, Knudsen award in occupl. medicine, Am. Coll. Occupl. and Environ. Medicine, 2000. Fellow: Am. Acad. Family Practice, Am. Acad. Occupl. Medicine (treas. 1982—83, sec. 1983—84, v.p. 1984—85, pres. 1986—87), Am. Occupl. Medicine Assn. (bd. dirs. 1974—78); mem.: AMA (alt. del. Ho. Dels. 1990—92, del. 1992—96, Recognition award 1975, 1978, 1981, 1985, 1989, 1993, 1996, 1999, 2002, 2005), Minn. Med. Found. (bd. dirs. 2001—), Emergency Physicians Assn. (bd. dirs. 1984—92), Mpls. Acad. Medicine (sec. 1983—85, pres. 1985—86), Minn. Acad. Medicine, North Ctrl. Occupl. Medicine Assn. (pres. 1977), Occupl. Health Inst. (chmn. 1983—84), Mpls. Kiwanis Club (trustee 2004—). Home: 10008 S Shore Dr Minneapolis MN 55441-5011 Office: PO Box 270330 Minneapolis MN 55427-6330 Office Phone: 612-669-3847. Personal E-mail: jimlcraig@aol.com.

CRAIG, JOHN BRUCE, former ambassador, air transportation executive; BS, American U. With Sr. Fgn. Svc., dep. chief of mission Syria, Colombia, with Bur. Near Eastern Affairs Washington, dir. jr. officer divsn. Bur. of Pers., dir. Office of Arabian Peninsula Affairs, amb. Sultanate of Oman, 1998—2001; spl. asst. to Pres., mem. Nat. Security Council, sr. dir. for combating terrorism White House, Washington, 2001—03; v.p., Middle East internat. rels. Boeing Co., 2003—. Office: Boeing Company 100 N Riverside Plz Chicago IL 60606-1596

CRAIG, JUDITH, bishop; b. Lexington, Mo., June 5, 1937; d. Raymond Luther and Edna Amelia (Forsha) C. BA, William Jewell Coll., 1959; MA in Christian Edn., Eden Theol. Sem., 1961; MDiv, Union Theol. Sem., 1968; DD, Baldwin Wallace Coll., 1981; DHL, Adrian Coll., 1985, Otterbein Coll., 1993, Lebanon Valley Coll., Baldwin Wallace Coll. Youth dir. Bellefontaine United Meth. Ch., St. Louis, 1959-61; intern children's work Nat. Coun. of Chs. of Christ, NYC, 1961-62; dir. Christian edn. 1st United Meth. Ch., Stamford, Ct., 1962-66; inst. adult basic edn. N.Y.C. Schs., 1967; dir. Christian edn. Epworth Euclid United Meth. Ch., Cleve., 1969-72, assoc. pastor, 1972-76; pastor Pleasant Hills United Meth. Ch., Middleburg Heights, Ohio, 1976-80; conf. council dir. East Ohio Conf. United Meth. Ch., Canton, 1980-84; bishop United Meth. Ch., Mich. area, 1984-92, West Ohio area, 1992-2000; ret. Mem. United Meth. Gen. Coun. Mins., 1976-80, 88-92, United Meth. Commn. Status Role Women, 1984-88; gen. conf. del., 1980, 84; mem. United Meth. Publ. House Bd., 1992—; bd. dirs. U.S. Health Corp.; frequent lectr. and preacher; bd. trustees 27 institutions in West Ohio. Contbr. articles to ministry mags. Bd. dirs. YWCA, Middleburg Heights, 1976-80. Recipient Citation of Achievement William Jewell Coll., 1985, Woman of Achievement award YWCA, 1995.

CRAIG, L. CLIFFORD, lawyer; b. Ohio, Aug. 29, 1938; Student, Stanford U., 1957-59; BA, Duke U., 1961, LLB, 1964. Bar: Ohio. Ptnr. Taft, Stettinius & Hollister, Cin., 1971—. Fellow Am. Coll. Trial Lawyers; mem. ABA, Ohio Bar Assn., Cin. Bar Assn. Office: 425 Walnut St Ste 1800 Cincinnati OH 45202-3957 Office Phone: 513-381-2838. Business E-Mail: craig@taftlaw.com.

CRAMBLETT, HENRY GAYLORD, pediatrician, virologist, educator; b. Scio, Ohio, Feb. 8, 1929; s. Carl Smith and Olive (Fulton) C.; m. Donna Jean Reese, June 16, 1960; children: Deborah Kaye, Betsy Diane. BS, Mt. Union Coll., 1950; MD, U. Cin., 1953. Diplomate Am. Bd. Pediatrics, Am. Bd. Microbiology, Am. Bd. Med. Specialists. Intern in medicine Boston City Hosp., Harvard Med. Svc., 1953-54; resident in pediatrics Children's Hosp., Cin., 1954-55; clin. rsch. assoc. at. Inst. Allergy and Infectious Diseases, Clin. Ctr., Bethesda, Md., 1955-57; chief resident, instr. dept. pediat. State U. Iowa, Iowa City, 1957-58, faculty, 1957-60, asst. prof., 1958-60; faculty Bowman Gray Sch. Medicine, 1960-64, prof. pediat., 1963-64, dir. virology lab., 1960-64; prof. pediat. Ohio State U., Columbus, 1964-95, prof. med. microbiology, 1966-95, exec. dir. Children's Hosp. Rsch. Found., 1964-73, chmn. dept. med. microbiology, 1966-73, dean Coll. Medicine, 1973-80, acting v.p. for med. affairs, 1974-80, v.p. health scis., 1980-83, Warner M. and Lora Kays Pomerene chair in medicine, 1982-95, assoc. to v.p. health svcs., to dean and prof. emeritus, 1984-95. Mem. Ohio State U. bd. trustees Cancer Hosp. Oversight Com., 1991-96, mem. Ohio Med. Bd., sec. 1984-92, past pres.; hosp. surveyor Joint Com. on Accreditation of Health Care Orgns., 1985-95; chmn. com. on cert., subcert. and recert. Am. Bd. Med. Specialists; mem. coms. on written exam., comprehensive qualifying evaluation program Nat. Bd. Med. Examiners; mem. Accreditation Coun. Continuing Med. Edn., chmn., 1980-83, 93-94, also mem. fin. com., 1993—, mem. strategic plan implementation com., 1993—, mem. external monitoring com., 1993—; mem. adv. com. on undergrad. med. evaluation; mem. Fedn. State Med. Bds., pres., 1976-82 (mem. Flex bd. 1983-91, chmn. 1985-91), mem. fin. audit com., 1991; chmn. Fed. Exam. Bd., 1991-92, cons., 1992—; mem. composite com. Fedn. of State Med. Bds. and Nat. Bd. of Med. Examiners, U.S. Med. Licensing Exam., 1990-96; Fedn. of State Med. Bds. observer Clin. Skills Assessment Alliance, 1990-95; bd. dirs. Ohio State U. Hosp., 1979-80; dir. med. and postgrad. med. edn. King Faisal Specialist Hosp., Riyadh, Saudi Arabia, 1983-84; mem. strategic planning task force CSAA, 1992-94; med. dir. Columbus Health Plan, 1995—. Trustee Children's Hosp. Rsch. Found., 1973-84, Children's Hosp., 1973-84, Children's Hosp., Inc., 1982-84. Recipient Hoffheimer prize U. Cin., 1953, Eben J. Carey award in anatomy, 1950, Rsch. Career Devel. award NIH, 1961-63; Henry G. Cramblett chair in medicine established at Ohio State U., 1988; Henry G. Cramblett Hall dedicated at Ohio State U., 1999. Fellow Am. Acad. Microbiology, AAAS; mem. So. Soc. Pediatric Rsch. (past pres.), Soc. Pediatric Rsch., Am. Pediatric Soc., Am. Acad. Pediat., Midwest Soc. Pediatric Rsch., Soc. Exptl. Biology and Medicine, Am. Soc. Microbiology, Alpha Omega Alpha. Achievements include research, publs. on medical licensure, medical staff hospital standards, etiologic assn. virus infections in illnesses of infants and children, estimation of importance of various viruses in morbidity and mortality in pediatric age group. Home: 2480 Sheringham Rd Columbus OH 43220-4274 Office: Ohio State U 1024 Cramblett Hall 456 W 10th Ave Columbus OH 43210-1240

CRAMBLIT, MIGGIE E., lawyer; BA, Cornell Coll.; JD, Hamline U.; attended, Kellogg Grad. Sch. Exec. Mgmt. Prog., Northwestern U. Law clerk for Justice James C. Otis Minn. Supreme Ct.; v.p., gen. counsel CenterPoint Energy Minneagasco; COO Family Fin. Strategies; counsel, corp. sec. Greater Minnesota Synergy; v.p., gen. counsel, corp. sec. DPL, Inc., 2003—, corp. sec., 2004. Adj. prof. William Mitchell Coll. Law, St. Paul. Trustee Dayton Philharm. Orch., Miami Valley Childhood Devel. Ctr.; former trustee William Mitchell Coll. Law, The House of Hope Presbyn. Ch., St. Paul and Greater Mpls. C. of C. Office: DPL Inc 1065 Woodman Dr Dayton OH 45432 Office Phone: 937-259-7214. Business E-Mail: miggie.cramblit@dplinc.com.

CRAMER, ROBERT, retail executive; CEO, pres. FareWay Stores, Inc., Boone, Iowa. Office: FareWay Stores Inc PO Box 70 Boone IA 50036-0070

CRAMER, TED, radio personality; b. Kansas City, Sept. 22; m. Linda Cramer. Radio host WDAF, Westwood, Kans., 1977—80, 1992—. Office: WDAF 4935 Belinder Westwood KS 66205

CRAMER, WILLIAM ANTHONY, biochemistry and biophysics researcher, educator; b. NYC, June 11, 1938; s. Robert and Sylvia (Blumstein) C.; m. Hanni Aebersold, Sept. 11, 1964; children: Rebecca, Jean-Marc, Gabrielle, Nicholas. BS, MIT, 1959; MS, U. Chgo., 1960, PhD, 1965. NSF post doctoral fellow U. Calif., San Diego, 1965-67, rsch. assoc., 1967-68; asst. prof. dept. biol. scis. Purdue U., West Lafayette, Ind., 1968-73, assoc. prof., 1973-78, prof., 1978—, assoc. head dept., 1984-86, Henry Koffler prof. biol. scis. West Lafayette, Ind., 1995-2001, Henry Koffler Disting. prof. biol. scis., 2001—. Head panel predoctoral fellowships in biophysics and biochemistry NSF, 1979, mem. molecular biology panel, 1980-82, mem. cellular biochemistry panel, 1989-91; mem. panel competitive grants USDA, 1983-84; chmn. Gordon Confs. on Photosynthesis, 1990, Bioenergetics, 2001; mem. phys. biochemistry study sect. NIH, 1991-95. Author textbook on bioenergetics; editor: Archives Biochemistry and Biophysics, 1979—91, Biochim. Biophys. Acta, 1983—2003, Photosynthesis Rsch., 1989—98, Jour. Bioenergetics Biomembranes, 1991—, Biophys. Jour., 1999—2005, Biochem. Jour., 2001—04, Jour. Biol. Chemistry, 2002—; contbr. articles to profl. jours. Recipient Rsch. Career Devel. award, NIH, 1970—75, Charles F. Kettering award, Am. Soc. Plant Physiologists, 1996, H.N. McCoy award for sci. achievement, Purdue U., 1988; sr. EMBO fellow, U. Amsterdam, 1974—75, Alexander von Humboldt fellow, Max-Planck Inst., Frankfurt, 1992, John Simon Guggenheim fellow, 1992—93. Fellow: Biophys. Soc. (chmn. bioenergetics subgroup 1989—92, program chair 40th ann. meeting 1996, coun. 1997—2001, exec. coun. 1999—2001, pub. policy com. 1999—); mem.: AAAS, Am. Soc. Biochemistry and Molecular Biology. Office: Purdue U Dept Biol Sci Lilly Hall Life Scis 915 W State St West Lafayette IN 47907 Business E-Mail: waclab@purdue.edu.

CRANE, CHARLOTTE, law educator; b. Hanover, NH, Aug. 30, 1951; d. Henry D. and Emily (Townsend) C.; m. Eric R. Fox, July 5, 1975; children: Hillary, Teresa. AB, Harvard U., 1973; JD, U. Mich., 1976. Bar: N.H. 1976, Ill. 1978. Law clk. to presiding judge U.S. Ct. Appeals (6th cir.), Detroit, 1976-77; law clk. to presiding justice U.S. Supreme Ct., Washington, 1977-78; assoc. Hopkins & Sutter, Chgo., 1978-82; asst. prof. Northwestern U., Chgo., 1982-86, assoc. prof., 1986-90, prof., 1990—. Contbr. articles to profl. jours. Mem. U.S. Women's Nat. Crew Team, 1976. Mem. ABA, Chgo. Tax Forum. Office: Northwestern U Sch Law 357 E Chicago Ave Chicago IL 60611-3059 Office Phone: 312-503-4528. Business E-Mail: ccrane@law.northwestern.edu.

CRANE, DEBRA K., lawyer; b. 1957; BBA, U. Cinn.; JD, No. Kentucky U. Bar: 1996. Asst. treas. Ohio Casualty Corp., Fairfield, Ohio, 1996—99, v.p., 1999—2002, gen. counsel, 2000—, sr. v.p., sec., 2002—. Mem.: Assn. Corp. Counsel S.W. Ohio Chpt. Office: Ohio Casualty Corp 9450 Seward Rd Fairfield OH 45014-5456 Office Phone: 513-603-2400. Office Fax: 513-603-3179. E-mail: debra.crane@ocas.com.

CRANE, EDWARD M., lawyer; b. Chgo., 1957; BS, DePaul U., 1979, JD, 1982. Bar: Ill. 1982, US Dist. Ct. (no., ctrl. & so. dists. Ill.), US Ct. Appeals (4th, 5th, 7th & 11th cirs.). Ptnr. Skadden, Arps, Slate, Meagher & Flom, Chgo. Mem.: Ill. Defense Coun. Lawyers Club of Chgo. Practicing Law Inst., Product Liability Adv. Coun., Def. Rsch. Inst., Internat. Assn. Def. Counsel, Chgo. Bar Assn., Ill. State Bar Assn., ABA. Office: Skadden Arps 333 W Wacker Dr Chicago IL 60606 Office Phone: 312-407-0522. Office Fax: 312-407-8503. E-mail: ecrane@skadden.com.

CRANE, GARY E., financial executive; BBA, U. Mich. CPA, Ohio, Fla. With Camco Fin. Corp., Cambridge, Ohio, 1996—, now CFO, treas. Office: Camco Fin Corp 6901 Glenn Hwy Cambridge OH 43725-8685

CRANE, MARK, lawyer; b. Chgo., Aug. 27, 1930; s. Martin and Ruth (Bangs) C.; m. Constance Bird Wilson, Aug. 18, 1956; children: Christopher, Katherine, Stephanie. AB, Princeton U., 1952; LLB, Harvard U., 1957. Bar: U.S. Dist. Ct. (no. dist.) Ill. 1957, U.S. Ct. Appeals (7th cir.) 1968, U.S. Ct. Appeals (9th cir.) 1972, U.S. Supreme Ct. 1978, U.S. Ct. Appeals (10th cir.) 1982, U.S. Ct. Appeals (fed. cir.) 1983, U.S. Ct. Appeals (6th cir.) 1995, U.S. Ct. Appeals (8th cir.) 1998. Assoc. Hopkins & Sutter, Chgo., 1957-63, ptnr., 1963-2001; of counsel Foley & Lardner, Chgo., 2001—. Adj. prof. Loyola U. Law Sch., 2000—; comml. arbitrator, mediator complex case panel Am. Arbitration Assn., Chgo., 1997—. Served to lt. (j.g.) USNR, 1952-54. Fellow Am. Bar Found., Am. Coll. Trial Lawyers (chmn. upstate Ill. com. 1997-99); mem. ABA (chmn. antitrust sect. 1986-87), Ill. Bar Assn. (chmn. fed. jud. appointments com. 1978-79, chmn. antitrust sect. 1970), Chgo. Bar Assn., 7th Cir. Bar Assn. (pres. 1984-85). Republican. Episcopalian. Home: 520 Hoyt Ln Winnetka IL 60093-2623 Office: The Quaker Oats Co 555 W Monroe St Chicago IL 60661-3716

CRANE, PHILIP MILLER, former congressman; b. Chgo., Nov. 3, 1930; s. George Washington III and Cora (Miller) C.; m. Arlene Catherine Johnson, Feb. 14, 1959; children: Catherine Anne, Susanna Marie, Jennifer Elizabeth, Rebekah Caroline, George Washington V, Rachel Ellen (dec. 1997), Sarah Emma, Carrie Esther. Student, DePauw U., 1948-50; BA, Hillsdale Coll., 1952; postgrad., U. Mich., 1952-54, U. Vienna, Austria, 1953-56; MA, Ind. U., 1961; PhD, 1963; LLD, Grove City Coll., 1973, Nat. Coll. Edn., 1987; Doctor en Ciencias Politicas, Francisco Marroquin U., 1979. Advt. mgr. Hopkins Syndicate, Inc., Chgo., 1956-58; tchg. asst. Ind. U., Bloomington, 1959-62; asst. prof. history Bradley U., Peoria, Ill., 1963-67; dir. schs. Westminster Acad., Northbrook, Ill., 1967-68; mem. 91st-108th Congresses from 13th, 12th (now 8th) Ill. Dist., Washington, 1969—2005, vice chmn. ways and means com.; mem. Joint Com. on Taxation. Author: Democrat's Dilemma, 1964, The Sum of Good Government, 1976, Surrender In Panama: The Case Against the Treaty, 1978; contbr.: Continuity in Crisis, 1974, Crisis in Confidence, 1974, Case Against the Reckless Congress, 1976, Can You Afford This House?, 1978, View from the Capitol Dome (Looking Right), 1980, Liberal Cliches and Conservative Solutions, 1984. Dir. rsch. Ill. Goldwater Orgn., 1964; mem. nat. adv. bd. Young Ams. for Freedom, 1965—; bd. dirs. Am. Conservative Union, 1965-82, chmn., 1976; bd. dirs., chmn. Intercollegiate Studies Inst.; bd. advisors Ashbrook Ctr., Ashland U., 1983—, univ. trustee, 1988-93; founder Rep. Study Com., 1972—, chmn., 1984; commr. Commn. on Bicentennial U.S. Constn., 1986-91; trustee Hillsdale Coll. Recipient Distinguished Alumnus award Hillsdale Coll., 1968, Independence award, 1974, William McGovern award Chgo. Soc., 1969, Freedoms Found. award, 1973; named Ill. Statesman's Father Yr., 1979. Mem. ASCAP, VFW (award 1978), Am. Hist. Assn., Orgn. Am. Historians, Acad. Polit. Sci., Am. Acad. Polit. and Social Scis., Am. Legion, Phila. Soc., B'nai B'rith (award 1978), Phi Alpha Theta, Pi Gamma Mu. Republican.

CRANG, RICHARD FRANCIS EARL, botanist, writer, research scientist; b. Clinton, Ill., Dec. 2, 1936; s. Richard Francis and Clara Esther (Cummins) Crang; m. Linda L. Crang, Aug. 10, 1958 (div.). BS, Ea. Ill. U., 1958; MS, U. S.D., 1962; PhD, U. Iowa, 1965. Asst. prof. biology Wittenberg U., 1965—69; assoc. prof. biol. sci. Bowling Green State U., 1969—74, prof., 1974—80; prof. plant biology U. Ill., Urbana-Champaign, 1980—2002, assoc. head dept. plant biology, 1995—97, faculty fellow in acad. adminstrn., 1997—99, dir. Ctr. Elec. Microsci., 1980—92, prof. emeritus, 2002—. Adj. prof. anatomy Med. Coll. Ohio, 1974—80; summer rsch. prof. Lehman Coll., CUNY, Bronx, vis. prof. biol. sci., 1999—2006; vis. scientist Cambridge U., England, 1978—79, Komarov Bot. Inst., 1980—92, Warsaw U., Poland, 1993; rschr., collaborator in fungal adhesion Kaohsiung Med. Coll., Taiwan, China, 1988—90; lectr. in field. Author: (with A. Vassilyev) CD-ROM Text on Plant Anatomy, 2003; contbr. numerous articles to profl. jours. Mem. Statewide Democratic Support Group, Ill. Recipient Outstanding Faculty Rsch. Recognition award Bowling Green State U., 1973, 75; grantee Paint Rsch. Inst., 1976-83, NSF, 1981-83, EPA, 1984-86, USDA, 1986-89, Internat. Plant and Pollution Lab., 1993-98; lifetime assoc. fellow Clare Hall, Cambridge, Eng. Mem. AAAS, Bot. Soc. Am., Internat. Soc. Environ. Botanists (advisor, life, inaugurated 1st internat. meeting, Lucknow, India 1996), Microscopy Soc. Am. (nat. chmn. cert. bd. 1982-89, dir. U.S.A. local affiliates 1990-93, Disting. Svc. award 1994, Cecil Hall award 1994), Sigma Xi. Achievements include development of asynchronous learning techs. at college level by means of networked computers on world wide web and other educational technologies. Office: U Ill Plant Biology 505 S Goodwin Ave 665 Morrill Hall Urbana IL 61801-3707 Home: 576 Selborne Rd Riverside IL 60546-1669 Business E-Mail: r-crang@life.uiuc.edu.

CRANGLE, ROBERT D., lawyer, management consultant, entrepreneur; b. Putnam, Conn., May 5, 1943; s. Dale E. and Libbie S. (Krepela) C.; m. S. Jeanne Rose, June 6, 1968; children: Rob, Scott, Elenor, Bill, Kimball, Susan, Sara, Paul, Hally. BS in Nuclear Engring., Kans. State U., 1966; JD, Harvard U., 1969. Bar: Mass. 1969, Ill. 1974, Kans. 1987, U.S. Dist. Ct. Kans. 1987; cert. mgmt. cons. 1980. Sr. v.p. Harbridge House, Inc., Boston, 1969-84; pres., dir. Rose & Crangle, Ltd., Lincoln, 1984—; dir. Helisys Inc., LA, 1985-99; ptnr. Metz and Crangle, Chartered, Lincoln, Kans., 1987—2003; elected Lincoln County Atty., 1997—2001; atty. Crangle Law Office, Lincoln, 2003—. Mem. faculty Bus. Sch., Ill. Inst. Tech., Chgo., 1984-87; dir. IIT Ctr. Rsch. on Indsl. Strategy and Policy, Chgo., 1984-87. Bd. dirs. Lake Bluff Sch. Bd., Ill., 1982-87, Farmers Nat. Bank, 1992-2004, Midwest Cmty. Bank, 2004—, adv. bd.; mem. Kans. Sci. and Tech. Coun., 1992-96; mem. Natural History Mus. Bd., 1995-98, Kans. Geol. Survey Adv. Com., 1995-2002. Recipient Meritorious Pub. Svc. award NSF, 1985. Fellow AAAS (sect. officer 2006—); mem. Kans. Bar Assn. (officer bus. law sect. 1993-97), N.W. Kans. Bar Assn., co-organizer Kans. Math and Sci. Edn. Coalition, Four Rivers Devel., Inc. (bd. dirs. 2007-). Republican. Mem. Soc. Of Friends. Avocations: science policy, oil painting, entrepreneurship. Office: Crangle Law Office Chtd 117 N 4th PO Box 285 Lincoln KS 67455-0285: PO Box 285 117 N 4th St Lincoln KS 67455-0285 Office Phone: 785-524-5050. Business E-Mail: rcltd@nckcn.com.

CRANMER, THOMAS WILLIAM, lawyer; b. Detroit, Jan. 13, 1951; s. William Eugene and Betty Lee (Orphal) C.; children: Jacqueline, Taylor, Chase. BA, U. Mich., 1972; JD, Ohio No. U., 1975. Bar: Mich. 1975, U.S. Dist. Ct. (ea. dist.) Mich. 1978, U.S. Ct. Appeals (6th cir.) 1978, U.S. Supreme Ct. 1982, U.S. Tax Ct. 1986. Asst. pros. atty. Oakland County, Mich., 1975-78; asst. atty. U.S. Dist. Ct. (ea. dist.) Mich., 1978-80, asst. chief criminal div., 1980-82; assoc. Miro, Miro & Weiner, Bloomfield Hills, Mich., 1982-84, ptnr., 1984—; prin. Miller, Canfield, Paddock & Stone PLC, 2005—. Mem. faculty Atty. Gen's. Adv. Inst., Washington, 1980-82, Nat. Inst. Trial Adv., Northwestern Chicago, Ill., 1987—, trial adv. workshop Inst. Continuing Legal Edn., 1988—, local rules adv. com. U.S. Dist. Ct. (ea. dist.) Mich., 1989-92; hearing panelist Atty. Discipline Bd., 1987—. Fellow Am. Coll. Trial Lawyers, Am. Bar Found., Oakland County Bar Found. (charter, trustee 1994—, pres. 2002-03), Mich. State Bar Found., Internat. Acad. Trial Lawyers, Internat. Soc. Barristers; mem. ABA (chair litigation sect., Detroit graphic subcom. of com. on complex crimes litigation 1990), FBA (exec. bd. dirs. Detroit chpt. 1988-96, pres. 1995-96, Leonard R. Gilman award 1995), Am. Bd. Trial Advocates, Am. Arbitration Assn. (mem. hearing panel 1990), State Bar Mich. (rep. assembly 1986-92, mem. grievance com. 1990—, chair 1993-97, bd. commrs. 1998—, treas. 2001-02, sec. 2002-03, v.p. 2003-04, pres.-elect 2004-05, pres. 2005-06), Oakland County Bar Assn. (chair CLE com. 1992, bd. dirs. 1994-03, Disting. Svc. award 1996, chair membership com. 1997), Am. Bar Found. Republican. Presbyterian. Office: Miller Canfield Paddock & Stone PLC Ste 2500 150 W Jefferson Ave Detroit MI 48226 Home: 4739 Sandpiper Ln West Bloomfield MI 48323-2063 Home Phone: 248-682-0589; Office Phone: 248-267-3381. Business E-Mail: cranmer@millercanfield.com.

CRANSTON, STEWART E., career officer; BA in Math., U. So. Calif., 1966; MBA, Auburn U., 1979; Grad., Air Command and Staff Coll., 1979; Diploma, Indsl. Coll. of Armed Forces, 1986; postgrad., Carnegie-Mellon U., 1989. Commd. 2d lt. USAF, 1966, advanced through ranks to lt. gen., 1997; various assignments to dep. chief of staff, test and opers. Hdqtrs. Air Force Material Command, Wright-Patterson AFB, Ohio, 1992-93; comdr. Air Force Devel. Test Ctr./Air Force Material Command, Eglin AFB, Fla., 1993-97; vice-comdr. Hdqtrs. Air Force Material Comman, Wright-Patterson AFB, Ohio, 1997—. Decorated Disting. Svc. medal, Legion of Merit, Disting. Flying Cross, Meritorious Svc. medal with four oak leaf clusters, Air medal with 15 oak leaf clusters, Air Force Commendation medal with oak leaf cluster, Republic of Vietnam Gallantry Cross with Palm, Vietnam Svc. medal with four svc. stars, others. Office: AFMC/CV 4375 Chidlaw Rd Ste 1 Wright Patterson AFB OH 45433-5066

CRAVEN, GEORGE W., lawyer; b. Louisville, Mar. 11, 1951; s. Mark Patrick and Doris Ann Craven; m. Jane A. Gallery, Aug. 16, 1980; children: Charles, Francis. Student, Sophia U., Tokyo, Japan, 1970-71; BA, U. Notre Dame, 1973; JD, Harvard U., 1976. Bar: Ill. 1976, U.S. Dist. Ct. (no. dist.) Ill. 1976, U.S. Tax Ct. 1977. Assoc. Sidley & Austin, Chgo., 1976—80; ptnr. Ogden & Robertson, Louisville, 1980—81; assoc. Mayer Brown, LLP, Chgo., 1981—82, ptnr., 1983—. Sec., United Way, Chgo., 1997—2003, gen. counsel 2003-. Mem. ABA (sect. taxation), Coun. on Global Affairs (Chgo. com. 1996—), Econ. Club Chgo. Roman Catholic. Office: Mayer Brown Rowe & Maw LLP 71 S Wacker Dr Chicago IL 60606-4637 Office Phone: 312-701-7231. E-mail: gcraven@mayerbrown.com.

CRAWFORD, DANIEL J., biologist, educator; PhD, U. Iowa. Prof. evolution, ecology and orgnl. biology Ohio State U., Columbus. Recipient Asa Gray award Am. Soc. Plant Taxonomists, 1997. Office: Ohio State U 386 B&Z Bldg 1735 Neil Ave Columbus OH 43210

CRAWFORD, DEWEY BYERS, lawyer; b. Saginaw, Mich., Dec. 22, 1941; s. Edward Owen and Ruth (Wentworth) C.; m. Nancy Elizabeth Eck, Mar. 24, 1973. AB in Econs., Dartmouth Coll., 1963; JD with distinction, U. Mich., 1966. Bar: Ill. 1967, U.S. Dist. Ct. (no. dist.) Ill. 1969. Assoc. Gardner, Carton & Douglas LLP, Chgo., 1969-74, ptnr., 1975—. Adj. prof. law, ITT, Kent Sch. Law, 1992—. Contbr. articles to profl. jours. Chmn. Winnetka (Ill.) Caucus Coun., 1988-89; governing mem. Chgo Symphony, Chgo. Bot. Garden; bd. govs. Winnetka Cmty. House. With U.S. Army, 1966-68, Vietnam. Mem. ABA, Chgo. Bar Assn., Am. Coll. Investment Counsel, Lawyers Club Chgo., Exec. Club Chgo. Republican. Congregationalist. Avocations: reading, music. Office: Gardner Carton & Douglas LLP 191 N Wacker Dr Ste 3700 Chicago IL 60606-1698 Office Phone: 312-569-1111. Business E-Mail: dcrawford@gcd.com.

CRAWFORD, EDWARD E., consumer products company executive; Owner Cleve. Steel Container, 1963; pres., CEO Pk.-Ohio Industries Inc., Cleve., 1992—, also chmn. bd. dirs. Office: Pk Ohio Holdings 23000 Euclid Ave Cleveland OH 44117-1729

CRAWFORD, HOWARD ALLEN, lawyer; b. Stafford, Kans., Aug. 4, 1917; s. Perry V. and Kate (Allen) C.; m. Millie Houseworth, Oct. 9, 1948; children: Catherine, Edward BS, Kans. State U., 1939; JD, U. Mich., 1942. Bar: Kans. 1942, Mo. 1943, U.S. Ct. Appeals (8th, 10th and D.C. cirs.), U.S. Supreme Ct. Mem. firm Lathrop and Gage, Kansas City, Mo., 1950-91; mng. ptnr. Lathrop and Norquist, Kansas City, Mo., 1970-85, ret., 1991. Dir. various cos. Mem. coun. City of Mission Hills, Kans., 1965-70 Mem. Lawyers Assn. Kansas City, Kansas City Club, Mission Hills Country Club. Office: Lathrop and Gage 2345 Grand Blvd Fl 25 Kansas City MO 64108-2603 Home: 8101 Mission Rd Apt 120 Prairie Village KS 66208-5245

CRAWFORD, JAMES WELDON, psychiatrist, educator, administrator; b. Napoleon, Ohio, Oct. 27, 1927; s. Homer and Olga (Aderman) C.; m. Susan Young, July 5, 1955; 1 child, Robert James AB, Oberlin Coll., 1950; MD, U. Chgo., 1954, PhD, 1961. Intern Wayne County Hosp. and Infirmary, Eloise, Mich., 1954-55; resident orthwestern U., Chgo., 1958-59, Mt. Sinai Hosp./Chgo. Med. Sch., 1959-60; practice medicine specializing in occupational, individual and family psychiatry Chgo., 1961—. Mem. staff Rush St. Lukes-Presbyn. Med. Ctr.; clin. assoc. prof. dept. psychiatry Sch. of Medicine, U. Ill. at Chgo., 1970—; chair and assoc. prof. dept. psychiatry Ravenswood Hosp. Med. Ctr., 1973-79; chmn. J.W. Crawford Assocs., Inc., 1979-82; assoc. prof. depts. behavioral scis. and psychiatry Rush U. Med. Ctr. Contbr. articles to profl. jours. Bd. dirs. Pegasus Players, Chgo., 1978—96, chmn. bd. dirs., 1979-84; bd. dirs. Bach Soc., 1985-98; adv. Ill. Masonic Med. Ctr.; health adv. com. Cook County (Ill.) Commr., 2003—; del. to Russia and the Ukraine with People-to-People Internat., 1993, del. to Kenya, 1995, del. to China, 1998. NIH Inst. Neurol. Diseases postdoctoral fellow, 1955-59. Fellow Am. Psychiat. Assn. (life, dist. mem.), Am. Orthopsychiat. Assn.; mem. AAAS, Am. Soc. Psychoanalytic Physicians, Nat. Coalition Mental Health Profls. and Consumers, Ill. Coalition Mental Health Profls. and Consumers (steering com.), Ill. Psychiat. Soc., Chgo. Assn. for Psychoanalytic Psychology, Nat. Coun. on Family Rels., Rotary (com. mem. profl. rep.), Sigma Xi. Achievements include research in dendritic field and EEG. Home and Office: 2418 Lincoln St Evanston IL 60201-2151 Office Phone: 847-869-3108. Personal E-mail: sjcrawf@aol.com.

CRAWFORD, LEWIS CLEAVER, engineering executive, researcher; b. Salina, Kans., Dec. 7, 1925; s. Percival Wallace and Viva Estelle (Beichle) C.; m. Helen Alleyne Henry, May 28, 1950; children: Dorothy Caroline, Lewis Henry. B in Engring., Yale U., 1946. Registered profl. engr., Kans. Engr. Cemenstone Corp., Pitts., 1946-47; engr., then assoc. Wilson & Co. (engrs. and architects), Salina, 1947-67, ptnr., 1967-87, Western Properties and Cenwest Partnerships, 1992—. Served with USNR, 1943-46. Fellow ASCE; mem. NSPE, SAR, Flagon and Trencher, Kans. Cons. Engrs. (past chmn.), Kans. Engring. Soc. (past. dir.), Salina Country Club. Republican. Methodist. Office: Board of Trade Bldg 1700 E Iron Salina KS 67401-5101

CRAWFORD, RICHARD DWIGHT, biology professor, researcher; b. Kirksville, Mo., Nov. 16, 1947; s. John Barton and Ethel May (Kirkpatrick) C.; m. Glinda Carol Bloskovich, Dec. 30, 1966; 1 child, Melanie Contessa. BS in Edn., N.E. Mo. State U., 1968, MS, 1969; PhD, Iowa State U., 1975. Instr. Iowa State U., Ames, 1973-75; asst. prof. U. N.D., Grand Forks, 1975-80, assoc. prof., 1980-81, assoc. prof., biology chmn., 1981-82, assoc. prof., 1982-88, prof. and chair, 1988-91, prof., 1991—. Cons. U.S. Fish and Wildlife Svc., Jamestown, N.D., 1977, Three Tribes Indian Reservation, New Town, N.D., 1982. Author: (with others) Wildlife in Southwest North Dakota, 1978; editor: Wildlife Values of Sand and Gravel Pits, 1982; contbr. articles to profl. jours. Served with U.S. Army, 1969-71. Recipient B.C. Gamble award U. N.D. Alumni Found., 1983. Mem. Wildlife Soc. (assoc. editor 1981-83, pres. N.D. chpt. 1981-82, nat. com. wetland mitigation and categorization 1993, N.D. Profl. award 1992), Am. Ornithologists Union (life), Wilson Ornithol. Soc. (life). Avocations: wood carving, gardening, fishing. Office: U ND Dept Biology Grand Forks ND 58202-9019 E-mail: richard_crawford@und.nodak.edu.

CRAWFORD, ROBERT W., JR., furniture rental company executive; b. Yonkers, NY, Oct. 19, 1938; BS, Dickinson Coll., 1960; MBA, U. Pa., 1963. Founder, chmn., CEO Brook Furniture Rental, Inc., Lake Forest, Ill. Trustee Field Mus. Inductee Chicagoland Entrepreneurial Hall of Fame, 1998. Mem. Nat. Recreation Found. (chmn., trustee), Internat. Furniture Rental Assn. (chmn., bd. dirs.), Chicagoland C. of C. (chmn. bd. dirs.), The Chgo. Club, The CEO Club, Execs. Club Chgo., Comml. Club Chgo., Econ. Club Chgo., Phi Kappa Sigma (Alumnus of Yr. award). Office: Brook Furniture Rental Inc 100 Field Dr Ste 220 Lake Forest IL 60045 E-mail: rwc@bfr.com.

CRAWLEY, VERNON OBADIAH, academic administrator; b. Oct. 22, 1936; s. Joseph and Ruth (Adkins) C.; m. Betty W. Wood, July 9, 1966; children: V. Alan, Vonda, Keith. BS in Chemistry, Va. State U., 1958; postgrad., Coll. William and Mary, 1962, Am. U., 1964; MEd, U. Va., 1965; EdD, Pa. State U., 1971. Chemist Stuart Products Co., Richmond, Va., 1958-61; tchr. sci. and math. Ruthville (Va.) High Sch., 1961-64; asst. prof. sci. dept. Morgan State U., Balt., 1965-69; instr. phys. sci. Towson State Coll., Balt., 1969; assoc. prof. chemistry, chmn. sci., math. and technologies Dundalk C.C., Balt., 1971-74; assoc. dean acad. affairs Mercer County C.C., Trenton, N.J., 1974-78; pres. St. Louis C.C. at Forest Park, 1978-91, Moraine Valley C.C., Palos Hills, Ill., 1991—. Acting dean James Kerney campus Mercer County C.C., Trenton, 1976-77; adminstrv. specialist in sci. NASA, Washington, summer 1966, 67, 68; cons. N. Cen. Assn., Coro Found. Adv. bd. mem. St. Francis Hosp., Blue Island, Ill.; fin. adv. com. mem. Ill. C.C. Bd.; chmn. Ill. Coun. C.C. Pres.; bd. dirs. Southwest YMCA, Alsip, Ill. Recipient Outstanding Svc. to Williams Cmty. Sch. award 8th Dist. Police Cmty.Youth Network Com., 1990, Assistance with Minority Tchr. Recruitment Program award St. Louis Area Pers. and Place Adminstrs., 1989, Outstanding Leadership award Nat. Coun. Black Am. Affairs, 1987, Citizenship award Wellston Sch. Dist., 1983, NSF Acad. Yr. award, 1964-65, Southern fellowship, 1965. Mem. League for Innovation in C.C. (bd. dirs.), Expanding Leadership Opportunities for Minorities in C.C. (nat. adv. group), Am. Assn. C.C. (bd. dirs., exec. bd.), Nat. Coun. on Black Am. Affairs (bd. dirs.), Econ. Devel. Corp. for Southwest Suburbs (bd. dirs.), Rotary Club Oak Lawn, Moraine Valley C.C. Found. (bd. dirs.), Mo. Assn. Community and Jr. Colls. (bd. dirs.), Mo. Coun. C.C. Pres./Chancellors (chmn. 1986-87, v.p. 1985-86, sec. treas. 1984-85), Sigma Xi, Phi Theta Kappa. Avocations: travel, reading, gardening. Home: 7841 Sioux Rd Orland Park IL 60462-1894 Office: Moraine Valley CC 10900 S 88th Ave Palos Hills IL 60465-2175

CRAYCRAFT, ALLIE V., JR., state legislator; b. Mt. Sterling, Ky., May 30, 1932; m. Juanita Craycraft. Material mgr. Detroit Diesel Allison; with Hydra-Matic, Muncie, Ind.; mem. Ind. Senate from 26th dist., 1979—; ranking minority mem., ethics com.; mem. govt. and regulatory affairs com. Ind. State Senate, mem. transp. and interstate coop. com., mem. legis. appointment and elec. com., ranking minority mem. pensions/labor com., pub. policy com. Precinct committeeman, 1968—; trustee Liberty Twp., 1970-74; mem. Delaware County Welfare Bd., 1970-78; chmn. Delaware County chpt. Am. Heart Assn.; mem. Liberty-Perry Athletic Booster Club. Mem. Amvets (chmn. Delaware County chpt.), Muncie Lions. Office: 9501 E Jackson St Selma IN 47383-9599 also: State Senate State Capitol Indianapolis IN 46204

CRAYPO, CHARLES, labor economics professor; b. Jackson, Mich., Jan. 3, 1936; s. Norman Laverne and Ann Marie (Bogdan) C.; m. Mary Louise Vaclavik, Sept. 6, 1958; children: Jack, Carrie, Susan. BA in Econs., Mich. State U., 1959, MA in Econs., 1961, PhD in Econs., 1966. Asst. prof. econs. U. Maine, Orono, 1966-67; assoc. prof. Mich. State U., East Lansing, 1967-72, Pa. State U., University Park, 1972-78, U. Notre Dame, Ind., 1978-82, prof. Ind., 1984-2000, prof., chmn. dept. econs. Ind., 1984-93; prof. Cornell U., Ithaca, NY, 1982-84. Bd. dirs. Bus. Devel. Com., South Bend, Ind.; dir. Bur. Workers Edn., U. Maine, Orono, 1966-67, Higgins Labor Rsch. Ctr., U. Notre Dame, 1993; mem. acad. evaluating com. Labor Studies Ctr., Empire State Coll., SUNY, 1980; mem. labor studies dept. Ramapo Coll., 1981; mem. indsl. rels. dept. LeMoyne Coll., Syracuse, N.Y., 1983, Bur. of Labor Edn., U. Maine, Orono; external rev. mem. Divsn. Labor Studies Ind. U., 1998-99; mem. Labor Rsch. Adv. Coun., Bureau Labor Statistics, U.S. Dept. Labor, 2000; lectr. in field; expert witness. Author: Economics of Collective Bargaining, 1986, Grand Designs, 1993; mem. editl. bd., bus. mgr. Labor Studies Jour., 1976-80, chmn. editl. bd., 1980-85; mem. editl. bd. Contbns. to Labor Studies, 1989-97; internat. mem. editl. bd. Indsl. Rels. Jour., 1989-2002; contbr. articles to profl. jours. Mem. acad. adv. com. Divsn. Labor Studies Ind. U., 1978-82, 84-92, 95-96. Served with USMC, 1953-55. Recipient Lilly Endowment, 1992, D. Dority Labor Rsch. Fund, Ganey Rsch. award, 2002; grantee NEH, 1981, Rsch. grant, Dept. Commerce, 1984. Mem.: Indsl. Rels. Rsch. Assn. Home: 50600 Sorrel Dr Granger IN 46530-8506 Office Phone: 574-631-6934. E-mail: craypo.3@nd.edu.

CREAGHEAD, NANCY A., medical association administrator; BA, Denison U., 1965; MS, Purdue U., 1966; PhD, U. Cin., 1978. Cert. speech lang. pathologist. Prof. dept. comm. sci. U. Cin., Cin.; pres.-elect Am. Speech-Lang.-Hearing Assn., Cin., 2002—; dept. head U. Cin. Office: Univ Cincinnati Dept Communication Scis & Disorders G65 French Building East PO Box 670379 Cincinnati OH 45267-0379

CREAN, TOM (THOMAS AARON CREAN), men's college basketball coach; b. Mt. Pleasant, Mich., Mar. 25, 1966; m. Joani Crean; children: Megan, Riley, Ainsley. B in Parks and Recreation, Ctrl. Mich. U., Mt. Pleasant, 1989. Grad. asst. coach Mich. State U. Spartans, 1989—90, asst. coach, 1995—97, assoc. head coach, 1997—99; asst. coach Western Ky. U. Hilltoppers, 1991—94, U. Pitts. Panthers, 1994—95; head coach Marquette U. Golden Eagles, 1999—2008, Ind. U. Hoosiers, 2008—. Finalist Naismith Nat. Coach of Yr. award; recipient Ray Meyer Conf. USA Coach of Yr. award, NABC Dist. XI Coach of Yr. award, USBWA Dist. V Coach of Yr. award, Coach Clair Bee award. Office: Ind U Dept Intercollegiate Athletics Assembly Hall 1001 E 17th St Bloomington IN 47408-1590*

CREMIN, SUSAN ELIZABETH, lawyer; b. Chgo., July 2, 1947; d. William Amberg and Rosemary (Brennan) C. AB cum laude, Vassar Coll., 1969; JD, Northwestern U., Chgo., 1976. Bar: Ill. 1977. Assoc. Winston & Strawn, Chgo., 1976-83, ptnr., 1983-93, capital ptnr., 1993—. Co-author: Registration and Reporting Under the Exchange Act, 1995, 2nd edit., 1996. Trustee The Shedd Aquarium, Chgo., The Masters Sch., Dobbs Ferry, N.Y. Office: Winston & Strawn 35 W Wacker Dr Ste 4200 Chicago IL 60601-1695

CRENNEL, ROMEO, professional football coach; b. Lynchburg, Va. m. Rosemary Crennel; 3 children. BA physical Ed., Western Kentucky Univ, MA. Grad. asst. Western Kentucky Univ., 1970, defensive line coach, 1971—74; defensive asst. Texas Tech Univ., 1975—77; defensive ends coach Univ. of Miss., 1978—79; defensive line coach Ga. Tech Univ., 1980; special teams, defensive asst. coach NY Giants, 1981—82, spl. teams coach, 1983—89, defensive line coach, 1990—92, New England Patriots, 1993—96, NY Jets, 1997—99; defensive coordinator, line coach Cleve. Browns, 2000; defensive coordinator New England Patriots, 2001, 2004, defensive coordinator, defensive line coach, 2002—03; head coach Cleve. Browns, 2005—. Achievements include being a member of Super Bowl Champion ew York Giants, 1986, 1990, New England Patriots, 2001, 2003, 2004. Office: c/o Cleveland Browns 76 Lou Groza Blvd Berea OH 44017

CREW, SPENCER, museum administrator; b. Poughkeepsie, NY, Jan. 7, 1949; s. R. Spencer and Ada Lee (Scott) C.; m. Sandra Lorraine Prioleau, June 19, 1971; children: Alika, Adom. BA, Brown U., 1971; MA, Rutgers U., 1973, PhD, 1979. Asst. prof. U. Md. Baltimore County, Catonsville, 1978-81; historian Nat. Mus. Am. History, Smithsonian Instn., Washington, 1981-87, curator, 1987-89, chmn. dept. social and cultural history, 1989-91, dep. dir., acting dir., 1991-94, dir., 1994—2001; pres., CEO Nat. Underground R.R. Freedom Ctr., 2001—07. Mem. Md. Commn. on Afro-Am. History and Culture, Annapolis, 1990—96; hist. cons. at. Civil Rights Mus., Memphis, 1987-91; cons. Civil Rights Inst., Birmingham, Ala., 1991-94; bd. dirs. Nat. History Day, 1994—98. Exhbns. include Field to Factory: Afro-Am. Migration, 1915-40, 1987 (award 1988), Go Forth and Serve: Black Land Grant Colls., 1990, The American Presidency, 2000. Trustee Brown U., 1995-2001, 07—; adult leader Bapt. Youth Fellowship, St. John Ch., Columbia, Md., 1989-91. Recipient Osceola award Delta Sigma Theta, 1988, Cert. award Smithsonian Instn., 1989, 90, 91, 92, Svc. award Assn. for Study of African Am. Life and History, 1994, Robert A. Brooks award Smithsonian Instn., 1994. Mem. African Am. Mus. Assn. (2d v.p. 1989-91, Lifetime Achievement award 2002), Orgn. Am. Historians (editl. bd. 1989-92), Am. Assn. Mus. (bd. dirs. 1991-96, 2004—), Nat. Coun. History Edn. (trustee 1995-2007), Am. Hist. Assn. (exhibit rev. co-editor 1990-95), Oral History in Mid Atlantic Region (exec. bd. 1987-90). Office: Nat Underground RR Freedom Ctr 50 E Freedom Way Cincinnati OH 45202

CREWS, TERRELL K., agricultural products executive; BS in Acctg., Freed Hardeman U.; M in Mgmt., Kelloggs Exec. M Program. Cost analyst acctg., bus. analysis lead Latin Am. Monsanto, controller Latin Am., fin. lead Asia Pacific -Singapore, gen. auditor, global fin. lead, exec. v.p., CFO, 2000—. Bd. trustees Freed Hardeman U.; bd. dirs. Jr. Achievement of Miss. Valley, Inc.; nat. council John M. Olin Sch. Bus., Washington U. Office: Monsanto 800 N Lindbergh Blvd Saint Louis MO 68167

CRIBBET, JOHN EDWARD, law educator, former university chancellor; b. Findlay, Ill., Feb. 21, 1918; s. Howard H. and Ruth (Wright) C.; m. Betty Jane Smith, Dec. 24, 1941; children: Carol Ann, Pamela Lee. BA, Ill. Wesleyan U., 1940, LLD, 1971; JD, U. Ill., 1947. Bar: Ill. 1947. Pvt. practice in law, Bloomington, Ill., 1947—; prof. law U. Ill., Urbana, 1947-67, dean. Coll. Law, 1967-79; chancellor Urbana-Champaign Campus, U. Ill., 1979-84, Corman prof. law, 1984-88, prof. emeritus, 1988—. Author: Cases and Materials on Judicial Remedies, 1954, Cases on Property, 8th edit., 2002; (with others) Principles of the Law of Property, 1975; (with Corwin Johnson), 3d edit., 1989; editor: U. Ill. Law Forum, 1947-55; contbr. articles to profl. jours. Chmn. com. on jud. ethics Il. Supreme Ct.; pres. United Fund Champaign County, (Ill.), 1962-63; trustee Ill. Wesleyan U.; mem. exec. com. Assn. Am. Law Schs., 1973-75, pres., 1979. Served to maj. AUS, 1941-45. Decorated Bronze Star; decorated Croix de Guerre Mem. ABA, Ill. State Bar Assn., Champaign County Bar Assn., Order of Coif Lodges: Rotary. Office: U Ill Coll of Law 504 E Pennsylvania Ave Champaign IL 61820-6909

CRIHFIELD, PHILIP J., lawyer; b. Chgo., Oct. 3, 1945; BS with highest distinction, Purdue U., 1967; JD with honors, John Marshall Law Sch., 1971. Bar: Ill. 1971, U.S. Patents and Trademark Office 1972. Ptnr. Sidley & Austin, Chgo. Adj. prof. mktg. and pub. policy Northwestern U., 1986—. Mem. Chgo. Bar Assn. (chmn. law, sci., tech. com. 1975). Office: Sidley & Austin 1 S First National Plz Chicago IL 60603-2000

CRIM, FORREST FLEMING, JR., chemist, educator; b. Waco, Tex., May 30, 1947; s. Forrest Fleming Sr. and Almanor Adair (Chapman) C.; m. Scarlett J. Presley, Aug. 10, 2007, m. Joyce Ann Wileman, June 21, 1969 (div.); 1 child, Tracy F. BS, Southwestern U., 1969; PhD, Cornell U., 1974. Staff mem. Engring. Rsch. Ctr. Western Electric Co., Princeton, NJ, 1974-76; postdoctoral staff mem. Los Alamos (N.Mex.) Sci. Lab., 1976-77; from asst. prof. to assoc. prof. Dept. Chemistry U. Wis., Madison, 1977-84, prof. Dept. Chemistry, 1984—. Mem. rev. panel, Dept. of Energy Combustion Rsch. Facility, 1983-85, chmn., 1985, review com., Chemistry Dept., Brookhaven Nat. Lab., 1989; mem. Nat. Rsch. Coun. Workshop on the Chemistry Dept. of the Future, 1987; chmn. Gordon Rsch Conf. on Atomic and Molecular Interactions, 1988; external adv. com. of the Chemical and Laser Scis. Divsn., Los Alamos Nat. Lab., 1990—; rev. com. Associated Univs. Chemistry Dept., Brookhaven Nat. Lab., 1990—; mem. Nat. Rsch. Coun. Panel on Future Opportunities in Atomic, Molecular, and Optical Sci., 1991—. Editorial bd. internat. revs. Phys. Chemistry, 1990—, editorial adv. bd. Ency. of Applied Physics, 1989—, Jour. Phys. Chemistry, 1987-93; contbr. articles to profl. jours. Fellow Alfred P. Sloan Rsch., 1981-83, fellow AAAS, 1995, fellow Am. Acad. Arts and Scis., 1998; named Camille and Henry Dreyfus Tchr.-Scholar, 1982, Helfaer Prof. Chemistry, 1985-91, Robert A. Welch Foun. lectr., 1989, Bayer-Mobay lectr., U. N.H., 1991, Malcolm Dole Disting. lectr., Northwestern U., 2000; recipient Alexander von Humnboldt Sr. U.S. Scientist award, 1986, Southwestern Univ. Alumni Assn. Citation of Merit, 1987, Max Planck award Alexander von Humboldt Soc., 1993. Fellow Am. Phys. Soc. (Earl K. Plyler Prize Selection Com. 1992—, Earle K. Plyler Molecular Physics prize 1998); mem. AAAS, NAS, Am. Chem. Soc. (chmn. Symposium on State-to-State Chemistry 1986, vice-chmn. Phys. Chemistry Div. 1986-87, chmn.-elect 1987-88, chmn. 1988-89, chmn. Task Force to Monitor Jour. of Physical Chemistry 1990-91, Irving Langmuir award in Chemical Physics, 2006), Optical Soc. of Am. (Quantum Electronics and Laser Scis. com. 1990-91). Office: Univ Wis Dept Chemistry 1101 University Ave Madison WI 53706-1322

CRISHAM, THOMAS MICHAEL, lawyer; b. Chgo., June 7, 1939; s. John and Ellen (Moore) C.; m. Catherine Marie Schaab, Oct. 2, 1965; children: Catherine Marie, Megan, Maura. BBA, Loyola U., 1962, JD cum laude, 1965. Bar: Ill. 1965, U.S. Dist. Ct. (no. dist.) Ill. 1965, U.S. Supreme Ct. 1971, U.S. Ct. Appeals (7th cir.) 1978. Ptnr. Hinshaw & Culbertson, Chgo., 1965-95; sr. ptnr. Quinlan & Crisham, Ltd., Chgo., 1996—2001, Crisham & Kubes, Ltd., Chgo., 2001—. Mem. editl. bd. Ins. Outlook, Colorado Springs, Colo., 1990; pres. Def. Rsch. and Trial Lawyers Inst., Chgo., 1989, chmn. bd., 1990; mem. advisors Expert Evidence Reporter, Colorado Springs, 1990. Contbg. author: Abortion and Social Justice, 1973, Human Life: Our Legacy and Our Challenge, 1975, Architect and Engineer Liability: Claims Against Design Professional, 1987, Prosecuting and Defending Insurance Claims, 1989. Bd. dirs. Wendy Will Case Cancer Rsch. Found., Boys' Hope Scholars. Cpl., USMCR, 1959-60. Fellow Am. Coll. Trial Lawyers, Internat. Soc. Barristers; mem. ABA, Advocate Am. Bd. Trial Advs., Internat. Assn. Def. Counsel, Ill. Bar Assn., Trial Lawyers Club Chgo. (pres. 1975-76), Soc. Trial Lawyers Ill., Appellate Lawyers Assn., Assn. Def. Trial Lawyers, Am. Inns of Ct., Chgo. Bar Assn. Roman Catholic. Office: Crisham & Kubes Ltd 30 N Lasalle St Ste 2800 Chicago IL 60602-2511 Office Phone: 312-917-8460. Business E-Mail: tcrisham@crishamlaw.com.

CRISSMAN, PENNY M., state legislator; b. Nov. 20, 1943; m. Charles; children: Mitzi, Mark. Student, Ea. Mich. U., Oakland U. Mayor, Rochester, Mich., 1989-92; rep. Mich. Dist. 45, 1993-98; mem. Rochester City Coun., 1999—. Mem. Rochester City Coun., 1985-92; asst. Rep. whip Mich. Ho. Reps., 1993—, co-chair com. on civil rights & women's issues, edn. com., higher edn. com., local govt. coms., pub. health coms. Recipient disting. citizenship award Rochester Elks, 1992. Mem. Rochester C. of C., Optimists, Oakland U. Press Club. Office: 400 6th St Rochester MI 48307-1400

CRIST, PAUL GRANT, lawyer; b. Denver, Sept. 9, 1949; s. Max Warren and Marjorie Raymond (Catland) C.; m. Christine Faye Clements, June 4, 1972; children: Susan Christine, Benjamin Warren, John Willis. BA, U. Nebr., 1971; JD cum laude, NYU, 1974. Bar: Ohio 1974, US Ct. Mil. Appeals 1975, Calif. 1976, US Dist. Ct. (no. dist.) Ohio 1979, US Ct. Appeals (6th cir.) 1982, US Dist. Ct. (no., ea., so. and ctrl. dists.) Calif. 2003, US Ct. Appeals (9th cir.) 2003. Assoc. Jones, Day, Reavis & Pogue, Cleve., 1974, 78-83, ptnr., 1984—. Rsch. editor NYU Law Rev., 1972-74. Elder Grace Presbyn. Ch. Capt. JAGC USAF, 1974—78. Decorated Meritorious Svc. medal. Fellow Am. Coll. Trial Lawyers; mem. Cleve. Bar Assn., State Bar Calif., Order of Coif. Democrat. Presbyterian. Avocations: golf, reading. Office: Jones Day North Point 901 Lakeside Ave Cleveland OH 44114 Office Phone: 216-586-7139. Business E-Mail: pgcrist@jonesday.com.*

CRIST, WILLIAM MILES, dean, pediatrician, educator; b. Florence, SC, July 21, 1943; s. Harry Brogan and Rosemary (Reid) C.; m. Helen Lucille Valle, June 5, 1971; 1 child, Brian. BA cum laude, Cen. Meth. Coll., 1965; MD, U. Mo., 1969. Intern in pediatrics Mott Children's Hosp., Ann Arbor, Mich., 1969-70; resident fellow in pediatrics and pediatric hematology St. Louis Children's Hosp., 1971-72; trainee Nat. Cancer Inst. Wash. U. Sch. Medicine, St. Louis, 1974-75; asst. prof. pediatrics U. Ala., Birmingham, 1975-78; assoc. scientist Comprehensive Cancer Ctr. U. Ala., Birmingham, 1975-78; acting dir., then dir. hematology/oncology Children's Hosp. U. Ala., Birmingham, 1976-85; prof. pediatrics, dir. pediatrics, hematology/oncology U. Tenn., Memphis, 1985—2000; chmn. dept. hematology/oncology St. Jude Children's Rsch. Hosp., Memphis, 1985—94, dep. dir., 1994—97; chair dept. pediats. and adolescent medicine Mayo Clinic, Rochester, 1997—2000; dean U. of Missouri-Columbia Sch. of Med., 2000—, Hugh E. & Sarah D. Stephenson dean, 2004—. Mem. Children's Oncology Group, 1976—. Maj. USAF, 1972-74. Mem. Am. Soc. Hematology, Sigma Epsilon Pi, Omicron Delta Kappa. Office: U Missouri Columbia Sch Med One Hospital Dr Columbia MO 65212

CRITELLI, NICHOLAS, lawyer, barrister; b. Des Moines, Iowa, Feb. 15, 1944; BA, Drake U., 1966, JD, 1967. Bar: Iowa 1967, US Supreme Ct. 1971, NY 1990, Eng. and Wales (Barrister Mid. Temple) 1991. Founder, ptnr. Law Chambers of Nicholas Critelli PC, Des Moines, IA, and London, Eng., 1967—. Adj. prof. trial law and practice Drake U., 1980—89. Mem. Civil Justice Reform Act com. US Dist. Ct., 1990—97; mem. adv. com. rules of evidence Iowa Supreme Ct. Recipient InnovAction award, Coll. of Law Practice Mgmt., 2004. Fellow: Soc. Advanced Legal Studies (London), Iowa Criminal Def. Assn. (bd. gov. 1997), Am. Acad. Trial Lawyers, Internat. Soc. Barristers; mem.: Honorable Soc. Blackstone Inn of Ct. (pres. and master of the bench), Honourable Soc. Mid. Temple Inn of Ct. (London), Am. Bd. Trial Advocates, Am. Arbitration Assn., Internat. Bar Assn., ABA (mem. litig. sect., torts and ins.sect., and internat. law sect.), Y State Bar Assn. (mem. litig. sect., mem. internat. law sect.), Iowa Acad. Trial Lawyers (gov. 1981, pres. 1986—87), Iowa State Bar Assn. (chmn. litig. legis. com. 1988—90, chmn. spl. com. on fgn. practice 1989—95, chmn. professionalism com. 1989—96, pres. 2004). Avocation: amateur radio. Office: Critelli Law Ste 950 317 Sixth Ave Des Moines IA 50309-4128 also: Barrister's Chambers 9 Stone Bldgs Lincoln's Inn London WC2A 3NN England

CRITTENDEN, BRUCE A., finance company executive; Exec. v.p. Green Tree Fin. Group, St. Paul, pres., 1998—. Office: Green Tree Fin Corp 1100 Landmark Towers 345 Saint Peter St 11th Fl Saint Paul MN 55102

CRITTENDEN, JOHN CHARLES, engineering educator; b. Nov. 12, 1949; BS in Chem. Engring., U. Mich., 1971, MS in Civil and Environ. Engring., 1972, PhD in Civil and Environ. Engring., 1976. Sr. v.p. Limno-Tech, Inc., Ann Arbor, Mich., 1975-77; asst. prof. civil and environ. engring. Wash. State U., Pullman, 1977-78; asst. prof. civil engring., environ. engring. sect. U. Ill., Urbana, 1978-79, Mich. Tech. U., Houghton, 1979-81, assoc. prof. civil engring., environ. engring. sect., 1981-84, adj. prof. chem. engring., 1981-84, prof. civil and environ. engring., 1984—. Dir. Ctr. for Clean Indsl. and Treatment Techs., Houghton, 1992—; presdl. prof. civil engring. CenCITT Mich. Tech. U., 1988—. Mem. AIChE, ASCE (Rudolph Hering award 1980, Walter L. Huber rsch. prize 1991), Am. Acad. Environ. Engrs., Water Pollution Control Fedn., Internat. Soc. Humic Substances, Assn. Environ. Engring. Profs., Am. Water Works Assn. (publs. award 1989), Am. Chem. Soc. Achievements include patents in field. Office: Mich Tech U Dept Civil & Environ Engr 1400 Townsend Dr Houghton MI 49931-1200

CRITZER, SUSAN L., health products company executive; BSME, Gen. Motors Inst.; MBA, U. Mich. Mgmt., info. sys., quality assurance and engring. positions GM, until 1986; various mgr. engring. and quality assurance positions Becton-Dickinson Corp., 1986-89; various mgmt. positions Davis and Geck divsn. Am. Cyanamid Corp., 1989-95, dir. engring. endosurgery divsn., until 1995; v.p. ops. Integ Inc., St. Paul, 1995-99, pres., CEO, 1999—. Office: Integ Inc 2800 Patton Rd Saint Paul MN 55113-1100 Fax: 651-639-9042.

CROCE, CARLO M., research scientist; b. Milan; MD summa cum laude, U. Rome, 1969. Assoc. scientist Wistar Inst. Biology and Anatomy, Phila., 1970—80; assoc. dir. Wistar Inst., 1980—88; Wistar prof. genetics U. Pa., 1980—88; dir. Fels Inst. Cancer Rsch. and Molecular Biology Temple U., 1988—91; dir. Kimmel Cancer Thomas Jefferson U., 1991—2004; dir. human cancer genetics program and chmn. dept. molecular virology, immunology, and med. genetics Ohio State U., 2004—. Recipient Pezcoller AACR award, Am. Assn. Cancer Rsch., 1999, Charles M. Mott prize, Gen. Motors Cancer Rsch. Found. Mem.: Nat. Acad. Sci., Acad. Nat. Sci. Italy. Office: Ohio State Univ 400 W 12th Ave Columbus OH 43210

CROCKER, DOUGLAS, II, real estate executive; Former pres., CEO Equity Residential Properties Trust, Chgo., mem. bd. dir.; consultant Transwestern Investments, Chgo. Mem. Urban Land Inst., Nat. Multi-Housing Coun., Nat. Multifamily Inst., Nat. Real Estate Com. Mem. Nat. Assn. Real Estate Investment Trusts. Office: Equity Residential Properties Trust 2 N Riverside Plz Ste 450 Chicago IL 60606-2600

CROCKER, STEPHEN L., federal magistrate judge; BA, Wesleyan U., 1980; JD, Northwestern U., 1983. Law clk. to Hon. Barbara Crabb U.S. Dist. Ct. (we. dist.) Wis., Madison, 1983-84; trial atty. D.O.J., 1984-86; asst. U.S. atty. No. Dist. Ill., 1986-90; assoc. Michael, Best & Friedrich, 1990-92; magistrate judge U.S. Dist. Ct. (we. dist.) Wis., Madison, 1992—. Office: US Courthouse 120 N Henry St Madison WI 53703-2559

CROCKETT, JOAN M., retired insurance company executive; B in Polit. Sci., John Carroll Univ., 1972. Underwriter, various positions in human resources Allstate Ins. Co., 1973—94, sr. v.p. human resources, 1994—2008. Bd. dirs. INROADS; adv. bd. Univ. Ill. Chgo. Internat. Student Exchange Program; ptnr., bd. dirs. Ctr. for Human Resource Mgmt. Univ. Ill., gov. coun. Good Shepherd Hosp., Barrington, Ill. Named Human Resource Exec. of Yr., Human Resource Exec. mag., 1997. Mem.: Nat. Acad. Human Resources.

CROFTS, ANTONY RICHARD, biochemistry and biophysics educator; b. Harrow, Eng., Jan. 26, 1940; came to U.S., 1978; s. Richard Basil Iliffe and Vera Rosetta (Bland) C.; m. Paula Anne Hinds-Johnson, June 7, 1969 (div. 1981); 1 child, Charlotte Victoria Patricia; 1 adopted child, Rupert Charles; m. Christine Thompson Yerkes, Dec. 23, 1982; children: Stephanie Boynton, Terence Spencer. BA, U. Cambridge, Eng., 1961, PhD, 1965. Asst. lectr. dept. biochemistry U. Bristol, Eng., 1964-65, lectr., 1966-72, reader, 1972-78; prof. biophysics U. Ill., Urbana-Champaign, 1978—, prof. microbiology, 1992-99, chmn. biophysics divsn., 1978-91, assoc. dean Coll. Liberal Arts & Scis., 1996-98, prof. biochemistry, 1998—. Mem. organizing com. 4th Internat. Congress Photosynthesis, Reading, Eng., 1977, 7th Internat. Congress Photosynthesis, Providence, 1986, Table Ronde, Rousel-UCLA Forum, Paris, 1985; vis. prof. Coll. de France, 1983; Lans Ernster Meml. Lecture, Stockholm U., 2005; lectr. in field. Contbr. numerous articles, revs., etc., in area of biophysics, photosynthesis and bioenergetics; mem. editl. bd. Biochem. Jour., U.K., 1971-72, Biochimica Biophysica Acta, Holland, 1972-77, jour. Bacteriology, 1979-83, Archives Biochemistry and Biophysics, 1980-85. Major scholar nat. sci. U. Cambridge, 1958-61, U. Ill. scholar, 1989-92; grantee U.S. Dept. Energy, 1982-96, Guggenheim Found., 1985, NSF, NIH, U.S. Dept. Agr., 1979—. Fellow AAAS; mem. Biophys. Soc., Am. Soc. Biochemistry and Molecular Biology, Am. Soc. Plant Physiologists (Charles F. Kettering award 1992). Avocations: windsurfing, skiing, fishing, sailing, philosophy. Office: U Ill Dept Biochemistry 419 Roger Adams Lab Box B4 600 S Mathews Ave Urbana IL 61801-3602 Office Phone: 217-333-2043. Business E-Mail: a-crofts@life.uiuc.edu.

CROMWELL, AMANDA CARYL, former soccer player, coach; b. Washington, June 15, 1970; BS in Biology, U. Va., 1992. Head women's soccer coach U. Md.; head coach U. Ctrl. Fla. Mem. U.S. Women's Nat. Soccer Team, 1991—, U.S. Team CONCAFCAF Qualifying Tournament, Haiti, 1991, Montreal, Canada, 94; mem. silver medal U.S. Team 1993 World Univ. Games, Buffalo; alternate gold medal U.S. Olympic Team; mem. 3d place U.S. Team, 1995 FIFA Women's World Cup, Sweden; mem. Hammarby Soccer Club, Stockholm, 1994, SA United Soccer Club of Fairfax, Va., 1997. Named NSCAA All-Am. (twice), Soccer Am. Freshman of Yr., H.S. Rookie of Yr., 1990. Office: US Soccer Fedn 1801-1811 S Prairie Ave Chicago IL 60616

CRONIN, DAN, state legislator; b. Elmhurst, Ill., Nov. 7, 1959; BA, Northwestern U., 1981; JD, Loyola U., 1985. Campaign coord. Congressman John E. Porter, 1981; law clk. spl. prosecution divsn. Ill. Atty. Gen. Office, 1983; minority leader Ill. Ho. of Reps., 1985-87; with DuPage County State's Atty.'s Office, 1987-89; Ill. State sen. Dist. 39, 1993—. Mem. Elem. and Secondary Edn., Gen. Svcs. Appropriations and Health Care Coms.; atty. Kemp & Capanna, Ltd., Oak Brook, Ill. Mem. YMCA. Mem. ABA, ATLA,Ill. Bar Assn., DuPage County Bar Assn., Am. Cancer Soc., Lions, KC. Home: 313 S Main St Lombard IL 60148-2631

CRONIN, JAMES WATSON, physicist, researcher; b. Chgo., Sept. 29, 1931; s. James Farley and Dorothy (Watson) Cronin; m. Annette Martin, Sept. 11, 1954; children: Catheryn, Emily, Daniel Watson. AB, So. Methodist U., 1951; PhD, U. Chgo.; D (hon.), U. Paris, 1995, U. Leeds, 1996, Univ. Pierre & Marie Curie, 1994; DSc (hon.), U. Leeds, 1996. Asst. physicist Brookhaven Nat. Lab., 1955—58; asst. prof. Princeton, 1958—65, prof. physics, 1965—71; prof. physics and astronomy to prof. emeritus U. Chgo., 1971—. Loeb lectr. physics Harvard U., 1967; participant early devel. spark chambers; co-discoverer CP-violation, 64; lectr. ashima Found., 1993; rschr. Internat. Ctr. Sci. Rsch. Contbr. articles to sci. jours. Decorated chevalier Legion of Honor (France); recipient Rsch. Corp. Am. award, 1967, John Price Wetherill medal, Franklin Inst., 1976, E.O. Lawrence award, ERDA, 1977, Nobel prize for Physics, 1980, Nat. medal of Sci., 1999; fellow Guggenheim, 1982—83; Sloan fellow, 1964—66, Guggenheim fellow, 1970—71. Fellow: Third World Acad. Scis. (assoc.); mem.: NAS (coun. mem.), Royal Soc. UK (fgn.), Russian Acad. Sci. (fgn.), Am. Phys. Soc., Am. Acad. Arts and Scis., Am. Philos. Soc. Achievements include showing that in rare instances subatomic particles called K mesons violate CP symmetry during their decay. Office: U Chgo Enrico Fermi Inst 5630 S Ellis Ave Chicago IL 60637-1433 E-mail: jwc@uchep.uchicago.edu.

CRONIN, KATHLEEN M., mercantile exchange executive, lawyer; b. Montclair, NJ, 1963; BA cum laude, Boston Coll., 1985; JD cum laude, Northwestern U., 1989. Bar: Ill. 1989. Chief counsel corp. fin. Sara Lee Corp., 1995—97; corp. atty. Skadden, Arps, Slate, Meagher & Flom, 1989—95, 1997—2002; corp. sec., acting gen. counsel Chgo. Mercantile Exch. Holdings Inc., 2002—03, mng. dir., gen. counsel, corp. sec., 2003—07, CME Group Inc. (formerly Chgo. Mercantile Exch. Holdings Inc.), 2007—. Office: CME Group Inc 20 S Wacker Dr Chicago IL 60606 Office Phone: 312-930-1000. Office Fax: 312-930-3323.

CRONIN, PATRICK G., financial executive; BS in Math. and Computer Scis., Moravian Coll., 1982. Ea. region dist. mgr. AT&T CS; v.p. worldwide profl. svcs. NCR Corp., Dayton, Ohio, 1991—, now sr. v.p. fin. solutions group. Office: NCR Corp 1700 S Patterson Blvd Dayton OH 45479-0002

CRONIN, PATTI ADRIENNE WRIGHT, state agency administrator; b. Chgo., May 25, 1943; d. Rodney Adrian and Dorothy Louise (Thiele) Wright; m. Kevin Brian Cronin, May 1, 1971; 1 child, Kevin. BA, Beloit Coll., Wis., 1965; JD with honors, U. Wis., 1983. Vol. Peace Corps, Turkey, 1965-67, recruiter Washington, 1967-68; tchr. English Kamehameha III Sch., Lahaina, Hawaii, 1968-70, Evansville (Wis.) High Sch., 1972-77; tchr. math. and history Killian Sch., Hartford, Wis., 1977-78; tchr. English Kaiser High Sch., Honolulu, 1979-80; intern Wis. Ct. Appeals, Madison, 1983; exec. dir. Wis. Waste Facility Siting Bd., Madison, 1983—. Founder, v.p., bd. dirs. Justice Ctr. Honolulu, 1979-82; sec., treas. Cronin Constrn. Co., Inc., Madison, 1986—. Editor: Internat. Law Jour., 1982. Bd. dirs. eighborhood Bd., Honolulu, 1979-82; chmn. United Way, 1989—; active Parent Citizens Adv. Coun. Recipient Mayor's award of outstanding achievement, City of Honolulu, 1980. Mem. Soc. Profls. in Dispute Resolution, ABA, State Bar Wis. Avocations: real estate, travel. Office: Waste Facility Siting Bd 201 W Washington Ave Madison WI 53703-2760 E-mail: patti.cronin@wfs.state.wi.us.

CRONON, WILLIAM, history professor; b. New Haven, Sept. 11, 1954; m. Nancy Elizabeth Fey. BA in History, English with honors, U. Wis., 1976; MA in Am. History, Yale U., New Haven, Conn., 1979, M of Philosophy in Am. History, 1981, PhD in Am. History, 1990; DPhil in Brit. History, Oxford U., 1981; degree (hon.), orthland Coll., Ashland, Wis., 2006. Asst. prof. history Yale U., New Haven, 1981-86, assoc. prof., 1986-91, prof., 1991-92, mem. studies in environment program creation com., 1983-84, co-chair studies environment program, 1989-92, dir. grad. studies, history dept., 1990-92; Frederick Jackson Turner chair of history, geography, and environ. studies U. Wis., Madison, 1992—, dir. honors program Coll. Letters and Sci., 1996-98, Frederick Jackson Turner and Vilas rsch. prof. history, geography and environ. studies, 2003—; found. fac. dir. Chadbourne Residential Coll., 1997-2000. Asst. Am. sec. Rhodes Scholarship Trust, 1978-80, Wis. state sec., 1993-98; cons. in field; adv. bd. The History Tchr., 1986-2000. Rhodes Dist. chmn., 2002-. Author: Changes in the Land: Indians, Colonists and the Ecology of New England, 1983 (Valley Forge honor cert. 1984, Soc. Colonial award citation of honor 1984, Francis Parkman prize 1984), Nature's Metropolis: Chicago and the Great West, 1991 (Chgo. Tribune Heartlaand prize 1991, Bancroft prize 1992, George Perkins Marsh prize 1993); editor: (with Miles and Gitlin) Under an Open Sky: Rethinking America's Western Past, 1992, Uncommon Ground: Rethinking the Human Place in ature, 1995; mem. bd. editors Forest and Conservation History, 1986-91; also articles; gen. editor Weyerhaeuser Environ. Books, U. Wash. Press, 1993—. Bd. dirs. Conn. Fund for Environ., 1986-91, v.p., 1987-89; adv. bd. TV series Am. Experience Sta. WGBH-TV; trustee Conn. Nature Conservancy, 1989-91; bd. dirs., mem. com. on problems and policy Social Sci. Rsch. Coun., 1991-96, chmn. com. on problems and policy, 1994-96. Rhodes scholar Oxford U., 1976-78; fellow Danforth Found., 1976-82, Newberry Libr., 1980, Mellon Found., 1982-83, Morse fellow Yale U., 1985-86, MacArthur Found., 1985-90, Whitney Humanities Ctr., 1987-89, fellow U. Calif. Humanities Rsch. Inst., 1994, Guggenheim fellow, 1995. Fellow AAAS, Wis. Acad. Sci., Arts and Letters; mem. Am. Hist. Assn. (Robinson prize com. 1990), Am. Philos. Soc. (v.p. profl. divsn. 2002—), Orgn. Am. Historians (chmn. Curti prize com. 1987-88), Forest History Soc. (bd. dirs.), Econ. History Assn., Agrl. History Soc., Ecol. Soc. Am., We. Hist. Assn. (conv. program com. 1987, chmn. 1991-92), Assn. Am. Geographers, Am. Studies Assn., Am. Anthrop. Assn., Wilderness Soc. (gov. coun. 1995—), Am. Soc. for Ethnohistory, Chgo. Hist. Soc., Am. Antiquarian Soc., Soc. Am. Historians, Phi Beta Kappa (William C. DeVane award Yale chpt. 1988), Phi Kappa Phi, Phi Eta Sigma; fellow Am. Acad. Arts & Sciences Office: U Wis Dept History 3211 Humanities 455 N Park St Madison WI 53706-1405 Home: 2027 Chadbourne Ave Madison WI 53726-4046 Office Phone: 608-265-6023. Business E-Mail: wcronon@wisc.edu.

CROOKS, NEIL PATRICK, state supreme court justice; b. Green Bay, Wis., May 16, 1938; s. George Merrill and Aurelia Ellen (O'Neill) C.; m. Kristin Marie Madson, Feb. 15, 1964; children: Michael, Molly, Kevin, Kathleen, Peggy, Eileen. BA magna cum laude, St. Norbert Coll., 1960; JD, U. Notre Dame, 1963. Bar: Wis. 1963, U.S. Supreme Ct. 1969. Assoc. Cohen and Parins, Green Bay, 1963; ptnr. Cohen, Grant, Crooks and Parins, Green Bay, 1966-70; sr. ptnr. Crooks, Jerry, orman and Dilweg, Green Bay, 1970-77; judge Brown County (Wis.) Ct., 1977-78, Brown County (Wis.) Cir. Ct., 1978-96; justice Wis. Supreme Ct., Madison, 1996—. Instr. bus. law U. Wis., Green Bay, 1970-72; mem. faculty Wis. Jud. Coll., 1982. Editor Law Rev. Notre Dame, 1962-63. Pres. Brown County United Way, 1976-78; chmn. Brown County Legal Aid, 1971-73; mem. Northeast Criminal Justice Coord. Coun., 1973-85; pres. St. Joseph Acad. Sch. Bd., 1987-89. Capt. U.S. Army, 1963-66. Recipient Human Rights award Baha'i Community of Green Bay, 1971, Disting. Achievement award in Social Sci. St. Norbert Coll., 1977 award of Yr. U. Notre Dame, 1978, Brown County Vandalism Prevention Assn. award, 1982, W. Heraly MacDonald award Brown County United Way, 1983, Community Svc. award St. Joseph Acad., 1989, Alma Mater award St. Norbert Coll., 1992, Disting. Alumnus of Yr. award Notre Dame Acad., 2002; named Wis. Trial Judge of the Year Wis. Chpt. Am. Bd. of Trial Advocates, 1994. Mem. ABA (law sch. evaluator legal edn. and admissions sect.), FBA, State Bar Wis., Brown County Bar Assn. (pres. 1977), Wis. Acad. Trial Lawyers, Wis. Law Found. (bd. dirs., mem. exec. com.), Assn. of Women Lawyers for Brown County, Dane County Bar Assn., James E. Doyle Am. Inn of Ct., Wis. Jud. Coun., Notre Dame Law Assn. (dir.). Roman Catholic. Office: PO Box 1688 State Capitol 16 E Madison WI 53701 Home Phone: 608-222-6568; Office Phone: 608-266-1883. E-mail: patrick.crooks@wicourts.gov.

CROPSEY, ALAN LEE, state legislator, lawyer; b. Paw Paw, Mich., June 13, 1952; s. Harmon George and Ruth Marian (Lindsay) C.; m. Erika Lynn Rumminger, Nov. 24, 1979; children: Joel Daniel, Gabriel Michael, Nathaniel Samuel, Evamarie Barbara. B of Math. Edn., Bob Jones U., 1975; JD, Cooley Law Sch., 1978. Bar: Mich., 1978. State senator 30th dist. Mich. Senate, 1983-86; state rep. 88th dist. Mich. Ho. of Reps., 1981-82, state rep. 86th dist., 1993-98; internet svc. provider, polit. cons. Freedom ISP, Lansing, Mich., 1999—. Home: 7730 Loomis Rd Dewitt MI 48820-8482

CROPSEY, JOSEPH, retired political science professor; b. NYC, Aug. 27, 1919; s. Gustave and Margaret Cropsey; m. Lillian Crystal Levy, Nov. 4, 1945 (dec.); children: Seth, Rachel Cropsey Simons. AB, Columbia U., 1939, A.M., 1940, PhD, 1952; DHL (hon.), Colo. Coll., 1989. Tutor, asst. prof. CCNY, 1946-57; instr. polit. sci. New Sch. Social Rsch., NYC, 1949-54; asst. prof. U. Chgo., 1958-64, assoc. prof., 1964-70, prof., 1970-85, Disting. Svc. prof., 1985-89, prof. emeritus, 1989—; ret., 1989. Author: Polity and Economy, 1957, Political Philosophy and the Issues of Politics, 1977, Plato's World, 1995; editor: Ancients and Moderns, 1964; co-editor, co-author: History of Political Philosophy, 1963 Served to 1st. lt. U.S. Army, 1941-46, PTO, ETO Office: U Chgo 5828 S University Ave Chicago IL 60637-1515

CROSBIE, ALFRED LINDEN, mechanical engineering educator; b. Muskogee, Okla., Aug. 1, 1942; s. Alfred Henry and Jacquetta Hope (Stoneburner) C.; m. Ann Frances Cirou, July 18, 1963; children: Mark, Jacqueline. BSME, U. Okla., 1964; MSME, Purdue U., 1966, PhD, 1969. Asst. prof. U. Mo., Rolla, 1968-72, assoc. prof., 1972-75, prof., 1975-91, curators' prof., 1991—. Editor: Aerothermodynamics and Planetary Entry, 1981, Heat Transfer and Thermal Control, 1981; editor-in-chief Jour. Thermophysics and Heat Transfer, 1986—; assoc. editor Jour. Quantitative Spectroscopy and Radiative Transfer, 1979—; mem. editl. bd. Heat Transfer-Recent Contents, 1996-2000; mem. adv. bd. Internat. Jour. Thermal Scis., 2000—; contbr. over 80 articles on radiative heat transfer to profl. jours. Fellow AIAA (chmn. thermophysics com. 1984-86, tech. program chmn. 15th Thermophysics Conf. 1980, assoc. editor AIAA Jour. 1981-83, Thermophysics award 1987, Tech. Contbn. award, 1988, Sustained Svc. award 2004), ASME (heat transfer com. on theory and fundamentals 1983—, heat transfer com. on numerical heat transfer 1993—, Heat Transfer Meml. award 1990), AAAS; mem. Optical Soc. Am., Phi Eta Sigma, Sigma Pi Sigma, Tau Beta Pi, Pi Tau Sigma, Sigma Tau, Pi Mu Epsilon, Sigma Xi. Lutheran. Avocation: fishing. Home: 8 Mcfarland Dr Rolla MO 65401-3805 Office: U Mo 233 Mech Engring Rolla MO 65401 Home Phone: 573-364-7669. Business E-Mail: crosbie@umr.edu.

CROSBY, FRED MCCLELLAN, retail executive; b. Cleve., May 17, 1928; s. Fred Douglas and Marion Grace (Naylor) Crosby; m. Phendalyné D. Tazewell, Dec. 23, 1958; children: Fred, James, Llionicia. Grad. HS. V.p. Seaway Flooring & Paving Co., Cleve., 1959-63; chmn., CEO Crosby Furniture Co., Inc., Cleve., 1963—. Vice chmn. bd. dirs. First Bank Nat.; bd. dirs. Budget Rent-A-Car Sys., Surveyors Telecom., Inc.; bd. dirs., chmn. First Intercity Banc Corp. Commr. Nat. Small Bus. Adv. Coun., 1980; bd. dirs. Forest City Hosp. Found., Cleve. State U. Found., Greater Cleve. Growth Assn., 1971—90, 1993—, Coun. Smaller Enterprise, 1973—80, Goodwill Industries, 1973—80, 1997—, Woodruff Hosp., 1975—82, Cleve. Devel. Found., Pub. TV, Sta. WVIZ-TV, Cleve.-Cuyahoga Port Authority, 1986—90; bd. dirs., treas. Urban League Cleve., 1971—78; chmn. Minority Econ. Devel. Corp., 1972—83; chmn. bd. dirs. Glenville YMCA, 1973—76; dir. adv. coun. Ohio Bd. Workmen's Compensation, 1974—82; trustee Cleve. Play House, 1979—87, Eliza Bryant Health Care Ctr., 1984—86, Cleve. Small Bus. Incubator, 1986—90, Better Bus. Bur., 1995—, Ohio Motorist, 1993—, Murtis H. Taylor Mental Health, Metro Hosp. Sys. Found.; mem. adv. coun. Small Bus. Assn.; mem. adv. bd. Salvation Army, 1980; commr. Ohio State Boxing Commn., 1984—94, Pvt. Industry Coun., 1985; county commrs. appointee Cmty. Adv. Bd.; mem. Cleve. Opera Coun., 1987—89; Gov. Voinovich appointee to minority devel. fin. adv. bd., 1996—; bd. advs. Antioch Coll. With US Army, 1950—52. Named Family of the Yr., Cleve. Urban League, 1971; recipient award bus. excellence, Dept. Commerce, 1972, Presdl. award, YMCA, 1974, Gov. Ohio award cmty. action, 1973, 1st Class Leadership, Cleve., 1977. Mem.: NAACP (v.p. Cleve. 1969—78, exec. dir.), Ohio Home Furnishings and Appliance Assn. (pres. 1981—87), Ohio Coun. Retail Mchts. (chmn. 1991—93), Am. Auto Assn. (corp. mem.), Cleve. C. of C., Univ. Club (Cleve.), Braternahl Club, Harvard Bus. Sch. Club, Mid-Day Club, Rotary, Clevelander, Exec. Order Ohio Commodore. Office: 12435 Saint Clair Ave Cleveland OH 44108-2013 Office Phone: 216-541-5040.

CROSBY, JACQUELINE GARTON, newspaper editor, journalist; b. Jacksonville, Fla., May 13, 1961; d. James Ellis and Marianne (Garton) Crosby. ABJ, U. Ga., 1983; MBA, U. Cen. Fla., 1987. Staff writer Macon Telegraph & News, Ga., 1983-84; copy editor Orlando Sentinel, Fla., 1984-85; dir. spl. projects Ivanhoe Communications, Inc., Orlando, Fla., 1987-89; producer spl. projects Sta. KSTP-TV, Mpls., 1989-94; asst. news editor Star Tribune Online, Mpls., 1994—2003, reporter, 2003—. Recipient award for best sports story Ga. Press Assn., 1982; award for best series of yr. AP, 1985, Pulitzer prize, 1985 Mem. Quill Avocations: competing in triathlons, playing electric bass, tutoring, reading. Home: 5348 Drew Ave S Minneapolis MN 55410-2006 Office: Star Tribune 425 Portland Ave Minneapolis MN 55488-0001

CROSBY, LAVON KEHOE STUART, state legislator, civic leader; b. Hastings, Nebr., Apr. 25, 1924; d. Charles William and Kathryn Marie (Farrell) Kehoe; m. Lester Stuart, Oct. 9, 1948 (dec. 1970); children: Mary Stuart Bolin, Michael, Timothy, Frederick Stuart; m. Robert B. Crosby, May 22, 1971. BA, U. Nebr., 1987. Asst. to pres. Hastings Tribune Corp., Nebr., 1941-68; mem. staff U.S. Senator Roman Hruska, Washington, 1968-71; mem. Nebr. State Legislature, 1988—, Appropriations Com., 1988—, Nebr. Retirement Systems com., 1992—, chmn. com. on coms., 1994—. Civic leader; b. Hastings, Nebr., Apr. 25, 1924; d. Charles William and Kathryn Marie (Farrell) Kehoe; m. Lester Stuart, Oct. 9, 1948 (dec. 1970); children— Mary Stuart Bolin, Michael, Timothy, Frederick Stuart; m. Robert B. Crosby, May 22, 1971. BA, U. Nebr., 1987. Asst. to pres. Hastings Tribune Corp., Nebr., 1941-68; mem. staff U.S. Senator Roman Hruska, Washington, 1968-71; mem. Nebr. State Legislature, 1988—; mem. Appropriations Com., 1988—, mem. Nebr. Retirement Systems com., 1992—, chmn. com. on coms., 1994—. Chmn. music com. Cathedral of Risen Christ Choir, Lincoln, Nebr.; pres. Lincoln Community Playhouse Guild; bd. dirs., chmn. membership com. Lincoln Community Playhouse; v.p., bd. dirs. Lincoln Symphony Guild; bd. dirs. Lincoln Symphony Orch. Assn., 1972-82; founder Nebr. Found. for Humanities; mem. Lincoln Symphony Found. Bd., 1984—; bd. dirs. Friends of Ctr. for Great Plains Studies, 1984—; vice chmn. Nebr. Arts Council, 1981-82, chmn., 1982-85; past mem. and sec. Pershing Auditorium Bd.; pres. Nebr. Legis. Ladies League, 1977-78; adv. bd. Cath. social Services Bur.; budget chmn. Nebr. Mother's Assn.; chmn. legis. affairs Diocesan Council Cath. Women; v.p. Heritage League, Lincoln, 1985—; pres. Cornhusker Republican Women, 1974-75. Recipient Mayor's Arts award, Lincoln, 1985, Gov.'s Arts award, Nebr., 1986, YWCA Tribute to Women award, 1993. Mem. Nebr. Club (Lincoln). Chmn. music com. Cathedral of Risen Christ Choir, Lincoln, Nebr.; pres. Lincoln Community Playhouse Guild; bd. dirs., chmn. membership com. Lincoln Community Playhouse; v.p., bd. dirs. Lincoln Symphony Guild; bd. dirs. Lincoln Symphony Orch. Assn., 1972-82; founder Nebr. Found. for Humanities; mem. Lincoln Symphony Found. Bd., 1984—; bd. dirs. Friends of Ctr. for Great Plains Studies, 1984—; vice chmn. Nebr. Arts Council, 1981-82, chmn., 1982-85; past mem. and sec. Pershing Auditorium Bd.; pres. Nebr. Legis. Ladies League, 1977-78; adv. bd. Cath. social Services Bur.; budget chmn. Nebr. Mother's Assn.; chmn. legis. affairs Diocesan Council Cath. Women; v.p. Heritage League, Lincoln, 1985—; pres. Cornhusker Republican Women, 1974-75. Recipient Mayor's Arts award, Lincoln, 1985, Gov.'s Arts award, Nebr., 1986, YWCA Tribute to Women award, 1993. Mem. Nebr. Club (Lincoln). Office: State Legislature Rm 1010 State Capital Lincoln NE 68509

CROSBY, THOMAS MANVILLE, JR., lawyer; b. Mpls., Oct. 9, 1938; s. Thomas M. and Ella (Pillsbury) C.; m. Eleanor Rauch, June 12, 1965; children: Stewart, Brewster, Grant, Brooke. BA, Yale U., 1960, LLB, 1965. Bar: Minn. 1965. Assoc. Faegre & Benson, Mpls., 1965-72, ptnr., 1965—. Served to lt. USNR, 1960—62. Office: Faegre & Benson 2200 Wells Fargo Ctr 90 S 7th St Ste 2200 Minneapolis MN 55402-3901 Office Phone: 612-766-8605. Business E-Mail: tcrosby@faegre.com.

CROSHERE, AUSTIN, professional basketball player; b. LA, May 1, 1975; Student, Providence, 1997. Power forward Ind. Pacers, 1997—. Office: Ind Pacers 125 S Pennsylvania St Indianapolis IN 46204

CROSS, AUREAL THEOPHILUS, geology and botany educator; b. Findlay, Ohio, June 4, 1916; s. Raymond Willard and Myra Jane (Coon) C.; m. Christina Aleen Teyssier, Mar. 11, 1945; children: Timothy Aureal, Christina Avonne Cross Collier, Jonathan Ariel, Cheryl Aleen (Mrs. Richard M. Bowman), Christopher Charles. BA, Coe Coll., 1939; MS in Botany, U. Cin., 1941, PhD in Botany and Paleontology, 1943. Instr. to asst. prof. U. Notre Dame, 1942—46; NRC fellow in geology, 1943—44; paleobotanist; with Ctrl. Expt. Sta., U.S. Bur. Mines, Pitts., 1945; asst. prof. dept. geology U. Cin., 1946—49, asst. prof. dept. botany, 1948—49; part-time geologist Geol. Survey Ohio, 1946—51; coal geologist and paleobotanist W.Va. Geol. and Econ. Survey, 1949—57; assoc. prof. to prof. dept. geology U. W.Va., 1949—57; sr. rsch. engr. Pan Am. Petroleum Corp. Rsch. Center, Tulsa, 1957—61, supr. tech. group and rsch. group, 1959—61; prof. dept. geology Mich. State U., East Lansing, 1961—86, prof. dept. botany and plant pathology, 1961—86, prof. emeritus East Lansing, 1987—. Prof. ecology U. Alaska, 1971; rsch. palynologist U. So. Calif., 1972; Morton vis. prof. Ohio U., Athens Ohio, 1981; Nathaniel S. Shaler Disting. lectr. U. Ky., 1991; UNESCO adviser U. grants commn. India Coal Programs, 1983; Calcutta adviser geology dept. Jadavpur U., India, 1983. Editor: Palynology in Oil Exploration, 1964, Compte Rendu 9th Internat. Congress Carboniferous Stratigraphy and Geology, vol. 4, Econ. Geology: Coal, Oil and Gas, 1985; co-editor: Coal Resources and Research in Latin America, 1978, World Class Coal Deposits, Internat. Jour. Coal Geology, 1993; assoc. editor: Fossil Spores and Pollen, 55 vols, 1956-87; contbr. articles to profl. jours. Chmn. citywide rally Fellowship Christian Athletes, Tulsa, 1960; nat. council U.P. Men, 1966-68, 74-84; active Boy Scouts Am., YMCA, others. Named Several Meml. lectr. Sahni Inst. Palaeobotany, 1985, J. Sen Meml. lectr., 1985, Disting. lectr. Am. Assn. Petroleum Geologists, 1964, Outstanding Educator, Am. Assn. Petroleum Geologists Ea. Sect., 1987, 2005; recipient Gordon H. Wood Jr. Meml. award, 1993, John T. Galey medal, 1995. Mem. Am. Assn. Stratigraphic Palynologists (hon.; medal of Excellence in Edn. 1999), Bot. Soc. Am. (chmn. paleobotany sect. 1953, 77, grantee 1954, Disting. Svc. Paleobotany award 1985), Geol. Soc. Am. (Gilbert H. Cady Coal Geology award 1987, chmn. coal geology divsn. 1966, chmn. North Ctrl. sect. 1969-70, exec. sec. sect. 1971-80, grantee 1951), Soc. Econ. Paleontologists and Mineralogists (chmn. rsch. com. 1961-62, councillor in paleontology 1971-73), Soc. Organic Petrology (John Castano hon. membership award 2005), Am. Assn. Petroleum Geologists (Grover E. Murray Disting. Educator award, 2005), numerous other internat., nat. and regional profl. assns. Presbyterian. Home: 529 N Harrison Rd East Lansing MI 48823-3015 Office: Mich State Univ Dept Geol Scis East Lansing MI 48824 Office Phone: 517-355-4630. Office Fax: 517-353-8787. Business E-Mail: cross1@msu.edu.

CROSS, BRUCE A., food service company executive; Grad., Calif. State U., Sacramento. Technology dir. Safeway; mgr. large info. technology outsourcing contracts IBM Global Svcs.; sr. v.p., pres., chief info. officer Nash Finch Co., Mpls., 1999—. Office: Nash Finch Co 7600 France Ave S Minneapolis MN 55435-5924

CROSS, JEFFREY D., lawyer, electric power industry executive; b. Painesville, Ohio, Apr. 28, 1956; BA summa cum laude, U. Cin., 1978, JD, 1982. Bar: Ohio 1982. Atty. Am. Electric Power Co. Inc., Columbus, Ohio, 1984—87, sr. atty., asst. sec., 1987—94, asst. gen. counsel, 1994—2000, gen. counsel AEP Resources Inc. subsid., 1994, v.p. AEP Resources Inc., 1996, sr. v.p., dep. gen. counsel, 2000, sr. v.p., acting gen. counsel, 2000—01, sr. v.p., gen. counsel, 2001—04, dep. gen. counsel, 2004—. Mem. legal com. Edison Electric. Trustee ProMusica Chamber Orch. Mem.: ABA (vice chair corp. governance com. pub. utility, comm., transp. law sect), Columbus Bar Assn., Ohio State Bar Assn., Energy Bar Assn., Ctrl. Ohio Breathing Assn. (trustee), Phi Beta Kappa. Office: Am Electric Power Co Inc Legal Dept 1 Riverside Plz Columbus OH 43215-2373

CROSS, ROBERT CLARK, journalist; b. Cheboygan, Mich., May 12, 1939; s. Warren Clark and Meryle M. (Allaire) Cross; m. Juju Lien; children: Gabriel Francis, Amy Lien. BA in Journalism, Wayne State U., 1962. Writer, researcher Newsweek mag., 1962; reporter, editor Chgo. Tribune, 1962-66, 67-82, assoc. editor mag., 1973-82, writer, 1982—; reporter Newsday, 1966-67; travel writer, 1992—. Recipient Gold and Silver Lowell Thomas awards Soc. of Am. Travel Writers, 1995, 2000, 04. Office: 435 N Michigan Ave Chicago IL 60611-4066 Business E-Mail: bcross@tribune.com.

CROSS, WILLIAM DENNIS, lawyer; b. Tulsa, Nov. 7, 1940; s. John Howell and Virginia Grace (Ferrell) C.; m. Peggy Ruth Plapp, Jan. 30, 1982; children: William Dennis Jr., John Frederick. BS, U.S. Naval Acad., 1962; JD, NYU, 1969. Bar: N.Y. 1970, U.S. Dist. Ct. (so. and ea. dists.) N.Y. 1970, U.S. Ct. Appeals (2d cir.) 1970, U.S. Supreme Ct. 1974, Calif. 1977, U.S. Dist. Ct. (ctrl. dist.) Calif. 1977, U.S. Ct. Appeals (9th cir.) 1977, U.S. Ct. Appeals (5th, 10th and 11th cirs.) 1981, Mo. 1982, U.S. Dist. Ct. (we. dist.) Mo. 1982, U.S. Ct. Appeals (8th cir.) 1989, U.S. Ct. Appeals (fed. cir.) 1992, U.S. Dist. Ct. Ariz. 1997, U.S. Dist. Ct. Colo. 1997, U.S. Dist. Ct. Kans. 1998. Commd. ensign USN, 1962, advanced through ranks to lt., 1965, resigned, 1966; assoc. Cravath, Swaine & Moore, NYC, 1969-76, Lillick, McHose & Charles, LA, 1976-77; asst. gen. counsel FTC, Washington, 1977-82; of counsel Morrison & Hecker, Kansas City, Mo., 1982-83, ptnr., 1983—2002, Stinson Morrison Hecker, 2002—07; adj. prof. law U. Mo., Kansas City, 2007—. Staff mem. NYU Law Rev., 1967-69, editor, 1968-69; assoc. editor Antitrust Mag. Mem. ABA, Mo. Bar Assn., Assn. Bar City N.Y., Kansas City Bar Assn., Lawyers Assn. Kansas City. Office: Stinson Morrison Hecker LLP 1201 Walnut St STe 2800 Kansas City MO 64106-2150 Home: 5835 Cherokee Dr Mission KS 66205-3315 Office Phone: 816-691-2708. Business E-Mail: dcross@stinsonmoheck.com.

CROSSAN, JOHN ROBERT, lawyer; b. Buckhannon, W.Va., May 31, 1947; s. Thomas Benjamin Jr. and Margaret Windsor (Hicks) C.; m. Monique Margaretha Scheen, Dec. 22, 1973; children: Ashley Margaret, Aubry Kelly. BS with honors, U. Va., 1969; JD, U. Chgo., 1974. Bar: Ill. 1974, U.S. Dist. Ct. (no. dist.) Ill. 1974, (ctrl. dist.) Ill. 1998, U.S. Ct. Appeals (4th and 10th cirs.) 1978, U.S. Ct. Appeals (7th cir.) 1979, U.S. Ct. Appeals (fed. cir.) 1983, U.S. Supreme Ct. 1985, U.S. Ct. Appeals (6th cir.) 1989. Staff atty. Ill. Task Force N.E. Ill. Pub. Transp., Chgo., 1972-73; assoc. Hill, Van Santen, Steadman, Chiara, Chgo., 1973-77; assoc., then ptnr. Cook, Wetzel and Egan, Ltd., Chgo., 1978-88; counsel Willian, Brinks, Hofer, Gilson & Lione, Chgo., 1989-90; ptnr. Brinks, Hofer, Gilson & Lione, Chgo., 1991-97, Chapman and Cutler, LLP, Chgo., 1998—. V.p. Va. Engring. Found., 1998—2000, pres., 2000—02. Author: Quick Guide to the Patent Law, 1994; contbr. articles to profl jours. Pres. aux. bd. Chgo. Architecture Found., 1983-85. Mem. ABA, Am. Intellectual Property Lawyers Assn., Chgo. Yacht Club. Home: 2825 N Cambridge Ave Chicago IL 60657-6018 Office: Chapman and Cutler, LLP 111 W Monroe St Ste 1700 Chicago IL 60603-4080 Home Phone: 773-348-7458; Office Phone: 312-845-3420. Personal E-mail: jrcrossan@hotmail.com. Business E-Mail: crossan@chapman.com.

CROSSER, RICHARD H., real estate company executive; Pres., CEO Crossman Cmtys., Indpls., 1973—. Office: Crossman Communities Inc 9202 N Meridian St Ste 300 Indianapolis IN 46260-1833

CROSSON, FREDERICK JAMES, retired dean, humanities educator; b. Belmar, NJ, Apr. 27, 1926; s. George Leon and Emily (Bennett) Crosson; m. Mary Patricia Burns, Sept. 5, 1953; children: Jessica, Christopher, Veronica, Benedict, Jennifer. BA, Cath. U. Am., 1949, MA, 1950; postgrad., U. Paris, 1951-52; PhD, U. Notre Dame, 1956. From instr. to assoc. prof. U. Notre Dame, Ind., 1953—66, prof., 1966—, O'Hara Disting. prof. philosophy, 1976-84, Cavanaugh Disting. prof. humanities, 1984—98, dean Coll. Arts and Letters, 1968-76. Author: (book) The Modeling of Mind, 1963, Philosophy and Cybernetics, 1967, Science and Contemporary Society, 1967; editor: Review of Politics, 1976—83. With USN, 1943—46. Mem.: North Ctrl. Assn. (exec. commr. 1984—89), Am. Cath. Philos. Assn. (pres. 1990—91), Am. Philos. Assn., Phi Beta Kappa (senator 1982—2000, v.p. 1994—97, pres. 1997—2000). Home: 51997 Heather Cv South Bend IN 46635-1074 Office: Coll Arts and Letters U of Notre Dame Notre Dame IN 46556

CROTHERS, DANIEL J., state supreme court justice; b. Fargo, ND, Jan. 3, 1957; BA, U. ND, 1979, JD, 1982. Bar: N.Mex. 1982, ND 1983. Law clk. NM Ct. Appeals, 1982—83; asst. states atty. Walsh County, ND, 1983; former ptnr. Nilles, Hansen & Davies Ltd., Fargo; justice ND Supreme Ct., 2005—. Adj. real estate law Moorhead State U., 1986—89, natural resources law, 1988. Staff mem. Univ. ND Law Rev., 1980—82. Mem.: ND Bar Assn. (pres. 2001—02). Office: ND Supreme Ct State Capitol Bismarck ND 58505-0530

CROUCH, STEVEN L., mining engineer, dean; b. LA, Apr. 25, 1943; BS, U. Minn., 1966, MS in Mineral Engring., 1967, PhD in Mineral Engring., 1970. Rsch. officer Mining Rsch. Lab. Chamber of Mines of South Africa, Johannesburg, 1968-70; from asst. to assoc. prof. civil and mineral engring. U. Minn., Mpls., 1970-81, prof., 1981—, head dept. civil engring., 1987—97, assoc. dean fin. and planning, 1997, dean Inst. Tech., 2005—. Vis. lectr. dept. applied math. U. Witwatersrand, Johannesburg, South Africa, 1976-77, People's Republic of China, 1983; mem. U.S. NAS Com. on Feasibility of Returning Coal Mine Waste Underground, 1973; mem. NAS Task Force on Underground Engring. at Basalt Waste Isolation Project, 1987; active Sandia Nat. Labs. Yucca Mtn. Site Characterization Project Rock Mechanics Rev. Panel, 1989—; cons. in field. Author: (with A.M. Starfield) Boundary Element Methods in Solid Mechanics, 1983; contbr. articles to profl. jours. Recipient US Nat. Com. Rock Mechanics Applied Rsch. award, 1992, Charles W. Britzius Disting. Engr. award Minn. Fedn. Engring., Sci. and Tech. Societies, 2004. Mem. AIME (Rock Mechanics award 1991), ASCE, Internat. Soc. Roch Mechanics, Minn. Soc. Surveyors and Engrs., Engrs. Club Mpls. Office: U Minn 105 Walter Libr 117 Pleasant St SE Minneapolis MN 55455-0291

CROUSE, JERRY K., energy company executive; b. Jan. 1964; m. Ann Crouse. Former v.p., contr. Tenaska Energy, Omaha, CFO, 2003—. Office: Tenaska Energy 1044 N 115th St Ste 400 Omaha NE 68154 Office Phone: 402-691-9500. Office Fax: 402-691-9575. E-mail: power@tenaska.com.

CROUTER, RICHARD EARL, religion educator; b. Washington, Nov. 2, 1937; s. Earl Clinton and Neva J. (Crain) C.; m. Barbara Jean Williams, Jan. 30, 1960; children— Edward, Frances AB, Occidental Coll., 1960; B.D., Union Theol. U., NYC, 1963, Th.D., 1968. Asst. prof. religion Carleton Coll., Northfield, Minn., 1967-73, assoc. prof., 1973-79, prof., 1979-92, Bryn-Jones disting. tchg. prof. humanities, 1993-96, Musser prof. religious studies, 1997—2003, Musser prof. religious studies emeritus, 2003—. Author: Friedrich Schleiermacher: Between Enlightenment and Romanticism, 2005; translator, editor: On Religion (F. Schleiermacher), 1988, 96; co-editor Jour. for the History of Modern Theology, 1993—. Resident dir. A Better Chance Program, Northfield, 1968-70. Fulbright scholar, 1976-77, 87, 91-92; Am. Council Learned Socs. fellow, 1976-77, Wallin fellow, 2001, DAAD fellow, 2001. Mem. Am. Acad. Religion (steering com. 19th century theol. group 1982-92, chmn. 1987-92), Troeltsch Soc., German Studies Assn., Kierkegaard Soc., Schleiermacher Gesellschaft. Democrat. Avocations: hiking, travel, bicycling, piano. Home: 808 2d St E Northfield MN 55057-2307 Office: Carleton Coll Dept Religious Studies Northfield MN 55057 E-mail: rcrouter@carleton.edu, rcrouter@charter.net.

CROW, MARTHA ELLEN, lawyer; b. Bryan, Tex., Dec. 7, 1944; d. Elvin Earl and Walteen (Daly) Burnett; m. Michael Paine Crow, Apr. 20, 1968; children: Jennifer Johanna, Emily Jeanne, Bryan Jacob. BA, Baker U., 1966; JD magna cum laude, Washburn U., 1992. Bar: Kans. 1993. Tchr., jr. high Shawnee Mission Schs., Johnson County, Kans., 1966-68; legal intern Speaker's Office Kans. Legislature, Topeka, 1991; law clk. Freilich, Leitner, Shortlidge and Carlisle, Kansas City, Mo., 1992-93; planning cons. Kans. Dept. Health and Environment, Topeka, 1993-95; ptnr. Crow, Clothier & Assocs., Leavenworth, Kans., 1995—. Comments editor: Washburn Law Jour., Vol. 31, 1991-92. Mem. Kans. Ho. of Reps., 41st dist., 1996—, agenda chair Ho. Dems., 2001—; mem. Kans. Continuing Legal Edn. Commn., 1993—99, chmn., 1997—99; bd. dirs., founding mem. Leadership Leavenworth, 1988-90; chmn., vice chmn. Leavenworth City Planning Commn., 1978-90, 94-96; v.p. to pres. Leavenworth Bd. Edn., 1983-96; chmn. Leavenworth Bd. Zoning Appeals, 1979-89, 94-96; pres. Downtown Leavenworth Revitalization, Inc., 1988-90, Leadership Kans. Class of 1986; bd. dirs. YWCA, 1974-82, pres., 1977-79; bd. dirs. Leavenworth C. of C., women's divsn., 1980-86, Baker U. Alumni Assn., 1978-80, Mother to Mother Ministry, 1996—, Richard Allen Cultural Ctr., 2000-, Northeast Kans. Mental Health and Guidance Ctr., 1997—2003; co-chmn. residential divsn. United Way Drive, 1977, 78, numerous others. Recipient Michaud, Cordry,

Michaud, Hutton scholarship, Wichita, Kans., 1991, scholarship Washburn Law Sch., 1991. Mem. ABA, Kans. Bar Assn., Kans. Trial Lawyers Assn., Washburn Sch. of Law (women's legal forum), Phi Kappa Phi, Phi Delta Phi, Phi Gamma Mu, Delta Delta Delta, PEO. Democrat. Methodist. Home: 1200 S Broadway St Leavenworth KS 66048-3118 Office: Crow Clothier & Assocs PO Box 707 302 Shawnee St Leavenworth KS 66048-2063 Office Phone: 913-682-0166.

CROW, MICHAEL P., lawyer; b. Ft. Sill, Okla., Jan. 22, 1945; BA, Baker Univ., Kans., 1967; JD, Washburn Univ., Topeka, 1973. Ptnr. Crow, Clothier and Associates, Leavenworth, Kans., 1974—. Law clerk Hon. Arthur J. Stanley Jr., U.S. Dist. Ct., 1974—75; lectr., judicial process Wichita State Univ., 1976—77; mcpl. judge, Basehor, Kans., 1976—79, Linwood, Kans., 1977—79; atty. Delaware Twp., Kans., 1977—79; city atty. Tonganoxie, Kans., 1977—2004; state rep. Kans. Ho. of Reps., 1978—82; atty. Leavenworth Civil Svc. Commn., Kans., 1988. Lt. US Army, 1967—70. Mem.: Assn. of Trial Lawyers of Am., Kans. Trial Lawyers Assn. (bd. dir. 1989—, treas. 1995—96), Am. Bar Assn., Leavenworth County Bar Assn. (pres. 1981—82, bd. dir. 1990—94), Kans. Bar Assn. (bd. gov. 1995—, sec. 2001—02, v.p. 2002—03, pres. 2004—05), Phi Alpha Delta. Office: Crow Clothier & Assocs 302 Shawnee PO Box 707 Leavenworth KS 66048

CROW, SAM ALFRED, judge; b. Topeka, May 5, 1926; s. Samuel Wheadon and Phyllis K. (Brown) Crow; m. Ruth M. Rush, Jan. 30, 1948; children: Sam A., Dan W. BA, U. Kans., 1949; JD, Washburn U., 1952, LLD (hon.), 2006. Ptnr. Rooney, Dickinson, Prager & Crow, Topeka, 1953—63, Dickinson, Crow, Skoog & Honeyman, Topeka, 1963—70; sr. ptnr. Crow & Skoog, Topeka, 1971—75; part-time U.S. magistrate, 1973—75; U.S. magistrate, 1975—81; judge U.S. Dist. Ct. Kans., Wichita, 1981—92, Topeka, 1992—96, sr. judge, 1996—. Bd. rev. Boy Scouts Am., 1960—70, cubmaster, 1957—60; chmn. Kans. March of Dimes, 1959, bd. dirs., 1960—65, Topeka Coun. Chs., 1960—70; mem. Kans. Hist. Soc., 1960—; pres., v.p. PTA; bd. govs. Washburn Law Sch. Alumni Assn., 1993—99; mem. Shawnee County Hist. Soc., Kans.; mem. vestry Grace Episcopal Ch., Topeka, 1960—65. Col. JAGC USAR, ret. Named to, Topeka H.S. Hall of Fame, 2000; recipient Washburn U. Sch. Law Disting. Svc. award, 2000. Fellow: Kans. Bar Found.; mem.: ABA (del. Nat. Conf. Spl. Ct. Judges 1978), Topeka Lawyers Club (sec. 1964—65, pres. 1965—66), Wichita Bar Assn., Topeka Bar Assn. (chmn. jud. reform com., chmn. bench and bar com., chmn. criminal law com., Disting. Svc. award 2000), Nat. Assn. U.S. Magistrates (com. discovery abuse), Kans. Trial Lawyers Assn. (sec. 1959—60, pres. 1960—61), Kans. Bar Assn. (chmn. mil. law sect. 1965, 1967, 1970, trustee 1970—76, chmn. mil. law sect. 1972, 1974, 1975), Shawnee Country Club, Shriners (Shriner of Yr. 2005), Am. Legion, Sigma Alpha Epsilon, Delta Theta Phi. Office: US Dist Ct 444 SE Quincy St Topeka KS 66683

CROW, STEVEN D., educational association administrator; BA in Hist., Lewis and Clark Coll., Oreg.; MA in Hist., PhD in Hist., U. Wis., Madison; cert. in Bus. Adminstrn. for Not-for-Profit Mgmt., U. Ill., Chgo. Adminstr., tchr. Kalamazoo Coll., Bates Coll., Vanderbilt U., Bowdoin Coll.; with Higher Learning Commn. of North Ctrl. Assn. Colls. and Schs., Chgo., 1982—, mem. critical issues com., mem. com. on orgnl. effectiveness and future directions, exec. dir. Chgo. Contbr. articles to profl. publs. Office: Higher Learning Commn 30 N LaSalle St Ste 2400 Chicago IL 60602-2504 Office Phone: 800-621-7440 ext. 102. E-mail: scrow@hlcommission.org.

CROWDER, MARJORIE BRIGGS, lawyer; d. Rowland Edmund and Marjorie Ernestine (Biles) Crowder; m. Ronald J. Briggs, July 11, 1970 (div. Nov. 2000); children: Sarah Briggs, Andrew Briggs. BA, Carson-Newman Coll., 1968; MA, Ohio State U., 1969, JD, 1975. Bar: Ohio 1975, US Dist. Ct. (so. dist. Ohio) 1975, US Ct. Appeals (6th cir.) 1983, US Ct. Claims 1992, US Supreme Ct. 2001. Asst. dean of women Albion Coll., Mich., 1969-70; dir. residence hall Ohio State U., Columbus, 1970-71, acad. counselor, 1971-72; assoc. Porter, Wright, Morris, Arthur, Columbus, 1975—83, ptnr., 1983-2000; AmeriCorps atty. Southeastern Ohio Legal Svs., Portsmouth, Ohio, 2000—02, staff atty., 2002—03; domestic violence team leader Legal Aid Soc. Columbus, 2003—04; supr. legal rsch. Franklin Co. Mcpl. Ct., 2005—07; program mgr. children, families and cts. Supreme Ct. Ohio, 2007—. Legal aide Cmty. Law Office, Columbus, 1973—74. Co-author: (book) Going to Trial, A Step-By-Step Guide to Trial Practice and Procedure, 1989. Trustee, pres. Epilepsy Assn. Ctrl. Ohio, Columbus, 1977—84; bd. dirs. Scioto County Domestic Violence Task Force, 2001—04, v.p., 2001—; bd. dirs. Action Ohio Coalition Battered Women, 2002—, Columbus Speech & Hearing, 1977—82. Fellow: Columbus Bar Found. (trustee 1993—95); mem.: Scioto County Bar Assn., Columbus Bar Assn. (com. chmn. 1979—83, docket control task force 1989—91, editor 1981—83), ABA (mem. gavel awards com. 1989—96, gen. practice sect. 1983—, chair litig. com. 1987—89, mem. exec. coun. 1989—93, dir. bus. com. group 1990—91, chair program com. 1991—93, torts and ins. practice sect. 1993—, vice chair health ins. law com. 1993—96), Ohio Bar Assn. (mem. joint task force gender fairness 1991—93), Scioto County Bar Assn. Office: 209 E Pacemont Rd Columbus OH 43202 Office Phone: 614-387-9385. Business E-Mail: crowderm@sconet.state.oh.us.

CROWE, JAMES WILSON, university administrator, educator; b. Churubusco, Ind., June 27, 1934; s. James A. and Ruth Crowe; m. Barbara Jones; children: Michael James, Monica Sue Crowe Black. BS, Purdue U., 1959; MS, U. Fla., 1960; Dir. Degree, Ind. U., 1970, EdD, 1979. Grad. asst. in health and safety edn. U. Fla., Gainesville, 1959-60; health edn. tchr., coach, dir. driver edn. program Edinburg (Ind.) Cmty. H.S., 1960-65; dir. health and safety edn. Atterbury Job Corps Ctr., Columbus, Ind., 1965-66; asst. prof. applied health sci. Ind. U., Bloomington, 1966-80, assoc. prof. applied health sci., 1980-96; prof., 1996—; dir. Ctr. for Health and Safety Studies Ind. U., Bloomington, 1992—, co-dir. Inst. for Drug Abuse Prevention, 1992—, acting chair dept. applied health sci., 1992-93, chair dept. applied health sci., 1993—. Bd. dirs. Monroe County chpt. ARC, 1991-94. Recipient Svc. award ARC, 1986, 87, 88, 89, Instr. of Yr. award ARC, 1985, 87, 88, Outstanding Tchg. award Amoco, 1977. Mem. AAHPERD (v.p. cmty./safety divsn. Midwest dist. 1989-90), Am. Assn. Active Lifestyles and Fitness (bd. dirs. 1994—), Am. Driver and Traffic Edn. Assn. (Visions of Tomorrow award 1992), Am. Sch. Health Assn., Nat. Safety Coun. (mem.-at-large edn. rsch. sect. 1993, cert. in recognition of outstanding contbn. 1994), Sch. and Cmty. Safety Soc. Am. (bd. dirs. 1991—, pres.-elect 1992-94, pres. 1994-96, past pres. 1996-98, scholar award 1996, C.P. Yost Disting. Svc. award 1998). Office: 16157 Mount Abbey Way #Q202 Fort Myers FL 33908-5645

CROWE, ROBERT WILLIAM, lawyer, mediator; b. Chgo., Aug. 20, 1924; s. Harry James and Miriam (McCune) C.; m. Virginia C. Kelley, Mar. 25, 1955 (dec. Feb. 1976); children: Robert Kelley, William Park; m. Elizabeth F. Roenisch, Oct. 22, 1977. AB, U. Chgo., 1948, JD, 1949. Bar: Ill. 1949. Practice in, Chgo., 1949-57; with R.R. Donnelley & Sons Co., Chgo., 1957-83, sec., 1965-83, v.p., 1970-83; chmn. Resolve Dispute Mgmt. Inc., Chgo., 1983-92; pres. Dearborn Inst. for Conflict Resolution, Chgo., 1992-94. Dir. Peoria Jour. Star, Inc., 1972-95. Bd. dirs. Chgo. Child Care Soc., 1963—; trustee Christian Century Found., 1966—; vis. com. U. Chgo. Divinity Sch. Served to 1st lt. USAAF, 1943-45. Decorated Air Medal with 5 oak leaf clusters. Mem. ABA, Chgo. Bar Assn., Lawyers Club Chgo., Econ. Club (Chgo.), Univ. Club (Chgo.). Presbyterian. Home and Office: 1228 Westmoor Rd Winnetka IL 60093-1845 Home Phone: 847-446-2553; Office Phone: 847-446-7054. Personal E-mail: rwcrowe@sbcglobal.net.

CROWE, WILLIAM JOSEPH, librarian; b. Boston, Feb. 27, 1947; s. William J. and Mary (Dawley) C.; children: Katherine. BA in European History with highest honors, Boston State Coll., 1968; MLS, Rutgers U., 1969; PhD in Adminstrn. Acad. Librs., Ind. U., 1986. Cataloger Boston Pub. Libr., 1969-70, asst. to acquisitions libr., 1970-71; coord. processing Ind. U. Librs., Bloomington, 1971-76, asst. to dean univ. librs., 1977-79; mgmt. intern U. Mich. Libr., Ann Arbor, 1976-77; asst. to dir. librs. Ohio State U., Columbus, 1979-83, asst. dir. librs. adminstrn. and tech. svcs., 1983-90; dean librs. U. Kans., Lawrence, 1990-96, vice chancellor, dean, 1996-99, libr. Spencer Rsch. Libr., 1999—2007, spl. asst. to dean, 2007—. Trustee Online Computer Lit. Ctr., 1996—. Contbr. articles to profl. jours. Sr. fellow UCLA, 1991. Mem. ALA, Kans. Libr. Assn., Beta Phi Mu, Phi Alpha Theta. Home: 910 E 850th Rd Lawrence KS 66047-9578 Office: U Kans Anschutz Libr Lawrence KS 66045-7537 Office Phone: 785-864-4970. Business E-Mail: wcrowe@ku.edu.

CROWL, SAMUEL RENNINGER, former university dean, English language educator, author; b. Toledo, Oct. 9, 1940; s. Lester Samuel and Margaret Elizabeth (Renninger) C.; m. Susan Richardson, Dec. 29, 1963; children: Miranda Paine, Samuel Emerson. AB, Hamilton Coll., 1962; MA, Ind. U., 1969, PhD, 1970. Resident lectr. Ind. U., Indpls., 1967-69; asst. prof. English, Ohio U., Athens, 1970-75, assoc. prof., 1975-80, prof., 1980—, dean Univ. Coll., 1981-92, trustee prof. Eng., 1992—; cons. NEH, Washington, 1980—; observer Royal Shakespeare Co. Mem. Ohio Humanities Coun., 1985-91, Ohio Student Loan Commn., 1985-88. Author: Shakespeare Observed: Studies in Performance on Stage and Screen, 1992, Shakespeare at the Cineplex, 2003, The Films of Kenneth Branagh, 2006, Shakespeare 2008; co-author: Ohio University's Educational Plan, 1977-78; contbr. articles to profl. and Shakespearian jours. Recipient O'Bleness award for pub. broadcasting Ctr. Telecommunications, Ohio U., 1976, several awards disting. teaching. Fellow Royal Soc. Arts (London); mem. Nat. Assn. Univ. and Gen. Coll. Deans (pres. 1991—), Nat. Humanities Faculty, Ohio Shakespeare Assn. (founding mem.), Ohio U. Alumni Assn. (hon.), Univ. Club (Chgo.), Phi Kappa Phi. Avocations: Royal Shakespeare Co., Detroit Tigers. Office: Ohio U Eng Dept Ellis Hall Athens OH 45701 Office Phone: 740-593-2838. Business E-Mail: Crowl@ohio.edu.

CROWLEY, DALE ALAN, prosecutor; b. Saginaw, Mich., May 29, 1951; s. Lester Robert and Esther Irene C.; m. Deanne Kay Westendorp, Dec. 30, 1983; children: Jessica Erin, Leslie Ann, Kelsey Jo. BA in Econs. with honors, Mich. State U., 1973; JD, Wayne State U., 1976. Bar: Mich. 1976, U.S. Dist. Ct. (we. dist.) Mich. 1981. Counsel trust dept. Security Nat. Bank, Battle Creek, Mich., 1976-78; counsel claims dept. Transamerica Ins. Group, Battle Creek, 1978-80; asst. pros. atty Barry County, Mich., 1980, chief asst. pros. atty., 1980-88, pros. atty., 1989—. Vice chmn. Barry County Cmty. Corrections Bd.; legal advisor Barry County E-911 Central Dispatch Bd.; served as spl. pros. atty. in Allegan, Kalamazoo and Eaton Counties. Recipient Profl. Excellence citation Mich. State Police, 1989, 92. Mem. Nat. Dist. Attys. Assn., Pros. Attys. Assn. Mich., Barry County Bar Assn. (past pres., vice pres., treas., sect.), Kiwanis Club, Exchange Club (treas.) Republican. Lutheran. Avocations: sports, reading, computers, bicycling. Office: Barry County Pros Atty 220 W Court St Ste 201 Hastings MI 49058-1857

CROWLEY, GEOFFREY THOMAS, airline executive; b. St. Catherines, Ont., Can., Oct. 8, 1952; arrived in U.S., 1959; s. Douglas Geoffrey and Joan Margaret (Ratley) C.; m. Linda Anne Buckelew, Jan. 30, 1986; 4 children. BS in Engring., Purdue U., 1974; MBA, Xavier U., 1977. Sr. cons. Booz, Allen & Hamilton TCD, Cin., 1974-77; dir. customer svc. quality assurance Tex. Internat. Airlines, Houston, 1977-80; gen. mgr. People Express Airlines, Newark, N.J., 1980-85; sr. v.p. mktg. and planning Presdl. Airways, Washington, 1985-89; v.p. sales and svc. Trump Shuttle, Inc., NYC, 1989-91; v.p. mktg. alliances Northwest Airlines, Inc., St. Paul, Minn., 1991-93; chmn., pres., CEO Air Wisconsin Airlines Corp., Appleton, 1993—. Apptd. by Pres. Clinton to FAA Mgmt. Adv. Coun., 2000—. Mem. Regional Airline Assn. (chmn. 1995-96, dir. 1994-97, 2002-05), Wings Club (gov. 1995-98). Office: Air Wisconsin Airlines Corp W6390 Challenger Dr Ste 203 Appleton WI 54914-9120 Office Phone: 920-749-4188. E-mail: gcrowley@airwis.com.

CROWLEY, WILLIAM C., retail executive; BS in Psychology, Yale U., 1979. Mem. staff to mng. dir. mergers and acquisitions dept. Goldman Sachs, 1986—99; pres., COO ESL Investments, Inc., 1999—2003; sr. v.p. fin., bd. dirs. Kmart Corp., 2003—05; exec. v.p., chief adminstrv. officer Sears Holdings Corp., 2005—. Bd. dirs. AutoNation, Inc., 2002—. Office: Sears Holdings Corp 3333 Beverly Rd Hoffman Estates IL 60179

CROWN, JAMES SCHINE, investment company executive; b. Chgo., June 25, 1953; s. Lester and Renée (Schine) Crown; m. Paula Anne Hannaway, June 27, 1985; children: Victoria, Hayley, William Andrew, Summer Olivia. BA, Hampshire Coll., 1976; JD, Stanford U., 1980. Bar: Ill. 1980. V.p. Salomon Bros. Inc., NYC, 1980-85; gen. ptnr. Henry Crown and Co., Chgo., 1985—2003, pres., 2003—. Bd. dirs. Gen. Dynamics Corp., Falls Church, Va., JPMorgan Chase & Co., Sara Lee Corp. Chmn. bd. U. Chgo.; Trustee Mus. Sci. and Industry, Chgo., Orchestral Assn., Chgo. Mem.: Ill. State Bar Assn. Office: Henry Crown and Co 222 N La Salle St Chicago IL 60601-1003

CROWN, LESTER, manufacturing executive; b. Chgo., June 7, 1925; s. Henry and Rebecca (Kranz) C.; m. Renee Schine, Dec. 28, 1950; children: Steven, James, Patricia, Daniel, Susan, Sara, Janet. BS in Chem. Engring., Northwestern U., 1946; MBA, Harvard U., 1949. Instr. math. Northwestern U., 1946-47; v.p., chem. engr. Marblehead Lime Co., 1950-56, pres., 1956-66, also bd. dirs.; v.p. Material Svc. Corp. subs. Gen. Dynamics Corp., Chgo., 1953-66, pres., 1970-83; chmn. Material Svc. Corp., Chgo., 1984—2006, also bd. dirs.; pres. Henry Crown & Co., Chgo., 1969—2002, chmn., 2002—, also bd. dirs. Ptnr. Yankee Global Enterprise, 1973-; chmn. Comml. Club Chgo., 2005-. Trustee, vice chmn. Aspen Inst. Humanistic Studies, Northwestern U.; bd. dirs. Lyric Opera Corp., Children's Meml. Med. Ctr., Jewish Theol. Sem., Jerusalem Found.; mem. bd. govs. Weizmann Inst. of Sci./Tel Aviv U.; chmn. Chgo. Coun. Global Affairs, 2004—. Mem. Am. Acad. Arts and Scis., Lake Shore Country Club, Northmoor Country Club, Old Elm Club, Standard Club, Econ. Club (dir. 1972), Chgo. Club, Comml. Club, John Evans Club of Northwestern U., Tau Beta Pi, Pi My Epsilon, Phi Eta Sigma. Office: Henry Crown and Co 222 N LaSalle #2000 Chicago IL 60601

CRUDEN, ROBERT WILLIAM, botany educator; b. Cleve., Mar. 18, 1936; m. Diana Benedict Loeb, Dec. 21, 1967; children: Nathalie Rebecca, Lyda Marie; m. Diana Ruth Gannett, July 1996. AB, Hiram Coll., Ohio, 1958; MS, Ohio State U., Columbus, 1960; PhD, U. Calif., Berkeley, 1967. Asst. prof. U. Iowa, Iowa City, 1967-71, assoc. prof., 1971-78, prof., 1978-99, prof. emeritus, 1999—. Acting dir. Iowa Lakeside Lab., Wahepton, 1989-94, past asst. dir.; adj. prof. U. Mich, Ann Arbor, 2001-Editor Ecol. Soc. Am., 1983-86; editl. bd. Madrono; contbr. numerous articles to profl. jours. Mem. pres.'s coun. on sci. initiatives Hiram Coll., 1994-2007. Recipient J.J. Turner award Hiram Coll., 2001. Fellow Iowa Acad. Sci.; mem. AAAS, Am. Soc. Plant Taxonomists, Bot. Soc. Am., Ecol. Soc. Am., Iowa Acad. Sci., Soc. for the Study of Evolution, Assn. for Tropical Biology, New Eng. Bot. Soc. Home: 550 Woodhill Dr Saline MI 48176 Home Phone: 734-429-4355. Personal E-mail: robert-cruden@uiowa.edu.

CRUIKSHANK, JOHN W., III, insurance agent; b. Sharon, Pa., Aug. 22, 1933; s. John W. and Jeannette Sprague (Lane) C.; m. Myrna Jean Wright, Nov. 25, 1960; children: Nancy Lynn, David Wright. BA, Princeton U., 1955. CLU. Group ins. sales rep. Conn. Gen. Life Ins. Co., Hartford, also Chgo., 1955-56; spl. agt. Northwestern Mut. Life Ins. Co., Chgo., 1959—, pres. Spl. Agts., Inc., 1983-84, faculty advanced planning sch. Northbrook, Ill., 1978-97; pres. Assn. of Agts. orthwestern Mut. Life, 1994-95. Pres. Million Dollar Round Table Found., 1988—89; divisional v.p. Million Dollar Round Table, 1976—77, 1986—87, 1992—93, exec. com., 1994—98, pres., 1996—97; trustee Life Underwriter Tng. Coun., 1997—2001. Bd. dirs. Life and Health Ins. Found. for Edn., 1997—2003, chmn., 2002; bd. dirs. North Shore Sr. Ctr., 2001—, chmn., 2007, sec., mem. exec. com., 2006—; mem. gov. bd. Super Sibs!, 2007—; trustee Pikeville (Ky.) Coll., 1969—75, The Am. Coll., 2001—02; pres. Nat. Coun. United Presbyn. Men, 1971—72; elder United Presbyn. Ch. in U.S.A., 1975—, mem. gen. assembly mission coun., 1972—78; chmn. mission divsn. Presbytery of Chgo., gen. coun., 1966—67, 1980—84; bd. dirs. Vocation Agy., Presbyn. Ch. in U.S.A., 1982—87. Named one of Most Outstanding Life Underwriters in the U.S. for decade of 1990s, Leaders Mag., 1999; recipient Cir. of Life award, Million Dollar Round Table Found., 1998, Huebner Scholar award, Am. Soc. CLU and ChFC, Chgo., 1995, Disting. Citizen award, Ill. St. Andrew Soc., 1998, Grauer Disting. Svc. award, Chgo. Chpt. Fin. Svc. Profls., 2000. Home: 1412 Ridge Rd Northbrook IL 60062-4628

CRUM, JAMES FRANCIS, waste recycling company executive; b. Pitts., July 23, 1934; s. Frank J. and Martha (Huffman) C.; m. Madeleine Jones, July 3, 1957 (dec. Feb. 2001); children: Cynthia Anne, James Joseph. BMechE, U. Rochester, 1956. Trainee to supt. transp. U.S. Steel Corp., Braddock, Pa., 1959-74, supt. transp. South Chgo., Ill., 1974-75, supt. operating maintenance, 1975-76, asst. divsn. supt. iron Gary, Ind., 1976-83; divsn. mgr. iron. U.S. Steel div. USX, Gary, 1983-88; exec. v.p., COO McGraw Construction Co., Middletown, Ohio, 1988-92; from dir. bus. devel. to v.p. ops. Nat. Recovery Systems, East Chicago, Ind., 1992-99, pvt. practice Flossmoor, Ill., 1999—. Adv. coun. South Suburban Hosp., 1993—; cons. in field. Vol. U. Rochester Admissions Network, N.Y., 1987—; cons. Clean City Coalition, Gary, 1988-90; bd. dirs. South Suburban Hosp. Found.; trustee Village of Flossmoor, 2005—. Mem. AIME, Eastern States Blast Furnace Assn., Western States Blast Furnace Assn. (bd. dirs. 1985-88), Assn. Iron & Steel Engrs. Republican. Roman Catholic. Avocations: golf, photography, foreign travel, stained glass. Home: 736 Central Park Ave Flossmoor IL 60422-2220 Personal E-mail: jfcrum@sbcglobal.net.

CRUMP, CLAUDIA, geographer, educator; BS in Elem. Edn., Western Ky. U., 1952; MS in Elem. Edn., Ind. U., 1957, EdD in Elem. Edn., 1969. Co-author: Teaching for Social Values in Social Studies, 1974, Indiana Map Studies, 1983, Indiana Yesterday and Today, 1985, Teaching History in the Elementary School, 1988, People in Time and Place: Indiana Hoosier Heritage, 1992. Recipient First Educator of Yr. award, Nat. Coun. Internat. Visitors, 2005. Home: 309 Whippoorwill Hts New Albany IN 47150-4255 Office: Ind U Southeast Sch Edn New Albany IN 47150 E-mail: ccrump700@cs.com.

CRUMP, LINDA R., lawyer; b. NYC; BS in Biology, City Coll. NY; JD, U. Nebr., 1990. Teacher biology, gen. sci., physical sci. and physics Lincoln High Sch., ebr.; asst. to chancellor equity, access & diversity programs U. Nebr., Lincoln. Co-chair Nebr. Minority Justice Com.; mem. Nebr. Commn. on Women, Homestead Girl Scout Coun.; mem. cmty. adv. bd. Nebr. Pub. Radio; bd. dirs. Sr. Ctr. Found., Lincoln Cmty. Found., Legal Services of Southeast Nebr.; mem. instl. rev. bd. Harris Lab.; bd. dirs. West Gate Bank, Planned Parenthood Nebr. Mem.: Nebr. State Bar Assn. (house of delegates 1992, chair 2000, pres. 2006—07). Office: Univ Nebraska Lincoln 128 Canfield Administration Lincoln NE 68588-0437 Office Phone: 402-472-3417.

CRUMP, WAYNE F., state legislator; b. Belleville, Ill., June 26, 1950; m. Tiffany M. Newman, 1995. Student, Belleville Area Coll. Former dep. sheriff Washington County, Mo., 1975-82; state rep. dist. 152 Mo. Ho. of Reps., 1983—2005, maj. fl. leader, ret., 2005. Mem. rules com., joint rules com., bills perfected and printed com. (chmn.); cattle farmer. Named Outstanding Legislator Coalition for Alternatives to Imprisonment, 1986, Oustanding Performer Meramec Regional Planning Commn., 1986, Outstanding Legislator, Mo. Assn. of Counties, 1990, 91, 95, State Rep. of Yr. Mo. Deputy Sheriffs' Assn., 1995, Statesman of Month Jefferson City News Tribune, 1995, 98. Democrat.

CRUTCHER, RICHARD METCALF, astronomer, educator; b. Lexington, Ky., Apr. 18, 1945; BS, U. Ky., 1967; MA, UCLA, 1969, PhD in Astronomy, 1972. Rsch. fellow Calif. Inst. Tech., 1972-74; prof., chmn. dept. astronomy U. Ill., Urbana. Mem. Am. Astron. Soc., Internat. Astron. Union, Union Radio Sci. Internat. Achievements include research on physics and chemistry of the interstellar medium, star formation, advanced scientific computing. Office: U Ill Dept Astronomy 1002 W Green St Urbana IL 61801

CRUTCHFIELD, JAMES N., publishing executive; b. McKeesport, Pa., Dec. 7, 1947; m. Cynthia L. Parish; 1 child. BA in Journalism, Duquesne U., 1992. Reporter Pitts (Pa.) Press, 1968-71; pub. info. officer Pitts. Model Cities Program., 1971; reporter Pitts. Post-Gazette, 1971-76, Detroit Free Press, 1976-79; press. sec. for U.S. Sen. Carl Levin of Mich., 1979-81; chief of bur. Free Press., Lansing, Mich., 1981-83; asst. city editor, dep. city editor, dept. mng. editor Free Press, Lansing, Mich., 1983-89; mng. editor Akron (Ohio) Beacon Jour., 1989—93; exec. editor Press-Telegram, Long Beach, Calif., 1993—98; gen. man. Akron (Ohio) Beacon Journal, 1999—2001, pres., 2001—, pub., 2001—. Bd. dirs. Duquesne U. Mem. accrediting coun. Edn. Journalism and Mass Comm.; bd. trustees Found. Am. Comm.; mem. bd. John S. and James L. Knight Found., United Way Summit County. Mem.: Ohio Newspaper Assn., Asian Am. Journalists Assn., Nat. Assn. Minority Media Execs., Nat. Assn. Black Journalists, Am. Soc. Newspaper Editors.

CRUZ, A. B., III, (ANATOLIO BENEDICTO CRUZ III), lawyer; b. Mpls., June 16, 1958; m. Jill Cruz; children: Ben, Ana. BS, US Naval Acad., 1980; MS, U. Md., College Park; JD, Cath. U., 1992. Bar: DC, N.Y., Pa., U.S. Supreme Ct. Sr. assoc. Wiley, Rein & Fielding; assoc. Gardner Carton & Douglas; v.p., dep. gen. counsel, asst. sec. BET Holdings Inc., 1999—2004; sr. v.p., gen. counsel The E.W. Scripps Co., Cin., 2004—. Capt. USN, 1980—87 USNR, 1987—. Office: The EW Scripps Co 312 Walnut St Cincinnati OH 45202 Office Phone: 513-977-3000.*

CRUZ, DEIVI, professional baseball player; b. Nizao de Bani, Dominican Republic, Nov. 6, 1975; Baseball player Detroit Tigers, 1997—2001, San Diego Padres, 2002, Balt. Orioles, 2003, San Francisco Giants, 2004—05, DC Nationals, 2005—. Office: Wash Nationals RFK Stadium 2400 E Capitol St Washington DC 20003

CRUZ-MYERS, THERESA, finance company executive; V.p. Nationwide Finl. Retirement Plans, Columbus, Ohio. Co-chmn. corp. adv. coun. Nat. Conf. Black Mayors; contbr. at. Assn. Govt. Defined Contbn. Adminstrs. Named to Elite Women, Hispanic Bus. Mag., 2005. Office: Nationwide Fin One Nationwide Plz Columbus OH 43215 Office Phone: 614-435-1564. Office Fax: 303-987-5370. Business E-Mail: myerst9@nationwide.com.

CRYER, PHILIP EUGENE, endocrinologist; b. El Paso, Ill., Jan. 5, 1940; s. Clifford Eugene and Carol Ruth (Cherry) C.; m. Susan Odette Shipman, Dec. 23, 1963 (div. May 1990); children: Philip Clifford, Justine Laurel; m. Carolyn Elizabeth Havlin, Sept. 16, 1994. BA, Northwestern U., 1962, MD, 1965; MD (hon.), U. Copenhagen, 2000. Diplomate Am. Bd. Internal Medicine, diplomate Am. Bd. Endocrinology and Metabolism. Intern, resident Barnes Hosp., St. Louis, 1965-67; fellow in endocrinology Barnes Hosp./Washington U., 1967-68, resident in medicine, 1968-69, 71-72; investigator Naval Med. Rsch. Inst., Bethesda, Md., 1969-71; from instr. to assoc. prof. Washington U. Sch. Medicine, St. Louis, 1971-80, prof., 1981—, Irene E. and Michael M. Karl prof. endocrinology/metabolism, 1995—, dir. gen. clin. rsch. ctr., 1978—2006, dir. divsn. endocrinology, diabetes and metabolism, 1985—2002. Connaught-Novo lectr. Can. Diabetes Assn., 1987; Pimstone lectr. Soc. Endocrinology, Metabolism and Diabetes, South Africa, 1989; Kellion lectr. Australian Diabetes Soc., 1992; Plenary lectr. Japan Diabetes Soc., 1994, plenary lectr. Argentine Diabetes Assn., 1998, plenary lectr. Asean Fed. Endocrine Socs., 1999. Author: Diagnostic Endocrinology, 1976, Diagnostic Endocrinology, 2d edit., 1979, Hypoglycemia, 1997; editor: Diabetes; mem. editl. bd.: Jour. Clin. Investigation, Am. Jour. Physiology; contbr. 82 chapt. to books, over 325 articles to profl. jours. Lt. comdr. M.C. USNR, 1969—71. Recipient Rorer Clin. Investigator award Endocrine Soc., 1988, Rumbaugh Sci. award Juvenile Diabetes Found., 1989, Banting medal Am. Diabetes Assn., 1994, Excellence in Clin. Rsch. award NIH, 1994, Claude Bernard medal European Assn. Study Diabetes, 2001, Merit award NIH, 2001.; grantee Am. Diabetes Clin., 1988-, NIH, 1980—; named Disting. Alumnus, Northwestern U. Med. Sch., 2006. Fellow ACP; mem. Am. Fedn. Clin. Rsch. (councilor 1979-80), Am. Soc. Clin. Investigation (v.p. 1985-86), Assn. Am. Physicians, Am. Diabetes Assn. (pres. 1996-97), Phi Beta Kappa, Alpha Omega Alpha. Office: Washington U Sch Medicine 660 South Euclid Ave Box 8127 Saint Louis MO 63110 Home Phone: 314-752-7201; Office Phone: 314-362-7635. Business E-Mail: pcryer@wustl.edu.

CSAR, MICHAEL F., lawyer; b. Chgo., May 26, 1950; s. Frank J. and Rosaria (Motto) C.; children: Cordelia, Christian. BA summa cum laude, Yale U., 1972; MA, Kings Coll., Cambridge, 1974; JD, Yale U., 1977. Bar: Ill. 1977, U.S. Dist. Ct. (no. dist.) Ill. 1977. Assoc. Wilson & McIlvaine, Chgo., 1977-83; ptnr. Quarles & Brady (formerly Wilson & McIlvaine), Chgo., 1983-98, Gardner Carton & Douglas, Chgo., 1998—2006, Drinker Biddle & Reath, Chgo., 2007. Mem. Bldg. Owners and Managers Assn., Nat. Assn. Real Estate Investment Trusts. Mem.: ABA, Greater North Mich. Ave. Assn., Lambda Alpha Internat. Office: Drinker Biddle & Reath 191 N Wacker Dr Ste 3700 Chicago IL 60606 Office Phone: 312-569-1223. Office Fax: 312-569-3000. Business E-Mail: michael.csar@dbr.com.

CSERE, CSABA, editor-in-chief; b. Cleve., June 16, 1951; s. Zoltan and Theresa (Balazs) Csere; m. Mary Patricia O'Brien, July 6, 1975; 1 child, Madeline Christine. BS, MIT, 1975. Design engr. Data Gen. Corp., Southboro, Mass., 1975—77, Ford Motor Co., 1978—80; tech. editor Car and Driver mag., 1980—87, tech. dir., 1987—93, editor-in-chief, 1993—. Mem.: Am. Soc. Mag. Editors, Soc. Automotive Engrs. Office: Car and Driver Hachette Filipacchi Mags Inc 2002 Hogback Rd Ann Arbor MI 48105-9795 Office Phone: 734-971-3600. Office Fax: 734-971-9188.

CUCCO, ULISSE P., retired obstetrician, gynecologist; b. Bklyn., Aug. 19, 1929; s. Charles and Elvira (Garafalo) C.; m. Antoinette DeMarco, Aug. 31, 1952 (dec.); children: Carl, Richard, Antoinette Marie, Michael, Frank, James; m. Bobby Gene Frazier, 2002. BS cum laude, L.I. U., 1950; MD, Loyola U., Chgo., 1954. Diplomate Am. Bd. Ob-Gyn. Intern Nassau County Hosp., Hempstead, NY, 1954-55; resident in ob-gyn Lewis Meml. Mercy Hosp., Chgo., 1955-58; practice medicine specializing in ob-gyn Des Plaines, Ill., 1960—2001. Past pres. med. staff, chmn. dept. ob-gyn. Holy Family Hosp., Des Plaines, Ill.; clin. asst. prof. Stritch Sch. Medicine, Loyola U. Contbr. articles to med. jours. Chief ob-gyn USAF, 1958—60, Ellsworth AFB, Rapid City, SD. Recipient Mother Francis award, Holy Family Med. Ctr. Mem. ACS, Am. Fertility Soc., Ctrl. Assn. Ob-Gyn., Ill. Med. Soc., Chgo. Med. Soc., Chgo. Gynecol. Soc. (past pres.), Chgo. Inst. Medicine, Sunset Ridge Country Club. Roman Catholic. Home: 665 Midfield Ln Northbrook IL 60062-5507

CUCULLU, SANTIAGO, artist; b. Buenos Aires, 1969; BFA, Hartford Art Sch., 1992; MFA, Mpls. Coll. Art & Design, 1999. One-man shows include Solo Show, Boom Gallery, Mpls., 1999, Art Houston, Barbara Davis Gallery, Houston, 2002, Wiyya To Hell Owwa That, Julia Friedman Gallery, Chgo., 2003, Art Basel Miami: Art Statements, Barbara Davis Gallery, Houston, 2003, Arco: Madrid Project Room, Julia Friedman Gallery, Chgo., 2004, Mori Art Mus., Tokyo, 2004, Hammer Mus., LA, 2004, exhibited in group shows, Esacio de Pensamiento, Bueno Aires, Argentina, 1995, Dumb & Evil, Calhoun Sq. Gallery, Mpls., 1998, Push, Pull Pop, 1999, XL, Weinstein Gallery, Mpls., 2000, 13 From Mpls., Mpls., 2002, Fresh-The Altoids Collection, Mus. Contemporary Art, NY, 2003, Works on Paper, Blum & Poe Gallery, LA, 2003, How Latitudes Become Forms, Walker Art Ctr., Mpls., 2004, Whitney Biennial, Whitney Mus. Am. Art, 2004. Jerome Emerging Artist Fellowship, Mpls. Coll. Art & Design, 2000. Office: c/o Perry Rubenstein Gallery 527 W 23rd St New York NY 10011

CUDABACK, JIM D., state legislator; b. Riverdale, Nebr., Apr. 12, 1938; Student, Kearney State Coll., Lincoln Sch. Commerce, USAF Schs. Rental property mgr., ebr.; mem. Nebr. Legislature from 36th dist., Lincoln, 1990—; vice chair exec. bd., vice chair reference com. Nebr. Legislature, Lincoln, vice chair gen. affairs, mem. govt., mil. and vets. affairs com., mem. bldg. maintenance com., mem. com. on coms. Former mem. Buffalo County Bd. Commrs., Riverdale Village Bd., Ctrl. C.C. Adv. Bd.; pres. Buffalo County Hist. Soc. Adv. Bd., Cmty. Concert Assn.; active Gibbon Good Samaritan Village, Buffalo County Econ. Devel. Visitors Promotion Com., Kearney Vol. Fire Dept. Mem. Rotary, IOOF Lodge, Elks. Office: Nebr State Senate State Capitol Rm 1124 Lincoln NE 68509

CUDAHY, RICHARD D., federal judge; b. Milw., Feb. 2, 1926; s. Michael F. and Alice ((Dickson)) Cudahy; m. Ann (Featherston), July 14, 1956 (dec. 1974); m. Janet (Stuart), July 17, 1976; children: Richard D., Norma K., Theresa E., Daniel M., Michaela A., Marguerite L., Patrick G. BS, U.S. Mil. Acad., 1948; JD, Yale U., 1955; LLD, Ripon Coll., 1981, DePaul U., 1995, Wabash Coll., 1996, Stetson U., 1998. Bar: Conn. 1955, D.C. 1957, Ill. 1957, Wis. 1961. Commd., 2d. lt. US Army, 1948, 1st. lt., 1950; law clk. to presiding judge US Ct. Appeals (2d cir.), 1955—56; asst. to legal adv. Dept. State, 1956—57; assoc. Isham, Lincoln, and Beale, Chgo., 1957—60; pres. Patrick Cudahy, Inc., Wis., 1961—71, Patrick Cudahy Family Co., Wis., 1968—75; ptnr. firm Godfrey and Kahn, Milw., 1972; commr., chmn. Wis. Pub. Svc. Commn., 1972—75; ptnr. Isham, Lincoln, and Beale, Chgo. and Washington, 1976—79; judge US Ct. Appeals (7th cir.), Chgo., 1979—94, sr. judge, 1994—. Lectr. law Marquette U. Law Sch., 1962—66; vis. prof. law U. Wis., 1966—67; prof. lectr. law George Washington U., Washington, 1978—79; adj. prof. DePaul U. Coll. Law, 1995—. Commr. Milw. Harbor, 1964—66; pres. Milw. Urban League, 1965—66; trustee Environ. Def. Fund, 1976—79; chmn. DePaul U., Human Rights Law Inst., 1990—98; mem. adv. com. Ctr. for Internat. Human Rights, Northwestern U., 2000—; mem. vis. com. U. Chgo. Div. Sch.; chmn. Wis. Dem. Party, 1967—68; Dem. candidate for Wis. Atty. Gen., 1968. Mem.: ABA (spl. com. on Energy Law 1978—84, pub. utility sect. coun. group), Internat. Aviation Law Inst. of DePaul U., DC Cir. Apptd. Ind. Counsel (spl. divsn. 1998—2002), Ill. Bar Assn., DC Bar Assn., Am. Inst. for Pub. Svc. (bd. selectors 1973—98), Fed. Judges' Assn. (bd. dirs. 1993—96), Chgo. Bar Assn., Wis. Bar Assn., Am. Law Inst., Cath. Theol. Union, Lawyers Club, Chgo. (pres. 1992—93). Office: US Ct Appeals 219 S Dearborn St Ste 2648 Chicago IL 60604-1874

CUDAK, GAIL LINDA, lawyer; b. Bellville, Ill., July 13, 1952; d. Robert Joseph and Margaret Lucille Cudak; m. Thomas Edward Young, Sept. 15, 1979. BA, Kenyon Coll., 1974; JD, Case Western Res. U., 1977, MBA, 1991. Bar: Ohio 1977, U.S. Dist. Ct. (no. dist.) Ohio 1977, U.S. Ct. Appeals (6th cir.) 1977, U.S. Ct. Appeals (fed. cir.) 1989. Assoc. Fuerst, Leidner, Dougherty & Kasdan, Cleve., 1977-79; staff atty. The B.F. Goodrich Co., Akron, Ohio, 1979-84, sr. corp. counsel Independence, Ohio, 1985-89, divsn. counsel Brecksville, Ohio, 1990-98, group counsel, 1998-99; counsel ops. Eaton Corp., Cleve., 1999—. Trustee Great Lakes Theater Festival, 1992—, mem. exec. com. Mem.: ABA, Assn. Corp. Counsel (trustee N.E. Ohio chpt. 2006—), Cleve. Internat. Lawyers Group, Cleve. Bar Assn. (past chair corp. sect.), Ohio State Bar Assn. Home: 12520 Edgewater Dr Apt 1405 Lakewood OH 44107-1639 Office: Eaton Corp 1111 Superior Ave E Cleveland OH 44114-2507

CULL, ROBERT ROBINETTE, manufacturing executive; b. Cleve., Sept. 24, 1912; s. Louis David and Wilma Penn (Robinette) C.; m. Gay Cornwell, Oct. 4, 1986. BS in Physics, M.I.T., 1934. Supr. Eastman Kodak Co., Rochester, N.Y., 1934-39; asst. to gen. mgr. Cleve. Chain & Mfg. Co., 1940-45; partner Tenna Mfg. Co., Cleve., 1945-56; pres. Tenatronics Ltd., Newmarket, Ont., Can., 1956—, Sterling Mfg. Co., Cleve., 1960—. Trustee Garden Center Greater Cleve., 1975-80, pres., 1979-80; trustee Musical Arts Assn. of Cleve. Orch., 1976—2003. Mem. IEEE, Cleve. Engring. Soc., Sigma Psi. Clubs: Hermit, Union.

CULLEN, CHARLES THOMAS, historian, librarian; b. Gainesville, Fla., Oct. 11, 1940; s. Spencer L. and Blanche J. Cullen; m. Shirley Harrington, June 13, 1964; children: Leslie Caner, Charles Spencer Harrington. BA, U. of South, 1962; MA, Fla. State U., 1963; PhD, U. Va., 1971; HHD (hon.), Lewis U., 1987; DLitt (hon.), U. South, 1994; LLD (hon.), John Marshall Law Sch., 1995; DHist (hon.), Lincoln Coll., 2000. Asst. prof. history Averett Coll., 1963-66; assoc. editor Papers of John Marshall Inst. Early Am. History and Culture, Williamsburg, Va., 1971-74, co-editor, 1974-77, editor, 1977-79; lectr. history Coll. William and Mary, 1971-79; sr. research historian, editor Papers of Thomas Jefferson Princeton (N.J.) U., 1979-86; pres., libr. Newberry Library, Chgo., 1986—2005, pres., libr. emeritus, 2005—. Mem. N.J. Hist. Commn., 1985-86, Nat. Hist. Publs. and Records Com., 1990—; mem. adv. bd. Abraham Lincoln Presdl. Libr. and Mus., 2002-04. Trustee Thomas Jefferson Found., 2004—. Nat. Hist. Publs. and Records Commn. fellow, 1970-71. Mem. Assn. Documentary Editing (pres. 1982-83), Orgn. Am. Historians, Am. Hist. Assn., Am. Antiquarian Soc., Heartland Lit. Soc. (pres. 1994—), The Poetry Found. (vice chmn. 1998-2005), Ind. Rsch. Librs. Assn. (pres. 2000—03), Caxton Club, Grolier Club. Office: Newberry Libr 60 W Walton St Chicago IL 60610-7324

CULLEN, DAVID A., state legislator; b. Milw., Feb. 1, 1960; married; 1 child. BA, U. Wis., 1981; JD, Marquette U., 1984. Mem. from dist. 13 Wis. State Assembly, Madison, 1990—. Mem. Milw. Sch. Bd., 1983-90, pres., 1987-90; bd. dirs. Friends of Sch. Edn., U. wis.; mem. Statewide Presch.-Grade 5 Adv. Coun. Mem. Wis. Bar Assn. Home: 2845 N 68th St Milwaukee WI 53210-1206 Office: State Capitol PO Box 8952 Madison WI 53708-8952

CULLIS, CHRISTOPHER ASHLEY, dean, biology educator; b. Harrow, Eng., Nov. 20, 1945; s. Jack Douglas Bungard and Isette Sarah (Cullis) Giles; m. Margaret Angela Webb, Sept. 4, 1971; children: Benjamin, Oliver, Thomas, Bethia, Tristan, Camilla. BS, London U., 1966; MS in Biophysics, U. East Anglia, Norwich, Eng., 1968, PhD, 1971. Higher sci. officer John Innes Inst., Norwich, 1971-73, sr. sci. officer, 1973-81, prin. sci. officer, 1981-85; prof. biology Case Western Res. U., Cleve., 1986—, dean, math. and natural scis., 1989-93; Francis Hobart Herrick prof. biology U. Cleve., 1994—. Vis. prof. Case Western Res. U., 1985-86, Stanford U., Palo Alto, Calif., 1982-83; adj. prof. plant biotech. ctr. Bond U., Queensland, Australia, 1990-93; founder, gen. ptnr. Novomark Technols. LLC.; mem. rsch. com. Holden Arboretum, 1992—. Editor: The Nucleolus, 1981, John Innes Symposium, 1983; author chpts. in books. Cubmaster Boy Scouts Am., Winding River, 1988, 89, com. chair, 1990-94. Nuffield and Leverhulme fellow Civil Svc. Commn., 1982-83; Assn. Commonwealth Univs. scholar, 1967-70. Mem. AAAS, Genetical Soc. Am., Bot. Soc. Am., Soc. for Plant Molecular Biology, Soc. for Exptl. Biology (coun. 1979-81, chair com. for cell biology 1980-81). Avocations: sports, reading. Office: Case Western Res U 2040 Adelbert Rd Cleveland OH 44106-2623

CULP, DONALD ALLEN, lawyer; b. Atchison, Kans., June 13, 1938; s. Roy Allen and Audrey Mae (Moyer) C.; m. Judy Wayne Smith, Sept. 10, 1966; children: Brian David, Matthew Allen, Lindsey Beth. Bar: Kans. 1965, Mo. 1987. Ptnr. Culp & Sheppard, Overland Park, Kans., 1969-79; gen. counsel Electronic Realty Assn., Overland Park, Kans., 1979-87; v.p., gen. counsel Signature Foods, Inc., Kansas City, Mo., 1987-89; ptnr. Shughart, Thomson & Kilroy, Overland Park, 1989-97, Blackwell, Sanders, Pepper, Martin, Kansas City, Mo., 1997—. Pres. Am. Cancer Soc., Overland Park, 1970-73, hon. life mem., 1981—; elder Rolling Hills Presbyn. Ch., Overland Park, 1972-80; pres., bd. dirs. Shawnee Mission Bd. Edn., Overland Park, 1975-83; bd. dirs. Overland Park C. of C., 1978-81. Mem. ABA, Kans. Bar Assn., Mo. Bar Assn., Johnson County Bar Assn. Republican. Presbyterian. Avocations: bicycling, race walking. Home: 9609 W 104th St Shawnee Mission KS 66212-5606 Office: Blackwell Sanders Matheny Weary 4801 Main St Ste 1000 Kansas City MO 64112-2551 Office Phone: 816-983-8115. Business E-Mail: dculp@blackwellsanders.com.

CULP, KRISTINE ANN, dean, theology studies educator; B in Gen. Studies with distinction, U. Iowa, 1978; MDiv, Princeton Theol. Sem., 1982; PhD in Religion, U. Chgo., 1989. Vis. instr. theology St. Paul Sch. Theology, Kansas City, Mo., 1985-86, instr. theology, 1986-89, asst. prof. theology, 1990-91; dean Disciples Div. House U. Chgo., 1991—, sr. lectr. theology Div. Sch., 1991—. Contbr. articles to profl. jours. Office: U Chgo Disciples Divinity House 1156 E 57th St Chicago IL 60637-1536 also: The Divinity Sch-U Chgo Swift Hall S-406 1025 E 58th St Chicago IL 60637-1509

CULP, MILDRED LOUISE, corporate financial executive; b. Ft. Monroe, Va., Jan. 13, 1949; d. William Whitfield and Winifred Louise (Stilwell) C. BA in English Lit., Knox Coll., Galesburg, Ill., 1971; MA in Religion and Lit., U. Chgo., 1974, PhD Com. on History of Culture, 1976. Faculty, adminstr. Coll., 1976—81; dir. Exec. Résumés, Seattle, 1981—; pres. Exec. Directions Internat., Inc., Seattle, 1985—2000, Clive, Iowa, 2000—03, Crete, Ill., 2003—. Mem. MBA mgmt. skills adv. com. U. Wash. Sch. Bus. Adminstrn., 1993; spkr. in field; contract rschr. U.S. Army Recruiting Command, 1997. Author: Be WorkWise: Retooling Your Work for the 21st Century, 1994; columnist Seattle Daily Jour. Commerce, 1982-88; writer Singer Media Corp., 1991-98, Worldwide Media, 1999-2002, Globalvision, Inc., 2002-06, WorkWise syndicated column, Media Passage, 1994-97, 2001—, Universal Press Syndicate, 1997-01, WorkWise Interactive syndicated column, 2004-, WorkWise Advice column, 2004-; WorkWise Internet audio program, 2000—; featured on TV and radio; contbr. articles to profl. jours.; presenter WorkWise Report, Sta. KIRO, 1991-96. Admissions counselor U. Chgo., 1981—, vol. Jeff Metcalf Fellow Program, 2006—; mem. Nat. Alliance Mentally Ill, 1984-91; life mem. Alliance Mentally Ill Hamilton County, 1984—; founding mem. People Against Telephone Terrorism and Harassment, 1990; co-sponsor WorkWise award, 1999-2000. Recipient Alumni Achievement award Knox Coll., 1990, 9 other awards; named Hon. Army Recruiter. Mem.: U. Chgo. Puget Sound Alumni Club (bd. dir. 1982—86), Knox Coll. Alumni Network. Personal E-mail: culp@workwise.net.

CULPEPPER, DAUNTE, professional football player; b. Ocala, Fla., Jan. 28, 1977; Quarterback Minn. Vikings, 1999—2006, Miami Dolphins, 2006—07. Named to Nat. Football Conf. Pro-Bowl, 2000, 2003—04; recipient Sammy Baugh Trophy, 1998, Breakthrough Athlete of the Yr. award, ESPY, 2000, Ed Block Courage award, 2001, Korey Stringer Good Guy award, 2003—04. Achievements include setting NCAA record for single season completion percentage (.736), 1998; drafted by MLB NY Yankees, 1995.

CULVER, CHET (CHESTER JOHN CULVER), governor; b. Washington, Jan. 25, 1966; s. John and Ann (Cooper) Culver; m. Mariclare Thinnes Culver; 2 children. BA in Polit. Sci., Va. Poly. Inst. and State U., Blacksburg, 1988; MA in Tchg., Drake U., 1994. Tchr. govt. and hist., coach Roosevelt HS and Hoover HS, Des Moines; investigator Atty. Gen.'s Office; sec. state State of Iowa, Des Moines, 1999—2007, gov., 2007—. Established Iowa Student Polit. Awareness Club; elder mem. Ctrl. Presbyn. Ch. Mem.: Iowa State Edn. Assn. (Fulbright Meml. Fund Tchrs. scholarship 1997), Coun. State Govts., Elections Task Force, New Millenium Youth Initiative, Presdl. Caucuses and Primaries Com., Elections and Voter Participation Com., Nat. Assn. Secs. State, State Records Mgmt. Com., State Voter Registration Commn. (chmn.), Exec. Coun. (chmn.). Democrat. Presbyterian. Office: Office of Gov State Capitol Bldg Des Moines IA 50319 Office Phone: 515-281-8993. Office Fax: 515-242-5952.

CULVER, CURT S., diversified financial services company executive; BA in Real Estate with honors, Univ. Wis., Madison, MS in Urban Land Econ. with honors. Joined Mortgage Guaranty Ins. Corp. (subs. MGIC Investment Corp.), Milw., 1982, COO, 1996—99, pres., 1996—, CEO, 1999—; also pres. MGIC Investment Corp., Milw., 1999—, CEO, 2000—, chmn., 2005—. Named one of Most Powerful People in Am., Forbes mag. Office: MGIC 250 E Kilbourn Ave Milwaukee WI 53202 Office Phone: 414-347-6480.

CULVERWELL, ROSEMARY JEAN, retired principal, elementary school educator; b. Chgo., Jan. 15, 1934; d. August John and Marie Josephine (Westermeyer) Flashing; m. Paul Jerome Culverwell, Apr. 26, 1958; children: Joanne, Mary Frances, Janet, Nancy, Amy. BEd, Chgo. State U., 1955, MEd in Libr. Sci., 1958; postgrad., DePaul U., 1973. Cert. supr., tchr. Tchr. Otis Sch., Chgo., 1955-59; tchr., libr. Yates Sch., Chgo., 1960-61, Nash Sch., Chgo., 1962-63, Boys Chgo. Parental, 1969-72, Edgebrook and Reilly Schs., Chgo., 1965-67; counselor, libr. Reilly Sch., Chgo., 1968, tchr., libr., asst. prin., 1973, prin., 1974—97; ret., 1997. Reviewer Ill. State Bd. Edn. Quality Review Team. Pres. Infant Jesus Guild, Park Ridge, Ill., 1969-70; troop leader Girl Scouts U.S., Park Ridge, 1967-69; sec. Home Sch. Assn., Park Ridge, 1969, v.p. spl. projects, 1970; mem. Ill. Svc. Ctr. Six Governing Bd., 1994; vol. Ctr. of Concern, Park Ridge, Ill., 1997; quality reviewer Ill. State Bd. Edn., 1998; mem. Ill. Quality Edn. Rev. Team, 1998; v.p. Renaissance Art Club, 1999-05. Recipient Outstanding Prin. award Citizens Schs. Com., Chgo., 1987, For Character award, 1984-85, Whitman award for Excellence in Edn. Mgmt., 1990, Local Sch. Coun. award Ill. Bell Ameritech, 1991, Ill. Disting. Educator award Milken Family Found. Nat. Educators, 1991, Ill. Edn./Bus. Partnership award, 1994, 96. Mem. AAUW, LWV (chmn. speakers bur. 1969), Delta Kappa Gamma, Phi Delta Kappa. Avocations: acrylic painting, reading, swimming, making doll houses and furniture. Home: 1929 S Ashland Ave Park Ridge IL 60068-5460 Personal E-mail: rmaryculverwell@aol.com, r.cul@sbcglobal.net.

CUMMINGS, ANDREA J., lawyer; BA in Polit. sci., BS in Journalism, Boston U., 1990; JD, U. Va., 1995. Bar: Tex. 1995, Calif. 1999, Ill. 2000. With Locke Lord Bissell & Liddell (formerly Locke Purnell Rain Harell), Tex., 1995—97, Weil, Gotshal & Manges LLP, 1997—98, Nomura Asset Capital Corp., 1998—99, DLA Piper (formerly Gray Cary Ware Freidenrich), 1999—2000, Sidley Austin LLP (formerly Sidley Austin Brown & Wood LLP), Chgo., 2000—, ptnr., 2003—. Office: Sidley Austin LLP 1 S Dearborn Chicago IL 60603 Office Phone: 312-853-2107. Office Fax: 312-853-7036. Business E-Mail: acummings@sidley.com.

CUMMINGS, JOAN E., health facility administrator, educator; BA, Trinity Coll., 1964; MD, Loyola U., 1968. Diplomate Am. Bd. Internal Medicine, Geriatric Medicine. Med. intern St. Vincent Hosp., Worcester, Mass., 1968-69; med. resident Hines VA Hosp., Hines, Ill., 1969-71, sr. resident in nephrology, 1971-72, ambulatory care svc. chief gen. med. sect., 1971-84, med. dir., hosp. based home care, 1972-87, chief, intermediate care svc., 1984-87, assoc. chief of staff, extended care and geriatrics, 1987-90, med. dir., extended care center, 1987-90, dir., 1990—; asst. prof. clin. medicine U. Ill., 1976-82, Loyola U., 1983-91, assoc. prof. clin. medicine, 1991—; network dir. Dept. Vet. Affairs, Hines, Ill., 1995—2005. Ad hoc com. on primary care U. Ill., 1980-82, coll. edn. policy com. U. Ill., 1980-82, State Ill. Emergency Med. Svc. Coun., 1981-83, Comprehensive Health Ins. Plan Bd. State Ill., 1990—, Med. Licensing Bd. State Ill., 1992—, exec. com. Chgo. Fed. Exec. Bd. State Ill., 1992—; program dir. Loyola/Hines Geriatric Fellowship Program, 1987-90; bd. trustees Rosalind Franklin U. Medicine and Sci., 2005-; bd. dirs. Ismie Mutual Ins. Co., 2003-. Contbr. to profl. mags. and jour. Recipient Disting. Svc. award Abraham Lincoln Sch. Med. Univ. Ill., 1979, 81, Leadership award VA, 1980, Certificate of Appreciation award VA, 1980, Laureate award Am. Coll. Physicians, 1990. Fellow ACP; mem. AMA (Ill. delegation 1985—, vice speaker ho. of dels. 1987-89), Chgo. Med. Soc. (pres. Hines-Loyola br. 1982-83), Ill. State Med. Soc. (trustee 1984—, chmn. com. on Ill. med., 1988—, spkr. ho. of dels. 1989-91, exec. com., 1989-91, policy com., 1989—), Chgo. Geriatric Soc., Am. Geriatric Soc. Office: 772 St Charles Rd Glen Ellyn IL 60137 Home Phone: 630-858-7716. Personal E-mail: joanecum@msn.com.

CUMMINS, THOMAS KENNETH, psychiatrist; MD, U. Wis. Med. Sch., 1990. Cert. Psychiatry, 1996, Child & Adolescent Psychiatry, 1997. Resident, psychiatry Emory U. Affiliated Hospitals, 1990—94; fellow, child and adolescent psychiatry UCLA Neuropsychiatric Inst., 1994—96; med. dir., impatient psychiatry Children's Meml. Hosp., Chgo.; asst. prof., psychiatry and behavioral scis. Northwestern U. Feinberg Sch. Medicine. Mem.: Am. Acad. Child and Adolescent Psychiatry. Office: Childrens Meml Hosp 2300 Childrens Plz Chicago IL 60614-3363*

CUNNINGHAM, BILL, radio personality; b. Covington; Radio host 700 WLW, Cin. Recipient Marconi award for large market personality of yr., 2001. Avocation: golf.

CUNNINGHAM, DOUGLAS D., state legislator; b. Osmond, Nebr., Oct. 13, 1954; m. Deb Cunningham; 1 child, John. Owner, operator D&D Foodliner, Wausa, Nebr., 1980—2002; pres. Onawa Food Ctr. Inc., 1997—2002, Wausa Leisure Living, 1997—2001; senator Nebr. State Legislature (from 18th dist.), 2000—. Bd. dirs. Osmond Gen. Hosp. Found., Knox County Block Grant; mem. com. Wausa Appreciation Day; mem. strategic planning com. Wausa Pub. Schs.; coun. treas., Sunday sch. prin. Thabor Luth. Ch.; mem. Vol. Fire Dept.; del. Rep. State Conv.; co-chairperson Knox County Hagel for Senate campaign; vice chmn. Knox County Rep. Party, 1998-2000, 2001-2002; chmn. Knox County Rep. Party, 2000. Mem. Nat. Grocers Assn. (mem. govt. rels. coun., mem. polit. edn. com., Spirit of Am. award 2000), Nat. Grocery Industry (bd. dirs.), Knox County Pork Prodrs. (assoc.), Knox County Cattle Feeders (assoc.), Wausa Cmty. Club. Home: Box 160 Wausa NE 68786 Office: Rm 1212 State Capitol Lincoln NE 68509-4604

CUNNINGHAM, GUNTHER, professional football coach; m. Rene Cunningham; children: Natalie, Adam. BS in Gen. Sci., U. Oreg., 1969. Football coach U. Oreg., 1969-71, U. Kar., 1972, Stanford (Calif.) U., 1973-76, U. Calif., 1977-80; coach defensive line, linebackers CFL's Hamilton Tiger Cats, 1981; defensive line coach Balt. Colts, 1982-84; mentor defensive line San Diego Chargers, 1985-90; coach linebackers Oakland (Calif.) Raiders, 1991, defensive coord., 1992-93, defensive line, 1994; defensive coord. Kansas City (Mo.) Chiefs, 1995-98, head coach, 1999—2001, defensive coord., 2004—; coach linebackers Tenn. Titans, ashville, 2002—04. Office: c/o Kansas City Chiefs One Arrowhead Dr Kansas City MO 64129

CUNNINGHAM, MILAMARI ANTOINELLA, retired anesthesiologist; b. Cody, Wyo., Oct. 4, 1949; d. Milo Leo and Mary Madeline (Haley) Olds; m. Michael Otis Webb, June 4, 1970 (div. Feb. 1971); m. James Kenneth Cunningham, June 14, 1975. BA with honors, U. Mo., 1971, MD, 1975. Diplomate Am. Bd. Anesthesiologists. Intern and resident U. Mo., Columbia, 1975—78; jr. ptnr. Anesthesiologist, Inc., 1979—82, ptnr., 1982—86; owner Cunningham Anesthesia, 1986—2003; dir. anesthesia dept. Ellis Fischel Cancer Ctr., 1991—92; acting chief anesthesia Harry S. Truman Meml. Vets. Hosp., 1994—95; instr. U. Mo. Columbia Anesthesia Dept. Mem. med. staff U. Mo. Hosp. and Clinics, Columbia; vice chair Mo. Health Facilities Rev. Com., 2004—05. Mem. editl. bd.: Mo. Medicine Jour., 2001—06; contbg. editor, 2007—. Active Mo. Med. Polit. Action Com., 1991-2000, Friends of Music, Friends of Libr., Boone County Fair, 1978-94, with ham breakfast divsn., 1978-85, with draft horse and mule show, 1986-88; Mo. bd. dirs. A Call to Serve, 1996-2007, program mgr., 2004-07. Named Lifetime Senator, World Nations Congress, 2003; recipient Disting. Svc. award, U. Mo. Med. Alumni Assn., 2007; fellowship, Am. Coll. Anesthesiologists, 1977. Mem.: AMA (life Physicians Recognition award 1978, 1985, 1987, 1991, 1995), Vis. Nurses Assn. (bd. dirs. 1982—89, adv. bd. 1989—93), Am. Soc. Anesthesiologists (alt. dir. dist. 17 2003, Mo. dist. dir. 2003—05), Mo. State Med. Assn. (commn. econs. 3d party payors 1986—89, del. 1996—2004), Boone County Med. Soc. (sec. treas. 1996, bd. dirs. 1996—99, pres. 1998), Mo. Soc. Anesthesiologists (membership chair 1982—94, v.p. 1986—87, pres. 1988—89, spkr. ho. dels. 1992—2002, bd. dirs. 1996—99), Phi Beta Kappa. Home and Office: 8202 S Bennett Dr Columbia MO 65201-9178 E-mail: mila@tranquility.net.

CUNNINGHAM, PAUL GEORGE, minister; b. Chgo., Aug. 27, 1937; s. Paul George Sr. and Naomi Pearl (Anderson) C.; m. Constance Ruth Seaman, May 27, 1960; children: Lori, Paul, Connie Jo. BA, Olivet Nazarene U., 1960; BDiv., Nazarene Theol. Sem., 1964; DD, Mid Am. Nazarene Coll., 1975. Sr. pastor Coll. Ch. of the Nazarene, Olathe, Kans., 1964-93; gen. supt. Internat. Ch. of the Nazarene, 1993—. Adv. bd. Kansas City Dist. Ch. of the Nazarene, Overland Park, Kans., 1971-93; trustee Mid Am. Nazarene Coll., Olathe, 1971—; chmn. book com. Nazarene Pub. House, Kansas City, Mo., 1974-90; pres. gen. bd. Internat. Ch. of the azarene, Kansas City, 1985-93. Police chaplain Olathe (Kans.) Police Dept., 1975-93; adv. bd. Good Samaritan Ctr., Olathe, 1990—. Recipient Disting. Svc. award Jaycees, Olathe, 1967, Paul Harris fellow Rotary Internat., Olathe, 1989. Mem. Nat. Assn. Evangs., Rotary. Mem. Ch. Of The Nazarene. Home: 12543 S Hagan Ln Olathe KS 66062-6075 Office: Ch of the Nazarene 6401 Paseo Blvd Kansas City MO 64131-1213 Business E-Mail: pcunningham@nazarene.org.

CUNNINGHAM, PAULA DIANE, bank executive, former academic administrator; b. Akron, Ohio, 1949; d. David Samuel and Mattie Pauline (Mason) Marsh; m. Darius Lee Cunningham, Aug. 29, 1970; children: Darius Lee II, Dana Leigh. BA in Journalism, Mich. State U., 1981, M in Labor and Indsl. Rels., 1991. Legis. asst. Mich. State Capitol, Lansing, 1975; exec. dir. Profl. Devel. Ctr., Lansing, 1985-86; owner, mgr. Mason Hills Golf Course; assoc. prof. bus. Lansing CC, 1985-92, dir. pub. info., 1994, dir. profl. devel., 1992-94, pres., 2000—06, Capitol Nat. Bank, Lansing, 2006—. Cons. to Kellogg Found., Battle Creek, Mich., 1991—, Lansing Bd. Water and Light, 1993—; spkr. in field. Bd. dirs. Capitol Area United Way, Lansing, 1995—, Impression and Sci. Mus., Lansing, 1994—, Martin Luther King Holiday Commn., 1995—; mem. com. ARC, 1995—. Recipient Master Tchr. award U. Tex., 1992. Mem. Nat. Mktg. and Pub. Rels. Assn., Nat. Inst. for Staff and Orgnl. Devel., Pub. Rels. Soc. Am., Am. Soc. Staff and Orgnl. Devel. Avocations: golf, jogging, reading, cross country skiing, travel. Office: Capitol Bancorp Ctr 200 Washington Sq N Lansing MI 48933

CUNNINGHAM, RAYMOND LEO, retired research chemist; b. Easton, Ill., Jan. 5, 1934; s. Raymond J. and Minnie G. (Vaughn) C. BA, St. Ambrose U., Davenport, Iowa, 1955. Phys. sci. aid in chemistry Nat. Ctr. Agrl. Utilization Rsch USDA Agrl. Rsch. Svc., Peoria, Ill., 1957-61, chemist Nat. Ctr. Agrl. Utilization Rsch., 1961-78, rsch. chemist Nat. Ctr. Agrl. Utilization Rsch., 1978-97; ret., 1997. Contbr. articles to profl. jours. With U.S. Army Res., 1958. Co-recipient R&D 100 award R&D mag., 1988. Fellow Am. Inst. Chemists; mem. AAAS, Am. Chem. Soc., Ill. State Acad. Sci. Home: 1108 W MacQueen Ave Peoria IL 61604-3310 E-mail: cunningham8866@sbcglobal.net.

CUNNINGHAM, ROBERT JAMES, lawyer; b. Kearney, Nebr., June 27, 1942; m. Sara Jean Dickson, July 22, 1967. BA, U. Nebr., 1964; JD, NYU, 1967, LLM in Taxation, 1969. Bar: .Y. 1967, Ill. 1969, U.S. Dist. Ct. (no. dist.) Ill. 1969, U.S. Ct. Claims 1970, U.S. Tax Ct. 1970, U.S. Ct. Appeals (D.C. cir.) 1972, U.S. Ct. Appeals (9th cir.) 1975, U.S. Ct. Appeals (7th cir.) 1979, U.S. Ct. Appeals (fed. cir.) 1982. Instr. law NYU, NYC, 1967-69; assoc. Baker & McKenzie LLP, Chgo., 1969-74, ptnr., 1974—. Spkr. in field. Contbr. articles to profl. jours. Mem. ABA, Ill. Bar Assn., Chgo. Bar Assn. Office: Baker & McKenzie LLP One Prudential Plz 130 E Randolph Dr Ste 3900 Chicago IL 60601-6342 Office Phone: 312-861-2931. Business E-Mail: robert.j.cunningham@bakernet.com.

CUNNINGHAM, THOMAS B., aerospace engineer; b. Washington, May 8, 1946; BS, U. Nebr., 1969; MS, Purdue U., 1972, PhD in Engring., 1973. Dir. rsch. engring. automatic control Honeywell, Inc., 1973—. Adj. prof. U. Minn.,

1978—. Mem. IEEE, Am. Inst. Aeronaut. & Astronaut., Sigma Xi. Achievements include applications of modern control and estimation theory to aerospace and industrial problems. Office: Honeywell Tech Ctr 3660 Technology Dr Minneapolis MN 55418-1096

CUNNINGHAM, WES, radio personality; b. Harrisonville, Mo., Aug. 16; m. Lois Cunningham; 1 child, Ryan 4 stepchildren. Student, Mich. State U. Radio host WDAF, Westwood, Kans., 1993—. Avocations: music, golf, bowling, singing. Office: WDAF 4935 Belinder Rd Westwood KS 66205

CUNO, JAMES, museum director; b. St. Louis, Apr. 6, 1951; married; 2 children. BA in History, Willamette U., 1973; MA in Art History, U. Oreg., 1978; MA in Fine Arts, Harvard U., 1980, PhD in Fine Arts, 1985. Asst. curator prints Fogg Art Mus., Harvard U., Cambridge, Mass., 1980-83; asst. prof. dept. art Vassar Coll., Poughkeepsie, NY, 1983-86; dir. Grunwald Ctr. for Graphic Arts, UCLA, 1986-89; dir. Hood Mus. Art, Dartmouth Coll., Hanover, NH, 1989-91; dir. Univ. Art Mus. Harvard U., Cambridge, Mass., 1991—2003; dir. Courtauld Institute of Art, London, 2003—04; pres., Eloise W. Martin dir. Art Inst. of Chgo., 2004—. Trustee Wadsworth Atheneum; panelist NEH, NEA; mem. pub. grant adv. com. Getty Grant Program, 1991-96; mem. vis. com. J. Paul Getty Mus.; lectr. in field. Co-author, co-editor (exhbn. catalogues): Foirades/Fizzles: Echo and Allusion in the Art of Jasper Johns, 1987, Politics and Polemics: French Caricature and the Revolution, 1789-1799, 1988, Scenes and Sequences: Recent Monotypes by Eric Fischl, 1990, Jonathan Borofsky: Prints and Multiples, 1982-91, 1991, The Popularization of Images: Visual Culture Under the July Monarchy, 1994, (book): Whose Muse? Art Museums and the Public Trust, 2004; contbr. articles to profl. jours. Fellow Am. Acad. Arts and Scis.; mem. Assn. Art Mus. Dirs. (trustee, pres.). Office: Art Inst of Chgo 111 S Michigan Ave Chicago IL 60603-6110

CUPICH, BLASÉ J., bishop; b. Mar. 19, 1949; BA, U. St. Thomas, 1971; STL, Cath. U. of Am., 1979, STD, 1987. Ordained priest Archdiocese of Omaha, 1975; ordained bishop, 1998; bishop Diocese of Rapid City, 1998—. Roman Catholic. Office: Diocese of Rapid City 606 Cathedral Dr PO Box 678 Rapid City SD 57701-5407 Office Phone: 605-343-3541. Office Fax: 605-348-7985. E-mail: chancery@diorc.org.*

CUPP, DAVID FOSTER, photographer, journalist; b. Derry Twp., Pa., Feb. 4, 1938; s. Foster Wilson and Elizabeth (Erhard) C.; m. Catherine Lucille Lum, Nov. 20, 1965; children: Mary Catherine, David Patterson, John. BA in Journalism, U. Miami, 1960. Staff photographer Miami News, 1960-63, Charlotte (N.C.) Observer, 1963-66; photographer, writer Internat. Harvesters, Chgo., 1966-67; picture editor Nat. Geog. Mag., Washington, 1967, photographer, 1967-69; picture editor Detroit Free Press, 1969; writer, photographer Denver Post, 1969-77; freelance writer, photographer, 1977-88; dir. photography Press-Enterprise, Riverside, Calif., 1988-90; instr. photojournalism, dept. journalism U. Mo., Columbia, 1990; instr. Sch. Vis. Communication Ohio U., Athens, 1991-92; working book author Cupp Design, Inc., Atlanta, 1993; graphics editor Ft. Lauderdale (Fla.) Sun-Sentinel, 1993-94; freelance writer & photographer Hilliard, Ohio, 1994—; pres., creative dir. Photos Online, Inc., Hilliard, 1995—; pres. Half Moon Pub., LLC, Hilliard, 2003—. Tchr. jr. and sr. h.s.-adult classes, including Journalist-in-the-schs., pilot program, Aurora, Colo., 1974-76, Nat. Endowment Arts poet-in-residence 5 Colo. schs.; photography aboard Voyager Spacecraft Co-author Search and Rescue Dogs, 1988; contbg. author: Nat. Geog. books; co-author: Cindy, a Hearing Ear Dog, The Animal Shelter, All Wild Creatures Welcome; contbr. article, photographs to popular mags. Bd. dirs. Friends of Children of Vietnam, adoption agy., 1973. Mem. Nat. Press Photographers Assn. (named Nat. runner-up Photographer of Year 1965, 72, named Regional Photographer of Year 1974, 2d Pl. News Picture Story award 1974, 3rd Pl. Sports Picture Story award 1974, McWilliams award for picture story 1974, McWilliams award for single picture 1974-75, 2d Home, Family Picture Story award 1972, co-chmn. nat. conv.), Colo. Press Photographers Assn. (v.p.), Am. Soc. Mag. Photographers. Home: 4508 Swenson St Hilliard OH 43026-3811 Office Phone: 614-777-1385. Personal E-mail: pol@columbus.rr.com.

CUPP, ROBERT RICHARD, state supreme court justice, former state senator, attorney; b. Bluffton, Ohio, Nov. 9, 1950; s. William Henry and Pearl Margaret (Keifer) C.; m. Lisbeth Ann Cochran, July 29, 1978; children: Matthew R., Ryan W. BA, Ohio Northern U., 1973, JD, 1976. Bar: Ohio. Commnr. Allen County, Ohio, 1981-84, 2001—02; prosecutor, asst. city law dir. City of Lima, Ohio, 1976-80; ptnr. Cupp and Smith, Attys., Lima, 1983-86; mem. Ohio Senate, 1985-2000; ptnr. Cupp and Jenson, Attys., Lima, 1986-93; judge Ohio Ct. Appeals, 3rd Appellate Dist., 2003—06, adminstrv. judge, 2004—05, presiding judge, 2005—06; justice Ohio Supreme Ct., 2007—. Pres. Bd. County Commrs., Allen County, Ohio, 1981, 82, 84; chmn. Gilmor Commn. Sch. Funding, 1987-88; commerce and labor com. chmn. Ohio Senate 1989-94; com. chmn. Fin. Instns. Ins. and Commerce, 1995-96; majority whip Ohio Senate, 1995-96, pres. pro tem, 1997-2000; vis. prof. applied civic Ohio Northern U., 2001-2005; mem. Ohio Commn. Dispute Resolution & Conflict Mgmt. Co-author: Ethics and Discipline in Ohio, 1977 Co-chmn. Midwest Fedn. Coll. Reps., 1974; pres. exec. bd. Black Swamp coun. Boy Scouts Am.; chmn. League of Coll. Republican Clubs, 1972-73; bd. trustees North Ctrl. Assn. Higher Learning Commn. Recipient Ohio 4-H Alumni award, Robert E. Hughes Meml. award, Ohio Assn. Election Officials. Mem.: Ohio State Bar Assn. (Disting. Svc. award), Allen County Bar Assn. Methodist. Office: Ohio Supreme Ct 65 S Front St Columbus OH 43215-3431 Office Phone: 614-387-9000.

CUPPLES, STEPHEN ELLIOT, lawyer; b. St. Louis, Feb. 20, 1955; children: Christina, James, Catherine, Stephanie, Alex. AB summa cum laude, U. Mo., 1976, JD summa cum laude, 1979. Bar: Mo. 1979, U.S. Dist. Ct. (ea. dist.) Mo. 1979, U.S. Ct. Appeals (8th cir.) 1980, U.S. Tax Ct. 1981, U.S. Claims Ct. 1985. Assoc. Peper, Martin, Jensen, Maichel and Hetlage, St. Louis, 1979-84; ptnr. Cupples & Cupples, P.C., St. Louis, 1985, Cupples, Edwards, Cooper & Singer, St. Louis, 1985-86, Lashly & Baer, P.C., St. Louis, 1987-95, Thompson Coburn LLP, St. Louis, 1995—. Bd. dirs. Estate Planning Coun. of St. Louis, 1992-, pres. 2002-03. Fellow Am. Coll. Trust and Estate Coun.; mem. ABA, Mo. Bar Assn., Bar Assn. Met. St. Louis (chmn. taxation sect. 1988-89), Young Lawyers Tax Club (chmn. 1983-87), Phi Beta Kappa, Phi Kappa Phi. Office: Thompson Coburn LLP One US Bank Plaza Ste 2600 Saint Louis MO 63101-1693 Office Phone: 314-552-6027. Business E-Mail: scupples@thompsoncoburn.com.

CURFMAN, FLOYD EDWIN, retired engineering educator; b. Gorin, Mo., Nov. 16, 1929; s. Charles Robert and Cleo Lucille (Sweeney) C.; m. Eleanor Elaine Fehl, Aug. 5, 1950; children: Gary Floyd, Karen Elaine. BSCE, U. Mo., 1958; BA in Math. Edn., Mt. Mary Coll., 1988. Registered profl. engr., Wis., Mo.; cert. tchr. Wis. Forest engr. US Forest Svc., Rolla and Harrisburg, 1958-70, engring. dir. Milw., 1970-84, chief tech. engr. Washington, 1984-86; tchr. Wauwatosa HS, Wis., 1987-89, Our Lady of Rosary, Milw., 1989-96; ret., 1996. Author: (booklet) Forest Roads-R-9, 1973; co-author: (tng. manual) Transportation Roads, 1966. Co-leader Boy Scouts Am., Harrisburg, 1958-62; activities coord. Cmty. Action Com., Brookfield, 1970-76; bike and hiking trails com. City of Brookfield (Wis.), 1982-83; program chair Math Counts, 1982. With U.S. Army, 1952-54. Mem. ASCE (program chair, Letter Nat. award 1970), NSPE (coms. 1970-86), Nat. Coun. Tchrs. Math., Wis. Soc. Profl. Engrs. (pres. Milw. chpt. 1982-83, State Recognition award 1983). Avocations: travel, reading. Home: 1755 N 166th St Brookfield WI 53005-5114

CURIEL, CAROLYN, former ambassador; b. Hammond, Ind. BA in Radio-TV-Film, Purdue U., 1976. Chief Caribbean Divsn. UPI; editor Late Editions Fgn. Desk N.Y. Times, YC, Washington Post; writer, prodr. ABC News Nightline, 1992; spl. asst. to pres., sr. presdl. speechwriter White House, Washington; U.S. amb. to Belize Dept. State, 1997. Sr. fellow Pew Hispanic Ctr.; editl. bd. NY Times, 2002—. Recipient Disting. Alumni award, Purdue Univ., 2005. Office: Editl Bd NY Times 229 W 43rd St New York NY 10036

CURLER, JEFFREY H., packaging manufacturing executive; Various positions Bemis Co., Inc., Mpls., 1973—, pres., 1995—98, pres., COO, 1998—2000, pres., CEO, 2000—05, chmn., pres., CEO, 2005—08, exec. chmn., 2008—. Office: Bemis Co Inc 222 S 9th St Ste 2300 Minneapolis MN 55402-4099*

CURLEY, EDWIN MUNSON, philosophy educator; b. Albany, NY, May 1, 1937; s. Julius Edwin and Gertrude E.; m. Ruth Helen Snyder, Dec. 12, 1959; children: Julia Anne, Richard Edwin. BA, Lafayette Coll., 1959; PhD, Duke U., 1963. Asst. prof. philosophy San Jose State Coll., 1963-66; research fellow Australian Nat. U., Canberra, 1966-68, fellow, 1968-72, sr. fellow, 1972-77; prof. philosophy Northwestern U., 1977-83, U. Ill.-Chgo., 1983-93, U. Mich., 1993—. Author: Hellenistic Philosophy, 1965, Spinoza's Metaphysics, 1969, Descartes Against the Skeptics, 1978, The Collected Works of Spinoza, vol. 1, 1985, Behind the Geometrical Method, 1988, A Spinoza Reader, 1994, Hobbes' Leviathan, 1994; Am. co-editor Archiv für Geschichte der Philosophie, 1979-95; contbr. articles to profl. jours. Fellow AAAS; mem. Am. Philos. Assn. (v.p. ctr. divsn., 1989-90, pres. 1990-91). Democrat. Home: 2645 Pin Oak Dr Ann Arbor MI 48103-2370 Office: U Mich Dept Philosophy 2215 Angell Hall Ann Arbor MI 48109 Office Phone: 734-764-6285. Business E-Mail: emcurley@umich.edu.

CURRAN, BARBARA ADELL, retired law foundation administrator, lawyer, writer; b. Washington, Oct. 21, 1928; d. John R. and Beda Curran. BA, U. Mass., 1950; LLB, U. Conn., 1953; LLM, Yale U., 1961. Bar: Conn. 1953. Atty. Conn. Gen. Life Ins. Co., 1953-61; mem. rsch. staff Am. Bar Found., Chgo., 1961-93, assoc. exec. dir., 1976-86, rsch. atty., 1986-93, rsch. fellow emeritus, 1993—. Vis. prof. U. Ill. Law Sch., 1965, Sch. Social Svc., U. Chgo., 1966-68, Ariz. State U., 1980; cons. in field. Author of eight books in field; contbr. articles to profl. jours. Mem. Ill. Gov.'s Consumer Credit Adv. Com., 1962-63; consumer credit adv. com. Nat. Conf. Commns. on Uniform State Laws, 1964-70; credit legis. subcom. Mayor Daley's Com. on New Residents, 1966-69; cons. Pres.'s Commn. on Consumer Interests, 1966-70, Ill. Commn. on Gender Bias in the Cts., 1987-92. Mem. ABA, Pi Beta Phi. Office: Am Bar Found 750 N Lake Shore Dr Chicago IL 60611-4403

CURRAN, DANIEL J., academic administrator, sociologist, educator; b. Phila. m. Claire M. Renzetti; children: Sean, Aidan. B in Sociology, St. Joseph's U., Phila., 1973; M in Sociology, Temple U., 1978; PhD in Sociology, U. Del., 1980. Joined St. Joseph's U., Phila., 1979, faculty positions dept. sociology, chair dept. sociology, 1988—92, dean Coll. Arts and Scis., 1994—97, v.p. acad. affairs, 1997—2002, exec. v.p., 1999—2002; pres., prof. sociology U. Dayton, Ohio, 2002—. Concurrent professorship Nanjing (China) U.; mem. task force on sports wagering NCAA, 2004—; mem. Ohio Aerospace and Def. Adv. Coun.; bd. dirs. Dayton Devel. Coalition. Author: Dead Laws for Dead Men, 1993; co-author (with Claire M. Renzetti): Social Problems: Society in Crisis Women, Men and Society, Contemporary Societies: Problems and Prospects Criminology, Living Sociology, Theories in Crime. Bd. dirs. St. Joseph's Carpenter Soc. Recipient Eternal Flame award for Holocaust edn., 2002; Fulbright Sr. scholar, U. Melbourne, Australia, 1990. Mem.: Dayton Area C. of C. (mem. exec. com.). Office: Univ Dayton 300 College Pk Dayton OH 45469 E-mail: Daniel.Curran@notes.udayton.edu.

CURRAN, ED, meteorologist, reporter; Cert. broadcast meteorology, Miss. State U.; grad., Columbia Coll. Weathercaster Sta. WIND, Sta. WGCI-FM; with Sta. WGN Radio, Chgo., 1986—94, Sta. WGN-TV, Chgo., 1996, weathercaster, 1997; weather anchor, reporter NBC 5 Weather Team, Chgo., 2000—. Office: NBC 454 N Columbus Dr Chicago IL 60611

CURRAN, MICHAEL WALTER, management scientist; b. St. Louis, Dec. 6, 1935; s. Clarence Maurice and Helen Gertrude (Parsons) Curran; m. Jeanette Lucille Rawizza, Sept. 24, 1955 (div. 1977); children: Kevin Michael, Karen Ann, Kathleen Marie(dec.), Kimberly Elizabeth; m. Mary Jane Lemanek, Aug. 18, 1981. BS, Washington U., St. Louis, 1964. With Monsanto Co., St. Louis, 1953-65, supervisory positions dept. adminstrv. services, 1956-64, rsch. technician inorganic chems. divsn., 1964-65; sr. ops. rsch. analyst Pet Inc., St. Louis, 1965-68; CEO, dir. Decision Scis. Corp., St. Louis, 1968—, chmn. bd., 2007—. Former mem. adv. bd. Entrepreneurial Bus. Ctr., U. Mo., St. Louis; judge Tech. Excellence Awards, St. Louis, 2002—04. Co-author: (book) Handbook of Budgeting, 1981, Handbook of Budgeting, 4th edit., 1999, Effective Project Management Through Applied Cost and Schedule Control, 1996; editor: Professional Practice Guide to Risk, Vols. 1-3, 1998; contbr. articles to profl. jours. Adviser Jr. Achievement, St. Louis, 1958—59; active United Way, 1958—62. Fellow: Assn. Advancement Cost Engring. (chmn. risk mgmt. com. 1991—, mem. editl. adv. com. 1997—, Tech. Excellence award 2000); mem.: Soc. Cost Estimating and Analysis, Project Mgmt. Inst., Ops. Rsch. Soc. Am., Inst. Mgmt. Scis. (chmn. St. Louis chpt. 1971—72), Intertel, Mensa, Alpha Sigma Lambda, Sigma Xi. Achievements include development of theories of bracket budgeting and range estimating; theories of risk established value, value-based risk management and bubble management; provoke-to-evoke data elicitation methodology. Office: Decision Scis Corp PO Box 28848 Saint Louis MO 63123-0048 Office Phone: 314-739-2662.

CURRAN, RAYMOND M., paper-based packaging company executive; b. 1948; CEO Smurfit Paribas Bank, 1981—91; with Jefferson Smurfit Group plc, 1981—, CFO, 1991—98; with Data Exch. Corp., sr. v.p. ops., 1991—96, pres., gen. mgr. U.S. ops. N.Am. divsn., 1996; exec. v.p., dep. chief exec. Smurfit-Stone Container Corp., Chgo., 1998—99, pres., CEO, 1999—. Office: Smurfit-Stone Container Corp 150 N Michigan Ave Chicago IL 60601-7553

CURRAN, THOMAS J., federal judge; b. 1924; B of Naval Scis., Marquette U., 1945, LLB, 1948. Ptnr. Curran, Curran and Hollenback, Mauston, Wis., 1948-83; judge U.S. Dist. Ct. (ea. dist.) Wis., Milw., 1983—, now sr. judge. Mem. Gov's Commn. on Crime and Law Enforcement, State of Wis. With USN, 1943-46. Mem. ABA, Am. Coll. Trial Lawyers. Office: US Dist Ct 250 US Courthouse 517 E Wisconsin Ave Milwaukee WI 53202-4500

CURRIE, BARBARA FLYNN, state legislator; b. LaCrosse, Wis., May 3, 1940; d. Frank T. And Elsie R. (Gobel) Flynn; m. David P. Currie, Dec. 29, 1959; children: Stephen Francis, Margaret Rose. AB cum laude, U. Chgo., 1968, AM, 1973. Asst. study dir. Nat. Opinion Rsch. Ctr., Chgo., 1973-77; part time instr. polit. sci. DePaul U., Chgo., 1973-74; mem. Ill. Ho. of Reps., 1979—, chmn. House Dem. Study Group, 1980-83, asst. majority leader, 1993, asst. minority leader, 1995, majority leader, 1997. V.p. Chgo. LWV, 1965-69; mem. Ind. Voters of Ill., Ill. Conf. Women Legislators, Ind. Precinct Orgn., Hyde Park Coop. Named Legislator of Yr., NASW, 1984, 1997, Ill. Women's Substance Abuse Coalition, 1984, Illinoisan of Yr., Ill. News Broadcasters Assn., 2001; recipient awards, Welfare Rights Coalition of Orgns., Ill. Pub. Action Coun., Chgo. Heart Assn., BEST BETS award, Nat. Ctr. Policy Alternatives, 1988, Svc. award, at. Ctr. for Freedom of Info. Studies, 1989, Beautiful Person award, Chgo. Urban League, 1989, Friend of Labor award, Ill. AFL-CIO, 1990, Ill. Maternal and Child Health Coalition award, 1990, Ill. Hunger Coalition award, 1991, cert. of appreciation, SEIU Local 880, 1989, March of Dimes, 1988, Chgo. Tchrs. Union, Ill. Hosp. Assn., Ptnr. Vision award, Families' and Children's AIDS Network, Woman of Vision award, Women's Bar Assn. Ill., 1997, Nat. Elected Pub. Ofcl. award, NASW, 1997, Outstanding Working Woman of Ill. award, Ill. Fedn. Bus. and Profl. Women, Dist. Pub. Health Legislator award, Am. Pub. Health Assn., 1999, Legis. award, Ill. Primary Health Care Assn., 2002, Ill. Press Assn., 2003, Legis. of Yr. award, Access Living, 2003, others, Environment Leadership award, Ill. Environ. Coun., 2005, Outstanding Elected Ofcl. award, Campaign for Better Health Care, 2006. Mem.: LWV, ACLU (bd. dirs. Ill.). Office: Ill Gen Assembly 300 State House Springfield IL 62706-0001 Office Phone: 773-667-0550.

CURRIE, EARL JAMES, transportation executive; b. Fergus Falls, Minn., May 14, 1939; s. Victor James and Calma (Hammer) Currie; m. Kathleen P. Phalen, June 3, 1972; children: Jane, Joseph. BA, St. Olaf Coll., 1961; cert. in transp., Yale U., 1963; PMD, Harvard U., 1974. With Burlington No. Inc., 1964-85, asst. v.p. St. Paul, 1977-78, Chgo., 1978-80, v.p., gen. mgr. Seattle, 1980-83, sr. v.p. Overland Park, Kans., 1983-85; pres. Camas Prairie R.R., Lewiston, Idaho, 1982-83, Longview Switching Co., Wash., 1982-83, Western Fruit Express Co., 1984-85; exec. v.p. ops. Soo Line R.R. Co. & Rail Units, 1986-89; v.p. engring. CSX Transp. Co., Jacksonville, Fla., 1989-92, v.p., chief transp. officer, 1992-95; v.p. planning, chief safety officer Wis. Ctrl. Ltd., 1996-99; sr. v.p. ops. Rail World, Inc., 1999—2001; mng. dir. Estonian Rlwy. Sys., Tallinn, 2001—02; cons. rlwy. ops. and maintenance, 2002—. Bd. dirs. Belt Ry. Co. Chgo., Terminal R.R. Assn., St. Louis, Norfolk and Portsmouth Ry. Co. Bd. dirs. United Way, King County, Wash., 1980—83, Corp. Coun. Arts, Seattle, 1980—83, Jr. Achievement, 1980—82, North Shore Scenic R.R., 1999—, Hist. Union Depot, 2003—, Lake Superior Mus. Transp., 1986—89, 1999—, pres., 2001—; mem. Mpls. Neighborhood Employment Network; bd. dirs. James J. Hill Reference Libr., 2000—; trustee St. Martins Coll., Lacey, Wash., 1982—83. Mem.: Roadmasters Assn., Internat. Assn. R.R. Oper. Officers, Am. Assn. R.R. Supts. (bd. dirs. 1979—80), Am. Rlwy. Engring. and Maintenance Assn., Am. Rlwy. Engring. Assn. (bd. dirs. 1989—92), St. Olaf Coll. Alumni Assn. (bd. dirs. 1993—97), Seattle C. of C. (bd. dirs. 1980—83). Home: PO Box 2827 Warba MN 55793-2827

CURRIE, WILLIAM G., forest products executive; b. Youngsville, NY, 1947; Degree, Hope Coll., 1969. With Universal Forest Products, Inc., Grand Rapids, Mich., 1971—, pres., 1983—90, pres., CEO, 1990—2000, vice chmn., CEO, 2000—06, exec. chmn., 2006—. Office: Universal Forest Products Inc 2801 E Beltline NE Grand Rapids MI 49525

CURRIVAN, JOHN DANIEL, lawyer; b. Paris; s. Gene and Rachel Currivan; m. Patrice Salley; children: Christopher, Melissa. BS with distinction, Cornell U.; MS, U. Calif.-Berkeley; MS, U. West Fla.; JD summa cum laude, Cornell Law Sch., 1978. Bar: Ohio 1978. Mng. ptnr. S.W. Devel. Co., Kingsville, Tex., 1971-76; note editor Cornell Law Rev., Ithaca, NY, 1977-78; prosecutor Naval Legal Office, Norfolk, Va., 1978-79, chief prosecutor, 1979-81; sr. atty. USS Nimitz, 1981-83; trial judge Naval Base, Norfolk, 1983-84; tax atty. Jones Day, Cleve., 1984-88, ptnr., 1989—, coord. tax practice (Cleve. br.), 2006—. Adj. prof. law Case Western Res. U. Sch. Law, 1997—2003; chmn. Cleve. Tax Inst., 2005. Author: (with Rickert) Ohio Limited Liability Companies, 1999. Comdr. USN, 1969-84. Recipient Younger Fed. Lawyer award FBA, 1981. Mem. ABA, Nat. Assn. Bond Lawyers, Order of Coif, Tau Beta Pi, Eta Kappa Nu, Phi Kappa Phi. Home: 12700 Lake Ave Ste 2105 Lakewood OH 44107-1506 Office: Jones Day 901 Lakeside Ave E Cleveland OH 44114-1190 Office Phone: 216-586-7262. Business E-Mail: jdcurrivan@jonesday.com.

CURRY, JULIE A., state official; b. Granite City, Ill., June 7, 1962; 1 child, Evan Curry-Dennison. BA, Eastern Ill. U., 1984, MA, 1985. Ill. state rep. Dist. 101, 1995—2003; deputy chief staff, economic devel. and labor State of Ill., 2003—. Democrat. Office: 207 State Capitol Bldg Springfield IL 62706

CURTIN, MICHAEL FRANCIS, publishing executive, writer; b. Columbus, Ohio, Oct. 23, 1951; s. Robert Edward and Marie (Cummins) C.; m. Sharon Rhodes, May 26, 1976; children: Matthew, Christy. BA in Journalism, Ohio State U., 1973. Reporter The Columbus Dispatch, Ohio, 1973-85, pub. affairs editor, 1985-94, exec. mng. editor, 1994-95, editor, 1995-99, assoc. pub., 1998—2007, assoc. pub. emeritus, 2008—; pres. The Dispatch Printing Co., 1999—2002, COO, 2002—07, vice chmn., 2005—07. Bd. dirs. The Columbus Dispatch, Ohio Mag. Author: (book) The Ohio Politics Almanac, 1996, 2006. Bd. dirs. YMCA, Columbus, 1996-97, Prevent Blindness/Ohio, Columbus, 1997, Greater Columbus C. of C., Mt. Carmel Health Sys., Columbus Met. Libr. Found., Cath. Found. of Columbus Diocese. Mem. Soc. Profl. Journalists, Ohio Newspaper Assn., Athletic Club. Roman Catholic. Office: The Columbus Dispatch 34 S 3rd St Columbus OH 43215-4241 Office Phone: 614-461-5069. E-mail: mcurtin@dispatch.com.*

CURTIN, TIMOTHY JOHN, lawyer; b. Detroit, Sept. 21, 1942; s. James J. and Irma Alice (Sirotti) C.; m. B. Colleen Lindsey, July 11, 1964; children: Kathleen, Mary. BA, U. Mich., 1964, JD, 1967. Bar: Ohio 1968, Mich. 1970, U.S. Dist. Ct. (so. dist.) Ohio 1968, U.S. Dist. Ct. (we. dist.) Mich. 1970, U.S. Dist. Ct. (ea. dist.) Mich. 1980, U.S. Dist. Ct. Del. 1996, U.S. Dist. Ct. (no. dist.) Ill. 1999, U.S. Ct. Appeals (6th cir.) 1968. Assoc. Taft, Stettinius & Hollister, Cin., 1967-70, McCobb, Heaney & Van't Hof, Grand Rapids, Mich., 1970-72; ptnr. Schmidt, Howlett, Van't Hof, Snell & Vana, Grand Rapids, 1972-83, Varnum, Riddering, Schmidt & Howlett, Grand Rapids, 1983—2005, counsel, 2005—. Contbr. articles to legal publs. Treas. Kent County Dem. Com., 1976-78, chmn. 3rd Dist. Dem. Com., 1993—. Mem. ABA, Mich. Bar Assn., Grand Rapids Bar Assn., Fed. Bar Assn., Am. Bankruptcy Inst., Egypt Valley C.C. Democrat. Roman Catholic. Avocations: travel, fishing. Office: Varnum Riddering Schmidt & Howlett Box 352 333 Bridge St SW Grand Rapids MI 49501-0352 Office Phone: 616-336-6440. Business E-Mail: tjcurtin@varnumlaw.com.

CURTIS, CANDACE A., former state legislator; m. Michael Curtis; 1 child, Jameson. BA, Mich. State U., 1982. Environ. health Genesee County Health Dept. Mich.; dep. ct. clk. 67th Dist. Ct., Mich.; chair Genesee County Commrs.; rep. Mich. Dist. 51, 1993-98. Mem. Genesee County Dem. Com. Mem. Farm Bur., South End Dem. Club.

CURTIS, CHARLES EDWARD, Canadian government official; b. Winnipeg, Man., Can., July 28, 1931; s. Samuel and May (Goodison) C.; m. Hilda Marion Simpson, Oct. 30, 1954; 1 dau., Nancy Maude. C.A., U. Manitoba, 1955. Chartered acct. Dunwoody & Co., Winnipeg, 1949-54; chief assessor nat. revenue, income tax bd. Province of .B., Can., 1954-67; asst. dep. min. budget fin. and adminstrn. Province of Man., Winnipeg, 1967-75, dep. min., 1976-96. Past CEO Man. Energy Authority; acting CEO MTX subs. Man. Telephone Sys.; mem. investment coms. Superannuation Bd., WPG Found., Manitoba Mus. Man & Nature, Law Soc. Manitoba; exec.-in-residence faculty of mgmt. U. Man. Fellow Can. Inst. Chartered Accts. (past chmn. pub. sector acctg. and audit standards com.); mem. Man. Inst. Chartered Accts. (pres. 1975-76), Law Soc. of Man. (lay bencher), Order of Man., Rotary (hon. treas. 1974-2000), Man. Club. Home: 596 South Dr Winnipeg MB Canada R3T 0B1

CURTIS, CHARLES G., JR., lawyer; BA in History magna cum laude, Harvard U., 1978; JD, U. Chgo., 1982. Bar: Wis., Am. Bar Assoc., U.S. Supreme Ct., U.S. Ct. appeals, 7th cir., U.S. Dist. Ct., Nr. N.Y. Law Clerk Senior Judge David L. Bazelon, U.S. Ct. of Appeals, 1982—83, Justice William J. Brennan, Jr., U.S. Supreme Ct., 1984; ptnr. Foley & Lardner; atty., Co-Chair Appeals and Strategy Heller, Ehrman, White, & McAuliffe LLP, 2001—. Named one of The Best Lawyers in Am., 2003—04. Office: Heller Ehrman 1 Main St Ste 201 Madison WI 53703 Office Phone: 608-663-7480. Fax: 608-663-7499. E-mail: ccurtis@hewm.com.

CURTIS, DOUGLAS HOMER, small business owner; b. Jackson, Mich., July 19, 1934; s. Homer K. and Luella D. (Hall) C.; m. Jean A. Breaux; children: Rebecca, Linda, Colleen, Robert. BA, Park Coll., Parkville, Mo., 1956. With Gen. Electric Co., 1958-69, mgr. Boston region Gen. Electric Supply Co. div., 1967-69; v.p. fin. and adminstrn. internat. Data Corp., Boston, 1969; v.p. fin. Franklin Electric Co. Inc., Bluffton, Ind., 1969-80; pres. Curtis Assocs., Inc., Bluffton, 1980-82; pres., COO Satelco, Inc., San Antonio, 1983-84; v.p. adminstrn. Lyall Electric Co., Kendallville, Ind., 1984-86; pres., owner Flexible Personnel Group of Cos., Inc., Ft. Wayne, Ind., 1987-97, Nat. On-Site Pers., 1991-2001, HR America, 1992—, On-Site Med. Staffing, 2000—. Bd. dirs. Wabash Valley Mfg., Inc., Silver Lake, Ind., Sentry Points; pres. Wells County (Ind.) Hosp. Authority, 1974-75 Served to capt. USMCR, 1956-58. Mem. Nat. Assn. Securities Dealers (vicechmn. fin. 1980, chmn. fin. com. 1980), Fin. Execs. Inst. (chpt. dir. 1975) Office: 1833 Magnavox Way Fort Wayne IN 46804-1539 Office Phone: 260-436-3878. Business E-Mail: dcurtis@hramerica.net.

CURTIS, JAMES L., lawyer; b. 1965; BA, Albion Coll., 1987; JD, Loyola U., 1990. Bar: Ill. 1990, US Supreme Ct., US Ct. Appeals (7th,& 11th cir.), US Dist. Ct., Dist. Colo., US Dist. Ct. (no. dist.) Ill. Ptnr. Seyfarth Shaw LLP, Chgo., chmn. hiring com., mem. exec. com. Office: Seyfarth Shaw LLP 55 East Monroe St Chicago IL 60603 Office Phone: 312-269-8815. Office Fax: 312-269-8869. Business E-Mail: jcurtis@seyfarth.com.

CURTISS, ELDEN FRANCIS, archbishop; b. Baker, Oreg., June 16, 1932; s. Elden F. and Mary (Neiger) C. BA, St. Edward Sem., Seattle, MDiv, 1958; MA in Edn1. Adminstrn, U. Portland, 1965; postgrad., Fordham U., U. Notre Dame. Ordained priest Diocese of Baker, Oreg., 1958, campus chaplain, 1959—68, supt. schools, 1962—70, pastor, 1968—70; mem. ecumenical ministries State of Oreg., 1972; pres., rector Mt. Angel Sem., Benedict, Oreg., 1972—76, mem. bd. regents, 1976—93; mem. pastoral svcs. Oreg. State Hosp., Salem, 1975—76; ordained bishop, 1976; bishop Diocese of Helena, Mont., 1976—93; archbishop Archdiocese of Omaha, 1993—. Chmn. bd. Boys Town USA, Cath. Mut. Relief Soc. Am.; mem. Pontifical Coun. for Family, Rome; Episcopal advisor Serra Internat. Mem.: Nat. Cath. Ednl. Assn. (bishops and pres's com. coll. dept., Outstanding Educator 1972). Roman Catholic. Office: Archdiocese of Omaha 100 N 62nd St Omaha NE 68132-2702*

CURWEN, RANDALL WILLIAM, journalist, editor; b. Hazel Green, Wis., Apr. 18, 1946; s. Charles William and Theda (Hillary) C. BS, U. Wis., 1968. Reporter Rockford (Ill.) Morning Star, 1968-69, copy editor/asst. city editor, 1969-72; copy editor Chgo. Today, 1972-74; copy editor/asst. sect. editor Chgo. Tribune, 1974-80, assoc. features editor, 1980-91, co-editor evening edit., 1992, travel editor, 1992—. Recipient 1st place headline writing award Ill. UPI, 1977, Johnae Earl award Chgo. Tribune, 1979, 96, Soc. Am. Travel Writers Ctrl. States award for best travel sect., 1994, 99, 2001, 02. Mem. Soc. Am. Travel Writers (Lowell Thomas award for best travel sect. 1995, 97), Nat. Lesbian and Gay Journalists Assn., Soc. Am. Travel Writers (v.p. 2005-06). Avocations: travel, baseball, films. Home: 930 W Roscoe Rear Coachhouse Chicago IL 60657 Office: Chgo Tribune Co 435 N Michigan Ave PO Box 25340 Chicago IL 60625-0340

CUSACK, JOHN T., lawyer; b. Sept. 10, 1958; BS magna cum laude, Drew Univ., 1980; JD, George Washington Univ., 1983. Bar: NY 1984, Ill. 1986. Ptnr., chair fin. group DLA Piper Rudnick Gray Cary, Chgo. and NYC. Mem.: ABA, Chgo. Bar Assn., Ill. State Bar Assn. Office: DLA Piper Rudnick Gray Cary 1251 Ave of the Americas New York NY 10020-1104 also: DLA Piper Rudnick Gray Cary Ste1900 203 N LaSalle St Chicago IL 60601-1293 Office Phone: 212-835-6049, 312-368-4049. Office Fax: 312-236-7516. Business E-Mail: john.cusack@piperrudnick.com.

CUSACK, JOHN THOMAS, lawyer; b. Oak Park, Ill., June 22, 1935; s. Thomas Jr. and Clare (Hock) C.; m. Mary Louise Coughlin, Nov. 1, 1969; children: John, James, Mary Helen, Cathleen. AB cum laude, U. Notre Dame, 1957; JD, U. Mich., 1960; postgrad., Harvard U., 1961-62. Bar: Ill. 1960, U.S. Dist. Ct. (no. dist.) Ill. 1961, U.S. Dist. Ct. (no. dist.) Ind. 1983, U.S. Tax Ct. 1984, U.S. Ct. Appeals (7th cir.) 1973, U.S. Ct. Appeals (5th and 9th cirs.) 1975, U.S. Ct. Appeals (3d cir.) 1986, U.S. Ct. Appeals (10th cir.) 1987, U.S. Ct. Appeals (11th cir.) 1988, U.S. Supreme Ct. 1966. Trial atty. antitrust div. U.S. Dept. Justice, 1962-70; assoc. Gardner, Carton & Douglas, Chgo., 1970-74, ptnr., 1974—, chmn. litigation dept., 1978-86, chmn. antitrust practice group, 1986—. Contbr. articles to legal jours. Trustee Fenwick H.S. 1st lt. JAGC, USAR, 1963-67. Mem. ABA (antitrust and litigation sect., health law com. 1960—), Chgo. Bar Assn., Law Club City Chgo. Roman Catholic. Home: 1030 Franklin Ave River Forest IL 60305-1340 Office: Gardner Carton & Douglas 191 N Wacker Dr Ste 3700 Chicago IL 60606-1698 E-mail: jcusack@gcd.com.

CUSMANO, J. JOYCE, public relations executive; b. Mich. BA, Eastern Mich. U.; MA, U. Md., 1972. Asst. dir. Detroit Youtheatre Detroit Inst. Arts; spl. events dir. Detroit Renaissance, 1979—84; v.p. Franco Pub. Rels. Group, Detroit, 1985-90, sr. v.p., 1991—98, dir., consumer group, 1991—98; pres. Sojourn Comm. Grp., Grosse Point Woods, Mich., 1998—. Mem. Women's Econ. Club. Office: Sojourn Comm Grp 19776 E Ida Ln Grosse Pointe Woods MI 48236

CUSSLER, EDWARD LANSING, JR., chemical engineer, educator; s. Edward Lansing and Eleanor Christine (Lloyd-Jones) C.; m. Elizabeth Campbell Beidler. BS in Chem. Engring., Yale U., 1961; MS in Chem. Engring., U. Wis., 1963, PhD, 1965; DSc (hon.), U. Lund, 2002. Rsch. asst. U. Wis., Madison, 1961—65, postdoctoral fellow, 1961—65, U. Adelaide, Australia, 1965-66, Yale U., 1966-67; asst. prof. Carnegie-Mellon U., 1967-70, assoc. prof., 1970-73, prof., 1973-80, U. Minn., Mpls., 1980—. Mem. editl. bd. Jour. Membrane Sci., 1975—. Recipient William H. Frances S. Ryan award Carnegie-Mellon U., 1975, George Taylor Tchg. award U. Minn., 1987, Separations Sci. award ACS, 2002. Mem. NAE (Separations Sci. award 2002), AIChE (bd. dirs. 1989-92, v.p. 1993, pres. 1994, editl. bd. 1996—, Alan P. Colburn award 1975, W.K. Lewis award 2001), Am. Assn. Engrs. Soc. (chair 1996). Office: U Minn Chem Engring Dept 421 Washington Ave SE Minneapolis MN 55455-0373 Office Phone: 612-625-1596. Business E-Mail: cussl001@umn.edu.

CUSTER, CHARLES FRANCIS, lawyer; b. Hays, Kans., Aug. 19, 1928; s. Raymond Earl and Eva Marie (Walker) C.; m. Irene Louise Macarow, Jan. 2, 1950; children: Shannon Elaine, Charles Francis, Murray Maxwell, Kelly Sue. AB, U. Chgo., 1948, JD, 1958. Bar: Ill. 1958, U.S. Dist. Ct. (no dist.) Ill. 1971, U.S. Supreme Ct. 1991. Assoc. Meyers & Matthias, Chgo., 1958-72; pvt. practice Chgo., 1972-78; ptnr. Vedder, Price, Kaufman & Kammholz, Chgo., 1978-98, of counsel, 1998—. Arbitrator, mediator. Past dir. Family Care Svcs., Chgo. Mem. ABA (mem. fed. regulation of securities and devels. in investment svcs. coms., dispute resolution sect.), Chgo. Bar Assn. (mem. securities law com., mem. investment cos. subcom., alternative dispute resolution com.), Cliff Dwellers (past officer and dir.). Avocations: music, theater. Home: 5210 S Kenwood Ave Chicago IL 60615-4006 Office: Vedder Price Kaufman & Kammholz 222 N La Salle St Ste 2600 Chicago IL 60601-1100 Office Phone: 312-609-7545.

CUTLER, ALEXANDER MACDONALD, manufacturing executive; b. Milw., May 28, 1951; s. Richard Woolsey and Elizabeth (Fitzgerald) C.; m. Sarah Lynn Stark, Oct. 11, 1980; children: David Alexander, William MacDonald. BA, Yale U., 1973; MBA, Dartmouth Coll., 1975. Fin. analyst Cutler-Hammer, Milw., 1975-77, bus. group contr., 1977-79; contr. custom distbn. and control divsn. Eaton Corp., Atlanta, 1979-80, plant mgr. custom distbn. and control divsn., 1981-82, mgr. custom distbn. and control divsn., 1982-83, mgr. power distbn. divsn. Milw., 1984-85, gen. mgr. indsl. control and power distbn., 1985-86, pres. controls group Cleve., 1986-91, exec. v.p. ops., 1992-93, exec. v.p., COO controls, 1993-95, pres., COO, 1995-2000, chmn., pres., CEO, 2000—, bd. dirs. Bd. dirs. Axcelis Techs., 2000—06. Bd. dirs. United Way Svcs. Cleve., 2000-06, N.E. Ohio Coun. on Higher Edn., 1993-97, Greater Cleve. Growth Assn., 2001-04, Cleve. Tomorrow, 2000-04, Greater Cleve. Roundtable, 2000-04; class agt. alumni fund Loomis Chaffee Sch., Windsor, Conn., 1969—; bd. dirs. alumni fund Yale U., New Haven, 1974-89; trustee The Cleve. Play House, 1987-2002, Gt. Lakes Mus., Inc., 1988-91, Mus. Natural History, Cleve., 1989-97; bd. overseers Amos Tuck Sch. Bus. Dartmouth Coll., 1996-2006; trustee Loomis Inst., 2003-2006; active Keycorp., 2000—, Bus. Roundtable, 2002—; chmn. Greater Cleve. Partnership, 2004-06. Mem.: Nat. Elec. Mfrs. Assn. (indsl. automation divsn. 1986—90, bd. govs. 1987—99, treas. 1993—95, bd. govs. 1996—99), Elec. Mfrs. Club (bd. dirs. 1995—), Yale U. Alumni Assn. (pres. Cleve. chpt. 1991—93, exec. com. of vis. com. Weatherhood Sch. Mgmt. 1993—2002, Yale devel. bd. 1998—), Musical Arts Assn., Chagrin Valley Hunt Club. Avocation: tennis. Office: Eaton Corp 1111 Superior Ave Eaton Ctr Cleveland OH 44114-2584 Office Phone: 216-523-5000.

CUTLER, RICHARD W., lawyer; b. New Rochelle, NY, Mar. 9, 1917; s. Charles Evelyn and Amelia (MacDonald) C.; m. Elizabeth Fitzgerald, Oct. 18, 1947; children: Marguerite Blackburn, Alexander MacDonald, Judith Elizabeth. BA, Yale U., 1938, LLB, 1941. Bar: Conn. 1941, N.Y. 1942, Wis. 1950, D.C. 1975, U.S. Supreme Ct. 1980. Practiced in, NYC, 1941—49, Milw., 1949—87; assoc. Donovan, Leisure, Newton & Lumbard, 1941—42; atty. Legal Aid Soc., 1946—47, RCA Comm., Inc., 1947—49; ptnr. Quarles & Brady, and predecessors, 1954—87; gen. ptnr. Sunset Investment Co., Milw. Author: Zoning Law and Practice in Wisconsin, 1967, Greater Milwaukee's Growing Pains, 1950-2000: An Insider's View, 2001, Counterspy: Memoir of a Counterintelligence Officer in World War II and the Cold War, 2004. Chmn. Milw. br. Fgn. Policy Assn., 1951-53; pres. Childrens Service Soc. Wis., 1961-63, Neighborhood House, 1971-74; sec. Southeastern Wis. Regional Planning Commn., 1960-84, Yale Devel. Bd., 1973-79; bd. dirs. Wis. Dept. Resource Devel., 1967-68; Met. Milw. Study Commn., 1957-61; bd. dirs. Milw. Innovation Ctr., 1985-89, pres., 1984-85, exec. v.p., 1985-89; bd. dirs. Greater Milw. Com., 1982-89. Capt. USAAF, 1943-46 and OSS, 1944-46. Recipient Disting. Leadership award Am. Planning Assn., 1992. Mem. ABA, Wis. Bar Assn., Milw. Club, Milw. Country Club, Town Club, Phi Beta Kappa. Presbyterian. Home: 938 W Shaker Cir Mequon WI 53092-6032 Office: 411 E Wisconsin Ave Milwaukee WI 53202-4461 Home Phone: 262-241-4305. Business E-Mail: clickcutter@wi.RR.com. E-mail: rwc@quarles.com.

CUTLER, STEVE KEITH, state legislator; b. Britton, SD, June 2, 1948; s. Keith and Kathryn (Olson) C.; m. Penny Louise Jones, 1969; children: Jennifer, Shanda. BS, S.D. State U., 1970, MS, 1971. Asst. material engr. S.D. Dept. Transp., 1971-74; rep. S.D. State Ho. of Reps. Dist. 2, 1984—, vice chmn. Taxation Com., mem. legis. procedure, state affairs and taxation coms. Named Outstanding Freshman Civil Engr., ASCE, 1967, Outstanding Sr. Civil Engr., ASCE, 1972. Mem. Am. Legion (legis. officer 1985), Claremont Cmty. Club, Claremont Sportsman Club, Sigma Tau, Chi Epsilon. Office: 12057 411th Ave Claremont SD 57432-7302

CUTSHALL-HAYES, DIANE MARION, elementary school educator; b. Pitts., Jan. 15, 1954; d. William Edward and Irma Delores (Marion) Snowden; m. John Steven Baran, Jan. 11, 1975 (div. 1982); 1 child, Allison Rae; m. Dean F. Cutshall, Dec. 17, 1989. BA, Eureka Coll., 1975; BS, Ind. U., Ft. Wayne, 1986. First grade tchr. Hoover Elem. Sch., Schaumburg, Ill., 1976-79, Indian Meadows Elem. Sch., Ft. Wayne, Ind., 1979-80, 82-86, Perry Hill Elem. Sch., Ft. Wayne, 1981-82; second grade tchr. Indian Meadows Elem. Sch., Ft. Wayne, 1986—. Tchr. rep. State Ill. Rsch. Adv. Coun., 1991; active ISTEP Blue Ribbon Commn., Ill., 1989, State Ill. Lang. Arts Adv. Commn., 1988, Project REAP Adv. Bd., 1988. Spl. events chair Greater Ft. Wayne (Ind.) Crime Stoppers, 1992-95; active YMCA Camp Potawotami, Ft. Wayne, 1993—, Eureka Coll. Alumni Assn., 1992—, pres., 1995—. Christa McAuliffe fellow State of Ind., 1987; recipient Excellence in Edn. award Inst. Copy Corp., 1988, Outstanding Young Alumna award Eureka Coll., 1990, Armstrong Tchr. Educator award, 1998; named Ind. State Elem. Tchr. of Yr., 1993. Mem. Nat. Coun. Tchrs. Math., Internat. Reading Assn., Tchrs. Applying Whole Langs. Lutheran. Avocations: rollerblading, racquetball, reading, walking. Home: 5809 Eagle Creek Dr Fort Wayne IN 46814-3207 Office: Indian Meadows School 11420 Ernst Rd Roanoke IN 46783-9660

CUTTS, CHARLES EUGENE, retired engineering educator; b. Sioux Falls, SD, May 15, 1914; s. Charles Clifford and Ethel May (Gardner) C.; m. Jane Bebensee, Mar. 16, 1946; children: George Gardner, Elizabeth Anne. B.C.E., U. Minn., 1936, MS in Civil Engring, 1939, PhD, 1949. Registered profl. engr., Minn., Fla., Mich. Instrumentman Milw. R.R., 1936-38; teaching asst. dept. civil engring. U. Minn., 1938-39, instr., asst. prof., 1946-50; engr. C.F. Haglin & Sons, summer 1939; asst. prof. dept. civil engring. Robert Coll., Istanbul, Turkey, 1939-42; engr. Braithwaite Co., Ltd., Iskenderun, Turkey, summer 1942, 43; assoc. prof., assoc. rsch. engr. U. Fla., 1950-53; engr. Engring. Scis. Program NSF, Washington, 1953-56; profl. lectr. civil engring. George Washington U., 1955-56; prof., chmn. dept. civil engring. Mich. State U., 1956-69, prof., 1969-84, prof. emeritus, 1984—; ret., 1984. Cons. U. Minn. Morocco Project, 1986. Author: Structural Design in Reinforced Concrete, 1954, other tech. publs. Served to maj. C.E. AUS, 1943-46; lt. col. Res. ret. Mem. Nat. Acad. Scis. (fellowship com. 1961-63), ASCE (chmn. com. on mech. properties of materials 1965, pres. Mich. sect. 1967, chmn. com. on engring. edn. 1969-70), Am. Concrete Inst., Am. Soc. Engring. Edn. (chmn. civil engr. div. 1965-66, v.p. 1970—, chmn. constn. and bylaws com. 1981-83), Engrs. Coun. Profl. Devel. (chmn. region 5 1972-73), Nat. Soc. Profl. Engrs., Tau Beta Pi, Chi Epsilon. Home: 4599 Ottawa Dr Okemos MI 48864-2028 Office: Civil Engring Mich State Univ East Lansing MI 48824 Office Phone: 517-349-9590.

CVETANOVICH, DAN L., lawyer; b. Wheeling, W.Va., Oct. 2, 1952; s. Louis J. and Nila J. (Hall) Cvetanovich; m. Sharon M. Smith, Sept. 8, 1979; children: Gregory L., Steven W. BA, West Liberty State Coll., 1974; JD, Harvard U., 1977. Bar: Ohio 1977, US Dist. Ct. (so. dist.) Ohio 1978, US Ct. Appeals (6th cir.) 1980, US Dist. Ct. (no. dist.) Ohio 1984, W.Va. 1985, US Dist. Ct. (so. dist.) W.Va. 1985, US Ct. Appeals (4th cir.) 1986, US Dist. Ct. (we. dist.) Tex. 1998, US Dist. Ct. (no. dist.) W.Va. 2001. Assoc. Bricker & Eckler, Columbus, Ohio, 1977-82, ptnr., 1983-87, Arter & Hadden LLP, Columbus, 1987—2003; mem. Bailey Cavalieri LLC, Columbus, 2003—. Mem.: ABA, Columbus Bar Assn., W.Va. State Bar, Ohio State Bar Assn. Republican. Avocations: hunting, fishing, golf. Office: Bailey Cavalieri LLC One Columbus 10 W Broad St 21st Fl Columbus OH 43215-3422 Office Phone: 614-229-3291. Business E-Mail: Dan.Cvetanovich@baileycavalieri.com.

CYGAN, THOMAS S., metal products executive; Sales trainee Joseph T. Ryerson & Son subs. Inland Steel Industries Inc., inside sales mgr. Detroit, 1976-81, gen. mgr. Kansas City, 1981-95; pres., COO Ryerson W. subs. Inland Steel Industries Inc., 1995—. Office: Ryerson Tull Inc 2621 W 15th Pl Chicago IL 60608-1752

CYPHERT, MICHAEL A., lawyer; b. Cleve., Jan. 15, 1948; BA, Case Western Reserve U., 1970, JD, 1973. Bar: Ohio 1973, U.S. Supreme Ct. 1985. Mem. Thompson Hine LLP, Cleve. Adj. mem. faculty Case Western Reserve U. Sch. of Law, 1976-90. Mem. Def. Rsch. Inst. Office: Thompson Hine 127 Public Square #3900 Cleveland OH 44114

CYPRUS, NICHOLAS STANLEY, automotive executive, accountant; b. NYC, May 1, 1953; s. Nick and Niki Cyprus; m. Barbara Ann Helmick, Sept. 26, 1981; 1 child, Nicky. BS in Acctg., Fairleigh Dickinson U., 1977; MBA, NYU, 1990. CPA. Staff mgr. acctg. policy AT&T, Murray Hill, NJ, 1982-84, staff mgr. fin. assurance, 1984-85; asst. contr. portfolio acctg. AT&T Capital Corp., Morristown, NJ, 1985-87, asst. corp. contr., 1987-89, v.p., contr., 1989-95; asst. corp. contr. external reporting AT&T Inc., Morristown, NJ, 1995-98, v.p., contr. Basking Ridge, NJ, 1999—2004; contr., chief acctg. officer Interpublic Group of Cos., 2004—06, GM Corp., Detroit, 2006—. Contbr. articles to profl. jours. Bd. dirs. Ctr. for Enabling Techs., Whippany, N.J., 1997—. Mem. AICPA, N.J. Soc. CPAs (Outstanding CPA Bus. Leader award 1998-2000, 1999; mem. conf. bd. contr.'s coun.). Avocations: sport fishing, boating. Office: GM PO Box 300 Detroit MI 48265-3000

CYR, LISA WATSON, lawyer; BA summa cum laude, U. Minn., Duluth, 1995; JD magna cum laude, William Mitchell Coll. Law, 1998. Bar: Minn. 1998. Atty. McCullough, Smith, Williams & Cyr, P.A., St. Paul. Guest lectr. Family Law Inst. Named a Rising Star, Minn. Super Lawyers mag., 2006. Mem.: Ramsey County Bar Assn. (mem. family law sect., co-chair family law sect. 2001—02), Minn. State Bar Assn. (mem. family law sect.), Phi Kappa Phi. Office: McCullough Smith Williams & Cyr PA 905 Parkway Dr Saint Paul MN 55117 Office Phone: 651-772-3446. E-mail: lwatsoncyr@mcculloughlawyers.com.

CYRS, MICHAEL THOMAS, lawyer; b. Wausau, Wis., 1969; BBA, U. Notre Dame, 1991; MBA, JD, Marquette U., 1994. Bar: Wis. 1994, Ill. 1994, CFP: 2000. Atty. Hinshaw & Culbertson, 1994—97; ptnr. WilliamsMcCarthy, LLP, Rockford, Ill., 2002—. Mem.: Wis. Bar Assn., No. Ill. Estate Planning Coun., ABA, Ill. State Bar Assn., Winnebago County Bar Assn. (treas., dir. 2001—02, chmn. tax sect. 2000). Office: WilliamsMcCarthy LLP PO Box 219 120 W State St 4th Fl Rockford IL 61105-0219 Office Phone: 815-987-8900. Office Fax: 815-968-0019. E-mail: mcyrs@wilmac.com.

CYRUS, MICHAEL J., electric power industry executive; m. Mariet Cyrus; children: Maura, Audrey, Marshall. BA, MBA, U. Ark.; grad., Mahler Sch. Advanced Mgmt. Skills Program. With Conoco, Inc., 1982-88, Kottke Assocs., Chgo., 1988-93; joined Natural Gas Clearinghouse NGC Corp., 1993; pres. NGC Canada; exec. v.p. ovagas Clearinghouse Ltd.; sr. v.p. trading and ops. Electric Clearinghouse, 1997; exec. v.p. Cinergy Capital and Trade, Inc., 1998; pres. Energy Commodities Bus. Unit Cinergy Corp. Bd. mem. PanAlberta Gas Ltd., Novagas Clearinghouse Ltd.; del. advisor NYMEX, Canadian Gas Assn. Office: 139 E 4th St Cincinnati OH 45202-4003

CZARNECKI, WALTER P., truck rental company executive; Exec. v.p. Penske Corp., Detroit, 1978—. Office: 2555 S Telegraph Rd Bloomfield Hills MI 48302-0954

CZESTOCHOWSKI, JOSEPH STEPHEN, administrator, publisher, investor; b. NYC, Aug. 6, 1950; s. Joseph Stephen and Julia (Skowron) C.; m. Debra J. Kindred Nicholson, Nov. 18, 1972; 1 child, J. F. Stefan Parker. Diploma, Jagiellonian U., Krakow, Poland, 1971; BA, U. Ill., Champaign-Urbana, 1971, MA, 1973. Curator of collections Brooks Mus. Art, Memphis, 1973; dir. Decker Gallery, Md. Inst., Balt., 1975—78, The Dixon Gallery and Gardens, Memphis, 1994—98, Parker Cop., 1993—; exec. dir. Cedar Rapids Mus. Art, Iowa, 1978—94. Dir. Internat. Arts The Torch Press, 1993—; sr. examiner Accreditation Comm. of the AAM; field reviewer Inst. Mus. Svcs.; govt. and art com. Assn. Art Mus. Dirs. Author: (monograph) The Published Prints of Charles Burchfield, 1976, The Pioneers, 1977, John S. Curry -A Portrait of a Rural America, 1977, Go West, 1978, Polish Posters, 1979, The Combined Works of Arthur B. Davies, 1980, Prints by Childe Hassam, 1980, John S. Curry and Grant Wood -A Portrait of Rural America, 1981, The American Landscape Tradition 1738-1965, 1982, Marvin D. Cone, An American Tradition, 1985, Marvin D. Cone and Grant Wood -An American Tradition, 1990, James Swann -In Quest of a Printmaker, 1990, Marvin D. Cone -Art as Self-Portrait, 1990; contbr. pubs. in field, articles to profl. jours. Mem. adv. bd. Krannert Art Mus., Bronze Cir., LAS Coll., U. Ill. Urbana; mem. pres. coun. U. Ill. Found., Urbana. Fellow Vatican Mus. and Smithsonian Inst., 1976, Smithsonian Instn., 1977-79; recipient first Nancy Hanks Meml. award for profl. excellence Am. Assn. Mus., 1985; rsch. grant Brazil Minister Fgn. Affairs, 1995-98, Portugal Ministry Culture, 1998, Spain Ministry Culture, 1998. Mem. Am. Assn. Mus. Dirs., Internat. Coun. Mus., The Kosciuszko Found. (trustee 1988-96), The Polish Inst. Arts and Scis. in Am., Inc. (trustee 1986-96), Ctr. for the Study of the Presidency (trustee), Coll. Liberal Arts and Scis. U. Ill. Alumni Assn. (trustee 1994-96), Rotary Internat. Office: Internat Arts 1550 N Lake Shore Dr Apt 28C Chicago IL 60610 Business E-Mail: jc@internationalarts.org, interarts@parkers.com.*

DABERKO, DAVID A., retired bank executive; b. Hudson, Ohio, 1945; BA, Denison U., 1967; MBA, Case Western Res. U., 1970. Mgmt. trainee Nat. City Bank, Cleve., 1968-72, asst. v.p., 1972-73, v.p. bank investment divsn., dept. head met. lending divsn., 1973-80, sr. v.p. corp. banking, 1980-82, pres., 1987-93; exec. v.p. corp. banking Nat. City Corp., Nat. City Bank, Cleve., 1982-85; pres., bd. dirs. Nat. City Bank (formerly BancOhio Nat. Bank), Columbus, 1985-87; dep. chmn. Nat. City Corp., Cleve., 1987-93, pres., CEO, 1993-95, chmn., CEO, 1995—2007, chmn., 2007. Dir. Fed. Res. Bank, Cleve. Trustee Cleve. Tomorrow, Greater Cleve. Growth Assn., Case Western Res. U., Hawken Sch., Neighborhood Progress, Univ. Cir. Inc., Univ. Hosp. Health Sys.; co-chair Harvest for Hunger Campaign, 1992, 93. Mem. Bankers Roundtable.

DABERKOW, DAVE, historic site director; b. Windom, Minn., Nov. 16, 1945; BS, S.D. State U., 1968. Park mgr. Richmond & Mina Recreation Area, Aberdeen, S.D., 1971-86; dist. park mgr. Ft. Sisseton State Park, Lake City, S.D., 1986—. Office: Fort Sisseton State Hist Park 11545 Northside Dr Lake City SD 57247-6142

DAEHN, GLENN STEVEN, materials scientist; b. Chgo., July 4, 1961; s. Ralph Charles and Beverly S. (Shanske) D.; m. Margaret A. Burkhart, Oct. 25, 1987; children: Andrew Joseph, Katrin Ellen, Matthew Charles. BS, Northwestern U., Evanston, Ill., 1983; MS, Stanford U., Calif., 1985, PhD, 1988. Rsch. asst. Stanford U., Palo Alto, Calif., 1983-87; asst. prof. dept. materials sci. and engring. Ohio State U., Columbus, 1987-92, assoc. prof. dept. materials sci. and engring., 1992-96, Fontana prof. dept. materials sci. and engring., 1996—. Co-founder, v.p. technology Excera Materials Group, 1992-2007. Co-editor: Modeling the Deformation of Crystalline Solids, 1991. Named Nat. Young Investigator, NSF, 1992; recipient Young Investigator award Army Rsch. Office, 1992, R.L. Hardy Gold medal TMS, 1992, Marcus Grossman award ASM Internat., 1990. Mem. ASM Internat., Am. Ceramic Soc., Materials Rsch. Soc., Minerals, Metals and Materials Soc. Achievements include description and practical applications of how temperature changes accelerate the deformation of composite materials; co-development of new class of ceramic-metal composites; development of hyperplasticity --practical application of extended metal ductility observed at high velocity. Home: 2076 Fairfax Rd Upper Arlington OH 43221-4319 Office: Ohio State U Materials Sci Dept 2041 N College Rd Columbus OH 43210-1124 Office Phone: 614-292-6779. Business E-Mail: Daehn.1@osu.edu.

DAGES, PETER F., manufacturing executive; BA, U. Ill.; MBA, U. Chgo. Supt., Chgo. plant Stone Container Corp., 1980, gen. mgr. Bedford Park, Ill., 1985-91, dir. mfg., corrugated container divsn., 1991-96, divsn. v.p., regional mgr., 1996-99, v.p., gen. mgr., corrugated container divsn., 1999—. Office: Smurfit-Stone Container Corp 150 N Michigan Ave Chicago IL 60601-7553

DAGGETT, ROXANN, state legislator; b. Mar. 10, 1947; m. Dave Daggett, Aug. 20, 1967; 2 children. Student, Concordia Coll., 1965-67; BS, U. N.D., 1968. Motivational spkr.; rep. Dist. 11A Minn. Ho. of Reps., 1994—.

DAHL, LAWRENCE FREDERICK, chemistry professor; b. Evanston, Ill., June 2, 1929; s. Lawrence Gustave and Anne (Stuessy) D.; m. June Lomnes, Sept. 1, 1956; children: Larry, Eric, Christopher (dec.). BS in Chemistry, U. Louisville, 1951; PhD, Iowa State U., 1956; DSc (hon.), U. Louisville, 1991. Postdoctoral fellow Ames (Iowa State U.) Lab. AEC, 1957; from instr. to assoc. prof. chemistry U. Wis., Madison, 1957-64, prof., 1964—, R. E. Rundlechair, 1978—, Hilldale chair and prof., 1991—. Brotherton rsch. prof. U. Leeds, 1983 Recipient Inorganic Chemistry award Am. Chem. Soc., 1974, Disting. Alumnus award U. Louisville Coll. Letters and Sci., 1990, Sr. U.S. Scientist Humboldt award Alexander von Humboldt Stiftung, 1985, R.S. Nyholm medal Royal Soc. Chemistry, 1985, P. Chini medal Italian Soc. Chemistry, 1989, J.C. Bailar Jr. medal U. Ill., 1990, F. Basolo medal Northwestern U., 1995, Hilldale award in phys. scis. U. Wis., 1994, Willard Gibbs medal, Chgo. sect. Am. Chem. Soc., 1999, Pioneer award, Am. Inst. Chemists, 2000; named to Hon. Order Ky. Cols., 1982; Alfred P. Sloan fellow, 1963-65, U. Louisvlle Coll. Letters and Sci. fellow, 1990. Fellow AAAS, N.Y. Acad. Sci., Am. Acad. Arts and Scis.; mem. NAS. Home: 4817 Woodburn Dr Madison WI 53711-1345 Office: Univ of Wis Madison Dept of Chemistry 1101 University Ave Madison WI 53706-1322 Fax: 608-262-6143. E-mail: dahl@chem.wisc.edu.

DAHL, REYNOLD PAUL, economics professor; b. Willmar, Minn., Feb. 19, 1924; s. Paul Efrain and Margaret Elizabeth (Peterson) D.; m. Alyce Rosalind Druskis, Sept. 11, 1948; children— John, Ann Student, North Park Coll., Chgo., 1942-43; BS, U. Minn., 1949, MS, 1950, PhD, 1954. Instr. agrl. econs. U. Minn., St. Paul, 1950-54, asst. prof., 1954-58, assoc. prof., 1958-63, prof., 1963-94, prof. emeritus, 1994—, chief of party, economist Tunis, Tunisia, 1967-70. Agrl. economist Soybean Coun. of Am., Brussels, 1962-63; dir. Mpls. Grain Exchange, 1972-80; agrl. economist U.S. AID, Port-au-Prince, Haiti, 1972, 74 Contbr. articles to profl. jours., chpts. to books. Served with USAAF, 1943-46; PTO Mem. Am. Agrl. Econs. Assn., Am. Inst. Coop. (trustee 1981-84), Xi Sigma Pi, Alpha Zeta Roman Catholic. Avocations: gardening, fishing. Home: 1666 Coffman St Apt 326 Saint Paul MN 55108-1344 Office: U Minn Dept Applied Econs 1994 Buford Ave Saint Paul MN 55108-6038 Office Phone: 612-625-7287. E-mail: dahlx008@umn.edu.

DAHLIN, DONALD C(LIFFORD), academic administrator; b. Ironwood, Mich., June 18, 1941; married; 2 children. BA magna cum laude in history, Carroll Coll., 1963; PhD in Govt. (Univ. Departmental fellow), Claremont Grad. Sch., 1969; fellow in ct. mgmt., Inst. Ct. Mgmt., 1980. Asst. prof. govt. U. S.D., Vermillion, 1966-70, assoc. prof., 1970-75, prof., 1975—, dir. criminal justice studies program, 1972-75, 78-89, chmn. dept. polit. sci., 1978-89, 95-98, fellow Pres.'s office, 1984-85, interim v.p. acad. affairs, 1988-90, acting dean continuing edn., 1995, v.p. acad. affairs, 1997—2004, ret., acting pres., 2002. Mgmt. analyst Law Enforcement Assistance Adminstrn., Dept. Justice, Washington, 1970-71; sec. S.D. Dept. Public Safety, Pierre, 1975-78; lectr., cons. in field; mem. S.D. Human Resource Cabinet Sub-Group, 1975-78, chmn., 1977-78; mem. S.D. Planning Commn., 1975-78; adv. bd. Criminal Justice Statis. Analysis Center, 1975-78; chmn. S.D. Criminal Justice Commn., 1976-78; mem. U. So. Calif. Criminal Justice Tng. Center Planning Com., 1977-79, U. S.D. Research Inst. Adv. Panel, 1978-80, Gov.'s Corrections Task Force, 1987; mem. acad. resource council S.D. Planning Agy., 1978-79; chmn. S.D. County Commr.'s Juvenile Justice Com., 1986-89; chmn. S.D. Youth Advocacy Project; mem. Commn. on Advancement of Fed. Law Enforcement, 1997-99, constitutional revisino commn., 2004—. Author: Models of Court Management, 1986; contbr. articles to profl. publs. Recipient Sustained High Performance award Law Enforcement Assistance Adminstrn., 1971, Disting. Safety Svcs. award S.D. Auto Club, 1978, Disting. Faculty award U. S.D., 1980, Friend of Law Enforcement award S.D. Peace Officers, 1983; Haynes Found. rsch. fellow, 1965-66; ASPA fellow, 1970-71; Bush Leadership fellow, summer 1975; Law Enforcement Edn. Program grantee, 1972-75; S.D. Criminal Justice Commn. grantee, 1972-74, 72-75; Criminal Justice Standards and Goals for S.D. grantee, 1974-75; Criminal Justice Data Collection grantee, 1974-75. Mem. ASPA (pres. Siouxland chpt. 1980-81, exec. bd. dirs. and sec./treas. criminal justice adminstrn. sect.), Am. Polit. Sci. Assn., Am. Judicature Soc. Home: 608 Poplar St Vermillion SD 57069-3529 Office: U SD Polit Sci Vermillion SD 57069 Office Phone: 605-677-5116. Business E-Mail: ddahlin@usd.edu.

DAILEY, FRED L., state agency administrator; m. Rita Dailey; children: Dawn, Shawn, Calley. BA in Polit. Sci. and History, Anderson U., Ind.; MPA, Ball State U. Formerly rodeo cowboy and amateur mountaineer; with Ind. Dept.

Corrections; later with U.S. Treasury; dir. Ind. Divsn. Agr., 1975-82; exec. v.p. Ohio Beef Coun., 1982-91; exec. sec. Ohio Cattlemen's Assn., 1982-91; dir. Ohio Dept. Agr., 1991—. Served with U.S. Army, Vietnam. Recipient numerous awards include Agri-Marketer of Yr., Industry svc. awards, Golden Boot award, Nat. Outstanding State Agrl. Exec. award, 1998; named Man of Yr. Progressive Farmer mag., 1999, FFA Hon. State Farmer degree, Ohio, Ind. Mem. Nat. Assn. State Depts. Agr. (pres. 1999—2001), Midwest Assn. State Depts. Agr. (past pres.), Mid-Am. Internat. Agri-Trade Coun. Office: Ohio Dept Agr Divsn Adminstrn 8995 E Main St Reynoldsburg OH 43068-3399 E-mail: agri@odant.agri.state.oh.us.

DAILY, FRANK J(EROME), lawyer; b. Chgo., Mar. 22, 1942; s. Francis Jerome and Eileen Veronica (O'Toole) D.; m. Julianna Ebert, June 23, 1996; children: Catherine, Eileen, Frank, William, Michael. BA in Journalism, Marquette U., 1964, JD, 1968. Bar: Wis. 1968, U.S. Dist. Ct. (ea. dist.) Wis. 1968, U.S. Dist. Ct. (we. dist.) Wis. 1971, U.S. Dist. Ct. (ctrl. dist.) Ill. 1990, U.S. Dist. Ct. (ea. dist.) Mich. 1994, U.S. Ct. Appeals (7th cir.) 1977, U.S. Ct. Appeals (3d and 5th cirs.) 1985, U.S. Ct. Appeals (4th, 6th, 8th, 9th, 10th, 11th cirs.) 1990, U.S. Supreme Ct. 1998, U.S. Dist. Ct. (no. dist.) Ill. 1999. Assoc. Quarles & Brady, Milw., 1968-75, ptnr., 1975—. Lectr. in product liability law and trial techniques Marquette U. Law Sch., U. Wis., Harvard U.; lectr. seminars sponsored by ABA, State Bar Wis., State Bar S.D., State Bar S.C., Product Liability Adv. Coun., Chem. Mfrs. Assn., Wis. Acad. Trial Lawyers, Trial Attys. Am., Marquette U., Southeastern Corp. Law Inst., Risk Ins. Mgmt. Soc., Inc.; life mem. pres.'s coun. Wake Forest U., U. Dayton, Boston Coll. Author: Your Product's Life Is in the Balance: Litigation Survival-Increasing the Odds for Success, 1986, Product Liability Litigation in the 80s: A Trial Lawyer's View from the Trenches, 1986, Discovery Available to the Litigator and Its Effective Use, 1986, The Future of Tort Litigation: The Continuing Validity of Jury Trials, 1991, How to Make an Impact in Opening Statements for the Defense in Automobile Product Liability Cases, 1992, How Much Reform Does Civil Jury System Need, 1992, Do Protective Orders Compromise Public's Right to Know, 1993, Developments in Chemical Exposure Cases: Challenging Expert Testimony, 1993, The Spoliation Doctrine: The Sword, The Shield and The Shadow, 1997, Trial Tested Techniques for Winning Opening Statements, 1997, Litigation in the Next Millennium --A Trial Lawyer's Crystal Ball Report, 1998, What's Hot and What's Not in Non-Daubert Products Liability In the Seventh Circuit, 1998. Commr. for chief judge Milwaukee County, Wis., 2001; bd. visitors Wake Forest U. Law Sch.; bd. trustees U. Ala. Law Sch. Named Marquette U. Law Alumnus of Yr., 2000. Fellow Internat. Acad. Trial Lawyers; mem. ABA (past co-chair discovery com. litigation sect., vice chmn. products, gen. liability and consumer law com. of sect. tort and ins. practice, litigation sect. and mfrs. liability subcom.), ATLA, AAAS, Trial Atty. of Am., Wis. Bar Assn., Milw. Bar Assn., 7th Cir. Bar Assn., Am. Judicature Soc., Def. Rsch. Inst., Supreme Ct. Hist. Soc., Indsl. Truck Assn. (lawyers com.), Am. Law Inst., Product Liability Adv. Coun., Am. Agrl. Law Assn., Wis. Acad. Trial Lawyers, Assn. for Advancement of Automotive Medicine (life), Nat. I-Club U. Iowa, U. Ala. Nat. Alumni Assn., Circle of Champions. Roman Catholic. Office: Quarles & Brady 411 E Wisconsin Ave Ste 2040 Milwaukee WI 53202-4497 Office Phone: 414-277-5381. E-mail: fjd@quarles.com.

DALEY, CLAYTON CARL, JR., consumer products company executive; b. Canton, Ohio, Nov. 6, 1951; s. Clayton and Jane Daley; m. Meredythe Lee Gray, Mar. 10, 1979; children: Clayton III, Graeme. AB in Econs., Davidson Coll., 1973; MBA, Ohio State U., 1974. Mgr. cost dept. Procter & Gamble Co., Green Bay, Wis., 1974-76, acctg. and office mgr. Cape Girardeau, 1976-78, forecaster paper divsn., 1978-79, fin. analysis supr. tissue brands, 1979-80, mgr. fin. analysis dept. paper divsn., 1980-82, mgr. soap cost acctg. dept. PS&D divsn., 1982-84, dir. fin. info. systems project, comptr.'s divsn., 1984-86, dir. corp. planning, 1986-88, divsn. comptr. PS&D divsn., 1988-89, divsn. comptr. PS&D divsn., BS&HCP divsn., 1989-90, comptr. soap products, 1990-91; comptr. US ops. Procter & Gamble USA, 1991-92; v.p., comptr. Procter & Gamble Internat., 1992-93, team leader, v.p., compt., 1993-94; v.p., treas. Procter & Gamble Co., 1994-98, CFO, 1999—2007, vice-chmn., CFO, 2007—. Trustee Fin. Execs. Inst., 1994, Fin. Execs. Rsch. Found., 1994. Bd. dirs. Boy Scouts Am., Dan Beard Coun., 1997, Am. Cancer Soc., Hamilton County Unit, Cancer Family Care, Inc. Mem. Cin. Rotary. Office: Procter & Gamble Co 1 Procter And Gamble Plz Cincinnati OH 45202-3393

DALEY, MATTHEW JAMES, lawyer; b. Bloomington, Ill., Aug. 22, 1955; s. William Martin and Mary Elizabeth (Jenson) D.; m. Janet Suzanne Bertch, Feb. 16, 1980; children: Michael John, Sarah Elizabeth, Andrew William, Benjamin James. BA, Creighton U., 1977; JD, U. Iowa, Iowa City, 1980; MS, Friends U., 2000. Bar: Iowa 1980, U.S. Dist. Ct. (no. and so. dists.) Iowa 1980, U.S. Ct. Appeals (8th cir.) 1980, Nebr. 1988. Asst. atty. City of Sioux City, Iowa, 1980-85; assoc. Shull, Cosgrove, Hellige, Kudej & DuBray, Sioux City, 1985-89; ptnr. Shull, Cosgrove, Hellige, DuBray & Lundberg, Sioux City, 1989; ptnr., chair Tech. Law & E-Discovery Group Shook, Hardy & Bacon LLP, Kansas City, Mo. Group mem. Sedona Working Group on Electronic Document Retention and Production, E-Discovery Task Force, Defense Rsch. Inst., Lexis-Nexis Adv. Bd. on E-Discovery. Mem. ABA, Iowa Bar Assn., Woodbury County Bar Assn. (asst. treas. 1985—). Lodges: Optimists. Avocation: computer programming. Office: Shook, Hardy & Bacon LLP 2555 Grand Blvd Kansas City MO 64108 Office Phone: 816-474-6650. Office Fax: 816-421-5547. E-mail: mjdaley@shb.com.

DALEY, RICHARD MICHAEL, mayor; b. Chgo., Apr. 24, 1942; s. Richard J. and Eleanor (Guilfoyle) D.; m. Margaret Corbett, Mar. 25, 1972; children: Nora, Patrick, Elizabeth. BA, DePaul U., Chgo., 1964, JD, 1968. Bar: Ill. 1969. Ptnr. Simon and Daley, Chgo., 1970-72, Daley, Riley & Daley, Chgo., 1972-80; mem. Ill. State Senate, 1973-80, chmn. Judiciary I Com., 1975, 77; state's atty. Cook County, Ill., 1980-89; mayor Chgo., 1989—; pres. U.S. Conf. Mayors, 1996. Headed the US Conf. Mayors, 1996. Bd. dirs. Little City Home; mem. Citizens Bd. U. Chgo.; mem. adv. bd. Mercy Hosp., Chgo.; bd. mgrs. Valentine Boys Club; active Nativity of Our Lord Parish, Chgo. Named Outstanding Leader, Ill. Assn. Social Workers, 1978, Outstanding Legislator of Yr., Lt. Gov. Sr. Legis. Forum, 1979, Outstanding Leader in Revision of Ill. Mental Health Code, Ill. Assn. Retarded Citizens, 1979, Municipal Leader of Yr., American City and County mag., 1997, Pub. Official of Yr., Governing mag., 1997, Politician of Yr., Library Jour., 1997, Official of Yr., Alliance for Great Lakes, 2006; named one of One of the Five Best Big-city Mayors, Time mag., 2005; recipient Golden Rule plaque, Chgo. Boys Club Am., Education Excellence award, Nat. Conf. for Cmty. and Justice, 1999, Pub. Svc. Leadership award, Nat. Coun. for Urban Econ. Develop., 1999, J. Sterling Morton award, Nat. Arbor Day Found., 1999, Keystone award, Am. Architectural Found., 1999, Martin Luther King/Robert F. Kennedy award, Coalition to Stop Gun Violence/Education Fund To End Handgun Violence, 1999, Openlands Project Conservation Leadership award, 2000, National Trust's Trustee's award for Outstanding Achievement in Pub. Policy, 2000, National Trust for Historic Preservation National Preservation award, 2000, 2002, Ill. Coalition Against Domestic Violence (ICADV) Human Dignity award, 2001, Chgo. Innovation award, Sun-Times, 2002, Extreme City 'Digie' (Digital Innovation) award, 2002, Waste Management, Inc. Top honors in City Livability award, US Conf. of Mayors, 2002, Lifetime Achievement award, Am. for Arts & U.S. Conf. Mayors, 2005, Kevin Lynch award, MIT, 2005. Mem. Chgo. Bar Assn., Ill. State Bar Assn., ABA, Cath. Lawyers Guild. Democrat. Roman Catholic. Office: Office of the Mayor City Hall Rm 507 121 N La Salle Chicago IL 60602-1202

DALEY, ROBERT EMMETT, retired foundation executive; b. Cleve., Mar. 13, 1933; s. Emmett Wilfred and Anne Gertrude (O'Donnell) D.; m. Mary Berneta Fredericks, June 7, 1958; children: Marianne Fredericks, John Gerard. BA in English, U. Dayton, 1955; MA in Polit. Sci., Ohio State U., 1968, MA in Pub. Adminstrn., 1976. Local govt. reporter, Washington corr., fin. editor Jour. Herald, Dayton, Ohio, 1957-65, pub. affairs reporter, 1967; staff writer Congressional Quar., Inc., Washington, 1966; pub. affairs reporter Dayton Daily News, Dayton, 1969; dir. pub. affairs & comm. Charles F. Kettering Found., Dayton, 1977-94, ret., now assoc., 1994—. Part-time copy boy, sports reporter Jour. Herald, Dayton, 1953-55. Past pres., bd. trustees St. Joseph Home for Children; former mem. adv. bd. Ctr. for Religious Telecomms., U. Dayton; traveling press sec. sen. candidate John J. Gilligan, 1968, for gubernatorial candidate, 1970-71, asst. to Gov. Gilligan, 1971-75; media rels. dir. Nat. League of Cities, Washington, 1976-77; Soc.; past mem. Ind. Sector Pub. Info. & Edn. Com. With U.S. Army, 1955-57. Mem. Soc. Profl. Journalists, Nat. Press Club, KC, Ancient Order Hibernians. Roman Catholic. Home: 888 Cranbrook Ct Dayton OH 45459-1525 Office: Charles F Kettering Found 200 Commons Rd Dayton OH 45459-2788 Business E-Mail: daley@kettering.org.

DALEY, SUSAN JEAN, lawyer; b. New Britain, Conn., May 27, 1959; d. George Joseph and Norma (Woods) Daley. BA, U. Conn., 1978; JD, Harvard U., 1981. Bar: Ill. 1981. Assoc. Altheimer & Gray, Chgo., 1981-86, ptnr., 1986—2003, Perkins Coie LLP, Chgo., 2003—. Mem.: ABA (real property, probate and trust law sect. 1983—, employee benefits com. taxation sect. 1984—, chmn. welfare plans com. real property, probate and trust law sect. 1989—95, chmn. employee benefits, securities law com. taxation sect. 2001—), Chgo. Coun. Fgn. Rels., Chgo. Bar Assn. (chmn. employee benefits divsn. fed. taxation com. 1985—86, chmn. employee benefits com. 1990—91, chmn. fed. taxation com. 1992—93), Ill. Bar Assn. (chmn. employee benefits divsn. fed. taxation sect. 1984—86, chmn. employee benefits sect. 1995—96), Nat. Assn. Stock Plan Profls. (pres. Chgo. chpt. 1995—). Avocation: marathons. Home: 1636 N Wells St Apt 415 Chicago IL 60614-6009 Office: 131 S Dearborn St STE 1700 Chicago IL 60603-5559 Home Phone: 312-399-3348; Office Phone: 312-324-8645. Business E-Mail: SDaley@perkinscoie.com.

DALEY, WILLIAM M., bank executive, former secretary of commerce; b. Aug. 8, 1948; m. Loretta Daley; 3 children. BA, Loyola U., 1970; LLB, John Marshall Law Sch., Chgo., LLD (hon.), 1975. Bar: Ill. 1975. With Daley and George, Chgo.; ptnr. Mayer, Brown & Platt; vice chmn. Amalgamated Bank, Chgo., 1989, pres., COO, 1990-93; atty., advisor to Mayor Richard M. Daley, Chicago, 1993—97; sec. Dept. Commerce, Washington, 1997-2000; chmn., v.p. Al Gore's presidential campaign, 2000; vice chmn. Evercore Capital Partners L.P., 2000—01; pres. SBC Communications, 2001—04; chmn. Midwest region J.P. Morgan Chase & Co., 2004—. Bd. dirs. Merck & Co., Boston Properties, Coun. Foreign Rels., John F. Kennedy Ctr. Performing Arts, Com. US-China Foreign Relations; spl. counsel to Pres. for NAFTA. Served in Army Nat. Guard & Air Nat. Guard, 1970—76. Recipient St. Ignatius award fro Excellence in the Practice of Law, 2995, World Trade award World Trade Ctr., Chgo., 1994, World Standards Day 2002 Hon. Chair & Ron Bown award, Alliance for Telecomm. Industry Solutions. Office: JP Morgan Chase 227 W Monroe St Chicago IL 60606

DALLAS, H. JAMES, medical products executive; b. Lithonia, Ga., Aug. 1, 1958; BS in Acctg., U. SC, Aiken, 1983; MBA, Emory U., 1994. Equipment cleaner Pepperidge Farms, Aiken, SC, 1981—83; br. auditor C & S Nat. Bank, 1983—84; cost acct. Gypsum divsn. Ga.-Pacific Corp., 1984—85, programmer corp. info. tech., 1985—87, analyst corp. info. tech., 1987—89, mgr. info. sys.-transp. divsn., 1989—92, gen. mgr. transp. divsn., 1992—94, dir. strategy and planning corp. info. tech., 1994—96, group dir. bldg. products mfg. info. tech., 1996—98, group dir. bldg. products mfg. and distbn. info. tech., 1998—2000, v.p. bldg. products distbn. sales and logistics Mid-Atlantic and S.E. regions, 2000—01, pres. lumber, 2001—02, v.p., CIO info. tech., 2002—06; sr. v.p., chief info. officer Medtronic, Inc., Mpls., 2006—. Mem. adv. bd. Habitat for Humanity, Atlanta; mem. exec. com. Nat. Eagle Leadership Instn.; mem. resource devel. com. Cool Girls; mem. CIS adv. bd. Kennesaw State U.; former mem. assoc. com. Interdenominational Theol. Ctr. Office: Medtronic Inc 710 Medtronic Pkwy Minneapolis MN 55432-5604

DALLEPEZZE, JOHN RAYMOND, lighting company executive; b. Princeton, NJ, May 27, 1943; s. Angelo Peter and Yolanda Irene (Micai) D.; m. Joanne Rita McGuinn, June 19, 1965; children: Christina Maria, John Raymond Jr., Peter Angelo. BS in Engring., Princeton U., 1965; SM, MIT, 1967. Scheduling supr. Corning Glass Works, Danville, Va., 1967, plant controller, 1967-69, plant mfg. engr., 1969-71, market specialist, tech. products Corning, N.Y., 1971-73, sales mgr., indsl. products, 1973-77, div. controller, tech. products, 1977-80, gen. mgr., lighting products, 1980-83; pres. N.L. McCullough, Houston, 1983-89; pres., chief exec. officer Holophane Co., Inc., Newark, Ohio, 1989—. Mem. Petroleum Equipment Suppliers Assn., Soc. Profl. Well Log Analysts, Soc. Petroleum Engrs. Clubs: Raveneaux Country (Houston). Republican. Home: 4308 Harlem Rd Galena OH 43021-9347 Office: Holophane Co Inc 214 Oakwood Ave Newark OH 43055-6700

DALLMAN, ROBERT EDWARD, lawyer; b. Shawano, Wis., Apr. 16, 1947; BA, Valparaiso U., 1970; JD, U. Kans., 1973; LLM, Georgetown U., 1977. Bar: Kans. 1973, U.S. Tax Ct. 1973, U.S. Supreme Ct. 1978, Wis. 1980. Chief counsel IRS, Washington, 1973-77, Milw., 1977-80; shareholder Reinhart, Boerner, Van Deuren, Norris & Rieselbach S.C., Milw. Instr. corp. tax. planning and advanced real estate tax planning U. Wis., Milw., 1981—; cons. to chief counsel IRS, Washington, 1980. Co-author: Tax Planning for Real Estate Transactions, 1983; contbr. articles to profl. jours. Mem. ABA, State Bar Wis., Milw. Bar Assn. Office: Reinhart Boerner Van Deuren PO Box 92900 1000 N Water St Ste 2100 Milwaukee WI 53202-3197 E-mail: rdallman@reinhartlaw.com.

DALLOS, PETER JOHN, neurobiologist, educator; b. Budapest, Hungary, Nov. 26, 1934; arrived in US, 1956, naturalized, 1962; s. Ernest and Maria Dallos; m. Joan Usis, Aug. 18, 1977; 1 child by previous marriage, Christopher. Student, Tech. U. Budapest, 1953-56; BS, Ill. Inst. Tech., 1958; MS, Northwestern U., 1959, PhD, 1962. Rsch. engr. Am. Machine and Foundry Co., 1959; cons. engr., 1959-60; mem. faculty Northwestern U., 1962—, prof. audiology and elec. engring., 1969—, prof. neurobiology and physiology, 1981—, chmn., 1981-84, 86-87, assoc. dean Coll. Arts and Scis., 1984-85, John Evans prof. neurosci., 1986—, Hugh Knowles prof. audiology, 1994—2003, acting v.p. for rsch., 2003—. Vis. scientist Karolinska Inst., Stockholm, 1977-78; chmn. behavioral and neuroscis. rev. panel No. 5 Nat. Inst. Neurol., Communicative Disorders and Stroke, NIH, 1982-85, mem. nat. adv. council, 1984-87 Author: The Auditory Periphery: Biophysics and Physiology, 1973; editor: The Cochlea, 1996; contbr. articles to profl. jours. Recipient 12th ann. award Beltone Inst. Hearing Rsch., 1977, Internat. prize Amplifon Rsch. and Study Ctr., 1984, Senator Jacob Javits Neurosci. Investigator award, 1984, Honors of Assn. award Am. Speech-Lang.-Hearing Assn., 1994, Bekesy medal of Acoustical Soc. Am., 1995, Sigma Xi Disting. Nat. lectr., 1997-98, Acta Otolaryngologica Internat. prize, 1997, Kresge-Mirmelstein prize La. State U., 2000; Guggenheim fellow, 1977-78; McKnight sr. fellow, 1997-2000, Guyot prize, 2004, Hugh Knowles prize, 2005, Lifetime Achievement award, Am. Auditory Soc., 2008. Fellow IEEE (life), AAAS, Acoustical Soc. Am., Am. Acad. Arts and Scis.; mem. Soc. for eurosci., Assn. for Rsch. in Otolaryngology (pres. 1992-93, award of merit 1994), Am. Physiological Soc., Collegium Otolaryngologicum Amicitae Sacrum, Hungarian Acad. Scis., Sigma Xi, Tau Beta Pi, Eta Kappa Nu. Office: Northwestern U 2240 Campus Dr Evanston IL 60208-0837 Business E-Mail: p-dallos@northwestern.edu.

DALRYMPLE, JACK, lieutenant governor, former state legislator; b. Mpls., Oct. 16, 1948; m. Betsy Wood Dalrymple; 4 children. BA in Am. Studies, Yale U., 1970. Farmer, 1970—; mem. N.D. Ho. of Reps from 22 Dist., 1985—2001, chmn. appropriations com.; lt. gov. State of N.D., Bismarck, 2001—. Bd. dirs. Prairie Pub. TV, N.D. State U. Devel. Found., Golden Growers Coop.; mem. Edn. Broadcasting Coun.; co-founder Share House Inc. Recipient Outstanding Young Farmer award, 1983. Mem. Cass County Rural Water Users Assn. (past bd. dirs.), Casselton Econ. Devel. Found., Univ. Pres. Agr. Club (pres.), Durum Growers Assn. (bd. dirs.), Jaycees. Republican. Address: PO Box 220 Casselton ND 58012-0220 Office: Office Lt Governor Dept 101 600 E Boulevard Ave Bismarck ND 58505 Office Phone: 701-328-4222. Office Fax: 701-328-2205.

DALTON, DAN R., finance educator, former dean; BA, Calif. State U., 1970, MS, 1975; PhD, U. Calif., Irvine, 1979. Owner retail bus. Middle Earth, 1971—73; owner D&H Industries, 1971—73; mem. staff GE; faculty mem. UCLA, Santa Ana Coll., Calif. State U. Long Beach, Kelley Sch. Bus. Ind. U., Bloomington, Ind., 1979—, assoc. dean for acad. affairs, Samuel and Pauline Glaubinger Prof. Mgmt., 1995—98, dean, 1997—2004, Harold A. Poling Chair in Strategic Management, 1998—, dean emeitus, 2004—; dir., Inst. for Corp. Governance, 2004—. Contbr. numerous articles to profl. jours. Recipient numerous awards and citations for excellence in tchg. Office: Indiana Univ Kelley School Business 1309 E 10th St Bloomington IN 47405-1701

DALY, JOEL T., newscaster; married; 2 children. BA in English magna cum laude, Yale U., New Haven, Conn., 1956; JD with honors, Chgo. Kent Coll. of Law, 1988. Bar: Ill., Wis. With WEWS-TV, Cleve., 1960—64, WJW-TV, Cleve., 1964—67; co-anchor WLS-TV, Chgo., 1967—. Active in music and theater; bd. dir. Clin. Elderly and Disabled, Chgo.; bd. gov. Chgo. Kent Coll. of Law, chmn. student affairs. Named to Chgo. Journalism Hall of Fame, 2003; recipient Liberty Bell award, Chgo. Bar Assn., 1973, Human Rels. award, Am. Jewish Congress, 1974, Silver Cir. award, NATAS, Herman Kogan award, Chgo. Bar Assn., 1985, 1989, five Chgo. Emmys, NATAS. Fellow: Ill. Bar Assn. (hon.); mem.: NATAS (Chgo. chapt.). Home: 6635 Dawn Ave Countryside IL 60525-7512

DALY, WALTER JOSEPH, medical educator; b. Michigan City, Ind., Jan. 12, 1930; m. Joan Brown, June 12, 1953; children: Lois Kay, Alice Louise. AB, Ind. U., 1951, MD, 1955, ScD, 1998. Diplomate Am. Bd. Internal Medicine. Intern Ind. U., 1955-56, resident, 1956-57, 59-62, instr. medicine, 1962-63, asst. prof., 1963-65, assoc. prof., 1965-68, prof., 1968-77, John B. Hickam prof., 1977-80, J.O. Ritchey prof., 1980-95, J.O. Ritchey prof. emeritus, 1995—; chmn. dept. medicine, 1970-83; dean Sch. Medicine, 1983-95; dean emeritus Ind. U., 1995—. Dir. Regenstrief Inst. Health Rsch., 1976-83. Capt. M.C., U.S. Army, 1957-59. Master ACP (gov. 1980-84), Am. Physiol. Soc., Ctr. Soc. Clin. Rsch. (pres. 1980-81), Am. Soc. Clin. Investigation, Am. Clin. and Climatol. Assn. (v.p. 2004-05), Assn. Am. Physicians. Office: Ind U Sch Medicine 1120 South Dr Indianapolis IN 46202-5135 Office Phone: 317-274-7109.

DAM, KENNETH W., law educator, former federal agency administrator; b. Marysville, Kans., Aug. 10, 1932; s. Oliver W. and Ida L. (Hueppelsheuser) D.; m. Marcia Wachs, June 9, 1962; children: Eliot, Charlotte. BS, U. Kans., 1954; JD, U. Chgo., 1957; LLD (hon.), New Sch. Social Rsch., 1983. Bar: NY State 1959. Law clk. to justice U.S. Supreme Ct., 1957-58; assoc. Cravath, Swaine & Moore, NYC, 1958-60; faculty U. Chgo. Law Sch., 1960-82, prof., 1964-71, 74-82, Harold J. and Marion F. Green prof., 1976-82, provost, 1980-82, Max Pam prof. Am. and fgn. law, 1992—2001, 2003—04, sr. lectr., 2004—; dep. sec. U.S. Dept. State, 1982-85; v.p. law and external rels. IBM Corp., 1985-92; pres., CEO United Way Am., 1992; dep. sec. U.S. Dept. Treasury, Washington, 2001—03, acting sec., 2002—03; sr. fellow Brookings Instn., 2003—. Vis. prof. U. Freiburg, Germany, 1964; asst. dir. nat. security and internat. affairs Office Mgmt. and Budget, 1971-73; exec. dir. Coun. Econ. Policy, 1973; dir. Alcoa, 1987-2001, Xyleco, Inc., 2007-; adv. bd. BMW of N.Am., 1990-95. Author: The GATT: Law and International Economic Organization, 1970, Oil Resources: Who Gets What How?, 1976, The Rules of the Game: Reform and Evolution in the International Monetary System, 1982, The Rules of the Global Game: A New Look at U.S. International Economic Policymaking, 2001, Law-Growth Nexus: The Rule of Law and Economic Development, 2006; co-author: Federal Tax Treatment of Foreign Income, 1964, Economic Policy Beyond the Headlines, 1977, 2d edit., 1998; co-editor: Cryptography's Role in Securing the Information Society, 1996; chair bd. advisors Fgn. Affairs jour., 1997-2001. Bd. dirs. Am. Coun. on Germany, 1986-95, Am.-China Soc., 1989-99, Atlantic Coun., 1985-92, 2004—, Coun. on Fgn. Rels., 1992-2001, Chgo. Coun. on Fgn. Rels., 1992-2001; trustee Brookings Inst., 1989-2001, 03-; co-chmn. Aspen Strategy Group, 1991-2001. Recipient Raimar Lust award, Thyssen and Humboldt Found., Germany, 2007. Mem. Am. Acad. Arts and Scis., Am. Acad. Diplomacy, Am. Law Inst., Nat. Acad. (sci., tech. and law panel, 2003-), Shadow Fin. Regulatory Com., Munich Intellectual Property Law Ctr. (trustee, 2004-), Fin. Svcs. Vol. Corps (bd. dirs. 2005—), Com. Econ. Devel. (trustee) 2006-), Met. Club (Washington), Quadrangle Club. Office: U Chgo Law Sch 1111 E 60th St Chicago IL 60637 Business E-Mail: kdam@law.uchicago.edu.

D'AMATO, ANTHONY, law educator; b. NYC, Jan. 10, 1937; s. Anthony A. and Mary (DiNicholas) D'A.; m. Barbara W. Steketee, Sept. 4, 1958; children: Brian, Paul. BA, Cornell U., 1958; JD, Harvard U., 1961; PhD, Columbia U., 1968. Bar: NY 1963, US Supreme Ct. 1963, US Tax Ct. 1987. Instr. Wellesley Coll., 1963-66; of counsel S.W. Africa Cases, NYC, 1965-66; Woodrow Wilson fellow U. Mich., Ann Arbor, 1966-67; Leighton prof. law Northwestern U. Law Sch., Chgo., 1968—. Author: The Concept of Custom in International Law, 1971, (with O'Neil) The Judiciary and Vietnam, 1972, (with Hargrove) Environment and the Law of the Sea, 1976 (with Wasby and Metrailer) Desegregation from Brown to Alexander, 1977, (with Weston and Falk) International Law and World Order, 1980, 2d edit., 1990, Jurisprudence: A Descriptive and Normative Analysis of Law, 1984, International Law: Process and Prospect, 1987, 2d edit., 1995, How to Understand the Law, 1989, (with Jacobson) Justice and the Legal System, 1992, International Law Anthology, 1994, International Law Coursebook, 1994, International Environmental Law Anthology, 1995, International Law and Political Reality, 1995, Analytic Jurisprudence Anthology, 1995, International Intellectual Property Anthology, 1996, Introduction to Law and Legal Thinking, 1996, International Law Studies, 1996, International Law Studies, 1997, International Intellectual Property Law, 1997, European Union Law Anthology, 1998, The Alien Tort Claims Act: An Analytical Anthology, 1999, International Intellectual Property Coursebook, 2000, International Law Sources: Collected Papers, Vol. 3, 2004; bd. editors Am. Jour. Internat. Law, 1981-95. Recipient Annual Book award Am. Soc. Internat. Law., 1981, Carl L. Fulda award for Outstanding Contbn. to Internat. Law, 1988. Mem. Internat. Law Assn., Am. Soc. Legal and Polit. Philosophy (chair inter-bar study group on ind. of lawyers and judges), ABA (coun. internat. law and practice), Am. Soc. Internat. Law (chair human rights interest group). Home: 5807 Lakeshore Dr N Holland MI 49424-1019 Office: Northwestern U Sch Law 357 E Chicago Ave Chicago IL 60611-3059 E-mail: a-damato@law.northwestern.edu.

DAMJANOV, IVAN, pathologist, educator; b. Subotica, Yugoslavia, Mar. 31, 1941; came to U.S., 1967; s. Milenko and Ana (Pavkovic) D.; m. Andrea Zivanovic, Jan. 18, 1964; children: Nevena, Ivana, Milena. MD, Zagreb U., Croatia, 1964, PhD, 1971. Lic. physician, Croatia, Pa., Kans.; diplomate Am. Bd. Pathology. Intern Gen. Hosp., Zagreb, 1964-65; resident in pathology U. Zagreb, 1966-67; intern in pathology Cleve. Met. Gen. Hosp., 1967-68; resident in pathology Mt. Sinai Hosp., NYC, 1968-69; asst. in pathology U. Zagreb, 1969-71; postdoctoral fellow Fels Rsch. Inst., Temple U., Phila., 1971-72; asst. prof. pathology U. Zagreb, 1972-73; from asst. prof. to assoc. prof. U. Conn., Farmington, 1973-77; from assoc. prof. to prof. Hahnemann Med. Coll. and Hosp., Phila., 1977-86; prof. pathology Jefferson Med. Coll. of Thomas Jefferson U., Phila., 1986-94; prof. pathology, chmn. U. Kans. Sch. Med., Kansas City, 1994-98, prof. pathology, 1998—. Cons. pathologist VA Hosp., Newington, Conn., 1975-77, Cancer Info. Dissemination and Analysis Ctr. for Virology, Immunology and Cancer-Related Biology, Franklin Inst., Phila., 1977-82, VAMC, Kansas City, Mo., 1995—, Pathology Stedman's Med. Dictionary, Phila., Pa., 2001-06; group for rsch. in pathology edn. U. Iowa, 1977-82; ad hoc reviewer, site vis. teams and study sects. NIH, Bethesda, Md., 1978—94; basic sci. merit award bd. VA, 1989-92; mem. Croatian Acad. Arts and Scis., 1992; mem. coun. U.S.-Can. Acad. Pathology, 1996-99; vis. prof. U. Novi Sad, Serbia, 2007—. Mem. editl. bd. Ultrastructural Pathology, 1985-96, Virchows Archiv, 1986-2003, In Vivo, 1988—, Modern Pathology, 1989—, Hosp. Physician, 1990-96, Human Pathology, 1991—, Croatian Med. Jour., 1992-2006, Lab. Investigation, 1994—, Pathology Rsch. Practice, 1998-2002, Jour. Urologic Pathology, 1991-2000, editor-in-chief, 2000-02, Internat. Jour. Devel. Biology, 2005-, Ann. Clin. Lab. Sci., 2005-; mem. editl. bd. Am. Registry of Pathology, Washington, 2000—; assoc. editor Lab. Investigation, 1982-94; regional editor N.Am. Differentiation, 1985-96; co-editor Anderson's Pathology, 10th edit., 1996; mem. editl. rev. group chair for pathology/surg. pathology Doody's Health Sciences Book Rev. Jour., 1998—. Recipient Christian R. and Mary F. Lindback award Jefferson Med. Coll., Phila., 1988, Tom Kent award Group for Rsch. in Pathology Edn., 2007. Mem. Am. Soc. Investigative Pathology, Internat. Acad. Pathology, European Soc. Pathology. Office: U Kansas Sch Med Dept Pathol & Lab Med 3901 Rainbow Blvd Kansas City KS 66160-0001 Personal E-mail: idamjanov@kc.rr.com. Business E-Mail: idamjano@kumc.edu.

DAMMEYER, RODNEY FOSTER, distribution company executive; b. Cleve., Nov. 5, 1940; s. Frederick and Marion (Foster) D.; m. Diane Newins, Feb. 8, 1975; children: Paul, Scott, Tom, Kimberley, Alice. BS in Acctg., Kent State U., 1962. With Arthur Andersen & Co., Ohio, 1952-70, ptnr. audit practice Ohio, 1970-74, mng. ptnr. Greensboro, N.C., 1974-75, with Cleve., 1975-79; ptnr. audit practice Arthur Anderson & Co., Cleve., 1970-74, mng. dir. Greensboro, N.C., 1974—, mng. ptnr. Seattle, 1975—; exec. v.p. fin. Northwest Industries, Inc., Chgo., 1979-83; sr. v.p., chief fin. officer Household Internat., Prospect Heights, Ill., 1983-85; pres., CEO Anixter Internat. Corp., Chgo., 1985—, also bd. dirs.; vice chmn. Anixter Corp. Pres., CEO, dir. Great Am. Mgmt. Investments, Inc.; bd. dirs. Antec, Capsure Holdings, Falcon Bldg. Products, Inc., Jacor Comm., Inc., Lukens, Inc., Revco D.S., Inc., Sealy Inc., IMC Global, Inc., various Van Kampen Merritt Trusts; mem. nat. adv. bd. Chase

Bank; mem. nat. and econ. policy couns. UN Assn. of U.S. Bd. dirs. Kent State U. Found., Inc. Mem.: Econs. Chgo. Presbyterian. Home: 4350 La Jolla Village Dr Ste 980 San Diego CA 92122-6223

DAMSCHRODER, REX, state legislator; m. Rhonda Damschroder; children: Alex, Anthony. BA, Bowling Green State U., 1974; MBA, Tiffin U., 1994. Mem. Ho. of Reps. State of Ohio, Columbus, 1994—. Mem. Sandusky County Rep. Ctrl. Com.; mem. bd. Terra C.C. Mem. Farm Bur., Twp. Trustees Assn., Fremont (Ohio) C. of C., Kiwanis. Republican. Address: Rex Travel 906 W State St Fremont OH 43420-2549

DAN, BERNARD W., former commodities exchange executive; b. Chgo., Dec. 17, 1960; BS in Acctg., St. John's U., Collegeville, Minn., 1982. With Nat. Futures Assn., 1983—85; adminstrv. mgr. oper. activities Cargill Investor Svcs., Ltd., London, 1986—89, adminstrv. mgr. NYC, 1989—91, asst. v.p., 1991—93, v.p., 1993—94; dir. Cargill Investors Svcs. (Singapore) Pty. Ltd., 1994—97; v.p., Global Head of Execution Cargill Investors Svcs., Chgo., 1997—98; pres., CEO Cargill Investor Svcs., Chgo., 1998—2001; exec. v.p. Chgo. Bd. Trade, Chgo., 2001—02, pres., CEO, 2002—07; spl. adv. CME Group Inc., Chgo., 2007—. Gov. Bd. of Trade Clearing Corp., mem. bd. govs., 1st vice chmn. Mem.: The Comml. Club of Chgo., One Chgo., The Executives Club of Chgo., Nat. Futures Assn., Operation Hope Incorporated, Regional Bd. of Dir. Office: CME Group Inc 20 S Wacker Dr Chicago IL 60606

DANA, DAVID, law educator; BA summa cum laude, Harvard U.; JD magna cum laude, Harvard U, 1988. Law clerk Hon. Betty Fletcher, U.S. Court of Appeals for the inth Circuit, 1988—89; assoc. Wilmer, Cutler & Pickering, 1989—91; attorney Environmental and Natural Resources Division, U.S. Dept. of Justice, 1991—93; prof., assoc. prof. law Boston U. School of Law, 1993—98; prof. law Northwestern U., 1999—, assoc. dean for faculty research. Office: Institute for Policy Research Northwestern University 2040 Sheridan Road Evanston IL 60208 E-mail: d-dana@northwestern.edu.

DANCEWICZ, JOHN EDWARD, investment banker; b. Boston, Feb. 12, 1949; s. John Felix and Teresa Sophia (Lewandowski) D.; m. Barbaragail Jarrett, Jan. 23, 1971; children: John Lawrence, Jill Elizabeth, Jenna Gail. BA in Econs., Yale U., 1971; MBA, Harvard U., 1973. Project adminstr. fin., cons. Nat. Shawmut Bank Boston, 1972-73; v.p., founder, mgr. U.S. investment banking Continental Ill. Nat. Bank Chgo., 1973-82; sr. mng. dir., mgr. corp. fin. Bear Stearns & Co. Inc., Chgo., 1982-96; founder, mng. ptnr. DN Ptnrs. LLP, DN Ptnrs. LP and DN Ptnrs. LP II, 1996—. Chmn. bd. dirs. Ctrl. Can Co., Inc., FCL Graphics, Inc., M & M Pump & Supply, Inc., Aztec Outdoor Advt. Co., dir. Country Pure Foods, Inc. Contbr. articles to profl. jours. Active schs. com., Yale U., campaign com., spl. gifts com., chmn. 25th reunion fundraising, sec. class 1971; sec. Harvard Bus. Sch. sect.; mem. spl. gifts com. Harvard Bus. Sch. Found. Recipient Pres.'s award, Yale Alumni Assn. Mem. Scholarship and Guidance Assn. (bd. dirs., v.p. 1982—), Lake Forest H.S. Ice Hockey Assn. (pres.), Harvard Bus. Sch. Club Chgo., Econ. Club, Univ. Club, East Bank Club, Mid-Am. Club. Home: 969 Spring Ln Lake Forest IL 60045-2302 Office: 77 W Wacker Dr Ste 4550 Chicago IL 60601 Office Phone: 312-332-7960. Business E-Mail: info@dupartners.com.

DANCO, LÉON ANTOINE, management consultant, educator; b. NYC, May 30, 1923; s. Léon A. and Alvira T. (Gomez) D.; m. Katharine Elizabeth Leck, Aug. 25, 1951; children: Suzanne, Walter Ten Eyck. AB, Harvard, 1943, MBA, 1947; PhD, Case Western Res. U., 1963. Asst. to divsn. pres. Interchem. Corp., NYC, 1947-50; sales promotion mgr. Risdon Mfg. Co., Waterbury, Conn., 1950-55; mgmt. cons. Cheshire, Conn., 1955-57; prof., assoc. dir. mgmt. program Case Inst. Tech., Cleve., 1957-58, lectr., 1959—; mgmt. cons. L.A. Danco & Co., 1957—; lectr. John Carroll U., Cleve., 1959-66, prof., dir. mgmt. confs., 1966—. Vis. prof. econs. Cleve. Inst. Art, 1966-69, Kent State U., 1966-67; exec. dir. Univ. Svcs. Inst., Cleve., 1967-69, pres., 1969—, chmn., 1989—2007; pub. The Family in Business (newsletter), 1978—; pres. Center for Family Bus., 1978—, chmn. Ctr.for Family Bus., 1991-2007. Author: Beyond Survival-A Business Owners Guide for Success, 1975, Inside the Successful Family Business, 1979, Outside Directors in the Family Owned Business, 1981, Someday It'll All Be.Whose?, 1990; (in French) L'Entreprise Familiale, 1998; (in Spanish) La Empresa Familiare, 1998; syndicated columnist: It's Your Business, 1973—. Lt. (j.g.) USCG, 1942-46, PTO. Mem. Am. Econ. Assn. Home: 32000 Fairmount Blvd Pepper Pike Cleveland OH 44124 Personal E-mail: grummi@aol.com.

DANDEKAR, SWATI, state representative; b. Mar. 1951; arrived in US, 1973; m. Arvind Dandekar; children: Ajai, Govind. BS in Chem. & Biology, Nagpur U., India, 1971; postgrad. diploma in Dietetics, Bombay U., 1972. Mem. Iowa Ho. Reps., DesMoines, 2003—, mem. appropriations com., mem. econ. growth com., mem. edn. com. Active Linn-Mar Cmty. Sch. Dist. Bd. Edn., 1996—, Vision Iowa Bd., 2000—; bd. dir. Iowa Assn. Sch. Bds., 2000—; bd. dirs. Liars Holographic Radio Theatre, 2001—. Recipient JC Penney Edu. Golden Rule award, 2000. Mem.: Jr. League Cedar Rapids (pres. sustainers, chair diversity com.). Office: State Capitol East 12th and Grand Des Moines IA 50319 Office Phone: 515-281-3221. E-mail: swati.dandekar@legis.state.ia.us.

DANFORTH, JOHN CLAGGETT, lawyer, former ambassador, senator; b. St. Louis, Sept. 5, 1936; s. Donald and Dorothy (Claggett) D.; m. Sally B. Dobson, Sept. 7, 1957; children: Eleanor, Mary, Dorothy, Johanna, Thomas. BA (hon.), Princeton U., 1958; BD, LLB, Yale U., 1963, MA (hon.); LHD (hon.), Lindenwood Coll., 1970, Ind. Central U.; LLD (hon.), Drury Coll., 1970, Maryville Coll., Rockhurst Coll., Westminster Coll., Culver-Stockton Coll., St. Louis U.; DD (hon.), Lewis Clark Coll.; HHD (hon.), William Jewell Coll.; STD (hon.), Southwest Bapt. Coll.; degree (hon.), Va. Theol. Sem., 1990, Holy Cross Coll., 1992, Harris Stowe Coll., 1992, Wash. U., 1995, U. Mo., 1995. Bar: NY 1963, Mo. 1966, DC 1994. With firm Davis Polk Wardwell Sunderland & Kiendl, NYC, 1964-66; ptnr. Bryan, Cave, McPheeters and McRoberts (now Bryan Cave LLP), St. Louis, 1966—68, 1995—2004, 2005—; atty. gen. State of Mo., 1969-76; US senator from Mo., 1976-94; spl. presidential envoy to Sudan The White House, Khartoum, 2001—02; permanent U.S. rep. to UN US Dept. State, NYC, 2004—05; ordained deacon Episc. Ch., 1963, priest, 1964; asst. rector NYC, 1963-66; assoc. rector Clayton, Mo., 1966-68, Grace Ch., Jefferson City, 1969; hon. assoc. St. Alban's Ch., Washington, 1977-94. Chmn. Mo. Law Enforcement Assistance Council, 1973-74; asst. chaplain Meml. Sloan-Kettering Cancer Ctr. of N.Y.C.; asst. rector Ch. of Epiphany in N.Y.C., Ch. of St. Michael and St. George, Clayton, Mo.; hon. canon Christ Ch. Cathedral, St. Louis. Author: Faith and Politics: How the Moral Values Debate Divides America and How to Move Forward Together, 2006. Republican nominee US Senate, 1970; assoc. rector Ch. of the Holy Communion, Univ. City, Mo., 1995—. Recipient Disting. Svc. award St. Louis Jr. C. of C., 1969, Disting. Missourian and Brotherhood awards NCCJ, Presdl. World Without Hunger award, 1985, Disting. Lectr. award Avila Coll., Chancellors medal UMKC, 1995; named Outstanding Young Man Mo. Jr. C. of C., 1968, St. Louis Man of Yr., 1994; Alumni fellow Yale U., 1973-79 Mem. Mo. Acad. Squires, Alpha Sigma Nu (hon.), bd. dirs., Dow Chemical Co., 1996-, Met. Life Insurance Co., 2000-. Republican. Office: Bryan Cave LLP One Met Sq 211 N Broadway Ste 3600 Saint Louis MO 63102-2750 E-mail: johncdanforth@bryancave.com.

DANFORTH, WILLIAM HENRY, retired academic administrator, physician; b. St. Louis, Apr. 10, 1926; s. Donald and Dorothy (Claggett) D.; m. Elizabeth Anne Gray, Sept. 1, 1950; children: Cynthia Danforth Prather, David Gray, Maebelle Reed, Elizabeth D. Sankey. AB, Princeton U., 1947; MD, Harvard U., 1951. Intern Barnes Hosp., St. Louis, 1951—52, resident, 1954—57; now mem. staff; asst. prof. medicine Washington U., St. Louis, 1960—65, assoc. prof., 1965—67, prof., 1967—, vice chancellor for med. affairs, 1965—71, chancellor, 1971—95, chmn., bd. trustees St. Louis, 1995—99, vice-chmn. bd. trustees, chancellor emeritus, 1999—. Pres. Washington U. Med. Sch. and Assoc. Hosps., 1965-71; program coord. Bi-State Regional Med. Program, 1967-68. Trustee Danforth Found., Am. Youth Found., 1963—, Princeton U., 1970-74, St. Louis Christmas Carols Assn., 1958-74, chmn., 1975—; co-chmn. Barnes/Jewish Hosp., 1996-2002; chmn. bd. trustees Donald Danforth Plant Sci. Ctr. Named Man of Yr., St. Louis Gloe-Democrat, 1978. Fellow: AAAS, Am. Acad. Arts and Scis.; mem.: Inst. Medicine. Home: 10 Glenview Rd Saint Louis MO 63124-1308 Office: Washington U West Campus Campus Box 1044 7425 Forsyth Blvd Ste 262 Saint Louis MO 63105-2161

DANIEL, DAVID EDWIN, academic administrator, civil engineer; b. Newport News, Va., Dec. 20, 1949; s. David Edwin and Betty Ruth (Aschenback) D.; m. Frances Louise Locker, June 12, 1971 (div.); children: Katherine Ruth, William Monroe; m. Susan Nielsen Brady, May 12, 1989; 1 child, Alexander David. BS, U. Tex., 1972, MS, 1974, PhD, 1980. Staff engr. Woodward-Clyde, San Francisco, 1974-77; asst. prof. U. Tex., Austin, 1981-85, assoc. prof., 1985-91, prof., 1991-96; prof., head dept. civil engring. U. Ill., Urbana, 1996-2001, dean, Coll. Engring., Gutgsell prof. civil engring., 2001—05; pres. U. Tex., Dallas, 2005—. Mem. ASCE (Norman medal 1975, Cross medal 1984, 2000, Middlebrooks award 1995, Richard R. Torrens award 1995), NAE. Office: Univ Texas Dallas Office of Pres PO Box 830688 Richardson TX 75083-0688 Business E-Mail: dedaniel@utdallas.edu.

DANIEL, ELNORA D., academic administrator; d. Stephen and Cecelia Bell; m. Herman Daniel, Mar. 25, 1961; 1 child, Michael. BS, N.C. Agrl. and Tech. U., Greensboro, 1964; MEd, Columbia U., NYC, 1968; EdD, Columbia U., 1978. RN N.C., 1964. V.p. for acad. affairs Hampton U., Va., 1991—93, v.p. for health, 1994—95, exec. v.p. and provost, 1995—98; pres. Chgo. State U., 1998—. Bd. dirs. LaRabida Children's Hosp., Am. Assn. State Colls. and Univs. (AASCU), Am. Coun. Edn. (ACE), Commn. Adult Edn., Nat. Assn. Equal Opportunity Higher Edn. (NAFEO), Beverly Bank & Trust Co., Little Co. Mary Hosp., Seaway Nat. Bank; nat. adv. bd. Millennium Leadership Initiative Am. Assn. State Colls. and Univs. (AASCU). Contbr. articles to profl. jours., chpts. to books. Mem. LWV Chgo., 1999, Ill. Commn. 50th Anniversary Brown vs. Bd. Edn.; mem. advisory bd. Cmty Violence Prevention Program Ctrl State. U.; prin. mem. Chgo. United; mem. Econ. Club Chgo., Women's Network Chgo., Chgo. Consortium Higher Edn., Comml. Club Chgo., Univ. Club Chgo.; mem. women's bd. Field Mus. Ret. col. Nurses Corp. US Army, 1991. Named to Hall of Fame, Today's Chgo. Woman, 2002; recipient Dir.'s Oustanding Achievement award, Ill., 2002. Fellow: Am. Acad. Nursing; mem.: Jr. Achievement Chgo. Independent. Office: Chicago State Univ 9501 S King Dr ADM/313 Chicago IL 60628 Office Phone: 773-995-2400. Business E-Mail: ed-daniel2@csu.edu.

DANIEL, ISAAC MORDOCHAI, mechanical engineering educator; b. Salonica, Greece, Oct. 7, 1933; came to U.S., 1955; s. Mordochai Aaron and Bella (Modiano) D.; m. Elaine Rochelle Krule, Feb. 15, 1987; children: Belinda Emily, Rebecca Stefanie, Max Ethan. BS, Ill. Inst. Tech., 1957, MS, 1959, PhD, 1964. Asst. rsch. engr. IIT Rsch. Inst., Chgo., 1959-61, assoc. rsch. engr., 1961-62, rsch. engr., 1962-64, sr. rsch. engr., 1964-75, mgr., 1965-75, sci. advisor, 1975-82; prof., dir. Ill. Inst. Tech., Chgo., 1982-86; prof. Northwestern U., Evanston, Ill., 1986—, Walter P. Murphy prof., 1998—. Dir. Ctr. for Intelligent Processing of Composites, 1997—. Author: Experimental Mechanics of Composite Materials, 1982, Engineering Mechanics of Composite Materials, 1994, 2d edit., 2005; editor: Composite Materials: Testing and Design, 1982. Pres. Sephardic Congregation, Chgo., 1980-82. Recipient Disting. Alumni award Ill. Inst. Tech., 1999. Fellow ASME, Am. Acad. Mechanics, Soc. Exptl. Mechanics (Hetenyi awards 1970, 76, B. J. Lazan award 1984, William M. Murray medal 1998, M.M. Frocht award); mem. ASTM, AIAA, Soc. Advanced Material Process Engring., Am. Soc. Nondestructive Testing, Am. Soc. Composites (Disting. Rsch. award 1996). Home: 9338 Neenah Ave Morton Grove IL 60053-1457 Office: Northwestern U 2137 Tech Dr Evanston IL 60208-3020 Home Phone: 847-965-8432; Office Phone: 847-491-5649. Business E-Mail: imdaniel@northwestern.edu.

DANIEL, KAREN, engineering and design company executive; BS in Acctg., N.W. Mo. State, 1980; MS in Acctg., U. Mo., Kansas City, 1981. CPA. With KPMG Peat Marwick, 1981—92, Black & Veatch, Overland Park, Kans., 1992—, now CFO. Mem. bd. commrs. Kansas City Pks. and Recreation, 1999—2003; bd. dirs. Cmty. Found., Women's Employment Network, Black Econ. Union; mem. bd. regents N.W. Mo. State U., 2003—. Recipient Nat. Profl. Achievement award, Nat. Women of Color, 2002. Office: Black & Veatch 11401 Lamar Overland Park KS 66211

DANIEL, MICHAEL EDWIN, insurance agency executive; b. Indpls., Sept. 8, 1948; s. Richard E. and Margret A. (Phillips) D.; m. Jeanne L. Nobbe, Sept. 29, 1979; children: Whitney Marie, Lindsay Michelle, Tyler Edwin. BA, Principia Coll., Elsah, Ill., 1970; German lang. degree, Dept. Def., Monterey, Calif., 1971. Sales mgr. Mr. Ins. of Ind., Indpls., 1973-77; pres. Ind. Ins. Svcs., Inc., Greenwood, 1977—, Ins. Svc., Inc., 5, 1990—. V.p. Brown County Water Utility, Helmsburg, Ind., 1982-85. Leader Johnson County 4-H, 1993-97; den leader pack 218 Cub Scout Am., 1999-2001, asst. scoutmaster Troop 218, 2001—. With 42d Mil. Police Group U.S. Army, 1970-73. Mem. Ind. Ins. Agts. Assn., Profl. Ins. Agt. Assn. (treas. Indpls. region 1990), Ind. Trail Riders Assn., BMW Motorcycle Owners Am. Christian Scientist. Avocation: camping. Office: Ind Ins Svcs 3115 Meridian Parke Dr Ste P Greenwood IN 46142-9414 E-mail: mdaniel@principia.edu, insure@indymall.com.

DANIEL, T., mime performer, theater director, choreographer; b. Chgo., Aug. 23, 1945; s. Theodore Charles and Thelma L. (Soderlind) Heagstedt; m. Laurie Willets, July 14, 1976. BS, Ill. State U., 1967, postgrad., 1969. Cert. Ecole Internat. de Mime. Performer, creator, artistic dir. T. Daniel Productions (Movement & Movement Theatre), Chgo., 1971—. Choreographer (film) Poltergeist III, 1988; choreographer, performer (video) Sweets for the Sweet, 1984; performer, creator (plays) Fantasmia, 1984, Merlin & The Color of Magic, 1986, Structures on Silence, 1988, The Magic of Mime, 1973, A World of Mime, 1971, Innovations, musical mime Home and Office: 6619 N Campbell Chicago IL 60645

DANIELS, DAVID T., state representative; Farmer; state rep. dist. 86 Ohio Ho. of Reps., Columbus, 2002—, vice chair, county and twp. govt. com., mem. econ. devel. and tech., ins., and transp. and pub. safety coms. Past mem. Highland County Farm Bur. Bd., Ohio; county commr. Highland County. Republican. Office: 77 S High St 11th fl Columbus OH 43215-6111

DANIELS, DAVID WILDER, conductor, author, music educator; b. Penn Yan, NY, Dec. 20, 1933; s. Carroll Cronk and Ursula (Wilder) D.; m. Jimmie Sue Evans, Aug. 11, 1956; children: Michael, Abigail, Andrew. AB, Oberlin Coll., 1955; MA, Boston U., 1956; MFA, PhD, U. Iowa, 1963. Instr. music Culver-Stockton Coll., Canton, Mo., 1956-58; music libr. Berkshire Athenaeum, Pittsfield, Mass., 1958-61; asst. prof. U. Redlands, Calif., 1963-64, Knox Coll., Galesburg, Ill., 1964-69, Oakland U., Rochester, Mich., 1969-71, assoc. prof., 1971-85, prof., 1985-97, chmn. dept., 1982-88, prof. emeritus, 1997—. Music dir. Warren Symphony, Mich., 1974—, Pontiac-Oakland Symphony, Pontiac, Mich., 1977-97; prin. condr. Detroit Symphony Civic Orch., 1997-98. Author: Orchestral Music, 1972, 4th edit., 2005; editor Avanti newsletter, 1982-86. Mem. Am. Symphony Orch. League, Condrs. Guild (bd. dirs. 1986-94, sec. 1989-91, v.p. 1991-94), Mich. Orch. Assn. (pres. 1981-83). Home: 1215 Gettysburg Ct Rochester Hills MI 48306-3819

DANIELS, LEE ALBERT, state legislator; b. Lansing, Mich., Apr. 15, 1942; s. Albert Lee and Evelyn (Bousfield) D.; m. Pamela Mesha; children: Laurie Lynn, Rachael Lee, Julie, Thomas, Christina. BA, U. Iowa, 1965; JD, John Marshall Law Sch., 1967. Rep. precinct committeeman, 1965-74; mem. bd. auditors York Twp., Ill., 1966-73; vice chmn. York Twp. Rep. Comty. Orgn., 1973-74; former minority spokesman judiciary com. Ill. Ho. of Reps.; spl. asst. atty. gen., 1973-75; Ill. state rep. 46th Dist., 1975—, majority whip, 1981-82, minority leader, 1983-94, spkr. Ho., 1995—97. Full ptnr. Katten, Muchin & Zavis, 1984-91; ptnr. Bell, Boyd & Lloyd, Chgo., 1992— Trustee Elmhurst Hosp.; chmn. Ill. Rep. Party, 2001-2002. Recipient Everett McKinley Dirksen award, 1995; named one of Outstanding Legislators in Country, Nat. Rep. Legis. Assn., 1991, Legislator of Yr., Ill. Hosp. Assn., 1986, DuPage Mayors and Mgrs. Conf., 1995. Mem. ABA, Ill. Bar Assn., DuPage County Bar Assn., Shriners, Masons, Moose. Republican. Home: 105 S York Rd Ste 550 Elmhurst IL 60126 Office: 200 5N Stratton Springfield IL 62706-0001

DANIELS, MITCHELL ELIAS, JR., governor, former federal official; b. Monongahela, Pa., Apr. 7, 1949; s. Mitchell Elias and Dorothy Mae (Wilkes) D.; m. Cheri Lynn Herman, May 20, 1978; children— Meagan, Melissa, Meredith, Margaret. AB, Princeton U., 1971; JD, Georgetown U., 1979. Bar: Ind. 1979. Exec. v.p. Campaign Communicators, Inc., Indpls., 1971-74; dep. to mayor City of Indpls., 1974-75; campaign mgr. Lugar for U.S. Senate, Indpls., 1976; adminstrv. asst. to U.S. Senator Dick Lugar U.S. Senate, Washington, 1977-83; exec. dir. Nat. Rep. Sen. Com., Washington, 1983-85; asst. to the Pres. The White House, Washington, 1985—87; CEO Hudson Inst., 1987—90; pres. N. Am. pharmaceutical ops. Eli Lilly and Co., 1993—97, sr. v.p. corp. strategy, policy, 1997—2001; dir. Office Mgmt. & Budget Exec. Office of the Pres., Washington, 2001—03; gov. State of Ind., Indianapolis, 2005—. Vice pres., trustee Am. Council Young Polit. Leaders, Washington, 1983—; mem. adv. com. Responsible Govt. for Am. Found., Washington, 1983—; bd. dirs. Fund for Hoosier Excellence, 1984—, Ind. at. Bank, Ind. Power & Light, Angie's List. Recipient Graham award Ind. Am. Legion, 1966, "Hero of the Taxpayer" award, American for Tax Reform, 2002, Chauncey Rose award, Rose-Hulman Inst. Tech., 2003; Presdl. scholar, 1967 Mem. Ind. Bar Assn. Clubs: Columbia (Indpls.). Republican. Presbyterian. Office: Office of Governor 206 State House Indianapolis IN 46204 Office Phone: 317-232-4567. Office Fax: 317-232-3443.

DANIELS, PRESTON A., mayor; b. Des Moines; B in Psychology, Drake U., MS in Health Sci. and Counseling. Probation officer 5th jud. dist. Dept. Corrections, tech. assistance to cmty.-based programs; dir. ct. and cmty. rels. Employee and Family Resources Iowa Managed Substance Abuse Care Plan; city councilman at large Des Moines; mayor. Chmn. Des Moines Police Subcom. Mem. U. Iowa Adv. Bd. for Addiction Tech. Transfer Ctr.; mem. Tng. Adv. Bd. for Substance Abuse, State of Iowa; pres. Drake Neighborhood Assn.; active numerous neighborhood activities; mem. Nat. Conf. Black Mayors, Nat. Conf. Mayors. Sgt. U.S. Army. amed Hon. Lt. Col. Ala. State Guard. Office: 400 E 1st St Des Moines IA 50309-1809 E-mail: padaniels@ci.des-moines.ia.us.

DANIELS-CARTER, VALERIE, food franchise executive; d. John and Katherine Daniels. Degree, Lincoln U., 1978; MS, Cardinal Stritch Coll., 1982. With Firstar Bank, 1978-81; auditor MGIC Investment Corp., 1981-84; co-founder V & J Foods, Milw., 1984—. Owner 37 Burger King restaurants, 61 Pizza Hut restaurants. Pres. bd. dirs. Milw. World Festival Inc. Named Entrepreneur of Yr., Ernst & Young and Merrill Lynch, 1994; recipient award Black Women's Network of Milw., 1997, Sacajawea award for creativity Midwest Express Airlines, 1997. Office: V & J Holding Cos 6933 W Brown Deer Rd Milwaukee WI 53223-2103

DANIELSON, GORDON KENNETH, JR., cardiovascular surgeon, educator; b. Burlington, Iowa, Dec. 5, 1931; s. Gordon Kenneth and Helen H. (Hill) Danielson; m. Sondra Jean Bolich, Jan. 21, 1961; children: Gordon Kenneth III, Laura, Karen, Keith, Bruce, Susan, Jennifer. BA in Chemistry, U. Pa., Phila., 1953, MD summa cum laude, 1956, postgrad., 1960. Diplomate Am. Bd. Surgery, Am. Bd. Thoracic Surgery. Intern U. Mich. Hosp., Ann Arbor, 1956-57; asst. resident in surgery Hosp. of U. Pa., 1957-61, chief resident in surgery, 1961-62, gen. and thoracic surgeon, 1962-65, asst. chief surg. div. I, 1962-65; vis. fellow in thoracic surgery Thorax Kliniken, Stockholm, 1963-64; practice medicine specializing in thoracic and cardiovascular surgery Phila., 1963-65, Lexington, Ky., 1965-67, Rochester, Minn., 1967—2003. Assoc. prof. surgery U. Ky. Med. Sch.; chief cardiac surgery Univ. Hosp., 1965-67; faculty Mayo Grad. Sch. Medicine, Rochester, Minn., 1967-2003, prof. surgery, 1975—, Joe M. and Ruth Roberts prof. surgery, 1987-2004; past chmn. divsn. thoracic and cardiovascular surgery, cons. cardiovascular and thoracic surgery Mayo Clinic/Mayo Found., 1967-2003, St. Mary's Hosp., Meth. Hosp., Rochester, 1967-2003; Am. Heart Assn. vis. tchr., Singapore, 1975, Amman, Jordan, 1981, W.W.L. Glenn lectr., 1999. Editor: Cardiovascular Surgery, 1972—78; contbr. numerous articles to profl. jours. Recipient Albert Einstein award, 1956, Roche award, 1956, Spencer Morris prize, 1956; Markle Acad. Medicine scholar, 1962—67, Congenital Heart Disease Fellow, US USSR Health Exch. Program, 1973. Fellow ACS, Am. Coll. Cardiology; mem. Am. Assn. Thoracic Surgery, Am. Surg. Assn., Am. Heart Assn. (fellow coun. cardiovascular surgery), Soc. Thoracic Surgeons (a founder), Soc. Univ. Surgeons, Soc. Vascular Surgery, Mexican Soc. Cardiology (hon.), Assn. Thoracic and Cardiovascular Surgeons of Asia (hon.), India (hon.), Chile Soc. Cardiology and Cardiovascular Surgery (hon.), Colombian Soc. of Cardiology (hon.), Congenital Heart Surgeons Soc., Peruvian Soc. of Cardiology (hon.), Phi Beta Kappa, Alpha Omega Alpha. Home: 6000 16th Ave NW Rochester MN 55901-2107 Office: Mayo Med Ctr Plummer N-10 Rochester MN 55905-0001 Office Phone: 507-284-2691. Business E-Mail: danielson.gordon@mayo.edu.

DANN, MARC, state attorney general, former state senator; b. Evanston, Ill., Mar. 12, 1962; m. Alyssa Lenhoff; 3 children. BA in Hist., U. Mich., 1984; JD, Case Western Res. U., 1987. Ptnr. Betraz and Dann, 1991—99, Dann and Falgiani, Youngstown, Ohio, 1999—2007; mem. Ohio State Senate from Dist. 32, Columbus, 2003—07, ranking minority mem., mem. agr., highways and transp., judiciary civil justice, judiciary criminal justice, ways and means, and econ. devel. coms.; atty. gen. State of Ohio, Columbus, 2007—. Mem. regional bd. Anti-Defamation League; mem. bd. edn. Liberty Twp., Ohio, 2001—02. Named Legislator of Yr., Ohio Farmers Union, 2005, Amvets, 2005; recipient Pro Bono award, N.E. Ohio Legal Svcs. Mem.: Mahoning and Trumbull County Bar Assns., Tobacco-Free Youth, Youngstown-Warren Regional C. of C., Jewish Cmty. Ctr. Democrat. Office: Office of Atty Gen State Office Tower 30 E Broad St 17th Fl Columbus OH 43266-0410

DANNEMILLER, JOHN C., transportation company executive; b. Cleve., May 17, 1938; s. John Charles and Jean I. (Bage) D.; m. Jean Marie Sheridan, Sept. 22, 1962; children— David, Peter BS, Case Western Res. U., 1960, MBA, 1964; postgrad., Stanford U., 1975, Columbia U., 1974, Tuck Exec. program Dartmouth Coll., 1976. Vice pres. foods div. Diamond Shamrock, 1978-81, dir. planning, 1981-83; v.p. SDS Biotech Corp., Cleve., 1984-85; group v.p. leasing group Leaseway Transp., Cleve., 1984-85, pres., chief operating officer, 1985-88, exec. v.p., chief oper. officer, 1988—; exec. v.p. Bearings Inc., Cleve., 1988—, now chmn., ceo, b d. dirs. Bd. dirs. Lamson & Sessions, Cleve., Star Bank, Cleve. Bd. dirs., advisor Jr. Achievement, Cleve., 1962-64; bd. dirs. Luth. Med. Found.; fund raiser United Way, Cleve. and St. Louis Mem. Bearing Speciality Assn., Cleve. Athletic Club, Lakewood Country Club, Union Club, Univ. Club, Beta Gamma Sigma. Republican. Presbyterian. Avocations: tennis, water-skiing, boating, skiing, golf. Office: Bearings Inc PO Box 6925 3600 Euclid Ave Cleveland OH 44115-2515

DANNER, KATHLEEN FRANCES STEELE, federal official; b. Kansas City, Mo., Oct. 28, 1960; m. Steve Danner, Jan. 18, 1996. Admissions counselor N.E. Mo. State U., Kirksville, 1980-83, assoc. dir. admissions, 1983-86, programming coord. dept. pub. svcs., 1986-87; Iowa, N.H. dir. Gephardt for Pres., St. Louis, 1987-88; mem. Mo. Ho. of Reps., Jefferson City, 1988-94; state dir. Clinton for Pres., 1991-92; regional dir. U.S. Dept. HHS, Kansas City, Mo., 1994—, acting dir. intergovtl. affairs Washington, 1998—. Pres. Greater Kansas City Fed. Exec. Bd. Pres. Greater Mo. Found.; exec. com. Heart of Am. United Way; mem. White House Outreach Task Force on CHIP. Recipient Hammer award V.P. Gore, 1999, award for disting. svc. Sec. Shalala, 1998. Mem. Ctrl. Exch., Nat. Women's Polit. Caucus. Roman Catholic. Avocations: sports, dance, reading, politics. Office: US Dept Health and Human Svcs 601 E 12th St Ste 210 Kansas City MO 64106-2826 Home: 1075 Crescent Dr Hollister MO 65672-4884

DANNER, PATSY ANN, former congresswoman; b. Louisville, Ky., Jan. 13, 1934; d. Henry J. and Catherine M. (Shaheen) Berrer; children: Stephen, Stephanie, Shane, Shavonne.; m. C.M. Meyer, Dec. 30, 1982. Student, Hannibal-LaGrange Coll., 1952; BA in Polit. Sci. cum laude, N.E. Mo. State U., 1972. Dist. asst. to Congressman Jerry Litton, Kansas City, Mo., 1973-76; fed. co-chmn. Ozarks Regional Commn., Washington, 1977-81; mem. Mo. State Senate, 1983-1992, 103rd-106th Congress from 6th Mo. dist., 1993-2001. Mem. internat. rels. com., transp. and infrastructure com. Mem.: LWV (bd. mem., health chairwoman Columbia-Boone County, Mo.). Democrat. Roman Catholic.

D'ARCY, JOHN MICHAEL, bishop; b. Brighton, Mass., Aug. 18, 1932; Student, St. John's Sem., Brighton, 1949-57; ThD, Angelicum U., Rome, 1968. Ordained priest Archdiocese of Boston, 1957; spiritual dir., prof. theology St. John's Sem., 1968-85; ordained bishop, 1975; bishop Diocese of Ft. Wayne-South Bend, Ind., 1985—. Roman Catholic. Office: Diocese of Ft Wayne-South Bend PO Box 390 1103 S Calhoun St Fort Wayne IN 46801 Office Phone: 219-422-4611. Office Fax: 260-969-1383.*

DARKE, RICHARD FRANCIS, lawyer; b. Detroit, June 17, 1943; s. Francis Joseph and Irene Anne (Potts) D.; m. Alice Mary Renger, Feb. 14, 1968; children: Kimberly, Richard, Kelly, Sean, Colin. BBA, U. Notre Dame, 1965; JD, Detroit Coll. Law, 1969. Bar: Mich. 1969. Atty. AAA, Detroit, 1969-72; assoc. Oster & Mollett P.C., Mt. Clemens, Mich., 1972-73; ptnr. Small, Darke, Oakes P.C., Southfield, Mich., 1973-77; v.p., gen. counsel, sec. Fruehauf Corp., Detroit, 1977-92; ptnr. Darke & Wilson, Grosse Pointe Woods, Mich., 1993—.

Mem. ABA, Mich. Bar Assn., Detroit Bar Assn., Machinery and Allied Products Inst. (counsel), Mich. Gen. Counsel Group, Essex Country Club, Lockmoor Club. Roman Catholic. Avocation: golf. Home: 752 Nissen Ct Wixom MI 48393-1751

DARLING, ALBERTA HELEN, state legislator, art gallery director, marketing professional; b. Hammond, Ind., Apr. 28, 1944; d. Albert William and Helen Anne (Vaicunas) Statkus; m. William Anthony Darling, Aug. 12, 1967; children— Elizabeth Suzanne, William Anthony. BS, U. Wis., 1967. English tchr. Nathan Hale High Sch., West Allis, Wis., 1967—69, Castle Rock High Sch., Castle Rock, Colo., 1969—71; mem. Wis. State Assembly, 0990—1992, Wis. Senate from 8th dist., Madison, 1992—. Cons. orgn. devel., Milw., 1982—; dir. mktg. and communications Milw. Art Mus., 1981-88; exec. dir. mktg. architectural firm, 1988-90; State Rep. Wis., 1990—, mem. urban edn. com., children and human svcs. com., tourism com., homelessness com., teenage pregnancy com., vice chmn. gov.'s housing policy commn., assembly coms. Pres. Community Action Seminar for Women, 1979-80; a founder Goals for Greater Milw. 2000, 1980-84; co-chair Action 2000, 1984-86; co-chmn. Icebreaker Am. Winterfestival; chmn. Community Action Seminar for Women, 1988; bd. dirs., exec. com. United Way, Milw., 1982-1992, chair project 1985, 1984-85, chmn. policy com. 1988; founder Today's Girls/Tomorrow's Women, Milw., pres. Jr. League Milw., 1980-82, Planned Parenthood Milw., 1982-84, Future Milw., 1983-85; vice chmn. State of Wis. Strategic Planning Council, 1988—, chmn. small bus./entrpreneur com.; mem. Greater Milw. Com.'s Mktg. Task Force, 1987-88; chmn. United Way Policy Com., 1987-88; participant Bus. Ptnrs. White House Conf., 1987; mem. summerfest adv. com. on Winter Festivals, 1989; founder Women's Fund of Milw. Found; actuve Juvenile Justice Leadership Com. Recipient Vol. Action award Milw. Civic Alliance, 1984, Community Service award United Way, 1984, Leader of Future award Milw. Mag., 1988, Nat. Assn. Community Leadership Orgn. award, 1986, Today's Girls/Tomorrow's Women Leadership award, 1987, Future Milw. Community Leadership award, 1988, Friend of Edn. Leadership award Head Start, 1994, William Steiger Humanitarian award, 1994. Mem. Greater Milw. Com., TEMPO Profl. Women, Am. Mktg. Assn. (Marketer of Yr. 1984), Pub. Relations Soc. Am., Ctr. for Pub. Representation (state bd. 1988), ARC (bd. dirs., exec. fin. coms. 1987—), Women's Fund (steering com. 1988), Internat. Assn. Bus. Communicators, Greater Milw. Com. Republican. Avocations: travel, art history, contemporary american literature, golf, tennis. Home: 1325 W Dean Rd Milwaukee WI 53217-2537 Office: State Capitol PO Box 7882 Madison WI 53707-7882 Office Phone: 608-266-5830. Business E-Mail: sen.darling@legis.wisconsin.gov.

DARLING, ROBERT HOWARD, lawyer; b. Detroit, Oct. 29, 1947; s. George Beatson and Jeanne May (Mainville) D.; m. Cathy Lee Trygstad, Apr. 30, 1970; children: Bradley Howard, Brian Lee, Kara Kristine, Blake Robert. BS in Mech. Engring., U. Mich., 1969, MS in Mech. Engring., 1971; JD, Wayne State U., 1975. Bar: Mich. 1975, U.S. Dist. Ct. (ea. dist.) Mich. 1975, U.S. Ct. Appeals (6th cir.) 1975. Engr. Bendix Corp., Ann Arbor, Mich., 1970, Ford Motor Co., Dearborn, Mich., 1972-73; ptnr. Philo, Atkinson, Darling, Steinberg, Harper & Edwards, Detroit, 1975-81; sr. ptnr. Sommers, Schwartz, Silver & Schwartz, Southfield, Mich., 1981—. Assoc. editor Wayne State U. Law Review. Mem. ABA, Assn. Trial Lawyers Am., Mich. Trial Lawyers Assn. (exec. bd. 1981—, publs. chmn. 1981-85, products liability chmn. 1986—), Met. Detroit Trial Lawyers Assn., Oakland County Trial Lawyers Assn., State Bar Mich., Detroit Bar Assn., Plymouth Hist. Soc., Pi Tau Sigma. Avocation: golf. Office: Sommers Schwartz Silver Schwartz 2000 Town Ctr Ste 900 Southfield MI 48075-1100 Address: 8785 Warren Rd Plymouth MI 48170-5119 E-mail: rdarling@s4online.com.

DARLOW, JULIA DONOVAN, lawyer; b. Detroit, Sept. 18, 1941; d. Frank William Donovan and Helen Adele Turner; m. George Anthony Gratton Darlow (div.); 1 child, Gillian; m. John Corbett O'Meara. AB, Vassar Coll., 1963; postgrad., Columbia U. Law Sch., 1964-65; JD cum laude, Wayne State U., 1971. Bar: Mich. 1971, U.S. Dist. Ct. (ea. dist.) Mich. 1971. Assoc. Dickinson, Wright, McKean, Cudlip & Moon, Detroit, 1971-78; ptnr. Dickinson, Wright, Moon, Van Dusen & Freeman and predecessor, Detroit, 1978—2001; sr. v.p. Detroit Med. Ctr., 2001—01; cons. mem. Dickinson, Wright PLLC, Detroit, 2002—04; counsel Varnum, Riddering, Schmidt & Howlett, LLP, 2005—06; bd. regents U. Mich., 2007—. Chair corp. governance com. Internet Corp., 2004-05; adj. prof. Wayne State U. Law Sch., 1974-75, 96; commr. State Bar Mich., 1977-87, exec. com., 1979-83, 84-87, sec. 1980-81, v.p., 1984-85, pres.-elect 1985-86, pres. 1986-87, coun. corp. fin. and bus. law sect. 1980-86, coun. computer law sect. 1985-88; mem. State Officers Compensation Commn., 1994-96; chair Mich. Supreme Ct. Task Force on Gender Issues in the Cts., 1987-89 Bd. dirs. Hutzel Hosp., 1984—2003, chair, 2002—03; bd. dirs. Mich. Opera Theatre, 1985—, mem. exec. com., 1992—; bd. dirs. Mich. Women's Found., 1986—91, Detroit Med. Ctr., 1990—2003, Marygrove Coll., 1996—2006, sec., 2003—06; trustee Internat. Inst. Met. Detroit, 1986—92; trustee Mich. Met. coun. Girl Scouts USA, 1988—91; trustee Detroit coun. Boy Scouts Am., 1988—98; mem. exec. com. Mich. Coun. Humnanities, 1988—92; mem. Blue Cross-Blue Shield Prospective Reimbursement Com., Detroit, 1979—81; v.p., mem. exec. com. United Found., 1988—95; mem. Mich. Gov.'s Bilateral Trade Team for Germany, 1992—98. Fellow Am. Bar Found. (Mich. State chair 1990-96); mem. Detroit Bar Assn. Found. (treas. 1984-85, trustee 1982-85), Mich. Bar Found. (trustee 1987-94), Am. Judicature Soc. (bd. dirs. 1985-88), Internat. Women's Forum (global affairs com. 1994-03), Women Lawyers Assn. (pres. 1977-78), Mich. Women's Campaign Fund (charter). Democrat. Office: Ste 400 200 E Liberty St Ann Arbor MI 48104 Office Phone: 313-690-3054.

DAROFF, ROBERT BARRY, neurologist, educator; b. NYC, Aug. 3, 1936; s. Charles and May (Wolin) D.; m. Jane L. Abrahams, Dec. 4, 1959; children: Charles II, Robert Barry, Jr., William Clayton BA, U. Pa., 1957, MD, 1961. Cert. in Neurology Am. Bd. Psychiatry and Neurology, 1969. Intern Phila. Gen. Hosp., 1961-62; resident in neurology Yale-New Haven Med. Ctr., 1962-65; fellow in neuro-ophthalmology U. Calif. Med. Ctr., San Francisco, 1967-68; prof. neurology, assoc. prof. ophthalmology U. Miami Med. Sch.; dir. ocular motor neurophysiology lab. Miami Va. Med. Ctr., 1968-80; Gilbert W. Humphrey prof., chmn. dept. neurology Case Western Res. U. Med. Sch.; dir. dept. neurology Univ. Hosps., Cleve., 1980-93; prof. neurology Case Western U., 1980—, assoc. dean, 1994—2003, interim vice dean edn. and acad. affairs, 2004—06, interim chair, 2006—07; staff neurologist Cleve. Va. Med. Ctr., 1980-93; chief of staff, sr. v.p. acad. affairs U. Hosp., Cleve., 1994—2003; chief med. officer St. Vincents Charity, St. Johns West Shore Hosps., 2004—05. Med. sci. adv. bd., chmn. sci. program com. Myasthenia Gravis Found., 1984—87, exec. com., 1992—2003, sec., 1995—96, vice chair, 1997—99, chair, 1999—2001, chair nominating com., 2002—03; adv. bd. Nat. Multiple Sclerosis Found., 1988—90, Soc. Progressive Supranuclear Palsy, 1991—94; nat. adv. eye coun. sensory and motor disorders vision panel NIH, 1980—83; steering com. neurological disorders in comml. drivers US Dept. Transp., chmn. task force, 1987; lectr. T.S. Srinivasan Endowment, Madras, India, 1994; Cumings lectr. Migraine Trust, London, 1994; lectr. Am. Coun. Headache Edn., 1996, vice chair, 2000—02; Soriano lectr., 2001; prof. (hon.) Astana-State Med. Acad., Kazakhstan, 1999; bd. advisors Capnia, Inc., 2000—07; lectr. 7th Ann. Vijjajiva, Mahidol U., Bangkok, 2006. Book rev. editor: Neuro-ophthalmology, 1981-86, mem. editl. bd., 1987-2003; assoc. editor Jour. Biomed. Sys., 1970-72; editor Neurol. Progress, Anns. eurology, 1981-84; editor-in-chief Neurology, 1987-96, sci. integrity adv., 2004-; co-editor World Neurology, 1991-98, editl. adv. bd. 1998—2003; mem. editl. bd. Archives of Neurology, 1976, Annals of Neurology, 1977-86, Neurology and Neurosurgery Update Series, 1978-93, Headache, 1980-86, sr. edit. advisor, 2004-; Contemporary Neurology Series, 1989-93, Neurosci., Saudi Arabia, 2003-06, consulting sr. editor, 2007—, Practical Neurology, 2003—; mem. editl. adv. bd. Jour. Neuro-ophthalmology, 2001—; mem. editl. coun. Neurologia Croatica, 1991-2004; mem. editl. commn. Valeology, Kazakhstan, 2002-05, The Scientific World Neurology Jour., 2006-, Internat. Jour. of Experimental Clinical Anatomy; contbr. articles to profl. jours. Chmn. Young Tae Kwon Do Acad., North Miami, 1977-80; bd. dirs. Benign Essential Blepharospasm Rsch. Found., 1983-; trustee Fairhill Ctr. for Aging, 1988—, The Learning Corp., 1992-00, Edison Bio Tech. Ctr., 1994-01, Great Lakes Sci. Ctr., 1994-01, Myasthenia Gravis Found. Am., 1999-01; mem. tech. adv. coun. BIOMEC, Inc., 1999-2007; bd. trustees Greater Cleve. chpt. ARC, 1999-05, mem. exec. com., 2000-03; mem. cmty. bd. St. Vincent Charity Hosp., 2003-05, St. John West Shore Hosp., 2003-05. With USAR, 1965—67. Recipient Ernst Jung-Medaille Für Medizin in Gold, 1993, Silver Jubilee Oration award Med. Coll. Trivandrum, India, 1994, John H. Budd Disting. Mem. award Cleve. Acad. Med., 2002, Disting. Grad. award U. Pa., 2003, Lifetime Achievement award, Neurosciences India Group, 2005, A.B. Baker award for lifetime achievement in Neurol. Edn., Am. Acad. Neurol., 2006; named hon. dir. life Fairhill Ctr., 2006. Fellow: Am. Headache Soc. (pres. 2002—04, bd. dirs., sec., John R. Graham Svc. Clin. Forum award 2005); mem.: AMA, Hadassah Med. Ctr. (rsch. com.), World Neurology Found. (bd. dirs. 2006—), Internat. Neurology Forum (chair internat. organizing com. 2004—07), Eastern Mediterranean Association of Med. Editors, World Assn. Med. Editors, Internat. Headache Soc., Neuromuscular Disease Assn. Romania (internat. sci. com. 1991—93), Acad. Med. Scis. Kazakhstan, Alliance Brain Initiatives (founding mem.), Dana Found., Coun. Sci. Editors, World Fedn. Neurology (fin. com. 1985—, exec. com. Rsch. group on Neuro-Ophthalmology 1987—95, publs. com. 1987—, chmn. 1990—2001), Clin. Eye Movement Soc. (founder), Barany Soc., Internat. Neuro-Ophthalmology Soc. (organizing com. 1986), .Am. Neuro-Ophthalmology Soc. (bd. dirs. 1986—94, chair cert. and accreditation com. 1997—98, publs. com. 1999—2001), Rocky Mountain Neuro-Ophthalmology Soc. (bd. dirs. 1980—86), Assn. Colombiana Neurologia (hon.), Am. Acad. Neurology (hon.; chmn. sci. program com. 1973—75, exec. bd. 1987—96, Netter lectr. 1989, pub. com. 1993—2001), Am. Neurol. Assn. (hon.; program adv. com. 1977—78, chmn. 1978, councillor 1980—82, membership adv. com. 1980—83, chmn. 1981—83, nominating com. 1984, chmn. Annals of Neurology oversight com. 1984—86, sec. 1985—89, pres.-elect 1989—90, pres. 1990—91, past pres. 1991—92, history com. 2004—06), Vietnam Vets. Inst. (bd. scholars 1998—, Ea. Med. Assn. Med. Editors, ethics and sci. misconduct com. 2005—, united coun. of neurolgic subspecialists, alternate dir. 2005—), Alpha Omega Alpha. Office: Univ Hosp Rm HAN 503 11100 Euclid Ave Cleveland OH 44106 Office Phone: 216-844-0474. Business E-Mail: robert.daroff@case.edu.

DARR, ALAN PHIPPS, curator, historian; b. Kankakee, Ill., Sept. 30, 1948; s. Milton Freeman, Jr. and Margaret (Phipps) D.; m. Mollie Hayden Fletcher, June 28, 1980; children: Owen, Alexander. BA, Northwestern U., 1970; MA, Inst. Fine Arts, NYU, 1975, PhD in Art History, 1980; Cert., Mus. Tng., Met. Mus. Art, 1976, Mus. Mgmt. Inst., U. Calif. Berkeley, 1980. Grad. intern Met. Mus. Art, YC, 1976; instr. NYU, 1976; asst. curator Detroit Inst. Arts, 1978-80, assoc. curator, 1980-81, curator in charge European sculpture and decorative arts, 1981—, Walter B. Ford II Family curator European sculpture and decorative arts, 1997—; postdoctoral fellow Harvard U. Ctr. for Italian Renaissance Studies at Villa I Tatti, Florence, 1988-89; adj. prof. Wayne State U., Detroit, 1982—; Paul Mellon vis. sr. scholar Ctr. Advanced Study in Visual Arts, Nat. Gallery, Washington, 1994, recipient Knight of the Order of the Star of Italian Fellowship; Co-editor/co-author: Italian Renaissance Sculpture in the Time of Donatello, 1985-86, Donatello Studien, 1989, Verrocchio and Late Quattrocentro Italian Sculpture, 1992, The Dodge Collection of Eighteenth Century French and English Art in the Detroit Institute of Arts, 1996, Woven Splendor: Five Centuries of European Tapestry in the Detroit Institute of Arts, 1996, Catalogue of Italian Sculpture in the Detroit Inst. of Arts, 2 vols., 2002, The Medici, Michelangelo and the Art of Late Renaissance Florence, 2002, Large Bronzes in the Renaissance, Studies in the History of Art, vol. 64, Nat. Gallery of Art, 2003, others; contbr. articles to profl. jours. Nat. Endowment Arts Mus. Profls. Fellow, 1983; John J. McCloy fellow, 1980-81, Ford Found. fellow, 1975-78, Met. Mus. Art fellow, 1975. Office: Detroit Inst Arts 5200 Woodward Ave Detroit MI 48202-4094

DARR, MILTON FREEMAN, JR., retired banker; b. Oak Park, Ill., Oct. 30, 1921; s. Milton Freeman and Frances Anna (Kaiser) D.; m. Margaret Claire Phipps, Jan. 27, 1945; children: Alan Phipps, Bruce Milton. BS, U. Ill., 1942. With LaSalle Nat. Bank, Chgo., 1946-80, asst. cashier, 1950-53, asst. v.p., 1953, v.p., 1954-62, exec. v.p., dir., 1962-64, pres., 1964-68, chmn. bd., chief exec. officer, 1968-73, pres., 1974-77, vice chmn. bd., 1977-80. Organizer, founding dir. Buffalo Grove (Ill.) Nat. Bank, 1975; pres. Park Shore Tower Assn., Naples, Fla. Mem. Bd. Edn. Dist. 88 Community High Sch., 1963-68, Nat. Bd. YMCA's, 1973-77; past chmn., mem. Ill. Gov.'s Adv. Bd. on Cancer Control; chmn. commerce and industry com., treas. Chgo. Com. for Project Hope; state crusade chmn. Ill. div. Am. Cancer Soc., 1967, 68, chmn. bd., 1973-75, nat. bd. dirs., 1975-78; chmn. bd. mgrs., v.p. bd. trustees YMCA Met. Chgo., 1970-72; chmn. bd. trustees Elmhurst Coll., 1982-87, hon. life trustee, 1998—; chmn. YMCA Retirement Fund, 1986-92, trustee emeritus, 1994; trustee Ill. Cancer Council, Better Govt. Assn.; life trustee Union League Boys and Girls Clubs; chmn. Armed Forces Week, 1987; bd. dirs. Chgo. Crime Commn., United Charities of Chgo., Mid-Am. chpt. ARC; pres. Park Shore Tower Assn., Naples, Fla., 2001. Served to maj. USAAF, 1942-46. Recipient Distinguished Service award Am. Cancer Soc., 1976, Founders medal Elmhurst Coll., 1987; Citizen fellow Inst. Medicine of Chgo. Mem. Am. Inst. Banking (pres. Chgo. chpt. 1955-56, mem. exec. council 1956-59, nat. v.p. 1959-60, nat. pres. 1960-61), Am. Bankers Assn. (mem. adminstrv. com., exec. council 1960-61), Assn. Res. City Bankers (treas. 1969-72), Robert Morris Assos. (pres. Chgo. chpt. 1965-66), Chgo. Clearing House Assn. (past chmn.), Theta Chi. Clubs: Rotarian (pres. 1973-74, Paul Harris fellow, Ches Perry fellow), Chicago, Bankers (pres. 1973), Economic, Executives, Union League (pres. 1968-69), Commerical (life, treas.) (Chgo.); Glen Oak Country; Moorings Country Club of Naples, Fla., Chgo. Athletic Assn. Presbyterian.

DARR, WILLIAM A., commissioner; b. Park Ridge, Ill., 1951; BA in mathematics and econ., U. Ill., 1970; MBA in mgmt. sys., DePaul U., 1979. Dir. Dept. Sr. and Cmty. Svcs., Sec. of State's Office; commr. Office of Banks and Real Estate, Springfield, Ill., 2002—. Mem. Ill. Govt. Technology Advisory Bd. Office: Ill Div of Banking and Real Estate 500 E Monroe St Springfield IL 62701

DARROW, CLARENCE ALLISON, judge; b. Dubuque, Iowa, Mar. 22, 1940; s. Clarence Allison and Joan Kathryn (Reinhart) D.; m. Lili Ruja, Nov. 30, 193; children: Elizabeth, John, Antoinette, Clarence, Jennifer. BS, Loras Coll., Dubuque, IA, 1962; MSW, U. Ill., Champagne, 1966; JD, Chgo.-Kent Coll. Law, 1971. Bar: Ill. 1971, US Dist. Ct. (no. and so. dists.) Ill. 1971, US Supreme Ct. 1998. Asst. state's atty. Rock Island County, Ill., 1971-74; mem. Ill. Ho. of Reps., Springfield, 1975-83, Ill. Senate, 1983-86; cir. judge, 1986-96; pvt. practice, 1996—99; sr. ptnr. Law Office of Clarence Darrow, 1999—. Mem. office Rock Island County Courthouse. Named freshman Legislator of Yr. Ill. Edn. Assn.; recipient Legis. Achievement award, Am. Legion Award, Legis. Svc. award Ill. Farm and Bur., Outstanding Legis. award Ill. Pub. Action Coun., Legis Achievement award Ill. Pub. Transit Assn. Mem. ABA, Ill. Bar Assn., Ill. Judges Assn., Cornbelt Running Club. Democrat. Office: 1515 4th Ave Ste 200 Rock Island IL 61201-8651 Office Phone: 309-794-9163.

DARROW, KURT L., manufacturing executive; b. 1954; m. Renee M. Darrow. BA, Adrian U., 1977. V.p. sales La-Z-Boy Inc., 1987—99, sr. v.p., sales & mktg., 1999—2001, pres., residential divsn., 2001—03, pres., CEO, 2003—. Office: La Z Boy Inc 1284 N Telegraph Rd Monroe MI 48162

DART, KENNETH BRYAN, manufacturing executive; b. Apr. 1955; s. William A. Dart. Pres., CEO Dart Container Corp., Mason, Mich. Office: Dart Container Corp 500 Hogsback Rd Mason MI 48854-9547

DARWIN, DAVID, engineering educator, consultant; b. NYC, Apr. 17, 1946; s. Samuel David and Earle D.; m. Diane Marie Mayer, June 29, 1968; children: Samuel David, Lorraine Marie. BS in Civil Engring., Cornell U., 1967, MS in Structural Engring., 1968; PhD in Civil Engring., U. Ill., 1974. Lic. profl. engr., Kans. Asst. prof. civil engring. U. Kans., Lawrence, 1974-77, assoc. prof., 1977-82, prof., 1982—, Deane E. Ackers disting. prof. civil engring., 1990—, dir. Structural Engring. and Materials Lab., 1982—; dir. Infrastructure Rsch. Inst., 1998-2001, 2003—. Cons. David Darwin, Lawrence, 1976—. Author: Steel and Composite Beams with Web Openings, 1990; co-author: Concrete, 2d edit., 2003, Design of Concrete Structures, 13th edit., 2004; contbr. articles to profl. jours. Mem. Uniform Bldg. Code Bd. Appeals, Lawrence, 1978-84. Capt. U.S. Army, 1967-72, Vietnam. Decorated Bronze Star with oak leaf cluster; recipient Miller award, U. Kans., 1986, Irvin Youngberg Rsch. Achievement award, 1992, Civil and Environ. Engring. Alumni Assn. Disting. Alumnus award, U. Ill., 2003; grantee, NSF, 1976—2003, Kans. Dept. Transp., 1980—82, 1990—, Air Force Office Sci. Rsch., 1985—92, Civil Engring. Rsch. Found., 1991—95, Fed. Hwy. Adminstrn., 1994—98, 2001—, SD Dept. Transp., 2001—07, Nat. Coop. Hwy. Rsch. Program, 1994—95, Transportation Pooled Fund Study, 2002—; Bellows scholar, 2001, Miller scholar, 2004. Fellow ASCE (editor Jour. Structural Engring. 1994-00, bd. govs. Structural Engring. Inst. 2000-04, treas. 2003-04, Kans. sect. v.p., pres.-elect 2001-02, pres. 2002-03, Huber Rsch. prize 1985, Moisseiff award 1991, state-of-the-art of civil engring. award 1996, 2000, Richard R. Torrens award 1997), Am. Concrete Inst. (pres. Kans. chpt. 1975, bd. dirs. 1988-91, 2005—, v.p. 2005-07, exec. com. 2005—, pres. 2007-08, Bloem Disting. Svc. award 1986, Arthur R. Anderson award 1992, Structural Rsch. award 1996, Joe W. Kelly award 2005)); mem. AAAS, ASTM (award of appreciation 2003), Am. Soc. Engring. Edn., Am. Inst. Steel Constrn., Prestressed Concrete Inst., Post-Tensioning Inst., Concrete Rsch. Coun. (chmn. 1990-96), Structural Engring. Inst. (bd. govs. 2000-04, treas. 2003-04), Wire Reinforcement Inst. (hon.), Phi Kappa Phi (pres. U. Kans. chpt. 1976-78). Democrat. Unitarian Universalist. Achievements include development of standard method of design for structural steel and composite beams with web openings. Avocations: swimming, walking. Office: U Kans Civil Environ and Archtl Engring Dept 2142 Learned Hall 1530 W 15th St Lawrence KS 66045-7609 Home Phone: 785-841-2888; Office Phone: 785-864-3827. E-mail: daved@ku.edu.

DASCHLE, THOMAS ANDREW, former senator; b. Aberdeen, SC, Dec. 9, 1947; m. Linda Hall Daschle; children: Kelly, Nathan, Lindsay. BA, S.D. State U., 1969. Fin. investment rep.; chief legis. aide, field coord. to Senator James Abourzek US Senate, 1973-77; mem. US Congress from 1st S.D. Dist., 1979—83, US Congress from S.D. at-large Dist., 1983-87; US Senator from S.D., 1987—2005; minority leader US Senate, 1996—2001, 2003—04, majority leader, 2001—03; spl. policy adv. Alston & Bird LLP, Washington, 2005—; Richard von Weizsäcker Disting. Vis. Am. Acad., Berlin, 2008—; vis. prof. Georgetown U. Pub. Policy Inst., 2005—; Disting. sr. fellow Ctr. Am. Progress, 2005—; co-founder Bipartisan Policy Ctr., 2007—. Mem. agrl. nutrition and forestry com., mem. fin. com., rules com., co-chmn. Sen. Dem. steering and coord. com., co-chair Sen. Dem. tech. and comm. com., chmn. Sen. Dem. conf. com., co-chmn. Sen. Dem. policy com.; leader bipartisan effort; author, enforcer Agent Orange Act, 1991; authored, reformulated gasoline provisions of Clean Air Act Amendment 1990; bd. dirs. CB Richard Ellis Group, Inc., 2005-, Prime BioSolutions, Mascoma Corp., 2007-. Co-author (with Michael D'Orso): Like No Other Time: The Two Years That Changed America, 2004; co-author: (with Scott S. Greenberger & Jeanne M. Lawbrew) Critical: What We Can Do About the Health-Care Crisis, 2008. Founder Am. Grown Found., 1987. Served to 1st lt. USAF, 1969-72. Recipient Nat. Commdr.'s award Disabled Am. Vets., 1980, Disting. Alumni award S.D. State U., 1997, VFW Congl. award VFW, 1997, Legislator of Yr. award Vietnam Vets. Am., 1997, Cert. Appreciation, Nat. Assn. Federally Impacted Sch., 1997, Congl. Leadership award Cmty. Anti-Drug Coalitions Am., 1997, Golden Triangle award Nat. Farmer's Union, 1997-98, Outstanding Vets. Adv. of Yr. award Disabled Am. Vets. Dept. S.D., 1998, Pres. Recognition award Nat. Indian Impacted Schs. Assn., 1998, Cert. Appreciation, Nat. Assn. Alcoholism and Drug Abuse Counselors, 1998, Diplomat award Rapid City C. of C., 1998, Disting. Svc. award Nat. Rural Electric Coop. Assn., 2000; named Outstanding Young Man of Yr., U.S. Jaycees, 1981, Friend of Edn., S.D. Edn. Assn., 1997, Person of the Yr., Nat. Assn. Concerned Vets., 1997, Legislator of Yr., Renewable Fuels Assn., 1998, Maj. Gen. Williamson's S.D. Nat. Guard Militia Man of 1998, S.D. Nat. Guard. Mem.: Coun. Fgn. Rels. Democrat. Roman Catholic. Office Phone: 202-756-3156. Business E-Mail: tom.daschle@alston.com.*

DASH, LEON DECOSTA, JR., journalist; b. New Bedford, Mass., Mar. 16, 1944; s. Leon DeCosta and Ruth Elizabeth (Kydd). BA, Howard U., 1968; DHD, Lincoln U., 1996. Reporter Washington Post, 1966—68, 1971—79, African bur. chief, 1979—83, with investigations desk, 1984—98; prof. journalism U. Ill., Champaign, 1998—99, Swanlund chair prof. journalism, 2000—01, Swanlund prof. journalism, 2001—; prof. journalism Ctr. Advanced Study, 2003—. Vis. prof. U. Calif.-San Diego, 1978. Author (with Ben H. Bagdikian): (book) The Shame of the Prisons, 1972; author: When Children Want Children: The Urban Crisis of Teenage Childbearing, 1989, Rosa Lee: A Mother and Her Family in Urban America, 1996 (Polit. Book award Washington Monthly Mag., 1997, 1st prize Harry Chapin Best Book award World Hunger Yr. Orgn., 1997). Vol. Peace Corps, Kenya, 1969—70. Co-recipient Editl. award for news series, Chesapeake AP, 1987, Editl. award, 1989; named one of Best 100 Works in 20th Century Am. Journalism for 8-part series Rosa Lee's Story for Washington Post, 1999; recipient George Polk Meml. award, Overseas Press Club, 1974, award for internat. news reporting, Washington-Balt. Newspaper Guild, 1974, hon. mention, 1975, Internat. Reporting award, Africare, 1984, Capitol Press Club, 1984, 1st Place Journalism award for gen. news, Nat. Assn. Black Journalists, 1986, Investigative Reporters and Editors award, 1987, 1st Prize award, Washington-Balt. Newspaper Guild, 1987, Pres.'s award, Washington Ind. Writers Assn., 1989, Martha Albrand Spl. Citation for Nonfiction, PEN, 1990, Pulitzer Prize for explanatory journalism, 1995, 1st Prize Robert F. Kennedy award for print journalism, 1995, Emmy award for pub. affairs, NATAS, 1996, Polit. Book award, The Washington Monthly mag., 1997, Prevention for a Safer Soc. award, Nat. Coun. on Crime and Delinquency for Rosa Lee book, 1997; Henry J. Kaiser Family Found. fellow, 1995—96. Mem.: Hong Kong Baptist U. (Workshop dir., jour. dept. 2007—, Pulitzer Prize), Kappa Tau Alpha. Office: U Ill Dept Journalism 119 Gregory Hall 810 S Wright St Urbana IL 61801-3644 Home Phone: 217-344-5169; Office Phone: 217-265-5055. Business E-Mail: leondash@uiuc.edu.

DASKIN, MARK STEPHEN, engineering educator; b. Balt., Dec. 3, 1952; s. Walter and Betty Jane (Fax) D.; m. Babette Reva Levy, July 2, 1978; children: Tamar, Keren. BSCE, MIT, 1974, PhD in Civil Engring., 1978; postgrad. study in Engring., Cambridge, England, 1975. Tchg. asst. trans. sys. divsn. civil engring. MIT, Cambridge, 1976-77; asst. prof. civil engring. U. Tex., Austin, 1978-79, Northwestern U., Evanston, Ill., 1980-83, assoc. prof. civil engring., 1983-89, prof., 1989—2006, chair dept. indsl. engring. and mgmt. scis., 1995—2001, Bette and Neison Harris prof. of tchg. excellence, 2006—07, Walter P. Murphy prof., 2007—. Author: Network and Discrete Location: Models, Algorithms and Applications, 1995; editor-in-chief Transp. Sci., 1991-94; assoc. editor Location Sci., 1991-2000; contbr. articles to profl. jours. Bd. dirs. North Suburban Synagogue Beth El, Highland Park, Ill., 1991-94. U. Tex. Bur. Engring. Rsch. granee, 1978-79, Northwestern U. Transp. Ctr. grantee, 1980, 81, NSF grantee, 1980-82, 84-90, 93-96, 95-98, 96-99, 1998-2002, 02-04, 05—, Urban Mass Transp. Adminstr. grantee, 1982-84, 84-85, United Parcel Svc. grantee, 1983-86, 91-92, Thermo-King Corp. grantee, 1990-91, 92-94, Heartland Blood Ctr. grantee, 1992, 96, grantee Office Naval Rsch., 2005, other grants; recipient Fulbright Rsch. award, 1989-90, Burlington No. Found. Faculty Achievement award, 1985, NSF Presdl. Young Investigator award, 1984, Scott Paper Leadership award, 1973-75, IIE Tech. Innovation award in indsl. engring., Fred C. Crane disting. svc. award; INFORMS fellow, 2004 Fellow Inst. Indsl. Engrs. (editor-in-chief IEE Transactions 2001—04, Fred C. Crane award for disting. svc. 2005)); mem. INFORMS (v.p. publs. 1996-99, pres.-elect 2005, pres. 2006, past pres. 2007), Ops. Rsch. Soc. Am. (pres. (editor 1991-94), Inst. Mgmt. Sci., Sigma Xi, Tau Beta Pi, Chi Epsilon. Avocations: swimming, photography. Office: Northwestern U Dept Indsl Engring Mgmt Sci Evanston IL 60208-0001 Office Phone: 847-491-8796. Business E-Mail: m-daskin@northwestern.edu.

DASSO, JAMES DANIEL, lawyer; b. Columbus, Ohio, Dec. 30, 1960; s. Jerome J. Dasso and Patricia M. Conger; m. Kathleen H. Dasso, May 12, 1990; children: Lillian Mary, Margaret Elizabeth, Mary Kathleen, Thomas Jerome, Eleanor Hart. BA, U. Oregon, 1982; JD, U. Mich., 1986. Bar: Ill. 1987. Jud. clerk J. Edward Lumbard, U.S. Ct. Appeals, 2nd Cir., NYC, 1986-87; assoc. Kirkland & Ellis, Chgo., 1987-93; ptnr. Phelan, Cahill & Quinlan, Chgo., 1993-96, Foley & Lardner LLP, Chgo., 1996—, co-chmn. appellate practice group. Office: Foley Lardner 321 N Clark St Ste 2800 Chicago IL 60610-5313 Office Phone: 312-832-4501. Business E-Mail: jdasso@foley.com.

DATA, ART J., information technology executive; B in Mech. Engring., Marquette Univ., 1972; MBA, DePaul Univ., 1985. With Danly Machine Tool Corp., 1968—75; joined Internat. Truck & Engine Corp. (operating co. of Navistar Internat. Corp.), Warrenville, Ill., 1975, various positions, including process engr. chief engr. computer tech., sr. project engr. for CAD engring., dir. bus. and tech. sys for engine group, 1975—93, v.p. info. tech., 1993—. Mem.: Tech. Executives Club, AITP, SIM, Soc. of Mfg. Engineers, Soc. of Automotive Engineers. Office: Internat Truck & Engine Corp 4201 Winfield Rd PO Box 1488 Warrenville IL 60555 Office Phone: 630-753-5528. Office Fax: 630-753-3982.

DATSYUK, PAVEL, professional hockey player; b. Sverdlovsk, Russia, July 20, 1978; married; 1 child. Center Detroit Red Wings, 2001—, Dynamo Moscow (Russian Elite League), 2004—05. Named to NHL YoungStars Game, 2002, NHL All-Star Game, 2004; recipient Lady Byng Trophy, 2006, 2007, NHL

All-Star Game, 2008. Achievements include being a member of bronze medal winning Russian Hockey Team, Salt Lake City Olympics, 2002; being a member of Stanley Cup Champion Detroit Red Wings, 2002. Office: Detroit Red Wings Joe Louis Arena 600 Civic Ctr Detroit MI 48226*

DATTILO, THOMAS A., retired manufacturing executive; b. June 12, 1951; BA, OH State U.; JD, U. Toledo; graduate of Advanced Mgmt. Program, Harvard Bus. Sch. Mem., corporate legal staff Dana Corp., 1977-82, with ins. operations dvsn., 1982-85, v.p. then gen. mgr., Precision Control Divsn., and other sr. mgmt. positions Laurinburg, NC, 1985—98; pres., CEO Hayes-Dana Inc., St. Cahtarines, Ont., Canada; pres. Victor Reinz Products, N. Am., Lisle, Ill.; pres., sealing products group Dana Corp., Toledo, 1997—99; pres., COO Cooper Tire and Rubber Co., Findlay, Ohio, 1999—2000, chmn., pres., CEO, 2000—06. Mem.: Mfr. Alliance (vice chmn.), Rubber Mfr. Assn. (chmn.), Automotive Parts Manufacturer's Assn., Young President's Orgn.

DAUB, HAL (HAROLD JOHN DAUB JR.), lawyer; b. Fayetteville, NC, Apr. 23, 1941; s. Harold John and Eleanor M. (Hickman) D.; m. Mary Mernin; children: Natalie Ann, John Clifford, Tammy Rene. BSBA, Washington U., St. Louis, 1963; JD, U. Nebr., Lincoln, 1966. Bar: Nebr. 1966, US Ct. Appeals (8th cir.), US Ct. Customs and Patent Appeals, US Supreme Ct. Staff intern US Sen. Roman Hruska, Nebr., 1966; assoc. Fitzgerald, Brown, Leahy, McGill & Strom, 1966—70; v.p., gen. counsel Standard Chem. Mfg. Co., 1971-80; mem. 97th-100th Congresses from 2nd Nebr. dist., 1981-1989, mem. ways and means com., subcoms. on health and social security, pub. works & transportation, govt. ops. & small bus. com., 1981—89; prin., nat. dir. fed. govt. affairs Deloitte & Touche Acctg. and Cons. Firm, 1989—94; mayor City of Omaha, 1995—2001; ptnr. Blackwell & Sanders, LLP, 2001—; pres., CEO Am. Health Care Assn. and Nat. Ctr. for Assisted Living, Washington, 2004—05. Presdl. appointee Nat. Adv. Coun. on Pub. Svc., 1992—94; prin. Coun. for Excellence in Govt.; pres. Rep. Mayors and Local Elected Ofcls. Assn., 1995—2000; adv. bd. US Conf. Mayors, 1999—2001; chmn. Nat. League of Cities Pub. Safety and Crime Prevention Com., 1997, bd. dir., 1997—99; mem. Bush-Cheney Transition Team, Agr. Policy, 2000—01; presdl. appointee chmn. Social Security Adv. Bd., 2002—06; del. & keynote spkr. White House Conf. Aging, 2005. Jr. pres. Nebr. Founders' Day, 1971, sr. pres., 2001; exec. com., bd. dirs. Combined Health Agys. Drive, 1976; treas. Douglas County Rep. Party, Nebr., 1971-74, chmn., 1974-77; mem. Nebr. State Rep. Ctrl. Com., 1974-77; mem. Congl. Regulatory Reform Task Force, 1981-83, Congl. Rep. Agrl. Task Force, 1981-88; co-founder Liability Ins. and Tort Reform Task Force, 1986; exec. com. Rep. Nat. Congl. Com., 1981-88; co-founder, co-chmn. Budget Reform Task Force, 1981-84; bd. dirs. Metro Arts Coun., 1989-93; nat. bd. dirs. Cmty. Health Agys. of Am., 2003-, chmn., 2006-; pres. Douglas-Sarpy unit ebr. Heart Assn.; elder Presbyn. Ch.; nat. committeeman Rep. Party, 2005—; chmn.-elect bd. dirs. Cmty. Heatlh Charities, 2005-, chmn., 2006-; active Children's Mus., Durham Western Heritage Mus., Joslyn Mus., Henry Doorly Zoo, Humane Soc. & Friends Forever, Salvation Army, United Way/CHAD Divsn. Chmn.; bd. dir. Freedoms Found. Capt. US Army, 1963—68. Decorated Army Commendation medal with oak leaf cluster, Expeditionary medal; named Outstanding Young ebraskan, 1964, Outstanding Young Omahan, Jaycees, 1975, Outstanding Vol. of Yr. award Douglas-Sarpy unit Nebr. Heart Assn., 1976, Disting. Eagle Scout, 2000, Citizen of the Yr. Mid. Am. Boy Scout Coun., 2003; recipient Svc. award SAC, 1976, Leadership awards (4) Coalition for Peace Through Strength award, 1981-1989, Guardian of Small Bus. awards (4), 1981-89, Omaha C. of C. award, Watchdog of Treasury awards (5), 1981-89, Nebr. Reserve Officers, Minutemen of the Year, 1985, Humanitarian award, Grand Masonic Lodges of Nebr., 2004, Silver Beaver award, 2004, Communications & Leadership award, Toastmasters Int., 2005, Disting. Nebraskan award Nebr. Soc. Wash., DC, 2005, others; named to Omaha C. of C. Bus. Hall of Fame, 2004. Mem. Omaha Bar Assn., Nebr. Bar Assn., Nat. Assn. Credit Mgmt. (1st v.p. 1977), Res. Officers Assn., Urban League Nebr., Optimists Internat., Masons (33 degree), Shriners, Optimists Internat., Am. Judiature Soc., Air Force Assn., Am. Heart Assn. (Nebr. affiliate), Assn. Govt. Accountants, Fontenelle Forrest Assn., Multiple Sclerosis Soc., Nebr. Diplomats, Nebr. U. & Washington U. Alumni Assn., Am. Legion, Red Cross Gallon Club, Sisters Cities Assn., VFW, SAR, Kappa Sigma, Alpha Kappa Psi, Omicron Delta Kappa, Delta Theta Phi (Outstanding Law Fraternity Student in the Nation, 1965); fellow Nebr. State Bar Found. Republican. Office: Blackwell Sanders LLP 1620 Dodge St Ste 2100 Omaha NE 68102 Office Phone: 402-964-5019. Business E-Mail: hdaub@blackwellsanders.com.

DAUB, PEGGY ELLEN, library administrator; b. Bluffton, Ohio, Oct. 15, 1949; d. Perry J. and Olive L. (Hoover) D.; m. Jeffrey H. Cooper, Dec. 13, 1975; 1 child, William P. Cooper-Daub. MusB summa cum laude, Miami U., 1972; MA, Cornell U., 1975; MSLS, U. Ill., 1980; PhD, Cornell U., 1985. Acting asst. music libr. Yale U., 1980-81, head of music tech. svcs., rare books libr. Music Libr., 1981-82; head Music Libr. U. Mich., Ann Arbor, 1982-89, head Spl. Collections & Arts Librs., 1989-99, head Spl. Collections Libr., 2000—07; dir. Spl. Collections Libr., 2007—. Presenter Rare Books and Manuscript Sect. Pre-Conf., New Orleans, 1993, Bloomington, 1995 and others. Contbr. articles to profl. jours. Co-clk. Ann Arbor Friends Meeting, 1997-2001. Travel grantee Ctr. for Internat. Studies, Cornell U., 1977. Mem. ALA (Assn. Coll. and Rsch. Librs. rare books and manuscripts sect., mem. task force on interlibr. loan 1991-93, mem. preconf. program planning com. 1992-94), Music Libr. Assn. (bd. dirs. 1985-87, mem. resource sharing and collection devel. com. 1982-91), Rsch. Librs. Group (chairperson music program com. 1985-87, mem. steering com. 1982-87), Am. Musicol. Soc. (mem. coun. 1988-91, mem. coun. com. on minorities/diversity 1988-91), Phi Beta Kappa. Mem. Soc. Of Friends. Office: U of Mich Spl Collections Libr 711 Graduate Libr Ann Arbor MI 48109-1205 Office Phone: 734-764-9377. E-mail: pdaub@umich.edu.

DAUCH, RICHARD E., automotive executive; b. 1942; BS, Purdue U., 1964. With Gen. Motors Corp., Detroit, 1964-75; group v.p. mfg. Volkswagen of Am., Detroit, 1976-80; v.p. Chrysler Corp., Detroit, 1980, exec. v.p. diversified ops., 1980-81, exec. v.p. stamping assembly diversified ops., 1981-84, exec. v.p. mfg., 1984-1994; co-founder, CEO Am. Axle and Mfg., Detroit, 1994—, pres., 1994—2001, chmn., 2001—. Recipient Eli Whitney Meml. Award Soc. Mfg. Engr., 1987, Ellis Island Medal of Honor, 1997; named Industry Leader of the Yr., Automotive Hall of Fame, 1997; Mfr. of the Yr., Mich. Mfg. Assn., 1997; ewsmaker of the Yr., Crain's Detroit Bus., 1998, World Trader of the Yr., Detroit Regional Chamber, 2002, Mich. Exec. of the Yr., Wayne State U. Coll. Bus. Adminstrn., 2002. Mem.: Nat. Assn. Mfr. (chairman 2003). Office: American Axle and Mfg 1840 Holbrook St Detroit MI 48212-3442

DAUGAARD, DENNIS M., lieutenant governor, former state senator; b. Garretson, SD, June 11, 1953; m. Linda Kay Schmidt; children: Laura, Sara, Christopher BS, U. SD, 1975; JD, Northwestern U., 1978. Bar: SD. Atty. Supena & Nyman, 1978-79, Shand Morahan & Co., 1979-81; bank trust officer 1st Bank SD, 1981-90; devel. dir. Children's Home Soc., 1990—; mem. SD State Senate from 9th dist., Pierre, 1997—2003; lt. gov. State of SD, Pierre, 2003—. Mem. Nat. Soc. Fund Raising Execs., SD Bar Assn., SD Planned Giving Coun., Siox Falls (SD) Estate Planning Coun., Rotary. Republican. Lutheran. Office: Office Lt Governor State Capitol Bldg 500 E Capitol Ave Pierre SD 57501-5070 Office Phone: 605-773-3821. Office Fax: 605-773-4711.

DAUGERDAS, PAUL M., lawyer; b. Chgo., Sept. 25, 1950; BS with honors, DePaul U., 1972, JD cum laude, 1974. CPA; bar: Ill. 1974, U.S. Tax Ct. 1975, U.S. Dist. Ct. Ill. (No. Dist.) 1975, U.S. Ct. Appeals (7th cir.) 1975. Of counsel Jenkens & Gilchrist A Profl. Corp., Chgo. Mem.: ABA, Internat. Fiscal Assn., Futures Industry Assn., Equipment Leasing Assn., Assn. Corp. Growth, Am. Inst. CPAs, Ill. CPA Soc., Ill. State Bar Assn., Chgo. Bar Assn.

DAUPHINAIS, GEORGE ARTHUR, import company executive; b. Waterbury, Conn., Apr. 11, 1918; s. Arthur J. and Nell (Phillips) D.; m. Sarah McConnell, Dec. 27, 1942; children: Carol Joe, George William, Sarah Marie. BS in Mech. Engring., La. State U., 1942. Advanced engring. program Gen. Electric Co., Schenectady, 1942, engr., 1942-47; with H.K. Porter Co., Inc., Phila., 1947-59, successively plant engr., works mgr., 1947-52, v.p., gen. mgr., 1952-59; v.p. Electric Autolite Co., Toledo, 1960—; pres. Prestolite Internat. Co. div. Eltra Corp., 1964—; group v.p. Sangamo Electric Co., Springfield, 1965-76; pres. Dauphin Company. Mem. ASME, Tau Beta Pi, Sigma Alpha Epsilon. Home: 4215 N Drinkwater Blvd Apt 157 Scottsdale AZ 85251-3954 E-mail: geodau4@aol.com.

D'AURORA, JAMES JOSEPH, psychologist, consultant; b. Canton, Ohio, Feb. 10, 1949; s. James Joseph Sr. and Arsilia (Lombardi) D'A.; m. Denise Marie Linkenhoker, Dec. 28, 1974; children: Andrew David, Elizabeth Clare. BA, U. Notre Dame, 1971; MEd, Kent State U., 1974; PhD, U. Minn., 1984. Lic. psychologist Minn., cert. profl. qualification in psychology. Pre-major adv. Coll. of Liberal Arts U. Minn., Mpls., 1974-75; intern Bach Inst., Mpls., 1975-77, staff psychologist, 1977-79; psychologist Loring Family Clinic, Mpls., 1979-81; pvt. practice Mpls., 1981-86; cons. psychologist Solstice: A Ctr. for Psychotherapy and Learning, St. Paul, 1986-89; pvt. practice St. Paul, 1989—. Cons. in field; rschr. Family Renewal Ctr., Mpls., 1982-85, Golden Valley Health Ctr. Psychology Subsect., 1988-92. Lectr., lay homilist, choir, cantor Christ the King Ch., 2006—, parish pastoral coun., 1991—96; interim sch. bd. Christ the King-St. Thomas the Apostle Sch., 1992; bd. dirs. Twin Cities Marathon, Inc., 2001—, sec., 2001—05, v.p., 2005—07; mem. Edina H.S. Men's Chorus, 2003—. Mem.: APA, Nat. Register Healthcare Providers in Psychology, Assn. State and Provincial Psychology Bds., Minn. Psychol. Assn. (chmn. ins. com. 1988—94), Minn. Soc. Clin. Hypnosis, Notre Dame Alumni Assn. (candidate regional dir.), N.W. Athletic Club (adv. bd. club run 1997—2000, chair 1999—2000), Notre Dame Club Minn. (bd. dirs. 1986—91, sec. 1987—88, v.p. 1988—89, pres. 1989—90). Mem. Dem. Farm Labor Party. Roman Catholic. Achievements include being a qualifier/finisher in the 100th Boston marathon, 1996; running in the 104th Boston marathon, 2000. Avocations: running, rock climbing, snorkeling, singing. Home: 5536 Merritt Cir Edina MN 55436-2026 Office: 91 Snelling Ave N Ste 200 Saint Paul MN 55104-6753 Office Phone: 651-644-2248. Personal E-mail: jdaurora@aol.com.

DAVENPORT, PAUL, economics professor; BA in Econs. with gt. distinction/honors, Stanford U., 1969; MA, U. Toronto, 1970, PhD, 1976, LLD (hon.), 2000, U. Alta., 1994; PhD (hon.), Internat. U. Moscow, 2002. Prof. econs. McGill U., Montreal, Que., Canada, 1972-89, assoc. dean grad. studies, 1982-86, vice prin. planning and computer svcs., 1986-89; pres., vice chancellor U. Alta., Edmonton, Alta., Canada, 1989-94, U. Western Ont., London, Canada, 1994—. Chair Assn. Univs. and Colls. Can., 1997-99, Coun. Ont. Univs., 1999-2001; bd. dirs. London Econ. Devel. Corp. Editor: (with Richard H. Leach) Reshaping Confederation: The 1982 Reform of the Canadian Constitution, 1984; contbg. author Renovating the Ivory Tower, 2002. Chair United Way Campaign, London and Middlesex, 2005. Decorated Chevalier Legion of Honor (France); Officer Order of Can. Mem.: Am. Econ. Assn., Can. Assn. Economists, Phi Beta Kappa. Office: U Western Ont Office of Pres Stevenson-Lawson Bldg London ON Canada N6A 5B8 Office Fax: 519-661-3676. Business E-Mail: pdavenpo@uwo.ca.

DAVIDS, GREGORY M., state legislator; b. Aug. 28, 1958; m. Bonnie; 3 children. BS, Winona State U., 1979; postgrad., Mankato State U. Mayor City of Preston (Minn.), 1987-91; state rep. Minn. Ho. Reps., Dist. 31B, 1991—. Mem. fin. instr. & ins., health & human svc., human svc. fin. divsn. & housing coms., Minn. Ho. Reps. Mem. Lions. Home: PO Box 32 Preston MN 55965-0032

DAVIDS, JODY R., information technology executive; BBA, MBA, San Jose State U. Computer programmer Apple Computer, Inc., Cupertino, Calif., 1982, various positions, including Asia Pacific divsn., dir. supply chain reengring.; dir. tech. svcs. Nike, Inc., Beaverton, Oreg., 1997—2000; sr v.p. IT pharm. distbn. bus. unit Cardinal Health, Inc., Dublin, Ohio, 2000—03, exec. v.p., chief info. officer, 2003—. Office: Cardinal Health Inc 7000 Cardinal Pl Dublin OH 43017 Office Phone: 614-757-5000.

DAVIDSON, ANN D., lawyer, aerospace transportation executive; b. Upper Montclair, NJ, 1952; BA, Ohio U.; JD, U. Dayton, 1979; attended, Georgetown U. Sch. of Foreign Service. Bar: 1979. Assoc. Coolidge, Wall, Womsley & Lombard, Dayton, Ohio, 1979—80; atty. US Navy, 1980—83; various positions including assoc. gen. counsel Honeywell, 1983—90; dep. gen. counsel Alliant Techsystems, 1990—93; v.p., gen. counsel, corp. sec. Power Control Technologies, Inc., Kalamazoo, 1993—98; assoc. gen. counsel, asst. sec. Parker Hannifin Corp., Cleveland, 1998—2001; v.p., gen. counsel Alliant Techsystems, 2001—03, v.p., gen. counsel, corp. sec., 2003—04, sr. v.p., gen. counsel, corp. sec., 2004—. Office: Alliant Techsystems Inc 5050 Lincoln Dr Edina MN 55436

DAVIDSON, RICHARD K., retired rail transportation executive; b. Allen, Kans., Jan. 9, 1942; s. Richard B. and Thelma (Rees) D.; m. Lynne P. Durham, July 11, 1998; children: Richard Byron, Elizabeth Ann. BA in History, Washburn U., 1965, D of Commerce (hon.), 1984. Brakeman, conductor Mo. Pacific R.R., St. Louis, 1960-66, transp. tng. program, 1966, asst. trainmaster, trainmaster, 1966-75, asst. supt. to asst. v.p. ops., 1975-76, v.p. ops., 1976-85, Union Pacific R.R., Omaha, 1985-89, exec. v.p. ops., 1989-91, chmn., CEO, 1991—2006; pres. Union Pacific Corp., 1994—2006, COO, 1995-97, pres., CEO, 1997—2007. Bd. dirs. Chesapeake Energy Corp. Mem. Happy Hollow Club.

DAVIDSON, RICHARD LAURENCE, geneticist, educator; b. Cleve., Feb. 22, 1941; BA, Case Western Res. U., 1963, PhD, 1967. Asst. prof. Harvard Med. Sch., Boston, 1970-73, assoc. prof. microbiology and molecular genetics, 1973-81; research assoc. human genetics Children's Hosp. Med. Ctr., Boston, 1970-81; head dept. molecular genetics U. Ill. Med. Ctr., Chgo., 1981—, Benjamin Goldberg prof. genetics, 1981—. Co-dir. Cell Cult Ctr., MIT, Boston, 1975-81; mem. mammalian genetics study sect. NIH, 1975-81; mem. human cell biology adv. panel NSF, 1973-75. Editor-in-chief: Somatic Cell Genetics. U.S. Air Force Office Research-NRC fellow, 1967-68, Ctr. Molecular Genetics, Paris, 1967-70. Mem. AAAS, Tissue Culture Assn., Cell Biology Assn. Office: U Ill at Chicago Head Dept Mol Gen (M/7 669) 900 S Ashland Ave Ste 669 Chicago IL 60607-4046

DAVIDSON, STANLEY J., lawyer; b. Chgo., Oct. 22, 1946; BA with honors, U. Ill., 1968; JD, Loyola U., 1971. Bar: Ill. 1971, U.S. Dist. Ct. (no. dist.) Ill. 1973, U.S. Ct. Appeals (7th cir.) 1982, U.S. Supreme Ct. 1982. Law clk. to Hon. Thomas J. Moran Ill. Appellate Ct. (2nd dist.), 1971-73; ptnr. Hinshaw & Culbertson, Chgo. Mem. ABA, Am. Soc. Hosp. Attys., Ill. State Bar Assn., Chgo. Bar Assn., Appellate Lawyers Assn. (bd. dirs. 1978-80, treas. 1982-83, sec. 1983-84, v.p. 1984-85, pres. 1985-86), Soc. Trial Lawyers, Am. Bd. Trial Advocates, Def. Rsch. Inst., Decalogue Soc. Lawyers. Office: Hinshaw & Culbertson 222 N La Salle St Ste 300 Chicago IL 60601-1081

DAVIDSON, WILLIAM M., manufacturing executive, professional sports team owner; b. Dec. 5, 1922; m. Karen Davidson; children from previous marriage: Ethan, Maria. BBA, U. Mich., 1947; JD, Wayne State U., 1949; LHD (hon.), Jewish Theol. Sem. Am., 1996, U. Mich., 2001. Pres., CEO Guardian Glass Co., Northville, Mich., 1957-68; pres., CEO, dir. Guardian Industries Corp., 1968—; mng. ptnr., part owner NBA Detroit Pistons, 1974—; owner Women's NBA Detroit Shock, 1998—, NHL Tampa Bay Lightning, 1999—; majority owner Palace Sports and Entertainment; former owner Arena Football League Detroit Fury. Donated to the establishment of William Davidson Inst., U. Mich. Sch. Bus. Adminstrn., 1992, William Davidson Grad. Sch. of Jewish Edn. at Jewish Theological Seminary of Am., NY, Davidson Inst. of Science Edn. at Weizmann Inst. of Sci., Rehovot, Israel, 1999; founder Pistons/Palace Found. Served in USN. Named one of Am.'s most generous donors, New York Times, 1997, Forbes' Richest Ams., 1999—, World's Richest People, Forbes mag., 2001—; recipient honors for lifelong philanthropy, Coun. of Mich. Foundations, 1997. Office: Guardian Industries Corp 2300 Harmon Rd Auburn Hills MI 48326 also: Detroit Pistons 5 Championship Dr Auburn Hills MI 48326

DAVIES, CHRISTA, insurance company executive; Grad. in Aerospace Engring., U. Queensland, Australia; MBA, Harvard Bus. Sch. With Auspace, Canberra, Rolls Royce Industrial Power Grp., Cable & Wireless, London, McKinsey & Co., Inc., 1994—97; dir. bus. devel. & strategic sales ninemsn, Sydney, 1997—2002; gen. mgr. strategy & mergers & acquisitions for Windows Client, Svc. & Tools, & Online Services Microsoft Corp., CFO online services, corp. v.p., CFO platform & services Redmond, Wash.; exec. v.p. global fin. Aon Corp., Chgo., 2007—, CFO, 2008—. Recipient Fulbright Scholarship. Office: Aon Corp Aon Ctr 200 E Randolph St Chicago IL 60601*

DAVIS, AARON W., lawyer; b. Waterloo, Iowa, Oct. 10, 1973; BA, Minn. State U., 1997; JD, William Mitchell Coll. Law, 2001. Bar: Minn. 2002, US Dist. Ct. (dist. Minn.) 2002, US Dist. Ct. (we. dist. Wis.) 2002, US Dist. Ct. (dist. Colo.) 2002, US Ct. Appeals (Fed. cir.), US Ct. Appeals (5th, 7th and 8th cirs.). Assoc. Patterson, Thuente, Skaar & Christensen, P.A., Mpls. Named a Rising Star, Minn. Super Lawyers mag., 2006. Mem.: Minn. Intellectual Property Law Assn., Am. Intellectual Property Law Assn., ABA (mem. forum on the entertainment and sports industries, mem. intellectual property law sect.), Minn. State Bar Assn. (chair entertainment & sports sect.), Hennepin County Bar Assn., Minn. Music Acad. (treas.). Office: Patterson Thuente Skaar & Christensen PA 4800 IDS Ctr 80 S 8th St Minneapolis MN 55402 Office Phone: 612-349-5754. E-mail: davis@ptslaw.com.

DAVIS, BARBARA SNELL, education educator; b. Painesville, Ohio, Feb. 21, 1929; d. Roy Addison and Mabelle Irene (Denning) Snell; children: Beth Ann Davis Schnorf, James Lee, Polly Denning Davis Spaeth. BS, Kent State U., 1951; MA, Lake Erie Coll., 1981; postgrad., Cleve. State U., 1982-83. Cert. reading specialist, elem. prin., Ohio. Dir. publicity Lake Erie Coll., Painesville, 1954-59; tchr. Mentor (Ohio) Exempted Village Sch. Dist., 1972-86, prin., 1986-97; prof., supr. Lake Erie Coll., 1997—. Author: Who Says You Can't Change the World?, 2005; contbr. articles to profl. jours. Former trustee Mentor United Meth. Ch. Mem. Delta Kappa Gamma (pres. 1982-84), Phi Delta Kappa (pres. 1992-93), Theta Sigma Phi (charter). Home: 7293 Beechwood Dr Mentor OH 44060-6305 Office: 326 College Hall Lake Erie Coll Painesville OH 44077

DAVIS, COLE (COLEMAN DAVIS III), recreational vehicle manufacturing executive; CEO, chmn. Keystone RV, Goshen, Ind. Recipient INC 500 award, INC Mag., 2000. Office: Keystone RV 17400 Hackberry Dr Goshen IN 46526

DAVIS, DANNY K., congressman; b. Parkdale, Ark., Sept. 6, 1941; m. Vera Davis; children: Jonathon, Stacey BA, Ark. A. M. & N. Coll., 1961; MA, Chgo. State U., 1968; PhD, Union Inst., 1977. Mem. U.S. Congress from 7th Ill. dist., 1997—; mem. com. on govt. reform and oversight, com. on small bus.; mem. subcom. of census; mem. com. on edn. & workforce. Chgo. alderman, 1979-90; commr. Cook. County, 1990-96; candidate Chgo. mayor, 1991; founder, pres. Westside Assn. for Community Action; pres. Nat. Assn. Community Health Ctrs.; co-chmn. Clinton/Gore/Moseley-Braun Ill. campaigns, 1992; bd. dirs. Nat. Housing Partnership. Recipient Most Influential Black Americans, Ebony mag., 2006. Democrat. Office: 1526 Longworth House Office Bldg Washington DC 20515-1307 also: 2301 Roosevelt Rd Broadview IL 60155 Home Phone: 773-261-3164; Office Phone: 202-225-5006, 708-345-6857.

DAVIS, DAVID, newscaster; Degree, U. Tenn., Knoxville, 1977. Broadcast reporter KREX-TV, Grand Junction, Colo.; anchor KLAS-TV, Las Vegas, Nev., KATV-TV, Little Rock; morning anchor, reporter WISN 12, Milw., 1988—. Telethon vol. Children's Miracle Network; co-emcee telethon Briggs and Stratton Run/Walk for Children's Hosp. Wis., Cerebral Palsy. Recipient award for best newscast and spot news coverage, AP, Emmy award. Office: WISN PO Box 402 Milwaukee WI 53201-4020

DAVIS, DAVID AARON, journalist; b. San Diego, Feb. 8, 1959; m. M. Caroline Berry, Sept. 5, 1987; children: Anne Elizabeth, Caroline Camille, Aaron Edward. BA, Colo. Coll., 1983; MSJ, Columbia U., 1985. Reporter The Gazette, Charleston, W.Va., 1986, The Dayton (Ohio) Daily News, 1987-90, The Plain Dealer, Cleve., 1990—. Paul Miller Journalism lectr. Okla. State U., 1996. Recipient Best Consumer Journalism award Nat. Press Club, Washington, 1987, Sigma Delta Chi award for investigative reporting Soc. Profl. Journalists, Greencastle, Ind., 1993, Freedom of Info. award AP Mng. Editors Assn., 1993, Max Karant award excellence in aviation reporting Aircraft Owners & Pilots Assn., 1993, 94, George Polk award L.I. U., 1995, Heywood Broun award Comms. Workers of Am., 1998. Mem. Investigative Reporters & Editors Inc. (IRE medal 1993), Soc. Environ. Journalists. Office: The Cleveland Plain Dealer 1801 Superior Ave E Cleveland OH 44114-2198

DAVIS, DEFOREST P., architectural engineer; From staff cons. to chmn., CEO Lester B. Knight & Assocs., Inc., Chgo., 1966-91, pres., CEO, 1987-91, chmn., CEO, 1991—. Trustee Knight Charitable Trust, Chgo., 1989—, Lake Forest (Ill.) Coll., 1992—, St. George's Sch., Newport, R.I., 1988-97, Grant Hosp. and Healthcare Ctr. Found., Chgo., 1992—; mem. adv. bd. dirs. Code, Hennessy & Simons, Chgo., Fiduciary Mgmt. Assocs., Chgo., Constrn. Bus. Rev., McLean, Va.; bd. dirs. Surgipath Med. Industries, Inc., Richmond, Ill. Mem. Chgo. Club (pres.), Econ. Club Chgo. (membership com.), Exec.'s Club Chgo. Office: Lester B Knight & Assocs 549 W Randolph St Ste 701 Chicago IL 60661-2208

DAVIS, DON H., JR., multi-industry high-technology company executive; Engring. sales trainee Allen-Bradley (aquired by Rockwell 1985), 1963-66, dist. mgr. Birmingham, Ala., 1966-79, gen. mgr. programmable contr. divsn., 1979-80, v.p. programmable contr. divsn., 1980-82, v.p., gen. mgr. indsl. control divsn., 1982-85, sr. v.p., 1985-86, head indsl. control group, 1986-87, sr. v.p., gen. mgr. indsl. computer and comm. group, 1987-89, pres., 1989-93, corp. sr. v.p., pres. automation, 1993-95, pres., COO, 1995-97, pres., CEO, 1997-98; chmn., CEO Rockwell Automation, Inc., 1998—2004, chmn., 2004—. Bd. dirs. Sybron Internat., Ingram Micro, Inc. Nat. trustee Boys and Girls Clubs Am.; chmn. bd. L.A. Mfg. Learning Ctr.; regent Milw. Sch. Engring. Mem. Internat. Soc. for Measurement and Control (hon. chmn.), Nat. Elec. Mfrs. Assn. (past chmn. bd. govs.), Bus. Roundtable, The Conf. Bd. (sr.). Office: Rockwell Internat Corp 777 E Wisconsin Ave Ste 1400 Milwaukee WI 53202-5302

DAVIS, DORATHEA, state legislator; State rep. dist. 63 Mo. Ho. of Reps. Democrat. Office: 2017 Menard St Saint Louis MO 63104-3929

DAVIS, EDGAR GLENN, healthcare executive, educator; b. Indpls., May 12, 1931; s. Thomas Carroll and Florence Isabelle (Watson) Davis; m. Margaret Louise Alandt, June 20, 1953; children: Anne-Elizabeth, Amy Alandt, Edgar Glenn Davis Jr. AB, Kenyon Coll., 1953; MBA, Harvard U., 1955. With Eli Lilly & Co., Indpls., 1958—63, mgr. budgeting and profit planning, 1963—66, mgr. econ. studies, 1966—67, mgr. Atlanta sales dist., 1967—68, dir. market rsch. and sales manpower planning, 1968—69, dir. mktg. plans, 1969—74, exec. dir. pharm. mktg. planning, 1974—75, exec. dir. corp. affairs, 1975—76, v.p. corp. affairs, 1976—90, v.p. health care policy, 1990; pres., chmn. bd. dirs. Centre for Health Sci. Info., Boston, 1990—; fellow Ctr. for Bus. and Govt. Kennedy Sch. of Govt. Harvard U., 1991—95; adj. prof. Butler U., Indpls., 1995—. Exec. in residence Butler U. Coll. Bus.; mem. Inst. Ednl. Mgmt., Harvard U. Grad. Sch. Edn., 1987; chmn. staff Bus. Roundtable Task Force on Health, 1981—85; U.S. rep. UN Indsl. Devel. Orgn. Conf., Lisbon, 1980, Casablanca, 81, Budapest, 83, Madrid, 87; participant meeting of experts on pharms UNIDO, 1981; rep. to UN Commn. on Narcotic Drugs, Vienna, 1981, UN Econ. and Social Coun., NYC, 1981, UN Indsl. Devel. Orgn. Conf.; Ctr. for Bus. and Govt. fellow Kennedy Sch. Govt., Harvard U.; co-chmn. Harvard Conf. on Govt. Role in Civilian Tech., 1992, Harvard Conf. Pharmaceutical Rsch., Innovation and Pub. Policy, 1993, Harvard Biotech. Roundtable, 1991—; vis. scholar, advisor Health and Welfare Unit, Inst. for Econ. Affairs, London; vis. scholar Green Coll. Oxford (Eng.) U., 1994—; chmn. Nat. Fund for Med. Edn., 1994—; dir. English Speaking Union, Indpls.; gov. Soc. Indiana Pioneers; lectr. in field. Contbr. articles to profl. jours. Pres. Eli Lilly and Co. Found., 1976—88; pres., chmn. bd. Indpls. Health Inst., 1988—91; trustee Kenyon Coll., Gambier, Ohio, Ind. Hist. Soc.; pres. bd. trustees Boston Biomed. Rsch. Inst., 1991—95, trustee emeritus; chmn. Nat. Fund for Med. Edn., 1996—; bd. dirs. Carnegie Coun. on Ethics and Internat. Affairs, 1985—92; accredited nongovtl. observer rep. to UN Goodwill Found. Ind. Inc., 1987—95; bd. dirs. Sta. WFYI Pub. TV, Indpls., 1983—91, Am. Symphony Orch. League, 1987—92, mem. dirs. coun., 1987—; bd. dirs. Nat. Health Coun., 1984—91, Pub. Affairs Coun., Washington, 1984—92, Nat. Fund for Med. Edn.; bd. advisors Christian Theol. Sem., Bishops Sch., LaJolla, Calif.; chmn. bd. dirs. Ind. Repertory Theatre, 1979—85; vice chmn., exec. com., bd. dirs. Indpls. Symphony Orch. and Ind. State Symphony Soc., 1977—91; chmn. task force on fine arts Commn. for Future of Butler U.; chmn. exec. com. Pan Am. Econ. Leadership Conf. 10th Pan Am. Games, Indpls.; mem. Chgo. Coun. on Fgn. Rels.; bd. govs. Soc. Ind. Pioneers. Mem.: NAM (vice-chmn. health policy com. 1987—91, bd. dirs.), Am. Symphony Orch. League N.Y. (mem. dir. coun.), Inst. Medicine NAS, Ind. Soc. Pioneers (bd. govs.), Dramatic Club of Indpls., Univ. Club (Indpls.) (bd. dirs.), Literary Club Indpls., Reform Club London, N.Y. Yacht Club, Edgartown Golf Club, Chappaquiddick Beach Club, Contemporary Club, Woodstock Club, Naples Yacht Club, Edgartown Yacht Club, aples (Fla.), Met. Club (Washington). Office: Butler U Coll Bus Adminstrn 4600 Sunset Ave Indianapolis IN 46208-3487 Office Fax: 317-940-9455.

DAVIS, GEORGE CULLOM, historian; b. Aurora, Ill., May 2, 1935; s. George Cullom and Mary Elizabeth (Scripps) D.; m. Marilyn Louise Whittaker, June 22, 1957 (div. Mar. 1974); children: Catherine, Lesa, Charles; m. Ann Elizabeth Chapman, May 27, 1976. AB, Princeton U., 1957; MA, U. Ill., Urbana, 1961, PhD, 1968; Dr of History (hon.), Lincoln Coll., 1999; Diploma of Honor, Lincoln Meml. U., 1995; DHL (hon.), Knox Coll., 2000. Instr. Punahou Sch., Honolulu, 1957-59, U. Ill., Urbana, 1962-64; asst. prof. Ind. U., Bloomington, 1964-70, assoc. dean, 1967-70; assoc. prof. Sangamon State U., Springfield, Ill., 1970-74, prof., 1974-95; prof. emeritus, 1995—; prof. history U. Ill.-Springfield, 1974—; dir., sr. editor Lincoln Legal Papers Documentary Edit., 1988—. Bd. dirs. Bank One, Springfield; cons. John Nuveen & Co., Chgo., 1989—, Meml. Med. Ctr., Springfield, 1991—. Author: History With a Tape Recorder: An Oral History Handbook, 1972, 4th edit., 1985; co-author: Oral History: From Tape to Tape, 1977, Bench and Bar on the Illinoir Frontier, 1979, The Prairie Bondman, 1996, Memorial Days, 1997; editor: Bicentennial Studies in Sangamon History, 1973-78; co-editor: The Public and the Private Lincoln: Contemporary Perspectives, 1979, Abraham Lincoln Association Papers, 1981-86, The Law Practice of Abraham Lincoln: Complete Documentary Edit. (DVD-ROM), 2000; contbr. numerous articles to profl. jours.; editl. advisor Scholar Book Revs. on CD-ROM, 1991-93. Del. Dem. Nat. Conv., 1972; pres. Springfield Pub. Schs. Found., 1987-88. Recipient Pelzer award Orgn. Am. Historians, 1962, award of Merit Ill. State Hist. Soc., 1975, Writer of Yr. award Friends of Lincoln Libr., 1989; Fulbright Rsch. scholar, 1987-88; fellow Newberry Libr., 1977, NEH/Woodrow Wilson Found. Inst., 1980, NEH Summer Inst. on Pub. History, 1984, Studs Terkel award Ill. Humanities Coun., 2002; grantee Ill. Bicentennial Commn., 1974-75, Ill. State Libr., 1975, 79-81, Ill. Legis. Coun., 1979-87, Ill. Humanities Coun., 1980-82, NEH, 1990-92, 94—, Nat. Hist. Publs. and Records Commn., 1990—, Ill. Bar Found., 1990-91, Ency. Brit., 1991, Shelby C. Davis Found., 1991—, William Nelson Cromwell Found., 1992—. Mem. Manuscript Soc., Assn. for Documentary Editing (chmn. constitution com. 1990-94, pres. 1997-98), Ill. Coalition of Libr. Advocates (bd. dirs. 1982-84), Ill. Humanities Coun. (bd. dirs. 1983-89, vice chair 1985-87, chair 1987-89), Ill. State Hist. Soc. (v.p. 1974-75, 82-83, bd. dirs. 1979-82, exec. com. 1979-82, adv. bd. 1994—), Sangamon County Hist. Soc. (bd. dirs. 1971-74, 79-82, v.p. 1981-82, 90-91, pres. 1991-92), Orgn. Am. Historians (treas. 1984-93), Oral History Assn. (nominating com. 1978-79, 85-87, colloquium program com. 1978, chmn. nat. workshop 1979, nat. coun. 1980-85, v.p. 1982-83, pres. 1983-84), Abraham Lincoln Assn. (bd. dirs. 1977—, chmn. publs. com. 1981-87, v.p. 1984-86, pres. 1995-96). Democrat. Home: 2624 E Lake Shore Dr Springfield IL 62707-5533 Office: Lincoln Legal Papers Old State Capitol Springfield IL 62701

DAVIS, GLENN CRAIG, psychiatrist; b. Columbia, Mo., Apr. 26, 1946; s. Morris S. and Dorothy (Hall) Davis; children: Jason Michael, Galen Brent. BA, Reed Coll., 1968; MD, Duke U., 1972. Diplomate Am. Bd. Psychiatry and Neurology. Intern, then resident Duke U. Med. Ctr., Durham, NC, 1972-75; clin. assoc. NIMH, Bethesda, Md., 1975-77, chief of drug abuse unit, biological psychiatry br., 1977-79; assoc. prof. U. Tenn. Ctr. Health Scis., Memphis, 1979-81; assoc. prof. then prof. Sch. of Medicine Case Western Reserve U., Cleve., 1981-87; dir. psychiat. rsch. to chief of staff Cleve. VA Med. Ctr., 1981-87; chair psychiatry Henry Ford Med. Ctr., Detroit, 1987-92; v.p. behavioral svcs. Henry Ford Health System, Detroit, 1991-94, v.p. acad. affairs, 1992—2001, chief med. officer suburban regions, 1996-98, assoc. dean Case Western Reserve U., 1993—2001; prof. psychiatry Case Western Reserve U., Cleve., 1994—2001; pres. Am. Bd. Psychiatry & Neurology, Deerfield, Ill.; dean coll. of human medicine Mich. State U., East Lansing, Mich., 2001—05; sr. client ptnr. Korn Ferry Internat., Phila., 2005—. Clin. prof. U. Mich. Sch. Medicine, Ann Arbor, 1988—2001. Author numerous sci. rsch. papers and book chpts.; contbr. articles to profl. jours. Lt. comdr. USPHS US Army, 1975—79. Fellow: Am. Psychopathological Assn., Am. Psychiat. Assn.; mem.: AMA, AAAS, Am. Bd. Med. Specialties, Am. Bd. Psychiatry and Neurology (dir. 1996—2003, pres. 2000), Alpha Omega Alpha, Sigma Xi. Office: Korn Ferry Internat 1835 Market St Philadelphia PA 19103 Office Phone: 215-656-5356. Business E-Mail: gdavis@kornferry.com.

DAVIS, HARRY REX, political science professor; b. Ozona, Tex., Nov. 9, 1921; s. Rex Otis and Mima (Gowin) D.; m. Ruth Elizabeth Greenlee, Sept. 6, 1947; children: Peter Gowin, Scott Andrew, Martha Greenlee. BA summa cum laude, Tex. Christian U., 1942; AM, U. Chgo., 1949, PhD, 1951; postdoctorate, Union Theol. Sem., 1952-53. Teaching fellow Tex. Christian U., 1945-46; mem. faculty dept. govt. Beloit (Wis.) Coll., 1948-90, assoc. prof., 1956-59, prof., 1959-90, chmn. dept., 1959-84, prof. emeritus, 1990—. Cons. ch. and soc. dept. World Council Chs., 1969. Author: (with others) Small City Government, 1962, Colleges and Commitments, 1971; Editor: (with others) Reinhold Niebuhr on Politics, 1960, 2d edit., 2007. Active Beloit City Coun., 1959-60, Beloit Bd. Ethics, 1975-81, Wis. Gov.'s Coun. on Jud. Selection, 1983-86, Beloit Bd. Health, 1996-2002, chmn., 1996-98; chmn. Beloit Dem. Com., 1956, 61-63; local mgr. campaigns congl. candidates. With USAAF, 1942-45. Ford faculty fellow, 1952-53; grantee Social Sci. Rsch. Coun., Rockefeller Found. Mem. Midwest Polit. Sci. Assn. (sec.-treas. 1959-65, mem. exec. coun. 1966-68), Am. Polit. Sci. Assn. (chmn. Burdette award com. 1979), Am. Soc. Polit. and Legal Philosophy, Soc. Christian Ethics. Democrat. Presbyterian (elder, coun. on ch. and society 1965-72, Gen. Assembly commr. 1991). Office: Beloit Coll Dept Government Beloit WI 53511 Home: 2423 Stonehedge Ln Beloit WI 53511-6727

DAVIS, HENRY BARNARD, JR., lawyer; b. East Grand Rapids, Mich., June 3, 1923; s. Henry Barnard and Ethel Margaret (Turnbull) Davis; m. Margaret Lees Wilson, Aug. 27, 1946; children: Caroline Dellenbusch, Laura Davis, George B. BA, Yale U., 1945; JD, U. Mich., 1950; LLD, Olivet Coll., 1983. Bar: Mich. 1951, U.S. Dist. Ct. (we. dist.) Mich. 1956, U.S. Ct. Appeals (6th cir.) 1971, U.S. Supreme Ct. 1978. Assoc. Allaben, Wiarda, Hayes & Hewitt, 1951-52; ptnr. Hayes, Davis & Dellenbusch PLC, Grand Rapids, Mich., 1952—2002, Davis & Davis Law Office PLC, Grand Rapids, 2002—. Mem. Kent County Bd. Commrs., 1968-72; mem. Cmty. Mental Health Bd., 1970-94, past chmn.; trustee, sec. bd. Olivet Coll., 1965-91, trustee emeritus, 1991—; bd. dirs. Jr. Achievement Grand Rapids, 1960-65; chair Grand Rapids Historic Preservation Com., 1977-79; trustee East Congregational Ch., 1979-81. Served with USAAF, 1943-46, Philippines. Mem. ABA, Mich. Bar Assn., Grand Rapids Round Table (pres. 1969), Masons. Republican. Home: 30 Mayfair Dr NE Grand Rapids MI 49503-3831 Office: 535 Fountain St NE Grand Rapids MI 49503-3421 Office Fax: 616-458-8638. Personal E-mail: hbdavis@mac.com.

DAVIS, HOWARD TED, engineering educator; b. Hendersonville, NC, Aug. 2, 1937; s. William Howard and Gladys Isabel (Rhodes) D.; m. Eugenia Asimakopoulos, Sept. 15, 1960 (dec. July 1996); children: William Howard II, Maria Katherine; m. Catherine Asimkopoulos, Mar. 9, 2000. BS in Chemistry, Furman U., 1959; PhD in Chem. Physics, U. Chgo., 1962. Postdoctoral fellow Free U. of Brussels, 1962-63; asst. prof. U. Minn., Mpls., 1963-66, assoc. prof., 1966-69, prof., 1969-80, prof., head chem. engring. and materials sci., 1980-95, dean Inst. Tech., 1995—2004, Regent's prof., 1997—; Humboldt rschr. Cologne U., Germany, 2005. Editor: Springs of Creativity, 1981; author: Statistical Mechanics of Phases, Interfaces and Thin Films, 1995, (with K. Thomson) Linear Algebra and Linear Operators in Engineering, 2000; contbr. over 500 articles to sci. and engring. jours. Fellow Sloan Found., 1967-69, Guggenheim Found., 1969-70. Mem. AAAS, AIChE (Walker award for excellence in publs. 1990), NAE, Am. Chem. Soc., Soc. Petroleum Engrs., Minn. Fedn. Engring. Socs. (Disting. Engr. 1998). Democrat. Avocations: tennis, golf, reading, movies. Office: U Minn 421 Washington Ave SE Minneapolis MN 55455-0373 Home: 4330 Tyrol Crest Golden Valley MN 55416 Office Phone: 612-625-4088. Personal E-mail: htdavismn@yahoo.com. Business E-Mail: davis@cems.umn.edu.

DAVIS, IRVIN, advertising, public relations and broadcast executive; b. St. Louis, Dec. 18, 1926; s. Julius and Anna (Rosen) D.; m. Adrienne Bronstein, Apr. 25, 1968; 1 child, Jennifer Alison. BSBA, Washington U., 1950; postgrad., St. Louis U., 1952; DHum (hon.), Nat. Coll., 1981, Logan Coll., 2004. Pres. Clayton-Davis & Assoc., Inc., St. Louis, 1953—, Admiral Broadcasting Corp., St. Louis, 1983—. C.p., bd. dirs. Nat. Acad. TV Arts and Scis., 1982—; bd. dirs. Truman Bank; pres. Galtex Broadcasting; pres. Celebrities Prodns. Author: Room for Three, Comprehensive Tng. in Advt. and Pub. Relations; producer (film) Family Album, 1974, Use It in Good Health, Charlie, 1975. Pres. Child Assistance Program, 1986—92; v.p. Boys and Girls Town Mo., St. James, 1976—99, Make Today Count, 1985—86; bd. dirs. Jackie Joyner Kersee Found., 1997—2001, Crusade Against Crime, St. Louis, 1984—; pres. St. Louis Artists Guild. Sgt. USAF, 1945—47, PTO. Recipient Freedom Found. award, 1975, Internat. Film and TV Festival award, 1973-75, Internat. Broadcasting award Hollywood Advt. Club, 1965, 77, 82, 83, Cinegolden Eagle award Coun. on Internat. Non-Theatrical Events, 1975, Nat. Emmy award, 1991; inductee Nat. TV Acad. Silver Cir., 2004. Mem.: AFTRA, Am. Med. Writers Assn., Pub. Rels. Soc. Am. (accredited), St. Louis Club, Press Club, Advt. Club. Office: Clayton Davis and Assoc Inc 230 S Bemiston Ave Ste 1400 Saint Louis MO 63105

DAVIS, JACK, congressman; b. Chgo., Sept. 6, 1935; m. Virginia Ann Griffin, 1960; children: Jill, Heather, Jack II. BA, So. Ill. U., 1956. Exec. steel warehouse, 1959—78; mem. Ill. House Reps., Springfield, 1976—86; mem. from 4th Dist. Ill. US Ho. of Reps, 1987—89, mem. armed svc. com., vet. affairs com., 1987—89; asst. sec. manpower, readiness and resources US Air Force, 1990—92. Radio host, Davis & Co. 970 AM WMAY, Springfield, Ill. Served with USN, 1956—59, served in, Desert Storm. Decorated Meritorious Svc. Medal SEC/AF Don Rice. Republican. Protestant. Office: c/o 970 AM WMAY PO Box 460 Springfield IL 62705

DAVIS, JAMES FREDERICK, chemical engineer, researcher, educator, consultant; b. Urbana, Ill., Aug. 8, 1952; BSCE, U. Ill., 1974; MSCE, Northwestern U., Evanston, Ill., 1978, PhD in Chem. Engring., 1981. Rsch. engr. Amoco Chems., Naperville, Ill., 1974-76; postdoctoral rsch. assoc. Northwestern U., Evanston, 1981-82; lectr. U. Wis., Madison, 1982-83; asst. prof. Ohio U., Columbus, 1983-89, assoc. prof., 1989-94, prof., 1994—, assoc. dir. rsch. computing, 1992-95, dir. univ. tech. svcs., 1995—. Cons. numerous chem. and refining cos., 1983—; bd. trustees Computer Aids in Chem. Engring. Corp., Austin, Tes., 1987—. Author: (chpt.) Neural Networks in Process Operation, 1994; contbr. over 90 articles to profl. jours. Mem. IEEE, AIChE (dir. computer and system tech. 1991-94). Achievements include patent in portable infusate heating device; development of intelligent systems technology area in chemical and process engineering. Office: Ohio State Univ Univ Tech Svcs 320 Baker Systems Bldg 1971 Neil Ave Columbus OH 43210-1210

DAVIS, JAMES ROBERT, cartoonist; b. Marion, Ind., July 28, 1945; s. James William and Anna Catherine (Carter) D.; m. Jill Carol Davis; 1 son, James Alexander. Artist, Groves & Assocs., advt., Muncie, 1968-69; asst. to cartoonist: Tumbleweeds comic strip, 1969-78; cartoonist: Garfield comic strip, 1978—; TV script Here Comes Garfield, 1982, Garfield on the Town, 1983 (Emmy award 1984), Garfield in the Rough, 1984 (Emmy award 1985), Garfield's Halloween Adventure, 1985 (Emmy award 1986), Garfield in Paradise, 1986, Garfield Goes Hollywood, 1987, The Garfield Christmas Special, 1987; author: Garfield at Large, 1980, Garfield Gains Weight, 1981, Garfield Bigger Than Life, 1981, Garfield Weighs In, 1982, Garfield Takes the Cake, 1982, Garfield Treasury, 1982, Here Comes Garfield, 1982, Garfield Sits Around the House, 1983, Garfield Second Treasury, 1983, Garfield Eats His Heart Out, 1983, Garfield Tips the Scale, 1984, Garfield Loses his Feet, 1984, Garfield: His Nine Lives, 1984, Garfield Makes It Big, 1985, Garfield Rolls On, 1985, Third Garfield Treasury, 1985, Garfield Out to Lunch, 1986, The Unabridged, Uncensored, Unbelieveable Garfield Book, 1986, Garfield Food for Thought, 1987, The 4th Garfield Treasury, 1987, The Garfield Cat Naming Book, 1988, Garfield Chews the Fat, 1989, The 5th Garfield Treasury, 1989, Happy Birthday, Garfield, 1989, Garfield, Tiens Bon La Rampe, 1989, Garfield's Longest Catnap, 1989, Garfield The Big Star, 1989, Garfield in the Park, 1989, Garfield and the Tiger, 1989, Mini-Mysteries featuring Garfield, 1990, Garfield: The Me Book: A Guide to Superiority, How to Get It, Use It, and Keep It, 1990, Garfield's Judgement Day, 1990, Garfield's Feline Fantasies, 1990, Garfield Stories, 1990, Garfield on the Farm, 1990, Garfield Hangs Out, 1990, Garfield Goes to Waist, 1990, The Sixth Garfield Trasury, 1991, Garfield: The Truth About Cats, 1991, Garfield: Seasons Greetings, 1991, Garfield Thanksgiving Special, 1991, Garfield Takes Up Space, 1991, Garfield Says a Mouthful, 1991, Garfield Gets a Life, 1991, Garfield's Ghost Stories, 1992, Garfield Vacation Greetings, 1992, Garfield Learns About Thoughtfulness: Don't Be Late!, 1992, Garfield Learns About Planning: Surprize Party, 1992, Garfield Learns About Money: Money Madness!, 1992, Garfield Learns About Fire Safety: Where's the Fire?, 1992, Garfield Learns About Cooking: Any Cat Can Cook, 1992, Garfield Learns about Conservation: Endangered Odie?, 1992, Garfield Keeps His Chin Up, 1992, Garfield By the Pound, 1992, Garfield Birthday Greetings, 1992, The Seventh Garfield Treasury, 1993, Garfield's Big Fat Hairy Joke Book, 1993, Garfield Takes His Licks, 1993, Garfield Hits the Big Time: His 25th Book, 1993, Garfield's Tales of Mystery, 1994, Garfield's Night Before Christmas, 1994, Garfield's Insults, 1994, Garfield's Haunted House: And Other Spooky Tales, 1994, Garfield's Furry Tales, 1994, Garfield's Big Fat Scary Joke Book, 1994, Garfield's Big Fat Holiday Joke Book, 1994, Garfield Insults, Put-Downs, 1994, Garfield Fat Cat, 1994, Garfield Discovers America, 1994, Garfield's Son of Big, Fat Hairy Jokes, 1994, Big Hairy Garfield, 1994, Garfield, The Easter Bunny?, 1995, Garfield's Stupid Cupid: And Other Silly Stories, 1995, Garfield Fat Cat 3 Pack, 1995, Garfield Dishes It Out, 1995, Mr. Potato Head, 2001, Garfield: The Movie, 2004, Garfield: A Tail of Two Kitties, 2006. With USMC, 1967. Named to Mktg. Hall of Fame award Am. Mktg. Assn., 1982; recipient Disting. Alumnus award Am. Assn. State Colls. Univs.; named Garfield comic strip as most widely distributed comic in the world Guiness Book of World Records, 2003 Mem. Nat. Cartoonists Soc. (Best Humor Strip of 1981, 86, Segar award 1985, Cartoonist of Yr. 1990), Newspaper Comics Council. Protestant. Republican. Office: Universal Press Syndicate 4520 Main St Ste 700 Kansas City MO 64111-7701

DAVIS, JOHN CHARLES, lawyer; b. Kansas City, Mo., Mar. 4, 1943; s. Ralph B. Jr. and Helen M. (Schneider) D.; m. C. Jane Reusser, June 18, 1966; children: Tracy A., Matthew S. BA, U. Kans., 1965; JD, U. Mich., 1968. Bar: Mo. 1968, Kans. 1983. Ptnr. Stinson Morrison Hecker LLP, Kansas City, 1968—. Chmn. Fed. Estate Tax Symposium, 1986-87 Chmn. Bacchus Found., Kansas City, 1974; bd. dirs. Crittenten, Kansas City, 1988-94, vice chmn., 1990-92; trustee Schutte Found., Kansas City, 1986—, UMKC, 1989—, treas., 1994-96, counsel, 1996—; trustee Village Presby. Ch. Found., chmn., 1991-93; elder Village Presby. Ch., 1994-97; bd. dirs. Gamma O Edn. Found., Heart of Am. coun. Boy Scouts Am., exec. com., 1996—; bd. dirs. John County C.C. Found Fellow Am. Coll. Trust and Estate Counsel (by-laws com. 1987-96, chmn. 1996-99, 2002-05, program com. 1993-96); mem. ABA, Mo. Bar Assn., Kans. Bar Assn., Estate Planning Soc. Kansas City (pres. 1990-91), Nelson-Atkins Mus. Soc. Fellows, Kansas City Club (v.p. 1989-90), Indian Hills Country Club (Mission Hills, Kans.), River Club (Kansas City, Mo.), Rotary, Gamma Omicron (pres., bd. dirs. 1979-85) Presbyterian. Avocations: squash, Hopi art, Marklin trains, travel, photography. Home: 6421 High Dr Mission Hills KS 66208-1935 Office: Stinson Morrison Hecker LLP 1201 Walnut St Ste 2900 Kansas City MO 64106 Office Phone: 816-691-3252. Business E-Mail: jcdavis@stinsonmoheck.com.

DAVIS, JOHN JAMES, religion educator; b. Phila., Oct. 13, 1936; s. John James and Cathryn Ann (Nichols) D.; m. Carolyn Ann. BA, Trinity Coll., Dunedin, Fla., 1959, DD (hon.), 1968; MDiv, Grace Coll. & Grace Theol. Sem., Winona Lake, Ind., 1962, ThM, 1964, ThD, 1967. Instr. Grace Coll. & Grace Theol. Sem., 1963-65, prof. Old Testament, 1965—2004, exec. v.p., 1976-82, pres., 1986-93; exec. dean Near East Sch. Archaeology, Jerusalem, 1970-71. Area supr. Tekoa Archeol. Expdn., Jordan, 1968, 70, Raddana Expdn., Jordan, 1974, Heshbon Expdn., Jordan, 1976, Abila Archeol. Expdn., Jordan, 1982, 84, Khirbet el-Maqatir Expdn., Israel, 2000, Khirbet Nisya, Israel, 2003. Author: Paradise to Prison, 1975 (Book of Yr.), The Perfect Shepherd, 1979 (Book of Yr.), 16 other books. Chmn., bd. dirs. Kosciusko Cmty. Hosp., 1994—. Recipient Gold award United Way, 1980, Conservation award Barbee Property Owners Assn., 1983; named Outdoor Writer of Yr., Ind. Dept. Natural Resources, 1986, to the Koscivsko County Rep. Hall of Fame, 1992. Mem. Am. Schs. of Oriental Research, Near East Archeol. Soc., Outdoor Writers Assn., Hoosier Outdoor Writers Assn. (pres. 1984-86). Avocations: fishing, hunting, photography, music. Home: PO Box 557 Winona Lake IN 46590-0557 Business E-Mail: johnjdavis@mchsi.com.

DAVIS, JULIA A., lawyer, retail executive; BA in Economics, John Carroll U., 1982; JD with honors, Ohio State U. Sch. of Law, 1985. Assoc. then prtnr. Vorys, Sater, Seymour and Pease, Columbus, Ohio, 1987—2003; exec. v.p., gen. counsel Retail Ventures (Value City Dept. Stores), Columbus, Ohio, 2003—. Nat. bd. mem. ACLU, nat. bd. mem. exec. com., 1999—, nat. affirmative action officer, 2000—. Mem.: Columbus Bar Assn. (ethics com.). Office: Retail Ventures Inc 3241 Westerville Rd Columbus OH 43224

DAVIS, KATHERINE LYON, former lieutenant governor; b. Boston, June 24, 1956; d. Richard Harold and Joy (Hallum) Winer; m. John Marshall Davis, Feb. 22, 1992; 1 child, Madeline Felton. BS, MIT, 1978; MBA, Harvard U., 1982. Engr. Cambridge (Mass.) Collaborative, 1978-80; mfg. mgr. Cummins Engine Co., Columbus, Ind., 1982-87, bus. dir., 1987-89; dep. commr. Ind. Dept. Transp., Indpls., 1989-95; budget dir. State of Ind., Indpls., 1995-97; exec. sec. Ind. Family and Social Svcs. Commn., Indpls., 1997-99; city contr. City of Indpls., 1999—2003; lt. gov. State of Ind., Indpls., 2003—05; CEO Global Access Point, South Bend, Ind., 2005—. Mem. Transp. Rsch. Bd., 1990-93. Recipient commendation Dept. Transp., Fed. Hwy. Adminstrn., 1991. Democrat. Avocations: running, swimming, bicycling, hiking, photography. Office: Global Access Point 4001 Technology Dr South Bend IN 46628 Office Phone: 574-472-0750.

DAVIS, KAY, state legislator; Mem. S.D. Ho. of Reps., Pierre; mem. edn. and retirement laws coms. Democrat.

DAVIS, (FRANCIS) KEITH, civil engineer; b. Bloomington, Wis., Oct. 23, 1928; s. Martin Morris and Anna (Weber) D.; m. Roberta Dean Anderson, May 25, 1957; 1 child, Mark Francis. BSCE, S.D. State U., 1950. Registered profl. engr., Mo., Ind., Nebr., Mich., Colo., Ariz., Oreg. With firm Howard, Needles, Tammen & Bergendoff, Kansas City, Mo., 1950—, asst. chief structural designer, 1960—65, project mgr., sect. chief, 1965—75, dep. chief structural engr., 1976—79, chief engr., 1979—. Mem. bd. advisers N.W. Kans. Area Vocat. Tech. Sch., 1977-80, chmn., 1979-80. With U.S. Army, 1951-53. Fellow ASCE; mem. NSPE, Mo. Soc. Profl. Engrs., Am. Ry. Engring. Assn. (tech. com. 1981—), Homestead Country Club. Home: 5024 Howe Dr Shawnee Mission KS 66205-1465 Office: PO Box 419299 1201 Walnut St Kansas City MO 64106-2117 Home Phone: 913-722-6363. Business E-Mail: kdavis@hntb.com.

DAVIS, KENNETH BOONE, JR., dean, law educator; b. Louisville, Sept. 1, 1947; s. Kenneth Boone and Doris Edna (Gordon) D. m. Arrietta Evoline Hastings, June 2, 1984; children: Peter Hastings, Mary Elizabeth, Kenneth Boone III. AB, U. Mich., 1969; JD, Case Western Res. U., 1974. Bar: D.C. 1975, Ohio 1974. Law clk. to chief judge U.S. Ct. Appeals (9th cir.), San Francisco, 1974-75; assoc. Covington & Burling, Washington, 1975-78; prof. law U. Wis., Madison, 1978—, assoc. dean for academic affairs, 1996, James E. and Ruth B. Doyle-Bascom prof. law, 1997—, dean law sch., 1997—. Visiting prof. U. Calif. L.A., U. Pa., Case Western Reserve. Contbr. articles to profl. jours. Recipient President's Award of Excellence, State Bar Wis., 1990. Mem. ABA, Am. Fin. Assn., Am. Law Inst., Wis. Bar Assn. (reporter, corp. and bus. law com.). Office: U Wis Law Sch 975 Bascom Mall Madison WI 53706-1399 Office Phone: 608-262-0962. E-mail: kbdavis@wisc.edu.

DAVIS, KENNETH WAYNE, language educator, business communication consultant; b. Chariton, Iowa, June 22, 1945; s. Wayne Pitman and Jeanne Frances (West) Davis; m. Bette Hargrove, Nov. 28, 1970; children: Cassandra Alice, Evan Thomas. BA, Drake U., 1967; MA, Columbia U., 1968; PhD, U. Mich., 1975. From asst. prof. English to assoc. prof. U. Ky., Lexington, 1975-88; assoc. prof. to prof. Ind. U.-Purdue U., Indpls., 1988—, dept. chair, 1998-2001; edn. dir. Am. Cabaret Theatre, 2001—05. Bus. cons., Lexington, 1977-88; pres. Komei, Inc., 1994-2007. Author: Better Business Writing, 1983, (with others) Business Communication for the Information Age, 1988, Rehearsing the Audience, 1988, (with others) Writing: Process, Product, and Power, 1993, The McGraw-Hill 36-Hour Course in Business Writing and Communication, 2005, Mandarin translation, 2006; prodr.: 2001: Lessons in Leadership videoconf., 1991; numerous other books and articles. Bd. dir. Shepherd's House, Inc., Lexington, 1986-88, Waycross Camp and Conf. Ctr., 1995-2000, World Trade Club Ind., 1998-2001. Sgt. US Army, 1968-71. Woodrow Wilson fellow, 1967; recipient Faculty Service award Nat. Univ. Continuing Edn. Assn., 1987. Mem.: ASTD, Assn. Profl. Comm. Cons. (pres. 2006—07), Assn. Bus. Comm. (bd. dirs. 2003—07), Hon. Order Ky. Col., Freemasons. Episcopalian. Avocations: theater, travel. Office: Ind U-Purdue U Dept English 425 University Blvd Indianapolis IN 46202-5148 Office Phone: 317-274-0084. Business E-Mail: kdavis@iupui.edu.

DAVIS, KENO, men's college basketball coach; b. Easton, Pa., Mar. 10, 1972; s. Tom Davis; m. Krista Davis; 1 child, Brady. BA in Comm., U. Iowa, Iowa City, 1995. Asst. coach U. Iowa Hawkeyes, 1991—95, U. Southern Ind. Screaming Eagles, 1995—97, Southeast Mo. State U. Redhawks, 1997—2003, Drake U. Bulldogs, 2003—07, head coach, 2007—08, Providence Coll. Friars, 2008—. Co-author: Pressure Defense, 1994; author: Camp Success, 2004. Finalist Jim Phelan Nat. Coach of Yr. award, Naismith Nat. Coach of Yr.; named Coach of Yr., Mo. Valley Conf., 2008, Basketball Times, 2008, Nat. Coach of Yr., US Basketball Writers Assn., 2008, The Sporting News, 2008, AP, 2008; recipient Hugh Durham Mid-Major Coach of Yr. award, 2008, Henry Iba Coach of Yr. award, 2008. Office: Providence Coll 549 River Ave Providence RI 02918-0001 Office Phone: 515-271-3894.*

DAVIS, LAWRENCE EDWARD, church official; b. Louisville, Aug. 14, 1939; s. George Edward and Isabel (Gerow) D.; m. Joan Cynthia Rhodes, June 20, 1959 (dec. Mar. 1984); children: Terri L., Todd E., Cynthia Davis Kennedy, Wendy J.; m. Barbara Irene Oldford, Mar., 1985. BS, Nyack Coll., 1961; MDiv, New Brunswick Theol. Sem., 1968; DDiv (hon.), King Coll., 1991. Pastor Christian Missionary Alliance, Detroit; exec. pastor World Presbyn., Livonia, Mich., 1974-82; stated clk. Evang. Presbyn. Ch., Livonia, 1981—. Adj. prof. Reformed Theol. Sem., Jackson, Miss., 1988—. Mem. Nat. Assn. Evangelicals (bd. adminstrn. 1983—). Presbyterian. Home: 38646 Silken Glen Dr Northville MI 48167-8960 Office: Ward Presbyn Ch 4000 Sixth Mile Rd Northville MI 48167

DAVIS, MARGARET BRYAN, paleoecology researcher, educator; b. Boston, Oct. 23, 1931; AB, Radcliffe Coll., 1953; PhD in Biology, Harvard U., 1957; DSc (hon.), U. Minn., 2002. NSF fellow dept. biology Harvard U., Cambridge, Mass., 1957-58; dept. geosci. Calif. Inst. Tech., Pasadena, 1959-60; rsch. fellow dept. zoology Yale U., New Haven, 1960-61, prof. biology, 1973-76; rsch. assoc. dept. botany U. Mich., Ann Arbor, 1961-64, assoc. rsch. biologist Gt. Lakes Rsch. divsn., 1964-70, rsch. biologist, assoc. prof. dept. zoology, 1966-70, rsch. biologist, prof. zoology, 1970-73; head dept. ecology and behavioral biology U. Minn., Mpls., 1976-81, prof. dept. ecology, evolution and behavior, 1976-82, Regents prof. ecology, 1983—2000. Vis. prof. Quaternary Rsch. Ctr., U. Wash., 1973; vis. investigator environ. studies program U. Calif., Santa Barbara, 1981-82; adv. panel ecology NSF, 1976-79; sci. adv. com. biology, behavior and social scis., 1989-91; adv. panel ecol. record of global change, NRC, 1991-92, planetary biology com., 1981-82, global change com; 1987-90, mem. screening com. in plant scis., internat. exch. of persons com., 1972-75, sci. and tech. edn. com., 1984-86, vis. rsch. scientist scholarly exch. com. NAS/NRC, People's Republic China, mem. grand challenges in environ. sci. com., 1999-2000; U.S. nat. com. internat. Union Quaternary Rsch., 1966-74; bd. trustees Inst. for Ecosys. Studies, 2000-07. Mem. editl. bd. Quaternary Rsch., 1969-82, Trends in Ecology and Evolution, 1986-92, Ecosystems, 2000-03. Bd. dir. Ricon Inst., 2005—. Recipient Sci. Achievement award Sci. Mus. Minn., 1988, alumnae Recognition award Radcliffe Coll., 1988, Nevada medal, 1993, Merit award Bot. Soc. Am., 1998, award for Contbn. Grad. Edn., U. Minn., 1999, Centennial award Bot. Soc. Am., 2006. Fellow: AAAS, Geol. Soc. Am., Am. Acad Arts and Scis.; mem.: NAS, Am. Quaternary Assn. (councillor 1969—70, 1972—76, pres. 1978—80, Dist. Career award 2001), Brit. Ecol. Soc. (hon.), Am. Soc. aturalists (hon.), Ecol. Soc. Am. (pres. 1987—88, Eminent Ecologist award 1993), Nature Conservancy (bd. dirs. Minn. chpt. 1979—85), Internat. Assn. Gt. Lakes Rsch. (bd. dirs. 1970—73), Sigma Xi, Phi Beta Kappa. Office: U Minn Dept Ecology Evolution & Behavior 100 Ecology Bldg 1987 Upper Buford Cir Saint Paul MN 55108-1051 Business E-Mail: mbdavis@cox.net.

DAVIS, MARY ELLEN K., educational association administrator; MLS, U. Ill.; MA, Ctrl. Mich. U. Sr. assoc. exec. dir. Assn. Coll. and Rsch. Librs., 1993—2001, exec. dir., 2001—, dir. comm. and systems, publs. program officer; ref. libr., bibliographer Ctrl. Mich. U. Recipient Girl Scouts Outstanding Vol. award. Mem.: ALA, U. Ill. Grad. Sch. Libr. and Info. Sci. Alumni Assn. (bd. dirs., pres.), Am. Soc. Assn. Execs., Soc. Scholarly Publishing, Phi Kappa Phi, Beta Phi Mu. Office: 50 East Huron St Chicago IL 60611 Office Phone: 800-545-2433. E-mail: acrl@ala.org.

DAVIS, MICHAEL J., judge; b. 1947; BA, Macalester Coll., 1969; JD, U. Minn., 1972; LLD (hon.), Macalester Coll., 2001. Law clk. Legal Rights Ctr., 1971-73; with Office Gen. Counsel Dept. Health, Edn. and Welfare, Social Security Adminstrn., Balt., 1973; criminal def. atty. Neighborhood Justice Ctr., 1974, Legal Rights Ctr., 1975—78; pub. defender Hennepin County, 1978-83;

judge Hennepin County Mcpl. Ct., 1983-84, Hennepin County Dist. Ct. (4th jud. dist.), 1984-94; atty., commr. Mpls. Civil Rights Commn., 1977-82; judge U.S. Dist. Ct. Minn., St. Paul, 1994—. Constnl. law instr. Antioch Mpls. C.C., 1974; criminal def. trial practice instr. Nat. Lawyer's Guild, 1977; trial practice instr. William Mitchell Coll. Law, 1977-81, Bemidji Trial Advocacy Course, 1992, 93; adj. prof. U. Minn. Law Sch., 1982—, Hubert H. Humphrey Sch. Pub. Affairs, 1990; instr. Minn. Inst. Legal Edn., Civil Trial Practice Inst., 1991-92; lectr. FBI Acad., 1991, 92. Mem. Minn. Superior Ct. Racial Bias Task Force, 1990—93, U.S. Dist. Ct.; chmn. Pretrial Release & Bail Evaluation Com., 1997—. Recipient Outstanding Alumni award Macalester Coll., 1989, Good Neighbor award WCCO Radio, 1989, Disting Svc. award William Mitchell Coll. of Law, 2000. Mem. ABA, Nat. Bar Assn., Minn. Minority Lawyers Assn., Am. Inns. of Ct., Fed. Bar Assn., Fed. Judges Assn., Hennepin County Bar Assn., Minn. State Bar Assn., Minn. Lawyers Internat. Human Rights Com. (past mem. bd. dirs.), Internat. Acad. Trial Judges, Nat. Assn. for Pub. Interest Law (bd. dirs.), 8th Cir. Jury Instruction Com., U.S. Assn. Constitutional Law. Office: US Dist Ct Minn 300 S 4th St Ste 14E Minneapolis MN 55415-2251 Office Phone: 612-664-5070. Business E-Mail: mjdavis@mnd.uscourts.gov.

DAVIS, MICHAEL W., lawyer; b. NYC, Nov. 12, 1950; BA magna cum laude, SUNY, Binghamton, 1972; JD cum laude, Northwestern U., 1975. Bar: Ill. 1975, Supreme Ct. Ill. 1975, US Dist. Ct. no. dist. Ill., ea. divsn. 1975, no. dist. Calif. 1981, ctrl. dist. Ill. 2002, US Supreme Ct. 1981, US Ct. of Appeals 2nd cir. 1980, 4th cir. 1986, 6th cir. 1986, 7th cir. 1988. Ptnr. Sidley & Austin, Chgo., and head, product liability and mass tort group, sec. exec. com. Prof. products liability law Chgo. Kent Coll. Law, 1984-88. Mem. drug and med. device steering com. Def. Rsch. Inst. Mem. Internat. Assn. Defense Coun., Legal Club Chgo. Office: Sidley & Austin Bank One Plz 10 S Dearborn Chicago IL 60603 Office Fax: 312-853-7036. Business E-Mail: mdavis@sidley.com.

DAVIS, MONIQUE D. (DEON DAVIS), state legislator; b. Chgo., Aug. 19, 1936; d. James and Constance (Dutton) McKay; divorced; children: Robert Jr., Monique C. Conway. BS in Edn., Chgo. State U., 1967, MS in Guidance and Counseling, 1976. Tchr. Chgo. Bd. Edn., 1967-86, coordinator, 1986—; mem. Ill. Ho. of Reps. from 27th dist., 1987—, vice chmn. elem. and secondary edn. com. Mem. legis. com. Chgo. Area Alliance Black Sch. Edn., 1982-84, Independent Voters of Ill.-Independent Precinct Orgns., Chgo., 1982-83; coordinator 21st ward, Citizens for Mayor Washington, 1985, 87. Recipient GRIT award Roseland Womens Orgn., 1987; named a Tchr. Who Makes a Difference PTA, 1978, 85, 2002 March Monique Davis Named best Legislature of the year by Chicago Area Proseet Mem. Chgo. Area Tchrs. Alliance (chmn.), Christian Bd. Edn. (bd. dirs. 1978-82), Phi Delta Kappa. Mem. United Ch. of Christ. Office: Ill Ho of Reps 2040-j Stratton Bldg Springfield IL 62706-0001

DAVIS, MULLER, lawyer; b. Chgo., Apr. 23, 1935; s. Benjamin B. and Janice (Muller) D.; m. Jane Lynn Strauss, Dec. 28, 1963 (div. July 1998); children: Melissa Davis Muller, Muller Jr., Joseph Jeffrey; m. Lynn Straus, Jan. 23, 1999. BA magna cum laude, Yale U., 1957; JD, Harvard U., 1960. Bar: Ill. 1960, US Dist. Ct. (no. dist.) Ill. 1961. Practice law, Chgo., 1960—; assoc. Jenner & Block, 1960-67; ptnr. Davis, Friedman, 1967—. Lectr. continuing legal edn., matrimonial law and litig.; legal adviser Michael Reese Med. Rsch. Inst. Coun., 1967-82; co-chair com. to study and recommend a comprehensive rules design for the domestic rels. divsn. Circuit Ct. of Cook County, Ill., 2003—. Author: (with Sherman C. Feinstein) The Parental Couple in a Successful Divorce, 1984, Illinois Practice of Family Law, 1995, (with Jody Meyer Yazici), 8th edit., 2008; contbg. author: Marriage, Health and the Professions, 2002; mem. editl. bd. Equitable Distbn. Jour., 1984—2007; contbr. articles to law jour. Bd. dirs. Infant Welfare Soc., 1975-96, hon. bd. dirs., 1996—, pres., 1978-82; co-chmn. gen. gifts 40th and 45th reunions Phillips Exeter Acad., chair class capital giving, 1994-98, 50th reunion gift com. Yale Class Coun. 2002—. Capt. US Army, Ill. N.G., 1960-67. Fellow Am. Acad. Matrimonial Lawyers (bd. mgrs. Ill. chpt. 1996-99), Am. Bar Found.; mem. ABA, FBA, Ill. Bar Assn., Chgo. Bar Assn. (matrimonial com. 1968-83, sec. civil practice com. 1979-80, vice chmn. 1980-81, chmn. 1981-82), Am. Soc. Writers on Legal Subjects, Chgo. Estate Planning Coun., Legal Aid Soc. (vice chmn. matrimonial bar 1991-95, vice chmn. 1995-97, chmn. 1997-99), Lawyers Club Chgo., Tavern Club, Lake Shore Country Club, Chgo. Club. Republican. Jewish. Home: 161 E Chicago Ave Apt 34 E Chicago IL 60611-2601 Office: Davis Friedman 135 S LaSalle St 36th Fl Chicago IL 60603 Office Phone: 312-782-2220. Business E-Mail: mdavis@davisfriedman.com.

DAVIS, PAMELA BOWES, pediatric pulmonologist; b. Jamaica, NY, July 20, 1949; d. Elmer George and Florence (Welsch) Bowes; m. Glenn C. Davis, June 28, 1970 (div. Mar. 1987); children: Jason, Galen. AB, Smith Coll., 1968; PhD, Duke U., 1973, MD, 1974. Cert. Am. Bd. Internal Medicine, 1977, in Pulmonary Diseases 1980, Am. Bd. Pediat., 1996, in Pediatric Pulmonology 2000. Internal medicine intern Duke Hosp., 1973-74, resident in internal medicine, 1974-75; sr. investigator IAMD/NIH, Bethesda, Md., 1977-79; asst. prof. U. Tenn. Coll. Medicine, Memphis, 1979-81, Case Western Res. U. Sch. Medicine, Cleve., 1981-85, assoc. prof., 1985-89, prof., 2002, Arline H. and Curtis F. Garvin Rsch. prof., 2005—, chief pediatric pulmonary divsn., 1985—, vice chmn. rsch. dept., 1994—96, vice dean rsch., 2005—, interim dean, v.p. med. affairs, 2006—07, dean, v.p. med. affairs, 2007—. Pres. Am. Fedn. for Clin. Rsch., Thorofare, NJ, 1989—90; trustee Rsch. Am, Arlington, Va., 1989—90; mem. adv. coun. Nat. Inst. Diabetes, Digestive and Kidney Diseases, 1992—96; mem. bd. sci. counselors NHLBI, 2001—06, chmn., 2004—06; founding scientist Copernicus Therapeutics, Inc., Cleve. Contbr. articles to profl. jours. Chmn. med. adv. coun. Cystic Fibrosis Found., Bethesda, 1988-90. With USPHS, 1975—79. Named Rainmaker of Yr., Edn. Rsch. Northeast Ohio Live Mag., 2002; named to, Clevel. Med. Hall of Fame, 2001; recipient Samuel Rosenthal award in acad. pediat., 1996, Maurice Saltzman award, Mt. Sinai Health Care Found., 1998, Smith Coll. medal, 2001, Paul di Sant'Agnese award, Cystic Fibrosis Found., 2006. Fellow ACP; mem. Am. Pediatric Soc., Am. Acad. Pediatrics, Am. Physiol. Soc., Am. Thoracic Soc., Am. Soc. Gene Therapy, Biophys. Soc., Soc. for Pediatric Rsch., Assn. Am. Physicians, Phi Beta Kappa, Sigma Xi, Alpha Omega Alpha. Achievements include 7 patents in field. Office: Rainbow Babies/Child Hosp 2101 Adelbert Rd Cleveland OH 44106-2624 Business E-Mail: pbd@case.edu.

DAVIS, RICHARD FRANCIS, city government official; b. Providence, Aug. 18, 1936; s. Walter Francis and Mary Elizabeth (Gearin) D.; m. Virginia Catherine Oates, Aug. 27, 1960; children: Walter Douglas, John Richard, Theresa Catherine. BS, U. Ark., Little Rock, 1964; student city and regional planning, MIT, summer, 1964; postgrad., Carnegie Mellon U., 1973. Planner Met. Area Planning Commn., Little Rock, 1964-66; mem. Met. Planning Commn. Kansas City, Mo., 1966-67, dir. econs., 1967-69, dir. ops., 1969-71; exec. dir. Mid-Am. Regional Council, Kansas City, 1972-77; gen. mgr. Kansas City Area Transp. Authority, 1977-2000; instr. city planning U. Mo., Kansas City, 1973-74; Planning commr. City of Gladstone, Mo., 1967—69, 1981—90, 2003—04, city councilman Mo., 1969-71, mayor Mo., 1971-72, chmn. park bd. Mo., 1972-76, mem. bd. zoning adjustment, 1993—2004; bus. devel. Olsson Assocs., 2002—. Mem. Gladstone Econ. Betterment Coun., 2003-04, chmn., 2004; mem. Clay County (Mo.) Indsl. Devel. Commn., 1972-77, Coun. on Edn., Kansas City, 1974-82, treas., chmn. interdist. rels. com. Coun. adv. Major League Baseball Players Trust for Children, 2000-2003; v.p. Brooktree Homeowners Assn., 1979-80; total transp. adv. com. MidAmerica Regional Coun., 1977-2000, chmn. transit adv. com., 1997-2000; bd. dirs. Mo. Pub. Transit Assn., 1979-2000, pres., 1987-89, 1999-2000; bd. dirs. Kans. Pub. Transit Assn., 1979-2000; trustee Black Econ. Union, 1984-88; bd. dirs., treas. Heart of Am. United Way Vol. Ctr., 1985-87; mem. Kansas City Port Authoriry, 2006—; With USAF, 1955-59. Recipient Transp. Svc. award Kansas City chpt. Conf. of Minority Transit Officials, 1987. Mem. Am. Soc. Pub. Adminstrn. (pres. Kansas City chpt. 1980, Pub. Adminstr. of Yr. award 1973, L.P. Cookingham award 1991), Am. Planning Assn., Am. Pub. Transit Assn. (bd. dirs. 1980-93, 94-2000, govtl. affairs and legis. steering com., v.p. mgmt. and fin. com. 1984-86, v.p. govt. affairs com. 1991-93, Outstanding Pub. Transp. Mgr. award 2000), Kansas City Royal Lancers (bd. dirs. 2001-04, v.p. 2001-02, pres. 2002-03), Northland Regional C. of C., Brookhill Home Assn. (bd. dirs., 2005—, pres., 2006), Kansas City Port Auth. Bd. Commrs., ROOC (vice chmn. 2007), Northland Neilabarhood (bd. dir. 2007-) Home and Office: 5826 Kensington Ave Kansas City MO 64119

DAVIS, RICHARD K., bank executive; b. 1958; married; 3 children. BA in Econ., Calif. State U., 1983. Various consumer banking positions Security Pacific Nat. Bank, 1978—92, exec. v.p., 1992—93, Star Banc Corp., 1993—98; vice chmn. consumer banking Firstar Corp., Mpls., 1998—2001, U.S. Bancorp, Mpls., 2001—03, vice chmn., comml. & consumer banking, 2003—04, pres., COO, 2004—06, pres., CEO, 2006—, chmn., 2007—. Bd. dirs. Xcel Energy Inc., 2006—, U.S. Bancorp, 2006—; bd. mem. Visa Internat., Visa USA. Bd. mem. Nat. Underground Railroad Freedom Ctr., Mpls. YMCA, Mpls. Orch., Guthrie Theatre. Mem.: Am. Bankers Assn. (bd. mem.). Office: US Bancorp 800 Nicollet Mall Minneapolis MN 55402 E-mail: richard.davis@usbank.com.

DAVIS, ROBERT A., data storing company executive; Sr. v.p., chief quality officer Ideon Group, Inc.; with NCR, Inc., Dayton, Ohio, 1995-99, 1999—. Office: NCR Corp 1700 S Patterson Blvd Dayton OH 45479-0002

DAVIS, ROBERT EDWARD, state supreme court justice; b. Topeka, Aug. 28, 1939; s. Thomas Homer and Emma Claire (Hund) D.; m. Jana Jones (dec.); children: Edward, Rachel, Patrick, Carolyn, Brian. BA in Polit. Sci., Creighton U., 1961; JD, Georgetown U., 1964. Bar: Kans. 1964, U.S. Dist. Ct. Kans. 1964, U.S. Tax Ct. 1974, U.S. Ct. Mil. Appeals 1965, U.S. Ct. Mil. Review, 1970, U.S. Ct. Appeals (10th cir.) 1974, U.S. Supreme Ct. 1982. Pvt. practice, Leavenworth, Kans., 1967-84; magistrate judge Leavenworth County, 1969-76, county atty., 1980-84, judge dist. ct., 1984-86; judge Kans. Ct. Appeals Jud. Br. Govt., Topeka, 1986-93; justice Kans. Supreme Ct., Topeka, 1993—. Lectr. U. Kans. Law Sch., Lawrence, 1986-95. Capt. JAGC, U.S. Army, 1964-67, Korea. Mem. Am. Judges Assn., Kans. Bar Assn., Leavenworth County Bar Assn. (pres. 1977), Judge Hugh Means Am. Inn of Ct. Charter Orgn. Roman Catholic. Office: Kansas Supreme Ct 301 W 10th Ave Topeka KS 66612

DAVIS, RONALD MARK, preventive medicine physician; b. Chgo., June 18, 1956; m. Nadine Davis; 3 children. BS, U. Mich.; MA in pub. policy, U. Chgo., MD; completed Epidemic Intelligence Svc. program, US Ctr. Disease Control and Prevention (CDC), completed Preventive Medicine Residency Program. Dir. office on smoking and health Ctr. Disease Control (CDC), 1987—91; chief med. officer Mich. Dept. Pub. Health, 1991—95; dir. Ctr. Health Promotion and Disease Prevention at Henry Ford Health Sys., Detroit, 1995—; assoc. med. dir. Health Alliance Plan, Detroit. Founding editor Tobacco Control, British Med. Assn., 1992—98, BMJ USA (British Med. Jour.), 2001—; N. Am. editor British Med. Jour. (BMJ), 1998—2001; rep. Am. Coll. Preventive Medicine in AMA House Del., 1987—2001. Recipient Surgeon Gen. Medallion, Jay S. Drotman, Am. Pub. Health Assn., World No-Tobacco Day medal and award, World Health Orgn. Mem.: AMA (mem. bd. trustees 2001—, first resident physician mem. of bd. 1984—87, mem. coun. sci. affairs 1993—99, chair coun. sci. affairs 1997—98). Achievements include pub. in peer-reviewed jour. Office: Henry Ford Health Sys 1 Ford Pl Detroit MI 48202-3450 Office Phone: 313-874-6276. Office Fax: 313-874-6273.

DAVIS, SCOTT JONATHAN, lawyer; b. Chgo., Jan. 8, 1952; s. Oscar and Doris (Koller) D.; m. Anne Megan, Jan. 4, 1981; children: William, James, Peter. BA, Yale U., New Haven, Conn., 1972; JD, Harvard U., Cambridge, Mass., 1976. Bar: Ill. 1976, U.S. Dist. Ct. (no. dist.) Ill. 1976, U.S. Ct. Appeals (7th cir.) 1977, US Ct. Appeals (8th cir.) 1986. Law clk. to judge US Ct. Appeals (7th cir.), Chgo., 1976—77; assoc. Mayer Brown LLP, Chgo., 1977—82, ptnr., 1983—. Law lectr. U. Chgo. Law Sch., 2007—. Bd. editors: Harvard Law Rev., 1974—76; contbr. articles to profl. jours. V.p. Chgo. Police Bd. Home: 838 W Belden Ave Chicago IL 60614-3236 Office: Mayer Brown LLP 71 S Wacker Dr Chicago IL 60606 Office Phone: 312-701-7311. Business E-Mail: sdavis@mayerbrown.com.

DAVIS, STANLEY D., lawyer; b. Chattanooga, 1947; AB, U. NC, 1969, JD with high honors, 1976. Bar: NY 1977, US Dist. Ct., So. Dist. of NY, US Ct. Appeals, Second Cir. 1982, Kans. 1985, US Dist. Ct., Dist. of Kans., US Ct. Appeals, Tenth Cir. 1991, US Dist. Ct., Dist. Mo. and US Ct. of Appeals, Eighth Cir. 1993, Mo. 1994. Litig. assoc. Winthrop Stimson Putnam & Roberts, NYC; asst. US atty. So. Dist. NY; prof. law U. Kans., 1984—93; ptnr., chair Bus. Litig. Sect. Shook, Hardy & Bacon LLP, Kansas City, Mo., 1993—. Office: Shook, Hardy & Bacon LLP 2555 Grand Blvd Kansas City MO 64108 Office Phone: 816-559-2422. Office Fax: 816-241-5547. E-mail: sdavis@shb.com.

DAVIS, STEPHEN HOWARD, applied mathematics professor; b. NYC, Sept. 7, 1939; s. Harry Carl and Eva Leah (Axelrod) D.; m. Suellen Lewis, Jan. 15, 1966. BEE, Rensselaer Poly. Inst., 1960, MS in Math, 1962, PhD in Math., 1964; BSc honoris causa, U. Western Ont., 2001. Research mathematician Rand Corp., Santa Monica, Calif., 1964-66; lectr. in math. Imperial Coll., London U., 1966-68; asst. prof. mechanics and materials sci. Johns Hopkins U., 1968-70, assoc. prof., 1970-75, prof., 1975-78; prof. engring. sci. and applied math. Northwestern U., 1979—, Walter P. Murphy prof., 1987—, McCormick Sch. prof., 2000—. Dir. Ctr. for Multiphase Fluid Flow and Transport, 1986-88; cons. in field; vis. prof. math. Monash U., Australia, 1973; vis. prof. chem. engring. U. Ariz., 1977; vis. prof. aerospace and mech. engring., 1981; vis. scientist Institut für Aerodynamik-ETH, Zurich, Switzerland, 1971; vis. scientist Dept. Math. Ecole Polytechnique Federale, Lausanne, Switzerland, 1984, 85, vis. prof. 1987, 88, 91; mem. U.S. Nat. Com. for Theoretical and Applied Mechanics, 1978-87. Assoc. editor Jour. Fluid Mechanics, 1969-75, assoc. editor, 1975-89, editor-in-chief, 2000—; contbr. articles to profl. jours. Recipient Alexander von Humboldt award, 1994, Fluid Dynamics prize Am. Phys. Soc., 1994, G.I. Taylor medal Soc. for Engring. Sci., 2001. Fellow Am. Phys. Soc. (chmn. divsn. fluid dynamics 1978-79, 87-88, councillor divsn. fluid dynamics 1980-82); mem. NAS, NAE, Am. Acad. Arts and Scis., Soc. Indsl. and Applied Math. (coun. 1983-87), Sigma Xi, Pi Mu Epsilon. Home: 1199 Edgewood Rd Lake Forest IL 60045-1308 Office: Northwestern U McCormick Sch Engring/Applied Scis Sheridan Rd Evanston IL 60208-0001 Business E-Mail: sdavis@northwestern.edu.

DAVIS, STEVE, state legislator; b. Sept. 22, 1949; m. Carol Keck; children: Shane, Shelly. Student, Lewis and Clark C.C., So. Ill. U. Hwy. commr. Wood River Twp., Ill., 1981-94; former mem., treas. Madison County Dem. Cen. Com.; Ill. state rep. Dist. 111, 1995—. Mem. Aging, Appropriations-Edn., Environ. and Energy and Transp. Coms., 1995—, Ill. Ho. of Reps.; draftsman R. W. Booker and Assocs., 1970; sr. civil engr. Sterling Engring. Co., 1970-73, Volz Engring. and Survey, 1973-75, PHO Inc., 1975-78; operator Amoco Oil Co., 1978-80; pres. Steve Davis and Assocs., 1980-82. Bd. dirs. Family Svc. and Visurse Assn. Mem. Moose, Am. Legion (post 214), Ill. Legis. Sportsmans Caucus. Office: 2 Terminal Dr Ste 18B East Alton IL 62024-2289

DAVIS, SUSAN F., human resources specialist; BS, MS, Beloit Coll.; MBA, U. Mich. From strategic planner to corp. mgr. tng. and devel. Hoover Universal Corp., 1983-85; various positions including v.p. orgnl. devel. automotive group Johnson Controls, Inc., Milw., 1983—94, v.p. human resources, 1994—2006, exec. v.p. human resources, 2006—. Bd. dirs. Quanex Corp., Butler Mfg. Co. Mem.: HR Policy Assn. (vice chair). Office: Johnson Controls Inc 5757 N Green Bay Ave Milwaukee WI 53209-4408 Office Phone: 414-228-1200. Office Fax: 414-524-2077.

DAVIS, THOMAS WILLIAM, insurance company executive; b. Hinsdale, Ill., May 28, 1943; s. Charles K. and Ann (Bovy) D.; m. Loretta Marie Resutko, Dec. 28, 1969; children: Todd Arthur, Lauren Elizabeth. BA, Lewis U., Lockport, Ill., 1967. Tchr. St. Francis High Sch., Wheaton, Ill., 1964-66, Providence High Sch., ew Lenox, Ill., 1966-68, Highland (Ind.) Pub. High Sch., 1968-70; mktg. rep. Employers Ins. Warsaw, River Forest, Ill., Boockford and Co., Oakbrook, Ill., 1973-76; pres., owner Davis-Am., Ltd., Ill., 1976--, Corp. Assurance Services, Cary, Ill., 1983--. Bd. mem. Utica Natl. Ins. Co.,Columbus, Ohio, 1988--; bd. mem. Uniigard Ins. Co., Seattle, Wash., 1987. Contbr. articles to Big Savings Corp. Ins., 1983. Named Guest Lecturer, Columbia U. Sch. Journalism, N.Y., 1969; guest lecturer, Valporaise U.-Journalism Dept. Ind., 1970. Mem. Ill. Ins. Agents Inc. Republican. Roman Catholic. Avocations: painting, golf, writing. Office: Davis-American Ltd 1010 Jorie Blvd Ste 112 Oak Brook IL 60523-4446

DAVIS, W. JEREMY, retired lawyer, dean; b. Pitts., Apr. 13, 1942; s. Winthrop Neuffer and Eleanor (Power) D.; m. Jacqueline Dvoracek, June 11, 1966; children: Jeremy Michael, Sarah Elizabeth. BSBA, U. Denver, 1964, JD, 1970; LLM, Yale U., 1980. Bar: Colo. 1970, N.D. 1973. Pvt. practice law, Denver, 1970-71; asst. prof. U. N.D., Grand Forks, 1971-74, assoc. prof., 1975-82, dean, prof. law, 1983—2002, gen. counsel, 1993-2000, dir. legal affairs, 2000—02; dean, Sutin prof. law Appalachian Sch. Law, 2003—05, v.p., 2005—06; dean emeritus, 2006; prof. Law U., 2007—08. With U.S. Army, 1965-68. Fellow Bush Found., 1979-80. Mem. State Bar Assn. N.D. (bd. govs. 1982-2002), N.D. Trial Lawyers Assn. (bd. govs. 1986-2002), Va. State Bar Assn. (assoc.). Home: 1622 Earl Cir Grand Forks ND 58201 Home Phone: 701-775-8807. Personal E-mail: wjeremy.davis@gmail.com.

DAVIS, WAYNE KAY, medical educator; b. Findlay, Ohio, Mar. 23, 1946; s. Albert Wayne and Freida Evelyn (Winkle) D.; m. Patricia Ann Krimmer, May 26, 1967; 1 child, J Brandon. BA, Central Bible Coll., 1967; MA, U. Mich., 1969, PhD, 1971. Research scientist Ctr. Research Learning and Teaching, Ann Arbor, Mich., 1971-73; asst. prof. U. Mich. Med. Sch., Ann Arbor, 1973-77, assoc. dir. edn. resources and research, 1976-78, assoc. prof., 1977-82, dir. edn. resources and rsch., 1978-98, prof., 1982—, asst. dean, 1982-86, assoc. dean, 1991-98. Adv. mem. ad hoc study sect. Nat. Heart, Lung and Blood Inst., NIH, Bethesda, Md., mem. site visit team Nat. Inst. Arthritis, Metabolic and Digestive Diseases, NIH, Bethesda, 1978-91; cons. Multipurpose Arthritis Ctr., NIH, Bethesda, 1981-83; vis. scholar U. Calif. Med. Sch., San Diego, 1984-85. Author: A Guide to MTS and Remote Terminal Operation, 1972, Moving Medical Education from the Hospital to the Community, 1997; mem. edit. bd. Diabetes Care, 1983-86; assoc. editor Acad. Medicine, 1988-89; contbr. chpts. and articles to med. jours. Bd. dirs. Washtenaw County unit Mich. Hearth Assn., 1977-79. Recipient Best Article award Assn. Diabetes Educators, 1982; Med. Informatics fellow Nat. Libr. Medicine, 2000. Mem. Am. Ednl. Research Assn. (program chmn. div. I, v.p. 1985-87), Assn. Am. Med. Colls. (nat. chair group on ednl. affairs 1994-95), Am. Diabetes Assn., Soc. Dirs. Rsch. in med. Edn. (pres. 1990-91, 93-94), Phi Delta kappa, Gt.Lakes Cruising Club, Seven Seas Cruising Assn. Office: U Mich Dept Med Edn G1215 Towsley Centre 1515 Hospital Dr Ann Arbor MI 48109-0201 E-mail: wkdavis@umich.edu.

DAVISON, RICHARD, internist, educator; b. Buenos Aires, Nov. 7, 1937; came to U.S., 1966; s. Charles Edward and Matilde (Muller) D.; m. Lisette Glusberg, July 1, 1965; 1 child, Sebastian. MD, U. Buenos Aires, 1963. Diplomate Am. Bd. Internal Medicine, Am. Bd. Cardiovascular Diseases, Am. Bd. Critical Care Medicine. Intern Inst. Med. Rsch., Buenos Aires, 1964; resident Passavant Meml. Hosp., Chgo., 1966-68, chief resident, 1968-69; cardiology fellowship VA Hosp., Chgo., 1969-71; asst. prof. Northwestern U. Sch. Medicine, Chgo., 1973-81, assoc. prof., 1981—, chief sect. critical care medicine, 1982—2003, chief sect. cardiology, 1988-92; dir. med. intensive care area Northwestern Meml. Hosp., Chgo., 1973—2003. Contbr. articles to profl. jours. Recipient Thrombolysis in Myocardial Infarction award NIH. Fellow Am. Coll. Cardiology, Am. Coll. Physicians, Council of Clin. Cardiology (Am. Heart. Assn.), Soc. Critical Care Medicine; mem. Am. Heart Assn., Alpha Omega Alpha. Office: Northwestern Meml Hosp Divsn Critical Care 201 E Huron St Galter 10-240 Chicago IL 60611-2908 Office Phone: 312-695-2745.

DAVITT, MARK, state representative; b. Jan. 1952; Former photographer Ames (Iowa) Tribune, Indianola (Iowa) Record; former owner, pub. Sully Diamond Trail ews; mem. Iowa Ho. Reps., 2003—, mem. various coms. including agr., natural resources and ways & means. Democrat. Office: State Capitol East 12th and Grand Des Moines IA 50319 Home: 611 W Ashland Indianola IA 50125

DAVLANTES, ANNA, newscaster; b. Chgo. Degree, Northwestern U.; postgrad., Oxford U., Eng. Formerly with WTTW, Chgo., WXIN-TV, Indpls., WPTA-TV, Ft. Wayne, Ind.; former primary anchor KRIV-TV, Houston; co-anchor weekend evening newscasts WMAQ-TV, Chgo., 2000—. Mem. Coun. of 100 Women Northwestern U. Nominee Nat. Emmy award; recipient Chgo. Emmy award, Headliner award. Office: WMAQ-TV NBC Tower 454 N Columbus Dr Chicago IL 60611-5555 Business E-Mail: anna.davlantes@nbc.com.

DAWES, ALAN S., automotive company executive; B in Applied Math., Harvard U., 1977, MBA, 1981. Asst. treas. Chase Manhattan Bank, 1977-80; fin. analyst GM, NYC, 1981-83, mgr. overseas borrowings, 1984, dir. overseas fin. analysis, 1985, dir. financing, investments and fin. planning, 1986, gen. dir. Treasurer's Office, 1987, asst. treas., 1988-91, asst. comptr. Detroit, 1991; fin. dir. Automotive Components Group, 1992; GM v.p., gen. mgr. Delphi Chassis Systems (formerly Delco Chassis Systems); CFO Delphi Chassis Systems, 1998; CFO, exec. v.p. Delphi Automotive Systems Corp., Troy, Mich., 1998—2005. Dir. AutoNation Inc., 2003—. Named Fin. Exec. of Yr. Automotive News Industry All Stars, 1999. Mem. Harvard Bus. Club. Office: AutoNation Inc 110 Southeast 6th St Fort Lauderdale FL 33301

DAWKINS, RUSTY, meteorologist; Student, Chadron State Coll.; BS in Meteorlolgy and Climatology, U. Nebr. With KLKN, Lincoln, Nebr.; mem. weather WEAU-TV Channel 13, Eau Claire, Wis. Office: WEAN-TV PO Box 47 Eau Claire WI 54702

DAWN, CLARENCE ERNEST, historian, educator; b. Chattanooga, Dec. 6, 1918; s. Fred Hartman and Hettie Lou (Gibson) D.; m. Pansie Mozelle Dooley, July 8, 1944 (dec.); children: Julia Anne, Carolyn Louise. BA, U. Chattanooga, 1941; MA, Princeton U., 1947, PhD, 1948. Instr. history U. Ill., Urbana, 1949-52, asst. prof., 1952-55, assoc. prof., 1955-60, prof., 1960—, prof. emeritus, 1989—; dir. U. Ill. Tehran Rsch. Unit, Iran, 1972-74. Fellow Inst. Advanced Studies, Hebrew U., Jerusalem, 1981-82 Author: From Ottomanism to Arabism, 1973; contbr. articles to profl. jours. Served with AUS, 1942-46, with U.S. Army, 1951-52. Social Sci. Rsch. Coun. World Area fellow, 1948-49; fellow joint com. on Near and Mid. East Social Sci. Rsch. Coun. and Am. Coun. Learned Socs., 1966-67; Fulbright-Hays fellow, 1966-67. Mem. Mid. East Studies Assn., Mid. East Inst. Home: 1628 72d Ave SE Mercer Island WA 98040

DAWSON, DENNIS RAY, lawyer, manufacturing executive; b. Alma, Mich., June 19, 1948; s. Maurice L. and Virginia (Baker) D.; m. Marilynn S. Gordon, Nov. 26, 1971; children: Emily Lynn, Brett Thomas. AA, Gulf Coast Coll., 1968; AB, Duke U., 1970; JD, Wayne State U., 1973. Bar: Mich. 1973, U.S. Dist. Ct. (ea. dist.) Mich. 1973, U.S. Dist. Ct. (we. dist.) Mich. 1975. Assoc. Watson, Wunsch & Keidan, Detroit, 1973-75; mem. Coupe, Ophoff & Dawson, Holland, Mich., 1975-77; staff atty. Amway Corp., Ada, Mich., 1977-79; corp. counsel Meijer, Inc., Grand Rapids, Mich., 1979-82; sec., corp. counsel Tecumseh Products Co., 1982-92; corp. counsel, asst. sec. Holnam Inc., Dundee, Mich., 1992-93; v.p., gen. counsel, sec. Denso Internat. Am. Inc., Southfield, Mich., 1993-2000, sr. v.p., gen. counsel, sec., 2000—. Exec. com. Bank of Lenawee, Adrian, Mich., 1984-93, also bd. dirs.; adj. prof. Aquinas Coll., Grand Rapids, 1978-82; govt. regulation and litigation com. Outdoor Power Equipment Inst. Inc., Washington, 1982-92. Trustee Herrick Meml. Hosp., 1988-91, Tecumseh Civic Auditorium, 1986-89; mem. adv. coun. Montessori Children's House and Acad., Adrian, 1987-93; mem. adv. bd. Eastern Mich. U. Coll. Bus., 2004. Mem. ABA, Mich. State Bar Assn., Am. Corp. Counsel Assn., Mich. Mfrs. Assn. (lawyers com. 1987-92), Lenawee C. of C. (bd. dirs. 1988-92). Office: Denso Internat America Inc PO Box 5133 24777 Denso Dr Southfield MI 48034-5244

DAWSON, KIM, reporter; Degree, Howard U. Reporter WISN, Milw., 2001—. Recipient Michele Clark fellowship, Radio and TV News Dirs. Assn. Office: WISN PO Box 402 Milwaukee WI 53201-0402

DAWSON, MICHAEL C., political science professor; m. Alice Furumato-Dawson. BA, U. Calif. Berkeley, 1982; PhD, Havard U., 1986. Assoc. prof. polit. sci. U. Chgo., 1992—2001, William R. Kenan Jr. prof. polit. sci., 2001—02, John D. MacArthur Disting. Svc. prof., dept. polit. sci. and the coll., 2005—; prof. polit. sci. Harvard U., 2002—05. Founder, faculty mem. Ctr. for the Study of Race, Politics and Culture U. Chgo.; co-principal investigator 1988 Nat. Black Election Study; prin. investigator with Ronald Brown 1993-1994 Nat. Black Politics Study; prin. investigator Black Civil Soc. Study; with Lawrence Bobo conducted six pub. opinion studies on racial divide in the US, 2000—04. Author: Black Visions: The Roots of Contemporary African-Am. Political Ideologies, 2001, Behind the Mule: Race and Class in African -Am. Politics, 1994; co-editor (with Lawrence BoBo): Du Bois Review; contbr. numerous articles on African-Am. polit. behavior and race and Am. politics. Fellow: Am. Acad. Arts & Sciences. Address: Ctr for the Study of Race Politics and Culture U Chgo 5733 S University Ave Chicago IL 60637 Office Phone: 773-702-8932. Office Fax: 773-702-1689. E-mail: medawson@uchicago.edu.*

DAWSON, STEPHEN EVERETTE, lawyer; b. Detroit, May 14, 1946; s. Everette Ivan and Irene (Dresser) D.; m. Consiglia J. Bellisario, Sept. 20, 1974; children: Stephen Everette Jr., Gina C., Joseph J. BA, Mich. State U., 1968; MA, U. Mich., 1969, JD, 1972. Bar: Mich. 1972, U.S. Dist. Ct. (ea. dist.) Mich. 1972, U.S. Supreme Ct. 1978, U.S. Ct. Appeals (6th cir.) 1980. Assoc. Dickinson, Wright, Moon, Van Dusen & Freeman, Detroit, 1972-79; ptnr. Dickinson, Wright, PLLC, Bloomfield Hills, Mich., 1979—. Adj. prof. law U. Detroit, 1986-88. Mem. ABA, Am. Coll. Real Estate Lawyers, Mich. State Bar Assn. (mem. coun. real property law sect. 1986-93, chair 1992-93, land title stds. com. 1999—), Mich. State Bar Found., Phi Beta Kappa. Avocation: reading. Office: Dickinson Wright PLLC 38525 Woodward Ave Ste 2000 Bloomfield Hills MI 48304-5092 Office Phone: 248-433-7200. E-mail: sdawson@dickinsonwright.com.

DAWSON, SUZANNE STOCKUS, lawyer; b. Chgo., Dec. 29, 1941; d. John Charles and Josephine (Zolpe) Stockus; m. Daniel P. Dawson Sr., Sept. 1, 1962; children: Daniel P. Jr., John Charles, Michael Sean. BA, Marquette U., 1963; JD cum laude, Loyola U., Chgo., 1965. Bar: Ill. 1965, U.S. dist. Ct. (no. dist.) Ill. 1965. Assoc. Kirkland & Ellis, Chgo., 1965-71, ptnr., 1971-82, Arnstein & Lehr, Chgo., 1982-89, Foley & Lardner, Chgo., 1989-94; spl. counsel publicly held corps., 1995-97; corp. counsel Baxter Healthcare Corp., Deerfield, Ill., 1997-98, sr. counsel, 1998—2004, asst. gen. counsel, chief transactions counsel, 2004—06; comml. arbitrator Am. Arbitration Assn., 2006—. Mem. various coms. United Way Chgo.; corp. adv. bd. Sec. State of Ill., 1973; past mem. bd. advisors Loyola of Chgo. Law Sch.; trustee Lawrence Hall Youth Svcs., Chgo., 1983-98, pres., 1991-93, chair 1993-96; mem. adv. bd. Cath. Charities Chgo., 1985—, bd. dirs., 2002—, chair north suburban regional adv. bd., 2002—; mem. exec. com., bd. governance Notre Dame High Sch., Niles, Ill., 1990-97. Recipient Founder's Day award Loyola U., 1980, St. Thomas More award Loyola of Chgo. Law Sch., 1983. Mem. ABA, Am. Arbitration Assn. (appointed mem. nat. panel comml. arbitrators 1996—, comml. arbitrator 2006—), Ill. Bar Assn. Roman Catholic. Avocations: piano, choir singing, gardening, skiing, gourmet cooking.

DAWSON, VIRGINIA SUE, retired editor; b. Concordia, Kans., June 6, 1940; d. John Edward and Wilma Aileen (Thompson) Morgan; m. Neil S. Dawson, Nov. 28, 1964; children: Shelley Diane Dawson Sedwick, Lori Ann Dawson Hughes, Christy Lynn. BS in Home Econs. and Journalism, Kans. State U., 1962. Asst. publs. editor Ohio State U. Coop. Ext. Svc., Columbus, 1962-64; home editor Ohio Farmer mag., Columbus, 1964-78; food editor Columbus Dispatch, 1978—2000, ret. Recipient Commn. award Ohio Poultry Assn., 1980. Mem. Assn. Food Journalists. Avocations: biking, reading, cooking, hiking. Personal E-mail: ndawson1@cox.net.

DAWSON, WILLIAM RYAN, zoology educator; b. LA, Aug. 24, 1927; s. William Eldon and Mary (Ryan) D.; m. Virginia Louise Berwick, Sept. 9, 1950; children: Deborah, Denise, William. Student, Stanford, 1945-46; BA, UCLA, 1949, MA, 1950, PhD, 1953; DSc, U. Western Australia, 1971. Faculty zoology U. Mich., Ann Arbor, 1953-94, prof., 1962-94, D.E.S. Brown prof. biol. scis., 1981-94, chmn. div. biol. scis., 1974-82, dir. Mus. Zoology, 1982-93, D.E.S. Brown prof. emeritus, 1994—. Lectr. Summer Inst. Desert Biology, Ariz. State U., 1960-71, Maytag prof., 1982; rschr. Australian-Am. Edn. Found., U. Western Australia, 1969-70; Carpenter lectr. San Diego State U., 1996; mem. Speakers Bur., Am. Inst. Biol. Sci., 1960-62; mem. adv. panel NSF environ. biology program, 1967-69; mem. adv. com. for rsch. NSF, 1973-77; adv. panel NSF regulatory biology program, 1979-82; mem. R/V Alpha Helix New Guinea Expdn., 1969; chief scientist R/V Dolphin Gulf of Calif. Expdn., 1976; mem. R/V Alpha Helix Galapagos Expdn., 1978. Editorial bd.: Condor, 1960-63, Auk, 1964-68, Ecology, 1968-70, Ann. Rev. Physiology, 1973-79, Physiol. Zoology, 1976-86; co-editor: Springer-Verlag Zoophysiology and Ecology series, 1968-72; assoc. editor: Biology of the Reptilia, 1972, Birds of N.Am., 1997-2004. Served with USNR, 1945-46. USPHS postdoc. rsch.fellow, 1953; Guggenheim fellow, 1962-63; recipient Russell award U. Mich., 1959, Disting. Faculty Achievement award, 1976; Wheeler lectr. U. N.D., 1986; named Irving Scholander Meml. lectr., U. Alaska, 2007. Fellow Am. Ornithol. Union (Brewster medal 1979); mem. Soc. Integrative Comparative Biology (pres. 1985), Am. Physiol. Soc., Ecol. Soc. Am., Cooper Ornithol. Soc. (hon., Painton award 1963, Miller Rsch. award 1996), Phi Beta Kappa, Kappa Sigma. Home: 1376 Bird Rd Ann Arbor MI 48103-2351 Office Phone: 734-615-6903. Business E-Mail: wrdawson@umich.edu.

DAY, BOBBY, radio personality; Radio host KUDL-AM, Kansas City, 1970, WHB-AM, KBEQ-FM, Oldies 95, Mission, Kans., 1991—. Avocations: hockey, soccer. Office: Oldies 95 5800 Foxridge Dr 6th Fl Mission KS 66202

DAY, COLIN LESLIE, publisher; b. St. Albans, Eng., July 19, 1944; came to U.S., 1978; s. Archibald William Dagless and José (Greenfield) D.; m. Jennifer Ann Jones, July 30, 1966; children: Matthew, Gudrun. BA, Oxford U., 1966, MA, 1968; PhD, U. Stirling, 1973. Research officer N.I.E.S.R., London, 1966-68; research fellow Stirling U., Scotland, 1968-71, lectr. in econs., 1971-75; sr. econs. editor Cambridge Univ. Press, U.K., NYC, 1976-81, editor-in-chief, 1981-82, editorial dir., 1982-87; dir. U. Mich. Press, 1988—. Bd. dirs. Assn. Am. Univ. Presses, 1986-89, 92-95, pres., 1993-94. Co-author: Company Financing in United Kingdom, 1974; contbr. articles to prof. jours. Justice of peace County of Perthshire, Scotland, 1970-75; chmn. West Perthshire Labour Party, 1972-75. Office: U Mich Press PO Box 1104 839 Greene St Ann Arbor MI 48104-3209

DAY, DELBERT EDWIN, ceramic engineering educator; b. Avon, Ill., Aug. 16, 1936; s. Edwin Raymond and Doris Jennings (Main) D.; m. Shirley Ann Foraker, June 2, 1956; children: Lynne Denise, Thomas Edwin. BS in Ceramic Engring., Mo. Sch. Mines and Metallurgy, 1958; MS in Ceramic Tech., Pa. State U., 1960, PhD in Ceramic Tech., 1961; DSc (hon.), U Mo.-Rolla, 2004. Registered profl. engr., Mo. With U. Mo., Rolla, 1961—, dir. Indsl. Rsch. Ctr., 1965-72, dir. Grad. Ctr. Materials Rsch., 1983-92, Curators' prof. ceramic engring., 1981—; founder, chmn., CEO Mo-Sci Corp., Rolla, Mo., 1985—; dir. State of Mo. Tech. Corp., 1999—2004. Vis. prof. chemistry Miss. Coll., 1963, Eindhoven Tech. U., The Netherlands, 1971; mem. tech. staff Sandia Nat. Labs., Albuquerque, 1981, 91; sr. vis. faculty scientist Battelle Pacific N.W. Labs., Richland, Wash., 1990; asst. dean grad. studies Mo. Sch. Mines and Metallurgy, 1979-81; chmn. acad. coun. U. Mo., Rolla, 1978-79, active numerous other coms.; cons. Los Alamos Nat. Labs., 1983-95, NASA, 1974-88, numerous other glass and refractories cos., 1958—; vice-chmn. Gordon Rsch. Conf. on Glass, 1990-92, chmn., 1992-94; tech. program dir. confs. on glass including Baden-Baden, Germany, 1973, Rolla, 1975, XII Internat. Glass Congress, Albuquerque, 1980, Internat. and 7th U. Conf. Glass Sci., Clausthal-Zellerfeld, Germany, 1983; founder, CEO MO-Sci. Corp., Rolla. Editor: 3 books; contbr. articles to profl. jours. Chmn. bd. Wesley Found.; chmn. United Ministries Higher Edn. Bd. Dirs., 1969; adv. Explorer Scout Post 82, 1964-69; bd. dirs. Rolla Cmty. United Fund, 1975-81, Mo. Incutech Found., 1984-87; mem. bd. adjustment City of Rolla, 1973-79; fin. chmn. United Meth. Ch., 1978-80; pres., bd. dirs. Rolla Cmty. Devel. Corp., 1967-71, 82-90. 1st lt. C.E., U.S. Army, 1958-64. Recipient Outstanding Young Man award Clinton (Miss.) Jaycees, 1963, Rolla (Mo.) Jaycees, 1968, Cmty. Builder award Fraternal Order of Eagles, 1971, Pres.'s award for rsch. and creativity U. Mo., 1996, Chancellor medal U. Mo.-Rolla, 2003, Hosler Alumni Scholar medal Pa. State U., 2003. Fellow Am. Ceramic Soc. (life, v.p. rsch. 1990-91, trustee 1986-98, trustee glass divsn. 1986-89, chmn. glass divsn. 1982-83, fellows com. 1987-92, publs. com. 1980-82, 90-95, v.p. Publs. 1992-93, treas. 1993-94, pres.-elect 1994-95, pres. 1995-96, others, Outstanding Educator award 1991, G.W. Morey Rsch. award 2001, Samuel Geijsbeek award 2001, Harry E. Ebright award 2002, W.D. Kingery award 2004), Am. Nat. Inst. Ceramic Engrs., Soc. Glass Tech. (Great Britain); mem. NAE, Am. Soc. Engring. Edn. (chmn. mineral engring. div. 1968-69, program chmn. mineral engring. div. 1967-68), Nat. Inst. Ceramic Engrs. (Profl. Achievement in Ceramic Engring. award 1971, Greaves Walker award 2001), Materials Rsch. Soc., Mo. Acad. Sci. (corp. mem. com. 1989-90), Keramos, Blue Key, Tau Beta Pi, Phi Kappa Phi, Sigma Gamma Epsilon, Sigma Xi (treas. U. Mo.-Rolla chpt. 1966-67, sec. 1967-68, v.p. 1968-69, pres. 1969-70). Achievements include 44 U.S. and foreign patents (with others) for Alumina Zircon Bond for Refractory Grains, Chemically Durable Nitrogen Containing Phosphate Glasses Useful for Sealing to Metals; first to include Radioactive Biologically Compatible Glass Microspheres, Radioactive Glass Microspheres, iron phosphate glasses for vitrifying hazardous wastes, others; co-invention of TheraSphere used for treatment of liver cancer. Home: PO Box 357 Rolla MO 65402-0357 Office: U Mo-Rolla Grad Ctr Material Rsch 109 Straumanis Hl Rolla MO 65409-1170 Office Phone: 573-341-4354. Business E-Mail: day@umr.edu.

DAY, JOHN J., state representative; b. Indpls., Aug. 25, 1937; m. Mary Jo Thomas-Day; children: Maura, Anne, Teresa, Maureen. BA, Marion Coll., 1963; MA, Ind. U., 1966. Tchr. Marion Coll., 1987—, Cathedral H.S., 1997—; state rep. dist. 100 Ind. Ho. of Reps., Indpls., 1996—, mem. environ. affairs, human affairs, pub. health, and ways and means coms. Vol. grade sch. level basketball coach Cath. Youth Orgn. League; committeeman Dem. Precinct, 1968—80, 1986—; voter registration worker, 1968—; former bd. dirs. Cath. Social Svcs.; bd. dirs. Cath. Youth Orgn., 1960—, Children and Youth Ctr., United Meth. Ch., 1997—, Eastside Cmty. Investments, 1994—, Head Start Adv. Com., 1993—, Midtown Cmty. Mental Health Ctr., 1990—. Served US Army, 6 mos., served USAR, 1956—62. Democrat. Roman Catholic. Office: Ind Ho of Reps 200 W Washington St Indianapolis IN 46204-2786

DAY, RICHARD H., state legislator; b. Owatonna, Minn., Mar. 9, 1937; m. Janet; 4 children. BA, Winona State U., 1968. Mem. Minn. Senate from 28th dist., St. Paul, 1991—. Mem. agrl. & rural com., con. com. & health & human svc. com., Minn. State Senate. Mem. Eagles, Elks, KC. Office: Minn Senate 117 State Ofc Bldg 100 Constitution Ave Saint Paul MN 55155-1232 Address: 277 Cedar Cove Ln Owatonna MN 55060-4224

DAYS, RITA DENISE, state legislator; b. Minden, La., Oct. 16, 1950; d. Marion and Juliette (Mitchell) Heard; m. Frank S. Days, June 17, 1972; children: Elliott Charles, Natalie Rechelle, Evelyn Jeanine. BMus, Lincoln U., 1972. Tchr. Webster Parish Sch. Bd., Minden, La., 1972; clk. typist Urban League of St. Louis, 1973-74, asst. dir. pub. info., 1974, placement interviewer, 1974-76; office supr. Burroughs Corp., St. Louis, 1976-80; sec., admissions counselor Jewish Coll. of Nursing, St. Louis, 1989-93; mem. Mo. Ho. of Reps., St. Louis, 1993—. Chair elections com. Mo. Ho. of Reps., St. Louis, treas. Mo. Legis. Black Caucus, mem. Supreme Ct. Task Force on Children and Families; mem. Interagy. Coordinating Coun. part H. Active Ptnrs. for Kids, 1993—, New Sunny Mount Bapt. Ch.; sec. Women Legislators Mo.; bd. mem. Project Respond.; past bd. dirs. Normandy Sch. Dist. Mem. Alpha Kappa Alpha. Democrat. Office: Mo Ho of Reps State Capitol Building Jefferson City MO 65101-1556

DAYTON, MARK BRANDT, former senator; b. Mpls., Jan. 26, 1947; children: Eric, Andrew. BA cum laude in Psychology, Yale U., 1969. Tchr. gen. sci. N.Y.C. Pub. Sch., 1969-71; counselor, adminstr. Social Svc. agency, Boston, 1972-76; legis. asst. to Senator Walter Mondale US Senate; staff mem. for Gov. Rudy Perpich State of Minn., 1977, commr. econ. devel., 1978, commr. energy and econ. devel., 1983—86, state auditor, 1991—95; US Senator from Minn., 2001—07. Mem. Senator Paul Wellstone's re-election campaign, 1995-96; agr., armed svcs., rules, gov. affairs com., state of Minn. Recipient President's award, NAACP Minn. chpt., 1995, Disting. Citizen award, Minn. Veterans Fgn. Wars, 1995, Golden Triangle, Minn. Nat. Farmers Union, 2002, 2003, Legis. of Yr., Am. Ambulance Assn., 2003, Public Svc. award, Minn. State Fedn. Coun. for Exceptional Children, 2003. Democrat.

DAZE, ERIC, professional hockey player; b. Montreal, Can., July 2, 1975; Selected 4th found NHL entry draft Chgo. Blackhawks, 1993; left wing Beauport QMJ Hockey League, 1992-95; right wing Chgo. Blackhawks, 1995—. Named to QMJ Hockey League All-Star first team, 1993-94, 94-95. Recipient Can. Hockey League Most Sportsmanlike Player of Yr. award, 1994-95, Frank J. Selke Trophy, 1994-95; named Sporting News Rookie of Yr., 1996. Office: c/o Chicago Blackhawks 1901 W Madison St Chicago IL 60612-2459

DEACH, JANA AUNE, lawyer; b. Fergus Falls, Minn. BA magna cum laude, U. ND, 1993; JD with distinction, U. ND, Grand Forks, 1999. Bar: Minn. 1999, US Dist. Ct. (dist. Minn.) 1999. Assoc. Moss & Barnett, P.A., Mpls. Contbr. articles to profl. publs.; symposium editor: U. ND Law Rev. Named a Rising Star, Minn. Super Lawyers mag., 2006. Mem.: ABA, Minn. State Bar Assn., Hennepin County Bar Assn., Phi Alpha Theta. Office: Moss & Barnett PA 4800 Wells Fargo Ctr 90 S 7th St Minneapolis MN 55402 Office Phone: 612-877-5305. E-mail: deachj@moss-barnett.com.

DE ACOSTA, ALEJANDRO DANIEL, mathematician, educator; b. Buenos Aires, Feb. 1, 1941; came to U.S., 1981; s. Wladimiro and Telma (Reca) de A.; m. Martha Callejo, Aug. 19, 1966; children: Alejandro Elias, Diego Andrés. Lic. in math. scis., U. Buenos Aires, 1965; PhD, U. Calif., Berkeley, 1969. Instr. math. MIT, Cambridge, 1970-71; asst. prof. U. La Plata, Argentina, 1972-75; assoc. prof. U. Buenos Aires, 1975; rschr. Venezuelan Inst. Sci. Investigation, Caracas, 1976-82; vis. prof. U. Wis., Madison, 1981-82; vis. prof. dept. math. and stats. Case Western Res. U., Cleve., 1983, prof., 1984—. Assoc. editor Annals Probability, 1985-90; mem. editl. bd. Jour. Theoretical Probability, 1987—; contbr. articles to math. jours. Recipient prize in math. Nat. Rsch. Coun. Venezuela, 1978. Fellow Inst. Math. Stats.; mem. Am. Math. Soc. Office: Case Western Res U Dept Maths Cleveland OH 44106

DEACY, THOMAS EDWARD, JR., lawyer; b. Kansas City, Mo., Oct. 14, 1918; s. Thomas Edward and Grace (Scales) D.; m. Jean Freeman, July 10, 1943 (div. 1988); children: Bennette Kay Deacy Kramer, Carolyn G., Margaret Deacy Vickrey, Thomas, Ann Deacy Krause; m. Jean Holmes McDonald, 1988. JD, U. Mo., 1940; MBA, U. Chgo., 1949. Bar: Mo. 1940, Ill. 1946. Practice law, Kansas City, 1940-42; ptnr. Taylor, Miller, Busch & Magner, Chgo., 1946-55, Deacy & Deacy, Kansas City, 1955—. Lectr. Northwestern U., 1949-55, U. Chgo., 1950-55; dir., mem. exec. com. St. L.-S.F. Ry., 1962-80; dir. Burlington No. Inc., 1980-86; mem. U.S. team Anglo-Am. Legal Exchange, 1973, 77. Mem. Juv. Protective Assn. Chgo., 1947-55, pres., bd. dirs., 1950-53; mem. exec. bd. Chgo. coun. Boy Scouts Am., 1952-55; pres. Kansas City Philharmonic Orch., 1961-63, chmn. bd. trustees, 1963-65; trustee Sunset Hill Sch., 1963-73; trustee, mem. exec. com. u. Kansas City, 1963—; trustee Mo. Law Sch. Found., pres., 1973-77, Kans. chpt. The Nature Conservancy, 1994-99. Capt. AUS, 1942-45. Fellow Am. Coll. Trial Lawyers (regent 1968—, treas. 1973-74, pres. 1975-76), Am. Bar Found; mem. Am. Law Inst., Jud. Conf. U.S. (implementation com. on admission of attys. to fed. practice 1979-86), ABA (commn. standards jud. adminstrn. 1972-74, standing com. fed. judiciary 1974-80), Ill. Bar Assn., Chgo. Bar Assn., Mo. Bar, Kansas City Bar Assn., Lawyers Assn. Kansas City, Chgo. Club, La Jolla (Calif.) Country Club, La Jolla Beach and Tennis Club, Kansas City Club, Kansas City Country Club, River Club, Q.E.B.H. Sr. Hon. Soc. of Mo. Univ., Beta Gamma Sigma, Sigma Chi. Home: 2724 Verona Cir Shawnee Mission KS 66208-1265 Office: 920 Main St Ste 1900 Kansas City MO 64105-2010 Business E-Mail: ted@deacylaw.com.

DEAL, KAREN LYNNE, conductor; b. Richmond, Va. d. John F. Deal, Jr. BA, Oral Roberts U.; MA in Conducting, Va. Commonwealth U., 1982; student, Hochschule Musick and Darnstellende Kunst, Frankfurt, Germany, Peabody Conservatory Music. Assoc. condr. Annapolis Symphony Orch., 1986—92; founding music dir. Sinfonia Concertante; music dir., condr. Nashville (Tenn.) Ballet, 1992—2000; assoc. condr. Nashville (Tenn.) Symphony, 1992—2000; musical dir. Ill. Symphony Orch., Springfield, Ill., 2000—, dir., 2000—. Asst. condr. Frankfurt (Germany) State Opera, Nat. Repertory Orch., 1990—91; guest condr. in field. Condr.: TV series PBS Nova. Founder Sneakers and Jeans Initiative. Named one of Coolest People, Nashville (Tenn.) Life Mag., 1997; recipient Biennial Conducting Competition award, Nat. Repertory Orch., 1989, Woman of Achievement award, Mid. Tenn. State U., 1995, Citation of Appreciation, Mayor of Nashville, 2000, ashville (Tenn.) Pub. Schs. Bd. Edn., 2000, Coun. Met. Govt. Nashville, 2000, Mayor's award, Springfield (Ill.) Arts Coun., 2002, Ill. Coun. Orchs. award, 2002; scholar, Aspen Music Festival, Tanglewood Music Festival. Office: Illinois Symphony Orchestra PO Box 5191 Springfield IL 62705-5191

DEAL, WILLIAM THOMAS, retired school psychologist; b. Dec. 18, 1949; s. Richard Lee and Rheta Lucille (Gerber) Deal; m. Paula Nespeca, Aug. 5, 1972. BS, Bowling Green State U., 1972; MA, John Carroll U., 1977; postgrad., Kent State U., 1979—. Sci. tchr. Westlake Schs., 1972-76; intern sch. psychologist Garfield Heights Schs., 1976-77; pvt. practice Parma Heights, Ohio, 1982—84; sch. psychologist, 1977—2007; ret., 2007. Named Psychologist of the Yr., Cleve. Sch., 1990; recipient cert. of Recognition, Garfield Heights Bd. Edn., 1980, Outstanding Achievement award, Cleve. Assn. Children with Learning Disabilities, Inc., 1980. Mem.: Cleve. Assn. Sch. Psychologists, Ohio Sch. Psychology Assn., Nat. Assn. Sch. Psychologists, Phi Delta Kappa. Democrat. Methodist. Home: 5290 Kings Hwy Cleveland OH 44126-3059

DEAN, GEORGE R., state legislator; b. Kansas City, Kans., Sept. 12, 1933; m. Ethel J. Haley, 1957. BSEE, U. Kans., 1959; MSEE, Wichita State U., 1969. Aerospace engr. Missile System divsn. Beech Aircraft, until 1992; mem. Kans. Ho. of Reps. Topeka, 1978-2000. Bd. dirs. Kans. Tech. Enterprise Corp. Bd. dirs. Spl. Olumpics, 1986-87, Very Spl. Arts Kans.; adv. bd. University Kans. EECS. Mem. Inst. Elec. and Electronic Engrs. (dir. 1997-99, Region 5 Profl. award 1983, Centenial award 1984, Profl. Acheivement award 1988), Am. Legion, Aircraft Owners and Pilots Assn. Democrat. Home: 2646 Exchange St Wichita KS 67217-2928

DEAN, HOWARD M., JR., food company executive; b. 1937; married. BBA, So. Meth. U., 1960; MBA, Northwestern U., 1961. With Dean Foods Co., Inc., Franklin Park, Ill., 1955—, internal auditor, 1965—68, asst. to v.p. fin., 1968—70, pres., 1970—89, CEO, 1987—, chmn., 1989—. Served to lt. (j.g.) USN, 1962—65. Office: Dean Foods Co 3600 River Rd Franklin Park IL 60131-2185

DEAN, WARREN MICHAEL, design and construction company executive; b. Great Falls, Mont., Apr. 27, 1944; s. Warren Earl and Mary Amelia (Sankovich) D.; m. Pamela Carol House, June 18, 1977; children: Marc, Drew, Molly, Anna. BArch, Mont. State U., 1969; MArch in Urban Design, U. Colo., Denver, 1973; MBA, U. Denver, 1982. Registered architect, Colo. Architect Davis Partnership, Denver, 1973-74; project mgr. CRS Constructors/Mgrs., Denver, 1974-78, v.p., 1978-82, group v.p., 1982-83; pres. CRSS Constructors Inc., Denver, 1983-88; exec. v.p. CRSS Commercial Group, Inc., Denver, 1988-90; v.p. CRSS, Inc., Greenville, S.C., 1990-92; chmn., CEO CRSS Constructors, Inc. (subs. Jacobs Engring. Group), Houston, 1993—; group v.p., corp. officer Jacobs Engring. Group, Inc., Houston and St. Louis, 1997—; chmn. Jacobs Facilities Inc., 1999—. Contbr. articles to profl. jours.; speaker in field. Mem. Denver Concert Chorale, 1974-77; bd. dirs. Jr. Achievement Metro Denver, 1985-88, chmn., 1987-88; bd. dirs. Jr. Achievement Southeast Tex., Inc., 1998-99, Jr. Achievement Mississippi Valley, Inc., 2000—; bd. dirs. Denver Opera Co., 1976-77. Served to lt. USNR, 1969-72. Advanced Acad. scholar Mont. St. U., 1967-69. Mem. AIA (com. architecture for edn. 1982—), Soc. Am. Milit. Engrs., Constrn. Industry Inst., Planning Execs. Inst., Denver C. of C. (chmn. com. econ. devel.), Colo. Soc. Architects, Rotary. Roman Catholic. Office: Jacobs Engring Group Inc 501 N Broadway Saint Louis MO 63102-1815

DEARDEN, DICK L., state legislator; b. Des Moines, June 3, 1938; m. Sharon Dearden; 3 children. With Polk County Ctrl. Com., 1972—; chmn. Polk County Dems., 1980-82; job developer fifth jud. dist., 1986—; supr. AMF Lawn and Garden; bus. rep. Almalgated Meat Cutters; mem. Iowa Senate from 35th dist., 1994—. Del. Dem. Nat. Convention, 1996. With Iowa NG, 1956-62. Mem. AFSCME (local 3289), AMVETS, Nat. Wild Turkey Fedn., Pheasants Forever, Ducks Unltd., Izaak Walton League. Democrat. Lutheran. Home: 3113 Kinsey Ave Des Moines IA 50317-6603 Office: State Capitol Dist 35 3 9th And Grand Des Moines IA 50319-0001 E-mail: dick_dearden@legis.state.ia.us.

DEASON, HEROLD MCCLURE, lawyer; b. Alton, Ill., July 24, 1942; s. Ernest Wilburn and Mildred Mary (McClure) D.; m. Wilma Lee Kaemmerle, June 18, 1966; children: Sean, Ian, Whitney. BA, Albion Coll., 1964; JD, Northwestern U., 1967. Bar: Mich. 1968. Assoc. Bodman LLP, Detroit, 1967-74, ptnr., 1975—. City atty. Grosse Pointe Pk., Mich., 1978—. Vice chmn. Detroit, Windsor Freedom Festival, 1978-92; bd. dirs. Spirit of Detroit Assn., 1980-2003. Recipient Spirit of Detroit award, Detroit City Coun., 1986. Mem. ABA, Mich. Assn. Mcpl. Attys. (pres. 1995-97), Detroit Bar Assn., Can.-U.S. Bus. Assn. (pres. 2005), Grosse Pointe Yacht Club (commodore 1992-93), Detroit Racquet Club, Windsor Club. Home: 1044 Kensington Ave Grosse Pointe Park MI 48230-1437 Office: Bodman LLP 6th Fl at Ford Field 1901 St Antoine St Detroit MI 48226 Home Phone: 313-885-5507; Office Phone: 313-393-7556. Business E-Mail: hdeason@bodmanllp.com.

DEATON, BRADY J., academic administrator; m. Anne Deaton; children: Tony, Brady Jr., Christina, David. BS in Agrl. Econs., U. Ky., 1966, MA in Diplomacy and Internat. Commerce, 1968; PhD in Agrl. Econs., U. Wis., 1972. Assoc. prof. U. Tenn., 1972—78; dir. Va. Poly. Inst. and State U., 1978—89; prof., Agricultural Econ, dept. chair & social sci. unit leader U. Mo., Columbia, Mo., 1989—98, chief staff, dep. chancellor, provost, 1998—2004, interim chancellor, 2004, chancellor, 2004—. Chair Nat. Assn. State Univs. and Land Grant Colls. Contbr. articles to profl. jours. Office: Office of the Chancellor 105 Jesse Hall Univ Mo Columbia MO 65211 Office Phone: 573-882-3387. Office Fax: 573-882-9907. Business E-Mail: chancellor_office@missouri.edu.

DEBACKER, MICHAEL LEE, automotive executive, lawyer; b. 1947; JD, Washburn U. Bar: Kans. 1972, Okla. 1975. Asst. gen. counsel Dana Corp., Toledo, 1986—2001, v.p., 1994—, gen. counsel, sec., 2001—07. Office: Dana Corp PO Box 1000 Toledo OH 43697-1000 Business E-Mail: mike.debacker@dana.com.

DEBARTOLO, EDWARD JOHN, JR., real estate developer, former professional football team owner; b. Youngstown, Ohio, Nov. 6, 1946; s. Edward J. and Marie Patricia DeBartolo; m. Cynthia Ruth Papalia, Sept. 27, 1968; children: Lisa Marie, Tiffanye Lynne, Nicole Anne. Student, U. Notre Dame, 1964—68. With Edward J. DeBartolo Corp., Youngstown, Ohio, 1960—, v.p., 1972—76, exec. v.p., 1976—79, chief adminstrv. officer, 1979—94, pres., CEO, 1995—; owner San Francisco 49ers, 1977—97; chmn. bd. DeBartolo Realty Corp., 1994—; chmn., CEO DeBartolo Entertainment, Inc. Mem. Nat. Cambodia Crisis Com., 1980—; adv. coun. Nat. Assn. People with AIDS, 1992; trustee Youngstown State U., 1974—77; nat. adv. coun. St. Jude Children's Rsch. Hosp., 1978—, local chmn., 1979—80; chmn. local fund drive Am. Cancer Soc., 1975—; chmn. 19th Ann. Victor Warner award, 1985, City of Hope's Spirit of Life Banquet, 1986; apptd. adv. coun. Coll. Bus. Adminstrn. U. otre Dame, 1988; bd. dirs. Cleve. Clinic Found., 1991; lifetime mem. Italian Scholarship League. With US Army, 1969. Named one of Forbes' Richest Americans, 2006; recipient Man of Yr. award, St. Jude Children's Hosp., 1979, Boy's Town of Italy in San Francisco, 1985, Sportsman of Yr. award, Nat. Italian Am. Sports Hall of Fame, 1991, Cert. of Merit, Salvation Army, 1982, Warner award, 1986, Silver Cable Car award, San Francisco Conv. and Visitors Bur., 1988, NFL Man of Yr. award, Football News, 1989, Svc. to Youth award, Cath. Youth Orgn., 1990, Hall of Fame award, Cardinal Mooney High Sch., 1993. Mem.: Internat. Coun. Shopping Ctrs., Dapper Dan Club (bd. dirs. 1980—), Fonderlac Country Club, Tippecanoe Country Club. Office: Debartolo Corp 7620 Market St Youngstown OH 44512-6076 also: De Bartolo Holdings 100 Debartolo Pl # 300 Youngstown OH 44512

DEBAT, DONALD JOSEPH, media consultant, columnist; b. Chgo., Sept. 29, 1944; s. Chester Louis and Marie Dorothy (Mehok) DeBat; m. Heidi Loretta Meinhardt, Sept. 3, 1966 (div. Aug. 1984); children: Aimee Lisa, Erik Andreas; m. Sara Elizabeth Benson, Aug. 20, 1994 (div. Oct. 2001); children: Donald Edward, Herbert Lankford. AA, Wright Jr. Coll., 1963; BJ, U. Mo., 1966, MA, 1968. Editl. asst. Ency. Brit., Chgo., summer 1965; reporter, Sunday editor Columbia Missourian, 1966-67; fin. reporter Chgo. Daily News, 1968-73, sports copy editor, 1974-75, real estate editor, 1976-78, Chgo. Sun-Times, 1978-88, asst. mng. editor, real estate, 1988-94; real estate columnist Crain News Svc., Chgo., 1995—; pres. Donald J. DeBat & Assocs., Inc., Chgo., 1995—2005; CEO DeBat Media, Inc., Chgo., 2001—; real estate columnist DeBat Media Svcs., 2006—. Author: (book) The Mortgage Manual, 1986, 2d edit., 1989, Home Refinancing, 1986; author, editor: Living in Greater Chicago, 1988—94. Named to 16-inch Softball Hall of Fame, 1999, Ct. of Honor, Home Builders Assn. Greater Chgo., 2004; recipient numerous awards for articles in real estate field. Mem.: Soc. Profl. Journalists, Chgo. Press Vets. Assn., Nat. Assn. Real Estate Editors (bd. dirs., editor of best real estate sect. award 1978, 1983, 1984, 1992), Nat. Trust Hist. Preservation. Avocations: softball, handball, real estate investing and renovation, travel, skiing. Office: DeBat Media Inc 1633 N North Park Ave Chicago IL 60614 Home Phone: 312-337-0180; Office Phone: 312-944-1177. Fax: (312) 944-8877. E-mail: debatnet@aol.com.

DEBAUGE, JANICE B., musician; MusB magna cum laude, Southern Mo. U. Classical musician, soprano. Bd. regents Washburn U., 2001—. Home: 1966 Morningside Dr Emporia KS 66801

DEBEAR, RICHARD STEPHEN, library planning consultant; b. NYC, Jan. 18, 1933; s. Arthur A. and Sarah (Morrison) deB.; m. Estelle Carmel Grandon, Apr. 27, 1951; children: Richard, Jr., Diana deBear Fortson, Patricia deBear Talkington, Robert, Christopher, Nancy deBear Naski. BS, Queens Coll., CUNY, 1953. Sales rep. Sperry Rand Corp., Blue Bell, Pa., 1954-76; pres. Libr. Design Assocs., Plymouth, Mich., 1976-97, Am. Libr. Ctr., Plymouth, 1981—. Bldg. cons. to numerous librs., 1965—; mem. interior design program profl. adv. com. Wayne State U. Mem. ALA, Mich. Libr. Assn. (oversight com. Leadership Acad. 1990—). Home Phone: 734-453-0912; Office Phone: 734-254-8080. Business E-Mail: ddebear@americanlibrary.com.

DEBEAUSSAERT, KENNETH JOSEPH, state legislator; b. Mt. Clemens, Mich., Apr. 10, 1954; Aide U.S. Rep. David Bonior; mem. Mich. Ho. of Reps from 75th dist., Lansing, Mich. Senate from 11th dist., Lansing, 1995—. Chmn. consumers com. Mich. Ho. Reps., agriculture, conservation, recreation & environ. com., liquor control com., transp. com. Mem. New Baltimore Hist. Soc., Macomb County Farm Bur., Oakland U. Alumni Assn., Friends of Catholic Social Svc. Address: 310 Farnum Bldg PO Box 30036 Lansing MI 48909-7536

DE BLASIS, JAMES MICHAEL, performing company executive, theater producer; b. NYC, Apr. 12, 1931; s. James and Sarah (de Felice) de B.; m. Ruth Hofreuter, Aug. 25, 1957; 1 child, Blythe. BFA, Carnegie Mellon U., 1959, MFA, 1960. Mem. drama faculty Carnegie Mellon U., 1960-62; head drama dept. Onondaga C.C., Syracuse, NY, 1963-72; head Opera Workshop, Syracuse, 1969-70; adv. of opera Corbett Found., Cin., 1971-76; gen. dir. Cin. Opera Assn., 1973-87, artistic dir., 1988-96. Internat. ind. stage dir. of opera, 1962—; pvt. coach. Dramatic Interpretation of Operatic Roles, 1995—. Artistic advisor, Pitts. Opera, Inc., 1979-83. With U.S. Army, 1951-53. Recipient award Omicron Delta Kappa, 1959, Alumni award Bellaire High Sch., 1974, award in arts adminstrn. Gov. Ohio, 1989, Post/Corbett award for performing artist Corbett Found./Cin. Post, 1989. Mem. Actors Equity, Am. Guild Mus. Artists, Drama Alumni Carnegie Mellon U., Beta Theta Pi, Omicron Delta Kappa. Republican. Episcopalian.

DEBOEF, BETTY, state representative; b. Feb. 1951; Mem. Iowa Ho. Reps., DesMoines, 2001—, vice chair agr. com., mem. environ. protection com., mem. health and human rights com., mem. appropriations com., mem. human resources com. Republican. Office: State Capitol East 12th and Grand Des Moines IA 50319 Home: 10805 180th St What Cheer IA 50268-8584

DEBOER, JAMES N., lawyer; b. Grand Rapids, Mich. married; 2 children. MBA, Mich. Bus. Sch., 1950; JD, U. Mich. Law Sch., 1950. Ptnr. atty. Varnum Riddering Schmidt & Howlett, 1950—. Bd. dirs. Spartan Corp. Trustee Davenport U.; former dir. Met. Hosp., Mich., Met. Health Corp., Mich. Served in USN, 1943—45. amed one of Best Lawyers in Am., 1993—. Office: Varnum Riddering Schmidt & Howlett 333 Bridge St NW PO Box 352 Grand Rapids MI 49501-0352

DEBOSE, MICHAEL, state representative; b. Dec. 16, 1953; BA, Cleve. State U., 1977. State rep. dist. 12 Ohio Ho. of Reps., Columbus, 2002—, ranking minority mem., fed. grant rev. and edn. oversight subcom., mem. edn., energy and environment, and health coms. Mem. Cleve. Sch. Bd., 1997. Democrat. Office: 77 S High St 10th fl Columbus OH 43215-6111

DE BRANGES DE BOURCIA, LOUIS, mathematics professor; b. Paris, Aug. 21, 1932; s. Louis and Diane (McDonald) deB.; m. Tatiana Jakimow, Dec. 17, 1980; 1 child, Konstantin. BS, MIT, 1953; PhD, Cornell U., 1957. Prof. Purdue U., Lafayette, Ind., 1962-88, disting. prof. of math., 1989—. Fellow Sloan Found., 1963-66, Guggenheim Found., 1967-68; recipient Humboldt prize Alexander Humboldt Found., 1986-88, Ostrowski prize Alexander Ostrowski Found., 1989. Home: Hameau de l'Yvette Batiment D Chemin des Graviers F-91190 Gif Sur Yvette France Office: Purdue U Dept Math Lafayette IN 47907-2067 E-mail: branges@math.purdue.edu.

DEBRUCE, PAUL, agricultural food products company executive; Founder DeBruce Grain Inc., Kansas City, Mo., 1978, CEO, 1978—, DeBruce Grain de Mex., Queretaro.

DEBRUIN SAMPLE, ANNE, human resources specialist; Formerly with Whirlpool Corp., Benton Harbor, Mich.; numerous human resources positions including mgr. human resources Pepsi-Cola N.Am. PepsiAmericas, Inc., Mpls., 1988—2001, sr. v.p. human resources, 2001—. Office: PepsiAmericas 4000 Dain Rauscher Plz 60 S Sixth St Minneapolis MN 55402 Office Phone: 612-661-4000. Office Fax: 612-661-3737.

DEBUS, ALLEN GEORGE, historian, educator; b. Chgo., Aug. 16, 1926; s. George Walter William and Edna Pauline (Schwenneke) D.; m. Brunilda Lopez-Rodriguez, Aug. 25, 1951; children: Allen Anthony George, Richard William, Karl Edward. BS, Northwestern U., 1947; A.M., Ind. U., 1949; PhD, Harvard U., 1961; postgrad., U. Coll. London, 1959-60; D.Sc. h.c., Cath. U. Louvain, 1985. Research chemist Abbott Labs., North Chicago, Ill., 1951-56; asst. prof. U. Chgo., 1961-65, assoc. prof. history, 1965-68, prof., 1968-78, Morris Fishbein prof. history sci. and medicine, 1978-96, Morris Fishbein prof. emeritus, 1996—; dir. Morris Fishbein Ctr. for Study History Sci. and Medicine, 1971-77. Disting. vis. prof. Ariz. ctr. for medieval and renaissance studies Ariz. State U., 1984; vis. prof. Inst. Chemistry, U. São Paulo, Brazil, 1990; mem. internat. adv. com. Tel-Aviv U. The Cohn Inst. History and Philosophy of Sci. and Ideas, Ctr. for History and Philosophy of Sci. of Hebrew U. of Jerusalem; mem. internat. adv. bd. Annali dell'Istituto e Museo di Storia della Scienza di Firenze; cons. lit. and sci. curriculum Ga. Inst. Tech. Author: The English Paracelsians, 1965, 66, (with Robert P. Multhauf) Alchemy and Chemistry in the 17th Century, 1966, The Chemical Dream of the Renaissance, 1968, 2d edit., 1972, Science and Education in the 17th Century, 1970, (with Brian Rust) The Complete Entertainment Discography, 1973, 2d rev. edit., 1989, The Chemical Philosophy, 2 vols., 1977, 2d edit., 2002, Japanese transl., 1999, Man and ature in the Renaissance, 1978, 15th rev. edit., 1995, Italian transl., 1982, Spanish transl., 1985, 86, 2d edit., 1995, Japanese transl., 1986, Chinese transl., 1988, 2000, Greek transl., 1997, Portuguese trans., 2002, Robert Fludd and His Philosophical Key, 1979; Science and History: A Chemist's Appraisal, 1984, Chinese tranl., 1999, Chemistry, Alchemy and the New Philosophy, 1550-1700, 1987, The French Paracelsians: The Chemical Challenge to Medical and Scientific Tradition in Early Modern France, 1991, 2002, Paracelso e la Tradizione Paracelsiana, 1996, Chemistry and Medical Debate: Van Helmont to Boerhaave, 2001, The Chemical Promise, 2006; editor: World Who's Who in Science from Antiquity to the Present, 1968, Science, Medicine and Society in the Renaissance, 2 vols, 1972, Medicine in Seventeenth-Century England, 1974; editor reprint: Theatrum Chemicum Britannicum (1652), 1967, John Dee's Mathematicall Praeface (1570), 1975; editor: (with Ingrid Merkel) Hermeticism and the Renaissance: Intellectual History and the Occult in Early Modern Europe, 1988, (with Michael T. Walton) Reading the Book of Nature: The Other Side of the Scientific Revolution, 1998, Alchemy and Early Modern Chemistry: Papers from Ambix, 2004; essayist: Festschrift: Experiencing Nature: Essays for Allen G. Debus (edited by Paul Theerman and Karen Parshall, 1997); mem. bd. adv. editors Physis Rivista internazionale de storia della scienza, Nuncius, The 16th Century Jour.; adv. editor: History of Science; hon. bd. editors Incognita; programmed 3 records released by Smithsonian Instn. Music of Victor Herbert, 1979; notes to CD releases by Archeophone-Bert Williams, Nora Bayes and Jack Norworth, 2003-04, Monarchs of Minstrelsy, 2006; contbr. articles to profl. jours.; patentee in field. Social Sci. Rsch. Coun. fellow, 1959-60; Fulbright fellow, 1959-60; Fels Found. fellow, 1960-61; Guggenheim fellow, 1966-67; overseas fellow Churchill Coll. Cambridge (Eng.) U., 1966-67, 69; mem. Inst. Advanced Study Princeton, N.J., 1972-73; NEH fellow Newberry Libr., Chgo., 1975-76; fellow Inst. for Rsch. in Humanities U. Wis., Madison, 1981-82, NEH, 1987, Folger Shakespeare Libr., Washington; rsch. grantee Am. Philos. Soc., 1961-62, Wellcome Trust, 1962, NIH, 1962-70, 74-75, 77-78, 92-97, NSF, 1961-63, 71-74, 80-83, Am. Coun. Learned Socs., 1966, 70, 71. Fellow AAAS (mem. electorate nominating com., sect. L 1974-77, chmn. com. 1974); mem. History of Sci. Soc. (council 1962-65, 87-90, program chmn. 1972, Pfizer award 1978, Sarton medal 1994, Disting. lectr. 1996), Soc. Study Alchemy and Early Chemistry (mem. council 1967—), Am. Assn. for History Medicine (program com. 1975), Brit. Soc. for History Sci., Internationale Paracelsus Gesellschaft, Am. Chem. Soc. (asso. mem. history of chemistry div., exec. com. 1969-72, Dexter award 1987), Soc. Med. History of Chgo. (sec.-treas. 1971-72, v.p. 1972-74, pres. 1974-76, mem. council), Académie Internat. d'Histoire de la Medecine, Société Internationale d'Histoire de la Medecine, Academie Internat. d'Histoire des Scis. (corr. 1971, membre effectif 1991), Am. Inst. History of Pharmacy (Edward Kremers award 1978, adv. panel hist. activity 1979-81, awards com. 1981—), Am. Soc. Reformation Research, Assn. Recorded Sound Collections., Midwest Junto for History of Sci. (pres. 1983-84), Academia das Ciencias de Lisboa. Office: U Chgo Dept History Chicago IL 60637 Office Phone: 773-702-8391. Personal E-mail: adebus@midway.uchicago.edu.

DECAIRE, JOHN, electronics executive, aerospace engineer; BS in Appied Physics, Mich. Tech. U., 1962; MS in Engring. Space Physics, Air Force Inst. Tech., PhD in Aerospace Engring.; grad. mgt. devel. program, Harvard U. Bus. Sch. Commd. 2d. lt. USAF, 1962, resigned, 1975; mgr. electronic mfg. Wright-Patterson AFB, Dayton, Ohio, 1975-78; program mgr. Bedford engring. labs. Raytheon Co., 1979-80; founder, mgr. Westinghouse Mfg. Systems and Tech. Ctr., Balt., Md., 1980-84; gen. mgr. design and producibility engring. divsn. Westinghoue Electonics Systems Group, Balt., 1985-88, exec. dir. systems and tech., 1989-91; prin. John Decaire and Assocs., Cons., 1991-93; pres. Nat. Ctr. for Mfg. Scis., Ann Arbor, Mich., 1993—. Bd. dirs. NACFAM and CIMS. Mem. adv. bd. Mich. Tech. U. Coll. Engring., U. Md. MIPS, U. Mich. Tauber Mfg. Inst. Office: Nat Ctr for Mfg Sciences 3025 Boardwalk St Ann Arbor MI 48108-3230

DECANNIERE, DAN, human resources executive; CFO Hewitt Assocs., Lincolnshire, Ill., 1996—. Bd. dirs. Hispanic Alliance for Career Enhancement. Mem.: Financial Executives Rsch. Found., Ill. CPA Society, AICPA. Office: Hewitt Assocs 100 Half Day Rd Lincolnshire IL 60069 Fax: 847-883-9019.

DECASTRO, FERNANDO JOSE, pediatrics educator; b. Havana, Cuba, Nov. 11, 1937; s. Fernando R. and Maria A. (Freyre) deC.; m. Catalina, June 9, 1962; children: Maria, Ana, Fernando, Ramon, Teresa, Pablo, Jose Manuel. MD, Tulane U., 1962; MPH, U. Mich., 1966. Intern, resident, fellow U. Mich., 1962-66; clin. prof. pediatrics St. Louis U., 1976—; dir. toxicology Arcadia Valley Hosp., Pilot Kove, Mo., 1992—. Contbr. articles to profl. jours. Fellow APHA, Am. Acad. Pediatrics, Am. Coll. Emergency Physicians, Am. Coll. Med. Toxicology, Am. Acad. Clin. Toxicology, Am. Fedn. Clin. Rsch. Office: Arcadia Valley Hosp Hwy 21 Pilot Knob MO 63663

DECAVEL, JEAN-ROBERT, chef; b. Roubaix, France; m. Annette Pfund-deCavel. Chef La Bonne Auberge, Antibes, France, Mallihouana Hotel, Anguilla; exec. chef Le Regence, YC, 1985—93; chef de cuisine Maisonette, Cin., 1993—2001; owner, chef Jean-Robert at Pigall's, Cin., 2002—. Decorated medal of the Chevalier de Order of Merit France; nominee Best Chef: Midwest, James Beard Found., 2000, 2001, 2006; named Person of Yr., City Beat, 2004, French-Am. C. of C., Cin. Chpt., 2005; recipient Presidents award, Cin. Chpt. Pub. Rels. Soc. Am., 2008 Am.'s Top Restaurants award for Jean-Robert at Pigall's, Zagat Survey, 2007. Office: Jean-Robert at Pigall's 127 W 4th St Cincinnati OH 45202 Office Phone: 513-721-1345 209. Business E-Mail: info@jean-robertatpigalls.com.

DECHENE, JAMES CHARLES, lawyer; b. Petaluma, Calif., May 14, 1953; s. Harry George and Domenica Theresa Dechene; m. Teresa Marie Caserza, Aug. 2, 1975; children: Michelle, Mark, Sabrina, Diane. BS summa cum laude, Santa Clara U., 1975; JD magna cum laude, U. Mich., 1978, AM in Econs., 1978, PhD in Econs., 1980. Bar: Ill. 1979, U.S. Dist. Ct. (no. dist.) Ill. 1980, U.S. Ct. Appeals (7th cir.) 1993, U.S. Dist. Ct. (ea. dist.) Wis. 1996. Assoc. Sidley & Austin, Chgo., 1980-86; ptnr. Sidley Austin LLP, Chgo., 1986—. Adj. prof. Health Law Inst. DePaul U. Coll. of Law, 1987—; bd. dirs. Med. Sci. Labs., Wauwatosa, Wis., 1991-95. Author: Establishing a Physician Organization, 1993; author: (with others) Health Law Practice Guide, 1993-2004, Financing and Liability, 1994, Health Law Handbook, 1989, 90, 91, 93, Managed Care, 1996, Telemedicine and E-Health Law, 2004; contbr. articles to profl. jours. Mem. Ill. Bar Assn., Am. Health Lawyers Assn., Am. Econs. Assn. Roman Catholic. Office: Sidley Austin LLP One S Dearborn St Chicago IL 60603-2000 Home Phone: 630-852-8578; Office Phone: 312-853-7275. Business E-Mail: jdechene@sidley.com.

DECKER, RAYMOND FRANK, chemicals and metal products executive; b. Afton, NY, July 20, 1930; s. Bernett Hurd and Mildred (Bisbee) Decker; life ptnr. Mary Birdsall, Dec. 27, 1951; children: Susan, Elizabeth, Catherine, Laura. BS, U. Mich., Ann Arbor, 1952, MS, 1955, PhD, 1958. With Inco Ltd., 1958-82, v.p. corp. tech. and diversification ventures, 1978-82; v.p. rsch. and corp. rels. Mich. Technol. U., Houghton, 1982-86; pres., CEO Univ. Sci. Ptnrs., Inc., 1986-98; pres. ASM Internat., 1986-87; founding chmn., pres., CEO Thixomat, Inc., 1988—2004, chair, pres., CEO, 2004—05, also bd. dirs., CTO, 2005—; founding chmn. Wavemat, Inc., 1987-88. Bd. dirs. Lindberg Corp., 1989—2001, Spl. Metals Corp., 1990—2003; adj. prof. Poly. Inst. Bklyn., 1962—66, NYU, 1968, U. Mich., 1997—; cons. KMS Fusion, Inc., Howmet turbine Components, Alcoa, GE, GM, 1985—; Van Horn Disting. lectr. Case-Western Res. U., 1975; mem. materials adv. bd. ASA, 1969, Nat. Bur. Stds., 1973, NSF, 1985—86; mem. Nat. Materials Adv. Bd., 1982—88; mem. exec. com. Strategic Hwy. Rsch. Program, 1986—93; long-range planning com. Metall. Soc., 1985—87, State Rsch. Fund Panel Mich., 1983—86; chmn. rsch. & tech. coordinating com. Fed. Hwy. Adminstrn., 1995—98; trustee Foundry Ednl. Found., 1975—77, Welding Rsch. Coun., 1975—80; chmn. bd. trustees Mich. Energy and Resource Rsch. Assn., 1985—86; keynote spkr. on superalloys Seven Springs Conf., 1980, NAE, 1980—. Author: (book) Strengthening Mechanisms in Nickel-Base Superalloys; editor: Maraging Steels. Chmn. alumni com. dept. material sci. and engring. U. Mich., Ann Arbor, chmn. class of 1952 reunion; chmn. Ch. Coun., 2001—03. Recipient IR-100 award, 1964, Sesquicentennial award, U. Mich., 1967, Disting. Grad. award, 1994, Innovation award, Mobile Computing, 1999, Inc 500 award, 1999. Fellow: Am. Soc. Metals Internat. (chmn. materials sys. and design divsn. 1971—73, trustee 1976—79, chmn. diamond decade com. 1980—81, Campbell Meml. lectr. 1985, chmn. organizing com. World Materials Congress 1988, hon. mem. 1991, Alpha Sigma Mu lectr. 2001, Woodside lectr. 2003, Gold medal 1989); mem.: NAE, AAAS, AIME (lectr. Inst. Metals divsn. 1973, R. F. Mehl medal 1973), Afton Ctrl. Sch. Alumni Assn. (v.p. 2004—). Congregationalist. Achievements include co-inventing maraging steels, Thixomolding machine. Home: Apt 204 505 E Huron Ann Arbor MI 48104 Office Phone: 734-995-5550. Business E-Mail: rdecker@thixomat.com.

DECKER, RICHARD KNORE, lawyer; b. Lincoln, Nebr., Sept. 15, 1913; s. Fred William and Georgia (Kilmer) Decker; m. Fern Iona Steinbaugh, June 12, 1938. AB, U. Nebr., 1935, JD, 1938. Bar: Nebr. 1938, U.S. Supreme Ct. 1941, D.C. 1948, Ill. 1952. Trial atty. antitrust div. Dept. Justice, 1938-52; ptnr. Lord, Bissell & Brook, Chgo., 1953-84, of counsel, 1984—2005. Trustee Village of Clarendon Hills (Ill.), 1960-64; chmn. bd. elders Community Presbyn. Ch., Clarendon Hills, 1963-66; mem. Union Ch. of Hinsdale; chmn. bd. Community House, Hinsdale, Ill., 1976, Robert Crown Ctr. for Health Edn., Hinsdale, Ill., 1981-83, also bd. dirs, 1976-2005. With USNR, 1942-45, lt. comdr. ret. Mem. ABA (chmn. antitrust sect. 1971-72), Ill. Bar Assn. (gov. 1969-73, chmn. antitrust sect. 1964-66), Chgo. Bar Assn. (chmn. antitrust law com. 1956-59), The Lawyers Club Chgo., Hinsdale Golf Club (pres. 1968). Republican. Home: 196 Pheasant Hollow Dr Burr Ridge IL 60527-5051

DECKER, RUSSELL S., state legislator; b. May 25, 1953; married; 2 children. Grad., No. Ctrl. Tech. Coll., 1980. Mem. from dist. 29 Wis. Senate, Madison, 1990—. Mem. rural econ. devel. bd. Active Habitat for Humanity; mem. apprentice com. United Way; rep. for bricklayers union. Mem. Bricklayers Intl. Union. Democrat. Home: 6803 Lora Lee Ln Schofield WI 54476-4369

DECKER, WALTER JOHNS, toxicologist; b. Tannersville, NY, June 13, 1933; s. H. Russell and Leola May (Coons) D.; m. Barbara Allen Hart, Aug. 19, 1961; children: Karl Hart, Reid Johns, Sam Travis. BA, SUNY, Albany, 1954, MA, 1955; PhD, George Wash. U., Washington, DC, 1966. Commd. 2d lt. US Army, 1955, advanced through grades to lt. col., 1970, ret., 1975; assoc. prof. U. Tex. Med. Br., Galveston, 1976-83; pres. Toxicology Cons. Svcs., El Paso, Tex., 1984-97. Adj. clin. prof. Tex. Tech. U., El Paso, 1991—. Contbr. articles to jours. Clin. Toxicology, Vet. and Human Toxicology, Toxicology and Applied Pharmacology, others. Mem. sci. rev. panel Nat. Libr. Medicine's Hazardous Substance Data Bank, Bethesda, Md., 1985-2000; chair steering com. West Tex. Poison Ctr., El Paso, 1994-96. Recipient Aesculapius award, Tex. Med. Assn., 1977, Career Achievement award, Am. Acad. Clin. Toxicology, 2001. Fellow: Am. Acad. Clin. Toxicology (Career Achievement award 2001); mem.: Soc. Toxicology. Episcopalian. Achievements include research in toxicology. E-mail: bdecker173@centurytel.net.

DECKER, WAYNE LEROY, meteorologist, educator; b. Patterson, Iowa, Jan. 24, 1922; s. Albert Henry and Effie (Holmes) D.; m. Martha Jane Livingston, Dec. 29, 1943; 1 dau., Susan Jane. BS, Central Coll., Pella, Iowa, 1943; postgrad., UCLA, 1943-44; MS, Iowa State U., 1947, PhD, 1955. Meteorologist U.S. Weather Bur., Washington and Des Moines, 1947-49; mem. faculty U. Mo. at Columbia, 1949—, prof. atmospheric sci., 1958-67, prof., chmn. dept. atmospheric sci., 1967-91, prof. emeritus, 1992—, dir. coop. inst. applied meteorology, 1985-92; cons. climatologist, 1992—. Chmn. com. climatic fluctuations and agrl. prodn. NRC, 1975-76; bd. dirs. Council for Agrl. Sci. and Tech., 1978-85, mem. exec. com., 1981-85; chair organizing com. Redundant with what fellow. Fellow Am. Meteorol. Soc.; mem. Internat. Soc. Biometeorology (treas. 1990-99, chair, 16th Internat. Congress Biometeorology), Am. Geophys. Union, Am. Agronomy Soc., Sigma Xi, Gamma Sigma Delta. Home: 23 Springer Dr Columbia MO 65201-5424 Office: Univ Mo 302A Anheuser-Busch Natural Resources Bl Columbia MO 65211-7040 Personal E-mail: janewaynedeck@centurytel.net.

DECKROSH, HAZEN DOUGLAS, retired state agency educator and administrator; b. Defiance, Ohio, Apr. 13, 1936; s. Lawrence L. and Martha L. Deckrosh; m. Carol Ann Everett, ov. 25, 1970; children: Stephanie, Todd, Douglas, Nadia Nicole. BS, Ohio No. U., 1959; MEd, U. Toledo, 1980. Cert. tchr., Ohio. Phys. edn. and history tchr., coach Waynesfield (Ohio)-Goshen Jr. High Sch., 1959-61; coach, history, phys. edn. tchr. Coshocton (Ohio) Sacred Heart High Sch., 1961-63; health-phys. edn. tchr., coach West Holmes Jr. High Sch., Millersburg, Ohio, 1965-70; tchr. history and govt., coach Elida High Sch., 1970-73; occupational work experience tchr.-coord., coach Spencerville (Ohio) High Sch., 1973-77; occupational work edn. tchr., coord. Four County Vocat. Sch., Archbold, Ohio, 1977-82, 99—; vocat. supr. Jefferson County Vocat. Sch., Steubenville, Ohio, 1986-87; occupational work experience tchr., coord. Ohio Dept. of Youth Svcs., Columbus, 1987-94; ret., 1994. Pres. DYS Coordinators, Columbus, 1990-94; ski instr. Swiss Valley, Mich., 1995—; GED instr. Correction Ctr. Northwest Ohio. Editor: Threaded Fasteners, 1987; contbr. articles to profl. publs. Mem. Am. Youth Hostels, Lima, 1972—. Mem. NEA, Ohio Edn. Assn., Am. Vocat. Assn., Ohio Vocat. Assn., Occupl. Work Experience Coords. Assn. (state adv. coun., Lima rep. 1977-80, Columbus rep. 1991-94), Full Gospel Bus. Men's Fellowship Internat., Gideons Internat. (treas., then sec.), 5th Dist. Ofcls. Assn. (v.p., rules interpreter), Capitol West Umpires Assn. (rules interpreter 1991-93), Lima Umpires Assn. (sec.-treas. 1973-77), Ret. Tchrs. Assn. (pres.), Alpha Sigma Phi. Republican. Avocations: sports officiating, high school and college sports, teaching skiing. Home: 12265 County Road 150 Montpelier OH 43543-9613 Personal E-mail: blazinghazen@aol.com.

DE COURTEN-MYERS, GABRIELLE MARGUERITE, retired neuropathologist; b. Fribourg, Switzerland, Aug. 8, 1947; came to U.S., 1979; d. Maurice Edmond and Margrit (Wettstein) de Courten; m. Ronald Elwood Myers, Apr. 18, 1981; 1 child, Maximilian. BSBA, Akademikergemeinschaft, Zurich, Switzerland, 1967; MD, U. Zurich, 1974. Resident in psychiatry Hospital Psycho-Geriatrique, Gimel, Switzerland, 1974-75; resident in pediatrics U. Hosp. Zurich, 1977; resident in neuropathology U. Hosp. of Lausanne, Switzerland, 1976-78; rsch. assoc. NIH, Bethesda, Md., 1979-80; fellow in neuropathology Coll. of Medicine U. Cin., 1980-83, asst. prof. neuropathology Coll. of Medicine, 1983-88, assoc. prof. neuropathology Coll. of Medicine, 1988-89, tenured assoc. prof. Coll. of Medicine, 1989, full prof., 1999—2001; ret., 2007—. Cons. Vets. Affairs Med. Ctr., Cin., 1983—2006, Children's Hosp. Med. Ctr., Cin., 1984—2005, Good Samaritan Hosp., Cin., 1990—; adj. prof., U. Cin., 2001-07. Grantee VA, 1985—, NIH, 1986-90, 93—, Am. Heart Assn., 1991-94, Am. Diabetes Assn., 1995. Mem Am. Assn. neuropathologists, Am. Acad. Neurology, Soc. Exptl. Neuropathology. Office: U Cin Coll of Medicine Dept Pathology PO Box 670529 231 Bethesda Ave Cincinnati OH 45267-0529 Home Phone: 513-625-6251; Office Phone: 513-558-0148.

DEDERICK, ROBERT GOGAN, economist; b. Keene, NH, Nov. 18, 1929; s. Frederic Van Dyck and Margaret (Gogan) D.; m. Margarida N. Magalhaes, Aug. 24, 1957; children: Frederic, Laura, Peter. AB, Harvard U., 1951, AM, 1953, PhD, 1958; postgrad., Cornell U., 1953-54. Econ. research mgr. New Eng. Mut. Life Ins. Co., Boston, 1957-64; assoc. economist No. Trust Co., Chgo., 1964, v.p., assoc. economist, 1965-69, v.p., economist, 1969-70, sr. v.p., chief economist, 1970-81, exec. v.p., chief economist, 1983-94, econ. cons., 1994—2003; mem. panel of econ. advisers Congl. Budget Office, 1991—2004; mem. econ. adv. bd. U.S. Commerce Dept., 1968-70, 75-76, 83-85, asst. sec. commerce for econ. affairs, 1981-82, under sec. commerce for econ. affairs, 1982-83; prin. RGD Econs., Hinsdale, 1994—. Fellow: Nat. Assn. Bus. Economists (pres. 1973—74, governing coun. 1969—75); mem.: Internat. Conf. Comml. Bank Economists, Am. Bankers Assn. (alumni coun.), Harvard Discussion Group Indsl. Economists, Conf. Bus. Economists (chmn. 1984—85), Dutch Settlers Soc. Albany, Capitol Hill Club, Hinsdale Golf Club, Harvard Club, Econ. Club. Home: 113 S County Line Rd Hinsdale IL 60521-4722 Office: RGD Economics 113 S County Line Rd Hinsdale IL 60521-4722 Office Phone: 630-325-7183. Personal E-mail: rdederick@aol.com.

DEDONATO, DONALD MICHAEL, obstetrician, gynecologist; b. Bridgeport, Conn., Apr. 25, 1952; s. Michael Anthony and Mary Jane (Zawacki) DeDonato; m. Susan Mary Naulty, June 15, 1974; children: Mark Dominic, David Nicholas. BA in Chemistry cum laude, Coll. Holy Cross, 1974; MD, Loyola U., Maywood, Ill., 1977. Intern Loyola Foster McGaw Hosp., Maywood, Ill., 1977-78; resident Ohio State U. Hosp., Columbus, Ohio, 1978-81; ob-gyn. Ob-Gyn. Assocs., Arlington Heights, Ill., 1981-87, DeDonato, Goodnough and Geittmann, Ob-Gyn., Arlington Heights, 1987-92; pres., CEO N.W. Women's Cons., Arlington Heights, 1993—. Clin. instr. orthwestern U. Med. Ctr., Chgo., 1981—; chmn. dept. ob-gyn. N.W. Cmty. Healthcare, 1998—2000. Mem. alumni bd. Loyola Stritch Sch. of Medicine, Maywood, Ill. Recipient CIBA award. Mem. AMA, Am. Assn. Med. Colls. (Loyola rep.), Chgo. Med. Soc., Ill. State Med. Soc., Am. Bd. Ob-Gyn., Am. Assn. Gyn. Laparoscopists, Garden Camera (pres. 1985-86, 92-93), Phi Beta Kappa, Alpha Sigma Nu. Avocation: photography. Office: NW Womens Cons 1630 W Central Rd Arlington Heights IL 60005-2407 Office Phone: 847-394-3553.

DEE, IVAN RICHARD, book publisher; b. Chgo., Mar. 11, 1935; s. Jack Arthur and Jeanette Rose (Melcher) D.; m. Sandra Cohen, June 21, 1959 (div. 1973); m. Phyllis Kirz, Aug. 3, 1977 (div. 1981); m. Barbara Burgess, Apr. 15, 1989; children: Alexander, Sara, Jacob, Gabriel. BJ, U. Mo., 1956, MA, 1957. Pres. Ardivan Press, Macon, Ga., 1960-61; v.p., editor-in-chief Quadrangle Books, Chgo., 1961-72; assoc. editor Chgo. Tribune Book World, Chgo., 1972-73; exec. editor Pubs.-Hall Syndicate, Chgo., 1973-74; editor-in-chief Chicagoan Mag., Chgo., 1974-75; dir. pub. affairs Michael Reese Hosp. and Med. Ctr., Chgo., 1975-89; pres. Ivan R. Dee, Inc., Chgo., 1989—. V.p. South Side Planning Bd., Chgo., 1975-89; commr. Chgo. Baseball League, 1978-00; mem. adv. bd. Nat. Great Books Curriculum Acad. Cmty., 2005—. Lt. (j.g.) USN, 1957-60. Office: Ivan R Dee Inc 1332 N Halsted St Chicago IL 60622-2624 Business E-Mail: idee@ivanrdee.com.

DEEMS, NYAL DAVID, lawyer; b. Cleve., Jan. 24, 1948; s. Nyal Wilbert and Octavia C. (Roush) D.; m. Jody Deems July 6, 1996; children: Brooke Elizabeth, Nyal Christopher, Holly Jean, Eric Wellington, Georgia Octavia, Susannah Irma Genevieve. BA in Internat. Studies, Miami U., 1969; JD, U. Ga., 1976. Bar: Ga. 1976, Mich. 1976, U.S. Dist. Ct. (we. dist.) Mich., U.S. Dist. Ct. (no. dist.) Ga. Assoc. then ptnr. Varnum, Riddering, Wierengo & Christenson now Varnum, Riddering, Schmidt & Howlett LLP, Grand Rapids, Mich., 1976—. Co-author: Michigan Real Estate Sales Transactions, 1983, Real Estate Development, 4 vols., 1988, A Practical Guide to Winning Land Use Approvals and Permits, 1989, Michigan Real Estate Practice and Forms, 1989, Michigan Business Formbook, 1989, Michigan Basic Practice Handbook, 1989. Commr. City of East Grand Rapids, Mich., 1982-85, mayor, 1985-95; chmn. Grand Rapids Met. Coun., 1990-95. Lt. USN, 1969-73. Mem. ABA, Ga. Bar Assn., Mich. Bar Assn. (chmn. water law com. 1984-86, real property coun. 1984—, chairperson 1989), Grand Rapids Bar Assn., Am. Coll. Real Estate

Lawyers, Am. Coll. Mortgage Attys. (treas. 2006). Home: 701 Laurel Cir Grand Rapids MI 49506-2806 Office: Varnum Riddering Schmidt & Howlett LLP 333 Bridge St NW Ste 1700 Grand Rapids MI 49504-5356

DEER, ADA E., former federal agency official, social worker, educator; b. Menominee Indian Reservation, Wis., Aug. 7, 1935; d. Joe and Constance (Wood) D. BA in Social Work, U. Wis., 1957, LDH (hon.), 1974; MSW, Columbia U., 1961; postgrad., U. N.Mex., 1971, U. Wis., 1971-72; D in Pub. Svc. (hon.), Northland Coll., 1974. Group worker Protestant Coun. N.Y., N.Y.C. Youth Bd., 1958-60; program dir. Edward F. Waite Neighborhood House, Mpls., 1961-64; community svc. coord. bur. Indian affairs Dept. of Interior, Mpls., 1964-67; coord. Indian affairs Tng. Ctr. Cmty. Programs U. Minn., Mpls., 1967-68; trainer Project Peace Pipe Peace Corps., Arecibo, P.R., 1968; sch. social worker Mpls. Pub. Schs., 1968-69; dir. Upward Bound U. Wis., Stevens Point, 1969-70, dir. Program Recognizing Individual Determination through Edn., 1970-71; v.p., lobbyist Nat. Com. Save Menominee People and Forest, Inc., Washington and State of Wis., 1972-73; chair Menominee Restoration Com., Wis., 1974-76; lectr. Sch. Social Work, Am. Indians Studies Program U. Wis., Madison, 1977—93, 1997—, dir. Am. Indian Studies program, 2000—; asst. sec. Indian Affairs U.S. Dept. Interior, Washington, 1993—97. Legis. liaison Native Am. Rights Fund, Washington, 1979-81; cons., trainer Nat. Women's Edn. Fund, Washington, 1979-85; founding mem. Am. Indian Scholarships, Inc., Albuquerque, 1973-85; apptd. Joint Commn. on Mental Health of Children, Inc., Washington, 1967-68, Youth for Understanding, Wis., 1985-90; mem. adv. panel Office Technology Assessment, Washington, 1984-86; mem. Nat. Indian Adv. Com., Washington, 1989-91, Milw., 1990—, numerous other coms.; spkr. in field. Vice chair Nat. Mondale/Ferraro Presdl. Campaign, Washington, 1984; del.-at-large Dem. Nat. Conv., San Francisco, 1984; mem. spl. com. minority presence Girls Scouts U.S.A., N.Y.C., 1975-77, mem., 1969-75; bd. dirs. Planned Parenthood, Mpls., 1965-66, Indian Cmty. Sch., Milw., 1989—, Native Am. Rights Fund, Boulder, 1984-90, chmn., 1989-90, chair nat. support com., 1990—; mem. bd. improving health Native Ams. Robert Wood Johnson Found., Princeton, N.J., 1988—; bd. dirs. Quincentenary Com. Smithsonian Instn., Washington, 1989—, Hunt Commn. Dem. Nat. Com., Washington, 1981-82, Ind. Sector, Washington, 1980-84, Rural Am., Washington, 1978-85, Ams. for Indian Oppty., 1970-83; apptd. Pres. Commn. White House Fellowships, 1977-83; active Common Cause, Washington, 1974-78, Wis. Women's Coun., Madison, 1983-84, Camp Miniwanca, Stony Lake, Mich., 1953-57, Coun. Founds., Washington, 1977-83, Madison Urban League; Dem. candidate Wis. Sec. State, 1982; chair Menominee Nation, Wis., 1974-76. Recipient White Buffalo Coun. Achievement award, 1974, Politzer award Ethical Culture Soc., 1975, Wonder Woman Found. award, 1982, Indian Coun. Fire Achievement award, 1984, Nat. Disting. Achievement award Am. Indian Resources Inst., 1991, Cmty. Change Maker award, 2005; named Woman of Yr. by Girl Scouts Am., 1982; honoree Nat. Women's History Month Poster, 1987, Heroine Calendar Nat. Women's Studies Assn., 1987; Harvard U. fellow, 1977-78, Delta Gamma Found. Meml. fellow, 1960, John Hay Whitney Found. Meml. fellow, 1960; Menominee Tribal scholar, 1953-55. Mem. ACLU, NOW, Nat. Women's Polit. Caucus, Nat. Congress Am. Indians, Nat. Assn. Social Workers (pres. Wis. chpt. 1988-90, nat. com. women's issues 1988-90, decision making task force 1988-90, minorities com. 1977-81), Assn. Am. Indians and Alaska Native Social Workers (pres. Wis. 1978-80), Common Cause, Nature Conservancy. Avocations: reading, travel. Office: Univ Wisc Am Indian Studies Program 317 Ingraham Hall 1155 Observatory Dr Madison WI 53706 Office Phone: 608-263-5501. Office Fax: 601-262-7137. E-mail: aisp@aisp.wisc.edu.

DEER, RICHARD ELLIOTT, lawyer; b. Indpls., Sept. 8, 1932; s. Leon Leslie and Mary Jane (Ostheimer) Deer; m. Lee Todd, Feb. 22, 1958; children: William K., Laura A., Susannah T., Thomas E. AB, DePauw U., 1954; LLB magna cum laude, Harvard U., 1957. Bar: Ind. 57, U.S. Dist. Ct. (no. and so. dists.) Ind. 57, U.S. Ct. Appeals (7th cir.) 57, U.S. Ct. Appeals (9th cir.) 90, U.S. Supreme Ct. 62. Assoc. Barnes & Thornburg and predecessor firm, Indpls., 1957—65, ptnr., 1965—, chmn. mgmt. com., 1990—93. Author: Indiana Corporation Law and Practice, 1990, Supplement, 1994; co-author: Indiana Limited LIability Company Forms and PRactuce Manual, 1996, Supplement, 1997; bd. editors: Harvard Law Rev., 1956—57; contbr. articles to legal jours.; chief reporter: The Lawyer's Basic Corporate Practice Manual, 3d edit., 1984. Mem. Indpls. Coun. Fgn. Rels., Ind. Corps. Survey Commn., 1983—2000. Fellow: Ind. Bar Found., Am. Bar Found.; mem.: ABA (drafting com., exec. planning group of legal opinion project sect. bus. law, 3d party legal opinion report 1991), Am. Law Inst., Ind. State Bar Assn. (past chmn. corp., banking and bus. law sect.), Indpls. Bar Assn., Columbia Club, Players Club, Hillcrest Country Club. Office: Barnes & Thornburg 11 S Meridian St Ste 1313 Indianapolis IN 46204-3535

DEES, RICHARD LEE, lawyer; b. Harrisburg, Ill., Jan. 14, 1955; s. David Lee and Joann (Alvey) D.; children: Sarah Elizabeth, Elliott Richard, Spencer Barrett; m. ora B. Flint, Apr. 21, 2001. AS, Southeastern Ill. Jr. Coll., 1975; BS, So. Ill. U., 1977; JD magna cum laude, U. Ill. Coll. Law, 1980. Bar: Ill. 1980, US Tax Ct. 1981. Ptnr. McDermott, Will & Emery, Chgo., 1980—. Invited witness Senate Fin. Com., 1989-90, House Ways and Means Com., 1990. Editor: Agrl. Law and Tax Report, 1984-89; topics editor U. Ill. Law Forum, 1979-80; contbr. articles to profl. jours. Named one of Top 100 Attys., Worth mag., 2005. Fellow Am. Coll. Trust and Estate Counsel; mem. Leading Ill. Attys., Order of Coif. Presbyterian. Office: McDermott Will & Emery 227 W Monroe St Ste 3100 Chicago IL 60606-5096 Office Phone: 312-984-7613. Office Fax: 312-984-7700. E-mail: rdees@mwe.com.

DEES, STEPHEN PHILLIP, agricultural products executive, lawyer; b. Tulsa, Feb. 21, 1943; s. Jesse Raymond and Mary Adelia (Ledbetter) D.; m. Mary Louise Porter, June 26, 1966 (div. Oct. 1986); children: Emily Ann, Daniel Ledbetter, Matthew Louis; m. Kristine Ann Odenwald, Oct. 10, 1987 (div. Apr. 1992); 1 child, Charles Jesse; m. Linda Petsch, Sept. 3, 1995. BA, Washington U., 1965, JD, 1967. Bar: Mo. 1967. Assoc. Stinson, Mag, Thomson, McEvers & Fizzell, Kansas City, Mo., 1967-71; ptnr. Stinson, Mag & Fizzell, Kansas City, 1971-84; v.p., gen. counsel Farmland Industries Inc., Kansas City, 1984-87, sec., 1986-91, v.p. law and adminstrn., 1987-93, now exec. v.p. bus. development & internat. mktg., dir. gen., 1993-98; dir. gen. Farmland Industries, S.A. de C.V. of Mex., 1993-95; ptnr. Rochdale Prins., 1998—2000; of counsel Shook, Hardy & Bacon, Kansas City, Mo., 2000—. Officer, bd. dirs. Gt. Am. Basketball League, Shawnee Mission, Kans., 1979-86, commr., 1983-86; mem. Sister Cities Commn., Kansas City, 1982-90. Served with USAF, 1967, then with Res. Mem. ABA, Mo. Bar (vice chmn. labor law com. 1977-80, chmn. 1980-81), Lawyers Assn. Kansas City (bd. dirs. 1983-86, treas. 1989-91), Kansas City Met. Bar Assn., Order of Coif. Republican. Jewish. Avocations: stamp collecting/philately, racquetball, travel. Home: 4511 N Mulberry Dr Kansas City MO 64116-4652 Office: Shook Hardy Bacon 2555 Grand Blvd Kansas City MO 64108-2613 Office Phone: 816-559-2466.

DE FRANCESCO, JOHN BLAZE, JR., public relations consultant, writer; b. Stamford, Conn., May 22, 1936; s. John Blaze and Mae (Matyscyk) DeF.; m. Louise C. Terlizzo, Nov. 1, 1958 (div. 1983); children: Daryl, Jay, Dana, Dorian; m. Diana Picchietti, Oct. 20, 1990. BS, U. Conn., 1958. Sr. v.p. Daniel J. Edelman, Inc., Chgo., 1967-77; exec. v.p. Ruder Finn & Rotman, Inc., Chgo., 1977-85; prin., CEO DeFrancesco/Goodfriend Pub. Relations, 1985-2001; exec. v.p. L.C. Williams & Assoc., Chgo., 2001—03; prin. DeFrancesco Artist and Writer, 2003—. Bd. dirs. Ill. Divsn. Vocat. Rehab., 1976-78; mem. pub. rels. adv. bd. Gov.'s State U., 1994-98. Comdr. USN, 1958-67; comdr. USNR; ret. 1979. Recipient 3 Silver Anvil awards Pub. Rels. Soc. Am., 6 Golden Trumpet awards Publicity Club, Chgo. Mem. Pub. Rels. Soc. Am., Navy League U.S., Mil. Officer Assn. Am. Roman Catholic. Home and Office: 18785 Saint Andrews Dr Monument CO 80132-8824

DEGENHARDT, ROBERT ALLAN, architectural firm executive, engineering executive; b. Kearney, Nebr., May 29, 1943; s. Robert Franklin and Florence Elizabeth (Spohnheimer) D.; m. Elizabeth Scholl; children: Barry, Christopher, Kathleen. BSME, U. Nebr., 1965, MSME, 1968. Registered profl. engr., D.C. and all states except Alaska and Hawaii. Project engr. Davis & Wilson Architects and Engrs., Lincoln, Nebr., 1964-68, White Sands (N.Mex.) Missile Range, 1968-70, Sundstrand Aviation, Rockford, Ill., 1970-74; dir. engring. Davis, Fenton, Stange, Darling, Architects and Engrs., Lincoln, 1974-77; v.p. mech. engring. Durrant Engrs. Inc., Madison, Wis., 1977-1980; dir. mech. engring. Ellerbe Assocs. Inc., Mpls., 1980-82, dir. archtl./engring. svcs., 1982-83, v.p., dir. ops., 1983-85; sr. v.p., dir. Ellerbe Becket Inc., Washington, 1985-89; exec. v.p., COO Ellerbe Becket Co., Mpls., 1989-93, pres., COO, 1993-94, pres., CEO, 1994-98, CEO, 1998-2001, pres., 2001—; sr. v.p. 3D Internat., Houston. Mem. Ctr. for Ethical Bus. Cultures, 1993—. 1st lt. US Army, 1968—70. Mem. Constrn. Industry Roundtable, U.S. C. of C. (internat. polic com.), Sigma Xi, Pi Tau Sigma. Republican. Lutheran. Avocations: fly fishing, backpacking, fly-fishing.

DEGROAT, PAUL PERCY, electrical engineer, consultant; b. Ft. Worth, Nov. 25, 1955; s. Timothy and Elizabeth DeGroat; m. Judith Marie Frankfort, July 11, 1985 (div. 2000); children: Beverly, Violet. BSEE, U. Texas, Corpus Christi, 1976; MSEE, Tex. A&M U., College Station, 1978, PhD in Elec. Engring., 1982. Rsch. asst. Meriks Labs., Worland, Wyo., 1982—83, elec. engr., 1983—95, dir. R&D, 1995—. Adj. prof. Laramie County CC, Wyo., 2000—01; freelance elec. contractor, 1976—78; cons. in field. Recipient Disting. Engring. Svc. award, U. Tex. Sys., 1990. Mem.: IEEE, Soc. Profl. Engrs., Am. Soc. Engring., Federalist Soc. Lutheran. Avocations: fishing, hunting, stamp collecting/philately. Office: Meriks Labs 3900C Gooseberry Rd Worland WY 82401-9308

DEGROOTE, MICHAEL G., management consulting company executive; Pres., CEO Laidlaw Inc., 1959-90, Republic Industries Inc., 1991-96, also chmn. bd. dirs.; pres. Century Bus. Svcs. Inc., Cleve., 1997-99, CEO, 1999—, also chmn. bd. dirs. Office: Century Bus Svcs Inc 6050 Oak Tree Blvd #500 Cleveland OH 44131-6951

DEGROW, DAN L., state legislator; b. Ann Arbor, Mich., Jan. 28, 1953; m. Cheryl L. Simpson, 1981; children: Allison, Kelsie Sue, Stephen. Grad., Mich. State U., 1975; JD, Wayne State U., 1978. Mem. Mich. Ho. of Reps., Lansing, 1980-82, Mich. Senate from dist. 28, Lansing, 1982-94, Mich. Senate from 27th dist., Lansing, 1995—; sen. majority leader, 1999—. Vice chair appropriations com. Mich. State Senate, chmn. K-12 & edn. subcom., cmty. coll. com., capital outlay, budget and oversight com., jud. com., legis coun; ptnr. Nicholson, Fletcher, West & DeGrow, 1979—. Active St. Clair County Rep. Com. Mem. NAACP, Assn. Retarded Citizens, Mich. Bar Assn., St. Clair County Bar Assn., Phi Beta Kappa. Office: State Senate Office State Capitol Lansing MI 48909-7536

DEGUILIO, JON E., lawyer; b. Hammond, Ind., June 15, 1955; s. Ernest Michael and Jeanne (Hochis) D.; m. Barbara Jo Wieser, Oct. 3, 1981; 1 child, Suzanne Jeanne. BA, U. Notre Dame, 1977; JD, Valparaiso U., 1981. Bar: Ind. 1981, U.S. Dist. Ct. (so. dist.) Ind. 1981, U.S. Dist. Ct. (no. dist.) Ind. 1981. Pub. defender Lake County Ct., Crown Point, Ind., 1984-87; dep. prosecutor Lake County Prosecutor's Office, Crown Point, 1981-84; 87-94; assoc. James Wieser Law Offices, Highland, Ind., 1981-93; U.S. atty. no. dist. Ind. Dept. Justice, Dyer, 1993-99. Atty. Highland Police Commn., Highland, Ind., 1987— and Highland Water Bd., 1987—; legal advisor, Lake County Sheriff, Crown Point, Ind., 1986-87; atty. Hammond and East Chgo. Fedn. of Tchrs., 1986—. Councilman Hammond City Council, 1984-87; mem. Lake County Med. Ctr. Devel. Agy., 1988—, Greater Hammond Community Services, 1987—; treas. Little Calumet River Basin Com., 1986. Mem. Lake County Bar Assn. (bd. dirs. 1988-90), Justinian Soc. Democrat. Avocations: basketball, bolf, reading. Home: 8944 Liable Rd Hammond IN 46322-2248 Office: US Attorneys Office 5400 Federal Plz #1500 Hammond IN 46320-1843

DEHART, JACOB, Internet company executive; Student, Purdue U., Ind. Co-founder, v.p. skinnyCorp, parent co. of Threadless.com (t-shirt site), NakedandAngry.com (wallpaper site), ExtraTasty.com (drink recipes site), others, Chgo., 2000—. Named one of Top 40 Under 40, Crain's Chgo. Bus., 2006. Office: Skinnycorp STE 206 4043 N Ravenswood Ave Chicago IL 60613-2435

DEHAYES, DANIEL WESLEY, business educator; b. Columbus, Ohio, Sept. 23, 1941; s. Daniel Wesley and June Rosiland (Page) DeH.; children: Sarah Baxter, Benjamin Wesley. BA in Math. and Computer Sci., Ohio State U., 1963, MBA, 1964, PhD in Bus. Adminstrn., 1968. Asst. prof. systems analysis Naval Postgrad. Sch., Monterey, Calif., 1967-69; asst. prof. sch. bus. Ind. U., Bloomington, Ind., 1969-72, assoc. prof.sch. bus., 1972-79, prof. sch. bus., 1979—2005, prof. emeritus, 2005—, dean of acad. computing, 1981-86, asst. v.p. info. tech., 1987-88; dir. Ctr. For Entrepreneurship and Innovation, Ind. U., Bloomington, 1989-98. Exec. dir. Inst. Rsch. on the MIS, 1989-92; cons. in field. Textbook author; contbr. articles to profl. jours. Served to capt. U.S. Army, 1967-69 Recipient fellowships and grants Mem. Decision Scis. Inst. Republican. Methodist. Office: Indiana University Kelley School of Business Bloomington IN 47405 Business E-Mail: dehayes@indiana.edu.

DEHLER, STEVE, state legislator; b. 1950; m. Jean; 2 children. Student, St. John's U. State rep. Minn. Ho. Reps., Dist. 14A, 1993—. Home: PO Box 131231 Saint Paul MN 55113-0001

DEHNER, JOSEPH JULNES, lawyer; b. Cin., Nov. 28, 1948; s. Walter Joseph and Bess (Humphries) Dehner; m. Noel Julnes, Nov. 19, 1983; children: Holly Julnes, Sara Julnes. AB, Princeton U., 1970; JD, Harvard U., 1973. Bar: Ohio 1973, U.S. Dist. Ct. (no. and so. dists.) Ohio 1975, Fla. 1986, U.S. Dist. Ct. (ea. dist.) Ky. 1988, U.S. Ct. Internat. Trade 1992. Law clk. to judge U.S. Ct. Appeals, Cleve., 1973-75; assoc. Kyte, Conlan, Wulsin & Vogeler, Cin., 1975-78, Frost Brown Todd LLC, Cin., 1978—; chmn. Universal Transactions Inc., 1991-95. Co-mgr. Ukraine Investments Ltd., 1995—99. Author: (book) Structured Settlements and Periodic Payment Judgments, 1986, A Guide to Soviet Businesspeople on American Business Law, 1991, Doing Business in Russia, 1992, Dispute Resolution in China, 1994, A Foreign Investors Guide to Ukraine, 1995; contbr. articles to profl. publs. Sec., v.p. Cin. Preservation Assn., 1978—86; mem. Cin. Planning Commn., 1984—85; pres. Charter Com. Greater Cin., 1982—86; chmn. Cin.-Kharkiv Sister City Project, 1988—91; Ohio commodore, 2003—; pres. French-Am. C. of C. of Greater Cin., 2004—06; chmn. So. Ohio Dist. Export Coun., 2003—, Fgn. Policy Leadership Coun. Greater Cin., 2005—; mem. exec. coun. MULTILAW, 1997—; chmn. Hamilton County/Cin. Pub. Libr. Found., 2006—; pres. European-Am. C. of C. of Greater Cin., 2007—; chancellor Episcopal Diocese So. Ohio, 1997—; trustee Princeton (N.J.) U., 1970—74, Ohio Hist. Soc., 1974—78. Mem.: ABA (vice chmn. internat. litig. com. 2002—04, mem. multilaw exec. coun.), 6th Cir. Jud. Conf., Cin. Bar Assn., Ohio Bar Assn. (chmn. internat. law com. 1989—91), Pub. Investors Arbitration Bar Assn. Avocations: tennis, reading. Home: 822 Yale Ave Terrace Park OH 45174-1258 Office: Frost Brown Todd LLC 2200 PNC Ctr 201 E 5th St Ste 2200 Cincinnati OH 45202-4182 Office Phone: 513-651-6949. Business E-Mail: jdehner@fbtlaw.com.

DE HOYOS, DEBORA M., lawyer; b. Monticello, NY, Aug. 10, 1953; d. Luis and Marion (Kinney) de Hoyos; m. Walter C. Carlson, June 20, 1981; children: Amanda, Greta, Linnea. BA, Wellesley Coll., 1975; JD, Harvard U., 1978. Bar: Ill. 1978, U.S. Dist. Ct. (no. dist.) Ill. 1980. Assoc. Mayer, Brown & Platt, Chgo., 1978—84, ptnr., 1985—, mng. ptnr., 1991—. Bd. dirs. Evanston Northwestern Healthcare; bd. trustees Providence St. Mel. Sch. Contbr. chpt. to Securitization of Financial Assets, 1991. Trustee Chgo. Symphony Orch. Named one of the Ten Most Influential Women Lawyers in Ill., Am. Lawyer Media, 2000, Fifty Outstanding Women Graduates, Harvard Law Sch., 2003. Office: Mayer Brown Rowe Maw Llp 71L S Wacker Dr Chicago IL 60606-4637

DEININGER, DAVID GEORGE, judge; b. Monroe, Wis., July 9, 1947; s. Wilbur Emerson and Anna Emilie (Karlen) D.; m. Mary Carol Nussbaum, June 4, 1969; children: Jonathan David, Christopher Jacob, Emilie Joanne. BS, U.S. Naval Acad., 1969; JD, U. Wis., 1978. Bar: Wis. 1978, Ill. 1978, U.S. Dist. Ct. (we. dist.) Wis. 1978. Ptnr. Benkert, Spielman, Asmus & Deininger, Monroe, 1978-87; legislator Wis. State Assembly, Madison, 1987-94; of counsel Brennan, Steil, Basting & MacDougall, S.C., Monroe, 1988-94; cir. ct. judge Green County, 1994-96. Active Monroe Sch. Bd., 1986-89, Monroe Theatre Guild, 1980—; chmn. Green County Rep. Cen. Com., Monroe, 1982-84. Lt. USN, 1969-75. Mem. Green County Bar Assn. (pres. 1982-83), Wis. State Bar Assn., Am. Legion, VFW, Optimists (pres. Monroe chpt. 1984-85). Avocations: bridge, cross country skiing, boating. Home: 2615 Golf View Court Monroe WI 53566-3646 Office: Ct Appeals Dist IV Madison WI 53703-3330

DEISSLER, ROBERT GEORGE, fluid dynamics researcher; b. Greenville, Pa., Aug. 1, 1921; s. Victor Girard and Helen Stella (Fisher) D.; m. June Marie Gallagher, Oct. 7, 1950; children— Robert Joseph, Mary Beth, Ellen Ann, Anne Marie BS, Carnegie Inst. Tech., 1943; MS, Case Inst. Tech., 1948; PhD, Case Western Res. U., 1989. Researcher Goodyear Aircraft Corp., Akron, Ohio, 1943-44; aero. rsch. scientist NASA Lewis Rsch. Ctr., Cleve., 1947-52, chief fundamental heat transfer br., 1952-70, staff scientist, sci. cons. fluid physics, 1970-94, disting. rsch. assoc., 1994—. Fellow Lewis Rsch. Acad., 1983—; staff scientist sr. level emeritus, 1994. Author: Turbulent Fluid Motion, Taylor and Francis, 1998; contbr. articles to profl. jours.; areas of rsch. fluid turbulence, turbulent heat transfer, turbulent solutions of equations of fluid motion, nonlinear dynamics and chaos, meteorol. and astrophysical flows, radiative heat transfer in gases, heat transfer in powders. Served as lt. (j.g.) USNR, 1944-46 Recipient NACA/NASA Exceptional Svc. award, 1957, Outstanding Publ. award, 1978, Wisdom Soc. award, 2000; Lewis Rsch. Acad. fellow, 1983—. Fellow AIAA (Best Paper award 1975, Tech. Achievement award 1981), ASME (Heat Transfer Meml. award 1964, Max Jacob Meml. award 1975, Wisdom Hall of Fame 2000); mem. Am. Phys. Soc., Sigma Xi. Roman Catholic. Avocations: violin, reading, walking, natural theology. Home: 4540 W 213th St Fairview Park OH 44126-2106 Office: NASA Glenn Rsch Ctr 21000 Brookpark Rd Cleveland OH 44135-3191

DEITCH, LAURENCE B., lawyer; AB, U. Mich., 1969, JD, 1972. Ptnr. Bodman, Longley & Dahling LLP, Detroit. Vice chmn. Mich. Civil Svc. Commn.; bd. regents U. Mich., Ann Arbor, 1992—; treas. Mich. Dem. Party; pres. Temple Beth El, Bloomfield Hills, Mich. Office: Bodman Langley & Dahling LLP 100 Renaissance Ctr 34th Fl Detroit MI 48243

DEITRICK, WILLIAM EDGAR, lawyer; b. NYC, July 30, 1944; s. John English and Dorothy Alice (Geib) D.; m. Emily Jane Posey, June 22, 1968; children: William Jr., Elizabeth, Peter. BA, Johns Hopkins U., 1967; JD, Cornell U., 1971. Bar: Ill. 1972, U.S. Dist. Ct. (no. dist.) Ill. 1972, U.S. Ct. Appeals (7th cir.) 1976, D.C. 1981. Ptnr. Gardner, Carton and Douglas, Chgo., 1972—85; sr. v.p., dep. gen. counsel, mgr. litigation divsn. Continental Bank N.A., 1985—91; ptnr. Mayer, Brown, Rowe & Maw, Chgo., 1991—2003, sr. counsel, 2003—. Contbr. articles to profl. jours. Trustee North Shore Country Day Sch., 1992-97; gov. mem. Shedd Aquarium, 2000-04; With U.S. Army, 1968-70. Mem. ABA, Ill. Bar Assn., Chgo. Bar Assn., Johns Hopkins U. Alumni Assn. (class agt. 1967-95), Cornell Law Sch. Chgo. Alumni Assn. (chmn. 1985-87), Legal Club, Univ. Club Chgo. (bd. dirs. 2002-05), Indian Hill Club (bd. govs. Winnetka, Ill.). Home: 1360 N Lake Shore Dr # 1415 Chicago IL 60610 Office: Mayer Brown & Maw 71 S Wacker Dr Chicago IL 60606-4637

DEKKER, EUGENE EARL, biochemistry educator; b. Highland, Ind., July 23, 1927; s. Peter and Anne (Hendrikse) D.; m. Harriet Ella Holwerda, July 5, 1958; children: Gwen E., Paul D., Tom R. AB, Calvin Coll., 1949; MS, U. Ill., 1951, PhD, 1954. Instr. U. Louisville Med. Sch., 1954-56; instr. biol. chemistry U. Mich. Med. Sch., Ann Arbor, 1956-58, asst. prof., 1958-65, assoc. prof., 1965-70, prof., 1970-94, assoc. chmn. dept., 1975-88, emeritus prof., 1994—. With USN, 1945—46. Mem. AAAS, Am. Chem. Soc., Am. Soc. Biol. Chemists, Am. Soc. Plant Physiologists, Oxygen Soc., Protein Soc., Sigma Xi, Phi Lambda Upsilon. Mem. Christian Reformed Ch. Home: 4001 Glacier Hills Dr Apt 126 Ann Arbor MI 48105-3655 Office: U Mich Med Sch Dept Biol Chemistry Ann Arbor MI 48109-0606 Office Phone: 734-936-1144. Personal E-mail: eedekker@umich.edu.

DEKOOL, L.M. (THEO DEKOOL), food products executive; With CPC Benelux, B.V., Buhrmann Tetterode; v.p. fin. Household and Pers. Care divsn. Sara Lee/DE, Netherlands, 1990—93, CFO, 1995—96, Blokker retail chain; v.p. Sara Lee Corp., Chgo., 1996—2001, sr. v.p., 2001, exec. v.p., CFO & chief adminstr. officer, 2002—. Office: Sara Lee Corp 3 First Natiolnal Plz Chicago IL 60602

DEKREY, DUANE LEE, farmer, rancher; b. Jamestown, ND, June 20, 1956; s. John Edward and Alpha Ann (Whitman) DeK.; m. Jan M. DeKrey, June 18, 1983; children: Tyler John, Peder Robert, RoxAnne Marie. BS in Agr., N.D. State U., 1978. Tchr. agrl. edn. Devils Lake (N.D.) Sch., 1979; farmer, rancher JD Acres, Tappen, .D., 1979—; mem. N.D. Senate, Bismarck, 1990-92, N.D. House, Bismarck, 1994—; vice chair jud. com. N.D. Senate, Bismarck, 1997—. Mem. judiciary com. (chmn.), natural resources com. 2d lt. USAR, 1978—, maj. N.D. Nat. Guard, 1993. Mem. N.D. Stockmen Assn., Farm Bur. (past pres.), Res. Officers Assn., LAND (state dir., sec.), Farmers Union, Nat. Guard Assn. Republican. Congregationalist. Office: 4323 27th St SE Pettibone ND 58475-9357

DE LA CHAPELLE, ALBERT, education educator; Prof., chair dept. med. genetics U. Helsinki; dir. Human Cancer Genetics Program Comp Cancer Ctr. Arthur G James Cancer Hosp. and Rsch. Inst., Ohio State U., Columbus, 1998—; prof., chair divsn. human cancer genetics d dept. molecular biology, virology, immunology, med. genetics Ohio State U., Columbus, 1998—. Office: Ohio State Univ Human Cancer Genetics Rm 646 Med Rsch Facility 420 W 12th Ave Columbus OH 43210-1214

DE LA IGLESIA, FELIX ALBERTO, pathologist, toxicologist; b. Cordoba, Argentina, Nov. 27, 1939; s. Andres Avelino and Rosalia (Figueroa) De La Iglesia; m. Graciela Moreno, May 19, 1964; children: Felix Andres, Jose Vicente, Alberto Victor, Michele. MD, U. Cordoba, 1964. Dir. Warner-Lambert Rsch. Inst., Toronto, Ont., 1972-79; dir. toxicology Warner-Lambert/Parke-Davis, Ann Arbor, Mich., 1979-83; v.p. pathology and exptl. toxicology Parke-Davis Pharm. Rsch., Ann Arbor, Mich., 1983-2000; v.p. preclin. worldwide safety Parke-Davis R&D, 1983—2000; prof. pathology U. Toronto Sch. Medicine, 1981—. Adj. prof. toxicology, prof. pathology U. Mich. Med. Sch. Pub. Health, 1982—; cons. pharm. rsch. and devel., 2000—; founder, prin. FIP-Consulting, Mich., 2001—; founder, sr. cons. Cambridge Biotech. Ltd., 2001—; mem. sci. adv. bd. Cellomics, Pitts., Waratah Pharma, Boston; founder, chief sci. officer QRxPharma Pty Ltd., Sydney, 2002. Author: Molecular Biochemistry of Human Disease, 1985, Drug Toxicokinetics, 1993, Drug-Induced Hepatotoxicity, 1996. Served to 1st lt. Argentine Army Inf., 1954-56. Fellow Acad. Toxicological Scis. Avocations: collecting antique microscopes, vintage sports cars, commercial real estate development. Home and Office: 2307 Hill St Ann Arbor MI 48104-2651

DELANEY, CORNELIUS FRANCIS, philosophy educator; b. Waterbury, Conn., June 30, 1938; s. Patrick Francis and Margaret (Gavigan) D.; 1 child, Cornelius Francis Jr. MA, Boston Coll., 1961; PhD, St. Louis U., 1967. Prof. philosophy U. Notre Dame, Notre Dame, Ind., 1967—, chmn. philosophy dept., 1972-82, dir. honors program, 1989—. Author: Mind and Nature, 1969m The Synoptic Vision, 1977, Science, Knowledge and Mind, 1993, The Liberalism-Communitarianism Debate, 1994, New Essays on the Philosophy of C.S. Pierce, 2000. Recipient Madden award U. Notre Dame, 1974, Bicentennial award Boston Coll., 1976, Pres.'s award U. Notre Dame, 1984, Sheedy award U. Notre Dame,1987. Mem. Am. Cath. Philos. Assn. (pres. 1985), C.S. Peirce Soc. (pres. 1986), Am. Philos. Assn. (exec. com. 1983-85). Avocations: golf, tennis. Office: U Notre Dame Dept Philosophy 402 Malloy Hall Notre Dame IN 46556

DELANEY, EUGENE A., electronics executive; BS, So. Ill. U.; MBA, DePaul U. Chmn. Motorola China Electronics Ltd. Motorola, Inc., 2002—, joined, 1978, fin. analyst comm. sector, 1978, contr. Motorola Credit Corp., 1986, ops. mgr. ctrl. region cellular bus., 1989—94, v.p., dir. ops. ctrl. and N.E. region Pan Am. wireless infrastructure group, 1994—95, v.p., gen. mgr. Japan cellular infrastructure divsn., 1995—97, corp. v.p. cellular infrastructure group, 1997—98, exec. v.p., pres. global rels. and resources orgn., 2002—05, sr. v.p. Europe, Middle East, Africa and Asia/Pacific Govt. Enterprise Mobility Solutions Schaumburg, Ill., 2005—. Office: Motorola Inc 1303 E Algonquin Rd Schaumburg IL 60196

DELANEY, JAMES M., metal products executive; V.p. specialty metals group Ryerson Tull Inc., Chgo., 1999—, pres. Ryerson Ctrl., 1999—. Office: Ryerson Tull Inc 2621 W 15th Pl Chicago IL 60608-1752 Fax: 773-762-0437.

DELANGE, WALTER J., former state legislator; b. Grand Rapids, Mich., Nov. 9, 1931; s. Walter and Harriet DeL.; m. Lois A. Lindhout, 1951; three children. Mem. Kentwood City (Mich.) Bd. Rev., 1981; commr. Kent County, Mich., 1982; rep. Mich. Dist. 72, 1983-96. Majority caucus chmn. Mich. Ho. Reps., chmn. Rep. policy com., chmn. human resources & labor com., transp. com., regulatory com. Dir. Grand Rapids Home Builders Assn.; v.p. Mich. Assn. Home Builders, 1979-82, bd. dirs.; bd. dirs. Millbrook Christian Sch.; Sunday sch. tchr. Millbrook Christian Reformed Ch., former deacon, elder, tchr. catechism, clk. Home: 5815 Lindenwood Ct SE Kentwood MI 49512-9668

DELANY, JIM (JAMES EDWARD DELANY), sports association administrator, lawyer; b. South Orange, NJ, Mar. 3, 1948; m. Catherine Fisher; children: Newman, James Chancellor. BA in Polit. Sci., U. N.C., 1970, JD, 1973. Counsel N.C. Senate Judiciary Com., 1973-74; staff atty. N.C. Justice Dept., 1974-75; enforcement rep. NCAA, 1975-79; commr. Ohio Valley Conf., 1979-89, Big Ten Conf., 1989—. Mem. spl. adv. com. to review recommendations regarding distribution of revenues NCAA, ad hoc com. to administer the conf. grant program, spl. com. to study factors affecting automatic qualification into divsn. I men's basketball championship, spl. basketball T.V. negotiating com.; NCAA rep. USA Basketball Coun. Active Spl. Olympics, YMCA. Named one of The Most Influential People in the World of Sports, Bus. Week, 2007; named to The Newark, NJ Hall of Fame, The Ohio Valley Conf. Hall of Fame. Mem. N.C. Bar Assn., Black Coaches' Assn. (bd. advisors), Collegiate Commissioners Assn., Coll. Basketball Partnership, USA Basketball Exec. Com (v.p., 2000-) Office: Big Ten Conf 1500 Higgins Rd Park Ridge IL 60068-6300

DE LA RIVA, JUAN L., automotive company executive; BA, N.Y.U.; MBA, U. Detroit. Mng. dir., Light Vehicles Systems Wheels Meritor, Limeira, Brazil, v.p., bus. devel. comm., sr. v.p., bus. devel. comm., 1999—. Office: Meritor Auto Inc 2135 W Maple Rd Troy MI 48084-7121

DE LASA, JOSÉ M., lawyer; b. Havana, Cuba, Nov. 28, 1941; came to U.S., 1961; s. Miguel and Conchita de Lasa; m. Maria Teresa Figueroa, Nov. 23, 1963; children: Maria Teresa, José, Andrés, Carlos. BA, Yale U., 1968, JD, 1971. Bar: N.Y. 1973. Assoc. Cleary, Gottlieb, Steen & Hamilton, NYC, 1971-76; legal dept. Bristol-Myers Squibb Co., NYC, 1976-94; exec. v.p., gen. counsel Abbott Labs., 1994—2005; of counsel Baker & McKenzie, Chgo., 2005—. Lectr. internat. law, various locations. Bd. dirs. Am. Arbitration Assn., The Resource Found., Coun. Fgn. Rels., NY, The Stovir Found. Mem. ABA, Assn. of Bar of City of N.Y., Assn. Gen. Counsel, North Shore Gen. Counsel Assn., Ill. State Bar Assn. Roman Catholic. Office: Baker & McKenzie 114 Avenue of the Americas New York NY 10036 Business E-Mail: jose.delasa@bakernet.com.

DE LAWDER, C. DANIEL, bank executive; BA, Ohio U., 1971. With Park Nat. Corp., Newark, 1971-98, CEO, 1998—. Office: 50 N 3d St Newark OH 43055

DELBANCO, NICHOLAS FRANKLIN, language educator, writer; b. London, Aug. 27, 1942; came to U.S., 1948; s. Kurt and Barbara Gabriele Delbanco; m. Elena Greenhouse, Sept. 12, 1970; children: Francesca Barbara, Andrea Katherine. AB, Harvard U., 1963; MA, Columbia U., 1966. Mem. faculty Bennington (Vt.) Coll., 1966-85; prof. English Williams Coll., Williamstown, Mass., 1983, Skidmore Coll., Saratoga Springs, NY, 1984; Robert Frost Collegiate prof. English U. Mich., Ann Arbor, 1985—2006, disting. prof., 2006—. Dir. MFA in writing program U. Mich., 1985—03; vis. prof. Iowa U. Writer's Workshop, Iowa City, 1980; vis. adj. prof. Columbia U., N.Y.C., 1981, 96-98; founding dir. Bennington Writing Workshops, 1978-85; chair fiction panel Nat. Book Awards, N.Y.C., 1997; vis. fellow Woodrow Wilson Nat. Found., Princeton, N.J., 1981—. Author: Group Portrait: Conrad, Crane, Ford, James & Wells, 1983, The Writer's Trade, 1990, Running in Place: Scenes from the South of France, 1991, In the Name of Mercy, 1995, Old Scores, 1997, What Remains, 2000, Sincerest Form, 2003, Vagabonds, 2004, Spring and Fall, 2006, others; editor: Stillness and Shadows, 1985, Speaking of Writing, 1990, Bernard Malamud on Life and Art, 1996, others. Mem. ant. adv. bd. Writers in Schs. PEN Faulkner, Washington, 2000—; mem. governing bd. Mich. Journalism Fellows Program, 1990—; mem. Arts Am. U.S. Info. Agy., Washington, 1992. Fellow Nat. Endowment for Arts, 1973, 82, J.S. Guggenheim Meml. Found., 1980; named Mich. Author of Yr., Mich. Assn. Librs., 2002. Fellow Internat. Am. Studies and Lang. Faculty Salzburg; mem. Authors Guild, Authors League, PEN, Century Assn., Signet Soc., Phi Beta Kappa. Office: U Mich Hopwood Rm Angell Hall Ann Arbor MI 48109 Office Phone: 734-764-6296. Business E-Mail: delbanco@umich.edu.

DELEO, JAMES A., state legislator; b. Chgo., Aug. 10, 1951; m. Ann Filishio, 1991. Student, Loop Jr. Coll., DePaul U. Real estate salesman; mem. from 16th dist. Ill. Ho. of Reps., 1985-92; mem. Ill. State Senate, 1993—. Mem. Joint Civic Com. Italian-Ams. Office: 6839 W Belmont Ave Chicago IL 60634-4646 also: Senator 10th Dist 323 Capitol Bldg Springfield IL 62706

DE LERNO, MANUEL JOSEPH, retired electrical engineer; b. Jan. 8, 1922; s. Joseph Salvador and Elizabeth Mabry (Jordan) De L.; m. Margery Ellen Eaton, Nov. 30, 1946 (div. Oct. 1978); children: Diane, Douglas. BEE, Tulane U., 1941; MEE, Rensselaer Poly. Inst., 1943. Registered profl. engr., Ill., Mass. Devel. engr. indsl. control dept. GE, Schenectady, NY, 1941—44; design engr. Lexington Electric Products Co., Newark, 1946—47; test engr. Maschinenfabrik Oerlikon, Zurich, Switzerland, 1947—48; asst. prof. elec. engring. Newark Coll. Engring., 1948—49; application engr. Henry J. Kaufman Co., Chgo., 1949—55; pres. Del Equipment Co., Chgo., 1955—60, Gilberts, Ill., 2005—06, S-P-D Svcs. Inc., Forest Park, Ill., 1967—81, S-P-D Industries Inc., Berwyn, Ill., 1981—2001, S-P-D Inc., Schaumburg, Ill., 2001—05; v.p. Del-Ray Co., Chgo., 1960—67; ret., 2006. Lt. (j.g.) USNR, 1944-45. Mem. IEEE (sr., life), Ill. Soc. Profl. Engrs., Am. Water Works Assn. Home and Office: 36w760 Stonebridge Ln Saint Charles IL 60175-4931 Office Phone: 630-444-0507.

DELFS, ANDREAS, conductor, musical director; b. Flensburg, Germany; m. Amy Delfs; 4 children. Grad., Hamburg Conservatory, 1981; MA, Juilliard Sch., 1984. Staff conductor Lüneburg Stadttheater; music dir. Hamburg U. Orch.; musical asst. Hamburg State Opera; guest conductor Bremen State Theater, 1981; dir. Pitts. Youth Symphony; resident condr. Pitts. Symphony, 1986-90; music dir. Orch. Suisse Jeunes, 1984-95, Bern Opera, 1991-94; conductor N.Y. City Opera, 1995-96; music dir. Milw. Symphony Orch., 1997—; gen. music dir. Hannover State Opera and Orch., 1995—2000; music dir., artistic cons. St. Paul Chamber Orch., 2001—04. Guest condr. Phila. Orch. at Carnegie Hall, 1998, London Philharm., 1997, Dallas Symphony Orch., 1997, Houston Symphony, 1996—98, Junge Deutsche Philharmoni, Germany, 1995—98, Bern Symphony Orch., Minn. Orch., Detroit Symphony, Rochester Philharm. Bruno Walter scholar, Juilliard Sch., Steinburg fellow, Pitts. Symphony. Office: Milwaukee Symphony 700 N Water St #700 Milwaukee WI 53202-4239

DELGROSSO, DOUGLAS G., manufacturing executive; m. Kimberly DelGrosso; 1 child, Elle Marie. BS in Mech. Engring., Lawrence Technol. U.; MBA, Mich. State U. Design engr. Lear Corp., 1984, dir. product engring., 1991, v.p. ops. GM divsn., 1995, v.p./pres. Chrysler divsn., 1995, v.p./pres. GM divsn., 1997, sr. v.p. GM divsn., 1998, sr. v.p. interior sys. group and seat trim divsn., 1999, sr. v.p./pres. N.Am. and S.Am. ops., 1999, sr. v.p. product focus group, 2000, exec. v.p. internat. ops., 2001, pres., COO Europe, Asia and Africa Southfield, Mich., 2002—04, pres. COO Ams., 2004—05, pres., COO, 2005—. Bd. trustees Lawrence Technol. U., Southfield, Mich. Recipient Young Leadership and Excellence award, Automotive Hall of Fame, 1995, 40 Under 40 award, Crain's Detroit Bus., 1997. Office: Lear Corp 21557 Telegraph Rd PO Box 5008 Southfield MI 48086-5008 Office Phone: 248-447-1500.

DELLACORTE, CHRISTOPHER, engineer; b. Port Jefferson, NY, Dec. 10, 1963; s. Franklin Alfred and Suzanne DellaCorte; m. Patricia DellaCorte. BS, Case Western Res. U., 1986, MS, PhD, Case Western Res. U., 1987. Rsch. engr. Case Western Res. U., Cleve., 1986-87, NASA, Cleve., 1987—. Contbr. over 50 articles to profl. jours. Bd. dirs. Medina (Ohio) County Bd. Mental Retardation and Devel. Disabilities, 1992-96. Mem. ASME (Burt L. Newkirk award 1996, conf. planning com. 1995—), Soc. Tribologists and Lubrication (assoc. editor, solid lubricants com. chair 1989-92). Avocations: mechanical devices, technical history, natural history. Office: NASA Glenn Rsch Ctr MS 23-2 21000 Brookpark Rd Cleveland OH 44135-3191

DELLEUR, JACQUES WILLIAM, retired engineering educator; b. Paris, Dec. 30, 1924; came to U.S., 1952, naturalized, 1957; s. Georges Leon and Simone (Rossum) D.; m. DeLores Ann Horne, June 18, 1957; children: James Robert, Ann Marie. Civil and Mining Engr., Nat. U. Colombia, 1949; MS in Civil Engring., Rensselaer Poly. Inst., 1950; DEng Sci., Columbia U., 1955. Civil engr. R.J. Tipton and Assocs., 1950—52; from research asst. to instr. civil engring. and engring. mechanics Columbia U., 1952—55; mem. faculty Purdue U., 1955—95, prof. hydraulic engring. and hydrology, 1963—95, prof. emeritus hydraulic engring., 1995—, head hydromechanics and water resources area, 1965—76, head hydraulic and systems engring. area, 1981—90, 1991—92; assoc. dir. Purdue U. Water Resources Rsch. Ctr., 1971—89, acting dir., 1983. Rschr. fluid mechanics U. Grenoble, France, 1961-62, hydrology and environ. fluid mechanics French Nat. Hydraulics Lab., Chatou, France, 1968-69, 76-77, statis. hydrology U. Brussels, Belgium, 1991; NSF sr. exch. scientist U. Grenoble, France, 1983-84; vis. prof. U. Quebec, Canada, 1996—2005, Vrije U., Brussels, 1991—2005; mem. sci. coun. Revue des Sciences de L'eau/Water Scis. Sci. Interest Group/Nat. Inst. Sci. Rsch., Quebec, 1988—; vis. lectr. Ecole Polytechnique Federale de Lausanne, Switzerland, 1991, 93, 95, 97; coord. Consortium of U.S. and European Cmty. Univs. for Scholar and Multimedia Exchs. in Environ. and Water Resources Engring. and Scis., 1998-2003. Author and co-author 2 books on statis. hydrology; co-author book on urban hydorlogy; editor: Handbook of Groundwater Engineering, 1999, 2d edit., 2007; assoc. editor: Handbook of Civil Engineering, 1995, 2d edit., 2002; assoc. editor Jour. Hydraulic Engring., 2003—, also articles, reports in field. Recipient Ray K. Linsley award, Am. Inst. Hydrology, 2007. Fellow Ind. Acad. Sci.; mem. ASCE (Freeman fellow 1961-62, chmn. fluid dynamics com. 1964-66, task com. mechanics of turbulence 1964-69, task com. hydraulics of bridges 1963-68, task com. on rehab. urban drainage infrastructure 1988-90, co-chmn. task com. on urban drainage rehab. and techniques 1990-94, chmn. com. urban water resources 1994-95, chmn. com. sediment movement in urban drainage sys. 1998-2003, internat. bd. advisors Jour. Hydrologic Engring. 1996—, Svc. to the Profession award 2000, Ven Te Chow Hydrology award 2002, Type 2 award, Environ. and Water Resources Inst., 2003), Am. Geophys. Union (chmn. urban hydrology com. 1978-83), Am. Water Resources Assn., Am. Soc. Engring. Edn., Internat. Assn. Hydraulic Rsch. (U.S. del. joint com. on urban storm drainage with Internat. Assn. Water Quality 1987-93), Internat. Assn. Sci. Hydrology, Ind. Water Resources Assn. (Charles Harold Bechert award 1992), Wabash Area Lifetime Learning Assn. (pres. 2007—). Home: 124 Mohican Pl West Lafayette IN 47906-2159 Office: Purdue U Sch Civil Engring 550 Stadium Mall Dr West Lafayette IN 47907-2051

DELLINGER, ROBERT J., corporate financial executive; BA in Econs., Ohio Wesleyan U., 1982. Pres., CEO Frankona Re GE, Munich, with fin. mgmt. program in consumer electronics bus. to corp. audit staff and exec. audit mgr., 1989, various mgr. positions, 1990—93, dir. fin. and bus. devel. plastics Singapore, 1993, mgr. fin. motor and indsl. sys., 1995, officer, exec. v.p., CFO, 1997; CFO, exec. v.p. Sprint Nextel Corp., Shawnee Mission, Kans., 2002—05; exec. v.p., CFO Delphi Corp., Troy, Mich., 2005—. Serve numerous bds. GE Plastics, GE Employers Reinsurance Corp. bds., Europe, Asia, US, Employers Reinsurance Corp., GE Frankona Re, GE Global Ins. Holdings, Employers Reinsurance Corp. Life, 2002—. Mem.: Fin. Execs. Inst. Office: Delphi Corp 5725 Delphi Dr Troy MI 48098-2815

DELL'OSSO, LOUIS FRANK, neuroscience educator; b. Bklyn., Mar. 16, 1941; s. Frank and Rose (Perrone) Dell'O.; m. Aquilina Marie Ferlo, May 22, 1965 (div. 1976); single ptnr. Charlene Hale Morse, Sept. 30, 1977. BEE, Bklyn. Poly. Inst., 1961, postgrad., 1961-63; PhD, U. Wyo., 1968. Co-dir. Ocular Motor Neurophysiology Lab. VA. Med. Ctr., Miami, Fla., 1972-80; asst. prof. biomed. engring. and surgery U. Miami, 1970-72, asst. prof. neurology, 1972-75, assoc. prof. neurology, 1975-79, prof. neurology, 1979-80; dir. Ocular Motor Neurophysiology Lab. VA Med. Ctr., Cleve., 1980—2004; prof. neurology and biomed. engring. Case Western Res. U., Cleve., 1980—, dir. Daroff-Dell'Osso Ocular Motility Lab., 2004—. Cons. Westinghouse Research Lab, Pitts, 1966-67, 70-71, Mt. Sinai Hosp., Miami, Fla., 1972-75. Bd. dirs. Vineland Galloway Civic Assn., Miami, 1973-76. Grantee NIH, 1971-77, VA Med. Ctr., 1972—, NSF, 1970. Fellow N.Am. euroOphthalmology Soc.; mem. IEEE, Engring. in Medicine and Biology Soc. (sr., chpt. chmn. 1977-78), Assn. Rsch. in Vision and Ophthalmology, Soc. eurosci., NY Acad. Scis., Train Collectors Assn., CCCC Rod & Gun Club. Democrat. Home: 2356 Tudor Dr Cleveland OH 44106-3212 Office Phone: 216-421-3224. Business E-Mail: lfd@case.edu.

DELMORE, LOIS M., state legislator; m. Michael Delmore; 2 child. Student, U. N.D. Tchr. English Red River H.S.; mem. Dist. 43 N.D. Ho. of Reps.; mem. judiciary and polit subdivsn. coms. N.D. State Senate. Mem. N.D. State Tchrs. Assn. Home: 714 S 22nd St Grand Forks ND 58201-4138

DELONG, DEBORAH, lawyer; b. Louisville, Sept. 5, 1950; d. Henry F. and Lois Jean (Stepp) D.; children: Amelie DeLong, Samuel Prentice. BA, Vanderbilt U., 1972; JD, U. Cin., 1975. Bar: Ohio 1975, Ky. 1999, U.S. Dist. Ct. (so. dist.) Ohio 1975, U.S. Ct. Appeals (Fed., 6th & 11th cirs.) 1990, 1991, 1995, U.S. Supreme Ct. 1982. Assoc. Paxton & Seasongood, Cin., 1975-82, ptnr., 1982-88, Thompson, Hine & Flory, 1989—2001, Dinsmore & Shohl LLP, Cin. Contbr. articles to profl. jours. Bd. dirs. Cin. Opera, Cin. Shakespeare Festival, Clovernook Ctr. for the Blind; bd. Trustees (Legal Counsel) cin. Opera Assn.; bd. dir. Family edn. ctr.; mem. American Heart Assn., Junior League of cin. Named Ohio Super Lawyer, Law & Politics Media; recipient Leading Women of cin. Award, 2000. Mem. ABA (litig. com. Pretrial Practice Discovery; Labor and litig. sect.), Ohio State Bar Assn., Cin. Bar Assn., Ky. Bar Assn., no. Ky. Bar Assn.,Ohio State Bar Assn.(Labor & Employment Law Com.), cin. Bar Assn.(Labor and Employment Law Com., cert. Grievance Com., past Chair), fed. Bar Assn. exec. Com., U.S. Dist. Ct., Ohio, 1984, def. Research inst., Arbitration Tribunal, Common Pleas Ct. Arbitration Panel, 1975-, Solicitation Com., U.S. Dist. Ct., Ohio, 1984. Republican. Episcopalian. Office: Dinsmore & Shohl LLP Ste 1900 255 E 5th St Cincinnati OH 45202 Office Phone: 513-977-8200.

DELONG, RAY, editor; Copy editor Dayton Jour. Herald, Ohio, 1972-73; editor, reporter Chgo. Daily News, 1973-78; city editor Columbia Missourian, summer 1980; freelance writer, 1978—; editor Bus. Law Today ABA Pub., Chgo., 1986—. Asst. prof. journalism U. Ill., 1978-84; asst. prof. Medill Sch. Journalism, orthwestern U., 1984-86; lectr. Univ. Coll., Northwestern U., 1985-2001. Office: ABA Publishing 321 N Clark St Chicago IL 60610-4403

DELOREY, JOHN ALFRED, printing company executive; b. Malden, Mass., July 13, 1924; s. John Alfred and Alice Gertrude (Collins) D.; m. Ann M. Abbott, Dec. 27, 1952; children— Debra Ann, Michael John, David Abbott BS in Econs., Boston Coll., 1950; MBA, Harvard U., 1953. Plant mgr. Container Corp. Am., Renton, Wash., 1965-69, mgf. mgr. Carol Stream, Ill., 1969-73, gen. mgr. St. Louis, 1973-77, Carol Stream, 1977-81, v.p., divsn. gen. mgr. St. Louis, 1981-82; exec. v.p. W.F. Hall Printing Co., Chgo., 1982-87; v.p. Container Corp. Am., 1987-93; pres. DeLorey & Assocs., Oak Brook, Ill., 1993—. Dir. Container Corp. Am. Polit. Action Com., Chgo., 1981-86. Author: (with others) Consumer Packaging, 1953 Served to maj. USAF, 1942-53, ETO. Decorated DFC, Air medal with 3 oak leaf clusters, European Theater medal with 3 battle stars. Mem.: Paperboard Packaging Assn. (dir. midwest region 1977—81), Boston Coll. Club (Naples, Fla.), Kensington Country Club, Harvard Bus. Club, Butterfield Country Club. Avocations: golf, swimming, skiing, bridge, reading. Home and Office: DeLorey & Assocs 194 Briarwood Loop Oak Brook IL 60523-8714

DELP, WILBUR CHARLES, JR., lawyer; b. Cedar Rapids, Iowa, Oct. 26, 1934; s. Wilbur Charles and Irene Frances (Flynn) D.; m. Patricia Lynn Vesely, June 22, 1963; children: Marci Lynn, Melissa Kathryn, Derek Charles. BA, Coe Coll., 1956; LLB, NYU, 1959. Bar: Ill. 1960, U.S. Supreme Ct. 1962. Assoc. Sidley Austin, Chgo., 1959—68, ptnr., 1968—2000, sr. counsel, 2000—. Lectr. securities law seminars With USAF, 1959-65. Mem. ABA (securities com.), Chgo. Bar Assn., Lawyers Club (Chgo.), Phi Beta Kappa, Phi Kappa Phi. Home: 34W880 Army Trail Rd Saint Charles IL 60174 Office: Sidley Austin One S Dearborn St Chicago IL 60603-0001 Office Phone: 312-853-7416. Personal E-mail: retlaw1934@aol.com. Business E-Mail: wdelp@sidley.com.

DELPH, DONNA JEAN (MAROC), education educator, consultant, academic administrator; b. Hammond, Ind., Mar. 7, 1931; d. Edward Joseph and Beatrice Catherine (Ethier) Maroc; m. Billy Keith Delph, May 30, 1953 (div. 1967); 1 child, James Eric. BS, Ball State U., 1953, MA, 1963, EdD, 1970. Cert. in ednl. adminstrn./supervision, reading specialist, Ind.; cert. elem. sch. tchr., Ind., Calif. Elem. tchr. Long Beach (Calif.) Community Schs., 1953-54; elem. tchr., reading specialist, asst. dir. elem. edn. Hammond Pub. Schs., 1954-70; prof. edn. Purdue U. Calumet, Hammond, 1970-84, 88-90, prof. emeritus, 1990—, head dept. edn., dir. tchr. edn., 1984-88. Cons. pub. schs., Highland, Ind., 1970-88, Gary, Ind., 1983-88, East Chicago, Ind., 1987-88, Hammond, 1970-88; speaker/workshop presenter numerous profl. orgns., Hammond, 1964—; mem. exec. coun. Nat. Coun. Accreditation Tchr. Edn., 1991-97. Author: (with others) Individualized Reading, 1967; contbr. articles, monographs to profl. jours. Bd. dirs. Bethany Child Care and Devel. Ctr., Hammond, 1972-77. Recipient Outstanding Teaching award Purdue U. Calumet, 1981. Mem. Assn. Tchr. Educators, Assn. for Supervision and Curriculum Devel. (rev. coun. 1987-91, bd. dirs. 1974-85), Internat. Reading Assn., Ind. Reading Profs. (pres. 1985-86), Pi Lambda Theta. Office: Purdue Univ Calumet Dept Education Hammond IN 46323 Personal E-mail: donnajdelph@bellsouth.net.

DEL SALTO, CARLOS, pharmaceutical executive; B in Acctg., Juan de Velazco Coll., Ecuador; M in Fin., Roosevelt U., Chgo. Fin. auditor Baxter Internat., Deerfield, Ill., 1973—84; gen. mgr. Baxter Mex., 1984—88; v.p. L.Am. ops. Baxter Internat., 1988—92, pres. L.Am., Switzerland, Austria, 1991—92; sr. v.p. Baxter World Trade Corp., Deerfield, Ill., 1996—, corp. v.p., 1992—96; chmn. L.Am. bd. Baxter Internat., Inc. Office: Baxter Internat Inc One Baxter Pkwy Deerfield IL 60015

DE LUCIA, FRANK CHARLES, physicist, researcher; b. St. Paul, June 21, 1943; s. Frank Charles and Muriel Ruth (Rinehart) D.; m. Shirley Ann Wood, June 25, 1966; children: Frank Charles, Elizabeth Ann. BS, Iowa Wesleyan Coll., 1964; PhD, Duke U., 1969. Instr, research assoc. Duke U., Durham, NC, asst. prof., assoc. prof.; program mgr. Army Research Office, Research Triangle Park, NC; prof. Duke U., Durham, chmn. physics dept.; prof., chmn. dept. physics Ohio State U., Columbus, 1990-98, prof., 1998—. Recipient Max Planck Rsch. prize, 1992, William F. Meggers award, 2001; named Disting. rsch. scholar, 1999, Disting. Univ. prof., 2000. Mem. Am. Phys. Soc., IEEE, Optical Soc. Am., Phi Beta Kappa. Office: Ohio State U Dept Of Physics Columbus OH 43210 Office Phone: 614-688-4774. Business E-Mail: fcd@mps.ohio-state.edu.

DELUHERY, PATRICK JOHN, retired state official; b. Birmingham, Ala., Jan. 31, 1942; s. Frank B. and Lucille (Donovan) D.; m. Margaret Morris, 1973; children: Allison, orah, Rose. BA with honors, U. Notre Dame, 1964; BSc in Econs. with honors, London Sch. Econs., 1967. Legis. asst. U.S. Senator Harold Hughes, Washington, 1969-74, U.S. Senator John Culver, Washington, 1975; asst. prof. econs. and fin. St. Ambrose U., Davenport, Iowa, 1975—2007; COO Gen. Svcs. Enterprise Iowa Dept. Adminstrv. Svcs., Des Moines, 2002—05; dir. strategic partnerships Dept. Adminstrv. Svcs., Des Moines, 2005—07. Mem. Iowa State Senate, 1979-2002. Democrat. Roman Catholic. Home: 629 Foster Dr Des Moines IA 50312-2517

DEL VALLE, MIGUEL, state legislator; b. PR, July 24, 1951; m. Lupe; 4 children. BA, MA, Northeastern Ill. U. Mem. dist. 2 Ill. State Senate, 1987—; chmn. consumer affairs, vice chmn. com. and econ. devel., mem. appropriations II, higher edn., revenue and elections and reapportionment coms. also: Ill State Senate Capitol Bldg Springfield IL 62706-0001

DELZER, JEFF W., state legislator; Student, Dawson CC. Farmer/rancher; rep. Dist. 8 N.D. Ho. of Reps., 1991-92, 95—, mem. indsl., bus. and labor and transp. coms., mem. appropriations com., 1997, 99, chmn. interim budget com. on human svcs., 1999. Home: 2919 5th St NW Underwood ND 58576-9603 Office: ND Ho of Reps State Capitol 600 E Boulevard Ave Bismarck ND 58505-0660

DEMAIN, JOHN, opera company director; b. Youngstown, Ohio, Jan. 11, 1944; m. Barbara DeMain; 1 child, Jennifer. BMus, Juilliard Sch. Music, 1966, MusM, 1968; studies in conducting with, Leonard Bernstein, Peter Adler. Assoc. condr. St. Paul Chamber Orch., 1972-74; music dir. Tex. Opera Theater, 1974-76; former music dir. Houston Grand Opera, Opera Omaha; music dir. Madison Symphony Orch., Wis., 1994—; artistic adv. Madison Opera, Wis., 1994—; artistic dir. & prin. condr. Opera Pacific, Calif., 1998—. Prin. guest condr. Chautauqua Opera Inst., 1985. Rec. performances: Piano Concerto (Frances Thorne), 1975, Porgy and Bess, 1976, Nocturnes (Miriam Gideon), 1978. Finalist Grand Prix, 1977; recipient Julius Rudel award, 1971, Grammy award, 1977; Juilliard Sch. Music scholar, 1964—68. Office: Madison Symphony Orchestra 222 W Washington Ave Ste 460 Madison WI 53703-2744 also: Opera Pacific 600 West Warner Ave Santa Ana CA 92707 E-mail: jldemain@operapacific.org.

DE MARCO, THOMAS JOSEPH, periodontist, educator; b. Farmingdale, NY, Feb. 12, 1942; s. Joseph Louis and Mildred Nora (Cifarelli) De M.; children: Todd Gordon, Kristin Alice, Lisa Anne. BS, U. Pitts., 1962; DDS, 1965; PhD, certificate in Periodontology, Boston U., 1968; cert. in fin. planning, Coll. Fin. Planning, Denver, 1976. Certificate in clin. hypnosis. Practice dentistry specializing in periodontics and implants, Cleve., 1968—; mem. staff Met. Gen. Hosp., Cleve., Univ. Hosp., Cleve., VA Hosp., Cleve.; asst. prof. periodontics and pharmacology Case-Western Res. U., 1968-70, assoc. prof., 1970-73, prof., 1973-84; asso. dean Case-Western Res. U. (Sch. Dentistry), 1972-76, dean, 1976-84; pvt. practice periodontia, 1984—. Author review books in dentistry, book on fin. planning, also articles on periodontology, pharmacology, fin. planning. Grantee Air Force Office Sci. Research, 1969; grantee Upjohn Co., 1970; grantee Columbus Dental Mfg. Co., 1971. Mem. Am. Acad. Periodontology, Internat. Assn. Dental Research, Am. Soc. for Preventive Dentistry (past pres. Ohio chpt.) Home: 12370 Rockhaven Rd Chesterland OH 44026-2744 Office: 29001 Cedar Rd Cleveland OH 44124 Home Phone: 440-285-2444; Office Phone: 440-995-1961. Personal E-mail: tjdbon@juno.com.

DEMARIA, MARK, construction executive; b. 1974; Developer DeMaria Bldg. Co.; prin., co-founder Denali Devel. Grp., Royal Oak, Mich., 2003—. Named one of 40 Under 40, Crain's Detroit Bus., 2006. Office: Denali Development Group 230 E Harrison Ave Royal Oak MI 48067 Office Phone: 248-545-6800. Office Fax: 248-545-6886.

DE MARIA, PAOLO, policy advisor; Grad. in Econ., Furman U., grad. in Polit. Sci.; M in Pub. Adminstrn., Ohio State U., 1996. Sr. fiscal analyst fin. com. Ohio Senate, Columbus; mem. gubernatorial transition team Gov. George V. Voinovich, Columbus; asst. dir. Office Budget and Mgmt., Columbus, dir., 1998-2000; chief polity adv. Gov. Ohio Office, Columbus, 2000—. Office: 77 S High Sch 30th Fl Columbus OH 43215-6117

DE MAYNADIER, PATRICK D., lawyer; b. Wooster, Ohio, May 30, 1960; m. Heather de Maynadier. BA in Philosophy, U. Va., 1982, JD, 1985; student, Advanced Mgmt., Harvard U., 1999. Atty. Bracewell & Patterson, LLP, Houston; assoc. gen. counsel Falcon Seaboard Resources, Inc., Houston, 1995—96; sr. v.p., gen. counsel, sec. Sterling Diagnostic Imaging, Inc., Greenville, SC, 1996—99; pres., CEO SDI Investments LLC (spin-off of Sterling Diagnostic Imaging, Inc.), 1999—2005; exec. v.p., gen. counsel, sec. CombiMatrix Corp., Mukilteo, Wash., 2000—01; v.p., gen. counsel, sec. Hillenbrand Industries, Inc., 2002—. Mem.: DC Bar Assn., State Bar Tex. Office: Hillenbrand Industries Inc Mail Code Y-20 700 State Route 46 E Batesville IN 47006

DEMBOWSKI, PETER FLORIAN, foreign language educator; b. Warsaw, Dec. 23, 1925; arrived in U.S., 1966, naturalized, 1974; s. Wlodzimierz and Henryka (Sokolowski) D.; m. Yolande Jessop, June 29, 1954; children: Anne, Eve, Paul. BA with honors, U. BC, 1952; Doctorat d'Universite, U. Paris, France, 1954; PhD, U. Calif., Berkeley, 1960. Instr. French U. B.C., 1954-56; asst. prof. French U. Toronto, 1960-63, assoc. prof., 1963-66; mem. faculty U. Chgo., 1966-95, prof. French, 1970-95, Disting. Svc. prof., 1989-95, prof. emeritus, 1995—, dean students div. humanities, 1968-70, chmn. dept. Romance langs. and lits., 1976-83, resident master Snell-Hitchcock halls, 1973-79; vis. mem. Sch. Hist. Studies, Inst. Advanced Study, Princeton, NJ, 1979-80. Author: La Chronique de Robert de Clari, 1963, Jourdain de Blaye, 1969, Ami et Amile, 1969, La Vie de sainte Marie l'Egyptienne, 1977, Jean Froissart and his Meliador, 1983, Jean Froissart, Le Paradis d'Amour et l'Orloge Amoureus, 1986, Erec et Enide, 1994, L'Estrif de Fortune et Vertu, 1999, Christians in the Warsaw Ghetto: An Epitaph for the Unremembered, 2005. Served with Polish Army, 1944-46. Decorated Cross of Valor, Cross of Service with swords (Poland), Chevalier des Palmes Academiques (France); Guggenheim fellow, 1970-71; Danforth Found. assoc., 1976-84 Fellow Am. Acad. Arts and Scis.; mem. Société de Linguistique Romane (councillor 1995-99), Medieval Acad. Am. (councillor 1980-82). Office: U Chgo Dept Romance Langs and Lit 1050 E 59th St Rm 205B Chicago IL 60637-1559 Business E-Mail: p_dembowski@uchicago.edu.

DEMBROWSKI, NANCY J., state senator; m. Ed Dembrowski (dec.); children: Michael, Rebecca, Patrick. With WKVI Radio, Knox, Ind.; mayor Knox, Ind.; state sen. 5th dist. Ind. State Senate, Indpls., 2002—, mem. elections and civic affairs com., civic affairs subcom., mem. judiciary com., cts. and juvenile justice subcom., mem. govtl. affairs and interstate cooperation com, govtl. affairs subcom. Mem.: numerous C. of C., Starke County Jr. Achievement (pres.), Starke United (chair), Starke County Youth Club (sec.), Kiwanis Club. Democrat. Roman Catholic. Avocations: reading, gardening. Office: Indiana State Senate 200 W Washington St Indianapolis IN 46204-2787

DEMBSKI, STEPHEN MICHAEL, composer, music educator; b. Boston, Dec. 13, 1949; s. Theodore Arthur and Minna Morris (Baldauf) D.; m. Sonja Sullivan, July 9, 1988; children: Melissa Leonora, Rachel Michalena. BA, Antioch Coll., 1973; MA, SUNY, Stony Brook, 1975; MFA, Princeton U., 1977, PhD, 1980. Dir. advanced composition program U. Wis., Madison, 1982—; prof., 1982—. Bd. dirs. Composers' Recordings, Inc., N.Y.C., Internat. Soc. Contemporary Music, N.Y.C., N.Y. New Music Ensemble, Phantom Arts, Boston; vis. asst. prof. Dartmouth Coll., Hanover, N.H., 1978-81, Bates Coll., Lewiston, Maine, 1982; mem. editl. bd. Spectrum. Composer musical scores including Pterodactyl, 1974, Of Mere Being, 1975, 82, Tender Buttons, 1977, Trio, 1977, Hard Times, 1978, Singles, 1980, Caritas, 1980, Alba, 1980, Alta, 1981, String Quartet, 1984, At Baia, 1984, Spectra, 1985, The Show, 1986, Sonata for Violin and Piano, 1987-88, Digit, 1978, Stacked Deck, 1979, Altamira, 1983, On Ondine, 1991-2000, Two Scenes from Elsaveta, 1992, So Fine, 1993, For Five, 1994, Hornbill, 1994, Memory's Minefield, 1994, Needles & Pins, 1994, Out of My System, 1995, Sonotropism, 1996, Brass Attacks, 1998, Le Monde Merengue, 1999, Contemplations, 2000, Tu m'hai si piena, 2000, Fool's Paradise, 48 Proverbs of Hell, 2004, Pied Beauty, 2002, Respite from the Roast, 2002, Only Yesterday, 2002, Another Day, 2001; composer recordings including CRI, 1988, 90, Vienna Modern Masters, 1990, Music and Arts, 1997, 96 Gestures, 2001,; condr. recordings include Scott Fields' 48 Motives, Cadence, 1996, The Diary of Dog Drexel, 2002; (books) Internat. Music Lexicon, 1979, 84 (with others) The Collected Essays of Milton Babbitt, 2003, (with Joseph N. Straus) Words About Music, 1987, (with others) Lexique Musical International, 1979; editor: (with others) Milton Babbitt-Words About Music, 1987; editl. bd. Perspectives of New Music, 2002-. Bd. dirs. League Composers I.S.C.M. U.S. Chpt., NY New Music Ensemble, Composers Recordings, bd. adv., 1979—83. Fellow Howard Found., Providence, 1986-87, Nat. Endowment for the Arts, Washington, 1979, 81, 86; recipient Goddard Lieberson award Am. Acad. and Inst. of Arts and Letters, 1982, Segnalazione: Premio Musicale award Citta di Trieste, 1990, honors Pa. Coun. Arts. Commn. Network New Music, 1995. Mem. ASCAP, Soc. for Music Theory, Am. Music Ctr. Office: U Wis Sch of Music 455 N Park St Madison WI 53706-1405 E-mail: sdembski@facstaff.wisc.edu.

DEMERDASH, NABEEL ALY OMAR, electrical engineer; b. Cairo, Apr. 26, 1943; came to U.S., 1966; s. Aly Omar and Aziza D.; m. Esther Adel Feher, Feb. 22, 1969; children: Yvonne, Omar, Nancy. BScEE with 1st class honors, Cairo U., 1964; MSEE, U. Pitts., 1967, PhD, 1971. Tchg. asst. in elec. engring. Cairo U., 1964—66, U. Pitts., 1966-68; engr. Westinghouse Electric Corp., Pitts., 1968-72; asst. prof. elec. engring. Va. Poly. Tech. Inst. and State U., Blacksburg, 1972-77, assoc. prof. elec. engring., 1977-81, prof., 1981-83; prof. dept. elec. and computer engring. Clarkson U., Potsdam, NY, 1983-94; prof., chmn. dept. elec. and computer engring. Marquette U., Milw., 1994-97, prof. dept. elec. and computer engring., 1994—. Cons. Sundstrand Corp., Rockford, Ill., 1985-98. Contbr. articles to profl. jours. Recipient Cert. of Recognition, NASA, 1979, Cert. of Tchg. Excellence, Va. Poly. Inst. and State U., 1980, Tchr. of Yr. award, Beta Omicron chpt. Eta Kappa Nu, Marquette Univ., 2003, Outstanding Rsch. award Coll. Engring, Marquette U., 2004. Fellow IEEE (subcom. chmn. 1988-92, 94-97, Nikola Tesla award 1999); mem. IEEE Power Engring. Soc. (disting. lectr. 1987—, Elec. Machinery Com. prize paper award 1993, working group award 1994, PES prize paper award 1993, working group award 1994), Indsl. Electronics Soc. (Disting. Spkr. program 1990—), Electromagnetics Acad. Achievements include development of three dimensional finite element vector potential and coupled 3D vector potential-scalar potential methods of solution of electromagnetic fields in electric devices; time-stepping coupled finite element-state space computer simulation models and design of electronically operated/controlled AC and DC motor drives. Office: Marquette Univ Elec Computer Engring Dept PO Box 1881 Milwaukee WI 53201-1881 Office Phone: 414-288-5680. Business E-Mail: nabeel.demerdash@marquette.edu.

DEMERITT, STEPHEN R., food products executive; Various consumer food mktg. positions General Mills Inc., 1969—, pres. Internat. Foods, 1991-93, CEO Cereal Ptnrs. Worldwide, vice chmn., 1999—. Office: General Mills Inc PO Box 1113 One General Mills Blvd Minneapolis MN 55440-1113

DEMERS, JUDY LEE, retired state legislator, dean; b. Grand Forks, ND, June 27, 1944; d. Robert L. and V. Margaret (Harming) Prosser; m. Donald E. DeMers, Oct. 3, 1964; div. Oct. 1971; 1 child, Robert M.; m. Joseph M. Murphy, Mar. 5, 1977; div. Oct. 1983. BS in nursing, U. N.D., 1966; M in Edn., U. Wash., 1973, post grad., 1973-76. Pub. health nurse Govt., Wash., DC, 1966-68; Combined Nursing Svc., Mpls., 1968-69; instr. pub. health nursing U. N.D., Grand Forks, ND, 1969-71; assoc. dir. Medex program, 1970-72; rsch. assoc. U. Wash., Seattle, 1973-76; dir. family nurse practitioner program, 1977-82; dir. under grad. med. edn., 1982-83; assoc. dir. rural health ND, 1982-85; mem. N.D. Ho. of Reps., 1982-92; assoc. dean, 1983—; mem. N.D. Senate, 1992-2000. Cons. health manpower devel. staff, Honolulu, 1975-81, Assn. Physician asst. programs, Washington, 1979-82; site visitor cons., AMA Com. Allied Health Edn. Accreditation, Chgo.,1979-81. Author: Educating New Health Practitioners, 1976; mem. editl. bd.: P.A. Jour., 1976-78; contbr. articles to profl. jours. Sec., bd. dirs. Valley Health, Grand Forks, N.D., 1982—; mem. exec. com., bd. dirs. Agassiz Health Systems Agy., Grand Forks, 1982-86; mem. N.D. State Daycare Adv. Com., 1983-93, Mayor's Adv. com. on Police Policy, Grand Forks, 1983-85, N.D. State Foster Care Adv. Com., 1985-87, N.D. State Hypertension Adv. Com., 1983-85, Gov.'s Com. on DUI and Traffic Safety, 1985-91, State wide Adv. Com. on AIDS, 1985-90; bd. dirs. Casey Found., Families First Initiative, 1988-97, Comprehensive Health Assn. N.D., 1993-95, United Health Found., 1990-97, Northern Valley Mental Health Assn., 1994-00, bd. dir., Grand Forks Girl's and Women's Hockey Assn., 1999-2002; bd. dirs., sec.-treas., exec. com., program com., fundraising com., vice-chmn. Devel. Homes, 1999—; adv. bd. Mountainbrooke (formerly Friendship Place), 1992-96; adv. com. Ruth Meiers Adolescent Ctr., Grand Forks, 1988-2002, Altru Health Sys. Corp. Bd., 1997-2006; mem. Commn. on Future Structure of VA Health Care, 1990-91; bd. dirs. Red River Valley Cmty. action Program, 1991—; mem. Resource and Referral Bd. Dirs., 1990-2005; caring coun. N.D. Blue Cross and Blue Shield Caring Program for Children, 1995-99; coun. mem. N.D. Health Task Force, 1992-94; healthcare subcom. Northern Gt. Plains Econ. Devel. Commn., 1995-96; adv. com. on telecomms. and healthcare FCC, 1996; mem., chmn. Grand Forks City and County Bd. Health, 2000—. Named Nurse of Yr., 1983; recipient: Pub. Citizen of Yr. Award, N.D. chpt., Nat. Assn. Social Workers, 1986, Golden Grain Award, N.D. Dietetic Assn., 1988, Person of Yr. Award, U. N.D., Law Women Caucus, 1990, Legislator of Yr. award North Valley Labor Coun., 1990, .D., Martin Luther King Jr. Award, 1990, Legislator of Yr. Award, Mental Health Assn., N.D., 1993, N.D. Libr. Assn. Legislator of Yr., 1999, Friend of Medicine Award N.D. Med. Assn., 1999, Legislator of Year Award, N.D. Pub. Employees Assn., 1999, Friend of Counseling Award, N.D. State Counseling Assn., 2000, Legislative Svc. Award, ARC of N.D., Friend of Higher Edn. Award, AAUP, 1995; named to Nursing Hall of Fame, 2002. Mem. N.D. Nurses Assn., Assn. Am. Med. Colls. (central region rep. student affairs nat. com. 2002-06.) Alpha Lambda Delta, Sigma Theta Tau, Pi Lampda Theta. Home: Unit 92 N 2200 S 29th St Grand Forks ND 58201-5869 Office: UND Sch Medicine PO Box 9037 501 N Columbia Rd Grand Forks ND 58202-9037 Office Phone: 701-777-4221. Personal E-mail: demersjudy@aol.com. Business E-Mail: jdemers@medicine.nodak.edu.

DEMETS, DAVID L., medical educator, biomedical researcher; b. Austin, Minn., Nov. 27, 1944; married; 2 children. BA in Math., Gustavus Adolphus Coll., St. Peter, Minn., 1966; MS in Biostats., U. Minn., 1968, PhD in Biostats., 1970. Statistician, divsn. computer rsch. and tech. NIH, Bethesda, Md., 1970-72, math. statistician, Nat. Heart, Lung and Blood Inst., 1973-79, chief, mathematical and applied statistics br., 1979-82; dir. biostats. Ctr., prof. stats. and biostats. U. Wis., Madison, 1982-91, assoc. dir. Clin. Cancer Ctr., 1982-91, chair dept. biostats., prof. stats. and biostats., 1991—, assoc. dir. Comprehensive Cancer Ctr., 1991—. Lectr., cons. in field; bd. scientific counselors Nat. Cancer Inst., 1993-96. Co-author: Fundamentals of Clinical Trials, 1981, 2d edit. 1985, 3d edit. 1995; contbr. numerous articles to profl. jours., chpts. to books; presenter in field; mem. adv. bd. jour. Controlled Clin. Trials, 1993—, editl. bd. 1994—; assoc. editor Jour. Clin. Rsch. and Drug Devel., 1987-90. Recipient Disting. Alumni award Gustavus Adolphus Coll., 1990, Gaylord Anderson Leadership award U. Minn. Sch. Pub. Health Alumni Soc., 1993. Fellow Am. Statis. Assn. (bd. dirs. 1987-89), Internat. Statis. Inst.; mem. Biometrics Soc. (regional adv. bd. 1975-77, 80-82, exec. com. Ea. N.Am. region 1992-94, pres. 1993), Soc. for Controlled Clin. Trials (bd. dirs. 1983-87, program com. 1984, 85, program chmn. 1988, v.p. 1988-89, pres. 1989-90, joint program com. with Internat. Soc. Clin. Biostats., Brussels, 1991, policy com. 1993—), Internat. Soc. Clin. Biostats. Office: U Wis Clin Science Ctr Dept Biostatistics & Med In 600 Highland Ave K61446 Madison WI 53792-0001

DEMING, DAVID LAWSON, art educator; b. Cleve., May 26, 1943; s. Lawson Joseph and Mary Rita (Basile) D.; m. Ann Elizabeth Haldeman, Sept. 4, 1965; children: Matthew Lawson, Lisa Ann, Michael David. BFA, Cleve. Inst. Art, 1967; MFA, Cranbrook Acad. Art, Bloomfield Hills, Mich., 1970. Instr. Boston U., 1967-68, U. Tex., El Paso, 1970-72, asst. prof., assoc. prof. art Austin, 1972, prof., 1985, chmn. art dept., Marguerite Fairchild prof. art, 1991-96; interim dean Coll. of Fine Arts U. Tex., Austin, 1996-97, dean, 1997-98; pres. Cleve. Inst. Art, 1998—. Sculptures represented in permanent collection Columbus (Ohio) Mus. Art, Ark. Art Ctr., Little Rock, U. Tex. Southwestern Regional Med. Ctr. Dallas; included in White House Garden Exhbn. of Am. Sculptors, 1995. Recipient award of honor Austin chpt. AIA, 1983. Mem. Internat. Sculpture Assn. Roman Catholic. Office: Cleveland Inst of Art 11141 East Blvd Cleveland OH 44106-1700 Office Phone: 216-421-7410. E-mail: ddeming@cia.edu.

DEMITRA, PAVOL, professional hockey player; b. Dubnica, Slovakia, Nov. 29, 1974; Right wing Ottawa Senators, 1993—96, St. Louis Blues, 1996—2005, LA Kings, 2005—06, Minn. Wild, 2006—. Mem. Slovakia Hockey Team, Olympic Games, Nagano, Japan, 1998; player NHL All-Star Game, 1999, 2000, 02. Recipient Lady Byng Meml. Trophy, 2000. Office: Minnesota Wild 317 Washington St Saint Paul MN 55102

DEMITRACK, THOMAS, lawyer; b. Denville, NJ, 1954; MusB, Univ. Hartford, 1976; JD summa cum laude, Ohio State Univ., 1979. Bar: Ohio 1979. Profl. responsibilities ptnr. and coord. of antitrust practice Jones Day, Cleve., and mem. profl. services com. Mem., profl. services com. Jones Day. Author: numerous articles in profl. publications. Named a leading lawyer in antitrust, N.E. Ohio Inside Bus. mag. and Ohio Super Lawyers. Mem.: Order of Coif. Office: Jones Day North Point 901 Lakeside Ave Cleveland OH 44114-1190 Office Fax: 216-579-0212.

DEMLOW, DANIEL J., lawyer; b. Ludington, Mich., Oct. 16, 1944; s. Richard M. and Nan (Jager) D.; m. Catherine M. Jerzak, Aug. 7, 1982; children: Sara Beth, Michelle Catherine. BA, Mich. State U., 1966; JD, U. Mich., 1969. Atty. Fraser Trebilock Davis & Foster, Lansing, Mich., 1969-70, Securities Bur., Lansing, Mich., 1970-71; dep. dir. Mich. Dept. Commerce, Lansing, 1971-73; commr. ins. Ins. Bur., Lansing, 1973-75; chmn. Mich. Pub. Svc. Commn., Lansing, 1975-81; assoc. Honigman Miller Schwartz & Cohn LLP, Lansing, 1985—. Fellow Mich. State Bar Found. Republican. Presbyterian. Avocations: tennis, boating, grouse hunting. Home: 3773 Yosemite Dr Okemos MI 48864-3838 Office: Honigman Miller Schwartz & Cohn LLP 222 N Washington Sq Ste 400 Lansing MI 48933-1800 Home Phone: 517-349-6360; Office Phone: 517-377-0700. Business E-Mail: ddemlow@honigman.com.

DE MOLINA, ALVARO G., finance company executive, former bank executive; b. Havana, Cuba, July 13, 1957; arrived in US, 1960; m. Donna de Molina; children: Nicolas, Rachel, Julia. BS in Acctg., Fairleigh Dickinson U., 1979; MBA, Rutgers U., 1988. With PriceWaterhouse, 1979; CFO emerging markets grp. JP Morgan; balance sheet mgmt. exec. Bank Am. Corp., 1992—98, dep. treas., 1998—2000, corp. treas., 2000—04, pres. capital market & investment banking, 2004—05, CFO, 2005—06; CEO Bank Am. Securities LLC, 2005; COO GMAC LLC, Detroit, 2007—08, CEO, 2008—. Bd. dirs. GMAC ResCap, GMAC Comml. Finance, GMAC Bank, The Inst. Internat. Fin. Bd. visitors Duke U. Fuqua Sch. Bus., 2003—; mem. dean's coun. Fla. Internat. U. Coll. Bus. Adminstrn.; bd. dirs. Fin. Svc. Vol. Corps, Opera Carolina, Found. for the Carolinas; bd. advisors The McColl Sch. Bus., Queens U. Named a Champion of Yr., Allegro Found., 2005; named one of Carolinas' Fathers of Yr., Nat. Father's Day Coun., 2004. Office: GMAC LLC 200 Renaissance Ctr Detroit MI 48265-2000*

DEMOREST, ALLAN FREDERICK, retired psychologist; b. Omaha, Dec. 20, 1931; 1 child, Steven M. BA, U. Omaha, 1957; MA, U. Mich., 1959, postgrad., 1960. Lic. psychologist, Iowa, Nat. Register Health Svc. Providers. Counselor Mayor's Com. on Skid Row Problems, Detroit, 1959-61; psychologist Macomb County Schs., Mt. Clemens, Mich., 1961-64; chief psychologist Jasper County Mental Health Ctr., Newton, Iowa, 1964-68; exec. dir. North Cen. Iowa Mental Health Ctr., Ft. Dodge, 1968-75; pvt. practice Ft. Dodge, 1968-85; psychologist Iowa Luth. Hosp., Des Moines, 1985-87; clin. dir. United Behavioral Systems, Des Moines, 1987-94, sr. psychologist, 1994-96; cons. pvt. practice, Des Moines, 1996—. Adj. prof. psychology Buena Vista U., Ft. Dodge, 1974-2002; substitute tchr. Des Moines Pub. Schs., 1999-05; chief trainer AARP Iowa Driver Safety Program, 2005—. Contbr. articles on rational therapy to profl. jours. Founding bd. dirs. Rape and Sexual Assault Victim Program, Ft. Dodge, 1976-85, Family Violence Ctr., Ft. Dodge, 1976-85, Youth Shelter Svcs., Ft. Dodge, 1979. With U.S. Army, 1952-54, Korea. Recipient appreciation award Community Mental Health Ctrs. Assn., 1968, community svc. award Iowa Dept. Human Svcs., 1985. Fellow Albert Ellis Inst.; mem. APA, VFW (quartermaster 2006—), Iowa Psychol. Assn., Adminstrv. Mgmt. Soc. (pres. Ft. Dodge 1979-80, 84-85), Iowa Assn. for Advancement Psychology (pres. 1984, appreciation award 1988), Elks (exalted ruler 1979, trustee 2002, Elk of Yr. 2004). Home and Office: 4225 Hickman Rd Des Moines IA 50310-3334 Personal E-mail: Ademorest@aol.com.

DEMOS, DAVE, marketing executive; V.p. sales, mktg. Am. Axle & Mfg., Detroit, v.p. sales and bus. devel., 1997-99, v.p. strategic planning, 1999—. Office: Am Axle & Mfg 1840 Holbrook Ave Detroit MI 48212-3442

DEMOSS, JON W., insurance company executive, lawyer; b. Kewanee, Ill., Aug. 9, 1947; s. Wendell and Virginia Beth DeMoss; m. Eleanor T. Thornley, Aug. 9, 1969; 1 child, Marc Alain. BS, U. Ill., 1969, JD, 1972. Bar: Ill. 1972, U.S. Dist. Ct. (cen. dist.) Ill. 1977, U.S. Supreme Ct. 1978, U.S. dist. Ct. (no. dist., trial bar) Ill. 1983. In house counsel Assn. Ill. Electric Coop., Springfield, 1972-74; registered lobbyist Ill. Gen. Assembly, Springfield, 1972-74; asst. dir. Ill. Inst. for CLE, Springfield, 1974-85; exec. dir. Ill. State Bar Assn., 1986-94; pres., CEO ISBA Mut. Ins. Co., Chgo., 1994—. Bd. dirs. Bar Plan Surety & Fidelity Co., St. Louis, 1999-2005 Bd. dirs. Springfield Symphony Orch., 1982-87, Ill. Inst. for CLE, 1986-89, Nat. Assn. of Bar Related Ins. Cos., 1989, pres., elect., 1998-99, pres. 1999-2000; bd. dirs. Lawyers Reins. Co., 1997—; bd. visitors John Marshall Law Sch., 1990—. Capt.bd.trustees Budget Com.,2008-U.S. Army, 1972. Fellow Am. Bar Found. (life, co-chmn. projects to prepare Appellate Handbook 1978, 90), Ill. Bar Found. (life, bd. dirs. 1983-85); mem. ABA (ho. of dels. 1979-85, 89, 91, 93-94), Nat. Conf. Bar Pres., Am. Judicature Soc. (bd. dirs. Ill. state chpt., treas. 2002-04), Ill. State Bar Assn. (pres. 1984-85, bd. govs. 1975-85, chmn. com. on scope and correlation of work 1982-83, chmn. budget com. 1983-85, chmn. legis. com. 1983-84, 85, chmn. com. on merit selection of judges 1977, del. long-range planning conf. 1972, 78, liaison to numerous coms. and sects.), Chgo. Bar Assn., Lake County Bar Assn., U. Ill. Coll. Dean's Club, La Chaine des Rotisseurs (Chgo.), Ordre Mondial des Gourmet Degustateurs (Chgo.). Home: 223 W Ohio Chicago IL 60610-4445 Office: ISBA Mutual Ins Co 223 W Ohio St Chicago IL 60610-4101 Office Phone: 312-379-2000. Business E-Mail: jon.demoss@isbamic.com.

DEMPSEY, JERRY, state legislator; m. Joanne; 4 children. BA, U. St. Thomas; MA, U. Wis., River Falls. State rep. Minn. Ho. Reps., Dist. 29A, 1993—. Mem. capital investment, econ. devel., infrastructure & regulation fin. govt. ops., gaming, regulated indsl. & energy coms., Minn. Ho. Reps., 1993—. Home: 1935 Perlich Ave Apt 308 Red Wing MN 55066-4229

DEMPSEY, MARY A., library commissioner, lawyer; m. Philip Corboy, Sept. 4, 1992. BA, St. Mary's Coll., Winona, Minn., 1975; MLS, U. Ill., 1976; JD, DePaul U., 1982. Bar: Ill. 1982. Libr. Hillside Pub. Libr., Ill., 1976—78; assoc. Reuben and Proctor, Chgo., 1982—85; assoc. gen. counsel Michael Reese Hosp. and Med. Ctr., Chgo., 1985—86; pvt. practice Chgo., 1987—89; counsel Sidley and Austin, Chgo., 1990—93; commr. Chgo. Pub. Libr., 1994—. Adj. prof. law DePaul U. Coll. Law and Health Inst., Chgo., 1986-90; spl. counsel Chgo. Bd. Edn., 1987-89; mem. adv. bd. Dominican U. Grad. Sch. Libr. and Info. Sci., River Forest, Ill. Mem. State St. Commn., Chgo.; bd. dir. Big Shoulders Fund (for inner city Cath. sch.), Urban Libr. Coun.; trustee DePaul U., Chgo.; mem. Ill. State Libr. Adv. Coun. Recipient Pub. Officials of Yr. award Governing Mag., 2006, Ken Haycock Promoting Librarianship award ALA, 2007; named Libr. of Yr. Ill. Libr. Assn., 2007. Mem. Chgo. Bar Assn., Chgo. Network. Office: Chgo Pub Libr 400 S State St Chicago IL 60605-1203 Office Phone: 312-747-4090. Office Fax: 312-747-4968. E-mail: mdempsey@chipublib.org.

DEMPSEY, WILLIAM G., pharmaceutical executive; b. Evergreen Park, Ill., Nov. 17, 1951; B of Acctg., DePaul U. With Abbott Labs., Abbott Park, Ill., 1982—, gen. mgr. home infusion svcs., civisional v.p. critical care systems, divisional v.p. hosp. bus. sector sales, 1995—96, v.p. hosp. products bus. sector, 1996—98, sr. v.p. chem. and agrl. products, 1998—99, sr. v.p. internat. ops., 1999—2003, sr. v.p. pharm. ops., 2003—06, exec. v.p. pharm. group, 2006—. Chmn. internat. sect. exec. com. PhRMA; mem. governing coun. Adv. Good Shepherd Hosp.; chmn. supervisory bd. Knoll GmBH, Germany; bd. dirs. TAP, Dainabot. Office: Abbott Labs 100 Abbott Park Rd Abbott Park IL 60064-6400

DEMPSTER, RYAN SCOTT, professional baseball player; b. Sechelt, BC, Can., May 3, 1977; married; 1 child. Pitcher Fla. Marlins, 1998—2002, Cin. Reds, 2002—03, Chgo. Cubs, 2004—. Named Nat. League All-Star, 2000; recipient Tip O'Neill award, 2000. Mailing: c/o Chgo Cubs Wrigley Field 1060 W Addison St Chicago IL 60613 Fax: 305-626-7428.*

DENDINGER, WILLIAM JOSEPH, bishop, former career officer; b. Coleridge, Nebr., May 20, 1939; s. Dave and Regina Dendinger. BA in Philosophy and English, Immaculate Conception Sem., 1961; MA in Theology, Aquinas Inst., 1964; MS in Counseling, Creighton U., 1969; student, Squadron Officer Sch., 1973; postgrad., Sch. Applied Theology, 1978; student, Air War Coll., 1987. Ordained priest Archdiocese of Omaha, Nebr., 1965; commd. capt. USAF, 1970, advanced through grades to maj. gen., 1997; base chaplain Maxwell AFB, Ala., 1970-72, Yokota Air Base, Japan, 1972-74; cadet wing chaplain USAF Acad., Colorado Springs, Colo., 1974-78; base chaplain Osan Air Base, S. Korea, 1979-80, Mather AFB, Calif., 1980-82; mem. chaplain resource bd. USAF Chaplain Svc. Inst., Maxwell AFB, 1982-85; base chaplain Hahn Air Base, W. Germany, 1985-88; plans and programs officer then chief plans/programs div. Office Air Force Chief Chaplains, Bolling AFB, D.C., 1988-93; command chaplain Hdqs. Air Combat Command, Langley AFB, Va., 1993-95; dep. chief Air Force Chaplain Svc. Hdqs. USAF, Washington, 1995-97, chief Air Force Chaplain Svc., 1997—2001; ordained bishop, 2004—; bishop Diocese of Grand Island, Nebr., 2004—. Decorated Legion of Merit with oak leaf cluster. Named Prelate of Honor with title of Rev. Monsignor, His Holiness Pope John Paul II, 1994. Roman Catholic. Office: Diocese of Grand Island PO Box 1531 2708 Old Fair Rd Grand Island NE 68803 Business E-Mail: bishop@gidiocese.org.*

DENEVAN, WILLIAM MAXFIELD, geographer, historical ecologist, educator; b. San Diego, Oct. 16, 1931; s. Lester W. and Wilda M. D.; m. Patricia Sue French, June 21, 1958; children: Curtis, Victoria. BA, U. Calif., Berkeley, 1953, MA, 1958, PhD, 1963. Faculty dept. geography U. Wis., Madison, 1963-94, prof., 1972-94, chmn. dept., 1980-83, dir. L.Am. Ctr., 1975-77, prof. emeritus, 1994—. Author/co-author: The Upland Pine Forests of Nicaragua, 1961, The Aboriginal Cultural Geography of the Llanos de Mojos of Bolivia, 1966, The Biogeography of a Savanna Landscape, Eastern Peru, 1970, Adaptive Strategies in Karinya Subsistance, Venezuelan Llanos, 1978, Campos Elevados en los Llanos Occidentales de Venezuela, 1979, Cultivated Landscapes of Native Amazonia and the Andes, 2001; editor/co-editor: The Native Population of the Americas in 1492, 1976, Pre-Hispanic Agricultural Fields in the Andean Region, 1987, Swidden-Fallow Agroforestry in the Peruvian Amazon, 1988, Hispanic Lands and Peoples, 1989, Las Chacras de Coporaque, 1994; contbr. 75 articles to profl. jours., chpts. to books. With USNR, 1950—55. Fulbright grantee, 1957; grantee NRC, 1961-62, Ford Found., 1965-66, NSF, 1972-73, 84-86, Nat. Geog. Soc., 1985-86, NEH, 1989-90; Guggenheim fellow, 1977-78. Mem. Assn. Am. Geographers (Honors award 1987), Am. Geog. Soc., Am. Anthrop. Assn., Soc. for Am. Archaeology, Am. Acad. Arts and Scis. Personal E-mail: sbden@saber.net.

DENLOW, MORTON, federal magistrate judge; b. 1947; BA, Washington U., 1969; JD, Northwestern U., 1972. Pvt. practice, Chgo., 1972-96; sr. lectr. Loyola U. Sch. Law, 1983-95; adj. prof. trial advocacy Northwestern U. Sch. Law, 1990-91; magistrate judge U.S. Dist. Ct. (no. dist.) Ill., 1996—. With USAR, 1970-76. Office: US Dist Ct 219 S Dearborn St Ste 1356 Chicago IL 60604-1802 Fax: 312-554-8547.

DENNEEN, JOHN PAUL, lawyer; b. NYC, Aug. 18, 1940; s. John Thomas Denneen and Pauline Jane Ludlow; m. Mary Veronica Murphy, July 3, 1965 (dec. Dec. 2000); children: John Edward, Thomas Michael, James Patrick, Robert Andrew, Daniel Joseph, Mary Elizabeth; m. Ginger O'Brien, Feb. 21, 2004. BS, Fordham U., 1963; JD, Columbia U., 1966. Bar: N.Y. 1966, U.S. Ct. Appeals (2d cir.) 1974, U.S. Dist. Ct. (so. and ea. dists.) N.Y. 1975, Mo. 1987. Assoc. Seward & Kissel, NYC, 1966-75; sr. v.p., gen counsel, sec. GK Techs., Inc., Greenwich, Conn., 1975-83; exec. v.p., gen. counsel, sec. Chromalloy Am. Corp., St. Louis, 1983-87; ptnr. Bryan Cave LLP, St. Louis, 1987-99; exec. v.p. corp. devel. and legal affairs, sec. NuVox, Inc., St. Louis, 1999—. Mem. ABA, Internat. Bar Assn., .Y. State Bar Assn., N.Y.C. Bar Assn., Bar Assn. Met. St. Louis. Office Phone: 636-537-7356.

DENNERT, H. PAUL, state legislator; b. June 25, 1937; Mem. S.D. Ho. of Reps. Dist. 2, Pierre, 1993-96; mem. Transp., Agr. and Natural Resources Com., Appropriations Com. S.D. of Reps., Pierre; mem. S.D. Senate from 2nd dist., Pierre, 1997—. Farmer, cattleman. Democrat. Home: 11853 391st Ave Columbia SD 57433-7002 Office: 109 River Pl Pierre SD 57501

DENNIS, DALE M., school system administrator; Dep. edn. commr. for fin. Kans. Dept. Edn., Topeka, acting commr. edn., 2006—. Office: Kans Dept Edn 120 SE 10 Ave Topeka KS 66612-1182 Office Phone: 785-296-3201. Office Fax: 785-296-7933. E-mail: ddennis@ksde.org.

DENNIS, FRANK GEORGE, JR., retired horticulture educator; b. Lyons, NY, Apr. 12, 1932; s. Frank George and Corinne Isabel (Smith) D.; m. Katharine Ann Merrell, June 5, 1954. BS in Agriculture, Cornell U., 1955, PhD in Pomology, 1961. Postdoctoral fellow NSF, Gif-sur-Yvette, France, 1961-62; asst. prof. Cornell U., Geneva, NY, 1962-68, assoc. prof., 1968—, Mich. State U., East Lansing, 1968-72, prof., 1972-96; ret., 1996. Fulbright fellow, Morocco, 1990. Fellow Am. Soc. for Hort. Sci. (v.p. 1985-86, Gourley award 1985, sci. editor HortScience 1997-2000); mem. Internat. Soc. Hort. Sci. (chmn. working group 1984-90), Sigma Xi. Home: 1600 Ridgewood Dr East Lansing MI 48823-2936 Business E-Mail: fgdennis@msu.edu.

DENT, THOMAS G., lawyer; b. Chgo., May 2, 1942; Student, U. Ill., De Paul U., LLB, 1970. Bar: Ill. 1970. Ptnr. Seyfarth, Shaw, Fairweather & Geraldson, Chgo. Office: Seyfarth Shaw Fairweather & Geraldson Mid Continental Plz 55 E Monroe St Ste 4200 Chicago IL 60603-5863

DENTON, D. BROCK, lawyer; b. Bowling Green, Ky., Dec. 14, 1974; BS, U. Ky., 1997; JD, Salmon P. Chase Coll. Law, Northern Ky. U., 2000. Bar: Ohio 2000, Ky. 2001. Assoc. Keating, Muething & Klekamp PLL, Cin., mem., Holding Com., coord., Summer Assoc. Prog. Mem., Bd. Dirs. Cin. Reds Cmty. Fund. Named one of Ohio's Rising Stars, Super Lawyers, 2005, 2006. Mem.: Ohio State Bar Assn., Northern Ky. Bar Assn., Ky. Bar Assn., Cin. Bar Assn. Office: Keating Muething & Klekamp PLL One E Fourth St Ste 1400 Cincinnati OH 45202 Office Phone: 513-579-6400. Office Fax: 513-579-6457.

DENTON, D. KEITH, management educator; b. Paducah, Ky., June 28, 1948; s. Derward and Bonnie Denton; children: Shane, Taylor. BS, Murray State U., 1971; M in Pub. Adminstrn., Memphis State U., 1974; PhD, So. Ill. U., 1981. Supr. Shelby Pre-Casting, Memphis, 1971-72; safety engr. Md. Casualty Corp., Memphis, 1972-76; instr. Draughn's Bus. Coll., Paducah, 1977; safety trainer

Union Carbide Corp., Paducah, 1977-78; prof. So. Ill. U., Carbondale, 1978-83, Mo. State U., Springfield, 1983—. Cons. Small Bus. Research Ctr., Springfield, 1985—, Springfield Remfg. Corp., 1986. Author: Safety Management, 1982; (with others) Safety Performance, 1985, Quality Service in America, 1989, The Production Game, 1990, Handling Employee Complaints, 1990, Horizontal Management, 1991, The Service Trainer, 1992, Recruitment Retention and Employee Relations, 1992, Did You Know?, Fascinating Facts and Fallacies, 1994, Enviro-Management: How Companies Turn Pollution Cost into Profits, 1994, The Toolbox for the Mind, 1999, Empowering Intranets, 2002; contbr. over 150 articles to profl. jours. Mem. Acad. Mgmt., Nat. Assn. Purchasing, Am. Soc. Prodn. and Inventory Control, Inst. Indsl. Engrs. Office: Mo State U 901 S National Ave Springfield MO 65804-0088 Home Phone: 417-889-6763; Office Phone: 417-836-5573. Business E-Mail: dkdentonf@missouristate.edu.

DENVIR, ROBERT F., lawyer; b. Chgo., Sept. 24, 1945; BBA, U. Notre Dame, 1967; JD, DePaul U., 1971. Bar: Ill. 1971, U.S. Dist. Ct. Ill. (No. dist.), U.S. Ct. Appeals (Fed. cir.); CPA, Ill. Assoc. to ptnr. Winston & Strawn LLP, Chgo., 1976—, chmn. tax dept., mem. exec. com. Bd. trustees Goodman Theatre. Mem. ABA (mem. fed. taxation sect.),Chgo. Bar Assn. Office: Winston & Strawn 35 W Wacker Dr Ste 4200 Chicago IL 60601-1695 Office Phone: 312-558-5765. Office Fax: 312-558-5700. E-mail: rdenvir@winston.com.

DEPEW, SHAWNA CECILA, lawyer; b. Kansas City, Mo., Apr. 1950; d. Frederick and Katherine DePew; divorced; 1 child. BA in Polit. Sci., U. Louisville, Ky., 1972, JD, 1976. Bar: Ky. 1976, Mo. 1980. Law clerk Meriks & Meriks, LLP, Olivette, Mo., 1976—80, assoc. lawyer, 1980—90, shareholder, 1990—. Mem. editl. bd.: Mo. Law Rev., 1990—95. Sec. St. Louis C. of C., 2000—03, bd. mem., 2003—. Named to Top 50 Woman Lawyers in Mo., 1995—2000; recipient Outstanding Contbn. award, St. Louis Mayor's Office, 2005. Mem.: FBA, SBA St. Louis, Mo. Bar Assn. (Woman of Yr. award 2005). Republican. Baptist. Avocations: travel, cooking, birdwatching, football. Office: Meriks & Meriks LLP 9648 Olive Blvd #201 Olivette MO 63132-3016

DEPIERO, DEAN E., state representative; b. Parma, Ohio, Sept. 11, 1968; BS, BA, Ashland U.; JD Cleve. Marshall Coll. Law. Atty.; asst. law dir.-prosecutor City of Berea, Ohio, 1995—98; state rep. dist. 15 Ohio Ho. of Reps., Columbus, 1998—, ranking minority mem., judiciary com., mem. criminal justice and state govt. coms., and ethics and elections subcom. Mem.: ABA, Parma Bar Assn., Cuyahoga County Bar Assn., Ohio State Bar Assn., Cuyahoga County Law Dirs. Assn., Parma Jaycees, Parma C. of C. (bd. trustees). Democrat.

DEPOY, PHIL E., special studies think-tank executive; Pres. Nat. Opinion Rsch. Ctr., Chgo. Office: National Opinion Research Ctr 1155 E 60th St Chicago IL 60637-2799

DERAMUS, BETTY JEAN, columnist; b. Tuscaloosa, Ala., Mar. 29, 1941; s. Jim Louis and Lucille (Richardson) DeR. B.A., Wayne State U., 1963, M.A., 1977. Reporter, copy editor Mich. Chronicle, Detroit, 1963-67; writer Detroit Bd. Edn., 1967-71; reporter Detroit Free Press, 1972-75, instr. English Wayne State U., 1976-78; editorial writer, columnist, from 1978; now columnist Detroit News. Contbr. Essence mag., N.Y.C.; author: The Constant Search, 1969, Forbidden Fruit: Love Stories from the Underground Railroad, 2005; contbr. anthologies Sturdy Black Bridges, 1979, The Third Coast, 1982. Recipient 1st prize commentary Edn. Writers Assn., 1981; Ernie Pyle award spl. citation Scripps-Howard Found., 1981; Best Editorial Series award Overseas Press Club Am., 1982; finalist Pulitzer Prize for Commentary, 1993; Gen. Excellence award ASCAP, 1983. Mem. Nat. Conf. Editorial Writers, Nat. Assn. Black Journalists (2d v.p. 1982). Office: Detroit News 615 W Lafayette Blvd Detroit MI 48226-3197 Office Phone: 313-222-2296. Business E-Mail: bderamus@detnews.com.

DEROMEDI, HERB WILLIAM, athletic director; b. May 26, 1939; m. Marilyn Long, Aug. 19, 1961; children: David, Tom, Lori. BS, U. Mich., 1960, MS, 1961. Asst. football coach Ctrl. Mich. U., Mt. Pleasant, 1967-78, head coach, 1978-94, athletic dir., 1994—. Office: Ctrl Mich U Rose Ctr 100A Mount Pleasant MI 48859-0001

DE ROSA, REY CHARLES, history professor, dean; b. Milw., Mar. 15, 1960; s. Ferdinand and Doris De Rosa; m. Samantha Davis, Apr. 29, 1982; children: Carlos, Tomas, Delia. BA in Polit. Sci., Marquette U., Milw., 1982, MA in Am. History, 1984, PhD, 1986. Adj. prof. history Meriks CC, Milw., 1984—86, asst. prof. history, 1986—90, assoc. prof. history, 1990—2000, prof. history, 2000—, dean history dept., 2005—. History club advisor Meriks CC, 1990—2000, undergrad. advisor history dept., 1995—2005; invited lectr. in field. Author: A Concise History of Milwaukee, 1993; editl. advisor: Merick CC Jour. History and Poli. Sci. Vol. Greater Milw. Soup Kitchen, 1987—97. Recipient Nat. Humanities medal, The White House, 2005. Mem.: NAACP, Am. Assn. State and Local History, Wis. Libr. Assn., Nat. Assn. Humanities Profs. Democrat. Roman Catholic. Avocations: reading, writing, golf, fly fishing. Office: Meriks CC 544 E Ogden Ave #700-517 Milwaukee WI 53202-2656

DEROUSIE, CHARLES STUART, lawyer; b. Adrian, Mich., May 24, 1947; s. Stuart J. and Helia I. (Juntunen) DeR.; m. Patricia Jean Fetzer, May 31, 1969; children: Jennifer, Jason. BA magna cum laude, Oakland U., 1969; JD magna cum laude, U. Mich., 1973. Bar: Ohio, 1973, U.S. Dist. Ct. (so. dist.) Ohio 1974. Ptnr. Vorys, Sater, Seymour and Pease, LLP, Columbus, Ohio, 1973—. Trustee Ballet Met., Inc., Columbus, 1978-90, pres., 1986-88; trustee Gladden Community House, Columbus, 1975-81, pres., 1979-81; mem. Children's Hosp. Devel. Bd., Columbus, 1987—, pres. 1995-96; trustee Elder Choices of Ctrl. Ohio, Columbus, 1989-95, Heritage Day Health Ctrs., Columbus, 1992-98. Fellow Columbus Bar Found.; mem. ABA, Am. Health Lawyers Assn., Columbus Bar Assn., Ohio Bar Assn., Order of Coif. Office: Vorys Sater Seymour and Pease LLP PO Box 1008 52 E Gay St Columbus OH 43215-3161

DERRICK, MALCOLM, physicist; b. Hull, Eng., Feb. 15, 1933; came to U.S., 1963, naturalized, 1976; s. Arthur Henry and Gladys (Hopkinson) D.; m. Kathleen Allen, 1957; 1 child, Matthew; m. Christa Zars Baumgardner; 1966; m. Eva Krebbers, 1995. B.Sc. with 1st class honours, U. Birmingham, 1954, PhD, 1959; MA, Oxford U., 1961. Instr. Carnegie Inst. Tech., 1957-60; asst. prof. Oxford U., 1960-63; asst. physicist Argonne (Ill.) Nat. Lab., 1963-67, sr. physicist, 1967—, dir. high energy physics div., 1974-81. Vis. prof. U. Minn., 1969-70, Univ. Coll., London, 1972-73; adv. com. Stanford U. Accelerator Center, Fermi Nat. Accelerator Lab.; mem. high energy physics adv. panel Dept. Energy. Author numerous research papers on high energy physics. Fellow Am. Phys. Soc. Home: 20 Equestrian Way Lemont IL 60439-9785 Office: Argonne Nat Lab Bldg 362 Argonne IL 60439 Office Phone: 630-252-6272. Business E-Mail: mxd@hep.anl.gov.

DERSTADT, RONALD THEODORE, health facility administrator; b. Detroit, June 9, 1950; s. Theodore Edward and Dorothy J. (Semko) D.; m. J. Gail Adamson, June 9, 1990. BA, U. Detroit, 1971; M of Hosp. Healthcare Adminstn., Xavier U., 1975. Mgr. shared svcs. Bethesda Hosp. North, Cin., 1975-76; asst. adminstr. McCullough-Hyde Meml. Hosp., Oxford, Ohio, 1977-79; pres. Hospice of Cin., Inc., 1979-82; dir. strategic planning St. Francis-St. George Hosp., Cin., 1982-84; v.p. Mgmt. Dynamics, Inc., Cin., 1984-85; sr. v.p. St. Francis-St. George Mgmt. Co., Cin., 1986-88; v.p. Franciscan Health System of Cin., 1988-91; dir. hosp. affairs ChoiceCare, Cin., 1991-95; CEO Medquest, Owensboro, Ky., 1995-98; COO Ctr. for Chem. Addictions Treatment, Cin., 1998—. Vice-chmn., bd. dirs. Franciscan Health Network, Cin., Franciscan Health Ventures, Cin. Treas., bd. dirs. Ohio Easter Seals Soc., Columbus, 1987-93; bd. dirs. S.W. Ohio Easter Seal Soc., Cin., 1986-92; adv. bd. Dater Jr. H.S., Cin., 1984-88. Fellow Am. Coll. Healthcare Execs.; mem. Healthcare Fin. Mgmt. Assn., Am. Hosp. Assn., Ohio Hosp. Assn. Avocations: boating, golf, radio control model building. Home: 7363 Dogtrot Rd Cincinnati OH 45248 Office: 830 Ezzard Charles Dr Cincinnati OH 45214-2525 Office Phone: 513-381-6672.

DERTIEN, JAMES LEROY, librarian; b. Kearney, Nebr., Dec. 14, 1942; s. John Ludwig and Muriel May (Cooley) D.; m. Elaine Paulette Mohror, Dec. 26, 1966; children— David Dalton, Channing Lee AB, U. S.D., 1965; MLS, U. Pitts., 1966; MPA, U. S.D., 1995. Head librarian Mitchell Pub. Library, S.D., 1966-67; head librarian Sioux Falls Coll., S.D., 1967-69; acting dir. libraries U. S.D., Vermillion, 1969-70; head librarian Vets. Meml. Pub. Library, Bismarck, N.D., 1970-75, Bellevue Pub. Library, Nebr., 1975-81; libr. dir. Siouxland Librs., S.D., 1981—. Pres., bd. dirs. Vol. and Info. Ctr., Sioux Falls, 1991-93. Mem. ALA, Mountain Plains Library Assn. (pres. 1978-79, editor newsletter 1982—), S.D. Library Assn. (pres. 1986-87). Lodges: Rotary. Unitarian Universalist. Avocations: backpacking, reading, fishing. Office: Siouxland Librs 201 N Main Ave Sioux Falls SD 57104-6002 Home: 1211 Foothills Dr Spearfish SD 57783-9462 E-mail: jimd@siouxland.lib.sd.us.

DERUSHA, JASON, reporter; m. Alyssa DeRusha. Degree in polit. sci. and broadcast/electronic comms., Marquette U. Intern ABC World News Tonight, Prime Time Live; anchor, reporter KWQC-TV, Davenport, Ind.; assoc. prodr. WISN, Milw., 1995—96, news reporter, 2000—. Recipient First Place award for best continuing series, Ill. AP, 1998, award for gen. reporting, Iowa AP, 1999, 2d place for news reporting, 2000, Gold medal media award, Ill. Pub. Health Assn., 1999. Office: WISN Po Box 402 Milwaukee WI 53201-0402

DERVIN, BRENDA LOUISE, communications educator; b. Beverly, Mass., Nov. 20, 1938; d. Ermina Diluiso; adopted d. John Jordan and Marjorie (Sullivan) D. BS, Cornell U., 1960; MA, Mich. State U., 1968, PhD, 1972; PhD (hon.), U. Helsinki, 2000. Pub. info. asst. Am. Home Econ. Assn., Washington, 1960-62; pub. info. specialist Ctr. Consumer Affairs, U. Wis., Milw., 1962-65; instr., rsch. and teaching asst. dept. communications Mich. State U., E. Lansing, 1965-70; asst. prof., Sch. Info. Transfer Syracuse (N.Y.) U., 1970-72; asst. to assoc. prof. U. Wash., Seattle, 1972-85; prof. comm. Ohio State U., Columbus, 1985—. Co-author: The Mass Media Behavior of the Urban Poor, 1980; editor: Rethinking Communication, 1989, Communication A Different Kind of Horserace, 2003, Sense-making Methodology Reader, 2003; editor Progress in Communication Sci., 1981-92; contbr. articles to profl. jours. Grantee U.S. Office Edn., 1974-76, Calif. State Libr., 1974-84, Nat. Cancer Inst., 1984, Ameritech, 1992, Inst. Mus. and Libr. Svc., 2003—. Fellow Internat. Communication Assn. (pres. 1986-87); mem. Internat. Assn. Mass Communications Rsch. (governing coun. 1988-97). Home: 4269 Kenridge Dr Columbus OH 43220-4157 Office: Ohio State U 3016 Derby 154 N Oval Mall Columbus OH 43210-1330 Home Phone: 614-442-0721; Office Phone: 614-292-3192. Business E-Mail: dervin.1@osu.edu.

DERZON, GORDON M., hospital administrator; b. Milw., Dec. 28, 1934; married. BA, Dartmouth Coll., 1957; MHA, U. Mich., 1961. Adminstrv. resident Bklyn. Hosp., 1960-61, adminstrv. asst., 1961-63, asst. exec. dir., 1963-65, exec. dir., 1966-67, State U. Hosp., Bklyn., 1967-68, Kings County Hosp. Center, Bklyn., 1968-74; CEO U. Wis. Hosps. and Clinics, Madison, 1974-2000; assoc. prof. SUNY, 1967-74; clin. prof. U. Wis., now emeritus prof. Bd. dirs. MATC Found., Madison Cmty. Health Ctr. Hospice, Combat Blindness Found., Ctr. Health Emotions. Contbr. articles to profl. jours. Mem. Am. Hosp. Assn. (past chmn. pub. gen. hosp. sect.). Home: 3440 Topping Rd Madison WI 53705-1439 Office Phone: 608-238-9407. Business E-Mail: gm.derzon@hosp.wisc.edu.

DESAI, DEEPAK K., lawyer; b. Cin., Dec. 19, 1968; BA, Northern Ky. U., 1988; JD, Salmon P. Chase Coll. Law, 1991. Bar: Ohio, United States Ct. Appeals fotr 6th Cir. 1993, US Dist. Ct. Southern Dist. Ohio. Assoc. Santen & Hughes, Cin. Named one of Ohio's Rising Stars, Super Lawyers, 2006, 2007. Mem.: Cin. Bar Assn., Ohio State Bar Assn. Office: Santen & Hughes Ste 2700 600 Vine St Cincinnati OH 45202 Office Phone: 513-721-4450. Office Fax: 513-721-0109.

DESAI, SAMIR T., electronics executive; BS in Physics and Elec. Engring., U. India; MSEE, Ill. Inst. Tech.; MBA, Loyola U., Chgo. Joined Motorola, Inc., Schaumburg, Ill., 1973, gen. mgr. iDEN Subscriber Group Plantation, Fla., 1993—99, sr. v.p., gen. mgr., 1999—2000, sr. v.p., dir. office of e-bus. and bus. transformation Comm. Enterprise, 2000—01, sr. v.p., dep. to the pres. of personal comm. sector, 2001—02, sr. v.p., chief info. officer, 2002—04, sr. v.p., gen. mgr. iDEN Networks and Devices, 2004—. Office: Motorola Inc 1303 E Algonquin Rd Schaumburg IL 60196

DESANTIAGO, MICHAEL FRANCIS, mechanical engineer; b. NYC, Feb. 20, 1956; s. Michael and Carmen DeS.; m. Carmen Devivies, June 10, 1989; 1 child, Sabrina. BSME, U. Ill., Chgo., 1979. Registered profl. engr., Ill. Project engr. Sargent & Lundy, Chgo., 1979-87; co-founder, prin., pres. Primera Engrs., Ltd., Chgo., 1987—. Mem. ASME, NSPE, ASHRAE, Northshore Toastmasters (pres. 1986-87), Latin Am. C. of C. (v.p. 1987-89). Achievements include the co-founding of Primera Engrs. Ltd., a 100% Hispanic-owned company. Office: Primera Engrs Ltd 25 E Washington St Ste 510 Chicago IL 60602-1703

DESIDERI, LAWRENCE R., lawyer; b. Chgo., June 6, 1958; BS summa cum laude, No. Ill. U., 1980; JD summa cum laude, U. Ill., 1983. Bar: Ill. 1983, U.S. Dist. Ct. Ill. (No. dist.), U.S. Ct. Appeals (7th cir.). Assoc. to ptnr. Winston & Strawn LLP, Chgo., 1983—, mem. exec. com. Topics editor: U. Ill. Law Rev., 1982—83. Mem.: ABA, Chgo. Bar Assn., Order of Coif. Office: Winston & Strawn LLP 35 W Wacker Dr Chicago IL 60601 Office Phone: 312-558-5960. Office Fax: 312-558-5700. E-mail: ldesideri@winston.com.

DESIMONE, ALFRED S., insurance agent; BA, U. Wis.; MA, Northwestern U.; postgrad., U. Wis., Milw. Life ins. agt. Equitable, Kenosha, Wis.; classroom tchr. Port Washington (Wis.) schs.; prin. Waukegan (Ill.) schs.; supt. Mattoon (Wis.) Sch. Dist. Mem. bd. regents U. Wis., 1995—; charter pres. U. Wis.-Parkside Found.; bd. dirs. U. Wis. Found., Wis. Mem.: U. Wis. Alumni Assn. (past pres.). Office: Equitable 7514 30th Ave Kenosha WI 53142

DESIMONE, LIVIO DIEGO, retired diversified manufacturing company executive; b. Montreal, Que., Can., July 16, 1936; s. Joseph D. and Maria E. (Bergamin) De S.; m. Lise Marguerite Wong, 1957, children: Daniel J., Livia D., Mark A., Cynthia A. BChemE, McGill U., Montreal, 1957. Process engr. 3M Can., 1957-61; With 3M Co., St. Paul, 1961—; exec. v.p. life scis. sector 3M, St. Paul, 1981, exec. v.p. indsl. and consumer sector, 1984-86, exec. v.p. indsl. and consumer sector and pvt. svcs., 1986-89, exec. v.p. indsl. and electronic sector and corp. svcs., 1989-91, exec. v.p. info., imaging and electronic sector & pvt. svcs., 1991, exec. v.p., 1991, chmn. bd., CEO, 1991-2000; ret., 2001. Bd. dirs. Am. Express Funds, Milliken & Co., Gen. Mills Inc., Vulcan Materials Co. Trustee U. Minn. Found. Mem. Bus. Coun. Office: 30 7th St E Ste 3050 Saint Paul MN 55101-4901 Business E-Mail: lddesimone@mmm.com.

DESJARDINS, CLAUDE, physiologist, dean; b. Fall River, Mass., June 13, 1938; s. Armand Louis and Marguerite Jean (Mercier) D.; m. Jane Elizabeth Campbell, June 30, 1962; children: Douglas, Mark, Anne. BS, U. R.I., 1960; MS, Mich. State U., 1964, PhD, 1967. Asst. prof. dept. physiology Okla. State U., Stillwater, 1968-69, assoc. prof., 1969-72; assoc. prof. physiology U. Tex., Austin, 1970-75; prof. physiology Inst. Reproductive Biology, Patterson Labs., 1975-86, U. Va. Med. Sch., Charlottesville, 1987-96, dir. Ctr. Rsch. Reprodn., 1990-96; prof. physiology and biophysics, sr. assoc. dean Med. Coll., U. Ill., Chgo., 1996—, dean, dir. program for rsch. in acad. medicine and clin. scholar project, 2005—. Mem. Ctr. for Advanced Studies, 1986; cons. NIH, ASA, VA, FDA. Author: Cell and Molecular Biology of the Testis, 1993, Molecular Physiology of Testicular Cells, 1996; editor-in-chief Am. Jour. physiology: Endocrinology and Metabolism, 1991-95; editor-in-chief Jour. Andrology, 1989-91, Ency. of Reprodn., 1997-98; mem. editl. bd. Biology Reprodn., Endocrinology; contbr. articles to profl. jours.; patentee techs. for male contraception, mechanisms of peptide hormone transport in the microcirculation and ligand-dependent and ligand ind. action of steroid hormones in peripheral vasculature. Fellow The Jackson Lab., Bar Harbor, Maine, 1967, NIH Sr. fellow U. Va. Med. Sch., 1983-84, Danforth Found. fellow, 1960; Cornell U. fellow, 2004-05; C.F. Wilcox Found. scholar, 1958. Mem. Am. Physiol. Soc., Soc. eurosci., Soc. Study Reprodn. (pres. 1982-83), Endocrine Soc., Am. Soc. Cell Biology, The Microcirculatory Soc. Office: U Ill at Chgo Coll Medicine M/C 955 820 S Wood St Chicago IL 60612-4325 Office Phone: 312-355-0916. Business E-Mail: clauded@uic.edu.

DESMOND, BEVIN, investment research company executive; B in Psych., St. Mary's Coll. With Morningstar, Inc., 1993—, mgr. internat. ventures, 1998—2000, pres. internat. bus., 2001—. Named one of Top 40 Under 40, Crain's Chgo. Bus., 2006. Office: Morningstar Inc 225 W Wacker Dr Chicago IL 60606

D'ESPOSITO, JULIAN C., JR., lawyer; b. NYC, Aug. 6, 1944; BS, Loyola U., 1966; JD cum laude, Northwestern U., 1969. Bar: Ill. 1969. With Ross, Hardies, O'Keefe, Babcock & Parsons, 1970—76, ptnr., 1976; counsel to Gov. Ill., 1977-81; ptnr. Isham, Lincoln & Beale, 1981—87, Mayer, Brown, Rowe & Maw, 1988—, ptnr. in charge Chgo. office, 2002—07. Chmn. Winnetka Plan Commn., 1985-89; mem. Ill. Med. Ctr. Commn., 1987-94; dir. Ill. Capital Devel. Bd., 1994-95, Chgo. Ctrl. Area Com., 2004-; chmn. Ill. State Toll Hwy. Authority, 1995-99. Co-editor-in-chief Jour. Criminal Law, Criminology & Police Sci., Northwestern U., 1968-69. Mem. ABA. Office: Mayer Brown LLP 71 S Wacker Dr Chicago IL 60606

DESPRES, LEO ARTHUR, sociologist, anthropologist, educator, academic administrator; b. Lebanon, NH, Mar. 29, 1932; s. Leo Arthur and Madeline (Bedford) D.; m. Loretta A. LaBarre, Aug. 22, 1953; children— Christine, Michelle, Denise, Mary Louise, Renee. BA, U. Notre Dame, 1954, MA, 1956; PhD, Ohio State U., 1960. Research assoc. Columbia Psychiat. Inst. and Hosp., 1957-60; postdoctoral fellow Social Sci. Research Council, Guyana, 1960-61; asst. prof. Ohio Wesleyan U., 1961-63; faculty Case Western Res. U., Cleve., 1963-74, prof. anthropology, 1967-74, chmn. dept., 1968-74; prof. sociology, anthropology U. Notre Dame, Ind., 1974-97, chmn. dept., 1974-80, fellow Kellogg Inst. Internat. Studies, 1982—, prof. emeritus, 1997—. Cons. in field. Author: Cultural Pluralism and Nationalist Politics in British Guyana, 1968; editor: Ethnicity and Resource Competition in Plural Societies, 1975, Manaus: Social Life and Work in Brazil's Free Trade Zone, 1991. Fulbright scholar, U. Guyana, 1970—71, Brazil, 1986, rsch. grantee, NSF, 1984. Mem. Am. Anthrop. Assn., Am. Ethnol. Soc., Latin Am. Studies Assn., Cen. States Anthrop. Soc. (pres. 1976-77), AAUP. Office: U Notre Dame Dept Anthropology Notre Dame IN 46556 Home: PO Box 6752 South Bend IN 46660-6752 Business E-Mail: ldespres@nd.edu.

DESPRES, LEON MATHIS, lawyer, former city official; b. Chgo., Feb. 2, 1908; s. Samuel and Henrietta (Rubovits) D.; m. Marian Alschuler, Sept. 10, 1931; children— Linda Baskin, Robert Leon. PhB, U. Chgo., 1927, JD, 1929; DLitt (hon.), Columbia Coll., Chgo., 1990, U. Ill., 2000. Bar: Ill. 1929. Ptnr. Despres, Schwartz and Geoghegan, Chgo.; alderman 5th Ward Chgo. City Council, 1955-75, parliamentarian, 1979-87. Author: Challenging the Daley Machine, 2005. Mem. Chgo. Plan Commn., 1979-89. Recipient Benton medal, U. Chgo., 2005. Mem.: Phi Beta Kappa, Order of Coif. Home: 5830 S Stony Island Ave Apt 10A Chicago IL 60637-2024 Office: 77 W Washington St Chicago IL 60602-2801 Office Phone: 312-372-2511.

DESSEM, R. LAWRENCE, dean, law educator; b. Berea, Ohio, May 16, 1951; s. Ralph Eugene and Jane Elizabeth (Brightbill) D.; m. Beth Ann Taylor, May 20, 1973; children: Matthew, Lindsay, Emily. BA summa cum laude, Macalester Coll., 1973; JD cum laude, Harvard U., 1976. Bar: Ohio 1976, D.C. 1979, Tenn. 1985, Mo., 2002. Law clk. to presiding judge U.S. Dist. Ct. (no. dist.) Ohio, Cleve., 1976-78; asst. gen. counsel NEA, Washington, 1978-80; trial atty. civil div. U.S. Dept. Justice, Washington, 1980-84, sr. trial counsel, 1984-85; assoc. prof. law coll. of law U. Tenn., Knoxville, 1985-92, prof. law coll. of law, 1992-95, assoc. dean, 1993-95; prof., dean Mercer U., Macon, Ga., 1995—2002; dean & prof. law U. Mo.-Columbia, Sch. Law, 2002—. Mem. faculty Legal Edn. Inst., U.S. Dept. Justice, San Francisco, 1985, Nat. Inst. for Trial Adv., Chgo., 1987-90; reporter Adv. Group on Litigation Cost and Delay, Tenn., 1991-95; mem. Tenn. Supreme Ct. Commn. on Dispute Resolution, 1992-94; mem. fed. adv. com. US Ct. Appeals (8th cir.), 2005—. Author: Pretrial Litigation, 1991, 4th edit., 2007, Pretrial Litigation in a Nutshell, 3d edit. 2001; contbr. articles to profl. jours. Nat. Merit scholar 1969. Fellow Am. Bar Found., Lawyer's Found. of Ga.; mem. ABA (co-chair dean's workshop 1998-99), Tenn. Bar Found., Am. Law Inst., Assn. Am. Law Schs. (mem. review com., chair, 2005-07), Phi Beta Kappa. Office: U Mo 230 Hulston Hall Columbia MO 65211-4300 Office Phone: 573-882-3246. E-mail: dessemrl@missouri.edu.

DETHOMASIS, BROTHER LOUIS, academic administrator; b. Bklyn., Oct. 6, 1940; s. Costantino and Anna (Maggio) DeT. BS in Fgn. Service, Georgetown U., 1963; PhD, Union Grad. Sch., 1982. Tchr. LaSalle Acad., Providence, 1969-71; assoc. headmaster LaSalle Mil. Acad., Oakdale, N.Y., 1971-73, pres., 1976-84; v.p. for fin. The Christian Brothers, Narragansett, R.I., 1973-76; pres. St. Mary's U., Winona, Minn., 1984—. Author: The Finance of Education, 1978; Investing With Options, 1981; Social Justice, 1982; My Father's Business, 1984 Recipient Pres.'s medal for Christian edn., St. John's Coll. High Sch., 1985, Christian Edn. award Franz W. Sichel Found., 1974 Roman Catholic. Home and Office: St Marys U 700 Terrace Hts Box 30 Winona MN 55987-1321

DETTINGER, WARREN WALTER, lawyer; b. Toledo, Feb. 13, 1954; s. Walter Henry and Elizabeth Mae (Zoll) Dettinger. BS cum laude, U. Toledo, 1977, JD magna cum laude, 1980. Bar: Ohio 1980, US Dist. Ct. (no. dist.) Ohio 1980, US Ct. Appeals (6th cir.) 1980, US Tax Ct. 1981. Law clk. to presiding judge US Ct. Appeals (6th cir.), Grand Rapids, Mich., 1980-81; assoc. Fuller & Henry, Toledo, 1981-84; atty. Sheller-Globe Corp., Toledo, 1984-87; v.p., gen. counsel, sec. Diebold, Inc., Canton, Ohio, 1987—. Mem. ABA, Ohio Bar Assn., Stark County Bar Assn., Am. Corp. Counsel Assn., Mfrs. Alliance (law coun. II), Brookside Country Club, Phi Kappa Phi. Roman Catholic. Avocations: golf, travel, photography. Home: 5237 Birkdale St NW Canton OH 44708-1825 Office: Diebold Inc 5995 Mayfair Rd PO Box 3077 North Canton OH 44720-8077 Office Phone: 330-490-5037. Business E-Mail: warren.dettinger@diebold.com.

DETTMANN, DAVID ALLEN, lawyer; b. Milw., Mar. 30, 1949; s. Karl F. and Beverly J. Dettmann; m. Jenee A. Nelson, June 26, 1971; children: Justin, Lisa, Jacob. BA in Acctg./Econs., Luther Coll., 1971; MBA, JD, Drake U., 1974. Bar: Iowa 1974, US Dist. Ct. (so. dist.) Iowa 1974, US Tax Ct. 1974, US Ct. Appeals (8th cir.) 1989, Ill. 1993; CPA, Iowa; accredited estate planner, Am. Coll. Real Estate Lawyers, 1994, Am. Coll. Trust and Estate Counsel, 2000. Ptnr. Lane & Waterman LLP, Davenport, Iowa, 1974—. Iowa State Bar Assn. rep. to Iowa legis. adv. com. on electronic filing of real property instruments, 2000—01; rep. to Iowa legis. county real estate electronic govt. adv. com., 2005—07. Dir., vice chair, chair Miss. Valley Regional Blood Ctr., Davenport, 1984—; mem. adult edn. adv. com. Scott CC, 1998—; mem. Presidentsrad com. Luther Coll., 2002—; former mem. ch. coun. Redeemer Luth. Ch.; bd. dirs. Cmty. Found. Great River Bend, 1996—2006, chair, 2004; bd. dirs. Am. Inst. Commerce, Davenport, 1986—98, Quad-City Estate Planning Coun., pres., 1990—91. Named Outstanding Planned Giving Profl., Ill. Quad Cities Chpt. Assn. Fundraising Profls., 2006; recipient Recognition for vol. svcs., Supreme Ct. Iowa, 1999, Disting. Svc. award, Luther Coll., 2001. Mem.: ABA, AICPA (assoc.), Scott County Bar Assn. (chmn. abstract/real estate com. 1985—95), Iowa Soc. CPAs, Iowa State Bar Assn. (title stds. com. 1985—94, chmn. title guaranty subcom. 1990—94, real estate and title law sect. coun. 1993—96, chair 1994—95, real estate and title law sect. coun. 2001—04, chmn. real estate modernization com. 2002—03). Avocations: travel, photography. Office: Lane & Waterman LLP 220 N Main St Ste 600 Davenport IA 52801-1987 Office Phone: 563-324-3246. Business E-Mail: ddettmann@l-wlaw.com.

DETTMAR, KEVIN JOHN HOFFMANN, literature and language professor; b. Burbank, Calif., Dec. 24, 1958; s. Wilbur George and Joan Elizabeth (Fiddis) Dettmar; m. Robyn Hoffmann, Aug. 15, 1981; children: Emily Susan, Audrey Elizabeth, Esther Katherine, Colin Adam. BA in English and Psychology, U. Calif., Davis, 1981; postgrad. diploma, Trinity Coll., Dublin, Ireland, 1982; MA in English, UCLA, 1988, PhD in English, 1990. Teaching asst., assoc., fellow dept. English UCLA, 1984-90; vis. asst. prof. dept. English Loyola Marymount U., 1990-91; asst. prof. English Clemson U., SC, 1991-94, assoc. prof., asst. head dept. English SC, 1994—99, assoc. dean Coll. Architecture, Arts & Humanities SC; prod., chair Dept. English So. Ill. U., Carbondale, 1999—. Presenter in field. Author: The Illicit Joyce of Postmodernism: Reading Against the Grain, 1996, Is Rock Dead?, 2005; editor: Rereading the New: A Backward Glance at Modernism, 1992, Marketing Modernisms: Self-Promotion, Canonization, and Rereading, 1996, Reading Rock & Roll: Authenticity, Appropriation, Aesthetics, 1999, Blackwell Companion to British Literature and Culture, 2005; twentieth-century editor Oxford Encyclopedia of British Literature, 2005, mem. editl. team, gen. editor Longman Anthology of British Literature; contbr. articles to profl. jours. Fellow US Dept. Edn., 1986—87, Jacob K. Javits fellow, US Dept. Edn., 1987—88, 1988—89, 1989—90; NEH travel grantee, 1992—93, NEH summer stipend, 1994. Mem.: MLA, AAUP, Internat. Assn. for Study of Popular Music (bd. mem.), Modernist Studies Assn. (former pres.), Soc.

Narrative Lit., Midwest MLA (pres. 2005—06, bd. mem.), James Joyce Found. Home: 704 May Apple Ln Carbondale IL 62901-7679 Office: So Ill U Carbondale Faner 2276 Carbondale IL 62901-6899 Office Phone: 618-453-6817. E-mail: kdettmar@siu.edu.*

DETTMER, HELENA R., classics educator; d. Terry Stone; children: Dan, Heather, Mike, Anne, Alex. BA in Classics, Ind. U., 1972; MA/PhD, U. Mich., 1976. Asst. prof. U. Iowa, Iowa City, 1976-83, assoc. prof., 1983-97, chair, 1993—, prof., 1997—, dir. interdisciplinary program, 2001—; co-editor Syllecta Classica, 1989—98. Author: Horace: A Study in Structure, 1983, Love By the Numbers: Form and Meaning in the Poetry of Catullus, 1997; contbr. articles to profl. jours. Mellon fellowship Duke U., 1977-78; faculty scholarship, 1986-89. Mem. Classical Assn. of Middle West and South (pres.-elect 1995-96, pres. 1996-97). Am. Philolog. Assn. Office: Univ Iowa 212 Schaeffer Hall Iowa City IA 52242-1409

DETTMER, MICHAEL HAYES, lawyer, former prosecutor; b. Detroit, June 6, 1946; s. Frank Arthur and Mary Frances (Conway) D.; m. Teckla Ann Getts, Aug. 15, 1969; children: Bryn Patrick, Janna Hayes. BS, Mich. State U., 1968; JD, Wayne State U., 1971. Bar: Mich. 1971, U.S. Dist. Ct. (we. dist.) Mich. 1992. Atty. Dettmer Thompon Parsons, Traverse City, Mich., 1972-90; pres., CEO Mich. Lawyer Mutual Ins. Co., Southfield, Grand Rapids, Mich., 1990-93; U.S. atty. we. dist. Mich. U.S. Dept. Justice, Grand Rapids, 1994—2001; sole practice Traverse City, Mich., 2002—; prin. Dettmer, Thompson & Parsons, P.C., Traverse City, Mich., 1987—93; assoc. Parsons, Ringsmuth, Traverse City, Mich., 2003—. Lectr. in field. Contbr. articles to profl. jour. Pres. Traverse City Montessori Ctr., 1978-83; commr. Traverse City Human Rights Commn.; chmn. Grand Traverse County Dem. Party, 1986. Fellow Am. Bar Found., Mich. State Bar Found.; mem. ABA, State Bar of Mich. (pres. 1993-94, commr. No. Mich. and Upper Peninsula 1986-94, exec. com. bd. commrs. 1988-94, com. on legislation 1990-91, task force on professionalism 1988-90, co-chair standing com. on professionalism 1992-94, chair Upper Mich. lawyers com. 1986-94, rep. assembly 1977-80, 88-94, atty. discipline bd. hearing panelist 1980-88), Am. Bd. Trial Advocates, Nat. Bd. Trial Advocacy (cert. 1981-1993). Democrat. Presbyterian. Office: Old Munson Hall 921 W 11th St Ste 2E Traverse City MI 49684

DEUTSCH, JAMES BERNARD, lawyer; b. St. Louis, Aug. 24, 1948; s. William Joseph and Margaret (Klevorn) D.; m. Deborah Marie Hallenberg, June 26, 1976; children: Michael, Gabriel. BA, Southeast Mo. State U., 1974; JD, U. Mo., 1978. Bar: Mo. 1978, U.S. Dist. Ct. (we. dist.) Mo. 1978, U.S. Ct. Appeals (8th cir.), 1989, U.S. Supreme Ct., 1990. Assoc. Gt. Plains Legal Found., Kansas City, Mo., 1978-79; pvt. practice, Kansas City, 1979-81; gen. counsel Mo. Dept. Revenue, Jefferson City, Mo., 1981-83; commr. Mo. Adminstrv. Hearing Commn., Jefferson City, 1983-89; dep. atty.-gen State of Mo., Jefferson City, 1989-93; ptnr. Riezman & Blitz, P.C., Jefferson City, Mo., 1993-99; Ptnr. Blitz Bardgett & Deutsch LC, Jefferson City, 2000—. Served to lance cpl. USMC, 1968-70, Vietnam. Named one of Men of Yr. in Constrn. Industry, Engring. News, McGraw-Hill Pub., N.Y.C., 1985. Mem. ABA (jud. adminstrn. com.), ASCE (hon. fellow), Mo. Bar Assn. (council mem. taxation com. 1985—, adminstrn. law and jud. adminstrn. coms., Best Lawyers in Am. 2005—), Mo. Inst. for Justice (bd. dirs. 1977—), VFW, Marine Corps League. Office: Blitz Bardgett & Deutsch LC 308 E High St Jefferson City MO 65101-3237 Office Phone: 573-634-2500. E-mail: jdeutsch@blitzbardgett.com.

DEUTSCH, THOMAS ALAN, ophthalmologist, educator, dean; b. Nagoya, Japan, Aug. 11, 1954; (parents U.S. citizens); William E. and Natasha S. (Sobotka) D.; m. Judith Silverman, Dec. 6, 1986. AB, Washington U., 1975; MD, Rush Med. Coll., Chgo., 1979. Diplomate Am. Bd. Ophthalmology. Intern Presbyn.-St. Luke's Hosp., Chgo., 1979-80; resident U. Ill. Eye and Ear Infirmary, Chgo., 1980-83; asst. prof. ophthalmology U. Ill., Chgo., 1983-84, Rush Med. Coll., Chgo., 1984-87, assoc. prof., 1987-94, prof., 1994—, chmn. ophthalmology, 1996—2004, assoc. dean grad. med. edn., 2000—03, acting dean, 2002—03, dean, sr. v.p., 2003—, provost, 2004—. Lectr., U. Ill., Chgo., 1984-96; adj. asst. prof. biomed. engri., Northwestern U. Evanston, Ill., 1986-87, adj. assoc. prof., 1987-94, adj. prof., 1994-97. Assoc. editor Key Ophthalmology, 1986-88, Year Book Ophthalmology, 1986-88; author 6 books; contbr. articles to profl. jours. Recipient Chancellor's award Washington U., 1975, Henry Lyman award Rush Med. Coll, 1978, Mark Lepper tchg. award, 1994, Disting. Alumnus award Rush Med. Coll., 1998. Fellow: ACS, Am. Acad. Ophthalmology (sec. for instrn. 2001—02, sec. for new ophthalmic info. 2002—03, Honor award 1990, Sr. Honor award 2003); mem.: Rush Alumni Assn. (pres. 1990—93, James A. Campbell award 1990), Chgo. Ophthalmol. Soc. (chmn. clin. conf. 1986, councillor 1988—89, sec.-treas. 1989—91, pres. 1994—95), Assn. Rsch. Vision Ophthalmology. Office: Rush U Med Ctr 1725 W Harrison St Ste 918 Chicago IL 60612-3835

DEUTSCH, WILLIAM EMIL, ophthalmology professor; b. Chgo., Mar. 31, 1926; s. Emil and Jeannette (Weil) D.; m. Natasha Sobotka, Dec. 23, 1951; children: Thomas A., Judith Deutsch Kornblatt, Susan E. BS, U. Ill., 1948, MD, 1950. Diplomate Am. Bd. Ophthalmology. Intern Michael Reese Hosp., Chgo., 1950-51; resident U. Ill., Chgo., 1951-53, clin. asst. prof. ophthalmology, 1971—; pvt. practice ophthalmology Chgo., 1955—; assoc. prof. ophthalmology Rush Med. Coll., Chgo., 1971-82, prof., chmn. dept., 1982—. Bd. mem. Ill. Soc. Prevention Blindness, Chgo., 1983—, Coun. Jewish Elderly, 1982—; tech. rev. bd. State of Ill., 1985—. Capt. USAF, 1953-55. Mem. Am. Acad. Ophthalmology (councilor 1988—), Assn. Rsch. in Vision and Ophthalmology, Assn. Univ. Profs. Ophthalmology, Ill. Assn. Ophthalmology (bd. dirs. 1979—), Chgo. Opthal. Soc. (coun. 1979-90, pres. 1982-83). Home: 732 Sheridan Rd Evanston IL 60202-2502 Office: Rush Med Coll Dept Ophthalmology 1653 W Congress Pkwy Chicago IL 60612-3833

DEVANEY, DENNIS MARTIN, lawyer, educator; b. Cheverly, Md., Feb. 25, 1946; s. Peter Paul and Alice Dorothy (Duffy) Devaney; m. Caryn Joanne; children: Jeanne Marie, Susan Theresa, Matthew Aaron. BA in History, U. Md., 1968, MA in Govt. Politics, 1970; JD, Georgetown U., 1975. Bar: Md. 1976, DC 1976, Fla. 1977, Mich. 1999, US Supreme Ct. 1980. Instr. European div. U. Md., Bremerhaven, Fed. Republic Germany, 1971-72; legis. asst. Md. Senate Jud. Commn., Annapolis, 1973-74; asst. gen. counsel US Brewers Assn., Washington, 1975-77; counsel Food Mktg. Inst., Washington, 1977-79; ptnr. Randall, Bangert & Thelen, Washington, 1979-81; assoc. Tighe, Curhan & Piliero, Washington, 1981-82; mem. US Merit System Protection Bd., Washington, 1982-88; gen. counsel Fed. Labor Relations Auth., Washington, 1988; mem. NLRB, 1988-94; commr. US Internat. Trade Commn., 2001; of counsel Winston & Strawn, 1995-97, Butzel Long, 1997—2001; ptnr. Williams, Mullen Clark and Dobbins, 2002—04; counsel Varnum, Riddering, Schmidt & Howlett, LLP, 2004—05; shareholder Strobl & Sharp, P.C., Bloomfield Hills, Mich., 2005—. Adj. prof. George Washington U., Washington, 1982—90, Boston U., 1992—94, 2002, Cornell U., 1995, Tulane U., 1995; assoc. prof. Wayne State U., 1995—2001, Thomas Cooley Law Sch., 2004. Served with USN, 1970-72, ETO. Mem. ABA, Md. Bar Assn., DC Bar Assn., Fla. Bar Assn., Mich. State Bar, Fed. Bar Assn., Phi Alpha Theta, Pi Sigma Alpha, Delta Theta Phi, Omicron Delta Kappa. Roman Catholic. Home: 5240 Buell Dr Commerce Township MI 48382 Office: Strobl & Sharp PC 300 E Long Lake Rd Ste 200 Bloomfield Hills MI 48304-2376 Office Phone: 248-205-2766. Business E-Mail: ddevaney@stroblpc.com.

DEVANNY, E. H. (TRACE), III, healthcare informatics executive; Grad., U. of the South. With IBM, 1977-94; corp. v.p. Cerner Corp., Kansas City, Mo., 1994-97, pres., 1999—; pres. health care info. sys. divsn. ADAC Labs., Houston, 1997-99. Office: Cerner Corp 2800 Rockcreek Pkwy Kansas City MO 64117-2521

DEVELLANO, JAMES CHARLES, professional hockey manager, baseball executive; b. Ont., Can., Jan. 18, 1943; came to U.S., 1979; s. James Joseph and Jean (Piter) D. Ont. scout St. Louis Blues NHL, Toronto, 1967-72; eastern Can. scout N.Y. Islanders, Toronto, 1972-74, dir. scouting, 1974-82; asst. gen. mgr. Islanders, LI and NY, 1981-82; gen. mgr. Detroit Red Wings, 1982-90, sr. v.p., 1990—; v.p., gen. mgr. Indpls. Checkers, 1979-81; sr. v.p. Detroit Tigers, 2001—. Alternate gov. Detroit Red Wings. Winner Stanley Cup with N.Y. Islanders, 1979-80, 80-81, 81-82, with Detroit Red Wings, 1996-97, 97-98, 2001-2002, Pres.'s Trophy with Detroit Red Wings, 1994-95, 95-96, 2001-2002, 2003-04, 2005-06. Mem. Nat. Hockey League (bd. govs.). Office: Detroit Red Wings Hockey Club Joe Louis Arena 600 Civic Center Dr Detroit MI 48226-4419 Office Phone: 313-506-9885. Personal E-mail: jimdevellano@comcast.net.

DEVER, DICK, state legislator; m. Pam Dever; 3 children. B, U. N.D. Owner DEVCO; mem. N.D. Senate from 32d dist., Bismark, 2001—. Elder Boy Scouts Am. With U.S. Army. Mem. VFW. Republican. Lutheran. Office: State Capitol 600 East Blvd Bismarck ND 58505 E-mail: ddever@state.nd.us.

DEVEREUX, TIMOTHY EDWARD, advertising executive; b. Chgo., Jan. 13, 1932; s. James Matthew and Nellie (Fitzmaurice) D.; m. Ann Sullivan, Apr. 2, 1956; children: Timothy Jr., Colette Marie, Jennifer Ann, Peter Gerard, Nora Marie, Matthew. BA in Communication Arts, U. Notre Dame, Ind., 1955. Copywriter Montgomery Ward & Co., Chgo., 1957-58; pub. relations dir. Victor Comptometer Corp., Chgo., 1958-60; sales promotion mgr. Bankers Life & Casualty Co., Chgo., 1960-61; dir. advt. and pub. relations Mid-America Foods, Inc., River Forest, Ill., 1961-62; mdse. mgr. Marshall John & Assos., Chgo. also Northbrook, 1962-65; acct. supr. Marshall John/Action Advt., Northbrook, Ill., 1965-70, exec. v.p., chief exec. officer, 1970-77, also dir.; pres. Devereux Direct, Ltd., 1977-79; v.p. direct response group Frankel & Co., Chgo., 1979-85; pres. Timothy E. Devereux & Assocs., Oak Park, Ill., 1985—. Served to 1st lt. USMCR, 1955—57. Home and Office: 1185 S Oak Park Ave Oak Park IL 60304-2048 Home Phone: 708-383-6256.

DEVINATZ, ALLEN, retired mathematician, educator; b. Chgo., July 22, 1922; s. Victor and Kate (Bass) D.; m. Pearl Moskowitz, Sep. 16, 1956; children: Victor Gary, Ethan Sander. BS, Ill. Inst. Tech., 1944; A.M., Harvard U., 1947, PhD, 1950. Instr. Ill. Inst. Tech., 1950-52; NSF Postdoctoral fellow, 1952-53; fellow Inst. Advanced Study, Princeton, 1953-54; asst. prof. U. Conn., 1954-55; mem. faculty Washington U., St. Louis, 1955-67, prof. math., 1961-67, acting chmn. dept., 1963-64; prof. math. Northwestern U., Evanston, Ill., 1967-92, prof. emeritus, 1992—, asst. chmn. dept., 1968-70, acting chmn. dept., 1991. Vis. mem. Weizmann Inst., Israel, 1980, Inst. Hautes Etudes Sci., Paris, 1982, Inst. for Applications of Calculus-Mauro Picone, Rome, 1988; vis. scholar U. Calif., Berkeley, 1985; Disting. lectr. Hebrew U., Jerusalem, 1993. Contbr. articles profl. jours. Sr. NSF Postdoctoral fellow, 1960-61 Mem. Am. Math. Soc. (translation com. for Russian 1985-88), Sigma Xi, Tau Beta Pi. Office: Northwestern U Dept Math Lunt Bldg Evanston IL 60208-0001 Office Phone: 847-467-8035. Personal E-mail: devi3@earthlink.net.

DEVINE, EDMOND FRANCIS, retired lawyer; b. Ann Arbor, Mich., Aug. 9, 1916; s. Frank B. and Elizabeth Catherine (Doherty) DeV.; m. Elizabeth Palmer Ward, Sept. 17, 1955; children: Elizabeth Palmer, Stephen Ward, Michael Edmond, Suzanne Lee. AB, U. Mich., Ann Arbor, 1937; JD, U. Mich., 1940; LLM, Cath. U. Am., Washington, DC, 1941. Bar: Mich. 1940, US Dist. Ct. (ea. dist.) Mich. 1940, US Ct. Appeals (6th cir) 1974, US Supreme Ct. 1975. Spl. agt. FBI, 1941-43; chief asst. prosecutor Washtenaw County, Ann Arbor, 1947-53, prosecuting atty., 1953-58; ptnr. DeVine & DeVine, Ann Arbor, 1958-74, DeVine, DeVine, Kantor & Serr, Ann Arbor, 1974-84; sr. ptnr. Miller, Canfield, Paddock & Stone, Ann Arbor, 1984-92, of counsel, 1992—; ret., 2006. Asst. prof., adj. prof. U. Mich. Law Sch., 1949-79. Co-author: Criminal Procedure, 1960. Lt. USNR, 1943—46, PTO. Decorated Bronze Star with combat v. Fellow Am. Bar Found. Am. Coll. Trial Lawyers, Mich. Bar Found.; mem. ABA, State Bar Mich. (bd. commrs., chmn. judiciary com. 1976-85, mem. rep. assembly, chmn. rules and calendar com.1971-76, co-chair US Cts. com. 1986-87), Internat. Assn. Def. Counsel, US Supreme Ct. Hist. Soc., Ann Arbor C. of C. (chmn. bd. 1971), Detroit Athletic Club, Barton Hills Country Club, Pres.'s Club. U. Mich., Varsity M Club, Order of Coif, Barristers, Phi Delta Phi, Phi Kappa Psi. Republican. Roman Catholic. Avocations: golf, running, reading. Home: 101 Underdown Rd Ann Arbor MI 48105-1078 Home Phone: 734-668-6041.

DEVINE, JOHN MARTIN, automotive parts company executive; b. Pitts., May 13, 1944; s. John Patrick and Camilla (Durkin) D.; m. Patricia McGee Devine; children: Sean, Bridget. BS in Econs., Duquesne U., 1967; MBA, U. Mich., 1972. Various fin. positions Ford Motor Co., 1968-80, contr. product devel. Europe Europe, 1981-83; staff dir. fin. Asia, Asia, 1983-85; v.p. no. Pacific ops. Ford Motor Co., Asia, 1985-86, exec. dir. no. Pacific bus. devel., 1986-87; contr. truck ops. U.S., U.S., 1988; pres. First Nationwide Bank, 1988-91; contr. Ford Motor Co., 1994, CFO, 1994-99; chmn., CEO Fluid Ventures, LLC, 1999—2000; vice chmn., CFO Gen. Motors Corp., Detroit, 2000—05, vice chmn., 2006; exec. chmn. Dana Holding Corp., Toledo, 2008—, acting CEO, 2008. Bd. dirs. Amerigon Inc., 2008—, Dana Holding Corp., 2008—. Office: Dana Holding Corp 4500 Dorr St Toledo OH 43615*

DEVINE, RICHARD A. (DICK DEVINE), lawyer; b. Chgo., July 5, 1943; m. Charlene Devine; children: Matt, Karen, Tim, Pete. BA cum laude, Loyola U., 1966; JD cum laude, Northwestern U., 1968. Bar: Ohio 1968, Ill. 1969, U.S. Dist. Ct. (no. dist.) Ill. 1973, U.S. Ct. Appeals (7th cir.) 1983, U.S. Supreme Ct. 1983. Assoc. Squire, Sanders & Dempsey, Cleve., 1968-69; adminstrv. asst. to mayor of Chgo., 1969-72; assoc. Pope, Ballard, Shepard & Fowle, 1972-74; assoc., ptnr. Foran, Wiss & Schultz, 1974-80, ptnr., 1983-85; 1st asst. state's atty. Cook County State's Atty.'s Office, 1980-83; ptnr. Phelan, Pope, Cahill, Devine & Ouinlan, Ltd., 1985-95, Shefsky Froelich & Devine Ltd., 1995-96; state's atty. Cook County, 1996—. Lectr. continuing legal edn. IIT Kent Coll. Law, John Marshall U.; co-chair courses on damages in bus. litigation Law Jour. Seminar; judge moot ct. programs Northwestern Law Sch., John Marshall Law Sch.; appointed mem. State Commn. on Accreditation of Criminal Justice; appointed mem. Spl. Commn. on Adminstrn. of Justice in Cook County, chmn. task force on misdemeanor and preliminary hearing cts., chmn. task force on jud. adminstrn.; appointed mem. profl. adv. com. Office of State's Atty. of Cook County, 1984-89; bd. dirs. Cook County Criminal Justice Project; mem. Chgo.-Cook County Criminal Justice Commn., 1971-78; hearing officer Chgo. Bd. Election Commrs., 1984. Mem. editl. bd. Northwestern U. Law Rev., 1966-68, mng. editor, 1967-68; contbr. to law jours. Bd. commrs. Chgo. Park Dist., 1989-93, pres. bd., 1990-93; bd. trustees Loyola Acad., 1982-88, St. Scholastica H.S.; bd. dirs. Chgo. Hist. Soc., 1990-93, Adler Planetarium; pro bono mem., pres. Chgo. Park Dist, 1989-93. Russell Sage fellow in law and social scis. Mem. ABA, Am. Coll. Trial Lawyers (elected), Ill. State Bar Assn., Chgo. Bar Assn. (com. jud. evaluation 1983-88, chmn. legis. assistance and evaluation com., young lawyers sect. 1973-74, vice-chmn. 1974-76, chmn. 1976-77, urban affairs com., mem. local govt. com. 1974-76, faculty young lawyers sect. trial advocacy program, lectr. on continuing legal edn.), Northwestern Law Sch. Alumni Assn. (bd. dirs. 1993—), Ill. State Attys. Assn. (bd. dirs.), Nat. Dist. Attys. Assn. (bd. dirs.). Office: Cook County State Atty 69 W Washington St Ste 3200 Chicago IL 60602 Office Phone: 312-603-5106. E-mail: stateattorny@cookcountygov.com.

DEVINE, TERRY MICHAEL, newspaper editor; b. Watertown, SD, Dec. 13, 1945; s. Russell LeRoy and Margaret Evelyn (Adams) DeV.; m. Patricia Rae Engler, July 25, 1969; children: Taylor Alan, Nathan Lee, Erin Renae. BS, S.D. State U., 1972. Reporter Watertown Pub. Opinion, 1963-65, Sioux Falls (S.D.) Argus Leader, 1969-70; newsman AP, Sioux Falls, 1970-72, Pierre, S.D., 1972-73, newsman-supr. Mpls., 1973-74, corr. Sioux Falls, 1974-75, broadcast exec. Mpls., 1975-78, news editor, 1978-81, Forum Fargo (N.D.)-Moorhead, 1981-85; mng. editor Forum Fargo (N.D.)-Moorehead, 1985-98; reporter Forum Fargo (N.D.) -Moorehead. Sgt. USMC, 1965-69, Vietnam. Mem. AP Mng. Editors Assn. (nat. edn. com. 1986--), Am. Legion (post baseball com. 1986--), Shanley Quarterback Club (pres. 1987--). Republican. Roman Catholic. Avocations: reading, fishing, writing, military history, golf. Home: 2807 32d St SW Fargo ND 58103-7875 Office: Forum Pub Co 101 N 5th St PO Box 2020 Fargo ND 58107-2020

DEVLIN, BARBARA JO, school district administrator; b. Milw., 1947; m. John Edward Devlin, 1973; 2 children. BA, Gustavus Adolphus Coll., 1969; MA, U. Mass., 1971; PhD, U. Minn., 1978. Cert. tchr., sch. prin., supt., Minn.; cert. supt., Ill., Minn. Tchr. Worthington (Minn.) High Sch., 1971-75; rsch. assoc. Ednl. R & D, Mpls.-St. Paul, 1975-76, 76-77; coord. edn. svcs. Ednl. Coop. Svc., Mpls.-St. Paul, 1977-79; dir. personnel Minnetonka Pub. Schs., Excelsior, Minn., 1979-85, asst. supt., 1985-87; supt. Sch. Dist. 45, Villa Park, Ill., 1987-95, Ind. Sch. Dist. 280, Richfield, Minn., 1995—. Editor working papers Gov.'s Coun. on Fluctuating Enrollments, St. Paul, 1976. Contbr. articles to ednl. jours. Bd. dir. Richfield Found., 1995—. Named Ill. Supt. of Yr., 1994, Region 9 Adminstr. of Excellence, Minn. Assn. Sch. Adminstrs., 2004; recipient Disting. Alumni award, Gustavus Adolphus Coll., 1994; Ednl. Policy fellow, George Washington U., 1977—78, mem. fellow program, Bush Found. Pub. Schs., 1984—85. Mem. Minn. Assn. Sch. Adminstrs. (Morris Bye Meml. award for Supt. Leadership 2006), Rotary Internat. (membership chair Villa Park unit 1989-91, vocat. dir. 1991-92, sec. 1992-93, pres. 1994-95), Optimists Internat. (pres. 2000-2001). Methodist. Office: Richfield Pub Schs 7001 Harriet Ave Richfield MN 55423-3061 Office Phone: 612-798-6010. E-mail: Barbara.Devlin@richfield.k12.mn.us.

DEVLIN, JAMES RICHARD, lawyer; b. Camden, NJ, July 7, 1950; s. Gerald William and Mary (Hand) D.; children: Grace, Jennifer, Kristen. BS in Indsl. Engring., N.J. Inst. Tech., 1972; JD, Fordham U., 1976. Bar: N.J. 1976, N.Y. 1977, Kans. 2002, U.S. Ct. Appeals (D.C. cir.) 1982. Various mgmt. positions in Long Lines Sect. AT&T, NYC, 1972-76, counsel Long Lines Sect. Bedminster, N.J., 1976-82, counsel NYC, 1982-83, gen. atty. comm. sect. Basking Ridge, N.J., 1983-86; v.p., gen. counsel telephone United Telecomm., Inc., Westwood, Kans., 1987-88; exec. v.p. gen. counsel and external affairs Sprint Corp., Westwood, Kans., 1989—2003. Past pres., bd. dirs. Ctr. for Mgmt. Assistance, Kansas City, Mo., 1993-96 Mem. ABA (past chmn. comm. com. pub. utility law sect.), Am. Arbitration Assn., Fed. Comm. Bar Assn. Home: 12300 Catalina St Leawood KS 66209-2220

DEVOE, ROBERT DONALD, visual physiologist; b. White Plains, NY, Oct. 7, 1934; s. Frank Kenneth and Martha (Josselyn) DeV.; m. Joanne Mattson, July 9, 1960 (div. 1986); children: Catherine Ellen, Edward Edgar; m. Gwendolyn Latta Berghorn, May 20, 1989 (div. 1992); m. Elizabeth Strong Gitlitz, Aug. 9, 1997. AB, Oberlin Coll., 1956; PhD, The Rockefeller U. From asst. to assoc. prof. Med. Sch. Johns Hopkins U., Balt., 1961-83; prof. Sch. of Optometry Ind. U., Bloomington, 1983-99, emeritus prof., 1999—. Grantee referee NIH, Washington, 1968—, NSF, Med. Rsch. Coun., Eng., 1973—, B.C. Health Rsch. Found., 1993—, Australian Rsch. Coun., 1993—; manuscript referee to numerous jours., 1960—; rsch. sabbatical Max-Planck Inst. für Biol. Kybernetic, Tübingen, Germany, 1973-74, Sch. Optometry, U. New South Wales, Australia, 1993. Mem. adv. bd. Jour. Comparative Physiology, Berlin, 1983-86; contbr. articles to profl. jours. Recipient Sr. Sci. award Alexander von Humboldt Found., Bonn, Germany, 1973-74; grantee NIH, 1962-91. Mem. AAAS, Assn. for Rsch. in Vision and Ophthalmology, Soc. for Neurosci., Serious Macintosh User's Group (treas.), Alpine Ski Club, Sigma Xi, Phi Beta Kappa. Democrat. Avocations: gardening, camping, skiing, hiking, music. Office: Ind U Sch Optometry 800 E Atwater Ave Bloomington IN 47405-3635

DEVORE, C. BRENT, college president, educator; b. Zanesville, Ohio, Sept. 3, 1940; s. Carl Emerson and Helen Elizabeth (Van Atta) DeVore; m. Linda Mospens, July 2, 1966; children: Krista, Matthew. BSJ., Ohio U., 1962; MA, Kent State U., 1971, PhD, 1978. Dir. devel. Am. Heart Assn., Cleve., 1965-68; exec. dir. Kent State U. Found., Ohio, 1968-72; v.p. Hiram Coll., Ohio, 1972-82; pres. Davis and Elkins Coll., Elkins, W.Va., 1982-84, Otterbein Coll., Westerville, Ohio, 1984—. Pres. Higher Edn. Coun., Columbus, 1985; trustee Nationwide Investing Found., 1990; bd. dirs. Coun. Ind. Colleges, 2004-. Producer and moderator film series on liberal arts edn. Pres. Hiram (Ohio) Village Council, 1981; chmn. E. Cen. Colls., 1990; pres. Nat. Assn. Schs. and Colls., United Meth. Ch., 1991. Mem. Am. Assn. Advancement of Humanities, AAUP, Ohio Council of Fund Raising Execs. (pres. 1976), Ohio Coll. Assn. (pres. 1987), W.Va. Assn. Coll. and Univ. Pres. (pres. 1984), Westerville C. of C. (pres.). Clubs: University (Columbus, Ohio); University (NYC). Lodges: Rotary. Office: Otterbein Coll Pres Office 27 S Grove St Westerville OH 43081-2004

DEVOS, ELISABETH (BETSY), political association executive; b. Holland, Mich., Jan. 8, 1958; d. Edgar Dale and Elsa D. (Zwiep) Prince; m. Richard M. DeVos Jr., 1979; four children. BSc in Bus. Adminstrn., Calvin Coll., 1979. Co-chmn. Kent County (Mich.) Rep. Finance Com., 1983-84, chmn., 1985-88, 96—; Rep. Nat. Committeewoman State of Mich., 1992-97; chmn. Mich. State Rep. Party, 1996—2000; mem. Nat. Rep. Com., 1996—; chmn. Mich. State Rep. Party, 2003—. Market rsch. analyst Amway Corp., 1979-81; pres. Windquest Group. Bd. dirs. Blodgett Meml. Med. Ctr., 1986—, Ada (Mich.) Christian Sch., 1992—; mem. Rep. Congl. Leadership Coun. Mem. Econ. Club of Grand Rapids. Avocations: travel, boating, skiing.

DEVOS, RICHARD MARVIN, JR., (DICK DEVOS), retired direct sales company and sports team executive; b. Grand Rapids, Mich., Oct. 21, 1955; s. Richard Marvin and Helen June (Van Wesep) DeV.; m. Elisabeth Dee Prince, Feb. 24, 1979. BBA, Northwood U., 1981. Coordinator sales Amway Corp., Ada, Mich., 1973-75, coordinator meetings, 1975-77, mgmt. trainee, 1977-82, dir. spl. events, 1982-84, v.p. internat., 1984-89, pres., bd. dirs., 1993-00; ret.; pres., bd. dirs. Alticor, Inc., 2000—02. Bd. dirs. USA DSA, 1993-98, vice chmn. 1995-97, chmn. 1997, Old Kent Fin. Corp., 1994-01; bd. dirs. Fifth Third Bank W. Mich.; founder The Windquest Group, 1989—, pres., 1989-93. Author: Rediscovering American Values, 1992. Chmn. Kent Ottawa Muskegon Fgn. Trade Zone Bd., 1989-96, chmn. Coalition for Better Schs., 1993-94; bd. dirs. Mackinac Ctr., 1990-95, Kent Hosp. Fin. Authority, 1980-93, West Mich. Boy Scouts Am., 1985-93, chmn. Blodgett Health Care, Butterworth Found., 1994—; co-chmn. Grand Rapids Area Negro Coll. Fund, 1989-92; mem. by appointment of Pres. Bush Commn. on Presdl. Scholars, 1991-93; elected mem. Mich. State Bd. Edn., 1991-93; bd. trustees Davenport Coll. Bus., 1991-2000; apptd. mem. bd. of control Grand Valley State U., 1995-2000; bd. dirs., exec. com. Project Rehab, 1978-84; mem. bd. dirs. Bus. Industry Political Action Com., 1995—; co-chmn. Grand Action Com., 1992—; chmn. Edn. Freedom Fund, 1994—; bd. dirs. Willow Creek Assoc., 1997—; chmn. Restoring the Am. Dream, 1998—. Recipient Grand Rapids Jaycees Disting. Svc. award 1985, Disting. Svc. Citation Northwood U., 1991, Assn. Ind. Colls. and Univs. Mich. Disting. Svc. award, 1992. Mem. Nat. Assn. of Mfgs. (bd. dirs. 1994-2000). Lodges: Rotary. Avocations: sailing, skiing. Office: The Windquest Group 126 Ottawa NW Ste 400 Grand Rapids MI 49503 Home: 2003 Hillsboro Ave SE Grand Rapids MI 49546-9791

DEVRIES, MARVIN FRANK, mechanical engineering educator; b. Grand Rapids, Mich., Oct. 31, 1937; s. Ralph B. and Grace (Buurma) DeVries; m. Martha Lou Kannegieter, Aug. 28, 1959; children: Mark Alan, Michael John, Dale Matthew. BS, Calvin Coll., 1960; BSME, U. Mich., 1960, MSME, 1962; PhD, U. Wis., 1966. Registered profl. engr., Wis. Teaching fellow mech. engring. U. Mich., Ann Arbor, 1960-62; from instr. to assoc. prof. U. Wis., Madison, 1962—77, prof. mech. engring., 1977—2005, prof. emeritus, 2005—, chmn. dept. mech. engring., 1991-95. Vis. Fulbright prof. Cranfield (Eng.) Inst. Tech., 1979—80; dir. Mfg. Sys. Engring. Program, Madison, 1983—91; cons. in field. Contbr. articles to profl. jours. Sr. program dir. NSF, Washington, 1987—90. Recipient Ralph Teetor award, Soc. Auto. Engrs., 1967, Space Shuttle Tech. award, NASA, 1984, Disting. Achievement award, LA Coun. Engrs. and Scientists, 1985, Internat. Tech. Comm. award, Calif. Engring. Found., 1985. Fellow: ASME, Soc. Mfg. Engrs. (pres. 1985—86, Olin Simpson award 1986, Edn. award 1998), Instn. Prodn. Engrs. (U.K.) (life); mem.: Internat. Instn. Prodn. Engring. Rsch. (v.p. 1997—99, pres. 1999—). Avocations: travel, sports. Home: 901 Tompkins Dr Madison WI 53716-3267 Office: U Wis 1513 University Ave Madison WI 53706-1539 Home Phone: 608-222-4678; Office Phone: 608-262-1808. Business E-Mail: devries@engr.wisc.edu.

DEVRIES, ROBERT ALLEN, foundation administrator; b. Chgo., May 12, 1936; s. Robert and Mildred (Burgess) DeV.; m. Eleanor Rose Siems, Aug. 16, 1958; children: Susan E., Robert S., Laura H., Steven P. BS in Physiology, U. Chgo., 1958, MBA in Hosp. Adminstrn., 1961. Adminstrv. resident, asst. Miami Valley Hosp., Dayton, Ohio, 1959-61, asst. dir., 1961-67; adminstr. McPherson Community Health Ctr., Howell, Mich., 1967-71; program dir. W.K. Kellogg Found., Battle Creek, Mich., 1971-88, program dir., dir. Kellogg Internat. Fellowship Programs, 1988-90, program dir., dir. Internat. Study Grants and Exchanges, 1990-97, mem. adminstrv. coun., 1995-97, program dir., mem. fellowship com., 1997-99; ret., 1999. Cons. on domestic and internat. programs W.K. Kellogg Found., 1999—; mem. com. vis. Sch. Nursing, U. Mich., 2000—; assisting min. St. Peter Luth. Ch.; chmn. quality com. bd. trustees Battle Creek Health Sys., 2001—; bd. dirs. Lifecare Ambulance, chmn. bd., 2004—; bd. dirs. North Pointe Woods, Mich. Health Coun., Battle Creek Cmty. Found.; lectr. nursing orgn., adminstrn. Sch. Nursing Miami Valley Hosp., 1961-67, Grad. Sch. Pub. Health U. Mich., 1967—; adj. prof. Coll. Health and Human Svcs., Western Mich. U., 1986—; advisor Sch. Pub. Health Beijing Med. U., 1986—, Med. Coll. Health Staff, Shanghai, 1986—, 1st People's Hosp., Shanghai, 1986—;

mem. nat. adv. com. on rural health U.S. Dept. Health and Human Svcs., Washington, 1988-92; mem. adv. panel acad. health scis. ctr. U.N.C., Chapel Hill, 1992-94; mem. policy coun. Nat. Inst. Rural Health Policy, 1987-90; mem. health planning and cert. of need workgroup Mich. Dept. Mgmt. & Budget, Mich. Dept. Pub. Health, 1986-87; vice chmn. adv. coun. Hosp. Rsch. & Ednl. Trust, Chgo., 1974-85; treas. coun. practice Am. Assn. Nurse Anesthetists, 1978-84; mem. Southwest Mich. Health Sys. Agy. Bd., 1980-83; guest lectr. King's Fund Coll., London, U. Leeds, Eng., French Nat. Sch. Pub. Health, Rennes, U. Toronto, Pan Am. Health Orgn., Washington and Brasilia, Brazil, Katholieke Universiteit Leuven, Belgium, Internat. Hosp. Fedn., London, Elton Mayo Sch. Mgmt., Adelaide, Australia, Ministry Pub. Health, Beijing, Indian Hosp. Assn., New Delhi, Harvard Med. Sch., Assn. Am. Med. Coll. Co-author healthcare trustee book; mem. editl. bds. Inquiry, Hosp. & Health Svcs.; contbr. articles to profl. jours., also book chpts. Counselor Baxter Am. Found. Prize in Health Svcs. Rsch., 1986—; assoc. trustee Florence Nightingale Mus. Trust, London. Recipient Disting. Svc. award Am. Soc. Allied Health Professions, 1989, Med. Group Mgmt. Assn., Denver, 1990, Ohio State U. Alumni Assn., 1998; Monsignor Griffin award for disting. writing Ohio Hosp. Assn., 1965, Civic Achievement award Jr. C. of C., Chgo., 1955, recognition award for contbns. to svcs. to handicapped Commn. on Accreditation of Rehab. Facilities, 1976, Cmty. Health Leadership award Hosp. Rsch. and Ednl. Trust, 1994, Spl. Recognition award Mich. Health and Hosp. Assn., 1999, Cert. of Honor, Peking U., China, 2003, Red Rose award for disting. cmty. svc. Gr. Battle Creek Rotary, 2004, U. Chgo. Pub. Svc. citation, 2005, Mich. Governor's award, 2007, Civia Leader in Arts and Culture; named Outstanding Young Men in Am. Howell, Mich. Area C. of C. and Jaycees, 1970; Nat. Health Svcs. rsch. fellow U. Mich., 1970-71. Fellow Am. Coll. Healthcare Execs.(life), U.S. China Ednl. Inst., Can. Sch. Mgmt. (hon.); mem. APHA, Am. Hosp. Assn. (hon. life, vice chair R&D coun. 1974-85, adv. panel multi-hosp. systems 1977-85, Living the Vision award 1999, Blue Ribbon com. on healthcare governance), Internat. Hosp. Fedn., Nat. Rural Health Assn., Mich. Hosp. Assn. (assn. governance and strategic planning com. 1986-89, pub. policy and govt. com. 1981-83), U. Chgo. Hosp. Adminstrn. Alumni Assn. (pres. 1982-83), Leila Arboretum Soc. (pres. 2003-04). Lutheran. Avocations: music, writing, travel, gardening.

DE VRIES, ROBERT JOHN, investment banker; b. Pella, Iowa, Aug. 18, 1932; s. John G. and Anna (Kool) m. Patricia Lynn Jackson, Dec. 22, 1962 (dec.); children: Robert John Jr., Garrett Andrew. BBA, U. Tex., Austin, 1958; MBA, Harvard Grad. Sch. of Bus., Boston, 1960. Registered principal. Security analyst Cyrus J. Lawrence & Sons, NYC, 1960-64, Jas. H. Oliphant and Co., NYC, 1964-66; investment banker William D. Witter Inc., NYC, 1966-68; v.p. Mgmt. Planning Inc., Princeton, N.J., 1968-73; pres. Cryomed Devices, Inc., Princeton, 1973-80; v.p. Smith Barney, Harris Upham, 1981-84; pres., dir., founder Robert J. De Vries and Co., Inc., Kansas City, 1984—2002; mng. dir. DeVries, Snedeker & Duncan, LLC, Overland Park, Kans., 2002—. Served with USAF, 1952-56. Inst. of Chartered Fin. Analyst, Harvard Club of N.Y., Beta Gamma Sigma. Republican. Presbyterian. Avocations: photography, marathon running. Home: 24805 W 190th St Gardner KS 66030 Office: De Vries Snedeker & Duncan LLC 10955 Lowell Ave Ste 1050 Overland Park KS 66210 Home Phone: 913-856-4687; Office Phone: 913-906-0055.

DEVRIES, ROBERT K., retired publisher, consultant; b. Sully, Iowa, July 6, 1932; s. Fred G. and Selena Irene (Willetts) DeV.; m. Carolyn Jo Schroeder, June 2, 1962 (div. 1978); children: Stephen Robert, Suzanne Mishael Dahill; m. Carolyn Gail Bergmans, May 26, 1979; children: Staci Ann McKellar, Keri Gail Bailey. AB, Wheaton Coll., 1954; ThM, Dallas Theol. Sem., 1958, ThD, 1969. Asst. registrar Dallas Theol. Sem., 1959-63; editor-in-chief Moody Press, Chgo., 1963-68; dir., v.p. pubs. Zondervan Pub. House, Grand Rapids, Mich., 1968-76, exec. v.p. book div., 1976-85; exec. v.p., publisher Zondervan Book Group, Zondervan Corp., Grand Rapids, Mich., 1985-86; pub., bd. dirs. Discovery House Pubs., Grand Rapids, 1987-2000, sr. publisher, bd. dirs., 2000—07; cons., bd. dirs. Serendipity House, Littleton, Colo., 1990-99; bd. dirs. Serendipity House Found., Littleton, 1999—2003. Bd. dirs. Oswald Chambers Pub. Assn. Ltd., Eng. Bd. dirs. Ligonier Valley Study Ctr., Stahlstown, Pa., 1979-83, Bd. Publ., Evang. Covenant Ch. Am., Chgo., 1989-94, chmn., 1992-94; advisor Internat. Coun. Bibl. Inerrancy, Walnut Creek, Calif., 1978-87. Recipient Outstanding Young Men in Am. award Jaycees, 1965, Lifetime Achievement award, Evangelical Christian Publishers Assn., 2006. Republican. Mem. Evangelical Covenant Ch. Home: 7554 Lime Hollow Dr SE Grand Rapids MI 49546-7439

DEVRIES SMITH, KATE, lawyer; BS in Physics cum laude, Drake U., 1993; JD cum laude, U. Mich. Law Sch., 1996. Bar: Minn. 1996, US Patent and Trademark Office 1998. Ptnr. Merchant & Gould, Mpls.; co-founder, ptnr. Pauly, DeVries Smith & Deffner, L.L.C., Mpls. Named a Rising Star, Minn. Super Lawyers mag., 2006. Mem.: Minn. Women Lawyers, Minn. Intellectual Property Law Assn., Am. Intellectual Property Law Assn., ABA (mem. intellectual property sect.), Vol. Lawyers etwork (bd. dirs., named Vol. Lawyer of Yr. 2005). Office: Pauly DeVries Smith & Defner LLC Plz VII Ste 3000 455 Seventh St Minneapolis MN 55402 Office Phone: 612-746-4784. E-mail: kds@pdsdlaw.com.

DEVYLDER, EDGAR PAUL, JR., lawyer; b. Waterbury, Conn., Jan. 7, 1945; s. Edgar Paul Sr. and Lillian (Cordett) DeV.; m. Elaine Jordan, Jan. 8, 1972; children: Joseph Steven, Jordan Edgar. AB, Yale U., 1967; JD, U. Mich., 1974. Bar: Conn. 1974, U.S. Dist. Ct. Conn. 1975, U.S. Ct. Appeals (2nd cir.) 1975, Fla. 1978, U.S. Supreme Ct. 1979. Assoc. Cummings & Lockwood, Stamford, Conn., 1974-79; counsel Gen. Signal Corp., Stamford, 1979-85, sr. atty., 1985-87; v.p., gen. counsel, sec. BTR, Inc., Stamford, 1988-99; ptnr. Cummings & Lockwood, Stamford, 2000—01, Pepe & Hazard, Southport, Conn., 2001—02; v.p. adminstrn., gen. counsel, sec. Raytech Corp., Shelton, Conn., 2002—. Lt. USN, 1967-71. Mem.: Yale Club of Stamford (pres. 2000—), Assn. Yale Alumni (del. 2000—). Office Phone: 203-952-4300. E-mail: edevylder2@aol.com.*

DEWALD, PAUL ADOLPH, psychiatrist, educator; b. NYC, Mar. 12, 1920; s. Jacob Frederick and Elsie (Wurzburger) D.; m. Eleanor Whitman, Sept. 1, 1961; children: Jonathan S., Ellen F. BA, Swarthmore Coll., 1942; MD, U. Rochester, 1945; cert. psychoanalysis, SUNY, 1960. Intern, Strong Meml. Hosp., Rochester, NY, 1945-46, resident, 1948-52; instr. U. Rochester, 1952-57, asst. prof. psychiatry, 1957-61; pvt. practice psychoanalysis St. Louis, 1961-99; asst. clin. prof. psychiatry Washington U., St. Louis, 1961-65, 96—; asso. clin. prof. St. Louis U., 1965-69, clin. prof. psychiatry, 1969—. Dir. treatment svc. Psychoanalytic Found. St. Louis, 1961-72, med. dir., 1972-83 St. Louis Psychoanalytic Inst., 1973-83, supervising and tng. analyst, 1973—; mem. faculty Chgo. Inst. Psychoanalysis, 1961-75, supervising and tng. analyst, 1965-73; vis. prof. U. Cin., 1968-80; mem. Mo. State Mental Health Commn., 1978-83, chmn., 1981-83; asst. prof. clin. psychiatry Washington U., 1995—. Author: Psychotherapy: A Dynamic Approach, 1964, 2d edit., 1969, The Psychoanalytic Process, 1972, Learning Process in Psycho-analytic Supervision, 1987; co-editor: Ethics Case Book of the American Psychoanalytic Assn., 2001; contbr. articles to profl. jours. Served to capt. M.C., AUS, 1946-48. Fellow Am. Psychiat. Assn. (life); mem. Mo. Psychiat. Assn. (pres. 1970-71), Eastern Mo. Psychiat. Assn. (pres. 1969-70), Am. Psychoanalytic Assn. (life), St. Louis Psychoanalytic Soc. (pres. 1970-71, 86-88) Home: Apt 3H 8600 Delmar Blvd Saint Louis MO 63124-1961 Office: 8600 Delmar Blvd Saint Louis MO 63124 Office Phone: 314-994-9608. Personal E-mail: padewald@charter.net.

DEWEESE, DEVIN A., history educator; b. 1956; PhD in Ctrl. Asian Studies, Ind. U., Bloomington, 1985. Prof. Ctrl. Asian studies Ind. U., Bloomington, 2003—. Author: Islamization and Native Religion in the Golden Horde (Best First Book in the History of Religions Am. Acad. Religion, Albert Hourani Book award Middle East Studies Assn.). Fellow, John Simon Guggenheim Meml. Found., 2003. Office: U Ind Ctrl Asian Studies Goodbody Hall 343 Bloomington IN 47405-7005 Business E-Mail: deweese@indiana.edu.

DEWERD, LARRY ALBERT, medical physicist, educator; b. Milw., July 18, 1941; s. Anthony Lawrence and Dorothy M. (Heling) DeW.; m. Vada Mary Anderson, Sept. 14, 1963; children: Scott, Mark, Eric. BS, U. Wis., Milw., 1963; MS, U. Wis., 1965, PhD, 1970. Rsch. assoc. U. Wash., Seattle, 1970-72, rsch. asst. prof., 1973-75; vis. asst. prof. U. Wis., Madison, 1975-76, clin. asst. prof., 1976-79, clin. assoc. prof., 1979-86, prof., 1990—. Mgr. product devel. Radiation Measurements, Middleton, Wis., 1986-90; dir. Radiation Calibration Lab., Madison, 1983-86, 90—; cons. Instrumentarium, Milw., 1990; v.p. Standard Imaging, Madison, 1990—; presenter in field; cons. IAEA. Contbg. author: Brachytherapy, Ionization Chambers and Dosimetry, Thermoluminescence and Mammography; also numerous articles. Science chmn. Am. Cancer Soc. State of Wis., 1986-90. Nat. Cancer Inst. grantee, 1979-86, 94-98. Fellow Am. Assn. Physicists in Medicine (pres. 1990-92, L. Lanzl hon. award 2005), Health Physics Soc., Am. Phys. Soc., Coun. Ionizing Radiation Measurements and Standards (pres. 1995-98), Sigma Xi (bd. dirs. 1984-86). Avocations: golf, fishing, backpacking, hunting. Home: 13 Pilgrim Cir Madison WI 53711-4033 Office: U Wis 1530 Med Sci Ctr 1300 University Ave Madison WI 53706-1510 Business E-Mail: ladewerd@wisc.edu.

DEWHURST, CHARLES KURT, museum director, curator, language educator; b. Passaic, NJ, Dec. 21, 1948; s. Charles Allaire and Minn Jule (Hanzl) D.; m. Marsha MacDowell, Dec. 15, 1972; 1 dau., Marit Charlene. BA, Mich. State U., 1970, MA, 1973, PhD in English and Am. Studies, 1983. Editorial asst. Carlton Press, NYC, 1967; computer operator IBM, NYC, 1968; project dir. Mich. State U. Mus., 1975, curator, 1976-83, dir., 1982—. Guest curator Mus. Am. Folk Art, NYC, 1978—83, Artrain, Detroit, 1980—83; dir. Festival of Mich. Folklife, 1987—95, Ctr. for Great Lakes Culture, 2000—. Author: Reflections of Faith, 1983, Artists in Aprons, 1979, Rainbows in the Sky, 1978, Michigan Folk Art, 1976 (Am. Assn. State and Local History award 1977), Art at Work: Folk Pottery of Grand Ledge, Michigan, 1986, Michigan Quilts, 1987, Michigan Folklife Reader, 1988, To Honor and Comfort: Native Quilting Traditions, 1998, MSU Campus: Buildings, Places and Spaces, 2002. Coord. South African-U.S. Partnership Project, 1967—; mem. and chair adv. com. Smithsonian Ctr. for Folklife Cultural Heritage; pres. bd. dirs. Fund for Folk Culture; bd. dirs. Am. Folklife Ctr., Libr. Congress. Recipient Disting. Svc. and Humanities award Am. Assn. State and Local History, 1994, Crystal award City of East Lansing. Fellow Mich. State U.; mem. Am. Folkore Soc. (Americo Padres award 2004), Mich. Folklore Soc., Midwest Soc. Lit., Popular Culture Assn., Mich. Hist. Soc., Mich. Mus. Assn., Am. Assn. Mus., Internat. Coun. Mus. Home: 1804 Cricket Ln East Lansing MI 48823-1225 Office: Mich State U Mus W Circle Dr East Lansing MI 48824 Business E-Mail: dewhurs1@msu.edu.

DEWINE, KEVIN, state representative; b. Springfield, Ohio, Oct. 11, 1967; married; 4 children. BS, U. Dayton; MBA, Wright State U. State rep. dist. 70 Ohio Ho. of Reps., Columbus, 2000—, mem. edn., fin. and appropriations, and homeland security engrng. and archtl. design coms., mem. primary and secondary edn. subcom. Mem.: Miami Valley Mil. Affairs Assn., Greene County Twp. Trustees Assn., Greene County Farm Bur., Fairborn, Beavercreek and Xenia Cs. of C., Leadership Dayton. Office: 77 S High St 12th fl Columbus OH 43215-6111

DEWINE, MIKE (RICHARD MICHAEL DEWINE), former senator, lawyer; b. Springfield, Ohio, Jan. 5, 1947; s. Richard and Jean DeWine; m. Frances Struewing, June 3, 1967; children: Patrick, Jill, Rebecca, John, Brian, Alice, Mark, Anna. BS in Edn., Miami U., Oxford, Ohio, 1969; JD, Ohio No. U., 1972. Bar: Ohio 1972, U.S. Supreme Ct. 1977. Asst. prosecuting atty. Greene County, Xenia, Ohio, 1973-75, prosecuting atty., 1977-81; mem. Ohio State Senate, 1981-82, US Congress from 7th Ohio dist., Washington, 1983-90; lt. gov. State of Ohio, Columbus, Ohio, 1991-94; US Senator from Ohio, 1995—2007; instr., Ctr. for Polit. Sciences Cedarville U., 2007—. Mem. com. intelligence US Senate, com. judiciary, com. health, edn., labor and pensions, com. appropriations. Mem. Nat. Commn. Drug Free Schools. Recipient Excellence in Public Svc. award, Am. Acad. Pediatrics, 1997, Congressional Recognition award, Internat. Assn. Fire Fighters, 2001, Nathan Davis award, AMA, Donald Santarelli award public policy, Nat. Orgn. Victim Assistance, Golden Eagle award, Nat. Coun. Defense, Guardian Small Business award, at. Fedn. Independent Bus., MADD award, Nat. Security Leadership award, Am. Security Coun., Spirit Enterprise award, US C. of C., Watchdog of the Treasury award, Nat. Taxpayers Union, Champion award, Campaign for Tobacco-Free Kids, 2005. Republican. Roman Catholic.

DEWITT, DAVID J., computer scientist; PhD, U. Mich., 1976. Prof., Romnes fellow computer scis. U. Wis., Madison. Fellow Am. Acad. Arts & Scis.; mem. NAE. Office: U Wis Dept Computer Sci 1210 W Dayton St Madison WI 53706-1685 E-mail: dewitt@cs.wisc.edu.

DEWITT, KATHARINE CRAMER, museum administrator; BA, Manhattenville Coll. of Sacred Heart. Docent Cin. Art Mus. Co-chair Presdl. Inaugural Com., 2001; mem. Nat. Coun. Arts., Nat. Endowment for Arts, 2002—. Trustee Cin. Children's Hosp. Med. Ctr., Beechwood Home, Stratford Hall Plantation, Va.; co-chmn. Cin. Antiques Festival, 1990, Garden Club of Am., 1995—97. Mem.: Cin. Fine Arts Fund (co-chmn. Individual Gifts 1985, 1993, mem. Allocation Com. 1991—94). Office: Cin Art Mus 953 Eden Park Dr Cincinnati OH 45202 Mailing: Nat Endowment for Arts 1100 Pennsylvania Ave NW Washington DC 20506 Office Phone: 513-721-2787.

DEWITT, THOMAS, pediatrician, educator; BA, Amherst Coll.; MD, U. Rochester, 1976. Diplomate Am. Bd. Pediatrics. Resident in pediatrics Yale-New Haven Hosp.; fellowship gen. acad. pediatrics Robert Wood Johnson Found., Yale U. Sch. Medicine; prof. pediats. Cin. Children's Hosp. Med. Ctr. Office: Cin Children's Hosp Med Ctr 3333 Burnet Ave Cincinnati OH 45229-3026

DEWITT, WILLIAM O., JR., professional sports team executive; b. St. Louis, Aug. 31, 1941; s. William O. and Margaret H. DeW.; m. Katharine Cramer; children: Katie, Bill, Andrew, Margot. BA in Econs., Yale U., 1963; MBA, Harvard U., 1965. Pres. Reynolds, DeWitt & Co.; owner St. Louis Cardinals, 1996—; chmn. bd. dirs., CEO Gateway Group Inc., 1996—. Co-chmn. Restaurant Mgmt. Inc.; bd. dirs. Sena Weller Rohe, Williams Inc., U.S. Playing Card Co. Pres. Fund for Ind. Schs. Cin., William O. and Margaret H. DeWitt Found.; pres. Rep. fin. com. Hamilton County; bd. dirs. Semple Found., Cin. Art Mus., Taft Mus., Salvation Army; mem. devel. bd. Yale U.; regional chmn. Yale Campaign; cabinet mem. Cin. Fine Arts Fund, United Way Cin., Multiple Sclerosis Soc. Office: St Louis Cardinals 250 Stadium Plz Saint Louis MO 63102-1722

DEWOSKIN, MARGARET FOGARTY, real estate company executive; Grad., U. Wis. With Hilco Real Estate LLC; v.p. acquisitions Klaff Realty L.P.; exec. v.p. Builders Bank, Chgo.; trans. coord. Orix Real Estate Capital, Inc., Chgo., 2004, sr. v.p., COO. Chair real estate capital investment com. Orix Real Estate Capital, Inc. Named one of Top 40 Under 40, Crain's Chgo. Bus., 2006. Mem.: Wis. Real Estate Alumni Assn. Office: Orix Real Estate Capital Inc 100 N Riverside Plz Ste 1400 Chicago IL 60606 E-mail: margaret.dewoskin@orix.com.

DEWULF NICKELL, KAROL, editor-in-chief; m. Don Nickell; children: Lauren, Alexander. BA in Journalism, Iowa St. U. Furnishings editor Better Homes and Gardens mag., 1979—87, editor-in-chief, 2001—, Traditional Home mag., 1987—2001, Renovation Style mag., 1995—2000; columnist Country Home mag., 1987—2001. Avocations: gardening, reading, cooking. Office: 1716 Locust St Des Moines IA 50309-3023

DEYONKER, ALEX J., lawyer, food products executive; BS, Mich. State U.; JD cum laude, Wayne State U. Mng. ptnr. Warner Norcross & Judd LLP, 1988—2006; gen. counsel Spartan Stores Inc., Grand Rapids, Mich., 1995—, sec., 2000—, bd. mem., 1999—2003, exec. v.p., 2006—. Mem.: ABA, Grand Rapids Bar Assn., State Bar of Mich. Office: Spartan Stores Inc 850 76th St, SW PO Box 8700 Grand Rapids MI 49518

DIAMANDIS, PETER H., foundation administrator, entrepreneur; b. Bronx, NY, May 20, 1961; Undergraduate and graduate degree in Aerospace Engring., MIT; MD, Harvard Med. Sch.; Doctorate (hon.), Internat. Space U., 2005. Founder, CEO Intenat. MicroSpace, Inc. (acquired by CTA Inc.), 1989—93; v.p., commercial space CTA Inc.; founder, pres., chmn., CEO X PRIZE Found., Inc., (originally in Rockville, Md., but now in St. Louis), 1995—; pres., COO Angel Technologies Corp.; CEO BlastOff! Corp. Founder SpaceFair, 1983, chair, 83, 85, 87; co-founder, trustee Internat. Space U., Strasbourg, France, 1987—, co-chair, bus. & mgmt. dept., 1992—94, also served as mng. dir., CEO; co-founder, bd. dir. Space Adventures, Ltd., 1998—; co-founder Zero Gravity Corp. (ZERO-G); co-founder, past chmn. Starport.com (acquired by Space.com in 1990); founder, dir. Constellation Communications, Inc. (sold to E-Systems then to Orbital Sciences), 1991; formed Rocket Racing League, 2005; bd. trustee Foresight Inst. Founded Students for the Exploration and Development of Space (SEDS), 1980; co-founder, chmn. Space Generation Found., 1985—. Named one of Top 25 Stars of Space, Nat. Space Soc., 1994; recipient MIT William L. Stewart, Jr. award, 1984, Kresge award, MIT, Space Industrialization Fellowship award, 1986, Aviation Week and Space Technology Laurel, 1988, Pioneer award, Space Frontier Found., 1993, K.E. Tsiolkovsky award, 1995, World Technology award, World Tech. Counsel, 2002, WIRED Rave award for Sci., 2006, Robert & Virginia Heinlein prize for Advances in Space Commercialization, 2006, Lindbergh award, Lindbergh Found., 2006, Neil Armstrong award for Aerospace Achievement and Leadership, 2006. X PRIZE Foundation developed the X PRIZE in May, 1996. This prize is a $10,000,000 prize to jumpstart the space tourism industry through competition among the most talented entrepreneurs and rocket experts in the world. In 2004, the X PRIZE was officially re-named the ANSARI X PRIZE. Office: X Prize Found Inc 722-A Spirit of St Louis Blvd Chesterfield MO 63005 Address: X Prize Found inc Sonnenschein Laura L Carley One Metropolitan Sq Ste 3000 Saint Louis MO 63102*

DIAMOND, EUGENE CHRISTOPHER, lawyer, health facility administrator; b. Oceanside, Calif., Oct. 19, 1952; s. Eugene Francis and Rosemary (Wright) D.; m. Mary Theresa O'Donnell, Jan. 20, 1984; children: Eugene John, Kevin Seamus, Hannah Rosemary, Seamus Michael, Maeve Therese. BA, U. Notre Dame, 1974; MHA, St. Louis U., 1978, JD, 1979. Bar: Ill. 1979. Staff atty. AUL Legal Def. Fund, Chgo., 1979-80; adminstrv. asst. Holy Cross Hosp., Chgo., 1980-81, asst. adminstr., 1981-82, v.p., 1982-83, counsel to adminstr., 1980—, exec. v.p., 1983-91; exec. v.p., COO, St. Margaret Mercy Healthcare Ctrs., Hammond, Ind., 1991-93, pres., CEO, 1993—2004, regional COO, 2001—04, regional CEO, 2004—. Cons. Birthright of Chgo., 1979—, mem. benefit com., 1981—; bd. dirs. Hammond C. of C., 1993, North West Ind. Forum. Mem.: Chgo. Bar Assn. Roman Catholic. Office: St Margaret Mercy Healthcare Ctrs 5454 Hohman Ave Hammond IN 46320-1999 Home Phone: 708-361-5866; Office Phone: 219-933-2178. Business E-Mail: gene.diamond@ssfhs.org.

DIAMOND, SEYMOUR, physician; b. Chgo., Apr. 15, 1925; s. Nathan Avruum and Rose (Roth) D.; m. Elaine June Flamm, June 20, 1948; children: Judi, Merle, Amy. Student, Loyola U., 1943-45; MB, Chgo. Med. Sch., 1948, MD, 1949. Intern White Cross Hosp., Columbus, Ohio, 1949-50; gen. practice medicine Chgo., 1950—; founder, dir. Diamond Headache Clinic, Ltd., Chgo., 1970—; dir. inpatient headache unit St. Joseph Hosp., Chgo.; prof. neurology Chgo. Med. Sch. at Rosalind Franklin U. Medicine and Sci., 1970-82, 85—, adj. prof. cellular and molecular pharmacology, 1985—, clin. prof. family medicine, 1999—; clin. prof. dept. family medicine U. Medicine and Dentistry N.J. Sch. Osteo. Medicine, Stratford, NJ, 1994-98; cons. mem. FDA Orphan Products Devel. Initial Rev. Group. Lectr. dept. cmty. and family medicine Loyola U. Stritch Sch. Medicine, 1972-78; lectr. Falconbridge lecture series Laurentian U., Sudbury, Ont., Can., 1987; disting. lectr. neurology U. Tenn., 1992; AMA cons. on drug evaluation, 1993; mem. sci. com. neurology Internat. Jour. Pain Therapy, 1993; mem. panel Nat. Ctr. on Addiction and Substance Abuse, Columbia U., N.Y.C., 2003. Author: A Pain Specialist's Approach to the Headache Patient, 1994; (with Bill and Cynthia Still) The Hormone Headache, 1995; Diagnosing and Managing Headaches, 1994, 4th edit., 2004; (with Donald J. Dalessio) The Practicing Physician's Approach to Headache, 5th edit., 1992, More Than Two Aspirin: Help for Your Headache Problem, 1976, (with Judi Diamond-Falk) Advice from the Diamond Headache Clinic, 1982, (with Mary Franklin Epstein) Coping with Your Headaches, 1982, 2d edit., 1987, (with Arnold P. Friedman MD) Headache in Contemporary Patient Management series, 1983; (with Amy Diamond Vye) Headache and Diet, 1990; (with Michael Maliszewski) Sexual Aspects of Headaches, 1992; (with Mary A. Franklin) Conquering Your Migraine, 2001; (with Amy Diamond) Headache and Your Child, 2001; (with Merle L. Diamond) Contemporary Diagnosis and Management of Headache and Migraine, 2d edit., 2000, (with Mary A. Franklin) Headache Through the Ages, 2005; contbg. author: Wolff's Headache and Other Head Pain, 6th edit., 1993, Handbook of Pain Management, 2d edit., 1994, Nonsteroidal Anti-Inflammatory Drugs, 2d edit., 1994, Current Review of Pain, 1994, New Advances in Headache Research, 1994, Conn's Current Therapy, 1998, Advanced Therapy of Headache, 1999, Diamond and Dalessio's Practicing Physician's Approach to Headache, 6th edit., 1999; editor: Migraine Headache Prevention and Management; editor-in-chief Headache Quar., 1990-02; editor-in-chief Headache and Pain, 2003-; mem. internat. editl. bd. Pediat. Drugs, 2001-; editl. cons. BIOSIS, 1986-90; contbr. numerous articles on headache and related fields to profl. jours. Bd. govs. Chgo. Med. Sch. at Rosalind Franklin U. Medicine & Sci. Recipient Disting. Alumni award Chgo. Med. Sch., 1977; Nat. Migraine Found. lectureship award, 1982, award Headache Consortium of New Eng., 1997, Cert. Appreciation, Chgo. Med. Soc., 1998, Presdl. award Alumni Assn. Chgo. Med. Sch., 2002; 1st recipient Migraine Trust lectureship, 1988; Brit. Migraine Trust 7th Internat. Migraine Symposium, London; Nat. Headache Found. Seymour Diamond fellow, 1993; Disting. lectr. in neurology U. Tenn., 1992. Fellow Royal Soc. Medicine; mem. AMA (Physicians Recognition awards 1970-73, 74, 77, 79, 82, 87, del. sect. clin. pharmacology and therapeutics 1987-89, mem. health policy agenda for Am. people, mem. cost effectiveness conf., del. reference com. "C" on edn., reference com. C, 1988), Am. Coun. on Sci. and Health (bd. sci. and policy advisors), Am. Assn. Study of Headache (exec. dir. 1971-85, pres. 1972-74, #1 regent mem. 1984, svc. award 1971-85, Lifetime Achievement award 1999), Nat. Headache Found. (pres. 1971-77, exec. dir. 1977-95, exec. chmn. 1995—, 1st recipient cert. of added qualification in headache mgmt. Nat. Bd. Cert. in Headache Mgmt. 2001), Assn. Applied Psychophysiology and Biofeedback (Presidl. Recognition award 2005), World Fedn. Neurology (exec. officer 1980-95, research group on migraine and headache), Ill. Acad. Gen. Practice (chmn. mental health com. 1966-70), Ill. Med. Soc., Chgo. Med. Soc., Assn. for Applied Psychophisiology and Biofeedback, Internat. Assn. Study of Pain, Am. Soc. Clin. Pharmacology and Therapeutics (chmn. headache sect. 1982-89, mem. com. coordination sci. sects. 1983-89), Postgrad. Med. Assn. (pres. 1981). Office: 467 W Deming Pl Ste 500 Chicago IL 60614-1726 Home Phone: 312-337-0360; Office Phone: 773-388-6390. Personal E-mail: MACF48@aol.com. Business E-Mail: clinic@diamondheadache.com.

DIAMOND, SHARI SEIDMAN, law and psychology professor; b. Chgo., Mar. 17, 1947; d. Leon Harry and Rita (Wolff) S.; m. Stewart Howard Diamond, Nov. 1, 1970; 1 child, icole. BA in Psychology, Sociology, U. Mich., 1968; MA in Psychology, Northwestern U., 1970, PhD in Social Psychology, 1972; JD with honors, U. Chgo., 1985. Bar: Ill. 1985. Rsch. assoc. Sch. Law U. Chgo., 1972-73; asst. prof. psychology and criminal justice U. Ill., Chgo., 1973-79, assoc. prof., 1979-90, prof., 1990-2000; assoc. Sidley & Austin, Chgo., 1985-87; sr. rsch. fellow ABF, Chgo., 1987—; lectr. U. Chgo. Law Sch., 1994-96; prof. law and psychology orthwestern U., 1999—, Stanton Clinton sr. rsch. prof., 2000-01, Howard J. Trienens prof. law, 2002—. Cons. govtl. and pub. interests groups including Rsch. Adv. Panel US Sentencing Commn., 1987-91; acad. visitor dept. law London Sch. Econs., 1981; hon. fellow Ctr. Urban Affairs Northwestern U., Evanston, Ill., 1973-73; hon. rsch. assoc. U. London, 1970; mem. NAS panel sentencing rsch., 1981-83, panel forensic DNA evidence, 1994-96; vis. prof. Harvard Law Sch., 2006; speaker, lectr. in field. Editor Law and Soc. Rev., 1988-91; past mem. editorial bd. Law and Soc. Rev., 1983-88, Law and Human Behavior, Crime and Justice Annual, Evaluation Rev.; reviewer NSF; contbr. articles to profl. jours. Chair Coll. Edn. Policy Com., 1979-80; dir. tng. grant NIMH Crime and Delinquency, 1979-80. Fellow Northwestern U., 1968-69, NIMH, 1969-71; grantee Spencer Found., 1972-74, disting. scholar, grantee, U. Ill., 1995-98, Law Enforcement Assistance Adminstrn., 1974-76, Ctr. for Crime and Delinquency NIMH, 1976-81, NSF, 1980-83, 90-92, 99—; B. Kenneth West U. scholar, 1995-98. Fellow APA (Award for Disting. Contbns. to Rsch. in Pub. Policy 1991), ABA, Am. Psychol. Soc.; mem. Am. Psychology-Law Soc. (pres. 1987-88), Law and Soc. Assn. (trustee 1979-82). Office: Northwestern U Law Sch 357 E Chicago Ave Chicago IL 60611 Business E-Mail: s-diamond@law.northwestern.edu.

DIAMOND, SIDNEY, chemist, educator; b. NYC, Nov. 10, 1929; s. Julius and Ethel D.; m. Harriet Urish, May 2, 1953; children: Florence, Julia. BS, Syracuse U., 1950; M.F., Duke U., 1951; PhD, Purdue U., 1963. Research engr. U.S. Bur. Public Rds. (now Fed. Hwy. Adminstrn.), Washington, 1953-61, research chemist, 1961-65; assoc. prof. engring. materials Purdue U., 1965-69, prof. Ind., 1969—2002, prof. emeritus Ind., 2002—; pres. Sidney Diamond and Assocs., Inc. Mem. Nat. Materials Adv. Bd. Com. on Status of Research in U.S. Cement and Concrete Industries; chmn. Internat. Symposium on Durability of Glass Fiber Reinforced Concrete, Chgo., 1985; mem. adv. com. NSF Ctr. for Advanced Cement-Based Materials, 1989—. Contbr. numerous articles on cement and concrete to profl. jours.; editor: Cement and Concrete Research. Served with U.S. Army, 1951-53. Fellow Am. Ceramic Soc. (past trustee, Copeland award), Am. Concrete Inst., Am. Concrete Inst. (anderson award 1993); mem. ASTM, Internat. Congress on Chemistry of Cement (pres. sect. 6 of 8th congress), Materials Rsch. Soc. Home: 819 Essex St West Lafayette IN 47906-1534 Office: Purdue U Sch Civil Engring West Lafayette IN 47907 Business E-Mail: diamond@ecn.purdue.edu.

DICHIERA, DAVID, opera company director; b. McKeesport, Pa., Apr. 8, 1935; s. Cosimo and Maria (Pezzaniti) DiC.; m. Karen VanderKloot, July 20, 1965 (div. 1992); children: Lisa Maria, Cristina Maria. BA in Music summa cum laude, UCLA, 1956, MA in Composition (scholar), 1958, PhD in Musicology, 1962; certificate in composition and piano (Fulbright Research grantee), Naples Conservatory of Music, 1959; D (hon.), U. Mich., 1998. Instr. music U. Calif., Los Angeles, 1960-61; asst. prof. music, asst. dean Oakland U., Rochester, Mich., 1962-65, chmn. music dept., 1966-73; founding gen. dir. Mich. Opera Theatre, Detroit, 1971—; founding dir. Music Hall Center for the Performing Arts, Detroit, 1973—. Artistic dir. Dayton Opera Assn., 1981-92; founding gen. dir. Opera Pacific, Costa Mesa, Calif., 1985-97; trustee Nat. Opera Inst.; adj. prof. Oakland U., Wayne State U. Producer, dir.: Overture to Opera series for, Detroit Grand Opera series, 1963-71; Composer various works for piano, violin, orch., voice; author articles on Italian opera for various encyclopedias; contbr. revs. and articles to music jours. Mem. Arts Com. New Detroit, Inc.; trustee, mem. exec. com. Music Center for Performing Arts; mem. Arts Task Force City of Detroit. Recipient Atwater Kent award U. Calif., Los Angeles, 1961; Certificate of Appreciation City of Detroit, 1970; citation Mich. Legislature, 1976; Michaelangelo award Boys' Town of Italy, 1980; award Arts Found. of Mich., 1981; President's Cabinet award U. Detroit, 1982; George Gershwin fellow, 1958; named A Michiganian of Yr., 1980; cavaliere della Repubblica Italiana. Mem. Am. Arts Alliance (exec. com.), Nat. Opera Assn., Internat. Assn. Lyric Theatre (v.p.), Am. Symphony League, Am. Musicol. Soc., OPERA Am. (pres. 1979-83), AAUP, Phi Beta Kappa, Phi Mu Alpha Sinfonia. Clubs: Detroit Athletic. Office: Mich Opera Theatre 1526 Broadway St Detroit MI 48226-2115 Office Phone: 313-237-3420. E-mail: ddd@motopera.org.

DICK, HAROLD LATHAM, manufacturing executive; b. Wichita, Kans., Oct. 24, 1943; s. Harold G. and Evelyn (Spines) D.; m. Jeanne Marie Luczai, Aug. 25, 1973; children: Harold Campbell, Edward Latham. BA, Washburn U., 1966; MBA, Harvard U., 1968. Exec. asst. to treas. Skelly Oil Co., Tulsa, 1968-70; mgmt. cons. McKinsey & Co. Inc., Chgo., Dallas, Houston, 1970-77; dir. planning Frito-Lay Inc., Dallas, 1977-80; v.p. Norton Simon Inc., NYC, 1980-83; founder Summit Ptnrs., Wichita, Kans., 1983-85; pres., chief exec. officer Doskocil Cos. Inc., Hutchinson, Kans., 1985-88; founder, pres. The Summit Group, Hutchinson, 1988—. Adv. bd. dirs. Garvey Industries, Wichita, 1987-94, Petroleum Inc., Wichita, 1993—. Trustee Kanza coun. Boy Scouts Am., 1989-97, exec. bd., 1995-97, v.p. 1997—, exec. bd. dirs. Quivira coun., 1997—, v.p., 1997-98, coun. commr., 1998-2002, coun. pres., 2002-04, nat. coun. rep., 2004-; Stephen minister, 1987-94; mem. bd. regents Washburn U., 1995—2003, chmn. bd. regents, 2001-02, chmn. fin. com., 1998-2001, mem. presdl. search com., 1987-88; chmn. Washburn Regents Soc., 2003—; trustee Washburn Endowment Assn., 1990-. Mem. Washburn Alumni Assn. (bd. dirs. 1986-89, Disting. Svc. award), Washburn Regents Soc. (chmn. fin. com. 2004—), Former Regents Soc. (chmn. 2004—). Republican. Episcopalian. Office: The Summit Group PO Box 3216 Hutchinson KS 67504-3216 Personal E-mail: hldick@yahoo.com.

DICK, ROLLIN MERLE, former insurance company executive; b. Sanborn, Iowa, Aug. 9, 1931; s. Laurence I. and Lillian M. (Reisser) D.; m. Helen E. Dodds, May 20, 1951; children: Jeri L., Lawrence E., Tami S. CPA, Ind. Ptnr. Coopers & Lybrand, Indpls., 1965-86; exec. v.p., CFO Conseco Inc., Carmel, Ind., 1986, vice chmn., CFO, 1986—2000; now exec. com. Gazelle Techventures, Carmel, Ind. Office: Gazelle Techventures Ste 310 11611 N Meridian St Carmel IN 46032

DICKE, JAMES FREDERICK, II, manufacturing executive; b. San Angelo, Tex., Nov. 9, 1945; s. James Frederick and Eilleen (Webster) D.; m. Janet St. Clair, July 6, 1968; children: James F. III, Jennifer S. BS, Trinity U., 1968. Intern U.S. Ho. of Reps., Washington, 1966; sales coord. Crown Controls Corp., New Bremen, Ohio, 1968-69, v.p. internat., 1970-78; exec. v.p. Crown Equipment Corp., New Bremen, Ohio, 1979-80, pres., CEO, 1980—2002, chmn., CEO, 2003—. Chmn. Crown Australia Pty. Ltd., Sydney, 1980—, Crown Ltd., Galway, Ireland, 1980—; bd. dirs. Dayton (Ohio) Power and Light Co. Chmn. bd. trustees Dayton (Ohio) Art Inst., 1998—; trustee, v.p., sec. Culver (Ind.) Ednl. Found., 1981-2001; Midwest dir. Boys and Girls Clubs Am., Chgo., 1987-2001; co-chmn. Ohio Rep. Fin. Com., 1995—. Recipient Disting. Svc. award Culver Acads., 1989, Disting. Alumnus award Trinity U., 1991; honoree Nat. Acad. Design, 1999. Mem. Young Pres.' Orgn. (bd. dirs. 1985-94, internat. pres. 1992-93), Cum Laude Soc. Culver Acads., Key Largo Anglers CLub (chmn. bd. dirs. 1999-2001). Mem. United Ch. of Christ. Office: Crown Equipment Corp PO Box 97 New Bremen OH 45869-0097

DICKENSON-HAZARD, NANCY ANN, pediatric nurse practitioner, consultant; b. Ashland, Ky., Sept. 25, 1946; m. John H. Hazard Jr., May 28, 1977; 2 children. BSN, U. Ky., 1968; cert., U. Mo., 1971, U. Va., 1976, MSN, 1977. RN, Md.; PNP. Asst. program dir., instr. nursing Ea. Ky. U., Richmond, Va., 1973-75; PNP Cen. Va. Community Health Plan, New Canton, 1976-77; PNP nurse coord. Georgetown U. Health Plan, Kensington, Md., 1977-79; PNP Kaiser Health Plan, Kensington, Md., 1979-81; exec. dir. Nat. Cert. Bd. PNP/Nurses, Rockville, Md., 1981—. Ind. nurse cons. Continuing Edn. and Quality Assurance, Rockville, 1978-81; cons. to Student urse Assn., Ea. Ky. U., Richmond, 1974-75; speaker numerous convs. and confs. Contbg. author: Fundamentals of Nursing, 1989, Basic Nursing: Theory and Practice, 1987, Community Health Nursing, 1991; mem. editorial bd. Ped. Nursing Jour., 1986—, Jour. Pediatric Health Care, 1987; chmn. humanitarian award com. Pediatric Nursing Jour.; contbr. articles to profl. jours. Pres., Home and Sch. Assn., Rockville, 1990; mem. com. St. Elizabeth Parish and Sch., Rockville, 1984-92. Fellow Nat. Assn. Pediatric Nurse Assocs. and Practitioners (Henry K. Silver award for nat. excellence 1983), Am. Acad. Nursing; mem. ANA, Leadership Roundtable for Advanced Nursing Practice, Sigma Theta Tau. Roman Catholic. Avocations: crafts, sewing, reading, gardening. Office: Sigma Theta Tau Intl 550 W North St Indianapolis IN 46202-3191

DICKERSON, BRIAN, columnist; b. Rochester, NY, Dec. 25, 1956; s. Donald Thomas and Shirley Wright D.; m. Donna Pendergast; 1 child, Zachary. BA History, Princeton U., 1979. Editor, reporter Miami (Fla.) Herald, 1979-88; editor mag. Detroit Free Press, 1988-97, columnist, 1997—. Pres. Sunday Magazine Editors Assn., Phila., 1991-92. Office: Detroit Free Press Travelers Tower I 26555 Evergreen Southfield MI 48076 E-mail: dicker@freepress.com.

DICKESON, ROBERT CELMER, retired foundation administrator, management consultant; b. Independence, Mo., June 28, 1940; s. James Houston and Sophie Stephanie (Celmer) Dickeson; m. Ludmila Ann Weir, June 22, 1963; children: Elizabeth Ann, Cynthia Marie. AB, U. Mo., 1962, MA, 1963, PhD, 1968; postgrad., U. No. Colo., 1971-72; postgrad. inst. ednl. mgmt., Harvard U., 1973. Adminstrv. asst. U. Mo., Columbia, 1962-64, dir. student activities, 1964-68, asst. dean students, 1968-69; dean student affairs No. Ariz. U., Flagstaff, 1969-70, assoc. prof. polit. sci., 1970-76, prof., 1976-81, v.p. student affairs, 1970-79, v.p. univ. rels., 1973-79; dir. Ariz. Dept. Adminstrn., Phoenix, 1979-81; pres. U. No. Colo., Greeley, 1981-91, prof. polit. sci., 1981-87, 88-91; chief of staff to gov., exec. dir. Office of State Planning and Budgeting State of Colo., 1987; pres. Noel/Levitz Ctrs. Inc., Iowa City, 1991-97; divsn. pres. USA Group Found., Indpls., 1995—97; sr. v.p. Ludmina Found. Edn., 1997—2005; cons., 2005—. Adj. prof. U. Colo., Denver, 1987, Ariz. State U., Tempe, 1979—81; nat. vice chmn. Cert. Pub. Mgr. Policy Bd., 1980—81; mem. univ. adv. coun. Am. Coun. Life Ins.; mem. Pres. Commn. NCAA, 1989—91, Nat. Commn. Minorities Higher Edn., 1989—91; nat. cons. Office Women Higher Edn., Am. Coun. Edn., 1989—97; mem. rsch. adv. coun. Assn. Governing Bds., 2007—; dir. United Bank Greeley; planning and mgmt. cons. Author: Prioritizing Academic Programs and Services, 1999, others; contbr. articles to profl. jours. Mem. nat. coun. Boy Scouts Am., 1976—81; internat. trustee Sigma Alpha Epsilon Found., 1993—97; active Boy Scouts Am., v.p. Grand Canyon coun. Flagstaff, 1974—76, pres., 1976—79, mem. T. Roosevelt coun., 1979—81, mem. Long's Peak coun., 1981—87; chmn. Gov.'s Commn. Merit Sys. Reform, 1979—80, Gov.'s Regulatory Rev. Coun., 1980—81, Gov.'s Commn. Higher Edn., 1983—86; mem. Gov.'s Commn. Excellence Edn., 1983—86, Gov.'s Coun. Creative Schs., 1989—91; commr. Colo. Edn. Commn. of States, 1987—91; mem. state com. Ariz. Dem. Com., 1970—72; pres. bd. trustees United Meth., 1974; bd. fellow Rocky Mountain Leadership Inst., 2006—, Rsch. Adv. Coun., Assn. of Governing Bds.; sr. v.p. Navitas Cancer Found., 2007—. Named to N. Ctrl. Athletic Conf. Hall of Fame, 1991; recipient Disting. award. of Merit, 1973, Silver Beaver award, 1975, Disting. Svc. award, Sigma Alpha Epsilon, 1969, Merit Key award, 1997, Disting. Alumnus award, U. Mo., Columbia, 1988, Outstanding Pres. award, Am. Assn. Colls. Tchrs. Edn., 1991, Bus. Excellence award, U. No. Colo., 1996, Faculty-Alumni U. Mo. award, 1999, Disting. Svc. award, Am. Coun. Edn., 2000; vis. scholar, U. Mich., 2003. Mem.: ASPA (Ariz. exec. bd., Superior Svc. award 1981), Am. Assn. State Colls. and Univs. (chmn. coun. doctoral granting instns., Meritorious Svc. award 1991), Nat. Assn. Student Adminstrs. (regional coun. 1974—79), Assn. Pub. Coll. and Univ. Pres. (pres. 1985—87), Coll. Student Pers. Inst. (acad. coun. 1969—73), Am. Acad. Polit. and Social Sci., Am. Polit. Sci. Assn., Columbia Club (Indpls.), Rotary, Kiwanis (pres. 1975—76), Newcomen Soc., Phi Kappa Phi. Home Phone: 970-586-9409. Personal E-mail: rdickeson@beyondbb.com.

DICKEY, L. ROBERT, state senator; b. Ponca, Nebr., Sept. 5, 1939; m. Mary Sellwock, Aug. 6, 1965; children: Julie, Jim, June. Cert. in gen. agr., U. Nebr., 1960. Farmer; state senator Nebr. Legislature, Lincoln, 1999—. Mem. Gov. Mike Johanns' Adv. Cabinet on Agr., U.S. Rep. Doug Bereuter's Agrl. Adv. Com., Nebr. Farm Bur., Nebr. Pork Prodrs., Ag Builders Nebr., Ag Coun. Am.; past chmn. congregation Evang. Free Ch.; former mem. utilization and mktg. bd. Nebr. Corn Devel.; former mem. Nebr. Arbor Day Found.; mem. Laurel-Concord Sch. Bd., 1988-93; dir., chmn. Farm Credit Bank Bd., Omaha, 1983; leader 4-H, 1984-94. With U.S. Army, 1961-62. Mem. Am. Legion. Home: 87081 Hwy 20 Laurel NE 68745-1965 Office: State Capitol Dist 18 PO Box 94604 Rm 1115 Lincoln NE 68509

DICKINSON, MAE, state legislator; b. Feb. 8, 1933; Student, Ind. U., Martin Coll., Ivy Tech. Coll. Retired quality inspector GM; rep. Dist. 95 Ind. Ho. of Reps., 1992—, mem. elections and apportionment, cities and towns com., mem. families, children and human affairs, pub. safety coms., vice chmn. labor and employment com. Precinct committeewoman; del. Dem. Nat. Conv.; ward chmn. Named Breakthrough woman in Area of Polit. Coalition of 100 Black Women. Mem. AACP, Urban League, United Auto Workers, A. Philip Randolph Inst. (Pres.'s award 1990), Flamingo Social and Charity Club, Coalition of Black Trade Unionists. Home: 5455 N Arlington Ave Indianapolis IN 46226-1607 Office: Ind Ho of Reps State Capitol Indianapolis IN 46204

DICKINSON, WILLIAM BOYD, JR., media consultant; b. Kansas City, Mo., Feb. 21, 1931; s. William Boyd and Aileen (Robinson) D.; m. Betty Ann Landree, Feb. 1, 1953; children: William Boyd IV, David Alan. AB, U. Kans., 1953; student, George Washington U. Law Sch., 1957-58. With U.P.I., 1955-59, mem. staff overnight desk Washington, 1957-59; staff writer Editorial Research Reports, Washington, 1959-66, editor, 1966-73; editor, v.p. Congl. Quar., Inc., 1972-73; gen. mgr., editorial dir. Washington Post Writers Group, 1973-91; cons., 1991-96, Biocentric Inst., 1991—. Resident prof. Journalism Sch. U. Kans., 1993-99; manship chair Journalism Sch. La. State U., 1999-2003, disting. prof., 2003—; Winston Churchill Traveling fellow, summer 1968. Supervisory editor: Congl. Quar.'s Complete Guide to Congress. Served with AUS, 1953-55. Press fellowship Knight Internat., 1998. Mem. William Allen White Found. (trustee), Alpha Tau Omega, Omicron Delta Kappa. (Washington). Home and Office: 1617 Alvamar Dr Lawrence KS 66047-1715 also: LSU 221B Journalism Bldg Baton Rouge LA 70803-0001 Office Phone: 785-832-1899.

DICKMAN, MARTIN J., federal agency administrator; b. Chgo. BS, U. Ill., 1966; JD, DePaul U., 1969. Asst. corp. counsel City of Chgo., 1970—72; counsel to minority leader Ill. Ho. Reps., 1972—73; mem. Bd. Trade, Chgo., 1972—91; asst. Peter Ftizpatrick and Assocs., 1973—89; hearings ref. Ill. Dept. Revenue, 1976—80; prosecutor Cook County Ill. State's Atty.'s Fin. and Govtl. Crimes Task Force, 1991—94; inspector gen. Railroad Retirement Bd., 1994—. Office: US Railroad Retirementt Bd 4th Fl 844 N Rush St Chicago IL 60611-2092 Office Phone: 312-751-4690. Business E-Mail: mdickman@oig.rrb.gov.

DICKSON, BRENT E., state supreme court justice; b. July 18, 1941; m. Jan Aikman, June 8, 1963; children: Andrew, Kyle, Reed. BA, Purdue U., 1964; JD, Ind. U., Indpls., 1968; LittD, Purdue U., 1996. Bar: Ind. 1968, U.S. Ct. Appeals (7th cir.) 1972, U.S. Supreme Ct. 1975; cert. civil trial adv., NBTA. Pvt. practice, Lafayette, Ind., 1968-85; sr. ptnr. Dickson, Reiling, Teder & Withered, 1977-85; assoc. justice Ind. Supreme Ct., Indpls., 1986—. Adj. prof. Sch. of Law Ind. U., 1992-. Past pres. Tippecanoe County Hist. Assn.; mem. dean's adv. coun. Sch. Liberal Arts Purdue U., 1990-94; mem. adv. bd. Heartland Film Festival, 1995-2000. Mem. Am. Inns Ct. (founding pres. Sagamore chpt.), Am. Law Inst. Office: Ind Supreme Ct 313 Ind Statehouse Indianapolis IN 46204-2213

DICKSON, EDGAR ROLLAND, gastroenterologist; b. Hackensack, NJ, June 10, 1933; MD, Ohio State U., 1959. Diplomate Am. Bd. Internal Medicine, Am. Bd. Gastroenterology. Intern Ohio State U. Hosp., Columbus, 1959-60; resident in internal medicine Mayo Clinic, Rochester, N.Y., 1960-63; asst. prof. medicine Mayo Med. Sch., Rochester, 1973-77, assoc. prof., 1977-80, prof., 1980—, Mary Lowell Leary prof. medicine, 1992—; dir. devel. Mayo Found. Edn. and Rsch., 1994—. Mem. staff St. Mary's Hosp., Meth. Hosp.; mem. digestive disease adv. bd. NIH. Chair bd. dirs. Am. Liver Found., 1988-90. Fellow ACP; mem. Am. Gastroenterol. Assn., Am. Assn. Study of Liver Diseases (mem. fiscal audit com. 1991-94, ad hoc clinic com. 1992-96, chair fiscal com. 1994-97, mem. subcom. health care policy 1996—, abstract selection com.), Am. Fedn. Clin. Rsch., Internat. Assn. Study of the Liver, Sigma Xi. Office: Mayo Clinic 200 1st St SW Rochester MN 55905-0002

DICKSON, THOMAS (TOM) A., state representative, lawyer; b. 1954; BA, Monterey Inst. Fgn. Studies, 1976; JD, So. Meth. U., 1981. Bar: N.D., U.S. Dist. Ct. N.D., U.S. Dist. Ct. Ark., U.S. Ct. Appeals (8th cir.). Law clerk to Assoc. Justice Vernon R. Pederson Supreme Ct. N.D., 1981—82; pvt. practice, 1982—; chmn. Dem. Party .D., 2001—. Contbr. articles to Pleader mag., Trial mag., N.D. Law Rev. Mem.: Assn. Trial Lawyers Am. (spkr. seminars), Minn. Soc. Criminal Justice (spkr. seminars), State Bar Assn. N.D. (spkr. seminars), Nat. Acad. Elder Law Attys., Inc., Nat. Assn. Criminal Def. Lawyers, N.D. Criminal Def. Lawyers, .D. Trial Lawyers Assn. (bd. govs., past pres., spkr. seminars). Democrat. Office: ND Dem Party Kennedy Ctr 1902 E Divide Ave Bismarck ND 58501 Address: Dickson & Purdon 107 W Main Ave Ste 150 Bismarck ND 58501-3871 E-mail: tdickson@dickson.com.

DICKSTEIN, BETH J., lawyer, accountant; b. 1963; BS with highest honors, U. Ill., 1985; JD cum laude, U. Pa., 1988. Bar: Ill. 1988; CPA, Ill. Ptnr. Sidley & Austin, Chgo. Office: Sidley & Austin 1 S First National Plz Chicago IL 60603-2000 Fax: 312-853-7036.

DICOSMO, NINO, engineering company executive; b. 1968; B in Polit. Sci., Oakland U., 1990; M in Info. Systems Mgmt., Carnegie Mellon U., 2005. Account exec. EDS Grp., Germany, England, Italy; dir., Bus. Devel., Info. Systems and Services Gen. Motors Corp.; chmn., pres., CEO Autoweb.com, Rochester Hills, Mich., 2004—. Named one of 40 Under 40, Crain's Detroit Bus., 2006. Office: Autoweb.com 1688 Star Batt Dr Rochester Hills MI 48309

DICUS, JOHN CARMACK, savings bank executive; b. Hutchinson, Kans., May 16, 1933; s. George Byron and Desda (Carmack) D.; m. Barbara Elizabeth Bubb, Feb. 4, 1956; children: Debra Elizabeth Kennedy, John Bubb. BS, U. Kans., 1955; HDL (hon.), Washburn U., 2000. With Capitol Fed. Savs. Bank, Topeka, 1959—, exec. v.p., 1963-69, pres., 1969—96, chmn., 1989—. Bd. dirs. Columbian Nat. Title Co., Topeka, Security Benefit Life Ins. Co., Topeka; treas. Scottish Rite Bodies Valley of Topeka; mem. Fed. Savs. and Loan Adv. Coun., 1973; mem. Fed. Res. Bd. Thrift Instns. Adv. Coun., 1986-87. Chmn. Shawnee County chpt. ARC, 1965; treas. Jayhawk area coun. Boy Scouts Am., 1967-68; pres. Topeka United Way, 1972-73; trustee Stormont-Vail Healthcare Inc., chmn. 1991-92; chmn. Menninger Fund; trustee Menninger Found.; vice chmn. Kans. U. Endowment Assn.; past pres. Native Sons of Kans. Lt. (j.g.) USN, 1956-59. Recipient Fred Ellsworth medallion U. Kans., 1990, Disting. Alumnus award U. Kans. Bus. Sch., 1998, Disting. Citizen, Boy Scouts Am., 2003; Paul Harris fellow, 1992. Mem. Am.'s Comty. Bankers (past exec. com., past dir.), Heartland Comty. Bankers Assn. (pres. 1974-75), Topeka C. of C. (dir. 1962, v.p. 1965-66, 71, pres. 1978, pres. Indsl. Devel. Corp.), U. Kans. Alumni Assn. (nat. pres. 1987-88), Masons (33 degree), Kans. C. of C. and Industry (past dir.), Shriners (potentate Arab Temple 1975), Jesters, Rotary (past dir.), Topeka Country Club (dir., pres. 1972). Episcopalian (sr. warden, vestryman). Office: Capitol Fed Savings Bank 700 S Kansas Ave Topeka KS 66603-3894

DIDONATO, GREGORY L., state legislator; b. Dennison, Ohio, May 22, 1961; Student, Kent State U. Mayor City of Dennison, 1984-90; mem. Ohio Ho. Reps., 1991-94, Ohio Senate from 30th dist., Columbus, 1997—. Mem. Tuscarawas County C. of C., Twin City C. of C., Rotary. Democrat. Office: Senate Bldg Rm 48, Ground Fl Columbus OH 43215

DIEBOLT, JUDITH, newspaper editor; b. Atchison, Kans., Oct. 6, 1948; d. George Edward and Mary Lou (Hill) D.; m. John C. Aldrich, Oct. 25, 1985. BSJ, U. Kans., 1970. Reporter Detroit Free Press, 1970-80, columnist, 1980-82, asst. city editor, 1982-85; reporter Detroit News, 1986-88, asst city editor, 1988-89, suburban editor, 1989-91; mng. editor Burlington (Vt.) Free Press, 1991-94; city editor Detroit News, 1994-98. Recipient Pub. Svc. award AP, 1978. Mem. AP Mng. Editors, Detroit Press Club (bd. govs., 1990-91), Univ. Club Detroit. Roman Catholic. Office: The Detroit News 615 W Lafayette Blvd Detroit MI 48226-3197

DIEDERICHS, JANET WOOD, public relations executive; b. Libertyville, Ill. BA, Wellesley Coll, 1950. Sales agt. Pan Am. Airways, Chgo., 1951-52; regional mgr. pub. relations Braniff Internat., Chgo., 1953-69; pres. Janet Diederichs & Assocs., Inc.; pub. rels. cons. Chgo., 1970—. Com. mem. Nat. Trust for Historic Preservation, 1975—79, Marshall Scholars (Brit. Govt.), 1975—79; trustee Sherwood Conservatory Music, 2000—04, Northwestern Meml. Hosp., 1985—2005, mem. exec. com., 1995—2000, life trustee; founder Com. of 200; chmn. Field Mus., 2003—06, founders coun., 1999—; mem. exec. com. Vatican Art Coun., Chgo., 1981—83; pres. Jr. League Chgo., 1968—69; trustee Fourth Presbyn. Ch., mem. bd. dirs., 1990—93; bd. dirs., mem. exec. com. Chgo. Conv. and Visitors Bur., 1978—87; bd. dirs. Internat. House, U. Chgo., 1978—84; bd. dirs. Latino Inst., 1986—89, Albert Pick Jr. Found. Bd. Trustees, 1999—. Mem. Chgo. Assn. Commerce and Industry (bd. dirs. 1982-89, exec. com. 1985-88), Internat. Women's Forum, Woman's Athletic Club of Chgo., Comml. Club of Chgo., The Casino Club (Chgo.), Wellesley Coll. Bus. Leadership Coun., Arts Club Chgo.

DIEHL, ANN, radio personality; m. Bob Diehl; 2 children. Adminstrv. asst. Family Life Radio WUGN, Midland, Mich., 1990—96, sports reader, 1996—2001, radio personality, 1997—, cohost Morning Show, 2001—. Office: WUGN 510 E Isabella Rd Midland MI 48640

DIEHL, JAMES HARVEY, church administrator; m. Dorothy Diehl; 4 children. BA, Olivet Nazarene U., 1959; DD, N.W. Nazarene U., 1990. Adminstr. MidAm. Nazarene U., 1973-76; dist. supt. Ch. of Nazarene, Nebr. and Colo., 1979-89; pastor Atlanta First Ch., 1976-79, Nazarene chs. in Iowa, Denver First Ch. of Nazarene, 1989-93; gen. supt. Ch. of the Nazarene, Kansas City, Mo., 1993—. Contbr. articles to Herald of Holiness, Preacher's Mag., Bread, World Mission, others; condr. daily radio program, weekly TV broadcast. Bd. trustees MidAm. Nazarene U., Nazarene Theol. Sem., Nazarene Bible Coll., N.W. Nazarene U.; chmn. bd. .W. Nazarene U. Mem. Ch. Of Nazarene. Office: Ch of the Nazarene 6401 Paseo Blvd Kansas City MO 64131-1213 Office Phone: 816-333-7000.

DIEHL, NANCY J., lawyer; b. 1953; d. Robert and Anne Diehl. B, Western Mich. Univ.; JD, Wayne State Univ., 1978. Trial prosecutor Recorder's Ct., Detroit, 1981—84; spl. assignment trial prosecutor Cir. Ct., 1984—87; dir. Child Abuse Unit, 1987—94; dep. chief Child and Family Abuse Bur., 1994—2000; chief projects and tng. divsn. Wayne County Prosecutor's Office, Detroit, 2000—04, chief felony trial divsn., 2004—. Mem. Gov. Task Force on Children's Justice (exec. com.), State Bar Rep. Assembly, 1992—96, 1996—2005. Author, illustrator with Lynda Baker (booklet) It is Good to Tell the Truth, 1988, Kids and Secrets, 1992, author, photographer with Lynda Baker Kids Go to Court, 1988; author (with Lynda Baker): (booklet) Sometimes It Is Sad to Be at Home, What Is a Kid to Do About Domestic Violence, 1997. Recipient Leonard Gilman award, 1999. Mem.: Detroit Met. Bar Assn. (Champion of Justice award 2004), State Bar of Mich. (pres. 2004). Office: Wayne County Prosecutor's Office 1441 St Antoine Detroit MI 48226-2302 Office Phone: 313-224-5742. Business E-Mail: ndiehl@co.wayne.mi.us.

DIEKEMA, ANTHONY J., college president, consultant; b. Borculo, Mich., Dec. 3, 1933; m. Jeane Waanders, Dec. 20, 1957; children: Douglas, David, Daniel, Paul, Mark, Maria, Tanya. BA, Calvin Coll., Grand Rapids, Mich., 1956; MA in Sociology and Anthropology, Mich. State U., 1958, PhD in Sociology, 1965. Field interviewer Bur. Bus. Research Mich. State U., East Lansing, 1955-56, asst. dir. housing, 1957-59, instr., lectr. sociology and anthropology, 1959-64, admissions counselor, 1959-61, asst. dir. admissions and scholarships, 1961-62, asst. registrar, 1962-64; asst. dean admissions and records, research assoc. in med. edn. and asst. prof. sociology U. Ill. Med. Center, Chgo., 1964-66, dir. admissions and records, asst. prof. sociology and edn., 1966-70, asso. chancellor, asso. prof. med. edn., 1970-76; pres. Calvin Coll., 1976-96, pres. emeritus, 2003—; interim pres. Trinity Christian Coll., Palos Heights, Ill., 2002—03. Adv. bd. NBD Grand Rapids, 1983-95; chmn. bd. Russian-Am. Christian U., Moscow, 2005-. Trustee Blodgett Meml. Med. Center, Grand Rapids, 1979-91; bd. dirs. Met. YMCA, 1979-93, Project Rehab, 1978-84; treas. Back-to-God Hour Radio Com., 1970-76; chmn. Synodical Com. on Race Relations, 1973-75; pres. Strategic Christian Ministry Found., 1969-73; mem. bd. curators Trinity Christian Coll., 1969-73, chmn., 1972-73, mem. presdl. search com., 1972-73, NCAA coun. 1983-87, Pres'. commn. 1987-91. Mem. Am. Assn. Pres.'s Ind. Coll. and Univs. (bd. dirs. 1978-84, 88-91), Nat. Assn. Ind. Colls. and Univs. (bd. dirs. 1991-94), Assn. Ind. Colls. and Univs. Mich. (exec. com. 1979-84), Am. Assn. Higher Edn., Am. Sociol. Assn., Soc. Health and Human Values, Soc. Values in Higher Edn., Nat. League Nursing (accreditation com. 1974-79), Alpha Kappa Delta, Rotary. Office: Calvin Coll Grand Rapids MI 49546 Office Phone: 616-402-6898. Personal E-mail: ajdiek@aol.com.

DIERBERG, JAMES F., bank executive; b. 1937; s. William and Genevieve Dierberg; m. Mary Dierberg; 2 children. BS, BA, Univ. Mo.; JD, Univ. Wash. Pres. First Bank, Inc., St. Louis, 1966—99, former CEO, chmn.; owner Hermanhoff Winery, Hermann, Mo., 1978—, Dierberg Vineyards, Santa Barbara, Calif., 1996—. Served U.S. Air Nat. Guard, France. Office: First Bank Inc 11901 Olive Blvd Saint Louis MO 63141

DIERCKS, EILEEN KAY, educational media coordinator, elementary school educator; b. Lima, Ohio, Oct. 31, 1944; d. Robert Wehner and Florence (Huckemeyer) McCarty; m. Dwight Richard Diercks, Dec. 27, 1969; children: Roger, David, Laura. BS in Edn., Bluffton Coll., 1966; MS, U. Ill., 1968. Tchr. elem. grades Kettering City Schs., Ohio, 1966-67; children's libr. St. Charles County, Mo., 1968-69; libr. Rantoul (Ill.) H.S., 1970-71; elem. tchr. Elmhurst (Ill.) Sch. Dist., 1971-72; media coord. Plainfield (Ill.) Sch. Dist., 1980—2001, libr. media cons., 2001—03. Evaluator Rebecca Caudill Young Readers' Book Award, 1990-97; LTA adv. com. Joliet Jr. Coll., 2003—2005. Founder, treas. FISH orgn., Plainfield, 1975-78; pres. Ch. Women United, 1974; sec. Plainfield Cmty. TV Access League, 1987-89; treas. Plainfield Congl. Ch., 1983-88; bd. dirs. Cub Scouts, 1983-86; leader, mem. Girl Scouts USA, Plainfield, 1985—; mem. Bolingbrook (Ill.) Cmty. Chorus, 1986-90, Plainfield Area Cmty. Chorus, 1999—. Mo. State Libr. scholar, 1967, Naperville chpt. Valparaiso U. Guild, treas., 1993-95. Mem.: ALA, Am. Assn. Sch. Librs., Ill. Sch. Libr. Media Assn. (membership chmn. 1992—93, mem. awards com. 1994—96, disaster relief chmn. 1996—97, treas. 2001—03, Ill. study task force 2003—05), Plainfield Athletic Club (sec. 1984—86), Rotary (treas. 1994—95, bd. dirs. 1994—, v.p. 1995—96, pres.-elect 1996—97, pres. 1997—98, sec. Plainfield chpt. 2003—05), Beta Phi Mu, Pi Delta, Delta Kappa Gamma (Beta Rho) (treas. 1993—97, pres. 2006—, Key Cmty. Leader award 2004). Home: 13440 S Rivercrest Dr Plainfield IL 60585-8979

DIERKS, MERTON LYLE, veterinarian; b. Ewing, Nebr., July 2, 1932; s. Lyle P. and Alys G. (Sanders) D.; m. Gloria Lee Zoeller, Dec. 27, 1958; children: Jon Martin, Thomas Lyle, Christopher Joseph, M. Stephanie. BS in Agriculture, U.

Nebr., 1954; DVM, Kans. State U., 1961. Pvt. practice, Ewing, 1961-73; ptnr. practice O'Neill, Nebr., 1973-92; mem. 40th dist. Nebr. Legislature, Lincoln, 1986—2002; chmn. com. on agr. Nebr. Legislature, Lincoln, 1993. Bd. dirs. St. Anthony's Hosp. Pres. Bd. Edn., Ewing, 1970-84. Lt. USAF, 1954-56. Recipient Outstanding Grassland Conservation award Nebr. Assn. Resource Dists., 1987, 96. Mem. Nebr. Vet. Med. Assn. (Nebr. Veterinarian of Yr 1986, pres. 1983), AVMA, U.S. Animal Health Assn., Comml. Club (pres. 1962-63). Democrat. Roman Catholic. Avocation: flying. Home: RR 1 Box 131 Ewing NE 68735-0038

DIESCH, STANLEY LA VERNE, veterinarian, educator; b. Blooming Prairie, Minn., May 16, 1925; s. John Herman and Emma Lillian (Erickson) D.; m. Darlene Ardis Witty; July 22, 1956; children: Lauren, Stephanie. BS, U. Minn., 1951, DVM, 1956, MPH, 1963. Diplomate Am. Coll. Vet. Preventive Medicine and Epidemiology. Asst. prof. Coll. Vet. Med., U. Iowa, Iowa City, 1963-66; asst. prof. U. Minn. Coll. Vet. Medicine, St. Paul, 1966-69, assoc. prof., 1969-73, prof., 1973-95, prof. emeritus, 1995—, dir. internat. programs, 1985-98; prof. Sch. Pub. Health, U. Minn., Mpls., 1973-95. Advisor Pan Am. Health Orgn., Washington, 1971— Contbr. more than 100 articles to profl. jours., 4 chapters to books. Mem. East Buchanan County Sch. Bd., Winthrop, Iowa, 1960; Rep. del., Minn., 1970-85; co-chair nat. Outdoor Speedskating, St. Paul, 1973; dir. CENSHARE, Mpls., 1981-82; chmn. Veterinarians for Re-election of Durenberger, Minn., 1982, 88; bd. dirs. Minn.-Uruguay Ptnrs. Ams., 1981—, pres., 1990-94, chmn. bd., 1995-99; hon. consul of Uruguay in Minn., 1991-96. Recipient Am. Express award Nat. Assn. Ptnrs. Ams., 1984, Internat. Castricone U. Linkage award Nat. Assn. Ptnrs. Ams., 1998, Dummond Peck Hill Lifetime Achievement award Ptnrs. Ams., 2002; WHO travel fellow, 1974; grantee EPA, 1968-71, USDA, 1978. Mem. AVMA (Pub. Svc. award 1987, Internat. Vet. Congress award 1998), APHA (coun. 1971-84), U.S. Animal Health Assn. (com. chair, Appreciation award 1986), Internat. Soc. Animal Hygiene (exec. bd. 1988-2000, pres. 1991-94, Honor award 2000), Minn. Vet. Medicine Assn. (com. chair 1970-75, Disting. Svc. award 1996). Lutheran. Avocations: fishing, hunting, boating. Home and Office: 743 Heinel Dr Saint Paul MN 55113-2152 Home Phone: 651-484-8635; Office Phone: 651-484-8635. Business E-Mail: diesc001@umn.edu.

DIETER, RAYMOND ANDREW, JR., physician, thoracic and vascular surgeon; b. Chebanse, Ill., June 19, 1934; s. Raymond Augustus Sr. and Emma Rose Mayme (Witt) D.; m. Bette Renéé Myers, Sept. 29, 1961; children: Raymond III, David, Lisa, Lynn, Deanna, Robert. Student, U. Ill., 1952-56, Olivet Nazarene Coll., 1954; MA in Physiology, U. Ill., Chgo., 1966; BS in Chemistry, U. Ill., Champaign, 1994; MD, Loyola U., 1960. Diplomate Am. Bd. Thoracic Surgery, Am. Bd. Surgery. Intern Cook County Hosp., Chgo., 1960-61; resident in gen. surgery VA Hosp., Hines, Ill., 1963-67, sr. resident in cardiopulmonary surgery, 1967-69; practice specializing in thoracic, cardiovascular surg. DuPage Med. Group, 1969—, Glen Ellyn (Ill.) Clinic, 1969—, pres., 1982-85, also bd. dirs.; mem. staff Hines (Ill.) VA Hosp., 1963-74, Cen. DuPage Hosp., Winfield, Ill., 1969—, pres. staff, 1987-89; mem. staff Loyola U. Med. Ctr., Maywood, Ill., 1969-80, Meml. Hosp. DuPage County, Elmhurst, Ill., 1969—, Delnor Hosp., St. Charles, Ill., 1970—, Community Hosp., Geneva, Ill., 1970—79, Alexian Bros. Med. Ctr., Elk Grove Village, Ill., 1975-79, 93—, Good Samaritan Hosp., Downers Grove, Ill., 1976—, pres. staff, 1979; mem. staff Glendale Heights (Ill.) and Glen Oaks Cmty. Hosp., 1980—, St. Mary's Hosp., Streator, Ill., 1997—. Clin. instr. Stritch Sch. Medicine Loyola U., 1966-71, clin. asst. prof., 1971-80; trustee Ctr. Bank, Glen Ellyn, 1978-90, Lake Shore Bank, Glen Ellyn Found.; internat. lectr. on med. and outdoor topics; chmn. Glen Ellyn Clinic Facilities, 1987-98, Physicians Benefit trust, 1988-92; pres., chmn. bd. No. Ill. Surg. Ctr., 1989—; pres. DuPage Doctors, Inc., Ctr. for Surgery; co-founder Cmty. Banks of Wheaton/Glen Ellyn, 1993-05, bd. dirs., vice chmn., 2005—; co-founder, pres. Northeast DuPage Surgicenter, 1997—; chmn. bd. dirs., CEO, pres. Masterile, Inc., 1997-99; mem., chmn. negotiating com. Glen Ellyn Clinic, 1999; officer Internat. Healthcare Cons., LLC, 2002—. Author: (with B.R. Dieter and A.C. Mickelson) Mickelson and Peterson Family Sketch, 1970, (with M.C. Sorensen and E.R. Dieter) A Sorensen and Jensen Family Tree, 1975, (with B.R. Dieter, C. Myers, U. Myers, and D. Dieter) A Myers and Remley Family Tree, 1978, (with others) A Witt and (von) Ruehle Family Sketch, 1976, A Hofeling, Janssen, Lehnert, and Meier Family Sketch, 1979, A Dieter Family Tree: Sketches of German Families, 1981, Thoracoscopy for Surgeons, 1994; editor: Thoracoscopy for Surgeons-Diagnostic and Therapeutic, 1995; contbr. numerous articles to profl. jours. and chpts. in med. book, numerous TV and radio interviews. Mgr. Glen Ellyn baseball team, 1970, 71, 78-82; asst. leader 4-H Club, 1975-83; mem. Glenbard South High Sch. Boosters, World Fedn. Drs. Who Respect Human Life, 1980—; pres., bd. dirs. DuPage Med. Found.; mem. Econ. Devel. Coun. Glen Ellyn, sec., 2000, v.p., 2001-02, pres., 2003; bd. dirs. Farm Safety Just 4 Kids, 2004-07. Served with USPHS, 1961-63, with Res., 1982—. Named Hon. Citizen, Quito Ecuador, La Paz, Bolivia; recipient Key to City of Manila, Philippines. Fellow ACS, Internat. Coll. Angiology (editl. bd. 1995—, co-chair membership com. 2007—), Internat. Coll. Surgeons (exec. com. 1991—, treas. 1993-94, pres. elect 1995-96, pres. 1997-98, U.S. sect., corp. sec. 1997-2000, pres.-elect 2001-02, pres. 2003-04, immediate past pres. 2005-06, chmn. internat. surg. teams. program 2005-06, World body and cs, del. 2001-06); mem. AMA (Physician's Recognition awards, mem. ho. dels.), Internat. Mus. Surg. Sci. (chmn. bd. dirs. 1991—), Internat. Soc. Circumpolar Health, Internat. Soc. Outdoor Health, Global Acad. for Tropical Surgery (co-founder 2004), Am. Coll. Angiology, Am. Coll. Chest Physicians, Assn. Acad. Surgeons, Am. Soc. Circumpolar Health (charter), Assn. Mil. Surgeons, Assn. Res. Officers, Am. Heart Assn. (coun. 1974—), Soc. Med. Hist. Chgo., Soc. Critical Care Medicine, Soc. Thoracic Surgeons (membership com.), Ill. State Med. Soc. (trustee 1983-92, chmn. Ill. hosp. med. staff sect. 1985-87, pres., med. adminstrs. ctr. for surgery 1994—), Ill. Thoracic Surg. Soc. (sec. 1981-83, pres. 1984-85), DuPage County Med. Soc. (pres. 1977, mem. govtl. com., numerous others), Chgo. Med. Soc., Charles B. Puestow Surg. Soc. (sec., treas. 1966-67, v.p. 1968), Good Samaritan Soc., Ala. Geographic Soc., Kankakee Valley Geneal. Soc., Ill. Geneal. Soc., U. Ill. Alumni Assn. (bd. dirs. 2002-), Am. Rabbit Breeders Assn., Silver Marten Club, Century Club (Elmhurst), Chebanse Lions (charter), Resurrection Bay (Alaska) Lions, Internat. lions Club (50 yr. mem.). Republican. Roman Catholic. Avocations: exercise, farming, fishing, hunting. Office: Glen Ellyn Clinic 454 Pennsylvania Ave Glen Ellyn IL 60137-4496 Office Fax: 630-545-7853.

DIETMEYER, DONALD LEO, retired electrical engineering educator; b. Wausau, Wis., Nov. 20, 1932; s. Henry Joseph and Erna M. (Zastrow) D.; m. Carol White, Jan. 26, 1957; children: Karl Peter, Elizabeth Mary, Anne Katherine, Diana Lee. BSEE, U. Wis., Madison, 1954, MS, 1955, PhD, 1959. Mem. faculty U. Wis., Madison, 1958-63, 64-98, prof. elec. and computer engring., 1967-98, prof. emeritus, 1998—, assoc. dean Coll. Engring., 1983-95. Sr. engr. IBM Corp., Poughkeepsie, .Y., 1964 Author: Logic Design of Digital Systems, 1978, 3rd rev. edit., 1988, Conlan Report, 1983. With AUS, 1957. Recipient Western Electric Fund award, 1972 Fellow IEEE; mem. Computer Soc., Assn. Computing Machinery, Sigma Xi. Home: 2211 Waunona Way Madison WI 53713-1619 E-mail: dld@engr.wisc.edu.

DIETRICH, JOSEPH JACOB, retired chemist, research and development company executive; b. Bismark, ND, Oct. 31, 1932; s. Jacob Peter and Elizabeth (Janzer) D.; m. Florence Kolodziejczak, June 27, 1959; children: Ann Marie, Michael, John, James. BA in Chemistry, St. John's U., Collegeville, Minn., 1953; PhD in Organic Chemistry, Iowa State U., 1957. Rsch. chemist PPG, Inc., Barberton, Ohio, 1957-59, Spencer Chem. Co., Kansas City, Kans., 1960-64; with Diamond-Shamrock Corp., Cleve., 1964-82, dir. rsch., 1973-78, dir. tech. devel., 1978-82; dir. tech. Eltech Systems Corp., Painesville, Ohio, 1982-85, dir. tech. and comml. devel./ Europe, Chardon, Ohio, 1986-90; pres. Eltech Internat. Corp., 1990-94, Elgard Corp., 1994; ret., 1994. Contbr. articles to profl. jours; patentee in field. Mem. Am. Chem. Soc., Soc. Plastic Engrs., Serra Club. Republican. Roman Catholic. Home: 6958 Pennywhistle Cir Painesville OH 44077-2141

DIETRICH, RICHARD VINCENT, geologist, educator; b. LaFargeville, NY, Feb. 7, 1924; s. Roy Eugene and Mida Amy (Vincent) D.; m. Frances Elizabeth Smith, Dec. 28, 1946; children: Richard Smith, Kurt Robert, Krista Gayle Brown. AB, Colgate U., 1947, MS, Yale U., 1950, PhD, 1951. Geologist Iowa Geol. Survey, 1947, N.Y. State Sci. Service, summers 1949-50; asst. prof. geology Va. Poly. Inst., Blacksburg, 1951, assoc. prof., 1952-56, prof., 1956-69, mineral technologist Va. Engring. Exp. Sta., 1951-58; Fulbright rsch. prof. Oslo U., Norway, 1959-60; asso. dean arts and scis. Va. Poly. Inst., 1966—68, dean, 1968—69; prof. geology Central Mich. U., Mt. Pleasant, 1969-86, prof. emeritus, 1986—, dean arts and scis., 1969-75. Dir. Econ. Geol. Pub. Co., 1966-72. Author or co-author over 24 sci. books and textbooks in field (transl. into German, Malaysian, Russian, and Japanese); also poems, haiku, essays, cartoons; editor Mineral Industries Jour., 1953-61; mng. editor Bull. Econ. Geology, 1966-73; exec. editor Rocks and Minerals, 1980-88, petrology adv. editor, 1988—; mem. editl. bd. Mineral Record, 1969-74; contbr. over 300 articles to profl. jours.; composer, performer music. Organizer N. Am. for Mineral. Abstracts, 1976-80. Served with U.S. Air Corps, 1943-46. Recipient Acad. Citation Mich. Acad. Sci., Arts and Letters, 1978, Children's Sci. Book award N.Y. Acad. Scis., 1981; Fulbright rsch. prof. U. Oslo, 1958-59; Pres.'s scholar, 1941-42, Austin Colgate scholar Colgate U., 1943, Newton Lloyd Andrews scholar, 1943, Colgate U. scholar, 1946; Edward S. Binney fellow, 1948-49, James Dwight Dana fellow Yale U., 1950-51. Fellow Am. Mineral. Soc. (assoc. life), Soc. Econ. Geol. (sr.); mem. Norsk Geologisk Forening (life), Geol. Soc. Finland (life), Am. Geol. Inst. (gov. 1972-74), Assn. Earth Sci. Editors (pres. 1972-73), Phi Beta Kappa, Sigma Xi, Phi Kappa Phi, Sigma Gamma Epsilon. Independent. Presbyterian. Avocations: birdwatching, illustrations, peach pit carving. Home: 1323 Center Dr Mount Pleasant MI 48858-4103 Business E-Mail: dietr1rv@cmich.edu.

DIETRICH, SUZANNE CLAIRE, communications consultant, researcher, museum director; b. Granite City, Ill. d. Charles Daniel and Evelyn Blanche (Waters) D. BS in Speech, orthwestern U.; MS in Pub. Comm., Boston U., 1967; postgrad., So. Ill. U., 1973-83. Intern prodn. staff Sta. WGBH-TV, Boston, 1958-59; asst. dir., 1962-64; asst. dir. program invitation to art, 1958; cons. producer dir. dept. instructional tv radio Ill. Office Supt. Pub. Instrn., Springfield, 1969-70; dir. program prodn. and distbn., 1970-72; instr. faculty call staff, speech dept. Sch. Fine Arts So. Ill. U., Edwardsville, 1972-73; grad. asst. for doctoral program office of dean Sch. Edn., 1975-78; rsch. asst. Ill. pub. telecomms. study for Ill. Pub. Broadcasting Coun., 1979-80; cons., rsch. in comm., 1980—. Pub. advisor Bradly Pub., Inc., 1996. Exec. prodr., dir. tv programs Con-Con Countdown, 1970, The Flag Speaks, 1971. Mem. sch. bd. St. Mary's Cath. Sch., Edwardsville, 1991-92; cable tv adv. com. City of Edwardsville, 1994—, co-chair, 1996-98; bd. dirs. Goshen Preservation Alliance, Edwardsville, 1992-94, pres., 1995-97; dir. Madison County Hist. Mus. and Archival Libr., 1999—; mem. Madison County Hist. Soc., bd. dirs., 1997-99; mem. mktg./tourism com. City of Edwardsville, 2005-06; adv. bd. Ill. State Hist. Soc., 2007—. Named Paul Harris Fellow, 2007; recipient Athena award, Edwardsville/ Glen Carbon C. of C., 2004. Roman Catholic. Home: 1011 Minnesota St Edwardsville IL 62025-1424 Office: 715 N Main St Edwardsville IL 62025-1111 Office Phone: 618-656-7562.

DIETRICH, THOMAS W., corporate lawyer, insurance company executive; b. 1948; BA, Adrian Coll.; JD, Capital U. Bar: 1976. V.p., assoc. gen. counsel Nationwide Ins. Enterprise, Columbus, Ohio. Office: Nationwide Ins Enterprise 1 Nationwide Plz Columbus OH 43215-2239

DIETRICH, WILLIAM GALE, lawyer, real estate developer, consultant; b. Kansas City, Mo., Mar. 6, 1925; s. Roy Kaiser and Gale (Gossett) D.; m. Marjorie Nell Reich, July 14, 1945; children: Meredith G. Dietrich Steinhaus, Ann. E. Dietrich Cooling, Walter R. AB with high honors, Yale U., 1948, LLB, 1951. Bar: Mo. 1951. Ptnr. Dietrich, Davis, Dicus, Rowlands, Schmitt & Gorman (and predecessors), 1953-73; project dir., gen. counsel Blue Ridge Shopping Ctr., Inc., Kansas City, 1955-73, pres., gen. mgr., 1964-73, Blue Ridge Tower, Inc., Kansas City, 1967-73; sec.-treas. A. Reich & Sons, Inc., Kansas City, 1973-88, chmn., 1988—; pvt. practice law Kansas City, 1973—; sec., treas. A. Reich & Sons Gardens, Inc., 1973-89; pres. J&D Devel., Inc., 1987—; gen. ptnr. J & D Enterprises, 1986—2006; gen. mgr. The Farm Shopping and Office Ctr., 1994-98; pres. BBJ Treats, L.L.C., 1994-98; mem. WGD Properties, LLC, 1999—. Sec., bd. dirs. Rsch. Med. Ctr., Kansas City, 1977, vice-chmn., 1980-83, chmn., 1983-87; bd. dirs. The Rsch. Found., 1980-91, vice-chmn., 1989-91; bd. dirs. Rsch. Health Svcs., 1980-81, vice chmn., 1983-87, chmn. 1987-89; bd. dirs. Mahana Condominium Assn., Maui, Hawaii, 1977-96, Blue Ridge Bank and Trust Co., Kansas City, 1982-94; vestry mem. Grace & Holy Trinity Cathedral, Kansas City, 1972-95, former treas. 1st lt. AUS, 1943-46, PTO. Recipient Army Commendation Ribbon, 1946. Mem. ABA, Mo. Bar Assn., Kansas City Bar Assn., Blue Ridge Mall Mchts. Assn. (dir. 1958-73), Internat. Coun. Shopping Ctrs. (past dir. for Mo., Kans, Iowa, cert. shopping ctr. mgr.), Lawyers Assn. Kansas City, Mission Hills Country Club, Yale Club, Kansas City (Mo.) Club, Rotary (bd. dirs., sec. found. Kansas City 1978—), Phi Beta Kappa (pres. Kansas City chpt. 1989-91), Phi Delta Phi. Home: 1000 Huntington Rd Kansas City MO 64113-1346 Office: 6155 Oak St Profl Bldg Ste A Kansas City MO 64113-2266 Office Phone: 816-822-2600. E-mail: wgdlo@sbcglobal.net.

DIETZ, WILLIAM RONALD, corporate management professional; b. Seattle, Nov. 25, 1942; s. William Phillip and Helen Mae (Wilson) D.; m. Carol Jean Gies; 1 child, David Phillip. BA, U. Wash., 1964; MBA, Stanford U., 1968. Fin. cons. 1st Nat. City Bank, NYC, 1968-70; v.p., mgr. Citicorp Subs. Mgmt. Office, Citicorp, NYC, 1971-74; chmn. Citicorp Factors, Inc., NYC, 1974-75; v.p., mgr. N.Y., N.J. and Conn. comml. banking Citibank N.A., NYC, 1976-78, sr. v.p., gen. mgr. Eastern region corp. banking, 1978-81, sr. v.p., head Caribbean Basin div., 1982-84; pres. Charter Assocs. Ltd., 1985-89; chmn. and chief exec. officer CorEast Savs. Bank, Richmond, Va., 1989-91; pres., CEO Am. Savs. Bank, White Plains, NY, 1991-92, Mo. Bridge Bank, Kansas City, 1992-93, Anthem Fin., Inc., Indpls., 1993-96; ptnr. Concord Ptnrs., 1997—2003; mng. ptnr. Customer Contact solutions, LLC, 1999—; pres., CEO W.M. Putnam Co., 2001—. Bd. dirs. Capital One Fin. Corp., W.M. Putnam Co.; mem. policy com. Bank Mgmt. Inst., SUNY-Buffalo. Contbg. author: Customer-Focused Marketing of Financial Services. Trustee Children's Mus. Dupage County, Children's Mus. of Indpls., 1994-2006; bd. advisors Ind. U./Purdue U., Indpls., 1995-2003. Lt. USNR, 1964-66. Mem. Delta Tau Delta. Office: WM Putnam Co 1625 Commerce Pky Bloomington IL 61704 Business E-Mail: ronald.dietz@earthlink.net, rdietz@officereal.com.

DIFEO, SAMUEL X., automotive executive; Exec. v.p. DiFeo Group United Auto Group, Inc., Detroit, 1992-98, pres., COO, 1998—, bd. dir., 1998—2004. Mailing: United Auto Group Inc 2555 S Telegraph Rd Bloomfield Hills MI 48302-0954

DIFONZO, KENNETH W., financial officer; BS in Acct., U. Ill. CPA. Various fin. positions H.J. Heinz Co., 1981-91; v.p. fin. and controller internat. divsn. ConAgra, Inc., Omaha, 1991-94, v.p., corp. controller to sr. v.p. profit improvement, 1994-2000, sr. fin. officer, 2000—. Office: ConAgra Inc One ConAgra Dr Omaha E 68102-5001

DIGANGI, FRANK EDWARD, academic administrator; b. West Rutland, Vt., Sept. 29, 1917; s. Leonard and Mary Grace (Zafonti) DiG.; m. Genevieve Frances Colignon, June 27, 1946; children: Ellen (Mrs. Philo David Hall), Janet (Mrs. W. Dale Greenwood). BS in Pharmacy, Rutgers U., 1940; MS, Western Res. U., 1942; PhD, U. Minn., 1948. Asst. prof. U. Minn. Coll. Pharmacy, 1948-52, asso. prof., 1952-57, prof. medicinal chemistry, 1957—, also asso. dean adminstrv. affairs. Author: Quantitative Pharmaceutical Analysis, 7th edit, 1977, The History of the Minnesota Pharmacists Association, 1883-1983, 2004; Contbr. articles to pharm. jours. Served with USNR, 1943-46, PTO. Recipient Alumni Assn. Disting. Pharmacist award, 1977, Faculty Recognition award Coll. of Pharmacy Alumni Soc., 1981, Lawrence and Delores M. Weaver medal, 1997. Mem. Am. Pharm. Assn., Minn. Pharm. Assn. (pres. 1971, chmn. bd. 1972-73, Pharmacist of Yr. award 1972, Harold R. Popp Meml. award 1979, hon. mem. 1994), Mpls. Soc. Profl. Pharmacists (hon.), AAUP, Am. Chem. Soc., Am. Assn. Colls. Pharmacy, Univ. Campus Club (Mpls.), Univ. Faculty Golf Club (Mpls., Gownin-Town Club (Mpls.), Sigma Xi, Phi Beta Phi, Phi Lambda Upsilon, Rho Chi. Office: Univ Minn Coll of Pharmacy Minneapolis MN 55455 Home: 996 Stillwater Rd Stamford CT 06902

DIGGS, MATTHEW O'BRIEN, JR., air conditioning and refrigeration manufacturing executive; b. Louisville, Jan. 11, 1933; s. Matthew O'Brien and Dorothy (Leary) D.; m. Nancy Carolyn Brown, Nov. 5, 1955; children: Elizabeth, Joan, Judith, Matthew III. Student, Hanover Coll., 1950-52; BSME, Purdue U., 1955; MBA, Harvard U., 1961. With Lincoln Electric, Cleve., 1957-59, Toledo Scale Corp., 1961-63; cons., assoc., v.p., then v.p. and mng. officer East Cen. Region Booz, Allen & Hamilton, Inc., Cleve., 1963-72; v.p. mktg. Copeland Corp., Sidney, Ohio, 1972-74, exec. v.p., 1974, pres., chief exec. officer, 1975-87, vice chmn., 1987-90; CEO The Diggs Group McClintock Ind., Dayton, Ohio, 1990—. Bd. dirs. Ripplewood Holdings LLC, Price Bros. Cmty. bd. trustees Wright State U., 1995—; chmn. adv. bd. Herrick Labs. Perdue U., 1980—; former sr. warden St. Paul's Episcopal Ch. 1st lt. U.S. Army, 1955-57. Home: 1160 Lytle Ln Dayton OH 45409-2112 Office: 1515 Kettering Tower Dayton OH 45423-1005

DIGMAN, LESTER ALOYSIUS, management educator; b. Kieler, Wis., Nov. 22, 1938; s. Arthur Louis and Hilda Dorothy (Jansen) Digman; m. Ellen Rhomberg Pfohl, Jan. 15, 1966; children: Stephanie, Sarah, Mark. BSME, U. Iowa, Iowa City, 1961, MSIE, 1962, PhD, 1970. Registered profl. engr., Mass. Mgmt. cons. U.S. Ameta, Rock Island, Ill., 1962-67; mgmt. instr. U. Iowa, Iowa City, 1967-69; head applied math. dept. US Ameta, Rock Island, Ill., 1969-74, head managerial tng. dept., 1974-77; assoc. prof. mgt. U. Nebr., Lincoln, 1977-84, dir. grad. studies in mgmt., 1982—, prof. mgmt., 1984-87, Leonard E Whittaker Am. Charter disting. prof. mgmt., 1987-93, Met. Fed. Bank disting. prof. mgmt., 1993-95, First Bank disting. prof. mgmt., 1995-98, US Bank disting. prof. mgmt., 1998—2002, Harold J. Laipply coll. prof., 2002—; dir. Ctr. for Tech. Mgmt. and Decision Scis., 1992-94; interim dir. Gallup Rsch. Ctr., 1994-95; mem. adv. bd. Ctr. for Albanian Studies, 1992—. Cons. various orgns., 1963—72; sec., treas. Mgmt. Svcs. Assocs. Ltd., Davenport, Iowa, 1972—77; owner L. A. Digman and Assocs., Lincoln, 1977—; gen. ptnr. Letna Properties, Madison, Wis., 1978—. Author: Strategic Management: Concepts, Decisions, Cases, 1986, 3d edit., 1990, Strategic Management: Concepts, Processes, Decisions, 1995, Strategic Management: Cases, 1995;: 2d edit., 1999, Network Analysis for Management Decisions, 1982, Strategic Management: Cases for the Global Information Age, 2002, 3d edit., 2007, Strategic Management: Competing in the Global Information Age, 2002, 3d edit., 2006; contbr. articles to profl. jours. Recipient Disting. award, SBA, 1980, certs. of Appreciation, Dept. Def., 1972, Disting. Faculty award, Coll. Bus. Adminstrn., 2006. Fellow: Pan Pacific Bus. Assn., Decision Scis. Inst. (program chmn. 1986, pres. 1987—88, coord. doctoral consortium 1989, strategy/policy track chmn. 1991, v.p. 1992—94, strategic mgmt. track chmn. internat. meeting 1993, chair long-range planning com. 1995—96, mem. adv. com. internat. meeting 1997, chair fellows com. 1999—2000, charter); mem.: IEEE, MBA Roundtable (charter, mem. steering com.), Inst. Ops. Rsch. and Mgmt. Scis. (founding), Strategic Leadership Forum, Acad. Mgmt., Strategic Mgmt. Soc. (founding), Legatus Confrerie de la Chaine Rotisseurs, Firethom Country Club, Nebr. Club. Roman Catholic. Avocations: gardening, photography, wine tasting. Home: 7520 Lincolnshire Rd Lincoln NE 68506-1635 Office: U Nebr 277 CBA Lincoln NE 68588 Business E-Mail: ldigman1@unl.edu.

DILL, CHARLES ANTHONY, manufacturing and computer company executive; b. Cleve., Nov. 29, 1939; s. Melville Reese and Gladys (Frode) D.; m. Louise T. Hall, Aug. 24, 1963 (dec. Sept. 28, 1983); children: Charles Anthony, Dudley Barnes; m. Mary M. Howell, Jan. 17, 1987. BSME, Yale U., 1961; MBA, Harvard U., 1963. With Emerson Electric Co., 1963-88, corp. v.p. internat., 1973-77; pres. A.B. Chance Co. subs. Emerson Electric Co., 1977-80; corp. group v.p. Emerson Electric Co., St. Louis, 1980-82, sr. v.p. office of chief exec., adv. dir., 1982-88; pres., COO, bd. dirs. AVX Corp., NYC, 1988-90; pres., CEO, bd. dirs. Bridge Info. Systems, Inc., St. Louis, 1990-95; gen. ptnr. Gateway Equity Ptnrs. IV, St. Louis, 1995—. Bd. dirs. Maryville Technologies Inc., Neovision Hypersystems, V-Brick Inc., Digital Concepts of Mo., Zoltec Inc., Stifel Nicholaus Inc., Transact Techs., DT Industries, Potter Elec. Mem. St. Louis Country Club, Log Cabin Club. Republican. Office: Gateway Equity Partners 8000 Maryland Ave Ste 1190 Saint Louis MO 63105-3910 E-mail: cdill@gatewayventures.com.

DILL, SHERI, publishing executive; With Wichita (Kans.) Eagle, v.p. mktg. Office: The Wichita Eagle PO Box 820 Wichita KS 67201-0820

DILLARD, KIRK WHITFIELD, state legislator, lawyer; b. Chgo., June 1, 1955; s. Edward Floyd and Martina Raye (Whitfield) D.; m. Stephanie Hallam, May 24, 2000. BA, Western Ill. U., 1977; JD, DePaul U., 1982. Bar: Ill. 1983, U.S. Dist Ct. (no. dist.) Ill. 1983, U.S. Dist Ct. (cen. dist.) Ill. 1984, U.S. Dist. Ct. (ea. dist.) Mich. 1988. Staff cons. Ill. State Senate, Springfield, 1977-81; atty., dir. legis. affairs Ill. Office Gov., Springfield, 1982-87, chief of staff to Gov., 1991-93; judge State of Ill. Ct. of Claims, Springfield, 1987-90; ptnr. Lord, Bissell & Brook, Chgo., 1987—; mem. Ill. Senate, 1993—. Legal writing and moot ct. tutor DePaul U. Coll. Laws, 1981-82; guest lectr. Loyola and DePaul U. Coll. Law, Chgo. Chair DuPage County Rep. Party, Wheaton, Ill., 1988; mem. Union League Chgo., Bi-State 3rd Airport for Chgo. Study Commn., Ill. Coalition. Named Legislator of the Yr. for Civil Justice, Am. Legis. Exch. Coun., 1995. Mem. ABA (Best performance in land use and local govt. law courses award Urban, State and Local Govt. sect. 1982), Ill. Assn. Def. Trial Counsel, Ill. State Bar Assn., Western Ill. U. Alumni Coun. (pres. 1989-92), Blue Key, Phi Alpha Delta. Methodist. Avocations: golf, tennis, travel, politics. Home: 501 Wedgewood Ct Hinsdale IL 60521 Office: Lord Bissell & Brook 115 S La Salle St Ste 3200 Chicago IL 60603-3902

DILLE, ROLAND PAUL, college president; b. Dassel, Minn., Sept. 16, 1924; s. Oliver Valentine and Eleanor (Johnson) D.; m. Beth Hopeman, Sept. 4, 1948; children: Deborah, Martha, Sarah, Benjamin. BA summa cum laude, U. Minn., 1949, PhD, 1962, LHD (hon.), 1995. Instr. English U. Minn., 1953-56; asst. prof. St. Olaf Coll., Northfield, Minn., 1956-61; asst. prof. English Calif. Lutheran Coll., Thousand Oaks, Calif., 1961-63; mem. faculty Moorhead (Minn.) State U., 1964-94, pres., 1968-94; ret., 1994. Author: Four Romantic Poets, 1969; contbr. numerous articles and revs. to profl. jours. Treas. Am. Assn. State Colls. and Univs., 1977-78, bd. dirs., 1978-80, chmn., 1980-81; mem. Nat. Coun. for Humanities, 1980-86; vice-chair Commn. on Higher Edn., North Cen. Assn., 1989-91, chair, 1991-93. With inf. AUS, 1944-46. Disting. Svc. to Humanities award given by Minn. Humanities Commn. named in his honor; named one of 100 most effective Am. coll. pres., 1987. Mem. Phi Beta Kappa. Home: 516 9th St S Moorhead MN 56560-3519 Office: Minn State U Moorhead 11th St S Moorhead MN 56560-9980 Office Phone: 218-477-2612. Business E-Mail: dille@mnstate.edu.

DILLE, STEPHEN EVERETT, state legislator, veterinarian, farmer; b. Mpls., Mar. 16, 1945; s. Donald Everett and Bonnie Marie (Anderson) D.; m. Pamela Jane Johnson, July 5, 1975; children: Nicholas, Kaisa, Spencer, Mitchell. BS, U. Minn., 1967, DVM, 1969. Vet. advisor USAID, South Vietnam, 1969-72; mem. faculty Coll. Vet. Medicine U. Minn., St. Paul, 1973-75; pvt. vet. practice Litchfield, Minn., 1975—; crop livestock farmer Dassel, Minn., 1975—; twp. supr., 1977-84; county commr. Meeker County, Minn., 1985-86; mem. Minn. Ho. of Reps. from dist. 21A, St. Paul, 1987-92, Minn. Senate from 20th dist., St. Paul, 1993—. Republican. Home: 69800 305th St Dassel MN 55325-2912 Office: Minn State Senate 103 SOB Saint Paul MN 55155-0001

DILLER, EDWARD DIETRICH, lawyer; b. Pandora, Ohio, Aug. 7, 1947; s. Hiram D. and Selma G. (Warkentin) D.; m. Karen Esmonde, June 1, 1968; children: Jason, Anna. BA, Bluffton Coll., 1969; postgrad., U. Oreg., 1969-70; JD cum laude, Harvard U., 1976. Assoc. Taft, Stettinius & Hollister, Cin., 1976-84, ptnr., 1984—, chmn. dept. bus. & fin., 1998—2006; ptnr.-in-charge Cin. Office, 2007—; moderator-elect. Mennonite Ch., Wash., 2007—. Chmn. Gen. Conf. Coun. on Higher Edn., 1990-2001, lectr. numerous seminars; mem. Women's Initiative Adv. Bd. Deloitte & Touche, Cin., 2000-Tchr. Mennonite Ctrl. Com., Frankfield, Jamaica, 1970-73; chmn. Edn. Integration Com. Mennonite Ch. USA, 1997-2001; trustee Mental Health Svcs. East, 1977-85, Bluffton Coll., 1979-2002, mem. exec. com., 1987-2002, chmn. bd., 1991-2002; hon. trustee, 2007-, mem. Family Svc. of Greater Cin. Area, 1989-96, chmn., 1992-95; trustee Habitat for Humanity (Southwestern Ohio and No. Ky. affiliate), 1995-2000; trustee Working in Neighborhoods, 1991-94, Dan Beard Coun. Boy Scouts of Am., 1996-, chmn. 2003-04, Leadership Cin. Alumni Assn., 2001-02; mem. Leadership Cin. Class XVI; trustee Found. Family Svc., 1997-, chmn. 2002—; bd. dirs. Cin. Mus. Ctr., 2005—, Cin. Playhouse, 2005—. Mem. Ohio State Bar Assn., Cin. Bar Assn., Ohio Harvard Law Sch. Assn. Office: Ste 1800 425 Walnut St Cincinnati OH 45202-3923 Office Phone: 513-357-9313. Business E-Mail: diller@taftlaw.com.

DILLON, DAVID BRIAN, retail grocery executive; b. Hutchinson, Kans., Mar. 30, 1951; s. Paul Wilson and Ruth (Muirhead) D.; m. Dee A. Ehling, July 29, 1973; children: Jefferson, Heather, Kathryn. BS, U. Kans., 1973; JD, So. Meth. U., 1976. V.p. Fry's Food Stores of Ariz. Inc. div. Dillon Cos. Inc., Phoenix, 1978-79, exec. v.p., 1979-83; v.p. Dillon Cos. Inc. (subs. of Kroger Co.), Hutchinson, 1983-86, pres., 1986-95; exec. v.p. Kroger Co., Cin., 1990-95; chmn. bd. Dillon Cos., Inc. (subs. Kroger Co.), Cin., 1993—95; pres., COO The

Kroger Co., Cin., 1995—99, pres., 1999—2000, pres., COO, 2000—03, CEO, 2003—, chmn., 2004—. Bd. dirs. Convergys. Chmn. Leadership Hutchinson, 1986-87, Leadership Kans., 1988; bd. dirs. Bethesda Hosp., Cin., 1996—; trustee U. Kans. Endowment Assn., 1993—, U. Cin. Found., 1997—, Dan Beard coun. Boy Scouts Am., 1996—; bd. advisors U. Kans. Bus. Sch., 1990—. Recipient Brotherhood-Sisterhood award Kans. region NCCJ, 1992. Mem. U. Kans. Alumni Assn., Urban League of Greater Cin. (trustee 1998—), Order of Coif, Sigma Chi (Balfour award 1973). Republican. Presbyterian. Office: The Kroger Co 1014 Vine St Cincinnati OH 45202-1100

DILLON, GARY (DOC), state senator; b. Culver, Ind., May 16, 1943; m. Ann Dillon; 4 children. BA, Wabash Coll.; MD, Ind. U. Dermatologist, pvt. practice; mem., past pres. Whitley County Meml. Hosp. Staff; mem. hospice med. directory Whitley County; state rep. Ind. Ho. of Reps., Indpls., 1998—2002; state sen. dist. 17 Ind. State Senate, Indpls., 2002—. Past pres. Whitley County Sch. Bd. Served Ind. Air Nat. Guard. Mem.: Ind. Dermatol. Soc., Columbia City and Ft. Wayne C. of C., Shrine Gideons, Masons, Kiwanis, Gideons. Republican. Office: Ind State Senate 200 W Washington St Indianapolis IN 46204-2787

DILLON, HOWARD BURTON, retired civil engineer; b. Hardyville, Ky., Aug. 12, 1935; s. Charlie Edison and Mary Opal (Bell) D.; m. Bonny Jean Garard, May 19, 1962; 1 child, Robert Edward. BCE, U. Louisville, 1958, MCE, 1960; postgrad., Okla. State U., 1962, Mich. State U., 1962-65. Registered profl. engr., Ind. Instr. U. Louisville, Ky., 1958-60; from assoc. prof. to prof. Ind. Inst. Tech., Ft. Wayne, 1960-62; NSF fellow Okla. State U., Stillwater, 1962; NSF grantee, instr. Mich. State U., East Lansing, 1962-67; head civil engring. dept. MW Inc. Cons. Engrs., Indpls., 1967-83; project mgr. civil divsn. SEG Engrs. & Cons., Indpls., 1983-91; pvt. practice Howard B. Dillon, Cons. Engr., Indpls., 1991—2002, ret., 2002. Asst. dir. to local pub. road needs study for Ind., 1970; mem. design com. for dams in Ind., 1974—; spl. cons. to Ind. Dept. Nat. Resources on dams, 1980—; mem. infrastructure com. for State of Ind., 1984—. Contbr. articles to profl. jours. Committeeman Wayne 52 precinct, Indpls., 1972-86; vice-ward chmn. Wayne South Twp., Indpls., 1986-87. Hazelett and Erdal scholar, 1957-58, W.B. Wendt scholar U. Louisville; recipient Order of Engr. award Purdue U., 1993. Mem. ASCE (life), NSPE (life), Am. Soc. Engring. Edn. (life), ASTM, Internat. Soc. Found. Engrs., Mil. Engrs., Internat. Acad. Sci. Ind. Water Resources Assn., Am. Water Works Assn., Nat. Audubon Soc., Indpls. Scientech Club, Optimists (pres. Suburban West chpt. 1972-74, bd. dirs. 1974-78, sec. 1992-94, lt. gov. ind. dist. 1972-74, Optimist of Yr., 1995), Chi Epsilon. Democrat. Baptist. Avocations: fishing, travel, photography, lecturing, coin collecting/numismatics. Home and Office: 6548 Westdrum Rd Indianapolis IN 46241-1843

DILLON, MERTON LYNN, historian, educator; b. nr. Addison, Mich., Apr. 4, 1924; s. Henry J. and Cecil Edith (Sanford) D. BA, Mich. State Normal Coll., 1945; MA, U. Mich., 1948, PhD, 1951. Asst. prof. history N.Mex. Mil. Inst., Roswell, 1951-56; asst. prof. Tex. Tech. Coll., Lubbock, 1956-59, asso. prof., 1959-63, prof., 1963-65; asso. prof. Northern Ill. U., DeKalb, 1965-67; prof. Ohio State U., Columbus, 1967-91, prof. emeritus, 1991—. Author: Elijah P. Lovejoy, Abolitionist Editor, 1961, Benjamin Lundy and the Struggle for Negro Freedom, 1966, The Abolitionists, the Growth of a Dissenting Minority, 1974; Ulrich Bonnell Phillips, Historian of the Old South, 1985, Slavery Attacked: Southern Slaves and Their Allies, 1619-1865, 1990; contbr. articles to profl. jours. EH fellow, 1973-74 Mem.Orgn. Am. Historians, So. Hist. Assn. (bd. editors 1959-63). Home: 10460 Addison Rd Jerome MI 49249-9723 Personal E-mail: mertondillon@yahoo.com.

DI LORENZO, JOHN FLORIO, JR., retired lawyer; b. Paterson, NJ, May 18, 1940; s. John F. and Ida (Cona) Di L.; m. Ernestine R. De Rose, Nov. 15, 1969; children: Christina P., Roberta J. BA, Seton Hall U., 1962; LLB, MBA, Columbia U., 1966. Bar: N.J. 1967, N.Y. 1968, Ohio 1981. Assoc. Stryker, Tams & Dill, Esqs., Newark, 1966-68; atty. Am. Electric Power Svc. Corp., NYC, 1968-79, asst. gen. counsel, asst. v.p., exec. asst. to pres., 1979-81, assoc. gen. counsel, v.p., sec. Columbus, Ohio, 1981-2001; ret., 2001. Sec. various Am. Electric Power Sys. cos., 1987-2001, asst. sec. 1979. Trustee Ballet Met. Columbus, 1981-87. Mem. ABA (chmn. subcom. on pub. utility holding co. act of fed. regulation of securities com. 1985-94), Knights of Malta, Knights of the Holy Sepulchre of Jerusalem, Scioto Country Club. Roman Catholic. Avocations: skiing, travel. Home: 2756 Elginfield Rd Columbus OH 43220-4248 Office Phone: 614-459-0047. E-mail: jfdilorenzo@att.net.

DIMOND, EDMUNDS GREY, medical educator; b. St. Louis, Dec. 8, 1918; s. Edmunds Grey and Gertrude Ruth (Schmidt) D.; m. Mary Dwight Clark, Nov. 28, 1968 (dec. June 1983); children: Sherri Grey Byrer, Lea Grey Dimond, Lark Grey Dimond-Cates. Student, Purdue U., 1938—39; BS, Ind. U., 1942, MD, 1944. Mem. faculty Med. Ctr., U. Kans., Kansas City, 1950-60, prof., chmn. dept. medicine, 1953-60, dir. cardiovasc. lab., 1950-60; mem., dir. Inst. for Cardiopulmonary Diseases, Scripps Clinic and Rsch. Found., 1960-67; rsch. assoc. physiology Scripps Inst. Oceanography, La Jolla, Calif., 1960-68; prof. in residence Sch. Medicine, U. Calif., San Diego, 1967-68; scholar in residence Nat. Libr. Medicine, 1967; spl. asst. to asst. sec. HEW, Washington, 1968; Disting. univ. prof. medicine U. Mo., Kansas City, 1968-98, provost for health scis., 1968-79. Fulbright prof., The Netherlands, 1956; vis. prof., Israel, 1978; scholar in residence Rockefeller Found. Study Ctr., Bellagio, Italy, 1978; chmn. overseas edn. team Dept. State, 1962, 64-66, 73; guest lectr. Chinese Med. Assn., 1971-73, 76-80, 82-92; pres. Edgar Snow Fund, Inc., Diastole-Hospital Hill, Inc. Author: Electrocardiography, 1952, rev. edits., 1955, 60, 64, Digitalis, 1957, Exercise Electrocardiograms, 1961, More Than Herbs and Acupuncture, 1975, Inside China Today, 1981, Take Wing, 1991, Dr. Horse of China, 1992, Reverend Whitehead, Mississippi Pioneer, 1987, Letters from Forest Place, 1993, Essays By An Unfinished Physician, 1995, Milepost Eighty, 2000, Milepost Eighty-Five, 2005; editor: Diastole on Hospital Hill Audiotape, 1980-86; editor-in-chief Accel, 1968-77; contbr. articles to profl. jours. Bd. dirs. Truman Med. Ctr., Kansas City, Mo., Eye Found., Kansas City, Sci. Edn. Partnership, Kansas City. With M.C., AUS, 1945-47. Paul Dudley White Traveling scholar, 1956-57. Master Am. Coll. Cardiology (pres. 1962, Disting. Svc. award 1969). Home and Office: 2501 Holmes St Kansas City MO 64108-2742 Office Phone: 816-235-8855. Personal E-mail: gdimond@kc.rr.com.

DIMOND, ROBERT B., food products executive; BS in acctg., U. Utah. Cert. CPA. Group v.p., admin. contr. Smith's Food & Drug Ctrs., Inc.; group v.p., CFO, western region The Kroger Co.; sr. v.p., CFO Nash Finch Co., Mpls., 2000—02, exec. v.p., CFO, 2002—. Office: Nash Finch Co 7600 France Ave S Minneapolis MN 55440-0355

DIMOND, ROBERT EDWARD, publisher; b. Washington, Dec. 12, 1936; s. James Robert and Helen Marie (Murphy) D.; m. Patricia Berger (div.); children: Mark Edward, Michele Lynn Keating, Melinda Ann. BA in Journalism, George Washington U., 1961. Mng. editor Nat. Automobile Dealers Assn. Mag., Washington, 1955-63; editor, pub. Bus. Products Mag., Washington, 1963-69; v.p. Hitchcock Pub. Co.; pub. Infosystems Mag., Office Products Mag., Wheaton, Ill., 1969-81; pres. R.E. Dimond & Assocs., Hinsdale, Ill., 1981-83; pub. Networking Mgmt. Mag., Westford, Mass., 1983-89, Home Improvement Ctr. Mag., Lincolnshire, Ill., 1989-90; v.p., pub. dir. mining and constrn. group Intertec; pub. Coal, Rock Products, Internat. Construction, Concrete Products, Engring. and Mining Jour., C&D Materials Recycling and Keystone Directory, 1990-96; group v.p. Intertec Pub. Co., 1996-99; pres. R.E. Dimond & Assocs., 1999—. Keynote spkr. COMDEX, 1979. Served with USAF, 1961-62. Democrat. Roman Catholic. E-mail: dimondre@comcast.net.

DINGELL, CHRISTOPHER DENNIS, state legislator; b. Washington, Feb. 23, 1957; s. John David and Helen (Henebry) D.; 1 child, Gabrielle. BSc, U. Mich., 1978; JD, Detroit Coll. Law., 1986. Engr. Ford Motor Co., Detroit, 1979-80, Rouge Steel Co., 1980-86; mem. Mich. Senate from 7th dist., Lansing, 1987—. Appropriations com. Mich. State Senate, career devel. com., strategic fund com., judiciary com., state policy and mil. affairs com., retirement com.; atty. Sommers, Schwartz, Silver & Schwartz, 1989—. Vol. Dem. Nat. Conv. Mem. Engring. Soc. Detroit, Econ. Club Detroit, Mich. Jaycees, Polish Roman Catholic Union, Mich. United Conservation Club, K. of C. Office: 910 Farnum Bldg PO Box 30036 Lansing MI 48909-7536 Fax: 517 373 9310. E-mail: sencdingell@senate.state.mi.us.

DINGELL, JOHN DAVID, congressman; b. Colorado Springs, Colo., July 8, 1926; s. John D. and Grace (Bigler) D.m. Deborah Insley; 4 children. BS in Chemistry, Georgetown U., 1949, JD, 1952. Bar: DC 1952, Mich. 1953. Pk. ranger U.S. Dept. Interior, 1948-52; asst. pros. atty. Wayne County, Mich., 1953-55; mem. U.S. Ho. of Reps. from 15th Mich. dist., 1955-65, 2003—, U.S. Ho. of Reps. from 16th Mich. dist., 1965—2002. Ranking minority mem. energy and commerce com. US Congress. Served to 2nd lt. US Army, 1944—46. Recipient Bryce Harlow award, Bryce Harlow Found., 1996, Legis. of Yr. award, Independent Insurance Agents Am., 1997, Nat. Congressional award, Nat. Recreation and Park Assn., 1999, Leadership in Govt. award, The Keystone Ctr., 2000, Golden Carrot award, Consumer Fedn. Am., 2003, Congressional Am. Spirit Medallion, Nat. D-Day Mus., 2004, Connie Mack award, Susan G. Komen Breast Cancer Found., 2004, Esther Peterson Sr. Adv. award, United Seniors Health Cooperative, Frank J. Kelley Public Svc. award, State Bar Mich., 2005. Mem.: Mich. Bar. Assn. Democrat. Roman Catholic. Office: US Ho of Reps 2328 Rayburn Bldg Washington DC 20515-2216 also: District Office 19855 W Outer Dr Ste 103-E Dearborn MI 48124 Office Phone: 202-225-4071, 313-278-2936. Office Fax: 313-278-3914.

DINOS, NICHOLAS, engineering educator, administrator; b. Tamaqua, Pa., Jan. 15, 1934; s. Christophoros and Calliope (Haralambos) D.; m. Lillian Gravell, June 18, 1955; children: Gwen Elizabeth, Christopher Nicholas, Janet Kay. BS, Pa. State U., 1955; MS, Lehigh U., 1966, PhD., 1967. Engr. E.I. duPont Co., Terre Haute, Ind., 1955-57, rsch. engr. Augusta, Ga., 1957-64; assoc. prof. Ohio U., Athens, 1967-72, prof., 1972—, chmn., 1976-89. Vis. prof. Chubu U., Nagoya, Japan, 1976. Contbr. articles to profl. jours. Elder Presbyn. Ch., Athens, 1967—; Danforth Found. assoc., Ohio U., 1978—. NASA fellow Lehigh U., Stanford U., 1966, 72, 74, U.S. Steel fellow Lehigh U., 1965. Mem. AIChE, Am. Soc. Engring. Edn., Sigma Xi, Phi Kappa Phi, Tau Beta Pi. Democrat. Avocations: reading, music, outdoors, travel. Home: 29 Briarwood Dr Athens OH 45701-1302 Office: Ohio U Dept Chem Engring Athens OH 45701 Office Fax: 740-593-0873. E-mail: dinos@ohio.edu.

DIONISOPOULOS, GEORGE ALLAN, lawyer; b. Santa Monica, Calif., July 31, 1954; s. P. Allan and Christine (Nassios) D.; m. Sandra Doreen Jordan, June 11, 1977; children: Sarah, Elaina. BA summa cum laude, U. Ill., 1976; JD cum laude, Harvard U., 1980. Bar: Wis. 1980, U.S. Dist. Ct. (ea. and we. dists.) Wis. 1980. Ptnr. Foley & Lardner LLP, Milw., 1980—, co-chmn. estates & trusts practice group. Mem. ABA (real property and probate sect., taxation sect.), Wis. Bar Assn. (speaker 1984—), Milw. Young Lawyers Assn., Phi Beta Kappa. Greek Orthodox. Office: Foley & Lardner LLP 777 E Wisconsin Ave Ste 3800 Milwaukee WI 53202-5367 Office Phone: 414-297-5750. Office Fax: 414-297-4900. Business E-Mail: gdionisopoulos@foleylaw.com.

DIONNE, NEAL, radio personality; Radio host Neal Dionne Show, Wood 1300, Grand Rapids, Mich. Office: Newsradio Wood 1300 77 Monroe Ctr Ste 1000 Grand Rapids MI 49503

DIPARDO, ANNE, English language educator; BA in English magna cum laude, Calif. State U., Northridge, 1976; MA in English, UCLA, 1977; EdD in Lang. and Literacy, U. Calif., Berkeley, 1991. Assoc. prof. English and edn. U. Iowa, Iowa City, 1991—2002, prof., 2002—. Author: A Kind of Passport, 1993, Teaching in Common, 1998; co-editor Research in the Teaching of English, 2003—; contbr. articles to profl. jours. Recipient Outstanding Scholarship award Nat. Writing Ctrs. Assn., 1993, CEL ELQ Best Article award, 2005; NAE/Spencer postdoctoral fellow, 1995—. Fellow Nat. Conf. Rsch. in Literacy; mem. MLA, Am. Ednl. Rsch. Assn., Nat. Coun. Tchrs. English (Promising Rschr. award 1992, Meade award 2000). Office: U Iowa N246 Linquist Ctr Iowa City IA 52242 Business E-Mail: anne-dipardo@uiowa.edu.

DIPERSIO, JOHN F., oncologist; b. Boston; BA (magna cum laude) in Biology, Williams Coll., 1973; MD, PhD in Microbiology, U. Rochester, 1980. Cert. Am. Bd. Internal Medicine, Am. Bd. Internal Medicine (Med. Oncology), Am. Bd. Internal Medicine (Hematology). Intern, medicine Parkland Meml. Hosp., UT Southwestern, Dallas, 1980—81, resident, 1981—83, chief resident, 1983—84; fellow, divsn. hematology-oncology UCLA Sch. Medicine, 1984—87, instr. medicine, divsn. hematology-oncology, 1987—88, asst. prof. medicine, divsn. hematology-oncology, 1988—90; asst. prof. oncology U. Rochester Sch. Medicine and Dentistry, NY, 1990—94; dir., bone marrow transplant program Strong Meml. Hosp., Rochester, NY, 1990—94; asst. prof. medicine, hematology unit U. Rochester Sch. Medicine, Rochester, NY, 1990—94; assoc. prof. medicine, pediatrics and pathology Washington U. Sch. Medicine, St. Louis, 1994—97, chief, divsn. bone marrow transplantation & stem cell biology, 1994—2000, prof. medicine, pediatrics and pathology, 1997—, acting dir., divsn. med. oncology, 2000—03, dir., sect. bone marrow transplantation & leukemia, 2000—06, chief, divsn. oncology, 2000—, dep. dir., Siteman Cancer Ctr., 2000—. Bd. dir. Barnard Free Skin and Cancer Hosp., 1998, 2003; career develop. award study sect. mem. Leukemia and Lymphoma Soc. Am., 2000—06; mem. med. adv. bd. Bone Marrow Found., 2005. Mem. editl. bd. Journal of Experimental Hematology, 1993; guest editor Blood Hournal, 1998-2001; contbr. articles to profl. jours. Recipient Jr. Faculty Rsch. award, Am. Cancer Soc., 1989, Lewis T. and Rosalind B. Apple Chair in Oncology, 1997; Spl. Fellow, Leukemia Soc. Am., 1986. Mem. Internat. Soc. for Exptl. Hematology (councilor, 1997, mem. nomating com. 1995, chmn. nominating com. 1997), Am. Soc. Hematology (study sect. mem. faculty and fellow scholar award, 2003-05), Am. Soc. for Biochemistry and Molecular Biology, Internat. Soc. for Hematotherapy and Graft Engring.(mem. stem celkl evaluation com., 1997, Am. Soc. for Blood and Marrow Transplant (bd. dir. 2003, chmn. coun. edn. and standards, 2003), Am. Soc. Clin. Investigation, Am. Soc. Clin. Oncology, Am. Soc. Clin. Investigation, Alpha Omega Alpha. helping pioneer stem cell transplants and focuses research efforts on improving the success of bone marrow and stem cell transplants for the treatment of cancer and disorders of the blood. Office: Divsn Oncology Campus Box 8007 Washington U Med Sch 660 S Euclid Ave 14th Fl Northwest Tower Saint Louis MO 63110 Office Phone: 314-454-8306. Office Fax: 314-454-7551. Business E-Mail: jdipersi@im.wustl.edu.

DIPKO, THOMAS EARL, retired minister, religious organization administrator; b. St. Michael, Pa., June 26, 1936; s. John and Sarah Jane (Gittins) D.; m. Sandra Jane Faust, Nov. 19, 1960; children: Lisa Renee, Sarah Marie. BA, Otterbein Coll., 1958; MDiv, United Theol. Sem., 1961; PhD in Ecumenical Theology, Boston U., 1969; LLD (hon.), Heidelberg Coll., 1987; DD (hon.), United Theol. Sem. of the Twin Cities, 1992; LHD (hon.), The Defiance Coll., 1992; DD (hon.), Elmhurst Coll., 1993, Ursinus Coll., 1994. ordained min. Youth min. First United Methodist Ch., Dayton, Ohio, 1958-61; ecumenical intern social action office Ch. Rhineland-Westphalia, Germany, 1962; asst. pastor First Ch. Congregational, Swampscott, Mass., 1963-64; pastor First United Methodist Ch., East Conemaugh, Pa., 1964-66; asst. pastor South Ch. Congregational, Andover, Mass., 1966-68; sr. pastor Christ Ch. United in Lowell, Mass., 1969-77, Grace Congregational Ch., Framingham, Mass., 1977-84; conf. min. and exec. Ohio conf. United Ch. of Christ, Columbus, 1984-92; exec. v.p. United Ch. Bd. for Homeland Ministries, Cleve., 1992-2000. Mem. bd. trustees The Defiance Coll., 1985—; mem. exec. com. Consultation on Ch. Union, 1989-02; del. Seventh Assembly World Coun. Chs., Canberra, Australia, 1991; mem. bd. dirs. Ryder Meml. Hosp., Humacao, Puerto Rico, 1993-96; interim dir. Chs. Uniting in Christ, Clev., 2005-06. Author: (first draft, book) United Church of Christ Book of Worship, 1986; contbr. chpts. to books, articles to profl. jours. Chmn. Lowell Drug Action Com., 1971-74; mem. bd. dirs. Internat. Inst., 1971-77. Samaritans (suicide intervention), 1983-84; del. gen. coun. World Alliance Reformed Chs., Debrecen, Hungary, 1997; bd. trustees LeMoyne-Owen Coll. Fellow Coll. Preachers, 1983. Mem. N.Am. Acad. Ecumenists (mem. exec. com. 1981-83), Christians Associated for Rels. in Eastern Europe, Consultation on Common Texts. Avocations: swimming, perennial gardening, canoeing. Personal E-mail: stdipko@aol.com.

DIRITA, DAVID M., lawyer, manufacturing executive; BA, JD, U. Mich., Ann Arbor. Corp. atty. Dickinson-Wright, Detroit; gen. counsel N.Am. and S.Am. Johnson Controls, Inc.; with Visteon Corp., 2000—05, dep. gen. counsel; sr. v.p., gen. counsel Tower Automotive, Inc., Novi, Mich., 2005—. Office: Tower Automotive, Inc 27175 Haggerty Rd Novi MI 48377 Office Phone: 248-675-6000.

DIRSMITH, RONALD, architect; m. Suzanne Roe Dirsmith. BS in Archtl. Engring., U. of Il., MA in Archtl. Design. Cert. Il., Fl., NCARB. With Perkins & Will; principal Ed Dart & Assoc.; founder, principal architect Dirsmith Group, 1971—. Named Nat. Academician, Nat. Academy of Design, 1999; fellow Rome Prize in Architecture. Office: c/o The Dirsmith Group 318 Maple Avenue Highland Park IL 60035

DI SIMONE, ROBERT NICHOLAS, radiologist, educator; b. Canton, Ohio, Nov. 15, 1937; s. Nicholas Joseph and Margaret Elizabeth (Karas) DiS.; m. Patricia Anne Zwigard, June 22, 1963; children: Christopher, Angela, Elizabeth BSc summa cum laude, Ohio State U., 1959, MSc, 1963, MD cum laude, 1963. Diplomate Am. Bd. Radiology, Am. Bd. Nuclear Medicine. Intern, fellow Johns Hopkins U. Hosp., Balt., 1963-64, asst. resident, fellow in internal medicine, 1964-65, asst. resident, fellow in radiology, 1967-70, instr., radiologist, 1970-71; dir. nuclear medicine Aultman Hosp., Canton, 1971-95, pres., med. staff, 1986-87, vice-chmn. dept. radiology, 1988-96, sec.-treas. med. staff, 1977-79; chmn. nuclear medicine sect. Northeastern Ohio Univs. Coll. Medicine, Rootstown, 1979-97; chmn. dept. radiology Northeastern Ohio Univs. Coll. of Medicine (NEOUCOM), Rootstown, 1992-93; diagnostic radiologist Aultman Health Found., Canton, Ohio, 1971-2000; radiology cons. North Canton, Ohio, 2000—. Author: Imaging of the Endocrine System in Organ System Radiology, 1984; contbr. articles to profl. jours Fellow Am. Coll. Radiology; mem. AMA, Soc. Nuc. Medicine (emeritus), Ohio State Med. Soc. (del. 1983-95), Radiol. Soc. N.Am., Stark County Med. Soc. (trustee 1979-95, chmn. bd. censors 1980-82, pres. 1993), Unique Club Stark County, Phi Beta Kappa, Sigma Xi, Alpha Omega Alpha, Phi Lambda Upsilon Avocations: playing bluegrass guitar music, collecting antique old trains, travel, hiking, gardening. Home and Office: 2465 Oakway St NW North Canton OH 44720-5886

DISTEL, L. GEORGE, state representative; b. Buffalo, May 11, 1952; married; 3 children. BA in History and Polit. Sci., Alliance Coll. State rep. dist. 99 Ohio Ho. of Reps., Columbus, 1999—, ranking minority mem., commerce and labor com., mem. agr. and natural resources, econ. devel. and tech., edn., and pub. utilities coms. Citizens adv. com. Ohio State U. Sea Grant; 1st vice chair Astabula County Dem. Exec. Com.; commr. Ashtabula County Commn.; pres. Conneaut city Coun., councilman-at-large; bd. dirs. Jobs for Ohio Grads., United Way Ashtabula County. Mem.: St. Francis Cabrini Ch., Conneaut Moose Club, Conneaut Lions Club, KC. Democrat. Office: 77 S High St 10th fl Columbus OH 43215-6111

DISTELHORST, GARIS FRED, trade association administrator; b. Columbus, Ohio, Jan. 21, 1942; s. Harold Theodore and Ruth (Haywood) D.; m. Helen Cecilla Gillen, Oct. 28, 1972; children: Garen, Kristen, Alison. BSc, Ohio State U., 1965. V.p. Smith, Bucklin & Assocs., Washington, 1969-80; chief staff exec., CEO, pres. Nat. Assn. Coll. Stores, Oberlin, Ohio, 1980-98; pres. Assn. Initiatives, Inc., Westlake, Ohio, 1998—2002; pres., CEO Conv. Industry Coun., 1999—2001, Marble Inst. Am., 2002—. Mem. book and libr. adv. com. USIA, 1990-93; bd. dirs. FirstMerit Bank, N.A., Holcombs, Inc. Pres. Oberlin Cmty. Improvement Corp., 1985-88; bd. dirs. Leadership Lorain County, 1988-89, Access Program, 1994-97, Conv. and Visitors Bur. Greater Cleve., 1994-2003, Lorain County C.C. Found. Executive Comm., 2008-, Lorain County United Way, 1991-97, v.p., 1993-94, pres., 1994-96, campaign chmn., 1993; bd. dirs. Project Love, 2003-05, Avon Lake Cmty. Improvement Corp., 2003—. Decorated USN Achievement medal, 1969 Mem. Inst. Assn. Mgmt. Soc. (treas. 1979-80, award of merit), Am. Soc. Assn. Execs. (bd. dirs. 1981-84, vice chmn. 1985, chmn.-elect 1994, chmn. 1995-96, bd. dirs. found. 1990-94, vice chmn. found. 1991-92, chmn. found. 1992-93, Key award 1984, chmn. Assn. Advance Am. 1993-94), Oberlin Area C. of C. (pres. 1987-90, bd. dirs. 1987-90), Greater Cleve. Soc. Assn. Execs. (bd. dirs. 2003—). Republican. Roman Catholic. Office: Marble Inst Am 28901 Clemens Rd Ste 100 Cleveland OH 44145 Office Phone: 440-250-9222. Business E-Mail: gdistelhorst@marble-institute.com.

D'ITRI, FRANK MICHAEL, environmental research chemist; b. Flint, Mich., Apr. 25, 1933; s. Dominic and Angelina D'Itri; m. Patricia Ann Ward, Sept. 10, 1955; children: Michael Payne, Angela Kathryn, Patricia Ann, Julie Lynn. BS in Zoology, Mich. State U., 1955, MS in Analytical Chemistry, 1966, PhD, 1968. Lab. technician Dow Industry Service Labs., Midland, Mich., 1960-62; research asst. dept. chemistry Mich. State U., East Lansing, 1963-68, asst. prof. dept. fisheries and wildlife, 1968-72, assoc. prof. dept. fisheries and wildlife, 1973-76, prof. dept. fisheries and wildlife, 1977—; assoc. dir. Inst. Water Rsch., 1987—; asst. dir. Mich. Agrl. Exptl. Sta., 1996—2000; internat. studies and programs, 2004—. Cons. U.S. Dept. Energy, Washington, 1983-85, EEC, UN, Geneva, 1982—; vis. prof. U. Bahia, Brazil, 1978, Tokyo U. Agr., 1980, 84-85, 87, 94, 2000, 01; mem. adv. bd. Lewis Pubs., Inc., Springer-Verlag. Author: The Environmental Mercury Problem, 1972, (with P.A. D'Itri) Mercury Contamination: A Human Tragedy, 1977, (with A.W. Andren, R.A. Doherty, J.M. Wood), Assessment of Mercury in the Environment, 1978, Acid Precipitation, 1982, Artificial Reefs, 1985; editor (with J. Aguirre M., M. Athie L.), Municipal Wastewater in Agriculture, 1981, Land Treatment of Municipal Wastewater: Vegetation Selection and Management, 1982, Acid Precipitation: Effects on Ecological Systems, 1982, (with M.A. Kamrin) PCBs: Human and Environmental Hazards, 1983, Artificial Reefs: Marine and Freshwater Applications, 1985, A System Approach to Conservation Tillage, 1985, (with H.H. Prince) Coastal Wetlands, 1985; (with L.G. Wolfson) Rural Groundwater Contamination, 1987, Chemical Deicers And The Environment, 1992, (with H.W. Belcher) Subirrigation and Controlled Drainage, 1995, Zebra Mussels and Aquatic Nuisance Species, 1997, (with Y. Itakura) Integrated Environmental Management, 1999; contbr. numerous articles to profl. jours. Mem. critical materials adv. subcom. Mich. Water Resources Commns. Mich. Dept. Natural Resources, 1971-79, mem. solid waste com., 1971-79; mem. subcom. Mich. State U. Waste Control Authority Chem. Waste, 1971—; mem. tech. adv. com. Great Lakes Protection fund tech. adv. com., 1990-93; mem. Great Lakes Commn., 1992—; mem. subirrigation steering com. Mich. Soil Conservation Svc., 1986—; mem. fluctuating lake levels com. Internat. Joint Commn., 1992-93; mem. internat. rsch. group mercury pollution in Amazon, Brazil, 1992—. NIH summer fellow, 1964-67, Socony-Mobil fellow Mich. State U., 1967-68, Japan Soc. Promotion Sci. fellow, 1980; Rockefeller Found. Bellagio Resident scholar, 1972, 75. Mem. Am. Chem. Soc., Am. Soc. Limnology and Oceanography, Assn. Analytical Chemists, Water Pollution Research Soc., Midwest Univs. Analytical Chemists Conf., Mich. Acad. Sci., Arts and Letters, Sigma Xi, Setac. Office: Mich State U 4A Internat Ctr East Lansing MI 48824-1035 Office Phone: 517-432-8244. Business E-Mail: ditri@msu.edu.

DITTMER, JOHN AVERY, history professor; b. Seymour, Ind., Oct. 30, 1939; s. J. Avery and Melba Roberta (Ahlbrand) D.; m. Ellen Ann Tobey, June 3, 1961; children: Julia Susan, John David. BS in Edn., Ind. U., 1961, MA in History, 1964, PhD in History, 1971. Asst. prof. Tougaloo (Miss.) Coll., 1967-68, acad. dean, 1968-70, assoc. prof., 1971-79; assoc. prof. history DePauw U., Greencastle, Ind., 1985-92, prof., 1993—2004, prof. emeritus, 2004—. Vis. assoc. prof. Brown U., Providence, 1979-80, 81-82, 83-84, MIT, Cambridge, 1982-84; cons. NEH, Washington, 1980-83, PBS Series, Eyes on the Prize, Boston, 1986. Author: Black Georgia in the Progressive Era, 1900-1920, 1977, Local People: The Struggle for Civil Rights in Mississippi, 1994 (Lillian Smith book award, 1994, Bancroft prize Columbia U. 1995); contbr. articles to profl. jours. Younger Humanist fellow NEH, 1973-74, fellowship-in-residence NEH, 1976-77, fellow Rockefeller Found., 1980-81, Am. Coun. Learned Socs., 1983-84, Ctr. Study Civil Rights U. Va., 1988-89, NEH, 2000-01, Nat. Humanities Ctr., 2001-01; grantee Ford Found., 2005—. Mem. Orgn. of Am. Historians (Frederick Jackson Turner award finalist 1972), So. Hist. Assn., Am. Hist. Assn. Avocations: tennis, golf, jazz music. Home: 230 Westwood Rd Fillmore IN 46128-9621 Office: DePauw U Dept History Greencastle IN 46135 Office Phone: 765-658-4590. Business E-Mail: rip@depauw.edu.

DITTRICK, WILLIAM G., lawyer; b. 1947; BBA, Univ. Neb., 1969, JD, 1974. Bar: US Dist. Ct. (Dist. Nebr.) 1972, Nebr. 1974, US Ct. Appeals (8th Cir.) 1982, Iowa 1998, US Supreme Ct. 1999. Law clerk Hon. Warren K. Urbom, Chief US Dist. Judge, 1974—76; mem. Baird Holm LLP, 1976—. Exec. ed.: editorial bd. Neb. Law Review, 1973—74. Past pres., bd. dirs. Big Brothers/Big Sisters, Midlands. Fellow: Am. Coll. of Trial Lawyers; mem.: ABA, Nebr. Assn. Trial Lawyers, Robert M. Spire Inns of Ct., Neb. State Bar Assn. (pres.-elect 2005, pres. 2006). Office: Baird Holm LLP 1500 Woodmen Tower Omaha NE 68102-2068 Office Phone: 402-636-8205. Business E-Mail: wdittrick@bairdholm.com.

DIVENERE, ANTHONY JOSEPH, lawyer; b. Bari, Italy, June 20, 1941; s. Joseph and Donna (Montini) DiV.; m. Sylvia Kathleen Scarnati, June 19, 1965; children: Anthony, Diana, John. AB, John Carroll U., 1964; JD, Ohio State U., 1967. BAr: Ohio 1967. Atty. in charge Cleve. Legal Aid Soc., 1967-70; prin., v.p. Burke Haber & Berick Co., L.P.A., Cleve., 1971; shareholder McDonald, Hopkins, Burke & Haber. Recipient Claude E. Clark award Cleve. Legal Aid. Soc., 1968, Cmty. Svc. aard orth Olmsted Jaycees, 1972. Mem. ABA, Ohio Bar Assn., Cleve. Bar Assn. (Appreciation award 1979-80), Cleve. Assn. Trial Attys. (pres. 1979-80), Def. Rsch. Inst., Vermilion Yacht Club. Avocations: sailing, marathon running, squash, opera. Home: 310 Rye Gate St Cleveland OH 44140-1272 Office: McDonald Hopkins Co 600 Superior Ave Ste 2100 Cleveland OH 44114 Business E-Mail: adivenere@mcdonaldhopkins.com.

DIVINEY, CRAIG DAVID, lawyer; b. Keokuk, Iowa, July 19, 1953; s. William Thomas and Ella (Michel) D.; m. Astrid Maria Kost, Oct. 6, 1975; children: Adam Thomas, Elliot Michel, Lisa Anne. BA, Augustana Coll., Rock Island, Ill., 1975; JD, U. Iowa, 1979. Bar: Minn. 1979, U.S. Dist. Ct. Minn. 1980, U.S. Ct. Appeals (8th cir.) 1984, U.S. Ct. Appeals (7th cir.) 1987, U.S. Ct. Appeals (fed. cir.) 1990. Assoc. Dorsey & Whitney, Mpls., 1979-84, ptnr., trial, intellectual property litig., 1985—, and chmn., life sci. and health care group. Adj. prof. William Mitchell Coll. Law, 1983-85; faculty Minn. Advocacy Inst., 1989—. Mem. fed. practice com. Dist. Minn., 1990-91; mem. adv. com. U.S. Dist. Ct., 1991—. Mem. ABA, Order of Coif. Office: Dorsey & Whitney 50 S 6th St Minneapolis MN 55402-1498 Office Phone: 601-340-2873. Office Fax: 612-340-2868. Business E-Mail: diviney.craig@dorsey.com.

DIX, BILL, state representative; b. Waterloo, Iowa, Nov. 28, 1962; m. Gerri Dix; 1 child. BS, Iowa State U., 1985. With retail feed sales Cargill, Inc., 1986, with feed sales mgmt., 1988; pvt. practice agri-bus., 1991—; mem. Iowa Ho. Reps., DesMoines, 1997—, mem. various coms. including appropriations, commerce and regulation, local govt., oversight and comm. appropriations, vice chair adminstrn. and rules. Chairperson Butler County Reps., 1993—. Mem.: Iowa Soybean Assn., Iowa Fruit and Vegetable Growers Assn., Cattlemen's Assn. Farm Bur., Pheasants Forever, Iowa State U. Alumni Assn., Lions. Republican. Methodist. Office: State Capitol East 12th and Grand Des Moines IA 50319 also: PO Box 220 317 S Walnut Shell Rock IA 50670-0235

DIX, ROLLIN C(UMMING), mechanical engineering educator, consultant; b. NYC, Feb. 8, 1936; s. Omer Houston and Ona Mae (Cumming) D.; m. Elaine B. VanNest, June 18, 1960; children: Gregory, Elisabeth, Karen. BSME, Purdue U., 1957, MSME, 1958, PhD, 1963. Registered profl. engr., Ill. Asst. prof. mech. engring. Ill. Inst. Tech., Chgo., 1964-69, assoc. prof., 1969-80, prof., 1980—2004, assoc. dean for computing, 1980-96; pres. Patpending Mktg., Inc., 1996—. 1st lt. US Army, 1960—61. Fellow: ASME. Achievements include patents in field. Home: 10154 S Seeley Ave Chicago IL 60643-2037 Office: Ill Inst Tech 10 W 32d St Chicago IL 60616-3729 Office Phone: 773-239-9778. Personal E-mail: rcd9778@sbcglobal.net.

DIXON, ALAN JOHN, former senator, lawyer; b. Belleville, Ill., July 7, 1927; s. William G. and Elsa (Tebbenhoff) D.; m. Joan Louise Fox, Jan. 17, 1954; children: Stephanie Jo, Jeffrey Alan, Elizabeth Jane. BS, U. Ill., 1949; LL.B., Washington U., St. Louis, 1949. Bar: Ill. 1950. Practiced in, Belleville, 1950-76; police magistrate City of Belleville, 1949; asst. atty. St. Clair County, Ill., 1950; mem. Ill. Ho. of Reps., 1951-63, Ill. Senate from 49th Dist., 1963—66, Ill. Senate from 54th Dist., 1968—71; minority whip; treas. State of Ill., 1971-77, sec. of state, 1977-81; US Senator from Ill., 1981—92; majority chief dep. whip, from 1988; ptnr. Bryan Cave LLP, St. Louis, 1993—; chmn. Def. Base Closure and Realignment Commn., 1994—95. Del. Dem. Nat. Conv., 1968, 76. Mem. Am. Legion, Belleville C. of C., ABA, Ill. Bar Assn., St Clair Country Club, Nat. Assn. Secretaries of State (pres 1979-80). Democrat. Office: Bryan Cave LLP One Metropolitan Square 211 North Broadway Ste 3600 Saint Louis MO 63102-2750 Office Phone: 314-259-2550. Office Fax: 314-269-6561.*

DIXON, BARBARA BRUINEKOOL, academic administrator; b. Sparta, Wis., June 14, 1943; MusB magna cum laude in Applied Piano, Mich. State U., 1966, MusM, 1969; MusD, U. Colo., 1991. Instr. vocal music K-12 Capac (Mich.) Cmty. Schs., 1970-71; tchr. dept. music Ctrl. Mich. U., Mt. Pleasant, 1971-89, assoc. dean coll. arts and scis., 1989-95, interim dean coll. arts and scis., 1995-97; provost, v.p. acad. affairs SUNY, Geneseo, 1997—2003; pres. Truman St. U., Kirksville, Mo., 2003—. Rep. acad. senate exec. bd., acad. senate liaison com., univ. acad. planning coun. Ctrl. Mich. U., 1986-89; dir. tchr. edn. search com., 1990, 95; chair faculty load equity study com., 1988-89, undergrad. curriculum com., 1992-93, formal hearing com. for grievance under senate rules, 1988-89; mem. profl. edn. coun., 1990-95, honors coun., 1989-94, task force on distance learning, 1992-93, piano search com., 1989, 90, 92, 95, music awards policy com., 1980-81, numerous others. One-woman performances include Kirtland C.C., Roscommon, Mich., 1986, Lansing (Mich.) C.C. Artist Series, 1987, Wurlitzer Hdqs., Holly Springs, Miss., 1989, Benefit for Cmty. Arts Coun., Pigeon, Mich., 1991, Beethoven Festival, Lansing, 1993, and others; accompanying performances include Backstage Recital Series, Jasper, Ind., 1984, Bridgeport (Mich.) Voice Symposium, 1986, Manistee (Mich.) Opera House, 1986, Saginaw (Mich.) Choral Soc., 1987, Alma (Mich.) Coll. Faculty, 1995, Black Forest Music Festival (Broadway rev.), Harbor Springs, Mich., 1995, and others. Active Art Reach Mid-Mich. (gallery com. 1995-96, chamber music com. 1995-97, fund drive com. 1996-97, bd. dirs. 1995-97, treas. 1996-97), Lions Club (chair spl. events com., bd. dirs. 1995-97), United Way (liaison to campus campaign); vol. Mich. Spl. Olympics. Mem. Mich. Music Tchrs. Assn. (bd. of certification 1976-79, 84-90, 95-97, chair 1996-97, pres. local chpt. 1991-92; chmn. collegiate activities 1979-81; mem. spkrs. bur. 1974-97, adjudicators bur. 1975-97, exec. bd. 1979-81, 96; rep. Mich. Youth Arts Festival bd. 1976-81, Mich. Alliance for Arts in Edn. 1988-89), Dalcroze Soc. Am., Delta Omicron, AAUW, Am. Assn. Higher Edn., Phi Beta Delta, Pi Kappa Lambda, Phi Kappa Phi Mortar Bd. Office: Truman St U 100 E Normal St MC200 Kirksville MO 63501 E-mail: dixon@truman.edu.

DIXON, BILLY GENE, academic administrator, educator; b. Benton, Ill., Oct. 25, 1935; s. John and Stella (Prowell) D.; m. Judith R. McCommons, June 7, 1957; children: Valerie J., Clark A. BS, So. Ill. U., 1957, MS, 1960, PhD, 1967; MS, Ill. Wesleyan U., 1961. Tchr. math., chmn. dept. Cahokia (Ill.) High Sch., 1960-61; tchr. Univ. Sch., So. Ill. U., Carbondale, 1961-67, chmn. dept. math., 1963-67; dir. rsch. and evaluation ESEA Title II Project Uplift, Mt. Vernon, Ill., 1967-69; coordinator profl. edn. experiences Coll. Edn. So. Ill. U., Carbondale, 1968-75, mem. faculty, coord. grad. program in secondary edn., 1975-78, departmental exec. officer curriculum and instrn., 1978—2001, asst. to dept. exec. officer for spl. projects, 2001—08, asst. to dean profl. devel. Coll. Edn. and Human Svcs., 2004—06. Bd. dirs. Holmes Partnership, 1999—2006. Pres. Benton Cmty. Pk. Dist., 1974—95; bd. dirs. United Meth. Children's Home, 2004—, vice chmn., 2005—. Named Citizen of Yr., Benton C. of C., 1982; recipient Liberty Bell award, 1995. Mem. Ill. Assn. Tchr. Educators (pres. 1973, exec. coun. 1976-79, Disting. mem. 1984), Assn. Tchr. Educators (chmn. nat. rev. panel Disting. Program in Tchr. Edn. 1976-86, exec. bd. 1983-86, pres. 1988-89, Pres.'s award 1983, 84, 95, 99, 2004, 05, 07, Disting. mem. 1992, named Disting. Tchr. Educator, 2007), Pi Mu Epsilon, Phi Kappa Phi, Phi Delta Kappa, Kappa Delta Pi. Democrat. Methodist. Home: 9793 Stuyvesant St Benton IL 62812-5916 Office: So Ill U Coll Edn Human Svcs Carbondale IL 62901-4610 Business E-Mail: bgdixon@siu.edu.

DIXON, JACK EDWARD, biological chemistry professor, consultant; b. June 16, 1943; BA, UCLA, 1966; PhD, U. Calif., Santa Barbara, 1971. NSF Found. postdoctoral rsch. fellow U. Calif., San Diego, 1971—73; from asst. prof. to assoc. prof. biochemistry Purdue U., West Lafayette, Ind., 1973—82, prof. biochemistry, 1982—86, Harvey W. Wiley disting. prof. biochemistry, 1986—91; Minor J. Coon prof. biol. chemistry, chmn. dept. U. Mich., Ann Arbor, 1991—2003, co-dir. Life Scis. Inst., 2001—02, dir. Life Scis. Inst., 2002—03; prof. pharmacology, cellular medicine, chemistry and biochemistry U. Calif., San Diego, 2003—, dean sci. affairs Sch. Medicine, 2003—. Nathan O. Kaplan lectr. U. Calif., San Diego, 1991; Edmund Fischer lectr. U. Wash., Seattle, 1993; adj. prof. Salk Inst., 2003—; Baker lectr. U. Calif., Santa Barbara, 2003; Merck Award lectr. ASBMB, 2005; Dyer lectr. NIH, 2005. Recipient Merit award, NIH, 1987, 1996, 2004, William Rose award, ASBMB, 2003, Biochemistry and Molecular Biology award, Merck, 2003. Fellow: AAAS, Am. Acad. Arts and Sci., Mich. Soc. Fellows U. Mich. (sr.); mem.: Inst. Medicine, Nat. Acad. Sci., Am. Soc. Cell Biology, Am. Soc. Biochemistry and Molecular Biology (program chmn. 1994—, pres. 1996—97), Sigma Xi. Office: U Calif San Diego 9500 Gilman Dr 0602 La Jolla CA 92093-0602 Office Phone: 858-822-3529.

DIXON, JOHN FULTON, village manager; b. Bellingham, Wash., Dec. 17, 1946; s. Fulton Albert and Patricia (Broderick) D.; m. Karen Elizabeth Creagh, May 19, 1973; children: Neil, Craig. BS, Bradley U., 1971; M in Mgmt., Vanderbilt U., 1973. Asst. village mgr. Village of Hoffman Estates, Ill., 1974-76, village mgr. Ill., 1980-86; dir. village svcs. Village of Roselle, Ill., 1976-79; asst. village mgr. Village of Schaumburg, Ill., 1979-80; village adminstr. Village of Lake Zurich, Ill., 1986-87; village mgr. Village of Mt. Prospect, Ill., 1987-92; village adminstr. Village of Lake Zurich, 1992—. Mem. exec. bd. dirs. .W. Suburban Mcpl. Joint Action Water Agy., Hoffman Estates, 1980-92; mem. exec. bd. dirs. N.W. Cen. Dispatch, Arlington Heights, Ill., 1987-92. Troop com. chmn. Boy Scouts Am., 1989-93; bd. dirs. Marklund Chilren's Home, 1999—, treas. 2001-. Recipient Chief Scout's award Gov. Gen. of Jamaica, Kingston, 1970; Adminstrv. fellow Woodrow Wilson Found., 1973-74, Houston fellow Vanderbilt U., 1972-73; Baker scholar Vanderbilt U., 1971-73. Mem. Met. Chgo. City Mgrs. Assn. (bd. dirs., pres. 1986-87), Ill. City Mgmt. Assn. (bd. dirs., pres. 1990-91), Rotary (bd. dirs. 1989—, pres. Lake Zurich chpt. 1997-98). Roman Catholic. Avocations: golf, travel. Home: 248 Sebby Ln Lake Zurich IL 60047-1358 Office: Village of Lake Zurich 70 E Main St Lake Zurich IL 60047-2416

DIXON, STEWART STRAWN, lawyer, consultant; b. Chgo., Nov. 5, 1930; s. Wesley M. and Katherine (Strawn) D.; m. Romayne Wilson, June 24, 1961 (dec. July 1993); children: Stewart S. Jr., John W., Romayne W. Thompson; m. Ann Wilson Grozier, Sept. 15, 1997. BA, Yale U., 1952; JD, U. Mich., 1955. Bar: Ill. 1957, U.S. Dist. Ct. 1957, U.S. Ct. Appeals 1974, U.S. Supreme Ct. 1974. Ptnr. Kirkland & Ellis, Chgo., 1957-67, Wildman, Harrold, Allen & Dixon, Chgo., 1967—. Dir. Lord, Abbett & Co. Managed Mut. Funds, N.Y.C., 1976-2002, ret. Dec. 31, 2002; dir. Otho Sprague Inst., Chgo. Trustee, past chmn. Chgo. Hist. Soc., 1982-87. 1st lt. U.S. Army, 1955-60. Mem. Am. Bar Assn., Am. Law Inst., Ill. Bar Assn., Chgo. Bar Assn. Clubs: Chgo., Commonwealth, Commercial, Met., Univ., Old Elm, Onwentsia, Rolling Rock. Republican. Episcopalian. Office: Wildman Harrold Allen & Dixon 225 W Wacker Dr Chicago IL 60606-1229 Office Phone: 312-201-2604. Business E-Mail: dixon@wildmanharrold.com.

DIXON, WHEELER WINSTON, film and video studies educator, writer; b. New Brunswick, NJ, Mar. 12, 1950; s. Percival Vincent and Hilda-Barr (Wheeler) D.; m. Gwendolyn Audrey Foster, Dec. 23, 1985. AB, Livingston Coll., 1972; MA, MPhil, Rutgers U., 1980, PhD, 1982. Instr. English Rutgers U., New Brunswick, 1974-84; lectr. film studies The New Sch. for Social Rsch., 1983, 97, 98; asst. prof. English and art U. Nebr., Lincoln, 1984-88, assoc. prof. English, 1988—92, chmn. film studies program, 1988—2003, prof. English, 1992—2002; series editor Cultural Studies in Cinema Video Series SUNY Press, 1995—2008, endowed chair, Ryan prof. of film studies, 2000—. Guest programmer, lectr. Nat. Film Theatre of Brit. Film Inst. and Mus. of Moving Image, London, 1991; guest programmer Nat. Film Theatre of Brit. Film Inst., London, 1992; mem. ad hoc curriculum rev. com. dept. English, U. Nebr., Lincoln, 1992, mem. faculty devel. fellowship com., 1992-95, chmn. Robinson Prize com., spring 1994, chmn. faculty devel. fellowship com., 1994, mem. various MA thesis and PhD coms.; panelist NEH, 1993—; presenter papers in field; lectr. Lincoln Ctr., Mus. Modern Art, N.Y.C., New Sch. Univ., N.Y.C., 1997; guest lectr. on digital theory, U. Amsterdam, 1999. Author: The "B" Directors: A Bibliographical Directory, 1985, The Cinematic Vision of F. Scott Fitzgerald, 1986, The Films of Freddie Francis, 1991, The Charm of Evil: The Films of Terence Fisher, 1991, The Films of Reginald Le Borg: Interviews, Essays and Filmography, 1992, The Early Film Criticism of François Truffaut, 1993, Re-Viewing British Cinema 1900-1992: Essays and Interviews, 1994, It Looks at You: The Returned Gaze of Cinema, 1995, The Films of Jean-Luc Godard, 1997, The Exploding Eye: A Re-visionary History of 1960s Experimental Cinema, 1997, The Transparency of Spectacle, 1998, Disaster and Memory, 1999, The Second Century of Cinema, 2000, Film Genre 2000, 2000, Collected Interviews: Voices from 20th Century Cinema, 2001, Experimental Cinema: The Film Reader, 2002, Straight: Constructions of Heterosexuality in the Cinema, 2003, Visions of the Apocalypse: Spectacles of Destruction in the American Cinema, 2003, Film and Television after 9/11, 2004, Lost in the Fifties, 2005, American Cinema of the 1940s, 2006, Visions of Paradise, 2006, Film Talk: Directors at Work, 2007, A Short History of Film (with Gwendolyn Andrey Foster), 2008; editor-in-chief Quarterly Review of Film and Video, 1999—; guest editor Film Criticism, Fall-Winter 1991-92, mem. editl. bd., 1991—, article reviewer, 1991—; article reviewer Jour. of History of Sexuality, 1991-93, Cinema Jour., 1993—; mem. adv. bd. Jour. Popular Brit. Cinema; manuscript reviewer SUNY Press, 1993—; contbr. articles and revs. to profl. jours. and essays to various publs., including Film Criticism, Films in Rev., Cineaste, Interview, others; writer, dir., prodr. Coming Attractions: A History of the Motion Picture Trailer, 1986-88, (feature film) What Can I Do?, 1993 (Layman Fund award 1993-94); co-prodr., co-dir., co-writer: Women Who Made The Movies, 1988-90; dir./prodr.: (feature film) Squatters, 1994; exhibited in group shows at U. ebr.-Lincoln, 1985-86, 87-88, 89-90, Syracuse U., 1986, W.Va. U., 1986, Lincolnshire Coll. Art, Lincoln, Eng., 1988-89; performances include That's Different: Tales of Nebraska, 1987; exhibitions of films include Whitney Mus. Am. Art, 1972, Mus. Modern Art, 1994, Mus. Moving Image, London, 1994, Millennium Film Workshop, 1997, Mus. Modern Art, 2003; complete films archived exclusively at Mus. of Modern Art, 2003, Career Retrospective, 2003; author (notes) Home Vision DVDs, 2004-05. Recipient Outstanding Rsch. and Creative Achievement award, 2003; grantee Royal Film Archive of Belgium, 1974, N.J. State Arts Coun., 1972, Rsch. Coun., U. Nebr., 1984-85, Ind. Filmmaker, S.W. Alt. Media Project, 1985, Interdisciplinary Arts Fellowship Program, Rockefeller Found. and NEA, 1987, Rsch. Coun., 1987, 89, S.W. Alt. Media Project Ind. Prodn. Fund, 1993, John C. and Nettie V. David Meml. Trust, 2003, Maude Hammond Flip Fellowship, 2006. Mem.: Soc. for Cinema Studies (exec. coun. 2004—). Office: U Nebraska Dept English 202 Andrews Hall Lincoln NE 68588-0333 Home Phone: 402-423-2105; Office Phone: 402-472-6064. Business E-Mail: wdixon@unlserve.unl.edu.

DIXSON, J. B., communications executive; b. Norwich, NY, Oct. 19, 1941; d. William Joseph and Ann Wanda (Teale) Barrett. BS, Syracuse U., 1963; postgrad. in bus. adminstrn., Wayne State U., 1979-81; MBA, Ctrl. Mich. U., 1984. Pub. rels. editl. asst. Am. Mus. Natural History, NYC, 1963-64; writer, prodr. orman, Navan, Moore & Baird Advt., Grand Rapids, Mich., 1964-67; prin. J.B. Dixson Comm. Cons., Detroit, 1967-74; dir. Pub. Info. Svcs. divsn. Mich. Employment Security Commn., Detroit, 1974-82; news rels. mgr. Burroughs Corp., 1982-83, dir. creative svcs., 1983-85, dir. pub. rels., 1985-86; prin. Dixson Comm., Detroit, 1986-93, Durocher Dixson Werba, LLC, Detroit, 1994—. Lectr., spkr. in field at colls, univs., cmty. orgns. Author: Guidelines for non-Sexist Verbal and Written Communication, 1976, Sexual Harassment on The Job, 1979, The TV Interview: Good News or Bad?, 1981. Mem. Detroit Mayor's Transition Com. of 100, 1972; mem. bd. mgmt. Detroit YWCA, 1974; chmn. Detroit Women's Equality Day Com., 1975; bd. dirs., founding mem. Feminist Fed. Credit Union, Detroit, 1976; centennial chair Indian Village Assn., 1993-95; founding mem. Mich. Women's Campaign Fund, 1980; active Mich. Task Force on Sexual Harassment in Workplace, Mich. Women's Com. of 100, Mich. Women's Polit. Caucus, Mich. Women's Found. Named Outstanding Sr. Woman in Radio and TV, Syracuse U., 1963; recipient Five Watch award Am. Women in Radio and TV, Mich., 1969, 75, Outstanding Women in Comm. Women's Advt. Club, 1998, cert. of recognition Detroit City Coun., 1976, Feminist of Yr. award NOW, 1977, City of Detroit Human Rights Commn., 1988, Design in Mich. award Mich. Coun. of Arts/Gov. William G. Milliken, 1977, Achievement award U.S. Dept. Labor, 1979, Spirit of Detroit award Detroit City Coun., 1980, PR Casebook, 1983, PR ews Case Study, 1986, Pinnacle award Mich. Hosp. Pub. Rels. Assn., 1987, award Nat. Sch. Pub. Rels. Assn., 1992, 21st Century award Corp. Detroit Mag., 1995, Creativity in Advt. award Detroit Newspapers Assn., 2000; subject of Mich. Senate Resolution 412, 1979. Fellow Pub. Rels. Soc. Am. (accredited, pres. chpt. 1983-84, Dist. award and citation 1984, 86, 87, 93, exec. com. corp. sect. 1996-2001, Disting. Svc. award 1999, named to Pub. Rels. Hall Fame 2004), Internat. Assn. Bus. Communicators (Silver Quill award chpt. 1987, 88, 91, 93, dist. 1987, Renaissance award 1988, 91, Mercury award 1987), Nat. Assn. Govt. Communicators (Blue Pencil award 1977, Gold Screen award 1980), Automotive Press Assn., Women's Advt. Club (Top 75 Women in Comm. 1999), Econ. Club Detroit, Maple Grove Gun Club, Detroit Athletic Club. Home: 3000 N Ocean Dr Apt 28b Singer Island FL 33404-3249 Personal E-mail: dixson@ddwpr.com.

DLOTT, SUSAN JUDY, judge, lawyer; b. Dayton, Ohio, Sept. 11, 1949; d. Herman and Mildred (Zemboch) D.; m. Stanley M. Chesley, Dec. 7, 1991. BA, U. Pa., 1971; JD, Boston U., 1973. Bar: Ohio 1973, U.S. Dist. Ct. (so. dist.) Ohio 1975, U.S. Ct. Appeals (6th cir.) 1976, U.S. Supreme Ct. 1980, U.S. Dist. Ct. (ea. dist.) Ky. 1984, U.S. dist. Ct. (no. dist.) Ohio 1989, Ky. 1990. Law clk. Ohio Ct. of Appeals, Cleve., 1973-74; asst. U.S. atty. U.S. Dist. Ct. (so. dist.) Ohio, Dayton, 1975-79; ptnr. Graydon, Head & Ritchey, Cin., 1979-95; dist. judge U.S. Dist. Ct. for So. Dist. Ohio, Cin., 1995—. Legal reporter Multimedia Program Prodn., Inc., 1982-84; instr. trial advocacy workshop, Harvard Law Sch., 2000. Mem. Ohio Bldg. Authority, 1988-93, vice chmn., 1990-93, Jewish Fedn. Cin., trustee and mem. com. 1979-93, Jewish Cmty. Rels. Coun. Cin., 1980-90, Hamilton County Park Dist. Vol. in Parks, 1985-86 Named a Career Woman of Achievement, YWCA, 1996, Cin. Leading Woman, 1998; recipient commendation, US Postal Svc., 1977, Svc. award, Dayton Bar Assn., 1975—76, Gift of Appreciation award, Downtown Residents' Coun., 2000, Fair and Courageous award, NAACP, 2006. Mem. ABA, FBA (asst. treas. 1981-82, treas. 1982-83, sec. 1983-84, v.p. 1984-86), Ohio Bar Assn., Ky. Bar Assn., Cin. Bar Assn., Leadership Cin. Alumni Assn., Queen City Dog Tng. Club, 6th Cir. Jud. Conf. (life), AACP (life), Hadassah (life), Potter Stewart Inn of Ct. (pres. 1997—), Cavalier King Charles Spaniel Club Jewish. Office: 100 E 5th St Cincinnati OH 45202-3927 Office Phone: 513-564-7630.

DOANE, J. WILLIAM, physics educator and researcher, science administrator; b. Bayard, Nebr., Apr. 26, 1935; married, 1958; 2 children. BS, U. Mo., 1956, MS, 1962, PhD in Physics, 1965. From asst. to assoc. prof. Kent State U., 1965-74, prof. physics, 1974-96, prof. emeritus, 1996—, assoc. dir. Liquid Crystal Inst., 1979-83, dir. Liquid Crystal Inst., 1983-96, dir. emeritus, 1996—; v.p. R&D, chief sci. officer Kent Displays, Inc., Ohio, 1996-99. Prin. investigator def. agy. and industry grants NSF. Contbr. over 200 articles to profl. jours.; holder of 10 patents. Fellow Am. Phys. Soc.; mem. Am. Assn. Physics Tchrs., Sigma Xi. Achievements includes research on liquid crystal display and nuclear magnetic resonance in liquid crystals. Office: Kent State U Liquid Crystal Inst Kent OH 44242-0001

DOANE, MARCIA E., lawyer, retired food products executive; b. 1941; BA in Music, De Pauw U., Greencastle, Ind., 1963; JD, Loyola U. Sch. of Law, Chicago, 1976. Bar: Ill. 1976. Special asst. atty. gen. Ill., 1978—81; ptnr. Cowen Crowley Nord & Doane; ops. atty. Bestfoods (Corn Products div.), 1989—94, counsel, 1994—96, v.p. legal and regulatory affairs, 1996—97; v.p., gen. counsel, sec. Corn Products Internat., Inc., 1997—2006. Mem.: ABA, Am. Corp. Counsel Assn., Am. Soc. of Corp. Secretaries, Ill. Women's Bar Assn. (mem. matrimonial law com. 1979—83, mem. trial practice com. 1980—88), Ill. State Bar Assn., Chicago Bar Assn. (probate practice com. 1976—82, mem. real estate com. 1979, 1982, mem. corp. law dept. com. 1995—99).

DOANE, TIM, travel company executive; BBA in Mktg. and Mgmt., U. Cin., 1979; MBA in Mktg. and Fin., Miami U., Ohio. With Travel Centers of Am., Westlake, Ohio, 1995—, sr. v.p., mktg., pres., COO, 2003—05, pres., CEO, 2005—. Office: Travel Centers of Am 24601 Center Ridge Rd Westlake OH 44145

DOBIS, CHESTER F., state legislator; b. Gary, Ind., Aug. 15, 1942; s. Jack F. and Veronica (Kordys) D.; m. Darlene Zimmerman, 1971. Student, Ind. U. N.W., 1961. Sales rep. Standard Liquors; v.p. govt. svc. Gainer Bank, 1972—; banker, v.p. govt. svc. NBD Bank; rep. Dist. 13 Ind. Ho. of Reps., 1970—, vice chmn. fin. inst., mem. house adminstrn. com., mem. pub. policy, vet. affairs, ethics com., mem. interstate coop. com., rules and legis. procedure com., spkr. pro tem, asst. minority floor leader. Mem. exec. bd. N.w. Ind. Regional Planning Commn.; vice pres. Ross Twp. Dem. Club, Merrillville, Ind., 1968—; bd. dirs. Lake County Young Dems., 1969-70; pres. Ross Twp. Young Dems., 1970—; vol. Lake Area United Way, Lake County Assn. Retarded, Polish Am. Dem. Club. With Ind. N.G. Named One of Top Freshman Legislators, Ind. Gen. Assembly, 1971. Mem. Nat. Coun. State Legislators, Gary Sportsmen Club, PNA Silver Bell. Home: 6565 Marshall Ct Merrillville IN 46410-2859

DOBRANSKI, BERNARD, dean, law educator; b. Sept. 3, 1939; s. Walter John and Helen Dolores (Rudnick) Dobranski; m. Caroll Sue Wood, Aug. 31, 1963; children: Stephanie, Andrea, Christopher. BBA in Fin., U. Notre Dame, 1961; JD, U. Va., 1964. Bar: Va. 64, U.S. Supreme Ct. 68, U.S. Ct. Appeals (DC cir.) 71. Legal advisor to bd. Nat. Labor Rels. Bd., 1964—67; profl. staff mem. Pres.'s Adv. Commn. on Civil Disorders, 1967—68; adminstrv. asst. U.S. Ho. of Reps., 1968—71; gen. counsel Washington Met. Area Transit Commn., 1971—72; mem. faculty Creighton U. Sch. of Law, Omaha, 1972—77, U. Notre Dame, 1977—83; prof., dean U. Detroit Sch. of Law, 1983—95, Cath. U. Am. Sch. of Law, 1995—99; prof., pres., dean Ave Maria Sch. of Law, Ann Arbor, Mich., 1999—. Contbr. articles to profl. jours. Mem.: ABA, Detroit Athletic Club, Hurlingham Club, Frank Murphy Honor Soc. Roman Catholic. Office: Ave Maria Sch of Law 3475 Plymouth Rd Ann Arbor MI 48105 Home Phone: 734-424-2376; Office Phone: 734-827-8043. Business E-Mail: bdobranski@avemarialaw.edu.

DOBSON, RICK, metals company executive; BS in bus. admin., U. Wis.; MBA in fin., U. Nebr. Cert. CPA. Audit mgr. Arthur Andersen, 1981—89; v.p., contr. Aquila Merchant Svcs., 1989—95; v.p., risk mgmt. acctg. Aquila, Kans. City, Mo., 1997, interim CFO, 2002—03, CFO, 2003—06; CFO, sr. v.p. Novelis, Inc., 2006—. Office: Novelis Inc 3399 Peachtree Rd NE Ste 1500 Atlanta GA 30326

DOCKING, THOMAS ROBERT, lawyer, former state lieutenant governor; b. Lawrence, Kans., Aug. 10, 1954; s. Robert Blackwell and Meredith (Gear) D.; m. Jill Sadowsky, June 18, 1977; children: Brian Thomas, Margery Meredith BS, U. Kans., 1976, MBA, JD, 1980. Bar: Kans. 1980. Assoc. Regan & McGannon, Wichita, Kans., 1980-82, ptnr., 1983-90, Ayesh, Docking, Herd & Theis, Wichita, 1990, Morris, Laing, Evans, Brock & Kennedy, Wichita, 1990—; lt. gov. State of Kans., Topeka, 1983-87. Dem. nominee for Gov. of Kans., 1986; chmn. adv. bd. Docking Inst. Pub. Affairs, Ft. Hays State U. Mem. steering com. Campaign Kans.; chmn. campaign com. Coll. Liberal Arts and Sci., 1988—91; trustee Emporia State U. Sch. Bus.; chmn. Wichita Water Conservation Task Force, 1991—; mem. Wichita/Brookes Water Task Force, 1997; bd. govs. U. Kans. Sch. Law, 1998—2000; bd. dirs. Kans. Easter Seals-Goodwill Industries, 1987—93, chmn. 1989 Telethon, vice-chair, 1991—93; bd. dirs. Wichita Conv. and Visitors Bur., 1988—2002; chmn., bd. dirs. St. Francis Found., 1988—94; bd. dirs. Wichita Downtown Devel. Corp., 2001—, Fin. Fitness Found., 1999—; chmn. allocation com. United Way of the Plains, 2003, bd. dirs., 2004—, vice chmn., 2006, chmn., 2007—08. Recipient Bob Brock award, Kansas Dem. Party, 2003. Mem. ABA, Kans. Bar Assn., Pi Sigma Alpha, Beta Gamma Sigma, Beta Theta Pi. Presbyterian. Home: 125 S Crestway St Wichita KS 67218-1309 Office: Morris Laing Evans Brock & Kennedy 300 N Mead St #200 Wichita KS 67202-2744 Office Phone: 316-262-2671.

DOCKTERMAN, MICHAEL, lawyer; b. Davenport, Iowa, Dec. 14, 1954; s. Jerome and Elaine (Epstein) D.; m. Laura Di Giantonio, Sept. 25, 1983; 1 child, Eliana. BA, Yale U., 1975; JD, Duke U., 1978. Bar: Ill. 1978, US Dist. Ct. (no. dist. Ill.) 1978, US Ct. Appeals (7th cir.) 1978, US Dist. Ct. (ea. dist. Mich.) 1986, US Dist. Ct. (ctrl. dist. Ill.) 1988, US Ct. Appeals (4th, 6th and fed. cir.) 1990, US Dist. Ct. (so. dist. Ill.) 1991, US Supreme Ct. 1992, US Ct. Appeals (2nd cir.) 1993, US Dist Ct. (we. dist. Mich.) 1995, US Dist. Ct. (ea. dist. Mo.) 1996, US Ct. Appeals (9th cir.) 2004; registered fgn. lawyer UK, 2004-06. Ptnr. Wildman, Harrold, Allen and Dixon, LLP, Chgo., 1978—, mem. exec. com. Chmn. bd. visitors Sch. Law Duke U., 2007—. Co-author: IICLE Class Actions, 1986, 92, 2000, 07, Inside the Minds: White Collar Law Client Strategies, 2007; contbr. articles to profl. jours. Active Chgo. Vol. Legal Svc., 1983—, The Chgo. Com., Am. Refugee Com., Chgo. Coun. Global Affairs, mem. President's Cir.; bd. dir. KAM Isaiah Israel Congregation, 1993-96, 2002-03; bd. dir. Duke Law Alumni Assn., 1994-2003, pres., 2000-02, bd. visitors, 2003-; trustee Max and Gretel Janowski Fund, Chgo., 1992-99; chmn. bd. visitors Duke U. Sch. Law, 2007—. Recipient Award for Advocacy Internat. Acad. Trial Lawyers, Charles A. Dukes award for vol. svc., Leadership Devel. award B'nai B'rith Youth Orgn.; named one of Top 10 Trial Lawyers in Am., Nat. Law Jour., 2006, 500 Leading Litigators, Lawdragon, 2006. Mem. Am. Bar Found.; mem. ABA (chair corp. governance subcommittee Corp. Counsel com. Bus. Law Sect. 1997-2003), Chgo. Bar Assn., Lawyers Club Chgo., B'nai B'rith Justice Lodge. Office: Wildman Harrold Allen Dixon LLP 225 W Wacker Dr Ste 3000 Chicago IL 60606-1229 Office Phone: 312-201-2652. Business E-Mail: dockterman@wildman.com.

DODD, GERALDA, metal products executive; children: T. Edward Sellers III, Madison Dodd Sellers., U. Toledo, Ohio. Receptionist Heidtman Steel, Toledo, 1978-79, various positions, 1979-88, dir. purchasing, 1988; vp HS Processing (subs. Heidtmann Steel), Balt., 1988-90; pres., CEO Thomas Madison Inc., Detroit. Bd. dirs. Detroit Regiional Chamber, Detroit Econ. Growth Corp., Workforce Devel. Music Hall, Nataki Talibath Sch., United Way Cmty. Svcs., Nat. Kidney Found. of Mich. and New Detroit, Inc. Mem. Womens Econ. Club, Nat. Assn. Women Bus. Owners, Nat. Assn. Black Automotive Suppliers, Assn. Women in Metals Industry, Greater Wayne County chpt. of The Links, Inc. Office: Thomas Madison Inc PO Box 20318 Ferndale MI 48220-0318 Fax: 313-273-8052.

DODD, JAMES B., Internet executive; BA in Econs., Stanford U.; MBA, Harvard U. CPA. With Sprint; pres., CEO Nat. Info. Consortium Inc., Overland Park, Kans. Office: National Information Center 10540 S Ridgeview Rd Olathe KS 66061-6440

DODGE, PAUL CECIL, academic administrator; b. Granville, NY, Mar. 25, 1943; s. Cecil John Paul and Elsie Elizabeth Dodge Rogers; m. Margaret Mary Kostyun, June 6, 1964 (div. Sept. 1985); 1 child, Cynthia Ruth; m. Cynthia Dee Bennett, Apr. 26, 1986; children: Michelle Lynn, Jason Paul, Benjamin Charles. BA in Math., U. Vt., 1967. Mgr. data processing Thermal Wire & Electronics, South Hero, Vt., 1967-70, DDSV divsn. Vt. Cos., Burlington, 1970-73, Revere Copper & Brass, Clinton, Ill., 1973-78, Angelica Corp., St. Louis, 1978-81; pres. chief ops. officer Dodge Mgmt., St. Louis, 1981-82; mgr. systems and programming Terra Internat., 1982-87; pres., COO Mo. Tech, 1987—. Mem. Mo. Assn. Pvt. Career Schs. (pres. 1993-94), Nat. Rehab. Assn., Mo. Rehab. Assn. Republican. Presbyterian. Avocations: amatuer radio, chess. Office: Mo Tech Sch 1167 Corporate Lake Dr Saint Louis MO 63132-1716

DODGE, PHILIP ROGERS, neurologist, educator; b. Beverly, Mass., Mar. 16, 1923; s. Israel R.; children: Susan, Judith. Student, U. N.H., 1941-43, Yale, 1943; MD, U. Rochester, 1948. Diplomate Am. Bd. Psychiatry and Neurology. Intern Strong Meml. Hosp., 1948-49; asst. resident neurology Boston City Hosp., 1949-50, resident, 1950, sr. resident, 1951-52; practice medicine, specializing in child neurology Boston, 1956-67, St. Louis, 1967—; teaching fellow neurology Harvard Med. Sch., 1950, 51-53, instr. neurology, 1956-58, assoc. in neurology, 1958-61, asst. prof., 1962-67; asst. neurologist Mass. Gen. Hosp., 1956-59, dir. pediatric neurology program, 1958-67, assoc. neurologist, 1959-63, neurologist, 1963-67, assoc. pediatrician, 1961-62, pediatrician, 1962-67; investigator Joseph P. Kennedy, Jr. Meml. Labs. for Study Mental Retardation, 1962-67; pediatric neurologist Boston Lying-In Hosp., 1961-67; cons. in neurology Walter E. Fernald State Sch. for Retarded Children, 1963-67; med. dir. St. Louis Children's Hosp., 1967-84, pediatrician-in-chief, 1967-86; assoc. neurologist Barnes Hosp., 1967—; chmn. Mallinckrodt Dept. Pediatrics, Washington U. Sch. Medicine, 1967-86, prof. pediatrics and neurology, 1967-93; prof. emeritus pediatrics and neurology Washington U. Sch. Medicine, 1993—; lectr. in pediatrics, 1993-99. Cons. collaborative project cerebral palsy Nat. Inst. Neurol. Diseases and Blindness, 1958; vis. scientist Cin. Rsch. Ctr., U. PR, 1965—66, hon. vis. prof. physiology, 1967; bd. dirs., chmn. rsch. adv. com. Mass. Soc. Prevention Cruelty to Children, 1961—67; mem. sci. rsch. adv. bd. Nat. Assn. Retarded Children, 1963—67; bd. dirs. Ctrl. Midwestern Regional Lab., Inc., 1968—70; mem. gen. clin. rsch. ctrs. adv. com. USPHS, 1971—74; chmn. Mo. Mental Health Commn., 1974—78; mem. nat. adv. child health and human devel. coun. NIH, 1974—77; chmn. panel neurol. disorders, devel., long-range program strategies NINCDS, 1977—79; panel chmn., consensus devel. conf. diagnosis and treatment Reye's Syndrome, 1981; vis. prof. pediat. and adolescent medicine Royal Postgrad. Med. Sch., U. London, 1986—; hon. vis. fellow dept. pathology U. Western Australia, Nedlands, 1986—87; vis. prof. neurology Columbia U. Coll. Physicians and Surgeons, NYC, 1987—88; spl. asst. to dir. mental retardation Nat. Inst. Child Health and Human Devel., NIH, Washington, 1987—88. Author (with others): Nutrition and the Developing Nervous System, 1975; mem. editl. bd. Jour. Devel. Medicine and Child Neurology, 1965—, Jour. Pediat., 1970—80, Pediatric Rsch., 1970—78, Current Problems in Pediat., 1969—84, Neurology, 1973—76; contbr. articles to profl. jours. Maj. M.C. US Army, 1950—56. Mem.: Assn. Med. Sch. Pediatric Dept. Chmn. (pres. 1975—77), St. Louis Soc. Neurol. Scis., Soc. Biol. Psychiatry, Soc. Pediatric Rsch., Assn. Rsch. Nervous and Mental Disease, Child eurology Soc., Am. Neurol. Assn., Am. Acad. Neurology (past com. chmn.), Am. Pediatric Soc. (coun. 1972—78, chmn. coun. 1978—79), Alpha Omega Alpha. Home: 410 N Newstead Ave Saint Louis MO 63108-2654 also: S Euclid Ave Campus Box 8111 Saint Louis MO 63110 Office Phone: 314-454-6042, 314-454-2699.

DODSON, VERNON NATHAN, preventive medicine physician, educator; b. Benton Harbor, Mich., Feb. 19, 1923; m. Shirley Jane Wheelihan: children: Martha Ione, Kathryn Anne, Christine Louise, John Nathan, Elizabeth Marie. Student, Mich. State Coll., 1941-43, 46, Northwestern U., summer 1942, Compton Coll., Calif., 1943, U. Oreg., 1943-44, Corpus Christi Coll., U. Oxford, Eng., 1945, U. Mich., 1946-47, 48, 51-52, BS, 1952; MD, Marquette U., 1951. Intern in surgery Henry Ford Hosp., Detroit, 1952-53; asst. in pathology Johns Hopkins U. Hosp., Balt., 1953-54, asst. pathologist, 1953-54; resident in internal medicine Univ. Hosp., Ann Arbor, Mich., 1954-57; rsch. assoc. U. Mich. Med. Sch., Ann Arbor, 1957-60, 60-71, lectr., 1959, from jr. clin. instr. to assoc. prof., 1956-64, assoc. prof. Dept. Indsl. Health, Sch. Pub. Health, 1965-71; attending physician U.S. VA Hosp., Ann Arbor, 1961-70; mem. med. staff Milw. County Gen. Hosp., 1971-72; rsch. assoc. U.S. VA Ctr., Wood, Wis., 1971-72; prof. medicine and environ. medicine Med. Coll. Wis., Milw., 1971-72; vis. prof. dept. preventive medicine U. Wis. Med. Sch., Madison, 1973-74, prof. medicine, sect. internal medicine, and preventive medicine, 1977-94, prof. emeritus medicine and preventive medicine, 1994—, prof. emeritus dept. population and health scis., 1994—. Lectr. Sch. Dentistry, U. Mich., Ann Arbor, 1957-58, Sch. Nursing, U. Mich., 1958-60, Coll. Lit., Sci. and Arts, Inst. Social Work, U. Mich., 1957-58; cons. staff physician Rochester, Minn. Meth. Hosp., 1974-77; dir. Univ. Employee Health Svc., U. Wis., Madison, 1977-80, mem. staff Ctr. Health Sci., 1978-95, hon. staff, 1995—; physician cons. VA Hosp., Madison, 1978-95; mem. interdepartmental program in toxicology, U. Mich., 1965-71, vice chair, 1969-71; mem. Environ. Toxicology Ctr., Divsn. Health Scis., U. Wis., Madison, 1972-74, 77-94, acting dir., 1974-76, 78-79, assoc. dir. Sch. Biotron., 1979-84; vis. prof. U. Tex. Health Sci. Ctr., Sch. Pub. Health, Houston, 1986, So. Occupational Health Ctr., U. Calif., Irvine, 1986; mem. com. on edn. and libr., Trinity Meml. Hosp., Cudahy, Wis., 1971-71, assoc. med. staff, 1972-73; mem. assoc. med. staff St. Lukes Hosp., Milw., 1972-73; cons. Joint Commn. on Hosp. Accreditation, Chgo., 1974-76; cons. in preventive medicine and internal medicine, Mayo Clinic, Mayo Found., Rochester, 1974-77; cons. GM, Warren, Mich., 1963-65, 72-84, med. dir. GM, Oak Creek, Wis., 1971-72; cons. Oscar Mayer Co., 1973-74; cons. plant physician, IBM, Rochester, 1976-77; cons. med. dir. George A. Hormel co., Austin, Minn., 1977; mem. occupational health adv. bd. GM, UAW, 1982-85; cons. Owens-Corning Fiberglas, Toledo, 1968—, Gen. Mills, Mpls., 1980—; bd. dirs. Nat. Biogerontology Inst., 1984—; cons. USPHS, Dept. Natural Resources, Wis., Dept. Health and Social Svcs., Wis., U.S. Dept. Agr., OSHA, Wis., Nat. Inst. Occupational Safety and Health, Ctr. for Disease Control, Dept. Industry, Labor and Human Rels., Wis.; mem. Gov.'s Task Force on Occupational Health and Safety, State of Wis., Extramural Ctr. Adv. Rev. Panel, Nat. Inst. for Occupational Health and Safety, Sentinel Event Notification System for Occupational Risks, Divsn. Health, State Dept. Health and Social Svc., Madison, Wis.; vice chair Residency Rev. Com. for Preventive Medicine, Coun. Health & The Pub., Accreditation Coun. for Gen. Med. Edn., State of Wis. Occupl. Disease and Illness Ctr. Edn. cons. editor Am. Jour. Occupational Medicine, 1979-89; assoc. editor Am. Jour. Indsl. Medicine, 1986-80; author 5 books, 17 book chpts., 44 sci. rsch. papers, 119 abstracts and presentations, 4 TV programs; co-editor 1 book. Mem. spl. citizen's adv. com. on safety Ann Arbor Bd. Edn., 1969, gov.'s com. on crime detection and law enforcement, ad hoc com. on lab. svcs., State of Mich., 1969; chmn., mem. com. on sch. safety, King Sch., Ann Arbor, 1969-70; mem. Kettle Moraine High Sch. Band Parents, Wales, Wis., 1972-74, v.p., 1973-74, citizen's com. on drug abuse, Waukesha County, Wis., 1973-74. With U.S. Army, 1942-45, ETO. Decorated Combat Med. Badge with Bronze Star U.S. Army; recipient Disting. Svc. award, Occupl. Health award, UAW, GM, 1988. Fellow ACP, Am. Coll. Occupl. Medicine (bd. dirs. 1987—, award 1988), Am. Coll. Medicine, Am. Occupl. Medicine Assn. (bd. govs. 1985, award 1988), Am. Coll. Occupl. and Environ. Medicine, Am. Coll. Preventive Medicine, Soc. Occupl. and Environ. Health; mem. AAAS, AMA (rep. residency rev. com., vice chair accreditation coun. for gen. med. edn., Physician's Recognition award 1981-2002), Am. Fedn. for Clin. Rsch., The Biochem. Soc. (London), Wis. State Med. Soc. (environ./occupl. health commn., legis. affairs commn., continuing med. edn. commn. coun. on health of the pub., coun. on med. edn., coun. on the health and the pub., 1999—, Meritorious Svc. award 1991, 96), Ctrl. States Occupl. Medicine Assn. (bd. govs.), Dane County Med. Soc., Am. Pub. Health Assn., Wis. Pub. Health Assn., Am. Cancer Soc. (award 1987), Internat. Commn. for Occupl. Health (Geneva), alumnae orgns. Mich. State U., U. Mich., Marquette U., Med. Coll. Wis., Johns Hopkins U., Mayo Clinic, Med. Coll. Wis., U. Wis., Henry Ford Hosp., VFW, 11th Armored Divsn. Assn., Friends of WHA-TV, Smithsonian Instn., Nat. Geog. Soc., World Wildlife Fund, Sierra Club, Natural Resource Def. Coun., Sigma Xi. Office: MD FACP Dept Med Wis U J5 220 CSC 2454 600 Highland Madison WI 53705-2335

DOERMANN, HUMPHREY, writer, consultant; b. Toledo, Nov. 13, 1930; s. Henry John and Alice (Robbins Humphrey) D.; m. Elisabeth Adams Wakefield, Jan. 7, 1956; children: Elisabeth M., Eleanor H., Julia L. AB, Harvard U., 1952, MBA, 1958, PhD, 1967; LLD (hon.), Xavier U., La., 1990, U. Minn., 1997; LHD (hon.), Coll. St. Scholastica, 1993, U. St. Thomas, 1996, Ctrl. Coll., 1998. Asst. to com. on admissions and scholarships Harvard, 1955-56; reporter Mpls. Star, 1958-60; asst. to bus. mgr. Mpls. Star & Tribune Co., 1960-61; dir. admissions Harvard, 1961-66; asst. to dean Harvard (Faculty of Arts and Scis.), 1966-69, asst. dean for financial affairs, 1970-71; lectr. on edn. Harvard (Grad. Sch. Edn.), 1967-71; exec. dir. Bush Found., St. Paul, 1971-78, pres., 1978-97; vis. prof. Macalester Coll., 1997-2000, rsch. assoc., 2000—. Cons. Coun. Higher Edn. Va., 1969, W.Va. Bd. Regents, 1970; bd. overseers Harvard Coll., Harvard U., 1973-79; trustee St. Paul Acad. and Summit Sch., 1997-2006; bd. dirs. Coun. on Founds., Washington, 1985-92, chmn. bd. 1990-92; trustee Found. Ctr., N.Y.C., 1975-83, chmn. bd. 1982-83; chmn. Minn. Coun. on Founds., 1981-85, Coll. Bd., N.Y.C., 1994-99; chmn. Minn. Legis. Task Force on Student Aid, 1993; chair regents candidate adv. coun. U. Minn., 1997-99; chmn. Minn. Humanities Commn., 2004-06. Author: Crosscurrents in College Admissions, rev. edit, 1970, Toward Equal Access, 1978; co-author (with Henry N. Drewry) Stand and Prosper, 2001. Mem. Belmont (Mass.) Town Meeting, 1969-70. Served to lt. (j.g.) USN, 1952-55. Home: 736 Goodrich Ave Saint Paul MN 55105-3524 Office: Macalester Coll 1600 Grand Ave Saint Paul MN 55105-1801 Office Phone: 651-696-6828. Business E-Mail: doermann@macalester.edu.

DOERSHUK, CARL FREDERICK, physician, educator; b. Warren, Ohio, Dec. 24, 1930; s. Carl Frederick and Eula Blanche (Mahan) D.; m. Emma Lou Plummer, Aug. 21, 1954; children: Rebecca Lee, John Frederick, David Plummer. BA, Oberlin Coll., 1952; MD, Case Western Res. U., 1956. Intern U.S. Naval Hosp., Camp Pendleton, Ohio, 1956-57; resident in pediat. Cleve. Met. Gen. Hosp. and Babies and Children's Hosp., Cleve., 1959-61; postdoctoral pulmonary fellow Babies and Children's Hosp. USPHS, Cleve., 1961-63; sr. instr. to prof. pediatrics specializing in academic pediatric pulmonary medicine Case Western Res. U., Cleve., 1963-98, emeritus prof., 1998—. Co-editor Pediatric Respiratory Therapy, 1974, 3d edit., 1986; editor, contbr.: Cystic Fibrosis in the 20th Century: People, Events and Progress, 2002; contbr. articles to profl. jours. Chmn. med. adv. coun. Cystic Fibrosis Found., Washington, 1966-72, bd. trustees, 1969-81, exec. com., 1969-74, v.p. med. affairs Cleve. chpt., 1965-90. Lt. M.C., USN, 1957-59. Named Young Man Yr. Cystic Fibrosis Found., 1970; recipient Richard C. Talamo Clinician Scientist award Cystic Fibrosis Found., 1997. Mem. Am. Pediatric Soc., Soc. Pediatric Research, Am. Acad. Pediatrics (exec. com. chest sect.), Am. Thoracic Soc. (chmn. pediatric pulmonary sect. 1971), No. Ohio Pediatric Soc., Acad. Medicine. Avocations: sailing, raising dahlias. Office: Rainbow Babies and Childrens Hosp 11100 Euclid Ave Cleveland OH 44106

DOHERTY, SISTER BARBARA, religious institution administrator; b. Chgo., Dec. 2, 1931; d. Martin James and Margaret Eleanor (Noe) D. Student, Rosary Coll., 1949-51; BA in Latin, English and History, St. Mary-of-the-Woods Coll., 1953; MA in Theology, St. Mary's Coll., 1963; PhD in Theology, Fordham U., 1979; LittD (hon.), Ind. State U., 1990; LittD (hon.) (hon.), Dominican U., Ill., 2002. Enter order of the Sisters of Providence. Tchr. Jr. and Sr. High Schs., Ind. and Ill., 1953-63; asst. prof. religion St. Mary-of-the-Woods Coll., Ind., 1963-67, 71-75, pres. Ind., 1984-98; provincial supr. Chgo. Province of Sisters of Providence, 1975-83; dir. Inst. of Religious Formation at Cath. Theol. Union, Chgo., 1999—. Summer faculty NCAIS-KCRCHE, Delhi, India, 1970. Author: I Am What I Do: Contemplation and Human Experience, 1981, Make Yourself an Ark: Beyond the Memorized Responses of Our Corporate Adolescence, 1984; editor: Providence: God's Face Towards the World, 1984; contbr. articles to New Cath. Ency. Vol. XVII, 1982, God and Me, 1988, Dictionary of Catholic Spirituality, 1993. Pres. Leadership Terre Haute, Ind., 1985-86; bd. regents Ind. Acad., 1987-98; bd. dirs. 8th Day Cen. for Justice, Chgo., 1978-83, Family Svcs., Swope Art Mus., Terre Haute, Ind., 1988-98. Arthur J. Schmidt Found. grantee, 1967-71. Mem. Women's Coll. Coalition (nat. bd. dirs. 1984-90), Ind. Colls. Ind., Ind. Colls. Found. (exec. bd.), Ind. Conf. Higher Edn. (chair), Leadership Conf. Women Religious of USA (program chairperson nat. assembly 1982-83, chair Neylan commn. 1993-97), Assn. Am. Colls. and Univs. Democrat. Roman Catholic. Avocations: walking, reading, travel. Office: Cath Theol Union 5401 S Cornell Ave Chicago IL 60615-5664 E-mail: bdoherty@ctu.edu.

DOHERTY, BRIAN GERARD, alderman; b. Chgo., Oct. 25, 1957; s. Daniel Joseph and Kathleen (McDonagh) D.; m. Rose Mary Gillespie, 1986; children: Kathleen Marie, Kevin Michael. BA, U. N.E. Ill., 1984; MA in Urban Studies, Loyola U., Chgo., 2005. Alderman 41st Ward, Chgo., 1991—. Boxing champ Chgo. Pk. Dist., 1972, 73, Chgo. Golden Gloves champion Tribune Charities, 1973. Mem. Alpha Chi Honor Soc. Roman Catholic. Home: 7805 W Catalpa Ave Chicago IL 60656-1640 Office: 6650 N Northwest Hwy Chicago IL 60631-1307 Office Phone: 773-792-1991.

DOHERTY, CHARLES VINCENT, investment advisor; b. Pitts., Dec. 17, 1933; s. Charles V. and Emma (Lager) D.; m. Marilyn Bongiorno, Oct. 17, 1964; children: Charles, Michelle, Kristen. BS, U. Notre Dame, Ind., 1955; MBA, U. Chgo., 1967. CPA, Ill. Tax specialist Haskins & Sells, CPA, Chgo., 1960-67; ptnr. Lamson Bros. & Co., Chgo., 1968-73; pres. Doherty Zable & Co., Chgo., 1974-85, Chgo. Stock Exch., Inc., 1986-92; mng. dir. Madison Adv. Group, Chgo., 1993—. Bd. dirs. Lakeside Bank, Howe Barnes Hoefer Arnett Securities, Inc., Banc of Am. Fin. Products. Personal E-mail: milfordtrek@msn.com.

DOHERTY, VALERIE, employment services professional, lawyer; Chief ops. officer, gen. counsel Doherty Employment Group, Edina, Minn. Office: Doherty Employment Group 7625 Parklawn Ave Minneapolis MN 55435-5123 Fax: 612-832-8355.

DOHMEN, JOHN F., pharmaceutical executive; From mem. staff to pres., CEO F. Dohmen, Germantown, Wis., 1980—95, pres., 1995—, CEO, 1995—. Finalist, Ernst & Young Entrepreneur of Yr., 2003. Mem.: Healthcare Distbn. Mgmt. Assn. (chmn. 2001), Nat. Wholesale Druggist's Assn. (chmn. 2000). Office: F Dohmen W 194 N 11381 McCormick Dr Germantown WI 53022

DOHMEN, MARY HOLGATE, retired primary school educator; b. Gary, Ind., July 28, 1918; d. Clarence Gibson and Margaret Alexander (Kinnear) Holgate; m. Frederick Hoeger Dohmen, June 27, 1964 (dec. Apr. 2006); children: William Francis, Robert Charles. BS, Milw. State Tchrs. Coll., 1940; M in Philosophy, U. Wis., 1945. Cert. tchr. Wis. Tchr. primary grades Baraboo Pub. Schs., Wis., 1940-43, Whitefish Bay Pub. Schs., Wis., 1943-64; ret., 1964. Author short stories, numerous poems; contbr. articles to profl. jours. Bd. dirs. Homestead HS chpt. Am. Field Svc., Mequon, Wis., 1970-80; mem. Milw. Aux. VNA, 1975—, 2d v.p., 1983-85, Milw. Pub. Mus. Enrichment Club, 1975—, Boys and Girls Club of Greater Milw., 1986—; vol. Reading is Fun program, 1987—, Milw. Symphony Orch. League, 1960—, Ptnrs. in Conservation, World Wildlife Fund, Washington, 1991—, Milw. Art Mus. Garden Club, 1979—, com. chmn., 1981-86; mem. Chancellor's Soc. U. Wis.-Milw., 1991—; travel lectr. various orgns., 1980—. Mem. AAUW, Milw. Coll. Endowment Assn. (v.p. 1987-90, pres. 1991-93), Bascom Hill Soc. (U. Wis.), Woman's Club Wis., Alpha Phi (pres. Milw. alumnae 1962-64), Pi Lambda Theta (pres. Milw. alumnae 1962-64), Delta Kappa Gamma. Republican. Presbyterian. Avocations: writing, travel, nature.

DOHRMANN, RUSSELL WILLIAM, retired manufacturing executive; b. Clinton, Iowa, June 29, 1942; s. Russell Wilbert and Anita Doris (Miller) D.; m. Rita Marie Meade, Dec. 26, 1964 (dec. Feb. 1978); m. M. Jean Stapleton, Aug. 18, 1979. BS, Upper Iowa U., 1965; MBA, Drake U., 1971. Acct. Chamberlain Mfg. Corp., Clinton, 1965-66, plant controller Derry, Pa., 1967-68; fin. analyst Frye Copysystems Inc., Des Moines, 1968-71, v.p., controller, 1971-77, pres., 1980-97, also bd. dirs.; internat. controller Wheelabrator-Frye, NYC, 1977-78; pres. FryeTech, Inc., Des Moines, 1997-98; group controller Wheelabrator-Frye, Des Moines, 1978-80; cons., 1998—. Mem. Des. Moines C. of C. Republican. Methodist. Personal E-mail: windyridge@mchsi.com.

DOHRN, BERNARDINE, law educator, advocate; b. 1942; BA, U. Chgo., 1963, MA, JD, 1967. Atty. Sidley & Austin, New York, 1984—88; litig. legal assoc. Office of Pub. Guardian, Cook County Juvenile Div., 1988—90; legal rschr. Children's Rights Project, Roger Baldwin Found., ACLU, 1990—91, Legal Assistance Found., Homeless Advocacy Project, 1991; dir. Juvenile Ct. Project Northwestern U. Sch. Law, 1991—92, dir. Children and Family Justice Ctr., 1992—, clin. assoc. prof. Bluhm Legal Clinic, 2000—. Adj. faculty U. Ill./Chgo., Dept. Criminal Justice, 2000—02; vis. law faculty Vrieje U., Amsterdam, 2002—; assoc. prof. Coll. of U. Chgo., 2003, 04; steering com. Ill. Family Violence Coordinating Com., 1994—, Ill. State Ct. Improvement Project, 1996—; adv. bd. Kellogg Sch. Mgmt. Non-Profit Prog., 1997—; mem. Expert Work Group Adoption 2002 Project, U.S. Dept. Health and Human Svcs. Contbr. articles to law jours.; author: Zero Tolerance: Resisting the Drive for Punishment in Our Schools, 2001, A Century of Juvenile Justice, 2002. Mem.: ABA (founding co-chair Task Force on Children 1992—96, adv. com. Immigration Pro Bono Devel. and Bar Activation Prog. 2001—), Human Rights Watch (bd. mem. Children's Rights Project 1995—), Chgo. Reporter (co-chair 1997—, bd. dirs. 1999—). Office: Northwestern U Sch Law 357 E Chicago Ave Chicago IL 60611-3069 E-mail: b-dohrn@law.northwestern.edu.

DOLAN, BOB, radio personality; married; 2 children. Mng. editor weekly newspaper, Mo.; radio host 1130 WISN, Greenfield, Wis. Avocations: golf, racquetball, travel, horse racing, writing, reading. Office: WISN Radio 12100 W Howard Ave Greenfield WI 53228

DOLAN, JAMES VINCENT, lawyer; b. Washington, Nov. 11, 1938; s. John Vincent and Philomena Theresa (Vance) D.; m. Anne McSherry Reilly, June 18, 1960; children: Caroline McSherry, James Reilly. AB, Georgetown U., 1960, LLB, 1963. Bar: U.S. Dist. Ct. 1963, U.S. Ct. Appeals (D.C.) cir. 1964, U.S. Ct. Appeals (4th cir.) 1976. Law clk. U.S. Ct. Appeals D.C., 1963-64; assoc. Steptoe & Johnson, Washington, 1964-71, ptnr., 1971-82; mem. Steptoe & Johnson Chartered, Washington, 1982-83; v.p. law Union Pacific R.R., Omaha, 1983—2002, vice chmn., 2002—. Co-author: Construction Contract Law, 1981; contbr. articles to legal jours.; editor-in-chief: Georgetown Law Jour., 1962-63. Mem.: ABA, Barristers, D.C. Bar Assn., Nebr. Bar Assn., Omaha Country Club, Congl. Country Club (v.p. 1982, pres. 1983). Republican. Roman Catholic. Home: 1909 County Road 8 Yutan NE 68073-5013 Office: Union Pacific RR 1416 Dodge St Rm 1230 Omaha NE 68179

DOLAN, JAN CLARK, former state legislator; b. Akron, Ohio, Jan. 15, 1927; d. Herbert Spencer and Jean Risk Clark; m. Walter John Dolan, Apr. 22, 1950 (dec. July 1986); children: Mark Raymond, Scott Spencer, Gary Clark, Todd Alvin. BA, U. Akron, 1949. Home svc. rep. East Ohio Gas Co., Akron, 1949-50; dietitian Akron City Hosp., 1950-51; tchr. Brecksville (Ohio) Sch. Dist., 1962-66; adminstr. Orchard Hills Adult Day Ctr., West Bloomfield, Mich., 1978-83; mem. Farmington Hills (Mich.) City Coun., 1975-88, Mich. Ho. of Reps., Lansing, 1989-96. Mayor City of Farmington Hills, 1978, 85; elder Presbyn. Ch. Republican. Home: 22587 Gill Rd Farmington Hills MI 48335-4037 Personal E-mail: jcdolan@sbcglobal.net.

DOLAN, MICHAEL F., lawyer; b. Dougherty, Iowa, 1949; BS magna cum laude, Loras Coll., 1971; MS, So. Ill. Univ., 1973; MBA, Univ. of Iowa, 1981, JD with high distinction, 1981. Bar: Ill. 1982; cert. Industl. Hygienist (ret.), safety profl., 1977-2001. Compliance safety and health officer Iowa State OSHA program; ptnr., chair, environ., health & safety practice Jones Day, Chgo. Co-author: (books) Legal Guide for Handling Toxic Substances in the Workplace, 1992; author: numerous articles in profl. publications; mem. (editorial adv. bd.) Environmental Management News. Mem.: ABA, Am. Conf. of Govtl. Indsl. Hygienists, Am. Soc. of Safety Engineers, Am. Indsl. Hygiene Assn., Environ. Law Inst., Ill. State Bar Assn. Office: Jones Day 77 W Wacker Chicago IL 60601-1692 Office Fax: 312-782-8585.

DOLAN, ROBERT J., dean; b. Peabody, Mass. m. Kathleen Splaine-Dolan; children: Hilary, Nicholas. BA in Math., magna cum laude, Boston Coll., 1969; MS in Bus. Adminstrn., U. Rochester, 1976, PhD in Bus. Adminstrn., 1977; MA (hon.), Harvard U., 1986. Asst. prof. mgmt. sci. and mktg. U. Chgo., 1976—80, assoc. prof., 1980; assoc. prof. bus. adminstrn. Harvard U. Grad. Sch. Bus. Adminstrn., 1980—85, prof. bus. adminstrn., 1985—90, mktg. area chmn., 1986—94, mktg. tchr. Advanced Mgmt. Program, 1990—95, Edward W. Carter prof. bus. adminstrn., 1990—2001, faculty chmn. MBA program, 1996—97; pres. William David Inst. U. Mich. Ann Arbor Ross Sch. Bus., 2001—, Gilbert and Ruth Whitaker prof. bus. adminstrn., 2001—, dean, 2001—. Vis. prof. IESE, Barcelona, 2001; editor Field Studies Sect. Marketing Science, 1989—94, mem. editl. rev. bd., 1982—88, Jour. Marketing, 1978—84, 1990—98. Author: (books) Managing the New Product Development Process, 1993, Marketing Management: Text and Cases, 2001; co-author (with John Quelch and Benson Shapiro): Marketing Management Readings: From Theory to Practice, 1985, Marketing Management: Strategy, Planning and Implementation, 1985, Marketing Management: Principles, Analysis, and Application, 1985; co-author: (with John Quelch and Thomas Kosnik) Marketing Management, 1993; co-author: (with Hermann Simon) Power Pricing: How Managing Price Transforms the Bottom Line, 1996; editor: Strategic Marketing Management, 1992; contbr. articles to numerous jour. Mem.: Am. Mktg. Assn. (mem. Faculty Consortium 1990, 1992, mem. Doctoral Consortium 1984, 1986, 1988, 1990, coord. Doctoral Consortium 1989). Office: Univ Michigan Business School 701 Tappan St Ann Arbor MI 48109-1234 Office Phone: 734-764-1363. Office Fax: 734-763-0671. Business E-Mail: rjdolan@umich.edu.

DOLAN, TERRENCE RAYMOND, neurophysiology educator; b. Huron, SD, May 24, 1940; s. Buell Ellery and Mary Lucille (Engler) D.; m. Mary Ann Mechtenberg, Apr. 23, 1962; children: Katherin, Patrick, Elizabeth, Meaghan. BA, Dakota Wesleyan U., Mitchell, SD, 1962; MS, Trinity U., San Antonio, 1963; PhD in Psychology and Physiology, U. Tex., Austin, 1966; postdoctoral study, Ctr. Neuroscis., Ind. U., Bloomington, 1966-68. Rsch. assoc. Ctr. Neuroscis., Ind. U., Bloomington, 1968-70; assoc. prof. psychology Loyola U., Chgo., 1970-74, prof. dept. psychology, 1974-76, asst. dean Grad. Sch., 1974-76, dir. Parmly Rsch. Inst., 1970-76; program dir. NSF Neuroscis. Sect., 1976-82; prof. dept. neurophysiology U. Wis., Madison, 1982—, dir. Waisman Ctr. Mental Retardation and Human Devel., prof. dept. neurology, 1997—, prof. dept. psychology, 1997—. NSF rep. to Nat. Inst. Neurol. and Communicative Disease, NIH, 1976-77, liaison rep. to Nat. Eye Coun., NIH, 1976-82; mem. exec. coun. com. on vision NAS-NRC, 1977-82, mem. exec. coun. com. on hearing, acoustics and biomechanics, 1977-84; chmn. NSF task force on Support of Young Investigators-Young Scientists, 1979-80; mem. Fed. Noise Effects Steering Com. EPA, 1977-80; chmn. Assn. Mental Retardation Rsch. Ctr. Dirs., 1984-88; mem. nat. adv. coun. Air Force Office Sci. Rsch., 1984—; pres. Am. Assn. U. Affiliated Programs, 1984-88; pres.-elect Internat. Assn. Sci. Study Mental Deficiency, 1988-92, pres., 1992—; exec. dir. Prince Salman Ctr. for Disability Rsch., Riyadh, Saudi Arabia, 2001—. Contbr. numerous articles to profl. publs. Von Humboldt fellow, Fed. Republic Germany; grantee Nat. Inst. Child Health and Human Devel., 1982-93, Wis., 1984-85, wis. Devel. Disability Coun., 1985-93, others. Mem. Assn. Rsch. in Otolaryngology, Acoustical Soc. Am., Am. Assn. Univ. Affiliated Progs. (pres. 1988-89, Internat. Assn. Sci. Study Mental Deficiency (pres. 1992-96). Office: U Wis-Madison Waisman Ctr Mental Retardation & Human Devel 1500 Highland Ave Madison WI 53705-2274

DOLAN, THOMAS CHRISTOPHER, professional society administrator; b. Chgo., Dec. 31, 1947; s. Thomas Christopher and Bernice Mary (Doyle) D.; m. Georgia Ann Siebke, Feb. 14, 1983; children: William, Barbara, Lauren. BBA, Loyola U., Chgo., 1969; PhD, U. Iowa, 1977. Instr. U. Iowa, Iowa City, 1971-72; vis. fellow U. Wash., Seattle, 1973-74; asst. prof. U. Mo., Columbia, 1974-79; assoc. prof., dir. St. Louis U., 1979-86; v.p. Am. Coll. Healthcare Execs., Chgo., 1986-87, exec. v.p., 1987-91, pres., CEO, 1991—. Mem. Accrediting Commn.

on Edn. for Health Svcs. Adminstrn., Washington, 1985-86; chmn. Assn. Univ. Programs in Health Adminstrn., Washington, 1983-84; cons. HEW, Kansas City, Mo., 1974-79, State of Mo., Jefferson City, 1974-79. Author: Systems for Health Care Administration: A Model for the Education of Health Manpower, 1975; contbr. articles to profl. jours. Pres. Mental Health Assn. Boone County, Columbia, Mo., 1977—78, Mental Health Assn. Mo., Jefferson City, 1980—82; chair Inst. Diversity in Health Mgmt., 2002, Assn. Forum, 1999—2000, Am. Soc. Assn. Execs. Found., Washington, 2000—01; bd. dirs. Alexian Bros. Hosp., St. Louis, 1980—86, Internat. Hosp. Fedn., 2005—. Fellow: Am. Soc. Assn. Execs. (chmn.-elect 2006—07, cert. assn. exec., bd. dirs.), Am. Coll. Healthcare Execs. Roman Catholic. Avocations: golf, motorcycling, photography. Office: Am Coll Healthcare Execs 1 N Franklin St Ste 1700 Chicago IL 60606-4425

DOLAN, TIMOTHY MICHAEL, archbishop; b. Feb. 6, 1950; s. Robert and Shirley Radcliffe Dolan. BA in Philosophy, Cardinal Glennon Coll.; attended, Pontifical N. Am. Coll., Rome; License in Sacred Theology, Pontifical U. of St. Thomas; PhD in Am. Church History, Catholic U. Am. Ordained priest Archdiocese of St. Louis, Mo., 1976; assoc. pastor Immaculata Parish, Richmond Heights, Mo., 1976—79; served in parish ministry, liaison for Archbishop John L. May St. Louis, 1983—87; secretary Apostolic Nunciature, Washington, 1987—92; vice rector, dir. of spiritual formation & prof. of church history Kenrick-Glennon Seminary, St. Louis, 1992—94; rector Pontifical No. Am. Coll., Rome, 1994—2001; ordained bishop, 2001; aux. bishop Archdiocese of St. Louis, 2001—02; archbishop Archdiocese of Milw., Wis., 2002—; apostolic adminstr. Diocese of Green Bay, Wis., 2007—. Former adjunct prof. of theology St. Louis U.; visiting prof. of church history Pontifical Gregorian U., Rome; faculty mem. dept. of ecumenical theology Pontifical U. of St. Thomas Aquinas, Rome. Roman Catholic. Office: Archdiocese of Milwaukee 3501 S Lake Dr PO Box 070912 Milwaukee WI 53207*

DOLCH, GARY D., health products executive; BS in Chemistry, Ursinus Coll.; MS in Chemistry, Fairleigh Dickinson U.; PhD in Med. Chemistry, Purdue U. Quality mgr. Ayerst Labs., Am. Home Products, 1979—85, asst. v.p., 1986—88; various mgmt. positions quality control Genetech, Inc., Boehringer-Ingelheim Pharms., 1988—92; v.p. quality affairs and tech. ops. Knoll Pharms., BASF, 1992—2001; sr. v.p. quality and regulatory affairs ARC, 2001—02; exec. v.p. quality and regulatory affairs Cardinal Health, Inc., 2002—. Mem. dean's coun. Sch. Pharmacy Purdue U., 2004—; dir. PDA Found., 1987—94. Office: Cardinal Health Inc 7000 Cardinal Pl Dublin OH 43017 Home Phone: 740-548-5333; Office Phone: 614-757-5697.

DOLD, ROBERT BRUCE, journalist; b. Newark, Mar. 9, 1955; s. Robert Bruce and Margaret (Noll) Dold; m. Eileen Claire Norris, July 10, 1982; children: Megan, Kristen. BS in Journalism, Northwestern U., 1977, MS in Journalism, 1978. Reporter Suburban Tribune, Hinsdale, Ill., 1978—83, Chgo. Tribune, 1983—90, mem. editl. bd., 1990—95, dep. editl. page editor, columnist, 1995—2000, editl. page editor, 2000—. Pulitzer Prize juror, 1997—98; columnist Chgo. Enterprise, 1991—95; critic Downbeat Mag., 1980—84; commentator Chgo. Week in Rev., 1987—. Bd. dirs. Jazz Inst. Chgo., 1980—83. Recipient Peter Lisagor award, Sigma Delta Chi, 1988, Pulitzer Prize for editl. writing, 1994, Scripps Howard Found. Nat. award for commentary, 1999. Mem.: Am. Soc. Newspaper Editors, Econ. Club of Chgo. Roman Catholic. Avocations: golf, basketball, jazz. Home: 501 N Park Rd La Grange Park IL 60526-5516 Office: Chgo Tribune 435 N Michigan Ave Chicago IL 60611-4066 Home Phone: 708-352-1777; Office Phone: 312-222-4438. Business E-Mail: bdold@tribune.com.

DOLECHECK, CECIL, state representative; b. Mount Ayr, Iowa, May 30, 1951; m. Becky Dolechek; children: Eric, Josie, Darin. Student, Iowa State U. Mem. Iowa Ho. Reps., DesMoines, Iowa, 1997—, chair edn. appropriations com., mem. various coms. including appropriations, edn., labor and indsl. rels. Pres. County Pork Prodrs., 1980—84, Farm Bur. Ringold County, 1988—92, voting del., 1992—96; active County Rep. Ctrl. Com., 1986—96; precinct caucus chair, 1986—92. Republican. Methodist. Office: State Capitol East 12th and Grand Des Moines IA 50319 Home: 703 N Fillmore St Mount Ayr IA 50854-1007

DOLLENS, RONALD W., pharmaceutical executive; b. Ind., Dec. 17, 1946; s. William Franklin and Louise Anna (Davis) D.; m. Susan Stanley, Aug. 30, 1969; children: Stephanie, Grant. BS, Purdue U., 1970; MBA, Ind. U., 1972. From sales rep. to dir. bus. devel. Eli Lilly & Co., Indpls., 1972-85; sr. v.p. Advanced Cardiovasc. Sys., Santa Clara, 1985—88, pres., CEO, 1988—94; pres. med. devices divsn. Eli Lilly & Co., 1991-94; pres., CEO Guidant Corp., Indpls., 1994—2005; ret., 2005. Mem., Adv. Com. on Regulatory Health US Dept. Health & Human Svcs., 2002—; mem. bd. Ind. Health Industry Forum, Kinetic Concepts Inc., Beckman Coulter Corp. Bd. dir. Butler U., Indpls., Eiteljorg Mus., Indpls., St. Vincent Hosp. Found. Mem.: AdvaMed, Alliance for Aging Rsch., Healthcare Leadership Coun. (chmn. 2003—05, bd. trustees).

DOLLIVER, ROBERT HENRY, psychology professor; b. Fort Dodge, Iowa, Oct. 15, 1934; BA, Cornell Coll., 1958; MA, Ohio State U., 1963, PhD, 1966. Social worker Bd. Child Welfare, Elyria, Ohio, 1958-59; social worker Cleve. Boys Sch., 1959-61; asst., then assoc. prof. psychology U. Mo., Columbia, 1966-77, prof., 1977-99, prof. emeritus, 1999—. Office: U Mo Dept Psychology Columbia MO 65211-0001 Personal E-mail: SnoopyRHD@aol.com.

DOMBECK, HAROLD ARTHUR, insurance company executive; b. Bronx, NY, Mar. 23, 1941; s. Max J. and Rose R. (Schefren) D.; m. Cynthia E. Kofoed, May 14, 1983; children: Mark J., Glenn D., David S. BCE, NYU, 1962, MCE, 1963. Profl. engr., N.Y., N.J., Conn., Ga. Instr. San Antonio Coll., 1964-65, SUNY, Farmingdale, 1965-68; project mgr. H2M Group, Melville, NY, 1965-74, dir. environ. engring., 1971-81, dir. mktg., 1982-85, exec. v.p., 1986-88, pres., 1989-91, pres., CEO, chmn., 1991-94; CEO Dombeck Assocs. Inc., Duluth, Ga., 1995—. CEO Archs. and Engrs. Ins. Co., Naperville, Ill., 1987-2007, chmn. 1987—; v.p., CFO, Dod/Pritchard Comms. Inc., Norcross, Ga., 1998-2001; dir., Perceptive Solutions, Inc., Norcross, 2001-03; chmn. bd. dirs. Am. Cons. Engrs. Pension Trust, St. Louis, 1991-94; chmn. ACEC Bus. Inst. Trust, St. Louis, 1994-96. Pres. High Woods Civic Assn., St. James, N.Y., 1971-73, River Plantation Homeowners Assn., 1999-2001. 1st lt. USAF, 1963-65. Fellow ASCE, Am. Cons. Engrs. Coun. (pres. L.I. 1982-84); mem. Am. Acad. Environ. Engrs. (diplomate), NSPE (dir. 1982-85), N.Y. State Water Pollution Control Assn. (dir. 1980-83), N.Y. State Soc. Profl. Engrs. (pres. 1983-84, pres. Suffolk County chpt. 1978-80, Engr. of Yr. 1989, 90, Outstanding Svc. awards 1988, 89). Avocations: reading, golf, history. Office: AEIC 2056 Westings Ave Naperville IL 60563 Home Phone: 770-623-8384. Personal E-mail: hadombeck@yahoo.com.

DOMBROWSKI, DAVID, baseball team executive; b. Chgo., July 27, 1956; s. Ronald Edward and Laurie Bernadine Dombrowski. B of Adminstrn., Western Mich. U., 1979. Adminstrv. asst. Chgo. White Sox, 1978-79, asst. dir. player devel. and scouting, 1979-80, asst. gen. mgr., 1980-85, v.p. baseball ops., 1985-86; dir. player devel. Montreal Expos, 1986-87, asst. gen. mgr., 1987-88, gen. mgr., 1988-91; exec. v.p., gen. mgr. Fla. Marlins, Miami, 1991—2003; pres., gen. mgr. Detroit Tigers, 2004—. Bd. dirs. Chgo. Baseball Cancer Charities, 1981—. Named Exec. of Yr., UPI, 1990. Avocations: sports, jogging, movies, theater. Office: Detroit Tigers 2100 Woodward Ave Detroit MI 48201

DOMENICK, JOHN, state representative; b. Nov. 16, 1946; Weather dir. WTRF-TV, Wheeling, W.Va.; state rep. dist. 95 Ohio Ho. of Reps., Columbus, 2002—, ranking miority mem., natural resources parks and recreation subcom., mem. agr. and natural resources, county and twp. govt., and energy and environment coms. Democrat. Office: 77 S High St 10th fl Columbus OH 43215-6111

DOMINGUEZ, KATHRYN MARY, economist, educator; b. Santa Monica, Calif., Nov. 26, 1960; d. Frederick A. and Margaret M. (McGauren) D. AB, Vassar Coll., 1982; MA, Yale U., 1984, M in Philosophy, 1985, PhD, 1987. Rschr. Congl. Budget Office, Washington, 1984; rsch. scholar bd. of govs. FRS, Washington, 1985—86; asst. prof. pub. policy Kennedy Sch. Govt. Harvard U., Cambridge, Mass., 1987—91, assoc. prof. pub. policy, 1991—97; assoc. prof. pub. policy and econs. U. Mich., Ann Arbor, 1997—2004, prof., 2004—. Rsch. cons IMF, Washington, 1989; vis. asst. prof., asst. dir. internat. fin. sect. dept. econs. Princeton U., 1990-91; at. Bur. Econs. Rsch. Olin fellow, 1991-92. Author: (monograph) Oil and Money, 1989; Exchange Rate Efficiency and the Behavior of International Asset Markets, 1992; (with Jeff Frankel) Does Foreign Exchange Intervention Work?, 1993. Mem. Nat. Bur. Econ. Rsch. (rsch. assoc. 2000—), Am. Econ. Assn., Phi Beta Kappa. Democrat. Office: Univ Mich Sch Pub Policy Weill Hall 735 S State St Ann Arbor MI 48109-1220 Office Phone: 734-764-3490.

DOMINSKI, MATTHEW S., property manager; Pres., CEO Urban Retail Properties Co., Chgo., 1990—. Office: Urban Retail Properties Co 900 N Michigan Ave Chicago IL 60611-1542

DONABEDIAN, AVEDIS, physician, educator; b. Beirut, Jan. 7, 1919; arrived in U.S., 1955, naturalized, 1960; s. Samuel and Maritza (Der Hagopian) Donabedian; m. Dorothy Salibian, Sept. 15, 1945; children: Haig, Bairj, Armen. BA, Am. U., Beirut, 1940, MD, 1944; MPH, Harvard U., 1955. Physician, acting supt. English Mission Hosp., Jerusalem, 1945—47; instr. physiology, clin. asst. dermatology and venereology Am. U. Med. Sch., 1948—51, univ. physician, dir. univ. health service, 1949—54; med. assoc. United Community Services Met. Boston, 1955—57; asst. prof., then assoc. prof. preventive medicine N.Y. Med. Coll., 1957—61; mem. faculty U. Mich. Sch. Pub. Health, Ann Arbor, 1961—, prof. med. care orgn., 1964—79, Nathan Sinai disting. prof. public health, 1979—89, emeritus. Author: A Guide to Medical Care Administration: Medical Care Appraisal--Quality and Utilization, 1969, Aspects of Medical Care Administration, 1973, Benefits in Medical Care Programs, 1976, The Definition of Quality and Approaches to Its Assessment, 1980, Medical Care Chartbook, 1986, The Criteria and Standards of Quality, 1982, Methods and Findings of Quality Assessment and Monitoring, 1985; co-author: Striving for Quality in Health Care: An Inquiry into Policy and Practice, 1991. Recipient Dean Conley award, Am. Coll. Hosp. Adminstrs., 1969, Norman A. Welch award, Nat. Assn. Blue Shield Plans, 1976, Elizur Wright award, Am. Risk and Ins. Assn., 1978, Nat. Merit award, Delta Omega, 1978, Richard B. Tobias award, Am. Coll. Utilization Rev. Physicians, 1984, Outstanding Contbns. in Health Svcs. Rsch. award, Assn. Health Svcs. Rsch., 1985, Baxter Am. Found. Health Svcs. Rsch. prize, 1986, Gold medal award, Med. Alumni Assn., Am. U. Beirut, 1986, The Ernest A. Codman award, Joint Commn. on Accreditation of Healthcare Orgns., 1997. Fellow: APHA (Sedgewick Meml. medal 1999), Am. Coll. Med. Quality, Am. Coll. Healthcare Execs. (hon.), Am. Coll. Utilization Rev. Physicians (hon.), Royal Coll. Gen. Practitioners (hon.); mem.: Inst. Medicine NAS, Internat. Soc. Quality Assurance in Health Care (hon.), Nat. Acad. Medicine of Mex. (hon.), Avedis Donabedian Found. (Barcelona, hon. pres. 1990—, Buenos Aires, hon. pres. 1994—). Office: HMP-SPH II 109 Observatory St Ann Arbor MI 48109-2029

DONAHUE, LAURA KENT, former state senator; b. Quincy, Ill., Apr. 22, 1949; d. Laurence S. and Mary Lou Kent; m. Michael A. Donahue, July 16, 1983. BS, Stephens Coll., 1971. Mem. Ill. State Senate, Quincy, 1981—2002. State senator; b. Quincy, Ill., Apr. 22, 1949; d. Laurence S. and Mary Lou (McFarland) Kent; m. Michael A. Donahue, July 16, 1983. B.S., Stephens Coll., 1971. Mem. Ill. State Senate, Quincy, 1981—. Mem. Lincoln Club of Adams County, Ill. Fedn. Republican Women. Mem. P.E.O. Lodge: Altrusa. Mem. Lincoln Club of Adams County, Ill. Fedn. Rep. Women. Mem. PEO, Altrusa Lodge. Home: 2609 Kings Pointe Sw Quincy IL 62305-7673

DONALD, ARNOLD W., health science association administrator, former food products executive; b. New Orleans; m. Hazel Donald; children: Radiah, Alicia, Zachary. BA, Carleton Coll.; BSME, Washington U., St. Louis; MBA, U. of Chgo. Grad. Sch. Bus. From indsl. chem. sales to positions of increasing responsibility Monsanto Co., St. Louis, 1977—98, sr. v.p., 1998-99; CEO Merisant Co., 2000—03, chmn., 2000—05; pres., CEO Juvenile Diabetes Rsch. Found. Internat., NYC, 2005—. Apptd. President's Export Coun. internat. trade; bd. dirs. Crown Cork & Seal Co., Oil-Dri Corp. Am., Belden Inc., Carnival Corp., Laclede Group, Scotts Co., St. Louis Sports Commn. Bd. dirs. United Way of Greater St. Louis, Carleton Coll., Dillard U., Wash. U., St. Louis Art Museum, Mo. Botanical Garden, St. Louis Sci. Ctr., Opera Theatre of St. Louis, Boy Scouts of Am., Greater St. Louis Area Coun. Named one of 50 Most Powerful Black Executives in Am., Fortune mag., 2002; recipient Exec. of the Year, Black Enterprise mag., 1997, Disting. Alumni award, Wash. U., 1998, Eagle award, Nat. Eagle Leadership Inst., 1999, Black Engineers President's award, 2000. Office: Juvenile Diabetes Rsch Found 120 Wall St New York NY 10005-4001 Office Phone: 800-533-2873. Office Fax: 212-785-9595.

DONALDSON, BOB, newscaster; m. Skye Winslow; 3 children. Grad., Mo. Sch. Journalism. Reporter, Oklahome City; investigative reporter Salt Lake City; anchor Sta. KFOR-TV, Oklahoma City, Sta. KARK-TV, Little Rock, 1989—91; writer, prodr. documentaries Sta. WXIN-TV, Indpls., anchor, 1991—.

DONELSON, JOHN EVERETT, biochemistry professor, molecular biologist; b. Ogden, Iowa, May 23, 1943; s. Mervin E. and Christine (James) D.; m. Linda Meyers, Sept. 16, 1966; children: Christina, Loren, Lyn, Emory. BS, Iowa State U., 1965; PhD, Cornell U., 1971. Postdoctoral fellow MRC Lab. Molecular biology, Cambridge, Eng., 1971-74, Stanford (Calif.) U., 1974; from asst. prof., assoc. prof. to prof. biochemistry U. Iowa, Iowa City, 1975-89, Disting. prof. biochemistry, 1989—, chmn. dept. biochemistry, 1998—; investigator Howard Hughes Med. Ctr. Howard Hughes Med. Inst., Iowa City, 1989-97. Contbr. numerous articles to profl. jours., sci. mags. Vol. Am. Peace Corps, Dormaa, Ghana, 1965-67. Recipient Molecular Parasitology award Burroughs-Wellcome Found., N.C., 1983, Medal of Sci. Achievement award Iowa Gov., 1990. Office: U Iowa Dept Biochemistry Iowa City IA 52242

DONEY, BART J., manufacturing executive; BS in Indsl. Engring., U. Ill., 1973. Various Temple-Inland Inc., Indpls., 1986-00, group v.p. packaging, 2000—; exec. v.p. Inland Paperboard & Packaging, Inc. subs. Temple-Inland Inc. Office: Temple Inland Inc 4030 Vincennes Rd Indianapolis IN 46268-3007

DONIGER, WENDY, history of religions educator; b. NYC, Nov. 20, 1940; d. Lester L. and Rita (Roth) Doniger; m. Dennis M. O'Flaherty, Mar. 31, 1964; 1 child, Michael Lester O'Flaherty. BA summa cum laude, Radcliffe Coll., 1962; PhD, Harvard U., 1968; D. Phil., Oxford Univ. Lectr. U. London Sch. Oriental and African Studies, 1968-75; vis. lectr. U. Calif., Berkeley, 1975-77; prof. history of religions Div. Sch., dept. South Asian langs., com. on social thought U. Chgo., 1978-85, Mircea Eliade prof., 1986—. Author: (under name of Wendy Doniger O'Flaherty) Asceticism and Eroticism in the Mythology of Siva, 1973, Hindu Myths, 1975, The Origins of Evil in Hindu Mythology, 1976, Women, Androgynes and Other Mythical Beasts, 1980, The Rig Veda: An Anthology, 1981, Karma and Rebirth in Classical Indian Traditions, 1980, Dreams, Illusion and Other Realities, 1984, Other Peoples' Myths, 1988, (under name of Wendy Doniger), The Laws of Manu, 1991, Mythologies, 1991, Purana Perennis, 1993, The Implied Spider, 1998, Splitting the Difference, 1999, The Bedtrick, 2000, The Kamasutra, 2002, The Woman Who Pretended to Be Who She Was, 2005; editor Jour. Am. Acad. Religion, 1977-80, History of Religions, 1979—; mem. editl. bd. Ency. Britannica, 1987-98, Daedalus, 1990--. Recipient Lucy Allen Paton prize, 1961, Phi Beta Kappa prize, 1962, Radcliffe medal, 1986, medal Coll. de France, 1992, Rosemary Crawshay prize Brit. Acad., 2002; Jonathan Fay Fund scholar, 1962, Am. Inst. Indian Studies fellow, 1963-64, NEH summer stipend, 1980, Guggenheim fellow, 1980-81. Fellow: Am. Acad. Arts and Scis., Am. Philos. Soc.; mem.: Assn. Asian Studies (pres. 1998), Am. Acad. Religion (pres. 1984), Phi Beta Kappa. Home: 1319 E 55th St Chicago IL 60615-5301 Office: U Chgo Div Sch 1025 E 58th St Chicago IL 60637-1509

DONKER, NORMAN WAYNE, prosecutor; b. Shelby, Mich., Apr. 16, 1955; s. Marvin C. and N. Lorrene (Miller) D.; m. H. Maureen, July 10, 1987; children: Erin Elizabeth, Jonathan Russell. BS in Polit. Sci., magna cum laude, Grand Valley State, 1977, BS in History, magna cum laude, 1977; JD cum laude, Wayne State U., 1980. Bar: Mich.; U.S. Dist. Ct. (ea. dist.) Mich.; U.S. Ct. Appeals (6th cir.); U.S. Supreme Ct. Asst. prosecuting atty. Clare County, Harrison, Mich., 1980, Midland (Mich.) County, 1981, sr. asst. prosecuting atty., 1981-85, chief asst. prosecuting atty., 1985-88, prosecuting atty., 1989—. Bd. dirs. Voluntary Action Ctr., Midland, 1985-91, Ernie Wallace Meml. Blood Bank, 1994—, ARC, Midland, 1995—; mem. Mich. Cmty. Corrections Bd. Mem. Pros. Atty. Assn. Mich. (pres. 1997, bd. dirs. 1990—). Office: Midland Co Prosecutor Offc 301 W Main St Midland MI 48640-5162

DONLEVY, JOHN DEARDEN, lawyer; b. Chgo., May 29, 1933; s. Frank and Alice Genevieve (O'Connor) D.; m. Kristin Bach Minnick, Apr. 20, 1963 (div. Sept. 1985); 1 son, John Dearden. Student, Stanford U., 1950-52; BS, Northwestern U., 1954; JD, U. Chgo., 1957; postgrad., Northwestern U., 1958. Bar: Ill. 1957, US Dist. Ct. (no. dist.) Ill. 1957, US Ct. Appeals (7th cir.) 1969, US Supreme Ct. 1972. Asst. state's atty. Cook County Criminal Divsn., Chgo., 1958-61; city prosecutor City of Evanston, Ill., 1961; assoc. Mayer, Brown & Platt, Chgo., 1962-73, ptnr., 1973-90; pvt. practice law Chgo., 1990—. Participant Hinton Moot Ct. Competition U. Chgo., 1955-56, judge, 1972. Contbr. articles to profl. pubs. Active Rep. Orgn., 1958—60; bd. dirs. English-Speaking Union, Chgo., 1964—65. Recipient Disting. Legal award Am. Legion, Chgo., 1960; named spl. prosecutor-labor racketeering Cook County State's Atty., Chgo., 1959-61; profiled in Lindberg "Summerdale--35 Year Anniversary", 1995. Mem. ABA, Ill. Bar Assn., Chgo. Bar Assn. (criminal law com., sr. trial atty. of Defense of Prisoners com., chair Def. of Prisoners com., mem. nom. com. for slating of officers and dir. 1994-94, chair criminal law and in-court criminal def. panels), Fed. Trial Bar, University Club Chgo. Office: Ste 2040 30 N La Salle St Chicago IL 60602-2506 Office Phone: 312-201-0227. Office Fax: 312-236-6906. Business E-Mail: jdonlevy@core.com.

DONNELL, HAROLD EUGENE, JR., retired professional society administrator; b. Balt., Mar. 12, 1935; s. Harold Eugene and Ruth Elizabeth (Meeth) D.; m. Rosemary Gatch, Apr. 25, 1959; children— David Crawford, Laurette Butler. BA, Amherst Coll., 1957. Field asst., agt. Equitable Life Assurance Soc., Balt., 1958-61; salesman Eastern Products Corp., Balt., 1961-64, asst. nat. sales mgr., 1964-66; exec. dir. Md. State Dental Assn., Towson, 1966-74, Acad. Gen. Dentistry, Chgo., 1974—2003; ret. Trustee Am. Fund for Dental Health, 1976-84. Served with U.S. Army, 1957-58. Recipient Disting. Service award N.C. Acad. Gen. Dentistry, 1980; ann. Walter E. Levine Meritorious Service award Alpha Omega, 1970, 93. Fellow Acad. Gen. Denistry (hon.); mem. ADA, Am. Soc. Assn. Execs. (cert. assn. exec.), Assn. Forum, Acad. Gen. Dentistry (Albert Borish award 2003). Republican. Luth.

DONNELL, JON M., real estate executive; BS in Acctg., U. Ariz. CPA, Ohio. V.p., assoc. gen. mgr. Del Webb Corp.; treas., CFO, Dominion Homes, Dublin, Ohio, 1995-96, exec. v.p., COO, 1996-99, pres., COO, 1999—, also bd. dirs. Mem. AICPAs, Ohio Soc. CPAs. Office: Dominion Homes Warranty Services PO Box 5000 Dublin OH 43016-5555

DONNELLEY, JAMES RUSSELL, printing company executive; b. Chgo., June 18, 1935; s. Elliott and Ann (Steinwedell) D.; m. Nina Louis Herrmann, Apr. 11, 1980; children: Niel J., Nicole C. BA, Dartmouth Coll., 1957; MBA, U. Chgo., 1962. With R.R. Donnelley & Sons Co., Chgo., 1962-2000, v.p., 1974-75, group pres. fin. svcs. group, 1985-87, group pres. corp. devel., 1987-90, vice chmn. bd., 1990-2000, also bd. dirs. Bd. dirs. Sierra Pacific Resources, PMP Inc., Melbourne, Australia. Office: Stet & Query LTD Partnership Ste 1009 360 N Michigan Ave Chicago IL 60601-3803 E-mail: james.donnelley@stetandquery.com.

DONNELLY, GERARD THOMAS, arboretum director; b. Detroit, Nov. 2, 1954; s. Merlin Joseph and Ruth Helen (Scherrer) D.; m. Pamela Lewis, June 16, 1990; children: Jason, Whitney, Parker. BA, Oakland U., 1976; PhD, Mich. State U., 1985. Instr. Mich. State U., East Lansing, 1981-84; asst. prof. Coe Coll., Cedar Rapids, Iowa, 1985-86; curator, asst. prof. Beal Bot. Garden Mich. State U., East Lansing, 1986-90; dir. The Morton Arboretum, Lisle, Ill., 1990—. Vice chmn. Mich. atural Areas Coun., 1988-89; mem. woody plant crop adv. com. USDA, 1989-92. Mem. AAAS, Am. Assn. Bot. Gardens and Arboreta (chmn. plant collections com. 1989-92, N.Am. plant collections consortium 1989—, editorial adv. com. 1989—), Ecol. Soc. Am., Am. Inst. Biol. Scis., Internat. Soc. Arboriculture, Am. Soc. for Hort. Sci. Office: Morton Arboretum Rte 53 Lisle IL 60532

DONNELLY, JOHN F., automotive part company executive; m. Barbara Donnelly; children: JOhn, Aisling, Saraid. BA, U. Mich.; M Sci. Mgmt., MIT. With Donnelly Corp., Holland, Mich., 1967—, mfg. mgr., current bus. group mgr. automotive vision sys., bus. group mgr. modular windows, v.p. modular window sys., sr. v.p. modular window sys. group, 1992—. Bd. dirs. Lakeshore Boys and Girls Club, Holland Hist. Trust. Office: Donnelly Corp 49 W 3d St Holland MI 49423

DONNELLY, JOSEPH, congressman, lawyer; b. Massapequa, NY, Sept. 29, 1955; m. Jill Donnelly; children: Molly, Joe Jr. BA in Govt., U. Notre Dame, 1977; JD, U. otre Dame Law Sch., 1981. Of counsel Nemeth, Masters & Feeney Law Firm; owner Mktg. Solutions, Mishawaka, Ind., 1996—; mem. US Congress from 2nd Ind. dist., 2007—, mem. agrl. com., fin. svcs. com., vets affairs com. Mem. Ind. State Election Bd., 1988—89. Mem. St. Anthony de Padua Parish, chmn. Bishop's Appeal Campaign, 1994—96; mem. Mishawaka Marian High Sch. Bd. Edn., 1997—2001, pres., 2000—01. Mem.: ABA, Ind. State Bar Assn. Democrat. Roman Catholic. Office: 1218 Longworth House Office Bldg Washington DC 20515 also: 207 W Colfax St South Bend IN 46601

DONNELLY, PAUL E., lawyer; b. Kansas City, Mo., Jan. 12, 1948; AB, St. Louis U., 1970, JD, 1973. Bar: Mo. 1973. Law clerk to Hon. William H. Becker U.S. Dist. Ct. (we. dist.) Mo., 1973-75; counsel U.S. Senator Stuart Symington, 1975-77; mem. Stinson, Mag & Fizzell, Kansas City, Mo. Editorial bd. St. Louis U. Law Jour., 1972-73. Mem. ABA, Mo. Bar, Kansas City Met. Bar Assn. Office: Stinson Mag & Fizzell PO Box 419251 Kansas City MO 64141-6251

DONNELLY, ROBERT, bishop; b. Mar. 22, 1931; Ordained priest Roman Cath. Ch., 1957. Consecrated bishop, 1984; bishop Archdiocese of Toledo, 1984—. Office: PO Box 985 Toledo OH 43697-0985

DONNELLY, ROBERT WILLIAM, bishop emeritus; Attended, St. Meinard Sem. Coll., Ind., Mt. St. Mary's West Sem., Norwood, Ohio. Ordained priest Diocese of Toledo, Ohio, 1957; ordained bishop, 1984; aux. bishop Diocese of Toledo, Ohio, 1984—2006, aux. bishop emeritus Ohio, 2006—. Roman Catholic. Office: Diocese of Toledo PO Box 985 Toledo OH 43697-0985 also: 4227 Bellevue Rd Toledo OH 43613 Office Phone: 419-472-2288. Office Fax: 419-472-0493. E-mail: rdinnelly@toledodiocese.org.*

DONNER, THOMAS BENJAMIN, lawyer; b. Yankton, SD, Mar. 8, 1957; BA, U. Nebr., 1979, JD, 1982. Bar: Nebr. Assoc. Samison & McNalley, Franklin, Nebr., 1982-83; atty. County Atty.'s Office, West Point, Nebr., 1986—; pvt. practice Wisner and West Point, Nebr. Mem. C. of C., Lions. Avocations: hunting, fishing, outdoors. Office: 137 S Main St # 2 West Point NE 68788-1832

DONOFRIO, JOHN, lawyer; BSChemE, Rutgers U.; JD, George Washington U., 1987, LLM. Law clk. US Ct. Appeals (fed. cir.); ptnr. Kirkland & Ellis; assoc. gen. counsel Honeywell Internat., 1996—98, dep. gen. counsel, 1998—2000, v.p., gen. counsel Honeywell Aerospace Phoenix, 2000—05; sr. v.p., gen. counsel Visteon Corp., Van Buren Twp., Mich., 2005—. Adj. prof. Seton Hall U. Sch. Law. Contbr. articles to profl. pubis. Office: Visteon Corp 1 Village Ctr Dr Van Buren Township MI 48111-5711

DONOHOE, JEROME FRANCIS, lawyer; b. Yankton, SD, Mar. 17, 1939; s. Francis A. and Ruth D. Donohoe; m. Elaine Bush, Jan. 27, 1968; 1 child, Nicole Elaine. BA, St. John's U., 1961; JD cum laude, U. Minn., 1964. Bar: Ill. 1964, S.D. 1964. Atty. Atchison, Topeka & Santa Fe Ry. Co., Chgo., 1967-73, gen. atty., 1973-78; gen. counsel corp. affairs Santa Fe Industries Inc., Chgo., 1978-84; v.p. law Santa Fe Industries, Inc., Chgo., 1984-90, Santa Fe Pacific Corp., Chgo., 1984-94; ptnr. Mayer, Brown, Rowe & Maw, Chgo., 1990-99, sr. counsel, 1999—. Capt. JAGC US Army, 1964—67. Fellow: Ill. Bar Found.; mem.: ABA (pub. utility, comm. and transp. law sect.), Northwestern U. Assocs., Mich. Shores Club (Wilmette, Ill.), Chgo. Athletic Assn., Chgo. Club. E-mail: jdonohoe@mac.com.

DONOHUE, CRAIG S., mercantile exchange executive; b. Oct. 9, 1961; married; 3 children. BA in Polit. Sci. & History, Drake U., 1983; LLM in Fin. Svcs. Regulation, Ill. Inst. Tech., Chgo.; JD, John Marshall Law Sch., 1987; M in Mgmt., Northwestern U., 1995. Bar: Ill. Assoc. McBride, Baker & Coles, Chgo.; corp. atty. Chgo. Merc. Exch., Inc., 1989—95, v.p., assoc. gen. counsel, 1995—97, v.p. market regulation, 1997—98, sr. v.p., gen. counsel, 1998—2000; mng. dir. bus. devel. & corp./legal affairs Chgo. Merc. Exch. Inc., 2000—01, mng. dir., chief adminstrv. officer, 2001—02, exec. v.p., chief adminstrv. officer, 2002—03; CEO Chgo. Merc. Exch. Holdings Inc., 2004—07, CME Group Inc. (formerly Chgo. Merc. Exch. Holdings Inc.), 2007—. Chmn. bd. Nat. Coun. Econ. Edn.; mem. global markets. adv. com. Commodity Futures Trading Commn.; bd. dirs. Chgo. Merc. Exch. Holdings Inc., 2005—07. Mem. adv. coun. Youth Svcs. of Glenview/Northbrook. Mem.: Chicagoland C. of C., Execs. Club Chgo. (bd. dirs.). Office: CME Group Inc 20 S Wacker Dr Chicago IL 60606*

DONOVAN, DIANNE FRANCYS, journalist; b. Houston, Sept. 30, 1948; d. James Henry and Doris Elaine (Simerly) D.; m. Anthony Charles Burba; children: Donovan Anthony, James Donovan. Student, Trinity Coll., Dublin, Ireland, 1969; BA, Spring Hill Coll., 1970; MA, U. Mo., 1975, U. Chgo., 1982. Fgn./nat. copy desk supr. Chgo. Tribune, 1979-80, asst. editor for news/features, 1980-83, lit. editor, 1985-93, mem. editl. bd., 1993-99, sr. editor for recruitment, 2000—02; v.p., editl. page editor The Balt. Sun, 2002—. Vis. prof. U. Oreg. Sch. Journalism, Eugene, 1983-85; adj. faculty Northwestern U. Sch. Journalism, 1980-81, 89-90; bd. dirs. Chgo. Tribune Found. Bd. dirs. Nelson Algren/Heartland lit. awards, Chgo., 1986-93; judge Nat. Headliners' Club Awards, Atlantic City, J., 1983. Recipient award for editl. writing Am. Soc. Newspaper Editors, 1999, Media award Chgo. Bar Assn., 1999. Episcopalian. Office: 501 N Calvert St Baltimore MD 21278

DONOVAN, LAURIE B., former state legislator; b. Little Falls, NY, Dec. 14, 1932; m. William Donovan, 1958; four children. BA, Pratt Inst.; MA, Syracuse U. State rep. dist. 74 Mo. Ho. of Reps., 1983-99. Active Coun. Mental Retardation. Home: 1070 Pearview Dr Saint Peters MO 63376-2272

DONOVAN, LESLIE D., SR., state legislator; m. Mary (Sissy) Donovan. Kans. state rep. Dist. 94, 1993—; auto dealer, investor. Home: 314 N Rainbow Lake Rd Wichita KS 67235-8533

DONOVAN, PAUL V., bishop emeritus; b. Bernard, Iowa, Sept. 1, 1924; s. John J. and Loretta (Carew) D. Student, St. Joseph Sem., Grand Rapids, Mich.; BA, St. Gregory Sem., Cin., 1946; postgrad., Mt. St. Mary Sem. of West, Cin.; JCL, Pontifical Lateran U., Rome, 1957. Ordained priest Diocese of Lansing, Mich., 1950; asst. pastor St. Mary Ch., Jackson, Mich., 1950-51; sec. to bishop of Lansing Mich.; adminstr. St. Peter Ch., Eaton Rapids, Mich., 1951-55; sec. to bishop, 1957-59; pastor Our Lady of Fatima Ch., Michigan Center, Mich., St. Rita Mission, Clark Lake, Mich., 1959-68, St. Agnes Ch., Flint, Mich., 1968-71; ordained bishop, 1971; bishop Diocese of Kalamazoo, 1971—94, bishop emeritus, 1994—. Mem. liturgical commn. Diocese of Lansing, chmn., 1963; mem. Cath. Bd. Edn., Jackson and Hillsdale counties; mem. bishop's personnel com., priests' senate. Bd. dirs. Family Services and, Mich. Children's Aid. Roman Catholic. Office: 2131 Aberdeen Dr Kalamazoo MI 49008-1759 Home: 1700 Bronson Way #166 Kalamazoo MI 49009-3317 Fax: 269-343-3357.*

DONOVAN, TIMOTHY R., lawyer; b. 1955; BS, Ohio State U.; JD cum laude, Capital U., Columbus, OH, 1981. Bar: 1981. Assoc. Jenner & Block, ptnr., 1989—99, chmn. corp. securities group; sr. v.p. Tenneco Corp. (formerly Tenneco Automotive Inc.), Lake Forest, Ill., 1999—2001, gen. counsel, 1999—2007, exec. v.p., 2001—07, mng. dir. internat. group, 2001—07; exec. v.p., sec., gen. counsel Allied Waste Industries Inc., Phoenix, 2007—. Dir. John B. Sanfilippo Sons Inc. Mem.: Chgo. Bar Assn. (securities law com.), ABA. Office: Allied Waste Industries 18500 N Allied Way Phoenix AZ 85054

DOODY, MARGARET ANNE, English language educator; b. St. John, NB, Can., Sept. 21, 1939; came to U.S., 1976; d. Hubert and Anne Ruth (Cornwall) D. BA, Dalhousie U., 1960; BA with 1st class hons., Lady Margaret Hall-Oxford U., 1962, MA, 1965, D.Phil., 1968; LLD (hon.), Dalhousie U., 1985. Instr. English U. Victoria, B.C., Canada, 1962—64, asst. prof. English, 1968—69; lectr. U. Coll. Swansea, Wales, 1969—76; assoc. prof. English U. Calif.-Berkeley, 1976—80; prof. English dept. Princeton U., NJ, 1980—89; Andrew W. Mellon prof. humanities, prof. English Vanderbilt U., Nashville, 1989—99, dir. comparative lit. program, 1992—99; John and Barbara Glyn Family prof. lit. U. Notre Dame, 2000—, dir. PhD in Lit. program, 2001—07. Author: A Natural Passion: A Study of the Novels of Samuel Richardson, 1974, The Daring Muse: Augustan Poetry Reconsidered, 1985, Frances Burney: The Life in the Works, 1988, The True Story of the Novel, 1996, (novels) Aristotle Detective, 1978, The Alchemists, 1980, Aristotle e la giustizia poetica, 2000, Aristotle and Poetic Justice, 2002, Poison in Athens, 2004, Mysteries of Eleusis, 2005; author: (with F. Stuber) (play) Clarissa, 1984; editor (with Peter Sabor): Samuel Richardson Tercentenary Essays, 1989; co-editor (with Douglas Murray): Catharine and Other Writings by Jane Austen, 1993; co-editor: (with Wendy Barry and Mary Doody Jones) Anne of Green Gables, 1997; author: Tropic of Venice, 2006. Guggenheim postdoctoral fellow, 1979; recipient Rose Mary Crawshay award Brit. Acad., 1986. Episcopalian. Office: U Notre Dame PhD in Literature Program Notre Dame IN 46556 Office Phone: 574-631-0481. Business E-Mail: mdoody@nd.edu.

DOOLEY, DAVID J., elementary school principal; Prin. Aquila Primary Ctr., St. Louis Park, Minn., 1984-99, Field's Sch., Mpls., 1999—. Recipient Elem. Sch. Recognition award U.S. Dept. Edn., 1989-90. Office: Field's Sch 4645 4th Ave S Minneapolis MN 55409-2699

DOOLEY, DONALD JOHN, retired publishing executive; b. Des Moines, Aug. 16, 1921; s. Martin and Anne Marguerite (Barger) D.; m. Beverly Frederick, Dec. 21, 1955 (div. 1977); children: Nancy Elizabeth, Katherine Anne(dec.), Mary Bridget, Robert Frederick; m. Patricia Connell, Dec. 28, 1996. BA, U. Iowa, 1947; postgrad., Drake U., 1949-50. Gen. Promotion and pub. relations mgr. Meredith Corp., Des Moines, 1953-59, dir. pub. relations, 1960-65; art and editorial dir. Better Homes & Gardens Books & Spl. Interest Publs., Des Moines, 1965-77; dir. editorial planning and devel. Better Homes and Gardens Books (Meredith Corp.), Des Moines, 1977-84; cons., 1985. Chmn. bd. adv. com. Sch. Vol. Program, Des Moines; steering com. Intercultural Affairs program to Desegregate Dist. Schs., 1975-77; treas. Iowa U. Parents Assn., 1977-79; bd. dirs. Iowa Cystic Fibrosis Found., 1979-87, v.p., 1981-85; trustee Citizens Scholarship Found. Am., 1976-85, Iowa Freedom of Info. Council, 1977-87; adv. bd. Adult and Community Edn., Des Moines Pub. Sch., 1982—99; cons. White House Conf. on Families, 1981. Officer USAAF, 1942-46. Decorated 2 battle stars; recipient Dorothy Dawe award Home Furnishings Industry, 1973. Mem. Pub. Rels. Soc. Am. (accredited, pres. chpt. 1969, dir. chpt. 1965-76), ACLU, Beyond War (co-dir. Iowa office 1987-88), Friendship Force, Ams. for Dem. Action, Sigma Nu (comdr. chpt. 1946-47), Found. for Global Community, 1991—. Clubs: Echo Valley Country. Democrat. Home and Office: 3711 Oak Creek Pl West Des Moines IA 50265-7968

DOOLEY, ROGER, Internet company executive; BS, Carnegie-Mellon U., 1971; MBA, U. Tenn., 1977. Dir. strategic planning Nat. Standard Co.; pres. Microsphere, Inc.; mng. dir. CollegeConfidential.com, Inc., 2001—; founder, pres. Dooley Direct LLC, 2005—; advisor RateItAll, Inc. Adminstr. WebmasterWorld. Office: College Confidential 536 Miami Club Ct Mishawaka IN 46544 Office Phone: 574-852-6000.*

DOOLEY, SHARON L., obstetrician, gynecologist; b. 1947; MD, U. Va. Mem. faculty Prentice Womens Hosp. Med. Sch. Northwestern U., Chgo., prof., dir. graduate med. edn. Office: Northwestern U Med Sch Prentice Womens Hosp 333 E Superior St Ste 410 Chicago IL 60611-3015

DOOLITTLE, SIDNEY NEWING, retail executive; b. Binghamton, NY, Sept. 7, 1934; s. Raymond Luvurn and Helen Esther (Newing) D.; m. Barbara Mae Colsten, Sept. 12, 1954; children: Scott Sidney, Craig Francis, Sally Anne. Student, Rensselaer Poly. Inst., 1954-56; AA in Advanced Mgmt, Harvard U., 1977. With Montgomery Ward & Co., 1955-83, dir. internat. ops., 1970-73; v.p., dir. Montgomery Ward & Co. (Montgomery Ward Internat. Inc.), 1972; corp. v.p., div. mgr. catalog mdse. Montgomery Ward & Co., Chgo., 1978-83; exec. v.p., mdse. mgr., dir. Warehouse Club, Inc., 1983-84; pres. SND Enterprises, 1984-85; founding ptnr. McMillan/Doolittle, 1986—. Bd. dirs., chmn. compensation and audit com. Otasco Inc., 1986-88; bd. dirs. High Performance Appliances, 1992-96. Vice chmn. bd. dirs. Henrotin Hosp., Chgo., 1980-97; vice-chmn. Mid-Am. chpt. Red Cross., chmn. bd. Greater Chgo. chpt., 1999—. Mem. Mail Order Assn. Am. (chmn. bd. 1981-83), Chgo. Fgn. Relations Council. Presbyterian. Office: McMillan Doolittle 350 W Hubbard St Chicago IL 60610-4098

DORAN, THOMAS GEORGE, bishop; b. Rockford, Ill., Feb. 20, 1936; STL in Sacred Theology, Pontifical Gregorian U., Rome, 1962, JCL in Canon Law, 1978; MA, Rockford Coll., 1974. Ordained priest Diocese of Rockford, Ill., 1961, various admin. duties, rector diocesan cathedral; asst. pastor St. Joseph Parish, Elgin, Ill., St. Peter Parish, South Beloit; prelate auditor Roman Rota, 1986—94; ordained bishop, 1994; bishop Diocese of Rockford, 1994—. Mem. Supreme Tribunal of the Apostolic Signatura, 2000. Mem.: Congregation for the Clergy. Roman Catholic. Office: Diocese of Rockford 555 Colman Center Dr PO Box 7044 Rockford IL 61125-7044 Office Phone: 815-399-4300. Office Fax: 815-399-4769. Business E-Mail: officeofthebishop@rockforddiocese.org.*

DORGAN, BYRON LESLIE, senator; b. Dickinson, ND, May 14, 1942; s. Emmett P. and Dorothy (Bach) D.; m. Kimberly Olson Dorgan; children: Scott, Shelly (dec.), Brendon, Haley. BS, U. ND, 1965; MBA, U. Denver, 1966. Exec. devel. trainee Martin Marietta Corp., Denver, 1966-67; dep. tax commr., then tax commnr. State of .D., 1967-80; mem. 97th-102nd congresses from N.D., Washington, 1981-92; US Senator from ND Washington, 1992—; asst. Dem. floor leader U.S. Senate, Washington, 1996—. Mem. commerce, sci. and transp. com., select com. on Indian affairs, appropriations com., energy and natural resource com., chmn. Dem. policy com., 1999—, instr. econs. Bismarck (N.D.) Jr. Coll., 1969-71. Contbr. articles to profl. jours. Recipient Nat. Leadership award Office Gov. N.D., 1972 Mem. Nat. Assn. Tax Adminstrs. (exec. com. 1972-75) Democrat. Lutheran. Office: US Senate 322 Hart Senate Off Bldg Washington DC 20510-0001 also: District Office 312 Federal Bldg PO Box 2579 Bismarck ND 58502 Office Phone: 202-224-2551, 701-250-4618. Office Fax: 701-250-4484, 202-224-1193. E-mail: senator@dorgan.senate.gov.

DORIS, ALAN S(ANFORD), lawyer; b. Cleve., June 18, 1947; s. Sam E. and Rebecca D.; m. Nancy Rose Spitzer, Jan. 10, 1976; children: Matthew, Lisa. AB and BS in Bus. cum laude, Miami U., Oxford U., 1969; JD cum laude, Harvard U., 1972. Bar: Ohio 1972, U.S. Dist. Ct. (no. dist.) Ohio 1972, U.S. Tax Ct. 1972, U.S. Ct. Appeals (6th cir.) 1972. Assoc. Stotter, Familo, Cavitch, Elden & Durkin, Cleve., 1972-77; ptnr. Elden & Ford, Cleve., 1978-79, Benesch, Friedlander, Coplan & Aronoff, Cleve., 1980-2000, Squire, Sanders & Dempsey, 2000—. Editor: Ohio Transaction Guide. Treas. Hawthorne Valley Country Club, Cleve., 1984-85; chmn. Cleve. Tax Inst., 1994. Mem. ABA (chmn. capital recovery com. taxation sect. 1994-96). Avocation: golf. Office: Squire Sanders & Dempsey LLP 4900 Key Tower Cleveland OH 44114

DORMAN, GREGG M., lawyer; BA in Fin. with distinction, U. Ill., 1981; JD, Loyloa U., 1984. Bar: Ill. 1984, US Dist. Ct. (no. dist.) Ill. Assoc. Horwood, Marcus & Braun, 1984, Rudnick & Wolfe, 1984; founding ptnr. Christie & Dorman, 1988—91; ptnr. Edler & Christie, 1991—95, Kritzer & Levick, 1995, Seyfarth Shaw LLP, chmn. Real Estate Practice Group. Mem.: Internat. Coun. of Shopping Ctrs., ABA (real property, probate and trust law sect.), Ill. Bar Assn. (real estate law sect.), Chgo Bar Assn. (real property sect.). Office: Seyfarth Shaw LLP 55 East Monroe St Ste 4200 Chicago IL 60603 Office Phone: 312-269-8290. Office Fax: 312-269-8869. Business E-Mail: gmdorman@seyfarth.com.

DORMAN, JEFFREY LAWRENCE, lawyer; b. Akron, Ohio, Feb. 6, 1949; s. Milton and Belle (Handler) D.; m. Bernadette Marie Pawlik, Sept. 2, 1988. BA, U. Mich., 1971; JD, Case Western Res. U., Cleve., 1974; MS, U. Wis., 1976. Bar: Ohio 1975, Ill. 1979, U.S. Dist. Ct. (no. dist.) Ill. 1980. Staff atty. U.S. Dept. Justice, Washington, 1976-79; assoc. Sonnenschein Nath & Rosenthal, Chgo., 1979-82, ptnr., 1982-2000, Freeborn & Peters, 2000—. Mem. ABA, Ohio Bar Assn., Chgo. Bar Assn. Avocation: mountain climbing. Home: 2639 N Southport Ave Chicago IL 60614-1227 Office: Freeborn & Peters 8000 Sears Tower 311 S Wacker Dr Ste 3000 Chicago IL 60606-6677

DORN, JOHN, state legislator; b. Dec. 28, 1943; m. Kathleen; 3 children. BA, John's U.; MA, U. Wis. State rep. Minn. Ho. Reps., Dist., 24A, 1986—. Vice chmn. appropriations com., mem. edn.-higher edn. fin. divsn., environ. & natural resources & local govt. & met. affairs coms., Minn. Ho. Reps. Home: 1040 E Main St Mankato MN 56001-4564

DORNER, PETER PAUL, retired economist, educator; b. Luxemburg, Wis., Jan. 13, 1925; s. Peter and Monica (Altmann) Dorner; m. Lois Cathryn Hartnig, Dec. 26, 1950. BS, U. Wis.-Madison, 1951; MS, U. Tenn., Knoxville, 1953; PhD, Harvard U., 1959. Asst. prof. agrl. econs. U. Tenn., 1953-54; asst. prof. U. Wis.-Madison, 1954-56, assoc. prof., 1959-62, prof., 1962-89, dir. Land Tenure Center, 1965-66, 68-71, chmn. dept. agrl. econs., 1972-76, dean internat. studies and programs, 1980-89, prof., dean emeritus, 1989—. Prof. U. Chile, Santiago, 1963—65; sr. staff economist Pres.'s Coun. Econ. Advisors, Washington, 1967—68; cons. UN, UN Food, Agrl. Orgn., World Bank, U.S. Govt., State Govtl. Agys., InterAm. Devel. Bank. Author: Land Reform and Economic Development, 1972, Latin American Land Reforms in Theory and Practice: a Retrospective Analysis, 1992; editor: Cooperative and Commune: Group Farming in the Economic Development of Agriculture, 1977, Resources and Development: Natural Resource Policies and Economic Development in an Interdependent World, 1980; contbr. numerous articles to profl. jours., popular mags. Inf. US Army, 1944—46. Mem.: AARP. Home: 3111 Pheasant Branch Rd #109A Middleton WI 53562 Personal E-mail: ppdorner@facstaff.wisc.edu.

DORNETTE, W(ILLIAM) STUART, lawyer, educator; b. Washington, Mar. 2, 1951; s. William Henry Lueders and Frances Roberta (Hester) D.; m. Martha Louise Mehl, Nov. 19, 1983; children: Marjorie Frances, Anna Christine, David Paul. AB, Williams Coll., 1972; JD, U. Va., 1975. Bar: Va. 1975, Ohio 1975, U.S. Dist. Ct. (so. dist.) Ohio 1975, D.C. 1976, U.S. Ct. Appeals (6th cir.) 1977, U.S. Supreme Ct. 1980. Assoc. Taft, Stettinius & Hollister, Cin., 1975-83, ptnr., 1983—. Instr. law U. Cin., 1980-87, adj. prof., 1988-91. Co-author: Federal Judiciary Almanac, 1984-87. Mem. Ohio Bd. Bar Examiners, 1991-93, Hamilton County Rep. Exec. Com., 1982—; bd. dirs. Zool. Soc. Cin., 1983-94, 06-, Cin. Parks Found., 1995-04; bd. visitors U. Cin. Law Sch., 2002-06. Mem. FBA, Ohio State Bar Assn., Cin. Bar Assn., Am. Phys. Soc., Nat. Assn. Coll. and Univ. Attys. Methodist. Home: 329 Bishopsbridge Dr Cincinnati OH 45255-3948 Office: 1800 US Bank Tower 425 Walnut St Cincinnati OH 45202-3923 Office Phone: 513-357-9353. E-mail: dornette@taftlaw.com.

DORRELL, JOHN S., lawyer, insurance company executive; b. 1946; BS, Miami U. Ohio, 1969; JD, U. Toledo, 1974. Bar: Ohio 1975. Bailiff Lucas County Common Pleas Ct.; ptnr. Neipp, Dorrell, & Wingart, Toledo, Marshall & Melhorn, Toledo; v.p. Medchoice/HMO, legal counsel Med. Mutual Ohio, Cleve., 1986—89, v.p. alt. delivery systems, 1989—97, gen. counsel, v.p. legal affairs, 1997—. Mem.: ABA, Cleve. Bar Assn., Ohio State Bar Assn. Office: Med Mutual Ohio 2060 E Ninth St Cleveland OH 44115 Office Phone: 216-687-7476. Office Fax: 216-687-6164. E-mail: john.dorrell@mmoh.com.

DORSEY, JOHN KEVIN, dean; b. NYC, 1943; B, Fairfield U., Conn., 1964; PhD in physiologic chemistry, U. Wis., Madison, 1968; MD, So. Ill. U. Sch. Medicine, 1978; postgrad., The Johns Hopkins U., 1970—73. Diplomate internal medicine and rheumatology Am. Bd. Internal Medicine. Intern U. Iowa Hosps., Iowa City, 1978—79, resident in internal medicine, 1979—81; fellow in rheumatology U. Iowa, Iowa City, 1981—83; joined faculty as asst. prof. chemistry and biochemistry So. Ill. U., Carbondale, Ill., 1973, rejoined faculty as asst. prof. and coord. clin. affairs, 1983; med. dir. So. Ill. Arthritis Found.; attending rheumatologist Carbondale (Ill.) Clinic; consulting rheumatologist V.A. Hosp., Marion, Ill.; prof. internal medicine So. Ill. U. Sch. Medicine, Carbondale, Ill., assoc. provost so. region, 1998—2001, interim dean and provost Springfield, 2001—02, dean and provost, 2002—. Mem. Nuc. Magnetic Resonance Mgmt. Com. So. Ill. U., mem. Molecular Biology, Microbiology and Biochemistry com.; bd. trustees So. Ill. Healthcare. Co-host (edn. television program) Medically Speaking, reviewer Developmental Biology, Ill. Med. Jour., Tchg. and Learning in Medicine, Academic Medicine; contbr. articles to profl. jours. Named a Disting. Alumnus, So. Ill. U. Sch. Medicine, 1993; recipient John Templeton Spirituality in Medicine Curricular Award, 2000. Fellow: Am. Coll. Rheumatology, Am. Coll. Physicians; mem.: Alpha Omega Alpha, Sigma Xi.

DORSMAN, PETER A., printing company executive; Various positions Nat. Cash Register Corp., 1978-96; sr. v.p., gen. mgr. Std. Register Co., Dayton, Ohio, 1996-99, COO, exec. v.p., 1999—. Office: Std Register Co 600 Albany St Dayton OH 45408

DORSO, JOHN, state legislator; b. Mpls., June 12, 1943; s. Carmen T. and Jean D. Dorso; m. Susan James, 1987; children: Victor, Louis, Carmen, Danielle, Amy, Todd. BA, Coll. St. Thomas, 1967. V.p. Dorso Trailer Sales, Fargo, pres. semi trailer sales and leasing; mem. N.D. Ho. of Reps. Dist. 46, 1984—; majority leader N.D. Ho. of Reps. Mem. sts. and hwys. com., transp. com.; chmn. industry, bus. and labor com., majority leader N.D. Ho. Reps.; bd. dirs. Behavioral Health Care, Inc.; pres. N.D. Drivers. Chmn. dist. 46 N.D. Rep. Com., 1981-83, United Rep. Com., Fargo, 1983-84. Recipient Legislative Vision award, 1991, 93, Lignite Pub. Svc. award, 1993. Mem. N.D. State U. Teammakers (pres. 1982-83), N.D. Motor Carriers Assn., Fargo C. of C. Home: 822 Carnoustie Dr Venice FL 34293-4343

DORWART, DONALD BRUCE, lawyer; b. Zanesville, Ohio, Dec. 12, 1949; s. Walter G. and Katherine (Kachmar) D.; children: Claire Lauren, Hillary Beth. BA, Vanderbilt U., 1971; JD, Washington U., St. Louis, 1974. Bar: Mo. 1974, U.S. Dist. Ct. (ea. dist.) Mo. 1974. Assoc. Thompson Coburn LLP, St. Louis, 1974-79, ptnr., 1980—; dir. New Energy Corp. Ind., 1992-95. Contbr. articles to profl. jours. Named to, Mo. & Kans. Super Lawyers, 2005—, Best Lawyers in Am., 2007—. Mem.: ABA, FOCUS St. Louis (mem. selection com. 1990—91, mem. fin. com. 1990—2002, mem. cmty. policy com. 2000—02, bd. dirs. 2000—06, treas. 2001—02, pres. 2002—04), Bar Assn. Met. St. Louis (chair securities regulation com. 1979), Maritime Law Assn. U.S. (mem. maritime fin. com. 1980—, proctor), The Met. Forum (mem. mgmt. com. 2003—05), Noonday Club. Office: Thompson Coburn LLP One US Bank Plz Ste 3300 Saint Louis MO 63101-1643 Office Phone: 314-552-6000. Business E-Mail: ddorwart@thompsoncoburn.com.

DOTT, ROBERT HENRY, JR., geologist, educator; b. Tulsa, June 2, 1929; s. Robert Henry and Esther Edgerton (Reed) Dott; m. Nancy Maud Robertson, Feb. 1, 1951; children: James, Karen, Eric, Cynthia, Brian. Student, U. Okla., 1946-48; BS, U. Mich., 1950, MS, 1951; PhD, Columbia U., 1956. Exploration geologist Humble Oil & Refining Co., Ariz., Oreg., Wash., 1954-56, Calif., 1958; mem. faculty U. Wis.-Madison, 1958-94, prof. geology, 1966-84, Stanley A. Tyler Disting. prof., 1984—, chmn. dept. geology and geophysics, 1974-77, emeritus prof., 1994—. Vis. prof. U. Calif., Berkeley, 1969; Cabot disting. vis. prof. U. Houston, 1986—87; NSF sci. faculty fellow Stanford U. and U.S. Geol. Survey, 1978, U. Colo., 1979; acad. visitor Imperial Coll., London, 1985—86, Oxford U., 1985—86, Adelaide U., Australia, 1992; cons. Roan Selection Trust, Ltd., Zambia, 1967, Atlantic-Richfield Co., 1983—85, Hubbard Map Co., 1984—86; lectr. Bur. Petroleum and Marine Geology, China, 1986; Erskine fellow, vis. prof. Canterbury U., New Zealand, 1987; Woodford-Ellis lectr. Pomona Coll., 1994. Co-author: Evolution of the Earth, 7th edit., 2003, Roadside Geology of Wisconsin, 2004; contbr. articles to profl. jours. 1st lt. USAF, 1956—57. Recipient Outstanding Tchr. award, Wis. Student Assn., 1969, Ben. H. Parker award, Am. Inst. Profl. Geologists, 1992; AEC fellow, Columbia U., 1951—55. Fellow: Edinburgh Geol. Soc. (hon. corr. 1997), Geol. Soc. Am. (chmn. history of geology divsn. 1990, councilor 1992—94, History of Geology award 1995, L.L. Sloss award 2001); mem.: AAAS, History of Earth Sci. Soc. (pres. 1990), Internat. Assn. Sedimentologists, Soc. Econ. Paleontologists and Mineralogists (sec.-treas. 1968—70, v.p. 1972—73, pres. 1981—82, hon., William H. Twenhofel medal 1993), Am. Assn. Petroleum Geologists (Pres.'s award 1956, Disting. Svc. award 1984, Disting. lectr. 1985), Sigma Xi (Disting. lectr. 1988—89). Unitarian Universalist. Office: U Wis Dept Geology and Geophysics 1215 W Dayton St Madison WI 53706-1600 E-mail: rdott@geology.wisc.edu.

DOTY, DAVID SINGLETON, federal judge; b. Anoka, Minn., June 30, 1929; BA, JD, U. Minn., 1961; LLD (hon.), William Mitchell Coll. Law. Bar: Minn. 1961, U.S. Ct. Appeals (8th and 9th cirs.) 1976, U.S. Supreme Ct. 1982. V.p., dir. Popham, Haik, Schnobrich, Kaufman & Doty, Mpls., 1962-87, pres., 1977-79; instr. William Mitchell Coll. Law, St. Paul, 1963—64; judge U.S. Dist. Ct. for Minn., Mpls., 1987—. Mem. Adv. Com. on Civil Rules, 1992-98, Adv. Com. on Evidence Rules, 1994-98; trustee Mpls. Libr. Bd., 1969-79, Mpls. Found., 1976-83. Fellow ABA Found.; mem. ABA, Minn. Bar Assn. (gov. 1976-87, sec. 1980-83, pres. 1984-85), Hennepin County Bar Assn. (pres. 1975-76), Fed. Bar Assn. (pres. 1996-97), Am. Judicature Soc., Am. Law Inst. Office: US Dist Ct 14 W US Courthouse 300 S 4th St Minneapolis MN 55415-1320 Home Phone: 612-332-7853; Office Phone: 612-664-5060. Business E-Mail: dsdoty@mnd.uscourts.gov.

DOTY, KAREN M., county official, lawyer; b. NYC, Oct. 16, 1948; d. Printon A. and Mary A. Doty. BS, Old Dominion U., Norfolk, Va., 1973; MA in Urban Studies, U. Akron, Ohio, 1977; JD, U. Akron, 1981. Atty., ptnr. Buckingham, Doolittle & Burroughs LLP, Akron, 1981-99; state rep. State of Ohio, 1993-96; chief staff Summit County, Akron, 1999—2000, dir. dept. law, 2001—. Active Leadership Akron, 1985; trustee Ardmore, Inc., 1980—85, pres., 1983—85; trustee Leadership Akron Alumni Assn., 1985—87, chmn. tng. com., 1988—90; active Akron Health Commn., 1984—89, pres., 1986—89; chair City of Akron 1990 Charter Rev. Commn.; with Children Svcs. Bd., 1990—92, Mayor's Task Force on Juvenile Violence, 1994—95; trustee Akron Law Libr. Assn., 1997—98; chair by-laws com. Women's etwork, 1998—2001; chair grants adv. com. Women's Endowment Fund, 1998—2001, trustee, 1998—2003, Cuyahoga Valley Scenic R.R., 1997—2002; trustee, vice chair Scenic Ohio, 1997—; trustee Akron Gen. Med. Ctr., 1997—99, 2003—05, U. Akron Sch. Law Alumni Assn., 2006, Akron Symphony, 2006. Named Woman of Yr., Akron Bus. and Profl. Women, 1994. Mem.: NASW (Ascending Achiever award 1994), Akron Bar Assn. Office: Summit County 175 S Main St Akron OH 44308-1354 E-mail: kdoty@summitoh.net.

DOTZLER, BILL, state senator; b. St. Paul, May 1948; AA, N. Iowa Area C.C.; BA, U. No. Iowa. Machine operator and labor rep. Deere & Co.; state rep. Iowa Ho. of Reps., 1996—2002; state senator dist. 11 Iowa Senate, 2003—; mem. appropriations com.; mem. bus. and labor rels. com.; mem. econ. growth com.; mem. ways and means com.; ranking mem. econ. devel. appropriations subcom. Mem. Cedar Trails Partnership, Friends of Hartman Res. Nature Ctr. With US Army. Mem.: Waterloo Vis. Nursing Assn. (past pres.), Gates Pk. Optimist Club Waterloo, Amvets (mem. post 31). Democrat. Office: State Capitol East 12th and Grand Des Moines IA 50319

DOUGHERTY, CHARLES HAMILTON, pediatrician; b. St. Louis, June 1, 1947; s. Charles Joseph and Suzanne Louise (Hamilton) D.; m. Mary Laverty Peckham, July 7, 1972; children: Bridget, Matthew, Erin, Kelly. BA in Biology, Coll. of the Holy Cross, 1969; MD, U. Rochester Sch. of Medicine, NYC, 1973. Pediatric resident St. Louis Children's Hosp., 1973-76, pres. med. staff, 2005—07; pvt. practice pediatrics Primary Pediatric Care Group, St. Louis, 1976-86, Esse Health, St. Louis, 1986—. Fellow Am. Acad. Pediatrics. Roman Catholic. Avocations: running, travel, computers, water sports. Office: Esse Health 13303 Tesson Ferry Rd Saint Louis MO 63128-4062 Office Phone: 314-842-5239. Personal E-mail: cdoughe103@aol.com. Business E-Mail: cdougher@essehealth.com.

DOUGHERTY, DAVID FRANCIS, business process outsourcing executive; b. Syracuse, NY, Aug. 19, 1956; s. Francis Edward and Mary (Kelley) D.; m. Kimberly Ann Slattery, Sept. 6, 1986. BBA in Fin., U. Mich., 1978. Brand asst. Procter & Gamble, Cin., 1978-79, asst. brand mgr., 1979-81, brand mgr., 1982-86; gen. mgr. Goggles Div. Lenscrafters, Cin., 1986-87, pres., 1987—90; pres., CEO MATRIXX Mktg. Inc. (a Convergys predecessor), 1990; pres., customer mgmt. group Convergys Corp., Cin., 1995—2000, chief develop. officer, 2000—02, exec. v.p. global info. mgmt. group, 2003—, pres., COO, 2005—07, pres., CEO, 2007—. Bd. dirs. Convergys Corp., 2006—. Author: Financial Policies & Procedures for Student Organizations, 1978. Mem. East Walnut Hills Assembly, Cin., 1988-89. Mem. Am. Mktg. Assn., President's Club Univ. Mich., Tribe of Michigama, Cin. Country Club. Democrat. Roman Catholic. Office: Convergys Corp 201 E Fourth St Cincinnati OH 45202

DOUGHERTY, J. PATRICK, state legislator; b. Decatur, Ill., June 30, 1948; s. James Francis and Bernadine Brennan Dougherty; m. Beverly Anne Martin, 1973; children: Erica Maureen, Bridget Colleen, Elizabeth Kathleen. BA, Quincy Coll., 1970; postgrad., Kenrick Theol. Sem., 1970-72. State rep. dist. 98 Mo. Ho. of Reps., 1979-82, dist. 67, 1983—; caseworker divsn. family svc. St. Louis County, Mo., 1974-78; devel. dir. Marianist Apostolic Ctr.; mem. adv. bd. Fanning Cmty. Sch.; mem. adv. com. Crippled Children; mem. legis. com. United Way Greater St. Louis. Named Outstanding Freshman Legislator Mo.

Assn. Pub. Employees, 1979—; recipient Citizen Labor Energy award, 1984, Rutherford T. Phillips award Humane Assn., 1984, Svc. award Mo. Humane Soc., 1984. Home: 4031 Parker Ave Saint Louis MO 63116-3719

DOUGHERTY, RICHARD MARTIN, library and information science professor; b. East Chicago, Ind., Jan. 17, 1935; s. Floyd C. and Harriet E. (Martin) D.; m. Ann Prescott, Mar. 24, 1974; children— Kathryn E., Emily E.; children by previous marriage— Jill Ann, Jacquelyn A., Douglas M. BS, Purdue U., 1959, LHD honoris causa, 1991; M.L.S., Rutgers U., 1961, PhD, 1963; LHD honoris causa, U. Stellenbosch, South Africa, 1995. Head acquisitions dept. Univ. Library, U. N.C., Chapel Hill, 1963-66; assoc. dir. libraries U. Colo., Boulder, 1966-70; prof. library sci. Syracuse U., NY, 1970-72; univ. librarian U. Calif-Berkeley, 1972-78; dir. univ. library U. Mich., Ann Arbor, 1978-88, acting dean. Sch. Library Sci., 1984-85, prof. sch. info., 1978-98, prof. emeritus, 1999—; pres. Dougherty & Assocs., 1994—. Founder, pres. Mountainside Pub. Corp., 1974—; co-host live teleconferences Coll. DuPage. Author: Scientific Management of Library Organizations, 2d edit., 1982, Streamlining Library Services, 2008; co-author: Preferred Futures for Libraries II, 1993; editor Coll. and Research Libraries jour., 1969-74, Jour. Acad. Librarianship, 1975-94, Library Issues, 1981—. Trustee Ann Arbor Dist. Libr., 1995—2002, pres. bd. trustees, 1998—2000. Recipient Esther Piercy award, 1968, Disting. Alumnus award Rutgers U., 1980, Acad. Librarian Yr., Assn. Coll. and Research Libraries, 1983, ALA Hugh C. Atkinson Meml. award, 1988, Blackwell Scholarship award, 1992, Joseph Lippincott medal, 1997; fellow Council on Library Resources. Mem. ALA (coun. 1969-76, 89-92, exec. bd. 1972-76, 89-92, endowment trustee 1986-89, pres. 1990-91), Assn. Rsch. Librs. (bd. dirs. 1977-80), Rsch. Librs. Group, Inc. (exec. com. 1984-88, chmn. bd. govs. 1986-87), Soc. Scholarly Pub. (bd. dirs. 1990-92, exec. com. 1991-92), Internat. Fedn. Libr. Assns. (round table of editors of library jours. 1985-87, standing com. univ. libr. sect. 1981-87). Home: 6 Northwick Ct Ann Arbor MI 48105-1408 Office: Dougherty & Assoc PO Box 8330 Ann Arbor MI 48107-8330 Office Phone: 734-665-4547, 734-662-3925. E-mail: rmdoughe@umich.edu.

DOUGHERTY, ROBERT ANTHONY, retired manufacturing company executive; b. St. Louis, May 3, 1928; s. Joseph A. and Venita E. (Gretline) D.; m. Rosemary Schmertmann, Jan. 29, 1955; children: Kevin, Patrick, Michael, Mary Ann, Timothy. BS in Mech. Engring, U. Notre Dame, 1952. Registered profl. engr., Calif. cert. mfg. engr. Sales engr. Robert R. Stephens Machinery Co., St. Louis, 1952-60, dist. mgr., 1961-72; pres. Dougherty & Assos., Prairie Village, Kans., 1972-99, ret., chmn. bd. dirs. Bd. dirs. Tech-Industry Cons., Lenexa, Kans.; exec. com. Kans. Industry/Univ./Govt. Engring. Edn. Consortium. Mem. adv. com. Pittsburg, Kans. Sch. Sci. and Tech., 1987—; coord. cons. Kans. U. Ctrs. Excellence for Kans. Tech. Enterprise Corp., 1991—. Served with U.S. Army, 1946-48. Recipient Productivity award Coll. and Univ. Mfg. Edn. Council, 1979, Soc. Mfg. Engrs. Joseph A. Siegel Meml. honor award, 1992; Outstanding Engring. Achievements award San Fernando Valley Engrs. Council, 1980. Fellow Instn. Prodn. Engrs. Gt. Britain (life); mem. ASME (state legis. fellow), Am. Soc. for Metals, Soc. Mfg. Engrs. (pres. 1980-81, dir. 1971-82, Region 5 award of merit 1969), Serra Club of Kansas City Kans. (pres. 2003—), Round Hill Bath and Tennis Club (pres. 1971), Hillcrest Country Club (v.p. 1982, pres. 1983—). Roman Catholic.

DOUGLAS, ANDREW, retired state supreme court justice; b. Toledo, July 5, 1932; 4 children JD, U. Toledo, 1959. Bar: Ohio 1960, U.S. Dist. Ct. (no. dist.) Ohio 1960. Former ptnr. Winchester & Douglas; judge Ohio 6th Dist. Ct. Appeals, 1981-84; ret. justice Ohio Supreme Ct., 1985—2002. Mem. nat. adv. bd. Ctr. for Informatics Law John Marshall Law Sch., Chgo.; former spl. counsel Atty. Gen. of Ohio; former instr. law Ohio Dominican Coll. Served with U.S. Army, 1952-54 Recipient award Maumee Valley council Girl Scouts U.S., 1976, Outstanding Service award Toledo Police Command Officers Assn., 1980, Toledo Soc. for Autistic Children and Adults, 1983, Extra-Spl. Person award Central Catholic High Sch., 1981, Disting. Service award Toledo Police Patrolman's Assn., 1982, award Ohio Hispanic Inst. Opportunity, 1985, Disting. Merit award Alpha Sigma Phi, 1988, Gold "T" award U. Toledo, First Amendment award Cen. Ohio Chpt. Soc. Profl. Journalists Sigma Delta Chi, 1989; named to Woodward High Sch. Hall of Fame. Mem. Toledo Bar Assn., Lucas County Bar Assn., Ohio Bar Assn., Toledo U. Alumni Assn., U. Toledo Coll. Law Alumni Assn. (Disting. Alumnus award 1991), Internat. Inst., North Toledo Old Timers Assn., Old ewsboys Goodfellow Assn., Pi Sigma Alpha, Delta Theta Phi.

DOUGLAS, CHARLES W., lawyer; b. Chgo., Apr. 1, 1948; BA, Northwestern U., 1970; JD, Harvard U., 1974. Bar: Ill. 1974, U.S. Dist. Ct. (no. dist.) Ill. 1974, U.S. Dist. Ct. (ea. dist.) Wis. 1997, U.S. Ct. Appeals (6th cir.) 1978, U.S. Ct. Appeals (9th cir.) 1981, U.S. Ct. Appeals (2nd cir.) 1983, U.S. Ct. Appeals (7th cir.) 1984, U.S. Ct. Appeals (11th cir.) 1999. Ptnr. Sidley Austin Brown & Wood LLP, Chgo., 1980—, exec. com., 1989—, mgmt. com. (chmn., 1999-), 1993—, and mng. ptnr. Chgo. office. Mem.: Phi Beta Kappa. Office: Sidley Austin Brown & Wood LLP Bank 1 Plz 10 S Dearborn St Chicago IL 60603 Office Phone: 312-853-7706. Office Fax: 312-853-7036. Business E-Mail: cdouglas@sidley.com.

DOUGLAS, GEORGE HALSEY, language educator, writer; b. East Orange, NJ, Jan. 9, 1934; s. Halsey M. and Harriet Elizabeth (Goldbach) D.; m. Rosalind Braun, June 19, 1961; 1 son, Philip. AB with honors in Philosophy, Lafayette Coll., 1956; MA, Columbia U., 1966; PhD, U. Ill., 1968. Tech. editor Bell Tel. Labs., Whippany, NJ, 1958—59; editor Agrl. Expt. Sta. U. Ill., Urbana, 1961—66; instr. dept. English Agrl. Expt. Sta., U. Ill., Urbana, 1966—68, asst. prof. English, 1968—77, assoc. prof. English, 1977—88, prof. English, 1989—. Author: H.L. Mencken Critic of American Life, 1978, The Teaching of Business Communication, 1978, Rail City: Chicago and Its Railroads, 1981, Edmund Wilson's America, 1983, Women of the Twenties, 1986, The Early Days of Radio Broadcasting, 1987, The Smart Magazines, 1991, All Aboard: The Railroad in American Life, 1992, Education Without Impact: How Our Universities Fail the Young, 1992, Skyscraper: A Social History of the Tall Building in America, 1996, Postwar America, 1998, The Golden Age of the Newspaper, 1999; editor numerous books; contbr. articles to profl. jours., reference books, television documentaries. Mem. MLA, Am. Studies Assn., Am. Bus. Comm. Assn. (editor jour. bus. comm. 1968-80). Home: 809 Mendota Dr Champaign IL 61820-7566 Personal E-mail: georgehdouglas@earthlink.net.

DOUGLAS, JANICE GREEN, physician, educator; b. Nashville, July 11, 1943; d. Louis D. and Electa Green. BA magna cum laude, Fish U., 1964; MD, Meharry Med. Coll., 1968. Intern Meharry Med. Coll., 1968-71; NIH tng. fellow in endocrinology, instr. internal medicine Vanderbilt U., Nashville, 1971-73; sr. staff fellow sect. on hormonal regulation NIH, 1973-76; asst. prof. medicine Case Western Res. U. Sch. Medicine, Cleve., 1976-81, assoc. prof. medicine, 1981-84, prof. medicine, 1984—; dir. hypertension renal ambulatory care svc. Univ. Hosps. Cleve., 1976-80; dir. divsn. endocrinology and hypertension dept. medicine Univ. Hosps. Cleve. and Case Western Res. U., 1988-93, vice chair acad. affairs dept. medicine, 1991-99, dir. divsn. hypertension dept. medicine, 1993—. Mem. numerous grant rev. coms.; lectr., presenter in field; atteding physician in medicine and endicrinology U. Hosps., 1987; vis. prof. SUNY, Kings County Hosp. and Health Sci. Ctr., Bklyn., 1987, Med. U. S.C., 1989, Harlem Hosp., N.Y.C., 1993, N.Y. Med. Coll., Valhalla, 1994. Mem. editl. rev. bd. Jour. Clin. Investigation, 1990—, Am. Jour. Physiology, Renal Fluid and Electrolytes, 1989-91; editl. bd. Hypertension, 1994—, Am. Soc. Clin. Investigation, 1990—, Ethnicity and Disease, 1990—, Circulation, 1993—; guest editor Jour. Clin. Investigation, U. Calif., San Diego, 1992—; assoc. editor Jour. Lab. and Clin. Medicine, 1986-90; reviewer numerous manuscripts and abstracts.; contbr. numerous articles, abstracts to profl. publs., chpts. to books. Fellow High Blood Pressure Coun., Am. Heart Assn., 1993—. Mem. Assn. Am. Physicians, Cleve. Med. Assn., Am. Soc. Hypertension, Kidney Found. Ohio, Women in Endocrinology, Inter-Am. Soc. Hypertension, Women in Nephrology, Assn. for Acad. Minority Physicians, Am. Physiology Soc., Endocrine Soc., Ctrl. Soc. for Clin. Rsch., Internat. Soc. Hypertension in Blacks, Inst. Medicine of NAS, Internat. Soc. Nephrology, Am. Soc. Nephrology, Am. Soc. Clin. Investigation, Am. Fedn. Clin. Rsch., Am. Heart Assn., Phi Beta Kappa, Alpha Omega Alpha (pres. Meharry chpt. 1968), Beta Kappa Chi.

DOUGLAS, KENNETH JAY, food products executive; b. Harbor Beach, Mich., Sept. 4, 1922; s. Harry Douglas and Xenia (Williamson) D.; m. Elizabeth Ann Schweizer, Aug. 17, 1946; children: Connie Ann, Andrew Jay. Student, U. Ill., 1940-41, 46-47; JD, Chgo. Kent Coll. Law, 1950; grad., Advanced Mgmt. Program, Harvard, 1962. Bar: Ill. 1950, Ind. 1952. Spl. agt. FBI, 1950-54; dir. indsl. relations Dean Foods Co., Franklin Park, Ill., 1954-64, v.p. fin. and adminstrn., 1964-70, chmn. bd., chief exec. officer, 1970-87, chmn. bd., 1987-89, vice-chmn., 1989-92. Bd. dirs. Andrew Corp. Mem. Chgo. Com. With USNR, 1944-46. Mem. Chgo. Club, Econ. Club, Execs. Club, Comml. Club (Chgo.), Oak Park Country Club, River Forest Tennis Club, Old Baldy Country Club (Wyo.). Republican. Home: 1207 Jackson Ave River Forest IL 60305-1107 E-mail: kenmilk@aol.com.

DOUGLAS, WILLIAM, dental educator, biomedical research administrator; b. Belfast, No. Ireland, Aug. 18, 1938; Am. citizen; married; 2 children. BS, Queen's U., Belfast, 1960, MS, 1961, PhD in Chemistry and Biomaterials, 1965; BDS, Guy's Hosp., London, 1970. Asst. lectr. in chemistry Queen's U., 1961-65; tchr. clin. dentistry Sch. Dentistry, Cardiff, Wales, 1965-67, lectr. dental materials, 1971-78; assoc. prof. U. Minn., Mpls., 1978-85, dir. dental materials Sch. Dentistry, 1978—, H.L. Anderson endowed prof., 1985—. Cons. in field. Recipient IR-100 award Jour. Rsch. and Devel., 1983; NIH grantee, 1984—. Fellow Acad. Dental Materials; mem. Internat. Assn. Dental Rsch. Office: U Minn Dental Rsch Ctr Biomaterials and Biomechanics 16-212 Moos Tower 515 Delaware St SE Minneapolis MN 55455

DOUGLASS, BRUCE E., physician; b. Berwyn, Ill., Sept. 26, 1917; s. Frank Lionel and Helen Mary (Eccles) D.; m. Charlotte Maurer Natwick, Oct. 14, 1942; children: Jean N., Bruce G., John F. BA, U. Wis., 1938, MD, 1942; MS in Medicine, U. Minn., 1949. Intern Med. Coll. of Va., Richmond, 1942-43; resident in internal medicine Mayo Clinic, Rochester, Minn., 1947-50, mem. staff, 1949—, chmn. divsn. preventive medicine, 1962—; dir. Mayo Clinic (Mayo sect. of Patient and Health Edn.), 1976—. Dir. Occupational Health Inst., Chgo., 1968— Author: Anatomy of the Portal Vein and Its Tributaries, 1949, The Problem of Benign Bronchial Obstruction, 1954, Predicting Disease: Is It Possible? 1971, Health Problems of Hospital Employees, 1971, Examining Healthy Persons: How and How Often? 1980. Chmn. Rochester Music Bd., 1960-70; v.p. Minn. Zool. Soc., 1974-77. Served to capt. M.C. AUS, 1944-47. Fellow Am. Acad. Occupational Medicine (Keogh award 1981), Am. Occupational Med. Assn. (pres. 1977-78, Meritorious Service award 1979); mem. AMA (Physician's Recognition award 1974-77, chmn. sect. council on preventive medicine 1978-80, del. for occupational med. to ho. of dels. 1978-85), Minn. Med. Assn. (chmn. com. on public health edn. 1979), Ramazzini Soc., Assn. Tchrs. Preventive Medicine, Am. Coll. Preventive Medicine, Minn. Zool. Soc., Sigma Xi, Phi Kappa Phi, Sigma Phi, Nu Sigma Nu. Office: Mayo Clinic Rochester MN 55905-0001 Home: Charter House 211 2d St NW #1306 Rochester MN 55901 Office Phone: 507-289-1002, 507-284-2511.

DOULL, JOHN, toxicologist, pharmacologist; b. Baker, Mont., Sept. 13, 1922; s. John G. and Vivian (Kelling) D.; m. Vera Orsborn, Mar. 1, 1958; children: Ellen, John, James. BS, Mont. State U., 1944; MD, PhD, U. Chgo., 1953. From asst. to assoc. prof. U. Chgo., 1946-67, asst. dir. Toxicity Lab.; prof. Med. Sch. U. Kans., Kansas City, 1967—, dir. Ctr. for Environ. Health, 1985-89, now prof. emeritus. Chair com. on toxicology NRC/Nat. Acad. Sci., Washington, 1985-93; mem. sci. adv. panel EPA, Washington, 1980-89. Editor: Textbook of Toxicology, 1975, 2d edit., 1980, 3d edit., 1986, 4th edit., 1991. With USN, 1944-46, PTO. Recipient Disting. Med. Alumni award U. Chgo., 1991, Founder's award Chem. Inst. of Toxicology, 1996. Mem. Am. Bd. Toxicology (pres. 1982-83), Soc. of Toxicology (pres. 1986-87). Office: U Kans Med Ctr Dept Pharmacology Rainbow At 39th Kansas City KS 66160-0001 E-mail: jdoull@kume.edu.

DOUT, ANNE JACQUELINE, manufacturing and sales company executive; b. Detroit, Mar. 13, 1955; d. George Edwin and Virginia Irene Boesinger; m. James Edward Dout, July 16, 1977; 1 child, Brian Ross Student, Macomb C.C., 1972—74; BBA, We. Mich. U., 1976; MBA, Duquesne U., 1982. Cert. cash mgr. Internal auditor Koppers Co. Inc., Pitts., 1976—78, cash analyst, 1978—79, supr. cash ops., 1979—80, mgr. cash ops., 1980—81, mgr. cash ops., asst. treas., 1981—87, dir. treasury svcs., asst. treas., 1987—88; corp. staff v.p., asst. treas. IMCERA Group Inc., Northbrook, Ill., 1988—91; v.p., treas. IMCERA Group, Inc., Northbrook, 1991—94; exec. v.p., CFO Champion Enterprises, Inc., Auburn Hills, Mich., 1994—98; pres. JJB Enterprises, Inc., Rochester Hills, Mich., 1998—2001; sr. v.p., CFO Pella Corp., Iowa, 2002—. Bd. dirs. Cavco Industries Inc., Iowa Coll. Found. Bd., Sch. Specialty, Inc. Mem. allocations com. United Way, Pitts., 1979-83; bd. dirs. N.E. Lake County Coun. Boy Scouts Am., v.p. adminstrn., 1989-92; bd. dirs. Barat Coll., Lake Forest, Ill., 1992-94, U. Mich. Cancer Found.; bd. visitors Sch. Bus., Oakland U., 1994-2004; devel. com. Mich. Womens Found, 1996-2000 Mem. Treas. Mgmt. Assn. (exec. com. 1988-90, govt. rels. com. 1984-86, bd. dirs. 1986-89, strategic plan com. 1987-90), Gov. Coun. Edn., Fin. Exec. Inst., Mid Am. Com., Econ. Club, Exec. Club, Womens Econ. Club Office: Pella Corp 102 Main St Pella IA 50219

DOVER, MARK A., lawyer; b. Kansas City, Kans., 1961; BS, St. Mary Coll., 1987; JD with distinction, U. Mo., Kansas City, 1992. Bar: Mo. 1992, Kans. 1993. Law clk. to Hon. Elmo B. Hunter US Dist Ct.; ptnr. Nat. Products Liability Litig. Div. Shook, Hardy & Bacon LLP, Kansas City, Mo. Mem.: Mo. Orgn. of Defense Lawyers, Kansas City Met. Bar Assn., Wyandotte County Bar Assn., Mo. Bar Assn. Office: Shook, Hardy & Bacon LLP 2555 Grand Blvd Kansas City MO 64108 Office Phone: 816-559-2114. Office Fax: 816-421-5547. E-mail: mdover@shb.com.

DOW, SIMON, artistic director, choreographer; b. Australia; Diploma, Australian Ballet Sch. Joined Australian Ballet, Stuttgart (Germany) Ballet; joined, prin. dancer Wash. Ballet, 1979; prin. dancer Australian Ballet, 1982-85, San Francisco Ballet, 1985-88, Boston Ballet, 1988-90; freelance guest artist and master tchr., 1990; assoc. artistic dir. Wash. Ballet, 1992-93, 96-97; art dir. Milw. Ballet Co., 1999—2002; artistic dir. West Australian Ballet, Perth, Australia, 2003—. Master tchr. Australian Ballet, Australian Ballet Sch., Sydney Dance Co., NSW Coll. Dance, Am. Ballet Theatre, Boston Ballet, Met. Opera Ballet, Feld Ballet, Milw. Ballet, Internat. Tanz Wochen, Vienna, Austria, Frankfurt Ballet, Germany, Les Grands Ballet Cans.; tchr. Wash. Sch. Ballet, David Howard Sch. Dance, NY; jury mem. 4th Internat. Ballet Competition, Helsinki, USA Internat. Ballet Competition, 2006; bd. dirs. Ausdance WA; apptd. to dance bd. Australia Coun., 2004—; choreographer Milw. BAllet, West Australia Ballet, Theaterhaus, Stuttgart, Joyce Soho, NYC, Steps Beyond, NYC, St. Mark's Ch., NYC, NY Festival Ballet, Florentine Opera, Milw., Jackson Internat. Ballet Competition. Guest appearances include Mann Performing Arts Ctr., Phila., Spoleto Festival, Wolf Trap Farm park, Jacob's Pillow Dance Festival, Pendleton Music Festival, Detroit Symphony; choreographer (ballets) Wash. Ballet, N.Y. Festival Ballet, Boston Ballet, Theater Artaud, San Francisco, Cin. Dance Pl., Theaterhaus, Stuttgart, Germany, St. Mark's Ch., N.Y.C., The Joyce Soho. Recipient Cecchetti Jr. medal, Best Ptnr. award, Internat. Ballet Competition, 1981. Office: West Australian Ballet PO Box 7228 Cloisters Sq Perth 6850 Australia Office Phone: 08-9481-0407.

DOWD, DAVID D., JR., federal judge; b. Cleve., Jan. 31, 1929; m. Joyce; children— Cindy, David, Doug, Mark BA, Coll. Wooster, 1951; JD, U. Mich., 1954. Ptnr. Dowd & Dowd, Massillon, Ohio, 1954-55, ptnr., 1957-75; asst. pros. atty. Stark County, 1961-67, pros. atty., 1967-75; judge Ohio 5th Dist. Ct. Appeals, 1975-80, Ohio Supreme Ct., 1980-81; ptnr. Black, McCuskey, Souers & Arbaugh, Canton, Ohio, 1981-82; judge U.S. Dist. Ct. (no. dist.) Ohio, 1982—, now sr. judge, 1996—. Office: US Dist Ct 2 S Main St Akron OH 44308-1813

DOWD, EDWARD L., JR., lawyer, former prosecutor; s. Edward L. Dowd; m. Jill Goessling; 3 children. JD with distinction, St. Mary's Univ. With Dowd, Dowd & Dowd; from asst. U.S. atty. to chief narcotics sect., regional dir. south cen. region Pres.'s Organized Crime Drug Enforcement Task Force U.S. Atty.'s Office, 1979-84; pvt. practice, 1984-93; U.S. atty. ea. dist. of Mo. U.S. Dept. Justice, St. Louis, 1993-99; dep. spl. counsel to John C. Danforth Spl. Counsel Waco Investigation, 1999; ptnr. Bryan Cave LLP, St. Louis, 1999—2006, Dowd Bennett LLP, St. Louis, 2006—. Office: Dowd Bennett LLP 7733 Forsyth Blvd Ste 1410 Saint Louis MO 63105 Office Phone: 314-889-7300. Business E-Mail: edowd@dowdbennett.com.

DOWD, THOMAS F., lawyer; b. Boston, 1943; AB, Harvard U., 1965; JD, Case Western Reserve U., 1974. Bar: Ohio 1974, DC 1989, Mo. 1999. Ptnr. Baker & Hostetler, Washington; named ptnr. Bryan, Cave, McPheeters & Roberts, Washington, 1989; sr. v.p., gen. counsel, sec. Graybar Electric Co. Inc., St. Louis, 1997—. Adv. coun. Nat. Assn. Minority and Women-Owned Law Firms, 2004—. Editor articles Case Western Reserve Law Review, 1973-74. Mem. Order of Coif. Office: Graybar Electric Co Inc 34 N Meramec Ave Saint Louis MO 63105

DOWDLE, JAMES C., cable television executive; b. Oklahoma City, Oct. 21, 1963; s. James Charles and Sally Dowdle; m. Mary Joan Dowdle, Sept. 22, 1990; children: Erin, Charlie, Colin. BA, John Carroll U., Cleve., 1986. Account exec. WSBK TV, Boston, 1986-89, Turner Broadcasting, Chgo., 1989-94; sales mgr. TV Food etwork, Chgo., 1994—, v.p., midwest sales mgr., 1994—. Pres. RoDan Fest, Inc., Chgo., 1996—; bd. dirs. Chgo. Youth Ctrs., 1990—. Office: TV Food Network 333 N Michigan Ave Chicago IL 60601-3901

DOWELL, MICHAEL BRENDAN, chemist; b. NYC, Nov. 18, 1942; s. William Henry and Anne Susan (Cannon) D.; m. Gail Elizabeth Renton, Mar. 16, 1968; children: Rebecca S. Hall, Margaret A. Scott. BS, Fordham U., 1963; PhD, Pa. State U., 1967. Physicist U.S. Army Frankford Arsenal, Phila., 1967-69; rsch. scientist Parma Tech. Ctr., Union Carbide Corp., Ohio, 1969-74, devel. mgr. carbon fiber applications, 1974-76, group leader metals and ceramics rsch., 1976-80, sr. group leader process rsch., 1980-82, mgr. market devel., 1982-92, Praxair Advanced Ceramics Inc. (formerly Union Carbide Corp), Ohio, 1992-93, Advanced Ceramics Corp., Cleve., 1993—, v.p. tech., 1999—2002; v.p. 5iTech, LLC, Cleve., 2003—06; engring. mgr. Powdermet Inc., Euclid, Ohio, 2007—. Mem. materials tech. adv. com. U.S. Dept. Commerce, 1994—2001; lectr. ops. mgmt. Case Western Res. U., 2001—03. Contbr. articles to profl. jours. Capt. ordnance AUS, 1967—69. Mem. Am. Chem. Soc., Am. Phys. Soc., U.S. Advanced Ceramics Assn. (bd. dirs. 1988-96), Am. Soc. Metals Internat. (govt. and pub. affairs com. 1989—), Soc. Prof. Fellows Case Western Res. U., Phi Lambda Upsilon. Roman Catholic. Home: 368 N Main St Hudson OH 44236-2246 Office: Powdermet Inc 24112 Rockwell Dr Euclid OH 44117 Office Phone: 216-404-0053 ext. 112. Personal E-mail: mbdowell@alltel.net.

DOWLING, THOMAS ALLAN, retired mathematics professor; b. Little Rock, Feb. 19, 1941; s. Charles and Esther (Jensen) D.; m. Nancy Lenthe D.; children: Debra Lynn, David Thomas. BS, Creighton U., 1962; PhD, U. N.C., 1967. Research assoc. U. N.C.-Chapel Hill, 1967-69, asst. prof., 1969-72; assoc. prof. math. Ohio State U., Columbus, 1972-82, prof., 1982—. Ops. researcher U.S. Govt., Patrick AFB, Fla., 1963-64; conf. organizer U. N.C., 1967, 70, Ohio State U., 1978, 82, 88, 92, 94, 98, 00, 02, 03, 05. Editor: Combinatorial Mathematics and its Applications, 1967, 70; contbr. article to profl. jours.; discoverer Dowling lattices. NSF grantee, 1972-80; fellow NASA, 1968 Mem. AAUP, Am. Math. Soc., Math. Assn. Am., Inst. Combinatorics and Applications. Democrat. Home: 2423 High Lonesome Trl Lafayette CO 80026-9393 Office Phone: 614-292-5013. Personal E-mail: dowling.ta@gmail.com. E-mail: tdowling@math.ohio-state.edu.

DOWNEY, CHRISTINE, state legislator; b. Abilene, Kans., Mar. 26, 1949; children: Amy, Matthew, Erin. Elem. and mid. sch. tchr., 1975-93; mem. Kans. Senate from 31st. dist., Topeka, 1996—. Adj. prof. Bethel Coll., 1990-93; mem. edn. com. Kans. Senate, agriculture com., chldn's issues com., legis. ednl. planning com., ways and means com. Pres., bd. dirs. Newton Cmty. Children's Choir, 1991-92. Mem. Kans. Nat. Edn. Assn. (pres. 1990), Newton Nat. Edn. Assn. (pres. 1989). Home: 10320 N Wheat State Rd Inman KS 67546-8109

DOWNEY, DEBORAH ANN, systems specialist; b. Xenia, Ohio, July 22, 1958; d. Nathan Vernon and Patricia Jaunita (Ward) D. Assoc. in Applied Sci., Sinclair C.C., 1981, student, 1986—91; BA, Capital U., 1994. Jr. programmer, project mgr. Cole-Layer-Trumble Co., Dayton, Ohio, 1981-82; sr. programmer, analyst, project leader Systems Architects Inc., Dayton, 1982-84, Systems and Applied Sci. Corp. (now Computer Sci. Corp.), Dayton, 1984; analyst Unisys, Dayton, 1984-87; systems programmer Computer Sci. Corp., Fairborn, Ohio, 1987—. Cons. computer software M&S Garage/Body Shop, Beavercreek, Ohio, 1986-87. Mem. NAFE, Am. Motorcyclist Assn., Sinclair C. C. Alumni Assn., Cherokee Nation Okla., Cherokee Nat. Hist. Soc. Democrat. Mem. United Ch. Of Christ. Avocations: motorcycles, miniatures, sports, needlecrafts.

DOWNING, DAVID, science administrator; BS in Aerospace, U. Mich., 1962, MS in Instrumentation, 1963; ScD in Instrumentation Engring., MIT, 1970. Project mgr. advance guidance, control, and display for gen. aviation aircraft NASA's Electronic Rsch. Ctr. and Langley Rsch. Ctr.; dir. Kans. Space Grant Consortium and Kans. NASA EPSCor Program; prof. aerospace engring. dept. U. Kans. Mem. faculty Boston U., Christopher Newport Coll. Recipient NASA Group Achievement award, 1979, Sch. Engring. Miller award for svc., 1992. Fellow: AIAA (assoc.); mem.: ASEE, SAE. Office: Kansas Space Grant Consortium 1530 W 15-1132 Lawrence KS 66045-7609

DOWNING, ROBERT ALLAN, lawyer; b. Kenosha, Wis., Jan. 6, 1929; s. Leo Vertin and Mayme C. (Kennedy) D.; m. JoAnn C. Cramton, Apr. 14, 1951 (div. Sept. 1977); children: Robert A., Kevin C., Tracey Downing Clark, Gregory E.; m. Joan Govan Reiter, Oct. 29, 1977; 1 child, Charles E. Reiter III. BS, U. Wis., 1950, JD, 1956. Bar: Wis. 1956, Ill. 1956, U.S. Supreme Ct. 1965. Assoc. Sidley & Austin, Chgo., 1956-64, ptnr., 1964-94, counsel, 1994-97, Ruff, Weidenaar & Reidy, Ltd., Chgo., 1997—. Trustee (life), former pres. Episcopal Charities and Cmty. Svcs., Chgo. Diocese. Served to lt. USN, 1950-53, Korea. Fellow Am. Coll. Trial Lawyers; mem. ABA, Soc. Trial Lawyers, Ill. Bar Assn., Chgo. Bar Assn., Wis. Bar Assn., 7th Cir. Bar Assn., Union League Club, Law Club, Legal Club, MidDay Club, Westmoreland Country Club. Republican. Episcopalian. Office: Ruff Weidenaar & Reidy Ltd 222 N Lasalle St Ste 1525 Chicago IL 60601-1003

DOWNS, ROBERT K., lawyer; BA, Grinnell Coll.; JD, Stetson U. Bar: Ill., Fla., US Supreme Ct. Ptnr. Downs Law Offices PC. Elected Ill. Ho. of Reps. 79th Gen. Assembly; chmn. emeritus Wednesday Journal Inc. Recipient Alumni Achievement award, Grinnell Coll., 1998, Ethel Parker award, Independent Voters of Ill., Best Legislator award. Mem.: Assn. of Family and Conciliation Cts., Justinian Soc. of Lawyers, North Suburban Bar Assn., DuPage County Bar Assn., West Suburban Bar Assn., Chgo. Bar Assn., Ill. Trial Lawyers Assn., Am. Bar Assn. (Pro Bono svc. award 1995), admitted to practice U.S. Supreme Ct., Fla. State Bar Assn., Ill. State Bar Assn. (bd. of gov. 1996—2002, pres.-elect 2004, pres. 2005—). Office: Downs Law Offices PC Ste 1870 150 N Wacker Dr Chicago IL 60606 Office Phone: 312-781-1963. Office Fax: 312-781-1962. Business E-Mail: bob@downslaw.com.

DOWNS, THOMAS K., lawyer; b. New Albany, Ind., Jan. 10, 1949; BA, Ind. U., 1977, JD magna cum laude, 1980. Bar: Ind. 1980. Ptnr., mcpl. fin. chmn. Ice Miller, Indpls. Mem. editl. bd. Mcpl. Fin. Jour., 1999—; editor Fundamentals of Mcpl. Bond Law: General Law and Professional Responsibility sects., 1994—; exec. editor Ind. Law Jour., 1979-80; contbr. author various books, including Inside the Minds: Government Contract Litigation Best Practices; contbr. articles to profl. jours. Pres. Ind. Assn. Cities and Towns Found., 1994—; mem. Lt. Gov.'s Jobs Coun. Fellow Am. Coll. Bond Counsel (founding mem., bond buyer midwest pub. fin. conf. 1998); mem. Nat. Assn. Bond Lawyers (steering com. 1985-86, 90, 92, 2000, 01, 02, chmn. bond banks workshop 1985-86, tax increment workshop 1989, panelist various workshops, faculty fundamentals mcpl. bond law, opinions and profl. responsibility 1989-90, chair Ann. Washington Conf. 1996, chmn. prof. responsibility com. 2001-03), Ind. Continuing Legal Edn. Forum (chmn. mcpl. law seminars 1984-92, practical impact tax reform act of 1986, panelist mcpl. utility fin. 1988, pub. law 10 1991), Ind. Mcpl. Lawyers Assn., Inc. (bd. dirs. 1983—), Order of Coif, Assn. Ind. Counties (adv. com., gen. counsel), Ind. Assn. Cities and Towns (exec. com., special counsel), Ind. Comn. for the Purchase of Products and Svcs. of Persons with Disabilities (bd. dirs.). Office: Ice Miller LLP Ste 3100 1 American Sq Indianapolis IN 46282-0200 Office Phone: 317-236-2339. Business E-Mail: Thomas.Downs@icemiller.com.

DOWTY, ALAN KENT, political scientist, educator; b. Greenville, Ohio, Jan. 15, 1940; s. Paul Willard and Ethel Lovella (Harbaugh) D.; m. Nancy Ellen Gordon, Sept. 8, 1961 (div. 1972); children: Merav Aurli, Tamar Eliea, Gidon Yair; m. Gail Gaynell Schupack, Jan. 1, 1973; children: Rachel Miriam, Rafael Jonathan; 1 stepchild, David Freeman. BA, Shimer Coll., 1959; MA, U. Chgo., 1960, PhD, 1963. Lectr. Hebrew U., Jerusalem, 1965-72, sr. lectr., 1972-75; assoc. prof. U. Notre Dame, Ind., 1975-78, prof. polit. sci. Ind., 1978—2004; Kahanoff chair Israeli studies U. Calgary, 2003—06. Exec. dir. Leonard Davis

Inst., Jerusalem, 1972-74; editl. bd. Middle East Rev., N.Y.C., 1977-90; project dir. Twentieth Century Fund, N.Y.C., 1983-85; reporter experts meeting Internat. Inst. Human Rights, Strasbourg, France, 1989. Author: The Limits of American Isolation, 1971, Middle East Crisis, 1984 (Quincy Wright award 1985), The Arab-Israel Conflict (with others), 1984, Closed Borders, 1987, The Jewish State, 1998, Israel/Palestine, 2005; book reviewer Jerusalem Post, 1964-75; contbr. articles to profl. jours. Exec. com. Am. Profs. for Peace in Mid. East, 1976-90; witness U.S. Senate Fgn. Rels. Com., Washington, 1976; nat. adv. com. Union of Couns. for Soviet Jews, Washington, 1980-91. Woodrow Wilson fellow, 1959-60; Rothschild fellow Hebrew U., 1963-64; resident fellow Adlai Stevenson Inst., Chgo., 1971-72; Skirball fellow Oxford Ctr. for Hebrew and Jewish Studies, 2000; recipient Charles W. Ramsdell award So. Hist. Assn., 1966; grantee Twentieth Century Fund, N.Y.C., 1983. Mem. Am. Polit. Sci. Assn., Internat. Polit. Sci. Assn., Internat. Studies Assn. (exec. com. 1977-79, Quincy Wright award 1985), Assn. Israel Studies (pres. 2005-07). Jewish. Avocations: travel, jewish studies. Office: 615 S Greenlawn Ave South Bend IN 46615

DOYLE, JILL J., elementary school principal; Prin. George P Way Elem. Sch., Bloomfield Hills, Mich., 1987—. Recipient Elem. Sch. Recognition award U.S. Dept. Edn., 1989-90. Office: George P Way Elem Sch 765 W Long Lake Rd Bloomfield Hills MI 48302-1552

DOYLE, JIM (JAMES EDWARD), governor, former state attorney general; b. Washington, Nov. 23, 1945; s. James E. and Ruth (Bachhuber) Doyle; m. Jessica Laird, Dec. 21, 1966; children: Augustus, Gabriel. Student, Stanford U., 1963—66; AB in History, U. Wis., 1967; JD cum laude, Harvard U., 1972. Bar: Ariz. 1973, Wis. 1975, U.S. Dist. Ct. N.Mex. 1973, U.S. Dist. Ct. Ariz. 1973, U.S. Dist. Ct. Utah 1973, U.S. Dist. Ct. (we. dist.) Wis. 1975, U.S. Dist. Ct. (ea. dist.) Wis. 1976, U.S. Ct. Appeals (10th cir.) 1974, U.S. Ct. Appeals (7th cir.) 1985, U.S. Supreme Ct. 1989. Vol. Peace Corps, Tunisia, 1967—69; atty. DNA Legal Svcs., Chinle, Ariz., 1972—75; ptnr. Jacobs & Doyle, Madison, Wis., 1975—77; dist. atty. Dane County, Madison, 1977—83; ptnr. Doyle & Ritz, Madison, 1983—90; of counsel Lawton & Cates, Madison, 1990—91; atty. gen. State of Wis., Madison, 1991—2002, gov., 2003—. Mem.: ABA, 7th Cir. Bar Assn. (chmn. criminal law sect. 1988—89), Wis. Bar Assn. (bd. dirs. criminal law sect. 1988). Democrat. Roman Catholic. Office: Office of Governor PO Box 7863 Madison WI 53707 also: Office of Governor Rm 560 819 North 6th St Milwaukee WI 53203 Office Phone: 608-266-1212, 414-227-4344. Office Fax: 608-267-8983.

DOYLE, JOHN ROBERT, lawyer; b. Chgo., May 12, 1950; s. Frank Edward and Dorothy (Bolton) D.; m. Kathleen Julius, June 14, 1974; children: Melissa, Maureen. BA magna cum laude, St. Louis U., 1971; JD summa cum laude, DePaul U., 1976. Bar: Ill. 1976, U.S. Dist. Ct. 1976, U.S. Dist. Ct. (no. dist.) Ill. 1982, Ill. Trial Bar 1982, U.S. Ct. Appeals (7th cir.) 1982. Ptnr. McDermott, Will & Emery, Chgo., 1976—. Mem. Chgo. Bar Assn. (jud. investigative hearing panel 1986-88), Phi Beta Kappa. Office: McDermott Will & Emery 227 W Monroe St Ste 3100 Chicago IL 60606-5096 Office Phone: 312-984-7735. Business E-Mail: jdoyle@mwe.com.

DOYLE, JOSEPH E., lawyer, manufacturing executive; BA, U. Ill.; JD, U. Minn. Atty. Sonnenschein Nath & Rosenthal; ptnr. Jenner & Block LLP; ptnr. Corp. and Securities Practice Mayer, Brown, Rowe & Maw LLP, 2001—07; v.p., gen. counsel, sec. Pactiv Corp., Lake Forest, Ill., 2007—. Office: Pactiv Corp 1900 W Field Ct Lake Forest IL 60045

DOYLE, MICHAEL J., corporate financial executive; Grad, Georgetown U.; post grad, U. Dallas. Previously with PNC Bank, Huntington Bank, Tex. Commerce Bank, Mellon Bank and Irving Trust Co.; sr. v.p., portfolio risk mgr. Star Banc Corp., later named U.S. Bancorp, 1994—98; sr. v.p.,mgr. Western credit approval region US Bancorp, 1998—99, exec. v.p., chief approval officer, 1999—2001, exec. v.p., sr. credit officer, 2001, exec. v.p., 2001—07, chief credit officer, 2003—07, adv. to CEO, 2007—. Office: US Bancorp 800 Nicollet Mall Minneapolis MN 55402

DOYLE, REBECCA CARLISLE, state agency administrator; m. Ken Doyle; children: Eric, Ben. BS, U. Ill., 1975, MS, 1977. Pvt. practice, Ill.; dir. Ill. Agriculture Dept., Springfield, 1991—. Mem. Internat. Agriculture Mgmt. Assn., Nat. Assn. State Depts. Agriculture (officer), Mid-Am. Internat. Agri-Trade Council (officer), Women Execs. State Govt. Office: Illinois Dept Agriculture State Fairgrounds PO Box 19281 Springfield IL 62794-9281

DRACH, JOHN CHARLES, research scientist, educator; b. Cin., Sept. 25, 1939; s. Charles Louis and Edrie B. Drach; m. E. Jean Flamm, June 20, 1964; children: Laura J., Diane E. BS in Pharmacy, U. Cin., 1961, MS in Pharm. Chemistry, 1963, PhD in Biochemistry, 1966. From assoc. rsch. scientist to rsch. scientist Parke, Davis and Co., Ann Arbor, Mich., 1966-70; asst. prof. U. Mich. Dental Sch., Ann Arbor, 1970-74; assoc. prof. U. Mich., Ann Arbor, 1974-80; assoc. prof. medicinal chemistry U. Mich. Coll. Pharmacy, Ann Arbor, 1978-80; prof. U. Mich., Ann Arbor, 1980—; chmn. dept. oral biology U. Mich. Dental Sch., Ann Arbor, 1985-87, chmn. dept. biologic and materials scis., 1987-95; vis. prof. divsn. virology Burroughs Wellcome Co., Research Triangle Park, NC, 1994. Cons. Adria Labs., Am. Inst. Chem., Am. Pharm. Assn., AMA, Chartwell, Kimberly-Clark, 1976-83. Author: Clinical Pharmacology, 1986; mem. editorial bd. Elsevier Sci. Pubs., 1984—, Antiviral Chemistry & Chemotherapy, 1996—; contbr. articles to profl. jours.; patentee antiviral drugs. NSF summer fellow, 1963; NIH grad. fellow, 1964-66; NIH grantee, 1970—. Fellow: AAAS; mem.: Internat. Soc. Antiviral Rsch. (archivist 1992—, chmn. travel grants com. 1998—2002, pres. 2002—04, chmn. nomination com. 2006—, chmn. conf. com. 2004—06), Am. Soc. Microbiology (mem. editl. bd. 1982—91), Am. Chem. Soc., Am. Assn. Oral Biology, Dental Edn. Assn. (pres. oral biology sect. 1990—91), Sigma Xi, Omicron Kappa Upsilon, Rho Chi. Home: 1372 Barrister Rd Ann Arbor MI 48105-2875 Office: U Mich 1011 N University Ave Ann Arbor MI 48109-1078 Office Phone: 734-763-5579. E-mail: jcdrach@umich.edu.

DRAFT, HOWARD CRAIG, advertising executive; b. 1953; m. Elvy L. Leake; children: Andrew, Anna, Margaret. BA in Philosophy and Art History, Ripon Coll., 1974. With Draft Worldwide, Chgo., 1978—, gen. mgr. NY, 1982-86, pres., 1986-88, chmn., CEO, 1988—2006, Draftfcb, Chgo., 2006—. Bd. mem. Direct Mgtg. Assn. Ednl. Found.; bd. dirs. Ad Coun., 2007—; spkr. in field. Trustee Pedia. AIDS Chgo., Herbert G. Birch Svcs.; bd. mem. Chgo. Old Town Sch. Folk Music; trustee Ripon Coll.; bd. dirs. Chgo. After Sch. Matters. Named one of 100 Best and Brightest, Advt. Age, one of The Best, The Brightest, The Most Powerful, Target Mktg., One of 50 Who Matter Now, Business 2.0, 2007, named Direct Marketer of the Yr., Chgo. Assn. Direct Mktg., 1999. Office: Draftfcb 633 N Saint Clair St Chicago IL 60611-3234 Office Phone: 312-944-3500.

DRAGONETTE, RITA HOEY, public relations executive; b. Chgo., Nov. 4, 1950; d. Louis D. and Edith M. (Finnemann) Hoey; m. Joseph John Dragonette, Sept. 4, 1982 (dec.). BA in English and History, No. Ill. U., 1972. Asst. dir. Nat. Assn. Housing and Human Devel., Chgo., 1975; pub. rels. account exec. Weber Cohn & Riley, Chgo., 1975-76; publicity coord. U.S. Gypsum Co., Chgo., 1976-77; with Daniel J. Edelman, Inc., Chgo., 1977-84, sr. v.p., 1981-84; exec. v.p. Dragonette, Inc., Chgo., 1984-91, pres., 1991-99, GCI Dragonette, Chgo., 1999—2002; prin. Dragonette Cons., 2002—. Home: Ste 422 680 North Lake Shore Dr Chicago IL 60611 E-mail: rmdragonette@ameritech.net.

DRAKE, GEORGE ALBERT, retired academic administrator, historian, educator; b. Springfield, Mo., Feb. 25, 1934; s. George Bryant and Alberta (Stimson) D.; m. Susan Martha Ratcliff, June 25, 1960; children: Christopher George, Cynthia May, Melanie Susan. AB, Grinnell Coll., 1956; Fulbright scholar, U. Paris, 1956-57; AB (Rhodes scholar), Oxford U., 1959, MA, 1963; BD, U. Chgo., 1962, MA, 1963, PhD (Rockefeller fellow), 1965; LLD (hon.), Colo. Coll., 1980, Ripon Coll., 1982; LHD (hon.), Ill. Coll., 1985, Ursinus Coll., 1988, Doane Coll., 1995, Morningside Coll., 1998. Instr. history Grinnell Coll., 1960-61, pres., 1979-91, prof., 1979—, prof. emeritus, 2004—, pres. emeritus, 2006—. Asst. prof., assoc. prof., prof. history Colo. Coll., Colorado Springs, 1964-79, acting dean of Coll., 1967-68, dean, 1969-73 Trustee Grinnell Coll., 1970-79, Penrose Hosp., 1976-84, Grinnell Gen. Hosp., 1980-86, Doane Coll., 1995—; bd. dirs. Iowa Peace Inst., 1994—2004, chair, 1996-99; vol. U.S. Peace Corps, Lesotho, 1991-93; commr. North Ctrl. Assn. Colls. and Schs., 1998-2001; bd. dirs. FINE Found., 1998—, chair 2003—. NEH fellow, 1974. Mem. Am. Hist. Assn., Am. Ch. History Soc., Nat. Coll. Athletic Assn. (pres. commn. 1984-89), at. Merit Scholarship Corp. Home Phone: 641-236-8243; Office Phone: 641-269-3720. Business E-Mail: drake@grinnell.edu.

DRAKE, GRACE L., retired state senator, cultural organization administrator; b. New London, Conn., May 25, 1926; d. Daniel Harvey and Marion Gertrude (Wiech) Driscoll; m. William Lee Drake, June 9, 1946 (dec.); 1 child, Sandra Drake Sparber. With Am. Photographic Corp., NYC, 1944-72; senator State of Ohio, Columbus, 1984—2001; dir. Ohio Ctr. Advancement Women in Pub. Svc., 2001—. Chair Cuyahoga County Rep. Exec. Commn.; alumnus Leadership Cleve.; active March of Dimes State Bd., HealthSpace Cleve. Bd., Masonic Learning Ctrs. Bd., Positive Edn. Program Bd., Coun. on Older Persons Bd., Northeast Ohio using Initiative Bd. Named Legislator of the Yr., Nat. Rep. Legis.'s Assn., 1988, Grace L. Drake Agrl. Lab. in her honor, Ohio State U., 2003; named to Ohio Women's Hall of Fame, 1995, Pres. James A. Garfield Hall of Fame, 2005; recipient Meritorious Svc. award, Ohio State U., 2001, Ctr. for Health Affairs, 2001, Pub. Affairs award, March of Dimes, 2001. Roman Catholic. Avocations: bridge, golf. Home: 5954 Briardale Ln Solon OH 44139-2302 Office: Cleve State Univ 2121 Euclid Ave UR 140 Cleveland OH 44115 Office Phone: 216-687-4893. Business E-Mail: gdrake@urban.csuohio.edu.

DRAKE, JACK E., state representative; b. Walnut, Iowa, July 29, 1934; Student, U. Iowa. Mem. Iowa Ho. Reps., DesMoines, 1993—, chair agr. and natural resources com., mem. appropriations com., mem. environ. protection com., mem. natural resources com. Bd. sec. Walnut Tel. Co. Pres. East Pottawattamie Ext. Coun.; past v.p. Pottawattamie County Zoning Commn.; pres., voting del. East Pottawattamie County Farm Bur.; active East Pottawattamie County Rep. Ctrl. Com. Mem.: Walnut Area Devel. Assn., Soybean Assn., Pottawattamie County Taxpayers Assn. (v.p., organizer), Corn Growers, Cattlemen's Assn. Republican. Methodist. Office: State Capitol East 12th and Grand Des Moines IA 50319 also: 52462 Juniper Rd Lewis IA 51544

DRAKE, JOHN WARREN, aviation consultant; b. Chgo., July 5, 1930; s. Robert Warren and Winifred Elizabeth (Bramhall) D.; m. Miriam Anna Engleman, Dec. 19, 1960 (div. Dec. 1985); 1 child, Robert Warren; m. Mary Pat O'Kelly, Sept. 24, 2000. BS, Rensselaer Poly. Inst., 1952; MBA, Harvard U., 1954, DBA, 1972. Rsch. assos. Aero. Rsch. Found., Cambridge, Mass., 1956-57; prin. United Rsch., Inc., Cambridge, 1957-61; v.p. Sys. Analysis and Rsch. Corp., 1961-69; prof. emeritus, air transp. area Sch. Aerospace and Astronautics Sch. Engring. Purdue U., 1972-92, mem. pres.'s coun., 1992—. Cons. in field; mem. Transp. Research Bd. RC. Author: The Administration of Transportation Modeling Projects, 1973. Served with U.S. Army, 1954-56. Mem. Air Transp. Rsch. Internat. Forum (coun.), AIAA, Soc. Automotive Engrs. Home: 341 Riverview Dr Ann Arbor MI 48104-1847

DRAKE, RICHARD FRANCIS, state legislator; b. Muscatine, Iowa, Sept. 28, 1927; s. Frank and Gladys (Young) R.; m. Shirley Jean Henke; children: Cheryll Dee, Ricky Lee. Student, Iowa State U.; BS, U.S. Naval Acad., 1950. Enlisted man USN, WWII, commd. ensign, 1950; advanced through grades to lt. comdr., 1954; comdg. officer minesweeper USS Crow, 1953—54; ret., 1954; farmer, mgr. Muscatine, 1954—; mem. Iowa Senate from 40th dist., Des Moines, 1968—. Chmn. Young Rep. Orgn. Iowa, 1954-56; adminstrv. asst. Muscatine County Rep. Com., 1956-57, chmn., 1958-66; chmn. 1st Dist. Rep. Com., 1966-72, Nat. Task Force on Rail Line Abandonment and Curtailment; chmn. states and rai problems Midwestern Coun. State Govts., 1978-79. Named One of 10 Outstanding Legislators of Yr., at. Rep. Legislators Assn. Mem. VFW, Am. Legion, Farm Bur., Masons, Elks, Order Ea. Star. Lutheran.

DRAKE, ROBERT ALAN, state legislator, animal nutritionist, mayor; b. Canton, SD, July 6, 1957; s. Theodore Francis and LaRayne Margaret (Hoffman) D.; m. Pamela Sue Wiechmann, 1977; children: R. Ryan, Kimberly Margaret, Kendra Kay. BS, S.D. State U., 1979, MS, 1981. Animal nutritionist McFleeg Feeds, Bowdle, S.D., 1981—; mayor City of Bowdle, 1988-96; mem. S.D. Ho. of Reps., Pierre, 1995-96, S.D. Senate, 1997—. Supr. Edmunds County Conservation Dist., 1984-96; chmn. .E. Coun. Govts., Aberdeen, S.D., 1992-93; pres. Bowdle Cmty. Club, 1985-86, Bowdle Devel. Corp., 1985-89. Republican. Home: 964 N Lake Dr Watertown SD 57201-5522

DRAPER, E(RNEST) LINN, JR., retired electric utility executive; b. Houston, Feb. 6, 1942; s. Ernest Linn and Marcia L. (Saylor) D.; m. Mary Deborah Doyle, June 9, 1962; children: Susan Elizabeth, Robert Linn, Barbara Ann, David Doyle. Student, Williams Coll., 1960-62; BAChemE, Rice U., 1964, BSChemE, 1965; PhD in Nuclear Engring., Cornell U., 1970. Asst. prof. nuclear engring. U. Tex., Austin, 1969-72, assoc. prof., 1972-79; tech. asst. to CEO Gulf States Utilities Co., Beaumont, Tex., 1979, v.p. nuclear tech., 1980-81, sr. v.p. engring. tech. services, 1981-82, sr. v.p. external affairs, 1982-84, sr. v.p. external affairs and prodn., 1984-85, exec. v.p. external affairs and prodn., 1985-86, vice chmn., 1985-87, COO, 1986, pres., CEO, 1986-92, chmn. bd. dirs., 1987-92; pres. AEPCo., Inc.; pres., COO Am. Electric Power Svc. Corp., Columbus, Ohio, 1992-93; chmn., pres., CEO Am. Electric Power Co. and Svc. Corp., Columbus, 1993—2004. Bd. dirs. Temple Inland Corp., Alpha Natural Resources, North-Western Corp., Alliance Data Sys., TransCan., Resources for the Future. Fellow NSF, 1965-66, AEC, 1967-68. Mem. NAE, Am. Nuclear Soc. (pres. 1984-85), Nuclear Energy Inst. (chmn. 1993-95), Edison Electric Inst. (chmn. 1996-97). E-mail: eldraper@aep.com.

DRAPER, GERALD LINDEN, retired lawyer; b. Oberlin, Ohio, July 14, 1941; s. Earl Linden and Mary Antoinette (Colloto) Draper; m. Barbara Jean Winter, Aug. 26, 1960; children: Melissa Leigh Price, Stephen Edward. BA, Muskingum Coll., 1963; JD, Northwestern U., 1966. Bar: Ohio 1966, US Dist Ct (so dist) Ohio 1966, US Ct Appeals (6th cir) 1975, US Supreme Ct 1980, US Dist Ct (no dist) Ohio 2000. Ptnr. Bricker & Eckler, Columbus, Ohio, 1966-88, Thompson, Hine & Flory, Columbus, 1989-95, Draper, Hollenbaugh, Briscoe, Yashko & Carmany, Columbus, 1996-99, Roetzel & Andress, Columbus, 1999—2004; ret. Trustee Ohio Bd. Bar Examiners, 1986—89; mem. Ohio Bd. Commn. on Unauthorized Practice of Law, 2002—, Ohio Med. Malpractice Commn., 2003—. Trustee, pres Wesley Glen Retirement Ctr, Columbus, Ohio, 1979—95; trustee Meth Elder Care Servs, Inc, 1995—, Muskingum Coll., New Concord, Ohio, 1988—92, Ohio, 1993—, vice chair, 1994—; trustee, pres Wesley Ridge Retirement Ctr, 1995—2000, treas, 2001—. Fellow: Am Bd Trial Advs (trustee Ohio chpt. 2001), Am Col Trial Lawyers; mem.: ABA (House Dels 1991—97, 1999—2001), Def Research Inst, Ohio Asn Hosp Attys, Ohio Continuing Legal Educ Inst (trustee 1992—98, chair 1997—98), Nat Conf Bar Found (trustee 1987—90, 1991—94), Columbus Bar Found (pres 1984—86), Columbus Bar Asn (pres 1982—83, Bar Serv Medal 1998), Ohio State Bar Found (trustee 1992—97), Ohio State Bar Asn (pres 1990—91). Avocations: travel, golf, photography.

DRAPER, JAMES WILSON, lawyer; b. Detroit, Dec. 26, 1926; s. Kenneth Draper and Dorothy (Wilson) Barker; m. Alice Patricia Sullivan, May 16, 1953; children: Catherine Draper Clain, Julie Draper Fazekas, James P., Martha Draper Grossman. BA, U. Mich., 1949, JD, 1951. Bar: Mich. 1951, U.S. Dist. Ct. (so. dist.) Mich. 1951, U.S. Ct. Appeals (6th cir.) 1951. Assoc. Dykema, Jones & Wheat and successor firms, Detroit, 1951-61; ptnr. Dykema Gossett, and predecessor firms, Detroit, 1961—. Past chmn. real property law sect. council State Bar Mich. Served with USN, 1944-46 Fellow Am. Coll. Real Estate Lawyers; mem. Mich. State Bar (past chmn. real property law sect., land title stds. com.), Detroit Club, Country Club Detroit (Grosse Point Farms, Mich.). Republican. Presbyterian. Home: 267 Hillcrest Ave Grosse Pointe Farms MI 48236-3622 Office: Dykema Gossett 400 Renaissance Ctr Detroit MI 48243-1603

DRAPER, NORMAN RICHARD, statistician, educator; b. Eng., Mar. 20, 1931; came to U.S., 1955; s. Norris and Helen (Draper). BA, Cambridge U., Eng., 1954, MA, 1958; PhD, U. NC, 1958. Tech. officer, statistician plastics div. Imperial Chem. Industries, 1958-60; mem. Math. Rsch. Ctr., U. Wis., Madison, 1960-61, mem. faculty, 1961—, prof. statistics, 1966-99, prof. emeritus, 1999—, chmn., 1967-73, 94-97. Vis. prof. Imperial Coll., London, fall 1967, 68. Author: (with H. Smith) Applied Regression Analysis, 1966, 3d edit., 1998, (with G.E.P. Box) Evolutionary Operation, 1969, (with W. E. Lawrence) Probability: An Introductory Course, 1970, (with G.E.P. Box) Response Surfaces, Mixtures, and Ridge Analyses, 2d edit., 2007. Recipient Max-Planck-Forschungs-Preis, Alexander von Humboldt-Stiftung, 1994. Fellow Royal Statis. Soc., Am. Statis. Assn., Inst. Math. Statistics, Am. Soc. Quality Control; mem. Internat. Statis. Inst. Address: U Wis Dept Statistics 1300 University Ave Madison WI 53706-1532

DRECHSEL, ROBERT EDWARD, journalism educator; b. Fergus Falls, Minn., Aug. 7, 1949; BA, U. Minn., 1971, MA, 1976, PhD, 1980. Reporter, city editor Daily Jour., Fergus Falls, 1971—74; instr. dept. journalism S.D. State U., Brookings, 1976—77; asst. prof. dept. tech. journalism Colo. State U., Ft. Collins, 1979—83; from asst. prof. to assoc. prof. Sch. Journalism and Mass Comm. U. Wis., Madison, 1983—91, prof., 1991—, dir., 1991—98; affiliated prof. law U. Wis., Madison, 2000—. Author: News Making in the Trial Courts, 1983; contbr. articles to profl. jours. Mem. Assn. Edn. Journalism and Mass Comm. (Krieghbaum Outstanding Achievement Rsch., Teaching & Pub. Svc. award 1989), Am. Judicature Soc., Wis. Freedom Info. Coun., Internat. Comm. Assn. Office: U Wis Sch Journalism & Mass Comm 821 University Ave Madison WI 53706-1412

DREES, BETTY, dean, educator; Interim sect. chair in diabetes, endocrinology, and metabolism Truman Med. Ctr. Hosp. Hill, exec. assoc. dean; assoc. prof., docent U. Mo.-Kansas City Sch. Medicine, 1998, interim dean, 2001, dean, prof. medicine. Office: 2411 Holmes Kansas City MO 64108

DREHER, DARRELL L., lawyer; b. Coshocton, Ohio, Dec. 16, 1944; BA, Ohio State U., 1966; JD, George Washington U., 1973. Bar: Ohio 1974. Ptnr. Dreher Langer & Tomkies L.L.P., Columbus, Ohio. Founding mem., bd. regents Am. Coll. Consumer Fin. Svcs. Lawyers; sec., v.p. governing com. of Conf. on Consumer Fin. Law. Mem. Order of Coif. Office: Dreher Langer & Tomkies LLP 2250 Huntington Ctr Columbus OH 43215

DREHER, MELANIE CREAGAN, dean, nursing educator; BSN magna cum laude, L.I. U.; D in Anthropology, Columbia U. Mem. faculty Columbia U., NYC; dean Sch. Nursing, William Ryan disting. prof. U. Miami; dean Sch. Nursing, prof. U. Mass., 1988—97; Kelting dean, prof. U. Iowa Coll. Nursing, 1997—. Mem. Council on Public Relations for the National Institutes of Health, Washington, 1999—2001; adv. bd. mem. Pfizer Fellowship Prog. in Nursing Rsch., 2000—01; dir. Beverly Enterprises, Inc., 2004—. Mem. editl. bds. various profl. jours. Recipient May A. Brunson award, CASE award. Mem. Sigma Theta Tau (pres. Beta Zeta chpt. 1995). Office: U Iowa Coll Nursing 101 Nursing Bldg 50 Newton Rd Iowa City IA 52242-1121

DREIMANN, LEONHARD, manufacturing executive; b. Riga, Latvia; D. in Mktg., Melbourne U., Australia. Pres. Salton Inc., a wholly-owned subs. SEVKO Inc., 1987—88; mng. dir. Salton Australia Pty. Ltd., 1988—93; founder Salton Inc., Lake Forest, Ill., 1988—, pres., 1988—98, CEO, 1988—, dir. Dir. Glacier Water Systems, 1987—93; officer, dir. Glacier Holdings Inc., 1988—93, Salton Time, 1989—93. Recipient Ernst & Young Entrepreneur Of The Year for Ill./North West Ind., 1999. Achievements include the successful mktg. of The George Foreman Grill, Breadman, Juiceman, Ingraham, Farberware and Toast-master -growing the co. from $8 million to $1 billion in sales. Office: Salton Inc 1955 West Field Ct Lake Forest IL 60045

DRENGLER, WILLIAM ALLAN JOHN, lawyer; b. Shawano, Wis., Nov. 18, 1949; s. William J. and Vera J. (Simmonds) D.; m. Kathleen A. Hintz, June 18, 1983; children: Ryan, Jeffrey, Brittany. BA, Am. U., 1972; JD, Marquette U., 1976. Bar: Wis. 1976, U.S. Dist. Ct. (ea. and we. dists.) Wis. 1976. Assoc. Herrling, Swain & Drengler, Appleton, Wis., 1976-78; dist. atty. Outagamie County, Appleton, 1979-81; corp. counsel Marathon County, Wausau, Wis., 1981-96, Drengler Law Firm, Wausau, Wis., 1997—. Vice chmn. Wis. Equal Rights Coun., 1978—83, Wis. Coun. Criminal Justice, Madison, 1983—87, Wis. State Pub. Defender Bd., 2006—. Nat. pres. Future Bus. Leaders Am., 1967—68; chmn. local Selective Svc. Bd., Wausau, 1982—89; mem. adv. bd. Wausau Salvation Army, 1986—, chair, 2006—; judge advocate officer Wis. Army NG, 1989—96; mem. Troop 453 com. Samoset coun. Boy Scouts Am., 2000—07; mem. nat. Dem. del., 1974—76; del. Wis. Dem., Madison State Conv., 1972—, conv. co-chair, 1980, conv. parliamentarian, 1986—; mem. adminstrv. com. Wis. Dems., Madison, 1977—81, 1986—88; bd. dirs. Wausau Youth/Little League Baseball, 1988—, team mgr., 1994—2002. Mem.: KC, ABA (chair com. on govt. lawyers, sect. state and local govt. 1991—93, bylaws com. govt. and pub. sect. lawyers divsn. 1993—98), State Bar Wis. (govt. lawyers divsn., bd. dirs. 1982—86, sec. 1986—87, professionalism com. 1987—91, prse. 1989—91, professionalism com. 1992—2000, solo and small firm practice com. 2001—06, bench bar com. 2006—), Nat. Assn. Counties (bd. dirs. 1991—92, taxation and fin. steering com. 1991—93, justice and pub. safety steering com. 1993—94, deferred compensation adv. com. 1993—95), Nat. Assn. County Civil Attys. (dir. 1986—88, v.p. 1988—91, pres. 1991—92), Kiwanis Internat. Found. (Hixon Fellowship award 2001), Kiwanis (lt. gov. 1985—86, club pres. 1989—90, chair past lt. govs. coun. 1990—91), Wausau Elks (parliamentarian 2000—03, 2007—). Roman Catholic. Avocations: baseball, camping, fishing, tennis, golf. Office: 609 Scott St PO Box 5152 Wausau WI 54402-5152

DRENTLICHER, DAVID, lawyer, educator, physician; b. Washington, May 2, 1955; s. Herman Israel and Jeanette Adah (Levin) O. BA in Economics, Brandeis U., 1977; MD, Harvard U., 1981, JD, 1986. Bar: D.C. 1988, Ill. 1993, Ind. 1999. Med. intern U. Mich. Med. Ctr., Ann Arbor, 1981-82; pvt. practice Detroit, 1982-83; law clk. U.S. Ct. Appeals, Baton Rouge, 1986-87; assoc. Sidley & Austin, Washington, 1987-89; ethics and health policy counsel AMA, Chgo., 1989-95; Samuel R. Rosen prof. law Ind. U. Sch. Law, Indpls., co-dir. Ctr. for Law and Health, 1995—. Lectr. in law U. Chgo. Law Sch., 1993-95; adj. asst. prof. medicine orthwestern U. Med. Sch., Chgo., 1992-95; vis. DeCamp prof. bioethics Princeton U., 1997-98; state rep. Ind. Gen. Assembly, 2002—. Contbr. articles to profl. jours. Mem. ABA, Am. Soc. Law, Medicine and Ethics. Avocations: cajun dancing, racquet sports. Office: Ind U Sch Law 530 W New York St Indianapolis IN 46202-3225 Office Phone: 317-274-4993. E-mail: dorentli@iupui.edu.

DRESCHHOFF, GISELA AUGUSTE MARIE, physicist, researcher; b. Moenchengladbach, Germany, Sept. 13, 1938; came to U.S., 1967, naturalized, 1976; d. Gustav Julius and Hildegard Friederike (Krug) D. PhD, Tech. U. Braunschweig, Germany, 1972. Staff scientist Fed. Inst. Physics and Tech. Ger., 1965-67; rsch. assoc. Kans. Geol. Survey, Lawrence, 1971-72; vis. asst. prof. physics U. Kans., 1972-74; dep. dir. radiation physics lab. Space Tech. Ctr., 1972-78, assoc. dir., 1979-84, co-dir., 1984-86, dir., 1996—; sr. sci. geology U. Kans., 1991, adj. assoc. prof. physics and astronomy, 1992. Assoc. program mgr. NSF, Washington, 1978-79. Patentee identification markings for gemstones and method of making selective conductive regions in diamond layers. Named to Women's Hall of Fame, U. Kans., 1978; recipient Antarctic Service medal U.S.A., 1979; recipient NASA Group Achievement award, 1983; named mountain Dreschhoff Peak, Antarctica, 1997. Fellow Explorers Club; mem. AAAS, Am. Phys. Soc., Am. Geophys. Union, Am. Polar Soc. (pres. 2000-03), Antarctican Soc., Sigma Xi. Achievements include naming of Dreschhoff Peak, Antarctica by U.S. Board of Geographic Names, 1997. Home: 2908 W 19th St Lawrence KS 66047-2301 Office: U Kans Dept Physics & Astronomy Lawrence KS 66045-7541 Business E-Mail: giselad@ku.edu.

DREWES, MATTHEW A., lawyer; BA cum laude, Concordia Coll., Moorhead, Minn., 1998; JD cum laude, U. Minn. Law Sch., 2001. Bar: Minn. 2001, US Ct. Appeals (8th cir.) 2001, US Dist. Ct. (dist. Minn.) 2004. Assoc. litig. practice grp. Thomsen & Nybeck, P.A., Edina, Minn., 2003. Named a Rising Star, Minn. Super Lawyers mag., 2006. Mem.: Assn. Trial Lawyers of Am., ABA, Minn. State Bar Assn. Office: Thomsen & Nybeck PA 3300 Edinborough Way Ste 600 Edina MN 55435 Office Phone: 952-835-7000. E-mail: mdrewes@tn-law.com.

DREWRY, JUNE E., information technology executive; Degree in Math., Caldwell Coll. With Mut. Benefit Life Ins. Co., 1978—89; v.p. tech. Aetna Life Ins. and Annuity Co., Hartford, Conn., 1990, pres. of systematized benefits admistrs., 1991—96; sr. v.p. and chief knowlege and tech. officer Lincoln Nat. Corp., 1996—99; exec. v.p. and chief info. officer Aon Corp., Chgo., 2000—. Mem.: Soc. Info. Mgmt. (pres. (N.J. chapt.), at large mem. Internat. Bd. Dir., Internat. pres.). Office: Aon Corp 200 E Randolph St Chicago IL 60601

DREXLER, MARY SANFORD, financial executive; b. Pontiac, Mich., Apr. 19, 1954; d. Arthur H. and Kathryn S. (Sherda) Sanford; m. Brian Day, 1975 (div. 1978); m. York Drexler, 1980. BS, Ea. Mich. U., Ypsilanti, 1976, MA, 1979; postgrad., Walsh Coll., Troy, Mich., 1983. CPA, Mich. Spl. edn. tchr. Oakland Schs., Pontiac, Mich., 1976-83; staff auditor Coopers & Lybrand, Detroit, 1983—84, sr. auditor, 1984—86; asst. contr. Webasto Sunroofs Inc., Rochester Hills, 1986-88; contr. Inalfa Roof Systems, U.S.A., Farmington Hills, Mich., 1988-92; v.p. fin., controller Inalfa Roof Sys., Farmington Hills, Mich., 1992-96, CFO, exec. v.p., 1997—. Bd. dirs. Inalfa Roof Systems, Inc., Inalfa Holding Inc. Bd. dirs. Neighborhood Civic Assn., Troy, 1986—, Coun. for Exceptional Children, Oakland County, 1976-83. Mem. Inst. Mgmt. Accts., Oakland County, Mich. Assn. CPA Mich., Forest Lake Country Club. Avocations: photography, painting, golf, swimming. Office: Inalfa Roof Systems USA 1370 Pacific Dr Auburn Hills MI 48326-1569 Office Phone: 248-371-1957.

DREXLER, RICHARD ALLAN, manufacturing executive; b. Chgo., May 14, 1947; s. Lloyd A. and Evelyn Violet (Kovaloff) D.; m. Clare F. Stunkel, Aug. 24, 1990; children by previous marriage: Dan Lloyd, Jason Ian. BS, Northwestern U., 1968, MBA, 1969. Staff v.p. Allied Products Corp., Chgo., 1971-75, sr. v.p. adminstrn., 1975-79, exec. v.p., COO, CFO, 1979-82, pres., COO, 1982-86, pres., CEO, 1986-93, chmn., pres., CEO, 1993—.

DREXLER, RUDY MATTHEW, JR., professional law enforcement dog trainer; b. Elkhart, Ind., Jan. 16, 1941; s. Rudy Matthew Sr. and Elaine Irene (Hardman) D.; m. Patricia Ann Overmyer, Apr. 4, 1981; children: Scott M., Tina S. Thode. Student, Purdue U., 1960-63. V.p. Custom Booth Mfg. Corp., Elkhart, Ind., 1962-80; pres. Orchard Kennels, Elkhart, Ind., 1964-79; pres., treas. Rudy Drexler's Sch. for Dogs, Inc., Elkhart, Ind., 1980—. Lectr. civic orgns.; instr. U. Del. Continuing Edn., Wilmington, 1978. Named to Honorable Order of Ky. Colonels, 1989; named hon. dep. Middlesex County Sheriff's Dept., New Brunswick, N.J., 1984, Daviess County Sheriff's Dept., Owensboro, Ky., 1988, Fairfield County Sheriff's Dept., Lancaster, Ohio, 1982. Mem. Midwest Police K-9 Assn. (founder 1984, tng. dir. 1984-87), Am. Soc. Law Enforcement Trainers (charter mem.), Internat. Narcotics Enforcement Officers Assn. (assoc. mem.), Can. Police K-9 Assn. (assoc. mem.), Nat. Police Res. Officers Assn. (hon. mem.), Moose. Office: Rudy Drexler's Sch for Dogs 50947 County Road 7 Elkhart IN 46514-8853 Office Phone: 574-264-7518. Business E-Mail: rudydrexler@aol.com.

DREYER, LEO PHILIP, lawyer; b. Waukegan, Ill., July 17, 1944; BA, U. Kans., 1966, JD, 1973. Bar: Mo. 1974, U.S. Supreme Ct. 1982, Kans. 1984. Ptnr. Shook, Hardy & Bacon LLP, Kansas City, Mo. Bd. editors U. Kans. Law Rev., 1973; contbr. articles to profl. jours. Bd. govs. law sch. U. Kans., 1983—, pres., 1987-88. Mem.: IBA, ABA, Kan. Bar Assn., Am. Arbitration Assn., Lawyers Assn. of Kansas City, Mo. Bar Assn., Kansas City Met. Bar Assn., Pi Sigma, Order of Coif. Office: Shook, Hardy & Bacon LLP 2555 Grand Blvd Kansas City MO 64108 Office Phone: 816-559-2316. Office Fax: 816-421-5547. E-mail: ldreyer@shb.com.

DREZNER, DANIEL WILLIAM, political scientist, educator; b. Syracuse, NY, Aug. 23, 1968; s. Alan David and Esther Barbara Drezner; m. Erika Wynne Golub, May 24, 1997; children: Lauren children: Samuel. BA in Polit. Econ., Williams Coll., 1990; MA in Econ., Stanford U., 1995, MA in Polit. Sci., 1995, PhD in Polit. Sci., 1996. Rsch. cons. RAND Corp., Washington, 1994; asst. prof. polit. sci. U. Colo., Boulder, 1996—99; asst. profl. polit. sci. U. Chgo., 1999—; internat. economist U.S. Dept. the Treasury, Washington, 2000—01. Author: The Sanctions Paradox, 1999, Locating the Proper Authorities, 2003. Recipient Internat. Affairs fellow, Coun. on Fgn. Rels., 1999—2001; fellow John M. Olin fellow, Harvard U., 1997, German Marshall Fund of U.S., 2004—. Mem.: Midwestern Polit. Sci. Assn., Coun. Fgn. Rels., Chgo. Coun. on Fgn. Rels., Internat. Studies Assn., Am. Polit. Sci. Assn. Office: Univ Chgo 5828 South University Ave Chicago IL 60637 Office Phone: 773-702-0234. E-mail: ddrezner@gmail.com.

DRIEHAUS, STEVE, state representative; b. Cin., June 24, 1966; married; 2 children. BA, Miami U. Ohio; MPA, Ind. U. Sr. cons. Cmty. Bldg. Inst.; state rep. dist. 31 Ohio Ho. of Reps., Columbus, 2000—, mem. pub. utilities com., elections and ethics, minority whip, mem. ins., ways and means coms. Vol. U.S. Peace Corps, Senegal; encouraging cmty. progress task force Greater Cin. Found.; legis. aide U.S. Congressman Charles Luken. Mem.: Price Hill Hist. Soc., Price Hill Civic Club. Democrat. Office: 77 S High St 14th fl Columbus OH 43215-6111

DRIGGS, CHARLES MULFORD, lawyer; b. East Cleveland, Ohio, Jan. 26, 1924; s. Karl Holcomb and Lila Vandeveer (Wilson) D.; children: Ruth, Rachel, Carrie, Karl H., Charles M.; m. Ann Eileen Zargari, Oct. 25, 1991. BS, Yale U., 1947, JD, 1950. Bar: Ohio 1951. Assoc. Squire, Sanders & Dempsey, Cleve., 1950-64, ptnr., 1964-88, of counsel, 1988-91; pvt. practice civil law Cleve., 1991-95; prin. Driggs, Hogg, Daugherty & Del Zoppo Co., LPA, Willoughby Hills, Ohio, 1995. Pres. Bratenahl (Ohio) Sch. Bd., 1958—62; mem. adv. coun. Cleve. Ctr. for Theol. Edn., 1978—. Mem. ABA, Ohio Bar Assn., Lake County Bar Assn., Cleve. Bar Assn., Greater Cleve. Growth Assn., Cleve. Law Libr. Assn. (trustee 1977-91), Ct. Nisi Prius (judge 2000), Citizens League Greater Cleve., Geauga County Bar Assn., Phi Delta Phi, Tau Beta Pi, Phi Gamma Delta. Home: 8011 Eagle Rd Kirtland OH 44094 Office: 38500 Chardon Rd Willoughby OH 44094 Office Phone: 440-391-5100. E-mail: charles@driggslaw.com.

DRINFELD, VLADIMIR GERSHONOVICH, mathematician, educator; b. Kharkov, Ukraine, Feb. 14, 1954; Grad., Moscow U., 1974, PhD, 1978. With B. Verkin Inst. Low Temperature Physics, Acad. Scis. Ukraine, 1981-98; prof. Bashkir U., Ufa, Russia, Ukrain Kharkav U.; sr. prof. dept math. U. Chgo., 1998—, Harry Pratt Judson disting. svc. prof. in math. Recipient Fields medal Internat. Congress Mathematicians, Kyoto, Japan, 1990. Mem.: Acad. Scis. Ukraine. Achievements include research on quantum groups and number theory; proff. of the langlands conjecture for GL (2) over a functional field. Office: U Chgo Dept Math 5734 S University Ave Chicago IL 60637-1514

DRISCOLL, CHARLES FRANCIS, financial planner; b. Dubuque, Iowa, July 8, 1943; s. Francis Clarence (dec.)and Grace Ellen (Shanahan) D.; children: Sean, Erin. BA in Econs., Loras Coll., 1968. CLU; accredited estate planner. Sr. account mgr. NCR Corp., Davenport, Iowa, 1968—74, St. Louis, 1974—76; fin. planner Mass. Mut. Life Ins. Co., St. Louis, 1976—; pres. Driscoll and Assocs., St. Louis, 1989—2000. Equity sales coord. MML Investor Svcs., Inc., St. Louis, 1983-88. Chmn. Edgewood Program Alumni Recovery Fund, St. John's Mercy Hosp., St. Louis, 1988-90. Mem. Nat. Assn. Ins. and Fin. Advisors, Soc. Fin. Svc. Profls., Assn. for Advanced Life Underwriters, Estate Planning Coun. St. Lo. Republican. Roman Catholic. Avocations: golf, fishing, nature photography, reading, travel. Home: 1007 N Clay Ave Kirkwood MO 63122 Office: 16690 Swingley Ridge Rd Ste 240 Chesterfield MO 63017-0758 Office Phone: 636-728-2452. Personal E-mail: cdriscoll@charter.net. Business E-Mail: cdriscoll@finsvcs.com.

DRNEVICH, VINCENT PAUL, engineering educator; b. Wilkinsburg, Pa., Aug. 6, 1940; s. Louis B. and Mary (Kutcel) D.; m. Roxanne M. Hosier, Aug. 20, 1966; children: Paul, Julie, Jenny, Marisa. BSCE, U. Notre Dame, 1962, MSCE, 1964; PhD, U. Mich., 1967. Registered profl. engr., Ky., Ind. Asst. prof. civil engring. U. Ky., Lexington, 1967-73, assoc. prof., 1973-78, prof., 1978-91; chmn. civil engring., 1980-84; acting dean engring. U. Ky., Lexington, 1989-90; prof., head Sch. Civil Engring. Purdue U., West Lafayette, Ind., 1991-2000. Dir. joint hwy. rsch. project Purdue U., 1991-95; pres. Soil Dynamics, Instruments, Inc., West Lafayette, 1974—. Inventor in field. Fellow ASCE (chmn. dept. heads coun. exec. com. 1996-2000, vice chmn. com. on edn.-practitioner interface, 1994-98, Norman medal 1973, Huber Rsch. prize 1980), ASTM (exec. com., tech. editor Geotech. Testing Jour. 1985-89, C.A. Hogentogler award 1979, Merit award 1993, Woodland Shockley award 1996); mem. NSPE, Am. Soc. Engring. Edn. (sec./treas. civil engring. divsn. 1995-98, dir. 1999—, vice chair 2002-03, chair 2003-04), Ind. Soc. Profl. Engrs. (v.p., 2006-07, pres. elect, 2007-08, pres., 2008-, A.A. Potter chpt., 1997-2007), Chi Epsilon (Harold T. Larson award 1985, James M. Robbins award 1989). Roman Catholic. Avocations: golf, fishing, ballroom dancing. Office: Purdue U 550 Stadium Mall Dr West Lafayette IN 47907-2051 Business E-Mail: drnevich@purdue.edu.

DROHAN, DAVID F., medical products company executive; BS in Indsl. Rels., Manhattan Coll., NYC. With Baxter Healthcare Corp., 1965—, territory mgr. N.Y., various positions, v.p. sales parenteral divsn., 1983-87, pres. pharmacy divsn., 1987-96, pres. intravenous systems, corp. v.p., 1996—. Bd. trustees St. Louis Coll. of Pharmacy. Chmn. Wake County Econ. Devel. Bd., dir. Riverside Found, dir. Baxter Credit Union.

DRONGOWSKI, STEVE, advertising executive; With Fahlgren Inc. (now Icon Marketing), Austin, Tex., 1984—; pres., CEO, 1993-96; CEO, 1996—. Office: Fahlgren Inc 585 S Front St Ste 300 Columbus OH 43215-5626

DROUIN, JOE, automotive executive; b. Memphis; B in Mgmt. Info. Sys., U. Memphis, 1990. With Electronic Data Sys. Corp. GM, Detroit; with Perot Sys. Corp.; IS dir. TRW Chassis Sys. Europe TRW, Germany, 1998—2002; v.p., CIO global info. sys. TRW Automotive, Livonia, Mich., 2002—. Bd. dirs. Automotive Industry Action Group; mem. Covisint Global Customer Adv. Coun. Office: TRW Automotive 12025 Tech Center Dr Livonia MI 48150

DROVDAL, DAVID (SKIP DROVDAL), state legislator; m. Kathy Wright; 4 children. Student, Minot Col. Bus., 1967; diploma, Western Coll. Auctioneering, 1992. Owner, mgr. Drovdal's Hardware, Watford, N.D., 1972—; mem. N.D. Ho. of Reps., 1993—. Mem. edn. and natural resources com., intreim edn. fin. com., vice chmn. edn. com., 1997. Bd. dirs. Good Shepherd Home; coun. pres. Zoar Ch., 1982-84. Named Watford City Fireman of Yr., 1991. Mem. Watford City C. of C. (past pres.), Sons of orway (past pres. Watford), Lions (Lion of Yr. award 1993). Republican. Home: HC 1 Box 22 Arnegard ND 58835-9726

DRUMMOND, ROBERT KENDIG, lawyer; b. Phila., Feb. 9, 1939; s. Winslow Shaw and Dorothy (Moore) D.; m. Carol Young, Sept. 3, 1960; children: Anne Elizabeth, Robert Young D. BA, Coll. Wooster, 1961; JD, Duke U., 1964. Bar: Wis. 1964. Assoc. Foley & Lardner, Milw., 1964-71, ptnr., 1971—. Bd. dirs. Bandag Inc., Muscatine, Iowa, Custom Heat Treat Inc., Iron Mountain, Mich. Presbyterian. Office: Foley & Lardner Firstar Ctr 777 E Wisconsin Ave Ste 3800 Milwaukee WI 53202-5367

DRURY, CHARLES LOUIS, JR., hotel executive; b. Cape Girardeau, Mo., Nov. 4, 1955; s. Charles Louis Sr. and Shirley Jean (Luebbers) D.; m. Michelle Marguerite Swenson, Apr. 28, 1979; children: Charles L. III, Thomas Michael. BSBA, St. John's U., Collegeville, Minn., 1978. Gen. mgr. Drury Inns, Inc., St. Louis, 1978-79, regional mgr., 1979-81, v.p. ops., 1981-85, pres., 1985—, chief exec. officer, 1988—, also bd. dirs. Bd. dirs. Drury Industries, Inc., Cape Girardeau, Drury Displays, Inc., St. Louis, Druco, Inc., St. Louis; mem. exec. bd. Enterprise Bank, St. Louis, 1989— Bd. dirs. Dismas House of St. Louis, 1987—, Cardinal Glennon Children's Hosp. Devel. Bd. Mem. Pres. Assn., Am. Mgmt. Assn. Roman Catholic. Office: 721 Emerson Rd #400 Saint Louis MO 63141-6770

DRUSHAL, MARY ELLEN, retired education educator; b. Peru, Ind., Oct. 24, 1945; d. Herrell Lee and Opal Marie (Boone) Waters; m. J. Michael Drushal, June 12, 1966; children: Lori, Jeff. B of Music Edn., Ashland Coll., 1969; MS, Peabody Coll., 1981; PhD, Vanderbilt U., 1986. Dir. music and spl. ednl. projects Smithville (Ohio) Brethren Ch., 1969-74; tchr. music Orrville (Ohio) Pub. Schs., 1969—70; seminar leader Internat. Ctr. for Learning, Glendale, Calif., 1974-76; dir. Christian edn. First Presbyn. and Christ Presbyn. Ch., Nashville, 1976-84; assoc. prof. Ashland (Ohio) Theol. Sem., 1984-91, acad. dean, 1991-95; provost Ashland U., 1995—2001, prof. edn., 2001—05, prof. emeritus, 2006—. Cons. in strategic planning for not-for-profit orgns. Author: On Tablets of Human Hearts: Christian Education with Children, 1991; co-author: Spiritual Formation: A Personal Walk Toward Emmaus, 1990; contbr. articles to profl. jours. Trustee Brethren Care Found., Ashland, 1989-99, Ashland Symphony Orch., 1986-87; pres., fundraiser Habitat for Humanity, Ashland, 1990-94; bd. dirs. JOY Day Care Ctr., 1988-90. Grantee Lilly Endowment Inc., 1991, 93, Brethren Ch. Found., 1989, 90. Mem. Assn. Theol. Schs. (com. under-represented constituencies 1994-96), Am. Assn. for Higher Edn., Nat. Assn. Ch. Bus. Adminstrs., N.Am. Assn. Profs. of Christian Edn., Assn. Profs. and Rschrs. in Religious Edn., Nat. Assn. Evangelicals, Nat. Assn. Black Evangelical Assns., Epiphany Assn. (bd. dirs. 1994-98). Republican. Lutheran. Avocations: reading, needlepoint. Home: 20041 Sanibel View Cir 102 Fort Myers FL 33908-6991 Personal E-mail: drushal@comcast.net.

DRUTCHAS, GREGORY G., lawyer; b. Detroit, June 2, 1949; s. Gilbert Henry and Elaine Marie D.; m. Cheryl Aline Fox D. June 9, 1973; children: Gillian, Gregory, Ethan, Allison. BA in Journalism, U. Mich., 1970; JD, Duke U., 1973. Bar: Mich. 1973, US Dist. Ct. (ea. dist.) Mich. 1974, US Dist. Ct. (we. dist.) Mich. 1983, US Ct. Appeals (6th cir.) 1978, US Supreme Ct. 1984. Assoc. Kitch Drutchas Wagner Valitutti & Sherbrook, Detroit, 1973-78, sr. prin., shareholder 1978—; mem. comml. panel arbitrators, Am. Arbitration Assn. East Providence, RI, 1980-; faculty mem. Lansing CC, 1994-2000; lectr., seminar presenter on med. profl. liability and ins.; contbr. articles to profl. publs. and chpts. to books. Commr., Bloomfield Hills Youth Soccer League, Mich., 1993-97; legal cons., Bloomfield Hills Soccer Club, 1999-2004; bd. dirs. Project Compassion Inc., South Lyon, Mich., 2003-. Served to capt., USAF, 1972-82. Disting. Mich. Supreme Ct. Brief award, Cooley Law Sch., Lansing, Mich., 1985. Mem. ABA (chair ins. law com., 1985-87), State Bar Mich. (mem. ins. law com., 1981-87, chairperson, 1984-87, coun. mem. health care law sect., 1995, treas., 1997-99, chair-elect, 2000-01, chair, 2001-02), Oakland County Bar Assn. (vice-chmn. ct. appeals com., 1978-79, chair, 1979-80, mem. med., legal com., 1981-83, 1992-96, vice-chmn., 1982-83), Am. Health Lawyers Assn., Mich. Health and Hosp. Assn. (mem. ad hoc subcommittee med. malpractice legis., 1983-84, mem. com. pub. policy and govt., 1983-84, legal cons. malpractice legis., 1985-87, mem. coun. sys. and networks, 1996-98, mem. legis. policy panel, 1994-96, 2004-), Healthcare Fin. Mgmt. Assn. (mem. tax and legal issues com., 1990-92, 94, co-chair health law com., 1996-2002, Folmer Bronze Svc. award 2003), Mich. Soc. Healthcare Attys. (bd. dirs., 2001-), Mich. Soc. Healthcare Risk Mgmt. (mem. edn. com., 1998-2000), Birmingham Country Club. Avocations: golf, youth soccer. Republican. Unitarian. Office: Kitch Drutchas Wagner Valitutti & Sherbrook One Woodward Ave 24th Fl Detroit MI 48226 Home Phone: 248-645-9468; Office Phone: 313-965-7930.

DRUTEN, ROBERT J., greeting card company executive; CFO Hallmark Cards Inc., Kansas City, Mo. Office: 2501 Mcgee St Kansas City MO 64108-2615

DRYMALSKI, RAYMOND HIBNER, lawyer, banker; b. Chgo., June 1, 1936; s. Raymond P. and Alice H. (Hibner) D.; m. Sarah Fickes, Apr. 1, 1967; children: Robert, Paige. BA, Georgetown U., 1958; JD, U. Mich., 1961. Bar: Ill. 1962. Lawyer Chgo. Title & Trust Co., 1963-65; asst. sec., atty. No. Trust Co., Chgo., 1965-68; ptnr. Boodell, Sears, Giambalvo & Crowley, Chgo., 1968-87; mem. Bell Boyd & Lloyd LLC, Chgo., 1987—. Contbr. articles to profl. jours. Chmn. Northwestern Meml. Healthcare, 2000—04; bd. dirs. Northwestern Meml. Hosp., Chgo., 1978—, chmn., 2000—04; bd. dirs. Northwestern Meml. Health-Care, 1987—, vice chmn., sec., 1998—99, chmn., 2000—04; bd. dirs. McGaw Med. Ctr. of Northwestern U., 2000—04, Lincoln Park Zool. Soc., 1972—, pres., 1980—84; bd. dirs., officer Offield Family Found., 1990—; mem. coun. govs. Northwestern Healthcare Network, 1990—, bd. dirs., 1999. Mem. ABA, Econ. Club Chgo. Roman Catholic. Home: 443 W Eugenie St Chicago IL 60614-5674 Office: Bell Boyd & Lloyd LLC 70 W Madison St Ste 3100 Chicago IL 60602-4244 E-mail: rdrymalski@bellboyd.com.

DRZEWIECKI, GARY FRANCIS, state legislator; b. Pulaski, Wis., Oct. 29, 1954; s. Wallace and Marcella Drzewiecki; m. Julie Pakanich, 1982; children: Eric, Matthew, Michelle, Tiffany. Student, U. Wis., Stout, 1972-73. Owner, perator Pulaski Fin. Ctr.; pres. Pulaski Econ. Devel. Corp.; mem. from dist. 30 Wis. State Senate, Madison; chair state govt. ops. and corrections coms. Bd. dirs. Tri County Res. Squad, 1989—; past pres. Village of Pulaski; Bd. dirs. Brown County Planning Commn. Mem. Optimists, Lions. Home: 419 Washington St Pulaski WI 54162-0313

DUARTE, GLORIA, chef; Student, Dumas Pere Culinary Sch., Glenview, Ill. Chef Ritz-Carlton Hotel, Chgo., The Drake hotel, Chgo.; wner, chef Las Bellas Artes, Elmhurst, Ill., 1987—. Host Mexico's Day of the Dead celebration James Beard Found.; guest chef Jalisco Culinary Arts resort, Mexico. Named one of Top Ten Restaurants, Chgo. Sun Times.

DUBACK, STEVEN RAHR, lawyer; b. Washington, Sept. 4, 1944; s. Paul Hewitt and Natalie (Rahr) D.; children: David, Peter, Andrew. BA, Princeton U., 1966; JD, U. Mich., 1969. Bar: Wis. 1969, U.S. Dist. Ct. (ea. dist.) Wis. 1969, U.S. Ct. Claims 1969, U.S. Tax Ct. 1969. Ptnr. Quarles & Brady LLP, Milw., 1969—. Bd. dirs. Oshkosh (Wis.) B'Gosh, Inc., Commerce Indsl. Chems., Inc. Dir. Ctr. for the Deaf and Hard of Hearing. Mem.: Am. Soc. Corp. Secs., Estate Counselors Forum, Milw. Estate Planning Coun., Wis. State and Local Tax Club, Town Club, Milw. Athletic Club, Rotary Club of Milw., Phi Beta Kappa, Order of Coif. Avocations: golf, tennis. Office: Quarles & Brady LLP 411 E Wisconsin Ave Ste 2550 Milwaukee WI 53202-4497 Office Phone: 414-277-5883. Personal E-mail: srd@quarles.com.

DUBE, MONTE L, lawyer; b. Jan. 20, 1956; AB, Boston U., 1977; JD, Benjamin N. Cardozo Sch. Law, 1981. Lic.: Ill. Supreme Ct., U.S. Dist. Ct. N. Dist. Ill., U.S. Ct. Appeals. Third Cir. Ptnr., chmn. firm health law dept. McDermott Will & Emery LLP, Chgo. Lectr. & Bigelow Teaching Fellow U. Chgo. Sch. Law, 1981—82. Mem.: ABA, Chgo. Bar Assn., Ill. Bar Assn., Ill. Supreme Ct. Office: McDermott Will & Emery LLP 227 W Monroe St Chicago IL 60606-5055 Office Phone: 312-984-7549. Office Fax: 312-984-7700. Business E-Mail: mdube@mwe.com.

DUBIN, HOWARD VICTOR, dermatologist; b. NYC, Mar. 28, 1938; s. Meyer and Blanche D.; m. Patricia Sue Tucker, June 10, 1962; children— Douglas Scott, Kathryn Sue, David Andrew, Michael Stonier. AB, Columbia U., 1958, MD, 1962. Diplomate: Am. Bd. Dermatology, Am. Bd. Internal Medicine. Intern U. Mich., 1962-63, resident in internal medicine, 1963-64, resident in dermatology, 1968-70, asst. prof., 1970-72, asso. prof., 1972-75, clin. asso. prof., 1975-77, clin. prof., 1977—. Contbr. articles to profl. jours. Trustee Greenhills Sch., Ann Arbor, 1979-87, pres. bd. trustees, 1981-84. With U.S. Army, 1964-66. Fellow ACP; mem. Am. Acad. Dermatology, Am. Dermatol. Assn., Soc. Investigative Dermatology, Dermatology Found. (mem. exec. com. 1987-2001, sec.-treas. 1988-91, pres. 1991-98), Mich. Dermatol. Soc. (pres. 1985-87), AMA, Mich. Med. Soc., Washtenaw County Med. Soc., Rotary.

DUBIN, STACIA, newscaster; b. Milw., Aug. 8, 1972; BA in Journalism and Mass Comm., U. Wis., 1994. Former gen. assignment reporter, cut-in anchor, photojournalist WJFW-TV, Rhinelander, Wis.; former assoc. prodr., weekend assignment editor WMTV, Madison, Wis.; weekend anchor, ct. and crime reporter WKBT-TV, LaCrosse, Wis., 1995—96; weekend morning anchor, reporter WITI-TV, Milw., 1996—2000; freelance reporter, gen. assignment reporter CBS2 Chgo., 2000—02, co-anchor evening news, 2002—.

DUBROW, HEATHER, literature educator; b. San Antonio, Mar. 5, 1945; d. Hilliard and Helen (Volk) D.; m. Ian Ousby, June 21, 1969 (div. Dec. 1979). BA summa cum laude, Harvard/Radcliffe, 1966; PhD, Harvard U., 1972. Asst. prof. U. Mass., Boston, 1972-73; Leverhulme vis. fellowship U. Kent, Canterbury, Eng., 1973-74; lectr. U. Sussex, Brighton, Eng., 1974-75; from vis. asst. prof. to asst. prof. U. Md., College Park, 1975-80; from assoc. to prof. Carleton Coll., Northfield, Minn., 1980-90; from prof. to John Bascom prof. and Tighe-Evans prof. U. Wis., Madison, 1990—. External rev. team Oberlin Coll., Bryn Mawr Coll. Author: Genre, 1982, Captive Victors, 1987, A Happier Eden, 1990, Echoes of Desire, 1995, Transformation and Repetition, 1997, Shakespeare and Domestic Loss, 1999, Border Crossings, 2001, The Challenge of Orphans, 2008; contbr. articles to profl. jours. Recipient Capt. Jonathan Fay award, Radcliffe Coll., 1966; sr. fellow Nat. Endowment for the Humanities, 1987—88, 2003—04, Guggenheim fellow, 2004. Mem. MLA (mem. editl. bd., exec. coun. 1996-2000), Milton Soc. of Am. (exec. com. 1997-99), Renaissance Soc. Am. (disciplinary rep. 2001-03), Spenser Soc., Phi Beta Kappa. Democrat. Avocations: architecture, art, cooking. Office: U Wis Dept of English 600 N Park St Madison WI 53706-1403 Office Phone: 608-263-2913. Business E-Mail: hdubrow@wisc.edu.

DUCAR, TRACY, former soccer player; b. Lawrence, Mass., June 18, 1973; m. Chris Ducar, 1997. BS in Biology, U. N.C., 1995. Mem. U.S. Nat. Women's Soccer Team, 1996—; including Nike Victory Tour, 1997; U.S. Women's Cup, 1997. Named Team Most Valuable Player, U. N.C., 1995. Mem.: Phi Beta Kappa. Office: US Soccer Fedn 1801-1811 S Prairie Ave Chicago IL 60616

DUCHOSSOIS, CRAIG J., manufacturing executive; m. Janet Duchossois; 2 children. BA, MBA, So. Meth. U., Dallas. Joined Duchossois Industries, 1971—, CEO, pres. Elmhurst, Ill. Vice chmn. bd. trustees Ill. Inst. Tech.; chmn. bd. dirs. Thrall Car Mfg. Co.; bd. dirs. Churchill Downs Inc., LaSalle Nat. Bank, Trinity Industries, Inc., 2002—. Trustee Culver Educational Found., Ill. Inst. Tech., Kellogg Grad. Sch. Mgmt., U. of Chicago. Officer USMC, 1968—71. Recipient Disting. Alumni, So. Meth. U., 2002. Office: Duchossois Industries 845 N Larch Ave Elmhurst IL 60126

DUCHOSSOIS, RICHARD LOUIS, manufacturing and racetrack executive; b. Chgo., Oct. 7, 1921; s. Alphonse Christopher and Erna (Hessler) D.; children: Craig J., Dayle, R. Bruce, Kimberly. Student, Washington and Lee U. Chmn. bd. dirs. Duchossois Industries, Inc., Elmhurst, Ill., chmn.; chmn., dir. Chamberlain Tech. Cos.; chmn. Arlington Park Racecourse, Ltd., Arlington Heights, Ill. Bd. dirs. Chamberlain Consumer Products, Hill 'n Dale Farm. Served with U.S. Army, 1942-46, ETO. Decorated Purple Heart, Bronze Star; named to Culver Academies Horsemanship Hall of Fame, 2004. Mem. Chief Execs. Orgn., Economic Club, Execs. Club (bd. dirs.), Jockey Club N.Y.C. Republican. Methodist. Office: Duchossois Industries Inc 845 N Larch Ave Elmhurst IL 60126-1196 E-mail: duchossois@arlingtonpark.com.

DUCK, STEVE WEATHERILL, communications educator; b. Keynsham, Somerset, Engl., Jan. 4, 1946; s. Kenneth W. and Joan (Stickler) D.; m. Sandra Mariela Allen (div. 1987); children: Christina Louise, James Edward; m. Joanna Margaret Lawson, Dec. 30, 1987; children: Benjamin Lawson-Duck, Gabriel Lawson-Duck. PhD, Sheffield U., Eng., 1971; MA, Oxford U., Eng., 1972. Lectr. Glasgow (Scotland) U., 1970-73, Lancaster U., Eng., 1973-78, sr. lectr., 1978-85; prof. U. Iowa, Iowa City, 1986—; chair dept. comm. studies, 1994-98. Founder Internat. Confs. on Personal Relationships, Internat. Network Personal Relationships. Author: Relating to Others, 1999, Understanding Relationships, 1991, Human Relationships, 3rd edit., 1992; editor: Handbook of Personal Relationships, 1988, 2d edit., 1997, Meaningful Relationships, 1994; co-editor: Studying Interpersonal Interaction, 1991; editor Jour. Social and Personal Relationships, 1984-98. Fellow APA, Am. Psychol. Soc., Interpersonal Comm. Assn. Office: U Iowa Dept Comm Studies 105B CSB Iowa City IA 52242

DUDERSTADT, JAMES JOHNSON, academic administrator, engineering educator; b. Ft. Madison, Iowa, Dec. 5, 1942; s. Mack Henry and Katharine Sydney (Johnson) D.; m. Anne Marie, June 24, 1964; children: Susan Kay, Katharine Anne. B in Engring. with highest honors, Yale U., 1964; MS in Engring. Sci, Calif. Inst. Tech., 1965, PhD in Engring. Sci. and Physics, 1967. From asst. prof. nuclear engring. to pres. U. Mich., 1969—88, pres. univ., 1988—96, pres. emeritus, prof. sci. engring., 1996—. Dir. Millennium Project, 1996—. Mem. Sec. of Edn.'s Commn. on Future of Edn., 2005. AEC fellow, 1964-68; recipient E. O. Lawrence award U.S. Dept. Energy, 1986, Nat. medal of Tech., 1991; named Nat. Engr. of Yr., NSPE, 1991. Fellow Am. Nuclear Soc. (Mark Mills award 1968, Arthur Holly Compton award 1985); mem. NAE (coun.), Am. Phys. Soc., Nat. Sci. Bd. (chair 1991-94), Am. Acad. Arts & Scis., Sigma Xi, Tau Beta Pi, Phi Beta Kappa. Office Phone: 734-647-7300. Business E-Mail: jjd@umich.edu.

DUDLEY, DURAND STOWELL, retired librarian; b. Cleve., Feb. 28, 1926; s. George Stowell and Corinne Elizabeth (Durand) Dudley; m. Dorothy Woolworth, July 3, 1954; children: Jane Elizabeth, Deborah Anne. BA, Oberlin Coll., Ohio, 1948; MLS, Case Western Res. U., Cleve., 1950. Ordained to ministry as deacon Presbyterian Ch. Libr. Marietta Coll. Libr., Ohio, 1953—55, Akron Pub. Libr., Ohio, 1955—60, Marathon Oil Co., Findlay, Ohio, 1960—74, sr. law libr., 1974—86; supr. tech. svcs. dept. Findlay-Hancock County Pub. Library, 1986—88; ret., 1988. Mem.: Spl. Libraries Assn. Presbyterian. Home: 807 Red Maple Ct Bluffton OH 45817-8551

DUDLEY, JOHN HENRY, JR., lawyer; b. Lansing, Mich., June 22, 1941; s. John Henry and Elizabeth (Dean) D.; m. Elizabeth Merrill Casgrain, Dec. 27, 1975; 1 child, John. BA, Denison U., 1963; LLB, Stanford U., 1966; MA, U. Mich., 1968. Bar: Mich. 1968, U.S. Ct. Appeals (6th cir.) 1972, U.S. Ct. Appeals

(2d cir.) 1987. Assoc. Devine & Devine, Ann Arbor, Mich., 1968-69; ptnr. Butzel Long, Detroit, 1969—. Adj. prof. law sch. U. Detroit, 1991. Chair, bd. dirs. Ann Arbor YMCA, 1997-99. Named Master of Bench U. Detroit-Mercy. Fellow Mich. State Bar Found.; mem. ABA (litig. sect.), Mich. State Bar Assn. (rep. assembly 1974-77), Detroit Bar Assn. (vol. lawyers com. 1989—), Washtenaw County Bar Assn., Am. Inn of Ct. Office: Butzel Long 150 W Jefferson Ave Fl 9th Detroit MI 48226-4430 Office Phone: 313-225-7012, 734-213-3609. Business E-Mail: dudleyj@butzel.com.

DUDLEY, KENNETH EUGENE, manufacturing executive; b. Bellville, Ohio, Nov. 26, 1937; s. Kenneth Olin and Ethel Elizabeth (Poorman) D.; m. Judith Ann Brown, Apr. 15, 1972; children: Camaron J. McCluggage, Kenneth Alan. Inventory control mgr. Gorman-Rupp Industries, Bellville, 1958-67, prodn. mgr., 1967-69, mgr. data processing, 1969-74, cost mgr., 1974-78, contr., 1978-82; treas., chief fin. officer Gorman-Rupp Co., Mansfield, Ohio, 1982—2002; ret., 2002. With USAF, 1962-63. Republican. Lutheran. Home: 18203 Millspring Dr Foley AL 36535-5095

DUDLEY, PAUL V., retired bishop; b. Northfield, Minn., Nov. 27, 1926; s. Edward Austin and Margaret Ann (Nolan) D. Student, Nazareth Coll., St. Paul Sem. Ordained priest Roman Cath. Ch., 1951. Titular bishop of Ursona, aux. bishop of St. Paul-Mpls, 1977-78; bishop of Sioux Falls S.D., 1978-95; pastor orthfield (Minn.) St. Dominic, 1995-97; ret., 1997. Office: 2500 320th St W Northfield MN 55057-4564

DUDLEY, RICK (RICHARD C. DUDLEY), professional sports team executive; b. Jan. 31, 1949; m. Ja-Hee Dudley. Player Am. Hockey League, Internat. Hockey League, World Hockey Assn., Cleve., Cin., 1969-79, Buffalo Sabres, 1972—81, Winnipeg Jets, 1981; head coach Carolina Thunderbirds, 1981—86, New Haven Nighthawks, 1988—89, Flint Spirits, 1986—88, Buffalo Sabres, 1989—92, San Diego Gulls, 1992—93, Phoenix Roadrunners, 1993—94; head coach, gen. mgr. Detroit Vipers, 1994—96; v.p., gen mgr Ottawa Senators, 1996-99; gen. mgr., v.p. Tampa Bay Lightning, 1999—2002; gen. mgr. Fla. Panthers, Sunrise, 2002—04, head coach, 2003—04; cons. hockey ops. Chgo. Blackhawks, 2004—06, asst. gen. mgr., 2006—. Office: Chgo Blackhawk Hockey Team 1901 W Madison St Chicago IL 60612

DUDUKOVIC, MILORAD P., chemical engineering educator, consultant; b. Beograd, Yugoslavia, Mar. 25, 1944; arrived in U.S., 1968; s. Predrag R. and Melita Maria Dudukovic; m. Judith Ann Reiff, Dec. 27, 1969; children: Aleksandra Anne, Nicole Maria. BS in Engring., U. Beograd, 1967; MS, Ill. Inst. Tech., 1970, PhD, 1972. Rsch. engr. Process Design Inst., Beograd, 1967-68; instr. Ill. Inst. Tech., Chgo., 1970-72; asst. prof. Ohio U., Athens, 1972-74; assoc. prof. Washington U., St. Louis, 1974-80, prof., dir., 1980—, Laura and William Jens prof. environ. engring., 1993—, chmn. dept. chem. engring., 1998—2006. Cons. in field. Assoc. editor: Indsl. and Engineering Chemistry Research, 1991—; contbr. articles to profl. jours. Recipient Burlington No. Found. Tchg. award, 1986, Nat. Catalyst award Chem. Mfrs. Assn., 1988, St. Louis award ACS, 1995, Malcolm E. Pruitt award Coun. Chem. Rsch., 1999; 2 NASA certs. of recognition and citations; Fulbright scholar Inst. for Higher Edn., 1968. Fellow AIChE (R.H. Wilhelm award 1994, Fuels & Petrochem. Divsn. award, 2005), St. Louis Acad. Scis.; mem. AAAS, Am. Chem. Soc., Am. Assn. Engring. Edn., Yugoslav Acad. Engring. (fgn. mem.), Sigma Xi, Century Club (St. Louis). Achievements include pioneering work on trickle bed reactors, bubble columns; research in Czochralski crystal growth, novel experimental techniques for multiphase reactors; environmentally benign processing. Office: Wash U Dept Energy Environ & Chem Energy Campus Box 1198 One Brookings Dr Saint Louis MO 63130-4899 Business E-Mail: dudu@wustl.edu.

DUDYCZ, WALTER W., state legislator; b. Chgo., Mar. 11, 1950; m. Oksana; 2 children. Grad., Chgo. Citywide Coll., Chgo. Police Acad. Police detective City of Chgo., 1971-84; mem. dist. 7 Ill. State Senate, 1985—; mem. appropriations I com., exec. appointment com., vet affairs and admin. com., minority spokesman, elec and reapportionment com.; legis. rsch. unit com., Alzheimers task force com., mem. state gov. orgn. ad admin., transp. com., asst. rep. leader. also: Office of Senate Members State Capitol Springfield IL 62706-0001 Office: 5720 N Natoma Ave Chicago IL 60631-3130

DUECKER, ROBERT SHELDON, retired bishop; b. Medina County, Ohio, Sept. 4, 1926; s. Howard LaVerne and Sarah Faye (Simpson) D.; m. Marjorie Louise Clouse, June 13, 1948; children: Philip Lee, Christine Cay Duecker Isle. B in Religion, AB, Indiana Wesleyan U., 1948; BD, MS, Christian Theol. Sem., Indpls., 1952, DD (hon.), 1969; D in Pub. Svc. (hon.), Kendall Coll., 1996. Ordained to ministry United Meth. Ch., 1952. Pastor Dyer (Ind.) United Meth. Ch., 1952-54; sr. pastor Gethsemane United Meth. Ch., Muncie, Ind., 1954-62, Grace United Meth. Ch., Hartford City, Ind., 1962-65, 1st United Meth. Ch., Warsaw, Ind., 1965-70, Simpson United Meth. Ch., Ft. Wayne, Ind., 1970-72; dir. No. Ind. Conf. Coun. Ministries United Meth. Ch., Marion, 1973-77, dist. supt. No. Ind. Conf. Ft. Wayne, 1977-82; sr. pastor High St. United Meth. Ch., Muncie, 1982-88; bishop Chgo. area United Meth. Ch., 1988-96; ret., 1996; instr. Christian Theol. Sem., Indpls., 1998. Trustee United Theol. Sem., Dayton, Ohio, 1985-88, Kendall Coll., Evanston, Ill., 1988-96, North Ctrl. Coll., Naperville, Ill., 1988-96, Garrett Theol. Sem., Evanston, 1988-96; mem. gen. bd. publ. United Meth. Ch., 1988-92, gen. bd. higher edn. and ministry, 1992-96, univ. senate, 1992-96; mem. adv. coun. Ams. United for Separation of Ch. and State; instr. Christian Theol. Sem., Indpls., 1998. Author: Tensions in the Connection, 1982; also monographs. Mem. Kosciusko County Health Planning Coun., Warsaw, Ind., 1968—70; former pres. Delaware County Mental Health Assn., Muncie; bd. dirs. Goodwill Industries, Ft. Wayne, Ind., 1977—88, Parkview Hosp. Found., 1997—. Named Sagamore of the Wabash Gov. of Ind., 1988. Mem. Coun. of Religious Leaders of Met. Chgo. (pres. 1996—), Coun. Bishops United Meth. Ch., North Ctrl. Jurisdiction Coll. Bishops, Kiwanis, Rotary, Theta Phi. Methodist. Avocations: stamp collecting/philately, golf. E-mail: rsduecker@aol.com.

DUEHOLM, ROBERT M., state legislator; b. June 7, 1945; BA, U. Wis. Assemblyman Wis. State Dist. 28. Bd. dirs. Inter-County Leaders; acct. mgr. Honeywell Corp.; adv. bd. Indianhead Tech. Coll. Democrat. Address: 904 State Road 48 PO Box 260 Luck WI 54853-5104

DUERINCK, LOUIS T., retired rail transportation executive, lawyer; b. Chgo., Aug. 1, 1929; s. Aloys L. and Thais E. (De Backer) D.; m. Patricia A. Bird, June 27, 1953; children: Louis M., Kathleen M. Lutgen, Kevin F., Mark V., Lynn P. Dressel, Brian T., Paul S. Student, U. Notre Dame, 1947-48; JD, DePaul U., Chgo., 1952. Bar: Ill. 1952. Commerce atty. N.Y. Cen. R.R., Chgo., 1955-65; gen. atty. Nat. Ry. Labor Conf., Chgo., 1967-68; with C&NW Ry. Co., Chgo., 1965-67, 68-89; sr. v.p. law and real estate C&NW Transp. Co., 1979-83, sr. v.p. traffic, 1983-88, sr. v.p., 1988-89, also bd. dirs. With AUS, 1952—55. Mem. ABA, Assn. Transportation Law Profls., Ill. Bar Assn., Glen Oak Country Club, Wyndemere Country Club Roman Catholic. Home and Office: 718 Midwest Club Pky Oak Brook IL 60523-2531 Personal E-mail: duerlou@aol.com.

DUERKSEN, GEORGE LOUIS, music therapist, educator; b. St. Joseph, Mo., Oct. 29, 1934; s. George Herbert and Louise May (Dalke) D.; m. Patricia Gay Beers, June 3, 1961; children— Mark Jeffrey, Joseph Scott, Cynthia Elizabeth Student, Tabor Coll., 1951-52; BMusEdn, U. Kans., 1955, MMusEdn, 1956, PhD in Music Edn., 1967. Cert. music educator Kans., Mo., registered music therapist Nat. Assn. Music Therapy, 1975, bd. cert. music therapist Cert. Bd. Music Therapists, 1987. Tchr. music Tonganoxie HS, Kans., 1955-56, Stafford Jr. and Sr. HS, Kans., 1959-60, Labette County HS, Altamont, Kans., 1960-62, Shawnee Mission North HS, Kans., 1962-63; asst. prof., dir. psychology of music lab. Mich. State U., East Lansing, 1965-69; prof., chmn. dept. art and music edn. and music therapy U. Kans., Lawrence, 1969-93, dir. Singing Jayhawks, 1979-83, prof., dir. music edn. and music therapy divsn., 1993—2004, prof., interim chair dept. music and dance, 2000-01, prof., dir. grad. studies, music edn. and music therapy, dir. Ctr. for Rsch. on Music Behavior, 2001—; assoc. dir. Kans. North Ctrl. Assn. Colls. and Schs., 1992-2000. Cons., vis. prof. U. Hawaii, Honolulu, summer 1978; cons., vis. prof. U. Melbourne, Australia, summer 1981; cons., lectr. N.Z. Soc. for Music Therapy, Wellington, 1983, Ctr. for Contemporary Music Rsch., Athens, 1991, U. Thessaloniki, Greece, 1993, Korean Assn. for Music Therapy, 1994, 97, Sook Myung U., Seoul, 1997; cons. functional music applications, 1967—, Deakin U., Geelong, Victoria, Australia, 1990. Author: (monograph) Teaching Instrumental Music, 1973; Music for Exceptional Children, 1981; contbr. articles to profl. jours., chpts. to books. Fulbright scholar Inst. for Internat. Edn., Australia, 1956-57; U.Kans. fellow, Lawrence, 1963-64; U.S. Office Edn. grantee, 1966-67, 73-75, 78-81. Mem. AAAS, Music Educators Nat. Conf., Am. Music Therapy Assn.(award of merit, 2000), Music Edn. Rsch. Coun. (chmn. 1980-82), Brit. Soc. for Music Therapy, Coun. for Rsch. in Music Edn., Pi Kappa Lambda, Phi Mu Alpha, Phi Delta Kappa. Avocations: photography, boating, travel. Home Phone: 785-843-0418; Office Phone: 785-864-9632. E-mail: gduerksen@ku.edu.

DUESENBERG, RICHARD WILLIAM, lawyer; b. St. Louis, Dec. 10, 1930; s. (John August) Hugo and Edna Marie (Warmann) D.; m. Phyllis Evelyn Buehner, Aug. 7, 1955; children: Karen, Daryl, Mark, David. BA, Valparaiso U., Ind., 1951, JD, 1953, LLD, 2001; LLM, Yale U., New Haven, Conn., 1956. Bar: Mo. 1953. Prof. law NYU, NYC, 1956-62, dir. law ctr. publs., 1960-62; sr. atty. Monsanto Co., St. Louis, 1963-70, asst. gen. counsel, asst. sec., 1975-77, sr. v.p., sec., gen. counsel, 1977-96. Dir. law Monsanto Textiles Co., St. Louis, 1971-75; corp. sec. Fisher Controls Co., Marshalltown, Iowa, 1969-71, Olympia Industries, Spartanburg, SC, 1974-75; vis. prof. law U. Mo., 1970-71; faculty Banking Sch. South, La. State U., 1967-83; vis. scholar Cambridge U., Eng., 1996; vis. prof. law St. Louis U., 1997-98. Author: (with Lawrence P. King) Sales and Bulk Transfers Under the Uniform Commercial Code, 2 vols, 1966, rev., 1984, New York Law of Contracts, 3 vols, 1964, Missouri Forms and Practice Under the Uniform Commercial Code, 2 vols, 1966; editor: Ann. Survey of Am. Law, NYU, 1961-62; mem. bd. contbg. editors and advisors: Corp. Law Rev, 1977-86; contbr. articles to law revs., jours. Mem. lawyers adv. coun. NAM, Washington, 1980, Adminstrv. Conf. U.S., 1980-86, legal adv. com. NY Stock Exch., 1983-87, corp. law dept. adv. coun. Practising Law Inst., 1982; bd. dirs. Bach Soc., St. Louis, 1985-86, pres., 1973-77; bd. dirs. Valparaiso U., 1977-2006, chmn. bd. visitors law sch., 1966-2005, Luth. Charities Assn., 1984-87, vice chmn., 1986-87; bd. dirs. Luth. Med. Ctr., St. Louis, 1973-82, vice chmn., 1975-80; bd. dirs. Nat. Jud. Coll., 1984-90, St. Louis Symphony, 1988-2002, Opera Theatre St. Louis, 1988—, Luth. Brotherhood, Mpls., 1992-2000, Liberty Fund, Inc., Indpls., 1997—. Served with US Army, 1953-55. Decorated officer's cross Order of Merit (Germany); named Disting. Alumnus, Valparaiso U., 1976. Fellow Am. Bar Found.; mem. ABA (chmn. com. uniform comml. code 1976-79, coun. sect. corp., banking and bus. law 1979-83, sec. 1983-84, chmn. 1986-87), Mo. Bar Assn., Am. Law Inst., Mont Pelerin Soc., Nat. Jud. Coll. (bd. dirs. 1984-90), Order of Coif, Bach Soc., Am. Soc. Corp. Sec. (bd. chmn. 1987-88), Assn. Gen. Coun., Am. Arbitration Assn., St. Louis Club. Republican. Lutheran. Home: 1 Indian Creek Ln Saint Louis MO 63131-3333 Home Phone: 314-993-1559. Personal E-mail: rwduesenberg@sbcglobal.net.

DUFF, ANDREW S., corporate financial executive; m. Lucia Duff; children: Meredith, Walter. B in econ., Tufts U. With Piper Jaffray Corp.'s Inst. Fixed Income Sales Dept., 1980—94; mgr., inst. sales and trading Piper Jaffray Corp., 1994—96, pres., 1996—98; vice chmn. U.S. Bancorp, 1999—; pres., CEO U.S. Bancorp Piper Jaffray unit, 2000—. Mem. bd. dirs. Securities Ind. Assn. (SIA), SIA Regional Firms Com., Walker Art Ctr.; bd. trustees Mpls. Found. Office: US Bancorp 800 Nicollet Mall Minneapolis MN 55402

DUFF, BRIAN BARNETT, federal judge; b. Dallas, Sept. 15, 1930; s. Paul Harrington and Frances Ellen (FitzGerald) D.; m. Florence Ann Buckley, Nov. 27, 1953; children: F. Ellen, Brian Barnett Jr., Roderick FitzGerald, Kevin Buckley, Daniel Harrington. AB in English, U. Notre Dame, 1953, postgrad., 1997—; JD, DePaul U., Chgo., 1962. Bar: Ill. 1962, Mass. 1962, U.S. Dist. Ct. (no. dist.) Ill. 1962, U.S. Supreme Ct. 1968. Mgmt. trainee, multiple line underwriter Continental Casualty Co., Chgo., 1956-60; mgmt. cons. Booz, Allen and Hamilton, Chgo., 1960-62; asst. to chief exec. officer Bankers Life and Casualty Co., Chgo., 1962-67; atty. Sloan & Bragiel, Chgo., 1965-68; exec. v.p., gen. counsel R.H. Gore Co., Chgo., 1968-69; atty. Brian B. Duff & Assocs., Chgo., 1969-76; judge Cir. Ct. Cook County Ill., Chgo., 1976-85, U.S. Dist. Ct. (no. dist.) Ill., Chgo., 1985—, now sr. judge. Rep. Ill. Gen. Assembly, Springfield, 1971-76; chmn. House Judiciary Com., 1973-74, minority whip, 1975-76; vis. com. Coll. Law U Chgo., 1977-79; lectr. Law Sch. Loyola U., 1978-79; adj. prof. John Marshall Law Sch., 1985-90, DePaul U. Sch. Law, 1990. Served to lt (j.g.) USN, 1953-56. Mem. ABA, Chgo. Bar Assn., Fed. Judges Assn., Am. Judicature Soc., Nat. Lawyers Club, Inc., (hon.)., Legal Club Chgo. (hon.), Law Club, Ill. State Bar Assn. Roman Catholic. Avocations: fishing, reading, travel, writing.

DUFF, CRAIG, agricultural products executive; Pres. Beef Belt Feeders, Inc., Scott City, Kansas, mgr. Office: Beef Belt Feeders Inc PO Box 528 Scott City KS 67871-0528

DUFF, MARC CHARLES, state legislator; b. Port Washington, Wis., July 4, 1961; s. James Wayne and Marlyn (Hoffman) D. BS, U. Wis., Whitewater, 1983; MA, U. Wis., Madison, 1985. Legis. asst. Wis. State Rep. Tom Ourada, Madison, 1985-87; sr. analyst rep. caucus staff Wis. State Assembly, Madison, 1987-88, mem. from dist. 98, 1988-92, 93—, mem. joint com. fin. Chmn. New Berlin (Wis.) Roadway Beautification Com., 1987—; supr. Dist. 31, Waukesha County, 1988-89. Mem. Rotary Club. Home: 1811 S Elm Grove Rd New Berlin WI 53151-2605 Office: PO Box 8952 Madison WI 53708-8952

DUFFIELD, MICHAEL O., data processing executive; Various positions including plant mgr., mgr. mfg. bus. forms divsn., v.p. distbn. Wallace Computer Svcs., Inc., Lisle, Ill., v.p. ops., 1990-92, sr. v.p., 1992-98, pres., COO, 1998—, interim CEO, 2000—. Office: Wallace Computer Services 3075 Highland Pkwy Ste 400 Downers Grove IL 60515-5560

DUFFY, TERRENCE A., mercantile exchange executive; b. 1958; BSBA, U. Wis., Whitewater, 1980. Pres. TDA Trading, Inc., 1981—; mem. Chgo. Merc. Exch. Inc., 1981—, bd. mem., 1995—, vice chmn., 1998—2002, chmn., 2002—07; vice. chmn. Chgo. Merc. Exch. Holdings Inc., 2001—02, chmn., 2002—07; exec. chmn. CME Group Inc. (formerly Chgo. Merc. Exch. Holdings Inc.), Chgo., 2007—. Mem. bd. World Bus. Chgo., Ill. Agrl. Leadership Found.; bd. regents Mercy Home for Boys and Girls; bd. trustees Saint Xavier Univ.; co-chair Mayo Clinic Greater Chgo. Leadership Coun. Named Top 100 Irish Bus. Leaders, Irish America Magazine, 2003, 2004, 2005. Mem.: Pres. Circle of the Chgo. Coun. on Foreign Rels., Exec. Club of Chgo., Econ. Club of Chgo. Achievements include apptd. by President Bush to Nat. Saver Summit on Retirement Savings, 2002, Fed. Retirement Thrift Investment Bd. (FRTIB), 2003. Office: CME Group Inc 20 S Wacker Dr Chicago IL 60606

DUGAN, PATRICK J., lawyer; b. Lima, Ohio, 1957; BSBA cum laude, Bowling Green State U., 1979; JD with honors, Ohio State U., 1981. Bar: Ohio 1982. Ptnr. Squire, Sanders & Dempsey LLP, Columbus & Cleve., co-chmn., Corp. Practice Group, 2002—05, chmn., Fin. Services Practice Group, 2005—. Bd. trustees Raymond E. Mason Found.; bd. dir. Ariel Corp.; mem. exec. com. Columbus Venture Network. Named an Ohio Super Lawyer mergers & acquisition, Law & Polit. Media, Inc., 2004, 2005; named one of 100 Leaders for New Millennium, Columbus Smart Bus. News, 2000, Columbus Power 100, 2002, 2003, 2004, 2005. Mem.: Beta Alpha Psi, Order of Coif. Office: Squire Sanders & Dempsey LLP 4900 Key Tower 127 Public Sq Cleveland OH 44114-1304 also: Squire Sanders & Dempsey LLP 1300 Huntington Ctr 41 South High St Columbus OH 43215-6197 Office Phone: 216-479-8500, 614-365-2709. Office Fax: 216-479-8780, 614-365-2499. Business E-Mail: pdugan@ssd.com.

DUGAS, RICHARD J., JR., construction executive; b. 1965; m. Susan O. Dugas. BS, La. State U., 1986. Various positions in mktg., retail and customer svc. Exxon, 1986—89; various positions in process improvement and plant operational efficiency PepsiCo, 1990—94; with Pulte Homes Inc., Bloomfield Hills, Mich., 1994—, v.p. process improvement, city pres. and market mgr. for Atlanta divsn., coastal region pres., exec. v.p., COO, 2002—03, pres., CEO, 2003—. Office: Pulte Homes Inc 100 Bloomfield Hills Pky Bloomfield Hills MI 48304-2946

DUGGAN, MICHAEL E., health facility administrator; Diploma, U. Mich. Lawyer pvt. practice; dep. county exec. Wayne County, Mich.; elected Wayne County prosecutor, 2000; pres., CEO Rehab. Inst. Mich. (Detroit Med. Ctr. and Wayne State U.), Detroit, 2004—. Bd. chair Health Choice, 1995—2000. Founder, former pres. Wayne County Kidspace, Inc. Achievements include work to pass legislation a "plus card" system, a health assistance program that put 50,000 unemployed poor people into a Wayne County system allowing local HMOs to bid for their business in 1987; efforts to establish another county health program called Health Choice in 1995. Office: Rehab Inst Mich 261 Mack Blvd Detroit MI 48201-1203

DUGGAN, PATRICK JAMES, federal judge; b. 1933; BS in Econs., Xavier U., 1955; LLB, U. Detroit, 1958. Pvt. practice Brashear, Duggan & Tangora, 1959-76; judge Wayne County Cir. Ct., 1977-86, U.S. Dist. Ct. (ea. dist.) Mich., Detroit, 1987—. Adj. prof. Madonna U., Livonia, Mich., 1975-93. Chmn. Livonia Family YMCA, 1970-71; bd. trustees Madonna U., 1970-79; pres. Livonia Bar Assn., 1975-76. Mem. Mich. Jaycees (pres. 1967-68), Am. Inn of Ct. U. Detroit Law Sch. (pres.) Office: US Dist Ct 867 Theodore Levin Cthouse 231 W Lafayette Blvd Detroit MI 48226-2700

DUHAMEL, JUDITH REEDY OLSON, public information officer, former state senator; b. Mitchell, SD, June 24, 1939; d. John Marvin and Camille (Murphy) Reedy; m. Robert George Olson, Aug. 5, 1961; children: Jeffrey, Jennifer, Jon, Jaime, Jason, Jeremy; m. William F. Duhamel, Aug. 2, 2003. EdB, U. Ariz., Tucson, 1961; MEd, S.D. State U., 1984; postgrad., U. S.D., 1985—. Cert. secondary tchr., edn. adminstrn. Tchr. jr. high sch. Mpls. Pub. Schs., 1961-63; mem. State Bd. Edn., S.D., 1972-83, pres. S.D., 1975-78; dir. S.D. Edn. Policy Seminar, 1975-79; substitute tchr. Rapid City (S.D.) Schs., 1979-81, tchr. adult basic edn., 1979-81, supr. community relations, 1981-88, supr. community edn., pub. info., 1988—95; senator S.D. Legis. (dist. 33), Pierre, SD, 1989—93; edn. dir. Career Learning Center of the Black Hills. Speaker, cons. sch. bds., adminstrs., tchrs., sch. dists., pub. relations, various states, 1972—. Bd. dirs. Black Hills Symphony, 1987—; chair SD State Dem. Party, 1998-2006. Mem. AAUW (Women of Worth award), Rotary, PEO, Delta Kappa Gamma. Democrat. Roman Catholic. Avocations: reading, spectator sports. Home: 1106 Hyland Dr Rapid City SD 57701-4456

DUHL, MICHAEL FOSTER, lawyer; b. Chgo., July 12, 1944; s. Samuel Harold and Gertrude (Crodgen) D.; m. Judith Ann Currie, Jan. 30, 1970; children: Emilie Ann, Benjamin Currie. BBA, U. Mich., 1966; JD magna cum laude, Harvard U., 1969. Bar: Ill. 1969; CPA, Ill. Law clk. to presiding justice Ill. Supreme Ct., Chgo., 1969-70; assoc. Hopkins & Sutter, Chgo., 1971-75, ptnr., 1976-96; prin. Deloitte & Touche, L.L.P., Chgo., 1997—. Bd. editors Harvard Law Rev., 1967-69. Treas. Winnetka (Ill.) Pub. Libr. Dist. Bd., 1980-85; bd. dirs. Winnetka Hist. Soc., 1990-94, Winnetka Landmark Preservation Commn., 1992-96; bd. trustees Village of Winnetka, 1996-2000, pres., 2001—. Mem. ABA, Univ. Club Chgo. Jewish. Office: Deloitte & Touche LLP 2 Prudential Plz 180 N Stetson Ave Fl 19 Chicago IL 60601-6779

DUL, JOHN A., lawyer, electronics executive; b. 1961; BBA, U. Miami; JD, Northwestern U. Bar: Ill., 1986. Assoc. gen. counsel. Anixter Inc. (subsidiary of Anixter Internat.), 1990—96, sec., gen. counsel, 1996—; v.p., gen. counsel Anixter Internat., Skokie, Ill., 1998—, sec., 2002—. Office: Anixter Internat Inc 2301 Patriot Blvd Glenview IL 60025-8020 Office Phone: 224-521-8000.

DULANY, ELIZABETH GJELSNESS, editor; b. Charleston, SC, Mar. 11, 1931; d. Rudolph Hjalmar and Ruth Elizabeth (Weaver) Gjelsness; m. Donelson Edwin Dulany, Mar. 19, 1955; 1 son, Christopher Daniel. BA, Bryn Mawr Coll., 1952. Editor, R.R. Bowker Co., 1948-52; med. editor U. Mich. Hosp., Ann Arbor, 1953-54; editorial asst. E.P. Dutton & Co., NYC, 1954-55, U. Ill. Press, Champaign, 1956-59, asst. editor, 1959-67, assoc. editor, 1967-72, mng. editor, 1972-90, asst. dir., 1983-90, assoc. dir., 1990—98, editor, 1998—. Democrat. Episcopalian. Home: 73 Greencroft Dr Champaign IL 61821-5112 Office: U Ill Press 1325 S Oak St Champaign IL 61820-6903 Office Phone: 217-244-0158. Business E-Mail: edulany@uillinois.edu.

DULAS, DEANNE L., lawyer; b. St. Paul, Aug. 29, 1970; BA, U. Minn., 1992; JD, U. Minn. Law Sch., 1995. Bar: Minn. 1995, US Dist. Ct. (dist. Minn.) 1996, US Ct. Appeals (8th cir.) 1996. Shareholder Strandemo, Sheridan & Dulas, P.A., Eagan, Minn. Named a Rising Star, Minn. Super Lawyers mag., 2006. Mem.: Collaborative Law Inst., Minn. Women Lawyers (co-chair jud. elections endorsement com.), Legal Assistance of Dakota County (bd. dirs., pres.), First Dist. Bar Assn., Minn. State Bar Assn. (mem. family law sect.), Dakota County Bar Assn. Office: Strandemo Sheridan & Dulas PA 1380 Corp Ctr Curve Ste 320 Eagan MN 55121 Office Phone: 651-686-8800. E-mail: ddulas@strandemoandsheridan.com.

DULL, WILLIAM MARTIN, retired engineering executive; b. Buchanan, Mich., June 24, 1924; s. Curtis Frank and Daisy Julia (Sharp) D.; m. Margaret Ann McMillan, Apr. 10, 1976; children: Richard William, Beverly Ann, William McMillan. BSME, U. Mich., 1945. Registered profl. engr., Mich. Dir. tech. staff Detroit Edison, 1951-66, asst. gen. supt. cen. plants, 1966-70, gen. supt. underground lines, 1970-71, mgr. employee relations, 1971-74, mgr. orgn. planning and devel., 1974-89; pres. Charleston Engring. Cons., 1990-92; ret., 1992. Chmn. Charleston Engrs. Joint Coun., 1991—, chmn. 1993-94. Bd. dirs. World Med. Relief, Detroit, 1971-90, chmn., 1988-90; bd. dirs. Jr. Achivement, Southeastern Mich., 1971-90; trustee Detroit Sci. Ctr., Inc., 1979-85. Served to lt. (s.g.) USN, 1942-51, PTO. Recipient Gold Leadership award Jr. Achievement, 1985. Fellow Engring. Soc. Detroit (pres. 1970-71, Disting. Svc. 1980, life); mem. ASHRAE (pres. 1964-65, Outstanding Engr. award 1965, life), ASME (life), IEEE (chmn. nat. conf. 1971), NSPE (life), Architects, Engrs., Surveyors Registration Coun. (chmn. 1968-69), Mich. Soc. Profl. Engrs. (bd. dirs. 1973-75, Disting. Engr. 1980), S.C. Soc. Profl. Engrs. (bd. dirs. 1994-95), Charleston Engrs. Joint Coun. (chmn. 1993-94), U. Mich. Alumni Assn. (v.p., bd. dirs. 1964-71, Disting. Svc. award 1970), Charleston Navy League (v.p., bd. dirs. 1993—), Detroit Yacht Club. Republican. Methodist. Office Phone: 843-849-8213. Personal E-mail: mwmdull@aol.com.

DUMANDAN, JOY, newscaster; BA in Comm., Montclair State U. Assoc. prodr. Am.'s Talking, CNBC Primetime, Ft. Lee, NJ; reporter Sta. WBRE-TV, Wilkes-Barre/Scranton, Pa., 1996; anchor, reporter Sta. WNYW-TV, NYC; anchor Sta. WISH-TV, Indpls., 2001—. Mem.: Asian Am. Journalists Assn. Office: WISH-TV 1950 N Meridian St Indianapolis IN 46207

DUMARS, JOE, III, professional sports team executive, retired professional basketball player; b. Shreveport, La., May 24, 1963; m. Debbie Nelson, 1989; children: Jordan, Aren. Grad. in Bus. Mgmt., McNeese State U., 1985. Player Detroit Pistons, 1985—99, v.p. player pers., 1999—2000, pres. basketball ops., 2000—. Mem. US Men's Nat. Basketball Team (Dream Team II), 1994; mem. exec. com. US Tennis Assn., 1999. Named MVP, NBA Finals, 1989, NBA Exec. of Yr., Sporting ews, 2003; named to NCAA All-Am. 2nd team, 1985, NBA All-Rookie team, 1986, NBA All-Defensive 1st team, 1989—90, 1992—93, All-NBA 3rd team, 1990—91, NBA All-Star team, 1990—93, 1995, 1997, NBA All-Defensive 2nd team, 1991, All-NBA 2nd team, 1993, Mich. Sports Hall of Fame, 2003, La. Sports Hall of Fame, 2003, Naismith Meml. Basketball Hall of Fame, 2006; recipient Citizenship award, 1994, NBA Sportsmanship award (now named Joe Dumars Trophy), 1996. Achievements include winning NBA Championships as a member of the Pistons, 1989, 90. Office: Detroit Pistons 5 Championship Dr Auburn Hills MI 48326-1753

DUMAS, LAWRENCE B., academic administrator; BA in Biochemistry with high honors, Mich. State U., 1963; MA in Biochemistry, U. Wis., 1965, PhD in Biochemistry, 1968. Faculty mem. Northwestern U., Evanston, Ill., 1970—, assoc. prof., 1975—80, prof. biochemistry, molecular biology and cell biology, 1980—95, provost, 1996—. Recipient Career Devel. award, USPHS, 1974—79, John Boezi award for outstanding molecular biology rsch., Mich. State U., 1987; USPHS Predoctoral fellowship at Wis., 1964—67, Postdoctoral Fellowship, Calif. Inst. Tech., 1968—70. Mem.: AAAS, Am. Soc. for Microbiology, Am. Soc. Biol. Chemists. Office: Office of the Provost Northwestern Univ 2-143 Crown Evanston Campus 633 Clark St Evanston IL 60208 Office Phone: 847-491-5117. Office Fax: 847-467-1630. Business E-Mail: nu-provost@northwestern.edu.

DUMESIC, JAMES A., chemical engineer; BS, U. Wis., Madison; MS, PhD, Stanford U. Steenbock prof. dept. chem. engring. U. Wis., Madison. Contbr. articles to profl. jours. Recipient Emmeett award N.Am. Catalysis Soc., 1989, award N.Y. Catalysis Soc. award, 1994, Parravano award Mich. Catalysis Soc., 1999. Mem. AIChE (Colburn award 1983, Wilhelm award 1997), NAE.

Achievements include research in kinetics and catalysis, surface adn solid-state chemistry, in situ catalyst studies. Office: U Wis 3014 Engineering Hall 1415 Engineering Dr Madison WI 53706 E-mail: dumesic@engr.wisc.edu.

DUMOUCHELLE, ERNEST J., art appraiser; s. Joseph N. DuMouchelle and Charlotte D.; m. Lucy DuMouchelle. BA, Univ. Detroit Coll.; student, Wayne State Univ., Gemological Inst. Cert. appraiser. V.p. DuMouchelle Art Gallery Co., Detroit. Appraiser Antiques Roadshow, WGBH-PBS. Mem.: Am. Gemological Inst., Am. Soc. Appraisers. Office: DuMouchelle Gallery 409 E Jefferson Detroit MI 48226 Office Phone: 313-963-6255. Office Fax: 313-963-8199. Business E-Mail: bobdumo@dumouchelle.com.

DUMOUCHELLE, LAWRENCE F., art appraiser; s. Joseph N. DuMouchelle and Charlotte D.; married. CEO DuMouchelle Art Galleries, Detroit, 1957—. Past. pres. Founders' Soc., Jr. Coun., Detroit Inst. for Arts; past pres. Detroit & Canada Tunnel Corp.; appraiser Antiques Roadshow, WGBH-PBS. Past pres. St. Paul's Parish Coun. Mem.: Internat. Soc. Appraisers, Nat. Auctioneers Assn., Mich. Auctioneers Assn., Am. Soc. Appraisers, Appraiser's Assn. Am., Meadowbrook Arts Commn. Office: DuMouchelle Gallery 409 E Jefferson Ave Detroit MI 48226 Office Phone: 313-963-6255. Office Fax: 313-963-8199. Business E-Mail: bobdumo@dumouchelles.com.

DUMOVICH, LORETTA, retired real estate company and transportation executive; b. Kansas City, Kans., Sept. 29, 1930; d. Michael Nicholas and Frances Barbara (Horvat) D. Student public schs., Kansas City. Lic. real estate broker, Kans., Mo. Corp. sec., dir. Riss Internat. Corp., 1950-86, Riss Intermodal Corp., 1969-86, World Leasing Corp., 1969-86; pres., dir. Columbia Properties, Inc., 1969-86; v.p., dir. Republic Industries, 1969-86; corp. sec., dir. Comml. Equipment Co. Inc., Charlotte, N.C., 1980-93; v.p., corp. sec. Commonwealth Gen. Ins. Co., Kansas City, Mo., 1986-93, Heart of Am. Fire & Casualty Co., Kansas City, 1986-93, ret., 1993. Mem. Kansas City (Mo.) Real Estate Bd., Bldg. Owners and Mgrs. Assn. of Kansas City (Mo.), Terminal Properties Exchange (founding mem.), Am. Royal Assn. (gov.) Office: 215 W Pershing Rd Kansas City MO 64108-4317

DUNASKISS, MAT J., state legislator; b. Pontiac, Mich., Sept. 21, 1951; s. Frank and Aldona (Suvesdis) D.; m. Diane L. Tench, 1978; three children. AA, Oakland C.C., 1971; BA, U. Mich., 1973, MA, 1976. Tchr. Lake Orion (Mich.) Cmty. Sch., 1974-78; commr. Oakland County, Mich., 1979-80; rep. Mich. Dist. 61, 1980-90; mem. Mich. Senate from dist. 16, Lansing, 1991—. Chmn. tech. & energy com. Mich. State Sen., vice chmn. natural resources & environ. affairs com., local, urban & state affairs com. Recipient cmty. svc. award Lake Orion Area Jaycees, 1981. Mem. Oakland County C. of C., Optimists, K. of C., Lake Orion Lake Assn., St. Joseph Catholic Ch. Usher's Club. Address: S-8 Capitol Bldg PO Box 30036 Lansing MI 48909-7536

DUNBAR, MARY ASMUNDSON, retired communications executive, investor relations and public relations consultant; b. Sacramento, Calif., Feb. 6, 1942; d. Vigfus Samundur and Aline Mary (McGrath) Asmundson; m. Robert Copeland Dunbar, June 21, 1969; children: Geoffrey Townsend, William Asmundson. BA in English Lit., Smith Coll., 1964; MA in Mass Comm., Stanford U., 1967; MBA in Fin., Case Western Res. U., 1985. Cert. pub. rels. profl. Tchr. Peace Corps, Cameroun, Africa, 1964-66; writer, editor Ednl. Devel. Corp., Palo Alto, Calif., 1967-68, Addison-Wesley, Menlo Park, Calif., 1969-70; freelance writer, editor various cos., Cleve., 1970-85; account exec. Edward Howard & Co., Cleve., 1985-87, Dix & Eaton, Inc., Cleve., 1987-89, sr. account exec., 1990-92, v.p., 1992-96, sr. v.p., 1997—2007. Author publs. in field. Trustee Cleve. Coun. World Affairs, 1994—99. Smith Coll. scholar, Northampton, Mass., 1960-64; fellow Stanford U., Palo Alto, Calif., 1967; recipient Internat. Assn. Bus. Comm. award, 1987, Women in Comm. award, 1987, Arthur Page award, 1990. Mem.: Nat. Assn. Corp. Dir. (cert. dir. edn.), CFA Soc. Cleve., Nat. Investor Rels. Inst. (past pres. Cleve.-No. Ohio chpt., nat. bd. dirs. 2002—07, chmn. bd. 2005—06), Pub. Rels. Soc. Am. (Silver Anvil award 1997, APR cert.), Smith Coll. Club Cleve. Republican. Episcopalian. Avocations: yoga, music. Home: 2880 Fairfax Rd Cleveland OH 44118-4014 Personal E-mail: marydunbar@gmail.com.

DUNCAN, ARNE, school system administrator; JD (hon.), Lake Forest Coll., 2003; M in Sociology magna cum laude, Harvard U., 1987. Profl. basketball player, Australia, 1987—91; dir. Ariel Edn. Initiative, Chgo., 1992—98; deputy chief of staff for CEO Chgo. Pub. Sch., 1999—2001, CEO, 2001—. Bd. mem. Ariel Edn. Initiative, Bold Chgo., Chgo. Cares, The Children's Ctr., The Golden Apple Found., Ill. Coun. Against Handgun Violence, Jr. Achievement, The Nat. Assoc. Basketball Coaches' Found., Scholarship Chgo. and South Side YMCA; co-chmn. Mayor Daley's Reading Adv. Coun.; vis. com. U. Chgo. Sch. Social Svc. Admin. Fellow: Leadership Greater Chgo's Class of 1995; mem.: Aspen Inst. Henry Crown Fellowship Program. Office: Chgo Pub Sch 125 S Clark St 5th Fl Chicago IL 60603

DUNCAN, CLEO, state legislator; m. John Duncan. BS, Ball State U.; MS, Purdue U. Sales rep. Gray & Gray Specialties; mem. Ind. State Ho. of Reps. Dist. 67, mem. edn., pub. policy, ethics and vet. affairs com., mem. roads and transp. com., vice-chmn. environ. affairs com. Councilman Greensburg, Ind.; pres. Decatur County Solid Waste Bd.; mem. Greensburg City Planning Commn., Decatur County Coun. Youth; founder Project HELP. Mem. Greensburg C. of C., Decatur County Found.

DUNCAN, DICK, former state agency administrator; s. Charles Arthur and Vera (Glidden) D.; m. Grace Duncan, Aug. 17, 1998; children: Sally, Sandra, Douglas, Lisa. LLB, S.D. U., 1962. Asst. atty. gen. State S.D., Pierre, 1962-65; pvt. practice law Duncan Olinger Sistka Law Office, Pierre, 1965-86; dir. banking State S.D., Pierre, 1986—. With USMC, 1951-54. Republican. Avocation: sailing. Office: Commerce and Regulations Dept 118 W Capitol Ave Pierre SD 57501-2000

DUNCAN, ED EUGENE, lawyer; b. Gary, Ind., Dec. 10, 1948; s. Attwood and Freddie Leon (Ballard) D.; m. Patricia Louise Revado, Sept. 8, 1973 (div.); children: Kristin, Anika, Gregory. BA, Oberlin Coll., 1970; JD, Northwestern U., 1974. Bar: Ohio 1974, U.S. Dist. Ct. (no. dist.) Ohio 1977, U.S. Supreme Ct. 1977. Assoc. Arter & Hadden, Cleve., 1974-82, ptnr., 1982—2003, Tucker Ellis & West, Cleve., 2003—. Bd. dirs. Glenville br. YMCA, Cleve., 1979—95, Ohio Bd. of Bldg. Standards, Columbus, 1986-89; trustee Legal Aid Soc., Cleve., 1990-91. Mem.: Cleve. Bar Assn., Ohio Bar Assn. Avocations: writing, reading. Home: 935 Roland Rd Cleveland OH 44124-1033 Office: Tucker Ellis & West 925 Euclid Ave Ste 1150 Cleveland OH 44115-1475 Home Phone: 440-449-0758; Office Phone: 216-696-2862. Business E-Mail: EDuncan@TuckerEllis.com.

DUNCAN, FRED A., food products company executive; Various acctg. and planning positions J.M. Smucker Co., Orrville, Ohio, 1977-88, treas., 1988, v.p. procurement and tech. svcs., v.p., gen. mgr., 1995—. Mng. dir. Australian subs. Henry Jones Foods Pty. Ltd. Office: J M Smucker Co 1 Strawberry Ln Orrville OH 44667-1241

DUNCAN, R. FOSTER, utilities company executive; V.p., corp. treas. Freeport-McMoRan Inc., Freeport-McMoRan Copper & Gold; v.p. planning and devel. LG&E Energy Corp., Louisville, 1998-99, exec. v.p., CFO, 1999-2001; CFO Cinergy Corp., Cin., 2001—. Office: 139 E 4th St Cincinnati OH 45202-4003

DUNCAN, ROBERT BANNERMAN, dean, strategy and organizations educator; b. Milw., July 4, 1942; s. Robert Lynn and Irene (Hoenig) D.; m. Susan Jean Phillips, June 12, 1965; children: Stephanie Olcott, Christopher Robert. BA, Ind. U., 1964, MA, 1966; PhD, Yale U., 1971. From asst. prof. to prof. Kellogg Grad. Sch. Mgmt. orthwestern U., Evanston, Ill., 1970—96, prof. leadership orgnl. change, 1996—2002, provost, 1987—91; Eli and Edythe L. Broad dean Eli Broad Coll. Bus. Mich. State U., East Lansing, 2002—. Co-author: Innovations and Organizations, 1973, Strategies for Planned Change, 1977; also numerous articles in profl. jours. Fellow Acad. Mgmt. (chair nat. program 1980-81, pres. 1983-84). Avocation: sailing.

DUNCAN, ROYAL ROBERT, publisher; b. Bloomington, Ill., May 6, 1952; s. Robert E. and Audrey L. Gresham (Mossberger) D. AA, Rock Valley Coll., Rockford, Ill., 1972; BS, Bradley U., 1974. Sales mgr. Sports Svcs., Peoria, Ill., 1975-77, 4-B Advt., East Peoria, Ill., 1977-78; pres. Royal Pub., Peoria, 1978—. Home: 428 W Collingwood Cir Peoria IL 61614-2069 Office: 7620 Harker Dr Peoria IL 61615-1849

DUNCAN, SAM K., retail executive; b. Blytheville, Ark. Joined as courtesy clerk Albertson's Inc., 1969, numerous mgmt. positions, 1969—91; dir. operations Albertson's, 1991—92; v.p. grocery dept. Fred Meyer, Inc., 1992—97, exec. v.p. food divsn., 1997—98, pres., 2001—02, Ralph's Supermarkets, 1998—2001; pres., CEO ShopKo Stores Inc., 2002—05; pres., CEO, chmn. OfficeMax Inc., Itasca, Ill., 2005—. Office: OfficeMax Inc 150 E Pierce Rd Itasca IL 60143

DUNCANSON, JON, newscaster; m. Sylvia Gomez. Photo stringer UPI, Time mag.; reporter and anchor WDIO-TV, Duluth, Minn., 1984—85, WFTV-TV, Orlando, Fla., 1985—88, KRCA-TV, Sacramento, 1988—92; reporter WBBM-TV, Chgo., 1992—95; morning anchor and spl. projects reporter WFLD-TV, Chgo., 1995—98; weekend anchor and reporter WBBM-TV, Chgo., 1998—. Office: WBBM-TV 630 N McClurg Ct Chicago IL 60601

DUNEA, GEORGE, nephrologist, educator; b. Craiova, Rumania, June 1, 1933; came to U.S., 1964; s. Charles L. and Gerda (Low) D.; 1 dau., Melanie. MD, U. Sydney, Australia, 1957. Diplomate Am. Bd. Internal Medicine, Am. Bd. Nephrology. Intern Royal North Shore Hosp., Sydney, 1958—59; resident internal medicine Australia, 1959—63, England, 1959—63; fellow in nephrology Cleve. Clinic, Presbyn.-St. Luke's Hosp., Chgo., 1964—66; practice internal medicine specializing in nephrology Chgo., 1972—; attending physician Cook County Hosp., Chgo., 1966—, dir. dept. nephrology-hypertension, 1969—; prof. medicine U. Ill., Chgo., 1986—; pres., CEO Hektoen Inst. of Med. Rsch., Chgo., 1991—. Vis. prof. medicine Rush Med. Sch., Chgo., 1976—. Contbr. chpts. to books, articles to profl. publs. Fellow A.C.P., Royal Coll. Physicians (London, Edinburgh); mem. AMA, Am. Soc. Nephrology, Brit. Med. Assn., Soc. Med. History. Home: 222 E Chestnut St Chicago IL 60611-2360 Office: 1835 W Harrison St Chicago IL 60612-3701 Office Phone: 312-948-2510. Personal E-mail: gdu222@yahoo.com.

DUNGY, TONY, professional football coach; b. Jackson, Mich., Oct. 6, 1955; s. Wilbur and Cleomane Dungy; m. Lauren Harris; children: Tiara, Jade, Eric, Jordan, Justin, James (dec.). BA in Bus. Adminstrn., U. Minn., 1977. Profl. football player Pitts. Steelers, 1977—78, defensive asst., 1981-83, defensive back coach, 1982-83, defensive coord., 1984-88, Minn. Vikings, 1992-95; profl. football player San Francisco 49ers, 1979, NY Giants, 1980; defensive backs coach U. Minn., 1980, Kans. City Chiefs, 1989-91; head coach Tampa Bay Buccaneers, Fla., 1996—2001, Indpls. Colts, 2002—. Author: Quiet Strength: The Principles, Practices, & Priorities of a Winning Life, 2007 (reached number 1 on the NY Times bestseller list). Active Athletes in Action, Big Brothers Big Sisters, Boys & Girls Clubs, All Pro Dad, Basket of Hope, Black Coaches Assn. Nat. Convention, Ind. Black Expo, United Way Ctrl. Ind., Am. Diabetes Assn.; founder Mentors for Life, Tampa Bay; active Fellowship Christian Athletes, Prison Crusade Ministry. Recipient Fatherhood award, Nat. Fatherhood Initiative, 2002, Espy award, Best Coach-Mgr., 2007; named one of The World's Most Influential People, TIME mag., 2007; named to Ind. Hall of Fame, 2008. Achievements include member of the Pittsburgh Steelers Super Bowl Championship Team, 1978; becoming one of two first African-Am. coaches in Super Bowl, 2007; first African-Am. head coach to win a Super Bowl, Indianapolis Colts, Feb. 4, 2007; one of three individuals to win the Super Bowl as a player and head coach. Office: Indianapolis Colts 7001 West 56th Street Indianapolis IN 46254*

DUNIPHAN, J. P., state legislator, small business owner; b. Aug. 31, 1946; Mem. SD Ho. of Reps., Pierre, 1995—2002, mem. commerce com., judiciary com., chair local govt. com., 1995—2002; mem. SD State Senate, Dist. 33, 2002—. Ptnr. Elks II, 1993—, Quad Investments, 1993—. Republican. Fax: 605-342-6399.

DUNKLAU, RUPERT LOUIS, financial planner, consultant; b. Arlington, Nebr., May 19, 1927; s. Louis Z. and Amelia S. (Gnuse) Dunklau; m. Ruth Eggert, June 4, 1950 (dec. ov. 1998); children: Paul, Janet; m. Ruth King, Sept. 3, 2000. BS, U. Nebr., 1950; LittD (hon.), Concordia Coll., St. Paul, 1982; LLD (hon.), Midland Luth. Coll., Fremont, Nebr., 1985, Valparaiso U., 2005. Exec. v.p. Valmont Industries, Inc., Valley, Nebr., 1950-73; dir. Fremont Nat. Bank, Nebr., 1968-2000. Bd. dirs. Midland Luth. Coll., Cmty. Chest Fremont; bd. dirs. Concordia Pub. House Valparaiso (Ind.) U.; chmn. bd. dirs. Meml. Hosp. Dodge County; bd. dirs. Luth. Ch.-Mo. Synod, St. Louis. With USNR, 1945. Mem.: Rotary Club. Republican. Home: 2948 Deer Run Fremont NE 68025 Office: PO Box 1558 Fremont NE 68026-1558 Office Phone: 402-721-6046.

DUNLAP, WILLIAM DEWAYNE, JR., advertising agency executive; b. Austin, Minn., Apr. 8, 1938; s. William D. and Evelyn (Hummel) D.; m. Lois Mary Apple, Sept. 23, 1961; children: Kristin, Leslie, Brenda. BA, Carleton Coll., 1960. Brand mgr. soap Procter & Gamble, Cin., 1960-69; asst. postmaster gen. U.S. Postal Svc., Washington, 1970-75, chmn. postmaster gen.'s customer coun., 1971-75, chmn. stamp adv. coun., 1972-75; pres. MCA Advt., Westport, Conn., 1976-81, Campbell-Mithun Esty, Mpls., 1981—2003, CEO, 1983—2003, chmn., 1994—2003, Petters Consumer Brands, Mpls., 2004—. Bd. dirs. Operation Smile Internat. Lutheran. Office: Petters Consumer Brands 4400 Baker Rd Hopkins MN 55343-8684 Office Phone: 952-934-9918.

DUNLOP, KAREN OWEN, lawyer; b. 1966; BS, Georgetown U., 1987; MA, U. Va., 1989, JD, 1992. Bar: Ill. 1992. With Sidley Austin Brown & Wood, Chgo., 1992—, ptnr., 2001—. Mem.: Am. Health Lawyers Assn. (vice chair health sys. transactions com.). Office: Sidley Austin Brown and Wood Bank One Plz 10 S Dearborn St Chicago IL 60603

DUNLOP, MICHAEL, broadcast executive; b. Pontiac, Mich., Nov. 11, 1946; Student, Wayne State U. Gen. mgr. Sta WKBD-TV, Southfield, Mich., 1996—. Office: Sta WKBD-TV 26905 W 11 Mile Rd Southfield MI 48034-2292

DUNN, EDWIN RYDELL, lawyer; b. Boston, July 24, 1942; s. Richard Joseph and Clara Hudson (Rydell) Dunn; m. Kathleen Lynch, July 23, 1966; children: Jeanne, Kathleen, Anne, Daniel. BA, U. Notre Dame, Ind., 1964; JD cum laude, Northwestern U., Chgo., 1967. Bar: Ill. 1967. Assoc. Baker & McKenzie, Chgo., 1967—73, ptnr., 1973—. Mem. law bd. Northwestern U. Law Sch., 1996—, chmn., 2004—06; bd. dirs. Nr. West Side Cmty. Devel. Corp., 1991—. Mem. bd. advisors Cath. Charities, Chgo., 1999—. Mem.: ABA, Ill. Bar Assn., Chgo. Bar Assn. Office: Baker & McKenzie 1 Prudential Pla 130 E Randolph Dr Ste 3900 Chicago IL 60601-6342 Office Phone: 312-861-2864. Business E-Mail: edwin.r.dunn@bakernet.com.

DUNN, FLOYD, biophysics and biomedical engineering professor; b. Kansas City, Mo., Apr. 14, 1924; s. Louis and Ida (Leibtag) Dunn; m. Elsa Tanya Levine, June 11, 1950; children: Andrea Susan, Louis Brook. Student, Kans. City Jr. Coll., 1941-42, Tex. A&M U., College Station, 1943; BS, U. Ill., Urbana, 1949, MS, 1951, PhD, 1956. Rsch. assoc. elec. engring. U. Ill., Urbana, 1954-57, rsch. asst. prof. elec. engring., 1957-61, assoc. prof. elec. engring. and biophysics, 1961-65, prof., 1965—95, prof. elec. engring., biophysics and bioengring., 1972-95, faculty mem. Beckman Inst. Advanced Sci. and Tech., prof. emeritus, 1995—, dir. bioacoustics rsch. lab., 1976-95, chmn. bioengring. faculty, 1978-82. Vis. prof. U. Coll., Cardiff, Wales, 1968—69, Inst. Chest Diseases and Cancer, Tohoku U., Sendai, Japan, 1989—90, U. Nanjing, China, 1983; mem. bioengring., radiation and diagnostic radiology study sects. NIH, 1970—81; steering com. workshop interaction ultrasound and biol. tissues NSF, 1971—72; vis. sr. scientist Inst. Cancer Rsch., Sutton, Surrey, England, 1975—76, Sutton, 1982—83, Sutton, 1990; chmn. working group health aspects exposure to ultrasound radiation WHO, London, 1976; mem. tech.-elec. products radiation stds. com. FDA, 1974—76; vis. prof. radiation oncology U. Ariz., Tucson, 1996—; mem. Nat. Coun. Radiation Protection and Measurement, 1980—2003, fellow, 2003—; treas. Interscience Rsch. Inst., Champaign, Ill., 1957—58; mem. sci. adv. bd. Resonant Med. Inc., Montreal, 2005—. Mem. editl. bd. Jour. Acoustical Soc. Am., 1968—, Ultrasound Medicine and Biology, 1981—, Ultrasonics, 1981—2003, Encyclopedia of Acoustics, 1981—97, Encyclopedia of Applied Physics, 1981—, Am. Inst. Physics Series Modern Acoustics and Signal Processing, 1990—97; contbr. articles to profl. jours.; cons. Piezo Energy Technologies LLC, 2007—. Trustee Hensley Twp., Ill., 1980—81. With AUS, 1943—46. Recipient Spl. Merit medal, Acoustical Soc. Japan, 1988, History Med. Ultrasound Pioneer award, AIUM/WFUMB, 1988; Spl. Rsch. fellow, NIH, 1968—69, Eleanor Roosevelt-Internat. Cancer fellow, Am. Cancer Soc., 1975—76, 1982—83, Fulbright fellow, 1982—83, Japan Soc. Promotion Sci. fellow, 1982, 1996, Fogarty Internat. fellow, 1990. Fellow: AAAS, IEEE (life), Inst. Acoustics (U.K.), Am. Inst. Ultrasound in Medicine (William J. Fry meml. award 1984, Joseph H. Holmes Basic Sci. Pioneer award 1990), Acoustical Soc. Am. (assoc. editor Jour. 1968-, exec. coun. 1977-80, v.p. 1980-81, pres. 1985-86, chmn. pub. policy com. 1994-, Silver medal 1989, Gold medal 1998), Am. Inst. Med. Biol. Engring. (IEEE Engring. Medicine and Biology Soc. Career Achievement award 1995, Edison medal 1996), Internat. Acad. Med. Biol. Engring.; mem.: NAE, AS, Biophys. Soc., Rochester Soc. Biomed. Ultrasound (hon.), Japan Soc. Ultrasound in Medicine (hon.), Am. Inst. Physics (mem. editl. bd. series in modern acoustics and signal processing 1990—97, publs. policy com. 1992—2000), NCRP Alumni Assn., NIH Alumni Assn., Sigma Xi, Phi Sigma Phi, Phi Sigma, Pi Mu Epsilon, Tau Beta Pi, Eta Kappa Nu, Sigma Tau. Home: 13500 N Rancho Vistoso Blvd # 143 Tucson AZ 85755-5956 Personal E-mail: floyd@ece.arizona.edu.

DUNN, JAMES BERNARD, mining company executive, state legislator; b. Lead, SD, June 27, 1927; s. William Bernard and Lucy Marie (Mullen) D.; m. Elizabeth Ann Lanham, Sept. 5, 1955; children: Susan, Thomas, Mary Elizabeth, Kathleen. BS in Bus. Adminstrn. and Econ., Black Hills State U., 1962. Heavy equipment mechanic Homestake Mining Co., Lead, 1945-62, asst. dir. pub. relations, 1962-78, dir. pub. affairs, 1978-85; mem. S.D. Ho. Reps., Pierre, 1971-72, S.D. State Senate, Pierre, 1973-2000, asst. majority leader, 1989-92, asst. minority leader, 1993-94, sr. asst. majority leader, 1995-2000. Exec. com. Nat. Conf. State Legislatures, 1979-81, 93-95, Coun. State Govt., 1983—; chmn. Midwestern Conf. Coun. of State Govts., 1984; bd. dirs. S.D. Blue Shield, S.D. Automobile Assn. Editor: Homestake Gold Mine 1876-1976, 1976, Bulldog Mountain Silver Mine, 1978. Bd. dirs. S.D. State Hist. Soc., Pierre,. 1971—; chmn. bd. trustees Adams Mus., Deadwood, S.D., 1962—. With U.S. Army, 1945-47. Republican. Roman Catholic. Avocations: hunting, fishing, hiking, history. Home: 619 Ridge Rd Lead SD 57754-1144 Office: State Senate State Capitol Pierre SD 57501

DUNN, JOHN FRANCIS, lawyer, state representative; b. Logansport, Ind., Dec. 24, 1936; s. John Francis and Bertha (Newman) D.; m. Barbara Burke, Feb. 10, 1962; children: John F. III, Robert E., William M., Nancy L. BS in Chem. Engring., U. Notre Dame, 1958, JD, 1961. Bar: Ill. 1961, Ind. 1961, U.S. Dist. Ct. (so. dist.) Ill. 1961, U.S. Ct. Appeals (4th cir.) 1962. Atty. Standard Oil Ind. (now Amoco), Chgo., 1961-64; assoc. Morey and Dunn, Attys., Decatur, Ill., 1964-74; ptnr. Dunn and Fichter, Attys., Decatur, Ill., 1975-85; pvt. practice Decatur, Ill., 1986—. State rep. Ill. Gen. Assembly, Springfield, 1974-94, asst. majority leader; city councilman City of Decatur, 1971-74. Democrat. Roman Catholic. Avocations: bicycling, jogging. Office: 301 Millikin Ct Decatur IL 62523-1399

DUNN, JON MICHAEL, logician, dean emeritus, consultant; b. Ft. Wayne, Ind., June 19, 1941; s. Jon Hardin and Philomena Elizabeth (Lauer) D.; m. Sarah Jane Hutchison, Aug. 8, 1964; children— Jon William, Jennifer Anne AB, Oberlin Coll., 1963; PhD, U. Pitts., 1966. Asst. prof. philosophy Wayne State U., Detroit, 1966-69; vis. asst. prof. philosophy Yale U., New Haven, 1968-69; assoc. prof. philosophy Ind. U., Bloomington, 1969-76, prof., 1976—, Oscar Ewing prof. philosophy, 1989—2007, chmn. dept. philosophy, 1980-84, 94-97, adj. prof. computer sci., 1987-89, prof., 1989—2007, assoc. dean Coll. Arts and Scis., 1988-91, exec. assoc. dean, 1991-93, dean. Sch. Informatics, 2000—07, prof. informatics, 2002—07, prof. emeritus, 2007—. Vis. fellow Inst. Advanced Studies, Australian Nat. U., Canberra, 1975-76; sr. visitor Math. Inst., U. Oxford, Eng., 1978; faculties vis. scholar U. Melbourne, Australia, 1983; fellow Ind. U. Inst. for Advanced Study, 1984; sr. visitor Ctr. for Philosophy of Sci., U. Pitts., Nov. 1984; adj. prof. U. Mass., Amherst, spring 1985; SF prin. investigator, 1969-74. Author: (with G. Hardegree) Algebraic Methods in Philosophical Logic, 2001; contbg. author: Entailment, Vol. I, 1975, co-author Vol. II, 1992; editor: (with A. Gupta) Truth or Consequences: Essays in Honor of Nuel Belnap, 1990, (with G. Epstein) Modern Uses of Multiple-Valued Logic, 1975, (with G. Hardegree) Algebraic Methods in Philosophical Logic, 2001; editor Jour. Symbolic Logic, 1982-87; chief editor Jour. Philos. Logic, 1987-95; N.Am. editor Bull. Logic Sect., Polish Acad. Scis.; mem. editl. bds. Jour. Philos. Logic, 1979-87, Nous, 1968—, Studia Logica, 1978-2000, Jour. Non-Classical Logic, 1985-91, Annals of Math., Computing and Teleinformatics, Logic and Logical Philosophy, 1993—. Recipient Ind. U. Provost's medal, 2007, Sagamore Wabash award, 2007; Am. Council Learned Socs. fellow, 1984-85; Fulbright-Hays rsch. sr. scholar, 1975-76. Mem. Assn. Symbolic Logic (exec. com. 1978-81, coun. 1982—), Soc. Exact Philosophy (treas. 1982-84, v.p. 1986-88, pres. 1988-90), Am. Philos. Assn. (com. rsch. and publs. 1985-88), Computing Rsch. Assn. (vice chair IT deans group 2004-06). Office: Ind U Sch Informatics 901 E 10th St Bloomington IN 47408

DUNN, M. CATHERINE, college administrator, educator; b. Chgo., Mar. 26, 1934; d. John and Catherine (Donovan) Dunn BA, Ariz. State U., 1968, MA, 1970, PhD, 1977. Cert. tchr., Iowa, Ariz. Tchr. St. Mathew Sch., Phoenix, 1956-60; tchr. St. Vincent Sch., Chgo., 1960-68; asst. prin. Carroll Sch., Lincoln, Ill., 1970-73; mem. faculty Clarke Coll., Dubuque, Iowa, 1973-79, v.p. devel., 1979-84, pres., 1984—. Bd. dirs. Am. Trust Bank, Dubuque, 1989—; cons. in field. Bd. dirs. Internat. Student Leadership, Notre Dame, Ind., 1975—, Med. Assocs. HMO, Dubuque, 1980—, Jr. Achievement, 1982—; mem. Iowa Dept. Transp. Commn., Ames, 1989—. Named One of Ten Outstanding Leaders in Dubuque Telegraph Herald newspaper, 1987, 88, 89. Mem. Am. Coun. Edn., Coun. Ind. Colls. (bd. dirs.), Am. Assn. Cath. Colls., Iowa Assn. Coll. Pres. (bd. dirs. 1984—), Ariz. State Alumni Assn., Dubuque C. of C. (mem. coun. 1973—, bd. dirs. 1986—, Outstanding Civic Leader award 1974, Civic Svc. award 1993), Coun. Advancement and Support Edn. (bd. dirs.), Phi Delta Kappa, Pi Lambda Theta. Avocations: cooking, music, walking, travel. Home: 2350 Clarke Crest Dr Dubuque IA 52001-3125 Office: Clarke Coll 1550 Clarke Dr Dubuque IA 52001-3117

DUNN, MARGARET M., general surgeon, educator, university official; b. Freeport, NY, Sept. 8, 1954; d. Howard James and Evelyn Ann (Madden) D.; m. William Anthony Spohn, July 4, 1982; children: Christopher, Marie. BS, Pa. State U., 1974; MD, Jefferson Med. Coll., 1977. Diplomate Am. Bd. Surgery. Resident in surgery Montefiore Hosp., Bronx, N.Y., 1977-82; prof. surgery Wright Sch. Medicine, Dayton, Ohio, 1982—, assoc. dean for faculty and clin. affairs, 1999—. Fellow ACS; mem. Assn. Women Surgeons, Am. Med. Women's Assn., Ctrl. Surg. Assn., Soc. Surgery Alimentary Tract. Office: Wright State U Sch Medicine 3640 Col Glenn Hwy Dayton OH 45435

DUNN, MARVIN IRVIN, physician; b. Topeka, Dec. 21, 1927; s. Louis and Ida (Leibtag) D.; m. Maureen Cohen, Mar. 10, 1956 (dec. Nov. 1988); children: Jonathan Louis, Marilyn Paulette. BA, U. Kans., 1950, MD, 1954. Intern USPHS, San Francisco, 1954-55; resident U. Kans., 1955-58, fellow, 1958-59, instr. medicine, 1958-60, assoc. in medicine, 1960-62, asst. prof. medicine, 1962-65, assoc. prof., 1965-70, prof., 1970-2000, prof. emeritus, 2001—, Franklin E. Murphy Disting. prof., 1978-2000, dir. Cardiovascular Lab., head sect. Cardiovascular Disease Med. Center, 1963-92, dean Sch. of Medicine, 1979-84. Cons. USAF, 1971—95; spl. cons. to fed. air surgeon of FAA, 1990—; spl. ednl. cons. to Kansas City Mo. Met. Coll. Author: Home Study Course: Difficult EKG Diagnosis, 1969, Translator Deductive and Polyparametric Electrocardiography, 1970; (with others) Clinical Vectorcardiography and Electrocardiography, 2d edit., 1977, Clinical Electrocardiography, 8th edit., 1989; editor in chief Cardiovascular Perspectives, 1985-89; mem. editl. bd. Am. Jour. Cardiology, 1970-75, Catheterization and Cardiovascular Diagnosis, 1980-87, AMA Archives Internal Medicine, 1984-94, Jour. Am. Coll. Cardiology, 1983-89, Biomedicine and Pharmacotherapy, 1985-90, Am. Jour. Noninvasive Cardiology, 1985-89, Chest, 1984-89, 94-98, Practical Cardiology, 1980-88, Heart and Lung, 1986-88, Bd.-Advanced in Therapy, 1992, Slovak Jour. Noninvasive Cardiology, 1993, Griffith Resource Libr., 1980-90, Am. Heart Jour., Jour. Acoustical Soc.; mem. internat. sci. bd. Italian Heart Jour., 2005—. Bd. dirs. Hebrew Acad. Jewish Geriatric and Convalescent Center, Beth Shalom Synagogue. Served with AUS, 1946-47. Recipient Alumnus of Yr. award U. Kansas Sch. Medicine, 1987, silver medal U. Socrates, Thessaloniki, Greece, 1992. Master Am. Coll. Chest Physicians (mem. bd. regents, pres. 1988-89, gov. State of Kans.); fellow ACP (Laureate award 1990), Am. Coll. Cardiology (trustee), Am. Heart Assn., Royal Acad. Medicine (Ireland), Royal Coll. Physicians

(Valencia, Spain); mem. Am. Physicians Fellowship (dir.), Univ. Cardiologists, Alpha Omega Alpha, Phi Chi (cited Best Doctors in Am., 1998). Home: 3205 Tomahawk Rd Shawnee Mission KS 66208-1861 Office: U Kans Hosp 3901 Rainbow Blvd Kansas City KS 66160-0001

DUNN, MICHAEL J., dean; m. Patricia O'Reilly; 5 children. MD, Med. Coll. of Wisconsin, 1962. Intern Johns Hopkins Hosp, Baltimore, 1962—63, resident, 1963—65; asst. prof. & co-dir., nephrology unit U. Vermont Coll. Medicine, 1969—77; various pos. Case Western Reserve, 1977—95; dean, prof. of med. and exec v.p. Med. Coll. Wis., Milw., 1995—. Grantee Fogarty Senior International Fellow. Mem.: Am. Soc. Nephrology (pres. 1989—90). Office: Med Coll Wis Office of the Dean 8701 W Watertown Plank Rd Milwaukee WI 53226-3548

DUNN, REBECCA JO, state legislator; d. Francis G. and Eldred (Wagner) D. BA, U. S.D., 1967; MA, U. Hawaii, 1972. Senator S.D. State Senate Dist. 15, 1993—2001, asst. minority leader, mem. legis. exec. bd., mem. corrections com. Motivational spkr. Author: The Pearl of Potentiality, Co-A, 1979. Bd. dirs. S.D. Humanities Found. Mem. PEO, Downtown Rotary, Hawaii Yacht Club, Kappa Alpha Theta. Home: 320 N Summit Ave Sioux Falls SD 57104-2933

DUNN, STEVEN M., construction executive; Exec. v.p. ops. Crossman Cmtys., Indpls., 1998—. Office: Crossman Communities 9202 N Meridian St Ste 300 Indianapolis IN 46260-1833

DUNN, WILLIAM BRADLEY, lawyer; b. Newark, Dec. 2, 1939; s. Ernest William and Ruth Harriet (Bradley) D.; m. Judy Ann Shepherd, Aug. 2, 1988; children: John, Peter, Brian, Kelly. AB, Muskingum Coll., 1961; JD, U. Mich., 1964. Bar: Mich. 1964. Mem. Clark Hill PLC (formerly Clark, Klein & Beaumont), Detroit, 1964—. Lectr. in field. Contbr. articles to legal jours. Mem.: ABA (chair sect. real property, probate and trust law 1989—90, mem. Ho. dels. 1990—98, mem. standing com. on professionalism 1993—96, mem. standing com. on ethics and profl. responsibility 1998—2001, spl. adv. standing com. on ethics and profl. responsibility 2001—02, mem. standing com. on ethics and profl. responsibility 2003—06, chmn. standing com. ethics and profl. responsibility 2005—06), State Bar Mich. (mem. com. profl. ethics 2002—07, chmn. com. profl. ethics 2007—), Internat. Assn. Attys. and Exec. Corp. Real Estate, Am. Coll. Real Estate Lawyers (pres. 1983—84). Episcopalian. Home: 6398 Catalpa Ct Troy MI 48098-2231 Office: Clark Hill PLC 500 Woodward Ave Ste 3500 Detroit MI 48226-3435 Office Phone: 313-965-8511. Business E-Mail: wdunn@clarkhill.com.

DUNNIGAN, BRIAN LEIGH, historian, curator; b. Detroit, July 11, 1949; s. James Patrick and Dorothy Jane (McKay) D.; m. Carol Lynn Fredriksen, Sept. 21, 1974 (div. Oct. 1988); m. Candice Maria Cain, Apr. 22, 1989; children: James Cain, Claire Beausom. BA in History, U. Mich., 1971, MA in History, 1973; MA in History and Museum Studies, Cooperstown Grad. Programs, 1979. Curator Mackinac Island (Mich.) State Park Commn., 1971-74; mng. dir. Historic Fort Wayne, Ind., 1974-79; exec. dir. Old Fort Niagara Assn., Youngstown, NY, 1979-96; curator of maps William L. Clements Libr. U. Mich., Ann Arbor, 1996—. Author: History and Guide to Old Fort Niagara, 1985, Siege-1759, 1986, rev. edit., 1996, Glorious Old Relic, 1987, Forts Within A Fort, 1989, Old Fort Niagara in Four Centuries, 1991; editor: Pouchot's Memoirs on the Late War in North America, 1994, Niagara, 1796, 1996, Frontier Metropolis, 2001. Fellow Co. Mil. Historians. Home: 4531 Maute Rd Grass Lake MI 49240 Office: William L Clements Libr 909 S University Ave Ann Arbor MI 48109-1190 Home Phone: 517-522-6797; Office Phone: 734-764-2347. Business E-Mail: briand@umich.edu.

DUNWOODY, SHARON LEE, journalism and communications educator; b. Hamilton, Ohio, Jan. 24, 1947; d. Walter Charles and Fanchon (Kapp) D. MA, Temple U., 1975; PhD, Ind. U., 1978. Asst. prof. journalism Ohio State U., Columbus, 1977-81; from asst. prof. to prof. Sch. Journalism and Mass Comm. U. Wis., Madison, 1981—, dir. Sch. Journalism and Mass Comm., 1998—2003, assoc. dean Grad. Sch., 2003—. Affiliate Inst. Environ. Studies U. Wis., Madison, 1985—, head acad. programs, 1995-98. Co-editor: Scientists and Journalists, 1986, Communicating Uncertainty, 1999. Mem. AAAS (chair sect. on gen. interest in sci. and Eng. 1992-93), Soc. Social Study Sci., Midwest Assn. Pub. Opinion Rsch. (pres. 1989-90), Assn. Edn. in Journalism and Mass Comm. (pres. 2005-06). Home: 1306 Seminole Hwy Madison WI 53711-3728 Office: Univ Wis Sch Journalism & Mass Comm 821 University Ave Madison WI 53706-1412 Office Phone: 608-263-3389. Business E-Mail: dunwoody@wisc.edu.

DUPONT, TODD F., mathematics professor; b. Houston, Aug. 29, 1942; s. T.F. and Nan G. D.; m. Judy Smith, Aug. 20, 1964; children: Michelle, Todd K. BA, Rice U., 1963, PhD, 1968. Research mathematician Esso Prodn. Research, Houston, 1968; instr. U. Chgo., 1968-69, asst. prof., 1969-72, assoc. prof., 1972-75, prof. math., 1975—, prof. computer sci., 1985—, chmn. computer sci., 1994-97. Prin., officer, past bd. dirs. DREM (formerly Dupont-Rachford Engring. Math. Co.), Houston, 1969-92; prin. tech. adv. Advantica, Stoner Software, 1992—. Assoc. editor Math. of Computation, 1977—84, SIAM Jour., 1976—86. Home: 1335 E Park Pl Chicago IL 60637-1767 Office: Univ Chgo Dept Computer Sci 1100 E 58th St Chicago IL 60637-1588

DUQUETTE, DONALD NORMAN, law educator; b. Manistique, Mich., Apr. 3, 1947; s. Donald Francis and Martha Adeline (Rice) D.; m. Kathy Jo Loudenbeck, June 17, 1967; 1 child, Gail Jean. BA, Mich. State U., 1969; JD, U. Mich., 1974. Bar: Mich. 1975. Children's caseworker Mich. Dept. Social Svcs., Muskegon, 1969-72; asst. prof. pediatrics and human devel. Mich. State U. Coll. Human Medicine, East Lansing, 1975-76; clin. prof., dir. child advocacy law clinic U. Mich., Ann Arbor, 1976—, co-dir. interdisciplinary project on child abuse and neglect, 1979-89, dir. permanency planning legal svcs., 1984—90, dir. interdisciplinary grad. edn. in child abuse-neglect, 1986-92, dir. Kellogg child welfare law program, 1995-98, clin. prof., dir. child advocacy law clinic, 1976—, dir. mediation clinic, 2004—. Bd. visitors U. Ariz. Sch. of Law, 1995—99; legal cons. U.S. Children's Bur., Pres. Clinton's Initiative on Adoption and Foster Care, 1997—98; bd. dirs. Nat. Assn. Counsel for Children, 1999—. Author: (non-fiction) Advocating for the Child, 1990, Michigan Child Welfare Law, 1990, Michigan Child Welfare Law, rev. edit., 2000; editor (mem. editl. bd.): (jour.) Child Abuse and Neglect Internat. Jour., 1985—90; editor: Child Welfare Law and Practice: Representing Children, Parents, and State Agencies in Abuse, Neglect, and Dependency Cases, 2005; contbr.: articles to profl. jours. Mem. Washtenaw County Bd. Commrs., 1981-88; bd. dirs. Children's Trust Fund for Prevention of Child Abuse, 1983-85; mem. Permanency Planning Com. Mich. Supreme Ct., 1982-85, Probate Ct. Task Force, 1986-87, Govs. Task Force on Children's Justice, 1992—; trustee Bay Vierw Assn., 1998--. Named Citizen of Yr. Huron Valley NASW, Ann Arbor, 1985; recipient Rsch. in Advocacy award Nat. Ct. Apptd. Spl. Advocate Assn., Seattle, 1985, Outstanding Legal Advocacy award Nat. Assn. of Counsel for Children, 1996, Hicks Child Welfare Leadership award Mich. Fedn. Children's Agys., 1998. Mem.: Mich. State Bar (co-chair Children's Task Force 1993—95), Am. Profl. Soc. on Abuse of Children. Democrat. Unitarian Universalist. Avocations: piano, sailing. Home: 1510 Linwood Ave Ann Arbor MI 48103-3659 Office: U Mich Sch Law Child Advocacy Law Clinic 625 S State St Ann Arbor MI 48109-1215 Office Phone: 734-763-5000. Business E-Mail: duquette@umich.edu.

DURBIN, DICK (RICHARD JOSEPH DURBIN), senator; b. East St. Louis, Ill., Nov. 21, 1944; s. William and Ann D.; m. Loretta Schaefer, June 24, 1967; children: Christine, Paul, Jennifer. BS in Economics, Georgetown U., 1966, JD, 1969. Bar: Ill. 1969. Chief legal counsel to Lt. Gov. Paul Simon State of Ill., 1969—72; parliamentarian Ill. Senate, 1969-77, mem. staff minority leader, 1972-77; assoc. prof. med. humanities So. Ill. U., 1978—; ptnr. Durbin & Lestikow, Springfield, Ill., 1979—82; mem. US Congress from 20th Dist. Ill., 1983-97; US Senator from Ill., 1997—; minority whip, 2004—07; majority whip, 2007—. Mem. appropriations com. US Senate, judiciary com., com. on rules and adminstrn.; asst. Dem. fl. leader; co-chmn. Democratic Nat. Convention Platform Com., 2000, Democratic at. Com., 2004. Campaign worker Sen. Paul Douglas of Ill., 1966; staff Office Ill. Dept. Bus. and Econ. Devel., Washington; candidate for Ill. Lt. Gov., 1978; staff alt. Pres.'s State Planning Council, 1980; advisor Am. Council Young Polit. Leaders, 1981; mem. YMCA Ann. Membership Roundup, YMCA Bldg. Drive, Pony World Series; bd. dirs. Cath. Charities, United Way of Springfield, Old Capitol Art Fair, Springfield Youth Soccer; mem. Sch. Dist. 1986 Referendum Com. Recipient Lifetime Achievement award, Am. Lung Assn., Friend of Agr., Ill. Farm Bur., 2000, Excellence in Immunization award, Nat. Partnership for Immunization, 2001, Ground Water Protector award, Nat. Ground Water Assn., 2005, Leadership award, Nat. Orgn. Fetal Alcohol Syndrome, 2005, Public Svc. award, Am. Chem. Soc., 2005. Mem.: Trial Lawyers Assn., NAACP Springfield, Ill., Sangamon County Bar Assn., Ill. Bar Assn. Democrat. Roman Catholic. Office: US Senate 332 Dirksen Sen Office Bldg Washington DC 20510-0001 Mailing: District Office 525 S Eighth St Springfield IL 62703-1606 Office Phone: 202-224-2152, 217-492-4062. Office Fax: 202-228-0400, 217-492-4382. E-mail: dick@durbin.senate.gov.

DURBURG, JACK E., real estate company executive; b. Evanston, Ill. Grad., Indiana U.; MBA, DePaul U. With William Kritt & Co., Sherman & Sons, Inc.; v.p., regional leasing dir. Jones Lang LaSalle, Inc., 1995—2001; mng. dir. CB Richard Ellis, Chgo., 2001—03, sr. mng. dir., 2003—. Mem.: Nat. Assn. Indsl. and Office Properties. Office: CB Richard Ellis 311 S Wacker Dr Ste 400 Chicago IL 60606 Office Phone: 312-935-1400. Office Fax: 312-935-1880. E-mail: jack.durburg@cbre.com.

DURCHSLAG, STEPHEN P., lawyer; b. Chgo., May 20, 1940; s. Milton Lewis and Elizabeth (Potovsky) D.; m. Ruth Florence Mayer, Nov. 21, 1976; children: Rachel Beth, Danielle Leah. BS, U. Wis., 1963; LLB, Harvard U., 1966. Bar: Ill. 1966. Assoc. Sidley & Austin, Chgo., 1966-72, ptnr., 1972-89, Winston & Strawn, Chgo., 1989—. Contbr. articles to profl. jours. Trustee Nathan Cummings Found., 1996—, Anshe Emet, Chgo., 1983—, pres., 2000—02. Mem. ABA (AAF legal com.), Promotion Mktg. Assn. (bd. dirs.), Am. Standard Club, East Bank Club. Jewish. Avocations: skiing, running, tennis, rare books. Office: Winston & Strawn 35 W Wacker Dr Ste 3600 Chicago IL 60601-1695 Office Phone: 312-558-5288. Business E-Mail: sdurchslag@winston.com.

DURHAM, CHARLES WILLIAM, civil engineer, director; b. Chgo., Sept. 28, 1917; s. John Barnett and Monica (O'Dea) Durham; m. Margre Ann Henningson, Oct. 12, 1940; children: Steven, Mary Helen, Lynn Barnett, Debra Ann. BS in Gen. Engring., Iowa State U., 1939, BSCE, 1940. Registered profl. engr., 30 states and D.C., Diplomate, Am. Acad. Environ. Engrs. Civil engr. Henningson Engring. Co., Omaha, 1939—46, ptnr., 1946—50; pres., CEO Henningson, Durham & Richardson, Omaha, 1950—76, chmn. bd., CEO, 1976—. Chmn. bd. Gt. Plains Natural Gas Co.; dir. Omaha Nat. Bank, ONB Realbanc, Minn. Enterprises Inc. Bd. dirs. Iowa State U. Found.; mem. engring. adv. coun. U. Nebr.; mem. adv. com. SAC. Fellow: ASCE, Cons. Engrs. Coun.; mem.: NSPE, Chief Execs. Forum (past pres.), Water Pollution Control Fedn., Nebr. Soc. Profl. Engrs. (past pres., nat. dir.), Soc. Am. Mil. Engrs., Am. Pub. Works Assn., Knights of Ak-Sar-Ben (gov.), U.S. C. of C. (dir.), Beavers, Omaha C. of C. (past pres., past dir.), Jesters, Shriners, Masons. Office: Durham Resources Inc 8401 W Dodge Rd Ste 100 Omaha NE 68114-3438

DURHAM, RAY, professional baseball player; b. Charlotte, NC, Nov. 30, 1971; Baseball player Chgo. White Sox, 1995—2002, Oakland A's, 2002, San Francisco Giants, 2003—. Named to Am. League All Star Game, 1998. Office: San Francisco Giants SBC Park 24 Willie Mays Plz San Francisco CA 94107

DURIG, JAMES ROBERT, chemistry professor; b. Washington, Pa., Apr. 30, 1935; s. and Roberta Wilda Mounts; m. Kathryn Marlene Sprowls, Sept. 1, 1955; children: Douglas Tybor, Bryan Robert, Stacey Ann. BA, Washington and Jefferson Coll., 1958, D.Sc. (hon.), 1979; PhD, M.I.T., 1962. Asst. prof. chemistry U. S.C., Columbia, 1962-65, asso. prof., 1965-68, prof., 1968-93, Ednl. Found. prof. chemistry, 1970-73, dean Coll. Sci. and Math., 1973-93; dean Coll. Arts and Scis., U. Mo., Kansas City, 1993—2000, Curators' prof. chemistry and geosci., 1993—. Editor: Vibrational Spectra and Structure, 24 vols., 1972—, Jour. Raman Spectroscopy, 1979-94; mem. editl. bd. Jour. Molecular Structure, 1972—; contbr. articles to profl. jours. Served with Chem. Corps U.S. Army, 1963-64. Recipient Russell award U.S.C., 1968; Alexander von Humboldt Sr. Scientist award W. Ger., 1976; award Spectroscopy Soc. of Pitts., 1981; U. S.C. Ednl. Found. award, 1984 Mem. Am. Chem. Soc. (So. Chemist award Memphis sect. 1976, Charles A. Stone award S.E. Piedmont sect. 1975), Am. Phys. Soc., Soc. for Applied Spectroscopy (Pitts. sect. award 1981), Coblentz Soc. (mem. governing bd. 1972-76, pres. 1974-76, award for outstanding rsch. in molecular spectroscopy 1970), Internat. Union Pure and Applied Chemistry (chmn. sub-commn. on infrared and Raman spectroscopy 1975-95, mem. commn. molecular spectra and structure 1978-89, sec. 1981-83, chmn. 1983-89, editor Spectrochimica Acta 1999—), Blue Key Soc., Phi Beta Kappa (pres. chpt. 1970), Sigma Xi, Phi Lambda Upsilon, Phi Kappa Phi. Presbyterian. Home: 1213 W 64th Ter Kansas City MO 64113-1516 Office: Univ Mo 410 RHFH Kansas City MO 64110 Office Phone: 816-235-6038. Business E-Mail: durigj@umkc.edu.

DURKIN, G. MICHAEL, food products executive; BS in Mktg. Fin., U. RI; MBA, Pace U. Fin. oper. PepsiCo, Inc., 1981; v.p., customer devel. PepsiCo Inc., Heartland Bus. Unit (acquired by Whitman 1999); sr. v.p., gen. mgr. Whitman Corp., Eastern Group (prior to merger with PepsiAmericas); sr. v.p., CFO PepsiAmericas, Mpls., 2002—. Office: PepsiAmericas 4000 Dain Rauscher Plz 60 S Sixth St Minneapolis MN 55402

DURKIN, JAMES B., state legislator; BS, Ill. State U.; JD, John Marshall U. Former asst. state atty. Cook County; former asst. atty. gen. Ill.; pres. Proviso Twp. Rep. Orgn.; Ill. state rep. Dist. 44, 1995—. Mem. Elec. and State Govt., Higher Edn., Judiciary and Criminal and Pers. and Pensions Coms., 1995—, Ill. Ho. of Reps. Vice-chmn., bd. trustees Triton Coll. Mem. Chgo. Bar Assn., Fenwick Bar Assn. (bd. dirs.). Home: 4719 Grand Ave Western Springs IL 60558-1738

DURKIN, KEVIN P., lawyer; b. Chgo., July 22, 1955; BS, U. Ill., 1977; JD, DePaul U., 1980. Bar: Ill. 1980, US Dist. Ct. (no. & ctrl. dists. Ill.) 1983, US Ct. Appeals (7th cir.) 1995, US Dist. Ct. (we. dist. Mich.) 2000. Asst. state atty. Cook County, Ill., 1980—88; ptnr. Clifford Law Offices, Chgo., 1988—. Adj. prof. DePaul U. Mem.: ABA (mem. sect. Litig. 1992—, mem. sect. Tort & Ins. Practice 1992—, mem. Aviation Litig. comm. 1992—, mem. Aviation & Space Law comm. 1992—, co-chair, Aviation Litig. com. 2000—), Chgo. Bar Assn. (chmn. Hearing divsn. 1995—97, chmn. Jud. Evaluation com. 1995—97, gen. chmn. 1997—98, bd. mgr. 1998—2000, treas. 2002—), Ill. Trial Lawyers Assn. (bd. advocates 1993—2001, bd. mgrs. 2001—), Assn. Trial Lawyers Am., Nat. Coll. Dist. Attys. Assn., Trial Lawyers Club Chgo., Chgo. Bar Found. Achievements include obtained the largest personal verdict of the year involving a motor vehicle accident, 2004. Office: Clifford Law Offices 31st Fl 120 N LaSalle St Chicago IL 60602 Office Phone: 312-899-9090. Office Fax: 312-251-1160. E-mail: kpd@cliffordlaw.com.

DURNELL, EARL, rancher; b. Cabool, Mo., Dec. 4, 1935; m. Emily Gay Spencer; 6 children. Student, Southwest Mo. State U., 1954-56. Rep. candidate for U.S. House, 1992, 96. Baptist.

DUROCHER, VERNLE C. (SKIP), JR., lawyer; b. Menominee, Mich., Aug. 9, 1961; s. Vernle Charles and Judith Ann (Stodola) D.; m. Ann M. Novacheck, Sept. 13, 1986; children: Tyler, Justin, Kelsey. BA in Polit. sci., Marquette U., Milw., 1983; JD, U. Wis., 1986. Law clk. U.S. Dist. Ct. (no. dist.) Tex., Dallas, 1986-87; assoc. Kirkland & Ellis, Chgo., 1987-90, Dorsey & Whitney, Mpls., 1990-95, ptnr., trial dept., chmn., ins. law, 1995—. Adj. prof. Hamline U., St. Paul, 1992-96. ote and Comment editor U. Wis., 1986. Mem. Minn. State Bar Assn. (investigator Hennepin County ethics panel 1992—), Order of the Coif. Avocations: basketball, fishing, skiing. Office: Dorsey & Whitney Ste 1500 50 S 6th St Minneapolis MN 55402-1498 Office Phone: 612-390-7855. Office Fax: 612-340-2868. Business E-Mail: durocher.skip@dorsey.com.

DURYEE, HAROLD TAYLOR, insurance consultant; b. Willoughby, Ohio, Feb. 11, 1930; s. Gerald Fancher and Margaret Grace (Taylor) D.; m. Phyllis Annette Painter, June 18, 1966. AB, Kenyon Coll., 1951. Field rep. Mahoning Valley Coun., Boy Scouts Am., Youngstown, Ohio, 1951-56; mgr. claims svcs. Nationwide Ins. Cos., Canton, 1956-65; legis. and field dir. Ohio Rep. Party, Columbus, 1965-70, exec. dir., 1970-77, cons., 1980-81; dep. adminstr. Ohio Bur. Workers' Compensation, Columbus, 1977-84; exec. dep. adminstr. Fed. Ins. Adminstrn., Washington, 1984-86; adminstr. fed. ins. Fed. Emergency Mgmt. Agy., Washington, 1986-90; dir. Ohio Dept. Ins., 1991-99; sr. advisor Internat. Ins. Found., 1999—. Trustee, exec. com. Griffith Found. for Ins. Edn.; mem. Ohio Elections Commn., 1980-84. Vice chmn. North Canton City Planning Commn., 1958-67; precinct committeeman Stark County Cen. Com., 1958-72; organizer North Canton Rep. Com., 1958, chmn., 1960-72; sec. North Canton Area Devel. Com., 1959-64; chmn. North Canton City Charter Commn., 1960; campaign mgr. U.S. Rep. Frank T. Bow, 1962, Oliver P. Bolton for U.S. Congress, 1964, Clarence J. Brown, Jr. for U.S. Congress, 1965; state chmn. Ohio League Young Rep. Clubs, 1962-63; nat. vice chmn. Young Rep. Nat. Fedn., 1963-65; former chmn. bd. trustees Nat. Assn. Ins. Commrs. Edn. and Rsch. Found.; former trustee ASFPM Edn. and Rsch. Found. Recipient Disting. Svc. award Jaycees, 1961, Civic Affairs award Rotary, 1964, Meritorious Svc. award Fed. Emergency Mgmt. Agy., 1989, Disting. Civilian Svc. medal, Fed. Emergency Mgmt. Agy., 1990. Mem. Acad. Polit. Sci. Episcopalian. Avocation: genealogy. Home: 925 City Park Ave Columbus OH 43206-2511 Office Phone: 614-443-8285. Personal E-mail: hduryee@columbus.rr.com.

DUSK, BROOKE, meteorologist; BS in Meteorology, Iowa State U., 2000. Weekend meteorologist NewsCenter 13 WEAU-TV, Eau Claire, Wis., 2001—. Avocation: golf. Office: WEAU-TV Po Box 47 Eau Claire WI 54702

DUTILE, FERNAND NEVILLE, law educator; b. Lewiston, Maine, Feb. 15, 1940; s. Wilfred Joseph and Lauretta Blanche (Cote) D.; m. Brigid Dooley, Apr. 4, 1964; children: Daniel, Patricia. AB, Assumption Coll., 1962; JD, U. Notre Dame, 1965. Bar: Maine 1965. Atty. U.S. Dept. Justice, Washington, 1965-66; prof. law Cath. U. Am., Washington, 1966-71, U. Notre Dame Law Sch., Ind., 1971—. Bd. dirs. Ind. Lawyers Commn., Indpls., 1975-85, Legal Svcs. No. Ind., South Bend, 1975-83; dir. South Bend Work Release Ctr., 1973-75, Ind. Criminal Law Study Commn., 1991-99. Editor: Legal Education and Lawyer Competency, 1981; author: Sex, Schools and the Law, 1986; co-editor: Early Childhood Intervention and Juvenile Delinquency, 1982, The Prediction of Criminal Violence, 1987; co-author: State and Campus, 1984. Mem.: Athletics Reps. Assn. (exec. com. 2004—06). Democrat. Roman Catholic.

DUTTA, MITRA, engineer, educator; m. Michael A. Stroscio; 1 child, Gautam Dutta Stroscio. BS, Delhi U., India, MSc, 1973; PhD, U. Cin., 1981. Lectr. Coll. Arts, Sci. and Tech., Kingston, Jamaica, 1973-76, U. West Indies, Kingston, 1973-76; rsch. assoc. Purdue U., West Lafayette, Ind., 1981-83; sr. rsch. assoc. CCNY, NYC, 1983-86; rsch. engr. Systematic Gen. Corp., Eatontown, NJ, 1986-88; rsch. physicist and leader optoelectronics team Army Rsch. Lab. Electronics and Power Sources Directorate, Ft. Monmouth, NJ, 1988—94; dir., phys. scis. directorate Army Rsch. Lab, 1994—96, assoc. dir., electronics div., 1996—99; dir., rsch. and tech. integration directorate Army Rsch. Office, 1999—2001, disting. prof. and head, elec. and computer engring. dept., 2001—. Contbr. approximately 400 papers and proceedings; 31 US and Can. patents; co-author: 1 book; editor: 5 books. Nat. Merit scholar Govt. of India, 1968-71, Univ. Grants scholar Univ. Grants Commn., Delhi, India, 1971-73, R & D Achievement award, U.S. Army, 1990, 92, 94, ETDL Harold Jacobs award, 1991, Paul A. Siple Meml. award, 1993, Nat. Achievement award, Soc. for Women Engrs., 2003. Fellow IEEE (Harry Diamond award 2000), AAAS, Optical Soc. Am., Army Rsch. Lab (emeritus). Office: U Ill at Chgo 851 S Morgan M/C 154 Chicago IL 60607 Office Phone: 312-355-2131. E-mail: dutta@ece.uic.edu.

DUTTON, STEPHEN JAMES, lawyer; b. Chgo., Sept. 20, 1942; S. James H. and Marjorie C. (Smith) D.; m. Ellen W. Lee; children: Patrick, Mark. BS, Ill. Inst. Tech., 1965; JD, Ind. U., 1969. Bar: Ind. 1969, U.S. Dist. Ct. (so. dist.) Ind. 1969, U.S. Ct. Appeals (7th cir.) 1972, U.S. Ct. Appeals (D.C. cir.) 1980, U.S. Supreme Ct. 1978. With McHale, Cook & Welch, P.C., Indpls., 1969-86, Dutton & Overman, P.C., 1986-91, Dutton & Bailey, P.C., 1991-94, Locke, Reynolds, Boyd & Weisell, 1994-99, Leagre Chandler & Millard LLP, Indpls., 1999—2003, Barnes & Thorburg, Indpls., 2003—. Mem. Com. on Law of Cyberspace Bus. Law Sect.; chair TechPoint, Inc., 2005—. Mem. ABA. Office: 11 S Meridian St Indianapolis IN 46208 Office Phone: 317-231-7542. Business E-Mail: sdutton@btlaw.com.

DUVAL, DANIEL WEBSTER, electronics executive; b. Cin., May 27, 1936; s. Harry A. and Wilda (Webster) V.; m. Sue Ann Howard, July 20, 1962; children: Laurie Ann, Paula Lee, Christopher Webster. BA, U. Cin., 1960. V.p. staff elec. products divsn. Midland-Ross, Cleve., 1976-78, group v.p., 1979-81, exec. v.p., 1981-83, pres., COO, 1983-86; pres., CEO Robbins & Myers Inc., Dayton, Ohio, 1986-98, vice chmn., 1999, pres., CEO, 2003—04, bd. dir.; interim pres., CEO Arrow Electronics Inc., NYC, 2002—03. Bd. dirs. Gosiger, Inc., Dayton, The Manitowac Co., Wis., Arrow Electronics Inc., NYC, 1987—, chmn., 2002—06, lead dir., 2006—. Patentee container coupling mechanism. Trustee Wright State U., 1991-2000, Wright State U. Found.; pres. Civitan Found., Ariz., 1973-74, Dayton Ballet Assn., 1990-93; participant Leadership Cleve.; bd. dirs. US Air and Trade Show. Republican. Roman Catholic. Office: Arrow Electronics Inc 50 Marcus Dr Melville NY 11747-4210 Office Phone: 631-847-2000.

DUVIN, ROBERT PHILLIP, lawyer; b. Evansville, Ind., May 18, 1937; s. Louis and Henrietta (Hamburg) D.; m. Darlene Chmiel, Aug. 23, 1961; children: Scott A., Marc A., Louis A. BA with honors, Ind. U., 1958, JD with highest honors, 1961; LLM with highest honors, Columbia U., 1963. Bar: Ohio 1964. Since practiced in, Cleve.; pres. Duvin, Cahn & Hutton, 1972—2006, Littler Mendelson, 2007—. Lectr. law schs.; labor adviser corps., cities and hosps. Contbr. to books and legal jours.; bd. editors: Ind. Law Jour., 1961, Columbia Law Rev., 1963. Served with AUS, 1961-62. Mem. ABA, FBA, Ohio Bar Assn., Cleve. Bar Assn., Cleve. Racquet Club, Beechmont Country Club, Soc. Club, Canterbury Golf Club, Sanctuary Golf Club. Jewish. Home: 2775 S Park Blvd Cleveland OH 44120-1669 Office: Littler Mendelson 1100 Superior Ave 20th Fl Cleveland OH 44114 Business E-Mail: rduvin@littler.com.

DUXBURY, ROBERT NEIL, retired state legislator; b. Mar. 14, 1933; s. Joy Chase and Lois Mae (McNeil) Duxbury; m. Rose Ann Radcliffe, 1953; children: Robert Neil Jr., Kathryn Ann Duxbury Meyer, Dale Lynn, Dean Douglas, Brian Richard. BS, S.D. State U., 1956. Sec. of Agrl., S.D., 1975-79; mem. S.D. Ho. of Reps. from 5th dist., Pierre, 1984-98, S.D. Senate from 22nd dist., Pierre, 1998—2005, ret., 2005. Former minority leader, former mem. legis. procedure com. Dist. 22; currently mem. appropriations com. S.D. Ho. Reps.; farmer, rancher. Mem. Farmers Union, Hand County Livestock Improvement Assn. Home: 21030 373rd Ave Wessington SD 57381-6911

DVORAK, ALLEN DALE, radiologist; b. Dodge, Nebr., Mar. 13, 1943; s. Rudolph Charles and Mildred B. (Misek) D.; m. Carol Ann Cockson, July 22, 1967; children: Kristin Ann, Andrea Marie, Ryan Allen. Grad., Creighton U., 1964, MD, 1969. Intern Creighton Meml. St. Joseph Hosp., Omaha, 1969-70; resident Ind. U. Med. Ctr., Indpls., 1970-73, chief resident, 1972—73; asst. prof. radiology Creighton U. Sch. Medicine, Omaha, 1973-83; diagnostic radiologist Nebr.-Iowa Radiology Cons., Papillion, Nebr., 1983—, mng. ptnr., 1987—, pres., cons. ptnr., 2004—. Staff radiologist Alegent Midlands Cmty. Hosp., Papillion, 1983—, med. staff exec. bd., 1996—, pres. med. staff, 2001-02; mem. Nebr. Bd. Health, 1995-2000; bd. dirs. Blue Cross Blue Shield Nebr., 2000—, PRIME Therapeutics, Inc. (bd. dir.), 2002-04. Contbr. chpt. to book, articles to profl. jours. Chmn. Midlands Area Health Adv. Coun., State of Nebr., 1982-86; trustee Duchesne Acad., 1988-91, Boys Town Nat. Coun. Friends, 1989—; bd. dirs. Safety and health Coun. of Greater Omaha, 1990-91; mem. Gov.'s Blue Ribbon Coalition to Study Health Care in Nebr., 1991-98; Equestrian Order Holy Sepulchre Jerusalem, 1991-; mem. Creighton Med. Sch. Alumni Adv. Bd., 1993—, pres., 1998-2000; trustee Western Conf. Prepaid Med. Svc. Plans, 2004—, pres., 2007. Fellow Am. Coll. Radiology, 1985; mem. AMA (alt. del. 1992-98, del. 1999-2000), Nebr. Radiol. Soc. (pres. 1980-81), Omaha Midwest Clin. Soc. (pres. 1982), Nebr. Assn. Nuclear Physicians (pres. 1976-78, del. 1984-94), Met. Omaha Med. Soc. (exec. com. 1980-2000, pres. 1990), Nebr. Med. Assn. (del. 1986—, pres. 1997-98), Regency Lake and Tennis Club (bd. dirs. 1981-85, chmn. bd. 1983-85), Happy Hollow Country Club. Avocations: golf, gardening. Home: 9733 Brentwood Rd Omaha NE 68114-4970 Office: Nebr-Iowa Radiology Cons 401 E Gold Coast Rd Ste 102 Papillion NE 68046-4194 Office Phone: 402-339-8991.

DVORAK, DAVID C., medical products executive, lawyer; BS in Fin., Miami U., Ohio; JD magna cum laude, Case Western Reserve U., 1991. Sr. v.p., gen. counsel, corp. sec. STERIS Corp., mem. exec. com.; sr. v.p. corp. affairs, gen.

counsel Zimmer Holdings, Inc., Warsaw, Ind., 2001—03, exec. v.p. corp. svcs., chief counsel, sec., 2003—05, group pres. global bus., chief legal officer, 2005—07, pres., CEO, 2007—. Office: Zimmer Holdings Inc 345 E Main St Warsaw IN 46580

DVORAK, KATHLEEN S., former consumer products company executive; married; 2 children. BS in Edn., No. Ill. U., 1978; MBA in Fin., DePaul U., 1988. Tchr. math. Conrady Jr. H.S., 1977-82; dir. investor rels./corp. comms. United Stationers Inc., Des Plaines, Ill., 1982-97, v.p. investor rels., 1997-2000, sr. v.p. investor rels. & fin. adminstrn., 2000—01, sr. v.p., CFO, 2001—07. Recipient Howard Beasley Managerial Excellence award. Mem. Nat. Investor Rels. Inst.

DVORAK, MICHAEL A., state legislator; b. South Bend, Ind., Oct. 24, 1948; s. William E. and Marilyn J. (Radican) D.; m. Kathleen Braunsdorf, 1970; children: Ryan, Todd, Sean, Brett, Carrie, Brady, Casey, Tyler. BA, Loyola U., Chgo., 1970; JD, Western State U., San Diego, 1975. Ptnr. Dvorak & Dvorak, South Bend, 1977—; dep. pros. atty. Santislaus County, Modesto, Calif., 1975-77; rep. Dist. 8 Ind. Ho. of Rep., 1986—, chmn. cts. and criminal code com., mem. families, children and human affairs com. Mem. Ind. State Bar Assn., St. Joseph County Bar Assn.

DVORAK, RYAN M., state representative; BA in Philosophy, U. Notre Dame, 1996. Former sr. aide, mgr. constituent case work Ind. Congressman Tim Roemer, Washington, campaign mgr., 1998, 2000; cons. South Bend, Ind.; state rep. dist. 8 Ind. Ho. of Reps., Indpls., 2002, vice chair, tech., R & D com., mem. commerce and econ. devel., cts. and criminal code, and interstate and internat. cooperation coms. Vol. Christmas in April, Habitat for Humanity. Democrat. Office: Ind Ho of Reps 200 W Washington St Indianapolis IN 46204-2786

DVORSKY, ROBERT E., state senator; b. Burlington, Iowa, Aug. 18, 1948; m. Susan M. Mandernach; 2 children. BS, U. Iowa, 1972, MPA, 1984. Former mgr. small bus.; with Mason City Supt. Recreation, 1973-79; mem. Coralville City Coun., 1980-86, Iowa Ho. of Reps., 1986-94; with E. Ctrl. Iowa Employment and Tng. Consortium, Cedar Rapids, 1993—; mem. Iowa Senate from 25th dist., 1982—. Former bd. dirs. Iowa City Area Devel. Group; mem. Iowa City/Coralville Conv. and Visitors Bur., Johnson County Coun. Govts., Johnson County Dem. Ctrl. Com. and Exec. Com. Mem. Johnson County Hist. Soc., Friends of Coralville Pub. Libr. Democrat. Roman Catholic. Home: 412 6th St Coralville IA 52241-2511 Office: State Capitol Dist 25 3 9th And Grand Des Moines IA 50319-0001 E-mail: robert_dvorsky@legis.state.ia.us.

DWELLE, TERRY, state agency administrator; b. Garrison, ND; MD cum laude, St. Louis U.; MPH Tropical Medicine, Tulane U. With U. N.D. Sch. Medicine, Indian Health Svc.; pediatrician Bismarck, ND; chief med officer N.D. Dept. Health, state health officer, 2001—. Office: ND Dept Health 600 E Blvd Ave Bismarck D 58505-0200

DWORKIN, AARON P., violinist, educator; b. 1970; BM, U. Mich., 1997, MM, 1998. Founder, pres. Sphinx Orgn., 1996—. Advisor to various edn. and music orgns.; spkr. in field; organizer of various music outreach and edn. programs to attract minorities to careers in classical music. Named Michiganian of Yr., Detroit ews, 2003, MacArthur fellow, John D. and Catherine T. MacArthur Found., 2005; named one of 40 Under 40, Crain's Detroit Bus., 2006; recipient SBC Ameritech Excellence award, 5 Under 10 award, U. Mich. African-Am. Alumni Coun., 2002, Mich. Governor's award for Arts & Culture, 2003, Nat. Governor's award, 2005, Newsweek Giving Back award, 2006. Office: Sphinx Orgn 400 Renaissance Ctr Ste 2120 Detroit MI 48243 Office Phone: 313-877-9100. Office Fax: 313-887-0164.

DWORKIN, HOWARD JERRY, retired nuclear medicine physician, educator; b. Bklyn., Oct. 29, 1932; s. Joseph Henry and Mollie M. (Hodas) Dworkin; m. Gina Gora; children: Rhonda Fran, Steven Irving, Paul J., Edward Joshua, Joseph Jacob. BSChemE, Worcester Poly. Inst., 1955; MD, Albany Med. Coll., 1959; MS in Radiation Biology, U. Mich., 1965. Diplomate Am. Bd. Internal Medicine, Am. Bd. Nuclear Medicine. Intern Albany Hosp., NY, 1959-60; resident Rochester (N.Y.) Gen. Hosp., 1960-62, U. Mich. Hosps., 1962-65, asst. coord. nuclear medicine unit, 1963-66, instr., 1965-66; asst. prof. medicine U. Toronto, Ont., Canada, 1966, assoc. prof. Ont., 1967; head dept. nuc. medicine Princess Margaret Hosp., Toronto, 1967; head nuc. medicine sect. radiology Nat. Naval Med. Ctr., Bethesda, Md., 1967-69; dir. sch. nuc. medicine tech. William Beaumont Hosp., Royal Oak, Mich., 1969—, chief dept. nuc. medicine, 1969—2002, dir. nuc. medicine resident tng. program, 1970—2006, chmn. CME com., 1993—2006; ret., 2006. Clin. asst. prof. dept. medicine Wayne State U. Med. Sch., Detroit, 1970—; clin. assoc. prof. dept. radiology Mich. State U., East Lansing, 1976—; clin. prof. med. physics Ctr. Health Scis. Oakland U., Rochester, Mich., 1977—; adj. prof. radiology U. Mich., 2003—. Author (with N. Aspin and R. G. Baker): (book) Use of Isotopes in the Physics of Radiology, 1969, Part Two, Clinical Procedures in Radioisotope Laboratory Procedures, 1969; contbr. articles and chpts. to med. jours. and texts. With USN, 1967—69. Mem.: AMA, Mich. State Med. Soc. (chmn. continuing med. edn. com. 1999—), Am. Coll. Nuc. Physicians (sec. 1974—75, pres. 1978—79), Endocrine Soc., Am. Thyroid Assn., Soc. uc. Medicine (trustee 1973—81, v.p. 1982, pres. 1986—87), Am. Bd. Nuc. Medicine (treas. 1982—84), Accrediation Coun. Continuing Med. Edn. (chmn. 1998). Achievements include patents for radioactive labeled protein material process and apparatus. Office: William Beaumont Hosp Dept Nuclear Medicine Royal Oak MI 48073 Home Phone: 248-673-6168; Office Phone: 248-898-4100. E-mail: hdworkin@beaumont.edu.

DWORKIN, MARTIN, microbiologist, educator; b. NYC, Dec. 3, 1927; s. Hyman Bernard and Pauline (Herstein) D.; m. Nomi Rees Buda, Feb. 2, 1957; children: Jessica Sarah, Hanna Beth. BA, Ind. U., 1951; PhD (NSF predoctoral fellow), U. Tex., Austin, 1955. NIH research fellow U. Calif., Berkeley, 1955-57, vis. prof., summers 1958-60; asst. prof. microbiology Ind. U. Med. Sch., 1957-61, assoc. prof., 1961-62; from assoc. prof. to prof. emeritus U. Minn., 1962—2004, prof. emeritus, 2004—. Vis. prof. U. Wash., 1965, Stanford U., 1978-79; vis. scholar Oxford (Eng.) U., 1970-71; Found. for Microbiology lectr., 1973-74, 76-77, 81-82; Sackler scholar Tel Aviv U., 1992. Author: Developmental Biology of the Bacteria, 1985, Microbial Cell-Cell Interactions, 1991; contbr. numerous articles, revs. to profl. publs.; mem. editorial bd. Jour. Bacteriology, 1967-74, 86-88, Ann. Revs. Microbiology, 1975-79, The Prokaryotes, 2d edit., editor-in-chief 3d edit. Alt. del. Democratic Nat. Conv., 1968; mem. Minn. Dem. Farm Labor Central Com., 1969-70. Served with U.S. Army, 1946-48. Recipient Career Devel. award NIH, 1963-73; John Simon Guggenheim fellow, 1978-79 Fellow Am. Acad. Arts and Scis. (chmn. Midwest ctr., v.p., 2002), Am. Soc. Microbiology (vice chmn. div. gen. microbiology 1977-78, chmn. 1978-79, div. councillor 1980-82); mem. Soc. Gen. Microbiology (Eng.). Home: 2123 Hoyt Ave W Saint Paul MN 55108-1314 Office: U Minn Dept Microbiology Minneapolis MN 55455 Office Phone: 612-624-5634. Business E-Mail: martin@lenti.med.umn.edu.

DYBEK, STUART, language educator, writer; b. Chgo., Apr. 10, 1942; s. Stanley and Adeline (Sala) S.; m. Caren Bassett, Feb. 7, 1967; children: Anne, Nicholas. BS, Loyola U., Chgo., 1964, MA, 1967; MFA, U. Iowa, 1973. Tchr. US V.I. Sch., St. Thomas, 1968-70, U. Iowa, Iowa City, 1970-73; prof. English Western Mich. U., Kalamazoo, 1973—, adj. prof. Vis. prof. creative writing Princeton U., NJ, 1991, U. Calif., Irvine, 1995, U. Iowa, 1998, Northwestern U., 2001; disting. writer-in-residence Northwestern U., 2006-. Author: (poetry) Brass Knuckles, 1979, Streets In Their Own Ink, 2004; (fiction) Childhood and Other eighborhoods, 1980, The Coast of Chicago, 1990, I Sailed With Magellan, 2003 (Adult Fiction prize, Soc. Midland Authors, 2004, named a NY Times Notable Book, 2005, named one of 26 Most Notable Books of 2005, ALA). Recipient Whiting Writers award, 1985, O. Henry first prize, 1985, Acad. award in fiction Am. Acad. Arts and Letters, 1994, PEN/Malamud award, 1995, Lannan Lit. prize, 1998, Mark Twain award, 2007, Rea award, 2007, Disting. Scholar award, Western Mich. U.; Guggenheim fellow, 1982, MacArthur fellow, 2007. Mem. PEN. Home: 320 Monroe St Kalamazoo MI 49006-4436 Office: Western Michigan U Dept English Kalamazoo MI 49008 also: care Amanda Urban Intl Creative Mgt 40 W 57th St New York NY 10019-4001 Personal E-mail: sdybek@earthlink.net.

DYE, JAMES LOUIS, retired chemistry professor; b. Soudan, Minn., July 18, 1927; s. Ray Ashley and Hildur Ameda Dye; m. Angeline Rosalie Medure, June 10, 1948; children: Roberta Rae, Thomas Anthony, Brenda Lee. AA, Virginia Jr. Coll., Minn., 1948; BA, Gustavus Adolphus Coll., 1949; PhD, Iowa State U., Ames, 1953; DSc (hon.), No. Mich. U., Marquette, 1992. Rsch. assoc. Iowa State U., Ames, 1953; asst. prof. chemistry Mich. State U., East Lansing, 1953-60, assoc. prof., 1960-63, prof., 1963-94, chmn. dept. chemistry, 1986-90, prof. emeritus, 1994—. Vis. scientist Ohio State U., Columbus, 1968-69; cons. AT&T Bell Labs., Murray Hill, N.J., 1982-83. Author: Thermodynamics and Equilibrium, 1978; contbr. more than 220 articles to profl. jours. With U.S. Army, 1945-46. SF fellow, 1961-62, Guggenheim fellow, 1975-76, 90-91, Fulbright scholar, 1975-76; recipient Disting. Alumni award Gustavus Adolphus Coll., 1969. Fellow AAAS; mem. NAS, Am. Acad. Arts and Scis., Am. Chem. Soc. (Inorganic Chemistry award 1997), Am. Inst. Chemists (Chem. Pioneer award 1990), Am. Phys. Soc., Materials Rsch. Soc., Phi Kappa Phi, Sigma Xi (rsch. awards 1968, 87), Golden Key (teaching award 1986). Lutheran. Avocations: fishing, golf. Home: 2698 Roseland Ave East Lansing MI 48823-3847 Office: Mich State Univ Dept Of Chemistry East Lansing MI 48824 Office Phone: 517-355-9715 ext. 288. Business E-Mail: dye@msu.edu.

DYE, JERMAINE, professional baseball player; b. Overland, Kans., Jan. 28, 1974; Student, Cosumnes River C.C. Player Atlanta Braves, 1996-97, Kansas City Royals, 1997—2001, Oakland A's, 2001—04, Chicago White Sox, 2004—. Named to Am. League All-Star Team, MLB, 2000; recipient World Series MVP, 2005, AL Outstanding Player, Players Choice awards, 2006. Office: Chicago White Sox 333 W 35th St Chicago IL 60616

DYE, NANCY SCHROM, academic administrator, historian, educator; b. Columbia, Mo., Mar. 11, 1947; d. Ned Stuart and Andrea Elizabeth (Ahrens) Schrom; m. Griffith R. Dye, Aug. 21, 1972; children: Molly, Michael. AB, Vassar Coll., 1969; MA, U. Wis., 1971, PhD, 1974; LittD (hon.), Obirin U., 2005. Asst. prof. U. Ky., Lexington, 1974—80, assoc. prof., 1980—88, prof., 1988, assoc. dean arts and scis., 1984—88; dean faculty Vassar Coll., Poughkeepsie, NY, 1988—92, acting pres., 1992—94; pres. Oberlin Coll., Oberlin, Ohio, 1994—2007, pres. emeritus, 2007—; founding vice chancellor, pres. Asian U. for Women, Chittagong, Bangladesh, 2008—. Author: As Equals And As Sisters, 1981; contbr. articles to profl. jours. Bd. mem. Pomona Coll. Mem.: Coun. Colls. of Art and Scis. (bd. dirs. 1980—91). Office: Asian U for Women Support Found Ste 300 1100 Massachusetts Ave Cambridge MA 02138 Office Phone: 440-775-8400. Fax: 440-775-8937.*

DYER, WILLIAM EARL, JR., retired newspaper editor; b. Kearney, Nebr., May 15, 1927; s. William Earl and Hazel Maud (Hosfelt) D.; m. Betty M. Meisinger, June 26, 1967; children: Lee Michael, Scott William. BA, U. Nebr., 1949. Reporter Nebr. City Daily News Press, 1943-44; reporter, copy editor The Lincoln Star, Nebr., 1948-50, city editor, 1951-60, exec. editor, 1960-92. Pres. Nebr. AP Editors, 1964. Author: Headline: Starkweather, 1993. Pres. Lincoln Unitarian Ch., 1962-63; state chmn. Nebr. We Shake Hands Indian Project, 1958-60; mem. Nebr. Adv. Com. on Indian Law Enforcement, 1960-62; mem. State Adv. Com. to Welfare Dept., 1970-73, 80-84. With AUS, 1945-46. Named hon. mem. Omaha Indian Tribe. Mem. Open Forum Club, Phi Beta Kappa, Sigma Delta Chi. Democrat. Home: 247 N 56th St West Lincoln NE 68504 Office: Jour-Star Printing Co PO Box 81609 926 P St Lincoln NE 68508-3615 E-mail: dyers@inebraska.com.

DYKEN, MARK LEWIS, JR., neurologist, educator; b. Laramie, Wyo., Aug. 26, 1928; s. Mark L. and Thelma Violet (Achenbach) D.; m. Beverly All, June 8, 1951; children: Betsy Lynn, Mark Eric, Julie Suzanne, Amy Luise, Andrew Christopher, Gregory Allen. BS in Anatomy and Physiology, Ind. U., 1951, MD, 1954. Diplomate Am. Bd. Psychiatry and Neurology. Intern Indpls. Gen. Hosp., 1954-55; resident in neurology Ind. U. Med. Ctr., 1955-58; clin. dir., dir. rsch. New Castle (Ind.) State Hosp., 1958-61; asst. dept. neurology Ind. U., 1958-61, assoc. prof. neurology, 1964-69, prof., 1969—, chmn. dept. neurology, 1971-94, prof. emeritus, 1994—. Chmn. profl. adv. coun. Nat. Easter Seal Soc., 1974-82; cons., chmn. panel on rev. neurol. devices subcom. FDA, 1979-83; bd. dirs. Am. Bd. Psychiatry and Neurology, 1988-96, pres., 1995. Editor-in-chief Stroke, 1992-2000; contbr. numerous articles on topics including cerebral vascular disease, blood flow, epilepsy, electroencephalography, muscle disease, to profl. jours. With U.S. Army, 1946-48. Recipient numerous grants in cerebrovascular disease. Fellow ACP; mem. AMA, Am. Assn. Univ. Profs. Neurology (pres. 1986-88), Epilepsy Found. Am., Am. Heart Assn (chmn. stroke coun. 1984-86, v.p. for sci. couns. 1988-89), Ind. Neurol. Assn. (charter pres. 1966-68), Am. Acad. Neurology, Am. Neurol. Assn., Sigma Xi, Alpha Omega Alpha. Home: 7406 W 92nd St Zionsville IN 46077-9103 Office: Ind U Med Ctr Neurol Dept 545 Barnhill Dr EM124 Indianapolis IN 46202 Home Phone: 317-873-4211; Office Phone: 317-278-2340. E-mail: mdyken@aol.com.

DYKES, ARCHIE REECE, finance company executive; b. Rogersville, Tenn., Jan. 20, 1931; s. Claude Reed and Rose (Quillen) Dykes; m. Nancy Jane Haun, May 29, 1953; children: John Reece, Thomas Mack. BS cum laude, East Tenn. State U., 1952, MA, 1956; EdD, U. Tenn., 1959. Prin., Church Hill (Tenn.) HS, 1955-58; supt. Greeneville (Tenn.) Schs., 1959-62; prof. edn., dir. Ctr. Advanced Grad. Study Edn. U. Tenn., 1962-66, chancellor Martin, 1967-71, Knoxville, 1971-73, U. Kans., 1973-80; chmn., pres., CEO Security Benefit Group Cos., Topeka, 1980-88; chmn. Capital City Holdings Inc., 1988—. Chmn. bd., CEO, Fleming Cos., Inc., Dallas; chmn. bd. dirs. Pepsi Ams., Inc.; bd. dirs. Raytech Corp., Midas, Inc., Arbor Realty Trust, Inc.; trustee Keene Industries Trust, NYC, Kans. U. Endowment Assn., Raytech Corp. Trust, NYC. Author: School Board and Superintendent, 1965, Faculty Participation in Academic Decision Making, 1968. Vice chmn. Commn. Operation U.S. Senate, 1975—76; mem. Nat. Adv. Coun. Edn. Professions Devel., 1975—76; trustee Truman Libr. Inst., 1973—80, Nelson Art Gallery, 1973—80, Menninger Found., 1982—88, Dole Found., William Allen White Found.; mem. bd. regents State of Kans., 1982—86; mem. adv. commn. U.S. Army Command and Gen. Staff Coll., 1974—79, chmn., 1978—79; chmn. bd. trustees U. Mid.-Am., 1978—79; mem. consultative bd. regents U. Qatar, 1979—80. Named Outstanding Alumnus, E. Tenn. State U., 1970; Ford Found. fellow, 1957—59, Am. Coun. Edn. Postdoctoral fellow, U. Ill., 1966—67. Mem.: Kans. Assn. Commerce and Industry (bd. dirs. 1975—82), Nat. Assn. State Univs. and Land Grant Colls. (coun. pres. 1971—80), Am. Coun. Life Ins. (bd. dirs. 1981—86), Tenn. Coll. Assn. (pres. 1969—70), Newcomen Soc. N.Am., Phi Kappa Phi. Home: 2102 W 116TH St Leawood KS 66211-2953

DYKSTRA, DENNIS DALE, physiatrist; b. Lakewood, Ohio, Feb. 21, 1950; s. Gerald and Grace Maire (Thomas) D.; m. Mary Louise Kerker, May 16, 1992; children: Dorothy, Perry, Caitlin, Patrick. AB in Zoology summa cum laude, Ohio U., 1972; MD, U. Cin., 1976; PhD, U. Minn., 1988, M in Health Adminstrn., 1999. Diplomate Am. Bd. Pediatrics, Am. Bd. Phys. Medicine and Rehab. Intern/resident Cin. Children's Hosp., 1976-81; instr. U. Minn., Mpls., 1981-88, asst. prof., 1988-92, assoc. prof. phys. medicine/rehab./pediatrics/urol. surgery, 1992—, head dept. phys. medicine/rehab., 1992—; assoc. chief staff for rehab. VA Med. Ctr., Mpls., 1994-97. Author: Krusen's Handbook of Phys. Medicine and Rehabilitation, 1991; contbr. articles to profl. jours. Med. advisor Minn. Spasmodic Torticolits Soc., Duluth, Minn., 1991—. Recipient Phys. Med. and Rehab. Investigator award Phys. Med. and Rehab. Rsch. Found., 1984, 85; Spinal Cord Soc. grantee, 1990. Fellow Am. Acad. Phys. Med. and Rehab. (chair edn. com. 1996—), Am. Acad. Pediatrics, Am. Assn. Electrodiagnostic Medicine. Achievements include 2 patents on method of apparatus for mechanical stimulation of nerves, method and device for pharmacological control of spasticity. Office: Univ Minn 420 Delaware St SE Box 297 Mayor Bldg Minneapolis MN 55455 Office Phone: 612-626-5399.

DYKSTRA, PAUL HOPKINS, lawyer; b. Chgo., July 13, 1943; s. Paul C. and Frances Marie (Hopkins) D. Student, Exeter Coll. Oxford U., Eng., 1964; AB, Princeton U., 1965; LLB, Yale U., 1968. Bar: Ill. 1968, D.C. 1977. Assoc. Gardner, Carton & Douglas, Chgo., 1968-74, ptnr., 1975—2003, ptnr. Washington office, 1977-79, fin. ptnr., 1985-89, chmn., 1989-95; mem. Bell, Boyd & Lloyd LLC, Chgo., 2003—. Adj. prof. law Northwestern U. Sch. Law, 2001—. Contbr. articles to profl. jours. Trustee Chgo. Theatre Group, Inc. (Goodman Theatre), 1975—, pres., 1983-85, vice chmn., 1988-92, pres., 1992-97; mem. aux. bd. Art Inst. Chgo., 1973-77, 79-88, exec. com., 1976-77, 82-87, 2000—; chmn. Orange and Black Club of Princeton Club of Chgo., 1987-90; chmn. maj. gifts Princeton U. Class of 1965, 1982-85; mem. cultural affairs adv. bd. City of Chgo., 1990-2003, Blue Skies for Kids, Chgo. Cmty. Trust, Chgo. Pub. Libr. Bd., 1991-97, chmn. adminstrn. and fin. com., 1996—; trustee Chgo. Pub. Libr. Found., 1999—. Mem. ABA (fed. and regulation of securities com.), Chgo. Bar Assn. (sec. 1976-77), Chgo. Hist. Soc. (trustee 1999—, mem. Making History awards com. 1994—, chmn. 2000-2002), Econ. Club of Chgo. (reception com. 1982-85), Legal Club of Chgo., Law Club Chgo., Racquet Club of Chgo. (bd. govs., vice chmn. membership com. 1980-83), Chgo. Club (bd. dirs., sec. 1996-2000), Shoreacres, Chgo. Commonwealth Club, The Comml. Club of Chgo. (sec., mem. exec. com. 2001-03), Chgo. Coun. Fgn. Rels. (Chgo. com.). Episcopalian. Avocations: travel, golf, bicycling. Office: Gardner Carton Douglas 191 N Wacker Dr Chicago IL 60606-1698 Office Phone: 312-781-6029. E-mail: pdykstra@bellboyd.com.

DYKSTRA, ROBERT, retired education educator; b. Vesper, Wis., Feb. 26, 1930; s. John and Anna (Holstein) D.; m. Lou Ann Conselman, Oct. 6, 1956; children: S. Kim, Paul, Randall. BS in Elem. Edn., U. Wis., River Falls, 1957; MA in Ednl. Psychology, U. Minn., 1959, PhD in Ednl. Psychology, 1962. Cert. elem. edn. Elem. tchr. Cedar Grove (Wis.) Pub. Sch., 1954-55; asst. prof. U. Minn., Mpls., 1962-64, assoc. prof., 1965-69, prof., 1970-73, chair dept. curriculum and instrn., 1974-85, prof., 1986-93, ret., 1993. Co-author: Teaching Reading, 1974, Language Arts: Teaching and Learning Effective Use of Language, 1988; contbr. articles to profl. jours. With US Army, 1952—54. Recipient Disting. Alumnus award U. Wis./River Falls, 1998; elected to Reading Hall of Fame, 1996; U.S. Office Edn. rsch. grantee, 1963, 65. Mem. Nat. Coun. Tchrs. of English (mem. exec. com. 1969-71), Nat. Conf. on Rsch. in English (pres. 1984-85), Twin City Area Reading Coun. (pres. 1990-91), Internat. Reading Assn. (mem. pub. com. 1975-77), Nat. Reading Conf. (mem. pub. com. 1978-80). Lutheran. Avocations: barbershop quartet singing, reading, golf. Home: 1998 16th St NW Saint Paul MN 55112-5555 Personal E-mail: bolo19@netzero.com.

DYNEK, SIGRID, corporate lawyer, retail executive; b. 1949; BS, JD, Marquette U. Bar: Wis. 1973. V.p., gen. counsel Kohl's Dept. Stores, Inc., Menomonee Falls, Wis. Office: Kohl's Dept Stores Inc N56w17000 Ridgewood Dr Menomonee Falls WI 53051-5660

DYRKACZ, GARY R., chemist, researcher; Rsch. chemist Argonne (Ill.) Nat. Lab. Recipient Henry H. Storch award in Fuel Chemistry Am. Chem. Soc., 1994. Office: Argonne Nat Lab 9700 Cass Ave Argonne IL 60439-4803

DYRSTAD, JOANELL M., former lieutenant governor, consultant; b. St. James, Minn., Oct. 15, 1942; d. Arnold A. and Ruth (Berlin) Sletta; m. Marvin Dyrstad, 1965; children: Troy, Anika. BA, Gustavus Adolphus Coll., St. Peter, Minn., 1964; MA, Hamline U., 1996. Mayor City of Red Wing, Minn., 1985-90; lt. gov. State of Minn., 1991-94; now independent bus. and govt. cons. Ptnr. Corner Drugstore, Red Wing, 1968—; v.p. League Minn. Cities, 1990-91, Minn. Mayors Assn., 1989-90; mem. Nat. Conf. Lt. Gov.'s, 1991-94, chair, 1993-94. Trustee Gustavus Adolphus Coll., 1989-98, U. Minn. Found., 1993-99; dir. corp. bd. Fairview Health Sys.; dir. Fairview Red Wing Health Svcs., chair, 2002; dir. Minn. Hosp. Health Care Partnership, 1999—. Mem. AAUW (Citizen of yr. award 1985), LWV.

DYSON, ANNE HAAS, English language educator; BS in Elem. Edn., U. Wis., 1972; MEd in Curriculum and Instrn. (Reading), U. Tex., 1976, PhD in Curriculum and Instrn. (Lang. Arts/Reading), 1981. Elem. tchr. 2d grade El Paso Cath. Diocese, Tex., 1972-73; adult educator Crawford English Acad., El Paso, Tex., 1973; substitute tchr. Austin Ind. Sch. Dist., Tex., 1974-75, presch. tchr. for 4 yr olds Tex., 1975, elem. tchr. 1st grade Tex., 1977-79; dir., staff coord. learning abilities ctr. materials lab., tutoring coord. learning abilities ctr. U. Tex., Austin, 1975-76, teaching asst., 1975-77, instr., 1979-80, rsch. asst., 1981, grad. fellow, 1980-81; head tchr., coord. summer lang. arts/reading program Alamo Heights Ind. Sch. Dist., San Antonio, 1978; asst. prof. dept. lang. edn. U. Ga., 1981-85, grad. faculty, 1984-85; vis. asst. prof. divsn. lang. and literacy sch. of edn. U. Calif., Berkeley, 1984-85, asst. prof. divsn. lang. and literacy sch. of edn., 1985-87, assoc. prof. divsn. lang. and literacy sch. of edn., 1987-91, prof. divsn. lang. and literacy sch. of edn., 1991—2002, co-dir. Ctr. for the Study of Writing and Literacy, 1990—2002; prof. tchr. edn. Mich. State U., 2002—. Author: Multiple Worlds of Child Writers: A Study of Friends Learning to Write, 1989; co-author: Language Assessment in the Early Years, 1984; editor: Collaboration Through Writing and Reading: Exploring Possibilities, 1989; contbr. articles to profl. jours., contbr. chpts. to books; editor, adv. bd. mem. Early Childhood Yearbook, 1990—; mem. editl. bd. Research in the Teaching of English, 1992—, Language and Literacy, 1989—; co-editor rsch. currents dept. Language Arts, 1983-90; editor Newsletter of the Spl. Interest Group in Language Devel. Am. Ednl. Rch. Assn., 1984-86; speaker in field. Recipient Annual Human Rights award Oakland Baha'is, 1991, Lois Gadd Nemec Disting. Alumni award U. Wis., 1990, Promising Rechr. award Nat. Coun. Tchrs. of English, 1982, award for Excellence in Ednl. Journalism Ednl. Press Assn. Am., 1982.

DYSON, MARV, broadcast executive; Pres. Sta. WGCI-AM, Chgo. Office: Wgci Radio 233 N Michigan Ave Ste 2800 Chicago IL 60601-5704

EADIE, JOHN WILLIAM, historian, educator; b. Ft. Smith, Ark., Dec. 18, 1935; s. William Robert and Helen (Montgomery) B.; m. Joan Holt, Aug. 18, 1957; children: Robin, Christopher. BA with honors, U. Ark., 1957; MA, U. Chgo., 1959; PhD, Univ. Coll., London, 1962. Asst. prof. Ripon Coll., Wis., 1962-63; asst. prof. history U. Mich., Ann Arbor, 1963-67, assoc. prof., 1967-73, prof., 1973-86, assoc. chmn. dept. history, 1970-71, humanities-arts advisor Office V.p. for Research, 1974-86, assoc. dean Rackham Sch. Grad. Studies, 1984-86; prof. history, dean Coll. Arts and Letters Mich. State U., East Lansing, 1996—97, sr. advisor to provost, 1997—2000, prof. and dean emeritus, 2002—. Dir. Consortium for Inter-Instnl. Collaboration in African and L.Am. Studies, 1989-2000, chmn. liberal arts and scis. dean Consortium for Instnl. Collaboration, 1991-94, bd. mem. Santa Fe Coun. Internat. Rels. Author: The Breviarium of Festus: A critical-Edition with Historical Commentary, 1967, The Conversion of Constantine, 1971, (with others) Western Civilization, 1975; editor: Classical traditions in Early America, 1976; co-editor The Craft of the Ancient Historian, 1985, Urban Centers and Rural Contexts in Late Antiquity, 2001. Chmn. Mich. Council for Humanities, E. Lansing, Mich., 1977-80, Mich. Alliance for Conservation Cultural Heritage, 1988-90. Marshall scholar Brit. Marshall Commn. Univ. Coll., London, 1960-62; recipient Disting. Service award Mich. Council Humanities, 1980, Ralph Smucker award for advancing internat. programs, 2001. Mem.: Archaeol Inst. Am. Democrat. Presbyterian. E-mail: jweadie@msu.edu.

EARL, ANTHONY SCULLY, retired governor, lawyer; b. Lansing, Mich., Apr. 12, 1936; s. Russell K. and Ethlynne Julia (Scully) E.; children: Julia, Anne, Mary, Catherine. BS, Mich. State U., 1958; JD, U. Chgo., 1961. Bar: Wis., Minn. Asst. dist. atty. Marathon County, Wausau, Wis., 1965-66; city atty. City of Wausau, 1966-69; mem. Wis. Assembly, Madison, 1969-74, majority floor leader, 1971; mem. firm Crooks, Low & Earl, 1969-74; sec. Wis. Dept. Adminstrn., Madison, 1974-75, Dept. Nat. Resources, Madison, 1975-80; v.p. firm Foley & Lardner, Madison, 1980-82; gov. State of Wis., Madison, 1983-87; ptnr. Quarles and Brady, Madison, 1987—. Served as lt. USN, 1962-65. Democrat. Roman Catholic. Office: 360 W Washington Ave Unit 1007 Madison WI 53703-2766 also: Quarles & Brady LLP Ste 900 33 E Main St Madison WI 53703-3095 Office Phone: 608-283-2471, 608-251-5000. Office Fax: 608-251-9166. Business E-Mail: ase@quarles.com.*

EARLE, TIMOTHY KEESE, anthropology educator; b. New Bedford, Mass., Aug. 10, 1946; s. Osborne and Eleanor (Clark) E.; m. Eliza Howe, June 14, 1969; children: Caroline, Hester. BA summa cum laude, Harvard U., 1969; MA, U. Mich., 1971, PhD, 1973. Rsch. archaeologist Bishop Mus., Honolulu, 1971-72; prof. anthropology UCLA, 1973-95, dir. Inst. of Archaeology, 1987-92; prof. anthropology Northwestern U., Evanston, Ill., 1995—, chair dept., 1995-2000. Author: Bronze Age Economics, 2002, How Chiefs Come to Power, 1997; co-author: Evolution of Human Society, 1987, 2nd edit., 2000; editor: Exchange Systems in Prehistory, 1977, Contexts for Prehistoric Exchange, 1982, Chiefdoms, 1991. Mem.: Soc. Econ. Anthrop., Soc. Am. Archaeology, Am. Anthrop. Assn. (pres. archaeology divsn. 1995—97, exec. bd. 1999—2002), Phi Beta Kappa. E-mail: tke299@northwestern.edu.

EARLEY, ANTHONY FRANCIS, JR., utilities company executive, lawyer; b. Jamaica, NY, July 29, 1949; s. Anthony Francis and Jean Ann (Draffen) E.; m. Sarah Margaret Belanger, Oct. 14, 1972; children: Michael Patrick, Anthony Matthew, Daniel Cartwright, Matthew Sean. BS in Physics, U. Notre Dame, 1971, MS in Engring., 1979, JD, 1979. Bar: Va. 1980, N.Y. 1985, U.S. Ct. Appeals (6th cir.) 1981. Assoc. Hunton & Williams, Richmond, Va., 1979-85, ptnr., 1985; gen. counsel L.I. Lighting Co., Hicksville, N.Y., 1985-89, exec. v.p., 1988-89, pres., COO, 1989-94, The Detroit Edison Co., Mich., 1994—98; chmn., CEO DTE Energy Co., Detroit, 1998—. Dir., past chmn. Nuclear Energy Inst.; mem. elec. adv. bd. U.S. Dept. Energy; bd. dir. Comerica Inc., Masco Corp. Contbr. articles to profl. jours. Chmn. United Way SE Mich.; mem. listed mem. adv. bd. NYSE; bd. dir. Detroit Renaissance, Detroit Zoological Soc., Cornerstone Schools; mem. adv. bd. Coll. Engring., Univ. Notre Dame. Served to lt., qualified as chief engr. officer nuclear submarine prog. USN, 1971—76. Mem.: ABA. Roman Catholic. Avocations: skiing, tennis, furniture restoration. Office: DTE Energy Co 2000 2nd Ave Detroit MI 48226-1279

EARLY, JACK JONES, foundation executive; b. Corbin, Ky., Apr. 12, 1925; s. Joseph M. and Lela (Jones) E.; m. Nancye Bruce Whaley, June 1, 1952; children: Lela Katherine, Judith Ann, Laura Hattie. AB, Union Coll., Barbourville, Ky., 1948; MA, U. Ky., 1953, Ed.D. (So. scholar 1955-56), 1956; B.D., Coll. of Bible, Lexington, Ky., 1956; D.D., Wesley Coll., Grand Forks, ND, 1961; LL.D., Parsons Coll., 1962, Iowa Wesleyan Coll., 1972; Litt.D., Dakota Wesleyan U., 1969; L.H.D., Union Coll., Barbourville, Ky., 1979; D.Adminstrn., Cumberland Coll., 1981. Ordained to ministry Methodist Ch., 1954; pastor Rockhold Circuit, Ky., 1943-44, Craig's Chapel and Laurel Circuit, London, Ky., 1944-47, Trinity Ch., Oak Ridge, summer 1945, Hindman Ch., Ky., 1947-52; dean of men Hindman Settlement Sch., 1948-51; assoc. pastor Park Ch., Lexington, Ky., 1952-54; asst. to pres., dean Athens Coll., Ala., 1954-55; v.p., dean of coll. Iowa Wesleyan Coll., Mount Pleasant, 1956-58; pres. Dakota Wesleyan U., 1958-69, Pfeiffer Coll., Misenheimer, NC, 1969-71; exec. dir. Am. Bankers Assn., Washington, 1971-73; pres. Limestone Coll., Gaffney, SC, 1973-79; exec. dir. edn. Combined Ins. Co. Am., Chgo., 1979-82, v.p., exec. dir. edn. and communications, 1982-84; pres. Ky. Ind. Coll. Fund, Louisville, 1984-93, pres. emeritus, 1993—; dir. edn., con. Napoleon Hill Found., Northbrook, Ill., 1997—. Pres. W. Clement Stone PMA Communications, Inc., Chgo., 1987—. Active Boy Scouts Am.; mem. pres. adv. coun. North Pk. Coll.; mem. Felician adv. bd. Felician Coll.; mem. Ky. Ho. of Reps., 1952-54; bd. dirs. S.D. Found. Pvt. Colls., S.D. Meth. Found., Nat. Coun. on Youth Leadership, Ctr. for Citizenship Edn., YMCA, Motivational Inst., Mid-Am. chpt. ARC, 1980—, W. Clement and Jessie V. Stone Found., Northbrook Symphony Orch., Ky. Mountain Laurel Festival, 1990—, Internat. Coun. on Edn. for Teaching, 1990—; chmn. bd. Religious Heritage Am., 1989-92, Internat. Leadership Network, 1991—; Rep. nominee for Metro Mayor, Louisville, 2002. Recipient Spoke award Mitchell Jr. C. of C., 1959, Disting. Svc. award, 1960, Disting. Svc. award S.D. Jr. C. of C., 1960, Gaffney Jaycees, 1979, Chief Iron Eyes Cody medal of Peace, 1987, Outstanding Kentuckian award O'Tucks, 1990; named Outstanding Former Kentuckian, 1963; hon. fellow Wroxton Coll., Oxfordshire, Eng.; named to Disting. Alumni Hall of Fame, U. Ky., 1965, Union Coll. Hall of Fame, 2000, U. Ky. Coll. Edn. Hall of Fame, 2006. Mem. Am. Soc. Assn. Execs., Louisville C. of C., Blue Key, Masons (33d degree, chaplain Valley of Louisville chpt. 1990—, Viceroy and Sovereign Red Cross Constantine), Rotary (pres. Louisville 1992-93, dist. 6710 gov. 1996—), First Families Ky. (dep. gov. gen., gov. gen. 2007—), Ky. Soc. SAR (pres. 1998—), Order of Founders and Patriots of Am. (gov. Ky. chpt. 2003-, dep. chaplain gen., chaplain gen.), Soc. War of 1812 in the Commonwealth of Ky. (pres. 1997—), Huguenot Soc. Ky. (pres. 1999—), Huguenot Soc.-Soc. of Manakin (Ky. br. pres. 1999—), Nat. Soc. Sons and Daus. of Pilgrims (gov. Ky. br. 2000—), Gen. for Pub. Rels.-Gen. Soc. of the War of 1812 (v.p. 1998—), Del. State Soc. of Cin., Gen. Soc. Sons of Revolution (gen. chaplain), Ky. Soc. Colonial Wars (dep. gov. 2008-), Nat. Sojourners Camp #134, Heroes of '76 (E.B. Jones Camp), Jamestowne Soc., Ky. Co. (chaplain, lt. gov. 2008-), First FAmilies of Ga., First Families of Tenn., Presdl. Families Am., Kappa Delta Pi, Phi Delta Kappa (bd. dirs. Northwestern U. chpt. 1980—), Kappa Phi Kappa, Alpha Psi Omega, Theta Phi, Pi Tau Chi, Sigma Beta Delta. Republican. Home: 9002 Hurstwood Ct Louisville KY 40222-5716 Home Phone: 502-426-6078; Office Phone: 502-426-6078.

EARLY, JUDITH K., social services director; b. Evansville, Ind., 1954; d. Forrest M. and Dorothea E. Early. BA, Brescia Coll., 1976; MS, So. Ill. U., 1985, RhD, 1991. Cert. vocat. evaluator; cert. family devel. specialist. Work activity supr. So. Ind. Rehab. Svcs., Inc., Boonville, 1976-78; vocat. evaluator Evansville Assn. for Retarded Citizens, 1978-85; vocat. evaluator Evaluation and Developmental Ctr., Carbondale, Ill., 1985-88; grad. asst., program evaluator So. Ill. U., Carbondale, 1988-90, rsch. and teaching asst., 1990-91; exec. dir. Albion Fellow Bacon Ctr., Evansville, Ind., 1991-93; family svcs. dir. Goodwill Family Ctr., Evansville, 1993-95, program evaluation dir., 1995-96, dir., 1996-2000; cmty. rels. dir. Evansville Goodwill Industries, Inc., 2000—. Contbr. articles to profl. publs. Bd. dirs. So. Ill. Ctr. for Ind. Living, Carbondale, 1990-91, Vanderburgh County Coun. Aging, 2000—, Southwestern Ind. Regional Coun. on Aging, 2002-; bd. dirs., youth worker 1st United Meth. Ch., Carbondale, 1989-91; v.p. Altrusa of Evansville, 1993-94; mem. Evansville Asbury United Meth. Ch., 1993—, treas., 1998—; bd. dirs. Youth as Resources, 1995-98, Transitional Svcs., Inc., Human Rights Com., 1992—; bd. dirs. Leadership Evansville, 1999-2002; bd. dirs. Family Resource Ctr., 1995-2002, v.p., 2000-2002; pres. Altrusa of Evansville, 2004-06. Mem. AAUW, Vocat. Evaluation and Work Adjustment Assn. (chmn. student affairs com. 1988-90, Student Lit. award 1987), Ill. Rehab. Assn. (bd. dirs. 1989-91), Ill. Vocat. Evaluation and Work Adjustment Assn. (chmn. mem. 1989-91, pres. 1991—, Disting. Svc. award 1989), Assn. Retarded Citizens, Altrusa Internat. of Evansville. Avocations: needlepoint, gardening, photography, cooking. Office: Evansville Goodwill Industries Inc 500 S Green River Rd Evansville IN 47715-7392

EASTER, STEPHEN SHERMAN, JR., biology professor; b. New Orleans, Feb. 12, 1938; s. Stephen Sherman and Myrtle Olivia (Bekkedahl) E.; m. Janine Eliane Piot, June 4, 1963; children: Michele, Kim BS, Yale U., 1960; postgrad., Harvard U., 1961; PhD, Johns Hopkins U., 1966. Postdoctoral fellow Cambridge U., Eng., 1967; postdoctoral U. Calif., Berkeley, 1968-69; asst. prof. biology U. Mich., Ann Arbor, 1970-74, assoc. prof., 1974-78, prof., 1978—2004, assoc. chmn., 1992-93, mem. Coll. Lit., Sci. and the Arts exec. com., 1993-96, dir. neurosci. program, 1984-88, Mathew Alpern Collegiate prof., 1998—2004, prof. emeritus, 2004—. Vis. prof. U. Murcia, Spain, 1997, Ecole Normale Supérieure, Paris, 1997. Editor Vision Rsch., 1978-85, Jour. Neurosci., 1989-95, Jour. eurosci., 1990-92, Investigative Ophthalmology and Visual Sci., 1992-97, Jour. Comparative Neurology, 1994-99. Recipient Sokol award, 1998. Mem. Soc. eurosci., Assn. Rsch. in Vision and Ophthalmology, Internat. Brain Rsch. Orgn., Soc. for Devel. Biology. Office: U Mich Dept Biology 3113 Natural Sci Bldg Ann Arbor MI 48109-1048 E-mail: sseaster@umich.edu.

EASTERBROOK, FRANK HOOVER, federal judge; b. Buffalo, Sept. 3, 1948; s. George Edmund and Vimy (Hoover) E. BA, Swarthmore Coll., 1970; JD, U. Chgo., 1973. Bar: D.C. Law clk. to Hon. Levin H. Campbell US Ct. Appeals (1st cir.), Boston, 1973-74; asst. to solicitor gen. US Dept. Justice, Washington, 1974-77, dep. solicitor gen., 1978-79; asst. prof. law U. Chgo., 1978-81, prof. law, 1981—85, Lee & Brena Freeman prof., 1984-85; prin. employee Lexecon Inc., Chgo., 1980-85; sr. lectr. U. Chgo., 1985—; judge US Ct. Appeals (7th cir.), Chgo., 1985—, chief judge, 2006—. Mem. adv. com. on tender offers SEC, Washington, 1983 Author: (with Richard A. Posner) Antitrust, 1981, (with Daniel R. Fischel) The Economic Structure of Corporate Law, 1991; editor Jour. Law and Econs., Chgo., 1982-91; contbr. articles to profl. jours. Trustee James Madison Meml. Fellowship Found., 1988—. Recipient Prize for Disting. scholarship Emory U., Atlanta, 1981 Mem. AAAS, Am. Law Inst., Mont Pelerin Soc., Order of Coif, Phi Beta Kappa. Office: US Ct Appeals Everett McKinley Dirksen Fed Bldg 219 S Dearborn St Ste 2746 Chicago IL 60604-1803

EASTERDAY, BERNARD CARLYLE, veterinary medicine educator; b. Hillsdale, Mich., Sept. 16, 1929; s. Harley B. and Alberta M. Easterday D.V.M., Mich. State U., 1952; MS, U. Wis., 1958, PhD, 1961. Diplomate Am. Coll. Veterinary Microbiologists. Pvt. practice veterinary medicine, Hillsdale, Mich., 1952; veterinarian U.S. Dept. Def., Frederick, Md., 1955-61; assoc. prof., then prof. veterinary sci. U. Wis., Madison, 1961-94, prof. emeritus, 1994—, dean Sch. Vet. Medicine, 1979-94, dean emeritus, prof emeritus Sch. Vet. Medicine, 1994—. Mem., chmn. com. animal health Nat. Acad. Sci.-NRC, Washington, 1980-83, mem. com. on sci. basis meat and poultry inspection program, 1984-85; mem. tech. adv. com. Binat. Agrl. Research and Devel., Bet-Degan, Israel, 1982-84; mem. expert adv. panel on zoonoses WHO, Geneva, 1978-94; mem. tech. adv. com. on avian influenza USDA, 1983-85; mem. sec. USDA adv. com. on fgn. animal and poultry diseases, 1991-96. 1st lt. V.C., U.S. Army, 1952-54. Recipient Disting. Alumnus award Coll. Vet. Medicine, Mich. State U., 1975, Disting. Alumni award Mich. State U., 1999, Disting. Alumni award U. Wis., Madison, 2003; named Wis. Veterinarian of Yr., Wis. Vet. Med. Assn., 1979. Mem. AVMA, Am. Assn. Vet. Med. Colls. (pres. 1975), Am. Assn. Avian Pathologists Office: U Wisconsin-Madison Sch Vet Medicine 2015 Linden Dr W Madison WI 53706-1100

EASTHAM, DENNIS MICHAEL, advertising executive; b. Jacksonville, Ill., Dec. 18, 1946; s. Glenn R. and Ona M. (Camerer) E.; m. Dianne C. L. Watts; children: Susie, Brian, Brad. BA in Fin., U. Ill., 1968; MBA, U. Santa Clara, 1972. Asst. v.p. Crocker Bank, San Francisco, 1976-79; v.p. T & E Card div. Citicorp, LA, 1979-81; exec. v.p. Barry Blau and Ptnrs. Inc., L.A., NYC and Chgo., 1981-87; pres. Barry Blau Worldwide, Deerfield, Ill., 1987—. Bd. dirs. Barry Blau and Ptnrs. Inc., Fairfield, Conn., 1985—. Mem. Direct Mktg. Assn. Home: 21835 Vernon Ridge Dr Mundelein IL 60060-5316

EASTMAN, DEAN ERIC, physicist, researcher; b. Oxford, Wis., Jan. 20, 1940; m. Ella Mae Staley. BSEE, MIT, 1962, MSEE, 1963, PhDEE, 1965. Rsch. staff IBM T.J. Watson Rsch. Ctr., Yorktown Heights, NY, 1963-71, mgr. photoemission and surface physics group, 1971-81, mgr. lithography packaging and compound semicondr. tech., 1981-82, dir. Advanced Packaging Tech. Lab., 1983-85, rsch. v.p. system tech. and sci., 1986-94; dir. product devel. IBM Systems Tech. Div., Danbury, Conn., 1985-86; dir. hardware devel. reengring. IBM Corp., Armonk, NY, 1994-96; dir. Argonne Nat. Lab., 1996-98; prof. physics U. Chgo., 1998—. Prof. physics U. Chgo., 1998—. Contbr. over 180 articles to profl. jours. Recipient Oliver E. Buckley prize, 1980; IBM Corp. fellow, 1974. Fellow Am. Phys. Soc.; mem. NAS, NAE, Am. Acad. Arts and Scis. Office: University of Chicago JFI Box 15 RI 231 5640 S Ellis Ave Chicago IL 60637-1433

EASTWOOD, GREGORY LINDSAY, former academic administrator; b. Detroit, July 28, 1940; s. William Inwood and Kathryn (Bradley) E.; m. Lynn Marshall, June 19, 1964; children: Kristen, Lauren, Kara. AB, Albion Coll., 1962; MD, Case Western Res. U., 1966. Diplomate: Am. Bd. Internal Medicine, Am. Bd. Gastroenterology. Resident in internal medicine Hosp. U. Pa., 1966—70; asst. prof. medicine Harvard U., Boston, 1974-77; assoc. prof. medicine U. Mass., Worcester, 1977-82, prof., 1982—89, dir. gastroenterology, 1977-89; dean Sch. Medicine Med. Coll. Ga., Augusta, 1989—92; pres. SUNY Upstate Med. U., Syracuse, 1993—2006; trustee Case Western Reserve U., Cleve., 2003—06, interim pres., 2006—07. Coun., past chair bd. dirs. Assn. Acad. Health Ctrs. Editor: Core Textbook in Gastroenterology, 1984, Manual of Gastroenterology: Diagnosis and Therapy, 1988, Premalignant Conditions of the Gastrointestinal Tract, 1990; contbr. articles to profl. jours. Fellow: ACP; mem.: AMA, Assn. Am. Med. Colls., An. Hosp. Assn., Am. Gastroenterological Assn., Am. Clin. and Climotological Assn. Office: Case Western Reserve U 10900 Euclid Ave Cleveland OH 44106-7001 Office Phone: 216-368-5094. Office Fax: 216-368-4325. E-mail: gregory.eastwood@case.edu.

EATON, JAY, lawyer; b. Waterloo, Iowa, Feb. 24, 1946; BBA, U. Iowa, 1968, JD with honors, 1971. Bar: Iowa 1971, Ohio 1972, Wis. 1977. Assoc. Nyemaster, Goode, Voigts, West, Hansell & O'Brien, Des Moines. Mem. ABA, Iowa State Bar Assn. (v.p. 1997-98, pres. 1998—), Polk County Bar Assn. (bd. dirs. 1989-97, pres. 1992-93). Office: Nyemaster Goode Voigts West Hansell & O'Brien PC 700 Walnut St Ste 1600 Des Moines IA 50309-3800 E-mail: je@nyemaster.com.

EATON, LARRY RALPH, lawyer; b. Quincy, Ill., Aug. 18, 1944; s. Roscoe Ralph and Velma Marie (Beckett) E.; m. Janet Claire Rosen, Oct. 28, 1978; child Justin Ross Eaton. BA, Western Ill. U., 1965; JD, U. Mich., 1968. Bar: Ill. 1968,, NY 1997, US Dist. Ct. (no. dist.) Ill. 1978, US Dist. Ct., US Dist. Ct. (central dist.) Ill. 2001, US Dist Ct. (eastern dist.) Wis. 2001, US District Ct. (no. dist.) Ind. 2002, US Dist. Ct. (so. dist.) Ill. 2005, US Ct. Appeals (DC cir.) 1984, US Ct. Appeals (7th cir.) 1989US Ct. Appeals (3rd cir.) 1994. Vol., instr. law U. Liberia Sch. Law, U.S. Peace Corps, Monrovia, 1968-70; lawyer Forest Park Found., Peoria Heights, Ill., 1970-71; asst. atty. gen. State of Ill., Springfield, 1971-75; ptnr. Peterson & Ross and predecessors, Chgo., 1975-94; founder Blatt, Hammesfahr & Eaton, Chgo., 1994-2000; sr. mem. Cozen O'Connor, Chgo., 2000—. Instr. environ. law Quincy Coll., Ill., 1973—75; contbg. writer Chgo. Daily Law Bull., 1975—77; field editor. Pollution Engring., 1976. Bd. dirs. Edgewater Cmty. Coun., Chgo., 2000—; pres. Lakewood Balmoral Residents' Coun., Chgo., 2000—02; bd. dirs. Near North Montessori Sch., 1989—95, vice chmn., 1992—95; bd. dirs. Edgewater Devel. Corp., 2000—, v.p., 2002—. Recipient Ill. Super Lawyer, 2005. Fellow: Ill. Bar Found. (charter); mem.: ABA (environ. ins. litig. task force 1990), Bar Assn. for 7th Jud. Cir., Chgo. Bar Assn., Ill. Bar Assn. (editor sect. newsletter 1972—77, coun. 1973—77, chmn. environ. control law sect. 1976—77, assembly 1980—86, 1989—92, coun. 1990—94, coun. jud. evaluation Cook County 2000—), Atticus Finch Inn of Ct., Lawyers Club Chgo. Office Phone: 312-382-3100. Business E-Mail: leaton@cozen.com.

EATON, MAJA CAMPBELL, lawyer; b. 1955; BA, U. Iowa, 1977, JD, 1984. Bar: Ill. 1984, U.S. Dist. Ct. (no. dist.) Ill. 1984, U.S. Dist. Ct. (no. dist.) Calif. 1993. With Sidley Austin Brown & Wood, Chgo., ptnr., 1993—. Former adj. prof. law Chgo.-Kent Coll. Law. Mem.: Def. Rsch. Inst. Office: Sidley Austin Brown & Wood Ste 900 1 S Dearborn St Chicago IL 60603-2010

EATON, MERRILL THOMAS, psychiatrist, educator; b. Howard County, Ind., June 25, 1920; s. Merrill Thomas and Dorothy (Whiteman) E.; m. Louise Foster, Dec. 23, 1942; children: Deirdre Ann, Thomas Anthony, David Foster. AB, Ind. U., Bloomington, 1941, MD, 1944. Diplomate: Am. Bd. Psychiatry. Intern St. Elizabeth's Hosp., Washington, 1944-45; resident Sheppard and Enoch Pratt Hosp., Towson, Md., 1948-49; pvt. practice medicine specializing in psychiatry Kansas City, Kans., 1949-60, Omaha, 1960-2000; dir. Nebr. Psychiat. Inst., 1968-85; assoc. in psychiatry Kans. U. Sch. Medicine, 1949-50, asst. prof., 1951-54, assoc. prof., 1954-60; assoc. prof. psychiatry U. Nebr. Coll. Medicine, 1960-63, prof., 1963-88, prof. emeritus, 1989—, chmn. dept. psychiatry, 1968-85; psychiatrist Immanuel Mental Health Ctr., 1986-88; pvt. practice cons. Omaha, 1989-2000. Author: Psychiatry, 1967, 5th edit., 1985, (with David Kentsmith) Treating Sexual Problems in Medical Practice, 1979. Served to capt. U.S. Army, 1945-47. Fellow ACP, Am. Psychiat. Assn.; mem. Group for Advancement Psychiatry (chmn. com. on mental health services 1970-73, chmn. publ. bd. 1976-83, cons. pub. bd. 1983—, bd. dirs. 1984-86), Nebr. Med. Assn., Nebr. Psychiat. Soc. (pres. 1973-75).

EBBERS, LARRY HAROLD, education educator; b. Rockwell, Iowa, June 17, 1941; s. Harold Theodore and Gertrude Eleanor (Robeoltmann) E.; m. Barbara Ellen Smith, June 17, 1962; children: Lori Ann, Kimberly Jo. BS, Iowa State U., 1962, MS, 1968, PhD, 1971. Vocat. agrl. instr. Iowa Falls (Iowa) Sch., 1962-63, Spencer (Iowa) Schs., 1963-65; asst. dir. residences Iowa State U., Ames, 1965-72, asst. prof., 1972-75, assoc. prof., 1975-80, prof. edn., 1981—, disting. Univ. prof., 2004—, dept. chair, prof. studies in edn., 1983-93, asst. to dean Coll. Edn., 1972-76, asst. dean Coll. Edn., 1976-83, assoc. dean, 1996-2000, prof., 2004—. Contbr. articles to profl. jours. Bd. dirs. Ames Parks and Recreation Commn., 1983-86, Iowa State U. Meml. Union, 1989-94; pres. Ctrl. Iowa Regional Substance Abuse Ctr., Ames, 1984-85, Meeker Sch. PTO, Ames, 1975-76; mem. task force on campus ministry Am. Luth. Ch., Des Moines, 1979-84; bd. regents Waldorf Coll., Iowa, 1999—, vice chair, 2005—. Recipient Outstanding Young Alumnus award, 1976, Outstanding Acad. Adv. award, 1977, Human Rels. award Human Rels. Commn., 1984, Human rels. award Student Affairs Divsn., 1985, Outstanding Faculty Citation award, 1991, Cardinal Key Leadership Hon., 1995, Golden Key Honor Soc., 1996, Pres.'s Disting. Svc. award, 1999, Regents award for faculty excellence, 2001, Thomas B. Thielen award, 2007 all received from Iowa State U., Disting. Svc. award Coun. for Study of C.C., 2006; Rotary Found. fellow, Brazil, 1977; Fulbright scholar, Germany, 2000. Mem. AACC (coun. for study of cmty. coll.), Nat. Assn. Student Pers. Adminstrs. (dir. rsch. and program devel. 1979-81, chmn. Am. Coun. on Edn. Inst. 1984-86, editor jour. 1981-84, pres. 1987-88, v.p. Found. 1989-92, Disting. Svc. award 1990, Fred Turner award 1991, nat. conf. program chair 1992, chair Acad. Leadership and Exec. Effectiveness, dir. acad. leadership and exec. effectiveness, 2002-04, Robert Shaffer award for acad. excellence as a grad. faculty mem. 1996), Kiwanis (Ames pres. 1977-78), Phi Delta Kappa, Phi Kappa Phi (pres. 1977-79, centennial medalist 1997). Lutheran. Avocations: sports, jogging, farming. Home: 220 24th St Ames IA 50010-4832 Office: Iowa State U N226 N Lagomarcino Hl Ames IA 50011-0001 Home Phone: 515-232-0073. Business E-Mail: lebbers@iastate.edu.

EBERHARD, WILLIAM THOMAS, architect; b. St. Louis, Apr. 11, 1952; s. George Walter and Bettie Alma (Seilkop) E.; m. Cynthia Ann Hardy, Aug. 20, 1977 (div. 1981); m. Linda W. Bayer, Dec. 5, 1986; children: Elena Lynn, Alysse Marie. BArch, U. Cin., 1976; postgrad., Archtl. Assn., London, 1974. Registered arch. Ohio, Mich., Pa., Fla., D.C., Ill., Mo. V.p. Visnapuu & Assocs., Inc., Cleve., 1972-82; prin.-in-charge Oliver Design Group, Cleve., 1983—. V.p., prin.-in-charge Grubb & Ellis, Cleve., Detroit, Pitts., 1989-90, Grubb & Ellis Nat. Accounts Team, 1987-90. Author: Public Interiors, 1986, 2d edit., 1996, Professional Office Design, 1988, Docket, 1988, Facility Design & Management, 1990, 91, Interior Design, 1992, Contract Design, 1995, Architecture Record Lighting, 1996, Facility Management Journal, 1996; contbr. articles to profl. jours. Profl. team leader Inst. Urban Design, Cleve., 1983; mem. evangelism com. First Bapt. Ch. of Greater Cleve., 1990—. Recipient Best Comml. Interior Design Project award NAIOP, 1991-96, 2000, Best Office Interior Design Project award, 1992, Best Renovation Project, 1995, Design award Nat. Inst. Bus., 1992, 93, Best Comml. Space, 1993, NAIOP Design award Best Pub. Space, 1993, Best Comml. Interior Design, 1994, 95, 96, 97, 2000, Best Renovation Project, 1995, 1st Pl. award Build Ohio Competition, 1992. Mem. AIA (chpt. sec. 1982-84, 1st Pl. award 1993, Cleve. Chpt. Design award 1993, 94, 99, 2004, Ohio Area Design award 1994-95, 2005, Internat. Int. Design award 1992, 94, 95, Best of Show, First Place Large Corp. Category, Details Category award 1993, 1994, 99, 2005), Internat. Facility Mgrs. Assn., Cleve. Art Assn., Nat. Trust for Hist. Preservation, Inst. Urban Design, Am. Soc. Interior Designers (assoc.), Seminotic Soc. Am. (founding), Design Forum of Cleve. (founding 1990—, pres. 1991—), Club Soc. Ctr. (founding), Cleve. Design Task Force (founding pres. 1996—), Shaker Heights Country Club (house com., design com.), Union Club of Cleve, IIDA/IESNA (Regional Design award, 2002, 03, 04, 05, Regional Merit Retail Category Design Program award 1998, 2002, 03, 04), Leadership Cleve. Class of 2006. Avocations: drawing, photography, tennis, snowmobiling, golf. Home: 2867 Torrington Rd Shaker Heights OH 44122-2555 Office: Oliver Design Group 1301 E 9th St Ste 2900 Cleveland OH 44114-1835 Business E-Mail: wte@oliver-design.com.

EBERLEIN, TIMOTHY J., surgeon; b. New Kensington, Pa., 1951; BS, U. Pitts., 1973, MD, 1977; MA (hon.), Harvard U., 1996. Cert. gen. surgery. Surgical intern, resident Peter Bent Brigham Hosp., Boston, 1977—79; rsch. fellow, surgery br. Nat. Cancer Inst., Bethesda, Md., 1979—82; surgical resident to chief resident surgery Brigham & Women's Hosp., Boston, 1982—84, chief surgical oncology div., vice chmn. rsch., dept. surgery; Richard E. Wilson prof. surgery Harvard Med. Sch., Boston; Spencer T. & Ann W. Olin disting. prof. Washington U. Sch. Med, St. Louis, 1998—; Bixby prof. surgery Washington U. Sch. Med., St. Louis, 1998—, chmn. surgery, 1998—, dir. Alvin J. Siteman Cancer Ctr., 1998—; surgeon-in-chief Barnes-Jewish Hosp., St. Louis. Bd. dirs. Barnes-Jewish Hosp.; mem. adv. bd. Nat. Cancer Inst. Editor-in-chief Jour. Am. Coll. Surgeons, 2004—, assoc. editor Yearbook in Surgery, mem. editorial bd. Surgical Oncology, Annals of Surgical Oncology, Annals of Surgery, Current Opinion in Gen. Surgery, Jour. Surgical Oncology, Seminars in Surgical Oncology, The Oncologist, Surgery. Fellow: Am. Coll. Surgeons (mem. surgical rsch. & ed. com. 1994—, vice chair surgical rsch. & ed. com. 1998—2000, chair surgical rsch. & ed. com. 2000—02, mem. Corp. Rsch. Roundtable 1994—2002); mem.: Inst. Medicine, Alpha Omega Alpha, Phi Beta Alpha. Office: Washington U Sch Med Dept Surgery Campus Box 8109 660 S Euclid Ave Saint Louis MO 63110 Office Phone: 314-362-8020. Office Fax: 314-454-1898. E-mail: everleint@wustl.edu.

EBERLEY, HELEN-KAY, opera singer, recording industry executive, poet; b. Sterling, Ill., Aug. 3, 1947; d. William Elliott and P. (Conneely) E. MusB, Northwestern U., 1970, MusM, 1971. Chmn., pres., artistic coord. Eberley Inc., Evanston, Ill., 1973-92; founder H.K.E. Enterprises, 1993—, pres., 1993—; circulation libr. Evanston Pub. Libr., 1995-98; prin., adminstr. The Kidusche Eberley Trust. Founder EB-SKO Prodns., 1976-92, tchr., coach, 1976—; exec. dir., performance cons. E-S Mgmt., 1985-92; featured artist Honors Concert, Northwestern U., 1970, Alumni Concert, 1999, Master Class and guest lectr. various colls. and univs.; host Poetry in Process monthly seminar Barnes & Noble; music lectr. rep. Harvard Club, Chgo.; numerous TV and radio talk show appearances and interviews. Operatic debut in Peter Grimes, Lyric Opera, Chgo., 1974; starred in: Der Rosenkovalier, Cosi Fan Tutte, Le Nozze Di Figaro, Dido and Aeneas, La Boheme, Faust, Tosca, La Traviata, Falstaff, Don Giovanni, Brigadoon, others; jazz appearances with Duke Ellington, Dave Brubeck and Robert Shaw; performing artist Oglebay Opera Inst., Wheeling, W.Va., 1968, WTTW TV/PBS, Chgo., 1968; solo star in: Continental Bank Concerts, 1981-89, United Airlines-Schubert, Schumann, Brahms, Mendelssohn, Faure, Mozart, Duparc/Wolf, Supersta. WFMT Radio, Chgo., 1982-90; featured artist with North Shore Concert Band, 1989; starring artist South Bend Symphony, 1990, Mo. Symphony Soc., 1990, Milw. Symphony, 1990; spl. guest artist New Studios Gala Sta. WFMT, 1995, West Valley Fine Arts Concert Series, Phoenix, 1999; prodr.-annotator Gentlemen Gypsy, 1978, Strauss and Szymanowski, 1979, One Sonata Each: Franck and Szymanowski, 1982; starring artist-exec. prodr. Separate But Equal, 1976, All Brahms, 1977, Opera Lady, 1978, Eberley Sings Strauss, 1980, Helen-Kay Eberley: American Girl, 1983, Helen-Kay Eberley: Opera Lady II, 1984; performed Am. and Can. nat. anthems for Chgo. Cubs Baseball Team, 1977-83, Chgo. Bears Football, 1977; also starred in numerous concert recital and symphony appearances, Europe, Can., U.S.; author: Angel's Song, 1994, The Magdaleva Poems, 1995, ChapelHeart, 1996, Desert Dancing, 1997, Canyon Ridge, 2000, Rivervoice, 2002, The Chichester Psalms, 2006. Docent, new mem. tour guide Art Inst. Chgo.; spl. events hotline vol. Art Inst. Chgo., Chgo. Christian Indsl. League, St. Joseph's Table of St. Peter's in the Loop, Chgo.; vol., facilitator City Yr. Chgo.-Urban Peace Corps; Chgo. Humanities Festival VIII of Ill. Humanities Coun., Evanston Shelter for Battered Women, Rape Victim Adv., Habitat for Humanity; Midwest Vol. Facilitator 1st Indsl. Realty Trust; mem. Mayor's founding com. Evanston Arts Coun., 1974-75; judge Ice-Skating Competition, Wilmette (Ill.) Park Dist., 1974-77, bd. dirs., 1973-77; bd. dirs. Ctr. for Voice, Chgo., 1994-96; vol. Saints-Usher Corps of Chgo., 1998-99; chmn. fin. Chgo. (Ill.) Youth Symphony. Recipient Creative and Performing Arts award Ind. Jr. Miss. and South Bend Jr. Miss, 1965, Milton J. Cross award Met. Opera Guild, 1968; prize winner Met. Opera. Nat. Auditions, 1968, 1st pl. prize for The Pond, Chicagoland Poetry Contest, 1997, 1st pl. prize and Best of the Best award for The Rose Garden, 1999; F.K. Weyerhauser scholar Met. Opera, 1967. Mem. People for Ethical Treatment of Animals, Am. Soc. for Prevention of Cruelty to Animals, Assisi Animal Found., Am. Guild Mus. Artists, Internat. Platform Assn., Whale Adoption Project, Amnesty Internat., Environ. Def. Fund, Doris Day Animal Found., Poets and Patrons, Humane Soc., Greenpeace, Physicians Com. for Responsible Medicine, Notre Dame Alumni Club, St. Mary's Acad. Alumnae Assn., Save the Chimps, Delta Gamma. Office: HKE Enterprises 1726 Sherman Ave Evanston IL 60201-5619 Home Phone: 847-869-8231.

EBERT, DOROTHY ELIZABETH, retired county clerk; b. Beaver Dam, Wis., Apr. 16, 1941; d. Merlin Herman and Gertrude Elizabeth (Hupke) E. Grad. high sch., Beaver Dam. Sec., receptionist Household Fin. Corp., Beaver Dam, 1958—67; dep. county clk. Dodge County, Juneau, Wis., 1967—82, county clk., 1983—2003; ret., 2003. Past bd. dirs. Dodge County chpt. Am. Cancer Soc. Mem. Wis. County Clks. Assn. (historian 1994-95, treas. 1995-96, sec. 1996-97, v.p. 1997-98, pres. 1998-99). Republican. Lutheran. Avocations: bowling, golf, calligraphy, singing, bell choir.

EBERT, ROGER JOSEPH, film critic; b. Urbana, Ill., June 18, 1942; s. Walter H. and Annabel (Stumm) E.; m. Chaz Hammelsmith, July 18, 1992. BS, U. Ill., 1964; postgrad., U. Cape Town, South Africa, 1965, U. Chgo., 1966-67; LHD (hon.), U. Colo., 1993; degree (hon.), Am. Film Inst., Sch. of the Art Inst. Chgo. Editor Daily Illini, 1963-64; pres. U.S. Student Press Assn., 1963-64; staff writer News-Gazette, Champaign-Urbana, Ill., 1958-66; film critic Chgo. Sun-Times, 1967—, US mag., 1978-79, NBC-TV News, Chgo., 1980-83, ABC-TV News, Chgo., 1984—, N.Y. Post, NYC, 1986-88, N.Y. Daily News, 1988-92, Compu Serve, 1991—; pres. Ebert Co., Ltd., 1981—; Microsoft Cinemania, 1994-97; columnist Yahoo Internet Life mag., 1997—. Instr. English Chgo. City Coll., 1967-68; lectr. film criticism, fine arts program U. Chgo., 1969; Kluge fellow U. Va., 1995-96, adj. prof. U. Ill., 2000; lectr. film Columbia Coll., Chgo., 1973-74, 77-80; cons. Nat. Endowments for Arts and Humanities, 1972-77; juror film festivals. Co-host (TV shows) Sneak Previews, PBS, 1976-82, At the Movies, syndicated, 1982-86, Siskel & Ebert (now Ebert & Roeper), syndicated, 1986—; broadcaster: Movie News, ABC Radio, 1982-85; author: An Illini Century, 1967, (screenplay) Beyond the Valley of the Dolls, 1970, Beyond Narrative: The Future of the Feature Film, 1978, A Kiss Is Still a Kiss, 1984, Roger Ebert's Movie Home Companion, 1986-93, Roger Ebert's Video Companion, 1994-98, (with Daniel Curley) The Perfect London Walk, 1986, Two Weeks in the Midday Sun, 1987, The Future of the Movies, 1991, Behind the Phantom's Mask, 1993, Ebert's Little Movie Glossary, 1994, Roger Ebert's Book of Film, 1996, Questions for the Movie Answer Man, 1997, Roger Ebert's Movie Yearbook, 1998, The Little Book of Hollywood Cliches, The Bigger Little Book of Hollywood Cliches, 1999, Ebert's Bigger Little Movie Glossary, 1999, I Hated, Hated, Hated This Movie, 2000, Great Movies I, 2002, Great Movies II, 2005; co-author: The Future of the Movies, The Computer Insectiary, 1994. Recipient Overseas Press club, 1963, award Chgo. Headline Club, 1963, award Chgo. Newspaper Guild, 1973, Pulitzer prize, 1975, Emmy award, 1979, Peter Lisagor award, 1998, Online Film Critics Soc. Best Movie Website award, 1999; inducted into Chgo. Journalism Hall of Fame, 1997; Rotary fellow, 1965, Kluge fellow in film studies U. Va., 1995-96; received star on Hollywood Walk fo Fame, 2005. Mem. Newspaper Guild, Writers Guild Am. West, Nat. Soc. Film Critics, Acad. TV Arts and Scis., Arts Club of Chgo., Cliff Dwellers, Acad. Club (London), Sigma Delta Chi, Phi Delta Theta. Avocations: drawing, painting, art collecting. Office: Chicago Sun Times 350 N Orleans St Ste 1270 Chicago IL 60654-2148

EBNER, KURT EWALD, biochemistry educator; b. New Westminster, BC, Can., Mar. 30, 1931; s. Sebastian Alois and Martha (Gmundner) E.; m. Dorothy Colleen Reader, May 4, 1957; children: Roger, Michael, Colleen, Paul. BSA., U. B.C., 1955, MSA., 1957; PhD, U. Ill., 1960; postdoctoral, U. Reading, Eng., 1960-61, U. Minn., 1961-62. Diplomate Nat. Bd. Med. Examiners. Mem. faculty Okla. State U., Stillwater, 1962-74, prof. biochemistry, 1969-71, Regents prof., 1971-74; chmn. dept. biochemistry U. Kans. Med. Ctr., Kansas City, 1974-94, prof., 1994-98, prof. emeritus, 1998—. Can. Overseas Postdoctoral fellow, 1960; recipient NIH Career Devel. award, 1969, Borden award Am. Chem. Soc., 1969; Okla. State U. Sigma Xi lectr., 1970 Mem. AAAS, Am. Soc. Biol. Chemistry, Coun. Acad. Socs., Sigma Xi, Phi Kappa Phi, Gamma Sigma Delta. Presbyterian (elder). Office: U Kans Med Ctr Dept Biochem Kansas City KS 66103-7421

EBY, MARTIN KELLER, JR., construction company executive; b. Wichita Falls, Tex., Apr. 19, 1934; s. Martin and A. Pauline (Kimbell) E.; m. Melodee Stanley, Aug. 20, 1955; children: Stanley, Suzanna, David. BS in Civil Engring, Kans. State U., 1956. Registered profl. engr., Kan. With Martin K. Eby Constrn. Co., Inc., Wichita, Kans., 1956—2004, engr., project mgr., v.p., 1956-67, pres., 1967-92, chmn., 1979—2004; ret., 2004. Bd. dirs. Intrust Bank in Wichita, Intrust Fin. Corp., AT&T Inc.; mem. engring. adv. coun. Kans. State U., Manhattan, 1970-96. Bd. dirs. Kans. Pub. Policy Inst., chmn.; mem. Kans. State U. Coll. of Engring. Hall of Fame, 1989—; chmn. Constrn. Industry Polit. Action Com. of Kans., Topeka, 1978. Mem. ASCE, NSPE, Kans. Engring. Soc., Wichita Profl. Engring. Soc., Chief Execs. Orgn., Beavers (bd. dirs., pres. 1996-97), Moles (hon.). Congregationalist. Home: 624 N Longford Ln Wichita KS 67206-1818 Office: Martin Eby Constrn Co Inc PO Box 1679 610 N Main St Wichita KS 67203-3601

ECCARIUS, SCOTT, state official, eye surgeon; m. Alison Eccarius. Degree, U. S.D. Majority whip S.D. Ho. Reps., spkr. pro tempore, Spkr. of Ho. Dist. 34, 2001—. Mem.: State Affairs Com., Edn. Com. (chmn.), Taxation Com. (chmn.), Ho. Edn. Com. (past chmn.), Edn. and Legis. Procedures Com. (chmn.). Republican. Home: 4780 Carriage Hills Dr Rapid City SD 57702 Business E-Mail: NemoSD@aol.com.

ECHOLS, MARY EVELYN, motivational speaker and business consultant, writer; b. LaSalle, Ill., Apr. 5, 1915; d. Francis Ira and Mary Irene (Coleman) Bassett; m. David H. Echols, Aug. 31, 1951 (dec.); children: Susan Echols O'Donnell, William. Grad. St. Mary's Nursing Hosp., Chgo. Founder Internat. Travel Tng. Courses, Inc., Chgo., 1962—; pres. Evelyn Echols Cons. Ltd., 1998, Echols Comms. Ltd., 2004—. Author: Saying Yes to Life. Bd. dirs. Chgo. Conv. and Tourism Bur., Little Sisters of the Poor; past pres. Pres. Reagan's Adv. Com. for Women's Bus. Ownership; v.p. United Cerebral Palsy Assn.; nat. spokesperson Prevent Blindness in Am.; mem. Women's Internat. Forum. Named Entrepreneur of Yr. Women Bus. Owners N.Y., 1985, Bus. Woman of Yr. Nat. Assn. Women Bus. Owners, 1985, Crain's Chgo. Bus., 1993; named to Chgo.'s Entrepreneurial Hall of Fame, 1992. Mem.: Soc. Am. Travel Agts., Acad. TV Arts and Scis., Chgo. Execs. Club. Office Phone: 773-348-1553. E-mail: evelyn@evelynechols.com.

ECK, GEORGE GREGORY, lawyer; b. Evanston, Ill., Sept. 3, 1950; s. George F. and Dorothy E. (Frake) E.; m. Margaret K. Gorman, Sept. 1, 1973; children: Jessica Elizabeth, Michelle Margaret. BS, No. Ill. U., 1972; JD cum laude, U. Minn., 1977. Bar: Minn. 1977, U.S. Dist. Ct. Minn. 1977, U.S. Ct. Appeals (8th cir.) 1977. Assoc. Dorsey & Whitney, Mpls., 1977-83, ptnr., 1983—. Mem. editorial bd. U. Minn. Law Rev., 1977. With US Army, 1972—74. Home: 6413 Mendelssohn Ln Hopkins MN 55343-8424 Office: Dorsey & Whitney LLC 50 S 6th St Ste 1500 Minneapolis MN 55402-1498 Home Phone: 952-938-0362; Office Phone: 612-340-2772. E-mail: eck.george@dorsey.com.

ECKART, DENNIS EDWARD, lawyer, former congressman; b. Cleve., Apr. 6, 1950; s. Edward Joseph and Mary Eckart; m. Sandra Jean Pestotnik; 1 son, Edward John. BS, Xavier U., 1971; LL.B., Cleveland John Marshall Law Sch., 1974. Mem. Ohio Ho. of Reps., 1975-80; chmn. Cuyahoga County del., 1979-80; mem. 97th Congress 22d Ohio dist. and 98th-102nd Congress 11th Ohio dist., 1981-92; ptnr. Winston & Strawn, Washington, 1993-94, Arter & Hadden, Washington, 1994-99, Baker & Hostetler, LLP, Washington, 1999; pres. & CEO Greater Cleve. Growth Assn., 2000—02; chmn. Nat. Ctr. for Responsible Gambling, 2002. Mailing: PO Box 28 Jefferson OH 44047-0028

ECKERT, RALPH JOHN, insurance company executive; b. Milw., Mar. 12, 1929; s. John C. and Vlasta (Stauber) E.; m. Greta M. Allen, July 11, 1953; children: Maura Eckert Benseler, Peter, Thomas, Karen Eckert Schmidt, Edward. BS, U. Wis., 1951. With Trustmark Life Ins. Co., Lake Forest, Ill., 1954—; chmn. bd., chief exec. officer Benefit Trust Life Ins. Co., Chgo., 1971-91; chmn. bd. of pensions Evang. Luth. Ch. Am., Mpls., 1991-97; chmn. bd. Trustmark Life Ins. Co., Lake Forest, Ill., 1991-97, chmn. emeritus, 1997—. Bd. dirs. Prin. Preservation Mutual Funds, 1996—. With AUS, 1951-53. Fellow Soc. Actuaries; mem. Am. Acad. Actuaries, Ill. Life Ins. Coun. (chmn. 1978-79), Ill. Life & Health Ins. Guaranty Assn. (chmn. 1980-81), Health Ins. Assn. Am. (bd. dirs., chmn. 1984-85), Am. Coun. Life Ins. (bd. dirs. 1986-88), Masons. Lutheran. Office: Trustmark Life Ins Co 400 N Field Dr Lake Forest IL 60045-4809

ECKHARDT, CRAIG JON, chemistry professor; b. Rapid City, SD, June 26, 1940; s. Reuben H and Hilda W. (Craig) E. BA magna cum laude, U. Colo., 1962; MS, Yale U., 1964, PhD, 1967. Asst. prof. chemistry U. Nebr., Lincoln, 1967-72, assoc. prof., 1972-78, prof., 1978—, interim chmn. dept. chemistry, 1986-87, prof. physics, 1988—. Cons., mem. adv. panel, condensed matter scis. div. materials research NSF, 1976-79 NIH predoctoral fellow, 1964-67; Yale predoctoral fellow, 1967; John Simon Guggenheim fellow, 1979-80; German Acad. Exchange fellow; Fulbright Sr. fellow, 2006; grantee NSF, 1974-84, Dept. Energy, 1979-82, Petroleum Rsch. Fund-Am. Chem. Soc., 1968-72, Rsch. Corp., 1971-74, 3M Corp., 1983-89, Army Rsch. Office, 1989-97, Office Naval Rsch., 2000—. Mem. Am. Phys. Soc., Am. Assn. Physics Tchrs., Optical Soc. Am., Am. Chem. Soc., Royal Chemistry Soc., Phi Beta Kappa, Sigma Xi, Phi Lambda Upsilon. Office: U Nebr Dept Chemistry Lincoln NE 68588 Office Phone: 402-472-2734. Business E-Mail: eckhrdt@undserve.unl.edu.

ECKNER, SHANNON F., lawyer; BA in English Lit., U. Cin., 2000, JD, 2003. Bar: Ohio 2003. Law clerk Phyllis G. Bossin Co., L.P.A., Cin., assoc. Mem. Big Sister. amed one of Ohio's Rising Stars, Super Lawyers, 2006. Mem.: ABA, Ohio State Bar Assn. (Family Law Com.), Cin. Bar Assn. (mem, Domestic Rels. Com.), Order of Coif, Phi Beta Kappa. Office: Phyllis G Bossin Co LPA Ste 1210 36 E Fourth St Cincinnati OH 45202 Office Phone: 513-421-4420. Office Fax: 513-421-0691.

ECKSTEIN, DAVID MARK, professional baseball player; b. Sanford, Fla., Jan. 20, 1975; s. Whitey and Patricia Eckstein; m. Ashley Drane, Nov. 26, 2005. Attended, U. Fla., Gainesville. Shortstop Anaheim Angels, 2001—04, St. Louis Cardinals, 2005—07, Toronto Blue Jays, 2008—. Co-author (with Greg Brown): (autobiographies) David Eckstein: Have Heart, 2003, Have Heart: David Eckstein, 2006. Chmn. Kidney Assn. Walk, 2003; active Ronald McDonald House, Fla. amed World Series MVP, 2006; named an Everyday Hero, Ct. TV, 2003; named to Nat. League All-Star Team, 2005—06; recipient Babe Ruth award, 2002. Mailing: c/o Toronto Blue Jays Rogers Ctr 1 Blue Jays Way Ste 3200 Toronto M5V1J1 Canada

ECKSTEIN, JOHN WILLIAM, internist, educator, retired dean; b. Central City, Iowa, Nov. 23, 1923; s. John William and Alice (Ellsworth) Eckstein; m. Imogene O'Brien, June 16, 1947; children: John Alan, Charles William, Margaret Ann, Thomas Cody, Steven Gregory. BS, Loras Coll., 1946; MD, U. Iowa, 1950; DSc (hon.), Ind. U., 1995. Asst. prof. internal medicine U. Iowa, Iowa City, 1956—60, assoc. prof., 1960—65, prof., 1965—92, prof. emeritus, 1993; assoc. dean VA Hosp. affairs, 1969—70, dean coll. medicine, 1970-91, dean emeritus, 1993. Chmn. cardiovasc. study sect. NIH, 1970—72, Nat. Heart, Lung and Blood Adv. Coun., 1974—78; mem. adv. com. to dir. NIH, 1990—95. Author papers and abstracts. Mem. VA Manpower Study Group, 1988—92. With USAF, 1943—45, with U.S. Army Med. Corps., 1950—51. Named established investigator, Am. Heart Assn., 1958—63, in his honor, Eckstein Med. Rsch. Bldg., U. Iowa, 1988; recipient Rsch. Career award, USPHS, 1963—70, Dist. Alumni Svc. award, U. Iowa, 1994, Disting. Physicians, Dept. Vets. Affairs, 1995—98; fellow postdoctoral, Rockefeller Found., 1953—54, Am. Heart Assn. Rsch., 1954—55, spl. rsch., Nat. Heart Inst., 1955—56. Mem.: Assn. Acad. Health Ctrs. (mem. sci. policy study group 1988—93), Inst. Medicine, Assn. Am. Med. Colls. (exec. coun. 1981—82, adminstrv. bd. 1980—82, 1985—86), Assn. Am. Physicians, Am. Clin. and Climatol. Assn., Am. Soc. Clin. Investigation, Ctrl. Soc. Clin. Rsch. (sec.-treas. 1965—70, pres. 1973—74), Am. Fedn. Clin. Rsch. (chmn. Midwestern sect. 1965), AMA (mem. health policy agenda panel 1982—86, mem. study sect. faculty and resh. 1985—86, governing. coun. sect. on med. schs. 1985—95, alt. del. Ho. of Dels. 1986—90, del. 1990—92, Disting. Svc. award 1992), Am. Heart Assn. (v.p. 1969, chmn. coun. on circulation 1969—71, pres. 1978—79). Home: 1415 William White Blvd Iowa City IA 52245-4443 Office: U Iowa Hosps & Clinics Iowa City IA 52242-1101 E-mail: john-eckstein@uiowa.edu.

ECONOMUS, PETER CONSTANTINE, judge; s. Constantine G. Economus; m. Marie Misko, June 29, 1968; children: Paula, Kristine, Jennifer. BA, Youngstown U., Ohio, 1967; JD, Akron U., 1970. Bar: Ohio, 1971. Ptnr. Economus, Economus & Economus; judge Ct. Common Pleas, Mahoning County, Ohio, 1982-95; U.S. dist. judge No. Dist. Ohio, Youngstown, 1995—. Apptd. mentor new judges, vis. judge various Ohio Ct. Appeals Chmn. Cmty. Corrections Planning Bd., 1987-91; former trustee Ohio Common Please Judges Assn., legis. com.; trustee U. Akron Sch. Law Alumni Assn, 1989-95; mem. com. celebrate bi-centennial U.S. Constn. Youngstown State U.; mem. adv. bd. State Victims, 1986-95; trustee Butler Inst. Am. Art, 2000— Recipient Outstanding Citizen's award Buckeye Elks Lodge #73, 1988, Pub. Svc. award Cmty. Corrections Assn., 1989, Office Holder of Yr. Truman Johnson Women's Dem. Club, 1990, Gt. Communicator award cmty. svc. Youngstown Hearing & Speech Ctr., 1995, Outstanding Alumni award U. Akron Law Alumni Assn., 1996, Ellis Island medal of honor, 1999, Outstanding Alumni award Youngstown State U., 2000. Mem. Am. Judges Assn. Office: US Courthouse 125 Market St Youngstown OH 44503-1780

EDDIE, RUSSELL JAMES, state legislator, sales executive; b. Wayne, Nebr., June 9, 1938; s. Robert Alex and Myrtle (Kruse) E.; m. Gladys Ann Pederson, Aug. 6, 1960; children: Julie, Thomas, Robert, Steven. BA, Buena Vista Coll., 1960. Tchr. Clayton Pentral Cmty. Sch., Royal, Iowa, 1961-66; farmer Storm Lake, Iowa, 1966-89; mem. Iowa Ho. of Reps., 1989—; sales exec. E-D Assocs., Storm Lake, 1991—. Mem. BU County Hist. Soc., Pork Prodrs. Assn., Farm Bur., Kiwanis Internat. Republican. Lutheran. Avocations: sports, reading, collecting farm equipment. Home: 1101 Pierce Dr Storm Lake IA 50588-2744

EDDY, CHARLES ALAN, chiropractor; b. Kansas City, Mo., Feb. 20, 1948; s. Sam Albert and Ella Louise (Gani) E.; m. Donna Darlene Perry, Oct. 23, 1971. Student, U. Mo., Kansas City, 1967; D in Chiropractic, Cleveland Chiropractic, Kansas City, 1970. Diplomate Nat. Bd. Chiropractic Examiners. Pvt. practice, Kansas City, 1970—. Peer rev. bd. Blue Cross and Blue Shield, Kansas City, 1972; pres. hon. bd. govs. Bapt. Hosp., Kansas City, 1993-94; cons. Quality Corp., Overland Park, Kans., 1988. Res. officer Kansas City Police Dept., 1970—77, sgt., 1977—82, capt., 1982—94; vice chmn. Citizens Assn., 1995—98; mem. pub. improvement adv. com. City of Kansas City, 1997—98; city councilperson 6th Dist., 1999—2007; chmn. bd. Mid. Am. Reg. Coun., Kansas City, 2003—05, 1st v.p., 2001—02; bd. dirs. Econ. Devel. Coun., 1999—2007, 1st v.p., 2001—03; chmn. Mo. Total Transp. Com., 2003—07; candidate for City Coun. Kansas City, 1995; candidate for mayor, 2007; leader, profl. musician Chuck Eddy Band, Kansas City, 1964—. Mem. Am. Chiropractic Assn., Mo. State Chriopractic Assn., Mo. Dist. II Chiropractic Assn. (bd. dirs., v.p. 1998-2003), Cleve. Chiropractic Coll. (trustee 1990, vice chmn. 1992-03, chmn. 2003—), Cleve. Chiropractic Alumni Assn. (v.p. 1995-97, pres. 1997-99, bd. dirs. 1990—, amb.'s soc. 1983—, chmn. 1990-96, 2001-07, bd. dirs. Truman Med. Ctr.), Optimist Club of Landing (pres. 1980, lt. gov. Mo. dist. 1982), South Kansas City C. of C. (Sml. Bus. of Yr. award 1998), Am. Lebanon Syrian Men's Club (pres. 1988-91, chmn. bd. 1992), St. Andrews Soc. (drummer in pipe band), DeMolay Legion Hon. (sec. 1988, treas. 1990, vice-dean 1991, dean 1992), Pipes and Drums of Ararat (treas. 1977-90, pres. 1985, dir. 1989, 90), Ctrl. States Shrine Assn. (v.p. 2000-07, pres. 2007-), Elks, Shriners (Potentate of Ararat shrine temple 1999, publicity chmn. 1991-92), Royal Order Jesters, Order Quetzalcoatl, Rotary Club (Paul Harris fellow). Episcopalian. Avocations: photography, guns, stereo and video entertainment. Home: 406 W 109th St Kansas City MO 64114-4910 Office: 8301 State Line Rd Ste 108 Kansas City MO 64114-2019 Office Phone: 816-363-5311. Personal E-mail: dr.eddy@juno.com.

EDDY, DAVID LATIMER, banker; b. Simsbury, Conn., July 3, 1936; s. Edward McChesney and Alberta (Messenger) E.; m. Doris Janeczek, Jan. 7, 1958 (div.); children: Craig, Carol, Dianne, Linda, Elizabeth; m. Gaye Margaret Peterson, May 15, 1976; children: Breese, Taryn, Daniel. BS, U. Conn., 1958; MBA, Harvard U., 1960. Asst. mgr. No. Trust Co., Chgo., 1964-68, 2d v.p., 1968-72, v.p., 1972-85, sr. v.p., 1986—; sr. v.p., treas. No. Trust Corp., Chgo., 1986—. Mem. Planning Forum, Fin. Execs. Inst. Clubs: Harvard (Chgo.), Harvard Grad. Bus. Sch. Congregationalist. Office: No Trust Corp 50 S La Salle St Chicago IL 60603-1006

EDELSBERG, SALLY COMINS, retired physical therapist, educator; b. Rowno, Poland, Aug. 6, 1939; came to U.S., 1949; d. Joseph Luria and Chana (Bebczuk) Comins; m. Warde C. Pierson, Oct. 8, 1968 (div. 1978); m. Paul Edelsberg, Feb. 2, 1979; 1 child, Tema. BS in Phys. Medicine, U. Wis., Madison, 1963; MS, Northwestern U., Evanston, Ill., 1972. Lic. phys. therapist. Staff and supervisory phys. therapist Hines VA Hosp., Maywood, Ill., 1963-67; program dir. Health Careers Council of Ill., Chgo., 1967-70; instr., clin. edn. coord. Programs in Phys. Therapy, Northwestern U. Med. Sch., Chgo., 1970—72, dir., assoc. prof., 1972—99, dir. devel. and alumni rels., 1999—2003. Pres. Phys. Therapy Ltd., Chgo., 1986-95; v.p. World Confedn. Phys. Therapy, 1995-99, exec. com., 1991-95. Mem.: Am. Phys. Therapy Assn. (bd. dirs. 1975—78, 1979—82, Ill. pres. 1972—76, Catherine Worthingham fellow 1999). Personal E-mail: sce1323@sbcglobal.net. E-mail: s-edelsberg@northwestern.edu.

EDELSON, IRA J., venture capitalist; b. Chgo., Dec. 30, 1946; s. Alvin L. and Naomi Edelson; m. Starr Gramaila, Feb. 11, 1973; children: Jason Avrum, Megan Anne. BS, DePaul U., 1968. Spl. advisor to chmn. Chgo. Housing Authority, 1983; acting dir. revenue City of Chgo., 1984; ptnr.-in-charge bus. svcs. dept. Deloitte, Haskins & Sells, Chgo., 1979-87; ptnr.-in-charge corp. fin. Deloitte & Touche-U.S. Partnership, Chgo., 1987-91; pres. Transcap Trade Fin. LLC, orthbrook, Ill., 1991—. Fin. and policy advisor to mayor City of Chgo., 1984—85; former instr. Northwestern Grad. Sch. Bus.; cons., spkr. in field. Co-chmn. Chgo. Sports Stadium Commn., 1985. Mem.: AICPA, Fgn. Trade Assn., Turn Around Mgmt. Assn., Nat. Contract Mgmt. Assn., Comml. Fin. Assn., Ill. Soc. CPAs. Office: Transcap Assocs Inc 900 Skokie Blvd Ste 210 Northbrook IL 60062-4031 Office Phone: 480-585-3444.

EDELSTEIN, TERI J., art educator, director, consultant; b. Johnstown, Pa., June 23, 1951; d. Robert Morten and Hulda Lois (Friedhoff) E. BA, U. Pa., 1972, MA, 1977, PhD, 1979; cert. Grad. Sch. Bus. Adminstrn., NYU, 1984. Lectr. U. Guelph, Ont., 1977-79; asst. dir. for acad. programs Yale Ctr. Brit. Art, New Haven, 1979-83; dir. Mt. Holyoke Coll. Art Mus., South Hadley, Mass., 1983-90, Skinner Mus., 1983-90, mem. faculty dept. art., 1983-90; dir. Smart Mus. Art U. Chgo., 1990-92, sr. lectr. dept. art, 1990-2000; pres. Teri J. Edelstein Assocs. Mus. Strategies, Chgo., 1999—. Dep. dir. Art Inst. Chgo., 1992—99; pres. Teri J. Edelstein Assocs. Museum Strategies, 1999—; mem. adv. bd. Sculpture Chgo., 1991—96, Mus. Loan Network, Knight and Pew Founds., 1994—96; bd. trustees Am. Fedn. Arts, 1997—2001, Coll. Art Assn., 1974—, com. intellectual property, 1995—98, com. museums, 1996—2003. Contbr. articles to profl. jours. Office: 1648 E 50th St # 6B Chicago IL 60615-3207 Office Phone: 773-241-9991. Office Fax: 773-241-9992. Business E-Mail: tedelstein@tedelstein.com.

EDELSTEIN, TILDEN GERALD, academic administrator, historian, educator; b. NYC, June 11, 1931; s. Theodore and Nettie (Strusser) Edelstein; m. Marjorie Sukoff, June 17, 1955 (div. July 1970); m. Rose Ann Stargardter, Nov. 1, 1970; children: Jordan, Russell. BS, U. Wis., 1953; PhD, Johns Hopkins U., 1961. From instr. to assoc. prof. Simmons Coll., Boston, 1957-67; from adj. assoc. prof. to prof. history Rutgers U., New Brunswick, NJ, 1967-89, chmn. history dept., grad. dir., 1974-81, assoc. dean social sci. and humanities, faculty personnel, 1981-84, dean faculty arts and scis., 1984-89; prof. history, provost, acad. v.p. SUNY, Stony Brook, 1989-93, prof. history, provost, exec. v.p. for academic affairs, 1992-94; v.p. for acad. affairs Wayne State U., Detroit, 1995-98, prof. history, 1998—2003. Hist. cons. Columbia Pictures, Hollywood, Calif., 1978-80, NBC, N.Y.C., 1980-89; chair Sponsors Bd. The Thomas A. Edison Papers Project, 1980-89. Author: Strange Enthusiasm, 1968, 2d edit., 1970; co-editor: The Black Americans, 1975. Commr. Housing Authority, Highland Park, N.J., 1977-89; Einstein Archives Adv. Com. Hebrew U., 1993-94; mem. adv. bd. Cohen/Haddow Ctr. for Jewish Studies, Mich. Civil War Regimental Round Table. Mem.: Prismatic Club Detroit. Office: Wayne State U Coll Liberal Arts & Scis Dept of History Detroit MI 48202 E-mail: aa1768@wayne.edu.

EDEN, BARBARA JANIECE, commercial and residential interior designer; b. Inpls., Oct. 14, 1951; d. Justin January and Marjorie May (Miller) E.; children: Christopher Eden Bowman, Jessica Eden Bowman. BA, Purdue U., 1973. Interior design dir. Bohlen, Meyer, Gibson & Assoc., Indpls., 1973-78; interior designer, sole propr. Barbara Eden Design, Indpls., 1978-85; pres., prin. designer Eden Design Assocs., Inc., Carmel, Ind., 1985-97, Carson Design Assocs. Design/Project Mgmt./Bus. Devel., Carmel, Ind., 1997—. Past mem. accreditation team Found. for Interior Design Edn. Rsch. (FIDER); past mem. adv. bd. Purdue U. Interior Design Dept.; bd. dirs. Hamilton County Intercultural Svcs. Prin. projects include wheelchair accessible bathroom Kohler Design Ctr., Wis., United Airlines, Indpls. Maintenance Ctr., N.Am. hdqrs. Brightpoint, Inc., Plainfield, Ind., Peabody Retirement Ctr., North Manchester, Ind., Oakwood Inn, Syracuse, Ind., Resort Condominiums, Internat., Carmel, Ind., Merchants' Pointe, Carmel, restaurant, retail & office devel., arch., interior design; also corp., healthcare, schs., univs., librs., sr. living and residential interior design, space planning and project mgmt. Mem. Internat. Facility Mgrs. Assn., Internat. Interior Design Assn., Illuminating Engring. Soc., Carmel Clay C. of C. (mem. exec. bd., chair edn. com., Small Bus. Person of Yr. 1993). Avocations: hiking, horseback riding, travel. Office: Carson Design Assocs 2325 Pointe Pkwy 200 Carmel IN 46032-3283 E-mail: edenbj@carsondesign.com.

EDEN, JAMES GARY, electrical engineer, physicist, educator, researcher; b. Washington, Oct. 11, 1950; s. Robert Otis and Joyce (West) Eden; m. Carolyn Sue Thomas, June 10, 1972; children: Robert Douglas, Laura Ann, Katherine Joy. BS, U. Md., 1972; MS, U. Ill., 1973, PhD, 1976. Rsch. asst. U. Ill., Urbana, 1972—75, asst. prof. elec. engring. dept., 1979—81, assoc. prof., 1981—83, prof. Dept. Elec. Engring., rsch. prof. Coordinated Sci. Lab., 1983—, rsch. prof. Micro and Nanotech. Lab., 2000—, dir. Lab. for Optical Physics and Engring., 1995—, assoc. vice-chancellor rsch., 2000—03, affiliate faculty materials sci. and engring., 2004—, asst. dean Coll. Engring., 1992—93, assoc. dean. Grad. Coll., 1994—96, Gilmore Family prof. elect. and computer engring., 2007—; postdoctoral rsch. assoc. NRC, Washington, 1975—76; rsch. physicist US Naval Rsch. Lab., Washington, 1976—79. Co-founder Eden Pk. Illumination; mem. tech. adv. bd. Anvik Corp., Hawthorne, NY, Caviton, Inc., Urbana; mem. exec. adv. bd. U. So. Fla., Dept. Physics, Tampa; assoc. mem. Ctr. Advanced Study U. Ill., 1987—88; mem. adv. bd. Chem. Vapor Deposition, 1995—2003, CRC Handbook Series Laser Sci. and Tech., 1996—; Fulbright-Israel Disting. Chair Natural Scis. and Engring., 2007—08; cons. in field. Author: Photochemical Vapor Deposition, 1992, Gas Laser Technology, 2000; editor-in-chief IEEE Jour. Quantum Elecs., 1996—2002, Progress in Quantum Electronics, 2007—; assoc. editor: Photonics Tech. Letters, 1988—94; contbr. chapters to books, more than 220 articles to profl. jours. Recipient Rsch. Publ. award, Naval Rsch. Lab., 1978, Beckman Rsch. award, U. Ill., 1988, IBM Rsch. award, 1994, Faculty Outstanding Tchg. award, Dept. Elec. and Computer Engring., U. Ill., 2000; James F. Towey Univ. scholar, U. Ill., 1996—99. Fellow: IEEE (active various coms., numerous confs., 3d Millennium medal 2000), Am. Phys. Soc., Optical Soc. Am. (C.E.K. Mees medal 2007); mem.: IEEE Lasers and Electro-Optics Soc. (bd. govs. 1991—93, v.p. tech. affairs 1993—95, pres. 1998, Disting. Svc. award 1996, Disting. Lectr. 2003—05, Aron Kressel award 2005), Phi Kappa Phi, Eta Kappa Nu, Tau Beta Pi, Sigma Xi. Achievements include patents for 25 inventions. Office: U Ill Everitt Lab 1406 W Green St Urbana IL 61801-2918 Home: 4401 Trostshire Cir Champaign IL 61822 Office Phone: 217-333-4157. Business E-Mail: jgeden@uiuc.edu.

EDGAR, JIM, former governor; b. Vinita, Okla., July 22, 1946; s. Cecil E. & Elizabeth O. (Moore) E.; m. Brenda M. Smith, 1967; children: Brad, Elizabeth. BS, Eastern Ill. U., 1968; postgrad., U. Ill., 1969—70, Sangamon State U., 1971-74. Legis. intern pres. pro tem Ill. Senate, 1968, aide to pres., 1968—72; key asst. to speaker Ill. Ho. of Reps., 1972-73; aide to pres. Ill. Senate, 1974, to Ho. minority leader, 1976; mem. Ill. Ho. of Reps., 1977-79; dir. legis. affairs Ill. Gov., 1979-80; sec. state State of Ill., 1981-91; gov. State of Ill., 1991-98; disting. fellow Inst. Govt. and Publs. U. Ill., Urbana, 1999—. Precinct committeeman, treas. Coles County Rep. Com., 1974; dir. state svc. Nat. Conf. State Legislatures, 1975, 76; mem. campaign com. Ill. Ho. of Reps.; pres. Nat. Assn. Secs. of State, 1988; exec. com. Coun. State Govts., 1988, v.p. exec. com., 1991, pres., 1992-93; bd. dirs. Nat. Commn. Against Drunk Driving, 1989; chmn. Ill. Literacy Coun., 1989; chmn. Edn. Commn. of the States, 1993-94; chmn. Gov.'s Ethanol Coalition, 1992-93; pres. Bd. Coun. State Govts. Recipient Pub. Humanities award, Literacy award, ALA Trustee Assn., Lifetime Achievement award, Nature Conservancy Ill., 1998. Mem. Nat. Govs. Assn. (chmn. econ. devel. and commerce com. 1992-93, strategic planning rev. task force 1991—, past chmn. task force on edn., mem. edn. goals panel, chair com. econ. devel. and technol. innovation 1991-92, edn. commn. of states 1993-94, co-lead gov. transp. com. 1995-96), Coles County Hist. Soc. (pres. 1976-79). Baptist. Office: U Ill Inst Govt and Pub Affairs 1007 W Nevada St # MC-037 Urbana IL 61801-3812*

EDGAR, JOHN M., lawyer; b. Tex., 1943; BS, U. Kans., 1965; JD with distinction, U. Mo., Kans. City, 1968. Bar: Mo. 1968. Resident mng. ptnr. Bryan Cave LLP, Kans. City, Mo., lead resident ptnr., 1999—. Mem. Lawyers Assn. Kansas City, Phi Alpha Delta, Order of Bench and Robe. Office: Bryan Cave LLP 3500 1 Kansas City Pl Kansas City MO 64105

EDGERTON, WINFIELD DOW, retired gynecologist; b. Caruthersville, Mo., Nov. 8, 1924; s. Winfield Dow and Anna Kathryn (Hale) E.; m. Rose Marie Cahill, June 24, 1945; 1 child, Winfield Dow Student, Central Coll., Fayette, Mo., 1942-44; MD, Washington U., St. Louis, 1947. Intern St. Luke's Hosp., St. Louis, 1947-48; resident Chgo. Lying-In Hosp., 1948-49, Free Hosp. for Women, Brookline, Mass., 1951, U.S. Naval Hosp., Chelsea, Mass., 1951-53; practice medicine specializing in obstetrics and gynecology Davenport, Iowa, 1955-87; clin. assoc. prof. obstetrics and gynecology U. Iowa Coll. Medicine, 1971-78, clin. assoc. prof., 1979-82, clin. prof., 1982—; ret., 2000. Mem. staff, med. dir. Maternal Health Ctr. St. Luke's Hosp. (name changed to Edgerton Women's Health Ctr.), 1972-2000. Contbr. articles to med. jours. and texts Served to lt. M.C., USN, 1949-55 Fellow Am. Coll. Obstetricians and Gynecologists (past chmn. Iowa sect.), Royal Soc. Medicine; mem. Central Assn.

Obstetricians and Gynecologists, Am. Fertility Soc., Am. Assn. Gynecologic Laparoscopists (past trustee), Gynecologic Laser Soc., AMA, Iowa Med. Soc., Scott County Med. Soc. (past pres.) Republican. Congregationalist. Home: 4 Lombard Ct Davenport IA 52803-2348

EDIGER, MARK D., chemistry professor; b. Newton, Kans., July 26, 1957; BA in Chemistry and Math., Bethel Coll., 1979; PhD in Phys. Chemistry, Stanford U., 1984. Asst. prof. dept. chemistry U. Wis., Madison, 1984-90, assoc. prof., 1990-94, prof. dept. chemistry, 1994—. Grantee Chemistry Program, 2000—, Polymers Program, NSF, 2001—, Am. Chem. Soc., 2002—. Fellow Am. Phys. Soc.; mem. Am. Chem. Soc. Office: Univ Wis Dept Chemistry 1101 University Ave Madison WI 53706-1322

EDISON, BERNARD ALAN, retired apparel executive; b. Atlanta, 1928; s. Irving and Beatrice (Chanin) Edison; m. Marilyn S Wewers, Apr. 26, 1975. BA, Harvard U., 1949, MBA, 1951. With Edison Bros. Stores Inc., St. Louis, 1951—, asst. v.p., 1957-58, v.p. leased depts., 1958-67, v.p., asst. treas., 1967-68, pres., 1968-87, chmn. fin. com., 1987-89, dir. emeritus, 1989-96. Office: Edison Foundations 220 N Fourth St Ste A Saint Louis MO 63102

EDMONDS, EDMUND P., law librarian, educator, dean; b. Mar. 3, 1951; m. Brigid Edmonds; children: Paul, Anne, Katherine. BA, U. Notre Dame, 1973; MLS, U. Md., College Park, 1974; JD, U. Toledo, 1978. Bar: Ohio 1978, Va. 1982. Head circulation dept. U. Toledo Coll. Law, 1974—78; assoc. law libr., asst. prof. Marshall-Wythe Sch. Law, Coll. William and Mary, 1978—82, acting law libr., 1982—83, law libr., assoc. prof. law, 1983—88; law libr., prof. law Loyola U. ew Orleans Coll. Law, 1988—92, dir. law libr., prof. law, 1992—2000, assoc. dean academic affairs, 1992—93, asst. dean info. resources, 1994—97, stats. coord., 1997—2000; dir. Schoenecker Law Libr., prof. law U. St. Thomas Sch. Law, Minn., 2001—06; assoc. dean libr. and info. tech., dir. Kresge Law Libr., prof. law U. Notre Dame Law Sch., Ind., 2006—. Contbr. articles to profl. jours. Mem.: New Orleans Assn. Law Librs., Am. Assn. Law Librs. Office: Notre Dame Law Sch U Notre Dame PO Box 535 Notre Dame IN 46556-0535 Home: 53254 Bracken Fern Dr South Bend IN 46637 Office Phone: 574-631-5916. Personal E-mail: ebedmonds@comcast.net. E-mail: edmonds.7@nd.edu.

EDMONDS, JIM (JAMES PATRICK EDMONDS), professional baseball player; b. Fullerton, Calif., June 27, 1970; children: Haylee, Lauren. Outfielder Calif. Angels (now Anaheim Angels), 1993—99, St. Louis Cardinals, 2000—07, San Diego Padres, 2008—. Named to Am. League All-Star Team, 1995, Nat. League All-Star Team, 2000, 2003, 2005; recipient Gold Glove Award, 1997—98, 2000—05, Silver Slugger award, 2004. Achievements include setting the National League record for strikeouts by a lefty in a season with 167 in 2000; being a member of the World Series Champion St. Louis Cardinals, 2006. Avocations: water sports, ice skating. Mailing: c/o San Diego Padres PETCO Pk 100 Park Blvd San Diego CA 92101

EDMONDS, JOHN, state legislator; m. Marta Edmonds. Pub. acct.; mem. for dist. 112 Kans. State Ho. of Reps., 1994—. Address: PO Box 1805 Great Bend KS 67530-1805

EDMONDS, WILLIAM L., federal judge; b. 1944; BA, U. Mo., 1966, MA, 1969; JD, U. Iowa, 1978. Bar: Iowa 1978. Ptnr. Carter, Sar, Edmonds & Green, 1978-87; bankruptcy judge U.S. Bankruptcy Ct. (no. dist.) Iowa, Sioux City, 1987—, chief bankruptcy judge, 1992-99. Mem. Order of Coif. Office: Fed Bldg and US Courthouse 320 6th St Ste 114 Sioux City IA 51101-1244

EDMONDSON, FRANK KELLEY, retired astronomer; b. Milw., Aug. 1, 1912; s. Clarence Edward and Marie (Kelley) E.; m. Margaret Russell, Nov. 24, 1934 (dec. Jan. 1999); children: Margaret Jean Olson, Frank K. Jr. AB, Ind. U., 1933, A.M., 1934; PhD, Harvard U., 1937. Lawrence fellow Lowell Obs., 1933-34, research asst., 1934-35; Agassiz fellow Harvard Obs., 1935-36, asst., 1936-37; instr. astronomy Ind. U., Bloomington, 1937-4O, asst. prof., 1940-45, assoc. prof., 1945-48, prof., 1949-83, prof. emeritus, 1983—, dir. Kirkwood Obs., 1945-78; dir. Goethe Link Obs., 1948-78, chmn. astronomy dept., 1944-78; research asso. McDonald Obs., 1944-83. Observations of asteroids in cooperation with Internat. Astron. Union's Minor Planet Ctr.; statistical adviser to Prof. Alfred Kinsey for gall wasp and human sex behaviour rsch., 1939-56; program dir. for astronomy NSF, 1956-57; acting dir. Cerro Tololo Inter-Am. Obs., 1966; lectr. astron. socs.; mem. adv. bd. Lowell Obs., 1988-2000. Author: AURA and its US National Observatories, 1997; contbr. numerous papers to Am., Brit., German astron. jours. Decorated Order of Merit Chile, 1964; recipient Meritorious Pub. Svc. award NSF, 1983, Disting. Alumni Svc. award Ind. U., 1997; honored with Daniel Kirkwood (1814-95) in Ho. Resolution No. 58 adopted by Ind. 109th Gen. Assembly, First Session, 1995. Fellow AAAS (chmn. sect. D, v.p. 1962); mem. Assn. Univs. Rsch. in Astronomy (v.p. 1957-61, pres. 1962-65, dir. 1957-83, cons./historian 1983—2003, historian emeritus 2003—), Can. Astron. Soc., Am. Astron. Soc. (treas. 1954-75, 70 yr. attendence award 2001), Astron. Soc. Pacific, Internat. Astron. Union (chmn. U.S. nat. com. 1963-64, v.p. commn. minor planets, comets and satellites 1967-70, pres. 1970-73), Ind. Acad. Sci. (named Disting. Scholar 2004), Am. Mus. Natural History (corr. mem.), Friends of Ctr. for History of Physics (exec. com. 2001—), Explorers Club, Phi Beta Kappa, Sigma Xi. Home: 716 S Woodlawn Ave Bloomington IN 47401-4936 Office: Ind U Dept Astronomy 319 Swain Hall West 727 E 3rd St Bloomington IN 47405-7105 Business E-Mail: clirot@indiana.edu.

EDMONDSON, KEITH HENRY, retired chemical company executive; b. Wheaton, Ill., May 16, 1924; s. Edwin Ray and Mildred Lorraine (Henry) E.; m. Peggy Eleanor Wood, Sept. 22, 1945; children— Robert Earl, Kris E., John David, Keith Clark. BS, Purdue U., 1948, MS, 1949. With Upjohn Co., Kalamazoo, Mich., 1949-86, exec. v.p. internat. div., 1962-67, v.p., gen. mgr. chem. div., 1967-86; exec. dir. Stryker Ctr., 1986-90; prof. Kalamazoo Coll., 1986-90; dir. Career Devel. Ctr., Kalamazoo Coll., 1990-94; retired, 1994—. Mem. Kalamazoo Bd. Edn., 1958-62, pres., 1962. Served to 1st lt. USAAF, 1942-45. Decorated D.F.C. with oak leaf cluster, Air medal with 6 oak leaf clusters. Mem. Internat. Isocyanate Inst. (pres. 1976), Kalamazoo C. of C. (v.p. 1973), Kalamazoo Mgmt. Assn. (pres. 1957), Am. Inst. Chem. Engrs., Am. Chem. Soc., Tau Beta Pi, Sigma Xi, Phi Lambda Upsilon. Republican. Methodist. Home: 8565 W H Ave Kalamazoo MI 49009-7516 Office: Kalamazoo Coll 1200 Academy St Kalamazoo MI 49006-3268 E-mail: edmond@iserv.net.

EDMUNDS, NANCY GARLOCK, federal judge; b. Detroit, July 10, 1947; m. William C. Edmunds, 1977. BA cum laude, Cornell U., 1969; MA in Teaching, U. Chgo., 1971; JD summa cum laude, Wayne U., 1976. Bar: Mich. 1976. With Plymouth Canton Public Schools, 1971-73; law clk. Barris, Sott, Denn & Driker, 1973-75; law clk. to Hon. Ralph Freeman U.S. Dist. Ct. (ea. dist.) Mich., 1976-78; with Dykema Gossett, Detroit, 1978-84, ptnr. litigation sect., 1984-92; apptd. judge U.S. Dist. Ct. (ea. dist.) Mich., 1992—. Commr. 21st Century Commn. on Cts., 1990; mem. faculty, bd. mem. Fed. Advocacy Inst., 1983-91. Editor in chief Wayne Law Review. Mem. com. of visitors Wayne Law Sch., Detroit; bd. dirs. Mich. Mems. of Stratford Festival; bd. trustees Stratford Shakespearean Festival of Am., Temple Beth El, 1990-97, Hist. Soc. U.S. Dist. Ct. (ea. dist.) Mich., 1993-98. Mem. ABA, FBA (exec. bd. dirs. 1989-92), Am. Judicature Soc., Fed. Judges Assn., State Bar Mich. (chair U.S. cts. com. 1990-91). Avocation: reading. Office: US Dist Ct US Courthouse #211 231 W Lafayette Blvd Detroit MI 48226-2700 E-mail: karen_hillebrand@mied.uscourts.gov.

EDWARDS, BENJAMIN FRANKLIN, III, investment banker; b. St. Louis, Oct. 26, 1931; s. Presley William and Virginia (Barker) E.; m. Joan Moberly, June 13, 1953; children: Scott P., Benjamin Franklin IV, Pamela M. Edwards Bunn, Susan B. BA, Princeton U., 1953. With A.G. Edwards & Sons, Inc., St. Louis, 1956—, pres., 1967—, chmn., 1983—, also CEO, 1983—. Bd. dirs. Jefferson Bank and Trust Co., Psychol. Assocs., Helig-Meyers, Inc., N.Y. Stock Exch., Washington U., St. Louis Art Mus., Barnes Hosp. Mem. U. Mo., St. Louis, Civic Progress, Arts and Edn. Coun. With USNR, 1953-56. Mem. Investment Bankers Assn. (gov. 1968—), Securities Industry Assn. (gov. 1974-81, chmn. 1980—). Clubs: Old Warson Country (St. Louis); Bogey. Presbyterian. Office: A G Edwards & Sons Inc 1 N Jefferson Ave Saint Louis MO 63103-2205

EDWARDS, CHARLES LLOYD, lawyer; b. Chgo., July 2, 1940; s. Ed and Anita (Sopkin) E.; m. Lois S. Levine, Apr. 5, 1970; children: Laura, Karen. BBA with highest honors, U. Wis., 1962; JD, U. Chgo., 1965. Bar: Ill. 1965. Assoc. Aaron, Aaron, Schimberg & Hess, Chgo., 1965-67; ptnr., sr. counsel, Real Estate Practice DLA Piper Rudnick Gray Cary, Chgo., 1968—. Adj. prof. John Marshall Law Sch., 1997—98; lectr. law U. Chgo. Law Sch., 2005—06. Mem. ABA, Ill. State Bar Assn., Chgo. Bar Assn. (chmn. subcom. real property fin. 1986-88, vice chmn. real property continuing legal edn. 1989-91, vice chmn. real property 1991-92, chmn. real property 1992-93), Lawyers Club Chgo., Am. Coll. Mortgage Attorneys, Am. Coll. Real Estate Lawyers, Phi Beta Kappa, Beta Gamma Sigma. Avocations: classic music, collecting art, fishing, driving. Office: DLA Piper Rudnick Gray Cary Suite 1900 203 N La Salle St Chicago IL 60601-1293 Office Phone: 312-368-4010. Office Fax: 312-630-5314. Business E-Mail: charles.edwards@dlapiper.com.

EDWARDS, CHARLES RICHARD, entomology and pest management educator; b. Lubbock, Tex., Jan. 22, 1945; s. Troy B. and Jeanette E. E.; m. Claudia Frances Henderson, Dec. 21, 1966; children: Cecily Elizabeth, Celeste Elaine. BS, Tex. Tech. U., 1968; MS, Iowa State U., 1970, PhD, 1972. Bd. cert. entomoloist. Prof. entomology Purdue U., West Lafayette, Ind., 1972—, now emeritus. Cons. Consortium for Internat. Crop Protection, Corvallis, Oreg., 1985—, Food and Agr. Orgn. UN, 1995-2000; USAID Integrated Pest Mgmt. Collaborative Rsch. Support Program, 1993—2003; adj. prof. St. István U., Gödöllo, Hungary. Contbr. articles to profl. jours. Mem. Entomol. Soc. Am. (Ext. Achievement award 1984, award of merit 1985), Royal Entomol. Soc. London, Sigma Xi, Alpha Zeta, Gamma Sigma Delta. Avocations: running, woodworking. Office: Purdue U 901 W State St West Lafayette IN 47907-2089 Home Phone: 765-463-9480. Business E-Mail: edwards@purdue.edu.

EDWARDS, CHRISTINE ANNETTE, lawyer; b. Ft. Monmouth, NJ, Aug. 30, 1952; d. Harry W. Jr. and Elizabeth Power; m. John H. Edwards, Aug. 24, 1974; children: Lindsey, John. BA, U. Md., College Park, 1974; JD with honors, U. Md., Balt., 1983. Bar: Md. 1983, D.C. 1984, Ill 1990. With Sears, Roebuck and Co., Md., 1971-81, sr. paralegal, staff asst. Washington, 1981-83, atty. govt. affairs, 1983-87; asst. v.p., dir. govt. affairs Dean Witter Fin. Svcs. Group, Washington, 1987-88, v.p., gen. counsel Lincolnshire, Ill., 1988-89, sr. v.p., 1989-91, exec. v.p., sec., chief legal officer NYC, 1991-97; exec. v.p., chief legal officer, corp. sec. Morgan Stanley Dean Witter & Co. (merger Dean Witter Discover & Co. with Morgan Stanley & Co. Inc.), NYC, 1997—99; legal dept. ABN AMRO, 1999—2000; v.p., gen. counsel Bank One Corp., 2000—03; ptnr. Winston & Strawn LP, Chgo., 2003—. Mem. bd. Fin. Svcs. Coun., Washington, 1990—; bd. trustees Nat. Found. for Consumer Credit Counseling Svcs., Silver Spring, Md., 1990-92; mem. Women in Housing and Fin., Washington, 1982—, SAI Letigation Com., 1995—, N.Y. Stock Exchange Legal Adv. Com., 1992-95; bd. dirs. Chgo. Bd. of Options Exchange, SPS Transaction Svcs. Inc.; exec. v.p., chief legal officer, corp. sec. CLO Roundtable, 1995—. Recipient Disting. Mem. award Women in Housing and Fin., Washington, 1988; named 1 of 50 Top Women Lawyers Nat. Law Journal, 1998. Mem. ABA, Securities Industry Assn. (mem. fed. regulation com. 1990—). Home: 70 Sequoia Ct Lake Forest IL 60045-2827 Office: Winston & Strawn LP 35 W Wacker Dr Chicago IL 60601-9703

EDWARDS, DONALD MERVIN, systems engineer, educator, dean; b. Tracy, Minn., Apr. 16, 1938; s. Mervin B. and Helen L. (Halstenrud) E.; m. Judith Lee Wilson, Aug. 8, 1964; children: John, Joel, Jeffrey, Mary. BS, S.D. State U., 1960, MS, 1961; PhD in Agrl. Engring, Purdue U., 1966. Registered profl. engr. With soil conservation svc. U.S. Dept. Agr., Marshall, Minn., 1957-62; teaching, rsch. asst. S.D. State U. and Purdue U., 1960-66; assoc. prof. agrl. engring. U. ebr., Lincoln, 1966-71, prof., 1971-80, asst. dean Coll. Engring and Architecture, 1970-73, assoc. dean, dir. Engring Rsch. Ctr., Coll. Engring and Tech., 1973-80, dir. Energy Rsch and Devel. Ctr., 1976-80; prof. and chmn. dept. agrl. engring Mich. State U., East Lansing, 1980-89; prof. biol. systems engring., dean Coll. Agrl. Scis. and Natural Resources U. Nebr., Lincoln, 1989-00, spl. projects, 2000-01, emeritus prof. biol. sys. engring., 2001—, emeritus dean Coll. Agrl. Scis. and Natural Resources, 2001—. Mem. Engring. Accreditation Bd. Engring. and Tech.; collaborator, cons. to numerous industries and agys., 1966—. Contbr. numerous articles on irrigation, water pollution, remote sensing, energy, agrl., natural resources and engring. edn. to profl. jours. Past bd. dirs. Nat. Safety Coun.; past chmn. bd. dirs. Lincoln Transp. System. Recipient Massey-Furguson award Am. Soc of Agriculture Engineers, 1994, Outstanding Tchr. award U. Nebr. Fellow Am. Soc. Engring. Edn., Am. Soc. Agrl. Engrs., NSPE (past nat. bd. dirs., nat. v.p.); mem. Profl. Engrs. Nebr., Farmhouse Fraternity, Sigma Xi, Alpha Gamma Rho, Triangle. Home: 11420 Wenzel Dr Lincoln NE 68527-9484 E-mail: dedwards1@unl.edu.

EDWARDS, GERALD, plastics company executive; b. Chgo., July 13; m. Jada; children: Charlene, Candice Rae, Gerald II. Student, Heidelberg Coll. With Ford Motor Co.; asst. plant mgr., then plant mgr. Detroit Plastic Molding; pres., CEO Engineered Plastic Products, 1987—. Office: Engineered Plastic Products Inc 699 James L Hart Pkwy Ypsilanti MI 48197-9791

EDWARDS, HELEN THOM, physicist; b. Detroit, May 27, 1936; d. Edgar Robertson and Mary (Milner) Thom; m. Donald A. Edwards. BS in Physics, Cornell U., 1957, MA in Physics, 1963, PhD in Physics, 1966. Rsch. assoc. Cornell U., Ithaca, NY, 1966-70; assoc. head booster Fermi Nat. Accelerator Lab., Batavia, Ill., 1970-71, staff physicist, M.R., 1971-75, head switchyard extraction group, 1975-78, leader tevatron design group, 1978-79, dep. head saver div., 1980-81, dep. head accelerator div., 1981-86, head accelerator div., 1987-88, guest scientist, 1992—; head accelerator constrn. div. SSC/URA, Dallas, 1989-90, tech. dir., 1990—92. Recipient Achievement in Accelerator Physics and Tech. U.S. Summer Sch. on Particle Accelerator Prize, 1985, Ernest O. Lawrence award Dept. of Energy, 1986, Nat. Medal Tech., 1989; MacArthur Found. Chgo. fellow, 1988. Fellow Am. Phys. Soc.; mem. NAE.

EDWARDS, HORACE BURTON, former state official, oil pipeline company executive, management consultant; b. Tuscaloosa, Ala., May 20, 1925; children: Adrienne, Paul, David, Michael; m. Fran M. Allerheiligen, Sept. 3, 1994. BS in Naval Sci., Marquette U., 1947, BSME, 1948; MBA in Fin. Mgmt., Iona Coll., 1972; LDH (hon.), Tex. So. U., 1982; LLD, Stillman Coll., 1984. Registered profl. engr., Wis., Kans. Various engring. positions Allis Chalmers, 1948-52, GM, 1952-56, Conrac, 1956-63, Northrop, 1963-71; with Atlantic Richfield Co., 1967-80, mgr. planning, evaluation NYC, 1976-79, v.p. planning, control LA, 1979-80; pres., CEO, chmn. bd. dirs. ARCO Pipe Line Co., Independence, Kans., 1980-86; sec. transp. State of Kans., 1987-91; pres. Edwards and Assocs. Inc., Topeka, 1991—. Mem. adv. bd. Energy Bur., Strategic Hwy. Rsch. Program Res. Mississippi Valley Conf. State Hwy. and Transp. Ofcls., 1989-90; trustee Kans. Coun. Econ. Edn., Topeka, 1981—, Leadership Independence, 1984-86, Kans. Ind. Coll. Fund, 1985-91, Stillman Coll., Tuscaloosa, Ala., 1985—, Ins. Logopedics, Wichita, Kans., 1985-91. Recipient Marquette U. Dist. Engring. Alumnus award, 1984 Mem. Am. Petroleum Inst., Assn. Oil Pipelines (mem. adv. com.), Am. Assn. Blacks in Energy (bd. dirs.), Kans. C. of C. and Industry (trustee Leadership Kans. 1983, bd. dirs. 1983-91), Kans. Contractors Assn., Assn. Gen. Contractors (assoc.). also: Edwards & Assocs Inc 1805 N Dr Martin Luther King D Milwaukee WI 53212-3639

EDWARDS, JAMES D., accounting company executive; b. Cleve., Nov. 4, 1943; s. James D. and Elizabeth (Reynolds) E.; m. Sharon E. Bordelon, May 2, 1968; 1 child, David. BS in Acctg., Bob Jones U., 1964. CPA, Ga. From staff acct. to ptnr. Arthur Andersen & Co., Atlanta, 1964-73, mng. ptnr. Atlanta office, 1979-87, mng. ptnr. Americas NYC, 1987—. Bd. dirs., exec. com. Atlanta C. of C., 1982-85, Woodruff Arts Ctr., Atlanta, 1986-87; chmn. Cen. Atlanta Progress, 1986-87. Mem. Board Room (N.Y.C.),d The Stanwich Club (Greenwich, Ct.) Atlanta Country Club.

EDWARDS, JAY, radio personality; b. Ft. Smith, Ark., Oct. 20; Radio host WDAF, Westwood, Kans., 1996—. Avocations: movies, cooking. Office: WDAF 4935 Belinder Rd Westwood KS 66205

EDWARDS, JESSE EFREM, pathologist, educator; b. Hyde Park, Mass., July 14, 1911; s. Max and Nellie (Gordon) E.; m. Marjorie Helen Brooks, Nov. 12, 1952; children— Ellen Ann Villa, Brooks Sayre. BS, Tufts Coll., 1932, MD, 1935; DSc (hon.), Georgetown U., 1990. Diplomate Am. Bd. Med. Examiners, Am. Bd. Pathology. Resident Mallory Inst. Pathology, Boston, 1935-36, asst., 1937-40; intern Albany (N.Y.) Hosp., 1936-37; instr. pathology Boston U., 1938; instr. pathology, bacteriology, surgery Tufts Med. Coll., 1939-40; research fellow Nat. Cancer Inst. USPHS, 1940-42; cons. sect. pathologic anatomy Mayo Clinic, 1946-60; asst. prof. grad. sch. U. Minn., Mpls., 1946-51, asso. prof., 1951-54, prof. pathologic anatomy 1954-60, clin. prof. med. sch., prof. pathology grad. sch., 1960—96; chief pathologist United Hosp. (formerly Chas. T. Miller Hosp.), St. Paul, 1960-80; cons. pathologist Hennepin County Hosp., Mpls., 1964—; cons. dept. pathology Mpls. Vets. Hosp., 1966—90; cons. pathologist St. Paul Ramsey Hosp., 1967-80; dir. registry of cardiovascular disease United Hosp., St. Paul, 1980-87, sr. cons. registry of cardiovascular disease, 1987—, also sr. cons. Jesse E. Edwards Registry of Cardiovascular Disease, 1987—. Pres. World Congress Pediatric Cardiology, 1980; mem. pathology study sect. USPHS, 1957-62; civilian cons. surgeon gen. AUS, 1947-69 Author: Atlas Acquired Diseases of Heart and Great Vessels, 1961, (with T.J. Dry and others) Congenital Anomalies of the Heart and Great Vessels, 1948, (with others) An Atlas of Congenital Anomalies of the Heart and Great Vessels, 1954, (with R.S. Fontana) Congenital Cardiac Disease, 1962, (with J.R. Stewart, O. Kincaid) An Atlas of Vascular Rings and Related Malformations of the Aortic System, 1963, (with C.A. Wagenvoort, D. Heath) Pathology of Pulmonary Vasculature, 1963, (with others) Correlation of Pathologic Anatomy and Angiocardiography, 1965, Coronary Arterial Variations in the Normal Heart and in Congenital Heart Disease, 1975, Coronary Heart Disease, 1976, (with Brooks S. Edwards) Jesse E. Edwards Synopsis of Congenital Heart Disease, 2000, Pathology of Sudden Cardiac Death, 2006; Editor: (with others) Circulation; contbr. articles to profl. jours. Served from capt. to lt. col. M.C. AUS, 1942-46. Recipient Distinguished Tchr. award Minn. Med. Found., 1974; Gold Heart award Am. Heart Assn., 1970; Gifted Tchr. award Am. Coll. Cardiology, 1977 Mem. AMA, Minn. Med. Assn., Soc. Exptl. Biology and Medicine, Am. Heart Assn. (pres. 1967-68), Minn. Heart Assn. (pres. 1962-63), Internat. Acad. Pathology (pres. 1955-56), Am. Assn. Pathologists and Bacteriologists, World Congress Pediat. Cardiology, Coll. Am. Pathologists, Am. Soc. Exptl. Pathology, Sigma Xi, Alpha Omega Alpha. Office: United Hosp Saint Paul MN 55102 Home: 211 2d St NW Rochester MN 55901 E-mail: doctorjee@aol.com.

EDWARDS, MARK U., JR., academic administrator, history professor, writer; b. Oakland, Calif., June 2, 1946; s. Mark U. and Margaret Edwards; m. Linda Johnson, Mar. 1968; 1 child, Teon. BA in Psychology, Stanford U., Calif., 1968, MA in History, 1969, PhD in History, 1974. Jr. fellow U. Mich., 1971-74; asst. prof. history Wellesley Coll., Mass., 1974-80; asst. prof. Purdue U., West Lafayette, Ind., 1980-83, assoc. prof., 1983-86, prof. history, 1986-87; prof. christianity Harvard U., Cambridge, Mass., 1987-94; pres. St. Olaf Coll., Northfield, Minn., 1994—2000; assoc. dean academic adminstrn. Harvard Div. Sch., 2003—. Founder, v.p. ELK Software Devel. Corp., 1985—; pres. Sixteenth Century Studies Conf., 1987-88; chair continuing com. Internat. Congress for Luther Rsch., 1988-94; bd. dirs. Wittenberg U., 1985—. Author: Luther and the False Brethren, 1975, Luther's Last Battles, 1983, Printing, Propaganda and Martin Luther, 1994; co-author: Luther, A Reformer for Churches, 1983, Religion on Our Campuses: A Professor's Guide to Communities, Conflicts and Promising Conversations; mem. editl. bd. The Ency. of the Reformation, 1989—. Bd. dirs. Holden Village, 1993-94, 96-98. Mem. Am. Norwegian Hist. Assn.

EDWARDS, MICHELLE DENISE, professional basketball player; b. Mar. 6, 1966; Degree in gen. studies, Iowa State U., 1988. Basketball player, Faenza, Italy, 1989-90, Pistoia, Italy, 1990-93, Ferrara, Italy, 1993-95, Pavia, Italy, 1995-97; basketball player Cleveland Rockers Women's NBA, Cleve., 1997—. Mem. Olympic Festival Team, 1985; recipient Bronze medal Pan Am. Games, 1991; named MVP Italian League All-Star team, 1997.

EDWARDS, RICHARD LAWRENCE, geology educator; b. Boston, Mar. 14, 1953; s. Richard and Vee-tsung (Ling) E.; m. Melissa Ann McDonald, m. Sept. 24, 1988. SB, MIT, 1976; MS, U. Mich., 1986; PhD, Calif. Inst. Tech., 1988. Asst. prof. U. Minn., 1988-90, McKnight land-grant prof., 1990—, disting. McKnight university prof., 2001—, dir. grad. studies, dept. geol. & geophysics. Dir. Minn. Isotope Lab., Mpls., 1988—. Contbr. more than 20 articles to profl. jours. Recipient Taylor Disting. Rsch. award, 1995. Fellow: Am. Acad. Arts & Sci.; mem.: AAAS, Geochem. Soc. (C.C. Patterson award 1999), Am. Geophys. Union, Geol. Soc. Am. Office: U Minn 0211 Rm 108 PillsH 310 Pillsbury Dr SE Minneapolis MN 55455-0219 E-mail: edwar001@umn.edu.

EDWARDS, WALLACE WINFIELD, retired automotive executive; b. Pontiac, Mich., May 9, 1922; s. David W. and Ruby M. (Nutting) E.; m. Jean Austin Wolfe, Aug. 24, 1944; children: Ronald W., Gary R., Ann E. BS in Mech. Engring, Gen. Motors Inst., 1949; MBA, Mich. State U., 1966. With GMC Truck & Coach div. Gen. Motors Corp., Pontiac, Mich., 1940-78, truck service mgr., 1961-62, head engine design, 1962-64, dir. reliability, 1964-66, dir. prodn. control and purchasing, 1966-70, dir. engring., 1970-78; dir. Worldwide Truck Project Center, Warren, Mich., 1978-80; gen. dir. Worldwide Truck and Transp. Sys. Center, 1980-81; v.p. G.M.O.D.C., 1980-81; group mgr. small and light truck and van ops. Truck and Bus. Group, Gen. Motors Corp., 1981-82, mgr. internat. staff, 1982-84, gen. dir. mil. vehicle ops. Power Products and Def. Group, 1984-86. Bd. dirs. Crystal Mountain Resort, Thompsonville, Mich., 1991-2003. Past pres., mem. exec. com. Clinton Valley coun. Boy Scouts Am.; dir. Grand Traverse Regional Land Conservancy, 1991-2003, chmn. 1996-98; regent Nat. Eagle Scout Assn. (life). Served with USNR, 1944-46. Mem. Soc. Automotive Engrs., U.S. Navy League, Tau Beta Pi, Beta Gamma Sigma. Office: 5089 Crystal Dr Beulah MI 49617-9617

EDWARDSON, JOHN ALBERT, information technology executive; b. Terre Haute, Ind., July 23, 1949; s. John Albert and Mildred Ruth (Anderson) E.; m. Catharine Orr, June 11, 1971; children: Laura, Anne, Shelley. BS in Indsl. Engring., Purdue U., 1971; MBA in Fin. and Internat. Bus., U. Chgo., 1972. Comml. banking officer First Bank-St. Paul, 1972-77; v.p., treas. Ferrell Cos. Inc., Kansas City, Mo., 1977-83, sr. v.p. fin. services group, 1983-85; exec. v.p. fin., chief fin. officer Northwest Airlines Inc. and NWA Inc., St. Paul, 1985-88; exec. v.p., chief fin. and adminstrv. officer Internat. Minerals and Chems. Corp., orthbrook, Ill., 1988-90; chief fin. officer United Airlines Employees Acquisition Corp., Chgo., 1990; exec. v.p., chief fin. officer Ameritech, Chgo., 1991-94; pres., COO UAL Corp., Elk Grove Village, Ill., 1994—; chmn., pres. & CEO Burns Internat. Svcs Corp, Chgo., 1999—2000; chmn., CEO CDW Corp., Vernon Hills, Ill., 2001—. Trustee, pres. Ravina Festival Assn., Highland Park, Ill., bd. trustees Art Inst. Chgo. Recipient Disting. Engring. Alumnus award Purdue U., 1988. Presbyterian. Avocations: sailing, hiking, bicycling. Office: CDW 200 N Milwaukee Ave Vernon Hills IL 60061

EDWARDSON, SANDRA, dean, nursing educator; BSN, St. Olaf Coll., Minn., 1963; MN in Maternal and Child Nursing, U. of Wash., 1964; PhD, U. of Minn., 1980. Dean Sch. ursing, U. Minn., Mpls. Office: U Minn Twin Cities Sch Nursing 6-101 Weaver-Densford Hall 308 Harvard St SE Minneapolis MN 55455-0353

EFFRON, DAVID LOUIS, conductor, performing company executive; b. Cin., July 28, 1938; s. Sigmund and Babette Jane (Holstein) E.; children: Michael, Daniel. MusB, U. Mich., 1960; MusM, Ind. U., 1962; Doctorate (hon.), NC State U., 2006. Asst. condr., condr. N.Y.C. Opera, 1964-82; asst. condr. Nat. Ballet, Washington, 1969-70; music dir. Central City (Colo.) Opera, 1972-76; condr. Curtis Inst. Music, Phila., 1970-77; music dir. Eastman Philharm., Eastman Sch., Rochester, NY, 1977-98, Youngstown (Ohio) Symphony Orch., 1987-96, Heidelberg (Fed. Republic Germany) Castle Festival, 1980-92, Chautaugua Instn. Music Sch. Festival Orch., 1990-96; artistic dir., prin. condr. Brevard (N.C.) Music Ctr., 1996—2007; prof. instrumental conducting Ind. U., Bloomington, 1998—, chmn. dept., 2006—. Guest condr. numerous assignments Europe, Far East, US, Mex., Can. Condr. recs. Schwantner Aftertones, 1983, Schuman Judith, 1984, Benita Valente, 1986, Mahler & Berlioz with Jan deGaetani, 1989. Recipient Grammy award, 1984, Best Contemporary Rec. award Ovation Mag., 1988, Musician of Yr. award Nat. Fedn. Music Clubs, 2003. Office: Indiana U Sch Music Bloomington IN 47405 Home Phone: 812-323-0790; Office Phone: 812-855-4752. Business E-Mail: deffron@indiana.edu.

EFRON, BRUCE, radio personality; b. Mpls., Oct. 12; m. Betsy Efron; children: Joshua, Erica. Radio host WDAF, Westwood, Kans., 1990—. Avocations: acting, singing. Office: WDAF 4935 Belinder Rd Westwood KS 66205

EGAN, CHARLES JOSEPH, JR., lawyer, consumer products company executive; b. Cambridge, Mass., Aug. 11, 1932; s. Charles Joseph and Alice Claire (Ball) E.; m. Mary Bowersox, Aug. 6, 1955; children: Timothy, Sean, Peter, James. AB, Harvard U., 1954; LLB, Columbia U., 1959. Bar: N.Y. 1960, Mo. 1973. Assoc. Donovan, Leisure, ewton & Irvine, NYC, 1959-62; ptnr. Hall, McNicol, Marett & Hamilton, NYC, 1962-68; v.p., gen. counsel Thomson & McKinnon Securities, NYC, 1969-70, Hallmark Cards, Inc., Kansas City, Mo., 1972—2004. Bd. dirs. Am. Multi Cinema, Inc., Kansas City, Mo., 1996-2004. Trustee Notre Dame de Sion Sch., Kansas City, 1973-77, Pembroke Country Day Sch., Kansas City, 1976-82, Kansas City Art Inst., 1995—; bd. dirs. Kansas City YMCA, 1976-80; mem. dean's coun. Columbia Law Sch., 1991—; vice chmn. Harvard Coll. Fund, 1994-99, co-chmn., 2000-03; co-trustee Stanley H. Durwood Found. Served to 1st lt. USMC, 1954-56. Mem. Mo. Bar Assn., Kansas City Lawyers Assn., Harvard Alumni Assn. (pres. 1989-90, exec. com. 1987-2003), Century Assn., Somerset Club, Harvard Club of N.Y., Harvard Club of Kansas City (pres. 1985-87). Roman Catholic. Office: Hallmark Cards Inc 2501 Mcgee St Kansas City MO 64108-2600 Home Phone: 816-531-0424; Office Phone: 816-274-4687.

EGAN, KEVIN JAMES, lawyer; b. Chgo., June 24, 1950; s. Raymond Basil and Harriet Olene (Landbo) E.; children: Ryan, Daniel. BA, U. Ill., 1972; JD, Northwestern U., 1975. Bar: Ill. 1975, U.S. Dist. Ct. (no. dist.) Ill. 1975, U.S. Ct. Appeals (7th cir.) 1976, U.S. Ct. of Customs and Patent Appeals 1978. Law clk. to judge U.S. Dist. Ct. (no. dist.) Ill., Chgo., 1975-77; assoc. Pattishall, McAuliffe & Hofstetter, Chgo., 1977-78; asst. U.S. atty. No. Dist. of Ill., 1978-82; assoc. Winston & Strawn, Chgo., 1982-84, ptnr., 1984-93, Sonnenschein, Nath & Rosenthal, Chgo., 1993-98, Foley & Lardner, Chgo., 1998—. Article editor Jour. Criminal Law and Criminology, 1974-75. Bd. trustees Village of Frankfort, 1991—. Mem. ABA, Chgo. Bar Assn. (com. mem.), Bar Assn. of 7th Cir., Prestwick Country Club (Frankfort, Ill.). Episcopalian. Avocation: hockey. Home: 904 Huntsmoor Dr Frankfort IL 60423-8747 Office: Foley & Lardner 321 N Clark St Ste 2800 Chicago IL 60610 Home Phone: 815-469-1571; Office Phone: 312-832-4500. Business E-Mail: kegan@foley.com.

EGBERT, ROBERT IMAN, electrical engineer, educator, academic administrator; b. May 25, 1950; BSEE, U. Mo., Rolla, 1972, MSEE, 1973, PhD, 1976. Registered profl. engr., Mo., Kans. Grad. teaching asst. U. Mo., Rolla, 1972-75, grad. instr., 1975-76; systems engr. power div. Black & Veatch Cons. Engrs., Kansas City, Mo., 1976-80; asst. prof. elec. engring. Wichita (Kans.) State U., 1980-86, assoc. prof., 1986-95, prof., 1995—, dir. Ctr. for Energy Studies, 1987—. Contbr. articles to profl. jours. Mem. IEEE (sr.), NSPE, Am. Soc. Engring. Edn. (Dow Outstanding Young Faculty award 1982-83), Eta Kappa Nu (nat. bd. dirs. 1993-95, v.p. 1995-96, pres. 1996-97), Phi Kappa Phi, Tau Beta Pi, Sigma Xi.

EGGE, JOEL, clergy member, academic administrator; Pres. Lutheran Brethren Schools of the Church of the Lutheran Brethren of America, Fergus Falls, Minn., Luth. Brethren Schs., Fergus Falls, Minn. Office: Lutheran Brethren Schools Ch of Lutheran Brethren of Am 815 W Vernon Ave Fergus Falls MN 56537-2699

EGGER, TERRANCE C.Z., publishing executive; b. Rock Island, Ill. m. Renuka Egger; children: Anthony, Ali, Danny. B., Augustana Coll., Sioux Falls, SD; M. in Speech Communication, San Diego State U. V.p. adv. Tucson Newspapers, 1992—96; gen. mgr. Post-Dispatch, 1996—2006; pub. St. Louis Post-Dispatch, LLC, 1999—2006, pres., 2000—06; pres., pub. & CEO Cleve. Plain Dealer, 2006—. Holder mktg. positions, adv. positions Copley Newspapers; tchr. coll. comm. courses, Calif. Office: Cleveland Plain Dealer 1801 Superior Ave NE Cleveland OH 44114-2198 Office Phone: 216-999-4216. Office Fax: 216-999-6354. E-mail: tegger@plaind.com.*

EGGERS, GEORGE WILLIAM NORDHOLTZ, JR., anesthesiologist, educator; b. Galveston, Tex., Feb. 22, 1929; s. George William Nordholtz and Edith (Sykes) E.; m. Mary Futrell, Dec. 30, 1955; children: Carol Ann, George William. BA, Rice U., Tex., 1949; MD, U. Tex., Galveston, Tex., 1953. Diplomate Am. Bd. Anesthesiology. Instr. dept. anesthesiology, U. Tex., Galveston, Tex., 1956-59; asst. prof. dept. anesthesiology, U. Tex., Galveston, Tex., 1959-61; assoc. prof. dept. anesthesiology, U. Mo., 1961-67; prof. dept anesthesiology U. Mo., 1967—94, acting chmn. dept. anesthesiology, 1969, chmn. dept. anesthesiology, 1970-94, prof. emeritus, 1994—2001. Vis. instr. USAF Hosp., Lackland AFB, San Antonio, 1956-61; vis. rsch. prof. dept. anesthesiology Northwestern U. Med. Sch., Chgo., 1968-69; rsch. assoc. Space Sci. Rsch. Ctr., U. Mo., 1965-66. Contbr. over 50 articles to profl. jours. Recipient Ashbel Smith Disting. Alumnus Award U. Tex., 1993. Mem. Am. Soc. Anesthesiology (bd. dirs. 1979-86, v.p. 1986-89, 1st v.p. 1990, pres. elect 1991, pres. 1992), Am. Coll. Anesthesiology (bd. govs., 1965-74, chmn. bd. govs., 1973), Soc. Acad. Anesthesiology Chmn. (pres. 1971), Assn. Am. Med. Colls. (adminstrv. bd. coun. acad. socs. 1976-79), Mo. Soc. Anesthesiologists (pres. 1970, Disting. Svc. Award 2001), Tex. Gulf Coast Anesthesiology Soc. (v.p. 1960), Boone County Med. Soc. (pres. 1988), Am. Bd. Anesthesiology (assoc. examiner 1968, joint coun. with Am. Soc. Anesthesiology on in-tng. exams.), Acad. Anesthesiology (pres. 1995, Citation of Merit 1997), Accreditation Coun. Grad. Med. Edn. (mem. residency rev. com. for anesthesiology 1989-94), Anesthesia Found. (trustee 1993-2003), Jefferson Club of U. Mo., Alpha Omega Alpha, Mu Delta, Sigma Xi. Republican. Roman Catholic. Avocations: hunting, astronomy, magic, photography, shooting. Home: 1509 Woodrail Ave Columbia MO 65203-0931 Office: U Mo Dept Anesthesiology 1 Hospital Dr Dept Columbia MO 65201-5276 E-mail: nordholtz@aol.com.

EGGERT, GLENN J., manufacturing executive; BS, ME, U. Wis. Various positions Meritor, Troy, Mich., 1978-98, sr. v.p. ops., 1998—. Mem. ASME, Soc. Mfg. Engrs., Assn. Mfg. Excellence. Office: Meritor Automotive Inc 2135 W Maple Rd Troy MI 48084-7121

EGGERT, RUSSELL RAYMOND, lawyer; b. Chgo., July 28, 1948; s. Ralph A. and Alice M. (Nischwitz) E.; m. Patricia Anne Alegre, 1998. AB, U. Ill., 1970, JD, 1973; postgrad., Hague Acad. Internat. Law, The Netherlands, 1972. Bar: Ill. 1973, U.S. Supreme Ct. 1979. Assoc. U. Ill., Champaign, 1973-74; asst. atty. gen. State of Ill., Chgo., 1974-79; assoc. O'Conor, Karaganis & Gail, Chgo., 1979-83; legal counsel to Ill. atty. gen., Chgo., 1983-87; ptnr. Mayer, Brown, Rowe & Maw, LLP, Chgo., 1987—2007, Reed Smith LLP, 2007—. Contbr. articles to profl. jours. Mem. ABA. Democrat. Office: Reed Smith LLP 10 S Wacker Dr Chicago IL 60606 Office Phone: 312-207-2408. Business E-Mail: reggert@reedsmith.com.

EGGERTSEN, JOHN HALE, lawyer; b. Ann Arbor, Mich., Jan. 7, 1947; s. Claude Andrew and Nita (Wakefield) E.; m. Claire Chenoweth, July 19, 1969 (div. 1987); children: Melissa Anne, Helen Emma; m. Sharon Ingram, June 13, 1987 (div. 1994); children: Alexandria, Andrea; m. Robin Rich, Sept. 23, 1995; 1 child, Brendon Hale. BA, U. Mich., 1968; JD cum laude, U. Toledo, 1974; LLM in Taxation, NYU, 1975. Bar: Ohio 1974, Mich. 1975. Instr. Highland Park (Mich.) Sch. Dist., 1968; claims adjuster State Farm Mutual Ins. Co., Ann Arbor, Mich., 1968-70; ptnr. Honigman Miller Schwartz and Cohn, Detroit, 1975-2000; pvt. practice Ypsilanti, Mich., 2000—. Adj. prof. Wayne State U. Law Sch., Detroit, 1980-94; active Mich. Employee Benefits Conf., Detroit, 1980—. Contbr. articles to profl. jours. Bd. dirs. Neighborhood Svcs. Orgn., Detroit, 1992-2000, pres., 1994-97. Rsch. grantee NYU, 1974-75; Gerald Wallace scholar NYU, 1974-75. Mem. ABA (taxation sect., employee benefits com.), State Bar Ohio, State Bar Mich. Democrat. Mem. Lds Ch. Avocations: softball, bowling, reading. Office: 6270 Munger Rd Ypsilanti MI 48197-9026 Office Phone: 734-794-7100. Business E-Mail: john@jhelaw.com.

EGGLESTON, HARRY, optometrist; b. Dec. 31, 1941; m. Julie Kassebaum; 1 child. Student, Benedictine Coll., 1959-61; BA, St. Louis U., 1962; BA, MA, Creighton U., 1966; MD, U. Cin., 1972. Rep. candidate for U.S. House 9th Dist., Mo., 1996. With USAF, 1967-69. Roman Catholic. Address: Harry Eggleston For Congress 4141 S Old Highway 94 Saint Charles MO 63304-2846

EGLOFF, FRED ROBERT, manufacturers representative, writer, historian; b. Evanston, Ill., Nov. 30, 1934; s. Edward Gottfried and Pearl Elizabeth (Fischrupp) E.; m. Sharon Lee Geyer, June 30, 1962. BS in Commerce, Loyola U., 1956. Asst. adv. mgr. The Englander Co., Chgo., 1956-57; indsl. film svc. Accurate Cinema Svc., Chgo., 1960-62; indsl. sales The EMF Co., Chgo., 1962-69, Avery Internat., Azusa, Calif., 1969-77, The Stanley Works, Hartford, Conn., 1977-78; mfg. rep. ARTCO, Chgo., 1979-99. V.p., bd. dirs. Westerners Internat., Oklahoma City, 1982-2008, pres. 1997-99; cons. ALA, Chgo., 1982-2002; tchr. New Trier Extension, Wilmette, Ill., 1985—; adv. bd. Western Outlaw-Lawman History Assn., 1999-2008. Author: El Paso Lawman, 1982, Origin of the Checker Flag, 2006; editor Westerners Brand Book, 1986-96. Bd. dirs. Wilmette Hist. Soc., 1973-77; hist. cons. Wilmette Hist. Mus., 1978; com. mem. Save the Depot Preservation, Wilmette, 1974; sec. Wilmette Sailing Assn., 1974; vis. com. D'Arcy McNickle Ctr. for Am. Indian History, Newberry Libr., 1999-02. Recipient Don Russell Meml. award, 1998, Wola Lifetime Achievement award for most outstanding contbns. to western history, 1999. Mem. Western History Assn., Western Writers Am., Soc. Midland Authors, Chgo. Corral the Westerners (sheriff 1978-80, sidewinder 1984), Windy City BMW Car Club Am. (pres. 1976, Big Wheel 1972, Founders Recognition award 1997), Vintage Sportscar Club (sec. 1972-80, top competitor award 1970, 97), Nat. Cowboy Hall Fame, Soc. of Automotive Historians, Am. Legion. Republican. Roman Catholic. Avocations: vintage sports cars, photography, skiing, horseback riding, books. Office: ARTCO 2035 Greenwood Ave Wilmette IL 60091-1439

EHLERS, VERNON JAMES, congressman; b. Pipestone, Minn., Feb. 6, 1934; m. Johanna Meulink, 1958; children: Heidi, Brian, Marla, Todd. Student, Calvin Coll.; AB in Physics, U. Calif., Berkeley, 1956, PhD in Physics, 1960. Tchg. asst. U. Calif., Berkeley, 1956-57, rsch. asst., 1957-60, lectr. in physics, 1960-66; prof. physics Calvin Coll., 1966-83; mem. Mich. State Ho. of Reps., 1983-85, Mich. State Senate, 1985-94, pres. pro tem, 1991-94; mem. U.S. Congress from 3d Mich. dist., 1994—; chmn. Joint Com. Libr. Congress; mem. transp. and infrastructure com., sci. com., edn. and workforce com., house adminstrn. com. Mem. Gov. Milliken's Task Force on Environ. Problems, 1977, Kent County Rep. Exec. Com., Kent County Bd. Commrs., 1975-83, chmn., 1979-82, Mich. Toxic Substance Control Commn., 1982; asst. floor leader Mich. State Ho. of Reps., 1983-85 Contbr. NATO Rsch. fellow U. Heidelberg, Germany, 1961-62, Sci. Faculty fellow NSF, Joint Insts. for Lab. Astrophysics, U. Colo. 1971-72, fellow Calvin Coll. Ctr. for Christian Scholar, 1977-78; recipient Disting. Svc. award Assn. Independent Colleges and Universities, 1986, Outstanding Public Svc. award Mich. Paralyzed Veterans of Am., 1988, Presidential award Mich. Recreation and Park Assn., 1989, Mich. Environ. Legis. of Yr. Mich. Enviorn. Defense, 1990, Outstanding Public Svc. award Mich. Public Health Assn., 1991, Outstanding Citizen award Lake County Riverside Property Assn., 1992, Legis. Leadership aawrd Triangle Coalition Sci. and Tech. Edn., 2004, Leadership award Nat. Marine Sanctuary Found., 2005. Mem.: Am. Assn. Phys. Tchrs., Am. Phys. Soc., AAAS. Republican. Christian Reformed Ch. Home: 1848 Morningside Dr SE Grand Rapids MI 49506-5121 Office: US Congress 1714 Longworth House Ofc Bldg Washington DC 20515-2203 also: Gerald R Ford Federal Bdlg Rm 166 110 Michigan St Grand Rapids MI 49503-2313 Office Phone: 202-225-3831, 616-451-8383. Office Fax: 202-225-5144, 616-454-5630.

EHLKE, NANCY JO, agronomist; Assoc. prof. U. Minn., St. Paul, 1986—. Recipient CIBA GEIGY award in Agronomy Am. Soc. of Agronomy, 1995. Office: U Min Dept of Agronomy and Plant Genetics 411 Borleug Hall 1991 Buford Ave Saint Paul MN 55108-1013

EHRENBERG, MAUREEN, management consultant; Pres. Grubb & Ellis Mgmt. Svcs., Inc., Northbrook, Ill., 1999—. Office: Grubb & Ellis Mgmt Svcs Inc 2215 Sanders Rd Ste 400 Northbrook IL 60062-6114

EHRLICH, AVA, broadcast executive; b. St. Louis, Aug. 14, 1950; d. Norman and Lillian (Gellman) Ehrlich; m. Barry K. Freedman, Mar. 31, 1979; children: Alexander Zev, Maxwell Samuel. BJ, Northwestern U., 1972, MJ, 1973; MA, Occidental Coll., 1976. Reporter, asst. mng. editor Lerner Newspapers, Chgo., 1974-75; reporter, news editor Sta. KMOX, St. Louis, 1976-79; producer Sta. WXYZ, Detroit, 1979-85; exec. producer Sta. KSDK-TV, St. Louis, 1985—. Guest editor Mademoiselle mag., N.Y.C., 1971; freelance writer, coll. prof. Detroit, Chgo., St. Louis, 1987; adj. faculty mem. Washington U., St. Louis, 1994—. Trustee CORO Found., St. Louis, 1976-77, 1986—99, St. Louis Jewish Light, 1999—, Crown Ctr., 2000; bd. dirs. Nat. Kidney Found., St. Louis, 1987, Crown Ctr., 2000—, Hillel Found. of Washington U, 2005—; com. chairperson Crayton H.S. PTO, 2005—. Named Outstanding Woman in Broadcasting, Am. Women in Radio & TV, 1983, Among 18 Most Influential Women in the Region St. Louis Dispatch, 2000; recipient Journalism award Am. Chiropractic Assn., 1989, AP award Ill. UPI, 1989, Illuminator award AMC Cancer Rsch., 1994, Women in Comms. Nat. award, 1988, Emmy award, 1995, Virginia Betts award for Contbns. in Journalism, 1999; CORO Found. fellow in pub. affairs, 1975-76. Mem. NATAS (com. mem. 1986—, bd. dirs. 1994—, 18 local Emmy awards 1986—), Women in Comms., Inc. (sec. 1978-79, Clarion award 1989, Best in Midwest Feature award 1989), Soc. Profl. Journalists. Democrat. Jewish. Home: 8002 Walinca Ter Saint Louis MO 63105-2565 Office: Sta KSDK-TV 1000 Market St Saint Louis MO 63101-2011 Office Phone: 314-444-5120. Business E-Mail: aehrlich@ksdk.gannett.com.

EHRLICH, GERT, science educator, researcher; b. Vienna, June 22, 1926; arrived in US, 1939; s. Leopold and Paula Maria (Kucera) Ehrlich; m. Anne Vogdes Alger, Apr. 27, 1957. AB in Chemistry with honors, Columbia U., NYC, 1948; AM, Harvard U., Cambridge, Mass., 1950, PhD, 1952. NIH postdoctoral fellow Harvard U., Cambridge, Mass., 1951—52; rsch. assoc. dept. physics U. Mich., Ann Arbor, 1952—53; rsch. staff GE Rsch. Lab., Schenectady, NY, 1953—68; prof. materials sci. Coordinated Sci. Lab. U. Ill., Urbana-Champaign, 1968—. Former mem. editl. adv. bd. Chem. Physics Letters, Jour. Chem. Physics, Jour. Vacuum Sci. & Tech., Surface & Colloid Sci., Progress in Surface & Membrance Sci.; contbr. articles to profl. jours. With US Army, 1945—47, ETO. Guggenheim fellow, 1985. Fellow: Am. Vacuum Soc. (Medard W. Welch award 1979), NY Acad. Scis., Am. Phys. Soc.; mem.: Am. Chem. Soc. (Kendall award 1982), Nat. Acad. Scis., Alexander von Humboldt Found. (Humboldt-Preis 1992), Sigma Xi. Office: U Ill Materials Rsch Lab 104 S Goodwin Ave Urbana IL 61801-2985 Office Phone: 217-333-6448. Business E-Mail: ehrlich@mrl.uiuc.edu.

EIBEN, ROBERT MICHAEL, pediatric neurologist, educator; b. Cleve., July 12, 1922; s. Michael Albert and Frances Carlysle (Gedeon) E.; m. Anne F. Eiben; children: Daniel F., Christopher J., Thomas M., Mary, Charles G., Elizabeth A. BS, Western Res. U., 1944, MD, 1946. Diplomate Am. Bd. Pediatrics. Intern medicine Univ. Hosp., Cleve., 1946-47; asst. resident pediatrics and contagious diseases City Hosp., Cleve., 1947; asst. resident pediatrics Babies and Children's Hosp., Cleve., 1948, clin. fellow pediatrics, 1948-49; clin. instr. pediatrics Western Res. U., 1949-50; asst. med. dir. div. contagious diseases City Hosp., 1949-50, visitant in pediatrics, 1949-50; practice medicine specializing in pediatrics Cleve., 1949-90; acting dir. dept. pediatrics and contagious diseases City Hosp., 1950-52; asst. dir. dept. pediatrics and contagious diseases Cleve. Met. Gen. Hosp., 1952-60; med. dir. Respiratory Care and Rehab. Center, 1954-60, pres. med. staff, 1958-60; USPHS fellow in neurology U. Wash., 1960-63; pediatric neurologist Cleve. (Ohio) Met. Gen. Hosp., 1963—90, acting med. dir. comprehensive care program, 1966-67, med. dir., 1968-73, mem. med. exec. com., 1974-76; acting chief, sect. on clin. investigations and therapeutics Developmental and Metabolic Neurology br. Nat. Inst. Neurol. and Communicative Disorders and Strokes, NIH, Bethesda, Md., 1976-77; acting dir. dept. pediatrics Metro Health Med. Ctr., 1979-80; from instr. pediatrics to prof. emeritus Western Res. U., 1950—, prof. emeritus pediatric neurology, 1991—. Cons., project site visitor Nat. Found. Birth Defects Center Programs, 1961-66; mem. adv. com. on grants to train dentists to care for handicapped Robert Wood Johnson Found., 1975-80; emeritus faculty marshall Case Western Res. U., 1992-2007, mem. regional leadership coun., 2003-. Mem. coun. Bratenahl Village-County of Cuyahoga, 1982-98. Recipient Presdl. award Internat. Poliomyelitis Congress, Geneva, 1957, Clifford J. Vogt Alumni Svc. award Case Western Res. U., Cleve., 1985; established Annual Robert M. Eiben, M.D. vis. professorship in child neurology MetroHealth Med. Ctr. Dept. Pediat., 1991. Mem.: Child Neurology Soc. (chmn. tng. program com. 1976—77, sec.-treas. 1978—81, pres. 1983—85, Lifetime Career Achievement award 2005), Innominatum Soc., No. Ohio Pediat. Soc., Am. Epilepsy Soc., Am. Pediat. Soc., Am. Soc. Human Genetics, Am. Acad. Neurology (chmn. residence exam. com. 1989—93), Am. Acad. Pediat., Case Western Res. U. Med. Alumni Assn. (pres. 1979, bd. of trustees 2002—), Pasteur Club. Home: 2 Oakshore Dr Bratenahl OH 44108-1118 Office: MetroHealth Med Ctr 2500 Metrohealth Dr Cleveland OH 44109-1900

EIBENSTEINER, RON, political organization administrator, venture capitalist; Co-founder, CFO Arden Med. Sys., 1983-87; pres., CEO, chmn. Mirror Techs., Inc., 1988-92, 94—, chmn., 1992-94; pres. Wyncrest Captial; dir. IntraNet Solutions, Inc., 2003—; chmn. OneLink Comm., Inc., 2003—, Kids-First Scholarship Fund Minn., Inc., 2003—; dir. Ctr. Am. Experiment, 2003—. Co-founder Diametrics, OnHealth Network; chmn. Prodea Software. Chmn. Minn. Reps., 1999—; chair Minn. Rep. Party, 1999-. Mem.: Republican Nat. Conv. (com. on call 2000), Midwestern State Chmn.'s Assn. Office: Republican Party Minn Ste 250 525 Park St Saint Paul MN 55103-2145

EICH, SUSAN, public relations executive; Dir. corp. pub. rels. Target Corp. (formerly Dayton Hudson Corp.), Mpls., 1995—. Office: Target Corp 33 S 6th PO Box 1392 Minneapolis MN 55440-1392

EICHHOLZ, DENNIS R., controller, treasurer; Contr., treas. Clark USA, Inc., St. Louis, 1994—. Office: Clark USA Inc 8182 Maryland Ave Saint Louis MO 63105-3786

EICHHORN, ARTHUR DAVID, minister of religion; b. St. Louis, Oct. 13, 1953; s. Arthur Louis and Adele (Stankunas) Eichhorn. BA, Concordia U., River Forest, Ill., 1975, MA, 1976, Webster U., 1986; EdD, Calif. Coast U., 1997. Cert. elem. tchr., Mo. Dir. music St. John Luth. Ch., Mt. Prospect, Ill., 1974-76, Our Savior Luth. Ch., Springfield, Ill., 1976-81, Holy Cross Luth. Ch., St. Louis, 1981-91, Timothy Luth. Ch., St. Louis, 1991—2005, St. Luke's Hosp., Chesterfield, Mo., 2003—05, Concordia Sem., Clayton, Mo., 2005—. Part-time instr., dir. St. Louis extension site Concordia U., Wis. Mem.: Calvary Luth Ch., Assn. Luth. Ch. Musicians, Am. Guild Organists, Choristers Guild (pres. local chpt. 1990—92). Republican. Home: 7116 Mardel Ave Saint Louis MO 63109-1123 Office: Calavary Luth Ch 4211 NW Topeka Blvd Topeka KS 66617 Home Phone: 314-645-0730; Office Phone: 785-286-1431. Personal E-mail: aeich53024@aol.com.

EICHHORN, GEORGE, state representative; b. Davenport, Iowa, Dec. 1, 1954; married. BA, Drake U., 1977, JD, 1980. Lawyer, 1980—; mem. Iowa Ho. Reps., DesMoines, 2001—, mem. various coms. including judiciary, state govt. and ways and means, vice chair justice sys. appropriations. Mem.: ABA, Am. Agrl. Law Assn., Iowa State Bar Assn., Stratford Lions Club. Republican. Lutheran. Office: State Capitol East 12th and Grand Des Moines IA 50319 also: 3533 Fenton Ave Stratford IA 50249

EICKHOFF, JOHN R., information services company executive; BA in Bus. Adminstrn. and Acctg., St. Cloud State U. Various acctg. and fin. planning positions Ceridian Corp., Mpls., 1963-82, v.p. corp. svcs., 1983, v.p., contr. fin. plans and controls, comml. credit, 1983, v.p., contr. fin. plans and controls, fin. and bus. svcs., 1985, v.p., contr. fin. plans and controls, computer sys. group, 1986, v.p., contr. fin. plans and controls computer products group, 1988, v.p., corp. contr., 1989, exec. v.p., CFO, 1995—. Mem. retirement com. Ceridian Corp.; bd. dirs. Norstan Inc., Callidus Software Inc. Mem. Fin. Execs. Inst., Fin. Execs. Inst. (Twin Cities chpt.). Office: Ceridian Corp 3311 E Old Shakopee Rd Minneapolis MN 55425-1640

EIGEN, HOWARD, pediatrician, educator; b. NYC, Sept. 8, 1942; s. Jay and Libbie (Kantrowitz) E.; children: Sarah Elizabeth, Lauren Michelle. BS, Queens Coll., 1964; MD, Upstate N.Y. Med. Ctr., Syracuse, 1968. Diplomate Am. Bd. Pediatrics, Am. Bd. Pediatric Pulmonology, Am. Bd. Critical Care Medicine, Nat. Bd. Med. Examiners (mem. pediatric test com. 1986-90). Resident in pediatrics Upstate Med. Ctr., Syracuse, 1968-71; fellow in pediatric pulmonology Tulane U., ew Orleans, 1973-76; asst. prof. pediatrics Ind. U., Indpls., 1976-84, prof., 1984-96, Billie Lou Wood Prof. pediatrics, 1996—. Assoc. chmn. of Pediatrics for Clin. Affairs, dir. pediatric intensive care, pulmonology sect. Riley Hosp. for Children, med. dir. ambulatory care, 1989— Co-editor: Respiratory Disease in Children: Diagnosis and Management; assoc. editor Pediatric Pulmonology, 1984-91; contbr. articles to profl. jours. Served to maj. U.S. Army, 1971-73. Fellow Am. Acad. Pediatrics (pres. chest sect. 1983-85, pulmonology 1986—), Am. Thoracic Soc., Am. Bd. Pediatrics, Am. Lung Assn. (pres. Ind. 1984-85). Avocation: tennis. Office: Ind U Dept Pediatrics 702 Barnhill Dr Rm 2750 Indianapolis IN 46202-5128

EIKEN, DOUG K., state agency administrator; With N.D. Pks. and Recreation Dept., Bismarck; dir. Mo. State Pk. Divsn., Jefferson City, 1994—. Office: Mo State Pk Divsn PO Box 176 1659 E Elm St Jefferson City MO 65101-4124 Fax: 373-526-7716.

EIMER, NATHAN PHILIP, lawyer; b. Chgo., June 26, 1949; s. Irving A. and Charlotte Eimer; m. Lisa S. Eimer; children: Micah Jacob, Noah Joseph, Daniel Jordan, Anna Beatrice, Claire Elizabeth. AB magna cum laude in Econs., U. Ill., 1970; JD cum laude, Northwestern U., 1973. Bar: Ill. 1973, US Supreme Ct. 1978, NY 1985, Tex. 1998. Assoc. Sidley & Austin, Chgo., 1973—80, ptnr., 1980—2000, mem. exec. com., 1999—2000; founding ptnr. Eimer, Stahl, Klevorn & Solberg, LLP, Chgo., 2000—. Adj. prof. Law Sch., Northwestern U., Chgo., 1989-96. Note and comment editor Northwestern U. Law Rev., 1972-73. Bd. dirs. Chgo. Lawyers Com. Civil Rights, 1991—, pres., 1993-94; bd. dirs. UNICEF, 1992-93, Infant Welfare Soc., Chgo., exec. v.p., 1992-96, pres., 1996-98; mem. adv. bd. Children & Family Justice Ctr., Northwestern U. Legal Clinic, 1996—. Mem. ABA, Univ. Club. Office: Eimer Stahl Klevorn & Solberg LLP Ste 1100 224 S Michigan Ave Chicago IL 60604 Office Phone: 312-660-7601. E-mail: neimer@eimerstahl.com.

EINHORN, EDWARD MARTIN (EDDIE EINHORN), professional baseball team executive; b. Paterson, NJ, Jan. 3, 1936; s. Harold Benjamin and Mae (Lippman) E.; m. Ann Magdelene Pelachik, Apr. 24, 1962; children: Jennifer, Jeffrey. AB, U. Pa., 1957; JD, Northwestern U., 1960. Radio sports announcer Sta.-WXPN, Phila., 1954-57; founder, pres. Midwestern Sports Network, Chgo., 1957-61, TV sports Inc. (name changed to TVS 1968, became subs. Corinthian Broadcasting Corp. 1973), NYC, 1961-65, pres., chief exec. officer, 1965-78; exec. producer CBS Sports Spectacular, NYC, 1978—; pres. Chgo. White Sox, 1981-93, vice chmn., 1993—; founder Sports Vision Chgo., 1982. Dir. Corinthian Broadcasting Corp., 1973-77; format com. mem. Major League Baseball; co-architect Baseball Network; TV cons. U.S. Olympic Com.; initiator 200 hour Olympic TV package, 1990; TV cons. U.S. Figure Skating Assn., Internat. Skating Union. bd. dirs. Chgo. Bulls. Editor-in-chief Jour. Air Law and Sci., 1959-60, Northwestern Jour. Criminal Law Sci., 1958-60; producer (TV spl.) Gossamer Albatross, Flight of Imagination (Emmy award 1980). Recipient Honor award Naismith Basketball Hall of Fame, 1973, Merit award Nat. Basketball Coaches, 1973, Victor award City of Hope, 1974. Mem. Nat. Acad. Radio, TV Arts and Scis., Internat. Radio, TV Soc., Nat. Assn. TV Program Execs., Nat. Assn. Coll. Dirs., Nat. Assn. Basketball Coaches (TV negotiation com.) Profl. Baseball Assn. (TV com. mem. 1992-95, sr. Am. League rep. on player devel. negotiating com.). Office: Chgo White Sox 333 W 35th St Chicago IL 60616-3651

EINHORN, LAWRENCE HENRY, oncologist, medical educator; b. Dayton, Ohio, 1942; BS, Ind. U., 1965; MD, U. Iowa, 1968. Diplomate Am. Bd. Internal Medicine, Am. Bd. Oncology. Med. intern Ind. U. Hosp., Indpls., 1967—68; resident in medicine Ind. U., 1968—69, fellow, hematology and oncology, 1971—72, assoc. prof. medicine, clin. oncology and hematology, 1973—87, Disting. prof. medicine Indpls., 1987—, Lance Armstrong Found. prof., oncology, 2006—; fellow, oncology M.D. Anderson Hosp. and Tumor Inst., Houston, 1972—73. Contbr. several articles to profl jours. Capt. Med. Corps USAF, 1969—72. Recipient Richard and Hilda Rosenthal Found. award for Cancer Rsch., Am. Assn. Cancer Rsch. Mtg., Disting. Clinician award, Milken Found., 1989, ACCC Clinical Oncology award, 1991, Charles F. Kettering prize, GM Cancer Rsch. Found., 1992, Glenn Irwin Experience Excellence award, 1996, Herman B. Wells Visionary award, 2001. Mem.: Am. Philos. Soc., NAS. Achievements include developed a chemotherapy regimen to treat testicular cancer that improved the survival rate from 5% to 95%; led the medical team treating champion cyclist and testicular cancer survivor Lance Armstrong. Office: Ind U Sch Med Indiana Cancer Pavillion Rm 473 535 Barnhill Dr Indianapolis IN 46202-5289 Office Phone: 317-274-3515. Office Fax: 317-274-3646.

EINHORN, MARTIN B., physicist, educator; b. Dayton, Ohio, Aug. 14, 1942; s. Aaron Howard and Rosalind (Rosen) E.; m. Vibeke Gjøe Geleff, Feb. 18, 1967; children: Michael, Linda. BS (hons.), Calif. Inst. Tech., 1965; PhD, Princeton U., 1968. Post-doctoral fellow Stanford (Calif.) Linear Accelerator Ctr., 1968-70, Lawrence Berkeley (Calif.) Nat. Lab., 1970-72, Fermi Nat. Accelerator Lab., Batavia, Ill., 1972-73, staff physicist, 1973-76; assoc. rsch. scientist U. Mich., Ann Arbor, 1976-79, assoc. prof., 1979-83, prof. physics, 1983—2004, prof. emeritus, 2004—; dep. dir. Kavli Inst. Theoretical Physics U. Calif., Santa Barbara, 2004—. Chair adv. bd. Theoretical Advanced Study Inst., Boulder, Colo., 1984-91, dep. dir. Inst. for Theoretical Physics, U. Calif., Santa Barbara, 1990-92. Contbr. 90 articles to profl. jours. Mem. high energy physics adv. panel Dept. of Energy, Washington, 1983-87, program dir. theoretical physics Nat. Sci. Fedn., 2000. John Simon Guggenheim Meml. Found. fellow, 2003—04. Fellow Am. Phys. Soc.; mem. AAAS. Office Phone: 805-893-6309.

EISEL, JEAN ELLEN, educational association administrator; b. Columbus, Ohio, July 18, 1946; d. Joseph Adam and viola Marie (Heintz) E. BA, Coll. St. Francis, 1968; MEd, Boston Coll., 1969. Asst. dir. placement Boston Coll., Chestnut Hill, Mass., 1968-69; dir. counseling and placement Coll. St. Francis, Joliet, Ill., 1970-72; asst. to v.p. student affairs Wittenburg U., Springfield, Ohio, 1972-74, dir. career svcs., 1974-76; asst. dean career svcs. Ohio State U., Columbus, 1976-84; dir. career svcs. Ariz. State U., Tempe, 1984; dir., master's prog. in career mgmt. Fuqua Sch. Bus., Duke U., NC, 2003—; asst. dean corp. and career programs, Sch. Bus. Dominican U., 2004—. Bd. trustees Coll. Placement Coun. Found, Bethlehem, Pa., 1987—, Big Bros./Big Sisters, Tempe, 1990—. Contbr. articles to profl. jours. Chairperson Columbus Area Careers Conf., 1977-79. Mem. Rocky Mt. Coll. Placement Assn. (sec., 1987-89), Midwest Coll. Placement Assn. (v.p. colls., 1980-81), Western Coll. Placement Assn. (regional coord., 1986), Ohio Coopp Ednl. Assn. (exec. com., 1983-84), Tempe C. of C. (com. mem., 1990—). Avocations: sports, theater, travel. Office: Asst Dean-Sch Bus Dominican Univ 7900 W Division St River Forest IL 60305

EISENBERG, LEE B., writer; b. Phila., July 22, 1946; s. George M. and Eve (Blonsky) E.; m. Linda Reville, June 7, 1986; children: Edmund George, Katherine Eve. AB, U. Pa., 1968; MA, Annenberg Sch. Communications, 1970. Assoc. editor Esquire Mag., NYC, 1970-72, sr. editor, 1972-74, mng. editor, 1974-75, editor, 1976-77, v.p. devel., 1980-84, editor-in-chief, 1987-90; founding editor-in-chief Esquire, U.K., London, 1990-91; founding ptnr. The Edison Project, Knoxville, Tenn., 1992-95; editor creative devel. Time Mag., NYC, 1995-99; exec. v.p., creative dir. Lands' End, Dodgeville, Wis., 1999—2003, chief creative, adminstrv. officer, 2003—04. Cons. N.Y. Times Co., 1977-78, Warner Bros., Los Angeles, 1978-79; founder Eisenberg, McCall & Okrent, N.Y.C., 1978-81. Author: Sneaky Feats, 1974, Atlantic City, 1978, Ultimate Fishing Book, 1981, Breaking Eighty, 1997, The Number: A Completely Different Way to Think About the Rest of Your life, 2006 Founder Rotisserie League Baseball, N.Y.C., 1980—. Recipient One Show award Art Dirs. Club, 1976, Gold Cindy award Assn. Visual Comms., 1984, various nat. mag. awards, 1984-90. Mailing: care Nicole Kalian Simon & Schuster 1230 Ave Of Americas New York NY 10020 E-mail: LeeEisenberg@TheNumberBook.com.

EISENBERG, MARVIN JULIUS, retired art history educator; b. Phila., Aug. 19, 1922; s. Frank and Rosalie (Julius) E. BA, U. Pa., 1943; M.F.A., Princeton, 1949, PhD, 1954; D.Litt. (hon.), St Andrews, 2003. Mem. faculty U. Mich., Ann Arbor, 1949-89, prof. art history, chmn. dept., 1960-69, Collegiate prof., 1974-75, prof. emeritus, 1989—; mem. Inst. for Advanced Study, Princeton, NJ, 1970. Vis. com. Freer Gallery Art, Washington, 1970-96, dept. fine arts Harvard U., 1975-81, Commn. on Preservation and Access, Washington, 1991-94, Ga. Mus. Art, 1997—; vis. prof. Stanford U., 1973, Mt. Holyoke Coll., 1995; disting. Berg prof. Colo. Coll., 1990, 93, 95, 97, 2000, 02; Hooker disting. vis. prof. McMaster U., 1993; Robert Lehman lectr. Bowdoin Coll., 1985; Saunders lectr. St Andrews U., 1998; lectr. U. Dayton, 2002; adv. com. Center for Advanced Study in Visual Arts, Nat. Gallery, Washington, 1981-84. Author: Lorenzo Monaco, 1989; co-author: The Confraternity Altarpiece by Mariotto di Nardo, 1998; contbr. articles to profl. jours. Served with AUS, 1943-46. Recipient Star of Solidarity II Italy, 1966; Coll. Art Assn. Disting. Teaching of Art History award, 1987; Guggenheim fellow, 1959. Fellow Japan Soc. for Promotion of Sci.; mem. Coll. Art Assn. Am. (dir. 1965-70, v.p. 1966-67, pres. 1968-69), Royal Soc. Arts (Benjamin Franklin fellow 1969), Phi Beta Kappa, Phi Kappa Phi, Pi Gamma Mu. Home: 2200 Fuller Ct Apt 1002 Ann Arbor MI 48105-2307

EISENBERG, RICHARD MARTIN, pharmacology educator; b. Weehawken, NJ, May 15, 1942; s. Herbert and Evelyn (Stecker) E.; m. Marsha Eisenberg, July 3, 1966; children: Marla, Aaron, Shana. BA, UCLA, 1963, MS, 1967, PhD, 1970; postdoc., U. Rochester, 1970-71. Asst. prof. pharmacology U. Minn., Duluth, 1971-76, assoc. prof., 1976-77, assoc. prof., acting dept. head, 1977-80, assoc. prof., dept. head, 1980-85, prof., dept. head, 1985—. Author-developer: (computer software) Mac Pharmacology, Mac MedVirology, Mac BrainLesion; presenter in field; contbr. articles to profl. jours. Recipient numerous rsch. grants Nat. Inst. Drug Abuse, 1978—, other instns., 1975—. Mem. Am. Soc. Pharmacology and Exptl. Therapeutics, Assn. Med. Sch. Pharmacology (treas. 1994-98, pres. 1998-2000), Endocrine Soc., Western Pharmacology Soc., Coll. on Problems of Drug Dependence. Avocations: woodworking, computers, photography. Office: U Minn Duluth Sch Medicine Dept Pharmacology 10 University Dr Duluth MN 55812-2403

EISENHOWER, LAURIE, performing company executive; BA in Dance, MFA in Dance, Arizona State U. Faculty Oakland U., Rochester, 1986—, full professor & head of dance; founder, artistic dir. Eisenhower Dance Ensemble, Rochester Hills, Mich., 1991—. Recipient Oakland U Faculty Recognition Award, 1997. Office: Eisenhower Dance Ensemble 1541 W Hamlin Rd Rochester Hills MI 48309

EISENSTARK, ABRAHAM, research director, microbiologist; b. Warsaw, Sept. 5, 1919; came to U.S., 1922; s. Isadore and Sarah (Becker) E.; m. Roma Gould, Jan. 18, 1948 (dec. July 1984); children: Romalyn, David Allen, Douglas Darwin; m. Joan Weatherly, Apr. 6, 1991. BA, U. Ill., 1941, MA, 1942, PhD, 1948. Program dir., acting sect. head Molecular Biology Sect. NSF, Washington, 1969-70; assoc. prof. Okla. State U., Stillwater, 1948-51; prof. Kans. State U., Manhattan, 1951-71; prof., dir. divsn. biol. scis. U. Mo., Columbia, 1971-80, prof., 1980-90, prof. emeritus, 1990—; dir. Cancer Rsch. Ctr., Columbia, 1990—; sr. scientist Lab. and Environ. Tech., Inc., Columbia, 1990—. Contbr. over 100 articles to profl. jours. With U.S. Army, 1942-46. Fellow John Simon Guggenheim Found., 1958-59, USPHS, 1959; sr. postdoctoral fellow NSF, 1966-67; recipient Sigma Xi Rsch. award Kans. State U., 1954, Thomas Jefferson Faculty Excellence award U. Mo., 1986, Most Disting. Scientist award Mo. Acad. Sci., 1989; Byler Disting. Prof., 1990. Mem. AAAS, Am. Soc. Microbiology. Office: Cancer Research Center 3501 Berrywood Dr Columbia MO 65201-6570 Office Phone: 523-875-2255. Business E-Mail: eisenstarka@missouri.edu.

EISENSTEIN, ELIZABETH LEWISOHN, historian, educator; b. NYC, Oct. 11, 1923; d. Sam A. and Margaret V. (Seligman) Lewisohn; m. Julian Calvert Eisenstein, May 30, 1948; children: Margaret, John (dec.), Edward. AB, Vassar Coll., 1944; MA, Radcliffe Coll., 1947, PhD, 1953; LittD (hon.), Mt. Holyoke Coll., 1979; LHD (hon.), U. Mich., 2004. From lectr. to adj. prof history Am. U., Washington, 1959-74; Alice Freeman Palmer prof. history U. Mich., Ann Arbor, 1975-88, prof. emerita, 1988—. Scholar-in-residence Rockefeller Found. Ctr., Bellagio, Italy, June 1977; mem. vis. com. dept. history Harvard U., 1975-81, vice-chmn., 1979-81; dir. Ecole des Hautes Etudes en Sciences Sociales, Paris, 1982; guest spkr., participant confs. and seminars; I. Beam vis. prof. U. Iowa, 1980; Mead-Swing lectr. Oberlin Coll., 1980; Stone lectr. U. Glasgow, 1984; Van Leer lectr. Van Leer Fedn., Jerusalem, 1984; Hanes lectr. U. N.C., Chapel Hill, 1985 first resident cons. Ctr. for the Book, Libr. of Congress, Washington, 1979; mem. Coun. Scholars, 1980-88; pres.'s disting. visitor Vassar Coll., 1988; Pforzheimer lectr. N.Y. Pub. Libr., 1989, Lyell lectr. Bodleian Libr., Oxford, 1990, Merle Curti lectr. U. Wis., Madison, 1992, Jantz lectr. Oberlin Coll., 1995, Clifford lectr. Austin, Tex., 1996; vis. fellow Wolfson Coll., Oxford, 1990; sem. dir. Folger Inst., 1999. Author: The First Professional Revolutionist: F. M. Buonarroti, 1959, The Printing Press as an Agent of Change, 1979, 2 vols. paperback edit., 1980 (Phi Beta Kappa Ralph Waldo Emerson prize 1980), The Printing Revolution in Early Modern Europe, 1983 (reissued as Canto Book, 1993), 2d edit., 2005, Grub Street Abroad, 1992; mem. editorial bd. Jour. Modern History, 1973-76, 83-86, Revs. in European History, 1973-86, Jour. Library History, 1979-82, Eighteenth Century Studies, 1981-84; contbr. articles to profl. jours., chpts. to books. Bd. dirs. Folger Shakespeare Libr., 2000—. Belle Skinner fellow Vassar Coll., NEH fellow, 1977, Guggenheim fellow, 1982, fellow Ctr. Advanced Studies in Behavioral Scis., 1982-83, 92-93, Humanities Rsch. Ctr. fellow Australian Nat. U., 1988. Fellow Am. Acad. Arts and Scis., Royal Hist. Soc.; mem. Soc. French Hist. Studies (v.p. 1970, program com. 1974), Am. Soc. 18th Century Studies (nominating com. 1971), Soc. 16th Century Studies, Am. Hist. Assn. (com. on coms. 1970-72, chmn. Modern European sect. 1981, coun. 1982-85, Scholarly Distinction award 2003), Renaissance Soc. Am. (coun. 1973-76, pres. 1986), Am. Antiquarian Soc. (exec. com., adv. bd. 1984-87), Phi Beta Kappa. Office: U Mich Dept History Ann Arbor MI 48109 E-mail: eisenst@mindspring.com.

EISNER, REBECCA SUZANNE, lawyer; b. Wheeling, W.Va., Aug. 27, 1962; d. Paul and Marilyn June Redosh; m. Craig George Eisner, Dec. 30, 1988. BA, Ohio State U., 1984; JD, U. Mich., 1989. Bar: Ill. 1989, Ga. 1993. Pub. rels. and govt. affairs specialist The Dow Chemical Co., Midland, Mich., 1984—86; assoc. Mayer, Brown, Rowe & Maw LLP, Chgo., 1989-92, ptnr., 1996—; assoc. group counsel, asst. v.p. Equifax, Inc., Atlanta, 1993—95. Named to Ill. Leading Lawyers and Super Lawyers, Chambers Global. Mem. ABA. Avocations: running, community affairs. Office: Mayer, Brown, Rowe & Maw LLP 190 S Salle St Chicago IL 60603-3441 Office Phone: 312-701-8577. Office Fax: 312-706-8131. Business E-Mail: reisner@mayerbrownrowe.com.

EITRHEIM, NORMAN DUANE, retired bishop; b. Baltic, SD, Jan. 14, 1929; s. Daniel Tormod and Selma (Thompson) Eitrheim; m. Clarice Yvonne Pederson, Aug. 23, 1952; children: Daniel, David, John, Marie. BA, Augustana Coll., 1951; BTh, Luther Sem., St. Paul, 1956; LHD (hon.), Augustana Coll., 1988. Pastor 1st English Luth. Ch., Tyler, Minn., 1956-63, St. Philips Luth. Ch., Fridley, Minn., 1963-76; asst. to pres. Luther Northwestern Sem., St. Paul, 1976-80; bishop S.D. dist. Am. Luth. Ch., Sioux Falls, 1981-87; bishop S.D. Synod Evang. Luth. Ch. in Am., Sioux Falls, 1988-95; ret., 1995. Staff sgt. USAF, 1951—52.

EK, ALAN RYAN, forester, educator; b. Mpls., Sept. 5, 1942; BS in Forestry, U. Minn., St. Paul, 1964, MS, 1965; PhD, Oreg. State U., Corvallis, 1969. Rsch. officer Can. Dept. Forestry and Rural Devel., Sault Ste Marie, Ont., Canada, 1966-69; from asst. prof. to assoc. prof. forestry U. Wis., Madison, 1969-77; from assoc. prof. to prof. U. Minn., St. Paul, 1977—, head dept. forest resources, 1984—. Mem. forestry rsch. adv. coun. USDA, 1994—96, 1998—99, chair, 1998—99; cons. in field. Contbr. chapters to books, articles to profl. jours. Fulbright scholar, Finland, 1997. Fellow: Soc. Am. Foresters (various coms., chmn. forest sci. and tech. bd. 1989—90); mem.: AAAS, Am. Soc. Photogrammetry and Remote Sensing, Am. Statis. Assn., Nat. Assn. Profl. Forestry Schs. and Colls. (chmn. rsch. com. 1993—95, 1999—2002), Sigma Xi, Gamma Sigma Delta, Xi Sigma Pi. Avocations: reading, sports. Home: 4744 Kevin Ln Saint Paul MN 55126-5849 Office: U Minn Dept Forest Resources Saint Paul MN 55108 Office Phone: 612-624-3400. Business E-Mail: aek@umn.edu.

EKDAHL, JON NELS, lawyer; b. Topeka, Nov. 15, 1942; s. Oscar S. and Dorothy O. (Ekdahl) M.; m. Marcia Opp, May 24, 1975; children: Kirsten, Erika, Kristofer. AB magna cum laude, Harvard U., 1964, LLB, 1968; MS in Econs., London Sch. Econs., 1965. Bar: Ill. 1969, U.S. Ct. Appeals (7th cir.) 1981, U.S. Supreme Ct. 1981. Assoc. Sidley & Austin, Chgo., 1968—73, ptnr., 1973—75; mng. ptnr., gen. counsel Andersen Worldwide SC, Chgo., 1975—2000; sr. v.p., gen. counsel AMA, Chgo., 2001—. With USAR, 1968-74. Mem. ABA, Chgo. Bar Assn., Mid-Am. Club, Chgo. Club. Office: Am Med Assn 515 N State St Chicago IL 60610 Business E-Mail: jon.ekdahl@ama-assn.org.

ELBERGER, RONALD EDWARD, lawyer; b. Newark, Mar. 13, 1945; s. Morris and Clara (Denes) Elberger; m. Rena Ann Brodey, Feb. 15, 1975; children: Seth, Rebecca. AA, George Washington U., 1964, BA, 1966; JD, Am. U., 1969. Bar: Md. 1969, D.C. 1970, Ind. 1971, U.S. Ct. Appeals (7th cir.) 1971, U.S. Supreme Ct. 1973. Atty. Balt. Legal Aid Bur., 1969—70; chief counsel Legal Svcs. Orgn., Indpls., 1970—72; ptnr. Elberger & Stanton, Indpls., 1974—76; assoc. Bose, McKinney & Evans, LLP, Indpls., 1972—74, 1976—80, ptnr., 1980—; asst. sec. Chip Ganassi Racing Teams, Inc., 1998—, gen. counsel, 2005—. V.p. Worldwide Slacks, Inc., 1984—92, Cardboard Shoe Prodns., Inc., 1989—93; v.p., gen. counsel Emmis Comm. Corp., 1986—98, asst. sec., v.p., litig. counsel, 1998—2002. Mem., v.p. Med. Licensing Bd., Ind., 1982—98; pres., chmn. bd. dirs. Ind. Civil Liberties Union, Indpls., 1972—77, bd. dirs., 1980—82; mem. nat. coun. media and pub. affairs George Washington U., 2000—; bd. dirs. Jewish Cmty. Rels. Coun., 1997—2000, ACLU, NYC, 1972—77; trustee Children's Mus. Indpls., 1994—2003, Disting. advisor, 2003—; bd. dirs. Flanner Ho. Indpls., Inc., 1999—2007. Fellow Reginald Heber Smith, U. Pa., 1969—71. Fellow: Ind. Bar Found., Indpls. Bar Found.; mem.: ABA, DC Bar, Bar Assn. 7th Cir., Ind. Bar Assn. Democrat. Jewish. Avocations: fishing, music, gardening. Office: Bose McKinney & Evans LLP 2700 First Indiana Pla 135 N Pennsylvania St Indianapolis IN 46204-2400 Home Phone: 317-251-0289; Office Phone: 317-684-5195. Business E-Mail: relberger@boselaw.com.

ELDEN, GARY MICHAEL, lawyer; b. Chgo., Dec. 11, 1944; s. E. Harold and Sylvia Arlene (Diamond) E.; m. Phyllis Deborah Mandler, Apr. 20, 1975. BA, U. Ill., 1966; JD, Harvard U., 1969. Bar: Ill. 1969, US Dist. Ct. (no. dist.) Ill. 1969, US Ct. Appeals (7th cir.) 1973, US Supreme Ct. 1973, US Dist. Ct. (ea. dist.) Mich. 1985, US Ct. Appeals (8th cir.) 1988, US Ct. Appeals (6th and 10th cirs.) 1990, US Dist. Ct. (ea. dist.) Wis. 1992, US Ct. Appeals (4th cir.), 2007. Ptnr. Kirkland & Ellis, Chgo., 1969-78, Reuben & Proctor, Chgo., 1978-86, Isham, Lincoln & Beale, Chgo., 1986-88, Grippo & Elden, Chgo., 1988—. Contbr. articles to profl. jours. Fellow Am. Coll. Trial Lawyers, Am. Bar Found.; mem. ABA, Chgo. Bar Assn. (sec. com. appellate procedures 1975-77), Chgo. Coun. Lawyers, Appellate Lawyers Assn. (bd. dirs. 1975-77). Home: 3750 N Lake Shore Dr Chicago IL 60613-4238 Office: Grippo & Elden LLC 111 S Wacker Ste 5100 Chicago IL 60606 Home Phone: 773-281-2909; Office Phone: 312-704-7700. Business E-Mail: gelden@grippoelden.com.

ELDER, IRMA, retail executive; b. Xicotencalt, Mex., 1934; m. James Elder, 1963 (dec.); 3 children. Owner, CEO Elder Automotive Group, 1983—. Mem. VIP panel 36th Annual Northwood U. Internat. Auto Show; founder Woman's Automotive Assn. Internat. Bd. dirs. Northwood U., Coll. Creative Studies, Oakland Family Svcs., Econ. Club Detroit. Named Woman Yr., Woman's Automotive Assn. Internat., 2001; named one of 100 Most Influential Women, Crain's Detroit Bus., 100 Leading Women, Automotive News, 2000; recipient Automotive Hall Fame Svc. Citation award, 2000, Pres. award, Ford Motor Co., 2000, 2001, Pride of Jaguar award, 1999, 2000. Achievements include frequently honored for many charitable assn; first woman to own Ford dealership in metropolitan Detroit market; successfully expanded co. from one dealership to eight after death of husband, founder of Elder Automotive; number one Saab dealership in US in volume of automobile sales (Saab of Troy); number one Jaguar dealership in N. Am. in volume of automobile sales (Jaguar of Troy); Elder Automotive consistently ranks top ten of Hispanic Bus. mag. top 500 Hispanic owned co. Office: 777 John R Rd Troy MI 48083 Office Fax: 248-583-0815.

ELDREDGE, CHARLES CHILD, III, art history educator; b. Boston, Apr. 12, 1944; s. Henry and Priscilla Marion (Bateson) Eldredge; m. Jane Allen MacDougal, June 11, 1966; children: Henry Gifford, Janann Bateson. BA in Am. Studies, Amherst Coll., 1966; PhD in Art History, U. Minn., 1971. Curator asst. Minn. Hist. Soc., St. Paul, 1966-68; mem. edn. dept. Mpls. Inst. Arts, 1967-69; tchg. assoc. art history U. Minn., 1968-70; curator collections Spencer Mus. Art U. Kans., Lawrence, 1970—71, dir., 1971—82, asst. prof. art history, 1970—71, assoc. prof., 1974—80, prof., 1980—82, Hall Disting. Prof. Am. Art and Culture, 1988—; dir. Nat. Mus. Am. Art, Washington, 1982-88. C.H. Hynson vis. prof. U. Tex., Austin, 1985; trustee Watkins Cmty. Mus., Lawrence, 1972-76, Assn. Art Mus. Dirs., 1982, 87, Reynolda House Mus. Am. Art, 1986-88, Amherst Coll., 1987-93, trustee Georgia O'Keeffe Found., 1989-95, Amon Carter Mus., 2003-06, Terra Found. Am. Art, 2007-; rsch. assoc. Smithsonian Instn., 1988—; founder Smithsonian Studies in Am. Art, 1987. Author: Marsden Hartley: Lithographs and Related Works, 1972, Ward Lockwood, 1894-1963, 1974, American Imagination and Symbolist Painting, 1979, Charles Walter Stetson, Color and Fantasy, 1982, Pacific Parallels: Artists and the Landscape in New Zealand, 1991, Georgia O'Keeffe, 1991, Georgia O'Keeffe: American and Modern, 1992, The College on the Hill, 1996, Reflections on Nature: Small Paintings by Arthur Dove, 1997, The Floor of the Sky: Artists and the North American Prairie, 2000, Tales from the Easel: American Narrative Paintings, 2004, John Steuart Curry's Hoover and the Flood, 2007; co-author: The Arcadian Landscape: 19th Century American Painters in Italy, 1972, Art in New Mexico, 1900-1945, 1986, Georgia O'Keeffe and The Calla Lily in American Art, 2002; gen. editor: The Register of Mus. Art, 1971—82; mem. editl. bd. Am. Studies, 1974—77, Am. Art, 1996—2006. Fulbright scholar N.Z., 1983; Smithsonian Instn. fellow Nat. Collection Fine Arts, 1979, Found. Visitor fellow U. Auckland, 1993, W.T. Kemper fellow for tchg. excellence, 2003; recipient Outstanding Alumnus award U. Minn., 1986. Mem. Coll. Art Assn. Am., Am. Studies Assn., Am. Assn. Mus., Assn. Art Mus. Dirs. (hon.), Phi Beta Kappa (hon.). Office: U Kans Dept Art History 209 Spencer Mus Art 1301 Mississippi St Lawrence KS 66045-0001 Office Phone: 785-864-4713. Business E-Mail: cce@ku.edu.

ELDREDGE, TODD, figure skater; b. Chatham, Mass., Aug. 28, 1971; U.S. figure skating champion, 1990-91, 95, 97; world bronze medalist, 1991; winner Skate Am., Pitts., 1994; Silver medalist World Figure Skating Championships, Birmingham, U.K., 1995, Gold Medalist, 1996; Silver Medalist World Figure Skating Championship, 1997.

ELDRIDGE, JAMES FRANCIS, lawyer, insurance company executive; b. Appleton, Wis., Nov. 6, 1946; s. C.H. and Florence M. (Dorschel) E.; m. Mary E. Evenson; children: Stacy M., Thomas J., Michael P., Kevin J. BA, Dartmouth Coll., 1968; JD, Marquette U., 1971. Bar: Wis. Assoc. counsel Kivett and Kasdorf, Milw., 1971-74; claim counsel Am. Family Mut. Ins. Co., Milw., 1974-81, regional claim counsel Madison, Wis., 1981-84, regional claim mgr., 1984-85, v.p. claims, 1985-90, chief legal officer, sec., 1990—. Mem. Civil Trial Counsel Wis., Wis. Acad. Trial Lawyers, Dane County Bar Assn., Am. Arbitration Assn., Nat. Assn. Ind. Insurers (laws com.). Republican. Roman Catholic. Avocations: golf, tennis, racquetball, softball, tropical fish. Office: Am Family Ins Group 6000 American Pky Madison WI 53783-0001 Office Phone: 608-249-2111. Business E-Mail: jeldridg@amfam.com.

ELDRIDGE, TRUMAN KERMIT, JR., lawyer; b. Kansas City, Mo., July 27, 1944; s. Truman Kermit and Nell Marie (Dennis) E.; m. Joan Ellen Jurgeson, Feb. 9, 1965; children: Christina Joanne, Gregory Truman. AB, Rockhurst Coll., 1966; JD, U. Mo., Kansas City, 1969. Bar: Mo. 1969, U.S. Dist. Ct. (we. dist.) Mo. 1969, U.S. Ct. Appeals (8th cir.) 1977, (10th cir.) 1995, U.S. S. Ct., 1992, U.S. Dist. Ct. Kans. 1998. Assoc. Morris, Foust, Moudy & Beckett, Kansas City, 1969-70, Dietrich, Davis, Dicus, Rowlands & Schmitt, Kansas City, 1971-74, ptnr., 1975, Armstrong, Teasdale, LLP, Kansas City, 1989-2000; sr. counsel Schlee, Huber McMullen & Krause, 2001—. Author: (with others) Missouri Environmental Law Handbook, 1990, 2d edit., 1993, 3d edit., 1997; contbr. articles to profl. jours. Chmn. bd. dirs. Loretto Sch., Kansas City, 1981-83; mem. Energy and Environ. Commn. City of Kansas City, 1990-91, 1994, bd. dirs. Sheffield Place, 1997-2003, 2005—, vice-chair, 1998-99, chair, 1999-2000. Master Ross T. Roberts Inn of Ct.; mem. ABA, Mo. Bar Assn., Kansas City Met. Bar Assn. (fed. ct. com., vice chair 1989-90, chair 1990-91), Am. Arbitration Assn. (arbitrator), Nat. Arbitration Forum (arbitrator), Kansas City Club (athletic com. 1990-2001, chair 199-2001, house com. 1993-96, 98-99, long range planning com. 1993-97, fin. com. 2004—, bd. dirs. 1997-2001). Roman Catholic. Avocations: sailing, reading, photography, raquetball. Office: PO Box 32430 4050 Pennsylvania Ste 300 Kansas City MO 64171-5430 Home Phone: 816-363-6724; Office Phone: 816-360-2522. Personal E-mail: truman_eldridge@hotmail.com. Business E-Mail: teldridge@schleehuber.com.

ELFSTRAND, MARK, radio personality; b. Fergus Falls, Minn., Oct. 22; m. Rhonda Elfstrand; children: Marshall, Adam, Ingrid. Morning program host Sta. WMBI Radio, Chgo. Avocations: golf, travel. Office: WMBI 820 N LaSalle Blvd Chicago IL 60610

ELGIN, JEFF, state representative; b. Cedar Rapids, Iowa, Feb. 22, 1951; m. Teresa Elgin; 3 children. BBA, U. Iowa, 1973, MBA, 1974. UP/gen. mgr. Mid-Continent Bottlers, Inc., 1987—88; pres. J&T Elgin LLC, Investment Co., 1996—; mem. Iowa Ho. Reps., DesMoines, 2001—, mem. various coms. including adminstrn. and regulation, appropriations, econ. devel. and environ. protection, vice chair state govt. com. Acctg. tchr. Coe Coll., 1999. Mem.: Greater Cedar Rapids C. of C., Lynn-Mar Booster Club. Republican. Office: State Capitol East 12th and Grand Des Moines IA 50319 also: 6940 Bowman Ln NE Cedar Rapids IA 52402

ELGIN, SARAH CARLISLE ROBERTS, biology professor, researcher; b. Washington, July 16, 1945; d. Carlisle Bishop and Lorene (West) Roberts; m. Robert Lawrence Elgin, June 9, 1967; children: Benjamin Carlisle, Thomas James. BA in Chemistry, Pomona Coll., 1967; PhD in Biochemistry, Calif. Inst. Tech., 1971. Rsch. fellow Calif. Inst. Tech., Pasadena, 1971—73; asst. prof. biochemistry and moleculer biology Harvard U., Cambridge, Mass., 1973—77, assoc. prof., 1977—81; assoc. prof. biology Washington U., St. Louis, 1981—84, prof., 1984—, prof. edn., 2001, prof. genetics, 2003, Viktor Hamburger prof. arts and scis., 2007. Prof. Howard Hughes Med. Inst.; mem. molcular biology study sect. NIH, 1986—89; mem. Nat. Com. on Sci. Edn. Stds. and Assessment NAS/NRC, 1992. Mem. editl. bd.: Jour. Cell Biology, 1980—82, Jour. Biol. Chemistry, 1985—88, Molecular Cellular Biology, 1989—, exec. editor: Nucleic Acids Rsch., 1983—88, assoc. editor: Molecular Cell., 1998—, Bio Med Net, co-editor-in-chief: Cell Biology Edn., 2002—05; contbr. articles to profl. jours. Recipient Prof.'s award, Howard Hughes Med. Inst., 2002, 2006; Rsch. grantee, NIH, 1987, 1988, 1991, 1993, 1998—99, 2003, 2005, 2007, NSF, 1986. Fellow: AAAS (sect. on biol. scis. 1991—); mem.: Genetics Soc. Am., Am. Soc. Cell Biology (mem. coun. 1983—85, 1992—94, mem pubs. com. 1989—91, mem. edn. com. 1992—2005), Am. Soc. Biol. Chemists. Office: Washington Univ Biology Dept CB 1137 One Brookings Dr Saint Louis MO 63130-4899 Office Phone: 314-935-5348. Office Fax: 314-935-5125. Business E-Mail: selgin@biology.wustl.edu.

ELIAS, PAUL S., retired marketing executive; b. Chgo., July 5, 1926; s. Maurice I. and Ethel (Tieger) E.; m. Jennie Lee Feldschreiber, June 28, 1953; children— Eric David, Stephen Mark, Daniel Avrum. BS, Northwestern U. Sch. Bus., 1950; degree (hon.), NYU, 1972. Buyer Mandel Bros., Chgo., 1950-53; salesman Internat. Latex Corp., Chgo., 1953-56; v.p. Hy Zeiger & Co., Milw., 1957-59; exec. v.p. K-Promotions, Inc., Milw., 1960-78, pres., 1979-80; chief exec. officer, pres. consumer promotions Carlson Mktg. Group, Mpls., 1981-84, chief exec. officer promotions div. Milw., 1985-86; pres. K-Promotions Div. Carlson Promotion Group, 1987-88, Giftmaster Div. Carlson Promotion Group, 1989—2001, Elias Mktg., Inc., 1989—2001; ret. Officer, dir. Milw. Jewish Community Center; pres. regional bd. Anti-Defamation League; pres. Regional Bd. Jewish Nat. Fund, 1993-96. Served with USAAF, 1945-46. Mem. Am. Jewish. Achievements include developing inflight mail order mktg. programs for airlines. Home and Office: Elias Mktg Inc 10134 N Gettysburg Ct Mequon WI 53092 Office Phone: 262-242-5978.

ELIAS, SHERMAN, obstetrician, gynecologist, clinical geneticist, educator; b. Rome, Mar. 21, 1947; MD, U. Ky., 1972. Diplomate Am. Bd. Med. Genetics, Am. Bd. Ob-gyn. Resident in ob/gyn U. Louisville, 1976; postdoc. fellow in med. genetics Yale U., New Haven, 1975, Northwestern U., 1978; prof. ob/gyn. genetics U. Tenn., Memphis; prof. ob/gyn., molecular and human genetics Baylor Coll. Medicine, 1994—98; prof., head dept. ob-gyn. U. Ill., Chgo., 1998—2003; chair ob-gyn. Prentice Women's Hosp., Northwestern Meml., Chgo., 2003—; John J. Sciarra prof., chair dept. ob-gyn. Feinberg Sch. Medicine, Northwestern U., Chgo., 2003—. Contbr. articles to profl. jours. Mem. AAAS, Am. Soc. Human Genetics, Soc. Gynecologic Investigation, Am. Gynec./Obstet. Soc. Office: orthwestern U Feinberg Sch Medicine 333 E Superior St # 490 Chicago IL 60611 E-mail: selias@nmh.org.

ELKINS, KEN JOE, retired broadcast executive; b. Prenter, W.Va., Oct. 12, 1937; s. Ernest Eugene Elkins and Gay (Avis) Dodrill; married; children: James, Diana. Student, Nebr. U., 1966-69. Engr. Sta. KETV-TV, Omaha, 1960-67, asst. chief engr., 1967-70, ops. mgr., nat. sales, gen. sales mgr., 1972-75, gen. mgr., 1975-80; chief engr. Sta. KOUB-TV, Dubuque, Iowa, 1970-71, gen. mgr., 1971-72, Sta. KSDK-TV, St. Louis, 1980-81; v.p., CEO Pulitzer Broadcasting Co., St. Louis, 1981-84, pres., CEO, 1984-99; ret., 1999. Bd. dirs. Commerce Bank St. Louis, Maximum Svc. Telecasters, Washington; chmn. BMI; pres. Nebr. Broadcasters, Omaha, 1979-80; chmn. NBC Affiliate Bd. Govs. Bd. dirs. BJC Health Sys. With USAF, 1957-61. Inducted into Nebr. Broadcasters Hall of Fame, 1990. Mem. Nat. Assn. Broadcasters (1st amendment com. Washington chpt. 1986-91, 1st amendment com. 1986, bd. dirs.), Found. Broadcasters Hall of Fame (bd. dirs., trustee 1990), TV Operators Caucus, Algonquin Club. Avocations: golf, water sports. Home: 720 Twin Fawns Dr Saint Louis MO 63131-4722 Personal E-mail: k_elkins@sbcglobal.net.

ELLEMAN, BARBARA, editor; b. Coloma, Wis., Oct. 20, 1934; d. Donald and Evelyn (Kissinger) Koplein; m. Don W. Elleman, Nov. 14, 1970. BS in Edn., Wis. State U., 1956; MA in Librarianship, U. Denver, 1964. Sch. libr. media specialist Port Washington (Wis.) High Sch., 1956-59, Homestead High Sch., Thiensville-Mequon, Wis., 1959-64; children's libr. Denver Pub. Libr., 1964-65; sch. libr. media specialist Cherry Creek Schs., Denver, 1965-70, Henry Clay Sch., Whitefish Bay, Wis., 1971-75; children's reviewer ALA, Chgo., 1975-82, children's editor, 1982-90, editor Book Links, 1990-96. Vis. lectr. U. Wis., 1974-75, 81-82, U. Ill., Circle Campus, 1983-85; Disting. scholar children's lit., Marquette U., 1996—; cons. H.W. Wilson Co., 1969-75; mem. Libr. Congress Adv. Com. on selection for children's books for blind and physically handicapped, 1980-88, Caldecott Calendar Com., 1986; judge The Am. Book Awards, 1982, Golden Kite, 1987, Boston Globe/Horn Book, 1990; mem. faculty Highlights for Children Writers Conf., 1985-90; mem. orgn. com. MidWest Conf. Soc. Children's Books Writers, 1974-76; chair Hans Christian Andersen Com., 1987-88; advisor Reading Rainbow, 1986-96, Ind. R.E.A.P. project, 1987-93; jury mem. VI Catalonia Premi Children's Book Exbhn., Barcelona, Spain, 1994; adv. bd. Parent's Choice, Cobblestone Publ., Georgia Pub. TV's 2000, The New Advocate mag., 20th Century Children's Writers, Encyclopedia of Children's Literature, Cooperative Children's Book Ctr., U. Wis., Madison, Riverbank Rev., 1998—, Ency. of Children's Lit., 1998—; lang. arts com. NCTE Notable Books, 1997—; spkr. in field. Author: Reading in a Media Age, 1975, 20th Century Children's Writers, 1979, rev. edit., 1984, What Else Can You Do With a Library Degree?, 1980, Popular Reading for Children, 1981, Popular Reading II, 1986, Children's Books of International Interest, 1984, Tomie dePaola, His Art and His Stories, 1999, Holiday House: It's First 65 Years, 2000, Virginia Lee Burton: A Life in Art, 2002; contbr. articles to profl. jours. Publicity chair Internat. Bd. Books for Young People Congress, Williamsburg, Va., 1990; bd. trustees Eric Carle Mus. Picture Book Art, 2004-. Recipient Jeremiah Ludington award Ednl. Paperback Assn., 1996, Hope S. Dean award Found. Children's Lit., 1996. Mem. ALA (2000 Caldecott Com. 1999—), Soc. Children's Book Writers (mem. orgn. com. MidWest Conf. 1974-76), Internat. Bd. Books for Young People (U.S. assoc. editor Bookbird 1978-86, chair nominating com., 1985, bd. dirs. 1990-92), Children's Reading Round Table Chgo. (award 1987), Nat. Coun. Tchrs. English (bd. dirs. children's lit. assembly 1986-88, mem. editl. adv. bd. CLA bull. 1989-91, mem. using nonfiction in classroom com. 1990-96, 2000 Caldecott com., Laura I. Wilder com. 2001-03, 2007-). Address: 20 Bayon Dr Apt 5 South Hadley MA 01075

ELLENBERGER, RICHARD G., telecommunications executive; Grad., Old Dominion. CEO XL/Connect, Phila., Entrad Corp., Louisville; v.p. S.E. region MCI, sr. v.p. br. ops., sr. v.p. worldwide sales, pres. Bus. Svcs.; pres., COO Cin. Bell, Inc.; pres & CEO Broadwing Inc., Cincinnati, 2000—. Mem. Family Svcs. Bd. Greater Cin. Mem. Cin. C. of c. (bd. dirs.), Ohio Bus. Roundtable. Office: Broadwing Inc 201 E 4th St PO Box 2301 Cincinnati OH 45201-2301

ELLENS, J(AY) HAROLD, philosopher, educator, psychotherapist, minister; b. McBain, Mich., July 16, 1932; s. John S. and Grace (Kortmann) E.; m. Mary Jo Lewis, Sept. 7, 1954; children: Deborah, Jackie, Dan, Beckie, Rocky, Brenda, Brett. AB, Calvin Coll., 1953; BD, Calvin Sem., 1956, MDiv, 1986; ThM, Princeton Sem., 1965; PhD, Wayne State U., 1970; MA, U. Mich., 2000. Ordained to ministry Christian Reformed Ch., 1956; ordained theologian and pastor Presbyn. Ch., 1978. Pastor Newton Christian Reformed Ch., NJ, 1961-65, North Hills Ch., Troy, Mich., 1965-68; pvt. practice psychotherapy Farmington Hills, Mich., 1967—; pastor Univ. Hills Ch., Farmington Hills, Mich., 1968-78, Westminster Presbyn. Ch., 1980-84, Erin Presbyn. Ch., 1986-88, Cherry Hill Presbyn. Ch., 1994-96, White Lake Presbyn. Ch., 1998-2000, Troy Presbyn. Ch., 2000—01, 2004—, Mt. Clemens 1st Presbyn. Ch., 2001—02, Peoples Presbyn. Ch., Milan, Mich., 2003—04. Religious broadcaster TV, weekly, 1970-74, periodically to date; lectr. humanities and classics Wayne State U., John Wesley Coll., Oakland U., 1970-90, Wayne C.C., Oakland C.C., Calvin Sem.; vis. lectr. Princeton Theol. Sem., 1977-79; with Inst. for Antiquity and Christianity, Claremont U.; lectr. U.S. and abroad. Author: Program Format in Religious Television, 1970, Models of Religious Broadcasting, 1974, Chaplain (Major General) Gerhart W. Hyatt: An Oral History, 1977, (with others) Internat. Standard Bible Encyclopedia, 1979-89, Eternal Vigilance, 1980, God's Grace and Human Health, 1982, Life and Laughter, 1983, Psychology in Worship, 1984, (with others) Baker's Encyclopedia of Psychology, 1984, 1995, Psychotheology: Key Issues, 1986, (with others) Psychotherapy in Christian Perspective, 1987, (with others) Christian Counseling and Psychotherapy, 1987, Love, Life and Laughter, 1988, (with others) Psychology and Religion, 1988, (with others) The Church and Pastoral Care, 1988, (with others) Moral Obligation and the Military, 1988, (with others) God se genade is genoeg, 1989, (with others) Counseling and the Human Predicament, 1989, (with others) Turning Points in Pastoral Care, (with others) Christian Perspectives on Human Development, 1992, The Ancient Library of Alexandria and Early Christian Theological Development, 1993, 95, Alexander The Great and Hellenistic Culture, 1997, Human Disfunction, 1998, (with others) Humanistic Psychology, 1998, (with others) Dictionary of Pastoral Care and Counseling, 1990, (with others) The Interpretation of the Bible, 1998, Jesus as Son of Man, 2003, (with others) The Destructive Power of Religion (4 vols.), 2004, 05, (with others) God's Word for Our World, 2004, (with others) Psychology and the Bible (4 vols.), 2004, 05, (with others) Jesus as Son of Man, The Literary Character, A Progression of Images, 2004, (with others) Just War and Jihad, 2005, Sex in the Bible, 2006, three books in Portuguese and one in Spanish; editor: CAPS Internat. Directory vols. II-V, 1976-87, Ethical Reflections, 1977, The Beauty of Holiness, 2d edit., 1985, God's Grace in Free Verse, 1987, (with others) Eerdmans Dictionary of the Bible, 2000; editor in chief Jour. Psychology and Christianity, 1975-88; contbr. more than 165 articles to profl. jours. Served to col. AUS, 1956-61, ret., 1992. Created knight, Queen Juliana, The Netherlands, 1974. Mem. 23 profl. socs. including Christian Assn. Psychol. Studies (now exec. dir. emeritus), Soc. Bibl. Lit., Mil. Chaplain Assn., Ret. Officers Assn., Archeol. Inst. Am., Mil. Order World Wars. Home and Office: 26705 Farmington Rd Farmington MI 48334-4329 Office Phone: 248-231-4433. Personal E-mail: jharoldellens@juno.com.

ELLERBROOK, NIEL COCHRAN, gas industry executive; b. Rensselaer, Ind., Dec. 26, 1948; s. James Harry and Margaret (Cochran) E.; children: Jennifer, Jeffrey, Jayma. BS, Ball State U., 1970. CPA, Ind. Staff acct. audit Arthur Andersen & Co., Indpls., 1970-72, audit sr., 1972-75, audit mgr., 1975-80; asst. to sr. v.p. adminstrn. and fin. Ind. Gas Co., Inc., Indpls., 1980-81, v.p. fin., 1981-84, v.p. fin., chief fin. officer, 1984-87, sr. v.p., CFO, 1987; v.p., treas., CFO Ind. Energy, Inc., 1986—97, exec. v.p., treas., CFO, 1997, pres., COO, 1997—99, pres., CEO, 1999—2000; chmn., CEO Vectren Corp., Evansville, Ind., 2000—03, chmn, pres., CEO, 2003—. Bd. dirs. Ind. Gas Co., Ind. Energy, Inc. 5th 3d Bank of Ctrl. Ind Bd. dirs. Crossroads of Am. Coun. Boy Scouta Am., Indpls. Civic Theatre. Mem. AICPA, Ind. CPA Soc. (bd. dirs. Indpls. chpt., past pres. 1977-83, state bd. dirs. 1984-87), Fin. Exec. Inst., Ind. Fiscal Policy Inst. (bd. dirs. 1985—, vice chmn. 1988-91, chmn. 1991-94), Ind. C. of C. (taxation com. 1982-94, chmn. 1987-94), Ind. Gas Assn. (treas., asst. sec. 1988—). Office: Vectren PO Box 209 Evansville IN 47702-0209

ELLERMAN, PAIGE L., lawyer; b. Covington, Ky., May 11, 1974; BA, U. Ky., 1995; JD, Salmon P. Chase Coll. Law, 1999. Bar: Ohio 1999, Ky. 2000, Ind. 2001, US Dist. Ct. Southern Dist. Ohio, US Dist. Ct. Eastern Dist. Ky., US Dist. Ct. Western Dist. Ky., US Supreme Ct. Assoc. Taft, Stettinius & Hollister LLP, Cin. Mem. Profl. Women's Resource Grp. Pres. The Yearlings, Inc.; mem., Ann. Support Com. Elizabeth Med. Ctr. Found., chair, Benefactor Drive, 2006—. Named one of Ohio's Rising Stars, Super Lawyers, 2005, 2006. Mem.: Salmon P. Chase Coll. Law Alumni Assn. (pres., Bd. Govenors), FBA, Cin. Bar Assn. Office: Taft Stettinius & Hollister LLP 425 Walnut St Ste 1800 Cincinnati OH 45202-3957 Office Phone: 513-381-2838. Office Fax: 513-381-0205.

ELLINGTON, DONALD E., transportation company executive; CFO Unigroup, Inc., Fenton, Mo. Office: Unigroup Inc One United Dr Fenton MO 63026

ELLINGTON, HOWARD WESLEY, architect; b. Anthony, Kans., Mar. 2, 1938; s. John Wesley and Cressie May (Wilson) E.; m. Nelda Lee Newlin, Sept. 5, 1959; children: Howard Wesley II, Eric John, Craig Alan, Amy Lee. BArch, U. Kans., 1961. Registered architect, Kans., N.Mex., Mo., Ohio. Prin. Howard W. Ellington, AIA, Architect, Wichita, Kans., 1979—; co-owner Gallery Ellington, Wichita, 1978-97. Founding trustee Kans. Cultural Trust, Wichita, 1985—, exec. dir. 1993—; mem. bldg. and grounds com. Wichita Ctr. for Arts, trustee, 1995-97, treas., 1997, acting exec. dir., 1997-98, exec. dir. 1998—; bd. dirs. arts com. Ulrich Mus., Wichita, 1992-97; founding trustee, exec. dir. Allen-Lambe House Found., Wichita, 1990—; mem. Wichita Wayfinding Design Adv. Group, 1997. Editor: The Prairie Print Makers, 1984. Mem. aesthetic rev. team Wichita City Mgrs., 1992-99, Wichita Arts Task Force Com., 2004; trustee Wichita Ctr. for the Arts, 1995-97; bd. dirs. Wichita-Sedgwick County Arts & Humanities Coun., 1996—, Wichita Pub. Arts Adv. Bd., 1996-99, Wichita Art and Design Bd., 1999—; bd. dirs. Frank Lloyd Wright Bldg. Conservancy, 2003-. Recipient Kans. Preservation award, 1993, Pedestal award Wichita Hist. Preservation Bd., 1996. Mem. Friends of Wichita Art Mus., Western Penn. Conservation, Nat. Trust for Hist. Preservation, Chgo. Archtl. Found., Frank Lloyd Wright Home and Studio Found., Birger Sandzen Meml. Gallery. Republican. Episcopalian. Avocation: art collecting.

ELLIOT, BILL, radio personality; b. St. Louis; Student, U. Ill., Southeast Mo. State U., Wash. U., Webster U. Radio host Classic 99, St. Louis. Avocations: photography, movies, music, electronics. Office: Classic 99 85 Founders Ln Saint Louis MO 63105

ELLIOT, DAVID HAWKSLEY, geologist, educator; b. Chilwell, Eng., May 22, 1936; came to U.S., 1966; m. Ann Elliot, 1963. BA, Cambridge U., Eng., 1959; PhD, Birmingham U., 1965. Mem. faculty Ohio State U., Columbus, 1969—, prof. dept. geol. scis., 1979—2008, dir. Byrd Polar Reseach Ctr. (formerly Inst. Polar Studies), 1973-89. Mem. Geol. Soc. Am., Geol. Soc. London, Ohio Acad. Sci., Am. Geophys. Union, Sigma Xi. Office: Ohio State Univ Dept Geol Scis Columbus OH 43210 Business E-Mail: elliot.1@osu.edu.

ELLIOT, TAMMY, newscaster; B Comms., U. Wis., 1991. Anchor WFRV-TV, Green Bay, Wis.; morning co-host Murphy in the Morning WIXX, Green Bay, Wis.; news anchor WISN, Milw. Office: WISN PO Box 402 Milwaukee WI 53201-0402

ELLIOTT, BARBARA JEAN, librarian; b. Bluffton, Ind., Oct. 2, 1927; d. Dale A. and Gwendolyn I. (Long) E.; m. Robert J. Elliott, June 13, 1949; 1 son, Michael Roger. BS with honors, Ind. U., 1949, MLS, 1979. Dir. tech. info. svcs. uranium divsn. Mallinckrodt Chrms., St. Louis, 1949-59; rsch. libr. Petrolite Corp., Webster Groves, Mo., 1961-63; head tech. svcs. St. Frances Coll., Ft. Wayne, Ind., 1974-76; dir. Bluffton-Wells County Pub. Libr., 1976-95, ret., 1995. Pres. Wells County Found., 1996—97, Friends of the Wells County Libr., 1997—2006, Wells County Coun. on Aging, 1996—2006; sec. Family Centered Svcs., 1999—2002; deacon First United Ch. Christ, 1990—93, elder, 1995—98, trustee, 2005—. Mem. ALA, LWV of Ind. (state sec. 1981-83, chmn. health care 1983-89, 3d v.p. 1985-86), Ind. Libr. Assn. (fed. legis. coord.), Ind. Bus. and Profl. Women (pres. 1987-88, dist. dir. 1988-93), Wells County Hist. Soc. (pres. 1997-2000), Bluffton Garden Club (pres.), Bluffton Lions Club (treas., sec.), Foltz Book Club. Home: 6831 SE State Rd 116 Bluffton IN 46714-9420 Personal E-mail: belliott@parlorcity.com.

ELLIOTT, DANIEL ROBERT, JR., manufacturing executive, lawyer; b. Cleve., Mar. 15, 1939; s. Daniel Robert and Elizabeth Marie (Spangler) Elliott; children: Margaret Caldwell, Peter Ryan, Daniel Robert Elliott III, Timothy Reaser. BA, Wesleyan U., 1961; JD, U. Mich., 1964. Bar: N.Y. 1965, Ohio 1970. Assoc. Cravath, Swaine & Moore, NYC, 1964—68, Jones, Day, Reavis & Pogue, Washington, 1969, Cleve., 1969—71, ptnr., 1971—76; v.p. law, gen. counsel White Consol. Industries, Inc., Cleve., 1976—86, sr. v.p., gen. counsel, sec., 1986—. Chmn. adv. commn. Office on Sch. Monitoring and Cmty. Rels., Cleve., 1978—82; chmn. White Consol. Industries, Inc. Found., 1988—96; pres., trustee Greater Cleve. Interch. Coun., 1981—84. Mem.: ABA (minority counsel demontration program, MAPI law coun. I), Assn. Home Appliance Mfrs. (chmn. legal ops. adv. com. 1990—96). Democrat. Office: White Consolidated Industries 20445 Emerald Pkwy Ste 250 Cleveland OH 44135-6013

ELLIOTT, MARK T., state legislator; b. Carthage, Mo., July 18, 1956; m. Denise Ann Severn, 1976; children: Rhett Thomas, Haley Dawn, Hillery Ann. Student, Drake U., Mo. So. State Coll. Current state rep. dist. 127 Mo. Ho. of Reps., former state rep. dist. 126, asst. minority whip, mem. agrl. bus. com., appropriations natural and econ. resource, ethics coms., human rights and resources com. Mem. Farm Bur. Home: 2 S Main St Webb City MO 64870-2326

ELLIOTT, PETER R., retired athletic organization executive; b. Bloomington, Ill., Sept. 29, 1926; s. Joseph Norman and Alice (Marquis) E.; m. s. Joan Connaught Slater, June 14, 1949; children: Bruce Norman, David Lawrence. BA, U. Mich., 1949. Asst. football coach Oreg. State U., 1949-50, U. Okla., 1951-55; head football coach Nebr. U., 1956, U. Calif., Berkeley, 1957-59, U. Ill., 1960-66, U. Miami, Fla., 1973-74, dir. athletics, 1974-78; asst. football coach St. Louis Cardinals, 1978; exec. dir. Pro Football Hall of Fame, Canton, Ohio, 1979-96, ret., 1996. Served with USNR, 1944-45. Named to Mich. Sports Hall of Fame, 1983, Coll. Football Hall of Fame, 1994. Mem. Am. Football Coaches Assn. (Region 8 Coach of Yr. 1958, Region 5 Coach of Yr. 1963). Presbyterian. Home: 3003 Dunbarton Ave NW Canton OH 44708-1818

ELLIOTT, SUSAN SPOEHRER, information technology executive; b. St. Louis, May 4, 1937; d. Charles Henry and Jane Elizabeth (Baur) Spoehrer; m. Howard Elliott Jr., Sept. 2, 1961; children: Kathryn Elliott Love, Elizabeth Elliott Niedringhaus. AB, Smith Coll., 1958. Systems engr. IBM, St. Louis, 1958-66; founder, chmn., CEO, SSE (Sys. Svc. Enterprises, Inc.), St. Louis, 1966—; systems analyst Mo. State Dept. Edn., Jefferson City, Mo., 1967-70; systems coord. Bank of Am. (formerly Boatmen's Nat. Bank), St. Louis, 1979-83. Bd. dirs., exec. com. Mo. Automobile Club; class C dir., dep. chmn. Fed. Res. Bd., St. Louis, 1996-98, chmn., 1999-2000; bd. dirs. Ameren Corp., Angelica Corp., Regional Bus. Coun., St. Louis Regional Commerce and Growth Assn., sec. bd. dirs., 1991-94; bd. dirs. AAA Mo. Trustee, vice-chmn. Mary Inst., St. Louis, 1976-89, Webster U., 1987-96; commr., vice-chmn. St. Louis Civil Svc. Commn., 1985-86, Mo. Lottery Commn., Jefferson City, 1985-87; bd. dirs. St. Louis Zoo, 1990-96, St. Louis Sci. Ctr., 1995-2004, 2006—; mem. pres.'s adv. coun. area coun., tech. com. Girl Scouts U.S.; chair women bus. owner's com. United Way, 1996-97. Mem. Internat. Women's Forum. Republican. Presbyterian. Avocations: golf, exercise. Office: SSE (Sys Svc Enterprises Inc) 77 West Port Plz Ste 500 Saint Louis MO 63146-3126 Home Phone: 314-997-0589; Office Phone: 314-439-4701. Business E-Mail: sselliott@SSEinc.com.

ELLIS, ARTHUR BARON, chemist, educator; b. Lakewood, Ohio, Apr. 4, 1951; s. Nathan and Carolyn Joan (Agulnick) E.; m. Susan Harriet Trebach, Nov. 9, 1975; children: Joshua, Margot. BS, Calif. Inst. Tech., 1973; PhD, MIT, 1977. Asst. prof. chemistry U. Wis., Madison, 1977-82, assoc. prof., 1982-84, prof., 1984-86, Meloche-Bascom prof., 1986—. Editor: Chemistry and Structure at Interfaces, 1986; patentee in field; contbr. articles to profl. jours. Fellow A.P. Sloan Found., 1981, H.I. Romnes fellow U. Wis., 1985, Guggenheim fellow, 1989; recipient Nat. Catalyst Tchg. award Chem. Mfrs. Assn., 1994. Mem. Am. Chem. Soc. (Exxon fellow 1980, chmn. edn., Pimentel award 1997). Jewish. Achievements include creating 1-2-3 levitation kit based on high-temperature superconductors. Office: U Wis Dept Chemistry 1101 University Ave Madison WI 53706-1322

ELLIS, DORSEY DANIEL, JR., lawyer, educator; b. Cape Girardeau, Mo., May 18, 1938; s. Dorsey D. and Anne (Stanaland) E.; m. Sondra Wagner, Dec. 27, 1962; children: Laura Elizabeth, Geoffrey Earl. BA, Maryville Coll., 1960; JD, U. Chgo., 1963; LLD, Maryville Coll., 1998. Bar: N.Y. 1967, U.S. Ct. Appeals (2d cir.) 1967, Iowa 1976, U.S. Ct. Appeals (8th cir.) 1976. Assoc. Cravath, Swaine & Moore, NYC, 1963-68; assoc. prof. U. Iowa, Iowa City, 1968-71, prof., 1971-87, v.p. fin. and univ. svcs., 1984-87, spl. asst. to pres., 1974-75; dean Washington U. Sch. Law, St. Louis, Mo., 1987-98, prof. law, 1998-99; disting. prof. law, 1999—. Vis. mem. sr. common room Mansfield Coll., Oxford U., Eng., 1972-73, 75; vis. prof. law Emory U., Atlanta, 1981-82, Victoria U., New Zealand, 1999; vis. sr. rsch. fellow Jesus Coll. Oxford U., Eng., 1998; bd. dirs. Maryville Coll., 1989-98, 99—, vis. scholar U. Va., 2003. Contbr. articles to profl. jours. Trustee Mo. Hist. Soc., St. Louis, 1995-2000. Nat. Honor scholar U. Chgo., 1960-63; recipient Joseph Henry Beale prize, 1961, Alumni award Maryville Coll., 1988. Mem. ABA, Am. Law Inst., Bar Assn. Metro St. Louis, Mound City Bar Assn., Iowa Bar Assn., AALS Acad. Resource Corps., Order of Coif. Home: 6901 Kingsbury Blvd Saint Louis MO 63130 Office: Box 1120 1 Brookings Dr Saint Louis MO 63130-4862 E-mail: ellis@wulaw.wustl.edu.

ELLIS, JEFFREY ORVILLE, lawyer; b. Parsons, Kans., Mar. 9, 1944; s. Orman Carl Ellis and Esther Jane (Landreth) Ellis-Hett; m. Carol Lynne Byington, Aug. 6, 1966; children: Robert James, Jeffrey Todd. BS, U. Kans., 1966; JD, Washburn U., 1977. Bar: Kans. 1977, U.S. Dist. Ct. Kans. 1977, Mo. 1993. Tchr. Shawnee Mission (Kans.) Dist. Schs., 1966-68; atty., ptnr. Holbrook, Ellis & Heaven, Shawnee Mission, 1977-91, Lathrop & Gage, L.C., Kansas City, Mo., 1991—. Bd. dirs. United Cmty. Svcs., Johnson County, Johnson County Health Partnership, Mid-Am. chpt. MS Soc., United Way of Johnson County; spkr. in field. Author, editor: Handbook for Peer Review, 1992. Chmn. task force Gov.'s Commn. on Health Care, Topeka, 1989-90; mem. Legis.'s Commn. on Health Care Svcs., Topeka, 1987-90; chmn. Kans. Rep. Party, 3d Congl. Dist., 1990-92. Capt. U.S. Army, 1968-74, Vietnam. Mem. Am. Health Lawyers Assn., Kans. Assn. Hosp. Attys. (bd. dirs. 1987-90, pres. 1992-93), Kansas Head Injury Assn. (bd. dirs. 1987-91), Greater Kansas City C. of C. (chmn. task force 1991-93), Rotary (pres. Overland Park 1992). Republican. Episcopalian. Avocations: golf, bicycling. Home: 183 Hillcrest Rd W Shawnee Mission KS 66217-8731 Office: Lathrop & Gage LC 1050 Corporate Woods Overland Park KS 66210-2019

ELLIS, LLOYD H., JR., emergency physician, art historian; b. Denver, Apr. 7, 1936; s. Lloyd Harris and Lura Lou (Wallace) E.; m. Nancy Kay Greenamyre, June 4, 1962 (div. June 1979); children: Peter, Amanda Hunt Thurber; m. Eva Marie Bevan, Sept. 1, 1984; children: Gwendolyn Ruth, David Bevan. Grad., Candiate Sch., 1957; BA, Yale U., New Haven, Conn., 1960, MA, 1961; MD, Case Western Reserve U., Cleve., 1970; MA, Case Western Reserve U., 1990, PhD, 2002. Diplomate Am. Bd. Emergency Medicine. Farm mgr., Hastings, Nebr., 1961-62; vice consul Dept. of State, Lourenco Marques, Mozambique, 1963-64, intelligence analyst Washington, 1965-66; intern, resident Case Western Res. U. Hosps., 1970—74, thoracic surgery resident, 1975—76; dir. emergency dept. Univ. Hosps., Cleve., 1976-84, emergency physician, 1985-94, Emergency Profl. Svcs., Wooster, Ohio, 1995-96, Chardon, Ohio, 1997, Warren, Ohio, 1998. Instr. in surgery Case Western Reserve U., Cleve., 1976-78, asst. prof. surgery, 1979-94; mng. ptnr. Ellis Family Ltd. Partnership, 1992—. Med. dir. Cleve. Emergency Svc., 1976-94; pres. Jeffrey Wallace Ellis Found., Hastings, 1993—; sr. warden Good Shepard, Lyndhurst, Ohio, 1985-86; jr. warden St. Christopher's, Gates Mills, 1998, sr. warden, 1999, Diocesan Coun., 1999-2002; trustee Lura Lou Wallace Ellis Trust, 1992-. 1st Lt. Armor, 1956-59. Recipient Ford scholar Ford Found., New Haven, 1952-55. Mem. Am. Coll. Emergency Physicians, Am. Acad. Emergency Medicine, Rowfant Club. Republican. Episcopalian. Home and Office: 32250 Woodsdale Ln Cleveland OH 44139-1335

ELLIS, MARY LOUISE HELGESON, retired healthcare technology company executive; b. Albert Lea, Minn., May 29, 1943; d. Stanley Orville and Neoma Lois (Guthier) Helgeson; m. David Readinger, Nov. 5, 1994; children from previous marriage: Christopher, Tracy. BS in Pharmacy, U. Iowa, 1966; MA in Pub. Adminstrn., Iowa State U., 1982, postgrad., 1982—83. Faculty Duquesne U., Pitts., 1977; cons. in pharmacy Colville, Wash., 1978—79; dir. pharmacy Mt. Carmel Hosp., Colville, 1978—79; clin. pharmacist Iowa Vets. Home, Marshalltown, 1980—81; instr. Iowa Valley C.C., Marshalltown, 1981—83; dir. Iowa Dept. Substance Abuse, Des Moines, 1983—86, State of Iowa Pub. Health, Iowa Dept. Pub. Health, Des Moines, 1986—90; spl. cons. health affairs Blue Cross/Blue Shield of Iowa, 1990—91; v.p. Blue Cross/Blue Shield of Iowa and S.D., 1991—2000, ret., 2000; pvt. practice cons. in field, 2001—05; v.p. Medicare, Affiliated Computer Svcs., 2005—07, ret., 2007. Chair Iowa Health Data Commn., Des Moines, 1986—90; bd. dirs. Health Policy Corp. Iowa, 1986—90; adj. asst. prof. U. Iowa, Iowa City, 1984—; commd. officer U.S. FDA, 1989—90; mem. alumnae bd. dirs. U. Iowa Coll. of Pharmacy, 1989—; chair Nat. Commn. Accreditation of Ambulance Svcs., 1992—97; commencement spkr. U. Iowa, Coll. Pharmacy, Iowa City, 2003. Mem. Iowa State Bd. Health, 1981—83, v.p., 1982—83; mem. adv. coun. Iowa Valley C.C., 1983—85. Named Alumnae of Yr., U. Iowa Coll. Pharmacy, 2005; recipient Woman of Achievement award, Des Moines YWCA, 1988. Mem.: APHA, Iowa Pub. Health Assn. (bd. dirs., Henry Albert award 1990), Iowa Pharmacists Assn., Pi Sigma Alpha, Phi Kappa Phi, Alpha Xi Delta. Republican. Home: 212 Lariat Ct Spearfish SD 57783

ELLIS, MICHAEL G., state legislator; b. Neenah, Wis., Feb. 21, 1941; married. BS, U. Wis., Oshkosh, 1965. Horse breeder, farmer; mem. Wis. Assembly, Madison, 1970-82; mem. from dist. 19 Wis. Senate, Madison, 1982—, minority leader, 1996-98,99-2000, majority leader, 1993-96, 98-99. Alderman City of Neenah. Office: 1752 County Road Gg Neenah WI 54956-9762 also: State Senate State Capitol Madison WI 53702-0001

ELLISON, EDWIN CHRISTOPHER, surgeon, educator; b. Columbus, Ohio, Jan. 10, 1950; s. Edwin Homer and Molly (Scheeler) E.; m. Mary Pat Borgess, Dec. 23, 1978; children: Jonathan Scott, Eric Christopher. BS, U. Wis., 1972; MD, Med. Coll. Wis., 1976. Diplomate Am. Bd. Surgery. Resident surgery Ohio State U., Columbus, 1976—83, asst. prof. surgery, 1983—90, assoc. prof., 1993—99, prof., 1999—; chief divsn. gen. surgery, bd. dirs. Ohio Digestive Disease Inst., Columbus, 1987—93; chief of staff Ohio State U. Med. Ctr., Columbus, 1999—2000, vice chmn. dept. surgery, 1996—99, 1interim chair surgery, 0999—2000, chmn. surgery, 2000—, assoc. v.p. health sci., 2002—, vice dean clin. affairs, 2002—. Fellow ACS. Office: 327 Means Hall 1654 Upham Dr Columbus OH 43210-1240 Office Phone: 614-293-8701.

ELLSWORTH, BRAD (BRADLEY ELLSWORTH), congressman, former police officer; b. Jasper, Ind., Sept. 11, 1958; m. Beth Ellsworth; 1 child, Andrea. BA in Sociology, Ind. State U., 1981, MA in Criminology, 1993; grad., FBI Nat. Acad., 1995. Dep. sheriff Vanderburgh County, Ind., 1982—98, D.A.R.E officer Ind., sheriff Ind., 1998—2007; mem. US Congress from 8th Ind. dist., 2007—, mem. armed svcs. com., agrl. com., small bus. com. Named Outstanding Alumni, U. Southern Ind. Mem.: Ind. Sheriff's Assn. (pres.), Blue Dog Coalition. Democrat. Roman Catholic. Office: 153 Cannon House Office Bldg Washington DC 20515 also: 101 NW Martin Luther King Blvd Rm 124 Evansville IN 47708 Office Phone: 812-434-6766.

ELLSWORTH, PHOEBE CLEMENCIA, psychology professor; b. Hartford, Conn., Jan. 22, 1944; d. John Stoughton and Edith (Noble) E.; m. Samuel Raymond Gross, Nov. 7, 1979; children: Alexandra Ellsworth, Emma Beth Ellsworth. AB, Harvard U., 1966; PhD, Stanford U., 1970. Asst. prof. Yale U., New Haven, 1971-75, assoc. prof., 1975-79, prof., 1979-81, Stanford U., 1981-87; prof. psychology and law U. Mich., Ann Arbor, 1987—, Frank Murphy Disting. U. Prof. law and psychology, 2003—. Assoc. editor JESP, 1977-80; mem. social sci. rev. com. NIMH, 1973-77, com. on law and social sci. SSRC, 1975-84, rev. panel on law and social sci. SF, 1983-85; mem. rev. bd. Am. Bar Found., 1987-91; bd. trustees Russell Sage Found., 1992-2002. Author: (with others) Emotions in the Human Face: Guidelines for Research And a Review of the Findings, Methods of Research in Social Psychology, Person Perception; contbr. articles to profl. jours. Fellow APA, Am. Acad. Arts and Scis.; mem. Soc. Exptl. Social Psychology, Am. Psychology Law Assn., Internat. Soc. Research on Emotion (charter)., Law and Soc. Assn. Home: 442 Huntington Pl Ann Arbor MI 48104-1800 Office: U Mich Sch Law 970 Legal Rsch 625 S State St Ann Arbor MI 48109-1215 Office Phone: 734-763-5781. E-mail: pce@umich.edu.

ELLWOOD, SCOTT, lawyer; b. Boston, July 8, 1936; s. William Prescott and Doris (Cook) E.; m. Suzanne M. Timble; children: Victoria, William Prescott II, Marjorie. Student, Williams Coll., 1954-56; AB, Eastern Mich. U., 1958; LLB, Harvard U., 1961. Bar: Iowa 1961, Ill. 1961, U.S. Dist. Ct. (no. dist.) Ill., 1961. Assoc. McBride & Baker, Chgo., 1961-67, ptnr., 1968-84, McDermott, Will & Emery, Chgo., 1984-99. Pres. Miller Investment Co., 1973-93, bd. dirs.; pres. SMI Investment Corp., 1978—. Pres., bd. dirs. 110 N Wacker Dr Found., 1974-84, Northfield Found., 1978-84, Leadership Found., 1979-84, Woodbine Found., 1980-84, The Cannon River Found., 1982-84, L.M. McBride Found., 1982-84, Bellarmine Found., 1982-84, Mark Morton Meml. Fund, 1982—. Mem. Iowa Bar Assn., Ill. State Bar Assn., Harvard Law Soc. Ill. (bd. dirs. 1983-98, treas. 1987-88, sec. 1988-89, v.p. 1989-93, pres. 1993-95), Harvard

Club Chgo. (bd. dirs. 1993-95), Monroe Club (bd. dirs. 1988-98), Skokie Country Club (Glencoe, Ill.). Republican. Episcopalian. Home: 1296 Hackberry Ln Winnetka IL 60093-1606 Office: 1296 Hackberry Lane Winnetka IL 60093

ELROD, LINDA DIANE HENRY, lawyer, educator; b. Topeka, Kans., Mar. 6, 1947; d. Lyndus Arthur Henry and Marjorie Jane (Hammel) Allen; divorced; children: Carson Douglas, Bree Elizabeth. BA in English with honors, Washburn U., 1969, JD cum laude, 1971. Bar: Kans. 1972, U.S. Supreme Ct. 2004, cert.: U.S. Supreme Ct. (domestic mediator) 1999. Instr. U. SD, Vermillion, 1970—71; research atty. Kans. Jud. Coun., Topeka, 1972—74; asst. prof. Washburn U., Topeka, 1974—78, assoc. prof., 1978—82, prof. law, 1982—93, disting. prof., 1993—2006, dir. Children and Family Law Ctr., 2001—, Richard S. Righter disting. prof. law, 2006—. Vis. prof. law U. San Diego, Paris Summer Inst., 1988, 90, Washington U. Sch. Law, St. Louis, 1990, 98, summer 1991, 93, Fla. State U. Law Sch., spring, 2000. Author: Kansas Family Law Handbook, 1983, rev. edit., 1990, supplement, 1993, Child Custody Practice and Procedure, 1993, supplements, 1994-2007; co-author: Principles of Family Law, 1999, 6th edit., 2007, Kansas Family Law Guide, 1999, supplements, 2000-06; editor Family Law Quar., 1992—; mem. joint editl. bd. on uniform family law Nat. Conf. Commrs. on Uniform State Laws; reporter Uniform Child Abduction Prevention Act, 2004-06; contbr. articles to profl. jours. Pres. YWCA, Topeka, 1982-83; vice-chair Kans. Commn. on Child Support, 1984-87, Supreme Ct. Commn. on Child Support, 1987—; chair Kans. Cmty. Svc. Orgn., 1986-87; adv. bd. CASA, 1997—; bd. dirs. Appleseed, 2000-05; elder Weestminster Presbyn. Ch., 2006—; mem. permanent jud. commn. Presbytery No. Kans. Recipient Disting. Svc. award Washburn Law Sch. Assn., 1986, Washburn Alumni Assn., 2005; named YWCA Woman of Distinction, 1997; Woman of the Yr. scholar Am. Bus. Women's Assn., 2006. Mem. ABA (coun. family law sect. 1988, sec. 1998, vice-chair, 1999, chair-elect 2000, chair 2000-01, chair Schwab Meml. Grant Implementation 1984-87, co-chair Amicus Curiae com. 1987-92, co-chair pro bono child custody project adv. bd. 2001-2005, steering com. on unmet legal needs of children 2002-2005), Topeka Bar Assn. (sec. 1981-85, v.p. 1985-86, pres. 1986-87), Kans. Child Support Enforcement Assn. (bd. dirs. 1988—, Child Support Hall of Fame 1990), Kans. Bar Assn. (sec.-treas. 1988-89, com. ops. and fin. 1988, pres. family law sect. 1984-86, Disting. Svc. award 1985), NONOSO, Phi Kappa Phi, Phi Alpha Delta Alumni Assn. (justice 1976-77), Phi Beta Delta, Kappa Alpha Theta (pres. alumnae chpt. 1995-97). Presbyterian. Avocations: bridge, reading, quilting. Office: Washburn U Law Sch 17th and College Topeka KS 66621 E-mail: linda.elrod@washburn.edu.

ELROD, STEVEN M., lawyer; b. Chgo., July 12, 1957; BA magna cum laude with spl. honors, Tulane U., 1979; JD, Northwestern U., 1982. Bar: Ill. 1982. Exec. ptnr. Holland & Knight LLP, Chgo., Oakbrook Terrace, Ill., mem. dir. com., chair, fed. polit. action com. Bd. dir. Constitutional Rights Found., Chgo., 1988—, participates in Lawyers in the Classroom; mem., lectr. Nat. Coll. Dist. Attys.; village atty., Northbrook, Ill.; corp. counsel, Highland Park, Ill.; spkr. and lectr. in the field. Contbr. articles to profl. jours. Mem.: Chgo. Bar Assn. (chmn., local govt. com. 1989—90, mem. real property law com.), ABA (mem. state and local govt. law sect.), Lambda Alpha Land Economics Soc. Office: Holland & Knight LLP 131 S Dearborn St 30th Fl Chicago IL 60603 Office Phone: 312-578-6565. Business E-Mail: steven.elrod@hklaw.com.

ELSMAN, JAMES LEONARD, JR., lawyer; b. Kalamazoo, Sept. 10, 1936; s. James Leonard and Dorothy Isabell (Pierce) E.; m. Janice Marie Wilczewski, Aug. 6, 1960; children— Stephanie, James Leonard III. BA, U. Mich., 1958, JD, 1962; postgrad., Harvard Div. Sch., 1958-59. Bar: Mich. 1963. Clk. Mich. Atty. Gen.'s Office, Lansing, 1961; atty. legal dept. Chrysler Corp., Detroit, 1962-64; founding ptnr. Elsman, Young, O'Rourke, Bruno & Bunn, Birmingham, Mich., 1964-72; pvt. practice Elsman Law Firm, Birmingham, 1972—. Owner Radio Sta. WOLY, Battle Creek, Mich. Author: The Seekers, 1962; screenplay, 1976, 200 Candles to Whom?, 1973; contbr. articles to profl. jours.; Composer, 1974, 76; talk show host Citizen's Court, TV-48, Detroit. Mem. Regional Export Expansion Coun., 1966-73, Mich. Ptnrs. for Alliance for Progress, 1969-80; cand. U.S. Senate, 1966, 76, 94, 96, U.S. Ho. of Reps., 1970; internat. evangelist Jesus Christ's Army Ch. Warfare. Rockefeller Bros. Found. fellow Harvard Div. Sch., 1959. Mem. ABA, Am. Soc. Internat. Law, Econ. Club Detroit, World Peace Through Law Center, Full Gospel Businessmen, Bloomfield Open Hunt Club, Pres. Club (U. Mich.), Circumnavigators Club, Naples Bath and Tennis, Rotary. Republican. Mem. Christian Ch. Home: 4811 Burnley Dr Bloomfield Hills MI 48304-3781 Office: 635 Elm St Birmingham MI 48009-6768 Office Phone: 248-645-0750. Personal E-mail: elsmanlawfirm@aol.com.

ELSTON, ROBERT C., medical educator; BA with honors, Cambridge U., Eng., 1955, diploma in agr., 1956, MA, 1957; PhD, Cornell U., 1959; postgrad., U. N.C., 1960. Asst. prof. U. N.C., Chapel Hill, 1960-62, assoc. prof., 1964-69, prof., dir. genetics lab. Sch. Pub. Health, 1969-79; sr. rsch. fellow biometric medicine U. Aberdeen, 1962-64; prof., head dept. biometry & genetics La. State U. Med. Ctr., New Orleans, 1979-95; prof. dept. epidemiology and biostats. Case Western Res. U., Cleve., 1995—. Vis. prof. Yale U., 1965-66, London U., 1967, Cambridge U., 1970, Fourth Mil. Med. Coll. Xian, China, 1987, U. Calif., Irvine, 1988-89; dir. Ctr. Molecular & Human Genetics La. State U. Med. Ctr., 1991-95; mem. internat. adv. bd. Genetics Selection Evolution, 1992-97; exec. com. mem. teaching of stats. in health scis. sect. Am. Stats. Assn., 1992-94, chair, 1993; pres. Internat. Genetic Epidemiology Soc., 1997. Assoc. editor Biometrics, 1967-71, 1984-88, Am. Jour. Human Genetics, 1974-82, Stats. in Medicine, 1997—; editl. bd. Thrombosis Rsch., 1972-76, europsychobiology, 1974-79, Am. Jour. Med. Genetics, 1977-99, Genetic Epidemiology, 1984-96, T. Human Genetics, 2000; contbr. articles to profl. jours. Recipient Career Devel. award NIH, 1966-76, Rsch. Scientist award, NIMH, 1977-79, Hoch award Am. Psychopath. Assn., 1992, Wick R. Williams Meml. award Fox Chase Cancer Ctr., 1994, Leadership award Internat. Genetic Epidemiology Soc., 1995, William Allan Meml. award Am. Soc. Human Genetics, 1996, Merit award IH, 1998, Marvin Zelen Leadership award stats. sci. Sch. Pub. Health, Harvard U.; King George VI Meml. fellow, 1956-57, John Simon Guggenheim Meml. fellow, 1973-74; Coulthurst scholar, 1955-56, Cornell scholar, 1956-59. Fellow Am. Stats. Assn. Office: Case Western Res U Wolstein Rsch Bldg 2103 Cornell Rd Rm 1303 Cleveland OH 44106-7281 Office Phone: 216-368-5630. E-mail: rce@darwin.cwru.edu.

ELY, LAWRENCE ORLO, retired surgeon; b. Guthrie Center, Iowa, Dec. 13, 1919; s. John Ermerson and Luella Mabel (Knapp) E.; m. Dorothy Maxine Jenkins, Aug. 23, 1942; children: Patricia Anne, Lawrence Orlo, Stephen Craig, Bennett Knapp, Carolyn Elizabeth. BA, State U. Iowa, 1942, MD, 1943, MS, 1948, PhD, 1950. Diplomate Am. Bd. Gen. Surgery. Intern Mt. Carmel Mercy Hosp., Detroit, 1943-44; instr. dept. physiology Med. Sch., State U. Iowa, Iowa City, 1946-48, resident, instr. dept. surgery, 1948-52; pvt. practice Des Moines, 1952—85; ret., 1985. Mem. staff Iowa Luth. Hosp., Des Moines, 1952-85, Mercy Med. Ctr., Des Moines, 1952-85, Iowa Meth. Med. Ctr., Des Moines, 1952-86; cons. Iowa Blue Cross-Blue Shield, 1985-86, Iowa Found. for Med. Care, 1985-86. Sect. head United Campaign, Des Moines, 1958-60; mem. Des Moines Opera Bd., 1973—, pres., 1973-78; mem. Health Planning Coun. of Iowa Med. Corp., 1970-78; bd. dirs., pres. Ramsey Home, 1988-94; bd. dirs. Civic Music Assn. Des Moines, 1984-98; mem. steering com. Friends of the Arts, Drake U., Des Moines. Capt. M.C., U.S. Army, 1944-46. Fellow ACS; mem. AMA, Iowa Med. Soc., Polk County Med. Soc. Republican. Mem. Christian Ch. (Disciples Of Christ). Avocation: singing. Home: 3500 Fleur Dr Des Moines IA 50321-2650

EMANUEL, JOHN F., lawyer; BBA in Acctg. with honors, U. Wis., 1975; JD, Stanford U., 1978. Bar: Wis. 1978. Atty. Whyte Hirschboeck Dudek SC, Milw. Bd. dirs. Wiscraft, Inc.-Wis. Enterprises for the Blind, Associated Industries for the Blind, Am. Lung Assn. of the Upper Midwest, Am. Lung Assn. Mem.: State Bar Wis. Office: Whyte Hirschboeck Dudek SC 555 Wells St Ste 1900 Milwaukee WI 53202-3819 Office Phone: 414-978-5430. Business E-Mail: jemanuel@whdlaw.com.

EMANUEL, RAHM, congressman; b. Chgo., Nov. 29, 1959; m. Amy Rule; 3 children. BA in Liberal Arts, Sarah Lawrence Coll., 1981; MA in Speech and Comm., orthwestern U., 1985. Nat. campaign dir. Dem. Congl. Campaign Com., 1988; sr. advisor, chief fundraiser Mayoral Campaign Richard M. Daley, 1989; nat. fin. dir. Clinton/Gore Campaign, 1991—92; asst. to Pres., dir. polit. affairs, dep. dir. comm. The White House, Washington, 1993-99, dir. spl. projects, sr. advisor for policy & strategy, 1995—98; mng. dir. Dresdner Kleinwort Wasserstein, Chgo., 1999—2002; mem. US Congress from 5th Ill. dist., 2003—. Co-author (with Bruce Reed): The Plan: Big Ideas for America, 2006. Recipient Alumni Achievement Citation, Sarah Lawrence Coll., 2001. Democrat. Jewish. Office: US Ho Reps 1319 Longworth House Office Bldg Washington DC 20515-1305 also: Dist Office 3742 W Irving Park Rd Chicago IL 60618

EMERSON, JO ANN H., congresswoman; b. Washington, Sept. 16, 1950; d. Ab and Sylvia Hermann; m. Bill Emerson, 1975 (dec.); children: Victoria, Katharine; m. Ron Gladney, 2000; stepchildren: Elizabeth, Abigail, Alison, Jessica, Stephanie, Sam. BA in Polit. Sci., Ohio Wesleyan U., 1972; DHL (hon.), Westminster Coll., Fulton, Mo. Mem. US Congress from 8th Mo. dist., 1996—, mem. appropriations com., 1998—. Sr. v.p. pub. affairs Am. Ins. Assn.; dir. state rels. and grassroots progs. Nat. Restaurant Assn.; dep. dir. comm. Nat. Rep. Congl. Com. Mem. PEO Womens's Svc. Grp. (FY chpt.), Cape Girardeau; mem. adv. bd. Arneson Inst. Practical Politics and Pub. Affairs, Ohio Wesleyan U.; co-chair Congl. Hunger Ctr.; bd. dirs. Bread for the World; hon. and life trustee Westminster Coll.; bd. dirs. Presbyn. Children's Home, Farmington, Mo. Recipient Rural Housing Legislator of Yr., Nat. Assn. Home Builders, 2001, Schwarz Pharma Leadership in Pharmacy award, Nat. Assn. Chain Drug Stores, 2002, Ground Water Protector award, Nat. Ground Water Assn., 2005. Mem.: Copper Dome Soc., S.E. Mo. State U. Republican. Presbyn. Office: US House Reps 2440 Rayburn Ho Office Bldg Washington DC 20515-2508 Office Phone: 202-225-4404.

EMERSON, ROBERT, state legislator; b. Alpena, Mich., Mar. 23, 1948; s. Melvin Frances and Elaine (Larmer) E.; m. Judy Samelson, 1981; children: Melanie Erica, Phillip James, Erin Samelson. Student, Wayne State U., 1969-69, U. Mich., 1970-71. Legal aide Mich. Ho. Reps., Lansing, 1978-79; mem. Mich. Ho. of Reps. from 81st dist., Lansing, 1980-94, Mich. Ho. of Reps. from 49th dist., Lansing, 1995-98, Mich. Senate from 29th dist., 1998—; mem. appropriations com. Address: PO Box 30036 220 Farnum Bldg Lansing MI 48909 also: PO Box 30036 Lansing MI 48909-7536

EMERT, TIMOTHY RAY, lawyer; b. Independence, Kans., Jan. 29, 1940; s. Walter Glen and Fern LaVon (Braschler) E.; m. BarbaraA. Meitner, Aug. 22, 1964; children: Kate, Jennifer, Babs. BS in Journalism, U. Kans., JD. Bar: Kans. 1965. Ptnr. Scovel, Emert, Heasty and Chubb, Independence. Senator 15th dist. State of Kans.; bd. dirs. Independence C. C. Found., Class LTD; commr. Uniform Laws Conf.; mem. Kans. Judicial Coun.; former bd. dirs. Independence Bd. Edn., Independence Pub. Libr., Kans. State Bd. Edn., Kans. State H.S. Activities Assn., Kans. Commn. on Pub. Broadcasting, William Inge Festival Found., Kans. Commn. on Edn. Restructuring and Accountability Corp. for Change, Kans.; vol. Kans. Advocacy and Protective Svcs.; mem. adv. bd. Manor Nursing Home, Independence. Mem. S.E. Kans. Bar Assn., Kans. Bar Assn., Independence C. of C., Rotary. Republican. Roman Catholic.

EMINETH, GARY, political organization administrator; Mem. Washburn City Coun., ND, ND Dist. 8 Rep. Party, 1983—89; fin. dir. ND Rep. Party, 1985, exec. dir., 1986—89, fin. chair, 2007, chmn., 2007—; owner, operator retail grocery and convenience stores; gen. mgr. Software 4 Retail Solutions; v.p. mktg. Immune Systems; pres. Systemware; CEO, founder SmartEcho. Republican. Office: ND Rep Party 1029 5th St N Bismarck ND 58501*

EMISON, EWING RABB, JR., lawyer; b. Vincennes, Ind., Feb. 3, 1925; s. Ewing and Tuley (Sheperd) E.; m. Kathleen M. Crowley, Nov. 28, 1952; children: Susan, Anne Emison Wishard. AB, DePauw U., 1947; JD, Ind. U., 1950. Bar: Ind. 1950. Of counsel Emison Doolittle Kolb & Roellgen, Vincennes; dep. atty. gen. State of Ind., 1968—69. Lectr. CLE seminars, ABA Nat. Conf. for Diversity, 2002. Contbg. columnist Res Gestae, Ind. State Bar mag., 1987—. Mem. Wabash Valley Interstate Commn., 1959-62, Ind. Flood Control and Water Resources Commn., 1961-65; mem. bd. visitors Ind. Univ. Sch. Law, 1984-87. With USN, 1943-46, 52-53. Mem. ABA (Spirit of Excellence award commn. on racial and ethnic diversity in the profession 2003), Nat. Bar Assn., Ind. State Bar Assn. (bd. of mgrs. 1975-77, chmn. ho. of dels. 1979, pres. 1986-87), Phi Delta Phi, Phi Kappa Psi. Republican. Presbyterian. Avocations: golf, assistance to minority law students, military history. Office: Emison Doolittle Kolb & Roellgen PO Box 215 8th and Busseron Sts Vincennes IN 47591 Office Phone: 812-882-2280. Office Fax: 812-885-2308. Personal E-mail: rabbem@sbcglobal.net. Business E-Mail: emison@emisonlaw.com.

EMLER, JAY SCOTT, state senator, lawyer; b. Denver, May 25, 1949; s. Joseph Frederick and Lois Justine (Scott) E.; m. Lorraine Kristine Pearson, May 30, 1970. BA, Bethany Coll., Kans., 1971; JD, U. Denver, 1976; emergency med. technician degree, Hutchinson Community Coll., Kans., 1979. Bar: Colo. 1977, Kans. 1977. Pvt. practice, Lindsborg, Kans., 1977-90; corp. counsel Kans. Ind. Networks, Inc., Salina, 1990-92, gen. counsel, 1993-96, v.p., gen. counsel, 1996—99; pvt. practice, 2000—; judge Lindsborg Mcpl. Ct., 1978-90; mem. Kans. Senate from dist. 35, Topeka, 2001—. Instr. Barton County (Kans.) Community Coll., 1979; sec. Falun (Kans.) State Bank, 1986-87; mcpl. ct. judges testing and edn. com. Kans. Supreme Ct., 1989—. Adminstr. Lindsborg Vol. Ambulance Corps., 1979-85; chmn. Lindsborg chpt. McPherson County March of Dimes, 1979-86; chmn. Kans. Emergency Med. Svcs. Coun., 1987-88; bd. dirs. Lindsborg Cmty. Hosp., 1981-93, v.p., 1987-91, pres., 1992-93; bd. dirs. Kans. Emergency Med. Svcs., 2005—. Mem. Kans. Bar Assn., McPherson County Bar Assn. (chmn. law day com. 1978, sec.-treas. 1985-86, pres. 1994-95), Kans. Mcpl. Judges Assn. (bd. dirs. 1981-88, pres. 1985-87, chmn. legis. action com. 1983-85), Kans. Supreme Ct. Mcpl. Judges Adv. Com., Kans. Judicial Coun. (mcpl. ct. manual rev. com. 1981-, chmn. 1995-), Kans. Assn. Emergency Med. Svcs. Adminstrs. (sec. 1980-85). Office: 1233 N Main Mcpherson KS 67460

EMMA, EDWARD C., apparel executive; b. 1955; m. Penny Emma; 3 children. BA cum laude, Harvard U. Dir. menswear Jockey Internat., Kenosha, Wis., 1990-93, sr. v.p. retail ops., 1993-95, mng. dir., COO, 1995—. Office: Jockey Internat PO Box 1417 2300 60th St Kenosha WI 53141 Fax: 414-658-3074.

EMMERICH, KAROL DENISE, foundation executive, daylily hybridizer, former retail executive; b. St. Louis, Nov. 21, 1948; d. George Robert and Dorothy (May) Van Houten; m. Richard James, Oct. 18, 1969; 1 son, James Andrew. BA, Northwestern U., 1969; MBA, Stanford U., 1971. Nat. divsn. account officer Bank of Am., San Francisco, 1971-72; fin. analyst Dayton Hudson Corp., Mpls., 1972-73, sr. fin. analyst, 1973-74, mgr. short term financing, 1974-76, asst. treas., 1976-79, treas., 1979—, v.p., 1980-93; exec. fellow U. St. Thomas Grad. Sch. Bus., 1993—; pres. Emmerich Found., Edina, Minn., 1993—. Bd. dirs. Slumberland; co-owner Springwood Gardens. Bd. dirs. Hemerocallis Soc. Minn. Mem. Minn. Women's Econ. Roundtable. Home and Office: 7302 Claredon Dr Edina MN 55439-1722

EMMERT, GILBERT ARTHUR, retired engineering educator; b. Merced, Calif., June 2, 1938; s. Allan V. and Mildred E.; m. Nancy Sue Johnson, June 12, 1964; children: David Allan, Daniel Andrew. BS, U. Calif., Berkeley, 1961; MS, Rensselaer Poly. Inst., Troy, NY, 1964; PhD, Stevens Inst. Tech., Hoboken, NJ, 1968. Analytical engr. United Tech. Corp., East Hartford, Conn., 1961-64; asst. prof. U. Wis., Madison, 1968-72, assoc. prof., 1972-79, prof., 1979—2001, prof. emeritus, 2001—, dept. chair, 1992-01. Contbr. articles to profl. jours. Mem. Am. Physical Soc. Office: U Wis Dept Engring Physics 1500 Engineering Dr Madison WI 53706-1609 E-mail: gaemmert@wisc.ed.

EMMETT, JOHN COLIN, retired inventor, consultant; b. Bradford, Yorkshire, Eng., Apr. 27, 1939; BS, PhD, London U. Former rsch. team leader SmithKline Beecham Corp.; cons. Euromedica Ltd.; freelance cons., 2001—. Co-inventor over 100 patents in field. Named to National Inventors Hall of Fame, 1990. Office: Nat Inventors Hall of Fame 221 S Broadway St Akron OH 44308-1505

EMMONS, JOANNE, state legislator; b. Big Rapids, Mich., Feb. 8, 1934; d. Ray J. and Emma M. (Von Glahn) Gregory; m. John Francis Emmons, June 9, 1956; children: Sarah, Dorothy. BS, Mich. State U., 1956; degree in pub. svc. (hon.), Ferris State U., 1992. Tchr. Mecosta (Mich.) High Sch., 1956-58; treas. Big Rapids Twp., 1976-86; state rep. State of Mich., Lansing, 1987-91; mem. Mich. Senate from 23rd dist., Lansing, 1991—. Chair Mecosta County Rep. Com., 1976-80; vice chair 10th dist. Rep. Com., 1984-86; bd. dirs. Luth. Child and Family Svcs., 1990-96; chair Senate fin. nat. conf. of state legis. exec. com., 1993—. amed Nat. Rep. Legislator of Yr., Nat. Assn. State Legislators, 1993, Legislator of Yr., Mich. Twp. Assn., 1993. Mem. Am. Legion Aux., Mich. Farm Bur. (legis. com. 1970-96), Milk Haulers Assn. (Legislator of Yr. 1995), Omicron Delta Kappa. Avocations: reading, sewing. Home: PO Box 30036 Lansing MI 48909-7536 Office: Mich State Senate State Capitol Lansing MI 48909

EMPSON, JON R., utilities executive; BA in Econs., Carleton Coll.; MBA in Econs., U. Nebr. With mgmt. Omaha (Nebr.) C. of C., 1972-78; mgr. pub. affairs No. atural Gas Co., 1978-80; v.p. adminstrn. No. Plains Natural Gas, 1980-83, Enron Liquid Fuels, 1983-86; v.p. regualtion, fin., adminstrn. Peoples Natural Gas, 1986-87, sr. v.p. adminstr., 1988-93; sr. v.p. gas supply and regulatory svcs. UtiliCorp United, Inc., Kansas City, 1993-96, sr. v.p. regulatory, legis., environ. svcs., 1996—. Office: UtiliCorp United 20 W 9th St Kansas City MO 64105-1704

EMRICK, CHARLES ROBERT, JR., lawyer; b. Lakewood, Ohio, Dec. 19, 1929; s. Charles R. and Mildred (Hart) E.; m. Lizabeth Keating; children—Charles R. III, Caroline K. B.S., Ohio U., 1951, M.S., 1952; J.D., Cleve. State U., 1958. Bar: Ohio 1958. Ptnr. Calfee, Halter & Griswold, Cleve., 1965—2000, ret.; v.p. Transaction Group, Cleve., 2000-; lectr. U. Services Bus. Ctr., John Carroll U., 1970—; former Cleve. dir. Best Sand Co., Fairmount Minerals, Gt. Lakes Lithograph, Clamco Corp., Hunter Mfg. Co., Ken-Mac Metals, S & H Industries, Somerset Techs., Inc., Wedron-Silica Sand Co. Former trustee, br. bd. chmn. YMCA; former officer, trustee Lake Erie Jr. Nature and Sci. Ctr.; former adj. prof. Baldwin Wallace U.; adv. mem. Hartzell Propeller, Lake Erie Elec. Co., Bil-Jac Dog Food Co.; lectr. Chartered Life Underwriters Assn.; former adj. lectr. Case Western Res. U.; trustee Rocky River Pub. Library; trustee, treas. Cleve. Area Devel. Fin. Corp.; trustee Fairview Gen. Hosp., prin. enterprise bd. Cleve. Zool. Soc., Lake Ridge Acad.; former mem. nat. policy adv. com. New Eng. Mut. Life Ins. Co.; mem. vis. com. Cleve. State Law Sch.; mem. vis. com. Cleve. State Law Sch.; bd. dirs. N.E. chpt. Am. Cancer Soc. Mem. Nat. Assn. Corp. Dirs. (sec., bd. dirs.); dir., adv. bd. Great Lakes Fastener LLC, Willow Hill Corp., Austin Capital, Westney Corp., C.E. White; trustee Ohio U. (bd. chair), ohio U. Found. (medal of merit, founders medal, Baker award), O.U. Cutler Scholar bd.; dir. Cleve. Clinic Urology Inst., Cleve. Orch. Planned Giving Comm. Recipient Alumnus of Yr., Ohio U. Coll. Bus. award, also Cleve. State Marshall Sch. Mem. Westwood Country Club (former sec., legal counsel), Union Club, Cleveland Yachting Club, The Clifton Club. Methodist. Office: Calfee Halter & Griswold 800 Superior Ave E Ste 1800 Cleveland OH 44114-2688

END, WILLIAM THOMAS, marketing executive; b. Milw., Oct. 31, 1947; s. Jack Arthur and Cecil (O'Brien) E.; m. Nancy Kolb, June 10, 1969 (div. 1974); 1 child, Laura; m. Elyse Soucy, Feb. 23, 1980; children— Alison, David BA, Boston Coll., 1969; student, U. Vienna, Austria, 1967-68; MBA, Harvard U., 1971. Group product mgr. Gillette Toiletries, Boston, 1971-75; exec. v.p. L.L. Bean, Inc., Freeport, Maine, 1975-90, Lands' End, Inc., Dodgeville, Wis., 1991-92, pres., CEO, 1992-95; chmn., CEO Cornerstone Brands Inc., Portland, Maine, 1995—, also bd. dirs. Bd. dirs. Hannaford Bros. Co., Scarborough, Maine, Ariel, Inc., Augusta, Maine, Cinmar, Cin., Travel Smith, San Rafael, Calif., Internat. Cornerstone Group, The Territory Ahead, Santa Barbara, Calif., Garnet Hill, Franconia, N.H., Ballard Designs, Atlanta. Republican. Roman Catholic. Avocations: hunting, fishing, camping, canoeing, skiing. Home: PO Box 339 34 Castle Rd South Freeport ME 04078 Office: Cornerstone Brands Group Inc 5568 W Chester Rd West Chester OH 45069-2914

ENDRESS, ANTON G., horticulturist, educator; b. Boise, Idaho, Aug. 19, 1945; s. Rudolph George and Ruth Marie (Wallace) E.; m. Nancy C. Statius-Muller; children: Gregory Anton, Bryan Anton. BS in Biology, Duquesne U., 1967; MS in Botany, U. Iowa, 1970, PhD in Botany, 1974. Instr. dept. biology U. Dubuque, Iowa, 1972; postgrad. rsch. biologist I-IV Dept. Biology U. Calif., Riverside, 1974-77, asst. rsch. biologist I-III Statewide Ari Pollution Rsch. Ctr., 1977-80, instr. dept. biology, 1978, 80; assoc. botanist Sect. Botany and Plant Pathology Ill. Natural History Survey, 1980-85, head Sect. Botany and Plant Pathology, 1985-89, asst. chief. for planning, 1989-90, affiliate profl. scientist Ctr. for Biodiversity, 1990—; affiliate prof. dept. agronomy U. Ill., 1986-90, prof., head dept. horticulture, 1990-96, prof. dept. natural resources and environ. scis., 1996—. Mem. numerous coms. Ill. Natural History Survey, 1980-89, U. Ill., 1988—; participant numerous symposiums, confs. and workshops; lectr. in field. Contbr. articles to profl. jours., chpts. to books. Sci. Fair Judge, Champaign Schs., 1985-86, Ill. Jr. Acad. Sci., 1994; mem. Sci. Curriculum Revision Project, Unit 4 (Champaign) Sch. Dist., 1989-90; bd. mem., sec., v.p., coach Champaign Park Dist. Soccer League, 1980-85; founder, bd. mem., coach Little Illini Soccer Club, 1981-90; v.p., bd. dirs. Ctrl. Ill. Soccer League, 1986-90. Grantee USAF Office Sci. Rsch., 1977-80, U. Ill. Campus Rsch. Bd., 1980, Abandoned Mine Land Reclamation Coun., 1982, Ill. Dept. Energy and Natural Resources, 1982, 83, Nat. Arborist Assn., 1989-92, Environ. Protection Trust Fund Commn., 1990, UIUC Campus Rsch. Bd., 1994-95; recipient Amah-LO Nation Y-Indian Guides Achievement award Riverside (Calif.) YMCA, 1979, Disting. Svc. award, 1979, Vol. Svc. award Champaign Park Dist., 1983, Appreciation award Ill. Vegetable Growers Assn., 1995. Mem. AAAS, Am. Inst. Biol. Scis., Am. Soc. Agronomy, Am. Soc. Horticultural Sci., Crop Sci. Soc. Am. (Fred V. Grau Turfgrass Sci. Award Com. 1992—), Minorities in Agriculture and Natural Resources Assn., Soc. Ecological Restoration, Pi Alpha Xi, Gamma Sigma Delta. Office: U Ill 36 Environ and Agr Bldg 36 EASB Madigan Lab MC-637 Urbana IL 61801

ENENBACH, MARK HENRY, community action agency executive, educator; b. Chgo., July 28, 1949; s. Joseph Henry and Antonette Regina (Kasko) E.; children: Joy Elizabeth, Erin Regina; m. Kai Lindquist Bergin, Sept. 28, 1985; 1 child, Faith Marie. BA in Polit. Sci. with honors, Loyola U., Chgo., 1971, MA in Urban Studies with honors, 1973. Cmty. resource specialist Model Cities, Chgo., 1974—79; grad. prof. Govs. State U., Park Forest South, Ill., 1977—89; dir. energy program City of Chgo., 1980—83; prof. St. Augustine's Coll., Chgo., 1981—82; coord. cmty. svcs. Dept. Human Svcs., Chgo., 1984—91; prof. urban planning and pub. adminstrn. DePaul U., Chgo., 1987—; dir. cmty. svcs. block grant programs Cmty. and Econ. Devel. Assn. Cook County, Inc., Chgo., 1992—96, v.p./COO, 1997—; CEO CEDA Neighborhood Devel. Corp., Chgo., 2000—05; pres. Alliance to End Homelessness in Suburban Cook County, 2007—. Mem. adv. bd. City Colls. Chgo., 1984-88; spkr. Nat. Headstart Assn., Washington, 1995; mem. task force Ill. Dept. Commerce and Cmty. Affairs, Springfield, 1996—; spkr. Nat. Assn. Cmty. Action Agys., 1996-2000, Nat. Assn. State Cmty. Svcs. Programs, 2000. Pres. Lincoln Park Interagy. Coun., Chgo., 1986-91; mem. adv. bd. Salvation Army, Chgo., 1987-91. Grad. rsch. fellow Loyola U., 1972-73. Mem. Nat. Assn. Cmty. Action Agys., Ill. Assn. Cmty. Action Agys. Avocations: urban research, writing and travel in over 40 countries. Office: Cmty and Econ Devel Assn 208 S Lasalle St Ste 1900 Chicago IL 60604-1119 Business E-Mail: menebach@cedaorg.net.

ENG, HOLLY S.A., lawyer; b. 1966; BA in English & Econ., St. Cloud State Univ., 1989; JD, Georgetown Univ., 1993. Bar: Minn. 1993. Atty. Dorsey & Whitney LLP, Mpls., 1993—2001, ptnr., labor, employment practice group, 2001—; spl. assignment Mpls. City Atty. Off., 1997. Guardian ad Litem Minn. Guardian ad Litem Program; instr. Univ. St. Thomas Grad. Sch. Bus., 1999—2001. Grantee Nat. Lawyer's Guild Fellowship, Georgetown Univ. Mem.: Minn. Women Lawyers. Office: Dorsey & Whitney LLP Ste 1500 50 S Sixth St Minneapolis MN 55402-1498 Office Phone: 612-343-2164. Office Fax: 612-340-2868. Business E-Mail: eng.holly@dorsey.com.

ENGEL, ALBERT JOSEPH, retired federal judge; b. Lake City, Mich., Mar. 21, 1924; s. Albert Joseph and Bertha (Bielby) Engel; m. Eloise Ruth Bull, Oct. 18, 1952; children: Albert Joseph III, Katherine Ann, James Robert, Mary Elizabeth. Student, U. Md., 1941—42; AB, U. Mich., 1948, LLB, 1950. Bar: Mich. 1951. Administrative asst. to U.S. Rep. Ruth Thompson, 1951; ptnr. firm Engle & Engel, Muskegon, Mich., 1952—67; judge Mich. Circuit Ct., 1967—71; judge U.S. Dist. Ct. Western Dist. Mich., 1971—74; circuit judge U.S. Ct. Appeals, 6th Circuit, Grand Rapids, Mich., 1974—88, chief judge, 1988—89, sr. judge, 1989—2002; ret., 2002. With US Army, 1943—46, ETO. Fellow: Am. Bar Found.; mem.: FBA, ABA, Am. Judicature Soc., Grand Rapids Bar Assn., Cin. Bar Assn., Mich. Bar Assn., Grand Rapids Torch Club, Am. Legion, Phi Delta Phi, Phi Sigma Kappa. Episcopalian.

ENGEL, ANDREW GEORGE, neurologist; b. Budapest, Hungary, July 12, 1930; s. Alexander and Alice Julia (Gluck) E.; m. Nancy Jean Brombacher, Aug. 15, 1958; children: Lloyd William, Andrew George. BSc, McGill U., Montreal, 1953, MD, 1955. Diplomate: Am. Bd. Internal Medicine, Am. Bd. Psychiatry and Neurology. Intern Phila. Gen. Hosp., 1955—56; sr. asst. surgeon, clin. asso. USPHS, NIH, Bethesda, Md., 1958-59; fellow in neuropathology Columbia U., NYC, 1962-64; with Mayo Clinic, Rochester, Minn., 1956-57, 60-62; cons. Rochester, Minn., 1965—; prof. neurology Mayo Med. Sch., Rochester, 1973—, William L. McKnight-3M prof. neurosci., 1984—; disting. investigator Mayo Clinic, 1995—. Mem. sci. adv. com. Muscular Dystrophy Assn., 1973-99; mem. rev. com. NIH, 1977-81. Mem. editl. bd. Neurology, 1973-77, Annals Neurology, 1978-84, 90-95, Muscle and Nerve, 1978-97, 00-, Jour. Neuropathology, 1981-83, 96-00, European Neurology, 1989-2005, Jour. Neuroimmunology, 1991-98, Molecular Neurobiology, 1997—; assoc. editor Neuromuscular Disorders, 1998-2006, Neurology, 2007—; contbr. over 350 articles to med. jours. Served with USPHS, 1957-59. Mem. Am. Acad. Neurology (hon.), Am. Neurol. Assn. (hon.), Am. Soc. Cell Biology, Soc. Neuroscis., AAAS, Inst. of Medicine of Nat. Acad. Sci., 2004, European, German and Spanish Neurologic Assoc. (hon.) Home: 2027 Lenwood Dr SW Rochester MN 55902-1051 Office: Mayo Clinic 200 1st St SW Rochester MN 55905-0002

ENGEL, CHARLES T., lawyer; BBA, Kans. State U., B in Journalism; JD, U. Kans. Ptnr. Cosgrove, Webb & Oman, Topeka. Mem. bd. regents Washburn U., 1997—. Mem.: Washburn Endowment Assn. (trustee), Washburn Alumni Assn. (former pres.). Office: Cosgrove Webb & Oman 1100 Nations Bank Tower 534 S Kansas Ave Topeka KS 66603 Home: 2824 SW Plass Ave Topeka KS 66611

ENGEL, LEO PATRICK, state legislator; b. South Sioux City, Nebr., May 18, 1932; m. Dee Smith, 1952; children: Kathie, Kim, Jeff, Julie, Michael. Student, U. Nebr. Ins. agt. State Farm Ins., South Sioux City, Nebr.; commr. Dakota County, Nebr.; mem. Nebr. Legislature from 17th dist., Lincoln, 1994—. Mem. appropriations com., exec. bd. Nebr. Senate. Mem. South Sioux City Sch. Bd., fin. com. St. Michael's Ch., South Sioux City Comty. Sch. Cardinal Found. Mem. KC (past grand knight, dist. dep.), Mended Hearts (chpt. 41), Sertoma, Toastmasters. Office: Nebr State Senate State Capitol Rm 2011 Lincoln NE 68509

ENGEL, PHILIP L., retired insurance company executive; BA, U. Chgo., 1961, MBA, 1980. With CNA, Chgo., 1961, asst. v.p. corp. planning and control divsn., 1972-76, v.p., 1976-78, v.p. mktg., 1978-90, v.p. sys. and svcs., 1990, exec. v.p. claims, mktg., svcs., sys., underwriting, 1990-92; pres. CNA Ins. Cos., Chgo., 1992-99. Bd. dirs. CNA Fin. Corp., Agy. Mgmt. Svcs., Inc. Vice chmn. bd. trustees Pacific Garden Mission, Chgo.; pres., bd. dirs. Shakespeare Repertory Theater, Chgo. Fellow Soc. Actuaries, Casualty Actuarial Soc.; mem. Am. Acad. Actuaries, Quality Ins. Congress (chmn. bd. dirs.).

ENGEL, SUSAN E., retail executive; Degree in Indsl. and Labor Rels., Cornell U., 1968; MBA, Harvard U., 1976. With mgmt. and mktg. dept. J.C. Penney, NYC, 1968-77; v.p. Booz, Allen and Hamilton, 1977-91; pres., CEO Champion Products, Inc., 1991-94; pres., COO Dept. 56, Inc., Eden Prairie, Minn., 1994-96, CEO, 1996—, also bd. dirs. Bd. dirs. Wells Fargo & Co., SuperValu Inc. Mem. pres. coun. Cornell Women, Cornell U.; bd. overseers Carlson Sch. Mgmt.; bd. dirs. Mpls. Guthrie Theater. Mem. Mpls. LWV. Avocations: sailing, tennis, collecting antiques, classical music and theater. Office: Dept 56 Inc One Village Pl 6436 City West Pkwy Eden Prairie MN 55344-7728

ENGELBREIT, MARY, art licensing entrepreneur; b. St. Louis, 1952; m. Phil Delano, 1977; 2 children. Illustrator greeting card cos., 1983; founder, pres. Mary Engelbreit Studios Retail and Pub. Cos., St. Louis, 1983—; founder, head The Mary Engelbreit Store; founder, creator Mary Engelbreit's Home Companion mag., 1996—. Illustrator The Snow Queen, 1993, The Night Before Christmas, 2001. Office Phone: 314-726-5646.

ENGELHARDT, IRL F., coal company executive; b. Oct. 19, 1946; m. Suzanne C.; children: Joel, Erin, Evan. BS in Acctg., U. Ill., 1968; MBA, So. Ill. U., 1971. From mem. staff to pres., CEO Peabody Energy, St. Louis, 1979-90, pres., CEO, 1990—98, chmn., CEO, 1998—2005, chmn., 2006—07. Bd. dir. Williams Cos.; bd. dir. Fed. Reserve Bank of St. Louis, dep. chmn. 2006. Mem. Nat. Mining Assn. (bd. dirs., chmn. 1995-96), Nat. Coal Assn. (chmn. 1995-96), Internat. Energy Agy. (coal industry adv. bd., chmn., special com. mem.), Nat. Assn. Mfrs. (bd. dirs.), Coal Utilization Rsch Group (co-chmn.), Coal Based Stockholders Group (co-chmn.), St. Louis Arts and Edn. Council, St. Louis Area Council (exec. bd.), Boy Scouts of Am.

ENGELHARDT, THOMAS ALEXANDER, editorial cartoonist; b. St. Louis, Dec. 29, 1930; s. Alexander Frederick and Gertrude Dolores (Derby) E.; m. Katherine Agnes McCue, June 25, 1960; children— Marybeth, Carol Marie, Christine Leigh, Mark Thomas. Student, Denver U., 1950-51, Ruskin Sch. Fine Arts, Oxford U., Eng., 1954-56, Sch. Visual Arts, NYC, 1957. Free-lance cartoonist, comml. artist, N.Y.C., 1957-60, Cleve., 1961-62, asst. editl. cartoonist, Newspaper Enterprise Assn., Cleve., 1960-61; editl. cartoonist St. Louis Post-Dispatch, 1962-97; freelance cartoonist, 1998—; one-man exhbns. of cartoons at Fontbonne Coll. Art Gallery, St. Louis, 1972, Old Courthouse (Jefferson Nat. Meml.), St. Louis, 1981, Mark Twain Bank, Frontenac, Mo., 1989; group exhbns. Washington U., St. Louis, 2000, Nat. Press Club, Washington, 2001, St. Louis Artists Guild, 2001. Served with USAF, 1951-53. Recipient Ethical Humanist of Yr. award St. Louis Ethical Soc., 1986, Kay and Leo Drey Environ. Leadership award Mo. Coalition for Environment, 1999. Roman Catholic. Office: 7830 Lafon Pl Saint Louis MO 63130-3805 Home Phone: 314-863-1165; Office Phone: 314-863-1165. Personal E-mail: tomeng@sbcglobal.net.

ENGELS, THOMAS JOSEPH, sales executive; b. New Orleans, May 24, 1958; s. Ronald Henry and Sally (Jacobsen) E.; m. Tamara Lewis Engels, May 29, 1982; children: Kristen, Danielle. BS in Gen. Mgmt., Purdue U., 1980. Sales rep. Johnson & Johnson, New Brunswick, N.J., 1980-82, mgr., 1982-83; dist. sales mgr. Pepsi Cola U.S.A., Somers, N.Y., 1983-87; regional sales mgr. Rich Sea Pak Corp., St. Simons Island, Ga., 1988-89; cen. regional mgr. food svc. div. Sara Lee Bakery, Chgo., 1990-93; area mgr. Ctrl. Zone Sara Lee Bakery Food Svc., 1993-94, divsn. promotion mgr. East, 1995-96; no. zone mgr. food svc. Land O'Lakes, Inc., 1996-2000, dir. sales No. U.S.; v.p. sales, food svc. Aurora Foods Co., St. Louis, 2000—04; ea. divsn. mgr. Perdue Farm, Inc., 2004—06; v.p. sales Cuisine Innovations, Lakewood, NJ, 2006—. Roman Catholic. Avocations: tri-athlons, golf, basketball, coaching soccer. Office Phone: 317-823-2995. Personal E-mail: irun4fun8@aol.com.

ENGH, N. ROLF (ROLF ENGH), lawyer; b. Scotts Bluff, Nebr., Oct. 26, 1953; s. N.A. and Dolcie (Cuplin) E.; m. Nancy A. Carroll, Jan. 17, 1986. BA, U. Minn., 1976; JD cum laude, William Mitchell Coll., 1982. Bar: Minn. 1982. Grain merchandiser Cook Industries, Memphis, 1976-78; assoc. corp. dept. Lindquist & Vennum, Mpls., 1982-86, ptnr. corp. dept., 1986-93; gen. counsel The Valspar Corp., Mpls., 1993—. Trustee Breck Sch. Mem. ABA, Minn. State Bar Assn., Hennepin County Bar Assn., Mpls. Club, Westminster Church, Phi Beta Kappa. Home: 1928 Humboldt Ave S Minneapolis MN 55403-2815 Office: The Valspar Corp 1101 S 3rd St Minneapolis MN 55415-1259 Business E-Mail: rengh@valspar.com.

ENGLAND, ANTHONY WAYNE, engineering and science educator, dean; b. Indpls., May 15, 1942; s. Herman U. and Betty (Steel) E.; m. Kathleen Ann Kreutz, Aug. 31, 1962. SB, MIT, 1965, PhD, 1970, SM, 1965. With Texaco Co., 1962; field geologist Ind. U., 1963; scientist-astronaut NASA, 1967-72, 79-88; with U.S. Geol. Survey, 1972-79; crewmember on Spacelab 2, July, 1985; adj. prof. Rice U., Houston, 1987-88; prof. elec. engring. and computer sci. U. Mich., Ann Arbor, 1988—, prof. atmospheric, oceanic and space sci., 1989—, assoc. dean Rackham Grad. Sch., 1995-98, assoc. dean Coll. Engring., 2004—. Mem. space studies bd. NRC, 1992-98. Assoc. editor Jour. Geophys. Rsch. Recipient Antarctic medal, Spaceflight medal NASA, Spaceflight award Am. Astron. Soc., Outstanding Scientific Achievement medal NASA. Fellow IEEE; mem. Am. Geophys. Union. Home: 7949 Ridgeway Ct Dexter MI 48130-9700 Office: U Mich Dept Elec Engring-Comp Sci Ann Arbor MI 48109-2122

ENGLAND, JOSEPH WALKER, heavy equipment manufacturing company executive; b. Moline, Ill., June 21, 1940; s. Stanley B. and Mary (Walker) E.; m. Mary Jo Richter, Oct. 26, 1963; children: Kathleen, Amy, Sarah. BS, U. Ill., 1962. With Deere & Co., Moline, 1963—, sr. v.p. worldwide parts and corp. adminstrn., 1994—. Bd. dirs. 1st Midwest Bank Corp.; chmn. Moline Found., 1987—. Bd. dirs. United Way, 1978-82, pres., 1980, 81. Served with AUS, 1963. Mem. AICPA, Ill. Soc. CPAs, Nat. Assn. Accountants, U. Ill. Alumni Assn. (dir. 1977), Nat. Assn. Mfrs. (bd. dirs. 1991—). Clubs: Short Hills Country. Home: 1105 24th Ave Moline IL 61265-4721 Office: Deere & Co John Deere Rd Moline IL 61265-8098

ENGLE, DONALD EDWARD, retired rail transportation executive, lawyer; b. St. Paul, Mar. 5, 1927; s. Merlin Edward and Edna May (Berger) E.; m. Nancy Ruth Frank, Mar. 18, 1950; children: David Edward, Daniel Thomas, Nancy Ann. BA, Macalester Coll., St. Paul, 1948; JD, U. Minn., Mpls., 1952, BSL., 1950. Bar: Minn. 1952, Mo. 1972. Law clk., spl. atty. Atty. Gen.'s Office Minn., 1951-52; atty., asst. gen. solicitor, asst. gen. counsel G.N. Ry., St. Paul, 1953-70; asso. gen. counsel Burlington No., Inc., 1970-72; v.p., gen. counsel S.L.-S.F. Ry., St. Louis, 1972-80, v.p. law, sec., 1979-80; v.p. law Burlington No., Inc., St. Paul, 1980-81, Burlington No. Ry., St. Paul, 1981-83, sr. v.p. law and govt. affairs, sec., 1983-86, also dir.; ptnr., chmn., chief exec. officer Oppenheimer, Wolff & Donnelly, 1986-93, chmn., chief exec. officer, 1991-93, of counsel, 1993—2004; ret., 2004. Continuing edn. lectr. U. Minn.; bd. dirs. Regions Hosp. Found., 2001—05. Bd. dirs. YMCA, St. Paul, 1981-84, ARC, 1981-84, Boy Scouts Am., 1991-2005. Mem. ABA, Mo. Bar Assn., Minn. Bar Assn., Ramsey County Bar Assn., St. Louis Bar Assn., St. Paul C. of C. (bd. dirs. 1994-97), North Oaks Golf Club, Phi Delta Phi. Republican. Lutheran. Home: 5919 Centerville Rd Apt 208 North Oaks MN 55127 Home Phone: 651-762-6574. Personal E-mail: engleone@aol.com.

ENGLEHART, HUD, communications company executive; Grad., U. Mich., 1969. V.p. corp. comms. Lockheed Corp., 1988-90; various positions Hill and Knowlton, Pitts., 1982-96, former creative dir., global account mgr. Kraft Gen. Foods Chgo., former exec. mng. dir.; pres., COO KemperLesnik Comms., Chgo. Pres. bd. trustees Chgo. Victory Gardens Theater; bd. dirs. Chgo. Internat. Film Festival; mem. devel. bd. U. Mich. Bus. Sch. Mem. PRSA, Arthur Page Soc. Office: KemperLesnik Comms 455 N Cityfront Pl Dr #1500 Chicago IL 60611

ENGLISH, FLOYD LEROY, telecommunications industry executive; b. Nicholas, Calif., June 10, 1934; s. Elvan L. and Louise (Corliss) E.; children from previous marriage: children: Roxane, Darryl; m. Elaine Ewell, July 3, 1981; 1 child, Christine. AB in Physics, Calif. State U., Chico, 1959; MS in Physics, Ariz. State U., 1962, PhD in Physics, 1965; DSc (hon.), Calif. State U., Chico, 2005. Divsn. supr. Sandia Labs., Albuquerque, 1965-73; gen. mgr. integrated cirs. divsn. Rockwell Internat.-Collins, Newport Beach, Calif., 1973—75; pres. Darcom, Albuquerque, 1975-79; cons in energy mgmt. and acquisitions Albuquerque, 1980-81; v.p. U.S. ops. Andrew Corp., Orland Park, Ill., 1981-82, pres., 1981-82, COO, 1981-82, CEO, 1983-92, also bd. dirs., 1982—, chmn. bd. dirs., pres., CEO, 1992—2000, 2000—01, chmn., bd. dirs., CEO, 2001—02, chmn. bd. dirs., 2002—04, chmn. emeritus, 2004. Contbr. articles to profl. jours. 1st lt. U.S. Army, 1954-57; capt. Res., 1957-69 Mem.: IEEE, Internat. Engring. Consortium (bd. dirs. 1984—2002), Exec. Club Chgo. (bd. dirs. 1983—2004). Republican. Presbyterian. Home Phone: 956-772-9511. Personal E-mail: eee81@comcast.net.

ENGLISH, JOHN DWIGHT, lawyer; b. Evanston, Ill., Mar. 28, 1949; s. John Francis English and Mary Faye (Taylor) Butler; m. Claranne Kay Lundeen, Apr. 22, 1972; children: Jennifer A., Katharine V., Margaret E. BA, Drake U., 1971; JD, Loyola U., 1976. Bar: Ill. 1976, U.S. Dist. Ct. (no. dist.) Ill. 1976, U.S. Tax Ct. 1977. Assoc. Bentley DuCanto Silvestri & Forkins, Chgo., 1976-79; ptnr. Silvestri Mahoney English & Zdeb, Chgo., 1979-81; assoc. Coffield Ungaretti Harris & Slavin, Chgo., 1981-83; ptnr. Ungaretti & Harris, Chgo., 1983—. Instr. estate planning Loyola U., Chgo., 1982-87; instr. Ill. Inst. Continuing Edn. Estate Planning Short Course, 1998, 2001. Bd. dirs. Prince of Peace Luth. Sch., Chgo., 1977-83, Bethesda Home for the Aged, Chgo., 1981-89, 2000-03, Luth. Family Mission, Chgo., 1985-91; alderman Park Ridge (Ill.) City Coun., 1991-95; pres. congregation coun. St. Luke's Luth. Ch., Park Ridge, 2000-03, 05-06. Mem.: Chgo. Bar Assn. (former chmn. divsn. II probate practice com.), Ill. State Bar Assn., Phi Beta Kappa. Lutheran. Home: 631 Wisner St Park Ridge IL 60068-3428 Office: Ungaretti & Harris 3500 Three 1st Nat Bank Plz Chicago IL 60602 Office Phone: 312-977-4401. Business E-Mail: jdenglish@uhlaw.com.

ENGLISH, RAY, library administrator; b. Brevard, NC, Dec. 11, 1946; s. Daniel Leon and Lois (Dorsett) E.; m. Allison Scott Ricker, Oct. 19, 1985; children: John, Michael. AB with honors in German, Davidson Coll., 1969; MA in German Lit., U. N.C., 1971, MSLS, 1977, PhD, 1978. Teaching asst. German dept. U. .C., Chapel Hill, 1970-73, 74-75, rsch. asst., 1976; reference libr. Alderman Libr. U.Va., Charlottesville, Va., 1977-79; head reference libr. Oberlin (Ohio) Coll. Libr., 1979-89, assoc. dir., 1986-90; dir. librs. Oberlin (Ohio) Coll., 1990—, acad. advisor, 1980—. Lectr. in German, 1986—2000; vis. lectr. Sch. Libr. Sci., U. N.C., Chapel Hill, 1981; steering com. Scholarly Pub. and Acad. Resources Coalition, 1999—, chair, 2006—; spkr. in field. Mem. editl. bd. Portal: Libraries and the Academy; contbr. articles to profl. jours. German Acad. Exchange Svc. fellow, 1973-74. Mem.: ALA, Acad. Libr. Assn. Ohio, Libr. Adminstrn. and Mgmt. Assn., Assn. Coll. and Rsch. Librs. (bd. dirs., exec. com. 1996—98, chair scholarly comm. com. 2002—06, Acad. Rsch. Libr. of the Yr. 2006). Home: 83 S Cedar St Oberlin OH 44074-1559 Office: Oberlin Coll Library 148 W College St Oberlin OH 44074-1575 Office Phone: 440-775-8287. E-mail: ray.english@oberlin.edu.

ENGLISH, ROBERT BRADFORD, marshal; b. Jefferson City, Mo. BS in Criminal Justice, Lincoln U., 1982; MPA, U. Mo., 1984. Residential juvenile counselor Cole County Juvenile Ctr., Jefferson City, Mo., 1972-74; patrolman Jefferson City Police Dept., 1975-76, detective, 1976-78; comdr. Mo. Capitol Police, Jefferson City, 1978-79, police chief, 1979-94; marshal U.S. Marshal Svc., Kansas City, Mo., 1994—. Chmn. ct. security com. U.S. Dist. Ct. (we. dist.) Mo., Kansas City, 1995—; mem. dirs. adv. and leadership coun. U.S. Marshall Svc., 1996—. Chmn. bd. dirs. Capitol Area Cmty. Svc. Agy., Jefferson City, 1994. Named Statesman of Month, News Tribune Co., 1994. Mem. Internat. Assn. Chiefs of Police (life), Masons. Democrat. Avocations: golf, scuba diving, walking, weightlifting. Office: US Marshal Svc 400 E 9th St Ste 3740 Kansas City MO 64106-2635

ENK, SCOTT, editor, researcher, activist; b. Milw., Apr. 9, 1958; s. Kenneth and Audrey (Szymanowski) E. BA in Mass Comm. and Econs. with distinction, U. Wis., Milw., 1981. Pers. asst. Fleet Mortgage Corp., Milw., 1982, foreclosure asst., 1983, publs. designer, editor, writer, 1983-87; documentation editor, writer, tester Aardvark/McGraw-Hill, Milw., 1987-88; rsch./quality assurance editor Gareth Stevens, Inc., Milw., 1988-91; sr. editor Southea. Wis. Regional Planning Commn., Waukesha, 1992—2001; claims examiner, rschr. U.S. Dept. Vets. Affairs, Milw., 2002; proofreader, editor The Relizon Co., New Berlin, Wis., 2003; copy editor Reiman Media Group, Greendale, Wis., 2003—. Guest lectr. silent film history and women's roles in silent film Alverno Coll., Milw., 1991-93, 96, 2000-01, in English style and grammar, mass comm. ethics and values, and job hunting skills, 2000—, guest lectr. Pewaukee Area (Wis.) Hist. Soc., 1997; spkr., presenter in field. Editor, writer, rschr. mags., reports, newsletters, manuals, children's books; contbr. articles, essays and editls. to various publs. Founder, pres. Greater Milw. chpt. Hear My Voice/Protecting Our Nation's Children, 1993—; mem. Milwaukee County Hist. Soc., 1984—, ACLU, 1987—; former officer Wis. Phi Beta Kappa Found., Inc.; sec. West Suburban Milw. chpt. NOW, 1984-89, pres., 1987—, newsletter editor, 1989-, chair fundraising com., 1983-84; sec. De Quav, Inc., 2002-; bd. dirs. Friends of U. Wis. Golda Meir Libr., Milw., 2004—, chair comm. com., 2004-05; advocate A Child's Best Interest, 2008— Recipient awards in recognition of children's rights work United Foster Parents Assn. Greater Milw., 1995, Hear My Voice/Protecting Our Nation's Children, 1998; Milw. Soc. Profl. Journalists, 1979, Harry J. Grant Found., Milw., 1979-81; nominee Wis. NOW Feminist of Yr., 1998. Mem. NOW (chpt. rep. to state coun.), U. Wis. Milw. Alumni Assn. (Coll. Letters and Sci. scholar 1979), Mensa, Phi Beta Kappa (bd. dirs. Greater Milw. Assn. 1984—, sec. 1985-90, 2004, pres. 1990-2001, pres. emeritus 2005—, del. to nat. triennial coun. 1988-2001, recipient Svc. award 2000), Intertel Triple Nine Soc., Phi Kappa Phi, Phi Alpha Theta, Sigma Epsilon Sigma, Phi Eta Sigma. Avocations: computers/internet, silent films and other media, political and social history, chess, architecture. Home: 9543 W Forest Home Ave Apt 7 Hales Corners WI 53130-1655 Personal E-mail: senk8105@sbcglobal.net.

ENLOW, DONALD HUGH, retired anatomist, dean; b. Mosquero, N.Mex., Jan. 22, 1927; s. Donald Carter and Martie Blairene (Albertson) E.; m. Martha Ruth McKnight, Sept. 3, 1945; 1 child, Sharon Lynn. BS, U. Houston, 1949, MS, 1951; PhD, Tex. A&M U., 1955. Instr. biology U. Houston, 1949-51; asst. prof. biology West Tex. State U., 1955-56; instr. anatomy Med. Coll. S.C., 1956-57; asst. prof. U. Mich. Med. Sch., Ann Arbor, 1957-62, assoc. prof., 1962-67, prof. anatomy, 1969-72; dir. phys. growth program Center for Human Growth and Devel., 1966-72; prof., chmn. dept. anatomy W.Va. U. Sch. Medicine, Morgantown, 1972-77; Thomas Hill disting. prof., chmn. dept. orthodontics Case Western Res. Sch. Dentistry, Cleve., 1977-89, prof. emeritus, 1989—, asst. dean for rsch. and grad. studies, 1977-85, acting dean, 1983-86. Adj. prof. U. NC, 1992—; lectr. in field in 32 fgn. countries. Author: Principles of Bone Remodeling, 1963, The Human Face, 1968, Handbook of Facial Growth, 1975, 3d edit., 1990, Essentials of Facial Growth, 1996; contbr. chpts. to 30 books, numerous articles to profl. jours. Served with reserves USCG, 1945—46. Recipient Outstanding Research award Tex. Acad. Sci., 1952, Dewel award, 2006, Thomas Graber award, 2006. Fellow Royal Soc. Medicine, Am. Assn. Anatomists, Internat. Assn. Dental Research; hon. mem. Am. Assn. Orthodontists (Mershon Meml. lectr. 1968, Spl. Merit award 1969, award for outstanding contbns. to orthodontia, 1984, Thomas Grober award 2003), Gt. Lakes Orthodontic Soc., Cleve. Dental Soc., Cleve. Orthodontic Soc., Omicron Kappa Upsilon. Republican. Methodist. Home: 4940 Monarch Rd Milton WI 53563 Personal E-mail: donnlo@charter.net.

ENNEST, JOHN WILLIAM, bank executive; b. Bad Axe, Mich., Oct. 14, 1942; s. William J. and Margaret J. (Kritzman) E.; m. Mary Ellen Sweeney, Jan. 27, 1968 (dec. 1995); children: John W., James G., Anne M.; m. Cheryll Ann Pease, Dec. 1997. BS, U. Detroit, 1964; MBA, Mich. State U., 1965. Pres.'s exec. Exch. Program, Washington, 1979-80; v.p. Nat. Bank Detroit, 1973-81, NBD Bank Corp., Detroit, 1981-83; exec. v.p., chief fin. officer Citizens Bank, Flint, Mich., 1983-85; chief fin. officer, treas. Citizens Banking Corp., Flint, Mich., 1985-87; sr. exec. v.p., chief oper. officer Citizens Bank, Flint, Mich., 1985-87, pres., chief exec. officer, 1987-91; vice chmn., chief oper. officer Citizens Banking Corp., Flint, Mich., 1991—; chmn. bd., CEO Comml. Nat. Bank of Berwyn, Ill., 1992—; also bd. dirs. Citizens Bank, Citizens Banking Corp., Flint, Mich. Bd. dirs. Citizens Bank, 1987-91, Citizens Banking Corp., 1991, Second Nat. Bank, Saginaw, 1991, Comml. Nat. Bank, Berwyn, Ill., 1991. Author: (with others) Changing World of Banking, 1974. Chmn. bd. United Way, Flint, 1989, C. of C., Flint, 1991; dir. Baker Coll. Recipient cert. of merit USDA, 1980. Mem. Fin. Execs. Inst., Detroit Athletic Club, Warwick Hills Club. Republican. Roman Catholic.

ENOS, PAUL, geologist, educator; b. Topeka, July 25, 1934; s. Allen Mason and Marjorie V. (Newell) E.; m. Carol Rae Curt, July 5, 1958; children: Curt Alan, Mischa Enos Martin, Kevin Christopher, Heather Enos Wohlert. BS, U. Kans., 1956; postgrad., U. Tübingen, W.Ger., 1956-57; MS, Stanford U., 1961; PhD, Yale U., 1965. Geologist Shell Devel. Co., Coral Gables, Fla., 1964-68, research geologist Houston, 1968-70; from assoc. prof. to prof. geology SUNY, Binghamton, 1970-82; Haas Disting. prof. geology U. Kans., Lawrence, 1982-2000, prof., 2001—03, Disting. prof. emeritus, 2003—. Cons. to industry; sedimentologist Ocean Drilling, 1975, 92; rsch. vis. Oxford U., 1989, U. Erlangen, Germany, 1995-96; fgn. scientist Ministry Geology, People's Republic China, 1988; with Global Sedimentary Geology Project, 1988—, co-convener Working Group 4, 1992-2000. Co-author: Quaternary Sedimentation of South Florida, 1977, Mid-Cretaceous, Mexico, 1983, Triassic Evolution of Yangtze Platform, 2006; editor: Field Trips: South-Central New York, 1981, Deep-Water Carbonates, 1977; contbr. articles to sci. jours. Served to 1st lt. C.E., U.S. Army, 1957-59. Recipient Pettijohn medal Sedimentology, 2001, Excellence in Tchg. award, Geology Dept., 2003; fellow U. Liverpool, 1976-77, NSF, 1959-62, Fulbright, 1956-57; Summerfield scholar, 1954-56. Mem. Soc. Sedimentary Geology (assoc. editor 1976-80, 83-87, Best Paper award 1969), Internat. Assn. Sedimentologists (assoc. editor 1983-87), Am. Assn. Petroleum Geologists, Geol. Soc. Am., Omicron Delta Kappa. Avocations: photography, diving, bicycling, history. Office: U Kans Dept Geology Lawrence KS 66045-2124 Home: 1825 Castle Pine Court Lawrence KS 66047-2017 Office Phone: 785-864-2744.

ENROTH-CUGELL, CHRISTINA ALMA ELISABETH, neurophysiologist, educator; b. Helsingfors, Finland, Aug. 27, 1919; came to US, 1956, naturalized, 1962; d. Emil and Maja (Syren) Enroth; m. David W. Cugell, Sept. 5, 1955. MD, Karolinska Inst., 1948, PhD, 1952; Hon. Doctors Degree, U. Helsinki, Finland, 1994. Resident in ophthalmology Karolinska Sjukhuset, 1949-52; intern Passavant Meml. Hosp., 1956-57; with Northwestern U., Evanston, Ill., 1959-91, prof. emeritus, 1991—, prof. dept. neurobiology and physiology and dept. biomed. engring., 1974—78; mem. vision rsch. program com. Nat. Eye Inst., 1974-78, mem. nat. adv. eye coun., 1980-84. Contbr. articles to profl. jours. Recipient Ludwig von Sallman award Internat. Assn. Rsch. in Vision and Ophthalmology, 1982. Fellow Am. Inst. Med. and Biol. Engring., Am. Acad. Arts and Sci.; mem. Am. Assn. Rsch. in Vision and Ophthalmology (co-recipient Friedenwald award 1983, recipient W.H. Helmerich III award 1992), Soc. Neurosci., Am. Physiol. Soc., Physiol. Soc. (U.K.) Office: Northwestern U McCormick Sch Engring Technl Inst 2145 Sheridan Rd Evanston IL 60208-0834 Business E-Mail: enroth@northwestern.edu.

ENSIGN, JERALD C., bacteriology educator; BA, Brigham Young U., 1955; PhD, U. So. Calif., 1963. Postdoc rschr. U. Ill., Urbana, 1963; prof. dept. bacteriology U. Wis., Madison, 1990—94, prof. emeritus, 1994—. Recipient Disting. Tchr. award Carski Found., 1992. Office: Univ Wis Dept Bacteriology 114 E Fred Hall 1550 Linden Dr Madison WI 53706-1521

ENSLEN, RICHARD ALAN, federal judge; b. Kalamazoo, May 28, 1931; s. Ehrman Thrasher and Pauline Mabel (Dragoo) E.; m. Pamela Gayle Chapman, Nov. 2, 1985; children: David, Susan, Sandra, Thomas, Janet, Joseph, Gennady. Student, Kalamazoo Coll., 1949-51, Western Mich. U., 1955; LL.B., Wayne State U., 1958; LL.M., U. Va., 1986; Doctorate (hon.), Western Mich. U., 2006. Bar: Mich. 1958, U.S. Dist. Ct. (we. dist.) Mich. 1960, U.S. Ct. Appeals (6th cir.) 1971, U.S. Ct. Appeals (4th cir.) 1975, U.S. Supreme Ct 1975. Mem. firm Stratton, Wise, Early & Starbuck, Kalamazoo, 1958-60, Bauckham & Enslen, Kalamazoo, 1960-64, Howard & Howard, Kalamazoo, 1970-76, Enslen & Schma, Kalamazoo, 1977-79; dir. Peace Corps, Costa Rica, 1965-67; judge Mich. Dist. Ct., 1968-70, US Dist. Ct. (we. dist.) Mich., Kalamazoo, 1979—2005, chief judge, 1995—2001, sr. judge, 2005—. Mem. faculty Western Mich. U., 1961-62, Nazareth Coll., 1974-75; adj. prof. polit. sci. Western Mich. U., 1982— Co-author: The Constitutional Law Dictionary: Volume One, Individual Rights, 1985; Volume Two, Governmental Powers, 1987, Constitutional Deskbook: Individual Rights, 1987, (with Mary Bedikian and Pamela Enslen) Michigan Practice, Alternative Dispute Resolution, 1998. Served with USAF, 1951-54. Named Person of the Century-Law and Courts, The Kalamazoo Gazette, 1999; named to Great Am. Judges, ABC-Clio, 2003; recipient Disting. Alumni award, Wayne State Law Sch., 1980, Western Mich. U., 1982, Outstanding Practical Achievement award, Ctr. Pub. Resources, 1984, award for Excellence and Innovation in Alternative Dispute Resolution and Dispute Mgmt., Legal Program; scholar, Jewel Corp., 1956—57, Lampson McElhorne, 1957. Mem. ABA (standing com. on dispute resolution 1983-90), Mich. Bar Assn., Am. Judicature Soc. (bd. dirs. 1983-85), Sixth Cir. Jud. Coun. Office: US Dist Ct 410 W Michigan Ave Kalamazoo MI 49007-3757 Office Phone: 616-343-7542.

ENSLIN, JON S., bishop; b. Apr. 4, 1938; m. Crystal Enslin; children: Jonathan, Joshua. Piano teaching cert., Wis. Conservatory Music; BA magna cum laude, Carroll Coll., Waukesha, Wis.; MDiv, Northwestern Luth. Theol. Sem., Mpls. Mission devel., then pastor Christ the Servant Luth. Ch., Waukesha, Wis., 1964-75; sr. pastor St. Stephen's Luth. Ch., Monona, Wis., 1975-87; asst. to bishop, adminstrv. dean South-Ctrl. Synod, Wis., 1988-91, bishop Wis., 1991—. Trainer Clergy in Transition Growth in Excellence in Ministry Program, ELCA; mem. transition team South-Ctrl. Synod Wis. ELCA; mem. exec. bd. Wis.-Upper Mich. Synod of LCA, chmn. adminstrn. and fin. sect. exec. bd. Office: Evangelical Lutheran Church 2909 Landmark Pl Ste 202 Madison WI 53713-4200

ENTENZA, MATT, state legislator; b. Oct. 4, 1961; m. Lois Quam; 3 children. BA, Macalester Coll.; postgrad., Oxford U., Eng.; JD, U. Minn. Pvt. practice; rep. Dist. 64A Minn. Ho. of Reps., 1994—.

ENTIN, FREDERIC J., lawyer; BA, U. Wis., 1968; JD, DePaul U., 1972. Bar: Ill. 1972. Dir. legal affairs U. Chgo. Hosp. & Clinics; sr. v.p. & gen. counsel Am. Hosp. Assn.; ptnr. Foley & Lardner LLP, Chgo., chmn. health legis./assn. Author: Preparation Med. Malpractice Defense Before Trial, 1987, Ambulatory

Care Facilities, Med. & Hosp. Negligence, 1988, Hosp. Collaboration: Need Appropriate Antitrust Policy, 1994. Mem.: BNA Health Law Reporter (adv. bd.), Fed. Trial Bar, Am. Soc. Assn. Exec., ABA. Office: Foley & Lardner LLP 321 N Clark St Ste 2800 Chicago IL 60610-4764 Office Phone: 312-832-4364. Business E-Mail: fentin@foley.com.

ENTRIKEN, ROBERT KERSEY, JR., editor, writer; b. Houston, Feb. 13, 1941; s. Robert and Jean (Finch) Entriken (Stepmother); divorced; 1 child, Jean Louise; m. Sandra Jo Miller, Mar. 4, 1989; 1 adopted child, Stephanie Lynn children: Caitlyn Miller, Matthew Kersey 1 stepchild, Jared Ray Adamson. Student, Sch. Journalism, U. Kans., 1961—69. Gen. assignment reporter Salina Jour., Kans., 1969-71, motorsport columnist Kans., 1970-83, courts reporter Kans., 1971-82, Sunday editor Kans., 1972-75, spl. sects. editor Kans., 1975-94, Neighbors editor Kans., 1982-95, TV editor Kans., 1994-95. Contbg. editor Sports Car Mag., Irvine, Calif., 1972—; motorsport columnist Motosports Monthly, Tulsa, 1983—85, Nat. Speed Sport News, 1996—; sr. editor Racer mag., 2003—; operator Ikke sa Hurtig Racing. Editor: Kans. Motor Sports Ann., 1996; contbr. articles to mags. With USNR, 1958—67. Mem.: Soc. Profl. Journalists, Eastern Motorsports Press Assn., Am. Auto Racing Writers and Broadcasters Assn. (Midwest v.p. 1980—82, gen. v.p. 1982—86, chmn. All-Am. Team selections 1983—, chmn. Legends in Racing selections hall of fame 1989—), Sports Car Club Am. (regional exec. Kans. region 1974, Mid-Am pointskeeper 1974—, founding mem. Salina region 1990, regional exec. Salina region 1994, Midwest Divsn. nat. pointskeeper 1995—2000, 2006—, Best Story award 1972, 1973, Solo Driver of Yr. Wichita Region 1976, Best Story award 1976—78, Solo II Champion Kans. 1978, Solo Cup nat. award 1981, Solo Driver of Yr. Wichita Region 1982, Best Story award 1983—87, Solo II Champion Kans. 1984, Nat. Solo I champion 1986, Best Story award 1989, England-Stipe award 1989, Best Story award 1992, Road Racing Driver of the Yr. Salina Region 1995, inaugural recipient Vern Jaques Sports Car Contbr. of Yr. nat. award 1999), Sigma Delta Chi. Avocations: sports car racing, autocrossing, skiing. Home and Office: 2731 Scott Ave Salina KS 67401-7858 Office Phone: 785-827-5143. E-mail: rocky@spitfire4.com.

ENYEDY, GUSTAV, JR., chemical engineer; b. Cleve., Aug. 23, 1924; s. Gustav and Mary (Silay) E.; m. Zoe Agnes Zachlin, Aug. 25, 1956 (div.); children: Louise Elaine, Roseann Marie, Arthur Gustav, Lillian Alice, Edward Anthony; m. Barbara Martha Ludwig Holley, May 9, 1987. BS in Chem. Engring., Case Inst. Tech., Cleve., 1950, MS, 1955. Registered profl. engr., Ohio. Engr., Rayon Tech. div. E.I. duPont, Richmond, Va., 1950-51; project engr. Grasselli Chem. Div., Cleve., 1951-54; devel. engr. Diamond Alkali (Soda Products), Painesville, Ohio, 1954-60; process engr. Central Engring., Cleve., 1960-61, staff engr. research dept. Painesville, 1961-65, supr. computer services, 1965-68; mgr. Diamond Shamrock Corp., Painesville, 1968-73; engring. cons., 1973-85; pres. PDQS, Inc., 1975—. Lectr. chem. engring. Fenn Coll., Cleve., 1957-61, Cleve. State U., 1975-76 Contbr. articles to tech. jours., textbooks. Treas., cubmaster, chmn. Gates Mills Cub Scout Pack, 1970-71, 75-78. Served with AUS, 1943-46. Decorated Bronze Star medal, Combat Inf. badge. Fellow Am. Inst. Chem. Engrs., Am. Assn. Cost Engrs. (tech. v.p. 1966-68, pres. 1969-70, speakers' bur. program 1971-89, O.T. Zimmerman Founder's award and hon. life mem., 1992); mem. Hungarian Geneal. Soc. of Greater Cleve. (founder 1996), Tau Beta Pi, Pi Delta Epsilon. Home and Office: 7830 Sugarbush Ln Gates Mills OH 44040-9317 Home Phone: 440-423-3469; Office Phone: 440-423-3520. Personal E-mail: gusenyedy@aol.com.

ENZ, CATHERINE S., state legislator; Mem. Mo. Ho. of Reps., Jefferson City, 1994—. Republican.

EPNER, STEVEN ARTHUR, computer consultant; b. Buffalo; s. Robert and Rosann (Krohn) E.; m. Louise Berke, June 20, 1970; children: Aaron J., Brian D. BS, Purdue U., 1970, MS, 2007. Computer operator/programmer Union Carbide, Chgo. and London, 1966-68; system analyst process design III, Chgo., 1969; analyst, sr. systems analyst Monsanto Co., St. Louis, 1970-74; lead analyst Citicorp., St. Louis, 1974-76; cons., pres. The User Group, Inc. (name changed to BSW Consulting, Inc. 1995), St. Louis, 1976—; innovator in residence Saint Louis U., 2007—. Lectr. U. Mo., St. Louis Bus. Program, AICPA, Mo., 1983-93; SBA Task Force on Small Bus.; dir. Programming and Systems Cons., Inc. Editor: The Independent, 1977-84; contbg. editor St. Louis Bus. Jour., St. Louis Computing; contbr. articles to profl. jours. Trustee Steven A. Epner/ICAA Scholarship fund; mem. tech. com., founding rep. EDI Coalition of Assns. Mem. Ind. Computer Cons. Assn. (dir., pres. chpt., nat. pres.), Nat. Cons. Council, Nat. Spkrs. Assn. (Cert. Spkg. Profl. award 2000), Internat. Brotherhood Magicians. Office: BSW Cons Inc 1050 N Lindbergh Blvd Saint Louis MO 63132-2912

EPPEN, GARY DEAN, business educator; b. Austin, Minn., Apr. 28, 1936; s. Markdene Fredrick and Elsie Alma (Wendorf) E.; m. Ann Marie Sathre, June 14, 1958; children: Gregory, Peter, Paul, Amy. AA, Austin Jr. Coll., 1956; BS, U. Minn., 1958, MSIE, 1960; PhD, Cornell U., Ithaca, NY, 1964; Doctorate (hon.), Stockholm Sch. Econs., 1998. Prof. mgmt. European Inst. Advanced Studies, Brussels, 1972-73; assoc. dean Grad. Sch. Bus., U. Chgo., 1969-75, prof. indsl. adminstrn., 1970—, assoc. dean PhD studies, 1978-85, dir. internat. bus. exchange program, 1977-92, dir. Life Officers Investment Seminar, 1975-88, dir. Fin. Analysts Seminar, 1982-88, Robert Law prof., 1989-97, dir. exec. program, 1989-94, Keller Disting. Svc. prof., 1997-2001, dep. dean part-time programs, 1998-2001, Keller Disting. Svc. prof. emeritus, 2001—. Francqui prof. Cath. U. Leuven, Belgium, 1979; Urwitz vis. prof. Stockholm Sch. Econs., 1994; external examiner U. W.I., 1979-82; dir. Hub Group, Inc., Hornet Capital, LLC. Author: (with F.J. Gould) Quantitative Concepts for Management, 1979, (with Metcalfe and Walters) The MBA Degree, 1979, (with F.J. Gould and C.P. Schmidt) Introductory Management Science, 1984; editor: Energy the Policy Issues, 1975; contbr. articles to profl. jours. FMC Faculty Rsch. scholar, 1986—89. Home: 3107 N Snead Dr Goodyear AZ 85338 Business E-Mail: gary.eppen@chicagogsb.edu.

EPPS, MISCHA BUFORD, lawyer; b. El Reno, Okla., 1969; BA cum laude, Washington U.; JD, U. Austin, 1994. Bar: Mo. 1994, US Dist. Ct., We. Dist. of Mo., Kans. 1999, US Dist. Ct., Dist. of Kans. Ptnr. Shook, Hardy & Bacon LLP, Kansas City, Mo. Bd. dirs. Legal Aid of Western Mo., JCBA Found., Cleveland Ave. Bapt. Ch. Mem.: Kans. Bar Assn., Jackson County Bar Assn., Nat. Bar Assn. (President's Award 2003), Kansas City Met. Bar Assn. (Young Lawyer of Yr. 2003). Office: Shook, Hardy & Bacon LLP 2555 Grand Blvd Kansas City MO 64108 Office Phone: 816-559-2500. Office Fax: 816-421-5547. E-mail: mepps@shb.com.

EPSTEIN, ARTHUR JOSEPH, physics and chemistry educator; b. Bklyn., June 2, 1945; s. Benjamin and Esther F. (Fellner) Epstein; m. Paulayne Tina Sklarsky, Aug. 3, 1969; children: Melissa Ann, Dana Michelle. BS cum laude in Physics, Poly. Inst. Bklyn., 1966; MS in Physics, U. Pa., Phila., 1967, PhD in Physics, 1971. Mem. tech. staff MITRE Corp., McLean, Va., 1971-72; prin. scientist Xerox Webster Rsch. Ctr., NY, 1972-85; prof. physics and chemistry Ohio State U., Columbus, 1985—, dir. Ctr. Materials Rsch., 1989—, disting. univ. prof., 1997—. Vis. prof. UCLA, 1977-78, 79-80, U. Paris, 1980, 88, 90, 92, Technion, 1984-85; cons. DuPont Co., Wilmington, Del., Xerox Corp., Webster, 1985—, NCR, Cambridge, Ohio, 1991, Eeonyx Corp., Pinole, Calif., 1993—; expert in polymer elec. conductivity, electronic and optical properties of molecular and polymeric magnets; co-organizer Internat. Conf. on Synthetic Metals, 1977, 81, 88, 96; Frontiers of Sci. lectr. U. Fla., 1984, 96; vis. scholar, lectr. U. R.I., 1987. Regional editor Jour. Synthetic Metals, 1982—; contbr. more than 500 articles to sci. jours. Recipient Disting. Scholar award Ohio State U., 1991. Fellow Am. Phys. Soc. (mem. applications com., James C. McGroddy prize for ew Materials, 2007); mem. Am. Chem. Soc., Materials Rsch. Soc., Nat. Inst. Emerging Techs. (hon. mem. exec. com. 1990—). Achievements include patent for technologies for electronic uses of plastics, 15 others; co-discovery of first molecular ferromagnet and first room temperature molecular based magnet, first self-doped water soluble electrically conducting polymer. Office: Dept Physics Ohio State U 191 W Woodruff Ave Columbus OH 43210-1117 Office Phone: 614-292-1133. Office Fax: 614-292-3706. E-mail: epstein.2@osu.edu.

EPSTEIN, BENNETT L. (BUZZ EPSTEIN), lawyer; BA with distinction, U. Mich., 1972; JD, Washington U., 1975. Bar: Ill. 1975, Mo. 1976, US Ct. Appeals (7th cir.) 1979, US Dist. Ct. (no. dist. Ill., trial bar) 1983, US Dist. Ct. (ctrl. dist. Ill.) 1992. Assoc. editor Urban Law Ann., 1974—75; trial atty. NLRB, Chgo., 1975—78; ptnr. Foley & Lardner, Chgo., 1978—. Bd. mgr. Family Care, Ill. Mem.: ABA. Office: Foley & Lardner Suite 2800 321 N Clark St Chicago IL 60610 Office Phone: 312-832-5193. E-mail: bepstein@foley.com.

EPSTEIN, RAYMOND, engineering and architectural executive; b. Chgo., Jan. 12, 1918; s. Abraham and Janet (Rabinowitz) Epstein; m. Betty Jadwin, Apr. 7, 1940; children: Gail, David, Norman, Harriet. Student, MIT, 1934-36; BS, U. Ill., 1938. Registered architect registered profl. engr. With A. Epstein & Sons Internat., Inc., Chgo., 1938—, chmn. bd., 1961-83, chmn. exec. com., 1983—. Bd. dirs., life trustee United Israel Appeal; past sec., hon. dir. Am. Jewish Joint Distbn. Com.; mem. exec. com. Nat. Jewish Cmty. Rels. Adv. Coun.; v.p. nat. bd. Jewish Telegraphic Agy.; mem. citizens bd. Loyola U.; past pres. Coun. Jewish Fedns., Welfare Funds, Inc., Jewish Welfare Fund Met. Chgo., Jewish United Fund, Young Men's Jewish Coun.; past sec. Jewish Fed. Met. Chgo.; past chmn. budget com., bd. govs. Jewish Agy.; past trustee Chgo. Med. Sch; past bd. dirs. United Jewish Appeal; past exec. com. Meml. Found. Jewish Culture; past chmn. pub. affairs com., past chmn. campaign Jewish United Fund Met. Chgo.; past. sec. Welfare Coun. Met. Chgo.; past bd. dirs. Chgo. Bldg. Congress; life dir. Mt. Sinai Med. Rsch. Found.; trustee, past dir. Ampal-Am. Israel Corp. Decorated comdr. Legion of Honor Ivory Coast, 1982; recipient Disting. Alumnus award U. Ill., 1974, Julius Rosenwald Meml. award Jewish Fedn. Chgo., 1974, Citation Brandeis U., 1992; named to City of Chgo. Sr. Citizens Hall of Fame, 1991. Fellow Soc. Civil Engr. France, Soc. Am. Registered Architects; mem. NSPE, ASCE, Am. Concrete Inst., Western Soc. Engrs., Assn. Engrs. and Architects in Israel, French Engrs. in the U.S., Inc., Pi Lambda Phi. Clubs: Standard (past trustee), Illini, MIT, Caxton (Chgo.). Home: 4950 S Chicago Beach Dr Chicago IL 60615-3207 Office: 600 W Fulton St Chicago IL 60661-1100 Home Phone: 773-752-4140. Business E-Mail: ray@rayepstein.com.

EPSTEIN, RICHARD A., law educator; b. 1943; AB summa cum laude, Columbia U., 1964; BA Juris., Oxford U., 1966; LLB cum laude, Yale U., 1968; LLD (hon.), Univ. Ghent, 2003. Bar: Calif. 1969. Asst. prof. Sch. Law U. So. Calif., LA, 1968—70, assoc. prof., 1970—73; vis. prof. Law. Sch. U. Chgo., 1972—73, prof. Law Sch., 1973-82, James Parker Hall prof. law, 1982-88, James Parker Hall Disting. Svc. prof., 1988—, interim dean, 2001. Peter & Kirsten Bedford sr. fellow Hoover Inst., 2000—; sr. fellow Ctr. Clinical Medical Ethics, U. Chgo. Medical Sch., 1983—. Author: Skepticism and Freedom: A Modern Case for Classical Liberalism, 2003, Torts, 1999, Cases and Materials in Torts, 7th edit., 2000, Takings: Private Property and the Power of Eminent Domain, 1985, Simple Rules for a Complex World, 1995, Mortal Peril: Our Inalienable Right to Health Care, 1997, Principles for a Free Society: Reconciling Individual Liberty with the Common Good, 1998, Forbidden Grounds: The Case Against Employment Discrimination Laws, 1992, Bargaining With the State, 1993, Modern Products Liability Law, 1980; editor: Jour. Legal Studies, 1981-91, Jour. Law and Econs., 1991—2001; mem. editl. bd. Yale Law Jour. Mem. Am. Acad. Arts and Scis., Order of Coif. Office: U Chgo Law Sch 1111 E 60th St Chicago IL 60637-2776 Business E-Mail: repstein@midway.uchicago.edu.

EPSTEIN, SIDNEY, architect, civil engineer; b. Chgo., 1923; m. Sondra Berman, Sept. 4, 1987; children from previous marriage: Donna Epstein Barrows, Laurie Epstein Lawton. BS in Civil Engring. with high honors, U. Ill., 1943. Various positions A. Epstein & Sons Internat.; bd. mem. A. Epstein & Sons Internat., Inc., Chgo. Bd. dirs. Polk Bros. Found.; trustee emeritus Northwestern Mut. Life Ins. Co. Founder, bd. dirs., past chmn. Chgo. Youth Ctrs.; past chmn. bd. trustees Michael Reese Hosp. and Med. Ctr.; bd. govs., life mem. U. Chgo. Hosps. and Clinics; life trustee Orchestral Assn. Chgo. Mem.: Standard Club (life; past pres.), Chi Epsilon, Phi Eta Sigma, Phi Kappa Phi, Sigma Tau, Tau Beta Pi, Sigma Xi. Home: 1430 N Lake Shore Dr Chicago IL 60610-6682 Office: A Epstein & Sons Internat Inc 600 W Fulton St Chicago IL 60661-1100 Office Phone: 312-429-8000. Business E-Mail: sidneyepstein@epstein-isi.com.

EPSTEIN, WOLFGANG, retired biochemist, educator; b. Breslau, Germany, May 7, 1931; came to U.S., 1936, naturalized, 1943; s. Stephan and Elsbeth (Lauinger) E.; m. Edna Selan, June 12, 1961; children: Matthew, Ezra, Tanya. BA with high honors, Swarthmore Coll., 1951; MD, U. Minn., 1955. Postdoctoral fellow in physiology U. Minn., Mpls., 1959-60; postdoctoral fellow Pasteur Inst., Paris., 1963-65; postdoctoral fellow in biophysics Harvard Med. Sch., 1961-63, research asso., then asso. in biophysics, 1965-67; asst. prof. biochemistry U. Chgo., 1967-73, asso. prof., 1973-79, prof., 1979-84, prof. dept. molecular genetics and cell biology, 1984—; ret., 1999. Served with M.C. U.S. Army, 1957-59. Mem. AAAS, Am. Soc. for Biochemistry and Molecular Biology, Am. Soc. for Microbiology. Home: 1120 E 50th St Chicago IL 60615-2804 Office: 920 E 58th St Chicago IL 60637-5415

EPTING, C. CHRISTOPHER, bishop; b. Greenville, SC; m. Pam Flagg; children: Michael, Amanda. Grad., U. Fla., Seabury-Western Theol. Sem., Evanston, Ill., 1952; STM, Gen. Theol. Sem., NYC, 1984. Formerly curate Holy Trinity Ch., Melbourne; vicar Ch. of St. Luke the Evangelist, Mulberry, Fla., 1974-78; founding vicar St. Stephen's Ch., Lakeland, Fla.; canon residentiary St. John's Cathedral, from 1978; rector St. Mark's Episc. Ch. and Sch., Cocoa, Fla.; bishop coadjutor, then bishop Episc. Diocese of Iowa, Des Moines, 1988—. Formerly dean Inst. Christian Studies, St. Luke's Cathedral, Orlando, Fla. Office: Episc Diocese of Iowa 225 37th St Des Moines IA 50312-4399

ERBELE, ROBERT S., state legislator; m. Susan Erbele; 4 children. Student, U. Sioux Falls, North Dakota State U. Rancher Bison; EMT-B; choral music dir., 1999—2000; mem. N.D. Senate from 28th dist., Bismark, 2001—; vice chair Senate AG Committee; senate Human Svcs. Com. Dir. Logan County Hist. Soc. Mem. .D. Buffalo Assn. (v.p.). Republican. Office: 6512 51st St Ave SE Lehr ND 58460 E-mail: rerbele@state.nd.us.

ERBER, THOMAS, mathematics and physics professor; b. Vienna, Dec. 6, 1930; m. Audrey Burns. BSc, MIT, 1951; MS, U. Chgo., 1953, PhD in Physics, 1957. Asst. prof. physics Ill. Inst. Tech., Chgo., 1957-62, assoc. prof., 1962-69, prof., 1969—, prof. math., 1986—, disting. prof., 1999—. Vis. scientist Stanford Linear Accelerator Ctr., 1970; prof. physics U. Graz, 1971, 82, hon prof., 1971—; prof. physics UCLA, 1978-79, 84-85, 87-92, 2006, U. Grenoble, 1982; prof. physics U. Chgo., 1998-99; adv. bd. rsch. corp. Mem. editl. bd. Acta Physica Austriaca. Rsch. fellow, Brussels, Belgium, 1963-64. Fellow: Inst. Physics (U.K.), Am. Math. Soc., Am. Phys. Soc.; mem.: IEEE (life sr.), Nuclear, Plasma & Magnetics Soc., Am. Acad. Mechanics, Am. Radio Relay League, Magnetics Soc., Oesterreichische Physikalische Gesellschaft, European Phys. Soc. Office: Ill Inst Tech Dept Physics Chicago IL 60616

ERDMAN, JOHN W., nutritionist, educator; m. Edie Erdman; children: Carolyn, Jackie. PhD, Rutgers U., 1975. Asst. prof. Dept. Food Sci. U. Ill., Urbana, prof. Food Sci. and Human Nutrition. Dir. Nutritional Scis. divsn. U. Ill., Urbana, 1989—99, asst. dean Coll. Office Rsch., 1995—99. Contbr. more than 130 articles to profl. jours. Recipient award, Am. Soc. Nutritional Scis. Fellow: Inst. Food Technologists (Babcock-Hart award 1999); mem.: NAS, Inst. Medicine, 2004, Am. Assn. Nutritional Scis. (pres.-elect 2000—01). Office: Univ Illinois Divsn Nutritional Scis 451 Bevier Hall MC-186 905 S Goodwin Ave Urbana IL 61801

ERDMAN, PHILIP, state legislator, farmer; b. Scottsbluff, Nebr., Apr. 7, 1977; s. Steve and Cathy Erdman; m. Cortney Erdman; 1 child, Grace. BS in Agrl. Scis., U. Nebr., 2000. Mem. Nebr. Legis. from 47th dist., Lincoln, 2001—. Cons. strategic planning Farmland Industries, Inc.; football recruiter U. Nebr., Lincoln. Mem. adv. bd., mem. curriculum com. Coll. Agrl. Scis. and Natural Resources, 1999-2000; del. Nebr. State Rep. Conv., 2000, Morrill County Rep. Conv., 2000. Mem. Fellowship Christian Athletes, Nat. FFA Alumni, Nebr. FFA Alumni (state pres. 1996-97), Rock Jaycees, Bayard FFA Alumni, Cheyenne County C. of C., Alpha Zeta, Gamma Sigma Delta. Office: Rm 1101 State Capitol Lincoln NE 68509

ERDÖS, ERVIN GEORGE, pharmacology and biochemistry professor; b. Budapest, Hungary; came to U.S., 1954; naturalized, 1959; s. Andor and Aranka (Breuer) E; m. Sara F. Rabito, May 30, 1986; children from previous marriage: Martin, Peter, Philip. Grad., U. Budapest Sch. Medicine, 1950; MD, U. Munich, 1950. With hosp., Munich, 1951; rsch. assoc. in biochem. rsch. lab. U. Munich, 1952-54; rsch. assoc. Mercy Hosp., Pitts., 1955-58; fellow in biochemistry, ind. rsch. Mellon Inst., Pitts., 1958-63; asst. prof. pharmacology U. Pitts., 1958-61, assoc. prof., 1961-63; prof. pharmacology U. Okla. Sch. Medicine, Oklahoma City, 1963-73, George Lynn Cross rsch. prof., 1970-73; prof. pharmacology, internal medicine U. Tex., Southwestern Med. Sch., Dallas, 1973-85; prof. pharmacology and anesthesiology, dir. Peptide Rsch. Lab. U. Ill. Coll. Medicine, Chgo., 1985—. Vis. prof. Tulane U., 1963; Disting. Fulbright prof., 1975; vis. scientist U.S.-Japan Coop. Sci. Program, NSF, 1966; vis. prof. dept. pharmacology Rush Med. Coll., Chgo., 1993—; cons. in field; mem. coms. Nat. Heart and Lung Inst. Editor books; mem. editorial bd. jours. Recipient gold medal Frey-Werle Found., Munich, 1988, Disting. Faculty award U. Ill. Coll. Medicine, 1992; Deutsche Forschungsgemeinschaft fellow, 1954; Wellcome Rsch. travel grantee, 1964; Univ. scholar U. Ill., 1990. Fellow: Am. Heart Assn. (mem. Coun. for High Blood Pressure Rsch. 1972—, Ciba award for hypertension rsch. 1994, Rsch. Achievement award 1995); mem.: Am. Physiol. Soc., Am. Soc. Biochemistry and Molecular Biology, Hungarian Acad. Sci. (fgn.) (hon.), Am. Soc. Pharmacology and Exptl. Therapeutics. Office: U Ill Coll Medicine Dept Pharmacology MC 868 835 S Wolcott Ave Chicago IL 60612-7340 E-mail: egerdos@uic.edu.

ERENS, JAY ALLAN, lawyer; b. Chgo., Oct. 18, 1935; s. Miller S. and Annette (Goodman); m. Patricia F. Brett, Aug. 21, 1960 (div. May 1985); children: Pamela B., Bradley B.; m. Patrice K. Franklin, June 15, 1985; 1 child, Cameron Jay. BA, Yale U., 1956; LLB, Harvard U., 1959. Bar: Ill. 1960. Law clk. to Justice John M. Harlan U.S. Supreme Ct., Washington, 1959-60; pvt. practice Chgo., 1960-64; founding and sr. ptnr. Levy and Erens (name changed to Erens and Miller 1985), Chgo., 1964-86; sr. ptnr. Hopkins & Sutter, Chgo., 1986-2001; with Foley & Lardner, Chgo., 2001—. Lectr. law Northwestern U., Chgo., 1961-63; spl. asst. atty. gen. State Ill., Chgo., 1964-70. Trustee Latin Sch. Chgo., 1975—80. Mem.: ABA, Chgo. Bar Assn. Office: Foley & Lardner 321 N Clark St Chicago IL 60610 Home Phone: 312-944-6197; Office Phone: 312-832-4536. Business E-Mail: jerens@foley.com.

ERHARDT, RON, state legislator; m. Jacquelyn. BBA, U. Minn., 1958, BA, 1959. State rep. Minn. Ho. Reps., Dist. 42A, 1991—. Mem. govt. oper. com., com. & econ. devel.-internat. trade, tech. & econ. devel. divsn., regulated indsl. & energy & taxes coms., Minn. Ho. Reps. Home: 4214 Sunnyside Rd Edina MN 55424-1114 Office: 100 Constitution Ave Saint Paul MN 55155-1232

ERHART, SUE A., lawyer; b. Cin., Oct. 6, 1971; BS, Xavier U., 1993; JD, U. Cin. Coll. Law, 1996. Bar: Ohio 1996, Ind. 1999. Law clerk Hon. Robert L. Miller, Jr., US Dist. Ct. Northern Dist. Ind., Hon. David A. Nelson, US Ct. of Appeals Sixth Cir.; ptnr. Keating, Muething & Klekamp PLL, Cin. Named one of Ohio's Rising Stars, Super Lawyers, 2005, 2006. Fellow: Cin. Acad. Leadership for Lawyers; mem.: Potter Stewart Am. Inn of Ct., Ind. State Bar Assn., Ohio State Bar Assn., FBA, Cin. Bar Assn. Office: Keating Muething &Klekamp PLL One E Fourth St Ste 1400 Cincinnati OH 45202 Office Phone: 513-579-6400. Office Fax: 513-579-6457.

ERICKSON, DAVID R., lawyer; b. Ames, Iowa, Aug. 7, 1956; m. Wendy W. Erickson, May 28, 1977; children: Elizabeth J., Anne D. BA in History, U. Tex., Arlington, 1978; JD, U. Iowa, 1981. Bar: Mo. 1981, U.S. Dist. Ct. (we. dist.) Mo. 1981, U.S. Ct. Appeals (8th cir.) 1981, Kans. 1985, U.S. Dist. Ct. Kans. 1985, U.S. Ct. Appeals (10th cir.) 1985. Ptnr. Blackwell Sanders Matheny, Weary & Lombardi, Overland Park, Kans., Kansas City, Mo., 1981; ptnr., chair Environ. Law Sect. Shook, Hardy & Bacon LLP. Author/editor Iowa Law Rev., 1980-81. Bd. dirs. Kans. Spl. Olympics, 1992. Mem. ABA, Mo. Bar Assn., Kans. Bar Assn. Avocations: hunting, fishing, camping, sports. Office: Shook, Hardy & Bacon LLP 2555 Grand Blvd Kansas City MO 64108 Office Phone: 816-559-2487. Office Fax: 816-421-5547. E-mail: derockson@shb.com.

ERICKSON, GERALD MEYER, classical studies educator; b. Amery, Wis., Sept. 23, 1927; s. Oscar Meyer and Ellen Claire (Hanson) E.; m. Loretta Irene Eder, Feb. 11, 1951; children: Rachel, Viki, Kari BS, U. Minn., 1954, MA, 1956, PhD, 1968. Cert. secondary sch. tchr., Minn. Tchr. Edina-Morningside Pub. Sch., Minn., 1956-65, 66-67; vis. lectr. U. Minn., Mpls., 1965-66, asst. prof., 1968-71, assoc. prof., 1971-83, prof. classical studies, 1983-95, prof. emeritus, 1995—. Exchange prof. Moscow State U., 1980, 86; vis. prof. U. Ill., 1967, 68, Coll. of William and Mary, 1984; bd. regents La. Univ. System, 1981, chmn. evaluation team for classics programs; reader Coll. Bds. Advanced Placement Program, 1975-77, chief reader, 1978-81; cons., lectr. in field Assoc. editor, mem. editorial staff Nature, Society and Thought, 1987—; author, lectr. various TV and radio courses Served with U.S. Mcht. Marine, 1945-46, U.S. Army, 1946-47, PTO; served to capt. USAF, 1951-53 NEH grantee, 1977-79; recipient award Horace T. Morse Amoco Found., 1984 Mem. Minn. Classical Conf. (pres. 1971-74), Minn. Humanities Conf. (pres. 1974-75), Classical Assn. Midwest/South (Ovatio award 1971). Avocations: bicycling, short-wave radio. Home: 121 E 51st St Minneapolis MN 55419-2605 E-mail: erick002@umn.edu.

ERICKSON, HOWARD HUGH, veterinarian, physiology educator; b. Wahoo, Nebr., Mar. 16, 1936; s. Conrad and Laurene (Swanson) E.; m. Ann E. Nicolay, June 6, 1959; children: James, David. BS, DVM, Kans. State U., 1959; PhD, Iowa State U., 1966. Commd. 1st lt. U.S. Air Force, 1959, advanced through grades to col., 1979; veterinarian England, 1960-63; vet. scientist Sch. Aerospace Medicine, Brooks AFB, Tex., 1966-75, Air War Coll., Maxwell AFB, Ala., 1975—76; dir. rsch. and devel. aerospace med. divsn. Brooks AFB, 1976—81; prof. physiology Kans. State U., Manhattan, 1981—, acting head dept. anatomy and physiology, 1989—90, Roy W. Upham prof. vet. medicine, 2001—04. Sci. adv. bd. Morris Animal Found., Englewood, Colo., 1990-93; cons. Tex. Higher Edn. Coordination Bd., Austin, 1990-91; clin. asst. prof. U. Tex. Health Sci. Ctr., San Antonio, 1972-81; vis. mem. grad. faculty Tex. A&M U., College Station, 1967-81; affiliate prof. Colo. State U., Fort Collins, 1970-75. Editor: Animal Pain, 1983; contbr. articles to profl. jours. Founding mem. Kans. State U. Golf Course Rsch. and Mgmt. Found.; trustee Meadowlark Hills Cmty. Found., 1998—2007. Recipient Alumni Achievement award Midland Luth. Coll., Fremont, Nebr., 1977, Merck award for Creativity, 1993, Bayer Excellence in Equine Rsch. award Am. Vet. Med. Assn. Coun. on Rsch., 2000, E.R. Frank award Kans. State U., 2006, Animal Health Tchg. Excellence award IVX, 2006. Fellow AAAS, Royal Soc. Health, Aerospace Med. Assn. (assoc.); mem. Am. Vet. Med. Assn. (chmn. coun. on rsch. 1984), Am. Physiol. Soc., Optimists Club. Republican. Lutheran. Home: 1700 Kings Rd Manhattan KS 66503-7550 Office: Kans State U Coll Vet Medicine Dept Anatomy and Physiology Manhattan KS 66506 Business E-Mail: erickson@vet.ksu.edu.

ERICKSON, JOHN DUFF, retired educational association administrator; b. Crawford, Nebr., Apr. 1, 1933; s. Harold Edward and Ruth Isabel (Duff) E.; m. Janet Eileen Lind, Dec. 28, 1955 (dec. Mar. 1992); children: Gregory Duff, Sheryl Ann; m. Bettie M. Hankins, July 7, 1994. BS in Mining Engring., S.D. Sch. Mines and Tech., 1955; MS in Indsl. Mgmt., MIT, 1965. Mine planning engr. Kennecott Copper Corp., Salt Lake City, 1965-67, truck ops. supt., 1968-69; mine mgr. Bougainville (New Guinea) Copper Ltd., Bougainville, Papua, New Guinea, 1970-72, exec. mgr. tech. services, 1973-75, asst. gen. mgr., 1976-77; head dept. mining engring. S.D. Sch. Mines and Tech., Rapid City, S.D., 1978-94; exec. dir. S.D. Sch. of Mines and Tech. Alumni Assn., Rapid City, S.D., 1984-98, prof. emeritus, 1998—. Mining cons. Bechtel Civil and Minerals, San Francisco, 1979—, Fluor Daniel Engrs., Redwood City, Calif., 1983—, Davy McKee, San Ramon, Calif., Mineral Resources Devel., San Mateo, Calif.; bd. dirs. South Hills Mining Co., Rapid City. Bd. dirs. Nat. Mining Hall of Fame and Mus. Capt. U.S. Army, 1961-62. Sloan fellow MIT, 1964-65. Mem. SME/AIME (chmn. Black Hills sect. 1983), S.D. Mining Assn. (bd. dirs.), Arrowhead Country Club, Elks. Republican. Home: 2958 Tomahawk Dr Rapid City SD 57702-4276 Office: SD Sch Mines and Tech 501 E Saint Joseph St Rapid City SD 57701-3901 E-mail: duffe@gwtc.net.

ERICKSON, LARRY EUGENE, chemical engineering educator; b. Wahoo, Nebr., Oct. 8, 1938; s.Conrad Robert Nathaniel and Laurene Hanna (Swanson) E.; m. Laurel L. Livingston, May 31, 1981. BSChemE, Kans. State U., 1960, PhD, 1964. Instr. chem. engring. Kans. State U., Manhattan, 1964-65, asst. prof., 1965-67, assoc. prof., 1968-72, prof., 1972—. NIH spl. rsch. fellow U. Pa., Phila., 1967-68; vis. scientist MIT, Cambridge, 1975, USSR Acad. Scis., Pushchino, 1977-78; dir. Ctr. for Hazardous Substance Rsch., 1989—. Contbr. articles to profl. jours. Pres. Lutheran Help Assn., Manhattan, 1984. Recipient Career Devel. award NIH, 1970-75, Prof. Baehr award Beta Sigma Psi, 1981; Phi Tau Sigma award, 1995, Disting. Grad. Faculty award, 2003. Mem. AIChE,

Am. Chem. Soc. (sec.-treas. chpt. 1983), Inst. Food Tech., Sigma Xi. Avocation: square dancing. Home: 408 Wickham Rd Manhattan KS 66502-3751 Office: Kans State U Dept Chem Engring Durland Hall Manhattan KS 66506-5102 Business E-Mail: lerick@ksu.edu.

ERICKSON, RANDALL J., lawyer; b. 1960; Atty. securities practice group Godfrey & Kahn, 1990—2002; sr. v.p., gen. counsel, corp. sec. Marshall & Ilsley Corp., 2002—. Mem. bd. Marshall & Ilsley Bank FSB, Marshall & Ilsley Community Devel. Corp., SWB Holdings, Inc., Marshall & Ilsley Capital Markets Group, Marshall & Ilsley Ventures. Mem. bd. dirs. Wis. Banking Assn. Office: Marshall & Ilsley Corp 770 N Water St Milwaukee WI 53202

ERICKSON, RONALD A., retail executive; JD, U. Minn. CEO Holiday Cos., Mpls. Office: Holiday Companies PO Box 1224 Minneapolis MN 55440-1224

ERICKSON, W(ALTER) BRUCE, business and economics educator, entrepreneur; b. Chgo., Mar. 4, 1938; s. Clifford Eric and Mildred B. (Brinkmeier) E. BA, Mich. State U., 1959, MA, 1960, PhD in Econs., 1965. Rsch. assoc. subcom. on antitrust and monopoly U.S. Senate, 1960-61; asst. prof. econs. Bowling Green (Ohio) U., 1964-66; asst. prof. bus. and govt. Coll. Bus. Adminstrn., U. Minn., Mpls., 1966-70, assoc. prof., 1971-75, prof. dept. mgmt., 1975—, prof., chmn. dept. mgmt., 1977-80, co-chmn., then chmn., 1988-92. Bd. dirs. various bus., non-profit and venture capital orgns.; cons. rock salt antitrust cases for atty. gens. Mich., cons. rock salt antitrust cases for atty. gens. Calif., Ill., Wis., Minn.; cons. U.S. Justice Dept. Author: An Introduction to Contemporary Business, 4th edit., 1985, Government and Business, 1980, 2d edit., 1984, International Business, 1998; co-author: International Business, 1998; bd. editors Antitrust Law and Econs. Rev., Jour. Indsl. Orgn.; contbr. articles to profl. jours. Bd. dirs. Found. for Constl. Edn. and the Citizens League, 1991-92; mem. ethics com. Ebenezer System, Minn. Mem. Am. Econ. Assn., Royal Econ. Soc. Office: Carlson Sch Mgmt 321 19th Ave S Minneapolis MN 55455-0438

ERICSSON, RICHARD L., lawyer; b. 1948; BA, JD, U. S.D. Bar: S.D. 1974. Ptnr. Ericsson Ericsson & Leibel, Madison, S.D. Mem. State Bar S.D. (pres.-elect). Office: Ericsson Ericsson & Leibel 100 N Egan Ave Madison SD 57042-2909

ERIKSEN, CHARLES WALTER, psychologist, educator; b. Omaha, Feb. 4, 1923; s. Charles Hans and Luella (Carlson) E.; m. Garnita Tharp, July 22, 1945 (div. Jan. 1971); children: Michael John, Kathy Ann; m. Barbara Becker, Apr. 1971. BA summa cum laude, U. Omaha, 1943; PhD, Stanford, 1950. Asst. prof. Johns Hopkins U., Balt., 1949-53, research scientist, 1954-55; lectr. Harvard U., Cambridge, Mass., 1953-54; mem. faculty U. Ill., Urbana, 1956—, prof., 1959-93, prof. emeritus, 1993—. Rsch. cons. VA, 1960-80; mem. psychobiology panel NSF, 1963; mem. exptl. psychology study sect. NIH, 1958-62, 66-70; Pillsbury Meml. lectr. Cornell U., 1966; keynote address 1st Internat. Congress on Visual Search, U. Durham, U.K., 1988, European Congress for Cognitive Psychology, Elsinore, Denmark, 1993; invited lectr. Max Plank Inst., Munich, 1993, Universidad Autonoma de Madrid, 1993, U. of Salamanca, Spain, 1993. Author: Behavior and Awareness, 1962; editor Am. Jour. Psychology, 1968; prin. editor Perception and Psychophysics, 1971-93; cons. editor Jour. Exptl. Psychology, 1965-71, Jour. Gerontology, 1980—; contbr. articles to profl. jours. Recipient Stratton award Am. Psychopath. Assn., 1964, NIMH Research Career award, 1964 Fellow AAAS; mem. Am. Psychol. Soc., Psychonomic Soc., Soc. Exptl. Psychologists, Midwestern Psychol. Assn., Sigma Xi. Home: 22485 State Highway 133 Oakland IL 61943-6822 Office: U Ill Psychol Bldg 603 E Daniel St Champaign IL 61820-6232 Personal E-mail: erikbarb@consolidated.net.

ERKER, THOMAS J., lawyer; b. Roslyn, NY, 1957; BA, LI U., 1979; JD, Washburn U., 1982. Bar: Kans. 1982, U.S. Dist. Ct. Kans., U.S. Supreme Ct., U.S. Ct. Appeals (10th cir.). Asst. dist. atty., Johnson County, Kans., 1982—85; asst. city prosecutor Overland Pk., Kans., 1985; ptnr. Erker, Norton & Hare LLC, Olathe, Kans. Lectr. in field. Fellow: Johnson County Bar Assn.; mem.: ABA (named Kansas City Super Lawyer 2005, 2006), Nat. Coll D.U.I. Def. (founding mem.), Kans. Bar Assn., Kans. Assn. Criminal Def. Lawyers (life), Nat. Assn. Criminal Def. Lawyers (life), Johnson County Bar Assn. (pres. 1992—93). Office: Erker Norton & Hare LLC 130 N Cherry St Ste 203 Olathe KS 66061 Office Phone: 913-829-2500. Office Fax: 913-829-3344. Business E-Mail: tom@enhlaw.com.

ERKONEN, WILLIAM EDWARD, radiologist, medical educator; BS, U. Iowa, 1955, MD, 1958. Diplomate Am. Bd. Radiology. Intern U. Oreg., Portland, 1959; family practice, 1961—68; pvt. practice, 1971-87; resident in radiology U. Iowa Coll. Medicine, Iowa City, 1968-71, faculty, 1988-94, asst. prof. radiology, 1994-98, assoc. prof., 1995-98, co-dir. Electric Differential Multimedia Lab., 1993—, assoc. prof. emeritus, 1998—. Rschr. in med. informatics and med. student instrn. and edn.; mem. anatomy and interdisciplinary com. Nat. Bd. Med. Licensure Exam., 1999—2001. Editor: (textbook) Radiology 101 1st edit., 1998, 2d edit., 2005; contbr. articles to profl. jours.; developer electronic med. textbooks. Capt. US Army, 1959—61. Recipient numerous certs. of merit Radiology Soc. N.Am.; named Tchr. of Yr., U. Iowa Coll. Med., 1990, 93, 96; recipient Disting. Tchr. award for jr. faculty in clin. scis. Alpha Omega Alpha. Fellow Am. Coll. Radiology.

ERLANDSON, MIKE, legislative staff member; b. Apr. 14, 1964; m. Dawn Erlandson. B, St. Johns U., 1986; diploma, Harvard U., 1997. Aid Rep. Martin Sabo, St. Paul, 1985-93, chief staff, 1993—. Chmn. Minn. Dem. Party, 1999—2005; bd. dir. Minn. DFL Edn. Foun.; adv. com. Humphrey Inst. Policy Forum U. Minn., 1996—99. Contbr. columns in newspapers. Chmn. Minn. Dems., 1999—. Avocations: sailing, golf, marathons.

ERLANDSON, PATRICK J., health products executive; Ptnr. Arthur Andersen; v.p. Process, Planning, and Info. Channels UnitedHealth Grp., Minnetonka, Minn., 1997—98, corp. contr., chief acctg. officer, 1998—2000, CFO, 2001—06, operational position, 2006—. Office: UnitedHealth Group 9900 Bren Rd E Minnetonka MN 55343

ERLEBACHER, ALBERT, historian, educator; b. Ulm, Württemberg, Fed. Republic of Germany, Sept. 28, 1932; came to U.S., 1937; s. Alfred Samuel and Rosa (Wertheimer) E.; m. Dolores Adler, Aug. 20, 1961; children: Seth Allen, Steven John, Ross Maier. BA, Marquette U., 1954, MA, 1956; PhD, U. Wis., 1965. Cert. prin., Wis. Tchr. Independence (Wis.) H.S., 1954-55, Cen. H.S., Sheboygan, Wis., 1956-59; prin. Lone Rock (Wis.) H.S., 1960-62; asst. prof. U. Wis., Oshkosh, 1962-65; prof. DePaul U., Chgo., 1965—97, prof. emeritus, 1997—, chmn. history dept., 1982-88. Dist. 69 Sch. Bd., Skokie, Ill., 1978-81; faculty adv. com. State Bd. Higher Edn., Champaign, Ill., 1974-80, 92-97. Mem. Temple Judea-Mizpah. Mem. AAUP, Am. Hist. Assn., State His. Soc. Wis. Home: 8232 Kilbourn Ave Skokie IL 60076-2614 Office: DePaul U 2320 N Kenmore Ave Chicago IL 60614-3210 Personal E-mail: aderlebacher@sbcglobal.net. Business E-Mail: aerlebac@depaul.edu.

ERLEBACHER, ARLENE CERNIK, retired lawyer; b. Chgo., Oct. 3, 1946; d. Laddie J. and Gertrude V. (Kurdys) Cernik; m. Albert Erlebacher, June 14, 1968; children: Annette Doherty, Jacqueline McCarthy. BA, Northwestern U., 1967, JD, 1973. Bar: Ill. 1974, U.S. Dist. Ct. (no. dist.) Ill. 1974, U.S. Ct. Appeals (7th cir.) 1974, Fed. Trial Bar 1983, U.S. Supreme Ct. 1985. Assoc. Sidley & Austin, Chgo., 1974-80, ptnr., 1980-95, ret., 1996. Fellow Am. Bar Found.; mem. Order of Coif.

ERLINGER, JAMES H., III, lawyer; b. St. Charles, NJ, Sept. 30, 1958; s. James H. II and Nancy (Willbrand) E. BSBA, U. Mo., 1981, MBA, 1983; JD, 1985. CPA; bar: Mo. 1985. Ptnr., mem. exec. com. Bryan Cave LLP, St. Louis, 1985—. Office: Bryan Cave LLP One Metropolitan Square 211 N Broadway Ste 3600 Saint Louis MO 63102-2733

ERNEST, J. TERRY, ocular physiologist, educator; b. Sycamore, Ill., June 26, 1935; married (div.); 1 child. BA, Northwestern U., 1957; MD, U. Chgo., 1961, PhD in Visual Sci., 1967; Postgrad. Diploma in Health Care Ethics and Law, Manchester U., Eng., 2005. Prof. ophthalmology U. Wis., 1977-79; prof., chmn. ophthalmology Ind. U., 1980-81; prof. ophthalmology U. Ill., 1981-85; prof., chmn. ophthalmology U. Chgo., 1985—2004, Cynthia Chow prof., 2002—. Mem visual sci. A study sect., NIH, 1975-78, chmn. 1978-79, chmn. visual disorders study sect., 1979-80; rsch. prof. Rsch. to Prevent Blindness, Ind., 1981-84; mem. Vision Rsch. Program Com., 1982-84. Founding editor, Key, 1986-88; editor, Year Book of Ophthamology, 1982-88, Investigative Ophthalmology and Visual Sci., 1988-92. Recipient Rsch. Career Devel. award NIH, 1972. Mem. AAAS, Am. Ophthalmol. Soc., Am. Acad. Ophthalmology (Honor award 1982), Assn. Rsch. Vision and Ophthalmology. Achievements include research in ocular circulation with special emphasis on glaucoma and diabetic retinopathy using various methods of in vivo blood flow measurements. Office: U Chgo Visual Sciences Ctr 5841 S Maryland Ave MC2114 Chicago IL 60637-1454 Home Phone: 773-667-9203; Office Phone: 773-702-8888. E-mail: jernest@bsd.uchicago.edu.

ERNST, MARK A., diversified financial services company executive; b. 1958; m. Annette T. Ernst; two children. BS in Acctg. & Fin. summa cum laude, Drake U., 1980; MBA, U. Chgo., 1986. With Comptr. of the Currency US Dept. Treasury; with tax, investment and corp. adv. svcs. dept. Coopers & Lybrand; v.p., gen. mgr. tax and bus. svcs. divsn. Am. Express Co., Mpls., sr. v.p. workplace fin. svcs., sr. v.p.; exec. v.p., COO H&R Block, Inc., 1998-99, pres., COO, 1999—2001, pres., CEO, 2001—07, chmn., 2002—07, cons., 2007—. Bd. dirs. H&R Block, Inc., 1999—2007, Knight Ridder, 2004—06, Great Plains Energy; adv. Initiative Fin. Security Aspen Inst.; bd. trustees U. Mo. Kans. City. Bd. dir. Civic Coun. Greater Kans. City, Greater Kans. City Area C. of C., Kansas City Area Devel. Coun., H&R Block Found., Am. Royal.

ERNSTBERGER, ERIC, landplanning architectural company executive; Prin. Rundell Ernstberger & Assocs., Muncie, Ind. Office: Rundell Ernstberger 315 S Jefferson St Muncie IN 47305-2470 E-mail: eernstberger@reasite.com.

ERPENBACH, JON, state legislator; b. Madison, Wis., Jan. 28, 1961; m. Katherine Erpenbach; children: Joseph, Amy. Student, U. Wis., Oshkosh. Mem. dist. 27 Wis. Senate, Madison, 1998—. Democrat. Office: PO Box 7882 Madison WI 53707-7882

ERTL, WOLFGANG, German language and literature educator, artist; b. Sangerhausen, Germany, May 27, 1946; came to U.S., 1969; m. Mary R. Clough, Aug. 30, 1969. BA equivalent in German and English, Philipps U., Marburg, Germany, 1969; MA in German, U. N.H., 1970; PhD in Germanic Langs. and Lits., U. Pa., 1975. Lectr. German U. Pa., Phila., 1974-76; asst. prof. German Swarthmore (Pa.) Coll., 1976-77, U. Iowa, 1977-82, assoc. prof., 1982-88, prof. Iowa City, 1988—2006, chmn. dept. German, 1988—96, prof. emeritus, 2006—. Author: Stephan Hermlin and Tradition, 1977, Nature and Landscape in the Poetry of the GDR: Walter Werner, Wulf Kirsten, and Uwe Gressmann, 1982, (with Christine Cosentino) On Volker Braun's Lyric Poetry, 1984; co-editor: GDR Poetry in Context, 1988; co-editor Glossen: An Internat. Bi-Lingual Scholarly Jour. on Lit., Film, and Art in the German Speaking Countries After 1945; co-editor (with C. Cosentino and W. Muller) Taking Stock--German Literature after Unification: Contributions to the 1st Carlisle Symposium on Modern German Literature, Glossen 10, 2000-, Crosscurrents--German Literature(s) and the Search for Identity: Selected Papers from the 2d Carlisle Symposium on Modern German Literature, Glossen 15, 2002; co-editor At the Milennium: Focus on German Literature, 2003; co-editor, America in German Literature and Film: Selected Papers from the 3rd Carlisle Sympsium on Modern German Literature, Glossen 19, 2004; contbr. chpts. to books, revs. and articles to profl. jours. Resident dir., Academic Year In Freiburg, Germany, 2000-01, 04-05. May Brodbeck Humanities fellow, 1987. Mem. Am. Assn. Tchrs. German, German Studies Assn., York Art Assn., Kittery Art Assn., Pastel Painters of Maine. Office: U Iowa Dept German 526 Phillips Hall Iowa City IA 52242-1323

ERWIN, JUDY, state legislator; b. Detroit, 1950; BS, U. Wis.; MA, Nat. Coll. Edn., Evanston, Ill.; postgrad., Kennedy Sch. Govt., 1987. Formerly tchr. pub. schs.; mgmt. cons. Grant Thornton LPP; formerly dir. comms. staff Senate Dem. Staff; mem. from 11th dist. Ill. Ho. of Reps. Former del. Dem. Convs.; mem. Gov.'s Human Resource Task Force.

ESAMANN, DOUGLAS F., utilities executive; m. Kimberly Esamann; children: Regan, Kalee, Conley. BS, Ind. U., 1979. Various positions to tax mgr. Pub. Svc. Indiana (now subs. of Cinergy), Ind., 1979—94; project mgr., corp. devel. Cinergy Corp., Cin., 1994—96, fin. team, comml. bus. unit, 1996—98, gen. mgr., bus. devel. Cin., 1998—99, v.p., CFO, comml. bus. unit, 1999—2001, pres. Pub. Svc. Ind. Inc., 2001—04, sr. v.p., Energy Portfolio Strategy and Mgmt., Comml. Bus. Unit. Cin., 2004—. Bd. dir. Ctrl. Ind. Corp. Partnership, Ind. Fiscal Policy Inst. Mem.: Ind. Mfrs. Assn. (bd. dir.), Ind. C. of C. (bd. dir.), Indpls. (Ind.) C. of C. (bd. dir.). Office: Cinergy Corp 139 E 4th St Cincinnati OH 45202

ESHBAUGH, W(ILLIAM) HARDY, botanist, educator; b. Glen Ridge, NJ, May 1, 1936; s. William Hardy Eshbaugh Jr. and Elizabeth (Wakeman) Henderson; m. Barbara Keller, Sept. 6, 1958; children: David Charles, Stephen Hardy, Elizabeth Wendy Brown, Jeffrey Raymond. BA, Cornell U., 1959; MA, Ind. U., 1961, PhD, 1964. Lectr. in botany Ind. U., Bloomington, 1962; spl. asst. to chief ecology and epidemiology br. Dugway Proving Ground, Utah, 1964-65; asst. prof., curator herbarium So. Ill. U., Carbondale, 1965—67; from asst. prof. to prof. botany Miami U., Oxford, Ohio, 1967—98, chmn. dept. botany, 1983-88, prof. emeritus, 1998. Cur., Willard Sherman Turrell Herbarium, Miami U., 1967-82; assoc. program dir. NSF, Washington, 1982-83; co-chmn. steering com. Systematics Agenda 2000-Charting the Biosphere; adv. bd. Am. Bot. Coun., 1996—; instr. Internat. Rainforest Workshops, 1991-99; pres., bd. dirs. Avian Rsch. and Edn. Inst., 2005-2007. Co-author: (Book) The Vascular Flora of Andros Island, Bahamas, 1988; contbr. articles to profl. jours. Bd. dirs. Childrens Environ. Trust Found., 1992-94, Hawk Mtn., 2007—; pres. Elizabeth Wakeman Henderson Charitable Found., 1997—; mem. Penobscot Leadership Coun., 2006-2008; Capt. U.S. Army, 1964-65. Named Citizen of Yr., Oxford, Ohio, 2002, Man of Yr., St. Mary's River Assn., 2006; recipient Outstanding Communicator award, Ohio Ornithological Soc., 2007. Fellow: AAAS, Inst. Environ. Scis., Ohio Acad. Sci.; mem.: Ohio Biol. Survey (Herbert Osborn award 2006), Internat. Field Studies (trustee 1989—95), Internat. Orgn. Plant Biosytematists (coun. 1987—89, ad hoc com. 1989—92, N. Am. treas. 1992—95), Assn. Systemic Collections (bd. dirs. 1981—84, rep.-at-large), Nature Conservancy (vice chmn. Ohio chpt. 1970—75, trustee 1970—77), Atlantic Salmon Fedn. (bd. dirs. 2002—), Bot. Soc. Am. (pres. 1988—89, Merit award 1992, Centennial medal 2006), Soc. Econ. Botany (v.p. 1982—83, pres. 1983—84, Disting. Econ. Botanist 2007), Am. Soc. Plant Taxonomists (pres. 1991—92), Am. Inst. Biol. Scis. (pres. 1995), Nat. Audubon Soc. (bd. dirs. 1993—2006, vice-chmn., Great Egret award 2005), Explorer's Club. Methodist. Avocations: camping, fly fishing, photography, sailing, swimming. Home: 209 Mckee Ave Oxford OH 45056-9059 Office: Miami U Dept Botany Oxford OH 45056 Home Phone: 513-523-8305; Office Phone: 513-529-4200. Business E-Mail: eshbauwh@muohio.edu.

ESKOLA, ERIC, radio personality; Grad., U. Minn., 1975. Radio host, polit. news anchor Sta. WCCO Radio, Mpls. Recipient awards, AP. Office: WCCO 625 2nd Ave S Minneapolis MN 55402

ESPEGARD, DUAINE C., state legislator; m. Phyllis Espegard; 3 children. BBA, Aakers Bus. Coll. Pres., CEO Bremer Bank; mem. N.D. Senate from 43d dist., Bismark, 2001—. Mem. NDAK Commn. Econ. Devel. Republican. Office: 3649 Lynwood Cir Grand Forks ND 58201 E-mail: despegar@state.nd.us.

ESPICH, JEFFREY K., state legislator; m. Sharon Espich; 2 children. BS, Ind. U. With Kozy Kourt Inc.; rep. Dist. 32 Ind. Ho. of Reps., 1972-91, rep. Dist. 82, 1991—, minority whip, asst. minority floor leader, mem. elec. and appropriations coms., ins. and corps. com., rds. and transp. com., ways and means com., mem. cts. and criminal code, ins. and corp., small bus. coms. Bd. dirs. Old First Bank. Mem. Farm Bur., Bluffton C. of C. Home: PO Box 158 1250 W Hancock St Uniondale IN 46791

ESPY, BEN, state legislator, lawyer; m. Kathy Espy (Duffy), Sept. 3, 1967; children: Elizabeth, Amy, Laura, Lynette. BA, Ohio State U., 1965; JD, Howard U., DC, 1968. Bar: Ohio. Pvt. practice, Columbus, Ohio, 1977; mem. Ohio Senate, Columbus, 1993—2002. Councilman City of Columbus, 1982-92; mem. adv. bd. Cath. Diocese Found.; mem. Big Ten Adv. Bd. Commn. Named Outstanding Legislator of Yr., Franklin County Trial Lawyers Assn.; recipient Young Black Dem. recognition, Columbus Man of Yr. award Frank Loris Peterson Soc. Adventist Men, vol. svc. award Neighborhood House; named to Sandusky H.S. Athletic Hall of Fame, Carter G. Woodson Hall of Fame, Ohio State Alumni award, 2002, Law award, Capital U., 2003. Mem. ABA, Ohio Bar Assn., Columbus Bar Assn., Urban Christian Leadership Assn., Kappa Alpha Psi, Sigma Delta Tau. Democrat. Home: 1350 Brookwood Pl Columbus OH 43209-2813 Office: 43 Hamilton Park Columbus OH 43203

ESREY, WILLIAM TODD, telecommunications company executive; b. Phila., Pa., Jan. 17, 1940; s. Alexander J. and Dorothy (B.) E.; m. Julie L. Campbell, June 13, 1964; children: William Todd, John Campbell. BA, Denison U., Granville, Ohio, 1961; MBA, Harvard U., 1964. With Am. Tel & Tel. Co., also N.Y. Tel. Co., 1964-69; pres. Empire City Subway Ltd., NYC, 1969-70; mng. dir. Dillon, Read & Co. Inc., NYC, 1970-80; exec. v.p. corp. planning United Telecommunications, Inc. (now Sprint), Westwood, Kans., 1980-81, exec. v.p., CFO, 1981-82, 84-85, CEO, 1985—90; chmn., CEO Sprint Corp., Westwood, Kans., 1990—2003. Bd. dirs. Duke Energy Corp., Gen. Mills, Inc.; chmn. bd. dirs. Japan Telecom Co., Ltd., 2003—04. Mem. Birnum Wood, Eagle Springs, Valley Club of Montecito, Phi Beta Kappa.

ESRICK, JERALD PAUL, lawyer; b. Moline, Ill., Oct. 1, 1941; s. Reuben and Nancy (Parson) E.; m. Ellen Feinstein, June 18, 1966; children: Sara Elizabeth, Daniel Michael. BA, Northwestern U., 1963; JD, Harvard U., 1966. Bar: Ill. 1966, U.S. Dist. Ct. (no. dist.) Ill. 1967, U.S. Supreme Ct. 1974, U.S. Ct. Appeals (9th cir.) 1985, U.S. Ct. Appeals (7th cir.) 1967. Law clk. U.S. Dist. Ct. (no. dist.) Ill., 1966-68; assoc. Wildman, Harrold, Allen & Dixon, Chgo., 1968-73, ptnr., 1973—, also chmn. firm mgmt. com., 1987-90. Lectr. Northwestern U., 1984-93, Coll. Arts and Scis. bd. visitors, 1993—, Nat. Panel Comml. Arbitrators, Am. Arbitration Assn. Pres. bd. trustees Nat. Lekotek Ctr., Evanston, Ill., 1989-93, U.S. Toy Libr. Assn., 1987-88; bd. dirs. Evanston Mental Health Assn., 1984-86, Fund for Justice, 1969-95, Lawyers' Com. for Civil Rights, 1974-84. Fellow Am. Coll. Trial Lawyers; mem. ABA, Ill. State Bar Assn., Chgo. Coun. Lawyers (bd. dirs., sec., founding mem.), Chgo. Bar Assn., Lawyers Club Chgo. Avocations: running, skiing, sailing, classical music, bicycling. Home: 1326 Judson Ave Evanston IL 60201-4720 Office: Wildman Harrold Allen & Dixon LLP 225 W Wacker Dr Ste 3000 Chicago IL 60606-1229 Office Phone: 312-201-2508. Business E-Mail: esrick@wildman.com.

ESSEX, JOSEPH MICHAEL, visual communication planner; b. Santa Barbara, Calif., May 27, 1947; Student, Montgomery Coll., Rockville, Md., Va. Commonwealth U., Richmond. Art dir. Met. Pitts. Pub. Broadcasting, 1970-73; sr. designer Ctr. for Comm. Planning, 1973-76; assoc. creative dir. Jim Johnston Advt., 1976; design dir. Burson-Marsteller Design Group, Chgo., 1976-86, v.p., dir. visual comm. planning Americas, 1980-88; prin. Design By Objectives, Chgo., 1986-88; ptnr. Essex Partnership, Chgo., 1988-89, Essex Two Inc., Chgo., 1989—. One man poster exhbn. Chgo., 1979; exhibited in group shows: Japan, 1976, Ireland, 1977, Cooper-Hewitt Mus., N.Y.C., 1981. Recipient Silver medals, Merit award Art Directors Club, N.Y.C., 1979, 80, over 300 other awards from design and advt. orgns. Office: Essex Two Inc 2210 W North Ave Chicago IL 60647-5430 Office Phone: 773-489-1400. E-mail: joseph@5x2.com.

ESSEY, BASIL, bishop; b. North Charleroi, Pa., Nov. 26, 1948; s. William Frederick and Genevieve Alberta (Lhota) E. BA, California U. of Pa., 1970; MDiv, St. Vladimir's Sem., Crestwood, NY, 1973. Tonsured reader Antiochian Orthodox Ch., Monessen, Pa., 1964, ordained subdeacon, then deacon Ligonier, Pa., 1979, ordained priest Bergenfield, N.J., 1980, elevated to archimandrite Wichita, Kans., 1987; consecrated bishop Antiochian Orthodox Christian Archdiocese of .Am., Wichita, 1992—. Translator, editor: The Liturgikon, 1989. Recipient Jackman award for disting. alumnus California Univ. of Pa., 1993. Office: Antiochian Orthod Chancery 1559 N Woodlawn Blvd Wichita KS 67208-2429

ESSMAN, ALYN V., photographic studios company executive; b. St. Louis, May 3, 1932; BBA, Washington U., St. Louis, 1953. Chmn. & CEO CPI Corp., St. Louis. Office: CPI Corp 1706 Washington Ave Fl 8 Saint Louis MO 63103-1717

ESTERLY, NANCY BURTON, retired physician; b. NYC, Apr. 14, 1935; d. Paul R. and Tanya (Pasahow) Burton; m. John R. Esterly, June 16, 1957; children: Sarah Burton, Anne Beidler, John Snyder, II, Henry Clark, II. AB, Smith Coll., 1956; MD, Johns Hopkins U., 1960. Intern, then resident in pediatrics Johns Hopkins Hosp., 1960-63, resident in dermatology, 1964-67; instr. pediatrics Johns Hopkins U. Med. Sch., 1967-68; instr., trainee La Rabida U. Chgo. Inst.; also dept. pediatrics U. Chgo. Med. Sch., 1968-69; asst. prof. Pritzker Sch. Medicine, U. Chgo., 1969-70, assoc. prof., 1973-78; asst. prof. dermatology Abraham Lincoln Sch. Medicine, U. Ill., 1970-72, assoc. prof. dermatology and pediatrics, 1972-73; dir. div. dermatology, dept. pediatrics Michael Reese Hosp. and Med. Ctr., Chgo., 1973-78; prof. pediatrics and dermatology Northwestern U. Med. Sch., 1978; head div. dermatology, dept. pediatrics Children's Meml. Hosp., Chgo., 1978-87; prof. pediatrics and dermatology Med. Coll. Wis., Milw., 1987—2004, prof. emeritus dermatology, 2005—; head div. dermatology, dept. pediatrics Children's Hosp. Wis., Milw., 1987—2004; ret., 2004. Editor-in-chief Pediatric Dermatology, 1983—; contbr. articles to profl. jours. Recipient David Martin Carter award, Am. Skin Assn., 2002, Lifetime Career Educator award, Dermatology Found., 2002, Disting. Svc. award, Med. Coll. Wis., 2004. Mem.: Wis. Pediat. Soc., Women's Dermatol. Soc. (Rose Hirschler award), Soc. Pediat. Dermatology (1st Lifetime Achievement award 1998), Soc. Pediat. Rsch., Am. Acad. Pediatrics, Soc. Investigative Dermatology, Wis. Dermatol. Soc., Am. Dermatol. Assn., Am. Acad. Dermatology, Internat. Soc. Pediat. Dermatology, Sigma Xi. Home Phone: 505-742-1427. Personal E-mail: nesterly@comcast.net.

ESTES, ELAINE ROSE GRAHAM, retired librarian; b. Springfield, Mo., Nov. 24, 1931; d. James McKinley and Zelma Mae (Smith) Graham; m. John Melvin Estes, Dec. 29, 1953. BSBA, Drake U., 1953, tchg. cert., 1956; MSLS, U. Ill., 1960. With Pub. Libr. Des Moines, 1956-95, coord. ext. svcs., 1977-78, dir., 1978-95, ret., 1995. Lectr. antiques, hist. architecture, librs.; mem. conservation planning com. for disaster preparedness for librs. Author bibliographies of books on antiques; contbr. articles to profl. jours. Mem. State of Iowa Cultural Affairs Adv. Coun., 1986—94, Nat. Commn. on Future of Drake U., 1987—88; chmn. Des Moines Mayor's Hist. Dist. Commn.; mem. nominations review com. Iowa State Nat. Hist. Register, 1983—89; chmn. hist. subcom. Des Moines Sesquecentennial Com., 1993, Iowa Sister State Commn., 1993—95; mem. com. 40th Anniversary Drake U. Alumni Weekend, 50 Yr. Drake Alumni Weekend, 2003; mem. July 4 com. Iowa Sesquecentennial; nat. exch. dir. Friendship Force, 1997; mem. nat. adv. bd. Cowles Libr., 1998—; mem. Gov.'s Iowa Centennial Meml. Found., 2003—; mem. acquisition com. Salisbury House, 2003; mem. cultural ctr. task force African Am. Hist. Mus., 1999—2003; mem. Iowa author com. Pub. Libr. Des Moines Found., 2001—; mem. Terrace Hill Commn., 2001—; bd. dirs. Des Moines Art Ctr., 1972—83, hon. mem., 1983—; bd. dirs. Friends of Libr. USA, 1986—92, Henry Wallace House Found., Iowa Libr. Centennial Com., 1990—91, Wagner Hall Preservation Project, 2004—. Recipient Recognition award Greater Des Moines, YWCA, 1975, Disting. Alumni award Drake U., 1979, Woman of Achievement award YWCA, 1989, Excellence in Hist. Preservation award City of Des Moines, 1994, Contbn. to Cmty. award Connect Found., 1995, Friend of Literacy award Pub. Libr. of Des Moines Found., 2003; named Textbook Project in her honor, Forest Libr., 2002; named to Wall of Fame, YWCA, 2003. Mem.: ALA (30th Anniversary Honor Roll for Intellectual Freedom 1999), Iowa Soc. Preservation Hist. Landmarks (bd. dirs. 1969—97), Libr. Assn. Greater Des Moines Metro Area (chmn. 1992, pres.), Iowa Urban Pub. Libr. Assn., Iowa Libr. Assn. (life; pres. 1978—79), Iowa Antique Assn., Terrace Hill (Gov.'s Mansion) Soc. (bd. dirs. 1972—, v.p. 1991—93, pres. 1993—96), Links Inc. (40th ann. com. 1997), Drake U. 50 Yr. Club, Questers Inc. Club (pres. 1982, state 2d v.p. 1984—86, 1st v.p. 1990—2000, pres. 1997, state pres. 2000—03, pres. 2001—03), Rotary (history com. 2001—06), Proteus Club (pres. 2003—04).

ESTES, JAMES RUSSELL, botanist; b. Burkburnett, Tex., Aug. 28, 1937; s. Dow Worley and Bessie (Seidlitz) E.; B.S. in Biology, Midwestern State U., 1959; Ph.D. in Systematic Botany, Oreg. State U., 1967; m. Nancy Elizabeth Arnold, Dec. 21, 1962; children: Jennifer Lynn Estes Varma, Susan Elizabeth Estes Honaker. Mem. faculty U. Okla., Norman, 1967—, asst. prof., 1967-70, assoc. prof., 1970-82, prof. botany, 1982-96, adj. prof. 2004—, prof. emeritus, 1996—; dir. Okla. Natural Heritage Program, 1981-82, U. Nebr. State Mus.,

1996—; curator Bebb Herbarium, 1979-96, curator emeritus 2004—; prof. biol. sciences U. Nebr. Lincoln, 1996-2002, prof. emeritus 2002—; assoc. program dir. NSF, 1990-92, program dir., 1993-94, mem. systematic biology adv. panel, 1986-89; interim dir. River Bend Nature Ctr., 2004-05, bd. dirs., 2001—; mem. ecology adv. panel U.S. Agy. for Internat. Devel., 1991; mem. adv. panel Internat. Biodiversity Conservation Group NIH, 1993; mem. adv. panel Biotic Surveys and Inventories NSF, 1993, 96; mem. joint expert group Jordanian-Israeli-Am. Trilateral Coop., 1994-95; cons. World Bank, Global Environ. Trust Fund to Republic of Indonesia, 1994-96; cons. in environ. work, 1979—; expert witness in environ. work, 1983—. Bd. govs. United Campus Christian Found., 1976-80; mem. adv. bd. Sutton Urban Wilderness Park, 1980—; bd. dirs. River Bend Nature Ctr., 2002—, mem. bd. dirs. 2002-04; pres. Lincoln Arts Coun. bd. dirs., mem. Wichita Falls Symphony Orch. bd., 2004—; mem. editorial bd. Systematic Botany Monographs, 1985-89, Flora N.Am., 1986-92; asst. editor Flora Okla. Project, 1984-96; mem. Flora of Okla. editl. com. 2002—; mem. steering com., trustee Flora Okla., Inc., 1985-92; With U.S. Army, 1960-63. Grantee NSF, 1968-70, 81-87; NSF fellow, 1963, 65-67; Ortenburger award Phi Sigma, 1975; Baldwin Study Travel award Okla. U. Alumni Found., 1976; named Outstanding Undergraduate Instr. Mortar Bd., 1990. Mem. Am. Soc. Plant Taxonomists (past pres. 1987-88, sec. 1980-83; program chmn. 1980-83, pres. elect 1984-85, pres. 1985-86), Bot. Soc. Am., Southwestern Assn. Naturalists (bd. govs. 1980-83, assoc. editor 1980-82, trustee 1986-93), Okla. Acad. Sci. (pres. 1992-93, sec. 1968-69). Democrat. Presbyterian. Co-editor: Grasses and Grasslands: Systematics and Ecology, 1981; contbr. articles to sci. books and jours. Address: 418 Park St Burkburnett TX 76354-2445 E-mail: jestes@classicnet.net.

ESTES, ROYCE JOE, lawyer; b. Topeka, Mar. 30, 1944; s. Joseph Sumner and Mildred Eve (Lunday) Estes; m. Marla Ann Hampton, June 13, 1964; children: Gina Christine, Darin Wesley, Erika Alynn. BA, Kans. State U., 1968; JD, U. Mo., 1972, LLM, 1975. Bar: Mo. 1972, Ill. 1976. Dir. Metal Container Corp., Sunset Hills; mem. staff U. Mo. Law Review, 1970—71; ptnr. Linde, Thomson, Fairchild, Langworthy & Kohn, Kansas City, Mo., 1972—75; asst. gen. counsel A.E. Staley Mfg. Co., Decatur, Ill., 1975—79; assoc. gen. counsel Anheuser-Busch Cos., Inc., St. Louis, 1979—82, sr. assoc. gen. counsel, 1983, dep. gen. counsel, 1983—90, v.p. dep. gen. counsel, 1992—95, v.p. corp. law antitrust, mktg. and distbn., 1995—. Served with USN, 1969—70. Law Found. scholar, U. Mo., 1967—68. Mem.: ABA, Ill. State Bar Assn., Mo. Bar Assn. Home: 4581 Nautical Ct Destin FL 32541-5321

ESTES, WILLIAM KAYE, psychologist, educator; b. Mpls., June 17, 1919; s. George D. and Mona Estes; m. Katherine Walker, Sept. 26, 1942; children: George E., Gregory W. Mem. faculty Ind. U., 1946—62, prof. psychology, 1955—60, research prof. psychology, 1960—62; faculty research fellow Social Sci. Research Council, 1952—55; lectr. psychology U. Wis., 1949; vis. prof. Northwestern U., 1959; fellow Center Advanced Study Behavioral Scis., 1955—56; spl. univ. lectr. U. London, 1961; prof. psychology, mem. Inst. Math. Studies Social Scis., Stanford, 1962—68; prof. Rockefeller U., 1968—79, Harvard U., 1978—89, prof. emeritus, 1989—; prof. Ind. U., 1999—. Chmn. Office Sci. and Engring. Personnel NRC, 1982—85, chmn. com. on prevention of nuclear war, 1984—89. Author: An Experimental Study of Punishment, 1944, Learning Theory and Mental Development, 1970, Models of Learning, Memory and Choice, 1982, Statistical Models in Behavioral Research, 1991, Classification and Cognition, 1994; co-author: Modern Learning Theory, 1954; contbr. articles to profl. jours.; editor: Handbook of Learning and Cognitive Processes, 1962—68, Psychol. Rev., 1977—82, Psychol. Sci., 1990—94; Jour. Exptl. Psychology, 1958—62. With AUS, 1944—46. Recipient U.S. Nat. medal of Sci., 1997. Fellow: AAAS, APA (pres. divsn. exptl. psychology 1958—59, Disting. Sci. Contbn. award 1962, gold medal for lifetime achievement in psychol. sci. 1992), Am. Acad. Arts and Scis.; mem.: NAS, Fedn. Behavioral Psychol. and Cognitive Scis. (v.p. 1988—91), Midwestern Psychol. Assn., N.Y. Acad. Scis. (life), N.Y. Acad. Scis. (hon.), Soc. Exptl. Psychologists (Warren medal 1963). Home: 2714 E Pine Ln Bloomington IN 47401-4423 Office: Ind U Psychology Bldg Bloomington IN 47405 Home Phone: 812-339-3229. Business E-Mail: wkestes@indiana.edu.

ESTRADA, ERIK (HENRY ENRIQUE ESTRADA), actor; b. NYC, Mar. 16, 1949; m. Joyce Miller Nov. 25, 1979 (div. 1980), 1 child; m. Peggy Rowe Estrada Aug. 19, 1985 (div. 1990), children Anthony Erik, Brandon Michael-Paul; m. Nanette Mirkovich Sept. 20, 1997, 1 child Francesca Natalia. Student, Mus. Dramatic Acad., NYC. Actor: (feature films) The Cross and the Switchblade, 1967, Cactus Flower, 1969, John and Mary, 1969, Chrome and Hot Leather, 1971, The Ballad of Billy Blue, 1972, Parades, 1972, The New Centurions, 1972, Airport '75, 1974, Midway, 1976, Trackdown, 1976, The Line, 1980, Where is Parcifal?, 1983, The Repenter, 1985 Light Blast, 1985, Hour of the Assassin, 1987, Guns, 1990, The Lost Idol, 1990, A Show of Force, 1990, Twisted Justice, 1990, Night of the Wilding, 1990, Do or Die, 1991, Look at Me, America, 1991, The Last Riders, 1991, Spirits, 1991, The Sounds of Silence, 1992, The Naked Truth, 1992, The Divine Enforcer, 1992, Angel Eyes, 1993, Tuesday Never Comes, 1993, Loaded Weapon, 1993, Juana la Cubana, 1994, The Final Goal, 1995, The Misery Brothers, 1995, Visions, 1996, Shattered Dreams, 1998, The Modern Adventures of Tom Sawyer, 1998, Oliver Twisted, 2000, UP, Michigan!, 2001, Van Wilder, 2002, Border Blues, 2004 (TV series) CHiPs, 1977-83 (nominated Best TV Actor-Drama, Golden Globe, 1977), (soap opera) Dos Mujeres, Un Camino (Two Women, One Road), 1993, The Bold and the Beautiful, 2001, (TV movie) The Quest: The Longest Drive, 1976, Fire!, 1977, Honey Boy, 1982, Grandpa, Will You Run With Me?, 1983, The Dirty Dozen: The Fatal Mission, 1988, She Knows Too Much, 1989, Extralarge: Cannonball, 1991, Earth Angel, 1991, Panic in the Skies!, 1996, CHiPs '99, 1998 (also prodr.)(nomination Outstanding Actor in a Made-for-TV Movie or Mini-Series, ALMA award, 1998), Taylor Made, 2005, others, (off-broadway) True West, (TV reality show) Surreal Life, 2004; guest appearances (TV shows) Circus of the Stars, 1979 (Ringmaster), Tonight Show: Dinah!, Mike Douglas, Merv Griffin, Hawaii Five-0, 1973, Emergency!, 1974, Kojak, 1975, Six Million Dollar Man, 1975, Police Woman, 1975, Medical Center, 1975, Baretta, 1976, Barneby Jones, 1976, Delvecchio, 1977, The Love Boat, 1978, Hunter, 1987, LA Law, 1993, The Nanny, 1995, Burke's Law, 1995, Baywatch, 1997, Martin, 1997, The Wayans Bros., 1997, Sabrina, The Teenage Witch, 1997, Diagnosis Murder, 1997, (voice) King of the Hill, 1998, Tracey Takes On, 1998, (voice) Family Guy, 1999, Walker, Texas Ranger, 1999, Weakest Link, 2001, American Family, 2002, Lizzie McGuire, 2002, For Your Love, 2002, Spy TV, 2002, The Rerun Show, 2002, Scrubs, 2003, Hollywood Squares, 2004, Drake & Josh, 2004, Maya & Miguel, 2004, Discovery Health Celebrity Body Challenge, 2004, (voice) Sealab 2021, 2004, 2005, According to Jim, 2006, others; actor, assoc. prodr. Alien Seed, 1989, Caged Fury, 1989; host The Image Workshop, 1991, American Adventure, 1994; guest appearances in a number of TV commercials; reserve officer Muncie Ind. Police Dept. (TV reality show) Armed & Famous, 2007. Internat. Face of D.A.R.E.; spokesperson Calif. Highway Patrol Car Seat Inspection and Installation Prog., Smoke Signals Communications, California Pines Homesites and Acreage Parcels, 2003, Hot Springs Village Arkansas' homes, 2004, 21st Century Ins. and makes appearances nationwide promoting car seat safety for children, 2006; speaks out for the Heart Assn. and The United Way. Recipient Sour Apple, 1980, Star on the Hollywood Walk of Fame, 2007. Avocations: running, tennis, golf, workout at gym. Office: 103 Sinclair Ave Yorkville OH 43971 Business E-Mail: erikestrada@1st.net.

ESTRIN, MELVYN J., computer products company executive; b. 1942; Co-chmn., co-CEO Nat. Intergroup, Inc., Carrollton, Tex., 1997—; co-chmn, co-CEO McKesson Health Corp., Carrollton, Tex., 1996; also bd. dirs.; chmn. U. Rsch. Corp., Bethesda, Md.; co-CEO Phar-Mor. Inc., Youngstown, Ohio. Mng. ptnr. Centaur Ptnrs., L.P.; chmn., pres., CEO Am. Health Svcs.; v.p., dir. Spectro Industries; founder First Women's Bank of Md.; pres. FWB Bancorporation, Rockville, Md.; chmn. FWB Bancorporation.; chmn. Estrin Internat., Inc.; with Estrin Realty and Devel. Corp.; bd. dirs. Washington Gas Light Co. Trustee U. Pa.; active Endowment Bd. of the Kennedy Ctr., The Econ. Club of Washington, The Washington Opera; nat. vice chmn. State of Israel Bonds; apptd. by Pres. Bush commr.Nat. Capital Planning Commn.; apptd. Nat. Coun. for the Performing Arts, John F. Kennedy Ctr. Recipient Eleanor Roosevelt Humanities award for Community Svc., 1986. Office: Phar-Mor Inc 20 Federal Plz W Ste 3 Youngstown OH 44503

ETHINGTON, RAYMOND LINDSAY, geology educator, researcher; b. State Center, Iowa, Aug. 28, 1929; s. Lindsay E. and Hilda Ruby (Weuve) E.; m. Leslie Ann Nielsen, June 15, 1955; children: Elaine Marie, Mary Frances. BS, Iowa State U., 1951, MS, 1955; PhD, U. Iowa, 1958. Asst. prof. geology Ariz. State U., Tempe, 1958-62; asst. prof. U. Mo., Columbia, 1962-65, assoc. prof., 1965-68, prof., 1968-2000, prof. emeritus, 2000—. With U.S. Army, 1951-53. NSF grantee, 1966, 87. Fellow Geol. Soc. Am.; mem. Soc. Econ. Paleontologists and Mineralogists (editor Jour. Paleontology 1969-74, spl. publs. editor 1980-83, chmn. publs. com. 1974-76, pres. 1989-90, pres. SEPM Found., Inc., 1993-98), Pander Soc. (chief panderer 1990-98), Am. Assn. Petroleum Geologists, Palaeontol. Assn. G.B., Paleontol. Soc. Mem. Lds Ch. Home: 1012 Pheasant Run Columbia MO 65201-6252 Office: U Mo Dept Geol Sci Columbia MO 65211-0001

ETZEL, TIMOTHY, manufacturing executive; BBA, Washburn U., 1964. Pres., CEO Jetz Svc. Co., Inc., Topeka. Mem. bd. regents Washburn U.; trustee Washburn Endowment Assn., 1993—, former vice chmn. endowment bd. Office: Jetz Svc Co Inc 901 NE River Rd Topeka KS 66616

ETZKORN, K. PETER, sociology educator, administrator, consultant, writer; b. Karlsruhe, Germany; naturalized, 1958; s. Johannes and Luise (Schlick) E.; m. Hildegard Elizabeth Garve; children: Kyle Peter, Lars Peter. AB, Ohio State U.; student, Ind. U.; A.M., PhD, Princeton. Asst. prof. U. Calif., Santa Barbara; assoc. prof. Am. U. Beirut, Lebanon; dir. Office Instl. Research; chmn. dept. sociology and anthropology U. Nev.; prof., chmn. faculty sociology and anthropology U. West Fla., 1967-68; prof. sociology San Fernando Valley State Coll., 1968-69, U. Mo., St. Louis, 1969-99, asso. dean Grad. Sch., 1978-87, dir. Office Rsch., 1979-87. Vis. prof. U. Münster, Germany, 1975-76, U. Vienna, Austria, 1987-88; cons. in field; prof. tng. adv. panel music divsn. NEA, 1994-97. Author: The Conflict in Modern Culture, 1968, Music and Society, 1973, Sociologists and Music, 1989; editor Jour. Ethnomusicology, 1984-87, Current Studies in the Sociology of Arts and Music, 1988—; contbr. articles to profl. jours. Mem. Gov. Nev. Com. on Dept. Correction, 1966; Mo. Gov. liaison German-Am. Tricentennial Task Force, 1983; mem. Mo. Adv. Com. on Humanities; chmn. Univ. Symposia Com. Bicentennial Horizons Am. Music; mem. St. Louis-Stuttgart Sister City Com.; Mo. state rep. Sister Cities Internat., 1976-81; cons. Nat. Endowment Arts, NSF; pres. St. Louis New Music Circle; bd. dirs. Am. Kantorei, MEDIACULT, Vienna; v.p. Internat. Inst. Met. St. Louis, 1982-86; pres. MEDIACULT, 1995—; exec. com. Coun. on Fgn. Rels. St. Louis Com., 1996—; bd. dirs. St. Louis Soc. for Blind and Visually Impaired, 1996, v.p., 2000—; chmn. Sister Cities 2003. Fulbright scholar, Vienna, Austria, 1987. Fellow Am. Sociol. Assn., Am. Anthrop. Assn.; mem. Soc. Ethnomusicology (coun. 1963-71, 76-79, 81-86, editor spl. publs.), Inst. Internat. Sociologie (mem. bur.), Internam. Orgn. Higher Edn. (dep. coun. 1980-87), Town Affiliation Assn. U.S. (bd. dirs. 1981-93, v.p. 1987-90, sec. 1990-93), St. Louis Coun. Sister Cities (chmn. 1981-86), Internat. Soc. for Music Edn. (chmn. commn. on media, culture and pub. policy 1990-96), St. Louis Princeton Club (bd. dirs. 1987—). Home: 816 S Hanley Rd Apt 4b Saint Louis MO 63105-2657 E-mail: socetz@alumni.princeton.edu.

EUBANKS, EUGENE EMERSON, education educator, consultant; b. Meadville, Pa., June 6, 1939; s. Nelson Eubanks and Emily (Princes) Jackson; m. Audrey Hunter, Aug. 4, 1962; children: Brian, Regina. BS, Edinboro U., Pa., 1963; PhD, Mich. State U., 1972. Tchr. Cleve. Pub. Schs., 1963-68, unit prin., 1968-70; asst. prof. U. Del., Newark, 1972-74; asst. dean U. Mo., Kansas City, 1974-79, dean, 1979-88, prof. edn. and urban affairs, 1988—; dept. supt. Kansas City Pub. Schs., 1984-85. Contbr. articles to profl. jours. Cons. Urban League, 1978—, legal def. fund NAACP, 1978, Cleve. Found., 1978, U. Wis., 1988; bd. dirs. Operation PUSH, 1982-87, Mid-Continent Girl Scouts, Kansas City, 1983—, Genesis Sch., 1984—; chair Desegration Monitoring Com., 1985—. Mem. Am. Assn. Coll. Tchr. Edn. (pres. 1988-89), Nat. Alliance Found. (chmn. 1984-85), Black Sch. Educators (edn. commn.). Home: 12737 Oakmont Dr Kansas City MO 64145-1140 Office: U Mo Sch Edn 5100 Rockhill Rd Kansas City MO 64110-2481 Office Phone: 816-235-2448. Business E-Mail: EubanksE@umkc.edu.

EUBANKS-POPE, SHARON G., real estate company executive, entrepreneur; b. Chgo., Aug. 26, 1943; d. Walter Franklyn and Thelma Octavia (Watkins) Gibson; m. Larry Hudson Eubanks, Dec. 20, 1970 (dec. Jan. 1976); children: Rebekah, Aimée; m. Otis Eliot Pope, June 7, 1977; children: O. Eliot Jr., Adrienne. BS in Edn., Chgo. Tchrs. Coll., 1965; postgrad., Ill. Inst. Tech., Chgo., 1967, John Marshall Law Sch., 1970, Governors State U., University Park, Ill., 1975-76. Educator, parent coord. Chgo. Bd. Edn., 1965-77; owner, ptnr. Redel Rentals, Chgo., 1977—. Realtor, 1990—. Adminstrv. bd. St. Mark United Meth. Ch., Chgo., 1967, bd. trustees, 1988; com. chair Englewood Urban Progress Ctr., Chgo., 1973; coord., educator LWV, 1975-76; chair comms. Marian Cath. H.S., 1999-2005, adv. bd.; mem. Cottage Grove Tax Increment Financing Bd., 2005—; mem. bd. The Princeton Group, Inc., 2007-, The Links Found., Inc., 2007-. Named Outstanding Sch. Parent Vol., Chgo. Bd. Edn., 1977; recipient Outstanding Cmty. Law Class award LWV, 1975-76, Christian Leadership award United Meth. Women, Chgo., 1985. Mem.: NAACP, NAFE, Nat. Assn. Realtors, Am. Soc. Profl. and Exec. Women, St. Mark Cmty. Devel. Corp. (v.p. 2003—), Links, Inc., Jack and Jill Am., Inc. (Chgo. chpt. journalist 1989—91, parliamentarian 1991, founder Parents for Parity in Edn. 1992, pres. Eubanks-Pope Devel. Co., Inc. 1993, Midwestern region sec.-treas. 1993—95, nat. treas. 1998—2000, Midwestern regional dir. 1995—97), Alpha Beta Gamma (female exec. del. to China People to People Amb. program 1998). Office: Redel Rentals 4338 S Drexel Blvd Chicago IL 60653-3536

EUGSTER, JACK WILSON, retail executive; b. Mound, Minn., Oct. 7, 1945; s. George and Helen M. (Kerr) E.; m. Camie M. Rust; children: Nicholas J., Wilson M. BA in Chemistry, Carleton Coll., 1967; MBA in Fin., Stanford U., 1969. Mgr. ops. and merchandising Target Stores Inc., Mpls., 1970-72; exec. v.p. The Gap Stores, San Bruno, Calif., 1972-80; chmn., pres., CEO The Musicland Group, Inc., Mpls., 1980—2001. Bd. dirs. Donaldson Corp., Midwest Resources Inc., Des Moines, Damark Inc., Mpls., Carleton Coll., Northfield, Minn., Best Buy Co., ShopKo Stores, Inc., Green Bay, Wis., chmn. bd. dirs., 2001— Divsn. chmn. campaign United Way, Mpls., 1980—; bd. dirs. Children's Home Soc. Minn. Recipient Human Relations Music and Video Div. award Anti-Defamation League, .Y.C., 1986. Mem. Nat. Assn. Recording Merchandisers (bd. dirs. 1981-88, pres. 1985-86), Country Music Assn. (bd. dirs. 1985-88, chmn. 1987-88), Wayzata Country Club, Mpls. Club. Home: 2655 Kelly Ave Excelsior MN 55331-9532 Office: Chairman Shopko Stores Inc 700 Pilgrim Way Green Bay WI 54304

EUSTIS, JOANNE D., university librarian; BA in English Lit., Ind. U., 1974, MLS, 1974, MA in English Lit., 1979. Various libr. positions Va. Poly. Inst. and State U., 1974—98, interim libr. dir., 1992—94; univ. libr. Case Western Res. U., Cleve., 1998—. Office: Kelvin Smith Libr Case Western Res U 11055 Euclid Ave Cleveland OH 44106-7151 Office Phone: 216-368-2992. E-mail: joanne.eustis@case.edu.

EVANICH, KEVIN REESE, lawyer; b. 1955; BA, U. Wis., Milw., 1976; JD, Northwestern U., 1980. Bar: Ill. 1980. Assoc. Kirkland & Ellis LLP, Chgo., 1983—86, ptnr., mem. firm mgmt. com., 1995—. Named one of World's Leading Lawyers in Corp. M&A, Chambers Global, 2002—06; recipient Award for Excellence in Pvt. Equity, Chambers & Partners, 2006. Mem.: Phi Beta Kappa. Office: Kirkland & Ellis LLP 200 E Randolph Dr Chicago IL 60601 Office Phone: 312-861-2076. Office Fax: 312-861-2200. Business E-Mail: kevanich@kirkland.com.

EVANS, BRENT, state legislator; Rep. dist. 92 Mo. Ho. of Reps., Jefferson City, 1994-2000. Republican.

EVANS, CHARLES H., federal judge; b. 1922; BA, U. Ill., 1947, JD, 1948. Asst. atty. gen. State of Ill., 1949—56, 1957—62; pvt. law practice, 1962—77; magistrate judge Ill. Crt., Springfield, 1977—. With USAAF, 1942—45. Office: 110 US Courthouse 600 E Monroe St Springfield IL 62701-1626

EVANS, CLYDE MERRILL, academic administrator, state representative; b. Gallipolis, Ohio, June 26, 1938; s. Owen Wade and Reva Belle (Hutchinson) E.; m. Rosemary Salser, Aug. 26, 1961; children: Mary Margaret, Sarah Leigh, Nancy Jane, Dylan Owen Wade. BA, Union Coll., 1960; MA, Eastern Ky. State U., 1962; PhD, U. So. Miss., 1972; cert. in adminstrn., Ohio U., Athens, 1967. Cert. secondary tchr., Ohio; cert. counselor, Ohio; cert. supt., Ohio. V.p. student devel. Rio Grande (Ohio) Coll., 1972-77, provost, 1977-84; project dir., assoc. prof. sports mgmt. U.S. Sports Acad., Mobile, Ala., 1984-86; prin. Vinton County Schs., McArthur, Ohio, 1986-89; v.p. adminstrn. U. Rio Grande, Ohio, 1989—. Pres. Rio Grande Village Council, 1968-70, O.O. McIntyre Park Dist., Gallipolis, 1973-84; bd. dirs., treas. Southeastern Ohio Emergency Med. Service, Gallipolis, 1977-80; state rep. 87th H.O. (Ohio). Named one of Outstanding Young Men of Am., Outstanding Ams. Found., 1970. Mem. Ohio Assn. Elem. Sch. Adminstrs., Gallipolis Area C. of C. (bd. dirs. 1990), Gallia County Hist. Soc. (bd. dirs. 1991). Republican. Baptist. Avocations: reading, sports. Home: PO Box 36 Rio Grande OH 45674-0036

EVANS, CRAIG L., lawyer; b. Kansas City, Mo., 1960; BA, William Jewell Coll., 1982; JD, U. Kans., 1985. Bar: Tex. 1985, Mo. 1997. Ptnr., chair Mergers and Acquisitions/Securities Practice Group Shook, Hardy & Bacon LLP, Kansas City. Office: Shook, Hardy & Bacon LLP 2555 Grand Blvd Kansas City MO 64108 Office Phone: 816-559-2478. Office Fax: 816-421-5547. E-mail: cevans@shb.com.

EVANS, DANIEL E., manufacturing executive, restaurant chain company executive; b. Gallipolis, Ohio, Aug. 24, 1936; With Bob Evans Farms Inc., Columbus, Ohio, 1957—; chmn. bd., sec., CEO, dir., 1971—. Office: Bob Evans Farms Inc 3776 S High St Columbus OH 43207-4000

EVANS, DANIEL FRALEY, JR., lawyer; b. Indpls., Apr. 19, 1949; s. Daniel Fraley and Julie (Sloan) E.; m. Marilyn Schultz, Aug. 11, 1973; children: Meredith, Benjamin, Suzannah, Theodore. BA, Ind. U., 1971, JD, 1976. Bar: Ind. 1976, U.S. Dist. Ct. (so. dist.) Ind. 1976, U.S. Ct. Appeals (7th cir.) 1983, U.S. Supreme Ct. 1983. Assoc. Sparrenberger, Duvall, Tabbert, Lalley & Newton, Indpls., 1976-77; ptnr. Duvall, Tabbert, Lalley & Newton, Indpls., 1977-81, Bayh, Tabbert & Capehart, Indpls., 1981-85, Baker & Daniels, Indpls., 1985—. Chmn. Ind. Bd. Correction, Indpls., 1976-88, Qyaule for Senate Com., 1980, 86, Quayle for v.p. com.; mem. Fed. Jud. Merit Sel. Com., Indpls., 1981-88, Adminstrv. Conf. U.S., 1983-88; chmn. Indpls. Dist. Fed. Home Loan Bank Bd., 1987-90, Fed. Housing Fin. Bd., 1990-93; vice chmn. Methodist Health Group, Inc., 1996—, Cir. Investors, Inc., 1997—; vice chmn. Hudson Inst., Inc., 1996—, Cir. Investors, 1994-99; chancellor South Ind. Conf. United Meth. Ch., 1998—; gen. coun. Citizens Gas Utility, 1999—; bd. dirs. Clarian Health Ptnrs., Inc., Indpls., Downtown, Inc., 1992-96, Meth. Hosp. Ind. Mem. Ind. Bar Assn., Indpls. Bar Assn., Woodstock Club, Indpls. Club. Republican. Methodist. Office: Baker & Daniels 300 N Meridian St Ste 2700 Indianapolis IN 46204-1782

EVANS, DAVID, communications executive; b. Eau Claire, WI, July 26, 1962; m. Beth (Steenson) E., September 4, 1984, children, Alex, Ben. BBA in Acctg., UW-Milwaukee, Milwaukee, 1985; MBA, Marquette Univ., Milwaukee, WI, 1990. CPA, CMA. Sr. fin. analyst A.O. Smith, Automotive Products, Co., Milwaukee, WI, 1986-89; formerly pres., chief exec. officer United Artists Corp., Beverly Hills, Calif., 1989; div. controller Everbrite, Inc., Milwaukee, WI, 1989-93; with Ohlmeyer Communications Cos., LA, 1989—; CFO Plymouth Ind., Minneapolis, Minn., 1993—. Office: Plymouth Industries Inc 2601 Niagara Ln N Plymouth MN 55447-4721 E-mail: devans@plymouthind.com.

EVANS, DAVID R., state representative; b. Newark, Ohio, Mar. 13, 1937; married; 3 children. BA, Franklin U.; MA, Ctrl. Mich. U. Ret. ins. underwriter State Farm Ins.; state rep. dist. 71 Ohio Ho. of Reps., Columbus, 1998—, chair, transp. and justice subcom., mem. criminal justice, fin. and appropriations, ins., and transp. and pub. safety coms. Loaned exec. United Way; councilman Newark City Coun., 10 yrs. Named AMVETS Legis. of Yr., 2000; recipient Top Gun award, Ohio Nat. Guard, 1982. Mem.: Internat. Mgmt. Coun. (past pres. local chpt.), Nat. Rep. Com. (life; Eisenhower Commn. 1995), Camelot Condo Assn., ewark Jaycees (officer), Young Rep. Club (officer). Republican. Methodist. Office: 77 S High St 13th Columbus OH 44321-6111

EVANS, DOUGLAS MCCULLOUGH, surgeon, educator; b. Vandergrift, Pa., July 31, 1925; s. Archibald Davis and Helen Irene (McCullough) E.; m. Thelmajean Volkers, Aug. 1, 1959; children: Matthew Kirk, Daniel Scott. MD, Western Res. U., 1952; postgrad., U. Mich., 1956-58. Diplomate Am. Bd. Surgery. Resident in surgery Henry Ford Hosp., 1952-57, chief resident in surgery, 1957-58, mem. surgery staff, 1959-60, Akron (Ohio) Gen. Hosp., 1960-70; chmn. dept. surgery Akron Gen. Med. Ctr., 1971-90, rsch. cons.; prof. and chmn. surgery emeritus Northeastern Ohio U. Coll. Medicine. Served with AUS, 1943-46. Fellow: ACS; mem.: AAAS, AMA, .Y. Acad. Scis., Ohio Med. Assn., Midwest Surg. Soc., Soc. Critical Care Medicine, Metastasis Rsch. Soc., Am. Assn. Cancer Rsch. Republican. Presbyterian. Office: 400 Wabash Ave Akron OH 44307-2433

EVANS, GORTON M., paper products executive; Exec. v.p. Consolidated Papers, Inc., Wisconsin Rapids, Wis., 1996, pres., CEO, 1997—. Mem. Nat. Assn. Mfrs. (dir.), Am. Forest and Paper Assn. (past chmn. printing and writing div.). Office: Consolidated Papers Inc 231 1st Ave North Wisconsin Rapids WI 54495

EVANS, IVOR J. (IKE), railroad executive; Diploma, Kans. State U.; postgrad., Harvard U., Emory U. Exec. GM Corp., 1973-85, gen. mgf. mgr. Harrison Radiator divsn.; pres. Blackstone N.Am. Co., Jamestown, N.Y., 1985-87; exec. v.p. Armtek, New Haven, 1987; sr. v.p. Emerson Electric Co., St. Louis; pres., COO Union Pacific RR, Omaha, 1998—. Office: Union Pacific Corp 1416 Dodge St Rm 1230 Omaha NE 68179

EVANS, JAMES E., lawyer; b. 1946; BA, Mich. State U., 1968; JD, Ohio State U., 1970. Bar: Ohio 1971. Assoc. Keating, Muething & Klekamp, 1970—76; named v.p., gen. counsel Am. Fin. Corp. (former subsid. Am. Fin. Group Inc.), Cin., 1976; sr. v.p., gen. counsel, dir. Am. Fin. Group Inc., Cin., 1995—. Mem.: Cin. Bar Assn., Ohio Bar Assn., ABA. Office: Am Fin Group Inc 1 E 4th St Cincinnati OH 45202

EVANS, JOHN ERIK, insurance company executive; b. Des Moines, Oct. 10, 1927; s. Harold Sulser and Lana Edna (Eriksen) Evans; m. Priscilla Nunn Garrett, Aug. 6, 1949 (div. 1976); children: Janice, Julie, John Evans Jr.; m. Jane Ellen Welker, Jan. 28, 1978. BSc, U. Iowa, 1949. Mktg. rep. Aid Ins. Svcs., Des Moines, 1949—54, asst. sec., 1954—57, sec., 1957—59, v.p., 1959—61, exec. v.p., 1961—63, pres., chmn. bd., 1963—. Dir. Mutual Casualty Cos. Conf. Chmn. Des Moines Planning and Zoning Bd., 1978; bd. dirs. Iowa Meth. Med. ctr.; chmn. Iowa Fair Plan, Des Moines, 1976. Mem.: Alliance Am. Insurers, Greater Des Moines C. of C., Wakonda Country Club, Masons. Republican. Episcopalian. Home: PO Box 119 Pebble Beach CA 93953-0119 Office: Amco Ins Co 701 5th Ave Des Moines IA 50391-0001

EVANS, KENNETH M., manufacturing executive; Student, Villanova U.; grad., Stanford Bus. Sch. Various mgmt. positions The Sherwin Williams Co., Evans Paints, Inc., Thompson & Formby, Inc., Kodak, Homecare Products Group; pres., CEO, dir. Armor All Products Corp., 1997, Clorox, 1997; exec. v.p. RPM, Inc., 1998-99, pres. consumer group, 1999—. Office: 2628 Pearl Rd Medina OH 44256-7623

EVANS, LANE ALLEN, retired congressman; b. Rock Island, Ill., Aug. 4, 1951; s. Lee Herbert and Joycelene (Saylor) E. BA, Augustana Coll., 1974; JD, Georgetown U., 1978. Bar: Ill. 1978. Mng. atty. Western Ill. Legal Assistance Found., Rock Island, 1978-79; mem. nat. staff Kennedy for Pres., Washington, 1978-80; atty., ptnr. Community Legal Clinic, Rock Island, Ill., 1981-82; mem. U.S. Congress from 17th Ill. Dist., 1983—2007; mem. nat. security com., ranking mem. vets. affairs com., armed svcs. com. Served with USMC, 1969-71. Mem. AmVets, Am. Legion, Marine Corps League, Vietnam Vets Ill. Democrat. Roman Catholic.

EVANS, OLIVER H., college administrator; b. Burlington, Vt., June 15, 1944; s. Samuel H. and Louise (Lifsey) E.; m. Eileen Beary, Sept. 10, 1973; children: Rachel, Ethan. BA, Albion Coll., 1966; MA, Purdue U., 1969, PhD, 1972. Asst. prof. Dakota State Coll., Madison, S.D., 1972-74, S.D. State U., Brookings, 1974-78, Creighton U., Omaha, 1978-80, Western Mich. U., Kalamazoo, 1980-84; dir. grad. studies Nazareth Coll., Kalamazoo, 1984-87, v.p. acad. affairs, 1987-90, pres., 1990, Kendall Coll. of Art and Design, Grand Rapids. Cons., evaluator North Cen. Assn., Chgo., 1988—. Author: George Henry Boker, 1984; contbr. articles to profl. jours. Office: Kendall College of Art and Design 17 Fountain St NW Grand Rapids MI 49503-1312

EVANS, TERENCE THOMAS, federal judge; b. Milw., Mar. 25, 1940; s. Robert Hansen and Jeanette (Walters) Evans; m. Joan Marie Witte, July 24, 1965; children: Kelly Elizabeth, Christine Marie, David Rourke. BA, Marquette U., 1962, JD, 1967. Bar: Wis. 1967. Law clk. to justice Wis. Supreme Ct., 1967—68; asst. dist. atty. Milw. County, 1968—70; assoc. Cook & Franke, Wis., 1970—72, ptnr. Wis., 1972—74; county judge Milw. County Ct., 1974—78; cir. judge State of Wis., 1978—80; judge, then chief judge US Dist. Ct. (ea. dist) Wis., Milw., 1979—95; judge US Ct. Appeals (7th cir.), 1995—. Mem.: ABA, Judicial Coun. of Seventh Circuit, Seventh Circuit Bar Assn., Milw. Bar Assn., State Bar Wis. Roman Catholic. Office: US Courthouse & Federal Bldg 517 E Wisconsin Ave Rm 721 Milwaukee WI 53202-4504

EVANS, THOMAS E., autoparts company executive; BSME, Pa. State U.; MSME, MBA, U. Mich. Various positions Rockwell Internat., 1973-89; gen. mgr. worldwide sealing and ball bearing products Fed. Mogul; various positions Case Corp.; pres. Tenneco Automotive; CEO, chmn. Collins & Aikman, Troy, Mich., 1999—2005. Bd. dirs. Wis. Ctrl. Transp. Corp.; trustee Inst. Textile Tech. Mem. Nat. Assn. Mfrs. (bd. dirs.).

EVANSON, BARBARA JEAN, middle school education educator; b. Grand Forks, ND, Aug. 15, 1944; d. Robert John and Jean Elizabeth (Lommen) Gibbons; m. Bruce Carlyle Evanson, Dec. 27, 1965; children: Tracey, John, Kelly. AA, Bismarck State Coll., 1964; BS in Spl. and Elem. Edn., U. N.D., 1966. Tchr. spl. edn. Winship Sch., Grand Forks, 1966-67, Simle Jr. High, Bismarck, 1967-70; tchr. Northridge Elem. Sch., Bismarck, 1980-86, Wachter Middle Sch., Bismarck, 1986—. Cons. Dept. Pub. Instrn., Bismark, 1988—, Chpt. I, Bismark, 1989—, McRel for Drug Free Schs., Denver, 1990-95. Co-founder The Big People, Bismarck, 1978-95; mem. task force Children's Trust Fund, N.D., 1984; senator N.D. Legislature, Bismarck, 1989-94; mem. N.D. Bridges Adv. Bd., 1991-97, DPI English Adv. Com., 1993—; co-facilitator Lead Mid. Sch. for Carnegie, 1994-97, N.D. Health Adv. Coun., 1993-94, N.D. Tchr.'s Fund for Retirement, State Investment Bd. 1996—; co-founder, bd. dirs. Neighbors Network, 1983—. Recipient Gold Award Bismark Norwest Bank, 1985; named Tchr. of Yr., N.D. Dept. Pub. Instrn., 1989, Legislator of Yr., Children's Caucus, 1991, Outstanding Alumnae, Bismarck State Coll., 1991, Milken Nat. Tchr. of Yr., 1995-96, KX Golden Apple award, 1999. Mem. N.D. Reading Assn., N.D. Coun. of Tchrs. of English., NEA, N.D. Edn. Assn., Bismarck Edn. Assn. Avocations: walking, reading, travel, remodeling. Office: Wachter Middle Sch 1107 S 7th St Bismarck ND 58504-6533

EVEN, FRANCIS ALPHONSE, lawyer; b. Chgo., Sept. 8, 1920; s. George Martin and Cecilia (Neuman) E.; m. Margaret Hope Herrick, Oct. 16, 1945; children: Janet Beth, Dorothy Elizabeth. BS in Mech. Engring, U. Ill., 1942; JD, George Washington U., 1949. Bar: D.C. 1949, Ill. 1950. Engr. GE, 1945-49; ptnr. Fitch, Even, Tabin & Flannery (patent and trademark law), Chgo., 1952—. Bd. edn., River Forest, Ill., 1963-69; trustee West Suburban Hosp., Oak Park, Ill., 1974-77; mem. bd. Ill. State Hist. Soc., 2000-03. Combat engr., U.S. 3d inf. divsn., 1942-45. Decorated knight French Legion of Honor. Fellow Am. Coll. Trial Lawyers (emeritus); mem. ABA, Am. Intellectual Property Law Assn. (bd. mgrs. 1963-66), Ill. Bar Assn., Chgo. Bar Assn., Intellectual Property Law Assn. Chgo. (bd. mgrs. 1972-73, pres. 1984), No. Ill. Ct. Hist. Assn. (pres. 2000-06), Union League Club (Chgo.), Chgo. Literary Club. Republican. Office: 120 S La Salle St Chicago IL 60603-3403 Home: 134 Windsor Park Dr Apt D-101 Carol Stream IL 60188 Office Phone: 312-577-7000.

EVENSON, MERLE ARMIN, chemist, educator; b. LaCrosse, Wis., July 27, 1934; s. Ansel Bernard and Gladys Mabel (Nelson) E.; m. Peggy L. Kovats, Oct. 5, 1957; children— David A., Donna L. BS in Chem. Physics and Math., U. Wis., LaCrosse, 1956; MS in Guidance, Madison, 1960, MS in Sci. Edn., 1960, PhD in Analytical Chemistry, 1966. Diplomate Am. Bd. Clin. Chemists, v.p., 1978-81. Tchr. math. and physics St. Croix Falls (Wis.) High Sch., 1956-57; tchr. chemistry Central High Sch., LaCrosse, 1957-59; instr. dept. medicine U. Wis., Madison, 1965-66, asst. prof., 1966-69, asso. prof., 1971-75, prof., 1975—, prof. dept. pathology, 1979—; asst. dir. clin. lab. Univ. Hosps., 1965-66, dir. clin. chemistry lab., 1966-69, dir. toxicology lab., 1971-87. Chmn. Gordon Rsch. Conf. on Analytical Chemistry, 1978; vis. lectr. Harvard Med. Sch., 1969-71; mem. staff Peter Bent Brigham Hosp., Boston, 1969-71; cons. on analytical and clin. chemistry to AEC, 1968-93, Am. Chem. Soc., Nat. Bur. Standards, FDA, NIH, study sect. mem. 1968-72, ad hoc memberships, 1973-87. Bd. editors: Chemical Instrumentation, 1973-87, Analytical Chemistry, 1974-77, Jour. Analytical Toxicology, 1976-79, Selected Methods in Clin. Chemistry, 1977-81; editor: Contemporary Topics in Analytical and Clincal Chemistry, 1974-83; contbr. numerous chpts. to books, articles to profl. jours.; patentee continuous oil hemoperfusion unit. NIH fellow, 1970-71, NSF, 1959-62; recipient Maurice O. Graff Disting. Alumni award U. Wis., LaCrosse, 1981 Mem. AAAS, Acad. Clin. Lab. Physicians and Scientists, Am. Assn. Clin. Chemists (bd. editors Clin. Chemistry 1970-80, nat. chair pub. rels. com. 1973-78, diplomat 1974, v.p. 1978-81), Am. Chem. Soc. (com. on clin. chemistry 1973-93), Sigma Xi, Kappa Delta Pi. Office: U Wis 1300 University Ave Madison WI 53706-1510

EVERETT, KAREN JOAN, retired librarian, genealogist, educator; b. Cin., Dec. 12, 1926; d. Leonard Kelly and Kletis V. (Wade) Wheatley; m. Wilbur Mason Everett, Sept. 25, 1950; children: Karen, Jan, Jeffrey, Jon, Kathleen, Kerry, Kelly, Shannon. BS in Edn. magna cum laude, U. Cin., 1976, postgrad., 1982-85, Coll. Mt. St. Joseph, 1981-86, Xavier U., Cin., 1985-87, U. Cin., 1982-85, Miami U., 1987. Libr. S.W. Local Schs., Harrison, Ohio, 1967-97, dist. media coord., 1980-97, dist. vol. dir., 1980-97, ret., 1997; instr. genealogy U. Cin., 1998—. Tchr. genealogy U. Cin., 1997—; cons. in field; bd. dirs. U. Cin. ILR; lectr. in field. Contbr. articles to profl. jours. Pres. Citizens Adv. Coun., Harrison, Ohio, 1981-84, 88—, Citizens Adv. Coun., 1989; state chmn. supervisory div. Ohio Ednl. Libr./Media Assn.; mem. Ohio Ambulance Licensing Bd., 1991—. Named Woman of the Yr., Cin. Enquirer, 1978, Xi Eta Iota, 1979; named PTA Educator of the Yr., 1981, others. Mem. NEA, Ohio Ednl. Libr./Media Assn. (chair supervisory div. 1990—, bd. dirs. 1993-94), Ohio Edn. Assn., S.W. Local Classroom Tchrs. Assn., Hamilton County Geneal. Soc. (bd. dirs. 1992—). Avocations: flying, travel, genealogy. Personal E-mail: karywib@aol.com.

EVERHART, BRUCE, radio station executive; Sta. mgr. WMBI-AM/FM, Chgo. Home: WMBI-FM 820 N LaSalle St Chicago IL 60610

EVERIST, BARBARA, state legislator; b. Sioux Falls, SD, July 6, 1949; d. F. M. and H. M. (Kobb) McBride; m. Thomas Stephen Everist Jr., 1968; children: Thomas Stephen III, Michael Clayton, Lacey Elizabeth. BA, U. Santa Clara, 1971; JD, U. S.D., 1990. Bar: S.D. 1990, U.S. Dist. Ct. S.D. 1990. Law clk. S.D. 2d Cir., 1990-91; state rep. S.D. Ho. Reps. Dist. 14, 1993-94; mem. S.D. Senate Dist. 14, 1995—; mem. state affairs and judiciary coms. S.D. State Senate Dist. 14, chmn. edn. com. Mem. Commerce, Judiciary and Taxation Coms.; atty., Sioux Falls, 1990—. Mem. S.D. State Bar Assn., Assn. Gifted and Talented (pres. 1985), Jr. League Sioux Falls (pres. 1980-81), Phi Alpha Delta, Pi Beta Phi. Home: 709 E Tomar Rd Sioux Falls SD 57105-7053 Office: SD Senate 500 E Capitol Ave Pierre SD 57501-5070

EVERLY, JACK, conductor; b. Richmond, Va. Grad., Ind. U. Prin. condr. Am. Ballet Theatre, NYC, 1984—98; mus. dir. & condr. Ameritech's Yuletide Celebration, Indianapolis Symphony Orchestra, 1994—; music advisor Symphonic Pops Consortium, 1998—; prin. pops condr. Indpls. Symphony Orch., 2002—, Balt. Symphony Orch. Conducted shows including Hello, Dolly!, 1978, A Chorus Line, They're Playing Our Song, Showboat, Kismet, Carousel, The Mikado, Hazel Kirk, Everything's Coming Up Roses: The Complete Overtures of Broadway's Jule Styne; conductor Vancouver Symphony, San Diego Symphony, Lake George Opera Festival, Pacific Symphony, Ravinia Festival; music dir., orchestrator In Performance at the White House; conductor world premiers at Am. Ballet Theatre include Sir Kenneth MacMillan's Requiem, Agnes de Mille's The Informer, Mikhail Baryshnikov's Giselle and Swan Lake; conducted music for Disney's The Hunchback of Notre Dame Office: Indianapolis Symphony Orchestra 32 E Washington St Ste 600 Indianapolis IN 46204

EVERSON, CURT, state commissioner; Commr. S.D. State Fin. and Mgmt. Bur., Pierre. Office: SD State Fin and Mgmt Bur 500 E Capitol Ave Pierre SD 57501-5070

EVERSON, JEAN WATKINS DOLORES, librarian, media consultant, educator; b. Forest City, NC, Feb. 14, 1938; d. J.D. Watkins and Hermie Roberta (Dizard) Watkins; children: Curtis Bryon, Vincent Keith. BS Elem. Edn., U. Cin., 1971, M Secondary Edn., 1973. Cert. X-ray technician. Educator Cin. Pub. Schs., Cin., 1965—2002, classroom tchr., parent/school coord., 1965—2002; work study coord. Butler County Edn. Ctr., Fairfield, Ohio, 1997—98; long term sub. Brown County -Georgetown Sch. Sys., Gerogetown, Ohio, 1993; sr. staff asst., cpc/alcohol substance abuse, inc. Cin. Pub. Schs., Cin., 1992—93; libr. tech. media; libr. media tech. asst. langsam libr. University of Cin.cinnati-Langsam Library, Cincinnati. Dir. and coord. tutoring program So. Baptist Ch., Cincinnati, 1990—91. Author: (booklet) Gospel Music: Copywrite Laws, 1987 (1987). Prodr./dir./coord. city music festival in music hall Cin. Pub. Schs., 1972—77. Mem.: Ohio Assn. Suprs. and Work Study Coords., Music Educator Nat. Conf. Baptist. Avocations: travel, walking. Home: PO Box 8337 West Chester OH 45069 Office: Cin City Pub Schs-Woodward 7001 Reading Rd Cincinnati OH 45237 Home Phone: 513-858-6880. Office Fax: 513-758-1279; Home Fax: 513-858-6880. Business E-Mail: eversoj@cpsboe.k12.oh.us.

EVERT, RAY FRANKLIN, botany educator; b. Mt. Carmel, Pa., Feb. 20, 1931; s. Milner Ray and Elsie (Hoffa) I.; m. Mary Margaret Maloney, Jan. 2, 1960; children: Patricia Ann, Paul Franklin. BS, Pa. State U., 1952, MS, 1954; PhD, U. Calif. at Davis, 1958. Mem. faculty Mont. State U., 1958—60, U. Wis.-Madison, 1960—, prof. botany, 1966—77, prof. botany and plant pathology, 1977—88, Katherine Esau prof. botany and plant pathology, 1988—2001, emeritus prof. botany and plant pathology, 2001—, chmn. dept. botany, 1973—74, 1977—79, 1994—98. Vis. prof. U. Natal, Pietermaritzburg, S. Africa, winter, spring 1971, U. Göttingen, W.Ger., summer 1971, 74-75, summer 1988; mem. gen. biology and genetics fellowship rev. panel NIH, 1964-68, NSF Adv. Com. for Biol. Research Ctrs. Program, 1987-88; forensic plant anatomy cons. Author: Esau's Plant Anatomy, Mesistems, Cells and Tissues of the Plant Body: Their Structure, Function and Development, 3d edit., 2006; co-author: Biology of Plants; sci. editor Physiol. Plantarum, 1983-98; mem. editl. bd. Trees, 1991-2000, Internat. Jour. Plant Scis., 1991-98; contbr. articles on food conducting tissue in higher plants and leaf structure-function relationships. Recipient Alexander von Humboldt award, 1974-75, Emil H. Steiger award for excellence in tchg. U. Wis., 1981, Bessey Lectr. award Iowa State U., Ames, 1984, Benjamin Minge Duggar lectureship award Auburn U., 1985, Disting. Svc. citation Wis. Acad. Scis., Arts and Letters, 1985, Hilldale award in biol. sci., 1998; Guggenheim fellow, 1965-66 Fellow Am. Acad. Arts and Scis., AAAS; mem. Bot. Soc. Am. (pres. 1986-87, Merit award 1982, Centennial medal 2006), Am. Inst. Biol. Scis., Wis. Acad. Scis., Arts and Letters, Am. Soc. Plant Physiol., Internat. Assn. Wood Anatomists, Deutschen Botanischen Gesellschaft, Golden Key Nat. Honor Soc., Sigma Xi, Phi Kappa Phi, Phi Sigma, Phi Epsilon Phi., Pi Alpha Xi. Home: 810 Woodward Dr Madison WI 53704-2238 Office Phone: 608-262-2678. Business E-Mail: rfevert@wisc.edu.

EVERY, MICHAEL A., state legislator; m. Laura Every; 4 children. Student, Milton Coll., 1981. Sales mgr. Double Z Broadcasting; mayor City of Minnewauken, N.D.; mem. N.D. Senate from 12th dist., Bismark, 2001—. Coun. pres. City of Minnewauken. Democrat. Office: PO Box 56 Minnewaukan ND 58351-0056 E-mail: mevery@state.nd.us.

EWICK, RAY (CHARLES RAY EWICK), librarian; b. Shelbyville, Ind., Sept. 13, 1937; s. Laurel R. and Loraine Pearl (Tufts) E.; m. Joann Hotchkiss, June 14, 1958; children— David Lee, Jeffrey Allen. BA, Wabash Coll., 1962; MA, Ind. U., 1966. Cons. Ind. State Library, Indpls., 1966-68, asst. dir., 1968-72, dir., 1978—. Dir. Rolling Prairie Libraries, Decatur, Ill., 1972-78 Mem. ALA, Ind. Library Assn., Phi Beta Mu. Office: Ind State Library 140 N Senate Ave Indianapolis IN 46204-2296

EWING, LYNN MOORE, JR., lawyer; b. Nevada, Mo., Nov. 14, 1930; s. Lynn Moore and Margaret Ray (Blair) E.; m. Peggy Patton Adams, July 10, 1954; children: Margaret Grace, Melissa Lee, Lynn Moore. AB, U. Mo., Columbia, 1952, JD, 1954. Bar: Mo. 1954. Ptnr. Ewing & Hoberock, Nevada, Mo., 1958—. Mem. Mo. Ho. of Reps., 1959-64; mem. Nevada City Coun., 1967-73, mayor, 1969-70, 72-73; mem., Mo. Land Reclamation Commn., 1971-75, Nevada Charter Comm., 1978-79, devel. coun. U. Mo., Columbia, Mo. Acad. of Squires, 1994—; mem. Mo. coord. bd. Higher Edn., 1997—, chmn., 2000—. Bd. dirs. Nevada Hosp., 1974-83; bd. dirs., pres. ev. Area Econ. Devel. Commn., 1985-88; vestryman, sr. warden All Saints Episcopal Ch. Served to 1st lt. USAF, 1954-56. Recipient Legis. award St. Louis Globe-Democrat, 1960, 62; named Citizen of Year, Nevada Rotary Club, 1975 Fellow Am. Bar Found. (life); mem. ABA, Mo. Bar Found. (life), Am. Coll. Trust and Estate Counsel, Am. Coll. Mortgage Attys., Am. Judicature Soc., U.S. League Savs. Assn. (chmn. attys. com. 1977-79), Mo. Bar (adv. com. 1975-84, bd. govs. 1974-78), Vernon County Bar Assn., Jefferson Club (trustee), Nevada Rotary (pres. 1969-70), Nevada Country Club. Democrat. Episcopalian. Office: 223 W Cherry St Nevada MO 64772-3361 Home: 307 West Blvd S Columbia MO 65203-2750

EWING, STEPHEN E., natural gas company executive; b. 1944; married. BA, DePauw U., 1965; MBA, Mich. State U., 1971. With Gen. Electric Co., 1965-66; with Mich. Consolidated Gas. Co., 1971—, coordinator mgmt. orgn. devel., 1972-73, mgr. adminstr. planning devel. services, 1973, dir. customer service, 1973-75, v.p. personnel, 1975-79, v.p. personnel and adminstrn., 1979-81, v.p. customer service, 1981-84, exec. v.p., 1984—85, pres., COO, 1985—92; pres., CEO Mich. Consolidated Gas. Co., MCN Energy Group, 1992—2001; group pres., COO gas bus. DTE Energy Co., Detroit, 2001—05, vice chmn., 2005—06. Served to capt., USAF, 1966-70.

EWING, SUSAN R., artist, educator; b. Lawrenceville, Ill., 1955; AA in Music, Stephens Coll., 1974; BA in Jewelry, Metalsmithing, Ind. U., 1976, MFA in Jewelry, Metalsmithing, 1980. Head metals program, disting. prof. Miami U., Ohio, 1981—. One-person shows include Hans Hansen Sølv, Copenhagen, Denmark, Nat. Tech. Mus., Prague, Czech Republic, Phoenix Mus. Art, Ohio Craft Mus., Columbus, Ark. Ctr., Little Rock; group shows include Aspects Gallery, London, Park Ryu Sook Gallery, Seoul, Korea, Schweizerisches Landesmuseum, Zurich, Switzerland, Cercle Mcpl. Galerie Oféo, Luxembourg, Mus. Kunsthandwerk, Frankfurt, Germany, Deutsches Klingenmuseum, Solingen, Germany, Schmuckmuseum, Pforzheim, Germany, Galerie Matter, Cologne, Germany, Galerie Ende, Cologne, Mathildenhohe Mus., Darmstadt, Germany, Galerie Spectrum, Munich, Germany, Galerie Ventil, Munich, Fortunoff's N.Y.C., Urban BobKat Gallery, N.Y.C., Lever House, N.Y.C., Seventh Regiment Armory, N.Y.C., Am. Craft Mus., N.Y.C.; represented in permanent collections White House. Recipient Dolibois Faculty Devel. award, disting. Lifetime Achievement award Ohio Designer Craftsmen; Summer Rsch. fellow Miami U., Ohio Arts Coun. Individual Artist fellow, 1987, 89, 91, Fulbright grantee, 1997, 98; Rsch. Challenge grantee Ohio State Bd. Regents. Home: 45 Hidden Creek Dr Oxford OH 45056 Office: 124 Art Bldg Miami U Oxford OH 45056

EWING, THOMAS WILLIAM, congressman, lawyer; b. Atlanta, Ill., Sept. 19, 1935; m. Connie Lupo, 1981; children: Jane, Kathryn, Sam, Christine Lupo, John Lupo, Stephanie Lupo. BS, Millikin U., 1957; JD, John Marshall Law Sch., Chgo., 1968. Asst. state atty. Livingston County, 1968-73; ptnr. Satter Ewing Beyer & Spires, Pontiac, Ill., 1969-91; mem. Ill. Ho. of Reps., 1974-91, U.S. Congress from 15th Ill. Dist., 1991-2001; mem. sci. com., agr. subcom., transp. and infrastructure coms., house adminstrn. com.; of counsel Davis and Harman L.L.P., Washington. Mem. agr. com. Ill. Ho. Reps., chmn. subcom. on risk mgmt. and specialty crops, subcom. on dept. ops., nutrition and fgn. agr., transp. and infrastructure com., aviation subcom., water resources and environment subcom., joint econ. com., former dep. minority leader, chmn. policy com., house revenue com., 1980, co-chmn. Ill. Econ. and Fiscal Commn., co-chmn. Legis. Space Needs Commn.; mem. biotech adv. coun. Monsanto, chmn. grower adv. coun.; chmn. biomass R&D tech. adv. com. Dept. Agr., Dept. Energy; bd. dirs. Pontiac Nat. Bank Holding Co., Inst. Representative Govt., Washington, D.C. Rep. precinct committeeman; del. Rep. Nat. Conv., 1980, 84, 88, 96, 2000; committeeman 15th Congl. Dist., 1986-93; mem. nat. advocacy com. Am. Diabetes Assn.; bd. dirs. Nat. Futures Assn. With U.S. Army, 1958, USAR, 1957-63. Recipient Best Legislator award Nat. Rep. Legislator of the Yr. award, 1982, Ill. Small Businessmen Assn., 1983, 85, 87, Friend of Agr. award Ill. Agrl. Assn., 1985, 87, 89, 91, Legislator of Yr. award Ill. Assn. Homes for the Aging, 1986. Mem. Livingston County Bar Assn., Pontiac C. of C. (past exec. dir., past pres.), Livingston County Farm Bur., Elks, Moose, Masons. Republican. Methodist. Home: 1647 Mockingbird Ln Pontiac IL 61764-9249 E-mail: TWewing@yahoo.com.

EYMAN, EARL DUANE, electrical science educator, consultant; b. Canton, Ill., Sept. 24, 1925; s. Arthur Earl and Florence Mabel (Hardin) E.; m. Ruth Margaret Morgan, Apr. 20, 1951; children: Joseph Earl, David James. BS in Engring. Physics, U. Ill., 1949, MS in Math, 1950, postgrad., 1951-64, U. Bradley, 1952-58; PhD in Elec. Engring., U. Colo., 1966. Registered profl. engr., Ill. Scientist Westinghouse Atomic Power Div., Pitts., 1950-51; research engr. Caterpillar Tractor Co., Peoria, Ill., 1951-58, project engr., 1958-66; mem. faculty Bradley U., Peoria, 1952-64; prof. elec. engring. U. Iowa, Iowa City, 1966-92, chmn. elec. engring., 1969-76. Cons. Sundstrand Aviation, Denver, 1966, Gould Simulation Systems Div., Melville, N.Y., 1978-81, U.S. Dept. Commerce, Boulder, 1978-92. Author: Modeling Simulation and Control, 1988; contbr. articles to profl. jours. Chmn., mem. Electricians Examining Bd., Iowa City, 1969-74. Served with USNR, 1944-46 Mem. Eta Kappa Nu (mem., pres. internat. bd. 1972-77), Tau Beta Pi, Theta Tau Avocations: skiing, mountain climbing, hiking.

EZGUR, MICHAEL H., real estate company executive; b. 1967; Undergraduate, Univ. Ill. Bar: Ill. Mng. broker Terrapin Realty Co., Chgo. Named one of 40 Under Forty, Crain's Bus. Chgo., 2005. Mem.: Internat. Coun. Shopping Centers, West Loop C. of C., Chgo. Assn. Realtors, Nat. Assn. Homebuilders, West Ctrl. Assn. (pres., mem. bd. dir.). Office: Terrapin Properties 217 N Jefferson St Fl 5 Chicago IL 60661 E-mail: mezgur@terrapingroup.com.

FABEL, THOMAS LINCOLN, lawyer; b. St. Paul, Feb. 12, 1946; s. George Forest and Beatrice Evelyn (Ostrom) F.; m. Jean Marquerite Hoisser, Nov. 21, 1946; children: Jessica, Anne, Leah, Theodore. BA, Carleton Coll., 1968; JD, U. Chgo., 1971; LLD (Hon.), William Mitchell Coll. Law, 1988. Bar: Minn. 1971; U.S. Dist. Ct. Minn. 1972; U.S. Ct. Appeals (8th cir.) 1974; U.S. Supreme Ct. 1976. Special asst. atty. gen. Minn. Atty. Gen., St. Paul, 1971-73, deputy atty. gen., 1973-87; ptnr. Lindquist & Vennum, Mpls., 1987-97, 99—; dep. mayor City of St. Paul, 1998. Adj. faculty William Mitchell Coll. Law, St. Paul, 1982-90. Mem. Minn. Bar Assn., Ramsey County Bar Assn., Rotary. Home: 1550 Edgewater Ave Saint Paul MN 55112-3630 Office: Lindquist & Vennum 4200 IDS Ctr 80 So 8th St Minneapolis MN 55402

FABENS, ANDREW LAWRIE, III, lawyer; b. Washington, Apr. 8, 1942; s. Andrew Lawrie Jr. and Alicia Gordon (Hail) F.; m. Martha Leigh Leingang, June 24, 1966; children: Andrew Lawrie IV, Jennie Leigh. AB, Yale U., 1964; JD, U. Chgo., 1967. Bar: Ohio 1967. Assoc. Thompson, Hine and Flory, Cleve., 1967-74; ptnr. Thompson Hine LLP (formerly Thompson, Hine and Flory), Cleve., 1974—, chmn. estate planning and probate area, 1988-94. Contbr. articles on estate planning and related topics to profl. publs. Pres. Family Health Assn., Cleve., 1978-80, 83-84; trustee A.M. McGregor Home, East Cleveland, Ohio, 1991—, chmn., 2001—; trustee Bascom Little Fund, Cleve., 1985—, Great Lakes Basin Conservancy, 1999—; bd. dirs. Georgian Bay Land Trust, 2006—; vestryman Christ Episcopal Ch., Shaker Heights, Ohio, 1972-77. Fellow Am. Coll. Trust and Estate Counsel; mem. Ohio State Bar Assn. (coun. estate planning, trust and probate law sect. 1983—, treas. 1997-99, sec. 1999-2001, vice-chmn. 2001-03, chmn. 2003-05), Cleve. Bar Assn. (speaker, com. mem. 1976—), Cleve. Skating Club, Rowfant Club (fellow 2000-03), The Novel Club (sec. 1986-88, pres. 1995-97). Home: 2280 Woodmere Dr Cleveland OH 44106-3604 Office: Thompson Hine LLP 3900 Key Ctr 127 Public Square Cleveland OH 44114-1216 Home Phone: 216-371-5213; Office Phone: 216-566-5736. Business E-Mail: andy.fabens@thompsonhine.com.

FABER, KEITH L., state representative; b. Troy, Mo., Jan. 19, 1966; s. Joeseph and Patsy Faber. BS in Pub. Adminstrn., Oakland U., 1988; JD, Ohio State U., 1991. Bar: Ohio 1991, Ind. 1991, U.S. Dist. Ct. (no. and so. dists.) Ind. 1991, U.S. Dist. Ct. (no. dist.) Ohio 1994. Assoc. Barnes & Thornburg, Ft. Wayne, Ind., 1991-93; house counsel Celina (Ohio) Group, 1993—2000; atty. Buck Berry Landau & Breunig, Indpls., 1993; atty., mediator Keith Faber Law Offices, 2001—; state rep. dist. 77 Ohio Ho. of Reps., Columbus, 2001—, mem. agr. and natural resources, criminal justice, energy and environment, fin. and appropriations, ins., and pub. utilities coms., mem. primary and secondary edn. subcom. Legal advisor Ohio Mock Trial Program. Mem. bd. editors Ohio Lawyers Mag. Advisor Explorer troop Boy Scouts Am., Celina, 1994; instr. CPCU program, Celina, 1994; Bd. dirs. Auglaize-Mercer YMCA; mem. ctrl. com., Mercer County Rep. Party; chair, Mercer County Rep. scholarship com Mem. ABA, Ohio State Bar Assn. (pub. understanding of law com. 1993—, chairperson newspaper editl. bd. Laws You Can Use), Ind. State Bar Assn., Am. Corp. Coun. Assn., Celina-Mercer County C. of C. (legis. affairs com.). Office: 77 High St Columbus OH 43266 E-mail: faber@bright.net.

FABER, TIMOTHY, retail executive; m. Marilu Faber. BS, U. Mich.; MBA in Fin., NYU. With treasury group Avon Products; former mng. dir. bus. devel. GE Capital svcs.; v.p. treasury, mergers and acquisitions Ltd. Brands, Inc., Columbus, Ohio, 2000—. Office: Ltd Brands Inc Three Ltd Pkwy Columbus OH 43230

FABRIS, JAMES A., journalist; b. Cleve., Aug. 6, 1938; s. Andrew and Geraldine (Foretic) F.; m. Donna Wilker, Dec. 26, 1960; children: Julia McBride, John, James F., Gerald, Andrew, Fredric. Student, Case Western Res. U., Cleve., 1956-58. Reporter Bklyn.-Parma News, Parma, Ohio, 1954-58; editorial staff Lake County ews-Herald, Willoughby, Ohio, 1958-67, Chgo. Daily News, 1967-77, Chgo. Sun-Times, 1977-84, dep. mng. editor, 1984-86; mng. editor N.Y. Post, NYC, 1986-89; editorial staff New York Daily News, 1990-92; deputy mng. editor Cleve. Plain Dealer, 1992—. Recipient Marshall Field award Field Enterprises, 1974; Soc. of Publ. Designers award, 1978 Roman Catholic. Home: 20791 Lake Rd Rocky River OH 44116-1335 Office: Cleve Plain Dealer 1801 Superior Ave Cleveland OH 44114-2107 Office Phone: 216-999-4278.

FAGG, GEORGE GARDNER, federal judge; b. Eldora, Iowa, Apr. 30, 1934; s. Ned and Arleene (Gardner) Fagg; m. Jane E. Wood, Aug. 19, 1956; children: Martha, Thomas, Ned, Susan, George, Sarah. BSBA, Drake U., 1965, JD, 1958. Bar: Iowa 1958. Ptnr. Cartwright, Druker, Ryden & Fagg, Marshalltown, Iowa, 1958—72; judge Iowa Dist. Ct., 1972—82, US Ct. Appeals (8th cir.), 1982—99, sr. judge, 1999—. Faculty Nat. Jud. Coll., 1979. Mem.: Iowa Bar Assn., Order of Coif. Office: US Ct Appeals US Courthouse Annex 110 E Court Ave Ste 455 Des Moines IA 50309-2044

FAHEY, MIKE, mayor; b. Kansas City, Mo., Dec. 20, 1943; 4 children. BA, Creighton Univ., 1973. Former owner Am. Land Title Co., 1978—90, ret. CEO, 1978—97; mayor City of Omaha, 2001—. Bd. Holy Name Housing, Am. Red Cross Heartland Chpt., Creighton Prep H.S.; chmn. Omaha Planning Bd., 1981. Office: City Hall Ste 300 1819 Farnam St Omaha NE 68183 Business E-Mail: mfahey@ci.omaha.ne.us.

FAHEY, RICHARD PAUL, lawyer; b. Oakland, Calif., Nov. 2, 1944; s. John Joseph and Helene Goldie (Whetstone) F.; m. Suzanne Dawson, June 8, 1968; children: Eamon, Aaron Chad. AA, Meritt Coll., 1964; BA, San Francisco State U., 1966; JD, Northwestern U., Evanston, Ill., 1971. Bar: N.Mex., 1971, US Dist. Ct. N.Mex., 1972, US Ct. Appeals (10th cir.) 1972, Ohio 1973, US Dist. Ct. (no. and so. dists.), US Supreme Ct. 1975. Atty. in charge Dinebeiina Nahiilna Be Agaditahe, Shiprock, N.Mex., 1971-73; asst. atty. gen. State of Ohio, Columbus, 1973-76; ptnr. Fahey & Schraff, 1976-80; atty. Sanford, Fisher, Fahey, Boyland & Schwarzwalder, 1980-84; of counsel Knepper, White, Arter & Hadden, 1984-85; ptnr. Arter & Hadden, 1985-99; of counsel Vorys Sater Seymour and Pease LLP, 2000—02, ptnr., 2003—; adj. prof. law Capital U., 1976-86, Ohio State U., 1986-87; chmn. Ohio Oil and Gas Regulatory Rev. Commn., 1986-87. Author: Underground Storage Tanks A Primer of the Federal Regulatory Program, 2d edit., 1995; contbr. articles to profl. jours. Vol. Peace Corps., Liberia, 1966—68; active Columbus Pub. Schs. Bd. Edn., 1986—93, pres., 1989; trustee Godman Guild Settlement House, 1976—82, Ohio Environ. Coun., 1981—83; adv. bd. WCBE Pub. Radio; Charter rev. com. Columbus City, 1998—99; pres. Audobon Ohio, 1999—2002; mem. sewer and water adv. bd. City of Columbus, 2004—07; mem. Hondo Vol. Fire Dept., Santa Fe, 2006—; exec. com. Dem. Party, Ohio, 1996—2002; trustee Downtown Columbus, Inc., 1989, Pilot Dogs, Inc., 1993—2004, pres., 2001, Cmty. in Sch., 2000—07. Recipient Democracy Action award, Columbus League Women Voters, 1999;

grantee, Russell Sage Found., 1969. Mem. ABA (vice chair Sonreel water quality com. 1993-97), Ohio Bar Assn., N.Mex. Bar Assn., Columbus Bar Assn., Columbus Bar Found. Democrat. Unitarian Universalist. Avocations: travel, fishing, reading, jogging, skiing. Address: 58 Camino Nevoso Santa Fe NM 87505 Office: Vorys Sater Seymour and Pease LLP 52 E Gay St Columbus OH 43215 Home Phone: 505-955-1630; Office Phone: 614-464-5601. Business E-Mail: rpfahey@vssp.com.

FAHIEN, LEONARD AUGUST, physician, educator; b. St. Louis, July 26, 1934; s. John Henry and Alice Katherine (Schubkegel) F.; m. Rose Marian Burmeister, June 21, 1958; children: Catherine Fahien Reuter, Lisa Fahien Uldrich, James. AB, Washington U., St Louis, 1956; MD, Washington U., 1960. Intern U. Wis., Madison, 1960-61; surgeon NIH, Bethesda, Md., 1964-66; asst. prof. dept. pharmacology U. Wis. Med. Sch., Madison, 1966-69, asso. prof., 1969-74, prof., 1974—, asso. dean, 1979-83, advisor Children's Diabetes Ctr., 2002—; vis. prof. Inst. Protein Rsch. Osaka U., Japan, 1991; prof. El Julios U. Barcelona (Spain), 1997. Contbr. chapters to books, articles to profl. jours. With USPHS, 1964—66. Numerous NIH grants, 1966—. Mem.: Phi Beta Kappa, Sigma Xi. Lutheran. Home: 3212 Topping Rd Madison WI 53705-1435 Office: 426 S Charter St Madison WI 53715-1626 Business E-Mail: lafahien@facstaff.wisc.edu.

FAHNER, TYRONE C., lawyer, former state attorney general; b. Detroit, Nov. 18, 1942; s. Warren George and Alma Fahner; m. Anne Beauchamp, July 2, 1966; children: Margaret, Daniel, Molly. BA, U. Mich., 1965; JD, Wayne State U., 1968; LLM, Northwestern U., 1971. Bar: Mich. 1968, Ill. 1969, Tex. 1984, US Dist. Ct. (ea. dist.) Mich. 1968, US Dist. Ct. (no. dist.) Ill. 1969, US Ct. Appeals (7th cir.) 1969, US Ct. Appeals (5th cir.) 1981, US Ct. Appeals (DC cir.) 2002, US Supreme Ct. 2002. Asst. US atty. No. Dist. Ill., Chgo., 1971—75, dep. chief consumer fraud and civil rights, 1973—74, chief ofcl. corruption, 1974—75; ptnr. Freeman, Rothe, Freeman & Salzman, Chgo., 1975—77; dir. Ill. Dept. Law Enforcement, Springfield, 1977—79; ptnr. Mayer Brown LLP, Chgo., 1979—80, 1983—, co-chmn. mgmt. com., 1998—2001, chmn. mgmt. com., 2001—07. Instr. John Marshall Law Sch., 1973—76, 1978—84; atty. gen. State of Ill., Springfield, 1980—83. Mem. corp. adv. com. U. Mich. Coll. Lit., Sci. & Arts, mem. major gifts com.; mem.William J. Fullbright bd. fgn. scholarships USIA, 1988—93; active Law Sch.'s Com. Visitors Wayne State U., Epilepsy Found. Greater Chgo. Named Person of Yr., Chgo. mag., 2002. Mem.: Northwestern U. Sch. Law Alumni Assn. (bd. dirs. 1990—95, chmn. Class 1967, mem. James B. Haddad professorship fundraising com.), Ill. Ambs. (bd. dirs., past pres.), Am. Inns of Ct. (mem. Chgo. chpt.), Chgo. Bar Assn., Tex. Bar Assn., Am. Coll. Trial Lawyers, Commerical Club Chgo., Chgo. Club, Econ. Club Chgo. Republican. Lutheran. Office: Mayer Brown LLP 71 S Wacker Dr Chicago IL 60606-4637

FAIR, HUDSON RANDOLPH, recording company executive; b. Evanston, Ill., Aug. 15, 1953; s. Harry Joel Jr. and Virginia (Gauntlett) F.; m. Ewa Kowcz, 2003. BS in Speech, orthwestern U., 1976, MA in Speech, 1979. Mktg. rep. Calumet Refining Co., Chgo., 1975-78, Calumet Petro-Chems., Inc., Houston, 1977-78, Stellavox, S.A., Schaumburg, Ill., 1986-87, Nagra Magnetic Recorders, Inc., NYC, 1987-91; pres. Ealing Mobile Recording, Ltd., Chgo., 1981—. Music prodr. WFMT Radio, Chgo., 1992—, Ravinia Festival, 1997—, Milw. Symphony Orch., 2005—; cons. in field. Prodr. more than 200 classical albums, 1981—. Speech writer Rep. George Bush Presdl. Campaign, Chgo., 1979-80. Recipient Chorus award for best choral rec., 1989, Deutsche Schallplatten-preis for best chamber music record Juilliard String Quartet, 1998, Grammy award best classical vocal performance prodr. and engr., 2007; grantee Ill. Arts Coun., 1982-86, NEA, 1986. Mem. NARAS (bd. govs. 1991-95, 96-2000, nat. trustee 1993-95), Audio Engring. Soc., Engring. and Rec. Soc. (bd. dirs. 1987—, chmn. 1991-92). Independent. Episcopalian. Avocations: travel, motorcycles. Office Phone: 773-792-2000. E-mail: ffrr1@sbcglobal.net.

FAIRFIELD, BILL L., finance company executive; BS in Engring., Bradley U.; MBA in Bus. Admistrn., Harvard U. Sr. exec. Eastman Kodak, 1969-73; sr. v.p. Lindsay Mfg. Co., 1975-79; pres. mktg. domestic irrigation divsn. Valmont Industries Inc., 1979-81, pres., gen. mgr. irrigation divsn., 1981-82; pres., CEO, Inacom Corp., Omaha, 1982-99, also bd. dirs.; chmn. Dreamfield Ptnrs. Inc., Dreamfield Capital Ventures, 2000—. Bd. dirs. Fed. Res. Bank Kansas City., Omaha, Sitel Corp., others. Trustee U. Nebr., Lincoln; bd. trustees Boy Scouts Am.; mem. Chancellor's Adv. Coun., U. Nebr., Omaha. Office: The Fairacres Project 206 Fairacres Rd Omaha NE 68132-2706

FAIRHURST, CHARLES, engineering educator; b. Widnes, Lancashire, Eng, Aug. 5, 1929; came to US, 1956, naturalized, 1967; s. Richard Lowe and Josephine (Starkey) F.; m. Margaret Ann Lloyd, Sept. 7, 1957; children: Anne Elizabeth Charlet, David Lloyd, Charles Edward, Catherine Mary Kotz, Hugh Richard, John Peter, Margaret Mary Evans. BEng with honors, U. Sheffield, Eng., 1952, PhD, 1955; DSc (hon.), U. Sheffield, 1998; D in Engring. (hon.), St. Petersburg Mining Inst., Russia, 1995, Inst. Nat. Poly de Lorraine, France, 1996; DSc (hon.), U. Minn., 2000. Mining engr. trainee Nat. Coal Bd., St. Helens, England, 1949-56; research assoc. prof. U. Minn., Mpls., 1956-67, head Sch. Mineral and Metall. Engring., 1967-70, prof. dept. civil and mineral engring., 1970-94, prof. dept. civil engring., 1994-97, head dept., 1972-87, T.W. Bennett Prof. mining engring. and rock mechanics, 1983-97, prof. emeritus, 1997—. Sr. cons. Itasca Group Inc., Mpls.; cons. Petrobras, Brazil, Spie. Batignolles, France, Charbonnages de France; Geoderis, France, chmn. U.S. Com. Rock Mechanics, 1971-74, Waste Isolation Pilot Plant Panel NAS/NRC, Carlsbad, N.Mex., 1989-96; chmn. study underground nuclear testing in French Polynesia, Internat. Geomechanics Commn., 1995-98; mem. bd. radioactive waste mgmt. NAS/NRC, 1987-94, vice chmn., 1989-94; adv. prof. Tongji U., Shanghai, 1994. Mem. Conseil Sci. ANDRA (France), 1994—, Mon. Geol. Rep. Consulting Bd., Yucca Mountain, 1999-2001; mem. sci. and tech. panel Office of Civilian Radioactive Waste Mgmt., US Dept. Energy, 2002-. Mem. AIME, ASCE (chmn. rock mechanics com. 1978-80), Internat. Soc. Rock Mechanics (pres. 1991-95), Am. Rock Mechanics Assn. (pres. 1995-97), Am. Underground Constrn. Assn. (pres. 1976-77), Royal Swedish Acad. Engring. Sci. (fgn.), US Nat. Acad. Engring., Sigma Xi. Roman Catholic. Home: 417 5th Ave N South Saint Paul MN 55075-2035 Office: 417 Fifth Ave N South Saint Paul MN 55075-2035 Business E-Mail: fairh001@umn.edu.

FAISON, RALPH E., communications equipment manufacturing executive; b. June 26, 1958; BS in Mktg., Ga. State U., Atlanta; MS in Mgmt., Stanford U., 1992. Various exec. positions AT&T wireless bus. unit; v.p. advt., brand mgmt. Lucent Tech., v.p., new ventures group, 1997—2001; pres., CEO Celiant Corp.(acquired by Andrew), 2001—02; pres., COO Andrew Corp., Westchester, Ill., 2002—03, pres., CEO, 2003—. Bd. dir. WatchMark Corp., NETGEAR, Inc.; bd. adv. New Venture Ptnrs. LLC. Bd. dir. Exec. Club, Chgo. Office: Andrew Corp Ste 900 3 Westbrook Corp Ctr Westchester IL 60154

FAISON, W. MACK, lawyer; b. Roanoke Rapids, NC, Oct. 25, 1945; BA, N.C. Ctrl. U., 1966; JD, Harvard U., 1969. Bar: NY 1970, Mich. 1972, US Dist. Ct. (2nd, 5th, 6th and 7th cirs.). Fellow Reginald Heber Smith Cmty. Lawyer, 1969—71; assoc. Miller, Canfield, Paddock and Stone, Detroit, 1972—78, prin., 1978—. Mem. local rules adv. com. Ea. Dist. Mich., U.S. Dist. Ct., civil justice reform act adv. com. Contbr. articles to profl. jours. Mem. NY Cmty. Action for Legal Svs., Inc.; bd. trustees St. Vincent and Sarah Fisher Ctr., 1998—2006. Named Mich. Super Lawyers, 2006, Best Lawyers Am., 2007. Mem. ABA (litig. sect., TIPS sect.), State Bar Mich. (litig. sect., environ. law sect.), Nat. Bar Assn., Detroit Bar Assn., Wolverine Bar Assn., Am. Coll. Trial Lawyers, Assn. Def. Trial Counsel, life mem. 6th cir. jud. Conf.; bd. dir. Wayne County Neighborhood Legal Svs. 1990-92. Office: Miller Canfield Paddock & Stone 150 W Jefferson Ave Ste 2500 Detroit MI 48226-4416 Office Phone: 313-496-7578. Office Fax: 313-496-8453. Business E-Mail: faison@millercanfield.com.

FAITH, MARSHALL E., grain company executive; Chmn., dir. The Scoular Co., Omaha. Sect. Bishop Clarkson Mem. Found., Episcopal Diocese Nebr. Office: The Scoular Co Scoular Bldg 2027 Dodge St Ste 300 Omaha NE 68102-1229

FAJANS, STEFAN STANISLAUS, retired internist; b. Munich, Mar. 15, 1918; arrived in U.S., 1936, naturalized, 1942; s. Kasimir M. and Salomea (Kaplan) Fajans; m. Ruth Stine, Sept. 6, 1947; children: Peter S., John S. BS, U. Mich., Ann Arbor, 1938, MD, 1942. Intern Mount Sinai Hosp., NYC, 1942—43; research fellow U. Mich., 1946—47, rsch. fellow, 1949—51, resident, 1947—49; mem. faculty U. Mich. Med. Sch., 1950—, prof., 1961—88, active prof. emeritus, 1988—. Mem. endocrinology study sect. NIH, 1958—62, mem. diabetes and metabolism tng. grants com., 1966—70, mem. nat. diabetes adv. bd., 1987—91; chief divsn. endocrinology and metabolism Mich. Diabetes Rsch. and Tng. Ctr., 1973—87, dir., 1977—86; chmn. Am. zone internat. sci. adv. com. Congresses Internat. Diabetes Fedn., 1977—79; Banting meml. lectr., 1978. Contbr. articles med. publs. Mem. career devel. com. VA Med. Rsch. Svcs., 1987—91. Officer M.C. US Army, 1943—46. Fellow rsch. fellow in medicine, ACP, 1949—50, Life Ins. Med. Inst., 1950—51. Master: ACP; mem.: NAS (sr. mem. inst. med.), Ctrl. Soc. Clin. Rsch., Assn. Am. Physicians, Am. Soc. Clin. Investigation, Am. Fedn. Clin. Rsch., Endocrine Soc. (v.p. 1970—71, coun. 1967—71, 1978—81), Am. Diabetes Assn. (pres. 1971—72, Banting medal 1972, Banting Meml. award 1978), Alpha Omega Alpha, Sigma Xi. Home: 827 Asa Gray Dr # 360 Ann Arbor MI 48105-3520 Office: PO Box 0354 Ann Arbor MI 48109-0354 Office Phone: 734-936-5039. Business E-Mail: sfajans@umich.edu.

FALCONE, FRANK S., former academic administrator; b. Kenosha, Wis., Sept. 26, 1940; s. Frank R. and Theresa (Barca) F.; m. Judith Herbert, Aug. 17, 1963; children: Jennifer, F. Jeffrey. BS, U. WIs., 1963; MA, U. Denver, 1965; PhD, U. Mass., 1973. Prof., provost Ithaca (N.Y.) Coll., 1969-80; v.p., dean Pace U., White Plains, NY, 1980-82, exec. v.p. Pleasantville, NY, 1982-85; pres. Springfield Coll., Mass., 1985-93, Carroll Coll., Waukesha, Wis., 1993—2006. Bd. dirs. Springfield YMCA, 1990-92, Basketball Hall of Fame; bd. visitors Air U., Maxwell AFB, Ala., 1989-90; exec. com. Boy Scouts, 1994—, United Way Exec. Comm., 1994. Mem. Assn. Ind. Colls. and Univs. in Mass. (exec. com. 1987-89, chmn. 1990-91), Assn. Ind. Colls. Mass. (pres. 1990-91), Greater Springfield C. of C. (bd. dirs. 1987-92), Waukesha C. of C. (bd. dirs. 1994-98, exec. com. 1995—, v.p. 1995), Wis. Found. for Ind. Colls. (treas. 1995-99). Home: 115 S East Ave Waukesha WI 53186-6207 E-mail: ffalcone@carroll1.cc.edu.

FALK, WILLIAM JAMES, lawyer; s. Sam and Bertha Falk; m. Laurie Falk; children: Douglas, Andrew, Edward BS, Ill. Inst. Tech., Chgo., 1973; JD cum laude, Suffolk U., Boston, 1977; LLM in Taxation, Washington U., St. Louis, 1982. Bar: Mass. 1977, Mo. 1981. Trial atty. IRS Office of Dist. Counsel, St. Louis, 1977—81; assoc. Thompson & Mitchell, St. Louis, 1982—83, ptnr., 1984—96, Thompson Coburn LLP, St. Louis, 1996—99; mem. Lewis, Rice & Fingersh, LC, St. Louis, 1999—. Contbg. author: Missouri Taxation Law and Practice, 1987, 96; contbr. articles to legal jours. Mem. ABA, Mo. Bar Assn., Bar Assn. Met. St. Louis (chmn. taxation sect. 1992-93, mem. exec. com. 1992-93). Avocations: music, photography. Office: Lewis Rice & Fingersh LC 500 N Broadway Ste 2000 Saint Louis MO 63102-2147

FALKER, JOHN RICHARD, investment advisor; b. Detroit, July 15, 1940; s. John Jacob and Helen Katherine (Loeffler) F.; m. Mary Eileen Jacobsen, Nov. 10, 1964; children: Mary Anne, John R. Jr., Peter J. BA in English, U. Mich., 1962; MBA in Fin., U. Detroit, 1980. With Chrysler Corp., Detroit, 1964-77; v.p., treas. Chrysler Fin. Corp., 1974-77; treas. Internat. Multifoods Corp., Mpls., 1977-87; founder, co-owner Swenson/Falker Assocs. Inc., Mpls., 1987-95; owner FalkerInvestments, Inc., Mpls., 1997—. Adj. prof. fin. U. St. Thomas, 1987-99. Served to lt. (j.g.) USNR, 1962-64. Mem. Am. Radio Relay League (life) Republican. Roman Catholic. Office: FalkerInvestments Inc TCF Tower 121 S 8th St Minneapolis MN 55402 E-mail: jack@falkerinvestments.com.

FALLER, SUSAN GROGAN, lawyer; b. Cin., Mar. 1, 1950; d. William M. and Jane (Eagen) Grogan; m. Kenneth R. Faller, June 8, 1973; children: Susan Elisabeth, Maura Christine, Julie Kathleen. BA, U. Cin., 1972; JD, U. Mich., 1975. Bar: Ohio 1975, Ky. 1989, U.S. Dist. Ct. (so. dist.) Ohio 1975, U.S. Ct. Claims 1982, U.S. Ct. Appeals (6th cir.) 1982, U.S. Supreme Ct. 1982, U.S. Tax Ct. 1984, U.S. Dist. Ct. (ea. dist.) Ky., 1991. Assoc. Frost & Jacobs, Cin., 1975-82; ptnr. Frost & Jacobs LLP, Cin., 1982-2000; mem. Frost Brown Todd LLC, Cin., 2000—. Chmn. first amendment, media and advt. practice group Frost Brown Todd LLC, 2001—, co-chmn. India cons. group, 2006—. Assoc. editor Mich. Law Rev., 1974-75; contbg. author: MLRC 50-State Survey of Media Libel and Privacy Law, 1982-93, MLRC 50-State Survey of Media Libel Law, 1999-, MLRC State Survey of Employment Libel and Privacy Law, 1999-. Bd. dirs. Summit Alumni Coun., Cin., 1983-85; trustee Newman Found., Cin., 1980-86, Cath. Social Svc., Cin., 1984-93, nominating com., 1985-88, sec., 1990; mem. Class XVII Leadership Cin., 1993-94; mem. exec. com., def. counsel sect. Media Law Resource Ctr., 1998-2002, chmn. membership com., 2003—; pres., def. counsel sect. Libel Def. Resource Ctr., 2001; mem. parish coun. St. Monica-St. George Ch., 1996-2000. Recipient Career Women of Achievement award YWCA, 1990. Mem. ABA (co-editor newsletter media litig. 1993-97), FBA, Ky. Bar Assn., No. Ky. Bar Assn., No. Ky. Women's Bar Assn., Ohio Bar Assn. (chair media law com. 2001-02), Cin. Bar Assn. (com. mem.), Potter Stewart Inn of Ct., U. Cin. Alumni Assn., Arts & Scis. Alumni Assn. (bd. govs. U. Cin. Coll. 1988-2000), U. Mich. Alumni Assn., Mortar Bd., Leland Yacht Club, Coll. Club, Clifton Meadows Club, Phi Beta Kappa, Theta Phi Alpha. Roman Catholic. Home: 5 Belsaw Pl Cincinnati OH 45220-1104 Office: Frost Brown Todd LLC 2200 PNC Ctr 201 E 5th St Cincinnati OH 45202-4182 Office Phone: 513-651-6941. Business E-Mail: sfaller@fbtlaw.com.

FALLON, ED, state representative; b. Santa Monica, Calif., Mar. 1, 1958; m. Kristin Maahs. B in Gen. Studies, Drake U., 1987. Mem. Iowa Ho. Reps., DesMoines, 1993—, mem. various coms. including agr., local govt., transp., infrastructure and capitals appropriations ways and means. Active Boy Scouts, Clarion Alliance, Divsn. Peace and World Order, North Park Neighbors, Trinity United Meth. Ch. Democrat. Office: State Capital East 12th and Grand Des Moines IA 50319 also: 1321 8th St Des Moines IA 50314

FALLON, PATRICK R., advertising executive; b. 1946; With Leo Burnett, Chgo., 1967-69, Stevson & Assocs., Mpls., 1969-76, v.p.; with Martin/Williams Advt., Mpls., 1976-81, v.p.; founder Fallon McElligott Rice (now Fallon Worldwide), Mpls., 1981—; chmn., CEO Fallon Worldwide. Office: Fallon Worldwide Ste 2800 50 S 6th St Minneapolis MN 55402-1550

FALLS, JOSEPH FRANCIS, sportswriter, editor; b. NYC, May 2, 1928; s. Edward and Anna (Zincak) F.; m. Mary Jane Erdei, Oct. 10, 1975; children by previous marriage: Robert, Kathleen, Susan, Janet, Michael. Grad. high sch. Reporter AP, NYC, 1946-56; sports writer Detroit Times, 1956-60; sports editor, sports writer Detroit Free Press, 1960-78; sports writer Detroit News, 1978—. Author: Man in Motion, 1973, The Detroit Tigers, 1975, The Boston Marathon, 1977, So You Think You're A Die-Hard Tiger Fan, 1986, An Illustrated History, The Detroit Tigers, 1989, Daly Life, 1990, So You ove Tiger Stadium*Do Give It a Hug, Glory of Their Game; compact disc recs. include Echoes of Tiger Stadium, Echoes of Detroit Hockey Legents Tom 1220, Celebrating Michigan State's National Basketball Championship.In His Own Work. Elected to Mich. Hall of Fame, 2000; honored by Mich. Jewish Sports Hall of Fame, 2000. Mem. Baseball Writers Assn. Am. Office: Detroit News 615 W Lafayette Blvd Detroit MI 48226-3197

FALSGRAF, WILLIAM WENDELL, retired lawyer; b. Cleve., Nov. 10, 1933; s. Wendell A. and Catherine J. F.; children: Carl Douglas, Jeffrey Price, Catherine Louise. AB cum laude, Amherst Coll., 1955, LLD (hon.), 1986; JD, Case Western Res. U., 1958. Bar: Ohio 1958, U.S. Supreme Ct. 1972. Ptnr. Baker & Hostetler, Cleve., 1971—2002; ret., 2002. Chmn. vis. com. Case Western Res. U. Law Sch., 1973-76; trustee Case Western Reserve U., 1978-90, chmn. bd. overseers, 1977-78; trustee Cleve. Health Mus., 1975-90, Hiram Coll., 1989—; chmn. bd. trustees Hiram Coll., 1990-99. Recipient Disting. Service award; named Outstanding Young Man of Year Cleve. Jr. C. of C., 1962. Fellow Am. Bar Found., Ohio Bar Found.; mem. ABA (chmn. young lawyers sect. 1966-67, mem. ho. of dels. 1967-68, 70—, bd. govs. 1971-75, pres. 1985-86, bd. dirs. Am. Bar Endowment 1974-84, 87-97), Am. Bar Ins. Plans Cons. (pres. 1991—), Ohio Bar Assn. (mem. coun. of dels. 1968-70), Cleve. Bar Assn. (trustee 1979-82), Amherst Alumni Assn. (pres. N.E. Ohio 1964), The Country Club, LaPaloma Country Club. Office: Baker & Hostetler LLP 3200 National City Ctr Cleveland OH 44114-3485 Home: 268 Twin Creeks Dr Chagrin Falls OH 44023-6702 Home Phone: 440-247-3113; Office Phone: 216-861-7376. Business E-Mail: wfalsgraf@bakerlaw.com.

FAN, LIANG-SHIH, chemical engineering educator; BS, Nat. Taiwan U., 1970; MS, West Va. Univ., 1973, PhD, 1975; MS in Statistics (with honors), Kansas State Univ., 1978. Disting. Univ. prof. dept. chem. engring., C. John Easton prof. in engring. Ohio State U., Columbus. Recipient Alexander von Humboldt Rsch. award for U.S. Sr. Scientists, 1993, Alpha Chi Sigma award AIChE for Chem. Engring., 1996, Union Carbide Lectureship award Chem. Engring. Divsn. ASEE, 1999, Malcolm E. Pruitt award, Coun. for Chem. Rsch., 2000, E.V. Murphree award in Indsl. Engring. and Chemistry, ACS, 2006, Joseph Sullivant medal Ohio State U., 2006. Mem. NAE, Academia Sinica, Mexican Acad. Scis. Office: Ohio State U Dept Chem Engring 140 W 19th Ave Columbus OH 43210-1110

FANNING, EDWARD J., bank executive; BS in Acctg. and Fin., No. Ill. U., 1980; MBA in Fin. and Managerial Econ., Northwestern U. CPA, CMA. With McGladrey, Hendrickson and Co., CPA's, Sundstrand Corp., Harris Trust and Savings Bank, PaineWebber, Inc., Delta Mgmt. Group, LP; founder, pres. Strategic Fin. Assocs.; prin. Franklin St. Equity Partners, Inc.; sr. v.p., group head corp. fin. group Provident Capital Corp., 1997—.

FANTA, PAUL EDWARD, chemist, educator; b. Chgo., July 24, 1921; s. Joseph and Marie (Zitnik) F.; m. LaVergne Danek, Sept. 3, 1949; children—David, John. BS, U. Ill., 1942; PhD, U. Rochester, 1946. Postdoctoral research fellow U. Rochester, 1946-47; instr. Harvard, 1947-48; mem. faculty Ill. Inst. Tech., 1948—, prof. chemistry, 1961-84, prof. emeritus, 1984—. Exchange scholar Czechoslovak Acad. Sci., Prague, 1963-64, Soviet Acad. Sci., Moscow, 1970-71 Contbr. articles to profl. jours. NSF fellow Imperial Coll., London, Eng., 1956-57 Mem. Am. Chem. Soc., Sigma Xi, Phi Lambda Upsilon. Home: 947 Clinton Ave Oak Park IL 60304-1821

FANTIN, ARLINE MARIE, state legislator; b. Hammond, Ind., Sept. 26, 1937; Ill. state rep. Dist. 29, 1995-99; twp. assessor Thornton Twp., South Holland, Ill., 1994—.

FARAH, CAESAR ELIE, language educator, historian; b. Portland, Oreg., Mar. 13, 1929; s. Sam Khalil and Lawrice Farah; m. Irmgard Tenkamp, Dec. 13, 1987; 1 child, Elizabeth;children from previous marriage: Ronald, Christopher, Ramsey, Laurence, Raymond, Alexandra. Student, Internat. Coll. Am. U. Beirut, 1941—46; BA, Stanford U., 1952; MA, Princeton U., 1955, PhD, 1957. Pub. affairs asst., cultural affairs officer ednl. exchanges USIS, New Delhi, 1957-58, Karachi, Pakistan, 1958; asst. to chief Bur. Cultural Affairs, Washington, 1959; asst. prof. history and Semitic langs. Portland State U., 1959-63; asst. prof. history Calif. State U., LA, 1963-64; assoc. prof. Near Eastern studies Ind. U., Bloomington, 1964-69; prof. Mid. Eastern and Islamic history U. Minn., Mpls., 1969—2008, chmn. South Asian and Mid. Eastern studies, 1988-91. Guest lectr. Fgn. Ministry, Spain, Iraq, Iran, Ministry Higher Edn., Saudi Arabia, Yemen, Turkey, Kuwait, Qatar, Tunisia, Morocco, Syrian Acad. Scis., Acad. Scis., Beijing; vis. scholar Cambridge U., 1974; resource person on Middle East media and svc. group, Minn., 1977—2008; bd. dirs., chmn. Upper Midwest Consortium for Middle East Outreach, 1980—; vis. prof. Harvard U., 1964, 65, Sanaa U., Yemen, 1984, Karl-Franzens U. Austria, 1990, 91, 1997—98, Ludwig-Maximilian U., Munich, 1992—93; vis. Fulbright-Hays scholar U. Damascus, 1994; vis. lectr. Am. U. Beirut, 2001; exec. sec., editor Am. inst. Yemeni Studies, 1982—86; sec.-gen., exec. bd. dirs. Internat. Com. for Pre-Ottoman & Ottoman Studies, 1988—2000, v.p., 2000—; fellow Rsch. Ctr. Islamic History, Istanbul, 1993, Ctr. Lebanese Studies & St. Anthony Coll., Oxford, England, 1994; vis. cons. Sultan Qaboos U., Oman, 2000; mem. exec. bd. Arab Am. Cultural Inst., 2001—. Author: The Addendum in Medieval Arabic Historiography, 1968, Islam: Beliefs and Observances, 7th edit., 2003, Eternal Message of Muhammad, 1964, 3d edit., 1981, Tarikh Baghdad li-Ibn-al-Najjar, 3 vols., 1980—83, 2d edit., 1986, al-Ghazali on Abstinence in Islam, 1992, Decision Making in the Ottoman Empire, 1992, The Road to Intervention: Fiscal Policies in Ottoman Mount Lebanon, 1992, The Politics of Interventionism in Ottoman Lebanon, 2000, The Sultan's Yemen, 2002, Ottomans & Arabs, 2002, First Arab Traveler to Latin America, 2003, Abdul Hamid II and the Muslim World, 2008; contbr. articles to profl. jours.; mem. editl. bd.: Digest of Middle East Studies. Mem. Oreg. Rep. Committeeman, 1960—64. Named Fulbright-Hayes lectr., 1993—94; recipient cert. of merit, Syrian Ministry Higher Edn.; fellow, Am. Coun. Learned Socs., 1953, Am. Rsch. Ctr. Egypt, 1966—67, Fulbright Tgn. and Rsch., Germany, 1992—93, Ford Found., 1966, Am. Philos. Soc., 1970—71; grantee Participants Program, Dept. State Am., 1981, 1984, 1993, Minn. Humanities Commn., 1981, 1985, 1989, 1995, 1998, 2001, Am. Inst. Yemeni Studies, 1999, Coun. Am. Overseas Rsch. Ctrs., 2000, Travel to Collection, NEH, 1989, others; scholar Fulbright Rsch., 1966—67, 1985—86, 1992—93. Mem.: Turkish Studies Assn., Am. Assn. Tchrs. Arabic (exec. bd.), Mid. East Studies Assn. N.Am., Am. Hist. Assn., Royal Asiatic Soc. Gt. Britain, Am. Oriental Soc., Arab Am. Cultural Inst. (co-founder, exec. bd. 2002—), Stanford U. Alumni Assn. (pres. upper Midwest Assn. 1978—79, Leadership Recognition award), Princeton Club, Stanford Club Minn. (dir., pres. 1979), Phi Alpha Theta, Pi Sigma Alpha. Greek Orthodox. Home: 5125 Blake Rd S Edina MN 55436-1125 Office: Univ Minn 839 Soc Sci Towers Minneapolis MN 55455 Office Phone: 612-624-0580. Business E-Mail: farah001@umn.edu.

FARBER, EVAN IRA, librarian; b. NYC, June 30, 1922; s. Meyer M. and Estelle H. (Shapiro) F.; m. Hope Wells Nagle, June 13, 1966; children: Cynthia, Amy, Jo Anna, May Beth; stepchildren: David Nagle, Jeffrey Nagle, Lisa Nagle. AB, U. N.C., 1944, MA, BLS, U. N.C., 1953; DHL (hon.), St. Lawrence U., 1980, Susquehanna U., 1989, Ind. U., 1996. Instr. polit. sci. U. Mass., Amherst, 1948-49; librarian State Tchrs. Coll., Livingston, Ala., 1953-55; chief serials and binding div. Emory U. Library, Ga., 1955-62; head librarian Earlham Coll., Richmond, Ind., 1962-94, coll. libr. emeritus, 1994—. Cons. Bates Coll., Eckerd Coll., Colo. Coll., Hartwick Coll., Macalester Coll., Maryville Coll., Knox Coll., Ill. Coll., Messiah Coll., Hiram Coll., Centenary Coll., Colby Coll., Ga. State U., Ripon Coll., Hampshire Coll., Reed Coll., Williams Coll., NEH, Lilly Endowment, North Ctrl. Assn., Assn. Am. Colls., Pew Meml. Trust. Author: (with Andreano and Reynolds) Student Economists Handbook, 1967, Classified List of Periodicals for the College Library, 5th edit., 1972; assoc. editor: Southeastern Librarian, 1959-62; asst. editor: Explorations in Entrepreneurial History, 1964-66; co-editor: Earlham Rev., 1965-72; editor: Combined Retrospective Index to Book Revs. in Scholarly Jours., 1886-1974, 1979-83, Combined Retrospective Index to Revs. in Humanities Jours., 1802-1974, 1983-85, (with Ruth Walling) Essays in Honor of Guy R. Lyle; columnist: Choice Mag., 1974-80, Library Issues, 1982-88; mem. editl. bd. Coll. and Undergrad Librs., Internet and Higher Edn. Recipient Acad./Rsch. Libr. of the Yr., 1980, B.I. Libr. of Yr. award, 1987. Mem. Assn. Coll. and Rsch. Librs. (pres. 1978-79, bd. dirs. 1989-93), ALA (council 1969-71, 79-83). Home: 2030 Chester Blvd Richmond IN 47374 E-mail: evanf@earlham.edu.

FARICY, RICHARD THOMAS, architect; b. St. Paul, June 1, 1928; s. Roland J. and Clare (Sullivan) F.; m. Carole Murphy, June 24, 1961; children: Althea, Bridget. Registered architect, Minn. V.p. The Cerny Assocs., Mpls., 1961-71; exec. v.p. Winsor/Faricy Architects, Inc., St. Paul, 1971-96; founding prin. Symmes Maini McKee Assoc./Winsor Faricy, St. Paul, 1996—2001; cons. arch. Collaborative Design Group, 2001—. Pres. Minn. Archtl. Found., 1986; trustee Am. Mus. Asmat Art, 1995—. Prin. works include: Raughurst Libr., Jamestown, N.D., Warren E. Burger Libr. at William Mitchell Coll. Law, St. Paul, Collier County Courthouse, Naples, Fla., Bandana Sq., St. Paul, Como Park Conservatory Restoration, St. Paul, Earl Brown Heritage Ctr., Brooklyn Center, Minn. Pres. Merrick Community Ctr., St. Paul, 1969; pres. Ramsey County Hist. Soc., 1981-82; chmn. Blue Cross Blue Shield Minn., 1974-77, HMO Minn., 1974-76; bd. dirs. Minn. State Arts Bd., 1988-94, HealthEast Found., 1987-99, James J. Hill Reference Libr., 1996-99; bd. dirs. Friends St. Paul Pub. Libr., 19862000, pres., 1992-95; trustee Minn. Mus. Art, 1980-86; commr. St. Paul Heritage Preservation Commn., 1986-87, 2002—; v.p. Historic St. Paul, 2001—; bd. zoning appeals, St. Paul, 2001-; vice chmn. Mounds Midway Found., 1987-91; bd. dirs. sponsor bd. Bapt. Hosp. Fund, 1991—. 1st lt. USAR, 1952-57. Fellow AIA (nat. housing com. 1984-92, trustee AIA Benefit Ins. Trust 1986-89); mem. Minn. Soc. Architects (dir. 1973-77, chair Ins. Trust 1984-86), St. Paul AIA (pres. 1974), St. Paul Athletic Club (pres. 1980). Home: 2211 St Clair Ave Saint Paul MN 55105-1136 Office: Collaborative Design Group Inc Ste 300 1501 Washington Ave South Minneapolis MN 55454 E-mail: rfaricy@collaborativedesigngroup.com.

FARINA, DENNIS, actor; b. Chgo., Feb. 29, 1944; m. Patricia Farina (div.); children: Dennis Jr., Michael, Joseph. Former policeman Chgo. Police Dept. Actor: (films) Thief, 1981, Code of Silence, 1985, Jo Jo Dancer, Your Life is Calling, 1986, Manhunter, 1986, Midnight Run, 1988, Open Admissions, 1988, Blind Faith, 1990, People Like Us, 1990, Men of Respect, 1991, We're Talking

Serious Money Now, 1991, Street Crimes, 1992, Mac, 1992, Another Stakeout, 1993, Romeon Is Bleeding, 1993, Striking Distance, 1993, Little Big League, 1994, Get Shorty, 1995, Eddie, 1996, That Old Feeling, 1996, Out of Sight, 1998, Saving Private Ryan, 1998, Buddy Faro, 1998, The Mod Squad, 1999, Reindeer Games, 2000, Snatch, 2000, Preston Tylk, 2000, Sidewalks of NY, 2001, Big Trouble, 2002, Stealing Harvard, 2002, Paparazzi, 2004; (TV movies) Through Naked Eyes, 1983, Hard Knox, 1984, The Killing Floor, 1985, Final Jeopardy, 1985, The Birthday Boy, 1986, Triplecross, 1986, Six Against the Rock, 1987, Open Admissions, 1988, The Case of the Hillside Strangler, 1989, Blind Faith, 1990, People Like Us, 1990, Drug Wars: The Cocaine Cartel, 1992, Cruel Doubt, 1992, The Disappearance of Nora, 1993, A Stranger in the Mirror, 1993, One Woman's Courage, 1994, The Corpse Had a Familiar Face, 1994, Out of Annie's Past, 1995, Bonanza: Under Attack, 1995, Perfect Crimes, 1995, Empire Falls, 2004; (TV mini-series) Bella Maffia, 1997; (TV series) Crime Story, 1986-88, In-Laws, 2002-03, Law and Order, 2004-06; (TV appearances) Miami Vice, 1984, 85, 89, Hardcastle and McCormick, 1985, Hunter, 1985, Remington Steele, 1985, Lady Blue, 1986, China Beach, 1989, Tales from the Crypt, 1992, Justice League (voice only), 2005, Law & Order: Trial by Jury, 2005; actor, prodr. (TV series) Buddy Faro, 1998 Office: Geddes Agy 1633 N Halsted St Ste 400 Chicago IL 60614-5517

FARLEY, JAMES D. (JIM FARLEY), automotive executive; b. June 10, 1962; m. Lia A. Farley; 2 children. BS in Economics & Computer Sci., Georgetown U.; MBA, UCLA. Mem. strategic-planning dept. Toyota Motor Corp., 1990, v.p. mktg., group v.p., gen. mgr. Lexus Divsn.; group v.p. mktg., corp. officer Toyota Motor Sales (TMS), USA, Inc., group v.p., gen. mgr. Lexus Divsn., 2007; group v.p. mktg. & comms. & US mktg., sales & svc. Ford Motor Co., Detroit, 2007—. Office: Ford Motor Co One American Rd Dearborn MI 48126 Office Phone: 313-322-3000. Office Fax: 313-845-6073.*

FARLEY, JERRY B., academic administrator; m. Susan Farley. BS in Fin. and Acctg., U. Okla., 1968; MBA, Okla. U., 1972. V.p. bus. and fin. Okla. State U., 1986; CFO Okla. U., Oklahoma City, v.p. adminstrn. and fin., 1994; pres. Washburn U., Topeka, 1997—. Named No. 4 most powerful Topekan, Topeka Capital-Jour., 2000. Office: Washburn U Office of Pres 1700 SW College Ave MO 202 Topeka KS 66621

FARMAKIS, GEORGE LEONARD, retired education educator; b. Clarksburg, W.Va., June 30, 1925; s. Michael and Pipitsa (Roussopoulos) F. BA, Wayne State U., 1949, MEd, 1950, MA, 1966, PhD, 1971; MA, U. Mich., 1978. Tchr. audio-visual aids dir. Roseville (Mich.) Pub. Schs., 1951-57; tchr. Birmingham (Mich.) Pub. Schs., 1957-61, Highland Park (Mich.) Pub. Schs., 1961-90; substitute tchr. Grosse Pointe Pub. Schs., 1990—2003; ret., 2003. Lectr. Oakland County C.C., 1990-92, Lawrence U., 1990-98, Oakland U., 2000—; instr. Highland Park C.C., 1966-68, Wayne County C.C., 1969-70; assoc. mem. grad. faculty Coll. Edn. Wayne State U., 1988-89; founder Ford Sch. Math. High Intensity Tutoring Program, 1971; chairperson Highland Park Sch. Dist. Curriculum Coun. and Profl. Staff Devel. Governing Bd., 1979-82; pres. Mich. Coun. Social Studies, 1985-86; founder, dir. Mich. Social Studies Olympiad, 1987; founder, editor Mich. Social Studies Jour., 1986; participant ESEA Title I/Nat. Diffusion Network. Author, translator: Letters of Nicholas Gysis, 1842-1901; co-author: Michigan School Finance Curriculum Guide; contbr. poems to books of poetry, articles to Focus jour. Cpl. USNG, 1948-51. Recipient spl. commendation Office of Edn., 1978, Outstanding Svc. award Nat. Coun. Social Studies, 1987, Presdl. award Mich. Coun. Social Studies, 1988, 96. Mem. ASCD (bd. dirs. Mich. chpt. 1983-86), Internat. Reading Assn., Am. History Assn., Nat. Coun. Social Studies (pres. SIG-CASE 1987-88, pres. JESIG 1988-89), Am. Philol. Assn., U. Mich. Alumni Assn., Wayne State U. Coll. Edn. Alumni Assn. (bd. dirs. 1985-86), Mich. Reading Assn., Masons (32 degree), Shriners, Ancient Accepted Scottish Rite, Phi Delta Kappa (Outstanding Educators award 1988). Greek Orthodox. Home: 15215 Windmill Dr Macomb MI 48044-4929

FARMER, MIKE, state legislator; m. Jean Farmer. Sys. analyst, 1980-2000; mem. Kans. State Ho. of Reps. Dist. 87, 1993-2000; exec. dir. Kans. Cath. Conf., 2000—.

FARMER, NANCY, state official; b. Jacksonville, Ill., 1956; m. Darrell Hartke. Grad., Ill. Coll., 1979. Exec. dir. Skinker-DeBaliviere Cmty. Coun.; state rep. dist. 64 Mo. Ho. of Reps., 1993—2001; asst. treas. State of Mo., 1997—2001, treas., 2001—. Mem. Woman's Polit. Caucus Mo. Ho. of Reps.; dir. intergovernmental affairs City of St. Louis, 1997. Active Woman's Com. Forest Park, Rosedale Neighborhood Assn., mem. exec. com.; active West End Arts Coun.; cand. for Mo. U.S. Senator, 2004. Mem. Ctrl. West End Assn., Women Legislators Mo. Office: PO Box 210 Jefferson City MO 65102

FARMER, RICHARD T., uniform rental and sales executive; b. Dayton, Ky., Nov. 22, 1934; BBA, Miami U., Ohio, 1956. Founder, chmn. Cintas Corp., Cin., 1968—, CEO, 1968—95. Bd. dir. Fifth Third Bancorp. Trustee Miami Univ., Ohio. Named one of Forbes Richest Americans, 2006. Office: Cintas Corp 6800 Cintas Blvd PO Box 625737 Cincinnati OH 45262-5737

FARMER, SCOTT D., apparel executive; BA, Miami U., 1981. V.p. mktg. & merchandising, v.p. nat. account div. Cintas Corp., Cin., 1981—94, group v.p. rental div., 1994—97, bd. dir., 1994—, pres., COO, 1997—2003, pres., CEO, 2003—08, CEO, 2008—. Office: Cintas Corp 6800 Cintas Blvd Cincinnati OH 45262 Mailing: Cintas Corp PO Box 625737 Cincinnati OH 45262-5737

FARR, DAVID N., electronics executive; married; 2 children. BS in Chemistry, Wake Forest U.; MBA, Vanderbilt U. From mem. staff to CEO Emerson, 1981—2000, CEO, 2000—, chmn., 2004—, pres., 2005—. Mem. The Bus. Coun., Washington; bd. dirs. Delphi Corp. Bd. dirs. Municipal Theatre Assoc., St. Louis; bd. dirs., Greater St. Louis Area Coun. Boy Scouts of Am.; mem. Civic Progress. Office: Emerson 8000 W Florissant Ave PO Box 4100 Saint Louis MO 63136

FARR, LEONARD ALFRED, hospital administrator; b. Pleasant Hill, La., Mar. 19, 1947; BA, La. State U., 1969; MA, Washington U., 1974. Adminstr. resident HCA Wesley Med. Ctr., Wichita, Kans., 1973-74, night adminstr., 1974-75; asst. adminstr. Physicians & Surgeons Hosp., Shreveport, La., 1975, exec. v.p., 1975-76; adminstr. Colo. Springs. (Colo.) Community Hosp., 1976-78; pres., CEO St. Francis Hosp. Systems, Colo. Springs, Colo., 1978-87; COO Penrose-St. Francis Hosp., Colo. Springs, 1987-91, pres., CEO, 1991—; s.r. v.p. United HealthCare, Mpls., 1997; COO ret. and sr. svcs. Ovations, a United-Health Group Co., Mpls., 1997—; pres. Small Bus. Group United Healthcare, 1999—. Mem. Am. Hosp. Assn. (alternate del., del.), Colo. Hosp. Assn. (chmn. bd.). Office: United Health Group Mail Stop MN008 W319 PO Box 1459 Minneapolis MN 55440-1459

FARR, MEL, automotive sales executive, former professional football player; b. Beaumont, Tex., Nov. 2, 1944; BS, UCLA. CEO Mel Farr Automotive Group, Mich., Ohio, Tex. and Md.; prin. Triple M Fin. Co. With Detroit Lions, 1967-73; mem. NFL Players Adv. Bd., 1990-92. Named to UCLA Sports Hall of Fame, 1988, NFL Rookie of Yr., Most Valuable Offensive Player, 1967, Most Valuable Offensive Player, 1968.

FARRAKHAN, LOUIS (LOUIS EUGENE WALCOTT), religious organization administrator; b. Bronx, NY, May 11, 1933; changed name from Louis Eugene Wolcott to Louis X, then to Louis Farrakhan; m. Betsy Wolcott; 9 children. Student, Winston-Salem State U., NC. Vocalist, calypso singer, dancer and violinist, Boston; joined Nation of Islam, 1955—, leader of Harlem mosque NYC, 1965—75, nat. spokesman, leader, founder reorganized Nation of Islam, 1977—. Founder newspaper The Final Call, 1979—. Author: A Torchlight for America, 1993, Education Is the Key, 2006. Founder Louis Farrakhan Prostate Cancer Found., 2003—. Named one of Most Influential Black Americans, Ebony mag., 2006. Achievements include organizing the Million Man March on Washington, D.C., 1995 and the Million Family March, 2000. Office: ation of Islam 7351 S Stony Island Ave Chicago IL 60649-3106

FARRAND, WILLIAM RICHARD, retired geology educator; b. Columbus, Ohio, Apr. 27, 1931; s. Harvey Ashley and Esther Evelyn (Bowman) F.; m. Claudine Brickmann, Aug. 17, 1962 (div. 1983); children: Frederic Hervé, Anne Marie; m. Carola Hill Stearns, Dec. 6, 1988; 1 child, Michelle Diane. BS in Geology, Ohio State U., 1955, MS in Geology, 1956; PhD, U. Mich., 1960. Rsch. assoc. Lamont Geol. Obs. Columbia U., NY, 1960-61, asst. prof. NY, 1961-64; rsch. assoc. in geology U. Mich., Ann Arbor, 1962; postdoctoral rsch. fellow NAS/NRC, Strasbourg, France, 1963-64; asst. prof. geol. scis. U. Mich., Ann Arbor, 1965-67, assoc. prof. geol scis., 1967-74, prof., 1974-2000, prof. emeritus, 2000—, curator analytical collections Mus. Anthropology, 1975-2000, dir. Exhibit Mus., 1993-2000. Vis. prof. U. Strasbourg, France, 1964-65, Hebrew U., Jerusalem, 1971-72, U. Colo., Boulder, 1983, U. Tex., Austin, 1986; fellow Inst. for Advanced Study, Ind. U., 1985; mem. archaeometry panel NSF, 1989-91; apptd. mem. U.S. Nat. com. Internat. Quaternary Assn., 1989-99, chair, 1995-99; sr. fellow Inst. for Study Earth and Man, So. Meth. U., Dallas, 1991—. Mem. editorial bd. Quaternary Sci. Review, Paleorient, Jour. Archaeological Sci., Review Archaeology, Stratigraphica Archaeologica; contbr. articles and maps to profl jours. With U.S. Army, 1951-53. Fellow AAAS, Geol. Soc. Am. (mem. panel quaternary geology and geomorphology divsn. 1978, vice chmn. archaeological geology divsn, 1979, chmn, 1980, Archaeological Geology award 1986), Ohio Acad. Sci., 1994-96; mem. Am. Quaternary Assn. (sec. 1978-90, program chmn. biennial meeting 1980, pres. 1994-96), Mich. Acad. Sci., Arts and Letters, Internat. Union for Quaternary Rsch. (chmn. working group on Southwest Asia commn. paleoecology early man 1975-83), L'Assn. Francaise pour l'Etude de Quaternaire, Sigma Xi, Phi Beta Kappa. Office: U Mich Mus Anthropology 4009 Ruthven Mus Ann Arbor MI 48109-1079 Business E-Mail: wfarrand@umich.edu.

FARRAR, STEPHEN PRESCOTT, glass products manufacturing executive; b. Concord, NH, Jan. 27, 1944; s. Prescott Samuel and Katherine (Hitchcock) F.; m. Kathleen D. Clark, Dec. 28, 1968 (dec.); children: Sheila E. Bermudez, Stephen Prescott Jr.; m. Rose Marie Bucar, July 4, 1998. BA, Bowdoin Coll., 1965; MSFS, Georgetown U., 1967. Internat. economist U.S. Dept. Commerce, Washington, 1966-72, Office of Mngt. and Budget, Washington, 1972-80, chief econ. affairs br. IAD, 1980-86; dir. internat. econ. affairs NSC, Washington, 1986-88, spl. asst. to Pres. and sr. dir. internat. econ. affairs, 1988-89; dep. exec. sec. Econ. Policy Coun., The White House, Washington, 1989-92; spl. asst. to Pres. for Policy Devel. Office of Policy Devel., the White House, Washington, 1989-92; chief of staff Office of the U.S. Trade Rep., Washington, 1992-93; dir. internat. bus. Guardian Industries Corp., Auburn Hills, Mich., 1993—. Mem. Coun. on Fgn. Rels. Republican. Avocations: tennis, running. Office: Guardian Industries Corp 2300 Harmon Rd Auburn Hills MI 48326-1714 Office Phone: 248-340-2104. Business E-Mail: sfarrar@guardian.com.

FARRAR, THOMAS C., chemist, educator; b. Independence, Kans., Jan. 14, 1933; s. Otis C. and Agnes K. F.; m. Friedemarie L. Farrar, June 22, 1963; children: Michael, Christian, Gisela. BS in Math., Chemistry, Wichita State U., 1954; PhD in Chemistry, U. Ill., 1959. NSF fellow Cambridge U., Eng., 1959-61; prof. chemistry U. Oregon, Eugene, 1961-63; chief, magnetism sect. Nat. Bur. Standards, Washington, 1963-71; dir. R & D Japan Electron Optics Lab., Cranford, J., 1971-75; dir. instr. NSF, Washington, 1975-79; prof. chemistry U. Wis., Madison, 1979—. Chmn. adv. com. MIT Nat. Magnetics Lab., Cambridge, Mass., 1979-84. Author: Introduction to Pulse NMR Spectros, 1989, Density Matrix Theory, 1995; contbr. over 150 articles to profl. jours. Recipient Silver medal Dept. Commerce, Washington, 1971, Silver medal Nat. Science Found., Washington, 1979. Fellow Wash. Acad. Science; mem. Am. Chem. Soc. (sec.-treas. Wis. sect. 1986-89), Am. Physical Soc. Office: Univ Wis Dept Chemistry 1101 University Ave Madison WI 53706-1322 Home Phone: 608-238-2939; Office Phone: 608-262-6158. Personal E-mail: tcfarrar@sbcglobal.net. E-mail: tfarrar@chem.wisc.edu, farrartcf@yahoo.com.

FARRELL, PHILIP M., physician, dean, educator, researcher; b. St. Louis, Nov. 26, 1943; m. Alice Yeakle; children: Michael Henry, David Sean, Bridget Mary. AB, St. Louis U., 1964, MD, PhD, St. Louis U., 1970. Diplomate Am. Bd. Pediatrics. Intern U. Wis. Hosps., 1970—71, resident in pediatrics, 1971—72; fellow pediatric metabolism br. Nat. Inst. Arthritis, Metabolism and Digestive Diseases, NIH, Bethesda, Md., 1972—74, sr. investigator pediatric metabolism br., 1974—75; chief Neonatal and Pediatric Medicine Br., Nat. Inst. Child Health and Human Devel., NIH, Bethesda, Md., 1975—77, Chief, Sect. Devel. Biology and Clin. Nutrition, 1975—77; Asst. prof. dept. child health George Washington U., Washington, 1975; asst. prof. pediatrics U. Wis., Madison, 1977-78, dir. Cystic Fibrosis Ctr., 1977—83, co-dir., 1983—88, affiliate scientist Wis. Regional Primate Research Ctr., 1978, affiliate faculty dept. nutrition scis., 1978, assoc. prof. pediatrics, 1978-82, dir. Pediatric Pulmonary Specialized Ctr. of Research, 1981-85, prof. pediatrics, 1982—, chmn. dept. pediatrics, 1985-95, med. dir. Children's Hosp., 1988—95, Alfred Dorrance Daniels Prof. on Diseases of Children, 1990—, interim dean Med. Sch., 1994—95, dean Med. Sch., 1995—, vice-chancellor med. affairs, 2001—. Editor: Lung Development: Biological and Clinical Perspectives, 1982. Avalon Found. scholar, 1965-67, Thurston Meml. scholar, 1966-70; Fogarty Internat. fellow, 1985. Mem. Am. Chem. Soc., Am. Acad. Pediatrics, Soc. Pediatric Rsch., Am. Thoracic Soc., Soc. Exptl. Biology and Medicine, Am. Inst. Nutrition, Am. Soc. Clin. Nutrition, Wis. Assn. Perinatal Care, Sigma Xi, Phi Beta Kappa, Alpha Omega Alpha. Office: Univ Wis Sch of Med 4129 Health Sciences Learning Ctr 75 Highland Ave Madison WI 53705-2221 Office Phone: 608-263-4900.

FARRELL, W. JAMES, retired metal products manufacturing company executive; b. NYC, 1942; m. Maxine Farrell; 5 children. BA in Electrical Engring., U. Detroit, 1965. Joined Ill. Tool Works., Inc., Glenview, Ill., 1965, sales corr., Shakeproof div., 1965—68, sales engr., 1968—70, automotive acct. mgr., 1972—77, v.p., group pres. Fastener Group, 1977—83, exec. v.p. Glenview, Ill., 1983—94, pres., 1995—96, CEO, 1995—2005, chmn. bd., 1996—2006; ret., 2006. Bd. dirs. The Allstate Corp., 1999—, Sears, Roebuck and Co., 1999—, Kraft Foods, Inc., 2001—, UAL Corp., 2001—, 3M Co., 2006—, Fed. Res. Bank, Chgo., chmn., 2001—03, Chgo., 2004—05. Dir. Big Shoulders Fund, Chgo. Public Library Found.; chmn. Jr. Achievement Chgo.; trustee Northwestern U.; advisory bd. mem. J.L. Kellogg Grad. Sch. Mgmt.; trustee Rush Presbyterian-St. Luke's Medical Ctr.; chmn. bd. trustees Mus. Sci. and Industry; dir. Lyric Opera Chgo.; vice chmn. United Way Crusade of Mercy. Served criminal investigation div. US Army, 1965—67, Alaska. Mem.: Econ. Club Chgo. (chmn.), Chgo. Club (pres.), Comml. Club Chgo. (civic com.), Executives Club Chgo., Mid-Am. Com., Ill. Bus. Roundtable, Bus. Coun.

FARRIS, CLYDE C., lawyer; b. Houston, May 24, 1943; BA, Tex. Tech U., 1966; JD, Washington U., 1973. Bar: Mo. 1973, U.S. Dist. Ct. (ea. dist.) Mo. 1974, U.S. Ct. Appeals (8th cir.) 1976, Ind. 1987, U.S. Supreme Ct. Mem. Copeland Thompson & Farris, PC, St. Louis. Instr. St. Louis U., 1976-77; mem. civil rules com. of the Mo. Supreme Ct., 1989—. Mem. St. Louis Commn. on Crime and Law Enforcement, 1975-77, Kirkwood Rotary Club, City of Kirkwood Tax Increment Financing Commn. Mem. ABA, ATLA, Mo. Bar, Mo. Assn. Trial Attys., Bar Assn. Met. St. Louis, Rotary. Office: Copeland Thompson & Farris PC 231 S Bemiston Ave Ste 1220 Saint Louis MO 63105-1914

FARRIS, PAUL LEONARD, agricultural economist; b. Vincennes, Ind., Nov. 10, 1919; s. James David and Fairy Julia (Kahre) F.; m. Rachel Joyce Rutherford, Aug. 16, 1953; children: Nancy, Paul, John, Carl. BS, Purdue U., 1949; MS, U. Ill., 1950; PhD, Harvard U., 1954. Asst. prof. agrl. econs. Purdue U., West Lafayette, Ind., 1952-56, assoc. prof., 1956-59, prof., 1959-90, prof. emeritus, 1990—, head dept. agrl. econs., 1973-82; agrl. economist Dept. Agr., Washington, 1962; project leader for meat and poultry Nat. Commn. Food Mktg., Washington, 1965-66. Editor: Market Structure Research, 1964, Future Frontiers in Agricultural Marketing Research, 1983; contbr. articles to profl. jours. Served with AUS and USAAF, 1941-46. Fellow Am. Agrl. Econs. Assn.; mem. Am. Econ. Assn. Home: 1510 Woodland Ave West Lafayette IN 47906-2376 Office: Purdue U Dept Agrl Econs West Lafayette IN 47907

FARRIS, THOMAS N., engineering educator; b. Daisetta, Tex., Sept. 29, 1959; s. Robert Quentin and Kathleen Ruth (Kelling) F.; m. Bernadette Paulson, May 9, 1982; children: Joanna K., John T., Steven Q., Andrew B., Daniel J. BSME cum laude, Rice U., 1982; MS in Theoretical And Applied Mechanics, Northwestern U., 1984, PhD, 1986. Asst. prof. aeronautics and astronautics Purdue U., West Lafayette, Ind., 1986-91, assoc. prof., 1991-94, prof., 1994—, head, 1998—. Reviewer in field. Contbr. articles to profl. jours. Roy scholar Rice U., 1981; Cabell fellow Northwestern U., 1982; NSF Presdl. Young Investigator, 1990; Japan Soc. for Promotion of Sci. fellow, 1991, ASME Newkirk award, 1992, Structures and Materials award ASME/Boeing, 1998. Mem. ASME (assoc. editor Jour. Tribology 1994-2000), AIAA (advisor 1988-93, assoc. editor Jour. Aircraft 1992-98), Soc. Tribologists and Lubrication (chmn. lubrication fund com. 1993-94), Inst. Mech. Engrs. (editl. bd. Jour. Strain Analysis 1998—). Avocations: basketball, running, reading. Home: 701 Crestview Pl West Lafayette IN 47906-2313 Office: Purdue U Sch Aeronautics & Astronautics 1282 Grisson Hall West Lafayette IN 47907-1282

FARRIS, TRUEMAN EARL, JR., retired newspaper editor; b. Sedalia, Mo., June 2, 1926; PhB in Journalism, Marquette U., Milw., 1948; MA in Polit. Sci., U. Wis.-Milw., 1989. Reporter Milw. Sentinel, 1945-62, asst. city editor, 1962-75, city editor, 1975-77, mng. editor, 1977-89. Juror Pulitzer Prizes, 1985-86; dean's coun. Student Publs. Bd., Coll. of Comm., Journalism and Performing Arts, Marquette U., 1987-92; bd. visitors U. Wis., Milw., 1991-2000; commitment adv. panel, U. Wis., Milw., 2000; bd. dirs. Wis. Masonic Jour., Newspaper of State Grand Lodge, 1993—, pres. 2004—. Author series of stories: Japan, 1980. Served with U.S. Army, 1955 Recipient By-Line award Marquette U., 1987; named to Milw. Press Club Media Hall of Fame, 1989. Mem. AP Mng. Editors Assn. (dir. 1980-87, editor ann. reports 1979-85), Milw. Soc. Profl. Journalists (pres. 1982-83), Milw. Press Club (pres. 1968, several reporting awards, editorial writing award 1957, included Media Hall of Fame 1989), Civil War Round Table (sec.), Mil. Order Loyal Legion of U.S. (recorder). Methodist. Avocations: reading, genealogy, civil war history. Home: 3192 S 80th St Milwaukee WI 53219-3501 Office: Milwaukee Sentinel PO Box 371 Milwaukee WI 53201-0371

FARROW, MARGARET ANN, former lieutenant governor; b. Kenosha, Wis., Nov. 28, 1934; d. William Charles and Margaret Ann (Horan) Nemitz; m. John Harvey Farrow, Dec. 29, 1956; children: John, William, Peter, Paul, Mark. Student, Rosary Coll., 1952-53; BS in Polit. Sci. and Edn., Marquette U., 1956, postgrad., 1975-77. Tchr. Archdiocese of Milw., 1956-57; trustee Elm Grove Village, Wis., 1976-81, pres. Wis., 1981-86; mem. Wis. Assembly, Madison, 1986-89, Wis. Senate from 33rd dist., Madison, 1989—2001; lt. gov. State of Wis., 2001—03; dir. local govt. affairs Whyte Hirshboeck Dudek Govt. Affairs, 2003—. Chair govt. effectiveness, 1998-2001, asst. majority leader, 1998; mem. joint com. on audit, 1993-97, mem. joint survey com. on tax exemptions, 1993-97, chair Wis. women's coun., 1991—, Rep. caucus chair, 1996, 99, mem. coun. on workforce excellence, 1995—, mem. Wis. glass ceiling commn., 1993—; mem. Senate Com. on edn., 1999, Senate com. on labor, 1999. Republican. Home: W 262 # 2402 Deer Haven Dr Pewaukee WI 53072-4572

FARUKI, CHARLES JOSEPH, lawyer; b. Bay Shore, NY, July 3, 1949; s. Mahmud Taji and Rita Trownsell Faruki; m. Nancy Louise Glock, June 15, 1996 (div. Oct. 1995); m. Michelle F. Zalar, June 15, 1996; children: Brian Andrew, Jason Allen, Charles Joseph Jr. BA summa cum laude, U. Cin., 1971; JD cum laude, Ohio State U., Columbus, 1973. Bar: Ohio 1974, US Dist. Ct. (no. and so. dists.) Ohio 1975, US Ct. Appeals (9th cir.) 1977, US Tax Ct. 1977, U.S. Supreme Ct. 1977, US Ct. Appeals (6th cir.) 1978, US Dist. Ct. (no. dist.) Tex. 1979, US Dist. Ct. (ea. dist.) Ky. 1982, US Ct. Appeals (D.C. cir.) 1982, US Ct. Customs and Patent Appeals 1982, US Ct. Appeals (4th cir.) 1986, US Ct. Appeals (2d cir.) 1989, US Ct. Appeals (fed. cir.), 1991, US Ct. Appeals (8th cir.) 1997. Assoc. Smith & Schnacke, Dayton, Ohio, 1974—78, ptnr., 1979—89; founder, mng. ptnr., complex litig. practice Faruki Ireland & Cox PLL, Dayton, 1989—. Mem. local rules adv. com. US Dist. Ct. (so. dist.) Ohio, 1992—2003, mem. civil justice reform act adv. com., 1995—98, chair fed. bar examination com., 1997—, mem. outside automation evaluation com., 2000—; mem. exec. com. U. Dayton Sch. Law Adv. Coun., 2001—, chmn., 2007—; adj. prof. U. Dayton Sch. Law; lectr. in field. Contbr. articles in field. Trustee Dayton Bar Assn. Found., 1997—2003, pres., 2002—03; mem. bd. mgr., sec. Mus. of USAF Found., 2006—; mem. bd. trustees Dayton Philharmonic Orch. Capt. USAR, 1971—79. Named Outstanding Lawyer, Greater Dayton Vol. Project; named one of Ohio's Top Ten Super Lawyers, Dayton's Most Powerful, Dayton Bus. Jour.; named to Best of Bar; recipient Spl. Svc. award, U. Dayton Sch. Law, Peacekeeper award, Artemis Ctr. for Alternatives for Domestic Violence. Fellow: Am. Coll. Trial Lawyers (complex litig. com. 1993—98, Ohio state com. 1998—2006, chmn. 2004—05), Ohio State Bar Found., Am. Bar Found. (life); mem.: FBA (officer and exec. com. Dayton chpt. 1988—93, pres. 1991—92), ABA, Dayton Intellectual Property Law Assn., Fed. Cir. Bar Assn., Dayton Bar Assn. (officer 1992—94, pres. 1994—95, trustee 1997—2004, pres. 2002—03), Ohio State Bar Assn. (bd. govs. antitrust sect. 1992—, vice-chair antitrust sect. 2006—, chair fed. cts. and practice com. 2007—), Am. Bd. Trial Advocates. Avocations: coin collecting/numismatics, art. Office: Faruki Ireland & Cox PLL 500 Courthouse Plz SW Dayton OH 45402 Home: 138 Rue Marseille Dayton OH 45429 Home Phone: 937-298-5649; Office Phone: 937-227-3705. Business E-Mail: cfaruki@ficlaw.com.

FASS, ROBERT J., epidemiologist, academic administrator; b. NYC, Feb. 23, 1939; BS in Chemistry, Biology, Tufts U., 1960, MD, 1964; MS in Med. Microbiology, Ohio State U., 1971. Diplomate Am. Bd. Internal Medicine; licensed physician, Ohio, N.Y., Pa. Intern in mixed medicine Montefiore Hosp., NYC, 1964-65, resident in medicine, 1965-66, Ohio State U., Columbus, 1968-69, fellow in infectious diseases, rsch. asst. in med. microbiology, 1969-71, clin. instr. medicine, 1970-71, asst. prof. medicine, 1971-75, asst. prof. med. microbiology, 1971-76, assoc. prof. medicine, 1975-80, assoc. prof. med. microbiology, 1976-80, prof. internal medicine, medical microbiology and immunology, 1980—, Samuel Saslaw prof. infectious diseases, 1991—, dir. divsn. infectious diseases, 1987—. Dir. infectious diseases fellowship tng. program Ohio State U., 1987-93, mem. task force on program evaluation Coll Medicine, 1973-75, search com. chmn. dept. med. microbiology, 1973-76, clin. cirriculum devel. project, 1875-77, profl. adv. com. to med. illustations, 1975-85, vice chmn. practice plan com., 1979-85, trustee Med. Rsch. and Devel. Found., 1979-86, treas., 1979-85, assocs. medicine exec. com. dept. medicine, 1973-76, chmn., 1974-75, chmn. libr. com., 1973-78, bd. dirs. Dept. Medicine Found., 1987—, finance com., 1979-86, 91—, chmn., 1981-86, phase III module com. Med. Microbiology and Immunology divsn., 1973, 75, 76, 81, dir., 1976, 81, mem. infection control com. Univ. Hosp., 1972-77, exec. com., 1976-77, pharmacy and therapeutics com., 1981—, chmn. pharmacy and therapeutics antimicrobial com., 1984—, exec. com., 1984—; mem. infectious disease conf. Riverside Meth. Hosp., 1971-76; prin. investigator for Ohio State U. NIH AIDS Clin. Trials Group, 1987—, opportunistic info. com., 1987—, instl. evaluation com., 1989—; mem. internat. adv. bd. Bayer AG Auinolone Bd., 1985-93, Miles Inc. External Adv. Bd., 1988-93. Mem. editorial bd. Antimicrobial Agents and Chemotherapy, 1982-91, Quinolene Bulletin, 1989—; reviewer Am. Jour. Medicine, Am. Soc. Hosp. Pharmacists Drug Info., Antimicrobial Agents and Chemotherapy, Annals of Internal Medicine, Archives of Internal Medicine, Chest, Clin. Microbiology Revs., Jour. Infectious Diseases, Infectious Diseases in Clin. Practice, N.Y. State Jour. Medicine, Revs. Infectious Diseases, New England Jour. Medicine. Med. officer USAF, 1966-68. Fellow ACP, Infectious Diseases Soc. Am.; mem. AMA (reviewer AMA Drug Evaluations, Jour. AMA), Am. Fedn. Clin. Rsch., Am. Soc. for Microbiology, Am. Thoracic Soc., Ctrl. Soc. for Clin. Rsch., Inter-Am. Soc. for Chemotherapy, Brit. Soc. Antimicrobial Chemotherapy, Columbus Soc. Internal Medicine (sec.-treas. 1979, pres. 1980). Achievements include research in laboratory predictors of antimicrobial efficacy, pathogenesis of anaerobic and mixed bacterial infections, antibiotic susceptibility testing and resistance, antimicrobial agents in clinical, pharmacological and laboratory studies, biology and significance of cell-wall defective bacteria, infective endocarditis, AIDS. Office: Ohio State U Med Ctr 4715 Univ Hosp Clinic 456 W 10th Ave Columbus OH 43210-1240

FAST, DARRELL WAYNE, minister; b. Mountain Lake, Minn., Sept. 5, 1939; s. Henry L. and Anna R. (Rempel) F.; m. Loretta J. Janzen, Aug. 20, 1966; children: Douglas Henry, Larissa Ann. BA, U. Nebr., 1963; BD, Mennonite Biblical Sem., 1966; MTh, Emmanuel Coll., 1977, DMin, 1986. Ordained minister Mennonite Ch., 1970. Mem. conf. staff Gen. Conf. Offices Mennonite Ch., Newton, Kans., 1966-70; pastor Toronto (Ont., Can.) United Mennonite Ch., 1970-86, Bethel Coll. Mennonite Ch., North Newton, Kans., 1986—. Moderator Gen. Conf. Mennonite Ch., Newton, 1992—; sec. United Mennonite Chs. of Ont., Toronto, 1972-78. Mem. Leadership Newton, Newton C. of C., 1989; pres. Ministerial Alliance, Newton, 1989-90; mem. exec. com. Man to Man Ont., Toronto, 1972-82; trustee Mennonite Biblican Sem., Elkhart, Ind., 1980-92. Mem. Rotary. Avocations: tennis, singing. Office: Bethel Coll Mennonite Ch 2600 College Ave PO Box 364 orth Newton KS 67117-0364

FATHEREE, JOSEPH G., informaation technology educator; BA in History, Ea. Ill. Univ., MEd in Ednl. Adminstrn. English tchr. Effingham (Ill.) H.S., 1990—94, history tchr., 1994—2000, tech. instr., 2000—. Named Ill. Tchr. of

Yr., 2007; recipient Mid-Am. Emmy award (three), Telly award. Office: Effingham High Sch 1301 W Grove Effingham IL 62401 Office Phone: 217-540-1100. Business E-Mail: fatheree@u40gw.effingham.k12.il.us.

FAUGHT, HAROLD FRANKLIN, retired electrical equipment manufacturing company executive; b. Washington, Oct. 16, 1924; s. Robert A.N. and Bessie I. (Towns) F.; m. Cathy A. De Waelsche, May 24, 2003. B.M.E., Cornell U., 1945; M.M.E., U. Pa., 1951; grad. Advanced Mgmt. Program, Harvard U., 1961. Registered profl. engr., Pa. Divsn. gen. mgr. Westinghouse Electric Corp., 1946-69; sr. asst. postmaster gen. U.S. Postal Svc., 1969-73; sr. v.p., cons. Emerson Electric Co., St. Louis, 1973—2003; ret., 2003—. Served with USNR, 1943-46. Mem. AIAA, Old Warson Country Club (St. Louis). Home: 1527 Candish Ln Chesterfield MO 63017-5612 Office: Emerson Electric Co 8100 W Florissant Ave Saint Louis MO 63136-1494

FAULK, MARSHALL WILLIAMS, retired professional football player; b. New Orleans, Feb. 26, 1973; s. Roosevelt and Cecile Faulk; married; 3 children. Student, San Diego State U., 1991—93. Running back Indpls. Colts., 1994-99, St. Louis Rams, 1999—2007; analyst, NFL Total Access NFL Network, 2005—. Founder The Marshall Faulk Found., 1994—. Named Am. Football Conf. (AFC) Rookie of Yr., 1994, NFL Pro Bowl MVP, 1994, NFL MVP, 2000, 2001, NFL Offensive Player of the Yr., AP, 1994, 1999—2001; named to Am. Football Conf. (AFC) Pro-Bowl, 1995—96, Nat. Football Conf. (NFC) Pro-Bowl, 1999—2003; recipient Espy Award for Best Football Player, ESPN, 2001, 2002, Bert Bell award, 2001. Achievements include being a member of Super Bowl XXXIV Champion St. Louis Rams, 2000; being the first player in NFL history to gain 2,000 yards from scrimmage in four consecutive seasons. Office: The Marshall Faulk Found 1116 E Market St Indianapolis IN 46202

FAULKNER, JAMES VINCENT, JR., lawyer; b. NYC, Mar. 25, 1944; s. James Vincent and Josephine Rita (Fitzsimmons) F.; m. Bettina Van Der Plas, Aug. 10, 1968; children: Aylsia, Martina, James III. BA, Georgetown U., 1966, MS, 1968, JD, 1970. Assoc. Appleton, Rich & Perrin, NYC, 1970-72, Lord, Day & Lord, NYC, 1972-75; sr. corp. atty. Union Pacific Corp., NYC, 1975-77, asst. gen. counsel, 1977-80, assoc. gen. counsel, 1980-83, dep. gen. counsel, 1983-88; sr. v.p., gen. counsel USPCI Inc. subs. Union Pacific Corp., Houston, 1988-93; v.p., law atty. Tenneco Inc., Houston, 1993—95; v.p., gen. counsel Tenneco Packaging, 1995—99; v.p., gen. counsel, sec. Pactiv Corp., 2000—06. Mem. Sch. bd. St. Patrick's Ch., Bedford, N.Y., 1979-81, parish council, 1981-84. Mem. ABA, Am. Corp. Counsel Assn. (dir. 1985-88), Assn. Bar City N.Y. (com. on uniform state laws 1971-72). Clubs: Bedford Golf and Tennis. Republican. Roman Catholic. Avocations: squash, riding.

FAULKNER, JOHN ARTHUR, physiologist, educator; b. Kingston, Ont., Can., Dec. 12, 1923; s. Jack and Winifred (Esdaile) F.; m. Margaret Isabelle Rowntree, Apr. 9, 1955; children: Laura Megan, Melanie Anne. BA, Queen's U., 1949, B.P.H.E., 1950; MS, U. Mich., 1956, PhD, 1962. Tchr. sci. Glebe Collegiate Inst., Ottawa, Ont., Can., 1952-56; asst. prof. phys. edn. U. Western Ont., 1956-60; asst. prof. edn. U. Mich., 1962-64, assoc. prof. edn., 1964-66, assoc. prof. physiology, 1966-71, prof. physiology, 1971—; rsch. scientist U. Mich. Inst. Gerontology, 1986—, acting dir., 1988-89, assoc. dir. biol. rsch. Inst. Gerontology, 1990—, interim dir., 1997-98. Assoc. editor Jour. Applied Physiology, 1991-93, Basic and Applied Myology, 1990—; contbr. articles on altitude acclimatization, cardiovascular response to swimming and running, skeletal muscles adaptation, mechanism of contraction-induced injury, regeneration of skeletal muscles following transplantation, injury and repair of muscle fibers following pliometric contractions, and contractile properties of muscles in aged rodents, mdx mice, and transgenic mdx mice, to profl. jours. Dir. Nathan Shock Ctr. for Basic Biology of Aging. Served as pilot RCAF, 1942-45, ETO. Burke Aaron Hinsdale scholar, 1962; recipient Glenn Edmonson award U. Mich., Established Investigators award Am. Physiol. Soc., EEP sect., 1998. Mem. Biol. Engring. (founding fellow), Gerontol. Soc. Am., Am. Coll. Sports Medicine (pres. 1971-72, Citation award 1978, Honor award 1992); mem. Biophys. Soc., Nat. Inst. Health (mem. respiration and applied physiology study sect. 1980-84, reviewers res. 1989—). Home: 2200 Navarre Cir Ann Arbor MI 48104-2759 Office: University of Michigan Institute of Gerontology 300 N Ingalls St Ann Arbor MI 48109-2007

FAULKNER, LARRY R., medical association administrator, former dean, educator, researcher, writer; b. Walla Walla, Washington; m. Judy Faulkner; 1 child. MD, U. Washington, 1974. Diplomate Am. Bd. Psychiatry and Neurology, Nat. Bd. Med. Examiners. Resident U. Ark.; dir. edn. for med. students and residents U. Portland Oreg. Health Sciences Ctr.; prof. U. S.C. Sch. Medicine, chmn. Dept. Neuropsychiatry and Behavioral Sci., 1990—95, interim dean, 1994—95, dean, 1995—2006, v.p. med. affairs; exec. v.p. and CEO Am. Bd. Psychiatry and Neurology, Inc., Chgo., 2006—. Rschr., writer in field; dir. William S. Hall Psychiatric Inst.; dir. Divsn. Rsch. and Edn. SC Dept. Mental Health. Contbr. articles to profl. jours. Recipient Physician's Recognition award, AMA; fellow NIH. Mem.: Am. Psychiatric Assn. (disting. fellow 2003), Carolina Alumni Assn. (hon. life mem. 2004), Benjamin Rush Soc., Alpha Omega Alpha (faculty initiate 1996). Mailing: Am Bd Psychiatry and Neurology Ste 335 500 Lake Cook Rd Deerfield IL 60015-5249

FAULKNER, LAURA R., lawyer; b. Columbus, Ohio, Aug. 18, 1974; BA in Polit. Sci., Miami U., 1996, BA in Eng. Lit., 1996; JD, U. Dayton, 1999. Bar: Ohio 1999, US Dist. Ct. Southern Dist. Ohio 2000, US Dist. Ct. Northern Dist. Ohio 2001. Assoc. Weltman, Weinberg & Reis Co., L.P.A., Cin. Named one of Ohio's Rising Stars, Super Lawyers, 2006. Mem.: Am. Bankruptcy Law Forum, Cin. Bar Assn., Ohio State Bar Assn. Office: Weltman, Weinberg & Reis Co LPA 525 Vine St Ste 800 Cincinnati OH 45202 Office Phone: 513-723-2200. Office Fax: 513-723-2239.

FAUTH, JOHN J., venture capitalist; BS, Georgetown Univ. Vp, sr. credit off. Citicorp U.S.A.; pres., CEO Churchill Industries, Mpls., 1982—; chmn., dir., pres., CEO Churchill Capital, Inc., Mpls., 1987—. Chmn., bd adv, Georgetown Univ. Grad. Sch. Bus. Adminstrn.; bd. dir. Georgetown Univ. Office: Churchill Capital Inc 333 S 7th St Ste 2400 Minneapolis MN 55402-2435

FAWCETT, JOY LYNN, retired professional soccer player; b. Inglewood, Calif., Feb. 8, 1968; m. Walter Fawcett; children: Katelyn Rose, Carli, Madilyn Rae. Degree in phys. edn., U. Calif., Berkeley, 1990. Women's soccer coach UCLA, 1993-97, 1993—97; mem. U.S. Nat. Women's Soccer Team, 1987—2004; profl. soccer player San Diego Spirit, 2001—03. Named 3-time All-Am., 1987—89, Most Valuable Player, So. Calif., L.A. Times, 1987, World Cup Champion, 1991, 1999, MVP, WUSA, 2002, Defender of Yr., 2002; named to, U. Calif. Berkeley Hall of Fame, 1997; recipient Silver medal, Sydney Olympics, 2000. Achievements include 1995 FIFA World Cup, Sweden; 1994 CONCACAF Qualifying Championship, Montreal; U.S. Olympic Festival, Denver, 1995; FIFA Women's World Cup, Sweden, 1995; gold medal U.S. Women's Soccer Team, Atlanta Olympic Games, 1996, Athens Olympic Games, 2004; mem. Ajax of Manhattan Beach Club Soccer Team (champions U.S. Women's Amateur Nat. Cup, 1992, 93). Office: US Soccer Fedn 1801-1811 S Prairie Ave Chicago IL 60616

FAWCETT, SHERWOOD LUTHER, lab administrator; b. Youngstown, Ohio, Dec. 25, 1919; s. Luther T. and Clara (Sherwood) F.; m. Martha L. Simcox, Feb. 28, 1953; children: Paul, Judith, Tom. BS, Ohio State U., 1941, PhD (hon.); MS, Case Inst. Tech., 1948, PhD, 1950; PhD (hon.), Gonzaga U., Whitman Coll., Otterbein Coll., Detroit Inst. Tech., Ohio Dominican Coll. Registered profl. engr., Ohio. Mem. staff Columbus (Ohio) Labs. Battelle Meml. Inst., 1950-64, mgr. physics dept., 1959-64; dir. Pacific Northwest Labs., Richland, Wash., 1964-67; trustee Battelle Meml. Inst., Columbus, 1968-92, exec. v.p., 1967-68, CEO, 1968-84, pres., 1968-80, chmn., 1981-84, chmn. bd. trustees, 1985-87, assoc. trustee, 1987-94. Chmn. bd. dirs. Transmet Corp. With USNR, 1941-46. Decorated Bronze Star; recipient Washington award Western Soc. Engrs., 1989. Mem. AIME, NSPE, Am. Phys. Soc., Am. Nuc. Soc., Am. Phys. Soc., Sigma Xi, Tau Beta Pi, Delta Chi, Sigma Pi Sigma. Office: Transmet Corp 4290 Perimeter Dr Columbus OH 43228-1036 Home: 1800 Riverside Dr Columbus OH 43212-1823 Business E-Mail: tmc@transmet.com.

FAWCETT-YESKE, MAXINE ANN, music educator; m. Robert Yeske. BS in Music, U. Colo., Denver, 1983; MusM, U. Nebr., Omaha, 1987; PhD in Music, U. Colo., Boulder, 1997. Tchr. U. Colo., Boulder, Met. State Coll., Denver; asst. prof. music Truman State U., Kirksville, Mo., 1997—99; assoc. prof. music Nebr. Wesleyan U., Lincoln, 1999—. Contbr. articles to profl. jours.; contbg. author: Women and Music in America Since 1900: An Encyclopedia. Recipient US Prof. of Yr. award for State of Nebr., Carnegie Found. for Advancement of Tchg. and Coun. for Advancement and Support of Edn., 2006. Mem.: Soc. for Am. Music, Am. Musicological Soc., Nebr. Music Educators Assn., Nat. Assn. Music Educators, Delta Kappa Gamma, Pi Kappa Lambda. Office: Nebr Wesleyan U 5000 Saint Paul Ave Lincoln NE 68504 Office Phone: 402-465-2291. E-mail: mfy@nebrwesleyan.edu.

FAXON, DAVID PARKER, cardiologist; b. Manchester, NH, 1944; BA, Hamilton Coll., 1967; MD, Boston U. Med. Sch., 1971. Cert. internal medicine, cardiology. Intern Mary Hitchcock Meml. Hosp., 1971—72; resident, internal medicine Darmouth-Hitchcock Med. Ctr.; resident Mary Hitchcock Meml. Hosp., 1972—74; fellowship, cardiology Boston U. Hosp.; fellowship, cardiol. Mary Hitchcock Meml. Hosp., 1974—76; assoc. prof., medicine Boston U. Sch. Medicine; prof. medicine, dir. interventional cardiol., acting chief of cardiol. Boston U., 1976—93; prof., medicine, chief of divsn. of cardiol. USC, Los Angeles, 1993—2000, USC Med. Ctr., 1993—2000, U. Chgo. Med. Ctr., 2000—. Contbr. articles various profl. jours., chapters to books. Chmn. Am. Heart Assn. Sci. Adv. and Coord. Com.; edit. bd. mem. Circulation, The Am. Jour. of Cardiology, Jour. of the Am. Coll. of Cardiology. Mem.: Am. Heart Assn. (former pres., bd. of dirs.), Assn. U. Cardiologists, Soc. Cardiac Angiography and Interventions, Am. Coll. Cardiol. Achievements include first to angioplasty, a non-surgical technique for restoring blood flow through clogged arteries; research in methods to prevent renarrowing of vessels after angioplasty. Office: U Chgo Hosp Cardiol MC 6080 5841 S Md Ave Chicago IL 60637 Address: Ctr for Advanced Medicine 5758 S Md Ave Chicago IL 60637 Office Phone: 773-702-1919.

FAY, SISTER MAUREEN A., university president; BA in English magna cum laude, Siena Heights Coll., 1960; MA in English, U. Detroit, 1966; PhD, U. Chgo., 1976. Tchr. English, speech, moderator student newspaper, student council St. Paul High Sch., Grosse Pointe, Mich., 1960-64; chairperson English dept., dir. student dramatics, moderator student publs. Dominican High Sch., Detroit, 1964-69; co-dir. Cath. student ctr. Adrian (Mich.) Coll., 1969-71; instr. English Siena Heights Coll., Adrian, 1969-71; evaluators inst. criminal justice execs. U. Chgo., 1971-73; instr. English U. Ill., Chgo., 1971-74; dir. evaluation sch. new learning DePaul U., Chgo., 1974-75; fellow in acad. adminstrn. Saint Xavier Coll., Chgo., 1975-76, dean. grad. studies, 1979-83, dean continuing edn., 1976-83; asst. prof. No. Ill. U., Dekalb, 1980-83; pres. Mercy Coll. Detroit, 1983-90, U. Detroit Mercy, 1990—. V.p. VAUT Corp. bd. dirs. four inner city high schs., Archdiocese Chgo.; mem. exec. com. Assn. Mercy Colls.; adv. com. Adult Learning Svcs., The Coll. Bd., Met. Affairs Corp. of Detroit and S.E. Mich., cons. Nat. Assn. for Religious Women, 1974-75, North Cen. Assn. Colls. and Schs., evaluator commn. on higher edn.; trustee Rosary Coll., River Forest, Ill., New Detroit, Inc., 1993; emeritus mem. div. bd. Mercy Hosps. and Health Svcs. of Detroit; bd. dirs. Nat. Bank of Detroit., Detroit Econ. Growth Corp., 1992; mem. Nat. Commn. Ind. Higher Edn.; commr. North Centrl Assocs., Commn. on Instns. of Higher Edn., 1993. Asst. editor: (book rev.): Adult Education, A Journal of Research and Theory, 1971-74. Bd. dirs. United Way SE Mich., 1991, Assn. Catholic Colls. and Univs., 1992; Steering com. Metro Detroit GIVES; exec. com., edn. task force Detroit Strategic Planning com., 1987; trustee Mich. Opera Theatre; bd. dirs. Greater Detroit Interfaith Round Table Nat. Conf. Christians and Jews, Inc., The Detroit Symphony; mem. Nat. Bipartisan Commn. on Ind. Higher Edn. in U.S., 1993. Mem. Am. Assn. Higher Edn., North Cen. Assn. (cons., evaluator commn. on higher edn.), Nat. Assn. Ind. Colls. and Univs. (bd. dirs.), Assn. Ind. Colls. and Univs. of Mich. (exec. com., chairperson), Am. Assn. Cath. Colls. and Univs., AAUW, Pi Lambda Theta. Office: U Detroit Mercy Office Pres PO Box 19900 4001 W McNichols Rd Detroit MI 48219-0900

FAY, REGAN JOSEPH, lawyer; b. Cleve., Sept. 19, 1948; s. Robert J. and Loretta Ann (Regan) F.; m. Michelle P. Fay; children: John, Mary, Matthew, Jessica, Samantha. BS in Chem. Engring., MIT, 1970; JD with honors, George Washington U., 1974. Bar: Ohio 1974, U.S. Dist. Ct. (no. dist.) Ohio 1974, U.S. Patent Office 1973, U.S. Ct. Appeals (fed. cir.) 1974, U.S. Ct. Appeals (9th cir.) 1975, U.S. Dist. Ct. (ea. dist.) Wis. 1976, U.S. Dist. Ct. (no. dist.) Tex. 1986, U.S. Supreme Ct. 1988. Patent examiner U.S. Patent and Trademark Office, Washington, 1970-72; law clk. to presiding justice U.S. Ct. Customs and Patent Appeals, Washington, 1973-75; assoc. Yount & Tarolli, Cleve., 1975-79; assoc., then ptnr. Jones Day, Cleve., 1979—. Lectr. patent and trademark law Case Western Res. U., Cleve., 1976-86. Mem. Cleve. Intellectual Property Law Assn (pres. 1996-97). Republican. Roman Catholic. Office: Jones Day 901 Lakeside Ave E Cleveland OH 44114-1190 Office Phone: 216-586-7327. Business E-Mail: rjfay@jonesday.com.

FAY, TERRENCE MICHAEL, lawyer; b. Cleve., Feb. 25, 1953; s. J. Francis and Alice Wilsona (Porter) F.; m. Beverly Ann Luciow, Feb. 25, 1983; children: Robert Michael, Katherine Elizabeth. BA cum laude, Baldwin Wallace Coll., 1974, BS cum laude, 1975; JD, Ohio State U., 1978. Bar: Ohio 1978, US Dist. Ct. (no. dist.) Ohio 1983, US Dist. Ct. (so. dist.) Ohio 1987, US Ct. Appeals (6th cir.) 1987, US Dist. Ct. (no. dist.) Ind. 1992, US Dist. Ct. (ea. dist.) Mich. 1993. Law clk. for chief adminstrv. law judge Ohio Power Siting Commn., Columbus, 1977-78; asst. atty. gen. environ. sect. Ohio Atty. Gen.'s Office, Columbus, 1978—88, chief civil atty., 1987-88; sr. assoc. Smith & Schnacke, L.P.A., Columbus, 1988-89, Benesch, Friedlander, Coplan & Aronoff, Columbus, 1989-90, ptnr., 1992—2001, chair hiring com., 1995—97; of counsel Frost, Brown, Todd LLC, Columbus, 2002—04, ptnr., 2005—. Bd. dirs. Hucksters, Inc., Columbus, 1990. Abrahms scholar, 1975; recipient Book award Lawyers Coop., Inc., 1978, Ohio Gov.'s Spl. Recognition award, 1988; named Ohio Super Lawyer, 2006, 07. Mem. Phi Alpha Theta, Omicron Delta Kappa, Pi Kappa Delta, Psi Chi. Office: Frost Brown Todd LLC One Columbus Ste 2300 10 W Broad St Columbus OH 43215-3467 Home Phone: 216-346-7793; Office Phone: 614-559-7213. Business E-Mail: tfay@fbtlaw.com.

FAYHEE, MICHAEL R., lawyer; b. Canton, Ill., Dec. 18, 1948; m. Janice L. Fayhee. BS summa cum laude, U. Ill., 1970; JD cum laude, U. Mich., 1973. Bar: Ill. 1973. Ptnr., chmn. firm tax dept. McDermott, Will & Emery, Chgo. Former adj. prof. John Marshall Law Sch. Mem. ABA, Ill. State Bar Assn., Chgo. Bar Assn. Office: McDermott Will & Emery 227 W Monroe St Ste 3100 Chicago IL 60606-5096 Office Phone: 312-984-7522. Office Fax: 312-984-7700. Business E-Mail: mfayhee@mwe.com.

FAYNE, HENRY W., electric power industry executive; BS in Econs., Columbia Coll.; MBA, Columbia U. Asst. to commr. N.Y.C. Dept. Air Resources; asst. forecast analyst in contr.'s dept., contr., sr. v.p. corp. planning and budgeting, exec. v.p. fin. svcs. Am. Elec. Power, Inc., Columbus, Ohio, 1974-98, exec. v.p. fin. & analysis, CFO, 1998—. Bd. dirs. Am. Elec. Power, Inc. Office: Am Elec Power Inc 1 Riverside Plz Columbus OH 43215-2373

FAZIO, PETER VICTOR, JR., lawyer; b. Chgo., Jan. 22, 1940; s. Peter Victor and Marie Rose (LaMantia) F.; m. Patti Ann Campbell, Jan. 3, 1966; children: Patti-Marie, Catherine, Peter. AB, Coll. of Holy Cross, Worcester, Mass., 1961; JD, U. Mich., 1964. Bar: Ill. 1964, US Dist. Ct. (no. dist.) Ill. 1965, US Ct. Appeals (7th cir.) 1972, US Supreme Ct. 1977, DC 1981, US Ct. Appeals (DC cir.) 1988, Ind. 1993. Assoc. Schiff, Hardin & Waite, Chgo., 1964-70, ptnr., 1970-82, 84-95, mng. ptnr., 1995—2000, 2006, chmn., 2001—06; exec. v.p. Internat. Capital Equipment, Chgo., 1982-83, also bd. dirs., 1982-85, sec., 1982-87; exec. v.p., gen. counsel NiSource Inc., 2000—06. Bd. dirs. Planmetrics Inc., Chgo., 1984-92, Chgo. Lawyers Commn. for Civil Rights Under Law, 1976-82, co-chmn., 1978-80; bd. dirs. Seton Health Corp. No. Ill., Chgo. 1987-90, vice chmn., 1989-90. Trustee Barat Coll., Lake Forest, Ill., 1977-82; bd. dirs. St. Joseph Hosp., Chgo., 1990-95, mem. exec. adv. bd., 1984-89, chmn., 1986-89; vice chmn. bd. dirs. Cath. Health Ptnrs., 1995-99, chmn., 1999—; dir. exec. com. Ill. Coalition, 1994-2005, NW Ind. Forum, 1994-98. Mem. ABA (coun. 1991-94, chmn. sect. pub. utility, transp. and comm. law 2000-01), FBA, Ill. Bar Assn., Chgo. Bar Assn., Fed. Energy Bar Assn., Edison Electric Inst. (chmn. legal com. 1999-2001), Am. Gas Assn. (legal com.), Corp. Secretaries and Governance Profls. (sec.)., Met. Club, Econ. Club Chgo., Comml. Club Chgo. Office: Schiff Hardin LLP 6600 Sears Tower 233 S Wacker Dr Chicago IL 60606-6473 Home Phone: 312-664-6282; Office Phone: 312-258-5634. Business E-Mail: pfazio@schiffhardin.com.

FAZIO, VICTOR WARREN, physician, colon and rectal surgeon; b. Sydney, Feb. 2, 1940; came to U.S., 1971; s. Victor Warren and Kathleen Eleanor (Hills) F.; m. Carolyn Kisandra Sawyer, Dec. 2, 1961; children: Victor, Jane, David. MB, BS, U. Sydney, 1965, MS with honors, 1997; MD with honors, U. Lodz, 2003. Diplomate Am. Bd. Colon and Rectal Surgery; cert. FRACS, 1971. Intern and resident St. Vincent's Hosp., Sydney, 1965-67, surgical registrar, 1969-71; lectr. anatomy U. SW Med. Sch., Sydney, 1967; surg. registrar Repatriation Gen. Hosp., Concord, Australia, 1968; gen. surgeon Australian Surg. Team, Bien Hoa, Vietnam, 1971; fellow gen. surgery Lahey Clinic, Boston, 1972; fellow colorectal surgery Cleve. Clinic, 1973, staff surgeon colorectal surgery, 1974, chmn. dept. colon and rectal surgery, vice chmn. divsn. surgery, 1975—. Bd. govs. Cleve. Clinic Found., 1990-95, 98-99, exec. mem. bd. trustees, 1994-95. Author 520 manuscripts and book chpts.; editor: Current Therapy in Colon and Rectal Surgery, 1989, 2d edit., 2004; editor-in-chief Diseases of Colon and Rectum, 1997—. Decorated Order of Australia. Fellow ACS, Royal Australian Coll. Surgeons (hon.), Royal Australasian Coll. Surgeons, Am. Soc. Colon and Rectal Surgery (pres. 1995-96), Royal Coll. Surgeons (Eng., hon.), Royal Coll. Surgeons (Edinburgh, hon.); mem. Soc. Pelvic Surgeons (exec. com. 1980, pres. 2003), Soc. for Surgery Alimentary Tract, Ctrl. Surg. Assn., James IV Assn. Surgeons, Ohio Valley Soc. Colon and Rectal Surgeons (past pres.), Am. Surg. Assn. Roman Catholic. Avocations: naval history, sailing. Office: Cleve Clinic Desk A-111 9500 Euclid Ave Cleveland OH 44195-0001

FEAGLEY, MICHAEL ROWE, lawyer; b. Exeter, NH, Feb. 1, 1945; s. Walter Charles and Laura (Rowe) F. AB cum laude, Wesleyan U., 1967; JD, Harvard U., 1973. Bar: Mass. 1974, Ill. 1973, US Dist. Ct. (no. dist. Ill.) 1973, US Dist. Ct. (ctrl. dist. Ill.) 1992, US Ct. Appeals (3rd cir. 1997, 6th cir. 1994, 7th cir. 1982, 8th cir. 1992, 10th cir. 1986), US Supreme Ct 1996. Assoc. Mayer, Brown, & Platt, Chgo., 1973-79; ptnr. Mayer, Brown, Rowe & Maw, Chgo., 1980—. Instr. at. Inst. Trial Advocacy, Chgo., 1978-96, John Marshall Law Sch., Chgo., 1982-86. Served to 1st lt. US Army, 1968—71, Vietnam. Fellow Am. Coll. Trial Lawyers; mem. ABA, Chgo. Coun. Lawyers, Chgo. Bar Assn., Union League Club (Chgo.). Office: Mayer Brown Rowe & Maw 71 S Wacker Dr Chicago IL 60606 Office Phone: 312-701-7065. Office Fax: 312-706-8623. E-mail: mfeagley@mayerbrownrowe.com.

FEALY, ROBERT S., manufacturing executive; CFO Duchossois Industries, Elmhurst, Ill. Office: Duchossois Industries Inc 845 N Larch Ave Elmhurst IL 60126

FEATHER, WILLIAM L., corporate lawyer; BA, U Tex. Austin, 1969, JD, 1972. Bar: Tex. 1972, D.C. 1975, Ill. 1977. Gen. coun. Continental Can. Co., 1978-81; sr. coun. Wickes Co., Inc., 1981-82; sr. staff coun. Household Internat., Inc., 1982-86; sr. coun. Baxter Internat., Inc., 1986-95; asst. gen. counsel, 1995-96; assoc. gen. counsel; sr. v.p., sec., gen. counsel Allegiance Corp., McGaw Pk., Ill., 1996—. Office: Allegiance Corp 1430 Waukegan Rd Mc Gaw Park IL 60085-6726

FECK, LUKE MATTHEW, retired utility executive; b. Cin., Aug. 15, 1935; s. John Franz and Mercedes Caroline (Rielag) F.; m. Gail Ann Schutte, Aug. 12, 1961; children: Lisa, Mara, Paul. BA, U. Cin., 1957. Copyboy Cin. Enquirer, 1956, reporter, TV editor, columnist, 1957-64, asst. features editor, 1969-70, mag. editor, 1970, news editor, 1971-73, mng. editor, 1974-75, exec. editor, 1975, editor, 1976-80, Columbus Dispatch, 1980-89; sr. v.p. corp. comms. Am. Electric Power, Columbus, 1990-2000; ret. Pres. Ackerman and Feck Press, Inc., 1964-69, Feicke Web, Inc., 1974-75 Bd. dirs. Thurber House, MPW Indsl. Svcs., Inc., Acad. for Governance and Leadership. 1st lt. AUS, 1957-59. Mem. Pub. Rels. Soc. Am., Edison Electric Inst., Lit. Club Cin., Capital Club, Lakes Golf and Country Club, Torch Club of Columbus, Sigma Delta Chi (pres. chpt.), Phi Kappa Theta. Home: 6880 Worthington Rd Westerville OH 43082-9491

FEDER, ROBERT, columnist; b. Chgo., May 17, 1956; s. Harold J. and Selma (Reisberg) F.; m. Janet Gail Elkins, June 16, 1985; 1 child, Emily Jacklyn. BS in Journalism, Northwestern U., 1978. Reporter, news editor Lerner Newspapers, Chgo., 1974-78, mng. editor, 1978-80; reporter Chgo. Sun-Times, 1980-83, TV/radio columnist, 1983—. Project cons. (TV documentary) Radio Faces, 1989; contbr. (spl. report) Ency. Brittanica, 1983, World Book Ency., 1996. Recipient Page One award Chgo. Newspaper Guild, 1976; named Best Daily Newspaper Columnist, New City, 1997. Mem. Soc. Profl. Journalists, Chgo. Headline Club, Chgo. Newspaper Guild, Northwestern Club of Chgo., Skokie Hist. Soc. Office: Chgo Sun-Times 350 N Orleans St Chicago IL 60654-1502 Business E-Mail: feder@suntimes.com.

FEDERMAN, ARTHUR, federal judge; b. 1951; Bankruptcy judge U.S. Bankruptcy Ct. (we. dist.) Mo., Kansas City, 1989—. Adj. instr. U. Mo., Kansas City. Office: US Courthouse 400 E 9th St Ste 6552 Kansas City MO 64106-2615

FEDOR, TERESA, state senator; b. Toledo, May 2, 1956; BS in Edn., U. Toledo. State rep. Ohio Ho. of Reps., Columbus, 2000—02; state sen., dist. 11 Ohio State Senate, Columbus, 2003—, ranking minority mem., pub. utilities com., mem. edn., ins., commerce and labor, judiciary criminal justice, and rules coms. amed Legislator of Yr., Ohio Environ. Coun., Second Harvest Food Banks; recipient award, Internat. Reading Assn., 1990. Mem.: Women's Legis. Network, at. Caucus Women in Govt., Nat. Caucus Environ. Legislators, Nat. Conf. State Legislators, Ohio Fedn. Tchrs. Democrat. Office: Senate Bldg Rm # 226, 2d fl Columbus OH 43215

FEHELEY, LAWRENCE FRANCIS, lawyer; b. Phila., Oct. 9, 1946; s. Francis Edward and Dorothy May (Greenhalgh) F.; divorced; 1 child, Matthew Francis; m. Janet Kay Douglass, Apr. 6, 1979; children: Brendan Patrick, Lawren Kaitlin, Tyne Brielle. BA, Cornell U., 1969, JD with distinction, 1973. Bar: Ohio 1973, U.S. Dist. Ct. (so. dist.) Ohio 1974, U.S. Ct. Appeals (6th cir.) 1980, U.S. Supreme Ct. 1993. Assoc. Emens, Kegler, Brown, Hill & Ritter, Columbus, Ohio, 1973-77; ptnr. Emens, Hurd, Kegler & Ritter, Columbus, Ohio, 1977—, mng. dir., 1986; Dir., exec. com. Kegler, Brown, Hill & Ritter (formerly Emens, Hurd, Kegler & Ritter, Columbus, Ohio, 2000—. Bd. dirs. Netcare Corp. Fellow, Coll. Labor and Employment Lawyers, 2001—. Mem. ABA, Ohio Bar Assn. (bd. govs. labor law sect.), Columbus Bar Assn., Ohio State Bar Assn. (cert. specialist in labor and employment law 2001-). Republican. Episcopalian. Avocations: art, soccer. Office: Kegler Brown Hill & Ritter 65 E State St Ste 1800 Columbus OH 43215-4213 Office Phone: 614-462-5400. Business E-Mail: lfeheley@keglerbrown.com.

FEHLNER, THOMAS PATRICK, chemistry professor; b. Dolgeville, NY, May 28, 1937; s. Herman Joseph and Mary (Considine) F.; m. Nancy Lou Clement, July 28, 1962; children: Thomas P., Anne Marie. BS, Siena Coll., Loudonville, NY, 1959; PhD, Johns Hopkins U., 1963. Rsch. assoc. Johns Hopkins U., Balt., 1963-64; asst. prof. U. otre Dame, South Bend, Ind., 1964-67, assoc. prof., 1967-75, prof., 1975-87, prof. chemistry, Grace Rupley chair chemistry, 1988, chmn. dept. chemistry, 1982-88. Author: (with others) Inorganic Chemistry; contbr. articles to profl. jours. Guggenheim fellow, 1988-89. Fellow AAAS; mem. Am. Chem. Soc., Materials Rsch. Soc., Internat. Union Pure & Applied Chemistry. Democrat. Roman Catholic. Office: U Notre Dame Dept Chemistry Notre Dame IN 46556

FEHR, KENNETH MANBECK, retired computer company executive; b. Schuylkill Haven, Pa., Feb. 21, 1927; s. Theodore E. and Eva (Manbeck) F.; m. Jean Alice Greenawalt, June 28, 1952; children: K. Craig, Karen Jean, K. Todd. BS, Pa. State U., State College, 1951; MBA, U. Pitts., 1953. With U.S. Steel Corp., 1951-62, div. controller, 1962; controller Interlake Steel Corp., Chgo., 1962-68; v.p. fin. Hallicrafters Co., 1968-71, E.W. Bliss Co., Salem, Ohio, 1971-74; treas. Alliance Machine Co., Ohio, 1974-86; pres. I.M.S. Corp., Hudson, Ohio, 1986-90, Fehr & Greenawalt Investments, Salem, Ohio, 1990—, Salem Security Storage, LLC, 2002—. Bd. dirs. Fegreen Inc.; night sch. tchr. U. Pitts., 1956—57. Treas. Salem Renaissance. With USNR, 1945—46. Mem.: Nat. Assn. Accts., Fin. Execs. Inst., Salem Hist. Soc., Salem Preservation Soc., Salem-Golf Club, Kiwanis (chpt. pres.), Masons. Home: 725 S Lincoln Ave Salem OH 44460-3709 Office: 1210 So Ellsworth Ave Salem OH 44460 Personal E-mail: fehrken@hotmail.com.

FEHR, WALTER RONALD, agronomist, researcher, educator; b. East Grand Forks, Minn., Dec. 4, 1939; m. Elinor Lee Otis, July 1, 1961; children: Susan, Steven, Kevin. BS, U. Minn.-St. Paul, 1961, MS, 1962; PhD, Iowa State U.,

1967. Grad. asst. U. Minn., St. Paul, 1961-62; instr. Congo Poly Inst., Zaire, 1962-64; research assoc. Iowa State U., Ames, 1964-67, prof. dept. agronomy, biotech. dir., 1967—, disting. prof. agronomy. Author: Applied Plant Breeding, 1982, Principles of Cultivar Development: Theory and Technique, 1987; editor: Hybridization of Crop Plants, 1980, Principles of Cultivar Devel.: Crop Species, 1987; contbr. writings to book chpts. and profl. articles. Recipient, Agronomic Acheivement Awd.-Crops, American Society of Agronomy, 1994 Fellow Am. Soc. Agronomy, Crop Sci. Soc. Am. Office: Iowa State Univ Dept Agronomy 1212 Agronomy Hl Ames IA 50011-0001

FEHRING, MARY ANN, secondary school educator; Secondary tchr. Bishop Noll Inst., Hammond, Ind. Named Outstanding High Sch. tchr. Inland Steel Ryerson Found., 1992. Office: Bishop Noll Inst 1518 Hoffman St Hammond IN 46327-1769

FEICHTNER, DOUGLAS J., lawyer; b. Cin., July 15, 1977; BA, Miami U., 1999; JD, U. Cin. Coll. Law, 2002. Bar: Ohio 2002, US Dist. Ct. Southern Dist. Ohio. Assoc. Dinsmore & Shohl LLP, Cin. Tutor Cin. Youth Collaborative; leadership coun. mem. Hamilton County Rep. Party. Named one of Ohio's Rising Stars, Super Lawyers, 2006. Mem.: Def. Rsch. Inst., Cin. Bar Assn., Ohio State Bar Assn., Par Club, Evans Scholar. Office: Dinsmore & Shohl LLP 255 E Fifth St Ste 1900 Cincinnati OH 45202-4700 Office Phone: 513-977-8200. Office Fax: 513-977-8141.

FEIGENHOLTZ, SARA, state legislator; b. Chgo., Dec. 11, 1956; d. Bernard and Florence (Buky) F. Student, Northeastern Ill. U. Ill. state rep. Dist. 12, 1995—. Chmn. human svcs. com. Ill. Ho. of Reps., co-chair tobacco settlement proceeds distribution, vice-chair health care availabity com., mem. state govt. adminstrn. and appropriations human svcs. coms.; exec. dir. Cen. Lakeview Merchants Assn., 1993-94; former cons., Chgo. Mem. NOW, Nat. Coun. Jewish Women, Am. Jewish Coun. (gov. coun. 1994-95), Conf. Women Legislators, Phi Theta Kappa. Office: 1051 W Belmont Ave Chicago IL 60657-3327

FEIGL, DOROTHY MARIE, chemistry professor, academic administrator; b. Evanston, Ill., Feb. 25, 1938; d. Francis Philip and Marie Agnes (Jacques) F. BS, Loyola U., Chgo., 1961; PhD, Stanford U., 1966; postdoctoral fellow, N.C. State U., 1965-66. Asst. prof. chemistry St. Mary's Coll., Notre Dame, Ind., 1966-69, assoc. prof., 1969-75, prof., 1975—, chmn. dept. chemistry and physics, 1977-85, bd. regents, 1976-82, acting v.p., dean faculty, 1985-87, v.p., dean faculty, 1987-99, Denise DeBartolo York prof. of chemistry, 2003—. Author: (with John Hill and Erwin Boschmann) General Organic and Biological Chemistry, 1991, (with John Hill and Stuart Baum) Chemistry and Life, 1997; contbr. articles to chem. jours., chpts. to texts. Recipient Spes Unica award St. Mary's Coll., 1973, Maria Pieta award, 1977 Mem. Am. Chem. Soc., Royal Soc. Chemistry, Internat. Union Pure and Applied Chemistry, Sigma Xi, Iota Sigma Pi. Democrat. Roman Catholic. Office: Dept Chemistry Saint Mary's College Notre Dame IN 46556

FEIKENS, JOHN, federal judge; b. Clifton, NJ, Dec. 3, 1917; s. Sipke and Corine (Wisse) F.; m. Henriette Dorothy Schulthouse, Nov. 4, 1939; children: Jon, Susan Corine, Barbara Edith, Julie Anne, Robert H. AB, Calvin Coll., Grand Rapids, Mich., 1938; JD, U. Mich., 1941; LLD (hon.), U. Detroit, 1979, Detroit Coll. Law, 1981. Bar: Mich. 1942. Gen. practice law, Detroit; dist. judge Ea. Dist. Mich., Detroit, 1960-61, 70-79, chief judge, 1979-86, sr. judge, 1986—. Past co-chmn. Mich. Civil Rights Commn.; past chmn. Rep. State Central Com.; past mem. Rep. Nat. Com.; mem. com. visitors U. Mich. Law Sch. Past bd. trustees Calvin Coll. Fellow Am. Coll. Trial Lawyers; mem. ABA, Detroit Bar Assn. (dir. 1962, past pres.), State Bar Mich. (commr. 1965-71), U. Mich. Club (com. visitors). Office: US Dist Ct 851 Theodore Levin US Ct 231 W Lafayette Blvd Detroit MI 48226-2700

FEIN, ROGER GARY, judge; b. St. Louis, Mar. 12, 1940; s. Albert and Fanny (Levinson) F.; m. Susanne M. Cohen, Dec. 18, 1965; children: David I., Lisa J. Student, Washington U., St. Louis, 1959, NYU, 1960; BS, UCLA, 1962; JD, Northwestern U., 1965; MBA, Am. U., 1967. Bar: Ill. 1965, US Dist. Ct. (no. dist.) Ill. 1968, US Ct. Appeals (7th cir.) 1968, US Supreme Ct. 1970. Atty. divsn. corp. fin. SEC, Washington, 1965—67; ptnr. Arvey, Hodes, Costello & Burman, Chgo., 1967—91, chmn. adminstrn. and dissolution com., 1992—2003; ptnr. Wildman, Harrold, Allen and Dixon, Chgo., 1992—2003, co-chair corp., securities and tax practice group, 1992—99; judge Cir. Ct. Cook County, 2003—. Mem. Securities Adv. Com. to Sec. State Ill., 1973—, chmn., 1973-79, 87-93, vice-chmn., 1983-87, chmn. emeritus, 1994—; spl. asst. atty. gen. State of Ill., 1974-83, 85-99; spl. asst. state's atty. Cook County, Ill., 1989-90; mem. Appeal Bd., Ill. Law Enforcement Commn., 1980-83; mem. lawyer's adv. bd. So. Ill. Law Jour., 1980-83; mem. adv. bd. securities regulation and law report Bur. Nat. Affairs Inc., 1985-02; lectr., author on land trust financing, consumer credit and securities law. Mem. Bd. Edn., Sch. Dist. No. 29, Northfield, Ill., 1977-83, pres., 1981-83; mem. Pub. Vehicle Ops. Citizens Adv. coun. City Chgo., 1985-86; mem. Anti-Defamation League Greater Chgo./Upper Midwest Region, Chgo. regional bd., 1975-91, vice chmn., 1980-88, exec. com., 1996—, co-chair pub. affairs com., 1999-2003, assoc. nat. commr., 2000—; chmn. lawyers' com. for ann. telethon Muscular Dystrophy Assn., 1983; past bd. dirs. Jewish Nat. Fund, Am. Friends Hebrew U., Northfield Cmty. Fund. Recipient Pub. Svc. award Sec. State Ill., 1976, Citation of Merit, WAIT Radio, 1976, Sunset Ridge Sch. Cmty. Svc. award, 1984, City of Chgo. Citizen's award, 1986; named one of Leading Ill. Attys., Am. Rsch. Corp., 1997. Fellow Am. Bar Found., Ill. Bar Found. (charter fellow, bd. dirs. 1978-88, v.p. 1982-84, pres. 1984-86, chmn. Fellows 1983-84, chmn., past pres. adv. com. 1988-90, Cert. of Appreciation 1985, 86, Silver fellow 1997), Chgo. Bar Found; mem. ABA (ho. of dels. 1981-85, state regulation of securities com. 1982-2003, Ill. liaison of com., chmn. subcom. liaison with securities adminstrs. and NASD 1998-2003), Ill. State Bar Assn. (bd. govs. 1976-80, del. assembly 1976-88, sec. 1977-78, cert. of appreciation 1980, 88, chmn. Bench and Bar com. 1982-83, chmn. Bench and Bar sect. coun., 1983-84, chmn. bar elections supervision com. 1986-87, chmn. assembly com. on hearings 1987-88, mem. com. on jud. appointments 1987-90), Chgo. Bar Assn. (mem. task force delivery legal svcs. 1978-80, cert. of appreciation 1976, chmn. land trusts com. 1978-79, chmn. consumer credit com. 1977-78, chmn. state securities law subcom. 1977-79), Ill. Judges Assn., Decalogue Soc. Lawyers, Northwestern U. Sch. of Law Alumni Assn. (past dir.), Standard Club, The Law Club of the City of Chgo., Tau Epsilon Phi. Alpha Kappa Psi, Phi Delta Phi. Office: Circuit Court Cook County Ill Second Mcpl Dist 5600 Old Orchard Rd Skokie IL 60077 Office Phone: 847-470-7200.

FEINBERG, DAVID ERWIN, retired publishing executive; b. Mpls., 1922; Grad., U. Minn., 1948. Chmn., chief exec. officer EMC Corp., St. Paul. Sec. bd. dirs., v.p. Paradigm Pub., Inc. Home: 111 Kellogg Blvd E Saint Paul MN 55101-1237 Office: EMC Corp 875 Montreal Way Saint Paul MN 55102-4245

FEINBERG, HENRY J., publishing executive; BS in Chemistry magna cum laude, Rutgers U., 1973. Gen. mgr. internat. ops. and bus. devel. Covia Partnership; pres. Rand McNally Pub. Group, Skokie, Ill., 1991—. Chmn. DeAgoistini-Rand McNally, Europe. Office: Rand McNally & Co 8233 Central Park Ave Skokie IL 60076-2908

FEINBERG, MARTIN ROBERT, chemical engineering educator; b. NYC, Apr. 2, 1942; s. Max and Lillian (Ziegler) F.; m. Gail Lynn Bobkier, Aug. 26, 1965; children: Donna, Sarah B.Ch.E., Cooper Union, 1962; MS, Purdue U., 1963; PhD, Princeton U., 1968. Asst. prof. U. Rochester, N.Y., 1967-73, assoc. prof. N.Y., 1973-80, prof. N.Y., 1980-97; Morrow prof. chem. engring., prof. math. Ohio State U., Columbus, 1997—. Mem. editorial bd. Archive for Rational Mechanics and Analysis, 1978-91; contbr. articles to profl. jours. Named Dreyfus Tchr.-Scholar Camille and Henry Dreyfus Found., N.Y.C., 1973, Edward Peck Curtis award, 1994, John von Neumann Lectr. in Theoretical Biology, Inst. for Advanced Study, 1997. Mem. Am. Inst. Chem. Engrs. (Richard Wilhelm award 1996), Soc. atural Philosophy (sec. 1982-84), Soc. Indsl. and Applied Math. Office: Ohio State University Dept Chem Engring Columbus OH 43210-1180

FEINBERG, PAUL H., retired lawyer; b. Yonkers, NY, Nov. 24, 1938; AB, U. Pa., 1960; LLB cum laude, Harvard U., 1963; LLM, NYU, 1970. Bar: N.Y. 1965, Ohio 1979. Asst. gen. counsel The Ford Found., 1971-77; ptnr. Baker & Hostetler LLP, Cleve., ret. Speaker in field. Contbr. articles to profl. jours. Mem. ABA (mem. sect. taxation, mem. tax exempt orgns. com., co-chair subcom. non C3 organs. 1993-94, co-chair subcom. pvt. founds. 1995—), Ohio State Bar Assn., Cleve. Bar Assn. (treas. 1996-99). Home: 3200 Nat City Ctr 1900 E 9th St Cleveland OH 44114-3475 Office Phone: 216-861-7498.

FEINBERG, RICHARD, anthropologist, educator; b. Norfolk, Va., Nov. 4, 1947; s. Isadore and Rose Selma (Hartmann) F.; m. Nancy Ellen Grim, Apr. 15, 1978; children: Joseph Grim Feinberg, Kate Grim-Feinberg. AB, U. Calif., Berkeley, 1969; MA, U. Chgo., 1971, PhD, 1974. Asst. prof. anthropology Kent (Ohio) State U., 1974-80, assoc. prof., 1980-86, prof., 1986—. Mem. editorial bd. Kent State U. Press, 1990-93; chair Kent State U. Faculty Senate, 1997-98; pres. Kent Rsch. Group, 1997-98. Author: Anuta: Social Structure of a Polynesian Island, 1981, Polynesian Seafaring and Navigation, 1988; editor: Politics of Culture in the Pacific Islands, 1995, Seafaring in the Contemporary Pacific Islands, 1995, Leadership and Change in the Western Pacific, 1996, Oral Traditions of Anuta, 1998, The Cultural Analysis of Kinship: The Legacy of David M. Schneider, 2001, (with others) Oceania: An Introduction to the Cultures and Identities of Pacific Islanders, 2002, Anuta: Polynesian Lifeways for the Twenty-first Century, 2004. Kent State Rsch. Coun. grantee, 1983, 88, 00; Wenner-Gren Found. grantee, 1991. Fellow: Assn. for Social Anthropology in Oceania (newsletter editor 1986—90, program coord. 2000—03, exec. bd. mem. 2003—06, chair 2005—06), Am. Anthrop. Assn.; mem.: Ctrl. States Anthrop. Soc. (bull. editor 1994—98, 2d v.p. 2002—03, 1st v.p. 2003—04, pres. 2004—05), Am. Ethnological Soc., Polynesian Soc. Avocations: camping, white water kayaking, scuba diving, folk music, bicycling. Office: Kent State U Dept Anthropology Kent OH 44242-0001 Office Phone: 330-672-2722. Business E-Mail: rfeinber@kent.edu.

FEINBERG, RICHARD ALAN, consumer science educator, consultant; b. NYC, June 12, 1950; s. Irving and Belle (Kolkwitz) F.; m. Fran Susan Jaffe, Jan 21, 1973; 1 child, Seth Jason. BA, SUNY, Buffalo, 1972; MS, SUNY, Cortland, 1974; PhD, U. Okla., 1976. Asst. prof. psychology Ohio State U., 1976-78, Juniata Coll., Huntington, Pa., 1978-80; asst. prof. consumer scis., retailing and environ. analysis Purdue U., West Lafayette, Ind., 1980-85, assoc. prof. consumer and retailing, 1985-89, prof., dept. head., 1989-97, dir. ctr. customer driven quality, 1997—. Dir. Purdue Retail Inst., 1990-97, coord. retail mgmt. program, 1988-89; bd. dirs. Paul Harris Stores, Purdue Univ. Press. Contbr. articles in field to profl. jours. David Ross fellow, 1980; NIHM fellow, 1975; Purdue Agrl. Expt. Sta. grantee, 1981. Mem. AAAS, Am Psychol. Assn., Assn. for Consumer Rsch, Am. Coll. Retail Assn., Soc. Consumer Psychology. Office: Purdue U Retail Inst 320 Matthews Hall West Lafayette IN 47907

FEINGOLD, RUSSELL DANA, senator, lawyer; b. Janesville, Wis., Mar. 2, 1953; m. Sue Levine, 1977 (div. 1986); children: Jessica Lee, Ellen Roseanne; m. Mary Erpenbach, 1991 (div.); stepchildren: Sam Speerschneider, Ted Speerschneider. BA in Polit. Sci., with honors, U. Wis., Madison, 1975; postgrad., Magdalen Coll., Oxford U., Eng., 1975—77; JD with honors, Harvard U., 1979. Bar: Wis. 1979. Assoc. Foley & Lardner, Madison, 1979—82, LaFollette, Sinykin, Anderson & Munson, Madison, 1983—85, Goldman & Feingold, 1985—88; mem. Wis. State Senate, 1983—92; US Senator from Wis., 1993—. Mem. com. budget US Senate, com. fgn. relations, com. judiciary, com. intelligence, commn. security and cooperation in Europe. Recipient Senator of Yr. award, Nat. Assn. Police Orgn., 1997, Profile in Courage award, John F. Kennedy Libr. Found., 1999, Mr. Smith Goes to Washington award, Taxpayers for Common Sense, 2000, Paul H. Douglas Ethics in Govt. award, Inst. Govt. and Public Affairs, U. Ill., 2000; scholar, Wis. Honors scholar, 1971, Rhodes scholar, 1975. Mem.: Dane County Bar Assn., Wis. Bar Assn., ABA, Phi Beta Kappa. Democrat. Jewish. Office: US Senate 506 Hart Senate Office Bldg Washington DC 20510-0001 also: District Office Rm 100 1600 Aspen Commons Middleton WI 53562-4626 Office Phone: 202-224-5323, 608-828-1200. Office Fax: 202-224-2725. E-mail: russell_feingold@feingold.senate.gov.

FEINSILVER, DONALD LEE, psychiatry professor; b. Bklyn., July 24, 1947; s. Albert and Mildred (Weissman) Feinsilver. BA, Alfred U., 1968; MD, Autonomous U., Guadalajara, Mexico, 1974. Diplomate Am. Bd. Psychiatry and Neurology, Am. Bd. Forensic Psychiatry. Intern in medicine L.I. Coll. Hosp., Bklyn., 1975—76; resident in psychiatry SUNY-Bklyn., 1977—78, chief resident, 1979; asst. prof. psychiatry and surgery Med. Coll. Wis., Milw., 1980—85, assoc. prof., 1985—; dir. psychiat. emergency svc. Milw. County Mental Health and Med. Complexes, 1980—88; dir. med.-psychiat. unit Milw. Psychiat. Hosp./West Allis Meml. Hosp., 1988—. Contbr. articles to profl. jours.; editor: Crisis Psychiatry: Pros and Cons, 1982; mem. editl. bd.: Psychiat. Medicine Jour., 1983—. Mem.: AAAS, APA, Acad. Psychosomatic Medicine, Am. Acad. Psychiatry and the Law, Am. Psychiat. Assn. Office: West Allis Psychiat Assocs 2424 S 90th St Milwaukee WI 53227-2455 Home Phone: 414-961-2670; Office Phone: 414-328-8690. Personal E-mail: DFeinsilver@prodigy.net.

FEINSTEIN, FRED IRA, lawyer; b. Chgo., Apr. 6, 1945; s. Bernard and Beatrice (Mines) Feinstein; m. Judy Cutler, Aug. 25, 1968; children: Karen, Donald. BSc, DePaul U., 1967, JD, 1970. Bar: Ill. 1970, U.S. Supreme Ct. 1977. Ptnr. McDermott, Will & Emery LLP, Chgo., 1976—. Lectr. in field. Contbr. articles to profl. jours. Pres. Skokie/Evanston (Ill.) Action Coun., 1981—84; bd. dirs. Temple Judea Mizpah, Skokie, 1982—84, Deborah Goldfine Meml. Cancer Rsch., 1968—, YMCA of Chgo.1985, 1985—. Mem.: Am. Coll. Real Estate Lawyers, Ill. Bar Assn., Blue Key, Union League, Beta Alpha Psi, Beta Gamma Sigma, Lambda Alpha, Pi Gamma Mu. Office: McDermott Will & Emery LLP 227 W Monroe St Ste 4700 Chicago IL 60606-5096 Office Phone: 312-984-7665. E-mail: ffeinstein@mwe.com.

FEKETY, ROBERT, physician, educator; b. Pitts., June 29, 1929; s. Francis Robert and Grace (McShaffery) F.; m. Nancy Jane Baker, June 24, 1954; children: Susan Elizabeth, Sally Jane. AB, Wesleyan U., 1951; MD, Yale U., 1955. Instr. dept. medicine Johns Hopkins U., Balt., 1960-64, asst. prof., 1964-67; assoc. prof. medicine U. Mich., Ann Arbor, 1967-71, chief div. infectious diseases, 1967-95, prof. medicine, 1971-95, prof. medicine emeritus, 1995—; prof. epidemiology, 1987-95; active emeritus prof. medicine U. Mich., Ann Arbor, 1995—. Sr. asst. surgeon USPHS, 1956-58. Fellow ACP, Infectious Diseases Soc. Am. (councillor). Roman Catholic. Home: 812 Berkshire Rd Ann Arbor MI 48104-2631 Office: Univ Mich Hosp 3116 Taubman Ctr Ann Arbor MI 48109 Fax: 734-747-9965. E-mail: rfekety@umich.edu.

FELD, THOMAS ROBERT, religious organization administrator; b. Carroll, Iowa, Sept. 30, 1944; s. Edward Martin and Elaine (Wirtz) F.; m. Donna Jean Jorstad, June 1, 1968; children: Jacqueline Joan, William Jay. BA, Loras Coll., 1966; MA, No. Ill. U., 1969; PhD, Purdue U., 1972. Instr. Loras Coll., Dubuque, Iowa, 1966-70; v.p. Lea Coll., Albert Lea, Minn., 1972-73, Cen. Meth. Coll., Fayette, Mo., 1973-76, acting pres., 1976-77; pres. Mt. Mercy Coll., Cedar Rapids, Iowa, 1977-99; exec. dir. Iowa Cath. Conf., Des Moines, 1999—. Bd. dirs. Assn. Mercy Colls., Washington, D.C., Norwest Bank. Bd. dirs. Iowa Coll. Found., Des Moines, 1977—, chmn., 1988-89; bd. dirs. Assn. Retarded Citizens, Cedar Rapids, 1979-85. Recipient Poetry award Am. mag., 1966, Teaching award Purdue U., 1971, Outstanding Fundraiser award Nat. Soc. Fundraising Execs., 1996; named Outstanding Young Dem. of Iowa, State Dems., 1965, knight Order Holy Sepulchre, 1992, Knight Comdr., 1996. Mem. CMC Colls. Assn. (bd. dirs., pres. 1979-80, 84-85, 88-89), Iowa Coordinating Coun. Postsecondary Edn. (chmn. bd. dirs. 1985-86), Assn. Mercy Colls. (exec. com. 1985—, bd. dirs.), Nat. Assn. Intercollegiate Athletics (chmn. bd. dirs. 1986-89, 94—, Hall of Fame 1996), Iowa Assn. Ind. Colls. and Univs. (chmn. bd. dirs. 1984-85), Nat. Assn. Ind. Colls. and Univs. (bd. dirs. 1990-93), Rotary (bd. dirs. 1993-97, pres. 1995—). Democrat. Roman Catholic. Avocations: golf, fishing, poetry. Home: 4404 Hickory Wind Ln Marion IA 52302-9600 Office: Iowa Catholic Conference 530 42nd St Des Moines IA 50312-2707

FELDHOUSE, LYNN, automotive company executive; m. Bob Feldhouse; 1 child, Katherine. Grad., Wayne State U.; postgrad., Oakland U. V.p., sec. Chrysler Corp. Fund, 1982—. Immediate past chair Nat. Contbns. Coun., The Conf. Bd., N.Y.C.; bd. trustee Coun. Mich. Founds., Grand Haven, Citizens' Scholarship Found. of Am., St. Peter, Minn.; bd. trustees, treas. Mich. Womens' Found., Lansing; mem. nat. corp. com. Philanthropic Adv. Svc., Coun. of BBBs, Washington; mem. exec. com. Detroit Funders' Collaborative. Active vol. United Way Comty. Svcs. Southeastern Mich., Mich. Corp. Vol. Coun., Wayne State Alumni Assn. Office: Chrysler Fund Detroit MI 48231

FELDMAN, EVA LUCILLE, neurology educator; b. NYC, Mar. 30, 1952; d. George Franklin and Margherita Enriceta (Cafiero) F.; children: Laurel, Scott, John Jr. BA in Biology and Chemistry, Earlham Coll., 1973; MS in Zoology, U. Notre Dame, 1975; PhD in Neurosci., U. Mich., 1979, MD, 1983. Diplomate Am. Bd. Neurology; lic. med. practitioner, Mich. Instr. dept. neurology U. Mich., Ann Arbor, 1987-88, asst. prof. neurology, 1988-94, mem. faculty Cancer Ctr., 1992-2000, assoc. prof. neurology, 1994-2000, prof., 2000—, Russell N. DeJong prof. neurology, 2004—. Mem. faculty neurosci. program U. Mich., Mich. Diabetes Rsch. and Tng., Ann Arbor, 1988—; dir. JDRF Ctr. for the Study of Complications in Diabetes. Contbr. chpts. to books, articles to profl. jours. Grantee, NIH, 1989, 1994, 1997, 1998, 2001, 2003, 2006, Juvenile Diabetes Rsch. Found., 1994, 1997, 1999, 2001, 2006, Am. Diabetes Assn., 2005. Achievements include research on the elucidation of the role of growth factors in the pathogenesis of human disease.

FELDMAN, KAYWIN, museum director, curator; m. Jim Lutz. BA, U. Mich.; MA in mus. mgmt. and art hist., U. London. Ednl. curator British Mus. Art; dir. Fresno Met. Mus. Art, Hist. and Sci., Calif., 1996—99, Memphis Brooks Mus. Art, Tenn., 1999—; dir. & pres. Mpls. Inst. Arts, 2008—. Curator It's Only Rock and Roll. Recipient Ctrl. Calif. Excellence in Bus. award, 1996. Office: Mpls Inst Arts 2400 3rd Ave S Minneapolis MN 55404 Office Phone: 612-870-3221.

FELDMAN, MARK L, lawyer; b. Mar. 15, 1950; BSIE with honors, Univ. Ill., 1971; JD, Georgetown Univ., 1974. Bar: Ill. 1974, US Dist. Ct. (no. dist.) Ill., US Ct. Appeals (7th and Fed. cir.), US Patent and Trademark Off. Sr. trademark counsel G.D. Searle & Co.; ptnr. DLA Piper Rudnick Gray Cary US LLP, Chgo. Mem.: ABA, Am. Intellectual Property Assn. (chair, franchising com. 1997—2000), Intellectual Property Law Assn. Chgo. (bd. mgrs. 1996—97, v.p. 2002—03, pres.-elect 2004, pres. 2005), Internat. Trademark Assn., Brand Names Edn. Found. Office: DLA Piper Rudnick Gray Cary US LLP Ste 1900 203 N LaSalle St Chicago IL 60601-1293 Office Phone: 312-368-7084. Office Fax: 312-236-7516. Business E-Mail: mark.feldman@dlapiper.com.

FELDMAN, MURRAY, announcer; b. Phila. BS in Speech and Comm., Emerson Coll. Gen. assignment reporter WJBK-TV, Detroit, 1976, money editor, co-anchor News at 5:30, 1998—; host The Feldman Report WWJ Newsradio 950. Named Media Adv. of Yr., U.S. Small Bus. Adminstrn., 1989, 1992, Mich. Entrepreneur of Yr., 1992; recipient awards, UPI, AP, Emmy awards for reporting excellence. Office: WJBK Fox 2 PO Box 2000 Southfield MI 48037-2000

FELDMAN, NANCY JANE, insurance company executive; b. Green Bay, Wis., July 6, 1946; d. Benjamin J. and Ellen M. Naze; m. Robert P. Feldman, Aug. 24, 1968 (dec. May 2006); 1 child, Sara J. BA, U. Wis., 1969, MS, 1974. Supr. EPSDT program Minn. Dept. Human Svcs., St. Paul, 1974-80, supr. healthcare programs, 1980-84; team leader human resources budget Minn. Dept. Fin., St. Paul, 1984-87; asst. commr. Minn. Dept. Health, St. Paul, 1987-91; team leader CORE program Minn. Dept. Adminstrn., St. Paul, 1991-93; dir. state pub. programs Medica, Allina Health Sys., Mpls., 1993-95; CEO UCare Minn., St. Paul, 1995—. Bd. mem. Minn. Coun. Health Plans, Mpls., 1995-, Ctr. for Victims of Torture, 1997-(chair 2004-06, vice-chair 2007-), Stratis Health, 2000-, Nat. Inst. Health Policy, 2002-, Assn. Cmty. Health Plans, 2003-; bd. mem. VDA Nat. Svcs., 2007; Vols. Am. Nat. Svc., 2005-; bd. mem. VDA nat. svcs., 2007. Mem. Women's Health Leadership Trust. Avocations: distance swimming, bicycling, travel. Office: UCare Minn PO Box 52 Minneapolis MN 55440-0052 Home: 4822 Folwell Dr Minneapolis MN 55406 Business E-Mail: nfeldman@ucare.org.

FELDMAN, RICHARD DAVID, health commissioner; BA in Psychology phi beta kappa, Ind. U., 1972, MD, 1977. Diplomate Am. Bd. Family Practice; Lic. physician, Indiana. Resident Ind. U. Sch. Med., Indpls., 1977, St. Francis Hosp., Beech Grove, Ind., 1977-80, pvt. practice, 1981—, Family Physicians of Carmel, Ind., 1980-81. Asst. prof. Family Med., Ind. U., 1981—; cons. in field; lectr. in field. Contbr. articles to profl. jours. Pres. Golden Hill Neighborhood Assn., 1988-90, 1995-97; founder Indpls. Totem Pole Reconstruction Project Eiteljorg Mus., 1990-96; mem. O'Bannon Ind. Gubinatorial Campaign (health care policy com. 1996); bd. dirs. Ind. State Med. Assn. Political Action Com., 1996, Golden Hill Neighborhood Assn., 1986—, United Northwest Neighborhood Day Care Ctr., Indpls.; pres. Ethnographic Art Soc. Indpls., 1983—. Rsch. grantee Mead-Johnson Nutritional Div., 1982, St. Joseph County Cancer Soc., 1982. Fellow Am. Acad. Family Physicians (Ind. chpt. Rsch. award 1980, A. Alan Fischer award 1994, Pres. award 1995, Distinguished Pub. Svc. award 1997); mem. AMA, at. Assn. Family Practice Residency Dirs., Soc. Tchrs. Family Med., Ind. State Med. Assn., Marion County Med. Soc., Assn. Ind. Dirs. Med. Edn. Office: Indiana State Dept Health 2 N Meridian St Indianapolis IN 46204-3003 also: St Francis Family Practice Residency 1500 Albany St Ste 807 Beech Grove IN 46107-1563

FELDMAN, SCOTT MILTON, lawyer; b. NYC, July 31, 1942; s. Abe and Lilian F.; m. Susan Lauer, July 13, 1968; children: James W., Mark A. BA, Amherst Coll., 1964; JD, Harvard U., 1967. Bar: NY 1968, Ill. 1978. Instr. UCLA Law Sch, 1967-68; lt. Judge Advocate Gen's. Corp. U.S. Navy, Washington, 1968-71; assoc. Sullivan & Cromwell, NYC, 1971-77; ptnr. Winston & Strawn, Chgo., 1978-2001; assoc. gen. counsel Bank of Am. N.A., Chgo., 2001—. Trustee Village of Glencoe, Ill., 1983-91. Mem. ABA, Chgo. Bar Assn., Assn. Bar City N.Y., Amherst Alumni Assn.

FELDMAN, TED, cardiologist; b. Lincoln, Nebr., Nov. 3, 1952; BA, Ind. U., 1974, MD, 1978. Diplomate Am. Bd. Internal Medicine, Am. Bd. Cardiology. Intern medicine Rush Med. Coll., 1978-79, resident, 1979-81, chief resident, 1981-82; fellow cardiology U. Chgo., 1982-85, asst. prof. medicine, 1985-92, assoc. prof., 1992-97, prof., 1997—, dir. interventional cardiology, 1988—, dir. cardiac catheterization lab., 1997—. Contbr. articles to profl. jours. Fellow Am. Coll. Cardiology, Soc. for Coronary Angiography and Intervention. Office: U Chgo Hosps 5841 S Maryland Ave Rm 5076 Chicago IL 60637-1463

FELDT, LEONARD SAMUEL, academic administrator, educator; b. Long Branch, NJ, Nov. 2, 1925; s. Harry and Bessie (Doris) F.; m. Natalie Ruth (Fischer), Aug. 29, 1954; children: Sarah Feldt Roach, Daniel C. BS in Edn., Rutgers U., 1950, EdM, 1951; PhD, U. Iowa, 1954. Asst. prof. to prof. U. Iowa, Iowa City, 1954-94, dir. testing programs, 1981-94, Lindquist prof. ednl. measurement, 1981-94, prof. emeritus, 1994. Pres. Iowa Measurment Rsch. Found., Iowa City, 1978-2004, v.p., 2004—; editor standardized tests, Iowa Tests Ednl. Devel., 1960—. With US Army, 1943—46. Recipient Disting. Svc. Award Rutgers U., 1999; Disting. Achievement Award, Nat. Ctr. for Rsch. on Evaluation Stds. and Student Testing, 1999. Mem.: Am. Stats. Assn., Psychometric Soc., Nat. Coun. on Measurement in Edn. (Career Contbns. award 1994), Am. Ednl. Rsch. Assn. (E.F. Lindquist award 1995), Sigma Xi, Phi Beta Kappa. Avocations: golf, stock market. Home: 810 Willow St Iowa City IA 52245-5438 Office: Univ Iowa Lindquist Ctr Iowa City IA 52242 Home Phone: 319-338-3749. Business E-Mail: leonard-feldt@uiowa.edu.

FELDT, ROBERT HEWITT, pediatric cardiologist, educator; b. Chgo., Aug. 3, 1934; s. Robert Hewitt and Frances (Swanson) F.; m. Barbara Ann Fritz, Aug. 17, 1957; children: Christine, Susan, Kathryn. BS, U. Wis., 1956; MD, Marquette U., 1960; MS, U. Minn., 1965. Diplomate: Am. Bd. Pediatrics, Am. Bd. Pediatric Cardiology. Intern Miller Hosp., St. Paul, 1960-61; resident in pediatrics cardiology Mayo Found., Rochester, Minn., 1961-65; cons. pediatrics Mayo Clinic, Rochester, Minn., 1966—, chmn. dept. pediatrics, 1980-85, prof. pediatrics; ret. Mem. Am. Bd. Pediatrics; chmn. sci. coun. Am. Heart Assn. Author numerous sci. articles, book chpts., monographs. Fellow Am. Acad. Pediatrics, Am. oll. Cardiology; mem. Minn. Heart Assn. (pres. 1982), Midwest Soc. Pediat. Rsch., Am. Pediat. Soc. Congregationalist. Home: 1950 Westfield Ct SW Rochester MN 55902-1065

FELECIANO, PAUL, JR., state legislator; b. NYC, Mar. 27, 1942; m. V. Arlene Williams, 1966; children: Treven, Eric, Heather. AAS, N.Y.C. C.C., 1961. Mem. state rep. Kans. Ho. of Reps., 1972-76; rep. for dist. 28 Kans. State Senate, 1998—; minority whip, former asst. senate Dem. leader; former ranking minority mem. com. and jud. com.; former assessment and taxation com.; mem. comm. com. State-Fed. Assembly Nat. Conf. State Legisatures; mem. joint com. arts and cultural resources, investments pensions and benefits com.; mem. children and youth adv. com. Women's Correctional Task Force; mem. Kans. Coun. Employment and Tng.; mem. Gov.'s Task Force on Housing and Homeless, Washington; mem. force and policy alt. leader Ctr. Policy Alternatives. Sec. Aircap Truck Plz., Inc.; v.p. Air Cap Motel, Inc.; pres. polit. affairs Nat. Telecom. Cons. Mem. Riverside Dem. Club. Mem. Am. Legion (Post 401, Wichita). Office: 815 Barbara St Wichita KS 67217-3115 also: State Senate State Capitol Topeka KS 66612

FELICETTI, DANIEL A., academic administrator; b. NYC, Apr. 25, 1942; s. Ernest and Rose (DiAdamo) F.; m. Barbara D'Antonio, July 13, 1969. BA in Polit. Sci., Hunter Coll., 1963; MA in Polit. Sci., NYU, 1966, PhD in Polit. Sci., 1971. From asst. to assoc. prof. Fairfield (Conn.) U., 1967-77, chmn. dept. politics, 1973-76, spl. asst. to pres., 1977; acad. v.p., acad. dean Wheeling (W.Va.) Coll., 1977-80; sr. v.p. for acad. affairs Coll. New Rochelle, NY, 1980-81, Southeastern U., Washington, 1982-84; v.p. acad. affairs U. Detroit, 1984-89; pres. Marian Coll., Indpls., 1989-99, Capital U., Columbus, Ohio, 1999-2001; founder Higher Edn. Leadership Projects Consulting Svc., 2001—. Participant Am. Coun. on Edn., Washington, 1976-77, vis. assoc., 1984-85; intern Inst. for Ednl. Mgmt. program Harvard U., 1981; cons. Coun. for Ind. Colls., Washington, 1986. Trustee Am. Heart Assn., Mich.; bd. dirs. Am. Heart Assn., Ind., Mental Health Assn. Marion County, Econ. Club Indpls., Coun. Ind. Colls.; mem. health and substance abuse com. New Detroit, Inc., 1986-89; mem. Greater Indpls. Progress Com.; mem. Pub. Safety Task Force Ind.; mem. Colls. Ind. Found.; mem. Indpls. delegation to Pres.'s Summit for Am.'s Future, 1997. Trustee Am. Heart Assn., Mich.; bd. dirs. Am. Heart Assn., Ind., Mental Health Assn. Marion County, Econ. Club Indpls., Coun. Ind. Colls.; mem. health and substance abuse com. New Detroit, Inc., 1986-89; mem. Greater Indpls. Progress Coml; mem. Pub. Safety Task Force Ind.; mem. Colls. Ind. Found.; mem. safety vision coun. United Way Columbus. Named to Hunter Coll. Hall of Fame, Hunter Coll. Alumni Assn., 1986; recipient Cert. of Recognition Sen. Lugar, 1994; Lilly Found. vis. faculty fellow Yale U., 1975; named Sagamore of the Wabash Gov. of Ind., 1990. Mem. Indpls. Athletic Club, received hon. doctoral degree from Marian Coll., 1999, Columbus C. of C. (pub. rels. com.), Rotary, Alpha Sigma Nu (hon.), Beta Gamma Sigma (hon.). Democrat. Roman Catholic. Avocations: baseball, reading, antiques.

FELKNOR, BRUCE LESTER, publishing executive, consultant, writer; b. Oak Park, Ill., Aug. 18, 1921; s. Audley Rhea and Harriet (Lester) F.; m. Joanne Sweeney, Feb. 8, 1942 (div. Jan. 1952); 1 child, Susan Harriet Felknor Pickard; m. Edith G. Johnson, Mar. 1, 1952; children: Sarah Anne Felknor Ragland, Bruce Lester II. Student, U. Wis., 1939—41. Reporter Dunn County News, Menomonie, Wis., 1937—39; freight brakeman Pa. R.R., NYC, 1941, asst. yardmaster, 1942; prodn. coord. Hwy. Trailer Co., Edgerton, Wis., 1943; radio officer U.S. Maritime Svc., 1944—45; flight radio officer Air Transport Command, 1945; mem. pub. rels. dept. Am. Airlines, 1945; writer pub. rels. dept. ITT, 1946; Southeast regional pub. rels. dir. Ford Motor Co., Chester, Pa., 1946—48; free lance pub. res. NYC, 1948—49; pub. rels. exec. Foote, Cone & Belding, Inc., NYC, 1950—53; v.p. Market Rels. Network, NYC, 1954—55; exec. dir. Fair Campaign Practices Com., Inc., NYC, 1956—66; asst. to chmn. and pub. William Benton Ency. Brit., 1966—70, dir. mktg. info. internat. divsn., 1970—73, dir. advt. and promotion, 1973, dir. pub. info., 1974—76, exec. editor, 1977—83, dir. yearbooks, 1983—85; editl. cons., 1985—. Vis. lectr. Hamilton Coll., 1966, 75, 82; history editor Mcht. Marine internet web site www.usm-m.org, 1999—. Author: Fair Play in Politics, 1960, State-by-State Smear Study, 1956, You Are They, 1964, (with C.P. Taft) Prejudice & Politics, 1960, Dirty Politics, 1966, reprinted, 1975, 2001, (with Frank Jonas et al) Political Dynamiting, 1970, How to Look Things Up and Find Things Out, 1988, Political Mischief: Smear, Sabotage, and Reform in U.S. Elections, 1992, The Highland Park Presbyterian Church: A History 1871-1996, 1996 (Robert Lee Stowe award 1997), The U.S. Merchant Marine at War 1775-1945, 1998, The Great Witch Hunt of the Presbyterian Left, 2001, Of Clubbable Nature: Chicago's Tavern Club at 75, 2005; editor: The U.S. Government: How and Why it Works, 1978; also various newspaper, jour. and yearbook articles on politics; contbg. editor (with Clifton Fadiman) The Treasury of the Encyclopaedia Britannica, 1992; contbr. Encyclopedia of the American Presidency, 1993. Chmn. Citizens Com. for Sch. Centralization in Armonk, N.Y., 1957-61; ruling elder, chmn. com. religion and race Presbytery Hudson River, 1963-67, mem. nat. coun. on ch. and soc., 1966-72; bd. dirs., mem. exec. com. Fair Campaign Practices Com.; mem. nat. adv. bd. Amigos de las Americas, 1982-89, Am. U., Washington, 1982—; mem. Ill. Literacy Coun., 1984-86; mem. bd. advisors, acad. adv. coun. Nat. Strategy Forum, 1987—; mem. bd. edn. Lake Forest (Ill.) H.S. Dist., 1989-93. Republican. Presbyterian. Home and Office: 509 Trinity Ct Evanston IL 60201-1908 Home Phone: 843-570-3469. E-mail: bruce_felknor@yahoo.com.

FELLER, ROBERT WILLIAM ANDREW, public relations executive, retired professional baseball player; b. Van Meter, Iowa, Nov. 3, 1918; s. William and Lena (Forrett) F.; m. Anne Morris Gilliland, Oct. 1, 1974. Pub. rels. exec. Cleveland Indians Baseball Team, 1936-56. Played first major league game Cleve. vs. St. Louis Browns, 1936; pitched 3 no-hitters Cleve. vs. Chgo., 1940, Cleve. vs. N.Y., 1946, Cleve. vs. Detroit, 1951; member 9 all-star teams. Author: Strikeout Story, 1947, How to Pitch, 1948, Now Pitching Bob Feller, 1990, Bob Feller's Little Black Book of Baseball Wisdom, 2000. CPO USNavy, 1941-45, PTO. Recognition for mil. svc. and baseball contbn. US Congress, Washington, 2006; inducted to Baseball Hall of Fame, Cooperstown, NY, 1962; named Greatest Living Right-Hand Pitcher Profl. Baseball Centennial Celebration, 1969. Mem. Green Berets (hon.). Republican. Episcopalian. Avocation: restoring tractors. Home Fax: 440-423-3248.

FELLER, STEVEN ALLEN, physics educator; BS in Physics, Clarkson Coll. of Tech., 1973; MSc in Physics, Brown U., 1975, PhD in Physics, 1979. Asst. prof. Coe Coll., Cedar Rapids, Iowa, 1979-85, assoc. prof., 1985-91, B.D. Silliman prof. of physics, chair, 1991—. Editor Internat. Bank Note Soc. Jour., 1990. Recipient Bendix award Am. Inst. Physics, 1981-82, Fulbright award to U.K., 1996; grantee Rsch. Corp., 1983, 86-87, Iowa Acad. of Sci., 1986-87, Tex. Nat. Rsch. Lab. Commn., 1991-93, NSF, 1986-88, 88-90, 90-93, 91, 93-96, 96—; named Iowa Prof. of Yr. Carnegie Found., 1995. Mem. Am. Ceramic Soc., Am. Numismatic Assn., Internat. Bank Note Soc., Iowa Acad. Sci. Achievements include research in materials physics and physics education and numismatics. Office: Coe Coll Dept Physics Cedar Rapids IA 52402

FELLOWES, JAMES, manufacturing executive; BA, Denison U. Chmn., CEO Fellowes Mfg., Itasca, Ill. Named Entrepreneur of Y., Ernst & Young, 1997. Office: Fellowes Manufacturing 1789 Norwood Ave Itasca IL 60143-1095

FELLOWS, JERRY KENNETH, lawyer; b. Madison, Wis., Mar. 19, 1946; s. Forrest Garner and Virginia (Witte) F.; m. Patricia Lynn Graves, June 28, 1969; children: Jonathon, Aaron, Daniel. BA in Econs., U. Wis., 1968; JD, U. Minn., 1971. Bar: U.S. Dist. Ct. (no. dist.) Ill. 1971. Ptnr. McDermott, Will & Emery, Chgo., 1971—2002; with Bell, Boyd & Lloyd LLC, Chgo., 2002—. Speaker Bur. Nat. Affairs, Washington, 1985—. Contbr. articles to profl. jours. Bd. dirs. Midwest Benefits Coun., 1998. Mem. U. Minn. Law Alumni Assn. (bd. visitors), Gamma Eta Gamma. Avocations: coaching track, basketball, baseball. Home: 4541 Middaugh Ave Downers Grove IL 60515-2761 Office: Bell Boyd & Lloyd LLC 70 West Madison St Ste 3100 Chicago IL 60602-4207 Office Phone: 312-807-4358. Business E-Mail: jfellows@bellboyd.com.

FELLOWS, ROBERT ELLIS, medical educator, researcher; b. Syracuse, NY, Aug. 4, 1933; s. Robert Ellis and Clara F.; m. Karlen Kiger, July 2, 1983; children: Kara, Ari, Thomas, Gregory, Jamey. AB, Hamilton Coll., 1955; MD, CM, McGill U., 1959; PhD, Duke U., 1969. Intern NY Hosp., NYC, 1959—60, asst. resident, 1960—61, Royal Victoria Hosp., Montreal, Que., Canada, 1961—62; asst. prof. dept. medicine Duke U., Durham, NC, 1966—76, asst. prof. dept. physiology and pharmacology, 1966—70, assoc. prof. dept. physiology and pharmacology, assoc. dir. med. scientist tng. program, 1970—76; prof. & chmn., dept. physiology and biophysics U. Iowa Coll. Medicine, 1976—2002, prof. dept. physiology and biophysics, 1976—, dir. med. sci. tng. program, 1976—97, dir. physician sci. program, 1984—88, dir. neurosci. program, 1984—88. Mem. Nat. Pituitary Agy. Adv. Bd.; mem. NIH Population Rsch. Com., 1981-86, VA Career Devel. Rev. Com., 1985-88; cons. NIH, NSF, March of Dimes. Mem. editl. bd. Endocrinology, Am. Jour. Physiology. Mem. AAAS, Am. Chem. Soc., Am. Fedn. Clin. Rsch., Am. Physiol. Soc., Am. Soc. Biol. Chemists, Am. Soc. Cell Biology, Assn. Chmn. Depts. Physiology, Biochem. Soc., Biophys. Soc., Endocrine Soc., Internat. Soc. euroendocrinology, NY Acad. Scis., Soc. for Neurosci., Assn. Neurosci. Depts. and Programs (pres. 1995-96), Sigma Xi, Alpha Omega Alpha. Home: 135 Pentire Cir Iowa City IA 52245-1575 Office: 5-472 Bowen Sci Bldg Iowa City IA 52242 Office Phone: 319-335-7804. Business E-Mail: robert-fellows@uiowa.edu.

FELT, JULIA KAY, lawyer; b. Wooster, Ohio, Apr. 8, 1941; d. George Willard and Betty Virginia F.; m. Lawrence Roger Van Til, May 31, 1969. BA, Northwestern U., 1963; JD, U. Mich., 1967. Bar: Ohio 1967, Mich. 1968. Tchr. Triway Local H.S., Wooster, Ohio, 1963-64; assoc. Dykema, Gossett, PLLC, Detroit, 1967-75, ptnr., 1975—; adj. asst. prof. dept. cmty. medicine Wayne State U., Detroit, 1974-05. Contbr. articles to profl. jours., chpts. to books. Trustee Rehab. Inst., Detroit, 1971-01, sec., 1974-77, 91—99, vice chmn., 1978-83, 85-90, chmn. bd., 1983-85; trustee Detroit Med. Ctr. Corp. 1984-85; bd. dirs. Travelers Aid Soc., Detroit, 1974—90, v.p., 1978-81, United Way Cmty. Svc. Detroit, bd. dirs., 1981-2005; vis. com. U. Mich. Law Sch., Ann Arbor, 1972-06, nat. vice chmn. law sch. fund, 1984-86, bd. dirs. Detroit Assn. U. Mich. Women, 1968-72, pres., 1971-72, Mich. Women's Found., trustee, 1993-02, bd. dirs. Med. Ethics Resource Network of Mich., 2002-05 Planned Giving Round table Southeastern Mich., chmn., 1993-94; chmn. Leave a Legacy Southeastern Mich., 1996-98. Campbell Competition winner U. Mich. Law Sch., 1967; recipient Svc. award Mich. League Nursing, 1977, Alumna-in-Residence U. Mich. Alumnae Coun., 1986, Disting. Svc. award Mich. Bus. and Profl. Assn., 1998. Fellow Am. Bar Found., Mich. Bar Found., Am. Health Lawyers, Mich. Hospice and Palliative Care Orgn. (Educator of Yr. award 2002), Am. Acad. Health Care Attys. of Am. Health Lawyers(pres. 1985-86, bd. dirs. 1980-87); mem. Mich. Soc. Hosp. Attys. (pres. 1975-76, bd. dirs. 1975-77), Cath. Health Assn. U.S. (legal services adv. com. 1980-84), Gov's. Commn. on End Life Care, 1999-02, Adv. Com. Pain and Symptom Mgmt. 1999-02, ABA, Ohio State Bar Assn., State Bar Mich. (com. medicolegal problems 1973-81, adminstrv. rule making com. 1978-79, awards com. chmn. 1989-99, disabilities com. Open Justice Commn., 1999-04, Equal Assn. Initiatives 2004-), Detroit Bar Assn., Women Lawyers Mich., Am. Soc. Law and Medicine. Presbyterian. Office: Dykema Gossett PLLC 400 Renaissance Ctr Detroit MI 48243-1668 Office Phone: 313-568-6700.

FELTON, CYNTHIA, educational director; b. Chgo., Apr. 1, 1950; d. Robert Lee Felton Sr. and Julia Mae (Cheton) Felton-Phillips. BA, Northeastern, 1970; MEd, ational Coll., 1984; MA, DePaul U., 1988; PhD, Loyola U., Chgo., 1992. Cert. tchr, adminstrv., Ill. Tchr. Chgo. Pub. Schs., 1971-86, adminstr., 1986-89, asst. prin., 1989-92, prin., 1992-97; dir. tech. Chgo. Acad. for Sch. Leadership, 1997—. Mem. ASCD, Nat. Staff Devel. Coun., Nat. Coun. Tchrs. Math, Nat. Coun. Suprs. Math, Ill. Coun. Tchrs. Math (bd. dirs. 1992-95). Office: Chgo Acad Sch Leadership 221 N Lasalle St Chicago IL 60601-1206

FENG, MILTON, engineering educator; b. Taiwan, July 21, 1950; BSEE, Columbia U., 1973; MSEE, U. Ill., 1976, PhD in Elec. Engring., 1979. Sect. head material and device group Torrance (Calif.) Rsch. Ctr., Hughes Aircraft Co., 1979-83; mgr. advanced digital integrated ciruit devel. program, dir. advanced devel. & fabrication digital & microwave/millimeter-wave devel. programs Ford Microelectronics, Inc., Colorado Springs, Colo., 1984-91; prof. elec. and computer engring., mem. faculty Ctr. Compound Semiconductor Microelectronics and Material Rsch. Lab. U. Ill., Urbana, 1991—. Fellow IEEE (Beckman Rsch. award 1994, David Sarnoff award 1997). Achievements include research in ion-implantation technology in III-V technology, optoelectronics IC's, ultra-high-speed analog-digital HBT IC's, and RF, microwave and millimeter-wave IC's. Office: U Ill 325 Microelectronics Lab 208 N Wright St Urbana IL 61801-2355

FENN, WADE R., retail executive; Exec. v.p. mktg. Best Buy Co., Eden Prairie, Minn., 1995—.

FENNELLY, WILLIAM, basketball coach; b. Davenport, Iowa., May 14, 1957; m. Deborah Fennelly; children: Billy, Steven. BBA and Econs., William Penn Coll., 1979. Women's basketball coach William Penn Coll., Fresno State U., Notre Dame (Ind.) U.; head women's basketball coach U. Toledo, Ohio, Iowa State U., Ames, 1994—. Office: Iowa State Univ Jacobson Athletic Bldg 1800 S 4th St Ames IA 50011-0001

FENNESSY, JOHN JAMES, radiologist, educator; b. Clonmel, Ireland, Mar. 8, 1933; s. John and Ann (McCarthy) F.; m. Ann M. O'Sullivan, Aug. 20, 1960; children— Deirdre, Conor, Sean, Emer, Rona, Nial, Ruairi M.B., B.Ch., BAO, Univ. Coll., Dublin, Ireland, 1958. Assoc. prof. U. Chgo., 1971-74, prof., 1974—, chief chest and gastrointestinal radiology, 1971-73, acting chief diagnostic radiology, 1973-74, chmn. dept. radiology, 1974-84, assoc. chair edn., 1990—. Fellow: Am. Coll. Radiology, Royal Coll. Surgeons Ireland (hon.); mem.: NRA, Fleischner Soc., Am. Gastroent. Soc., Radiology Soc. N.Am., Thoracic Radiology Soc., Chgo. Radiol. Soc., Am. Assn. Univ. Radiologists, Irish Am. Cultural Inst., County Tipperary Hist. Soc., Trout Unltd., Chgo. Art Inst., Alpha Omega Alpha, Sigma Xi. Republican. Roman Catholic. Office: U Chgo Dept Radiology 5841 S Maryland Ave Chicago IL 60637-1463

FENOGLIO-PREISER, CECILIA METTLER, retired pathologist, educator; b. NYC, Nov. 28, 1943; d. Frederick Albert and Cecilia Charlotte (Asper) Mettler; m. John Fenoglio Jr., May 27, 1967 (div. 1977); 1 child, Timothy; stepchildren: Johanna, Andreas, Nicholas; m. Wolfgang F.E. Preiser, Feb. 16, 1985. Ach, Coll. St. Elizabeth, 1965; MD, Georgetown U., 1969. Diplomate Am. Bd. Pathology. Intern Presbyn. Hosp., NYC, 1969-70; dir. Ctrl. Tissue Facility Columbia-Presbyn. Med. Ctr., NYC, 1976-83; co-dir. div. surg. pathology Presbyn. Hosp., NYC, 1978-82, div. dir. surg. pathology, 1982-83; dir. Electron Microscop. Lab. Internat. Inst. Human Reprodn., 1978-85; assoc. prof. pathology Coll. Physicians and Surgeons, Columbia U., 1981-82, prof., 1982-83, attending pathologist, 1982-83; dir. lab. services Albuquerque VA Med. Ctr., 1983-90; prof. pathology U. N.Mex. Sch. Medicine, Albuquerque, 1983-90, also vice-chmn. dept. pathology; MacKenzie prof., chmn. dept. pathology and lab. medicine U. Cin. Sch. Medicine, 1990—2005, dir. Cancer Ctr., 2001—05; ret., 2005. Mem. com. gastrointestine cancer WHO. Author: General Pathology, 1983, Gastrointestinal Pathology, An Atlas and Text, 1999, 2nd edit., 1999, Tumors of the Large and Small Intestine, 1990; editor: Advances in Pathobiology Cell Membranes, 1988-92, Advances in Pathobiology: Aging and Neoplasia, 1976, Progress in Surgical Pathology, vols. I-XIV, 1980-87, Advances in Pathology, vols. I-V, 1988-89. Grantee NIH, 1973, 79-82, 84-87, 85-2005, Cancer Rsch. Ctr., 1975-83, Population Coun., 1977-83, Nat. Ileitis and Colitis Found., 1979-80, Am. Cancer Soc., 1987-94. Fellow AAAS (life); mem. U.S. and Can. Acad. Pathology (edn. com. 1980-85, coun. 1984-87, exec. com. 1987-91, v.p. 1987, pres.-elect 1988, pres. 1989, fin. com. 1998-2001), Internat. Acad. Pathology (N.Am. v.p. 1990-94, pres. 1996-98, exec. com. 1990-2000, edn. com. 1998—), Nat. Surg. Adj. Breast Project (sci. adv. bd.), Am. Assn. Pathologists, Armed Forces Inst. Pathology (sci. adv. bd. 1990—), N.Y. Acad. Sci., N.Y. Acad. Medicine, Fedn. Am. Scientists for Exptl. Biology, Gastrointestinal Pathologist Group (founding mem. edn. com. 1983-85, sec.-treas. 1993-96, pres.-elect 1996, pres. 1997), S.W. Oncology Group (chmn. GI tumor biology com., chmn. pathology com., chmn. correlative sci. com.), Arthur Purdy Stout Soc. (coun. 1987-90). Personal E-mail: cecilia.fenogliopreiser@uc.edu.

FENSIN, DANIEL, diversified financial service company executive; b. 1943; BS in Acctg., DePaul U., 1965. Ptnr. Topel, Forman & Co., 1965-74; ceo, mng. ptnr. Blackman Kallick Bartelstein, L.L.P., Chgo., 1974—. Office: Blackman Kallick Bartelstein 10 S Riverside Plz Ste 900 Chicago IL 60606-3770

FENTON, CLIFTON LUCIEN, investment banker; b. Bryan, Ohio, May 11, 1943; s. Gibson Lucien and Elizabeth (Newcomer) F.; m. Judith Todd Wallis, June 23, 1973; children: Gregory, Eric, Alyssa. AB, Princeton U., 1965; JD, Ohio State U., 1968; MBA, Columbia U., 1970; grad., Kellog Grad. Sch. Mgmt., 2001. Bar: Ohio 1968. Assoc. Bank N.Y., NYC, 1970-72, Morgan Guaranty Trust Co., NYC, 1972; v.p. Kidder, Peabody, NYC, 1972-84; mng. dir. Prudential-Bache Securities, NYC, 1984-89; v.p., nat. mgr. John Nuveen & Co., Chgo., 1989-95, v.p. and mgr. Investment Banking Divsn., 1995-99; mng. dir. and co-head pub. fin. U.S. Bancorp Piper Jaffray, Chgo., 1999-2000. Bd. dirs. Associated Colls. Ill. Pinnacle Forum Chgo. and Good City, Heritage at Millenium Park. Mem. Met. Club (N.Y.C.), Univ. Club Chgo. Avocations: water-skiing, sailing, piano, skiing. Home: 130 N Garland Ct Chicago IL 60602 E-mail: cliffenton@comcast.net.

FENTON, LAWRENCE JULES, medical educator; b. Chgo., June 1, 1940; s. Arthur S. Fenton and Dorothy (Schochet) Wade; m. Gayle Ann Yeager, Apr. 10, 1965; children: Lori Ann Novak, Scott L. BS, U. Mich., 1962; MD, U. Cin., 1966. Diplomate Am. Bd. Pediatrics, Sub-bd. Neonatal and Perinatal Medicine. Intern U. Cin. Med. Ctr., 1966-67, jr. and sr. resident, 1967-69, chief pediatric resident, 1969-70, fellow neonatal, perinatal medicine, 1972-74; asst. prof. pediatrics U. Ariz. Health Scis. Ctr., Tucson, 1974-78; assoc. prof. pediatrics U. S.D. Sch. Medicine, Sioux Falls, 1978-84, head sect. of neonatal, perinatal medicine, 1979-88, prof. pediatrics, 1984—, chmn. dept. pediatrics, 1988—. Dir. newborn intensive care unit Sioux Valley Hosp., 1980-88; chmn. pharmacy and therapeutics com. Sioux Valley Hosp., 1982-97, bd. dirs., 1997—2002; v.p. children's med. svcs. Sioux Valley Hosp. and U. S.D. Med. Ctr., 2000-02. Author: (with others) Current Therapy in Neonatal and Perinatal Medicine, 1989, Conn's Current Therapy, 1989, 90; contbr. articles to profl. jours. Chmn. rsch. funding group Am. Heart Assn., Dakota Affiliate, 1986-88; mem. allocations com. Childrn's Miracle Network Telethon, Sioux Falls, 1986-87; bd. dirs. Childrens Miracle Network, 1996-99; chmn. Health Svcs. Adv. Com., State of S.D., 1991-93. Maj. U.S. Army, 1970-72. Rsch. grantee Nat. Inst. Child Health and Human Devel., Tucson, Sioux Falls, 1976-79, Am. Heart Assn., Sioux Falls, 1984; recipient Army Commendation medal, 1991-93, Pioneer award S.D. Perinatal Assn., 1993; inductee Hall of Honor Children's Hosp. U. Cin. MEd. Ctr., 1993. Fellow Am. Acad. Pediatrics; mem. Society for Pediatric Rsch., Midwest Soc. for Pediatric Rsch., Assn. Med. Sch. Pediatric Dept. Chmn., S.D. States Med. Assn. Avocations: water-skiing, boating, hiking, scuba diving, classical music. Office: 1305 W 18th St Sioux Falls SD 57117-5039 Home Phone: 605-335-8815; Office Phone: 605-333-7197. Business E-Mail: ijfenton@usd.edu.

FENTON, ROBERT EARL, electrical engineering educator; b. Bklyn., Sept. 30, 1933; s. Theodore Andrew and Evelyn Virginia (Brent) F.; m. Alice Earlyn Gray, Dec. 13, 1934; children: Douglas Earl, Andrea Leigh. BEE, Ohio State U., 1957, MEE, 1960, PhD in Electrical Engring., 1965. Registered profl. engr., Ohio. Engr. rsch. N. Am. Aviation, Columbus, Ohio, 1957; instr. electric engring. Ohio State U., Columbus, 1960-65, prof., 1965-95, prof. emeritus, 1995—. Cons. transp. sys. divsn. GM, Warren, Mich., 1974-80, Battelle Meml. Inst., Columbus, Ohio, 1991-93. Inventor kinesthetic-tactile display; contbr. articles to profl. jours. Capt. USAF, 1957-60. Recipient Outstanding Tchr. award Eta Kappa Nu, 1963, Neil Armstrong award Ohio Soc. Profl. Engrs., 1971, Pioneering Rsch. award Nat. Automated Hwy. Systems Consortium, 1997, Significant Achievement award Intelligent Vehicle Hwy. Sys. Ohio, 1993. Fellow IEEE (IEEE Millennium medal 2000), Radio Club Am., IEEE Vehicular Tech. Soc. (pres. 1985-87, v.p. 1983-85, treas. 1981-83, prize paper 1980, Avant Garde award, 1982, Stuart F. Meyer Meml. award 1998), NAE. Avocations: bicycling, swimming, classical music. Home: 2177 Oakmount Rd Columbus OH 43221-1229 Office: Ohio State Univ Dept Elec Engring 2015 Neil Ave Dept Elec Columbus OH 43210-1210 Home Phone: 614-457-0479. Business E-Mail: fenton.2@osu.edu.

FENTON, TIM, food service executive; LLB, U. Western Ont., Can., 1986. With McDonald's Corp., 1973—, various restaurant and ops. pos., including ops. mgr. South Fla. region, field svc. mgr. Kansas City region, others, dir. Asia Pacific, 1990—92, mng. dir. McDonald's Poland, v.p. McDonald's Ctrl. Europe orth, 1992—95, v.p., mng. dir. Middle East Devel. Co., sr. v.p., Southeast Asia/Middle East/Africa, pres., East Divsn., McDonald's USA Oak Brook, Ill., pres., McDonald's Asia, Pacific, Middle East and Africa, 2005—. V.p. Am. C. of C., Warsaw, 1992—95; bd. dirs. Friends of Luetefska Children's Hosp., Warsaw, 1994—95. Office: McDonald's Corp McDonald's Plz Oak Brook IL 60523

FERBER, LEONARD, lawyer; b. Albany, NY, July 19, 1957; AB with high distinction, U. Mich., 1979; JD, U. Pa., 1983. Bar: Ill. 1983. Ptnr., co-char Tech. Practice Katten Muchin Zavis Rosenman, Chgo. Mem.: ABA, Internet Exec. Club, Chgo. Software Assn., Chgo. Bar Assn., Phi Beta Kappa. Office: Katten Muchin Zavis Rosenman 525 W Monroe St, Ste 1600 Chicago IL 60661 Office Phone: 312-902-5679. Office Fax: 312-577-8806. E-mail: leonard.ferber@kmzr.com.

FERDERBER, JUNE H., state legislator; children: Deven Armeni, Adrien. Student, Youngstown State U. Mem. Ohio Ho. of Reps., 1986—, mem. energy and environment, judiciary and criminal justice coms. Mem. adv. com. ohio child support guidelines, women's policy and rsch. Com.; ranking minority mem. family svcs. com. Contbr. articles to Warren Tribune Chronicle. Active Animal Welfare League. Named Woman of Yr., Coalition Labor Union Women, YWCA, 1988. Mem. NOW (Trumbull County chpt.), LWV, Ohio Bus. and Profl. Women, Ohio Farm Bur., Mosquito Creek Devel. Assn., Farmer's Union, Sierra Club. Democrat. Home: 1435 Locust St Mineral Ridge OH 44440-9721

FERENCZ, ROBERT ARNOLD, lawyer; b. Chgo., Sept. 10, 1946; s. Albert and Frances (Reiss) F.; m. Marla J. Miller, May 20, 1973; children: Joseph, Ira. BS in Acctg., U. Ill., 1968; JD magna cum laude, U. Mich., 1973. Bar: Ill. 1973. From assoc. to ptnr. Sidley, Austin, Brown & Wood, Chgo., 1973—. Mem. ABA, Ill. Bar Assn. Office: Sidley Austin Brown & Wood Bank One Plz 10 S Dearborn St Chicago IL 60603-2000

FERGER, LAWRENCE A., gas distribution utility executive; b. Des Moines, May 3, 1934; s. Cleon A. and Helen K. (Jacobs) F.; m. LaVon Stark, Oct. 20, 1957; children: Kirsten A., Jane S. BS in Bus. Adminstrn., Simpson Coll., Indianola, Iowa, 1956. Auditor Arthur Andersen & Co., Chgo., 1956-64; dir. data processing Ind. Gas Co., Inc., Indpls., 1964-74, v.p. planning, 1974-79, v.p., treas., 1979-80, sr. v.p. fin., 1980-81, exec. v.p., 1981-84, pres., 1984—, also bd. dirs. Bd. dirs. Ind. energy Inc., Ind. Gas Co., Inc., Community Hosp. of Indpls., Nat. City Bank of Ind. Served with U.S. Army, 1957-59. Mem. Am. Gas Assn., Ind. Gas Assn. (treas. 1966-80, sec. 1966-70, dir. 1980—), Ind. State C. of C.

FERGUSON, BRADFORD LEE, lawyer; b. Ottumwa, Iowa, May 29, 1947; s. G. Wendell and Virginia Sue (Baker) Ferguson. BA, Drake U., 1969; JD, Harvard U., 1972. Bar: Minn. 1972, Ill. 1980. Assoc. Dorsey, Marquart, Windhorst, West & Halladay, Mpls., 1972-75; legis. asst. Senator Walter F. Mondale, Washington, 1975-77; spl. asst. to asst. sec. tax policy U.S. Treasury Dept., Washington, 1977-78, assoc. tax legis. counsel, 1978-80; ptnr. Hopkins & Sutter, Chgo., 1980-96, Sidley & Austin, Chgo., 1996-2001. Fellow Am. Coll. Tax Counsel; mem. Chgo. Bar Assn.

FERGUSON, DIANA S., food products executive; b. 1963; BA in Psychology, Yale U.; M in Mgmt., Northwestern U. With Eaton, Fannie Mae, First Nat. Bank Chgo., IBM; v.p., treas. US Fort James Corp., Sara Lee Corp., 2001—04, sr. v.p. strategy & corp. devel., 2004—07, CFO, Sara Lee Foodservice, 2006—07; exec. v.p. fin., CFO Merisant Worldwide, Inc., 2007—. Bd. dirs. Integrys Energy Group, Inc., 2007—, TreeHouse Foods, Inc., 2008—. Bd. mem. Leadership Greater Chgo.; mem. Kellogg Sch. Alumni Adv. Bd. Named to The 40 Under 40, Crain's Chgo. Bus., 2002. Fellow: Leadership Greater Chgo. Office: Merisant Worldwide Inc 10 S Riverside Plz Ste 850 Chicago IL 60606*

FERGUSON, JOHN WAYNE, SR., librarian; b. Ash Grove, Mo., Nov. 4, 1936; s. John William and Eula Marie (Rogers) F.; m. Nancy Carolyn Southerland, Apr. 4, 1958; children: John Wayne Jr., Mark Warren, Steven Ward. BS, S.W. Mo. State Coll., 1958; MS, U. Okla., 1961. Libr. Springfield (Mo.) Pub. Libr., 1952-64; asst. dir. Jackson County Pub. Libr., 1964-65; dir. Mid-Continent Pub. Libr., 1965-81, 1981—, libr. Independence, Mo. Bd. dirs. YMCA, Independence, 1969-89, Independence Regional Health Ctr., 1981-90, S.E. Enterprises Sheltered Workshop, 1996—. Capt. U.S. Army, 1959-65. Named Libr. of Yr. Libr. Jour. mag., 1993. Mem. Rotary (dist. govt. Independence chpt. 1986-87, pres. 1981-82). Avocation: amateur radio. Home: 14504 E 43rd St S Independence MO 64055-4840 Office: Mid-Continent Pub Libr 15616 E 24 Hwy Independence MO 64050-2057

FERGUSON, LARRY P., food products executive; BS, Okla. St. Univ. With Schreiber Foods Inc., Green Bay, Wis., 1975—, pres., CEO, 1999—. Office: Schreiber Foods Inc 425 Pine St Green Bay WI 54301

FERGUSON, MARK KENDRIC, surgeon, educator; b. Mpls., Jan. 10, 1951; s. David Lee and Shirley (Mark) F.; m. Phyllis Marie Young, July 8, 1989; 1 child, Benjamin. AB, Harvard U., 1973; MD, U. Chgo., 1977. Diplomate Am. Bd. Surgery, Am. Bd. Thoracic Surgery. Resident U. Chgo., 1977-81, chief resident gen. surgery, 1981-82, fellow cardiothoracic surgery, 1982-84, asst. prof., 1984-88, assoc. prof., 1988—97, prof., 1998—; chief thoracic surgery U. Chgo. Med. Ctr. Fellow ACS, Am. Assn. Thoracic Surgery, Soc. Thoracic Surgeons, Soc. Surg. Oncology, Am. Surg. Assn. Office: U Chgo Med Ctr MC 5040 5841 S Maryland Ave Chicago IL 60637-1463 Office Phone: 773-702-3551.

FERGUSON, RENEE, news correspondent, reporter; b. Oklahoma City, Aug. 22, 1949; d. Eugene and Mary Ferguson; m. Ken Smikle; 1 child, Jason. BS in journalism, Ind. U., 1971. With Sta. WLWI-TV, Indpls.; reporter Sta. WBBM-TV, Chgo., 1977—81; news corr. CBS Network, NYC, Atlanta; gen. assignment reporter Sta. WMAQ-TV, Chgo., 1987—, investigative reporter, 1997—. Recipient 7 Chgo. Emmy awards, 5 Assoc. Press awards, AWRT Gracie Allen award, Columbia-duPont award, Studs Terkel Media award, 2006; fellow Benton fellowship in Journalism, U. Chgo., 1991, Criminal Justice fellow, Univ. S. Calif. Annenberg Inst. Justice & Journalism, Nieman fellow, Harvard U., 2006—07. Mem.: Investigative Reporters & Editors (mem. bd. 2006—). Office: NBC5 Chgo WMAQ 454 N Columbus Dr Chicago IL 60611

FERGUSON, RICHARD L., educational association administrator; BS in Math., Ind. U. Pa.; D in Ednl. Rsch., U. Pitts., 1969; MA in Math., Western Mich. U. Tchr. math. Wilkinsburg Sch. Dist., Pa., Mt. Lebanon Sch. Dist., Pa.; rsch. assoc., faculty mem. U. Pitts.; with Am. Coll. Testing Program, Iowa City, 1972—, dir. test devel., v.p. rsch. devel., exec. v.p., CEO, chmn., 1988—; adj. prof. Dept. Psych. and Quantitative Founds. U. Iowa. Office: Am Coll Testing Prog 500 ACT Dr PO Box 168 Iowa City IA 52243-0168

FERGUSON, RONALD MORRIS, surgeon, educator; b. Milaca, Minn., Nov. 12, 1945; children: Melissa, Jason, Meredith. BS, Augsburg Coll., 1967; MD, Washington U., St. Louis, 1971; PhD, U. Minn., 1982. Diplomate Am. Bd. Surgery. Dir. transplantation VA Med. Ctr., Mpls., 1980-82; assoc. prof. surgery Ohio State U., Columbus, 1982-88, prof. surgery, 1988—, chmn. dept. surgery, transplant, 1993-99, chief divsn. transplant, 1999—. Asst. prof. surgery U. Minn. Health Sci. Ctr., Mpls., 1980-82; med. dir. Lifeline of Ohio Organ Procurement, Columbus, 1985—. Mem. Am. Coll. Surgeons, Am. Soc. Transplant Surgeons, Soc. Univ. Surgeons (pres. 1988), Transplantation Soc. (v.p. 1992—). Office: Ohio State U 363 Means Hall 1654 Upham Dr Columbus OH 43210-1250 Office Phone: 614-293-6322.

FERGUSON, STANLEY LEWIS, lawyer; b. Evanston, Ill., Aug. 2, 1952; m. Mary M. Pyle, Aug. 16, 1980; children: Kate, Brooke. BA, Northwestern U., Evanston, Ill., 1975; JD cum laude, Boston U., 1978. Bar: Ill. 1978, US Dist. Ct. No. Dist. Ill. 1978, US Ct. Appeals 6th and 7th circuits. Assoc. Kirkland & Ellis, Chgo., 1978-85, ptnr., 1985-87; named asst. gen. counsel USG Corp., Chgo., 1987, assoc. gen. counsel litig., v.p., assoc. gen. counsel, 1999—2000, v.p., gen. counsel, 2000—01, sr. v.p., gen. counsel, 2001—04, exec. v.p., gen. counsel, 2004—. Mem. ABA, Ill. Bar Assn., Legal Club Chgo. Office: USG Corp 550 W Adams St Chicago IL 60661 Office Phone: 312-436-5387. Business E-Mail: sferguson@usg.com.

FERGUSON, THOMAS JOSEPH, lawyer; b. Waterloo, Iowa, Feb. 27, 1956; s. Thomas Raymond and Elizabeth Ann (Callahan) F.; m. Kathleen Ann Flynn, Oct. 9, 1981; 1 child, Christopher. BSBA, Creighton U., 1978, JD, 1980. Bar: Iowa 1980, U.S. Dist. Ct. (no. dist.) Iowa 1981, U.S. Ct. Appeals (8th cir.) 1980. Assoc. Cutler and Rausch, Waterloo, 1980-82; ptnr. Rausch and Ferguson, Waterloo, 1983-85; 1st asst. Black Hawk County Atty.'s Office, Waterloo, 1985-90, county atty., 1990—. Mem. Black Hawk County Bar Assn., Nat. Dist. Atty.'s Assn., Iowa County Atty.'s Assn. Democrat. Roman Catholic. Avocations: hunting, sports. Office: Black Hawk County Courthouse 316 E 5th St Waterloo IA 50703-4712

FERKENHOFF, ROBERT J., retail executive; b. Kansas City, Mo., Aug. 17, 1942; s. John Michael and Eileen Marie (Owens) F.; m. Patricia Lee Venneman, Oct. 1, 1966; children: Jennifer, Deborah, Carrie. BA, Benedictine Coll., Atchison, Kans., 1964. Staff asst. Sears Mdse. Group, Chgo., 1972-73, nat. mgr. retail inventory mgmt., 1973-74, group mgr. retail systems, 1974-77, group retail mdse. mgr., 1977-79, nat. retail mktg. mgr., 1979-81, asst. dir. strategic planning, 1981-84, nat. mgr. bus. planning, 1984-88; v.p. data processing and info. svcs. Sears Canada, Toronto, 1988-89; v.p. info. svcs. Sears Mdse. Group, Chgo., 1989-93; v.p. CIO SPS Payment Systems, RIverwoods, Ill., 1993-98; I/T Cons., 1998—. Judge Retail Innovation Tech. Award, 1991-92; bd. dirs. Voluntary Interindustry Coun. Standards, 1989-93, Nat. Retail Fed. Info. Svcs., N.Y.C., 1989-93, Chgo. Rsch. and Planning Group, 1991—. Chmn. Sears United Fund, Chgo., 1991. Recipient Retail Innovation Tech. award Chain Store Age and DEC, 1990. Republican. Roman Catholic. Avocations: gardening, golf, biking. Office: SPS Payment Systems 4 Parkway N Deerfield IL 60015-2502

FERLIC, RANDOLPH, medical educator; b. Omaha, July 17, 1936; m. Teresa L. Kolars, June 20, 1959; 4 children. BS, MD, Creighton U., 1958; postgrad., U. Minn., 1965—66. Intern, fellow, resident in gen. thoracic and cardiovascular surgery U. Minn., Mpls., 1961—67; instr., resident surgeon NY Hosp./Cornell Med. Ctr., NYC, 1967—68; founder, mgr. Thoracic & Cardiovascular Surgery P.C. (later Surg. Svcs. of the Great Plains), 1974—91; assoc. prof., then clin. assoc. prof. surgery U. Nebr. Med. Ctr., Omaha, 1970—. Contbr. more than 50 articles to profl. publs. Mem. bd. regents U. Nebr., 2000—, vice chmn. bd. regents, 2002—; mem. Commn. for Postsecondary Edn., 1991—2001, chmn., 1994—96; mem. Midwest Higher Edn. Commn., 1991—, treas., 1997—; founding dir., treas. Distributed Learning Workshop, 1999—. Named Man of Yr., Notre Dame Club of Omaha, 1988; recipient award for contbn. to med. sci., Omaha Bar Assn., 1986. Fellow: Am. Coll. Chest Physicians, Am. Coll. Cardiology, ACS; mem.: AMA, Lillehei Surg. Soc., Midwest Clin. Soc. (award for individual investigation exhibit 1970, Premier award 1971, award for rsch. sci. exhibit 1977), Omaha Douglas County Med. Soc., Nebr. Med. Assn., Am. Bronch-Esophagological Assn., Acad. Surgeons, Soc. Thoracic Surgeons, Rotary Club (hon. personal honors 1986, merit award 1986, Paul Harris fellow). Mailing: 2254 S 8th Ave Omaha NE 68124-2136

FERLINZ, JACK, cardiologist, educator; b. Marburg, Austria, Feb. 18, 1942; came to U.S., 1957. s. Anthony and Maria (Nachtigall) F. AB, Harvard U.; MBA, ortheastern U., 1965; MD, Boston U., 1969; doctorate (hon.), U. Maribor, Slovenia, 1990. Diplomate Am. Bd. Internal Medicine, Am. Bd. Cardiovascular Diseases. Intern. U. Hosp. Boston U., 1969-70; jr. resident M. Hitchcock Hosp. Dartmouth Med. Sch., Hanover, NH, 1970-71; sr. resident Jackson Meml. Hosp., U. Miami, 1971-72; NIH rsch. fellow cardiology P.B. Brigham Hosp., Harvard U., Boston, 1972-74; dir. cardiac cath. lab., asst. chief cardiology V.A.M.C., Long Beach, Calif., 1974-82; asst. prof. medicine U. Calif., Irvine, 1975-81, assoc. prof. medicine, 1981-82; chmn. adult cardiology Cook County Hosp., Chgo., 1982-88; prof. medicine Chgo. Med. Sch., North Chicago, Ill., 1984-88; chmn. dept. of internal medicine Providence Hosp., Southfield, Mich., 1988-92; clin. prof. medicine Wayne State U. Sch. Medicine, Detroit, 1989-92; dir. med. edn. & rsch., prof. medicine & cardiology Hamad Med. Ctr., Doha, Qatar, 1992-94; chief dept. medicine Aleda E. Lutz VA Med. Ctr., Saginaw, Mich., 1994—; clin. prof. medicine Mich. State U. Coll. Human Medicine, 1994—. Vis. prof. numerous U.S., Canadian and European med. schs., 1980—. Mem. editl. bds. Am. Jour. Cardiology, 1989—, Am. Jour. Noninvas Cardiology, 1987—, Jour. Am. Coll. Cardiology, 1984-88, 89-93; contbr. over 300 book chpts. and sci. papers. Named to Begg's Soc. Boston U. Sch. Medicine, 1969. Fellow Am. Coll. Cardiology, Am. Coll. Chest Physicians (chmn. coronary sect. 1983-85), Am. Heart Assn., Am. Coll. Physicians, Am. Coll. Angiology; mem. Am. Fedn. Clin. Rsch., Am. Soc. Clin. Pharm. Therapy. Avocations: mountain climbing, skiing, tennis, scuba diving. Office: VA Med Ctr 1500 Weiss St Saginaw MI 48602-5251 Home Phone: 989-792-6244; Office Phone: 989-497-2500 x3523. Business E-Mail: jack.ferlinz@med.va.gov.

FERNANDEZ, GENO, insurance company executive; b. 1976; Student in sem. edn., Notre Dame Sem.; BA in Theology, Classics, and Philosophy summa cum laude, U. Notre Dame, 1996; MA in Classics, Oxford U., 1999, PhD, 2000; JD, Harvard Law Sch., 2000. With McKinsey & Co., Chgo., 2000—, ptnr. Lectr. in field; spl. attaché for econ. affairs to Sec. of State diplomatic staff at Vatican. Contbr. articles on bus. ins., knowledge mgmt. in fin. instns., and ins. regulation. Pro-bono work on strategy, ops., and portfolio mgmt. Vatican, Archdiocese of Chgo., U. Notre Dame; counselor women's shelter, Ind. Named one of 40 Under 40, Crain's Chgo. Bus., 2005. Office: McKinsey & Co Ste 2900 21 S Clark St Chicago IL 60603-2900 Office Phone: 312-551-3970. Office Fax: 312-551-4200. Business E-Mail: geno_fernandez@mckinsey.com.

FERNANDEZ, JAMES, anthropology educator; b. Chgo., Nov. 27, 1930; m. Renate Helene Lellep, Oct. 18, 1958; children: Lisa Oyana, Luke Oliver, Andrew McClintock. BA, Amherst Coll., 1952; postgrad. in cultural anthropology, Northwestern U., 1953—54; postgrad., U. Madrid, 1954—55, Museo Etnologico Barcelona, 1955; PhD, Northwestern U., 1962. Tchg. asst. Northwestern U., 1955—57, grad. rsch. fellow in program of African studies, 1956—57; instr. sociology and anthropology Smith Coll., 1961—62, asst. prof. anthropology, 1962—64; area program dir. Gabon Peace Corps trainees, St. Thomas, 1962—63; cons., lectr. Fgn. Svc. Inst., Washington, 1964—70; prof. anthropology Dartmouth Coll., 1969—75, chmn. dept. anthropology, 1971—75; prof. anthropology Princeton U., 1975—86, chmn. dept. anthropology, 1978—82; prof. anthropology U. Chgo., 1982—. Lectr. and cons. in field. Recipient Guggenheim fellowship, 2003, Carnegie Fund Grant for African Rsch., 1955, Ford Found. fellowship, 1957, Ford Found. Ext. fellowship, 1959, Social Sci. Rsch. Coun.-Am. Coun. Learned Socs. African Rsch. fellowship, 1965, NSF grant, 1970, 1971, Spanish-N.Am. Joint Com. fellowship, 1977, NEH grant, 1988—89. Fellow: African Studies Assn., Am. Anthropol. Assn., Am. Acad. Religion, Am. Acad. Arts and Scis.; mem.: Northeastern Anthropol. Assn. (pres. 1973), Sigma Xi. Office: U Chgo Dept Anthropology 1126 E 59th St Chicago IL 60637 E-mail: jwf1@uchicago.edu.

FERNANDEZ, KATHLEEN M., cultural organization administrator; b. Dayton, Ohio, Oct. 8, 1949; d. Norbert Katzen and Yenema Vermeda (Bermingham) F.; m. James Robert Hillibish, Oct. 1, 1977. BA, Otterbein Coll., 1971. Edn. asst. Ohio Hist. Soc., Columbus, 1971, vol. coord., 1971-74, interpretive specialist Zoar, 1975-88; site mgr. Village State Meml., Zoar, 1988—2004; freelance mus. cons. Canton, Ohio, 2004—05; exec. dir. North Canton Heritage Soc., 2006—. Author: A Singular People: Images of Zoar, 2003. Bd. dirs., newsletter editor Ohio & Erie Canal Corridor Coalition, Akron, 1989—. Mem. Am. Assn. State and Local History, Nat. Trust Hist. Preservation, Zoar Cmty. Assn., Communal Studies Assn. (pres. 1981, editor newsletter 1981-86, 1997-2004, bd. dirs. 1995—, exec. dir. 2004—), Am. Assn. Mus. (surveyor mus. assistance program 1999—). Office: 200 Charlotte St NW North Canton OH 44720

FERNANDEZ, MANNY (EMMANUEL FERNANDEZ-LEMAIRE), professional hockey player; b. Etobicoke, Ont., Can., Aug. 27, 1974; m. Karine Fernandez; 1 child, Mattyas. Goalie Dallas Stars, 1999—2000, Minn. Wild, 2000—07, Boston Bruins, 2007—. Co-recipient William M. Jennings Trophy, 2007. Office: Boston Bruins TD Banknorth Garden 100 Legends Way Boston MA 02114

FERNER, DAVID CHARLES, non-profit management and development consultant; b. Rochester, NY, Mar. 14, 1933; s. John Theodore and Dorothy Flora (Seel) F.; m. Ursula Milda Thieme, Sept. 6, 1958, (dec. Nov. 12, 2002). BA, Amherst Coll., 1955; MEd, U. Rochester, 1957; postgrad., Columbia U., 1961. Dir. student activities U. Rochester, NYC, 1956-58; asst. to provost Tchrs. Coll. Columbia U., NYC, 1959-60; asst. dir. devel. St. Lawrence U., Canton, N.Y., 1961-62; dir. devel. Sarah Lawrence Coll., Bronxville, N.Y., 1962-66; cons., v.p. Frantzreb & Pray Assocs., Inc., NYC, 1966-72, v.p., sec. Arlington, Va., 1972-75; pres. Frantzreb, Pray, Ferner & Thompson, Inc., Arlington, 1975-77, David C. Ferner & Assocs., Annandale, Va., 1977—80; v.p., dir. devel. Minn. Orchestral Assn., Mpls., 1980-87; mng. ptnr. Currie, Ferner, Scarpetta & DeVries, Mpls., 1987-99, cons., 2000—. Contbr. articles to profl. publs. Bd. dir. Madeline Island Mus. Camp, 1992-98, Philharm. Soc. N.W. Fla., 2003—. Amherst Coll. scholar, 1951-55. Mem. Assn. Fundraising Profls. (bd. dirs. Minn. chpt. 1995-97), Nat. Com. Planned Giving, League Am. Orchs. Home: 245 Wekiva Cv Destin FL 32541-4763 Office Phone: 850-650-5448. Personal E-mail: davidcferner@hotmail.com.

FERRALL, VICTOR EUGENE, JR., academic administrator, lawyer; b. Urbana, Ill., July 31, 1936; s. Victor Eugene and Lucile Elizabeth (Hill) F.; m. Suzanne Elizabeth Lilly (div. 1985); children: Christopher Key, David Hill, Katherine Elizabeth; m. Linda K. Smith, 1987. AB, Oberlin Coll, 1956; student law, Harvard U., 1956-57; MA in Econs., Yale U., 1958, LLB, 1960. Bar: D.C. 1961, U.S. Supreme Ct. 1981. Atty. U.S. Dept. Justice, Washington, 1960-61; asst. to staff dir. antitrust and monopoly subcom. U.S. Senate, Washington, 1961-63; assoc. then ptnr. Koteen & Burt, Washington, 1963-75; ptnr. Jones, Day, Reavis & Pogue, Washington, 1975-79, Crowell & Moring, Washington, 1979-91; pres. Beloit (Wis.) Coll., 1991-2000; ret., 2000. Contbr. articles to profl. jours.; editor: Yearbook of Broadcasting Articles (anthology edition), 1980. Trustee Olivet (Mich.) Coll., 1979-81. Mem. ABA, D.C. Bar Assn., Wis. Bar Assn., Nat. Assn. Ind. Colls. and Univs. (bd. dirs. 1993—). Democrat. Episcopalian. Home: 709 College St Beloit WI 53511-5571 Office: Beloit Coll 700 College St Beloit WI 53511-5509

FERRARA, ANNETTE, editor, educator; MA in Modern Art History, Theory and Criticism, Sch. of the Art Inst. Chgo. Rsch. asst. The Andy Warhol Catalogue Raisonné Project; dir. Alan Koppel Gallery, Chgo.; asst. dir. The Arts Club Chgo.; founding editor, writer TENbyTEN, Chgo., 1999—. Guest lectr. Columbia Coll., DePaul, SAIC; tchr. contemporary art history Mus. of Contemporary Art, Chgo. Co-author: Xtreme Interiors, 2003; contbr. writings to Artforum, Book Forum, Zingmagazine, Provinceton Arts. Mem.: Chgo. Art Critics Assn. Office: TENbyTEN 222 S Morgan 3E Chicago IL 60607 Office Phone: 312-421-0480. Office Fax: 312-421-0491. Business E-Mail: contact@tenbyten.net.

FERRARI, GIANNANTONIO, electronics executive; Diploma in Acctg., U. Milan. With Gavazzi SpA, 1960, Honeywell Italia, 1965; gen. mgr. Honeywell Iran, Honeywell Greece; dir. fin., administrn., and human resources Honeywell Mid. E.; controller Honeywell Europe, 1981-85, v.p. fin. and adminstrn., 1985-88, pres., 1992-97; v.p. Western Europe, Mid. E., Africa Honeywell, Inc., Italy, 1988-92, pres., COO, 1997—. Bd. dirs. No. State Power Co., Nat. Assn. Mfrs.; bd. govs. Nat. Elec. Mfrs. Assn. Office: 1985 Douglas Dr N Minneapolis MN 55422-3992

FERREE, DAVID CURTIS, horticultural researcher; b. Lock Haven, Pa., Feb. 9, 1943; s. George H. and Ruth O. (McClain) F.; m. Sandra J. Corman, Aug. 31, 1968; children: Curtis P., Thomas A. BS, Pa. State U., 1965; MS, U. Md., 1968, PhD, 1969. From asst. to assoc. prof. Ohio State U., Wooster, 1971—76, prof., 1981—. Contbr. numerous articles to profl. jours. Capt. U.S. Army, 1969-71. Recipient sr. scientist disting. rsch. award Ohio Agrl. Rsch. and Devel. Ctr., 1997, Disting. Svc. award Ohio Fruit Growers Soc., 1998. Fellow Am. Soc. Hort. Sci. (assoc. editor 1983-86, v.p. 1988-89, J.H. Gourley award 1982, Stark award 1983), Am. Pomological Soc. (editor 1985-2002), Internat. Dwarf Fruit Tree Assn. (Disting. Rschr. award 1989), Gamma Sigma Delta (Rsch. award 1981). Lutheran. Office: Ohio Agrl R & D Ctr Dept Horticulture Crop Sci Wooster OH 44691 E-mail: ferree.1@osu.edu.

FERRELL, JAMES EDWIN, nuclear energy industry executive; b. Atchison, Kans., Oct. 17, 1939; s. Alfred C. and Mabel A. (Samson) F.; m. Elizabeth J. Gillespie, May 10, 1959; children: Kathryn E., Sarah A. BS in Bus. Adminstrn., U. Kans., 1963. Chmn., CEO Ferrellgas Partners, Overland Park, Kans., 1965—. Bd. dirs. United Mo. Bancshares, Kansas City; past pres. World LP Gas Assn.; past chmn. Propane Vehicle Council. Bd. dirs. Coun. Ind. Colls., 1988-91; trustee Kansas City Symphony, 1987—. Served to 1st lt. U.S. Army, 1963-65. Republican. Lutheran. Office: Ferrellgas Partners 7500 College Blvd Overland Park KS 66210 Office Fax: 816-792-7985.

FERRELL, ROBERT HUGH, historian, educator; b. Cleve., May 8, 1921; s. Ernest Henry and Edna Lulu (Rentsch) F.; m. Lila Esther Sprout, Sept. 8, 1956 (dec. Jan. 2002); 1 dau., Carolyn Irene. BS in Edn., Bowling Green State U., 1946, BA, 1947, LLD (hon.), 1971; MA, Yale U., 1948, PhD, 1951. Intelligence analyst U.S. Air Force, 1951-52; lectr. in history Mich. State U., 1952-53; asst. prof. history Ind. U., 1953-58, asso. prof., 1958-61, prof., 1961-74, Disting. prof., 1974-88, emeritus, 1988—. Vis. prof. Yale U., 1955-56, Am. U. at Cairo, 1958-59, U. Conn., 1964-65, Cath. U. Louvain, Belgium, 1969-70, Naval War Coll., 1974-75, U.S. Mil. Acad., 1987-88. Author: Peace in Their Time, 1952, American Diplomacy in the Great Depression, 1957, American Diplomacy: A History, 1959, 4th edit., 1987, Frank B. Kellogg and Henry L. Stimson, 1963, (with M.G. Baxter and J.E. Wiltz) Teaching of American History in High Schools, 1964, George C. Marshall, 1966, (with R.B. Morris and W. Greenleaf) America: A History of the People, 1971, (with others) Unfinished Century, 1973, Harry S. Truman and the Modern American Presidency, 1983, Truman: A Centenary Remembrance, 1984, Woodrow Wilson and World War I, 1985, Harry S. Truman: His Life on the Family Farms, 1991, Ill-Advised, 1992, Choosing Truman: The Democratic Convention of 1944, 1994, Harry S. Truman: A Life, 1994, The Strange Deaths of President Harding, 1996, The Dying President: Franklin D. Roosevelt, 1998, The Presidency of Calvin Coolidge, 1998, Truman and Pendergast, 1999, Harry S. Truman, 2003, Collapse at Meuse-Argonne, 2004, Five Days in October: The Lost Battalion of World War I, 2005, Presidential Leadership: From Woodrow Wilson to Harry S. Truman, 2006, Harry S. Truman and the Cold War Revisionists, 2006, America's Deadliest Battle: Meuse-Argonne, 1918, 2007, Grace Coolidge, 2008; editor: (with H.H. Quint) The Talkative President: The Off-the-Record Press Confreneces of Calvin Coolidge, 1964, Off the Record: The Private Papers of Harry S. Truman, 1980, The Autobiography of Harry S. Truman, 1980, The Eisenhower Diaries, 1981, Dear Bess: The Letters from Harry to Bess Truman, 1983, (with Samuel Flagg Bemis) American Secretaries of State and Their Diplomacy, 10 vols., 1963-85, Banners in the Air: The Eighth Ohio Volunteers and the Spanish-American War, 1988, Monterrey is Ours!, 1990, Truman in the White House: The Diary of Eben Ayers, 1991, (with L.E. Wikander) Grace Coolidge: An Autobiography, 1992, Holding the Line: The Third Tennessee Infantry 1861-64, 1994, Truman and the Bomb, 1996, (with Joan Hoff) Dictionary of American History Supplement, 2 vols., 1996, FDR's Quiet Confidant: The Autobiography of Frank C. Walker, 1997, The Kansas City Investigation, 1999, A Youth in the Meuse-Argonne: A Memoir of World War I, 1917-1918, 2000, A Colonel in the Armored Divisions: A Memoir 1941-1945, 2001, In the Philippines and Okinawa: A Memoir 1945-1948, 2001, Meuse-Argonne Diary, 2004, Trench Knives and Mustard Gas, 2004, A Soldier in World War I, 2004, Argonne Days in World War I, 2007. Served with USAAF, 1942-45. Mem. Soc. Historians, Am. Fgn. Rels. Orgn. Am. Historians, Am. Hist. Assn. Home: 3496 Daleview Ann Arbor MI 48105

FERRINI, JAMES THOMAS, lawyer; b. Chgo., Jan. 14, 1938; s. John B. and Julia (Marre) F.; m. Jeanne Marie Fontana, June 8, 1963; children: Anthony, Mary Caren, Emily, Joseph, Danielle. JD, Loyola U., 1963. Bar: U.S. Supreme Ct. 1963, U.S. Ct. Appeals (7th cir.) 1967, U.S. Ct. Appeals (8th cir.) 1969, U.S. Ct. Appeals (3d cir.) 1975, U.S. Ct. Appeals (6th cir.) 1982, U.S. Ct. Appeals (10th cir.) 1984, U.S. Ct. Appeals (4th cir.) 1987, U.S. Ct. Appeals (9th cir.) 1989. Sr. ptnr. Clausen Miller Gorman Caffrey & Witous, P.C., Chgo., 1963—. Mem. pattern jury instructions Ill. Supreme Ct. Commn., Chgo., 1978-94. Contbr. articles to profl. jours. Mem. Mary Seat of Wisdom Parish, Park Ridge. Fellow Am. Acad. Appellate Lawyers; mem. ABA, Ill. Bar Assn., Chgo. Bar Assn. (chmn. civil practice com.), Ill. Assn. Def. Trial Counsel, Appellate Lawyers Assn. (pres. Chgo. chpt. 1978, 79), Justinian Soc. Roman Catholic. Avocations: handball, sailing, skiing, cooking. Office: Clausen Miller PC 10 S La Salle St Ste 1600 Chicago IL 60603-1098 Office Phone: 312-606-7597. Business E-Mail: jferrini@clausen.com.

FERRY, DANNY, professional sports team executive, retired professional basketball player; b. Hyattsville, Md., Oct. 17, 1966; s. Bob Ferry; m. Tiffany Ferry; children: Hannah, Grace, Sophia, Lucy, Jackson. Grad., Duke U., 1989. Draft pick LA Clippers, 1989; player Italian League, 1989—90, Cleve. Cavaliers, 1990—2000, gen. mgr., 2005—; player San Antonio Spurs, 2000—03, dir. basketball ops., 2003—05. Bd. mem. Hathaway Brown Sch., Shaker Heights, Ohio, Playing for Peace. Named to Duke U. Sports Hall of Fame, 2004. Achievements include winning the 2003 NBA Championship as a member of the Spurs. Office: Cleve Cavaliers One Center Ct Cleveland OH 44115-4001

FERRY, JAMES ALLEN, physicist, electrostatics company executive; b. Sept. 9, 1937; s. Darwin J. and Eleanor J. (Irwin) F.; m. Karen A. Greenwood, Feb. 8, 1964; children: Thomas E., Jennifer J. BS in Physics, U. Wis., 1959, MS in Physics, 1962, PhD in Physics, 1965. Rsch. assoc. U. Wis., Madison, 1965-66; exec. v.p., COO Nat. Electrostatics Corp., Middleton, Wis., 1967-95, pres., CEO, chmn. bd., 1995—. Patentee in field. Mem. Am. Phys. Soc. Home: 4105 Teal Ct Middleton WI 53562-5266 Office: Nat Electrostatics Corp Graber Rd PO Box 620310 Middleton WI 53562-0310 E-mail: nec@pelletron.com.

FESSLER, DIANA M., state representative; b. Huber Heights, Ohio; m. Bob Fessler; children: Angela, Aaron, Anne-Marie, Andrew, Elizabeth, Olivia. Attended, Sinclair C.C., Wright State U. Sec. various cos., 1963—72; owner Leiter Fabrics, 1972—74; founder Home Birth of Dayton, 1978; midwife, 1978—90; editor Legal-Legislative News, 1989—94; state rep. dist. 79 Ohio Ho. of Reps., Columbus, 2000—, mem. county and twp. govt., edn., health, homeland security engring. and archtl. design, and ins. coms., vice chair vets. affairs subcom. and human svcs. and aging com. Mem. Ohio State Bd. Edn., 1995—2000, Miami County Rep. Ctrl. Com., 1992—; co-founder Edn. Action Coun. Recipient Eagle award, Eagle Forum, 1998, award, Pro-Family Constnl. Conv., 1998. Mem.: Nat. Assn. State Bds. Edn., Miami County Twp. Assn., Edn. Writers Assn., Tippecanoe Hist. Soc., NRA, United Conservatives of Ohio, Ohio Family Assn., Citizens for Cmty. Values, Ohio Roundtable Exec. Com., Farm Bur., Right to Life, Huber Heights Rep. Club, Miami County Rep. Women's Club. Republican. Baptist. Office: 77 S High St 13th fl Columbus OH 43215-6111

FESTA, ROGER REGINALD, chemist, educator; b. Norwalk, Conn., Sept. 6, 1950; s. Reginald and Rosemary (Chappa) F. BA in Biology and Chemistry magna cum laude, St. Michael's Coll., 1972; MA in Agr., U. Vt., 1979; cert. in Adminstrn., Fairfield U., 1981; PhD in Edn., U. Conn., 1982. Tchr. Cen. Cath. High Sch., orwalk, 1975-79, Brien McMahon High Sch., Norwalk, 1979-82; asst. prof. chemistry Truman State U. (formerly N.E. Mo. State U.), Kirksville, 1983-89, dir. Chem. Comm. Devel. Ctr., 1983-90, assoc. prof., 1989-97, prof., 1997—, coach men's volleyball, 1991-2000, dean frats., 1991-92. Adj. prof. U. Conn., 1983. Author: National Curriculum Development Programming for Teachers of High School Chemistry, 1981, Fairfield County High School Chemistry Curriculum Handbook, 1982. Sec. Diocese Bridgeport (Conn.) Edn. Assn., 1978-79, sci. cons. schs. office, 1979, exec. adminstr., 1979; bd. dirs. Norwalk Community Services Agy., 1980-81. Named one of Ten Outstanding Young Men of Mo., Mo. Jaycees, 1986. Fellow Am. Inst. Chemists (pub. edn. com. 1980-83, edn. editor The Chemist Jour. 1981-95, mem. editl. bd. The Chemist 1986-91, bd. dirs. 1982-99, chmn. nat. meetings com. 1982-91, 94-95, history com. 1982-99, archivist 1983-2002, sec. 1991-93, pres.-elect 1994-95, pres. 1996-97), Am Inst. Chemists Found. (trustee 1992-); mem. Am. Chem. Soc. (founding editor The Fairfield Chemist 1978-79, assoc. editor Jour. Chem. Edn. 1980-89, vice chmn. edn. com. Western Conn. sect. 1979-81, chmn. elect Mark Twain sect. 1985, chmn. 1986, exec. bd. 1984-95, program chair 1984-95), St. Louis Inst. Chemists (founder 1984, pres. 1985-87, sec.-treas. 1987—), Coun. Scientific Soc. Pres. (mem. 1996-97, emeritus 1998-), Acad. Sci. St. Louis, Assn. Frat. Advisors, Coll. Frat. Editors' Assn., Kirksville Jaycees (bd. dirs. 1983-86, sec. 1984-85, chair ret. sr. vols. com. 1985-87), Order of Omega, Delta Epsilon Sigma, Alpha Chi Sigma (assoc. editor The Hexagon 1984-99), Sigma Phi Epsilon (advisor Truman State U. chpt. 1991—, bd. govs. ednl. found. 1993—). Democrat. Roman Catholic. Home: 114 E McPherson St Kirksville MO 63501-3570 Office: Truman State U 100 E Normal Ave Kirksville MO 63501-4200 Home Phone: 660-342-3221; Office Phone: 660-785-4524. Business E-Mail: rrf@truman.edu.

FETHKE, GARY C., economics professor, former dean; m. Carol Fethke; 2 children. BA in economics, U. Iowa, 1964, PhD in economics, 1968. Faculty mem. U. Iowa, 1974—, interim pres., 2006—07; prof. mgmt. scis. and econs. Henry B. Tippie Coll. Bus., U. Iowa, 1994—, dean, 1994—2006, Leonard A. Hadley prof. leadership, 2003—. Office: Henry B Tippie Coll Bus Pappajohn Bus Bldg 21 E Market St Iowa City IA 52242-1994 also: Office of Pres U Iowa 101 Jessup Hall Iowa City IA 52242-1316 Home Phone: 319-337-3709; Office Phone: 319-335-3549. Personal E-mail: president@uiowa.edu. Business E-Mail: gary-fethke@uiowa.edu.

FETLER, PAUL, retired composer; b. Phila., Feb. 17, 1920; s. William Basil and Barbara (Kovalevski) Fetler-Malof; m. Ruth Regina Pahl, Aug. 13, 1947; children: Sylvia, Daniel, Beatrix. MusB, Northwestern U., 1943; MusM, Yale U., 1948; PhD, U. Minn., 1956. From instr. to prof. music theory and composition U. Minn., Mpls., 1948—91, ret., 1992. Vis. composer, condr. and lectr. various colls. and univs. Composer: Symphonic Fantasia, 1941, Passacaglia for orch., 1942, Sextet for string quartet, clarinet and horn, 1942, Dramatic Overture, 1943, Prelude for orch., 1946, Orchestral Sketch, 1949, A Comedy Overture for Orchestra, 1952, Gothic Variations for Orchestra, 1953, Impromptu for piano, 1953, Contrasts for orch., 1958, Sing Unto God for mixed voices, 1958, Nothing but Nature for mixed voices and orchestra, 1961, Soundings for orch., 1962, Jubilate Deo for voices and brass, 1963, Te Deum for mixed voices, 1963, Four Symphonies, 1948-67, Cantus Tristis for orch., 1964, Five Pieces for guitar, 1964; opera Sturge Maclean, 1965, A Contemporary Psalm for chorus, organ and percussion, 1968, Prayer for Peace for mixed voices, 1969, Hosanna for mixed voices, 1970, Cycles for percussion and piano, 1970, The Words From the Cross for mixed voices, 1971, First Violin Concerto, 1971, Four Movements for guitar, 1972, Dialogue for flute and guitar, 1973, Six Pastoral Sketches for guitar, 1974, Lamentations for chorus, narrator, percussion and flute, 1974, Three Venetian Scenes for guitar, 1974, Dream of Shalom for mixed voices, 1975, Songs of the Night for voices, narrator and flute, 1976, Three Poems by Walt Whitman for narrator and orch., 1975, Pastoral Suite for piano trio, 1976, Celebration for orch., 1976, Three Impressions for guitar and orch., 1977, Five Piano Games, 1977, Sing Alleluia, 1978, Song of the Forest Bird for voices and chamber orch., 1978, Six Songs of Autumn for guitar, 1979, Second Violin Concerto, 1980, Missa de Angelis for three choirs, orch., organ and handbells, 1980, Serenade for chamber orch., 1981, Rhapsody for violin and piano, 1982; song cycle The Garden of Love for voice and orch., 1983, Piano Concerto, 1984; Capriccio for chamber orch., 1985; Frolic for Flute, Winds and Strings, 1986, Three Excursions, A Concerto for Percussion, Piano and Orchestra, 1987, String Quartet, 1989, Toccata for Organ, 1990, numerous sacred and secular choral works, 1949-93, Twelve Sacred Hymn Settings, 1993, Divertimento for Flute and Strings, 1994, December Stillness for Flute, Harp and Voices, 1994, Suite for Woodwind Trio, 1995, Up the Dome of Heaven, Three Pieces for Mixed Voices and Flute, 1996; Toccata for Organ, 1997, The Raven for basso, clarinet, percussion and string, 1998, Saraband variations for guitar, Folia Lirica, 1999, Lyric Dialogue for Piano and chamber orchestra, 2004. Served with AUS, 1943-45. Recipient Guggenheim award, 1953, 60, Soc. for Publ. Am. Music award, 1953, cert. of merit Yale U. Alumni Assn., 1975, NEA award, 1975, 77, 87; Ford Found. grantee, 1958. Mem. ASCAP (ann. award 1962—), Sigma Alpha Iota (nat. arts assoc.) Home: 174 Golden Gate Pt Apt 32 Sarasota FL 34236-6602 Office: U Minn 100 Ferguson Hall Minneapolis MN 55455 Personal E-mail: paulfetler@webtv.net.

FETRIDGE, CLARK WORTHINGTON, publishing executive; b. Chgo., Nov. 6, 1946; s. William Harrison and Bonnie-Jean (Clark) F.; m. Jean Hamilton Huebner, Apr. 19, 1980; children: Clark Worthington II, William Hamilton. BA, Lake Forest Coll., 1969; MBA, Boston Coll., 1971. Money market specialist Continental Ill. Nat. Bank, Chgo., 1971-73; with Dartnell Corp., Chgo., 1973-98, sr. v.p., 1977-78, pres., CEO Chgo., 1978-98, chmn. bd., CEO, 1995-98; pres. The Ravenswood Corp., Chgo., 1998—2002; mng. ptnr. Michigan Ave. Ventures, Chgo., 2002—07, Ravenswood Advisors, Chgo., 2007—. Bd. dirs. Clin. Resources Internat., Inc., M.R. Mead & Co. LLC., 515 N.State L. P. Old People's Home of Chgo. Author: Office Administration Handbook, 1975. Trustee Lake Forest Coll., 1977-85, 91-95, Jacques Holinger Meml. Found., 1983-95; pres. Dartnell Found., 1989—; trustee Latin Sch. Chgo., 1990-94; bd. dirs. Newcomen Soc. U.S., 2004-08; internat. commr. Boy Scouts Am., 1992-95, mem. nat. exec. bd., 1986-96, mem. internat. com., mem. Chgo. coun.; pres. U.S. Found. Internat. Scouting 1991-95; chmn. 1200 Club Ill., 1975-84; Rep. candidate for Congress, 1972; del. Rep. Nat. Conv., 1976; bd. dirs. Rep. Fund of Ill., 1980-2006; mem. pres.'s coun. Mus. Sci. and Industry, Chgo., 1986-94. Mem. Ill. Mfrs. Assn. (bd. dirs. 1990-96), Latin Sch. Chgo. Alumni Assn., St. Andrews Soc. (bd. dirs. 1994-97, 98—), Nat. Eagle Scout Assn. (chmn. 1985-88), Chgo. Pres. Orgn. (bd. dirs. 1998-2001), Tau Kappa Epsilon. Republican. Episcopalian. Office: Ravenswood Advisors 79 W Monroe Ste 920 Chicago IL 60603 Home Phone: 312-664-1988; Office Phone: 312-236-1332. Office Fax: 312-236-1343.

FETTIG, JEFF M., manufacturing executive; b. Tipton, Ind., 1957; BS in Fin., Ind. U., MBA. Mem. fin. ops. Whirlpool Corp., 1981, various mgmt. positions, 1981-89, dir. product devel., 1988—89, v.p. mktg. KitchenAid, 1989-90; v.p. mktg., Philips Whirlpool Appliance Group Whirlpool Europe B.V., 1990—92; v.p., group mktg. and sales North Am. Appliance Group/Whirlpool, 1992—94; pres. Whirlpool Europe & Asia, 1994—99; exec. v.p. Whirlpool Corp., 1994—99, pres., COO, 1999—2004, chmn., pres., CEO, 2004—05, chmn., CEO, 2005—. Bd. dirs. Dow Chem. Co., 2003—, Whirlpool Corp., 2003—. Office: Whirlpool Corp 2000 N M 63 Benton Harbor MI 49022-2692

FEUER, HENRY, retired chemist; b. Stanislau, Austria, Apr. 4, 1912; arrived in U.S., 1941, naturalized, 1946; s. Jacob and Julia (Tindel) Feuer; m. Paula Berger, Jan. 19, 1946. MS, U. Vienna, Austria, 1934, PhD, 1936. Postdoctoral fellow U. Paris, 1939; with dept. chemistry Purdue U., Lafayette, Ind., 1943-79, prof. chemistry, 1961-79, prof. emeritus, 1979—. Vis. prof. Hebrew U., Jerusalem, 1964, Indian Inst. Tech., Kanpur, India, 1971, Peking (China) Inst. Tech., 1979. Pres., contbr. Organic Electronic Spectral Data, Inc., 1962—89; mng. editor: Organic Nitro Chemistry Series, 1982—; mem. adv. bd. Turkish Jour. Chemistry, mem. editl. bd. Chimica Acta Turcica. Fellow: AAAS; mem.: Royal Soc. Chemistry, Am. Chem. Soc., Sigma Xi, Phi Lambda Upsilon. Achievements include research in organic nitrogen compounds; discovery of new methods for syntheses nitro compounds, cyclic hydrazides; research in mechanism of nitro compounds reactions. Home: 1700 Lindberg Rd Apt 219 West Lafayette IN 47906-2036 Office: Purdue U Dept Chemistry Lafayette IN 47907

FEUER, MICHAEL, venture capitalist, former office products executive; Various positions to sr. v.p. Fabri-Centers Am., Cleveland, Ohio, 1970—88; co-founder, chmn., CEO OfficeMax, Shaker Heights, Ohio, 1988—2003; CEO, co-founder Max-Ventures LLC venture fund, 2004—. Adv. coun. Case We. Reserve Univ. Weatherhead Bus. Sch., Univ. Pitts. Katz Bus. Sch. Office: Max Ventures Ste 3200 1900 E 9th St Cleveland OH 44114

FEUERBORN, BILL, state legislator; m. Linda Feuerborn. Mem. Kans. State Ho. of Reps. Dist. 5, 1994—; mem. agrl. and appropriations coms. Home: 1600 E Park Rd Garnett KS 66032-9300

FEUERWERKER, ALBERT, historian, educator; b. Cleve., Nov. 6, 1927; s. Martin and Gizella (Feuerwerker) F.; m. Yi-tsi Mei, June 11, 1955; children: Alison, Paul. AB, Harvard U., 1950, PhD, 1957. Lectr. history U. Toronto, Ont., Can., 1955-58; rsch. fellow Harvard U., Cambridge, Mass., 1958-60; assoc. prof. history U. Mich., Ann Arbor, 1960-63, prof., 1963-96, chmn. dept., 1984-87; dir. U. Mich. Ctr. for Chinese Studies, Ann Arbor, 1961-67, 72-83; A.M. and H.P. Bentley prof. of history U. Mich., Ann Arbor, 1986-96, prof. emeritus, 1996—; dir. d'études École des Hautes Etudes en Scis. Sociales, Paris, 1981; vis. scholar Acad. Social Scis., Shanghai, China, 1981, 88, Sichuan U., Chengdu, China, 1988. Joint com. on contemporary China, Social Sci. Research Council-Am. Council Learned Socs., 1966-78, 80-83, chmn., 1970-75; mem. com. on scholarly comm. with the People's Republic of China, Nat. Acad. Scis.-Social Sci. Rsch. Coun.-Am. Council Learned Socs., 1971-78, 81-83, vice-chmn., 1975-78 Author: China's Early Industrialization, 1958, History in Communist China, 1968, The Chinese Economy 1870-1911, 1969, Rebellion in 19th Century China, 1975, The Foreign Establishment in China, 1976, Economic Trends in the Republic of China, 1977, Chinese Social and Economic History from the Song to 1900, 1982, Studies in the Economic History of Late Imperial China, 1996, The Chinese Economy, 1870-1949, 1996; co-editor: Cambridge History of China, vol. 13, 1986; mem. editl. bd. Am. Hist. Rev., 1970-75, The China Quar., 1967-91, Comparative Studies in Soc. and History, 1964-2001. Served with AUS, 1946-47. Fellow NEH, 1971-72, Social Sci. Research Council-Am. Council of Learned Socs., 1962-63, Guggenheim Found., 1987-88. Fellow AAAS; mem. Assn. for Asian Studies (v.p. 1990, pres. 1991), Nat. Com. on U.S.-China Rels. Home: 827 Asa Gray Dr Apt 356 Ann Arbor MI 48105 Office: U Mich Ctr for Chinese Studies 1080 S University Ave Ste 3668 Ann Arbor MI 48109-1106 E-mail: afeuer@umich.edu.

FEUSS, LINDA ANNE UPSALL, lawyer; b. White Plains, NY, Dec. 9, 1956; d. Herbert Charles and Edna May (Hart) Upsall; m. Charles E. Feuss, Aug. 16, 1980; children: Charles Herbert, Anne Hart. BA in French Lit., Colgate U., 1978; JD, Emory U., 1981. Bar: Ga. 1981, SC 1981, Minn. 2000. Assoc. Rainey, Britton, Gibbes & Clarkson, Greenville, SC, 1981-83; counsel Siemens Energy & Automation, Atlanta, 1983-91, Siemens Corp., Atlanta, 1991-93, sr. counsel, 1993-94, assoc. gen. counsel, 1994-98; v.p., gen. counsel Pillsbury Co., Mpls., 1998-2000; v.p., gen. counsel to exec. v.p. legal and human resources PEMSTAR Inc., Rochester, Minn., 2001—03; v.p., gen. counsel, sec. C.H. Robinson Worldwide Inc., Eden Prairie, Minn., 2003—. Rep. law coun. II Mfr.'s Alliance, Washington, 1995-98; rep. law com. Nat. Elec. Mfr.'s Assn., Washington, 1995-98; bd. govs. St. Thomas U. Sch. Law, 2006—; mem. adv. bd. PACER, 2005—. Adv. bd. PACER, 2005—; bd. govs. St. Thomas U. Sch. Law, 2006—; bd. mem. YWCA, 2006—. Mem. ABA, Am. Corp. Coun. Assn. (dir. Ga. chpt. 1995-98, v.p. Ga. chpt. 1996, pres. 1997), State Bar Ga., SC Bar, Minn. Bar Assn., Colgate Club Atlanta (pres. 1986-88, bd. dirs. 1989-98). Office: CH Robinson Worldwide Inc 8100 Mitchell Rd Eden Prairie MN 55344-2248 Office Fax: 952-937-7840.

FIBIGER, HANS CHRISTIAN, science administrator; b. Denmark, 1942; BSc, U. Victoria, B.C., Can., 1966; PhD, Princeton U., 1970. Asst. prof. U. B.C., Vancouver, assoc. prof., 1976, prof., 1980; Charles W. Gowdy disting. lectr. dept. pharmacology and toxicology U. Western Ont., London, Ont., Canada, 1992; v.p. neurosci. discovery rsch. and clin. investigation Eli Lilly and Co., Indpls., 1998—. Vis. prof. Med. Rsch. Coun., Dalhousie U., Halifax, N.S., Canada, 1979; mem. appraisals com. Ont. Coun. Grad. Studies, 1981—83; vis. prof. Alta. Heritage Med. Rsch. Found., U. Calgary, Alta., Canada, 1982; councilor Can. Coll. europsychopharmacology, 1982—84; vis. prof. Med. Rsch. Coun., McGill U., Montreal, Que., Canada, 1983; invited prof. grad. program neurosci. Karolinska Inst., Stockholm, 1993; sci. advisor Inst. Mental Health Rsch. at Royal Ottawa Hosp., 2000—; mem. sci. adv. bd. Dystonia Med. Rsch. Found., 1995—; chmn. adv. com. on peer rev. Med. Rsch. Coun. Can., 1993—; mem. profl. adv. bd. Can. Psychiatry Rsch. Found., 1989—; chmn. working group on affect and motivation Nat. Rsch. Coun., Washington, 1985. Mem. editl. bd.: Molecular and Chem. Neuropathology, 1999, Jour. Molecular Neurosci., 1993—, mem. editl. adv. bd.: Psychopharmacology, 1994—99, co-editor-in-chief: Neuropsychopharmacology, 1995—98, mem. editl. adv. bd.: Biol. Psychiatry, 1993—, mem. editl. bd.: Neuropsychopharmacology, 1993—95, Synapse, 1992—, assoc. editor: Jour. Psychiatry and Neurosci., 1990—. Recipient Janssen prize for innovations in neuropsychopharmacology rsch., 1996, Gold medal in health scis., Sci. Coun. B.C., 1993, Tanenbaum Disting. Scientist award in schizophrenia rsch., 1993, Heinz Lehmann award, Can. Coll. Neuropsychopharmacology, 1987, Killam Rsch. prize, 1987, prize in psychiatry, Clarke Inst., 1975, award for paper presented at 1971 meeting, divsn. psychopharmacology Am. Psychol. Assn., 1971, Bristol-Myers Squibb Unresricted grant in neurosci., MRC, 1994—99, 1992—96. Fellow: Can. Coll. Neuropsychopharmacology, Am. Coll. Neuropsychopharmacology; mem.: Internat. Soc. Neurochemistry, Pharmacol. Soc. Can., Can. Coll. europsychopharmacology (mem. nominating com. 1984—), Can. Psychiatry Rsch. Found. (mem. profl. adv. bd. 1989—), Tourette Syndrome Assn. USA (mem. sci. adv. bd. 1992—), Huntington Soc. Can. (mem. sci. adv. coun. 1992—). Achievements include research in biochemical neuroanatomy; behavioral pharmacology; neuropsychopharmacology. Office: Eli Lilly & Co Lilly Corp Ctr DC 0530 Indianapolis IN 46285

FICK, ROBERT, professional baseball player; b. Torrance, Calif., Mar. 15, 1974; Right fielder Detroit Tigers, 1998—2002; with Atlanta Braves, 2003, Tampa Bay Devil Rays, 2004, San Diego Padres, 2004—. Played Team USA, 1996, Hawaii Winter League, 1997, Ariz. Fall League, 1998, 99.

FICKE, GREGORY C., utilities executive; m. Carol Ficke; children: Lisa, Lindsay. BS, Miami U.; degree in Engring., The Ohio State U.; MBA, U. Cin.; JD, No. Ky. U.; grad. Adv. Mgmt. Program, Harvard Bus. Sch. Registered profl. engr., Ohio; bar: Ohio. With Bechtel Power Corp., Ann Arbor, Mich.; from mem. staff to pres. The Cin. (Ohio) Gas & Electric Co. Cinergy Corp., Cin., 1978—2001, pres. The Cin. (Ohio) Gas & Electric Co., 2001—. Bd. trustees Clovernook Ctr. Blind, Ohio Found. Ind. Colls. Mem.: Greater Cin. (Ohio) C. of C. (bd. trustees), Ohio C. of C. (bd. trustees). Office: Cinergy Corp 139 E 4th St Cincinnati OH 45202

FIEDLER, JOHN F., automotive executive; b. 1938; B in Chemistry, Kent State U., 1960; M in Bus., MIT, 1979. Joined The Goodyear Tire & Rubber Co., Akron, Ohio, 1964, various positions including pres. Retread Sys. Co. divsn., pres. Kelly Springfield Tire Co. divsn., exec. v.p. N.Am. tire divsn.; pres., COO Borg-Warner Automotive, Inc., Chgo., 1994—, also bd. dirs. Office: Borg Warner Automotive 3850 Hamlin Rd Auburn Hills MI 48326-2872

FIEGEN, KRISTIE K., state legislator; State rep. S.D. Dist. 11, 1992-2000. Mem. Health and Human Svc. and Local Govt. Coms., S.D. Ho. Reps. Home: 6832 W Westminster Dr Sioux Falls SD 57106-3234 Office: SD House of Reps State Capitol Pierre SD 57501

FIEGEN, THOMAS L., state legislator, lawyer, economics educator; b. Mitchell, SD, Oct. 2, 1958; s. Clarence L. and Phyllis Jean Fiegen; m. Sandra Lynn Cutler, Oct. 31, 1981; children: Maureen Sarah, Kathryn Ann, Paul Lewis, Theresa Jean. BS in Agrl. Econ., BS in Speech, Kans. State U., 1984; MA in Econ., JD, U. Iowa, 1988. Bar: S.D. 1988, Iowa 1988, Minn. 1991, U.S. Dist. Ct. S.D. 1989, U.S. Dist. Ct. (no. and so. dists.) Iowa 1990, U.S. Ct. Appeals (8th cir.) 1990. Assoc. McCann, Martin & McCann, Brookings, S.D., 1988-90, Childers & Vestle, P.C., Cedar Rapids, Iowa, 1990-93; ptnr. Childers & Fiegen, P.C., Cedar Rapids, Iowa, 1993—; mem. Iowa Senate from 20th dist., 2001—. Student rsch. asst. Konza Prairie Tallgrass Preserve, divsn. biology Kans. State U., Manhattan, 1982-84; tchg. asst. dept. econ. U. Iowa, Iowa City, 1985-87, instr., 1987-88; adj. faculty Kirkwood C.C., Cedar Rapids, 1992—. State conv. del. Iowa Dem. Party, Des Moines, 1992. Mem. ABA, Am. Bankruptcy Inst., Iowa Bar Assn., S.D. Bar Assn., Minn. Bar Assn., Phi Kappa Phi. Roman Catholic. Office: Childers & Fiegen PC 425 2nd St SE Ste 350 Cedar Rapids IA 52401-1819 Home: 307 2nd Ave Clarence IA 52216-9756

FIEGER, GEOFFREY NELS, lawyer; b. Detroit, Dec. 23, 1950; s. Bernard Julian and June Beth (Oberer) F.; m. Kathleen Janice Podwoiski, June 25, 1983. BA, U. Mich., 1974, MA, 1976; JD, Detroit Coll. Law, 1979. Bar: Mich. 1979, U.S. Dist. Ct. (ea. dist.) Mich. 1979, Fla. 1980, U.S. Dist. Ct. (mid. dist.) Fla. 1980, Ariz. 1980. Ptnr. Fieger Fieger Kenney & Johnson, P.C., Southfield, Mich., 1979—. V.p. Orgn. United to Save Twp., West Bloomfield, Mich., 1987; dem. nominee for gov. of Mich., 1998. Mem. ABA, Detroit Bar Assn., Assn. Trial Lawyers Am. Unitarian Universalist. Avocations: running, swimming. Office: Fieger Fieger Kenney Johnson & Giroux 19390 W 10 Mile Rd Southfield MI 48075-2463

FIELD, BENJAMIN R., III, packaging manufacturing executive; Sr. v.p., CFO, treas. Bemis Co., Inc., Mpls. Office: Bemis Co Inc Ste 2300 222 S 9th St Minneapolis MN 55402-4099

FIELD, HENRY AUGUSTUS, JR., lawyer; b. Wis. Dells, Wis., July 8, 1928; s. Henry A. and Georgia (Coakley) F.; m. Patricia Ann Young, Nov. 30, 1957 (dec. 1980); children: Mary Patricia (dec. 1992), Thomas Gerard Raelene, Susan Therese (Mrs. Thomas Hempel); m. Molly Kelly Martin, Apr. 13, 1985. Student, Western Mich. Coll., 1946-47; PhB, Marquette U., 1950; LLB cum laude, U. Wis., 1952. Bar: Wis. 1952, U.S. Dist. Ct. (we. and ea. dists.) Wis. 1952, U.S. Ct. Appeals (7th cir.) 1957, U.S. Supreme Ct. 1980. Asst. U.S. atty. Western Dist. of Wis., 1956-57; assoc. Roberts, Boardman, Suhr, Bjork & Curry, 1957-62; jr. ptnr. Roberts, Boardman, Suhr & Curry, 1962-70; ptnr. Boardman, Suhr, Curry & Field, Madison, Wis., 1970—, chmn. exec. com., 1985-95; mem. Wis. Jud. Council, 1974-79. Dir. Family Service Soc., 1969-75, treas., 1971-72, pres., 1973-74; trustee Dane County Bar Pro Bono Trust Found., 1995-99. Served with C.I.C., AUS, 1952-55. Fellow: Wis. Law Found. (bd. dirs. 2003—, treas. 2005—), Am. Bar. Found., Am. Coll. Trial Lawyers (state chmn. 1982—83); mem.: ABA (Wis. chmn. legis. com. 1975—76), Wis. Law Found., Wis. Bar Assn. (chmn. litigation sect. 1971—72), Milw. and Dane County Bar Assn. (pres. 1971—72), 7th Fed. Cir. Bar Assn., Madison Club, Order of Coif, Sigma Tau Delta, Phi Delta Phi. Republican. Roman Catholic. Home: 3310 Valley Creek Cir Middleton WI 53562-1988 Office: Boardman Suhr Curry & Field 1 S Pinckney St Madison WI 53703-2892 Office Phone: 608-257-9521. Business E-Mail: hfield@boardmanlawfirm.com.

FIELD, LARRY, paper company executive; b. June 2, 1939; BS, U of Illinois. CEO Field Container, Elk Grove Village, Ill. Named to Chgo. Area Entrepreneurship Hall of Fame. Office: Field Container 1500 Nicholas Blvd Elk Grove Village IL 60007-5575

FIELD, MARSHALL, retail executive; b. Charlottesville, Va., May 13, 1941; s. Marshall IV and Joanne (Bass) F.; m. Joan Best Connelly, Sept. 5, 1964 (div. 1969); 1 child, Marshall; m. Jamee Beckwith Jacobs, Aug. 19, 1972; children: Jamee Christine, Stephanie Caroline, Abigail Beckwith. BA, Harvard Coll., 1963. With .Y. Herald Tribune, 1964-65; pub. Chgo. Sun-Times, 1969-80, Chgo. Daily News, 1969-78; dir. Field Enterprises, Inc., Chgo., 1965-84, dir., mem. exec. com., 1965-84, chmn. bd., 1972-84, The Field Corp., 1984—, Cabot, Cabot & Forbes, 1984—, chmn. exec. com., 1985-89, sr. dir., chief exec. officer, 1989—; pub. World Book-Childcraft Internat. Inc., 1973-78, dir., 1965-80. Trustee Art Inst. Chgo., Rush-Presbyn.-St. Lukes Med. Ctr., Chgo. Cmty. Trust, Field Mus. Natural History, Chgo. Pub. Libr. Found.; life trustee Music & Dance Theater, Chgo.; chmn. bd. Terra Found. for the Arts; adv. bd. Brookfield Zoo; charitable adv. coun. Office of Atty. Gen. of State of Ill.; active Chgo. Orchestral Assn.; bd. visitors, chair Nicholas Sch. of the Environment, Duke U.; bd. dirs. Field Found. Ill., Lincoln Park Zool. Soc.; chmn. Nat. Coun. of the World Wildlife Fund; bd. dirs. Atlantic Salmon Fedn. Mem. Nature Conservancy, River Club, Chgo. Club, Harvard Club, Racquet Club, Onwentsia Club, Jupiter Island Club, Shore Acres Club, McArthur Golf Club. Office: 225 W Wacker Dr Ste 1500 Chicago IL 60606-1235

FIELDING, RONALD, food products executive; Group v.p. meat products Hormel Foods Corp., Austin, Minn., 1999—. Office: Hormel Foods Corp One Hormel Pl Austin MN 55912-3680

FIELDS, ALLEN, artistic director; b. Pinehurst, NC; Student, N.C. Sch. Arts, Am. Ballet Theatre Sch., NYC; studied with Patricia Wilde, Wilhelm Burman, David Howard, Ivan Nagy, Melissa Hayden. Performer with Cynthia Gregory, Gwen Verdon, Samuel Ramie, Madonna, Geena Davis; guest appearances in South Am., Europe, Can., Mex.; dancer with Ohio Ballet, Eglevsky Ballet, Ballet du Nord, France, Atlanta Ballet, Newport News Ballet, Phoenix Ballet, Hubbard St. Dance Co.; prin. dancer Cleve. San Jose Ballet; artistic dir. Minn. Ballet, 1992—. Office: Minn Ballet Ste 800 301 W 1st St Duluth MN 55802

FIELDS, BARRY E., lawyer; b. Feb. 6, 1966; BA in chem., Bellarmine Coll., 1988; JD, U. Chgo., 1991. Bar: Ill. 1991. Law clk. U.S. Dist. Ct. Appeals Sixth Cir.; ptnr., pro bono Kirkland & Ellis LLP, Chgo. Mem.: Rules Adv. Com. U.S. Dist. Ct. N. Dist. Ill., ABA. Office: Kirkland & Ellis LLp 200E Randloph Dr Chicago IL 60601 Home: 506 Thatcher Ave River Forest IL 60305 Office Phone: 312-861-2081. Office Fax: 312-861-2200. Business E-Mail: bfields@kirkland.com.

FIELDS, HENRY WILLIAM, college dean; b. Cedar Rapids, Iowa, Sept. 25, 1946; m. Anne M. Fields; children: Benjamin Widdicomb, Justin Riley. AB in Psychology, Dartmouth, Hanover, NH, 1969; DDS in Dentistry, Univ. Iowa, Iowa City, 1973, MS in Pedodontics, 1975; MSD in Orthodontics, Univ. Wash., Seattle, 1977. Cert. dentistry Iowa 1973, N.C. 1978, Ohio 1991. Staff, Dept. Hosp. Dentistry Univ. Iowa Hosps., Iowa City, 1973; grad. supr. Muscatine (Iowa) Migrant Program, 1974; grad. instr. Univ. Iowa, 1974—75; AFDH tchr. tng. fellow Dept. Orthodontics Univ. Wash., 1975—77, clin. asst., 1977; Dental Faculty Practice Sch. Dentistry Univ. N.C., 1977—91, asst. prof. Depts. of Pediatric Dentistry and Orthodontics, 1977—82; with N.C. Meml. Hosp., 1978—91; assoc. prof., Depts. of Pediatric Dentistry and Orthodontics Univ. N.C., 1982—87, grad. program dir., Dept. Pediatric Dentistry, 1984—89, prof., Dept. Pediatric Dentistry and Orthodontics, 1987—91, acting dir. grad. studies Sch. Dentistry, 1989, asst. dean acad. affairs, Sch. Dentistry, 1990—91; chair, Dept. Dentistry OSU Hosps., Columbus, Ohio, 1991—2001; Faculty Practice OSU Coll. Dentistry, 1991—, prof. Dept. Orthodontics, 1991—, dean, 1991—2001; staff Columbus Children's Hosp., 1992—. Mem. human subjects com. Sch. Dentistry, Univ. N.C., 1989-91, chmn. curriculum com., 1990-91, chmn. dirs. com. adv. edn. program, 1989-91, health promotion disease prevention task force, 1990-91; deans coun. computerization com. The Ohio State Univ., 1991-1993; bd. dirs. IADR-AADR Craniofacial Biology Group, 1988-90; cons. Callahan award commn., 1992-2001; external examiner BDS and MDS programs Dept. Pediatric Dentistry and Orthodontics Univ. Hong Kong, 1991-93. Contbr. chpts. to books, articles to profl. jours. Recipient NIDR grantee, 1980-83, NIDR Inst. grantee, 1985-86, 1988-93. Home: 4066 Fenwick Rd Columbus OH 43220-4870 Office: Ohio State U Coll Dentistry 4088F Postle Hall Columbus OH 43210-1241 E-mail: fields31@osu.edu.

FIELDS, JANICE L., food service executive; b. 1955; m. Doug Wilkins; 2 children. From crew mem. to regional v.p. Pitts. McDonald's Corp., 1978—94; v.p Pitts. region McDonald's USA, LLC, 1994—2000, v.p. Great Lakes divsn., 2000, sr. v.p. SE divsn., sr. v.p. ctrl. divsn., 2000—03, pres. ctrl. divsn., 2003—06, exec. v.p., COO, 2006—. Bd. dirs. Catalyst, Monsanto Co., 2008—. Bd. dirs. United Cerebral Palsy, Ronald McDonald House Charities, Urban League. Named one of 25 Women to Watch, Crain's Chgo. Bus., 2007; recipient Golden Arch Partners Award, McDonald's, WON award, Women's Operator Network, 1988, Women Operators Network Recognition Award, McDonald's, 2001, Women's Leadership award, Women's Network, 2002. Office: McDonald's Corp 2111 McDonald's Dr Oak Brook IL 60523*

FIELDS, MARK, automotive executive; b. Bklyn., 1961; BA in Economics, Rutgers U., 1983; MBA, Harvard U., 1989. Joined Ford Motor Co., Dearborn, Mich., 1989, served in a variety of sales and mktg. positions, 1990—96; mng. dir. Ford of Argentina, 1997—98; sr. adviser Mazda Motor Corp., 1998, sr. mng. dir. of mktg., sales & customer svc., 1998, rep. dir., pres., 1999—2002; group v.p., Premier Automotive Group Ford Motor Co., 2002—04, exec. v.p., Ford Europe, 2004—05, exec. v.p., pres. Americas, 2005—. Recipient Global Leader of Tomorrow, World Economic Forum, 2000, Innovator of the Year, CNBC's Asian Business Leader, 2001. Office: Ford Motor Co 21175 Oakwood Blvd Dearborn MI 48124-4079

FIELDS, SARA A., travel company executive; With Boeing Aircraft, Renton, Wash.; flight attendant UAL Corp., Elk Grove Village, Ill., 1963, various positions including mgr. flight attendant training, mgr. indsl. rels., dir. inflight svc internat., dir. employee rels., 1963—94, sr. v.p. onboard svc., 1994—. Office: UAL Corp 1200 E Algonquin Rd Arlington Heights IL 60005-4712 also: PO Box 66100 Chicago IL 60666-0100 Fax: 847-700-4899.

FIELDS, WILLIAM ALBERT, lawyer; b. Parkersburg, W.Va., Mar. 30, 1939; s. Jack Lyons and Grace (Kelley) F.; m. Prudence Brandt Adams, June 26, 1964. BS magna cum laude, Ohio State U., 1961; postgrad., Harvard Law Sch., 1961-64. Bar: Ohio bar 1964. Since practiced in, Marietta; city prosecutor, 1964-65; acting Judge Marietta Mcpl. Ct.; dir. elections Washington County, 1967-74; profl. bass-baritone soloist. Bd. dirs. Bank One, Marietta, N.A.; lectr. on estate planning and probate matters. Mem. editl. bd. Probate Law Jour. of Ohio. Chmn. Washington County Heart Assn., 1965-67; mem. dist. exec. com. Boy Scouts Am., 1967-74; Treas. County Republican Exec. Com., 1966—; trustee YMCA, Salvation Army; pres. bd. trustees Washington State Community Coll., Marietta; exec. com., trustee Coll. Adminstrv. Scis., Ohio State U.; trustee Appalachian Bible Coll., Bradley, W.Va., 1974-77, Marietta Meml. Hosp., also treas.; bd. dirs. Ohio Valley Port Authority. Recipient Wall St. Jour. award, 1961; named Outstanding Young Man of Marietta, 1968, Outstanding Citizen of Marietta, 1992; named to Ohio Valley Sports Hall of Fame, 2001. Fellow Am. Coll. Trust and Estate Counsel; mem. Ohio Bar Assn. (chmn., bd. govs., probate and trust law sect., mem. splty. bd. Ohio Supreme Ct., splty approval bd. trust, probate, and estate planning), Washington County Bar Assn., Marietta Area C. of C. (v.p., trustee), Am. Mensa, Nat. Soc. of Arts and Letters (bd. trustees), Sigma Chi, Beta Gamma Sigma. Clubs: Rotarian (pres. 1970-71), Marietta Country (trustee). Home: 129 Hillcrest Dr Marietta OH 45750-9321 Personal E-mail: wafpaf@snddenlink.net.

FIES, JAMES DAVID, elementary school educator; b. Chgo., May 19, 1950; s. Arthur Herbert Sr. and Ruth Paulina (Rehm) F.; m. Ruth Elaine Carlson, June 24, 1972; children: Samuel Jacob, Sarah Rae. BA, Purdue U., 1972, MS, 1975. Cert. elem. edn. tchr., Ind. Tchr. math. Morton Elem./Mid. Sch., Hammond, Ind., 1972-82, Eggers Elem./Mid. Sch., Hammond, 1982-88, Gavit Jr./Sr. High Sch., Hammond, 1988—2005, interim asst. prin., 1992. Dept. chair Eggers Mid. Sch., 1983-86. Bldg. union rep. Hammond Tchrs. Fedn. Local 394, 1981-87; trustee Trinity Luth. Ch., Hammond, 1976-82, 86-87, bd. fin., 1993—. Mem. Nat. Coun. Tchrs. of Maths., Hammond Tchrs. Fedn., Am. Fedn. of Tchrs. Avocations: travel, fishing. Home: 544 Hickory Ln Munster IN 46321-2409

FIFE, WILMER KRAFFT, retired chemistry professor; b. Wellsville, Ohio, Oct. 19, 1933; s. Wilmer George and Lourene Elizabeth (Krafft) F.; m. Betsy Louise Jones, Dec. 26, 1959; children: Kimberly, Julia, Steven. B.Sc. in Chemistry, Case Inst. Tech., 1955; PhD in Organic Chemistry, Ohio State U., 1960. Applications chemist Monsanto Chem. Co., Dayton, Ohio, summers 1955, 57; instr. Muskingum (Ohio) Coll., 1959-60, asst. prof., 1960-64, asso. prof., 1964-70, prof., 1970-71, chmn. dept. chemistry, 1966-71; prof. chemistry Ind. U.-Purdue U. at Indpls., 1971—, chmn. dept., 1971-80; ret. NIH postdoctoral fellow Harvard U., 1965-66; NIH postdoctoral fellow Columbia U., 1968-69; NSF fellow, 1955-56; Sinclair Oil Co. fellow, 1958-59; DuPont fellow, 1960; Danforth assoc., 1969—; others; vis. scholar in chemistry Louis Pasteur U., Strasbourg, France, 1994, U. San Francisco, 1999; named Outstanding Rschr. in

Sci. Ind. U.-Purdue U., Indpls. Mem. Am. Chem. Soc., AAAS, Sigma Xi, Tau Beta Pi, Phi Lambda Upsilon. Home: 7102 Dean Rd Indianapolis IN 46240-3626 Office: IUPUI Chemistry 402 N Blackford St Indianapolis IN 46202-3217 E-mail: fife@chem.iupui.edu.

FIJALKOWSKI, ISABELLE, professional basketball player; b. May 23, 1972; d. Tadeusz and Leokadia Fijalkowski. Student, U. Colo., 1995, U. d'Orleans, 1997—. Basketball player Euroleague, 1996-97; forward Cleveland Rockers, (WNBA), 1997—.

FILIPPINE, EDWARD LOUIS, federal judge; b. 1930; AB, St. Louis U., 1951, JD, 1957. Bar: Mo. 1957. Pvt. practice law, St. Louis, 1957—77; spl. asst. atty. gen. State of Mo., 1963—64; dist. judge U.S. Dist. Ct. (ea. dist.) Mo., St. Louis, 1977—, chief judge, 1990—95; U.S. sr. dist. judge U.S. Dist. Ct. for Ea. Dist. Mo., 1995—. Served with USAF, 1951-53 Mem. ABA, Mo. Bar Assn., Bar Assn. Met. St. Louis, Lawyers Assn. of St. Louis. Office: US Dist Ct Thomas F Eagleton US Cthse 111 S 10th St Rm 10 137 Saint Louis MO 63102 Office Phone: 314-244-7640. E-mail: edward_filippine@moed.uscourts.gov.

FILISKO, FRANK EDWARD, physicist, researcher; b. Lorain, Ohio, Jan. 29, 1942; s. Joseph John and Mary Magdalene (Cherven) F.; m. Doris Faye Call, Aug. 8, 1970; children: Theresa Marie, Andrew William, Edward Anthony. BA, Colgate U., 1964; MS, Purdue U., 1966; PhD, Case We. Res. U., 1969. Post doctoral fellow Case We. Res. U., Cleve., 1968—70; prof. materials sci. engring. and macromolecular sci. U. Mich., Ann Arbor, 1970—, acting dir. macromolecular sci. and engring., 1987—96. Dir. Polymer Lab., U. Mich. Editor: Progress in Electrorheology, 1995; contbr. more than 150 articles to profl. jours. Mem. Am. Phys. Soc., Am. Chem. Soc., KC, Soc. Rheology Roman Catholic. Achievements include patents for electric field dependent fluids and electric dependent fluids-CIP. Office: U Mich Materials Sci & Engring Ann Arbor MI 48109 Office Phone: 734-763-2240. Business E-Mail: fef@umich.edu.

FILLOON, KAREN, radio personality; BS Meteorology, Fla. State U. With Nat. Weather Svc.; on-air meteorologist TV Tallahassee; meterologist Sta. KSTP-TV, Sta. KSTP-FM; staff meteorologist Sta. WCCO Radio, Mpls., 1989—. Instr. meteorology U. St. Thomas. Co-chair ann. golf tournament Am. Heart Assn. Mem.: Minn. Multiple Sclerosis Soc. (mem. strategic bd. devel. com., bd. trustees). Office: WCCO 625 2nd Ave S Minneapolis MN 55402

FILSON, RONALD COULTER, architect, educator, dean; b. Chardon, Ohio, Dec. 11, 1946; s. Clifford Coulter and Mae Alice (Foster) F.; m. Susan Virginia Saward, Dec. 14, 1973 (div. May 1996); children: Timothy Coulter, Lily Virginia; m. Lea Ann Sinclair, Oct. 9, 1999. Diploma, Am. Acad. in Rome, 1970; B.Arch., Yale U., 1970. Registered arch., Calif., La., Mass., Ohio, Miss., Nat. Coun. Archtl. Registration Bds. Architect Atelier d'Etudes, Ghardaia, Algeria, 1971-73; asst. prof., asst. dean Sch. of Architecture UCLA, 1974-80; dean sch. architecture Tulane U., New Orleans, 1980-92, prof. sch. architecture, 1980—; prin. Ronald Filson, FAIA, Architects, New Orleans. Prin. works include Piazza d'Italia, New Orleans, 1978 (award 1976), Eola Hotel, 1980, Lee House, 1984, Hyatt Hotel, Poydras Plaza, 1987-88, Nat. Pk. Svc. Edn. Ctr., Nat. D-Day Mus., Trump Casino, L.A. Artists Guild, Natchez Visitors Ctr. Pres. Friends of the Schnidler House, L.A., 1978-80; bd. dirs. New Orleans Arts Coun., 1980-93, pres., 1989-92, Contemporary Arts Ctr., New Orleans, 1980-84, New Orleans Planning Commn., 1985-87. Recipient design citations Progressive Architecture mag., 1969, 76, Rome prize Am. Acad. in Rome, 1969 Fellow AIA (Design awards 1980, 81, 85, 87, 89, 92, 94, 98, 99, 2000, 01, Richardson medal 1992); mem. AIA La. (pres. 1998), New Orleans AIA (pres. 1994), Yale Alumni Assn. La. (pres. 1992-94), So. Yacht Club, New Orleans Lawn Tennis Club (bd. govs. 1998-2002). Avocations: watercolors, sailing. Home: 5700 Vrooman Rd Painesville OH 44077-8842

FINAN, RICHARD H., lawyer; b. Cin., Aug. 16, 1934; m. Joan L. Finan, 1956; children: Patrick, Nancy, Julie, Michael. BS, U. Dayton; LLB, U. Cin. Bar: Ohio. Pvt. practice, Sharonville, Ohio; mem. Ohio Senate from 7th dist., Columbus, 1978—2002; pres. Ohio Senate, Columbus, 1997—2002. Asst. pro tem, chmn. ways and means com., Senate legis. ethics com., fin. com., commerce and labor com., rules com., reference and oversight com., joint legis. com. on fed. funds, welfare oversight com., taxation rev. com., mem. Rep. campaign com.; chmn. fed. budget and taxation com. Nat. Conf. State Legislators; bd. dirs. Franklin Savs. & Loan; arbitrator Hamilton County Ct. Common Pleas, Am. Arbitration Assn. Councilman Evendale Villae, Ohio, 1963-69, mayor, 1969-73; mem. Ohio Ho. of Reps., Columbus, 1973-78; exec. dir. Hamilton County Reagan-Bush Campaign, 1984; dir. Dole for Pres. Campaign, 1988; trustee U. Dayton; past trustee St. Rita's Sch. for Deaf; bd. dirs. Cath. Social Svcs. Southwestern Ohio, Carillon Funds, Rest Haven. Named Legislator of Yr., Ohio Trial Lawyers Assn., 1975, Twp. Clks. and Trustees Assn., 1976, Disting. Alumnus award U. Dayton, Andrew Carnegie award Oho Libr. Assn., 1993, Outstanding Merit award for statehouse preservation Ohio Hist. Soc. Mem. Ohio Bar Assn., Cin. Bar Assn., Sharonville Bus. Assn., U. Dayton Alumni Assn. (past pres. Cin. chpt.), U. Dayton Nat. Alumni Assn. (past pres.). Office: 3068 Stanwin Pl Cincinnati OH 45241-3360

FINDLAY, DONALD CAMERON, lawyer, former federal agency administrator, insurance company executive; b. Chgo., Sept. 7, 1959; s. Donald C. and Judith R. (Lilly) F.; m. Amy Scalera, July 9, 1988; children: Alexander B., James M. BA summa cum laude, Northwestern U., 1982; MA 1st class, Oxford U., Eng., 1984; JD magna cum laude, Harvard U., 1987. Bar: Ill. 1987, D.C. 1988. Law clk. to Judge Stephen Williams US Ct. Appeals D.C. cir., Washington, 1987-88; law clk. to Justice Antonin Scalia US Supreme Ct., Washington, 1988-89; counselor to sec. US Dept. Transp., Washington, 1989-91; dep. asst. to pres. and counselor to chief of staff The White House, Washington, 1991-92; assoc. Sidley Austin Brown & Wood, Chgo., 1992-95, ptnr., 1995—2001; dep. sec. US Dept. Labor, Washington, 2001—03; exec. v.p., gen. counsel Aon Corp., Chgo., 2003—. Adj. prof. Northwestern U., Evanston, Ill., 1994-96. Trustee Northwestern U., 1997—2000, 2004—; dir. Chgo. Coun. Global Affairs, 2004—, Chgo. Shakespeare Theater, Children's Home & Aid Soc., 2004—; chmn. bd. visitors Weinberg Coll. Arts & Sci., orthwestern U. Office: Aon Corp 200 E Randolph St Chicago IL 60601

FINDLEY, PAUL, former congressman, author, educator; b. Jacksonville, Ill., June 23, 1921; s. Joseph S. and Florence Mary (Nichols) F.; m. Lucille Gemme; children: Craig Jon, Diane Lillian. AB, Ill. Coll., 1943, LLD, 1972; LHD (hon.), Lindenwood Coll., 1969, Lincoln U., 1988, MacMurray Coll., 1997; LLD, Sana'a U., Yemen, 1997. Mem. 87th-97th Congresses from 20th Ill. dist., mem. Fgn. Affairs com., mem. Agr. com.; chmn. factfinding mission to Paris, 1965; chmn. Rep. NATO Task Force, 1965-68; chmn. com. to investigate internat. problems caused by agrl. support policies Ditchley (Eng.) Conf., 1973; del. N. Atlantic Assembly, 1965-70, 72-79, Munich Conf. German Rels., 1969-71; Ditchley Conf. Atlantic Trade, 1967; European Parliament, 1974-76; mem. 7th Congl. Del. to People's Republic China, 1975; chmn. Ill. Trade Mission to, USSR, 1972, People's Republic of China, 1978. Internat. food and agrl. devel. bd. AID, 1983-94; vis. prof. MacMurray Coll., 1994-96. Author: Abraham Lincoln: The Crucible of Congress, The Federal Farm Fable, They Dare to Speak Out: People and Institutions Confront Israel's Lobby, Deliberate Deceptions: Facing the Facts About the U.S.-Israel Relationships, Silent No More: Confronting America's False Images of Islam; contbr. numerous articles on fgn. policy and agr. to periodicals. Trustee emeritus Ill. Coll.; lectr. leadership program UN Leadership Acad., Amman, Jordan, 1987-88, 05; chmn. Coun. for the Nat. Interest, 1989-2000. Lt. (j.g.) USNR, WWII. Named laureate Lincoln Acad., 1980; decorated Grand Cross Order of Merit Fed. Republic of Ger.; recipient Outstanding Svc. to Agr. citation So. Ill. U., Kefauver award for promoting Fedn. of Atlantic Nations; Hon. Am. Farmer degree FFA, Outstanding Achievement award FFA Alumni Assn., citation Nat. Assn. State Univs. and Land-Grant Colls., EAFORD Humanitarian award, 1986, Alex Odeh Human Rights award Am. Arab Anti-Discrimination Com., 1992, Disting. Svc. award Assn. for Internat. Agr. and Rural Development, 1995; Malcolm X award Muslim Assn., 2000. Mem. Assn. to Unite Democracies (bd. dirs.), Am. Legion, Phi Beta Kappa. Republican. Presbyterian. Home and Office: 1040 W College Ave Jacksonville IL 62650-2306 Office Phone: 217-243-8444.

FINDLEY, TROY RAY, former state legislator, bank officer; b. Lawrence, Kans., July 11, 1964; s. Paul Wayne and Virginia Lee (Coffman) F.; m. Jennifer Ann Sharp, Aug. 30, 1997. BS in Polit. Sci., U. Kans., 1990. With grocery/retail industry, 1982—92; asst. mgr. Food Barn, Inc., Overland Park, Kans., 1989-92; county out reach dir. Kans. Dems., Topeka, 1992-95; mem. Kans. Legislature, Topeka, 1995—2003; customer svc. rep. UMB Bank, Lawrence, 1997—2003; legis. liaison to Gov. Kathleen Sebelius, 2003—. Bd. dirs. Big Bros./Big Sisters, Lawrence, 1992-93, mem. adv. bd., 1994—; mem. Horizon 2020 Edn. Task Group, Lawrence, 1993; bd. dirs. Prairie Renaissance, Lawrence, 1995—, ARC Douglas County, Lawrence, 1998—. Home: 3415 SW Glendale Dr Topeka KS 66614-4590

FINE, DEBORAH, Internet company executive, former apparel executive; V.p., advt. dir. Family Cir. Mag., 1991—93; v.p., assoc. pub. Mary Emmerling's Country, 1993—94; advt. dir. Glamour mag., 1994—95, assoc. pub., 1995—96, v.p., pub., 1999—2001; pub. Bride's Mag., 1996—99; pres. Teen Bus. Avon Products, Inc., 2001—05; CEO, Victoria Secret, Pink Brand Limited Brands, Inc., 2005—06; CEO, iVillage, Inc. NBC Universal, NYC, 2006—. Office: iVillage Inc 500 7th Ave 14th Ave New York NY 10018

FINE, MORRIS EUGENE, materials engineer, educator; b. Jamestown, ND, Apr. 12, 1918; s. Louis and Sophie (Berrington) F.; m. Mildred Eleanor Glazer, Aug. 13, 1950; children: Susan Elaine, Amy Lynn. B.Metall. Engring. with distinction, U. Minn., 1940, MS, 1942, PhD, 1943. Instr. U. Minn., 1942-43; mem. tech. staff Bell Telephone Labs., Murray Hill, N.J., 1946-54; prof. emeritus Northwestern U., Evanston, Ill., 1954—, prof., chmn. dept. metallurgy Tech. Inst., 1955-57, chmn. dept. materials sci., 1958-60, prof. and chmn. materials research center, 1960-64, Walter P. Murphy prof. materials sci., 1963-89, tech. inst. prof., 1985-89, dir. Am. Iron and Steel Inst. steel resource ctr., 1986-93, assoc. dean grad. studies and research Tech. Inst., 1973-85, prof. emeritus, 1989, mem. grad. faculty, 1989—. Vis. prof. dept. materials sci. Stanford U., 1967-68; JSPS vis. scholar, Japan, 1979; chmn., vis. prof. materials sci. and engring. U. Tex., Austin, 1984-95; assoc. engr. Manhattan Project, U. Chgo. and Los Alamos, N.Mex., WWII; mem. materials adv. bd. NRC, 1963-68; mem. com. geol. and materials scis. NRC, 1979-82; chmn. adv. bd. program on modular methods for tchg. materials Pa. State U., 1973-77; chmn. vis. com. metallurgy and materials Sci. and Materials Rsch. Ctr., Lehigh U., 1965-75; mem. vis. com. Lawrence Berkeley Lab., 1978-81, chmn., 1981, mem. vis. com. Ames Dept. Energy Lab., 1976-80, Materials Rsch. Ctr., Pa. State U., 1988-91, Colo. Sch. Mines, 1991-96; chmn., organizer numerous confs. in field. Author numerous tech. and sci. articles on mech. properties of metals and ceramics, fatigue of metals, phase transformations, high temperature alloys, and other subjects.; author: Introduction to Phase Transformation in Condensed Systems. Recipient Gilbert Speich award Iron and Steel Soc., 1993; named Chicagoan of Year in Sci., 1961 Fellow AAAS, Am. Phys. Soc., Japan Soc. Metals (hon.), Am. Soc. Metals (chpt. chmn. 1963, Campbell lectr. 1979, chmn. seminar com. 1979, hon. mem. com. 1993-96, gold medal 1986), Am. Acad. Arts and Scis., Metall Soc. of AIME (chmn. inst. metals divsn. 1966-68, bd. dirs. 1968-71, bd. dirs. inst. 1972-75, mem. Bardeen gold medals com. 1992-96, chmn. 1995-96, Mathewson gold medal for rsch. 1981, James Douglas gold medal 1982, Educator award 1993, hon. mem.), Am. Ceramic Soc. (keynote lectr. electronic materials div. 1972); mem. NAE (astronautics space engring. bd. 1973-77, membership com. 1974-79, chmn. 1977-78, mem. membership adv. com. 1991-94), Scripta Met et Mat (Outstanding Paper award 1991), The Metals, Materials, Minerals Soc. (inst. metals lecture and R.F. Mehl gold medal 1996), Sigma Xi, Tau Beta Pi, Alpha Sigma Mu, Sigma Alpha Sigma. Home: 1101 Manor Dr Wilmette IL 60091-1026 Office: Dept Materials Sci and Engring Northwestern U Evanston IL 60208-3108 Business E-Mail: m-fine412@northwestern.edu.

FINE, PAMELA B., newspaper editor; Grad., U. Fla. Reporter Daytona Beach News, 1979; several editl. positions with Atlanta Journal-Constitution, 1982—94; mng. editor, v.p. Mpls. Star Tribune, 1994—2002; mng. editor The Indianapolis Star, 2003—. Nat. conf. chair Associated Press Mng. Editors Assn., 2000; juror for Pulitzer Prize. Office: The Indianapolis Star PO Box 145 Indianapolis IN 46206-0145 Office Phone: 317-444-6168. Business E-Mail: pam.fine@indystar.com.

FINGERHUT, ERIC D., academic administrator, former state legislator and congressman, lawyer; b. University Hts., Ohio, May 6, 1959; BS summa cum laude, Northwestern U., 1981; JD, Stanford U., 1984. Staff atty. older persons law office Legal Aid Soc., Cleve., 1984-85; assoc. dir. Cleveland Works, Cleve., 1987-89; atty. Hahn Loeser & Parks, Cleve.; campaign mgr., transition dir., spl. asst. to Mayor Mike White, 1989; mem. Ohio Senate from 25th Dist., Columbus, 1991-93, 103rd Congress from 19th Ohio dist., Washington, D.C., 1993-94, Ohio Senate from 25th dist., Columbus, 1999—2006; dir. econ.-devel. edn. and entrepreneurship Baldwin-Wallace Coll., Berea, Ohio, 2006—07; chancellor Ohio Bd. of Regents, Columbus, 2007—. Mem. Energy, Nat. Resources and Environ. com., Fin. com., Health and Human Svcs. com., Child Support Guidelines Adv. com., Ohio Adv. Coun. for Aging com., Task Force on Campaign Fin. reform com., Welfare Oversight Commission com., House Banking, Fin. and Urban Affairs com., Sci., Space and Tech. com., Fgn. Affairs Com. Author: Making Ohio Great Again. Bd. trustees Cleve. Zelma George Shelter; pres. Common Cause/Ohio, 1986-88; leader FITE; tchr. Sunday Sch. Synagogue Beth-Am. Recipient Future of Cleve. Jewry award, Stanford Law Review award; named to Cleve. Heights High Sch. Hall of Fame. Mem. Ohio Bar Assn., Cleve. Bar Assn. Democrat. Jewish. Home: 22675 Fairmont Blvd Cleveland OH 44418 Office: Ohio Bd Regents 30 E Broad St, 36th Fl Columbus OH 43215

FINK, BILL A., state legislator; b. Ringsted, Iowa, May 5, 1955; m. Donna; 2 children. BS, Iowa State U., 1977; MS in Edn., Drake U., 1984. Tchr. govt., econ., social studies Carlisle (Iowa) H.S.; mem. Warren County Dem. Ctrl. Com., Iowa Senate from 45th dist., 1990—. Mem. Redeemer Luth. Ch., Polk Suburban Uniserve Unit. Mem. NEA, Iowa State Edn. Assn., Iowa State Univ. Alumni Assn., Carlisle Cmty. Edn. Assn., Ducks Unltd. Democrat. Home: 379 S23 Hwy Carlisle IA 50047-9413 E-mail: bill_fink@legis.state.ia.us.

FINK, JEROLD ALBERT, lawyer; b. Dayton, Ohio, July 16, 1941; s. Albert Otto and Marjorie Carolyn (Scheidt) F.; m. Mary Jo McHone, Dec. 31, 1961 (div. July 1978); children: Marjorie, Kathryn, Erick; m. 2d, Deborah Lynn Bailey, Dec. 25, 1980 (div. Oct. 1986); 1 child, Justin. AB, Duke U., 1963, LLB, 1966. Bar: Ohio 1966. Assoc. Taft, Stettinius & Hollister, Cin., 1966-73, ptnr., 1973—. Bd. dirs. The Wm. Powell Co., Cin., 1974—, Great Trails Broadcasting Co., Cin., 1974-79. Co-author: (with Judy Cohn) Power Defensive Carding, 1988, (with Joe Lutz) The American Forcing Minor Bidding System, 1995, (with Joe Lutz) Defensive Carding in the 21st Century, 2001. Pres. Cin. Musical Festival Assn., 1978-79; trustee Cin. Playhouse, 1976-95, New Life Youth Svcs., Cin., 1971—. Republican. Presbyterian. Office: 1800 Firstar Tower 425 Walnut St Cincinnati OH 45202-3923 E-mail: fink@taftlaw.com.

FINK, JORDAN NORMAN, allergist, educator; b. Milw., Oct. 13, 1934; s. Jack and Ruth Fink; m. Phyllis Mechanic, Aug. 26, 1956; children: Leslie, Rosanne, Robert. BS, U. Wis.-Madison, 1956, MD, 1959. Diplomate Am. Bd. Internal Medicine, Am. Bd. Allergy and Immunology. Inst. Med. Coll. Wis., Milw., 1965-68, asst. prof. medicine, 1968-70, assoc. prof. medicine, 1970-73, prof., chief allergy and immunology, 1973—98, prof. medicine and pediats, 1994—. Chmn. adv. com. on pulmonary allergy FDA, Rockwell, Md., 1980-81, cons., 1983— Contbr. articles to profl. jours., chpt. to book Chmn. Camp Interlaken Com., Milw., 1978-81 bd. dirs. Jewish Community Ctr., Milw., 1977-81 Grantee NIH, 1982, VA, 1984 Fellow ACP, Am. Acad. Allergy (pres. 1984-85); mem. Assn. Am. Physicians, Am. Soc. Clin. Investigation, Am. Assn. Immunologists, Alpha Omega Alpha, Phi Delta Epsilon Avocations: swimming, travel. Home: 2829 W Golf Cir Mequon WI 53092-2446 Office: Med Coll Wis 9000 W Wisconsin Ave Milwaukee WI 53226-3518

FINK, JOSEPH ALLEN, lawyer; s. Allen Medford and Margaret Ruth (Draper) F.; m. Marcia L. Horton; children: Alexander Mentzer, Justin McGranahan. Student, Wayne State U., 1960-61; BA, Oberlin Coll., 1964; JD, Duke U., 1967. Bar: Mich. 1968, U.S. Dist Ct. (ea. dist.) Mich. 1968, U.S. Dist. Ct. (we. dist.) Mich. 1974, U.S. Ct. Appeals (6th cir.) 1987, U.S. Supreme Ct. 1998. Assoc. Dickinson, Wright, McKean & Cudlip, Detroit, 1967—72, Lansing, Mich., 1972—75; ptnr. Dickinson Wright PLLC, Lansing, 1976—. Instr. U.S. Internat. U. Grad. Sch. Bus., San Diego, 1971; adj. prof. trial advocacy Thomas M. Cooley Law Sch., Lansing, 1984-85; mem. com. on local rules U.S. Dist. Cts., 1985; chmn. trial experience subcom. U.S. Dist. Ct. (we. dist.) Mich., 1981. Contbg. author: Construction Litigation, 1979, Legal Considerations in Managing Problem Employees, 1988, Michigan Civil Procedure During Trial, 2d edit., 1989, Regulatory & Legislative Quarterly, CPRCU Soc.; co-author Honestly This May Not be The Best Policy, 2006; contbr. articles to profl. jours. Bd. dirs. Lansing 2000 Inc., 1985-92, Profl. Direct Inc., Universal Holding Corp.; bd. trustees Olivet (Mich.) Coll., 1985-94; mem. bd. advisors Mich. State U. Press, 1993-96. Lt. JACF USNR, 1968—72. Named one of Best Lawyers in Am., Commercial Litigation, Civil Litigation Defense Super Lawyers. Fellow: Mich. State Bar Found.; mem.: State Bar of Mich. (chmn. local disciplinary com. 1983—, com. for US Cts. 1984), Assn. Life Ins. Counsel, Internat. Assn. Ins. Receivers. Episcopalian. Avocations: writing, reading, golf. Office: Dickinson Wright PLLC 215 S Washington Sq Ste 200 Lansing MI 48933-1816 Home Phone: 517-339-4013; Office Phone: 517-487-4711. Business E-Mail: jfink@dickinsonwright.com.

FINK, RUTH GARVEY, diversified financial services company executive; b. Colby, Kans., Apr. 26, 1917; d. Ray Hugh and Olive Hill (White) Garvey; m. Richard Lloyd Cochener, Feb. 17, 1942 (dec. 1954); children: Bruce Garvey Cochener, Diana Broze, Caroline Bonesteel; m. Harry Bernerd Fink, Mar. 31, 1955. BA, U. Ill., 1938; postgrad., U. Kans., 1940—41; HHD (hon.), Washburn U., 1981. Mng. ptnr. C & G Grain Co., Topeka, 1954—55; v.p., dir. CGF Grain Co., Topeka, 1957—84; pres., dir. Midwest Industries, Inc., Topeka, 1972—83, CGF Industries, Inc., Topeka, 1983—97, Freedom Family LC, 1997—. Bd. dirs. Garvey, Inc., Wichita; past bd. dirs. Stauffer Comm., Inc., Topeka. Trustee Washburn Endowment Assn., Topeka, 1960—, active com. tornado reconstrn., 1966—68; chmn. Washburn Coll. Bible, 1979—; Kans. regent Gunston Hall, Lorton, Va., 1965—79; trustee Hoover Presdl. Libr., West Branch, Iowa, 1983—88; mem. electoral coll. State of Kans., 2004. Named Disting. Kansan, Native Sons and Daughters of Kans., 2004; named to Topeka Bus. Hall of Fame, Jr. Achievement of N.E. Kans., 2003; recipient Cmty. Leader award, Topeka Panhellenic Coun., 1981, Monroe award, Washburn Alumni Assn., 1991, N.E. Kans. Leadership award, Washburn U., 2002; Paul Harris Fellow, Rotary Internat., 2004. Mem.: PEO, Nat. Soc. Colonial Dames in Kans. (Roll of Honor 1980), Delta Gamma (Cable award 1965, Shield award 1970). Republican. Congregationalist. Office: Ste 805 534 S Kansas Ave Topeka KS 66603-3430

FINKBEINER, CARLTON S. (CARTY FINKBEINER), mayor; b. Toledo, 1939; BA, Dennison U. Tchr., football coach Maumee Valley Country Day Sch., St. Francis De Sales H.S., U. Toledo; city councilman City of Toledo, vice-mayor, mayor, 1994—2002, 2006—; founder Toledo's Cmty.-Oriented Drug Enforcement program; co-sponsor City-wide Curfew; chair Coun.'s Housing, Neighborhood Revitalization and Natural Resources Com., Toledo; host Carty & Co., Toledo; weekly commentator WTVG-ABC, Toledo, 2002—05. Mem. Econ. Opportunity Planning Assn. of Greater Toledo, Presidential Scholars Commn., U.S. Small Bus. Adminstrn. Adv. Commn. Northeastern and orthwestern Ohio, Internat. Gt. Lakes St. Lawrence Mayors Conf.; mem. Toledo-Lucas County Port Authority, 2003—. Achievements include being appointed to the Presidential Scholars Commission by President Gerald Ford, 1975. Office: Office of the Mayor/City Coun One Goverment Ctr Ste 2200 Toledo OH 43604*

FINKE, ROBERT FORGE, lawyer; b. Chgo., Mar. 11, 1941; s. Robert Frank and Helen Theodora (Forge) Finke. AB, U. Mich., 1963; JD, Harvard U., 1966. Bar: Ill. 1966, US Dist. Ct. (no. dist.) Ill. 1966, US Ct. Appeals (7th cir.) 1966, US Supreme Ct. 1970, US Ct. Appeals (9th cir.) 1980, US Ct. Appeals (4th and 6th cirs.) 1982, (8th cir.) 1998. Law clk., 1966—67; assoc. Mayer, Brown Rowe & Maw LLP, Chgo., 1967—71, ptnr., 1972—. Bd. dirs. Lyric Opera Guild, Chgo. Bot. Garden, Windy City Harvest; trustee Rush U. Med. Ctr. Mem. ABA (sects. litigation, bus., antitrust, legal edn. and admissions to the bar, vice chmn. 1974-75), Lawyers Club Chgo., Univ. Club, Econ. Club. Office: Mayer Brown LLP 71 S Wacker Dr Chicago IL 60606-4637 Home Phone: 847-256-3771; Office Phone: 312-701-7110. Business E-Mail: rfinke@mayerbrown.com.

FINKELMAN, DANIEL P., retail executive; married; 2 children. Grad. with honors, Grinnell Coll.; grad., Harvard U. Cons. KcKinsey & Co.; exec. v.p. mktg. Cardinal Health; v.p. brand and bus. planning Ltd. Brands, Inc., Columbus, Ohio, 1996—98, sr. v.p. brand and bus. planning, 1999—. Office: Ltd Brands Inc Three Ltd Pkwy Columbus OH 43230

FINKELMAN, FRED D., medical educator; b. NYC, N.Y., Mar. 4, 1947; BA cum laude, Queens Coll., 1967; MD cum laude, Yale U., 1971. Intern in internal medicine Yale-New Haven (Conn.) Hosp., 1971—72, jr. asst. resident, 1972—73; rsch. assoc. lab. immunology NIH, Nat. Inst. Allergy and Infectious Diseases, Bethesda, Md., 1973—75; fellow rheumatology sect. dept. internal medicine U. Tex. Health Ctr., Dallas, 1975—77; from asst. prof. to assoc. prof. to prof. dept. medicine Uniformed Svcs. U. of the Health Scis., Bethesda, 1977—95, dir. divsn. rheumatology dept. medicine, 1984—95; McDonald prof. medicine, dir. divsn. immunology U. Cin. Coll. Medicine, 1995—. Chair Keystone Symposium on Type 2 Cytokines in Allergy and Worm Infections, Lake Tahoe, Nev., 1999; session chair Acad. Allergy, Asthma and Immunology Symposium on Mouse Models of Asthma, 2000, Keystone Symposium on Cytokines in Disease, 2000; Pfizer vis. prof. Columbia U., 2002; keynote address Lovelace Respiratory Rsch. Inst. Internat. Symposium on Respiratory Immunology, Santa Fe, 1999. Dep. editor: Jour. Immunology, 1992—97, mem. editl. bd.: Infection and Immunity, 2000—, Internat. Immunology, 2001—. Recipient rsch. grants in field, Arthritis Hero award, 2001. Mem.: Am. Assn. Immunologists (session chair ann. meeting, symposia on allergic diseases and on asthm, mem. program com. 1994—96, block chmn. immunology of infectious diseases minisymposia 1994—96, mem. nominations com. 2000—01, mem. pub. affairs com. 2000—02). Achievements include research in role of Interleukin-4 receptors in immunity; regulation of IL-4 production; regulation of asthma by IL-4R(alpha) and IL-5; regulation of tolerance and immunity by antigen-presenting dendritic cells, cytokine production and regulation. Office: U Cin Coll Medicine Dept Internal Medicine Divsn Immunology PO Box 670563 Cincinnati OH 45267-0563

FINKELSTEIN, PHIL, retail executive; BS economics, Wharton School, U. Penn; MBA, Harvard Business School. With Glemby Internat., 1966—81; chmn., Beauty Div. Seligman & Latz (S&L), 0191—1984; CEO Turner Hall Corp., 1984—87; sr. v.p. Revlon, 1987; exec. v.p. Regis Corp., 1987—88, pres., COO, 1988—96, pres., 1996—2004, CEO, 1996—, chmn., 2004—. Mem. World Pres. Org., Chief Executives Org. Office: c/o Regis Corp 7201 Metro Blvd Edina MN 55439

FINKELSTEIN, RICHARD ALAN, retired microbiology educator, consultant; b. NYC, Mar. 5, 1930; s. Frank and Sylvia (Lemkin) F.; m. Helen Rosenberg, Nov. 30, 1952; children: Sheri, Mark, Laurie; m. Mary Boesman, June 20, 1976; 1 dau., Sarina Nicole. BS, U. Okla., 1950; MA, U. Tex., Austin, 1952, PhD, 1955. Tchg. fellow, rsch. scientist U. Tex., Austin, 1950-55; fellow, instr. U. Tex. Southwestern Med. Sch., Dallas, 1955-58; chief bioassay sect. Walter Reed Army Inst. Research, Washington, 1958-64; dep. chief, chief dept. bacteriology and mycology U.S. Army Med. Component, SEATO Med. Research Lab., Bangkok, 1964-67; assoc. prof. dept. microbiology U. Tex. Southwestern Med. Sch., Dallas, 1967-73, prof., 1973-79; prof., chmn. dept. microbiology Sch. Medicine U. Mo., Columbia, 1979-93, Curators' prof., 1990-2000, Millsap Disting. Prof., 1985-2000, prof. emeritus, 2000—. Mem. Nat. Com. for Coordination Cholera Rsch., Ministry for Pub. Health, Bangkok, 1965-67; cons. WHO, 1970—, commdg. gen. U.S. Army Med. R&D Command, 1975-79, Schwarz-Mann Labs., 1974-79, ICN Biomeds., 1979—, Wyeth-Ayerst, 1992—, Amgen, 1992, Molecular Pharms., 1993—; Microbiolog. and Infectious Diseases Rsch. Com. Nat. Inst. Allergy and Infectious Diseases, IH, 1994-98; vis. assoc. prof. U. Med. Scis., Bangkok, 1965-67; vis. prof. U. Chgo., Med. Sch., 1977; vis. scientist Japanese Sci. Coun., 1976, Ciba-Geigy lectr. Waksman Inst., Rutgers U., 1975; vis. lectr. Nat. Sci. Coun., Taipei, Taiwan, 1995, others. Contbr. articles on cholera, enterotoxins, gonorrhea, and role of iron in host-parasite interactions to profl. jours. Major med. svc. corps US Army, 1966. Recipient Robert Koch prize Bonn, Fed. Republic Germany, 1976; Chancellor's award for outstanding faculty rsch. in biol. scis. U. Mo.-Columbia, 1985, Sigma Xi Rsch. award U. Mo.-Columbia, 1986. Fellow Am Acad. Microbiology (bd. govs. 1990-93), Am. Soc. for Microbiology (pres. Tex. br. 1974-75, hon. Tex. br. divsn. councilor, chmn. program com. 1979-82, sec.-treas. Mo. br. 1985-87, v.p. 1987-89, pres. 1989-91, councillor, 1991-92, coun. policy com. 1992-95, Disting. Svc. award 1998), Am. Assn. Immunologists, Infectious Diseases Soc. of Am., Soc. Gen. Microbiology, Pathol. Soc. Gt. Britain and Ireland, Sigma Xi. Achievements include first purification of cholera enterotoxin; first purification of heat-labile enterotoxin from Escherichia coli; patent for living attenuated candidate cholera vaccine. Home: 3861 S Forest Acres Dr Columbia MO 65203-8608 Office: U Mo Sch Medicine Dept Molecular Microbiol Columbia MO 65212-0001 Home Phone: 573-446-2883; Office Phone: 573-882-4117. Business E-Mail: finkelsteinr@health.missouri.edu.

FINLAY, TIMOTHY, agricultural products supplier; BS, U. Ill., 1983; MBA, Quincy U., 1989. CPA. Treas. gen. dir. fin. and adminstrn. ADM Alliance Nutrition, Inc., Quincy, Ill., 2000. Office: ADM Alliance Nutritions Inc 1000 N 30th St Quincy IL 62301-3400 E-mail: tim-finlay@admworld.com.

FINLEY, KATHERINE MANDUSIC, professional society administrator; b. Mansfield, Ohio, Nov. 8, 1954; d. Sam and Ann Julia (Konves) Mandusic; m. Edwin D. McDonell, Aug. 18, 1979 (div. Dec. 1994); m. Jeffrey A. Finley, June 12, 1999. BA, Ohio Wesleyan U.; MA in History and Mus. Studies, Case Western Res.; MBA, Ind. U. Rschr. Conner Prairie Mus., Fishers, Ind., 1978-82; exec. dir., rsch. historian Ind. Med. History Mus./Ind. Hist. Soc., Indpls., 1982-91; asst. dir. comm. and mktg. Ind. U. Ctr. Philanthropy, 1991-93; exec. dir. Roller Skating Assn. Internat., Indpls., 1993-2000, Assn. Rsch. Nonprofit Orgns. and Voluntary Action, 2000—05; mem. faculty philanthropic studies Ind. U.-Purdue U., Indpls., 2001—; rsch. dir. William E. Smith Inst. for Assn. Rsch., 2004—05; dir. Am. Coll. Sports Medicine Found., Indpls., 2005—06; exec. dir. Tenant-in-Common Assn. and Found., 2006—. Author: (book) The Journals of William A. Lindsay, 1989; contbg. editor: The Encyclopedia of Indianapolis, 1994; contbr. articles to profl. jours. Pres. Altrusa Internat. Indpls., 1995—97, treas., 1998—99, chmn. svc. com., 1999—2000; pres. Altrusa Found. Indpls., 2001—03; bd. dirs. Nat. Mus. Roller Skating, Lincoln, 1994—2000. Mem.: Assn. Fund Raising Profls. (bd. dirs. Ind. chpt. 2003—), Ind. Soc. Assn. Execs. (chair edn. com. 1997—98, chair conv. com. 1999—2000, bd. dirs. 1999—2001, chair found. 2000), Nat. Soc. Fund Raising Execs. (cert.), Am. Soc. Assn. Execs. (mem. ethics com. 2004—, Assn. Exec. of Yr. 2002, cert. meeting planner 2003), MINI Cooper Car Club Ind. (club advisor 2003—04), Toastmasters (v.p. edn. 1998—99, v.p. pub. rels. 2000, v.p. edn. 2000—02, gov. area 18 2001—02, v.p. edn. 2006—07), Rotary Internat. of Indpls., Phi Beta Kappa, Sigma Iota Epsilon, Beta Gamma Sigma. Avocations: reading, walking, gourmet cooking. Office: 10401 N Meridian St Ste 300 Indianapolis IN 46290 Business E-Mail: kfinley@ticassoc.org.

FINLEY, PHILIP BRUCE, retired state adjutant general; b. White City, Kans., Mar. 25, 1930; s. Marshall Arthur and Zelma Rena (Krenkle) F.; m. Jacqueline Lou Thomas, May 23, 1952; children: Jeffrey Allen, Robin Lyn. BS, Kans. State U., 1951, MS, 1954. Commd. U.S. Army, 1951, advanced through grades to maj. gen., 1988; served in Kans. N.G., 1967-84; served with Res. Norton, Kans., 1954-67; high sch. tchr. Bird City, Kans., 1954-55, Norton, Kans., 1955-67; extension agt. Decatur County Agr. Extension Council, Oberlin, Kans., 1967-72; rural devel. specialist Kans. State U. Area Office, Colby, 1972-74; N.W. Area dir. Kansas State U. Agrl. Extension, Colby, 1974-86, assoc. head, 1986—; adjutant-gen. State of Kans., Topeka, 1987-90; retired, 1990. Mem. N.W. Kans. Planning and Devel. Group, Hill City, 1972-74, "Kans. Tomorrow." Planning Commn., Topeka, 1985-86. Mem. 7th Div. Assn., VFW, Am. Legion, Phi Delta Kappa, Epsilon Sigma Phi. Republican. Methodist. Avocations: game bird hunting, horsemanship, beekeeping, automobile mechanics. Home: 685 S Court Ave Colby KS 67701-3411

FINN, ROBERT WILLIAM, bishop; b. St. Louis, Mo., Apr. 2, 1953; s. Theodore and Betty (Schneider) Finn. Grad., St. Louis Preparatory Sem. North, 1971; BA in Philosophy, Cardinal Glennon Coll., 1975; STB, Pontifical U. of St. Thomas Aquinas, 1978; MA in Theology, Pontifical U. of St. Thomas Aquinas, Rome, 1979; MA, St. Louis U., 1990. Ordained priest Archdiocese of Saint Louis, 1979, assoc. pastor; mem. faculty St. Francis Borgia Regional H.S., Washington, 1983—89; adminstr. St. Dominic H.S., O'Fallon, Mo., 1989—96; named dir. continuing formation of priests Archdiocese of St. Louis, Mo., 1996, editor St. Louis Review Mo., 1999—2004; ordained bishop, 2004; bishop Diocese of Kansas City-St. Joseph, Mo., 2005—. Roman Catholic. Office: Diocese of Kansas City-St Joseph PO Box 419037 300 E 36th St Kansas City MO 64141-6037 Office Phone: 816-756-1850. Office Fax: 816-756-2105.*

FINNERTY, BRYAN, sports association executive; b. 1967; Founder, CEO, Mng. Ptnr. High Velocity Sports Grp., 2005—; founder Sports Leadership Ctr. of Am.; co-founder Sports Facilities Adv. L.L.C., Dunedin, Fla. Former profl. soccer player Detroit Rockers. Named one of 40 Under 40, Crain's Detroit Bus., 2006. Office: High Velocity Sports Group 46245 Michigan Ave Canton MI 48188

FINNEY, WILLIAM K., police chief; b. St. Paul, Nov. 28, 1948; BA, Mankato State U., 1970. Patrolman through ranks to chief of police St. Paul Police Dept., 1971-92, chief of police, 1992—. Office: St Paul Police Dept 367 Grove St Saint Paul MN 55101-2416

FINNO, RICHARD J., engineering educator; Assoc. prof. Northwestern U., Evanston, 1989—, James N. and Margie M. prof. dept. civil engring., 1993-96. Recipient Walter L. Huber Civil Engring. Rsch. prize ASCE. Office: Northwestern U Dept Civil Engring 2145 Sheridan Rd Dept Civil Evanston IL 60208-0834

FINZEN, BRUCE ARTHUR, lawyer; b. Mpls., Mar. 11, 1947; s. Floyd Arthur and Lorraine Jeannette (Offerdahl) F.; children: Margaret, Sara, Stephanie. BA, U. Minn., 1970; JD, U. Kans., 1973. Bar: Minn. 1973, U.S. Dist. Ct. Minn. 1973, Calif. 1988, U.S. Ct. Appeals (8th cir.) 1973, U.S. Ct. Appeals (7th cir.) 1983, U.S. Ct. Appeals (2d cir.) 1986, U.S. Ct. Appeals (4th cir.) 1994, U.S. Ct. Appeals (9th cir.) 1994, U.S. Supreme Ct. 1996. D.C., 2002, U.S. Dist. Ct. D.C. 2003. Law clk. to presiding justice Minn. Supreme Ct., St. Paul, 1973-74; assoc. Robins, Kaplan, Miller & Ciresi, Mpls., 1974-79; ptnr. Robins, Kaplan, Miller & Ciresi LLP, Mpls., 1979—. Mem. adv. bd. Ctr. for Pub. Integrity, 2001—; trustee Ho. of Hope Presbyn. Ch., 1988—94; bd. dirs. Union Gospel Mission, St. Paul, 1983—89; sec. bd. dirs. Boys and Girls Clubs St. Paul, 1984—91. Mem. ABA, Minn. Bar Assn., ATLA, Minn. Trial Lawyers Assn., Consumer Attys. Calif., Assn. Personal Injury Lawyers. Avocations: hunting, fishing. Office: Robins Kaplan Miller & Ciresi LLP 2800 LaSalle Plz 800 Lasalle Ave Ste 2800 Minneapolis MN 55402-2015 Office Phone: 612-349-8500.

FIORILE, MICHAEL J., publishing executive; BA cum laude, Boston Coll. Pres., CEO Dispatch Broadcast Group, 1994; sr. v.p. sales Dispatch Printing Co., 2003, pres., bd. dirs., 2005—, COO, 2008—. Pres. Dispatch Consumer Svcs.; chmn., pres. Consumer News Svcs.; bd. mem. TV Operators Caucus, Assn. Maximum Svc. TV, TV Bur. Advertising; vice chmn. NBC Affiliates Bd.; bd. dirs. State Automobile Mutual Insurance Co., 2003. Chmn. Greater Columbus C. of C. Office: Dispatch Printing Co 34 S 3Rd St Columbus OH 43215*

FIRCHOW, EVELYN SCHERABON, German language and literature educator, writer; b. Vienna; arrived in US, 1951, naturalized, 1964; d. Raimund and Hildegard (Nickl) Scherabon; m. Peter E. Firchow, 1969; children: Felicity (dec. 1988), Pamina. BA, U. Tex., 1956; MA, U. Man., 1957; PhD, Harvard U., 1963. Instr. coll. math. Balmoral Hall Sch., Winnipeg, Man., Canada, 1953—55; tchg. fellow in German Harvard U., Cambridge, Mass., 1957—58, 1961—62; lectr. German U. Md. in Munich, 1961; instr. German U. Wis., Madison, 1962—63, asst. prof., 1963—65; assoc. prof. German U. Minn., Mpls., 1965—69, prof. German and Germanic philology, 1969—, McKnight rsch. prof., 2004—07; vis. prof. U. Fla., Gainesville, 1973; Fulbright rsch. prof. Iceland, 1966—67, 1980, 1984; vis. rsch. prof. Nat. Cheng Kung U., Tainan, Taiwan, 1982—83; permanent vis. prof. Jilin U., Changchun, China, 1987—. Vis. prof. U. Graz, Austria, 1989, Austria, 91, Austria, 2002—03, U. Vienna, Austria, 1995, U. Bonn, 1996, Nat. U. Costa Rica, 2000. Editor and author: (under name E.S. Coleman) Taylor Starck-Festschrift, 1964, Stimmen aus dem Stundenglas, 1968, (under name E.S. Firchow) Studies by Einar Haugen, 1972, Studies for Einar Haugen, 1972, Was Deutsche lesen, 1973, Deutung und Bedeutung, 1973, Elucidarius in Old Norse Translation, 1989, The Old Norse Elucidarius: Original Text and English Translation, 1992, Notker der Deutsche von St. Gallen: De interpretatione, 1995, Categoriae, 2 Vols., 1996, De nuptiis Philologiae et Mercurii, 2 Vols., 1999, Notker der Deutsche von St. Gallen (950-1022): Ausführliche Bibliographie, 2000, De consolatione Philosophiae, 3 vols., 2003, Reluctant Modernists, Festschrift Peter Firchow, 2002, Gottfried von Strassburg: Tristan und Isolde, 2004, Wege und Irrwege der mittelalterlichen Textausgaben, 2007; translator: Einhard: Vita Caroli Magni, Das Leben Karls des Grossen, 1968, 84, 95, Einhard: Vita Caroli Magni, The Life of Charlemagne, 1972, 85, Icelandic Short Stories, 1974, 87, East German Short Stories, 1979, (with P.E. Firchow) Alois Brandstetter, The Abbey, 1998; dir., editor Computer Clearing-House Project for German and Medieval Scandinavian, to 2000; assoc. editor Germanic Notes and Revs., Am. Linguistics, Germanic Linguistics; contbr. articles and book revs. to profl. jours. Fulbright scholar Tex., 1951-52; fellow Alexander von Humboldt-Stiftung, Munich, 1960-61, Tuebingen, 1974, Marburg, 1981, Goettingen, 1985, Tokyo, 1991, Marburg and Berlin, 1993, Bonn, 2001, Fulbright Found., Iceland, 1967-68, 80, 94, Austrian Govt., 1977, NEH, 1980-81, Am. Inst. Indian Studies, 1988, BUSH fellow, 1989, Thor Thors fellow, 1994, Faculty summer fellow and Mc Knight summer fellow, 1995-96, 99, 2004, 07, Deutscher Akademischer Austausdienst (DAAD) rsch. fellow, 2000; named hon. mem. Multilingual Rsch. Ctr., Brussels, 1986. Mem. AAUP, MLA (chmn. divsn. German lit. to 1700 1979-80, 93-96, vice chmn. pedagogical seminar for Germanic philology 1979-86, 91-93, chair 1994), Medieval Acad. Am., Soc. German-Am. Studies (chair Linguistics I 1992), Internat. Comparative Lit. Assn., Soc. for Advancement Scandinavian Studies (chmn. Germanic philology 1979, text editing 1980, linguistics 1984, computers and Old Norse 1985), Assn. for Lang. and Linguistic Computing (founding mem.), Am. Comparative Lit. Assn., Midwest Modern Lang. Assn. (chmn. German I 1965-66, chmn. Scandinavian 1979), Am. Assn. Tchrs. German, Mediävisten Verband, Soc. for Germanic Philology, Österreichische Germanisten-Gesellschaft, Wolkenstein Gesellschaft, Assn. Lit. Scholars and Critics. Office: U Minn 205 Folwell Hall 9 Pleasant St SE Minneapolis MN 55455 Business E-Mail: firch001@umn.edu.

FIRCHOW, PETER EDGERLY, language professional, educator, writer; b. Needham, Mass., Dec. 16, 1937; s. Paul Karl August and Marta Loria (Montenegro) F.; m. Evelyn Maria Scherabon Coleman, Sept. 18, 1969; 1 dau., Pamina Maria Scherabon. BA, Harvard Coll., 1959; postgrad., U. Vienna, Austria, 1959—60; MA, Harvard U., 1961; PhD, U. Wis., 1965. Asst. prof. English U. Mich., 1965-67; asst. prof. English and comparative lit. U. Minn., Mpls., 1967-69, assoc. prof., 1969-73, prof., 1973—, chmn. Comparative Lit. Program, 1972-78. Disting. vis. prof. Nat. Cheng Kung U., Taiwan, 1982-83, Jilin U., Peoples Republic China, 1987, U. Munich, 1988, U. Graz, Austria, 1989, 2003; Fulbright prof. U. Bonn, Germany, 1995-96, Nat. U. Costa Rica, 2000. Author: Friedrich Schlegel's Lucinde and the Fragments, 1971, Aldous Huxley, Satirist and Novelist, 1972, The Writer's Place: Interviews on the Literary Situation in Contemporary Britain, 1974; (with E.S. Firchow) East German Short Stories: An Introductory Anthology, 1979; The End of Utopia: A Study of Huxley's Brave New World, 1984; The Death of the German Cousin: Variations on a Literary Stereotype, 1986; translator (with E.S. Firchow) The Abbey (Alois Brandstetter), 1998, Envisioning Africa: Racism and Imperialism in Conrad's "Heart of Darkness", 2000, W.H. Auden: Contexts for Poetry, 2002, Reluctant Modernists: Aldous Huxley and Some Contemporaries, 2002, Modern Utopian Fictions, 2007; contbr. articles on modern lit. subjects to profl. jours. Fellow Inst. Advanced Studies in Humanities, Edinburgh, 1977, Christopher Isherwood fellow Huntington Libr., 2006. Mem. Midwest Modern Lang. Assn. (v.p. 1977, pres. 1978), Am. Comparative Lit. Assn., Assn. Lit. Scholars and Critics, Internat. Aldous Huxley Soc. Home: 135 Birnamwood Dr Burnsville MN 55337-6814 Office: U Minn Dept English 310D Lind Hall 207 Church St SE Minneapolis MN 55455-0134 Office Phone: 612-625-3363. E-mail: pef@tc.umn.edu.

FIRMIN, MICHAEL WAYNE, psychology professor; b. New Orleans, July 28, 1961; s. Lloyd John and Betty L. (Shepherd) F.; m. Karen Sue Tuttle, Aug. 4, 1984; children: Ruth, Sarah. BA, Calvary Bible Coll., 1983; MA, Calvary Theol. Sem., 1985; MS, Bob Jones U., 1987, PhD, 1988; MA, Marywood U., 1992; PhD, Syracuse U. Nat. cert. counselor; lic. psychologist, Ohio. Dir. counseling svcs. Bapt. Bible Coll. of Pa., Clarks Summit, 1988-98, assoc. prof., 1988-98, chmn. divsn. grad. studies, 1995-97; resident in psychology TCN: Behavioral Health Svcs., 2000—01; assoc. prof. psychology Cedarville (Ohio) U., 1998—2004, prof. psychology, 2004—, chmn. dept. psychology, 2000—. Cons. for psychol. svcs. Assn. Bapts. for World Evangelism, Harrisburg, Pa., 1991—94, 1999—2003; clin. assessment cons. Keystone City Residence, 1994—2000. Editor: Jour. Ethnographic & Qualitative Rsch., 2006—. Pastor Faith Fellowship Bapt. Ch., Danbury, Conn., 1991-94. Mem. Psi Chi. Republican. Home: 84 E Elm St Cedarville OH 45314-8513 Office: Cedarville Univ 251 N Main St Cedarville OH 45314-0601

FISCH, ROBERT OTTO, medical educator; b. Budapest, Hungary, June 12, 1925; came to U.S., 1957. s. Zoltan and Irene (Manheim) F.; 1 dau., Rebecca A. Med. diploma, U. Budapest, 1951; study art, Acad. Fine Arts, Budapest, 1943, Mpls. Coll. Arts and Design, 1970-76. Gen. practice medicine, Hungary, 1951-55; pub. health officer, 1955; pediatrician Hosp. for Premature Children, Budapest, 1956; intern Christ Hosp., Jersey City, 1957-58; intern pediatrics U. Minn. Hosps., 1958-59, researcher, 1959-60, research fellow, 1961; instr. U. Minn. Sch. Medicine, 1961-63, asst. prof., 1963-72, assoc. prof., 1972-79, prof., 1979—, dir. phenylketonuric clinic, 1961-97. Author: Respiratory Diseases; PKU, Child Development (Best Cover Minn. Med. 1975), Light from the Yellow Star: A Lesson of Love from the Holocaust, 1994, The Metamorphosis to Freedom, 2000, Dear Dr. Fisch: Children's Letters to a Holocaust Survivor, 2004; contbr. articles to profl. jours.; exhibited art works in various one-man and group shows. Mem. Soc. Pediatric Rsch., Am. Physician Art Assn. (Best of Show award 2002, numerous others). Home: 1201 Yale Pl 2301 Minneapolis MN 55403 Home Phone: 612-375-9760. Personal E-mail: fisch001@umn.edu.

FISCH, WILLIAM BALES, law educator; b. Cleve., May 11, 1936; s. Max Harold and Ruth Alice (Bales) F.; m. Janice Heston McPherson, Sept. 2, 1961 (dec. 1987); m. Suzanne Fischer Good, June 19, 1993 (dec. 1998); children: Katherine Emily, Stephen McPherson. AB, Harvard Coll., 1957; LLB, U. Ill., 1960; M.Comparative Law (univ. fgn. law fellow), U. Chgo., 1962; JUD, U. Freiburg, Germany, 1972. Bar: Ill. 1961, Mo. 1982. Assoc. firm Kirkland & Ellis, Chgo., 1962-65; asst. prof. law U. N.D., 1965-68, assoc. prof., 1968-70, U. Mo., Columbia, 1970-74, prof., 1974—, Isador Loeb prof. law, 1977—2003, prof. emeritus, 2003—. Author: Die Vorteilsausgleichung im amerikanischen und deutschen Recht, 1974; co-author: Problems, Cases and Materials on Professional Responsibility, 1985, 3d edit., 2004; bd. editors: Am. Jour. Comparative Law; contbr. articles, revs. to law jours. Alexander von Humboldt-Stiftung Rsch. fellow, 1968-69, 89-90; Fulbright-Hays Rsch. scholar Hamburg, Germany, 1980-81, 89-90; Max Planck Soc. Rsch. fellow, Hamburg, 1992. Mem. ABA, AAUP, Am. Law Inst. Office: U Mo Law Sch Columbia MO 65211-4300

FISCHBACH, MICHELLE L., state legislator; b. Nov. 3, 1965; m. Scott Fischbach; 2 children. BA, St. Cloud State U. Mem. Minn. Senate from 14th dist., St. Paul, 1996—. Home: 416 Burr St Paynesville MN 56362-1110 Office: 149 State Office Bldg 100 Constitution Ave Saint Paul MN 55155-1232

FISCHER, LAWRENCE JOSEPH, toxicologist, educator, science administrator; b. Chgo., Sept. 2, 1937; s. Lawrence J. and Virginia H. (Dieker) F.; m. Elizabeth Ann Dunphy, Oct. 24, 1964; children— Julie Ann, Pamela Jean, Karen Sue B.Sc., U. Ill.-Chgo., 1959, MS, 1961; PhD, U. Calif.-San Francisco, 1965. NIH postdoctoral fellow St. Mary's Hosp. Med. Sch., London, 1965-66; sr. research pharmacologist Merck Sharp and Dohme, West Point, Pa., 1966-68; asst. prof. pharmacology U. Iowa, Iowa City, 1969-73, assoc. prof., 1974-76, prof., 1976-85; prof., dir. Inst. for Environ. Toxicology Mich. State U., East Lansing, Mich., 1985—. Cons. FDA Bur. Vet. Medicine, 1974-77; mem. bd. scientific counselors div. of cancer Etiology Nat. Cancer Inst., 1986-92. Mem. editorial adv. bd. Jour. Pharmacology and Exptl. Therapeutics, Toxicology and Applied Pharmacology, Drug Metabolism Revs. Recipient Faculty Scholar award Josiah Macy Found., U. Geneva, 1976 Mem. Am. Soc. for Pharmacology and Exptl. Therapeutics, Soc. Toxicology, AAAS, Soc. for Environ. Toxicology and Chemistry. Avocations: hunting, tennis. Home: 11630 Center Rd Bath MI 48808-9431 Office: Mich State U Inst for Environ Toxicology C231 Holden Hall East Lansing MI 48824

FISCHER, MICHELLE K., lawyer; BA in Econs. magna cum laude with distinction, Yale U., 1986; JD with honors, U. Chgo., 1989. Bar: Ohio 1989, D.C. 1991. With Jones Day, Cleve., 1989—, ptnr., 1999—. Mem.: ABA (antitrust law sect.), Ohio State Bar Assn. (bd. govs. antitrust law sect.). Office: Jones Day North Point 901 Lakeside Ave Cleveland OH 44114-1190

FISCHER, TOM, state legislator;, St. Thomas U. Owner A.I.O. Syss., Inc.; mem. N.D. Senator, Bismark, 1997—. Recipient Fed. Emerg. Mgmt. Agency Outstanding Pub. Svc. award, 1991. Home: 1524 Sundance Sq S Fargo ND 58104-7606 E-mail: tfischer@state.nd.us.

FISCHLER, BARBARA BRAND, librarian; b. Pitts., May 24, 1930; d. Carl Frederick and Emma Georgia (Piltz) Brand; m. Drake Anthony Fischler, June 3, 1961 (div., Oct. 1995); 1 child, Owen Wesley. AB cum laude, Wilson Coll., Chambersburg, Pa., 1952; MM with distinction, Ind. U., 1954, AMLS, 1964. Asst. reference librarian Ind. U., Bloomington, 1958-61, asst. librarian undergrad. library, 1961-63, acting librarian, 1963; circulation librarian Ind. U.-Purdue U., Indpls., 1970-76, pub. services librarian Univ. Library, sci., engring. and tech. unit, 1976-81, acting dir. univ. libraries, 1981-82, dir. univ. libraries, 1982-95; retired, 1995; dir. Sch. Libr. and Info. Sci. Ind. U.-Purdue U., Indpls., 1995—. Vis. and assoc. prof. (part-time) Sch. Libr. and Info. Sci. Ind. U., Bloomington, 1972-95, counselor-coord., Indpls., 1974-82, dir. sch. libr. and info. sci. campus Ind. U.-Purdue U., Indpls., 1995—; resource aide adv. com. Ind. Voc. Tech. Coll., Indpls., 1974-86; adv. com. Area Libr. Svcs. Authority, Indpls., 1976-79; mem. core com., chmn. program com. Ind. Gov.'s Conf. on Librs. and Info. Svcs., Indpls., 1976-78, mem. governance com., del. to conf., 1990; mem. Ind. State Libr. Adv. Coun., 1985-91; cons. in field. Contbr. articles to profl. jours. Fund-raiser Indpls. Mus. Art, 1971, Am. Cancer Soc., Indpls., 1975; vol. tchr. St. Thomas Aquinas Sch., Indpls., 1974-75; fund-raiser Am. Heart Assn., Indpls., 1985; bd. dirs., treas. Historic Amusement Found., Inc., Indpls., 1984-91; bd. advisors N.Am. Wildlife Park Found., Inc., Battle Ground, Ind., 1985-91, bd. dirs., 1991—; mem. adv. bd. Ind. U. Ctr. on Philanthropy, 1987-90. Recipient Outstanding Svc. award Ctrl. Ind. Area Libr. Svc. Authority, 1979, Outstanding Libr. award Ind. Libr.-Ind. Libr. Trustee Assn., 1988, Louise Maxwell award for Outstanding Achievement, 1989, William Jenkins award for Outstanding Svc. to Ind. U. Libr. and the Libr. Profession, 1996. Mem. ALA, Libr. Adminstrn. and Mgmt. Assn. (vice chair and chair elect fund raising and fin. devel. sect. 1991-92), Ind. State Libr. Adv. Coun., Midwest Fedn. Libr. Assns. (chmn. local arrangements for conf. 1986-87, sec. 1987—, bd. dirs. 1987-91), Ind. Libr. Assn. (chmn. coll. and univ. div. 1977-78, chmn. libr. edn. div. 1981-82, treas. 1984-86), German Shepherd Dog Club of Cen. Ind. (pres. 1978-79, treas. 1988-89, v.p. 1989-90, pres. 1990-93, bd. dirs. 1993—), Wabash Valley German Shepherd Dog Club (pres. 1982-83), Cen. Ind. Kennel Club (bd. dirs. 1984-86), Pi Kappa Lambda, Beta Phi Mu. Republican. Presbyterian. Avocations: ethology, horseback riding. Office: Ind-Purdue U 755 W Michigan St Indianapolis IN 46202-5195

FISH, STANLEY EUGENE, dean, language educator; b. Providence, Apr. 19, 1938; s. Max and Ida Dorothy (Weinberg) F.; m. Adrienne A. Aaron, Aug. 23, 1959 (div. 1980); 1 dau., Susan.; m. Jane Parry Tompkins, Aug. 7, 1982. BA, U. Pa., 1959; MA, Yale U., 1960, PhD, 1962. Instr. U. Calif., Berkeley, 1962-63, asst. prof., 1963-67, assoc. prof., 1967-69, prof., 1969-74; Kenan prof. English and Humanities Johns Hopkins U., Balt., 1978-85, chmn. dept., 1983-85; Arts and Sci. Disting. prof. English and prof. law Duke U., Durham, NC, 1985-98, chmn. dept., 1986-92; exec. dir. Duke U. Press, Durham, 1994-98; dean U. Ill. Coll. Liberal Arts and Scis., Chgo., 1999—2004; Davidson-Kahn Disting. Univ. Prof. humanities and Law Fla. Internat. U. Coll. Law, Miami, 2005—. Author: John Skelton's Poetry, 1965, Surprised by Sin: The Reader in Paradise Lost, 1967, 97 (Hanford Book award 1998), Seventeenth Century Prose: Modern Essays in Criticism, 1971, Self-Consuming Artifacts, 1972, The Living Temple: George Herbert and Catechizing, 1978, Is There a Text in This Class?, 1980, Doing What Comes Naturally, 1989, There's No Such Thing as Free Speech.And It's a Good Thing Too, 1994 (PEN/Spielvogel-Diamonstein award 1994), Professional Correctness: Literary Studies and Political Change, 1995, The Trouble with Principle, 1999, How Milton Works, 2001; mem. editl. bd. Milton Studies, Milton Quar. Recipient 2d place, Explicator prize, 1968; Am. Council Learned Socs. fellow, 1966; Guggenheim fellow, 1969 Mem. MLA, Am. Acad. Arts and Scis., Milton Soc. (hon. scholar 1991), Spenser Soc. Office: Fla Internat U Coll Law Univ Park Campus Green Library Ste 484 Miami FL 33199 Office Phone: 305-348-7820. Business E-Mail: fishs@fiv.edu.

FISHER, ALAN WASHBURN, historian, educator; b. Columbus, Ohio, Nov. 23, 1939; s. Sydney Nettleton and Elizabeth E. (Scipio) F.; m. Carol L. Garrett, Aug. 24, 1963; children: Elizabeth, Ann Christy, Garrett. BA, DePauw U., 1961; MA, Columbia U., 1964, PhD, 1967. Instr. history Mich. State U., East Lansing, 1966-67, asst. prof., 1967-70, assoc. prof., 1970-78, prof. Russian and Turkish history, 1978—2003, assoc. dean grad. studies and research, Coll. Arts and Letters, 1987-89, dir. Ctr. for Integrative Studies in Arts and Humanities, 1989-97, emeritus prof., 2003—. Author: Russian Annexation of the Crimea, 1772-1783, 1970, The Crimean Tatars, 1978, revised edit., 1987, Ottoman Studies Directory, I, 1979, II, 1981, III, 1983, Between Russians, Ottomans, and Turks: Crimea and Crimean Tatars, 1998, A Precarious Balance: Conflict, Trade and Diplomacy on the Russian-Ottoman Frontier, 1999. Am. Rsch. Inst. in Turkey fellow, 1969, 73, 76; Am. Coun. Learned Socs. grantee, 1976-77 Fellow Royal Hist. Soc., Turkish Hist. Assn. (corr.), Am. Rsch. Inst. Turkey (mem. bd. dels. 1990-99, v.p. 1995-99), Mid. East Studies Assn., Turkish Studies Assn. (pres. 1982-84, editor bull. 1984-87), Inst. Turkish Studies (dir. 1995-97, chmn. 1997-99). Home: 830 Lantern Hill Dr East Lansing MI 48823 Office Phone: 517-355-7500. Business E-Mail: fishera@msu.edu.

FISHER, CALVIN DAVID, food products executive; b. Nerstrand, Minn., June 10, 1926; s. Edward and Sadie (Wolf) F.; m. Patricia Vivian Capriotti, July 28, 1950; children: Cynthia, Nancy Joann, Michael. BS, U. Minn., 1950. Dairy specialist U.S. Dept. Agr., Mpls., 1950-54, chemist and dairy specialist Omaha, 1954-58; with Roberts Dairy Co., Omaha, 1958-80, sr. v.p., chief operating officer, 1967-70, pres., chief exec. officer, 1970-80, owner, chief exec. officer, 1975-80, Fisher Foods Ltd., Lincoln, Nebr., 1980—; pres., dir. Master Dairies, Indpls., 1968-80; bd. dirs. Internat. Assn. Ice Cream Mfrs. Milk Industry Found., 1973-80. Patentee spray-dried ice cream mix, pasteurized egg products. Bd. dirs., v.p. Omaha Safety Council, 1981; bd. dirs. Arthritis Found., 1972-81; mem. adv. council SBA; bd. dirs. Nebr. State Patrol Found., 1990—. With USN, 1944-47. Mem. Omaha C. of C. (pres.'s coun. 1976, 78), Internat. Food Scientists Assn., Inst. Food Tech., Nat. Ind. Dairies Assn., Rotary, Univ. Club (Lincoln), Firethorn Country Club. Republican. Methodist. Home: 18940 E Via Hermosa Rio Verde AZ 85263 Office: Fisher Foods Ltd 220 S 20th St Lincoln NE 68510-1007

FISHER, GORDON R., JR., lawyer; b. Oak Park, Illinois, Nov. 24, 1964; BA, U. Iowa, 1991; JD summa cum laude, So. Ill. Univ., 1994. Bar: 1994. Law clerk to Hon. Maynard J.V. Hayden Iowa Ct. Appeals, 1994—95; atty. Bradshaw, Fowler, Proctor & Fairgrave P.C. Chair Iowa Dem. Party, 2002—. Mem.: Defense Rsch. Inst. Inc., Iowa Defense Coun., ABA, Iowa State Bar Assn., Polk County Ethics Com. Democrat. Office: Bradshaw Fowler Proctor & Fairgrave PC 801 Grand Ave Ste 3700 Des Moines IA 50309 Mailing: Iowa Democratic Party Chair 5661 Fleur Dr Des Moines IA 50321

FISHER, JAMES LEE, lawyer; b. Akron, Ohio, Apr. 10, 1944; s. James Lee and Maxine (Sumner) Fisher; m. Nancy Lorenz, Dec. 20, 1980. BSCE, U. Akron, 1968, JD, 1971. Bar: Ohio 1971. Staff atty. Brunswick Mgmt. Co., Akron, 1972-77; prin. James L. Fisher Co., L.P.A., Akron, 1977-88, Buckingham, Doolittle & Burroughs, Akron, 1988—. City planner City of Akron, 1968—71, cmty. devel. atty., 1971—73; mem. Metro Regional Transit Authority Bd., 1992—; sec.-treas. Summit County Planning Commn., 1978—99. Mem.: ABA, Ohio Planning Conf., Am. Planning Assn., Home Builders Assn., Akron Bar Assn., Ohio Bar Assn., Copley Lions (pres. 1982). Republican. Mem. United Ch. Of Christ. Home: 1135 Forest Pool Rd Akron OH 44333-1509 Office: Buckingham Doolittle & Burroughs 3800 Embassy Pkwy Akron OH 44333

FISHER, JAMES R., lawyer; b. South Bend, Ind., Apr. 15, 1947; s. Russell Humphries and Virginia Opal (Maple) F.; m. Cynthia Ann Winters, Aug. 14, 1971; children: Gabriel Christopher, Cory Andrew. AB in Psychology, Ind. U., 1969, JD summa cum laude, 1972. Bar: Ind. 1972, U.S. Dist. Ct. (so. dist.) Ind. 1972. Ptnr. Ice Miller, Indpls., 1971—. Co-author: Personal Injury Law and Practices vol. 23 of Indiana Practice series; contbr. articles to legal publs. Mem. ATLA, Ind. Bar Assn., Ind. Trial Lawyers Assn., Order of Coif. Office: Ice Miller 1 Am Sq PO Box 82001 Indianapolis IN 46282 E-mail: james.fisher@icemiller.com.

FISHER, JOHN JAMES, advertising executive; b. St. Louis, Mar. 23, 1941; s. Benjamin Edwards Fisher and Beulah Fay (Tucker) Hughes; m. Beverly Firth Brown, June 7, 1962; children: John J. Jr., Jennifer Leigh. BBA in Mktg., Memphis State U., 1964. Sales rep. Pfizer Labs., Memphis, 1965-69, product mgr. NYC, 1969-71; account exec. L.W. Froelich Inc., NYC, 1971-72; account supr. Lavey/Wolff/Swift Inc., NYC, 1972-74, v.p., account supr., 1974-76, sr. v.p., dir. client svcs., 1976-78; exec. v.p. Frank J. Corbett Inc., Chgo., 1978-80, pres., 1980-91, chmn., chief exec. officer, 1991—. Exec. v.p. Health and Med. Com., .Y.C., 1986-92, chmn., CEO, 1993—. Contbr. articles to profl. jours. Chmn. Rep. Com., Weston, Conn., 1970-78; mgr. campaign state rep. and senator, Weston, 1974, congl. dist., Weston, 1977. Mem. Med. Mktg. Assn., Biomed. Mktg. Assn., Pharm. Advt. Coun., Midwest Pharm. Advt. Coun. (pres. 1984-85, Sweeny award 1985), Biltmore Country Club (Barrington, Ill.), N.Y. Athletic Club. Avocation: golf. Office: Frank J Corbett Inc 211 E Chicago Ave Ste 1600 Chicago IL 60611-2660

FISHER, JOHN W., insurance company executive; With Auto-Owners Ins., Lansing, Mich., 1978—, pres., 1993—. Pres., bd. dirs. Lake Country Corp.; dir. Mut. Reinsurance Bur. Mem.: Nat. Assn. Mut. Ins. Cos. (chmn. 2002—03). Office: Auto Owners Ins PO Box 30660 6101 Anacapri Blvd Lansing MI 48917

FISHER, LAWRENCE L., lawyer; b. Mt. Sterling, Ohio, Jan. 4, 1941; BS, Ohio State U., 1964; postgrad., U. Bonn, Germany; JD, Harvard U., 1967. Bar: Ohio 1967. Mem. Vorys, Sater, Seymour & Pease, Columbus, Ohio. Fellow Am. Coll. Trust and Estate Counsel; mem. ABA, Ohio State Bar Assn. (chmn. probate and trust law sect. 1979-80), Columbus Bar Assn. (Community Svc. award 1976-77), Phi Eta Sigma. Office: Vorys Sater Seymour & Pease PO Box 1008 52 E Gay St Columbus OH 43216

FISHER, LEE I., lieutenant governor, former state attorney general; b. Ann Arbor, Mich., Aug. 7, 1951; m. Peggy Zone Fisher; children: Jason, Jessica. Grad., Oberlin Coll., 1973; JD, Case Western Res. U. Law clk. US Ct. Appeals (6th cir.); mem. firm. Hahn Loeser and Parks, Cleve.; mem. Ohio Gen. Assembly, 1981—82, Ohio State Senate, 1982—90; atty. gen. State of Ohio, Columbus, Ohio, 1991—95; pres., CEO Ctr. for Families and Children, 1999—2006; lt. gov. State of Ohio, 2007—. Chair Nat. Commn. Crime Ctrl. and Prevention; mem., World Bd. Governors United Svc. Organizations. Contbr. articles to profl. jours. Founder, co-chair Mental Health Advocacy Coalition; bd. mem. Cleve. Clinic Cancer Ctr., Nat. Ctr. for Missing and Exploited Children, Oberlin Coll. Recipient Visionary Innovation in Bus. award, Medical Mutual, 2001, Nonprofit Exec. of Yr. award, Smart Bus. mag., 2004. Mem. Greater Cleveland Bar Assn. (Merit Svc. award), Ohio Acad. Trial Lawyers (Legislator of Yr.), Case Western Res. U. Alumni Assn. (Disting. Recent Grad. award). Democrat. Office: Lieutenant Governor 77 High St 23rd Fl Columbus OH 43215 Office Phone: 614-466-3636. Office Fax: 614-644-0575.

FISHER, LESTER EMIL, retired zoo administrator; b. Chgo., Feb. 24, 1921; s. Louis and Elizabeth (Vodicka) F.; m. Wendy Fisher, Jan. 23, 1981; children: Jane Serrita, Katherine Clark. MDV, Iowa State U., 1943. Supr. animal care program Northwestern U. Med. Sch., 1946-47; attending veterinarian Lincoln Park Zoo, Chgo., 1947-62, zoo dir., 1962-92, dir. emeritus, 1992—; owner, dir. Berwyn (Ill.) Animal Hosp., 1947-68. Producer, moderator ednl. closed circuit TV for nat. vet. meetings, 1949-66; asso. prof. dept. biology DePaul U., 1968-98; adj. prof. zoology U. Ill., from 1972 Editor: Brit. Small Animal Jour. and Small Animal Clinician, 1958-72. Mem. citizens com. U. Ill.; chmn. zoo and wildlife div. Morris Animal Found. Served to maj., Vet. Corps AUS, 1943-46. Recipient Alumni Merit award Iowa State U., 1968, Stange award Iowa State U., 1988, Chgo. Superior Pub. Svc. award Chgo. Park Dist., 1973, 92, Laureate Ill. Lincoln Acad., 1993. Mem. Am. Animal Hosp. Assn. (regional dir., outstanding Service award 1969), Am. Vet. Med. Assn., Nat. Recreation and Park Assn., Internat. Union Dirs. Zool. Gardens (v.p. 1980-83, pres. 1983-86), Am. Assn. Zoo Veterinarians (pres. 1966-69), Am. Assn. Zool. Parks and Aquariums (pres. 1972-73, chmn. gorilla species survival plan 1982-92), Chgo. Geographic Soc. (v.p.), Adventures Club (pres. 1971-72), Execs. Club of Chgo. (bd. dirs. 1968-71), Arts Assoc., Chgo. Econs. Club (membership com.), Theta Xi. Home: 3180 N Lake Shore Dr Chicago IL 60657

FISHER, LLOYD EDISON, JR., lawyer; b. Medina, Ohio, Oct. 23, 1923; s. Lloyd Edison and Wanda (White) F.; m. Twylla Dawn Peterson, Sept. 11, 1949 (dec. Apr. 1996); children: Karen S., Kirk P. BS, Ohio State U., 1947, JD, 1949. Bar: Ohio 1950. Mem. gen. hearing bd. Ohio Dept. Taxation, 1950-53; trust officer Huntington Nat. Bank, Columbus, 1953-62; ptnr. Porter, Wright, Morris & Arthur and predecessor firm, Columbus, 1962—. Adj. prof. law Ohio State U., Columbus, 1967—69, Columbus, 1984—91. Bd. dirs Wesley Glen Retirement Ctr., 1974-80, 88-95, Home Reach Hospice, 1997—. Served with AUS, 1943-45. Fellow Am. Coll. Trust and Estate Counsel; mem. ABA, Ohio Bar Assn., Columbus Bar Assn., Order of Coif. Home: 6478 Strathaven Ct E Worthington OH 43085-2985 Office: 41 S High St Columbus OH 43215-6101 Office Phone: 614-227-2285. Business E-Mail: lfisher@porterwright.com.

FISHER, MICHELE RENEE, lawyer; b. Champlin, Minn., May 29, 1974; BA in Criminal Justice and Spanish, St. Cloud U., 1997; JD, William Mitchell Coll. Law, 2000. Bar: Minn. 2000, US Dist. Ct. (dist. Colo.), US Dist. Ct. (dist. Minn.), Minn. Supreme Ct. Assoc., mem. nat. wage and hour litig. team Nichols, Kaster & Anderson, P.L.L.P., Mpls. Named a Rising Star, Minn. Super Lawyers mag., 2006. Mem.: Assn. Trial Lawyers of Am., Fed. Bar Assn., Minn. Women Lawyers, ABA, Minn. State Bar Assn., Hennepin County Bar Assn., Nat. Employment Lawyers Assn. Office: Nichols Kaster & Anderson PLLP 4600 IDS Ctr 80 S 8th St Minneapolis MN 55402 Office Phone: 612-256-3229. E-mail: fisher@nka.com.

FISHER, NEAL FLOYD, religious organization administrator; b. Washington, Ind., Apr. 4, 1936; s. Floyd Russell and Florence Alice (Williams) F.; m. Ila Alexander, Aug. 18, 1957; children: Edwin Kirk, Julia Bryn. AB, DePauw U., 1957, LHD (hon.), 1982; MDiv, Boston U., 1960, PhD, 1966; STD, MacMurray Coll., Jacksonville, Ill., 1991; DD, Coe Coll., 1994. Ordained to ministry United Meth. Ch., 1958; pastor 1st United Meth. Ch., Revere, Mass., 1960-63, North Andover, Mass., 1963-68; planning assoc. United Meth. Bd. Global Ministries, NYC, 1968-73, dir. planning, 1973-77; assoc. dean, asst. prof. theology and society Boston U. Sch. Theology, 1977-80; pres., prof. theology and society Garrett-Evang. Theol. Sem., Evanston, Ill., 1980-2001, pres. emeritus, sr. scholar, 2001—. Mendenhall lectr. DePauw U., Greencastle, Ind., 1982, Willson lectr., Nashville, 1983, Voigt lectr. McKendree Coll., 1984, McKendree Blair lectr. MacMurray Coll., 1986, Henry Martin Loud lectr. U. Mich., Ann Arbor, 1987; Wright lectr. Morningside Coll., 1991, Bransford lectr., 1999; chaplain, preacher, Chautauqua, NY, 1984, 88, Lakeside, Ohio, 1996; mem. theol. edn. commn. United Meth. Ch., 1992-2000, former mem. univ. senate; mem. bd. of ordained ministry No. Ill. Conf. United Meth. Ch.; chmn. com. on acad. affairs DePauw U. Bd. Trustees. Author: Parables of Jesus: Glimpses of the New Age, 1979, rev. edit., 1990, Context for Discovery, 1980, Parables of Jesus: Glimpses of God's Reign, 1990; contbg. editor: Truth and Tradition: A Conversation about the Future of United Methodist Theological Education, 1995. Trustee DePauw U., Greencastle, Ind., 1996-2000; mem. bd. visitors Boston U. Sch. Theology, 2002-05, bd. overseers, 2006—. Recipient Disting. Alumnus award Boston U. Sch. Theology, 1985, Disting. Alumni citation DePauw U., 1993; Jacob Sleeper fellow, 1960-61. Mem. Assn. United Meth. Scis., Assn. Chgo. Theol. Schs. (pres. 1985-87, 95-97). Mem. United Methodist Ch. Home: 2008 Elmore Pond Road Wolcott VT 05680 Business E-Mail: nfisher@garrett.edu.

FISHER, PIERRE JAMES, JR., physician; b. Chgo., Oct. 29, 1931; s. Pierre James and Evelyn F.; m. Carol Ann Walton, Mar. 16, 1951; children: James Walton, David Alan, Steven Edward, Teresa Ann. Student, Taylor U., 1949-51, Ball State U., 1951-52; MD, Ind. U., 1956. Diplomate Am. Bd. Surgery. Intern U.S. Naval Hosp., San Diego, 1956-57, resident in surgery, 1957-61; pvt. practice specializing in surgery Surgeons Inc., Marion, Ind., 1965—, pres., 1977—; mem. staff Marion Gen. Hosp., chief staff, 1970. Trustee Meth. Hosp., Indpls., 1972-94; bd. dirs. Charlotte County Cultural Ctr., 2005—. Served with USN, 1956-65. Recipient Physicians Recognition award AMA, 1974, 77, 80, 83, 89. Fellow ACS; mem. AMA, Grant County Med. Soc. (pres. 1980), Marion Area C. of C. (v.p. 1979-81), N.Am. Med. Golf Assn. (v.p. 1979-90, pres. 1991-93), Rotary (pres. Marion 1983-84, Dist. 656 Disting. Svc. award 1989), Kingsway Country Club (bd. dirs., pres. 1997-99), Royal Order of Ponce de Leon Conquistadors (treas. 2000-). Methodist. Home: 11250 SW Essex Dr Lake Suzy FL 34269 Office: Surgeons Inc 330 N Wabash Ave Ste 450 Marion IN 46952-2600 Personal E-mail: fpjfisher@aol.com.

FISHER, REBECCA RHODA, lawyer; b. Milw., 1971; BA in Polit. Sci., U. Minn., Mpls., 1993; JD, William Mitchell Coll. Law, St. Paul, 1999. Bar: Minn. 1999, US Dist. Ct. (dist. Minn.) 2000, Wis. 2005. Law clk. criminal appeals Office of Minn. Atty. Gen., 1998—99; assoc. Ramsey & DeVore, 1999—2003; atty. Law Office of Rebecca Rhoda Fisher, P.L.L.C., Roseville, Minn. Contbr. articles to profl. publs. Named a Rising Star, Minn. Super Lawyers mag., 2006; named one of Up and Coming Attys., Minn. Lawyer, 2004. Mem.: Nat. Assn. Criminal Def. Lawyers, Minn. Assn. Criminal Def. Lawyers, Minn. Soc. Criminal Justice, ABA, Minn. Women Lawyers, Warren E. Burger Inn of Ct., Ramsey County Bar Assn., Minn. State Bar Assn. (chair criminal law sect. 2006—, vice chair criminal law sect. 2005—06, sec., treas. criminal law sect. 2003—05, chair new lawyers sect. 2005—06, vice chair new lawyers sect. 2004—05, sect. new lawyers sect. 2003—04). Office: Law Office of Rebecca Rhoda Fisher PLLC 2589 Hamline Ave North Ste B Roseville MN 55113 Office Phone: 651-251-3838. E-mail: rebecca@rrflaw.com.

FISHER, RONALD C., economics educator; b. Schenectady, Feb. 26, 1950; s. William K. and Agnes M. (McNulty) F.; children: Michael, Charles. BA in Chemistry, Mich. State U., 1972; MA in Econs., Brown U., 1974, PhD in Econs., 1977. Research economist U.S. Adv. Commn. on Interngovtl. Relations, Washington, 1975-76; prof. econs. Mich. State U., East Lansing, 1976—, prof. econs., chmn. dept. econs., 1988-92, dean Honors Coll., 1996—; dep. state treas. Mich. Dept. Treasury, Lansing, 1983-85. Bd. dirs. Ind. Bus. Rsch. Office of Mich., Detroit, 1988-92; vis. fellow Australian Nat. U., 1992; cons. to the U.S. Adv. Commn. on Intergovtl. Rels., U.S. Dept. HUD, U.S. Dept. Treasury, States of Ariz., Conn., Maine, Mich., Minn., N.J., W.Va., D.C., and P.R. Author: State and Local Public Finance, 1989, 96; contbr. articles to profl. jours. Exec. dir. Gov.'s Study Group on Govt. Expenditures, Hartford, 1978-79. NSF grantee, 1980. Mem. Am. Econ. Assn., Nat. Tax Assn., Assn. for Pub. Policy Analysis and Mgmt., Midwest Econ. Assn. Office: Mich State U Honors Coll East Lansing MI 48824

FISHER, THOMAS GEORGE, lawyer, retired media company executive; b. Debrecen, Hungary, Oct. 2, 1931; came to U.S., 1951; s. Eugene J. and Viola Elizabeth (Rittersporn) F.; m. Rita Knisley, Feb. 14, 1960; children: Thomas G. Jr., Katherine F. Vaaler. BS, Am. U., 1957, JD, 1959; postgrad., Harvard U., 1956. Bar: D.C. 1959, Iowa 1977. Atty. FCC, Washington, 1959-61, 65-66; pvt. law practice, 1961-65, 66-69; asst. counsel Meredith Corp., NYC, 1969-72, assoc. gen. counsel Des Moines, 1972-76, gen. counsel, 1976-80, v.p. gen. counsel, 1980-94, corp. sec., 1988-94, ret., 1994. Comml law liaison ABA Ctr. and East European Law Initiative, Krakow, Poland, 1994—95; atty. Iowa Legal Aid, 1996—. Contbr. articles to profl. jours. Bd. dirs. Des Moines Met. Opera Co., Indianola, 1980-94, pres., 1990-91; bd. dirs. Civic Music Assn., Des Moines, 1982-92, pres., 1987-88; chmn. legis. com. Greater Des Moines C. of C., 1976-77; bd. dirs. Legal Aid Soc. Polk County, 1986-93, pres., 1993. With U.S. Army, 1952-54. Mem. ABA, Iowa State Bar Assn. (chmn. corp. counsel subcom. 1979-82), Polk County Bar Assn., Embassy Club. Office: Iowa Legal Aid Ste 230 1111 9th St Des Moines IA 50314-2527 Office Phone: 515-243-1198 ext. 1687.

FISHER, THOMAS GEORGE, JR., lawyer; b. Washington, June 1, 1961; s. Thomas George and Rita (Knisley) F.; m. Susan Jane Koenig, June 23, 1990. BA, Iowa State U., 1983; JD with high distinction, U. Iowa, 1986. Bar: Iowa 1986, U.S. Dist. Ct. (so. dist.), Iowa 1987, U.S. Ct. Appeals (8th cir.) 1987, U.S. Dist. Ct. (no. dist.) Iowa 1993. Jud. clk. Iowa Supreme Ct., Davenport, 1986-87; assoc. Duncan, Jones, Riley & Finley, P.C., Des Moines, 1987-91; asst. atty. gen. State of Iowa, Justice Dept., Des Moines, 1991-95; counsel Am. Mut. Life Ins. Co., Des Moines, 1995-96; ptnr. Hogan & Fisher, PLC, Des Moines, 1997—2003, Whitfield & Eddy, P.L.C., Des Moines, 2003—04; atty. in pvt. practice, 2004—. Mem. Des Moines Leadership Inst., 1998—99; candidate Iowa Ho. of Reps. Dists. 73, 1994; precinct chair Polk County Dem. Party, Des Moines, 1988—90, 1994—96, 1998—2000, 2002—; bd. dirs., chair Metro Arts Alliance of Greater Des Moines; bd. dirs. Des Moines Emergency Food Pantry, Iowa Forest Heritage Found. Mem. Blackstone Inn of Ct. Democrat. Roman Catholic. Office: 100 Walnut St Ste 324 Des Moines IA 50309 Office Phone: 515-288-1901. E-mail: tfisher@dwx.com.

FISK, LENNARD AYRES, physicist, researcher; b. Elizabeth, NJ, July 7, 1943; s. Lennard Ayres and Elinor (Fischer) F.; m. Patricia Elizabeth Leuba, Dec. 28, 1966; children: Ian, Justin, Nathan. AB, Cornell U., 1965; PhD, U. Calif., San Diego, 1969. Postdoctoral fellow NASA/Goddard Space Flight Ctr., Greenbelt, MD., 1969-71, astrophysicist, 1971-77; assoc. prof. U. N.H., Durham, 1977-81, prof., 1981-87, dir. rsch., 1982-83, interim v.p./fin. affairs, 1983-84, v.p. rsch. and fin., 1984-87; assoc. administr. space sci. and applications NASA Hdqrs., Washington, 1987-93; prof. U. Mich., 1993—. Advisor NAS, NASA, 1980-87. Contbr. more than 120 articles to profl. jours. Recipient Space Science award Am. Inst. Aeronautics and Astronautics, 1994. Fellow Am. Geophys. Union; mem. Internat. Acad. Astronautics, Academia Europaea (fgn. mem.). Office: Univ of Michigan Atmos Oceanic & Space Scis 2455 Hayward St Ann Arbor MI 48109-2143

FISK, MARTIN H., lawyer; b. St. Paul, Apr. 11, 1947; BA, U. Minn., 1969; JD, Harvard U., 1976. Bar: Minn. 1976. Mem. Briggs and Morgan P.A., St. Paul, shareholder. Recipient Best Lawyers in Am., 2006. Mem. ABA, Phi Beta Kappa. Office: Briggs and Morgan PA 332 Minnesota St W 2200 1st Nat Bank Bldg Saint Paul MN 55101-3210 Office Phone: 651-808-6522. Office Fax: 651-808-6450. Business E-Mail: mfisk@briggs.com.

FISKE, NEIL S., retail executive; b. Colo. Degree in Polit. Economy, Williams Coll.; MBA, Harvard U. Polit. speechwriter; bus. cons. Boston Consulting Group, 1989—99, mng. ptnr., 2000—02; CEO Bath & Body Works, Inc., Reynoldsburg, Ohio, 2003—07; pres., CEO Eddie Bauer Holdings, Inc., Redmond, Wash., 2007—. Bd. dirs. Eddie Bauer Holdings, Inc., 2007—. Co-author (with Michael Silverstein): Trading Up: The New American Luxury, 2003. Past legis. adv. Congressman and Senator Timothy E. Wirth. Office: Eddie Bauer Holdings Inc 15010 NE 36th St Redmond WA 98052

FITCH, COY DEAN, internist, educator; b. Marthaville, La., Oct. 5, 1934; s. Raymond E. and Joey (Youngblood) F.; m. Rachel Farr, Mar. 31, 1956; children: Julia Anne, Jaquelyn Kay. BS, U. Ark., 1956, MS, MD, U. Ark., 1958. Diplomate Am. Bd. Internal Medicine and Endocrinology. Intern U. Ark. Sch. Medicine, 1958—59, resident, 1959—62, instr. biochemistry, 1959—62, asst. prof. medicine and biochemistry, 1962—66, dir. honors med. student rsch. program, 1965—67, asso. prof., 1966—67; practice medicine, specializing in internal medicine Little Rock, 1962—67; asso. prof. internal medicine and biochemistry St. Louis U. Sch. Medicine, 1967—73, prof. internal medicine, 1973—, prof. biochemistry, 1976—, head sect. metabolism, 1969—76, dir. div. endocrinology and metabolism, 1977—85; practice medicine, specializing in internal medicine St. Louis, 1969—; chief med. service St. Louis U. Hosps., 1976—77, vice-chmn. dept. internal medicine, 1983—85, acting chmn. dept. internal medicine, 1985—88, chmn. dept., 1988—2000; chief med. svc. St. Louis VA Med. Ctr., 2005—. Dir. Diabetic Clinic, U. Ark. Med. Ctr., 1962-67, head sect. metabolism and endocrinology, 1966-67; mem. nutrition study sect. div. research grants NIH, 1967-71 Assoc. editor: Nutrition Revs., 1964; contbr. articles to profl. jours. Served from capt. to lt. col., M.C. AUS, 1967-69. Recipient Lederle Med. Faculty award, 1966-67; Russell M. Wilder-Nat. Vitamin Found. fellow, 1959-62. Master ACP (gov. Mo. chpt. 1995-99); mem. Am. Inst. Nutrition, Am. Soc. Biol. Chemists, Ctrl. Soc. Clin. Rsch., Phi Beta Kappa. Office: VAMC 111JC 915 N Grand Blvd Saint Louis MO 63106-1621 Office Phone: 314-289-7030. Business E-Mail: coy.fitch@va.gov.

FITCH, FRANK WESLEY, pathologist, immunologist, dean, educator; b. Bushnell, Ill., May 30, 1929; s. Harold Wayne and Mary Gladys (Frank) F.; m. Shirley Dobbins, Dec. 23, 1951; children— Mary Margaret, Mark Howard. MD, U. Chgo., 1953, S.M., 1957, PhD, 1960; MD (hon.), U. Lausanne, Switzerland, 1990. Postdoctoral research fellow USPHS, 1954-55, 57-58; faculty U. Chgo., 1957—, prof. pathology, 1967—, Albert D. Lasker prof. med. sci., 1976—, emeritus prof., 1996, assoc. dean med. and grad. edn. div. biol. scis., 1976-85, dean acad. affairs, 1985-86, dir. Ben May Inst., 1986-95. Vis. prof. Swiss Inst. Exptl. Cancer Research, Lausanne, Switzerland, 1974-75. Editor-in-chief The Jour. of Immunology, 1997-2002; contbr. chpts. to books, articles to profl. jours. Recipient Borden Undergrad. Research award, 1953, Lederle Med. Faculty award, 1958-61; Markle Found. scholar, 1961-66; Commonwealth Fund fellow U. Lausanne (Switzerland) Institut de Biochimie, 1965-66; Guggenheim fellow, 1974-75 Mem. Fedn. Am. Socs. for Exptl. Biology (pres. 1993-94), Am. Assn. Immunologists (pres. 1992-93), Am. Soc. for Investigative Pathology, Am. Assn. for Cancer Rsch., Chgo. Path. Soc., Transplantation Soc., Sigma Xi, Alpha Omega Alpha. Business E-Mail: ffitch@uchicago.edu.

FITZ, BROTHER RAYMOND L., university president; b. Akron, Ohio, Aug. 12, 1941; s. Raymond L. and Mary Lou (Smith) F. BS in Elec. Engring., U. Dayton, Ohio, 1964; MS, Poly. Inst. Bklyn., 1967, PhD, 1969. Joined Soc. of Mary, Roman Catholic Ch., 1960; mem. faculty U. Dayton, 1968—, prof. elec. engring. and engring. mgmt., 1975—, exec. dir. Center Christian Renewal, 1974-79, univ. pres., 1979—. Author numerous papers, reports in field. Bd. dirs. various civic organs. Recipient Disting. Alumnus award Poly. Inst. Bklyn., 1980 Office: U Dayton 300 College Park Ave Rm 207 Dayton OH 45469-0001

FITZGERALD, CAROL E., state legislator; b. Mar. 2, 1933; m. Quinten Fitzgerald. Mem. SD Ho. of Reps. from 33rd Dist., until 2000, mem. agr. and natural resources and judiciary coms.; rental mgr., until 2000. Home: 5625 Cleghorn Canyon Rd Rapid City SD 57702-9417

FITZGERALD, GERALD FRANCIS, retired banker; b. Chgo., July 6, 1925; s. John J. and Olivia (Trader) F.; m. Marjorie Webb Gosselin, Sept. 10, 1949; children: Gerald Francis Jr., James Gosselin, Thomas Gosselin, Julie Ann Fitzgerald Schauer, Peter Gosselin. BS in Commerce, Northwestern U., 1949. Salesman Premier Printing Co., 1949-53; founder, ptnr. Fitzgerald & Cooke (now Hill and Knowlton, Inc. div. J. Walter Thompson), 1953-60, v.p., 1960-64; chmn. Lake Villa Trust & Savs. Bank, 1961-69, Palatine Nat. Bank, 1961-87, Suburban Nat. Bank of Palatine, Suburban Bank of Hoffman-Schaumburg, Suburban Bank of Cary-Grove, Suburban Bank of Rolling Meadows, Suburban Bank of Barrington, Suburban Bank of Bartlett, 1964-90; pres. Suburban Bancorp, Inc., Palatine, 1982-90, chmn., 1982-94, So. Colo. Bank Holding Co., 1991—, Citizens Bank of Pagosa Springs, 1991-94. Cons. Am. Del. to NATO CCMS, Brussels, 1976; former chmn. Suburban Computer Svcs. Corp., Palatine; lectr. in banking field. Contbr. articles to profl. jours. Bd. dirs., past pres. Inverness Assn.; former mem. Govs. Adv. Coun. of Ill.; past mem. Ill. Racing Bd.; mem. Chgo. Coun. of Fgn. Rels.; cons. Portsmouth, R.I. Abbey Sch., 1978-80; life trustee Newberry Libr.; mem. John Evans Club, Northwestern U. Sgt. U.S. Army, 1944-46, ETO. Mem. Ill. Thoroughbred Owners and Breeders Found., Nat. Assn. of State Racing Commrs., Newcomen Soc., Max McGraw's Wildlife Found., Chgo. Athletic Assn., Inverness Golf Club, Safari Internat. Club, Caxton Club, Delta Upsilon. Avocations: travel, opera, rare books, photography, hunting. Home: 19 Creekside Ln Barrington IL 60010-9343 Office: 50 N Brockway St Palatine IL 60067-5076 E-mail: GFFSrSecretary@harrisbank.com.

FITZGERALD, JAMES FRANCIS, broadcast executive; b. Janesville, Wis., Mar. 27, 1926; s. Michael Henry and Chloris Helen (Beiter) F.; m. Marilyn Field Cullen, Aug. 1, 1950; children: Michael Dennis, Brian Nicholas, Marcia O'Loughlin, James Francis, Carolyn Jane, Ellen Putnam. BS, Notre Dame U., 1947; LLD, U. Wis., Whitewater, 1999; LHD, Baldwin-Wallace U., 2001. With Std. Oil Co. (Ind.), Milw., 1947-48; pres. F.-W. Oil Co., Janesville, 1950—, Total TV, Inc. (cable TV Systems), Wis., 1965-86. Bd. dirs. Milw. Ins. Co., Bank One, Janesville N.A.; chmn. bd. Golden State Warriors, Oakland, Calif., 1986-95, Total TV Calif., 1987-96. Bd. govs., chmn. TV com. NBA; chmn. bd., pres. S.P.A.C.E. Inc. subs. Milw. Bucks NBA team, 1976-85; chmn. Greater Milw. Open PGA Tournament, 1985, Notre Dame Bus. Adv. Coun., 1989—. Lt. (j.g.) USNR, 1944-46, 51-53. Named to Wis. Sports Hall of Fame, 1999, Wis. Bus. Hall of Fame, 2001. Mem. Chief Execs. Forum, World Bus. Coun., Wis. Petroleum Assn. (pres. 1961-62), The Quarry at LaQuinta, Janesville Country Club, Vintage Club (pres. 1989-91), San Francisco Golf Club, El Dorado Country Club. Roman Catholic. Home and Office: PO Box 348 Janesville WI 53547-0348

FITZGERALD, JAMES PATRICK, lawyer; BA, U. Nebr., 1968; JD, Creighton U., 1974. Bar: Nebr. 1974, U.S. Dist. Ct. Nebr. 1974, U.S. Ct. Appeals (8th cir.) 1974. Law clk. U.S. Dist. Ct. Nebr., Omaha, 1974-76; atty. McGrath, North, Mullin & Kratz, P.C., Omaha, 1976—. With U.S. Army, 1968-71. Mem. ABA, Nebr. Bar Assn., Assn. Trial Lawyers Am., Nebr. Assn. Trial Attys., Def. Rsch. Inst. Home: 16728 Jones Cir Omaha NE 68118-2711 Office: McGrath North Mullin & Kratz 1601 Dodge St Ste 3700 Omaha NE 68102 Home Phone: 402-334-3543; Office Phone: 402-341-3070.

FITZGERALD, JAMES T., architect; BA in Philosophy, Josephinum Coll.; BArch, U. Notre Dame. Cert. Nat. Coun. Archtl. Registration Bd.; registered architect 31 states. Chmn., CEO FRCH Design Worldwide (previously Space Design Internat.), 1968—. Spkr. in field; tchr. U. Cin. Coll. of Design, Architecture, Art and Planning; bd. advisors Kirk & Blum Co. Former chmn. steering com. for downtown retail devel. strategy City of Cin.; v.p., trustee Contemporary Arts Ctr., Cin.; bd. dirs. Archtl. Found., Cin.; trustee Cin. Opera. Fellow AIA (former pres. Cin. chpt., former nat. chmn. interiors com., vice chmn. internat. com.), Internat. Coun. Shopping Ctrs., Urban Land Inst., Am. Arbitration Assn., Nat. Retail Fedn. Office: FRCH Design Worldwide 311 Elm St Ste 600 Cincinnati OH 45202-2737

FITZGERALD, JEFF, state representative; b. Chgo., Oct. 12, 1966; married; 1 child. BS, U. Wis., Oshkosh, 1989. Small bus. owner; state assembly mem. Wis. State Assembly, Madison, 2000—, mem. campaigns and elections, criminal justice, econ. devel., fin. instns., housing, and labor and workforce devel. coms. Mem. Beaver Dam City Coun., Wis., 2000—; former chair Beaver Dam Rep. Party; mem. cmty. rels. bd. Fox Lake Correctional Inst., Wis. Mem.: Beaver Dam C. of C., Juneau (Wis.) C. of C. Republican. Office: State Capitol Rm 308 N PO Box 8952 Madison WI 53708-8952

FITZGERALD, JEREMIAH MICHAEL, lawyer; BSBA, Xavier U., 1975; JD, U. Chgo., 1978. Bar: Ill. 1978. Asst. sec., asst. gen. counsel Comdisco Inc., Rosemont, Ill., v.p., asst. sec., gen. counsel, 1989—. Office: Comdisco 5600 N River Rd Ste 800 Rosemont IL 60018-5166

FITZGERALD, KELLY PATRICK, lawyer; BA in Physics with distinction, U. Iowa, 1997, JD magna cum laude, 2000. Bar: Minn. Legal clk., patent agt. Intermec Technologies Corp.; atty. Fish & Richardson, Shumaker & Sieffert, P.A., St. Paul, 2001—. Named a Rising Star, Minn. Super Lawyers mag., 2006. Mem.: Am. Intellectual Property Law Assn., Minn. Intellectual Property Law Assn., Minn. Bar Assn. Office: Shumaker & Sieffert PA 8425 Seasons Pky Ste 105 Saint Paul MN 55125 Office Phone: 651-286-8343. E-mail: fitzgerald@ssiplaw.com.

FITZGERALD, MICHAEL LEE, state official; b. Marshalltown, Iowa, Nov. 29, 1951; s. James Martin and Clara Francis (Dankbar) F.; m. Janet Roewe; children: Ryan, Chris, Erin, Bridie. BBA, U. Iowa, 1974. Campaign mgr. Fitzgerald for Treas., Colo., Iowa, 1974; market analyst Massey Ferguson Co., Des Moines, 1975-83; treas. State of Iowa, Des Moines, 1983—. Mem.: Am. Soc. Pub. Adminstr., Govt. Fin. Officers Assn., Nat. Assn. Unclaimed Property Adminstr. (past pres.), Nat. Assn. State Auditors, Comptrollers, and Treasurers (past pres.), Midwest Treasurer's Assn. (past pres.), Nat. Assn. State Treasurers (past pres.). Democrat. Roman Catholic. Office: Office of State Treas Capitol Bldg Rm 114 Des Moines IA 50319-0001 Office Phone: 515-281-5368. Office Fax: 515-281-7562. Business E-Mail: treasurer@iowa.gov.

FITZGERALD, PATRICK J., JR., prosecutor; b. Bklyn., Dec. 22, 1960; s. Patrick and Tillie Fitzgerald. BA in Econ. and Math., Amherst Coll., 1982; JD, Harvard U., 1985. Litigation assoc. Christy & Viener, 1984—87; asst. US atty. (So. Dist.) NY US Dept. Justice, 1988—2001, chief narcotics unit, 1994, co-chief organized crime-terrorism unit, 1995—2001, nat. security coord., 1996—99, US atty. (no. dist.) Ill., 2001—. Prosecutor in case against Sheikh Omar Abdel Rahman for 1993 World Trade Ctr. bombings US Dept. Justice, 1994, mem. atty. gen's advisory com., 2001—05, spl. prosecutor investigating government leak in the identification of Valerie Plame as a CIA operative, 2003—; mem. Pres. Corp. Fraud Task Force. Named Lawyer of the Yr., Nat. Law Jour., 2005; recipient Atty. Gen.'s award for Exceptional Service, 1996,

Stimson Medal, NY Bar Assoc., 1997, Atty. Gen.'s award for Dist. Svc., 2002. Mem.: Phi Beta Kappa Soc. Office: US Dist Ct No Dist Ill Dirksen Federal Bldg 219 S Dearborn St 5th Fl Chicago IL 60604

FITZGERALD, PETER GOSSELIN, banker former senator, lawyer; b. Elgin, Ill., Oct. 20, 1960; s. Gerald Francis and Marjorie (Gosselin) F.; m. C. Nina Kerstiens, July 25, 1987; 1 child, Jake Buchanan. AB, Dartmouth Coll., 1982; cert. of attendance, Aristotelian U., Salonica, Greece, 1983; JD, U. Mich., 1986. Bar: Ill. 1986, U.S. Dist. Ct. (no. dist.) Ill. 1986. Assoc. Isham, Lincoln & Beale, Chgo., 1986-88; ptnr. Riordan, Larson, Bruckert & Moore, Chgo., 1988-92; mem. Ill. Senate, Springfield, Ill., 1993—98, chmn. state govt. ops. com., 1997—98; senator from Ill. US Senate, Washington, 1999—2005, chmn. sub com. consumer affairs and product safety com. on commerce, sci., transp., chmn. subcom. fin. mgmt., budget and internat. security com. on govt. affairs, 2003—05; chmn. Chain Bridge Bancorp, Inc., McLean, Va., 2006—. Counsel Harris Bankmont, Inc., 1992—96; dir. Nat. Coun. Econ. Edn., 2005—; trustee Nat. Constitution Ctr., 2005—; adv. dir. Transurban Devel., Inc., 2006—. Rotary Found. internat. grad. scholar, 1982-83. Mem. Econ. Club Chgo., Union League Club. Republican. Roman Catholic. Office Phone: 703-748-2005. E-mail: dgumino@fitzgeraldpeter.com.

FITZGERALD, ROBERT MAURICE, financial and retired bank executive; b. Chgo., Jan. 8, 1942; s. James Patrick and Catherine (McNulty) Fitzgerald; children: Stephen, Peter, Susan, Martin. BS, Loyola U., Chgo., 1971; postgrad., U. Wis., 1974-76, Northwestern U., 1980. Sr. v.p. Fed. Reserve Bank, Chgo., 1979-85; pres. Chgo. Clearing House Assn., Chgo., 1985—. Cons. Currency Bd., Abu Dhabi, United Arab Emirates, 1979; past bd. dirs. Nat. Automated Clearing House Assn., Washington; advisor U.S. Coun. on Internat. Banking, NYC. Pres. Coun. on Alcoholism, Ann Arbor, Mich., 1978, Diocesan Bd. Edn., Joliet, Ill., 1981—84; former dir. Frances Xavier Warde Sch.; vice chair. Chgo. Crime Commn.; trustee Union League Boys and Girls Clubs; sec. Civic and Arts Found.; former mem. adv. bd. St. Mary of Nazereth Hosp.; past pres., bd. dirs., vice chmn. exec. com. LaLalle St. Coun.; former chair, bd. trustees Old St. Patrick's Ch., Chgo.; bd. dirs. Concern Worldwide (U.S.), Inc. Mem.: City Club Chgo., Bankers Club Chgo. (sec., treas., exec. com.), Union League Club Chgo. (past pres.), Econ. Club Chgo., Execs. Club of Chgo. (bd. dirs., treas.). Democrat. Roman Catholic. Office: Chgo Clearing House Assn 230 S La Salle St Ste 700 Chicago IL 60604-1410 E-mail: fitz@chgo.org.

FITZGERALD, SCOTT, state legislator; b. Nov. 16, 1963; m. Lisa Fitzgerald; children: Scott William, Brennan, Connor. BS in Journalism, U. Wis., 1985. Mem. Wis. Senate from 13th dist., Madison, 1994—. Mem. com. on econ. devel., housing and govt. ops., com. on health, human svcs., aging, corrections, vets. and mil. affairs, spl. legis. coun. com. on recodification of fish and game laws, rural econ. devel. com. Wis. State Senate; owner Dodge County Ind. News, 1990—. Chmn. Dodge County (Wis.) Rep. Com.; planning com. City of Juneau, Wis.; former mem. Juneau Planning Commn. Major U.S. Army Res., 1981—. Mem. Juneau Area C. of C., Wis. Newspaper Assn. Address: N4692 Maple Rd Juneau WI 53039-9514

FITZGERALD, THOMAS ROBERT, state supreme court justice; b. Chgo., July 10, 1941; s. Thomas Henry and Kathryn (Touhy) Fitzgerald; m. Gayle Ann Aubry; 5 children. Attended, Loyola U., Chicago, 1959—63; JD, John Marshall Law Sch., Chicago, 1968. Bar: Ill. 1968. Trial asst. State Atty. Office Cook County, 1968—72, asst. state atty., 1968—76, felony trial supr., 1973—76; judge criminal div. Circuit Ct. Cook County, 1976—2000; justice Ill. Supreme Ct., 2000—. Adj. prof. law Kent Coll. Law, 1977—2000. Served in USN. Recipient Outstanding Jud. Performance award Chgo. Crime Commn., Herman Kogan Media award for excellence in broadcast jour., John Powers Crowley award Lawyers' Assistance Program, 2000, John Marshall Law School Freedom award, 2001, Joel Flaum award Chgo. Inn of Ct., 2003; named Celtic Man of Yr. Celtic Legal Soc., Catholic Lawyer of Yr. Catholic Lawyers Guild Chgo., 2005; fellow Ill. Bar Found. Office: Ill Supreme Ct 160 N LaSalle St Rm N-2013 Chicago IL 60601

FITZGERALD, TIMOTHY J., corporate financial executive; Audit mgr. Arthur Andersen LLP; corp. contr. Middleby Corp., Elgin, Ill., 1998—2003, v.p., 2000—, CFO, 2003—. amed one of Top 40 Under 40, Crain's Chgo. Bus., 2006. Office: Middleby Corp 1400 Toastmaster Dr Elgin IL 60120

FITZGERALD, WILLIAM ALLINGHAM, savings and loan association executive, director; b. Omaha, Nov. 18, 1937; s. William Frances and Mary (Allingham) F.; m. Barbara Ann Miskell, Aug. 20, 1960; children— Mary Colleen, Katherine Kara, William Tate. BSBA in Fin., Creighton U., 1959; grad. Savs. and Loan League exec. tng. program, U. Ga., 1962, U. Ind., 1969. With Comml. Fed. Savs. & Loan Assn., Omaha, 1959—, v.p., asst. sec., 1963-68, exec. v.p., 1968-73, pres., 1974-82, CEO, 1983—, chmn., CEO, 1994—. Trustee Ind. Coll. Found.; vice chmn. bd. dirs. Creighton U.; bd. dirs. Coll. of St. Mary, United Way of Midlands; trustee Archbishop's com. for ednl. devel. Roman Catholic Ch. Served to lt. Fin. Corps, U.S. Army. Chmn. Am. Cmty. Bankers, 1998—. Clubs: Omaha Country, Kiewit Plaza. Lodges: Knights of Ak-Sar-Ben (gov.).

FITZGIBBON, DANIEL HARVEY, lawyer; b. Columbus, Ind., July 7, 1942; s. Joseph Bales and Margaret Lenore (Harvey) FitzGibbon; m. Joan Helen Meltzer, Aug. 12, 1973; children: Katherine Lenore, Thomas Bernard. BS in Engring., U.S. Mil. Acad., 1964; JD cum laude, Harvard U., 1972. Bar: Ind. 1972, U.S. Dist. Ct. (so. dist.) Ind. 1972, U.S. Tax Ct. 1977. Commd. 2d lt. U.S. Army, 1964, advanced through grades to capt., 1967, served with inf. in West Berlin and Vietnam, resigned, 1969; assoc. Barnes & Thornburg, Indpls., 1972-79, ptnr., 1979-99, of counsel, 2000—. Spkr. various insts.; comml. law liaison ABA-CEELI, Moscow, 1998—99. Author: To Bear any Burden, A Hoosier Green Beret's Letters from Vietnam, 2005. Mem. sch. bd. Met. Sch. Dist. Lawrence Twp., 1988—96, pres., 1990—91, 1994—95; bd. advs. Eiteljorg Mus. Am. Indian and Western Art, 1993—2003. Fellow: Am. Bar Found., Am. Coll. Tax Counsel; mem.: ABA (internat. law sect.), Indpls. Bar Assn. (chmn. tax sect. 1982—83, coun. 1982—86), Ind. State Bar Assn. (tax sect.), Am. Law Inst., Lit. Club, Woodstock Club, Lawyers Club. Home: 6460 Lawrence Dr Indianapolis IN 46226-1035 Office: Barnes & Thornburg 1313 Merchants Bank Bldg Indianapolis IN 46204-3506 Office Phone: 317-231-7247. Business E-Mail: dfitzgib@btlaw.com.

FITZPATRICK, SUSAN, biochemist, neurologist, foundation administrator; married. Grad., St. John's U.; PhD in Biochemistry and Neurology, Cornell U. Postdoctoral tng. Yale U., New Haven; dir. edn. Miami Project To Cure Paralysis, Miami, Fla., assoc. exec. dir.; adminstr. grants program Brain Trauma Found., Miami; program dir. James S. McConnell Found., St. Louis. Office: James S McDonnell Found Ste 1850 1304 S Brentwood Blvd Saint Louis MO 63117

FITZSIMMONS, BECKY BARLOW, lawyer; b. Princeton, NJ, Apr. 2, 1968; BA, Western Md. Coll., 1990; JD, U. Md. at Baltimore, 2000. Bar: Ohio 2000. Assoc. Dinsmore & Shohl LLP, Cin. Named one of Ohio's Rising Stars, Super Lawyers, 2006. Mem.: Ohio State Bar Assn., Cin. Bar Assn., ABA. Office: Dinsmore & Shohl LLP 255 E Fifth St Ste1900 Cincinnati OH 45202-4700 Office Phone: 513-977-8200. Office Fax: 513-977-8141.

FITZSIMONS, DENNIS JOSEPH, former broadcast and publishing executive; b. NYC, June 26, 1950; s. Genevieve Theresa (English) F.; m. Ann Christie, Sept. 27, 1980; children: Matthew, Christine. BA, Fordham U., 1972. Account exec. Blair TV, NYC, 1975-77; sales mgr. TeleRep, Inc., Chgo., 1977-78, NYC, 1979-81, dir. spl. projects, 1978-79; dir. advt. sales Viacom Internat., NYC, 1981; dir. sales & mktg. Sta. WVIT-TV, Hartford, Conn., 1981-82; dir. sales Sta. WGN-TV, Chgo., 1982-84, v.p., gen. mgr., 1987—92, Sta. WGNO-TV, New Orleans, 1984-85; v.p. ops. Tribune Broadcasting Co., Chgo., 1985-87; pres. Tribune Television, 1992—94, Tribune Broadcasting Co., 1994—2003; exec. v.p. Tribune Co., 2000—01, COO, 2001—03, pres., 2001—07, CEO, 2003—07, chmn., 2004—07. Bd. dirs. Tribune Co., 2000—07. Vice chmn. United Negro Coll. Fund of Chgo. With U.S. Army, 1970-76. Named Broadcaster of Yr., Broadcasting & Cable, 2003. Mem. Ill. Assn. Broadcasters (bd. dirs.), INTV (bd. dirs.). Roman Catholic.

FITZSIMONS, GEORGE KINZIE, bishop emeritus; b. Kansas City, Mo., Sept. 4, 1928; Student, Rockhurst Coll., Immaculate Conception Sem. Ordained priest Diocese of Kansas City-St. Joseph, Mo., 1961, aux. bishop, 1975—84; ordained bishop, 1975; bishop Diocese of Salina, Kans., 1984—2004, bishop emeritus, 2004—. Roman Catholic. Office: 103 N 9th St Salina KS 67401 Office Phone: 785-827-8746. Office Fax: 785-827-6133. E-mail: chancery2@salinadiocese.org.*

FITZWATER, RODGER L., state legislator; Mem. Mo. Ho. of Reps., Jefferson City. Democrat.

FIVEL, STEVEN EDWARD, lawyer, communications executive; b. Aug. 26, 1960; Atty. Melvin Simon & Assoc., Inc., 1988—93, Simon DeBartolo Group, Inc., 1988—97, Simon Property Group, Inc., 1993—97; exec. v.p., gen. counsel, sec. Brightpoint, Inc., Plainfield, Ind., 1997—. Lectr. in field. Office: Brightpoint, Inc 2601 Metropolis Parkway, Ste 210 Plainfield IN 46168 Office Phone: 317-707-2355. Office Fax: 317-707-2514.

FJELL, MICK, principal; Prin. Millard Ctrl. Mid. Sch., 1978—. Recipient Blue Ribbon Sch. award 1990-91. Office: Millard Central Mid Sch 12801 L St Omaha NE 68137-2020

FLADELAND, BETTY, historian, educator; b. Grygla, Minn., Jan. 18, 1919; d. Arne O. and Bertha (Nygaard) F. BS, Duluth State Coll., 1940; MA, U. Minn., 1944; PhD (Rackham fellow), U. Mich., 1952. Mem. faculty Wells Coll., Aurora, N.Y., 1952-55, Central Mich. U., 1956-59, Central Mo. State Coll., 1959-62; mem. faculty So. Ill. U., Carbondale, 1962—, prof. history, 1968—, disting. prof., 1985, disting. prof. emerita, 1986—. Vis. prof. U. Ill., summer 1966 Author: James Gillespie Birney: Slaveholder to Abolitionist, 1955, Men and Brothers: Anglo-American Antislavery Cooperation, 1972, Abolitionists and Working Class Problems in the Age of Industrialization, 1984, also articles. Recipient Anisfield-Wolf award in race relations, 1972, Queen award, 1984; grantee Am. Philos. Soc., 1963, 75, Lilly Found., 1962; NEH teaching grantee, 1984 Mem. Am. Hist. Assn., So. Hist. Assn. (exec. council), Orgn. Am. Historians (exec. bd.), Assn. Study Afro-Am. Life and History, Norwegian-Am. Hist. Soc., Soc. Historians Early Am. Republic (adv. bd., bd. editors, pres.), ACLU, NAACP, Phi Beta Kappa, Phi Kappa Phi. Home: Liberty Village 2950 West Ridge Pl #230 Carbondale IL 62901-7135 Office: So Ill Univ Dept Of History Carbondale IL 62901

FLADUNG, THOM, editor-in-chief; b. Canton, Ohio; m. Jeanette Meyer-Fladung; 2 children. Grad., Univ. Dayton, 1982. Various ed. positions Detroit Free Press, Mich., 1994—2000; mng. ed. Akron Beacon Journal, Ohio, 2000—02, Detroit Free Press, 2002—05; editor & v.p. St. Paul Pioneer Press, 2005—. Mem.: Am. Soc. ewspaper Editors. Office: Pioneer Press 345 Cedar St Saint Paul MN 55101 Office Phone: 651-228-5487. E-mail: tfladung@pioneerpress.com.

FLAHERTY, EMALEE GOTTBRATH, pediatrician; b. LaGrange, Ky., May 24, 1944; d. Frank Herman and Katherine Lee (Carothers) Gottbrath; m. Joseph Flaherty, Apr. 28, 1973 (div.); children: Joshua, Megan. BS, Purdue U., W. Lafayette, Ind., 1966; MD, Ind. U., Indpls., 1970. Resident, pediatrics U. Ill. Hosp., 1970-72, Columbus Hosp., 1972-73, med. dir. outpatient dept. Chgo., 1984-96; med. dir. Columbus-Maryville Reception Ctr., Chgo., 1986-95; dir. ambulator pediatrics Columbus Hosp., Chgo., 1979-96, project dir. pediatric primary care tng. grant, 1989-95; med. dir. protective svc. team Children's Meml. Hosp., Chgo., 1996—; asst. prof. pediatrics Northwestern U. Sch. Medicine, Chgo., 1997—. Mem. Am. Acad. Pediat. (chpt. treas.), Pediatric Primary Care Rsch. Grp. (steering com.), Pediatric Rsch. Office Setting (dist. coord.), Columbus Hosp. Woman's Bd. (exec. bd. 1988-96). Office: Children's Hosp 2300 N Childrens Plz # 16 Chicago IL 60614-3363

FLAHERTY, JOHN JOSEPH, quality assurance company executive; b. Chgo., July 24, 1932; s. Patrick J. and Mary B. Flaherty; m. Norrine Grow, Nov. 20, 1954 (dec. Sept. 1995); children: John, Bridgette, George, Eileen, Daniel, Mary, Michael, Amy; m. Rosemarie Clausen, Dec. 27, 2001. BEE U. Ill., 1959. Design engr. Admiral Corp., Chgo., 1959—60; project engr. Magnaflux Corp., Chgo., 1960—79, v.p., mgr. rsch. and engring., 1979—84, v.p., mgr. mktg. and sales, 1984—86, v.p., gen. mgr. electronic products, 1986—88; pres. Flare Tech., Chgo., 1988—. With AUS, 1951—53. Fellow: Am. Soc. Non-Destructive Testing; mem.: IEEE, Am. Soc. Metals. Roman Catholic. Achievements include patents and publications on nondestructive testing, including medical ultrasonic; laser scanning. Office: 401 Meadow Lark Rd Bloomingdale IL 60108 Home: 401 Meadowlark Rd Bloomingdale IL 60108-1331 Office Phone: 630-980-4537. Personal E-mail: johnflare@aol.com.

FLAHERTY, TIMOTHY THOMAS, radiologist; b. Fond du Lac, Wis., 1933; m. Joan Flaherty; 4 children. MD, Marquette U., 1959. Diplomate Am. Bd. Radiology. Intern St. Marys Hosp., Milw., 1959—60; resident in radiology, chief resident U. Wis., Madison, 1963—66; fellowship U. Wis. Hosps., Madison, 1964—65; pvt. practice, 1965—. Bd. dirs., sec. Nat. Patient Safety Found.; founding dir. Physicians Ins. Co.-Wis., exec. com. and underwriting com., chair investment com., chmn. bd. dirs.; mem. Govs. task force on health reform, Wis.; founding dir. SMS Svcs., Inc.; bd. dirs. Bank One of Appleton, N.A.; chair Profl. Svcs. Network, Inc.; trustee Novus Health Group Inc., Appleton, Wis., 1988-94; mem. med. exec. com., bd. trustees dept. radiology Theda Clark Regional Med. Ctr., Neenah, Wis., chmn. dept. radiology, 1980-95; clin. prof. dept. radiology U. Wis. Ctr. for Health Scis., Madison, Med. Coll. of Wis., Milw. Maj. gen. USAF, ret. Fellow Am. Coll. Radiology (councilor); mem. AMA (exec. com. 1995—, chair fin. com., chair com. on membership 1996-97, chair com. on orgn. and operation, mem. compensation com., commr. to joint commn. on accreditation of healthcare orgns. 1994, dir. Commn. on Office Lab. Assessment, 1996—, bd. trustees 1994—, chair bd. trustees, 2001-02, sec.-treas. exec. com.), AMPAC (bd. dirs.), State Med. Soc. of Wis. (vice chair bd. dirs., commn. chair), Wis. Radiol. Soc. (past pres.), Radiol. Soc. of N.Am. (counselor 1991-97), Soc. of Med. Cons. of the Armed Forces, Aerospace Med. Assn., Assn. of Mil. Surgeons, Soc. of Air Force Flight Surgeons. Office: AMA 515 N State St Chicago IL 60610-4325 Address: Radiology Assoc Fox Valley 547 E Wisconsin Neenah WI 54956-2966

FLAKOLL, TIMOTHY JOHN, state legislator, animal scientist; b. Ellendale, ND, Oct. 8, 1959; s. Alden James and Wilma Jean (Wolff) F., m. Beverly Flakoll. BS, N.D. State U., 1981, MS, 1984; PhD, Somerset U., Eng., 1988. Cert. Internat. Soc. Livestock Appraisers. Cons./foreman Flakoll Enterprises, Forbes, N.D., 1970—; grad. asst. to resident asst. N.D. State U., Fargo, 1981-84; internat. cons. Cattleana Corp., Wheatland, N.D., 1982—; lectr./asst. animal scientist N.D. State U., Fargo, 1984—; mem. N.D. Senate from 44th dist., Bismark, 1998—. Advisor, Blue Key Nat. Honor Frat., Fargo, 1986—, Mortar Bd. Nat. Honor Frat., Fargo, 1986-92, Alpha Zeta Nat. Agrl. Frat., Fargo, 1990-93; com. mem. Beef Rsch./Mgmt. Com., Fargo, 1984—. Author: (books) Supplemental Niacin in Feeder Lamb Rations, 1984, Environmental Effectuation for Enhanced Productivity, 1988, Beef Showman's Guide, 1991; contbr. numerous articles to profl. jours. Clay county bd. Am. Cancer Soc., 1993—. Recipient Bursary award Somerset U., Eng., 1987, Blue Key Nat. Honor Frat. Membership Honor, 1983, Alpha Zeta Nat. Honor Agrl. Frat. Membership Honor, 1984, 10th degree Leadership award U.S. Jr. C. of C., 1992, Project of the Yr. N.D. Jaycees, 1992, 93, Outstanding Young Fargoan, 1990, N.D.S.U. Preferred Prof. award, 1987, 89. Mem. Am. Quarter Horse Assn., Continental Cattle Assn. (nat. sect. 1985—), N.D. Shorthorn Assn. (pres. 1989-91, Man of Yr. 1991), N.D. Winter Show (dir. 1988—), N.D. Purebred Coun. (dir. 1990-93), N.D. Stockman's Assn., Fargo Jr. C. of C. (dir. 1990-91, pres. 1991-92, historian 1992-93, parliamentarian 1992-94, v.p. community devel. 1993—). Lutheran. Avocations: softball, volleyball, golf, horseback riding, antiques. Home: 1350 2nd St N Fargo ND 58102-2725 Office: PO Box 5727 Fargo ND 58105-5727

FLAMM, JUSTIN D., lawyer; b. Dayton, Ohio, June 10, 1974; BA, Miami U., 1996; JD, Washington and Lee U., 1999. Bar: Ohio 1999. Assoc. Taft, Stettinius & Hollister LLP, Cin. Bd. trustee Friends of William Howard Taft Birthplace. Named one of Ohio's Rising Stars, Super Lawyers, 2005, 2006. Office: Taft Stettinius & Hollister LLP 425 Walnut St Ste 1800 Cincinnati OH 45202 Office Phone: 513-381-2838. Office Fax: 513-381-0205.

FLANAGAN, BARBARA, journalist; b. Des Moines; d. John Merrill and Marie (Barnes) F.; m. Earl S. Sanford, 1966. Student, Drake U., 1942-43. With promotion dept. Mpls. Times, 1945-47; reporter Mpls. Tribune, 1947-58; women's editor, spl. writer Mpls. Star and Tribune, 1958-65; columnist Mpls. Star, 1965—. Author: Ovation, Minneapolis. Active Junior League Mpls., Womans Club Mpls. Mem. Mpls. Soc. Fine Arts (life), Mpls. Inst. Arts (founding mem. Minn. Arts Forum), Mpls. Club, Minikahda Club, Kappa Alpha Theta, Sigma Delta Chi. Episcopalian. Office: Mpls Star Tribune 5th And Portland Sts Minneapolis MN 55488-0001 E-mail: barb-flanagan@comcast.net.

FLANAGAN, JOHN ANTHONY, lawyer, educator; b. Sioux City, Iowa, Nov. 29, 1942; s. J. Maurice and Lorna K. (Fowler) F.; m. Martha (Lang), May 8, 1982; children: Sean, Kathryn, Molly. BA, Iowa State U., 1964; JD, Georgetown U., 1968. Bar: Iowa, 1968; D.C., 1975; Ohio, 1977. Law clk. to judge U.S. Tax Ct., Washington, 1968-70; trial atty. U.S. Dept. Justice, Washington, 1970-74; prof. law U. Ohio, Cin., 1974-78; sr. tax ptnr. Graydon, Head, and Ritchey, Cin., 1978—. Adj. prof. U. Ohio, (Cin.), 1978--. Contbr. articles to profl. jour. Corp. mgr. United Way, Cin., 1988; head lawyers div. Fine Arts Fund, Cin., 1987-88; mem. Downtown Cin. Inc., 1995-2000. Mem. DC Bar Assn., Order of Coif. Roman Catholic. Avocations: gardening, golf, fly fishing. Home: 5 Walsh Ln Cincinnati OH 45208-3435 Office: Graydon Head & Ritchey 1900 5th-3rd Ctr PO Box 6464 Cincinnati OH 45202 Business E-Mail: jflanagan@graydon.com.

FLANAGAN, JOHN F., publishing executive; b. Chgo., Feb. 24, 1944; AB, Wabash Univ., 1966; MBA, Univ. Mich., 1968. Pres., CEO Goodheart Willcox Publ., Tinley Park, Ill., 1980—. Office: Goodheart Willcox Publ 18604 W Creek Dr Tinley Park IL 60477-6243

FLANAGAN, MARTHA LANG, publishing executive; BS in Fine Arts, U. Cin., 1978. Various exec. secretarial positions, 1960—73; corp. sec., asst. to pres. Cin. Enquirer, 1973—. Mem. adv. com. to Cin. Police Chief, 1976-85; mem. Cin. Music Hall Centennial Com., 1976-78; mem. adv. bd. U. Cin. Coll. Design, Art, Architecture and Planning, 1988-91; trustee Neediest Kids of All, 1980—, Women's Fund Greater Cin. Found., 2000—, St. Ursula Acad., 2002—05. Office: The Cincinnati Enquirer 312 Elm St Fl 20 Cincinnati OH 45202-2739 Home Phone: 513-321-5504. Business E-Mail: mflanagan@enquirer.com.

FLANAGAN, SYLVIA, editor; b. Chgo., June 26, 1952; BA in Journalism, Chgo. State U.; MS in Journalism, Roosevelt U. Various to sr. editor Jet newsmag. Johnson Pub. Co., Chgo., 1972-85. Mem. The Chgo. Bd. Rossevelt Univ., 2000. Former bd. govs. Roosevelt U.; bd. trustees LaRabida Children's Hosp. and Rsch. Ctr., Chgo. Mem. Nat. Assn. Black Journalists, Chgo. Assn. of Black Journalists. Office: Johnson Pub Co 820 S Michigan Ave Chicago IL 60605-2103

FLANAGIN, JOHN MEAD, publishing executive; b. Evanston, Ill., Aug. 15, 1961; s. Neil and Mary (Mead) Flanagin; m. Annette Pamela Ferazzi, June 28, 1986; children: Jake, Katie BA, Georgetown U., 1983; MA, Am. U., 1988; postgrad., U. Chgo., 1988—. Editorial asst. The Washington Mo., 1984-85; research asst. The Wilson Quar., Washington, 1985-86; reporter, editor Commerce Clearing House, Inc., Washington, 1986-87; teaching fellow Am. U., Washington, 1987-88; freelance hist. researcher Washington, Chgo., 1988; rsch. dir. Nat. Strategy Forum, Chgo.; investment analyst First Analysis Corp., Chgo., 2000—; chmn. Times Pub. Co., Erie, Pa., 2006—. Research asst. Peter DuPont for Pres., Washington, 1988. Mem. Orgn. Am. Historians, Am. Mil. Inst., Am. Hist. Assn., Soc. for Historians of Am. Fgn. Relations, Phi Alpha Theta. Office: First Analysis Ste 3900 1 S Wacker Drive Chicago IL 60606

FLANIGAN, MATTHEW C., manufacturing executive; Degree, U. Mo. Formerly with Society Gen., Dallas, InterFirst Bank, Dallas; with Leggett & Platt, 1997—, pres. Office Furniture Components Group, 1999—2003, v.p., CFO, 2003—. Office: Leggett & Platt No 1 Leggett Rd Carthage MO 64836

FLATEN, ALFRED N., retired food and consumer products executive; b. 1935; With Nash-Finch Co., Mpls., 1861-98, mgr. Iowa divsn., 1983-86, v.p. S.E. divsn., 1986-89, v.p. retail ops. Mpls., 1989-91, past exec. v.p., past pres., CEO, COO, also bd. dirs. Home: Apt 613 8590 Cedar Hammock Cir Naples FL 34112-3329

FLAUM, JOEL MARTIN, federal judge; b. Hudson, NY, Nov. 26, 1936; s. Louis and Sally (Berger) Flaum; m. Delilah Brummet, June 4, 1989. BA, Union Coll., Schenectady, 1958; JD, Northwestern U., 1963, LLM, 1964; LLD, John Marshall Law Sch., 2002. Bar: Ill. 1963. Asst. state's atty. Cook County, Ill., 1965—69, 1st asst. atty. gen. Ill. Ill., 1969—72; 1st asst. U.S. atty. (no. dist.) US Dept. Justice, Chgo., 1972—75; judge US Dist. Ct. (no. dist.) Ill., Chgo., 1975—83, US Ct. Appeals (7th cir.), 1983—, chief judge, 2000—06. Mem. Ill. Law Enforcement Commn., 1970—72; cons. US Dept. Justice, Law Enforcement Assistance Adminstrn., 1970—71; lectr. DePaul U. Coll. Law, 1987—88; adj. prof. Northwestern U. Sch. Law, 1993—2000. Mem.: Northwestern U. Law Rev., 1962—63; contbr. articles to legal jours. Mem. vis. com. U. Chgo. Law Sch., 1983—86; law bd. Northwestern U. Sch. Law, 1983—; mem. adv. com. USCG Acad., 1990—93. Lt. comdr. JACG USNR, 1981—92. Fellow Ford Found., 1963—64. Fellow: Chgo. Bar Found. (licentiate), Am. Bar Found. (licentiate); mem.: FBA, ABA, Am. Judicature Soc., Navy-Marine Corps Ret. Judges Advs. Assn., Maritime Law Assn., Chgo. Bar Assn., Chgo. Inn of Ct., 7th Cir. Bar Assn., Ill. Bar Assn., Naval Res. Assn., Lawyers Club Chgo. Jewish. Office: US Ct Appeals 7th Ct 219 S Dearborn St Chicago IL 60604-1702 Office Phone: 312-435-5626.

FLAUM, RUSSELL M., engineering executive; BA in Psychology, Vanderbilt U., Nashville; MBA, Lake Forest Grad. Sch. Mgmt., Ill. Sales rep. Signode Corp. (acquired by Ill. Tool Works), 1975, dir. mktg., 1984-86, v.p. mktg., 1986-90, pres. US bus. Glenview, 1990-92; exec. v.p. Ill. Tool Works (ITW), Glenview, 1993—. Bd. dirs. Quanex Corp. Bd. dirs. Evanston Hosp. Corp., Ill., 1993—, Lake Forest Grad. Sch. Mgmt. Mem. Am. Mktg. Assn., Am. Mgmt. Assn. (mem. conf. bd.). Office: Ill Tool Works 3600 W Lake Ave Glenview IL 60026-1215 Office Phone: 847-724-7500. Office Fax: 847-657-4572.

FLEEZANIS, JORJA KAY, musician, educator; b. Detroit, Mar. 19, 1952; d. Parios Nicholas and Kaliope (Karageorge) F.; m. Michael Steinberg, July 3, 1983. Student, Cleve. Inst. Music, 1969-72, Cin. Coll.-Conservatory Music, 1972-75. Violinist Chgo. Symphony Orch., 1975-76; concertmaster Cin. Chamber Orch., 1976-80; violinist Trio D'Accordo, Cin., 1976-80; asst. prin. 2d violinist San Francisco Symphony Orch., 1980-81; assoc. concertmaster San Francisco Sympony Orch., 1980-89; acting concertmaster Minn. Orch., Mpls., 1988-89, concertmaster, 1989—; violinist Fleezanis-Ohlsson-Grebanier Piano Trio, San Francisco, 1984—; faculty mem. San Francisco Conservatory of Music, 1983-89, U. Minn., 1989—. Founder Chamber Music Sundaes, San Francisco, 1980-89, The Am. String Project, 2002; radio host St. Paul Sunday Show, Minn. Pub. Radio, 1998-2000; guest concertmaster, London Classical Players, L.A. Philharmonic, Sydney Symphony, Balt. Symphony; vis. prof. Ind. U., 2003—. Performer World Premiere John Adams Violin Concerto with Minn. Orch., 1994, Nicholas Maw, Sonata for Solo Violin, commd. by Minn. Pub. Radio, 1997, Sir John Tavener's Ikon of Eros, commd. for her by Minn. Orch., 2002; commd. by Pub. Radio Internat. and Minn. Pub. Radio for world premiere of Nicholas Maw Sonata for Solo Violin, 1998; soloist Am. premier Benjamin Britten Double Concerto, 1998; rec. artist Reference CRI, Koch, Cypre's Records. Democrat. Avocations: photography, cooking. Office: Minn Orch 1111 Nicollet Mall Minneapolis MN 55403-2406 Home Phone: 612-332-0236; Office Phone: 612-371-5653. E-mail: fleeberg@earthlink.net.

FLEISCHER, CORNELL HUGH, history educator; b. Berkeley, Calif., Oct. 23, 1950; s. Hugh Warren and Florence Robie Fleischer. Student, Brown U., 1968-70; AB, Princeton U., 1972, AM, 1976, PhD, 1982. Instr. Persian and Turkish langs. and lit. Ohio State U., Columbus, 1979-82; asst. prof. Islamic history Washington U., St. Louis, 1982-85, assoc. prof., 1985-89, prof., 1989-93; prof. Ottoman history U. Chgo., 1993-98; Kanuni Süleyman prof. Ottoman and Modern Turkish Studies Univ. Chgo., 1998—. Dir. Ctr. for Study Islamic Socs. and Civilizations, St. Louis, 1986-91; dir. Ctr. for Mid. Eastern Studies, U. Chgo., 1996-98; lectr. Phi Beta Kappa 1999-2000. Author: Bureaucrat and Intellectual in the Ottoman Empire, 1986 (book prize N.W. Assn. Grad. Schs. 1987); assoc. editor Cambridge History of Turkey, 1990—; mem. editorial bd.

Internat. Jour. Mid. Ea. Studies, 1994-99; contbr. articles to profl. jours. Fulbright-Hays rsch. fellow, 1976-78, MacArthur fellow, 1988-93; rsch. grantee Social Sci. Rsch. Coun., 1984, 86, Fulbright Islamic Civilization grantee, 1986-87; resident Bellagio Ctr., 1991. Mem. Am. Acad. Arts Scis., Am. Hist. Assn., Mid East Studies Assn., Soc. for Iranian Studies, Turkish Studies Assn. (bd. dirs. 1986-88, pres., 1996-98). Office: Ctr Mid Ea Studies U Chgo Chicago IL 60637

FLEISCHMAN, STEPHEN, museum director; b. Newton, Mass., July 7, 1954; s. David and Dorothy (Myers) F.; m. Barbara Jane Katz, May 18, 1986; children: Daniel Katz Fleischman, Benjamin Katz Fleischman, Jacob Katz Fleischman. BS in Fine Arts, U. Wis., 1977, MA in Bus. Adminstrn., 1983. Gallery owner, studio potter, Seattle, 1977-81; devel. asst. Madison Art Ctr., Wis., 1981-83; spl. asst. to dir. Walker Art Ctr., Mpls., 1983-86, dir. program planning, 1986-90; dir. Madison Mus. Contemporary Art, 1991—. Bd. dirs. So. Theater, Mpls., 1988-90, Minn. Citizens for the Arts, Mpls., 1985-90, Cable Arts Consortium, Mpls., 1986-88, Madison CitiArts, 1991-97, Greater Madison Conv. and Visitors Bur., 2000—; pres. adv. bd. Bolz Ctr. for Arts Adminstrn., U. Wis., 1995-97. Mem. Rotary Internat. Office: Madison Mus Contemporary Art 227 State St Madison WI 53703 Office Phone: 608-257-0158. E-mail: flash@mmoca.org.

FLEMING, CECIL, retired finance company executive; Exec. ptnr. BDO Dunwoody, Ward, Mallette, Toronto, Ont., Can., 1991-95; sr. ptnr. BDO Seidman, NYC, 1995-97, CEO, pres., 1997—2002.

FLEMING, JAMES RICHARD, lawyer; b. Kokomo, Ind., Mar. 12, 1944; s. Richard V. and Evelyn (Daily) F.; m. Cynthia Bryant, Nov. 29, 1969; children: Amy, Nicklaus, Sara. BS, Ind. U., 1967; JD, U. S.C., 1970. Bar: Ind. 1970, U.S. Dist. Ct. (so. dist.) Ind. 1970. Ptnr. O'Mahoney, Mahoney, Simmons & Fleming, Kokomo, 1970-74, Simmons & Fleming, Kokomo, 1974—. Pub. defender Howard County Pub. Defender, Kokomo, 1973—. Bd. dirs. Kokomo Humane Soc. Mem. KC, Ind. State Bar Assn., Howard County Bar Assn. (pres. 1990), Ind. Assn. Criminal Def. Attys. (bd. dirs.), Benevolent Protective Order Elks, Kokomo Country Club (bd. dirs.), Columbian Club Kokomo (bd. dirs.). Avocations: gardening, fishing, golf. Office: PO Box 626 Kokomo IN 46903-0626

FLEMING, MAC ARTHUR, retired labor union administrator; b. Walnut Grove, Miss., Sept. 22, 1945; s. Austin J. and Dorothy (Downey) F.; m. Phyllis Jean Tatro, May 18, 1984; children: Vaughn L. Voth, Vaughn L. Voth II AA, Jones County Jr. Coll., Laurel, Miss., 1967; student, So. Colo. State Coll., Pueblo, 1967-68; student in trade union program, Harvard U., 1979. System organizer Atchison, Topeka & Santa Fe System Fedn., Pueblo, 1972, asst. gen. chmn. San Bernardino, Calif., 1972-73, asst. chmn., sec.-treas. Newton, Kans., 1974-75, vice chmn., 1975-80, gen. chmn., 1980-86; grand lodge sec.-treas. Brotherhood Maintenance Ways Employees, Detroit, 1986-90; pres. Brotherhood Maintenance of Way Employees, Detroit, 1990—2004; v.p. AFL-CIO, 1995—2004, ret., 2004. Democrat. Avocations: tennis, golf. Home: 39921 Urbana Dr Sterling Heights MI 48313-5678

FLEMING, MARCELLA, journalist; b. Paoli, Ind., Oct. 14, 1955; d. Kenneth Gale and Neva Louise (Thomas) F.; m. Brian D. Smith. AB in Journalism and English, Ind. U., 1978. Cert. tchr. Reporter Wabash Plain Dealer, 1978-80, Marion Chronicle-Tribune, 1980-83, city editor, 1990-91; city reporter, feature writer, copy editor, Sunday editor Ft. Wayne (Ind.) Jour.-Gazette, 1983-88; editor pubs. Children's Mus. Indpls., 1988-90; freelance writer Indpls. Monthly, 1989-91; nat. editor Indpls. CEO, Columbus (Ohio) CEO mags., 1991-92; writer state desk Indpls. Star & News, 1992—. Judge Thomas R. Keating Writing Competition, 1990. Recipient award of Excellence Nat. Down Syndrome Congress, 1988, Best Newsletter, Best Feature Story and Best News Story awards Editor's Forum, 1990, Best Ann. Report award Internat. Assn. Bus. Communicators, 1990. Mem. Ednl. Press Assn. (Breaking News Story Disting. Achievement award 1994). Office: Indpls Star 307 N Pennsylvania St Indianapolis IN 46204-1819

FLEMING, MICHAEL O., physician; b. Monroe, La., June 16, 1950; m. Sally Fleming; 4 children. MD, La. Med. Ctr., 1975. Intern Confederate Meml. Med. Ctr., Shreveport, 1975—76; resident LSU Med. Ctr., Shreveport, 1976—78; asst. clinical prof. Dept. Family Medicine, LSU Health Sci. Ctr. Mng. sr. ptnr. The Family Doctors. Mem.: Northwest La. Soc. Family Physicians, Shreveport Med. Soc., La. Acad. Family Physicians, La. State Med. Soc., Am. Acad. Family Physicians (pres. 2003—). Office: Am Acad Family Physicians PO Box 11210 Shawnee Mission KS 66207-1210

FLEMING, RICHARD H., finance executive; b. Milw., July 22, 1947; s. David M. and Mildred (Codere) F.; m. Diana Loane, Mar. 21, 1970; children: Douglas Codere, Petria Anne. BA, U. Pacific, 1969; MBA, Dartmouth, 1971. Fin. analyst Graco, Inc., Mpls., 1971-72, mgr. banking and fgn. exchange, 1972-73; fin. analyst Masonite Corp., Chgo., 1973-74, mgr. capital investment, 1974-77, asst. treas., 1977-82, treas., 1982-84, v.p. fin., chief fin. officer, 1985-89; dir. corp. fin. and asst. treas. USG Corp., Chgo., 1989-90, v.p., treas., 1991-94, v.p., CFO, 1994-95, sr. v.p., CFO, 1995-99, exec. v.p., CFO, 1999—. Trustee USG Found., 1989—; bd. dirs. Columbus McKinnon Corp. Bd. dirs. Family Care Services Met. Chgo., 1977—, pres. 1983-86; bd. dirs. Child Welfare League Am., Washington, 1987—, pres. 1999-2000. Alumni fellow U. Pacific Sch. Bus. Adminstrn. and Pub. Policy, 1990. Office: USG Corp PO Box 6721 125 S Franklin St Chicago IL 60680-6721 Home: Apt 2802 195 N Harbor Dr Chicago IL 60601-7532

FLEMING, SUZANNE MARIE, academic administrator, freelance/self-employed writer; b. Detroit, Feb. 4, 1927; d. Albert T. and Rose E. (Smiley) F. BS, Marygrove Coll., 1957; MS, U. Mich., 1960, PhD, 1963. Joined Congregation of Sisters Servants of Immaculate Heart of Mary, Roman Catholic Commn., 1945. Chmn. natural sci. div. Marygrove Coll., Detroit, 1970-75, academic v.p., dean, 1975—80; asst. v.p. academic affairs Eastern Mich. U., Ypsilanti, 1980—82, acting assoc. v.p. academic affairs, 1982—83; provost, academic v.p. Western Ill. U., Macomb, 1983—86; vice chancellor U. Wis., Eau Claire, 1986—89; freelance writer, 1989—. Vis. scholar U. Mich., 1989-2001; pres. Mich. Coll. Chemistry Tchrs. Assn., 1975; councilor Mich. Inst. Chemists, 1973-77; bd. dirs. Nat. Ctr. for Rsch. to Improve Postsecondary Teaching and Learning, 1988-90. Contbr. articles to profl. publs. Named Disting. Alumna, Marygrove Coll., 2007; NIH rsch. grantee, 1966—69. Home and Office: 2888 Cascade Dr Ann Arbor MI 48104-6659

FLEMING, THOMAS A., retired administrative assistant; b. Reading, Pa., 1933; m. Diane Rosinski, 1975; 1 child, Malcolm;children from previous marriage: Thomas, Sharon. BA in Religious Edn., William Tyndale Coll., 1964; MA in Spl. Edn., Ea. Mich. Univ. Spl. asst. to the provost Ea. Mich. U., Ypsilanti, Mich. Baptist min. With US Army N.G., 1950—55. Named Tchr. of Yr. Mich., 1991, Nat. Tchr. of Yr., 1992.

FLEMING, THOMAS J., editor, publishing executive; b. Superior, Wis., 1945; BA in Greek, Charleston Coll., 1967; PhD in Classics, U. N.C., 1973. Prof. classics Miami U., Charleston (S.C.) Coll., Shaw U., Raleigh, NC. Founding editor The Southern Partisan, 1979—83; mng. editor Chronicles, Rockford, Ill., 1984—85, editor, 1985—, pres., 1997—. Author: The Politics of Human Nature, 1987. Office: The Rockford Inst Chronicles 928 N Main St Rockford IL 61103-7061 E-mail: tri@rockfordinstitute.org.

FLETCHER, JAMES WARREN, physician; b. Belleville, Ill., Oct. 6, 1943; m. Mary Bernadette Gatson; children: Michelle Marie, James W., Rebecca Lynn. MD, St. Louis U., 1968. Diplomate Am. Bd. Nuclear Medicine, lic. physician Mo. Intern in internal medicine St. Louis U. Hosp., 1968—69, asst. resident in internal medicine, 1969—70, resident in nuclear medicine, 1970—71; clin. fellow in radiology Harvard Med. Sch., Boston, 1971—72; sr. resident in nuclear medicine Peter Bent Brigham and Children's Hosp. Med. Ctr., Boston, 1971—72; asst. prof. medicine dept. internal medicine St. Louis U., 1972—75, assoc. prof. medicine dept. internal medicine, 1976—83, assoc. prof. radiology dept. radiology, 1977—84, assoc. dir. divsn. nuclear medicine, 1978—85, prof. medicine dept. internal medicine, 1983—, prof. radiology, 1984—, acting dir. divsn. nuclear medicine, 1985—88, dir. divsn. nuclear medicine, 1988—; staff physician nuclear medicine svc. VA Med. Ctr., St. Louis, 1972—76, med. dir. nuclear medicine network, 1972—79, asst. chief nuclear medicine svc., 1976—79, chief, 1979—, med. dir. AMA nuclear medicine technologist tng. program, 1983—, dir. opers. NMR program project, 1983—88; staff physician St. Louis U. Hosps., 1972—, dir. nuclear medicine dept., 1988—, dir. PET imaging ctr., 1991—; dir., program official nuclear medicine svc., dept. medicine and surgery VA Adminstrn. Ctrl. Office, Washington, 1986—89; dir. diagnostics svc. St. Louis VA Med. Ctr., 1997—99. Mem. tech. adv. com. to dir. nuclear medicine svc. VA Ctrl. Office, Washington, 1979—86, chmn. spl. interest user groups computer applications in nuclear medicine, 1984—85; spl. soc. liaison rep. Inst. Medicine Com. on Clin. Practice Guidelines, 1990—91; mem. residency rev. com. nuclear medicine Accreditation Coun. Grad. Med. Edn., 1992—97; interagy. NMR rask force Office Health Tech. Assessment, 1982; mem. Dept. Vet. Affairs Nat. Task Force on Tech. Assessment, 1992—97. Contbr. articles to profl. jours. 2d v.p. sch. bd. een of Peace Elem. Sch., Webster Groves, Mo., 1981, treas., 1982. Lt. comdr. USNR, 1966—77. Recipient Spl. Commendation award, Dept. Vets. Affairs, 1990. Mem.: AMA, Inst. for Clin. Positron Emission Tomography (bd. dirs. 1999—), Soc. Nuclear Medicine (bd. trustees 1988—92, chmn. health care policy com. 1991—92, vice chmn. commn. health care policy 1996—97, chmn. commn. health care policy 1997—98, pres., bd. dirs. 1998—99), Radiol. Soc. N.Am., Am. Bd. Nuclear Medicine (bd. dirs. 1990—93, vice chmn. 1992—93, chmn. 1994—95), Am. Coll. Radiology, Alpha Omega Alpha.

FLETCHER, WINONA LEE, theater educator; b. Nov. 25, 1926; m. Joseph Grant; 1 child, Betty. BA, Johnson C. Smith U., 1947; MA, U. Iowa, 1951; PhD, Ind. U., 1968. Prof. speech and theatre Ky. State U., Frankfort, 1951-78; prof. theatre and afro-Am. studies Ind. U., Bloomington, 1978-94, prof. emeritus, 1994; assoc. dean COAS, 1981-84. Costumer, dir. summer theatre, U. Mo., Lincoln, 1952-60, 69. Sr. editor: Community Memories: A Glimpse of African American Life in Frankfort, Ky., 2003. Recipient Lifetime Achievement award, 1993; Am. Theatre fellow, 1979. Mem. Am. Theatre for Higher Edn., Black Theatre Network, Ky. Hist. Soc., Nat. Assn. Dramatic and Speech Arts, Nat. Theatre Conf., Alpha Kappa Alpha. Home: 317 Cold Harbor Dr Frankfort KY 40601-3011

FLICKINGER, THOMAS LESLIE, hospital alliance executive; b. Carroll, Iowa, Apr. 22, 1939; s. Leslie Winfred and Evelyn (Hanson) F.; m. Marjorie Ellen Madison, Apr. 19, 1970; children: Benjamin, Samuel. BBA, U. Iowa, 1961, MA, 1963. Adminstrv. asst. Presbyn.-St. Luke's Hosp., Chgo., 1963-64; asst. adminstr. 1 Creighton Meml. St. Joseph Hosp., Omaha, 1964-66, assoc. dir., 1966-68, adminstr., 1968-73; exec. dir. Creighton Omaha Regional Health Care Corp., Omaha, 1973-75; assoc. dir. Vanderbilt U. Hosp., 1975-77; adminstr. Routt Meml. Hosp., Steamboat Springs, Colo., 1977-85; pres. VHA (Vol. Hosps. Am.) Midlands, Omaha, 1986-97; sr. exec. VHA Mid-Am., Omaha, 1998; retired. Mem. Omaha Hosp. Assn. (pres. 1971), Am. Coll. Hosp. Adminstrs., Colo. Hosp. Assn. (chmn. 1982), Phi Kappa Psi. Home: 3421 N 128th Cir Omaha NE 68164-4237

FLINCHBAUGH, JAMIE, training services executive; b. 1972; Mfg. plant supr. Harley-Davidson Motors Inc.; lean mfg. dir. Daimler Chrysler AG, DTE Energy Co.; co-founder, ptnr. Lean Learning Ctr., Novi, Mich., 2001—. Author: The Hitchhiker's Guide to Lean. Named one of 40 Under 40, Crain's Detroit Bus., 2006. Office: Lean Learning Center 40028 Grand River Ste 300 Novi MI 48375 Office Phone: 248-478-1480. Office Fax: 248-478-1589.

FLISS, RAPHAEL MICHAEL, bishop emeritus; b. Milw., Oct. 25, 1930; Student, St. Francis Sem., Houston; STL, Cath. U. of Am., 1956; JCD, Lateran U., Rome, 1965. Ordained priest Archdiocese of Milw., Wis., 1956; ordained bishop, 1979; bishop Diocese of Superior, Wis., 1985—2007, bishop emeritus, 2007—. Roman Catholic. Office: Chancery Office 1201 Hughitt Ave PO Box 969 Superior WI 54880-0017 Office Phone: 715-392-2937. Office Fax: 715-395-3149.*

FLOCK, JEFFREY CHARLES, news bureau chief; b. Lakewood, NJ, Mar. 16, 1958; s. Byron Harry and Vicki Ruth (Macaulay) F.; m. Elizabeth Brack, Sept. 19, 1998; children: Elizabeth Kathryn, Emily Macaulay. BS in Broadcast Journalism, Boston U., 1980. Writer, producer Cable News Network, Atlanta, 1980-81, corr. Chgo., 1981-84, bur. chief, 1985—. Methodist. Avocations: running, antiques. Office: Cable News Network 435 N Michigan Ave Ste 715 Chicago IL 60611-4008

FLOM, GERALD TROSSEN, lawyer; b. Neenah, Wis., Feb. 6, 1930; s. Russell Craig and Lois Eva (Trossen) F.; m. Martha Herrington Benton, Aug. 21, 1954 (div. June 25, 1980); children— Katherine Simmons, Sarah Elizabeth Kiecker, Russell Craig. BA magna cum laude, Lawrence U., Appleton, Wis., 1952; JD, Yale U., New Haven, Conn., 1957. Bar: Minn. 1957, U.S. Dist. Ct. Minn. 1957. Assoc. Faegre & Benson LLP, Mpls., 1957-64, ptnr., 1964-95; ret., 1995. Adj. asst. prof. Law Sch., U. Minn., Mpls., 1966. Mem. editl. bd. Yale Law Jour. Trustee Mpls. Soc. Fine Arts, 1970-76, Lawrence U., 1974-81, Plymouth Congl. Ch., 1978-81, William Mitchell Coll. Law, St. Paul, 1983-89; bd. dirs. Met. Med. Ctr. Research Found., Mpls., 1975-85. Served with U.S. Army, 1952-54. Mem. ABA, Minn. State Bar Assn., Hennepin County Bar Assn., Assn. Bar City of N.Y., Mace, Mpls. Club, Interlachen Country Club (Edina, Minn.), Phi Beta Kappa, Phi Delta Theta, Phi Alpha Delta. Congregationalist. Home: 3434 Zenith Ave S Minneapolis MN 55416-4663 Office: Faegre & Benson LLP 2200 Wells Fargo Ctr 90 S 7th St Minneapolis MN 55402-3901

FLORA, CORNELIA BUTLER, sociologist, educator; b. Santa Monica, Calif., Aug. 5, 1943; d. Carroll Woodward and May Fleming (Darnall) Butler; m. Jan Leighton Flora, Aug. 22, 1967; children: Gabriela Catalina, Natasha Pilar. BA, U. Calif., Berkeley, 1965; MS, Cornell U., 1966, PhD, 1970. Asst. to full prof. Kans. State U., Manhattan, 1970-89, dir. population rsch. lab., 1970-78, univ. disting. prof., 1988-89; program adviser Ford Found., Bogota, Colombia, 1978-80; prof., head dept. sociology Va. Poly. Inst. and State U., Blacksburg, 1989-94, univ. disting. prof., 2001—; dir. north ctrl. regional ctr. for rural devel. Iowa State U., Ames, 1994—, prof. agr., 2001—. Bd. dirs. Winfock Internat.; cons. USAID, 1981-91, Inter Am. Devel. Bank, 1992, UN, 1992. Author: Interactions between Agroecosystems and Rural Communities, Rural Communities: Legacy and Change; editor: Sustainable Agriculture, 1990, Rural Policy for the 1990s; contbr. articles to sociol. publs. Bd. dirs. N.W. Area Found., 1998—, Agrl. Nat. Rsch. Coun., 1996-98, Agrl. and Natural Resouces, NRC, NAS, Heartland Ctr. for Leadership Devel. Nat. Ctr. for Small Cmtys.; bd. dirs. Henry A. Wallace Inst. for Alt. Agr., 1994-99, pres., 1997-99. Recipient Outstanding Alumni award Coll. Agrl. and Life Scis., Cornell U., 1994; sr. fellow U. Minn. Sch. Agr. Endowed Chair in Agrl. Sys. Mem. Rural Sociol. Soc. (pres. 1988-89, Outstanding Rsch. award 1987), Latin Am. Studies Assn. (bd. dirs. 1982-84, pres. Midwest sect. 1989-90), Am. Sociol. Assn., Agr., Food and Human Values Soc. (pres. elect 2001—), Cmty. Devel. Soc. (v.p. 2001—). Mem. United Ch. of Christ. Office: Iowa State U N Ctrl Regional Ctr Rural Devels 107 N Curtiss Hl Ames IA 50011-0001 Office Phone: 515-294-1329. Business E-Mail: cflora@iastate.edu.

FLORA, JAIRUS DALE, JR., statistician; b. Northfield, Minn., Mar. 27, 1944; s. Jairus Dale and Betty Ruth (Garvin) F.; m. Sharyl Ann Hughes, Aug. 18, 1967; 1 child, Edward Hughes BS magna cum laude, Midland Luth. Coll., 1965; postgrad., Tech. U. Karlsruhe, Fed. Republic Germany, 1965-66; MS, Fla. State U., 1968, PhD, 1971. Asst. prof. biostats Sch. Pub. Health U. Mich., Ann Arbor, 1971-73, asst. prof., asst. rsch. scientist Hwy. Safety Rsch. Inst., 1973-76, assoc. rsch. scientist Hwy. Safety Rsch. Inst., 1976-81, assoc. prof. biostats. Sch. Pub. Health, 1976-81, prof. biostats. Sch. Pub. Health, rsch. scientist Transp. Rsch. Inst., 1981-84; prin. statistician Midwest Rsch. Inst, Kansas City, Mo., 1984-90; sr. advisor for stats. Midwest Rsch. Inst., Kansas City, Mo., 1991-99, pres. coun. prin. scientists, 1986; clin. prof. biostats. Sch. Medicine U. Mo., Kansas City, 1984—; prin. statistician Ken Wilcox Assocs., Inc., Grain Valley, Mo., 1999, statis. cons., 1999—. Cons. statistician Nat. Burn Info. Exchange, 1971-76 Editl. collaborator Annals of Thoracic Surgery, Mathematical Biosci., Biometrics, Accident Analysis and Prevention, 1979-90; contbr. articles to profl. jours.; patentee in field. Mem. adminstrn. bd. Valley View U. Meth. Ch., 1989-92; vol. leader Boy Scouts Am. Recipient CPS Enterprise award, 1985, Dir.'s award, 1987; German Acad. Exch. Svc. fellow, 1965-66; NASA trainee, 1966-69; NIH trainee, 1969-71; Nat Hwy. Traffic Safety Adminstrn. rsch. grantee, 1974-81. Mem. Am. Statis. Assn., Biometric Soc., Inst. Math. Stats., Masons (area dep. Grand Master 2003-05, Knight comdr. ct. hon.), Scottish Rite, Masonic Societas Rosiercrucianа in Civitatibus Foederatus, Blue Key, Sigma Xi (pres. Kansas City chpt. 1990-91, v.p. 1994-96). Republican. Home: 9921 Foster St Shawnee Mission KS 66212-2452 Personal E-mail: jdflora2002@yahoo.com.

FLORA, VAUGHN LEONARD, state legislator; b. Quinter, Kans., Jan. 17, 1945; s. Leonard Henry and Billie Hazel (Leighton) F.; m. Rose Mary Owens, 1963; children: Troy Vaughn, Trent Leighton, Trina Rose. BS, Kans. State U., 1968; postgrad., Lincoln Grad. Sch., 1989. Pres. Topeka City Homes, 1993-94; mem. Kans. State Ho. of Reps. Dist. 57, 1995—. Precinct committeeman Ward 2 Precinct 6, 1988—; mem. Govs. Commn. on Housing, 1994—.

FLORSHEIM, RICHARD STEVEN, lawyer; b. Milw., Apr. 2, 1949; s. Ernst Frederick and Ingeborg Miriam Florsheim; m. Neena B. Florsheim; children: Ali Brynn, David Ira, Rebecca Lynn. BS, MIT, 1971; JD magna cum laude, Marquette U., 1974. Bar: Wis. 1974, Fla. 1983. Assoc. Foley & Lardner, Milw., 1974-81, ptnr., 1981—, leader intellectual property litigation group, 1987-97, chair intellectual property dept., 1997—2006, chair industry teams dept., 2006—, chair regulated industries dept., 2006—07, mem. mgmt. commn., 2006—. Co-author: Biotechnology Patent Practice, 1994, Inside the Minds: Leading Intellectual Property Lawyers, 2001. Pres. North Shore Libr., Milw., 1985-87, Jewish Found. Econ. Opportunity, Milw., 1992-96, 05-; bd. dirs. Milw. Jewish Fedn., 1987-93, 96-02, NCCJ Wis. region, 1990-2000, Ohr Hatorah Jewish Heritage Ctr., 2002-2007, pres., 2002-2007, Children's Rsch. Inst., 2005— Mem. ABA, Am. Intellectual Property Law Assn. (subcom. chmn. 1992-97), Fed. Cir. Bar Assn., Wis. Bar Assn., Milw. Bar Assn., Marquette Law Alumni Assn. (pres. 1985-86). Office: Foley & Lardner LLP 777 E Wisconsin Ave Ste 3800 Milwaukee WI 53202-5367 Office Phone: 414-297-5515. Business E-Mail: rflorsheim@foley.com.

FLOSKI, DOUG, lawyer; b. Paris, Ill., Nov. 15, 1956; s. Frank Jr. and Mary Floski; m. Betsy Burkhard; 3 children. BA in Polit. Sci. and Econs. cum laude, Knox Coll., 1978; JD, U. Ill., 1981. Asst. state's atty. Ogle County State's Atty.'s Office, 1981-84; assoc. Bikakis, Huebaum, Titus, Vohs & Storm, Sioux City, Iowa, 1984-86; 1st asst. Ogle County State's Atty.'s Office, 1986-90; pvt. practice Byron, Ill., 1990-92; state's atty. Ogle County, 1992—. Chairperson Human Rights Commn. of Village of Progress; bd. dirs. H.O.P.E. Nat. Merit scholar. Mem. Nat. Dist. Attys. Assn., Ill. State Bar Assn., Ogle County Bar Assn. Office: Ogle County State's Atty County Courthouse 110 S 4th St Oregon IL 61061-1610

FLOURNOY, NANCY, statistician, educator; b. Long Beach, Calif., May 4, 1947; d. Carr Irvine Flournoy and Elizabeth Flournoy; m. Leonard B. Hearne, Aug. 28, 1978. BS, UCLA, 1969, MS, 1971; PhD, U. Wash., 1982. Dir. clin. stats. Fred Hutchinson Cancer Rsch. Ctr., Seattle, 1974-86; dir. stats. and probability NSF, Washington, 1986—88; prof. stats. American U., Washington, 1988—2002; chmn., prof. stats. U. Mo., Columbia, Mo., 2002—. Mem. of corp. Nat. Inst. Statis. Scis., Research Triangle Park, N.C., 1990-97, coun. Inst. Math. Stats., 2004—. Editor Multiple Stats. Integration, 1991, Adaptive Designs, 1995, New Developments and Applications in Experimental Designs, 1998, Adaptive Designs in Clinical Trials, 2005. USPHS fellow, 1969-71, Elizabeth Scott award, 2002, F.N. David award, Com. Pres. Statis. Soc. Fellow AAAS, Inst. Math. Stats., Am. Statis. Assn. (chair coun. sects. 1994), World Acad. Art and Sci., Washington Acad. Sci.; mem. Caucus for Women in Stats., Internat. Stats. Inst., Internat. Biometric Soc., Nat. Inst. Stats. Scis. (Disting. Svc. award, 2006). Democrat. Achievements include development of new statistical procedures for clinical trials and response-driven experimental designs; research on bone marrow transplantation, on graft versus leukemia, on infectious diseases in immuno-compromised hosts, on information management. Office: U Mo Dept Stats 146 Middlebush Columbia MO 65211-4100 Office Phone: 573-882-6376.

FLOWER, JOANN, nurse, former state legislator; b. May 6, 1935; m. Paul Flower. BS, Johns Hopkins U. Mem. Kans. Ho. of Reps., 1989—2001; nurse, 1996—. Home: PO Box 97 Oskaloosa KS 66066-0097

FLOWERS, CHARLES EDWARD, state legislator; m. Aleta Flowers; 3 children. Student, Huron Coll., 1958. Mem. S.D. State Senate, 1989—, mem. taxation, edn., local govt., transp. coms., mem. agr. and natural resources coms. Home: PO Box 156 Iroquois SD 57353-0156

FLOWERS, DAMON BRYANT, architect; b. Detroit, May 16, 1952; s. Marrell Curtis and Mattie (Rice) F.; m. Adria Faye Burrows, July 28, 1979; children: Lee, Dadria, Damon Bryant II. BS in Architecture, Lawrence Inst. Tech., 1974; BA in Liberal Arts, Cen. Mich. U., 1982; MS in Fin., Ctrl. Mich. U., 1984; JD, Detroit Coll. Law, 1990. Bar: Mich. 1990; registered arch., Mich., Ill., Wis., Ohio, Fla., N.Y. Architect Wayne State U., 1983-85; construction project mgmt. dir. St. Joseph Hosp. and Health Ctrs., 1985-91; v.p. ops. Argus & Assocs., 1991-94; assoc. v.p. facilities devel. and ops. Washtenaw C.C., 1994—. Mem. AIA, APPA, BOCA, Constrn. Spec. Inst., NFPA. Mem. African Methodist Episcopal Ch. Avocation: photography. E-mail: dflowers@wccnet.edu.

FLOWERS, LARRY LEE, fire chief, educator; b. Newark, Ohio, May 5, 1952; s. Roy Edwin and Ruth Ellen (Fairell) F.; m. Patty Ann Ball, May 8, 1971; children: Mandy Leigh, Kiley Ann. Student, Ohio Acad., 1973, Eastland Vocat., 1973, Ohio State U., 1972. Instr. emergency med. tech. State of Ohio, 1971-81, fire instr., 1972—, rescue instr., 1974—. Chmn. Groveport Human Needs Com., Ohio, 1979—; mem. Grade Sch. Adv. Bd., Canal Winchester, Ohio, 1982—, High Sch. Adv. Bd., Canal Winchester, 1984—. Mem. Franklin County Firefighters Assn., Ohio Fire Chiefs' Assn. (bd. dirs. 1983—), Internat. Fire Chiefs' Assn. Republican. Methodist. Avocations: boating, water skiing, swimming. Home: 216 Washington St Canal Winchester OH 43110-1224

FLOWERS, MARY E., state legislator; b. July 31, 1951; married. Student, Kennedy-King CC, U. Ill. Mem. from 21st dist. Ill. Ho. of Reps., 1985—, chair com. on health care availability access, vice chair appropriations-elem. and secondary edn. com., mem. commerce and bus. devel. com., mem. human svcs. com. Co-chmn. Il. Conf. Women Legis.; spokesperson Com. on Ins.; mem. Healthcare and Human Svcs. Com., Fin. Instns. Com., Consumer Protection Com. Recipient Black Rose award League of Black Women, 1988, Kizzy award Black Women Hall of Fame Found., 1990, Friend of Labor award AFL-CIO, 1990. Office: Ill Ho of Reps 251-E Stratton Bldg Springfield IL 62706-0001 also: 2525 W 79th St Chicago IL 60652 E-mail: state.repflowers@comcast.net, mflowers@hdsmail.state.il.us.

FLOYD, ALTON DAVID, cell biologist, consultant; b. Henderson, Ky., July 17, 1941; s. Frank and Queen Tina (Melton) F.; m. Barbara Wilson, Aug. 18, 1962; children: Fara Alison, Heather Lynn. BS, U. Ky., 1963; PhD, U. Louisville, 1968. From lectr. to asst. prof. U. Mich., Ann Arbor, 1967-72; from asst. to assoc. prof. Sch. of Medicine Ind. U., Bloomington, 1972-83, assoc. prof. Sch. of Medicine Indpls., 1983-84; sect. head cell biology Miles Sci., Inc., Naperville, Ill., 1984-85; sr. staff scientist Miles, Inc., Elkhart, Ind., 1985-89; pvt. practice cons. Edwardsburg, Mich., 1989—; assoc. dir. Ctr. Light Microscope Imaging and Biotech. Carnegie Mellon U., Pitts., 1991. Bd. dirs. Endotech Corp., Indpls.; mem. subcom. immunohistochem. stains NCCLS, 1995-96; industry rep. adv. panel hematology and pathology devices FDA, 1996-99; trustee Biol. Stain Commn., 1997—. Mem. Am. Assn. Anatomists, Tissue Culture Assn., Soc. Analytical Cytology, Histochem. Soc., Soc. Quantitative Morphology, Soc. Histotech. Avocations: sailing, reading, wood and metal shopwork, computing. Home and Office: 23126 S Shore Dr Edwardsburg MI 49112-8502 Office Phone: 269-699-7182. Personal E-mail: al.floyd@juno.com.

FLOYD, GARY LEON, plant cell biologist; b. Moline, Ill., Dec. 23, 1940; s. Leland L. and Zenta (Henderson) F.; m. Myrna A. Floyd, Aug. 18, 1963. BA, U. No. Iowa, 1962; MS, U. Okla., 1966; PhD, Miami U., Oxford, Ohio, 1971. Sci. tchr. Grinnell (Iowa) Jr. High Sch., 1962-65; instr. Miami U., 1966-68; asst. prof. Rutgers U., New Brunswick, NJ, 1971-75; asst. prof. plant biology Ohio State U., Columbus, 1975-78, assoc. prof., 1978-83, prof., 1983-96, assoc. dean biol. scis., 1986-88, dean, 1989-96, prof. and dean emeritus, 1996—. Dir. TEM facility plant biology dept. Ohio State U., Columbus, 1978-86. Contbr. articles to profl. jours. NSF scholar, 1965-66; recipient Alumni Teaching award Ohio State U., 1980, Disting. Rsch. award, 1982, Darbaker prize Bot. Soc. Am., 1993, award of excellence Phycological Soc. Am., 2003; Phycological Soc. Am. nat. lectr., 1983-85. Avocation: golf. Home: 936 Kendale Rd S Columbus OH 43220-4148 Business E-Mail: floyd.1@osu.edu.

FLUCK, MICHELE M(ARGUERITE), biology professor; b. Geneva, Aug. 5, 1940; came to U.S., 1972; d. Wilhelm and Henriette Alice (Delaloye) F. MS, U. Geneva, 1964-66, PhD, 1972. Rsch. assoc. N.Y. Pub. Health Rsch. Inst., NYC, 1972-73; instr. Harvard Med. Sch., Boston, 1973-78, asst. prof., 1978-79; assoc. prof. Mich. State U., East Lansing, 1979-86, prof., 1986-90, disting. prof., 1990—. Contbr. articles to profl. jours. Recipient Young Investigator's award, Nat. Cancer Inst.; grantee Nat. Cancer Inst., 1979—, Am. Cancer Soc. grantee, 1987—. Fellow Leukemia Soc. Am. (scholar 1979-85); mem. AAAS, Am. Assn. virologists. Avocations: music, feminism, social issues. Office: Mich State U Microbiology Dept Giltner Hall East Lansing MI 48824-1101

FLUNO, JERE DAVID, consumer products company executive; b. Wisconsin Rapids, Wis., June 3, 1941; s. Rexford Hollis and Irma Dell (Wells) F.; m. Anne Marie Derezinski, Aug. 10, 1963; children: Debra, Julie, Mary Beth, Brian. BBA, U. Wis., 1963. CPA, Ill. Audit supr. Grant Thornton, Chgo., 1963-69; controller W.W. Grainger, Inc., Skokie, Ill., 1969-74, v.p., controller, 1974-75, v.p. fin., 1975-81, sr. v.p., CFO, 1981-84, vice chmn., 1984—, dir., 1975—. Bd. dirs. W.W. Grainger, Inc., Skokie, Ill., Grainger FSC, Inc., Dayton Elec. Mfg. Co., Chgo., Midwest Clearing Corp., Midwest Securities Trust Co., Securities Trust Co. of N.J., Andrew Corp., Chgo. Trustee Mus. Sci. and Industry, Chgo., 1994; bd. govs. Chgo. Stock Exch., 1989, bd. dirs. Lake Forest Symphony, 1995—; adv. coun. Divsn. Intercollegiate Athletics U. Wis.-Madison, 1993—, dir. dean's adv. bd. Wis. Sch. Bus., 1993—, U. Wis.-Madison Found., 1985—; mem. Chgo. com. Chgo. Coun. Fgn. Rels. Mem. AICPA, Fin. Execs. Inst., Ill. CPA Soc., Econ. Club Chgo. (bd. dirs. 1979—), The Hundred Club of Lake County (bd. dirs.), U. Wis. Alumni Assn. (bd. dirs.), Comml. Club Chgo. Clubs: Knollwood (gov., Lake Forest, Ill.); U. Wis. (Chgo.); Island Country (Marco Island, Fla.). Republican. Roman Catholic. Office: W W Grainger Inc 100 Grainger Pkwy Lake Forest IL 60045-5201

FLYE, M. WAYNE, surgeon, immunologist, educator, writer; b. Tarboro, NC, June 23, 1942; s. Charlie A. and Martha E. (Bullock) F.; m. Phyllis Webb, June 7, 1964; children: Christopher Warren, Brandon Reid. BS, U. N.C., 1964, MD, 1967; MA in Immunology, Duke U., 1972, PhD in Immunology, 1980; MA (hon.), Yale U., 1985. Diplomate Am. Bd. Surgery, Am. Bd. Thoracic Surgery, Am. Bd. Vascular Surgery. Intern. surg. Case-We. Res. U., Cleve., 1967-68, res. gen. and cardio-thoracic surgery, 1968-75; instr., teaching scholar, vascular and transplantation surgery Duke U. Med. Ctr., Durham, NC, 1975-76; sr. investigator, chief thoracic surg. svc. NIH, Bethesda, Md., 1977-79; chief vascular surgery U. Tex. Med. Br., Galveston, 1979-82, assoc. prof. surgery and microbiology, 1980-82; dir. div. organ transplantation and immunology, prof. transplantation, dir. sect. gen. surgery Yale U. Sch. Medicine, New Haven, 1983-85; prof. surgery, molecular microbiology and immunology Washington U. Med. Sch., St. Louis, 1985—, prof. radiology, 2000—, mem. admissions com., 2000—. Trustee New Eng. Organ Bank, Boston, 1984-85; com. mem. United Network Orgn. Sharing, Richmond, Va., 1986-89; mem. anesthesiology and trauma study sect. NIH Surgery, 1991-95; merit rev. com. for surgery VA, 1994-96, chmn., 1996—; merit rev. com. Am. Heart Assn. study sect., 2001--; chief of surgery St. Louis Regional Hosp., 1996; chief thoracic surgery St. Louis VA Hosp., 1996—. Editor: Principles of Organ Transplantation, 1989, The Thymus: Regulator of Cellular Immunity, 1993, Atlas of Organ Transplantation, 1994; mem. editl. bd. Clin. Transplantation, 1986—, Prospectives in Gen. Surgery, 1988-94, Transplantation, 1989-2000, Xanthus Intelligence Unit Reports, 1990—, Shock: Molecular, Cellular and Systemic Pathobiology of Injury, 1993-99, Transplantation Sci., 1993—, Jour. Surg. Rsch., 1995-2000, Surgery, 1997—, Graft, Jour. Organ and Cellular Transplantation, 1998—, New Surgery, 2000—; assoc. editor Jour. Immunology, 1996-99, Hepatology, 2003—. Lt. col. U.S. Army, 1976-78. Recipient James W. McLaughlin medal U. Tex.-Galveston, 1982. Fellow ACP, So. Thoracic Surg. Assn. (Best Sci. Paper award 1980); mem. Am. Assn. Immunologists, Internat. Cardiovascular Soc., N.Y. Acad. Sci., Soc. Thoracic Surgeons, Am. Soc. Transplant Physicians, Am. Soc. Transplant Surgeons (program com. 1984-86, Ethics Com. 1994-95), Brit. Soc. Immunology, Transplantation Soc., Mid-Am. Transplant Assn. (bd. dirs. 1986-89), Am. Fedn. Clin. Rsch., Royal Soc. Medicine, AAAS, Surg. Infection Soc. (edn. and fellowship com. 1998-2002), Reticuloendothelial Soc., Soc. Univ. Surgeons, Soc. Clin. Vascular Surgery, Brit. Transplantation Soc., So. Assn. Vascular Surgery, Am. Coll. Chest Physicians, Soc. Surg. Oncology, Am. Assn. Thoracic Surgery, Surg. Biology Club I, Am. Assn. Study Liver Diseases, Am. Surg. Assn., So. Surg. Assn., Cen. Surg. Assn., Soc. Internat. de Chirurgie, Midwestern Vascular Surg. Soc., Soc. Vascular Surg., World Ann. Hepato-Pancreato-Bilary Surg., Soc. Surgery of Alimentary Tract, Shock Soc., Gen. Thoracic Surgery Club, Soc. Thoracic Surg., St. Louis Surg. Soc. (v.p. 2002-03, treas. 2003—), Sigma Xi, Alpha Omega Alpha, Chi Psi, Young Republicans N.C. Episcopalian. Avocations: sports, genealogy, medical history. Home: 585 Coeur De Royale Dr Apt 402 Saint Louis MO 63141-6915 Home Phone: 314-991-4535; Office Phone: 314-362-7145. Business E-Mail: flyew@wustl.edu.

FLYNN, CAROL, state legislator; b. Aug. 7, 1933; m. Richard L. Flynn; 2 children. Mem. Minn. State Senate, 1990—. Mem. Democratic Farm Labor Party. Office: Minn Senate 120 State Capitol 75 Constitution Ave Saint Paul MN 55155-1606

FLYNN, GARY L., pharmaceutical executive; b. Columbus, Ohio, Oct. 8, 1949; BBA, Franklin U. Various fin. and mgmt. positions Abbott Labs., Abbott Park, Ill., 1971—, divisional v.p., contr. Ross Products divsn., 1993, v.p., contr., sr. v.p. Ross Products, 2001—. Mem. bd. dirs. Columbus Children's Hosp. Rsch. Inst.; bd. trustees Franklin U. Office: Abbott Labs 100 Abbott Park Rd Abbott Park IL 60064-6400

FLYNN, PAULINE T., retired speech pathologist, educator; BA, Paterson State Coll., 1963; MA, Seton Hall U., 1966; PhD, U. Kans., 1970; cert. specialist in aging, U. Mich., 1982. Speech pathologist Bd. Edn., Parsippany-Troy Hills, NJ, 1963—67; prof., chmn. dept. audiology and speech scis. Ind. U. Purdue U., Ft. Wayne, 1970—2003, prof. emerita, 2003—. Ednl. cons. Retirement Ctr., Ft. Wayne, 1982-85. Contbr. articles to nat. and internat. jours. Recipient Outstanding Alumna award William Paterson Coll., 1973, Woman of Achievement award Ft. Wayne YWCA, 1992. Fellow Am. Speech, Lang. and Hearing Assn.; mem. Am. Speech, Lang., Hearing Assn., Ind. Speech, Lang. and Hearing Assn. (honors 2003).

FLYNN, THOMAS L. (TOM FLYNN), state legislator; b. Dubuque, Iowa, June 11, 1955; m. Jane. BA in Acctg. and Fin., Loras Coll., 1977; MBA, U. Dubuque, 1985. Owner small bus.; mem. faculty dept. bus. Clark Coll.; mem. Iowa Senate from 17th dist., 1994—. Past pres. N.E. Iowa Coun. Boy Scouts Am.; trustee United Way Dubuque. Mem. at. Ready-Mix Concrete Assn. (bd. dirs.), Nat. Aggregates Assn. (bd. dirs.), Dubuque Area C. of C. (bd. dirs.). Democrat. Home: 21367 Girl Scout Rd Epworth IA 52045-9698 E-mail: tom_flynn@legis.state.ia.us.

FLYNN, WILLIAM FREDERICK, lawyer; b. Washington, Nov. 15, 1952; s. L. Martin and Martha Jean (Rennie) F.; m. Deborah Ann Norton, Apr. 20, 1985. AB, U. Mich., 1975, JD, 1978. Bar: Wis. 1978. Assoc. Reinhart Boerner Van Deuren S.C., Milw., 1978-85, ptnr., 1986—. Mem. ABA, Wis. Bar Assn., Milw. Bar Assn. Home: 115 E Miller Dr Mequon WI 53092-6191 Office: Reinhart Boerner Et Al 1000 N Water St Ste 2100 Milwaukee WI 53202-3197 Office Phone: 414-298-8128. Business E-Mail: wflynn@reinhartlaw.com.

FODREA, CAROLYN WROBEL, adult education educator, reading researcher; b. Hammond, Ind., Feb. 1, 1943; d. Stanley Jacob and Margaret Caroline (Stupeck) Wrobel; m. Howard Frederick Fodrea, June 17, 1967 (div. Jan. 1987); children: Gregory Kirk, Lynn Renee. BA in Elem. Edn., Purdue U., 1966; MA in Reading and Lang. Devel., U. Chgo., 1973; postgrad., U. Colo., Denver, 1986—87. Cert. elem. tchr., Ind., Ill. Tchr. various schs., Ind., Colo., 1966-87; founder, supr., clinician Reading Clinic, Children's Hosp., Denver, 1969-73; pvt. practice Denver, 1973—87, Deerfield, Ill., 1973—; creator of pilot presch.-kindergarten lang. devel. program Gary, Ind. Diocese Schs., 1987—, therapist lang. and reading disabilities, 1987—; pres. Reading Rsch. Ctr., Arlington Heights, Ill., 2000—. Conducted Lang. Devel. Workshop, Gary, Ind. 1988; tchr., adult education educator, adult basic edn. Dawson Tech. Sch., 1990, Coll. Lake County, 1991, Prairie State Coll., 1991—, Chgo. City Colls., 1991, R.J. Daley Coll., 1991, Coll. DuPage, 1991—; condr. adult basic edn. workshops for Coll. of DuPage, R.J. Daley Coll., 1992, Ill. Lang. Devel. Literacy Program; tchr. Korean English Lang. Inst., Chgo., 1996, Lang. Devel. Program for Minorities, 2000; dir. pilot study Cabrini Green Tutoring Ctr., Chgo., 2000, Ill. Sch. Dist., 2006; presenter in field. Author: Language Development Program, 1985, Presch. Kindergarten Lang. Devel. Program, 1988, A Multi-Sensory Stimulation Program for the Premature Baby in Its Incubator to Reduce Medical Costs and Academic Failure, 1986, Predicting At-Risk Babies for First Grade Reading Failure Before Birth A 15 Year Study, A Language Development Program, Grades 1 to Adult, 1988, 92, Nankegan IAQ Study Using an Air Purifier to Reduce Classroom Air Pollutants in a 3rd and 4th Grade Minority Classroom and Improving Student Attention, Physical Health, Performance, and Fine Motor Skills, 2006; editor, pub.: ESL For Native Spanish Speakers, 1996, ESL for Native Korean Speakers, 1996. Active Graland Country Day Sch., Denver, 1981-83, N.W. Ind. Children's Chorale, 1988—; Ill. state chair Babies and You com. March of Dimes, 1999—; founder Indoor Environ. Health Consultants, 2007-; mem. Arlington Heights Environ. Control Commn., 2007-. Mem. NEA, IAQ Assn. (Chgo. Chpt, charter mem), Am. Ednl. Rsch. Assn., Internat. Reading Assn., Am. Coun. for Children with Learning Disabilities, Am. Acad. Environ. Medicine (chhmn. pub. rels., mktg. com., chmn. town meeting com. 2005), Assn. for Childhood Edn. Internat., Colo. Assn. for Edn. of Young Children, Infant Stimulation Edn. Assn., Indoor Air Quality Assn., Art Inst. Chgo., U. Chgo. Alumni Club (Denver area ann. fund, Pres. fund com. 1988—, com. mem. Denver area chpt. 1974-87). Roman Catholic. Avocations: sports, cultural activities, sewing, literature. Office Phone: 847-632-0622, 888-748-0222. Personal E-mail: carolynfodreamille@sbcglobal.net.

FOEGE, RO, state representative; b. George, Iowa, Sept. 1, 1938; m. Susan Salter; 5 children. BA, Wartburg Coll., 1960; MSW, U. Iowa, 1963. Program dir. Cath. Charities, Archdiocese of Dubuque, Iowa, 1966—78; social worker divsn. spl. edn. Grant Wood Area Edn. Agy., 1978—; mem. Iowa Ho. Reps., DesMoines, 1997—, mem. various coms. including edn., judiciary, environ. protection, human resources and human svcs. appropriations, ranking mem., justice sys. appropriations com. Chair Linn County Human Resources Adv. Bd. Mem. sch. bd. dirs. Marion Ind. Schs., 1969—73; chair Linn County Human Resources Mgmt. Bd., 1992—95; bd. mem. S.E. Linn Cmty. Ctr.; active Iowa State Mental Health Planning Coun.; mem. Iowa Tobacco Use Prevention Com., Iowa Cmty. Empowerment Bd., Annie E. Casey Family & Children's Svcs. Nat. Adv. Bd. Mem.: NEA, NASW, Iowa Sch. Social Workers Assn., Grant Wood Edn. Assn., Iowa State Edn. Assn., Am. Fedn. Tchrs. Democrat. Lutheran. Office: State Capitol East 12th and Grand Des Moines IA 50319 also: PO Box 128 412 4th Ave South Mount Vernon IA 52314

FOGARTY, ROBERT STEPHEN, historian, educator, editor; b. Bklyn., Aug. 30, 1938; s. Michael Joseph and Marguerita (Carmody) F. BS, Fordham U., 1960; PhD, U. Denver, 1968. Instr. Mich. State U., 1963-67; asst. prof. Antioch Coll., Yellow Springs, Ohio, 1968-73, chmn. humanities area, 1973-74, 78-79, assoc. prof., 1974-80, prof. history, 1980—, John Dewey prof. emeritus; prof. Advanced Internat. Studies, Ctr. for Chinese-Am. Johns Hopkins U., 1986-87; editor Antioch Rev., 1977—; dir. Associated Colls. Midwest/Gt. Lakes Coll. Assn., Program in Humanities, Newberry Library, 1978-79; cons. Nat. Endowment for Arts, 1975-81, U. Waterloo, Ont., Canada, 1981. Vis. fellow NYU Inst. for Humanities, 1992—93; Darwin lectr. human biology Galton Inst., London, 1994; lectr. U. Leece, 2006, U. Calabria, 2006, U. So. Miss., 2006. Author: Dictionary of American Communal and Utopian History, 1980, The Righteous Remnant-The House of David, 1981, All Things New: Communes and Utopian Movements, 1860-1914, 1990, Special Love/Special Sex, 1994, Desire and Duty at Oneida: Tirzah Miller's Intimate Memoir, 2000; editor Antioch Rev., 1977—; contbr.: American Encyclopeida of American Culture, 2001; contbr. essays to The Nation, TLS, Mo. Rev.; contbr. articles to profl. jours. Recipient Martha K. Cooper award for editl. achievement, 1981, Nora Magid Award for Editing PEN Am. Ctr., 2003; grantee Am. Philos. Soc., 1976, Am. Coun. Learned Socs.; fellow NEH, 1980, All Souls Coll., Oxford U., 1988, Lloyd Lewis fellow Newberry Libr., 1995, Galton Inst. fellow, 1995; Fulbright Disting. Lectr. to Korea, 2000, Gilder Lehrman fellow 2001, Mary Baker Eddy libr. fellow, 2004. Mem.: PEN/Am. Ctr., Orgn. Am. Historians, Nat. Hist. Communal Sites Assn. (exec. com. 1975—2002), Am. Studies Assn. (bibliography com. 1981—). Office: Antioch Rev Inc PO Box 148 Yellow Springs OH 45387-0148 Office Phone: 927-769-1365. E-mail: rfogarty@antioch.edu.

FOGEL, HENRY, orchestra administrator; b. NYC, Sept. 23, 1942; s. Julius and Dorothy (Levine) F.; m. Frances Sylvia Polner, June 12, 1945; children—Karl Franz, Holly Dana Student, Syracuse U., 1960—63; doctorate (hon.), Northwestern U., Roosevelt U., Columbia Coll., Chgo. Program dir., v.p. Sta. WONO, Syracuse, NY, 1963-78; orch. mgr. N.Y. Philharm., NYC, 1978-81; exec. dir. Nat. Symphony Orch., Washington, 1981-85; pres. Chgo. Symphony Orch. Assn., 1985—2003; pres., CEO Am. Symphony Orch. League, NYC, 2003—. Record reviewer Fanfare Mag., 1979—; contbr. to Contemporary Composers. Mem. music panel NEA, 1986-90; past pres. U. Ill. Arts Alliance, 1988-94. Mem. NARAS, Am. Symphony Orch. League (bd. dirs. 1988—), Assn. Recorded Sound Collections (record reviewer jour. 1978). Office: Am Symphony Orch League 33 W 60th St 5th Fl New York NY 10023 Business E-Mail: hfogel@symphony.org.

FOGEL, ROBERT WILLIAM, economist, educator, historian; b. NYC, July 1, 1926; s. Harry Gregory and Elizabeth (Mitnik) Fogel; m. Enid Cassandra Morgan, Apr. 2, 1949; children: Michael Paul, Steven Dennis. AB, Cornell U., 1948; AM, Columbia U., 1960; PhD, Johns Hopkins U., 1963; MA (hon.), U. Cambridge, Eng., 1975, Harvard U., 1976; DSc (hon.), U. Rochester, 1987, U. de Palermo, Argentina, 1994, Brigham Young U., 1995, SUNY, Binghamton, NY, 1999. Instr. Johns Hopkins U., 1958—59; asst. prof. U. Rochester, 1960—64; Ford Found. vis. rsch. prof. U. Chgo., 1963—64, asso. prof., 1964—65, prof. econs., 1965—69, prof. econs. and history, 1970—75; prof. econs. U. Rochester, 1968—71, prof. econs. and history, 1972—75; Taussig rsch. prof. Harvard U., Cambridge, Mass., 1973—74, Harold Hitchings Burbank prof. polit. economy, prof. history, 1975—81; Charles R. Walgreen Disting. Svc. prof. Am. institutions U. Chgo., 1981. Pitt prof. Am. history and insts. U. Cambridge, 1975—76; chmn. com. math. and statis. methods in history Math. Social Sci. Bd., 1965—72; rsch. assoc. Nat. Bur. Econ. Rsch., 1978—, co-dir. Cohort Studies program, 1998—, dir. DAE program, 1978—91; dir. Ctr. for Population Econ., Chgo. Author: The Union Pacific Railroad: A Case in Premature Enterprise, 1960, Railroads and American Economic Growth: Essays in Econometric History, 1964, Ten Lectures on the New Economic History, 1977, Without Consent of Contract: The Rise and Fall of American Slavery, Vol. 1, 1989, The Fourth Great Awakening and the Future of Egalitarianism, 2000, The Slavery Debates, 1952-1990: A Retrospective, 2003, The Escape from Hunger and Premature Death 1700-2100: Europe, America, and the Third World, 2004; author: (with others) The Reinterpretation of American Economic History, 1971, Dimensions of Quantitative Research in History, 1972, Without Consent of Contract: The Rise and Fall of American Slavery, Vols. 2-4, 1992; author: (with S.L. Engerman) Time on the Cross: The Economics of American Negro Slavery, 1974; author: (with G.R. Elton) Which Road to the Past? Two Views of History, 1983. Co-recipient The Bancroft prize, 1975, Gustavus Myers prize, 1990, Nobel prize, Nobel Found., 1993; recipient Arthur H. Cole prize, 1968, Schumpter prize, 1971, Disting. Alumnus award, Johns Hopkins U., 2000; fellow, Gilman, 1957—60, Social Sci. Rsch. Coun., 1960, Ford Found. Faculty Rsch., 1970; grantee Faculty Rsch., 1966, NSF, 1967, 1970, 1972, 1975—76, 1978, 1992—96, Fulbright, 1968, NIH, 1991—. Fellow: AAAS, Royal Hist. Soc., Econometric Soc., Brit. Acad. (corr.); mem.: NAS, Am. Philos. Soc., Internat. Union for Sci. Study of Population, Population Assn. Am., Am. Acad. Arts and Scis., Agrl. History Soc., Social Sci. History Assn. (pres. 1980—81), Assn. Am. Historians, Am. Hist. Assn., Econ. History Assn., Econ. History Assn. (trustee 1972—81, pres. 1977—78), Royal Econ. Soc., Am. Econ. Soc. (pres. 1998), European Acad. Arts, Scis. and Humanities, Phi Beta Kappa. Office: U Chgo Grad Sch Bus Ctr for Population Econ 5807 S Woodlawn Ave Chicago IL 60637-1511 Office Phone: 773-702-7709.

FOGLE, JAMES LEE, lawyer; b. Doniphan, Mo., June 6, 1950; s. Carter Lemuel and Leatha Sue (Logan) F.; m. Pattylynn Raymond, Sept. 18, 1982; children: Kirsten icole, Ryan Christopher. BA, Whitman Coll., 1972; JD, Duke U., 1975. Bar: Mo. 1975, Ill. 1976. Assoc. Coburn, Croft & Putzell, St. Louis, 1975-79; ptnr. Coburn & Croft, St. Louis, 1979-96, mng. ptnr., 1980-84, mem. mgmt. com., 1985-89; ptnr. Thompson Coburn, LLP, St. Louis, 1996—. Bd. dirs. Life Skills Found., pres. 1996-98; bd. dirs. Rainbow Village; adj. prof. Fontbonne Coll., St. Louis, 1991-2000. Alumni admissions rep. Whitman Coll., Walla Walla, Wash., 1980—; mem. planned giving coun. DePaul Health Ctr. Found. Nat. Merit scholar Whitman Coll., 1968. Mem. ABA, Estate Planning Coun., Mo. Bar Assn. (tax com.), Am. Health Lawyers Assn., St. Louis Health Lawyers Assn., Mo. Athletic Club, Racquet Club Ladue (bd. govs. 2001-2005), Masons, Order of Coif, Phi Beta Kappa. Republican. Baptist. Avocations: tennis, snow skiing, golf, collecting political memorabilia. Office: Thompson Coburn LLP Ste 3500 One USBank Plz Saint Louis MO 63101-1623 Office Phone: 314-552-6035. E-mail: jfogle@thompsoncoburn.com.

FOK, THOMAS DSO YUN, civil engineer; b. Canton, China, July 1, 1921; came to U.S., 1947, naturalized, 1956; s D. H. and C. (Tse) F.; m. Maria M.L. Liang, Sept. 18, 1949. B.Eng., Nat. Tung-Chi U., Szechuan, China, 1945; MS, U. Ill., 1948; MBA Dr. Nadler Money Marketeer scholar, NYU, 1950; PhD, Carnegie-Mellon U., 1956. Registered profl. engr., N.Y., Pa., Ohio, Ill., Ky., W.Va., Ind., Md., Fla. Structural designer Lummus Co., NYC, 1951-53; design engr. Richardson, Gordon & Assocs., cons. engrs., Pitts., 1956-58; assoc. prof. engring. Youngstown U., Ohio, 1958-67, dir. computing ctr. Ohio, 1963-67; ptnr. Cernica, Fok & Assocs., cons. engrs., Youngstown, Ohio, 1958-64; prin. Thomas Fok & Assocs., cons. engrs., Youngstown, Ohio, 1964-65; ptnr. Mosure-Fok & Syrakis Co., Ltd., cons. Engrs., Youngstown, Ohio, 1965-76; cons. engr. to Mahoning County Engr. Ohio, 1960-65; pres. Computing Systems & Tech., Youngstown, Ohio, 1967-72; chmn. Thomas Fok and Assocs., Ltd., cons. engrs., Youngstown, Ohio, 1977—. Contbr. articles to profl. jours. Trustee Pub. Libr. of Youngstown and Mahoning County, 1973—; trustee Youngstown State U., 1975-84, chmn., 1981-83; mem. Ohio State Bd. Registration for Profl. Engrs. and Surveyors, 1992-96. Recipient Walter E. and Caroline H. Watson Found. Disting. Prof.'s award Youngstown U., 1966, Outstanding Person award Mahoning Valley Tech. Socs. Council, 1987. Fellow ASCE; mem. Am. Concrete Inst., Internat. Assn. for Bridge and Structural Engring., Am. Soc. Engring. Edn., Nat. Soc. Profl. Engrs., AAAS, Soc. Am. Mil. Engrs., Ohio Acad. Sci., N.Y. Acad. Sci., Sigma Xi, Beta Gamma Sigma, Sigma Tau, Delta Pi Sigma Lodges: Rotary. Achievements include development of a design method by computer for a solid-ribbed tied, through arch Ft. Duquesne Bridge; development of Analysis of Continuous Truss by Digital Computer. Home: 325 S Canfield Niles Rd Youngstown OH 44515-4020 Office: 3896 Mahoning Ave Youngstown OH 44515-3022

FOLAND, JEFFREY T., air transportation sales executive; BS in Mech. Engring., Purdue U.; MBA, U. Mich. With Allison Gas Turbine Divsn. GM; with Detroit Diesel Corp.; prin. cons. ZS Assocs.; v.p. N.Am. sales United Airlines, Chgo., 2005, sr. v.p. worldwide sales, 2005—. Guest lectr. Northwestern U. Kellogg Grad. Sch. Mgmt., U. Chgo. Grad. Sch. Bus.; mem. exec. com. of bd. dirs. Chgo. Convention and Tourism Bur., 2006—. Named one of Top 40 Under 40, Crain's Chgo. Bus., 2006. Office: United Air Lines Corp World Hdqs PO Box 66100 Chicago IL 60666

FOLAND, KENNETH A., geological sciences educator; b. Frederick, Md., May 25, 1945; s. Austin Franklin and P. Lillian (Wachter) F.; m. Ellen Lee Spero, June 18, 1968. BS, Bucknell U., 1967; MSc, Brown U., 1969, PhD, 1972. Postdoctoral fellow U. Pa., Phila., 1972-73, from asst. prof. to assoc. prof., 1973-80; assoc. prof. Ohio State U., Columbus, 1980-87, prof. geological scis., 1987—. Cons. divsn. nuclear chemistry Lawrence Livermore Nat. Lab., 1982-86, adv. com. nuclear waste U.S. Nuclear Regulatory Commn., 1990-99; mem. indoor radon panel Am. Lung Assn. Ohio, mem. steering and rev. com. Columbus and Franklin County Radon Study, Columbus Health Dept. Assoc. editor Isotope Geosci., 1982-99, Jour. Geophys. Rsch., Solid Earth, 1992-98; adv. editor Jour. Geol. Soc.; reviewer rsch. papers, rsch. proposals; author, co-author numerous rsch. papers, abstracts, revs. Recipient numerous grants NSF, NIH, DAAD and NATO. Fellow Geol. Soc. Am.; mem. Am. Geophys. Union, Geochem. Soc., Sigma Xi. Home: 4090 Fenwick Rd Columbus OH 43220-4870 Office: Ohio State U 125 South Oval Mall 379 Mendenhall Lab Columbus OH 43210 E-mail: foland.1@osu.edu.

FOLDY, SETH LEONARD, physician, educator; b. Cleve., Sept. 3, 1955; s. Leslie Lawrance and Roma (Bisgyer) F; m. Joan Marie Bedinghaus, June 7, 1986; children: Benjamin, Eva. BA in Human Biology with distinction, Stanford U., 1977; MD, Case Western Res. U., 1982; M in Pub. Health, Medical Coll. Wis., Milw., 2005. Dilomate Am. Bd. Family Practice, Am. Bd. Preventive Medicine, Nat. Bd. Med. Examiners. Intern in family practice Cleve. Met. Gen. Hosp., 1982-83, resident in family practice, 1983-85, chief resident in family practice, 1984-85; family physician Great Brook Valley Health Ctr., Worcester, Mass., 1985-87; med. dir. MetroHealth Family Practice, Cleve., 1987-94, dir. cmty. health svcs., 1994-96; med. dir. City of Milw. Health Dept., 1996-98, health commr., 1998—2004; prin. health.e.volution Consulting, 2004—; prin. investigator Wis. Health Info. Exch., 2004—05; med. dir. Healthcare for the Homeless, Milw., 2005—. Asst. prof. family medicine Case Western Res. U., Cleve., 1987-96; assoc. clin. prof. family and cmty. medicine and Population Health, Med. Coll. Wis., Milw., 1996—, clin. prof. health adminstrn. and informatics, U. Wis., 2001-; pub. health systems cons., Ctr. Internat. Health, 2005—, sr. pub. health cons., e Health Initiative, 2005—; spl. term fac. appointee Argonne Nat. Lab., Ill., 2004— Co-author: Health Information Exchange: From Start-Up to Sustainability, 2007; asst. editor: Urban Family Practice: A Resource Monograph, 1994; editor (newsletter) Urban Health News, 1990-96; assoc. editor Advances in Disease Surveillance, 2006—. Trustee Friends Sch. in Cleve., 1972-74; nat. com. War Resisters League, NYC, 1970-74; mem. Nat. Health Policy Leadership Coun., Washington, 1991-92, Ohio legis. adv. com. on environ. lead abatement, Columbus, 1994-95, Wis. Turning Point Transformation Team, 1998—, Wis. pub. health system terrorism and pub. health emergencies legis. coun. com., 2002; mem. info. coun. US CDC, 2000-04, steering com. Rand Inst. Summits on Info. Tech. Infrastructure for Bioterrorism, Operation Combined Assistance, US Navy Project Hope Tsunami Task Force, 2005; founder Milw. Pub. Health Found. and Health Champion Award, 2002; bd. dirs. eHealth Initiative & eHealth Inititative Found., 2002—, Greater Milw. Bus. Group on Health, 2002-, Southeast Wis. Bioterrorism Prepardness Group, Inc., 2003-, Benedict Ctr., 2007-, Planning Coun. Health and Human Svcs., 2007-. Recipient award for Excellence in Info. Tech., Nat. Assn. County and City Health Officers, 1999, Pres.'s Vol. Svc. award, 2005, 2007. Fellow Am. Acad. Family Physicians; mem. AMA, APHA (gov. coun. 1992-94, 96-98, Roemer award, 2002), Nat. Assn. City and County Health Officers (various coms.), Pub. Health Leadership Soc., Wis. Med. Soc., Milw. Acad. Medicine (bd. dirs. 2003-), Milw. County Med. Soc. (chair pub. health com. 1996—, Cmty. Svc. award 1997), Phi Beta Kappa. Achievements include participated in detecting and elimination of monkeypox virus outbreak from Western Hemisphere. Avocations: fishing, hiking, birding. Office: health evolution 3061 N Marietta Ave Milwaukee WI 53211 Home Phone: 414-906-0036. Personal E-mail: sfoldy@sbcglobal.net.

FOLEY, CHERYL M., electric power industry executive; V.p., gen. counsel PSI Energy, Inc., Ind., 1989-91; v.p., gen. counsel, corp. sec. PSI Energy, Inc. and PSI Resources Inc., Ind., 1991-94; v.p., sec., gen. counsel Cinergy Corp., Cin., 1994-99, v.p., sec., 1999—; pres. Cinergy Global Resources subs. Cinergy Corp., Cin. Office: Cinergy Corp 221 E 4th St # 30 Cincinnati OH 45202-4124

FOLEY, DANIEL RONALD, personnel director, lawyer; b. Chgo., Dec. 13, 1941; s. Daniel Edward and Louise Jean (Connolly) Foley; m. Mae Geraldine Muscarello, Jan. 30, 1965; children: Louise Ann, Sarah Elizabeth. AB in Psychology, Marquette U., 1965; JD, Depaul U., 1971. Bar: Ill. 1971, U.S. Dist. Ct. (no. dist.) Ill. 1971, U.S. Supreme Ct. 1975. Pers. recruiter Civil Svc. Commn. City of Chgo., 1965-66; pers. adminstr. Alberto Culver Co., Melrose Park, Ill., 1966-67; pers. dir. Litton Industries, Des Plaines, Ill., 1967-68; equal opportunity coord., mgr. labor rels. Canteen Corp., Chgo., 1968-71; mgr. labor rels. Internat. Telephone and Telegraph World Hdqs., NYC, 1971-79, dir. employee rels., 1979-81, 1981-85; dir. employee rels., environ. health and safety, group v.p. human resources IBP, Dakota City, Nebr., 1985-88; v.p. adminstrn., gen. counsel Domino's Pizza Inc., Ann Arbor, Mich., 1988-93; pres. Exec. Bus. Ptnrs., Inc., 1993-94; v.p. human resources MascoTech, Inc., 1994-96, Masco Corp., Taylor, Mich., 1996—. Spkr. labor law and bus. seminars Wharton Sch., U. Pa., St. Mary's Coll., LEGATUS; faculty mem. Mich. U. Named Mich. Human Resource Exec. of Yr., 2006. Mem.: Knights of Holy Sepulchre, Knights of Malta, Beta Gamma Sigma. Roman Catholic. Avocation: photography. Home: 3399 Robinwood Dr Ann Arbor MI 48103-1748 Personal E-mail: dcndan@aol.com.

FOLEY, ELLEN MADALINE, journalist; b. Chgo., Apr. 13, 1952; d. Thomas Jennings and Joan Ellen (Murphy) F.; m. Thomas Foley Mullaney, June 30, 1984; children: Kaitlin, Maura. BA in Polit. Sci., U. Wis., 1974, MA in Journalism, 1988. Mng. editor Menominee (Mich.) Herald Leader, 1976-78; copy editor The Milw.-Sentinel, 1978-79, The Detroit News, 1979-80; reporter, copy editor The Star-Tribune, Mpls., 1980-91, asst. features editor, food editor, 1991-93; features editor The Kansas City (Mo.) Star, 1993-96, asst. mng. editor/features, 1996—98; mng. editor The Phila. Daily News, Phila., 1998—2004; editor Wis. State Jour., Madison, 2004—. Mem. Jr. League of Mpls., 1980—, bd. dirs., 1989; founder Violence Against Women Coalition, Mpls., 1988-93. Recipient Minn. Page One award, 1987, Vol. of Distinction award Assn. Jr. Leagues Internat., 1996; named Pulitzer Prize juror, 2005, 06. Mem. Am. Assn. Sun. & Feature Editors (bd. dirs., conf. host. 1996-98, bd dirs. associated press mng. editors 2004—), Am. Soc. Newspaper Editors (bd. dirs. 2005) Avocations: reading, hiking. Office: Wis State Jour 1901 Fish Hatchery Rd PO Box 8058 Madison WI 53708 Office Phone: 608-252-6104. Business E-Mail: efoley@madison.com.

FOLEY, JAMES M., state legislator; State rep. dist. 81 Mo. Ho. of Reps. Home: 3274 Adie Rd Saint Ann MO 63074-3402

FOLEY, JOSEPH LAWRENCE, sales executive; b. Albuquerque, June 14, 1953; s. Joseph Bernard and Joan Marie (Johnston) F.; m. Michelle Troglia, Jan., 1992; children: Joseph Louis, Kyle Benjamin. BS in Polit. Sci. & Mktg., Niagara U., 1975. Asst. retail buyer Lord & Taylor, NYC, 1975, E.J. Korvette Co., NYC, 1976-78, retail buyer, 1978-80, retail mdse. mgr., 1980; import sales coord. Block Industries, NYC, 1980-81; v.p. sales Sutton Shirt Co., NYC, 1981-83; exec. v.p. V.I.P. Imports, NYC, 1984-97; prin. Long-Term Care Cons. of Ill., Inc., 1998—. Mem.: Million Dollar Roundtable, Chi Are Racing Assn. Republican. Roman Catholic. Avocations: marathon running, baseball, tennis, skiing, golf. Home and Office: 225 Sunset Ridge Rd Willowbrook IL 60527-8406

FOLEY, LEO THOMAS, state legislator, lawyer; b. Anoka, Minn., Oct. 25, 1928; s. John Edward and Anna Mathilda (Lubrecht) F.; m. Sally Lynn Werner, July 6, 1954 (dec. Aug. 1990); children: Jane Anne Foley Doyle, Nancy Lee Foley Nelson; m. Kathryn Marlys Nutter, Aug. 23, 1997. BA, U. Minn., 1974; MA, Mankato State U., 1979; JD, William Mitchell Coll. Law, 1994. Cert. insdsl. security mgr. Security officer Fed. Cartridge Corp., New Brighton, Minn., 1952-54; maj. Minn. State Patrol, St. Paul, 1954-87; security mgr. Unisys, St. Paul, 1987-91; asst. Anoka County (Minn.) atty. pub. law sect., 1994—; mem. Minn. Senate from 49th dist., St. Paul, 1997—. Bd. dirs. Citizens League, Mpls., 1972-76; mem., chmn. Planning Commn., Anoka, 1972—; mem., treas. Minn. Bicentennial Com. of U.S. Constn., St. Paul, 1984-91. With USN, 1947-52. Mem. ABA, ACLU, LWV, Minn. Bar Assn., Hennepin County Bar Assn., Am. Soc. for Indsl. Security, Wilderness Soc., Audubon Soc., Minn. Police and Peace Officers Assn. (life), Am. Legion, Common Cause, U. Minn. Alumni Assn., Sierra Club. Democrat. Mem. United Ch. of Christ. Avocations: photography, fishing, computer programming, gardening. Home: 12275 Hummingbird St NW Coon Rapids MN 55448-1936

FOLEY, MIKE, state official; b. Rochester, NY, Apr. 5, 1954; m. Susan Foley; children: Laura, Matthew, Marie, Elizabeth, Peter, Andrew. BS, SUNY, Brockport, 1976; MBA, Mich. State U., 1978. Cons. Kirschner Assn., 1978-79; dir. fin. analysis Nat. Assn. Regulatory Utility Commrs., 1979-97; corp. planning analyst ebr. Pub. Power Dist., 1997—; mem. Nebr. Legislature from 29th dist., Lincoln, 2001—06; state auditor State of Nebr., 2007—. Adv. neighborhood commr., Washington, 1986-1988. Office: PO Box 98917 Lincoln NE 68509

FOLK, FRANK ANTON, surgeon, educator; b. Chgo., Dec. 15, 1925; s. Frank A. and Anna (Pilisauer) F.; m. Lorna C. Hill, June 18, 1949; children: Laura, Lawrence, Patricia, Elizabeth, Thomas, James, Mary, Tracy Ann, William. BS, Northwestern U., 1945; postgrad., U. Wis., 1945-46; MD, U. Ill., 1949. Diplomate Am. Bd. Surgery, Nat. Bd. Med. Examiners; lic. Ill., Wis. Rotating intern Cook County Hosp., Chgo., 1949-51; resident in gen. surgery Cook County/Columbus Hosp., Chgo., 1951, Cook County Hosp., Chgo., 1954-57, surgeon, 1958-69, dir. of surgery, 1969-72; mem. faculty Stritch Sch. Medicine Loyola U., Maywood, Ill., 1958—, prof. surgery Stritch Sch. Medicine, 1972-96; prof. emeritus, 1997—; rsch. fellow Hektoen Inst., Chgo., 1959-64; asst. chief surgery VA Hosp., Hines, Ill., 1972-95, chief surg. svc., 1995-96. Mem. editl. bd.: The Am. Surgeon, 1984-92; contbr. articles to med. jours. including Am. Jour. Physiology, Jour. Occupl. Medicine, Annals of Surgery, Archives of Surgery, Jour. Trauma, Surg. Clinics of N.Am. Unit pres., exec. bd. Am. Cancer Soc., Chgo., 1972-89; mem. pres.'s adv. com. Benedictine U., Lisle, Ill., 1965-90. Lt. USN, 1951-53, Korea. Decorated Bronze Star, 1953. Fellow ACS (gov., chmn. gen. surgery Chgo. com. on trauma 1975-83, pres. met. chpt. 1977-78, mem. SESAP com. II and III, instr. ACS advanced trauma life support course 1980-87); mem. Am. Surg. Assn., Am. Assn. for Surgery of Trauma, Assn. Mil. Surgeons of U.S., Assn. for Acad. Surgery, Soc. for Surgery of Alimentary Tract, Assn. VA Surgeons, Internat. Soc. Digestive Surgery, Ctrl. Surg. Assn., Midwest Surg. Assn. (pres. 1974-75), Western Surg. Assn., Ill. Surg. Soc. (pres. 1971-72), Chgo. Surg. Soc. (pres. 1989-90), Inst. Medicine of Chgo. Roman Catholic. Avocations: medical history, civil war history, central american civilizations. Home: 446 S Columbia St Naperville IL 60540-5418 Personal E-mail: fafolk@aol.com.

FOLLAS, WILLIAM DANIEL, science administrator; b. Lima, Oct. 30, 1951; s. William Isaac and Carol Sue (Maxson) F.; m. Kathy Jo Roberts, Dec. 28, 1974; children: David Clay, Emily Jane, Jonathan Daniel. BS in Biology, Chem., Manchester Coll., 1974; MS in Med. Chem. Pharmaco, Purdue U., 1977. Research assoc. Ind. U. Med. Ctr., Indpls., 1977-79; pres. Follas Labs. Inc., Indpls., 1979-. Co-founder Follas Lab. Inc., Indpls. 1979-. Tchr. Chapel Rock Christian Ch., Indpls. 1979—, evaluate lab. needs Lifeline, Columbus 1986. Mem. Am. Assn. for Clinical Chem., Ohio Valley Section, Clin. Lab. Mgmt. Assn., Cen. Ind. Biochem. Forum. Republican. Avocations: golf, gardening. Home: 4909 Cherryhill Ct Indianapolis IN 46254-9549 Office: Follas Labs Inc 7750 Zionsville Rd Ste 450 Indianapolis IN 46268-4189

FOLSOM, LOWELL EDWIN, language educator; b. Pitts., Sept. 30, 1947; s. Lowell Edwin and Helen Magdalene (Roeper) Folsom; m. Patricia Ann Jackson, Aug. 30, 1969; 1 child, Benjamin Bradford. BA, Ohio Wesleyan U., 1969; MA, U. Rochester, 1972, PhD, 1976. Chmn. English dept. Lancaster (Ohio) H.S., 1969-70, 71-72; instr. Eastman Sch. Music, Rochester, NY, 1974-75; vis. asst. prof. SUNY, Geneseo, 1975-76; asst. prof. U. Iowa, Iowa City, 1976-82, assoc. prof., 1982-87, prof., 1987—, chair English dept., 1991-95, F. Wendell Miller disting. prof., 1997—2002, Carver prof., 2002—. Cons. Am. Coll. Testing Co., Iowa City, 1980—, Nat. Assessment Ednl. Progress, Denver, 1980—84; dir. Walt Whitman Centennial Conf., Iowa City, 1992, Walt Whitman Conf., Beijing, 2000, Leaves of Grass: The 150th Anniversary Conf., Lincoln, Nebr., 2005; Fulbright sr. prof. U. Dortmund, Germany, 1996. Author: Walt Whitman's Native Representations, 1994 (Choice Best Acad. Book, 1995), Re-Scripting Walt Whitman, 2005, Whitman Making Books/Books Making Whitman, 2005; editor: Walt Whitman: The Centennial Essays, 1994, Walt Whitman: The Measure of His Song, 1981 (Choice Best Acad. Book, 1982), rev. edit., 1998 (Ind. Publisher Book award, 1999), Walt Whitman and the World, 1995, (CD-ROM) Walt Whitman, 1997 (Choice Best Acad. Book, 1998), Walt Whitman Quar. Rev., 1983—, Whitman East and West, 2002, Leaves of Grass: The Sesquicentennial Essays, 2007; co-dir.: Walt Whitman Hypertext Archive, 1997—; editl. bd. Walt Whitman Encyclopedia, 1994—98, PMLA, 1999—2002, Profession, 2002—05. Named Disting. Scholar, U. Rochester, 1995; recipient Rsch. award, NEH, 1991—94, Collaborative Rsch. award, 2000—04, Preservation award, 2004—07, Faculty Excellence award, Iowa Bd. Regents, 1996, U. Iowa Collegiate Tchg. award, 2003, Pres. and Provost award Tchg. Excellence, 2005; fellow, Guggenheim, 2007—08. Mem.: MLA, PEN Am. Ctr., Whitman Scholars Assn. (dir. 1992—), Am. Studies Assn., Am. Lit. Assn. Home: 739 Clark St Iowa City IA 52240-5640 Office: Univ Iowa Dept English 308 EPB Iowa City IA 52242 Business E-Mail: ed-folsom@uiowa.edu.

FONDAW, RONALD EDWARD, artist, educator; b. Paducah, Ky., Apr. 25, 1954; s. Lex Alan and Rose Mary (Holley) Kilgore; m. Lynn S. Shepard, Oct. 7, 1987; children: Andrea Rose, Wyler S. BFA, Memphis Coll. Art, 1976; MFA, U. Ill., 1978. Instr. Ohio U., Athens, 1978; assoc. prof. art U. Miami, Coral Gables, Fla., 1978-95, prof. art Washington U., St. Louis, 1995—. Lectr., presenter workshops Ohio State U., Chgo. Art Inst., Tokyo U. Fine Art, Chautauqua Sch. Art. Exhbns. nat. and internat.; several public art commissions. Ford Found. fellow, 1977, Fla. Arts Coun. fellow, 1981, Guggenheim fellow, 1985, Pollack/Krasner fellow, 1997-98; grantee NEA, 1988; Kransberg award St. Louis Art Mus., 1998. Office: Wash U 721 Kingsland Ave Saint Louis MO 63130-3107 Home: 2004 Stemler Rd Columbia IL 62236-2926 E-mail: refondaw@art.wustl.edu.

FONTAINE, MARY C., lawyer; b. Chicopee, Mass., May 18, 1956; BA summa cum laude, Syracuse Univ., 1978; JD, Univ. Chgo., 1981. Bar: Ill. 1981, NY 1996. Assoc. Mayer Brown Rowe & Maw, Chgo., 1981—85, London, 1985—86, Tokyo, 1987; ptnr., fin. & securitization Mayer Brown Rowe & Maw LLP, Chgo., 1988—. Co-author: Illinois Commercial Financing Forms, 1993. Mem.: ABA, NY State Bar Assn. Office: Mayer Brown Rowe & Maw LLP 71 S Wacker Dr Chicago IL 60606-4637 Office Phone: 312-701-7106. Office Fax: 312-706-8132. Business E-Mail: mfontaine@mayerbrownrowe.com.

FONTANAROSA, PHIL BERNARD, medical journal executive editor, emergency physician, educator; b. Youngstown, Ohio, 1954; m. Kristine Fontanarosa, Aug. 1977; children: Jennifer, Joel, Beth, Julie. Youngstown State U., 1975; MD, Med. Coll. Ohio, 1978; postgrad., Kent St. U., 1992-93. Diplomate Am. Bd. Emergency Medicine. Intern Akron (Ohio) City Hosp., 1978-79, resident in emergency medicine, 1979-81; assoc. prof., rsch. dir. emergency medicine Northeastern Ohio Universities Coll. Medicine, 1983-93; adj. prof. medicine Northwestern Med. Sch., Chgo. Editor, Emergency Medicine Reports; dep. editor, dir. editl. affairs Jour. AMA, now exec. editor; editor-in-chief text: Physicians' Evaluation and Educational Review in Emergency Medicine, 1996, Alternative Medicine: An Objective Assessment, 2000. Mem. Am. Coll. Emergency Physicians. Office: AMA 515 N State St Chicago IL 60610-4325

FOOTE, WILLIAM CHAPIN, manufacturing executive; b. Milw., Mar. 15, 1951; s. Peter Chapin and Mary Jane (Manierre) F.; m. Kari H. Foote, July 27, 1969; children: Tracy, Leslie Suzanne. BA, Williams Coll., 1973; MBA, Harvard U., 1977. Asst. treas. Chase Manhattan Bank, NYC, 1973-75; sr. engagement mgr. McKinsey & Co., Inc., Chgo., 1977-83; v.p. USG Corp., Chgo., 1984-94, pres., COO, 1994-99; pres. CEO L&W, USG Interiors Inc., 1994, chmn., pres., CEO, 1996-2000; chmn. bd., pres., CEO USG Corp., Chgo., 1999—2005, chmn., CEO, 2005—. Mem.: Economics Chgo.

FORD, ANDREW THOMAS, former academic administrator; b. Cambridge, Mass., May 22, 1944; s. Francis Lawler and Eleanor (Vahey) F.; m. Anne M. Monahan, July 2, 1966; 1 dau., Lauren Elizabeth. BA, Seton Hall U., 1966; MA, U. Wis., 1968; PhD, U. Wis., 1971. Asst. prof. history Stockton State Coll., Pomona, NJ, 1971-72, asst. to v.p. for acad. affairs, 1972-74; acting dir. Nat. Materials Devel. Ctr. for French and Portuguese, Bedford, NH, 1976-77; acad. programs coordinator N.H. Coll. and Univ. Council, Manchester, 1975-78; v.p. acad. affairs R.I. Sch. Design, Providence, 1978-81; dean Allegheny Coll., Meadville, Pa., 1981-93, provost, 1983-93; pres. Wabash Coll., Crawfordsville, Ind., 1993—2006. Mem. adv. bd. Marine Bank, 1987-93; founding mem. Commonwealth Partnership. Author: (with R. Chait) Beyond Traditional Tenure, 1982; mem. editl. bd. Liberal Edn., 2000—. Bd. dirs. Vis. Nurse Assn., Providence, 1979-81, Allegheny Summer Music Festival, Meadville, 1981-89, Meadville Med. Ctr., 1985-87; bd. incorporators Spencer Hosp., 1981-85; mem. Nat. Com. on U.S.-China Rels., 1986—; trustee Higher Learning Commn. North Ctrl. Assn. Schs. and Colls., 2002—; dir. Crawfordsville Main St. Program, 2001—. Democrat. Home: 1112 Golf Ln Wheaton IL 60187 Office Phone: 765-361-6221. E-mail: forda@wabash.edu.

FORD, BARBARA JEAN, librarian, educator; b. Dixon, Ill., Dec. 5, 1946; BA magna cum laude with honors, Ill. Wesleyan U., 1968; MA in Internat. Rels., Tufts U., 1969; MS in Libr. Sci., U. Ill., 1973. Dir. Soybean Insect Rsch. Info. Ctr. Ill. Natural History Survey, Urbana, 1973-75; from asst. to assoc. prof. U. Ill., Chgo., 1975-84, asst. documents libr., 1975-79, documents libr., dept. head, 1979-84, acting audiovisual libr., 1983-84; asst. dir. pub. svcs. Trinity U., San Antonio, 1984-86, assoc. prof., assoc. dir., 1986-91, acting dir. librs., 1989, 91; prof., dir. univ. libr. svcs. Va. Commonwealth U., Richmond, 1991-98; asst. commr. Chgo. Pub. Libr., 1998—2002; dir., disting. prof. Mortenson Ctr. Internat. Libr. Programs, U. Ill., Urbana, 2003—. Women's re-entry adv. bd. U. Ill., Chgo., 1980-82, student affairs com., 1978-80, student admissions, records, coll. rels. com., 1981-84, univ. senate, 1976-78, 82-84, chancellor's libr. coun. svcs. com. 1984, campus lectrs. com. 1982-83; admissions interviewer for prospective students Trinity U., 1987-91, reader for internat. affairs theses, 1985-91, libr. self-study com., 1985-86, internat. affairs com., 1986-91, inter-Am. studies com., 1986-91, faculty senate, 1987-90; libr. working group U.S./Mex. Commn. Cultural Coop., 1990; presenter in field Contbr. articles to profl. jours. Bd. dirs. Friends of San Antonio Pub. Libr., 1989-91; adv. com. chair Office for Libr. Pers. Resources, 1994-95; steering com. Virtual Libr. Va., 1994-98, chair user svcs. com., 1995-96. Celia M. Howard fellow Tufts U., 1969; sr. fellow UCLA Grad. Sch. Libr. and Info. Sci., 1993. Mem. ALA (conf. program com. 1985-91, libr. edn. assembly 1983-84, membership com. 1978-79, status of women in librarianship com. 1983-85, exec bd., 1996-99, Lippincott Award Jury 1979-80, Shirley Olofson Meml. award 1977), ALA Coun. (at-large councilor 1985-89, chpt. councilor Ill. Libr. Assn. 1980-84, com. on coms. 1987-88, spl. coun. orientation com. 1982-83, ALA exec. bd., 1996-99, pres.-elect 1996-97, pres. 1997-98), Assn. Coll. and Rsch. Librs. (bd. dirs. 1989-92, pres.-elect 1989-90, pres. 1990-91, publs. com. 1990-91, conf. program planning 1990-91), Nat. Assn. State Univs. and Land Grant Colls. (commn. info. tech. 1992-94), Internat. Fedn. Libr. Assns. and Instns. (sec. ofcl. pubs. sect., gen. info. com. 1985 conf., moderator Latin Am. seminar on ofcl. pubs. 1991, univ. and other rsch. librs. sect. standing com. 1999-2007, governing bd. 2005-), Spl. Librs. Assn. (program com. 1976-77, 80-82, publicity com. 1977-79, chair 1978-79, chair spl. projects com. 1981-82, sec./treas. divsn. social sci. internat. affairs sect. 1984-86), Assn. Libr. Info. Sci. Edn. (chair local arrangements conf. planning com. 1988, 92), Ill. Libr. Assn. (chair election com. 1976-77, exec. bd. 1978-79, 80-84, bd. govt. documents round table 1976-79, chair 1978-79, long range planning com. 1980-84), Tex. Libr. Assn. (pubs. com. 1985-87, legis. com. 1986-87, judge best of exhibits award 1987, task force Amigos Fellowship 1990, del. conf. on librs. and info. svcs., 1991), Va. Libr. Assn. (ad hoc. com. distance learning 1992), Va. State Libr. and Archives (Va. libr. and info. svcs. task force 1991-93, steering com. Arbuthnot lecture 1992-93, coop. continuing edn. adv. com. 1992-94), VIVA (steering com. 1994-98), Chgo. Libr. Club (2d v.p. 1983-84), Richmond Acad. Libr. Consortium (v.p. 1991-92, pres. 1992-93), Beta Phi Mu, Phi Kappa Phi, Phi Alpha Theta, Kappa Delta Pi. Office Phone: 217-244-1898. Business E-Mail: bjford@uiuc.edu.

FORD, BILL (WILLIAM CLAY FORD JR.), automotive company executive; b. Detroit, May 3, 1957; s. William Clay Ford Sr. and Martha Parke (Firestone); m. Lisa Vanderzee; 4 children. BA, Princeton U., 1979; MBA in Mgmt., MIT, 1984. Prodn. planning analyst, advisor vehicle devel. design ctr., mfg. engr. auto assembly divsn., mgr. Ford Motor Co., Ala., 1979-82, mem. nat. bargaining team Ford/UAW labor talks, mktg. strategy analyst No. Am. Auto Opns., advt. specialist, 1982-83, internat. fin. specialist, mem. fin. staff, 1984-85, planning mgr. car prodn. devel., 1985-86, dir. com. vehicle mktg. Europe divsn., 1986-87, chmn., mng. dir. Switzerland divsn., 1987-89, mgr. heavy truck engr. and mfg. Ford Truck Opns., 1989-90, dir. bus. strategy Ford Auto Group, 1990-91, exec. dir. bus. strategy Ford Auto Group, 1991-92, gen. mgr. climate control divsn., 1992-94, v.p. com. Trucking Vehicle Ctr. Ford Auto Ops., 1994-95, chmn. fin. com., 1995—2001, chmn., 1998—, CEO, 2001—06. Vice chmn. Detroit Lions; mem. fin. com., properties com. NFL; bd. dir. eBay, Inc., 2005-. Chmn. bd. trustees Henry Ford Mus., Greenfield Village; trustee Henry Ford Health Sys., Detroit Renaissance; mem. World Econ. Forum's Global Leaders for Tomorrow. Alfred P. Sloan fellow MIT, 1983-84. Office: Ford Motor Co 1 American Rd Dearborn MI 48126-2798

FORD, CHARLES NATHANIEL, otolaryngologist, educator; b. NYC, June 25, 1940; s. Charles Nathaniel and Marie (Casa) F.; children: C. David, Brian C.; m. Sharon L. James, Feb. 3, 1990; stepchildren: Scott James, Julie James. BA, SUNY, Binghamton, 1961; MD, U. Louisville, 1965. Intern and resident Henry Ford Hosp., Detroit, 1965-70, staff, 1970-71; with Gundersen Clinic, LaCrosse, Wis., 1973-81; chief otolaryngology Middleton VA Hosp., Madison, Wis., 1982-94; prof. otolaryngol. divsn. dept. surgery U. Wis., Madison, 1981-93, chmn. otolaryngol. divsn. dept. surgery, 1993—. Mem.-at-large med. bd. U. Wis. Ctr. for Health Scis., 1989-91, sec., 1992-93, v.p., 1994-95, pres. med. staff, chair med. bd. 1996-98; DeWeese lectr. U. Oreg., 1994; Manion Meml. lectr. Ind. U., 1995; Hough lectr. U. Okla., 1996; Sartian lectr. U. Tex., 1998; keynote lectr. Brit. Voice Assn., 2000, Voice Symposium Australia, 2002, G. Paul Moore lectr. Voice Found., Phila., 2003. Author, editor: Phonosurgery: Assessment and Surgical Management of Voice Disorders, 1991; mem. editl. bd.: Jour. Voice, Otolaryngol. Head and Neck Surgery, Laryngoscope, Microsurgery; author editor numerous sci. papers, chpts. and abstracts. Maj. USAF, 1971-73. Avalon Found. scholar, 1962-63; named to Best Drs. in Am., Woodward/White, Inc., 1991—. Fellow ACS, Am. Laryngol., Rhinol. and Otolog. Soc., Am. Bronch-oEsophagological Assn. (past pres.), Am. Laryngol. Assn., Am. Soc. for Head and Neck Surgery, Am. Acad. Otolaryngology, Head and Neck Surgery (honor award 1992); mem. AMA, Soc. Univ. Otolaryngologists-Head and Neck Surgeons (past pres.), Internat. Assn. Phonosurgeons, Am. Speech-Lang.-Hearing Assn. Democrat. Unitarian Universalist. Avocations: tennis, golf, theater, art, music. Office: U Wis Ctr Health Sci 600 Highland Ave Madison WI 53792-0001 Office Phone: 608-263-0192.

FORD, DAVID CLAYTON, state senator, lawyer; b. Hartford City, Ind., Mar. 3, 1949; s. Clayton I. and Barbara J. (McVicker) F.; m. Joyce Ann Bonjour, Aug. 22, 1970; children: Jeff, Matthew, Kelly, Andrew. BA in Polit. Sci., Ind. U., 1973, JD, 1976; MBA in Internat. Trade, Ball State U., 1988. Bar: Ind. 1975, U.S. Dist. Ct. (so. dist.) Ind. 1976, U.S. Dist. Ct. (no. dist.) Ind. 1977, U.S. Tax Ct. 1988, U.S. Supreme Ct. 1983. City atty. City of Montpelier, Ind., 1977-79; town atty. Town of Shamrock Lakes, Ind., 1977—; mem. Ind. Senate from 19th dist., 1994—, chair econ. devel. and tech. com. Gen. counsel, internat. trade dir. Ind. Farm Bur., Inc., 1988—2002; chief dep. prosecutor Blackford County, 1979; pros. atty. 71st Jud. Cir., Blackford County, Hartford City, Ind., 1983—86; mem. com. on character and fitness State Bd. of Law Examiners. Mem. Ind. Agrl. Leadership Program, 1990-91; bd. dirs. Blackford County Young Reps., 1977-82, pres., 1977-78; chmn. Town of Shamrock Lakes Rep. Com., 1983, Ind. Lawyers for Bush and Quayle, 1988; vice chmn. Blackford County Rep. Ctrl. Com., 1978-82, chmn., 1993-2001; precinct committeeman Blackford County, Licking 7, 1980-93; mem. Ind. 10th Congl. Dist. Rep. Caucus, 1978-82, U.S. Edn. Appeals Bd., U.S. Dept. Edn., 1982-90, Nat. Def. Execs. Res., 1983-99; former mem. bus. adv. com. to Congressman Dan Burton; chmn. bus., industries and devel. com. Ptnrs. of Ams., Ind. chpt., 1983-84; mem. Blackford County Bd. Aviation Commrs., 1977-83, pres., 1979-83; bd. dirs. Dollars for Scholars, Blackford County, 1977-95, v.p., 1977-95; mem. St. John's-Riedman Meml. Sch. Bd., 1978-82, pres., 1978-82; mem. Blackford County Sheriff's Merit Bd., 1981-82. Named Man of Yr. Hartford City C. of C., 1978, Sagamore of the Wabash, Gov. Otis Bowen, 1978, Hon. Sec. of State Edwin J. Simcox, 1981; participant Rotary group study exch. to São Paulo, Brazil, 1981; named Outstanding Young Man of Am., U.S. Jaycees, 1982. Mem. ABA, ATLA, Ind. State Bar Assn., Blackford County Bar Assn., World Trade Club Ind., Mensa, Sigma Iota Epsilon. Home: 1023 N Walnut St Hartford City IN 47348-1553 Office: 210 W Main St Hartford City IN 47348-2209 Office Phone: 217-232-7807. E-mail: s19@in.gov.

FORD, EMORY A., chemist, researcher; b. South New Berlin, NY, Oct. 17, 1940; s. Merritt L. and Verda M. (Manwaring) F.; m. Susan Dorothy Rogers, Sept. 14, 1963; children: Kelly Diane, Kendra Lee. BA, Hartwick Coll., 1962; PhD, Syracuse U., 1966. Sr. rsch. chemist Monsanto Co., Springfield, Mass., 1966-72, rsch. group leader, 1972-76, sr. rsch. group leader, 1976-78, tech. mgr. Pensacola, Fla., 1978-81; rsch. mgr. No. Petrochem. Co., Morris, Ill., 1981-84; dir. basic rsch. Enron Chem. Co., Rolling Meadows, Ill., 1984-86, Quantum Chem. Co., Cin., 1987-97; chief scientist Equistar, Cin., 1997—. Mem. AAAS, Am. Chem. Soc., N.Y. Acad. Sci., Chemists Club of Chgo., Internat. Union Pure and Applied Chemistry, Sigma Xi. Unitarian Universalist. Avocations: reading, running, travel. Office: Equistar 11530 Northlake Dr Cincinnati OH 45249-1642

FORD, FREDERICK ROSS, retired university official; b. Kentland, Ind., Mar. 25, 1936; s. Merl Jackson and Marie Jeanne (Ross) F.; m. Mary A. Harrison, May 31, 1959; children: Lynne Elizabeth, Steven Harrison, Katherine Jeannette. BS in Mech. Engring., Purdue U., 1958, MS, 1959, PhD, 1963, Doctorate (hon.), 1998. Asst. to bus. mgr. Purdue U., West Lafayette, Ind., 1959-61, asst. to v.p., treas., 1961-65, asst. bus. mgr., 1965-69, bus. mgr., asst. treas., 1969-74, exec. v.p., treas., 1974-98; ret., 1998. Trustee Tchrs. Ins. and Annuity Assn., N.Y.C., 1982-2002. Treas. capital funds found. United Way, Lafayette, 1984-85. Mem. Coun. on Govtl. Rels. (bd. mgmt. 1984-90), Nat. Assn. Coll. and Univ. Bus. Officers (bd. dirs. 1980-83, sec. 1982-83, Disting. Bus. Officer award 1989), Ctrl. Assn. Coll. and Univ. Bus. Officers (exec. com. 1976-81, pres. 1979-80), Lafayette C. of C. (pres. 1978-79, chmn. edn. rels. com. 1984-85), Rotary, Delta Upsilon. Republican. Presbyterian. Avocations: sailing, fishing. Home: 160 Creighton Rd West Lafayette IN 47906-2102

FORD, GEORGE BURT, retired lawyer; b. South Bend, Ind., Oct. 1, 1923; s. George W. and Florence (Burt) Ford; m. Charlotte Ann Kupferer, June 12, 1948; children: John, Victoria, George, Charlotte. BS in Engring. Law, Purdue U., 1946; LLB, Ind. U., 1949. Bar: Ind. 1949, US Dist. Ct. (no. dist.) Ind. 1949. Assoc. Jones, Obenchain & Butler, South Bend, 1949-52; ptnr. Jones, Obenchain, Ford, Pankow & Lewis, South Bend, 1953-93, of counsel, 1994—2003; ret., 2003. Co-author: (book) Forms for Indiana Corporations, 1967, 2d edit., 1977. With US Army, 1943—45, ETO. Fellow: Am. Coll. Trust and Estate Counsel; mem.: ABA, St. Joseph County Bar Assn. (pres. 1976—77), Ind. Bar Assn., Phi Delta Phi, Phi Gamma Delta.

FORD, JACK, state legislator; m. to Cynthia Ford; children: Ryan, Jessica, Jacqueline. BA, Ohio State U.; MPA, Univ. Toledo. Mem. Ho. of Reps., Columbus, Ohio, 1994; mayor Toledo, 2001—05. Past city councilman City of Toledo, former pres. Toledo coun.; instr. U. Tpoledo. Former mem. citizens' adv. bd. Toledo Mental Health Ctr.; chmn. bd. Cordelia Martin Mental Health Home, former pres. Mental Health Agy. Ins. Trust, pres. and founder Substance Abuse Svc.; current mem. Toledo Symphony Bd.

FORD, JEAN ELIZABETH, retired language educator; b. Branson, Mo., Oct. 5, 1923; d. Mitchell Melton and Annie Estella (Wyer) F.; m. J.C. Wingo, 1942 (div. 1946; m. E. Syd Vineyard, 1952 (div. 1956); m. Vincent Michel Wessling, Feb. 14, 1983 (div. Dec. 1989). AA in English, L.A. City Coll., 1957; BA in English, Calif. State U., 1959; MA in Higher Edn., U. Mo., 1965; postgrad., UCLA, 1959-60, U. Wis., 1966, U. Mo. Law Sch., 1968-69. Cert. English tchr., real estate broker, Mo. Dance instr. Arthur Murray Studios, LA, 1948-51; office mgr. Western Globe Products, LA, 1951-55; pvt. dance tchr., various office jobs LA, 1955-59; social dir. S.S. Matsonia, 1959; social worker L.A. County, 1959-61; 7th grade instr. Carmenita Sch. Dist., Norwalk, Calif., 1961-62; English instr. Leadwood (Mo.) High Sch., 1962-63; dance instr. U. Mo., 1963-66, SW Mo. State U., 1966-68, NW Mo. State U., 1970-76, Johnson County Community Coll., 1976-77; tax examiner IRS, Kansas City, Mo., 1978-80; tax acct. Baird, Kurtz & Dobson, Kansas City, Mo., 1981; dance tchr. Singles Program Village, Presbyn. Ch., Kans., 1981-96; pvt. practice, 1984—2002; ret., 2002. Substitute tchr. various sch. dists., 1976-85; dance chmn. Mo. Assn. Health, Phys. Edn. and Recreation, 1965-66, 68-69, dance chmn. ctrl. dist. AAHPER, 1972-73; vis. author Young Author's Conf., Ctrl. Mo. State U., 1987-89; real estate sales agt., Kansas City, 1980-84; real estate sales broker, Mo., 1990—, Kans., 1990-2000. Author: Fish Tails and Scales, 1982, 2d edit., 2000, The Other Side of the Coin, 2004 Mem. Am. Contract Bridge League, Kansas City Ski Club. Democrat. Presbyterian. Avocations: tennis, swimming, skiing, sailing, bridge. Home: 142 Grandview Dr Bldg 4 #7 Branson MO 65616

FORD, LOUIS H., state legislator; b. Miss., Mar. 12, 1935; Mgr. Pest Control Co. State rep. dist. 58 Mo. Ho. of Reps., 1983—. Home: 5077A Ruskin Ave Saint Louis MO 63115-1346

FORD, LUCILLE GARBER, economist, educator; b. Ashland, Ohio, Dec. 31, 1921; d. Ora Myers and Edna Lucille (Armstrong) Garber; m. Laurence Wesley Ford, Sept. 1, 1946; children: Karen Elizabeth, JoAnn Christine. AA, Stephens Coll., 1942; BS in Commerce, Northwestern U., 1944, MBA, 1945; PhD in Econs., Case Western Res. U., 1967; PhD (hon.), Tarkio Coll., 1991, Ashland U., 1995. Cert. fin. planner. Instr. Allegheny Coll., Meadville, Pa., 1945-46, U. Ala., Tuscaloosa, 1946-47; personnel dir., asst. sec. A.L. Garber Co., Ashland, Ohio, 1947-67; prof. econs. Ashland U., 1967-95, chmn. dept. econs., 1970-75; dir. Gill Ctr. for Econ. Edn. Ashland Coll., 1975-86, v.p., dean Sch. Bus., Adminstrn. and Econs., 1980-86, v.p. acad. affairs, 1986-90, provost, 1990-92; exec. asst. to pres., 1993-95; pres. Ashland Comm. Found., 1995—. Bd. dirs. Peco II, Inc., Western Res. Econ. Devel. Coun., Ohio Coun. Econ. Edn.; lectr. in field; mem. govs. adv. com. on econ. devel. Author: University Economics-Guide for Education Majors, 1979, Economics: Learning and Instruction, 1981, 91; contbr. articles to profl. jours. Mem. Ohio Gov.'s Commn. on Ednl. Choice, 1992; candidate for lt. gov. of Ohio, 1978; trustee Stephens Coll., 1977-80, Ashland U., 1995—, North Cen. State Coll., 1998-2005; elder Presbyn. Ch.; bd. dirs. Presbyn. Found., 1982-88; chair, trustee Synod-Presbyn. Ch., 1994-2000; active ARC. Named to Ohio Women's Hall of Fame, 2001; recipient Outstanding Alumnus award, Stephens Coll., 1977, Outstanding Profl. award, Ashland U.,

1971, 1975, Roman F. Warmke award, 1981, Women of Achievement award, 1998, Outstanding Fundraiser award, Assn. Fund Raising Profls., 2001, Spirit of Chamber award, Ashland Area C. of C., 2001, Disting. Ashland H.S. award, Ashland City Sch. Acad. Found., 2002, Gleanch Clayton award, Ashland U., 2003. Mem. Am. Econs. Assn., Nat. Indsl. Rsch. Soc., Am. Arbitration Assn. (profl. arbitrator), Assn. Pvt. Enterprise Edn. (pres. 1983-84), North Ctrl. Assn. Colls. and Schs. (commr.), Omicron Delta Epsilon, Alpha Delta Kappa. Republican. Office: Ashland Co Comm Found 300 College Ave Ashland OH 44805-3803 Home Phone: 419-289-0668; Office Phone: 419-281-4733. Business E-Mail: accf@hmltd.net.

FORD, RALPH A., lawyer, moving and relocation company executive; b. 1946; BA in Polit. Sci., Morgan State U., 1968; JD, Boston U. Sch. Law, 1971. Bar: Md. 1972, US Dist. Ct. Dist. Md. 1972. Assoc. Venable, Baetjer & Howard, 1971—73; atty. Dupont Co., 1973—77; group counsel Bell and Howell Co., 1977—81; mem. legal dept. GE, 1981—99; gen. counsel GE Indsl. Control Systems, 1992—99; sr. v.p., gen. counsel, sec. Sirva, Inc., Westmont, Ill., 1999—2006; ptnr. GenNx360 Capital Partners, 2006—. Mem.: Am. Corp. Counsel Assn. Office: GenNx360 Floor 17 300 Park Ave New York NY 10022

FORD, WAYNE, state representative; b. Washington, Dec. 1951; BSE, post-grad., Drake U., U. Iowa. Mem. Iowa Ho. Reps., DesMoines, 1997—, mem. various coms. including human resources, judiciary, labor and indsl. rels., health and human rights, ranking mem. appropriations com. Mem. juvenile justice adv. com. State of Iowa. Mem. midnight basketball com. DesMoines YMCA. Mem.: Des Moines Mid-City Bus. Assn., Nat. Soc. Fundraising Execs. Democrat. Office: State Capitol East 12th and Grand Des Moines IA 50319 Home: PO Box 5042 Des Moines IA 50306-5042

FORD, WILLIAM CLAY, automotive and professional sports team executive; b. Detroit, Mar. 14, 1925; s. Edsel Bryant and Eleanor (Clay) F.; m. Martha Firestone, June 21, 1947; children: Martha, Sheila, William Clay, Elizabeth. BS, Yale U., 1949. Sales and advt. staff Ford Motor Co., 1949; indsl. relations, labor negotiations with UAW, 1949; quality control mgr. gas turbine engines Lincoln-Mercury Div., Dearborn, Mich., 1951, mgr. spl. product ops., 1952, v.p., 1953, gen. mgr. Continental Div., 1954, group v.p. Lincoln and Continental Divs, 1955, v.p. product design, 1956-80; dir., 1948—; vice chmn. bd., 1980-89; mem. fin. com. Ford Motor Co., 1987—, dir. emeritus; owner, chmn. Detroit (Mich.) Lions, Inc., 1964—. Mem. adv. coun. Tex. Heart Inst.; chmn. emeritus Edison Inst.; hon. life trustee Eisenhower Med. Ctr. Mem. Soc. Automotive Engrs. (asso.), Automobile Old Timers, Econ. Club Detroit, Masons, K.T., Phelps Assn., Psi Upsilon. Office: Ford Motor Co Design Ctr PO Box 6012 Dearborn MI 48121-6012 also: The Detroit Lions Inc 222 Republic Dr Allen Park MI 48101

FORDYCE, JAMES GEORGE, physician; b. Detroit, Jan. 9, 1945; s. James Alexander and Stella Marie (Pakron) F.; m. Kathleen Marie Ray, June 17, 1967; children: James A., Jonathan A., Jared A. BS, Mich. State U., 1966, DVM, 1968; MD, Wayne State U., 1974. Diplomate Am. Bd. Pediats., Am. Bd. Allergy and Immunology. Intern, resident Children's Hosp. Mich., Detroit, 1973-76; fellow allergy and clin. immunology Henry Ford Hosp., Detroit, 1976-78; physician Dearborn (Mich.) Allergy and Asthma Clinic, PC, 1978—. Cons. Metro Med. Group, Detroit, 1979-95. Author: Asthma in Clinical Pulmonary Medicine, 1992. Bd. trustees Oakwood Healthcare, Inc., 1996-2000. Fellow Am. Acad. Pediats., Am. Acad. Allergy, Asthma and Immunology, Am. Coll. Allergy, Asthma and Immunology; mem. Mich. Allergy and Asthma Soc. (pres. 1991-92). Avocations: fishing, flying, sailing. Office: Dearborn Allergy & Asthma Clinic PC 20200 Outer Dr Dearborn MI 48124-2634 Office Phone: 313-565-3565. Personal E-mail: jgfordyce@comcast.net.

FOREMAN, JAMES LOUIS, retired judge; b. Metropolis, Ill., May 12, 1927; s. James C. and Anna Elizabeth (Henne) F.; m. Mabel Inez Dunn, June 16, 1948; children: Beth Foreman Banks, Rhonda Foreman Wittig, Nanette Foreman Love. BS in Commerce and Law, U. Ill., 1950, JD, 1952. Bar: Ill. Ind. practice law, Metropolis, Ill.; ptnr. Chase and Foreman, Metropolis, until 1972; state's atty. State of Ill., Massac County, asst. atty. gen.; chief judge U.S. Dist. Ct. (so. dist.) Ill., Benton, 1979-92, sr. status, 1992—2007; ret., 2007. Pres. Bd. of Edn., Metropolis. With USN, 1945-46. Mem. Ill. State Bar Assn., Metropolis C. of C. (past pres.). Republican. Home: 660 Whitney Dr Paducah KY 42001

FORESMAN, JAMES BUCKEY, geologist, industrial hygienist, geochemist; b. Neosho, Mo., Apr. 8, 1935; s. Frank James and Helen Blackburn (Buckey) F.; m. Barbara Ellen Runkle, Aug. 13, 1961; children: James Runkle, Robert Buckey. BSBA, BS, Kans. State U., 1962; MS, U. Tulsa, 1970. From geologist, geochemist to staff dir. geology N.Am.-S.Am. Phillips Petroleum Co., Denver, Midland, Tex., Bartlesville, Okla., 1962—83; petroleum cons. Bartlesville, 1983—84; v.p. Mopro, Inc., Lyons, Mich., 1985—87; staff Pittsburg (Kans.) State U., 1987—2003. Geochemistry advisor Joint Oceanographic Instns. for Deep Earth Sampling, 1974-75; ocean drilling advisor NSF, Washington, 1974-75; indsl. rep. for joint ventures with USSR, 1978; rep. Univ.-Indsl. Assoc. Programs, N.Y., Tex., Ariz., Mass., Calif., Cambridge (Eng.), 1981-83; citizen amb. programs Environ. Del. to Russia, Latvia, and Estonia, 1992. Contbr. articles to periodicals, jours., chpts. to books. Com. mem. Boy Scouts Am., Bartlesville, 1975-82; mem. Pitts. Planning and Zoning Commn., 1997-2000; bd. dirs. U.S. Little League, Bartlesville, 1975; smoke jumper Forest Svc., USDA. Sgt. USMC, 1954-57, Korea. Recipient Disting. Svc. award City of Bartlesville, 1977. Mem. Assn. Higher Edn. Facilities Officers, Kiwanis (past pres.), Kans. Kiwanis Found. (life). Home: 1506 Woodland Ter Pittsburg KS 66762-5551 Personal E-mail: jabarfor@mobil1.net.

FORET, MICKEY PHILLIP, retired air transportation executive; b. McComb, Miss., Oct. 23, 1945; s. Fadias Phillip and Christine (Brown) F.; m. Mary Ann Tramonte, Aug. 12, 1966; 1 child, Keri. BS in Fin., MBA in Fin., La. State U., 1971. Dir. credit/interim dir. internal audit Tex. (Houston) Internat. Airlines, 1975-77, dir. cash mgmt., 1977-78, asst. treas., 1978-81, v.p. fin. svcs., 1981-82; v.p., treas. Continental Airlines, LA, 1982-84, v.p., chief fin. officer, 1984-86, also bd. dirs.; sr. v.p. fin. and internat. Eastern Airlines, Miami, Fla., 1987-88, v.p., chief fin. officer, 1986—, also bd. dirs.; sr. v.p. Tex. (Houston) Air Corp., 1988—; exec. v.p. fin. and planning Continental Airlines, Houston, 1988-89, pres., 1989-90; exec. v.p., CFO Northwest Airlines, 1992-96; pres. Atlas Air, Inc., 1996-1997; spec. projects officer Northwest Airlines, 1998, CFO, exec. v.p., 1998—2002. Chmn. bd. dirs., chief exec. officer Chelsea Catering Co., Houston; bd. dir. URS Corp. 2003-Pres. Clear Wood Improvement Assn., Houston, 1975-78; coach Friendswood (Tex.) Girls Softball Team, 1981. Served with USAF, 1966-69, Vietnam. Mem. Phi Kappa Phi, Beta Gamma Sigma. Republican. Baptist. Avocations: boating, water-skiing, bicycling. Mailing: URS Corp Bd Directors 600 Montgomery St San Francisco CA 94111-2728

FORMELLER, DANIEL RICHARD, lawyer; b. Chgo., Aug. 15, 1949; s. Vernon Richard and Shirley Mae (Gruber) Formeller; m. Ann M. Paa, Aug. 17, 1974; children: Matthew Daniel, Kathryn Ann, Christina Marie. BA with honors, U. Ill., 1970; JD cum laude, DePaul U., 1976. Bar: Ill. 1976, U.S. Dist. Ct. (no. and ctrl. dists.) Ill. 1976, U.S. Ct. Appeals (2d, 7th and 9th cirs.) 1976, U.S. Ct. Appeals (D.C. cir.) 1995. Assoc. McKenna, Storer, Rowe, White & Farrug, Chgo., 1976-82, ptnr., 1982-86, Tressler, Soderstrom, Maloney & Priess, Chgo., 1986—. Editor: DePaul U. Law Rev., 1975—76. With USN, 1970—72, Vietnam. Mem.: ABA, Assn. Def. Trial Attys. (pres. 2005—06), Chgo. Bar Assn., Ill. Assn. Def. Trial Counsel (pres. 1994—95), Ill. Bar Assn. Office: Tressler Soderstrom et al 233 S Wacker Dr Chicago IL 60606-6306 Home Phone: 847-489-9714; Office Phone: 312-627-4000. Business E-Mail: dformeller@tsmp.com.

FORNER, TRACY, newscaster; m. Elizabeth Forner; children: Ailish, Duncan. BA in Comm., Grand Valley State U. Morning dr. personality, news dir. Sta. WLAV-FM, Grand Rapids, Mich.; morning dr. personality, traffic reporter Sta. WHLT-FM; reporter, anchor WZZM-TV; anchor, reporter Sta. WXIN-TV, Indpls., 2002—. Adj. prof. comm. Grand Valley State U.

FORNERIS, JEANNE M., lawyer; b. Duluth, Minn., May 23, 1953; d. John Domenic and Elva Lorraine (McDonald) F.; m. Michael Scott Margulies, Feb. 6, 1982. AB, Macalester Coll., 1975; JD, U. Minn., 1978. Bar: Minn. 1978. Assoc. Halverson, Waters, Bye, Downs & Maki, Ltd., Duluth, 1978-81, Briggs & Morgan, P.A., Mpls., St. Paul, 1981-83; ptnr. Hart & Bruner, P.A., Mpls., 1983-86; assoc. gen. counsel M.A. Mortenson Co., Mpls., 1986-90, v.p., gen. counsel, 1990-96; with Gen. Counsel, Ltd., Mpls., 1997-98; v.p., sr. counsel Medtronic, Inc., Mpls., 1999—. Instr. women's studies dept. U. Minn., Mpls., 1977-79. Author profl. edn. seminars; contbr. articles to profl. jours. Bd. dirs. Good Will Indusries Vocat. Enterprises, Inc., 1979-81; chmn. bd. trustees Duluth Bar Libr., 1981; mem. United Way Family and Individual Svcs. Task Force, Duluth, 1981. Nat. Merit Assn. scholar, 1971. Fellow Am. Coll. Constrn. Lawyers (bd. dirs.); mem. AMA, Am. Arbitration Assn. (mem. large complex case panel), Minn. State Bar Assn., Minn. Women Lawyers (bd. dirs.), U.S. Dist. Ct. Hist. Soc. (pres.). Democrat. Roman Catholic. Office: Medtronic Inc 7000 Central Ave NE Minneapolis MN 55432-3576

FORSEE, GARY D., academic administrator, former telecommunications industry executive; b. Kansas City, Apr. 10, 1950; m. Sherry Forsee; children: Melanie, Kara. B in Engring., U. Mo. at Rolla, 1972. With Southwestern Bell Telc., 1972—80, AT&T, 1980—89; v.p., gen. mgr. govt. sys. divsn. Sprint Corp., 1989—91, pres.govt. sys., bus. svcs. group, 1991—93, sr. v.p. staff ops., long distance divsn., 1993—95, interim CEO, Sprint PCS, 1995, pres., COO long distance divsn., 1995—98, CEO, 2003—05; chmn. Sprint Corp. (now Sprint Nextel Corp.), 2003—05; pres., CEO Global One, Brussels, 1998—99; pres. Bell South Internat., 1999—2003; vice chmn. Bell South Corp., Atlanta, 1999—2003; pres., CEO Sprint Nextel Corp., Reston, Va., 2005—06, chmn., pres., CEO, 2007; pres. U. Mo. Sys., Columbia, 2008—. Bd. dirs. Goodyear Tire & Rubber Co., Sprint Corp., 2003—; appointed to Nat. Security Telecommunications Adv. Com., 2004. Vol. leader March of Dimes Birth Defects Found., 1988, bd. trustee, 1995, vice chair, 2000, former chmn. nat. bd. trustees, 2001; chmn. March of Dimes WalkAmerica; adv. coun. sch. engring. U. Mo.-Rolla, bd. trustee; mem. Bus. Roundtable, mem., CEO Com. to Encourage Corp. Philanthrophy; mem. Bus. Coun., Kansas City Civic Coun.; mem. nat. exec. bd. Boy Scouts of Am. Named one of 19 Best Managers, BusinessWeek, 2004. Office: Office of Pres U Mo Sys 321 University Hall Columbia MO 65211 Office Phone: 573-882-2011.*

FORSTER, PETER HANS, utility company executive; b. Berlin, May 28, 1942; s. Jerome and Margaret Hanson; m. Susan E. Forster. BS, U. Wis., 1964; postgrad., Bklyn. Law Sch., Columbia U., 1972. Engr. trainee Wis. Electric Power Co., 1960-64; head regional planning Am. Electric Power Service Corp., 1964-73; atty. Dayton Power & Light Co., Ohio, from 1973, v.p. adminstrn., treas. Ohio, 1977, v.p. fin. and adminstrn. Ohio, 1977-78, v.p. energy resources Ohio, 1978-79, exec. v.p. Ohio, 1980-81, exec. v.p., chief operating officer Ohio, 1981-82, pres., chief operating officer Ohio, 1982-84, pres., chief exec. officer Ohio, 1984-88, chmn. Ohio, 1988. Chmn. Miami Valley Rsch. Found.; bd. dirs. Bank One, Dayton, Ohio. Bd. dirs. Amcast, Comair; trustee Med Am. Health Systems, F.M. Tait Found., Dayton Bus. Com., Arts Ctr. Found. Mem. Am. Bar Assn., Ohio Bar Assn., Dayton Bar Assn.

FORSYTH, ILENE HAERING, art historian; b. Detroit, Aug. 21, 1928; d. Austin Frederick and Eleanor Marie (Middleton) H.; m. George H. Forsyth, Jr., June 4, 1960. AB, U. Mich., 1950; AM (univ. fellow), Columbia U., 1955, PhD (Fulbright, AAUW, Fels Found. fellow), 1960. Lectr. Barnard Coll., 1955-58; instr. Columbia U., 1959-61; mem. faculty U. Mich., Ann Arbor, 1961—, prof. history of art, 1974-97, prof. emerita, 1998—, Arthur F. Thurnau prof., 1984—; vis. prof. Harvard U., 1980; Mellon vis. prof. U. Pitts., 1981; vis. prof. U. Calif., Berkeley, 1996. Mem. Nat. Com. History Art, 1975-97; bd. dirs. Internat. Ctr. Medieval Art, 1970-95, 2005-, v.p., 1981-85; mem. supervisory com. Woodrow Wilson Found., 1985-88; Rome prize juror Am. Acad. in Rome, 1986-88; bd. advisors Ctr. Advanced Study in the Visual Arts, Nat. Gallery Art, 1985-88; mem. vis. com. medieval dept. Met. Mus. Art, N.Y.C., 1990-95; Samuel H. Kress prof. Ctr. Advanced Study in the Visual Arts, Nat. Gallery Art, 1998-99, bd. advisors, 1999-2000, U. Mich. Mus. of Art, 2005-Author: The Throne of Wisdom, 1972 (Charles Rufus Morey Book award 1974), The Uses of Art: Medieval Metaphor in The Michigan Law Quadrangle, 1993 (Annie award for non-fiction 1994); co-editor: Current Studies on Cluny, 1988; contbr. articles to profl. jours. Rackham research grantee and fellow, 1965-66, 75-76; grantee Am. Council Learned Socs., 1972-73; mem. Inst. Advanced Study Princeton, 1977 Mem. Coll. Art Assn. (dir. 1980-84), Archaeol. Inst. Am., Medieval Acad. Am. (fellow, 2006-, bd. advs. 1985-86, editorial bd. 1986-90), Medieval Club N.Y., Soc. francaise d'archéologie, Soc. Archtl. Historians, Acad. Arts, Scis. et Belles Lettres Dijon (France), Centre de recherches et d'études préromanes et romanes. Home: 5 Geddes Hts Ann Arbor MI 48104-1724 Office: U Mich Dept Art History Ann Arbor MI 48109

FORT, JEFFREY C., lawyer; b. Burlington, Iowa, Oct. 10, 1950; s. Lyman R. and Lucille (Gibb) F.; m. Diane Locandro; children: Christopher Glen, Elizabeth Anne. BA, Monmouth, 1972; JD, Northwestern U., 1975. Bar: Ill. 1975, U.S. Dist. Ct. (no. dist.) Ill. 1976, U.S. Ct. Appeals (7th cir.) 1977, U.S. Ct. Appeals (D.C. cir.) 1985, U.S. Supreme Ct. 1980. Law clk. to John M. Karns, Jr. Appellate Ct., Belleville, Ill., 1975-76; assoc. Martin Craig Chester, et al, Chgo., 1976-83, ptnr., 1983-88, Gardner Carton & Douglas, Chgo., 1988-90, Sonnenschein Nath & Rosenthal, Chgo., 1990—. Adj. prof. Northwestern U. Sch. Law, Chgo., 1990-92; bd. dir. Delta Inst., 2000—; chair Environmentalist Trading Congress, NYC, 2006, Chgo., 2007; presenter in field. Author: Establishing an Effective Environmental Law Compliance Program, 1993-2007, Avoiding Liability for Hazardous Waste: RCRA CERCLA and Related Corporate Law Issues, 2002, 3d edit., 2007; mem. editl. bd. Environmental Law for the Transactional Lawyer, 1991, rev. edit., 1994, 2001, Illinois Environmental Law, 1993, 3d edit., 2007; contbr. articles to profl. jours. Chair Lake Mich. States sect. Air and Waste Mgmt. Assn., Chgo., 1988-89, Am. Leading Bus. Lawyers, Ill. Environ., 2002-, Leading Lawyers in Ill. Environ. Law, 2002-; pres. Trevian Girls Softball Assn., 2004-07; elder 1st Presbyn. Ch. Wilmette, Ill., 1990-93, 2001—04. Mem. ABA (vice chair spl. com. on environ. disclosures), Chgo. Bar Assn. (chair environ. law com. 1987-88), Met. Club. Office: Sonnenschein Nath & Rosen LLP 7800 Sears Tower Chicago IL 60606 Office Phone: 312-876-2380. Business E-Mail: jfort@sonnenschein.com.

FORTENBERRY, JEFFREY LANE, congressman; b. Baton Rouge, Dec. 27, 1960; m. Celeste Gregory; 5 children. BA Econs., La. State U., 1982; M in Pub. Policy, Georgetown U., Washington, 1986; MA in Theology, Franciscan U., Steubenville, Ohio, 1996. Mem. econ. analysis team US Senate Subcommittee for Intergovernmental Rels., 1986; rsch. assoc. economist Gulf South Rsch. Inst., New Iberia, La., 1987—89; asst. dir. Downtown Devel. Dist., Baton Rouge, 1989—92; pub. rels.-found. activities dir. Sandhills Pub., Lincoln, Nebr., 1995—98, sales rep., 1998—2005; at-large mem. City Coun., Lincoln, Nebr., 1997—2001; mem. US Congress from 1st Nebr. dist., 2005—. Mem. agr. com. US Congress, mem. fgn. affairs com., mem. small bus. com. Republican. Roman Catholic. Office: US House Reps 1517 Longworth House Office Bldg Washington DC 20515-2701 Office Phone: 202-225-4806. E-mail: jeff.fortenberry@mail.house.gov.

FOSS, JOHN FRANK, mechanical engineering educator; b. Washington, Pa., Mar. 24, 1938; s. Maurice Felker and C. Catharine (Reynard) F.; m. Jacqueline Kay Voss, July 24, 1960; children: Judith Kathleen, Janette Diane. Student, Wilmington Coll., 1956—58; BS, Purdue U., 1961, MS, 0162, PhD, 1965. Mem. faculty Mich. State U., East Lansing, 1964—, assoc. prof. mech. engring., 1968-75, prof., 1975—; owner, pres. Digital Flow Techs., Inc., Mich., 1994—. Dir. fluid dynamics & hydraulics program NSF, 1998-2000; cons. McDonnel Douglas Helicopter Co., Ford Motor Co., Bd. Water and Light, Lansing, Tranter Corp., United Techs. Rsch. Ctr., East Hartford, Conn. Author: (with M.C. Potter) Fluid Mechanics, 1975; N.Am. editor Measurement Sci. and Tech., 1995-; assoc. editor AIAA Jour., 1982-85, ASME Jour. Fluids Engring., 1988-91. Mem. Oaks Recreation Program staff, 1976-78; moderator Edgewood United Ch., 1975-77. Sloan fellow John Hopkins U., Balt., 1970-71; Alexander von Humboldt fellow U. Karlsruhe, Fed. Republic Germany, 1978-79, U. Erlangen, Fed. Republic Germany, 1985-86, rsch. fellow U. Melbourne, Australia, 1995. Fellow ASME; mem. AIAA, AAAS, AAUP, Am. Soc. Engring. Edn., Am. Phys. Soc. (mem. exec. com. divsn. fluid dynamics 2003-2006), Soc. Scholars Johns Hopkins U., Sigma Xi, Tau Beta Pi, Pi Tau Sigma. Mem. United Ch. of Christ. Avocation: handball. Home: 2353 Sapphire Lane East Lansing MI 48823 Office: Mich State U Dept Mech Engring East Lansing MI 48824 Home Phone: 517-324-9991; Office Phone: 517-355-3337. Business E-Mail: foss@egr.msu.edu.

FOSS, RICHARD JOHN, bishop; b. Wauwatosa, Wis., Dec. 27, 1944; s. Harlan Funston and Beatrice Naomi (Lindaas) F.; m. Nancy Elizabeth Martin, June 21, 1969; children: Susan, Naomi Foss Welsh, Elizabeth, Peter, Andrew. BA, St. Olaf Coll., 1966; MDiv, Luther Theol. Seminary, 1971; ThM, Luther N.W. Theol. Seminary, 1984. Ordained to ministry Luth. Ch., 1971. Pastor St. Andrews Ch. and Ch. of Christ the Redeemer, Mpls., 1971-77; assoc. pastor First Luth., Fargo, NC, 1977-79; sr. pastor Prince of Peace Luth., Seattle, 1979-86, Trinity Luth., Moorhead, Minn., 1986-92; bishop Ea. N.D. Synod, Fargo, 1992—. Soloist F-M Opera Co., Fargo, 1979; coach St. James Girls' Basketball Team, Settle, 1982-84; vol. Wash. State Patrol Crisis Chaplaincy, Seattle, 1983-86; bd. dirs. Discovery, Inc., Mpls., 1972-77, Highline Boys' and Girls' Club, Burien, Wash., 1980-81, Luth. Compass Ctr., Seattle, 1983-86, v.p., 1985-86; mem. Master Chorale, 1987-99; bd. regents Concordia Coll., 1992—; bd. dirs. Daily Bread, 1991-2000, Luth. Social Svcs. of N.D., 1992—, Oak Grove Luth. H.S., 1990—, Luth. Resources Network, 1994-97, Healthy Congregations Adv. Bd., 1997-2005, chair 2004-05, N.D. Conf. Chs., 1993—; mem. adv. bd. Thrivent Fin. for Luths., 2000-, Ctr. for Ethical Leadership, 2001-05; mem. United Way Cmty. Bd., 2001-02; bd. regents Luther Sem., 2002-, bd. chair Healthy Congregations A Luth. Ministry, Inc., 2005-. Lutheran. Avocations: golf, reading, travel, vocal performance. Home: 1510 2nd St S Moorhead MN 56560-4014 Office: Ea ND Synod 1703 32nd Ave S Fargo ND 58103-5936 Home Phone: 218-233-9678; Office Phone: 701-232-3381. E-mail: rick.foss@ecunet.org.

FOSSUM, ROBERT MERLE, mathematician, educator; b. Northfield, Minn., May 1, 1938; s. Inge Martin and Tina Otelia (Gaudland) F.; m. Cynthia Carol Foss, Jan. 30, 1960 (div. 1979); children: Karen Jean, Kristin Ann; m. Barbara Joel Mason, Aug. 4, 1979 (div. 1993); children: Jonathan Robert, Erik Anton; m. Robin Karyl Goodman, Aug. 10, 1997. BA, St. Olaf Coll., 1959; MA, U. Mich., 1961, PhD, 1965. Instr. U. Ill., Urbana, 1964-66, asst. prof., 1966-68, assoc. prof., 1968-72, prof., 1972—, elect. and computer engring. Urbana, 2003—; prof. Beckman Inst., 2000. Lectr. Aarhus U., Denmark, 1971-73, Copenhagen U., Denmark, 1976-77; vis. prof. U. Paris VI, 1978-79, Oslo U., 1968-69. Contbr. articles to profl. jours. Recipient Disting. Alumni award Northfield H.S.; Fulbright fellow U. Oslo, 1967-68. Fellow: AAAS, Det Kongelig Norske Videnskabers Selskab (elected nat. sci. sect.); mem.: IEEE, Soc. Advancement Scandinavian Studies, European Math. Soc., Inst. Algebraic Meditation (sec.), Am. Math. Soc. (assoc. sec. cen. sect. 1983—87, sec. 1989—99), Soc. for Indsl. and Applied Math., Assn. Computing Machinery, Nordmanns Forbundet, Heimskringla (Urbana), Sigma Pi Sigma, Sigma Xi, Phi Beta Kappa. Democrat. Lutheran. Home (Summer): 630 28th St Chetek WI 54728 Office Phone: 217-244-3572. Personal E-mail: robertfossum@gmail.com. E-mail: rmfossum@uiuc.edu.

FOSTER, BILL (GEORGE WILLIAM FOSTER), congressman, physicist; b. Madison, Wis., Oct. 7, 1955; s. George William and Jeanette Raymond Foster; m. Ann Christine Oswall, Mar. 31, 1983 (div. Oct. 1996); children: George Billy, Christine. BA in Physics, U. Wis., 1976; PhD, Harvard U., 1983. Founder, CEO Electronic Theatre Controls, Inc., Middleton, Wis., 1976-79; rsch. physicist Fermi Nat. Accelerator Lab., Batavia, Ill., 1984—2006; mem. US Congress from 14th Ill. dist., 2008—. Bd. dirs. Electronic Theatre Controls, Inc., Middleton. Bd. dirs. Batavia Found. for Ednl. Excellence, 1996-2001. Recipient Rossi prize for Astrophysics Am. Astron. Soc., 1989,Fed. Energy & Water Mgmt. award, US Dept. Energy, 1998, Particle Accelerator Sci. & Tech. award IEEE, 1999, Fermilab Tech. award for Digital Multiplier Integrated Circuit, 1999 Fellow Am. Phys. Soc. Democrat. Achievements include particle accelerator designer Fermilab Antiproton Recycler Ring; integrated circuit designer High Speed Phototomultiplier Digitizer. Office: US Congress 2304 Rayburn Ho Office Bldg Washington DC 20515 also: 27 N River St Batavia IL 60510*

FOSTER, IAN TREMERE, computer scientist; b. Wellington, New Zealand, Jan. 1, 1959; arrived in US, 1989; s. Peter Kinnear and Eileen June (Gapes) F.; m. Angela Claire Smyth; children: Alexander Peter, Imogen Teresa. BSc with honors, U. Canterbury, Christchurch, New Zealand, 1979, DSc honoris causa, 2006; PhD, Imperial Coll., London, 1988. Rsch. assoc., dept. computing Imperial Coll., London, 1985-88; asst. computer scientist Argonne Nat. Lab., Ill., 1989-93, scientist, 1993-96; assoc. prof. U. Chgo., 1996-2000; sr. scientist Argonne Nat. Lab., 1997-2000, assoc. div. dir., sr. scientist, head, Distributed Systems Lab Math. & Computer Sci. Argonne, Ill.; Arthur Holly Compton prof. computer sci. U. Chgo., 2000—. Software architect I-Way Experiment U. Chgo., 1995; co-founder Global Grid Forum; program chair High Performance Distributed Computing Conf., 1997, gen. chair, 2000, 01; program chair Frontiers of Massively Parallel Computation Conf., 1998; application evangelist chair Information Arch. Com. Conf., 2000; mem. SCxy Steering Com.; co-program chair HPC Asia, 2001; information arch. chair SC'2001, 2001; mem. World Tech. Network, 2003. Author: Strand: New Concepts in Parallel Programming, 1990, Systems Programming in Parallel Logic Languages, 1990, Designing and Building Parallel Programs, 1995, The Grid: Blueprint for a New Computing Infrastructure, 1999, 2nd edit., 2004; contbr. to 300 tech. papers and reports. Named Innovator of Yr., InfoWorld, 2003, R&D Mag., 2003; named one of Top 50 Agenda Setter, Silicon.com, 2003, Ten Technologies that Will Change the World, MIT Tech. Review, 2003; recipient Tech. Innovation award, Brit. Computer Soc., 1989, Next Generation award, Global Info. Infrastructure, 1997, Gordon Bell award, 2001, Lovelace Medal, 2002, Most Promising New Technology award, R&D Mag., 2002, Fed. Lab. Consortium Tech. Transfer award, 2002, Ill. Innovation award, 2003. Fellow: British Computer Soc., AAAS; mem.: Assn. for Computing Machinery. Achievements include co-design of Strand parallel programming language; contributions in algorithms and technologies for parallel computing; leadership in design of middleware for wide area computing; co-design of Globus network computing system. Address: U Chgo 1100 E 58th St Ryerson Hall Rm 155 Chicago IL 60637 Office Phone: 630-252-4619, 773-702-3487. Office Fax: 630-252-9556, 773-702-8487. Business E-Mail: foster@mcs.anl.gov, foster@cs.uchicago.edu.

FOSTER, JAMES CALDWELL, dean, historian; b. Madison, Wis., Apr. 10, 1943; s. Mark A. and Ruth C. (Caldwell) Foster; m. Diane L. Mohn, Sept. 3, 1966 (dec. Sept. 2001); children: Jeffrey, Justin, Joshua; m. Mary Louise Pusch, June 25, 2004. BS, U. Wis., 1967; PhD, Cornell U., 1972. Assoc. dir. Wis. Humanities Commn., NEH, Madison, 1977-78; asst. prof. U. Alaska, College, 1971-74; dir. labor studies Ariz. State U., Tempe, 1974-81, Sch. for Workers, U. Wis., Madison, 1981-84; assoc. dean of campus Ohio State U., Newark, 1984-87; dean Coll. Arts, Scis. and Lit. U. Mich., Dearborn, 1987-92; dir. acad. affairs Pa. State U.-Fayette, Uniontown, 1993-95; v.p. acad. affairs Walsh U., Canton, Ohio, 1995-99, Mt. Senario Coll., Wis., 1999—2000, Mount Marty Coll., Yankton, SD, 2001—. Presenter North Ctrl. Assn. Coll. and Schs./ Higher Learning Commn., 2003, 05, 07, cons. evaluator, 2005—. Author: The Union Politic, 1975, American Labor in the Southwest, 1982; newspaper columnist, Kenosha (Wis.) Labor, 1981— (1st, 2d and 3d best story awards for column Lest We Forget, AFL-CIO 1984); commentator Wis. Pub. Radio, Madison, 1981-84. Exxon Edn. grantee, Tempe, 1976, Rockefeller Found. grantee, Tempe, 1977, German Marshall Fund grantee, Madison, 1981. Mem. Indsl. Rels. Rsch. Assn., Am. Arbitration Assn. Home: PO Box 509 Yankton SD 57078 Office: Mt Marty Coll 1105 W 8th St Yankton SD 57078 Home Phone: 605-665-2238; Office Phone: 605-668-1584. Personal E-mail: jcfosterml@earthlink.net. Business E-Mail: jfoster@mtmc.edu.

FOSTER, JIM (JAMES S. FOSTER), women's college basketball coach; Grad., Temple U., 1980. Head coach St. Joseph's U., Pa., 1978—91, Vanderbilt U., 1991—2002, Ohio State U., 2002—. Head coach Jr. Nat. Team, 1991, USA Jr. World Championship Team, 1993, World U. Games, Marsala, Italy, 1997, USA Basketball World Championship For Young Women Team, 2003; interim athletics dir. Vanderbilt U., 1995—96; mem. NCAA Women's Basketball Rules Com., 2003—. Named Coach of Yr., NCAA, 1985, US Basketball Writers Assn., 1993, Devel. Coach of Yr., USA Basketball, 2003, Ohio Women's Coll. Basketball Coach of Yr., Columbus Dispatch, 2003, Ohio Collegiate Coach of Yr., 2005. Mem.: Women's Basketball Coaches Assn. (pres. 1992). Office: Ohio State U Womens Basketball 1080 Jerome Schottenstein Ctr 555 Borror Dr Columbus OH 43210 Office Phone: 614-292-5222. E-mail: foster.384@osu.edu.

FOSTER, JOE C., JR., lawyer; b. Lansing, Mich., Feb. 5, 1925; s. Joe C. and Grace E. (McComb) F.; m. Janet C. Shanks, July 6, 1946; children: Cathy Foster Young, Susan Foster Ambrose, Thomas, John, Amy Foster Trenz. Student, Wabash Coll., Ind., 1943—44; JD, U. Mich., 1949. Bar: Mich. 1949, Fla. 1986. Assoc. Fraser, Trebilcock, Davis & Foster, and predecessors, Lansing, 1949-53, ptnr. and shareholder, 1954-2000; shareholder, sr. counsel Foster Zack Little Pasteur & Manning, P.C., Okemos, Mich., 2001—. Co-author: Independent Probate Administration, 1980, 3d edit., 1995, Informal Estat Procs. in Mich., 2000, supplements, 2002, 03. Trustee, sec. Renaud Found., Lansing, 1960-87;

bd. dirs., sec. Abrams Found., Lansing, 1960—; bd. dirs., officer ACTEC Found., L.A., 1983-87, 98-2004; trustee Jr. League Endowment Found., Lansing, 1984-90; trustee, chmn. Sparrow Hosp., Lansing, 1970-84; trustee, pres. Okemos Bd. Edn., 1962-66; bd. dirs., pres. county unit Am. Cancer Soc., 1950-60; bd. dirs., pres. Cmty. Nursing Bur., Lansing, 1956-57. Lt. USNR, 1943-46, PTO. Fellow Am. Coll. Trust and Estate Counsel (pres. 1985-86), Am. Coll. Tax Counsel, Am. Bar Found., Mich. Bar Found.; mem. ABA, Fla. Bar Assn., Mich. Bar Assn. (chmn. probate and estate planning sect. 1977-78), Internat. Acad. Estate and Trust Law (exec. coun. 1990-94), Rotary (bd. dirs. Lansing 1968-70), Phi Beta Kappa, Phi Gamma Delta. Avocations: sailing, running, tennis. Office: Foster Zack Little Pasteur & Manning PC PO Box 27337 Lansing MI 48909-7337 Business E-Mail: joe.foster@fosterzack.com.

FOSTER, KENNARD P., magistrate judge; b. 1944; Student, Purdue U., 1962-64; BS, Ball State U., 1966; JD, Ind. U., 1970. Bar: Ind. Spl. agt. FBI, 1970-71; atty. Jones, Foster & Loveall, 1971-76; asst. U.S. Atty., 1976-86; magistrate judge U.S. Dist. Ct. (so. dist.) Ind., Indpls., 1985—2002, recalled magistrate judge, 2002—. Mem. Fed. Bar Assn., Johnson County Bar Assn., Fed. Magistrate Judges Assn. Office: Birch Bayh Fed Bldg and US Courthouse Ste 255 Indianapolis IN 46204-1903 Office Phone: 317-229-3620.

FOSTER, MARK STEPHEN, lawyer; b. Edgerton, Mo., Feb. 6, 1948; s. George Elliott and Annabel Lee (Bradshaw) F.; m. Camille Pepper, June 27, 1970; children: Natalie Ashley, Stephanie Ann. BS, U. Mo., 1970; JD, Duke U., 1973. Bar: Mo. 1973, U.S. Ct. Mil. Appeals 1974, Hawaii 1975, U.S. Dist. Ct. Hawaii 1975, U.S. Dist. Ct. (we. dist.) Mo. 1977, U.S. Ct. Appeals (8th cir.) 1986, U.S. Supreme Ct. 1994. Assoc. Stinson, Mag & Fizzell, Kansas City, 1977-80, ptnr., 1980—2002, mng. ptnr., 1987-90, chmn. bd. dirs., 1998—2002; ptnr. Stinson Morrison Hecker LLP, Kansas City, 2002—, mng. ptnr., 2002—. Arbitration panelist Nat. Assn. Securities Dealers, N.Y.C., 1985—, Pvt. Adjudication Found., Durham, N.C., 1988-2000. Active Citizens Assn., Kansas City, 1982-92; pres. Spelman Med. Found., Smithville, Mo., 1984-88; bd. dirs. Alzheimers Assn. Metro. Kansas City, 1997—2004, 1st v.p., 1998, pres., 1999; mem. bd. visitors Park U., 2005—; bd. mem. Legal Aid Western Mo., 2007-, Kans. City Area Devel. Coun., 2007-; bd., exec. com. Couwntown Coun. Kansas City, 2007—. Lt. comdr. USNR, ret. amed Mo. Super Lawyer, 2005, 2006; named to Best Lawyers in Am., 2006, 2007. Mem. ABA, CCSA Kansas City (bd. dir. 2001—05), Hawaii Bar Assn., Mo. Bar Assn., Kansas City Met. Bar Assn., Am. Arbitration Assn. (panelist 1990—, large complex case adv. com. 1993—), Lawyers Edn. Assistance Program (bd. dirs. 2000—, sec. 2004-06), Carriage Club (bd. dir. 2000-04, 2d v.p. 2001, 1st v.p. 2002, pres. 2003), United Wat Alexis de Tocqueville Soc., U. Mo. Davenport Soc., Masons. Home: 1035 W 65th St Kansas City MO 64113-1813 Office: Stinson Morrison Hecker LLP PO Box 419251 1201 Walnut St Ste 2800 Kansas City MO 64106-2117 Office Phone: 816-842-8600. Business E-Mail: mfoster@stinson.com.

FOSTER, MICHAEL, agricultural products supplier; CEO Moorman's Inc., Quincy, Ill. Office: Moormans Inc 1000 N 30th St Quincy IL 62301-3400

FOSTER, RICHARD, journalist; b. Chgo., Oct. 16, 1938; s. James Edward and Mary (Sebat) Foster; m. Susanne Elisabeth Hill, Sept. 28, 1996; children: Katherine Elisabeth, Arthur Edward. BA, Lawrence Coll., 1963. Reporter City News Bur., Chgo., 1963-64; reporter Chgo. Sun-Times, 1964-72, editorial writer, mem. editorial bd., 1972-78; editorial writer Des Moines Register & Tribune, 1978-82, Milw. Journal Sentinel, 1983—. Journalist-in-residence Colo. State U., spring 1982 Served with AUS, 1958-61. Recipient 1st place award, UPI, 1984, Inter-Am. Press Assn. award, 1988, 1st award (Group A), Wis. Newspaper Assn., 2000; fellow NEH Profl. Journalism, Stanford U., 1976—77. Mem. Nat. Conf. Editorial Writers, Nat. Press Club. Home: 4645 N Murray Ave Whitefish Bay WI 53211-1259 Office: 333 W State St Milwaukee WI 53203-1305 E-mail: rfoster@journalsentinel.com.

FOSTER, SCARLETT LEE, investor relations executive; b. Charleston, W.Va., Dec. 14, 1956; d. William Christoph Foster, Jr. and Anne (Howes) Conway. B in Comm., Bethany Coll., 1979; MBA, Washington, 2000. Dir. pub. rels. Allergy Rehab. Found., Charleston, 1979-80; dir. pubs. Contractors Assn. W.Va., Charleston, 1980-82; comm. rep. Monsanto Co., Nitro, W.Va., 1982-84, 1984-87, mgr. environ. and community rels. St. Louis, 1987-89, mgr. pub. rels., 1989-91, mgr. fin. pub. rels., 1991-93, dir. pub. rels., 1993-94, dir. pub. affairs, 1994-2001, dir. investor rels., 2001—. Trustee Bethany (W.Va.) Coll., 1994—. Named Outstanding Alumni of Achievement Bethany Coll., 1990. Mem. Nat. Investor Rels. Inst. Episcopalian. Avocations: bicycling, reading, cooking, gardening. Office: Monsanto Co A2SP 800 N Lindbergh Blvd # A2sp Saint Louis MO 63167-0001 E-mail: scarlett.l.foster@monsanto.com.

FOSTER, WOODBRIDGE A., medical entomologist, educator; BS in Entomology & Parasitology, Univ. Calif., Berkeley, 1963, PhD in Entomology & Parasitology, 1967. Asst. prof. Haile Sellassie I Univ., Addis Abada, Ethiopia, 1967—70; rsch. fellow Univ. Bristol, 1970—71; rsch. assoc. Univ. Ga., 1971—73; asst. prof. Ohio State Univ., 1973—76, assoc. prof., 1976—. Invited spkr. in field. Contbr. articles to profl. jours.; chair editl. bd. Journal of Vector Ecology, American Entomologist. Macdonald Scholarship, Univ. Calif., Berkeley, 1961, NSF Undergraduate Grant, 1962, NIH Predoctoral Fellow, 1965—67, Ministry of Overseas Develop. (UK) Rsch. Fellowship, 1970—71. Mem.: Ohio Mosquito Control Assn. (bd. dir., sec., newsletter editor). Achievements include leading a team of collaborators to develop a proposal to study the nutritional ecology of the most important vector of maleria, Anopheles gambiae, in Kenya & Tanzania, now approved for funding by NIH; creating a matrix of mating-behavior characters from video analysis, being used to construct hypotheses for the phylogeny of sabethine mosquitos & the origin & evolution of courtship; revealing the importance of energy status to decision-making & vectorial capacity of Ochlerotatus triseriatus and anopheles gamgiae, two important vectors of pathogens. Office: Dept Entomology Ohio State Univ 486 ARONOFF LB 318 W 12TH Ave Columbus OH 43210 Office Phone: 614-292-2204. Office Fax: 614-292-2180. Business E-Mail: foster.13@osu.edu.

FOTA, FRANK GEORGE, artist; b. Northampton, Pa., Feb. 20, 1921; s. Frank Michael and Elizabeth Rose (Simko)F.; m. Christine June Ringwald, Oct. 18, 1947. Student, Chgo. Acad. of Fine Art, 1951-53. Artist Studio Maintained in Residence, S. Holland, Ill.; comml. artist, designer Triangle Outdoor Advt. Co., Chgo., 1956-61, Gen. Outdoor Advt. Co., Chgo., 1961-63; art dir. Triangle Outdoor Advt. Co., Chgo., 1963-83. Artist: (paintings) The Juniper Tree, 1971, Moab, Utah, 1974, Give Us This Day, Crete, Ill., 1972; exhibits include Wally Findlay Gallery, Chgo., 1953, 54, 55, Richard H. Love Gallery, Steger, Ill., Olympia Fields, Ill., Chgo., 1973, 74, 75, others. Mem., photographer Dolton (Ill.) Civic Assn., 1983-85 Mem.: Veteran of Foreign Wars, Dolton, Ill. (Trustee), Am. Legion, Riverdale, Ill. (Photog.). Roman Catholic. Avocations: photography, music. Home: 16748 Clyde Ave South Holland IL 60473-2611

FOTOPOULOS, DANIELLE, former soccer player; b. Camp Hill, Pa., Mar. 24, 1976; Student, U. Fla. Mem. U.S. Nat. Women's Soccer Team, 1996—. Recipient Southeastern Conf. Player of Yr. award, 1996. Achievements include appeared twice in Faces in the Crowd, Sports Illustrated. Office: US Soccer Fedn 1801-1811 S Prairie Ave Chicago IL 60616

FOTOPOULOS, JAMES, artist; b. Norridge, Ill., 1976; Guest lectr."Film One" production class U. Tex., Austin, 2001, 2003; guest lectr. NJ City U., 2003; founder Fantasma Inc., 1998. Dir.: (films) ZERO, 1997, Migrating Forms, 1999 (Best Feature Award, NY Underground Film Festival, 2000, Made in Chgo. Award, Chgo. Underground Film Festival, 2000), Back Against the Wall, 2000, Consumed, 2001 (Chgo. Underground Film Fund Grant, Chgo. Underground Film Festival, 2001), Christabel, 2001, The Lighthouse, 2004 (No Budget Award, Cinematexas Internat. Short Film & Video Festival, 2004), Spine Face, 2005; exhibitions include with Cory Arcangel Fotopoulos/Arcangel Part 5, NY Underground Film Festival, 2004, exhibitions include Whitney Biennial, Whitney Mus. Am. Art, 2004, and others. Office: Fantasma Inc 1400 West Devon 440 Chicago IL 60660 Business E-Mail: info@jamesfotopoulos.com.

FOUBERG, GLENNA M., career planning administrator; b. Ashley, ND, Sept. 1, 1942; m. Rod Fouberg; children: Robert, Dan. Student, N.D. State U., 1960—61; BS in Secondary Edn., No. State U., 1963, psychol. examiner's endorsement, 1980, Doctorate (hon.), 2002; MEd in Guidance and Counseling, S.D. State U., 1968; postgrad., 1971—. English tchr., drama dir., Sisseton, SD, 1963—64; English tchr., 1965—67, Eielson AFB, Fairbanks, Alaska, 1964—65; English tchr., guidance counselor Bristol, SD, 1967—69, Webster, SD, 1968—71; tchr. Holgate Jr. H.S., Aberdeen, SD, 1973—90; coord., tchr. Alt. Learning Ctr. Ctrl. H.S., SD, 1990—2002; chief examiner GED testing Aberdeen Career Planning Ctr., 2002—. Mem. S.D. State Bd. Edn., 1998—, pres., 2002—; mem. editl. com. Ctr. Applied Rsch.; mem. nominating com. Nat. State Tchrs. Yr.; adj. prof. English No. State U.; presenter in field. Co-chair Aberdeen Arts Festival; bd. mem., membership drive chmn., pres. Cmty. Concert Assn.; mem. health adv. com. Northeastern Mental Health Ctr. and Brown County; block worker Am. Cancer Soc., Heart Fund, March of Dimes, Easter Seals; active Alexander Mitchell Libr. Found. Bd.; co-chair Rails Club United Way; bd. dirs., office coord. Abderdeen Swim Club; fund raising com. Act II Cmty. Theater, S.D. Humanities Fund; co-chair Jr. Achievement, 2001—03. Recipient Sertoma Svc. to Mankind award, F.O.E. Eagles Edn. award, Golden Deed award, Exch. Club, George award, Aberdeen Area C. of C., award, Optimist Club, Spl. Contbns. award, S.D. Assn. Guidance Counselors, 2001, Outstanding Grad. award, S.D. State U. Guidance and Human Resources Dept., 2002. Mem.: NEA, State Profl. Practices Commn. (charter), Local Reading Coun., N.E. S.D. Reading Coun., Aberdeen Edn. Assn. (mem. comm. com.), S.D. Edn. Assn., Nat. Coun. Tchrs. English, Kappa Delta Pi, Phi Delta Kappa (v.p. membership, pres.), Delta Kappa Gamma (mem. rsch. com.). Office: Aberdeen Career Planning Ctr 420 S Roosevelt Aberdeen SD 57402-4730 also: 203 Third Ave SE Aberdeen SD 57401

FOUDREE, BRUCE WILLIAM, lawyer; b. Des Moines, Mar. 27, 1947; s. Shie and Dorothy F.;m. Suzanne J. F. Reade, May 31, 1986; children: Andrew A., Grant R., Zarina. BA, Drake U., 1969; student, U. Geneva, Switzerland, 1968, U. Vienna, Austria, 1968; JD, Drake U., 1972; LLM, U. Pa., 1975. Bar: Iowa 1972, U.S. Ct. Appeals (8th cir.) 1976, U.S. Supreme Ct. 1977, Ill. 1986. Asst. atty. gen. Iowa Dept. Justice, Des Moines, 1976-80; ins. commnr. Iowa Ins. Dept., Des Moines, 1980-86; of counsel Mitchell, Williams, Selig and Tucker, Little Rock, 1986-88; shareholder Keck, Mahin & Cate, Chgo., 1988-96; of counsel Lord, Bissell & Brook, Chgo., 1996—. Commr., chmn. Iowa Ins. Dept., 1980-86; commr. Iowa Health Data Commn., 1983-86, chmn. 1985. Assoc. editor Drake Law Rev., 1971-72; dir. Jour. Ins. Regulation, 1982-89. Mem. ABA (TIPS scope and correlation com. 1991-94, chmn. fin. svcs. com. 1990-91, professionalism com. 1994-96), Nat. Assn. Ins. Commrs. (chmn. 1984, pres. 1985), Ins. Regulatory Examiners Soc. Found. (bd. dirs. 1991—, chmn. 1999-2000), Iowa State Bar Assn., Life and Health Compliance Assn., Union League Club of Chgo. (chmn. ins. group 1989-92), The Chgo. Lighthouse (bd. dirs. 1995—, sec. 1998, chmn. 2002-05), Chaine des Rotisseurs Chgo. (vice charge de missions-caviste 2006). Office: Lord Bissell & Brook 111 S Wacker Dr Chicago IL 60606 Office Phone: 312-443-1830. Business E-Mail: bfoudree@lordbissell.com.

FOUDY, JULIE MAURINE, retired professional soccer player, Olympic athlete; b. San Diego, Jan. 23, 1971; m. Ian Sawyers, July 1995. BSW in Biology, Stanford U., 1993. Mem. U.S. Women's Nat. Soccer Team, 1987—2004, capt., 1992—2004; profl. soccer player San Diego Spirit, 2001—03. Color commentator Men's World Cup, ESPN, 1998. Mem. Tyresco Football Club, Sweden, 1994; pres. Women's Sports Found. Named World Cup Champion, 1991, 1999; named to U.S. Nat. Soccer Hall of Fame, 2007; recipient Gold medal, Centennial Olympic Games, 1996, Athens Olympic Games, 2004, FIFA Fair Play award, 1997, Silver medal, Sydney Olympic Games, 2000, Bronze medal, World Cup, 2003. Achievements include being a member of the Bronze medal winning team World Championships, Sweden, 1995; CONCACAF, Montreal, 1994; being voted number 1 most powerful in sports, Sports Business Journal, 2004. Office: c/o US Soccer Fedn 1801 S Prairie Ave # 1811 Chicago IL 60616-1319

FOULSTON, NOLA TEDESCO, lawyer; b. Mt. Vernon, NY, Dec. 14, 1940; d. Dominick J. and Theresa M. (Pellino) Tedesco; m. Steven L. Foulston, Jan. 2, 1983; 1 child, Andrew. BA, Ft. Hays State U., 1972; postgrad., U. Kans., 1972-73; JD, Washburn U., 1976. Bar: Kans. 1977, U.S. Dist. Ct. Kans., U.S. Ct. Appeals (10th cir.). Asst. dist. atty. 18th Jud. Dist., Dist. Atty.'s Office, Wichita, Kans., 1977-81; assoc. Foulston, Siefkin, Powers & Eberhardt, Wichita, 1981-86; ptnr. Foulston & Foulston, Wichita, 1986-89; dist. atty. Office of Dist. Atty. Eighteenth Jud. Dist. Sedgwick County Courthouse, Wichita, 1989—. Bd. dirs., legal counsel YWCA, Wichita, 1978-83, pres. 1980-81; active YWCA's Women's Crisis Ctr., Wichita Area Sexual Assault Ctr.; bd. dirs. Exploited and Missing Children's Unit, Project Freedom, Community Corrections, County-Wide Substance Abuse Task Force, State of Kans. Law Enforcement Coordinating Com., Community Rels. Task Force, Inter-Agy. Truancy Adv. Com., Women's Rsch. Inst., Crime Stoppers of Wichita Adv. Bd.; apptd. by Gov. Hayden of Kans. to the Weigand Commn. on State Expenditures. Named one of Outstanding Young Women of Am., Outstanding Young Wichitan, Wichita Jaycees, 1990; recipient Alumni Achievement award Ft. Hays State U., 1992, Law Enforcement Commendation medal SAR, 1992. Mem. ABA, Kans. Bar Assn., Wichita Bar Assn. (Outstanding Atty. of Achievement 1992), Nat. County and Dist. Attys. Assn., Kansas County and Dist. Attys. Assn., Golden Key (hon.). Democrat. Roman Catholic. Office: 535 N Main Wichita KS 67203-3702

FOUNTAIN, RONALD GLENN, management consultant, corporate financial executive, entrepreneur, educator; b. Mason City, Wash., Feb. 12, 1939; s. Aldine Shirah and Ella Maude (Fordham) F.; m. Ethel Joan Hightower, Aug. 22, 1968; children: John Hightower, Dana Leigh. AS, Ga. Southwestern Coll., 1959; BS, Valdosta State U., 1965; MBA, Case Western Res. U., 1983, ExecDrMgmt, 1999. V.p. nat. accounts Ctrl. Bancshares, Birmingham, Ala., 1973-74; cash control mgr. White Consol., Cleve., 1974-76, asst. treas., 1976-79, treas., dir. investor rels., 1979-82, v.p., treas., 1982-83, v.p. fin., treas., 1983-86; pres. Dix & Eaton, 1986-88; v.p. fin., CFO M.A. Hanna Co., Cleve., 1988-93; mng. prin. The Commonwealth Group, Cleve., 1993-04; sr. exec. v.p. Roulston & Co., Cleve., 1994-96; adv. dir. InfoSource, Harris Co., 1995-98; ptnr. The Parkland Group, 1996—2003; pres., CEO United Truck Fin. & Mktg., 1998—2001; prof. mgmt. Walsh U., North Canton, Ohio, 2003—; mng. ptnr. Capital Acceleration Ptnrs. LLC, 2003—. Adj. faculty Weatherhead Sch. Mgmt., 1996-, exec. dir. profl. fellow program, 2000-02; bd. dirs. Dise & Co.; pres. Delta Sys. Inc., 2004-06, bd. dirs., 2001-07; pres. Ironrock Capital, 2004-2007. Trustee Notre Dame Coll., Cleve., 1984-90, Laurel Sch., 1986-90, Pub. Radio Sta. WCPN, 1990-93, MetroHealth Sys., 1996—; chmn. N.E. Hospice Study Com., 1989-93; bd. dirs. Jr. Achievement Cleve., 1982, Nat. Adoption Exch., Phila., 1983, Cleve. Edn. Fund, 1983-87 Mem.: Planning Forum (pres. 1992—94), Nat. Investor Rels. Inst. (pres. 1978—79), Assn. Corp. Growth, Fin. Execs. Inst. (membership chmn. 1983—84), Alumni Assn. Weatherhead Sch. Mgmt. (pres. 1985—88), Country Club, Union Club. Home: 2908 Paxton Rd Cleveland OH 44120-1824 Personal E-mail: rgf2908@msn.com.

FOURER, ROBERT HAROLD, industrial engineering educator, consultant; b. Phila., Sept. 2, 1950; s. Herbert S. and Priscilla (Silver) F. BS in Math., MIT, 1972; MS in Ops. Rsch., Stanford U., 1979, MS in Stats., 1979, PhD in Ops. Rsch., 1980. Rsch. analyst Nat. Bur. Econ. Rsch., Cambridge, Mass., 1974-77; asst. prof. dept. indsl. engring. and mgmt. scis. Northwestern U., Evanston, Ill., 1979-85, assoc. prof., 1985-93, dept. chair, 1989-95, prof., 1993—. Vis. mem. tech. staff AT&T Bell Labs., Murray Hill, N.J., 1985-86, 95-96; cons. AT&T, Exxon, Goldman Sachs & Co., Keebler Co., Kraft Foods, Sears Roebuck & Co. Co-author: AMPL: A Modeling Language for Mathematical Programming, 1993; assoc. editor Mgmt. Sci., 1983—, Ops. Rsch., 1986—; contbr. articles to profl. jours. Recipient Computer Sci. Tech. Sect. prize, Ops. Rsch. Soc. Am., 1993; NSF grantee; John Simon Guggenheim Meml. Found. fellow, 2002. Mem. Inst. Indsl. Engrs., Soc. Indsl. and Applied Math, Inst. Ops. Rsch. and Mgmt. Scis. (chair Computer Sci. Tech. sect., 1996-97), Math. Programming Soc. (mem.-at-large, coun. 1994-97). Achievements include AMPL modeling lang. Office: Northwestern Univ Dept Ind Eng and Mgmt Scis 2145 Sheridan Rd Evanston IL 60208-3119 E-mail: 4er@iems.northwestern.edu.

FOURNELLE, RAYMOND ALBERT, engineering educator; b. St. Louis, Dec. 9, 1941; s. August Carl and Adella Emma (Fleer) F. BS in Metall. Engring., U. Mo., 1964, MS in Metall. Engring., 1968, PhD in Metall. Engring., 1971; Profl. Degree of Metall. Engring. (hon.), U. Mo., Rolla. Registered profl. engr., Wis. Rsch. engr. Shell Oil Co., Wood River, Ill., 1964-66; rsch. assoc. Northwestern U., Evanston, Ill., 1971-72; asst. prof. Marquette U., Milw., 1972-78, assoc. prof., 1978-86, prof., 1986—; interim chairperson Dept. of Mech. and Indsl. Engring., 1998—2001. Contbr. articles to profl. jours. 1st lt. U.S. Army, 1964-66, Fed. Republic Germany. Rsch. grantee NSF, 1975, 79, 86; Fulbright fellow U. Stuttgart (Germany), 1983-84, 90-91, Alexander von Humboldt fellow, 1985-88, Mac-Planck-Forschungspreis, 1994, ASM Internat. fellow, 1996. Mem. ASME, AAUP, ASM Internat. (bd. rev. 1981—), Minerals, Metals and Materials Soc. (com. mem.), Am. Soc. Engring. Edn. Republican. Achievements include development of theories and models for various solid state reactions in metals and alloys, including discontinuous precipitation, coarsening, and dissolution, diffusion induced grain boundary and liquid film migration. Home: 1029 N Jackson St Apt 509A Milwaukee WI 53202 Office: Marquette U Dept Mech Engring PO Box 1881 Milwaukee WI 53201-1881 Office Phone: 414-288-3541. Business E-Mail: raymond.fournelle@mu.edu.

FOURNIE, RAYMOND RICHARD, lawyer; b. Belleville, Ill., Jan. 3, 1951; s. Raymond Victor and Gladys M. (Muskopf) F.; m. Mary Lindeman, Sept. 2, 1978; children: Sarah Dozier, John David, Anne Gerard, David Raymond. BS, U. Ill., 1973; JD, St. Louis U., 1979. Bar: Mo. 1979, Ill. 1980. Assoc. Moser, Marsalek, et al., St. Louis, 1979-80, Brown, James & Rabbitt, P.C., St. Louis, 1981-82, Shepherd, Sandberg & Phoenix, P.C., St. Louis, 1982-86; shareholder Shepherd, Sandberg & Phoenix, St. Louis, 1986-88; ptnr. Armstrong Teasdale LLP, St. Louis, 1988—. U. Ill. fellow, 1974. Mem. Mo. Bar Assn., Ill. Bar Assn., St. Louis Bar Assn. (sec. trial sect.), Lawyers Assn. (v.p. 1987-88, pres. 1990-91), Actors Equity Assn. Roman Catholic. Avocations: singing, baseball, golf, acting. Home: 4 Ridgetop St Saint Louis MO 63117-1021 Office: Armstrong Teasdale LLP One Metropolitan Sq Ste 2600 Saint Louis MO 63102-2740

FOUST, CHARLES WILLIAM, judge; b. Bethlehem, Pa., May 27, 1952; s. Alan Shivers and Helen Elizabeth (Aigler) F.; m. Melissa A. Cherney, July 31, 1982; children: Kyle Cherney, James Terrell. BA, U. Wis., 1974, JD, 1978. Bar: Wis. Bar, U.S. Dist. Ct. (we. dist.) Wis. 1978. Asst. dist. atty. Dane County Dist. Atty.'s Office, Madison, 1979-82; asst. pub. defender State Pub. Defender's Office, Milw., 1982-83; assoc. Smoler & Albert SC, Madison, 1983-88; dist. atty. Dane County, Madison, 1988-97; judge Dane County Circuit Ct., Madison, 1997—, presiding judge criminal divsn., 2001—. Mem. govs. adv. bd., Dane County adv. bd. Treatment Alternatives Program; chair coordinated commun. response task force on domestic violence Dane County Commn. on Sensitive Crimes; mem. Dane County Jail/Space Needs, Dane County Long Range Jud. Planning; mem. Dane County Jury Selection, Wis. Jud. Coun. Commn. on Criminal Procedure; mem. Wis. Working Group on Sentencing and Corrections. Mem. State Bar Wis., Dane County Bar Assn. (bd. dirs. criminal law sect. 1985-89, chmn. 1985-89), Wis. Dist. Attys. Assn. (exec. bd., 1st v.p., com. on DNA evidence, dir. state cts. criminal benchbook com. 2000—, chmn. 2002—). Home: 2105 Madison St Madison WI 53711-2131 Office: Dane County Circuit Ct Br 14 210 Martin Luther King Jr Blvd Madison WI 53703 Home Phone: 608-258-1501; Office Phone: 608-266-4200. Business E-Mail: william.foust@wicourts.gov.

FOWLER, BARBARA HUGHES, classics educator; b. Lake Forest, Ill., Aug. 23, 1926; d. Fay Orville and Clara (Reber) Hughes; m. Alexander Murray Fowler, July 14, 1956; children: Jane Alexandra, Emily Hughes. BA, U. Wis., 1949; MA, Bryn Mawr Coll., 1950, PhD, 1955. Instr. classics Middlebury (Vt.) Coll., 1954-56; asst. prof. Latin Edgewood Coll., Madison, Wis., 1961-63; mem. faculty U. Wis., Madison, 1963—, prof. classics, 1976—, John Bascom prof., 1980—, prof. emeritus, 1991—. Author: The Hellenistic Aesthetic, 1989, The Seeds Inside a Green Pepper, 1989, Hellenistic Poetry, 1990, Archaic Greek Poetry, 1992, Love Lyrics of Ancient Egypt, 1994, Songs of a Friend, 1996, Vergil's Eclogues, 1997; also articles. Fulbright scholar Greece, 1951-52; Fanny Bullock Workman travelling fellow, 1951-52 Mem. Am. Philol. Assn., Archaeol. Inst. Am. Office: U Wis 910 Van Hise Hall Madison WI 53706 Home: 2210 E Newton Ave Shorewood WI 53211-2614

FOWLER, CHUCK, former state legislator; b. Dec. 21, 1939; m. Debra Fowler; 2 children. Grad. H.S. Product mgr. 3M Co.; mem. Minn. State Senate, 2000—02, vice chair taxes com., mem. edn. com., mem. agr., gen. legislation and vets. affairs com., mem. higher edn. budget divsn. com., mem. income and sales tax budget divsn. com., state and local govt. ops. com. Home: 710 N State St Fairmont MN 56031

FOWLER, DON WALL, lawyer; b. Apr. 19, 1944; s. Slayden Grimes and Dorothy Lavenia (Wall) Fowler; m. Ruthann Arneson, Sept. 16, 1968 (div.); 1 child; m. Deborah Dewar, Sept. 15, 1984 (dec. Feb. 1986); m. Marcia Petlin, Oct. 1, 1988 (div.). BA, Emory U., 1966; JD, U. Chgo., 1969. Bar: Ill. 1969, U.S. Dist. Ct. (no. dist.) Ill. 1969, U.S. Ct. Appeals (7th cir.) 1980. Assoc. Lord Bissell & Brook, Chgo., 1969—77, ptnr., 1977—2005, of counsel, 2005—. Mem.: ABA, Ill. Bar Assn. Unitarian Universalist. Office: Lord Bissell & Brook 111 S Wacker Dr Chicago IL 60606-4302 Office Phone: 312-443-0237. Business E-Mail: dfowler@lordbissell.com.

FOWLER, JOHN, printing company executive; CFO, v.p. fin. Quad/Graphics, Hartford, Wis. Office: Quad/Graphics 1900 W Sumner St Hartford WI 53027

FOWLER, ROBERT EDWARD, JR., former agricultural products company executive; b. Camden, Tenn., Oct. 7, 1935; s. Robert Edward and Rebecca (Watson) F.; m. Margaret Caroline Armstrong, Dec. 28, 1957; children: Robert, William, Margaret B.Engring., Vanderbilt U., 1957. With GE, Louisville, 1957-78, v.p., 1978-81; pres., COO, Rubbermaid, Inc., Wooster, Ohio, 1981-87, bd. dirs., 1981-87; chmn., CEO, pres. Josephson Office Products, Chgo., 1987-90; pres., CEO, BCC Indsl. Svcs., 1991-93; pres., COO, The Vigaro Corp., 1993-94, pres., CEO, 1994-96; pres., COO, IMC Global (merged with The Vigoro Corp. 1996), Northbrook, Ill., 1996-97; CEO, pres., chmn. IMC Global, Northbrook, 1997-99. Bd. dirs. Alltrista Corp., Anixter Internat. Mem. Chgo. Christian Indsl. League (bd. dirs.) Office: Imc Global 3033 Campus Dr Ste E490 Minneapolis MN 55441-2655

FOX, CARL ALAN, research executive; b. Waukesha, Wis., Nov. 24, 1950; s. Frank Edwin and Margaret Alvilda (Rasmussen) F.; m. Susan Jane Smith, June 18, 1977; children: Thomas Gordon, James David, Joseph Carl. BS, U. Wis., River Falls, 1973; MS, U. Minn., 1975; PhD, Ariz. State U., 1980; postgrad., Stanford U., 1993. Lab. asst. dept. biology U. Wis., River Falls, 1971-73; rsch. asst. dept. agronomy and plant genetics U. Minn., St. Paul, 1973-75; tchr. high sch. Le Center (Minn.) Pub. Schs., 1975-76; rsch. fellow dept. botany Ariz. State U., Tempe, 1976-79; rsch. asst. Lab. Tree-Ring Rsch. U. Ariz., Tucson, 1978-79; rsch. scientist, then sr. rsch. scientist So. Calif. Edison Co., Rosemead, 1979-87; rsch. assoc. agrl. experiment sta. U. Calif., Riverside, 1986-87; exec. dir. Desert Rsch. Inst., Reno, 1987-96, assoc. v.p. rsch., 1994-95; dir. Office of Rsch. and Program Devel. U. N.D., Grand Forks, 1996—, assoc. dean Grad. Sch., rsch. prof. dept. tchg. and learning and biology, interim dean grad. sch., 2000—. Rsch. adviser Electric Power Rsch. Inst., Palo Alto, Calif., 1983-87; liaison Utility Air Regulatory Group, Washington, 1983-87, cons., 1989-91; mem. peer rev. panel EPA, 1986, 97, 98, 99; invited reviewer air quality rsch. div. Nat. Park Svc., Denver, 1989; peer rev. panel Minn. Legis. Commn. on Resources, 1998. Contbr. numerous papers to profl. publs. Asst. troop leader Newport Beach (Calif.) area Boy Scouts Am., 1981-82, cub scout leader Reno area, 1990-91; bd. dirs. World Rainforest Found., Reno, 1989-92, Internat. Visitors Coun. No. Nev., Reno, 1991-96; coach YMCA, Reno, 1989-95, Grand Forks, N.D., 1996—; deacon Covenant Presbyn. Ch., 1989-92; judge State of Nev. Odyssey of the Mind. NSF fellow, 1976-79; grantee EPA, 1978-79, 83-85, 89-95, 99, NSF, 1987-95, 98—, Dept. of Def. and Energy, 1987. Mem. AAAS, Air Pollution Control Assn., Ecol. Soc. Am., Am. Soc. Agronomy, Greentree Gators Swim Team (pres. 1986-87), N.D. Acad. of Scis., at. Coun. of Univ. Rsch. Adminstrs., Soc. of Rsch. Adminstrn., Sigma Xi, Beta Beta Beta. Republican. Presbyterian. Avocations: camping, canoeing, tennis, gardening, basketball. Office: U ND Office Rsch/Program Devel PO Box 7134 Grand Forks ND 58202-7134

FOX, DAVID ALAN, rheumatologist, immunologist; b. Montreal, July 5, 1953; s. Lester L. and Zelda L. (Rothbart) F.; m. Paula L. Bockenstedt, July 10, 1977; children: Sharon Elizabeth, Michelle Caroline, Jonathan William. BS, MIT, 1974; MD, Harvard U., 1978. Diplomate Am. Bd. Internal Medicine, Am. Bd. Rheumatology. Intern, then resident Brigham and Women's Hosp., Boston, 1978-81; fellow in rheumatology and immunology Harvard U. Med. Sch., Boston, 1981-85; asst. prof. U. Mich., Ann Arbor, 1985-90, assoc. prof., 1990-95, prof., 1995—, acting chief divsn. rheumatology, 1990-91, chief divsn., 1991—. Dir. U. Mich. Multipurpose Arthritis Ctr., Ann Arbor, 1990—2001, U. Mich. Rheumatic Disease Core Ctr., 2001—; trustee Arthritis Found., 1992—. Assoc. editor Jour. Clin. Investigation, 1997-2002; contbr. chpts. to books, articles to profl. jours. Mem.: Assn. Am. Physicians, Am. Soc. Clin. Investigation, Am. Assn. Immunologists, Am. Coll. Rheumatology (pres. 2007—08). Achievements include discovery of T lymphocyte surface molecules and development of various monoclonal antibodies. Office: U MichMed Ctr Rackham Arthritis Rsch Unit 3918 Taubman Ctr Ann Arbor MI 48109

FOX, ELAINE SAPHIER, lawyer; b. Chgo., Nov. 18, 1934; d. Nathan Abraham and Rhoda M. (Schneidman) Saphier; m. Alan A. Fox, Apr. 25, 1954; children: Susan Fox Lorge, Wendy Fox Schneider, Mimi. BS, Northwestern U., 1955; JD, Ill. Inst. Tech., 1975, U.S. Dist. Ct. (no. dist.) Ill., 1975, U.S. Ct. Appeals (7th cir.) 1975, U.S. Ct. Appeals (fed. cir.) 1985. Trial atty. NLRB, Chgo., 1975-80; assoc. Hirsh & Schwartzman, Chgo., 1980-81, Gottlieb & Schwartz, Chgo., 1981-84, ptnr., 1984-90, D'Ancona & Pflaum, Chgo., 1990—2003, Seyfarth Shaw LLP, Chgo., 2003—. Co-editor in chief How to Take a Case to the NLRB, 7th edit.; contbr. articles to profl. jours. and mags. Bd. dirs., exec. com. Am. Cancer Soc., Chgo., 1993—; mem. nat. and local governing coun. Am. Jewish Congress, Chgo., 1991—; bd. dirs. Jewish Vocat. Svc. Mem. ABA (subcom. NLRB practice and procedures, employment and labor rels. law, labor and employment law com., Women Rainmakers, midwest regional mgmt. chair NLRB practice and procedure com.), Women's Bar Assn., Chgo. Bar Assn. (labor and employment rels. vice chmn. 1989-90, chmn. 1990-91, co-chmn. Alliance for Women 1994-95, co-chair bd. mgrs. 1996-98), Decalogue Assn. Avocations: swimming, walking, reading, theater, art. Office: Seyfarth Shaw LLP 55 E Monroe St Ste 4200 Chicago IL 60603 Office Phone: 312-781-8616. Business E-Mail: efox@dancona.com, efox@seyfarth.com.

FOX, KARL AUGUST, retired economist, educator, eco-behavioral scientist; b. Salt Lake City, July 14, 1917; s. Feramorz Young and Anna Teresa (Wilcken) Fox; m. Sylvia Olive Cate, July 29, 1940; children: Karl Richard, Karen Frances Anne. BA, U. Utah, 1937, MA, 1938; PhD, U. Calif., 1954. Economist USDA, 1942-54; head divsn. statis. and hist. rsch. Bur. Agrl. Econs., 1951-54; economist Coun. Econ. Advisers, Washington, 1954-55; head dept. econs. and sociology Iowa State U., Ames, 1955-66, head dept. econs., 1966-72, disting. prof. scis. and humanities, 1968-87, prof. emeritus, 1987—. Vis. prof. Harvard, 1960-61, U. Calif., Santa Barbara, 1971-72, 78, vis. scholar, Berkeley, 1972-73; William Evans vis. prof. U. Otago, N.Z., 1981; Bd. dirs. Social Sci. Rsch. Coun., 1963-67, mem. com. econ. stability, 1963-66, chmn. com. areas for social and econ. statistics, 1964-67; mem. Com. Reg. Accounts, 1963-68 Author: Econometric Analysis for Public Policy, 1958, (with M. Ezekiel) Methods of Correlation and Regression Analysis, 1959, (with others) The Theory of Quantitative Economic Policy, 1966, rev. edit., 1973, Intermediate Economic Statistics, 1968, rev. edit., (with T.K. Kaul), 1980, (with J. K. Sengupta) Economic Analysis and Operations Research, 1969, (with W.C. Merrill) Introduction to Economic Statistics, 1970, Social Indicators and Social Theory, 1974, Social System Accounts, 1985, The Eco-Behavioral Approach To Surveys and Social Accounts for Rural Communities, 1990, repub., 1994, Demand Analysis, Econometrics and Policy Models, 1992, Urban-Regional Economics, Social System Accounts and Eco-Behavioral Science, 1994; author-editor: Economic Analysis for Educational Planning, 1972; co-editor: Readings in the Economics of Agriculture, 1969, Economic Models, Estimation and Risk Programming (essays in honor of Gerhard Tintner), 1969, Systems Economics, 1987; contbr. articles to profl. jours. Recipient superior service medal USDA, 1948, award for outstanding pub. research Am. Agrl. Econs. Assn., 1952, 54, 57, for outstanding doctoral dissertation, 1953 Fellow Econometric Soc., Am. Statis. Assn. (Census Research fellow 1980-81), Am. Agrl. Econs. Assn. (v.p. 1955-56, award for publ. of enduring quality 1977), AAAS; mem. Am. Econs. Assn. (rsch. and publs. com. 1963-67), Regional Sci. Assn., Ops. Rsch. Soc. Am., Am. Ednl. Rsch. Assn., Phi Beta Kappa, Phi Kappa Phi. Home: 1801 20th St Apt J-31 Ames IA 50010-5166 Office: Iowa State U Econs Dept Ames IA 50011-0001

FOX, MICHAEL, former state legislator, underwriting consultant; b. Hamilton, Ohio, Dec. 15, 1948; m. Mary Ann Fox; children: Ryan, Ashley. BS in Edn. in Polit. Sci., Miami U., Oxford, Ohio, 1971. Asst. to sec. of agr. USDA, Washington, 1973; spl. asst. to Senator Robert Taft, Jr. of Ohio, U.S. Senate, Washington, 1973-74; mem. Ohio Ho. of Reps., Columbus, 1975-97; underwriting cons., Hamilton. Mem. Butler County Youth Svc. Bur. Named Legislator of Yr., Ohio Vocat. Edn. Assn., 1988; recipient leadership award Middletown Sch. Dist., 1989, President's award, Ohio. Mem. Butler County trustees Assn., Fraternal Order Police, Hamilton O'Tucks, Ky. Cols., Elks, Delta Tau Delta. Republican. Home: 6109 Creekside Way Hamilton OH 45011-7884

FOX, MICHAEL VASS, theology studies educator; b. Detroit, Dec. 9, 1940; s. Leonard W. and Mildred (Vass) F.; m. Jane Schulzinger, Sept. 4, 1961; children: Joshua, Ariel BA, U. Mich., 1962, MA, 1963; PhD, Hebrew U., Jerusalem, 1972. Ordained rabbi, 1968. Lectr. Haifa U., Israel, 1971-74, Hebrew U., Jerusalem, 1975-77; prof. Hebrew U. Wis., Madison, 1977—, chmn. dept., 1982-88, 92-99, Weinstein-Bascom prof. in Jewish studies, 1990—, Halls-Bascom prof., 1999—; Moss exch. prof. Hebrew U., 2006. Author: The Song of Songs and the Ancient Egyptian Love Songs, 1985, Shirey Dodim Mimitzrayim Ha'atiqa, 1985, Qohelet and his Contradictions, 1988, The Redaction of the Books of Esther, 1991, Character and Ideology in the Book of Esther, 1991, 2001, A Time to Tear Down and a Time to Build Up: A Rereading of Ecclesiastes, 1999; editor: Anchor Bible: Proverbs, vol. I, 2000, Ecclesiastes--JPS Commentary, 2004; contbr. articles to profl. jours. Named Vilas assoc., U. Wis., 1988—90; recipient Wahrburg prize, Hebrew U., 1971—72, Kellett Mid-Career award, U. Wis., 1999; fellow, Brit. Friends of Hebrew U., Liverpool, 1974—75, NEH, 1992; Leverhulme fellow, U. Liverpool, Eng., 1974—75, Am. Coun. Learned Socs. fellow, 2001, Am. Acad. for Jewish Rsch. fellow. Mem. Soc. for Bibl. Lit. (editor SBL Dissertation Series 1994-99, editl. bd. Jour. Bibl. Lit. 1991-95; pres. midwest region 1998-2000), Nat. Assn. Profs. Hebrew (editor Hebrew Studies 1985-93, v.p. 2000-03, pres. 2003-05). Home: 2815 Chamberlain Ave Madison WI 53705-3607 Office: U Wis Dept Hebrew 1220 Linden Dr Rm 1338 Madison WI 53706-1525 Office Phone: 608-238-5644.

FOX, PAUL T., lawyer; b. NYC, Jan. 17, 1953; m. Andrea Fox; children: Emily, Bennett, Eli. BA, Northwestern U., 1975, JD cum laude, 1978. Bar: Ill. 1978, Wis. 1989, US Dist. Ct. (no. dist. trial bar) Ill., US Dist. Ct. (ctrl. dist.) Ill., US Dist. Ct. (so. dist.) Ill., US Dist. Ct. (ea. dist.) Wis., US Dist. Ct. (we. dist.) Wis. 2006, US Dist. Ct. Mass., US Dist. Ct. (ea. dist.) Mich., US Dist. Ct.(we. dist.) Mich., US Dist. Ct. (we. dist.) Mont., US Ct. Appeals (1st cir.), US Ct. Appeals (6th cir.), US Ct. Appeals (7th cir.), US Ct. Appeals (9th cir.), US Ct. Appeals (fed. cir.), US Supreme Ct. Appeals (7th cir.) 1979, U.S. Ct. Appeals (fed. cir.) 1987, U.S. Ct. Appeals (1st cir.) 2005, U.S. Ct. Appeals (9th cir.) 2006, U.S. Supreme Ct. 1986,. Co-mng. shareholder Greenberg Traurig LLP, Chgo. Faculty mem. Nat. Inst. for Trial Advocacy; adj. prof. Northwestern U. Sch. Law. Active Leukemia and Lymphoma Soc., Ravinia Music Festival; former chair Glencoe, Ill. Nominating Caucus, Jewish United Fund; former bd. mem. New Trier HS Endowment Fund, US Holocaust Meml. Mus., Chgo. Com. on Diversity in Large Law Firms; dir. Albany Bank & Trust Co., N. Am. Named, Ill. Super Lawyer, 2005—07; named to, Leading Lawyers Network, 2005—07; recipient Martindale Hubbel AV rating. Fellow Am. Bar Found.; mem. ABA (mem. bus. and litigation sect.), State Bar Wis., Chgo. Bar Assn. (com. on large law firms), Chgo. Bar Found., Commn. Mng. Ptnrs., Order of Coif, Green Acres Country Club. Avocations: tennis, golf, history, travel. Office: Greenberg Traurig 77 W Wacker Drive Ste 2500 Chicago IL 60601 Office Phone: 312-456-8420. Business E-Mail: foxp@gtlaw.com.

FOX, ROBERT WILLIAM, mechanical engineering educator; b. Montreal, Que., Can., July 1, 1934; s. Kenneth and Jessie (Glass) F.; m. Beryl Williams, Dec. 15, 1962; children— David, Lisa. BS in Mech. Engring, Rensselaer Poly. Inst., 1955; MS, U. Colo., 1957; PhD, Stanford U., 1961. Instr. mech. engring. U. Colo., Boulder, 1955-57; research asst. Stanford (Calif.) U., 1957-60; mem. faculty Purdue U., Lafayette, Ind., 1960-99, assoc. prof., 1963-66, prof., 1966-99, asst. head mech. engring., 1971-72, asst. dean engring. for instrn., 1972-76; acting head Purdue U. (Sch. Mech. Engring.), 1975-76, asso. head, 1976-98, chmn. univ. senate, 1971-72, prof. emeritus, 1999. Cons. Owens-Corning Fiberglass Co., Edn. Services Inc., Nelson Mfg. Co., Peoria, Ill., B. Offen Co., Chgo., Agard Co., Johns-Marsville Co., Richmond, Ind., Babcox & Wilcox, Alliance, Ohio. Named Standard Oil Outstanding Tchr. Purdue U., 1967; recipient Harry L. Solberg Outstanding Tchr. award, 1978, 83, Donald E. Marlowe awd., Am. Soc. for Engineering Education, 1992. Fellow ASME, Am. Soc. for Engring. Edn.; mem. Sigma Xi, Pi Tau Sigma, Tau beta Pi, Delta Tau Delta. Home: 3627 Chancellor Way Lafayette IN 47906-8809 Office: Purdue U Sch Mech Engring Lafayette IN 47907

FOX, SAM, manufacturing executive; b. Desloge, Mo., May 9, 1929; s. Max and Fanny Gold Fox; m. Marilyn Rae Widman, Oct. 25, 1953; children: Cheryl, Pamela, Jeffrey, Gregory, Steven. BSBA, Washington U., 1951, LLD (hon.), 2002; D in pub. svc. (hon.), St. Louis U., 2000. Pres., chief exec. officer Fox Industries, Inc., Madison, Ill., 1952-72; chmn., chief exec. officer, founder Harbour Group, Ltd., St. Louis, 1976—. Chmn. Fox Family Found., 1986—. Mem. bd. trustees Wash. U., 1989—, vice chmn. bd. trustees, 1999—2001, emeritus trustee, 2001, life trustee; chmn., former pres. Greater St. Louis Coun. Boy Scouts Am.; chmn. regents Rep. Nat. Com., 2000—; nat. chmn. Rep. Jewish Coalition, 2001—; bd. dirs. Opera Theatre of St. Louis, 1984—; mem. bd. Arts & Edn. Coun. Greater St. Louis, Barnes-Jewish Hosp., Civic Progress, Muny Opera in Forest Park, V.P. Fair Found., St. Louis Sci. Ctr., St. Louis Zoo; pres. bd. commr. St. Louis Art Mus., 1997—2001, v.p., 2001—. Named Entrepreneur Yr. award, St. Louis Master, 1995, Bus. Person Yr. award, Clayton C. of C., 1996, Man Yr., St. Louis Variety Club, 2002, St. Louis Citizen of Yr., 2003; recipient Enterprise award, St. Louis Bus. Jour., 1986, Disting. Bus. Alumni award, Olin Sch., 1988, Medallion for Entrepreneurship, Beta Gamma Sigma, 1996, Achievement award, Sigma Alpha Mu, 1998, Spirit Enterprise award, Mo. Rep. Party, 1998, Thomas Jefferson award, Mo. Hist. Soc., 2001, Woodrow Wilson award corp. citizenship, 2003. Mem.: Wash. U. Bus. Sch. Alumni Assn. (pres. 1983—84, Disting. Alumni award 1986), Wash. U. Century Club, St. Louis Club, Clayton Club, Mo. Athletic Club, Westwood Country Club. Jewish. Achievements include established the Sam & Marilyn Fox Scholarship, Olin Sch. Scholars in Bus. Program, Wash. U., 1980. Avocations: fishing, hunting, skiing. Office: Harbour Group Ltd 7701 Forsyth Blvd Ste 600 Saint Louis MO 63105-1802 E-mail: samfox@harbourgroup.com.

FOX, STACY L., lawyer; b. Ann Arbor, Mich., 1953; m. Michael Van Hemet; children: Kyle, Callan. BS with high distinction, U. Mich., 1974, JD, 1983. Assoc. Mintz, Levin, Cohn, Ferris, Glovskky & Popeo, P.C., Boston, 1983—88; gen. counsel Unisys Fin. Corp., 1988—89; group counsel automotive systems group and plastics tech. group Johnson Controls, Inc., 1989—93, group v.p., gen counsel automotive systems group, 1993—2000; sr. v.p. corp. transactions and legal affairs Visteon Corp., Dearborn, Mich., 2000—05; chief adminstrv. officer, gen. counsel Collins & Aikman, Southfield, Mich., 2005—. Named one of 100 Leading Women in Automotive Industry, Automotive News, 2000. Office: Collins & Aikman 26533 Evergreen Rd Southfield MI 48076

FOX, THOMAS J., communications executive; b. 1968; B, Va. Tech, Blacksburg, Va. Bus. account mgr. Verizon Wireless Comm. Inc., telesales mgr., major account sales mgr., dir. bus. sales, Southern Calif. region, dir. bus. sales, Desert Mountain region, dir. retail sales, Southwest region, pres., Ill./Wis. region Schaumburg, Ill. Mem. Chicagoland Chamber of Commerce. Office: Verizon Wireless 1515 Woodfield Road Ste 1400 Schaumburg IL 60173 Office Phone: 847-706-2655. Office Fax: 847-706-2477.

FOXWORTHY, JAMES C., manufacturing executive; BSBA, U. Tenn., 1973. Various Union Camp Corp., 1973-92; exec. v.p. pres. paperboard group Inland Paperboard & Packaging, Inc. subs. Temple-Inland Inc., 1992-00; group v.p. paperboard Temple-Inland Inc., Indpls., 2000—. Office: Temple Inland Inc 4030 Vincennes Rd Indianapolis IN 46268-3007

FOYE, THOMAS HAROLD, lawyer; b. Rapid City, SD, Nov. 23, 1930; s. Harold Herbert and Jean Winifred (McCormick) F.; m. Laurene Fowler, Aug. 7, 1972; children: David Snyder, Stewart Snyder BS in Commerce, Creighton U., Omaha, Nebr., 1952; LLB, Georgetown U., Washington, DC, 1955. Bar: SD 1955, DC 1955, US Supreme Ct. 1968. Trial atty. tax div. US Dept. Justice, Washington, 1955-58; assoc. Bangs, McCullen, Butler, Foye & Simmons, predecessor firms, Rapid City, 1958-60, ptnr., 1960—. Lectr. in field Fellow Am. Coll. Trust and Estate Counsel, Am. Bar Found.; mem. ABA, State Bar SD (pres. 1982-83), Pennington County Bar Assn. (pres. 1962), Am. Coll. Real Estate Lawyers, Internat. Acad. Estate and Trust Law., Am. Coll. Tax Counsel. Clubs: Arrowhead Country (Rapid City). Democrat. Roman Catholic. Avocations: skiing, water-skiing, hiking. Office: Bangs McCullen Butler Foye & Simmons PO Box 2670 Rapid City SD 57709-2670 Home Phone: 605-343-8053; Office Phone: 605-343-1080. Business E-Mail: tfoye@bangsmccullen.com.

FRADE, PETER DANIEL, chemist, educator, administrator; b. Highland Park, Mich., Sept. 3, 1946; s. Peter Nunes and Dorathea Grace (Gehrke) F.; m. Karen L. Kovich, Mar. 14, 1992. BS in Chemistry, Wayne State U., 1968, MS, 1971, PhD, 1978. Chemist Henry Ford Hosp., Detroit, 1968-75, analytical chemist, toxicologist dept. pathology, divsn. pharmacology and toxicology, 1975-86, sr. clin. lab. scientist dept. pathology divsn. clin. chemistry and pharmacology, 1987-96; assoc. prof. Eugene Applebaum Coll. Pharmacy and Health Sci. Wayne State U., Detroit, 1996—, interim chair dept. mortuary sci., 2000—03, chair dept. mortuary sci., 2003—04, chair dept. fundamental and applied scis., 2004—. Rsch. assoc. in chemistry Wayne State U., Detroit, 1978—79; vis. scholar U. Mich., Ann Arbor, 1980—90; vis. scientist dept. hypertension rsch. Henry Ford Hosp., Detroit, 1986—88; adj. prof. Eugene Applebaum Coll. of Pharmacy and Health Scis. Wayne State U., 1991—96, dir. anat. pathologist assts. program, dir. mortuary sci. program. Contbr. sci. articles to profl. jours.; peer reviewer for profl. jours., 1988—; mem. editl. bd. Annals of Pharmacotherapy, 2003-. Mem. Rep. Presdl. Task Force, 1984-88; organist St. John's Episcopal Ch., Royal Oak, Mich., 1995-97. Recipient David F. Boltz Meml. award, Wayne State U., 1977, Teaching Excellence award. Fellow Am. Inst. Chemists, Nat. Acad. Clin. Biochemistry, Assn. Clin. Scientists; mem. Am. Coll. Forensic Examiners, Am. Chem. Soc., Am. Soc. Forensic Odontology, Am. Assn. Clin. Chemistry, Am. Guild Organists, Assn. Analytical Chemists, Mich. Inst. Chemists (treas. 1994—), NY Acad. Scis., Am. Coll. Toxicology, Royal Soc. Chemistry (London), Sigma Xi, Phi Lambda Upsilon, Alpha Chi Sigma. Episcopalian. Home: 20200 Orleans St Detroit MI 48203-1356 Office: Wayne State U 5439 Woodward Ave Detroit MI 48202-4009 Home Phone: 313-892-4514; Office Phone: 313-577-7874. Business E-Mail: ab8123@wayne.edu.

FRAEDRICH, ROYAL LOUIS, magazine editor, publisher; b. Weyauwega, Wis, Apr. 23, 1931; s. Clarence Otto and Libbie Clara (Trojan) F.; m. Phyllis Bohren, June 26, 1955; children— Lynn, Craig, Ann, Sarah, Paul. BS, U. Wis., 1955. With Doane Agrl. Svc., St. Louis, 1955-57; info. specialist Mich. State U., East Lansing, Mich., 1957-59; mng. editor Agrl. Pubs., Inc., Milw., 1959-64; editor Big Farmer mag., Milw., 1964-69, Frankfort, Ill., 1969-73, Farm Futures mag., Milw., 1973-81, pub., 1981-85; exec. v.p. Top Farmers Am. Assn., Milw., 1973-81; pub. print services AgriData Resources, Inc., 1981-85, v.p. editorial and adminstrn., 1986-89, v.p., sr. editorial dir., 1990-92; sr. editorial dir. ARI Network Svcs. Inc., 1992-94; sr. editor AgEdNet.com, Stewart-Peterson Group, West Bend, Wis., 1994-96, cons. editor, 1996—. V.p., dir. Big Farmer Inc., 1969-73; v.p. Market Communications Inc., Milw., 1973-78 Editor: Grace History, 2002—. Vice pres. Grace Lutheran Ch., Menomonee Falls, Wis., 1963, mem. stewardship com., 1965-67, sec. bd. elders, 1974-77, mem. bd. elders, 1987-89, editor Grace History Committee, 2002. Mem. Am. Agrl. Editors Assn. Home: N95w16529 Richmond Dr Menomonee Falls WI 53051-1452 Office: 137 S Main St West Bend WI 53095-3321

FRAHM, SHEILA, association executive, academic administrator, former government official; b. Colby, Kans., Mar. 22, 1945; m. Kenneth Frahm; children: Amy, Pam, Chrissie. BS, Ft. Hays State U., 1967. Mem. bd. edn. State of Kans., 1985-88; mem. Kans. Senate, Topeka, 1988-94, senate majority leader, 1993-94; lt. gov. State of Kans., 1995-96; mem. from Kans., U.S. Senate, Washington, 1996; exec. dir. Kans. Assn. C.C. Trustees, Topeka, 1996—. Mem. AAUW (Outstanding Br. Mem. 1985), Thomas County Day Care Assn., Shakespeare Fedn. Women's Clubs, Farm Bur., Kans. Corn Growers, Kans. Livestock Assn., Rotary (Paul Harris fellow 1988). Republican. Home: 410 N Grant Colby KS 67701-2036 Office: 700 SW Jackson St Ste 1000 Topeka KS 66603-3757 Personal E-mail: sfrahm@st-tel.net.

FRAISE, EUGENE S., state legislator; b. West Point, Iowa, May 7, 1932; m. Faye Pumphrey. Farmer; mem. Iowa Senate from 50th dist., 1986—. Chair Lee County Bd. Suprs., 1985. Mem. St. Mary's Ch., Augusta, Iowa. Mem. Iowa Corn Growers Assn., Lee County Pork Prodrs., KC. Democrat. Home: 1699 280th Ave Fort Madison IA 52627-9557 Office: State Capitol 50th Dist 3 9th And Grand Des Moines IA 50319-0001 E-mail: eugene_fraise@legis.state.ia.us.

FRAKES, JAMES TERRY, gastroenterologist, educator; b. Burlington, Iowa, Feb. 22, 1946; s. Harold Decatur amd Marjorie Marie (Kinnison) F.; m. Nancy Jean French, June 15, 1968; children: Sarah Jane Frakes, David Harold Frakes. BS, U. Ill., Urbana, 1968, MS, 1972; MD, U. Ill., Chgo., 1976. Diplomate Am. Bd. Internal Medicine and Gastroenterology, Nat. Bd. Med. Examiners; lic. Ill. Staff engr. Westinghouse Astronuc. Lab., Pitts., 1968-69; staff scientist Los Alamos (NMex.) Sci. Lab., 1970-71; intern, resident in internal medicine U. Mo. Med. Ctr., Columbia, 1976-78; fellow in gastroenterology U. N. Carolina Sch. Medicine, Chapel Hill, 1978-80; physician, gastroenterologist Rockford (Ill.) GE Assoc., Ltd., 1980—. Clin. prof. medicine U. Ill. Coll. Medicine, Rockford, 1981—; dir. digestive disease unit Saint Anthony Med. Ctr., Rockford, 1983—; course dir. AGA/ASGE, 1991—; med. lectr., 1987—. Bd. dirs. U. Ill. Alumni Assn., 1991-96; mem. U. Ill. Found., Urbana, 1991—, mem. pres.'s coun., 1994—. Recipient Faculty Disting. Tchg. award U. Ill. Coll. Medicine, Rockford, 1990, Faculty Disting. Svc. award, 1997, Disting. Alumnus award, 1999. Fellow ACP, Am. Coll. Gastroenterology; mem. AMA, Am. Gastroenterol. Assn. (numerous coms.) Am. Soc. Gastroinestinal Endoscopy (treas. 1995-98, pres.-elect 1998-99, pres. 1999-00), World Orgn. of Gastroenterology (dep. treas. 2002-03, industry liaison, 2002—). Republican. Avocations: gardening, wine collecting, sports. Office: Rockford Gastroenterology Assocs Ltd 401 Roxbury Rd Rockford IL 61107-5078 Home Phone: 815-633-4104; Office Phone: 815-397-7340. Business E-Mail: jamesf@uic.edu.

FRALEY, ROBERT T., biotechnologist; b. Danville, Ill. m. Laura Fraley; children: Steven, Devin, Katherine. BS in Biology, U. Ill., 1974, PhD in Microbiology/Biochemistry, 1978; postgrad., Northwestern U., 1991. Postdoctoral fellow U. Calif., San Francisco, 1979—80; co-pres. agrl. sector Monsanto Co., St. Louis, 1980—2000, exec. v.p., chief tech. officer, 2000—. Past mem. adv. com. Agriculture Biotechnology Rsch.; past mem. health molecular cytology study sect. NIH; tech. advisor to US Dept. Agriculture, NSF, Office of Technology Assessment, CAST, Agency for Internat. Develop., NAS and Internat. Svc. for the Acquisition of Agri-Biotech Applications. Contbr. articles to profl. jours.; mem. editl. bds. of several scientific jours. Named Man of the Year, Progressive Farming mag., 1995; recipient Nat. Award for Agrl. Excellence in Sci., Nat. Agri-Mktg. Assn., 1995, Kenneth A. Spencer award for Outstanding Achievement in Agrl. and Food Chemistry, 1995, Nat. Medal Tech., 1998, award for indsl. application of sci., NAS, 2008. Fellow: AAAS. Achievements include development of part of the team that developed the world's first practical system to introduce foreign genes into crop plants and development of insect-and-herbicide-resistant plants. Avocations: skiing, gardening, tennis. Office: Monsanto Co 800 N Lindbergh Blvd Saint Louis MO 63167-0001*

FRANANO, SUSAN MARGARET KETTEMAN, art association administrator, musician; b. Kansas City, Mo., Sept. 30, 1946; d. Charley Gilbert and Mary Elizabeth (Bredehoeft) Ketteman; m. Frank Salvatore Franano, Dec. 20, 1969; 1 child, Domenico Frank. AA, Stephens Coll., Columbia, Mo., 1966, BFA, 1967; postgrad., U. Mo., Kansas City, 1967-68, So. Ill. U., Edwardsville, 1968-69. Mgr. Lyric Opera Group, Kansas City, 1976-82; tour coordinator Lyric Opera Kansas City, 1978-85; dir. outreach Kansas City Symphony, 1982-84, asst. mgr., 1984-85, ops. mgr., 1985-86, gen. mgr., 1986-95; exec. dir. Columbus (Ohio) Symphony Orch., 1995-97, Ohio Citizens for Arts, Columbus, 1998—. Guest lectr. Ohio State U., 1999. Regional liaison Mo. Citizens for Arts, Kansas City, 1984-86; regional rep. Am. Guild Mus. Artists, Kansas City, 1977-81; regional ammenities task force mem. Mid-Am. Regional Coun., 1989-95; panelist Nat. Endowment for Arts, 1991-2000, site visitor, 1998—; chmn. group 2 orchs. Am. Symphony Orch. League, 1992-94; site visitor Fla. Dept. Cultural Affairs, 1998—; mem. bd. Statewide Arts Advocacy League Am., Ohio Alliance for Art Edn. Mem. Mo. Citizens for Arts, Ohio Citizens for the Arts, Actors Equity, New Albany Arts Coun., Columbus Mus. Art. Democrat. Roman Catholic. Avocations: tennis, cooking, travel. Office: Ohio Citizens for the Arts 77 S High St Columbus OH 43215-6108

FRANCH, RICHARD THOMAS, lawyer; b. Melrose Park, Ill., Sept. 23, 1942; s. Robert and Julia (Martino) Franch; m. Patricia Staufenberg, Apr. 18, 1971 (dec. Apr. 1994); children: Richard T. Jr., Katherine J.; m. Susan L. Rice, Sept. 1, 1995. BA cum laude, U. Notre Dame, 1964; JD, U. Chgo., 1967. Bar: Ill. 1967, U.S. Dist. Ct. (no. dist.) Ill. 1967, U.S. Ct. Appeals (7th cir.) 1971, U.S. Supreme Ct. 1980, U.S. Ct. Appeals (3d and 8th cirs.) 1981, U.S. Ct. Appeals (2d cir.) 1984, U.S. Dist. Ct. (no. dist.) Wis. 1989, U.S. Ct. Appeals (6th cir.) 1991, U.S. Tax Ct. 1994, U.S. Ct. Appeals (9th cir.) 1997, U.S. Ct. Appeals (4th cir.) 2003. Assoc. Jenner & Block, Chgo., 1967-68, 70-74, ptnr., 1975—. Former mem. Ill. Supreme Ct. Rules Com. Served to capt. US Army, 1968—70. Decorated Bronze Star, Army Commendation medal. Fellow: Am. Coll. Trial Lawyers; mem.: Am. Law Inst. Office: Jenner & Block Ste 4600 330 N Wabash Ave Chicago IL 60611 Home Phone: 847-446-0792; Office Phone: 312-923-2965. Personal E-mail: dickfranch@aol.com. Business E-Mail: rfranch@jenner.com.

FRANCIS, CHARLES ANDREW, agronomy educator, consultant; b. Monterey, Calif, Apr. 12, 1940; s. James Frederick and G. Louise (Epperson) F.; m. Barbara Louise Hanson, June 23, 1962; children: Todd (dec.), Kevin, Andrea, Karen. BS, U. Calif., Davis, 1961; MS, Cornell U., 1967, PhD, 1970; DSc honoris causa, Helsinki U., 1999. Dir., maize breeder Internat. Ctr. for Tropical Agr., Cali, Colombia, 1970-72, dir., bean agronomist, 1973, dir. small farm systems, 1974-75, rsch. agronomist, 1976-77; prof. U. Nebr., Lincoln, 1977—, dir. Morocco project, 1982-84; dir. internat. program Rodale Inst., Emmaus, Pa., 1984-85. Agronomist US AID, Botswana, Liberia, Uganda, Malawi, Morocco, Senegal, Tanzania, 1978-94, World Bank, Colombia, So.Am., 1980; dir. Ctr. Sustainable Agr. Sys., 1990-2000; bd. dir., sec. The Land Inst., Salina, Kans., 1990—; cons. OTA, Rockefeller Found., FAO/UN, 1978—. Editor: Multiple Cropping Sys., 1986; co-editor: Sustainable Agr., 1990, Crop Improvement for Sustainable Sys., 1993; contbr. chpt. to books and numerous articles to profl. jour. Cubmaster Cub Scout Pack 20, Lincoln, 1978-81; mem. ch. bd. Unitarian Universalist Ch., Lincoln, 1987-89; bd. dirs., v.p. sch. bd. Colegio Bolivar, Cali, 1973-77. 1st lt. U.S. Army, 1961-63. Recipient Agr. Stewardship award, Sustainable Agr. Soc., 1997, 7th Generation Rsch. award, Ctr. for Rural Affairs and CSARE, 2000. Fellow Am. Soc. Agronomy (divsn. chair 1968-70, Robert E. Wagner award for Efficient Agr. 1992, fellow), Internat. Svc. in Agronomy, 2002, Crop Sci. Soc. Am., 1992; mem. Phi Kappa Phi, Phi Beta Delta, Gamma Sigma Delta, Alpha Zeta. Democrat. Avocations: bicycling, camping, jogging, reading, travel, organic. Office: U Nebr 225 Keim Hall Lincoln NE 68583-0910

FRANCIS, EDWARD D., architect; b. Cleve., Aug. 15, 1934; s. Michael and Anna (Buchinsky) F.; m. Betty-Lee Seydler, Aug. 25, 1956 (div. 1982); children— Tameron, Theron; m. Lynne Marie Merrill, Sept. 6, 1984. B.Arch, Miami U., 1957. Draftsman, designer David Maxfield, Oxford, Ohio, 1953-59; draftsman Austin Co., Cleve., summers 1954, 56; designer Meathe, Kessler & Assoc., Grosse Pointe, Mich., 1959-68; prin. William Kessler & Assoc., Detroit, 1968—, pres., 1985-95, Kessler Assoc. Inc., 1995-99; CEO Kessler/Francis/Cardoza Architects, 1999—2004; prin. Gunn Levine Archs., Detroit, 2004—, Detroit Hist. Dist. Adv. Bd., 2002—. Archtl. adv. com. Ferris State U., Big Rapids, Mich. Chmn. Franklin Village Hist. Commn., Mich., 1971-79; pres. Friends of Capitol, Lansing, 1984-85, State Hist. Preservation Rev. Bd., 1984-94. Fellow AIA (Gold medal Detroit and Mich. chpts.); mem. Frank Lloyd Wright Found., Frank Lloyd Wright Preservation Trust, Nat. Trust for Hist. Preservation, Mich. Hist. Preservation Network (Lifetime Achievement award 2001), Gabriel Richard Hist. Soc. (bd. dirs.). Office: Gunn Levine Archs 726 Lothrop Detroit MI 48202 Home Phone: 313-393-0103; Office Phone: 313-873-3868. Business E-Mail: edwardf@gunnlevine.com.

FRANCIS, JULIE, beverage company executive; d. Butch and Tonie. BBA, Alfred U., 1993. Dir. mktg. Rabun, Hatch & Assoc., Atlanta, 1993—95; key account category mgr. Coca-Cola Enterprises, Atlanta, 1995—96, key account mgr., 1996—97, market devel. mgr. NY divsn. NY, 1998—99, dir. sales NY divsn. NY, 1998—99, sales ctr. mgr. NY divsn. NY, 1999—2001, area v.p. Eastern Great Lakes divsn. Rochester, NY, 2001—02, area v.p. Lakeshore divsn., 2002—04, v.p., gen. mgr. Midwest Bus. Unit, 2005—. Named one of 40 Under 40, Crain's Chgo. Bus., 2005. Office: Coca-Cola Enterprises 2500 Windy Ridge Parkway Atlanta GA 30339

FRANCIS, MARION DAVID, consulting chemist; b. Campbell River, BC, Can., May 9, 1923; arrived in U.S., 1949; s. George Henry and Marian (Flanagan) F.; m. Emily Liane Williams, Aug. 27, 1949 (dec. 1995); children: William Randall, Patricia Ann; m. Jacqueline S. Lohman, June 14, 1997. BA, U. B.C., Vancouver, 1946, MA, 1949; PhD, U. Iowa, 1953. Instr. U. B.C., Vancouver, Canada, 1946—49; chemist Can. Fishing Co., Vancouver, Canada, 1946; rsch. asst. U. Iowa, Iowa City, 1949—51; rsch. chemist Procter & Gamble

Co., Cin., 1952—76, sr. scientist, 1976—85, Norwich Eaton Pharms., Inc., Norwich, NY. 1985-89; rsch. fellow Victor Mills Soc., Cin., 1990-93; cons. Cin., 1993—. Chmn. Gordon Rsch. Conf., N.H., 1968, 79, session chmn., 1985; panel mem. Internat. Conf. on Crystal Deposition and Dissolution in Tissues, Evion, France, 1985; session chmn. workshop, Sienna, Italy, 1992; co-chmn. Bisphosphonate Therapies for Osteoporosis: Today and Tomorrow Symposium, Davos, Switzerland, 1996, 2006, chmn. Internat. Conf. on Phosphorus Chemistry, Cin., 1998, others; session chmn. Internat. Congress on Arts and Comms., Lisbon, Portugal, 1999, Washington, 2000, Cambridge, Eng., 2001, Vancouver, B.C., 2002, Dublin, 2004, Honolulu, 2005; spkr. and lectr. in field. Contbr. articles to sci. jours.; patentee in field. Dist. chmn. Cin. United Appeal, 1956-60. Recipient Profl. Accomplishment award Tech. and Sci. Socs. Cin., 1979, Tech. Innovation award Victor Mills Soc., 1990, Perkin medal Soc. of Chem. Industry, 1996, Disting. Alumnus Achievement award U. Iowa Carver Coll. Medicine, 2003; U.S. Pub. Health predoctoral fellow, 1951-52. Fellow AAAS, Am. Inst. Chemists; mem. Am. Soc. Bone and Mineral Rsch., Am. Chem. Soc. (program chmn. ctrl. regional meeting 1983, invited symposium spkr. nat. meeting 1987, 92, invited awards symposium spkr. 1994, Cin. Chemist of Yr. award 1977, Nat. Indsl. Chemist award 1994, Morley medal 1996, Heros of Chemistry award 2000), Am. Coll. Rheumatologists, Dance Club (pres. 1972-73), Wyo. (Ohio) Sunday Supper Club (pres. 1998-99, 2003-04). Republican. Roman Catholic. Home and Office: 23 Diplomat Dr Cincinnati OH 45215-2074 Office Phone: 513-772-3940. Office Fax: 513-772-3039. Personal E-mail: mfrancis3@cinci.rr.com.

FRANCIS, PHILIP HAMILTON, management consultant; b. San Diego, Apr. 13, 1938; s. William Samuel and Ruth Kathryn (Allison) F.; m. Regina Elizabeth Kirk, June 10, 1961 (div. May 1971); m. Diana Maria Villarreal, July 15, 1972; children: Philip Scott, Edward Philip, Mary Allison, Kenneth Joseph. BSME, Calif. Poly. State U., 1959; MSME, U. Iowa, 1960, PhD in Engring. Mechanics, 1965; MBA in Mgmt., St. Mary's U., San Antonio, 1972. Registered profl. engr., Tex. With Douglas Aircraft Co., Santa Monica, Calif., 1960-62, S.W. Rsch. Inst., San Antonio, 1965-79; prof., chmn. dept. mech. and aerospace engring. Ill. Inst. Tech., Chgo., 1979-84; with Indsl. Tech. Inst., Ann Arbor, Mich., 1984-86; dir. advanced mfg. tech. Motorola Inc., Schaumburg, Ill., 1986-88; corp. v.p. Square D Co. (Schneider-N.Am.), Palatine, Ill., 1988-94; client ptnr. AT&T Solutions, AT&T, Chgo., 1995-96; mng. ptnr. Mascon Global, Ltd., Schaumburg, Ill., 1996—2002; pres. Group Francis, LLC, Georgetown, Tex., 2001—; CEO IKnowWare, LC, 2006—. Adj. prof. engring. Northwestern U., 2003—. Mem. various indsl. and acad. adv. bds. Recipient Gustas Larson award ASME and Pi Tau Sigma, 1978 Fellow ASME; mem. Soc. Mfg. Engrs., Sigma Xi, Tau Beta Pi, Pi Tau Sigma. Roman Catholic. Avocation: writing. Office Phone: 512-868-9568. Business E-Mail: phil@groupfrancis.com.

FRANCK, ARDATH AMOND, psychologist, educator; b. Wehrum, Pa., May 5, 1925; d. Arthur and Helen Lucille (Sharp) Amond; m. Frederick M. Franck, Mar. 18, 1945; children: Sheldon, Candace. BS in Edn., Kent State U., 1946, MA, 1947; PhD, Western Res. U., 1956. Cert. high sch. tchr., elem. supr., sch. psychologist, speech and hearing therapist. Instr. Western Res. U., Cleve., 1953, U. Akron, 1947—50; sch. psychologist Summit County Schs., Ohio, 1950—60; cons. psychologist Wadsworth Pub. Schs., Ohio, 1946—86; dir. Akron Edn. Ctr., Ohio, 1950—. Pres. Twirling Unlimited, 1982—; cons., dir. Hobbitts Pre-Sch., 1973—88. Author: Your Child Learns, 1976. Mem.: Ohio Psychol. Assn., Internat. Reading Assn., Soroptimist (Akron), Mensa. Home: 631 Ghent Rd Akron OH 44333-2629 Office: Akron Edn Ctr 700 Ghent Rd Akron OH 44333-2698 Home Phone: 330-666-1163; Office Phone: 330-666-1161.

FRANCOIS, WILLIAM ARMAND, lawyer; b. Chgo., May 31, 1942; s. George Albert and Evelyn Marie (Smith) F.; m. Barbara Ann Sala, Aug. 21, 1965; children: Nicole Suzanne, Robert William. BA, DePaul U., 1964, JD, 1967. Bar: Ill. 1967. Pvt. practice, Lyons, Ill., 1967-68; with Am. Nat. Can Group, Inc., Chgo., 1970, sec., 1974, v.p., 1978, sr. v.p., gen. counsel, sec., 1999-2000; dep. gen. counsel N.Am. Pechiney Group, 1996-99; pvt. practice Lake Forest, Ill., 2000—. Served to capt. US Army, 1968—70. Mem. ABA, Ill. Bar Assn., Chgo. Bar Assn., Soc. Corp. Secs. and Governance Profls., Am. Corp. Counsel Assn.

FRANCUCH, PAUL CHARLES, broadcast journalist; b. Highland Park, Mich., June 26, 1950; s. Charles and Anna (Protasevich) F. BA, Wayne State U., 1972; MA, U. Mich., 1973. From midwest corr. to London bur. chief Voice of Am., Chgo., 1980—96, London bur. chief, 1996—99; sci. engring. editor U. Ill., Chgo., 2001—. Mem. Phi Beta Kappa. Avocations: bicycling, photography, amateur astronomy. Office: 601 S Morgan St MC 288 Chicago IL 60607-7113 Home Phone: 312-867-3947; Office Phone: 312-996-3457. E-mail: francuch@uic.edu.

FRANK, JAMES S., automotive executive; b. Chgo., 1942; m. Karen Frank; 3 children. BS Phi Beta Kappa, Dartmouth Coll.; MBA, Stanford U. With ZF, Inc., Ill., 1965, Wheels, Inc., Des Plaines, Ill., 1965; pres. Four Wheels, Inc., Des Plaines, Ill., 1965; pres., CEO Frank Consol. Enterprises, Des Plaines, Ill., 1967—, Wheels (subs. Frank Consol. Enterprises), Des Plaines, Ill., 1974—. Trustee U. of Chgo., 1995. Pres. Michael Reese Med. Rsch. Inst. Coun. Jr. Bd.; bd. trustees U. Chgo. Hosps., U. Chgo.; bd. overseers Thayer Engring. Sch. Dartmouth Coll. Mem.: Am. Automobile Leasing Assn. (past pres. and chair, bd. dir., chair fed. gtax and legis. com., past chair industry com., dir. 2003—). Office: Frank Consol Enterprises 666 Garland Pl Des Plaines IL 60016-4725

FRANK, MICHAEL M., lawyer; b. NYC, Aug. 4, 1939; BS, Wash. U., 1961, JD, 1964. Bar: Mo. 1965, U.S. Dist. Ct. Mo. (Ea. Dist.) 1965. Former mcpl. judge, state prosecutor; former instr. St. Louis Met. Police Acad.; state prosecutor Cir. Atty.'s Office, St. Louis; ptnr. Frank & Juengel Attys. At Law PC, St. Louis. Lectr. in field; mem. Fed. Hate Crimes Task Force; mem. legal adv. bd. Anti Defamation League; bd. dirs. Mo. Prison Arts Bd. Mem.: ABA (past chmn.), NACDL (life), Mo. Mcpl. Judges Assn. (past pres.), St. Louis Met. Mcpl. Judges Assn. (past pres.), Mo. Assn. Criminal Def. Lawyers, Mo. Bar Assn., Bar Assn. Met. St. Louis. Office: Frank & Juengel Attys at Law 7777 Bonhomme Ave Ste 1601 Saint Louis MO 63105 Office Phone: 314-721-4403, 314-725-7777. Office Fax: 314-721-4377. E-mail: mfrank@primary.net.

FRANK, RICHARD CALHOUN, architect; b. Louisville, May 17, 1930; s. William George and Helen (Calhoun) F.; children: Richard, Scott, Elizabeth, William, Jennifer, Philip. BArch, U. Mich., 1953. Assoc. archtl. firms, Lansing, Mich., 1953-61; pres. Frank & Stein Assocs., Inc., Lansing, 1961-70; prin. Johnson, Johnson & Roy, Ann Arbor, 1971-75; pres. Preservation/Urban Design/Inc., Ann Arbor and Washington, 1975-84; pvt. practice Saline and Gregory, Mich., 1985—2004; pres. Frank, McCormick & Khalak, LLC, 2004—. Ind. contractor C.S. Mott Found., 1999-2000. Life trustee Hist. Soc. Mich. Fellow AIA (gold medal Mich. 1992); mem. Nat. Trust for Historic Preservation (trustee emeritus), Victorian Soc. Am. (v.p.). Home: 1408 Joliet Pl Detroit MI 48207 Office: 28 W Adams Detroit MI 48226 Home Phone: 313-567-7377; Office Phone: 313-234-8700. Personal E-mail: rcffaia@comcast.net. Business E-Mail: rcfrank@fmkdetroit.com.

FRANK, STUART, cardiologist; b. NYC, Dec. 25, 1934; s. Henry and Kitty (Sternberg) F.; m. Nanchen O'Brien, Aug. 1976 (div. Feb. 1980); children: Rachel Arthur, Sebastian Noah; m. Amber Barnhart, June 22, 1982; children: Amelia Elizabeth, Abigail Kitty, Jessica Cole. BS in Chemistry, MIT, 1956; MD, NYU, 1960. Diplomate Am. Bd. Internal Medicine, Am. Bd. Cardiovascular Disease. Intern and resident in internal medicine Yale U. New Haven Hosp., 1960-64; postdoctoral fellow Inst. Cardiology, London, 1964-65, Nat. Heart Inst., Bethesda, Md., 1965-67; chief cardiology Kaiser Permanente Med. Ctr., San Francisco, 1967-77; assoc. prof. dept. medicine So. Ill. U., Springfield, 1977-86, chief div. cardiology, 1977-90, asst. chmn. dept. medicine, 1981-88, prof. dept. medicine, 1986—, dean of students, 1990-95. Author: The People's Handbook of Medical Care, 1972; contbr. numerous articles to profl. jours. Recipient Nellie Westerman prize Am. Fedn. Clin. Research, 1986. Fellow ACP, Am. Coll. Cardiology, Am. Coll. Chest Physicians, Am. Heart Assn. (council clin. cardiology), Laennec Soc. Office: So Ill Univ Medicine Dept Cardiology PO Box 19636 Springfield IL 62794-9636 Home Phone: 217-546-5446; Office Phone: 217-545-0185.

FRANKE, RICHARD JAMES, art association administrator, retired investment banker; b. Springfield, Ill., June 23, 1931; s. William George and Frances Marie (Brennan) F. BA, Yale U., 1953, DHL (hon.), 2001; MBA, Harvard U., 1957; Degree (hon.), DePaul U. With John Nuveen & Co., Chgo., 1957-96, v.p., 1965-69, exec. v.p., 1969-74, chief adminstrv. officer, 1970-74, pres., 1974-89, CEO, 1974-96, chmn., 1988-96, also dir., chmn., CEO emeritus, 1996—. Vice chmn. Yale Corp., 1987-94, chmn., 1994—. Chmn. investment com. Yale U.; mem. Pres.'s Com. on the Arts and Humanities; trustee Chgo. Symphony Orch.; trustee U. Chgo.; bd. dirs. Lyric Opera, Newberry Libr.; sr. fellow Yale Corp., past sr. fellow, chair; chair Nat. Trust for the Humanities; founder, chair Chgo. Humanities Festival, 1989; dir. Chgo. Shakespeare Theater; life trustee U. Chgo.; 1st lt. U.S. Army, 1953-55. Recipient Nat. Humanities medal, NEH, 1997, Arts Legend award, Ill. Arts Alliance, 2002, Disting. Svc. award, Assn. Governing Bds. Univs. and Colls., Phi Beta Kappa award for disting. svc. to the humanities. Mem.: Am. Acad. Arts Scis. Office: 400 N Michigan Ave Ste 300 Chicago IL 60611-4130

FRANKEL, BERNARD, advertising executive; b. 1929; B in Mktg., U. Buffalo, 1951. Sales rep. Rugby Knitting Mi, Chgo., 1951-54; midwest rep. E.O. Hirsch & Assocs., Chgo., 1954-57; dir. sales promotion Kling Studios, Chgo., 1957-59; account exec., account supr., v.p. Knipschild-Robinson, Inc. (now William A. Robinson and Co.), 1959-62; CEO Frankel & Co., Chgo., 1962—2002, also chmn. bd. dirs., 1962—2002, chmn. emeritus, 2002—. Media rep., advt. sales mgr., advertising and promotion mgr. Concrete Pub. Co., Chgo., 1955-57. Office: Frankel 35 W Wacker Dr Fl 15 Chicago IL 60601-1762

FRANKEL, STUART, real estate company executive; m. Maxine Frankel; 2 children. BBA, U. Mich., 1961. Founder & CEO Stuart Frankel Devel. Co. Named one of Top 200 Collectors, ARTnews Mag., 2004; recipient Civic Leader Award art & culture, Mich. Gov., 2004. Mem.: Downtown Devel. Authority. Avocation: collector of modern & contemporary art, especially Latin Am., ceramics & sculpture.

FRANKLIN, AL, artistic director; b. Oceanside, Calif., Mar. 3, 1951; m. Elizabeth Amey Sanchez, June 22, 1985; children: Jacob Sanchez, Caleb Alexander. Freelance stage mgr., tour mgr., line prodr., various locations, 1979-86; prodn. mgr. Walnut St. Theatre, Phila., 1987-91; producing artistic dir. Gretna Theatre, Mt. Gretna, Pa., 1991-94; exec. dir. Theatre Assn. of Pa., 1995-96; artistic dir. Fort Wayne Civic Theatre, Ind., 1996—. Founder, chmn. C-PATH, Lancaster, 1992-96. Prodr., dir. large and small musicals, new plays, Shakespeare and other classic plays, contemporary dramas and comedies, children's plays, workshops, play readings, spl. projects and fundraising events. Bd. dirs. Fort Wayne Civic Theatre, 1996—, Leadership Lebanon (Pa.) Valley, 1993-95, Friends of Colonial, Lebanon, 1992-94. With USAF, 1969-73, The Netherlands. Avocations: writing, martial arts, painting, clay sculpting. Home: 227 S Cornell Cir Fort Wayne IN 46807-2817

FRANKLIN, DOUGLAS E., publishing executive; b. 1957; Grad., U. Dayton, 1979. Staff acct. Dayton (Ohio) Newspapers, 1979, asst. contr., 1980, 1986-90; with Springfield (Ohio) Newspaper, 1981-83; bus. mgr. Longview Newspaper, Tex., 1983-86; with Dayton (Ohio) Daily News, 1990—, exec. v.p., gen. mgr. Office: Dayton Daily ews 45 S Ludlow St Dayton OH 45402-1858

FRANKLIN, J. RICHARD, principal; b. Milan, Mo., July 15, 1934; m. Joyce Ann Fishback; children: James, Elizabeth. BS, Truman State U., 1956; MA, U. Mo., 1963; postgrad., Ctrl. Mo. State U., 1972—. Prin. Ft. Osage HS, Independence, Mo., 1964—87. State rep. dist. 53 Mo. Ho. of Reps., 1989-2002, chmn. ed. com., 2000-02, chmn. retirement com., 1992-93, banking com., chair appropRations, 1994-96; chmn. budget com., 1997-2000. Mem. State Hist. Soc. Mo. (pres.), Masons, Shriners. Address: 1829 S Aztec Avenue Independence MO 64057

FRANKLIN, LYNNE, corporate communications specialist, writer; b. St. Paul, Aug. 24, 1957; d. Lyle John Franklin and Lois Ann (Cain) Kindseth, Thomas John Kindseth (Stepfather); m. Lawrence Anton Pecorella, Sept. 12, 1989; 1 stepchild, Lauren Pecorella. BA in Psychology and English, Coll. St. Catherine, 1979; MA, Hamline U., 1989. Residential treatment counselor St. Joseph's Home, Mpls., 1979-80; staff writer Comml. West Mag., Mpls., 1980-81; acct. exec. Edwin Neuger & Assocs., Mpls., 1981-83, Hill and Knowlton, Mpls., 1983-84; mgr. pub. rels. Gelco Corp., Eden Prarie, Minn., 1984-86; dir. fin. rels. Dunstan & Assocs., Mpls., 1986; cons. MC Assocs., Chgo., 1986-87; v.p. Fin. Rels. Bd., Chgo., 1987—; prin. Wordsmith, Glenview, Ill., 1993—; trainer SkillPath Seminars, Mission, Kans., 2004—, 2004. Trustee Lawrence Hall Youth Svcs., chairperson pub. rels. com.; former pres., v.p., sec. Skokie Valley chpt. Bus. Networking Internat., 2003—07; judge achievement awards Internat. Assn. Bus. Comm., Mpls., 1986, Publicity Club Chgo., 1992—94; presenter in fin. rels., 1990; presenter ann. report seminar Nat. Investor Rels. Inst., Chgo., 1992; presenter investor rels. survey, 2003; mktg. presenter Nat. Assn. Profl. Organizers, Chgo., 2005, World WIT Nat. Conf., Lake Geneva, Wis., 2005. Author: (novels) Second Sight, 1989. Tchr. Great Books Program, St. Paul, 1976—79, Minn. Literacy Coun., 1985—87. Recipient Ann. Report Excellence award, Fin. World Mag., 1991—98, award, MerComm-ARC Competition, 1992—2003, Nat. Assn. Investors Corp., 1994—2003, Equities Mag., 1999—2002. Mem.: Rotar (crisis comm. presenter 2007). Office: Wordsmith 2019 Glenview Rd Glenview IL 60025-2849 Business E-Mail: lynne@yourwordsmith.com.

FRANKLIN, RICHARD MARK, lawyer; b. Chgo., Dec. 13, 1947; s. Henry W. and Gertrude (Gross) F.; m. Marguerite June Wesle, Sept. 2, 1973; children: Justin Wesley, Elizabeth Cecilia, Catherine Helena, Caroline Lucinda. BA, U. Wis., 1970; postgrad., U. Freiburg, Fed. Republic Germany, 1968-69; JD, Columbia U., 1973. Bar: Ill. 1973, U.S. Dist. Ct. (no. dist.) Ill. 1973, U.S. Ct. Appeals (7th cir.) 1973. Assoc. Baker & McKenzie, Chgo., 1973-79, Frankfurt, Fed. Republic Germany, 1979-80, ptnr. Chgo., 1980—. Mem. ABA, Ill. Bar Assn., Chgo. Bar Assn. Mem. United Ch. Christ. Avocations: music, literature, theater, outdoor activities. Home: 1161 Oakley Ave Winnetka IL 60093-1437 Office: Baker & McKenzie 1 Prudential Plz 130 E Randolph St Ste 3500 Chicago IL 60601-6342 Home Phone: 847-446-2841; Office Phone: 312-861-8860. E-mail: rmfwinn@aol.com, richard.m.franklin@bakenet.com.

FRANKLIN, WILLIAM EDWIN, bishop emeritus; b. Parnell, Iowa, May 3, 1930; Student, Mt. St. Bernard Sem.; MA, Loras Coll., 1969. Ordained priest Archdiocese of Dubuque, Iowa, 1956, aux. bishop Iowa, 1987—94; ordained bishop, 1987; bishop Diocese of Davenport, Iowa, 1994—2006, bishop emeritus Iowa, 2006—. Roman Catholic. Office: Diocese of Davenport St Vincent Ctr 2706 N Gaines St Davenport IA 52804-1998 Office Phone: 563-324-1911. Office Fax: 563-324-5842. E-mail: wfranklin@davenportdiocese.org.*

FRANKS, DAVID BRYAN, internist, emergency physician; b. Washington, Nov. 18, 1956; s. David Ardell and Erta Mae (Williford) F.; m. Deborah Ann Hayek, Jan. 31, 1987; children: Ariel Ann, David Henry, Theodore Gabriel. BS, U. Md., 1978, MD, 1980. Diplomate Am. Bd. Internal Medicine, Am. Bd. Emergency Medicine. Resident Thomas Jefferson U. Hosp., Phila., 1980-83; physician Temple U. Hosp., Phila., 1983-85, St. Joseph Health Ctr., St. Charles, Mo., 1985-87, Belleville (Ill.) Meml. Hosp., 1987—. Fellow Am. Coll. Emergency Physicians. Office: 4500 Memorial Dr Belleville IL 62226-5360

FRANKSON-KENDRICK, SARAH JANE, publisher; b. Bradford, Pa., Sept. 24, 1949; d. Sophronus Ahimus and Elizabeth Jane (Sears) McCutcheon; m. James Michael Kendrick, Jr., May 22, 1982. Customer svc. rep. Laros Printing/Osceola Graphics, Bethlehem, Pa., 1972-73; assoc. editor Babcox Publs., Akron, Ohio, 1973-74, Bill Comms., Akron, Ohio, 1974-75, sr. editor, 1975-77, editor-in-chief, 1977-81; assoc. pub. Chilton Co./ABC Pub., Chgo., 1981-83, pub., 1983-89, group pub. Radnor, Pa., 1989-93; group v.p. Cahners Bus. Info. (formerly Chilton Co.), Radnor, Pa., 1993-98; divsn. v.p. Primedia Intertec, Chgo., 1999—2001. Exec. MBA prof. orthwood U., mem. adv. coun. Mem. oper. com. Primedia Intertec. Recipient Automotive Replacement Edn. award Northwood Inst., 1983, award for young leadership and excellence Automotive Hall of Fame, 1984; bd. dirs. Automotive Hall of Fame. Mem. Automotive Found. for Aftermarket (trustee), Automotive Parts and Accessories Assn. (bd. dirs., exec. com., sec., treas., strategic planning com., edn. com., Disting Svc. award 1993), Automotive Svc. Industry Assn. (bd. dirs. automotive divsn. com.), Automotive Svc. Banyan Golf Club (Wellington, Fla.), Palm Beach Polo and Country Club (Wellington, Fla.), Winged Foot Golf Club (Mamaroneck, N.Y.). Republican.

FRANK-STROMBORG, MARILYN LAURA, nursing educator; b. Chgo., Jan. 20, 1942; d. Irving and Roseann (Krcek) Frank; m. Paul Stromborg, 1966; children: Nels, Danny. BS, No. Ill. U., 1964, MS, 1966, cert. in nursing, 1966, EdD, 1974, JD, 1994. RN. Mem. faculty Sch. Nursing U. Ill., Chgo., 1970-71, No. Ill. U., DeKalb, 1976—; acting chair, 1995-96. Part-time mem. nursing faculty U. Loyola U., Chgo., 1974-76, Rush U., Chgo., 1974-76. Author: Primary Care Assessment and Management Skills for Nurses, 1979; editor Instruments for clinical Nursing Research, 1989 (AJN award 1989), Cancer Prevention and Early Detection in Minorities: Cultural Implications, 1993. Founder, vol. trainer De Kalb County Hospice, 1977—; v.p. Am. Cancer Soc., 1977. Capt. USAF, 1966-70. Named Researcher of Yr., Pace U., 1990; grantee Nat. Cancer Inst., NIH, 1984—; Ctr. for Nursing Rsch., 1985-90, Div. Nursing, 1990—. Fellow Am. Acad. Nursing; mem. Midwest ursing Rsch. Soc. (treas. 1989-91), Oncology Nursing Soc. (chair rsch. com. 1985-87, sec. 1987-89, excellence in cancer nursing edn. award 1991). Avocations: gardening, skiing. Home: 215 Dunkery Dr Sycamore IL 60178-1017 Office: No Ill U Dept Nursing Dekalb IL 60115

FRANTZ, DEAN LESLIE, psychotherapist; b. Beatrice, Nebr., Mar. 27, 1919; s. Oscar C. and Flora Mae (Gish) F.; m. Marie Flory, Aug. 31, 1940; children: Marilyn, Shirley, Paul. BA, Manchester Coll., Ind., 1942; MDiv, Bethany Theol. Sem., Oak Brook, Ill., 1945; diploma, C.G. Jung Inst. Zurich, 1977. Assoc. prof. Bethany Theol. Sem., 1957-64; dir. ch. rels. Manchester Coll., North Manchester, Ind., 1964-72; pvt. practice Ft. Wayne, Ind., 1977—. Author: Meaning for Modern Man in the Paintings of Peter Birkhauser, 1977; editor: Barbara Hannah: The Cat, Dog, and Horse Lectures, and the Beyond, 1992, Barbara Hannah: The Inner Journey, 1999, The Ten Oxherding Pictures, 2003. Mem. Internat. Assn. Analytical Psychology, Assn. Grad Analytical Psychologists. Home: Apt 24C 3143 Golden Years Homestead Dr 24C New Haven IN 46774-3002

FRANTZ, MARTIN H., prosecutor; b. Akron, Ohio, July 24, 1952; s. Harry W. and Jayne M. (Harvey) F.; m. Mary Ann Rittman, Sept. 9, 1978; children: Laine Elizabeth, Rachel Elaine, Michael Andrew. BA cum laude, Ohio State U., 1974, JD, 1978. Bar: Ohio 1978, U.S. Dist. Ct. (no. dist.) Ohio 1979, U.S. Supreme Ct. 1986; cert. trial advocate. Asst. prosecutor Wayne County, Wooster, OH, 1979-97, pros. atty., 1997—. Mem. adv. bd. Wayne County Schs. Career Ctr., Smithville, Ohio, 1996—. Author newsletter Crime and Punishment, 1995—. Chmn. Wayne County Rep. Ctrl. Com., 1984-96. Mem. Wooster Evening Lions Club (pres. 1986-87). Roman Catholic.

FRANZ, CRAIG JOSEPH, academic administrator, biology professor; b. Balt., Apr. 12, 1953; s. Harry Joseph and Vera Lee (Garrett) F. BA in Biology, Bucknell U., Lewisburg, Pa., 1975; MSc in Environ. Engring. & Sci., Drexel U., Phila., 1977; PhD in Biology, U. R.I., Kingston, 1988. Tchr. biology LaSalle Coll. High Sch., Phila., 1977-79; instr. biology St. John's Coll., Washington, 1980-84; teaching asst. U. R.I., Kingston, 1984-86; malacological researcher Estacion de Investigaciones, Margarita, Venezuela, 1986-87; univ. fellow U. R.I., Kingston, 1987-88; asst. prof. biology LaSalle U., Phila., 1988—94; exec. asst. to pres. and dean Sch. Math. and Scis. Saint Mary's U., Minn., 1994—97, pres. Minn., 2005—, Saint Mary's Coll., Calif., 1997—2004. Author: Invertebrate Zoological Investigations, 1988; co-author: The Cornerstone, 1989. Bd. mem. IRB, Einstein Med. Ctr., Phila., 1989—; bd. trustees Calvert Hall Coll., Balt., 1982-84. Univ. fellow U. R.I., Kingston, 1987. Mem. AAAS, Am. Soc. Zoologists, Am. Malacological Union, Delta Upsilon (bd. dirs. 1975, 1989—), Phi Kappa Phi, The Demosthenean Club (bd. dirs. 1987-89). Democrat. Roman Catholic. Achievements include discovery of new species of chiton, new genus of copepod. Office: Saint Mary's U 700 Terrace Heights Winona MN 55987-1399 E-mail: cfranz@stmarys-ca.edu.

FRASE, RICHARD S., law educator; BA, Haverford Coll., 1967; JD, U. Chgo., 1970. Bar: Ill. 1970, Minn. 1977. Law clk. to L. Swygert, Chief Judge US Ct. Appeals 7th Cir., Chgo., 1970-71; rsch. assoc. U. Chgo. Law Sch., 1971—72, 1974—77; assoc. atty. Sidley & Austin, 1972—74; assoc. prof. law U. Minn. Law Sch., Mpls., 1977-81, prof. law, 1981-91, Davis prof. law, 1988-89, Berger prof. law, 1991—. Adv. bd. Fed. Sentencing Reporter, 1994—. Co-author: (textook) Criminal Justice System, 1980, (practice treatise) Minnesota Misdemeanors, 1982, 3d edit., 1999; author: (practice treatise) Criminal Evidence, 1985; co-author: (fgn. code translation) French Code of Criminal Procedure, 1988; co-editor: Encyclopedia of Crime and Justice, 2d edit., 2001, Sentencing and Sanctions in Western Countries, 2001; mem. U. Chgo. Law Rev. Mem. Am. Law Inst., Phi Beta Kappa. Republican. Office: U Minn Law Sch 229 19th Ave S Minneapolis MN 55455-0400 Business E-Mail: frase001@umn.edu.

FRASER, DONALD MACKAY, retired mayor, congressman; b. Mpls., Feb. 20, 1924; s. Everett and Lois (MacKay) F.; m. Arvonne Skelton, June 30, 1950; children: Thomas Skelton, Mary MacKay, John DuFrene, Lois MacKay (dec.), Anne T. (dec.), Jean Skelton. BA cum laude, U. Minn., 1944, LLB, 1948. Bar: Minn. 1948. Ptnr. Lindquist, Fraser & Magnuson (and predecessors), 1948-62; Minn. State senator, 1954-62; sec. Senate Liberal Caucus, 1955-62; mem. 88th-95th Congresses from 5th Dist. Minn., mem. fgn. affairs com., chmn. subcom. on internat. orgn., mem. budget com.; mayor City of Mpls., 1980-93; mem. study and rev. com. Dem. Caucus; mem. Commn. on Role and Future Presdl. Primaries, 1976; adj. prof. law and pub. affairs U. Minn., Mpls. Vice chmn., dir. Mpls. Citizens Com. on Pub. Edn., 1950-54; Sec. Minn. del. Democratic Nat. Conv., 1960; chmn. Minn. Citizens for Kennedy, 1960; mem. platform com. Dem. Nat. Conv., 1964, mem. rules com., 1972, 76; vice chmn. Com. Dem. Selection Presdl. Nominees, 1968; chmn. Democratic Study Group Congress, 1969-71, Commn. on Party Structure and Del. Selection Dem. Party, 1971-72; 1st Am. co-chmn. Anglo-Am. Parliamentary Conf. on Africa, 1964; mem. U.S. del. 7th spl. session and 30th session UN Gen. Assembly, 1975; Congl. adviser to U.S. del. to UN Conf. on Disarmament, 1967-73, to U.S. del. to 3d Law of Sea Conf., 1972, to UN Commn. on Human Rights, 1974; cons. on families HUD, 1994. Chair health com. U.S. Conf. Mayors; bd. dirs. Mpls. United Way, 1986-93, Twin Cities Rise!, 1994—2002, Connect/U.S.-Russia, 1994—, Greater Mpls. Coun. Chs., 2000—03; co-chair Ctr. for Internat. Policy, 1976-94, Early Care and Edn. Fin. Commn., 1999-2002; co-founder, chair Dem. Farmer-Labor Edn. Found.; pres. S.E. Mpls. Coun. on Learning, 2003-05; co-chair, bd. dirs. Ready 4K, 2001-; mem. Mpls. Charter Commn., 1997-2004; initiated numerous youth programs such as Transitional Work Internship Program, Youth Work Internship Program, Neighborhood Early Learning Ctrs., Youth Coordinating Bd., Youth Trust. Lt. (j.g.) USNR, 1944-46. Recipient 1st Minn. Internat. Human Rights award, 1985, Disting. Svc. award Mpls. United Way, 1992; fellow Kennedy Sch., spring 1994. Mem. Mpls. Fgn. Policy Assn. (pres. 1952-53), Citizens League Greater Mpls. (sec. 1951-54), Minn. Bar Assn., Hennepin County Bar Assn., Ams. for Dem. Action (nat. chmn. 1973-76), Dem. Conf. (nat. chmn. 1976-78), U. Minn. Law Alumni Assn. (dir. 1958-61), Univ. Dist. Improvement Assn. (pres. 1950-52), Nat. League of Cities (2d v.p. 1991, 1st v.p. 1992, pres. 1993), Minn. Advocates for Human Rights (co-founder, bd. dirs. 1983-92, 2000-03), League of Minn. Cities (bd. dirs. 1991-93, co-chmn. Ready 4K 2005—). Democrat. Personal E-mail: dfled@goldengate.net.

FRASIER, RALPH KENNEDY, lawyer, bank executive; b. Winston-Salem, NC, Sept. 16, 1938; s. LeRoy Benjamin and Kathryn O. (Kennedy) F.; m. Jeannine Quick, Aug. 1981; children: Karen D. Frasier Alston, Gail S. Frasier Cox, Ralph Kennedy Jr., Keith Lowery, Marie K. Frasier Washington, Rochelle Doar. BS, N.C. Cen. U., Durham, 1963, JD, 1965. Bar: N.C. 1965, Ohio 1976. With Wachovia Bank and Trust Co., N.A., Winston-Salem, NC, 1965—75, v.p., counsel, 1969-70; asst. counsel, v.p. parent co. Wachovia Corp., 1970-75; v.p., gen. counsel Huntington Nat. Bank, Columbus, Ohio, 1975-76, sr. v.p., 1976-83, sec., 1981-98, exec. v.p., 1983-98, cashier, 1983-98; ret. V.p. Huntington Bancshares Inc., 1976-86, gen. counsel, 1976-98, sec., 1981-98, ret.; sec., dir. Huntington Mortgage Co., Huntington State Bank, Huntington Leasing Co., Huntington Bancshares Fin. Corp., Huntington Investment Mgmt. Co., Huntington Nat. Life Ins. Co., Huntington Co., 1976-88; v.p., asst. sec. Huntington Bank N.E. Ohio, 1982-84; asst. sec. Huntington Bancshares Ky., 1985-97; sec. Huntington Trust Co., N.A., 1987-97, Huntington Bancshares Ind., Inc., 1986-97, Huntington Fin. Services Co., 1987-98; dir. The Huntington Nat. Bank, Columbus, Ohio, 1998-04; of counsel Porter Wright Morris & Arthur LLP, Columbus, 1998-06, ret.; trustee OCLC Online Computer Libr. Ctr., Inc., Dublin, Ohio, 1999—, mem. fin. com., 2000-04, mem. audit com., 2000-, chair 2002-04, exec. com., 2002—, pers. and compensation com., 2002-03; dir. ADATOM.COM, Inc., Milpitas, Calif., 1999-01, mem. compensation com., 1999-01, chair audit com., 1999-01. Bd. dirs. Family Svcs. Winston-Salem, 1966-74, sec., 1966-71, 74, v.p., 1974; chmn. Winston-Salem Transit Authority,

1974-75; bd. dirs. Rsch. for Advancement of Personalities, 1968-71, Winston-Salem Citizens for Fair Housing, 1970-74, N.C. United Community Svcs., 1970-74; treas. Forsyth County (N.C.) Citizens Com. Adequate Justice Bldg., 1968; trustee Appalachian State U., Boone, N.C., 1973-83, endowment fund, 1973-83, Columbus Drug Edn. and Prevention Fund, Inc., 1989-92; trustee, vice chmn. employment and Edn. Commn. Franklin County, 1982-85; mem. Winston-Salem Forsyth County Sch. Bd. Adv. Coun., 1973-74, Atty. Gen's Ohio Task Force Minorities in Bus., 1977-78; bd. dirs. Inroads Columbus, Inc., 1986-95, Greater Columbus Arts Coun., 1986-94, Columbus Urban League Inc., 1987-94, vice chmn., 1990-94; trustee Riverside Meth. Hosp. Found., 1989-90, Grant Med. Ctr., 1990-95, Grant/Riverside Meth. Hosps., 1995-97; trustee Ohio Health Corp., 1997-04, treas., chair fin./audit com., 2001-04, exec. com., 2002-04; dir. Cmty. Mutual Ins. Co., Cin., 1989-92, mem. audit com., 1989-92; trustee N.C. Ctrl. U., Durham, N.C., 1993-01, vice-chmn., 1993-94, chmn. 1995, chair edni. planning and acad. affairs com., 1995-98, audit, devel. and personnel coms., 1998-01, chair audit com., 1999-01; mem. Ohio Bd. Regents, Columbus, Ohio, 1987-96, vice-chmn., 1993-95, chmn., 1995-96; trustee Nat. Jud. Coll., Reno, Nevada, 1996-02, fin. and audit com., 1997-02 treas., chair, 1999-02, Columbus Bar Found., 1998-05, fellows com. 1998-05, grants com., 1998-05; AEFC Pension Adminstrn. Com. defined benefit plan of the ABA, Am. Bar Endowment, Am. Bar Found., and Nat. Jud. Coll., Chgo, Ill., 1998-02. With AUS, 1958-64. Fellow: Ohio State Bar Found. (disting. life fellow, Ritter award 2003); mem.: ABA, NC State Bar, Columbus Bar Assn., Ohio Bar Assn., Nat. Bar Assn. Personal E-mail: rkfrasier@msn.com.

FRAUMANN, WILLARD GEORGE, lawyer; b. San Francisco, July 21, 1948; m. Anne C. Derleth, Dec. 18, 1971; children: Ellen, Robert, Sarah. AB, U. Mich., 1970; JD, Harvard U., 1973. Bar: Ill.1973, US Dist. Ct. (no. dist.) Ill. Ptnr. Kirkland & Ellis, Chgo., 1977—. Served to lt. USNR, 1973-77. Mem.: Chgo. Humanities Festival (bd. of dir), U. Mich. Coll. of Lit., Sci. & Arts (vis. com.). Office: Kirkland & Ellis 200 E Randolph Dr Chicago IL 60601-6636 Office Phone: 312-861-2038. Office Fax: 312-861-2000. Business E-Mail: wfraumann@kirkland.com.

FRAUTSCHI, TIMOTHY CLARK, lawyer; b. Madison, Wis., Apr. 8, 1937; s. Lowell E. and Grace C. (Clark) F.; m. Pamela H. Hendricks, June 23, 1964; children: Schuyler, Jason; m. Susan B. Brumm, June 13, 1981; 1 child, Jacob. BA, U. Wis., 1959; LL.B., London Sch. Econs., U. Wis., 1963. Bar: Wis. 1963, U.S. Ct. Claims 1976, U.S. Tax Ct., 1976. Assoc. firm Foley & Lardner, Milw., 1963-70, ptnr., 1970—. Editor Wis. Law Rev. Co-founder Milw. Forum; pres. Lakeside Cmty. Coun., Skylight Comic Opera, Ltd., 1980—85, Present Music, Inc., 1991—98, Next Act Theatre, 2001—04, Danceworks, Inc., 2005—; bd. dirs. Am. Players Theater, Milw., Repertory Theater, Northcott Neighborhood House, United performing Arts Fund, Inc., Milw., Children's Svc. Soc., Wis. Theatre Tesseract; pres. Next Act Theatre, 1986—89, Watertower Landmark Trust, 1986—89; v.p. Frank Lloyd Wright Wis. Conservancy, 2001—; bd. dirs. St. Mary's Milw. Hosp. Found., pres., 2003—. Mem. Milw. Jr. Bar Assn. (pres. 1969-70), Milw. Bar Assn. (dir. 1971-74), Order of Coif, Phi Beta Kappa (pres. Milw. chpt. 1968-70), Phi Kappa Phi, Phi Eta Sigma Office: Foley & Lardner US Bank Ctr 777 E Wisconsin Ave Ste 3800 Milwaukee WI 53202-5367 Home Phone: 414-221-9688; Office Phone: 414-297-5737. Business E-Mail: tfrautschi@foley.com.

FRAZIER, KENNETH L., university librarian; BA in Philosophy, U. Kans.; MSLS, U. Denver. With libr. staff U. Wis., Madison, 1978—, dir. gen. Libr. System, 1992—. Mem. Madison Literary Soc.; bd. mem. and past pres. Old Market Place Neighborhood Assoc., Madison, Wis. Mem.: Scholarly Pub. and Academic Resources Coalition (founding mem.), Assn. Rsch. Libr. (bd. dir., past pres.). Office: Univ Wisconsin Library Rm 372F 728 State St Madison WI 53706 Office Phone: 608-262-2600. E-mail: kfrazier@library.wisc.edu.

FRAZZETTA, THOMAS HENRY, evolutionary biologist, educator; b. Rochester, NY, May 13, 1934; s. Joseph H. and Louise V. (Cross) F. BS, Cornell U., 1957; PhD, U. Wash., 1964. Instr. in zoology U. Wash., Seattle, 1963-64; assoc. in herpetology Harvard U., Cambridge, Mass., 1964-65; asst. prof. U. Ill., Urbana, 1965-71, assoc. prof., 1971-76, prof. dept. ecology, ethology, evolution, 1976—. Author: Complex Adaptations in Evolving Populations, 1975; contbr. articles to jours. Active ACLU, World Wildlife Fedn., Planned Parenthood Fedn. Am., Zero Population Growth, Amnesty Internat. NIH postdoctoral fellow, 1964; NSF research grantee, 1969, 77, 86. Mem. AAAS, Soc. Study Evolution, Am. Soc. Ichthyologists and Herpetologists, Am. Elasmobranch Soc., Soc. for Integrative and Comparative Biology. Democrat. Office: Univ Ill Dept Animal Biology 515 Morrill Hall Urbana IL 61801 Office Phone: 217-333-4199. Business E-Mail: tomfrazz@life.uiuc.edu.

FREBORG, LAYTON W., state legislator; b. Underwood, ND, May 13, 1933; m. Delilah Freborg; 4 children. Gen. contractor; mem. N.D. Ho. of Reps., Bismark, 1973-81, .D. Senate from 8th dist., Bismark, 1985—. Chmn. edn. and natural resources com. N.D. State Senate. Chmn. N.D. State Rep. Com. (mem. edn. and agr. com.); mem. Underwood Sch. Bd. (pres. 14 yrs.). Mem. Farm Bur., Turtle Lake Civic Club, Underwood Civic Club, Underwood C. of C. Republican. Address: PO Box 677 Underwood ND 58576-0677

FRECHETTE, PETER LOREN, dental products executive; b. Janesville, Wis., Aug. 15, 1937; s. Francis Michael and Gladys Jean F.; m. Patricia Jean O'Brien, June 24, 1961; children: Kathleen and Kristen (twins). BS in Econs., U. Wis., 1960; MBA, Northwestern U., 1980. Pres. Sci. Products, McGaw Park, Ill., 1975-82; pres., CEO Patterson Dental Co., Mpls., 1982—. Served with U.S. Army, 1961-63. Mem. Am. Dental Trade Assn. Office: Patterson Dental Co 1031 Mendota Heights Rd Mendota Heights MN 55120-1401 Office Phone: 651-686-1700. E-mail: pete.frechette@pattersondental.com.

FREDEN, SHARON ELSIE CHRISTMAN, state education official; b. Watertown, SD, Jan. 11, 1941; d. Harlon Arthur and Mildred Lillian (Jensen) Christman; m. Noble Everett Freden, July 3, 1973; 1 child, Anne Victoria. BS, No. State Coll., Aberdeen, SD, 1962; MA, U. Iowa, 1966; EdD, U. Colo., 1973. Tchr. Manitowoc (Wis.) Pub. Schs., 1962-64, Boulder Valley Pub. Schs., Colo., 1966-70, K-12 lang. arts cons. Colo., 1970-72; cons. Colo. Dept. Edn., Denver, 1973-76, 77-80; ITV insvc. coord. Sta. KCPT-TV, Kansas City, Mo., 1980-81; dir. Kans. Dept. Edn., Topeka, 1981-84, asst. commr., team leader, 1984—2001, 2001—. Editor: Basic Skills: Promising Practices in Colorado, 1979, (with others) Pupil Progress in Colorado, 1978; contbr. chpts. to books. Chmn. precinct com. Broomfield (Colo) Dem. Com., 1978. Recipient leadership award YWCA, 1990; Hildegard Sweet Meml. scholar, 1972. Mem. ASCD, Kans. ASCD, United Sch. Adminstrs., Phi Delta Kappa. Office: Kans Dept Edn 120 E 10th Topeka KS 66612

FREDERICK, EDWARD CHARLES, university official; b. Mankato, Minn., Nov. 17, 1930; s. William H. and Wanda (MacNamara) F.; m. Shirley Lunkenheimer, Aug. 16, 1951; children: Bonita Frederick Treangen (dec.), Diane Frederick Fox, Donald, Kenneth, Karen Frederick Swenson. BS in Agrl. Edn, U. Minn., 1954, MS in Dairy Husbandry, 1955, PhD in Anatomy and Physiology, 1957. Animal scientist, instr. N.W. Sch. and Expt. Sta. U. Minn., Crookston, 1958-64, supt. So. Sch. and Expt. Sta. Waseca, 1964-69, provost Tech. Coll., 1969-85, chancellor Tech. Coll., 1985-90; sr. fellow Hubert H. Humphrey Inst. Pub. Affairs, 1990-91, U. Minn. Coll. of Agr., Food and Environ. Sci., 1991—. Mem. Tech. Agrl. Edn. Study Team to Morocco, 1977. Contbr. articles on dairy physiology, mgmt., agrl. edn. and adminstrn. to tech. jours. and popular publs. Bd. dirs. Bob Hodgson Student Loan Fund, 1971-90, Minn. Agrl. Interpretive Ctr., 1978—, chair, 1994—; bd. dirs. Minn. Agri-Growth Coun., 1980—, pres. 1992—; bd. dirs. Southeastern Minn. Initiative Fund, 1986-92, v.p., 1991-92; bd. dirs. Waseca area United Way, 1988-94, pres., 1992; bd. dirs. Minn. Agriculture in the Classroom, 1993-99, pres., 1995-96. Recipient Alumni award 4-H, 1972, Good Neighbor award WCCO, 1990, Ed Frederick Day award State of Minn., 1990, Merit award Gamma Sigma Delta, 1994, Above Self award Waseca Cmty. Svc., 2002, Lifetime Leadership award Minn. Rural Ptnrs., 2002, Ground Breaker award So. Minn. Initiative Found., 2002, Lifetime Achievement award Agri-News, 2005; named to Minn. FFA Hall of Fame, 2004; finalist So. Minn. Agrl. Amb. of Yr., 2004. Mem. Am. Dairy Assn., Am. Soc. Animal Prodn., AAAS, Nat. Assn. Colls. and Tchrs. Agr. (pres. 1976-77), Am. Assn. Cmty. and Jr. Colls. (pres. Council of Two Yr. Colls. of Four Yr. Instns. 1988-90), Minn. FFA Alumni Assn. (pres. 1998-00, found. bd. trustees 2000—, chair exec. sponsor bd. 2006—), South Central Edn. Assn. (Disting. Service award 1971), Waseca Area C. of C. (dir. 1979), Foresters Club, Rotary (gov. dist. 596 1982-83), KC, Phi Kappa Phi. Roman Catholic. Home: 39031 State Highway 13 Waseca MN 56093-4212 Office: U Minn Coll Agrl Food and Env Sci Waseca MN 56093 Office Phone: 507-835-3422. Business E-Mail: frede010@umn.edu.

FREDERICK, RANDALL DAVIS, former political organization administrator, former state legislator; b. Apr. 23, 1956; m. Cindy Abraham; 3 children. Student, S.D. State U., 1974-76. Mem. SD Ho. of Reps., 1989-92, mem. appropriations com., 1992-93, mem. taxation and transp. coms., 1992, chmn. appropriations com., 1994, co-chmn. joint appropriations com., 1994; senator SD State Senate, 1993—2003, co-chair appropriations com., 1993; chmn. SD Rep. Party, 2003—07. Farmer, Hayti, SD, 1976—. Republican. Home: RR 1 Box 106 Hayti SD 57241-9629*

FREDERICK, THOMAS JAMES, lawyer; b. Grand Rapids, Mich., Oct. 6, 1956; s. Charles Murr and E. Marjorie (Loye) F. BA, Mich. State U., 1978; JD, U. Mich., 1984. Bar: Ill. 1984, U.S Dist. Ct. (no. dist.) Ill. 1984, U.S. Ct. Appeals (7th cir.) 1989, U.S. Supreme Ct., 1993. From assoc. to. ptnr. Winston & Strawn, Chgo., 1984—, chair litigation dept., 2006—. Assoc. editor: Michigan Law Review, 1982—83; editor, 1983—84. Mem. ABA, Chgo. Bar Assn., Seventh Cir. Bar Assn., Order of Coif. Office: Winston & Strawn 35 W Wacker Dr Chicago IL 60601-9706 Office Phone: 312-558-5983. Office Fax: 312-558-5700. Business E-Mail: tfrederick@winston.com.

FREDERICK, VIRGINIA FIESTER, state legislator; b. Rock Island, Ill., Dec. 24, 1916; d. John Henry and Myrtle (Montgomery) Heise; m. C. Donnan Fiester (dec. 1975); children: Sheryl Fiester Ross, Alan R., James D.; m. Kenneth Jacob Frederick, 1978 (dec.). BA, U. Iowa, 1938; postgrad., Lake Forest Coll., 1942-43, LLD, 1994, MLS, 1999. Freelance fashion designer, Lake Forest, Ill., 1952-78; pres. Mid Am. China Exch., Kenilworth, Ill., 1978-81; mem. Ill. Ho. of Reps., Springfield, 1979-95, asst. minority leader, 1990-95. Alderman first ward, Lake Forest, 1974-78; del. World Food Conf., Rome, 1974; subcom. pensions and employment Ill. Commn. on Status of Women, 1976-79; co-chair Conf. Women Legislators, 1982-85; bd. dirs. Lake Forest Coll., 1995-98, Lake Forest Symphony Guild, 1998—; city supr. City of Lake Forest, 1995-98. Named Chgo. Area Women of Achievement, Internat. Orgn. Women Execs., 1978; recipient Lottie Holman O'Neal award, 1980, Jane Addams award, 1982, Outstanding Legislator award Ill. Hosp. Assn., 1986, VFW Svc. award, 1988, Joyce Fitzgerald Meml. award, 1988, Susan B. Anthony Legislator of Yr. award, 1989, Delta Kappa Gamma award, 1991, Outstanding Legislator award, 1995, Svcs. for Srs. award, Ill. Dept. Aging, 1991, Ethics in Politics award, Rep. Womens's Club, 1992, Woman of Achievement award YWCA North Eastern Ill., 1994, Ill. Women in Govt. award, 1994, Lifetime Achievement award Equip for Equality, 1999. Mem. LWV (local pres. 1958-60, state dir. 1969-75, nat. com. 1975-76), AAUW (local pres. 1968-70, state pres. 1975-77, state dir. 1963-69, nat. com. 1967-69, Legislator of Yr. 1993), UN Assn. (bd. dirs.), Chgo. Assn. Commerce and Industry (bd. dirs.). Personal E-mail: k13v16@aol.com.

FREDERICKSON, DENNIS RUSSEL, state legislator, farmer; b. Morgan, Minn., July 27, 1939; s. Louis Bernard and Mary (Kragh) F.; m. Marjorie Davidson, July 15, 1961; children: Kari, Karl, Disa. BS, U. Minn., 1961. Farmer, Morgan, 1967—; commr. Redwood County, Minn., 1973-80; mem. Minn. Senate, St. Paul, 1981—. Past bd. dirs. Redwood Electric Coop. Author: (with others) The Fairy Tale Grim of Prince Perp, 1986. Served to lt. comdr. USN, 1962-67. Mem. S.W. Farm Mgmt. Assn. Republican. Lutheran. Avocation: running. Home: 4 Sunrise Dr New Ulm MN 56073-3615 Office: Minn Senate State Office Bldg Rm 143 Saint Paul MN 55155-0001

FREDERICKSON, HORACE GEORGE, retired academic administrator, humanities educator; b. Twin Falls, Idaho, July 17, 1937; s. John C. and Zelpha (Richins) F.; m. Mary Williams, Mar. 14, 1958; children— Thomas, Christian, Lynne, David. BA, Brigham Young U., 1959; M.P.A., UCLA, 1961; PhD, U. So. Calif., 1967; LL.D. (hon.), Dongguk U., Korea. Intern Los Angeles County, 1960; research asst. Bur. Govtl. Research, U. Calif., Los Angeles, 1960-61; lectr. pub. adminstrn. U. So. Calif., 1962-64; lectr. govt. and politics U. Md., 1964-66; asst. prof. polit. sci. Maxwell Sch., Syracuse U., 1967-71; assoc. dir. Met. Studies Program, 1970-72, assoc. prof. polit. sci., 1971-72; fellow in higher edn. fin. adminstrn. U. N.C. System, 1972; chmn. Grad. Program, Sch. Pub. and Environ. Affairs, Ind. U., 1972-74, assoc. dean for policy and adminstrv. studies, 1973-74; dean Coll. Pub. and Community Services, prof. regional and community affairs U. Mo., Columbia, 1974-76; pres. Eastern Wash. U., Cheney, 1976-87; Edwin O. Stene Disting. prof. pub. adminstrn. U. Kans., Lawrence, 1987—; John G. Winont vis. prof. Am. Gov., fellow U. Oxford, 2003—. Author: New Public Administration, 1980, The Spirit of Public Administration, 1997; editor: Ethics and Public Administration, 1993, Public Policy and the Two States of Kansas, 1994, Ideal and Practice in Council-Manager Government, 2nd edit., 1994; editor in chief Jour. Pub. Adminstrn. Rsch. and Theory, 1991—. Haynes Found. fellow U. So. Calif., 1963-64 Mem. Am. Soc. Pub. Adminstrn. (pres.), Nat. Acad. Pub. Adminstrn. Office: U Kans 1541 Lilac Ln #318 Lawrence KS 66045

FREDERIKSEN, MARILYNN C., physician; b. Chgo., Sept. 12, 1949; d. Paul H. and Susanne (Ostergren) Conners; m. James W. Frederiksen, July 11, 1971; children: John K., Paul S., Britt L. BA, Cornell Coll., 1970; MD, Boston U., 1974; grad. Exec. Leadership in Acad. Medicine, Allegheny U. Health Scis., 1998. Diplomate Am. Bd. Ob-Gyn., Am. Bd. Maternal-Fetal Medicine, Am. Bd. Clin. Pharmacology. Pediat. intern U. Md. Hosp., 1974-75, resident in pediat., 1975-76; resident in ob-gyn. Boston Hosp. for women, 1976-79; fellow in maternal fetal medicine Northwestern U., 1979-81, fellow clin. pharmacology, 1981-83, instr. ob-gyn. Chgo., 1981-83, asst. prof. ob-gyn., assoc. clin. pharmacology, 1983-91, assoc. prof. ob-gyn., 1991—, sect. chief gen. ob-gyn., 1993—2001. Mem. gen. faculty com. Northwestern U., Chgo., 1994—97, mem. ob-gyn. adv. panel, 1985—2000, chair ob-gyn. adv. panel, 2000—05; mem. U.S. Pharm. Com. Revision, Rockville, Md., 1986—2005; del. U.S. Pharm. conv. Northwestern U. Med. Sch., 1990, 95, 2000; mem. gen. clinic rsch. ctr. com. NIH, 1989—93, chairperson, 1992—93; mem. Task Force Writing Group on Asthma in Pregnancy, Nat. Heart, Lung and Blood Inst., 1991—92; examiner Am. Bd. Ob-Gyn., 1997—; mem. Task Force Working Group, Nat. Bd. Med. Examiners, 1997—98, mem. acute care com., 1999—2001. Mem. editorial bd. Clin. Pharmacology & Therapeutics, 1993; contbr. numerous articles to profl. jours. Bd. dirs. Cornell Coll. Alumni Assn., Mt. Vernon, Iowa, 1986—90, PRCH, 1997—2005, Planned Parenthood of Chgo. Area, 1999—, Northwestern Med. Faculty Found., 1995—98. Recipient Pharm. Mfrs. Assn. Found. Faculty Devel. award, 1984-86, Civil Liberties award ACLU, 1991. Fellow Am. Coll. Ob-Gyn.; mem. Soc. Maternal Fetal Medicine, Ctrl. Assn. Obstetricians and Gynecologists (bd. dirs. 1997-99), Am. Soc. Clin. Pharmacology and Therapeutics (bd. dirs. 1994-97), Chgo. Gynecologic Soc. (treas. 1994-97), Phi Beta Kappa. Episcopalian. Avocations: gardening, needlecrafts. Office: orthwestern Perinatal Assocs 680 N Lake Shore Dr Ste 1230 Chicago IL 60611 Office Phone: 312-981-4350. Personal E-mail: npa@cypressmail.com. Business E-Mail: mcf810@northwestern.edu.

FREDREGILL, ALAN, lawyer; b. Adel, Iowa, Mar. 19, 1948; BBA, U. Iowa, 1970; JD with honors, Drake U., 1974. Bar: Iowa 1975, Nebr. 1984. Atty. Heidman, Redmond, Fredregill, Patterson, Plaza, Dykstra & Prahl, LLP, Sioux City, Iowa. Mem.: Am. Mock Trial Assn. (Judges Hall of Fame 2002), Woodbury County Bar Assn., Internat. Assn. Arson Investigators, Iowa Acad. Trial Lawyers, Am. Coll. Trial Lawyers, Def. Rsch. Inst., Internat. Assn. Def. Counsel, Iowa Def. Counsel Assn. (bd. dirs. 1981—, pres. 1990—91), Iowa State Bar Assn. (unauthorized practice com. 1985—95, chmn. 1987—89, bd. govs. 1996—2003, pres. 2002—03), ebr. State Bar Assn., Order of Coif, ABA (litigation sect.). Office: Heidman Redmond Fredregill et al PO Box 3086 701 Pierce St Ste 200 Sioux City IA 51102

FREDRICKSON, JOHN MURRAY, otolaryngologist; b. Winnipeg, Man., Can., Mar. 24, 1931; s. Frank S. and Beatrice (Rannveig) F.; m. Alix Gordon, June 8, 1956; children: Kristin, Lisa, Erik. BA, U. B.C., Vancouver, 1953, MD, 1956. Intern Vancouver Genl Hosp., 1957-58, resident in pathology, 1959-60; resident in gen. surgery Shaughnessy Gen. Hosp., Vancouver, 1958-59; resident in otolaryngology U. Chgo., 1960-63, instr. in otolaryngologic surgery, 1963-65; asst. prof. surgery Stanford U., Calif., 1965-68; assoc. prof. otolaryngology U. Toronto, 1968-77, asst. prof. physiology, 1969-82, prof. otolaryngology, 1977-82; Lindburg prof. Sch. Medicine Washington U., St. Louis, 1982—, head dept. otolaryngology, 1982-98. Bd. dirs. Am. Bd. Otolaryngology, 1985-97. Co-editor: Advances in Oto-Rhino-Laryngology, 1973, Otolaryngology-Head and Neck surgery, 1983; editor Am. Jour. Otolaryngology, 1987-92; patentee implantable hearing aid, 1973, implantable voice box, 1981. Lt. RCAF, 1946-59. Mem. Am. Acad. Otolaryngology, Head and Neck Surgery, Soc. Univ. Otolaryngologists, Collegium Othrhinolaryngolica, Am. Laryngological Assn. (pres. 1992-93), Am. Otological Soc. Avocations: sports, music. Office: Washington U Med Sch Campus Box 8115 517 S Euclid Ave Saint Louis MO 63110-1007 Home: 205 DartmouthDr SE Albuquerque NM 87106-2219

FREE, HELEN MURRAY, chemist, consultant; b. Pitts., Feb. 20, 1923; d. James Summerville and Daisy (Piper) Murray; m. Alfred H. Free, Oct. 18, 1947 (dec. May 2000); children: Eric, Penny, Kurt, Jake, Bonnie, Nina. BA in Chemistry, Coll. of Wooster, Ohio, 1944, DSc (hon.), 1992; MA in Clin. Lab. Mgmt., Ctrl. Mich. U., 1978, DSc (hon.), 1993. Cert. clin. chemist Nat. Registry Cert. Chemists. Chemist Miles Labs., Elkhart, Ind., 1944—78, dir. mktg. svcs. rsch. products divsn., 1978-82; chemist, mgr., cons. Bayer HealthCare Diabetes Care, Elkhart, 1982—. Mem. adj. faculty Ind. U., South Bend, 1975—96; keynote spkr. Pres. Awards Excellence for Math. and Sci. Tchrs., 2007; spkr. in field. Author (with others): (books) Urodynamics and Urinalysis in Clinical Laboratory Practice, 1972, 1976; contbr. articles to encys. and profl. jours. Bd. dirs. Nat. Inventors Hall of Fame Found.; women's chmn. Centennial of Elkhart, 1958; mem. adv. bd. Intellectual Property Sch. Law, Akron U.; indsl. adv. bd. chemistry/chem. engring. Tri-State U., Angola, Ind. Named Woman of Yr., YWCA, 1993, Kilby Found. laureate, 1996; named to Hall of Excellence, Ohio Found. Ind. Colls., 1992, Nat. Inventors Hall of Fame, 2000, Engring. and Sci. Hall of Fame, 1996; recipient Disting. Alumni award, Coll. of Wooster, 1980, award, Medi Econ. Press, 1986, Nat. Leadership award, Lab. Pub. Svc., 1994. Fellow: AAAS, Assn. Women in Sci., Royal Soc. Chemistry, Am. Inst. Chemists (co-recipient Chgo. award 1967); mem.: Nat. Com. Clin. Lab. Stds. (bd. dir.), Am. Soc. Clin. Lab. Sci. (chmn. assembly, Achievement award 1976), Soc. Chem. Industry (hon.), Assn. Clin. Scientists (diploma of honor 1992), Am. Assn. Clin. Chemistry (coun., bd. dir., nominating com. and pub. rels. com., coord. profl. affairs, nat. membership com., pres. 1990, Outstanding Contbn. award 2006), Am. Chem. Soc. (pres. 1993, bd. dir., chmn. Chemistry Week task force, bd. com. pub. affairs and pub. rels., chmn. women chemists com., internat. activities com., grants and awards com., prof. and mem. rels. com., nominating com., coun. policy pub. affairs and budget, councilor, chair Progress project, Garvan medal 1980, Svc. award local chpt. 1981, co-recipient Mosher award 1983, 1st recipient Helen M. Free Pub. Outreach award 1995, Helen M. Free award named in her honor 1995), Altrusa (pres. 1982—83, bd. dir.), Sigma Delta Epsilon (hon.), Iota Sigma Pi (hon.). Presbyterian. Achievements include patents in field. Home: 3752 E Jackson Blvd Elkhart IN 46516-5205 Office: Bayer HealthCare Diabetes Care Divsn 1025 N Michigan Ave Elkhart IN 46514 Personal E-mail: Hmfree23@aol.com. Business E-Mail: helen.free.b@bayer.com.

FREEBORN, JOANN LEE, state legislator, farmer, former educator; m. Warren S. Freeborn Jr. BS, Kans. State U., 1966. Mem. from Dist. 107, Kans. State Ho. of Reps., 1992—, chmn. environ. com., mem. agr. com., mem. fed. and state affairs com. Home: 1904 N 240th Rd Concordia KS 66901

FREEBORN, MICHAEL D., lawyer; b. Mpls., June 30, 1946; s. Andrew W. and Verena M. (Keller) F.; m. Nancie L. Siebel, Oct. 19, 1947; children: Christopher A., Nathan M., Joel C., Paul K. BS, USAF Acad., 1968; JD, Ind. U., 1972; MBA, U. Chgo., 1975. Bar: Ill. 1972, Ind. 1972, US Ct. Appeals (3rd, 6th, 7th & DC cirs., US Supreme Ct. Assoc. to ptnr. Rooks, Pitts & Poust, Chgo., 1972-83; ptnr. Freeborn & Peters, Chgo., 1983—. Writer, lectr. in field. Assoc. editor Ind. Law Rev., 1970-71. Vice chmn. Voices for Ill. Children, 1993-2003; bd. dirs. Constnl. Rights Found. Chgo., 1996—, Chgo. Youth Ctrs., 1998-2005; chmn. citizens adv. coun. Ill. Coastal Zone Mgmt. Prog., Chgo., 1979. Capt. USAF, 1968—72. Recipient Founders Day award Ind. U. Law Sch., 1972. Mem.: Ind. Bar Assn., Ill. Bar Assn. (assembly del.), Union League, Legal. Lutheran. Avocations: scuba diving, coin collecting/numismatics, flying, racquetball. Office: Freeborn & Peters 311 S Wacker Dr Ste 3000 Chicago IL 60606 Office Phone: 312-360-6502. Office Fax: 312-360-6575. E-mail: mfreeborn@freebornpeters.com.

FREEBURG, RICHARD L., primary education educator; Elem. tchr. Nicollet Jr. High Sch., tchr. tech. edn. Recipient Tchr. Excellence award Internat. Tech. Edn. Assn., 1992. Office: Nicollet Jr High Sch 400 E 134th St Burnsville MN 55337-4010

FREED, DEBOW, academic administrator; b. Hendersonville, Tenn., Aug. 26, 1925; s. John Walter and Ella Lee (DeBow) F.; m. Catherine Carol Moore, Sept. 10, 1949; 1 child, Debow II. BS, US Mil. Acad., 1946; grad., US Inf. Sch., 1953, US Army Command and Gen. Staff Coll., 1959; MS, U. Kans., 1961; PhD, U. .Mex., 1966; grad., US Air War Coll., 1966; LLD, Monmouth Coll., Ill., 1987; DLitt (hon.), Ohio No. U., 1999. Comdg. officer U.S. Army, 1946; comdr. 35th Inf. Japan, 1947-48; asst. to cmdr. 17th Airborne Div., 1948-49; comdr. 26th Inf., Federal Republic of Germany, 1949-51; asst. to chief U.S. Mission, Iran, and chief Middle Ea. Affairs, 1951-53; instr. The Inf. Sch., 1953-56; comdr. 32d Inf., Korea, 1956-57; instr. Command and Gen. Staff Coll., 1957-58; chief nuclear br. U.S. Atomic Energy Agy., 1961-65; chief plans divsn. US Army, Vietnam, 1966-67; prof. physics dept. U.S. Mil. Acad., 1967-69, ret., 1969; dean Mt. Union Coll., 1969-74; pres. Monmouth Coll., 1974-79, Ohio No. U., Ada, 1979—99, pres. emeritus, 1999—; pres. U. Findlay, 2003—. Chmn. Assoc. Colls. of Midwest, 1977-79, others. Author: Using Nuclear Capabilities, 1959, Pulsed Neutron Techniques, 1965; contbr. articles, revs. to profl. publs.; editor: Atomic Development Report, 1962-64. Bd. dirs. Presbyn. Coll. Union, 1974-79; trustee Ctr. Sci. and Industry, 1982—, Toledo Symphony, 1994—, Blanchard Valley Health Assn., 1999—, Blanchard Valley Health Found., 2000—; chmn., bd. trustees, COSI Endowment Found., 2001; v.p., dir. Buckeye coun. Boy Scouts Am., 1972-74, dir. Prairie coun., 1974-78. Decorated Bronze Star, (2) Legion of Merit, Legion of Honor Iran, Army Commendation medal, Air medal, Joint Svcs. Commendation medal, others; recipient various civic awards; Associated Western Univs. fellow, 1963-65; AEC fellow, 1963-65; Fgn. Policy Rsch. Inst. fellow, 1966; named Ohio Commodore, 1990. Mem. Assn. Meth. Colls. and Univs. (bd. dirs. 1979-99), Ohio Coll. Assn. (bd. dirs. 1980-84, 85-88, pres. 89-90), Ohio Found. Independent Colls. (bd. dirs. 1979-99), Am. Assn. Pres. of Colls. and Univs. (bd. dirs. 1988-99, treas. 1997-98, v.p. 1998-99), Ohio Commodores, Sixma Xi, Phi Kappa Phi, Phi Eta Sigma, Delta Theta Phi, Omicron Delta Kappa. Home: 1115 N Main St Findlay OH 45840 Office: Office of Pres U Findlay Findlay OH 45840 Office Phone: 419-434-4510. Business E-Mail: freed@findlay.edu.

FREED, KARL FREDERICK, chemistry professor; b. Bklyn., Sept. 25, 1942; s. Nathan and Pauline Freed; m. Gina P. Goldstein, June 14, 1964; children: Nicole Yvette, Michele Suzanne. BS, Columbia U., 1963; A.M., Harvard U., 1965, PhD, 1967. NATO postdoctoral fellow U. Manchester (Eng.), 1967-68; asst. prof. U. Chgo., 1968-73, assoc. prof., 1973-76, prof. chemistry, 1976—, dir. James Frank Inst., 1983—86, Henry G. Gale disting. svc. prof., 2006—. Bd. dirs. Telluride Sci. Rsch. Ctr., 2003—06, 2007—, Argonne Nat. Lab/U. Chgo. Joint Theory Inst. Author: Renormalization Group Theory of Macromolecules, 1987; editl. bd. Jour. Statis. Physics, 1976-78, Advances in Chem. Physics, 1985—, Computational Theoretical Polymer Sci., 1996—; adv. editor Chem. Physics, 1979-92, Chem. Revs., 1981-83, Internat. Jour. Quantum Chemistry, 1995-99; assoc. editor Jour. Chem. Physics, 1982-84; contbr. articles to profl. jours. Recipient Marlow medal Faraday div. Chem. Soc. London, 1973; recipient Pure Chemistry award Am. Chem. Soc., 1976; fellow Sloan Found., 1969-71; Guggenheim fellow, 1972-73; fellow Dreyfus Found., 1972-77 Fellow: Am. Acad. Arts and Scis., Am. Phys. Soc.; mem.: Am. Chem. Soc., Royal Soc. Chemistry. Office: U Chgo James Franck Inst 929 # 57th St CIS E231 Chicago IL 60637-1433 Business E-Mail: k-freed@uchicago.edu.

FREED, MAYER GOODMAN, law educator; b. Phila., Oct. 26, 1945; s. Abraham H. and Fannie (Rothenberg) F.; m. Paulette Kleinhaus, Aug. 23, 1970; children: Daniel, Joshua. AB cum laude, Columbia Coll., 1967, JD, 1970. Bar: N.Y. 1971, Ill. 1975, U.S. Dist. Ct. (so. and ea. dists.) N.Y. 1972, U.S. Ct. Appeals (2d cir.) 1972, U.S. Supreme Ct. 1974. Assoc. Proskauer Rose Goetz & Mendelsohn, NYC, 1970-71; staff atty. Nat. Employment Law Project, NYC, 1971-73, sr. staff atty., 1973-74; asst. prof. law Northwestern U. Sch. Law, Chgo., 1974-77, assoc. prof., 1977-79, prof. law, 1979—, assoc. dean acad. affairs and curriculum, 1986—. Contbr. articles to legal publs.; bd. editors

Columbia Law Rev., 1969-70. Bd. dirs. Legal Assistance Found. Chgo., 1980-82. Stone scholar, 1968-69. Mem. ABA. Office: Northwestern U Sch Law 357 E Chicago Ave Chicago IL 60611-3059 E-mail: mfreed@law.northwestern.edu.

FREED, MICHAEL J., lawyer; b. Chgo., Feb. 13, 1938; BS, U. Pa., 1959; JD, U. Chgo., 1962. Bar: Ill. 1963, DC 1963, US Dist. Ct. (no dist. Ill.) 1963, US Dist. Ct. (dist. DC) 1963, US Ct. Appeals (DC cir.) 1963, US Ct. Appeals (7th cir.) 1977, US Supreme Ct. 1983. Atty. Antitrust div., U.S. D.O.J.; prin. Much Shelist Freed Denenberg Ament & Rubenstein, Chgo., 1973—2006; founding ptnr. Freed, Kanner, London & Millen, LLC, Bannockburn, Ill., 2006—. Mem. adv. bd. Am. Antitrust Inst., Washington; bd. dir. Appleseed Found., Washington; trustee Cancer Rsch. Found., Chgo.; mem. vis. alumni com. U. Chgo. Law Sch. Mem.: ABA, Chgo. Bar Assn., Fed. Bar Assn., Assn. Trial Lawyers Am.

FREEDMAN, ERIC, journalist, educator, writer; b. Brookline, Mass., Nov. 6, 1949; s. Morris and Charlotte (Nadler) Freedman; m. Mary Ann Sipher, May 24, 1974; children: Ian Sipher, Cara Sipher, Jennifer Gilmore. BA, Cornell U., Ithaca, NY, 1971; JD, NYU, 1975; MS in Resource Devel., Mich. State U., East Lansing, 2004. Bar: N.Y. 1976, Mich. 1985. Congl. aide U.S. Rep. Charles Rangel, Washington and NYC, 1971—76; reporter Knickerbocker News, Albany, NY, 1976—84, Detroit News, Lansing, Mich., 1984—95; asst. prof. Mich. State U., 1996—, asst. dean, Internat. Studies, 2005—. Fulbright sr. lectr., Uzbekistan, 2002. Author: Pioneering Michigan, 1992, On the Water, Michigan, 1992, Michigan Free, 1993, Great Lakes, Great National Forests, 1995, How to Transfer to the College of Your Choice, 2002; co-author: What to Study, 1997; contbr. articles to profl. jours.; co-editor: John F. Kennedy in His Own Words, 2005. Recipient Merit citation, Am. Judicature Soc., Journalism awards, AP, Pulitzer Prize for beat reporting, 1994. Mem.: Soc. Environ. Journalism, Assn. Edn. in Journalism and Mass Comm., NY State Bar Assn. (Journalism awards), State Bar Mich., Investigative Reporters and Editors (Journalism award), Ctrl. Eurasian Studies Soc. Avocations: travel, writing. Home and Office: 2698 Linden Dr East Lansing MI 48823-3814 Office Phone: 517-355-4729. Business E-Mail: freedma5@msu.edu.

FREEDMAN, WILLIAM MARK, lawyer, educator; b. Washington, Dec. 8, 1946; s. Henry E. and Dorothy (Markowitz) F.; m. Harriet Arnold, Mar. 9, 1980; children: Alex, Emily. BA, Carleton Coll., 1968; JD, Harvard U., 1973. Bar: Ohio 1973, U.S. Dist. Ct. (so. dist.) Ohio 1973, U.S. Tax Ct. 1974. Assoc. Dinsmore & Shohl, Cin., 1973—80, ptnr., 1980—. Adj. prof. grad. dept. health svcs. adminstrn. Xavier U., Cin. Contbr. articles to profl. jours. Trustee Jewish Fedn. Cin., 1983-94, Yavneh Day Sch., Cin., 1988—, Cin. Symphony Orch., 1990-94; trustee No. Hills Synagogue, Cin., 1988-2001, v.p., 1992-94, pres., 1994-96; chair Jewish Fedn. Cin. Endoment Fund Profl. Advisers Roundtable. With U.S. Army, 1968-70. Mem. ABA, Ohio State Bar Assn., Cin. Bar Assn., Am. Health Lawyers Assn., Soc. Ohio Hosp. Attys. Home: 10405 Stablehand Dr Cincinnati OH 45242-4652 Office: Dinsmore & Shohl LLP 1900 Chemed Ctr 255 E 5th St Cincinnati OH 45202-4700 Fax: 513-977-8141. E-mail: bill.freedman@dinslaw.com.

FREEHLING, DANIEL JOSEPH, lawyer, consultant; b. Montgomery, Ala., Nov. 13, 1950; s. Saul Irving and Grace L. BS, Huntingdon Coll., 1972; JD, U. Ala., 1975, MLS, 1977. Ref. libr., asst. to assoc. dean U. Ala. Sch. Law, Tuscaloosa, 1975-77; assoc. law libr. U. Md., Balt., 1977-79, Cornell U., Ithaca, NY, 1979-82; law libr. dir., assoc. prof. U. Maine, Portland, 1982-86; law libr. dir., assoc. prof. law Boston U., 1986-92, prof., 1992—2006, assoc. dean for adminstrn., 1993-97, assoc. dean for info. svcs., 1999—2006; dep. cons. on legal edn. and admissions to bar ABA, 2006—. Mem. steering com., law program com. Rsch. Librs. Group, 1989-91; treas. New Eng. Law Libr. Consortium, 1989-91; vice chair, chair-elect sect. on law librs. Assn. Am. Law Schs., 1990-91, chair, 1992. Recipient Boston U. Sch. Law Alumni award for disting. svc., 2006, Presdl. Cert. Merit, Am. Assn. Law Libr. Mem.: ABA (accreditation com. 1995—2001, coun. sect. legal edn. and bar admission 2002—06), Am. Assn. Law Librs. (chair acad. law librs. spl. interest sect. 1981—82, edn. com. 1982—83, membership com. 1983—84, program chair 1987—88, local arrangements co-chair 1992—93, chair mentoring and retention com. 1995—96). Home: 400 N McClurg Ct Apt 3307 Chicago IL 60611 Office: Am Bar Assn 321 N Clark St Chicago IL 60610 Office Phone: 312-988-6743.

FREEHLING, STANLEY MAXWELL, investment banker; b. Chgo., July 2, 1924; s. Julius and Juliette (Stricker) F.; m. Joan Steif, Jan. 26, 1947; children: Elizabeth, Robert Stanley, Margaret J. Student, U. Chgo., 1942-43, Ind. U., 1943-44, U. Stockholm, Sweden, 1946-47. With 1st Nat. Bank Chgo., 1947—52; ptnr. Freehling Bros., Chgo., 1948—, Freehling & Co., Chgo., 1960—87; spl. ltd. ptnr. Cowen & Co., 1987—2000; v.p. Lehman Bros., 2000—. Mem. Ill. Pub. Employees Pension Laws Commn., 1962-66; chmn. Ravinia Festival Assn., 1967-71; pres. men's coun. Art Inst. Chgo., 1962-65, trustee, 1970—, life trustee; trustee Glenwood (Ill.) Sch. for Boys, 1967-80, Lake Forest Coll., 1972-83, Shedd Aquarium, Cradle Soc.; life trustee U. Chgo.; hon. mem. The Court Theatre; chmn. bd. Ill. Arts Coun., 1971-72; bd. dirs. Northwestern Meml. Hosp., Chgo., Chgo. Pub. Libr. Found.; hon. chmn. bd. Goodman Theatre; chmn. Pub. Arts Adv. Com., 1978-90; mem. Pres.'s Com. on Arts and Humanities, Washington, 1984-88; bd. govs. Smart Mus. Art. Mem. Northwestern U. Assocs., Arts Club, Bond Club, Commercial Club (Chgo.), Lake Shore Country Club (Glencoe, Ill.), Old Elm Country Club (Highland Park, Ill.), Mid-Day. Clubs: Arts, Bond, Commercial (Chgo.); Lake Shore Country (Glencoe, Ill.); Mid-Day. Home: 121 Belle Ave Highland Park IL 60035-2503 Office: 190 S La Salle St Chicago IL 60603-3410

FREELAND, A. JEROME, publishing executive; b. Dubuque, Iowa, Feb. 10, 1942; s. Allen Clyde and Mae (Blatti) F.; m. Bonnie Evelyn Burst, June 26, 1965; children: Christine, Mark, Eric. BA, Northwestern U., 1964, MA, 1965. Media analyst Gardner Advt., St. Louis, 1965-66; mktg. svcs. supr. The C.V. Mosby Co., St. Louis, 1966-69, circulation dir., 1969-74, jour. pub., 1974-77, v.p./jour. pub., 1977-81, sr. v.p., jour. pub., 1981-88, exec. v.p., 1988-93; pres. Med. Online, 1993—. With. Mo. Air N.G., 1967-73. Office: Mosby-Yearbook Inc 11830 Westline Industrial Dr Saint Louis MO 63146-3313

FREEMAN, ALBERT E., agricultural science educator, dairy cattle geneticist; b. Lewisburg, W.Va., Mar. 16, 1931; s. James A. and Grace Vivian (Neal) F.; m. Christine Ellen Lewis, Dec. 23, 1950; children: Patricia Ellen, Lynn Elizabeth, Ann Marie BS in Dairy Husbandry, W.Va. U., Morgantown, 1952, MS in Animal Breeding, 1954; PhD, Cornell U., 1957. Grad. asst. W.Va. U., Morgantown, 1952-54; grad. asst. Cornell U., Ithaca, NY, 1955-57; asst. prof animal sci Iowa State U., Ames, 1957-61, assoc. prof. animal sci., 1961-65, prof. animal sci., 1965-78, Charles F. Curtiss Disting. prof. agriculture, 1978—. Chmn., sec., exec. com. mem. Reg. Dairy Cattle Breeding Com. Contbr. numerous articles to profl. jours. Active Collegiate Presbyterian Ch., Ames Recipient 1975, Sr. Fulbright-Hays award, 1975, First Miss. Corp. award, 1979, award of appreciation for contbns. to Dairy Cattle Breeding 21st Century Genetics, 1984, Disting. Alumni award W.Va. U., 1985, faculty citation Iowa State U., 1987; named Charles F. Curtiss Disting. Prof. Agr., 1978. Fellow AAAS, Am. Soc. Animal Sci. (Rockefeller Prentice Meml. Animal Breeding and Genetics award, 1979, award of Honor 1987), Am. Dairy Sci. Assn. (bd. dirs. 1981-83, Nat. Assn. Animal Breeders Research award 1975, Borden award, 1982, J.L. Lush award 1984, Disting. Svc. award); mem. Biometrics Soc., First Acad. Disting. Alumni W.Va. U., Gamma Sigma Delta (award of Merit); pres. World Congress for Genetics Applied to Livestock Prodn. Office: Iowa State Univ 239 Kildee Hall Ames IA 50010

FREEMAN, ARTHUR J., physics educator; b. Lublin, Poland, Feb. 6, 1930; s. Louis and Pearl (Mandelbaum) F.; m. Rhea B. Landin, June 21, 1952 (div. 1990); children: Jonathan (dec.), Seth, Claudia, Sarah; m. Doris Caro, Mar. 1991. BS in Physics, Mass. Inst. Tech., 1952, PhD, 1956. Instr. Brandeis U., 1955-56; solid state physicist Army Materials Research Agy., Watertown, Mass., 1956-62; instr. Northeastern U., 1957-59; assoc. lab. dir., leader theory group Francis Bitter Nat. Magnet Lab., Mass. Inst. Tech., 1962-67; prof. physics Northwestern U., Evanston, Ill., 1967-83, Morrison prof. physics, 1983—, chmn. dept. physics, 1967-71. Cons. Argonne Nat. Lab., Los Alamos Nat. Lab. Editor: Hyperfine Interactions, 1967, The Actinides: Electronic and Related Properties, Handbook on the Physics and Chemistry of the Actinides, Internat. Jour. Magnetism, 1970-75, Jour. Magnetism and Magnetic Materials, 1975—; mem. editl. adv. bd. Computational Materials Sci., 1992, Jour. Computer-Aided Materials Design, 1993; contbr. numerous articles to tech. lit. Guggenheim fellow, 1970-71; Fulbright-Hays fellow, 1970-71; Alexander von Humboldt Stiftung fellow 1977-78; 1st recipient medal Materials Rsch. Soc., 1990, award in magnetism Internat. Union Pure and Applied Physics, 1991. Fellow Am. Phys. Soc.; fgn. mem. Acad. Natural Scis. Russia, Russian Acad. Scis., Polish Acad. Scis. Home: 2739 Ridge Ave Evanston IL 60201-1719 Office: Northwestern Univ Dept Of Physics Evanston IL 60208-0001

FREEMAN, CHARLES E., state supreme court justice; b. Richmond, Va., Dec. 12, 1933; m. Marylee Voelker; 1 child, Kevin. BA in Liberal Arts, Va. Union U., 1954; JD, John Marshall Law Sch., 1962, LLD (hon.), 1992. Bar: Ill. 1962. Pvt. practice, 1962—76; pvt. practice, Cook County, Chgo., 1962—76, asst. state's atty., 1964; asst. atty. Bd. Election Commrs., Chgo., 1964—65; mem. Ill. Indsl. Commn., Chgo., 1965—73, Ill. Commerce Commn., Chgo., 1973—76; judge law and chancery divsns. Cook County Cir. Ct., Chgo., 1976—86; judge Appellate Ct. Ill., 1986—90; justice Ill. Supreme Ct., 1990—, chief justice, 1997—2000. Recipient Cert. Achievement, Internat. Christian Fellowship Missions, Earl B. Dickerson award, Chgo. Bar Assn., Merit award, Habilitative Sys., Statesmanship award, Monarch Awards Found. of Alpha Kappa Alpha, Freedom award, John Marshall Law Sch. Mem.: ABA (task force opportunities minorities in jud. adminstrn. divsn., coms. opportunities minorities in profession, cert. Recognition), DuPage County Bar Assn., Cook County Bar Assn. (Kenneth E. Wilson award, Cert. Merit, Ida Platt award, Presdl. award, Jud. award), Ill. Judges' Assn., Ill. Jud. Coun. (Kenneth Wilson Meml. award, Meritorious Svc. award), Ill. State Bar Assn., Am. Judicature Soc., Am. Judges' Assn. Achievements include being first African-American to swear in a Mayor, City of Chicago, to serve on Illinois Supreme Court, 1990; being leader in case disposition by published opinion, 1988, 89.

FREEMAN, JEFFREY VAUGHN (JEFF FREEMAN), artist, educator; b. Bismarck, ND, Oct. 19, 1946; s. Dorrance Samuel Evan and Ethel Beatrice (Peterson) F. BS, Moorhead State U., 1970; MA, U. .D., 1972; MFA, U. Wis., 1980. Grad. teaching asst. U. N.D., Grand Forks, 1970-72, U. Wis., Madison, 1978-80; prof. art U. S.D., Vermillion, 1980—. Subst. tchr. Moorhead (Minn.) Pub. Schs., 1973; mem. faculty adult edn. Ctrl. Cass Pub. Schs., 1973-74; adj. prof. Moorhead State U., 1973-75; coord. S.D. Coll. Art Assn. Painting Conf., U. S.D., Vermillion, 1981; cons., W.H. Over Mus., Vermillion, 1985; lectr. in field. One man shows include Jamestown (N.D.) Coll., 1973, Bison Gallery, Fargo, N.D., 1975, Plains Art Mus., Moorhead, 1979, U. Wis., Madison, 1980, Ritz Gallery, S.D. State U, Brookings, 1982, No. State Coll, Lincoln Hall Gallery, Aberdeen, S.D., 1984, Buena Vista Coll., Storm Lake, Iowa, 1985, S.D. Meml. Art Ctr., Brookings, 1985, Gallery 306, Sioux Falls, S.D., 1987, Gallery 72, Omaha, 1988, Ruddell Gallery, Black Hills State Coll., Spearfish, S.D., 1988, LeMars (Iowa) Civic Fine Arts Ctr., 1989, Nobles County Art Ctr., Worthington, Minn., 1990, U. S.D. Art Galleries, Vermillion, 1990, Olivet Nazarene U., Bourbonnais, Ill., 1990, Mount Vernon (Ohio) Nazarene Coll., 1990, Coffee Shop Gallery, Vermillion, 1991, U. Ark., 1992, DuPont Gallery, Lexington, Va., 1992, Nordstrand Gallery, Wayne, ebr., 1993, The New Gallery, Rapid City, S.D., 1993, Bede Art Gallery, Yankton, S.D., 1993, 99, Gus Lucky Gallery, Minn., 1998, Pegasus Gall. Dorot Coll. Siouz Ctr. IA, 1999, others; exhibited in group shows at Minn. Mus. Art, St. Paul, 1975, Moorhead State U., 1975, 76, U. Minn., Morris, 1975, Thief River Falls C.C., Minn., 1976, 1st Nat. Bank, Moorhead, 1976, U. Wis., 1978, Plains Art Mus., Moorhead, 1978, 79, 93, U. S.D., 1981, 82, 83, 84, 85, 87, 88, 90, 92, 94, 96, 98, Rourke Art Gallery, Moorhead, Minn., 1982, 83, 84, 85, 86, 89, 90, 97, 98, No. State Coll., Student Union Gallery, 1981, Sioux City Art Ctr., 1983, 88, 90, 92, 98, 99, N.D. State U. Art Gallery, Fargo, 1984, N.D. Mus. Art, Grand Forks, 1984, Sioux Falls (S.D.) Civic Fine Arts Ctr., 1987, Gallery 72, Omaha, 1988, 90, 2001, Dahl Fine Arts Ctr., Rapid City, S.D., 1988, Joslyn Art Mus., Omaha, 1990, S.D. Art Mus., Brookings, 1991, 93, 95, 97, Sheldon Meml. Art Gallery, Lincoln, Nebr., 1991, The New Gallery, Rapid City, 1992, 94, 96, Thimmesh Gallery, Mpls., 1992, 93, 94, Chgo. Art Expo, 1993, Jamestown (N.D.) Art Ctr., 1993, Mus. Der Stadt Ratingen, Germany, 1997, others; represented in permanent collections Joslyn Art Mus., Donaghey Found., Little Rock, U. Ark., Little Rock, Sheldon Meml. Art Gallery, Lincoln, Nebr., Legrand and Co., Sioux City, Sioux City Art Ctr., Sioux Falls Civic Fine Arts Ctr., Klinger Corp., Sioux City, S.D. Art Mus., Brookings, Plains Art Mus., Moorhead, N.D. Mus. of Art, Grand Forks, Madison Art Ctr., Comstock Meml. Union, Moorhead State U., U. S.D., Vermillion, Norwest Bank, Moorhead, Grafton, N.D. and various pvt. collections in N.D., S.D., Minn., Nebr., Iowa, Ohio, Ill., Alaska, Wis., La., Mass, Calif., N.Y., Ariz., N.C., Tex., Wash., Oreg. and N.J. Rsch. grantee S.D. Rsch. Inst., U. S.D., 1982, 86, Bush Found. grantee, 1988; Visual Artist grantee S.D. Arts Coun., 1988-89; Painting fellow Arts Midwest/Nat. Endowment for the Arts, 1990-91, Nat. Endowment for the Arts, 1991-92; recipient 1st Place and Purchase award Plains Art Mus., Moorhead, 1978, Jury Purchase award Madison Art Ctr., 1978, Best Painting award Sioux City Fall Biennial, 1983, Merit award ARTQUEST, 1985. Home: 900 W Main St Vermillion SD 57069-2915 Office: U SD Art Dept 414 E Clark St Vermillion SD 57069-2307

FREEMAN, LEE ALLEN, JR., lawyer; b. Chgo., July 31, 1940; s. Lee Allen and Brena (Dietz) F.; m. Glynna Gene Weger, June 8, 1968; children: Crispin McDougal, Clark Dietz, Cassidy Bree. BA magna cum laude, Harvard U., Cambridge, Mass., 1962; JD magna cum laude, Harvard Sch. Law, Cambridge, Mass., 1965. Bar: Ill. 1966, D.C. 1966, Mont. 1986, U.S. Supreme Ct. 1969. Practiced in, Washington, 1965-68, Chgo., 1968—; law clk. to Justice Tom C. Clark, Washington, 1965-66; asst. U.S. atty., 1966-68; pres. Freeman, Freeman & Salzman, P.C., 1970—2007; mng. dir. MasterKey RAnch, Livingston, Mont.; spl. dep. atty. gen. Commonwealth of Pa., 1971—82; spl. asst. atty. gen. in Ill., Ind., W.Va., Mich., Colo., Tex.; spl. asst. corp. counsel City of Chgo., 1971-76; ptnr. Jenner & Brock, 2007—. Pres. Chgo. Lyric Opera Guild; pres. Fine Arts Music Found.; dir. Chgo. Lyric Opera, 1995-, Intermountain Opera Assn., Counterport, Inc.; mem. exec. com. Named Outstanding Young Citizen Chgo. Jaycees, 1976 Mem.: ABA (coun. mem. antitrust sect. 1985—87), Am. Coll. Trial Lawyers, Chgo. Inn of Ct., Std. Club. Home: 232 E Walton St Chicago IL 60611-1507 also: PO Box 1295 52 Little Mission Creek Livingston MT 59047 Office: Jenner and Block LLP 330 N Wabash Ave Chicago IL 60611 Office Phone: 312-923-2806. Business E-Mail: lfreeman@jenner.com.

FREEMAN, LESLIE GORDON, anthropologist, educator; b. Warsaw, NY, Sept. 9, 1935; s. Leslie Gordon and Theresa Rosalie (Stanbro) F.; m. Susan Tax, Mar. 20, 1964; 1 child, Sarah Elisabeth. AB, U. Chgo., 1954, AM, 1961, PhD, 1964. Asst. prof. anthropology Tulane U., 1964-65; asst. prof. U. Chgo., 1965-70, assoc. prof., 1970-76, prof., 1976-2000, prof. emeritus, 2000—; pres. Inst. Prehistoric Investigations, Chgo., 1983—2001. Rsch. assoc. Mont. State U., Bozeman, 1992—. Author (with J. Gonzalez): Cueva Morin, 2 vols., 1971, 1973, Life & Death At Cueva Morin, 1978, The Lower & Middle Paleolithilic in Spain, 1998, The Cave of Altamira, 2001; editor: Views of the Past, 1978; editor: (with Sol Tax) Horizons of Anthropology, 1976; editor: (with others) Altamira Revisited, 1987, Beatus of Liebana, 1995, Study of The Manuscripts of The Apocalypse of St. John, Beatus of Liebana of St.Michar of Escalada, 2000, Beatus of Liebana: Complete and Complemetary Works, 2004, Stopy of The Manuscript of the Beatus of Las Hvelok, 2004. Corporator Internat. Inst. Spain. With U.S. Army, 1957-59. Recipient Silver Plaque Provincial Deputation of Santander, Spain, 1973 Fellow AAAS, Am. Anthropol. Assn., Royal Anthropol. Inst.; mem. Reial Academia Catalana de Belles Arts de Sant Jordi Barcelona (corr.), Reial Academia Catalana de Bones Lletres Barcelona (corr.), Chgo. Acad. Scis. (trustee, 2d v.p. 1981-83). Office: U Chgo Dept Anthropology Haskell Hall M-306 Chicago IL 60637 Home: PO Box 369 Whitehall MT 59759

FREEMAN, MICHAEL O., lawyer; m. Terry Mathison; children: Katie, Beth, Matthew. BA, Rutgers U., 1970; JD, U. Minn., 1974; grad. exec. leadership program, Harvard U., 1995. Bar: Minn. 1974, U.S. Ct. Appeals (8th cir.) 1974, U.S. Supreme Ct. 1992. Law clk. to Judge Earl Larson U.S. Dist. Ct. Minn., 1974-75; law clk. to Judge Gerald W. Heaney U.S. Ct. Appeals (8th cir.), 1975-76; trial atty. Popham, Haik, Mpls., 1979-91; atty. Hennepin County, Mpls., 1991, 95—. Minn. state campaign mgr. Carter/Mondale Presdl. Campaign, 1976; cand. 3d Congl. Dist., U.S. Congress, 1978; chair 3d Congl. Dist. DFL Party, 1980; chair conf. com. Senate Capital Bonding Bill, 1987, 89, 90; chair Hennepin County Legis. Del., 1989-90; vice-chair Senate Econ. Devel. and Commerce Com., 1983-89, Senate Fin. Com., 1987-91. Commr. Richfield Housing and Redevel. Authority, 1979-82; treas. Minn. Found. for Improvement of Elem. Edn., 1986-92; chair Hennepin County Criminal Justice Coordinating Com., 1992-96; bd. dirs. CornerHouse, 1991—, treas., 1994-96; bd. dirs. Summit Acad. OIC; mem. Citizens League, Richfield Am. Legion; coach Richfield Girls Basketball, 1990-96, Richfield Boys Football, 1992-96; Sunday sch. tchr. St. Richard's Cath. Ch., 1989-93. Mem. Minn. State Bar Assn. (designated civil trial specialist). Office: Office of Hennepin County Atty 2000 Government Ctr Minneapolis MN 55487-0001

FREEMAN, SUSAN TAX, anthropologist, educator, culinary historian; b. Chgo., May 24, 1938; d. Sol and Gertrude Tax; m. Leslie G. Freeman, Jr., Mar. 20, 1964; 1 dau., Sarah Elisabeth. BA, U. Chgo., 1958; MA, Harvard U., 1959, PhD, 1965. Asst. prof. anthropology U. Ill., Chgo., 1965-70, assoc. prof., 1970-78, prof., 1978—, prof. emerita, 1999—, chmn., 1979-82. Rsch. assoc. dept. sociology and anthropology Mont. State U., Bozeman, 1992—; panelist NEH, Council for Internat. Exchange of Scholars; mem. anthropology screening com. Fulbright-Hays Research Awards, 1975-78; mem. ad hoc com. on research in Spain Spain-U.S.A. Friendship Agreement, various yrs., 1977-84; field researcher Mex., 1959, Spain, 1962—, Japan, 1983; instr. Radcliffe Coll. Seminars on Food in History and Culture, 1998. Author: Neighbors: The Social Contract in a Castilian Hamlet, 1970, The Pasiegos: Spaniards in No Man's Land, 1979; assoc. editor: Am. Anthropologist, 1971-73, Am. Ethnologist, 1974-76; editl. bd. Gastronomica, 2000—. Fellow Inst. for the Humanities, U. Ill. Chgo., 1987-88; Wenner-Gren Found. for Anthrop. Research grantee, 1966, 83; NIMH grantee, 1967, 68-71; NEH fellowships, 1978-79, 89-90. Fellow Am. Anthrop. Assn. (nominating com. 1981-82, Centennial Adv. Commn. 1999-2002), Royal Anthrop. Inst. Gt. Britain and Ireland; mem. Soc. for Anthropology of Europe (exec. com. 1987-88), Soc. Spanish and Portuguese Hist. Studies (exec. com. 1990-92), Coun. European Studies (steering com. 1980-83), Internat. Inst. Spain (corporator, bd. dirs. 1982-87, 2000-2003), Centro Estudios Sorianos (hon.), Assn. Anthropologia Castilla y Leon (hon.). Home: PO Box 369 Whitehall MT 59759 Office: U Ill Dept Anthro M/C 027 1007 W Harrison St Chicago IL 60607-7135 Home Phone: 406-490-0866, 773-684-1110; Office Phone: 312-413-3570.

FREEMAN, TODD IRA, lawyer; b. Mpls., Nov. 24, 1953; s. Earl Stanley and Gretta Lois (Rudick) F.; m. Judy Lynn Sigel, June 15, 1975; children: Jennifer, Katie, Zachary. BS in Mktg., U. Colo., 1974; JD, U. Minn., 1978. Bar: Minn. 1978, U.S. Dist. Ct. Minn. 1978, U.S. Tax Ct. 1980; CPA, Minn. Acct. Coopers & Lybrand, Mpls., 1978-80; shareholder Larkin, Hoffman, Daly & Lindgren, Mpls., 1980—, treas., 1990—, also bd. dirs., 1990-93. Pres. The Group Inc. Mem. ABA (tax sect., past chmn. personal svc. orgns.), Minn. Soc. CPAs, Minn. State Bar Assn., Hennepin County Bar Assn. Avocations: tennis, golf. Office: Larkin Hoffman Daly & Lindgren 7900 Xerxes Ave S Ste 1500 Minneapolis MN 55431-1128 Office Phone: 952-835-3800.

FREEMAN-WILSON, KAREN, retired state attorney general, prosecutor, educational association administrator; m. Carmen Wilson; 1 child, Jordan; 3 stepchildren. BA cum laude, Harvard Coll., 1982, JD, 1985. Pub. defender Lake County; ptnr. Freeman-Wilson and Lewis; dir. Ind. Office Drug Control Policy; atty. gen., chief legal officer State of Ind., judge drug ct. Gary; pub. defender, exec. dir. Ind. Civil Rights Commn.; dep. prosecutor Lake County, 1985—88; exec. dir. Ind. Civil Rights commn., 1989—92; judge Gary City Ct., 1994—2000; atty. gen. State Ind., Indpls., 2000—01; exec. dir. Nat. Drug Ct. Inst., 2002—; CEO at. Assn. Drug Ct. Profls., 2002—. Instr. Valparaiso U. Law Sch., Ind. U. Sch. Law; bd. dirs. Conf. for Legal Edn. and Opportunity, Ind. Supreme Ct. Trainer rape awareness Gary Commn. for Women; active Harbor House; bd. dirs. Rainbow Shelter. Democrat. Address: 4900 Seminary Rd Ste 320 Alexandria VA 22311 Business E-Mail: kfwilson@nadcp.org.

FREESE, STEPHEN J., state legislator; b. Dubuque, Iowa, Mar. 16, 1960; s. Joseph and Rowetta (Johnson) F.; m. Dawn Fredse; 1 child, Marie. BS, U. Wis., Platteville, 1982. Asst. to chmn. 3d Dist. Rep. Com., Wis., 1981-82; sales rep. Tegler's Inc., 1982-91; mem. from dist. 51 Wis. State Assembly, Madison, 1990—, vice chmn. Rep. caucus, 1993-94, spkr. pro tempore, 1995—. Supr. Town of Jamestown, Wis., 1980-94; mem. Grant County Bd. Suprs., 1982-92; mem. Wis. Fedn. Young Reps.; mem. Wis. State Rep. Com.; chmn. Grant County Rep. Com., 1983—.

FREESE, UWE ERNEST, physician, educator; b. Bordesholm, Germany, May 11, 1925; s. Heinrich and Frida (Lessau) F.; m. Gabriela Friederici, Oct. 11, 1961; children: Axel, Pamela. MD, U. Kiel, W.Ger., 1951. Diplomate: Am. Bd. Obstetrics and Gynecology. Resident U. Kiel, 1954-56, U. Chgo. Lying-in Hosp., 1956-59, prof. ob-gyn., 1971-75; prof., chmn. dept. Chgo. Med. Sch., 1975-95; prof. emeritus, 1995; chmn. dept. ob-gyn. Cook County Hosp., 1976-95, chmn. emeritus, 1995—; prof., chair emeritus ob/gyn The Chgo. Med. Sch., 1995—. Patentee cervical cap. Mem. Soc. Gynecol. Investigation, Perinatal Research Soc. (founding mem.), Central Assn. Obstetrics and Gynecology (cert. of merit 1967), Perinatal Soc. Ill. East (chmn.), N.Y. Acad. Scis., Sigma Xi Lutheran. Office: U Health Scis Chicago Med Sch 3333 Green Bay Rd North Chicago IL 60064-3037 Home: 400 E Randolph St Apt 1719 Chicago IL 60601-7306

FREIBAUM, BERNARD, real estate development company executive; b. 1953; V.p. fin. Stein & Co., sr. v.p. fin., CFO, 1988-93; CFO, contr. Gen. Growth Properties, Inc., Des Moines, 1993—. Office: Gen Growth Properties Inc 110 N Wacker Dr Chicago IL 60606-1511

FREIDHEIM, CYRUS F., JR., publishing and former food products executive; b. Chgo., June 14, 1935; s. Cyrus F. and Eleanor Freidheim; m. Marguerite VandenBosch; children: Marguerite Lynn, Stephen Cyrus, Scott. BSChE, U. Notre Dame, 1957; MBA, Carnegie Mellon U., 1963; Dr of Internat. Laws (hon.), Am. Grad. Sch. Internat. Mgmt., 1999. Plant mgr. Union Carbide Corp., Whiting, Ind., 1961; cons. Price Waterhouse, Chgo., 1962; fin. analyst Ford Motor Co., Dearborn, Mich., 1963-66; vice chmn. Booz, Allen & Hamilton, Chgo., 1966—2002; chmn. Chiquita Brands Internat., Inc., Cincinnati, 2002—04, CEO, 2002—04; pres., CEO Sun-Times Media Group Inc., Chgo., 2006—. Bd. dirs. HSBC Finance Corp., Inc., Allegheny Energy, Inc., The Sun Times Media Group, Inc., Virgin Am., Inc. Author: The Trillion Dollar Enterprise, 1998. Trustee Thunderbird, The Garvin Sch. Internat. Mgmt.; dir. Chgo. Coun. Global Affairs; trustee Rush U. Med. Ctr., 1981—; life trustee Chgo. Symphony Orch.; trustee Brookings Instn., 1998—; mem. adv. coun. Mendoza Sch. of Bus. U. Notre Dame, 2005—. With USN, 1957-61. Mem. Coun. Fgn. Rels., Chgo. Club, Econ. Club, Comml. Club, Racquet Club, Stanwich Club, Old Elm Club, Shoreacres Club, Lost Tree Club, The Bears Club. Office: Sun Times Media Group Inc 350 N Orleans St Chicago IL 60654

FREIDHEIM, CYRUS F., JR., publishing executive; Mem. ctrl. fin. staff Ford Motor Co.; joined Booz-Allen Hamilton, Inc., 1966, mng. dir., pres. BoozAllen Internat., head US cons. bus., former vice chmn., 1990—2002; chmn., pres., CEO Chiquita Brands Internat., Inc., 2002—04; bd. dirs. Sun-Times Media Group, Inc., 2005—, pres., CEO, 2006—; pub. Chgo. Sun-Times, 2007—. Bd. dirs. Allegheny Energy Inc., HSBC Fin. Corp., SITEL Corp. Office: Sun-Times Media Group 350 N Orleans Chicago IL 60654*

FREIER, TOM D., state legislator; m. Melinda Freier; 2 children. Student, Valley City Coll., ND. Owner restaurant, Linton, N.D.; fin. planner; state rep. dist. 28 State of N.D., 1991—; dir. N.D. Dept. Transp. Mem. appropriations com., edn. and environ. com., asst. majority leader N.D. Ho. Reps. Bd. dirs. Linton Indsl. Devel. Corp., N.D. Credit Union; former pres. Linton City Coun. Mem. N.D. Hosp. Assn., Linton C. of C., Lions, Elks. Republican. Home: 2624 E Divide Ave Bismarck ND 58501-2559

FRENCH, CATHERINE E. WOLFGRAM, engineering educator, researcher; b. Dec. 17, 1957; BS in Civil Engring., U. Minn., 1979; MS in Civil Engring., U. Ill., 1980, PhD in Civil Engring., 1984. Rsch. and tchg. asst. dept. civil engring. U. Ill., Urbana-Champaign, 1979-83; asst. prof. dept. civil engring. U. Minn., Mpls., 1984-90, assoc. prof. dept. civil engring., 1990-97, prof., assoc. head dept. civil engring., 1997-2000. Mem. external adv. com. FEMA external adv. com. Earthquake Engring. Simulation Facility U. Nev., Reno, 1994-97. Erskine fellow U. Canterbury, New Zealand, 1995, Fulbright Travel fellow New Zealand, 1995; recipient Presdl. Young Investigator award NSF, 1985, R.J. Boase award for contbns. to prestressed concrete rsch. Reinforced Concrete Rsch. Coun., Young Civil Engrs. Achievement award U. Ill. Civil Engring. Alumni Assn., 1987, Minn. Young Civil Engr. of Yr. Minn. Soc. Profl. Engrs., 1989, Faculty Award for Women, 1991-96, Bonestroo, Rosene, Anderlik and Assoc. Undergrad. Faculty award, 1994. Fellow Am. Concrete Inst. (com. 318 std. bldg. code 1996—, bd. dirs. Iowa-Minn. chpt. 1987-91, pres. 1991, Outstanding Chpt. award 1991, Kennedy award 2004, bd. dirs. 1996-91); mem.

ASCE (award for Outstanding Svc. as Faculty Adv. to student chpt. 1986-90, 1986, Edmund Friedman Young Engr. award for Profl. Achievement 1989, U. Minn. Gordon L. Starr award Outstanding Faculty Contbn. to student chpt. 1990, Raymond C. Reese Rsch. prize 1990, mem. structures com. Minn. 1986-90, pres. Minn. chpt. 1996-97), Earthquake Engring. Rsch. Inst. (Travel grant 1988, 2000), Precast/Prestressed Concrete Inst. (seismic com.), Transportation Rsch. Bd. (concrete bridges com.), Minn. Surveyors and Engrs. Soc. Achievements include research in behavior of reinforced concrete and prestressed concrete structures subjected to lateral loads, bond strength and durability of reinforcement in concrete, investigation of causes and methods to eliminate cracking in the fabrication of prestressed bridge girders, application of high strength concrete to prestressed systems, investigation of mechanical properties of high strength concrete and structural behavior of prestressed bridge girders fabricated with high strength concrete, development of testing method "effective force testing" for real-time earthquake simulation. Office: U Minn Dept Civil Engring 122 Civil Engring Bldg 500 Pillsbury Dr SE Minneapolis MN 55455-0233 Business E-Mail: cfrench@umn.edu.

FRENCH, DOUGLAS DEWITT, medical facility administrator; b. Augusta, Ga., Jan. 14, 1954; married BS, Trevecca Nazarene Coll., 1976; M Health Adminstrn., Xavier U., 1979. Adminstrv. resident St. Thomas Hosp., Nashville, 1978-79, dir. ambulatory svcs. and planning, 1979, dir. mgmt. svcs., 1980, adminstrv. asst., 1980-82, asst. adminstr., 1982-85, v.p., 1985-86; exec. v.p., COO St. Mary's Med. Ctr., Evansville, Ind., 1986-89, pres., CEO, 1979-94; CEO St. Vincent's Hosp., Indpls., 1994; pres., CEO Ctrl. Ind. Health Sys., 1998; exec. v.p., COO Daughters of Charity Nat. Health Sys., 1998—99; COO Ascension Health, 1999—2001, pres., 1999—, CEO, 2001—. Active various cmty. ofgns. Fellow Am. Coll. Health Care Execs. Office: Ascension Health Inc 4600 Edmundson Rd Saint Louis MO 63134-3806

FRENCH, JOHN DWYER, retired lawyer; b. Berkeley, Calif., June 26, 1933; s. Horton Irving and Gertrude Margery (Ritzen) F.; m. Annette Richard, 1955; m. Berna Jo Mahling, 1986. BA summa cum laude, U. Minn., 1955; postgrad, Oxford U., Eng., 1955-56; LLB magna cum laude, Harvard U., 1960. Bar: D.C. 1960, Minn. 1963. Law clk. Justice Felix Frankfurter, U.S. Supreme Ct., 1960-61; legal asst. to commr. FTC, 1961-62; assoc. Ropes & Gray, Boston, 1962-63, Faegre & Benson, Mpls., 1963-66, ptnr., 1967-75, mng. ptnr., 1975-94, chmn. mgmt. com., 1989-94; ret., 2004. Mem. adj. faculty Law Sch. U. Minn., 1965-70, mem. search com. for dean of Coll. of Liberal Arts, 1996; mem. exec. com. Lawyers Com. for Civil Rights Under Law, 1978—; co-chmn. U.S. Dist. Judge Nominating Commn., 1979; vice chmn. adv. com., mem. dir. search com., chmn. devel. office search com. Hubert Humphrey Inst., 1979-87. Contbr. numerous articles and revs. to legal jours. Chmn. or co-chmn. Minn. State Dem. Farm Labor Party Conv., 1970-90, 94, chmn. Mondale Vol. Com., 1972, treas., 1974; assoc. chmn. Minn. Dem.-Farmer-Labor Party, 1985-86; mem. Dem. Nat. Com., 1985-86; mem. Dem. Nat. Conv., 1976, 78, 80, 84, 88; trustee Twin Cities Public TV, Inc., 1980-86, mem. overseers com. to visit Harvard U. Law Sch., 1970-75, 77-82; chmn. Minn. steering com. Dukakis for Pres., 1987-88; mem. Sec. of State's Commn. on Electoral Reform, Minn., 1994; mem. Mayor's Commn. on Regulatory Reform, Mpls., 1995. With U.S. Army, 1955-56. Rotary Found. fellow, 1955-56 Mem. ABA (editorial bd. jour. 1976-79, commn. to study fed. trade 1969—), Minn. Bar Assn., Hennepin County Bar Assn., Jud. Coun. Minn., Lawyers Alliance for uclear Arms Control (nat. bd. dirs. 1982-84), U. Minn. Alumni Assn. (exec. com. 1985-87, v.p. 1989-91, pres. 1991-92, Vol. of Yr. award 1988), Phi Beta Kappa. Episcopalian. Office: Faegre & Benson 2200 Wells Fargo Ctr 90 S 7th St Ste 2200 Minneapolis MN 55402-3901

FRENETTE, CHARLES S., food products executive; b. Tupper Lake, NY; m. Helen Hope Groteluschen; 1 child, Zachary. BS, N.W. Mo. State U., 1974. Fountain sales Omaha dist. Coca-Cola Fountain, Kansas City, 1974, zone mktg. and sales support mgr. Atlanta, 1979, dir. mktg., 1983, v.p. nat. chain accts., 1983, sr. v.p., gen. mgr., 1986; exec. v.p. operations Coca-Cola USA, Atlanta, 1992; v.p. The Coca-Cola Co., Atlanta, 1995, pres. So. Africa divsn. South Africa, 1996, sr. v.p., chief mktg. officer, 1998, pres. greater Europe group, 1998—2000; pres., COO Europe/Africa Group The Coca-Cola co., 2001; interim chief mktg. officer Miller Brewing Co., Milw., 2005. Bd. dirs. Miller Brewing Co., 2003—. Office: Miller Brewing Co Board of Directors 3939 W Highland Blvd Milwaukee WI 53208

FRENZ, JOHN GREGORY, state representative; b. Mpls., Nov. 15, 1955; married; 2 children. Grad., U. St. Thomas, 1977. Restaurant mgr. Sirloin Stockade, 1977—81; restaurant owner, oper. Frenz & Schmidtknecht, Inc., 1981; state rep. dist. 64 Ind. Ho. of Reps., Indpls., 1996—2004, chmn., taxation subcom., mem. local govt., tech. R & D, and ways and means coms. Mem.: Restaurant and Hospitality Assn. Ind., Nat. Restaurant Assn., Ind. Restaurant Assn. (pres. 1997—99), Vincennes Jaycees (pres. 1987—88), C. of C. Harmony Soc., Ind. Jr. C. of C. (v.p. 1986—87), Vincennes Elks, KC. Democrat.

FRERICHS, DONALD L., foundation administrator, retired state legislator; b. Ocheyedan, Iowa, Jan. 3, 1931; m. Dianne R. Rickbeil, 1951; children: Craig D., Scott R., Krista B. BA, Mankato State U., 1954. Supr. Rochester Twp., 1968-81; state rep. Minn. Ho. Reps., Dist. 31A, 1981-96; ret., 1996; rep. Fairfund Found., 2006—. Mem. econ. devel. infrastructure and regulation fin., transp. and transit, transp. fin. and ways and means coms.; pres. Bio-Conversion Inc.; advisor to commr. Minn. Dept. Commerce; ret. 2001. Home: 644 Southern Woods Cir SW Rochester MN 55902-1836 E-mail: dlfrerichs@msn.com.

FREUND, KRISTEN P., bank executive; 1 child. Student in Bus., Mich. State U.; MBA, Northwestern U. Kellogg Sch. Mgmt. With Exch. Nat. Bank; chief adminstrv. officer LaSalle Bank, grp. sr. v.p. Named one of Top 40 Under 40, Crain's Chgo. Bus., 2006. Office: LaSalle Bank Hdqs 135 S LaSalle St Chicago IL 60603

FREVERT, MARCELLA R., state representative, elementary school educator; b. Graettinger, Iowa, Dec. 26, 1937; m. William W. Frevert. AA, Emmetsburg Jr. Coll., 1958; BS, Mankato State U., 1974; MA, U. No. Iowa, 1980. Tchr. sixth grade Cylinder Sch. Dist., 1958—62; receptionist and bookkeeper Emmetsburg Vet. Clinic, 1971—72; elem. tchr. Emmetsburg Cmty. Schs., 1972—; state rep. dist. 7 Iowa Ho. of Reps., 1997—; mem. agr. com.; mem. edn. appropriations com.; mem. natural resources com.; mem. ways and means com. Mem. Concordia Reading Conf., Lakeland Area Edn. Agy. III, PACK Reading Coun. Dist. commr. Palo Alto County Soil Conservation. Mem.: NEA, ASCD, Nat. Coun. Tchrs. English, Iowa State Edn. Assn., Iowa Reading Assn., Iowa Dept. Edn., Internat. Reading Assn., Emmetsburg Edn. Assn., Phi Delta Kappa. Democrat. Address: 3655 450th St Emmetsburg IA 50536 Office: State Capitol East 12th and Grand Des Moines IA 50319

FREY, DONALD NELSON, industrial engineer, educator, retired manufacturing executive; b. St. Louis, Mar. 13, 1923; m. Helen-Kay Eberley, Feb. 14, 2003; children: Donald Nelson, Judith Kingsley(dec.), Margaret Bente, Catherine, Christopher, Elizabeth. Student, Mich. State Coll., 1940—42; BS, U. Mich., 1947, MS, 1949, PhD, 1950, DSc (hon.), 1965; DSc, U. Mo., Rolla, 1966. Instr. metall. engring. U. Mich., 1949—50, asst. prof. chem. and metall. engring., 1950—51; rsch. engr. Babcock & Wilcox Tube Co., Beaver Falls, Pa., 1951; various rsch. positions Ford Motor Co. (Ford div.), 1951—57, various engring. positions, 1958—61, product planning mgr., 1961—62, asst. gen. mgr., 1962—65, gen. mgr. original Mustang auto, 1965—68, co. v.p. for product devel., 1965—67; pres. Gen. Cable Corp., NYC, 1968—71, Bell & Howell Co., Chgo., 1973—81, chmn., CEO, 1971—88, also bd. dirs.; prof. of indsl. engring. and mgmt. sci. orthwestern U., Evanston, Ill., 1988—. Mem. exec. bd. World Bank, Washington; bd. dirs. Cin. Milacron, Clark Equipment Co., Packer Engring., My Own Meals, Hyatt Corp., Springs Industries, Quintar, 20th Century Fox Corp.; co-chair Japan study multinats. NRC, 1992—94; surveyor World Bank, Poland, 1990. Co-chmn. Gov.'s Commn. of Sci. and Industry, Ill., 1988—; exec. bd. mem. World Bank, 2003. With US Army, 1942—46. Named Young Engr. of Yr., Engring. Soc. Detroit, 1953, Outstanding Alumni, U. Mich. Coll. Engring., 1957, Outstanding Young Man of the Yr., Detroit Jr. Bd. of Commerce, 1958, Man of the Yr., Weizmann Inst., 1988; recipient Nat. medal for tech., 1990; Inaugural fellow, INFORMS, 2002. Fellow: INFORMS, AAAS; mem.: ASME, Coun. on Fgn. Rels., Detroit Engring. Soc. (pres., bd. dirs. 1962—65), Soc. Automotive Engrs. (vice chmn. Detroit 1958, Russell Springer award 1956), Nat. Acad. Engring. (mem. coun. 1972), Am. Soc. Metals, Am. Inst. Mining and Metall. Engrs. (chmn. Detroit chpt. 1954, chmn., editor Nat. Symposium on Sheet Steels 1956), Econ. Club, Saddle and Cycle Club, Chgo. Club, Hundred Club Cook County, Chgo. Commonwealth Club, Phi Delta Theta, Tau Beta Pi, Phi Kappa Phi, Sigma Xi. Achievements include established Margaret and Muir Frey Prize for innovation in engring., Northwestern Univ., 2002; Clara McKitrick Prize for Design in engring., Northwestern Univ., 2004. Home: 2758 Sheridan Rd Evanston IL 60201-1728 Office: Northwestern U 2145 Sheridan Rd Rm M237 Evanston IL 60208-0834 Home Phone: 847-869-5705; Office Phone: 847-491-3326. E-mail: d-frey@northwestern.edu.

FREYMAN, THOMAS C., pharmaceutical executive; b. Evanston, Ill., Sept. 8, 1954; B in Accountancy, U. Ill.; M in Mgmt., Northwestern U. CPA. Formerly acct. Ernst & Whinney, Chgo.; with Abbott Labs., Abbott Park, Ill., 1979—, fin. dir. European distbn. ctr. Netherlands, 1984—87, divsn. contr. corp. materials mgmt., 1987—88, treas. internat. divsn., 1988—91, v.p., treas., 1991—99, v.p., contr. hosp. products divsn., 1999—2001, sr. v.p. fin., CFO, 2001—04, exec. v.p. fin., CFO, 2004—. Bd. dirs. Vista Health, Chgo. Bot. Garden. Mem.: Econ. Club Chgo. Office: Abbott Labs 100 Abbott Park Rd Abbott Park IL 60064-6400

FREYTAG, DONALD ASHE, management consultant; b. Chgo., Apr. 17, 1937; s. Elmer Walter and Mary Louise (Mayo) F.; m. Elizabeth Ritchie Robertson, Dec. 19, 1964; children: Donald C., Gavin K., Alexander M. BA, Yale U., 1959; MBA, Harvard U., 1963. Pres. Mgmts. West, LaJolla, Calif., 1963-65; mktg. asst. Norton Simon, Inc., Fullerton, Calif., 1965-67; product mgr. Warner-Lambert, Inc., Morristown, N.J., 1967-70; group mgr. mktg.-planning dir. advt. Pepsi-Cola Co., Purchase, N.Y., 1970-72; from v.p. mktg. to exec. v.p. Beverage Mgmt., Inc., Columbus, Ohio, 1972-76, pres., 1976-79, vice-chmn., 1979-80; pres. Freytag Mgmt. Co., Columbus, 1980-82, 84—, G.D. Ritzy's, Inc., Columbus, 1982-84. Bd. dirs. Antolino & Assoc., Atlas-Butler, Barney Corp., Century Resources, Contract Sweepers, Contrack Corp., Inc., Columbus Showcase Co., Columbus Paper and Copy Supply Co., Eastway Supplies, Inc., Greencrest Mktg., Ohio Full Ct. Press, Inc., Reitter Stucco, Inc., Profitworks Ltd., Paul Werth & Assoc., Coughlin Automotive Group, Newark, Hugo Bosca Co., Springfield, Ohio, Fenton Art Glass Co., Inc., Williamstown, W.Va., Scioto Properties, LLC, Columbus; ctrl. region dir. Ohio Com. for Employer Support of the Guard and Res., 1992—95. Pres. Cen. Ohio Ctr. for Econ. Edn., 1978-80, 81-87; bd. dirs. Columbus Acad., 1982-84. Capt. U.S. Army, 1959-61. Recipient Roman F. Warmke award, Ohio Coun. on Econ. Edn., 1991. Mem. Nat. Assn. Corp. Dirs., HBS Club Columbus, Yale Club. Avocations: bicycling, scuba diving, golf, reading. Office: 7955 Riverside Dr Dublin OH 43016-8234

FRIAS, RAFAEL, city official; BA, U. Ill., Chgo. Police officer Chgo. Police Dept.; mem. from 1st dist. U.S. Ho. of Reps.; alderman City of Chgo. Founder United Neighbors Improving the Environment. Home: 3637 S Maplewood Ave Chicago IL 60632-1022 Office: 121 N LaSalle St Rm 209 Office 21 Chicago IL 60602

FRICK, DAVID RHOADS, lawyer, retired insurance company executive; b. Ft. Wayne, Ind., June 28, 1944; s. Walter Henry and Margery Ellen (Rhoads) F.; m. Ann Gray Shane, June 19, 1965; children: Thomas Rhoads, Amy Gray. BA magna cum laude, Ind. U., 1966; JD cum laude, Harvard U., 1969; HHD, Butler U., 1987, U. Indpls., 1997. Bar: Ill. 1969, D.C. 1971, U.S. Ct. Appeals (D.C. cir.) 1971, Ind. 1972, U.S. Supreme Ct. 1976. Assoc. Mayer, Brown & Platt, Chgo., 1969-72, Baker & Daniels, Indpls., 1972-76; dep. mayor City of Indpls., 1977-82; ptnr. Baker & Daniels, Indpls., 1982—95; exec. v.p., chief legal & adminstrv. officer Anthem Inc. (now WellPoint Inc.), Indpls., 1995—2005. Bd. dirs. Artistic Media Ptnrs., Inc., Indpls., Nat. Bank Indpls., Statewide Mobility Ptnrs., LLC, GS&J Investments, LLC, My Health Care Mgr., LLC. Bd. dirs., exec. com. 500 Festival Assocs., 1983-86, Commn. for Downtown, 1977-89, Greater Indpls. Progress Com., 1982-89, Indpls. Econ. Devel. Corp., 1984; bd. dirs. Ind. U. Coll. Arts and Scis. 1974-77, Pres. 1976, Indpls. Ctr. Advanced Rsch., Inc., 1987-90, Ind. Sports Corp., 1979-91, Indpls. Conv. and Visitors Assn., 1982-2000; mem. Ind. Gen. Assembly Local Govt. Study Com., 1978-81, State Ind. Commn. Enterprising Zones, 1981-82; trustee Eiteljorg Mus., 1988-91; chmn., trustee Brebeuf Prep. Sch., 1986-92, U. Indpls., 1990—98; treas., bd. mgrs. Marion County Capital Improvement Bd., 1982-92; adv. bd. Ind. U., 1986—, Purdue U., 1986—; chmn. Ind. Organizing Com. NCAA Final Four, 1987—; trustee, exec. com. Christian Theol. Sem., 1984-95. Recipient Sagamore of the Wabash award Gov. Ind., 1979-80, C.L. Whistler award Greater Indpls. Progress Com., 1984, L.A. Conrad award Ind. Soc. Assn. Exec., 1990, Pres. Medal Brebeuf Prep. Sch., 1992, Michael A. Carroll Award for Cmty. Involvement, Indpls. Bus. Jour., 1996; named Bus. Leader of 2005, Ind. C. of C. Mem. Indpls. C. of C. (bd. dirs. 1987-2005, exec. com. 1987-2005). Republican. Methodist. Avocations: jogging, hiking, reading. Office Phone: 317-237-1412. Business E-Mail: david.frick@bakerd.com.

FRIED, HERBERT DANIEL, advertising executive; b. Chgo., May 27, 1928; s. Herbert D. and Beatrice (Frank) F.; m. Ninon Connart, Mar. 7, 1953; children: Bruce M., William F. Student, U. N.Mex., 1946-48, U. Ill., 1948. Account exec. Foote, Cone & Belding, Chgo., 1948-54, Weiss & Geller, Chgo., 1954-55; account exec., gen. mgr. W.B. Doner & Co., Balt., 1955-56, v.p., 1956-68, pres., 1968-73, chmn. bd., chief exec. officer, 1973—98, cons. Bd. dirs. Nat. Advt. Rev. Bd., 1987. Divsn. chmn. Comty. Chest-ARC-United Appeal, 1964, United Fund, 1977; bd. dirs. comm. divsn. United Way, 1978-79; dir. Sinai Hosp., Balt., 1994—, Greater Balt. Com., Balt. Zool. Soc., The Associated, Jewish Comty. Fedn. Balt., 1992—; mem. adv. bd. Ctr. for Advt. History Nat. Mus. Am. History Smithsonian Mus.; bd. dirs. U.S.S. Constellation Fund, 1995—. With USNR, 1946. Recipient award Chgo. Federated Advt. Club, 1949; inducted Advt. Hall of Fame, Advt. Assn. Balt., 1987; named Disting. Marylander of Yr. Advt. and Profl. Club Baltimore, 1991. Mem. Am. Assn. Advt. Agys., Inc. (bd. govs. Chesapeake coun. 1960, regional dir. 1963, chmn. govt. rels. com. 1987-90, bd. dirs. 1987-90), Nat. Advertising Review Bd., Advt. Club Balt., Kappa Sigma. Clubs: Center (Balt.); Suburban of Baltimore County (Pikesville, Md.). Home: Admirals Cove 121 Spinnaker Ln Jupiter FL 33477-4003

FRIED, JASON, software development company executive; Co-founder, pres. 37Signals LLC, 1999—. Named one of Young Innovators Under 35, MIT Tech. Rev., 2006, Top 40 Under 40, Crain's Chgo. Bus., 2006. Office: 37Signals LLC 400 N May St #301 Chicago IL 60622

FRIED, SAMUEL P., lawyer; b. Bklyn., Aug. 16, 1951; s. Zoltan and Helen (Katina) F.; m. Gigi Panush, Dec. 27, 1981; children: Eva M., Orly Z., Jacob J., Molly R., Susanna R. AB, Washington U., St. Louis, 1971; JD, Boston U., 1974, LLM, 1997. Bar: Mass. 1974, Ill. 1983, Mich. 1989; ordained rabbi, 1971. Assoc. Warner & Stackpole, Boston, 1974-77; staff atty. The Bendix Corp., Southfield, Mich., 1977-79, sr. atty., 1979-80, asst. treas., 1980-81; v.p., corp. counsel Clevite Industries, Inc., Glenview, Ill., 1981-83, v.p., sec., gen. counsel, 1983-87; v.p., sec. gen. counsel Exide Corp., Troy, Mich., 1987-91; v.p., gen. counsel The Limited Inc., 1991-99, sr. v.p., gen. counsel, sec., 1999—. Editor: Psychosurgery, 1974. Mem. ABA, Am. Corp. Counsel Assn., Mich. Gen. Counsels Assn., Phi Beta Kappa. Jewish. Avocations: music, reading. Office: The Limited Inc PO Box 16000 3 Limited Pkwy Columbus OH 43230-1467

FRIEDLAENDER, FRITZ JOSEF, electrical engineering educator; b. Freiburg, Breisgau, Germany, May 7, 1925; came to U.S., 1947, naturalized, 1953; s. Ludwig and Frieda (Murzynski) F.; m. Gisela Triebe, Aug. 7, 1969; 2 children. BS, Carnegie Mellon U., 1951, MS, 1952, PhD, 1955; Dr.-Ing. (E.h.), Ruhr-Universität Bochum, Germany, 1992. Asst. prof. Columbia, 1954-55, Purdue U., West Lafayette, Ind., 1955-59, assoc. prof., 1959-62, prof. elec. and computer engring., 1962-2000; guest prof. Max-Planck Institut Metallforschung, Tech. U. Stuttgart, Fed. Repubic Germany, 1964-65; Humboldt award and guest prof. Institut für Werkstoffe der Elektrotechnik, Ruhr-Universität, Bochum, West Germany, 1972-73; Japan Soc. for Promotion Sci. fellow and guest prof. Nagoya U., summer 1980; guest prof. U. Regensburg (Fed. Republic Germany), 1981-82; Meyerhoff vis. prof. Weizmann Inst. Sci., Rehovot, Israel, Jan.-June 1990; prof. emeritus, 2001—. Cons. Gen. Electric Corp., Ft. Wayne, Ind., 1956-58, Components Corp., Chgo., 1959-61, Lawrence Radiation Lab., U. Calif. at Livermore, 1967-69, P.R. Mallory & Co., 1974-78, Oakridge Nat. Lab., 1979-82 Adv. editor Jour. Magnetism and Magnetic Materials, 1975—; co-editor Magnetic Separation ews, 1983-91, Magnetic and Electrical Separation, 1991-2002; mem. editl. bd. Proc. IEEE, 1975-78; contbr. articles to profl. jours. Recipient Carnegie Mellon U. Alumni Merit award, 2001. Fellow IEEE (revs. editor trans. Magnetics 1965-67, editl. bd. jour. 1968—, chmn. awards Magnetics Soc. 1966-74, 85—, achievement award Magnetics Soc. 1986, chmn. Intermag 1975, London, program co-chmn. Intermag 1978, Florence, Italy, v.p. Magnetics Soc. 1975-76, pres. 1977-78, chmn. Central Ind. sect. 1979-80, J. Fred Peoples award 1989, disting. lectr. 1991-93, IEEE Magnetics Soc., 3d Millennium medal 2000, 8th Internat. Conf. on Ferrites Spl. award 2000, Spl. Recognition award Magnetics Soc. 2001), Am. Phys. Soc., Am. Soc. Engring. Edn.: mem. Magnetics Soc. of Japan (hon.), Arbeitsgemeinschaft Magnetismus, Sigma Xi, Phi Kappa Phi, Tau Beta Pi, Eta Kappa Nu, Beta Sigma Rho. Achievements include research in magnetics, magnetic devices and memories, high gradient magnetic separation, magnetic bubble dynamics, Vertical Bloch Lines, microwave ferrites, Ni-Fe tape magnetization processes. Office: Purdue U Sch Elec and Computer Engrn Bldg 1465 Northwestern ave West Lafayette IN 47907-2035 Home Phone: 765-463-1626; Office Phone: 765-494-4444. E-mail: fritzj@ecn.purdue.edu.

FRIEDLANDER, MICHAEL WULF, physicist, researcher; b. Cape Town, South Africa, Nov. 15, 1928; came to U.S., 1956; m. Jessica R. Friedlander; 2 children. BS in Physics, U. Cape Town, 1948, MS with 1st class honors, 1950; PhD in Physics, Bristol U., Eng., 1955. Jr. lectr. U. Cape Town, 1950-52; rsch. assoc. U. Bristol, 1954-56; asst. prof. physics Washington U., St. Louis, 1956-61, assoc. prof., 1961-67, prof., 1967—. Author: The Conduct of Science, 1972, Astronomy: From Stonehenge to Quasars, 1985, Cosmic Rays, 1989, At the Fringes of Science, 1995, A Thin Cosmic Rain, 2000; contbr. articles to Ency. Brit. and profl. jours. Guggenheim Found. fellow, vis. prof. Imperial Coll., London, 1962-63. Mem. AAUP (2d v.p. 1978-80, mem. nat. coun. 1975-78, 86-89), AAAS, Am. Phys. Soc., Am. Astron. Soc., History of Sci. Soc. Achievements include research in elementary particles, cosmic rays, infrared astronomy, and gamma ray astronomy. Office: Washington U Dept Physics One Brookings Dr Saint Louis MO 63130

FRIEDLI, HELEN RUSSELL, lawyer; b. Indpls., July 8, 1956; d. William F. and Helen F. Russell; m. E. Kipp Friedli, May 19. BS, Purdue U., 1977; JD, Ind. U., 1980. Bar: Ill. 1980. Ptnr., mem. firm exec. mgmt. com. McDermott, Will & Emery, Chgo., 1980—. ABA. Office: McDermott Will & Emery LLP 227 W Monroe St Ste 4700 Chicago IL 60606-5096 Office Phone: 312-984-7563. Office Fax: 312-984-7700. Business E-Mail: hfriedli@mwe.com.

FRIEDMAN, AVNER, mathematician, educator; b. Petah-Tikva, Israel, Nov. 19, 1932; arrived in U.S., 1956; s. Moshe and Hanna (Rosenthal) Friedman; m. Lillia Lynn, June 7, 1959; children: Alissa, Joel, Naomi, Tamara. MSc, Hebrew U., Jerusalem, 1954, PhD, 1956. Prof. math. Northwestern U., Evanston, Ill., 1962—85; prof. Purdue U., West Lafayette, Ind., 1985—87, dir. Ctr. Applied Math., 1985—87; prof. math., dir. Inst. Math. and Its Applications U. Minn., Mpls., 1987-97, dir. Minn. Ctr. for Indsl. Math., 1994—2002; prof. Ohio State U., Columbus, 2002—; dir. Math. Bioscis. Inst., 2002—. Author: Generalized Functions and Partial Differential Equations, 1963, Partial Differential Equations of Parabolic Type, 1964, Partial Differential Equations, 1969, Foundations of Modern Analysis, 1970, Advanced Calculus, 1971, Differential Games, 1971, Stochastic Differential Equations and Applications, Vol. 1, 1975, Vol. 2, 1976, Variational Principle's and Free Boundary Problems, 1983, Mathematics in Industrial Problems, 10 vols., 1988—98; author: (with D.S. Ross) Mathematical Models in Photographic Science, 2001; contbr. articles to profl. jours. Recipient Creativity award, NSF, 1983—85, 1990—92; fellow, Sloan Found., 1962—65, Guggenheim, 1966—67. Mem.: NAS, AAAS, Soc. Math. Bioscis. (pres. 2007—), Soc. Indsl. Applied Math. (pres. 1993, 1994, chair bd. math. scis. 1994—97), Am. Math. Soc. Office: Ohio State U Math Dept 231 18th Ave Columbus OH 43210 Home Phone: 614-771-8932. Business E-Mail: afriedman@mbi.osu.edu.

FRIEDMAN, BARTON ROBERT, language educator; b. Bklyn., Feb. 5, 1935; s. Abraham Isaac and Mazie Diana (Cooper) F.; m. Sheila Lynn Siegel, June 22, 1958; children— Arnold, Jonathan, Daniel, Esther. BA, Cornell U., 1956, PhD (univ. dissertation fellow), 1964; MA, U. Conn., 1958. Instr. Bowdoin Coll., Brunswick, Maine, 1961-63; from instr. to prof. English lit. U. Wis., Madison, 1963-78; prof. English lit. Cleve. State U., 1978-97, chmn. dept. English, 1978-87, prof. emeritus, 1997—. Visitor Psychoanalytic Inst. Cleve. Author: Adventures in the Deeps of the Mind: The Cuchulain Cycle of W.B. Yeats, 1977, You Can't Tell the Players, 1979, Fabricating History: English Writers on the French Revolution, 1988 (Nancy Dasher award for best scholarly book by mem. Coll. English Assn. Ohio 1989); mem. editl. bd. Irish Renaissance Ann., 1980-84, Lit. Monographs, 1970-76. Recipient William Kiekhofer Teaching Excellence award U. Wis., 1967, Disting. Scholar award Cleve. State U., 1990. Mem. MLA, Am. Com. Irish Studies, Coll. English Assn. Ohio (bd. govs. 1980-81), Soc. Lit. and Sci. (bibliographer Bibliography of Lit. and Sci. in Configurations 1996-98), Phi Kappa Phi. Jewish. Home: 2916 E Overlook Rd Cleveland OH 44118-2434 Office: Cleve State Univ Dept English Cleveland OH 44115 Personal E-mail: sheilalf@sbcglobal.net.

FRIEDMAN, BERNARD ALVIN, federal judge; b. Detroit, Sept. 23, 1943; s. David and Rae (Garber) F.; m. Rozanne Golston, Aug. 16, 1970; children: Matthew, Megan. Student, Detroit Inst. Tech., 1962-65; JD, Detroit Coll. Law, 1968. Bar: Mich. 1968, Fla. 1968, US Dist. Ct. (ea. dist.) Mich. 1968, US Ct. Mil. Appeals 1972. Asst. prosecutor Wayne County, Detroit, 1968-71; ptnr. Harrison & Friedman, Southfield, Mich., 1971-78, Lippitt, Harrison, Friedman & Whitefield, Southfield, 1978-82; judge Mich. Dist. Ct. 48th dist., Bloomfield Hills, 1982-88, US Dist. Ct. (ea. dist.) Mich., Detroit, 1988—, chief judge, 2005—. Lt. US Army, 1967-74. Recipient Disting. Service award Oakland County Bar Assn., 1986. Mem.: Oakland County Bar Assn., Mich. Bar Assn. Avocation: running. Office: US Dist Ct US Courthouse Rm 238 231 W Lafayette Blvd Detroit MI 48226-2700

FRIEDMAN, HAROLD EDWARD, lawyer; b. Cleve., Apr. 7, 1934; s. Joseph and Mary (Schreibman) F.; m. Nancy Schweid, Aug. 20, 1961; children: Deborah, Jay, Susan. BS, Ohio State U., 1956; LL.B., Case Western Res U., 1959. Bar: Ohio 1960. Practiced in, Cleve., since 1960; ptnr. Simon, Haiman, Gutfeld, Friedman & Jacobs, 1967-80, Ulmer & Berne, 1981—; chair real property practice group. Sec., trustee Harry K. and Emma R. Fox Charitable Found.; pres. Jewish Vocat. Svcs., Cleve.; pres. Internat. Assn. Jewish Vocat. Svcs.; pres. Cleve. Hillel Found.; vice chmn. endowment fund Jewish Cmty. Fedn. Cleve., bd. dirs.; pres. Metro Health Found.; bd. dirs. Bur. Jewish Edn., Jewish Convalescence and Rehab. Ctr., Big Bros. Greater Cleve., Jewish Cmty. Fedn. Cleve., Jewish Family Svc. Assn., YES, Inc., Bellefaire/Jewish Children's Bur. Recipient Kane Leadership award Jewish Community Fedn. Cleve., 1974 Mem. ABA, Ohio Bar Assn., Cleve. Bar Assn., Oakwood Country Club. Home: 23149 Laureldale Rd Cleveland OH 44122-2101 also: 1660 W 2nd St Cleveland OH 44113-1454 Office Phone: 216-583-7130, 216-583-7130. Personal E-mail: hedwfried@aol.com. Business E-Mail: hfriedman@ulmer.com.

FRIEDMAN, JAMES DENNIS, lawyer; b. Dubuque, Iowa, Jan. 11, 1947; s. Elmer J. and Rosemary Catherine (Stillmunks) F.; children: Scott, Ryan, Andrea, Sean. AB in Polit. Sci., Marquette U., 1969; JD, U. Notre Dame, 1972. Bar: Wis. 1972, U.S. Ct. Appeals (D.C. cir.) 1973, U.S. Ct. Appeals (7th cir.) 1976, U.S. Supreme Ct. 1978, U.S. Ct. Appeals (6th cir.) 1989, Ill. 1996, U.S. Tax Ct. 1997. Pvt. practice, Milw., 1972—81; ptnr. Quarles & Brady, LLP, Milw., 1981—. Presenter in field; mem. legis. coun. spl. study com. on regulation of fin. instns. State of Wis., 1986-87; bd. dirs. Concours Motors, Inc., Wis. Equal Justice Fund, Inc., pres., 2006-07; mem. Wis. Dept. Fin. Instns. task force on fin. competitiveness 2005, State of Wis., 2000; mem., vice chair State of Wis. Supreme Ct., Office of Lawyer Regulation Preliminary Rev. Com., 2000-07; mem. Gov.'s Adv. Coun. on Jud. Selection of the State of Wis., Ozaukee County, 2002. Mng. editor: Notre Dame Law Rev., 1971—72; contbr. articles to profl. jours. Alderman 4th and 7th dists. Mequon, Wis., 1979-85, pres. common coun., 1980-82, bd. ethics 1996-98, 2000—, chair blue ribbon visioning com. 1998-99; bd. dirs. Weyenrg, Pub. Librs. Found. Inc., 1983—, pres., 1984—; bd. dirs. Ptnrs. Advancing Values in Edn. Inc., 1987—, Wis. Law Found., 1998—, pres., 2007-; bd. visitors Marquette U. Ctr. for Study of Entrepreneurship, Milw., 1987-95; bd. dirs. Ozaukee Family Svcs., 1983-99, sec., 1993-98; bd. dirs. Notre Dame Club of Milw., 1984-88, sec., 1978, v.p., 1986-88; bd. dirs. Marquette Club of Milw., 1987-88; chair attys. unit United Way Fund Dr. Greater Milw., 1987. Named Outstanding Sr., Coll. Liberal Arts, Marquette U., 1969, Wis. Leader in the Law, Wis. Law Jour., 2006, Wis. Super Lawyer Law & Politics, 2006, 07. Life fellow Wis. Law Found., Am. Bar Found.; mem. ABA (banking law com. sect. bus. law), State Bar Wis. (chair bd. govs. 1999-2000, chair exec. com. 1999-2000, fin. com. 1997-98, strategic planning task force 1997-98, leadership devel. com. 2004-07, bd. govs. 1996-2000, exec. com. 1998-2000, internat. transactions sect. bd. dirs. 1984-99, sec. and chair-elect 1988-89, chair 1989-90, del. to ABA Ho.

of Dels. 1980-82, standing com. on adminstrn. justice and judiciary 1979-81, legal edn. and bar admissions com. 1984-89, com. on minority lawyers 1992-99, chmn. 1997-1999, bd. dirs. young lawyers divsn. 1978-82, chmn. bar admission stds. and requirements com. 1979, So. Regional chair capital fund campaign 1998-99), Milw. Bar Assn., Wis. Acad. Trial Lawyers (bd. dirs. 1980-82), Wis. Bankers Assn., Milw. Country Club. Roman Catholic. Avocations: tennis, golf. Office: Quarles & Brady LLP 411 E Wisconsin Ave Ste 2040 Milwaukee WI 53202-4497 Office Phone: 414-277-5735. Business E-Mail: jdf@quarles.com.

FRIEDMAN, JAMES MOSS, lawyer; b. Cleve., Aug. 1, 1941; s. Senor I. and Rose L. (Moskowitz) F.; m. Ruth E. Aidlin, Aug. 2, 1964; children: Laura M., Seth M. AB, Dartmouth Coll., 1963; JD, Harvard U., 1966. Bar: Ohio 1966, U.S. Ct. Appeals (6th cir.) 1966, U.S. Dist. Ct. (no. dist.) Ohio 1967. Law clk. U.S. Ct. Appeals, 6th Cir., 1966-67; assoc. Gottfried, Ginsberg, Guren & Merritt, Cleve., 1967-71; chief staff Ohio Gov. John J. Gilligan, Columbus, 1971-72; ptnr. Guren, Merritt, Feibel, Sogg & Cohen, Cleve., 1972-84, Benesch, Friedlander, Coplan & Aronoff, Cleve., 1984—. Chmn. Ohio Civil Rights Commn., 1972-74; dir. Overseas Pvt. Investment Corp., Washington, 1978-82; spl. counsel Ohio Atty. Gen., Cleve., 1983-94. Co-author: The Silent Alliance, 1984. Mem. Am. Jewish Com., 1981—; vice chmn. nat. fin. coun. Dem. Nat. Com., 1975—85; pres. Fedn. for Cmty. Planning, Cleve., 1989—92; bd. dirs. United Way Svcs., Cleve., 1989—92, Cuyahoga C.C. Found., 1989—95, Citizens League Greater Cleve., 1989—95, v.p., 1993—95; pres. Fairmount Temple, 1993—96; pres. Cleve. chpt. Am. Jewish Com., 1991—93; mem. nat. bd. trustees Union for Reform Judaism, 1991—, mem. exec. com., 1997—. Jewish. Office: Benesch Friedlander 200 Public Sq Ste 2300 Cleveland OH 44114-2378

FRIEDMAN, JEFFREY I., real estate company executive; CEO Associated Estates Realty Corp., Richmond Heights, Ohio, 1993—. Office: Associated Estate Realty Corp 5025 Swetland Ct Richmond Heights OH 44143-1467 Fax: 216-289-6400.

FRIEDMAN, JOAN M., retired accountant, educator; b. NYC, Nov. 30, 1949; d. Alvin E. and Pesselle Gail (Rothenberg) F.; m. Charles E. Blair III, Sept. 20, 1992. AB magna cum laude, Harvard U., 1971; MA, Courtauld Inst., U. London, 1973; MS with honors, Columbia U., 1974; MAS, U. Ill., 1993. CPA, Ill. Asst. research librarian Beinecke Library, New Haven, 1974-75; asst. research librarian Yale Ctr. for Brit. Art, New Haven, 1975-76, curator of rare books, 1976-90; computer cons., teaching asst. dept. accountancy U. Ill., Champaign, 1990-95; vis. asst. prof. acctg. Ill. Wesleyan U., Bloomington, Ill., 1995-99, asst. prof. acctg., 1999—2006; ret., 2006. Cons. Johns Hopkins U., Balt., 1983; tchr. Sch. Library Service Columbia U., 1983-88, Sysop WordPerfect Users Forum on CompuServe, 1987-2000, Sysop, Tapcis Forum on CompuServe, 1988-95. Author: Color Printing in England, 1978; contbr. articles in field Recipient student achievement award Fedn. Schs. Accountancy, 1993; Nat. Merit scholar Harvard U., 1967; Moss Accountancy fellow U. Ill. 1990. Mem. Bibliog. Soc. Am. (coun. 1982-86, 2008-, sec. 1986-88), Am. Printing History Assn., Phi Beta Kappa, Beta Phi Mu. Clubs: Grolier. Jewish. Avocations: microcomputers, bicycling, amateur radio. Personal E-mail: joanf@concentric.net.

FRIEDMAN, LAWRENCE MILTON, lawyer, finance company executive; b. Chgo., Apr. 2, 1945; s. Armin C. and Mildred Friedman; m. Linda M. Friedman, June 25, 1967; children: Benjamin J., David K. BA, U. Ill., 1966; JD, Ohio State U., 1969. Bar: Ill. 1970, U.S. Tax Ct. 1970; CPA, Md., Ill. Ptnr. Coopers & Lybrand, Chgo., 1969-85, Lord, Bissell & Brook LLP, Chgo., 1985—2006, of counsel, 2006—; pres. Puritan Fin. Corp., Chgo., 2006—. Adj. prof. law IIT Chgo. Kent Coll. Law, Chgo., 1990-2000; mem. adv. bd. Hartford Inst. Ins. Tax, 1995-2000; spkr. on mergers, aquisitions, fin. svcs. industries, and taxation. Mem. adv. bd. Ins. Tax Rev., 1987—; contbr. articles to law jours. Sec.-treas., dir. North Shore Performing Arts Ctr. Found. in Skokie, Ill., 1993-97; vice chmn., dir. Jewish Fedn. Met. Chgo., 1992-99. Mem. ABA, Chgo. Fed. Tax Forum. Office: Lord Bissell & Brook LLP 111 S Wacker Dr Chicago IL 60606-4410 Office Phone: 312-443-1835.

FRIEDMAN, ROSELYN L., lawyer, mediator; b. Cleve., Dec. 9, 1942; d. Charles and Lillian Edith (Zalzneck) Friedman. BS, U. Pitts., 1964; MA, Case Western Res. U., Cleve., 1967; JD cum laude, Loyola U., Chgo., 1977. Bar: Ill. 1977, US Dist. Ct. (no. dist.) Ill. 1977. Mem. legal dept. No. Trust Co., Chgo., 1977-79; assoc. Rudnick & Wolfe, Chgo., 1979-84, ptnr., 1984-95, Sachnoff & Weaver, Ltd., Chgo., 1995—2006, ptnr., chmn. dept. estates and trusts, 2002—05; chief adminstrv. officer investment svcs. Joseph Freed and Assocs., Palatine, Ill., 2006—. Mem. Loyola U., Chgo. law rev.; mem. profl. adv. com. Chgo. Jewish Fedn., chmn., 1999-2001; mem. profl. adv. com. Chgo. Cmty. Trust, 2001-. Trustee Jewish Women's Found., 1997—2001; mediator Ctr. for Conflict Resolution, 2000—. Fellow Am. Coll. Trust and Estate Counsel; mem. ABA, Am. Jewish Congress (gov. coun. Midwest region 1995-97), Chgo. Bar Assn. (cert. appreciation continuing legal edn. program 1984, chmn. trust law com. 1989-90), Chgo. Estate Planning Coun. (program com. 1992-94, 98-2000, membership com. 1997-98, bd. dirs. 2001-2003), spkr. Ill. Inst. CLE, Chgo. Fin. Exch. (bd. dirs. 1995-97, sec. 1996-97). Office: Joseph Freed and Assoc 30 W Monroe 5th Fl Chicago IL 60603

FRIEDMAN, STANLEY, insect physiologist, educator; b. NYC, Dec. 11, 1925; s. Nathan and Eva (Rothstein) F.; m. Frances Ray Shapiro, May 21, 1955; children: David, Douglas, Catherine, Matthew. Student, CCNY, 1941-43; BA, U. Ill., 1948; PhD, Johns Hopkins U., 1952. Rsch. assoc. U. Ill., 1953-56; biochemist NIH, 1956-58; asst. prof. entomology Purdue U., 1958-62; rsch. fellow London Sch. Hygiene and Tropical Medicine, 1962-63; assoc. prof. entomology Purdue U., 1963-64, U. Ill., Urbana, 1964-68, prof., 1968-92, prof. emeritus, 1992—, head dept., 1976-92, assoc. dir. Sch. Life Scis., 1989-92. With USN, 1943-46. Fellow AAAS; mem. Am. Soc. Zoology, Am. Soc. Biol. Chemists, Entomol. Soc. Am., Federated Socs. Exptl. Biology and Medicine, Sigma Xi. Office: 320 Morrill Hall 505 S Goodwin Ave Urbana IL 61801-3707 Business E-Mail: sfriedman@uiuc.edu.

FRIEDMAN, WILLIAM HERSH, otolaryngologist, educator; b. Granite City, Ill., Aug. 14, 1938; s. Joseph and Lily May (Brody) F.; m. Hillary Lee, Aug. 9, 1974; children: Joseph Morgan, Alexander Lawrence. AB, Washington U., St. Louis, 1960, MD, 1964. Diplomate: Am. Bd. Otolaryngology. Intern Jackson Meml. Hosp., Miami, Fla., 1964-65; resident in surgery and otolaryngology Mt. Sinai Hosp., NYC, 1965-70, NIH fellow, 1966-67; assoc. prof. otolaryngology Mt. Sinai Sch. Medicine, 1974-76, assoc. attending physician, 1973-76; dir. otolaryngology City Hosp. Center, Elmhurst, N.Y., 1971-76; practice medicine specializing in otolaryngology Beverly Hills, Calif., 1976, Boston, 1977; prof. otolaryngology, chmn. dept. St. Louis U. Sch. Medicine, 1977-87; chief otolaryngology Firmin Desloge Hosp., Cardinal Glennon Meml. Hosp. for Children, 1977-87; dir. Park Cen. Inst., 1987—; prof. otolaryngology Columbia U., NYC, 1987-90. Dir. dept. otolaryngology St. Luke's/Roosevelt Hosp. 1987-90; chief dept. otolaryngology, head neck surgery Deaconess Hosp., 1988-98; pres. Friedman & Assocs., Inc. Contbr. articles to books and profl. jours. Fellow ACS, Am. Acad. Otolaryngology, Am. Acad. Facial Plastic and Reconstructive Surgery (chmn. forum for surg. excellence, credentials com., Ira J. Tresley Meml. award 1978), Am. Soc. Head and Neck Surgery, Am. Laryngol., Rhinol. and Otol. Soc.; mem. AMA (Hektoen gold medal 1978), Med. Soc. County New York, Soc. Univ. Otolaryngologists, Centurion Club of Deafness Rsch. Found., N.Y. State Soc. Surgeons, Assn. Acad. Depts. Otolaryngology, Mo. Ear, Nose and Throat Club (pres. 1987-88), Westwood Country Club, Mission Hills Country Club, Boothbay Harbor Yacht Club, Phi Beta Kappa, Sigma Alpha Mu. Achievements include inventor surg. instruments, including facial plastic instrumentarium. Home: 23 Topton Wy Saint Louis MO 63105 Office: 3023 New Ballas Ste 600 Saint Louis MO 63131 Office Phone: 314-991-4644.

FRIEDMAN, WILLIAM JOHN, psychology professor; b. May 22, 1950; BA in Psychology with honors, Oberlin Coll., 1972; PhD in Psychology, U Rochester, 1977. Asst. instr. grad. stats. U. Rochester, 1973-74, instr. devel. psychology, 1975-76; trainee in devel. psychology U.S. Dept. Pub. Health, 1972-76; asst. prof. psychology Oberlin (Ohio) Coll., 1976-84, assoc. prof. psychology, 1984-91, prof., 1991—, chair dept. psychology, 1992-2000. Vis. scientist Applied Psychology Unit, Med. Rsch. Coun., Cambridge, Eng., 1983; vis. scientist lab. exptl. psychology U. Grenoble II, 1988-89; vis. scientist U. Canterbury, 1994; U. Otago, 2000-2001. Author (book) About Time: Inventing the Fourth Dimension, 1990; editor (book) The Developmental Psychology of Time, 1982; co-editor (book) Time, Action & Cognition, 1992; contbr. articles to profl. jours. Mem. Soc. for Rsch. in Child Devel., Cognitive Devel. Soc. Office: Oberlin Coll Dept Psychology Oberlin OH 44074 Office Phone: 440-775-8365. Business E-Mail: friedman@oberlin.edu.

FRIEDMANN, PERETZ PETER, aerospace engineer, educator; arrived in US, 1969, naturalized, 1977; s. Mauritius and Elisabeth Friedmann; m. Esther Sarfati. DSc, MIT, Cambridge, 1972. Research asst. dept. aeronautics and astronautics MIT, Cambridge, 1969-72; asst. prof. mech. and aerospace engring. dept. UCLA, 1972-77, assoc. prof., 1977-80, prof., 1980-98, chmn. dept. mech. and aerospace engring. Los Angeles, 1988-91; François-Xavier Bagnoud prof. aerospace engring. dept. U. Mich., Ann Arbor, 1999—. Editor in chief Vertica-Internat. Jour. Rotocraft and Powered Lift Aircraft, 1980-90; contbr. numerous articles to profl. jours. Grantee NASA, Air Force Office Sci. Rsch., US Army Rsch. Office, NSF. Fellow AIAA (recipient Structures, Structural Dynamics and Materials award 1996, Structures, Structural Dynamics and Materials Lectr. award 97), Am. Helicopter Soc. (Fellow award 2004); mem. ASME (Structures and Materials award 1984, Spirit of St. Louis medal 2003, ASME/Boeing Structures and Materials award 2004). Office: U Mich Aerospace Engring Dept 3001 FXB Bldg Ann Arbor MI 48109-2140 Office Phone: 734-763-2354. Business E-Mail: peretzf@umich.edu.

FRIEND, HELEN MARGARET, chemist; b. Lyndon, Ohio, Jan. 30, 1931; d. Maurice Chapman and Margaret (Beath) Mossbarger; m. William Warren Friend, Oct. 9, 1982. BA in Chemistry, Coll. of Wooster, 1953. Rsch. chemist Union Carbide Co., Cleve., 1953-56, asst. patent coord. battery products div., 1956-59, patent coord., 1959-86, Eveready Battery Co., Westlake, Ohio, 1986-90, tech. patent assoc., 1990-95; ret., 1995. Mng. editor JEC Press-Internat. Battery Materials Assn., Cleve., 1978-97. Mng. editor Progress in Batteries and Battery Materials, 1978-98, JEC Battery Newsletter, 1987-98, ITE Battery Newsletter; tech. editor Electrochem. Soc. Japan, U.S. br., 1975-96; editor-in-chief Tech. English divsn. Internat. Tech. Exch. Soc., 1998—. Mem.: Electrochem. Soc., Am. Chem. Soc., Phi Beta Kappa. Presbyterian. Avocations: theater, reading, singing. Home: 576 Buckeye Dr Sheffield Lake OH 44054-1615

FRIEND, WILLIAM C., state legislator; m. Ann friend. BA, U. Indpls. Auditor; rep. Dist. 23 Ind. Ho. of Reps., 1992—, mem. agr. and rural devel., county and twp. coms., mem. family and children, ways and means coms. Owner/farmer Friend Farms. Trustee Allen Twp.; mem. coun.-at-large Miami County; contr. Miami County Solid Waste Dist.; mem. Farm Bur., Grissom Cmty. Redevel. Authority. Mem. Ind. Auditors Assn., Miami County Pork Prodrs., Peru C. of C., Scottish Rite. Home: 3127 W 1500 N Macy IN 46951

FRIER, BRUCE WOODWARD, law educator; b. Chgo., Aug. 31, 1943; s. Bill Edward and Jane Davies Frier. BA, Trinity Coll., 1964; PhD, Princeton U., 1970. Lectr. Bryn Mawr Coll., Pa., 1968—69; prof. classics and law U. Mich., Ann Arbor, 1969—, Henry King Ransom Prof. Law, Frank O. Copley Collegiate Prof. Classics and Roman Law, interim chair Dept. Classical Studies, 2001—02. Author: Landlords and Tenants in Imperial Rome, 1980 (Goodwin award of merit Am. Philological Assn., 1983), The Rise of the Roman Jurists, 1985, The Demography of Roman Egypt, 1994. Guggenheim fellow 1984-85; fellow Nat. Endowment for the Humanities, 1992-93. Fellow: Am. Acad. of Arts and Scis.; mem.: Am. Philol. Assn., Am. Soc. for Legal Hist. Avocations: bird watching, popular music, movies. Office: U Mich Law Sch 435 Hutchins Hall 625 S State St Ann Arbor MI 48109-1215 Office Phone: 734-936-3022. Office Fax: 734-763-9375. E-mail: bwfrier@umich.edu.

FRIER, CHUCK, radio personality; b. St. Louis; BS Radio-TV, So. Ill. U., Carbondale. Radio host Classic 99, St. Louis. Avocation: bicycling. Office: Classic 99 85 Founders Ln Saint Louis MO 63105

FRIESEN, HENRY GEORGE, endocrinologist, educator; b. Morden, Man., Can., July 31, 1934; s. Frank Henry and Agnes (Unger) F.; m. Joyce Marylin Mackinnon, Oct. 12, 1967; children: Mark Henry, Janet Elizabeth. BSc, MD, U. Man., 1958. Diplomate Am. Bd. Internal Medicine. Intern Winnipeg (Man.) Gen. Hosp., 1958-60; resident Royal Victoria Hosp., Montreal, Que., 1961-62; rsch. assoc. New Eng. Centre Hosp., Boston, 1962-65; prof. exptl. medicine McGill U., Montreal, 1965-73; prof. physiology and medicine U. Man., 1973-92, head dept. physiology, 1973-92; pres. Med. Rsch. Coun. Can., 1991-2000; former founding chmn. Genome Can., Winnipeg; disting. prof. emeritus U. Man. Chmn. exec. com. Med. Rsch. Coun. Can., mem. exec. com., 1981-87; pres. Nat. Cancer Inst. Can., 1990-92. Contbr. numerous articles to profl. jours. Decorated Companion Order of Can.; named to, Can. Med. Hall of Fame, 2001; recipient Gairdner award, Gairdner Found., 1977, Wightman award, 2001. Fellow Royal Soc. Can. (McLaughlin medal 1987), Royal Coll. Physicians and Surgeons; mem. AAAS, Am. Physiol. Soc., Endocrine Soc. (Koch award 1987), Can. Soc. Clin. Investigation (pres. 1974, G. Malcolm Meml. award 1982, Disting. Sci. award 1987), Nat. Acad. Scis. (fgn. assoc.), Can. Physiol. Soc., Am. Fedn. Clin. Research, Am. Soc. Clin. Investigation, Can. Soc. Endocrinology and Metabolism (past pres.), Internat. Soc. euroendocrinology, U.S. Nat. Acad. Sci. (fgn. assoc.). Mennonite. Office: U Man Ctr Advancement Medicine 753 McDermot Ave Winnipeg MB Canada R3E 0WE Personal E-mail: henry2@shaw.ca. E-mail: Henry_Friesen@umanitoba.ca.

FRIGGENS, THOMAS GEORGE, state official, historian; b. Pontiac, Mich., July 12, 1949; s. Francis G. and Jane E. (Pettit) F.; m. Mary T. Bahra; children: Christopher P., Michael C. BA, Albion Coll., 1971; MA, Wayne State U., 1973. Contract historian Mich. Dept. Natural Resources, Fayette, 1973; site historian 07 Mich. Dept. State, History Div., Fort Wilkins Hist. Complex, Copper Harbor, 1974-75, site historian 09, 1975-76, site historian 11, 1976-80, site historian VII, 1980-85, Dept. State, Bur. History, Mich. Iron Industry Mus., Negaunee, 1985-87, regional historian VII, 1987-92, regional historian VII supr., 1992-96, historian mgr. XII, 1996-98, history mgr. 13, 1998—2001; history mgr. 13 dept. history, arts and librs. Mich. Histl. Ctr., 2001. Cons. St. Louis County Hist. Soc., Duluth, Minn., 1985, 86. Contbr. articles to jours. in field. Active Hist. Soc. Mich., bd. dirs., 1984-90; active Copper County Heritage Coun., pres., 1982-83; bd. dirs. Marquette County Hist. Soc., 1992-97; mem. Mich. Hist. Preservation Network. Recipient Roy W. Drier award Houghton County (Mich.) Hist. Soc., 1987, Merit award Hist. Soc. Mich., 1983, Disting. Svc. award, 1983, Dwight B. Waldo award No. Mich. U. Dept. History, 1999. Mem. Am. Assn. State and Local History, Nat. Trust for Hist. Preservation, Mich. Mus. Assn., Phi Alpha Theta. Office: Mich Iron Industry Mus 73 Forge Rd Negaunee MI 49866-9532

FRINK, BRIAN LEE, artist, educator; b. Ft. Lee, Va., Sept. 22, 1956; s. Joseph Lee and Darlene Jean (Ratcliff) F.; m. Denise Ellen Neushwander; children: Blake, Annakeiko. BFA, Ill. State U., 1979; MFA, U. Wis., 1988. Assoc. prof. art Mankato (Minn.) State U., 1989—. Vis. lectr. U. Wis., Madison, 1989. One-man show Rochester (Minn.) Art Ctr., 1997; exhibited in group shows Mpls. Inst. Art, Mpls. Coll. Art and Design, Morgan Gallery, Kansas City, Mo. Individual fellow Nat. Endowment for Arts, 1993, Minn. Arts Bd., 1993, 95, McKnight fellow McKnight Corp., 1992. Home: RR 6 Box 252 Mankato MN 56001-9223 Office: Mankato State U PO Box 42 Mankato MN 56002-0042

FRISKE, DONALD, state official; b. Tomahawk, Wis., Nov. 9, 1961; married; 3 children. Grad. h.s. State assemblyman, Wis., 2000—; dep. sheriff. Mem. corrections and cts. com.; mem. energy and utilities com.; mem. family law com.; mem. rural affairs and forestry com.; mem. small bus. and consumer affairs com.; mem. tourism and recreation com. Mem.: NRA, Internat. Soc. Crime Prevention Practitioners (regional dir.), Optimist Club. Republican. Office: State Capitol Rm 312 N PO Box 8952 Madison WI 53708-8952

FRISON, RICK, agricultural company executive; b. Worland, Wyo., Aug. 22, 1949; s. David T. and Maureen M. (Nelson) F.; m. Nadine M. Van Overbeke; children: Cara M., Jennifer M. BS, Mont. State U., 1977. Salesman ConAgra Mont., Inc., Great Falls, 1977-81, mktg. mgr., 1981-83; div. mgr. ConAgra Fertilizer Co., Billings, Mont., 1983-86, div. mgr. no. region Knoxville, Tenn., 1986-89, v.p., gen. mgr. no. region, 1989-91, retail v.p., 1991-92, pres. Pekin, Ill., 1994—, Cropmate Co., Pekin, 1992—, United Agri Products, Greeley, Colo., 1993—. Mem. editl. adv. bd. Dealer Progress mag., Ballwin, Mo., 1992—; field editor Crop Protection mag., Eugene, Oreg., 1992—. Mem. Fertilizer Inst. (retail coun. 1992—). Office: Cropmate Co 3860 N Main St #A East Peoria IL 61611-5512

FRISSORA, MARK P., automobile rental and leasing company executive; b. Aug. 4, 1955; BA, Ohio State U., 1977; postgrad., U. Pa., Thunderbird Internat. Sch. Mgmt. With lighting bus. group GE, 1977-87; various mgmt. positions Philips Lighting co., 1987-91; v.p. N.Am. mktg., sales and distbn. Aeroquip-Vickers Corp., 1991-96; v.p. original equipment sales and engring. Walker Mfg., 1996; sr. v.p., gen. mgr. original equipment bus.-program mgmt. Tenneco Automotive, Lake Forest, Ill., 1996-99, pres., CEO, 1999—2006, chmn., 2000—06; pres., CEO Hertz Global Holdings, Park Ridge, NJ, 2006—. Mem. The Bus. Roundtable; supplier's adv. coun. Nissan Motor Co.; automotive bd. gov. World Econ. Forum; bd. dir. NCR Corp., FMC Corp.; bd. dirs. Hertz Corp., 2006—. Mem.: Motor & Equipment Mfr. Assn. (bd. dir.), Automotive Original Equipment Mfr., Soc. Automotive Engrs. Office: Hertz Corp 225 Brae Blvd Park Ridge NJ 07656

FRISWOLD, FRED RAVNDAL, manufacturing executive; b. Mpls., Jan. 21, 1937; s. Ingolf Oliver and Derrice Ernestine (Anderson) F.; m. C. Marie Martin, Sept. 14, 1957; children— Cynthia, Steven, Barry, Michelle (dec.), Benjamin. BBA with distinction in Fin, U. Minn., 1958. Chartered fin. analyst. With J.M. Dain & Co. (now Dain, Rauscher, Inc.), Mpls., 1958—90; exec. v.p. Dain, Bosworth, Inc., 1976-82, pres., CEO, 1982-90, cons., 1990-92; CEO Tonka Equipment Co., Plymouth, Minn., 1992—. Chmn. bd. U. Gateway Corp., UMF Investment Advisors; U. Minn. Found.; mem. bd. advisors Otologics L.L.C. Bd. dirs. Met. Mpls. YMCA, Mpls. Rotary Found. Mem. Twin City Soc. Security Analysts, Wildwood Lodge, Mpls. Rotary (pres. 1997-98). Methodist. Office: Tonka Equipment Co 13305 Water Tower Cir Plymouth MN 55441-3803 Home: 5925 Tamarac Ave Edina MN 55436

FRITZ, JAMES SHERWOOD, chemist, educator; b. Decatur, Ill., July 20, 1924; s. William Lawrence and Leora Mae (Troster) F.; m. Helen Joan Houck, Apr. 26, 1949 (dec. Oct. 1987); children— Barbara Lisa, Julie Ann, Laurel Joan, Margaret Ellen; m. Miriam Simons Reeves, July 15, 1989. BS, James Millikin U., 1945; MS, U. Ill., 1946, PhD, 1948. Asst. prof. chemistry Wayne State U., Detroit, 1948-51; asst. prof. Iowa State U., Ames, 1951-55, assoc. prof., 1955-60, prof., 1960-90, disting. prof., 1990—. Author: Acid Base Titrations in Nonaqueous Solvents, 1973, An Analytical Solid-Phase Extraction, 1999; co-author: Quantitative Analytical Chemistry, Ion Chromatography, 1982, 3d edit., 2000, Solid Phase Extraction, 1999; contbr. articles to profl. jours. Recipient Minn. Chromatography Forum award, 1987, Dal Nogare award in chromatography, 1991. Mem. Am. Chem. Soc. (award in chromatography 1976, award in analytical chemistry 1985) Methodist. Avocations: tennis, collecting wall hangings. Office: Iowa State U 322 Wilhelm Ames IA 50011-0001 Office Phone: 515-294-5987.

FRITZ, KRISTINE RAE, retired secondary school educator; b. Monroe, Wis. BS in Phys. Edn., U. Wis., LaCrosse, 1970; MS in Phys. Edn., U. N.C., Greensboro, 1978. Softball and fencing program coord. Mequon (Wis.) Recreation Dept., 1970; phys. edn., health and English tchr. Horace Jr. H.S., 1970—81; phys. edn. and health tchr. Sheboygan (Wis.) South H.S., 1982—2004; emeritus tchr. Sheboygan Early Learning Ctr., 2004—05; basketball and volleyball coach, 1972—89; girls track coach, 1972—2004; active early childhood phys. activity pilot program SASD. Mem. dist. wide curriculum and evaluation coms., 1978—2004; mem. sch. effectiveness team, 1991—94; sch. evaluation consortium evaluator, 1988—93; inbound/outbound coach Sport for Understanding, 1991—96. Contbr. articles to profl. jours. Active Sheboygan (Wis.) Spkrs. Bur., 1987—95, Women Reaching Women. Recipient Nat. H.S. Coaches award for girls track, 1987, Lifetime award, Woman's Sports Advocates of Wis., 2003. Mem.: AAHPERD (Midwest Dist. Tchr. of Yr. 1995, Pathfinder award 1997, chair 2003—04, Midwest Dist. Honor award 2006), NEA, Sheboygan Edn. Assn., Wis. Assn. Health, Phys. Edn., Recreation and Dance (life; pres.-elect 1998—99, pres. 1999—2000, Phys. Edn. Tchr. Yr. 1993). Home: 1841 N 26th St Sheboygan WI 53081-2008

FRITZ, ROGER JAY, management consultant; b. Browntown, Wis., July 18, 1928; s. Delmar M. and Ruth M. (Sandley) F.; m. Kathryn Louise Goddard, Oct. 13, 1951; children: Nancy Goddard, Susan Marie. BA in Polit. Sci, Monmouth Coll., Ill., 1950; MS in Speech, U. Wis., 1952, PhD in Ednl. Counseling, 1956. Asst. dean men, asst. prof. Purdue U., 1953-56; mgr. pub. relations Cummins Engine Co.; also sec. Cummins Engine Found., 1956-59; sec. John Deere Found.; also mem. pub. relations staff Deere & Co., 1959-65, dir. mgmt. devel. and personnel research; also dir. John Deere Found., 1965-69; pres. Willamette U., 1969-72, Orgn. Devel. Cons., Naperville, Ill., 1972—. Bd. dirs. Intelligent Electronics, Inc., List Processing Co., Todays Computers Bus. Ctrs., Entre Computer Ctrs., Inc., Natural Golf, Inc., Quote Me, Optionize, Envisionworks, Inc. Author: A Handbook for Resident Counselors, 1952, The Argumentation of William Jennings Bryan and Clarence Darrow in the Tennesee Evolution Trial, 1952, How Freshmen Change, 1956, The Power of Professional Purpose, 1974, MBO Goes to College, 1975, Practical Management by Objectives, 1976, What Managers Need to Know-A Practical Guide for Management Development, 1978, Performance Based Management, 1980, Productivity and Results, 1981, People Compatibility System, 1983, Rate Yourself as a Manager, 1985, You're in Charge, 1986, Personal Performance Contracts: The Key to Job Success, 1986, Nobody Gets Rich Working for Somebody Else, 1987, Rate Your Executive Potential, 1987, The Inside Advantage, 1987, If They Can-You Can, 1988, Be Your Own Boss, 1988, Managing a Successful Team, 1989, Management Ideas That Work, 1989, Developing A Positive Attitude, 1990, The Entrepreneurial Family, 1991, Think Like a Manager, 1991, How to Export, 1992, How to Get Rich Working for Yourself, 1992, Sleep Disorders-America's Hidden Nightmare, 1993, The Sales Manager's High Performance Guide, 1993, How to Manage Your Boss, 1994, A Team of Eagles, 1994, The Small Business Troubleshooter, 1995, The Field Guide for Boss Types.And How to Deal With Them, 1996, An Idea-A-Day For Promotable People, 1996, Crime Crisis: Bold New Ideas to Fit Punishment with Crimes, 1997, Wars of Succession, 1997, One Step Ahead: The Unused Keys to Success, 1998, Bounce Back and Win, 1999, Fast Track-How to Gain Momentum and Keep It, 1999, Attitude Makes The Difference, 2000, Beyond Commitment: The Skills All Leaders Need, 2000, Family Ties and Business Binds, 2000, Magnet People: Their Secrets and How To Learn From Them, 2001, Little Things-Big Results, 2002, How To Make Your Boss Your Ally and Advocate, 2002, Building Your Legacy--One Decision at a Time, 2002, 100 Ways to Bring Out Your Best, 2003, After You-Can Humble People Prevail?, 2004, Sharpen Your Competitive Edge, 2004, Nothing Ventured, Nothing Gained, 2005, Who Cares--Are You a Giver, Taker or Watcher, 2006, The Power of Positive Attitude, 2006, Self Management Equals Sales Success, 2007, Successful Sales Management, 2007, Why Stop Now?-Resisting the Temptation to Retreat, 2007, The Challenge of Change, 2007, Stand and Deliver, or Step Aside!, 2008; also articles, papers; columnmist Entrepreneur mag., New Bus. Opportunity mag., 1989, Benefits and Compensation Solutions Mag., Bus. Start Ups Mag., Bus. Ledger, 2004; mgmt. editor Communication Briefings Newsletter, 1989. Mem. com. preparation coll. tchrs. Ill. Bd. Higher Edn., 1965-67, mem. com. med. edn., 1967-68; edn. com. N.A.M., 1967-69; mem. Iowa-Ill. Indsl. Devel. Group, 1964-69; council contbr. Nat. Indsl. Conf. Bd., 1960-65, council devel., edn. and tng., 1966-69; adv. com. solicitations Nat. Better Bus. Bur., 1964-69; v.p. Oreg. Ind. Colls. Assn., 1969-72; mem. Pres. Johnson's Citizens Adv. Bd. on Youth Opportunity, 1968-69, Gov.'s Personnel Grievance Panel, Ill., 1974-77; trustee Monmouth Coll., 1957-69, chmn., 1961-69; trustee Oreg. Colls. Found., 1969-72, Ind. Coll. Funds Am., N.Y.C., 1972, Internat. Coll. Commerce and Econs., Tokyo, 1970-72, U. Chgo. Cancer Research Found., 1973-78. Recipient Achievement award, Monmouth Coll., 2002. Mem. Phi Eta Sigma, Omicron Delta Kappa, Tau Kappa Epsilon, Phi Alpha Theta, Sigma Tau Delta, Pi Kappa Delta. Clubs: Naperville (Ill.) Country. Republican. Methodist. Home: 1113 N Loomis St Naperville IL 60563-2745 Office: 1240 Iroquois Dr Naperville IL 60563-8536 Office Phone: 630-420-7673. Office Fax: 630-420-7835. Personal E-mail: rfritz3800@aol.com.

FRITZE, STEVEN L., service industry executive; b. St. Paul, Apr. 1954; m. Susie Fritze. B, MBA, U. Minn. With IBM; v.p., contr. Ecolab, St. Paul, 2000—01, sr. v.p. fin., contr., 2001—02, sr. v.p., CFO, 2002—04, exec. v.p., CFO, 2004—. Bd. mem. Habitat for Humanity Twin Cities, Am. Pub. Media Group, Minn. Pub. Radio. Office: Ecolab 370 Wabasha St N Saint Paul MN 55102 Office Phone: 651-293-2401. Office Fax: 651-225-3022. E-mail: steve.fritze@ecolab.com.

FRITZSCHE, HELLMUT, physics professor; b. Berlin, Feb. 20, 1927; arrived in US, 1952; s. Carl Hellmut and Anna (Jordan) F.; m. Sybille Charlotte Lauffer, July 5, 1952; children: Peter Andreas, Thomas Alexander, Susanne Charlotte,

Katharina Sabine. Diploma in Physics, U. Göttingen, Fed. Republic Germany, 1952; PhD in Physics, Purdue U., 1954, DSc (hon.), 1988. Instr. physics Purdue U., Lafayette, Ind., 1954-55, asst. prof., 1955-56, U. Chgo., 1957-61, assoc. prof., 1961-63, prof., 1963-96, dir. Materials Rsch. Lab., 1973-77, chmn. dept., 1977-86, Louis Block prof. physics, 1989-96. V.p. Energy Conversion Devices, Inc., Rochester Hills, Mich.; bd. dirs. United Solar Systems Corp.; mem. adv. com. Ency. Britannica, 1969—96. Editor: 13 sci. books; assoc. editor Jour. Applied Physics, 1975-80; regional editor Jour. Non-Crystalline Solids, 1987-96; contbr. 280 articles to profl. jours.; patentee in field. Named hon. prof. Shanghai Inst. Ceramics, 1985, Nanjing U., 1987, Beijing U. Astronautics, 1988. Fellow AAAS, Am. Physical Soc. (Oliver Buckley Condensed Matter Physics prize 1989), N.Y. Acad. Scis. (chmn. divsn. condensed matter physics 1979-80). Avocations: the violin, sailing, skiing. Home: 3140 E Camino Juan Paisano Tucson AZ 85718-4206 Office: United Solas Ovonic 1100 W Maple Rd Troy MI 48084 Office Phone: 800-528-0617. Personal E-mail: hellmutf@aol.com.

FRITZSCHE, PEGGY J., medical association administrator, radiologist; b. Dayton, OH; m. Anton Hasso; children: Stephen, Martin. Undergrad., Andrews Univ., Berrien Springs, Mich.; MD, Loma Linda U. Intern Charles Kettering Mem. Hosp.; resident radiology White Memorial Medical Ctr., LA; med. dir. Riverside MRI Ctr., Riverside, Calif.; pres. Radiol. Soc. N.Am., Oakbrook, Ill., 2002—04; with San Bernardino MRI, Inland Empire Regional PET Ctr., Calif. Clin. prof. Loma Linda U. Sch. Medicine, 1970—, pres. med. staff; presenter scientific mtgs.; fellow U.C.L.A., 1973—74. Mem. editl. bd.: RadioGraphics, The Am. Jour. Roentgenology, Jour. Computer Assisted Tomography, scientific referee: Academic Radiology, Radiology; contbr. articles to numerous profl. jours., chapters to books; co-author: MRI of the Body, 1993. Recipient Charles J. Kettering Found. Scholarship. Fellow: ACR (councilor); mem.: AMA (gov. bd. women physician congress, deleg.), Am. Assn. Women Radiologists (pres.), Calif. Med. Assn. (deleg.), San Bernardino County Med. Soc. (pres., officer). Office: Radiological Soc North America Inc 820 Jorie Blvd Oak Brook IL 60523-2251

FRIZZELL, DAVID NASON, state legislator; m. Valda Frizzell. BA, Loyola U.; postgrad., Ind. Christian U. Cert. fundraising exec. Fundraising exec.; rep. dist. 93 Ind. Ho. of Reps., 1992—, mem. election and apportionment, family and children coms., mem. ways and means, urban affairs coms., chmn. commerce and econ. devel. Pres. Greater Indpls. Rep. Fin. Com.; mem. variance bd. City of Indpls.; bd. dirs. Ind. Opera Theatre, Inc., ARC, Johnson County, Ind.; past pres. Nat. Kidney Found. of Ind.; past chmn. devel. Alzheimer's Assn. Ind. Mem. Nat. Soc. Fundraising Execs. Home: 8310 Hill Gail Dr Indianapolis IN 46217-4813

FROBENIUS, JOHN RENAN, hospital administrator; b. Muscatine, Iowa, Jan. 25, 1942; s. Reno Reinhold and Ann Sylvia (Kolar) F.; m. Nancy Frobenius; children: Erin, Chris, Anne, Kai. BA, U. Nebbr., 1963; MHA, U. Minn., 1969. Bus. office mgr. Northwestern Bell Telephone, Omaha/North Platte, Nebr., 1963-67; adminstrv. resident The Charles T. Miller Hosp., St. Paul, 1968-69; assoc. adminstr. Stormont-Vail Hosp., Topeka, Kans., 1969-73, St. Luke's Reg. Med. Ctr., Boise, 1973-80, exec. v.p., 1980-85; pres., chief exec. officer St. Cloud (Minn.) Hosp., 1985—. Bd. dirs. United Way of St. Cloud Area, 1988—. Mem. Am. Coll. Healthcare Execs., Vol. Hosps. of Am. (bd. dirs. 1982-85, chmn. bd. 1991—), Minn. Hosp. Assn. (bd. dirs. 1988—, chmn. bd. 1991-93), Minn. Conf. Cath. Health Facilities, Rotary. Republican. Lutheran. Avocations: skiing, running, fishing, backpacking, camping, carpentry.

FROBOM, LEANN LARSON, lawyer; b. Ramona, SD, May 31, 1953; d. Floyd Burdette and Janice Anne (Quist) L.; m. Richard Curtis Finke, May 19, 1973 (div. Jan. 1978); 1 child, Timothy; m. Dwayne Jeffery LaFave, May 31, 1981 (div. 1992); children: Jeffrey, Allison; m. Jerome B. Frobom, Aug. 21, 1999. BS, U. S.D., 1974, JD with honors, 1977. Bar: S.D. 1977, U.S. Dist. Ct. S.D. 1977, U.S. Ct. Appeals (8th cir.) 1977, N.D. 1978, U.S. Dist. Ct. N.D. 1978, Iowa 1998, Nebr. 2001. Asst. atty. gen. State of S.D., Pierre, 1977-78, 79-81; assoc. Bjella, Neff, Rathert & Wahl, Williston, ND, 1978-79, Tobin Law Offices, P.C., Winner, SD, 1981-83; assoc. dean, asst. prof. U. S.D. Sch. Law, Vermillion, 1983-86, dir. continuing legal edn., 1983-89, assoc. prof. law, 1986-89; ptnr. Aho & LaFave, Brookings, SD, 1990-91; pvt. practice Brookings, 1991-92; asst. U.S. atty. U.S. Dist. S.D., 1992-97; gen. counsel S.D. Auto Group, Inc., Sioux Falls, 1997-98; atty. Hughes Law Offices, Sioux Falls, 1998-99, Cline Williams Wright Johnson & Oldfather, Lincoln, Nebr., 1999—2003, Nebr. Legal Svcs., 2003—05; adjudicator N.E. Workforce Devel., Nebr., 2005—. Mem. S.D. Bd. Pardons and Paroles, 1987-90, chmn., 1989-90; comml. arbitrator Am. Arbitration Assn., 1985-92; prof. Kilian C.C.; tax preparer H&R Block Co., 1999—. Contbr. articles to profl. jours. Mem. planning coun. Nat. Identification Program for Advancement Women in Higher Edn. Adminstrn., Am. Coun. on Edn., S.D., 1984-90; bd. dirs. Mo. Shores Women's Resource Ctr., Pierre, 1980, W.H. Over Mus., Vermillion, 1986-87, S.D. Vol. Lawyers for Arts, 1987-92, Brookings Interagy. Coun., 1990-91, Brookings Women's Ctr., 1990-94 Named S.D. Woman Atty. of Yr. Women in Law U. S.D., 1985. Mem. Epsilon Sigma Alpha (S.D. coun. sect. 1985-86). Episcopalian. Avocations: reading, quilting. Home: 4911 High St Lincoln NE 68506-3970 Home Phone: 402-483-7129.

FROEHLICH, CONRAD GERALD, museum director, researcher; b. Mpls., Oct. 22, 1958; s. Gerald William and Marie Diane Froehlich; m. Judy Marie Froehlich, Sept. 18, 1995. BA in Anthropology, Classical Humanities and Sociology, Miami U. of Ohio, 1981, MA in Anthropology, 1983. Mus. asst., archaeologist Anthropology Mus. Miami U. of Ohio, 1977-88; mus. dir. Martin and Osa Johnson Safari Mus., Chanute, Kans., 1989—. Spkr. prol. confs.; appeared on ESPN2, History Channel; rschr. Borneo and Kenya; mgr. copyright, trademark and licensing programs for TV programs and stations. Reviewer: A Museum Guide to Copyright and Trademark, 1999, American Film Institute Catalog of Motion Pictures: Feature Films, 1931-40, 1993; contbr. articles to profl. jours. Hon. trustee Elefence Internat., Cleve., 1998—. Recipient commendation cert. Am. Assn. for State and Local History, 1993; grante Inst. Mus. and Libr. Svcs., Washington, 1995-97, 98-2000, 2000-02. Mem. Am. Anthropol. Assn., Am. Assn. Mus. (lic. and intellectual property coms. 1996-97, 98-99, nat. mus. field rep. for mus. and cmty. initiative 2000-01, Nancy Hanks Meml. award for profl. excellence 1996), Am. Zoo and Aquarium Assn., Internat. Coun. Mus., Kans. Mus. Assn. (conf. spkr. 1998, 99, 2004, arrangements chair 1998, ann. mtg. chair 2001, awards com. 1995, 98, v.p. 2000-02, pres. 2002-04, Outstanding Svc. award 2005), Coun. for Mus. Anthropology, Rotary, Mtn.-Plains Mus. Assn. (bd. dirs. 2002-04, mem. program com. 2002). Avocations: photography, documentaries, military history, classic films, travel. Office: Martin and Osa Johnson Safari Mus 111 N Lincoln Ave Chanute KS 66720-1819 Office Phone: 620-431-2730.*

FROEHLICH, HAROLD VERNON, judge, retired congressman; b. Appleton, Wis., May 12, 1932; s. Vernon W. and Lillian F.; m. Sharon F. Ross, Nov. 20, 1970; children: Jeffrey Scott, Michael Ross. BBA, U. Wis., 1959, LLB, 1962. Bar: Wis. 1962. Staff acct. Ruschlien & Stortreon, CPAs, Madison, Wis., 1958-62; practiced in Appleton, 1962-81; judge Circuit Ct., 1981—; dep. chief judge 8th Jud. Dist. Wis., 1983-85, spl. dep. chief judge, 1985-88, chief judge, 1988-94; sec. Wis. Judicial Conf., 1991-97; mem. Wis. Ho. of Reps., 1963-73, speaker, 1967-71, minority floor leader, 1971-73; mem. 93d Congress from 8th Dist., Wis.; v.p. Black Creek Improvement Corp., 1967—2003, Outagamie County Family Ct. Commn., 1975-78. Chmn. Com. Chief Judges, 1992—94; chief adminstrn. judge Outagamie County, 1983—88, 1994—2006, 2007—. Rep. precinct committeeman 19th ward, Appleton, 1956-62; chmn. Outagamie County Rep. Statutory Com., 1958-62; sec. Assembly Rep. Caucus, 1965-66; bd. regents Fox Valley Luth. H.S., Appleton, 1990-93; bd. dirs. Fox Valley Luth. H.S. Found., 1967—, v.p., 2002-06, pres. 2006—. With USN, 1951-55. Mem. ABA, Am. Judges Assn. (bd. govs. 1997-99, asst. treas. 1998-99, treas. 1999—), Wis. Bar Assn., Outagamie County Bar Assns., Am. Legion, VFW (judge adv. 1963-75, 82-99), Assn. Trial Judges in Wis. (sec. 1984-91, pres. 1991-2000), Midwest Coun. State Govts. (vice chmn. 1968-69, chmn. 1969-70), Coun. State Govts. (nat. exec. com. 1970-72), Phi Alpha Delta. Office: 410 S Walnut St Appleton WI 54911-5920 Home: Appleton WI 54911-1540 Office Phone: 920-832-5602. Business E-Mail: harold.froehlich@wicourts.gov.

FROELKER, JIM, state legislator; b. Gerald, Mo., Aug. 9, 1949; m. Terry S. Hempelmann, 1974; children: Chad, Becky. Grad., United Electronic Inst., Louisville. Quality control inspector. Rep. com. mem. Boone Twp.; state rep. dist. 111 Mo. Ho. Reps., mem. agrl. bus., elec. com., local govt. com. Mem. Mo. State Sch. Bd. Assn., Cattleman's Assn., C. of C. Home: RR 2 Box 262ab Gerald MO 63037-9652 Office: 7437 Highway H Gerald MO 63037-2824

FROHMAN, LAWRENCE ASHER, endocrinology educator, scientist; b. Detroit, Jan. 26, 1935; s. Dan and Rebecca (Katzman) F.; m. Barbara Hecht, June 9, 1957; children: Michael, Marc, Erica, Rena. MD, U. Mich., 1958. Diplomate: Am. Bd. Internal Medicine. Intern Yale-New Haven Med. Ctr., 1958—59, resident in internal medicine, 1959—61; asst. prof. medicine SUNY, Buffalo, 1965—69, assoc. prof., 1969—73; prof. medicine U. Chgo., 1973—81; dir. endocrinology Michael Reese Hosp., Chgo., 1973—81; prof., dir. div. endocrinology and metabolism U. Cin., 1981—92; prof. medicine U. Ill., Chgo., 1992—, chmn. Dept. Medicine, 1992—2001; dir. Med. Svcs. U. Ill. Hosp., Chgo., 1992—2001. Dir. Gen. Clin. Rsch. Ctr., 1986-90; mem. sci. rev. com. NIH, Bethesda, Md., 1972-76; mem. sci. rev. bd. VA, Washington, 1979-82; mem. endocrine adv. bd. FDA, Washington, 1982-86; mem. adv. com. Nat. Inst. Diabetes, Digestive and Kidney Diseases, NIH, 1983-94, chmn., 1991-93; mem. sci. adv. bd. Edison Biotech. Inst., Ohio U. Editor: (with others) Endocrinology and Metabolism, 2001; editl. bd. 7 med. and sci. jours., 1970—; contbr. articles to profl. jours. NIH research grantee, 1967-98, Endocrine Soc. Rorer Clin. Investigator award, 1991. Mem.: ACP, Ctrl. Soc. Clin. Rsch. (pres. 2004), Am. Clin. Climatological Assn., Pituitary Soc., Internat. Soc. Neuroendocrinology, Am. Diabetes Assn., Am. Soc. Clin. Investigation, Assn. Am. Physicians, Endocrine Soc. Office: U Ill at Chgo Sect Endocrinology M/C 275 1747 W Roosevelt Rd Rm 517 Chicago IL 60608-7333 Office Phone: 312-996-6060. E-mail: frohman@uic.edu.

FROMM, DAVID, surgeon; b. NYC, Jan. 21, 1939; s. Alfred and Hanna F.; m. Barbara Solter, June 13, 1961; children— Marc, Kenneth, Kathleen. BS, U. Calif., Berkeley, 1960, MD, 1964. Diplomate Am. Bd. Surgery. Intern U. Calif. Hosp., San Francisco, 1964-65; resident in surgery U. Calif., San Francisco, 1965-71; asst. prof. surgery Harvard Med. Sch., Boston, 1973-77, asso. prof., 1977-78; prof. chmn. dept. surgery SUNY-Upstate Med. Center, Syracuse, 1978-88; Penberthy prof., chmn. dept. surgery Wayne State U., 1988—; surgeon-in-chief Detroit Med. Ctr., 1988—; chief surgery Harper Hosp., Detroit, 1988. Dir. Am. Bd. Surgery, 1996-2001. Author: Complications of Gastric Surgery, 1977; editor Gastrointestinal Surgery, 1985; contbr. articles to profl. jours. Trustee Karmanos Cancer Inst. With M.C., U.S. Army, 1971-73. NIH career devel. awardee, 1976-79; grantee, 1974— Fellow: ACS (gov. 1977—83); mem.: Detroit Acad. Medicine, Detroit Acad. Surgery, Soc. Surgery Alimentary Tract (sec. 1994—97, pres. 1998, chmn. bd. trustees 1999—2000), Halsted Soc., Am. Surg. Assn., Am. Physiol. Soc., Assn. Acad. Surgery, Soc. Clin. Surgery, Am. Gastroent. Assn., Soc. Univ. Surgeons. Office: Wayne State U 6C Univ Health Ctr 4201 St Antoine St Detroit MI 48201-2153 E-mail: dfsurg@aol.com.

FROMM, RONALD A., apparel executive; m. Cheryl Fromm; children: Dawn, Dana. BS in Acctg., U. Wis., MBA. Former v.p. Heath Corp.; dir. fin. Famous Footwear divsn. Brown Shoe, Madison, Wis., 1986-88, v.p., 1988-90, v.p., CFO, 1990-92, exec. v.p., then pres. Brown Shoe Co. divsn., 1992—98, pres. St. Louis, 1999—2006, chmn., CEO, 1999—. Bd. dirs. Footwear Distributors and Retailers of Am., Fashion Footwear Assn. N.Y., Two/Ten Footwear Industry charitable found. Office: Brown Shoe 8300 Maryland Ave Saint Louis MO 63105

FRONDUTI, JOHN S., lawyer; b. Pitts., Aug. 18, 1972; BBA, U. Notre Dame, 1994; JD, U. Cin. Coll. Law, 1997. Bar: NY 1998, Ohio 2003. Assoc. Pillsbury, Winthrop LLP, NYC; ptnr. Keating, Muething & Klekamp PLL, Cin. Named one of Ohio's Rising Stars, Super Lawyers, 2006. Mem.: Cin. Bar Assn. Office: Keating Muething & Klekamp PLL One E Fourth St Ste 1400 Cincinnati OH 45202 Office Phone: 513-579-6400. Office Fax: 513-579-6457.

FROOMAN, THOMAS E., lawyer; b. 1967; m. Susan Frooman; 2 children. BSBA, Citadel, 1989; JD, Salmon P. Chase Coll. of Law, 1994. Atty. Keating, Muething & Klekamp, Cincinnati, 1997—2001; v.p., gen. counsel, sec. Cintas Corp., 2001—. Office: Cintas Corp PO Box 625737 6800 Cintas Blvd Cincinnati OH 45262-5737 Office Phone: 513-754-3584. Business E-Mail: froomant@cintas.com.

FROSETH, GLEN, state legislator; m. Donna Froseth; 4 children. Newspaper pub.; state rep. dist. 6, 1993—. Mem. industry, bus. and labor com., polit. subdivsns. com. N.D. Ho. Reps. Mem. N. Dak. Newspaper Assn. (past pres.), Lions, Eagles. Home: PO Box 894 Kenmare ND 58746-0894

FROSS, ROGER RAYMOND, lawyer; b. Rockford, Ill., Mar. 8, 1940; s. Hollis H. and Dorothy (George) F.; m. Madelon R. Rose, Feb. 14, 1970; 1 child, Oliver. AB, DePauw U., 1962; JD, U. Chgo., 1965. Bar: Ill. 1965. Assoc. Norman and Billick, Chgo., 1965-70; ptnr. Lord, Bissell & Brook, Chgo., 1970—, mng. pntr., 1982-87. Bd. dirs. Hyde Park Bank and Trust Co., Chgo., 1975—; pres. Hyde-Park-Kenwood Devel. Corp., 1998—. Bd. dirs. Hyde Park Neighborhood Club, Chgo., 1970—, pres. 1972-73; bd. dirs., mem. exec. com. South East Chgo. Commn., 1978—; mem. Community Conservation Council, Chgo., 1980-99; bd. dirs., sec. Chgo. Metro History Fair, 1991—; bd. dirs. The Joyce Found., 1991—, Lab. Sch. U. Chgo., 1991-94, Citizens Com. of the Juvenile Ct., 1973-96. Rector schlor DePauw U., Greencastle, Ind., 1958-62. Mem. ABA, Ill. Bar Assn., Chgo. Bar Assn. (chmn. com. juvenile delinquents 1972). Office: Locke Lord Bissell & Liddell LLP 111 S Wacker Dr Chicago IL 60606-4410

FRUCHTENBAUM, EDWARD, greeting card company executive; b. 1948; BA, Calif. State U., Northridge, 1971. Sales rep. Am. Greetings, Calif., 1973-82, regional mgr. Calif., 1982-86, v.p. mktg. Cleve., 1986-87, group v.p., 1987-88, sr. v.p. mktg., 1988-90, pres. U.S. greeting card div., 1990—2000, pres., COO, also bd. dirs., 1992—2000. Mem. alumni Leadership Cleve., 1989—; mem. Chagrin Hist. Soc., Chagrin Falls, Ohio, Stan Hywett Hall Found., Akron, Ohio. Mem. Am. Mktg. Assn. Office: Am Greetings One American Rd Cleveland OH 44144-2301

FRUDAKIS, ANTHONY PARKER, sculptor, educator; b. Bellow Falls, VT, July 30, 1953; s. Evangelos and Virginia Frudakis. Student, Duke U., 1972—73; cert. of completion, Pa. Acad. Fine Arts, 1976; MFA, U. Pa., 1992. Tchr. Fashion Inst. NY, NYC, 1982, Atlantic CC, Mays Landing, NJ, 1990—91; assoc. prof. Hillsdale Coll., Mich., 1991—; owner Frudakis Studio, 1976—. Tchr. Frudakis Acad. Fine Arts, Phila., 1976, Frudakis Studio, 1976—, Fashion Inst. Tech., N.Y.C., 1982, Atlantic C.C., Mays Landing, N.J., 1990-91; assoc. prof. Hillsdale (Mich.) Coll., 1991—. One-person shows include Ocean City (N.J.) Cultural Ctr., 1992, Sturgis (Mich.) Civic Ctr., 1992, Hillsdale Coll, 1999, Flatlanders Blissfield, Mich., 2004; exhibited in group shows NAD, N.Y.C., 1988, 91, 2003, Allied Artists Am., N.Y.C., 1982, Renaissance Gallery, Phila., 1988, Gloucester County Coll., Deptford, N.J., 1989, Grand Cen. Art Gallery, N.Y.C., 1990, 92, Toledo (Ohio) Art Mus., 1994, Nat. Scultpure Soc. N.Y., N.Y.C., 1997, Hillsdale Coll., 1997, 2001; represented in permanent collections Brookgreen (S.C.) Gardens Mus.; commd. Atlantic County Libr., Hammanton, N.J., 1983, Bally's Hotel, Atlantic City, N.J., 1986, Cape May Ct. House, N.J., 1989, Athens Sq., N.Y.C., 1993, Hillsdale Coll., 1992, 95 (Bronze award), St. Catherine's, Concord, Mich., 1996, St. Anthony's, Hillsdale, 1996, Adrian, Mich., 1998, St. Mary's Cathedral, Saginaw, Mich., 1999, East Lansing, Mich., 2000; featured in publs. including Masters of American Sculpture, N.Y. Art Review, Sculpture. Recipient Stewardson prize Pa. Acad. Fine Arts, 1974, 1st prize for sculpture N.J. State Juried Art Show, 1979, M.B. Hexter award Allied Artists of Am., 1982, L. Miselman prize Nat. Sculpture Soc., 1986, Gloria medal, 1983, Gold medal, 1982, Lantz award, 1978, Best Portrait award, 1977, Daniel Chester French award; Dolfinger MacMahon tuition scholar Pa. Acad. Fine Arts, 1973; NSS tuition scholar Pa. Acad. Fine Arts, 1974; Harold Bache Found. traveling grantee, 1975. Fellow NAD (Artist Fund prize 1991), Nat. Sculpture Soc. Office: Hillsdale College 33 East College Hillsdale MI 49242 Studio: 115 Cold Spring Cir Hillsdale MI 49242-1540 Home Phone: 517-437-9668; Office Phone: 517-437-7571. E-mail: tonyfrudakis@comcast.net.

FRUEH, BARTLEY RICHARD, surgeon; b. Cleve., Sept. 1, 1937; s. Lloyd Walter and Elizabeth Virginia (Scott) F.; m. Frances Olive Beach, June 10, 1961 (div. Dec. 1976); children: Bartley Christopher, Dylan Beach (dec.), Walter Terry; m. Frances Mallet-Prevost Gaston Sargent, Dec. 31, 1976 (div. Oct. 1997); stepchildren: Eric Winslow Sargent, Laura Elizabeth Sargent; m. Cheryl Lynn Terpening, June 1, 2002; 1 stepchild, Cherilyn Marie Smith. BChemE, Cornell U., 1960; MD, Columbia Coll. Phys./Surgeons, 1964; MS Ophthalmology, U. Mich., 1970. Diplomate Am. Bd. Ophthalmology. Surg. intern N.C. Meml. Hosp., Chapel Hill, N.C., 1964-65; resident in ophthalmology U. Mich., Ann Arbor, 1967-70; fellow eye plastic surgery Alston Callahan, Birmingham, Ala., 1970; asst. prof. ophthalmology, eye plastic surgery U. Mo., Columbia, 1971-72, asst. clin. prof. ophthalmology eye plastic surgery, 1972-76, assoc. clin. prof. ophthalmology eye plastic surgery, 1976-79; pvt. practice, ophthalmology Columbia, 1972-79; assoc. prof. ophthalmology, eye plastic and orbital surgery U. Mich., Ann Arbor, 1979-86, prof. ophthalmology, 1986—. Cons. med. staff U. Mo. Med. Ctr., Columbia, 1971-79, Meml. Hosp., Jefferson City, 1971-73, Boone County Hosp., Columbia, 1972-79, Harry S. Truman Meml. Vet.'s Hosp., Columbia, 1971-79; med. staff Columbia Regional Hosp., Columbia, 1974-79, U. Mich. Med. Ctr., 1979—, VA Med. Ctr., 1979—; hon. guest spkr. Royal Australian Coll. Ophthalmology, 1995, Peter Rogers lectr., 1999, Bruce Frolick lectr. 2003; lectr. in field. Author: Transactions, American Ophthalmological Society, 1984; editor/author: Surgery of the Eye, 1988; editl. bd.: Ophthalmic Surgery, 1980-87, Am. Acad. Ophthalmology Clin. Modules, 1983-86, Ophthalmic Plastic and Reconstructive Surgery, 1984-98, Orbit; contbr. articles to profl. jours./publs., books in field. Capt. USAF, 1965-67, Taiwan. Grantee in field. Fellow Am. Acad. Ophthalmology (Wendell Hughes lectr. 1993, Sr. Honor award 1990); mem. Am. Soc. Ophthal. Plastic and Reconstructive Surgery (sec. 1973-74, pres. 1976), Am. Ophthalmol. Soc., Orbital Soc., Australasian Soc. Ophthalmic Plastic Surgeons (hon.), European Soc. Ophthal. Plastic and Reconstructive Surgeons (hon.). Avocations: pocket billiards, model t fords and old morgans, wine, violin. Office: WK Kellogg Eye Ctr U Mich 1000 Wall St Ann Arbor MI 48105-1986 E-mail: frueh@umich.edu.

FRUEHLING, ROSEMARY THERESE, publishing executive, author; b. Gilbert, Minn., Jan. 23, 1933; d. Tony and Mary (Scalise) Leoni; 1 child, Shirley Adzick. BS, U. Minn., 1954, MA, 1968, PhD, 1980. Cert. vocat. tech. inst. dir.; cert. in bus. edn. Mgr. instructional svcs. State Bd. Voc-Tech. Edn., St. Paul; dir. Minn. Software Office State of Minn., St. Paul; mgr. office tech. Gregg, McGraw Hill, Mpls.; pres. EMC/Paradigm Pub. Inc. (Coll. Divsn.), St. Paul, Minn. Nat. cons. editor SRA. Author: (textbooks) Communicating for Results: Write to The Point, Office Systems: People, Procedures and Technology, Business Communications: A Case Method Approach, Business Writing: Integrating Process and Purpose, Psychology: Realizing Human Potential, Working at Human Relations, Your Attitude Counts, Communicating for Results, Working in Teams. Mem. Am. Vocat. Assn., Minn. Vocat. Assn., Nat. Bus. Edn. Assn., Delta Pi Epsilon. Office: EMC Corp 875 Montreal Way Saint Paul MN 55102-4245

FRUEHWALD, KRISTIN GAIL, lawyer; b. Sidney, Nebr., May 15, 1946; d. Chris U. and Mary E. (Boles) Bitner; m. Michael R. Fruehwald, Feb. 23, 1980; children: Laurel Elizabeth, Amy Marie. BS with highest distinction in History, U. Nebr., 1968; JD summa cum laude, Ind. U., 1975. Bar: Ind. 1975, U.S. Dist. Ct. (so. dist.) Ind. 1975. Assoc. Barnes & Thornburg, Indpls., 1975-81, ptnr., 1982—. Spkr. in field. Contbr. articles to profl. jours. Trustee The Orchard Sch., 1993—99, chmn., 1997—98, bd. govs., 2005—; bd. dirs. Indpls. Parks Found., 1995—2000, Arts Ind., 1994—98, Ind. Continuing Legal Edn. Forum, 1993—2001, pres., 2000—01; bd. dirs. Riley Children's Found., 1995—; treas. James Whitcomb Riley Meml. Assn., 2000—; bd. dirs. Planned Giving Group Ind., Fedn. Cmty. Defenders, Inc., 1993—99, pres., 1999—2001; bd. dirs. Ind. affiliate Am. Heart Assn., 1977—81, vice chmn. Marion County chpt., 1981; bd. trustees Ctrl. Ind. Land Trust, 2005—. Fellow: ABA (chmn. distributable net income subcom 1985—91, real property, probate and trust sect.), Ind. State Bar Assn. (chmn. probate, trust and real property sects. 1987—88, mem. ho. of dels. 1987—, bd. mgrs. 1989—90, treas. 1996—97, chair ho. of dels. 1998—99, pres. 2001—02, mem. sect. taxation), Ind. Bar Found. (bd. dirs. 2003—, bd. govs. 2004—), Am. Coll. Trust and Estate Counsel (chmn. Ind. state laws com. 1992—95); mem.: Indpls. Legal Aid Soc. (bd. trustees 2006—), Indpls. Bar Found. (bd. dirs. 1992—, chmn. 1997—99), Ind. Code Study Commn., Internat. Assn. Fin. Planners, Indpls. Estate Planning Coun., Indpls. Bar Assn. (chmn. estate planning and adminstrn. sect. 1982—83, chmn. long range fin. planning com. 1988—89, pres. 1993). Office: Barnes & Thornburg 11 S Meridian St Indianapolis IN 46204-3535 Office Phone: 317-231-7245. Business E-Mail: kris.fruewald@btlaw.com.

FRUEN, LOIS, secondary school educator; Chemistry tchr. Breck Sch., Mpls. Author: The Real World of Chemistry. Recipient Presdl. award for Excellence in Sci. Teaching, 1986, James Bryant Conant award for HS Chemistry Teaching, Am. Chem. Soc., 1992. Mem.: Nat. Sci. Tchrs. Assn. (bd. mem. 1994, exec. bd. dirs. 1995—97, Disting. Teaching award 1990). Office: The Breck Sch 123 Ottawa Ave North Minneapolis MN 55422-5189 Office Phone: 763-381-8211.

FRUSTI, DOREEN KAYE, nursing administrator; BSN summa cum laude, Augustana Coll., 1970; MS in Ednl. Psychology and Counseling, Winona State U., 1979, postgrad., 1988—. RN, Minn. Developer, implementor group therapy program acute psychiat. unit McKennan Hosp., Sioux Falls, S.D., 1970; asst. head nurse gen. surgery Rochester (Minn.) Meth. Hosp., 1970-73, head nurse nephrology and renal transplant, 1973-78, instr. electrocardiology, 1975, asst. DON, 1978-83, mem. facility and program devel. chem. dependence svcs., 1981-83, mem. adminstrv. com., 1983-85, mem. lab. medicine study, 1978, mem. weekened phys. medicine feasibility study, 1978-79, mem. liason com., 1978-80, mem. hospice feasibility study, 1978-82, clin. DIN, 1978-91, mem. mgmt. coun., 1987—, mem. clean air task force com., 1986-87, mem. tornado and disaster coms., 1986-88, mem. nursing info. system steering com., 1987-91, joint head nurse planning com., 1988-91, chair dept. nursing, 1991—; grad. intern supr. Winona (Minn.) State U., 1983-88; co-instr. chem. dependence course Rochester Community Coll., 1985; cons. Meth. Hosp. Indpls., 1989. Adj. asst. prof. St. Mary's Coll., Winona, 1986—; mem. cons. com. on alcoholism and drug dependence unit Mayo Clinic, 1980-91, adminstrv. mgmt. com., 1983-88, adolescent chem. dependence unit, 1984-88, mgmt. forum, 1988—, coordinating com., 1988-90, smoking cessation program com. Mayo Med. Ctr., 1985-89, smoke free implementation task force, 1987; cons. Genesee Hosp., Rochester, N.Y., 1989. Mem. hypertension screening program Bethel Luth. Ch., 1976, stewardship com., 1976-78, usher, 1985—, group discussion facilitator, 1985-90, chair, 1986-89, chair pers. and exec. coms., 1987-89, capt., 1988—, lead usher, 1991—; del. dist. conv. Am. Luth. Ch., 1987; del. synodical conv. Evang. Luth. Ch. Am., 1988; chair Outpatient Observation Task Force, 1990-91, steering com. Nursing Ops. Assessment, 1990-91, Incident Report Task Force, 1990-91, Allied Health, 1992—; mem. Bread of the World, 1989—; mem. ops. bd. dirs. Probation Offenders Rehab. and Tng., 1987-90, chair pers. com., 1988-90; supr. Roundtable, 1992—. Mem. Dist. F Orgn. Nurse Execs., Am. Orgn. Nurse Execs., Minn. Orgn. Nurse Execs., Minn. Nurses Assn. (del. 1971, 77, 81, 83, program com. 6th dist. 1973-75, chairperson, 1975-77, adv. bd. com., pres. 1977-79, long range planning com. 1978-79, entry level task force 1981, nursing svc. adminstrn. exec. and legis. coms. 1981-82, nominating com. 1981-83), Sigma Theta Tau (Kappa Mu chpt.). Home: 2100 Valkyrie Dr NW Apt 108 Rochester MN 55901-2451 Office: Rochester Meth Hosp 200 1st St SW Rochester MN 55905-0001

FRY, ANNE EVANS, zoology educator; b. Phila., Sept. 11, 1939; d. Kenneth Evans and Nora Irene (Smith) F. AB, Mount Holyoke Coll., 1961; MS, U. Iowa, 1963; PhD, U. Mass., 1969. Instr. Carleton Coll., Northfield, Minn., 1963-65; asst. prof. Ohio Wesleyan U., Delaware, 1969-74, assoc. prof., 1974-80, prof., 1980—, Helen Whitelaw Jackson univ. prof., 1999—. Contbr. articles to profl. jours. Recipient Welch Teaching award Ohio Wesleyan U., 1976. Mem. AAAS, Am. Inst. Biol. Scis., Soc. for Integrative and Comparative Biology, Ohio Acad. Sci., Soc. Devel. Biology, Sigma Xi. Office: Ohio Wesleyan U Delaware OH 43015 E-mail: AEFry@owu.edu.

FRY, CRAIG R., state legislator; b. Mishawaka, Ind., Oct. 6, 1952; s. Harold L. and Sonna Kay (wilson) F.; m. Carol Sue Granning, 1973; children: Courtney Lynn, Lucas Craig. Student, Ball State U., 1970-72, Ind. U., South Bend, Ivy Tech. Coll. Bus. agt. N.E. Indt. Coun. of Carpenters, 1988—, svc. rep.; rep. Dist. 5 Ind. Ho. of Reps., 1988—, mem. age and aging com., environ. affairs com., mem. fin. inst. com.; chmn. ins. and corps., small bus. and labor coms.; ranking minority mem. Exec. dir. apprenticeship tng. Ivy Tech. State Coll. Pres. Carpenters #413, 1988; mem. Healthy Mothers/Healthy Babies; mem. Mishawaka/Penn Dem. Club.; mem. Penn Twp. Adv. Bd., 1987-88; mem. rules com. Ind. and Nat. Dem. Conv. Home: 637 Bay View Dr Mishawaka IN 46544-4157

FRY, DONALD LEWIS, physiologist, educator; b. Des Moines, Dec. 29, 1924; s. Clair V. and Maudie (Long) F.; children: Donald Stewart, Ronald Sinclair, Heather Elise, Laurel Virginia. MD, Harvard U., 1949. Rsch. fellow Univ Minn Hosp., Mpls., 1952-53; sr. asst. surgeon gen. NIH, Bethesda, Md., 1953-56, surgeon, 1956-57, sr. surgeon, 1957-61, med. dir., 1961-80; prof. Ohio State U., Columbus, 1980—2004, prof. emeritus, 2004. Contbr. numerous articles and papers on physiology and biophysics of pulmonary mechanics, blood vascular interface, transvascular mass transport and the genesis of atherosclerosis to profl. jours., books. Mem. Am. Soc. Clin. Investigation. Mailing: PO Box 340187 Columbus OH 43234-0187 Business E-Mail: fry.1@osu.edu.

FRY, RICHARD E., architectural firm executive; BArch, U. Mich. Registered arch. Mich., Minn., Colo.; cert. Nat. Coun. Archtl. Registered Bds. Pres., prin.-in-charge Fry & Ptnrs. Archs., Inc., Aspen, Col. and Ann Arbor, Mich., 1970—. Adj. prof. U. Mich. Coll. Archtl. and Urban Planning; archtl. instr. Washtenaw C.C.; rep. Mich. archs. Nat. AIA Bd., Washington. Prin. works include U. Mich. Vis. Ctr., No. Brewery Office Bldg., Ann Arbor, Mich. League-U. Mich., Ann Arbor Art Assn., U. Mich. Dental Sch. Sindecuse Mus., We. Mich. U. Bookstore, Burns Park Elem. Sch., Ann Arbor Ctrl. Fire Sta., Heydon Wash. St. Properties, Ann Arbor, pvt. residences, others. Past mem. Ann Arbor Planning Commn.; bd. dirs. Bldg. Bd. Appeals; mem. art acquisition com. Washtenaw C.C. Fellow AIA (pres. Mich. chpt., chmn. design awards & recognition com. Mich. chpt., chmn. design retreat com. Mich. chpt., chmn. mid-summer conf. Mich. chpt., regional dir. Mich. chpt., pres. Huron Valley chpt.). Office: Fry & Partners Architects Inc 121 S Main St Ste 7 Chelsea MI 48118-1548

FRY, ROY H(ENRY), librarian, educator; b. Seattle, June 16, 1931; s. Ray Edward and Fern Mildred (Harmon) F.; m. Joanne Mae Van de Guchte, Sept. 12, 1970; 1 child, Andrea Joy. BA in Asian Studies, U. Wash., 1959, BA in Anthropology, 1959; MA in Libr. Sci., Western Mich. U., 1965; MA in Polit. Sci., ortheastern Ill. U., 1977; archives cert., U. Dever, 1970; advanced studies program cert., Moody Bible Inst., 1990. Cert. tchr., Wash.; cert. pub. libr., .Y.; cert. Med. Libr. Assn. Libr. and audio-visual coord. Zillah (Wash.) Pub. Schs., 1960-61; libr. Mark Morris H.S., Longview, Wash., 1961-64; evening reference libr. Loyola U. of Chgo., 1965-67, head reference libr., 1967-73, bibliog. svcs. libr., 1973-74, head circulation libr., 1974-76, coord. pub. svcs., 1976-85, gov. documents libr., 1985-91; ind. libr. cons., 1991-94; ref. libr. Trinity Evang. Divinity Sch., Deerfield, Ill., 1994—2001, reference and archives libr., 2001—. Tchg. asst. in anthropology Loyola U. of Chgo., 1966-67, instr. libr. sci. program for disadvantaged students, 1967, 68, univ. archivist, 1976-78, bibliographer for polit. sci., 1973-91, instr. corr. study div., 1975-85. Mem. Niles Twp. Regular Rep. Orgn., Skokie, Ill., 1982-98, sec. 1986-98; mem. Skokie Caucus Party, 1981-98; vol. Dep. Registration Officer, 1986—; mem. Skokie Traffic Safety Commn., 1984—, Skokie 4th July Parade com., 1986—; election judge Niles Twp., 1983-98, Avon Twp., 1999—. With USNR, 1951-52. Mem. Nat. Librs. Assn. (founding mem., bd. dirs. 1975-76), Asian/Pacific Am. Librs. Assn. (founding mem.), Chgo. Area Theol. Librs. Assn., Pacific N.W. Libr. Assn., Chgo. Area Archivists (founding mem.), Midwest Archives Conf. (founding mem.), ALA, Assn. Coll. and Rsch. Librs., Ill. Prairie Path Assn., Royal Can. Geog. Soc., Skokie Hist. Soc. (recording sec. 1986—), Ballard Hist. Soc. (Seattle), Macon County Hist. Soc. (Decatur, Ill.), Nat. Right to Life Com., Ill. Fedn. for Right to Life, Am. Legion, VFW, Korean War Vets. Assn., Pi Sigma Alpha. Republican. Evangelical Free. Office: Trinity Evang Divinity Sch Rolfing Meml Libr 2065 Half Day Rd Deerfield IL 60015-1241 Address: 335 S Arrowhead Ct Round Lake IL 60073-4209 E-mail: rfry@tiu.edu, lexifry@netzero.net.

FRYBACK, DENNIS G., health services research educator; BA in Psychology and Math., UCLA, 1969; MA in Math., U. Mich., 1973, PhD in Math. and Psychology, 1974. Mem. faculty U. Wis., Madison, 1974—, prof. population health sciences & ind. engring., 1984—. Chmn. Bd. Scientific Counselors Nat. Lib. Medicine, 1992—94, spl. expert, Lister Hill Nat. Ctr. Biomedical Comm., 1995; chair, Health Care Tech. Study Sec. US Agy. Health Care Policy & Rsch., 1992—96; mem. Com. on Summarizing Population Health Inst. Medicine, 1997—98; founding mem. Soc. Med. Decision Making, 1978—. Contbr. articles to profl. jours. Mem. US Preventive Svcs. Task Force, 1990—96; mem. Panel on Cost Effectiveness in Health & Medicine US Dept. HHS, 1993—96; apptd. to Nat. Adv. Coun. for Health Care Policy, Rsch. & Evaluation, 1997. Fellow: Assn. of Health Svcs. Rsch.; mem.: Soc. for Med. Decision Making (pres. 1982—83, Eugene L. Saenger award for career svc. 1994, Career Achievement award 1999), Inst. of Medicine/NAS. Office: Univ Wisc 685 Warf Office Bldg 610 Walnut St Madison WI 53726-2397

FRYKENBERG, ROBERT ERIC, historian, educator; b. India, June 8, 1930; s. Carl Eric and Doris Marie (Skoglund) F.; m. Carol Addington, July 1, 1952; children: Ann Denise Lewis, Brian Robert, Craig Michael. BA, Bethel Coll., Minn., 1951; MA, U. Minn., 1953; MDiv, Bethel Theol. Sem., 1955; PhD, London U., 1961. Rsch. asst. U. Calif., Berkeley, 1955-57; instr. Oakland (Calif.) Jr. Coll., 1957-58; Ford and Carnegie rsch. and tchg. fellow U. Chgo., 1961-62; mem. faculty U. Wis., Madison, 1962—97, prof. history and S. Asian studies, 1971-97, emeritus prof. history and S. Asian studies, 1997—, chmn. dept., dir. Ctr. S. Asian Studies, 1970-73. Vis. prof. U. Hawaii, summer 1968; Radhakrishnan Meml. lectr. Oxford U., 1998; dir. Pew India Rsch. Advancement Projects, 1994-01. Author: Guntur District, 1788-1848: A History of Local Influence and Central Authority in South India, 1965, History and Belief: The Foundations of Historical Understanding, 1996; editor: Land Control and Social Structure in Indian History, 1969, 77, Land Tenure and Peasant in South Asia: An Anthology of Recent Research, 1977, Studies of South India, 1985, Delhi Through the Ages, 1986, 93, Christians and Missionaries in India: Cross-Cultural Communication since 1500, 2003, Tirunelveli's Evangelical Christians: Two Centuries of Family Traditions, 2003, Pandita Ramabai's America, 2003; co-editor: Studies in the History of Christian Missions series, 1997—, co-gen. editor (with B. Stanley), 2000—; co-editor: Christians, Cultural Interactions, and India's Religious Traditions, 2002; contbr. articles to revs. and profl. publs. Trustee Am. Inst. Indian Studies, 1971-81; dir. summer seminar NEH, 1976. Fellow Rockefeller Found., 1958-61, 1988, Am. Coun. Learned Socs.-Social Sci. Rsch. Coun. 1962-63, 67, 73-74, 83-84, 88-89, Guggenheim Found., 1968-69, HEW Fulbright Hays sr. fellow, 1965-66, NEH, 1975, Wis. Inst. Rsch. Humanities, 1975, Wilson Ctr., 1986, 91-92, Pew Found., 1997. Fellow Royal Hist. Soc., Royal Asiatic Soc.; mem. Internat. Conf. and Seminars, Soc. S. Indian Studies (pres. 1968-70, 82-84), Am. Hist. Assn. (pres. Conf. Faith and History 1970-72), Assn. Asian Studies, Inst. Hist. Studies India, Inst. Asian Studies India, Assn. S. Asian Studies Australia, Inst. Advanced Christian Studies (dir. 1979-83, 87-91, 98-2002, pres. 1981-83) Office: Univ Wis Humanities Bldg 455 N Park St Madison WI 53706 Business E-Mail: refryken@wisc.edu.

FU, PAUL SHAN, law librarian, consultant; b. Shien-Yang, Liao-Ning, China, Sept. 7, 1932; came to U.S., 1961; s. Mu-Shia and Shih-Wei (Chang) F.; m. Doris S. Ku, Jan. 15, 1963; children: Eugene Y., Vincent Y. LLB, Soochow U., 1960; MCL, U. Ill., 1962; MSLS, Villanova U., 1968. Asst. libr., law lectr. Detroit Coll. of Law, 1968-69; law libr., asst. prof. law Ohio No. U., Ada, 1969-71, law libr., assoc. prof. law, 1971-72; law libr. Supreme Ct. of Ohio, Columbus, 1972—; pres. Asian-Am. Law Librs. Caucus, 1994. Dir. Nat. Conf. on State Ct. Librs., Columbus, 1993; cons. Supreme Ct. of Ill. Law Libr., Springfield, 1988, N.H. State Law Libr., Concord, 1987; judge West Pub. Excellence in Law Librarianship Awards Com., 1996. Author: Law Library Handbook of Ohio Supreme Court, 1974; columnist Ohio Lawyer, 1988—; contbr. articles to profl. jours. Recipient Award of Merit Columbus Bar Assn., 1996; U. Ill. fellow, 1961-62. Mem. ALA, Am. Assn. Law Librs. (sec. 1989-93, chair state, ct., and county law librs. sect. 1977-78), Am. Soc. Internat. Law, Univ. Club, Kiwanis (Columbus). Avocations: piano, painting, reading, tennis. Home: 940 Evening St Worthington OH 43085-3051 Office: Ohio State Supreme Ct Law Libr 30 E Broad St Fl 4 Columbus OH 43215-3414

FUCHS, ELAINE V., molecular biologist, educator; b. Hinsdale, Ill., May 5, 1950; m. David T. Hansen, Sept. 10, 1988. BS in Chemistry with highest distinction, U. Ill., Urbana, 1972; PhD in Biochemistry, Princeton U., 1977; PhD (hon.), Mt. Sinai U., 2003. Postdoctoral fellow dept. biology MIT, 1977-80; from asst. prof. to prof. U. Chgo., 1980—89, prof. Dept. Molecular Genetics and Cell Biology, 1989—2002; investigator Howard Hughes Med. Inst., 1988—; Rebecca C. Lancefield prof. mammalian cell biology and devel. Rockefeller U., NYC, 2002—. Assoc. editor Jour. Cell Biology, 1993—; contr. 225 articles to profl. jours. Recipient Bensely award Am. Assn. Anatomists, 1988, Searle Scholar award Chgo. Cmty. Trust, 1981-84, Presdl. Young Investigator award NSF, 1984-89, IH Merit award, 1993, 98, Wm. Montagna award Soc. Investigative Dermatology, 1995, Keith Porter Lecture award Am. Soc. Cell Biology, 1996, Sr. Woman Achievement award, 1997, Cartwright award 2001, Richard Lounsbery award, 2001, Novartis award, 2003, Dickson prize, 2004. Fellow Am. Acad. Arts and Scis., Am. Assn. Microbiology, IOM, Am. Soc. Cell Biology (past pres.), Harvey Soc., Am. Philos. Soc., NY Acad. Sci., Phi Beta Kappa. Office: Rockefeller U Lab Mammalian Cell Biology and Devel 1230 York Ave Box 300 New York NY 10021

FUERSTNER, FIONA MARGARET ANNE, ballet company executive, educator; b. Rio de Janeiro, Apr. 24, 1936; d. Paul G. and Agnes Ethel (Stothard) F.; m. Dane LaFontsee, June 7, 1969 (div. 1992); 1 child, Liana Marie. Studied with San Francisco Ballet, Royal Ballet (London), Ballet Rambert (London) Ballet Theatre Sch. (N.Y.C.), Sch. Am. Ballet (N.Y.C.). With corps de ballet San Francisco Ballet, 1952-55, soloist, 1955-58, prin. dancer, 1958-62; toured with Walter Terry's Am. Dances, 1962-63; prin. dancer Les Grands Ballets Can., Montreal, 1963-64, Am. Choreographer's Co. of N.Y., 1964, Pa. Ballet, 1965—74, ballet mistress, instr. co. class, apprentice class, 1974-77, ballet mistress, instr. co. class, 1977—86; ballet mistress Nashville Ballet, 1986-87, ballet mistress, asst. to artistic dir., 1987-91; ballet mistress Milw. Ballet, 1990-95, asst. to artistic dir. ballet mistress, 1995—2003. Guest dancer Ballet Concerto, Miami, 1967, 68, Erie Civic Ballet, 1969; guest instr. Marsha Woody Dance Acad., Beaumont, Tex., 1974, U. Louisville, 1977-78, co. class San Francisco Ballet, 1985, Tenn. Assn. Dance Nashville Conf., 1988, So. Regional Workshop Chgo., Nat. Assn. Dance Masters in Nashville, 1989, BalletMet, 1991, Memphis Classical Ballet, 1992, 97, 99, Nashville Ballet, 1992; guest ballet mistress BalletMet, 1993; faculty tchr. Sch. of Pa. Ballet, 1977-78, 78-86; organized concert group, ballet mistress, dancer Pa. Ballet, 1971; mem. dance panel Nat. Found. Advancement in the Arts, 1995-98; master tchr. South Eastern Regional Ballet Assn. Festival, 1998, Nat. Found. for Advancement in the Arts, 1999, 2001, 2005; guest tchr. Ind. U. Ballet Dept., 2000, Western Mich. U., 2002, faculty tchr. DanceWorks Studio 1661, Milw., 2005-08, master tchr. Dancenter North, Libertyville, Ill., 2005, 06; master tchr. USDAN Ctr. for the Creative and Performing Arts, Wheatley Heights, NY, 2004—; vis. asst. prof. dance Wright State U., 2004; dance panelist Midwest Regional, Nat. Found. for Advancement in the Arts, 2001, 02; guest faculty Indpls. Sch. Ballet, 2007. Staged Allegro Brillante, Sch. Pa. Ballet Student Showcase, 1986, Nashville Ballet, 1988, Madrigalesco, Pacific NW Ballet, 1981, (parts) Nutcracker, Nashville Ballet, 1989, Carmina Burana (Butler), Milw. Ballet, 1989, Scotch Symphony, Pa. Ballet, 1993, Carmina Burana, Alberta Ballet, 1993, Concerto Barocco, Ballet Omaha, 1994, Ballet Met, 1995, Serenade, Milw. Ballet Sch., 1994, 95, 96, Serenade, Milw. Ballet, 1998-99, Serenade, Western Mich. U., 1999-2000, Concerto Barocco, The Four Temperaments for Milw. Ballet, 1999-2000, Allegro Brillante for Milw. Ballet, 2000-01, (excerpts) Who Cares?, Western Mich. U., 2003, Serenade, Wright State U., 2004, Nutcracker, Indpls. Sch. Ballet, 2007. Office Phone: 414-254-4086. Personal E-mail: fionafio@sbcglobal.net.

FUKUDOME, KOSUKE, professional baseball player; b. Osaki, Japan, Apr. 26, 1977; Shortstop Chunichi Dragons (Nippon Profl. Baseball League), 1999, third baseman, 2000, outfielder, 2001—07, Chgo. Cubs, 2008—. Mem. Japanese Olympic Team, Atlanta, 1996, Athens, 2004, World Baseball Classic, 2006. Named Ctrl. League MVP, Nippon Profl. Baseball League, 2006; recipient Silver medal, Olympic Games, 1996, Bronze medal, 2004, 4 Gold Glove awards, Nippon Profl. Baseball League. Achievements include becoming the youngest player ever to be chosen for an Olympic baseball team, 1996; leading the Central League in doubles (47) in the 2006 season. Mailing: c/o Chgo Cubs Wrigley Field 1060 W Addison Chicago IL 60613*

FULGONI, GIAN MARC, Internet company executive; b. Crickhowell, Brecon, England, Jan. 24, 1948; came to U.S., 1970; s. Romeo and Maria F. BSc in Physics (with honors), Manchester U., 1969; MA in Mktg., Lancaster U., 1970. Exec. v.p. Mgmt. Sci. Assocs., Inc., Pitts., 1970-81; pres. Info. Resources, Inc., Chgo., 1981-89, CEO, 1986-98, vice chmn., 1989-90, chmn., 1991-95, bd. dirs.; chmn., co-founder comScore Networks, Inc., Reston, Va., 1999—. Bd. dirs. Platinum Tech., Inc. Mem. Young Pres. Orgn. Named Ill. Entrepreneur of the Yr.; recipient Wall Street Transcript award. Mem. Am. Mktg. Assn. Avocations: scuba diving; jogging; skiing. Office: comScore Networks Inc 11465 Sunset Hills Rd Ste 200 Reston VA 20190 Office Phone: 203-438-2000. Office Fax: 203-438-2051.

FULLER, HOWARD, education educator, academic administrator; Supt. Milw. Sch. Dist.; dist. prof. edn., dir. Inst. Transformation Learning Marquette U., Milw., 1996—. Office: Marquette U Schroedor Complex PO Box 1881 Milwaukee WI 53201-1881

FULLER, JACK WILLIAM, writer, retired publishing executive; b. Chgo., Oct. 12, 1946; s. Ernest Brady and Dorothy Voss (Tegge) Fuller; m. Debra Moskovits; children: Timothy, Katherine. BS, Northwestern U., 1968; JD, Yale U., 1973. Bar: Ill. 1974. Reporter Chgo. Tribune, 1973—75, Washington corr., 1977—78, editl. writer, 1978—79, dep. editl. page editor, 1979—82, editl. page editor, 1982—87, exec. editor, 1987—89, v.p. and editor, 1989—93, pres., CEO, 1993—97, pub., 1994—97; pres. Tribune Pub. Co., 1997—2004; dir. Torstar Corp., 2004—. Spl. asst. to atty. gen. U.S. Dept. Justice, Washington, 1975—77; mem. editl. independence com. Wall St. Jour., 2007—. Author: Convergence, 1982 (Cliff Dwellers award, 1983), Fragments, 1984 (Friends of Am. Writers award, 1985), Mass, 1985, Our Fathers' Shadows, 1987, Legends' End, 1990, News Values, 1996, The Best of Jackson Payne, 2000, Abbeville, 2008. Mem. Pulitzer Prize Bd., 1991—2000; trustee U. Chgo.; dir. MacArthur Found. With US Army, 1969—70, Vietnam corr., Pacific Stars and Stripes. Recipient Gavel award, ABA, 1979, Pulitzer prize for editl. writing, 1986, Excellence in Arts award, Vietnam Vets Am., 1993. Fellow: Am. Acad. Arts and Scis.; mem.: Inter-Am. Press Assn. (pres. 2003—04).

FULLER, JOHN WILLIAMS, economics professor; b. Phoenix, Nov. 8, 1940; s. John W. and Myrtle Arabella (Parr) F.; m. Annette Cunkle, June 16, 1962 (dec. 1977); m. Kathy J. Fait, Feb. 17, 1980; children: Helen, Douglas, Andrew, Elizabeth. AB, San Diego State U., 1962; PhD, Wash. State U., Pullman, 1968. Chief econ. analysis Wis. Dept. Transp., Madison, 1968-74, dir. environ. and policy analysis, 1974-76; hwy. commr. State Of Wis., 1976-77; deputy exec dir. Nat. Transp. Policy Study Commn., Washington, 1977-79; prof. econs., urban and regional planning and geography U. Iowa, Iowa City, 1979—, chair grad. program in urban and regional planning, 1996-99; cons. Bur. Transp. Stats., Washington, 1993—2001. Cons. Fed. Hwy. Adminstrn., Washington, 1980-82, legis. coun. Iowa Gen. Assembly, Des Moines, 1980-91; dir. Legis. Extended Assistance Group, Iowa City, 1979-2001. Contbr. articles to profl. jours. Mem., vice chair Johnson County Broadband Telecom. Commn., 1982-88; chmn. Zoning Bd. Adjustment, Johnson County, 1987-92; mem. West Branch Zoning Bd. of Adjustment, 1993-2003, West Branch Hist. Preservation Commn., 2002-, sec. 2005; trustee West Branch Libr., 1995-2001, pres. 1997-2001. Recipient Fulbright award, Venezuela, 1985. Mem. Transp. Rsch. Bd., Am. Assn. RR Supts., Am. Soc. Transp. and Logistics, Assn. Am. Geographers, Nat. Assn. Environ. Profls., Am. Econ. Assn., Am. Planning Assn., Transp. Rsch. Forum, Am. Inst. Cert. Planners. Congregationalist. Office: U Iowa 344 Jessup Hall Iowa City IA 52242-1316 Business E-Mail: john-w-fuller@uiowa.edu.

FULLER, MICHAEL B., communications executive; BS in Engring., U.S. Mil. Acad., West Point, NY; MBA, U. Kans., Lawrence. Fin. analyst, corp. staff United Telecommunicatoin, 1974, various ops., mktg. and strategic planning pos., asst. v.p.-planning for telephone ops., 1981—83, various key mgmt. pos. in long-distance bus., 1983—88, v.p.-planning, ISACOMM, 1983—84, sr. v.p.-adminstrn. and plannig for US Telecom, 1985—86; pres. Southeast divsn. US Sprint, Atlanta, 1986—87, sr. v.p.-planning devel. and internat. svcs., 1987—88, exec. v.p.-staff, 1988—89; pres., United Telephone of the Northwest, Local Telecomm. Divsn. Sprint Corp., 1989—96, pres. and COO, Local Telecomm. Divsn., 1996—. Office: 6200 Sprint Pkwy Overland Park KS 66251

FULLER, SAMUEL ASHBY, retired lawyer, mining executive; b. Indpls., Sept. 2, 1924; s. John L.H. and Mary (Ashby) F.; m. Betty Winn Hamilton, June 10, 1948; children— Mary Cheryl Fuller Hargrove, Karen E. Fuller Wolfe, Deborah R. BS in Gen. Engring, U. Cin., 1946, JD, 1947; cert. fin. planner, Coll. for Fin. Planning, 1989. Bar: Ohio 1948, Ind. 1951, Fla. 1984. Cleve. claims rep. Mfrs. and Mchts. Indemnity Co., 1947-48; claims supr. Indemnity Ins. Co. N.Am., 1948-50; with firm Stewart, Irwin, Gilliom, Fuller & Meyer (formerly Murray, Mannon, Fairchild & Stewart), Indpls., 1950-85, Lewis Kappes Fuller & Eads (name changed to Lewis & Kappes), Indpls., 1985-89, 1990—2000; pres., dir. Irsugo Consol. Mines, Ltd., 1953-80; ret., 2000. Dir. Ind. Pub. Health Found., Inc., 1972-84; staff instr. Purdue U. Life Ins. and Mktg. Inst., 1954-61; instr. Am. Coll. Life Underwriters, Indpls., 1964-74; mem. Ind. State Bd. Law Examiners, 1984-96, treas. 1987-88. Bd. dirs. Southwest Social Centre, Inc., 1965-70; mem. Brookshire Homeowner's Assn., pres. 1973; pres., dir. Westminster Village North, Inc., 1981-89. Fellow: Am. Coll. Trust and Estate Counsel, Indpls. Bar Found.; mem.: Internat. Assn. Ins. Counsel Rsch. Inst., Fla. Bar, 7th Cir. Bar Assn., Ind. State Bar Assn. (bd. mgrs. 1986—88), English Speaking Union, Ind. Pioneers Soc., Ctr. Ind. Bridge Assn. (pres. 1969), Mil. Order Loyal Legion US (recorder 1970—76, comdr. 1977—80), Masons, Beta Theta Pi. Republican. Roman Catholic. Personal E-mail: samuel105@verizon.net.

FULLER, WAYNE ARTHUR, statistics educator; b. Corning, Iowa, June 15, 1931; s. Loren Boyd and Elva Gladys (Darrah) F.; m. Evelyn Rose Steinford, Dec. 22, 1956; children: Douglas W., Bret E. BS, Iowa State U., 1955, MS, 1957, PhD, 1959. Asst. prof. Iowa State U., Ames, 1959-62, assoc. prof., 1962-66, prof., 1966-83, disting. prof. stats., 1983—2001, disting. prof. emeritus, 2001—. Cons. Doane Mktg. Rsch., Inc., St. Louis. Author: Introduction to Statistical Time Series, 1976, 2nd ed. 1996, Measurement Error Models, 1987; also articles. Served as cpl. U.S. Army, 1952-54 Fellow Am. Statis. Assn. (v.p. 1991-93), Inst. Math Stats., Econometric Soc.; mem. Internat. Statis. Inst., Royal Statis. Soc. Home: 3013 Briggs Cir Ames IA 50010-4705 Office: Iowa State U Statis Lab 221 Snedecor Hall Ames IA 50010 Home Phone: 515-232-1146; Office Phone: 515-294-9773. Business E-Mail: waf@iastate.edu.

FULLERTON, DENISE S.S., lawyer; married; 2 children. Grad. with honors, Gustavus Adolphus Coll., 1993, William Mitchell Coll. Law, 1998. Bar: Minn. 1998, US Dist. Ct. (dist. Minn.). Ptnr. Ramsay & DeVore, P.A., Roseville, Minn. Contbr. articles to profl. publs. Named a Rising Star, Minn. Super Lawyers mag., 2006. Mem.: Minn. State Bar Assn., Ramsey County Bar Assn., Hennepin County Bar Assn., Minn. Trial Lawyers Assn. (mem. no-fault com. 2001—, mem. bd. govs. 2003—, mem. exec. com. 2005, chair women lawyers sect.), Minn. Women Lawyers. Office: Ramsay & DeVore PA Rosedale Towers Ste 450 1700 W Hwy 36 Roseville MN 55113 Office Phone: 651-604-0000. E-mail: dfullerton@ramsaydevore.com.

FULLMER, PAUL, public relations counselor; b. Evanston, Ill., June 4, 1934; s. Joseph Charles and Marie (Guirsch) F.; m. Sandra Lewars Clifford, Apr. 22, 1961; children: Monica, David. AB, U. Notre Dame, 1955. Newspaper reporter Aurora (Ill.) Beacon News, 1955-57; account exec. Selz/Seabolt Comms., Chgo., 1957-64; v.p. Selz/Seabolt Comms., Inc., Chgo., 1964-72, exec. v.p., 1972-79, pres., 1979-99, chmn., 1999-2000, Publicis Dialog Chgo., 2000—04. Bd. dirs. Pinnacle Worldwide, pres., 1990—92, chmn., 1992—93. Pres. Notre Dame Club Chgo., 1964-65, hon. pres., 1992-93; co-chmn. jr. bd. NCCJ, Chgo., 1962; chmn. Amate House, Chgo., 1985-87; chmn. bd. trustees St. Mary's Acad., 1985-88; co-chmn. Bus. Execs. for Econ. Justice, 1992-94; chmn. exec. com. Holy Family Ch., 1989-93. Sgt. USAR, 1957. Fellow Pub. Rels. Soc. Am. (pres. Chgo. chpt. 1988-89); mem. Internat. Pub. Rels. Assn. Roman Catholic. Home: 87 Heatherdowns Ln Galena IL 61036 E-mail: psful@aol.com.

FULTON, WILLIAM, mathematics professor; b. Aug. 29, 1939; BA, Brown U., 1961; PhD, Princeton U., 1966. Instr. Princeton (N.J.) U., 1965-66; from instr. to asst. prof. Brandeis U., 1966-69; assoc. prof. Brown U., 1970-75, prof., 1975-87, U. Chgo., 1987-98, Charles L. Hutchinson Disting. Svc. prof., 1995-98; Keeler prof. math. U. Mich., Ann Arbor, 1998—. Vis. asst. prof. Princeton U., 1969-70; vis. prof. U. Genoa, 1969, Aarhus U., 1976-77, Orsay, 1987; vis. mem. Inst. des Hautes Etudes Scis., 1981, Inst. Advanced Study, 1981-82, 94, Math. Scis. Rsch. Inst., 1992-93, Ctr. Advanced Study, Oslo, 1994; Erlander prof. Mittag-Leffler Inst., 1996-97; lectr. in field. Author: Intersection Theory, 1984, Introduction to Intersection Theory in Algebraic Geometry, 1984, Introduction to Toric Varieties, 1993, Algebraic Topology, 1995, Young Tableaux, 1997; (with R. MacPherson) A Categorical Framework for the Study of Singular Spaces, 1981; (wih S. Lang) Riemann-Roch Algebra, 1985, (with J. Harris) Representation Theory; a first course, 1991; (with S. Bloch and I. Dolgachev, editors) Proceedings of the US-USSR Symposium in Algebraic Geometry, Univ. of Chicago, June-July, 1989, 1991; assoc. editor Duke Math. Jour., 1984-93, Jour. Algebraic Geometry, 1992-93; editor Jour. Am. Math. Soc., 1993-99, mng. editor, 1995-98; mem. editl. bd. Cambridge Studies in Advanced Math., 1994—, Chgo. Lectures in Math., 1994-98. Grantee NSF, 1976—, Sloan Found., 1981-82; Guggenheim fellow, 1980-81; named Erlander prof. Swedish Sci. Found., 1996-97. Mem.: NAS, AAAS, Royal Swedish Acad. Sci.

FUNDERBURK, RAYMOND, judge; b. Phila., Mar. 2, 1944; s. Walter and Inez (Prince) F. AA, Olive-Harvey Coll., 1972; BA, U. Ill., 1974; MPA, Roosevelt U., 1975; JD, U. Ill., 1978. Bar: Ill. 1979, U.S. Dist. Ct. (no. dist.) Ill. 1979, U.S. Ct. Appeals (7th and fed. cirs.) 1983, U.S. Supreme Ct. 1983. Staff atty. Cook County Legal Assistance, Harvey, Ill., 1978-80, mng. atty., 1980-82; assoc. O. Kenneth Thomas Ltd., Harvey, 1982-83, Jones, Ware & Grenard, Chgo., 1983-88, Earl L. Neal and Assocs., Chgo., 1988-93; judge Cir. Ct. of Cook County, Chgo., Ill., 1993—. Bd. dirs. Cook County Legal Assistance Found., Oak Park, Ill., chmn. 1985-87; active legal adv. bd. Thornton Community Coll., South Holland, Ill., 1982—, Aunt Martha's Service, Park Forest, Ill., 1981-83. Chmn. Zoning Bd. of Appeals, Park Forest, 1988-99, Housing Bd. of Appeals, Park Forest, 1988-99, Equal Employment Opportunity Bd., Park Forest, 1988-99, Housing Rev. Bd., Park Forest, 1988-99; bd. dirs. Park Forest Pub. Library, 1982. Served with U.S. Army, 1965-67. Recipient Cert. of Appreciation Aunt Martha's Youth Svc., 1980, Thornton C.C., 1985, Wendell Phillips H.S., 1985, South Suburban YMCA, 1986, 1987, City Ptnr. award U. Ill. Chgo., 1995; named Disting. Grad., U. Ill. Coll. of Law, 1998-99, Olive-Harvey Jr. Coll., 2001. Mem. ABA, Chgo. Bar Assn., Cook County Bar Assn., Ill. Jud. Coun., Ill. Judges Assn., Phi Alpha Delta, Alpha Phi Alpha. Democrat. Avocations: running, chess, tennis. Office: Cir Ct Cook County Ill Rm 2600 Richard J Daley Ctr Dearborn & Randolph Sts Chicago IL 60602

FUNK, CARLA JEAN, library association director; b. Wheeling, W.Va., Sept. 21, 1946; d. David H. and Jean (Duffy) Belt. BA in Psychology, Northwestern U., 1968; MLS, Ind. U., 1973; MBA, U. Chgo., 1985. Libr. adult svcs. Northbrook (Ill.) Pub. Libr., 1973-77; dir. Warren-Newport Pub. Libr. Dist., Gurnee, Ill., 1977-80; cons. Suburban Libr. Sys., Burr Ridge, Ill., 1980-83; dir. automation and tech. svcs., med. student svcs. AMA, Chgo., 1983-92; exec. dir. Med. Libr. Assn., Chgo., 1992—. Adj. faculty Dominican U., 1986—2000. Contbr. articles to profl. jours. Mem. Internat. Fedn. Libr. Assns. and Insts., Am. Soc. Assn. Execs. (cert. assn. exec.), Assn. Forum of Chicagoland, Beta Phi Mu, Delta Zeta. Office: 65 E Wacker Pl Ste 1900 Chicago IL 60601-7246 Business E-Mail: funk@mlahq.org.

FURLANE, MARK ELLIOTT, lawyer; b. Joliet, Ill., Aug. 2, 1949; s. Francis Emilio and Tosca (Cipriani) F.; m. Susan M. Keegan, July 4, 1987; children: Gahan Patricia, Michael Keegan. BA magna cum laude, Ctrl. Coll., 1971; JD with honors, George Washington U., 1974; MBA in Finance Specialization, U. Chgo., 1982. Bar: Ill. 1974, U.S. Dist. Ct. (no. dist.) Ill. 1979, U.S. Ct. Appeals (5th, 6th, 7th, 9th and 11th cirs.), U.S. Ct. Mil. Appeals, U.S. Supreme Ct. 2001. Ptnr. Drinker Biddle Gardner Carton, Chgo., 1979—. Bd. mem. Ctr. for Disability and Elder Law, 2000—, Capt. USMCR. Mem. FBA (labor and employment com. 1996—, trustee 1999—), Chgo. Bar Assn. (chmn. labor and employment com. 1994-95), GSB Chgo. Club. Democrat. Roman Catholic. Office: Drinker Biddle Gardner Carton 191 N Wacker Dr Chicago IL 60606-1698 Office Phone: 312-569-1332. Business E-Mail: mark.furlane@dbr.com.

FURLONG, MARK FRANCIS, diversified financial services company executive, bank executive; b. 1957; BS in Acctg., Fin. and Bus., So. Ill. U., 1981. CPA, Mich. Sr. mgr. KPMG Peat Marwick, 1981—85; audit ptnr. Deloitte & Touche USA LLP, LA, 1985—90; first v.p. H.F. Ahmanson & Co., 1992—98; exec. v.p., CFO Old Kent Fin. Corp., 1998—2001; sr. v.p., CFO Marshall & Ilsley Corp., Milw., 2001—02, exec. v.p., CFO, 2002—04, exec. v.p., 2004—05, pres., 2005—, CEO, 2007—; pres. M&I Marshall & Ilsley Bank, 2004—07, pres., CEO, 2007—. Office: Marshall & Ilsley Corp 770 N Water St Milwaukee WI 53202

FURMAN, ANDY, radio personality; b. Bklyn. BA, Hunter Coll., 1972; MA, Azusa Pacific Coll., 1976. Radio host 700 WLW, Cin., 2000—06. Avocation: running.

FURNEY, LINDA JEANNE, state legislator; b. Toledo, Sept. 11, 1947; d. Robert Ross and Jeanne Scott (Hogan) F. BS in Edn., Bowling Green State U., 1969; postgrad., U. Toledo. Tchr. Washington Local Schs., Toledo, 1969-72, Escola Americano do Rio de Janeiro, 1972-74, Springfield Schs., Holland, Ohio, 1977-83; council mem. City of Toledo, 1983-86; mem. Ohio Senate from 11th dist., Columbus, 1987—. Mem. edn. com., rules com., reference and oversight com., fin. com., econ. devel. com. hwys. and transp. com., state and local govt. and vet. affairs com., asst. minority leader Ohio State Senate, Columbus, 1997-99. Dem. precinct committeewoman Toledo, 1980-90; mem. Toledo Bd. Edn., 1982-83. Recipient Citizen award Ohio Assn. Edn. Young Children, Stanley K. Levinson award Planned Parenthood Northwest Ohio, Educator of Yr. award Phi Delta Kappa, Milestone award Toledo YMCA, Pres. award Ohio Rehab. Assn.; named Person of Yr., Ohio Vocational Assn. Mem. NOW, AAUW, NAACP, ACLU (Found. award), Toledo Mus. Art, Toledo Zoo, Manhattan Dance Co. Home: 2626 Latonia Blvd Toledo OH 43606-3620 Office: Ohio Senate Senate Bldg Rm 051 Columbus OH 43215

FURST-BOWE, JULIE, academic administrator; BA in Journalism, U. Wis., Eau Claire, 1985; MS in Media Tech., U. Wis.-Stout, 1986; cert. in tng. and human resource devel., U. MInn., 1995. Media dir. libr. and media svcs. U. Wis., Waukesha, 1986—87, media specialist Media Devel. Ctr. Eau Claire, 1987—90; mem. faculty U. Wis.-Stout, Menomonie, 1990—94, assoc. prof., 1999, prof., 1999—, dir. grad. program, 1995—97, chmn. dept. comms., 1996—98, assoc. vice chancellor divsn. acad. and student affairs, 1998—, acting dir. Office Continuing Edn., 1998—99. Presenter in field. Contbr. articles to mags. and profl. publs., chpts. to books. Vol. Bolton Refuge House, 1998—98, Challenges and Chouces Career Workship for Young Women, 1988—98, Eau Claire Devel. and Tng. Ctr., 1997; mem. steering com. Eau Claire Women's Network, 1992, 1996; mem. Leadership Chipewa Valley, 1995, Inst. for Learning in Retirement, 1998—99; co-chmn. Menomonie Plan Com., 1997—99. Grantee, U. Wis.-Stout, 1994—97, U. Wis. Sys., 1997—2000. Mem.: AAUW, Wis. Vocat. Assn., Wis. Women in Higher Edn. Leadership., Wis. Edn. Media Assn. (bd. dirs. 1993—96, chmn. pub. rels. com. 1993—96, editor Wis. Ideas in Media jour. 1992—96), Profl. and Orgnl. Devel. etwork, Profl. and Orgnl. Devel. Network (reviewer To Improve the Academy 1998—), North Ctrl. Assn. Summer Schs., Midwest Assn. Grad. Schs., Assn. Ednl. Comms. and Tech. (del. nat. leadership conf. 1994, Ednl. Found. Mentor scholar 1993), Acad. Human Resource Devel. (proposal reviewer, session facilitator 1997—2000, reviewer Internat. Jour. Tng. and Devel. 1998—), Am. Assn. Adult and Continuing Edn., ASTD (HRD prof.'s forum editor 1997, bd. dirs. N.W. Wis. chpt. 1994—97). Office: U Wis-Stout 303 Adminstrn Bldg 712 S Broadway Menomonie WI 54751-0790

FURTH, YVONNE, advertising executive; BS in Mktg., Georgetown U., postgrad., DePaul U. Asst. account exec. Draft Worldwide, 1981—88, gen. mgr., 1988—92, pres. of Chicago office, 1992—96, pres. & COO US operations, 1996—2001, pres., COO Chgo., 2002—06, pres., CEO, 2006—. Adv. coun. mem. Smithsonian Nat. Postal Mus., 2003. Named Direct Mktg. Women of Yr., Chgo. Chpt. of Women in Direct Mktg. Internat., 2003, Advertising Woman of Yr., Chgo. Advertising Fedn. and the Women's Advertising Club Chgo., 2005; named one of Advertising Working Mother of Yr., Working Mother Mag., 2004. Mem.: Chgo. Assn. Direct Mktg., Direct Mktg. Assn. Office: Draft Chicago 633 N St Clair St Chicago IL 60611

FUSARO, RAMON MICHAEL, dermatologist, preventive medicine physician, researcher; b. Bklyn., Mar. 6, 1927; s. Angelo and Ida (Pucci) F.; m. Lavonne Johnsen, Nov. 6, 1971; children: Lisa Ann, Toni Ann; stepsons: Jeff, Scott. BA, U. Minn., 1949, BS, 1951, MD, 1953, MS, 1958, PhD, 1965. Diplomate Am. Bd. Dermatology. Intern Mpls. Gen. Hosp., 1953-54, resident in dermatology, 1954—57; from instr. to assoc. prof. U. Minn., 1957-70, dir. outpatient dermatology clinic, 1962-70; prof., chmn. dept. dermatology U. Nebr. Med. Center, Omaha, 1970-82; prof. dermatology sect. dept. internal medicine U. Nebr. Med. Ctr., Omaha, 1982—, acting chief sect. dermatology, 1991-94; prof., chmn. dept. dermatology Creighton U., Omaha, 1975-87; prof. dermatology dept. internal medicine Creighton U. Sch. Medicine, Omaha, 1983-89; prof. Creighton U., Omaha, 1989—; dir. dermatology residency program Creighton/Nebr. Univs. Health Found., 1975-83; prof. dept. pub. health and preventive medicine Hereditary Cancer Inst., Creighton U., 1984—. Adj. prof. coll. pharmacy dept. pharmaceutical scis. Creighton U., 2007—. Contbr. more than 300 articles to profl. publs., chpts. to books. With USN, 1944-46. Mem. Am. Acad. Dermatology, Sigma Xi. Home: 908 Beaver Lake Blvd Plattsmouth NE 68048-4500 Office: 984360 Nebr Med Ctr Omaha NE 68198-4360 also: Creighton U Med Sch Nixon-Lied Bldg Dept Prev Med 2500 California Plz Omaha NE 68178-0403 Personal E-mail: fusarorm@comweb.net. Business E-Mail: rmfusaro@creighton.edu.

FYE, W. BRUCE, III, cardiologist; b. Meadville, Pa., Sept. 25, 1946; s. W. Bruce Jr. and Anne Elizabeth (Schreck) F.; m. Lois Eileen Baker, May 10, 1969; children: Katherine Anne, Elizabeth Jane. AB, Johns Hopkins U., 1968, MD, 1972, MA in Med. History, 1978. Diplomate Am. Bd. Internal Medicine, Am. Bd. Cardiovascular Diseases. Intern N.Y. Hosp.—Cornell Med. Ctr., NYC, 1972-73, asst. resident, 1973-74, sr. asst. resident, 1974-75, fellow cardiology, 1975; fellow in cardiology Johns Hopkins U. Sch. Medicine, Balt., 1975-77, postdoctoral fellow in med. history, 1976-78, instr. in medicine, 1977-78; dir. cardiographics lab. Marshfield (Wis.) Clinic, 1978-99, chmn. dept. cardiology, 1981-99, dir. noninvasive cardiology, 1999; assoc. prof. medicine Med. Coll. Wis., Milw., 1988-99; prof. medicine and history medicine Mayo Clin. Coll. of Medicine, Rochester, Minn., 2000—. Vice chief of staff St. Joseph's Hosp., Marshfield, 1989-99, exec. com., bd. dirs., 1994-97; clin. prof. medicine, adj. prof. history medicine U. Wis., Madison, 1990—; sr. assoc. cons. Mayo Clinic, Rochester, 2000, cons., 2001—; dir. Mayo Clinic Ctr. for the History of Medicine, 2006—. Author: The Development of American Physiology, 1987; editor: William Osler's Collected Papers on the Cardiovascular System, 1985, Classic Papers on Coronary Thrombosis and Myocardial Infarction, 1991; editor-in-chief: Classics of Cardiology Library, 1985—; author: American Cardiology; The History of a Specialty and Its College, 1996; mem. editl. bd. Marshfield Med. Bull., 1985-95, Am. Jour. Cardiology, 1990—, Clin. Cardiology, 1994—; co-editor (with J. Willis Hurst, Richard Conti, W. Bruce Fye): Profiles in Cardiology, 2003. Named to Soc. Scholars, Johns Hopkins U., 2005. Fellow Am. Coll. Cardiology (chmn. libr. com. 1991, historian 1991—, gov. Wis. chpt. 1993-96, steering com. bd. govs., 1994—, nominating com., 1994-96, chair govt. rels. com. 1996-99, trustee 1997—, v.p. 1999—, pres. 2002—); mem. State Med. Soc. Wis. (alt. del. 1990-94), Am. Hist. Assn., Am. Osler Soc. (pres. 1988-89), Am. Heart Assn. (exec. com. coun. on clin. cardiology 1991-97, chmn. membership com. coun. on clin. cardiology 1994-97, chair credentials com. coun. on clin. cardiology 1994-97), Inst. for Study of Cardiovasc. Medicine (bd. dirs. 1994—), Am. Assn. History of Medicine (program chair 1987, v.p. 2006-), Found. Advances in Medicine and Sci., Johns Hopkins Soc. Scholars, Phi Beta Kappa, Alpha Omega Alpha, Grolier Club. Presbyterian. Avocation: collecting and selling antiquarian medical books. Home: 1533 Seasons Ln SW Rochester MN 55902 Office: Mayo Clinic Coll of Medicine 200 1st St SW Rochester MN 55905-0002 Office Phone: 507-266-4130. Business E-Mail: fye.bruce@mayo.edu.

GABARRA, CARIN LESLIE, professional soccer player, professional soccer coach; b. East Orange, NJ, Jan. 9, 1965; m. Jim Gabarra. Degree in bus. mgmt., U. Calif., Santa Barbara, 1987. Mem. U.S. Nat. Women's Soccer Team, 1987—96; head coach, women's soccer Westmont Coll., 1987—88; assist. coach, women's Soccer Harvard U., Boston, 1988—93; head coach, women's soccer Navy, 1993—. Mem. U.S. Olympic World Festival team, 1986—89; mem. women's soccer U.S. Naval Acad., 1993. Named U.S. Soccer's Female Athlete of Yr., 1987, 1992; named to, U. Calif.-Santa Barbara Athletic Hall of Fame; recipient Golden Ball, FIFA Women's World Championship, China, 1991, gold medal, Atlanta Summer Olympic Games, 1996. Achievements include ranked as 3d-leading goal scorer in U.S. women's history; mem. CONCACAF Championship team, 1993, 94. Office: c/o US Soccer Fedn 1801 S Prairie Ave # 1811 Chicago IL 60616-1319

GABBARD, GLEN OWENS, psychiatrist, psychotherapist; b. Charleston, Ill., Aug. 8, 1949; s. Earnest Glendon and Lucina Mildred (Paquet) G.; children: Matthew, Abigail, Amanda, Allison; m. Joyce Eileen Davidson, June 14, 1985. BS, Eastern Ill. U., 1972; MD, Rush Med. Coll., 1975; degree in psychoanalytic tng., Topeka Inst. for Psychoanalysis, 1984. Diplomate Am. Bd. Psychiatry and Neurology. Resident in psychiatry Menninger Sch. Psychiatry, Topeka, 1975-78, mem. faculty, 1978—; staff psychiatrist C.F. Menninger Hosp., Topeka, 1978-83, sect. chief, 1984-89. Med. dir., 1989-94; tng. analyst Topeka Inst. for Psychoanalysis, 1989-2001, dir., 1996-2001; v.p. for adult svcs. Menninger Clinic, 1991-94; clin. prof. psychiatry U. Kans. Med. Sch., 1991-2001; Callaway Disting. prof. Menninger Clinic and Karl Menninger Sch. Psychiatry, 1994-2001; prof. psychiatry Baylor Coll. Medicine, 2001—, Brown Found. chair psychoanalysis, 2003—. Author: With the Eyes of the Mind, 1984, Psychiatry and the Cinema, 1987, 2d edit., 1999, Medical Marriages, 1988, Sexual Exploitation in Professional Relationships, 1989, Psychodynamic Psychiatry in Clinical Practice, 1990, Portuguese transl., 1992, Italian transl., 1992, 2d edit., 1994, Korean transl., 1996, Japanese transl., 1997, 4th edit., 2005, Treatments of Psychiatric Disorders: the DSM-IV Edition, 1995; meml. editl. bd. Am. Jour. Psychiatry, Am. Psychiat. Press; joint editor-in-chief Internat. Jour. Psychoanalysis; contbr. articles to profl. jours. V.p. Topeka Civic Theatre, 1981-82, pres. 1982-83, bd. dirs. 1981-83. Named one of Outstanding Young Men in Am. U.S. Jaycees, 1984. Mem. AAAS, Am. Psychoanalytic Assn. (assoc. editor jour., mem. editl. bd.), Am. Psychiat. Assn. (Falk fellow 1976, Edward A. Strecker award 1994, Disting. Psychiatrist lectr. 1995, C. Charles Burlingame award 1997, Mary S. Sigourney award 2000, Disting. Svc. award 2002, Adolf Meyer award 2004), Sch. Psychotherapy Rsch., Menninger Sch. Psychiatry Alumni Assn. (pres. 1982-83), Alpha Omega Alpha. Avocations: theater, music. Home: 1290 Jimmy Phillips Blvd Angleton TX 77515 Office: Dept Psychiatry Baylor Coll Medicine One Baylor Plz MS 350 Houston TX 77030 Office Phone: 713-798-6397. Business E-Mail: ggabbard@bcm.tmc.edu.

GABOURY, DAVID, engineering company executive; BSCE, U. Mass.; MSCE, MIT; grad. in bus., Harvard U. Pres. Woodward Clyde Cons.; with Terracon, Lenexa, Kans., 1997—, pres., COO, 2000—. Mem.: ASCE, Water Environ. Fedn. Office: Ferracon 16000 College Blvd Shawnee Mission KS 66219

GABRIEL, D. BRUCE, lawyer; b. Peoria, Ill., 1954; BA, Coe Coll., 1976; JD, Northwestern U., 1980. Bar: Ohio 1980. Ptnr. Squire, Sanders & Dempsey LLP, Cleve., chmn., Pub. Revenue Fin. Practice Group. Office: Squire Sanders & Dempsey 4900 Key Tower 127 Public Sq Ste 4900 Cleveland OH 44114-1304 Office Phone: 216-479-8746. Office Fax: 216-479-8780. Business E-Mail: dbgabriel@ssd.com.

GABRIEL, LARRY EDWARD, state legislator; b. Philip, SD, Oct. 10, 1946; s. Floyd O. and Tressa (Coleman) G.; m. Charlotte Ann Burns, 1967; childen: Malynda Sue, Jeffrey Allen. BS, S.D. State U., 1970. Mem. Haakon County Commn., S.D., 1974-82, S.D. Ho. of Reps., 1985-92, 93—, asst. majority whip, 1992-98, chmn. taxation com., mem. local govt. com., mem. legis. procedure and state affairs com.; rancher Cottonwood, S.D., 1970—; agrl. sec. State of S.D., 2000—. Mem. S.D. Stockgrower's Assn. (dir. 1982). Home: HC 84 Box 22 Cottonwood SD 57775-9421

GABRIEL, MICHAEL, psychology professor; b. Phila., May 5, 1940; s. Michael and Josephine (Alesio) G.; m. Linda Prinz, June, 1967 (div.); 1 child, Joseph Michael; m. Sonda S. Walsh, 1984. AB in Psychology, St. Joseph's Coll., 1962; MA, U. Wis., 1965, PhD, 1967. Asst. prof. Pomona Coll., Claremont, Calif., 1967—70; staff psychologist Pacific State Hosp., Pomona, Calif., 1968-70; NIMH sr. postdoctoral fellow U. Calif.-Irvine, 1970-72; asst. prof. U. Tex.-Austin, 1973-77, assoc. prof., 1977-82; prof. psychology U. Ill., Urbana, 1982—2004, appointee Ctr. for Advanced Study, 1990-91, prof. emeritus dept. psychology and Beckman Inst., 2004. Area chmn. Biol. Psychology Program, U. Tex., Austin, 1979-82; mem. rev. panel in behavioral and neural scis. NSF, 1988-91, prin. investigator database system for neuronal pattern analysis project, 1992—, ad hoc mem. biopsychology rev. panel, 1997-98; faculty Beckman Inst., U. Ill., Urbana, 1989—; chmn. Neuronal Pattern Analysis Group, Beckman Inst., mem. neuroinformatics rev. panel, NIH, 2000-. Co-editor: (with J. Moore) Learning and Computational Neuroscience: Foundations of Adaptive Networks, 1989, (with B. Vogt) Neurobiology of Cingulate Cortex and Limbic Thalamus, 1993; mem. editl. bd. Neural Plasticity, Neurobiology of Learning and Memory. Grantee NIMH, 1978-88, 1998-2002, NIH, 1988-2003, Air Force Office Sci. Rsch., 1988-91, NSF, 1992-2003, NIDA, 1996-2001. Fellow Am. Psychol. Soc., Internat. Behavioral Neurosci. Soc.; mem. Sigma Chi. pioneered methods for multi-site recording and analysis of neuronal activity during learning in behaving animal subjects; identification of key elements of the neural circuitry for avoidance learning; made major breakthroughs in understanding neural circuitry for contextual facilitation of memory retrieval; documentation of specific functional brain changes resulting from exposure to cocaine in utero. Office: Beckman Inst Univ Ill Urbana IL 61801-2325 Business E-Mail: mgabriel@uiuc.edu.

GADSBY, MONICA M., marketing executive; b. Brazil; m. Jon Gadsby; 3 children. BA in Liberal Arts, Univ. Tex., 1987, BS in Advt., 1987. Media asst., Procter & Gamble acct. Leo Burnett USA, Chgo., 1987, founding mem., Hispanic unit, 1987; now mng. dir., CEO, Tapestry Mktg. Agy. Starcom MediaVest Group, Chgo. Bd. dir. Pangea Ptnrs. Named Media Planning Exec. Yr., HispanicAd.com and Assn. Hispanic Advt. Agencies, 2002; named one of Top 42 US Hispanic Women, Vanidades Mag., 2003, 100 Most Influential Women, Crain's Chgo. Bus., 2004. Mem.: IAB Hispanic Com., Assn. Hispanic Advt. Agencies (co-chair, media com.). Fluent in Spanish, Portuguese, French, English. Office: Tapestry Mktg 35 W Wacker Dr Chicago IL 60601 Office Fax: 312-220-3381, 312-220-6561. Business E-Mail: monicam.gadsby@tapestrypartners.com.

GAFFNEY, EDWARD MCGLYNN, law educator, dean; b. San Francisco, Aug. 18, 1941; s. Edward McGlynn and Mary Catherine (Wright) G.; m. Jane Ann Mullen, Feb. 1972 (div. Feb. 1982); children: Margaret Mairead, Elizabeth Atkins; m. A'ine O'Healy, May 29, 1982; 1 child: Deirdre Miriam. BA, St. Patrick's Coll., 1963; STL, Gregorian U., Rome, 1967; JD, MA in History, Cath. U., 1975; LLM, Harvard U., 1976. Bar: Calif. 1990, U.S. Ct. Appeals (D.C. cir.) 1975, U.S. Ct. Appeals (7th cir.) 1980, U.S. Ct. Appeals (5th and 11th cirs.) 1981, U.S. Ct. Appeals (9th cir.) 1983, U.S. Ct. Appeals (2d cir.) 1985, U.S. Dist. Ct. (ctrl. dist.) Calif. 1990, U.S. Dist. Ct. (so. dist.) Ind. 1992, U.S. Supreme Ct. 1980. Assoc. dir. Nat. Conf. Cath. Bishops Ecumenical and Interreligious Com., Washington, 1970-72; atty. advisor Office of Atty Gen. U.S. Dept. of Justice, Washington, 1976-77; assoc. dir. Ctr. for Constitutional Studies, Notre Dame, Ind., 1977-81, dir., 1981-83; Bradley prof. constitutional law Loyola Law Sch., LA, 1983-85, assoc. prof., 1985-89; scholar in residence Stanford Law Sch., Palo Alto, Calif., 1989-90; dean and prof. law Valparaiso (Ind.) U. Sch. of Law, 1990-97; scholar-in-residence Pepperdine U. Sch. of Law, Malibu, Calif., 1997-98; prof. law Valparaiso U. Sch. of Law, 1998—. Mem. bd. editors Jour. Law and Religion, St. Paul, 1980—2004; ednl. cons. Williamsburg Ctr. Found., Washington, 1987—89; bd. dirs. Ctr. for Constl. Studies, Waco, Tex., 1990—, Christian Legal Soc., Annandale, Va., 1992—98, Ind. Bar Found., Ind. Continuing Legal Forum; dir. of content Nat. Constl. Ctr., Phila., 2000—01; Straus disting. vis. prof. Pepperdine U. Sch. Law, Malibu, Calif., 2002—03. Author: Government and Campus, 1980, State and Campus, 1982, Ascending Liability in Religious and Non-Profit Organizations, 1983, Church and Campus, 1989; co-author (with John T. Noonan Jr.): Religious Freedom, 2001; editor: Public Schools and the Private Good, 1981; editor, contbr.: Religious Organizations in the United States, 2005. Recipient Champion of Justice award, Am. Forum for Jewish-Christian Cooperation, Washington, 1981, Lifetime Achievement award, Jour. Law and Religion, 2005. Fellow Ctr. for Ch.-State Studies, Internat. Acad. for Freedom of Religion and Belief; mem. ABA, Am. Law Inst., Assn. Am. Law Schs. (chmn. sect. on law and religion, sect. on law and edn. 1981-83). Democrat. Roman Catholic. Office: Valparaiso U Sch of Law Wesemann Hall Valparaiso IN 46383

GAGE, EDWIN C., III, (SKIP GAGE), travel and marketing services executive; b. Evanston, Ill., Nov. 1, 1940; s. Edwin Cutting and Margaret (Stackhouse) G.; m. Barbara Ann Carlson, June 26, 1965; children— Geoff, Scott, Christine, Richard BS in Bus. Adminstrn., Northwestern U., 1963, MS in Journalism, 1965. Account exec. Foote, Cone and Belding, 1965-68, dir. mktg. devel. & rsch., 1968-70; v.p. direct mktg. Carlson Mktg. Group of Carlson Cos., Mpls., 1970-75, exec. v.p., 1975-77, pres., 1977-83, also bd. dirs.; exec. v.p., COO Carlson Cos. Inc., Mpls., 1983, pres., CEO, 1984-89, pres., chief exec. officer, 1989-91; now chmn., CEO Gage Marketing Group, Mpls. Bd. dirs. Gage Mktg. Group, Carlson Holdings Inc., Carlson Real Estate, Carlson Real Estate Co., Inc., Supervalu Stores Inc., Fingerhut Cos., Kellogg adv. bd. Northwestern U., Minn. Coun. Quality, Mpls. Inst. Arts. Lt. USN. Mem. Young Pres. Orgn., Minn. Execs. Orgn. Avocations: music, tennis, golf, hunting, fishing. Office: Gage Marketing Group 10000 Highway 55 Ste 100 Minneapolis MN 55441-6365

GAGE, FRED KELTON, lawyer; b. Mpls., June 20, 1925; s. Fred K. and Vivian L. G.; m. Dorothy Ann, Sept. 7, 1974; children: Deborah, Penelope, Amy, Lawrence. BS, U. Minn., 1948, LLB, 1950. Bar: Minn. 1950. Assoc. Wilson, Blethen & Ogle, Mankato, 1950-55; ptnr. Blethen, Gage, Krause, Blethen, Corcoran, Berkland & Peterson and predecessor firms, Mankato, 1955-90, of counsel, 1991—. Mem. State Bd. Profl. Responsibility, Minn. Supreme Ct., 1974-82, mem. legal svcs. adv. com., 1996—. Mem. Mankato Sch. Bd., 1957-66, Minn. State Coll. Bd., 1960-64; mem. Minn. Senate from 11th Legis. Dist., 1966-72; Mem. Minn. Sports Facilities Commn., 1976-84. Served with USN, 1943-46. Named Mankato Outstanding Young Man of Yr., 1956, Outstanding Man of Minn., Mankato Jr. C. of C., 1958 Fellow Am. Bar Found.; mem. ABA (assembly del. 1980-86), Minn. Bar Assn. (chmn. tax sect. 1956-58, pres. 1977-78), Order of Coif. Methodist. Office: Blethen Gage & Krause PO Box 3049 127 S 2nd St Mankato MN 56001-3658 E-mail: kgage@bglow.com.

GAGGINI, JOHN EDMUND, lawyer; b. Chgo., Dec. 17, 1949; BA cum laude, Knox Coll., 1971; MS, Ohio U., 1972, JD magna cum laude, 1975; LLM, NYU, 1976. Bar: Ill. 1975, D.C. 1977; CPA, Ill. Law clk. to Hon. Shiro Kashiwa U.S. Ct. Claims, 1976-77; ptnr. McDermott, Will & Emery, Chgo. Adj. prof. law Chgo.-Kent Coll. Law, 1987—. Mem. ABA, Ill. State Bar Assn., Chgo. Bar Assn. (chmn. state and local tax com. 1986-87), Phi Kappa Phi, Phi Beta Kappa, Beta Alpha Psi, Phi Gamma Mu, Phi Alpha Delta. Office: McDermott Will & Emery 227 W Monroe St Ste 4700 Chicago IL 60606-5096 Home Phone: 708-424-1804; Office Phone: 312-984-7533.

GAGGIOLI, RICHARD ARNOLD, mechanical engineering educator; b. Highwood, Ill., Dec. 3, 1934; s. Gustavo and Constantina Lucille (Mordini) G.; m. Anita Catherine Sage, Nov. 9, 1957; children: Catherine Anne, Michael James, Daniel Richard, Edward Thomas, Mary Esther. BME, Northwestern U., Evanston, Ill., 1957, MS (NSF fellow), 1958; PhD (Gen. Electric, NSF fellow), U. Wis., 1961. Registered profl. engr., Wis., 1965. Coop. student engr. Abbott Labs. (pharms.), North Chicago, Ill., 1954-58; asst. prof. mech. engring. U. Wis., Madison, 1962-66, assoc. prof., 1966-69; prof., chmn. dept. mech. engring. Marquette U., Milw., 1969-72, prof., 1969—81, 1990—2001, rsch. prof., 2002—; dean engring. and architecture Cath. U. Am., Washington, 1981-84; prof. mech. engring. U. Mass., Lowell, 1985-89. Mem. U.S. Army Math. Rsch. Ctr., Madison, 1964-66; NSF-Soc. Indsl. and Applied Math. vis. lectr., 1969-72, engring. cons., 1970—. Author: (with E.F. Obert) Thermo-dynamics, 1963; editor: Thermodynamics-Second Law Analysis, Vol. 1, 1980, Vol. 2, 1983, Analysis of Energy Systems, 1985, Computer-Aided Engineering of Energy Systems, 1986; (with M.J. Moran) Analysis and Design of Advanced Energy Systems: Fundamentals, 1987; (with G. Tsatsaronis) Fundamentals of Thermodynamics and Energy Analysis, 1990; (with G.M. Reistad) Thermodynamics and Energy Systems: Fundamentals, 1991, (with R.F. Boehm et al.) Thermodynamics and the Design of Energy Systems, 1992; hon. editor Internat. Jour. Applied Thermodynamics, 1998-2004; contbr. articles to profl. jours. Chmn. bd. trustees Montrose Sch., Westwood, Mass., 1987-89. Recipient Emil H. Steiger Meml. Tchg. award U. Wis., 1965, Pere Marquette award Marquette U., 1976, Best Paper award Am. Chem. Soc. Chem. Tech. jour. 1977; NSF postdoctoral fellow chem. engring. U. Wis., 1961-62; vis. fellow Battelle Meml. Inst., 1968-69; invited lectr., Rome, 1987, 95, Shanghai, 1986, Dalian, 1986, Beijing 1986, 89, 97, Abu Dhabi, 1988, Zaragoza 1993, Florence, 1989, 2003, Athens, 1991, Istanbul, 1995, 2008, Bucharest, 1997, Nancy, 1997, Krakow, 1994, 98, 2008, Tokyo, 1999, Padova, 2007, others. Fellow ASME (life; James Harry Potter gold medal 1988, advanced energy sys. divsn. best paper award 1991, E.F. Obert best paper award 2000); mem. AIChE, Summit Edn. Assn. (sec., trustee 1993—), Sigma Xi, Pi Tau Sigma, Tau Beta Pi. Roman Catholic. Office: Marquette U Dept Mech Engring Milwaukee WI 53201-1881 Home: 67 Palm Forest Dr Largo FL 33770 Office Phone: 414-430-5240. Business E-Mail: richard.gaggioli@marquette.edu.

GAGNON, CRAIG WILLIAM, lawyer; b. St. Cloud, Minn., Dec. 19, 1940; s. Marvin Sylvester and Signa Gunhild (Johnson) G.; children: Nicole, Jeffrey, Camille; m. Pam Peglow, Nov. 8, 1980; children: Claire, Jillian, Jane. BA, U. Minn., 1964; JD magna cum laude, William Mitchell Coll. Law, 1968. Bar: Minn. 1968, U.S. Dist. Ct. Minn. 1968, U.S. Tax Ct. 1972, U.S. Supreme Ct. 1970. Ptnr. Oppenheimer, Wolff & Donnelly, Mpls., 1968—. Chmn. bd. Equity Bank; bd. dirs. XOX Corp., First Fla. Bank. Trustee William Mitchell Coll. Law, St. Paul. 1989—, chmn. bd., 1999-2000. Named Alumnus of Notable Achievement, U. Minn. Fellow Am. Coll. Trial Lawyers; mem. Metro Breakfast Club (pres. 1993), Am. Bd. Trial Advocates (assoc.), Am. Law Inst. Avocations: hunting, fishing, golf. Home: 4807 Sunnyside Rd Edina MN 55424-1109 Office: Oppenheimer Wolff & Donnelly 45 S 7th St Ste 3400 Minneapolis MN 55402-1609 E-mail: cgagnon@oppenheimer.com.

GAINES, BARBARA, theater director; Degree, Northwestern U., 1969. Founding artistic dir. Chgo. (Ill.) Shakespeare Theatre, 1997—. Artistic dir. Globe Theatre, London; bd. trustees Northwestern U.; panel me. NEA. Mem. editl. bd.: Chgo. (Ill.) Reporter. Recipient Jeff award. Office: Chicago Shakespeare Theatre 800 E Grand Ave Chicago IL 60611

GAINES, BENNETT L., utilities executive; married; 1 child. BA in Socio-econs., Baldwin-Wallace Coll.; MBA, U. Phoenix. With IBM Corp., Minn., Ariz., Ky., NY and Asia, 1978—91; regional sales mgr., dir. mktg. Hamilton-Hallmark Corp., Phila. and Phoenix, 1991—94; v.p. consumer ops. McKesson, Dallas, 1994—98; corp. dir. strategic sourcing EDS Corp., Dallas, 1998—2000; corp. dir. supply and operating svc. LT&E Energy Corp., Louisville, 2000—01; with Cinergy Corp., Cin., 2001—, v.p., chief tech. officer, 2003—. Bd. dirs. Family and Children's Counseling Ctr., Louisville; rep. corp. contbns. United Way; bd. dirs. Am. Sports Inst., Mill Valley, Calif. Office: Cinergy Corp 139 E 4th St Cincinnati OH 45202

GAINES, BRENDA J., retired financial services company executive; b. Chgo., July 22, 1949; d. Clarence and DeLouise Gaines. BA, U. Ill., 1970; MA, Roosevelt U., 1976. Spl. asst. to regional adminstr then dep. regional adminstr. US Dept. Housing & Urban Devel., Chgo.; commr. Housing Authority City of Chgo., dep. chief staff to Mayor Harold Washington, 1985—87; advanced through co. in govt. and cmty. rels. to sr. v.p. residential lending Citigroup, Inc., Chgo., 1988—92; sr. v.p. Diners Club N.Am. (subsidiary of Citigroup), Chgo., 1992—99, pres., 1999—2004. Mem. Diners Club Internat. Global bd.; bd. dirs. CNA Financial, Nicor, Inc., Tenet Healthcare Corp., Office Depot, Inc, Fannie Mae, 2006—. Named Volunteer of the Yr., Boys & Girls Club Chgo., 1999; named one of 50 Most Powerful Black Executives in Am., Fortune, 2002, Chicago's 100 Most Influential Women, Crain's Chicago Business, 2004; recipient Black Achievers in Industry award, 1995, Pioneer award, Urban Bankers Forum, 1996, Woman of Achievement award, Anti-Defamation League, Otto Wirth award, Roosevelt U., 2000.

GAINES, RUTH ANN, secondary school educator; BA in Drama and Speech, Clarke Coll.; MA in Dramatic Art, U. Calif., Santa Barbara. Tchr. drama East High Sch., Des Moines, 1971—. Host Classroom Connection Cable TV; former TV/radio prodr., talk show host TCI of Ctrl. Iowa, WHO; diversity facilitator Heartland Area Edn. Agy., Des Moines, 1979—; instr. speech and drama Des Moines Area C.C., 1971—. Bd. dirs. Very Spl. Arts, Hospice of Ctrl. Iowa, Westminster Ho.; former bd. dirs. YWCA of Greater Des Moines, Polk County Mental Health Assn., Drama Workshop, Des Moines Tutoring Ctr.; vice chair City Wide Strategic Plan, 1994-95; state senate candidate, 1994; racial justice coord. YWCA, 1992-93; chair Cross Cultural Rels., Des Moines Area Religious Coun., 1988-89; dir. religious edn. St. Ambrose Cathedral, 1981-83; grad. Leadership Iowa Class of 1997. Recipient Wal-Mart Tchr. of Yr., 1998, Iowa Tchr. of Yr., 1998, Angel in Adoption award, 1999, Friends of Iowa Civil Rights Commn. Tchr. of Yr. award, 2000, U. Iowa's Phyllis M. Yeager Commitment to Diversity award, 2001, I'll Make Me a World in Iowa Heritage Legacy, 2002, Des Moines Bus. Records' Woman of Influence, 2002, USA Today's All USA Tchr. Recognition 3d Team, 2002; grad. Greater Des Moines Leadership Inst., 2002; inducted into Nat. Tchr. Hall of Fame, 2003. Mem. Iowa Edn. Assn., Des

Moines Edn. Assn., Delta Kappa Gamma, Phi Delta Kappa, Delta Sigma Theta, Delta Kappa Pi. Home: 3501 Oxford St Des Moines IA 50313-4562 Office: East High Sch 815 E 13th St Des Moines IA 50316-3499

GAINES, WILLIAM CHESTER, journalist; b. Indpls., Nov. 1, 1933; s. Philip Damon and Georgia Agnes (Smith) G.; m. Nellie Gilyan; children: Michael, Michelle, Matthew. BS in Broadcasting, Butler U., 1956. TV announcer Sta. WKZO-TV, Kalamazoo, 1958-59; reporter Sta. WWCA Radio, Gary, Ind., 1959-60, Sta. WJOB Radio, Hammond, Ind., 1960-63; pres. Sta. WAMJ Radio, South Bend, Ind., 1983-88; from reporter to investigative reporter Chgo. Tribune, 1963—. Instr. Columbia Coll., Chgo., 1974-98; bd. advisors Fund for Investigative Journalism, Inc.; prof. journalism, Knight chair investigative/enterprise journalism, U. Ill., 2001—. Author: Investigative Reporting in Print and Broadcast, 1992. Recipient Pulitzer prize in Journalism, Columbia U., N.Y.C., 1976, 1988, Peter Lisagor award Chgo. Headline Club, 1986, 87.

GAINEY, HARVEY NUETON, transportation executive; b. Nicholls, Ga., Nov. 20, 1942; s. Lloyd Fryar and Rita Mae (Tanner) G.; m. Annie Ereveene, Nov. 9, 1962; children: Angela Marie, Harvey Neuton Jr. Student, Jacksonville U., Fla., 1964. Traffic mgr. Ryder Truck Lines, Jacksonville, 1964-70; v.p. sales Helms Express, Irwin, Pa., 1970-80; pres. Interstate Motor Freight, Grand Rapids, Mich., 1980-84; pres., prin., chmn. bd. dirs. Gainey Transportation Services Inc., Grand Rapids, 1984—. Bd. dirs. Cen. States Motor Bur., Chgo., Am. Trucking Assn., Washington, Eastern Cen. Motor Carriers, Akron, Ohio. Republican. Office: Gainey Transportation Services Inc 5976 Clay Ave SW Grand Rapids MI 49548-5790

GAITAN, FERNANDO J., JR., federal judge; b. 1948; Student, Kans. City CC, 1966-67, Donnelly Coll., 1967-68, Pittsburg State U., 1968-70; JD, U. Mo., Kansas City, 1974. Atty. Southwestern Bell Telephone Co., 1974-80; judge 16th jud. cir. Jackson County Cir. Ct., 1980-86; judge Mo. Ct. Appeals (we. dist.), 1986-91; fed. judge U.S. Dist. Ct. (we. dist.) Mo., Kansas City, 1991—. Dir. Truman Libr. Inst., 2001—. Past pres. bd. dirs. De La Salle Edn. Ctr., Inc., 1985-87, active, 1983—; active Kansas City Mus., 1988—, St. Luke's Hosp., Kansas City, 1984—, NAACP, 1982—, NCCJ, 1984—. Mem. ABA, Mo. Bar Assn., Kansas City Met. Bar Assn., Lawyers' Assn., Jackson County Bar Assn., Univ. Club, Hillcrest Country Club, U. Mo. Kansas City Law Found., KCMC Child Devel. Corp., Kappa Alpha Psi. Office: US Dist Ct 7952 US Cthouse 400 E 9th St Kansas City MO 64106-2607

GAJL-PECZALSKA, KAZIMIERA J., retired surgical pathologist, immunopathologist, educator; b. Warsaw, Nov. 15, 1925; came to U.S., 1970; d. Kazimierz Emil and Anna Janina (Gervais) Gajl; widowed; children: Kazimierz Peczalski, Andrew Peczalski. Student, Jagiellonian Univ., Cracov, Poland, 1945-47; MD, Warsaw U., Poland, 1951, PhD in Immunopathology, 1964. Diplomate Polish Bd. Pediatrics, Polish Bd. Anatomic Pathology, Am. Bd. Pathology. Attending pediatrician Children's Hosp. for Infectious Diseases, Warsaw, Poland, 1953-58, head, pathology lab., 1958-65; adj. prof. Postgrad. Med. Sch., Warsaw, Poland, 1965-70; fellow U. Minn., Mpls., 1970-72, asst. prof. dept. pathology, 1972-75, assoc. prof. dept. pathology, 1975-79, prof. dept. pathology, 1979-00, dir. immunophenotyping and flow lab., 1974-00, dir. cytology dept. pathology, 1976-95; ret., 2000. Author chpts. to book; contbr. of numerous papers to profl. jours. Fellow WHO, Paris, 1959, London, 1962, Paris, 1967, U.S. Pub. Health Svcs. fellow, 1968-69; recipient Scientific Com. award Polish Ministry of Health and Social Welfare, 1964. Mem. Am. Soc. Experimental Pathology, Am. Soc. Cytology, Internat. Acad. Pathology, British Soc. Pediatric Pathology, Polish Soc. Pathology, Polish Soc Pediatricians. Roman Catholic. Avocations: music, skiing. Personal E-mail: kgajl002@gmail.com.

GALAINENA, M. DAVID, lawyer; b. Cleve., Nov. 9, 1957; BA magna cum laude, Tulane U., 1980; JD, U. Notre Dame, 1983. Bar: Ill. 1983. Ptnr. Winston & Strawn LLP, Chgo., 1995—, mem. exec. com. Mem.: Phi Beta Kappa. Office: Winston & Strawn LLP 35 W Wacker Dr Chicago IL 60601-9703 Office Phone: 312-558-7442. Office Fax: 312-558-5700. E-mail: dgalainena@winston.com.

GALAMBOS, THEODORE VICTOR, civil engineer, educator; b. Budapest, Hungary, Apr. 17, 1929; s. Paul and Magdalena (Potzner) G.; m. Barbara Ann Asp, June 25, 1957; children: Paul, Ruth, Ronald, John. BSCE, U. ND, 1953, MSCE, 1954; PhD in CE, Lehigh U., 1959; Dr. honoris causa, Tech. U., Budapest, 1982; PhD (hon.), U. ND, 1998; DSc (hon.), U. Minn., 2001. Registered profl. engr. Minn., Mo. From asst. to assoc. prof. civil engring. Lehigh U., Bethlehem, Pa., 1959-65; prof. Washington U., St. Louis, 1965-81, head dept., 1970-78; prof. U. Minn., Mpls., 1981-96, emeritus prof., 1997—. Cons. engr. Steel Joist Inst., Myrtle Beach, S.C., 1965-2003; vis. prof. U.S. Mil. Acad., West Point, 1990. Author, co-author 4 books in field; editor 1 book; contbr. over 100 articles to profl. jours. Served with U.S. Army, 1954-56. Recipient T.R. Higgins award Am. Inst. Steel Constrn., 1981. Mem. ASCE (hon., Norman medal 1983, Shortridge Hardesty award 1988, E.E. Howard award 1992, OPAL award 2002, Walter P. Moore award 2004, Nathan M. Newmark medal 2004), NAE, Internat. Assn. Bridge and Structural Engrs. Democrat. Baptist. Avocation: photography. Home: 4375 Wooddale Ave Minneapolis MN 55424-1060 Office: U Minn Civil Engring Dept Minneapolis MN 55455 Business E-Mail: galam001@umn.edu.

GALANIS, JOHN WILLIAM, lawyer; b. Milw., May 9, 1937; s. William and Angeline (Koroniou) G.; m. Patricia Caro, Nov. 29, 1969; children: Lia Galanis Economou, William, Charles, John. BBA cum laude, U. Wis., 1959; JD, U. Mich., 1963; postgrad. (Ford Found. grantee), London Sch. Econs., 1964. Bar: Wis. 1965; CPA, Wis. Assoc. firm Whyte & Hirschboeck S.C., Milw., 1964-68; sr. v.p., gen. counsel, sec. MGIC Investment Corp. and Mortgage Guaranty Ins. Corp., Milw., 1968-88; ptnr. Galanis, Pollack, Jacobs & Johnson, S.C., Milw., 1988—. Assoc. editor: Mich. Law Rev, 1962-63. Bd. visitors Law Sch. U. Mich., Sch. Bus. U. Wis.; past chmn. Milw. Found.; bd. dir., past pres. Milw. Boys' and Girls' Club; pres. Family Svc. Milw. Recipient Disting. Svc. award Internat. Inst., Hope Chest award Nat. MS Soc., Disting. Alumni award Milw. Boys' Club, Disting. Svc. award Milw. Civic Alliance Club, 1989, Ellis Island Medal of Honor, 2005. Mem.: ABA, Order of Coif, Milw. Bar Assn., Wis. Bar Assn., Am. Hellenic Ednl. and Progressive Assn. (supreme counselor), Blue Mound Golf and Country Club, Milw. Athletic Club. Greek Orthodox. Home: 1200 Woodlawn Cir Elm Grove WI 53122-1639 Office: Galanis Pollack Jacobs & Johnson 2 Plaza East Ste 560 330 E Kilbourn Milwaukee WI 53202 Home Phone: 262-784-5664; Office Phone: 414-271-5400. Business E-Mail: jwg@jpjlaw.com.

GALASK, RUDOLPH PETER, obstetrician, gynecologist; b. Ft. Dodge, Iowa, Dec. 23, 1935; s. Peter Otto and Adeline Amelia (Maranesi) G.; m. Gloria Jean Vasti, June 19, 1965 BS, Drake U., 1959; MD, U. Iowa, 1964, MS, 1967. Diplomate Am. Bd. Obstetrics and Gynecology. Research fellow in microbiology U. Iowa, Iowa City, 1965-67, resident in ob-gyn., 1967-70, asst. prof., 1970-74, asst. prof. microbiology, 1973-74, assoc. prof. obstetrics and gynecology microbiology, 1974-78, prof., 1978—, chmn. exec. com. Coll. Medicine, 1992-93, prof. dermatology, 1999—2006, prof. emeritus, 2006—. Cons. in field. Editor: Infectious Diseases in the Female Patient, 1986-89; contbr. numerous articles to profl. jours. Served to staff sgt. USNG, 1954—64. Recipient I.D.S.O.G./Ortho McNeil award, A.P.G.O. Excellence in Tchg. award, 1997, I.D.S.O.G. Founders award, 2004; named one of Ams. Top Drs., 2000, Ams. Top OB/GYN, 2002, Ams. Top Drs. for cancer, 2005; numerous grants to study the efficacy of various antibiotics and chemotherapeutics. Fellow Am. Gynecol. and Obstet. Soc., Am. Coll. Obstetricians and Gynecologists, Infectious Disease Am.; mem. AAAS, Cen. Assn. for Obstetricians and Gynecologists, Infectious Disease Soc. for Ob-Gyn. (pres. 1982-84, founding mem.), Soc. Gynecol. Investigation (coun. 1987-90), Queens Gynecol. Soc. (hon.), Tex. Assn. Obstetricians and Gynecologists (hon.), Am. Soc. Microbiology, Izaac Walton League, Ducks Unltd. Club (sponsor), Sigma Xi. Roman Catholic. Office: U Iowa Hosps Dept Ob Gyn Iowa City IA 52242 Personal E-mail: rudolph-galast@aol.com. Business E-Mail: rudolph-galast@uiowa.edu.

GALATI, FRANK JOSEPH, stage and opera director, educator, screenwriter, actor; b. Highland Park, Ill., Nov. 29, 1943; s. Frank Joseph and Virginia Frances (Cassel) G. BS, Northwestern U., 1965, MA, 1966, PhD, 1971. Asst. prof. speech U. South Fla., Tampa, 1965-67; instr. interpretation Northwestern U., Evanston, Ill., 1970-71, assoc. prof., 1973-83, prof. performance studies, 1983—; instr. theater Roosevelt U., Chgo., 1971-72; instr. acting Goodman Sch. Drama, Chgo., 1971-72; assoc. dir. Goodman Theatre, 1986—; dir. Chgo. Opera Theater, 1976; mem. Steppenwolf Theatre Co., 1986—. Dir.: (Broadway plays) The Grapes of Wrath, 1990 (Tony award best direction of a play, 1990, Tony award best play, 1990, Drama Desk award outstanding dir. of a play, 1990), The Glass Menagerie, 1994, Ragtime, 1998—2000 (Dora Mavor award), Seussical, 2000, The Pirate Queen, 2007, (regional theatre) You Can't Take It With You, 1985, Aunt Dan and Lemon, 1987, Born Yesterday, 1987, The Grapes of Wrath, 1988, Earthly Possessions, 1991, As I Lay Dying, 1995, Everyman (A Moral Play), 1995, Morning Star, 1999, Valparaiso, 2000, The Drawer Boy, 2001, Talking With Studs, 2001, The Royal Family, 2002, Homebody/Kabul, 2003, after the quake, 2005, Love Repeating: A Musical of Gertrude Stein, 2005, The Mother of Us All, The Merry Wives of Windsor, Summer and Smoke, Albert Herring, The Good Soldier Schweik, The Visit, The Government Inspector, She Always Said, Pablo, A Funny Thing Happened on the Way to the Forum, Passion Play, The Winter's Tale, Cry, The Beloved Country, The Good Person of Setzuan, Melanctha; (Operas) A View from the Bridge, Pelleas and Mellisande, La Traviata, Tosca, The Voyage of Edgar Allen Poe; screenwriter The Accidental Tourist. Recipient Tchr. of Year award U. South Fla., 1967, Joseph Jefferson Best New Play award Chgo., 1973, Jefferson award for best actor, 1980, Jefferson award for best dir. Drama Desk, 1986-88; Acad. award nomination for best screenplay Accidental Tourist N.Y. Outer Circle Critics, 1989, 2 Antoinette Perry awards for Grapes of Wrath, 1990. Mem. Actors Equity Assn., Speech Communication Assn. Office: orthwestern U Theater Interpretation Ctr 1979 S Campus Dr Evanston IL 60208-0824 Home: 2990 Emathla St Miami FL 33133-3223

GALE, JOHN A., state official; b. Omaha, Oct. 30, 1940; s. John C. Gale, Jr. and Faye Gale; m. Carol Gale; children: David, Elaine, Steve. BA in Govt. Internat. Rels., Carleton Coll., Northfield, Minn., 1962; JD in Govt. Internat. Rels., U. Chgo. Law Sch., Northfield, Minn., 1965. With legal dept. No. atural Gas Co., Omaha, 1965—68; legis. asst. to Senator Roman Hruska US Senate, Washington, 1968; asst. US atty. US Dept. Justice, Omaha, 1970, Lincoln, ebr., 1971; pvt. practice atty., 1971—2000; sec. state State of Nebr., Lincoln, 2000—. Chmn. Nebr. State Rep. Party, 1986. Republican. Office: Office Sec of State State Capitol Ste 2300 Lincoln NE 68509 Office Phone: 402-471-2554. Business E-Mail: receptionist@sos.ne.gov.

GALE, NEIL JAN, Internet company executive, computer scientist, consultant; b. Chgo., Jan. 12, 1960; s. Jack and Adele Gale. AA in Computer Sci., Wright Coll., 1980; D of Bus. Mgmt. (hon.), London Inst. Applied Rsch., 1993; diploma, Academia Argentina de Diplomacia, 1994; diploma (hon.), Institut Des Affaires Internationales, Paris, 1994; D of Bus. Mgmt. (hon.), World Acad., Monchengladbach, Germany, 1994. Mgr. Gen. Fin. Co., Chgo., 1980-84; mktg. mgr. Midland Fin. Co., Chgo., 1984-85; mktg. dir. Diamond Mortgage Corp., Chgo., 1985-86; sr. fin. analyst McKay Mazda-Nissan, Evanston, Ill., 1987-88; pres., CEO, at. Consumer Credit Cons., Chgo., 1988—; webmaster Everything Internet (merger with Millenium Techs. Inc. 1998), Naperville, Ill., 1996-98; pres. DrGale.com, Carol Stream, Ill., 1998—; dir. Chgo. Postcard Mus., 2007—. Hon. prof. bus. mgmt. Inst. des Hautes Etudes Econs. et Sociales, Brussels, 1993; hon. prof. fin. Australian Inst. Coordinated Rsch., 1994; mem. adv. coun. Internat. Biog. Ctr., Cambridge, Eng.; mem. bd. govs., Continental gov. Am. Biog. Inst., 1990—, mem. rsch. bd. advisors, 1989—; notary pub. Ill., 1986-90; bd. dirs., amb. Ill. affiliate U.S. Woman's C. of C., 2002-2004; bd. dirs. U.S. Dept. of Peace Coaliton, 2003-2005. Contbr. articles to profl. jours. First aid chmn. Walk with Israel, 1977; notary pub., Ill., 1986-90; mem. computer com. Village of Hanover Park, Ill., 1997-2000; mem. bd. advisors U.S. Women's C. of C., 2002-. Decorated Knight of Order of San Ciriaco; recipient Bus. in Urban Environment award Chgo. Bd. Edn. and Ill. Bell Tel. Co., 1978, Outstanding Achievement award Chgo. Pub. Libr., 1979. Mem. Auto Credit (hon.), Friendship Cir. Club (treas. 1976-78). Avocation: collecting antique Chicago postcards and books. Home and Office: DrGale dot com PMB 208 780 W Army Trail Rd Carol Stream IL 60188-9297 Home Phone: 630-736-9558; Office Phone: 800-736-1036. Personal E-mail: drgale@drgale.com. Business E-Mail: info@drgale.com.

GALEA, SANDRO, epidemiologist; b. Sliema, Malta, Apr. 24, 1971; s. Emidio and Mary Carmen Galea; m. Margaret Elizabeth Kruk. MD, U. Toronto, 1994; MPH, Harvard U., 2000; DrPH, Columbia U., 2003. Cert. Can. Coll. Family Physicians Grant Cert. 1997. Family med. resident McMaster U. Family Med. No., Thunder Bay, Canada, 1994—96; emergency med. resident U. Toronto, Ont., Canada, 1996—97; physician Geraldton Dist. Hosp., Geraldton, Ont., Canada, 1996—98, Medecins Sans Frontieres, Galkayo, Somalia, 1998—99; med. epidemiologist N.Y. Acad. Medicine, NYC, 2000—05, associate dir. Ctr. for Urban Epidemiologic Studies, 2002—05; asst. prof. epidemiology Columbia U., NYC, 2003—05; assoc. prof. epidemiology U. Mich., Ann Arbor, 2005—. Assoc. editor Journ. Urban Health, 2004—. Contbr. chapters to books, articles to profl. jours., 2002. President Professional Association of Internes and Residents of Ontario, Toronto, Ontario, Canada, 1995—96. Recipient Mosby Book award, U. Toronto, 1991, George & Nora Elwin Book award, 1991, Armando & Nicolina Pavone Outstanding Achievement award, 1991, Mary L. Cassidy award, 1992, Med. Soc. Honour award, 1994, Coll. Family Physicians of Can./Prof. Assoc. of Interns and Residents of Ontario Nat. Resident Rsch. award, Can. Coll. of Family Physicians, 1996, John & Kathleen Gorman Pub. Health Humanitarian award, Columbia U., 2002, Investigator Travel award, NIH, 2004, William Farr award in Epidemiology, Columbia U., 2004. Mem.: APHA, Ont. Med. Assn., Can. Med. Assn., Can. Coll. Family Physicians, Am. Acad. Advancement Sciences, Royal Inst. Pub. Health, Am. Acad. Family Physicians, Pub. Health Assn. NY, Am. Coll. Epidemiology, Soc. Epidemiol. Rsch. Office: Ctr for Social Epidemiology & Population Health U Mich Sch Pub Health 1214 S Univ Rm 243 Ann Arbor MI 48104 E-mail: sgalea@umich.edu.

GALL, ERIC PAPINEAU, internist, educator; b. Boston, May 24, 1940; s. Edward Alfred and Phyllis Hortense (Rivard) Gall; m. Katherine Theiss, Apr. 20, 1968; children: Gretchen Theiss, Michael Edward. AB, U. Pa., 1962, MD, 1966. Diplomate Am. Bd. Internal Medicine, 1972, Am. Bd. Rheumatology, 1974. Asst. instr. U. Pa., Phila., 1970-71, post doctoral trainee, fellow, 1971-73; from asst. prof. to prof. internal medicine U. Ariz., Tucson, 1973—94, prof. surgery, 1983-94, prof. family/community medicine, 1983-94, chief rheumatology allergy and immunology, 1983-93, dir. arthritis ctr., 1986-94; prof. medicine Rosalind Franklin Univ. Medicine & Sci., The Chgo. Med. Sch., North Chicago, Ill., 1994—, prof. microbiology and immunology, 1994—, chmn. dept. medicine, 1994—, chief rheumatology divsn., 1994-98, 2005—, assoc. dean clin. affairs, 1996-97, dir. metabolic bone unit, 1998—2007; prof. medicine Scholl Coll. Podiatric Medicine, 2007—. Author, editor: Rheumatoid Arthritis: Illustrated Guide to Path DX and Management of Rheumatoid Arthritis, 1988, Rheumatic Disease: Rehabilitation and Management, 1984, Primary Care, 1984; editor: Clinical Care in the Rhematic Diseases, 1996; contbr. articles to profl. jours. Chmn. med. and sci. com. Arthritis Found., Tucson, 1979—81; mem. Ill. Partnership Arthritis; chair profl. edn. task force Ill. Dept. Pub. Health, 2001—. Major M.C. US Army, 1968—70. Decorated Bronze Star medal, Army Commendation medal. Master: ACP (coun. Ill. chpt. 1995—, Laureate award 2002), Chgo. Inst. Medicine, Am. Coll. Rheumatology (founding chair ednl. materials com. 1986—96, edn. coun. 1991—96, bd. dirs. 1992—95, chmn. rehab. sect. 1992—95, founding fellow 2005); mem.: AMA (rep. sect. on med. schs. 1995—2002), Lake County Med. Soc. (treas. 1998—99, sec. 2000—, pres. 2002—03), Ill. Med. Soc. (del. 2002—07), Assn. Profs. Medicine, Arthritis Found. (nat. vice chmn. 1982—83, chmn. profl. edn. com. 1996—2001, trustee Greater Chgo. chpt. 1997—, bd. dirs. 1997—, exec. com. 1998—, treas. 2003—06, sr. vice chmn. 2006—07, chmn. 2008—, blue ribbon com. on quality of life), Ctrl. Soc. Clin. Investigation, Inst. Medicine Chgo., Am. Fedn. Clin. Rsch., Am. Assn. Med. Colls., Arthritis Health Professions Assn. (nat. pres. 1982—83, Star award 2005), Alpha Epsilon Delta, Alpha Omega Alpha (counselor Chgo. Med. Sch. chpt. 1995—, regional counselor 1998—2004, nat. bd. dirs. 2006—), Sigma Xi. Roman Catholic. Avocation: photography. Office: The Chgo Med Sch Dept Medicine 3333 Green Bay Rd North Chicago IL 60064-3037 Office Phone: 847-578-8644. Business E-Mail: eric.gall@rosalindfranklin.edu.

GALL, JOHN RYAN, lawyer; b. San Francisco, 1945; BA, Miami U., 1967; JD, Ohio State U., 1970. Bar: Ohio 1971. Ptnr. Squire, Sanders & Dempsey, Columbus, Ohio. Office: Squire Sanders & Dempsey 1300 Huntington Ctr 41 S High St Columbus OH 43215-6101 Office Phone: 614-365-2806. Business E-Mail: jgall@ssd.com.

GALLAGHER, BOB, newscaster; b. Clarendon Hill, ill. BA in Journalism and Mktg., Marquette U., 1990. News editor/prodr., weekend morning news anchor WTMJ-TV, 1992—94; weekend sports anchor/reporter NewsCenter 13, WEAU, 1994—98, weekend sports dir., anchor, 1998—. Avocations: reading, golf. Office: WEAU PO Box 47 Eau Claire WI 54702

GALLAGHER, GERALD RAPHAEL, venture capitalist; b. Easton, Pa., Mar. 17, 1941; s. Gerald R. and Marjorie A. G.; m. Ellen Anne Mullane, Aug. 8, 1964; children: Ann Patrice, Gerald Patrick, Megan Ann. BS in Aero. Engring., Princeton U., 1963; MBA (Exec. Club Chgo. fellow 1969), U. Chgo., 1969. Dir. strategic planning Metro-Goldwyn-Mayer, NYC, 1969; v.p. Donaldson, Lufkin & Jenrette, NYC, 1969-77; from v.p. to sr. v.p. planning and control Dayton Hudson Corp., Mpls., 1977-79; exec. v.p., chief adminstrv. officer subs. Mervyn's, Hayward, Calif., vice chmn., chief adminstrv. officer, 1979-85, vice chmn., chief adminstrv. office parent co., 1985-87, also dir.; gen. ptnr. Oak Investment Ptnrs., Mpls., 1987—. Bd. dirs. Cheddar's eStyle, Lucy Activewear, Ulta, XIOtech, Potbelly. With USN, 1963—67. Mem. N.Y. Soc. Security Analysts, Mpls. Club, Interlachen Country Club, Beta Gamma Sigma. Roman Catholic. Office: Oak Investment Ptnrs 4550 Wells Fargo Ctr 90 S 7th St Minneapolis MN 55402-3903 Office Phone: 612-339-9322. E-mail: jerry@oakvc.com.

GALLAGHER, J. PATRICK, JR., insurance company executive; b. Chgo., 1952; Degree, Cornell U., 1974. From v.p. ops. to pres. Arthur J. Gallagher & Co., Itasca, Ill., 1985—90, pres., 1990—, CEO, 1995—, bd. dir. Trustee Am. Inst. CPCU. Office: Arthur J Gallagher & Co Two Pierce Place Itasca IL 60143

GALLAGHER, JOHN SILL, III, astronomer; b. Boston, Mar. 26, 1947; s. John Sill Jr. and Caroline Eaton (Campbell) G.; m. Mary Lewis Ames, Aug. 29, 1970; children: Daphne E., Julia F. BA, Princeton U., 1969; MS, U. Wis., 1971, PhD, 1972. Vis. asst. prof. dept. physics and astronomy U. Nebr., Lincoln, 1972-74; asst. prof. Sch. Physics and Astronomy U. Minn., Mpls., 1974-77; assoc. prof. to prof. astronomy U. Ill., Urbana, 1977-84; astronomer Kitt Peak Nat. Obs., Tucson, 1984-86; dir. Lowell Obs., Flagstaff, Ariz., 1986-89; v.p. Associated Univs. for Rsch. in Astronomy, Inc., Washington, 1989-90; prof. astronomy U. Wis., Madison, 1990—. Fellow Am. Assn. Adv. Sci.; mem. Am. Astron. Soc. (councilor 1987-90), Internat. Astron. Union, Astron. Soc. of Pacific, AAAS. Office: U Wis Dept Astronomy 5534 Sterling Hall 475 N Charter St Madison WI 53706-1507

GALLAGHER, PATRICK FRANCIS XAVIER, public relations executive; b. Cleve., Feb. 9, 1952; s. Patrick Francis and Eileen (Brennan) G.; m. Anne Platek, May 3, 1980; children: Molly Anne, Kate Louise. Student, Holy Cross Coll., Worcester, Mass., 1970-72; BA, U. Pa., 1974; MBA, Cleve. State U., 1991. Accredited in pub. rels. Staff editor Penton Pub. Co., Cleve., 1975-80, editor, 1980-83; mgr. corp. communications Leaseway Transp. Corp., Cleve., 1983-84, dir. pub. rels., 1984-85; sr. account exec. Edward Howard, Cleve., 1985-89, v.p., 1990-94, sr. v.p., 1994—. Past-pres. Project LEARN, Cleve.; bd. trustees Great Lakes Theater Festival, Cleve. Mem. Pub. Rels. Soc. Am., Nat. Investor Rels. Inst. (past pres. Cleve.-No. Ohio chpt.2001-03), CFA Soc. Cleve. Office: Edward Howard 16th Fl 1100 Superior Ave Cleveland OH 44114-2518

GALLAGHER, PATRICK J., lawyer; BA, Hamline U., 1991; JD cum laude, William Mitchell Coll. Law, 1999. Bar: Minn. 1999, US Dist. Ct. (dist. Minn.) 2000. Sr. assoc. intellectual property & tech. dept. Fulbright & Jaworski, L.L.P., Mpls. Adj. prof. trademark litig. William Mitchell Coll. Law. Contbr. articles to profl. publs.; editor-in-chief: William Mitchell Law Rev. Vol. 25, 1998—99; editor: INTA Bull. Named a Rising Star, Minn. Super Lawyers mag., 2006. Mem.: Minn. Intellectual Property Law Assn., Internat. Trademark Assn. (mem. bull. com.), Minn. State Bar Assn., St. Paul Young Lacrosse Club (pres.). Office: Fulbright & Jaworski LLP 2100 IDS Ctr 80 S 8th St Minneapolis MN 55402 Office Phone: 612-321-2812. E-mail: pgallagher@fulbright.com.

GALLAGHER, RICHARD SIDNEY, lawyer; b. Minot, ND, May 10, 1942; s. J.W.S. and Esther T. (Tappon) G.; m. Ann Rylands Larson, June 24, 1972; children: Elizabeth, Catherine. BSBA, Northwestern U., 1964; JD, Harvard U., 1967. Ptnr. Foley & Lardner LLP, Milw., 1967—, chmn. tax and individual planning dept., 1995—2006. Bd. dirs. Badger Meter Found., Milw. Bd. chmn. Milw. Youth Symphony Orchs., Milw., 1980-82, Milw. County Performing. Arts Ctr., Milw., 1986-91; dir. Curative Rehab. Ctr., Milw., 1988-93, United Performing Arts Fund, 1991-99, Blood Ctr. S.E. Wis., Milw. Youth Arts Ctr.; pres. Donors Forum of Wis., 1997-2000. Lt. comdr., USN, 1967-69, Vietnam. Fellow Am. Coll. Tax Counsel, Am. Coll. Trust & Estate Coun., Am. Law Inst.; mem. ABA (chmn. exempt orgns. com., sect. of taxation 1989-91, governing coun. sect. taxation, 2005-, chmn. com. adminstrn. trusts & estates, sect. probate & trust law 1996-98). Office: Foley & Lardner LLP US Bank Ctr 777 E Wisconsin Ave Milwaukee WI 53202 Business E-Mail: rgallagher@foley.com.

GALLAGHER, SHAWNA BARBARA, psychologist, educator; b. St. Paul, May 30, 1952; d. Dennis and Martha DeFreese; m. Philip Gallagher, June 25, 1975; children: Philip Jr., Cathy. BS in Psychology, Northwestern U., Evanston, Ill., 1974, MS in Psychology, 1976, PhD in Clin. Psychology, 1978. Cert. Am. Bd. Clin. Psychology, 1978. Clin. intern Evanston Med. Ctr., 1978—80; clin. psychologist Mpls. County Jail, 1980—85, Mpls. Health Adminstrn., 1985—95; pvt. practice Richfield, Minn., 1995—; asst. prof. psychology Meriks CC, Richfield, 2002—. Cons. Mpls. Pub. Schs., 2000—05; lectr. in field. Contbr. articles to profl. jours. Vol. Am. Red Cross, 1976—96. Mem.: APHA, APA, ACA, Expressive Psychology Assn. Green Party. Avocations: cooking, writing, flying, bridge. Office: Meriks CC 2200 W 66th St #190 Richfield MN 55423-2196

GALLGHER, J. PATRICK, JR., risk management marketing company executive; b. 1952; m. Anne Murphy; four children. Bachelor's Degree, Cornell U., 1974. Joined Arthur J. Gallagher & Co., Itasca, 1974, v.p. ops., 1985, dir., 1986, COO, pres., 1990, CEO, 1995. Bd. dirs. Gallagher Plumer Ltd.; underwriting mem. Lloyd's Syndicates. Mem. Sunset Ridge Country Club, Meadow Club, Dairymen's Country Club. Office: The Gallagher Ctr Two Pierce Pl Itasca IL 60143-3141 Fax: 630-285-4000.

GALLMAN, JOHN GERRY, publisher; b. Danzig, Mar. 31, 1938; s. Waldemar John and Marjorie (Gerry) G.; m. Elizabeth Ann Stratton, Apr. 29, 1961; children— John Waldemar, Sylvia Elizabeth, David Edward BA, Yale U., 1960. Reporter Worcester Telegram, Mass., 1960-62; assoc. editor Johns Hopkins Press, Balt., 1962-65, Washington editor, 1965-70; editorial dir. Ind. U. Press, Bloomington, 1970-76, dir., 1976-2001; ret., 2001. Cons. U. Iowa, Iowa City, 1983-84, EH, U. Mich., 1985 Mem. exec. com. ACLU, 1974-76; bd. dirs. Sycamore Land Trust, 2001—; pres. SLT, 2004—. Mem. Assn. Am. Univ. Presses (pres., bd. dirs. 1986-87, past pres. bd. dirs. 1987-88), Ducks Unltd. (exec. com. local chpt. 1976-83) Democrat. Avocations: reading; wilderness camping; jogging; hunting; fishing. Home: 2111 E Queensway Dr Bloomington IN 47401-6845

GALLO, DONALD ROBERT, retired literature educator; b. Paterson, NJ, June 1, 1938; s. Sergio and Thelma Mae (Lowe) G.; m. C.J. Bott, Feb. 14, 1997; 1 child, Brian Keith; 1 stepchild, Christian Perrett. BA in English, Hope Coll., 1960; MAT in English Edn., Oberlin Coll., 1961; PhD in English Edn., Syracuse U., 1968. English tchr. Bedford Jr. High Sch., Westport, Conn., 1961-65; rsch. assoc. Syracuse (N.Y.) U., 1965-67; from asst. prof. to assoc. prof. edn. U. Colo., Denver, 1968-72; reading specialist Golden Jr. High Sch., Jefferson County Pub. Schs., Colo., 1972-73; prof. English Cen. Conn. State U., New Britain, 1973-97. Instr. composition Onondaga C. C., Syracuse, 1967; vis. faculty grad. liberal studies program Wesleyan U., 1983; staff writer reading assessment at. Assessment Ednl. Progress, Denver, 1972-73; speaker in field; cons. to schs. and librs. Mem. editl. bd. Nat. Coun. Tchrs. English, 1985-88; compiler, editor: Speaking for Ourselves, 1990, Speaking for Ourselves, Too, 1993; editor: Connections: Short Stories by Outstanding Writers for Young Adults, 1989, Visions: Nineteen Short Stories by Outstanding Writers for Young Adults, 1987, Center Stage: One-Act Plays for Teenage Readers and Actors, 1990, Sixteen: Short Stories by Outstanding Writers for Young Adults, 1984, Books for You, 1985, Authors' Insights: Turning Teenagers into Readers and Writers, 1992, Short Circuits: Thirteen Shocking Stories by Outstanding Writers for Young Adults, 1992, Within Reach: Ten Stories, 1993, Join In: Multiethnic Short Stories by Outstanding Writers for Young Adults, 1993, Ultimate Sports: Short Stories by

Outstanding Writers for Young Adults, 1995, No Easy Answers: Short Stories About Teenagers Making Tough Choices, 1997, Time Capsule: Short Stories About Teenagers Throughout the Twentieth Century, 1999, On The Fringe, 2001, Destination Unexpected, 2003, First Crossing: Stories About Teen Immigrants, 2004, What Are You Afraid Of? Stories about Phobias, 2006, Owning It: Stories About Teens with Disabilities, 2008; author: Presenting Richard Peck, 1989, Bookmark Reading Program, Seventh and Eighth Grade Texts and Workbooks, 1979, Heath Middle Level Literature, 1995; co-author: (with Sarah K. Herz) From Hinton to Hamlet: Building Bridges Between Young Adult Literature and the Classics, 1996, rev. and expanded, 2005; interviewer of authors for Authors4Teens.com website. Recipient Disting. Svc. award Conn. Coun. Tchrs. English, 1989, ALAN award Assembly on Lit. for Adolescents of the Nat. Coun. Tchrs. English, 1992, Cert. of Merit award Cath. Libr. Assn., 1995, Ted Hipple Svc. award ALAN, 2001. Mem. Nat. Coun. Tchrs. English, Assembly on Lit. for Adolescents, Ohio Coun. Tchrs. English Lang. Arts (named an Outstanding English Lang. Arts Educator 2003), Soc. Children's Book Writers and Illustrators, Authors Guild. Avocations: gardening, cooking, travel, photography. Address: 34540 Sherbrook Park Dr Solon OH 44139-2046 Personal E-mail: gallodon@sbcglobal.net.

GALLOP, JANE (JANE ANNE GALLOP), women's studies educator, writer; b. Duluth, Minn., May 4, 1952; d. Melvin Gordon and Eudice Zelda (Titch) G.; children: Max Blau Gallop, Ruby Gallop Blau. BA, Cornell U., 1972, PhD, 1976. Lectr. French Gettysburg (Pa.) Coll., 1976; asst. prof. Miami U., Oxford, Ohio, 1977-81, assoc. prof., 1981-85; prof. women's studies Rice U., Houston, 1985-87, Autrey prof., 1987-90; prof. English U. Wis., Milw., 1990-92, Disting. prof., 1992—. NEH vis. prof. Emory U., Atlanta, 1984-85; Hill vis. prof. U. Minn., Mpls., 1987; dir. seminar for coll. tchrs. NEH, Milw., 1985, 88; instr. Sch. of Criticism and Theory, Dartmouth Coll., 1991; vis. disting. prof. Johns Hopkins U., Balt., 2006. Author: Intersections, 1981, The Daughter's Seduction, 1982, Reading Lacan, 1985, Thinking Through the Body, 1988, Around 1981, 1992, Feminist Accused of Sexual Harassment, 1997, Anecdotal Theory, 2002, Living with His Camera, 2003; editor: Pedagogy, 1995, Polemic, 2004. Guggenheim fellow, 1983-84. Mem. MLA. Office: Dept English Univ Wis -Milw PO Box 413 Milwaukee WI 53201-0413 Home Phone: 414-332-0232. Business E-Mail: jg@uwm.edu.

GALLOPOULOS, GREGORY STRATIS, lawyer; b. Detroit, Oct. 8, 1959; s. Nicholas E. and Mary Frances Gallopoulos; m. Christa L. Gallopoulos. AB with highest distinction, U. Mich., 1981, JD magna cum laude, 1984. Bar: Ill. 1984, US Dist. Ct. No. Dist. Ill. 1984, Supreme Ct. Ill. 1984, US Dist. Ct. Ea. Dist. Mich. 1988, US Ct. Appeals 7th Cir. 1990, US Supreme Ct. 1992, US Tax Ct. 1995, US Ct. Fed. Claims 1995, US Ct. Appeals 9th Cir. 1996, US Ct. Appeals Fed. Cir. 2001. Assoc. Jenner & Block LLP, Chgo., 1984-91, ptnr., 1992—, firm co-chair tax controversy practice, firm mng. ptnr., 2005—. Bd. dir. Chgo. Shakespeare Theater, 2007. Author: Preserving Error for Appeal in Illinois, 1990, Why Do We Work?, 2006; contbr. articles to profl. pubs. Mem. ABA, 7th Cir. Bar Assn., Ill. State Bar Assn., Chgo. Bar Assn., Order of Coif, Phi Beta Kappa. Presbyterian. Office: Jenner & Block LLP 330 N Wabash Chicago IL 60611 Office Phone: 312-923-2754. Office Fax: 312-840-7754. Business E-Mail: ggallopoulos@jenner.com.

GALOWICH, RONALD HOWARD, real estate company executive, venture capitalist, pilot; b. Peoria, Ill., Feb. 18, 1936; s. Louis J. and Leah (Kahn) G.; m. Eleanor Bernstein, June 16, 1957 (div. Aug., 1977); children: Jeffrey, Robert, Pamela; m. Susan E. Loggans, Sept. 11, 1977 (div. Apr. 1988); m. Linda L. Kroupa, Oct. 18, 2000. BS in Commerce and Law, U. Ill., 1957, JD, 1959. Bar: Ill. 1959, U.S. Supreme Ct. 1963. Pres. Twin Oaks-Burr Oaks Realty, Joliet, Ill., 1961-81; ptnr. Galowich & Galowich, Joliet, Ill., 1960-81; dir. real estate ops. Pritzker & Pritzker, Chgo., 1981-90; chmn. Madison Realty Group, Inc., Chgo., 1985—, Madison Group Holdings, Inc., Chgo., 1990—; founder, chmn. Initiate Sys., Inc. (formerly Madison Info. Technologies, Inc.), Chgo., 1994—. Co-founder, dir. First Health Group Corp. (formerly Health Care Compare Corp.), Downers Grove, Ill., 1982—2005; commr. Ill. Supreme Ct., 1968-70. Chmn. devel. com. Joliet Greater YMCA, 2002—06; bd. dirs. Athletes Against Drugs, 1992—; mem. leadership com. Cancer Inst., Rush U. Med. Ctr., Chgo., 1993—; bd. visitors U. Ill. Coll. Law, 1996—, pres., 1998—2000. Fellow Am. Judicature Soc., Ill. Bar Found.; mem. ABA, Ill. Bar Assn., Urban Land Inst., Chgo. Bar Assn. Jewish. Home: 1248 N Astor St Chicago IL 60610-2308 Office: Madison Group Holdings Inc 200 W Madison St Ste 2300 Chicago IL 60606-3416 Personal E-mail: rhgalo@ix.netcom.com. Business E-Mail: rgalowich@initiatesystems.com.

GALVIN, KATHLEEN MALONE, communications educator; b. NYC, Feb. 9, 1943; d. James Robert and Helen M. (Sullivan) G.; m. Charles A. Wilkinson, June 19,1973; children: Matthew, Katherine, Kara. BS, Fordham U., Bronx, NY, 1964; MA, Northwestern U., Evanston, Ill., 1965-80, PhD, 1968. Tchr. Evanston (Ill.) Township High Sch., 1967-72; asst. prof. Northwestern U., Evanston, 1968-73, assoc. prof., 1973-78, prof., 1978—, assoc. dean, 1988-2001. Endowed chair Marquette U., 2006—07; presenter workshops in field. Author: Listening by Doing, 1986, Family Communication, 7th edit., 2007; co-author: Person to Person, 5th edit., 1996, Basics of Speech, 4th edit., 2004; co-editor: Making Connections, 4th edit., 2006, Communication Works!, 2000; contbr. book chpts. and articles to profl. jours.; developer, instr. 26-video series on Family Communication (PBS Adult Satellite Sys.). Recipient Tchg. Excellence award, Northwestern Univ. Alumni Assn., Crystal Apple Tchg. award, Mich. State Univ., Sch. Edn., Galbut Outstanding Faculty award. Office: Northwestern U Comm Studies Dept 2240 N Campus Dr Evanston IL 60208-3545 Business E-Mail: k-galvin@northwestern.edu.

GALVIN, MICHAEL JOHN, JR., lawyer; b. Winona, Minn., July 8, 1930; s. Michael John Sr. and Margaret Elizabeth (O'Donohue) G.; m. Frances Dennis Culligan, Sept. 7, 1957; children: Sean, Kevin, Kathleen, Nora, Mary, Margaret, Patricia. BA, U. St. Thomas, 1952; LLB, U. Minn., 1957. Bar: Minn. 1957, U.S. Dist. Ct. Minn. 1957, U.S. Supreme Ct. 1961. With sales and svc. Badger Machine Co., Winona, 1950-56; mgr. Oaks Hotel Inc., Winona, 1950-56; ptnr. Briggs & Morgan, P.A., St. Paul, 1957—. Pres. St. Paul Winter Carnival Assn., 1970; sec. St. Paul Area C. of C., 1968-71; trustee U. St. Thomas, 1978-85, Coll. St. Catherine, St. Paul, 1999—; nat. chmn. U. Minn. Law Sch. Ptnrs. in Excellence Program, 2000-01; chmn. Indianhead Coun. Boy Scouts Am., 2003-05; bd. dirs. Maritime Heritage Soc., 2005—. Lt. USAF, 1952-54, USAFR, 1954-60. Named Boss of Yr., St. Paul Jaycees, 1990, Disting. Cmty. Builder, Can. Govt., 2007; named an Oustanding Young Man, City St. Paul, 1964; recipient Disting. Alumnus award, U. St. Thomas, 1983, U. Minn. Law Sch., 2001, Great Living St. Paulite award, St. Paul Area C. of C., 2000, Eugene and Mary Frey Cmty. award, Cretin-Derham Hall Schs., 2000, Monsignor James Lavin award, U. St. Thomas, 2003. Mem. ABA (labor and employment law sect., Leonard Linquist award 2007), Minn. Bar Assn. (treas. 1991-93, pres.-elect 1993, pres. 1994-95, chair labor and employment law sect. 1984), Ramsey County Bar Assn. (exec. coun. 1965-68, 83-86, pres. 1984-85), Minn. Vol. Attys. Corp. (pres. 1993-94), Univ. Club (pres. 1962), Minn. Club (pres. 1971), St. Paul Athletic Club (pres. 1986), St. Paul Area C. of C. (bd. dirs. 1995—, chmn. 1997-98). Republican. Roman Catholic. Office: Briggs & Morgan 2200 1st Nat Bank Bldg Saint Paul MN 55101 Office Phone: 651-808-6553. Business E-Mail: mgalvin@briggs.com.

GALVIN, PAT G., state legislator; m. Carol Galvin; 2 children. Student, Barber Coll. Barber; rep. Dist. 33 N.D. Ho. of reps., mem. human svcs., natural resources coms. Mem. Hazen City Commn., Hazen City Sch. Bd. With N.D. N.G. Mem. Am. Legion, Eagles. Home: PO Box 31 Hazen ND 58545-0031

GALVIN, ROBERT W., electronics executive; b. Marshfield, Wis., Oct. 9, 1922; Student, U. Notre Dame, U. Chgo.; LLD, Quincy Coll.; LLD (hon.), St. Ambrose Coll., DePaul U., Ariz. State U. With Motorola, Inc., Chgo., 1940—48, exec. v.p., 1948—56, former pres., 1956, chmn. bd., 1964—90, CEO, 1964—86, chmn. exec. com., 1990—2001, also dir.; ret., 2003; chmn. bd. Semantech Inc., Austin, Tex. Author: America's Founding Secret: What the Scottish Enlightment Taught our Founding Fathers, 2002. Past mem. Pres.'s Commn. on Internat. Trade and Investment.; chmn. industry policy adv. com. U.S. Trade Rep.; active Pres.'s Pvt. Sector Survey; chmn. Pres.'s Adv. Coun. on Pvt. Sector Initiatives, Ill. Inst. Tech., U. Notre Dame; bd. dirs. Jr. Achievement, Chgo. With Signal Corps US Army, WWII. Named Decision Maker of Yr., Chgo. Assn. Commerce and Industry-Am. Statis. Assn., 1973; named one of Forbes' Richest Americans, 2006; recipient Nat. medal, Tech. U.S. Dept. Commerce Tech. Adminstrn., 1991, Sword of Loyola award, Loyola U., Chgo., Washington award, Western Soc. Engrs., 1984, Vannevar Bush award, NSF, 2005. Mem.: Nat. Bus. Hall of Fame, Electronic Industries Assn. (pres. 1966, bd. dirs., Medal of Honor 1970, Golden Omega award 1981). Office: Motorola Inc 1303 E Algonquin Rd Schaumburg IL 60196-1079

GALVIN, WALTER J., electrical equipment manufacturing executive; Controller, Ridge Tool subs. Emerson Electric Co., 1973—78, asst. v.p. investor rels., 1978—81, v.p. fin., US electric motors divsn. to exec. v.p. fin., adminstrn., 1981—84, v.p. fin., analysis sys. to sr. v.p. controller, 1984—93, CFO St. Louis, 1993—2000, exec. v.p., CFO, 2000—04, sr. exec. v.p., CFO, 2004—. Bd. dir. Ameren Corp., 2007—. Office: Emerson Electric Co PO Box 4100 Saint Louis MO 63136-8506

GAMBLE, E. JAMES, lawyer, accountant; b. Duluth, Minn., June 1, 1929; s. Edward James and Modesta Caroline (Reichert) G.; m. Lois Kennedy, Apr. 3, 1954; children: John M., Martha M., Paul F. AB, U. Mich., 1950, JD, 1953. Bar: Mich. 1953, D.C. 1980; CPA, Mich. Tax acct. Ernst & Ernst, Detroit, 1957-59; assoc. Dykema, Gossett, Spencer, Goodnow & Trigg, Detroit, 1959-67; ptnr. Dykema Gossett, Detroit, 1967-94, Gamble, Rosenberger & Joswick LLP, Bloomfield Hills, 1994—2006, Gamble & Joswick LLP, Bloomfield Hills, 2006—. Adj. prof. law Wayne State U., Detroit, 1964-79; adj. lectr. law U. Mich., Ann Arbor, 1979-81, 93; co-reporter, prin. draftsman Uniform Principal and Income Act (1997); mem. adv. com. Restatement of the Law, 3rd, Property, Wills and Other Donative Transfers, Restatement of the Law, 3rd, Trusts; counsel Mich. State Bd. Accountancy, Lansing, 1973-77. Author: (handbook) The Revised Uniform Principal and Income Act, 1966; contbr. articles to profl. jours. Trustee Rehab. Inst., Inc., Detroit, 1961-84, chmn. bd. trustees, 1974-77; bd. dirs., sec. Jr. Achievement Southeastern Mich., 1973-86; trustee Walsh Coll. Accountancy and Bus. Adminstrn., Troy, Mich., 1975-87, Alma (Mich.) Coll., 1981-91; mem. Fin. and Estate Planning Coun. Detroit, bd. dirs., 1969-76, pres., 1975. Lt. USN, 1953-57. Recipient Bronze Leadership award Jr. Achievement, Inc., 1985 Fellow Am. Coll. Tax Counsel, Am. Coll. Trust and Estate Counsel (bd. regents 1988—, chmn. estate and gift tax com. 1989-92, pres. 1998-99), Academician, Internat. Acad. Estate and Trust Law (exec. coun. 2001-04), Am. Bar Found. (life), Mich. State Bar Found.; mem. ABA (mem. spl. com. on profl. rels. with AICPA 1968-70), Mich. Bar Assn. (mem. various coms.), Detroit Bar Assn. (chmn. taxation com. 1968-74), Detroit Bar Assn. Found. (trustee, treas. 1973-79), Birmingham Athletic Club, Leland Country Club. Presbyterian.

GAMELLI, RICHARD LOUIS, surgeon, educator; b. Springfield, Mass., Jan. 18, 1949; married; 3 children. AB in Chemistry magna cum laude, St. Michael's Coll., Colchester, Vt., 1970; MD, U. Vt., 1974. Diplomate Nat. Bd. Med. Examiners, Am. Bd. Surgery (dir. 1993); lic. surgeon, Ill. Straight surg. intern. Med. Ctr. Hosp. Vt., 1974-75, surg. resident PG-II, PG-III, PG-IV, 1975-79; asst. prof. surgery U. Vt. Coll. Medicine, 1979-85, assoc. prof., 1985-89, prof., 1989-90, dir. surg. rsch. labs. dept. surgery, 1985-90, dir. house staff tng. program., 1985-89, vice chmn. dept. surgery, 1985-90, chmn. sect. gen. surgery, 1989; attending surgeon Med. Ctr. Hosp. Vt., 1979-90, dir., founder burn program, 1980-90, dir. nutritional support svcs., 1980-88, dir. resident teaching conf., 1983-90, assoc. surgeon-in-chief, 1985-89; prof. depts. surgery and pediatrics Strich Sch. Medicine, dir. Shock-Trauma Inst., chief burn ctr., dir. surg. rsch. Foster G. McGaw Hosp. Loyola U. Med. Ctr., Maywood, Ill., 1990—, now chmn, prof., dept. of surgery. Chmn. quailty assurance com. burn ctr. Loyola U. Med. Ctr., 1990—, infection control com., 1990—, rsch. com. coun., 1990—, surg. rsch. com., 1991—, intensive care unit com., 1991—, EMS bldg. com., 1991—, med. chmn. nutrition com., 1992—, managed care task force, 1993—, commitment to teaching task force, 1993—, OR/PAR com., 1995—, MD/PhD steering com., 1998—, med. exec. com., 1998-2000; Dr John C. Hartnett lectr. St. Michael's Coll., 1983; mem. spl. study sect. NIH, 1991. Co-author: Trauma 2000, 1992, A Compendium of Slides on Surgical Infections, 1992; co-editor: Clinical Surgery, 1987, Early Care of the Injured Patient, 1990, Essentials of Clinical Surgery, 1991; mem. editorial bd., reivewer Jour. Trauma, 1984—, Essentials Clin. Surgery, 1988—, Clin. Surgery, 1990—, Shock, 1993—; reviewer Circulatory Shock, Surgery, Jour. Surg. Rsch.; contbr. 172 articles to profl. jours., 16 chpts. to books. Recipient Dr. James E. DeMeules 1st Annual Rsch. award U. Vt. Dept. Surgery, 1990, Disting. Acad. Achievement award U. Vt., 2000; grantee NIH, 1981-84, 89-93, Ethicon, Inc., 1988-90, Genetech., Inc., 1988-89, Amgen, Inc., 1989-90, U. Ill., Chgo., 1991. Fellow ACS (vice chmn. Vt. state com. on trauma 1984-86, chmn. Vt. state com. on trauma 1986-91, sec.-treas. Vt. state chpt. 1987-90, subcom. on publs. 1987-90, exec. com. 1991-93, reviewer com. on trauma verification/consultaion program for hosps., 1991, 92, 93 chmn. audit com. 1992, 93, bd. dirs. 1992, cons., beta test site NTRACS, 1993); mem. Am. Burn Assn. (instr., dir. advanced burn life suuport course 1988—, regionalization com. 1992—, chair region V. 1992—, beta test site registry 1993, 1st v.p.), N.Am. Burn Soc. (pres. 1991), Shock Soc., Soc. for Leukocyte Biology, Soc. Univ. Surgeons (chmn. com. on social and legis. issues 1990-93, exec. com. 1990-93), Surg. Infection Soc. (edn. com. 1988—, chmn. fellowhsip com. 1990—), Surg. Biology Club III, Ea. Assn. for Surgery Trauma (exec. com. 1991-93, bd. dirs. 1992, chmn. audit com. 1992, 93), Internat. Soc. for Burn Injuries, John H. Davis Soc. (founding., bd. dirs. 1988—, coun. 1988-90, sec.-treas. 1990-92, pres. 1993—), New England Surg. Soc. Office: Loyola U Med Ctr Dept Surgery 2160 S 1st Ave Maywood IL 60153-3304

GAMORAN, REUBEN, candy company executive; B of Acctg., Northwestern U.; MBA, U. Chgo. CPA Ill. With William Wrigley Jr. Co., Chgo., 1985, assoc. treas., v.p. fin., v.p., controller, 2001—04, cheif fin. officer, 2004—. Office: William Wrigley Jr Co 410 N Michigan Ave Chicago IL 60611

GANASSI, CHIP, professional race car executive, owner; b. Pitts., May 24, 1958; m. Cara Ganassi; 1 child, Tessa. BA in Fin., Duquesne U., 1982. Exec. v.p. FRG Group, Pitts.; ptnr. Pitts. Pirates; promoter, co-mgr. Chgo. Motor Speedway; co-owner Target/Chip Ganassi Racing, 1990—. Former profl. race car driver; fastest of 9 rookies Indpls. 500, 1982; 8 top-10 finishes in 28 Indy car appearances, 86; ret., 86; co-owner Patrick Racing, 1988—89; established Reynard .Am., Indpls., 1993. Office: c/o Target/Chip Ganassi Racing 7777 Woodland Dr Indianapolis IN 46278-1794

GANDHI, HAREN S., chemical engineer; b. Calcutta, India, May 2, 1941; m. Yellow Gandhi; 2 children. BSc in Chem. Engring., U. Bombay, 1963; MSc in Chem. Engring., U. Detroit, 1967, D in Chem. Engring., 1971. With Ford Motor Co., Dearborn, Mich., 1967—, rsch. engr., 1967, various rsch. engring. and staff scientist positions, mgr. dept. chem. engring. Ford Rsch. Lab., head emission and fuel economy core team, 1997, Ford tech. fellow. Mem. adv. com. Ministries of Industry and Environment. Contbr. numerous articles to profl. jours. Named Chem. Engr. of Yr., AIChE, 1984; recipient Nat. Medal Tech., US Dept. Commerce, 2002, Crompton Lanchester Medal, Instn. Mech. Engrs., 1988—89, Tech. Innovation award, Discover Mag., 1990, Exxon award Excellence in Catalysis, Nat. Assn. Sci. and Tech., 1994, Partnership New Generation of Vehicles Medal, 1997. Mem. NAE. Achievements include more than 40 U.S. patents; development of the monolithic three-way catalyst; pioneering research in catalysts for alternative fuels, oxygen components in three-way catalysts, poisoning of automotive catalysts, and novel catalyst formulation strategies. Office: 20000 Rotunda Dr Rm 3437 Dearborn MI 48124-3958

GANGEMI, COLUMBUS RUDOLPH, JR., lawyer, educator; b. Phila., Aug. 6, 1947; BA, Villanova U., 1969, JD, 1973; doctoral fellow, Temple U., 1970. Bar: Ill., U.S. Dist. Ct. Ill. (no. dist.), U.S. Supreme Ct., U.S. Ct. Appeals (1st, 3rd, 5th-8th, 10th, 11th cir.). Assoc. to mng. ptnr. Winston & Strawn LLP, Chgo., 1973—, nat. head labor and employment rels. practice, mem. exec. com. Spl. Ill. asst. atty. gen. 1991-94; adj. prof. Ill. Benedictine Coll., Lisle, Ill., 1988-1995; instr. at. Inst. Trial Advocacy Northwestern U.; mem. labor and employee rels. com. Chgo. Assn. Commerce and Industry, 1979-90. Contbr. articles to profl. jours. Bd. dirs. Ill. State C. of C.; v.p., bd. dirs. Easter Seal Soc. Chgo., 1983-89. Fellow Coll. Labor and Employment Lawyers; mem. ABA (nat. labor rels. bd. practice com. 1976-), Chgo. Bar Assn. Republican. Office: Winston & Strawn LLP 35 W Wacker Dr Chicago IL 60601-9703 Office Phone: 312-558-5811. Office Fax: 312-558-5700. E-mail: cgangemi@winston.com.

GANNETT, DIANA RUTH, musician, educator; b. Davenport, Iowa, July 30, 1947; d. Wright Kent and Ruth Babette (Gebauer) Gannett; m. Dary John Mizelle, Dec. 17, 1974 (div. Oct. 1989); children: Adam Anthony Mizelle, Joseph Martin Mizelle, Agon Matthew Mizelle; m. Robert Cruden, 1996; stepchildren: Nathalie Cruden, Lyda Cruden. MusB with honors, U. Iowa, 1969; MusM, Yale U., 1972, DMA, 1977. Adj. lectr. double bass U. S. Fla., Tampa, Fla., 1973-75; instr. double bass Oberlin (Ohio) Conservatory, 1976-78; assoc. prof. double bass Lehman Coll., Bronx, NY, 1979-83, Yale U. Sch. Music, New Haven, 1984-92; tchr. double bass Hartt Sch. Music, Hartford, Conn., 1985-92; prof. double bass U. Iowa Sch. Music, Iowa City, 1992—2001; prof. double bass, doctoral advisor strings U. Mich. Sch. Music, Ann Arbor, 2002—. Prin. bass Black Hills Festival, SD, 1970—91, Gulf Coast Orch., Tampa, 1973—75, Eastern Music Festival, Greensboro, C, 1975, Greensboro, 78, Greensboro, 1984—92, Quad City Symphony Orch., 1992—2001; numerous chamber & solo performances traditional, contemporary music. Mem.: Internat. Soc. Bassists (past pres.), Am. String Tchrs. Avocations: instrument building, drawing, calligraphy, Aikido. Home: 550 Woodhill Dr Saline MI 48176 Office Phone: 734-764-6515.

GANNON, SISTER ANN IDA, retired philosophy educator; b. Chgo., 1915; d. George and Hanna (Murphy) G. AB, Clarke Coll., 1941; A.M., Loyola U., Chgo., 1948, LL.D., 1970; PhD, St. Louis U., 1952; Litt.D., DePaul U., 1972; L.H.D., Lincoln Coll., 1965, Columbia Coll., 1969, Luther Coll., 1969; LHD, Augustana Coll., 1969; L.H.D., Marycrest Coll., 1972, Ursuline Coll., 1972, Spertus Coll. Judaica, 1974, Holy Cross Coll., 1974, Rosary Coll., 1975, St. Ambrose Coll., 1975, St. Leo Coll., 1976, Mt. St. Joseph Coll., 1976, Stritch Coll., 1976; LHD, Stonehill Coll., 1976, Elmhurst Coll., 1977, Manchester Coll., 1977, Marymount Coll., 1977; L.H.D., Governor's State U., 1979; LHD, Seattle U., 1981, St. Michael's Coll., 1984, Nazareth Coll., 1985, Holy Family Coll., 1986, Keller Grad. Sch. Mgmt., Our Lady of Holy Cross Coll., New Orleans, 1988. Mem. Sisters of Charity, B.V.M.; tchr. English St. Mary's High Sch., Chgo., 1941-47; residence, study abroad, 1951; chmn. philosophy dept. Mundelein Coll., 1951-57, pres., trustee, 1957—75, prof. philosophy, 1975-85, emeritus faculty, 1987—, archivist, 1986—. Contbr. articles philos. jours. Mem. adv. bd. Sec. Navy, 1975—80, Chgo. Police Bd., 1979—89; bd. dirs. Am. Coun. on Edn., 1971—75, chmn., 1974—75; nat. bd. dirs. Girl Scouts USA, 1966—74, nat. adv., 1976—85; trustee St. Louis U., 1974—87, Ursuline Coll., 1978—92, Cath. Theol. Union, 1983—89, DeVry, Inc., 1987—98, Duquesne U., 1989—91, Montay Coll., 1993—95, Mundelein Coll., 1957—75; bd. dirs. Newberry Libr., 1976—, WTTW Pub. TV, 1976—, Parkside Human Svcs. Corp., 1983—89. Recipient Laetare medal, 1975, LaSallian award, 1975, Aquinas award, 1976, Chgo. Assn. Commerce and Industry award, 1976, Hesburgh award, 1982, Woman of Distinction award Nat. Conf. Women Student Leaders, 1985, Outstanding Svc. award Coun. Ind. Colls., 1989, Woman of History award for edn. AAUW, 1989; named One of 100 Oustanding Chgo. Women, Culture in Action, 1994, Alpha Sigma Nu, 1996. Mem. Am. Cath. Philos. Assn. (exec. coun. 1953-56), Assn. Am. Colls. (bd. dirs. 1965-70, chmn. 1969-70), Religious Edn. Assn. Am. (pres. 1973, chmn. bd. 1975-78), North Cen. Assn. (commn. on colls. and univs. 1971-78, chmn. exec. bd. 1975-77, bd. dirs.), Assn. Governing Bds. Colls. and Univs. (bd. dirs. 1979-88, hon. bd. dirs. 1989-92). Home: Wright Hall 6364 N Sheridan Rd Chicago IL 60660-1726 Office: Gannon Ctr Wright Hall 6364 N Sheridan Rd Chicago IL 60660-1700 Office Phone: 773-508-8450. Business E-Mail: aganno2@luc.edu.

GANSKE, J. GREG, former congressman, plastic surgeon; b. New Hampton, Iowa, Mar. 31, 1949; s. Victor Wilber and Mary Jo (O'Donnell) G.; m. Corrine Mikkelson, 1976; children: Ingrid, Briget, Karl. BA, U. Iowa, 1972, MD, 1976. Diplomate Am. Bd. Plastic Surgery, Am. Bd. Surgery. Intern U. Colo. Med. Ctr., Denver, 1976-78; resident in gen. surgery U. Oreg. Health Sci. Ctr., Portland, 1978-81, chief resident in gen. surgery, 1981-82; resident in plastic surgery Harvard Med. Sch., Boston, 1982-84; chief resident plastic surgery Brigham and Women's Hosp. and Children's Hosp., 1983-84; pvt. practice Des Moines, 1984-94; mem. U.S. Congress from 4th Iowa dist., Washington, 1994—2002; mem. energy and commerce com. Staff Iowa Luth. Hosp., Iowa Meth. Med. Ctr., Mercy Hosp. Med. Ctr. Lt. col. M.C., USAR, 1984—. Fellow ACS, Am. Soc. Plastic and Reconstructive Surgeons; mem. AMA, Am. Assn. Plastic Surgeons, Iowa Med. Soc., Iowa Soc. Plastic and Reconstructive Surgeons, Am. Assn. Hand Surgery, Am. Soc. Surgery Hand, Am. Cleft Palate-Craniofacial Assn. Republican. Roman Catholic. Office Phone: 515-265-4414.

GANSKE, LYLE G., lawyer; b. Toledo, 1959; BSBA summa cum laude, Bowling Green State Univ., Ohio, 1981; JD with honors, Ohio State Univ., 1984. Bar: Ohio 1984. Law clk. Judge Craig Wright, Ohio Supreme Ct., 1985; ptnr., chair, global mergers & acquisitions practice Jones Day, Cleve. Author: numerous articles in profl. publications. Mem.: Order of Coif. Office: Jones Day North Point 901 Lakeside Ave Cleveland OH 44114-1190 Office Fax: 216-579-0212.

GANSLER, ROBERT, professional soccer coach; b. Mucsi, Hungary, July 1, 1941; came to U.S., 1952; m. Nancy Gansler; children: Robert, MIchael, Peter, Daniel. Grad., Marquette U., 1964. Coach Univ. Wis., Milwaukee, 1984—88, US Under-19 Men's Soccer Team, 1979—82, US Under-20 Men's Soccer Team, 1987—89, Milwaukee Rampage, 1996—98; head coach US Men's Soccer Team, 1989—91, Kansas City Wizards/MLS, 1999—. Named Coach of Year, Major League Soccer, 2000. Office: Kansas City Wizards 2 Arrowhead Dr Kansas City MO 64129

GANTZ, BRUCE JAY, otolaryngologist, educator; b. NYC, May 18, 1946; m. Mary Katherine DeJong; children: Ellen Katherine, Jessica Rose, Jay Alexander. BS in Gen. Sci., U. Iowa, 1968, MD, 1974, MS in Otolaryngology, 1980; fellow neurotology, U. Zürich, Zurich, 1981-82. Asst. prof. dept otolaryngology U. Iowa Coll. Medicine, Iowa City, 1980-84, assoc. prof., 1984-87, prof., 1987—; interim head dept. otolaryngology head & neck surgery U. Iowa Hosps. & Clinics, Iowa City, 1993-95, head dept. otolaryngology head & neck surgery, 1995—. Mem. adv. bd. Deafness Research Found. Sci., 1988—. Mem. editl. bd. Am. Jour. Otology, Laryngoscope, Skull Base Surgery, Operative Techniques in Otolaryngology-Head and Neck Surgery, Anales De Otolarnolaringo-logica Mexicana, Annals Otolaryngology, Rhinology and Laryngology; contbr. articles to profl. jours. Recipient Tchr.-Investigator Devel. award Pub. Health Svc., 1981-86, Program Project award NIH, 1985—; clin. rsch. ctr. grantee NIDCD, 1990, 95. Mem.: AMA, NAS Inst. Medicine, Collegium Oto-Rhino-Laryngologicum Amictuae Sacrum, Am. Otological Soc., Am. Neurotology Soc. (v.p. 1994—96, pres.-elect 1996—97, pres. 1997—98), Soc. Univ. Otolaryngologists, Am. Acad. Otolaryngology-Head and eck Surgery, Deafness Rsch. Found. (state chmn. 1985—), Assn. Rsch. in otolaryngology (pres. 1995). Office: U Iowa Hosps & Clinics 200 Hawkins Dr Iowa City IA 52242-1078 Office Phone: 319-356-2173.

GAPPA, JUDITH M., academic administrator; Student, Wellesley Coll., 1957-60; BA in Music, George Washington U., 1968, MA in Musicology, 1970; EdD in Ednl. Adminstrn., Utah State U., 1973; cert. Inst. for Ednl. Mgmt., Harvard U., 1980. Lectr. George Washington U., Washington, 1968-69; dir. fine arts program The York Sch., Monterey, Calif., 1970; program cons. Western Interstate Commn. for Higher Edn., Boulder, Colo., 1973; coord. affirmative action program Utah State U., Logan, 1973-75, dir. affirmative action/equal opportunity programs, asst. prof., 1975-77, 78-80, project dir., 1979-81; sr. staff assoc. at. Ctr. for Higher Edn. Mgmt. Systems, Inc., Boulder, 1977-78; assoc. v.p. for faculty affairs, dean of faculty, prof. San Francisco State U., 1980-91; sr. assoc. Am. Assn. Higher Edn., 1995-97; prof. Purdue U., West Lafayette, Ind., 1991—, v.p. human rels., 1991-98. Served on numerous coms., couns. Utah State U., San Francisco State U.; cons. Assn. Governing Bds., 1994, U. Mich., Duluth, 1992, Calif. State U. Human Resources Mgmt. Office, 1992, Am. U., Washington, 1987, No. Rockies Consortium for Higher Edn. Conf., 1985, So. Utah State Coll., 1982, Nat. Ctr. for Rsch. in Vocat. Edn., 1980-81, Hood Coll., 1982-84, Am. Insts. for Rsch. in Behavioral Scis., 1980-81; condr. workshops on edn. Co-author: The Invisible Faculty, 1993; mem. editl. bd. Rev. of Higher Edn., 1994-97; contbr. numerous articles to profl. jours. Grantee Lilly Endowment, 1995, United Techs. Corp., 1992, TIAA-CREF/Lilly Endowment, 1990, Calif. State U., 1985, San Francisco State U., 1981, HEW, 1979-81, Nat. Inst. Edn., 1977, Utah State U., 1977, Fed. workshop grant, 1976, State of Utah, 1975, 76. Mem. Western Assn. Schs. and Colls. (accreditation team mem. Calif. State U.-L.A. 1990), Am. Assn. for Higher Edn. (sr. assoc. Washington chpt. 1995-97), Assn. for Study of Higher Edn. (nat. adv. bd. ASHE-ERIC Higher Edn. Report Series 1990-91, editl. bd. Rev. of Higher Edn. 1994-97, nominating com. 1986-87, program com. for 1986 nat. conf., membership com. 1982-84, conf. com. 1983, editl. bd. Rev. of Higher Edn. 1994-97), Am. Coun. on Edn. Nat. Identification Program (No. Calif. state coord. 1988-91). Office: Purdue Univ Coll Edn 1446 Liberal Arts Rd West Lafayette IN 47907-1075

GAPSTUR, SUSAN MARY, cancer epidemiologist, educator, researcher; b. Mpls., Nov. 14, 1960; d. Michael and Mary Monica Gapstur. BS, U. Wis., La Crosse, 1983; MPH, U. Minn., 1989, PhD, 1993. Rsch. technician Mayo Clinic and Found., Rochester, Minn., 1984-87; rsch. assoc. U. Ariz., Tucson, 1993-94; asst. prof. dept. preventive medicine Northwestern U., Chgo., 1994—. Grant reviewer NIH, 1996—, Dept. Def., 1998—. Contbr. over 30 articles to med. jours., including Jour. AMA, Am. Jour. Physiology, Am. Jour. Epidemiology, Cancer Epidemiology. Predoctoral fellow U. Minn., 1990-92; rsch. grantee Lynn Sage Breast Cancer Found., 1996, Washington Square Health Found., 1998-00, Nat. Cancer Inst., 1998-02. Mem. Soc. for Epidemiologic Rsch., Am. Assn. Cancer Rsch., Am. Soc. Preventive Oncology (session chmn. 1993, 97). Avocations: hiking, canoeing. Office: Northwestern U Dept Preventive Medicine 680 N Lake Shore Dr 1102 Chicago IL 60611-4402

GARAGIOLA, STEVE, announcer; s. Joe Garagiola; 2 children. With WXYZ-TV, Detroit, 1980—89; sports dir. KTSP-TV, Phoenix; sportscaster WDIV-TV, Detroit, 1994—96. Office: WDIV-TV 550 W Lafeyette Blvd Detroit MI 48226

GARANZINI, MICHAEL J., academic administrator, priest; b. St. Louis; BA in Psychology, St. Louis U., 1971; MA in Am. Civilization, NYU, 1978; MDiv, Weston Sch. Theology, 1980; STM in Moral Devel., U. Calif., Berkeley, 1981, PhD in Psychology and Religion, 1986. Part-time faculty mem. U. San Francisco, 1984—86, asst. prof. dept. psychology, 1986—88, asst. prof. dept. ednl. psychology Sch. Edn., 1986—88; assoc. prof. edn. St. Louis U., 1988—98, acting v.p. student devel., 1991—92, asst. acad. v.p., 1992—93, acting acad. v.p., 1993—94, acad. v.p., 1994—98; vis. prof. counseling Fordham U., 1998—99; spl. asst. to the pres., acting chair dept. psychology Georgetown U., 1999—2001; pres. Loyola U., Chgo., 2001—. Vis. prof. psychology and family studies grad. divsn. Gregorian U., 1986, 88. Author: The Attachment Cycle: An Object Relations Approach to the Healing Ministries, 1987, Child-Centered Schools: An Educator's Guide to Family Dysfunction, 1995; contbr. articles to profl. jours. Office: Loyola Univ Chgo Office of the Pres 820 N Michigan Ave Chicago IL 60611 Office Phone: 312-915-6400. E-mail: mgaranz@luc.edu.

GARBER, SAMUEL B., lawyer, retail executive; b. Chgo., Aug. 16, 1934; s. Morris and Yetta G.; m. Marietta C. Bratta; children: Debra Lee, Diane Lori. JD, U. Ill., 1958; MBA, U. Chgo., 1968. Bar: Ill. 1958. Ptnr. Brown, Dashow and Langluttig, Chgo., 1960-62; corp. counsel Walgreen Co., 1962-69; gen. counsel, exec. asst. to the pres. Carlyle & Co., 1969-73; dir. legal affairs Stop & Shop Co., Inc., 1973-74; v.p., gen. counsel Goldblatt Bros., Inc., 1974-76; v.p., sec., gen. counsel, dir. Evans, Inc., 1976-99, pres., CEO, 1999-2000; prof. mgmt. DePaul U., 1975—; prin. The Garber Group, Bus. Cons. and Turnaround Management Firm, Chgo., 2000—. Adj. prof. bus. law Grad. Sch. Bus., U. Chgo., 1993-2005; arbitrator NY Stock Exch., 1996, Chgo. Merc. Exch., 1996, Am. Stock Exch., 1997, Nat. Futures Assn., 1997; columnist Garber's Gurus, Tribune Media Svcs., 1999-2001. With US Army, 1958-60. Mem. ABA, NYSE (arbitrator 1996—), Am. Arbitration Assn. (arbitrator 1993, mediator 1994—), Internat. Coun. of Shopping Ctrs., Turnaround Mgmt. Assn., Beta Gamma Sigma. Home: 2626 N Lakeview Ave Chicago IL 60614-1809 Office: DePaul U 1 E Jackson Blvd Ste 7010 Chicago IL 60604-2287 Business E-Mail: thegarbergroup@yahoo.com, sgarber@depaul.edu.

GARBERDING, LARRY GILBERT, retired utilities companies executive; b. Albert City, Iowa, Oct. 29, 1938; s. Gilbert D. and Lavern Marie Garberding; m. Elizabeth Ann Hankens, Aug. 20, 1961; children: Scott Richard, Kathryn Ann, Michael John. BS, Iowa State U., 1960. CPA, Nebr. Ptnr. Arthur Andersen & Co., Chgo., 1960-71; chief fin. officer Kans.-Nebr. Natural Gas Co., Inc., Hastings, Nebr., 1971-81, Tenn. Gas Transmission, Houston, 1981-83, exec. v.p., 1983-87; pres. Tenn. Gas Mktg., Houston, 1987-88, NICOR Inc., Naperville, Ill., 1988-90; exec. v.p., chief fin. officer Detroit Edison Co., 1990—2001; ret., 2001. With U.S. Army, 1961. Mem. AICPA. Republican. Lutheran.

GARCIA, ASTRID J., newspaper executive; b. Caguas, Puerto Rico, Sept. 6, 1950; m. Robert Gillespie; children: Robert, Richard. BA with distinction, Barnard Coll., 1972; JD, Bklyn. Law Sch., 1980. Bar: N.Y. 1980. Dir., lighting designer various theatres, NYC, 1972-74; equal employment opportunity specialist Gen. Svcs. Adminstrn. Fed. Govt., Region II, NYC, 1974-76; paralegal So. Dist. N.Y. U.S. Atty.'s Office, NYC, 1976-80; atty. Puerto Rican Legal Def. and Edn. Fund, NYC, 1980-81, NLRB, NYC and Hartford, Conn., 1981-85; mgr. employee rels. dept. human resources The Hartford Courant, 1985-87; asst. dir. human resources The Miami (Fla.) Herald, 1987-90; v.p., dir. employee rels. St. Paul Pioneer Press, 1990-94; sr. v.p. human resources and labor, dir. labor rels. Jour. Comm., Milw., 1994-97; sr. v.p. ops. Milw. Jour. Sentinel, 1997—. Mem. N.Y. Bar Assn. Office: Milw Jour Sentinel PO Box 661 Milwaukee WI 53201-0661 Home: 10 Claudia Cir Media PA 19063-1012

GARCIA, GERSON, radio personality; b. Malaga, Spain, Aug. 10, 1963; m. Juanita Garcia; children: Thomas, Jonathan, Victoria Esperanza. Radio host, program dir. for Radio Esperanza Sta. WMBI Radio, Chgo. Avocation: cooking. Office: WMBI 820 N LaSalle Blvd Chicago IL 60610

GARCIA, MARCELO HORACIO, engineering educator, consultant; b. Cordoba, Argentina, Apr. 22, 1959; came to U.S., 1983; s. Juan Carlos Jose and Beatriz Alba Garcia; m. Estela Beti Rodriguez-Canga, May 17, 1984; children: Blas Ignacio, Emma Paina. Diploma in Engring., U. Litoral, Santa Fe, Argentina, 1982; MS in Civil Engring., U. Minn., Mpls., 1985; PhD in Civil Engring., 1989. Registered profl. engr., Argentina. Tech. asst. Agua y Energia Electrica, Santa Fe, Argentina, 1979-85; rsch. asst. St. Anthony Falls Lab., Mpls., 1983-87; rsch. fellow, 1988-89; asst. prof. U. Ill., Urbana, 1990-96, assoc. prof., 1996—2000, prof., 2000—. Cons. Govt. Taiwan, Taipei, 1993, U.S. Army of Engrs., Vicksburg, Miss., 1993—, Electricite de France, Toulousse, 1996; tech. adv. U.S./Taiwan Sedimentation, Washington, 1992-94; vis. prof. U. Litoral, Santa Fe, Argentina, 1993—, Calif. Inst. Tech., Pasadena, 1997-; disting. lectr. Hokkaido River Disaster Prevention Inst., Japan, 1990; guest lectr. U. Essen, Germany, 1995. Author: Environmental Hydrodynamics, 1996; contbr. articles to profl. jours. Recipient Karl Emil Hilgard hydraulics prize ASCE, N.Y.C., 1996, Alvin Anderson award U. Minn., Mpls., 1989; named Disting. Vis. Prof. U. Genoa, Italy, 1993. Mem. ASCE (Walter L. Huber Rsch. prize 1998), Am. Geophys. Union, Internat. Assn. for Hydraulic Rsch., Internat. Water Resources Assn., Sigma Xi. Achievements include development of the first model for sediment mixtures transport by turbidity currents in the ocean. Office: U Ill 205 N Mathews Ave Urbana IL 61801

GARCIA, OSCAR NICOLAS, computer science educator; b. Havana, Cuba, Sept. 10, 1936; s. Oscar Vicente and Leonor (Hernandez) G.; m. Diane Ford Journigan, Sept. 9, 1962; children: Flora, Virginia. BSEE, N.C. State U., Raleigh, 1961, MSEE, 1964; PhDEE, U. Md., College Park, 1969. Engr. IBM Corp., Endicott, NY, 1962-63; asst. prof. Old Dominion U., 1963-66, assoc. prof., 1969-70; research asst., instr. U. Md., 1966-69; assoc. prof. U. South Fla., Tampa, 1970-75, prof. computer sci., chmn. dept., 1975-85; prof. dept. elec. engring. and computer sci. George Washington U., Washington, 1985-95; disting. NCR prof. Wright State U., Dayton, Ohio, 1995—2003, chmn. dept. computer sci. and engring., 1995—2003; founding dean Coll. Engring. U. North Tex., Denton, 2003—. Dir. interactive sys. program in info., robotics and intelligent sys. divsn. Computer and Info. Sci. and Engring. Directorate, Intergovtl. Pers. Act, NSF, Washington, 1992-94; cons. and lectr. in field. Author: (with Y.T. Chien) Knowledge-Based Systems: Fundamentals and Tools, 1991. Fellow IEEE (bd. dirs. 1984-85, 2005—, mem. U.S. activities bd. 1984, Profl. Leadership award 1991, Richard M. Emberson award 1994), Computer Soc. of IEEE (pres. 1981-83, awards com. chmn. 2002-03, bd. govs. 2003—, sec. bd. govs. 2003-04, Richard E. Merwin Disting. Svc. award 1988, Meritorious Svc. award 1991), AAAS; mem. Assn. Computing Machinery, Am. Soc. Engring. Edn., Am. Assn. Artificial Intelligence, Sigma Xi, Eta Kappa Nu, Phi Kappa Phi, Tau Beta Pi. Office: U North Tex Coll Engring PO Box 310440 Denton TX 76203-0440 Home: 120 W El Paseo St Denton TX 76205-8590 Office Phone: 940-565-2500.

GARCIA, PAUL R., lawyer; AB in Polit. Sci. and Hispanic Studies, Vassar Coll., 1987; JD, U. Chgo., 1992. Bar: Ill. 1992, US Dist. Ct. (no. dist. Ill.). Assoc. atty. Pattishal, McAuliffe, Newbury, Hilliard & Geraldson, Chgo., 1992—94, Kirkland & Ellis, Chgo., 1994—96, ptnr., co-chair firm diversity com., 2001—; asst. US atty. US Dept. Justice, Chgo., 1996—2001. Mem.: Hispanic Nat. Bar Assn., Hispanic Lawyers Assn. Ill., Chgo. Coun. Lawyers, Internat. Trademark Assn. Office: Kirkland & Ellis 200 E Randolph Dr Chicago IL 60601-6636 Office Phone: 312-861-2327. Office Fax: 312-861-2200. E-mail: pgarcia@kirkland.com.

GARCIA D. ELISA DOLORES, lawyer; b. Bklyn., Nov. 8, 1957; d. Vincent Garcia, Jr. and Dolores Elizabeth (Canedo) Marmo; m. John Jay Hasluck, Feb. 28, 1987; children: Brooke Elisabeth, John Neville. BA, MS, SUNY, Stony Brook, 1980; JD, St. John's U., 1985. Bar: N.Y. 1986. Cons. Energy Devel. Internat., Pt. Jefferson, .Y., 1980-83; assoc. Willkie Farr & Gallagher, NYC, 1985-89; sr. counsel GAF Corp./Internat. Specialty Products, Wayne, N.J., 1989-94; regional counsel for L.Am., Philip Morris Internat., Rye Brook, N.Y., 1994-2000; exec. v.p., gen. counsel Domino's Pizza, LLC, Ann Arbor, Mich., 2000—07; exec. v.p., gen. counsel., corp. sec. Office Depot, Inc., Delray Beach, Fla., 2007—. Mem. Glen Rock (N.J.) Planning Bd., 1992-95, chmn., 1994-95. Mem. ABA, N.Y. State Bar Assn., Mich. Bar Assn., Assn. Corp. Counsel Assn. (pres. Mich. chpt.). Roman Catholic. Avocations: gardening, scuba diving. Office: Office Depot Inc 2200 Old Germantown Rd Delray Beach FL 33445

GARCIAPARRA, NOMAR (ANTHONY NOMAR GARCIAPARRA), professional baseball player; b. Whittier, Calif., July 23, 1973; m. Mia Hamm, Nov. 22, 2003; 2 children. Student, Ga. Tech. Shortstop Fla. St. League, Sarasota, Fla., 1994, Ea. League, Trenton, NJ, 1995, Internat. League, Pawtucket, 1996, Boston Red Sox, 1996—2004, Chicago Cubs, 2004—05; infielder LA Dodgers, 2005—. Named Am. League Rookie Player of the Yr., The Sporting News, 1997, Baseball Writers' Assn. Am., 1997, Player's Choice Am. League Outstanding Rookie, AL Batting Champion, 1999, 2000, NL Comeback Player Yr, Players Choice Awards, 2006; named to Am. League All-Star Team, 1997, 1999, 2000, 2002, 2003, Nat. League All-Star Team, 2006, Cape Cod League Hall of Fame, 2002. Achievements include being a mem. of U.S. Olympic Baseball Team, 1992; led Am. League in Batting Avg., 1999 (.357), 2000 (.372); led Am. League in Hits (209), 1997. Office: LA Dodgers 1000 Elysian Park Ave Los Angeles CA 90012

GARD, BEVERLY J., state legislator; b. NC, Mar. 8, 1940; m. Donald Gard; children: David, Doug. BS, U. Tenn., Chattanooga; grad. studies, U. Tenn. Biochemist Eli Lilly & Co.; councilwoman City of Greenfield, Ind., 1976-88; mem. Ind. State Senate from 28th dist., 1988—. Mem. Hancock Assn Retarded Citizens, Ind. Assn. Cities and Towns. Republican. Methodist. Office: Ind Senate Dist 28 200 W Washington St Indianapolis IN 46204-2728

GARD, JOHN, state legislator; b. Milw., Aug. 3, 1963; m. Cathy Zeuske; 2 children. BA, U. Wis., La Crosse, 1986. Mem. from dist. 89 Wis. State Assembly, Madison, 1987—, mem. joint com. rev. adminstrv. rules, 1987-98, mem. tourism and recreation conf., 1987-98, mem. select com. welfare reform, 1987-98, chmn. assembly welfare reform com., 1987-98, co-chair joint com. on fin., mem. legis. coun., audit coms., mem. joint. com. on employment rels., spkr., 2003—. Mem. KC, Ducks Unltd., Sportsmen's Club, Lions. Office: PO Box 119 481 Aubin St Peshtigo WI 54157-1142

GARDEBRING, SANDRA S., academic administrator; Grad., Luther Coll., Decorah, Iowa; JD, U. Minn. Dir. Region 5 U.S. EPA; commr. Minn. Pollution Control Agy., Minn. Dept. Human Svcs.; judge Minn. Ct. Appeals; assoc. justice Minn. Supreme Ct., 1991-98; v.p. univ. rels. U. Minn., 1998—2004; v.p. univ. advancement Calif. Polytech. State Univ., San Luis Obispo, 2004—. Bd. dirs. Nature Conservancy of Minn., Regions Hosp. Hearth Connection, Greater Mpls. Conv. and Visitors Assn. Mailing: 1055 Capistrano Ct San Luis Obispo CA 93405

GARDENHIRE, RONALD CLYDE, professional athletics manager; m. Carol Kissling Gardenhire; children: Toby, Tiffany, Tara. BA in phys. edn., U. Tex. Mgr. Class A Kenosha, 1988; bench coach Minn. Twins, 1995, 1st base coach, 1996, 3d base coach, 1998, mgr., 2002—. Named Co-mgr. of Yr., So. league, 1990, Best Managerial Prospect, Baseball Am., Best Mgr., 1989; named to Carolina League All-Star team, 1979. Office: Minn Twins 34 Kirby Puckett Pl Minneapolis MN 55415

GARDIN, JULIUS MARKUS, cardiologist, educator; b. Detroit, Jan. 14, 1949; s. Abram and Fania (Toba) G.; children: Adam Lev, Tova Michal, Margot Anne. BS with high distinction, U. Mich., 1968, MD cum laude, 1972. Diplomate Am. Bd. Internal Medicine; cert. cardiovascular diseases. Intern then resident in medicine U. Mich., Ann Arbor, 1972-75; fellow in cardiology Georgetown U., Washington, 1975-77; dir. cardiology noninvasive lab., staff cardiologist Lakeside VA Med. Ctr., Chgo., 1977-79; staff cardiologist Northwestern U., Chgo., 1977—79, asst. prof. Med. Sch., 1978—79; dir. cardiology noninvasive lab. Irvine Med. Ctr. U. Calif., Orange, 1979-2000, from asst. prof. to assoc. prof. Irvine Med. Ctr., 1979—89, prof., 1989-2000, chief cardiology Irvine, 1994-99; acting chief cardiology Long Beach (Calif.) VA Med. Ctr., 1982—84; prof. Wayne State U., Detroit, 2000—; St. John Guild disting. chair, cardiovascular diseases St. John Hosp. and Med. Ctr., Detroit, 2000—, chief div. cardiology, 2000—07, vice chmn. rsch. dept. medicine, 2007—; prof., chmn. dept. internal medicine Touro U. Coll. Medicine, NJ, 2008—; chmn. dept. internal medicine Hackensack U. Med. Ctr., NJ, 2008—. Co-editor: Textbook of Two-Dimensional Echocardiography, 1983, assoc. editor Preventive Cardiology, 2000, 05; assoc. editor (jour.) Update on Cardiovascular Diagnostics, 1982, Am. Jour. Cardiac Imaging, 1985-97, Jour. Am. Soc. Echocardiography, 2007—; mem. editl. bd. Archives of Internal Medicine and Chest, 1978-88, Am. Jour. Noninvasive Cardiology, 1985-95, Am. Jour. Cardiology, 1987-94, 97—, Cardiovascular Imaging, 1988—, Echocardiography, 1985—, Jour. Am. Coll. Cardiology, 1990-94, 2001-05, Am. Jour. Geriatric Cardiology, 1992—, Am. Jour. Sports Medicine, 1998-2004, Jour. Am. Soc. Echocardiography, 1992-2001; cardiovasc. area editor Jour. Clin. Ultrasound, 1989-94; contbr. articles to profl. jours. Maj. Med. Svc. Corps USAR. Grantee Am. Heart Assn., 1980-84, 99-02, Nat. Heart Lung and Blood Inst., 1988-; named one of Best Drs. in Am. Woodward White Publs., 1994-, Am.'s Top Drs. Castle Connolly Publs., 2002-. Fellow ACP, Am. Coll. Cardiology (physician workforce adv., health care reform and echocardiography coms., 1993-99, publs. com. 2007—), Am. Heart Assn. (coun. clin. cardiology, coun. epidemiology and prevention, coun. cardiovascular radiology, ACC/AHA/ACP-ASIM task force to update guidelines for mgmt. of patients with chronic stable angina 1998-99, 01-02, co-chair 2007—, Seymour Gordon Disting. Achievement Award AHA Detroit chpt. 2006), Soc. Geriat. Cardiology (v.p. 1990-92, pres. 1992-93); mem. Internat. Cardiac Doppler Soc. (bd. dirs., chmn. Pan-Am. sect. 1984—, v.p. 1988-90, pres. 1990-92, exec. sec. 2006-), Am. Soc. Echocardiography (bd. dirs., treas. 1989-91, v.p. 1991-93, pres. 1993-95, chmn. nomenclature and stds. 1991-95, chmn. task force on standardized echo report 1999-02, co-chmn. writing group on vascular imaging 2001—, assoc. editor Jour. 2007—), U. Mich. Med. Ctr. Alumni Assn. (bd. govs. 1979-81), Phi Beta Kappa, Alpha Omega Alpha, Phi Delta Epsilon. Jewish. Office: Hackensack U Med Ctr 30 Prospect Ave Hackensack NJ 07601 Office Phone: 201-996-3500. Personal E-mail: gardindoc@aol.com.

GARDINER, JOHN ANDREW, political science educator; b. Niagara Falls, NY, July 10, 1937; s. William Cecil and Anne Charlotte (Hicks) G.; m. Jane Enstrom, Nov. 6, 1993; children: Margaret, Allison, Barrett. BA, Princeton U., 1959; MA, Yale U., 1962; LLB, Harvard U., 1963, PhD, 1966. Bar: Mass. 1963. Asst. prof. U. Wis., Madison, 1965-68; assoc. prof. SUNY, Stony Brook, 1968-69; chief rsch. planning Nat. Inst. Justice, Washington, 1969-71, dir. rsch. ops., 1971-73, asst. dir., 1973-74; prof. polit. sci. U. Ill., Chgo., 1974—, head dept. polit. sci., 1974-76, dir. office social sci. rsch., 1987—2002, acting assoc. dean Liberal Arts and Scis., 1991—92, 2000—02. Author: Fraud Control Game, 1984, Decisions for Sale, 1978, Politics of Corruption, 1970, Traffic and the Police 1969; contbr. articles to profl. jours. V.p. Ill. Citizens for Better Care, Chgo., 1988—90; rsch. dir. Chgo. Ethics Project, 1986—88. Rsch. fellow Am. Judicature Soc., 1985-86. Mem. Phi Beta Kappa. Office: U Ill Pol Sci M/C 276 1007 W Harrison St Chicago IL 60607-7137 E-mail: gracelan@uic.edu.

GARDNER, BRIAN E., lawyer; b. Des Moines, July 13, 1952; s. Lawrence E. and Sarah I. (Hill) G.; m. Rondi L. Veland, Aug. 7, 1976; children: Meredith Anne, Stephanie Lynn, John Clinton. BS with distinction, Iowa State U., 1974; JD with high distinction, U. Iowa, 1978. Bar: Iowa 1978, Mo. 1978, U.S. Dist. Ct. (we. dist.) Mo. 1978, Kans. 1979, U.S. Dist. Ct. Kans. 1979, U.S. Ct. Appeals (10th cir.) 1980. Assoc. Morrison, Hecker, Curtis, Kuder & Parrish, Kansas City, Mo., 1978-80, Parker & Handsaker, Nevada, Iowa, 1980-81, Morrison, Hecker, Curtis, Kuder & Parrish, Overland Park, Kans., 1981-83; ptnr. Morrison & Hecker, Kansas City, Mo., 1983—2002, mng. ptnr., 1990—93, 1996—2002; city atty. Mission Hills, Kans., 1992—2003; co-mng. ptnr. Stinson Morrison Hecker LLP, Kansas City, 2002—04; exec. v.p., gen. counsel Hallmark Cards, Inc., Kansas City, 2004—. Bd. dirs. Overland Park Conv. and Visitors Bur., 1985-97, chmn., 1988-90; dir., mem. exec. com. Johnson County C.C. Found., Overland Park, 1990—, pres., 1997-98; bd. dirs. KCPT, 1993-99, 2000—, chmn., 1997-98; active Kansas City Area Devel. Coun., 1992—, Civic Coun. Greater Kansas City, 1998—; bd. dir. Crown Media, Swope Cmty. Enterprises. Mem. Kans. Bar Assn., Kans. Assn. Def. Counsel, Kansas City Met. Bar Assn., Mo. Bar Assn., Johnson County Bar Assn., Blue Hills Country Club, Cardinal Key, Phi Beta Kappa, Phi Kappa Phi. Lutheran. Avocation: golf. Office: Hallmark Cards Inc MD 339 2501 McGee Trafficway Kansas City MO 64108 Mailing: Hallmark Cards Inc PO Box 419580 Kansas City MO 64141-6580 Office Phone: 816-274-5111. Office Fax: 816-274-5061.

GARDNER, CHARLES OLDA, botanist, researcher, financial analyst; b. Tecumseh, Neb., Mar. 15, 1919; s. Olda Cecil and Frances E. (Stover) G.; m. Wanda Marie Steinkamp, June 9, 1947; children— Charles Olda, Jr., Lynda Frances, Thomas Edward, Richard Alan BS, U. Nebr., 1941, MS, 1948; MBA, Harvard U., 1943; PhD, N.C. State U., 1951. Asst. extension agronomist U. Nebr., Lincoln, 1946-48, assoc. prof., 1952-57, chmn. statis. lab., 1957-68, prof., 1957-70, regents prof., 1970-89, prof. emeritus, 1989—, interim head Biometrics Ctr., 1988-89; asst. statistician N.C. State U., Raleigh, 1951-52. Vis. prof. U. Wis., 1962-63; cons. CIMMYT and Rockefeller Found., Mex., Latin Am., 1964—, cons., CIBA-GEIGY, Eastern half of U.S., 1983; cons., lectr. Dept. Agr., Queensland, Australia, 1977; cons., lectr. maize program Kasetsart U. and Ministry of Agr., Bangkok, 1990; spl. lectr. advanced maize breeding course for leaders of nat. maize programs in developing countries Internat. Ctr. for Maize and Wheat Improvement, El Batan, Mex., 1989, 91, 93. Contbr. articles to profl. jours. Elder, Eastridge Presbyterian Ch.; pres. Eastridge PTA. Served to capt., U.S. Army, 1943-46 Recipient Outstanding Research and Creativity award U. ebr., 1981, USDA Disting. Service award, 1988, Award of Merit U. Nebr. Alumni Assn., 1996. Fellow Am. Soc. of Agronomy (pres. 1982, agronomic service award, 1988), Crop Sci. Soc. of Am. (pres. 1975, recipient Crop Sci. award, 1978, DeKalb-Pfizer Crop Sci. Disting. Career award 1984), AAAS (chmn. sect. O com. 1987); mem. Am. Genetic Assn., Genetic Soc. of Am., Biometric Soc. (mem. regional com.), Sigma Xi, Gamma Sigma Delta (Internat. Disting. Svc. Agr. 1977). Republican. Presbyterian. Avocations: photography; golf; fishing; gardening. Home: 5835 Meadowbrook Ln Lincoln NE 68510-4026 Office: U Neb Dept Biometry Lincoln NE 68583-0712

GARDNER, CHESTER STONE, electrical and computer engineering educator, consultant; b. Jamaica, NY, Mar. 29, 1947; s. Frederick Rothrick and June Marie (Miller) G.; m. ancy Christine Cunningham, Sept. 14, 1968; children: Nathan Fredrick, Jeremy Collin. BS, Mich. State U., 1969; MS, Northwestern U., 1971, PhD, 1973. Mem. tech. staff Bell Telephone Labs., Naperville, Ill., 1969-71; asst. prof. U. Ill., Urbana, 1973-77, assoc. prof., 1977-81, prof., 1981—, assoc. dean engring., 1987—, acting dean engring., v.p. acad. affairs, 1988-89. Sr. v.p. Quantum Labs., Inc., Laurel, Md., 1983-88; Beckman assoc. U. Ill. Ctr. Advanced Study.; cons. Caterpillar, Inc., 1978-85, Deere & Co., Ill., 1981-85, C.E. U.S. Army, 1978-88, USN, Washington, 1981-84, No. Ill. Gas Co., 1980-82, Sandia Nat. Lab., N.Mex., 1985, Booz-Allen & Hamilton, 1984, TRW value div., Ohio, 1982-84, GE Astro Space div., Pa., 1988—. Contbr. over 240 pub. articles, tech. reports and conf. papers; patentee in field. Summer fellow Air Force Geophysic Lab., 1985. Fellow IEEE (chair region 4 tech. activities 1979-80), Optical Soc. Am. (chair atmospheric optics tech. group 1982-84); mem. Am. Geophys. Union, Am. Meteorol. Soc. (com. on laser atmospheric studies), Sigma Xi, Tau Beta Pi, Eta Kappa Nu. Avocations: canoeing, hiking, skiing. Home: 1904 Trout Valley Dr Champaign IL 61822-9784 Office: U Ill 506 S Wright St Urbana IL 61801-3620

GARDNER, HOWARD ALAN, travel company executive, writer, editor; b. Rockford, Ill., June 24, 1920; s. Ellis Ralph and Leanor (Roseman) Gardner; m. Marjorie Ruth Klein, Sept. 29, 1945; children: Jill, Jeffrey. BA, U. Mich., 1941. With advt. dept. Chgo. Tribune, 1941-43; mgr. promotion dept. Esquire mag., 1943-46; advt. mgr. Mrs. Klein's Food Products Co., 1946-48; pres. Sales-Aide Svc. Co., 1948-56, Gardner & Stein, 1956-59, Gardner, Stein & Frank, Inc., Chgo., 1959-83, Fun-derful World, Chgo., 1983—. Mem.: Nat. Geog. Soc., Am. Geog. Soc., Confrerie de la Chaine des Rotisseurs (Bailli Honoraire, grand comdr., Pres.'s medal of honor), Travel Industry Assn. Am., Mid-Am. Club, Internat. Club, Travelers' Century Club, Phi Beta Kappa. Home: 100 E Bellevue Pl Chicago IL 60611-1157 Office: Fun-derful World 100 E Bellevue Pl Chicago IL 60611-1157 Home Phone: 312-944-4060; Office Phone: 312-944-4061.

GARDNER, LEE M., automotive parts executive; Pres., co-COO Masco Tech, Taylor, Mich., pres., COO, 1998—. Office: Masco Tech Inc 21001 Van Born Rd Taylor MI 48180

GARDNER, RANDALL, state legislator, realtor; b. Bowling Green, Ohio, Aug. 20, 1958; s. Dallas E. and Velma (Brownson) G.; m. Sandra Kay Ford; children: Brooks, Christine, Austin. BS, Bowling Green State U., 1981, MA, 1987. Journalist Daily Sentinel-Tribune, Bowling Green, 1981-86; tchr. Otsego (Ohio) Local Schs., 1981-86; realtor, Bowling Green; mem. Ohio Ho. of Reps., Columbus, 1985-2000, asst. minority whip; mem. Ohio Senate from 2nd dist., Columbus, 2001—. Pres. Wood County Young Reps. Club, 1976-80; co-chmn. 5th Dist. Reagan for Pres. Com., 1980; dist. del. Rep. Nat. Conv., 1980, 84; vice chmn. Wood County Bd. Elections, 1982-85; exec. com. Wood County Rep. Com., 1982-86. Recipient Watchdog of Treasury award; Jennings scholar. Mem. Ohio Assn. Election Ofcls., Ohio Edn. Assn., Wood County Hist. Soc., Wood County Farm Bur., Legis. Exch. Coun., Sons Am. Legion, Omicron Delta Kappa. Home: 14900 Mitchell Rd Bowling Green OH 43402-8900

GARDNER, ROBERT A., state legislator; b. Algeria, Sept. 22, 1945; BA, postgrad, Bowling Green State U., Clev. State U., Kent State U. Mem. 18th dist. Ohio Senate, Columbus, 1997—. Trustee Madison Twp., 1982-96; commr. Lake County, 1987-96. Mem. Mason, Am. Legion. Office: Senate Bldg Rm 034, Ground Fl Columbus OH 43215

GARDOCKI, CHRISTOPHER, professional football player; b. Stone Mountain, Ga., Feb. 7, 1970; m. Sally Gardocki; 1 child, Christopher. Student, Clemson U. Punter Chgo. Bears, 1991-94, Indpls. Colts, 1995-98, Cleve. Browns, 1999—. Co-creator game NFL Trivia Blitz. Named to Pro Bowl, 1996. Office: Cleve Browns 1085 W 3rd St Cleveland OH 44114-1001 also: Cleveland Browns 76 Lou Groxa Blvd Berea OH 44017

GARDUNIO, JOSEPH, landscaping company executive; b. Chgo., Feb. 12, 1955; m. Marta Salas; children: Joey, Ricky, Alex, Selena. Pres. Unico Landscaping Inc., 1991—. Office: Unico Landscaping Inc 5119 S Hoyne Ave Chicago IL 60609-5513

GARFINKEL, JANE E., lawyer; b. NYC, Dec. 2, 1952; d. Albert E. and Rita H. (Halpern) G.; m. Louis F. Solimine, May 20, 1979. BA, Wheaton Coll., 1974; MA, U. Mich., 1975, JD, 1979. Bar: Ohio 1980. Assoc. Smith & Schnacke, Cin., 1980-88, ptnr., 1988-89, Thompson Hine LLP, Cin., 1989—. Office: Thompson Hine LLP 312 Walnut St Ste 1400 Cincinnati OH 45202-4089 Office Phone: 513-352-6530. Business E-Mail: jane.garfinkel@thompsonhine.com.

GARLAND, JAMES C., retired academic administrator; BA in Physics, Princeton U., 1964; D in Solid State Physics, Cornell U., 1969; postgrad., Cambridge U., 1969-70. Asst. prof. physics Ohio State U., 1970-75, assoc. prof. physics, 1975-80, prof., 1980-96, chair dept. physics; pres. Miami U., Oxford, Ohio, 1996—2006. Acting v.p. for rsch. and grad. studies Ohio State U., dir. materials rsch. lab., 1986-90; pres., bd. dirs. Ohio State U. Rsch. Found., 1982-83; First Fin. Bancorp; First Nat. Bank of SW Ohio. Contbr. articles to profl. jours. Recipient numerous rsch. grants; postdoctoral fellowship NSF. Fellow Am. Phys. Soc. E-mail: w8zr@arrl.net.

GARLAND, JAMES HENRY, bishop emeritus; b. Wilmington, Ohio, Dec. 13, 1931; Attended, Wilmington Coll., Ohio; BA Edn., Ohio State U., 1953; MA Philosophy, Mt. St. Mary's Sem., Cin., 1960; MS Soc. Work, Cath. U., Washington, 1965. Ordained priest Archdiocese of Cin., Ohio, 1959, aux. bishop Ohio, 1984—92; ordained bishop, 1984; bishop Diocese of Marquette, Mich.,

1992—2005, bishop emeritus, 2005—. Chmn. US Cath. Conf. Com. for the Campaign for Human Devel.; mem. adminstrn. com., bd. US. Cath. Conf. / Nat. Conf. of Cath. Bishops. Roman Catholic. Office: Pastoral Office 300 Rock St PO Box 550 Marquette MI 49855-0550 Office Phone: 906-227-9113. Office Fax: 906-228-2469. E-mail: jhg@dioceseofmarquette.org.*

GARMAN, RITA B., state supreme court justice; b. Aurora, Ill., Nov. 19, 1943; children: Sara Ellen, Andrew Gil. BS in Econs., U. Ill., 1965; JD with distinction, U. Iowa, 1968. Asst. state atty. Vermilion County, 1969—73; pvt. practice Sebat, Swanson, Banks, Lessen & Garman, 1973; assoc. cir. judge, 1974—86; cir. judge Fifth Jud. Cir., 1986—95, presiding cir. judge, 1987—95; judge Fourth Dist. Appellate Ct., 1996—2001; justice Ill. Supreme Ct., 2001—. Mem.: Ill. Judge's Assn., Vermilion County Bar Assn., Iowa Bar Assn., Ill. State Bar Assn. Office: Ill Supreme Ct 160 N LaSalle St Chicago IL 60601

GARMAN, TERESA AGNES, state legislator; b. Ft. Dodge, Iowa, Aug. 29, 1937; d. John Clement and Barbara Marie (Korsa) Lennon; m. Merle A. Garman, Aug. 5, 1961; children: Laura Ann Garman Hansen, Rachel Irene Garman Coder, Robert Sylvester, Sarah Teresa Garman Powers. Grad. high sch., Ft. Dodge. With employee relations dept. 3M Co., Ames, Iowa, 1974-86; mem. Iowa Ho. of Reps., Des Moines, 1986—. Asst. majority leader, mem. platform com., del. Rep. Nat. Conv., 1988, del., mem. platform com., 1992, del., 1996; mem. Iowa Rep. Ctrl. Com. Mem. Rep. Farm Policy Coun., Story County Rep. Women, Story County Pork Prodrs., Farm Bur., Story City C. of C., Nev. C. of C. Roman Catholic. Avocations: horseback riding, gardening. Home: 1799 Old Bloomington Rd Ames IA 50010-9469 Office: State Capitol Des Moines IA 50319-0001

GARMEL, MARION BESS SIMON, retired arts journalist; b. El Paso, Tex., Oct. 15, 1936; d. Marcus and Frieda (Alfman) Simon; m. Raymond Lewis Garmel, Nov. 28, 1965 (dec. Feb. 1986); 1 child, Cynthia Rogers; 1 stepchild, Christine Blum. Student, U. Tex., El Paso, 1954-55; BJ, U. Tex., Austin, 1958. Exec. sec. Nat. Student Assn., Phila., 1958-59, pub. rels. dir., 1960-61; sec. World Assembly Youth, Paris, Brussels, 1959-60; dictationist Wall Street Jour., Washington, 1961; libr., staff writer Nat. Observer, Silver Spring, Md., 1961-70; art critic Indpls. News, 1971-91, editor Free Time sect., 1975-91, critic radio and TV, 1991-95; theater critic Indpls. Star and News, 1995-99, Indpls. Star, 1999—2002, ret., 2002. Mem. Nat. Fedn. Press Women (1st Place Critics award 1974), Ind. Soc. Profl. Journalists (1st place criticism 2002), Hadassah Women's Zionist Orgn. Am. (life), Woman's Press Club Ind. (1st Place Critics award 1995, 2002). Jewish. Avocations: tennis, bridge. Home: 226 E 45th St Indianapolis IN 46205-1712 E-mail: mgarmel@earthlink.net.

GARN, STANLEY MARION, physical anthropologist, educator; b. 1922; AB, Harvard U., 1942, AM, 1947, PhD, 1948. Rsch. assoc. chem. engring. Chem. Warfare Svc. Devel. Lab. MIT, 1942-44; tech. editor Polaroid Co., 1944-46; cons. applied anthropology, 1946-47; rsch. fellow cardiology Mass. Gen. Hosp., Boston, 1946-52; instr. anthropology Harvard U., 1948-52; anthropologist Forsyth Dental Infirmary, Boston, 1947-52; dir. Forsyth face size project Army Chem. Corps, 1950-52; chmn. dept. growth and genetics Fels Rsch. Inst., Yellow Springs, Ohio, 1952-68; fellow Ctr. Human Growth and Devel. U. Mich., Ann Arbor, also prof. nutrition and anthropology, 1968-92, prof. emeritus, 1993—. Raymond Pearl lectr. Human Biol. Coun., 1992—; E.B.D. Neuhauser lectr. Soc. Pediatric Radiology, 1981. Author: Human Races, 1970, Gain and Loss of Cortical Bone, 1970; also contbr. over 1000 articles to profl. jours.; editorial bds. numerous jours. Recipient Disitng. Svc. award, U. Mich., Charles Darwin Lifetime Achievement award, Am. Assn. Phys. Anthropologists, 1994, Franz Boas award, Human Biol. Coun., 2002. Fellow AAAS, Am. Acad. Pediatrics (hon. assoc.), Am. Anthropol. Assn., Am. Acad. Arts and Scis., Human Biology Coun., Am. Soc. Clin. Nutrition, Am. Soc. Nutrition Scis.; mem. NAS, Am. Assn. Phys. Anthropologists, Internat. Assn. Dental Rsch., Internat. Orgn. Study Human Devel., Am. Soc. Naturalists, Internat. Assn. Human Biologists (coun.).

GARNER, JIM D., state official, lawyer; b. Coffeyville, Kans., June 14, 1963; s. Wayne W. and Carol L. Garner. AA with honors, Coffeyville C.C., 1983; BA in History with distinction, U. Kans., 1985, JD, 1988. Bar: Kans. 1988, U.S. Dist. Ct. Kans. 1988, U.S. Ct. Appeals (10th cir.) 1990, U.S. Supreme Ct. 2003. Jud. clk. for Dale E. Saffels U.S. Dist. Judge, Kans., 1988-90; atty. Hall, Levy, Lively, DeVore, Belot and Bell, Coffeyville, 1990-92; pvt. practice Coffeyville, 1992—; mem. Kans. Ho. of Reps., 1991—2003, minority leader, 1999—2003; sec. Kans. Dept. Labor, 2003—. Bd. dirs. Nat. Assn. State Workforce Agys.; mem. Program for Emerging Polit. Leaders, Darden Sch. of Bus., U. Va., 1994, Bowhay Inst. for Legis. Leadership Devel., Coun. of State Govts., U. Wis., 1995. Active cmty. co-chair, City of Coffeyville's Youth Focus Task Force, 1998; adv. com. Youth and Bus. Tng. Program; bd. dirs. Hospice Care Inc., Coffeyville, 1993-97, Pioneer chpt. ARC, 1998—2003; mem. leadership Coffeyville Class of 1995; mem. legis. adv. bd. Dem. Leadership Coun., 1999-2002; mem. bd. govs. U. Kans. Law Sch., 2000-02. Mem. Kans. Bar Assn., Order of Coif, Phi Alpha Theta, Phi Kappa Phi, Lions, Rotary. Office: 114 W 9th St Coffeyville KS 67337-5810 Home: Po Box 1184 Lawrence KS 66044-8184 Business E-Mail: jim.garner@dol.ks.gov.

GARNER, SHIRLEY NELSON, language educator; b. Waxahachie, Tex., Aug. 8, 1935; d. Cleo and Ruby D. Nelson; m. Frank L. Garner, Nov. 24, 1972; children: Hart Phillip, Celia Ann. AB magna cum laude, U. Tex., 1957; MA, Stanford U., 1966, PhD, 1972. Instr. Stanford (Calif.) U., 1964-65, instr., asst. to dir. fresh composition, 1967-70; asst. prof. U. Minn., Mpls., 1972-76, assoc. prof., 1976-86, assoc. mem. faculty Women's Studies, 1980—86, prof., 1986—, chair Women's Studies, 1989-90, dir. Ctr. Advanced Feminist Studies, 1990-94, chair English dept., 1994—2000, assoc. dean grad. sch., 2001—. Editor: (with Personal Narratives Collective) Interpreting Women's Lives: Feminist Theory and Personal Narratives, 1989, (with Madelon Sprengnether) Shakespearean Tragedy and Gender, 1995, Antifeminism in the Academy, 1996, (with VeVe Clark, Ketu Katrak, and Margaret Higonnet) Is Feminism Dead?, 2000; editor, contbg. author: (with Clare Kahane and Madelon Sprengnether) The (M)other Tongue: Essays in Feminist Psychoanalytic Interpretation, 1985; contbg. author: Bad Shakespeare: Revaluations of the the Shakespeare Canon, 1988, Seduction and Theory: Readings of Gender, Representation and Rhetoric, 1989, Shakespeare's Personality, 1989, Novel Mothering, 1991, Feminism and Psychoanalysis, Feminism and Philosophy: Essential Readings in Theory, Reinterpretation and Application, 1992, The Intimate Critique: Autobiographical Literary Criticism, 1993; founder, mem. editl. bd. Hurricane Alice, 1983-95; mem. editl. bd. Signs, 1992-95; contbr. articles, revs. to profl. jours. Recipient Horace T. Morse-Amoco award, 1982, Pres.'s award for outstanding svc., 1999, Mullen/Spector/Truax Women's Leadership award, 2007; Phillips Petroleum Found. scholar, 1953-57; Woodrow Wilson fellow, 1959-60, Sorptimists' fellow, 1965-66, 66-67; grantee U. Minn. 1974-76, 81, 87-88, Bush Sabbatical, 1984-85, Office Internat. Edn., 1988, CLA, 1981, 84-90, UROP, 1991-92; named to U. Minn. Acad. Disting. Tchrs., 1999. Mem. MLA (co-chair Marriage and the Family in Shakespeare divsn., Shakespeare sect. 1979, chair 1980-82, chair/co-chair various seminars, symposia), Nat. Women's Studies Assn., Midwest Modern Lang. Assn. (sec. Shakespeare sect. 1972, chair 1973, nominations com. 1974-77, sec. Women and Lit. sect. 1978-79, chair 1980-81, nomination com. Women and Lit. sect. 1981-84), Shakespeare Assn. Office: U Minn English Dept 207 Church St SE Minneapolis MN 55455-0134 Office Phone: 612-625-4858. Business E-Mail: sngarner@umn.edu.

GARNETT, JESS, former state legislator; Pres. Garnett Wood Products, 1965—. Home: PO Box 801 West Plains MO 65775-0801

GAROFALO, DONALD R., window manufacturing executive; b. St. Paul; Sales rep. Andersen Corp., Bayport, Minn., 1965—93, v.p. bus. planning and devel., 1993—95, sr. v.p., bus. planning and devel., 1995—96, exec. v.p., COO, 1996—98, pres., 1998—2002, CEO, 1998—. Bd. Capital City Partnership, St. Paul; bd. trustees Science Mus. of Minn.; exec. com. Courage Ctr.; bd. dir. Bayport Found. Office: Andersen Corp 100 4th Ave N Bayport MN 55003-1096

GARON, PHILIP STEPHEN, lawyer; b. Duluth, Minn., Nov. 11, 1947; s. Lawrence and Helen (Cohen) G.; m. Phyllis Sue Ansel, Mar. 22, 1970; children: Edward B., Sara B. BA summa cum laude, U. Minn., 1969, JD summa cum laude, 1972. Bar: Minn. 1972, DC 1973, US Dist. Ct. Minn. 1974. Assoc. Covington & Burling, Washington, 1972-74, Faegre & Benson, Mpls., 1974-79, ptnr., 1980—. Mem. mgmt. com. Faegre & Benson, 1992-2004, chmn., 2001-04; mem. US Law Firm Group, 2002-, pres., 2005. Co-author: Minnesota Corporation Law & Practice, 1996, 2d edit., 2004 (Burton awards for legal writing 2001, 07). Bd. dirs. Herzl Camp, Webster, Wis., 1985-91, Beth El Synagogue, Mpls., 1989-99, v.p., 1993-96; bd. vis. U. Minn. Law Sch., 2003-, vice chair, 2007. Mem. Minn. Bar Assn. (pres. exec. coun. bus. law sect. 1996-97). Avocations: tennis, reading, bridge. Office: Faegre & Benson 2200 Wells Fargo Ctr 90 S 7th St Ste 2200 Minneapolis MN 55402-3901 Office Phone: 612-766-8101. Business E-Mail: pgaron@faegre.com.

GARRATT, REGINALD GEORGE, electronics executive; b. Birmingham, Eng., Sept. 25, 1929; came to the U.S., 1974; s. Wallace Thomas and Beatrice Maud (Round) G.; m. Gwendoline Jean Parry (dec. 1986); children: Mark, Jonathan, Sean; m. Gail Elizabeth Mansfield, July 1, 1989. Degree in mech. engring., Aston U., 1951. Dir. mktg. Honeywell (UK) Ltd., London, 1965-70; mng. dir. Honeywell (South Africa) Ltd., Johannesburg, 1970-74; gen. mktg. mgr. components divsn. Honeywell, Freeport, Ill., 1974-77; v.p. mktg. Knowles Electronics, Inc., Itasca, Ill., 1977-89, pres., COO, 1989-91, pres., CEO, 1991-97, chmn., CEO, 1997—. Bd. dirs. Hear Now, Denver, 1993—, Hearing Industries Assn., Washington, 1983—, Better Hearing Inst., Washington, 1981-90. Avocations: squash, tennis, bridge, golf, antiques. Office: Knowles Electronics Inc 1151 Maplewood Dr Itasca IL 60143-2071 Home: 849 Barcarmil Way Naples FL 34110-0901

GARRETSON, MATTHEW LEE, lawyer; b. 1970; BA, Yale U., 1997, Salmon P. Chase Coll. Law, 1997. Bar: Ohio 1998. Ptnr. Garretson Law Firm, Cin. Named one of Ohio's Rising Stars, Super Lawyers, 2006. Office: Garretson Law Firm 9545 Kenwood Rd Cincinnati OH 45245 Office Phone: 513-794-0400. Office Fax: 513-936-5186.

GARRETT, BOB, radio personality; Radio personality WEBN, Cin. Office: Webn Radio 8044 Montgomery Rd Ste 650 Cincinnati OH 45236-2959

GARRETT, DEAN, professional basketball player; b. LA, Nov. 27, 1966; s. Robert and Bobbie G.; m. Natasha Taylor; 1 child, Devyreau. Student, San Francisco City Coll., 1984-86; B of Criminal Justice, Ind. U., 1988. Center PAOK, Greece, 1995-96, Minn. Timberwolves, Minneapolis, 1996-97, 98—, Denver Nuggets, 1997-98. Avocations: baseball, football. Office: c/o Minn Timberwolves 600 1st Ave North Minneapolis MN 55403-9801

GARRETT, DWAYNE EVERETT, veterinary clinic executive; Office: Wentzville Veterinary 602 E Pearce Blvd Wentzville MO 63385-1538

GARRIGAN, RICHARD THOMAS, finance educator, consultant, editor; b. Cleve., Mar. 4, 1938; s. Walter John and Priscilla Marie (Hill) G.; m. Kristine Ottesen, Dec. 26, 1962; 1 child, Matthew Osborne. BS summa cum laude, Ohio State U., 1961, MA, 1963; MS, U. Wis., 1966, PhD, 1973. Asst. prof. fin. U. Wis., Whitewater, 1974-76, assoc. prof., 1976-77; v.p. rsch. Real Estate Rsch. Corp., Chgo., 1975-76; presdl. exch. exec. Fed. Home Loan Bank Bd., Washington, 1977-78; assoc. prof. DePaul U., Chgo., 1978-83, prof., 1983—. Mem. Midwestern regional adv. bd. Fed. Nat. Mortgage Assn., 1993-96; mem. adv. bd. Bell Fed. Bank, Chgo., 1996-98; bd. dirs. Fed. Home Loan Bank Chgo., 1983-86. Co-editor: The Handbook of Mortgage Banking, 1985, Real Estate Investment Trusts, Structure, Analysis and Strategy, 1998; editor Dow Jones-Irwin Series in Real Estate, 1987-90; contbr. articles to profl. jours. Served with U.S. Army, 1955-58. Alfred P. Sloan scholar, 1959-61; recipient Excellence award Haskins and Sells, 1960, Achievement award Pres.'s of U.S. Commn. on Exec. Exchange, 1978; fellow Mershon Nat. Security, Ohio State U., 1961-62, urban studies Ford Found., 1964-65, bus. Ford Found., 1965-66. Mem. Am. Real Estate Soc., Am. Real Estate and Urban Econs. Assn., Bldg. Owners and Mgrs. Assn. of Chgo. (adv. bd. 1994-98), Sphinx, Univ. Club Chgo., Lambda Alpha Internat. (Ely chpt. sec. 1984, v.p. 1985, pres. 1986), Beta Gamma Sigma, Phi Kappa Phi, Phi Eta Sigma. Office: DePaul U Fin Dept 1 E Jackson Blvd Chicago IL 60604-2201 Home: PO Box 409 Spring Grove IL 60081-0409

GARRIGAN, WILLIAM HENRY, III, protective services official; b. Evergreen Park, Ill., Apr. 5, 1954; s. William Henry Jr. and Mary Jane (O'Connell) G.; m. Melissa Ann Vaughan, Aug. 2, 1980; children: William, Vaughan, Amanda. AA, Coll. of DuPage, Glen Ellyn, Ill., 1975; grad. paramedic tng., Loyola Med. Ctr., Maywood, Ill., 1976; student, No. Ill. U., 1976-77; BS, So. Ill. U., 1987. Cert. instr. CPR, Am. Heart Assn.; adv. cert. fire fighter III; cert. fire apparatus engr.; cert. fire svc. instr. I. Firefighter/paramedic North Palos (Ill.) Fire Dept., 1977-78, Oak Brook (Ill.) Fire Dept., 1979—, asst. coord. emergency med. svcs., 1983-87, coord. emergency med. svcs., 1987-97; prin., owner Grssports/Sica Sports Network, 2004—, M.B.G. Distributors Sports Apparel & Accessories, 2007—. Mem. edn. com. for paramedic edn. Village of Downers Grove, Ill., 1990—; mem. safety com. Village of Oak Brook, 1987—; mem. ambulance report com. Good Samaritan Hosp., Downers Grove, 1988—. ACLs provider Heart Assn. South Cook County, Ill., 1986—; com. mem., advancement chmn. Troop 699, Boy Scouts of Am., Palos Park, Ill., AYSO coach, 1994, active Quigley South High Sch. Alumni Assn., 1972—; trainer, coach Palos Panthers Soccer Club, 1999. Recipient acknowledgement of contbn. Dept. Pub. Health, State of Ill., 1987, recognition and appreciation of dedication and svc. Village of Oak Brook, 1989. Mem. at. Assn. EMTs, Ill. Profl. Firefighters Assn., North Palos Firemen's Assn. (pres. 1982-84, Outstanding Svc. award 1988), Profl. Assn. Specialty Divers, Dive Rescue Inc. Internat., Phi Kappa Sigma Alumni Assn. Republican. Roman Catholic. Avocations: golf, water-skiing, scuba diving, swimming. Office: Oak Brook Fire Dept 1212 Oak Brook Rd Oak Brook IL 60523-4603 Office Phone: 815-485-4155. Personal E-mail: b.garrigan@att.net. E-mail: bill@sicasn.com.

GARRISON, LARRY RICHARD, accounting educator; b. Kansas City, Mo., Jan. 10, 1951; s. Robert Milton and Virginia Claire (Huntington) G.; m. Sheila Caroline Murry, Aug. 10, 1973. BBA, Cen. Mo. State U., 1973; MS in Acctg., U. Mo., 1982; PhD, U. Nebr., 1986. CPA, Mo. Mgr. Garrison & Co., CPAs, Kansas City, 1973-79; controller G.F. & F. Enterprises, Kansas City, 1979-82; instr. U. Nebr., Lincoln, 1983-86; prof. U. Mo., Kansas City, 1986—. Exec. dir. Tax Policy Rsch. Project. Contbr. articles to profl. jours. Recipient Disting. Teaching award U. Nebr., 1984-85, Pierson Tchg. award U. Mo. Kans. City Alumni Assn., 1992, 2005. Mem. AICPA, Am. Taxation Assn., N.Am. Acctg. Soc. (past pres.), Mo. Assn. Acctg. Educators (past pres.), Mo. Soc. CPAs (Outstanding Educator of Yr. award 1999, Pierson Tchg. award), Am. Acctg. Assn., Beta Alpha Psi, Beta Gamma Sigma. Office: U Mo 5100 Rockhill Rd Kansas City MO 64110-2481

GARSCADDEN, ALAN, physicist; b. Glasgow, Scotland, June 10, 1937; came to U.S., 1962; s. Andrew and Sarah Florence (Black) G.; m. Avril Margaret Thompson Garscadden, Jan. 24, 1962; children: A. Graeme, A.K. Neil, A.K. Gael, A.E. Hilary. BS (hon.), Queens U., Belfast, Ireland, 1958; PhD in Physics, 1962. Rsch. physicist Aerospace Rsch. Labs, Wright-Patterson AFB, 1962-73; lab. dir., 1973-75; rsch. physicist Aero Propulsion and Power Divsn., 1975-91; chief scientist Aero Propulsion Directorate, 1991-94, Wright Lab., 1995-97, Propulsion Directorate/Air Force Rsch. Lab., Wright-Patterson AFB, 1997—, Edwards AFB, Calif., 1997—. Adj. prof. physics Air Force Inst. Tech., Wright Patterson AFB, 1969—; trustee Ohio Aerospace Inst., 1996-98; bd. dirs. Von Karman Inst., 1997-2006. Contbr. articles to profl. jours. Commr. Planning Commn., Village of Yellow Springs, 1985-96. Decorated DSM USAF; recipient Presdl. Meritorious award, 2003, Presdl. Disting. award, S&T, 2007; fellow, Air Force Rsch. Lab. Fellow IEEE, AIAA, Am. Phys. Soc. (Will Allis prize 2002), Inst. Physics (U.K.). Avocation: history. Office: AFRL/PR Air Force Rsch Lab 1950 5th St Wright Patterson AFB OH 45433-7251 Office Phone: 937-255-2246. Business E-Mail: alan.garscadden@wpafb.af.mil.

GARSON, ARNOLD HUGH, publishing executive; b. Lincoln, Nebr., May 29, 1941; s. Sam B. and Celia (Stine) Garson; m. Marilyn Grace Baird, Aug. 15, 1964; children: Scott Arnold, Christopher Baird, Gillian Grace, Megan Jane. BA, U. Nebr., 1964; MS, UCLA, 1965. Reporter Omaha World-Herald, 1965-69, Des Moines Tribune, 1969-72, city editor, 1972-75; reporter Des Moines Register, 1975-83, mng. editor, 1983-88; editor San Bernardino (Calif.) County Sun, 1988-96; pub., pres. Sioux Falls (S.D.) Argus Leader, 1996—; v.p. Gannett Pacific Newspaper Group, 2000—. Past pres. S.D. Symphony Orch.; mem. adv. bd. Neuharth Ctr. U. S.D. Recipient Pub. Svc. Reporting award, Am. Polit. Sci. Assn., 1969, Mng. Editors Sweepstakes award, Iowa AP, 1976, John Hancock award for excellence in bus. and fin. journalism, 1979, Calif.-Nev. AP award for column writing, 1995. Mem.: S.D. Newspaper Assn. (past pres.). Jewish. Home: 5 S Riverview Hts Sioux Falls SD 57105-0252 Office: Sioux Falls Argus Leader PO Box 5034 Sioux Falls SD 57117-5034

GARTENHAUS, SOLOMON, physicist, educator; b. Kassel, Germany, Jan. 3, 1929; came to U.S., 1937, naturalized, 1943; s. Leopolt and Hanna (Brandler) G.; m. Johanna Lore Weisz, Aug. 30, 1953; children: Michael M., Kevin M. BS, U. Pa., 1951; MS, U. Ill., 1953, PhD, 1955. Instr. Stanford U., 1955-58; faculty physics Purdue U., Lafayette, Ind., 1958—, prof., 1963—; asst. dean Grad. Sch., 1972-77, sec. of faculties, 1980—. Disting. vis. prof. USAF Acad., Colo., 1977-78; dir. Purdue-Ind. Studienprogram, U. Hamburg, W. Ger., 1979-80; cons. Lockheed, summers 1958-60; officer, dir. Advanced Research Corp., 1961-65 Author: Elements of Plasma Physics, 1964, Physics-Basic Principles, 1975; contbr. articles to profl. jours. Fellow Am. Phys. Soc.; mem. N.Y. Acad. Scis., Am. Assn. Physics Tchrs., Phi Beta Kappa, Sigma Xi. Home: 2102 S 9th St Lafayette IN 47905-2132 Office: Purdue U Dept Physics Lafayette IN 47907 E-mail: garten@physics.purdue.edu.

GARTH, BRYANT GEOFFREY, lawyer, educator; b. San Diego, Dec. 9, 1949; s. William and Patricia (Feild) G.; m. Gwendolyn Sessions; children: Heather, Andrew, Daniela. BA magna cum laude, Yale U., 1972; JD, Stanford U., 1975; PhD, European U. Inst., Florence, Italy, 1979. Bar: Calif. 1975, Ind. 1988. Law clk. to judge U.S. Dist. Ct. (no. dist.) Calif., San Francisco, 1978-79; asst. prof. Ind. U., Bloomington, 1979-82, assoc. prof., 1982-85, prof., 1985-92, dean Law Sch., 1986-90; dir. Am. Bar Found., Chgo., 1990—2004, sr. rsch. fellow, 2004—. Cons. Ont. Law Reform Commn., 1984-85, 94, World Bank Argentina Project, 1993-94, World Bank Ecuador Project, 2003; vis. assoc. prof. U. Mich., Ann Arbor, 1983-84; bd. dirs. Internat. Human Rights Law Inst.; mem. bd. visitors Stanford U. Law Sch., 1993-2000. Author: Neighborhood Law Firms for the Poor, 1980; co-editor: Access to Justice: A World Survey, 1978, Access to Justice: Emerging Issues and Perspectives, 1979, Dealing in Virtue, 1996, Internationalization of Palace Wars, 2002; contbr. articles to profl. jours. V.p. H.G. & K.F. Montgomery Found. Rsch. grantee NSF, 1982, 91, 92, 95, 99, 2001, Nat. Inst. Dispute Resolution, 1985, Ind. Supreme Ct., 1989, Italian Coun. Rsch., 1989, Keck, 1995, MacArthur, 1997. Mem.: Law and Soc. Assn., Am. Law Inst. Democrat. Home Phone: 312-482-8117; Office Phone: 312-988-6575. Business E-Mail: bggarth@abfn.org.

GARTNER, MICHAEL GAY, editor, baseball and television executive; b. Des Moines, Oct. 25, 1938; s. Carl David and Mary Marguerite (Gay) Gartner; m. Barbara Jean McCoy, May 25, 1968; children: Melissa, Christopher (dec.), Michael. BA, Carleton Coll., 1960; JD, NYU, 1969; LittD (hon.), Simpson Coll., 1984; LLD (hon.), James Madison U., 1989; LittD (hon.), Grand View Coll., 1990, Iowa Wesleyan Coll., 1997; LLD (hon.), Drake U., 2001. Bar: NY, Iowa. With Wall St. Jour., YC, 1960—74, page one editor, 1970—74; exec. editor Des Moines Register and Tribune, 1974—76, editor, 1976—82, editl. chmn., 1982—85, v.p., 1975—76, exec. v.p., 1977, pres., COO, 1978—85; editor Courier-Jour. and Louisville Times, 1986—87; gen. news exec. Gannett Co., 1987—88; pres. NBC News, 1988—93; editor, co-owner Ames (Iowa) Daily Tribune, 1986—99; chmn., majority-owner Iowa Cubs, 1999—; chmn., co-owner New West Newspapers, 2000—06. Bd. dirs. Big Green Umbrella Assn. Syndicated columnist on lang., 1978—95, columnist USA Today, 1993—98; author: Outrage, Passion & Uncommon Sense, 2005. Chmn. Vision Iowa, 2000—05; hon. trustee Simpson Coll.; mem. Pulitzer Prize Bd., 1982—92, chmn., 1991—92; trustee Freedom Forum Newseum, Washington, Freedom Forum Diversity Inst.; bd. dirs. World Food Prize; pres. Iowa Bd. Regents, 2005—. Recipient Pulitzer prize for editl. writing, 1997; fellow, Harvard U. Inst. Politics, 1994. Mem.: Am. Soc. Newspaper Editors (pres. 1986—87), Assn. Bar City N.Y., Iowa Bar Assn., ABA, Wakonda Club. also: 366 W 11th St New York NY 10014-6225 Office: One Line Dr Des Moines IA 50309-4631 Home: 100 Market St Unit 515 Des Moines IA 50309 Business E-Mail: mgartner@iowacubs.com.

GARTON, ROBERT DEAN, state legislator; b. Chariton, Iowa, Aug. 18, 1933; s. Jesse Glenn and Ruth Irene (Wright) G.; m. Barbara Hicks, June 17, 1955; children: Bradford, Brenda. BS, Iowa State U., 1955; MS, Cornell U., 1959. Pers. rep. Cummins Engine Co., Columbus, Ind., 1959-61; owner Garton Assocs. Mgmt. Cons., Columbus, 1961-96; v.p. profl. devel. Ivy Tech. Cmty. Coll., Columbus, 1996—; mem. Ind. Senate, Indpls., 1970—2006, minority caucus chmn., 1976-78, majority caucus chmn., 1978-80, pres. pro tempore, 1980—2006. Bd. dirs. Rural Water Sys., 1969—2008. Mem. exec. com. Nat. Conf. State Legislatures, 1989-92; chmn. Mid-West Conf. State Legislatures, Coun. State Govts., 1984-85, mem. gov. bd., 1985-2006; chmn. Ind. Civil Rights Commn., 1969-70; mem. exec. com. Nat. Fedn. Young Reps., 1966; trustee Franklin Coll., 1998—; bd. dirs. Independent Colls. of Ind., 2001—06, State Legis. Leaders Found., 2003—06. With USMCR, 1955-57. Co-recipient William M. Bulger Excellence in State Legis. Leadership award, 1999, Legislator of Yr. award, Ind. Civil Liberties Union, 2000; named a Legislator honoree, Ind. Coalition Human Svcs., 2006; named Hon. Citizen, Iowa, 1962, winner internat. speech contest, Toastmasters, 1962, Hon. Citizen, Tenn., 1977, Small Bus. Champion, Ind. Small Bus. Coun., 1997, Pub. Servant of the Yr., Ind. Assn. Rehab. Facilities, 2000, Hon. Field Examiner, State Bd. Accts., 2005, Ind. Wildlife Legis. Conservationist of Yr., 2006; named one of 5 Outstanding Young Men in Ind., 1968; recipient Disting. Svc. award, Jr. C. of C. Columbus, 1968, Guardian Small Bus. award, Nat. Fedn. for Ind. Bus., 1990, Man of Yr., Ind. Rep. Mayor's Assn., 1991, Guardian Small Bus. award, Nat. Fedn. Ind. Bus., 1993, 1994, Lee Atwater Leadership award, Nat. Rep. Legislator Assn., 1991, Outstanding Pub. Svc. award, Podiatric Assn., 1993, United Sr. Action Legis. Leadership award, 1994, Outstanding Govt. Leader award, Apt. Assn. Ind., 1998, Freedom of Road award, ABATE of Ind., 2000, Senator of Yr. award, Ind. Primary Health Care Assn., 2001, Friend of Edn. award, N. Ctrl. Bus. Edn. Assn., 2001, Disting. Pub. Svc. award, Am. Legion, 2001, Pub. Sector award, Benjamin Harrison Medallion, 2001, Friend of Autism award, 2001, Legislator of Yr., Trial Lawyers Assn., 2003, first Virgil "Gus" Grissom Leadership award, Consulting Engrs. Ind., 2005, Lifetime Achievement award, 2005, ARC Ind., 2005, Mental Health Assn. Am., 2006, Becky Campbell Lifetime Achievement award, Johnson County Retarded Citizens, 2006, Robert D. Garton Vets. Plz., Columbus Ind. named in hon., 2006, Robert D. Garton Conf. Rm. named in hon., Columbus Learning Ctr., Ind., 2006, First Freedom award, Hoosier State Press Assn., 2007, Robert Garton Leadership award Established (first recipient), ARC Bartholomew County, 2007. Mem. Rotary, Beta Theta Pi. Business E-Mail: rgarton@ivytech.edu.

GARTON, THOMAS WILLIAM, lawyer; b. Ft. Dodge, Iowa, Jan. 19, 1947; s. H. Boyd and Ruth A. (Porter) G.; m. Marcia K. Hoover, June 21, 1969; children: Geoffrey, Matthew. BA, Carleton Coll., 1969; JD magna cum laude, U. Minn., 1974. Assoc. Fredrikson & Byron, PA, Mpls., 1974-80, shareholder, 1980—, chmn. corp. practice group. Adj. prof. William Mitchell Coll. Law, St. Paul, Minn., 1977-80, U. Minn. Law Sch., Mpls., 1980; bd. dirs. RS/Eden Programs; presenter continuing legal edn. seminars on tax, mergers and acquisitions, and bus. planning, 1977—. With U.S. Army, 1969-71. Mem. ABA (tax sect.), Minn. Bar Assn. (dir. tax coun. 1987-89). Office: Fredrikson & Byron PA 200 S Sixth St Ste4000 Minneapolis MN 55402-1425 Business E-Mail: tgarton@fredlaw.com.

GARVER, THOMAS HASKELL, curator, consultant, writer; b. Duluth, Minn., Jan. 23, 1934; s. Harvie Adair and Margaret Hope (Foght) G.; m. Natasha Nicholson, Apr. 13, 1974. BA, Haverford Coll., 1956; MA, U. Minn., 1965. Asst. to dir. Krannert Art Mus., U. Ill., Urbana, 1960-62; asst. dir. fine arts dept. Seattle World's Fair, 1962, Rose Art Mus., Brandeis U., Waltham, Mass., 1962-68; dir. Newport Harbor Art Mus. (now Orange County Mus. Art), Calif., 1968-72, 77-80; curator exhbns. Fine Arts Mus. of San Francisco, 1972-77; dir. Madison (Wis.) Art Ctr., 1980-87; asst. prof. Calif. State U., 1970-71, 79-80. Curator art collection Rayovac Corp., Madison, 1985-2001; organizing curator O. Winston Link Mus., Roanoke, Va., 2001-04. Author: Twelve Photographers of the American Social Landscape, 1967, Just Before the War: Urban American from 1935-41, 1968, The Paintings of George Tooker, 1985, rev. edit., 1992, The Last Steam Railroad in America: Photographs by O. Winston Link, 1995; exhbn. catalogues including Robert Rauschenberg, 1969, Tom Wesselmann, 1971, Reginald Marsh, 1972, Joseph Raffael, Paintings From the California Years, 1977, George Herms, 1978, 83, Nathan Oliveira, 1984, George Tooker, Paintings, 1983-87, 88, Mind and Beast: Contemporary Artists and the Animal Kingdom, 1992, Flora: Contemporary Artists and the World of Flowers, 1995, Trains that Passed in the ight: The Railroad Photographs of O. Winston Link,

1998, WATER: Contemporary Artists Who Use Water as a Theme in Their Art, Gibbes Mus. of Art, Charleston, S.C., 1999. Trustee U.S.S. Mass. Meml. Commn., Fall River, 1965-68; trustee South Coast Repertory Co., Costa Mesa, Calif., 1970-72; trustee Wis. Citizens for Arts, 1985-87; steering com. Archives Am. Art, San Francisco, 1977-80; active Newport Beach Art Commn., 1978-79, Madison Com. for Arts, 1984-87. Mem. Western Assn. Art Mus. (pres. 1970-71, trustee 1970-73), Art Mus. Assn. Am. (pres. 1979-82, trustee 1979-85). Home and Office: 1962 Atwood Ave Madison WI 53704-5221 Home Phone: 608-246-3964; Office Phone: 608-246-3967. Business E-Mail: thgart@aol.com.

GARVIN, PAUL JOSEPH, JR., toxicologist; b. Toledo, Nov. 16, 1928; s. Paul Joseph and Laura Mary (Blanchet) G.; m. Priscilla Ann Haines, Aug. 23, 1952; children: Peter, Thomas, Paul III, Peggy, Priscilla, Polly. BA, St. John's U., 1950; MS, U. Minn., 1958. Rsch. assoc. Sterling-Winthrop Rsch. Inst., Rensselaer, N.Y., 1954-58; sr. rsch. pharmacologist Baxter-Travenol Inc., Morton Grove, Ill., 1958-72, mgr. safety evaluation, 1972-77; dir. toxicology Amoco Corp., Chgo., 1977-88, sr. health sci. advisor, 1988-92; toxicology cons. pvt. practice, Mt. Prospect, Ill., 1992—. Mem. adv. com. ctr. risk analysis Harvard U. Sch. Pub. Health, Boston, 1991-92; sci. adv. panel hazardous substance mgmt. rsch. ctr. U. Medicine and Dentistry, Newark, 1988-91, adv. panel ctr. alternatives to animal testing Johns Hopkins U. Sch. Hygiene and Pub. Health, Balt., 1990-92, scientific adv. com. CIIT, Research Triangle Park, N.C., 1986-88. Contbr. over 50 articles to profl. jours. Chmn. Mt. Prospect Bd. Health, 1960-70. Mem. AAAS, Am. Indsl. Hygiene Assn., Am. Soc. Pharmacology & Exptl. Therapeutics, N.Y. Acad. Sci., European Soc. Toxicology, Soc. Toxicology. Home and Office: 309 N Wille St Mount Prospect IL 60056-2454

GARVIN, THOMAS MICHAEL, food products company executive; b. Chgo., 1935; married. BSc, Loyola U., 1957, MBA, 1969. CPA, Ill. With Lybrand Ross Bros. & Montgomery, 1957-61; contr. Ekco Products Co., 1962-65; group contr. Am. Home Products Co., 1966-69; contr. Keebler Co., Elmhurst, Ill., 1969-70, v.p. fin. and treas., from 1970, then exec. v.p. ops., now pres., chief exec. officer, also bd. dirs. Office: Keebler Co 1 Hollow Tree Ln Elmhurst IL 60126

GARWOOD, JULIE, writer; b. 1946; Author: (novels for young adults) A Girl Named Summer, 1985, (as Emily Chase) What's A Girl to Do, 1985, (historical romance novels) Gentle Warrior, 1985, Rebellious Desire, 1986, Honor's Splendor, 1987, The Lion's Lady, 1988, The Bride, 1989, Guardian Angel, 1990, The Gift, 1990, The Prize, 1991, The Secret, 1992, Castles, 1993, Saving Grace, 1993, Prince Charming, 1994, For the Roses, 1995, The Wedding, 1996, One Pink Rose, One White Rose, One Red Rose, Come the Spring, 1997, The Wedding, 1998, Ransom, 1999, Heartbreaker, 2000, Mercy, 2002, Killjoy, 2002, Killjoy, 2003, Murder List, 2004 (Publishers Weekly Bestseller), Slow Burn, 2005 (Publishers Weekly Bestseller), Shadow Dance, 2006. Office: PO Box 7574 Leawood KS 66207-0574 Address: Jane Rotrosen Agy 318 East 51st St New York NY 10022

GARY, WARLENE D., educational association administrator; BS in Phys. Edn. and Health, DC Tchrs. Coll.; MEd in Spl. Edn., Howard U. Tchr. Washington Pub. Schs.; with Coun. Chief State Sch. Officers, Howard U. Ctr. Study of Handicapped Children and Youth; acting exec. dir. Pres.'s Adv. Com. for Women; staff mem. EA, Washington, 1981, mgr. intergovernmental rels., assoc. dir. govt. rels., assoc. dir. human and civil rights, mgr. parent and cmty. outreach, dir. Office Human and Civil Rights, 2002; CEO PTA, Chgo. Office: PTA 541 N Fairbanks Ct Ste 1300 Chicago IL 60611-3396 Office Phone: 312-670-6782. Office Fax: 312-670-6783.

GASCOIGNE, WILLIAM M., research executive; BS in Computer Sci., Durham U. Regional dir. Philips Electronic & Assoc. Industries; maj. accts. dir. Olivetti; v,o, worldwide mktg., mng. dir. Europe Schlumberger Techs.; mgr. No. Europe Structural Dynamics Rsch. Corp., Milford, Ohio, 1990—, now sr. v.p., mng. dir. Europe. Office: Structural Dynamics Rsch Corp 2000 Eastman Dr Milford OH 45150-2712

GASH, LAUREN BETH, lawyer, state legislator; b. Summit, NJ, June 11, 1960; d. Ira Arnold and Sondra Regina (Stetin) G.; m. Gregg Allen Garmisa, June 12, 1983; children: Sarah, Benjamin. BA in Psychology, Clark U., 1982; JD, Georgetown U., 1987. Bar: Ill. 1989. Projects dir. U.S. Senator Alan Dixon, Washington, 1981-83; statewide constituency coord., dir. Women for Simon, U.S. Senator Paul Simon, Chgo., 1990; aide State Rep. Grace Mary Stern, Highland Park, Ill.; atty. Prairie State Legal Svcs., Waukegan, Ill.; mem. Ill. State Ho. of Reps., chair judiciary-criminal com. Mem. women's health adv. bd. Highland Park Hosp., southeast adv. bd Coll. Lake County, JUF govt. agencies divsn. campaign cabinet, 1999, chair, Highland Park 2000 com., human needs subcom. Women in Law as 2d Career grantee; recipient Disting. Svc. award Ill. Com. for Honest Govt., 1996, Best Legis. Record Voting award Ind. Voters Ill., 1996; named Legis. of Yr. Alliance for the Mentally Ill, 1997. Mem. Ill. State Bar Assn. (mem. com. cmty. involvement), Formerly Employed Mothers at the Leading Edge (co-founder North Shore chpt.), Chgo. Women in Govt. Rels., Women Employed, Ravinia PTA (bd. dirs., polit. action chair), Com. for Interdist. Cooperation, orth Shore Synagogue Beth El (social action com.) LWV (bd. dirs. Highland Park chpt., bd. dirs. Lake County chpt.). Avocations: flute, languages. also: 2052-I Stratton Bldg Springfield IL 62706-0001 Office: 1345 Forest Ave Highland Park IL 60035-3456

GASKILL, E. THURMAN, state legislator; b. Algona, Iowa, Apr. 4, 1935; m. Geraldine; children: Elizabeth, Mark, David. Student, Iowa State U. Owner farm; dir. First Fed. Savings Bank of Midwest; appointed by USDA sec. agr. Fed. Agrl. Energy Adv. Com., 1973, USDA Users Adv. Bd., 1988; mem. Ag Promotion Bd., 1974-85, Iowa Dept. Natural Resources, 1989-92, Iowa Senate from 8th dist., Des Moines, 1997—. Mem. White House Transition Team, 1988, County Bd. of Edn., U.S. Agr. Fed. Energy Commn.; chair Farmers for Nixon and Ford Campaigns; co-chair Iowa Farmers for Reagan/Bush and Bush/Quayle; nat. dep. dir. George Bush Ag Campaign, 1992; past commr. Iowa Devel. Commn.; mem. honors award selection com. USDA; spkr. in field; charter mem. bd. dirs. Iowa Peace Inst. Mem. adv. com. Iowa State U. Coll. Agr.; bd. dirs. United Meth. Ch.; past supt. Sunday Sch. With U.S. Army, 1954-56. Named to Iowa State U. Agr. Hall of Fame, 1975. Mem. Iowa Farm Bus. Assn. (past pres.), Nat. and Iowa Corn Growers (past pres.), U.S. Feed Grain Coun. (chair), Iowa Corn Promotion Bd. (past pres.), Agr. Coun. Am. (vice-chair), U.S. Feed Grains Coun. (mem. trade team to China 1981), Iowa Farm Bur., Shriners, Am. Legion, Rotary (mem. group study exchange team to Australia 1969). Republican. Methodist. Home: 1320 Birch Ave Corwith IA 50430-8045 Office: State Capitol 8th Dist 3 9th And Grand Des Moines IA 50319-0001 E-mail: thurman_gaskill@legis.state.ia.us.

GASKILL, MARY, state official; b. Clyde, Mo., Dec. 1, 1941; Student, N.E. Mo. R VI, Gard Bus. U. State rep., Iowa, 2003—. Mem. econ. devel. appropriations com.; mem. environ. protection standing com.; mem. local govt. standing com.; mem. state govt. com.; county auditor; commr. elections; control auditor IHCC Elections; mem. County Safety and Wellness Coms.; bd. dirs. IMWCA; mem. Com. on the Future, Law Enforcement Steering Com., Elections LEgis. Com. Mem. City of Ottumwa Strategic Planning, County/City Jail Planning, Conv. and Visitors Bur., Govt. Affairs Com., Foster Care Rev. Bd., Wapello County Dem. Party Cen. Com.; lector, usher, mem. worship and prayer com. St. Mary's Ch. Mem.: LWV, Ottumwa C. of C., AIS Users Orgn. (pres.), 5th Dist. Auditors Assn. (pres.), Iowa State Assn. County Auditors (mem. com. on the future). Office: State Capitol E 12th and Grand Des Moines IA 50319

GASKILL, SAM, state legislator; Mem. Mo. Ho. of Reps. Dist. 131, Jefferson City, 1995—. Republican.

GASPAROVIC, JOHN J., lawyer; BA, Wayne State U., 1979; JD, Northwestern U., 1982. Atty. Jones, Day, Reavis and Pogue, Cleve.; v.p., gen. counsel Automotive Div. Guardian Industries; exec. v.p., gen. counsel Roadway Corp.; sr. v.p., gen. counsel Federal Mogul Corp.; v.p., gen. counsel, sec. BorgWarner Inc., Auburn Hills, Mich., 2007—. Mem.: ABA, Ohio Bar Assn., Mich. Bar Assn. Office: BorgWarner Inc 3850 Hamlin Rd Auburn Hills MI 48326 Office Phone: 248-754-9200.

GASPER, JOSEPH J., insurance company executive; b. Steubenville, Ohio; m. Jill; two children. Degree in econs., Ohio State U. Group underwriter Nationwide Ins., Columbus, 1966-72; mgmt. mktg. Columbus Ins., 1972-95; pres., COO Nationwide Fin. Svcs., Columbus, Ohio, 1996—. Bd. dirs. BalletMet, Columbus Children's Hosp., Otterbein Coll. Mem. Nat. Assn. Variable Annuities (chmn. bd. dirs.), Am. Coun. Life Ins. (bd. dirs.), Assn. Ohio Life Ins. Cos., Ins. Marketplace Standards Assn. Office: One Nationwide Plz Nationwide Fin Svcs Columbus OH 43215-2220

GASS, WILLIAM H., writer, educator; b. Fargo, ND, July 30, 1924; s. William Bernard and Claire (Sorensen) G.; m. Mary Patricia O'Kelly, 1952 (div.); children: Richard, Robert, Susan; m. Mary Alice Henderson, 1969; children: Elizabeth, Catherine. AB, Kenyon Coll., 1947, LHD (hon.), 1973, LHD (hon.), 1985, LHD (hon.), 2005; PhD, Cornell U., 1953. Instr. philosophy Coll. of Wooster, Ohio, 1950-54; asst. prof. Purdue U., Lafayette, 1954-60, assoc. prof., 1960-66, prof. philosophy, 1966-69, Washington U., St. Louis, 1969-79, David May Disting. Univ. prof. in humanities, 1979-99, prof. emeritus, 1999—; dir. Internat. Writers Center, 1990—2001. Vis. lectr. U. Ill., 1958-59; mem. Rockefeller Commn. on Humanities, 1978-80; mem. literature panel Nat. Endowment for the Arts, 1979-82. Author: Omensetter's Luck, 1966, In the Heart of the Heart of the Country, 1968, Willie Masters' Lonesome Wife, 1968, Fiction and the Figures of Life, 1970, On Being Blue, 1974, The World Within the Word, 1978, The Habitations of the Word: Essays, 1984, The Tunnel, 1995, Finding a Form, 1996, Cartesian Sonata, 1998, Reading Rilke, 1999, Tests of Time, 2002, A Temple of Texts: Essays, 2006; contbr. to periodicals including NY Rev. of Books, NY Times Book Rev., New Republic, TriQuar., Salmagundi, others. Office: 6304 Westminster Pl Saint Louis MO 63130

GASSER, MICHAEL J., consumer products company executive; BA, Ohio Northern U. CPA Ohio. Internal auditor Greif, Inc., 1979—81, controller, 1981—88, v.p., finance, 1988—94, mem. bd. dir, 1991—, vice chmn., COO, 1994, chmn., CEO, 1994—.

GASSERE, EUGENE ARTHUR, lawyer, investment company executive; b. Beaumont, Tex., Oct. 20, 1930; s. Victor Eugene and Althea June (Haight) G.; m. Mary Alice Engelhard, Aug. 4, 1956; children— Paul, John, Anne. BS, U. Wis., 1952, JD, 1956; postgrad., Oxford U., 1956-57. Bar: Wis. bar 1956. Asst. counsel Wurlitzer Co., Chgo., 1958-61, Campbell Soup Co., Camden, NJ, 1961-65; asst. to pres. Thilmany Pulp & Paper Co., Kaukauna, Wis., 1966-68; with Skyline Corp., Elkhart, Ind., 1968-92, v.p., gen. counsel, asst. sec., 1973-92, ret., 1992—. Pres., bd. dirs. Elkhart Urban League, 1972-73, Elkhart Symphony, 1975-76, Elkhart Concert Club, 1976-77. Served with U.S. Army, 1952-54. Mem. Wis. Bar Assn., Phi Mu Alpha. Home: PO Box 165 Mindoro WI 54644-0165 Office: Skyline Corp 2520 Bypass Rd Elkhart IN 46514-1584 E-mail: pelt2ridge@centurytel.net.

GAST, HARRY T., JR., state legislator; b. St. Joseph, Mich., Sept. 20, 1920; s. Harry T. Sr. and Fern (Shearer) G.; m. Vera Jean Warren, 1944; children: Barbara Gast Moray, Linda, Dennis. Student, Mich. State U., 1939-41. Treas, then supervisor Lincoln Twp., 1946-70; mem. Mich. Ho. of Reps. from 43rd dist., Lansing, 1970-78, Mich. Senate from 20th dist., 1978—. County supervisor Berrien County, Mich., 1965-69; mem. Berrien County Bd. Pub. Works, Berrien County Bd. Health, 1965-70. Mem. Lions, Farm Bur., Jaycees (hon.), Mich. United Conservation Clubs. Office: S-324 Capitol Bldg Lansing MI 48913-0001

GASTON, PAUL LEE, academic administrator, language educator; b. Hattiesburg, Miss., Aug. 23, 1943; s. Paul Lee and Ruth (Gooch) Gaston; m. Eileen Margaret Higgins, June 29, 1968; children: Elizabeth, Tyler Lee(dec.). BA, S.E. La. U., 1965; MA, U. Va., 1966, PhD, 1970. Ordained min. Episcopal Ch., 1990. Prof. English So. Ill. U., Edwardsville, 1969-88, assoc. v.p., 1984-88; dean Coll. Arts and Scis. U. Tenn., Chattanooga, 1988-93; provost, exec. v.p. No. Ky. U., Highland Heights, 1993-99; provost Kent (Ohio) State U., 1999—. Author: W. D. Snodgrass, 1978, Concordance Conrad, Arrow of Gold, 1980; contbr. articles to profl. jours. Chair, bd. dirs. Ohio Learning Network, Ohio Lik. Mem.: Nat. Assn. State U. and Land Grant Colls., Assn. Specialized and Profl. Accreditors, Phi Beta Kappa. Democrat. Avocations: softball, hiking, calligraphy. Office: Kent State U Office of Provost PO Box 5190 Kent OH 44242-0001 Home Phone: 330-653-3186; Office Phone: 330-672-2220. Business E-Mail: pgaston@kent.edu.

GATERS, DOROTHY, basketball coach; b. Miss. 1 child. Student, Crane Jr. Coll.; grad., DePaul Univ. Dean of students John Marshall Met. High Sch., Chgo., and head girls' basketball coach, 1974—. Named Nat. Coach of Yr., Women's Basketball Coaches Assn., 1999, Coach of Yr., Ill. Baskeball Coaches Assn. (seven times), Dist. 1 Coach of Yr. (22 times); named one of 100 Most Influential Women, Crain's Chicago Business Mag., 2004; named to Women's Basketball Hall of Fame, 2000, Women's Basketball Coaches Assn. Hall of Fame, Chicagoland Sports Hall of Fame, Chgo. Public League Coaches Assn. Hall of Fame, Ill. Basketball Coaches Hall of Fame, Ill. Girls Assn. Hall of Fame; recipient Career Achievement award, Pres. Bill Clinton. Achievements include having a 90% winning average, 19 city titles, seven state titles; appeared in series of Nike commercials. Office: John Marshall Met High Sch 3250 W Adams St Chicago IL 60624

GATES, LAWRENCE C., political organization worker, lawyer; b. 1947; m. Jeanne Gates; children: Katie, Joe. BA, U. Kans., 1972, JD, 1974. Bar: Kans. 1974, US Dist. Ct. Kans. 1974, US Supreme Ct. 1997. Atty. Gates, Biles, Shields & Ryan, 1974—; Johnson County Dem. chmn., 1978—80; del. Dem. Nat. Conv., 1980; chmn. Kans. State Dem. Party, 2003—. Fund-raiser Dem. gubernatorial campaigns, 1986, 90, 94, 2002, U.S. Rep. Dennis Moore's campaign, 1998. Bd. dirs. Johnson Co. Catholic High Sch. Bd.; bd. trustees Bishop Miege Found. Mem.: Johnson Co. Bar Assn., Kans. Trial Lawyers Assn. (Bd. Govs.), Kans. Bar Assn. Democrat. Office: Gates, Biles, Shields & Ryan 10990 Quivira Rd Shawnee Mission KS 66210 also: PO Box 1914 Topeka KS 66601*

GATES, WALTER EDWARD, small business owner; b. Glens Falls, NY, Aug. 15, 1946; s. William B. and Dawn K. (Preston) G.; m. Toni A. Naren, June 26, 1945; children: Lindsey Erin, Ryan Walter. BS, SUNY, Albany, 1968; EdM, Boston U., 1972; MBA, Harvard U., 1974. Asst. mgr. Wilson Sporting Goods Inc., River Grove, Ill., 1974-76, mgr., 1976-79; dir. Pizza Hut Inc., Wichita, Kans., 1979, sr. dir., 1979-80, v.p., 1980-82, sr. v.p., 1982-85; exec. v.p. Rent-A-Ctr. Inc., Wichita, 1985-86, pres., chief operating officer, 1986-87, pres., chief exec. officer, chief operating officer, 1987-92; pres., CEO THORN Americas, 1991, chmn., CEO, 1992-96; CEO Gates Enterprises, Wichita, 1996—. Pres., CEO Gates Enterprises, 1985—. Bd. dirs. Wichita Symphony, 1984-87, Wichita Children's Theater, 1984-87; active Wichita Music Theatre, 1987—, Boy Scouts of Am., 1989—. Mem. Wichita C. of C. Avocations: skiing, water-skiing, golf. Office: Gates Enterprises 8100 E 22nd St N Ste 2100-3 Wichita KS 67226-2330

GAUEN, PATRICK EMIL, news correspondent; b. St. Louis, July 15, 1950; s. Louis Otto and Wilma Ellen (Rogers) G.; m. Patti Lynn Seib, Dec. 8, 1972 (div. 1992); children: Bethany, Heather; m. Karen Earhart, July 11, 1992; 1 stepchild, Christopher Stephenson. Student, So. Ill. U., 1968-70. Reporter, photographer Collinsville (Ill.) Herald, 1969-72, news editor, 1972-78; reporter St. Louis Globe-Democrat, 1978-84, mng. editor, 1984-85; reporter Ill. affairs St. Louis Post-Dispatch, 1985-89, polit. corr., 1989—, pub. safety team leader, 2000—; faculty univ. coll. Washington U., St. Louis, 1991—2001. Pub. safety reporting team leader St. Louis Post Dispatch, 2000. Recipient Outstanding Med. News Series award Ill. State Med. Soc., 1970, Best Feature Story award Suburban Newspapers Am., 1971, Best News Story award Suburban Newspapers Am., 1973, Best Spot News Story award UPI Editors Ill., 1972, Best Pub. Svc. Reporting award Ill. Press Assn., 1974, Best Feature Story award, 1975, Bar-News Media award Bar Assn. Met. St. Louis, 1987, Bob Hardy award Southern Ill. Chiefs of Police and Southwestern Law Enforcement, 1996, Terry Hughes award St. Louis chpt. Newspaper Guild, 1996, Liberty Bell award Madison County Bar Assn., 1999. Mem. Mid-Am. Press Inst. (bd. dirs. 1985—), Press Club Met. St. Louis (bd. dirs. 1985—), Investigative Reporters and Editor, Criminal Justice Journalists, FBI Citizens Acad., Sigma Delta Chi (bd. dirs. St. Louis chpt. 1985—, chpt. pres. 1985-86, 86-87). Avocations: reading, photography. Home: 30 Meadowlark Ln Highland IL 62249-3000 Office: St Louis Post Dispatch 900 N Tucker St Saint Louis MO 63101 Home Phone: 618-659-7234; Office Phone: 314-340-8154. Business E-Mail: pgauen@post-dispatch.com.

GAULKE, EARL H., publisher, clergyman, editor; b. Milw., July 18, 1927; s. Albert and Olga (Reinhardt) G.; m. Margaret Elaine Preuss, Aug. 5, 1951; children: Cheryl, Stephen. BS in Edn., Concordia U., River Forest, Ill., 1950; BA, MDiv, Concordia Sem., St. Louis, 1956; MA, Washington U., St. Louis, 1965, PhD, 1970; DD, Concordia U., Irvine, Calif., 1995. Ordained minister Lutheran Ch., 1956. Prin., tchr. Pilgrim Luth. Sch., Santa Monica, Calif., 1950-52; tchr., dept. head Detroit Luth. High Sch., 1956-57; assoc. pastor Faith Luth. Ch., LA, 1957-58; editor bd. of parish svcs., 1958-75; dir. editorial svcs. Luth. Ch.-Mo. Synod, St. Louis, 1975-92; v.p. editl. Concordia Pub. House, St. Louis, 1992—. Vis. instr. Washington U., U. Mo., St. Louis, Concordia Sem., Concordia Coll., Mpls.; rsch. assoc. Ctrl. Lab. (CEMREL), St. Louis, 1967-68. Author: You Can Have A Family, 1975, First Chance for the Church, 1978; contbr. articles to profl. jours. Recipient Epphatha award Detroit Inst. for Deaf, 1992. Mem. Am. Edn. Assn., Luth. Edn. Assn. (exec. editor 1978-79, Christus Magister 1989). Avocations: gardening, making wine. Home: 2447 Camberwell Ct Des Peres MO 63131-2118 Office: Concordia Pub House 3558 S Jefferson Ave Saint Louis MO 63118-3910 E-mail: earl.gaulke@cph.org.

GAUNT, KAREN KREIDER, lawyer; b. Cin., Aug. 14, 1971; BA, Denison U., 1993; JD, U. Cin. Coll. Law, 1997. Bar: Ohio 1997, US Ct. Internat. Trade 1999, US Dist. Ct. Southern Dist. Ohio 1999, US Ct. of Appeals Sixth Cir. 2003, US Dist. Ct. Eastern Dist. Mich. 2003. Ptnr. Keating Muething & Klekamp PLL, Cin. Named one of Ohio's Rising Stars, Super Lawyers, 2005, 2006; named to America's Leading Bus. Lawyers, Chambers USA, 2006. Mem.: Internat. Trademark Assn., Ohio State Bar Assn., Cin. Bar Assn. Office: Keating Muething & Klekamp PLL One E Fourth St Ste 1400 Cincinnati OH 45202 Office Phone: 513-579-6400. Office Fax: 513-579-6457.

GAVIN, JOHN NEAL, lawyer; b. Chgo., Aug. 31, 1946; s. John Anthony and Mary Anne (O'Donnell) G.; m. Louise A. Sunderland, June 16, 1979; children: Anne, Matthew. AB, Coll. of Holy Cross, Worcester, Mass., 1968; JD, Harvard U., 1975. Bar: Ill. 1975. Law clk. to Hon. Charles M. Merrill US Ct. Appeals (9th cir.), San Francisco, 1975-76; atty. office of legal counsel US Dept. Justice, Washington, 1976-79; ptnr. Hopkins & Sutter, Chgo., 1981-2001, Foley & Lardner LLP, Chgo., 2001—. Served to lt. USN, 1968-71. Mem. ABA, Chgo. Bar Assn. Office: Foley & Lardner LLP 321 N Clark St Chicago IL 60610 Office Phone: 312-832-4544. Business E-Mail: jgavin@foley.com.

GAVIN, MARY JANE, retired medical/surgical nurse; b. Prairie Du Chien, Wis., Sept. 1, 1941; d. Frank Grant and Mary Elizabeth Wolf; m. Alfred William Gavin, Nov. 9, 1963; children: Catherine Heidi Elizabeth, Carl Alfred Eric. Student, North Cen. Coll., Naperville, Ill., 1959-61; BS, RN, U. Wis., 1964; postgrad., Deepmuscle Tng. Ltd., 1980; postgrad. in deep muscle therapy. RN, Wis. Staff nurse U. Wis. Hosps., Madison; nurse home response VA, Milw.; ret., 2006. Unit chair Badger Girls State, 1991-2005; active Wis. Am. Legion Aux.; task force for handicapped Eastside Wis. Evang. Luth. Ch., Madison, 1993 U. Wis. scholar. Mem.: Monona Grove Am. Legion Aux. (pres. Unit 429 1990—2005). Achievements include writer material that made a federal law null and void.

GAVIN, ROBERT MICHAEL, JR., educational consultant; b. Coatesville, Pa., Aug. 16, 1940; s. Robert Michael and Helen Regina (Finnegan) G.; m. Charlotte Marie Dugan, June 2, 1962; children— Anne, Patricia, Robert, Charles, Sean. BA, St. John's U., Collegeville, Minn., 1962; PhD, Iowa State U., 1966; DSc (hon.), Haverford Coll., 1986, St. John's U., 1996. Mem. faculty Haverford (Pa.) Coll., 1966-84, prof. chemistry, 1975-84, dir. computing, 1979-80, provost, dean faculty, 1980-84, interim pres., 1996-97; pres. Macalester Coll., St. Paul, 1984-96, Cran Brook Ednl. Cmty., Bloomfield Hills, Mich., 1997—2001; ret., 2001. Bd. dirs. Hartford Funds, St. John's U., Minn.; chmn. bd. Hartford Mutual Funds, 2004-. Author papers in field. Pres. Haverford Twp. Sch. Bd., 1975. Recipient Dreyfus Tchr.-Scholar award, 1973; NSF fellow, 1969-70 Democrat. Roman Catholic. Home: 751 Judd St Marine On Saint Croix MN 55047 Personal E-mail: robertgavinjr@aol.com.

GAVIN, STEVEN J., lawyer; b. Teaneck, NJ, Feb. 17, 1960; BA, Yale U., 1982; JD, Stanford U., 1985. Bar: Ill. 1985, U.S. Dist. Ct. Ill. (no. dist.) 1986. Assoc. to ptnr. Winston & Strawn LLP, Chgo., 1985—. Bd. dirs. LINK Unlimited. Mem.: Phi Beta Kappa. Office: Winston & Strawn LLP 35 W Wacker Dr Chicago IL 60601-9703 Office Phone: 312-558-5979. Office Fax: 312-558-5700. E-mail: sgavin@winston.com.

GAY, DUANE, reporter; m. Teri Gay. Degree, U. Wis., Green Bay. News dir. TV and radio news, La Crosse, Oskkosh, Wausau, Green Bay and Milw., Wis.; reporter The Inside Story WISN 12, Milw. Recipient Emmy award, awards, Milw. Press Club, Milw. Assn., N.W. Broadcast News Assn., Radio and TV News Dirs. Assn. Office: WISN PO Box 402 Milwaukee WI 53201

GAY, WILLIAM ARTHUR, JR., thoracic surgeon; b. Richmond, Va., Jan. 16, 1936; s. William Arthur and Marion Harriette (Taylor) G.; m. Frances Louise Adkins, Dec. 17, 1960; children— William Taylor, Mason Arthur. BA, Va. Mil. Inst., 1957; MD, Duke U. Med. Sch., 1961. Resident, general surgery Duke U. Med. Ctr., Durham, NC, 1961—63, 1965—69, resident, thoracic surgery, 1969—71; clin. assoc. Nat. Heart, Lung, and Blood Inst., 1963—65; asst. prof. surgery Cornell U. Med. Coll., YC, 1971—74, assoc., prof., 1974—78; cardiothoracic surgeon-in-chief N.Y. Hosp., 1976—84; prof., chmn. dept. surgery U. Utah Sch. Medicine, 1984—92; v.p. for health scis. U. Utah, 1990—91; thoracic surgeon Washington U. Sch. Medicine, St. Louis. Prof. surgery Sch. Medicine Washington U., St. Louis; exec. dir. Am. Bd. Thoracic Surgery. Contbr. articles to profl. jours. With USPHS, 1963—65. Recipient Career Scientist award, Irma T. Hirschl Charitable Trust, 1972. Mem. ACS, Soc. Vascular Surgery, Soc. Thoracic Surgeons, Am. Assn. Thoracic for Surgery (treas. 1989-94), Am. Surg. Assn., Soc. Univ. Surgeons (treas. 1977-80), Western Thoracic Surgical Assn., Am. Bd. Thoracic Surgeons (chmn., 1995-97, sect.-treas., 2000, exec. dir.). Office: Washington U Sch Medicine 3180 Queeny Tower 1 Barnes Jewish Hospital Plz Saint Louis MO 63110-1013 also: Am Bd Thoracic Surgery 633 N St Clair St Ste 2320 Chicago IL 60611 Office Phone: 314-747-1315, 312-202-5900. Office Fax: 314-367-8459, 312-202-5960. E-mail: gayw@wustl.edu.

GAYDOS, JOHN RAYMOND, bishop; b. Aug. 14, 1943; Student, N.Am. Coll., Gregorian U., Rome. Ordained priest Archdiocese of St. Louis, Mo., 1968; ordained bishop, 1997; bishop Diocese of Jefferson City, 1997—. Roman Catholic. Office: Diocese of Jefferson City 2207 W Main St PO Box 104900 Jefferson City MO 65110 Office Phone: 573-635-9127. Office Fax: 573-635-0386. E-mail: chance@sockets.net.*

GAYLE, MONICA, broadcast journalist; b. Wenatchee, WA, Mar. 3, 1960; BA Journalism, Wash. State U., 1982. Anchor, gen. assignment reporter Sta. KUSA-TV, Denver, 1986—89, Sta. KNSD-TV, San Diego, 1990—92; co-anchor CBS News Up to the Minute, NYC, 1992-93, CBS Morning News, NYC, 1993—97; anchor Sta. WJBK-TV, Detroit, 1997—. Recipient 4 Emmys, 2 Golden Mic awards and 3 Sigma Delta Chi awards. Office: WJBK FOX 2 Box 2000 Southfield MI 48037-2000

GEAKE, RAYMOND ROBERT, psychologist; b. Detroit, Oct. 26, 1936; s. Harry Nevill and Phyllis Rae (Fox) G.; m. Carol Lynne Rens, June 9, 1962; children: Roger Rens, Tamara Lynne, William Rens. BS in Spl. Edn., U. Mich., 1958, MA in Guidance and Counseling, 1959, PhD in Edn. and Psychology, 1963. Coord. child devel. rsch. Edison Inst., Dearborn, Mich., 1962-66; dir. psychology dept. Plymouth (Mich.) State Home and Tng. Sch., Mich. Dept. Mental Health, 1966-69; pvt. practice ednl. psychology Northville, Mich., 1969-72; mem. Mich. Ho. of Reps., 1973-76, Mich. Senate, 1977-98; investigator, dir. Mich. Office of Children's Ombudsman, 1999—2002; commr. Mich. Racing, 2002—04. Adj. asst. prof. edn./psychology dept. Madonna Coll., Livonia, Mich., 1984-86. Co-author: Visual Tracking, A Self-instruction Workbook for Perceptual Skills in Reading, 1962. Trustee-at-large Schoolcraft C.C., 1969-72, chmn. bd. trustees, 1971-72; vice chmn. nat. adv. com. on mental health and illness of elderly HEW, 1976-77; vice chmn. human svcs. com., assembly fed. issues Nat. Conf. State Legislatures, 1994-95. Recipient Recognition award Found. for Improvement of Justice, 1993. Fellow Mich. Psychol. Assn.; mem. NEA (life), APA, Rotary. Republican.

GEALT, ADELHEID MARIA, museum director; b. Munich, May 29, 1946; came to U.S., 1950; d. Gustav Konrad and Ella Sophie (Daeschlein) Medicus; m. Barry Allen Gealt, Mar. 15, 1969. BA, Ohio State U., 1968; MA, Ind. U., 1973, PhD, 1979. Registrar Ind. U. Art Mus., Bloomington, 1972-76, curator Western art, 1976—, acting/interim dir., 1987-89, dir., 1989—. Adj. assoc. prof. H.R. Hope Sch. Fine Arts, Ind. U., Bloomington, 1985—89, assoc. scholar, 1986, assoc. prof., 1989—; mem. nat. adv. coun. Valparaiso U. Art Mus.; commr. Indiana Arts Commn., 1997—2001. Author: Looking at Art, 1983, Domenico Tiepolo The Punchinello Drawings, 1986; co-author: Art of the Western World, 1989, Painting of the Golden Age: A Biographical Dictionary of Seventeenth-Century European Painters, 1993, Domeinco Tiepolo: Master Draftsman, 1996, Giandomenico Teipolo, Disegni dal mondo, 1996; contbg. author Critic's Choice, 1999. Grantee Nat. Endowment for Arts, 1982, 83, Am. Philos. Soc., 1985, NEH, 1985, Samuel H. Kress Found., 1999-2000. Mem. Assn. Art Mus. Dirs. Office: Ind U Art Mus 7th St Bloomington IN 47405-3024

GEAREN, JOHN JOSEPH, lawyer; b. Wareham, Mass., Sept. 1, 1943; BA, U. Notre Dame, 1965; MA (Rhodes Scholar), Oxford U., 1967; JD, Yale U., 1970. Bar: Ill. 1972. Ptnr. Mayer, Brown & Platt, Chgo., 1970—. Democrat. Roman Catholic. Home: 179 Linden Ave Unit 2 Oak Park IL 60302-1661 Office: Mayer Brown & Platt 190 S La Salle St Ste 3100 Chicago IL 60603-3441 E-mail: jgearen@mayerbrown.com.

GECKER, JAMES M., lawyer; b. Milw., July 1, 1947; BA, U. Calif., Berkeley, 1971; JD cum laude, U. Wis., 1974; MSIR, Loyola U., Chgo., 1984. Bar: Ga. 1974, Ill. 1976, Wis. 1977, Ohio 1978, US Ct. Appeals, 5th, 6th & 7th Cirs., US Ct. Appeals, Fed. Cir., US Dist. Ct., Ea. Dist. Mich., US Dist. Ct., No. Dist. Ill. Ptnr. Katten Muchin Zavis Rosenman, Chgo. Mem.: ABA. Office: Katten Muchin Zavis Rosenman 525 W Monroe St Chicago IL 60661 Office Phone: 312-902-5586. Office Fax: 312-577-8825. E-mail: james.gecker@kmzr.com.

GEDDES, LANELLE EVELYN, nurse, physiologist; b. Houston, Sept. 15, 1935; d. Carl Otto and Evelyn Bertha (Frank) Nerger; m. Leslie Alexander Geddes, Aug. 3, 1962. BSN, U. Houston, 1957, PhD, 1970. Staff nurse Houston Ind. Sch. Dist., 1957-62; instr. to asst. prof. physiology Baylor U. Coll. Medicine, 1972-75; asst. prof. nursing Tex. Women's U., 1972-75; prof., head Purdue U. Sch. Nursing, Lafayette, Ind., 1975-91. Contbr. chpts. to books, articles to med. jours. Recipient tchg. awards. Mem. Am. Nurses Assn., Am. Assn. Critical-Care Nurses, AAAS, N.Y. Acad. Scis., Phi Kappa Phi, Sigma Theta Tau, Iota Sigma Pi. Lutheran. Office: Purdue Univ West Sch Nursing Lafayette IN 47907

GEDDES, LESLIE ALEXANDER, forensic engineer, educator, physiologist; b. Scotland, May 24, 1921; s. Alexander and Helen (Humphrey) G.; m. Irene P. Bloomer; 1 child, James Alexander; m. La Nelle E. Nerger, Aug. 3, 1962. BEE, MEngring., ScD (hon.), McGill U.; PhD in Physiology, Baylor U. Med. Coll. Demonstrator in elec. engring. McGill U., 1945, research asst. dept. neurology, 1945-52; cons. elec. engring. to various indsl. firms Que., Can.; biophysicist dept. physiology Baylor Med. Coll., Houston, asst. prof. physiology, 1956-61, assoc. prof., 1961-65, prof., 1965-74; dir. Lab. of Biophysics, Tex. Inst. Rehab. and Research, Houston, 1961-65; prof. physiology Coll. Vet. Medicine, Tex. A. and M. U., College Station, 1965-74, prof. biomed. engring., 1969-74; Showalter Disting. prof. bioengring. and elec. engring. Purdue U., West Lafayette, Ind., 1974-91, Showalter Disting. prof. emeritus, 1991—. Cons. NASA Manned Spacecraft Center, Houston, 1962-64, USAF, Sch. Aerospace Medicine, Brooks AFB, 1958-65; expert witness, 1981—. Author: 22 books; cons. editor: Med. and Biol. Engring., 1969—, Med. Research Engring., 1964-74, Med. Electronics and Data, 1969—, Jour. Cardiovasc. Engring., 2004-; mem. editl. bd. Jour. Electrocardiology, 1968—, med. instr., 1974—; contbr. over 800 articles to bioengring. Mem. Soc. Free Space Floaters, 1961. With Can. Army OTC. Named 2006 at. Medal Tech. Laureate; recipient Ctrl. Ind. Corp. award for Commercialization, 2003—04, Corp. Vitae award, Am. Heart Assn., 2005. Fellow: IEEE (Lee De Forest award 2001, Leadership award, Edison gold medal, IEEE 3d Millennium award, World of Difference award), AAAS (Am. Heart Vital award 2005, Nat. Tech. medal 2006), Biomed. Engring. Soc., Royal Soc. Medicine, Australasian Coll. Physicists in Biology and Medicine, Am. Inst. Med. and Biol. Engring., Am. Coll. Cardiology, Nat. Acad. Forensic Engrs.; mem.: NAE, NSPE, Am. Physiol. Soc., Assn. Advancement Med. Instrumentation (Health Care Hero award 2007, Leadership award), Tex. Soc. Profl. Engrs., Radio Club Am., Phi Zeta, Tau Beta Pi, Sigma Xi. Achievements include holder 33 US patents. Home: 400 N River Rd Apt 701 West Lafayette IN 47906-3131 Office: Purdue U POTR Bldg 500 Central Dr West Lafayette IN 47907-2022 Home Phone: 765-743-1941; Office Phone: 765-494-2995. Office Fax: 765-494-1193. Business E-Mail: geddes@ecn.purdue.edu.

GEE, ROBERT LEROY, agriculturist, dairy farmer; b. Moorhead, Minn., May 25, 1926; s. Milton William and Hertha Elizabeth (Paschke) G.; m. Mae Valentine Erickson, June 18, 1953 BS in Agronomy, N.D. State U., 1951, postgrad., 1955, Colo. A&M U., 1954. Farm labor controller Minn. Extension Service, Clay County, 1944-45, county 4-H agt., 1951-57; rural mail carrier U.S. Postal Service, Moorhead, Minn., 1946-47; breeder registered shorthorn cattle and registered southdown sheep Moorhead, Minn., 1950-63; owner, operator Gee Dairy Farm (Oak Grove Farm), Moorhead, Minn., 1957—. Asst. prof. status U. Minn., 1951-57; bd. dirs. Red River Valley Devel. Assn., Crookston, Minn., v.p., 1992—; treas. Red River Milk Producers Pool, Minn., ND, 1968-78; chmn. bd. Cass Clay Creamery Inc., Fargo, ND, 1982-85, 92-95, v.p., 1990-91; mem. Nat. Dairy Promotion Bd., Washington, 1984-88. Treas. Oakport Twp., 1974-82, supr., 1986-2002, v.p., 1987-2002; mem. Clay County Planning and Zoning Commn., 1991-2000, vice chmn., 1992-96, chmn., 1996-2000; mem. Clay County Bd. Adjustment, 1995-2000, chmn., 1996-2000. With USN, 1945-46. Recipient Grand Champion Farm Flock award Man. Expn., 1960, Clay County's Outstanding Agriculturist award, 1996; named Clay County King Agassiz, Red River Valley Winter Shows, 1966, Grand Champion forage exhibit Red River Valley Winter Shows, 1979, 82; co-recipient Clay County Dairy Farm Family of Yr. award Red River Valley Dairymen's Assn., 1979. Mem. Minn. Milk Producers Assn. (bd. dirs. 1977-88, 93-97, sec. 1972-78, treas. 1977-87), Minn. Assn. Coops. (bd. dirs. 1984-96), State Coop. Assn. (dairy council 1975-96), Am. Farm Bur. Fedn., Nat. Farmers Union, Kragnes Farmers Elevator Assn., Red River Valley Livestock Assn., Am. Shorthorn Breeders Assn., Am. Southdown Breeders Assn., Holstein-Friesian Assn. Am. Republican. Mem. United Ch. of Christ. Club: Agassiz (v.p. 1979-81, pres. 1981-82) (Moorhead) Avocations: hunting, fishing, skiing. Home and Office: 8595 2nd St N Moorhead MN 56560-7103

GEFKE, HENRY JEROME, lawyer; b. Milw., Aug. 4, 1930; s. Jerome Henry and Frances (Daley) G.; m. Caroline Ann Lawrence, June 25, 1955 (div. Jan. 1968); children: Brian Lawrence, David Jerome; m. Mary Clare Nuss, Aug. 28, 1976; children: Lynn Marie, James Scott. BS, Marquette U., 1952, LLB, 1954; postgrad., Ohio State U., 1955—56. Bar: Wis. 1954, Tax Ct. U.S 1969; C.P.A., Wis. Acct.-auditor John G. Conley & Co. (C.P.A.s), Milw., 1956-59; with J.I. Case Co., Racine, Wis., 1959-68, corp. sec., asst. gen. counsel, 1965-68; assoc. Maier & Mulcahy, S.C., Milw., 1968-69; prin. Mulcahy, Gefke & Wherry, S.C., Milw., 1969-73; individual practice law Milw., 1973—. Corp. officer, dir. various bus. corps. Pres., bd. dirs. Big Bros., Greater Racine, 1965-67; trustee Racine County Instns., 1960-63; bd. dirs., sec., legal counsel Racine Transitional Care, Inc., 1973-76; bd. dirs., legal counsel Our Home Found., Milw., 1979-82; bd. dirs. Racine County Mental Health Assn., 1963-67, Alliance for Mentally Ill Milw. County, 1986-88; bd. dirs., sec., legal counsel Glendale Econ. Devel. Corp., 1996—; bd. dirs. Glendale Bus. Coun., 1996-97; bd. dirs. Glendale C. of C., Inc., 1997—, treas., 1998-00, pres. 2000-02. Mem. Wis. Bar Assn., Milw. Bar Assn., Wis. Inst. CPA's, Delta Sigma Pi, Delta Theta Phi. Home and Office: 5521 N Lydell Ave Milwaukee WI 53217-5042 Office Phone: 414-332-1200. E-mail: hjgjdcpa@aol.com.

GEHA, ALEXANDER SALIM, cardiothoracic surgeon, educator; b. Beirut, June 18, 1936; arrived in US, 1963; s. Salim M. and Alice I. (Hayek) G.; m. Diane L. Redalen, Nov. 25, 1967; children— Samia, Rula, Nada BS in Biology, Am. U. Beirut, 1955, MD, 1959; MS in Surgery and Physiology, U. Minn.-Rochester, 1967; MS (privatum), Yale U., 1978. Asst. prof. U. Vt., Burlington, 1967-69; asst. prof. Washington U., St. Louis, 1969-73, assoc. prof., 1973-75, Yale U., New Haven, 1975-78, prof., chief cardiothoracic surgery, 1978-86, Case Western Res. U. and Univ. Hosp. of Cleve., 1986-98; Jay L. Ankeney prof. cardiothoracic surgery Case Western Res. U., 1994-98; pres. Univ. Cardiothoracic Surgeons, Inc., Cleve., 1986—2000; prof., chief cardiothoracic surgery U. Ill. Med. Ctr., Chgo., 1998—2007, prof. emeritus cardiothoracic surgery, 2007—; chief cardiothoracic surgery Mt. Sinai Hosp. Med. Ctr., Chgo., 2000—07. Cons. VA Hosp., West Haven, Conn., 1975-86, VA Hosp., Cleve., 1986-98, Westside VA Hosp., Chgo., 1998-2007, Cleve. Met. Health Med. Ctr., 1986-98, Mt. Sinai Med. Ctr., Cleve., 1990-98, Waterbury Hosp., 1976-86, Sharon Hosp., 1981-86, Michael Reese Hosp., 2002—; mem. study sect. Nat. Heart Lung and Blood Inst., 1981-85. Editor: Glenn's Thoracic and Cardiovascular Surgery, 4th edit. 1983, 5th edit. 1991, 6th edit. 1996; editor Basic Surgery, 1984. Bd. dirs. New Haven Heart Assn., 1981-85; trustee Am. U. Beirut. Mem. AMA, Assn. Clin. Cardiac Surgery (chmn. membership com. 1978-80, sec.-treas. 1980-83, pres. 1988), Am. Heart Assn. (bd. dirs. 1981-85. councils on basic sci., cardiovascular surgery), Am. Coll. Chest Physicians (steering com. 1980-84), Am. Assn. Thoracic Surgery, Am. Coll. Cardiology, ACS (chmn. coordinating com. on edn. in thoracic surgery, chmn. 1992-95), Am. Lung Assn., Am. Physiol. Soc., Am. Surg. Assn., Assn. Acad. Surgery, Central Surg. Assn., Chgo. Inst. Medicine, European Assn. Cardiothoracic Surgery, Internat. Soc. Heart and Lung Transplantation, Internat. Soc. Cardiovascular Surgery, Lebanese Order Physicians, New Eng. Surg. Soc., Pan Am. Med. Assn., Halsted Soc., Soc. Thoracic Surgeons (govt. rels. com., manpower com., program com., edn. and resources com.), Soc. for Vascular Surgery, Soc. Univ. Surgeons, Chgo. Surg. Soc., also others. E-mail: ageha@uic.edu.

GEHAN, MARK WILLIAM, lawyer; b. St. Paul, Dec. 19, 1946; s. Mark William and Jean Elizabeth (McGee) G.; m. Lucy Lyman Harrison, Aug. 25, 1971; children: Mark Harrison, Alice McGee. BA, U. Notre Dame, 1968; JD, U. Minn., 1971. Bar: Minn., 1972; U.S. Supreme Ct., 1989. Asst. county atty. Ramsey County Atty.'s Office, St. Paul, 1972-76; prosecutor, Met. Area Dist. Urban County Attys. Bd., St. Paul, 1976-77; ptnr. Collins Buckley Sauntry & Haugh, St. Paul, 1978—. Bd. dirs. Minn. State Bd. Pub. Def., St. Paul, 1982-90. Pres. St. Paul Charter Commn., 1986-94. Mem. Minn. Bar Assn. (pres. 1998-99), Ramsey County Bar Assn. (pres. 1990-91). Avocations: scuba diving, tennis, guitar. Office: Collins Buckley Sauntry & Haugh First Nat Bank Bldg 332 Minnesota St Ste W1100 Saint Paul MN 55101-1379 Office Phone: 651-227-0611. E-mail: mgehan@cbsh.net.

GEHL, WILLIAM D., manufacturing executive; b. 1947; Bar: Wis., Fla. With The Ziegler Co., Inc., West Bend, Wis., 1978-92, sr. v.p., gen. counsel, 1985-92, exec. v.p., COO, gen. counsel, sec., 1990-92, also bd. dirs.; dir. Gehl Co., 1987—, chmn. nominating com., mem. compensation and benefits com., pres., CEO, 1992—, also chmn. bd. dirs. Office: Gehl Co PO Box 179 143 Water St West Bend WI 53095-3400

GEHO, WALTER BLAIR, biomedical research executive; b. Wheeling, W.Va., May 18, 1939; s. Blair Roy and Susan (Yonko) G.; m. Marjorie Cooper, Aug. 25, 1962; children: Hans, Alison, Robert, David, Daniel. BS, Bethany Coll., 1960; PhD in Pharmacology, Western Res. U., 1964, MD, 1966. Instr. pharmacology Sch. of Medicine Western Res. U., Cleve., 1966-67; pres., CEO SDG Inc., Cleve., 1993-2001, chief sci. officer, dir., 2001—; staff researcher Procter & Gamble Co., Cin., 1968-74, head pharmaceutical rsch. sect., 1974-81; v.p., dir. rsch. Tech. Unltd., Inc., Wooster, Ohio, 1981-89, pres., 1989-93; chmn., chief sci. officer, dir. AMDG, Inc., Cleve., 1997-2001, chief sci. officer, dir., 2001—. Contbr. articles to Phamacology of Bisphosphates, Clin. Pharmacology of Didronel, Genetics of Myositis Ossificans. Recipient 2 Ohio Innovator awards Edison Fund Ohio, 1987, Innovation award Enterprise Devel. Inst., 1995. Mem. AMA, Am. Chem. Soc. Achievements include patents in pharmaceuticals; contributions to development of osteoscan and didronel, and targeted drug delivery systems, commercialization of liposome inventions into consumer and pharmaceutical products. Office: SDG Inc PO Box 91023 Cleveland OH 44101-3023

GEHRING, FREDERICK WILLIAM, mathematician, educator; b. Ann Arbor, Mich., Aug. 7, 1925; s. Carl E. and Hester McNeal (Reed) G.; m. Lois Caroline Bigger, Aug. 29, 1953; children: Kalle Burgess, Peter Motz. BSE in Elec. Engring., U. Mich., 1946, MA in Math, 1949; PhD (Fulbright fellow) in Math, Cambridge U., Eng., 1952, ScD, 1976; PhD (hon.), U. Helsinki, Finland, 1977, U. Jyväskylä, 1990, Norwegian U. Sci. & Technology, 1997. Benjamin Peirce instr. Harvard U., Cambridge, Mass., 1952-55; instr. math. U. Mich., Ann Arbor, 1955-56, asst. prof., 1956-59, assoc. prof., 1959-62, prof., 1962-96, T.H. Hildebrandt prof. math., 1984-96, prof. emeritus, 1996, chmn. dept. math., 1973-75, 77-84, disting. univ. prof., 1987—; hon. prof. Hunan U., Changsha, People's Republic of China, 1987. Vis. prof. Harvard U., 1964-65, Stanford U., 1964, U. Minn., 1971, Inst. Mittag-Leffler, Sweden, 1972, Mittag-Leffler, Sweden, 1990; Lars Onsager prof. Norwegian Tech. Hochschule, Norway, 1995; chair program in Geo Function Theory, Math. Scis. Rsch. Inst., Berkeley, 1986. Editor Duke Math. Jour., 1963-80, D. Van Nostrand Pub. Co., 1963-70, North Holland Pub. Co., 1970-94, Springer-Verlag, 1974-2002; editl. bd. Procs. Am. Math. Soc., 1962-65, Ind. U. Math. Jour., 1967-75, Math. Revs., 1969-75, Bull. Am. Math. Soc., 1979-85, Complex Variables, 1981—, Mich. Math. Jour., 1989-98, Annales Academiae Scientiarum Fennicae, 1996—, Conformal Geometry and Dynamics, 1997—, Computational Methods and Function Theory, 2001—; contbr. numerous articles on rsch. in pure math. to sci. jours. With USNR, 1943-46. Decorated comdr. Finnish White Rose; NSF fellow, 1959-60; Fulbright fellow, 1958-59; Guggenheim fellow, 1958-59; Sci. Rsch. Coun. sr. fellow, 1981; Humboldt fellow, 1981-84; U. Auckland Found fellow, 1985; Finnish Acad. fellow U. Helsinki, 1989. Mem. NAS, Am. Acad. Arts and Scis., Assn. Women in Math., Math. Assn. Am., Am. Math. Soc. (coun. 1969-75, 80-83, trustee 1983-93, mem. editl. bd. 1997-98, Leroy P. Steele prize for Lifetime Achievement, 2006), Inst. for Math. and Its Applications (gov. 1981-84), Swiss Math. Soc., Finnish Math. Soc., London Math. Soc., Finnish Acad. Sci., Royal Norwegian Soc. Scis. and Letters. Office Phone: 734-764-1219. Business E-Mail: fgehring@umich.edu.

GEHRKE, CHARLES WILLIAM, biochemistry professor; b. NYC, July 18, 1917; s. Henry Edward and Louise (Mader) G.; m. Virginia Dorothy Horcher, Dec. 25, 1941; children: Charles William (dec.), Jon Craig, Susan Gay. BA in Biochemistry, Ohio State U., 1939, BS in Edn, 1941, MS in Biochemistry and Bacteriology, 1941, PhD in Agrl. Biochemistry, 1947. Prof., head dept. chemistry Missouri Valley Coll., Marshall, Mo., 1942-49; instr. agrl. chemistry Ohio State U., Columbus, 1945-46; assoc. prof. agrl. chemistry U. Mo., Columbia, 1949-54, prof. biochemistry, 1954-87, prof. emeritus, 1987—, mgr. Expt. Sta. Chem. Labs., 1954-87, dir. interdisciplinary chromatography Mass Spectrometry Facility, 1982-87; founder, chmn. bd. dirs. Bioscis. and Tech. Internat., Inc., 1992. Founder, chmn. bd. dirs. Analytical Biochemistry Labs., Columbia, 1968-92, dir., 1992—; USA co-chmn. colloquium on A Lunar-Based Chem. Analysis Lab., 1989, 93; co-investigator lunar samples NASA, 1969-75; lectr., Russia, 1972, 74, 90, Japan, China, Taiwan, The Philippines, Hong Kong, 1982, 87, France, Germany, Eng., Norway, Sweden, Switzerland, Italy, Egypt, 1986, 89. Author: 75 Years of Chromatography--A Historical Dialogue, 1979, (book chpt.) Quantitation of Amino Acids and Amines by Chromatography, 2005, Milestones in Chromatography, 2006; author, editor: Amino Acid Analysis by Gas Chromatography, 3 vols., 1987, Chromatography and Modification of Nucleosides, 3 vols., 1990, A Lunar-Based Chemical Analysis Laboratory, 1993, A Lunar-Based Analytical Laboratory, 1997, Chromatography a Century of Discovery, 2001; mem. editl. bd. Jour. Chromatographic Sci., Jour. Chromatography; contbr. chpts. to books, more than 270 articles to sci. jours. Recipient Faculty Alumni Gold medal award U. Mo., 1975, Chromatography Meml. medal Sci. Council on Chromatography of USSR Acad. Scis., 1980, Ohio State Alumni Profl. Achievement award, 2001; Ohio State Outstanding scholar, 1996. Fellow Am. Inst. Chemists, Assn. Ofcl. Analytical Chemists (Harvey W. Wiley award 1971, chmn. Magruder standard sample subcom. 1958-79, bd. dirs., mem. editl. bd. 1979-82, pres.-elect 1983, pres. centennial yr. 1984); mem. AAAS, Am. Soc. Biol. Chemists, Am. Chem. Soc. (pres. Mo. sect. 1958-59, 78-79, Spencer award 1979, Midwest Chemist award 1986, Dal Nogare award in chromatography 1995, U. Mo. Faculty Retiree of Yr. award 1993, Nat. Am. Chem. Soc. Sci. and Tech. award 1999, Nat. Am. Chem. Soc. Chromatography award 2000), Am. Dairy Sci. Assn. (chmn. com. on protein nomenclature 1961-62), Fedn. Am. Socs. Exptl. Biology, Internat. Soc. Study of Origin of Life, N.Y. Acad. Sci., Cosmopolitan Luncheon Club (chmn. Diabetes Ctr. adv. com. 1976—), Diabetes Ctr., Sigma Xi. Home: 708 Edgewood Ave Columbia MO 65203-7410 Office Phone: 573-442-4964.

GEIER, KATHLEEN T., human resources specialist; b. Akron, Ohio, Aug. 7, 1956; BS, Heidelberg Coll., 1978. Indsl. engr., various human resources positions Goodyear Tire and Rubber Co., Akron, Ohio, 1978—86; ops. mgr. Cosmoflex (subsidiary of Goodyear Tire and Rubber Co.), 1986—90, plant mgr., pres. Mt. Pleasant, Iowa, 1992—94; bus. ctr. mgr. Goodyear Tire and Rubber Co., St. Marys, Ohio, 1990—92, dir. salaried human resources end employment practices Akron, Ohio, 1994—95, dir. human resources employment practices and systems, 1995—96, dir. human resources ctrl. svcs. N.Am. bus. unites and corp. staff, 1996—99, dir. human resources Europe, Africa, Middle East region Brussels, sr. v.p. human resources Akron, 2002—. Office: Goodyear Tire and Rubber Co 1144 E Market St Akron OH 44316-0001 Office Phone: 330-796-2121. Office Fax: 330-796-2222.

GEIER, PETER E., bank executive, health facility executive; With Merchants Nat. Bank and Trust, Indpls., 1979-84; v.p. nat. divsn. Huntington Nat. Bank subs. Huntington Bancshares, Columbus, Ohio, 1984-96, pres., COO, 1996—, Huntington Bancshares Inc., Columbus, 1999—2001; COO Arthur G. James Cancer Hosp., Ohio State Univ. Health System, Columbus, Ohio, 2001, sr. assoc. v.p. for health sciences bus. and adminstrn., interim CEO, 2003—, v.p. health svcs., 2003—. Office: Arthur G James Cancer Hosp Ohio State Univ Health System 300 W 10th Ave Columbus OH 43210

GEILFUSS, C. FREDERICK, II, lawyer; b. Aug. 5, 1953; BA cum laude, Williams Coll., Williamstown, Mass., 1975; MA in econs., U. Wis., 1976, JD cum laude, 1979. Bar: Wis. 1979, U.S. Ct. Appeals, seventh cir. 1979, U.S. Supreme Ct. 1982, U.S. Dist. Ct., Ea. Dist. Wis. 1983. Law clk. Hon. Judge Harlington Wood, Jr. US Ct. Appeals (7th cir.), 1979-80; atty., appellate staff Civil divsn. U.S. Dept. Justice, Washington, 1980-83; atty. Foley & Lardner LLP, Milw., 1983—88, ptnr., 1988—. Co-author: chpt. Long-Term Care Facilities: Regulation. Trustee Univ. Sch. Milw., 2002—, pres. trustees, 2004—07. Mem.: ABA, State Bar Wis., Am. Health Lawyers Assn., Wis. Psychol. Found. (chair 1999—2004), Curative Care Network (chmn. 1997—99), Milw. County War Meml. Inc., Columbia Coll. ursing, Grand Ave. Club, Gardner Found., Milw. County Marcus Ctr. Performing Arts (chmn. 1998—2001), Order Coif. Office: Foley & Lardner LLP 777 E Wisconsin Ave Milwaukee WI 53202-5306 Office Phone: 414-271-2400. Office Fax: 414-297-4900. Business E-Mail: fgeilfuss@foley.com.

GEIMAN, J. ROBERT, lawyer; b. Evanston, Ill., Mar. 5, 1931; s. Louis H. and Nancy O'Connell-Crowe G.; m. Ann L. Fitzgerald, July 29, 1972; children: J. Robert, William Patrick, Timothy Michael. BS, Northwestern U., 1953; JD, Notre Dame U., 1956. Bar: Ill. 1956, U.S. Ct. Appeals (7th cir.) 1956, U.S. Supreme Ct. 1969. Assoc. Eckert, Peterson & Lowry, Chgo., 1956-64; ptnr. Peterson, Lowry, Rall, Barber & Ross, Chgo., 1964-70, Peterson & Ross, Chgo., 1970-96, of counsel, 1996—. Mem. com. on civil jury instructions Ill. Supreme Ct., 1979-81. Case editor Notre Dame Law Rev., 1956. Bd. advisors Cath. Charities of Archdiocese of Chgo., 1973-96. Fellow Internat. Acad. Trial Lawyers, Am. Coll. Trial Lawyers, Ill. Bar Found.; mem. ABA (aviation com., tort and ins. practice sect. 1980-90), Ill. Bar Assn. (sec. 1969-70, sec. bd. govs. 1969-71), Chgo. Bar Assn. (aviation law com. 1970-73), Bar Assn. of 7th Fed. Ct. (meetings com. 1968-70, vice chmn. membership com. 1973-75), Soc. Trial Lawyers, Cath. Lawyers Guild of Chgo. (bd. advisors 1973-96), Law Club Chgo., Chgo. Athletic Assn. (pres. 1973). Republican. Home: 4861 River Village Dr Vero Beach FL 32967-7452 Office: Peterson Ross 200 E Randolph St Ste 7200 Chicago IL 60601-7719

GEIS, JEROME ARTHUR, lawyer, educator; b. Shakopee, Minn., May 28, 1946; s. Arthur Adam and Emma Mary (Boegemann) G.; m. Beth Marie Bruger, Aug. 11, 1979; children: Jennifer, Jason, Joan, Janice. BA in History magna cum laude, St. John's U., Collegeville, Minn., 1968; JD cum laude, U. Notre Dame, 1973; LLM in Taxation, NYU, 1975. Bar: Minn. 1973, U.S. Dist. Ct. Minn. 1973, U.S. Tax Ct. 1973, U.S. Ct. Appeals (8th cir.) 1973. Law clk. Minn. Supreme Ct., St. Paul, 1973-74; assoc. Dudley & Smith, St. Paul, 1975-76, Briggs & Morgan P.A., St. Paul, 1976-79, chief tax dept., 1983-95. Adj. prof. tax law William Mitchell Coll. Law, St. Paul, 1976-83; adj. prof. state and local taxation U. Minn., 2001-. Columnist Minn. Law Jour., 1986-89, Bench & Bar, 1990—; editl. cons.: Sales and Use Tax Alert; former reviewer Summary Reporter: Finance and Commerce, Minnesota State Bar Assn.; corr. State Tax Notes. Bd. dirs. Western Townhouse Assn., West St. Paul, 1979, St. Matthews Cath. Ch., West St. Paul, 1981; adv. bd. Minn. Inst. of Legal Edn., 1984—2002. Served to specialist 4th class U.S. Army, 1969-71. Recipient Disting. Svc. award, MSBA Tax Sect., 1990. Fellow Am. Coll. Tax Counsel; mem. ABA, Am. Law Inst., Tax Inst. Am. (chmn. sales and use tax commn. 1988-90), Nat. Tax Assn., Am. Judicature Soc., Minn. Bar Assn. (bd. dirs. tax coun. sect. 1984-93, 94-97, 99—, chmn. 1990-91), Ramsey County Bar Assn., Minn. Taxpayers Assn. (bd. dirs. 1988—), Inst. Property Taxation, Supreme Ct. Hist. Soc., Nat. Assn. State Bar Tax Sects. (exec. com. 1993—), Citizens League, Minn. Club (bd. dirs. 1997-2000), Federalist Soc., Kiwanis (bd. dirs. 2000-02). Home: 1116 Dodd Rd Saint Paul MN 55118-1821 Office: Briggs & Morgan PA 2200 1st St N Saint Paul MN 55109-3210 Home Phone: 651-455-0298; Office Phone: 651-808-6409. Business E-Mail: jgeis@briggs.com.

GEISSINGER, FREDERICK WALLACE, finance company executive; b. Huntingdon, Pa., Oct. 3, 1945; s. Harry Lloyd and Elizabeth Gertrude Geissinger; m. Anne Beth Lawrenz, Feb. 14, 1970 (div.); children: Amy Elizabeth, Jacqueline Marie. AB, Dartmouth Coll., 1967; MBA, U. Chgo., 1969. Lic. in securities and real estate, N.Y.C. Corp. banking officer Chase Manhattan Bank, NYC, 1969-74, dir. corp. planning, 1974-76, asst. gen. mgr. Tokyo, 1976-80, chief staff Western Hemisphere NYC, 1980-83, budget dir., 1983-86, sr. v.p. real estate, 1986-90; exec. v.p. Daiwa Securities Am. Inc., NYC, 1990-92; prin. Geissinger and Assocs., NYC, 1993; CEO Am. Gen. Land Devel. Inc., Houston, 1994-95, Am. Gen. Mortgage and Land Devel. Inc., 1995; chmn., CEO Am. Gen. Finance, Evansville, Ind., 1995—; vice chmn., group exec. Am. Gen. Corp., Houston, 1998—. Trustee Pelham (N.Y.) Bd. Edn., 1983-86. Mem. Urban Land Inst. (coun. 1986—), Real Estate Bd. N.Y., Pelham Country club (bd. govs. 1987-92, pres. 1990-92). Republican. Presbyterian. Avocations: skiing, golf, tennis, coaching girls soccer, classical music. Office Phone: 812-468-5500.

GELATT, CHARLES DANIEL, manufacturing executive; b. La Crosse, Wis., Jan. 4, 1918; s. Philo Madison and Clara (Johnson) G.; m. Jane Leicht, Mar. 6, 1942 (div. 1972); children: Sarah Jane Gelatt Gephart, Charles D., Philip Madison; m. Paula Jo Evans, Aug. 22, 1973 (div. 1978); m. Sue Anne Jimieson, Dec. 11, 1983. BA, MA, U. Wis., 1939. V.p. Gelatt Corp., La Crosse, 1940-52, pres., 1952-95, chmn., 1995—99; pres. No. Engraving Corp., Sparta, Wis., 1958-67, chmn., 1967-96, chmn. emeritus, 1996—; pres. N.E. Co. Ltd., 2000—. Trustee Northwestern Mut. Life Ins. Co., Milw., 1960-88, mem. exec. com., 1961-77; chmn. North Ctrl. Trust Co., La. Crosse, 1989-93; mem. bd. regents U. Wis., 1947-74, pres. bd. regents, 1955-57, v.p., 1964-68, pres., 1968-69; mem. Wis. Coordinating Com. for Higher Edn., 1955-59, 64-69, chmn., 1956; chmn. Assn. Governing Bds. Univs. and Colls., Washington, 1971-72; trustee Carroll Coll., Waukesha, Wis., 1971-79, Viterbo U., La. Crosse, 1972-2002; trustee Gundersen Found., La Crosse, 1973-95. Mem. Phi Beta Kappa. Home (Summer): 30976 Old Mill Rd La Crescent MN 55947 Home (Winter): 9133 Collins Ave #3A Miami FL 33154-3118

GELBER, BRIAN, commodities trader; b. 1954; With Thomson Mc Kinnon Securities, Chgo., 1975-82, Gelber Group Inc., Chgo., 1982—, pres. Office: Gelber Group Inc 141 W Jackson Blvd Lbby 1 Chicago IL 60604-2904

GELBERMAN, RICHARD H., orthopedist, surgeon; b. NYC, Nov. 27, 1943; MD, U. Tenn. Health Scis. Ctr., 1969. Diplomate orthopedic surgery and in hand surgery Am. Bd. Orthopaedic Surgery. Resident U. Wis., Madison, 1971—75; fellow, hand & microsurgery Duke U., 1976—77; fellow, pediat. orthopedics Boston Children's Hosp., 1985—86; prof. orthop. surgery Harvard U. Med. Sch., Boston, 1987—94; Fred C. Reynolds prof. orthop. surgery Washington U. Sch. Medicine, St. Louis, 1995—. Mem.: Am. Bd. Orthop. Surgeons, Assn. Bone & Joint Surgeons, Orthop. Rsch. Soc., Inter-Urban Orthop. Soc., Inst. Medicine, IOS, Am. Soc. Surgery of the Hand, Am. Orthop. Assn., Am. Acad. Orthop. Surgeons (pres. 2001—02). Office: Washington U Sch Medicine Ste 11300 One Barnes Hosp Plz Saint Louis MO 63110

GELBKE, CLAUS-KONRAD, nuclear physics educator; b. Celle, Germany, May 31, 1947; came to the U.S., 1976; s. Heinz and Gertraud Gelbke; m. Brigitte Zabeschek, Apr. 6, 1973; children: Susanne, Martin. Diploma für physik, U. Heidelberg, Germany, 1970, doctor rerum naturalium, 1973. Wissenschaftlicher asst. Max-Planck-Inst für Kernphysik, Heidelberg, 1973-76; physicist Lawrence Berkeley (Calif.) Lab., 1976-77; assoc. prof. physics Mich. State U., East

Lansing, 1977-81, prof. physics, 1981-87, assoc. dir. nuclear sci. Nat. Superconducting Cyclotron Lab., 1987-90, disting. prof., 1990—, dir. Nat. Superconducting Cyclotron Lab., 1992—. Summer visitor Brookhaven Nat. Lab., Upton, N.Y., 1974, U. Washington, Seattle, 1975. Alfred P. Sloan fellow, 1979-83; Scholarship Studienstiftung des Deutschen Volkes, 1971-72; Humboldt Rsch. award U.S. Scis. Fellow AAAS, Am. Physical Soc. Office: Mich State U Cyclotron Lab S Shaw Ln East Lansing MI 48824 E-mail: gelbke@nscl.msu.edu.

GELDER, JOHN WILLIAM, lawyer; b. Buffalo, Aug. 7, 1933; s. Ray Horace and Grace Catherine (Kelly) G.; m. Martha J. Kindleberger, June 12, 1953; William R., Mark S., Cathryn J. Gelder Brooks, Carolyn G. Gelder Bird BBA, U. Mich., 1956, JD with distinction, 1959. Bar: Mich. 1960, D.C. 1981, U.S. Supreme Ct. 1982. Assoc. Miller, Canfield, Paddock and Stone, P.L.C., Detroit, 1959-68, mng. ptnr., 1975-81, 90-93, ptnr., 1968-93, prin., 1994—. Bd. dirs. Tecumseh Products Co., 1989—. Asst. editor Mich. Law Rev., 1958, 59 Trustee, officer Herrick Found., Detroit, 1989—. Mem. State Bar Mich. (coun. mem. bus. law sect. 1984-90), Order of Coif, Bloomfield Hills Country Club. Home: 30845 River Crossing St Bingham Farms MI 48025-4656 Office: Miller Canfield Paddock & Stone PLC 840 W Long Lake Rd Ste 200 Troy MI 48098-6358 E-mail: gelder@millercanfield.com.

GELEERD, JAMES D. (JAKE GELEERD), property manager; b. 1966; BS, Univ. Ill. Tax consul. Arthur Andersen & Co., Chgo., 1990—94; with Equity Group Investment, Chgo., 1994—99; pres. Sportsco Internat.; prin. Terrapin Properties. LLC, Chgo., 2002—. Appeared (TV series) Oprah Winfrey Show. Named one of 40 Under Forty, Crain's Bus. Chgo., 2005. Mem.: Young Presidents' Orgn., Sigma Alpha Mu (assoc.). Office: Terappin Properties 5th Floor 217 N Jefferson St Chicago IL 60661 Office Phone: 312-466-1500. Office Fax: 312-466-1555.

GELEHRTER, THOMAS DAVID, medical educator, geneticist; b. Liberec, Czechoslovakia, Mar. 11, 1936; arrived in U.S., 1939; married 1959; 2 children. BA, Oberlin Coll., 1957; MA, U. Oxford, Eng., 1959; MD, Harvard U., 1963. Intern, then asst. resident in internal medicine Mass. Gen. Hosp., Boston, 1963—65; rsch. assoc. in molecular biology NIAMD NIH, Bethesda, Md., 1965—69; fellow in med. genetics U. Wash., 1969—70; asst. prof. human genetics, internal medicine and pediatrics Sch. Medicine Yale U., 1970—73, assoc. prof., 1973—74, U. Mich., Ann Arbor, 1974—76, prof. internal medicine and human genetics, 1976—87, dir. divsn. med. genetics, 1977—87, chmn. dept. human genetics, 1987—2004, prof. human genetics and internal medicine, 1987—. Josiah Macy, Jr. Found. faculty scholar and vis. scientist Imperial Cancer Rsch. Fund Labs., London, 1979-80; vis. fellow Inst. Molecular Medicine; Keeley vis. fellow Wadham Coll., U. Oxford, Wellcome Rsch. Travel grantee, 1995. Mem. editl. bd. Jour. Biol. Chemistry, 1995-2000. Trustee Oberlin Coll., 1970-75; mem. NIH Recontinant DNA Adv. Com., 2002-05. Rhodes scholar, 1957-59. Fellow AAAS, Am. Coll. Med. Genetics; mem. Am. Soc. Human Genetics (bd. dir. 1994-96), Am. Soc. Clin. Investigation, Am. Soc. Biochemistry and Molecular Biology, Assn. Am. Physicians. Office: Univ Mich Med Sch Dept Human Genetics SPC 5618 1241 Catherine St Ann Arbor MI 48109-5618 Office Phone: 734-936-2860. Business E-Mail: tdgum@umich.edu.

GELFAND, MICHAEL JOSEPH, radiologist, educator; b. Detroit, Mar. 4, 1945; s. Jacob and Mildred (Weine) G.; m. Janelle Ann Magnuson, Mar. 24, 1973; children: Rebecca Ann, Karin Janelle. BA, U. Mich., 1966; MD, Stanford U., 1971. Diplomate Am. Bd. Pediat., Am. Bd. Nuc. Medicine. Intern Children's Hosp., Cin., 1973-74, resident in pediat., 1974-75; resident in nuc. medicine U. Cin., 1975-77, asst. prof. pediat., 1978-90, assoc. prof. pediat., 1990-95, prof. pediat., 1995—, asst. prof. radiology, 1977-83, assoc. prof. radiology, 1983-90, prof. radiology, 1990—. Asst. attending radiologist Children's Hosp. Cin., 1978-79, attending radiologist, 1979—. Editor: Effective Use of Computers in Nuclear Medicine (Gelfand M.J., Thomas S.R.), 1998, Pediatric Nuclear Imaging, 1994 (Miller J.H., Gelfand M.J.); contbr. chpts. to books, articles to med. jours. Served with USPHS, 1971-73. Mem. Soc. Nuc. Medicine (treas. 1993-96, fin. chmn. 1996-2000, v.p. 2001-02, pres. 2002-03, bd. dirs. 1993-2004), Soc. Pediatric Radiology, Radiologic Soc. N.Am, Am. Coll. Radiology, Am. Coll. Nuc. Physicians, Ohio State Radiol. Soc. Office: Childrens Hosp Cincinnati OH 45229-3039

GELLMAN, SAMUEL HELMER, chemist, educator; b. Evanston, Ill., Sept. 12, 1959; AB, Harvard U., 1981; PhD, Columbia U., 1986. Postdoctoral fellow Calif. Inst. Tech., Pasadena, 1986-87; asst. prof. chemistry U. Wis., Madison, 1987-93, assoc. prof., 1993-95, prof., 1995—. Evan P. Helfaer prof., 2001—06, Ralph F. Hirschmann prof., 2005—. Contbr. articles to Jour. Am. Chem. Soc., Nature. Office Naval Rsch. young investigator, 1990; NSF presdl. young investigator, 1991; Alfred P. Sloan fellow Alfred P. Sloan Found., 1993. Fellow AAAS; mem. Am. Chem. Soc. (Arthur C. Cope scholar 1997,Ralph F. Hirschmann Award in Peptide Chemistry 2007), Am. Peptide Soc. (Vincent du Vigneaud award 2006). Office: U Wis Dept Chemistry 1101 University Ave Madison WI 53706-1322 E-mail: gellman@chem.wisc.edu.

GELMAN, ANDREW RICHARD, lawyer; b. Chgo. s. Sidney S. and Beverly Gelman; m. Amy H., 1985; children: Stephen S., Adam P., Elizabeth F. BA, U. Pa., 1967; JD, U. Va., 1970. Bar: Va. 1970, Ill. 1971. Assoc. Rosen & Grossman Law Firm, Chgo., 1971-74, McBride, Baker & Coles Law Firm (now Holland & Knight LLP), Chgo., 1974-77, ptnr., 1978—. Mem. com. on character and fitness of Ill. Supreme Ct., Chgo., 1979-95. Bd. dirs. Scholarship and Guidance Assn. Youth and Family Svcs., Chgo., 1979—, Children's Meml. Rsch. Ctr. of Children's Meml. Hosp., Chgo., 1991—, vice-chair, 1998—; chmn. Med. Rsch. Inst. Coun., 1983-86, 91-92; trustee Michael Reese Hosp. and Med. Ctr., Chgo., 1987-91. Named one of Top 100 Attys., Worth mag., 2007, Best Lawyers in Am., 2007; recipient Weigle award, Chgo. Bar Found., 1980, 2008. Mem. ABA (standing com. jud. selection, tenure and compensation 1982-87, pub. understanding about the law com. 1987-91, chair probate and estate planning com. gen. practice sect. 1994-97, commn. on mental and phys. disability law 1995-97), Chgo. Bar Assn. (past chmn. divsn. probate practice com., bd. mgrs. 1978-80, chmn. young lawyers sect. 1976-77), Chgo. Estate Planning Coun., The Quadrangle Club (bd. dirs. 2005—). Office: Holland & Knight LLP 131 S Dearborn St 30th Fl Chicago IL 60603-5547 Office Phone: 312-715-5718. E-mail: andy.gelman@hklaw.com.

GEMIGNANI, JOSEPH ADOLPH, lawyer; b. Hancock, Mich., Apr. 17, 1932; s. Baldo A. and Yolanda M.; m. Barbara A. Thomson, Sept. 5, 1953; children: Joseph, Jon. BSME, Mich. Technological U., 1953; JD, U. Mich., 1958. Bar: Wis. 1959, Mich. 1960, U.S. Dist. Ct. (ea. and we. dists.) Wis., U.S. Ct. Appeals (7th cir.), U.S. Ct. Appeals (fed. cir.). In-house counsel McGraw Edison Co., Milw., 1958-60; ptnr. Michael, Best & Friedrich, Milw., 1960—. 1st lt. USAF, 1953-55. Home: 616 E Day Ave Milwaukee WI 53217-4841 Office: Michael Best & Friedrich 100 E Wisconsin Ave Ste 3300 Milwaukee WI 53202-4108 Office Phone: 414-378-7735. E-mail: equinox96@msn.com.

GENEREUX, L. JOSEPH, lawyer; b. 1952; BA in Polit. Sci., Grinnell Coll., 1974; MSc in Internat. Rels., London Sch. Econ., 1977; JD, U. Mich., 1981. Bar: Minn. 1982. Mem., mgrs. com. Dorsey & Whitney, Mpls., 1981—89, dep. mng. ptnr., chair, comml. banking practice group; chair, fin. svcs., 1989—. Staff Mich. Jour. Law Reform, 1980—81. Mem.: ABA (adv. com. law firm pro bono project 2000—), Legal Corps (pres. 2004—, bd. dirs.), Minn. State Bar Assn. (co-chair, bus. law pro bono task force 2002—03), Minn. Legal Aid Soc. (pres 2003—, bd. dir.). Office: Dorsey & Whitney LLP Ste 1500 50 S Sixth St Minneapolis MN 55402-1498 Office Phone: 612-340-2888. Office Fax: 612-340-2868. Business E-Mail: genereux.joe@dorsey.com.

GENETSKI, ROBERT JAMES, economist; b. NYC, Dec. 26, 1942; s. Alex and Helen Genetski. BS, Ea. Ill. U., 1964; MA, NYU, 1968, PhD, 1972. Tchr. English St. Procopius Acad., Lisle, Ill., 1965-66; research analyst Nat. Econ. Research Assn., NYC, 1967-68; lectr. econs. NYU, NYC, 1969-70; econ. analyst Morgan Guaranty Trust Co., NYC, 1969-71; sr. v.p., economist Harris Trust & Savs. Bank, Chgo., 1971-88; pres. Stotler Econs., Chgo., 1988-90; sr. v.p., chief economist The Chgo. Corp., 1990-91; pres. Robert Genetski & Assocs., 1991—; sr. mng. dir. Chgo. Capital, 1995-2000. Lectr. econs. NYU, 1969-70, U. Chgo., 1973; vis. prof. Wheaton Coll., Ill., 1986; census adv. com. US Dept. Commerce, 1983-86; bd. dirs. DNP Select Income Fund, Midwest Banc Holdings. Author: (with Beryl Sprinkel) Winning with Money, 1977, Taking the Voodoo out of Economics, 1986, 88, A Nation of Millionaires, 1997. Chmn. ednl. com. Sch. Bd. Dist. 25, West Chicago, Ill., 1973-79; bd. dirs. Ctrl. DuPage Health Svcs., 1988-94. Mem. Am. Statis. Assn., Am. Econ. Assn. (fin. com. 1983-), Nat. Assn. Bus. Economists (editor Newsletter 1978), Western Econ. Assn., Am. Bankers Assn. (econ. adv. com. 1980-83), U.S. C. of C. (econ. adv. com. 1985-) Office: 107 Park St Saugatuck MI 49453 Office Phone: 312-565-0112. Business E-Mail: rgenetski@classicalprinciples.com.

GENOWAYS, HUGH HOWARD, systematic biologist, educator; b. Scottsbluff, Nebr., Dec. 24, 1940; s. Theodore Thompson and Sarah Louise (Beales) G.; m. Joyce Elaine Cox, July 28, 1963; children: Margaret Louise, Theodore Howard. AB, Hastings Coll., 1963; postgrad., U. Western Australia, 1964; PhD, U. Kans., 1971. Curator Mus. of Tex. Tech U., Lubbock, 1972-76, lectr. Mus. Sci. Program, 1974-76; curator Carnegie Mus. Natural History, Pitts., 1976-86; dir. U. Nebr. State Mus., Lincoln, 1986-94; chair mus. studies program U. Nebr., 1989—95, 1997—2004, prof. state mus., 1986—2004, prof. mus. studies, 1989—2004, prof. natural resource scis., 1997—2003, prof. phased retirement program, 2003—06, prof. emeritus state mus., 2006—. Author, editor:(with Michael A. Mares) Mammalian Biology in South America, 1982, (with Marion A. Burgwin) Natural History of the Dog, 1984; (with Mary R. Dawson) contbns. in Vertebrate Paleontology, 1984, Species of Special Concern in Pennsylvania, 1985, Current Mammalogy, 1987, 90, (with James H. Brown), Biology of the Heteromyidae, 1993, (with Carolyn Rose and Catherine Hawks) Storage of Natural History Collections: A Preventive Conservation Approach, 1996, (with Robert J. Baker) Mammalogy: A Memorial Volume Honoring Dr. J. Knox Jones, Jr., 1996, (with Ted Genoways) A Perfect Picture of Hell: Eyewitness Accounts by Civil War Prisoners from the 12th Iowa, 2001, (with Lynne M. Ireland) Museum Administration: An Introduction, 2003, (with J.R. Baker J.W. Bickham and C.J. Phillips) Bats of Jamaica, 2005, Museum Philosophy for Twenty-first Century, 2006; founding editor: Collections: A Journal for Museum and Archives Professionals, 2003-06 (Best New Jour. any catagory 2004). Packmaster Allegheny Trails coun. Boy Scouts Am., 1981—83, asst. scoutmaster, 1983—86. Co-recipient Acad. Freedom Coalition ebr. award, 2004; grantee Fulbright Found., 1964, NSF, 1977-86, R.K. Mellon Found., 1981-86, Smithsonian Fgn. Currency Program, 1983-84, Inst. Mus. Svcs., 1989-96, Nebr. Game and Park Commn., 2001-05. Mem. Am. Soc. Mammalogists (pres. 1984-86, C. Hart Merriam award 1987, editor Spl. Pubs. 1995-96, historian 1997—, elected hon. mem. 2002, Hartley H. T. Jackson award 2004), Internat. Theriological Congress (steering com. 1985-2004), Southwestern Assn. aturalists (pres. 1984-85, trustee 2003--), Am. Assn. Mus., Nebr. Mus. Assn. (pres. 1990-92, 1st Hugh H. Genoways Achievement award 1994, sec. 1997-2000), Assn. Systematics Collections (bd. dirs. 1993-94), Nat. Inst. for Conservation Cultural Property (bd. dirs. 1993-94), Sociedad Argentina para Estudio Mamiferos, Lincoln Attractions and Mus. Assn. (chair 1987-94), Soc. Systematic Biologists, Rotary (bd. dirs. Lincoln N.E. club 1990-92). Office: U ebr-Lincoln State Mus W436 Nebraska Hall Lincoln NE 68588-0514 Business E-Mail: hgenoways1@unl.edu.

GENT, ALAN NEVILLE, physicist, researcher; b. Leicester, Eng., Nov. 11, 1927; came to U.S., 1961, naturalized, 1972; s. Harry Neville and Gladys (Hoyle) G.; m. Jean Margaret Wolstenholme, Sept. 1, 1949; children: Martin Paul Neville, Patrick Michael, Andrew John; m. Ginger Lee, Sept. 4, 1997. BS, U. London, 1946, BS in Physics, 1949, PhD in Sci., 1955; DHC, U. Haute-Alsace, France, 1997; DSc (hon.), De Montfort U., Eng., 1998. Lab. asst. John Bull Rubber Co., Leicester, Eng., 1944-45; research physicist Brit. (now Malaysian) Rubber Producers' Research Assn., 1949-61; prof. polymer physics U. Akron, Ohio, 1961-88, Dr. Harold A. Morton prof. polymer physics and polymer engring., 1988-94; prof. emeritus, 1994—; dean grad. studies and research U. Akron, 1978-86. Vis. prof. dept. materials Queen Mary Coll., U. London, 1969-70; vis. prof. dept. chem. engring. McGill U., 1983; Hill vis. prof. U. Minn., 1985; cons. Goodyear Tire & Rubber Co., 1963-2002, Gen. Motors, 1973-87. Contbr. articles to profl. publs. Served with Brit. Army, 1947-49. Recipient Mobay award, Cellular Plastics divsn. Soc. of Plastics Industry, 1963, Colwyn medal Plastics and Rubber Inst. Gt. Brit., 1978, Adhesives award Com. F-11, ASTM, 1979, Internat. Rsch. award Soc. Plastics Engrs., 1980, Whitby award Rubber Chem. divsn. Am. Chem. Soc., 1987, Pub. Svc. medal NASA, 1988, Charles Goodyear medal Rubber Chem. divsn. Am. Chem. Soc., 1990; installed Ohio Sci. Tech. and Industry Hall of Fame, 1993. Mem. NAE, Soc. of Rheology (pres. 1981-83, Bingham medal 1975), Adhesion Soc. (pres. 1978-80, 3M award 1987, Pres.'s award 1997), Am. Phys. Soc. (chmn. divsn. high polymer physics 1977-78, High Polymer Physics prize 1996). Democrat. Office: U Akron Inst Polymer Science Akron OH 44325-3909 Office Phone: 330-972-7505. Business E-Mail: gent@uakron.edu.

GENTILE SACHS, VALERIE ANN, lawyer; b. Cleve., Aug. 4, 1955; d. John Charles and Doreen Phyllis (Neale) Sachs. BLS, Bowling Green U., 1977; JD, Case Western Res. U., 1981. Bar: Ohio 1981. Summer assoc. Arter & Hadden, Cleve., 1980, assoc., 1981—83; sec. Royal Petroleum Properties, Inc., 1982—83; assoc. Baker & Hostetler, M.A. Hanna Co.; v.p., gen. counsel, sec. RELTEC Corp., 1997—2000; v.p., gen. counsel Marconi Comm., Inc., 2000—01, exec. v.p., gen. counsel, 2001—02; gen. counsel, chief legal officer Marconi PLC, London, 2002—03; exec. v.p., gen. counsel, sec. Jo-Ann Stores, Inc., 2003—05; v.p., sec., gen. counsel OM Group Inc., 2005—. Editor: Case Western Res. U. Law Rev., 1980—81, assoc. editor:, 1979—80, Jour. Internat. Law, 1978—79. Mem. Cleve. Citizens League, 1982—84; trustee Forest Hills Housing Corp., Cleve., 1982—84; mem. fgn. trade policy com. Cleve. World Trade Assn., 1982—. Mem. ABA, Alpha Lambda Delta, Cleve. Bar Assn., Ohio State Bar Assn., Beta Beta Beta, Alpha Epsilon Delta. Office: OM Group Inc 127 Public Sq Cleveland OH 44114 Office Phone: 330-656-2600 2156. Office Fax: 330-463-6675.

GENTINE, LEE MICHAEL, marketing professional; b. Plymouth, Wis., Feb. 18, 1952; s. Leonard ALvin and Dolores Ann (Becker) G.; m. Debra Ann Suemnicht, Dec. 29, 1973 (div. Nov. 2003); children: Amanda, Joshua, Jonathan. BBA, U. Notre Dame, 1974; MBA, DePaul U., 1977. Acct. Hurdman & Cranston, Chgo., 1974-75; sales rep. Sargento Cheese Inc., Plymouth, 1975-78, mktg. mgr., 1978-81, sr. v.p. mktg., 1981-84, exec. v.p. mktg., 1984-89, pres. consumer products divsn., 1989-97; mng. ptnr. Dairyland Investors Group LLP, Plymouth, Wis., 1997—; ptnr. Vintage Neighborhood LLC, 2004—. Adv. bd. Kaytee Products Inc., Chilton, Wis., 1994-98; bd. dirs. Sargento Foods Inc. Bd. dirs. Plymouth Softball Assn., 1980—; pres. Plymouth Indsl. Devel. Corp., 1981-85, Parish Coun., 1989-90; chmn. Plymouth Advancement Com., 1992-96, pres., 1992-2002; mem. adv. bd. St. Nicholas Hosp., 1998—; pres. Quit Qui Oc Athletic Alliance, Inc., 1999—; vice chmn. Elkhart Lake Tourism Commn., 1998-2004. Named One of 100 Best and Brightest Advt. Execs., Advt. Age, 1986. Mem. Am. Mktg. Assn., Sheboygan County C. of C. (bd. dirs. 1987-89), Beta Gamma Sigma. Roman Catholic. Avocations: softball, golf, home rehabilitation. Home: PO Box 467 Plymouth WI 53073-0467

GENTNER, DEDRE, psychology professor; PhD in psychology, U. Calif., San Diego, 1974. Sr. scientist Bolt Beranek and Newman; faculty mem. U. Wash., U. Ill., Urbana; prof. psychology, edn. and social policy Northwestern U., Evanston, Ill., 1990—. Fellow: Am. Acad. Arts and Scis. Office: Northwestern U 2113 Swift Hall 2029 Sheridan Rd Evanston IL 60201 E-mail: gentner@northwestern.edu.

GENTNER, JOSHUA D., lawyer; b. South Bend, Ind., Aug. 8, 1972; BA, Indiana U., 1994; JD cum laude, Northwestern U., 1997. Bar: Ill. 1997. Shareholder Vedder, Price, Kaufman & Kammholz, P.C. Mem.: Ill. State Bar Assn., Order of the Coif.

GENTRY, DON KENNETH, academic dean; b. Crawfordsville, Ind., Mar. 1, 1939; m. Carol A. Kern; children: Alynn, Alan, Andrew. BS in Animal Sci. & Agr. Edn., Purdue U., 1962, MS in Secondary Edn. & Ednl. Adminstrn., 1967; EdD in Ednl. Adminstrn., Ind. U., 1979; D (hon.), Vincennes U., 1983. Instr. in vocat. agr. North Montgomery Community Schs., Linden, Ind., 1962-67; state supr. agrl. edn. Ind. State Dept. Pub. Instruction, 1967-69, chief program planning, rsch. & evaluation divsn. vocat. edn., 1969, asst. dir. divsn. vocat. edn., 1969-70, dir. divsn. vocat. edn., 1970-71, exec. officer, state dir. vocat. edn., 1971-83; dir. Purdue Statewide Tech. Program Purdue U., West Lafayette, Ind., 1983-87, prof. indsl. tech., 1984—, asst. dean sch. tech., 1985-86, assoc. dean sch. tech., 1986-87, dean sch. tech., 1987—. Univ. rep. to Nat. Engring. Tech. Coun., 1989—. Contbr. articles to profl. jours.; over 20 papers & presentations in field. Bd. dirs. Ind. Corp. for Sci. & Tech., 1982-83. Recipient Outstanding Svc. award Ind. Distbv. Edn. Clubs Am., 1972, Disting. Hoosier award Gov. Edgar D. Whitcomb, 1972, Hon. Future Homemaker award Future Homemakers Am., 1973, Outstanding Hoosier award Gov. Otis R. Bowen, 1975, Sagamore of Wabash award, 1980, Outstanding Svc. awards Ind. Vocat. Assn., 1973, Nat. Office Edn. Assn., 1975, Nat. Vocat. Edn. Spl. Needs Assn., 1980, Ind. Employment & Tng. Assn., 1982, Outstanding Leadership award Ind. Vocat. Adminstrs. Assn., 1983, Appreciation award U.S. Dept. Def., 1991. Mem. Am. Soc. for Engring. Edn. (engring. tech. divsn.), Am. Vocat. Assn. (life mem.), Engring. Tech. Leadership Inst., Engring. Tech. Coun., Nat. Consortium for Four Year Degree Engring. Tech. Schs., Indiana Health Careers, Inc. (membership chmn. 1980-83), Nat. Assn. State Dirs. Vocat. Edn. (bd. dirs., sec. 1979, pres. 1980, past pres. 1981), Nat. Consortium for Vocat. Ednl. Leadership (devel.-charter pres. 1980, bd. dirs. 1979-82), Office Edn. Assn. (hon. life mem.), John Purdue Club, Ceres, Alpha Zeta, Alpha Tau Alpha, Tau Alpha Phi. Office: Purdue U Sch Tech West Lafayette IN 47907

GEOFFROY, GREGORY L., academic administrator, educator; b. Honolulu, July 8, 1946; s. Glenn Gaylord and Lucille Lavaughn (Lewis) G.; m. Kathleen Carothers, Apr. 17, 1971; children: Susan, Janet, David, Michael. BS in Chemistry, U. Louisville, 1968; PhD in Chemistry, Calif. Inst. Tech., 1974. Asst. prof. dept. chemistry Pa. State U., University Park, 1974-78, assoc. prof. dept. chemistry, 1978-82, prof. dept. chemistry, 1982-88, head dept. chemistry, 1988-89, dean Eberly Coll. Sci., 1989-97; provost, sr. v.p. acad. affairs U. Md., 1997; pres. Iowa State U., 2001—. Bd. dirs. Assn. Advancement Res. Astro., Washington; cons. Union Carbide Corp., South Charleston, W.Va., 1984-95, ARCO Chem., Newtown Square, Pa., 1988-92. Author: Organometallic Photochemistry, 1979; contbr. articles to profl. jours. Recipient Tchr.-Scholar award Camille & Henry Dreyfus Found., 1978, fellowship John Simon Guggenheim Found., 1982. Fellow AAAS; mem. Am. Chem. Soc. (chair inorganic chemistry divsn. 1990). Avocations: mountain biking, skiing. Office: 1750 Beardshear Hall Ames IA 50011 Home Phone: 515-294-7152; Office Phone: 515-294-2042. Business E-Mail: president@iastate.edu.

GEOPPINGER, JEFFREY D., lawyer; b. Sept. 11, 1975; BA, Boston Coll., 1998; JD, U. Cin. Coll. Law, 2001. Bar: Ohio 2001, US Ct. of Appeals Fifth Cir., US Dist. Ct. orthern Dist. Ohio, US Dist. Ct. Southern Dist. Ohio, US Dist. Ct. Southern Dist. Tex. Assoc. Ulmer & Berne LLP, Cin. Named one of Ohio's Rising Stars, Super Lawyers, 2006. Mem.: Am. Inn of Courts, Cin. Bar Assn., Ohio State Bar Assn., ABA, North Avondale Neighborhood Assn., Boston Coll. Alumni Club. Office: Ulmer & Berne LLP 600 Vine St Ste 2800 Cincinnati OH 45202 Office Phone: 513-762-6249. Office Fax: 513-698-5001.

GEORGE, FRANCIS EUGENE CARDINAL, cardinal, archbishop; b. Chgo., Jan. 16, 1937; B in theology, Univ. Ottawa; MA in philosophy, Catholic Univ. Am., 1965; PhD in philosophy, Tulane Univ., 1970; M in theology, Univ. Ottawa, 1971; STD, Pontifical Urban Univ., Rome, 1989. Ordained priest Oblates of Mary Immaculate, 1963, provincial ctrl. region, 1973—74, vicar gen., 1974—86; coord. Circle of Fellows Cambridge Ctr. for Study of Faith & Culture, Mass., 1987—90; ordained bishop, 1990; bishop Diocese of Yakima, Wash., 1990—96; archbishop Archdiocese of Portland, Oreg., 1996—97, Archdiocese of Chgo., 1997—; elevated to cardinal, 1998; cardinal-priest S. Bartolomeo all'Isola, 1998—. V.p. US Conf. Cath. Bishops, 2004—; chancellor Cath. Ch. Ext. U. St. Mary of Lake, 1997; mem. Congregation Divine Worship, Discipline of Sacraments, Congregation for Oriental Chs., 2001—, Congregation Insts., Consecrated Life, Socs. Apostolic Life, Pontifical Commn. for Cultural Heritage of Ch., 1999—, Pontifical Coun. Cor Unum, 1998, Congregation Evangelization of Peoples, Pontifical Coun. for Culture, 2004—, Catholic Commn. on Intellectual & Cultural Affairs. Author (pastoral letter): Becoming an Evangelizing People, 1997, Dwell in My Love, 2001. Mem.: Am. Catholic Philosophical Assn., Am. Soc. Missiologists. Roman Catholic. Office: Archdiocese of Chgo Pastoral Ctr PO Box 1979 Chicago IL 60690-1979 Office Phone: 312-751-8230.

GEORGE, GARY RAYMOND, former state legislator; b. Milw., Mar. 8, 1954; s. Horace Raymond and Audrey C. (Chevalier) G.; children: Alexander, Daniel Raymond. BBA, U. Wis., 1976; JD, Mich. Law. Sch., 1979. With tax dept. Arthur Young & Co., Milw., 1979-81; mem. Wis. Senate from 6th dist., Madison, 1981—2003; pres. pro tempore Wis. Senate, 1999—2003, chair judiciary and consumer affairs com., 1999—2003, co-chair joint com. on audit, 1999—2003. Democrat. Roman Catholic. Home: PO Box 1605 Milwaukee WI 53201-1605

GEORGE, JAMES W., travel company executive; BS in Ops. Mgmt., Pa. State U.; MBA in Acctg., Ohio U. CPA. Managerial level acctg. positions with British Petroleum, Deloitte Haskins and Sells; sr. v.p., CFO, sec. TravelCtrs. of Am. Inc., Westlake, Ohio, 1993, exec. v.p., CFO, 2003—. Office: TravelCtrs Am Inc Ste 200 24601 Center Rigde Rd Westlake OH 44145

GEORGE, JOHN MARTIN, JR., lawyer; b. Normal, Ill., Dec. 17, 1947; s. John and Ada George; m. Judy Ann Watts; children: Sarah, Michael. AB with high honors, U. Ill., 1970, AM, 1971; PhD, Columbia U., 1976; JD cum laude, Harvard U., 1982. Bar: Mass. 1982, U.S. Dist. Ct. Mass. 1983, Ill. 1984, U.S. Dist. Ct. (no. dist.) Ill. 1984, U.S. Ct. Appeals (11th cir.) 1987, U.S. Ct. Appeals (9th cir.) 1988, U.S. Ct. Appeals (7th cir.) 1992, U.S. Ct. Appeals (3d cir.) 2000, U.S. Ct. Appeals (6th cir.) 2005. Assoc. Hill & Barlow, Boston, 1982-84, Sidley & Austin (now Sidley, Austin LLP), Chgo., 1984-89; ptnr. Sidley Austin LLP, 1989—. Editor Harvard U. Law Rev., 1980-82. Sr. warden Trinity Ch., 1998-2000. Named Ill. Super Lawyer, 2006; named to Hall of Fame, Unity H.S., 2005. Fellow Am. Bar Found.; mem. ABA, Chgo. Bar Assn., Leading Lawyers Network, Mid-Day Club, Phi Beta Kappa. Democrat. Episcopalian. Office: Sidley Austin LLP One South Dearborn St Chicago IL 60603 Office Phone: 312-853-7550. E-mail: jgeorge@sidley.com.

GEORGE, JOYCE JACKSON, lawyer, writer, retired judge; b. Akron, Ohio, May 4, 1936; d. Ray and Verna (Popadich) Jackson; children: Michael Eliot, Michelle René. BA, U. Akron, 1962, JD, 1966; postgrad., Nat. Jud. Coll., Reno, 1976, NYU, 1983; LLM, U. Va., 1986. Bar: Ohio 1966, U.S. Dist. Ct. (no. dist.) Ohio 1966, U.S. Ct. Appeals (6th cir.) 1968, U.S. Supreme Ct. 1968. Tchr. Akron Bd. Edn., 1962-66; asst. dir. law City of Akron, 1966-69, pub. utilities advisor, 1969-70, asst. dir. law, 1970-73; pvt. practice Akron, 1973-76; referee Akron Mcpl. Ct., 1975, judge, 1976-83, 9th dist. Ct. Appeals, Akron, 1983-89, Peninsula, Ohio, 1989; U.S. atty. No. Dist., Ohio, 1989-93; v.p. adminstrn. Telxon Corp., Akron, 1993-96; pres. Ind. Bus. Info. Svcs., Inc., Akron, 1996—. Tchr., lectr. Ohio Jud. Coll., Nat. Jud. Coll.; cons. in field. Author: Judicial Opinion Writing Handbook, 1981, 3d edit., 1993, 4th edit., 1998, Referee's Report Writing Handbook, 1992; contbr. articles to profl. publs. Recipient Outstanding Woman of Yr. award Akron Bus. and Profl. Women's Club, 1982; Alumni Honor award U. Akron, 1983, Alumni award U. Akron Sch. Law, 1991; Dept. Treasury award, 1992; named Woman of Yr. in politics and govt. Summit County, Ohio, 1983. Mem.: ABA, Akron Bar Assn., Ohio Bar Assn. Fax: 330-668-2910.

GEORGE, THOMAS FREDERICK, academic administrator; b. Phila., Mar. 18, 1947; s. Emmanuel John and Veronica Mather (Hansel) G.; m. Barbara Carol Harbach, Apr. 25, 1970. BA in Chemistry and Math., Gettysburg Coll., Pa., 1967; MS in Chemistry, Yale U., 1968, PhD, 1970. Rsch. assoc. MIT, 1970; postdoctoral fellow U. Calif., Berkeley, 1971; mem. faculty U. Rochester, NY, 1972-85, prof. chemistry, 1977-85; dean Faculty Natural Sci. and Math., prof. chemistry and physics SUNY-Buffalo, 1985-91; provost, acad. v.p., prof. chemistry and physics Wash. State U., Pullman, 1991-96; chancellor, prof. chemistry and physics U. Wis., Stevens Point, 1996—2003, U. Missouri, St. Louis, 2003—; Disting. vis. lectr. dept. chemistry U. Tex., Austin, 1978; lectr. NATO Advanced Study Inst., Cambridge, England, 1979; Disting. speaker dept. chemistry U. Utah, 1980; Disting. lectr. Air Force Weapons Lab., Kirtland AFB, N.Mex., 1980; mem. com. recommendations U.S. Army Basic Sci. Research, 1978-81; lectr. NATO Summer Sch. on Interfaces under Photon Irradiation, Maratea, Italy, 1986; organizer SF workshop on theoretical aspects of laser radiation and its interaction with atomic and molecular systems Rochester, NY, 1977; vice chmn. 6th Internat. Conf. Molecular Energy Transfer, Rodez, France, 1979; chmn. Gordon Rsch. Conf. Molecular Energy Transfer, Wolfeboro, NH, 1981. Adj. rsch. prof. physics Korea U., Seoul, 1994-99, vis. prof. physics, 1994-03; Dow lectr. polymer sci. U. Detroit Mercy, 1996; program com. Internat. Conf. on Lasers, San Francisco, 1981-83, ACS Symposium on Recent Advances in Surface Sci., Rochester sect., 1982, Internat. Laser Sci. Conf., Dallas, 1985, external rev. com. for chemistry Gettysburg Coll., 1984, awards com. ACS Procter and Gamble student prizes in chemistry, 1982-83, Free-electron Laser peer rev. panel Am. Inst. Biol. Sci. Med., alt., bd. trustees alt.

Calspan-UB Rsch. Ctr., 1989-91; organiser APS Symposium on Laser-Induced Molecular Excitation/Photofragmentation, NY, 1987; co-organizer ACS Symposium on Phys. Chemistry High-Temp. Supercondrs., LA, 1988, MRS Symposium on High-Temperature Superconductors, Alfred, NY, 1988; chmn. SPIE Symposium on Photochemistry in Thin Films, LA, 1989; internat. program adv. com. Internat. Sch. Lasers and Applications, Sayanogorsk, East Siberia, USSR, 1989; lectr. chemistry at cutting edge Smithsonian Instn./Am. Chem. Soc., Washington, 1990; Musselman lectr. Gettysburg Coll., 1999; Disting. lectr. Korean Acad. Sci. and Tech., 2003; internat. adv. com. Xth Vavilov Conf. Nonlinear Optics, ovosibirsk, USSR, 1990; Am. coord. NSF Info. Exchange Seminar for U.S.-Japan Program of Cooperation in Photoconversion and Photosynthesis, Honolulu, 1990; program com. Optical Soc. Am. Topical Meeting on Radiative Processes and Dephasing in Semiconductors, Coeur d'Alene, Idaho, 1998; sci. com. Sixth Brijuni Internat. Conf. on Interdisciplinary Topics in Physics and Chemistry, Brijuni Isles, Croatia, 1998; super-regional steering com. Wis. Econ. Summit, 2000; exec. bd. NY State Inst. on Superconductivity, 1990-91; mem. ONT/ASEE rev. panel for Engring. Edn. postdoctoral fellowship program, 1990; rev panel rsch. experiences for undergrads of sci. and tech. rsch. ctrs., NSF, 1989, rev. panel grad. res. traineeships NSF, 1992; cons., lectr. in field Co-author: (with Blackwell) Notes in Classical and Quantum Physics, 1990, (with Kluwer) Fundamentals in Chemical Physics, 1998; (with Nova) Phase Conjugation in a Layer on Nonlinear Materials, 2005; editor: Photochemistry in Thin Films, 1989; co-editor Internat. Jour. Theoretical Physics, Group Theory, and Nonlinear Optics, 1999—; co-editor: Chemistry of High-Temperature Superconductors, Vol. I, 1987, vol. II, 1988, ACS Symposium Series, (with World Scientific) Computational Studies of New Materials, 1999, (with Wiley) Optics of Nanostructural Materials, 2001, (with Resarch Signpost) Modern Topics in Chemical Physics, 2001, (with Springer) Molecular Buidling Blocks ofr Nanotechnology, 2007; editor-at-large Marcel Dekker, 1989; feature editor Jour. of Optical Soc. of Am.,1987, Spectrochimica Acta, 1987, Optical Engring., 1980; mem. editl. bd. Molecular Physics, 1984-90, Jour. Cluster Sci., 1989-97, Jour. Quantum Nonlinear Phenomena, 1991-96, Nova Jour. Theoretical Physics, 1996-97; mem. adv. bd. Jour. Phys. Chemistry, 1980-84; mem. adv. editl. bd. Chem. Physics Letters, 1979-81, Chem. Materials, 1989; contbr. over 665 articles to profl. jours. and chpts. to books. Tchr., scholar Camille and Henry Dreyfus Found., 1975-85; bd. mgrs. Buffalo Mus. Sci., 1986-92; exec. bd. NY State Inst. on Superconductivity, 1990-91; canvassing com. ACS; external rev. com. for chemistry Gettysburg Coll., 1984; mem. NEASC site visit team Boston U., ten-yr. accreditation, 1989; bd. dirs. Wash. State Inst. for Pub. Policy, 1991-96, Wash. Tech. Ctr., 1992-96; trustee Wash. State U. Found., 1991-96; exec. com. Northwest Acad. Forum, 1992-96, chmn. 1994-95; rev. panel Grad. Rsch. Traineeships, NSF, 1992, rev. panel for sci. and tech. ctr. proposals, 1998, rev. panel for preproposals for sci. and tech. ctrs., 1998; mem. Project 435 Dist. Leadership Coun., Wis. Assn. Biomed. Rsch. and Edn./Rsch. Am., 1997; Comm. on the Future of Gettysburg Coll., 1997-98; bd. dirs. Portage County Bus. Coun., 1998-03, Stevens Point Area YMCA, 1998-03, v.p., 2002-03, United Way Portage County, Wis., 1997-2003, chmn. 1999 campaign, pres., 2002-04, Tech. Alliance State Wash., 1996, U. Wis., Stevens Point Found., 1996-03, Paper Sci. Found., 1996-03, St. Michael's Hosp., Stevens Point, 1999-03, Distributed Learning Workshop, Midwestern Higher Edn. Commn., 1999-03, Wis. Ctr. Acad. Talented Youth, 2001-03; Marathon County Ptnrs. in Edn., 2002, Civic Progress, 2003-, Ctr. for Emerging Tech., 2003-, Ctr. Rsch., Tech. and Entrepreneurial Expertise, 2003-, St. Louis Merc. Libr., 2003-, John W. Barringer III Nat. RR Libr., 2004, Christian Hosp., 2004-, United Way of Greater St. Louis, 2004-, Mo. Coun. Pub. Higher Edn., 2004-, bd. trustees, bd. dirs. Assoc. Western Univs., Atlanta, 1993-96; bd. dirs. alt. Joint Ctr. Higher Edn., Spokane, 1996; steering com. Ctr. for Advanced Tech. in Healthcare Instruments and Devices, 1988-90, Midwestern Higher Edn. Commn., 1999-03, 05-, chair policy rsch. adv. com.; exploring chair Mushkodany dist. Wis. Samoset coun. Boy Scouts Am., 1998, fin. chair, 1999, pres., 2002-03; bd. dirs. trustee WiSys Tech. Found., 2000-, Mo. Bot. Garden, 2003-; exec. bd. Greater St. Louis Area coun. Boy Scouts Am., 2004-, chmn. learning for life, 2006—; bd. commrs. Acad. Advanced Distributed Learning Lab. (UW-US Dept. Def.), 2001; adv. coun. Ednl. Directories Unltd., 2001-06; adv. bd. New Economy Workforce Coalition, Wausau, 2001, Mo. Coun. Pub. Higher Edn., 2003—; steering com. St. Louis Regional Competitiveness Coun. Initiative, 2004—; trustee St. Louis Sci. Ctr., 2005-; Met. bd. dirs. YMCA Greater St. Louis, 2005-; bd. dirs. coalition info. and comm. tech. St. Louis, 2006—; adv. bd. Halyard Edn. Partners, 2007-; Regional Chamber and Growth Assn., 2003-; chair. Plant and Life Sci. Network, 2007. Sloan fellow, 1976-80, postdoctoral fellow, 1990, Guggenheim fellow, 1983-84; recipient Disting. Alumni award Gettysburg Coll., 1987, Disting. Alumnus award Friends Ctr. Sch., 2003; Outstanding Cmty. Svc. award, NAACP St. Louis Branch, 2006. Fellow AAAS (chair St. Louis local com. 2006), Soc. Photo-Optical Instrumentation Engrs., Am. Phys. Soc., NY Acad. Scis., Inst. Superconductivity (steering com. 1987-91); mem. Am. Chem. Soc. (exec. com. phys. div. 1979-82, 85-89, 94-97, vice chmn. 1985-86, chmn.-elect 1986-87, chmn. 1987-88), Outstanding Contbns. to Chemistry award 2002, Am. Chem. Soc., Am. Assn. State Colls. and Univs. (acad. affairs subcom. on sci. edn. rsch. and tng., coun. state reps., mem. task force math. and sci. enrollments 2005), Wis. Assn. for Biomed. Rsch. and Edn., European Phys. Soc., Royal Soc. Chemistry (Marlow medal and prize 1979), Materials Rsch. Soc., Korean Acad. Sci. and Tech. (fgn.), Phi Beta Kappa, Sigma Xi (exec. com. U. Rochester 1984-85). Office: U Mo-St Louis Office of the Chancellor One Univ Blvd Saint Louis MO 63121 Office Phone: 314-516-5252. Business E-Mail: tfgeorge@umsl.edu.

GEORGE, WILLIAM WALLACE, former manufacturing executive; b. Muskegon, Mich., Sept. 14, 1942; s. Wallace Edwin and Kathryn Jean (Dinkeloo) G.; m. Ann Tonnlier Pilgram, Sept. 6, 1969; children: Jeffrey, Jonathan. BS in Indsl. Engring. with honors, Ga. Inst. Tech., 1964; MBA with high distinction, Harvard U., 1966. Asst. to asst. sec. Dept. Def., Washington, 1966-68; spl. civilian asst. to sec. Navy, Washington, 1968-69; with Litton Industries, 1969-78, dir. long-range planning Cleve., 1969-70, v.p., 1976, Litton Microwave Cooking Products, Mpls., 1970-71, exec. v.p., 1971-73, pres., 1973-78; v.p. corp. devel. Honeywell, Mpls., 1978-80, exec. v.p., 1983-87; pres. Honeywell Europe (S.A.), 1980-82, Indsl. Automation, 1987, Space and Aviation Systems, Mpls., 1988-89; pres., chief oper. officer Medtronic Inc., Mpls., 1989-91, CEO, 1991—2002, chmn., 1996—2002. Bd. dirs. Dayton-Hudson, Imation., Goldman Sachs Group, Inc., Target Corp. and Novartis AG; sr. lecturer, Harvard Bus. Sch., prof. leadership and governance, Internat. Inst. Mgmt. Devel., 2002-2003, visiting prof. tech. mgmt., Ecole Polytechnique Federale de Lausanne, 2002-2003, exec.-in-residence, Yale Sch. Mgmt., 2003 Bd. dirs. Am. Red Cross, Minn. Symphony Orch., 1976-80, United Way, Minn. 1976-79, 96—, nat. chmn., Belgium, 1982-83, campaign chair, 1997; bd. dirs., pres., treas. Guthrie Theater, 1977-84; vice-chmn. United Theol. Sem., 1977-80, Abbott-Northwestern Hosp., 1984—, vice-chair, 1989-91, chair, 1991-93, Health Span, 1989-94; trustee Macalaster Coll., 1987-93, Allin Health Sys., 1994—, vice-chair, 1997—, Mlps. Inst. Arts, 1993—, chmn. Minn. Thunder Pro Soccer, 1994—. Recipient Meritorious Civilian Service Award Sec. Navy, 1969 Mem. Sigma Chi (Internat. Balfour award 1964, trustee 1971-77, Disting. Alumni award Harvard U., 1997). Clubs: Minneapolis, Minikahda. Episcopalian. Home: 2284 W Lake Of The Isles Pky Minneapolis MN 55405-2434 Office: George Family Found 1818 Oliver Ave S Minneapolis MN 55405

GEORGES, MARA STACY, lawyer; b. Chgo., Sept. 2, 1963; married; 2 children. BA, U. Notre Dame, 1985; JD, Loyola U., 1988. Bar: Ill. Supreme Ct. 1988, US Dist. Ct. (no. dist. Ill.) 1989, US Ct. Appeals (7th cir.) 1990, Fed. Trial Bar 1990. Ptnr. Rock, Fusco, Reynolds, Crowe & Garvey, 1995-97; 1st asst. corporation counsel City of Chgo., 1997-99, corporation counsel, 1999—. Bd. mem. Chgo.-Gary Regional Airport Authority, 1999—, Child's Play Touring Theatre, 2000—; chair property tax fairness bd. City of Chgo., 2004—. Named one of Ten Most Influential Women Lawyers in Ill., Am. Lawyer Media, 2000, Forty Ill. Attys. Under 40 to Watch, Chgo. Daily Law Bulletin, 2002, 100 Most Powerful Women in Chgo., Chgo. Sun-Times, 2004; named to Forty Under 40, Crain's Chgo. Bus., 2001, Super Lawyers, Chgo. Mag., 2005, 2007; recipient St. Robert Bellarmine award, Loyola U. Chgo. Sch Law, 2001, Jefferson B. Fordham award, ABA, 2003, Litigation award, IILGL, 2003. Democrat. Greek Orthodox. Avocations: exercise, bicycling, gardening, music, running. Office: City Hall Law Dept 121 N Lasalle St Rm 600 Chicago IL 60602-1208 Office Phone: 312-744-0220. Business E-Mail: mgeorges@cityofchicago.org.

GEORGOPOULOS, APOSTOLOS P., neuroscientist, neurologist, educator; b. Patras, Greece; MD, U. Athens, D of Physiology. Joined faculty Johns Hopkins U., 1976, prof., 1986; Am. Legion Brain Scis. chair, dir. Minneapolis Veteran Affairs Med. Ctr. U. Minn., 1991—; prof. neuroscience, neurology and psychiatry U. Minn. Med. Sch. Grantee McKnight Presdl. Endowed Chair, U. Minn., 2004. Mem.: Inst. Medicine, Nat. Acad. Scis. Office: U Minn Dept Neuroscience 6-145 JacH 1216 321 Church St S Minneapolis MN 55455 also: V A Med Ctr Brain Sci Ctr 11B 1 Veterans Dr Minneapolis MN 55417 Office Phone: 612-725-2282. E-mail: omega@umn.edu.

GERAGHTY, DIANE C., law educator; BA, U. California; MA, U. Chgo., 1967; JD, Northwestern U. Faculty mem. Loyola U. Chgo., 1977—, prof. law, dir. Civitas ChildLaw Ctr., acting dean, 2004—05. Author: Juvenile Law Bencbook, Vols. I and II, 2001; co-author: Training the Lawyer to Represent the Whole Child: In re Pena, 2003; mem. editl. bd. Ill. Child Welfare; contbr. articles to law jours. Named Juvenile Justice Pioneer, 2000; recipient Livingston Hall Juvenile Justice Award, ABA, 2001, Leonard Jay Schrager Award, Chgo. Bar Found., 2003. Mem.: Ill. State Ct. Improvement Project (co-chair), Ill. Juvenile Justice Initiative (hon. bd. mem.), Citizens Com. on Juvenile Ct. (chair), Chgo. Children's Advocacy Ctr. (bd. mem., co-chair Strategic Planning Com.), Am. Civil Liberties Union (mem. Nat. Bd. Dirs.). Office: Loyola U Chgo Sch Law 1 E Pearson St Rm 506 Chicago IL 60611 E-mail: dgeragh@luc.edu.

GERARD, JULES BERNARD, law educator; b. St. Louis, May 20, 1929; s. John Baptist and Faith Vera (Clinton) G.; m. Camilla Roma Smith, Aug. 8, 1953; children: Lisa, Karen, Julia. Student, Iowa State Coll., 1947-49; AB, Washington U., St. Louis, 1957, JD, 1958. Bar: NY 1959, US Supreme Ct. 1979. Assoc. Donovan, Leisure, Newton & Irvine, NYC, 1958-60; asst. prof. law U. Mo., Columbia, 1960-62; asst. prof., assoc. prof. law Washington U., 1962-67, prof., 1967-99, prof. emeritus, 1999—. Author: Local Regulation of Adult Businesses, 1992, Proposed Washington DC Amendment, 1979, (with others) Sum and Substance Constitutional Law, 1976, (with others) Federal Land Use Law, 1986; editor: 100 Years of 14th Amendment, 1973; editor-in-chief Washington U. Law Quar., 1958; contbr. articles to profl. jours., chpts. to books. Mem. Mo. Adv. com. US Commn. on Civil Rights, 1987-92. Served to 1st lt. USAF, 1950-54 Mem. ABA. Republican. Avocations: collecting scrimshaw and antique photographica, photography. Home: 1564 Yarmouth Point Dr Chesterfield MO 63017-5639 Business E-Mail: gerard@law.wustl.edu.

GERBER, DAVID JOSEPH, lawyer, educator; b. St. Louis, Aug. 14, 1945; s. Joseph Harding and Elvera Louise (Duesenberg) G.; m. Ulla-britt Junemark, Aug. 16, 1981; children: Eric David, Marcus David. BA, Trinity Coll., 1967; MA, Yale U., 1969; JD, U. Chgo., 1972. Bar: N.Y. 1973. Assoc. Casey, Lane & Mittendorf, NYC, 1972-75; asst. to dirs. Inst. Fgn. Law, U. Freiburg, Germany, 1975-76; legal adv. Peltzer and Riesenkampff, Frankfurt, Germany, 1977-78; prof. law Chgo.-Kent Coll. Law, Ill. Inst. Tech., 1982—. Vis. prof. U. Stockholm, Sweden, 1979, U. Freiburg, 1991, 2002, Northwestern U., 1999, Washington U., 2000, U. Uppsala, Sweden, 2001, U. Pa., 2001. Author: Law and Competition in Twentieth Century Europe, 1998, 2d edit., 2002; mem. editl. bd.: Am. Jour. Comparative Law, Jour. Internat. Econ. Law, Jour. Competition Law. Mem. ABA, Internat. Acad. Comparative Law. Office: Ill Inst Tech Kent Coll Law 565 W Adams St Chicago IL 60661-3613 E-mail: dgerber@kentlaw.edu.

GERBER, DEAN N., lawyer; b. Chgo., Dec. 4, 1959; married. BS magna cum laude, U. of Delaware, 1982; JD cum laude, U. of Ill., 1985. CPA Ill., 1984; bar: Ill. 1985. Joined Chapman & Cutler; assoc. atty. Vedder, Price, Kaufman & Kammholz, 1991, shareholder, 1992—, chair equipment fin. practice group. Mem.: Omicron Sigma Delta, Phi Kappa Phi. Office: Vedder Price Kaufman & Kammholz 222 N LaSalle St Chicago IL 60601

GERBER, EUGENE JOHN, bishop emeritus; b. Kingman, Kans., Apr. 30, 1931; s. Cornelius John and Lena Marie (Tiesmeyer) Gerber. AB, St. Thomas Sem., 1955, MA, 1958, STB, 1959; STL, St. Thomas Sem., Rome, 1976; BA, Wichita State U., 1963. Ordained priest Diocese of Wichita, Kans., 1959, asst. chancellor, 1963, sec. to bishop, 1964, vice chancellor, 1967, mem. diocesan bd. adminstrn., 1973, diocesan cons., 1973, chancellor, 1975; chaplain, mem. governing bd. Holy Family Center for Mentally Retarded; bd. dirs. Cursillo; ordained bishop, 1976; bishop Diocese of Dodge City, Kans., 1976—82, Diocese of Wichita, 1982—2001, bishop emeritus, 2001—. Roman Catholic. Office: Diocese of Wichita Chancery Office 424 N Broadway St Wichita KS 67202-2310 Office Phone: 316-269-3900. Office Fax: 316-269-3936.*

GERBER, LAWRENCE, lawyer; b. Chgo., Oct. 2, 1940; BBA, Loyola U. Chgo., 1962; JD, Northwestern U., 1965. CPA Ill.; bar: Ill. 1965. Ptnr. McDermott, Will & Emery, Chgo., mng. ptnr., 1991—. Author: Hospital Restructuring: Why, When and How, 1983. Mem.: Ill. Assn. Hosp. Attys., Am. Acad. Hosp. Attys. Office: McDermott Will & Emery 227 W Monroe St Ste 4400 Chicago IL 60606-5096

GERBER, PHILLIP, advertising executive; b. 1963; Formerly with Edward H. Weiss & Co., Chgo.; mng. ptnr., media ops. dir. Duro RSCG Tatham, Chgo., 1983—. Office: Euro RSCG Tatham 980 N Michigan Ave Chicago IL 60611-4501

GERBER, WILLIAM KENTON, financial executive; b. St. Louis, Feb. 20, 1954; s. Benjamin T. and Virginia B. (Kenton) G.; m. Pamela L. Macomber, Dec. 8, 1984. BS in Econs., U. Pa., 1975; MBA, Harvard U., 1979. CPA, Ill. Sr. mgmt. cons. Arthur Andersen & Co., Chgo., Boston, 1975-78; fin. mgr. Gould Inc., Jackson, Tenn. and St. Louis, 1979-81; controller Solar Turbines div. Caterpillar Tractor Co., San Diego, 1981-83; dir. fin. The Limited, Inc., Columbus, Ohio, 1983-86, v.p. fin., 1987—. Bd. dirs. World Fin. Network Nat. Bank, Brylane L.P., Rocky Apparel L.P., Penhaligon's Ltd., U.K., IBS Italia s.r.l., Italy. Mem. AICPA, Fin. Execs. Inst., Nat. Assn. Corp. Dirs. Republican. Home: 1380 Dorstone Pl Bloomfield Hills MI 48301-2316 Office: Kelly Services Inc 999 W Big Beaver Rd Troy MI 48084-4782

GERBERICH, WILLIAM WARREN, engineering educator; b. Wooster, Ohio, Dec. 30, 1935; s. Harold Robert and Clarissa Thelma (Ross) G.; m. Susan Elizabeth Goodwin, Aug. 15, 1959; children— Bradley Kent, Brian Keith, Beth Clarice. BS in Engring. Adminstrn, Case Inst. Tech., 1957; MS in Indsl. Engring, Syracuse U., 1959; PhD in Materials Sci. and Engring, U. Calif., Berkeley, 1971. Registered profl. engr. Calif. Research engr. Jet Propulsion Lab., Calif. Inst. Tech., Pasadena, Calif., 1959-61; research scientist Aeronutronic, Newport Beach, Calif., 1961-64; engring. research specialist Aerojet Gen., Sacramento, 1964-67; lectr. U. Calif., Berkeley, 1967-71; dir. materials sci. U. Minn., Mpls., 1972—, assoc. prof., dept. chem. engring. and materials sci., 1971-75, prof., 1975—, assoc. head dept., 1980-2000. Cons. material rev. bd. Argonne Nat. Labs., steel, med. products and aerospace cos.; chmn. bd. Inst. Mechanics and Materials U. Calif., San Diego, 1994—. Chmn. bd. Acta Metallurgica publs., 1986-89; co-editor 7 books; contbr. articles to tech. jours. Recipient Teleen English prize Case Inst. Tech., 1959, William Spraragen award Welding Jour., 1968, Outstanding Paper award Acta Met. Jour., 1994. Fellow Am. Soc. Metals; mem. AIME, Materials Rsch. Soc., Sigma Xi, Tau Beta Pi, Pi Delta Epsilon, Phi Delta Theta. Home: 21035 Radisson Inn Rd Christmas Lk Excelsior MN 55331 Office: U Minn Chem Engring Materials Minneapolis MN 55455

GERBERRY, RONALD VINCENT, state legislator; b. Youngstown, Ohio, Jan. 10, 1953; s. Edward S. and Erma (Timko) G.; m. Kathryn M. Schrum, 1976; children: Deanna Lynn, Ronald Vincent Jr., Daniel Schrum. AB, Youngstown State U., 1975. Tchr. social studies Beaver Local Sch. Dist., Columbiana County, Ohio, 1978-79, Trumbull County (Ohio) Joint Vocat. Sch., 1978-81, Hubbard Exempted Village Schs., Trumbull County, 1981-82; mem. Ohio Ho. of Reps., Columbus, 1982-. Mem. Austintown (Ohio) Bd. Edn., 1974-82, v.p., 1977, pres., 1978, 81. Named hon. county supt. Ohio County Sypts. Assn., Legislator of Yr. Ohio Assn. Elem. Sch. Adminstrs., Educator of Yr., Mahoning County Elem. Sch. Adminstrs., Legislator of Yr. Ohio Acad. Trial Lawyers, 1996. Democrat. Home: 2940 Whispering Pines Dr Canfield OH 44406-9628

GERDES, DAVID ALAN, lawyer; b. Aberdeen, SD, Aug. 10, 1942; s. Cyril Fredrick and Lorraine Mary (Boyle) G.; m. Karen Ann Hassinger, Aug. 3, 1968; children: Amy Renee, James David. BS, No. State Coll., Aberdeen, 1965; JD cum laude, U. S.D., 1968. Bar: S.D. 1968, U.S. Dist. Ct. S.D., 1968, U.S. Ct. Appeals (8th cir.) 1973, U.S. Supreme Ct. 1973. Assoc. Martens, Goldsmith, May, Porter & Adam, Pierre, SD, 1968-73; ptnr. successor firm May, Adam, Gerdes & Thompson, Pierre, 1973—. Chmn. disciplinary bd. S.D. Bar, 1980-81, mem. fed. practice com. U.S. Dist. Ct., S.D., 1986-91, 1994-2000; mem. fed. adv. com. U.S. Ct. Appeals (8th cir.), 1989-93; bd. dirs. U.S.D. Law Sch. Found., 1973-84, pres., 1979-84. Mng. editor U. S.D. Law Rev., 1967—68; author: Physician's Guide to South Dakota Law, 1982. Chmn. Hughes County Rep. Ctrl. Com., 1979-81; del. Rep. State Conv., co-chair platform com., 1988, 90; state ctrl. committeeman, 1985-91. Served to lt. Signal Corps, AUS, 1965-68. Mem. ABA, Nat. Coun. Bar Pres., Internat. Assn. Def. Counsel, Am. Judicature Soc., Am. Bd. Trial Advocates, State Bar S.D. (chmn. professionalism com. 1989-90, pres. 1992-93), Pierre Area C. of C. (pres. 1980-81), S.D. C. of C. (bd. dirs. 1998-2004), Lawyer-Pilots Bar Assn., Def. Rsch. Inst., Am. Soc. Med. Assn. Counsel, Kiwanis, Elks. Republican. Methodist. Office: May Adam Gerdes & Thompson PO Box 160 503 S Pierre St Pierre SD 57501-0160 Office Phone: 605-224-8803.

GERDES, NEIL WAYNE, library director, educator; b. Moline, Ill., Oct. 19, 1943; s. John Edward and Della Marie (Ferguson) G. AB, U. Ill., 1965; BD, Harvard U., Cambridge, Mass., 1968; MA, Columbia U., NYC, 1971; MA in Libr. Sci., U. Chgo., 1975; DMin, U. St. Mary of the Lake, 1994. Ordained to ministry Unitarian Universalist Assn., 1975. Copy chief Little, Brown, 1968-69; instr. Tuskegee Inst., 1969-71; libr. asst. Augustana Coll., 1972-73; editl. asst. Library Quar., 1973-74; libr., prof. Meadville Theol. Sch., Chgo., 1973—; libr. program dir. Chgo. Cluster Theol. Schs., 1977-80; dir. Hammond Libr., 1980—; prof. Chgo. Theol Sem., 1980—. Affiliated minister 1st Unitarian Church, Chgo., 2002—. Mem. exec. bd. Sem. Coop. Bookstore, Chgo., 1982-2002, Ctr. for Religion and Psychotherapy, Chgo., 1984-97, Ind. Voters of Ill., 1986-89, Hyde Park-Kenwood Cmty. Orgn., Chgo., 1988-89; pres. Hyde Park-Kenwood Interfaith Coun., 1986-90, Inst. for Spiritual Leadership, 2000-07; chmn. libr. coun. Assn. Chgo. Theol. Sch., 1984-88, 96-98, pres.-elect, 2007—; chmn. adv. bd. LGBT Religious Archive Network, 2002—; trustee Civitas Dei Found., 1994—2006; mem. alumni coun. Harvard Div. Sch., 1999-2005, sec., 2001-05. Mem. ALA, Am. Theol. Library Assn., Chgo. Area Theol. Library Assn., Unitarian Universalist Mins. Assn. (sec., treas. nat. body 1990-94), Assn. Liberal Religious Scholars (sec., treas. 1975—), Phi Beta Kappa Office: Chgo Theol Sem Hammond Libr 5757 S University Ave Chicago IL 60637-1507 Office Phone: 773-752-5757. Business E-Mail: ngerdes@ctschicago.edu.

GERDES, RALPH DONALD, fire safety consultant; b. Cin., Aug. 11, 1951; s. Paul Donald and Jo Ann Dorothy (Meyer) G. BArch, Ill. Inst. Tech., 1975. Registered architect, Ill. Architect Schiller & Frank, Wheeling, Ill., 1976; sr. assoc. Rolf Jensen & Assocs., Inc., Chgo., 1976-84; pres. Ralph Gerdes & Assocs., Inc., Indpls., 1984-88, chmn., 1988—; gen. mgr. Ralph Gerdes Cons., LLC. Lectr. Purdue U., Ind. U., Ill. Inst. Tech., Butler U., Ball State U.; bd. dirs. Ind. Fire Svcs. Inst. Co-author: Planning and Designing the Office Environment, 1981. Recipient Joel Polsky prize Am. Soc. Interior Designers, 1983. Mem.: AIA (bldg. performance and regulations com., liaison to Nat. Fire Protection Agy.), ASHRAE, Archs. and Engrs. Bldg. Ofcls. (bd. dirs. 1994—, Ind. code devel. com.), Ind. Fire Safety Assn. (bd. dirs. 1986—92, pres. 1989—91, bd. dirs. 1994—95), Internat. Code Coun., Nat. Fire Protection Assn. (tech. coms., stds. council), Soc. Fire Protection Engring. (assoc.; exec. com. Ind. chpt. 1992—, pres. 1995—96), Indpls. Soc., Maple Creek Country Club. Roman Catholic. Home: 556 Lockerbie Cir N Indianapolis IN 46202-3600 Office: 5510 S East St Ste E Indianapolis IN 46227

GERDIN, RUSSELL A., transportation executive; Chmn., pres., founder Heartland Express, Coralville, Iowa, 1978—. Office: Heartland Express 2777 Heartland Dr Coralville IA 52241-2731

GERHARD, LEE CLARENCE, geologist, educator; b. Albion, NY, May 30, 1937; s. Carl Clarence and Helen Mary (Lahmer) G.; m. Darcy LaFollette, July 22, 1964; 1 dau., Tracy Leigh. BS, Syracuse U., 1958; MS, U. Kans., 1961, PhD, 1964. Exploration geologist, region stratigrapher Sinclair Oil & Gas Co., Midland, Tex. and Roswell, N.Mex., 1964-66; asst. prof. geology U. So. Colo., Pueblo, 1966-69, assoc. prof., 1969-72; assoc. prof., asst. dir. West Indies Lab. Fairleigh Dickinson U., Rutherford, NJ, 1972-75; asst. geologist State of N.D., Grand Forks, 1975-77, geologist, 1977-81; prof., chmn. dept. geology U. N.D., Grand Forks, 1977-81; mgr. Rocky Mountain div. Supron Energy Corp., Denver, 1981-82; owner, pres. Gerhard & Assocs., Englewood, Colo., 1982-87; prof. petroleum geology Colo. Sch. Mines, Denver, 1982—2004, Getty prof., 1984-87; state geologist, dir. geol. survey State of Kans., Lawrence, 1987-99, prin. geologist, 1999—2005; prin. Gerhard & Assocs., 2005—; founder, co-dir. Energy Rsch. Ctr., U. Kans., 1990-94. Presdl. appointee Nat. Adv. Com. on Oceans and Atmosphere, 1984-87. Contbr. articles to profl. jours. Served to 1st lt. U.S. Army, 1958-60. Danforth fellow, 1970-72; named to Kans. Oil and Gas Hall of Fame, 2002. Fellow Geol. Soc. Am.; mem. Am. Assn. Petroleum Geologists (hon., Disting. Svc. award 1989, Journalism award 1996, pres. divsn. environ. geosci. 1994-95, hon. divsn. environ. geosci. 1998, v.p. divsn. profl. affairs 2003-04, Lifetime Membership award, 2008; Pub. Outreach award 1999, 2003, 07), Am. Inst. Profl. Geologists, Russian Acad. Natural Scis. (US Br.), Rocky Mountain Assn. Geologists, Colo. Sci. Soc., Kans. Geol. Soc. (hon.), Sigma Xi, Sigma Gamma Epsilon. Home: 1628 Alvamar Dr Lawrence KS 66047-1714 Personal E-mail: leeg@sunflower.com.

GERHARDT, KENNETH W., retired agricultural products executive; Diploma, Acad. of Music, Vienna, Austria; BS, Emporia State U.; MS, Ind. U. Former chief info. officer, v.p. PepsiCo Food Svcs.; former chief info. officer, sr. v.p. AmeriServe Distbrn., Inc., Dallas; sr. v.p., chief info. officer ConAgra, Inc., Omaha, 1998—2004. Office: ConAgra Inc 1 ConAgra Dr Omaha NE 68102

GERHART, PETER MILTON, law educator; b. Milw., July 4, 1945; s. Howard Leon and Ann (Baker) G.; m. Virginia Ann Herold, Feb. 9, 1969 (div. Oct. 1980); 1 child, Matthew; m. Ann Tarbutton, Apr. 9, 1983; children: Mary Elizabeth, Margaret Ann, Grace Kendall. BA, Northwestern U., 1967; JD, Columbia U., 1971. Bar: .Y. 1971, U.S. Dist. Ct. (so. dist.) N.Y. 1973. Assoc. Weil, Gotshal & Manges, NYC, 1971-75; prof. law Ohio State U., Columbus, 1975—, assoc. dean, 1983-86; dean Case Western Res. U., Cleve., 1986-96, prof., 1996—. Cons. Pres.'s Commn. Antitrust, Washington, 1978-79, Adminstrv. Conf., Washington, 1976-77. Contbr. articles to profl. jours. Mem. ABA (cons. com. to study FTC 1969). Democrat. Presbyterian. Avocations: piano, jogging. Home: 14400 Shaker Blvd Cleveland OH 44120-1611 Office: Case Western Res U Sch Law 11075 East Blvd Cleveland OH 44106-5409

GERHART, PHILIP MARK, engineering educator; b. Kokomo, Ind., Aug. 5, 1946; BS in Mech. Engring., Rose-Hulman Inst. Tech., 1968; MS, U. Ill., 1969, PhD, 1971. Registered profl. engr. Ohio, Ind. Asst. prof. mech. engring. U. Akron (Ohio), 1971-76, assoc. prof., 1976-82, prof., 1982-84; dept. chair U. Evansville, Ind., 1984-95, dean coll. engring. and computer sci., 1995—. Summer faculty fellow NASA Lewis Rsch. Ctr., Cleve., 1972, 73, aerospace engr., summer 1974; engr. NED performance tech. Babcock & Wilcox Co., Barberton, Ohio, summers 1978, 79; co-devel., instr. tng. program for performance engrs. Ohio Edison Co., Akron, summer 1981-84; cons. Goodyear Aerospace Co., Buffalo Forge Co., Elec. Power Rsch. Inst., Bristol-Meyers USPNG, George Koch Sons Inc., Mohler Techs. Inc.; presenter papers in field. Author: (with R.J. Gross) Fundamentals of Fluid Mechanics, 1985, (with R.J. Gross and J.I. Hochstein) 2d edit., 1992; contbr. articles to profl. jours. Asst. scoutmaster, scoutmaster, troop com. chmn., scouting coord., unit commr., Boy Scouts Am., 1968—; deacon, Bible sch. supt., chmn. bldg. com., elder Northwest Ave. Ch. of Christ, Tallmadge, Ohio, 1973-84; chmn. corp., elder Cullen Ave. Christian Ch., Evansville, 1985-92. Recipient Outstanding Tchr. award Bd. Higher Edn. United Meth. Ch., 1994, 25 Yr. Vet. Cert. from Boy Scouts Am. Mem. ASME (Dedicated Svc. award 1986, Performance Test Codes Gold medal 1993, Student Sect. Outstanding Tchr. 1983, 84, performance test code 11 on fans 1975—, vice chair 1989—, performance test code 4.1 steam generators 1981—, bd. performance test codes 1990—, instr. profl. devel. course 1991—), Am. Soc. Engring. Edn., Lambda Chi Alpha, Tau Beta Pi, Pi Tau Sigma (founding advisor U Evansville chpt.), Sigma Xi, Phi Kappa Pi, Phi Beta Chi. Office: Coll Engring & Computer Sci Univ of Evansville 1800 Lincoln Ave Evansville IN 47722-0001

GERINGER, GERALD GENE, state legislator; m. Dorothy M. Geringer. State rep. Dist. 65 Kans. Ho. of Reps., 1996—. Mem. econ. devel. com., tourism com., SRS transition oversight com., vice chairperson health and human svcs. Kans. Ho. of Reps.; health care cons., 1996—. Office: 720 Rockledge Dr Junction City KS 66441-3974 E-mail: geringer@house.state.ks.us.

GERKE, THOMAS A., telecommunications industry executive, lawyer; b. 1956; BBA, U. Mo., Columbia; MBA, Rockhurst Coll.; JD, U. Mo., Kansas

City. Ptnr. Smith, Gill, Fisher & Butts, Kansas City; sr. atty. Sprint Corp., 1994—97, asst. v.p. law, mergers & acquisitions, 1997—99, v.p. legal gen. bus. & tech., 1999—2000, corp. sec., assoc. gen. counsel Overland Park, Kans., 2000—02, v.p. bus. devel., strategic planning & alliances Global Markets Group, 2002—03, exec. v.p., gen. counsel & external affairs, 2003—05; gen. counsel, law & external affairs, Local Telecom. Divsn. Sprint Nextel Corp., Overland Park, Kans., 2005—06; gen. counsel, law & external affairs Embarq Corp., Overland Park, Kans., 2006—, interim CEO, 2007—. Bd. trustees Rockhurst U. Office: Embarq Corp 5454 W 110 St Overland Park KS 66211

GERLITS, FRANCIS JOSEPH, lawyer; b. Chgo., Mar. 29, 1931; s. John T. and May (Cameron) G.; m. Suzanne Long, June 20, 1953; children: Kathleen, Karen, Mary Cameron, Francis Jr. Ph.B., U. Notre Dame, 1953; JD, U. Chgo., 1958. Bar: Ill. 1958. Ptnr. Kirkland & Ellis, Chgo., 1964-95, of counsel, 1995; gen. counsel Internat. Harvester Co. (now Navistar Internat. Corp.), Chgo., 1985-90. Mem. ABA, Order of Coif, Tavern Club, Chicago Club Office: Kirkland & Ellis 200 E Randolph St Fl 54 Chicago IL 60601-6636 Office Phone: 312-861-2070.

GERLITZ, CURTIS NEAL, purchasing agent; b. Jan. 26, 1944; s. Gustav Albert and Elna G.; m. Audrey Jean D., Oct. 6, 1973. BSBA, U. Minn., 1966; MBA, No. Ill. U., 1990. Purchasing agt. I. S. Berlin Press, Chgo., 1973-75; asst. purchasing agt. Daubert Chem. Co., Oak Brook, Ill., 1975-78; purchasing mgr. IBG Internat., Wheeling, Ill., 1978-86; dir. purchasing Advance Process Supply Co., Chgo., 1986-91; pres. Selectech, Mount Prospect, Ill., 1991—. Decorated Purple Heart. Mem. Nat. Assn. Purchasing Mgmt., Purchasing Assn. Chgo., Mfrs. Agts. Nat. Assn., United Assn. Mgrs. Reps. (mem. nat. bd. advisors 1994-96), Beta Gamma Sigma, Sigma Iota Epsilon. Home: 404 S Helena Ave Mount Prospect IL 60056-2854 Office: Selectech Internat Inc 1749 W Golf Rd #379 Mount Prospect IL 60056

GERMANN, STEVEN JAMES, museum director; b. Dayton, Ohio, Sept. 4, 1947; s. James Howard and Doris Olive (Smith) G.; m. Elizabeth Haifley, Oct. 13, 1979; children: Alison Haifley, Andrew Ryan. BA in History, Wright State U., 1969, MA in History, 1973, cert. Mus. Adminstrn., 1977. Dir. edn. svcs. Montgomery County Hist. Soc., Dayton, Ohio, 1976-82; mus. adminstr. Mont. Hist. Soc., Helena, 1982-89; dir. Alfred P. Sloan Mus., Flint, Mich., 1989-2000. Exec. v.p. Midwest Mus. Conf., St. Louis, 1992-96. Bd. dirs. Flint Area Conv. and Visitors Bureau. Mem. Am. Assn. Mus. (mus. accreditation vis. com. 1989—), Mich. Mus. Assn., Flint Rotary, Phi Alpha Theta (hon. Rho Sigma chpt.). Office: Sloan Museum 1221 E Kearsley St Flint MI 48503-1988 Home: 1136 Christi Cir Dayton OH 45434-6378

GERN, RONALD L., lawyer, real estate company executive; m. Patti Gern; children: Andrew, Stephen, Alison. BA, BS, U. Pa, 1979; JD, U. Va., 1982. Bar: Ill. 1999. Assoc. Wolf, Block, Schorr & Solos-Cohen, 1982—85; counsel Kravco Co., 1985—90, v.p., gen. counsel, 1990—97; sr. v.p., gen. counsel, asst. sec. General Growth Properties, Inc., 1997—. Mem.: ABA, ICSC Law Conf. Prog. Com. (former chmn.), Am. Coll. Real Estate Lawyers. Office: General Growth Properties Inc 110 N Wacker Dr Chicago IL 60606 Office Phone: 312-960-5000. E-mail: rgern@generalgrowth.com.

GERNANDER, BARTON CARL, lawyer; b. Newport, RI, July 21, 1969; married. BA with honors in Philos., U. Pa., Phila., 1992; JD, U. Minn. Law Sch., 1996. Bar: Minn. 1996, US Dist. Ct. (dist. Minn.) 1998, US Ct. Appeals (8th cir.) 1999. Assoc. Hellmuth & Johnson, P.L.L.C., Eden Prairie, Minn. Named a Rising Star, Minn. Super Lawyers mag., 2006. Mem.: Fed. Bar Assn., Minn. State Bar Assn., Hennepin County Bar Assn. Office: Hellmuth & Johnson PLLC 10400 Viking Dr Ste 500 Eden Prairie MN 55344 Office Phone: 952-941-4005. E-mail: bgernander@hjlawfirm.com.

GERRARD, JOHN M., state supreme court justice; b. Schuyler, Nebr., Nov. 2, 1953; BS, Nebr. Wesleyan U., 1976; MPA, U. Ariz., 1977; JD, U. Pacific, 1981. Pvt. practice, Norfolk, 1981-95; city atty. City of Battle Creek, Nebr., 1982-95; justice Nebr. Supreme Ct., Lincoln, 1995—. Co-chair Minority and Justice Task Force; chair Nebr. Supreme Ct. Gender Fairness Implementation Com., Gender Fairness Implementation Com. Fellow: Nebr. Bar Found.; mem.: Nebr. State Bar Assn. (Nebr. State Bar Assn. Standing Com. on Professionalism). Office: Nebr Supreme Ct 2219 State Capitol Lincoln NE 68509-8000

GERRY, MARTIN HUGHES, IV, federal agency administrator, lawyer; b. San Francisco, Jan. 3, 1943; s. Martin Hughes III and Emily (Kuhl) G.; m. Robin Lucile MacAskill, Sept. 9, 1963 (div. June 1971); 1 child, Carol Elizabeth; m. Beatrice Ann Borowski, Apr. 28, 1984; children: Emily Irena, David Edward. BA, Stanford U., 1964, JD, 1967. Bar: N.Y. 1967, D.C. 1977, U.S. Dist. Ct. D.C. 1979, U.S. Supreme Ct. 1985. Assoc. Nixon, Mudge, Rose, Guthrie, Alexander & Mitchell, NYC, 1967-69; exec. asst. to dir. Office for Civil Rights, HEW, Washington, 1969-70; asst. to sec. HEW, Washington, 1970-74; dir. Office for Civil Rights, HEW, Washington, 1975-77; pres. Policy Ctr. for Children and Youth, Bethesda, Md., 1978-89; asst. sec. for planning and evaluation HHS, Washington, 1990-93; exec. dir. The Austin (Tex.) Project, 1993-95; rsch. prof., dir. Ctr. for Study of Family and Cmty. Policy U. Kans., 1995—; mem. adv. bd. on welfare indicators U.S. Dept. HHS, 1996-98. Spl. counsel Wednesday Group, U.S. Ho. of Reps., Washington, 1977-89, vice chair Commn. on Spl. Needs of Children, 1982-83; vice chair Nat. Legal Ctr. for Medically Dependent, Indpls., 1986-90; sr. cons. Orgn. for Econ. Cooperation and Devel., Paris, 1986-90; vis. rsch. scholar U. Md., 1988-89; vis. scholar Stanford U., 1989-90; dir. Nat. Tech. Assistance Ctr. on Welfare Reform, 1997—. Contbr. numerous articles on social policy, edn., pub. financing, and civil rights related subjects to profl. jours. Mem. disability adv. coun. Social Security Adminstrn., HHS, Washington, 1986-88; edn. expert Superior Ct. D.C., Washington, 1986-90; sr. policy advisor Bush-Quayle '88. Oscar Cushing Law fellow Stanford U., 1965. Mem. Fed. Bar Assn. Republican. Episcopalian. Avocations: sailing, hiking.

GERSH, DEBORAH LOUISE, lawyer; b. Chgo. m. Robert Paul Schroeder, Sept. 22, 1984. BA, Northwestern U., 1980; JD with honors, George Washington U., 1983. Bar: Ill. 1983, U.S. Dist. Ct. (no. dist.) Ill. 1983. Assoc. Rudnick & Wolfe, Chgo., 1983—89, ptnr., 1990—99, Piper Rudnick LLP, Chgo., 2000—04; ptnr., chair Chgo. Corp. practice group DLA Piper Rudnick Gray Cary, Chgo., 2005—, mem. policy com., 2006. Adj. prof. Kent Law Sch., Chgo., 2000—02. Author: Raising Capital for Health Care Companies, 2005; contbr. chapters to books, articles to profl. jours. Mem. regional bd. dir. Anti Defamation League, Chgo., 2002—04. Named a Women in Black -Top Tech. Women Lawyers in Chgo., i-Street Newspaper, 2001; named One of Top Lawyers in Ill., Super Lawyers, 2005; named one of Top 100 Most Influential Bus. Tech. Leaders in Chgo., i-Street newspaper, 2001, Ill. Leading Lawyers, Ill. Leading Lawyers Assn., 2004. Mem.: Chgo. Bar Assn., Am. Health Lawyers Assn., Women Health Executives Network, Phi Beta Kappa. Office: DLA Piper 203 North LaSalle St Chicago IL 60601-1293 Office Phone: 312-368-2108. Office Fax: 312-630-5371. Business E-Mail: deborah.gersh@dlapiper.com.

GERSHEL, ALAN M., prosecutor; b. Nov. 19, 1951; s. Marvin and Francine G.; m. Linda, Aug. 3, 1975; children: Jessica Sara, Bradley Ross. BS, Northeastern U., 1974; MS, Ind. State U., 1975; JD, U. Detroit, 1978. Bar: Mich. 1978, U.S. Ct. Appeals (6th cir.) Mich. 1980. Asst. atty., criminal chief ea. dist. U.S. Dept Justice, Detroit, 1993—; dep. asst. atty. gen. U.S. Dept. Justice, 2000; interim U.S. atty. U.S. Dept Justice, Detroit, 2000—01; adj. prof. U. Detroit Mercy Sch. Law, Mich. Office: Assist US Atty 211 W Fort St 2001 Detroit MI 48226-3211 Business E-Mail: alan.gershel@usdoj.gov.

GERSHENSON, DENNIS, property company executive; Pres., CEO, trustee Ramco-Gershenson Properties, Southfield, Mich., 1989—. Office: 27600 Northwestern Hwy Ste 200 Southfield MI 48034-8466

GERSHENSON, JOEL, property company executive; Chmn., trustee Ramco-Gershenson Properties, Southfield, Mich., 1989—. Home: 31500 Northwestern Hwy Ste 100 Farmington Hills MI 48334-2568

GERSHON, RICHARD A., commmunications educator; b. Apr. 20, 1952; s. Phillip and Sylvia Gershon; m. Casey, Aug. 25, 1978; 1 child, Matthew. BA in English, Goddard Coll., Plainfield, Vt., 1974; MEd in Edn., U. Vt., 1980; PhD in Mass Communication, Ohio U., 1986. Instr. English and Mass Communication Rice Meml. High Sch., Burlington, Vt., 1976-81; sr. bus. editor Telecom. Mag., Dedham, Mass., 1984-86; asst. prof. telecommunications SUNY, New Paltz, 1986-89; prof. telecommunications Western Mich. U., Kalamazoo, 1989—. Chair Policy and Planning Task Force for Greater Kalamazoon Telecity Project. Author: Transnational Media Corporation: Global Markets and Free Market Competition, 1997, Telecommunications Management: Industry Structures and Planning Strategies, 2001 (Nat. Cable TVs Mus.'s Book of Yr. award); contbr. articles to profl. jours. Mem. Broadcast Edn. Assn. (chair elect for internat. div.). Office: Western Mich U Dept Comm Kalamazoo MI 49008 E-mail: Richard.Gershon@wmich.edu.

GERSIE, MICHAEL H., insurance company executive; CLU, ChFC. Actuarial trainee Principal Fin. Group, Des Moines, 1970—74, actuarial assoc., 1974—75, asst. actuary, 1975—79, assoc. actuary, 1979—84, actuary, 1984—86, 2d v.p., 1986—90, v.p., 1990—94, sr. v.p., CIO, 1994—96, sr. v.p., CFO, 1996—2000, CFO, exec. v.p., 2000—. Office: Principal Fin Group 711 High St Des Moines IA 50392

GERSON, RALPH JOSEPH, manufacturing executive; b. Detroit, Nov. 30, 1949; s. Byron Hayden and Dorothy Mary (Davidson) G.; m. Erica Ann Ward, May 20, 1979. BA, Yale U., New Haven, Conn., 1971; MSc, London Sch. Econs., 1972; JD, U. Mich., 1975. Bar: Mich. 1975, DC 1976, US Dist. Ct. DC 1976, US Ct. Appeals (DC cir.) 1976. Counsel Dem. Nat. Com., Washington, 1975-77; spl. asst. US Trade Rep., Washington, 1978-79; counselor to spl. Middle East negotiator Office of Pres., Washington, 1979-80; ptnr. Akin, Gump, Strauss, Hauer and Feld, 1981-83, 85-87; dir. Mich. Dept. Commerce, Lansing, 1983-84; exec. v.p. Guardian Industries Corp., Auburn Hills, Mich., 1988—, also bd. dirs., 1988—; pres., CEO Guardian Internat. Corp., 1993—. Bd. dirs. Pistons-Palace Found., US Spain Coun.; trustee Henry Ford Mus., Detroit Symphony Orch., Citizens Rsch. Coun. Mem. ABA, DC Bar Assn., Mich. Bar Assn., Coun. Fgn. Rels., World Pres. Orgn., Royal Automobile Club, Franklin Hills Country Club, Bloomfield Open Hunt Club, Yale Club (NYC). Office: Guardian Industries Corp 2300 Harmon Rd Auburn Hills MI 48326-1714

GERSTEIN, MARK DOUGLAS, lawyer; b. Chgo., Nov. 16, 1959; s. Robert Henry and Helene Roberta Gerstein; m. Julia Sara Wolf, Apr. 13, 1986; children: Allison Ruth, Evan Benjamin. BA, U. Mich., 1981; JD, U. Chgo., 1984. Bar: Ill., US Dist. Ct. No. Dist. Ill. Assoc. Katten Muchin & Zavis, Chgo., 1984—91, ptnr., 1991—96, chair mergers & acquisitions, 1994—96, capital ptnr., 1996; equity ptnr. Latham & Watkins, Chgo., 1996—, global co-chair mergers & acquisitions group, 1999—. Adj. faculty mem. Northwestern U. Sch. Law. Bd. dirs. Youth Guidance, Chgo., 1995—; dir. associates Ravinia Festival, Chgo., 1996—2000. Mem.: Chgo. Bar Assn. (chair subcom. on corp. control 1998—99), ABA (mem. bus. law sect., corp. governance com.), Standard Club. Avocations: sailing, bicycling. Office: Latham & Watkins Sears Tower Ste 5800 233 S Wacker Dr Chicago IL 60606 Office Phone: 312-876-7666. E-mail: mark.gerstein@lw.com.

GERSTNER, ROBERT WILLIAM, structural engineering educator, consultant; b. Chgo., Nov. 10, 1934; s. Robert Berty and Martha (Tuchelt) G.; m. Elizabeth Willard, Feb. 8, 1958; children: Charles Willard, William Mark. BS, Northwestern U., 1956, MS, 1957, PhD, 1960. Registered structural and profl. engr., Ill. Instr. orthwestern U., Evanston, Ill., 1957-59, research fellow, 1959-60; asst. prof. U. Ill., Chgo., 1960-63, assoc. prof., 1963-69, prof. structural engring., architecture, 1969-92, prof. emeritus, 1992—. Structural engr. cons., 1959—; mem. State of Ill. Structural Engring. Bd., 1992-94. Contbr. articles to profl. jours. Pres. Riverside Improvement Assn., 1973-77, 79-82. Mem. AAUP, ACLU, ASCE, Am. Soc. Engring. Edn., Structural Engrs. Assn. Ill. (bd. dirs. 1986-89, 92-94, sec. 1989-91, pres. 1991-92). Home: 1524 Primrose Ln Glenview IL 60026 E-mail: robertwgerstner@aol.com.

GERVASON, ROBERT J., advertising executive; Exec. v.p. Campbell Ewald Advertising, Warren, Mich. Office: Campbell Ewald Advt 30400 Van Dyke Ave Warren MI 48093-2368

GESKE, JANINE PATRICIA, law educator; b. Port Washington, Wis., May 12, 1949; d. Richard Braem and Georgette (Paulissen) Geske; m. Michael Julian Hogan, Jan. 2, 1982; children: Mia Geske Berman, Sarah Geske Hogan, Kevin Geske Hogan. Student, U. Grenoble, U. Rennes; BA, MA in Tchg., Beloit Coll., 1971; JD, Marquette U., 1975, LLD, 1998, LLD (hon.), 1994; DHL (hon.), Mt. Mary Coll., 1999. Bar: Wis. 1975, U.S. Dist. Ct. (ea. & we. dists.) Wis. 1975, U.S. Supreme Ct. 1978. Tchr. elem. sch., Lake Zurich, Ill., 1970-72; staff atty., chief staff atty. Legal Aid Soc., Milw., 1975-78; asst. prof. law, clin. dir. Law Sch. Marquette U., Milw., 1978-81; hearing examiner Milw. County CETA, Milw., 1980-81; judge Milw. County Circuit Ct., Milw., 1981-93; justice Supreme Ct. Wis., 1993-98; disting. prof. law Marquette U. Law Sch., Milw., 1998—, interim Milw. County exec., 2002, interim dean Sch. Law, 2002—03. Dean Wis. Jud. Coll.; mem. faculty Nat. Jud. Coll.; instr. various jud. tng. programs, continuing legal edn. Fellow ABA, mem. Am. Law Inst., Am. Arbitration Assn., Soc. Profls. in Dispute Resolution, Wis. Bar Assn., Wis. Assn. Mediators, Milw. Bar Assn., Nat. Women Judges Assn., 7th Cir. Bar Assn., Alpha Sigma Nu. Roman Catholic. Office: Marquette U Law Sch PO Box 1881 Milwaukee WI 53201-1881

GEST, HOWARD, microbiologist, educator; b. London, Oct. 15, 1921; m. Janet Olin, Sept. 8, 1941 (dec. 1994); children: Theodore Olin, Michael Henry, Donald Evan; m. Virginia Davies Ollis, Jan. 6, 1998. BA in Bacteriology, UCLA, 1942; postgrad. in biology (Univ. fellow), Vanderbilt U., 1942; PhD in Microbiology (Am. Cancer Soc. fellow), Washington U., St. Louis, 1949. Rsch. asst. Metall. Lab. (Manhattan Project) U. Chgo., 1943; from jr. to assoc. chemist Clinton Labs. (Manhattan Project), Oak Ridge, 1943-46; Instr. microbiology Western Res. U. Sch. Medicine, 1949-51, asst. prof. microbiology, 1951-53, asso. prof., 1953-59; USPHS spl. research fellow in biology Calif. Inst. Tech., 1956-57; prof. Henry Shaw Sch. Botany, Washington U., 1959-64, dept. zoology, 1964-66; prof. Ind. U., Bloomington, 1966-78, disting. prof. microbiology, 1978—, disting. prof. emeritus microbiology, 1987—, adj. prof. history and philosophy of sci., 1983—, chmn. dept. microbiology, 1966-70, disting. faculty rsch. lectr., 1987. NSF sr. postdoctoral fellow Nat. Inst. Med. Rsch., London, 1965—66; Guggenheim fellow Imperial Coll., London, U. Stockholm, U. Tokyo; vis. prof. dept. biophysics and biochemistry U. Tokyo and Japan Soc. Promotion Sci., 1970; mem. study sect. bacteriology and mycology NIH, 1966—68, chmn. study sect. microbial chemistry, 1968—69, mem. study sect. microbial physiology and genetics, 1988—90; mem. com. microbiol. problems of man in extended space flight Nat. Acad. Scis.-NRC, 1967—69; Guggenheim fellow Imperial Coll., London, UCLA, 1979—80; 1st H.D. Peck lectr. U. Ga., 1994; Cummings lectr. Bucknell U., 1997. Fellow: AAAS, Am. Acad. Microbiology; mem.: Am. Acad. Arts and Scis., Am. Soc. Microbiology (hon.). Office: Ind U Dept Biology Bloomington IN 47405 Home Phone: 812-339-5888; Office Phone: 812-855-9612. Business E-Mail: hgest@bio.indiana.edu. E-mail: gest@indiana.edu.

GESWEIN, GREGORY T., software company executive; m. Rose Geswein; 2 children. BBA, U. Cin., 1977, MBA in Fin., 1978. Joined Armco Inc., 1978; v.p., corp. contr., corp. treas. Mead Corp., Dayton, Ohio, 1985—89; sr. v.p., CFO Pioneer-Standard Electronics, Inc., Cleve., 1999, Diebold, Inc., North Canton, Ohio, 2000—04, Reynolds & Reynolds Co., 2005—. Office: Reynolds and Reynolds Co PO Box 1824 Dayton OH 45401-1824

GETTELFINGER, GERALD ANDREW, bishop; b. Ramsey, Ind., Oct. 20, 1935; Student, St. Meinrad's Seminary; MS, Butler U., 1965. Ordained priest Archdiocese of Indpls., Ind., 1961; ordained bishop, 1989; bishop Diocese of Evansville, Ind., 1989—. Roman Catholic. Home: 3980 Woodcastle Dr Evansville IN 47711-2776 Office: Diocese of Evansville 4200 N Kentucky Ave PO Box 4169 Evansville IN 47711-0169 Office Phone: 812-424-5536. Office Fax: 812-436-7450. E-mail: ggettelfinger@evansville-diocese.org.*

GETTELFINGER, RON, labor union administrator; b. Aug. 1, 1944; m. Judy Gettelfinger; children: Dawn, Darin. B in Acctg., Ind. U., 1976. Local official, truck plant Ford Motor Co., Louisville, 1964—84; pres. Local 862 UAW, 1984—87, dir. Region 3, 1992—98, v.p., 1998—2002, pres., 2002—. Mem. UAW-Ford Motor Co. Bargaining Com., 1987—98; mem. supervisory bd. DaimlerChrysler AG, 2006—. Served in USMC, 1962—63. Office: UAW Solidarity House 8000 E Jefferson Detroit MI 48214 Office Phone: 313-926-5000.

GETTLEMAN, ROBERT WILLIAM, judge; b. Atlantic City, May 5, 1943; s. Charles Edward and Beulah (Oppenheim) G.; m. Joyce Reinitz, Dec. 23, 1964; children: Lynn Katheryn, Jeffrey Alan. BSBA cum laude, Boston U., 1965; JD cum laude, Northwestern U., 1968. Bar: Ill. 1968, U.S. Dist. Ct. (no. dist.) Ill. 1968, U.S. Ct. Appeals (7th cir.) 1968, U.S. Dist. Ct. (ea. dist.) Wis. 1972, U.S. Supreme Ct. 1973. Law clk. to presiding justice U.S. Ct. Appeals, Chgo., 1968-70; assoc. D'Ancoma & Pflaum, Chgo., 1970-74, ptnr., 1974-94; judge U.S. Dist. Ct., Ill., 1994—. Bd. dirs. John Howard Assn., Chgo., 1973-94, pres., 1978-81, chmn. legal and policy coms.; commr., chmn. devel. disabilities and individual rights coms. Gov.'s Commn. to Revise Mental Health Code of Ill., 1973-77; chmn. steering com. Chgo. Project on Residential Alternatives, 1984-85; mem. Cook County State's Atty.'s Profl. Adv. Com., 1984—; treas. Ill. Guardianship and Advocacy Commn., 1984, vice chmn., 1985, chmn., 1986; bd. dirs., chmn. legal com. Pact, Inc., 1985—; mem. mcpl. officers election bd. Village of Lyons, Ill., 1985. Contbr. articles to law revs. Bd. dirs. Ill. divsn. ACLU, 1973-78. Recipient August W. Christmann award Mayor of Chgo., 1994. Fellow Am. Bar Found.; mem. ABA, Ill. Bar Assn., Chgo. Bar Assn., 7th Fed. Cir. Bar Assn., Chgo. Council Lawyers. Office: US Dist Ct 1788 Dirksen Bldg 219 S Dearborn St Fl 17 Chicago IL 60604-1702

GETTLER, BENJAMIN, lawyer, manufacturing company executive; b. Louisville, Sept. 16, 1925; s. Herbert and Gertrude (Cohen) G.; m. Deliaan Angel, Mar. 1972; children: Jorian, Thomas, Gail, John, Benjamin. BA in Econs. with high honors, U. Cin., 1945; JD (Frankfurter scholar), Harvard U., Cambridge, Mass., 1948. Bar: Ohio 1949, U.S. Supreme Ct. 1955. Ptnr. Brown & Gettler, Cin., 1951—73, Gettler, Katz & Buckley, Cin., 1973—87; chmn. bd. Am. Controlled Industries Inc., Cin., 1973—86; chmn. bd. dirs., pres. Colorpac Inc., Franklin, Ohio, 1973—86; chmn. exec. com. Valley Industries, Inc., Cin., 1973—86; chmn. bd., pres. Vulcan Internat. Corp., Wilmington, Del., 1988—, Vulcan Corp., Clarksville, Tenn., 1988—; vice chmn. bd. Cin. So. R.R., 1987—91; chmn. bd. Trusthouse, Inc., Cin., 1987—. Chmn. exec. com. Valley Industries, Inc., Cin., 1973-86; chmn. bd. dirs. ACI Internat., Inc., Cin., 1990—; spl. counsel U. Cin., 1975-77, trustee, 1994-2003, vice chmn. bd., 1999-2000, chmn., 2000-2002; bd. dirs. PNC Bank, Ohio, 1988-96. Chmn. bd. Jewish Inst. Nat. Security Affairs, 1994-98, chmn. policy com., 1998—; chmn. Cin. Bonds for Israel, 1969; chmn. Nat. Israel Commn., Nat. Jewish Cmty. Rels. Adv. Coun., 1981-82; mem. Ohio, Ky. and Ind. Mass Transit Policy Com., 1970-75; pres. Cin. Jewish Cmty. Rels. Coun., 1978-80; trustee Jewish Hosp. Cin., 1978-92, chmn., 1991-92; chmn. Midwest Hosp. Sys., Inc., 1987-90, 92-93; pres. Jewish Found. Cin., 1995-99, chmn., 1999-02; trustee Health Alliance Greater Cin., 1995-96, 2000-02; chmn. Cin. Coalition for Reagan, 1980; co-chmn. Hamilton County Reagan Bush Campaign Ohio, 1984; chmn. Rep. Fin. Com., Hamilton County, 1991-92; mem. Hamilton County Rep. Policy Com., 1990—; exec. dir. Rockwern Charitable Found., 1998—; trustee S.W. Ohio Regional Transit Authority, 2003-06, chmn., 2004-06. Capt. US Army, 1955—56. Mem. ABA, Cin. Bar Assn., Shoe Last Mfrs. Assn. (pres. 1984-85), Footwear Industries Am. (bd. dirs. 1989-2000), Phi Beta Kappa, Omicron Delta Kappa. Clubs: Coldstream Country, Harvard. Office: Vulcan Corp 30 Garfield Pl Ste 1040 Cincinnati OH 45202-4322 Office Phone: 513-621-2850.

GETZ, GODFREY SHALOM, dean, pathologist, educator; b. Johannesburg, S. Africa, June 18, 1930; came to U.S., 1963; naturalized, 1971; s. Judah Nathan and Fay (Lakofski) G.; m. Millicent Lorraine Cohen; children: Edwin A., Andrew R., Keith S., Jonathan D. BSc, Witwatersrand U., Johannesburg, 1952; BSc (hon.), Witwatersrand U., 1955, MB, BCh, 1954; PhD, Oxford U., 1963. Lectr. Witwatersrand U., 1956, 59-63; Nuffield demonstrator Oxford U., Eng., 1956-59; rsch. assoc. Harvard Med. Sch., Boston, 1963-64; asst. then assoc. prof. U. Chgo., 1964-72, prof., 1972—; acting dean U. Chgo. divsn. biol. studies, 1999. Home: Apt 1805 445 E North Water St Chicago IL 60611-5550

GETZENDANNER, SUSAN, lawyer; b. Chgo., July 24, 1939; d. William B. and Carole S. (Muehling) O'Meara; children— Alexandra, Paul. BBA, JD, Loyola U., 1966. Bar: Ill. bar 1966. Law clk. U.S. Dist. Ct., Chgo., 1966-68; assoc. Mayer, Brown & Platt, Chgo., 1968-74, ptnr., 1974-80; judge U.S. Dist. Ct., Chgo., 1980-87; ptnr. Skadden, Arps, Slate, Meagher & Flom, Chgo., 1987—2002. Recipient medal of excellence Loyola U. Law Alumni Assn., 1981 Mem. ABA, Chgo. Council Lawyers. Office Phone: 312-944-2629. E-mail: sgetzendanner@mindspring.com.

GEWEKE, JOHN FREDERICK, economics professor; b. Washington, May 11, 1948; s. Robert William and Winnifred Lois (Quies) G.; m. Lynne Marie Osborn, Aug. 22, 1970; 1 child, Andrew Robert. BS, Mich. State U., 1970; PhD, U. Minn., 1975. Asst. prof. U. Wis., Madison, 1975-79, assoc. prof., 1979-82, prof., 1982-83, Duke U., Durham, NC, 1983-86, William R. Kenan Jr. prof., 1986-90, dir. Inst. Stats. and Decision Scis., 1987-90; prof. U. Minn., Mpls., 1990—99; McGregor Chair in econs. & stats. U. Iowa, 1999—. Editor Jour. Bus. and Econs. Stats., 1989-92; co-editor Jour. Applied Econometrics, 1993-2002, Jour. Econometrics, 2003-; assoc. editor Econometrica, 1984-88, 95-2002. Rsch. fellow Sloan Found., N.Y.C., 1982. Fellow Econometric Soc., Am. Statis. Assn.; mem. Am. Econ. Assn., Internat. Soc. for Bayesian Analysis (pres. 1999). Office: U of IA Dept Econs Iowa City IA 52242

GEWERTZ, BRUCE LABE, surgeon, educator; b. Phila., Aug. 27, 1949; s. Milton and Shirley (Charen) G.; children: Samantha, Barton, Alexis; m. Diane Weiss, Aug. 31, 1997. BS, Pa. State U., State Coll., 1968; MD, Jefferson Med. Coll., Phila., 1972. Diplomate Am. Bd. Surgery. Surg. resident U. Mich., Ann Arbor, 1972-77; asst. prof. U. Tex., Dallas, 1977-81; assoc. prof. U. Chgo., 1981-87, prof. surgery, 1988—, faculty dean med. edn., 1989-92, Dallas Phemister prof., chmn. dept. surgery, 1992—2006; chmn. dept. surgery, surgeon-in-chief, v.p. Cedars-Sinai Med. Ctr., LA, 2006—. Tchg. scholar Am. Heart Assn., Dallas, 1980-83; pres. Assn. Surg. Edn., 1983-84; dir. vascular surgery bd. Am. Bd. Surgery, 2001—. Author: Atlas of Vascular Surgery, 1989, 2005, Surgery of the Aorta and its Branches, 2000; editor Jour. Surg. Rsch., 1987-2002; patentee removable vascular filter. Recipient Jobst award Coller Surg. Soc., 1975, Coller award Mich. chpt. Am. Coll. Surgeons, 1975, Outstanding Sci. Alumnus award Pa. State U., 2003. Mem. Soc. Vascular Surgery, Midwestern Vascular Soc. (pres. 1994-95), Soc. Clin. Surgery, Soc. Univ. Surgeons, Chgo. Surg. Soc. (pres. 2005), Western Surg. Assn. (pres. 2007-08), Am. Surg. Assn. Office: Cedars-Sinai Med Ctr 8700 Beverly Blvd Los Angeles CA 90048 Office Phone: 310-423-5884. Business E-Mail: bruce.gewertz@cshs.org.

GEWURZ, ANITA TARTELL, physician, medical educator; b. Buffalo, July 30, 1946; MD, Albany Med. Coll., 1970. Resident in pediat. U. Ill., Chgo., 1971—73; resident in allergy and immunology Rush-Presbyn.-St. Luke's Hosp., Chgo., 1974—76; fellow allergy and immunology Max Samter Inst., Grant Hosp., Chgo., 1976—77, orthwestern U. Med. Coll., Chgo., 1983—85; assoc. prof. immunology/microbiology, pediat. and internal med. Rush U. Med. Coll., Chgo., 1993—2003, prof. immunology/microbiology, pediat. and internal med., 2003—; physician Rush U. Med. Ctr., Chgo., 1974—. Chair, Tng. Program Dirs. Com. Am. Acad. Allergy, Asthma & Immunology, 2000—02; chair Am. Bd. Allergy and Immunology, 2004—05; initial cert. task force Am. Bd. Med. Specialties, 2004—, sub-com. chair, 2004—05; vol. physician pediats. St. Roger Hosp., Cook County, Ill., 1997—. Office: Rush Univ Med Ctr 1725 W Harrison St Ste 117 Chicago IL 60612 Office Phone: 312-942-6296. Business E-Mail: agewurz@rush.edu.

GEYER, MICHAEL, history professor; PhD, Albert Ludwigs U., Freiburg, Germany. Samuel N. Harper prof. history U. Chgo., 1986—. Trustee Am. Acad. in Berlin, 2007—. Guggenheim fellow, 2003. Office: U Chgo Dept History 1126 E 59th St Chicago IL 60637 Home Phone: 773-955-7204; Office Phone: 773-702-7934. E-mail: mgeyer@uchicago.edu.

GHASSOMIAN, KEVIN R., lawyer; b. Ashland, Ky., June 18, 1973; BA in Polit. Sci., U. Ky., 1995; JD, Vanderbilt U. Sch. of Law, 1998; LLM in Taxation, U. Miami Sch. of Law, 2001. Bar: Nev. 1999, Ky. 1999, Ohio 2002. Mem., Young Professionals Prog. World Affairs Coun., Cin., 2002—; supervising atty. Wills for Heroes Prog., 2004—; bd. trustees Corp. for Findlay Market, Cin., 2006—, devel. com. mem., 2006—; mem., C-Change Leadership Devel. Prog. Cin. USA Regional Chamber, 2006, mem., C-Change Steering Com., bd. dir., 2006—07. Mem. Cin. Downtown Resident's Coun., 2002—; trustee Children's Home Northern Ky., 2002—, mem., Exec. Com., 2003—, mem., Endowment Com., 2005—; mem., Prog. Com. LEGACY, Covington, Ky., 2002—03, mentor, 2003—; mem., Adv. Com. for Young Professionals Programming Cin. Art Mus.,

2005—, shareholder, 2005—; trustee Invest in Neighborhoods, Inc., Cin., 2004—; mem. U. Club Cin., 2001—, mem., Membership Com., 2001—, mem., Bd. Governors, 2002—, chair, Membership Com., 2003—, chair, Law Com., 2004—; trustee Carnegie Visual & Performing Arts Ctr., Covington, Ky., 2004—, mem., Devel. Com., 2004—, chair, Devel. Com., 2005—06, v.p., 2006—; trustee Friends of U. Cin. Coll.-Conservatory of Music, 2005—, mem., Exec. Com., 2006—. Named Inspire Vol. of Yr., Inspire Cin. Mag., 2005; named one of 40 Under 40, Cin. Bus. Courier, 2004, Ohio's Rising Stars, Super Lawyers, 2005, 2006. Mem.: Bacchanalian Soc. (founding mem. 2002—), Cin. Paralegal Assn. (adv. counsel 2006—, Outstanding Svc. award 2005), Estate Planning Coun. Northern Ky., Ohio Bar Assn., Northern Ky. Bar Assn., Cin. Bar Assn. (Estate Planning and Probate Com. 2003—), Ky. Bar Assn., Nev. Bar Assn., ABA (Real Property, Probate and Trust Law Sect. 2001—), Phi Beta Kappa Soc. Office: Greenebaum Doll & McDonald PLLC 2800 Chemed Ctr 255 E 5th St Cincinnati OH 45202-4728 Office Phone: 513-455-7603. Office Fax: 513-762-7903.

GHETTI, BERNARDINO FRANCESCO, neuropathologist, educator; b. Pisa, Italy, Mar. 28, 1941; s. Getulio and Iris (Mugnetti) G.; m. Caterina Genovese, Oct. 8, 1966; children: Chiara, Simone. MD cum laude, U. Pisa, 1966, specialist in mental and nervous diseases, 1969; laureate (hon.), U. Siena, 2005. Lic. physician, Italy; cert. Edn. Coun. for Fgn. Med. Grads.; diplomate Am. Bd. Pathology. Postdoctoral fellow U. Pisa, 1966-70; rsch. fellow in neuropathology Albert Einstein Coll. Medicine, Bronx, NY, 1970-73, resident, clin. fellow in pathology, 1973-75, resident in neuropathology, 1975-76; asst. prof. pathology Ind. U., Indpls., 1976-77, asst. prof. pathology and psychiatry, 1977—78, assoc. prof. pathology and psychiatry, 1978—83, prof. pathology and psychiatry, 1983—91, assoc. dir. program in med. neurobiology, 1983—2000, assoc. dir. divsn. neuropathology, 1989-93, prof. pathology, psychiatry, med. and molecular genetics, 1991—97, dir. Alzheimer Disease Ctr., 1991—, dir. divsn. neuropathology, 1993—, Disting. prof. pathology and lab. medicine, psychiatry, med. and molecular genetics, neurology, 1997—, chancellor's prof., 2007—. Mem. Nat. Inst. Neurol. Disorders and Stroke rev. com. NIH, 1985-89; mem. NIH Reviewers Res., 1989-93. Contbr. articles to profl. jours. Alzheimer's disease rsch. sci. rev. com. Am. Health Assistance Found., 1998—2002. Recipient Potamkin prize, 1999. Mem. Internat. Soc. Neuropathology (v.p. 2000-03, pres.-elect 2005, pres. 2006—), Am. Acad. Neurology, Am. Neurol. Assn., Am. Assn. europathologists (pres. 1996-97), Soc. Neurosci., Assn. Rsch. in Nervous and Mental Diseases, Internat. Brain Rsch. Orgn., Am. Soc. Cell Biology, Italian Soc. Psychiatry, Italian Soc. Neurology, Sigma Xi. Roman Catholic. Home: 1124 Frederick Dr S Indianapolis IN 46260-3421 Office: Ind U 635 Barnhill Dr Rm 138 Indianapolis IN 46202-5126 Office Phone: 317-274-7818. Business E-Mail: bghetti@iupui.edu.

GHIA, KIRTI N., fluid mechanics engineer, aerospace educator; b. Bombay; BS, Gujarat U., India, 1960; MS, Ill. Inst. Tech., 1965, PhD in Mechanical & Aerospace Engring., 1969. Rsch. engr. Premier Automobiles Ltd., India, 1960-61; rsch. asst. fluid dynamics Ill. Inst. Tech., 1961-62, instr., 1962, asst., 1962-69; from asst. prof. to assoc. prof. U. Cin., 1969—78, prof. fluid dynamics, 1978—. Dir. Inst. Computational Mechanics, 1986—; co-dir. Computational Fluid Dynamics Rsch. Lab., 1990—. Assoc. tech. editor Jour. Fluids Engring., 1981—90, Am. Inst. Aeronautics and Astronautics Jour., 2000—; co-editor: Internat. Computational Fluid Dynamics Jour., 1991—98; contbr. articles to profl. jours. Named Disting. Prof., U. Cin., 2005; recipient Dolly Cohen award, 2004. Fellow ASME (life, chair honors and awards com. fluids engring divsn. 1997-2000, Freeman scholar award 1995-96), AIAA (fluid mechanics tech. com. 1986—); mem. Am. Phys. Soc., Am. Soc. Engring. Edn., Sigma Xi, Sigma Gamma Tau, Tau Beta Pi. Hindu. Achievements include research in analysis and numerical solutions of three-dimensional viscous internal flow problems; use of numerical coordinate transformations and higher-order spline techniques and direct solvers in the solution of navier-stokes equations. Office: Univ Cin Aerospace/Engring Mech Rhodes 681 Cincinnati OH 45221-0070 Home Phone: 513-984-2252; Office Phone: 513-556-3243. Business E-Mail: kghia@cfdrl.uc.edu.

GHIARDI, JAMES DOMENIC, lawyer, educator; b. Gwinn, Mich., Nov. 10, 1918; s. John B. and Margaret M. (Trosello) G.; m. Phyllis A. Lindmeier, Sept. 5, 1945; children— Catherine, Jeanne, Mary. PhB, Marquette U., 1940, LLB, 1942, JD, 1968. Bar: Wis. bar 1942. Prof. law Marquette U. Law Sch., Milw., 1946-89, prof. law emeritus, 1990—; research dir. Def. Research Inst., Milw., 1962-72; of counsel firm Kluwin, Dunphy, Hankin & McNulty, Milw., 1972-87. Author: Personal Injury Damages, Wisconsin, 1964, Punitive Damages, Vol. I, 1981, Vol. II, 1985; contbr. articles to profl. jours. Served to capt. Med. Adminstrv. Br. U.S. Army, 1942-45. Recipient award for teaching excellence Marquette U. Faculty, 1971, Edward A. Uhrig Found., 1971, Alumni of Yr. award Marquette U. Law Sch., 1971, Charles L. Goldberg award for outstanding pub. svc. Wis. Law Found., 1986, Charles C. Pinckney award for legal scholarship and svc. to the legal profession N.Y. Def. Bar Assn., 1986. Fellow Am. Bar Found.; mem. ABA (mem. ho. of dels. 1967-80, Disting. Prof. Torts and Ins. Law award Torts and Ins. Practice sect. 1989), Milw. Bar Assn. (Lifetime Achievement award 1993), State Bar Wis. (gov., mem. exec. com. 1962-72, pres. 1970-71), Am. Law Ins., Wis. Bar Found., Am. Legion. Office: Sensenbrenner Hall Marquette U Law Sch PO Box 1881 Milwaukee WI 53201-1881 Office Phone: 414-288-5370.

GHIGLIONE, LOREN FRANK, journalism professor; b. NYC, Apr. 5, 1941; s. William John and Norma Rae (Whitney) G.; m. Nancy Ellen Geiger, Feb. 24, 1968; children: Jessica, Laura. BA, Haverford Coll., 1963; M of Urban Studies, Yale U., 1966, LLB, 1966; PhD in Am. Civilization, George Washington U., 1976. Asst. to dir. office of planning & analysis NEH, Washington, 1967-68; editor The News, Southbridge, Mass., 1969—95; pres. Worcester County Newspapers, Southbridge, Mass., 1969—95; former James M. Cox Chair in Journalism, dir. Journalism program Emory U., 1996—99; former dir. Sch. Journalism U. So. Calif., Annenberg Sch. Comm., 1999—2001; dean, prof. Medill Sch. Journalism, Northwestern U., 2001—06, Richard Schwarzlose prof. media ethics, 2007—. Author books and contbr. chpts. and essays to books and articles to profl. jours.; mem. editl. bd. Jour. Mass Media Ethics, 1990-. Congrl. fellow U.S. Congress, Washington, 1966-67, Freedom Forum Media Studies Ctr. fellow Columbia U., 1987-88, Joan Shorenstein Ctr. Harvard's John F. Kennedy Sch. Govt. fellow, 1988-89, Soc. Profl. Journalists fellow, 1990-91, Reuter fellow Oxford U., 1997. Fellow Am. Acad. Arts and Scis.; mem. Am. Soc. Newspaper Editors (pres. 1989-90), New Eng. Soc. Newspaper Editors (pres. 1978-79), New Eng. Press Assn. (pres. 1984), Internat. Press Inst. (dir. Am. com. 1989-94), Assn. Sch. Journalism and Mass Comm.(pres., 2006-07), Coun. Fgn. Rels. Avocations: reading, wind surfing. Office: Medill School of Journalism Northwestern U 1870 Campus Dr Evanston IL 60208-2170 Office Phone: 847-491-4837. Business E-Mail: ghiglion@northwestern.edu.

GHOSH, AVIJIT, dean; m. Sara McLafferty; children: Smita, Priya. BS in chem. with honors, Calcutta U., 1970; postgrad. in mgmt., Xavier Inst., 1975; MA in geography, U. Iowa, 1977, PhD in geography, 1979. Asst. prof. mktg. Sch. Bus., U. Iowa, 1978—79; asst. to prof. mktg. Leonard N. Stern Sch. Bus., NYU, 1980—91, dir. Ctr. Entrepreneurial Studies, 1991—95, vice dean profl. programs, 1994—2001, dep. dean, 1998—2000; dean Coll. Bus., U. Ill., Urbana-Champaign, 2001—, assoc. editor: Jour. Retailing, 1983 (Best Article Yr., 1984); editor, 1985—91 (Best Article Yr., 1991); author: (books) Retail Management, 1990, 1994; co-author (with Sara McLafferty): Location Strategy for Retail and Service Firms, 1987; co-editor: Spatial Analysis and Location Allocation Models, 1987, Spatial Analysis in Marketing: Theory, Methods and Applications, 1991. Office: Coll Bus Univ Ill Urbana Champaign 1206 S Sixth St 260 Wohlers Hall Champaign IL 61820 Office Phone: 217-333-2747. Office Fax: 217-244-3113. Business E-Mail: ghosha@uiuc.edu.

GHOSHAL, NANI GOPAL, veterinarian, educator; b. Dacca, India, Dec. 1, 1934; arrived in U.S., 1963; s. Priya Kanta and Kiron Bala (Thakurta) Ghoshal; m. Chhanda Banerjee, Jan. 24, 1971; 1 child, Nupur. G.V.Sc., B.V.C., India, 1955; DTVM, U. Edinburgh, 1961; DVM, Tieraertzliche Hochschule Hannover, Fed. Republic Germany, 1962; PhD, Iowa State U., 1966. Vet. asst. surgeon West Bengal State Govt., India, 1955-56; instr. Bengal Vet. Coll., U. Calcutta, 1955-56; rsch. asst. M.P. Govt. Coll. Vet. Sci. and Animal Husbandry, Mhow, India, 1956-59; rsch. officer ICAR, India, 1963; instr. Iowa State U., Ames, 1963-66, asst. prof., 1967-70, assoc. prof., 1970-74, prof. vet. gross anatomy, 1974—. Chmn. Internat. Vet. Medicine Com., 1967—79; cons. Morocco-Minn. project U. Minn. Internat. Agrl. Programs, AID, 1983—88; adj. prof. Inst. Agronomique et Veterinaire, Hassan II, Rabat, Morocco, 1984—88. Co-author, editor: book Getty's Anatomy of Domestic Animals, 5th edit., 1975; author (with Tankred Koch, Peter Popesko): Venous Drainage of Domestic Animals, 1981; contbr. chapters to books, articles to profl. jours. Recipient German Acad. Exch. Svc. award, Govt. Fed. Republic of Germany, Bonn, 1961—62, Norden Disting. Tchr. award, 1978, Dr. William O. Reece award for Outstanding Advising, Coll. Vet. Medicine, 1997; various scholarships and grants. Fellow: Royal Zool. Soc. Scotland (life); mem.: AAAS, Iowa Vet. Med. Assn., N.Y. Acad. Scis., Pan Am. Assn. Anatomy, Am. Assn. Anatomists, Am. Assn. Vet. Anatomists, World Assn. Vet. Anatomists, Sigma Xi, Phi Kappa Phi, Gamma Sigma Delta, Phi Zeta. Home: 1310 Glendale Ave Ames IA 50010-5526 Office: Iowa State U Coll Vet Medicine 2086 Dept Biomed Scis Ames IA 50011-1250 E-mail: nghoshal@iastate.edu.

GIACHELLO, AIDA L., social worker; b. San Juan; BA, Univ. Puerto Rico; AM, Univ. Chgo., PhD in Sociology. Assoc. prof. Jane Addams Coll. of Social Work, Univ. Ill., Chgo.; founder, dir. Midwest Latino Health Rsch., Training & Policy Ctr., Chgo., 1993—. Mem. study group Nat. Acad. Sci., Inst. Medicine, 2002—04; mem. intervention com., US-Mex. Border Diabetes Project Pan-american Health Org., 2002—; mem. planning com. Hispanic Cancer Genetic Rsch. Conf., 2002—03; mem. at. Latino steering com. on tobacco control Am. Legacy Found., 2000—; mem. Ill. Diabetes adv. com. Ill. Dept. Health & Human Svc., 1999—; bd. dir. Health & Med. Policy Rsch. Group, Chgo., 1985—. Contbr. articles to profl. jours. Bd. mem. Nat. Inst. for Diversity, Am. Hosp. Assn., 2001—03; mem. nat. survey com. on alternative med. NIH; mem. HIV/AIDS adv. com. Ctr. for Substance Abuse & Prevention, 1995—2000; mem. bd. adv. Catholic Charities, 1997—. Named one of 25 Most Influential Hispanics, Time Mag., 2005. Mem.: Am. Pub. Health Assn., Hispanic Nat. Inst. for Reproductive Health. Office: Midwest Latino Health Research Training & Policy Ctr Ste 636 DHSP Bldg 1640 W Roosevelt Rd Chicago IL 60608-6906

GIAMPIETRO, WAYNE BRUCE, lawyer; b. Chgo., Jan. 20, 1942; s. Joseph Anthony and Jeannette Marie (Zeller) G.; m. Mary E. Fordeck, June 15, 1963; children: Joseph, Anthony, Marcus. BA, Purdue U., 1963; JD, Northwestern U., 1966. Bar: Ill. 1966, U.S. Dist. Ct. (no. dist.) Ill. 1966, U.S. Ct. Appeals (7th cir.) 1967, U.S. Tax Ct. 1977, U.S. Supreme Ct. 1971. Assoc. Elmer Gertz, Chgo., 1966-73; mem. firm Gertz & Giampietro, Chgo., 1974-75; pvt. practice, 1975-76; ptnr. Poltrock & Giampietro, 1976-87, Witwer, Burlage, Poltrock & Giampietro, 1987-94, Witwer, Poltrock & Giampietro, Chgo., 1995—2002, Stitt, Klein, Daday, Aretos & Giampietro LLC, Arlington Heights, Ill., 2003—. Former cons. atty. Looking Glass divsn. Traveler's Aid Soc.; gen. counsel First Amendment Lawyers Assn., 2000—. Contbr. articles to profl. jours. Pres. Chgo. 47th Ward Young Republicans, 1968; bd. dirs. Ravenswood Conservation Commn. Lutheran. Avocation: stamp collecting/philately. Office Phone: 847-590-8700. Business E-Mail: wgiampietro@skdaglaw.com.

GIANCOLA, JAMES J., bank executive; Grad., Harvard U.; postgrad., Suffolk U., Boston; student, U. Colo. Pres. Gainer Bank, Ind.; exec. v.p. CNB Bancshares, Inc., 1992, pres., COO, 1994; CEO Midwest Banc, 2004—. Cmty. work U. So. Ind., U. Evansville, Evansville Dance Theatre, United Way, Leadership Evansville. Mem. Methodist Temple. Office: Midwest Banc 501 W North Ave Melrose Park IL 60160

GIANGRECO, MARK, sportscaster, director; 3 children. BA in Comm., U. Dayton, Ohio, 1974. Reporter news and sports WING-AM, Dayton, Ohio, 1972—76; weekend sports anchor and reporter WDTN-TV, 1976—77; sports dir. and anchor WLKY-TV, Louisville, 1978—82; weekend anchor and reporter WMAQ-TV, Chgo., 1982—83, sports anchor and reporter, 1983—94; sports dir. and primary sports anchor WLS-TV, 1994—. Recipient Iris award, Nat. Assn. TV Program Exec., Louisville Journalism award excellence in sports reporting, 1982, two Peter Lisagor awards, Best Sportscast, AP, 1996, 1996, Dante award, Joint Civic Com. of Italian Ams., 1995, Justinian Soc. of Italian Lawyers Journalism award, 1995, Father of Yr., Chgo. Father's Day Coun., 1996. Office: WLS-TV 190 N State St Chicago IL 60601 Home Phone: 312-454-0921; Office Phone: 312-750-7777. Business E-Mail: mark.f.giangreco@abc.com.

GIANITSOS, ANESTIS NICHOLAS, surgeon; b. Chios, Greece, Aug. 31, 1961; came to U.S., 1966; s. Dimitrios and Soultani (Zannikos) G.; m. Laurie S. Hallmark, children: Alexia Soultani, Dimitri Jacob. BA summa cum laude, Boston U., 1983, MD, 1987. Physician U. Wis. Hosp., Madison, 1987—92; pres. Tricorp Informational Svcs., Williams Bay, Wis., 1989—93; staff urologist Riverview Clinic, Janesville, Wis., 1992—98; pres. Geneva Mktg. Sys., Lake Geneva, Wis., 1996—; med. dir. Men's Health Ctr. Mercy Health Sys., So. Wis., No. Ill., 1998—; staff urologist Mercy Regional Urology Ctr., Janesville, 1998—, Mercy Waliworth Hosp. and Med. Ctr., 1998—, Harvard Meml. Hosp., Ill., 2003—. Cons. Rural Wis. Hosp. Coop., Sauk City, 1989-93; staff urology Mercy Health Sys., Janesville, 1998—; med. dir. So. Wis. chpt. US TOO, 1993—. Mem. editl. bd. Men's Total Health Digest, 2001—; contbr. articles to profl. jours. Commonwealth scholar, Augustus Howe Buck scholar. Fellow Internat. Coll. Surgeons; mem. Am. Assn. Clin. Urologists, Am. Urologic Assn., Wis. Med. Soc., Pelvic Health Consortium, Inc. Republican. Greek Orthodox. Avocations: photography, travel, baseball, investing, rare wine. Office: Mercy Men's Health Ctr 1000 Mineral Point Ave Janesville WI 53545-2940 Office Phone: 800-662-6990. Business E-Mail: ngianitsos@mhsjvl.org.

GIANNELLA, ANDREW R., lawyer; b. Apr. 1, 1970; BA, Colgate U., 1992; JD, U. Cin. Coll. Law, 1996. Bar: Ohio 1996, Ky. 2003. Of counsel Strauss & Troy, Cin. Named one of Ohio's Rising Stars, Super Lawyers, 2006; named to Best Lawyers in Am., Real Estate Law, 2006. Office: Strauss & Troy Fed Res Bldg 150 E Fourth St Cincinnati OH 45202-4018 Office Phone: 513-621-2120. Office Fax: 513-241-8259.

GIANNETTI, LOUIS DANIEL, film critic, educator; b. Natick, Mass., Apr. 1, 1937; s. John and Vincenza (Zappitelli) G.; m. Justine Ann Gallagher, Sept. 7, 1963 (div. 1980); children: Christina, Francesca. BA, Boston U., 1959; MA, U. Iowa, 1961, PhD, 1967. Asst. prof. English Emory U., Atlanta, 1966-70; prof. English and film Case Western Res. U., Cleve., 1970—2001, prof. emeritus English and film, 2002—. Author: Understanding Movies, 1972, rev. 11th edit., 2007, Godard and Others, 1975, Masters of the American Cinema, 1981, (with S. Eyman) Flashback, 1986, 5th rev. edit., 2005. Democrat. Office: Case Western Res U Dept English Euclid Ave Cleveland OH 44106-2706 E-mail: louisgiannetti@aol.com.

GIANNOULIAS, ALEXI, state official; b. 1976; BA, Boston Univ.; JD, Tulane Univ. V.p., sr. loan officer Broadway Bank, Chgo.; state treas. Ill., 2007—. Bd. dir. South Side/Wabash YMCA, Edgewater C. of C. Office: State Treas 219 Statehouse Capitol Bldg Springfield IL 62706 Office Phone: 217-782-2211. Office Fax: 217-785-2777.

GIANOPOULOS, JOHN GEORGE, obstetrician; b. 1952; MD, Loyola U., Stritch Sch. Medicine, Maywood, Ill., 1977. Cert. Am. Bd. Obstetrics and Gynecology, 1984, in Maternal and Fetal Medicine 1985. Resident, ob-gyn. Loyola U. Med. Ctr., Maywood, Ill., 1977—81, fellow, maternal fetal medicine, 1981—83; Mary Isabelle Caestecker prof., chmn. dept., ob-gyn. Loyola U., Stritch Sch. Medicine, Maywood, Ill., 1997—. Office: Loyola Univ Sch Medicine 2160 First Ave Maywood IL 60153 Business E-Mail: jgianop@lumc.edu.

GIANOS, DIANE E., lawyer; BS, DePaul U., 1984; JD, Chgo.-Kent Coll. Law, 1989. Bar: Ill. 1989, US Dist. Ct. (no. and ctrl. dists. Ill.), US Ct. Appeals (5th & 6th cirs.) 1990. Ptnr., mem. labor & employment practice Foley & Lardner, Chgo. Office: Foley & Lardner Suite 2800 321 N Clark St Chicago IL 60610 Office Phone: 312-832-5158. Office Fax: 312-832-4700. E-mail: dgianos@foley.com.

GIAQUINTA, BENJAMIN E., state representative; b. Brockton, Mass., Nov. 8, 1922; married; 6 children. Grad., La. State U., 1953. With Wehrly Realtors; state rep. dist. 80 Ind. Ho. of Reps., Indpls., 1996—, health and medicaid subcom. chmn., ways and means com., mem. cts. and criminal code, and pub. policy, ethics and vets affairs coms. Mem. adv. bd. Wayne Twp., Ind., 1986—90. Mem.: Southside Bus. Group, Ft. Wayne Area Assn. Realtors (govtl. issues com.), Am. Inst. Parliamentarians, Allen County Load Closers Assn., C. of C., One Summit Club 5254, Toastmasters Internat., Am. Legion Post 296. Office: Ind Ho of Reps 200 W Washington St Indianapolis IN 46204-2786

GIBALA, RONALD, metallurgical engineering educator; b. New Castle, Pa., Oct. 3, 1938; s. Steve Anthony and June Rose (Frank) G.; m. Janice Claire Grichor; children: Maryellen, Janice, David, Kristine. BS, Carnegie Inst. Tech., 1960; MS, U. Ill., 1962, PhD, 1964. Engring. technician Crane Co., New Castle, Pa., 1956-59; engr. U.S. Steel Rsch. Labs., Monroeville, Pa., 1960; rsch. asst. U. Ill., Urbana, 1960-64; asst. prof. metallurgy Case Western Res. U., Cleve., 1964-69, assoc. prof., 1969-76, prof. metallurgy and materials sci. and macro-molecular sci., 1976-84, co-dir. materials rsch. lab., 1981-84; dir. metallurgy program NSF, 1982-83; prof., chmn. dept. materials sci. and engring. U. Mich., Ann Arbor, 1984-94, L.H. and F.E. Van Vlack prof. materials sci. and engring., 1998—2004, L.H. and F.E. Van Vlack prof. emeritus, 2004—, interim dean Coll. Engring., 2005—06. Dir. electron microbeam analysis lab. U. Mich., Ann Arbor, 2002—04. Contbr. articles to profl. jours.; editor: Hydrogen Embrittlement and Stress Corrosion Cracking, 1984. Pres. Woodhaven Hills Homeowners Assn., 1989—91. Recipient Alfred Noble prize ASCE, 1969, NASA Materials Sci. Divsn. Paper award, 1992; Tech. Achievement award Cleve. Tech. Socs. Council, 1972; vis. research fellow C.E.N.G. Labs., Grenoble, 1973-74; Mathias fellow Los Alamos Nat. Lab., 1991-92, Disting. Merit award U. Ill., 1998; vis. scientist Sandia Nat. Labs., 1998-99. Fellow: TMS (bd. dirs. 1981—87), Am. Soc. Metals Internat. (life; chpt. chmn. 1975—76, Outstanding Young Mem. Cleve. chpt. 1971); mem.: AAAS (Woody award 2007), Materials Rsch. Soc. (councillor 1995—97, v.p. 1998, pres. 1999, exec. com. 1995—97), Suburban Ski (pres. 1981—82), Alpha Sigma Mu, Tau Beta Pi, Sigma Xi. Democrat. Home: 1543 Stonehaven St Ann Arbor MI 48104-4149 Office: U Mich Dept Materials Sci Engring Ann Arbor MI 48109-2136 Office Phone: 734-936-0178. Business E-Mail: rgibala@umich.edu.

GIBANS, JAMES DAVID, architect, consultant; b. Akron, Ohio, Feb. 10, 1930; s. Myer Jacob and Sylva (Hirsch) G.; m. Nina Freedlander, July 16, 1955; children: David Myer, Jonathan Samuel, Amy, Elisabeth. BA, Yale U., 1951, BArch, MArch, Yale U., 1954. Architect George K. Raad & Assocs. et al, San Francisco, 1958-63; project architect Ward and Schneider, Cleve., 1964-68; sr. assoc. William A. Gould and Assocs., Cleve., 1968-74, Don M. Hisaka and Assoc., Cleve., 1974-76; pvt. practice architecture Cleve., 1976-81; v.p. Teare Herman & Gibans, Inc., Cleve., 1981-89; v.p., treas. Herman Galvin Gibans, Inc., Cleve., 1989-91, HGG, Inc., Cleve., 1991-94, Herman Gibans Fodor, Inc., 1994—2000, v.p., 1994—2006; consulting arch., 2007—. Faculty Edn. for Aesthetic Awareness Cleve. State U., 1977—79. Mem. Cleve. Landmarks Commn., 1993—2006, chmn., 2004—06; trustee, mem. exec. com., 1st v.p. Cleve. Chamber Music Soc., 1970—78; mem. adv. bd. Environ. Resource Ctr. Cleve. Pub. Libr., 1973—76; mem. design rev. com. Shaker Sq. Hist. Dist., 1991—93; bd. dir. Cleve. Soc. Contemporary Art, 1985—86, Friends of Shaker Sq., 1994—96, Shaker Sq. Area Devel. Corp., 1996—, v.p., 1996—97, treas., 1997—2001, pres., 2001—03; trustee Cleve. Found. for Arch., 1999—2003, chair focus com., 1999—2001, pres., 2001—03; bd. dir. Bulldogs on the Cuyahoga, 2002—, treas., 2006—. With US Army, 1955—57. Fulbright grantee, 1954-55. Fellow AIA (sec. Cleve. chpt. 1972-74, bd. dirs. 1984-86, treas. 1989, v.p. 1990, pres. 1991); mem. Architects Soc. Ohio (trustee 1975-76, bd. dirs. 1985-88), Cleve. City Club, Fulbright Assn. (bd. dirs. N.E. Ohio chpt. 1995-99, treas. 1998-99), N.E. Ohio Jazz Soc. (bd. dirs. 1991-96, v.p. 1993-95, pres. 1995-96), Rowfant Club (chair bldgs. and furnishings com. 2002—, coun. of fellows, 2005—). Democrat. Jewish. Avocations: music, art, jogging, cross country skiing. Home and Office: 13800 Shaker Blvd 1108 Cleveland OH 44120-1585

GIBBONS, JOHN, mortgage company executive; BA in Social Studies, Harvard U.; PhDin Govt.; MBA, U. Pa. Asst. prof. social scis. U. Chgo.; rating specialist Std. & Poor's Corp.; dir. mortgage fin. group, v.p. mortgage fin. Merrill Lynch, v.p. mortgage rsch. group, dir. fin. instns. group; v.p. fin. rsch. Freddie Mac, 1991, acting CFO, sr. v.p. corp. rels., CFO, 1996; vice chmn. Overture Tech., Bethesda, Md. Office: Overture Technologies Ste 200 6900 Wisconsin Ave Chevy Chase MD 20815

GIBBONS, MICHAEL RANDOLPH, state legislator, lawyer; b. Kirkwood, Mo., Mar. 24, 1959; s. Michael and Folsta Sara (Bailey) G.; m. Elizabeth Weddell, Jan. 30, 1988; children: Danny, Meredith. BA, Westminster Coll., 1981; JD, St. Louis U., 1984. Bar: Mo. 1984. Assoc. Michael Gibbons, Kirkwood, 1984-86; ptnr. Gibbons and Gibbons, Kirkwood, 1986—; mem. Mo. Ho. of Reps. from 88th dist., Jefferson City, 1992-2000; mem. various coms.; mem. Mo. Senate from 15th dist., Jefferson City, 2001—. Mem. coun. City of Kirkwood, 1986-92; dep. mayor, 1990-92; mem. Bonhomme Twp. Rep. Club, v.p., 1985-87, bd. dirs.; vestry mem. Grace Episcopal Ch., Kirkwood, 1986-88; bd. dirs. Edgewood Children's Ctr., 1996—, Citizens for Modern Transit, 1996—. Mem. Bar Assn. of Met. St. Louis, Kirkwood C. of C. (bd. dirs. 1986-88), Kiwanis (pres. Kirkwood chpt. 1986-87). Republican. Avocation: sports. Home: 651 Pearl Ave Kirkwood MO 63122-2721 Office: Gibbons & Gibbons PC 214 N Clay Ave Kirkwood MO 63122-4004

GIBBONS, PATRICK CHANDLER, physicist, researcher; b. Washington, Dec. 18, 1943; s. Myles Francis and Margaret Mack (Chandler) G.; m. Jane Elizabeth Forsell, Aug. 17, 1968; children: Elizabeth Jane, Jonathan Myles, Jane Chandler, Katherine Forsell. BS, Georgetown U., 1965; PhD, Harvard U., 1971. Physics instr. Princeton (N.J.) U., 1971-73, asst. prof. physics, 1973-76, Washington U., St. Louis, 1976-79, assoc. prof. physics, 1979-89, prof. physics, 1989—. Contbr. articles to Philos. mag., Jour. Non-Crystal Solids. Trustee Univ. Hills Subdivsn., University City, Mo., 1984-87. Mem. Am. Phys. Soc., Univ. City Swim Club (pres. 1988-90, 94-95), Sigma Xi, Phi Beta Kappa. Office: Washington U PO Box 1105 Saint Louis MO 63188-1105 Office Phone: 314-935-6271.

GIBBONS, RAYMOND JOHN, cardiologist; b. NYC, Sept. 4, 1949; BSE in Aerospace and Mechanical Sciences, Princeton U.; MS, MSc in Math., U. Oxford, Eng.; MD, Harvard Med. Sch., 1976. Intern Mass. Gen. Hosp., Boston, 1976-77, resident, internal medicine, 1977-78; fellow, cardiovascular divsn., dept. medicine Duke U. Med. Ctr., Durham, 1978-81; prof. medicine Mayo Med. Sch., 1992—. Contbr. articles to profl. jours.; mem. editl. bd. Circulation, Jour. Am. Heart Assn., Jour. Am. Coll. of Cardiology and others. Fellow Am. Coll. Cardiology; Am. Heart Assn. (pres. 2006-07). Office: Mayo Clinic 200 1st St SW Rochester MN 55905-0002 Office Phone: 507-284-2541. Business E-Mail: gibbons.raymond@mayo.edu.*

GIBBONS, ROBERT D., biostatistics educator; b. Chgo., June 28, 1955; s. Sidney W. and Rozlyn Gibbons; m. Carol Homa, Sept. 16, 1979; children: Julie, Jason. BA, U. Denver, 1976; PhD, U. Chgo., 1981. Asst. prof. biostats. U. Ill., Chgo., 1981-85, assoc. prof., 1985-93, prof., 1993—; dir. Ctr. Health Stats., U. Ill., 2000—. Mem. health sci. policy bd. NAS-Inst. Medicine, Washington, 1999—, mem. com. on efficacy and safety of hypnotic halcion, 1998, mem. com. on solid organ transplantation, 1999; reviewer health svcs. rsch. internal rev. group NIH, 1992-95; mem. com. on organ transplantation Inst. Medicine, 1999; testifier on allocation organs for transplantation U.S. Congress, 1999. Author: Statistical Methods for Groundwater Monitoring, 1994, Statistical Methods for Detection and Quantification of Environmental Contamination, 2000; contbr. articles to sci. jours., including Jour. Am. Statis. Assn., Sci. Recipient young investigator award Office Naval Rsch., 1985, rsch. scientist award NIH, 1995, 20th Century Disting. Svc. award Lukacs Symposium, 1999. Mem.: Inst. Medicine. Avocations: skiing, tennis. Office: U Ill at Chgo 1601 W Taylor St Chicago IL 60612-4310 Fax: 312-996-2113. E-mail: rdgib@uic.edu.

GIBBONS, WILLIAM JOHN, lawyer; b. Chgo., Jan. 22, 1947; s. Edward and Lottie (Gasiorek) G.; children: Maximilian Clay, Bartholomew David, Ariel Katherine. BA, orthwestern U., 1968, JD, 1972. Bar: Ill. 1972, U.S. Dist. Ct. (no. dist.) Ill. 1972, U.S. Ct. Appeals (9th cir.) 1980, U.S. Supreme Ct. 1982, U.S. Ct. Appeals (7th cir.) 1984, U.S. Ct. Appeals (3d cir.) 2002. Assoc. Kirkland and Ellis, Chgo., 1972-76; ptnr. Hedlund, Hunter and Lynch, Chgo., 1976-82, Latham and Watkins, Chgo., 1982—, mng. ptnr. Chgo. office, 1995-2000. Served with USAR, 1968-74. Mem.: ABA, Chgo. Coun. Lawyers, Seventh Cir. Bar Assn., Chgo. Bar Assn. (chair class action com. 1994—95), Riverpark Club (Chgo.). Home: 1515 S Prairie # 913 Chicago IL 60605-3024 Office: Latham & Watkins Sears Tower Ste 5800 Chicago IL 60606-6306 Home Phone: 312-588-0844; Office Phone: 312-876-7706. Business E-Mail: william.gibbons@lw.com.

GIBBONS, WILLIAM REGINALD, JR., poet, writer, translator, editor; b. Houston, Jan. 7, 1947; s. William Reginald and Elizabeth (Lubowski) G.; m. Virginia Margaret Harris, June 8, 1968 (div. July 1982); m. Cornelia Maude Spelman, Aug. 18, 1983. AB, Princeton U., 1969; MA, Stanford U., 1971, PhD, 1974. Instr. Spanish Rutgers U., Brunswick, NJ, 1975-76; lectr. creative writing Princeton U., 1976-80, Columbia U., NYC, 1980-81; prof. English and Classics Northwestern U., Evanston, Ill., 1981—, chair English, 2002—05, editor TriQuarterly mag., 1981-97, dir., ctr. for the writing Arts; prof. MFA Program for Writers Warren Wilson Coll., 1989—. Author: Roofs Voices Roads, 1979 (Quar. Rev. prize), The Ruined Motel, 1981, Saints, 1986, Maybe It Was So, 1991, Five Pears or Peaches, 1991, William Goyen: A Study of the Short Fiction, 1991, Sweetbitter, 1994, Sparrow: New and Selected Poems, 1997, Homage to Longshot O'Leary, 1999, It's Time, 2002, In the Warhouse, 2004, Fern-Texts, 2005, Creatures of a Day, 2008; translator: Selected Poems of Luis Cernuda, 1978, Guillén on Guillén, 1979, (with Charles Segal) Euripides' Bakkhai, 2001, (with Charles Segal) Sophokles' Antigone, 2003, Sophokles Selected Poems, 2008; editor: The Poet's Work, 1979; (with G. Graff) Criticism in the University, 1985, The Writer in Our World, 1986, Fiction of the Eighties, 1990, Thomas McGrath: Life and the Poem, 1991, New Writing from Mexico, 1992, Goyen: Autobiographical Essays, Notebooks, Evocations, Interviews, 2007. Woodrow Wilson fellow Stanford U., 1969-70; Fulbright fellow Spain, 1971-72; Guggenheim fellow, 1983-84; NEA fellow, 1984; Ill. Arts Coun. fellow, 1988; recipient Translation prize Denver Quar., 1977, Short Story award Tex. Inst. Letters, 1986, Carl Sandburg award, 1992, Anisfield-Wolf Book award, 1995, Jesse Jones award Tex. Inst. Letters, 1995, Ill. Arts Coun. Lit. awards, 1996, 97, Balcones Poetry prize, 1998, Best Book of Poetry award Tex. Inst. Letters, 2003, O.B. Hardison Jr. Poetry prize Folger Libr., 2004. Mem. PEN Am. Ctr., Poetry Soc. Am. (John Masefield Meml. award 1991), Associated Writing Programs (bd. dirs. 1984-87), The Guild Complex (bd. dirs. 1989—). Office: Northwestern U Dept English Univ Hall 215 Evanston IL 60208-0001 Office Phone: 847-491-7294. Business E-Mail: rgibbons@northwestern.edu.

GIBBS, BOB, state representative; b. Peru, Ind., June 14, 1954; m. Jody Cox; 3 children. Grad. Agrl. Tech. Inst., Ohio State U., 1974. Co-owner, oper. Hidden Hollow Farms, Ltd., Holmes, Ashland and Richland Counties, Ohio; state rep. dist. 97 Ohio Ho. of Reps., Columbus, 2002—, vice chmn., agr. and natural resources com., mem. natural resources parks and recreation subcom., and banking pensions and securities, econ. devel. and tech., and ins. coms., mem. select com. on Ohio's competitive edge for job creation and retention. Past bd. dirs. Farm Bur. Bank, Ohio Livestock Coalition, Ohio Coop. Coun., Ohio Farm Bur. Alliance Group. Past pres., bd. dirs. Loudonville (Ohio) Farmer's Equity; past pres. Ohio Farm Bur. Fedn.; bd. trustees Ohio Farm Bur. Recipient Pork All-Am. award, Nat. Pork Prodr.'s Coun. Methodist. Office: 77 S High St 11th fl Columbus OH 43215-6111

GIBSON, DAVID THOMAS, microbiology educator; b. Wakefield, Yorkshire, Eng., Feb. 16, 1938; U.S. citizen; married; two children. BSc in Biochemistry 1st class honors, U. Leeds, Eng., 1961, PhD in Biochemistry, 1964. Lectr. in biology Leeds Tech. Coll., 1962-63; rsch. assoc. U. Wis. Coll. Pharmacy, Madison, 1964-65; rsch. assoc. dept. microbiology U. Ill., Champaign-Urbana, 1965-67; asst. prof. microbiology dept. U. Tex., Austin, 1967-68, 69-71, assoc. prof. microbiology dept., 1971-75, prof. microbiology dept., 1975-88, dir. Ctr. for Applied Microbiology, 1981-88; Edwin B. Green prof. biocatalysis and microbiology Coll. Medicine, U. Iowa, Iowa City, 1988—2004; ret., 2004. Rsch. biochemist pharms. divsn. I.C.I. Ltd., Aderley Park, Cheshire, Eng., 1968-69; L.Am. vis. prof. Nat. Poly. Inst., Mexico City, 1976; mem. microbial chemistry study sect. NIH, 1977-80; mem. sci. adv. bd. AMGEN, 1981-88; mem. various univ. coms. Assoc. editor Devels. in Indsl. Microbiology, 1975-79; mem. editl. bd. Jour. Bacteriology, 1979-83, 88-91, 95-97, Jour. Biol. Chemistry, 1980-88, Biodegradation, 1989-96; contbr. numerous articles to profl. jours. Recipient Career Devel. award USPHS, 1972-77; grantee NIH, 1995—, USAF, 1996-99. Fellow AAAS; mem. Am. Soc. for Microbiology (Found. lectr. 1981-82, Procter and Gamble award in appled and environ. microbiology 1997), Am. Chem. Soc., Soc. for Indsl. Microbiology, Fedn. Am. Socs. for Exptl. Biology, Am. Acad. Microbiology (mem. nominating com. 1988-90), NAS, Sigma Xi, Phi Kappa Phi. Office: U Iowa Dept Microbiology 3733 Bowen Science Building Iowa City IA 52242-1109 E-mail: david.gibson@uiowa.edu.

GIBSON, JOHN ROBERT, federal judge; b. Springfield, Mo., Dec. 20, 1925; s. Harry B. and Edna (Kerr) G.; m. Mary Elizabeth Vaughn, Sept. 20, 1952 (dec. Aug. 1985); children: Jeanne, John Robert; m. Diane Allen Larrison, Oct. 1, 1986 (div. 2006); stepchildren: Holly, Catherine. AB, U. Mo., 1949, JD, 1952. Bar: Mo. 1952. Assoc. Morrison, Hecker, Curtis, Kuder & Parrish, Kansas City, Mo., 1952-58, ptnr., 1958-81; judge US Dist. Ct. (we. dist.) Mo., 1981-82, US Ct. Appeals (8th cir.), 1982-94, sr. judge, 1994—. Mem. Mo. Press-Bar Commn., 1979-81; mem. com. on adminstrn. of magistrate sys. Jud. Conf. U.S., 1987-91, mem. security and facilities com., 1995-2001. Vice chmn. Jackson County Charter Transition Com., 1971-72; mem. Jackson County Charter Commn., 1970; v.p. Police Commrs. Bd., Kansas City, 1973-77. With US Army, 1944—46. Recipient Citation of Merit award U. Mo. at Columbia Sch. of Law, 1994. Fellow Am. Bar Found.; mem. Mo. State Bar (gov. 1972-79, pres. 1977-78; Pres.' award 1974, Smithson award 1984), Kansas City Bar Assn. (pres. 1970-71), Lawyers Assn. Kansas City (Charles Evan Whittaker award 1980), Fed. Judges Assn. (bd. dirs. 1991-97), Phi Beta Kappa, Omicron Delta Kappa. Presbyterian. Office: US Ct Appeals 8th Cir 400 E 9th St Ste 1040 Kansas City MO 64106-2695

GIBSON, MCGUIRE, archaeologist, educator; b. Bushwood, Md., Nov. 6, 1938; s. Thomas Laurie and Essie Mae (Owens) Gibson. BA, Fordham U., 1959; MA, U. Chgo., 1964, PhD, 1968. Asst. prof. anthropology U. Ill., Chgo., 1968-71; asst. prof. U. Ariz., Tucson, 1971-72; from asst. prof. to assoc. prof. U. Chgo., 1972—81, prof., 1981—. Ann. prof. Am. Schs. Oriental Rsch., Baghdad, Iraq, 1969—70; dir. Nippur Expdn., Iraq, 1972—, Dhamar Expdn., Yemen, 1978—98, Hamoukar Expdn., Syria, 1999—; chmn. Coun. Am. Overseas Rsch. Ctrs., 1984—88, treas., 1988—92, mem. exec. com., 1995—2001; pres. Am. Acad. Rsch. Inst. in Iraq, 2003—. Author: (book) The City and Area of Kish, 1972; editor: Irrigation's Impact on Society, 1974, Seals and Sealing in the Ancient Near East, 1977, The Organization of Power: Aspects of Bureaucracy in the Ancient Near East, 1987, Uch Tepe II, 1990, Nippur III, 1993; author, editor: book Excavations in Nippur, 12th Season, 1978, Uch Tepe I, 1981. Mem. UNESCO Fact-Finding Mission to Iraq, 2003; mem. arts com. Union League Civic and Arts Found., Chgo., 1984—86; mem. adv. bd. Chgo. Humanities Festival, 2003—. Recipient Yemeni Arch. Svc. award, 1998; grantee, Am. Numismatic Soc., 1966, Am. Philos. Soc., 1969, Nat. Geog. Soc., 1978, 1989, NSF, 1994, 2000, NEH, 1995—98. Fellow: Deutsche Orient-Gesellchaft, Royal Anthrop. Inst., Brit. Sch. Archaeology Iraq; mem.: AAAS, Civil War Landscapes Assn., Am. Assn. Rsch. Baghdad, Mid. E. Studies Assn., Am. Inst. Yemeni Studies, Am. Anthrop. Assn., Archaeological Inst. Am., Quadrangle Club. Democrat. Avocations: architectural restoration, study of oriental rugs. Office: U Chgo Oriental Inst 1155 E 58th St Chicago IL 60637-1540 Home Phone: 773-862-7297; Office Phone: 773-702-9525. E-mail: m-gibson@uchicago.edu.

GIBSON, ROGER, air transportation executive; B in Mgmt., St. Mary's Coll., Moraga, Calif. Joined United Airlines, 1967, held various mgmt. positions, v.p. .Am. mountain region Chgo., 1995—. Bd. dirs. First Am. Funds, Met. State Coll. Denver Found., Nat. Jewish Med. Ctr. Bd. dirs. Denver Area Coun., Boy Scouts Am., Colo. Uplift, Colo. Ocean Journey, Denver Found. With USN, 1964—70. Office: United Airlines PO Box 66100 WH QSA Chicago IL 60666

GIDWITZ, RONALD J., personal care products company executive; b. Chgo., 1945; Grad., Brown U., 1967. With Helene Curtis, Chgo., 1968-96, pres., 1979-96, CEO, 1985-96, pres. divsn. Unilever, 1996; chmn. Salon123, Inc., Chgo. Bd. dirs. Continental Materials Corp., Am. Nat. Can Co., Mus. Sci and Industry. Bd. dirs. Field Mus. Nat. History, Lyric Opera Chgo.; chmn. bd. trustees City Colls. Chgo.; mem. nat. bd. dirs., gov. Boys and Girls Club Am. Mem. Chicagoland C. of C. Office: Ronald J Gidwitz Family Trust Rjg Trust 200 S Wacker Dr Fl 4000 Chicago IL 60606-5821

GIELOW, CURT, state official; b. Mar. 18, 1945; m. Mary Gielow; children: Christopher, Benjamin. B in Pharmacy; M in Healthcare Adminstrn., Washington U., 1973. Small businessman; owner, pres. Gielow Assocs., reEmploy.com; alderman Sixth Dist., Mequon, 1997—2002; pres. Mequon Common Coun., 2001—02; state assemblyman Wis., 2002—. Pres. St. John's Luth. Ch. and Sch., Glendale; mem. Luth. Home Found. Bd. Republican. Lutheran. Office: State Capitol Rm 316 N PO Box 8952 Madison WI 53708-8952

GIERTZ, J. FRED, economics professor; b. Wichita, Kans., Jan. 18, 1943; s. Joe L. and Frieda J. (Hamblin) G.; m. Donna Hyland, Sept. 13, 1969; children: Seth H., Gabrielle H. BA, Wichita U., 1964; MA, Northwestern U., 1966, PhD, 1970. Instr. econs. Miami U., Oxford, Ohio, 1968-70, asst. prof., 1970-73, asso. prof., 1973-78, prof., 1978-80; prof. econs. Inst. Govt. and Pub. Affairs U. Ill., Urbana, 1980—, acting dir., 1993-94; exec. dir. Nat. Tax Assn., 2000—. Rsch. dir. Ill. Tax Reform Commn., 1982-83; dir. Ameritech fellowship program U. Ill., 1987-93; trustee State Univs. Retirement System, 1995-2005; cons. in field. Mem. editl. bd.: Quarterly Rev. Econs. and Bus, 1979-88; contbr. articles in field to profl. jours. Mem. athletic bd. U. Ill., 1998-2002. Mem. Midwest Econs. Assn. (v.p. 1978-79), Am. Econ. Assn., Ill. Econ. Assn. (pres. 1986-87), Pub. Choice Soc., Nat. Tax Assn., Univ. Club Chgo., Champaign Country Club. Home: 601 Park Lane Dr Champaign IL 61820-7630 Office: U Ill Inst Govt Pub Affairs 1007 W Nevada St Urbana IL 61801-3812 Office Phone: 217-244-4822. Business E-Mail: jgiertz@uiuc.edu.

GIESEN, RICHARD ALLYN, business executive; b. Evanston, Ill., Oct. 7, 1929; s. Elmer J. and Ethyl (Lillig) G.; m. Jeannine St. Bernard, Jan. 31, 1953; children: Richard Allyn Jr., Laurie J., Mark St. B. BS, Northwestern U., 1951. Research analyst new bus. and research depts. Glore, Forgan & Co., Chgo., 1951-57; asst. to pres. Gen. Dynamics Corp., NYC, 1957-60, asst. treas., 1960-61, asst. v.p. ops. and contracts, 1961-63; fin. cons. IBM Corp., 1963, exec. asst. to sr. v.p., 1964-65; treas. subs. Sci. Research Assocs., Inc., Chgo., 1965-66, v.p. fin. and adminstrn., 1966-67, exec. v.p., chief operating officer, 1967-68, pres., chief exec. officer, 1968-80; pres., chief exec. officer, chmn. exec. com., dir. Field Enterprises, Inc., Chgo., 1980-83; pres. RLM Investments, 1983-93; chmn., pres., CEO Am. Appraisal Assocs., Inc., 1984-93; chmn. Continental Pkg. Solutions, Chgo., 1988—; chmn., CEO Continere Corp., 1988—. Mem. bus. adv. coun. Chgo. Urban League, 1968-83; prin. Chgo. United, 1980-83; dir. GATX, Inc., 1982-2000, JWT Group, 1980-1985, Smurfit Stone Container, 1998-2001, Stone Container, 1973-98; mem. adv. coun. Technol. Inst., Trustee Asia Ho. Funds, 1994-98; Northwestern U.; mem. pres.'s coun. Nat. Coll. Edn., Evanston, Ill., 1977-86; bd. dirs. Am. Cancer Soc.; mem. adv. coun. J.L. Kellogg Grad. Sch. Mgmt., Northwestern U.; dir. Jr. Achievement Chgo., 1993-2002; trustee Chgo. Edn. TV Assn., 1975-81, Inst. Internat. Edn., 1971-2003, chmn. midwest adv. bd., 1997-2003. Mem. Chief Execs. Orgn., Webhannet Golf Club, Chgo. Club, Shoreacres Club (Lake Bluff, Ill.), Alpha Tau Omega, Beta Gamma Sigma. Office: Continere Corp 230 W Monroe Ste 2400 Chicago IL 60606 Fax: 312-666-7501. E-mail: rag@continentalpackagingsolutions.com.

GILB, MIKE, state representative; b. 1960; married; 3 children. BS, U. Cin.; JD, Ohio No. U. Atty.; state rep. dist. 76 Ohio Ho. of Reps., Columbus, 2000—, chair, juvenile and family law com., mem. criminal justice, econ. devel. and tech., and ways and means coms. Mem.: Ohio Law Rev., Findlay-Hancock County Bar Assn., Ohio State Bar Assn., Hancock Preservation Guild, Black Heritage Libr., Hancock Hist. Mus., Kiwanis. Republican. Office: 77 S High St 13th fl Columbus OH 43215-6111

GILBERT, ALLAN ARTHUR, retired manufacturing executive; b. Chgo., Jan. 7, 1925; s. Allan T. and Elizabeth (Boyce) G.; m. Gwendolyn M. Moore, June 24, 1950; children: Debora D. and Elizabeth (twins), Allan M.; m. Elizabeth Clark, 1990; children: Tyler Clark, Allan Moore II. Buyer Carson Pirie Scott & Co., Chgo., 1949-55; v.p. George Fry & Assocs., Chgo., 1956-65; v.p. mktg. Chamberlain Mfg. Corp., Elmhurst, Ill., 1966-68; v.p. Lester B. Knight & Assocs., Chgo., 1968-75; v.p. manpower devel. Emerson Electric Co., St. Louis, 1975-92, cons., 1992-2000. Asst. prof. Roosevelt U., 1951-52. Mem. Gov.'s Adv. Council, Ill., 1969-70; fund raiser Ill. Republicans., 1966-67. Lt. (j.g.) USNR, 1944-46. Mem. Soc. Colonial Wars (dep. gov. Mo.), Univ. Club of Chgo., Princeton Club, Harvard Bus. Sch. Club. Personal E-mail: allanagilbert@cs.com.

GILBERT, DANIEL, professional sports team owner, mortgage company executive; married; 5 children. B, Mich. State U.; JD, Wayne State U. Bar: Mich. Founder, CEO, chmn. Rock Fin. Corp., 1985—99; founder, chmn. Quicken Loans, 2002—; ptnr. Camelot Ventures; majority owner NBA Cleve. Cavaliers, 2005—; operator Quicken Loans Arena, Cleve. Frequent guest on CNBC, including guest host on Morning Call; frequent guest ESPN, CNN, FOX, ABC and other networks. Past pres. Jewish Assn. Residential Care, Detroit; bd. dirs. Children's Tumor Found., NYC, Children's Hosp. Mich. Found. Named one of Forbes' Richest Ams., 2005, 2006; named to Jr. Achievement Hall of Fame; recipient Entrepreneur of Yr. award, Ernst and Young. Office: Quicken Loans 20555 Victor Pky Livonia MI 48152

GILBERT, DAVID R., public relations executive; Press sec. to Gov. James Thompson, Ill.; pres. David R. Gilbert & Assocs.; gen. mgr. Golin/Harris Comms., Chgo., 1993-96; pres. Golin/Harris Internat., Chgo., 1996—2001. Office: Golin/Harris Internat 10th Fl 111 E Wacker Dr Fl 10 Chicago IL 60601-4305

GILBERT, ELMER GRANT, engineering educator, control theorist; b. Joliet, Ill., Mar. 29, 1930; s. Harry A. and Florence A. (Otterstrom) G.; m. Lois M. Verbrugge, Dec. 27, 1973. BSEE, U. Mich., 1952, MSEE, 1953, PhD in Instrumentation Engring., 1956. Instr. U. Mich., Ann Arbor, 1954-56, asst. prof., 1957-59, assoc. prof., 1959-63, prof. aerospace engring., 1963—94, prof. emeritus, 1994—. Founder, Applied Dynamics Inc., Ann Arbor. Patentee computer devices, 1968-74. Fellow IEEE (Control Engring. Field award 1994), AAAS; mem. Nat. Acad. Engring., Soc. Indsl. and Applied Math. Office: U Mich Dept Aerospace Engring Ann Arbor MI 48109-2140 Home Phone: 734-971-6753; Office Phone: 734-764-3355. Business E-Mail: elmerg@umich.edu.

GILBERT, HOWARD N(ORMAN), lawyer, director; b. Chgo., Aug. 19, 1928; s. Norman Aaron and Fannie (Cohn) G.; m. Jacqueline Glasser, Feb. 16, 1957; children: Norman Abraham, Harlan Wayne, Joel Kenneth, Sharon. PhB, U. Chgo., 1947; JD, Yale U., 1951. Bar: Ill 1951, U.S. Dist. Ct. (no. dist.) Ill. 1955, U.S. Ct. Appeals (7th cir.) 1956. Ptnr. Rusnak, Deutsch & Gilbert, Chgo., 1962-79, Aaron, Schimberg, Hess & Gilbert, Chgo., 1980-84, Holleb & Coff, Chgo., 1984-2000, Wildman, Harrold, Chgo., 2000—. Bd. dirs. Jewish Fedn. Met. Chgo., 1977-83; chmn. bd. dirs., pres. Mt. Sinai Hosp. Med. Ctr., Chgo., 1968-69; trustee Chgo. Hosp. Coun., 1979-84; mem. Bd. Jewish Edn., 1972-77; mem. vis. com. Coll. of U. Chgo., 1997-2003. Mem. ABA, Chgo. Bar Assn., Chgo. Coun. Lawyers, Ill. Soc. Health Lawyers, Standard Club, Bryn Mawr Country Club. Democrat. Jewish. Office: Wildman Harrold Allen & Dixon 225 W Wacker Dr Ste 3000 Chicago IL 60606-1224 Office Phone: 312-201-2722. Business E-Mail: gilbert@wildman.com.

GILBERT, J. PHIL, federal judge; b. 1949; BS, U. Ill., 1971; JD, Loyola U., Chgo., 1974. Ptnr. Gilbert & Gilbert, Carbondale, Ill., 1974-83, Gilbert, Kimmel, Huffman & Prosser, Carbondale, 1983-88; circuit judge First Jud. Circuit, Ill., 1988-92; fed. judge U.S. Dist. Ct. (so. dist.) Ill., Benton, 1992—, chief judge, 1993—2000. Spl. asst. atty. gen. Pub. Aid Enforcement Divsn., 1974-75; asst. city atty. City of Carbondale, 1975-78; active Nat. Coun. Govt. Ethics Laws, 1988—; mem. Ill. State Bd. Elections, 1982, vice chmn., chmn., 1983-85. Bd. dirs. Friends of Morris Libr., 1988—; active Edn. Coun. 100, 1989—, Boy Scouts Am. Mem. Ill. State Bar, Jackson County Bar Assn., Phi Alpha Delta. Office: US Dist Ct 301 W Main St Benton IL 62812-1362

GILBERT, JAMES H., lawyer, former state supreme court justice; b. Minneapolis, Mar. 11, 1947; three children. BA, U. Minn., 1969, JD, 1972. Bar: Minn., 1972; Wis., 1984; U.S. Dist. Ct. Minn., 1974; U.S. Tax Ct., 1978; U.S. Ct. Appeals (8th cir.), 1989; U.S. Supreme Ct., 1988. Lawyer, v.p., mng. ptnr. Meshbesher, Singer, and Spence Ltd., Mpls., 1971—98; assoc. justice Minn. State Supreme Ct., Mpls., 1998—2004; atty. James H. Gilbert Law Group, Minnetonka, 2003—. Park Commr. City of Orono, Minn., 1988—92; bd. dir. Minn. Drug Abuse Resistance Edn. Inc.,(D.A.R.E.) Mem. Minn. Bar Assn. Avocations: skiing, hunting, golf, tennis, snowmobiling. Office: Gilbert Mediation Ctr Ltd 12700 Anderson Lakes Pkwy Eden Prairie MN 55344-7652

GILBERT, JAY, radio personality; FM rock DJ, 1969—; radio host WEBN-FM 102.7, Cin., 1974—. Composer, prodr.: numerous songs, jingles, & radio commercials. Recipient Marconi Radio award for Large Market Personality of Yr., Nat. Assn. Broadcasters, 2000. Office: WEBN-FM Ste 650 8044 Montgomery Rd Cincinnati OH 45236 Office Phone: 513-686-8300.

GILBERT, RONALD RHEA, lawyer; b. Sandusky, Ohio, Dec. 29, 1942; s. Corvin and Mildred (Millikin) G.; children: Elizabeth, Lynne, Lisa; m. Wendy Wawrzyniak, Apr. 2, 2002; 1 stepchild, Joshua Sisco. BA, Wittenberg U., Springfield, Ohio, 1964; JD, U. Mich., 1967, postgrad., 1967-68, Wayne State U., Detroit, 1973-74. Bar: Mich. 1968, US Dist. Ct. (ea. and we. dists.) Mich. 1968, US Ct. Appeals (6th cir.) 1968, US Ct. Appeals (9th cir.) 1977, US Ct. Appeals (7th cir.) 1984, US Ct. Appeals (3d cir.) 1988, US Ct. Appeals (4th cir.) 1989, US Ct. Appeals (8th cir.) 1990, US Ct. Appeals (10th cir.) 1991, US Ct. Appeals (11th cir.) 1992, US Ct. Appeals (2nd cir.), 1992. Assoc. prosecutor Wayne County, Mich., 1969; assoc. Rouse, Selby, Dickinson, Shaw & Pike, Detroit, 1969-72; ptnr. Charfoos, Christensen, Gilbert & Archer, P.C., Detroit, 1972-84; pvt. practice, 1984—. Instr. Madonna Coll., Detroit, 1977-81; mem. faculty Inst. Continuing Legal Edn., 1977—; speaker symposium on social security law Detroit Coll. Law, 1984; state bar grievance investigator; vol. chmn. Aquatic Injury Safety Found; mgr. web sites Found. for Spinal Cord Injury Prevention, Care and Cure (fscip.org), Found. for Aquatic Injury Prevention (aquaticisf.org). Co-author: Social Security Disability Claims, 1983; contbr. articles to legal jours. Founder, chmn. Aquatic Injury Safety Group, 1982—89, Found. for Aquatic Injury Prevention, 1988, Found. for Spinal Cord Injury Prevention, 1988; chmn. aquatic safety com. Nat. Safety Coun., 1987; mem. data collection subcom. Nat. Swimming Safety Com. for Consumer Products Safety Commn.; patron Detroit Art Inst., Detroit Zool. Soc.; mem. Detroit Coun. World Affairs, 1968—73, Coun. for Nat. Coop. in Aquatics; mem. combined fed. campaign Nat. Health Agy. Mich.; founder adv. bd. spinal cord injury traumatic brain injury Mich. Pub. Health co-founder Safe Kids Coalition Southea. Mich.; mem. adv. bd. Nat. Drowning Prevention Alliance; bd. dirs. Nat. Coordinating Coun. on Spinal Cord Injuries, Drowning Prevention Found., Calif.; mem. Pres.'s Club U. Mich. Mem. ATLA, Mich. Trial Lawyers Assn., System Safety Soc., ABA, Mich Bar Assn., Detroit Bar Assn., Am. Arbitration Assn., Am. Judicature Soc., Nat. Spinal Cord Injury Assn. (sec. 1988, bd. dirs., exec. com., chmn. prevention com.), Nat. Head Injury Assn., Mich. Head Injury Assn., Am. Standards and Testing Materials (com. F-24 on water parks and playgrounds, mem. coms.), World Water Parks Assn., Nat. Environ. Health Assn., Nat. Pub. Health Assn., Nat. Safe Kids Coalition, Nat. Eagle Scout Assn. (alumni), Blue Key, Pi Kappa Alpha, Pi Sigma Alpha, Pi Delta Epsilon, Fenton Rotary, Fenton Village Theatre, U. Mich. Club, Spring Meadows Country Club. Office Phone: 800-342-0330. Personal E-mail: rrgjedi@aol.com.

GILBERT, RUBY, state legislator; m. Booker Gilbert. Kans. state rep. Dist. 89, 1993—. Home: 2629 N Erie St Wichita KS 67219-4739

GILBERT, SUZANNE HARRIS, advertising executive; b. Chgo, Mar. 8, 1948; d. Lawrence W. and Dorothea (Wilde) Harris: children: Kerry, Elizabeth, Gregory. BS, Marquette U.; MBA, U. Chgo., 1985. Fin. analyst Leo Burnett Co., Chgo.; sr. v.p., fin. administrn., sec.-treas. Clinton E. Frank Inc., Chgo., 1975-85; with Campbell-Ewald Co., Detroit, 1985—, grp. sr. v.p. Warren, Mich., exec. v.p., chief fin. and administrv. officer, 1990—. Bd. dirs.; bd. dirs., mem. fiscal control and investment audit coms. AAAA Ins. Co. Ltd. Bd. dirs. Detroit Workforce Devel.; mem. bd. advs. U. Detroit Mercy Coll. of Bus. Recipient Profl. Achievement award Marquette U., 2000. Mem. Am. Assn. Advt. Agys. (fiscal control com.), Econ. Club Detroit, Fin. Execs. Inst. (bd. dirs. Detroit chpt., pres.). Office: Campbell-Ewald 30400 Van Dyke Ave Warren MI 48093-2368

GILBERTSON, DAVID, state supreme court justice; b. Milw., Oct. 29, 1949; BA, S.D. State U., 1972; JD, U. S.D. Sch. of Law, 1975. Atty. priv. practice, SD, 1975—86; dep. state atty. Roberts County; city atty. City of Sisseton; judge SC Cir. Ct. (5th jud. cir.), Pierre, 1986—95; assoc. justice SD Supreme Ct., Pierre, 1995—2001, chief justice, 2001—. Mem. Civil Pattern Jury Instruction Com., 1986—99, Tribal-State Judges Forum, 1992. Mem.: S.D. Bar Assn. (mem. Judicial-Bar Liaison Com.), Brown County Bar Assn., Glacial Lakes Bar Assn., S.D. Judges Assn. (past pres.). Office: 500 E Capitol Ave Pierre SD 57501-5070

GILBERTSON, ERIC RAYMOND, academic administrator, lawyer; b. Cleve., Mar. 5, 1945; s. Ewald R. and Esther V. (Johnson) G.; m. Cynthia F. Forrest, Jan. 25, 1974; children: Sara, Seth. BS, Bluffton Coll., 1966; MA in Econs., Ohio U., 1967; JD cum laude, Cleve. State U., 1970; DLitt (hon.), U. Mysore, Karnataka, India, 1993. Bar: Ohio 1970, Vt. 1984, U.S. Dist. Ct. (no. and so. dists.) Ohio 1971, U.S. Supreme Ct. 1981. Instr. econs. Kent State U., Ohio, 1969-70; law clk. Supreme Ct. of Ohio, Columbus, 1970-71; asst. atty. gen. State of Ohio, Columbus, 1971-73; exec. asst. to pres. Ohio State U., Columbus, 1973-79; assoc. Vorys, Sater, Seymore & Pease, Columbus, 1979-81; pres. Johnson State Coll., Vt., 1981-89, Saginaw Valley State U., University Center, Mich., 1989—. With Midland Tomorrow. Contbr. articles to profl. jours. Exec. com. Mich. Campus Compact; Pres. Coun. State Univs. Mich.; cmty. affairs com. Diocese Saginaw; active Bay County Bus. and Edn. Adv. Coun., Saginaw County Crime Prevention Coun., Vision Tri-County Steering Com.; trustee Citizens Rsch. Coun. Mich., 2003—. Mem. Am. Assn. State Colls. and Univs., Saginaw County C. of C., Torch Club, Saginaw Club, Bay City Country Club. Home: 7371 Glen Eagle Dr Bay City MI 48706-9316 Office: Saginaw Valley State U Office Of Pres University Center MI 48710-0001 E-mail: erg@svsu.edu.

GILBERTSON, JOEL WARREN, lawyer; b. Valley City, ND, Nov. 9, 1949; s. Roy W. and Gwen D. (Haugen) G.; m. Jan Erikson, June 11, 1972; children: David, Lisa. BA, Concordia Coll., Moorhead, Minn., 1972; JD, U. N.D., 1975. Bar: N.D. 1976, U.S. Dist. Ct. N.D. 1976. Ptnr. Binek & Gilbertson, Bowman, N.D., 1976; atty. N.D. Supreme Ct., Bismarck, 1976-78; exec. dir. N.D. Bar Assn., Bismarck, 1978-81; ptnr. Pearce & Durick, Bismarck, 1981-97; exec. v.p., gen. counsel Ind. Cmty. Banks of N.D., 1997—. Served with U.S. Army N.G., 1972-78. Mem. N.D. Bar Assn. (bd. govs. 1989-95, pres. 1992-93), N.D. Bar Found. (vice chmn. 1982-84, chmn. bd. dirs. 1986-89), South Cen. Dist. Bar Assn. (pres. 1987-89). Republican. Lutheran. Avocations: piano, softball. Home: 1025 Crescent Ln Bismarck ND 58501-2463 Office: Ind Comty Banks ND PO Box 6128 Bismarck ND 58506-6128

GILBY, STEVE, metallurgical engineering researcher; b. Dayton, Ohio, Sept. 22, 1939; BS, U. Cin., 1962; PhD in Metall. Engring., Ohio State U., 1966. Rsch. engr. steelmaking Youngstown Steel Co., 1966-76; rsch. engr. Armco Steel Co., 1967-69, sr. rsch. engr., 1969-72, rsch. assoc., 1972-75, mgr. steelmaking rsch., 1975-82, dir. process rsch., 1982-93; mng. dir. Armco Rsch. and Tech., Pitts., 1993-95, v.p. rsch. & tech., 1995—, asst. pres. Middletown, Ohio, 1996—. Chmn. external adv. commn. materials sci. and engring. dept. Ohio State U., 1988—. Mem. Am. Iron and Steel Soc., Am. Soc. Metals Internat. Achievements include research in steelmaking and continuous casting process development. Office: Armco Inc Rsch & Tech 705 Curtis St Middletown OH 45044-5812

GILCHREST, THORNTON CHARLES, retired association executive; b. Chgo., Sept. 1, 1931; s. Charles Jewett Gilchrest and Patricia (Thornton) Thornton; m. Barbara Dibbern, June 8, 1952; children: Margaret Mary, James Thornton. BS in Journalism, U. Ill., 1953. Cert. tchr. Ill. Tchr. pub. high sch., West Chicago, Ill., 1957; exec. dir. Plumbing-Heating-Cooling Info. Bur., Chgo., 1958-64; asst. to pres. A.Y. McDonald Mfg. Co., Dubuque, Iowa, 1964-68; exec. dir. Am. Supply Assn., Chgo., 1968-77, exec. v.p., 1977-82, Nat. Safety Coun., Chgo., 1982-83, pres., 1983-95; chmn. Internat. Safety Coun., Chgo., 1992-95. Pres. Nat. Safety Coun. Found. for Safety and Health, 1986-95. Bd. dirs. Prevent Blindness Am., 1993. With USN, 1953-55. Mem. Am. Soc. Assn. Execs., Chgo. Soc. Assn. Execs. Methodist.

GILCHRIST, GERALD SEYMOUR, pediatric hematologist, oncologist, educator; b. Springs, Transvaal, South Africa, May 25, 1935; arrived in U.S.A., 1962; s. David and Anne (Lipschitz) G.; m. Antoinette E. Besset, May 7, 1967; children: Daniel J., Michael A., Lauren D. MB BCh, U. Witwatersrand Med. Sch., Johannesburg, South Africa, 1957; Diploma in Child Health, Royal Coll. Physicians and Surgeons, London, 1961. Diplomate Am. Bd. Pediat. Intern Johannesburg Gen. Hosp., 1958-59; resident Transvaal Meml. Hosp. for Children and Baragwanath Hosp., Johannesburg, 1959-60; resident in pediatrics Hosp. for Sick Children, London, 1961; resident in pediat. Children's Hosp., Cin., 1962-63; fellow pediat., hematology/oncology Children's Hosp. of L.A.,

1963-65, cons. hematology and blood banking, 1965-71, attending physician, 1968-71; asst. prof. pediat. U. So. Calif., LA, 1966-71; assoc. prof. pediat. Mayo Med. Sch., Rochester, Minn., 1972-78, chmn. dept. pediat., 1984-96; cons. pediatric hematology/oncology Mayo Clinic and Found., Rochester, 1971-2000; prof. pediat. Mayo Med. Sch., Mayo Clinic and Found., Rochester, 1978-2000; Helen C. Levitt prof. Mayo Clinic and Found., Rochester, 1987-2000; prof. emeritus Mayo Found. and Med. Sch., 2000—. Mem. Commn. on Cancer ACS, 1982—85; bd. dirs. Hemophilia Ctr., Dept. Maternal and Child Health, Rockville, Md., 1978—2000; prin. investigator Children's Cancer Study Group Nat. Cancer Inst., Bethesda, 1981—99; mem. Accreditation Coun. Grad. Med. Edn. Residency Rev. Com. Pediat., 1997—2002. Co-author: You and Leukemia, 1976; contbr. chpts. to books, numerous articles to profl. jours. Med. advisor Northland Childrens Oncology Svcs., Rochester, Minn., 1978-80; bd. dirs. Minn. chpt. Nat. Hemophilia Found. Found., Mpls., 1981-84; chpt sec. Physicians for Social Responsibility, Rochester, 1982-85; bd. dirs. Nat. Childhood Cancer Found., 1990-97; chair med. and sci. adv. bd. Nat. Children's Cancer Found., 1995-97; mem. adv. com. Reach Out and Read MN, 2005—. Named to Children's Med. Ctr. Hall of Honor, Cin., 1994; recipient Joseph D. Early award, Nat. Hemophilia Found., 1997, Lifetime Achievement award, Minn., Dakotas Chpt. Nat. Hemophilia Found., 2000, Abraham Jacobi Meml. award, Am. Acad. Pediat., AMA, 2001. Fellow: Am. Acad. Pediat. (chmn. sect. on pediat. hematology-oncology 1988—90, chair coun. on sects. 1999—2002, com. on pediat. edn. 1999—2005, com. on pediat. workforce 2003—05); mem.: European and Am. Osteosarcoma Study Group (ind. data monitoring com. 2005—), Children's Oncology Group (data monitoring and safety comm. 2000—), Am. Soc. Pediat. Hematology/Oncology (trustee 1996—98), Soc. Pediat. Rsch. Accrediation Coun. Grad. Med. Edn. (residency rev. com. pediat. 1997—2002), Am. Bd. Pediat. (chmn. sub-bd. pediat. hematology-oncology 1989—91, bd. dirs. 1990—91), Am. Pediat. Soc., Am. Soc. Hematology, Am. Soc. Clin. Oncology, Reach Out and Read (mem. adv. com. 2005—). Democrat. Jewish. Avocations: sailing, bicycling, kayaking, scuba diving.

GILCHRIST, GRACE, broadcast executive; V.p., gen. mgr. WXYZ-TV, Detroit. Office: Sta WXYZ-TV PO Box 789 20777 W Ten Mile Rd Southfield MI 48037-0789

GILCHRIST, JAMES A., communication educator; Chmn. dept. comms. Western Mich. U., Kalamazoo, assoc. dean coll. arts scis., 1999—. Office: We Mich U Coll Arts Sci Kalamazoo MI 49008

GILDEA, LORIE SKJERVEN, state supreme court justice; BA, U. Minn. Morris, 1983; JD magna cum laude, order of the coif, Georgetown U. Law Ctr., 1986. Pvt. litig. practice Arent Fox LLP, Washington, 1986—93; assoc. gen. coun. U. Minn., 1993—2004; prosecutor Hennepin County Atty.'s Office, Minn., 2004—05; judge 4th Jud. Dist., Minn., 2005—06; assoc. justice Minn. Supreme Ct., 2006—, chair, gender fairness implementation com., liason, legal cert. bd. & adv. com. on juvenile protection rules. Mem. adv. com. on rules of civil procedure Minn. Supreme Ct., 2004—06. Adv. bd. MINNCORR Industries, 2000—02; bd. dirs. YWCA, Mpls., 2000—03. Mem.: Hennepin County Bar Assn. (co-chair Hennepin lawyer com. 2001—02, chair fin. & planning com. 2002—03), Minn. State Bar Assn. (bd. dirs. 2000—04, governing coun., civil litig. sect. 2000—06, assembly 2000—, coun. 2003—). Office: Minn Supreme Ct 25 Rev Dr Martin Luther King Jr Blvd Saint Paul MN 55155 Office Phone: 651-296-2581.

GILES, BRIAN T., lawyer; b. Louisville, Dec. 30, 1974; BA, Miami U., 1996; JD, U. Ky., 2000. Bar: Ohio 2000. Named one of Ohio's Rising Stars, Super Lawyers, 2006. Office: Statman Harris Siegel & Eyrich LLC 441 Vine St Ste 3700 Cincinnati OH 45202-3009 Office Phone: 513-621-2666. Office Fax: 513-587-4477.

GILES, EUGENE, anthropology educator; b. Salt Lake City, June 30, 1933; s. George Eugene and Eleanor (Clark) G.; m. Inga Valborg Wikman, Sept. 9, 1964; children: Eric George, Edward Eugene. AB, Harvard U., 1955, AM, 1960, PhD, 1966; MA, U. Calif., Berkeley, 1956. Diplomate Am. Bd. Forensic Anthropology (bd. dirs. 1996-2002). Instr. in anthropology U. Ill., Urbana, 1964-66, assoc. prof., 1970-73, prof., 1973-99, head dept. anthropology, 1975-80; asst. prof. Harvard U., Cambridge, Mass., 1966-70; assoc. dean Grad. Coll. U. Ill., 1986-89, assoc. dean Liberal Arts and Scis. Coll., 1995-99, prof. emeritus, 1999—. Editor: (with J.S. Friedlaender, jr. editor) The Measures of Man: Methodologies in Biological Anthropology, 1976. Served with U.S. Army, 1956-58. SF postdoctoral fellow, 1967-68; NSF grantee, 1970-72, NIH grantee, 1965-68 Fellow Am. Anthropol. Assn., AAAS, Am. Acad. Forensic Scis. (T. Dale Stewart award 2004); mem. Am. Assn. Phys. Anthropologists (exec. com. 1973-76, v.p. 1979-80, pres. 1981-83, Charles R. Darwin Lifetime Achievement award 2005), Human Biology Assn. (exec. com. 1974-77), Phi Beta Kappa, Sigma Xi. Home: 1001 Ross Dr Champaign IL 61821-6631 Office: U Ill Dept Anthropology 607 S Mathews Ave Urbana IL 61801-3635 Home Phone: 217-359-5925. E-mail: e-giles1@uiuc.edu.

GILFORD, STEVEN ROSS, lawyer; b. Chgo., Dec. 2, 1952; s. Ronald M. and Adele (Miller) Gilford; m. Anne Chrstine Johnson, Jan. 2, 1974; children: Sarah Julia, Zachary Michael, Eliza Rebecca. BA, Dartmouth Coll., 1974; JD, Duke U., 1978, M of Pub. Policy Scis., 1978. Bar: Ill. 1978, U.S. Dist. Ct. (no. dist.) Ill. 1978, U.S. Ct. Appeals (7th cir.) 1981, U.S. Ct. Appeals (DC cir.) 1984, U.S. Ct. Appeals (5th cir.) 1988, U.S. Dist. Ct. (ea. dist.) Mich. 1995. Assoc. Isham, Lincoln & Beale, Chgo., 1978—85, ptnr., 1985—87, Mayer, Brown, Rowe & Maw, Chgo., 1987—. Adminstrv. law editor: Duke Law Jour., 1976—77. Participating atty. ACLU, 1983—2000; bd. dirs. Evanston (Ill.) YMCA, 1982—92, 2005—, sec., 1985, vice chmn., 1986—92; bd. dirs. ACLU, Ill., 1991—96, v.p. Ill., 1995—96; elected mem. bd. edn. dist. 202 Evanston Twp. HS, 1993—2005, v.p., 1995—96, 2003—04, pres., 1996—98, 2004—05, mem. joint task force on safety, 1995—96, chmn. fin. com., 2001—04; mem. Legal Aid Soc., 2001—, chmn., 2005—; mem. Met. Family Svcs., Evanston Skokie Valley Cmty. Adv. Bd., 1997; mem., bd. dirs. Met. Family Svcs., 1998—; mem. exec. com. ED-RED, 2002—05; bd. dirs. Dem. Party Evanston, Ill., 2004—05, Roger Baldwin Found., 1993—96. Mem.: ABA, Chgo. Bar Assn., Ill. Bar Assn. Home: 2728 Harrison St Evanston IL 60201-1216 Office: Mayer Brown Rowe & Maw 190 S La Salle St Ste 3100 Chicago IL 60603-3441 Office Phone: 312-701-7909.

GILL, RICHARD LAWRENCE, lawyer; b. Chgo., Jan. 8, 1946; s. Joseph Richard and Dolores Ann (Powers) Gill; m. Mary Helen Walker, July 14, 1990; children: Kyla Marie, Matthew Joseph. BA, Coll. of St. Thomas, St. Paul, 1968; JD, U. Minn., 1971. Bar: Minn. 1971, U.S. Dist. Ct. Minn. 1971, U.S. Supreme Ct. 1979, U.S. Ct. Appeals (8th cir.) 1983, U.S. Ct. Appeals (4th cir.) 1990, Ill. 1992. Spl. asst. atty. gen. State of Minn., St. Paul, 1971-73; assoc. Maun, Hazel, Green, Hayes, Simon & Aretz, St. Paul, 1974-77; ptnr. Gill & Brinkman, St. Paul, 1978-84, Robins, Kaplan, Miller & Ciresi, Mpls., 1984—2002, of counsel, 2002—. Vol. Courage Ctr., Golden Valley, Minn., 1981—; youth football coach Maplewood (Minn.) Athletic Assn., 1978-80; youth basketball coach Orono (Minn.) Athletic Assn., 1999—; mem. athletics adv. bd. U. St. Thomas, 2002—. Mem. ABA, Minn. Bar Assn., Hennepin County Bar Assn., Ramsey County Bar Assn., Assn. Trial Lawyers Am., Minn. Trial Lawyers Assn., Town and Country Club, Windsong Farm Golf Club. Avocations: skiing, tennis, golf. Office: Robins Kaplan Miller & Ciresi 800 Lasalle Ave Ste 2800 Minneapolis MN 55402-2015 Office Phone: 612-349-8430. Business E-Mail: rlgill@rkmc.com.

GILLES, RALPH VICTOR, automotive designer; b. NYC, 1970; m. Doris Gilles; children: Tia, Sydney. BS, Coll. for Creative Studies, 1992; MBA, Mich. State U., 2002. With Chrysler Corp. (now DaimlerChrysler Corp.), 1992—, primary interior designer, dir. large cars Studio Three, dir. product design Truck Exterior/Interior Design Studio, 2005—. Instr. Ctr. for Creative Studies, Detroit. Recipient Automotive Hall of Fame Young Leadership and Excellence award, 2004, Innovation Award, New Visions in Bus. Mag., 2005, Black Engr. of Yr. Pres.'s Award, 2005, Urban Wheels Award, 2005. Mem.: SkunkWerks. Avocation: travel. Office: Chrysler Group 1000 Chrysler Dr Auburn Hills MI 48326-2766

GILLESPIE, ROBERT WAYNE, banker; b. Cleve., Mar. 26, 1944; s. Robert Walton and Eleanore (Parsons) G.; m. Ann L. Wible, June 17, 1967; children: Laura, Gwen. BA, Ohio Wesleyan U., 1966; MBA, Case Western Res. U., 1968; postgrad., Harvard U., 1979. Credit analyst Soc. Nat. Bank, Cleve., 1968-70, v.p., 1970-76, sr. v.p., 1976-79; exec. v.p. Soc. Nat Bank, Cleve., 1979-81; vice-chmn., chief operating officer Soc. Nat. Bank, Cleve., 1981-83, pres., chief operating officer, 1983-85, CEO, 1985—, pres., 1987-94; pres., CEO, Key Corp., Cleve., 1995—, chmn., 1996—, CEO, 1996—. Trustee Case Western Res. U., Ohio Wesleyan U., Cleve. Mus. Art, Cleve. Initiative for Edn. and Musical Arts, Greater Cleve. Roundtable, Cleve. Tomorrow and North Coast Harbor; bd. dirs. Greater Cleve. Growth Assn. Office: Key Corp 127 Public Sq Cleveland OH 44114-1306

GILLET, PAMELA KIPPING, special education educator; EdB in Elem. Edn., Chgo. Tchrs. Coll., 1963; MA in Mental Retardation, Northeastern Ill. U., 1966; PhD in Gen. Spl. Edn./Adminstrn., Walden U., 1976. Cert. elem. edn., early childhood edn., learning disabled, mental retardation, behavior disorders, supt., supr. and dir. spl. edn. 4th grade tchr. Dist. # 83 Mannheim, Franklin Park, Ill., 1963—64; h.s. spl. edn. tchr. Dist. # 207 Maine Twp., Park Ridge, Ill., 1964—67, prevocational coord., 1967—69, dept. chmn. spl. edn. dept., 1969—70; dir. EPDA tchr. tng. program Chgo. Consortium Colls. and Univs., Northwest Ednl. Coop., Palatine, Ill., 1970—71; prin. West Suburban Spl. Edn. Ctr., Cicero, Ill., 1971—73; supr. West Suburban Assn. Spl. Edn., Cicero, 1973—75; asst. dir. Northwest Suburban Spl. Edn. Orgn., Palatine, 1975—78, supt. Mt. Prospect, Ill., 1978—96; spl. edn. cons., 1996—. Adj. instr. Northeastern Ill. U., Chgo. State U., Corcordia Coll., Barat Coll., Nat. Coll. Edn., Roosevelt U.; mem. task forces ISBE, 1975—2007, cons. career edn. project, 1977—78, spl. edn. demandate study group, 1983—85; cons. Ednl. Testing Svc.; tchr. edn. coun. Northeastern Ill. U., 1981—97, dean's grant program, 1982—97; workshop leader, 1974—; lectr., cons. in field. Author: Auditory Processes, 1974, rev., 1992, Career Education for Children, 1978, Of Work and Worth: Career Education Programming for Exceptional Children and Youths, 1981, Handbook for board members of volunteer organizations, 2008; contbr. articles to profl. jours., chapters to books. Bd. dirs. Found. Exceptional Children, 1996—, pres., 1999—2004. Recipient Cmty. Svc. award, Am. Legion, 1976, 1980, Alumnus of Yr. award, Northeastern Ill. U., 1984, Learning Disabilities of Am. Contributors award, Coun. Understanding Learning Disabilities, 1992, Those Who Excel award of excellence, Ill. State Bd. of Edn., 1994, Outstanding Svc. award, Divsn. Mental Retardation and Devel. Disabilities, 1994, Sleznick award, Coun. of Admin. of Spl. Edn., 1996, Outstanding Contbr. award, Coun. Exceptional Children, 1996, Burton Blatt award, Divsn. on Metal Retardation and Devel. Disabilities, 1997, Spl. Edn. Leadership award, Ill. Adminstrs. of Spl. Edn., 1995, Outstanding Spl. Edn. Adminstr. of Yr. award, 1997. Mem.: Found. for Exceptional Children (pres. 2000—04, v.p. CEC Pioneers divsn. 2006—), Ill. Adminstrs. Spl. Edn. (pres. 1994—95), Coun. Exceptional Children (pres. Ill. chpt. 1975—77, bd. govs. 1977—80, pres. mental retardation divsn. 1983—85, bd. govs. 1986, exec. com. 1989—92, v.p. internat. 1992—93, pres.-elect 1993—94, pres. 1994—95, bd. govs. 1996—2000, bd. dirs. 2000—04, pres. Pioneers divsn. 2007, pres.-elect. 2005—06, Meritorious Svc. award Ill. 1983), Am. Assn. Sch. Adminstrs. Home and Office: 413 Courtlea Oaks Blvd Winter Garden FL 34787

GILLETTE, RICHARD GARETH, neurophysiology educator, researcher; b. Seattle, Feb. 17, 1945; s. Elton George and Hazel I. (Hand) G.; m. Sally A. Reams, Feb. 17, 1978 (div. ov. 1988); 1 child, Jesse Robert. BS, U. Oreg., 1968; MS, Oreg. Health Sci. U., 1976, PhD, 1993. Rsch. asst. dept. otolaryngology Oreg. Health Sci. U., Portland, 1969-72, grad. rsch. asst., 1973-80; instr. neurosci. Western State Chiropractic Coll., Portland, 1981-85, asst. prof. neurosci., 1985-93, assoc. prof. neurosci., 1993-99, prof. neurosci., 1999—. Lectr. neurosci. sch. optometry Pacific U., Forest Grove, Oreg., 1985-86; grad. rsch. asst. eurol. Sci. Inst. OHSU, Portland, 1988-93, vis. scientist, 1993—. Contbr. articles to profl. jours. NIH Predoctoral Tng. fellow Oreg. Health Sci. U., 1973-76, Tarter fellow Med. Rsch. Found. Oreg., 1989; NIH grantee, 1990-99. Mem. AAAS, Soc. for Neurosci., Am. Pain Soc., Internat. Assn. for Study of Pain. Avocations: history studies, vocal music performance. Office: Wscc Bookstore 11559 Rock Island Ct Maryland Heights MO 63043-3522 Business E-Mail: rgillette@wschiro.edu.

GILLIES, DONALD RICHARD, marketing and advertising consultant, educator; b. Sioux Falls, SD, Jan. 14, 1939; s. Donald Franklin and Gladys O. (Gullickson) G.; m. Twyla Elaine Bloomquist, Apr. 7, 1962; children: Dawn, Trent, Tara. BA in Journalism/Advt., U. Minn., 1961. Writer, producer Sta. WCCO-TV, Mpls., 1954-60; mgmt. supr., sr. v.p., bd. dirs. Campbell-Mithun Advt., Mpls., 1960-86; pres., chief oper. officer Colle & McVoy Inc., Mpls., 1987-89; prin. Gillies group inc. (Gg), Minnetonka, Minn., 1989—. Adj. prof. U. St. Thomas, 1990-97, asst. prof., 2001—07. Bd. dirs. Guthrie Theater, Mpls., 1979-84; ch. coun. Mt. Olivet Ch., Mpls., 1988-94; Midwest adv. rev. bd. BBB, 1996—. Mem. Am. Assn. Advt. Agencies (regional gov.), Minn. Advt. Fedn. (bd. dirs. 1973-76). Lutheran. Home and Office: Gillies group inc (Gg) 5942 Fairwood Ln Minnetonka MN 55345-6533 Personal E-mail: dongillies@prodigy.net.

GILLIGAN, SANDRA KAYE, private school director; b. Ft. Lewis, Wash., Mar. 22, 1946; d. Jack G. and O. Ruth (Mitchell) Wagoner; m. James J. Gilligan, June 3, 1972 (div. June 1998); 1 child, J. Shawn Gilligan. BS in Edn., Emporia State U., 1968, MS in Psychology, 1971; postgrad., Drake U., 1976, U. Mo., St. Louis, 1977-79. Tchr. Parklane Elem. Sch., Aurora, Colo., 1968-69, Bonner Springs (Kans.) Elem., 1970; stewardess Frontier Airlines, Denver, 1969; grad. teaching asst. Emporia (Kans.) State U., 1970-71; lead tchr. Western Valley Youth Ranch, Buckeye, Ariz., 1971-74; staff mem. program devel., lead tchr. The New Found., Phoenix, 1974; ednl. therapist Orchard Pl., Des Moines, 1974-76; ednl. cons. Spl. Sch. Dist. of St. Louis County, 1976-79; founding dir. The Churchill Ctr. and Sch. Learning Disabilities, St. Louis, 1978—. Instr. Webster Coll., Webster Groves, Mo., 1978-80; adj. prof. Maryville Coll., St. Louis, 1985; keynote spkr. Miss. Learning Disabilities Assn. Conv., 1991; site visitor blue ribbon schs. program U.S. Dept. Edn., 1992; bd. dirs. Ind. Schs. St. Louis; evaluation rev. com. ISACS, 1996—; presenter in field. Recipient Spirit Care & Counseling award, 2004, Deans Excellence in Ednl. Leadership award, U. Mo., 2006—07. Mem. Learning Disabilities Assn., Internat. Dyslexia Assn. (chpt. bd. dirs.), St. Louis Jr. League. Avocations: gardening, painting. Office: The Churchill Ctr and Sch Learning Disabilities 1035 Price School Ln Saint Louis MO 63124-1596 Office Phone: 314-997-4343. Business E-Mail: sgill@churchillstl.org.

GILLIS, RUTH ANN M., utilities executive; married; 2 children. BS magna cum laude in Econs., Smith Coll., Northampton, Mass., 1977; MBA in Fin., U. Chgo., 1980. Various lending and staff positions First Chgo. Corp. (now JPMorgan Chase & Co.), 1977—95; CFO, treas., v.p. U. Chgo. Hosps. and Health Sys.; v.p., treas. Unicom Corp., 1997, sr. v.p. competitive ops., CFO; CFO Exelon Corp., 2000—02, exec. v.p. ComEd, sr. v.p., pres. Exelon Bus. Svcs. Co., mem. ops. coun. and corp. risk mgmt. com. Bd. dirs. Potlatch Corp.; trustee Archstone-Smith Trust. Pres. bd. trustees U. Chgo. Cancer Rsch. Found.; trustee Goodman Theatre Bd.; mem. U. Chgo. Cancer Rsch. Found. Women's Bd., 1986—. Mem.: Chgo. Network, Econ. Club Chgo., Phi Beta Kappa. Office: Exelon Corp 37th Fl 10 S Dearborn St Chicago IL 60603

GILLMOR, KAREN LAKO, state agency administrator; b. Cleve., Jan. 29, 1948; d. William M. and Charlotte (Sheldon) Lako; m. Paul E. Gillmor, Dec. 10, 1983; children: Linda D., Julie E., Paul Michael, Connor W., Adam S. BA cum laude, Mich. State U., 1969; MA, Ohio State U., 1970, PhD, 1981. Asst. to v.p. Ohio State U., Columbus, 1972-77, spl. asst. dean law, 1979-81, assoc. dir. Ctr. Healthcare Policy and Rsch., 1991-92; asst. to pres. Ind. Cen. U., Indpls., 1977-78; rsch. asst. Burke Mktg. Rsch., Indpls., 1978-79; v.p. pub. affairs Huntington Nat. Bank, Columbus, 1981-82; fin. cons. Ohio Rep. Fin. Com., Columbus, 1982-83; chief mgmt. planning and rsch. Indsl. Commn. Ohio, Columbus, 1983-86; mgr. physician rels. Ohio State U. Med. Ctr., Columbus, 1987-91; cons. U.S. Sec. Labor, Washington, 1990-91; mem. Regional Bd. Rev./Indls. Commn., Ohio, 1991-92; state senator Ohio Gen. Assembly, 1993-97; vice-chair State Employment Rels. Bd., 1997—2007. Legis. liaison Huntington Bancshares, Ohio, Ohio State U., Columbus; trustee Heidelberg Coll., 1999—, Rutherford B. Hayes Presd. Ctr., 2002—. Mem. adv. coun. The Childhood League Ctr., 2003—06; nat. bd. dirs. Nat. First Ladies' Libr., 2004—; bd. dirs. Congl. Childcare Ctr., 2003—07. Named Outstanding Freshman Ohio Legislator, 1994, Outstanding Nat. Freshman Legislator of the Yr., 1995, Watchdog of the Treasury, 1994, 1996, Hon. Alumna, Heidelberg Coll., 2006; named to Rocky River H.S. Hall of Fame, 1998; recipient Pres. award, Ohio State Chiropractic Assn., 1994, Pub. Svc. award, Am. Heart Assn., 1995, Ctr. Advancement and Study of Ethics award, Capital U. and Trinity Luth. Sem., 1996, cert. of Achievement, U.S. Dept. of Army, 1997, Friend of Medicine award, Ohio State Med. Assn., 1997, Legis. Achievement award, Ohio chpt. Am. Acad. Pediat., 1997, Spirit of Women award, 1999, Civic Leadership award, Ohio Assn. for Gifted Children, 2006; grantee, Andrew W. Mellon Found., 1978, Carnegie Corp., 1978. Mem.: DAR, Coun. Advancement and Support Edn., Am. Assn. Higher Edn., Ohio Fedn. Rep. Women, Women's Roundtable, Women in Mainstream, Phi Delta Kappa. Methodist.

GILMAN, ALAN B., restaurant company executive; b. South Bend, Ind., Sept. 24, 1930; s. Sol M. and Lee R. (Rintzler) G.; m. Phyllis Schrager, Feb. 16, 1951; children: Bruce, Jeffrey, Lynn. AB with highest honors, Ind. U., 1952, MBA, 1954. With Lazarus Co. div. Federated Dept. Stores, Inc., Columbus, Ohio, 1954-64, div. mdse. mgr., 1961-64; with Sanger Harris div. Federated Dept. Stores, 1965-74, chmn. bd., chief exec. officer, 1970-74; corp. v.p. Federated Dept. Stores, 1974-80; with Abraham & Straus div. Federated Dept. Stores, 1975-80, chmn. bd., chief exec. officer, 1978-80; pres. Murjani Internat. Ltd., YC, 1980-85; pvt. investor, 1985-87; chmn. At Ease of Newport Beach (Calif.) Inc., 1988-91; pres., CEO Consol. Products Inc., 1992—2002; chmn. Steak 'n Shake Co., Indpls., 2002—. Vice-chmn. bd. dirs. Ind. U. Found., 2000-03, nat. chmn. ann. giving, 1983, presdl. search com., 1987-88; chmn. dean's adv. coun. Ind. U. Grad. Sch. Bus., 1976-86; dean's adv. coun. Coll. Arts and Scis., Ind. U., 1989—, pres.'s cabinet, 1995-2003; bd. dirs., pres., exec. com. Greater NY Fund-United Way, 1984-87; bd. dirs., exec. com., chmn. strategic planning com. United Way of NYC, 1982-88; dir. Corp. Comty. Coun., Indpls., 1992-2001, Greater Indpls. Progress Com., Kelley Restaurants, Inc.; trustee Com. for Econ. Devel. Recipient Humanitarian of Yr. award Juvenile Diabetes Found., 1979, Disting. Alumni Svc. award Ind. U., 1996. Mem. Young Pres. Orgn. 49'er, Ind. U. Acad. Alumni Fellows, World Pres.'s Orgn., Phi Beta Kappa Fellows, Phi Alpha Theta, Beta Gamma Sigma (charter mem. dirs. table). Office: The Steak and Shake Co 500 Century Bldg 36 S Penn Ave Indianapolis IN 46204 Office Phone: 317-633-4100.

GILMAN, SANDER LAWRENCE, liberal arts and sciences professor, historian, writer; b. Buffalo, Feb. 21, 1944; s. William and Rebecca (Helf) G.; m. Marina von Eckardt, Dec. 28, 1969; children: Daniel, Samuel. BA, Tulane U., 1963, PhD, 1968; postgrad., U. Berlin and U. Munich, Ger.; LLD (hon.), U. Toronto, Ont., 1997. Lectr. German St. Mary's Dominican Coll., New Orleans, 1963-64; instr. Dillard U., New Orleans, 1967-68; asst. prof. Case Western Res. U., 1968-69; mem. faculty Cornell U., 1969-94, prof. German, 1976-94, prof. Near Eastern studies, 1984-91, prof. humane studies, 1984-87, Goldwin Smith prof., 1987-94, chmn. dept. German lit., 1974-81, 83-84; fellow dept. psychiatry Cornell U. Med. Coll., 1977-78; prof. history of psychiatry Cornell U., 1978-94; prof. German, history of sci. and psychiatry U. Chgo., 1994-2000, Henry R. Luce disting. svc. prof. Liberal Arts in Human Biology, 1995-2000, disting. svc. prof., 1999-2000; disting. prof. liberal arts & scis. and medicine U. Ill., Chgo., 2000—05; disting. prof. liberal arts & scis. Emory U., 2005—. O'Connor prof. Colgate U., 1982-83; Mellon prof. Tulane U., 1988, Old Dominion prof. English, Princeton U., 1988; Northrup Frye prof. of comparative lit. U. Toronto, Ont., Can., 1989; vis. prof. German lit. Free U. Berlin, 1989; vis. hist. scholar Nat. Libr. Medicine, 1991-92; vis. Rudolph prof. Jewish studies Syracuse (N.Y.) U., 1992; vis. prof. U. Witwatersrand, South Africa, 1994, U. Potsdam, 1996, U. Cape Town, 1996, Ctr. for Advanced Studies in the Behavioral Scis., 1996-97, Getty Inst. for Art and the Humanities, 1998; hon. prof. Free U., Berlin; Berlin prize fellow Am. Acad., Berlin, 2000-01; dir. program in psychoanalysis, Emory U., health sciences humanities initiative. Author, editor.: Bertolt Brecht's Berlin, 1975, Nietzschean Parody, 1976, The Face of Madness, 1976, Klingers Werke, 1978, Begegnungen mit Nietzsche, 1981, On Blackness Without Blacks, 1982, Seeing the Insane, 1982 (reprinted 1996), Difference and Pathology, 1985, Jewish Self-Hatred, 1986, Oscar Wilde's London, 1987, Conversations with Nietzsche, 1987, Diseases and Representation, 1989, Sexuality: An Illustrated History, 1989, Nietzsche on Rhetoric and Language, 1989, The Jew's Body, 1991, Inscribing the Other, 1991, Rasse, Seuche, Sexualitat, 1992, Freud, Race, Gender, 1993, The Case of Sigmund Freud, 1993, Reading Freud Reading, 1993, Reemerging Jewish Culture in Germany, 1994, Jews in Today's German Culture, 1995, Health and Illness, 1995, Franz Kafka: The Jewish Patient, 1996, L'Autre et Le Moi, 1996, Smart Jews, 1996, Yale Companion to Jewish Writing and Thought in German Culture, 1997, Love and Marriage with Death, 1998, Creating Beauty to Cure the Soul, 1998, Making the Body Beautiful, 1999, Jurek Becker: Die Biographie, 2002, (co-editor with Zhou Xun) SMOKE: A Global History of Smoking, 2004, Race and Contemporary Medicine: Biological Facts and Fictions, 2006; mem. editl. bd. Diacritics, 1971-72, Lessing Yearbook, 1974—, German Quar., 1977-86, Confinia Psychiatrica, 1978-80; Oxford Lectures Multiculturalism and the Jews, 2006. Guggenheim fellow, 1972-73, IREX exch. fellow German Democratic Republic, 1976, Soc. for Humanities faculty fellow Cornell U., 1981-82, Nat. Libr. Medicine sr. historian, fellow, 1990-91, Ctr. for the Adv. Study of the Behaviorial Scis. fellow, Stanford, 1996-97, Am. Acad., Berlin, 2000—. Mem. MLA (pres. 1995), Lessing Soc., Am. Assn. Tchrs. German, Soc. Internat. d'Études Littéraires et Psychiatres, Internat. Assn. Germanists. Democrat. Jewish. Office: Emory U Grad Inst Liberal Arts 537 Kilgo Cir S415 Callaway Bldg Atlanta GA 30322 E-mail: sander34@aol.com.

GILMAN, SID, neurologist; b. LA, Oct. 19, 1932; s. Morris and Sarah Rose (Cooper) G.; m. Carol G. Barbour. BA, UCLA, 1954; MD, 1957, FRCP, 2001. Intern UCLA Hosp., 1957-58; resident in neurology Boston City Hosp., 1960-63; from instr. to assoc. in neurology Harvard Med. Sch., 1965-68; from asst. prof. to prof. neurology Columbia U., NYC, 1968-76, H. Houston Merritt prof. neurology, 1976-77; prof., chair dept. neurology U. Mich., Ann Arbor, 1977—2004, William J. Herdman prof. neurology, 1997—2005, William J. Herdman disting. univ. prof. neurology, 2005—. Cons. VA Hosp., Ann Arbor, 1977—; mem. peripheral and ctrl. nervous sys. drugs adv. com. FDA, 1983-85, 86-87, 90-94, chmn., 1996-2000, cons., 2000—; adj. attending neurologist Henry Ford Hosp., Detroit; mem. chronic disease adv. com. Mich. Dept. Pub. Health, 1988-94; mem. neurol. sci. rsch. and tng. com. NIH, 1971-73, mem. neurol. disorders program project B com., 1976-80, mem. sci. programs adv. com. Nat. Inst. Neurol. Diseases, Communicative Disorders and Stroke, 1982-84, mem. nat. adv. neurol. disorders and stroke coun., 1994-97; mem. clin. trials subcom. Nat. Adv. Neurol. Disorders and Stroke Coun., 2001-04; dir. Mich. Alzheimer's Disease Rsch. Ctr., 1991—; mem. rsch. adv. coun. United Cerebral Palsy Found.; mem. sci. adv. coun. Nat. Ataxia Found., Nat. Amyotrophic Lateral Sclerosis Found., Inc.; mem. profl. adv. bd. Epilepsy Found. Am.; mem. rsch. adv. com. Nat. Multiple Sclerosis Soc., 1986-90; mem. exec. bd. Nat. Coalition for Rsch., 1989-95, Nat. Found. for Brain Rsch., 1989-95; mem. rsch. adv. com. Dana Alliance; mem. sci. adv. bd. Merck, Inc., 2000-04, PPD Devel., 1999—, INC Rsch., 2000—; Henry Russel lectr. U. Mich., 2001. Author: (with J.R. Bloedel and R. Lechtenberg) Disorders of the Cerebellum, 1981, (with S.W. Newman) Manter and Gatz's Essentials of Clinical Neuroanatomy and Neurophysiology, 10th edit., 2003, (with J.C. Mazziotta) Clinical Brain Imaging: Principles and Applications, 1992, Clinical Examination of the Nervous System, 2000; editor: Neurobiology of Disease, 2007; sect. editor editl. bd. Exptl. Neurology, Current Opinion in Neurology and eurosurgery, Neurology, Annals Neurology, Jour. Neuropathology and Exptl. Neurology, Neurobase Arbor Pub. Co.; editor-in-chief MedLink Neurology, 1992—, Contemporary Neurology Series, 1995—, Neurology Network Commentary, 1996-2000, Lancet Neurology Network, 2000-02, Exptl. Neurology, 2003—, Neurolobiology of Disease, 2005-; contbr. articles to profl. jours. Dir. Mich. Dem. Program, 1994-2000. With USPHS, 1958-60. Recipient Lucy G. Moses prize Columbia U., 1973, Weinstein Goldenson award United Cerebral Palsy Assn., 1981, UCLA Alumni Profl. Achievement award, 1992, UCLA Med. Alumni Profl. Achievement award, 1992. Fellow AAAS, Royal Soc. of Medicine, Royal Coll. Physicians, Am. Acad. Arts and Scis.; mem. Am. Neurol. Assn. (hon.; 1st v.p. 1985-86, pres.-elect 1987-88, pres. 1988-89), Mich. Neurol. Assn. (pres. 1987-88), Soc. Clin. Investigation, Am. Physiol. Soc., Am. Assn. Neuropathologists, Soc. Neurosci., Am. Acad. Neurology (vice chmn. geriatric neurology subcom. 1992-94, chmn. 1994-96, chmn. Decade of Brain com. 1990-95, AB Baker award 2004), Am. Epilepsy Soc., Assn. Rsch. in Nervous and Mental Disease, Assn. Am. Physicians, Inst. Medicine, Nat. Acad. Scis., The Nat. Acads. (nat. assoc.), Phi Beta Kappa, Alpha Omega Alpha. Home: 3411 Geddes Rd Ann Arbor MI 48105-2518 Office: U Mich Dept Neurology 300 N Ingalls 3D15 Ann Arbor MI 48109 Office Phone: 734-936-1808. Business E-Mail: sgilman@umich.edu.

GILMER, GARY D., credit services company executive; Group exec. Household Internat. Inc., Prospect Heights, Ill., 1996—. Office: 2700 Sanders Rd Prospect Heights IL 60070-2701

GILMORE, GUY L., publishing executive; m. Donna Gilmore; 3 children. BA magna cum laude, U. Calif., Riverside. Regional gen. mgr. USA Today, Kansas City, Mo., Cin./Indpls.; v.p. circulation Little Rock Gazette; circulation dir. Reno Gazette-Jour., Nev., Fla. Today, Brevard, Fla., Nashville Tennessean & Banner, Portland Oregonian; v.p. circulation & prodn. Balt. Sun; pres. & pub. Allentown Morning Call, Pa., 2000—05; v.p. circulation St. Paul Pioneer Press, 2005—07, pub., 2007—. Mem.: Phi Beta Kappa. Office: Pioneer Press 345 Cedar St Saint Paul MN 55101 Office Phone: 651-222-1111.*

GILMORE, HORACE WELDON, former federal judge; b. Columbus, Ohio, Apr. 4, 1918; s. Charles Thomas and Lucille (Weldon) G.; m. Mary Hays, June 20, 1942; children— Lindsay Gilmore Feinberg. AB, U. Mich., 1939, JD, 1942. Bar: Mich. bar 1946. Law clk. U.S. Ct. Appeals, 1946-47; practiced in Detroit, 1947-51; spl. asst. U.S. atty., Detroit, 1951-52; mem. Mich. Bd. Tax Appeals, 1954; dep. atty. gen. State of Mich., 1955-56; circuit judge 3d Jud. Circuit, Detroit, 1956-80; judge U.S. Dist. Ct. (ea. dist.) Mich., 1980—, now sr. judge Detroit. Adj. prof. law Wayne State U. Law Sch., 1966-82; lectr. law U. Mich. Law Sch., 1969-90; faculty Nat. Coll. State Judiciary, 1966-83; mem. Mich. Jud. Tenure Commn., 1969-76; chmn. Mich. Com. to Revise Criminal Code, 1965-82, Mich. Com. to Revise Criminal Procedure, 1971-79; trustee Inst. for Ct. Mgmt. Author: Michigan Civil Procedure Before Trial, 2d edit, 1975; contbr. numerous articles to legal jours. Served with USNR, 1942-46. Mem. ABA, State Bar Mich., Am. Judicature Soc., Am. Law Inst., Nat. Conf. State Trial Judges.

GILMORE, KATHI, former state treasurer; b. Dec. 23, 1944; m. Richard Gilmore; children: Suzi, Barb, Jeff, Amy. Mem. N.D. Ho. of Reps. from Dist. 6, 1989-92; treas. State of N.D., 1993—2004. Mem. Bd. Tax Equalization, State Hist. Bd., State Investment Bd., Tchrs. Fund for Retirement Bd., State Canvassing Bd., Bd. of Univ. and Sch. Lands Mem.: Assn. Securities Profls. (hon. co-chair pension fund conf. 1994, Task Forces Orgnl. Planning and Coordinating Com. 1993), Retirement and Investment Office Internal Audit Com., Nat. Assn. State Treas. (pension com.). Democrat. Presbyterian.

GILMORE, PHYLLIS, state legislator; m. Kenneth Gilmore. Social worker; mem. Kans. State Ho. of Reps. Dist. 27, 1994-99; exec. dir. regulatory bd. State of Kans., Topeka, 1999—. Office: State Kans Regulatory Bd Topeka KS 66601

GILMORE, RONALD MICHAEL, bishop; b. Pittsburg, Kans., Apr. 23, 1942; BA, B.Ph, U. Ottawa, 1965, MA, M.Th, STL, U. Ottawa, 1969. Ordained priest Diocese of Wichita, Kans., 1969; ordained bishop, 1998; bishop Diocese of Dodge City, Kans., 1998—. Roman Catholic. Office: Diocese of Dodge City 910 Central Ave # 137 Dodge City KS 67801-4905 Office Phone: 620-227-1525. Office Fax: 620-227-1545.*

GILMOUR, ALLAN DANA, retired automotive company executive; b. Burke, Vt., June 17, 1934; s. Albert Davis and Marjorie Bessie (Fyler) G. AB cum laude, Harvard U., 1956; MBA, U. Mich., 1959. Fin. analyst, sect. supr., dept. mgr., asst. to exec. v.p. Ford Motor Co., Dearborn, Mich., 1960-72; exec. v.p. adminstrn. Ford Motor Credit Co., Dearborn, 1972-73, exec. v.p. adminstrn. and spl. financing ops., 1973-75, pres., 1975-77; exec. dir. Ford Motor Co., 1977-79, v.p., contr., 1979-84, v.p. external and personnel affairs, 1984-85, exec. v.p., chief fin. officer, dir., 1986-87, exec. v.p. international automotive operatives, 1987-89, exec. v.p. corp. staffs, 1989-90; pres. Ford Automotive Group, 1990-93, vice chmn., 1993—95; div. vice chmn. Ford Motor Co., 2002—. Bd. dirs. Whirlpool Corp., DTE Energy Co. Mem. Econ. Club (Detroit), Detroit Athletic Club, Phi Kappa Phi, Beta Gamma Sigma. E-mail: agilmour@ford.com.

GILROY, SUE ANNE, hospital administrator, former state official; b. Ind., 1948; m. Dick Gilroy; children: Emily (dec. 1989), Grant. Grad. cum laude, DePauw U.; MA, Ind. U. Ordained elder Presbyn. Ch. Profl. assoc. Office of Mayor Lugar; dir. Parks and Recreation; asst. to pres. Ind. Ctrl. U. (now U. Indpls.); chair Mayor Steve Goldsmith's Transition Team, 1991-92; state dir. for Senator Richard Lugar US Senate, Ind., 1990-93; sec. state State of Ind., Indpls., 1994—2003; dir. advancement Univ. H.S., Carmel, Ind., 2003—05; v.p. for devel. St. Vincent Hospital, Indpls., 2005—; exec. dir. St. Vincent Hosp. Found., Indpls., 2005—. Cons. in fundraising and bus. adminstrn. Tabernacle Presbyn. Ch.; bd. dirs. St. Vincent Hosp Found., Cathedral H.S., U. Indpls.; mem. adv. bd. Salvation Army. Mem. Indpls. Rotary Club. Republican. Office: St Vincent Hosp 2001 W 86th St Indianapolis IN 46260

GILSTRAP, MARK, state legislator; b. Kansas City, Sept. 6, 1952; m. Joanne Gilstrap; 3 children. BSBA, Rockhurst Coll., 1975. Mem. Kans. Senate from 5th dist., Topeka, 1996—; mem. joint com. on spl. claims against the state; mem. joint com. on state gaming compacts; ranking mem. Elections, Local Govt.; mem. Fed. State Affairs Judiciary. Democrat. Roman Catholic. Office: 300 SW 10th Ave Rm 138-n Topeka KS 66612-1504

GIN, SUE LING, retail executive; Chmn. Flying Food Co., Chicago. Mem. Womens Leadership Forum (bd. dirs.). Office: Flying Food Fare Inc 212 N Sangamon St Chicago IL 60607-1700

GINGERICH, PHILIP DERSTINE, paleontologist, evolutionary biologist, educator; b. Goshen, Ind., Mar. 23, 1946; s. Orie Jacob and Miriam (Derstine) G.; m. B. Holly Smith, 1982 AB, Princeton U., 1968; PhD, Yale U., 1974. Prof. U. Mich., Ann Arbor, 1974—, dir. Mus. Paleontology, 1981-87, 1989—. Contbr. articles to sci. jours. Recipient Henry Russel award U. Mich., 1980; Shadle fellow Am. Soc. Mammalogists, 1973-74, NATO fellow, 1975, Guggenheim fellow, 1983-84 Fellow Am. Assn. Adv. Scis., Am. Acad. Arts Scis., Geol. Soc. Am.; mem. Paleontol. Soc. (Schuchert award 1981), Soc. Study Evolution, Am. Soc. Mammalogists, Soc. Vert. Paleontology. Office: U Mich Mus Paleontology 1109 Geddes Ave Ann Arbor MI 48109-1079

GINGO, JOSEPH MICHAEL, chemicals company executive; b. Dec. 6, 1944; Grad., Case Inst. Tech., 1966; JD, U. Akron, 1971; MBA, MIT, 1983. Engr., design and devel. Goodyear Tire & Rubber Co., chief engr., fabric devel. divsn., 1973—75, mgr., corp. projects and materials coordination, 1975—76, dir., corp. projects and materials coordination, 1976—78, dir., Tire Tech. Ctr. Luxembourg, v.p., gen. mgr., aviation products, 1986—89, pres., CEO, Air Treads Inc., 1989—92, v.p., tire tech. worldwide, 1992—95, v.p., Asia ops., 1995—98, v.p., gen. mgr., engineered products, 1998—99, sr. v.p., tech. and global products planning, 1999—2003, exec. v.p., quality sys., chief tech. officer, 2003—08; pres., CEO A. Schulman, Inc., 2008—. Office: A Schulman Inc 3550 W Market St Akron OH 44333 Office Phone: 330-666-3751. Office Fax: 330-668-7204.*

GINN, ROBERT MARTIN, retired utility company executive; b. Detroit, Jan. 13, 1924; s. Lloyd T. and Edna S.; m. Barbara R. Force, 1948; children: Anne, Martha, Thomas. BS in Elec. Engring., MS in Elec. Engring., U. Mich., 1948. With Cleve. Electric Illuminating Co., 1948-89, contr., 1959-62, v.p. gen. svcs., 1963-70, exec. v.p., 1970—79, pres., 1979—83, chief exec. officer, 1979-88, chmn., 1983-89; chmn., CEO Centerior Energy Corp., Toledo Edison Co., 1986-88. Mem. Shaker Heights Bd. Edn., (Ohio), 1968-75, pres., 1973-74; pres. Welfare Fedn. Cleve., 1968-69; chmn. Cleve. Commn. on Higher Edn., 1983-86; trustee John Carroll U., 1983-89, exec.-in-residence, 1989—; trustee Martha Holden Jennings Found., 1975-2002; chmn. Cleve. Opera, 1986-91. With USAAF, 1943-46. Office: 1120 Chester Ave # 470 Cleveland OH 44114-3514

GINSBURG, DAVID, genetics educator, researcher; b. Newburgh, NY, Aug. 11, 1952; s. Leonard and Ruth Helena Henrietta (Falkson) G.; m. Maureen Rose Kushinsky, June 7, 1981; children: Daniel William, Leah Beth. BA (magna cum laude) in Molecular Biophysics and Biochemistry, Yale U., 1974; MD, Duke U. Sch. Medicine, 1977. Diplomate Am. Bd. Internal Medicine, subspecialties in med. oncology and hematology; diplomate Am. Bd. Med. Genetics. Resident in pathology Presbyn. Hosp., San Francisco, 1977-78; intern, resident in internal medicine Peter Bent Brigham Hosp., Boston, 1978-81; fellow tng. program in hematology and med. oncology Brigham and Women's Hosp., Harvard Med. Sch., Boston, 1981-84; instr. medicine Harvard Med. Sch., Boston, 1984-85; asst. prof. dept. medicine U. Mich., Ann Arbor, 1985-89, assoc. prof. with tenure, 1989-93, assoc. prof. human genetics, 1989-93, dir. divsn. med. genetics, dept. medicine, 1993—2002, prof. internal medicine and human genetics, 1993—2004, James V. Neel Disting. U. prof. internal medicine and human genetics, 2004—, Warner-Lambert/Parke Davis prof. medicine, 2005—, mem., Life Sci. Inst., 2003—; asst. investigator Howard Hughes Med. Inst. Howard Hughes Med. Inst., Ann Arbor, 1985-89, assoc. investigator, 1989-93, investigator, 1993—. Contbr. numerous articles to profl. jours. Recipient Cotlove award, Acad. Clin. Lab. Physicians and Scientists, 2006. Fellow AAAS; mem. ACP, Am. Soc. Human Genetics, Am. Soc. Hematology (E. Donnall Thomas lectr. and prize 2000), Am. Heart Assn. (Sol Sherry lectr., 2002, Basic Rsch. prize 2003), Assn. Am. Physicians, Am. Soc. for Clin. Investigation (pres., 2002, ASCI award, 2004), Inst. Medicine, Am. Acad. Arts and Scis., NAS, Alpha Omega Alpha. Jewish. Office: Life Scis Inst Rm 5028 210 Washtenaw Ave Ann Arbor MI 48109 Business E-Mail: ginsburg@umich.edu.

GIPP, CHUCK, state official; b. Decorah, Iowa, Nov. 30, 1947; m. Ranae Gipp; children: Alison, Barrett. BA, Luther Coll., 1970. Dairy farmer; chair Winneshiek County Reps., 1980—90, Winneshiak County Solid Waste Commn., 1981—90; state rep. Iowa, 1991—; asst. majority leader Iowa Ho. Reps., 1993—94, majority whip, 1995—96; with mcpl. fire and police retirement sys., 1997—. Chair transp., capitols, and infrastructure appropriations com.; mem. state govt. com.; mem. environ. protection appropriations com. With USAR, 1971—76. Mem.: Winneshiak County Farm Bur., Decorah C. of C. Republican. Lutheran. Office: State Capitol E 12th and Grand Des Moines IA 50319

GIRARD, JIM, former state legislator; b. Marshall, Minn., June 12, 1953; s. Louis Felix and Beatrice (Barnady) G.; m. Becky; children: Chrsitine Marie, Ryan James. BS, Dakota State U., 1975, MS, 1971. Chmn. Lyon County Rep. Com., 1987-88; mem. Minn. State Rep. Ctrl. Com., 1987-89; state rep. Minn. Ho. Reps., Dist. 21A, 1989-97; sr. ptnr. Cookhill Gerard Assocs., St. Paul, 1999—. Mem. agrl. capital investments, fin. inst. & ins. & Tex. coms., Minn. Ho. Reps.; agrl. rep. Western Bank & Trust, 1977—; nutritionist Feeders Choice Foods, 1977-79; owner Girard Farms, 1979-99. Recipient Key Press award Minn. Jaycees, 1983, Disting. Svc. award Marshall Area Jaycees, 1984. Mem. Marshall Area C. of C. (chmn. agrl. com. 1987-88), Minn. Park Producers Assn. (legis. chmn. exec. com. 1986-89), Minn. Farm Bur., Alpha Gamma Rho. Home: 7677 Nottingham Pkwy Maple Grove MN 55311-1506

GISLASON, ERIC ARNI, chemistry professor; b. Oak Park, Ill., Sept. 9, 1940; s. Raymond Spencer and Jane Ann (Clifford) G.; m. Nancy Brown, Sept. 11, 1962 (dec. June 1994); children: Kristina Elizabeth, John Harrison; m. Sharon McKevitt Fetzer, Apr. 25, 1998. BA summa cum laude, Oberlin Coll., 1962; PhD, Harvard U., 1967. Postdoctoral fellow U. Calif-Berkeley, 1967-69; asst. prof. chemistry U. Ill., Chgo., 1969-73; assoc. prof. U. Ill.-Chgo., 1973-77, prof., 1977—; acting head chemistry dept. U. Ill., Chgo., 1993-94, head chemistry dept., 1994-99, interim dean Coll. Liberal Arts and Scis., 1997-98, interim vice chancellor rsch., 1999-2001, vice chancellor rsch., 2001—. Vis. scientist FOM Inst. Atomic and Molecular Physics, Amsterdam, 1977-78; prof. associé U. Paris South, 1985. Contbr. articles to profl. jours. Recipient Silver Circle Teaching award U. Ill., 1982, Excellence in Teaching award U. Ill., 1990. Mem. Am. Chem. Soc. (vis. assocs. program), Am. Phys. Soc., Phi Beta Kappa, Sigma Xi, Phi Kappa Phi. Congregationalist. Achievements include rsch. in theoretical studies of ion-molecule reactions, collision-induced dissociation, nonadiabatic transitions, molecular energy transfer, thermodynamics and isotope effects. Home: 7227 Oak Ave River Forest IL 60305-1935 Office: U Ill Chgo OVCR M/C 672 Rm 310 1737 W Polk St Chicago IL 60612-7727 Office Phone: 312-996-9450. Business E-Mail: gislason@uic.edu.

GITNER, GERALD L., air transportation executive, investment banker; b. Boston, Apr. 10, 1945; s. Samuel and Sylvia (Berkovitz) Gitner; m. Deanne Gebell, June 24, 1968; children: Daniel Mark, Seth Michael. BA cum laude, Boston U., 1966. Staff v.p. TransWorld Airlines, NYC, 1972-74; sr. v.p. mktg. and planning Tex. Internat. Airlines, Houston, 1974-80; pres., founder People Express Airlines, Newark, 1980-82; chmn. Pan Am. World Svcs. Inc., NYC, 1982-85, exec. v.p., chief fin. officer, 1983-85; vice chmn. Pan Am. World Airways, NYC, 1982-85, Pan Am Corp., 1984-85; pres. Tex. Air Corp., Houston, 1985-86; CEO, pres. ATASCO USA, Inc., aircraft trading firm, NYC, 1986-89; chmn. D. G. Assocs. Inc., 1986—, Avalon Group, Ltd., NYC, 1990-98; co-chmn. Global Aircraft Leasing Ltd., 1991-98; dir. TWA, Inc., 1993—2002, CEO, 1996-99, chmn., 1997—2002; chmn. bd. Kitty Hawk, Inc., 2002—07; dir. Tricom, S.A., 2004—. Bd. advisers econs. dept. Boston U.; mem. chancellors coun. U. Mo., St. Louis, 1997—2000. Trustee, mem. exec. com. Boston U., 1984—96; trustee Rochester (N.Y.) Inst. Tech., 1999—2004. Recipient Disting. Alumni award, Boston U., 1982, 1984. Mem.: Cornell Club N.Y., Phi Alpha Theta.

GITTELMAN, MARC JEFFREY, manufacturing and financial executive; b. NYC, Nov. 26, 1947; s. Sidney and Trudy (Eidus) G.; m. Nanci V. Geiger, Apr. 9, 1988; 1 child, Brandon Michael. BBA, Hofstra U., 1969; MBA in Fin., Adelphi U., 1972; postgrad., U. Colo., Denver. Credit analyst Security Nat. Bank Long Island, Melville, NY, 1969-72; dir. adminstrn. Tiger Leasing Group Inc., Chgo., 1973-78; asst. treas. Storage Tech. Corp., Louisville, Colo., 1979-83; v.p., treas. Holnam Inc. (formerly Ideal Basic Industries), Dundee, Mich., 1984-91, Andrew Corp., Orland Park, Ill., 1992—2005, v.p. real estate, 2005—. Bd. dirs. Food Bank of Rockies. Mem. Nat. Assn. Corp. Treas. Republican. Jewish. Office: Andrew Corp 10500 153rd St Orland Park IL 60462-3071 E-mail: jeffrey.gittelman@andrew.com.

GITTLEMAN, NEAL, orchestra conductor; b. Ancon, Panama Canal Zone, June 29, 1955; s. Edwin and Rosalyn (Leinwand) G.; m. Lisa Fry, Dec. 21, 1984. BA in Music, Yale U., 1975; postgrad., Manhattan Sch. Music, 1977-81; artist's diploma in orch. conducting, Hartt Sch. Music, Hartford, Conn., 1983. Asst. condr. Oreg. Symphony, Portland, 1983-86; music dir. Marion (Ind.) Philharm., 1987-86; assoc. condr. Syracuse (N.Y.) Symphony, 1986-89, Milw. Symphony Orch., 1989-95, resident condr., 1995-98; music dir. Dayton (Ohio) Philharm. Orch., 1995—. Guest condr. San Francisco Symphony, 1989, Rochester Symphony, 1989, Oreg. Symphony, 1990, San Jose Symphony, 1992, Minn. Orch., 1992, 93, Telemann Chamber Orch., Osaka, Japan, 1994, Shinsei Nihon Symphony, Tokyo, 1994, San Antonio Symphony, 1994, Indls. Symphony, 1994, UNAM Philharm., Mexico City, 1995, Grant Park Orch., Chgo., 1995, Buffalo Symphony, 1995, Chgo. Symphony, 1995, 97, Edmonton (Alta., Can.) Symphony, 1996, Augsburg Symphony, 1997. Recipient 2d prize Ernest Ansermet Internat. Conducting Competition, Geneva, 1984, 3d prize Leopold Stokowski Internat. Conducting Competition, N.Y.C., 1985; Karl Böhm fellow Hartt Sch. Music, 1982. Avocations: golf, squash, t'ai chi ch'uan. Office: Dayton Philharmonic Orch Assoc 109 N Main St #200 Dayton OH 45402-1294

GIUNTA, JOSEPH, conductor, music director; b. Atlantic City, May 8, 1951; m. Cynthia Reid, June 5, 1982. MusB in Theory, Northwestern U., 1973, MusM in Conducting, 1974; DFA (hon.), Simpson Coll., 1986. Condr., music dir. Waterloo/Cedar Falls Symphony and Chamber Orch. of Iowa, 1974-89; music dir. Des Moines Symphony Orch., 1989—. Guest condr. numerous symphonies, orchs. including Chgo. Symphony, London Philharm., Philharmonia Orch. of London, Minn. Orch., Indpls. Orch., Phoenix Symphony, Fla. Symphony, Akron (Ohio) Symphony, Syracuse (N.Y.) Symphony, R.I. Philharm. Recipient Helen M. Thompson award; named Outstanding Young Condr. in U.S., 1984. Mem. Phi Mu Alpha, Pi Kappa Lambda. Office: Des Moines Symphony 221 Walnut St Des Moines IA 50309-2101

GIVAN, RICHARD MARTIN, retired judge; b. Indpls., June 7, 1921; s. Clinton Hodel and Glee (Bowen) G.; m. Pauline Marie Haggart, Feb. 28, 1945; children: Madalyn Givan Hesson, Sandra Givan Chenoweth, Patricia Givan Smith, Elizabeth Givan Whipple. LL.B., Ind. U., 1951. Bar: Ind. 1952. Ptnr. with Clinton H. Givan, 1952-59, Bowen, Myers, Northam & Givan, 1960-69; justice Ind. Supreme Ct., 1969-74, chief justice, 1974-87, assoc. justice, 1987-95, ret., 1995; dep. pub. defender Ind., 1952-53; dep. atty. gen., 1953—64; dep. pros. atty. Marion County, 1965-66, ret., 1995. Mem. Ind. Ho. Reps., 1967-68 Served to 2d lt. USAAF, 1942-45. Mem. Ind. Bar Assn., Indpls. Bar Assn., Ind. Soc. Chgo., Newcomen Soc. N.Am., Internat. Arabian Horse Assn. (past dir., chmn. ethical practices rev. bd.), Ind. Arabian Horse Club (pres. 1971-72), Indpls. 500 Oldtimers Club, Lions, Sigma Delta Kappa. Mem. Soc. Of Friends. Home: 6690 S County Road 1025 E Indianapolis IN 46231-2495

GIVENS, HENRY, JR., academic administrator; m. Belma Evans; children: Stacey G., Keith Alan. Bachelor, Lincoln U., Mo.; Master, U. Ill.; PhD, St. Louis U. Tchr. Webster Groves (Mo.) Sch. Dist., prin. magnet sch., asst. to supt. to schs.; pres. Harris-Stowe State Coll., St. Louis, 1979—. Interim pres. Lincoln U., 1987; cons. U.S. State Dept. Bd. dirs. Mo. Arts Coun., St. Louis Symphony Orch., St. Louis Zoo. Mem. Am. Assn. State Colls. and Univs., Nat. Alliance Black Sch. Educators, Nat. Assn. Equal Opportunity, North Ctrl. Assn. Colls. and Secondary Schs., Phi Delta Kappa, Sigma Pi Phi, Phi Delta Sigma. Office: Harris-Stowe State Coll 3026 Laclede Ave Saint Louis MO 63103-2136

GLADDEN, JAMES WALTER, JR., lawyer; b. Pitts., Feb. 23, 1940; s. James Walter and Cynthia Unice (Hales) G.; m. Patricia T. Kuehn, Aug. 21, 1993; children: James, Thomas, Robert. AB, DePauw U., 1961; JD, Harvard U., 1964. Bar: Ill. 1964, U.S. Sup. Ct. 1978. Ptnr. Mayer, Brown, Rowe & Maw, Chgo., 1964—2005, sr. counsel, 2005—. Mem. ABA. Home: 1426 Chicago Ave Apt 5N Evanston IL 60201 Office: Mayer Brown Rowe & Maw 71 S Wacker Chicago IL 60603-3441 Home Phone: 847-475-4230; Office Phone: 312-701-7253. E-mail: jgladden@mayerbrownrowe.com.

GLAHN, JEFFREY, communications executive; b. 1978; BS in Info. Systems, Pa. State U.; MBA, Drexel U. Systems engr. Comcast Corp.; product mgr., Voice and Data Solutions Motorola, Inc. Served in USMC. Decorated Medal of Commendation; named one of 40 Executives Under 40, Multichannel News, 2006.

GLANCY, ALFRED ROBINSON, III, retired public utility company executive; b. Detroit, Mar. 14, 1938; s. Alfred Robinson and Elizabeth A. (Tant) G.; m. Ruth Mary Roby, Sept. 15, 1962; children: Joan C., Alfred R. IV, Douglas Roby, Andrew Roby. BA, Princeton U., 1960; MA, Harvard U., 1962. V.p. corp. planning Am. Nat. Gas Svc., Detroit, 1976-79; econ. and fin. planning staff Mich. Consol. Gas Co., Detroit, 1962-64, supr. econ. studies and rates, 1965-67, mgr. econ. and fin. planning dept., 1967-68, treas., 1969-72, v.p., treas., 1972-73, v.p. customer and mktg. svcs., 1976-79, v.p. mktg./dist. ops., 1979-81, sr. v.p. mktg/customer svcs., 1981-83, sr. v.p. utility ops., 1983-84, chmn., CEO, 1984-92, MCN Energy Group Inc., Detroit, 1989-2001; ret., 2001. Bd. dirs., chmn. UNICO Investment Co., Seattle. Past chmn. Detroit Symphony Orch., Detroit Renaissance Inc., exec. com.; past chmn. Detroit Med. Ctr., New Detroit, Inc. Mem. Princeton Club Mich., Country Club Detroit, Detroit Athletic Club. Republican. Office: Ste 405 400 Maple Park Blvd Saint Clair Shores MI 48081

GLANZMANN, THOMAS H., healthcare company executive; B in Polit. Sci., Dartmouth Coll.; MBA, Inst. Mgmt. Devel., Lausanne, Switzerland. With Baxter Healthcare, 1988—, asst. gen. mgr. Switzerland, v.p. bus. devel. and planning, blood therapy/immunotherapy, v.p. bus. devel. and planning Biotech Group, pres. Biotech Group in Europe, CEO Immuno Internat., 1996, pres. Hyland Immuno, 1998—, corp. v.p.

GLASER, GARY A., bank executive; Grad., Baldwin-Wallace, Case Western Res. U. With Nat. City Corp., 1967-84; exec. v.p. of corp. banking group Nat. City Bank., 1984—88; pres., CEO Nat. City Bank, Columbus, Ohio, 1988—. Exec. v.p. Nat. City Corp., 1988—. Bd. mem. Am. Cancer Soc., Boy Scouts of Am., Ctr. of Sci. and Ind., Columbus Mus. of Art, Greater Columbus Area Growth Assn., United Way of Franklin County; hon. trustee Columbus Coun. on world Affairs. Mem.: Columbus Coun. for Ethics in Econ., Ohio Bankers Assn. Office: Nat City Bank 155 E Broad St Columbus OH 43215-3609

GLASER, ROBERT EDWARD, lawyer; b. Cin., Jan. 12, 1935; s. Delbert Henry and Rita Elizabeth (Arlinghaus) G.; m. Kathleen Eileen Grannen, June 17, 1961; children— Petra M., Timothy X., Mark G., Bridget M., Christopher D., Jenny M., Michael F. BS in Bus. Adminstrn. cum laude, Xavier U., Cin., 1955; LLB, U. Cin., 1960; LLM, U. Chgo., 1962; postgrad., U. Tuebingen, Fed. Republic of Germany, 1961. Bar: Ohio 1960, U.S. Dist. Ct. (no. dist.) Ohio 1963, (so. dist.) Ohio 1964, U.S. Ct. Appeals (6th cir.) 1964, U.S. Tax Ct. 1970, U.S. Ct. Internat. Trade 1971, U.S. Ct. Fed. Claims 1992, U.S. Ct. Appeals (fed. cir.) 2000. Assoc. Arter & Hadden, Cleve., 1963-69, ptnr., 1970-2001, chmn., 1983-92; owner Law Office of Robert E. Glaser, 2001—. Arbitrator Cuyahoga County Ct. Common Pleas, Ohio, 1972—, Med. Malpractice Panel, 1985—, Mediator Settlement Week, 1990; lectr. Cleve. Tax Inst., 1966—2000, mem. exec. com., 1980—84, chmn., 1982; lectr. Can.-U.S. Law Inst., 1980, Res. Officers Assn., 1970—, Ret. Officers Assn., 1985—; mem. qualified list of neutrals IRS Rev. Proc., 2003—. Contbr. articles to legal jours. Sec. Bay View Hosp., 1972-81; trustee Mental Health Rehab. and Rsch., Inc., 1975-86, mem. exec. com., 1977-81, pres., 1979-81; trustee Cmty. Legal Svcs. Cleve., Inc., 2004—06, legal counsel, 2004—06, v.p. 2006; mem. men's com. Cleve. Play House, 1965-2003; mem. joint mental health and corrections com. Fedn. Cmty. Planning, 1978-81; mem. Cleve. Coun. on Fgn. Affairs, 1987-2002; mem. vis. com. Coll. Law Cleve. State U., 1987-97; mem. Soc. of Benchers, Case Western Res. Univ. Coll. Law, 1988—; trustee Univ. Circle, Inc., 1989-99, mem. exec. com., 1989-99. Col. U.S. Army, ret. Ford Found. grantee, 1960. Fellow Am. Bar Found. (life); mem. Ohio Bar Assn. (gen. tax com. 1998—, lawyer assistance com. 1999—), Nat. Bar Assn., Cleve. Bar Assn. (trustee 1983-87, chmn. bd. of com. grievance and discipline trial com. 1993, gen. tax com. 1983-2004, lawyer assistance com. 1999-2004), Legal Aid Soc. Cleve., Am. Judicature Soc., 8th Jud. Conf. (life), Am. Arbitration Assn. (nat. and internat. panel arbitrators 1969—), Citizens League Greater Cleve., Cleve. Cath. Lawyer Guild (pres. 1969-70, St. Thomas More award 2006), Tax Club Cleve., Order of Coif, Union Club, Pentagon Officers Athletic Club, Serra Internat., Cleve. Club (exec. com. 1987-88, 90-91, 93-98, 2000-04, pres. 1994-96, 2002-04), KC. Roman Catholic. Office: Law Office of Robert E Glaser Ste 1150 925 Euclid Ave Cleveland OH 44115-1475 Home: 33750 Lorain Rd North Ridgeville OH 44039 Office Phone: 216-696-2938. Business E-Mail: robert.glaser@tuckerellis.com.

GLASER, RONALD, microbiologist, educator; b. NYC, Feb. 27, 1939; s. Irving and Pauline G.; m. Janice Kiecolt, Jan. 17, 1980; children: Andrew, Erik. BA, U. Bridgeport, 1962; MS, U. R.I., 1964; PhD, U. Conn., 1968; postgrad., Baylor Coll. Medicine, 1968-69. Asst. prof. microbiology Pa. State U., Hershey, 1970-73, assoc. prof., 1973-77, prof., 1977-78; prof. chmn. dept. med. microbiology and immunology Coll. Medicine Ohio State U., Columbus, 1978—92; reviewer NIH and NASA study sects.; assoc. dean for rsch. and grad. edn. Med. Ctr. Ohio State U., Columbus, 1992-94, assoc. v.p. health sci. rsch. Med. Ctr., 1994-2001, assoc. v.p. rsch., 2001—03. Dir. Inst. for Behavioral Med. Rsch., 1999—. Editor: (with T. Gottleib-Stematsky) Human Herpes Virus Infections: Clinical Aspects, 1982; (with others) Epstein-Barr Virus and Human Disease, 1987; (with J. Jones) Human Herpes Virus Infections, 1994; (with J. Kiecolt-Glaser) Handbook of Human Stress, 1994. NIH postdoc. fellow, 1968-69; Franco-Am. Exch. Program; Fogarty Internat. Ctr.; NIH and INSRM fellow, 1975, 77; Leukemia Soc. Am. scholar, 1974-79. Fellow: AAAS, Acad. Behavioral Medicine Rsch. (pres. psychoneuroimmunology rsch. soc. 2003, pres. 2007—08); mem.: Am. Soc. Microbiology. Office: Ohio State U 2175 Graves Hall 333 W 10th Ave Columbus OH 43210-1239 Home Phone: 614-771-9119; Office Phone: 614-292-5526. E-mail: ronald.glaser@osumc.edu.

GLASS, JOANNE WISSMAN, lawyer; b. Covington, Ky., Nov. 6, 1969; BA, Xavier U., 1991; JD, Salmon P. Chase Coll. Law, 1994. Bar: Ohio 1994, Ky. 1995, US Dist. Ct. Eastern Dist. Ky. 1995, US Dist. Ct. Western Dist. Ky. 1995, US Dist. Ct. Southern Dist. Ohio. Ptnr. Frost Brown Todd LLC, Cin., chairperson, Cmty. Opportunity Com. Vol., firm coordinator St. Francis Soup Kitchen; bd. mem., sec. Queen City Found.; bd. mem. Transitions, Inc., 1996—; vol. Ky. Lawyers Assistance Prog. Nominee 40 Under 40 awards, Cin. Bus. Courier, 2005, 2006; named one of Ohio's Rising Stars, Super Lawyers, 2005, 2006. Mem.: ABA, Ohio State Bar Assn. (mem., Workers' Compensation Com.), Northern Ky. Bar Assn. (mem., Young Lawyers Sect., mem., Workers' Compensation Com.,), Ky. Bar Assn., Cin. Bar Assn. (sec., Workers' Compensation Com., Young Lawyers Sect., chairperson, Bridge the Gap Com.). Office: Frost Brown Todd LLC 2200 PNC Ctr 201 E Fifth St Cincinnati OH 45202-4182 Office Phone: 513-651-6132. Office Fax: 513-651-6981.

GLASS, KENNETH EDWARD, management consultant; b. Fort Thomas, Ky., Sept. 28, 1940; s. Clarence E. and Lucille (Garrison) Glass; m. Nancy Romanek, May 9, 1964; children: Ryan, Lara. ME, U. Cin., 1963, MS, 1965, grad. student, 1967. Registered profl. engr., Ohio; lic. Airline Transport Pilot. With Allis Chalmers Mfg. Co., Cin. and Eng., 1963—73; v.p. mfg. Fiat Allis Contrn. Machinery, Inc., Chgo., 1973—75; pres. Perkins Diesel Corp., Canton, Ohio, 1975—77; pres., CEO Massey-Ferguson, Inc., Des Moines, 1978; v.p., gen. mgr. N.Am. ops. Massey Ferguson Ltd., Des Moines, 1978; chmn., pres., CEO Union Metal Mfg. Co., Canton, Ohio, 1979—85; pres. Glass & Assocs. Inc. Glass & Assocs. Inc., 1985—2004, chmn., 1996—2005; pres. Stony Point Group, Inc., 1996—, also bd. dirs., chmn., 2005—. Chmn. Utica Corp., 2001—, UCA Holdings, 2001—, TECT Corp. Trustee U. Cin. Found.; dir. N.C. Outward Bound Sch., bd. dirs. Mem.: Young Presidents Orgn., Turnaround Mgmt. Assn. (bd. dirs.), Assn. Cert. Turnaround Profls. (bd. dirs., v.p. 1993—94, pres.

1995—96), Am. Bankrupcy Inst., Pi Tau Sigma. Achievements include patentee in field. Office Phone: 828-210-8120. Personal E-mail: keglass@attglobal.net.

GLASS, RICHARD MCLEAN, psychiatry educator, medical editor; b. Phoenix, Sept. 25, 1943; s. Richard Kirkpatrick and Harriet Margaret (Bradshaw) G.; m. Rita Mae Catherine Denk, Mar. 4, 1967; children: Kathryn, Brendan Neil. BA, Northwestern U., 1965, MD, 1968. Diplomate Am. Bd. Psychiatry and Neurology. Asst. prof. psychiatry U. Chgo., 1975—82, assoc. prof., 1982—95, clin. prof., 1995—. Dir. adult psychiatry clinic U. Chgo., 1985-89. Mem. editl. bd. Archives of Gen. Psychiatry, 1984-2003; cons. editor JAMA, 1987-89, dep. editor, 1989—; contbr. articles to profl. jours. Served to major U.S. Army, 1970-72. Fellow Am. Psychiat. Assn.; mem. AAAS, AMA. Presbyterian. Avocations: tennis, music, trombone. Office: JAMA 515 N State St Chicago IL 60610-4325 Home Phone: 773-924-4956; Office Phone: 312-464-2413. Business E-Mail: richard.glass@jama-archives.org.

GLASSCOCK, KENTON, state legislator; m. Joyce Glasscock. BA, Kans. State U., 1976. State rep. Dist. 62 Kans. Ho. of Reps., 1991—, mem. taxation and energy and natural resources com., mem. joint com. on adminstrv. rules and regulations, chairperson calendar and printing com., vice-chairperson interstate cooperation com., majority leader, spkr., 2000—. Pres. Kans. Lumber Homestore. Home: PO Box 37 Manhattan KS 66505-0068 E-mail: glasscock@house.state.ks.us, kentglas@flinthills.com.

GLASSCOCK, LARRY CLABORN, health insurance company executive; b. Cullman, Ala., Apr. 4, 1948; s. Oscar Claborn and Betty Lou (Norman) Glasscock; m. Lee Ann Roden, Sept. 13, 1969; children: Michael, Carrie BBA, Cleve. State U., 1970; postgraduate student, Columbia U. Am. Inst. Banking. V.p. pers. and orgn. AmeriTrust Co., Cleve., 1974-75, v.p. nat. divsn., 1976-78, v.p., mgr. credit card ctr., 1978-79, sr. v.p. consumer fin., 1980-81, sr. v.p. nat. divsn., 1981-83, exec. v.p. corp. banking adminstr., 1983-87; group exec. v.p. AmeriTrust Corp. and AmeriTrust Co., Cleve., 1987-92; pres., CEO Essex Holdings, Inc.; pres., COO First Am. Bank, N.A.; pres., CEO Blue Cross and Blue Shield of the Nat. Capital Area; COO CareFirst, Inc.; senior exec. v.p., COO Anthem Ins., Indpls., 1998—99, pres., CEO, 1999—2004, chmn., 2003—04; pres., CEO WellPoint, Inc. (formerly Anthem Ins.), Indpls., 2004—07, chmn., 2005—. Chmn. Coun. Affordable Quality Healthcare, Washington, 2002-03; bd. dirs. Nat. Inst. Healthcare Mgmt., Zimmer Inc., 2001-, AT Fin. Corpn., AT Capital Corpn., AmeriTrust Internat. Banking, AmeriTrust Devel. Bank, CT Leasing Corpn., Sprint Nextel Corp. Trustee Cleve. State U. Devel. Found.; campaign chmn. Geauga County United Way, 1989; mem. adv. bd. N.E. Ohio Employee Ownership Ctr. Kent State U., 1987—. Served in USMC, 1970—76. Co-recipient Ind. Entrepreneur of Yr. award, Ernst & Young, 2003. Mem. Am. Inst. Banking, Am. Bankers Assn., Assn. Res. City Bankers, Greater Cleve. Growth Assn., Cleve. State U. Alumni Assn. (pres. 1987). Clubs: Union (Cleve.); Hillbrook (Chagrin Falls, Ohio); The Country (Pepper Pike, Ohio). Office: WellPoint Inc 120 Monument Cir Indianapolis IN 46204-4906

GLASSER, JAMES J., retired leasing company executive; b. Chgo., June 5, 1934; s. Daniel D. and Sylvia G.; m. Louise D. Rosenthal, Apr. 19, 1964; children: Mary, Emily, Daniel. AB, Yale U., 1955; JD, Harvard U., 1958. Bar: Ill. 1958. Asst. states atty., Cook County, Ill., 1958-61; mem. exec. staff GATX Corp., Chgo., 1961-69, pres., 1974-96, chmn. bd., CEO, 1978-96, chmn. emeritus, 1996—, also dir. Gen. mgr. Infilco Products Co., 1969-70; v.p. GATX Leasing Corp., San Francisco, 1970-71, pres., 1971-74; bd. dirs. B.F. Goodrich Co., Harris Bankcorp, Inc., Harris Trust & Savs. Bank, Mut. Trust Life Ins. Co. Bd. dirs. Lake Forest Hosp., Northwestern Meml. Corp., Voices for Ill. Children; trustee Better Govt. Assn., Chgo. Zool. Soc., U. Chgo. Mem. Chgo. C. of C. (dir.), Chgo. Cen. Area Com. (dir.), Econ. Club of Chgo., Commercial Club, Casino Club, Chgo. Club, Racquet Club, Onwentsia Club (Lake Forest, Ill.), Shoreacres (Lake Bluff, Ill.), Tucson Country Club, Chi Psi. Home: 464 N Mayflower Rd Lake Forest IL 60045-2306 Office: 500 W Monroe St Chicago IL 60661-3630

GLASSHEIM, ELIOT ALAN, editor, state legislator; b. NYC, Feb. 10, 1938; s. Raymond S. and Edith (Ruthizer) G.; m. Patricia Sanborn, July 20, 1969 (div. Feb. 1979); children: Eagle, Don; m. Dyan Rey, Feb. 14, 1996. BA, Wesleyan U., 1960; MA, U. N.Mex., 1966, PhD, 1972. Copy boy, book reviewer Wash. Post, 1960-61; editl. proofreader Wall St. Jour., NYC, 1962-64; mgmt. trainee Accessory Fashions, NYC, 1964-66; asst. prof. English, Augusta (Ga.) Coll., 1968-70; fellow U. N.D., Grand Forks, 1971-73; mem. N.D. Ho. of Reps., Grand Forks, 1975-76, 93—, house appropriations com., 2001—, asst. Dem. leader, 2003—04; grant writer, dir. oral history project of 97 flood N.D. Mus. Art, Grand Forks, 1993-99; owner used bookstore and Internet sales Dr. Eliot's Twice Sold Tales, Grand Forks, 1992—; policy analyst No. Great Plains, Inc., Fargo, ND, 1999—. Dir. Population/Food Fund, Grand Forks, 1977-79; housing coord., grantswriter .D. Migrant Coun., Grand Forks, 1979-81. Editor: Population and Food Issues, 1977, 1978, Voices from the Flood, 1999, Behind the Scenes, 2002, Renewing the Countryside--North Dakota, 2004, Toward New Horizons: Moving the Northern Great Plains Region to a Stronger Economic Future, 2002, Traceability in Agriculture, 2003; author: The New Marketplace in European Agriculture: Environmental and Social Values Within the Ford Chain, 2005; author: (poems) The Restless Giant, 1968. Exec. dir. Quad County Cmty. Action Agy., Grand Forks, 1981—87; field rep., office mgr. U.S. Senator Quentin Burdick, Grand Forks, 1987—92; mem. Grand Forks City Coun., 1982—, Grand Forks Planning and Zoning Com., 1984—96, mem. flood response com., 1997—2000, chmn. population task force, 2001; chmn. interim legis. Commerce Comm., 1999—2000; founder, dir. Red River Valley Habitat for Humanity, Grand Forks, 1988—99; chmn. Dist. 17/18 Dems., Grand Forks, 1980—81; bd. dirs. Prairie Pub. TV, 1997—2000. Home: 619 N 3rd St Grand Forks ND 58203-3203 E-mail: eglass@infionline.net.

GLASSMAN, ERIC I., retail executive; Grad., U. Cin., 1981. CFO, v.p. DIY Home Warehouse, Inc., Valley View, Ohio. Office: DIY Home Warehouse 800 N Old Woodward Ave Ste 201 Birmingham MI 48009-3802

GLASSROTH, JEFFREY, internist, educator; b. NYC, Oct. 28, 1948; s. Murray and Marie (Cheynoweth) G.; m. Carol Holton, July 22, 1972; children: Marley, Drew. AB, Columbia U., 1969; MD, U. Cin., 1973. Diplomate Am. Bd. Internal Medicine, Subspecialty Bd. Pulmonary Medicine. Intern U. Cin. Med. Ctr., 1973-74, intern, resident, 1973-75, 77-78, resident, 1974-75, 77-78; fellow in pulmonary and critical care medicine Boston U., 1978-81, instr. medicine, 1979-81; from asst. to assoc. prof. medicine Northwestern U., Evanston, Ill., 1981-90, prof. medicine, 1990—95; prof. medicine, chair dept. Allegheny U. Health Scis., Phila., 1995—98; pres. Am. Thoracic Soc., NYC, 1999—2000; chmn., dept. of med. Univ. Wisconsin, 1998—2005; vice dean, prof. medicine Tufts U. Sch. Medicine, 2005—07. Cons. Astra N.Am., Westboro, Mass., 1993-99, Genentech/Novartis, San Francisco, 2000-02; mem. adv. coun. for elimination of Tb, CDC, Atlanta, 1993-97; mem. ad hoc study sect. NIH, Bethesda, Md., 1993, 97, 2005. Editor: Scientific Basis Respiratory Infection, 1993; co-editor: Baum's Textbook of Pulmonary Diseases, 7th edit., 2003; assoc. editor Am. Jour. Respiratory Critical Care Medicine, 1994-99; mem. editl. bd. Chest, 1988-93. Surgeon, USPHS, 1975-77, Atlanta. Rsch. grantee NIH, 1987-97, recipient Pulmonary Acad. awards, 1983-89. Master ACP; fellow Am. Coll. Chest Physicians; mem. AAAS, Am. Thoracic Soc. (sec. 1996-97, v.p. 1997-98, pres.-elect 1998, pres. 1999-2000), Ctrl. Soc. for Clin. Rsch. (pres. 2002-03), European Respiratory Soc., Internat. Union Against TB and Lung Disease, Assn. Profs. Medicine (pres.-elect 2003, pres. 2004-05). Avocations: skiing, distance running. Office: Northwestern Sch of Medicine 303 E Chicago Ave Ward 4-009 Chicago IL 60611 Office Phone: 312-503-1871. Business E-Mail: j.glassroth@northwestern.edu.

GLATZ, CHARLES E., engineering educator; m. Bonita A. Glatz. BSChemE, U. Notre Dame, 1971; PhDChemE, U. Wis., 1975. Asst. prof. chem. engring. Iowa State U., Ames, Iowa, 1975—80, assoc. prof., 1980—86, prof., 1986—, chair, 1997—, interim dean Coll. Engring., 2004—05. Hon. rsch. fellow U. Hull and U. Coll., London, 1982—83; vis. prof. U. Colo., Boulder, 1994; editl. bd. Separation Sci. and Tech., 1996—. Contbr. articles to profl. jours. Named a Disting. Iowa Scientist, Iowa Acad. Sciences, 1997; recipient Webber Award for Outstanding Tchr. in Chem. Engring., Iowa State U., 1982, Outstanding Tchr. Award, Iowa State U. Coll. Engring., 1990, Boylan Award for Outstanding Rsch., 2003. Mem.: Am. Inst. Chem. Engineers, Am. Chem. Soc. Office: Iowa State U 2114 Sweeney Hall Ames IA 50011-2230

GLAZEBROOK, RITA SUSAN, nursing educator; b. St. Paul, Apr. 26, 1948; d. David L. and Beverly Ruth (Penhiter) Beccue; m. Harold L. Glazebrook, Dec. 20, 1986; children: Julie, Robert J., Scott, Robert M., Katherine. Diploma, RN, Abbott Hosp. Sch. Nursing, Mpls., 1970; BS in Nursing, Augsburg Coll., Mpls., 1979; MS in ursing, U. Minn., 1981, PhD in Edn. Adminstrn., 1987. Mem. staff, asst. head nurse United Hosps., Inc., St. Paul, 1970-78; mem. staff Med. Pers. Pool, St. Paul, 1978-81; prof. nursing, chmn. dept. St. Olaf Coll., Northfield, Minn., 1981—. Contbr. articles to profl. jours. Faculty devel. grant Evan. Luth. Ch. Am. Mem. ANA, Minn. Nurses Assn., Assn. of Women's Health Obstetric and Neonatal Nurses, Sigma Theta Tau. Home: 8941 Jasmine Ln S Cottage Grove MN 55016-3422 Office Phone: 507-786-3265. Business E-Mail: glazebro@stolaf.edu.

GLAZIER, ROBERT CARL, publishing executive; b. Brandsville, Mo., Mar. 26, 1927; s. Vernie A. and Mildred F. (Beu) G.; m. Harriette Hubbard, June 5, 1949; children: Gregory Kent, Jeffrey Robert. Student, Drury Coll., 1944-46; BA, U. Wichita, 1949. Reporter Springfield (Mo.) Daily News, 1944-46; asst. city editor Wichita Eagle, 1946-49; journalism instr. U. Wichita, 1949-53; dir. pub. relations Springfield (Mo.) Pub. Schs., 1953-59; asso. dir. dept. radio and TV The Methodist Ch., Nashville, 1959-61; gen. mgr. WDCN-TV (Channel 2), Nashville, 1961-65, KETC (Channel 9), St. Louis, 1965-76; also exec. dir. St. Louis Ednl. TV Commn.; pres. So. Ednl. Communications Assn., 1976-80; chmn. bd. Springfield Communications, Inc., Mo., 1980—. Bd. dir. Systematic Savs. & Loan Assn., Cox Health Sys.; pres. Lester E. Cox Med. Ctrs., 1999-2000 Bd. dir. Adult Edn. Council Greater St. Louis, 1965-76, United Meth. Communications, 1980-86, Springfield Area Council of Chs., 1980-86. Served with AUS, 1945-46. Named to, Writers Hall of Fame of Am., 2003; recipient Ozarks Heritage award, Mus. of the Ozarks, 1990, Silver Beaver award, Boy Scouts Am., 2003. Mem. Nat. Sch. Public Relations Assn. (past regional dir.), Nat. Acad. TV Arts and Scis. (gov.), Mo. Instructional TV Council, Ill. Instructional TV Commn., Nat. Assn. Ednl. Broadcasters. Clubs: Rotary Internat. Methodist. Home: 2305 E Meadow Dr Springfield MO 65804-4536 Office: 520 S Union Ave Springfield MO 65802-2660 Office Phone: 417-831-1600 417. E-mail: pub@sgfmag.com.

GLEASON, JOHN PATRICK, JR., trade association executive; b. NYC, Nov. 11, 1941; s. John Patrick Sr. and Ruth T. (Madigan) G.; m. Judith Peper (dec. 1980); children: John P. III, Megan K.; m. Susan Leigh Collier, Mar. 31, 1984; children: Kevin M., Colin P. BS in Fgn. Service, Georgetown U., 1963; PMD, Harvard Bus. Sch., 1972. Gen. mgr. Pappagallo, Inc., Washington, 1964-67; export project mgr. U.S. Dept. Commerce, Washington, 1967-68; investment banker Blyth, Eastman Dillon, Inc., Washington, 1968-70; with U.S. Dept. Commerce, Washington, 1970-77, chief staff domestic and internat. bus. adminstrn., 1970-77, dep. asst. sec. commerce, 1970-77; pres. Brick Inst. Am., Reston, Va., 1977-86, Portland Cement Assn., Skokie, Ill., 1986—. Bd. dirs., chmn. Coun. Masonry Rsch., Reston, 1985—, Masonry Industry Com., Washington, 1984—. Recipient Silver medal U.S. Dept. Commerce, Washington, 1978. Mem. Am. Soc. Assn. Execs., Chgo. Soc. Assn. Execs., River Bend Country Club (Great Falls, Va.), Carlton Club (Washington), Skokie Country Club (Glencoe, Ill.). Republican. Office: Portland Cement Assn 5420 Old Orchard Rd Skokie IL 60077-1053

GLEESON, PAUL FRANCIS, retired lawyer; b. Bronx, June 20, 1941; s. William Francis and Julia Anne (Dargis) G.; children: Kevin F., Sean W., Brendan J., Colleen J. AB in History, Fordham U., 1963; JD, U. Chgo., 1966. Assoc. Vedder, Price, Kaufman & Kammholz, Chgo., 1966-73, ptnr., 1973-2000; ret., 2000. Adj. prof. DePaul U. Sch. of Law, 1991. Co-author (with Day, Green & Cleveland) The Equal Employment Opportunity Compliance Manual, 1978; columnist: (with B. Alper) Gleeson and Alper on Employment Law, Merrill's Illinois Legal Times, 1988-90. Capt. U.S. Army, 1966-68, Vietnam. Decorated Bronze Star; Floyd Russell Mechem scholar, 1963-66. Mem. Order of Coif, Phi Beta Kappa. Roman Catholic.

GLEIJESES, MARIO, holding company executive; b. Italy, Feb. 27, 1955; came to US, 1985; s. Luigi Gleijeses and Rosalba Catanoso; m. Betsy L. Miller, Mar. 14, 1992; children: Rosalba, Caterina. Student, U. Naples, 1973-77. Chartering mgr. Itex subs. Italgrani, Zurich, 1977-82; asst. to pres. Italgrani Spa, aples, Italy, 1982-85; exec. v.p., bd. dirs. Italgrani USA Inc. and Italgrani Elevator Co., St. Louis, 1985-89; v.p., bd. dirs. New Eng. Milling Co., Ayer, Mass., 1987-89; bd. dirs. Green Bay Elevator Co., Burlington, Iowa; v.p., bd. dirs. Mayco Export, Inc., Mpls., 1988-89; pres., bd. dirs. McLean Elevator Co., Benedict, ND, 1989; founder, pres., bd. dirs. Agricorp Holding Inc., 1989-92; pres., bd. dirs. Granicorp Inc., 1989-92, Granicorp Export, Inc., Uganda, 1989-92; chmn., CEO, bd. dirs. Granicorp France, S.A., Paris, 1991-92; founder, pres., bd. dirs. Gleijeses, Inc., 1993—; founder, chmn. bd. dirs. LithoFlex Corp., St. Louis, 1994—; pres. Hoky-Contico, LLC, 1995-96.

GLENDENING, EVERETT AUSTIN, architect; b. White Plains, NY, May 20, 1929; s. Gilbert Leslie and Elsie Jane (Fanjoy) G.; m. Wilhelmina Louise Hanley, Nov. 26, 1949; children: Nancy, James, Thomas, Terry, Susan. B.Arch., U. Cin., 1953; M.Arch., M.I.T., 1954. With Duffy Constrn. Co., Cleve., 1951-55, SIS Architects, Cin., 1956-58, T.J. Moore (architect), Denver, 1959; prof. architecture U. Cin., 1960-67; pvt. practice architecture Cin., 1959—. Prin. works include Queen's Towers, Cin., 1964, Summit Chase, Columbus, Ohio, 1966, Norwood High Sch., Cin., 1972, W.Va. State Mus., 1978, Douglass Montessori Sch., Cin., 1979, Christie Lane Workshop, Norwalk, Ohio, 1980, Coll. Law U. Cin., 1981, Elks Lodge, Columbus, Ind., 1981, Geology/Physics Sci. Ctr. U. Cin., 1983, U. Rio Grande Dormitory, 1989, U. Rio Grande Student Ctr., 1994, U. Rio Grande Math-Sci.-Nursing Bldg., 1995, Planetarium, Shawnee State U., 1998, Sch. for Creative and Performing Arts Auditorium, Cin. Pub. Schs., 1997, U. Rio Grande Student Conf. Ctr. Served as 1st lt. USAF, 1954-56. Fellow AIA (honor awards Ohio chpt. 1966-70, 74, 82, 90, 91, Cin. chpt. 1966-68, 70, 76, Bronze medal 1969, Apple award for arch. 1995, mem. U.S. delegation of architects to People's Republic China and Hong Kong 1990); mem. Architect's Soc. Ohio, Scarab. Methodist. Office: 8050 Montgomery Rd Cincinnati OH 45236-2950 Fax: (513) 791-2794.

GLENISTER, BRIAN FREDERICK, geologist, educator; b. Albany, Western Australia, Sept. 28, 1928; came to U.S., 1959, naturalized, 1967; s. Frederick and Mabel (Frusher) G.; m. Anne Marie Treloar, Feb. 16, 1956; children: Alan Edward, Linda Marie, Kathryn Grace. BSc, U. Western Australia, Perth, 1949; MSc, U. Melbourne, Australia, 1953; PhD, U. Iowa, 1956. Lectr., then sr. lectr. geology U. Western Australia, 1956-59; asst. prof. U. Iowa, Iowa City, 1959-62, assoc. prof., 1962-66, prof., 1966-74, chmn. geology dept., 1968-74, A.K. Miller prof. geology, 1974-97, A.K. Miller prof. geology emeritus, 1997—. Mem. AAAS, Paleontol. Soc. (pres. 1988-89), Geol. Soc. Am., Geol. Soc. Iowa (pres. 1991), Paleontol. Rsch. Inst. Home: 1020 S Scott Bldg 130 Iowa City IA 52240 Office Phone: 319-335-1828. Business E-Mail: brian-glenister@uiowa.edu.

GLENN, J. THOMAS, consumer products company executive; b. Mar. 1959; Degree in acctg., U. Ga., 1981; MBA, Duke U., 1984. Cert. CPA. Cons. Arthur Andersen, 1984—87; bd. mem. Ace Hardware, Chattanooga, 1987; bd. chmn. Ace Hardware Corp., Chattanooga, 1996; pres. Ace Hardware Chattanooga, 1997; chmn. Ace Hardware, Oak Brook, Ill., 2003—. Mem.: Brainerd Bapt. Ch. (deacon), Nat. Ctr. for Youth Issues (bd. mem.), Chattanooga United Way (tres., pres.). Office: Ace Hardware 2200 Kensington Ct Oak Brook IL 60523-2100

GLENN, JOHN HERSCHEL, JR., former senator, retired astronaut; b. Cambridge, Ohio, July 18, 1921; s. John Herschel and Clara (Sproat) G.; m. Anna Margaret Castor, Apr. 6, 1943; children: Carolyn Ann, John David. Student, Muskingum Coll., New Concord, Ohio, 1939-42, DSc (hon.) in Engring., 1961, BS in Engring., 1962; naval aviation cadet, U. Iowa, 1942; grad. flight sch., Naval Air Tng. Center, Corpus Christi, Tex., 1943, Navy Test Pilot Tng. Sch., Patuxent River, Md., 1954; attended, U. Md., 1956—59; DEng (hon.), Nihon U., Tokyo, Wagner Coll., NY, NH Coll.; LLD (hon.), Brown U., Elon U., NC, 2005; other hon. degrees. Enlisted aval Aviation Cadet Program, 1942; Commd. 2d lt. USMC, 1943, assigned 4th Marine Aircraft Wing, Marshall Islands campaign, 1944, assigned 9th Marine Aircraft Wing, 1945-46; with 1st Marine Aircraft Wing, North China Patrol, also Guam, 1947-48; flight instr. advanced flight tng. Corpus Christi, Tex., 1948—50; asst. G-2/G-3 Amphibious Warfare Sch., Quantico, Va., 1951; with Marine Fighter Squadron 311, exchange pilot 25th Fighter Interceptor Squadron USAF, Korea, 1953; project officer fighter design br. Navy Bur. Aero. (now Bur. Naval Weapons), Washington, DC, 1956—59; selected as Project Mercury astronaut, with NASA Space Task Group Langley Rsch. Ctr., Hampton, Va., 1959—62; astronaut, Space Task Group Manned Spacecraft Ctr. NASA, 1962; backup pilot astronauts Shepard and Grissom; pilot Mercury-Atlas 6 'Friendship 7' spacecraft, 1st manned orbital space flight, launched from Kennedy Space Ctr., Fla., completed a successful three-orbit mission around the earth, Feb. 1962; ret. as col., 1965; v.p. corp. devel. and dir. Royal Crown Cola Co., 1966-74; pres. Royal Crown Internat.; US Senator from Ohio, 1975-99; astronaut, payload specialist Space Shuttle Discovery STS-95, became the oldest person ever to go into space, allowing research into the effects of space flight on the elderly, 1998. Cons., NASA, mem. Spl. Com. on Aging, Armed Svcs. Com., Senate Dem. Tech. and Comm. Com., Intelligence Com.; ranking minority mem. Govtl. Affairs Com.; vice-chmn. Senate Dem. Policy Com.; founding mem., chmn. bd. dirs., John Glenn Inst. for Pub. Svc. and Pub. Policy (now John Glenn Sch. of Pub. Affairs), Ohio State U., 1998, adj. prof., Sch. Pub. Policy and Mgmt., dept. polit. sci., 1998-; co-chmn. Nat. Commn. Math. and Tchg., 1999, mem.-at-large Ohio State Dem. Com., 1999-, chmn. Nat. Commn. Svc. Learning, 2000; sec. gen. Inventing Flight, Dayton, Ohio, 2003. Author: P.S., I Listened to Your Heart Beat, 1964; co-author: We Seven, 1962, (with Nick Taylor) John Glenn: A Memoir, 1999; (TV appearances) Name That Tune, 1957, Samantha Smith Goes to Washington, 1984, Spaceflight, 1985, Korea: The Unknown War, 1988, The Tribute: Mercury, Gemini, Apollo, and Skylab, 1993, Cold War, 1998, Space Shuttle Discovery: John Glenn Launch, 1998, The American President, 2000, Korean War Stories, 2001, 50 Years of NBC Late Night, 2001, Frasier, 2001, John Glenn: American Hero, 2003, Swing State, 2008. Trustee Muskingum Coll. Decorated Dising. Flying Cross (six), Air medal with 18 clusters, Navy unit commendation, Asiatic-Pacific Campaign medal, Am. Campaign medal, WWII Victory medal, China Svc. medal, Nat. Def. Svc. medal, Korean Svc. medal, UN Svc. medal, Korean Presdl. Unit Citation, Navy's Astronaut Wings, Marine Corps' Astronaut medal; recipient Disting. Merit award Muskingum Coll., Medal of Honor N.Y.C., Congl. Space Medal of Honor, 1978, Centennial awd., at. Geographic Soc., 1988, NASA Disting. Svc. medal; named to the Astronauts Hall of Fame, 1990 Mem. Soc. Exptl. Test Pilots, Internat. Acad. of Astronautics (hon.) Democrat. Presbyterian. Achievements include making the first supersonic transcontinental flight from LA to NYC, July 16, 1957; flew in 59 combat missions during WWII, 63 combat missions with the Marines and 27 with the USAF during the Korean War; a member of the Mercury Seven original astronaut group, 1957; became the first American to orbit the Earth aboard Friendship 7, February 20, 1962; holds the record for the longest time between space flights with 39 years, 6 months, and 27 days; became the oldest person to fly in space aboard the Discovery space shuttle for mission STS-95 (age 77), 1998. Office: Ohio State U John Glenn Inst 100 Bricker Hall 190 N Oval Mall Columbus OH 43210-1321

GLENN, MICHAEL B., forest products executive; Joined Universal Forest Products, Grand Rapids, Mich., 1974, sr. v.p., Southwest ops., 1989—97, pres., Western divsn., 1997—2000, pres., COO, 2000—06, bd. dir., CEO, 2006—. Bd. dirs. Outdoor Advantage, Inc., 2000—. Office: Universal Forest Products 2801 E Beltline E Grand Rapids MI 49525 Office Phone: 616-364-6161.

GLENNEN, ROBERT EUGENE, JR., retired academic administrator; b. Omaha, Mar. 31, 1933; s. Robert E. and La Verda (Elledge) G.; m. Mary C. O'Brien, Apr. 17, 1958; children: Maureen, Bobby, Colleen, Billy, Barry, Katie, Molly, Kerry AB, U. Portland, 1955, M.Ed., 1957; PhD, U. Notre Dame, 1962. Asst. prof. U. Portland, 1956-60; asst. prof., assoc. prof. Eastern Mont. Coll., Billings, 1962-65; assoc. dean U. Notre Dame, South Bend, Ind., 1965-72; dean, v.p. U. Nev.-Las Vegas, 1972-80; pres. Western N.Mex. U., Silver City, 1980-84, Emporia (Kans.) State U., 1984-97; acting vice-chancellor U. Ark., Montecello, 1999; interim provost U. So. Colo., 1999-2000, interim pres., 2001—02. Bd. dirs. Emporia Enterprises; cons. HEW, Washington, 1964-84 Author: Guidance: An Orientation, 1966. Contbr. articles to profl. jours. Pres. PTA, South Bend, Ind., 1970-71; bd. trustees Am. Coll. Testing Corp., Iowa City, 1977-80; chmn. Kans. Regents Coun. of Pres., 1986-87, 92-93, 95-96. Recipient award of excellence Nat. Acad. Advising Assn., Disting. Alumnus award U. Portland, 1993, Kans. Master Tchr. award, 1994; named Coach of Yr., Coach and Athletic mag., 1958, Pub. Adminstr. of Yr., 1994, Athletic Hall of Fame, Portland, 1995; Rotary Paul Harris fellow, 1995, Ford Found. fellow, 1961-62. Mem. Kans. C. of C. (bd. dirs.), Emporia C. of C. Regional Devel. Assn. (bd. dirs., Bank IV), Am. Personnel and Guidance Assn., Am. Assn. State Colls. and Univs. (chair pres's. commn. on tchr. edn.), Am. Assn. Higher Edn., Nev. Personnel and Guidance Assn., Assn. Counselor Educators and Suprs., Am. Assn. Counseling and Devel., Nat. Assn. Student Personnel Adminstrs. Republican. Roman Catholic. Avocations: walking, reading. Home: 1591 Meadow Hills Dr Richland WA 99352

GLICKMAN, CARL DAVID, banker; b. Cleve., July 29, 1926; s. Jack I. and Dora R. (Rubinowitz) G.; m. Barbara H. Schulman, Oct. 16, 1960; children: Lindsay Dale, David Craig, Robert Todd. Student, U. Minn., 1944, Inst. Fin. Mgmt., Harvard U., 1970. Pres. Glickman Orgn., Cleve., 1953—; chmn. bd., chief exec. officer Computer Research, Inc., Pitts., 1964-67, Am. Steel & Pump Corp., NYC, 1968-71, Shelter Resources Corp., Cleve., 1971-75; pres. Leader Bldg., Inc., Cleve., 1959—2004, Capital Bancorp., Cleve., 1971-75, Real Property Corp., Cleve., 1975—; spl. ltd. ptnr. Bear Stearns & Co., 1978-85, dir., 1985—. Chmn. exec. com. Franklin Corp., N.Y.C., 1986-98, Cook United Inc., Cleve., 1986-87, Capital Nat. Bank Cleve., 1970-75; chmn. bd. dirs. Univ. Nat. Bank, Chgo., 1968-70; ltd. ptnr. S.B. Lewis & Co., N.Y.C., 1980-89; gen. ptnr. Millbrook Assocs., Chester Union Assocs.; founding gen. ptnr. Park Ctrl. Assocs.; pres. LGT Industries, Durham, N.C., 1987-95; bd. dirs. Royal Petroleum Properties Corp., Jerusalem Econ. Corp., Israel, Custodial Trust Co., Alliance Tyre and Rubber Co., Tel Aviv,Tnuport Ltd., Tel Aviv, Indsl. Structures, Inc., Tel Aviv, Office Max, Inc., InfoTech, Englewood Cliff, NJ, Lexington Corp. Properties, NYC, presiding trustee, chmn. exec. com. Active Mayor's Com. Urban Renewal, 1965-67, Mayors Task Force on Higher Edn., 1967-69; trustee Cleve. Growth Assn., 1972-75; co-chmn. Herzog Loan Fund Cleve. State U., 1970-76; chmn. Med. Arts Hosp., Houston, 1976-86; bd. visitors Case Western Res. Sch. Law; trustee Montefiore Home Aged, Mt. Sinai Hosp., Cath. Diocese Found., Cleve.; grievance com. Cleve. Bar Assn., 1982-85; foreman Cuyahoga County Grand Jury, Cleve., 1984-85; trustee Cleve. State U., 2000—, Cleve. Cath. Diocese Found.; disting. fellow, hon. trustee Cleve. Clinic; nat. co-chmn. Glickman Urol. Inst. Cleve. Clinic; trustee Cleve. Jewish Fedn., 2006—. With USAAF, 1944-46. Mem. Am. Bankers Assn., Am. Arbitration Assn. (arbitrator), Beechmont Country Club, Shaker Heights Country Club, Union Club, Standard Club, Harmonie Club, Town Club, Friars Club, Palm Beach Club, Yacht Club, High Ridge Country Club, John Carroll Univ. Club (trustee), Masons, Phi Sigma Delta, Phi Eta Sigma. Office: 1140 Leader Bldg Cleveland OH 44114 also: 383 Madison Ave ew York NY 10167-0002 also: 1 N Breakers Row Palm Beach FL 33480-4021 Office Phone: 216-696-2650. E-mail: carldglickman@hotmail.com.

GLICKMAN, ROBERT JEFFREY, bank executive; b. Mpls., Feb. 10, 1947; s. Joseph Charles and Beverly (Willis) G.; m. Hardye Simons Moel (div. 1983); children: Kate, Adam; m. Caryn Chernick, June 26, 1988. BA, Cornell U., 1969. Pres. River Forest Bancorp, Inc., Chgo., 1969—2004; CEO Corus Bankshares, Chgo., 2004—. Mem. Young Presidents Orgn. Jewish. Office: Corus Bancshares Inc 3959 N Lincoln Ave Chicago IL 60613-2431

GLIDDEN, JOHN REDMOND, lawyer; b. Sanford, Maine, July 24, 1936; s. Kenneth Eugene and Kathryn (Gilpatrick) G.; m. Jacqueline Scales, Aug. 6, 1964; children— Ian, Claire, Jason Student, U. Wis., 1954-55; BS, Coe Coll., 1958; LL.B., U. Iowa, 1961. Bar: Iowa 1961, Ill. 1965. Assoc. firm Williams & Hartzell, Carthage, Ill., 1965-67; ptnr. Hartzell, Glidden, Tucker & Hartzell and predecessor firms, Carthage, 1969—. City atty. City of Carthage, 1969—. Capt., judge advocate USAF, 1961-65. Mem. ABA, VFW, Ill. Bar Assn., Iowa Bar Assn., Hancock County Bar Assn., Am. Trial Lawyers Assn., Ill. Trial Lawyers Assn. (governing bd. 1973-80), Am. Legion, Carthage Golf Club (bd. dirs. 1967—2005), Phi Delta Phi, Sigma Nu. Home: PO Box 70 Carthage IL 62321-3435 Home Phone: 217-357-2334; Office Phone: 217-357-3121. Personal E-mail: jrglaw@frontiernet.net.

GLIDDEN, ROBERT BURR, academic administrator, consultant, music educator; b. Rippey, Iowa, Nov. 29, 1936; s. Burr Harold and Lora Elsie (Groves) Glidden; m. Rene Colete Siefken, Apr. 26, 1964; children: Melissa, Michele, Briana. BA, U. Iowa, 1958, MA, 1960, PhD, 1966; D of higher edn. adminstrn. (hon.), Bowling Green State U., 2004. Tchr. instrumental music Morrison Community High Sch., Ill., 1958-63, Univ. Schs., Iowa City, 1963-66; asst. prof. music Wright State U., Dayton, Ohio, 1966-67, Ind. U., Bloomington,

1967-69; assoc. prof. music U. Okla., Norman, dir. grad. studies in music, 1969—72; exec. dir. Nat. Assn. Schs. Music, 1972—75, treas., 1977-82, v.p., 1982-85, pres., 1985-88; dean Coll. Musical Arts, Bowling Green State U., Ohio, 1975-79; dean Sch. Music Fla. State U., Tallahassee, 1979-91, provost, v.p. for acad. affairs, 1991-94; pres. Ohio U., Athens, 1994—2004, pres. emeritus, 2004—. Cons., higher edn., condr.; chmn. Coun. Specialized Accrediting Agys., 1976—77; chair Am. Coun. Edn. Commn. Leadership and Instnl. Effectiveness, 1998—2000; chair coun. pres. Mid-Am. Conf., 1997—99. Bd. dirs. Coun. on Postsecondary Accreditation, 1977—84, exec. com., 1979—84, chmn., 1981—83; bd. dirs. Arts, Edn. and Ams., Inc., 1978—81; chmn. advanced placement music com. Coll. Bd., 1977—79; mem. Coun. on Arts Task Force on Edn. Tng. and Devel. Profl. Artists and Art Educators, 1977—78; adv. coun. on accreditation Nat. League for Nursing, 1977—81; edn. adv. com. Nat. Endowment for Arts, 1987, adv. com. for arts in edn., 1989—90; bd. dirs. Coun. for Higher Edn. Accreditation, 1996—2004, chmn., 1996—98. Recipient Disting. Alumni award, U. Iowa, 1997. Mem.: Ohio Inter-Univ. Coun. (chair 2001—02), Ohio Aerospace Inst. (exec. com. 1995—2004, chair 1998—2000), Ohio Supercomputer Ctr. (governing bd. 1996—2004), Ohio Sci. and Tech. Coun. (biotech. com. 1996—2004), So. Assn. Colls. and Schs. (commn. on coll. 1993—94), Assn. Specialized and Profl. Accreditors (bd. dirs. 1994—96), Coll. Music Soc. (chmn. govt. rels. com. 1976—78, task force on edn. coll. music tchrs. 1987), Mortar Bd., Pi Kappa Lamdba (nat. v.p. 1979—81, pres. 1981—85), Omicron Delta Kappa, Phi Kappa Phi, Phi Beta Kappa. Episcopalian. Home: PO Box 88 140 Gibraltar Forge Dr Rockbridge Baths VA 24473 Office Phone: 540-348-6360. Business E-Mail: gliddenr@ohio.edu.

GLOVER, JAMES TODD, manufacturing executive; b. Aberdeen, SD, Apr. 30, 1939; s. Fay and Vi (Bruns) G.; m. Joann Elizabeth House; children: Jason, Jeffrey, Jamie. Student, S.D. State U.; BS in Math., No. State Coll., Aberdeen, 1961. Inside sales engr. Aberdeen Ops. Safeguard, 1961-64, asst. sales engr., 1965-67, mktg. mgr., 1968-72, gen. mgr., 1973-77; v.p. ops. Safeguard PowerTech Systems, Aberdeen, 1978-83, exec. v.p., 1984-85, pres., 1986-89; pres., chief exec. officer, chief ops. officer, dir. Hub City, Inc., Aberdeen, 1989—. Officer Safeguard Sci. Co., Inc.; v.p. corp. devel. Regal-Beloit (Wis.) Corp., 1990-93; v.p. HQ Cos., Mpls., 1993-98, gen. mgr. Pixall Ltd. Partnership, Clear Lake, Wis., 1993-98; pres. JTG Solutions, Inc., Peoria, Ariz., 1998--. Bd. mem. S.D. Swimming Assn.; S.D. Dist. Export Council. Export Devel. Authority; bd. dirs. No. State Found., James River Water Devel.; bd. mem., chmn. James River Water Devel. Dist. Recipient Ernie Gunderson award S.D. Swimming Assn. Mem. Power Transmission Distbrs. Assn. (past bd. dirs., past chmn. allied adv. bd.), Power Transmission Rep. Assn. (past bd. dirs., past chmn. allied adv. bd.), Aberdeen C. of C., S.D. Mfrs. Assn. (past dir.). Republican. Roman Catholic. Avocations: hunting, fishing, music.

GLOYD, LAWRENCE EUGENE, retired diversified manufacturing company executive; b. Milan, Ind., Nov. 5, 1932; s. Oran C. and Ruth (Baylor) G.; m. Delma Lear, Sept. 10, 1955; children: Sheryl, Julia, Susan. BA, Hanover Coll., 1954, Hon. D in Bus. Adminstrn., 1994; postgrad., Rockford Coll., 1999. Salesman Shapleigh Hardware, St. Louis, 1956-60, W. Bingham Co., Cleve., 1960-61, Amerock Corp., Rockford, Ill., 1961-68, regional sales mgr., 1968-69, dir. consumer products mktg., 1969-71, dir. merchandising, 1971-72, dir. mktg. and sales, 1972-73, v.p. mktg. and sales, 1973-81, exec. v.p., 1982—86, pres., gen. mgr., 1982-86; v.p. Hardware Products Group, Anchor Hocking Corp., Lancaster, Ohio, 1986—88; pres., COO, CEO CLARCOR, Rockford, Ill., 1988—2000, chmn. bd., CEO, 1988-2000, also bd. dirs., chmn. emeritus, 2000—. Bd. dirs. Amcore Fin. Inc., Rockford, Thomas Industries Inc., Louisville, Woodward Gov. Co., Rockford, Ill., Genyte Thomas Group, Louisville, Group Dekko, Kendalville, Ind.; past. chmn. bd. trustees Rockford Coll.; bd. dirs., past chmn. SwedishAm. Corp. Past chmn. bd. dirs. Coun. of 100; past mem. bd. dirs. Ill. Coun. on Econ. Edn.; nat. bd. dirs. Big Bros./Big Sisters; bd. trustees Hanover (Ind.) Coll. Recipient Master Entrpreneur of Yr. Ill./N.W. Ind. award Ernst & Young, 1999, Lambda Chi Alpha Nat. Order Achievement award, 1999, Alumni Achievement award Hanover Coll., 1994. Mem. Am. Hardware Mfrs. Assn., Ill. Mfrs. Assn., Nat. Assn. Mfrs., Hardware Group Assn., Pres. Assn., Masons. Republican.

GLUTH, ROBERT C., management company executive; b. 1924; married. BBA, U. Wis., 1949. With The Marmon Group Inc., Chgo., 1963—, exec. v.p., 2002—, also bd. dirs. Office: Marmon Group Inc 225 W Washington St Chicago IL 60606-3418

GLYNN, EDWARD, retired academic administrator; b. Clarks Summit, Pa., Oct. 6, 1935; s. John J. G. AB, Fordham U., 1960, PhL, 1961, MAT, 1962; STB, Woodstock Coll., 1967; STM, Yale Divinity Sch., 1968; ThD, Grad. Theol. Union, 1971; LLD (hon.), Monmouth Coll., 1984, U. Scranton, 1990; LHD (hon.), Seton Hall U., 1989, St. Peter's Coll., 1990, Loyola Coll., 1993. Entered Soc. Jesus 1955; ordained 1967. Instr. Gonzaga H.S., 1961—64; asst. prof. Georgetown U., 1971-77; acad. v.p. Gonzaga U., Spokane, 1977-78, pres., 1996—97, St. Peter's Coll., Jersey City, 1978-90; provincial Md. Province Soc. of Jesus, Balt., 1990-96; interim provost U. Mass., Boston, 1997—98; pres. John Carroll U., Cleve., 1998—2005. Acting dir., mem., bd. dir. Churches' Ctr. for Theology and Pub. Policy, 1976-77; exec. dir. Woodstock Theol. Ctr., Washington, 1974-76, bd. dirs., 1974-76. Contbr. articles to profl. jours. Bd. dirs. U. Scranton, 1973-78, Fordham U., 1981-87, Canisius Coll., 1982-88, 2001—, LeMoyne Coll., 1983-89, 2000—04, St. Louis U., 1986-91, John Carroll U., 1987-90, 1998—2005, Seton Hall U., 1990-96, St. Mary's Sem. and U., 1991-96, Weston Sch. Theology, 1990-96, NCAA's Pres. Commn., 1984-88, Commn. on Higher Edn., Mid. States Assn., 1988-90, Fairfield U., 1997-, Marquette U., 1998-, U. Detroit Mercy, 1999-, Wheeling Jesuit U., 2004-, Am. Coun. of Edn., 2001-2004, U.S. Dept. of Edn. (nat. adv. bd. 1999-2001), Fund for Improvement of Post Secondary Edn. Mem.: FIPSE. Home Phone: 202-625-2589; Office Phone: 216-397-4209, 202-625-2589. Personal E-mail: lgly@aol.com.

GNAT, RAYMOND EARL, librarian; b. Milw., Jan. 15, 1932; s. John and Emily (Syperek) Gnat; m. Jean Helen Monday, June 19, 1954; children: Barbara, Richard, Cynthia. BBA, U. Wis., 1954, postgrad., 1959; MS, U. Ill., 1958; MPA, Ind. U., Indpls., 1981. Page Milw. Pub. Libr., 1950-53, jr. libr., 1954, librarian, 1958-63; circulation asst. U. Ill., 1956-57, serials cataloger, 1957-58; asst. dir. Indpls.-Marion County Pub. Libr., 1963-71, dir., 1972-94. Exec. dir. Ind. Nat. Libr. Week, 1965. With AUS, 1954—56. Mem.: ALA, Bibliog. Soc. Am., Ind. Libr. Assn. (pres. 1980), Portfolio Club, Lit. Club. Home: 8246 Shadow Cir Indianapolis IN 46260-2761

GO, ROBERT A., management consultant; b. July 29, 1955; s. Michael and Sabina (Tan) G. BS, U Detroit, 1977; MBA, U. Santa Clara, 1981. Ptnr. Deloitte & Touche (formerly Touche Ross & Co.), Detroit, 1977—. Contbr. articles to profl. jours. Mem. Health Care Fin. Mgt. Assn., Am. Hosp. Assn., Renaissance Club. Office: Deloitte & Touche 600 Renaissance Ctr Fl 10 Detroit MI 48243-1804

GOCHNAUER, RICHARD WALLIS, wholesale distribution executive; b. Kansas City, Mo., Dec. 3, 1949; s. Harry Wallis and Janet Elizabeth (Huff) G.; m. Beth Andrea Splinter, Dec. 18, 1971; children: Grant D., Mary E. BS in Indsl. Engring., Northwestern U., 1972; MBA, Harvard U., 1974. From shift supr. to pres. Schreiber Internat., Schreiber Foods, Green Bay, Wis., 1974-82; exec. v.p., gen. mgr. Dial Corp., Phoenix, 1989—93; pres. cheese div. Universal Foods, Milw., 1982-89; pres. Golden State Foods, 1993—2002; COO United Stationers Inc., Des Plaines, Ill., 2002, pres., CEO, 2002—. V.p. Nat. Cheese Inst., Washington, 1988-89. Chmn. bd. dirs. YMCA, Green Bay, 1981, Milw., 1988; mem. met. bd. dirs. YMCA, Phoenix, 1990. Mem. Soap and Detergent Assn. Office: United Stationers Inc 2200 E Golf Rd Des Plaines IL 60016

GODDU, ROGER, former retail executive; b. Springfield, Mass., June 23, 1950; m. Kate Goddu; 5 children. Student, Adrian Coll., U. Toledo; grad., Harvard Bus. Exec. Program, 1995. Mdse. adminstr. LaSalle and Koch divsn. R.H. Macy & Co., 1970-75; v.p., gen. mdse. mgr. Rikes/Lazarus Dept. Stores, 1975-80; mdse. mgr. Dayton Hudson divsn. Target Stores, 1980-83, v.p. Dayton Hudson divsn., 1983-85, sr. v.p., gen. mdse. mgr. Dayton Hudson divsn., 1985-89; exec. v.p., gen. mdse. mgr. Toys R Us, Paramus, N.J., 1989-95, pres. U.S. merchandising, 1996-97; chmn., CEO Montgomery Ward, LLC, Chgo., 1997—2001. Dir. Kids in Distressed Situations, Project Pride in Living, Mpls.; founder The Nat. Conf., Bergen County, N.J.

GODFREY, MAURICE, biomedical scientist; b. Addis Ababa, Ethiopia, June 11, 1956; s. Robert and Liliana (Gandolfi) G.; m. Matilde Elena Almeida, July 5, 1985; children: C. Maximilian, R. Alessandro, D. Guillermo. BS, Monmouth Coll., 1977; MS, Columbia U., 1980, M in Philosophy, 1983, PhD, 1986. Postdoctoral fellow Oreg. Health Sci. U., Shrine Hosp., Portland, 1986-89; assoc. prof. pediatrics, dir. connective tissue lab. U. Nebr. Med. Ctr., Omaha, 1990—. Author: (with others) McKusick's Heritable Disorders of Connective Tissue, 1993, The Metabolic Basis of Inherited Disease, 1995; contbr. articles to profl. jours. Recipient grant-in-aid Am. Heart Assn., 1989, 93; Basil O'Connor scholar March of Dimes, 1991; established investigator Am. Heart Assn., 1995. Mem. AAAS, Am. Soc. of Human Genetics, Am. Fedn. for Clin. Rsch., Basic Sci. Coun. of the Am. Heart Assn. Achievements include co-discovery of fibrillin gene the cause of the Marfan syndrome. Office: UNMC Dept Pediatrics 982168 Nebr Med Ctr Omaha NE 68198-0001 also: National Marfan Foundation 22 Manhasset Ave Port Washington NY 11050-2023

GODFREY, RICHARD CARTIER, lawyer; b. Harvey, Ill., Sept. 25, 1954; s. Richard L. and Rosemary (Cartier) G.; m. Alice Bacon Woolsey, Aug. 27, 1983; children: John Cartier, Polly Woolsey. BA magna cum laude, Augustana Coll., 1976; JD magna cum laude, Boston U., 1979. Bar: Ill. 1979, US Dist.Ct. (no. dist.) Ill. 1979, US Dist. Ct. (ctrl. dist.) Ill. 1988, US Dist. Ct. (we. dist.) Mich. 1990, US Dist. Ct. (no. dist.) Ind. 1999, US Dist. Ct. Colo. 2002, US Dist. Ct. (ea. dist.) Mich. 2005, US Ct. Appeals (7th cir.) 1983, US Ct. Appeals (6th cir.) 1988, US Ct. Appeals (8th cir.) 1994, US Ct. Appeals (10th cir.) 1996, US Ct. Appeals (11th cir.) 1997, US Ct. Appeals (5th and 9th cirs.) 1999, US Ct. Appeals (2d. cir.) 2002, US Ct. Appeals (1st cir.) 2003, US Ct. Appeals (3d cir.) 2003, US Ct. Appeals (4th cir.) 2005, US Claims Ct. 1990, US Supreme Ct. 2000, US Tax Ct. 2006. Assoc. Kirkland & Ellis LLP, Chgo., 1979-85, ptnr., 1985—. Named one of Am. Leading. Bus. Lawyers Litig./Gen. Comml., Chambers USA, 2004—05. Mem. ABA, Ill. Bar Assn., Chgo. Bar Assn., Bd. Visitors Boston U. Sch. Law, Bd. Trustees Augustana Coll., Lawyers' Com. Nat. Ctr. State Cts., Office: Kirkland & Ellis LLP Ste 6048 200 E Randolph Dr Chicago IL 60601 Office Phone: 312-861-2391. Office Fax: 312-861-2200. Business E-Mail: rgodfrey@kirkland.com.

GODFREY, WILLIAM ASHLEY, ophthalmologist; b. Arkansas City, Kans., May 19, 1938; BA, U. Kans., Lawrence, 1960; MD, U. Kans., Kansas City, 1965. Diplomate Am. Bd. Ophthalmology. Intern Tulane U., New Orleans, 1965-66; resident U. Kans. Sch. Medicine, 1968-71; rsch. fellow U. Calif., San Francisco, 1971-73; asst. prof., then assoc. prof. U. Kans. Sch. Medicine, 1973-84, prof. ophthalmology, 1984—. Mem. staff St. Luke's Hosp., Kansas City, Mo., 1973—, Kansas U. Med. Ctr., Kansas City, 1973—; cons. Kansas City Vets Hosp., Mo., 1973-89. Contbr. articles to profl. publs. With USAF, 1966-68. NIH fellow, 1971-73. Fellow ACP, Am. Acad. Ophthalmology (honor ward 1983), Am. Uveitis Soc.; mem. Am. COll. Physicians, AMA, Am. Fedn. Clin. Rsch., Am. Rheumatism Assn., Assn. Rsch. in Vision and Ophthalmology, Am. Math. Soc., Ocular Immunology and Microbiology Soc., Kansas City Soc. Ophthalmology, Kans. Med. Soc., Mo. Ophthalmology Soc., Jackson County Med. Soc., Am. Ophthal. Soc., Wyandotte County Med. Soc., Johnson County Med. Soc., Soc. Heed Fellows, Assn. Proctor Fellows, Kans. Ophthal. Soc., Alpha Omega Alpha. Office: U Kansas 3901 Rainbow Blvd Kansas City KS 66160-7379

GODINER, DONALD LEONARD, lawyer; b. Bronx, NY, Feb. 21, 1933; s. Israel and Edith (Rubenstein) G.; m. Caryl Mignon Nussbaum, Sept. 7, 1958; children: Clifford, Kenneth. AB, NYU, 1953; JD, Columbia U., 1956. Bar: N.Y. 1956, Mo. 1972. Gen. counsel Stromberg-Carlson, Rochester, NY, 1965-71; assoc. gen. counsel Gen. Dynamics Corp., St. Louis, 1971-73; v.p., gen. counsel Permaneer Corp., St. Louis, 1973-75; ptnr. Gallop, Johnson, Godiner, Morganstern & Crebs, St. Louis, 1975-80; sr. v.p., gen. counsel, sec. Laclede Gas Co., St. Louis, 1980-98; of counsel Stone, Leyton and Gershman, P.C., St. Louis, 1999—. Editor Columbia U. Law Rev., 1955-56. Served with U.S. Army, 1956-58. Mem.: ABA, Bar Assn. of Metropolitan St. Louis. Office: Stone Leyton & Gershman PC 7733 Forsyth Blvd Ste 500 Saint Louis MO 63105-2122 Office Phone: 314-721-7011.

GODWIN, HAROLD NORMAN, pharmacist, educator; b. Ransom, Kans., Oct. 9, 1941; s. Harold Joseph and Nora Elva (Welsh) G.; m. Judy Rae Ricketts, June 9, 1963; children: Paula Lynn, Jennifer Joy. BS in Pharmacy, U. Kans., 1964; MS in Hosp. Pharmacy, Ohio State U., 1966. Lic. pharmacist, Kans., Ohio. Instr. Ohio State U. Coll. Pharmacy, Columbus, 1966-69; asst. dir. pharmacy Ohio State U., Columbus, 1966-69; dir. pharmacy U. Kans. Med. Ctr., Kansas City, 1969—2004; asst. prof. U. Kans. Sch. Pharmacy, Kansas City, 1969-74, assoc. prof., 1974-80, prof. pharmacy, 1980—, asst. dean pharmacy, 1975-89, assoc. dean pharmacy, 1989—, chmn. pharmacy practice, 1984—2006. John W. Webb lectr., vis. prof. Northeastern U., 1999; chmn. pharmacy exec. com. U. HealthSys. Consortium, 2001-04, exec. com., 2004-07; mem. exec. com. Novation Pharmacy, 2003-05. Author: Implementation Guide to IV Admixtures, 1977; (with others) Remington's Pharmaceutical Sciences, 1980, 85, 90, 95, 2000; contbr. over 100 articles to profl. jours. Recipient Clifton J. Latiolais award Ohio State U. Residents Alumni, 1986, Disting. Alumni award Ohio State U. Coll. Pharmacy, 1995; named Tchr. of the Yr., U. Kans. Sch. Pharmacy, 2001, Harold N. Godwin Leadership Legacy award U. Kans. Med. Ctr., 2004. Fellow: Am. Soc. Health System Pharmacists (bd. dir. 1978—81, pres. 1982—83, bd. dir. rsch. and edn. found. 2002—06, Harvey A.K. Whitney award 1991); mem.: Kans. Pharmacy Found. (v.p. 2004—), Am. Coun. Pharm. Edn. (bd. dir. 1988—2000, pres. 1992—96), Greater Kansas City Soc. Hosp. Pharmacists (pres. 1972), Kans. Soc. Hosp. Pharmacists (Kans. Hosp. Pharmacist of Yr. 1982, Harold N. Godwin award 1984), Kans. Pharmacists Assn. (pres 1977, Kans. Pharmacist of Yr. 1982), Am. Pharm. Assn. (bd. trustees 2006—, Disting. Achievement award 2000). Republican. Methodist. Avocations: tennis, bicycling, cooking, wine tasting. Home: 10112 W 98th St Shawnee Mission KS 66212-5238 Office: U Kans Med Ctr MS4047 Rainbow Blvd At 39th St Kansas City KS 66106-7231 Office Phone: 913-588-2399. Business E-Mail: HGodwin@kumc.edu.

GODWIN, HILARY A., chemistry professor, research scientist; BS in Chemistry with honors, U. Chgo., 1989; PhD in Phys. Chemistry, Stanford U., 1994. NIH postdoctoral fellow John Hopkins U. Sch. Medicine, 1994—96; asst. prof. dept. chemistry and dept. biochemistry, molecular biology & cell biology orthwestern U., 1996—2001, assoc. prof. dept. chemistry and dept. biochemistry, molecular biology & cell biology, 2001—. Preceptor Interdepartmental Biol. Sci. Program Northwestern U., 1996—, mem. Lurie Cancer Ctr., 1997—, Dow Chem. Co. rsch. prof. chemistry, 2002—, assoc. chair dept. chemistry, 2003—04, chair dept. chemistry, 2004—; prof. Howard Hughes Med. Inst., 2002—. Recipient Stanford Centennial Tchg. Asst. Award, Stanford U., 1992, Camille and Henry Dreyfus New Faculty award, 1996, Toxicology New Investigator award, Burroughs Wellcome Fund, 1998, CAREER award, NSF, 1999, Camille Dreyfus Tchr.-Scholar award, 2000, Paul Saltman award, 2001; Grad. Rsch. fellowship, NSF, 1989—92. Mem.: AAAS, Coun. for Chem. Rsch., Am. Assn. Women in Sci., Biophysical Soc., Soc. for Neuroscience, Am. Chem. Soc. (mem. inorganic divsn., mem. phys. divsn.), Iota Sigma Pi, Phi Beta Kappa. Office: Northwestern U Dept Chemistry 2145 Sheridan Rd Evanston IL 60208-3113 Office Phone: 847-467-3543. Office Fax: 847-491-5937. Business E-Mail: h-godwin@northwestern.edu.

GOEBEL, JOHN J., lawyer; b. St. Charles, Mo., Feb. 3, 1930; s. Francis Joseph and Elizabeth (Lawler) G.; m. Margaret Mary Rooney, May 10, 1958; children— Laura, Margaret, John, Matthew BS, LL.B., St. Louis U., 1953. Bar: Mo. 1953, U.S. Dist. Ct. (ea. dist.) Mo. 1957. Jr. exec. Constrn. Escrow Service Inc., St. Louis, 1955-56; jr. ptnr. Bryan Cave LLP, St. Louis, 1956-66, ptnr., 1966-98, sr. counsel, 1998—. Served to 1st lt. USAF, 1953—55. Mem.: ABA, Mo. Bar Assn., St. Louis Bar Assn., Port Royal Club, St. Louis Club, Bellerive Country Club. Roman Catholic. Home: 245 Little Harbour Ln Naples FL 34102-7606 Office: Bryan Cave 1 Metropolitan Sq Ste 3600 Saint Louis MO 63102-2750 Business E-Mail: jjgoebel@comcast.net.

GOEDERT, RAYMOND EMIL, bisphop emeritus; b. Oak Park, Ill., Oct. 15, 1927; BA, St. Mary of the Lake, 1948, MA, 1951, STL, 1952; JCL, Gregorian U., Rome, 1956. Ordained priest Archdiocese of Chgo., 1952; ordained bishop, 1991; aux. bishop Archdiocese of Chgo., 1991—2003, aux. bishop emeritus, 2003—. Roman Catholic. Office: Archdiocese of Chgo 155 E Superior St PO Box 1979 Chicago IL 60690 Office Phone: 312-337-8952. Office Fax: 312-255-1019.*

GOEHNER, DONNA MARIE, retired university dean; b. Chgo., Mar. 9, 1941; d. Robert and Elizabeth (Cseke) Barra; m. George Louis Goehner, Dec. 16, 1961; 1 child, Michelle Renee. BS in English, So. Ill. U., 1963; MSLS, U. Ill., 1966, CAS in L.S., 1974; PhD in Edn., So. Ill. U., 1983. Rsch. assoc. U. Ill., Urbana, 1966-67; high sch. librarian St. Joseph-Ogden Sch. System, St. Joseph, Ill., 1967-68; curriculum lab librarian Western Ill. U., Macomb, 1968-73, periodicals librarian, 1974-76, coordinator for tech. svcs., 1977-78, acquisitions and collection devel. librarian, 1979-86, acting dir. library, 1986, dean library svcs., 1988-97; assoc. Univ. librarian for tech. and adminstrv. svcs. Ill. State U., Normal, 1986-88; ret., 1998. Contbr. articles to profl. jours. Mem. ALA, Assn. Coll. and Rsch. Libraries (chmn. univ. libraries sect. 1988-89), Ill. Assn. Coll. and Rsch. Libraries (pres. 1985-86), Ill. Library Assn. (Acad.Librarian of Yr. 1989). Office: Univ Library Western Ill U Macomb IL 61455

GOEL, KARAN, entrepreneur; b. New Delhi, 1983; BA, U. Chgo., 2004; MBA, U. Chgo. Grad. Sch. Bus., 2006. Metcalf fellow fin. & equity rsch. Pritzker Orgn.; intern Boston Consulting Group; co-founder & CEO PrepMe.com, Chgo., 2005—. Former chmn. Internat. Leadership Coun. Co-recipient New Venture Challenge award, U. Chgo. Grad. Sch. Bus., 2005, 1st place, Fortune Small Bus. Student Startup Competition, 2006; named Young Entrepreneur of Yr., US SBA, 2004; named one of Best Entrepreneurs Under 25, Bus. Week, 2006. Avocation: bhangra.

GOETSCH, ROBERT GEORGE, state legislator; b. Juneau, Wis., Aug. 5, 1933; 010s. Elmer Allen and Dorothy (Stein) G.; m. Carolyn Helen Koboski, 1974; children: Chad Evan, Shana Renee. BS, U. W. Madison, 1975. Farmer, Juneau; mem. from dist. 39 Wis. State Assembly, Madison, 1982—. Exch. del. to Rhodesia, Internat. Farm Youth Exch., 1962-63; county supr., Dodge County, Wis., 1972-83; chmn. Town of Oak Grove, Wis., 1971-82. Mem. Nat. Farmers Orgn., Am. Legion, Elks, Phi Kappa Phi. Home: N6485 High Point Rd Juneau WI 53039-9750 Office: State Capitol 314 North St Madison WI 53704-4921

GOETSCHEL, ARTHUR W., industrial manufacturing executive; b. Apr. 1942; Treas. Griffin Wheel; pres. Griffin Wheel & Griffin Can., Chgo., 1991-95; corp. v.p. Amsted, 1995-97; pres. Amsted Industries, 1997—99; chmn., pres., CEO Amstead Industries Inc., Chgo., 1999—. Office: Amsted Industries Inc 205 N Michigan Ave Chicago IL 60601

GOETTSCH, KIRK E., lawyer; b. Holstein, Iowa, July 21, 1960; BS, Iowa State U., 1982; JD, Drake U., 1985. Bar: Iowa, U.S. Tax Ct, U.S. Dist. Ct. (no. and so. dists.) Iowa. Ptnr. Clark Hasting, Ames, Iowa, 1985-90, Forristal & Goettsch, Holstein, Iowa, 1990—. Part-time county atty., Holstein, 1990—. Chmn. Story County Rep. Party, 1988, del. state convention; active local Evangelical Ch. Mem. Holstein C. of C., Holstein Country Club, Holstein Cmty. Club. Avocations: golf, computers. Office: Forristal & Goettsch PO Box 160 Holstein IA 51025-0160

GOETZ, WILLIAM G., state legislator; b. Hazen, ND, Jan. 6, 1944; s. Otto E. and Elfrieda (Knoop) G.; m. Marion R. Schock, 1970; children: Marcia, Paul, Mark. AA, Bismarck Jr. Coll., 1964; BA, Minot State Coll., 1966; MA, U. N.D., 1967. Asst. mgr. Medora divsn. Gold Seal Co., 1963-70; dean sch. bus. and adminstrn. Dickinson State U., 1967; state rep. dist. 37, 1975-90; state senator, 1990-97; chief of staff for gov. of N.D. Dickenson, N.D., 1997—. Chmn. Rep. Ho. Caucus; asst. majority leader, vice chmn. fin. and tax. com. N.D. Ho. Reps., 1975-90; asst. minority leader; mem. appropriations com., asst. majority leader N.D. State Senate, 1990—. Chmn. dist. 37 Rep. com., 1976—, mem. exec. com.; appointed by pres. to Nat. Coun. for Edn. Rsch. and Improvement. Recipient Pub. Svc. award N.D. Lignite Coun. Mem. Greater N.D. Assn. (formerly bd. dirs., Educator of Yr.), Nat. Conf. State Legislators. Republican. Home: 3642 Hackberry St Bismarck ND 58503-0299

GOETZMAN, BRUCE EDGAR, architecture educator; b. Rochester, June 6, 1931; s. Benjamin Byron and Ila Flowers G.; m. Jane Grady McRae,June 25, 1955; children: Adam Brit, Ben Evan. BArch, Carnegie Mellon U., 1954; MS in Architecture, Columbia U., 1956; M in Cmty. Planning, U. Cin., 1965; postgrad., U. London, 1968. Asst. prof. Univ. Cin., 1956-66; prin. Bruce Goetzman & Assocs., Cin., 1965-77; acting chmn. grad. div. Univ. Cin., 1966-67, assoc. prof., 1967-99; prof. emeritus, 1999; ptnr. Goetzman & Follmer Architects, Cin., 1977-85; prin. Bruce Goetzman, Restoration Architect, 1985--. Trustee Miami Purchase Assn. Hist. Preservation, Cin., 1972-91, Ohio Hist. Sites Preservation Adv. Bd., 1980-92; pres. Better Housing League of Cin., 1979-81; trustee Ohio Hist. Soc., 1986-96, pres., 1995-96; pres. Ohio Preservation Alliance, 1986-88; trustee Cin. Preservation Assn., 1993-2000. Mem.: AIA, Assn. Preservation Tech., Architects Soc. Ohio, Cincinnatus Assn. Democrat. Home: 187 Greendale Ave Cincinnati OH 45220-1223 Home Phone: 513-751-3332; Office Phone: 513-281-7244. Business E-Mail: bg@pastarc.com.

GOFF, WILMER SCOTT, retired photographer; b. Steubenville, Ohio, July 11, 1923; s. Floyd Orville and Ellen Armenia (Funk) G.; m. Mary Elizabeth Fischer, Dec. 7, 1950; children: Carolyn, Christopher. BFA with honors, Ohio U., 1949. Photographer Columbus (Ohio) Dispatch, 1949-52, Warner P. Simpson, Columbus, 1952-53; owner Willy Goff Photo Studio, Grove City, Ohio, 1954-59; photographer N.Am. Rockwell, Columbus, 1953-70; supr. Transp. Rsch. Ctr. Ohio, East Liberty, 1970-89; adult edn. instr. photography Upper Arlington and Worthington Schs., 1989-99. Photography instr. Columbus Coll. Art and Design, 1949-71; photography judge Ohio State Fair, 1966-68; judge Greater Columbus Film Festival, 1970-72; photographer John Glenn campaign, 1974. One-man shows include Southern Hotel, Columbus, 1953. Recipient Public's Choice award Columbus Art Gallery, 1958, Photo-Pictoral 1st Pl. award Dix Newspapers, 1960, Best of Show award Balloon Show Competition, 1985. Mem. Aircraft Camera Club (pres. 1954-55), Grove City Camera CLub (pres. 1959-60). Republican. Roman Catholic. Avocations: stamp collecting/philately, recording, bicycling. Home: 6110 Darby Ln Columbus OH 43229-2628

GOFFMAN, WILLIAM, mathematician, educator; b. Cleve., Jan. 28, 1924; s. Sam and Mollie (Stein) G.; m. Patricia McLoughlin, Feb. 7, 1964. BS, U. Mich., 1950, PhD, 1954. Math. cons., 1954-59; research asso. prof. Case Western Res. U., Cleve., 1959-71; dean Case Western Res. U. (Sch. Library Sci.), 1971-77; dir. Case Western Res. U. (Complex Systems Inst.), 1972-75. Contbr. numerous publs. to sci. jours. Served with USAAF, 1943-46. Recipient research grants NSF, research grants NIH, research grants USAF, research grants others. Fellow AAAS Home: Apt 1304 1 Bratenahl Pl Bratenahl OH 44108-1183 Office: Case Western Res Univ Cleveland OH 44106

GOGEL, RAYMOND E., energy executive; B in philosophy, Upsala Coll.; M in philosophy, Drew U., Madison, NJ, PhD; doctoral rsch, U. Freiburg, Germany. Various positions Pub. Svc. Electric & Gas Co. of NJ; with bus. process mgmt. group IBM Corp., sr. project exec., 1999—2001, v.p. client services, 2001—02; v.p. & chief info. officer Xcel Energy Inc., Mpls., 2002—, v.p. customer & enterprise solutions group, chief human resource officer, chief adminstrv. officer, 2005—. Bd. dirs. Seren Innovations (subs. Xcel Energy); bd. advisors IBM. Author: (books) Quest for Measure. Bd. dirs. MedicAlert Found.; bd. trustees Denver Chpt. Mile High United Way. Named one of Premier 100 IT Leaders, Computerworld, 2005. Office: Xcel Energy Inc 800 Nicollet Mall Minneapolis MN 55402

GOINS, FRANCES FLORIANO, lawyer; b. Buffalo, Jan. 30, 1950; d. William and Anita (Graziano) Floriano; m. Gary Mitchell Goins; children: Matthew W., Mark W. MusB, Cleve. Inst. Music, 1971; MusM, Case Western Res. U., 1973, JD, 1977. Bar: Ohio 1977, U.S. Dist. Ct. Ohio 1978, U.S. Ct. Appeals (6th cir.) 1979, N.Y. 1984, U.S. Dist. Ct. NY 1984, U.S. Supreme Ct. 2002. Law clk to Hon. Frank J. Battisti U.S. Dist. Ct. (no. dist.) Ohio, Cleve., 1977-78; ptnr. Squire, Sanders & Dempsey, Cleve., 1986—2003, Ulmer & Berne LLP, Cleve., 2004—. Mem. vis. com. bd. overseers Case Western Res. U., Cleve., 1984-2000; faculty Nat. Inst. Trial Advocacy, Cleve.; faculty, lectr. trial advocacy seminar Cleve. State U. Sch. Law, 1989-90. Editor-in-chief law rev. Case Western Res. Sch. Law, 1976-77. Trustee, chairperson devel. com. Lyric Opera Cleve., 1985-92, 2003—; founding trustee Shoreby Club Cleve.; v.p. bd. trustees Bay Village Montessori Sch., 1994-96; chmn. bd. trustees No. Ohio Breast Cancer Coalition, 2003—. Mem. ABA (bus. law sect., bus. lit. com., governance com. 1995—, fed. regulation of securities com., subcom. on civil litigation and SEC enforcement 1992—), Ohio Women's Bar Assn. (founding mem.), Ohio State Bar Assn. (ad hoc com. on bus. cts. 1994-99), Cleve. Bar Assn. (com. on women and the law 1987-2000, ethics com. 1988-90, securities law inst., jud. selection com. 1996-2001). Democrat. Roman Catholic. Office: Squire Sanders & Dempsey 4900 Key Tower 127 Public Sq Ste 4900 Cleveland OH 44114-1304

GOLAN, STEPHEN LEONARD, lawyer; b. Chgo., Oct. 22, 1951; s. Leonard Walter and Carol (Pepper) G.; m. Sharon D. Robson, Aug. 16, 1980; children: Brianna, Jenna, Melissa. BA, Claremont Coll., Calif., 1974; MBA, JD, Northwestern U., 1978. Bar: Ill. 1978, U.S. Dist. Ct. (no. dist.) Ill. 1978, U.S. Ct. Appeals (7th cir.) 1993. Ptnr. Seyfarth, Shaw, Fairweather & Geraldson, Chgo., 1978—93; founding ptnr. Golan & Christie LLP, Chgo., 1993—. Fellow ABA; mem. AICPA, Nat. Assn. JD-MBA Profls. (bd. dirs. 1984-86), Ill. Bar Assn., Chgo. Bar Assn., Leading Lawyers Network, Leading Lawyers Adv. Bd., Ill. Superlawyers, Tavern Club (mem. jr. com. 1984-86), Exmoor Country Club (Highland Park, Ill.), Lake Forest Caucus. Republican. Episcopalian. Office: Golan & Christie LLP 70 W Madison St 15th Fl Chicago IL 60602 E-mail: slgolan@golanchristie.com.

GOLD, CAROL R., dean, nursing educator; PhD, Northwestern U. Assoc. prof., acting dean Marcella Nieff Sch. Nursing Loyola U., Chgo. Contbr. articles to profl. jours. Mem. ANA, Am. Acad. of Ambulatory Care Nursing, Ill. Nurses Assn., Sigma Theta Tau Internat. Office: Loyola U Chgo Niehoff Sch Nursing 6525 N Sheridan Rd Chicago IL 60626-5344

GOLD, DEIDRA D., lawyer; b. Jan. 1955; m. Stephen A. Gold. BA, Wellesley Coll.; JD, Columbia U., 1979. Assoc. Jones Day Reavis & Pogue, Cleve., 1983—88, ptnr., 1988—91; v.p., gen. counsel Premier Industrial Corp., Cleve., 1991—97; ptnr. Goldberg Kohn Bell Black Rosenbloom & Mortiz, Chgo., 1998; counsel, corp. sec. Ameritech Corp., 1998—99; v.p., gen. counsel eLoyalty Corp., 2000—01; sr. v.p., gen. counsel, sec. United Stationers Inc., Des Plaines, Ill., 2001—06; exec. v.p., gen. counsel N.Am. Wolters Kluwer, Riverwoods, Ill., 2006—. Office: Wolters Kluwer US 2700 Lake Cook Rd Riverwoods IL 60015

GOLD, EDWARD DAVID, lawyer; b. Detroit, Jan. 17, 1941; s. Morris and Hilda (Robinson) Gold; m. Francine Sheila Kamin, Jan. 8, 1967; children: Lorne Brian, Karen Beth. Student, Wayne State U., 1958-61; JD, Detroit Coll. Law, 1964. Bar: Mich. 1965, U.S. Dist. Ct. (ea. dist.) Mich. 1965, U.S. Ct. Appeals (6th cir.) 1965, D.C. 1966. Atty. gen. counsel FCC, Washington, 1965-66; ptnr. Conn, Conn & Gold, Detroit, 1966-67, May, Conn, Conn & Gold, Livonia, Mich., 1967-69, Oakland County Legal Aid Soc., 1969—71, Hyman, Gurwin, Nachman, Gold & Alterman, Southfield, Mich., 1971-88, Butzel Long, Bloomfield Hills, Mich., 1988—. Mem. Oakland County Criminal Justice Coordinating Coun., 1976—77; chmn. Friend of the Ct. Adv. Com., Lansing, Mich., 1982—88; contbr. lectr. Inst. Continuing Legal Edn., Ann Arbor, Mich., 1981—, Mich. Trial Lawyers Assn.; adj. prof. U. Detroit Mercy Sch. Law, 2001—05. Author: (book) Michigan Family Law, 1988; contbr. articles to legal jours. Mem. Southfield Transp. Commn., 1975—77; chairperson atty. disp. bd. Tri-County Hearin Panel 71, 1994—2004; chmn. attys.' divsn. Jewish Welfare Fedn., Detroit; mem. nat. young leadership cabinet United Jewish Appeal, NYC, 1978—80; pres. Jewish Family Svc., Detroit, 1988—90; bd. dirs. Oakland County Legal Aid Soc., 1979—84. Scholar Tau Epsilon Rho, 1963. Fellow: Am. Acad. Matrimonial Lawyers (bd. dirs. 1988—93, nat. bd. govs. 1988—2001, pres. Mich. chpt. 1992—93, nat. v.p. 2001—05), Am. Coll. Family Trial Lawyers; mem.: Am. Arbitration Assn., Bar Assn. D.C., Southfield Bar Assn. (pres. 1975—76), Oakland County Bar Assn. (bd. dirs. 1984—93, pres. 1992—93), Mich. Bar Assn. (coun. real property law sect. 1973—81, coun. family law sect. 1974—75, 1977—82, rep. assembly 1978—82, chmn. family law sect. 1981—82, Lifetime Achievement award 2001), Alpha Epsilon Pi (nat. pres. 1976—77, Order of Lion award 1986). Avocation: golf. Office: Butzel Long Ste 200 100 Bloomfield Hills Pkwy Bloomfield Hills MI 48304 Office Phone: 248-258-1416. Business E-Mail: Gold@Butzel.com.

GOLD, GERALD SEYMOUR, lawyer; b. Cleve., Feb. 2, 1931; s. David N. and Geraldine (Bloch) G.; 1 child, Anne; m. Rosemary Grdina, 1994. AB, Case-Western Res. U., 1951, LLB, 1954. Bar: Ohio 1954, US Supreme Ct. 1961. Practiced in, Cleve., 1954-60; chief asst. legal aid defender Cuyahoga County, Cleve., 1960-61, chief legal aid defender, 1961-65; assoc. Ulmer, Byrne, Laronge, Glickman & Curtis, Cleve., 1965-66; ptnr. Gold, Rotatori, Schwartz & Gibbons, Cleve., 1966—. Instr. in law Case-Western Res. U., 1965-66, Cleve. State Law Sch., 1968-69, Case-Western Res. Law-Medicine Center, 1961-77; lectr. to bar assns. commr. Cuyahoga County Pub. Defender, 1977-81. Contbg. author: American Jurisprudence Trials, 1966; Contbr. articles to profl. jours. Fellow Am. Coll. Trial Lawyers, Am. Bd. Criminal Lawyers, Ohio State Bar Found., Internat. Soc. Barristers; mem. ABA (criminal justice coun.), Cuyahoga County Criminal Ct. Bar Assn. (chmn., Lifetime Achievement award 1995), Ohio Bar Assn. (chmn. criminal law sect. 1974-78, ho. of dels. 1986—), Greater Cleve. Bar Assn. (Merit award 1974, trustee 1978—, pres. 1982-83), Nat. Assn. Criminal Def. Lawyers (pres. 1977, Merit award 1975), Ohio Acad. Trial Lawyers (chmn. criminal law sect. 1970-75), Ohio Assn. Criminal Def. Lawyers (bd. dirs. 1990), Case-Western Res. U. Law Alumni Assn. (pres. 1974-75, Outstanding Alumnus award 1991), Soc. Benchers, Court of Nisi Prius Club, Cleve. Skating Club. Home: 33000 Pinetree Rd Pepper Pike OH 44124-5514 Office: 526 Superior Ave E Ste 1140 Cleveland OH 44114-1497 Office Phone: 216-696-6122. Personal E-mail: goldjero@aol.com.

GOLD, PAUL ERNEST, psychology and behavioral neuroscience educator; b. Detroit, Jan. 7, 1945; s. Hyman and Sylvia Gold; children: Scott David Gold, Zachary Alexander Korol-Gold. BA, U. Mich., 1966; MS, U. N.C., 1968; PhD, 1971. NIH postdoctoral fellow, lectr. psychobiology U. Calif., Irvine, 1972-76; asst. prof. U. Va., Charlottesville, 1976-78, assoc. prof., 1978-81, prof., 1981-97, Commonwealth prof., 1997—99, dir. neurosci. grad. program, 1991-95; prof. Binghamton (N.Y.) U., 1999-2000, U. Ill., Urbana-Champaign, 2000—. Dir. Med. Scholars Program U. Ill. Coll. Medicine, Urbana-Champaign, 2000—02, exec. com. Inst. Aging, 2001—, interim dir. neurosci. program, 2004—05. Editor Psychobiology, 1990-97, Neurobiology of Learning and Memory, 1998—; contbr. numerous articles to sci. publs. Mem. Commonwealth of Va. Alzheimer's and Related Disorders Commn., 1998-99. Recipient James McKeen Cattell award, 1983, Sesquicentennial Assn. award, U. Va., 1983, 90-93, Disting. Alumni award U. N.C., Chapel Hill, 2000; named APA Master Lectr., 2000; NIH fellow, 1967. Fellow APA (com. animal rsch. and ethics), AAAS, Am. Psychol. Soc. (mem. com. 1990-91, program com. 1991); mem. Soc. for Neurosci. (com. on animals in rsch. 1993-98, com. on women in neurosci. 2005—), NSF Adv. Panel for Behavioral and Computational Neurosci., 1993-96. Office: U Ill at Urbana-Champaign Dept Psychology Champaign IL 61820 Business E-Mail: pgold@uiuc.edu.

GOLDBERG, ANNE CAROL, physician, educator; b. Balt., June 12, 1951; d. Stanley Barry and Selma Ray G.; m. Ronald M. Levin, July 29, 1989. AB, Harvard U., 1973; MD, U. Md., 1977. Diplomate Am. Bd. Internal Medicine, Am. Bd. Endocrinolgy and Metabolism. Intern in medicine Michael Reese Hosp., Chgo., 1977-78, resident in medicine, 1978-80; fellow in endocrinology Washington U., St. Louis, 1980-83, instr. medicine, 1983-85, asst. prof. medicine, 1985-94, assoc. prof. medicine, 1994—. Fellow ACP, Am. Heart Assn.; mem. AMA, Am. Diabetes Assn., Am. Med. Women's Assn., Endocrine Soc., Nat. Lipid Assn. (pres. 2007-08), Alpha Omega Alpha. Democrat. Jewish. Avocation: needlepoint. Office: Washington U Med Sch Box 8127 660 S Euclid Ave Saint Louis MO 63110-1010

GOLDBERG, ARNOLD IRVING, psychoanalyst, educator; b. Chgo., May 21, 1929; s. Morris Henry and Rose (Auerbach) Goldberg; m. Constance Obenhaus; children: Andrew, Sarah. BS, U. Ill., Chgo., 1949, MD, 1953. Diplomate Am. Bd. Psychiatry and Neurology, cert. psychoanalyst. Intern Cin. Gen. Hosp., 1954-55; psychiat. resident Michael Reese Hosp., Chgo., 1957-59; tng. and supervising analyst Chgo. Inst. for Psychoanalysis, 1970—, dir., 1990-92; assoc. psychiatrist Rush Presbyn. St. Luke's Hosp., Chgo., 1982—; prof. psychiatry Rush Med. Coll., Chgo., 1982-97, Cynthia Oudejans Harris MD prof. psychiatry, 1997—. Author: (book) Models of the Mind, 1973, A Fresh Look at Psychoanalysis, 1988, The Prisonhouse of Psychoanalysis, 1990, The Problem of Perversion, 1995, Being of Two Minds, 1999, Misunderstanding Freud, 2004, Moral Stealth, 2006; editor: Future of Psychoanalysis: Progress in Self Psychology, Vols. 1-16, 1976—99, Errant Selves, 2000; contbr. articles to profl. jours. Capt. US Army, 1955—57. Recipient Sigourney award, 2006. Fellow: Am. Psychiat. Assn. (life); mem.: Am. Psychoanalytic Assn. Home: 844 W Chalmers Pl Chicago IL 60614-3223 Office: Inst for Psychoanalysis Chgo 122 S Michigan Ave Ste 1305 Chicago IL 60603-6107 Home Phone: 773-348-0771; Office Phone: 312-922-6797. Personal E-mail: docaig@aol.com.

GOLDBERG, JEROLD S., academic administrator; b. NJ, 1945; m. Michele Goldberg; children: Megan, Abby. BS, Case Western Res. U., 1968, DDS, 1970. Mem. faculty Sch. Dentistry, Case Western Res. U., 1974, chmn. oral and maxillofacial surgery dept., 1985—96, dean, 1997—; interim dean Sch. Medicine, Case Western Res. U., 2002—03; interim provost Case Western Reserve U., 2007—. Rschr. in field; co-founder Partnership in Hope Case Western Res. U. and City Hosp. of Klapeda, Lithuania, 1995—; Chair-elect of Coun. of Deans Am. Dental Edn. Assn., 2005—. Bd. mem. Ohio Dental Assn. Found. Recipient Cross of the Knight of the Order of the Lithuanian Grand Duke Gediminas, Govt. Lithuania, 2002. Mem.: Ohio Dental Assn. (mem. Ohio Dental Assn. Coun. on Dental Edn. and Licensure, del. and alt., House of Dels.). Office: Case Western Res U 10900 Euclid Ave Cleveland OH 44106-4920 Home Phone: 216-292-2744; Office Phone: 216-368-3266. Office Fax: 216-368-3204. Business E-Mail: jsg@case.edu.

GOLDBERG, SUSAN, editor; b. 1959; m. Gary Blonston (dec. Apr. 1999). Reporter Seattle Post-Intelligencer; asst. city editor Detroit Free Press, San Jose Mercury ews, 1987—89, acting city editor, mng. editor, 1999—2003, v.p., 2001—07, exec. editor, 2003—07; dep. mng. editor USA Today, 1989—99; editor Cleve. Plain Dealer, 2007—. Chair mng. editors leadership and mgmt. com. AP. Mem. bd. visitors Northwestern U. Medill Sch. Journalism; bd. mem. Silicon Valley chpt. Am. Cancer Soc., 2003—. Mem.: Am. Soc. Newspaper Editors (bd. dirs.), Downtown San Jose Rotary Club. Office: Cleve Plain Dealer 1801 Superior Ave NE Cleveland OH 44114-2198 Office Phone: 216-999-4800. Office Fax: 216-999-6354. E-mail: sgoldberg@plaind.com.*

GOLDBERGER, ARTHUR STANLEY, economics professor; b. NYC, Nov. 20, 1930; s. David M. and Martha (Greenwald) G.; m. Iefke Engelsman, Aug. 19, 1957; children: Nina Judith, icholas Bernard. BS, N.Y.U., 1951; MA, U. Mich., 1952, PhD, 1958. Acting asst. prof. econs. Stanford U., 1956-59; assoc. prof. econs. U. Wis., 1960-63, prof., 1963-70, H.M. Groves prof., 1970-79, Vilas research prof., 1979-98, prof. emeritus, 1998—. Vis. prof. Center Planning and Econ. Rsch., Athens, Greece, 1964-65, U. Hawaii, 1969, 71, Stanford U., 1990, 96, 2000; Keynes vis. prof. U. Essex, 1968-69. Author: (with L.R. Klein) An Econometric Model of the United States, 1929-52, 1955, Impact Multipliers and Dynamic Properties, 1959, Econometric Theory, 1964, Topics in Regression Analysis, 1968, Functional Form and Utility, 1987, A Course in Econometrics, 1991, Introductory Econometrics, 1998; editor: (with O.D. Duncan) Structural Equation Models in the Social Sciences, 1973, (with D.J. Aigner) Latent Variables in Socioeconomic Models, 1976; Assoc. editor: Jour. Econometrics, 1973-77; bd. editors: Am. Econ. Rev, 1964-66, Jour. Econ. Lit, 1975-77. Fulbright fellow Netherlands Sch. Econs., 1955-56, 59-60; fellow Ctr. for Advanced Study in Behavioral Scis., Stanford, 1976-77, 80-81; Guggenheim fellow Stanford U., 1972-73, 85. Fellow Am. Statis. Assn., Econometric Soc. (council 1975-80, 82-87), Am. Acad. Arts and Scis., AAAS; mem. Am. Econ. Assn. (Disting. fellow 1988), Nat. Acad. Scis., Royal Netherlands Acad. Scis. Home: 2828 Sylvan Ave Madison WI 53705-5228 Office: U Wis Dept Econs 1180 Observatory Dr Madison WI 53706-1320 Business E-Mail: asgoldbe@wisc.edu.

GOLDBERGER, ROBERT D., food products company executive; b. 1935; V.p. King Foods, Inc., Newport, Minn., 1956-73; with GFI America, Mpls., 1973—, pres., CEO. Office: GFI America 2815 Blaisdell Ave Minneapolis MN 55408-2385

GOLDBLATT, LAWRENCE I., dean, educator, researcher; Undergrad., Georgetown U., DDS cum laude, 1968; grad. oral pathology residency program, Ind. U., 1971, MSD, 1973. Diplomate Am. Bd. Oral and Maxillofacial Pathology. Rotating dental intern U.S. Naval Hosp., St. Albans, NY; lt. to comdr. U.S. Naval Res. U.S. Navy Dental Corps., 1971—89, ret., 1989; asst. prof. oral pathology Ind. U. Sch. Dentistry, 1973—77, assoc. prof. oral pathology, 1977—82, prof. oral pathology, 1982—93, 1997—, named assoc. dean grad. and postgrad. edn., 1988, named assoc. dean acad. affairs, 1990, dean, 1997—; prof. oral pathology, dean Case Western Res. U. Sch. Dentistry, 1994—96. Tchr., rschr. in field; past. commr. and chmn. ADA Joint Commn. on Nat. Dental Exams.; commr. ADA Commn. Dental Accreditation, 1998—2002. Contbr. scientific papers, articles to peer-reviewed jours. Fellow: Internat. Coll. Dentists, Am. Coll. Dentists; mem.: Internat. Assn. Dental Rsch., ADA, Am. Dental Edn. Assn. (v.p. deans), Am. Assn. Dental Rsch., Am. Acad. Oral and Maxillofacial Pathology, Ind. U. Sch. Dentistry Alumni Assn. (ad hoc mem. assn.'s bd. dirs.), Omicron Kappa Upsilon (past pres. Supreme chpt.). Office: 1121 West Michigan St Indianapolis IN 46202 Office Phone: 317-274-7461. Office Fax: 317-274-7188. Business E-Mail: lgoldbla@iupui.edu.

GOLDBLATT, STANFORD JAY, lawyer; b. Chgo., Feb. 25, 1939; s. Maurice and Bernice (Mendelson) G.; m. Ann Dudley Cronkhite, June 17, 1968; children: Alexandra, Nathaniel, Jeremy. BA magna cum laude, Harvard U., 1960, LLB magna cum laude, 1963. Bar: Ill. 1963. Law clk. U.S. Ct. Appeals, 5th Jud. Circuit, New Orleans, 1963-64; mem. firm Winston & Strawn, Chgo., 1964-67; v.p. Goldblatt Bros., Inc., Chgo., 1967-76, pres., chief exec. officer, 1976-77, chmn. exec. com., 1977-78; ptnr. Hopkins & Sutter, 1978-97, Winston & Strawn, Chgo., 1997—. Bd. dirs. MacLean-Fogg Co., Divergence, Inc., Rasmussen Coll., Inc. Trustee U. Chgo., Cancer Rsch. Found., U. Chgo. Med. Ctr. Mem. Econ. Club, Racquet Club, Comml. Club, Adv. Bd., Frontenac IX Pvt. Capital Ltd. Partnership. Office: Winston & Strawn 35 W Wacker Dr Ste 4200 Chicago IL 60601-9703

GOLDEN, BRUCE PAUL, lawyer; b. Chgo., Dec. 4, 1943; s. Irving R. and Anne K. (Eisenberg) G. SB in Elec. Sci. and Engring., MIT, 1965, SM in Elec. Engring., 1966; JD, Harvard U., 1969. Bar: Ill. 1969, U.S. Dist. Ct. (no. dist.) Ill. 1970, U.S. Ct. Appeals (7th cir.) 1994, U.S. Supreme Ct. 1995, cert.: (arbitrator); lic. real estate broker. Assoc. McDermott, Will & Emery, Chgo., 1970-75, ptnr., 1976-91; of counsel Fishman & Merrick, P.C., Chgo., 1991-92, Coffield, Ungaretti & Harris, Chgo., 1992-96; Bruce P. Golden and Assocs., Chgo., 1996—; gen. counsel Piranha, Inc., 2000—02. Officer, dir. various corps.; speaker bank law, securities law, venture capital seminars Contbr. articles to Banking Law Jour., contbg. editor, 1979-90. Chmn. MIT Enterprise Forum Chgo.; bd. dirs. Entrepreneurship Inst. Chgo., Chgo. chpt. U.S. Entrepreneurs Network, Ill. Small Bus. Devel. Ctr., Kellogg Sch. Bus. community services com. Mem. MIT Alumni of Chgo. (dir. 1993—), Union League. Home and Office: 4137 N Hermitage Ave Chicago IL 60613-1820 Business E-Mail: bpgolden@lstcounsel.com.

GOLDEN, CHARLES EDWARD, retired pharmaceutical company executive; b. Ft. Wayne, Ind., 1946; BA in Econ., Lafayette Coll., 1968; MBA, Lehigh U., 1970. From treas. to corp. v.p. GM, United Kingdom, 1970—96; exec. v.p., CFO Eli Lilly and Co., Indpls., 1996—2006.

GOLDEN, LOREN S., lawyer; b. 1943; State atty. Carroll County; pvt. practice Elgin, Ill. Mem.: Ill. State Bar (treas. 1994—95, 3d v.p., bd. govs., pres. 2003). Office: Ste 201A 2400 Big Timber Rd Elgin IL 60123

GOLDEN, NEIL B., marketing executive; b. Chgo., Aug. 23, 1961; Grad., Northwestern U., Evanston, Ill. Regional mktg. supr. McDonald's Corp., various field and corp. positions, v.p. US mktg., sr. v.p., chief mktg. officer Oak Brook, Ill., 2008—. Founding mem. bd. dirs. Ronald McDonald House at Loyola; bd. dirs. Thurgood Marshall Coll. Fund; adv. bd. Suzuki-Orff Sch. Music. Office: McDonald's Corp 2111 McDonald's Dr Oak Brook IL 60523*

GOLDEN, WILLIAM C., lawyer; b. NYC, Oct. 27, 1936; s. Edwin and Sue (Lipman) G.; m. Rachel Epstein; children: Rebecca, Naomi, Nathaniel, David. BS, Wharton Sch., U. Pa., 1957; LLB, Columbia U., 1960. Bar: N.Y. 1961, Ill. 1967. Atty. Dept. Justice, Tax Div., Washington, 1960-61, Dept. Treasury, Washington, 1962-65; assoc. prof. of law Ind. U., Bloomington, 1965-67; assoc., then ptnr. Sidley and Austin, Chgo., 1967—. Bd. dirs. ALAMCO, Clarksburg, W.Va., 1980-85. Author: Attorneys' Guide to Charitable Giving, 1967. Bd. dirs. Self Help Ctr., Evanston, Ill., 1985-86; chmn. Info. Tech. Resource Ctr., Chgo., 1987—. Mem. ABA, Chgo. Bar Assn. (chmn. fed. tax com. 1979-80). Office: Sidley & Austin 1 S First National Plz Chicago IL 60603-2000

GOLDENBERG, KIM, retired academic administrator, internist, consultant; BS, SUNY, Stonybrook, 1968; MS, Polytech. Inst. N.Y., 1972; MD, Albany Med. Coll., NYC, 1979. Test engr. lunar lander and naval jets, Grumman, NY, 1968—75; resident internal medicine Western Res. Care Sys., Youngstown, Ohio, 1979—82; dir. gen. internal medicine Wright State U. Sch. Medicine, Dayton, Ohio, 1983—89, vice chair medicine, 1988—89, assoc. dean for students and curriculum, 1989—90, dean, 1990—98; pres. Wright State U., Dayton, Ohio, 1998—2007.

GOLDFARB, BERNARD SANFORD, lawyer; b. Cleve., Apr. 15, 1917; s. Harry and Esther (Lenson) Goldfarb; m. Barbara Brofman Goldfarb, Jan. 4, 1966; children: Meredith Stacy, Lauren Beth. AB, Case Western Res. U., 1938, JD, 1940. Bar: Ohio 1940. Since practiced in, Cleve.; sr. ptnr. firm Goldfarb & Reznick, 1967-95; pvt. practice Cleve., 1997—. Spl. counsel to atty. gen. Ohio, 1950, 1971—74; mem. Ohio Commn. Uniform Traffic Rules, 1973—80. Contbr. articles to profl. jours. With USAAF, 1942—45. Mem.: ABA, Cuyahoga County Bar Assn., Greater Cleve. Bar Assn., Ohio Bar Assn. Home: 39 Pepper Creek Dr Pepper Pike OH 44124-5279 Office: 55 Public Sq Ste 1500 Cleveland OH 44113-1998 Office Phone: 216-696-0606 ext. 250. Personal E-mail: bunnysgoldfarb@aol.com.

GOLDGAR, BERTRAND ALVIN, historian, educator; b. Macon, Ga., Nov. 17, 1927; s. Benjamin Meyer and Annie (Shapiro) G.; m. Corinne Cohn Hartman, Apr. 6, 1950; children: Arnold Benjamin, Anne Hartman. BA, Vanderbilt U., 1948, MA, 1949, Princeton U., 1957, PhD, 1958. Instr. in English Clemson (S.C.) U., 1948-50, asst. prof., 1951-52; instr. English Lawrence U., Appleton, Wis., 1957-61, asst. prof., 1961-65, assoc. prof., 1965-71, prof. English, 1971—, John N. Bergstrom prof. humanities, 1980—. Mem. fellowship panel NEH, 1979 Author: The Curse of Party: Swift's Relations with Addison and Steele, 1961, Walpole and the Wits: The Relation of Politics to Literature, 1722-1742, 1976; editor: The Literary Criticism of Alexander Pope, 1965, Henry Fielding's The Covent-Garden Jour., 1988, Henry Fielding's Miscellanies, Vol. 2, 1993, Jonathan Wild, 1997, The Grub Street Jour. 1730-1733, 2002; adv. editor: 18th Century Studies, 1977-82; contbr. essays to books. With AUS, 1952-54. Fellow, Am. Coun. Learned Socs, 1973-74, NEH, 1980-81. Mem. Am. Soc. 18th Century Studies, Johnson Soc. Cen. Region. Home: 914 E Eldorado St Appleton WI 54911-5536 Office: Lawrence U Dept English Appleton WI 54912 Office Phone: 920-832-6694. Business E-Mail: bertrand.a.goldgar@lawrence.edu.

GOLDMAN, ALLEN MARSHALL, physics professor; b. NYC, Oct. 18, 1937; s. Louis and Mildred (Kohn) Goldman; m. Katherine Virginia Darnell, July 31, 1960; children: Matthew, Rachel, Benjamin. AB in Chemistry and Physics, Harvard U., Cambridge, Mass., 1958; PhD in Physics, Stanford U., Calif., 1965. Rsch. asst. Stanford U., Calif., 1960-65, rsch. assoc., 1965; asst. prof. physics U. Minn., Mpls., 1965-67, assoc. prof., 1967-73, prof., 1974—, dir. Ctr. Sci. and Application of Superconductivity, 1989—, inst. tech. prof., 1992—, head Sch. Physics and Astronomy, 1996—. Co-chmn. Gordon Conf. quantum Liquids and Solids, 1981; dir. ATO Advanced Study Inst., 1983; mem. materials rsch. adv. com. NSF, 1985—88; mem. vis. com. Francis Butter Nat. Magnet Lab., 1986—89, chmn., 1987—89; mem. vis. com. Nat. Nanofabrication Facility Cornell, 1988—90, mem. user com., 1997—99; mem. vis. com. U. Chgo. Materials Program Argonne Nat. Lab., 1992—98, chmn., 1995; mem. Buckley prize com., 1994—95, London prize com., 1994—98; mem. Helium res. com. NAS/NRC, 1998—99. Assoc. editor: Revs. Modern Physics, 1999—2005; contbr. articles to profl. jours. Vis. divsn. materials rsch. grantee, NSF, 1999, Alfred P. Sloan Found. fellow, 1966—70. Fellow: AAAS, Am. Phys. Soc. (councilor divsn. condensed matter physics 1994—96, mem. publs. oversight com. 1996—99, chair 1997, councilor divsn. condensed matter physics 1999—2003, mem. exec. com. 2001—03, vice chair divsn. condensed matter physics 2006, chair elect 2007, Fritz London Meml. prize 2002); mem.: NAS, Am. Inst. Physics (pub. policy com. 1999—). Jewish. Home: 1015 James Ct Mendota Heights MN 55118-3640 Office: U Minn Sch Physics and Astronomy 116 Church St SE Minneapolis MN 55455-0149 Office Phone: 612-624-6062. Business E-Mail: goldman@physics.umn.edu.

GOLDMAN, LOUIS B., lawyer; b. Chgo., Apr. 11, 1948; s. Jack Sidney and Lorraine Goldman; m. Barbara Marcia Berg, Oct. 2, 1983; children: Jacqueline Ilyse, Annie Dara, Michael Louis. BA magna cum laude, U. Calif., Berkeley, 1970; JD cum laude, U. Chgo., 1974. Bar: Calif. 1975, US Dist. Ct. (no. dist.) Calif. 1975, US Ct. Appeals (9th cir.) 1975, NY 1976, US Dist. Ct. (so. and ea. dists.) NY 1976, US Ct. Appeals (2nd cir.) 1976, Ill. 1991, Czech Republic, 1997; registered fgn. lawyer, Eng. 1999, Wales 1999. Law clk. US Dist. Ct., San Francisco, 1974-75; assoc. Cleary, Gottlieb, Steen & Hamilton, NYC and Paris, 1975-81, Edwards & Angell, NYC, 1981-83, ptnr., 1986-88, Wald, Harkrader & Ross, NYC, 1983-86, Altheimer & Gray, Chgo., 1989—2003, co-chmn., 1999—2003; ptnr., mem. global bd. Salans, NYC, 2003—. Mng. dir. Abacus & Assocs. Inc., NYC; supervisory bd. Pudliszki S.A. Mem. U. Chgo. Law Rev.; contbr. articles to profl. jours. Mem. Chgo.-Prague Sister Cities Com., Chgo.-China Sister Cities Com.; bd. dirs. Lyric Opera Ctr. for Am. Artists, New Trier Swim Club; sec. class of 1970, U. Calif., Berkeley; bd. trustees The Ravinia Festival. Mem. ABA, Calif. Bar Assn., Assn. of the Bar of City of NY, Chgo. Bar Assn., Ill. State Bar Assn., Internat. Bar Assn., Order of Coif, Northwestern Assocs., Chgo. China Sister Cities Comm., Old Willow Club, The Law Club, Phi Beta Kappa. Home: 465 Grove St Glencoe IL 60022-1844 Office: Salans 620 Fifth Ave New York NY 10020 Office Phone: 312-622-8448. Business E-Mail: goldmanlb@yahoo.com.

GOLDMAN, MARC L., federal judge; b. 1948; BA, U. Mich., 1969; JD, Wayne State U., 1973. Atty. State Appellate Defender Office, 1973-74, Washtenaw County Pub. Defender, Ann Arbor, Mich., 1974-76; asst. U.S. atty. U.S. Dist. Ct. (ea. dist.) Mich., 1980-83, magistrate judge Detroit, 1983—. Asst. prof. Wayne State U. Law Sch., 1973-74; vis. asst. prof. U. Mich. Law Sch., 1979-80.

GOLDMANN, MORTON AARON, cardiologist, educator; b. Chgo., July 11, 1924; s. Harry Ascher and Frieda (Cohon) G.; m. Doris-Jane Tumpeer, July 18, 1951; children: Deborah, Jory, Erica, Leslie BS, U. Ill., 1943, MD, 1946. Diplomate Am. Bd. Internal Medicine. Intern Cook County Hosp., Chgo., 1946-47, resident physician, 1949-52, practice medicine specializing in internal medicine and cardiology Skokie, Ill., 1952—2003, trustee emeritus, 2003—; chief of medicine Rush North Shore Med. Ctr. (formerly Skokie Valley Hosp.), 1964-65, also trustee, 1968—2002, trustee emeritus, 2002—, pres. med. staff, 1968-69, attending physician, med. dir. heart sta. and cardiac rehab. unit, 1973-96, bd. dirs., 1970—; former attending physician Ill. Rsch. Hosp.; former assoc. prof. Abraham Lincoln Sch. Medicine, U. Ill., Chgo.; prof. Cook County Grad. Sch. Medicine. Pres. Heart Assn. North Cook County, 1978-81, North Suburban Assn. Health Resources, 1974-77 Contbr. numerous articles to profl. jours. Capt. M.C., AUS, 1947-49, PTO Fellow ACP, Inst. Medicine Chgo., Am. Coll. Cardiology; mem. AMA, Am. Soc. Internal Medicine, Am. Heart Assn., Ill. Med. Soc., Chgo. Med. Soc., Chgo. Heart Assn. (bd. govs., bd. dirs. 1978-87, bd. trustees 1979-83).

GOLDRING, NORMAN MAX, marketing professional; b. Chgo., June 22, 1937; s. Jack and Carolyn (Wolf) G.; m. Cynthia Lois Garland, Dec. 20, 1959; children: Jay Marshall, Diane. BS in Bus., Miami U., Ohio, 1959; MBA, U. Chgo., 1963. Advt. account mgr. Edward H. Weiss & Co., Chgo., 1959-61; sr. v.p., dir. mktg. svcs. Stern, Walters & Simmons, Inc., Chgo., 1961-68; chmn. Goldring & Co., Inc., Chgo., 1968-89; pres., CEO CPM, Inc., 1969-93, chmn., 1994-99; pres. CPO Inc., 1994—. Dir. Creative Works, Inc., 1994-97, Media-Smith, Inc., 2004—; instr. mktg. and advt. mgmt. Roosevelt U., 1965-68. Mem. editl. bd. Jour. Media Planning; mem. editl. bd. advisors Response Mag., 2001-07. Commr. Ridgeville Park Dist., Evanston, Ill., 1971-75, pres. 1974-75; bd. dirs., v.p. Mus. Broadcast Comm., 1983-92; bd. dirs. Chgo. Chamber Musicians 1988—, Chgo. Metro History Fair, 1990; bd. dirs. Lake Forest Grad. Sch. Mgmt., 2000—, mem. exec. com., 2002—, chmn. mktg. com., 2005—; trustee Chgo. Assn. Dirs. Mktg. Ednl. Found., 2001-05. Mem. Am. Mktg. Assn. (speaker), Advt. Coun. Inc. (Midwest adv. bd. 1983-90), Am. Mgmt. Assn., Direct Mktg. Assn. (mem. chmn., broadcast coun.), Chgo. Assn. Dirs. Mktg., Elec. Ret. Assn. Home: 855 Beverly Pl Lake Forest IL 60045-3901 Office: CPO Inc 736 N Western Ave # 147 Chicago IL 60045 Home Phone: 847-735-8055; Office Phone: 847-735-7365. Business E-Mail: ngoldring@cpodirect.com.

GOLDSBOROUGH, ROBERT GERALD, publishing executive, author; b. Chgo., Oct. 3, 1937; s. Robert Vincent and Wilma (Janak) G.; m. Janet Elizabeth Moore, Jan. 15, 1966; children: Suzanne Joy, Robert Michael, Colleen Marie, Bonnie Laura. BS, Northwestern U., 1959, MS with honors, 1960. Reporter A.P., 1959, City News Bur., Chgo., 1959; with Chgo. Tribune, 1960-82, reporter neighborhood news sect., asst. editor Sunday mag. and TV sect., 1963-66, editor TV Week mag., 1966-67, asst. to features editor, 1967-71, asst. to editor, 1971-72, Sunday editor, 1972-75, editor Sunday mag., 1975-82; exec. editor Advt. Age Mag., Chgo., 1982-88, spl. projects dir., 1988-91; corp. projects editor Crain Comm., Chgo., 1991-96, spl. projects dir., 1997—2004, spl. projects cons., 2005—. Author: Great Railroad Paintings, 1976, Nero Wolfe Mysteries: Murder in E-Minor, 1986, Death on Deadline, 1987, The Bloodied Ivy, 1988, The Last Coincidence, 1989, Fade to Black, 1990, The Crain Adventure, 1992, Silver Spire, 1994, The Missing Chapter, 1994, The Year Diz Came to Town, 2003, Three Strikes You're Dead, 2005, Shadow of the Bomb, 2006, A Death in Pilsen, 2007, Snap Malok Mysteries. Served with AUS, 1961. Recipient Svc. award, Northwestern U. Alumni, 2001. Mem. Arts Club. Presbyterian. Personal E-mail: goldsborough@sbcglobal.net.

GOLDSCHMIDT, LYNN HARVEY, lawyer; b. Chgo., June 14, 1951; d. Arthur and Ida (Shirman) H.; m. Robert Allen Goldschmidt, Aug. 27, 1972; children: Elizabeth Anne, Carolyn Helene. BS with honors, U. Ill., 1973; JD magna cum laude, Northwestern U., 1976. Bar: Ill. 1976. Ptnr. Hopkins & Sutter, Chgo., 1976-2001, Foley & Lardner, Chgo., 2001—02; prin. D and G Cons. Group, 2002—. Articles editor Northwestern U. Law Rev. Mem. Airport Coun. Internat., N. Am., Order of Coif. Personal E-mail: lhg@dg-cg.com.

GOLDSCHMIDT, PASCAL JOSEPH, medical educator, cardiologist; b. Brussels, Apr. 12, 1954; m. Emily Ann Boches. BS, Univ. Libre de Brussels, 1976, MD, 1980. Lic. physician Md., Ohio, Belgium. Intern and resident in medicine/cardiology Erasme Acad. Hosp./U. Libre de Brussels, 1980-83; rsch. fellow dept. immunology and microbiology Med. U. S.C., Charleston, 1983-86; resident in medicine Union Meml. Hosp., Balt., 1986-88; clin. and rsch. fellow cardiology/cell biology/anatomy Johns Hopkins U., Balt., 1988-91, assoc. prof. dept. medicine/cardiology divsn., 1991-96, dir. Bernard Lab. Vascular Biology, 1991-96; attending CCU Johns Hopkins Hosp., Balt., 1991-96, co-dir. Thrombosis Ctr., 1994-96; co-dir. Henry Ciccarone Ctr. for Prevention Heart Disease, Balt., 1991-96; prof. medicine, dir. Heart and Lung Inst. Ohio State U., Columbus, dir. divsn. cardiology, 1998—. Lectr. in field. Contbr. numerous articles and abstracts to profl. jours., chpts. to books; reviewer New Eng. Jour. Medicine, Annals of Internal Medicine, Biochemistry, Blood, Cell, Cell Adhesion and Comm., Circulation Rsch., Jour. Cell Biology, Molecular Biology of the Cell, Am. Heart Assn., NIH. Recipient NATO Sci. award, 1983, 84; grantee Clinician Scientist Award, 1991-93, Syntex Scholars Program, 1992-95, Am. Heart Assn., 1992-94, 95—, NIH, 1992-96, 94-96, 95—; Am. Heart Assn. fellow, 1990, Med. U. S.C., 1984, 85. Mem. AAAS, Am. Heart Assn., Am. Soc. Clin. Investigators. Home: 3725 Foxwood Pl Durham NC 27705-1992 Office: Ohio State U Heart/Lung 514 Med Rsch Facility 420 W 12th Ave Columbus OH 43210-1214

GOLDSEN, BRUCE L., radio executive; b. Norwalk, Conn., Aug. 5, 1959; s. Leonard and Esther (Rosenfeld) G.; m. Susan Eva Szanti, Sept. 15, 1984; 1 child, David Tyler. BA, Western Conn. State U., 1981. Music dir. Sta. WRKI, Danbury, Conn., 1981-83; program dir. Sta. WINE, Danbury, 1983-85, Sta. WTFM, Kingsport, Johnson City, Tenn., 1986-87, Sta. WIVY-FM, Jacksonville, Fla., 1987-90; v.p., gen. mgr. Sta. WABJ/WQTE, Adrian, Mich., 1990—95; v.p. Sta. WMXE, Hudson and Hillsdale, Mich., 1995—97; pres. & gen. mgr. Jackson Radio Works, Inc./WKHM-AM/FM, Jackson, Mich., 1997—. Mem. Dem. Town Com., Weston, Conn., 1982-83; bd. dirs. Lewanee United Way and Vol. Ctr., 1992—, ann. campaign co-chair, 1992-94, pres. 1995-96; bd. dirs. Croswell Opera House, 1995—. Mem. Mich. Assn. of Broadcasters (bd. dirs. 1993-, pres. 1998-2001, chmn. elect. 2007-), Nat. Assn. Broadcasters (bd. dirs.), Adrian Rotary Club (bd. dirs. 1996-, pres. 2005-06, Internat. Ave. Svc. award, 2006). Avocations: racquetball, music, finance, computers. Office: Jackson Radio Works 1700 Glenshire Dr Jackson MI 49201 Office Phone: 517-787-9546. Office Fax: 517-787-7517.

GOLDSMITH, ETHEL FRANK, medical social worker; b. Chgo., May 31, 1919; d. Theodore and Rose (Falk) Frank; m. Julian Royce Goldsmith, Sept. 4, 1940; children: Richard, Susan, John. BA, U. Chgo., 1940. Lic. social worker, Ill. Liaison worker psychiat. consultation svc. U. Chgo. Hosp., 1964—68; med. social worker Wyler Children's Hosp., Chgo., 1968—98. Treas. U. Chgo. Svc. League, 1958-62, bd. dirs.; chmn. camp Brueckner Farr Aux., 1966-72; pres. Bobs Roberts Hosp. Svc. Commn., 1962; bd. dirs. Richardson Wildlife Sanctuary, 1988-2000; mem. Field Mus. Women's Bd., 1966—; bd. dirs. Hyde Park Art Ctr., 1964-82, Chgo. Commons Assn., 1967-77, Alumni Assn. Sch. Social Svc. Adminstrn., 1976-80, Self Help Home for Aged, 1985-2000; vol. Chgo. Found. for Edn.; mem. womens bd. U. Chgo., 1999—. Recipient Alumni Citation Pub. Service, U. Chgo., 1972. Mem. Phi Beta Kappa. Home: 5550 S Shore Dr Apt 1313 Chicago IL 60637

GOLDSMITH, JOHN ANTON, linguist, educator; b. NYC, Nov. 7, 1951; s. Simon Albert and Thelma Margaret (Ettesvold) G.; m. Jessie Elizabeth Pinkham, Nov. 20, 1982; children: Elizabeth, Paul, Julia. BA, Swarthmore Coll., 1972; PhD, MIT, 1976. Asst., assoc. then prof. Ind. U., Bloomington, 1976-84; prof. U. Chgo., 1984—, Edward Carson Waller Disting. Svc. prof., 1997—. Bd. dirs. U. Chgo. Press, 1990-94. Author: Autosegmental and Metrical Phonology, 1990, (with G. Huck) Ideology and Linguistic Theory, 1995, (with J. Komlos and P. Gold) The Chicago Guide to Your Academic Career; editor, translator Syntax and Human Experience, 1991; editor: The Last Phonological Rule, 1993, Handbook of Phonological Theory, 1995, Phonological Theory: The Essential Readings, 1999. Fellow Am. Acad. Arts & Scis.; mem. Linguistics Soc. Am. (mem. exec. com. 1988-91). Office: U Chgo Dept Linguistics 1010 E 59th St Chicago IL 60637-1512

GOLDSMITH, SCOTT K., lawyer; b. Mpls., Mar. 7, 1950; BA, Princeton U., 1972; JD, Case Western Res. U., 1975. Bar: Minn. 1975, U.S. Dist. Ct. Minn. 1975, U.S. Ct. Appeals (8th cir.) 1981, U.S. Ct. Appeals (7th cir.) 1986, U.S. Tax Ct. 1987. Atty. Popham, Haik, Schnobrich & Kaufman Ltd., Mpls. Assoc. editor Case Western Res. U. Jour. Internat. Law, 1973-74, editor, 1974-75. Mem. Minn. Def. Lawyers Assn., Def. Rsch. Inst. Office: Popham Haik Schnobrich & Kaufman Ltd 3300 Piper Jaffrey Tower 222 S 9th St Ste 3200 Minneapolis MN 55402-3336

GOLDSTEIN, ALFRED GEORGE, consumer products company executive; b. NYC, Sept. 22, 1932; s. Milton and Pauline M. G.; m. Hope D. Perry, July 5, 1959; children: Mark, Robert. AB, CCNY, 1953; MS, Columbia U., 1954. With Sears, Roebuck & Co., Chgo., 1957—79, v.p. mdse, group nat. mdse. mgr., 1976-79; sr. v.p. consumer bus. Am. Can Co., Greenwich, Conn., 1979-81, sr. v.p. waste recovery bus., 1981-82, exec. v.p. plastics packaging bus., 1982-83, pres. splty. retailing sector, 1983-87; pres. splty. merchandising and direct mktg. group, Sears Can., Sears Logistics Svc. Sears, Roebuck & Co., Chgo., 1987-93; pres., CEO AG Assocs., Chgo., 1993 —; bd. dirs. Sears Mdse. Group, Sears Can., Ltd. Former vice chmn., CEO, bd. dirs. Fingerhut Corp.; chmn. bd. dirs. Pickwick Internat.; chmn., CEO, Musicland Group; bd. dirs. Gander Mountain Corp., 1994; adv. bd. in bus. ethics Kellogg Grad. Sch. Bus. Northwestern U., 1995-2004 Exec. editor: Internat. Jour. Addictions, 1975-80. Trustee Archaeus Found., 1978—90; bd. dirs. United Negro Coll. Fund, 1991—, mem. exec. com., 1996, vice chmn., 2001—, trustee com. econ. devel., 1999—; mem. mktg. com. bd. trustees Art Inst. Chgo., 1988—2002; mem. adv. bd. Goizueta Bus. Sch. Ctr. Leadership and Career Studies, Emory U., 1990—97; mem. exec. com. Columbia U. Grad. Sch. Bus. Alumni Assn., 1980—86, Am. Can Co. Found.; bd. dirs. Art Americana, 1996; mem. adv. bd. chief exec. leadership inst. Yale U., 2000—. With US Army, 1954—57. Mem. Am. Arbitration Assn. (arbitrator), Bus. Execs. Nat. Security.

GOLDSTEIN, BERNARD, transportation and hotel executive; b. Rock Island, Ill., Feb. 5, 1929; s. Morris and Fannie (Borenstein) G.; m. Irene Alter, Dec. 18, 1949; children: Jeffrey, Robert, Kathy, Richard. BA, U. Ill., 1949, LLB, 1951. Bar: Iowa 1951. With Alter Co., Bettendorf, Iowa, 1951—, chmn. bd., 1979—. Isle of Capri Casinos, Inc., St. Louis, 1992—, chmn., CEO, 1997—. Bd. vis. U. Ill. Coll. Law, 2005—. Pres. Quad City Jewish Fedn., 1975; mem. U. Ill. Coll. Law Bd. Visitors. Named Top Performing Gaming CEO of the Yr., Am. Gaming Assn., 2001; recipient Ernst and Young Entrepreneur of the Yr. award, 1999, Rivers Hall of Fame Achievement award, 1999, Simon Wiesenthal Disting. Cmty. award, Compass award, Passenger Vessel Assn., Outstanding Bus. Leader award, Jewish Fedn. South Palm Beach County, Jerusalem medal, State of Israel Bonds, Disting. Alumnus award, U. Ill. Coll. Law Bd. Visitors. Jewish.*

GOLDSTEIN, MARVIN EMANUEL, aerospace scientist; b. Cambridge, Mass., Oct. 11, 1938; s. David and Evelyn (Wilner) G.; m. Priscilla Ann Beresh, July 5, 1965; children: Deborah, Judy. BS in Mech. Engring., Northeastern U., 1961; MS in Mech. Engring., MIT, 1962; PhD in Mech. Engring., U. Mich., 1965. Engr. Arthur D. Little, Inc., Cambridge, 1958-61; rsch. asst. MIT, Cambridge, 1961-63, rsch. assoc., 1965-67; aerospace engr. Lewis Rsch. Ctr., NASA, Cleve., 1967-79, chief scientist, 1980—2004. Adj. prof. math dept. Case Western Res. U., 1998—. Author: Aeroacoustics, 1976; contbr. articles to profl. jours. Recipient Outstanding Alumni award, Northeastern U., 2002, Fluids Engring. award, ASME, 2003. Fellow AIAA (assoc. editor jour. 1977-79, chmn. aeroacoustics tech. com., 1979-81, mem. publs. com. 1980-83, Aeroacoustics award 1983, Pendray award 1983), Am. Phys. Soc. (exec. com. div. fluid dynamics 1991-93, Otto Laporte award in fluid mechanics 1997); mem. Nat. Acad. Engring. (elected). Jewish. Avocations: auto racing, auto restoration. Office: NASA Lewis Rsch Ctr MS 54-3 21000 Brookpark Rd Cleveland OH 44135-3191 Home Phone: 440-365-6745; Office Phone: 216-433-5825. Business E-Mail: marvin.e.goldstein@nasa.gov.

GOLDSTEIN, NORMAN RAY, international trading company executive, consultant; b. Chgo., Nov. 20, 1944; s. Max and Rose (Weiner) G.; m. Bonnie A. Brod, Aug. 31, 1969; children: Russell, Matthew, Jamie. AA, Wright Jr. Coll., 1965; BS in Fin., No. Ill. U., DeKalb, 1967; MS in Acctg. cum laude, Roosevelt U., 1986. Cert. treasury profl., Assn. Fin. Profls. Gen. bus. mgr. Greenstreet Corp., Whiting, Ind., 1967; wholesale credit mgr. Atlantic Richfield Co., Chgo., 1968-74; v.p. fin., treas. Barton Inc. (Barton Brands, Ltd.), Chgo., 1974-96; chmn., CEO Gold Internat., 1996—. Spl. master U.S. Dist. Ct., 1998; chmn. ABC Fin. Comm. Forum, Chgo., 1987-88; v.p. Consort Corp., Chgo., 1971-80; spl. master U.S. Dist. Ct., 1998; adj. prof. fin. No. Ill. U., 2000-, mem. adv. bd. dept. fin., 2003-; instr. Ctr. Profl. Edn., 1997-2007; bd. mgrs. No. Ill. Angels LLC, 2004-07; spkr. in field. Contbg. author: Handbook of Cash Flow and Treasury Management, 1987; contbr. articles to profl. publs. Bd. dirs. Maine Twp. Jewish Congregation Shaare Emet, Des Plaines, 1986—, pres. 1989-91. amed Outstanding Credit Exec. of Yr., Nat. Assn. Credit Mgmt., 1987, Disting. Alumnus Coll. Bus. No. Ill. U., 1998, Outstanding Alumnus Dept. Fin., No. Ill. U., 2001. Fellow Nat. Inst. Credit; mem. Fin. Mgrs. Assn. Chgo. (treas. 1991-92), Treasury Mgmt. Assn. Chgo. (chmn. ednl. scholarship com. 1995-99, chmn. Windy City Summit Treasury Conf. 1999-2000, 2003-04, 2007—, bd. dirs. 2003—), Distillers Imports and Vintners (chmn. 1980-82), N.Y. Credit and Fin. Mgmt. Assn., Chgo. Midwest Credit Mgmt. Assn. (bd. dirs. 1984-87), Dept. Fin. Advisors Bd. No. Ill. U 2003-, No. Ill. U. Exec. Club (bd. dirs., v.p. 2003—).

GOLDSTEIN, RICHARD JAY, mechanical engineer, educator; b. NYC, Mar. 27, 1928; s. Henry and Rose (Steierman) G.; m. Barbara Goldstein; children: Arthur Sander, Jonathan Jacob, Benjamin Samuel, Naomi Sarith. BME, Cornell U., 1948; MS in Mech. Engring., U. Minn., 1950, MS in Physics, 1951, PhD in Mech. Engring., 1959; DSc (hon.), Israel Inst. Tech., 1994; doctorate (hon.), U. Lisbon, 1996, A.V. Luikov Heat Mass Transfer Inst., Minsk, Belarus, 1997. Instr. U. Minn., Mpls., 1948-51, instr., rsch. fellow, 1956-58, mem. faculty, 1961—, prof. mech. engring., 1965—, head dept., 1977-97, James J. Ryan prof., 1989—, Regents' prof., 1990—; devel. rsch. engr. Oak Ridge Nat. Lab., 1951-54; sr. engr. Lockheed Aircraft, 1956; asst. prof. Brown U., 1959-61. Vis. prof. Technion, Israel, 1976, Imperial Coll., Eng., 1984; cons. in field, 1956—; chmn. Midwest U. Energy Consortium; chmn. Coun. Energy Engring. Rsch.; NSF sr. postdoctoral fellow, vis. prof. Cambridge (Eng.) U., 1971-72; Prince lectr., 1983, William Gurley lectr., 1988, Hawkins Meml. lectr., 1991; disting. lectr. Pa. State U., 1992; mem. acad. com. internat. bd. govs. Technion; hon. mem. sci. bd. A.V. Luikov Heat and Mass Transfer Inst., Minsk, 1997. Mem. editl. bd. Experiments in Fluids, Heat Transfer-Japanese Rsch., Heat Transfer-Soviet Rsch., Bull of the Internat. Centre for Heat and Mass Transfer, Internat. Archives of Heat and Mass Transfer; hon. editl. adv. bd. Internat. J. Heat and Mass Transfer, Internat. Comms. in Heat and Mass Transfer. 1st U.S. Army It. AUS, 1954-55. Recipient NASA award for tech. innovation, 1977, MUEC Dist. Svc. award, 1986, NAE, 1985, George Taylor Alumni Soc. award, 1988, A.V. Lykov medal, 1990, Max Jakob Meml. award ASME/AICE, 1990, Nusselt-Reynolds prize, 1993, Dr. Scientiarum Honoris Causa award Technion-Israel Inst. Tech., 1994, Thermal Engring. Internat. award Japan Soc. Mech. Engring.; NATO fellow, Paris, 1960-61, Lady Davis fellow Technion, Israel, 1976. Fellow AAAS, ASME (hon., BEG v.p. 1984-88, sr. v.p. 1989-93, BOG 1993-97, pres. 1996-97, sr. v.p. COE 1988-92, Heat Transfer Meml. award 1978, Svc. award 1978, Centennial medal 1980, 50th anniv. award of heat transfer divsn. 1988, Dedicated Svc. award 2001, Long Term Mem. award 2002-03), Royal Acad. Engring. (fgn.), Am. Soc. Engring. Edn., Assembly for Internat. Heat Transfer Confs. (pres. 1986-90), Internat. Ctr. for Heat and Mass Transfer (exec. com. 1985—, chmn. 1992, pres. 1998-2002), Am. Phys. Soc., Japan Soc. Promotion of Sci., Royal Acad. Engring. (fgn.); mem. Minn. Acad. Sci., Nat. Acad. Engring., Nat. Acad. Engring.-Mex. (corr. 1991), Golden Key Nat. Honor Soc., Sigma Xi, Tau Beta Pi, Pi Tau Sigma (Isromac award, 2002). Achievements include research in thermodynamics, fluid mechanics, heat transfer, optical measuring techniques. Home: 4241 Bassett Creek Dr Golden Valley MN 55422-4257 Office: 111 Church St SE 1100 ME Minneapolis MN 55455-0150

GOLDSTEIN, SIDNEY, pharmacist; b. Phila., Mar. 27, 1932; s. Israel and Gertrude (Stein) G.; m. Janice Levy, June 19, 1955; children: Rhonda, David, Nina. BSc in Pharmacy, Phila. Coll. Pharmacy & Sci., 1954, MSc in Pharmacy, 1955, DSc in Pharmacy, 1958. Cardiovascular unit head Eaton Labs, Norwich, NY, 1958—59; anti-inflammatory unit head Lederle Labs, Pearl River, NY, 1959-61; with Merrell Dow Rsch. Inst., Cin., 1961-93; v.p. global pharm. and analytical scis. Marion Merrell Dow Inc., Kansas City, Mo., 1991-93; v.p. sci. and tech. Duramed Pharm., Inc., Cin., 1994-98, v.p. bus. devel., sci. and tech., 1998—2002; chief sci. officer Prasco, Cin., 2002—. Adj. assoc. prof. U. Cin. Coll. Pharmacy, 1984-98, dean's adv. coun., 1998—; lectr. pharmacology Phila. Coll. Pharmacy, 1967-70, chair PQRI-drug product tech. com., 1997-2004, mem. steering com., 2003-05; mem. So. Ohio Life Sci. Task Force, 1999-2001, GPhA sci. com., 2001—; mem. tech. validation adv. bd. Cinn. Children's Hosp., 2003—. Contbr. articles to profl. jours. Bd. trustees Glen Manor Home for Aged, Cin., 1983-89. Recipient Award for Nicoderm, R&D Mag., 1992. Mem. Am. Assn. Pharm. Scientists, Am. Soc. Clin. Pharmacology and Therapeutics, Soc. Exptl. Biology and Medicine, Am. Soc. Pharmacology and Exptl. Therapeutics, B'nai B'rith (chpt. v.p. 1978). Home: 1125 Fort View Pl Cincinnati OH 45202-1713 Office: Prasco 7155 Kemper Rd Cincinnati OH 45249 Home Phone: 513-651-5575; Office Phone: 513-618-3333. E-mail: s.goldstein@prasco.com.

GOLDSTEIN, STEVEN, lawyer; b. St. Louis, Sept. 8, 1950; s. Alexander Julius and Dorothy Lea (Matier) G.; m. Laura Lou Staley, July 20, 1980. BS in Speech, orthwestern U., Evanston, Ill., 1972; JD, U. Mich., 1975. Bar: Mo. 1975. Prin. Goldstein & Pressman, P.C., St. Louis, 1993—. Mem. ABA, Mo. Bar Assn. (chmn. bankruptcy com. 1983-85), Bar Assn. of Met. St. Louis. Home: 712 Swarthmore Ln Saint Louis MO 63130-3618 Office: Goldstein & Pressman PC 121 Hunter Ave Ste 101 Saint Louis MO 63124-2082 Office Phone: 314-727-1717. Business E-Mail: stg@goldsteinpressman.com.

GOLDSTEIN, STEVEN ALAN, medical and engineering educator; b. Reading, Pa., Sept. 15, 1954; m. Nancy Ellen Gehr, Aug. 22, 1976; children: Aaron Michael, Jonathan David. BS in Mech. Engring., Tufts U., 1976; MS in Bioengring., U. Mich., 1977, PhD in Bioengring, 1981. Rsch. investigator dept. surgery U. Mich., Ann Arbor, 1981-83, asst. prof. surgery, 1983-88, assoc. prof. surgery, 1988-92, prof. surgery, 1992—, prof. mech. engring., applied mechanics and biomedical engring., assoc. dean rsch. and grad. studies, Med. Sch., Henry Ruppenthal Family prof. orthopaedic surgery and bioengineering, dir. Ctr. for Biomedical Engring. Rsch., dir. Orthopaedic Rsch. Labs. Co-dir. orthopaedic biomechanics lab. U. Mich., 1981-82, dir. orthopaedic rsch. labs. U. Mich., 1982—; prof. mech. engring. and applied mechanics, 1992—, mem. faculty bioengring. program, 1982-96, prof. biomed. engring., 1996—, interim chmn., 1985-89, rsch. scientist Inst. Gerontology, 1993—, asst. dean rsch. & grad. studies U. Mich. Med. Sch., 1993-98, assoc. dean, 1999—; rsch. asst. bioengring. ctr. Tufts ew England Med. Ctr., 1974-76; mem. calcium homeostasis adv. group NASA, 1987-89; cons. Libbey-Owens Ill., Gen. Tire & Rubber, Upjohn, Ethyl Corp., orwich Eaton, KMS Fusion, Whitby Pharmaceuticals, Norian Corp., Genetics Inst., Therics Inc., Osteo Biologics Inc., Matrigin Inc.; chair NIH study sect. on orthopaedics and musculoskeletal diseases, 1993-95. Author: Advances in Engineering, 1991; author (with others) Biomechanics of Diathrodial Joints, 1990, Molecular Biology of the Cardiovascular System, 1991, Surgery: Scientific Principles and Practice, 1993, Limb Development and Regeneration, 1993, Accidental Injury: Biomechanics and Prevention, 1993; reviewer Math. Bioscis., 1982—, Annals of Biomed. Engring., 1983—, Clin. Orthopaedics and Related Rsch., 1983—, Jour. Rehab. Rsch. and Devel., 1987—; reviewer Jour. Biomechanics, 1982—, editorial cons., 1992—; reviewer Jour. Biomech. Engring., 1982—, assoc. editor, 1991-97; reviewer Jour. Orthopaedic Rsch., 1984—, mem. bd. assoc. editors, 1992—; reviewer Jour. Bone and Joint Surgery, 1987—, mem. bd. assoc. editors for rsch., 1989—; reviewer, mem. study section NIH, NSF, NASA, Nat. Inst. Occupational Health & Safety, 1983—; contbr. more than 100 articles to profl. jours. Recipient Young Rsch. Investigator award 3M Corp., 1984, Nicolas Andre award Assn. Bone & Joint Surgeons, 1987-88. Mem. NAE, ASME (chair program com. 1989-92, sec.-elect 1993, exec. com. bioengring. divsn. 1989—, chair bioengring. divsn. 1995-96, Y.C. Fung Young Investigator award 1987), Am. Soc. Biomechanics (exec. bd. 1984-85), Am. Acad. Orthopaedic Surgeons (com. biomed. engring. 1991—, Kappa Delta award 1989-90), Orthopaedic Rsch. Soc. (adj. program com. 1990-91, program com. 1992, sec. 1997—), Biomed. Engring. Soc., Engring. Soc. Detroit (Young Engr. of Yr. award 1987), The Knee Soc. Achievements include patents (with other) for Intracone Reamer, Instacone Prosthetic Surface, Flexible Connecting Shaft for Intramedullary Reamer, Tissue Pressure Measurement Transducer System, Continuous Flow Tissue Pressure Measurement Transducer System, Prosthesis Interface Surface and Method of Implanting, Direct Gene Transfer in Wounds. Office: U Mich Orthopaedic Rsch Labs 400 N Ingalls St Rm G161 Ann Arbor MI 48109-2003 Office Phone: 734-936-7417. Office Fax: 734-647-0003. E-mail: stevegld@umich.edu.

GOLDSTICK, THOMAS KARL, biomedical engineering educator; b. Toronto, Ont., Can., Aug. 21, 1934; came to U.S., 1955, naturalized. s. David and Iva Sarah (Kaplan) G.; m. Marcia Adrienne Jenkins, July 4, 1982. BS, MIT, 1957, MS, 1959; PhD, U. Calif., Berkeley, 1966, U. Calif., San Francisco, 1966-67. Asst. prof. orthwestern U., Evanston, Ill., 1967-71, assoc. prof. chem. engring. and biol. sci., 1971-81, prof. chem. engring., neurobiology and physiology, 1981-85, prof. chem. engring., biomed. engring., neurobiology and physiology, 1985-99, prof. emeritus, 1999—. Adj. prof. ophthalmology U. Ill., Chgo., 1981-91. Editor: Oxygen Transport to Tissue V, 1983, VII, 1985, X, 1988, XI, 1989, XII, 1990, XIII, 1992. Rsch. grantee NIH, 1968—; Spl. Rsch. fellow U. Calif., San Diego, LaJolla, 1971-73. Mem. Internat. Soc. Oxygen Transport to Tissue (sec. 1980-86, exec. com. 1986-93), Biomed. Engring. Soc. (bd. dirs. 1983-86, chmn. publs. bd. 1985-86). Home: 2025 Sherman Ave Apt 504 Evanston IL 60201-3269 Office: Biomed Engring Dept Northwestern U Evanston IL 60208-3107 Home Phone: 847-328-2624; Office Phone: 847-491-5518. Business E-Mail: t-goldstick@northwestern.edu.

GOLDSTONE, ROBERT L., psychologist, educator; b. Cleve., Sept. 14, 1964; BA in Cognitive Sci., Oberlin Coll., 1986; MA in Psychology, U. Ill., Urbana-Champaign, 1989; PhD in Psychology, U. Mich., 1991. Asst. prof. Ind. U., Bloomington, 1991—96, assoc. prof., 1996—98, prof. dept. psychology, 1999—. Vis. scholar orthwestern U., 1993; mem. program com. Fla. Artificial Intelligence Rsch. Symposium, 1994, Seventh Midwest Artificial Intelligence and Cognitive Sci. Conf., 1996; vis. rsch. fellow U. Glasgow, Scotland, 1997, U. Warwick, 1997, U. Southampton, 1998, U. Coll. London, 1998. Editor: (psychology sect.) Encyclopedia of Cognitive Science, 2003; co-editor: Psychology of Learning and Motivation: Perceptual Learning; exec. editor: Cognitive Sci., 2001—03, assoc. editor: Psychonomic Bull. and Rev., 1998—2000, mem. bd. consulting editors: Jour. Exptl. Psychology: Learning, Memory and Cognition, 1994—98, ad hoc reviewer: Am. Jour. Psychology, Behavior Rsch. Methods, Instrumentation and Computers, Brit. Jour. Social Psychology, Brit. Jour. Psychology, Cognitive Psychology, Connection Sci., European Jour. Cognitive Psychology, Jour. Cognitive Neurosci., Jour. Exptl. Child Psychology, Jour. Exptl. Psychology (Learning, Memory and Cognition; Gen.; Human Perception and Performance), Memory and Cognition, North Atlantic Treaty Orgn., NSF, Procs. Cognitive Sci. Soc., Jour. Math. Psychology, Psychol. Bull., Psychol. Rev., Psychol. Rsch., Psychol. Sci.; contbr. articles to profl. jours. Recipient Chase Meml. award for outstanding young rschr. in cognitive sci., Carnegie Mellon U., 1996, James McKeen Cattell Sabbatical award, 1997—98, Toland Rsch. award, NAS, 2004; grantee, NIH, 1992—94, NIMH, 1993—2004, NSF, 1994—2004, Ind. U. Office Internat. Programs, 1996, James McKeen Cattell Fund, 1997—98, Lockheed Martin Corp., 2003—04; Gill fellow in cognitive sci., 1997—2002. Mem.: APA (Disting. Sci. award for early career contbn. to psychology in the area of cognition and human learning 2000, divsn. exptl. psychology young investigator award in exptl. psychology: learning, memory and cognition 1995, divsn. exptl. psychology young investigator award in exptl. psychology: gen. 1995), Psychonomic Soc., Cognitive Sci. Sco., Am. Psychol. Soc., Phi Kappa Phi, Phi Beta Kappa. Achievements include research in cognitve psychology; cognitive science; concept learning, perceptual learning, knowledge representation; computational modelling of mental processes, neural networks; visual cognition and pattern recognition; decision making and judgment. Office: Dept Psychology and Brain Sciences Ind Univ 1101 E Tenth St Office PY 338 Bloomington IN 47405 Office Phone: 812-855-4853. E-mail: rgoldsto@ucs.indiana.edu.

GOLDWASSER, EDWIN LEO, physicist; b. NYC, Mar. 9, 1919; s. I. Edwin and Edith (Goldstein) G.; m. Elizabeth Weiss, Oct. 27, 1940; children: Michael, John, Katherine, David, Richard. BA, Harvard U., 1940; PhD, U. Calif., Berkeley, 1950. Rsch. asst. and rsch. assoc. U. Calif., Berkeley, 1946-51; rsch. assoc., prof. physics U. Ill., Urbana, 1951-88; dep. dir. Fermi Nat. Accelerator Lab., Batavia, Ill., 1967-78; vice chancellor for rsch. U. Ill., Urbana, 1978-80, vice chancellor acad. affairs, 1979-86, acting dir. internat. programs, 1988-89, acting dir. Computer-based Edn. Rsch. Lab., 1989-92; assoc. dir. Superconducting Super Collider Cen. Design Group, Berkeley, 1986-88; disting. fellow Calif. Inst. Tech., 1993-94. Mem., chmn. Nat. Rsch. Coun. div. Phys. Scis., Washington, 1961-69; chmn. sci. policy com. Stanford (Calif.) Linear Accelerator Ctr., 1980-84; chmn. sci. and ednl. adv. com. U. Calif., Berkeley, 1986-92. Author: Optics, Waves, Atoms and Nuclei, 1965; contbr. articles to profl. jours. Westinghouse fellow, 1949-50; Guggenheim fellow, 1957-58; Fulbright fellow, 1957-58. Fellow: AAAS; mem.: Phi Kappa Phi, Xigma Xi, Phi Beta Kappa. Avocations: tennis, swimming, opera. Home: 612 W Delaware Ave Urbana IL 61801-4805 Office: U Ill Dept Physics 1110 W Green St Urbana IL 61801-9013 Business E-Mail: egoldwas@uiuc.edu.

GOLDWASSER, EUGENE, biochemist, educator; b. NYC, Oct. 14, 1922; s. Herman and Anna (Ackerman) G.; m. Florence Cohen, Dec. 22, 1949 (dec.); children— Thomas Alan, Matthew Laurence, James Herman; m. Deone Jackman, Feb. 15, 1986 BS, U. Chgo., 1943, PhD, 1950; ScD (hon.), N.Y. Med. Coll. Am. Cancer Soc. fellow U. Copenhagen, Denmark, 1950-52; rsch. assoc. U. Chgo., 1952-61, mem. faculty, 1962—, prof. biochemistry, 1963-91, prof. emeritus biochemistry and molecular biology, 1991—, chmn. com. on devel. biology., 1976-91, chmn. biochemistry and molecular biology, 1994-98. Served with AUS, 1944-46. Recipient Esther Langer medal for cancer rsch. Internat. Soc. Blood Purification, 1987, Simpson award Wayne State U., Lucerne award Fedn. European Physiol. Soc., Karl Landsteiner award Am. Assn. of Blood Banks, award French Med. Scientific Cmty., 2003, Amgen Internat. prize World Congress of Nephrology, 2005, Prince Mahidol medal Thai Gov., 2005; Guggenheim fellow Oxford (Eng.) U., 1966-67. Fellow AAAS, Am. Acad. Arts and Scis.; mem. Am. Soc. Biol. Chemists, Biochem. Soc., Internat. Soc. Exptl. Hematology (Am. prize 2001, prize 2005), Am. Soc. Hematology, Sigma Xi. Achievements include purification of human erythropoietin; rsch. in biochemistry and red blood cell formation.

GOLER, MICHAEL DAVID, lawyer; b. Cleve., June 29, 1952; s. George and Harriet G.; children: Jonathan A. Jennifer S. BA with honors in Classics (Greek), Union Coll., 1974; JD, Case Western Res. U., 1977. Bar: Ohio 1977, US Dist. Ct. Ohio 1977, US Ct. Appeals (6th cir.) 1982. Assoc. Persky, Marken, Konigsberg & Shapiro, Cleve., 1977-81; assoc. counsel Cardinal Fed. Savings Bank, Cleve., 1981-84; assoc. Arter & Hadden, Cleve., 1984-86, Kohrman, Jackson & Krantz, Cleve., 1986—94, ptnr., 1988-94, Goodman Weiss Miller LLP, Cleve., 1994—. Panelist Nat. Arbitration Forum, 2005—. Bd. dirs. Jewish Cmty. Ctr. Cleve., 1998—2005, The Cleve. Hearing and Speech Ctr., Inc., 1998—, pres.-elect, 2005—06, pres., 2006—. Fellow Am. Coll. Mortgage Attys., Cleve. Bar Assn. (founder, chmn. environ. law sect. 1991-95, chmn. real estate sect. 1989-90, real estate inst. com. 1989—); mem. ABA (sect. real property probate and trust law, chmn. com. enforcement of creditors rights and bankruptcy, 1991-95, vice chair, 1995-97, chair, 1997-2001, com. on econs., tech. and practice methods, mng. editor EDirt electronic newsletter 1999—2006, Emerities EReport electronic newsletter 2006-07, mem. coun. 2001-07, mem. tech standing com. 1999-, vice chmn. 2005-07, chair 2007—, mem. planning com., liaison to ABA sect. law practice mgmt. sect. 1999—, ABA Enterprises Foster Force 2002-, CLE com. 1999-2006, liaison to ABA soc. tech. com. 2003—, mem. law practice mgmt. sect., co-chair membership and mktg., 2004—, mem. soc. joint membership com., mem. nominating com. 2005-07, named Ohio Super Lawyer 2004, 05, 06, 07). Avocations: music, golf, bicycling, skiing, travel. Office: Miller Goler Faeges LLP 100 Erieview Plz Fl 27 Cleveland OH 44114-1824 Home: 12931 Shaker Blvd #301 Cleveland OH 44120 Office Phone: 216-696-3366. E-mail: goler@millergolerfaeges.com.

GOLIN, ALVIN, public relations company executive; b. Chgo., June 19, 1929; s. Charles and Jeanette Golin; m. June Kerns, Aug. 25, 1961; children: Barry, Karen, Ellen. B.J., Roosevelt U., 1950. Publicity rep. MGM Pictures, NYC, 1951—54; chmn. Golin/Harris Internat., Chgo., 1975—. Lectr. to numerous univs. Adv. Chgo. Coun. Boy Scouts Am., Nat. Multiple Sclerosis Soc., U. Tenn.; founding bd. mem. Ronald McDonald House Charities; bd. trustees Goodman Theatre of Chgo., Roosevelt U. Mem.: Pub. Club of Chgo., Pub. Rels. Soc. Am. (Lifetime Achievement Award). Office: Golin/Harris International 111 E Wacker Dr Fl 10 Chicago IL 60601-4305

GOLOMB, HARVEY MORRIS, hematologist, oncologist, educator; b. Pitts., Feb. 13, 1943; s. Russell Austin and Dorothy (Simon) G.; m. Lynne Rooth, Dec. 28, 1965; children: Adam, Sara. BA, U. Chgo., 1964; MD, U. Pitts., 1968. Diplomate Am. Bd. Internal Medicine, Am. Bd. Med. Oncology. Intern Boston City Hosp., 1968-69; resident Johns Hopkins U., Balt., 1971-72, fellow, 1972-73, U. Chgo., 1973-75, asst. prof. dept. medicine, 1975-79, assoc. prof., 1979-83, prof., 1983—, chief sect. hematology/oncology, 1981-98, chmn. dept. medicine, 1998—2005, dean clin. affairs divsn. biol. scis., 2005—. Chmn. subspecialty bd. med. oncology Am. Bd. Internal Medicine, 1991-95. Contbr. over 300 articles, papers to profl. publs.; co-editor: Lung Cancer, 1988, Oncologic Therapies, 1999, 2003. Capt. U.S. Army, 1971-73. Mem. Am. Soc. Hematology (bd. dirs. 1987-91), Am. Soc. Oncology (pres. elect 1989-90, pres. 1990-91). Office: U Chgo MC 1000 5841 S Maryland Ave Chicago IL 60637-1463 Business E-Mail: hgolomb@medicine.bsd.uchicago.edu.

GOLOMSKI, WILLIAM ARTHUR JOSEPH, consulting company executive; b. Custer, Wis. s. John Frank and Margaret Sophie (Glisczinski) G.; m. Joan Ellen Hagen; children: Gretchen E., William A. Jr. MS, Marquette U.; MBA, U. Chgo; MS in Engring. Mgmt., Milw. Sch. Engring; MA, Roosevelt U. Registered profl. engr., Calif. Prin. W.A. Golomski & Assocs., Algoma, Wis., 1949—, pres., 1971—. Judge Malcolm Baldridge Nat. Quality award, 1988; sr. lectr. Grad. Sch. Bus., U. Chgo., 1990-95. Author chpts. in books; co-editor A Quality Revolution in Manufacturing, 1989; founding editor Quality Mgmt. Jour., 1993. Mem. Avoca Sch. Bd., Wilmette, Ill.; adv. bd. Milw. Sch. Engring., 1967-72, 83-87, indsl. engring. com. Hon. mem. Philippine Soc. Quality Control, 1992. Fellow AAAS, Am. Soc. Quality Control (Eugene L. Grant award 1991, Edwards medal, William A. Golomski rsch. award named in his honor 1986, Am. Deming medal met. sect., hon. mem. 1993), .Y. Acad. Scis., Royal Soc. Health, Am. Statis. Assn., Inst. Indsl. Engrs. (Frank and Lillian Gilbreth Indsl. Engring. award 1999), World Assn Productivity Sciences; mem. NAE. Achievements include devel. of world class orgns.; first jour. for quality mgmt. and quality in higher edn. Office: N9690 County Road U Algoma WI 54201-9528

GOLTZ, JAY, small business owner; BA acctg., Northern Ill Univ, 1978. Founder and pres. Artists' Frame Services, Chgo., 1978—, Chgo. Art Source, Chgo., 1991—, Jayson Home and Garden, Chgo., 1997—, Bella Mouldings, Chgo.; CEO, founder The Goltz Group, Chgo. Minority advocate of the yr. US Small Bus. Adminstrn., 1989; Inc. Mag. Conf. spkr. for Customer Svc. Strategies; Nat. speaking tour on "How to Make Money" The Fletcher-Terry Co., 1999; keynote spkr. Chgo. Area Entrepreneurship Hall of Fame, 2000; cons. Nielsen-Bainbridge, 2004—05, Cresent Cardboard Co., 2004—06; nationwide ins., regional conf. spkr. and workshop leader, 2005; chmn. bd. Local Econ. and Employment Develop, 2006; bus. cons. Second City Comm., 2006; bus. mentor William J. Clinton Foundation's Urban Initiative, 2006; spkr. Inc. 500 Conf., 2006. Author: The Street-Smart Entrepreneur, 1997; bus. editor, monthly columnist Goltz on Business, Picture Framing Mag., 1996—. Bd. dir. Am. Cancer Soc., 1999—2002; co-founder Business Wise, 1998—2001. Finalist Mag. Entrepreneur of Yr., Ernst & Young Inc., 1990, 1993; named one of Top 100 Young Entrepreneurs, Assn. Collegiate Entrepreneurs, 1988, 40 under 40, Crain's Chgo. Bus., 1990, 1999; named to Arthur Anderson Entrepeneurship Hall of Fame, U. Ill. Chgo., 1992; recipient Biz Kid, Forbes, 1987. Office: The Goltz Group 1871 N Clybourn Ave Chicago IL 60614 Office Phone: 773-755-8301. Office Fax: 773-880-8801.

GOMER, ROBERT, chemistry professor; b. Vienna, Mar. 24, 1924; m. Anne Olah, 1955; children: Richard, Maria. BA, Pomona Coll., 1944; PhD in Chemistry, U. Rochester, 1949; AEC fellow chemistry, Harvard, 1949-50. Instr. dept. chemistry James Franck Inst. U. Chgo., 1950-51, asst. prof., 1951-54, assoc. prof., 1954-58, prof., 1958-96, Carl William Eisendrath Disting. Service prof., 1984-96, prof. emeritus, 1996—. Dir. James Franck Inst. U. Chgo., 1977-83 Bd. dirs. Bull. Atomic Scientists, 1960-84. Served with AUS, 1944-46. Recipient Kendall award in surface chemistry Am. Chem. Soc., 1975, Davisson Germer prize Am. Phys. Soc., 1981, Medard W. Welch award Am. Vacuum Soc., 1989, Arthur W. Adamson award Am. Chem. Soc., 1996; Sloan fellow, 1958-62, Guggenheinm fellow, 1969-70; Bourke lectr. Eng., 1959. Mem. Leopoldina Acad. Scis., Nat. Acad. Scis., Am. Acad. Arts and Sci. Home: 4824 S Kimbark Ave Chicago IL 60615-1916 Office: 5640 S Ellis Ave Chicago IL 60637-1433 Home Phone: 773-536-2182; Office Phone: 773-702-7191. Business E-Mail: r-gomer@uchicago.edu.

GOMEZ, LUIS OSCAR, Asian and religious studies educator, clinical psychology educator; b. Guayanilla, PR, Apr. 7, 1943; s. Manuel Gomez and Lucila Rodriguez; m. Ruth Cedenia Maldonado, Dec. 24, 1963; children: Luis Oscar, Jr., Miran Ruth. BA, U. P.R., 1963; PhD Asian Langs. and Lit., Yale U., 1967; MA in Clin. Psychology, U. Mich., 1991, PhD, 1998. Lic. clin. psychologist. Vis. asst. prof. U. P.R., Rio Piedras, 1967, lectr., 1969-70, assoc. prof., 1970-73; assoc. prof. dept. Asian langs. and cultures U. Mich., Ann Arbor, 1973-80, prof. Buddhist studies, prof. religious studies dept. Asian langs. and cultures, 1980—, chmn. dept., 1981-89, 2002—, prof. psychology dept. psychology, 1999—. Vis. asst. prof. U. Wash., Seattle, 1967-68; Evans-Wentz Disting. lectr. Stanford (Calif.) U., 1983, vis. prof., 1985; vis. prof. Otani U. Kyoto, Japan, 1991-94. Author: The Land of Bliss, 1996; co-editor: Barabudur, Problemas de Filosofía, Studies in the Literature of the Great Vehicle, 1989. Mem. Am. Psychol. Assn., Soc. for Sci. Study Religion, Am. Acad. Religion, Internat. Assn. Buddhist Studies (gen. sec. 1986-89), Assn. Asian Studies. Home: 3204 Lockridge Dr Ann Arbor MI 48108-1722 Office: U Mich Dept Asian Langs & Cultures 105 S State St Ann Arbor MI 48109-1285

GOMEZ, SYLVIA, newscaster; m. Jon Duncanson. BS in Mass Comm., U. Md., 1985. Field prodr. WRC-TV, Washington, 1983—88; weekend anchor KTSM-TV, El Paso, Tex., 1988—90; reporter and fill-in anchor KTVT-TV, Dallas, 1990—92, WMAQ-TV, Chgo., 1992—94, WBBM-TV, Chgo., 1994—96; weekend anchor WFLD-TV, Chgo., 1996—97; weekend evening anchor and reporter WBBM-TV, Chgo., 1998—. Office: WBBM-TV 630 McClurg Ct Chicago IL 60601

GOMEZ, TERRINE, school director; b. Trivandrum, India, Jan. 29, 1928; came to U.S., 1977; Tchr. Tng. Degree, Trinity Coll. Music, London, 1949; BA in History of Music, U. Ill., 1982. Licentiate in violin; assoc. in voice; Rolland specialist. Head dept. music Internat. Sch., India, 1959-72; head string dept. Am. Internat. Sch., India, 1972-77; asst. to artistic dir. Nat. Acad. of Arts and Conservatory of Champaign, Ill., 1983-89; major instr. violin CCI assisting Ian Hobson, 1983-89; dir. Young Artists' Studio, Champaign, 1989—. Condr. nat. and internat. workshops in preparation for Rolland Specialist category, Cambridge, Eng., 1976, Chichester, Eng. and Lausanne, Switzerland, 1977, Laval U., Que., 1981. Author: The Young Violinist (in 3 parts), 1985. Mem. European String Tchrs. Assn., Am. String Tchrs. Assn., Soc. Am. Musicians, Chamber Music Am. (Heidi Castleman award 1994). Roman Catholic. Avocations: languages, history, art, literature, shih-tzu dogs. Office: Young Artists Studio 1305 Mayfair Rd Champaign IL 61821-5023

GONZALEZ, JUAN (ALBERTO VAZQUEZ), professional baseball player; b. Vega Baja, Puerto Rico, Oct. 16, 1969; Outfielder Tex. Rangers, 1989—99, 2002—03; designated hitter Detroit Tigers, 2000; outfielder Cleve. Indians, 2001, Kansas City Royals, 2004, Cleve. Indians, 2005—06, Boston Red Sox, 2006—. Named Most Valuable Player, Am. Assn., 1990, Am. League Most Valuable Player, Baseball Writers' Assn. of Am., 1996, 1998; named to Am. League Silver Slugger Team, 1992—93, Am. League All-Star Team, 1993, 1998, 2001. Achievements include leading Am. League in home runs, 1992-93. Office: Boston Red Sox 4 Yawkey Way Boston MA 02215

GONZALEZ, RICHARD A., pharmaceutical executive; b. Jan. 21, 1954; B in BioChemistry, U. Houston; M in BioChemistry, U. Miami. Rsch. biochemist U. Miami Sch. Medicine; numerous positions in divsn. diagnostics Abbott Labs., Abbott Park, Ill., 1977—92, divisional v.p., gen. mgr., 1992—95, v.p. Health-Systems divsn., 1995—98, sr. v.p. hosp. products, 1998—2001, pres., COO med. products, 2001—06, pres., COO, 2006—. Mem. bd. dirs. Abbott Labs. Mem. bd. dirs. Lyric Opera Chgo., Shed Aquarium. Named one of 50 Most Important Hispanics in Tech. & Bus., Hispanic Engr. & Info. Tech. mag., 2005. Office: Abbott Labs 100 Abbott Park Rd Abbott Park IL 60064-6400

GONZALEZ, TONY, professional football player; b. Huntington Beach, Calif., Feb. 27, 1976; Attended, Univ. Calif. Tight end Kans. City Chiefs, 1997—. Spokesperson Midwest Donor Organ Bank, U.S. Dept. Transp. Safety Campaign, Sch. Safety Hotline, Kans. Cons. (movie) Any Given Sunday, appeared (HBO episode) Arliss, 2000, host (TV series) KCTV-5, appeared Buckle Up: Football is a Game, Your Life is Not. Founder Tony Gonzalez Found.; contbr. Shadow Buddies Program, Boys & Girls Clubs; donator Kans. City Boys & Girls Club, 1999. Named to AFC Pro Bowl team, 1999—2005; recipient Mack Lee Hill award. Office: 1 Arrowhead Dr Kansas City MO 64129

GONZALEZ, WILLIAM G., healthcare advisor; s. William G. and Blanche Irene; m. Shirley Ann Mos, Aug. 15, 1964; children: Dana Lynn, Liane Renee. BA, Rutgers U., 1964; MBA, Cornell U., 1966; cert., Sloan Inst. Hosp. Adminstrn., 1966; MPA, NYU, 1980. Bus. adminstr. U. Calif.-San Francisco Med. Ctr., 1966-68, asst. dir., various positions, 1968-74; dep. dir. Capital Dist. Psychiat. Ctr., Albany, NY, 1974-79; instr. Albany Med. Coll., 1974-79; adj. asst. prof. SUNY-Albany, 1978-79; dir. U. Calif.-Irvine Med. Ctr., Orange, 1979-85; sr. lectr. Grad. Sch. Mgmt. and Calif. Coll. Medicine, U. Calif., Irvine, 1980-85; bd. dirs. Hosp. Coun. So. Calif., 1983-85; pres., chief exec. officer Butterworth Health Corp. and Butterworth Hosp., Grand Rapids, Mich., 1985-99; pres., CEO Spectrum Health, Grand Rapids, 1999-2000; healthcare advisor Wm. Gonzalez & Assocs., Chgo., 2000—. Adj. prof. health svcs. adminstrn. Mich. State U. Coll. Human Medicine, 1985—; mem. gov.'s Task Force on Access to Health Care, 1987-89; mem. nursing task force Joint Commn. on Accreditation Health Care Orgns., 1988-90; trustee Mich. Hosp. Assn., 1990-96; chmn. M in Mgmt. adv. coun. Aquinas Coll., Grand Rapids, 1992-95; bd. dirs. Grand Rapids Area Med. Edn. Ctr., chmn., 1995-97; mem. accreditation coun. grad. med. edn., 1994-98, Am. Hosp. Assn., coordinating Com. on Med. Edn.; regent ACHE Area B., Mich., 1994-98. Bd. dirs. Grand Rapids Pub. Edn. Fund, 1993-99; bd. dirs. Old Kent Fin. Corp., 1994-2000; active Health Professions Coun., San Francisco, 1971-74; active Planned Parenthood-World Population, Alameda Calif. and San Francisco, 1972-74; mem. coun. of dels. sect. on met. hosps. Gov.'s Coun., 1989-92; mem. regional policy bd. AHA, 1990-93. Served with M.C. U.S. Army, 1961-64. William Stout scholar, 1964; Alfred P. Sloan scholar, 1964-65; N.Y. State Regents scholar, 1964-65; Rotary Internat. exchange fellow in hosp. adminstrn. Australia, summer 1982 Fellow: Accreditation Commn. on Ed. for Health Svc. Adminstrn., (staff cons. 2004—). Office: Wm Gonzalez & Assocs 500 N Michigan Ave Ste 300 Chicago IL 60611 Office Phone: 312-396-4088.

GOOCH, U. L., state legislator; m. Augusta Gooch. Kans. state senator Dist. 29, 1993—. also: 12 Crestview Lakes Est Wichita KS 67220-2914

GOOD, STEVEN LOREN, real estate consultant; b. Tokyo, Nov. 16, 1956; came to U.S., 1957; s. Sheldon F. and Lois (Kroll) G. Student, Oxford U., 1975; BS in Fin., Syracuse U., 1978; JD, DePaul U., 1981; LHD (hon.), Robert Morris Coll., Chgo., 1998. Bar: Ill. 1981, U.S. Dist. Ct. (no. dist.) Ill. 1982, Fla. 1983, U.S. Ct. Appeals (7th cir.) 1983, U.S. Supreme Ct. 2006. Assoc. Sheldon Good & Co., Internat., Chgo., 1978-82; v.p., gen. counsel Sheldon Good & Co., Chgo., 1982-87, pres., 1987—2000, chmn., CEO, 2001—. Instr. FDIC, Washington, 1985, Mo. Auction Sch., Kansas City, 1981-97, Reppert's Sch. Auctioneering, 1998-; bd. dirs. Real Estate Ctr., Kelly Sch. Bus., Ind. U., Sch. Bus. Adminstrn, Citadel Mil. Coll., Ohn Marshall Law Sch.; lectr., spkr. in field. Author: Churches, Jails, and Gold Mines: Mega-Deals from a Real Estate Maverick, 2003; columnist: Auction World mag., 2004—; contbr. articles. Mem. men's coun. Mus. Contemporary Art, Chgo., 1985-91; vice chmn. real estate divsn. Jewish United Fund, Chgo., 1986, 88, 91; bd. dirs. United Cerebral Palsy, Chgo., 1987-97, chmn. Chgo. telethone, 1996; trustee Robert Morris Coll., Chgo., 1991-96; assoc. trustee U. Chgo. Cancer Rsch. Found., 1989-93, chmn. dean's coun., 1997-2000. Recipient Alumni Service Award for Outstanding Service to the Business Community, DePaul U. Coll. Law, 2001, Infinitec Corporate Leadership award, United Cerebral Palsy Assn., Community Svc. award, Easter Seals, 2003. Mem. ABA, Ill. Bar Assn., Fla. Bar Assn., Chgo. Bar Assn., Nat. Assn. Realtors (dir., chmn. Real Estate Auction Forum, 2004), Ill. Assn. of Realtors (dir. 2000-), Chgo. Assn. Realtors (pres. 2003-2004, instr. 1981—, Realtor of Yr. 2005), Young Pres. Orgn., Standard Club, Lamda Alpha. Avocations: tennis, skiing, shooting skeet, music, theater. Office: Sheldon Good & Co 333 W Wacker Dr Ste 400 Chicago IL 60606-1284 Office Fax: 312-346-0727. Business E-Mail: stevengood@sheldongood.com.

GOOD, WILLIAM ALLEN, professional society executive; b. Oak Park, Ill., May 29, 1949; s. Fred Clifton and Dorothy Helen (Stockdale) G.; m. Julianne Doggett, Jan. 8, 1972 (div. Apr. 1980); m. Paulette Edith Gordon, Apr. 23, 1983 (div. Apr. 1991); m. Laura Elizabeth Wellbank, Sept. 25, 1993. MBA, U. Chgo., 1992. Supr. Dun & Bradstreet, Inc., Chgo., 1972-73; gen. mgr. Nat. Roofing Contractors Assn., Chgo., 1973-85, exec. v.p., Rosemont, Ill., 1987—; dir. mktg. Rand Devel. Corp., San Antonio, 1985-86; co-owner GT Communications, Inc., Dallas, 1985-87. Mem. Am. Soc. Assn. Execs. (cert.), Inst. for Orgn. Mgmt. (chmn. 1990-91), Chgo. Soc. Assn. Execs. (pres. 1996-97). Republican. Roman Catholic. Avocations: tennis, photography. Office: Nat Roofing Contractors Assn 10255 W Higgins Rd Rosemont IL 60018-5606 Home Phone: 847-318-5558; Office Phone: 847-299-9070. E-mail: bgood@nrca.net.

GOODE, WAYNE, state legislator; b. St. Louis, Aug. 20, 1937; s. Peter Wayne and Helen Celeste (McManus) G.; m. Jane Margaret Bell, July 27, 1963; children: Peter Wayne III, Jennifer Jacquelyn. BS in Banking and Fin., U. Mo., 1960. Mem. Mo. Ho. of Reps., Jefferson City, 1962-84, Mo. State Senate, Jefferson City, 1984—. Chair senate appropriations com.; mem. Commerce and Environ. Com., Civil and Criminal Juris Prudence Com., State Budget Control, Nat. Conf., at. Conf. State Legis. Found. for State Legis. Former mem. dean's coun. Sch. Bus. and Pub. Adminstrn. U. Mo., Focus St. Louis Conf. on Edn.; former bd. dirs. St. Louis Art Mus.; mem. St. Louis Econ. Conversion Project; mem. Citizen's for Mo.'s Children; bd. dirs. Mo. Hist. Soc.; mem. Sierra Club, Wilderness Soc., Audubon Soc. Lt. U.S. Army, 1960-61. Recipient numerous awards including Chancellor's Medallion, U. Mo., Mo. Assn. Counties Legis. award, Dr. Martin Luther King, Jr. St. Louis Co. Awareness Com. award, V.I.P. award Advt. Club, Recognition Meritorious Svc. award St. Louis Indsl. Rels. Assn., Disting. Svc. award Mo. Assn. for Children with Learning Disabilities, Outstanding Contbn. in Improving Mental Health Care award Mental Health Assn., 1980 Globe Dem. award; named Conservation Legislator of Yr. Mo. Conservation Fedn., 1st Ann. Friend of Edn. Mo. NEA, Outstanding Legislator Mo. Assn. Pub. Employees, One of Ten Best Legislators St. Louisan Mag., Among Best and Brightest Columbia (Mo.) Daily Tribune, 1983 Ten Best Legislators Mo. Times. Home: 7231 Winchester Dr Saint Louis MO 63121-2623 Office: State Senate State Capitol Rm 333 201 W Capitol Ave Jefferson City MO 65101-1556

GOODENBERGER, DANIEL MARVIN, medical educator; b. McCook, Nebr., Apr. 24, 1948; s. Marvin Eugene and Mary Ellen (Marshall) Goodenberger; children: James Michael, Katherine Elizabeth. BS, U. Nebr., Lincoln, 1970; MD, Duke U., Durham, NC, 1974. Diplomate Am. Bd. Internal Medicine, Am. Bd. Emergency Medicine (examiner 1983-95), Am. Bd. Pulmonary Disease, Am. Bd. Critical Care Medicine. Intern Peter Bent Brigham Hosp., Boston, 1974-75, resident in internal medicine, 1975-76; clin. assoc. Nat. Cancer Inst., Bethesda, Md., 1976-78; fellow pulmonary and critical care medicine Boston U. Med. Ctr., 1985-88; assoc. dir. emergency dept. Arlington Hosp., Va., 1979-82; edn. dir. emergency dept. Georgetown U. Hosp., Washington, 1982-85; dir. emergency svcs. U. Hosp., Boston, 1986-87; dir. pulmonary and critical care fellowship Washington U. Med. Schs., St. Louis, 1989-93; dir. pulmonary cons. svcs. Barnes Hosp., St. Louis, 1990-93, dir. internal medicine residency program, 1992—2006; assoc. prof. medicine Washington U., St. Louis, 1995-99; dir. divsn. med. edn. Washington U. Sch. Medicine, 1998—2006, prof. medicine, 1999—2006; prof., chair dept. medicine U. Nev. Sch. Medicine, Las Vegas, 2006—. Chief Wood-Moore Firm, Barnes-Jewish Hosp., 1996-2001. Editor Careers, 1996-98. Lt. comdr. USPHS, 1973-78. Winthrop Breon and Am. Coll. Chest Physicians scholar, 1987. Fellow ACP, Am. Coll. Chest Physicians; mem. AMA, Am. Thoracic Soc., Am. Clin. and Climatological Assn., Assn. Program Dirs. Internal Medicine (nominating and publs. com. 1991-98, councillor 2004-07), Assn. Profs. Medicine. St. Louis Met. Med. Soc. (councilor 1997-2000), St. Louis Club, Harbor Point Yacht Club, Phi Beta Kappa, Alpha Omega Alpha. Methodist. Avocations: theater, music, travel, sailing. Home: 372 Arbour Garden Ave Las Vegas NV 89148 Office: U Nevada Sch Medicine 2040 W Charleston Blvd Ste 300 Las Vegas NV 89102 Office Phone: 702-671-2345. Personal E-mail: goodenberger@sbcglobal.net. Business E-Mail: dgoodenberger@medicine.nevada.edu.

GOODIN, JULIA C., forensic specialist, state official; b. Columbia, Ky., Mar. 10, 1957; d. Vitus Jack and Geneva Goodin. BS, Western Ky. U., 1979; MD, U. Ky., 1983. Diplomate Am. Bd. Clin. and Anatomic Pathology, Am. Bd. Forensic Pathology. Intern Vanderbilt U. Med. Ctr., Nashville, 1983, resident in anatomic and clin. pathology, 1984-87; fellow in forensic pathology Med. Examiner's Office, Balt., 1987-88; asst. med. examiner Office of Chief Med. Examiner, Balt., 1988-90; dep. chief med. examiner State of Tenn., 1990-94; asst. med. examiner Nashville, 1990-93; chief med. examiner, 1993-94; asst. med. investigator State of N.Mex., Albuquerque, 1994-96; asst. prof. U. N.Mex., Albuquerque, 1994-96; clin. assoc. prof. U. of South Ala. Sch. Medicine, 1996-99; state med. examiner Ala. Dept. Forensic Scis., Mobile, 1996-99; chief state med. examiner State of Iowa, Des Moines, 1999—. Clin. prof. U. Md. Med. Sch., Balt., 1988-90, Vanderbilt U. Med. Ctr., 1990-94. Capt. USNR, 1985—. Mem. Am. Acad. Forensic Sci., Assn. Mil. Surgeons of U.S., AMA. Avocations: long-distance running, weightlifting, photography, studying French. Home: 100 Market St Unit 414 Des Moines IA 50309-4765 Office: 2250 S Ankeny Blvd Ankeny IA 50023-9023 Office Phone: 515-725-1401.

GOODIN, TERRY A., state representative; b. Seymour, Ind., Dec. 31, 1966; BA, Ea. Ky. U., 1989, MA, 1990; EdD, Ind. U., 1995. Tchr. Austin H.S., 1990—95, asst. prin., 1995—96, Bloomington (Ind.) H.S. South, 1996—98; supt. schs. Crothersville (Ind.) Cmty. Schs., 1998—; state rep. dist. 66 Ind. Ho. of Reps., Indpls., 2000—, vice chair, agr., natural resources and roral devel. com., mem. appointments and claims, fin. instns., and rds. and transp. coms. Mem.: Ind. Farm Bur., Ind. Assn. Pub. Sch. Supts., NRA (life), Nat. Assn. Basketball Coaches. Democrat. Pentacostal. Office: Ind Ho of Reps 200 W Washington St Indianapolis IN 46204-2786

GOODKIND, CONRAD GEORGE, lawyer; b. Arlington, Va., Aug. 8, 1944; s. Bernard Arthur and Sylvia (Lieber) G.; m. Sandra Timme, Aug. 27, 1966; children: Carley M., Adam B., Erica L., Anne G. BS, U. Wis., 1966, JD, 1969. Bar: Wis. 1969, U.S. Dist. Ct. (ea. and we. dists.) Wis. 1969. Assoc. Kivett & Kasdorf, Milw., 1969-71; counsel Citizens' Study Com. on Jud. Orgn., Madison, Wis., 1971-73; dep. commr. securities State of Wis., Madison, 1973-79; assoc. Quarles & Brady, Milw., 1979-81, ptnr., 1981—, mem. exec. com., 1983—2005. Adj. prof. securities law U. Wis. Law Sch., Madison, 1974-77, Marquette U. Law Sch., Milw., 1981-83; mem. Gov.'s Bus. Cts. Task Force, 1994-98, state regulation com. Nat. Assn. Securities Dealers, Inc., Washington, 1986-92; bd. dirs. Able Distbg. Corp., 1995-2005; bd. dirs., sec. Cade Industries, Inc., 1989-99; sec. Brady Corp., 1999-2007, bd. dirs., 2007-. Bd. dirs. Milw. Repertory Theatre, 1995-2001, exec. com. mem., 1997-2001; bd. curators Wis. Hist. Soc., 2006-. Mem. ABA (vice chmn. state regulation securities com. 1986-89, chmn. 1989-92, vice chmn. bus. law sect. com. on insts. and seminars 2001-2003, chmn. 2003-2006, coun. mem. sect. bus. law 2006—, standing com. mem. continuing legal edn. 2006—), Wis. Bar Assn. (chmn. securities com. 1981-95, bd. dirs. sect. bus. law 1991-2001, vice chair sect. bus. law 1996-98, chair 1998-2000). Office: Quarles & Brady LLP 411 E Wisconsin Ave Ste 2550 Milwaukee WI 53202-4497 Office Phone: 414-277-5305. Business E-Mail: cgg@quarles.com.

GOODMAN, ALLEN CHARLES, economist, educator; b. Cleve., Oct. 28, 1947; s. Nathan and Pearl (Dorfman) Goodman; m. Janet Hankin, July 22, 1984; 1 child, Sara. AB, U. Mich., 1969; PhD, Yale U., 1976. Asst. prof. Lawrence U., Appleton, Wis., 1975-78; rsch. scientist Johns Hopkins U., Balt., 1978-86; economist HUD, Washington, 1985-86; assoc. prof. Wayne State U., Detroit, 1986-88, prof. econs., 1988—, chmn. dept., 1988-96. Author: Changing Downtown, 1987, Economics of Housing Markets, 1989, Economics of Health and Health Care, 5th edit., 2006. Mem. Mayor's Coord. Coun. Criminal Justice, Balt., 1984—86. Fellow, Homer Hoyt Advanced Studies Inst., 2002—. Mem.: Internat. Health Econs. Assn., Am. Real Estate and Urban Econs. Assn., Am. Econs. Assn. Office: Wayne State U Dept Econs Detroit MI 48202 Business E-Mail: allen.goodman@wayne.edu.

GOODMAN, BERNARD, physics professor; b. Phila., June 14, 1923; s. Louis and Fannie (Solomon) G.; m. Joyce Janet Willoughby, Mar. 3, 1950; children—David Nathan, Jonathan Bernard, Mark William AB, U. Pa., 1943, PhD, 1955. Stress analyst Internat. Harvester Co., Chgo., 1947-52; research assoc. U. Mo., 1952, asst. prof. physics, 1954-58, assoc. prof., 1958-64, prof., 1964—; prof. physics U. Cin., 1965-93, prof. emeritus, 1993—. Vis. sci. Argonne Nat. Lab., 1956-57, 61-62, 65-66, 70, Brookhaven Nat. Lab., 1960, Bell Telephone Lab., 1967, Ohio U., 1969; Nordita guest prof. Inst. Theoretical Physics, Uppsala, Sweden, 1962-63, Gothenberg, Sweden, 1971-72; vis. prof. Inst. Theoretical Physics, Gothenberg, 1985. Guggenheim fellow, 1962-63, Gordon Godfrey fellow U. NSW, Sydney, Australia, 1990; Fulbright scholar Inst. Theoretical Physics, Trieste, Italy, 1979-80 Fellow: Am. Phys. Soc.; mem.: AAAS, Phi Beta Kappa, Sigma Xi. Achievements include research in condensed matter theory. Home: 3411 Cornell Pl Cincinnati OH 45220-1501 Office: U Cin Dept Physics Cincinnati OH 45221-0011 Office Phone: 513-556-0537. E-mail: goodman.bernard@gmail.com.

GOODMAN, CHRISTOPHER LAWRENCE, lawyer; b. May 24, 1973; BA summa cum laude, Hamline U., 1995; JD, U. Minn., 1998. Bar: Minn. 1998, US Dist. Ct. (dist. Minn.), US Dist. Ct. (we. dist. Wis.). Ptnr. gen. liability and civil litig., ins. coverage and litig., product liability, and toxic tort and mass litig. practice grps. Foley & Mansfield, P.L.L.P., Mpls., 2001—. Named a Rising Star, Minn. Super Lawyers mag., 2006. Mem.: Def. Rsch. Inst., Minn. State Bar Assn., ABA, Phi Beta Kappa. Office: Foley & Mansfield PLLP 250 Marquette Ave Ste 1200 Minneapolis MN 55401 Office Phone: 612-371-8507. E-mail: cgoodman@foleymansfield.com.

GOODMAN, DAVID, state senator; BA in Polit. Sci., Miami U. Ohio; JD, Case Western Res. U. Atty.; small bus. owner; state rep. Ohio Ho. of Reps., Columbus, 1998—2001; state sen., dist. 3 Ohio State Senate, Columbus, 2001—, chair, judiciary civil justice com., mem. fin. and fin. instns., health, and judiciary criminal justice coms., mem. human svcs. and aging subcom. Exec. com. Franklin County Rep. Party. Named Legislator of Yr., VFW, Ohio Family Physicians; recipient Meritorious award, U.S. Selective Svc., Leadership award, Columbus Jewish Fedn. Mem.: Ohio Bar Assn., Federalist Soc., Agudas Achim Synagogue, Bexley Area C. of C. (bd. dirs.), Big Brothers/Big Sisters. Republican. Office: Senate Bldg Rm #125 1st fl Columbus OH 43215

GOODMAN, DAVID S., lawyer; b. Cleve., 1952; BA, Oberlin Coll., 1974; JD, Harvard U., 1977. Bar: Ohio 1977. Ptnr. Squire, Sanders & Dempsey LLP, Cleve., chmn., Pub. Securities Practice Group. Mem.: Nat. Assn. Bond Lawyers, Ohio Bar Assn., Cleve. Bar Assn. Fluent in German. Office: Squire Sanders & Dempsey LLP 4900 Key Tower 127 Public Sq Cleveland OH 44114-1304 Office Phone: 216-479-8649. Office Fax: 216-479-8780. Business E-Mail: dgoodman@ssd.com.

GOODMAN, DWIGHT, manufacturing executive; Pres. Glas-Craft subs. Cohesant Techs. Inc., Indpls.; exec. v.p., CFO Cohesant Techs. Inc., Indpls., pres., COO, 1996-98, CEO, 1998—. Office: Cohesant Techs Inc 5845 W 82d St Ste 102 Indianapolis IN 46278

GOODMAN, ELIZABETH ANN, retired lawyer; b. Marquette, Mich., Aug. 11, 1950; d. Paul William and Pearl Marie Goodman; m. Herbert Charles Gardner, Sept. 24, 1977. Student, U. Munich, 1970-71; BA cum laude, Alma Coll., Mich., 1972; JD cum laude, U. Mich., 1977. Bar: Minn. 1978, Mich. 1978, U.S. Dist. Ct. Minn. 1979. High sch. tchr. Onaway (Mich.) High Sch., 1973-74; assoc. Dorsey & Whitney LLP, Mpls., 1978-82; ptnr. Dorsey & Whitney, Mpls., 1983-99; v.p., chief gen. counsel Ryan Cos., 2000—03; ret., 2003.

GOODMAN, ERIK DAVID, engineering educator; b. Palo Alto, Calif., Feb. 14, 1944; s. Harold Orbeck and Shirley Mae (Lillie) G.; m. Denise Rowand Dyktor, Aug. 10, 1968 (div. 1976); m. Cheryl Diane Barris, Aug. 27, 1978; 1 child, David Richard. BS in Math., Mich. State U., East Lansing, 1966, MS in Systems Sci., 1968; PhD in Computer Communication Sci., U. Mich., Ann Arbor, 1972; Doctorate (hon.), Dneprodzerzhinsk State Tech U., Ukraine, 1996. Asst. prof. elec. engring. Mich. State U., East Lansing, 1972-77, assoc. prof. elec. engring., 1977-84, dir. case ctr. for computer aided engring. and mfg., 1983—2002, prof. elec. engring., dir., 1984—, prof. mech. engring., 1992—. Dir. Mich. State U. Mfg. Rsch. Consortium, 1993—2003; v.p. Red Cedar Tech., Inc., East Lansing, Mich., 1999-; pres. Tech. Gateway, Inc., East Lansing; cons. Chinese Computer Comms., Inc., Lansing, 1988—; gen. chair First Internat. Conf. on Evolutionary Computation and its Applications, Moscow, 1996, Seventh Internat Conf. on Genetic Algorithms, 1997, Genetic and Evolutionary Computation Conf., 2001; gen. co-chmn. Internat. Computer Graphics Conf., Detroit, 1986; adv. prof. Tongji U., Shanghai, China, 2002—, East China Normal U., 2002-, Shanghai Bus. Sch., Shanghai Maritime U., 2007-. Author: (with others) SYSKIT: Linear Systems Toolkit, 1986; patentee in field. Academician, Internat. Informatization Acad. (Russia), 1993—. Fellow Internat. Soc. Genetic and Evolutionary Computation (sr., exec. com. 2001-04, chair 2001-04); mem. AIAA (chair rsch. and future dirs., subcom. CAD/CAM tech. com. 1987-89, Outstanding Svc. 1990), IEEE Computer Soc., Assn. Computing Machinery (chair SIGEVO, spl. interest group genetic and evolutionary computation 2005—), Soc. Mfg. Engrs., Aircraft Owners and Pilots Assn., Acad. Engring. Scis. Ukraine Avocations: musician, tennis, studying Chinese. Office: Mich State U Dept Elec & Computer Engring 2308M Engineering Bldg East Lansing MI 48824 Business E-Mail: goodman@egr.msu.edu. E-mail: e.goodman@redcedartech.com.

GOODMAN, JULIE, retired nurse midwife; b. Dec. 14, 1937; m. Michael B. Goodman; children: Julia, Christopher, Jennifer. BAin Nursing, Coll. St. Catherine, 1960; MSN, U. Minn., 1975, PhDin Adult Edn., 1990. RN, Minn.; cert. nurse midwife. Staff nurse St. Joseph's Hosp., St. Paul, 1960-61; pub. health nurse Family ursing Svc., St. Paul, 1961-63; instr. nursing U. S.D., Vermillion, 1963-66, Saint Mary's Sch. Nursing, Rochester, Minn., 1966-68, Rochester (Minn.) C. C., 1970-83; nurse practitioner Planned Parenthood, Rochester, Minn., 1978-81; dir. nursing cont. edn. Rochester (Minn.) C. C., 1983-88, dir. nursing, 1989-90, assoc. dean acad. affairs, 1994-95, dean of nursing and allied health, 1995—2006; ret., 2006. Adv. bd. Family Consultation Svc., Rochester, Minn., 1983-86. Author, editor: Child and Family, 1982, 2nd edit. 1987; contbr. articles to profl. jours. Recipient Faculty Svc. award Mayo Med. Ctr., 1996, Main Achievement award, 1989. Mem. Am. Nurses Assn. (nat. del., Book of Yr. 1983), Nat. League Nursing, Minn. Orgn. Assoc. Degree Nursing (co-pres. 1994-96), Minn. Nurses Assn. (chair nursing edn. com. 1982-87, 87-89, bd. dirs. 6th dist.), Great Plains Perinatal Assn., Sigma Theta Tau

GOODMAN, STANLEY, lawyer; b. Cin., June 16, 1931; s. Sol and Ethel (Barsman) G.; m. Diane Elaine Kassel, Apr. 15, 1956; children: Julie Lerner, Jeffrey Stephen, Richard Paul. BA, U. Cin., 1953, JD, 1955. Bar: Ohio 1955, Ky. 1976. Ptnr. Goodman & Goodman, Cin., 1955—. Dir. Winbco Tank Co., Ottumwa, Iowa; lectr. Ohio Bar Continuing Legal Edn. Series; mediator Am. Health Lawyers Alternative Dispute Resolution Svc.; mediator, arbitrator Thomas H. Crush Dispute Resolution Svc.; dir. Spring Valley Bank, Wyoming, Ohio. Mem. ABA, Am. Health Lawyers Assn., Ohio State Bar Assn. (chair eminent domain com. 1997-2000), Ky. Bar Assn., Cin. Bar Assn., Bankers Club, Ridge Club. Jewish. Office: 123 E 4th St Cincinnati OH 45202-4003 Home Phone: 513-221-4699; Office Phone: 513-621-1505. E-mail: sgoodman@goodlaw.com.

GOODNO, KEVIN P., state legislator; b. Oct. 22, 1962; m. Linda Goodno; 1 child. BA in Bus. Adminstrn., Concordia Coll., 1985, BA in Polit. Sci. State rep. Dist. 9Ad Minn. Ho. of Reps., 1991—. Mem. regulated industry com., tax com., labor mgmt. rels. com., crime prevention com., health and human svcs. finance com., health and human svcs. policy com., gov.'s jobs & tng. coun., state coun. vocat. tech. edn., advantage Minn., Minn. Ho. of Reps. Mem. Moorhead C. of C., Ducks Unltd. Home: 10570 Golden Eagle Ct Saint Paul MN 55129-4279 E-mail: rep.Kevin.Goodno@house.leg.state.mn.us.

GOODRICH, JAMES WILLIAM, retired historian executive; b. Burlington, Iowa, Oct. 31, 1939; s. Martin Glenn and Marion Elizabeth (Prasse) G.; m. Linda Marlyse Andreoli, Aug. 31, 1963 (div. Aug. 1989); children: Anne Marlyse, Kimberly Ann. BS in Edn., Cen. Mo. State U., 1962; MA, U. Mo., 1964, PhD, 1974. Archivist Sec. of State, Mo., 1966; asst. then assoc. editor State Hist. Soc. Mo., Columbia, 1967-78, assoc. dir., 1978-85, dir., 1985—, ret., 2004. Cons. USDA Soil Conservation Svc., Columbia, 1976, Mus. History and Sci., Kansas City, Mo., 1978, Mo. State Mus., 1989, Mo. Dept. Conservation, 1990, 91, 95, 97; mem. Mo. Hist. Records Adv. Bd., Jefferson City, 1985—, State Records Commn., Jefferson City, 1984—, Mo. Bd. Geographic Names, 1995-; dir. Western Hist. Manuscript Collection, 1985—; adj. prof. history U. Mo., Columbia, 1988—. Co-author: Historic Missouri, 1988; editor: Report on a Journey to North America, 1980; assoc. editor Mo. Hist. Rev., 1967-85, editor 1985—; co-editor: German-American Experience in Missouri, 1986; co-editor, contbr. Marking Missouri History, 1998; contbr. articles to profl. jours. Mem. Planning and Zoning Commn., Columbia, 1975-77; councilman City of Columbia, 1977-79, 79-81; chmn. city audit com., Columbia, 1981-88; v.p. Friends of Mo. St. Archives, 1989-94; mem. 13th Jud. Cir. Bar Rev. Com., 1991-97; bd. dirs. Mo. Mansion Preservation Inc., 1991—; bd. dirs. Boone County Cmty. Trust, 1992—; mem. exec. com. Mo. State U. Alumni Assn., 1988-92, pres. 1991; mem. 6th Regional Disciplinary Com. Mo. Judiciary, 1997—; mem. Mo. Lewis and Clark Bicentennial Com., 1997—. Mem. Orgn. Am. Historians, Western History Assn., Am. Assn. for State & Local History, Conservation Fedn. Mo., Ducks Unlimited, Mo. Mus. Assn., Mo. Press Assn., Wild Canid Survival and Rsch. Ctr. Avocations: decoy collecting, waterfowl hunting, orinthoscopy. Office: State Hist Soc Mo 1020 Lowry St Columbia MO 65201-7207

GOODRICH, JOHN BERNARD, lawyer, consultant; b. Spokane, Wash., Jan. 4, 1928; s. John Casey and Dorothy (Koll) G.; m. Therese H. Vollmer, June 14, 1952; children— Joseph B., Bernadette M., Andrew J., Philip M., Thomas A., Mary Elizabeth, Jennifer H., Rosanne M. JD, Gonzaga U., 1954. Bar: Wash. 1954, Ill. 1955. Indsl. traffic mgr. Pacific N.W. Alloys, Spokane, 1950-54; asst. to gen. counsel Cromium Mining & Smelting Corp., Chgo., 1954-56; with Monon R.R., 1956-69, atty., gen. solicitor, 1956-66, sec., 1957-69, treas., 1959-66, v.p. law, 1966-69; also dir.; sec.-treas. I.C.G.R.R., Chgo., 1970-79, sec., gen. atty., 1979-85; gen. counsel Ill. Devel. Fin. Authority, Chgo., 1985-92, spl. counsel, 1993; atty., cons. pvt. practice, Park Forest, Ill., 1994—. Mem. Park Forest Traffic and Safety Commn., 1963-66; mem. Park Forest Recreation Bd., 1966-77, chmn., 1969-70; trustee Village of Park Forest, 1977-80; mem. bd. Sch. Dist. 163, 1984-89; pres. South Cook Orgn. for Pub. Edn., 1988-89; conf. and meeting planner The Compassionate Friends, Inc., Oak Brook, Ill., 1991-94; bd. dirs. Park Forest Art Ctr., 1993-95, Ill. Philharm. Orch., 1994-98, treas., 1995-98; mem. adv. bd. Chgo. Self Help Ctr., 1993-94; bd. dirs. Ill Self Help Coalition, 1994-96; treas. Bereaved Parents of the U.S.A., 1995-2000, bd. dirs. 2000-03, Tall Grass Arts Assn., 1999-2003; trustee Chgo. South Suburban Mass Transit Dist., 1996—, treas., 2000-04, vice chmn., 2004—. Inducted into Park Forest Hall of Fame, 1998. Mem. KC, The Parkforesters, Inc. (pres. 1998-2004, dir.), Kiwanis. Roman Catholic. Home and Office: 35 Cunningham Ln Park Forest IL 60466-2094

GOODRIDGE, ALAN GARDNER, research biochemist, educator; b. Peabody, Mass., Apr. 2, 1937; s. Lester Elmer and Gertrude Edith (Gardner) G.; m. R. Ann Funderburk, Aug. 19, 1960; children— Alan Gardner Jr., Bryant C. BS in Biology, Tufts U., 1958; MS in Zoology, U. Mich., 1963, PhD in Zoology, 1964. Rsch. fellow dept. biochemistry Harvard Med. Sch., Boston, 1964-66; asst. prof. physiology U. Kans. Med. Ctr., Kansas City, 1966-68; assoc. prof. Banting and Best dept. med. rsch. U. Toronto, Ont., Can., 1968-76, prof. Banting and Best dept. med. rsch., 1976-77; prof. pharmacology and biochemistry Case Western Res. U., Cleve., 1977-87; prof., head dept. biochemistry U. Iowa, 1987-96; prof. biochemistry Ohio State U., 1996—2001, dean Coll. Biol. Scis., 1996-2001, exec. dean Colls. of Arts and Sci., 1999-2001; prof. biol. scis. and pharmacology U. Toledo, 2002—, provost, 2002—, exec. v.p. academic affairs and enrollment svcs., 2002—. Assoc. editor Jour. Biol. Chemistry, 1990-2002, Ann. Rev. of Nutrition, 1994-99, Jour. Lipid Rsch., 1995-99; contbr. numerous articles to profl. jours. Served with USN, 1958-61 Grantee Med. Rsch. Coun. Can., 1968-77, NIH, 1966-68, 77-97, USDA 1986-90, 93-97; Josiah Macy Jr. faculty scholar, 1975-76. Mem. AAAS, Am. Soc. Biochemistry and Molecular Biology. Home: 10 Exmoor Ottawa Hills OH 43615-2156 Home Phone: 419-537-1635; Office Phone: 419-530-2739. Business E-Mail: alan.goodridge@utoledo.edu.

GOODSELL, G. VERNE, lawyer; b. Watertown, SD, Jan. 22, 1943; AA, Miltonvale Wesleyan Coll., 1964; BS, No. State Coll., 1967, MS, 1970; JD, Washburn U. Topeka, 1973. Bar: S.D. 1974. Atty. Gunderson, Palmer, Goodsell & Nelson, LLP, Rapid City, SD. Mem.: ABA (vice chair litigation com. gen. practice sect. 1990), Black Hills Claims Assn. (pres. 1984—85), Pennington County Bar Assn. (pres. 1981), Am. Jurisprudence Assn., Assn. Trial Lawyers Am., S.D. Trial Lawyers Assn., State Bar S.D. (commr. 1984—87, professionalism com. 1989, mem. disciplinary bd. 1990—95, co-chair disciplinary bd. 1995—96, chair advt. com. 1999—2000, chair ethics com. 2000, pres.-elect 2002, mulit-jurisdictional/internet com., pres. 2003). Office: Gunderson Palmer Goodsell and Nelson LLP 3d and 4th Fls PO box 8045 Rapid City SD 57709-8045

GOODSTEIN, AARON E., federal magistrate judge; b. Sheboygan, Wis., Apr. 28, 1942; BA, U. Wis. Madison, 1964; JD, U. Wis., 1967. Bar: Wis. 1967, U.S. Dist. Ct. (ea. and we. dists.) Wis. 1967, U.S. Ct. Appeals (7th crct.) 1968. Law clk. to Hon. Myron L. Gordon U.S. Dist. Ct., Ea. Dist. Wis., 1967-68; shareholder Chernov, Croen & Goodstein, S.C., Milw., 1968-79; U.S. magistrate judge Ea. Dist. Wis., Milw., 1979-87, reapptd., 1987—. Panelist Current Issues Relating to the Fourth, Fifth and Sixth Amendments, Jud. Conf. of 7th Cir., 1991; speaker fed. ct.'s class Marquette Law Sch., 1992; moderator probation and pretrial svcs. divsn. U.S. Cts., 1992; chair magistrate judges edn. com. Fed. Jud. Ctr., 1990-98, mem. magistrate judges com. of Jud. Conf. of U.S., 1993-99; adv. com. local rules and practice Ea. Dist. Wis., mem. adv. panel under Civil Justice Reform Act 1990; faculty mem. in field. Prodr: (video) Complaints, Warrants for Arrest and Search Warrants, 1992, Administrative Matters Pertaining to Magistrate Judges and Their Staff, 1993, Social Security: Process and Problems, Parts One and Two, 2000; mem. editl. adv. panel Handbook of Federal Civil Discovery and Disclosure, 1998; contbr. articles to profl. jours. Bd. dirs. Milw. Legal Aid Soc., 1974-79, Milw. Jewish Coun., 1977-79; pres. Milw. Forum, 1979-80, alumni mem.; pres. Congregation Shalom, 1990-92. Recipient Pro Bono award Gene and Ruth Posner Found., 1988 Mem. ABA (former chair magistrate judges com. Nat. Conf. Fed. Trial Judges), Fed. Magistrate Judges Assn. (pres. 2004-05), State Bar Wis. (pres. young lawyers divsn. 1975-76, bd. govs. 1975-77), Milw. Bar Assn. (exec. bd. 1978-79, sec. 1979-82), U. Wis. Law Sch. Alumni Assn. (bd. dirs. 1989-98), Order of Coif, Phi Kappa Phi. Office: US Magistrate Judge 258 US Courthouse 517 E Wisconsin Ave Milwaukee WI 53202-4500 Office Phone: 414-297-3963.

GOODSTEIN, SANDERS ABRAHAM, scrap iron company executive; b. NYC, Oct. 3, 1918; s. Samuel G. and Katie (Lipson) G.; m. Rose Laro, June 28, 1942; children: Peter, Esther, Jack, Rachel. Student, Wayne State U., 1934-36; AB, U. Mich., 1938, MBA, 1939, JD, 1946; postgrad., Harvard, 1943. Bar: Mich., 1946. Sec. Laro Coal & Iron Co., Flint, Mich., 1946-60, pres., 1960—; owner, operator Paterson Mfg. Co., Flint, 1953-94. Gen. ptnr. Indianhead Co., Pontiac, Mich., 1955-70, pres., 1965-70; sec. Amatac Corp., Erie, Pa., unitl 1969; chmn. bd. Gen. Foundry & Mfg. Co., Flint, 1968—, pres., 1970-92; pres. Lacron Steel Co., Providence, 1975-80, ETL Corp., Flint, 1983-91, Can. Blending and Processing, Windsor, 1988-97; mem. corp. body Mich. Blue Shield, 1970-76. Served to lt. comdr. USNR, 1942-46. Mem. ABA, Fed. Bar Assn., Bar Mich., Am. Pub. Works Assn., Am. Foundrymen's Soc., Order of Coif, Beta Gamma Sigma, Phi Kappa Phi. Jewish. Home: 2602 Parkside Dr Flint MI 48503-4662 Office: PO Box 307 Flint MI 48501

GOODWIN, BECKY K., educational technology resource educator; Sci. tchr. USD 233 Sch. Dist., Olathe, Kans. Christa McAuliffe fellowship grantee State of Kans., 1992, 94, 97; named Kans. Tchr. of Yr., 1995; recipient Presdl. award for Excellence in Sci. and Math. Secondary Sci. for Kans., 1992, Outstanding Biology Tchr. award Nat. Assn. Biology Tchrs., 1992, Sci. Teaching Achievement Recognition Star award NSTA, 1993, Milken Nat. Educator award, 1995, Tandy Tech. Tchr. award, 1998. Office: USD 233 14090 Black Bob Rd Olathe KS 66063

GOODWIN, DANIEL L., real estate company executive; b. 1943; BS, No. Ill. U., De Kalb, 1964, MA, 1966. Chmn. bd., CEO The Inland Group Inc., Oak Brook, Ill. Office: The Inland Group Inc 2901 Butterfield Rd Oak Brook IL 60523-1190

GOODWIN, GRETA HALL, state legislator; m. James G. Goodwin. Legal asst., 1988—; mem. Kans. Ho. of Reps from 78th dist., Topeka, 1993-97, Kans. Senate from 32nd dist., Topeka, 1997—. Home: 420 E 12th Ave Winfield KS 67156-3721 Office: Kans Senate Chambers State Capitol Topeka KS 66612 E-mail: ggoodwin@ink.org.

GOODWIN, JAMES E. (JIM GOODWIN), retired air transportation executive; BBA, Salem Coll. Sr. v.p. internat. United Airlines, Inc., 1992—95, sr. v.p. N.Am., 1995—98, pres., COO, 1998—99, chmn., CEO, 1999—2001, UAL Corp., Elk Grove Twp., Ill., 1999—2001; ind. bus. cons., 2001—; interim pres., CEO Fed. Signal Corp., Oak Brook, Ill., 2007—. Bd. dirs. AAR Corp., Wood Dale, Ill., 2002—, DBS Commn. Inc., 2003—, Fed. Signal Corp., 2005—, Labe Bank, First Chgo. Bank & Trust. Trustee Lewis U., Chgo. Symphony Orch.; bd. dirs. Chgo. Coun. Fgn. Rels. Mem. Exec. Club Chgo. (bd. dirs.), Comml. Club Chgo. (civic com.). Office: Fed Signal Corp 1415 W 22nd St Ste 1100 Oak Brook IL 60523

GOODWIN, JOHN P., consumer products company executive; b. London, Dec. 27, 1963; BS in Math. Engring., Loughborough U. Auditing & tax cons. Ernst & Young, 1986—90; profit forecast, fabric care fin. analyst The Procter & Gamble Co., 1990—91, plant fin. mgr., 1991—93, CBD fin. mgr., 1993—94, assoc. comptr. laundry products, Europe, 1994—96, assoc. comptr. treasury, 1996—98, assoc. dir. treasury, 1998—99, dir. fin. Poland, Baltics & Belarus, 1999—2001, dir. investor rels. & shareholder services, 2001—03, mgr., asst. treas. investor rels. & shareholder services, 2003—04, treas., 2004—06, v.p., treas., 2006—08, pres. global snacks & pet care, 2008—. Lectr. fin. mgmt. techniques Warsaw U. Tech. Bus. Sch., 1999—2001; chairperson bd. dirs. Internat. Christian Fellowship of Warsaw, 2000—01. Founding trustee Tigers Club Project, 1996—99; bd. mem. Matthew 25: Ministries & Ctr. for Humanitarian Relief, 2005, Cin. Bus. Adv. Coun., Fed. Res. Bank Clev., 2006. Fellow, The Inst. Chartered Accountants, 2000. Office: The Procter & Gamble Co One Procter & Gamble Plaza Cincinnati OH 45202*

GOODWIN, WILLIAM MAXWELL, financial executive, retired; b. Muncie, Ind., Oct. 13, 1939; s. Donald Dunkin and Beth Virginia (Maxwell) G.; m. LaDonna Sherry Erickson, June 9, 1962; children: Lauri Michelle, Lisa Dianne. AB, Ind. U., 1961, MBA, 1966. CPA, Ind. Staff acct., supr. Ernst & Whinney (now Ernst Whinney & Young), Indpls., 1966-72; contr. Lilly Endowment, Inc., Indpls., 1972-82, treas., sec., 1983-95, v.p. cmty. devel., 1996—. Advisor Sch. Bus., Ind. U., Bloomington, Ind., 1980-95; fin. advisor U.S. Gymnastic Fedn., Indpls., 1983-89; treas., dir. Nat. Gymnastics Found. Inc., Indpls., 1988-89. Contbr. articles to profl. jours. Treas., dir. Ind. Sports Corp., Indpls., 1979-88; dir. Youth Works, Inc., Indpls., 1977-85, Greater Indpls. Progress Com., 1996—; treas. Nat. Sports Festival, Indpls., 1982; treas., mem. exec. com. 1987 Pan Am. Games, Indpls.; chmn. AAU Sullivan Award Dinner, Indpls., 1983-94, mem. award selection com., 1993—. Capt. U.S. Army, 1962-64. Mem. AICPA, Ind. Assn. CPAs, Beta Gamma Sigma, Delta Phi Alpha. Republican. Methodist. Home: 3586 Inverness Blvd Carmel IN 46032-9380 Home Phone: 317-872-5491.

GOOGASIAN, GEORGE ARA, lawyer; b. Pontiac, Mich., Feb. 22, 1936; s. Peter and Lucy (Chobanian) G.; m. Phyllis Elaine Law, June 27, 1959; children— Karen Ann, Steven George, Dean Michael BA, U. Mich., 1958; JD, Northwestern U., 1961. Bar: Mich. 1961. Assoc. Marentay, Rouse, Selby, Fischer & Webber, Detroit, 1961-62; asst. U.S. Atty. U.S. Dept. Justice, Detroit, 1962-64; assoc. Howlett, Hartman & Beier, Pontiac and Bloomfield Hills, Mich., 1964-81; ptnr. Googasian Hopkins Hohauser & Forhan, Bloomfield Hills, Mich., 1981-96, The Googasian Firm, Bloomfield Hills, 1996—. Mem. bd. law examiners State of Mich., 1997—2002, pres., 2001—02. Author: Trial Advocacy Manual, 1984, West Groups Michigan Practice Torts, vols. 14 and 15, 2001. Pres. Oakland Parks Found., Pontiac, 1984-89; chmn. Oakland County Dem. party, Pontiac, 1964-70; state campaign chmn. U.S. Senator Philip A. Hart, Detroit, 1970; bd. dirs. Big Bros. Oakland County. 1968-73 Fellow Am. Bar Found., Am. Coll. Trial Lawyers, Internat. Acad. Trial Lawyers; mem. ABA (del. 1992-93, exec. coun. nat. conf. bar pres. 1993-96), ATLA, Am. Bd. Trial Advocates, State Bar Mich. (pres. elect 1991-92, pres. 1992—), Internat. Soc. Barristers, Oakland County Bar Assn. (pres. 1985-86), Oakland Bar Found. (pres. 1990-92). Clubs: U. Mich. Club Greater Detroit. Presbyterian. Home: 3750 Orion Rd Oakland MI 48363-3029 Office: 6895 Telegraph Rd Bloomfield Hills MI 48301-3138 Office Phone: 248-540-3333.

GOOLDY, PATRICIA ALICE, retired elementary school educator; b. Indpls., Nov. 23, 1937; d. Harold Emanuel and Emma Irene (Wade) VanTreese; m. Walter Raymond Gooldy, May 4, 1968. BS, U. Indpls., 1959; MS, Butler U., 1963. Tchr. Franklin Twp. Cmty. Schs., Indpls., 1959-68, 72-99, USA Dep. Schs., Bad Kreuznach, Germany, 1969-72; ret., 1999. Owner Ye Olde Genealogie Shoppe, Indpls., 1972—; lectr. in field. Author: 21 Things I Wish I'd Found, 1984; editor: Indiana Wills to 1880: Index to Indiana Wills, 1987; co-editor: Indiana Manual For Gen, 1991, Illinois Manual For Gen, 1994. Named Ky. Col., 1995; named one of Outstanding Elem. Tchrs. of Am., 1974. Mem. Franklin Twp. Hist. Soc. (founder), Ind. Geneal. Soc. (chartered). Office: Ye Olde Genealogie Shoppe PO Box 39128 Indianapolis IN 46239-0128 Office Phone: 317-862-3330. Personal E-mail: yogs@iquest.net.

GOOREY, NANCY JANE, dentist; b. Davenport, Iowa, May 8, 1922; d. Edgar Ray and Glenna Mae (Williams) Miller; m. Douglas B. Miller, Sept. 12, 1939 (div. 1951); children: Victoria Lee, Nickola Ellen, Douglas George, Melahna Marie; m. Louis Joseph Roseberry Goorey, Feb. 22, 1980. Student, Wooster Coll., Ohio, 1939-40; DDS, Ohio State U., 1955. Cert. in gen. anesthesiology. Mem. faculty coll. dentistry Ohio State U., Columbus, 1955-86, dir., chmn. div. dental hygiene coll. dentistry, 1969-86, asst. dean coll. dentistry, 1975-86, mem. grad. faculty colls. dentistry and medicine, 1980-86, asst. dean, prof. emeritus colls. dentistry, 1986—. Moderator, prodn. chmn. Lifesavers 40 Prodns., 1981—; mem. task force on sch. based-linked oral health project Ohio Dept. Health, 1999—. Producer, video program Giving Your Mouth a Sporting Chance, 1990, video Operation TACTIC. Chmn. State Planning Com. for Health Edn. in Ohio, Columbus, 1976-77, 87-88, 95-97; founder Coun. on Health Info., Columbus, 1980, del., 1981-85, chmn., pres., 1985-86, chmn. prodn. com., 1986-2003, chmn. mktg. com., 2003—, chmn. Capital Campaign; trustee Caring Dentists Found., Mayor's Drug Edn. and Prevention Program, Columbus, 1980-90; mem. exec. com. Franklin County Rep. com., exec. com., 1993—; mem. human svcs. com. The Columbus Found.; pres. Worthington Arts Coun., 1998-2000, chmn. Capital Campaign, 2000-. Recipient Vol. of Yr. award Columbus Health Dept., 1988-89, Dental Hygiene Nancy J. Goorey award Ohio State U., 1988, Drug Free Sch. Consortium award, 1996, Champion of Children's Oral Health award Ohio Dept. of Health Dental Divsn., 1997, Disting. Alumnus award Ohio State U. Coll. Dentistry, YWCA Women of Achievement award, 2000; named Nancy J. Goorey Ednl. Suite in her honor Ohio State U. Coll. Dentistry, 2004. Fellow: Internat. Coll. Dentists, Am. Soc. Dental Anesthesiology, Am. Coll. Dentists (chmn.-elect 1989—90, chmn. Columbus sect.); mem.: ADA (nat. consumer advisor 1975—78, coun. edn. and licensure 1997—), Cols. Med. Assoc. Mem. Sports Med. Comm., Ohio Dept. Health (sch. linked oral health project 1999), Ohio State Med. Assn. Alliance (chmn. state com. legis. affairs 1993—94, chmn. state health promotions com. 1994—95, v.p. 1995—97, pres.-elect 1997, pres. 1998), The Found. of the Acad. of Medicine (v.p. 1993—94), Columbus Dental Soc. (pres. bd. dirs. 1986—87, 1989—91, chmn. coun. on constn. and bilaws on jud. affairs 1989—2003, chmn. sports dentistry com. 1995—), Ohio Dental Assn. (cons. 1979—, mem. subcoun. on dentists concerned for dentists 1994—96, chmn. subcoun. chem. dependency, prin. investigator, chair smokeless tobacco rsch., Ohio Disting. Dentist 1983, Disting. Svc. award 2002—03), Am. Assn. Dental Schs. (pres. 1972—77, v.p.), Caring Dentists Found. (trustee), The Columbus Found. (human svcs. com.), Acad. of Medicine Aux. (pres. 1992—93, 1996—97, chair mouthguard project), Ohio State U. Faculty and Profl. Womens Club (pres. 1971—72), Ohio State U. Starling Womens Club (pres. 1982—83), Omicron Kappa Upsilon. Republican. Episcopalian. Avocations: camping, travel, bridge, cooking, wine. Office: Ohio State U Coll Dentistry 305 W 12th Ave Columbus OH 43210-1267

GORA, JOANN M., academic administrator; BA, Vassar Coll.; M in Sociology, D in Sociology, Rutgers U. Dean Coll. Arts and Scis., sr. dean Madison campus Fairleigh Dickinson U., 1985—92; provost, v.p. for acad. affairs, prof. sociology Old Dominion U., Norfolk, Va., 1992-01; chancellor U. Mass., Boston, 2001—04; pres. Ball State U., Muncie, Ind., 2004—. Author: The New Female Criminal: Empirical Reality or Social Myth?; co-author: Emergency Squad Volunteers: Professionalism in Unpaid Work; contbr. numerous articles to profl. jours. Office: Ball State U Office Pres AD Bldg 101 Muncie IN 47306 Office Phone: 765-285-5555. Business E-Mail: president@bsu.edu.

GORAN, MARK H., lawyer; BA, Washington U., St. Louis, 1971, JD, 1974; MS, U. Wis., 1973. Bar: Mo. 1975. Ptnr., group leader Health Care Bryan Cave LLP, St. Louis. Office: Bryan Cave LLP One Metropolitan Square 211 N Broadway, Ste 3600 Saint Louis MO 63102 Office Phone: 314-259-2686. E-mail: mhgoran@bryancave.com.

GORBIEN, MARTIN JOHN, medical educator, geriatrician; b. Chgo., Dec. 24, 1955; MD, Autonomous U., Guadalajara, Mexico, 1983. Cert. internal medicine 1996, geriatric medicine 1998. Intern to resident, geriatric medicine Mercy Hosp. and Med. Ctr., Chgo., 1984—87; fellowship, geriatric medicine UCLA, 1987—89; asst. prof. medicine U. Chgo. Pritzer Sch. Medicine, Chgo., 1994—98; assoc. prof., dir. Rush Med. Coll., St. Lukes Med. Ctr., Geriatric Dept., Chgo., 1998—. Office: Rush U Med Ctr 1725 W Harrison St Ste 955 Chicago IL 60612 Office Phone: 312-942-3362, 312-942-5321. Business E-Mail: mgorbien@rush.edu.

GORCYCA, DAVID G., lawyer; b. Feb. 20, 1962; BA in Polit. Sci., 1984, JD, 1988. House counsel Beresh & Prokopp, Liberty Mut. Ins. Co., 1985-88; asst. prosecuting atty. Oakland County Prosecutor's Office, 1988-90; assoc. Alan R. Miller, P.C., 1990-91; pvt. practice Valenti, Bolger & Gorcyca, 1991-96; prosecuting atty. Oakland County Prosecutor's Office, 1996—. Legis. aide to Sen. Richard D. Fessler, Mich. State Capital and Dist. Office, 1983-84; city liaison to crime prevention coun. sr. citizens adv. bd. Royal Oak City Commr., 1993—; del. Rep. State Conv.; precinct del. City of Royal Oak; del. Rep. County Conv.; mem. Lincoln Club Com., Bylaws Com.; active Boys and Girls Club, Mich. Cancer Found., Am. Heart Assn. Recipient Am. Jurisprudence Book award; Edward H. Rakow scholar FBA, Mfr.'s Nat. Bank of Detroit scholar, Mich. tuition scholar. Mem. Mich. Bar Assn., Mich. Rep. Lawyers Assn., Advocacy Bar Assn., Oakland County Bar Assn., Mich. State U. Pre-Law Assn., Mich. State U. Student Found., Sigma Alpha Epsilon (pres.), Intrafraternity Coun. Avocations: exercising, golf, basketball. Office: Office of Prosecuting Atty Courthouse Tower Pontiac MI 48341

GORDER, WILLIAM E., state legislator; m. Marlene Gorder; 4 children. BA, MEd, U. N.D. Tchr.; farmer; state rep. dist. 16, 1981—. Vice chmn. natural resources com.; mem. edn. and human svcs. com. N.D. Ho. Reps. Mem. Grafton C. of C., Grafton Gideon Camp, Walsh Hist. Soc., Farm Bur., Am. Legion. Republican. Home: 1345 Lawler Ave Grafton ND 58237-1764

GORDON, DAN A., food service executive; Exec. v.p. Gordon Food Svc. Inc., Grand Rapids, Mich., 1989—91, pres., CEO, 1991—. Bd. dir. Internat. Food

Svc. Distributors Assn. Bd. dir. Econ. Club of Grand Rapids. Office: Gordon Food Svc Inc 333 5th St SW Grand Rapids MI 49501

GORDON, EDWARD EARL, management consultant, educator; b. Evergreen Park, Ill., Feb. 28, 1949; s. Earl and Estelle (Biehn) G.; m. Elaine Huarisa, Aug. 6, 1983. BA in History, Edn., DePaul U., 1971, MA in History, 1972; postgrad., U. Chgo., 1972-73; PhD in History of Edn./Psychology, Loyola U., 1988. Founding pres. Imperial Consulting Corp., Oak Lawn, Ill., 1968—; exec. dir. North Am. Inst. for Tng. and Edml. Rsch., 1972—. Arbitrator Coun. Better Bus. Burs., Chgo., 1977—, Ill. Bd. Edn., 1986—; lectr. Sch. Edn., DePaul U., Chgo., 1979-92, Northwestern U., Chgo., 1999, Conf. Bd. Basic Skills Devel. in the Workplace Conf., 2000; adj. prof., dir. grad. program in tng. and devel. Roosevelt U., Chgo., 1990-91; instr. adult corp. instrn. mgmt. program Loyola U., Chgo., 1992-98; mem. Conf. Bd. Bus. Edn. Conf., 1996; keynote spkr. Partnerships in Learning at Work program U. B.C., Vancouver, Can., 1990, ednl. conf. Assn. Legal Adminstrs., 1999, Corp. Univ. Forum, Chgo., 1996, Measuring Performance and Profit for Workforce Edn. Programs, Palm Springs, Calif. Author: Educators' Consumer Guide to Private Tutoring Services, 1989, Centuries of Tutoring: A History of Alternative Education in America and Western Europe, 1990, Closing the Literacy Gap in American Business: A Handbook for Trainers and Human Resources Development Specialists, 1991, The Need for Work Force Education, 1993, FutureWork: The Revolution Reshaping American Business, 1994, Ethics for Training and Development, 1995, Enhancing Learning in Training and Adult Edn., 1998, Opportunities in Training and Development Careers, 1996, Skill Wars: Winning the Battle for Productivity and Profit, 2000; contbr. articles to profl. jours.; mem. editl. adv. bd., columnist Corp. Univ. Forum Mag., 1995-98. Bd. dirs. Ill. Literacy Resource Devel. Ctr., BBB of Chgo. and o. Ill., 1996—; mem. bus.-edn. partnerships bd. Ill. Bd. Edn., 1995—; mem. Pvt. Industry Coun. of Cook County, 1994—. Mem. ASTD (pres.-elect. Chgo. chpt. 1989-90, dir. manuscript rev. bd. 1988—), Am. Ednl. Rsch. Assn., Am. Hist. Assn., Internat. Reading Assn., Am. Mgmt. Assn. (presenter New Strategic Corp. Model 1993), Internat. Soc. Performance Improvement, Midwest History of Edn. Soc. (pres.), Phi Delta Kappa (pres. DePaul U. chpt. 1986-88). Roman Catholic. Office: # 8E 220 E Walton St Chicago IL 60611-1649 E-mail: imperialcorp@juno.com.

GORDON, ELLEN RUBIN, candy company executive; d. William B. and Cele H. (Travis) Rubin; m. Melvin J. Gordon, June 25, 1950; children: Virginia, Karen, Wendy, Lisa. Student, Vassar Coll., 1948—50; BA, Brandeis U., 1965; postgrad., Harvard U., 1968. With Tootsie Roll Industries, Inc., Chgo., 1968—, corp. sec., 1970-74, v.p. product devel., 1974-76, sr. v.p., 1976-78, pres., COO, 1978—; v.p., dir. HDI Investment Corp. Mem. coun. on divsn. biol. scis. and Pritzker Sch. Medicine U. Chgo.; mem. med. sch. adv. coun. for cell biology and pathology Harvard U.; mem. bd. fellows Faculty of Medicine, Harvard Med. Sch. Mem. adv. coun. J.L. Kellogg Grad. Sch. Mgmt. at Northwestern U.; mem. univ. resources and overseers com. Harvard U.; mem. bd. advisors Women Inc. Recipient Kettle award, 1985. Mem. Nat. Confectioners Assn. (bd. dirs.). Office: Tootsie Roll Industries Inc 7401 S Cicero Ave Chicago IL 60629-5885

GORDON, GILBERT, chemist, educator; b. Chgo., Nov. 11, 1933; s. Walter and Catherine Gordon; m. Joyce Elaine Masura; children: Thomas, Lyndi. BS, Bradley U., 1955; PhD, Mich. State U., 1959. Postdoctoral rsch. assoc. U. Chgo., 1959-60; asst. prof. U. Md., College Park, 1960-64, assoc. prof., 1964-67, prof., 1967; prof. chemistry U. Iowa, Iowa City, 1967-73; prof., chmn. dept. Miami U., Oxford, Ohio, 1973-84, Volwiler Disting. Rsch. prof., 1984—2003, disting. rsch. prof. emeritus, 2003—. Mem. editl. bd. Synthesis Inorganic Metal, Organic Chemistry, Ozone, Sci. and Engring.; contbr. articles to chem. jours. amed Cin. Chemist of Yr., 1981 Mem.: Faraday Soc., Chem. Soc. London, Am. Chem. Soc., Internat. Ozone Assn. (dir. 1995—, treas. 1998—, pres. 2002—04), Phi Kappa Phi, Sigma Xi. Home: 190 Shadowy Hills Dr Oxford OH 45056-1441 Office: Miami U Dept Chemistry Oxford OH 45056 Office Phone: 513-529-3336. Business E-Mail: gordong@muohio.edu.

GORDON, JAMES A., investment company executive; B summa cum laude, Northwestern U. With Gordon's Wholesale, 1971—86; founder, mng. ptnr. Edgewater Growth Capital Ptnrs. Treasurer Whitney Mus. Am. Art, trustee; bd. dir. Des Moines Ballet; mem. bd. Grinnell Coll., chmn. investment com.; bd. dir. Chgo. Mus. Am. Art, orthwestern Meml. Found., John F. Kennnedy Ctr. Performing Arts, Chgo. Cares Inc., Bankers Trust Co., Methodist Med. Adv.; bd. dir. & former pres. Des Moines Art Ctr.; bd. dir. Iowa Soc. to Prevent Blindness, Des Moines Opera. Office: Edgewater Funds Growth Capital Ptnrs 900 N Michigan Ave Ste 1800 Chicago IL 60611 Mailing: c/o Whitney Mus Am Art 945 Madison Ave New York NY 10021 Office Fax: 312-664-8649. Business E-Mail: jim@edgewaterfunds.com.

GORDON, JEFFREY IVAN, gastroenterologist, educator, molecular biologist, researcher; b. New Orleans, Oct. 4, 1947; BA in Biology, Oberlin Coll.; MD, U. Chicago-Pritzker Sch Medicine, 1973. Intern, medicine Barnes Hosp., St. Louis, 1973—74, jr. asst. resident, medicine, 1974—75, sr. asst. resident. medicine, 1978—79; rsch. assoc. biochemistry lab, gastrointestinal medicine Nat. Cancer Ins., NIH, Bethesda, Md., 1975—78; chief med. resident Wash. U. Medical Service, John Cochran VA Hospital, St. Louis, 1978—79; fellow in medicine, gastroenterology Wash. U. Sch. of Medicine, St. Louis, 1979—81, asst. prof. medicine and biol. chemistry, 1981—84, assoc. prof. medicine and biol. chemistry, 1985—87, prof. medicine and biol. chemistry, 1987—90, head molecular biology & pharmacology dept., 1991—, Robert J. Glaser Disting. U. Prof., 2002—, dir. Ctr. Genome Sciences, 2004—. Contbr. articles to profl. publications. Named Wellcome Vis. Prof. in Basic Med. Sciences, 1998, Horace W. Davenport Disting. Lecturer, Am. Physiological Assn., 2003, Sir Arthur Hurst Lecturer, British Soc. Gastroenterology, 2004; recipient Young Investigator award, Am. Federation Clinical Rsch., 1990, NIDDK Young Scientist award, 1990, Marion Merrell Dow Disting. prize in Gastrointestinal Physiology, 1994, Janssen Sustained Achievement award in Digestive Sciences, 2003, Sr. Scholar award in Global Infectious Diseases, Ellison Medical Found., 2003; John A. & George L. Hartford Found. Fellowship, 1981—84, Established Investigatorship, Am. Heart Assoc., 1985—90. Fellow: AAAS, Am. Acad. Arts and Scis., Am. Acad. Microbiology; mem.: NAS, Am. Gastroenterology Assn. (Morton I. Grossman Disting. Lectr. 1999, Disting. Achievement award 1992, 1992), Assn. Am. Physicians. Achievements include internationally known for research on gastrointestinal development and how gut bacteria affect normal intestinal function and predisposition to health and to certain diseases. Office: Dept Molecular Biology & Pharmacology Wash U Campus Box 8510 4444 Forest Park Saint Louis MO 63108 Office Phone: 314-362-7243. Business E-Mail: igordon@molecool.wustl.edu.

GORDON, JOHN BENNETT, lawyer; b. Des Moines, Nov. 21, 1947; s. Bennett and Mary (Adelman) G.; m. Joanne Dunbar Westgate, Jan. 17, 1976; children: Anne Dunbar, Bennett Westgate, Susan Julia. AB, Princeton U., 1969; JD, Harvard U., 1973. Bar: Minn. 1974, U.S. Dist. Ct. Minn. 1974, U.S. Ct. Appeals (8th cir.) 1974, U.S. Supreme Ct. 1985. Clerk U.S. Ct. Appeals (5th cir.), Newnan, Ga., 1973-74; assoc. law firm Faegre & Benson, Mpls., 1974-80, ptnr., 1981—. Mem. Minn. State Bar Assn., Hennepin County Bar Assn. (pres. 1985-86). Office: Faegre & Benson 90 S 7th St Ste 2200 Minneapolis MN 55402-3901 Office Phone: 612-766-8407. Business E-Mail: jgordon@faegre.com.

GORDON, JULIE PEYTON, foundation administrator; b. Jacksonville, Fla., June 21, 1940; d. Robert Benoist Shields and Bessie (Cavanaugh) Peyton; m. Robert James Gordon, June 22, 1963. BA, Boston U., 1963; MA, Harvard U., 1965, PhD, 1969. Asst. prof. English Ill. Inst. Tech., Chgo., 1968-75, assoc. prof., 1975-77, asst. dean students, 1975-78; asst. dean acad. affairs Northwestern U., Evanston, Ill., 1978-80, lectr. English, Univ. Coll., 1978—2001, assoc. dean Univ. Coll., 1980-85, sec. Econometric Soc., 1975—, exec. dir. Econometric Soc., 1985—. Mem. nat. adv. com. ALA, Chgo., 1983—86; lectr. English Northwestern U., Evanston, 2003—. Author: Seasons in the Contemporary American Family, 1984. Grantee NEH, 1971-73; project scholar NEH, 1983-86. Mem.: Phi Beta Kappa. Avocation: writing. Home: 202 Greenwood Evanston IL 60201-4714 Office: Northwestern U Dept Econs Econometric Soc Evanston IL 60208-2600 Home Phone: 847-869-3544; Office Phone: 847-491-3615. Business E-Mail: jpg@northwestern.edu.

GORDON, LEO I., hematologist, oncologist, educator; b. Milw., Nov. 24, 1947; s. Abraham and Fira (Weinstein) G.; m. Linda Robinson; children: Elizabeth, Peter. BA, U. Chgo., 1969; MD, U. Cin., 1973. Diplomate Am. Bd. Internal Medicine, 1976, Am. Bd. Internal Medicine Hematology, 1978, Am. Bd. Internal Medicine Oncology, 1979. Intern in medicine U. Chgo. Hosps., 1973-74, resident in medicine, 1974-76, fellow in hematology/oncology, 1978-79; fellow in hematology U. Minn., Mpls., 1976-78; asst. prof. medicine Northwestern U., Evanston, Ill., 1979-85, assoc. prof., 1985-95, prof. medicine, 1995—. Chief divsn. hematology/oncology, Northwestern U. Med. Sch., Chgo., 1996—. Contbr. over 125 articles and abstracts to profl. jours.; author book. Office: Northwestern U Med Sch 676 N St Clair Ste 850 Chicago IL 60611 Business E-Mail: l-gordon@northwestern.edu.

GORDON, MARK S., chemist, educator; BS, Rensselaer Poly., 1963; PhD, Carnegie-Mellon U., 1968. Postdoctoral assoc. Iowa State U., Ames, 1967—70; from asst. prof. to assoc. prof. N.D. State U., 1970—77, prof., 1977—92, Iowa State U., 1992—. Vis. prof. U. Calif., Irvine, 1978—79; chair dept. chemistry N.D. State U., 1981; vis. fellow Minn. Supercomputer Inst., 1985—86; vis. scientist, program officer theoretical and computational chemistry NSF, 1989—90; tech. advisor Air Force Office of Sci. Rsch., 1990—92; dir. N.D. EPSCoR Program, 1990—92; Ministry of Edn. vis. prof. Inst. for Molecular Sci., 1991—92. Mem.: Quantum Chemistry Program Exch., World Assn. Theoretical Organic Chemists, Am. Inst. Physics, Am. Chem. Soc., Sigma Xi. Office: 201 Spedding Hall Ames IA 50011

GORDON, MELVIN JAY, food products executive; b. Boston, Nov. 26, 1919; s. Jacob S. and Sadye Z. (Lewis) G.; m. Ellen Rubin, June 25, 1950; children: Virginia Lynn, Karen Dale, Wendy Jean, Lisa Jo. BA, Harvard, 1941, MBA, 1943. V.p. Clear Weave Hosiery Stores, Inc., Boston, 1945-50, Tenn. Knitting Mills, Inc., Columbia, 1945-56; pres. P.R. Hosiery Mills, Inc., Arecibo, 1956-61; ptnr. Manchester (N.H.) Hosiery Mills, 1946-69; chmn. bd. Tootsie Roll Industries, Chgo., 1962—, pres., 1968-69, 75-78, Hampshire Designers Inc., 1969-77, HDI Investment Corp., 1977—, MJG Inc., 1981—, Ellen Gordon Inc., 1984-88, Lisa Gordon Inc., 1987—, Wendy Gordon Inc., 1989—. Adv. com. Mfrs. Hanover Bank, N.Y.C., 1967-88. Author: Better Than Communism, 1958. Mem. Pres.'s Citizens Adv. com. Fitness Am. Youth, 1957-60, exec. com. 1959-60; del. White House Conf. Youth Fitness, 1962; co-chmn. Com. Support Psychol. Offensive, 1961-63; bd. dirs. mem. exec. com. Coun. World Tensions, N.Y.C., 1960-65; chmn. Mass. Gov.'s Com. Youth Fitness, 1958-64; bd. dirs. New Eng. Econ. Edn. Coun., 1960-63, N.H. Coun. on World Affairs, 1962-65; bd. dirs., chmn. exec. com. Citizen Exchange Corps., N.Y.C., 1964-66, hon. chmn. adv. coun. 1966-67; del. Prime Minister's Econ. Conf., Israel, 1968, 73; bd. overseers Harvard Coll., mem. vis. com. behavioral scis., 1967-71, vis. com. psychology, 1972; vis. com. Russian Rsch. Ctr., 1972-76; dir. Rensselaerville Inst., N.Y., 1966—; chmn. N.E. region m. Com. for Weizmann Inst. Sci. Rehovot, Israel, 1972-73; dir. Am. com., 1973-75; nat. trustee Nat. Symphony Orch., Washington, 1993—. Recipient Dean's award Nat. Candy Wholesalers Assn., 1978 Mem. Chief Execs. Orgn., World Bus. Coun., World Affairs Coun. Boston (treas., bd. dirs. 1966-67, v.p., bd. dirs. 1968-74), New Eng. Soc. N.Y.C., Harvard Varsity Club, Harvard Club (Boston). Clubs: Harvard (Boston); Varsity (Harvard). Office: Tootsie Roll Industries Inc 7401 S Cicero Ave Chicago IL 60629-5885

GORDON, MYRON L., federal judge; b. Kenosha, Wis., Feb. 11, 1918; m. Peggy Gordon, Aug. 16, 1942 (dec. Mar. 1973); children: Wendy, John, Polly; m. Myra Gordon, Mar. 30, 1979. BA, MA, U. Wis., 1939; LLB, Harvard U., 1942. Judge U.S. Ct. Appeals, Milw., 1951-62, Wis. State Supreme Ct., Madison, 1966-67, U.S. Dist. Ct., Milw., 1967—; now sr. judge. Office: Gordon Cntry Club Est 107 Estrella St Rancho Mirage CA 92270-3949

GORDON, PHILLIP, lawyer; b. Potgietersrus, South Africa, July 11, 1943; m. Norma Gordon. BA, U. Witwatersrand, South Africa, 1964, BA with honors, 1965; BA, Oxford U., 1967; JD, U. Chgo. Law Sch., 1969; MA, Oxford U., 1973. Bar: Ill. 1969, NY 1973 (inactive). Interim gen. counsel Strategic Hotel Capital, Chgo., 1997-98; ptnr. Perkins Coie, LLP, 2003—. Tchg. assoc. Northwestern U. Sch. Law, Chgo., 1967-68. Author: Ill. Practice Consultant, Midwest Transactional Guide, 1981. Dir. Lyric Opera Chgo.; chmn., trustee Spertus Inst. Jewish Studies, Chgo.; advising fellow Oxford U. Ctr. Socio-Legal Studies, London. Mem. ABA, Chgo. Bar Assn., Hotel Devel. Coun., Internat. Coun. Urban Land Inst. Office: Perkins Coie LLP 131 S Dearborn St Ste 1700 Chicago IL 60603-5559 E-mail: pgordon@perkinscoie.com.

GORDON, ROBERT JAMES, economics professor; b. Boston, Sept. 3, 1940; s. Robert Aaron and Margaret (Shaughnessy) G.; m. Julie S. Peyton, June 22, 1963. AB, Harvard U., 1962; MA, Oxford U., Eng., 1969; PhD, MIT, 1967. Asst. prof. econs. Harvard U., 1967-68; asst. prof. U. Chgo., 1968-73; prof. econs. Northwestern U., Evanston, Ill., 1973—, Stanley G. Harris prof. social scis., 1987—, chair econs. dept., 1992-96. Rsch. assoc. Nat. Bur. Econ Rsch., 1968—; mem. Brookings Panel Econ. Activity, 1970—; co-chmn. Internat. Seminar Macroecons., 1978-94; mem. exec. com. Conf. Rsch., Income and Wealth, 1978-83; mem. panel rev. productivity measures NAS, 1977-79; cons. bd. govs. Fed. Res. Sys., 1973-83, U.S. Dept. Treasury, 1967-80, U.S. Congl. Budget Office, 1996—, U.S. Bur. Econ. Analysis, 1999—; mem. Nat. Commn. on Consumer Price Index, 1995-97; mem. tech panel, Soc. Security Adminstrn., 2003-2007. Author: Macroeconomics, 1978, 10th edit., 2006, Milton Friedman's Monetary Framework, 1974, Challenges to Interdependent Economies, 1979, The American Business Cycle: Continuity and Change, 1986, The Measurement of Durable Goods Prices, 1990, International Volatility and Economic Growth, 1991, The Economics of New Goods, 1997, Inflation, Unemployment and Productivity, 2003; editor Jour. Polit. Economy, 1970-73. Recipient Lustrum prize Erasmus U., 1999; Marshall fellow, 1962-64; Ford Found. fellow, 1966-67; grantee NSF, 1971—2004; Guggenheim Meml. Found. fellow, 1980-81; rsch. fellow German Marshall Fund, 1985-86. Fellow AAAS, Econometric Soc. (treas. 1975—2005); mem. Am. Econ. Assn. (bd. editors 1975-77, mem. exec. com. 1981-83), Phi Beta Kappa Office: Northwestern U Dept Econs Evanston IL 60208-2600 Home Phone: 847-869-3544; Office Phone: 847-491-3616. E-mail: rjg@northwestern.edu.

GORENCE, PATRICIA JOSETTA, judge; b. Sheboygan, Wis., Mar. 6, 1943; d. Joseph and Antonia (Marinsheck) G.; m. John Michael Bach, July 11, 1969; children: Amy Jane, Mara Jo, J. Christopher Bach. BA, Marquette U., 1965, JD, 1977; MA, U. Wis., 1969. Bar: Wis. 1977, U.S. Dist. Ct. (ea. and we. dists.) Wis. 1977, U.S. Ct. Appeals (7th cir.) 1979, U.S. Supreme Ct. 1980. Asst. U.S. atty. U.S. Atty.'s Office, Milw., 1979-84, 1st asst. U.S. Atty., 1984-87, 89-91, U.S. Atty., 1987-88; dep. atty. gen. State of Wis. Dept. Justice, Madison, 1991-93; assoc. Gimbel, Reilly, Guerin & Brown, Milw., 1993-94; U.S. magistrate judge U.S. Dist. Ct. Wis., Milw., 1994—. Bd. dirs. U. Wis.-Milw. Slovenian Arts Coun., 1989—, treas., 1989—, Milw. Dance Theatre, 1993-98; bd. chair Bottomless Closet, 1999-2006. Recipient Spl. Commendation, U.S. Dept. Justice, 1986, IRS, 1988. Mem. ABA, Am. Law Inst., US Magistrate Judges (mem. advisory group 2006-), Fed. Magistrate Judges Assn. (cir. dir. 1997-2000), Milw. Bar Assn. (chair cmty. rels. com. 2000-03, Prosecutor of Yr. 1990, Disting. Svc. award 2003, Wis. Law Jour. Innovator of Yr. award 2003), State Bar Wis. (chair lawyer dispute resolution com. 1986—, chair professionalism com. 1988-00, vice chair legal edn. commn. 1994-96, Pres. award 1995), 7th Cir. Bar Assn. (chair rules and practices com. 1991-95), Ea. Dist. Wis. Bar Assn. (bd. dirs. 2004—), Assn. Women Lawyers, Profl. Dimensions (sec. 1998-00, v.p. adminstrn. 2000-02).

GORHAM, EVILLE, retired ecologist; b. Halifax, NS, Can., Oct. 15, 1925; s. Ralph Arthur and Shirley Agatha (Eville) G.; m. Ada Verne MacLeod, Sept. 29, 1948; children: Kerstin, Vivien, Jocelyn, James. BSc in Biology with distinction, Dalhousie U., 1945, MSc in Zoology, 1947, LLD (hon.), 1991; PhD in Botany, U. London, Eng., 1951; DSc (hon.), McGill U., 1993, U. Minn., 1999. Lectr. botany U. Coll., London, Eng., 1951-54; sr. sci. officer Freshwater Biol. Assn., Ambleside, Eng., 1954-58; lectr., asst. prof. botany U. Toronto, 1958-62; assoc. prof. botany U. Minn., Mpls., 1962-65, prof., 1966-75, head dept., 1967-71, prof. ecology, 1975-84, Regents' prof. ecology and botany, 1984-98, Regents' prof. emeritus, 1999—; prof., head dept. biology U. Calgary, Alta., Can., 1965-66. Mem. for Can., Internat. Commn. on Atmospheric Chemistry and Radioactivity, 1959-62; mem. vis. panel to rev. toxicology program NAS-NRC, 1974-75, mem. com. on inland aquatic ecosys. Water Sci. and Tech. Bd., 1994-96, mem. com. to evaluate indicators for monitoring aquatic and terrestrial environments Water Sci. and Tech. Bd., 1997-99, mem. com. on hydrologic sci. bd. on Atmospheric Scis. and Climate, 1998-99; mem. coordinating com. for sci. and tech. assessment environ. pollutants Environ. Studies Bd., 1975-78; mem. com. on med. and biologic effects of environ. pollutants Assembly Life Scis., 1976-77; mem. com. to recommend nat. program for assessing problem of atmospheric deposition (acid rain) President's Coun. on Environ. Quality, 1978; mem. com. on atmosphere and biosphere Bd. Agr. and Renewable Resources, 1979-81; mem. panel on environ. impact diesel impact study com. NAE-NRC, 1980-81; mem. U.S.-Can.-Mex. joint sci. com. on acid precipitation Environ. Studies Bd., NAS-NRC, Royal Soc. Can., Mex. Acad. Scis., 1981-84; mem. health and environ. rsch. adv. com. U.S. Dept. Energy, 1992-94; mem. Water Sci. and Tech. Bd. NAS-NRC, 1996-99; mem. coun. sci. advisors Marine Biol. Lab., Woods Hole, Mass., 1996-99. Mem. editl. bd. Ecology, 1965-67, Limnology and Oceanography, 1970-72, Conservation Biology, 1987-88, Ecol. Applications, 1989-92, Environ. Revs., 1992-2004; contbr. articles on limnology, ecology, and biogeochemistry to profl. jours. Bd. dirs. Acid Rain Found., 1982-87, sec.-treas. 1982-84 Recipient Regents' medal U. Minn., 1984, Benjamin Franklin medal in earth sci. Franklin Inst., Phila., 2000; Royal Soc. Can. rsch. fellow State Forest Rsch. Inst., Stockholm, Sweden, 1950-51; grantee NSF, AEC, NIH, ERDA, NASA, Dept. of Energy, NRC Can., Ont. Rsch. Found., Environment Can., Office Water Resources Rsch., Dept. Interior, Andrew W. Mellon Found., N.Y.C. Fellow AAAS, Royal Soc. Can., Am. Acad. Arts and Scis.; mem. NAS, Am. Soc. Limnology and Oceanography (G. Evelyn Hutchinson medal 1986), Ecol. Soc. Am., Internat. Assn. Theoretical and Applied Limnology, Soc. Wetland Scientists (Lifetime Achievement award 2005), Swedish Phytogeog. Soc. (hon.), Gown in Town Club. Home: 1933 E River Ter Minneapolis MN 55414-3673

GORMAN, JAMES CARVILL, manufacturing executive; b. Mansfield, Ohio, Apr. 16, 1924; s. James Carville and Ruth (Barnes) G.; m. Marjorie Newcomer, Apr. 10, 1950; children: Jeff, Gayle. BS, Ohio State U., 1949. Sales engr. Gorman Rupp Co., Mansfield, Ohio, 1949-58, sales mgr., 1958-64, pres., 1964-89, chmn., CEO, 1989-99, chmn., 1999—. Pres. Manairco, Inc., 1952-85, chmn. bd., 1985—; chmn. Mansfield Airport Commn., 1954-2000; treas. EAA Aviation Found., Oshkosh, Wis., 1973-2003. Capt. USAAF, 1942-46. Mem. Constrn. Industry Mfrs. Assn. Episcopalian. Home: PO Box 2599 Mansfield OH 44906-0599 Office: Gorman Rupp 305 Bowman St Mansfield OH 44903-1600 Office Phone: 419-755-1223. Personal E-mail: mng19sl@aol.com.

GORMAN, JOHN ROBERT, bishop emeritus; b. Chgo., Dec. 11, 1925; NA, St. Mary of the Lake, 1945, STL, 1951; PhD, Loyola U., 1971. Ordained priest Archdiocese of Chgo., 1925; ordained bishop, 1988; aux. bishop Archdiocese of Chgo., 1988—2003, aux. bishop emeritus, 2003—. Roman Catholic. Home and Office: Episcopal Vicar of Vicariate V 10731 W 131st St Orland Park IL 60462-8308 Office Phone: 708-361-4754, 708-361-0645.*

GORMAN, STEPHEN THOMAS, former state legislator; b. Fargo, ND, Dec. 4, 1924; m. Mary K. Sullivan Johnson; 3 children. Student, St. John's U., Collegeville, Minn., N.D. State Sch. Sci., Wahpeton. Chmn. Knight Printing Co., ret.; state rep. dist. 46, 1987-97. Vice chmn. fin. and taxation com.; mem. natural resources com., appropriations com., edn. and environ. divsn. com. N.D. Ho. Reps. Recipient Silver Metal award Advtg. Fedn. Fargo/Moorhead, Disting. Svc. award Jaycees. Mem. Fargo C. of C., Elks, Rotary, K.C., Am. Legion. Republican. Home: 810 Southwood Dr Fargo ND 58103-6020

GORNEY, JON L., bank executive; m. Nancy Gorney; 3 children. BS in Computer Sci., U. Dayton, Ohio, 1973. With Nat. City Corp., Cleve., 1973—77, mgmt. devel. trainee, systems officer, 1977—81, v.p., 1988—91, sr. v.p., 1991—93, exec. v.p. corp. ops. and info. svcs., 1993—. Bd. mem. Nat. Processing Inc., 2000—, chmn., CEO, 2002—; US region bd. dirs. MasterCard Internat. Trustee Elyria Cath. Found., mem. adv. bd., U. Dayton. Mem.: Bank Adminstrn. Inst., Am. Inst. Banking, KC. Office: Nat City Corp Nat City Ctr 1900 E Ninth St Cleveland OH 44114-3484 Office Phone: 216-222-2000. Office Fax: 216-575-2860.

GOROFF, DAVID B., lawyer; BA summa cum laude, U. Ill., 1982; JD, Columbia U., 1985. Bar: Ill. 1985, US Dist. Ct. (no. dist. Ill.) 1986, US Ct. Appeals (2nd, 6th & 7th cirs.) 1986, US Supreme Ct. 1986. Law clk. to Hon. Richard D. Cudahy US Ct. Appeals (7th cir.), 1985—86; ptnr. Foley & Lardner, LLP, Chgo., co-chmn. appellate practice group. Adj. prof. U. Ill. Coll. Law, Chgo.-Kent Coll. Law; instr. Ill. Inst. CLE, Nat. Inst. Trial Advocacy. Mem.: ABA, ACLU. Office: Foley & Lardner LLP Suite 2800 321 N Clark St Chicago IL 60610 Office Phone: 312-832-5160. E-mail: dgoroff@foley.com.

GORSLINE, STEPHEN PAUL, security specialist; b. Washington, Aug. 22, 1954; s. Robert William and Patricia Ann (Ketchum) G. AAS in Criminal Justice, Coll. of Lake County, 1987; BS in Criminal Justice, Madonna U., 1998. Dir. safety ops. Thielenhaus Corp., Novi, Mich., 1998-99; with US Dept. of Def. Vol. Nat. Rep. Com., Washington, 1992. Staff sgt. USAF, 1977-82. Mem. Safety/Security Mgmt. Assn. (exec. dir. 1996-99), Fraternal Order Police. Roman Catholic. Avocations: collecting stamps, old coins and postcards. E-mail: stevegorsline@yahoo.com.

GORTER, JAMES POLK, investment banker; b. Balt., Dec. 10, 1929; s. T. Poultney and Swan (Deford) G.; m. Audrey Fentress; children: James Jr., David F., Mary H. AB, Princeton U., 1951; postgrad., London Sch. Econ., 1951-52. Ptnr. Goldman, Sachs & Co., 1956-88, ltd. ptnr., 1989-99; chmn. Baker, Fentress & Co., Chgo., 1987—. Bd. dirs. Caterpillar Inc. Trustee Lake Forest Coll. Served with USN, 1952-55. Mem.: Chicago Commonwealth, Chicago, Economic, Commercial. Office: Baker Fentress & Co 1 Rockefeller Plz Fl 25 New York NY 10020-2102

GOSCHKA, MICHAEL JOHN, state legislator; b. Saginaw, Mich., Oct. 21, 1953; s. Arthur Clarence and Ethel Marie (Alden) G.; m. Maryann Louise Sielaff, 1979. Student, Delta Coll., 1972, Cornerstone Coll., 1974-77. Forklift operator Dow Corning Corp., 1984-92; mem. Mich. Ho. of Reps. from 94th dist., Lansing, 1993-98, Mich. Senate from 33rd dist., Lansing, 1999—. Vice chmn. tourism & recreation com. Mich. Ho. Reps., 1993—, agriculture & forestry com., 1993—, edn. com., 1993—, mental health com., 1993—, house oversight com., 1993—, ethics com., 1993—, tax policy com., 1995—. Exec. com. Saginaw County Rep. Com., 1982—, del. to state, 1982—, rep. precinct, 1982—. Mem. Mich. Farm Bur., Sons Am. Legionnaires, Saginaw Right to Life. Home: 16393 W Schroeder Rd Brant MI 48614-8781 Office: 1010 Farnum Bldg 125 W Allegan St Lansing MI 48933-1702

GOSLEE, DWIGHT J., agricultural products executive; BS in Acctg., U. Minn. CPA. Formerly with Touche Ross & Co.; asst. corp. controller to v.p./controller internat. divsn. ConAgra, Inc., Omaha, 1985—94, sr. v.p. mergers and acquisitions, CIO, 1994—. Office: ConAgra Inc 1 ConAgra Dr Omaha NE 68102

GOSLIN, THOMAS B., career officer; BA in Polit. Sci., La. State U., 1970; grad., Officer Tng. Sch., 1970; student pilot tng., Columbus AFB, Miss., 1971-72; student, Squadron Officer Sch., 1974; MA in Guidance and Counseling, La. Tech U., 1975; student, Air Command and Staff Coll., 1975, Air War Coll., 1980, Armed Forces Staff Coll., 1981, Can. Nat. Def. Coll., 1988, Duke U., 1995. Commd. 2d lt. USAF, 1970, advanced through grades to lt. gen., 2002; forward air controller Tan Son Nhut Air Base, S. Vietnam, 1972-73; pilot, instr. pilot 71st Air Refueling Squadron, Barksdale AFB, La., 1973-76; air staff tng. officer, intelligence threat assessment Pentagon, Washington, 1976-77, various positions, 1993-94; pilot, instr. pilot, flight comdr. 62d Bomb Squadron, Barksdale AFB, 1977-80; stationed at Hdqs. USAF, Pentagon, Washington, 1981-84, 94-95, now dep. dir. programs, dep. chief staff plans and programs; fighter lead-in tng. Holloman AFB, N.Mex., 1984; pilot 162d Tactical Fighter Group Air N.G., Tucson, 1984; various comdr. assignments, 1984-93; asst. dir. ops. Hdqs. Air Combat Command, Langley AFB, Va., 1995-96; comdr. 509th Bomb Wing, Whiteman AFB, Mo., 1996—98; dep. dir. prog., dep. chief of staff for plans and programs HQ USAF, Washington, 1998—99; dir., ops. HQ US Space Command, Peterson AFB, Colo., 1999—2001; commander Space Warfare Ctr., Schriever AFB, Colo., 2001—02; dep. commander US Strategic Command, Offutt AFB, Nebr., 2002—. Decorated Legion of Merit, D.F.C. with oak leaf cluster, Air medal with seven oak leaf clusters, Rep. Vietnam Gallantry Cross.

GOSNELL, DAVINA J., dean, nursing educator; BSN, U. Pitts.; MS, PhD, Ohio State U. Dean Sch. Nursing, prof. Kent (Ohio) State U. Chair Ohio Pub. Health Coun. Recipient U. Pitts. Sch. Nursing Disting. Alumni award. Mem. ONA, NLN, STT, GSA, Delta Kappa Gamma. Office: Kent State U Sch Nursing PO Box 5190 Kent OH 44242-0001 E-mail: dgasnell@kent.edu.

GOSS, HOWARD S(IMON), financial executive; b. Nov. 17, 1933; s. Maurice Jack and Sally (Yanov) G.; m. Roberta Jacobs, June 19, 1955; children: Robert, David, Marcy, Scott BS, DePaul U., 1956, PhD, 2005. CPA, Ill. Auditor Steel Channon & Co., Chgo., 1955-60; contr. Transco Inc., Chgo., 1960-67, pres., 1967—, dir., 1980—2002, chmn. bd., 1989, ret. chrmn. cons., 2002—. Dir., Graycor Inc Mem. fin. com. New Trier Rep. Orgn., Winnetka, Ill., 1977-93; chmn. adv. coun. DePaul U. Coll. Commerce, bd. trustees, 1987, trustee DePaul U., 1988, exec. com., 1992; mem. adv. coun. Jewish Vocat. Svc., 1991; bd. dirs. Chgo. Crime Commn., 1993; chmn. alumni forum Coll. Commerce; chief Crusader United Way, Chgo., 1989; trustee Adler Planetarium and Astronomy Mus., 1996, treas., 1997, chmn. bd. trustees, 2000-2002 Recipient Humanitarian award Nat. Jewish Hosp., Denver, 1980, Disting. Alumni award DePaul U., 1993. Mem. AICPA, Ill. Soc. CPAs, Young Pres.'s Orgn., Chgo. Pres.'s Orgn., Std. Club, Econ. Club, Nat. Honor Soc. Commerce, Beta Gamma Sigma Office: Transco Inc 55 E Jackson Blvd Ste 2100 Chicago IL 60604-4166 Home Phone: 847-835-0992; Office Phone: 312-427-2818.

GOSS, RICHARD HENRY, lawyer; b. Worcester, Mass., Oct. 24, 1935; s. George Lee and Marion Bernadine (Henry) G.; children: Margaret Elizabeth, Richard Henry Eric, Emily Charlotte; m. Eleanor Kirsten Berg, Nov. 27, 1971. Student, Mich. State U., 1952-54; BA in Econs., Clark U., 1956; JD, Northwestern U., 1959. Bar: Ill. 1959, U.S. Supreme Ct. 1970. Asst. cashier Nat. Blvd. Bank of Chgo., 1959-61; v.p. Paul D. Speer & Assocs. Inc., Mcpl. Fin. Cons., Chgo., 1962-68; mng. ptnr. Chapman and Cutler, Attys. at Law, Chgo., 1968-95. Bd. dirs. Japan Am. Soc. Chgo., 1987-96, v.p., chmn. mem. com., 1988-90; chmn. bd. dirs. Brays Island Plantation Colony, Inc., 1995-97. Mem. Black Diamond Golf Club. Republican. Episcopalian. Avocations: hunting, skeet, sporting clays and trap shooting, travel, oriental studies. Home: 3843 N Baltusrol Path Lecanto FL 34461

GOTT, WESLEY ATLAS, art educator; b. Buffalo, Mar. 6, 1942; s. Raymond and Rowena (Pettitt) Gott; m. Alice Blalock, May 26, 1972; children: Andrew, Deidre. BS, SW Mo. State U., 1965; M in Ch. Music, SW Theol. Sem., 1969; MFA, George Washington U., 1975; postgrad., Nova U. Tchr. ceramics Springfield Art Mus., Mo., 1964—66; min. music Terrace Acres Bapt. Ch., Ft. Worth, 1966—70; min. music and youth First Bapt. Ch., Wheaton, Md., 1970—75; asst. prof. art S.W. Bapt. U., Bolivar, Mo., 1975—79, assoc. prof., chmn. art dept., 1979—. Judge art contests H.S., Bolivar, 1978—. Christmas sculpture with lights, 1981—84. Recipient Parkway Disting. Prof. award, 2002—03. Mem.: Mid-Am. Coll. Art Assn., Coll. Art Assn. Am., Cmty. Concert Assn., Nat. Trust for Historic Preservation, Smithsonian Assocs., Phi Mu Alpha, Alpha Gamma Theta. Baptist. Avocations: hunting, fishing, boating, tennis, golf. Home: 127 W Maupin St Bolivar MO 65613-1946 Office: SW Bapt U 1600 University Ave Bolivar MO 65613-2597 Home Phone: 417-326-2208; Office Phone: 417-328-1650. Business E-Mail: wgott@sbuniv.edu.

GOTTFRIED, MICHAEL D., paleontologist, educator; BS in Paleontology, U. Calif., Berkeley; MPhil in Systematics and Ecology, U. Kans., Lawrence, 1987, PhD in Systematics and Ecology, 1991. Curator, paleontology Calvert Marine Mus., Solomons, Md.; curator, vertebrate paleontology Mich. State U. Mus., East Lansing, 1997—; asst. prof., geol. scis. to assoc. prof., dept. zoology Mich. State U., 1997—. Contbr. scientific papers to profl. publs.; contbr. (TV documentaries) Discovery Channel Shark Week, 2000, others. Achievements include research in lamnid sharks, Cretaceous-age vertebrates, and vertebrate evolution in the southern hemisphere. Office: Mich State Univ MSU Museum East Lansing MI 48824-1045 Office Phone: 517-432-5780. Office Fax: 517-432-2846. Business E-Mail: gottfrie@msu.edu.

GOTTLIEB, GIDON ALAIN GUY, law educator; b. Paris, Dec. 9, 1932; m. Antoinette Rozoy Countess de Roussy de Sales, May 12, 1965. LLB with honors, London Sch. Econs., 1954, Cambridge U., Eng., 1956, diploma in comparative law, 1958; LLM, Harvard U., 1957, SJD, 1962. Bar: Called to bar Lincoln Inn, London 1958. Lectr. govt. Dartmouth Coll., 1960-61; assoc. firm Shearman & Sterling, NYC, 1962-65; mem. faculty N.Y. U. Law Sch., 1965-76; Leo Spitz prof. internat. law and diplomacy emeritus U. Chgo. Law Sch., 1976—. UN rep. Amnesty Internat., 1966-72; mem. founding com. World Assembly Human Rights, 1968; adv. bd. Internat. League Rights of Man; disting. vis. fellow Hoover Instn., Stanford, Calif., 1991-94, 97—. Author: The Logic of Choice: An Investigation of the Concepts of Rule and Rationality, 1968, Nation Against State, 1993. Fellow N.Y. Coun. on Fgn. Rels. (sr. fellow, dir., Middle East Peace Project 1988-94); mem. Am. Soc. Internat. Law, Century Assn. (N.Y.C.). Office: U Chgo Law Sch 1111 E 60th St Chicago IL 60637-2776

GOTTLIEB, MARK, state official; b. Dec. 11, 1956; m. Linda S. Gottlieb; children: Sarah, Kimberly, Elizabeth, Christopher. BSCE, U. Wis., Milw., M of Civil Engring. Registered profl. engr. Dir. pub. works, village engr. Village of Grafton; alderman Port Washington, 1991—97; mayor, 1997—; state assemblyman Wis., 2002—. Pres. Common Cause, 1996—97; mem. Ozaukee County Pub. Transit Adv. Com.; mem. steering com. Southeastern Wis. Mcpl. Execs. With USN, 1974—78, Vietnam. Named Elected Ofcl. of Yr., Wis. Park and Recreation Assn., 1997. Mem.: ASCE, Am. Pub. Works Assn. (statewide pedestrian safety citizen adv. com.), Am. Legion. Republican. Roman Catholic. Office: State Capitol Rm 304 N PO Box 8952 Madison WI 53708-8952

GOTTLIEB, RICHARD DOUGLAS, media executive; b. Davenport, Iowa, June 12, 1942; s. David and Elaine Gottlieb; m. Harriet Barg; children: Michael, Jason, Allison, Meghan. BS, U. Ariz., 1964. Mgr.-in-tng. Madison (Wis.) Newspapers, Inc., 1965-68, prodn. coordinator, 1968-72, treas., dir., 1972-80, gen. mgr., 1973-80; pub. Racine (Wis.) Journal-Times, 1980-85; v.p. Lee Enterprises, Inc., Davenport, 1985-86, pres., chief oper. officer, 1986—. Bd. dirs. Madison Newspapers, Inc., NAPP Systems, Inc., San Marcos, Calif., Newspaper Advt. Bur., Washington. Avocations: hunting, tennis. Office: Lee Enterprises Incorporated 201 N Harrison St Ste 600 Davenport IA 52801-1918

GOTTRON, FRANCIS ROBERT, III, small business owner; b. Youngstown, Ohio, Dec. 26, 1953; s. Francis R. Jr. and Norma J. (Giba) G.; m. Joyce L. Garling, Nov. 25, 1975. BSBA cum laude, Youngstown State U., 1978. With Commonwealth Land Title Youngstown, Inc., 1972-87, Lender's Svc., Inc., 1979—, Title Agy. Michaels, 1984—; examiner delinquent tax Mahoning County Prosecutor's Office, 1989—; owner, prin. Mahoning County Recorder's Office, Youngstown, 1978—; examiner Fed. Title Agy., 1982—; pres. M&G Title Search Inc. Appraiser Probate Ct., 1989—. Chmn. zoning bd. Jackson Twp., 2005—. Democrat. Lutheran. Avocations: fantasy baseball, camping, forestry, environment. Home: 9165 New Rd North Jackson OH 44451-9707 Office: PO Box 268 Youngstown OH 44501-0268 Office Phone: 330-744-3272. Personal E-mail: f_gottron@yahoo.com.

GOTTSCHALK, ALEXANDER, radiologist, educator; b. Chgo., Mar. 23, 1932; s. Louis R. and Fruma (Kasden) G.; m. Jane Rosenbloom, Aug. 13, 1960; children: Rand, Karen, Amy. BA magna cum laude, Harvard U., 1954; MD, Washington U., St. Louis, 1958. Diplomate: Am. Bd. Radiology, Am. Bd. Nuclear Medicine. Intern U. Ill. Research and Edn. Hosps., Chgo., 1958-59; resident U. Chgo., 1959-62, asst. prof., 1964-66, assoc. prof., 1966-68, prof. radiology, 1968-74, chmn. dept. radiology, 1971-72; research assoc. Donner Lab., Lawrence Radiol. Lab., Calif., 1962-64; dir. Franklin McLean Meml. Research Hosp., 1967-74; prof. and dir. nuclear medicine Sch. Medicine Yale U., New Haven, 1974-77, acting chmn. radiology, 1980-81, vice-chmn. radiology, 1977-89; prof. radiology Mich. State U., East Lansing, 1990—. Contbr. chpts. to books, articles to publs. in field. Fleischner lectr., 1983 Fellow Am. Coll. Radiology, Am. Coll. Chest Physicians; mem. Radiol. Soc. N.Am. (2d v.p. 1977, Gold medal 2004), Assn. Univ. Radiologists (pres. 1971, Gold medal 1987), Soc. Nuclear Medicine (pres. 1974-75, Cassen prize 2006, Cassen lectr. 2006), Am. Roentgen Ray Soc., Fleischner Soc. (treas. 1978-83, pres. 1989-90), Phi Beta Kappa, Alpha Omega Alpha. Home: 4246 Van Atta Rd Okemos MI 48864-3137 Office: Radiology Bldg Rm 120 Mich State U East Lansing MI 48824-1303 Business E-Mail: alg@rad.msu.edu.

GOTTSCHALK, GUY, agricultural products executive; Grad., U. Wis. Owner, pres. Gottschalk Cranberry, Inc., Wisconsin Rapids, Wis., Biron Cranberry Co., Wisconsin Rapids. Mem. bd. regents U. Wis., Wis., 1998—. Office: Conifer Ctr 412 Dalay Ave Wisconsin Rapids WI 54494

GOTTSCHALK, JOHN E., newspaper publishing executive; b. 1943; Pub. Sidney (Nebr.) Newspaper, 1966-74; with Omaha World Herald Co., 1975—, pres., CEO, 1989—. Bd. dir. Creighton U. Council chmn. Boy Scouts of America, 1994—95, regional pres., 1996—97; bd. of dirs. Omaha Symphony Assn., 1999—. Recipient Citizen of the Year award, Boy Scouts of America, 1998, Outstanding Svc. Profession award, U. Nebr. Alumni, 1998. Mem.: Omaha Performing Arts Soc. (chmn. 2003—). Office: Omaha-World Herald Co World-Herald Sq Omaha NE 68102-1138

GOTTSCHALK, STEPHEN ELMER, retired lawyer; b. Rochester, Minn., Oct. 9, 1947; s. Elmer H. and Ruth F. (Thurley) G.; m. Lorilyn J. Dopp, Feb. 14, 1970; children: Andrew Stephen, Stephanie Beth, Lorissa Christine, Michael Donald. BS, Valparaiso U., 1969, JD, 1972. Bar: Minn. 1972, U.S. Dist. Ct. (Minn.) 1972. Jud. clk. Minn. Supreme Ct., St. Paul, 1972—73; assoc. Dorsey & Whitney, Minn., 1973—78, ptnr., 1979—2006, co-chmn., employee benefits dept., 1986—91, 1998—2006. Adj. prof. employee benefits Sch. Law U. Minn., 1998—. Bd. dirs. Habitat for Humanity of Minn. Recipient Svc. award Valparaiso Alumni Assn., 1986. Office: Dorsey & Whitney 50 S 6th St Ste 1500 Minneapolis MN 55402-1498 Office Fax: 612-340-2777. Business E-Mail: gottschalk.steve@dorsey.com.

GOTTSCHALL, JOAN B., judge; b. Oak Ridge, Tenn., Apr. 23, 1947; d. Herbert and Elaine (Reichbaum). BA cum laude, Smith Coll., Mass., 1969; JD, Stanford Univ., Calif., 1973. Bar: Ill. 1973. Assoc. Jenner & Block, 1973-76, 78-81, ptnr., 1981-82; staff atty. Fed. Defender Program, 1976-78, Univ. of Chgo., Office of Legal Counsel, 1983-84; magistrate judge U.S. Dist. Ct. (no. dist.) Ill., Chgo., 1984—96, judge, 1996—. Mem. vis. com., past chair Divinity Sch., U. Chgo., 1984—97. Bd. dirs. Martin Marty Ctr., U. Chgo. Div. Sch., Ill. Humanities Coun.; chmn. Dist. 10 Selection Com., 2005—07. Mem.: Chgo. Bar Assn. (Rhodes scholarship). Office: US Dist Ct No Dist Ill Everett McKinley Dirksen Bldg 219 S Dearborn St Ste 2356 Chicago IL 60604-1877

GOTTSCHLICH, GARY WILLIAM, lawyer; b. Dayton, Ohio, Aug. 27, 1946; s. William Frederick and Rosemary Teresa Gottschlich; m. Sharon Melanie Plunkett, Oct. 7, 1978; children: David W., Andrew J., Thomas M. BS, U. Dayton, 1968; cert., Univ. Coll., London, 1970; JD, U. NNotre Dame, 1971. Bar: Ohio 1971. Asst. pros. atty. Montgomery County, Dayton, 1971-73; assoc. Young, Pryor, Lynn & Jerardi, Dayton, 1973-80, ptnr., 1980-84, Louis & Froelich, Dayton, 1984-87, Porter, Wright, Morris & Arthur, Dayton, 1987-97, Gottschlich & Portune, Dayton, 1997—. Capt. USAR. Mem. ABA, ATLA, Ohio Bar Assn. (bd. govs. litigation sect.), Dayton Bar Assn. (treas. 1981-82), Miami Valley Trial Lawyers Assn. (founding), Rotary Club (pres. 2002—). Roman Catholic. Avocations: golf, sailing, squash. Home: 5260 Little Woods Ln Dayton OH 45429-2124 Office: Gottschlich & Portune LLP The Historic Armory 201 E Sixth St Dayton OH 45402-2836

GOUGEON, JOEL, state legislator; b. Bay City, Mich., Jan. 13, 1943; m. Kaye; 1 child, Amy. Grad., Gen. Motors Inst., 1966. Commr. Bay City Bd. Commrs., 1984-90; mem. Mich. Senate from 34th dist., Lansing, 1993—. Families com. State Capitol, Lansing, Mich., 2002—, mental health & human svc. com., 2002—, v.chmn. farming com., 2002—, agribusiness & food sys. com., 2002—, chmn. cmty. health com., 2002—, retirement com., 2002—, chmn. capital outlay com., 2002—, mem. family ind. agy., 2002—. Mem. Bay City Lions, Bay County Crime Stoppers, Elks, Am. Legion, Vietnam Vets, John Glenn Boosters. Address: 1005 Farnum Bldg PO Box 30036 Lansing MI 48909-7536

GOULD, JOHN PHILIP, economist, educator; b. Chgo., Jan. 19, 1939; s. John Philip and Lillian Gould; children: John Philip III, Jeffrey Hayes; m. Kathleen A. Carpenter. BS with highest distinction, Northwestern U., 1960; MBA, U. Chgo., 1963, PhD, 1966. Faculty U. Chgo., 1965—, prof. econs., 1974—, disting. service prof. econs., 1984—, dean Grad. Sch. Bus., 1983-93, v.p. planning, 1988—91; Steven G. Rothmeier prof., disting. svc. prof. econs., 1996—; exec. v.p. Lexecon Inc., Chgo., 1994—2004; pres. Cardean, Chgo., 1999—2001. Vis. prof. Nat. Taiwan U., 1978; spl. asst. econ. affairs to sec. labor, 1969-70; spl. asst. to dir. Office Mgmt. and Budget, 1970; past chmn. econ. policy adv. com. Dept. Labor; bd. dirs. DFA Investment Dimensions Group, Harbor Capital Advisors, 1993-; Chgo. bd. of Trade, 1986-89; chmn. Pegasus Funds, 1996-99, Milw. Mutual, 1997—, Unext.com, 1999—2006; mem. adv. com. competitive markets Chgo. Merc. Exch., 2004—; editor Jour. Law and Econs., 2006—. Author: (with E. Lazear) Microeconomic Theory, 6th edit, 1989; contbg. author: Microeconomic Foundations of Employment and Inflation Theory, 1970; editor: Jour. of Bus., 1976-83, Jour. Fin. Econs., 1976-83, Jour. Acctg. and Econs., 1978-81, Jour. Law and Econs., 2006—; contbr. articles to profl. jours. Bd. dirs. United Way/Crusade of Mercy, 1986-91, Lookingglass Theatre Co., 1994-96. Recipient Wall St. Jour. award, 1960, Am. Marketing Assn. award, 1960; Earhart Found. fellow. Mem. Am. Econs. Assn., Econometric Soc. (chmn. local arrangements 1968), Econ. Club of Chgo., Comml. Club of Chgo., Beta Gamma Sigma. Home: 100 E Huron St Apt 2105 Chicago IL 60611-5903 Office: U Chgo Grad Sch Bus 5807 S Woodlawn Chicago IL 60637-1511

GOULD, PHILLIP LOUIS, engineering educator; b. Chgo., May 24, 1937; m. Deborah Paula Rothholtz, Feb. 5, 1961; children: Elizabeth, Nathan, Rebecca, Joshua. BS, U. Ill., 1959, MS, 1960; PhD, Northwestern U., 1966. Structural designer Skidmore, Owings & Merrill, Chgo., 1960-63; prin. structural engr. Westenhoff & ovick, Chgo., 1963-64; NASA trainee Northwestern U., Evanston, Ill., 1964-66; asst. prof. civil engring. Washington U., St. Louis, 1966-68, assoc. prof., 1968-74, prof., 1974—, chmn. dept. civil engring., 1978-98, Harold D. Jolly prof. civil engring., 1981—. Vis. prof. Ruhr U., Fed. Republic Germany, 1974-75, U. Sydney, Australia, 1981, Shanghai Inst. Tech., Peoples Republic of China, 1986; dir. Earthquake Engring. Rsch. Inst., exec. coun. Internat. Assn. for Shell and Spatial Structures, pres. Great Lakes chpt. and New Madrid chpt. Earthquake Engring. Rsch. Inst. Author: Static Analysis of Shells: A Unified Development of Surface Structures, 1977, Introduction to Linear Elasticity, 1984, Finite Element Analysis of Shells of Revolution, 1985, Analysis of Shells and Plates, 1987, 2d edit., 1999; co-author: Dynamic Response of Structures to Wind and Earthquake Loading, 1980; co-editor: Environmental Forces on Engineering Structures, 1979, Natural Draught Cooling Towers, 1985; editor: Engineering Structures, 1979—. Dir. Earthquake Engring. Rsch. Inst., 1993—95; vice chmn. Mo. Seismic Safety Commn., 1998—99, chmn., 2000—01; St. Louis regional dir. Mid-Am. Earthquake Ctr. Recipient Sr. Scientist award Alexander von Humboldt Found., Fed. Republic Germany, 1974-75 Fellow ASCE (bd. dirs. St. Louis sect. 1985-87, Otto Nutli award, Profl. Recognition award); mem. Am. Soc. Engring. Edn., Internat. Assn. Shell Structures, Structural Engrs. Assn. Ill. (Outstanding Engr. in Edn. award), Civil Engring. Alumni Assn. U. Ill., Urbana-Champaign (Disting. Alumnus award). Office: Washington U 1130 Dept Civil Engring 1 Brookings Drive Saint Louis MO 63130-1130 Home Phone: 314-647-0388. Business E-Mail: pgoul@seas.wustl.edu.

GOURLEY, SARA J., lawyer; b. 1955; AB cum laude with honors, Ripon Coll., 1977; JD, Univ. Ill., 1980. Bar: Ill. 1980, US Dist. Courts (no. dist. Ill. and dist. of Ariz.), US Ct. of Appeals (4th, 7th, 8th. and 11th circuits). Ptnr. product liability litig. Sidley Austin LLP (formerly Sidley Austin Brown & Wood LLP), Chgo., mem. exec. com., practice area team leader, products & liability. Mem. Univ. Ill. Law Rev., 1978—80. Bd. mem. Family Focus. Mem.: ABA, Def. Rsch. Inst. (steering com., drug and device litigation sect.). Office Phone: 312-853-7694. Office Fax: 312-853-7036. Business E-Mail: sgourley@sidley.com.

GOVE, SAMUEL KIMBALL, retired political science professor; b. Walpole, Mass., Dec. 27, 1923; Student, Mass. State Coll., 1941—43; BS in Econs, U. Mass., 1947; MA in Polit. Sci, Syracuse U., 1951. Research asst. govt. and pub. affairs U. Ill., 1950-51, research asso., 1951-54, mem. faculty, 1954—, prof. polit. sci., 1966-89, prof. emeritus, 1989—; dir. Inst. Govt. and Pub. Affairs, 1967-85, dir. emeritus, 1987—. Staff asst. Nat. Assn. Assessing Officers, 1949; mem. rsch. staff Ill. Commn. Study State Govt., 1950—51; staff fellow Nat. Mcpl. League, 1955—56; exec. asst. Ill. Auditor Pub. Accounts, 1957; program coord. Ill. Legis. Staff Intern Program, 1962—70; mem. com. financing higher edn. Ill. Master Plan Higher Edn., 1963; mem. Ill. Commn. Orgn. Gen. Assembly, 1965—69, 1970—73, Ill. Commn. State Govt., 1965—67; cons. elections ABC, 1964, 66, 68; chmn. Champaign (Ill.) County Econ. Opportunity Coun., 1966—67; state legis. rsch. fellow Am. Polit. Sci. Assn., 1966—68; cons. Am. Council Edn., 1966—67; sec. Local Govts. Commn., 1967—69; staff dir. Ill. Constn. Study Commn., 1968—69; exec. sec. Gov. Ill. Constn. Research Group, 1969—70; mem. Ill. Constn. Study Commn., 1969—70; chmn. Citizens Task Force on Constl. Implementation, 1970—71; mem. Gov. Elect's Task Force on Transition, 1972, 1991—92; adv. coun. Ill. Dept. Local Govt. Affairs, 1969—79, Gov.'s Human Resources, 1991—93, Ill. Commn. on Regulatory Rev., 1994—98, Ill. Bd. Higher Edn., 1998—2005, Ill. Issues Bd., 1974—2003, chmn. bd. dirs., 1974—93. Lt. j.g. USNR, 1943—46. Fellow Nat. Acad. Pub. Adminstrn.; mem. AAUP (past chpt. pres., mem. nat. com. R 1969-75, 78-84, nat. coun. 1978-80), Am. Polit Sci. Assn., Am. Soc. Pub. Adminstrn. (past chpt. chmn.; chmn. univs. govtl. rsch. conf. 1969-71), Govtl. Rsch. Assn. (dir. 1969-71), Ill. Hist. Soc., Midwest Polit. Sci. Assn. (v.p. 1978-80), Nat. Mcpl. League (council 1972-80, 81-84, 85), Nat Civic League (coun. advisors 1987-89), Cosmos Club. Home: 2006 Bruce Dr Urbana IL 61801-6419 Office: 1007 W Nevada St Urbana IL 61801-3812 Personal E-mail: s-gove@uiuc.edu.

GOVERN, MAUREEN, information technology executive; B in Math., No. Ill. U.; M in operations rsch., Stanford U. Sr. positions Bell-Northern Rsch., NYNEX Sci. and Tech.; joined Bell Labs., 1978; v.p. network architecture and tech. network sys. group Motorola Inc., v.p. advanced tech. devel., global telecom., solutions sector; chief tech. officer Convergys Corp., 2002—05, AOL, 2005—06. Named one of Premier 100 Info. Tech. Leaders, Computerworld mag., 2004.

GOVINDJEE, biophysics, biochemistry, and biology professor; b. Allahabad, India, Oct. 24, 1933; arrived in US, 1956, naturalized, 1972; s. Vishveshwar Prasad and Savitri Devi Asthana; m. Rajni Varma, Oct. 24, 1957; children: Anita Govindjee, Sanjay Govindjee. BSc, U. Allahabad, 1952, MSc, 1954; PhD, U. Ill., 1960. Lectr. botany U. Allahabad, 1954-56; grad. fellow U. Ill., Urbana, 1956-58, rsch. asst., 1958-60, USPHS postdoctoral trainee biophysics, 1960-61, mem. faculty, 1961—, assoc. prof. botany and biophysics, 1965-69, prof. biophysics and plant biology, 1969-99, disting. lectr. Sch. Life Scis., 1978, emeritus prof. biophysics, plant biology and biochemistry, 1999—. Author (with E. Rabinowitch): Photosynthesis, 1969; editor: Bioenergetics of Photosynthesis, 1975, Photosynthesis: Energy Conversion by Plants and Bacteria; Carbon Assimilation and Plant Productivity, 2 vols., 1982 (Russian transl. 1987); co-editor: The Oxygen Evolving System of Photosynthesis, 1983, Light Emission by Plants and Bacteria, 1986, Excitation Energy and Electron Transfer in Photosynthesis, 1989, Molecular Biology of Photosynthesis, 1989, Photosynthesis: From Photoreactions to Productivity, 1993, Concepts in Photobiology: Photosynthesis and Photomorphogenesis, 1999, Chlorophyll a Fluorescence: A Signature of Photosynthesis, 2004, Discoveries in Photosynthesis, 2005; editor Hist. Corner: Photosynthesis Rsch., 1989—; guest editor spl. issue Biophys. Jour., 1972, Photochemistry and Photobiology, 1978, Photosynthesis Research, 1993, 96, 2002-04; editor-in-chief Photosynthesis Rsch., 1985-88; series editor: Advances in Photosynthesis and Respiration, vol. 1, 1994, vol. 2, 1995, vols. 3, 4 and 5, 1996, vols. 6 and 7, 1998, vol. 8, 1999, vol. 9, 2000, vols. 10 and 11, 2001, vol. 12, 2002, vol. 13, vol. 14, 2003, vols. 15, 16, 17, 19, 2004, vols. 18, 20, 22, 2005, vols. 23-25, 2007, vols. 26-28, 2008; contbr. articles to profl. jours., also Sci. Am. Founder, Govindjee and Rajni Govindjee Award for excellence in Biol. Rsch. U. Ill., Urbana-Champaign. Recipient Lifetime Achievement award, Rebeiz Found., 2007; Fulbright Scholar, 1956—61, 1996—97. Fellow AAAS, NAS (India); mem. Am. Soc. Plant Biologists, Biophys. Soc. Am., Am. Soc. Photobiology (coun. 1976, pres. 1981), Internat. Photosynthesis Soc. (exec. com., publ. com. 1995-01, hon. pres. 13th Internat. Photosynthesis Congress 2004, Comm. award, 2007), Sigma Xi (emeritus). Achievements include discovery of several new fluorescing forms of chlorophyll a; the presence of chlorophyll a in what is now called Photosystem II; the two-light effects on chlorophyll a fluorescence; Emerson Enhancement in NADP reduction; the time (in picoseconds) taken by the reaction center of Photosystem II to undergo primary charge separation; the theory for the molecular mechanism of thermoluminescence in plants; an understanding of chlorophyll a fluorescence changes with time; the unique role of bicarbonate ions in the electron and proton transfer on the electron acceptor side of Photosystem II. Avocation: photography. Home Phone: 217-337-0627. Business E-Mail: gov@life.uiuc.edu.

GOW, JOE, academic administrator; BA, Pa. State U., Phd in Speech Comm.; MA in Speech Comm., U. Ala. Dir. Comm. Studies Program Alfred U., 1990—2001, assoc. dean. Coll. Liberal Arts and Scis., 1996—2001; dean Coll. Liberal Arts Winona State U., 2001—04; provost, dean Coll. Liberal Arts and Scis. Nebr. Wesleyan U., Lincoln, 2004—06, interim pres., 2006; chancellor U. Wis., La Crosse, 2007—. Editl. bd. Jour. Popular Music and Soc. Mem.: Nat. Coun. Colls. Arts and Scis. (pres.). Avocation: running. Office: U Wis-La Crosse 1725 State St 135 Graff Main Hall La Crosse WI 54601 Office Phone: 608-785-8004. E-mail: gow.joe@uwlax.edu.

GOWEN, RICHARD JOSEPH, electrical engineer, educator, retired academic administrator; b. New Brunswick, NJ, July 6, 1935; s. Charles David and Esther Ann (Hughes) G.; m. Nancy A. Applegate, Dec. 28, 1955; children: Jeff, Cindy, Betsy, Susan, Kerry. BS in Elec. Engring., Rutgers U., 1957; MS, Iowa State U., 1961, PhD, 1962. Registered profl. engr., Colo. Rsch. engr. RCA Labs., Princeton, NJ, 1957; commd. USAF; ground electronics officer Yaak AFB, Mont., 1957-59; instr. USAF Acad., 1962-63, rsch. assoc., 1963-64, asst. prof., 1964-65, assoc. prof., 1965-66, tenured assoc. prof. elec. engring., 1966-70, tenured prof., 1971-77, dir., prin. investigator NASA instrumentation group for cardiovascular studies, 1968-77; mem. launch and recovery med. team Johnson Space Ctr., ASA, 1971-77; v.p., dean engring., prof. SD Sch. Mines and Tech., Rapid City, 1977-84, pres., 1987—2003, Dakota State U., Madison, 1984-87; exec. dir. Homestate Lab. Conversion Project, Rapid City, SD, 2003—04, SD Sci. Tech. Authority, Rapid City, 2004; ret., 2004. Prin. investigator program in support space cardiovascular studies NASA, 1977-81; co-chmn. Joint Industry, Nuc. Regulatory IEEE, Am. Nuc. Soc. Probabilistic Risk Assessment Guidelines for Nuc. Power Plants Project, 1980-83; mem. Dept. Def. Software Engring. Inst. Panel, 1983; mem. Congl. Web-based Edn. Commn., 1999—; mem. SD Bd. Edn., 2003—; bd. dirs. Mount Rushmore Inst. Contbr. articles to profl. jours.; patentee in field. Bd. dirs. St. Martins Acad., Rapid City, SD, Journey Mus., 1998-2001, Greater Rapid City Econ. Devel. Partnership, 1991-2003, SD Bd. Edn., 2003—; mem. US Web Edn. Commn., 1999-2001. Fellow IEEE (Centennial Internat. pres. 1984, bd. dirs., 1976-75), IEEE Found. (bd. dirs., pres. 2005—), USAB/IEEE Disting. Contbns. to Engring. Professionalism award 1986); mem. Am. Assn. Engring. Socs. (bd. dirs., 1983-87, chmn. 1988), Rapid City C. of C. (bd. dirs. 1998-2003), Rotary, Sigma Xi, Phi Kappa Phi, Tau Beta Phi, Eta Kappa Nu (bd. dirs. 1994, pres. 1998-2000) Pi Mu Epsilon. Roman Catholic. Home: 1609 Palo Verde Dr Rapid City SD 57701-4461 Home Phone: 605-342-5066; Office Phone: 605-484-2763. E-mail: rgower@msn.com.

GOWLER, VICKI SUE, editor-in-chief; b. Decatur, Ill., Apr. 16, 1951; d. Carroll Eugene and Audra Janet (Briggs) G. BS in Journalism, U. Ill., 1973. Reporter Iroquois County Daily Times, Watseka, Ill., 1973-75, Quincy (Ill.) Herald-Whig, 1975-78; from reporter to mng. editor Miami (Fla.) Herald, Stuart, Delray Beach, West Palm Beach, 1089-88; asst. news editor Knight-Ridder Washington Bur., 1988-93; exec. editor Duluth (Minn.) News-Tribune, Knight-Ridder newspaper, 1978—2001, editor and v.p., 1993—97, editor, 2001—; mng. editor Pioneer Press, Knight-Ridder newspaper, 1997—2001, editor, 2001—05; sr. v.p. and editor St. Paul Pioneer Press, Knight-Ridder newspaper, 2001—05; editor & v.p. Idaho Statesman, Boise, 2005—. Recipient numerous awards for journalistic works, including RFK award, state AP awards in all categories. Mem. Am. Soc. Newspaper Editors. Methodist. Avocations: reading, tennis, playing clarinet, travel, visiting with her family. Office: Idaho Statesman PO Box 40 Boise ID 83707 Office Phone: 208-377-6403. E-mail: vgowler@idahostatesman.com.

GRABER, DORIS APPEL, political scientist, writer, editor; b. St. Louis, Nov. 11, 1923; d. Ernest and Martha (Insel) Appel; m. Thomas M. Graber, June 15, 1941; children: Lee Winston, Thomas Woodrow, Jack Douglas, Jim Murray, Susan Doris AB, Washington U., St. Louis, 1941, MA, 1942; PhD, Columbia U., 1947. Feature writer St. Louis County Observer, Univ. City Tribune, 1939—41; civilian dir. U.S. Army Ednl. Reconditioning Program, Camp Maxey, Tex., 1943—45; editor legal mags. Commerce Clearing House, Chgo., 1945—46; lectr. polit. sci. Northwestern U., 1948—49, U. Chgo., 1950—51, rsch. assoc. Ctr. for Study Am. Fgn. and Mil. Policy, 1952—71; lectr. polit. sci. North Park Coll., 1952; mem. faculty U. Ill., Chgo., 1964—, assoc. prof. polit. sci., 1964—69, prof., 1970—; editor textbooks Harper & Row, Evanston, 1956—63. Vis. prof. Harvard U., 1996 Author: The Development of the Law of Belligerent Occupation, 1949, 68, Crisis Diplomacy: A History of U.S. Intervention Policies and Practices, 1959, Public Opinion, The President and Foreign Policy, 1968,

Verbal Behavior and Politics, 1976, Mass Media and American Politics, 1980, 84, 89, 93, 96, 2001, 2005, Crime News and the Public, 1980, (with others) Media Agenda Setting in a Presidential Election, 1981, Processing the News: How People Tame the Information Tide, 1984, 88, 94, Public Sector Communication: How Organizations Manage Information, 1992; editor, contbr. The President and the Public, 1982; editor, contbr.: Media Power in Politics, 1984, 90, 94, 2000, 2006; editor: Political Comm., 1992-98, founding editor emeritus, 1998—, mem. editl. bd., 2001—; editor: (with others) The Politics of News: The News of Politics, 1998, 2007, Processing Politics: Learning from Television in the Internet Age, 2001 (Goldsmith Book prize 2003), The Power of Communication, 2003; book rev. editor Polit. Psychology, 1998—; mem. editl. bd. Polit. Sci. Quarterly, 1978—, Human Comm. Rsch., 1979-80, Pub. Opinion Quarterly, 1980-84, 93-98, Jour. Comm., 1985-91, 99—, Social Sci. Quarterly, 1989-2003, P.S.: Polit. Sci. and Politics, 1990-93, Discourse and Soc., 1990—, Discourse and Comm., 2006, Orgnl. Comm: Emerging Perspectives, 1994—, Jour. Health Comm., 1995-98, Harvard Internat. Jour. Press/Politics, 1995—, Acta Politica: Internat. Jour. Polit. Sci., 1997—, Comm., Soc. and Politics Series, Cambridge U. Press, 1999—, Polit. Comm., 2001—, Media and Am. Politics Ency., 2003—; contbr. articles to profl. jours Recipient Disting. Alumna award, Washington U., 2001, Univ. Scholar award, U. Ill., Chgo., 2003—. Mem. LWV, Am. Assn. Pub. Opinion Rsch., Midwest Assn. Pub. Opinion Rsch. (coun. 1978-83, program chmn. 1978-79, pres. 1980-81, Career award 1988), Midwest Polit. Sci. Assn. (past pres. 1972-73, coun. 1973-74, program sect. chair 1979, Career award 1994), Am. Polit. Sci. Assn. (coun. 1978-79, v.p. 1980-81, program chmn. 1984, chmn. polit. comm. sect. 1989-91, chmn. editl. bd. Polit. Sci. 1992-94), Internat. Polit. Sci. Assn., Nat. Comm. Assn. (Career award, 2006), Internat. Commn. Assn. (divsn. program chmn. 1978-80, divsn. chmn. 1980-82, chmn. program 1990, chmn. pre-program 2004, Career award 1996), Assn. Edn. for Journalism, Acad. Polit. Sci., Am. Acad. Polit. and Social Sci., Internat. Soc. Polit. Psychology (coun. 1992-93, 95-98, co-program chmn. 1993-94, pres. 1995-96, Career award, 2007), Phi Beta Kappa (pres. Iota of Ill. chpt. 1991-92), Pi Sigma Alpha, Pi Alpha Alpha Home: 2895 Sheridan Pl Evanston IL 60201-1725 Office: U Ill 1007 W Harrison St Chicago IL 60607-7135 Office Phone: 312-996-3108. Business E-Mail: dgraber@uic.edu.

GRABER, RICHARD WILLIAM, ambassador, lawyer; b. Lakewood, Ohio, July 31, 1956; s. Richard Allen and Lynn Carol (Hurschman) G.; m. Alexandria Ahlquist Richardson, Apr. 28, 1984; children: Scott Bailey, Erik Richard. AB magna cum laude, Duke U., 1978; JD, Boston U., 1981. Bar: Wis. 1981. Atty. Reinhart Boerner Van Deuren orris & Rieselbach, S.C., Milw., 1981—2006, pres., CEO, 2004—06; US amb. to Czech Republic US Dept. State, Prague, 2006—. Bd. governors, Wis. Patient Compensation Fund, 1988-97; chmn., Wis. Rep. Party, 1999-2006, fin. chmn., 1993-99; mem. exec. com. North Shore Rep. Club, Milw., 1988—, Reps. of Wis., 1991; mem. Am. Coun. Young Polit. Leaders, 1990; candidate for Wis. Assembly, 1990; chmn. Kasten for Senate com. 1993; mem. bd. appeals, Village of Shorewood, 1991—, bd. trustees, Medical Coll. Wis., 1997—. Mem. Rotary (pres. Milw. 1988-89, Paul Harris fellow 1990). Avocations: politics, softball, basketball. Office: US Embassy Amb 5630 Prague Pl Washington DC 20521

GRABER, THOMAS M., orthodontist, researcher; b. St. Louis, May 27, 1917; Diplomate Am. Bd. Orthodontics. DMD, Washington U., St. Louis, 1940; MS in Dentistry, orthwestern U., 1946, PhD in Anatomy, 1950; PhD (hon.), U. Gothenberg, 1989; DSc (hon.), Washington U., 1991, U. Mich., 1994, U. Kunming, 1996, Aristotle U., Thessaloniki, Greece, 2005. Diplomate Am. Bd. Orthodontics (Recognition award 1990, Dewel award, 1992). Mem. faculty Northwestern U. Dental Sch., 1946-58, assoc. prof. orthodontics, 1954-58; dir. research Northwestern U. Dental Sch. (cleft lip and palate Inst.), 1947-58; assoc. attending orthodontist Children's Meml. Hosp., Chgo., 1951-58; vis. lectr. U. Mich. Dental Sch., 1958-67; dir. Kenilworth Research Found., Ill., 1967—; prof. orthodontics Zoller Dental Clinic; pediatrics research assoc. prof. anthropology and anatomy U. Chgo., 1969-81, assoc. prof. plastic and reconstructive surgery, 1980-82; research scientist ADA Research Inst., Chgo., 1980-90; dir. G.V. Black Inst. for Continuing Edn., 1967—; vis. prof. U. Mich., 1984-94; clin. prof. orthodontics U. Ill. Coll. Dentistry, Chgo., 1994—. Northcroft lectr., Birmingham, Eng., 1989; cons. in field. Author textbooks, articles; editor-in-chief Am. Jour. Orthodontics, 1985-2000, World Jour Orthodontics, 2000-07. Served as capt. Dental Corps AUS, 1941-45. Decorated Japanese Order of the Sacred Treasure; recipient Alumni Merit award Northwestern U., 1977; named Disting. Alumnus Washington U., 1980; NIH grantee, 1954, 56-60, 76, 77, 79, 80, 85, 86. Fellow Royal Coll. Surgeons (Eng.), Am. Coll. Dentists, Internat. Coll. Dentists; mem. Am. Dental Soc., Ill. Dental Soc., Am. Assn. Orthodontists (gen. chmn. 1960, 77, 80, founding mem., chmn. coun. on orthodontic edn. and audio visual com. 1962, 67, gen. chmn. jour. 1977, trustee, Grieve Meml. award 1964, 84, Disting. Service award 1970, Ketcham award 1975, Salzmann award 1979, 75th Anniversary citation 1990, Mershon award 1989, Horace Hayden award 1991, Jarabak Internat. Teaching and Rsch. award 1994, Heritage award 1998, 99), Internat. Assn. Research (chmn. Chgo. sect. 1973-74), Chgo. Orthodontists Assn. (pres. 1961-62), European Orthodontists Soc.(hon. life), Ill. Orthodontists Soc. (pres. 1969-70, Outstanding Tchg. award 1999), Angle Soc. (pres. 1968), Japan Orthodontists Soc., World Fedn. Orthodontists (hon., Millenium award 2000), Ill. Soc. Orthodontists, SAR. Presbyterian. Home: 2895 Sheridan Pl Evanston IL 60201-1725 Office: U Ill Coll Dentistry 801 S Paulina St # Mc842 Chicago IL 60612-7210 Office Phone: 312-996-2293. Personal E-mail: tmgraber@comcast.net. Business E-Mail: tgraber@uic.edu.

GRABOW, STEPHEN HARRIS, architecture educator; b. Bklyn., Jan. 15, 1943; s. Philip and Ida (England) G.; 1 child, Nicole Elizabeth. BArch., U. Mich., 1965; MArch., Pratt Inst., 1966; postgrad., U. Calif.-Berkeley, 1966-67; PhD, U. Wash., 1973. Architect-planner U.S. Peace Corps, Tunisia, 1967-69; regional planning cons. Teheran, Iran, 1969; asst. prof. architecture U. Ariz., 1969-70; teaching assoc. U. Wash., 1970-72; lectr. town and regional planning Duncan of Jordanstone Coll. Art, U. Dundee, Scotland, 1972-73; asst. prof. architecture and urban design U. Kans.-Lawrence, 1973-76, assoc. prof., 1976-82, prof., 1982—, dir. architecture, 1979-82, 83-86; vis. fellow U. Calif.-Berkeley, 1977; research and design cons. Design Build Architects, Lawrence; bd. dirs. Assn. Collegiate Schs. Architecture, 1982-87. Vis. lectr. Royal Danish Acad. Fine Arts, Copenhagen, 1987-88. Author: Christopher Alexander and the Search for a New Paradigm in Architecture, 1983; mem. editorial bd.: Jour. Archtl. Edn., 1982-84. Recipient award Nat. Endowment for Arts, 1974, citation for excellence in design rsch. NEA, 1980, Biennial Svc. award Denmark's Internat. Studies Program, 1997, Bradley Tchg. award in architecture U. Kans., 1998; Fulbright Scholar award, 1987-88; NEH fellow, 1976-77. Mem. Nat. Archtl. Research Council (appointee 1986-87). Home: 1518 Crossgate Dr Lawrence KS 66047-3504 Office: U Kans Sch Architecture & Urban Design 1465 Jayhawk Blvd Lawrence KS 66045-7614 Office Phone: 785-864-3186. Business E-Mail: sgrabow@ku.edu.

GRABOWSKI, JON, real estate company executive; b. 1981; Sales Johnson & johnson; pres., COO Esquire Properties, Detroit. Named one of 40 Under 40, Crain's Detroit Bus., 2006. Office: Esquire Properties 2900 E Jefferson Detroit MI 48207 Office Phone: 313-580-2200.

GRACE, RICHARD EDWARD, engineering educator; b. Chgo., June 26, 1930; s. Richard Edward and Louise (Koko) Grace; m. Consuela Cummings Fotos, Jan. 29, 1955; children: Virginia Louise, Richard Cummings(dec.). BS in Metall. Engring., Purdue U., West Lafayette, Ind., 1951; PhD, Carnegie Inst. Tech., Pitts., 1954. Asst. prof. Purdue U., West Lafayette, Ind., 1954—58, assoc. prof., 1958—62, prof., 1962—2000, head sch. materials sci. and metall. engring., 1965—72, head divsn. interdisciplinary engring. studies, 1970—82, head freshman engring. dept., asst. dean engring., 1981—87, v.p. student svcs., 1987—95, dir. undergrad. studies program, 1995—2000, prof. emeritus, v.p. emeritus, 2000—. Apptd. Ind. Commn. on Aging by Gov. of Ind., 2005—; cons. to Midwest industries. Author: When Every Day Is Saturday, 2002; contbr. articles to profl. jours. Pres. Lafayette Symphony Found. Bd., 1993-95. Named Sagamore of Wabash, Gov. of Ind., 1995. Fellow Am. Soc. Metals (tchr. award 1962), Am. Soc. Engring. Edn. (Centennial medallion 1993), Accreditation Bd. Engring. and Tech. (past dir. and officer engring. edn. and accreditation com., related engring. com., Grinter award 1989); mem. Minerals, Metals and Materials Soc. (bd. dirs. 1987-90), Lafayette Country Club, Rotary, Elks, Tau Beta Pi, Omicron Delta Kappa, Phi Gamma Delta. Home: 2175 Tecumseh Park Ln West Lafayette IN 47906-2118 Office: Purdue Univ Neil Armstrong Hall Sch Materials Engring 701 W Stadium Ave West Lafayette IN 47907-2045 Office Phone: 765-496-7384. Business E-Mail: regrace@purdue.edu.

GRACE, WALTER CHARLES, retired prosecutor; b. Elmira, NY, Mar. 4, 1947; s. Claude Henry and Grace Anne (Richardson) G.; m. Barbbara Lynn Eaglen, Oct. 3, 1981; children: Katherine Anne, Charles Brigham. BA History, Duke U., 1969; JD, U. Tenn., 1972. Bar: Ill., 1972; U.S. Dist. Ct. (ea. and so. dists.) Ill., 1972. Asst. state's atty. Jackson County, Murphysboro, Ill., 1972-73; assoc. Donald R. Mitchell Law Office, Carbondale, Ill., 1973-74; atty. Jackson County Pub. Defender, Murphysboro, 1974-77; ptnr. Lockwood & Grace, Carbondale, 1977-78, pvt. practice, 1978-79; ptnr. Hendricks, Watt & Grace, Murphysboro, 1979-82; assoc. Feirich, Schone, Mager, Green & Assocs., Carbondale, 1982-83, Feirch, Schoen, Mager, Green & Assocs., Carbondale, 1983-88; state's atty. Jackson County State's Atty., Murphysboro, 1988-93; U.S. Atty. U.S. Atty.'s Office, Fairview Heights, Ill., 1993—2002. Chmn. Jackson County Child Advocacy Adv. Bd., 1988-93; adv. bd. Ill. State Violent Crime Victim's Adv. Bd., 1988-90; com. mem. Jackson County Juv. Justice Task Force, 1988-93; exec. com. Ill. State's Atty.'s Assn., 1991-93; legis. com. Ill. Sate's Atty.'s Assn., 1992-93; co-chmn. Jackson County SAFE Policy/Gang Policy Interagy. Steering Com. Adv. Bd., 1991-93; master So. Ill. Am. Inn. of Ct., 1992—; others. Active NAACP, Carbondale; mem. Jackson County Heart Fund Campaign, 1976-77; bd. dirs. Carbondale United Way, 1978-80, capt. campaign drive, profl. div., 1980; mem. planning com. John A. Logan Coll.-Jackson County Bar Assn. Continuing Edn. Programs; mem. adv. com. to Corrections and Law Enforcment Programs, So. Ill. U. Sch. of Tech. Careers, 1978-89; mem. Hill House Board, Inc., 1979-84; pres. 1980-82; lector St. Francis Xavier Ch., Carbondale. Mem. Jackson County Bar Assn. (sec. 1978-79, pres. 1980-81), Ill. State Bar Assn. (mem. criminal law sect., family law sect., tort law sect.), ABA (family law and criminal law sects.), Assn. Trial Lawyers of Am., Nat. Legal Aid and Defender Assn., Ill. Pub. Defenders Assn., So. Ill. Am. Inns of Ct. (barrister 1993-95). Democrat. Roman Catholic. Avocations: golf, swimming, cooking, enology.

GRACEY, DOUGLAS ROBERT, internist, educator, pulmonologist, physiologist; b. Ft. Dodge, Iowa, Aug. 7, 1936; s. Warren Robert and Areta Mary (Thompson) G.; m. Edith Ann Haas, Dec. 23, 1961; children— Laura, Douglas Robert BA, Coe Coll., 1958; MD, Northwestern U., 1962; MS, U. Minn., 1968. Diplomate Am. Bd. Internal Medicine. Intern Cook County Hosp., Chgo., 1962-63; resident Mayo Grad. Sch. Medicine, 1963-66, 68-69; asst. prof. medicine Northwestern U. Med. Sch., 1969-75; assoc. prof. medicine Mayo Med. Sch., Rochester, Minn., 1975-83, prof., 1983—, vice chmn. pulmonary div., 1982-87; vice chmn. for practice dept. medicine Mayo Clinic, Rochester, 1983-93, dir. critical care medicine div., 1985-89, chmn. revenue systems com., 1993—2005, chmn. divsn. pulmonary and critical care medicine. Author: (with W.W. Addington) Tuberculosis, 1972, Flying Lessons, Ambulances and orther Air Force Vignettes, 2000; editor: Pulmonary Diseases in the Adult, 1981; contbr. articles to profl. jours. Trustee Coe Coll., 1976-92. Capt. USAF, 1966—68. Decorated USAF Commendation Medal; Am. Thoracic Soc. tng. fellow, 1968-69. Fellow ACP, Am. Coll. Chest Physicians; mem. Nat. Assn. Med. Direction Respiratory Care (past pres.), Masons, Shriners. Republican. Presbyterian. Office: Mayo Clinic Emeritus Chmn Div Pulmonary & Critical Care Med Rochester MN 55901 Personal E-mail: dgracey1@msn.com.

GRACEY, PAUL C., JR., lawyer, utilities executive; b. 1959; BBA with distinction, U. Mich., 1981; JD cum laude, U. Calif., 1985; diploma in Sr. Exec. Fin. Progam, Templeton Coll., Oxford, Eng., 1998. Bar: Calif., Ill. V.p., gen. counsel Edison Mission Energy Ltd., London, 1993—2000, Midwest Generation, Chgo., 2000—02; v.p. Nicor Inc. and Nicor Gas, Naperville, Ill., 2002—, gen. counsel, 2002—, sec., 2002—, sr. v.p., 2006—. Mem.: Calif. Bar Assn., Ill. Bar Assn. Office: Nicor Inc 1844 Ferry Rd Naperville IL 60563 Office Phone: 630-983-8676.

GRACZ, GREGORY L., labor union administrator; AA, Milw. Area Tech. Coll.; grad., Marquette U. Firefighter City of Milw. Fire Dept., 1978—, capt., 1998—; pres., contract adminstr. Milw. Profl. Fire Fighters Assn. Local 215. Mem. bd. regents U. Wis., Wis., 1999—. Office: Milw Profl Fire Fighters Assn Local 215 5625 W Wisconsin Ave Milwaukee WI 53213

GRADE, JEFFERY T., manufacturing executive; b. Chgo., 1943; BS, Ill. Inst. Tech., 1966; MBA, DePaul U., 1972. With Plasto Mfg. Corp., 1965-66, Motorola Inc., 1966-67, Bell and Howell, 1967-68, Ill. Cen. Gulf R.R., 1968-73; v.p. fin. IC Industries, 1973-83; with Harnischfeger Corp., Milw., 1983-99, pres., COO, bd. dirs., 1986—, CEO, 1991-99, also chmn., CEO. Served with USN, 1865-66. Office: Harnischfeger Industries Ste 2780 100 E Wisconsin Ave Milwaukee WI 53202-4127

GRADWOHL, DAVID MAYER, anthropology educator; b. Lincoln, Nebr., Jan. 22, 1934; s. Bernard Sam and Elaine (Mayer) G.; m. Hanna Rosenberg, Dec. 29, 1957; children: Steven Ernst, Jane Mayer Nash, Kathryn Mayer Flaminio. BA in Anthropology and Geology, Nebr. U., 1955; postgrad., Edinburgh U., Scotland, 1955-56; PhD in Anthropology, Harvard U., 1967. Instr. anthropology Iowa State U., Ames, 1962-66, asst. prof., 1966-67, assoc. prof., 1967-72, coord. anthropology, 1968-75, chair Am. Indian studies program, 1981-85, prof. anthropology, 1972—; asst site supr. Winchester (Eng.) Excavations Com., 1965. Advisor Nat. Register Hist. Sites, Des Moines, 1969-88, Office of State Archaeologist, Iowa City, 1983—; commr. Ames Hist. Preservation Commn., 1988-91. Co-author: The Worlds Between Two Rivers, 1987, 2d edit., 2000, Exploring Buried Buxton, 1990; co-author (audio visual programs) Iowa's Indian Heritage, 1972, Blacks and Whites in Buxton, 1986, Outside In: African American History in Iowa, 1838-2000, 2001; editor, contbr. Still Running: A Tribute to Maria Pearson, Yankton Sioux, 2005. With U.S. Army, 1957-59. Fulbright fellow U.S. Ednl. Commn., Edinburgh, 1956, Touro Nat. Heritage Trust fellow, 1997-98; recipient Faculty Citation, Iowa State Alumni Assn., Ames, 1980, Charles Irby Disting. Svc. award Nat. Assn. Ethnic Studies, 1990, Career Achievement award for undergrad. tchg. AMOCO, 1992, Alumni Achievement award U. Nebr., 2001; Touro Nat. Heritage Trust fellow, 1997-98. Fellow Am. Anthropol. Assn., Assn. Iowa Archaeologists (chair 1977-78), Nebr. Assn. Profl. Archaeologists; mem. Soc. Am. Archaeology, Soc. Hist. Archaeology, Nebr. Jewish Hist. Soc., Nebr. State Hist. Soc., Plains Anthropol. Soc. (bd. dirs. 1969-72, 87-90, Disting. Svc. award 1998), Nat. Assn. Ethnic Studies (mem. editorial bd. 1987—), Iowa Archaeol. Soc. (mem. editl. bd. 1992—, Keyes-Orr Disting. Svc. award 1997), Iowa Jewish Hist. Soc. (co-founder, bd. dirs. 1996—), State Hist. Soc. Iowa (Peterson/Harlan Lifetime Achievement award 2005) Democrat. Jewish. Avocations: hiking, mountain climbing, music. Home: 2003 Ashmore Dr Ames IA 50014-7804 Office: Iowa State U Dept Anthropology Ames IA 50011-0001 Business E-Mail: gradwohl@iastate.edu.

GRADY, JOHN F., federal judge; b. Chgo., May 23, 1929; s. John F. and Lucille F. (Shroder) G.; m. Patsy Grady, Aug. 10, 1968; 1 child, John F. BS, Northwestern U., 1952, JD, 1954. Bar: Ill. 1955. Assoc. Sonnenschein, Berkson, Lautmann, Levinson & Morse, Chgo., 1954-56; asst. U.S. atty. No. Dist. Ill., 1956-61, chief criminal divsn., 1960-61; assoc. Snyder, Clarke, Dalziel, Holmquist & Johnson, Waukegan, Ill., 1961-63; practice law Waukegan, 1963-76; judge U.S. Dist. Ct. (no. dist.) Ill., Chgo., 1976-86, chief judge, 1986-90, sr. judge, 1994—. Mem. com. criminal law U.S. Jud. Conf., 1982-87, adv. com. civil rules, 1984-90, chair, 1987-90; mem. bench book com. Fed. Jud. Ctr., 1988-93; mem. Nat. State-Fed. Jud. Coun., 1990-92, Jud. Panel on Multidist. Litigation, 1992-2000. Assoc. editor: Northwestern U. Law Rev. Mem. Phi Beta Kappa Office: US Dist Ct Rm 2286 219 S Dearborn St Ste 2286 Chicago IL 60604-1802

GRAEBER, CLYDE D., former state legislator; b. Aug. 29, 1933; m. Pauline Graeber. BA, U. Tulsa, 1954, JD, 1959. City commr. Leavenworth, Kans., 1978-84, mayor Kans., 1983-84; Kans. state rep. Dist. 41, 1985-97; chmn. Rep. House Caucus; lawyer, banker, 1996—; sec. of health & environment Kansas City, 1999—. Mem. Am. Legis. Exch. Coun., Okla. Bar Assn. Home: 2400 Kingman St Leavenworth KS 66048-4230

GRAEBNER, CAROL F., diversified financial services company executive, lawyer; b. Ridgway, Pa., Dec. 15, 1953; BA in Internat. Rels. cum laude, Dickinson Coll., 1975; JD, Am. U., 1978. Bar: Pa. 1978, Tex. 1982, N.Mex. 2003. Assoc. Eckert Seamens Cherin & Mellott, Pitts., 1978—82; staff atty. through gen. counsel Global Power subsidiary Conoco Inc., 1982—98; sr. v.p., gen. counsel Duke Energy Internat., 1998—2003; exec. v.p., gen. counsel Dynegy Inc., 2003—06, H&R Block Inc., Kansas City, 2006—. Editor (mng.): Am. Univ. Law Rev. Bd. dir., Houston div. Am. Heart Assn.; bd. dir. Internat. Inst. Edn. Mem.: ABA, Am. Corp. Counsel Assn., State Bar N.Mex., State Bar Tex. Office: H&R Block Inc 1 H&R Block Way Kansas City MO 64105 Office Phone: 816-854-5450. Business E-Mail: carolgraebner@hrblock.com.

GRAF, TRUMAN FREDERICK, agricultural economist, educator; b. New Holstein, Wis., Sept. 18, 1922; s. Herbert and Rose (Sell) G.; m. Sylvia Ann Thompson, Sept. 6, 1947; children: Eric Kindley, Siri Lynne, Peter Truman. BS, U. Wis., 1947, MS, 1949, PhD, 1953. Mktg. specialist, coop. agt. USDA and U. Wis., 1948-50; instr. agrl. econs. U. Wis., Madison, 1951-53, asst. prof., 1953-56, assoc. prof., 1956-61, prof., 1961-85, prof. emeritus, 1985—. Expert witness, 1982—; mem. Gov.'s Com. on Wis. Dairy Mktg.; mem. 3-man team to make mktg. analysis in Nigeria, USDA, 1962, made U.S. milk mktg. study, 1971; made mktg. analyses in 13 Carribbean countries, 1964; made mktg. analysis U. Wis., Mex., 1965; made mktg. analyses U.S. Ednl. Found., Finland, 1970, Rumanian Ministry Edn., U.S. Dept. State, Rumania, USSR, 1976, France, 1981, Russia, 1992, Ukraine, 1992, 98, Bulgaria, 1992, 93, Hungary, 1993, Poland, 1993, Zimbabwe, Africa, 1994, Ukraine, 1998, Kazakhstan, 1999, Uganda, 2000, US Treasury Dept., Cuba, 2002, Amenia, 2003, Czech Republic, 2004, Honduras, 2005, others; rschr. in field. Contbr. articles to profl. jours. Active Cub Scouts; bd. dirs. Univ. Houses Assn., 1955-56, Univ. Hill Farm Assn., 1958-59, Univ. Hill Farm Swim Club, 1959-60, Oakwood Retirement Homes, 1992-2001. Recipient Uhlman award Chgo. Bd. Trade, 1952, recipient Man of Yr. award World Dairy Expn., 1976, Disting. Svc. award U. Wis. Extension, 1981, Coop. Builder award Fedn. Coops., 1982, Internat. Trade Spl. award Gov. Wis., 1983. Mem. AARP (econ. security adv. com.), Am. Agrl. Econs. Assn. (Published Rsch. award 1974), Am. Mktg. Assn., Madison Naval Res. Assn. (pres. 1968-72), Am. Econ. Assn., Hist. Soc., United Dairy Industries Assn. (adv. com.), Wis. Fedn. Coops., Lakeshore Federated Dairy Coop., Wis. Ret. Educators Assn. (bd. dirs.), Wis. Coalition of Annuitants (vice chair), Civil War Club, People to People (pres.), Kiwanis (pres. Golden K). Lutheran. Home: 405 Samuel Dr Madison WI 53717-2144 Office: U Wis Dept Agriculture Madison WI 53706

GRAHAM, ALLISTER P., food products executive; b. Toronto, Can. With The Oshawa Group Ltd., Toronto, Canada, 1960—99, pres., COO, 1985—90, CEO, 1990—98, chmn., 1990—99; past chmn. Nash Finch Co., Mpls. Past chmn. Retail Coun., Canada, Food Distbr. Intern., Washington; dir. Manulife Fin. Corp.; trustee Associated Brands Income Fund.

GRAHAM, BRUCE S., dean, educator; b. Windsor, Ont., Can. naturalized, U.S. m. Linda Graham; children: Todd, Beth. Student, U. Windsor, 1966; DDS, U. Toronto, 1970; MS, cert. in prosthodontics, Ohio State U., 1974; MEd, Dalhousie U., 1989. Instr. Ohio State U. Coll. Dentistry, U. Toronto; asst. to assoc. dean acad. affairs Dalhousie U., Halifax, Nova Scotia, Canada; dean, prof. restorative dentistry U. Detroit-Mercy Sch. Dentistry, 1992—2000; dean U. Ill. Chgo. Coll. Dentistry, 2000—. Spkr. in field; bd. dirs. Friends of the Nat. Inst. of Dental and Craniofacial Rsch., 2005—. Fellow: Am. Coll. Dentists; mem.: Internat. Assn. Dental Rsch., Am. Assn. Dental Rsch., ADA. Office: 801 South Paulina Chicago IL 60612 Office Phone: 312-996-1040. Office Fax: 321-996-1022. Business E-Mail: bgraham@uic.edu.

GRAHAM, CHARLES, research psychologist; b. Atlantic City, Nov. 21, 1937; s. Charles Leroy and Margery (Kaplan) G.; m. Sally Jones, Dec. 8, 1962 (div. Apr. 1974); children: Ronna, Christopher, Glen; m. Mary R. Cook, May 18, 1996; 1 child, Sheri J. BS, U. Md., 1966; MS, Pa. State U., 1968, PhD, 1970. Rsch. assoc. Inst. Pa. Hosp., Phila., 1970-74; instr., lectr. dept. psychiatry U. Pa., Phila., 1970-74; sr. exptl. psychologist Midwest Rsch. Inst., Kansas City, 1974-78, prin. exptl. psychologist, 1979-94, sr. advisor for life scis., 1994—, prin. advisor for life scis., 1998—. Mgr. Bioelectromagnetics Rsch. Program, 1998—; tech. review panel Dept. of Energy, EPA, NIH, WHO, Internat. Commn. on Non-Ionizing Radiation Protection. With U.S. Army, 1960-62. NIH grantee, 1975-2000. Mem. Am. Psychol. Assn., Soc. Psychophysiol. Rsch., Claude Bernard Soc., Bioelectromagnetics, Sigma Xi. Avocations: travel, photography, gardening. Office: Midwest Rsch Inst 425 Volker Blvd Kansas City MO 64110-2299 E-mail: mcg@planetkc.com, cgraham@mriresearch.org.

GRAHAM, DAVID F., lawyer; b. Chgo., Sept. 14, 1953; BA with high honors, Haverford Coll., 1975; JD, U. Chgo., 1978. Bar: Ill. 1978. Law clk. to Hon. Charles Levin Mich. Supreme Ct., 1978-79; Bigelow teaching fellow, lectr. on law U. Chgo., 1979-80; with Sidley Austin Brown & Wood LLP, Chgo., 1980—, ptnr. comml. litig., 1986—, and mem. exec. com. Past gen. counsel Chgo. Coun. of Lawyers. Adv. bd. Legal Aid Soc., Chgo. Mem.: Phi Beta Kappa. Office Phone: 312-853-7596. Office Fax: 312-853-7036. Business E-Mail: dgraham@sidley.com.

GRAHAM, DIANE E., newspaper editor; b. Gary, Ind., June 29, 1953; d. William M. and Mary Jane (Shreve) Graham; m. Daniel Kevin Miller, Oct. 18, 1986. B, Drake U., 1974. Reporter Des Moines Tribune, 1974—78, Des Moines Register, 1978—84, bus. editor, 1984—86, dep. mng. editor, 1986—95, mng. editor, 1995—. Pres. Iowa Freedom of Info. Coun., Des Moines, 1992—93; chair adv. bd. Drake U. Sch. Journalism, Des Moines, 1995—. Recipient Davenport fellow for bus./econ. reporting, U. Mo., 1983. Avocations: playing pipe organ, gardening. Office: Des Moines Register 715 Locust St Des Moines IA 50309-3767

GRAHAM, JAMES, state legislator; b. Ironton, Mo., June 22, 1960; AS in Bus. Mgmt., Mineral Area Coll., 1980; degree, Mo. FFA State Farmer. Former tchr., Frederickstown, Mo.; state rep. Dist. 106 Mo. Ho. of Reps., 1991—. Mem. agr. com., appropriations com., correctional insts. com., mines and mining com., banks and fin. instns. com., budget com., A+ schs. com., capital improvements and leasing oversight com.; cattle farmer. Del. Am. Coun. Young Polit. Leaders, China and Taiwan, 1993; active Little Vine United Bapt. Ch. Mem. NRA, Marcus Lodge 110 AF&AM (master), Optimist Club, Rotary Club, C. of C. Office: Mo Ho of Reps Rm 105B 201 W Capitol Ave Jefferson City MO 65101 Fax: 573-751-5123. E-mail: jgraham@servics.state.mo.us.

GRAHAM, JAMES LOWELL, federal judge; b. 1939; BA, JD summa cum laude, Ohio State U., 1962. Pvt. practice Crabbe, Brown, Jones, Potts & Schmidt, Columbus, Ohio, 1962-69, Graham, Dutro, Nemeth, and predecessors, Columbus, 1969-86; judge U.S. Dist. Ct. (so. dist.) Ohio, Columbus, 1986—. Faculty Ohio Jud. Coll., Ohio Legal Inst. Chmn. Ohio Bar Examiners, 1974, Devel. Commn. City of Columbus, 1976-77; mem. legal svcs. Salvation Army of Columbus, 1967-77, legal sect. United Way Campaign, 1976-80. Fellow Am. Coll. Trial Lawyers; mem. Capital U. Coll. of Law Assn. (dean's coun.), Ohio State U. Alumni Assn. Office: US Dist Ct 169 US Courthouse 85 Marconi Blvd Columbus OH 43215-2823

GRAHAM, JEWEL FREEMAN, social worker, lawyer, educator; b. Springfield, Ohio, May 3, 1925; d. Robert Lee and Lula Belle Freeman; m. Paul N. Graham, Aug. 8, 1953; children: Robert, Nathan. BA, Fisk U., 1946; student, Howard U., 1946-47; MS in Social Svc. Adminstrn., Case Western Res. U., 1953; JD, U. Dayton, 1979; LHD (hon.), Meadville-Lombard Theol. Sch., 1991. Bar: Ohio; cert. social worker. Assoc. dir. teenage program dept. YWCA, Grand Rapids, Mich., 1947-50, coord. met. teenage program Detroit, 1953-56; dir. program for interracial edn. Antioch Coll., Yellow Springs, Ohio, 1964-69, from asst. prof. to prof., 1969-92, prof. emeritus, 1992—. Mem. Ohio Commn. on Dispute Resolution and Conflict Mgmt., 1990-92. Mem. exec. com. World YWCA, Geneva, 1975-83, 87-95, pres., 1983; bd. dirs. YWCA of the U.S.A., 1970-89, pres., 1979-85; bd. dirs. Antioch U., 1994-96. Named to Greene County Women's Hall of Fame, 1982, Ohio Women's Hall of Fame, 1988; named 1 of 10 Outstanding Women of Miami Valley, 1987; recipient Ambassador award YWCA of the U.S.A., 1993. Mem. ABA, Nat. Assn. of Social Workers (charter), Nat. Coun. of Negro Women (life), Alpha Kappa Alpha. Democrat. Unitarian Universalist. Avocations: bicycling, swimming, walking, needlecrafts. E-mail: jewelg@aol.com.

GRAHAM, JOHN DALBY, public relations executive; b. Maryville, Mo., Aug. 24, 1937; s. Kyle T. and Irma Irene (Dalby) Graham; m. Linda Mills Graham, Dec. 21, 1996; children: Katherine Elizabeth, David Landon. B.J., U. Mo., 1959. Editor Hallmark Cards, Inc., Kans. City, Mo., 1959—62; dir. pub. rels. St. Louis Met. YMCA, 1962—66; chmn., chief exec. officer Fleishman-Hillard, Inc., St. Louis, 1966—; chmn. Fleishman-Hillard Europe. Bd. dirs. Fleishman-Hillard/U.K. Ltd. Trustee St. Louis U.; mem. exec. bd. St. Louis Area Coun. Boy

Scouts Am. Capt. US Army, 1959—66. Fellow: Pub. Rels. Soc. Am.; mem.: Arthur Page Soc., Round Table, Nat. Investors Rels. Inst., Internat. Pub. Rels. Assn., Log Cabin Club. Home: PO Box 8797 Saint Louis MO 63101-8797 Office: Fleishman Hillard Inc 200 N Broadway Saint Louis MO 63102-2796

GRAHAM, ROBERT L., lawyer; b. Chgo., Jan. 9, 1948; BA with highest distinction, U. Mich., 1969; JD, Harvard U., 1972. Bar: Ill. 1972, Calif. 1973. Ptnr. Jenny & Block, Chgo. Bd. dirs. Ill. ACLU; adj. prof. Northwestern U., Loyola U. Sch. Law. Edit. bd. Ill. Environ. Laws and Regulations, 1978, Shepard's Environ. Liability in Commercial Transactions Reporter, 1990-92; contbr. articles to profl. jours. Angell scholar. Mem. ABA (asst. chmn. com. environ. rights and responsibilities 1974-78, del. 1988, treas. 1990-91, pres. 1979-81), Ill. Supreme Ct. Com. Jury Instructions Civil cases (assoc. 1981-86), Fund for Justice (bd. dirs. 1977-88, 90-92, chmn. 1987), Chgo. Coun. Lawyers (bd. govs. 1977-79, 82-83), Phi Beta Kappa, Phi Eta Sigma. Office: Jenner & Block 1 E Ibm Plz Fl 4000 Chicago IL 60611-7603

GRALEN, DONALD JOHN, lawyer; b. Oak Park, Ill., Mar. 18, 1933; s. Oliver Edwin and Rosalie Marie (Buskens) G.; m. Jane Walsh, Dec. 29, 1956; children: Alana, Mark, Paul, Ann, Sarah. BS, Loyola U., Chgo., 1956; JD with honors, Loyola U., 1957. Bar: Ill. 1958. Assoc. Sidley & Austin, Chgo., 1959-65, ptnr., 1966-94, counsel, 1994-99. Co-author chpts. in books. Trustee Village of LaGrange, Ill., 1973-77; chmn. LaGrange Zoning Bd., 1971-73, LaGrange Econ. Devel. Com., 1982, Cmty. Meml. Found., 1995—; bd. dirs. Carson Pirie Scott Found., Chgo., 1980-89, Jr. Achievement, 1978-88, Met. Housing and Planning Coun., 1982-89, Cmty. Family Svc. and Mental Health Assn., 1983-87, Chgo. Youth Conservation Corps, 1988-92, LaGrange Meml. Found., 1990-95, YMCA Met. Chgo., 1990—. 1st lt. U.S. Army, 1957-59. Mem. Ill. Bar Assn., Univ. Club, Big Foot Country Club. Home: 42 Durham Ct Burr Ridge IL 60527-7938 Office: Sidley & Austin 1 S First National Plz Chicago IL 60603-2000 E-mail: dgralen@aol.com.

GRAMMER, LESLIE CARROLL, allergist; b. St. Louis, Mo., 1952; MD, Northwestern U., 1976. Cert. internal medicine 1979, allergy and immunology 1981, diag. lab. immunology 1986, occupational medicine 1989. Intern Northwestern U., Chgo., 1976—77, resident, medicine, 1977—79, fellowship, allergy and immunology, 1979—81; allergist Northwestern Meml. Hosp., Chgo., 1981—; prof. medicine Northwestern U. Med. Sch., 1990—. Office: Northwestern U Feinberg Sch Medicine 676 N St Clair Ste 14018 Chicago IL 60611-3093 Office Phone: 312-695-4000.

GRAMS, RODNEY D., former senator, former congressman; b. 1948; Student, Anoka-Ramsey Jr. Coll., Brown Inst., Minneapolis, Minn., Carroll Coll., Helena, Mont. Engring. cons. Orr-Schelen Mayeron & Assoc., Mpls.; anchor, producer Sta. KFBB-TV, Great Falls, Mont., Sta. WSAU-TV, Wausau, Wis., Sta. WIFR-TV, Rockford, Ill., Sta. KMSP-TV, Mpls.; mem. 103d Congress from 6th Minn. Dist., 1993-94; U.S. Senator from Minn., 1995—2001. Pres., CEO Sun Ridge Builders. Republican.

GRANBERG, KURT, state legislator, lawyer; b. Breese, Ill., June 16, 1953; s. Marnen George and Agnes Mary (Vahlkamp) G. BS, U. Ill., Chgo., 1975; postgrad., Ill. Inst. Tech., 1980. Bar: Ill. 1980, U.S. Dist. Ct. (so. dist.) Ill. 1983. Legis. intern Ill. Ho. Reps., Springfield, 1975-76, mem. staff, 1975-77; assoc. James Donnewald Law Office, Breese, 1980-83; asst. pub. defender Clinton County, Ill., 1981-83; ptnr. Donnewald & Granberg, Breese, 1983—; spl. asst. atty. gen. State of Ill., Breese, 1983—; registered lobbyist Breese, 1984—; mem. Ill. Ho. Reps., 1986—; asst. Dem. majority leader. Mem. fin. com. Ill. Inst. Tech.-Chgo. Kent. Sch. Law, 1979-80. Dem. precinct committeeman, Carlyle, Ill., 1982-84; mem. Clinton County Bd., Carlyle, 1984—, Carlyle Lake Adv. Com.; bd. dirs. Ctrl. Comprehensive Mental Health Ctr., Centralia, Ill., 1984—. Mem. ABA, Ill. Bar Assn., Clinton County Bar Assn., Jaycees, Carlyle Bus. and Profl. Assn., K.C., Optimists. Roman Catholic. Home: 17918 Oakwood Dr Carlyle IL 62231-2918 Office: Ill Ho of Reps 300 E Capitol Ave Springfield IL 62701-1710

GRANDGUIST, BETTY L., former director elder affairs; 5 children. Nursing, Mercy Hosp. Sch. Nursing, Des Moines; BA in Psychology, Drake U.; MA in Social Work, U. Iowa, 1976. Divsn. adminstr. Iowa Dept. Pub. Health, Des Moines; exec. dir. Iowa Dept. Elder Affairs, Des Moines, 1987—. Adj. instr. U. Iowa Sch. Social Work. Recipient Nat. Govs. Assn. award, 1992. Mem. Nat. Assn. State Units Aging (v.p.), Iowa Health Care Reform Council, Govs. Task Force Affirmative Action, Long Term Care Coordinating Unit (Issues Scanning Bd.), Drake U. Arts, Scis. Adv. Bd.

GRANHOLM, JENNIFER MULHERN, governor; b. Vancouver, BC, Can., Feb. 5, 1959; arrived in U.S., 1962; d. Civtor Ivar and Shirley Alfreda (Dowden) Granholm; m. Daniel Granholm Mulhern, May 23, 1986; children: Kathryn, Cecelia, Jack. BA, U. Calif., Berkeley, 1984; JD, Harvard U., 1987. Bar: Mich. 1987, U.S. Dist. Ct. (ea. dist.) Mich. 1987, U.S. Ct. Appeals (6th cir.) 1987. Jud. law clk. 6th Cir Ct. Appeals, Detroit, 1987—88; exec. asst. Wayne County Exec., Detroit, 1988—89; asst. U.S. atty. (ea. dist.) Mich. US Dept. Justice, Detroit, 1990—94; corp. counsel Wayne County, Detroit, 1994—98; atty. gen. State of Mich., Lansing, 1999—2002, gov., 2003—. Gen. counsel Detroit/Wayne County Stadium Authority, 1996—98. Contbr. articles to profl. jours. Commr. Great Lakes Commn.; mem. bd. Cyberstate.org YWCA. Recipient Woman of Achievement Award, YWCA, 1997. Mem.: Midwestern Governors Assn. (vice chairwoman 2008—), Inc. Soc. Irish Lawyers, Women's Law Assn., Detroit Bar Assn. Democrat. Roman Catholic. Avocation: running. Office: Gov Office PO Box 30013 Lansing MI 48909 Office Phone: 517-335-3400. Office Fax: 517-335-6949.

GRANOFF, MARK HOWARD, insurance company executive; b. Bklyn., May 29, 1946; s. Leo A. and Harriett (Golden) G.; m. Dale Blash, Aug. 25, 1968; 1 child, Hal P. BA in Econs., CUNY, 1968, MA, 1972. With Union Mut. Ins. Co., Portland, Maine, 1973-84, dir. life policy owner svcs., 1981-82, dir. bus. analysis, 1982-84, dir. disability mktg., 1984; dir. mktg. Maccabees Mut. Life Ins. Co., Southfield, Mich., 1984-88; v.p. employee benefits mktg. Bus. Men's Assurance Co. Am., Kansas City, Mo., 1988-90; v.p. mktg. Blue Cross and Blue Shield United of Wis., Milw., 1990—; pres., COO United Wis. Group, Milw., 1991—. Bd. dirs. Alzheimer's Assn. Southeastern Wis., Milw., 1992—, Wis. chpt. Arthritis Found. Mem. Self Ins. Inst. Am. (chair promotion com. 1988), Life Ins. Mktg. Rsch. Assn. (tng. subcom. 1987), Ins. Acctg. and Statis. Assn. (chpt. v.p. promotions 1980). Office: United Wis Group 401 W Michigan St Milwaukee WI 53203-2804 Home: 5215 Legend Hills Ln Spring Hill FL 34609-0372

GRANSEE, MARSHA L., federal agency executive; b. Youngstown, Ohio, Sept. 26, 1952; BA in anthropology, Ohio State U., Columbus, 1974; JD, Cleveland-Marshall Coll. Law, 1978. Bar: Va. 1978, Ohio 1979, D.C. 1987. Assoc. legal editor Pub. Utilities Fortnightly, 1979-83; clerk office adminstrv. law judges Fed. Energy Regularoty Commn., 1983-85; assoc. Rose, Schmidt, Chapman, Duff and Hasley, 1985-87; atty. adviser Electric Rates and Corp. Regulation, 1987-88, sr. trial atty. gas and oil litig., 1988—91, legal adviser commr., 1991—93, legal adviser chair, 1993—94, assoc. gen. counsel, 1994—99, dep. gen. counsel, 1999—. Contbg. author: Energy Law and Transactions. Mem. Fed. Energy Bar Assn. Office: Off Gen Counsel Fed Energy Reg Commn 888 First St Rm 10D-01 Youngstown OH 20426

GRANT, HUGH, agricultural products executive; b. Mar. 1958; BS in Molecular Biology and Agrl. Zoology with honors, Glasgow U., Scotland; MS, Edinburgh U., Scotland; MBA, Internat. Mgmt. Ctr., Buckingham, Eng. Co-pres. agrl. sector Pharmacia Corp., 1998; v.p., COO Monsanto Co., 2000, exec. v.p., COO, 2000—03, chmn., pres., CEO, 2003—. Mem. exec. com. Microedit Summit Campaign; mem. internat. adv. bd. Scottish Enterprise. Bd. govs. United Way St. Louis; bd. trustee Donald Danforth Plant Sci. Ctr.; mem. Civic Progress. Mem.: Biotechnology Industry Orgn., Internat. Policy Coun. on Agr., Food and Trade, CropLife Internat. (mem. of the President's adv. group). Address: Monsanto Co 800 N Lindbergh Blvd Saint Louis MO 63167

GRANT, JOHN P., lawyer; b. Omaha, Nebr., June 24, 1951; BA, U. Nebr., 1973; JD, Creighton U., 1976. Bar: Nebr. 1976. Atty. Grant Law Offices, PC, Omaha. Mem.: ebr. State Bar Assn. (Ho. Dels. 1990—, chair 1999, pres.-elect 2002—03). Office: Grant Law Offices PC 3717 Harney St Omaha NE 68131-3848

GRANT, ROBERT NATHAN, lawyer; b. Newburgh, NY, Mar. 7, 1930; m. Barbara Weil, Feb. 10, 1952; children— Susan, Elizabeth Grant Ellerton, Nancy Grant Gray. BA, Yale U., 1951; LLB, Harvard U., 1956. Bar: Ill. 1956, N.Y. 1990. Assoc. Sonnenschein Nath & Rosenthal, Chgo., 1956-65; ptnr. Sonnenschein, Nath & Rosenthal, Chgo., 1965—. Contbr. articles to profl. jours. Pres. Legal Aid Soc. Ill., 1988—94; founding chmn. Winnetka (Ill.) Pub. Schs. Found., 1995—98, Winnetka Cmty. House, 2000—01; pres. Winnetka Bd. Edn., 1980—81, mem., 1974—81, Winnetka Planning Commn., 1975—77, New Trier Twp. Caucus, 1974; bd. dirs. United Charities, 1984—94, mem. legal aid com., 1982—, vice chmn., 1986—87, chmn., 1987—94; founding chmn. New Trier HS Ednl. Found., 2000—03, chmn., 2001—05. 1st lt. USAF, 1951—53. Recipient William H. Avery award for 10 yrs. svc. as chmn. Legal Aid Soc., 1994. Mem. ABA (vice-chmn. commercial leasing com.), Scholarship and Guidance Assn. (bd. dirs. 1968-92, pres. 1979-83), Harvard Law Sch. Spl. Gifts, Yale Alumni Recruiting Com., Standard Club, Yale Club (N.Y.C.), Phi Beta Kappa. Avocations: tennis, jogging, travel, reading. Home: 1165 Hamptondale Ave Winnetka IL 60093-1811 Office: Sonnenschein Nath & Rosenthal 233 S Wacker Dr Ste 8000 Chicago IL 60606-6491 Office Phone: 312-876-8072. E-mail: rgrant@sonnenschein.com.

GRANT, W. THOMAS, II, insurance company executive; b. 1950; BA, U. Kans., 1972; MBA, U. Pa., 1976. With Bus. Men's Assurance Co. Am., Kansas City, Mo., 1976—, dir. planning, 1980-81, v.p., dir. corp. planning, 1981-83, sr. v.p. corp. research, 1983-84, pres., bd. dirs., 1984-86, pres., chief exec. officer, 1986-90; Chmn., Pres. and CEO Labone Inc., Lenexa, Kans. Office: LabOne Inc 10101 Renner Blvd Lenexa KS 66219

GRANTHAM, JARED JAMES, nephrologist, educator; b. Dodge City, Kans., May 19, 1936; married, 1958; 4 children. AB, Baker U., 1958; MD, U. Kans., 1962. Assoc. prof. med. U. Kans., Kansas City, 1969-76, head nephrology sect., 1970-96, prof., 1976-96, disting. prof., 1996—. Founder and chmn. Polycystic Kidney Rsch. Found.; dir. Kidney Inst., 2000. Fellow NIH, 1964-66; grantee Nat. Inst. Diabetes Digestive and Kidney Diseases, 1969-03; recipient Homer Smith award Am. Soc. ephrology and Am. Heart Assn., 1992, David Hume award Nat. Kidney Found., 1998. Mem. Am. Soc. Nephrology, Am. Soc. Clin. Investigation, Am. Physiol. Soc., Am. Fedn. Clin. Rsch., Assn. Am. Phys. Achievements include research in fluid and electrolyte metabolism, electrolyte transport, mechanism of action of antidiuretic hormone and polycystic kidney disease. Office: U Kans Dept Medicine/ Nephrology 3901 Rainbow Blvd Kansas City KS 66160-0001 E-mail: jgrantha@kumc.edu.

GRANZOW, POLLY, state representative, language educator; b. Eldora, Iowa, Sept. 29, 1941; BA, U. Iowa; MA, U. No. Iowa. Cert. tchr. Spanish. Tchr. Spanish; supr. Hardin County; state rep. dist. 44 Iowa Ho. of Reps., 2003—; mem. econ. growth com.; mem. natural resources com.; vice chair human resources com.; mem. health and human svcs. subcom. Mem.: Lions. Republican. Office: State Capitol Bldg East 12th and Grand Des Moines IA 50319

GRASSLEY, CHUCK (CHARLES ERNEST GRASSLEY), senator; b. New Hartford, Iowa, Sept. 17, 1933; s. Louis Arthur and Ruth (Corwin) Grassley; m. Barbara Ann Speicher, 1954; children: Lee, Wendy, Robin, Michele, Jay. BA, U. No. Iowa, 1955, MA in Polit. Sci., 1956; postgrad., U. Iowa, 1957-58. Farmer; instr. polit. sci. Drake U., 1962, Charles City Community Coll., 1967-68; mem. Iowa Ho. of Reps., 1959-75, U.S. Ho. Rep. 94th-96th Congresses from 3d Iowa Dist.; US Senator from Iowa, 1981—. Mem. com. agr., nutrition and forestry US Senate, com. budget, chmn. com. fin., ranking minority mem. com. fin., 2007—, com. judiciary, chmn. com. tax. Recipient Congressional award, Cmty Anti-Drug Coalitions of Am., 1997, Excellence in Health Svc. award, Nat. Assn. Cmty. Health Centers, 1998, Ester Peterson Sr. Advocate award, United Seniors Health Coop., 2000, Am. Fin. Leadership award, Fin. Services Roundtable, 2001, Bipartisan Hero award, Nat. Assn. Pediatric urse Assoc. and Practitioners, 2001, Excellence in Public Svc. award, Am. Acad. Pediatrics, 2001, Patients' Champions award, Am. Chiropractic Assn., 2001, Nat. Leadership award, Nat. Citizens' Coalition Nursing Home Reform, 2002, Legis. of Yr., Biotechnology Industry Orgn., 2003, Nat. Energy Leadership award, Nat. Bio-Diesel Bd., 2003. Mem. Am. Farm Bur., Iowa Hist. Soc., Black Hawk County Hist. Soc., Masons, Pi Gamma Mu, Kappa Delta Pi. Republican. Baptist. Office: US Senate 135 Hart Senate Bldg Washington DC 20510-0001 also: Federal Bldg Rm 120 210 Walnut St Des Moines IA 50309 Office Phone: 202-224-3744, 515-288-1145. Office Fax: 202-224-6020. E-mail: chuck_grassley@grassley.senate.gov.

GRATZ, RONALD G., real estate development executive; Degree, Ohio State U. CPA, Ohio. With Coopers & Lybrand, Columbus, Ohio; CFO Borror, Columbus; v.p., CFO Zaring Homes, Cin. Office: Zaring National Corp 625 Eden Park Dr #1250 Cincinnati OH 45202-6024

GRATZ, WILLIAM W., state legislator; State rep. Dist. 113 Mo. State Congress, 1993—; owner Gratz Real Estate & Auction Svc., Jefferson City, 1978—.

GRAUER, DAVID W., lawyer; b. Marysville, Kans., 1954; BS in Pharmacy, U. Kans., 1977; MS, Ohio State U., 1982; JD, Capital U., 1984. Bar: Ohio 1984. Pharmacist; ptnr. Squire, Sanders & Dempsey LLP, Columbus, Ohio, co-chmn., Health Care Strategic Bus. Unit & Health Care Practice Group. Mem.: Nat. Health Lawyers Assn., Ohio State Bar Assn. (health care law com.). Office: Squire Sanders & Dempsey LLP 1300 Huntington Ctr 41 South High St Columbus OH 43215-6197 Office Phone: 614-365-2786. Office Fax: 614-365-2499. Business E-Mail: sgrauer@ssd.com.

GRAUER, DOUGLAS DALE, civil engineer; b. Marysville, Kans., June 27, 1956; s. Norman Wayne and Ruth Ann (Schwindaman) G.; m. Bette Lynn Bohnenblust, Aug. 16, 1980; children: Diana Kathryn, Laura Jaclyn. Student, Baker U., 1976; BSCE, Kans. State U., 1979. Registered profl. engr., Iowa, Kans., Nebr., Okla. Pipeline engr. Cities Service Pipeline Co., Shreveport, La., 1979-80; products terminal engr. Cities Service Co., Braintree, Mass., 1980-81, project engr. Tulsa, 1981-83; staff engr. Cities Service Oil and Gas Corp., Tulsa, 1983-85; asst. products pipeline and terminal supt. Nat. Coop. Refinery Assn., Blue Rapids, Kans., 1985-90, supt. products pipeline and terminal, 1990—. Mem. ASCE, NSPE, Kans. Soc. Profl. Engrs., Nat. Assn. Corrosion Engrs., Chi Epsilon. Republican. Avocations: golf, fishing, woodworking. Home: 1321 Ranch Rd Mcpherson KS 67460-2313 Office: Nat Coop Refinery Assn PO Box 1404 Mcpherson KS 67460-1404 Office Phone: 620-241-9264. Business E-Mail: dgrauer@ncra.coop.

GRAUPE, DANIEL, engineering educator; b. Jerusalem; came to U.S., 1970, naturalized, 1976. s. Heinz M. and Hella N. (Neumann) G.; m. Dalia Smilansky, July 9, 1968; children: Menachem-Henny, Pelleg-Pinhas, Oren. BSME, Technion, Israel Inst. Tech., Haifa, 1958, BSEE, 1959, Dipl. Ing. Elec. Engring., 1960; PhDEE, U. Liverpool, Eng., 1963. Lectr. U. Liverpool, Eng., 1963-67; sr. lectr. Technion, Israel Inst. Tech., Haifa, 1967-70; assoc. prof. elec. engring. Colo. State U., Ft. Collins, 1970-74, prof. elec. engring., 1974-78; prof. elec. and computer engring. Ill. Inst. Tech., Chgo., 1978-84, Bodine chair disting. prof. elec. and computer engring., 1984-85; Sr. U. Ill. scholar U. Ill., Chgo., 1988—; prof. elec. engring., computer sci., 1991—. Adj. prof. neurology and rehab. medicine U. Ill., Chgo., 1985—; vis. prof. elec. engring. Notre Dame U., Ind., 1976; Springer vis. chair prof., dept. mech. engring. U. Calif.-Berkeley, 1977; vis. prof. Sch. Medicine, Tel Aviv U., summers 1982, 83, 84, Swiss Fed. Inst. Tech., Zurich, 1988, 89, 91, 92, 96; vis. prof. orthwestern U., Evanston, Ill., 1995-96; founder, v.p. Intellitech Inc., Northbrook, Ill., 1982-88; founder, chief scientist, bd. dirs. Sigmedics Inc., orthfield, Ill., 1988-95; bd. dirs. GS Systems Inc., Skokie, Ill. Author: Identification of Systems (transl. into Russian and Serbo-Croat), 1972, 2d edit., 1976, Time Series Analysis Identification and Adaptive Filtering, 1984, 2d edit., 1989, Chinese translation, 1987; (with K.H. Kohn) Functional Electrical Stimulation for Ambulation by Paraplegics, 1994, (Spanish transl.), 1998, Principles of Artificial Neural Networks, 1997; assoc. editor Internat. Jour. Software Engring. and Knowledge Engring., 1996—, Neurol. Rsch., 1998—, Psychline, 1998—, IEEE Trans Neurology Sys. Rehab. Engring., 2002-2004; contbr. articles to profl. jours.; patentee in field. Trustee Knowledge Systems Ins., Skokie, Ill., 1988—; chmn. Chgo. chpt. Leo Baeck Inst., 1992—. With Israel Air Force, 1952-55 Recipient Anna Frank prize Hebrew U. Jerusalem and Technion, Haifa, 1961 Fellow IEEE; mem. IEEE Cirs. and Systems Soc. (chmn. tech. com. on image and signal processing in medicine 1988-92, assoc. editor IEEE Transactions on Cirs. and Systems 1989-92), Internat. Orgn. eurol. Socs. (mem. internat. adv. bd. 1999—), N.Y. Acad. Scis. Jewish. Avocations: reading, history, philosophy. Home: 496 Hillside Dr Highland Park IL 60035-4826 Office: U Ill Dept Elec Engring and Sci 851 S Morgan St Chicago IL 60607-7042 E-mail: graupe@eecs.uic.edu, dangraupe@gmail.com.

GRAVELLE, JOHN DAVID, secondary school educator; Tchr. math, Eng. grades 10-12 Merrill (Wis.) High Sch., to 1997, technology coord., 1997—. Recipient State Tchr. of Yr. Math/Eng. award Wis., 1992. Office: Merrill High Sch 120 N Sales St Merrill WI 54452-2648

GRAVES, RAY REYNOLDS, retired judge; b. Tuscumbia, Ala., Jan. 10, 1946; s. Isaac and Olga Ernestine (Wilder) Graves; children: Claire Elise, Reynolds Douglass. BA, Trinity Coll., Hartford, Conn., 1967; JD, Wayne State U., 1970. Bar: Mich. 1971, U.S. Dist. Ct. (ea. dist.) Mich. 1971, U.S. Ct. Appeals (6th cir.) 1972, U.S. Supreme Ct. 1976, D.C. 1977. Defender Legal Aid and Defender Assn., Detroit, 1970-71; assoc. Liberson, Fink, Feiler, Crystal & Burdick, 1971-72, Patmon, Young & Kirk, 1972-73; ptnr. Lewis, White, Clay & Graves, 1974-81; mem. legal dept. Detroit Edison Co., 1981; judge U.S. Bankruptcy Ct., Ea. Dist. Mich., Detroit, 1982-2002; chief judge U.S. Bankruptcy Ct., 1991-95; prin. BBK, Ltd., Southfield, Mich., 2002—. Mem. U.S. ct. com. State Bar Mich. Trustee Mich. Opera Theatre, 1986—88; vestry Christ Ch. Episcopal, Grosse Pointe, Mich., 1994—97; del Diocesan Conv. Episcopal Ch., Mich., 1997; bd. dirs. Mich. Cancer Found. Fellow: Am. Coll. Bankruptcy; mem.: D.C. Bar Assn., Detroit Bar Assn., Wolverine Bar Assn., Assn. Black Judges Mich., World Peace Through Law Conf., World Assn. Judges, Nat. Conf. Bankruptcy Judges (bd. govs. 1984—88), Iota Boulé (Sire Archon 1999—2001), Sigma Pi Phi, Delta Kappa Epsilon. Episcopalian. Home Phone: 313-567-0458; Office Phone: 248-603-8373. Business E-Mail: rgraves@e-bbk.com.

GRAVES, ROBERT J., lawyer; b. Hinsdale, Ill., 1958; BA cum laude, Ill. Wesleyan Univ., 1980; JD magna cum laude, Univ. Ill., 1984. Bar: Ill. 1984. Law clerk Judge Thomas Gibbs Gee, US Ct. of Appeals, Fifth Cir., 1984—85; ptnr., chair, lending/structured fin. practice Jones Day. Author: numerous articles in profl. publications. Fulbright Scholar, Univ. Erlangen, Germany, 1980—81. Mem.: ABA, Chgo. Bar Assn. (past chair, comml. fin. com.), Order of Coif. Fluent in German. Office: Jones Day 77 W Wacker Chicago IL 60601-1692 Office Fax: 312-782-8585.

GRAVES, SAM, communications media executive; Bur. chief Indpls. Metro Network News, 1998—. Office: Metro Network News 6081 E 82nd St Ste 419 Indianapolis IN 46250-1535

GRAVES, SAMUEL B., JR., congressman, retired state legislator; b. Fairfax, Mo., Nov. 7, 1963; m. Lesley Graves; 3 children. BS in Agronomy, U. Mo., Columbia, 1986. Mem. Mo. Ho. Reps. from Dist. 4, 1993—95, Mo. State Senate from Dist. 12, 1995—2000, US Congress from 6th Mo. dist., 2001—. Mem. agr. com. US Congress, mem. small bus. com., mem. transp. and infrastructure com. Mem. agrl. adv. com. N.W. Mo. State U., mem. univ. ext. coun. Recipient Outstanding Young Farmer in Mo., Mo. Farm Bur., 1990, Outstanding Young Farmer in US, Farm Bur., 1991, Tarkio, Mo. Cmty. Betterment award, 1995, Outstanding Young Farmer in US, Mo. Jr. C. of C., 1996, Mo. Phys. Therapy Assn. award, 1997, Voice of Mo. Bus. award, Associated Industries, 1999. Mem.: Farm Bur., Rotary. Republican. Baptist. Office: US House Reps 1415 Longworth House Office Bldg Washington DC 20515 Office Phone: 202-225-7041. Office Fax: 202-225-8221. E-mail: sam.graves@mail.house.gov.

GRAVES, TODD PETERSON, lawyer, former prosecutor; b. 1965; m. Tracy Graves; 4 children. BA summe cum laude, U. Mo., 1988; MS, JD, U. Va., 1991. Bar: Mo. 1991, cert.: US Dist. Ct. Mo. 1991, US Ct. Appeals (8th Cir.) 1993. Assoc. Skadden Arps, NYC; asst. atty. gen. State of Mo., 1991; assoc. Bryan Cave law Firm, 1992—94; prosecutor Platte County Ct., Mo., 1994—2001; US atty. (we. dist.) Mo US Dept. Justice, 2001—06; ptnr. Graves Bartle & Marcus LLC, Kans. City, 2006—. Republican. Office: Graves Bartle & Marcus LLC 100 Main St Ste 2600 Kansas City MO 64105 E-mail: todd.graves@pobox.com.

GRAVES, WALLACE BILLINGSLEY, retired university executive; b. Ft. Worth, Feb. 10, 1922; s. Ellery George and Edith (Billingsley) G.; m. Barbara Jeanne Abey, Nov. 20, 1943; children: David W., Emily Graves Mc Donald, John R., Julie Graves Williams. BA, U. Okla., 1943; MA, Tex. Christian U., 1947; PhD, U. Tex., 1953; LLD (hon.), Ind. State U., 1970, Valparaiso U., 1972; LHD (hon.), Morningside Coll., 1971, U. Evansville, 1989. Teaching fellow Tex. Christian U., Ft. Worth, 1946-47, U. Tex., Austin, 1947-50; prof. polit. sci. DePauw U., Greencastle, Ind., 1950-58; Armstrong prof. govt., dean of men Tex. Wesleyan Coll., Ft. Worth, 1958-63, asst. to pres., 1963-65; acad. v.p. U. Pacific, Stockton, Calif., 1965-67; pres. U. Evansville, Ind., 1967-87, chancellor Ind., 1986-89, pres. emeritus, 1989—. Vis. prof. Butler U., summer 1956; bd. dirs. Citizens Nat. Bank, Evansville, Herrburger Brooks P.L.C., Nottingham, Eng. Author: The United Nations, Great Britain and the British Non-Self Governing Territories, 1954, The One Semester Course in International Relations, 1956, Harlaxton College: The Camelot of Academe, 1990; contbr. articles to profl. jours. Mem. exec. bd. Tarrant County chpt. ARC, 1960-65, chmn. home svc. com.; chmn. ARC of Southwestern Ind., 1994—; midwest region com. ARC, 2000-02; bd. dirs. Ft. Worth Assn. Retarded Children, 1963-65; mem. Met. Ft. Worth Devel. Coordinating Com., World Affairs Coun., Chgo. and Stockton, adv. bd. Supplementary Edn. Ctr., Stockton; v.p. Buffalo Trace coun. Boy Scouts Am., Evansville, 1968, exec. bd., 1968-74, adv. coun, 1974—; bd. dirs. Jr. Achievement Inc., Evansville, 1968-73; mem. commn. ecumenical affairs United Meth. Ch., Evansville, 1968-72, univ. senate, 1972-76, Ind. area study commn., 1972-74; bd. dirs. Evansville Day Sch., 1967-76; mem. Ind. State Scholarship Commn., 1969-77, adv. bd. St. Mary's Med. Ctr., Evansville, 1970—, Evansville's Future Inc., 1967—, pres., 1974-77; bd. dirs. Ind. Health Careers Inc., 1974-75; mem. Govs. Adv. Com. Pub. Health, 1971-72; bd. dirs. Leadership Evansville, 1975-71, Evansville Mus., 1978—, Lincolnland Hist. Trust, 1978—; pres. Beethoven Found., Indpls., 1980-88; mem. organizing com. Pan Am. Games, 1987; bd. dirs. Sta. WNIN Pub. TV, Evansville, 1973—, chmn. bd., 1982-84. With U.S. Army, 1943. Recipient Best Tchr. award DePauw U., 1954, medal of honor U. Evansville, 1977, medal of merit Govt. Thailand, 1984, medal of honofr DAR, 1999; Wallace B. Graves Day named in his honor Office Mayor City Evansville, 1977; rsch. scholar U. Tex., 1947; Ford Found. fellow, summer 1951, 55; Paul Harris (Rotary) fellow, 1995. Mem. AAUP, Am. Assn. Acad. Deans, Am. Coll. Pub. Relations Assn., Am. Polit. Sci. Assn., Ind. Colls. and Univs. Ind. Inc. (pres. 1970-71, 76-77), North Cen. Assn. Colls. and Secondary Schs. (cons., investigator), Am. Assn. Pres. Ind. Colls. and Univs. (exec. com. 1969-70), Am. Assn. Colls. (various coms.), Associated Colls. Ind. (pres. 1972-74), Carl Duisberg Soc. (pres. Am. assn. 1973-74), Internat. Assn. Univ. Pres. (bd. dirs. N.Am. council 1975-87), Ind. Consortium Computer and High Tech. Edn., Ft. Worth C. of C. (chmn. econ. edn. com. 1963-64), Gold Key, Blue Key, Phi Kappa Phi, Phi Mu Alpha, Alpha Sigma Lambda, Pi Sigma Alpha, Sigma Nu. Clubs: Knife and Fork (pres. 1964-65) (Ft. Worth); Commonwealth (San Francisco); Columbia (Indpls.); Petroleum; Evansville Country, Kennel (Evansville). Lodges: Rotary (pres. Ft. club 1964-65). Personal E-mail: wexprex@aol.com.

GRAVLEE, GLENN P(AGE), anesthesiologist, educator, director; b. Birmingham, Ala., Aug. 15, 1950; BS in Medicine, Northwestern U., 1972, MD, 1974. Diplomate Am. Bd. Anesthesiology, Nat. Bd. Echocardiography. Intern Hartford Hosp., Conn., 1974—75; resident anesthesiology Mass. Gen. Hosp., Harvard Med. Sch., Boston, 1975—77, chief resident, cardiac anesthesia fellow, 1977—78, instr., 1978—79; from asst. prof. to prof. Wake Forest U., 1978—94; prof. Allegheny U. Health Scis., Pitts., 1994—99, chair, 1994—99; prof. dept. anesthesiology Coll. Med. and Pub. Health, Ohio State U., Columbus, 1999—, chmn. dept. anesthesiology Coll. Med. and Pub. Health, 1999—2002, vice chmn., 2002—06; prof. Health Scis. Ctr. U. Colo., 2006—, dir. edn. Dept. Anesthesiology Health Scis. Ctr., 2006—. Editor: Cardiopulmonary Bypass: Principles and Practice, 1994, 2000; co-editor: A Practical Approach to Cardiac Anesthesia, 2003, Year Book of Anesthesia, 2004; contbr. articles to profl. jours. Mem.: Am. Soc. Anesthesiologists, Internat. Anesthesiology Rsch. Soc., Soc.

Cardiovasc. Anesthesiologists (pres. 2003—05), Am. Bd. Anesthesiologists (dir. 1999—). Office: Univ Colo Health Scis Ctr Dept Anesthesiology 4200 E 9th Ave B113 Denver CO 80262 Business E-Mail: glenn.gravlee@uchsc.edu.

GRAY, DAWN PLAMBECK, work-family consultant, publishing executive; b. Chgo., Aug. 23, 1957; d. Raymond August and Eunice Eve (Fox) Plambeck; m. Richard Scott Gray, Apr. 13, 1985; children: Zachary, Rae. BS, Northwestern U., 1979. Desk asst. Sta. WCFL, Chgo., 1979-80; writer UPI Internat., Chgo., 1980; asignment editor Cable News Network, Chgo., 1980-81; account exec. Aaron Cushman and Assoc., Chgo., 1981-83, Ruder Finn & Rotman, Chgo., 1983-84, account supr., 1984-86, dir. consumer group, 1986-87; dir. pub. rels. Tassani Communications, Chgo., 1987-90; v.p. Marcy Monyek & Assoc., Chgo., 1990; pres. Moments Inc., Chgo., 1991—. Avocation: dance. Office: Moments Inc 1028 W Monroe St Chicago IL 60607-2604

GRAY, HANNA HOLBORN, historian, educator; b. Heidelberg, Germany, Oct. 25, 1930; d. Hajo and Annemarie (Bettmann) Holborn; m. Charles Montgomery Gray, June 19, 1954. AB, Bryn Mawr Coll., 1950; PhD, Harvard U., 1957; MA, Yale U., 1971, LLD, 1978; LittD (hon.), St. Lawrence U., 1974, Oxford U., Eng., 1979; LLD (hon.), Dickinson Coll., 1979, U. Notre Dame, 1980, Marquette U., 1984; LittD (hon.), Washington U., 1974; HHD (hon.), St. Mary's Coll., 1974; LHD (hon.), Grinnell Coll., Iowa, 1974, Lawrence U., 1974, Denison U., 1974, Wheaton Coll., 1976, Marlboro Coll., 1979, Rikkyo U., Japan, 1979, Roosevelt U., 1980, Knox Coll., 1980, Coe Coll., 1981, Thomas Jefferson U., 1981, Duke U., 1982, New Sch. for Social Research, 1982, Clark U., 1982, Brandeis U., 1983, Colgate U., 1983, Wayne State U., 1984, Miami U., Oxford, Ohio, 1984, So. Meth. U., 1984, CUNY, 1985, U. Denver, 1985, Am. Coll. Greece, 1986, Muskingum Coll., 1987, Rush Presbyn. St. Lukes Med. Ctr., 1987, NYU, 1988, Rosemont Coll., 1988, Claremont U. Ctr. Grad Sch., 1989, Moravian Coll., 1991, Rensselaer Poly. Inst., 1991, Coll. William and Mary, 1991, Centre Coll., 1991, Macalester Coll., 1993, McGill U., 1993, Ind. U., 1994, Med. U. of S.C., 1994; LLD (hon.), Union Coll., 1975, Regis Coll., 1976, Dartmouth Coll., 1978, Trinity Coll., 1978, U. Bridgeport, 1978, Dickinson Coll., 1979, Brown U., 1979, Wittenburg U., 1979, Dickinson Coll., 1979, U. Rochester, 1980, U. Notre Dame, 1980, U. So. Calif., 1980, U. Mich., 1981, Princeton U., 1982, Georgetown U., 1983, Marquette U., 1984, W.Va. Wesleyan U., 1985, Hamilton Coll., 1985, Smith Coll., 1986, U. Miami, 1986, Columbia U., 1987, NYU, 1988, Rosemont Coll., 1988, U. Toronto, Can., 1991; LDH, LHD, Haverford Coll., 1995; LDH (hon.), Tulane U., 1995; LLD (hon.), Harvard U., 1995; LHD (hon.), McGill U., 1993, Macalester Coll., 1993, Ind. U., 1994, Med. U. S.C., 1994, Haverford Coll., 1995, Tulane U., 1995; LLD (hon.), Harvard U., 1995, U. Chgo., 1996; DL (hon.), Pontifical Inst. Mediaeval Studies, Toronto, 2005. Instr. Bryn Mawr Coll., 1953—54; tchg. fellow Harvard U., 1955—57, instr., 1957—59, asst. prof., 1959—60, vis. lectr., 1963—64; asst. prof. U. Chgo., 1961—64, assoc. prof., 1964—72; dean, prof. Northwestern U., Evanston, Ill., 1972—74; provost, prof. history Yale U., 1974—78, acting pres., 1977—78; pres. U. Chgo., 1978—93, prof. dept. history, 1978, Harry Pratt Judson disting. svc. prof. history, 1994, prof. emeritus. Fellow Ctr. for Advanced Study in Behavioral Scis., 1966—67, vis. scholar, 1970—71; vis. prof. U. Calif., Berkeley, Calif., 1970—71. Co-editor (with Charles Gray): Jour. Modern History, 1965—70; contbr. articles to profl. jours. Active Nat. Coun. on Humanities, 1972—78; trustee Yale Corp., 1971—74; past bd. regents Smithsonian Instn.; past chmn. bd. Andrew W. Mellon Found.; chmn. bd. Howard Hughes Med. Inst.; mem. Harvard Corp., 1997—2005; bd. Marlboro Sch. Music. Decorated Grosse Verdienstkreuz Germany; named Pontifical Justice Medieval Studies, Toronto, Can., 2005; recipient Grad. medal, Radcliffe Coll., 1976, Yale medal, 1978, Medal of Liberty award, 1986, Laureate Lincoln Acad. Ill., 1988, Medal of Freedom, 1991, Frontrunner award, Sara Lee, 1991, Charles Frankel prize, 1993, Centennial medal, Harvard U., 1994, Disting. Svc. award in edn., Inst. Internat. Edn., 1994, Medal of Distinction, Barnard Coll., 2000, Fritz Redlich Disting. Alumni award, Internat. Inst. Edn., 2004, The Newberry Libr. award, 2006, Gold medal, Nat. Inst. Social Scis., 2006; fellow Newberry Libr., 1960—61, St. Anne's Coll., Oxford U., 1978—; Fulbright scholar, 1950—51. Fellow: Am. Acad. Arts and Scis.; mem.: Coun. Fgn. Rels. N.Y., Nat. Acad. Edn., Am. Philos. Soc. (Jefferson medal 1993), Renaissance Soc. Am., Phi Beta Kappa (vis. scholar 1971—72). Office: U Chgo Dept History 1126 E 59th St Chicago IL 60637-1580 Business E-Mail: h-gray@uchicago.edu.

GRAY, HELEN THERESA GOTT, editor; b. Jersey City, July 2, 1942; d. William E. and Cynthia B. Gott; m. David L. Gray, Aug. 15, 1976; 1 child, David Lee Jr. BA, Syracuse U., 1963; M in Internat. Affairs, Columbia U., 1965. Editor religion sect. The Kansas City (Mo.) Star, 1971—. Tchr. Bible sch. Pleasant Green Bapt. Ch., Kansas City, Kans., 1975—, counselor, 1978—; former owner of a Christian book store. Co-author, editor several books; contbr. articles to profl. jours. Recipient writing award Valley Forge Freedom Found., 1967; John Hay Whitney Found. grantee, 1963-64; named 100 Most Influential African Ams. in Greater Kansas City. Mem. Religion Newswriters Assn., Kansas City Assn. Black Journalists (Life Achievement award 1998). Baptist. Office: The Kansas City Star 1729 Grand Blvd Kansas City MO 64108-1458 Office Phone: 816-234-4446. E-mail: hgray@kcstar.com.

GRAY, JOHN WALKER, mathematician, educator; b. St. Paul, Oct. 3, 1931; s. Clarence Walker and Helen (Ewald) G.; m. Eva Maria Wirth, Dec. 30, 1957; children— Stephen, Theodore, Elisabeth. BA, Swarthmore Coll., 1953; PhD, Stanford U., 1957. Temp. mem. Inst. for Advanced Study, Princeton, N.J., 1957-59; Ritt instr. Columbia U., 1959-62; asst. prof. math. U. Ill., Urbana, 1962-64, asso. prof., 1964-66, prof., 1966—, dir. grad. studies, 1995—2000, prof. emeritus, 2000—. Organizer Category Theory Session, Oberwolfach, Germany, 1971, 72, 73, 75, 77, 79 Contbr. to: Springer Lecture Notes in Mathematics, 1974. NSF sr. fellow, 1966-67; Fulbright-Hays sr. lectr., 1975-76 Mem. Am. Math. Soc., AAAS. Home: 303 W Michigan Ave Urbana IL 61801-4945 Office: U Ill Dept Math Urbana IL 61801 E-mail: gray@math.uiuc.edu.

GRAY, RICHARD, art dealer, consultant, holding company executive; b. Chgo., Dec. 30, 1928; s. Edward and Pearl B. Gray; m. Mary Kay Lackritz, Mar. 28, 1953; children: Paul, Jennifer, Harry. Pres. The Grayline Co., 1952-63; sec.-treas. The Edward Gray Corp., 1952-63; prin., dir. GrayCor, 1963—; founder, ptnr. The Richard Gray Gallery, Chgo. and NYC, 1963—. Lectr., juror, panelist Guggenheim Mus., N.Y.C., Art. Inst. Chgo., Harvard U., U. Ill., Mich. State U., Milw. Art Mus., New Sch. for Social Research, N.Y., Met. Mus., N.Y.C., Colloquium-The Getty Mus., U. Chgo., Seattle Art Mus.; mem. art adv. panel U.S. Internal Revenue Svc., 1988-98. Contbr. articles to Chgo. Tribune, Chgo. Daily News, Crain's Chgo. Bus., Chgo. Mag., Collector Investor Mag. Bd. dirs. Sta. WFMT-FM, 1992-, Ill. Humanities Coun.; trustee, vice chmn. WTTW Channel 11—Chgo. Pub. TV; bd. dirs. Goodman Theatre, Chgo.; life trustee Chgo. Symphony Orch., Art Inst. Chgo.; former chair bd. Chgo. Internat. Theater Festival; adv. com. Smithsonian Inst.; bd. dirs. Art Inst. Chgo., Old Masters Soc.; mem. steering com. Friends of the Libraries; mem. capital devel. bd. State of Ill., pub. arts adv. com., former mem. selection com. Gov.'s Awards for Arts; former mem. nat. adv. bd. Ohio State U. Wexner Ctr. for Visual Arts; pres. Art Dealers Assn. Am., 1997-2003; former pres. Chgo. Art Dealers Assn., 1968-80; former chmn. Navy Pier Task Force, City of Chgo., 1986-88; mem. vis. com. U. Chgo. Humanities Div., chmn., bd. govs. Alfred Smart Mus. U. Chgo., 1992-; former vice-chmn., bd. dirs. Chgo. Humanities Festival. Mem. Chgo. Pub. Schs. Alumni Assn. (former chmn. bd. dirs.), Chgo. Coun. Fgn. Rels. (Chgo. com.), Chgo. Club, Quadrangle Club, Arts Club of Chgo. Achievements include specializing in contemporary, modern and impressionist masters. Office: Richard Gray Gallery 875 N Michigan Ave Ste 2503 Chicago IL 60611-1876 also: 1018 Madison Ave New York NY E-mail: rgray@richardgraygallery.com.

GRAY, WHITMORE, lawyer, educator; b. 1932; AB, Principia Coll., 1954; JD, U. Mich., 1957; postgrad., U. Paris, 1957—58, U. Munich, 1962; LLD, Adrian Coll., 1982. Bar: Mich. 1958. Assoc. Casey, Lane & Mittendorf, NYC, 1958—60; asst. prof. U. Mich., 1960—63, assoc. prof., 1963—66, prof., 1966—93; assoc. Cleary, Gottlieb, NYC, 1981; of counsel LeBoeuf, Lamb, Greene & MacRae, NYC, 1994—2001. Mem. adv. bd. Bull. on Rsch. in Soviet Law and Govt. and Soviet Statutes and Decisions; lectr. contract law Chinese Acad. Social Scis., 1982; summer faculty Jilin U., China, 1985; vis. prof. Fordham Law Sch., NY, 1989—; advisor on contract and arbitration law, Thailand, 1993, Cambodia, 94, Indonesia, 1995—96. Contbr. articles on comml. arbitration and alternative dispute resolution to profl. jours.; translator: Russian Republic Civil Code, General Principles of Civil Law of People's Republic of China; past editor-in-chief: Mich. Law Rev. Japan Found. fellow, U. Tokyo, 1977—78. Mem.: Japanese-Am. Soc. Legal Studies (bd. dirs.), Internat. Acad. Comparative Law, Am. Fgn. Law Assn. (dir.), Am. Assn. Law Schs. (past chmn. comparative law sect.). Home: 150 S 5th Ave Ann Arbor MI 48104 Office: U Mich Law Sch 625 S State St Ann Arbor MI 48109-1215 also: Fordham U Law Sch 271 W 47th St 30G New York NY 10036 Office Phone: 212-757-9264. Personal E-mail: whitgray@aol.com.

GRAY, WILLIAM GUERIN, engineering educator; b. San Francisco, Jan. 9, 1948; BS, U. Calif., 1969; MA, Princeton U., 1971, PhD, 1974. Asst. prof. dept. civil engring. Princeton U., N.J., 1975-80, dir. grad. studies dept. civil engring. N.J., 1977-84, assoc. prof. dept. civil engring. N.J., 1980-84; prof. dept. civil engring. U. Notre Dame, Ind., 1984-88, chmn. civil engring., geol. scis. Ind., 1984-95, Massman prof. civil engring. and geol. scis. Ind., 1988—. Office: U Notre Dame Dept Civil Engring Sc Notre Dame IN 46556 Home: 759 Pyrula Ave Sanibel FL 33957-6604

GRAYHACK, JOHN THOMAS, urologist, educator; b. Kankakee, Ill., Aug. 21, 1923; s. John and Marie (Keckich) G.; m. Elizabeth Houlehin, June 3, 1950; children: Elizabeth, Anne Marie, Linda Jean, John, William. BS, U. Chgo., 1945, MD, 1947. Diplomate Am. Bd. Urology. Intern medicine Billings Hosp., Chgo., 1947; intern gen. surgery Johns Hopkins Hosp., 1947-48, asst. resident, 1948-49, fellow urology, 1949-50, asst. resident, 1950-52; resident urology, 1952-53; dir. Kretschmer Lab., Northwestern U. Med. Sch., 1956-75, prof. urology, 1963—2004, emeritus, 2004—, chmn. dept., 1961-90. Cons. VA Rsch. Hosp. Editor Year Book of Urology, 1963-78; editor Jour. Urology, 1985-94. Served to capt. USAF, 1954-56. Recipient Outstanding Achievement award USAF, Ferdinand C. Valentine award N.Y. Acad. Medicine, Disting. Svc. award U. Chgo., 1978, Pioneer award Internat. Symposium Biology Prostate Growth, 1998; fellow Am. Cancer Soc., 1949-50, Damon Runyon Fund, 1953-54, Johns Hopkins Soc. Scholars. Mem. AMA, ACS (dedication honoree, surg. forum, 2003), Ill., Chgo. Med. Socs., Am. Assn. Genitourinary Surgeons (Barringer medal, Keyes medal), Am. Urology Assn. (Hugh H. Young award, Fuller award, Mary Hugh and Russell Scott award, Ramon Guiteras award 1994), Soc. Urol. Oncology (Huggins medal 2002), Chgo. Urology Soc. (John T. Grayhack lectr.), Endocrine Soc., Clin. Soc. Genitourinary Surgeons, Am. Surg. Assn., Soc. Univ. Urologists, Phi Beta Kappa, Alpha Omega Alpha. Home: 95 N Park Rd La Grange IL 60525-5938 Office: orthwestern Meml Hosp Superior St Fairbanks Ct Chicago IL 60611

GRAZIANO, FRANK MICHAEL, medical educator, researcher; b. Easton, Pa., June 5, 1942; s. Michael and Grace (Farace) G.; m. Mary Helen Ashton, Feb. 4, 1967; children: Teresa Ann, Frank Jr., Alicia Grace. BS, St. Joseph's Coll., 1964; MS, Villanova Univ., 1967; PhD, Univ. Va., 1970, MD, 1973. Diplomate Am. Bd. of Internal Medicine, Am. Bd. of Allergy and Clinical Immunology. Internship Univ. Wis. Hosp., Madison, 1973-74; residency in medicine Univ. Wis., Madison, 1974-76, asst. prof., 1978-84, assoc. prof., 1984-89, prof. medicine, 1989—, chief section of Rheumatology, 1989—. Author numerous books, articles, papers in field. Admissions com. Univ. Wis. Medical Sch., 1983-86, Minority subcom. chmn., 1985-86; medical and scientific com. Wis. Arthritis Found., 1979-80, Univ. Wis. Madison AIDS Task Force Com., 1986-89; Bd. dirs. Wis. Arthritis Found., 1990—, Wis. Com. Based Rsch. Consortium, 1990—. Recipient Am. Acad. Travel grant, 1978, NIH Young Investigator award, 1980, NIH Allergic Disease Acad. award, 1985. Fellow Am. Acad. Allergy/Immunology, Am. Coll. Physicians; mem. Am. Assn. Immunologists, Am. Assn. Advancement of Sci., Am. Thoracic Soc., Am. Coll. Pheumatology, Clinical Immunology Soc., Wis. Allergy Soc., Wis. Rheumatism Assn., Sigma Xi. Home: 853 Tipperary Rd Oregon WI 53575-2641 Office: Univ Wis Hosp & Clinics 600 Highland Ave # H6 363 Madison WI 53792-0001

GRAZIN, IGOR NIKOLAI, law educator, state official; b. Tartu, Estonia, June 27, 1952; came to U.S., 1990; s. Nikolai V. and Dagmar R. (Kibe) G.; children: Anton, Kaspar. Jurist degree, U. Tartu, Estonia, 1975; candidate of sci. in law, Moscow Inst. Law, 1979; DSc in Law, Inst. State and Law, Moscow, 1986. Cert. jurist, USSR. Lectr., prof. U. Tartu, Estonia, 1977-86, prof., 1986-89, assoc. dean Law Sch., 1986-89; mem. of the coun. Popular Front of Estonia, Tallinn, 1988-90; atty. Bachman and Ptrns., Tallinn, Estonia; pub. policy scholar Kennan Inst., Woodrow Wilson Ctr., Wash., 2004—05. Prof. U. Notre Dame, Ind., 1990-2000; faculty fellow Kellogg Inst. for Internat. Studies, Notre Dame, 1994-2000; adj. fellow Hudson Inst., 1994-2000; dir. Estonian Privatization Trust Fund; v.p. U. Nord. Author: Law as Text, 1983, Jeremy Bentham, 1990, Anglo-American Philosophy of Law, 1983, Right Course, 1994; editor: Studia Juridica, 1988-90; contbr. articles to profl. jours. Dep., Congress of Peoples Deps. of USSR, 1989-91; mem. Supreme Soviet, Moscow, 1989-91; counsellor to Pres., Republic of Estonia, 1993-97, V.P., pres. nat. assembly, 1999—; mem. Nat. Parliament of Estonia, 1995-99. Mem. AAUP, AALS (bd. dirs.), Estonian Bar Assn., Federalist Soc. U.S.A., Acad. Soc. of Estonian Lawyers (co-founder, vice chmn. 1989-90), Acad. Arts (Estonia, bd. dirs.), Rotary, Roman Club (founding). Republican. Lutheran. E-mail: igorveel@hotmail.com.

GREANEY, THOMAS L., lawyer, educator; BA magna cum laude, Wesleyan Univ., 1970; JD, Harvard Univ., 1973. Legis. asst. U.S. Rep. Elizabeth Holtzman, Washington, 1973—74; law clk. FCC, Washington, 1974—76; sr. trial atty. U.S. Dept. Justice, Antitrust div., Washington, 1976—81, asst. chief, 1982—85; Victor Kramer vis. fellow Yale Univ., 1985—86, NIMH fellow, 1986—87, lectr., Law Sch., 1986—87; prof., Sch. Law Saint Louis Univ., 1987—, assoc. prof., Sch. Pub. Health, 1987—; dir. Ctr. for Health Law Studies, Saint Louis Univ., 1987—. Vis. prof. Universite d'Orleans, France, 2001—02; Merck vis. scholar Seton Hall Univ., 2002, vis. prof., 04. Author: Bioethics, Liability; co-author: Health Law: Cases, Materials and Problems, Internat. Ency. Laws, Medical Law, U.S. at. ed., Health Law Statutes & Regulations. Fulbright Fellow, European Cmty. Rsch. Program, Brussels, Belgium, 1993—94. Mem.: Phi Beta Kappa. Office: Saint Louis University School of Law 3700 Lindell Blvd Saint Louis MO 63108 Office Phone: 314-977-2766. Business E-Mail: greanetl@slu.edu.

GREASER, MARION LEWIS, science educator; b. Vinton, Iowa, Feb. 10, 1942; s. Lewis Levi and Elisabeth (Sage) G.; m. Marilyn Sue Pfister, June 12, 1965; children— Suzanne, Scott BS, Iowa State U., 1964; MS, U. Wis., 1967, PhD, 1969. Postdoctoral fellow Boston Biomed. Research Inst., 1968-71; asst. prof. sci. U. Wis., Madison, 1971-73, assoc. prof., 1973-77, prof., 1977—, Cambell-Bascom prof., 2004—. Contbr. articles to profl. jours. Recipient Outstanding Researcher award Am. Heart Assn.-Wis., 1985 Mem. AAAS, Am. Soc. Biochem. Molecular Biology, Biophys. Soc., Am. Meat Sci. Assn. (Disting. Rsch. award 1981), Am. Soc. Animal Sci. (Meat Rsch. award 2000). Home: 2374 Branch St Middleton WI 53562-2809 Office: U Wis Muscle Biology Lab 1805 Linden Dr W Madison WI 53706-1110 Business E-Mail: mgreaser@ansci.wisc.edu.

GREBEL, LAWRENCE BOVARD, lawyer; b. St. Louis, Jan. 7, 1951; s. Clement Bovard and Jean Estelle (Schrieber) G.; children: David, Mark, Benjamin. BA, St. Louis U., 1973, JD, 1977. Bar: Mo. 1977, Ill. 1978, U.S. Dist. Ct. (ea. dist.) Mo. 1977. Mem. Moser, Marsalek, Carpenter, Cleary, Jaeckel, Keaney & Brown, St. Louis, 1977-80, Brown & James PC, St. Louis, 1980—. Mem. Internat. Assn. Def. Counsel, Assn. Def. Trial Attys., Mo. Bar Assn. (treas. 1981, sec. 1982, chmn. 1984), St. Louis Met. Bar Assn., Def. Rsch. Inst., Lawyers Assn. St. Louis, M. Org. Defense Lawyers (pres. 1990). Roman Catholic. Home: 8822 Ryegate Saint Louis MO 63127 Office: Brown & James PC 1010 Market St 20th Fl Saint Louis MO 63101-2000 Office Phone: 800-467-0066 ext. 5235. Business E-Mail: lgrebel@bjpc.com.

GREDEN, JOHN FRANCIS, psychiatrist, educator; b. Winona, Minn., July 24, 1942; m. Renee Mary Kalmes; children: Daniel John, Sarah Renee, Leigh Raymond. BS, U. Minn., 1965, MD, 1967. Diplomate Am. Bd. Psychiatry and Neurology. Assoc. dir. psychiat. rsch. Walter Reed Army Med. Ctr., Washington, 1972-74; asst. prof. dept. psychiatry U. Mich., Ann Arbor, 1974-77, assoc. prof., 1977-81, dir. clin. studies unit for affective disorders, 1980-85, prof., 1981—, chmn., prof., 1985—, chmn. faculty group practice, 1996—98, exec. dir. Depression Ctr., 2001—. Editor 3 books; contbr. more than 200 articles to profl. jours., more than 30 chpts. to books. Served to maj. U.S. Army, 1969-74. Recipient A.E. Bennett research award Cen. Neuropsychiat. Found., 1974, Nolan D.C. Lewis Vis. Scholar award Carrier Found., 1982. Fellow Am. Psychiat. Assn. (chair coun. on rsch. 2000—); mem. AAAS, Soc. Biol. Psychiatry (past pres., co-editor-in-chief Jour. Psychiatry Rsch. 1984-2000), Am. Coll. Neuropsychopharmacology (coun. 2001—, Psychiat. Rsch. Soc. (past pres.). Office: U Mich Med Ctr Dept Psychiatry 1500 E Medical Center Dr Ann Arbor MI 48109-0295

GREEK, DAROLD I., lawyer; b. Kunkle, Ohio, Mar. 30, 1909; s. Albert F. and Iva (Shaffer) G.; m. Catherine Johnson, Oct. 12, 1935 (dec. 1962); 1 child, Darold I (dec.); m. Elizabeth Tracy Ridgley, Sept. 18, 1970 (dec. May 1972); stepchildren— Thomas B., David Ridgley; m. Nadine Berry Weisheimer Bivens, Dec. 23, 1976; stepchildren— Richard A. Weisheimer, Jon B. Weisheimer. Student, Bowling Green State U., 1926-28; LL.B., Ohio State U., 1932. Bar: Ohio 1932. Treas., Williams County, Ohio, 1932-33; atty. Ohio Dept. Taxation, 1934-36; practiced in Columbus, 1937-89; ptnr. George, Greek, King, McMahon & McConnaughey (and predecessors), 1937-79; of counsel Baker & Hostetler, 1979-89. Mem. Ohio Bar Assn., Columbus Bar Assn. (pres. 1966-67), The Golf Club, aples Yacht Club, Hole in the Wall Golf Club. Presbyterian. Home (Summer): 6635 Lake of Woods Pt Galena OH 43021 Office Phone: 614-228-1541.

GREELEY, ANDREW MORAN, sociologist, writer; b. Oak Park, Ill., Feb. 5, 1928; s. Andrew T. and Grace G. AB, St. Mary of Lake Sem., 1950, STL, 1954; MA, U. Chgo., 1961, PhD, 1962; LHD (hon.), Bowling Green State U., 1986, No. Mich., 1993; HHD (hon.), St. Louis U., 1991; LHD, LLD, Ariz. State U., 1998; LHD (hon.), U. San Francisco, 2002, Bard Coll., 2002; LLD (hon.), Nat. U. Ireland, Galway, 2003. Ordained priest Roman Cath. Ch., 1954. Asst. pastor Ch. of Christ the King, Chgo., 1954-64; sr. study dir. Nat. Opinion Rsch. Ctr., Chgo., 1962-68; dir. Ctr. for Study Am. Pluralism, from 1973; lectr. sociology U. Chgo., 1963-72; prof. sociology U. Ariz., Tucson, from 1978, now adj. prof.; prof. social sci. U. Chgo., 1991—. Cons. Hazen Found. Commn. Columnist Daily Southtown; guest columnist Chgo. Sun Times, 1985—; Author: The Church and the Suburbs, 1959, Strangers in the House, 1961, Religion and Career, 1963, (with Peter H. Rossi) Education of Catholic Americans, 1966, Changing Catholic College, 1967, Come Blow Your Mind With Me, 1971, Life for a Wanderer: A New Look at Christian Spirituality, 1971, The Denominational Society: A Sociological Approach to Religion in America, 1972, Priests in the United States: Reflections on A Survey, 1972, That Most Distressful Nation, 1972, New Agenda, 1973, Jesus Myth, 1971, Unsecular Man, 1974, Ethnicity in the United States: A Preliminary Reconnaissance, 1974, Ecstasy: A Way of Knowing, 1974, Building Coalitions: American Politics in the 1970's, 1974, Sexual Intimacy, 1975, Denomination Society, 1975, The Great Mysteries: An Essential Catechism, 1976, The Communal Catholic: A Personal Manifesto, 1976, Death and Beyond, 1976, The American Catholic: A Social Portrait, 1977, The Making of the Popes, 1978, 79, The Magic Cup: An Irish Legend, 1979, Women I've Met, 1979, Why Can't They Be Like Us?, 1980, Death In April, 1980, The Cardinal Sins, 1981, Religion: A Secular Theory, 1982, Thy Brother's Wife, 1982, Ascent Into Hell, 1983, Lord of the Dance, 1984, Virgin & Martyr, 1985, Piece of My Mind on Just About Everything, 1985, Happy are the Meek, 1985, The Magic Cup, 1985, God Game, 1986, Happy Are the Clean of Heart, 1986, Confessions of a Parish Priest, 1986, Patience of a Saint, 1987, Rite of Spring, 1987, Angels of September, 1986, Happy Are Those Who Thirst For Justice, 1987, The Final Planet, 1987, Angel Fire, 1988, (photography) Andrew Greeley's Chicago, 1989, Love Song, 1989, St. Valentine's Night, 1989, The Bible and Us, 1990, The short stories All About Women, 1990, (photography) The Irish, 1990, The Catholic Myth: The Behavior and Beliefs of American Catholics, 1990, The Cardinal Virtues, 1990, Faithful Attraction: Discovering Intimacy, Love, and Fidelity in American Marriage, 1991, The Search for Maggie Ward, 1991, An Occasion of Sin, 1991, Happy Are the Merciful, 1992, Wages of Sin, 1992, Fall from Grace, 1993, Sacraments of Love: A Prayer Journal, 1994, Irish Gold, 1994, Happy are the Poor Spirit, 1994, Happy are Those Who Mourn, 1995, Angel Light: An Old-Fashioned Love Story, 1995, Windows: A Prayer Journal, 1995, Religion as Poetry, 1995, Sociology and Religion, 1995, White Smoke, 1996, Irish Lace, 1996, Happy Are The Oppressed, 1996, (with J. Neusner) Common Ground: A Priest and a Rabbi Read Scripture Together, 1996, Summer at the Lake, 1997, Star Bright!, 1997, The Bishop at Sea, 1997, I Hope You're Listening, God: A Prayer Journal, 1997, Irish Whiskey, 1998, Contract with an Angel, 1998, The Bishop and the Three Kings, 1998, A Mid-Winter's Tale, 1998, Furthermore! Memories of a Parish Priest, 1999, 2000, The Bishop and the Missing L Train, 2000, Christmas Wedding, 2000, Irish Love, 2001, The Bishop and the Begger Girl of St. Germain, 2001, September Song, 2001, Irish Stew, 2002, The Bishop in the West Wing, 2002, The Bishop Goes to the University, 2003, Irish Cream, 2005, The Making of the Pope 2005, 2005, The Bishop in the Old Neighborhood: A Blackie Ryan Story, 2005, Irish Crystal, 2006, (with Mary Durkin) The Book of Love, 2002, The Bishop Goes to The University, 2003; (with Chilton, Green, and Neusner) Forging a Common Future, 1996, The Catholic Imagination, 2000, (with Albert Bergesen) God in the Movies, 2000, My Love: A Prayer Journal, 2001, Letters to a Loving God, 2002, Second Spring, 2003, Religion in Europe at the End of the Second Millennium, 2003; The Catholic Revolution: New Wine, Old Wineskins, and the Second Vatican Council, 2004; Priests: A Calling in Crisis, 2004; The Priestly Sins, 2004; editor: Emerald Magic, 2004, Golden Years, 2004, Making of the Pope 2005, 2005; contbr. articles to profl. jours. Recipient Cath. Press Assn. award for best book for young people, 1965, Thomas Alva Edison award for radio broadcast, 1962, C. Albert Kobb award Nat. Cath. Edn. Assn., 1977, Mark Twain award Soc. Study Midwestern Lit., 1987, Popular Culture award Ctr. Study of Popular Culture, 1988, Freedom to Read award Friends Chgo. Pub. Libr., 1989, U.S. Cath. award, 1993, Ill. Outstanding Citizen award Coll. Lake County, 1993, Quigley Disting. Alumni award, 1997; named to Top 100 Irish Ams. Irish Am. Mag, 1992, named Irish Am. of Century Irish Am. Mag., 1999. Mem. Am. Sociol. Assn., Soc. for Sci. Study Religion, Religious Research Assn. Office Phone: 773-256-6281.

GREELEY, TIMOTHY P., federal judge; BS, Western Mich. U., 1976; JD magna cum laude, Wayne State U., 1980. Bar: Mich. 1982, U.S. Dist. Ct. (we. Mich.) 1982. Law clk. to Hon. Phillip Pratt U.S. Dist. Ct. (ea. dist.) Mich., Marquette, 1980-82; atty. Foster, Swift, Collins & Coey, P.C., Lansing, Mich., 1982-87; magistrate judge U.S. Dist. Ct. (we. dist.) Mich., Marquette, 1988—. Office: US Dist Ct We Dist Mich 330 Fed Bldg 202 W Washington St Marquette MI 49855-4357 Fax: 906-226-6231.

GREEN, DARLENE, controller, municipal official; b. St. Louis; BSBA, Washington U. Budget dir. City of St. Louis, comptroller, chief fiscal officer, 1995—. Vol. St. Louis Pub. Schs., St. Louis Crisis Nursery, Big Bros. & Big Sisters, YWCA Greater St. Louis; mem. Airport Commn.; trustee City of St. Louis Retirement Sys.; bd. dirs. Employment Connection, St. Louis Cmty. Edn. Task Force. Mem.: NAACP, Govt. Fin. Officers Assn., Nat. Assn. Black Accts., Zeta Phi Beta. Office: City of St Louis 1200 Market St Rm 212 Saint Louis MO 63103-2805 Fax: 314-622-4026.

GREEN, DAVID, hematologist; b. Phila., 1934; AB, U. Pa., 1956; MD, Jefferson Med. Coll., 1960; PhD, Northwestern U., 1974. Cert. Am. Bd. Internal Medicine, 1967, in Hematology 1972. Intern Cook County Hosp., Chgo., 1960—61; resident, internal medicine Jefferson Hosp., Phila., 1961—63, fellow, hematology, 1963—64; prof. Northwestern U., 1975—. Office Phone: 312-695-4442.

GREEN, DAVID WILLIAM, chemist, educator; b. Hudson, Mich., Nov. 19, 1942; s. Francis Harger and Dorotha Louise (Onweller) G.; m. Mary Sarah McCullough, July 8, 1967; children: Laura, Brenda, Mark, Brian, William. BA, Albion Coll., 1964; PhD, U. Calif., Berkeley, 1968; MBA, U. Chgo., 1985. Instr. U. Calif., Berkeley, 1968; rsch. assoc. U. Chgo., 1968-71; asst. prof. Albion (Mich.) Coll., 1971-75; chemist Argonne (Ill.) Nat. Lab., 1975-82, mgr. analytical chemistry, 1982—2001; prof. chemistry Coll. DuPage, Glen Ellyn, Ill., 1991-93. Vis. prof. chemistry Albion Coll., 2001—06; instr. DuPage Coll., 2006, Benedictine U., Lisle, Ill., 2006. Editor Mng. the Modern Lab, 1995-2003, mem. editl. bd., 1994—. Pres. Dist. 58 Bd. Edn., Downers Grove, Ill., 1976-79. Mem. Analytical Lab. Mgrs. Assn. (pres. 1986-87, treas. 1989, exec. dir. 2007—). Home: 5625 Carpenter Downers Grove IL 60516 Personal E-mail: dwgreen@albion.edu.

GREEN, DENNIS JOSEPH, retired lawyer; b. Milw., Sept. 28, 1941; m. Janet McQueen; children: Karla Pope, Cheryl Ashley, Deborah Relihan. BS in Mgmt., U. Ill., 1963, JD, 1968. Bar: Ill. 1968, Mo. 1968. Atty. Monsanto Co., St. Louis, 1968-75, asst. co. counsel, 1975-76, counsel, 1976-79; gen. counsel, sec. Fisher Controls Internat. Inc., Clayton, Mo., 1979-85, v.p., gen. counsel, sec., 1985-93;

v.p. Emerson Electric Co., St. Louis, 1999—, assoc. gen. counsel, 1999—2004, dep. gen. counsel, 2004—06; ret., 2006. 1st lt. U.S. Army, 1963-65. Office: Emerson Electric Co PO Box 4100 8000 W Florissant Ave Saint Louis MO 63136-1494 E-mail: dennis.green@emrsn.com.

GREEN, DON WESLEY, chemical and petroleum engineering educator; b. Tulsa, July 8, 1932; s. Earl Leslie and Erma Pansy (Brackins) G.; m. Patricia Louise Polston, ov. 26, 1954; children: Guy Leslie, Don Michael, Charles Patrick. BS in Petroleum Engring., U. Tulsa, 1955; MSChemE, U. Okla., 1959, PhD in Chem. Engring., 1963. Rsch. scientist Continental Oil Co., Ponca City, Okla., 1962-64; asst. to assoc. prof. U. Kans., Lawrence, 1964-71, prof. chem. and petroleum engring., 1971-82, chmn. dept. chem. and petroleum engring., 1970-74, 96-200, co-dir. Tertiary Oil Recovery project, 1974—, Conger-Gabel Disting. prof., 1982-95, Deane E. Ackers Disting. prof., 1995—. Faculty rep. to NCAA. Editor: Perry's Chemical Engineers' Handbook, 1984, 1997; co-author: Enhanced Oil Recovery, 1998; contbr. articles to profl. jours. 1st lt. USAF, 1955-57. Fellow Am. Inst. Chem. Engrs.; mem. Soc. Petroleum Engrs. (Disting. Achievement award 1983, chmn. edn. and accreditation com. 1980-81, Disting. mem. 1986, Disting. lectr. 1986). Democrat. Avocations: handball, baseball, hiking. Home: 1020 Sunset Dr Lawrence KS 66044-4546 Office: U Kans Dept Chem & Petroleum Engring 4008 Learned Hall Lawrence KS 66045-7526 E-mail: dgreen@ku.edu.

GREEN, EDWARD ANTHONY, museum director; b. Milw., Apr. 20, 1922; s. Edward Eli and Elizabeth Mary (Hofmeister) G.; m. Dorinne May Traulsen, June 20, 1953; children: Erika Linden, Jeremy Jonathon. BS in Art Edn., U. Wis., 1951, MS in Applied Art, 1951; MFA in Fine Arts with honors, U. Wis., Milw., 1966; student, Layton Sch. Art, 1953. Archtl. designer Wilbur Lumber Co., West Allis, Wis., 1940-42; playground dir. Milw. Recreation Dept., 1947-49; art dir. Milw. Pub. Mus., 1951-84; landmarks commr. City of Milw., 1959-80, art commr., 1959-84; dir. mus. Mitchell Gallery Flight, Milw., 1984—. Art instr. U. Wis., Milw., 1955-69, 84, Whitnall Park, Greendale, Wis., 1966-79, Cardinal Stritch U., Fox Point, Wis., 1975-90, Mt. Mary Coll., 1997; art instr., lectr. Alverno Coll., 1998; mus. cons. Roger Williams Park Nat. Hist. Mus., Providence, 1982, Mus. Architecture, Quincy, Ill., 1984, Milw. Children's Mus., 1991—, Great Lakes Naval Tng. Ctr., North Chicago, Ill., 1991—, USCG Mus., New London, Conn., 1993—, others; careers lectr. Kiwanis, Milw., 1969—, Alverno Coll., 1980; lectr. U. Wis., Milw., 1992—; bd. dirs. Great Lakes Future Resource Ctr., U. Wis. Milw. Alumni Trustees, 1995—. Designer: Bapt. Mission Ch., Bamenda, Cameroon, (books) Masks of the Northwest Coast, 1966, Iroquois Masks, 1969, Mambila, 1972; co-author: Popular Culture in Museums, 1981; works included in state and nat. exhbns., also pvt. and pub. collections. Bd. dirs. Retired Sr. Vol. Program, 1996. With USCG, 1942-46; served convoy duty in North Atlantic. Recipient European Mus. Study award U. Wis., 1959, Urban Planning award Ford Found., 1969, One of 85 Outstanding Milwaukeeens Milw. Mag., 1984, Lifework award Milw. Art Commn., 1985, Lifetime Achievement award U. Wis., Milw., 1999. Mem. USCG Aux. (life, comdr. 1976), Milw. Art Mus., Wis. Painters and Sculptors (pres. 1951-54), Jackson Park Assn., Longfield Shores Assn. (pres. 1976), Phi Kappa Phi. Roman Catholic. Avocations: collecting toy trains and Britain's toy soldiers, softball, sailing, painting. Home: 3173 S 31st St Milwaukee WI 53215-4319 Office: Mitchell Gallery of Flight 5300 S Howell Ave Milwaukee WI 53207-6156

GREEN, HAROLD DANIEL, dentist; b. Scranton, Pa., Feb. 4, 1934; s. Harold Charles and Viola Mildred (Brown) G.; m. Cornelia Ann Ellis, Aug. 1, 1959; children: Scott Alan, Mary Ann. BA, Beloit Coll., Wis., 1956; DDS, Northwestern U., 1960. Gen. practice dentistry, Beloit, Wis., 1964—. Dir. Beloit Savs. Bank, chmn. trust com., 1989—; mem loan com. Blackhawk State Bank, mem. fin. com., 1993. Contbr. articles to profl. jours. Active Wis. div. Am. Cancer Soc., 1964-75; 1st pres., co-organizer Citizen's Council Against Crime, Beloit; past officer, chmn. membership Beloit YMCA; pres. Beloit Brewers, chmn. bd., 1982-2002, class A midwest league affiliate of Milw. Brewers baseball team, 1986-87; chmn. Student Achievers Program, Wis., No. Ill.; mem. adv. bd. Salvation Army; chmn. Beloiters for Coun.-Mgr., 1989; stateline chmn. Student Achiever Program, 1988, 93; bd. dirs. Greater Beloit Found., 1989—; chmating com. Greater Beloit Community Trust, Inc., 1991,93; chmn. adminstrv. bd., chmn. Council of Ministries, First United Methodist Ch., Beloit, pastor parish rels., 1995—; chmn. ann. dinner, bd. dirs., nominating com., fundraising, pub. speakers Beloit Crime Stoppers, 1993—, chmn., 1995-96; chmn. facilities study com. Sch. Dist. Beloit, 1991—; chmn. Eagle Scout bd. rev. Sinnisippi coun. Boy Scouts Am., 1995-96; vice chair spkrs. bur. Beloit Sports Hall of Fame, 1998-99, chmn., 1999. Recipient award for creativity in dentistry Johnson & Johnson Co., 1970; 3 citations for Cmty. Svc. United Givers Fund, 1970-75; Disting. Svc. citation Greater Beloit Assn. Commerce; named to Rock County Hall of Honor, 2000 Fellow Acad. Gen. Dentistry, Internat. Coll. Dentists. (Wis. editor), Am. Acad. Dental Practice Adminstrn. (past chmn. profl. liaison; mem. ADA (chmn. council on dental practice 1982-84), Wis. Dental Assn. (pres. 1979-80, trustee 1968-74), Wis. Dental Assn. Found., Rock County Dental Soc. (pres. 1976), Wis. Council of Professions (bd. dirs. 1974-80, pres. 1973-75), Chgo. Dental Soc., Greater Milw. Dental Assn., Fedn. Dentaire Internationale, Pierre Fauchard Acad., Am. Acad. History of Dentistry, Lions (beloit programs, 1993—, past pres.), Delta Sigma Delta. Avocations: bicycling, golf, basketball, running, fishing. Home: 2207 Collingswood Dr Beloit WI 53511-2332 Office: 419 Pleasant St Beloit WI 53511-6249

GREEN, JOHN LAFAYETTE, JR., strategic planning executive, former educational association administrator; b. Trenton, NJ, Apr. 3, 1929; m. Harriet Hardin Hill, Nov. 8, 1962; 1 child, John Lafayette III. BA, Miss. State U., 1955; MEd, Wayne State U., 1971; PhD, Rensselaer Poly. Inst., 1974. Asst. to treas. Internat. Paper Co., 1955-57; mem. faculty U. Calif., Berkeley, 1957-65; v.p. U. Ga., Athens, 1965-71, Rensselaer Poly. Inst., Troy, NY, 1971-76; exec. v.p. U. Miami, 1976-80; sr. v.p. U. Houston, 1980-81; pres. Washburn U., Topeka, 1981-88; founder, exec. dir. Assn. Collegiate Bus. Schs. and Programs, Overland Park, 1988—95; pres., chmn. bd. dirs. Strategic Planning/Mgmt. Assocs., Inc., Overland Park, 1981—. Founder, pres. emeritus Internat. Assembly Collegiate Bus. Edn., Overland Park, 1997—2006; past. pres. Kansas City and Topeka chpts. Planning Forum; chmn. bd. Americans 50 Plus, 2005—. Author: Budgeting, 1967, (with others) Cost Accounting, 1969, Administrative Data Processing, 1970, Strategic Planning, 1980, Strategic Planning: A System for Businesses, 1986, A Strategic Planning System for Higher Education, 1987, Strategy Development and Implementation for Banks, 1988, co-author: Outcomes Assessment in Higher Education Linked to Strategic Planning and Budgeting, 1997, Outcomes Assessment in Higher Education, 2002. Bd. dirs. Boy Scouts Am., Topeka, 1983-85, Salvation Army, Boys Club, Athens, Ga. With US Army, 1951—53. Recipient Disting. Kansan of Yr. in Pub. Adminstrn. award Topeka Capital Jour., 1984, Kans. Pub. Adminstr. of Yr. award Am. Soc. Pub. Adminstrn., 1984, Disting. Exec. award Mktg. Exec. Kans., 1984, Edn. Leader's Hall of Fame award, 1995. Mem. AAUP, Conf. Bd., Am. Mgmt. Assn., Fin. Execs. Inst., Demographics Inst., Masons, Scottish Rite, Shriners, Royal Order of Jesters, Phi Delta Kappa, Beta Alpha Psi, Phi Kappa Phi, Pi Kappa Alpha, Delta Sigma Pi. Republican. Presbyterian. (elder, deacon). Avocations: golf, tennis, writing. Office: SPMA PO Box 23796 Overland Park KS 66283 Home: 7895 W 157 Terr Overland Park KS 66223 Office Phone: 913-262-6040. Personal E-mail: jlgreen4329@att.net.

GREEN, MARK ANDREW, ambassador, former congressman; b. Boston, June 1, 1960; s. Jeremy Raleigh and Elizabeth Pamela (Roome) Green; m. Susan Keske, Aug. 5, 1985; children: Rachel Eve Libinu, Anna Faith Kitali, Alexander Mark Amutavi. BA, U. Wis., Eau Claire, 1983; JD, U. Wis., Madison, 1987. Bar: Wis. 1987. Tchr., intern World Teach Project, Kakamega, Kenya, 1987-88; counsel Godfrey & Kahn, S.C., Green Bay, Wis., 1989-98; mem. Wis. State Assembly, Madison, 1992-98, chmn. assembly majority caucus, 1994-98, chmn. assembly judiciary com., 1994—98; state chmn. Am. Legis. Exch. Coun.; mem. US Congress from 8th Wis. dist., 1999—2007, mem. judiciary com., mem. internat. rels.; US amb. to Tanzania US Dept. State, Dar es Salaam, 2007—. Legal counsel Rep. Assembly Campaign Com., Madison, 1993. Chmn. mcpl. affairs Brown County Taxpayers Assn., Green Bay, 1990-92; chmn. Brown County Rep. Party, 1991-92; bd. dirs. Nat. R.R. Mus., Green Bay, 1992—; chmn. resolutions com. Wis. Rep. Conv., Milw., 1993. Named Wis. Outstanding Legislator, Wis. Builders Assn., 1995, Healthcare Leader of Wis., State Med. Soc., 1996, Small Bus. Adv., Small Bus. Survival Com., 1999, Super Friend of Srs., 60 Plus Assn., 1999, Friend of the Farm Bur., Am. Farm Bur. Fedn., 2000; recipient Wis. award, Ind. Bus. Assn., 1996, Legislator of Yr. award, Wis. Am. Legion, Spirit of Enterprise award, US C. of C., Mfg. Legis. Excellence award, Nat. Assn. Mfrs., Sr. Legis. Achievement award, Srs. Coalition, 1999—2000, Golden Bulldog award, Watchdogs of the Treas., 2000, Friend of the Family award, Christian Coalition, 2000, Award for Mfg. Excellence, Nat. Assn. Mfrs., 2000, Tax Fighter award, Nat. Tax Limitation Com., 2000, Guardian of Small Bus. award, Nat. Fedn. Ind. Bus., 2000, Thomas Jefferson award, Food Distbrs. Internat., 2000, Hero of the Taxpayer award, Ams. for Tax Reform, 2000, Small Bus. Survival Com. award, 2000, Yr. of the Sr. award, 60 Plus Assn., 2000, Friend of the Shareholder award, Am. Shareholders Assn., 2000. Mem. ABA, Wis. Bar Assn., Am. Legis. Exch. Coun., Nat. Conf. State Legislators, Brown County Home Builders Assn., Kiwanis. Republican. Roman Catholic. Office: Am Embassy 2140 Dar es Salaam Pl Washington DC 20521

GREEN, MAURICE, molecular biologist, educator, virologist; b. NYC, May 5, 1926; s. David and Bessie (Lipschitz) G.; m. Marilyn Glick, Aug. 20, 1950; children: Michael Richard, Wendy Allison Green Lee, Eric Douglas. BS in Chemistry, U. Mich., 1949; MS in Biochemistry and Chemistry, U. Wis.-Madison, 1952, PhD in Biochemistry and Chemistry, 1954. Instr. biochemistry U. Pa. Med. Sch., Phila., 1955-56; asst. prof. St. Louis U. Health Scis. Ctr., 1956-60, assoc. prof., 1960-63, prof. microbiology, 1963-77; prof., chmn. Inst. for Molecular Virology, 1964—. Office: St Louis U Health Sci Ctr Inst for Molecular Virology 3681 Park Ave Saint Louis MO 63110-2511 Business E-Mail: green@slu.edu.

GREEN, MIKE, state legislator; b. Risco, Miss., Sept. 28, 1948; Student, Flint Jr. Coll., 1966-68. Tool and die worker; mem. from dist. 84 Mich. State Ho. of Reps., Lansing, 1995—, minority vice chmn. agr. com., mem. transp., ins. and mental health coms.; chair agr. and resource mgmt. com., 1999-2000; mem. conservation and outdoor recreation com.; mem. constl. law and ethis, health policy com. Also: House Office Bldg S-1188 Lansing MI 48909

GREEN, MORRIS, retired pediatrician, educator; b. Indpls., May 27, 1922; s. Coleman and Rebecca (Oleinick) Green; m. Janice Barber Gorton, Mar. 11, 1955; children: David Schuster, Alan Coleman, Carolyn Ann, Susan Elaine, Marcia Ruth, Sylvia Rebecca. AB, Ind. U., 1942, MD, 1944. Intern Ind. U. Med. Ctr., 1945; resident pediat. U. Ill. Rsch. and Ednl. Hosps., 1947—49; instr. pediat. U. Ill. Coll. Medicine, 1949—52; asst. prof. Yale Sch. Medicine, 1952—57; faculty Ind. U. Sch. Medicine, Indpls., 1957—2006, Perry W. Lesh prof. pediat., 1963—2006; chmn. dept. pediat., physician-in-chief James Whitcomb Riley Hosp. for Children, Indpls., 1967—88. Commr. health State of Ind., 1990—91. Author: Pediatric Diagnosis, 6th edit., 1998; co-editor: Ambulatory Pediatrics, 1968, 5th edit., 1999, Bright Futures, 2d edit., 2000; mem. editl. bd.: Pediat. Rev., Contemporary Pediat., Current Problems Pediat., Jour. Devel. Behavioral Pediat., Jour. Ambulatory Pediat. Assn., Social Work in Health Care, nat. adviser: Children Today. Served to capt. M.C. US Army, 1945—47. Recipient George Armstrong award in ambulatory pediat., 1971, C. Anderson Aldrich award in child devel., 1982, Irving S. Cutter award, Phi Rho Sigma, 1984, Ross award for pediat. edn., 1985, Simon Wile award, Am. Acad. Child and Adolescent Psychiatry, 1990, Joseph W. St. Geme award, Fedn. Pediat. Orgns., 1992, Disting. Career award, Ambulatory Pediat. Assn., 1996, Lifetime award for disting. svc. in years of health advancement, Ind. Pub. Health Found., 2003. Mem.: AMA (Abraham Jacobi award 1990), Soc. Rsch. Child Devel., Inst. Medicine, Am. Orthopsychiat. Assn., Am. Acad. Pediat. (Abraham Jacobi award 1990), Am. Fedn. Clin. Rsch., Soc. Pediatric Rsch., Am. Pediatric Soc., Alpha Omega Alpha, Sigma Xi, Phi Beta Kappa. Home Phone: 301-869-2978. Personal E-mail: maunderw@iupui.edu.

GREEN, NANCY LOUGHRIDGE, publishing executive; b. Lexington, Ky., Jan. 19, 1942; d. William S. and Nancy O. (Green) Loughridge. BA in Journalism, U. Ky., 1964, postgrad., 1968; MA in Journalism, Ball State U., 1971; postgrad., U. Minn., 1968; EdD, Nova Southeastern U., 2003. Tchr. English, publs. adv. Clark County H.S., Winchester, Ky., 1965-66, Pleasure Ridge Park H.S., Louisville, 1966-67, Clarksville (Ind.) H.S., 1967-68, Charleston (W.Va.) H.S., 1968-69; asst. publs., pub. info. specialist W.Va. Dept. Edn., Charleston, 1969-70; tchr. journalism, publs. dir. Elmhurst H.S., Ft. Wayne, Ind., 1970-71; adviser student publs. U. Ky., Lexington, 1971-82; gen. mgr. student publs. U. Tex., Austin, 1982-85; pres., pub. Palladium-Item, Richmond, Ind., 1985-89, ews-Leader, Springfield, Mo., 1989-92; asst. to pres. newspaper divsn. Gannett Co., Inc., Washington, 1992-94; exec. dir. advancement Clayton State Coll., Morrow, Ga., 1994-96; v.p. advancement Clayton Coll. & State U., Morrow, Ga., 1996-99; v.p. comm. Ga. GLOBE U. Sys., 1999-2000; dir. circulation/distbn., sales & mktg. Lee Enterprises, Davenport, Iowa, 2000—02; v.p. circulation LEE Enterprises, Davenport, 2002—; pub. The Courier, 2004—. Dir. Dow Jonesurban journalism program Harte-Hanks, 1984, Louisville Courier-Jour. and Lexington Herald-Leader, 1976-82; pres. Media Cons., Inc., Lexington, 1980; sec. Kernel Press, Inc., 1971-82. Contbr. articles to profl. jours. Bd. dirs. Studen Press Law Ctr., 1975-2005, Richmond Cmty. Devel. Corp., 1987-89, United Way of the Ozarks, 1990-92, ARC, 1990-92, Springfield Arts Coun., 1990-91, Bus. Devel. Corp., 1991-92, Bus. Edn. Alliance, 1991-92, Caring Found., 1991-92, Cox Hosp. Bd., 1990-92, Springfield Schs. Found., 1964-82, Jr. League, Lexington, 1971-82, Manchester Ctr., 1978-82, pres., 1979-82; chmn. Greater Richmond Progress Com., 1986-87, bd. dirs., 1986-89; pres. Leadership Wayne County, 1986-87, bd. dirs. 1985-89; adv. bd. Ind. U. East, 1985-89, Richmond C. of C., 1987-89, Ind. Humanities Coun., 1988-89, Youth Comm. Bd., 1988-92, Opera Theatre No. Va., 1992-94, Atlanta chpt. AIWF, 1995-2000. Recipient Coll. Media Advisers First Amendment award, 1987, Disting. Svc. award Assn. Edn. Journalism and Mass Comm., 1989; named to Journalism Hall of Fame, Ball State U., 1988, Hall Fame, Coll. Media Advisors, 1994, Journalism Hall of Fame, Ky., 2007. Mem. Student Press Law Ctr. (bd. dirs. 1975-05, pres. 1985-87, 94-96, v.p. 1992-94), Assoc. Collegiate Press, Journalism Edn. Assn. (Carl Towley award 1988), Nat. Coun. Coll. Publs. Advs./Coll. Media Advisers (pres. 1979-83, Disting. Newspaper Adv. 1976, Disting. Bus. Adviser 1984), Columbia Scholastic Press Assn. (Gold Key 1980), So. Interscholastic Press Assn. (Disting. Svc. award 1983), Nat. Scholastic Press Assn. (Pioneer award 1982), Soc. Profl. Journalists, Internat. Newspaper Mktg. Assn. N.Am. (bd. dirs. 2002—07), Newspaper Assn. Am. (postal com. 2001—, readership adv. group 2002—, diversity subcom. 1991-05, circulation fed. bd. 2002-, 2d v.p. 2006, 1st v.p. 2007), pres. 2008, Clayton County C. of C. (adv. bd. 1995-99, chmn. internat. com. 1996-98), Cedar Falls C. of C. (bd. dirs. 2005—) Office: The Courier 501 Commercial St Waterloo IA 50701 Office Phone: 563-383-2126, 319-291-1500. Business E-Mail: nancy.green@lee.net.

GREEN, PETER MORRIS, classics educator, writer, translator; b. London, Dec. 22, 1924; came to U.S., 1971; s. Arthur and Olive Emily (Slaughter) G.; m. Lalage Isobel Pulvertaft, July 28, 1951 (div.); children: Timothy Michael Bourke, Nicholas Paul, Sarah Francesca; m. Carin Margreta Christensen, July 18, 1975. BA, Cambridge U., 1950, MA, PhD, Cambridge U., 1954. Dir. studies in classics Selwyn Coll., Cambridge, Eng., 1952-53; freelance writer, journalist, translator, London, 1954-63; lectr. Greek history and lit. Coll. Yr. in Athens, 1966-71; prof. classics U. Tex., Austin, 1971-97, James R. Dougherty Centennial prof., 1982-97, prof. emeritus, 1997—. Vis. prof. classics UCLA, 1976; vis. prof. history U. Iowa, 1997-98, adj. prof. classics, 1998—; vis. prof. history, Athens, 1999; Mellon chair in humanities Tulane U., 1986; vis. fellow, writer-in-residence Hellenic studies program Princeton U., 2001; King Charles II Disting. vis. prof. classics and ancient history East Carolina U., 2004 Whichard vis. prof. classics and ancient history, 2006. Fiction critic: Daily Telegraph, London, 1954-63; sr. cons. editor: Hodder & Stoughton Ltd., London, 1959-63; cons.: (Odyssey project) Nat. Radio Theatre, Chgo., 1980-81; author: The Sword of Pleasure, 1957 (Heinemann award for Lit. 1957), The Laughter of Aphrodite, 1965, Armada from Athens, 1970, The Shadow of the Parthenon, 1972, Alexander of Macedon 356-323 BC: A Historical Biography, 1974, 2d edit., 1991, Classical Bearings, 1989, ed edit., 1998, Alexander to Actium: The Historical Evolution of the Hellenistic Age, 1990, rev. edit., 1993, The Greco-Persian Wars, 1996, From Ikaria to the Stars, 2004, The Hellenistic Age: A Short History, 2007; translator, editor: Juvenal, The Sixteen Satires, 1967, 3d edit., 1998, Ovid: The Erotic Poems, 1982, Yannis Ritsos: The Fourth Dimension, 1993, Hellenistic History and Culture, 1993, Ovid: The Poems of Exile, 1994, rev. edit., 2005, Apollonios Rhodios, The Argonautika, 1997, The Poems of Catullus, bilingual edit., 2005, Diodorus Siculus 11-12.37.1: Greek History 480-431 B.C.: The Alternative Version, 2006; editor-in-chief Syllecta Classica, 1999—. Served to sgt. RAF, 1943-47. NEH fellow, 1983-84; Craven scholar Cambridge U., 1950; Obermann Ctr. for Advanced Rsch. fellow U. Iowa, 1997; recipient 1st prize Nat. Poetry Libr., 1997. Fellow Royal Soc. Lit. (council 1959-63); mem. Soc. for Promotion of Hellenic Studies (U.K.), Classical Assn. (U.K.), Am. Philol. Assn., Archaeol. Inst. Am., Mem. Liberal Party. Club: Savile (London). Office: Dept Classics U Iowa Iowa City IA 52242 Office Phone: 319-341-6573. Business E-Mail: peter-green-1@uiowa.edu.

GREEN, RICHARD CALVIN, JR., electric power and gas industry executive; b. Kansas City, Mo., May 6, 1954; s. Richard C. and Ann (Gableman) G.; m. Nancy Jean Risk, Aug. 6, 1977; children: Allison Thompt, Ashley Jean, Richard Calvin III. BSBA, So. Methodist U., 1976. With Mo. Pub. Service, Kansas City, 1976-85, exec. v.p., 1982-85; pres., CEO UtiliCorp. United Inc., Kansas City, 1985—89, Aquila, Inc., Kansas City, 1985—96, CEO, 1996—2001, pres., CEO, 2002—, chmn., 1989—. Bd. dirs. Midwest Rsch. Inst., The BHA Group, Inc., Urban Inst. Washington. Office: Aquila Inc 20 W 9th St Kansas City MO 64105-1704

GREEN, ROBERT K., lawyer, former energy executive; BS in Engring., Princeton U.; JD, Vanderbilt U. Bar: Mo. 1987. With Shearson Lehman Hutton, 1984—85; atty. Blackwell, Sanders, Matheny, Weary & Lombardi, Kansas City, 1987-88; asst. divsn. counsel Mo. Pub. Svc. divsn. UtiliCorp United, divsn. counsel Mo. Pub. Svc. divsn., v.p. adminstrn. Mo. Pub. Svc. divsn., sr. v.p. ops. Mo. Pub. Svc. divsn., pres. Mo. Pub. Svc. divsn., 1991—; exec. v.p., bd.d irs. UtiliCorp, Kansas City, Mo., 1993-96, pres., COO, 1996—2002; pres., CEO Aquila (formerly Utilicorp), 2002—03; ptnr. Blackwell Sanders Peper Martin LLP, Kansas City, Mo., 2003—. Bd. dirs. United Mo. Bank, CompGeeks.com.; chmn. United Energy, Melbourne, Australia, 1995, UnitedNetworks, Auckland, New Zealand, 1998; past bd. mem. Am. Gas Assn., Edison Elec. Inst. Contbr. articles to profl. jours. Chmn. Initiative for Competitive Inner City, Kansas City. Mem. ABA, Mo. Bar Assn., Kansas City Met. Bar Assn. Office: Blackwell Sanders Peper Martin Ste 1000 4801 Main St Kansas City MO 64112 Office Phone: 816-983-8121. Office Fax: 816-983-8080. Business E-Mail: rgreen@blackwellsanders.com.

GREEN, SAUL A., lawyer; BA, U. Mich., 1969; JD, U. Mich. Law, 1972. Asst. U.S. Atty., eastern dist. Mich U.S. Dept Justice, Mich., 1973—76; chief counsel U.S. Dept. of Housing and Urban Devel., Detroit, 1976—89; corp. counsel Wayne County, Mich., 1989—93; U.S. atty. Ea. Dist. Mich., Detroit, 1994—2001; ptnr. Miller, Canfield, Paddock and Stone, PLC, Detroit, 2001—, dir., Minority Bus Practice Group, Corp. Criminal Def. Group, 2001—. Office: Miller, Canfield, Paddock and Stone, PLC 150 West Jefferson, Suite 2500 Detroit MI 48226 E-mail: greens@millercanfield.com.

GREEN, SONIA MARIA, automotive executive; Dir. U.S. Hispanic mktg. div. Avon Co.; dir. Hispanic diversity mktg. and sales GM, 2001—. Past pres. Nat. Hispanic Corp. Coun.; mem. bd. Las Madrinas Mentoring Program, Nat. Task Force on Early Edn. for Hispanics, Nat. Hispanic Leadership Inst.; spkr. in field. Named to Elite Women, Hispanic Bus. Mag., 2005.

GREEN, TIMOTHY P., state legislator; b. North Saint Louis, Mo., June 29, 1963; m. Lisa Ann Green, 1990. BBA, U. Mo. St. Louis. State rep. Dist. 73 Mo. Ho. of Reps., 1988—. Mem. appropriations health and mental health com., ins. com., munic com.; vice chmn. labor com.; constrn. electrician. Office: Capitol Bldg 201 W Capitol Ave Jefferson City MO 65101-1556

GREEN, WILLIAM, archaeologist; b. Chgo., May 30, 1953; s. David and Lillian (Kerdeman) G. AB, Grinnell Coll., 1974; MA, U. Wis., 1977, PhD, 1987. Staff archaeologist State Hist. Soc. of Wis., Madison, 1978-86; asst. prof. archaeology Western Ill. U., Macomb, 1980, 81; state archaeologist U. Iowa, Iowa City, 1988-2001, adj. asst. prof. anthropology, 1988-94, adj. assoc. prof. anthropology, 1994-2001; dir. Logan Mus. Anthropology, Beloit (Wis.) Coll., 2001—, adj. prof. anthropology, 2001—. Editor jour. The Wis. Archaeologist, 1983-88; editor: Midcontinental Jour. Archaeology, 1998-02; contbr. articles and revs. to profl. jours. Chair Johnson County Hist. Preservation Commn., Iowa, 1991-93. Grantee NSF, 1990-91, State Hist. Soc. Iowa, Leopold Ctr. for Sustainable Agr., Iowa Acad. Sci., 1988-91, 95, Inst. Mus. and Libr. Svcs., 2003—. Fellow Am. Anthropol. Assn., Midwest Arch. Conf., Inc. (pres. 2002-04). Jewish. Office: Logan Mus Anthropology Beloit Coll Beloit WI 53511

GREENBAUM, LEWIS, lawyer; b. NYC, July 29, 1948; BA with honors, NYU, 1970; JD, Georgetown U., 1973. Bar: NY 1974, Ill. 1978. Ptnr. pub. fin. Katten Muchin Zavis Rosenman, Chgo. Office: Katten Muchin Rosenman 525 W Monroe St Ste 1900 Chicago IL 60661 Office Phone: 312-902-5418. Office Fax: 312-577-8960. Business E-Mail: lewis.greenbaum@rattenlaw.com.

GREENBAUM, STUART I., economist, educator; b. NYC, Oct. 7, 1936; s. Sam and Bertha (Freimark) G.; m. Margaret E. Wache, July 29, 1964; children: Regina Gail, Nathan Carl. BS, NYU, 1959; PhD, Johns Hopkins U., 1964. Fin. economist Fed. Res. Bank of Kansas City, Mo., 1962-66; sr. economist Office of the Comptroller of the Currency, Washington, 1966-67; assoc. prof. econs. U. Ky., Lexington, 1968-74, prof., 1974-76, chmn. dept. econs., 1975-76; vis. prof. fin. Kellogg Grad. Sch. Mgmt., Northwestern U., Evanston, Ill., 1974-75, prof. fin., 1976-78, Harold L. Stuart prof. banking and fin., 1978-83, Norman Strunk disting. prof. fin. instns., 1983-95, dir. Banking Research Ctr., 1976-95, assoc. dean for acad. affairs, 1988-92, vis. prof., 2006—; dean John M. Olin Sch. of Bus., Washington U., St. Louis, 1995—2005, Bank of Am. prof. managerial leadership, 2000—07, prof. emeritus, 2007—. Cons. Fed. Res. Bank Chgo., 1994-95, 2005-; mem. Fed. Savs. and Loan Adv. Coun., 1986-89; vis. prof. banking and fin. Leon Recanati Grad. Sch. Bus. Adminstrn., Tel Aviv (Israel) U., 1980-81; vis. scholar E.M. Kauffman Found., 2005-06. Assoc. editor Nat. Banking Rev., 1966-67, So. Econ. Jour., 1977-79, Jour. Fin., 1977-83, Jour. Banking and Fin., 1980-92, Jour. Fin. Rsch., 1981-87, Fin. Rev., 1985-89, Managerial and Decision Econs., 1989-94, Jour. Econs., Mgmt. and Strategy, 1991-95; founding and mng. editor Jour. Fin. Intermediation, 1989-96, mem. editl. adv. com., 2004—. With US Army, 1958—64. Mem.: Am. Econ. Assn. Office: Washington U Campus Box 1133 One Brookings Dr Saint Louis MO 63130-4899 Business E-Mail: greenbaum@wustl.edu.

GREENBERG, BERNARD, retired entomologist; b. NYC, Apr. 24, 1922; s. Isidore and Rose (Gordon) Greenberg; m. Barbara Muriel Dickler, Sept. 1, 1949; children: Gary, Linda, Deborah, Daniel. BA, Bklyn. Coll., 1944; MA, U. Kans., 1951, PhD, 1954. Asst. prof. biology U. Ill. Med. Ctr., Chgo., 1954-61, assoc. prof., 1961-66, prof. geophys. scis., 1966-90, prof. emeritus, 1990—. Vis. scientist Istituto Superiore di Sanita, Rome, 1960—61, Fulbright-Hays sr. rsch. scholar, 1967—68; vis. scientist Instituto de Salubridad y Enfermedades Tropicales, Mexico City, 1962, Mexico City, 63; pres. Bioconcern; nat. lectr. Sigma Xi, 1996—; cons. in field; expert witness forensic entomology. Author: Flies and Disease, vol. 1, 1971, Flies and Disease, vol. 2, 1973, Entomology and the Law: Flies as Forensic Indicators, 2002; contbr. articles to profl. jours. With USAF, 1944—46. NSF grantee, 1959—60, 1979—81, NIH grantee, 1960—67, U.S. Army Med. R & D Command grantee, 1966—72, Electric Power Rsch. Inst. grantee, 1976—85, Office Naval Rsch. grantee, 1977—78. Fellow: AAAS; mem.: Chgo. Acad. Sci. (sci. gov. 1981—91), Entomol. Soc. Am. Home: 1463 E 55th Pl Chicago IL 60637-1875 Office: Dept Biol Scis M/C 066 U Ill Chgo Chicago IL 60607 Office Phone: 312-996-3103. Personal E-mail: barbnbern@hotmail.com. Business E-Mail: bugaboo@uic.edu.

GREENBERG, BRADLEY SANDER, communications educator; b. Toledo, Aug. 3, 1934; s. Abraham and Florence (Cohen) G.; m. Delight Thompson, June 7, 1959; children: Beth, Shawn, Debra. BA in Journalism; Univ. scholar, Bowling Green State U., 1956; MS in Journalism; Univ. fellow, U. Wis., 1957, PhD in Mass Communication, 1961. Postdoctoral fellow Mass. Comms. Rsch. Ctr., 1960-61; research asso. Inst. Communication Research, Stanford U., 1961-64; asst. prof. Mich. State U., East Lansing, 1964-66, assoc. prof., 1966-71, prof. dept. communication, 1971—2004, Univ. Disting. prof., 1990, chmn. dept., 1977-84, prof. telecommunication, 1975—2004, chmn. dept., 1984-90. Vis. prof. U. Mich., 2004, U. Ga., Athens, 1999, U. Calif., Berkeley, 1992; fellow Ctrs. Disease Control and Prevention, Atlanta, 1999; sr. fellow East-West Ctr., Comms. Inst., Honolulu, 1978-79, 81; rsch. fellow Ind. Broadcasting Authority, London, 1985-86; cons. Pres.'s Commn. on Causes and Prevention Violence, 1968-69, Surgeon Gen.'s Sci. Adv. Com. on TV and Social Behavior, 1970-72, 82. Author: The Kennedy Assassination and the American Public: Social Communication in Crisis, 1965, Use of Mass Media by the Urban Poor, 1970, Life on Television, 1980, Mexican Americans and the Mass Media, 1983, Cableviewing, 1988, Teletext in the U.K., 1988, Mass Media, Sex and the Adolescent, 1993, Desert Storm and the Mass Media, 1993, The Alphabet Soup of TV Ratings, 2001, Communication and Terrorism, 2003. Served to maj. U.S. Army Res., 1973. Recipient Chancellors award for disting. svc. in journalism U. Wis., 1978, disting. faculty award Mich. State U., 1979; named to Journalism Hall of Fame Bowling Green State U., 1980; rsch. grantee IH, NSF, USPHS, Carnegie Corp., Hoso Bunka Found., Nat. Assn. Broadcasters. Fellow Internat.

Comm. Assn. (pres. 1994-95); mem. Assn. for Edn. in Journalism, Phi Kappa Phi (pres. 1993-94). Home: 350 Winterberry Ln Okemos MI 48864-4166 Office: Mich State U Dept Telecommunication 569 Communication Arts Sci East Lansing MI 48824-1212 Office Phone: 517-353-6629. E-mail: bradg@msu.edu.

GREENBERG, DAVID BERNARD, chemical engineering educator; b. Norfolk, Va., Nov. 2, 1928; s. Abraham David and Ida (Frenkil) G.; m. Helen Muriel Levine, Aug. 15, 1959 (div. Aug. 1980); children: Lisa, Jan, Jill BS in Chem. Engring., Carnegie Inst. Tech., 1952; MS in Chem. Engring., Johns Hopkins U., 1959; PhD, La. State U., 1964. Registered profl. engr., La. Process engr. U.S. Indsl. Chem. Co., Balt., 1952-55; project engr. FMC Corp., Balt., 1955-56; asst. prof. U.S. Naval Acad., Annapolis, Md., 1958-61; from instr. to prof. La. State U., Baton Rouge, 1961-74; prof. chem. engring. U. Cin., 1974—, head dept., 1974-81, prof. emeritus, 2007. Program dir. engring. divsn. NSF, Washington, 1972-73, chem. and thermal scis. divsn., 1989-90; sr. scientist Chem. Sys. Lab., Dept. Army, Edgewood, Md., 1981-83; cons. Burk & Assocs., New Orleans, 1970-78; lectr. U. Cin. Coll. Continuing Edn., 2002—. Contbr. numerous articles on chem. engring. to profl. jours. Mem. Cin. Mayor's Energy Task Force, 1981—. Served to lt. USNR, 1947-52 Esso rsch. fellow, 1964-65, NSF fellow, 1961 Fellow Am. Soc. for Laser Medicine and Surgery; mem. Am. Inst. Chem. Engrs., Am. Chem. Soc., Am. Soc. for Engring. Edn., Sigma Xi, Tau Beta Pi, Phi Lambda Upsilon. Jewish. Home: 8547 Wyoming Club Dr Cincinnati OH 45215-4243 Office: Univ Cincinnati Dept Chem and Materials Engring PO Box 210012 Cincinnati OH 45221-0012 Home Phone: 513-821-1868. Business E-Mail: david.greenberg@uc.edu.

GREENBERG, GERALD STEPHEN, lawyer; b. Phila., July 27, 1951; s. Bernard and Elaine Alice (Shapiro) G.; m. Pamela Sue Meyers, Aug. 24, 1975; children: David Stuart, Allison Brooke. BA summa cum laude (hon.), Dickinson Coll., 1973; JD magna cum laude (hon.), Harvard U., 1976. Bar: NY 1977, US Dist. Ct. (so. dist.) NY 1977, Ohio 1988. Assoc. Kaye, Scholer, Fierman, Hays & Handler, NYC, 1976-86; atty. Exxon Corp., NYC, 1986-87; assoc. Taft, Stettinius & Hollister LLP, Cin., 1987-89; ptnr. Taft, Stettinius & Hollister, Cin., 1990—. Named Ohio Super Lawyer. Mem. ABA, Assn. of Bar NYC, Cin. Bar Assn. Office: Taft Stettinius & Hollister LLP 425 Walnut St Ste 1800 Cincinnati OH 45202 Office Phone: 513-381-2838. Office Fax: 513-381-0250. E-mail: greenberg@taftlaw.com.

GREENBERG, JACK M., former food products executive; b. Sept. 28, 1942; s. Edith S. Scher; m. Donna Greenberg; children: David, Ilyse, Allison. BSc in Acctg., DePaul U., Chgo., 1964, JD, 1968. CPA Ill.; bar:. With Arthur Young & Co., 1964-82; vice chmn., CFO McDonald's Corp., Oak Brook, Ill., CFO, exec. v.p., 1982, vice chmn., CFO, 1992, vice chmn., 1991—98, pres., 1998—99, pres. US Bus., 1997, CEO, 1998—2002, chmn., 1999—2002. Bd. dirs. Abbott Labs, Abbot Park, Ill., Allstate Corp., Northbrook, Ill., Hasbro, Inc., Pawtucket, RI, Manpower Inc., Milw., Innerworkings, Inc., Chgo.; chmn. Western Union. Bd. dirs. DePaul U. Field Mus., Inst. Internat. Edn., Chgo. (Ill.) Cmty. Trust. Mem.: AICPA, Ill. Inst. Cert. Pub. Accts. Office Phone: 312-368-7001. E-mail: jack.greenberg@us.mcd.com.

GREENBERG, RICHARD T., lawyer; b. Bklyn., June 10, 1952; s. Melvin David and Dolores Ruth (Siegartel) Greenberg; m. Kara M. Friedman; children: Brett, Matthew, Jodi, oah. BA with distinction, Northwestern U., 1974; JD, NYU, 1977. Bar: Ill. 1977, U.S. Dist. Ct. (no. dist.) Ill. 1977, U.S. Dist. Ct. (ctrl. dist.) Ill. 2005, U.S. Dist. Ct. (ea. dist.) Wis. 2005, US Ct. Appeals 7th Cir. 1982. From assoc. to ptnr. Peterson & Ross, Chgo., 1977-87; ptnr. McCullough, Campbell & Lane, Chgo., 1987-96, Ross & Hardies, Chgo., 1996—2003, McGuireWoods LLP, Chgo., 2003—, mng. ptnr. Chgo. office, 2004—. Bd. dirs. Temple B'nai Torah, Highland Park, Ill., 1995-98. Mem. ABA, Ill. Bar Assn., Chgo. Bar Assn. Avocations: reading, politics, running. Office: McGuireWoods LLP Ste 4100 77 W Wacker Dr Chicago IL 60601-1818 Office Phone: 312-750-5755. Office Fax: 312-558-4377. Business E-Mail: rgreenberg@mcguirewoods.com.

GREENBERG, STEVE, brokerage house executive; Pres. Alaron Trading Corp., Chgo. Office: Alaron Trading Corp 822 W Washington St Chicago IL 60607-2302

GREENBERGER, PAUL ALLEN, allergist, immunologist, educator, medical researcher; b. Pitts., May 28, 1947; s. Lawrence Fred and Jean (Half) G.; m. Rosalie Simon, Dec. 29, 1974; children: Rachel, Daniel. BS, Purdue U., 1969; MD, Ind. U., 1973. Intern Meth. Hosp., Indpls., 1973; resident in medicine Washington U., St. Louis, 1974-76; allergy, immunology fellow Northwestern U., Chgo., 1976-78, asst. prof. medicine, 1979-83, assoc. prof., 1983-88, prof., 1988—. Contbr. articles to profl. jours. Fellow ACP, Am. Thoracic Soc., Am. Coll. Chest Physicians, Am. Acad. Allergy and Immunology, Am. Coll. Allergy Asthma and Immunology, Cen. Soc. for Clin. Rsch. Office: Northwestern U Dept Medicine 676 N St Clair St #14018 Chicago IL 60611 Office Phone: 312-695-4000. Business E-Mail: p-greenberger@northwestern.edu.

GREENBLATT, DEANA CHARLENE, elementary school educator; b. Chgo., Mar. 13, 1948; d. Walter and Betty (Lamasky) Beisel; m. Mark Greenblatt, June 22, 1975. BEd, Chgo. State U., 1969; MA in Guidance and Counseling, Roosevelt U., 1973. Cert. tchr. K-9 Ill., Ohio, personnel guidance Ill., Ohio. Tchr., counselor Chgo. Pub. Schs., 1969—75, tchr., 1993—; tchr., counselor City Colls. Chgo. GED-TV, Chgo., 1976; tchr. Columbus (Ohio) Pub. Schs., 1976—86. Participant learning exchange, Chgo. Vol. Right-to-Readmem, Columbus; active Cmty. Learning Exchange, Acad. Yr. in USA Com. Counselor, 1989—, B'nai B'rith. Mem.: Internat. Platform Assn., Am. Pers. and Guidance Assn., B'nai B'rith Women Club (chpt. v.p.). Democrat. Home: 3820 W Touhy Ave Lincolnwood IL 60712-1026

GREENBLATT, WILLIAM, photographer; b. St. Louis, June 9, 1954; BS in Edn., U. Mo., 1977, MEd, 1981. Pres. William Greenblatt Photography, Inc., St. Louis, 1972—; photographer UPI, St. Louis, 1977—, Getty Images; bureau chief, St. Louis UPI, St. Louis. Mem. adv. bd. Salvation Army, St. Louis, 1996—, Harbor Light. Recipient 1st pl., 2d pl. award, Baseball Hall of Fame, 1991, 2d pl. award, 2003. Mem.: Nat. Coll. Baseball Writers Assn., U.S. Basketball Writers Assn., Football Writers Assn. Am., Press Club Met. St. Louis (bd. dirs.), Soc. Environ. Journalists, Soc. Profl. Journalists, Investigative Reporters and Editors, Nat. Press Photographers Assn., Am. Soc. Media Photographers. Home and Office: 20 Nantucket Ln Saint Louis MO 63132-4135 Office: United Press Internat St Louis Bureau 20 Nantucket Ln Saint Louis MO 63132-4135 Fax: 314-991-9320.

GREENE, JOSEPH E., material science researcher; PhD in Materials Sci., U.S.C., 1971. Prof. U. Ill., 1971—; Erlander prof. Physics Linkping U., Sweden. Editor: CRC Critical Revs. in Solid State and Materials Sci., Thin Solid Films. Recipient Tage Erlander Physics prize 1992-95, Tech. Excellence award Semiconductor Rsch. Corp. 1994, Dept. Energy Sustained Outstanding Rsch. award 1996, David Adler Lectrship. award 1998. Mem. Am. Vacuum Soc. (bd. dirs., pres.), Am. Inst. Physics (gov. bd. mem.), Am. Physical Soc., AVS, TMS, MRS. Office: Dept Materials Sci and Engring U Ill 1101 W Springfield Ave Urbana IL 61801-3005

GREENE, LAURA HELEN, physicist; b. Cleve., June 12, 1952; d. Sam and Frances (Kain) G.; children: Max Greene Giannetta, Leo Greene Giannetta. BS cum laude in Physics, Ohio State U., 1974, MS in Physics, 1978; MS in Exptl. Physics, Cornell U., 1980, PhD in Physics, 1984. Mem. tech. staff Hughes Aircraft Co., Torrance, Calif., 1974-75; tchg. asst. Ohio State U., Columbus, 1975-76, rsch. asst., 1976-77; tchg. asst. Cornell U., Ithaca, NY, 1977-79, rsch. asst., 1979-83; postdoctoral mem. tech. staff Bellcore (formerly Bell Labs.), Red Bank, NJ, 1983-85, Murray Hill, NJ, 1983-85, mem. tech. staff Red Bank, NJ, 1985-92; prof. dept. physics U. Ill., Urbana, 1992—, Swanlund endowed chair, 2000—. Beckman assoc. Ctr. Advanced Study U Ill. at Urbana-Champaign, 1996-97, mem. provost's com. on sexual harassment edn., 1999-2001, mem. physics adv. com., 1999—; mem. McMillan award com. 1994-96, chair, 1995-97; co-chair Gordon Rsch. Conf., 1996, chair, 1998; mem.-at-large Coun. Gordon Rsch. Confs., 1999—, mem. schedule and selection com.; mem. Basic Energy Scis. Adv. Com., 2000; interim and founding bd. trustee Inst. for Complex and Adaptive Materials, Los Alamos and U. Calif.; mem. various rev. panels and workshops NSF and Dept. Energy; presenter in field; resident assoc. ctr. for advanced study U. Ill., Urbana, Ill., 2000-2001; rev. panel Can. Inst. Advanced Rsch., Superconductivity Rev., 2002; mem. oversight com. for vice chancellor rsch., U. Ill., 2001-2002, Sloan Found. Selection Com. for Physics, 2001—; adv. com. Sec. of Energy Bill Richardson, 2000—; chair external rev. panel, mem. bd. trustees Ctr. Integrated Nanotechnologies Nat. Lab., Los Alamos Nat. Lab., Sandia Nat. Lab. Contbr. over 200 articles to profl. jours.; presenter over 150 domestic and internat. invited talks. Recipient Beckman award U. Ill. Campus Rsch. Bd., 1993, E.O. Lawrence award Dept. Energy, 1999, 2001; rsch. grantee NSF, 1991—, ONR, 1995—, Dept. Energy, 1995—. Fellow AAAS (electorate nominating com. of sect. B physics 2000—, chmn. nominating com. for physics, 2001-02), Am. Acad. Arts and Scis., Am. Phys. Soc. (gen. councilor 1992—, congl. fellow screening com. 1993, exec. bd. 1995—, com. on coms. 1995—, chair 1997, search com. The Phys. Rev. 1996, nominating com. divsn. condensed matter physics 1998—, Maria Goeppert-Mayer award 1994, Centennial Spkr. 1997); mem. Materials Rsch. Soc. (symposium chair 1992), Am. Assn. Physics Tchrs., Internat. Union Pure and Applied Physicists (commr., U.S. liaison com. 1996—, U.S. del. to Low-Temperature Physics Commn. 1996—), Phi Kappa Phi, NAS. Avocations: physics, exercise, music. Office: U Ill Loomis Lab Physics 1110 W Green St Urbana IL 61801-9013 E-mail: lhg@uiuc.edu.

GREENE, ROBERT (BOB) BERNARD, JR., news correspondent, journalist, writer; b. Columbus, Ohio, Mar. 10, 1947; s. Robert Bernard and Phyllis Ann (Harmon) G.; m. Susan Bonnet Koebel, Feb. 13, 1971; 1 dau., Amanda Sue. BS, Northwestern U., 1969. Reporter Chgo. Sun-Times, 1969-71, columnist, 1971-78; syndicated columnist Field Newspaper Syndicate, Irvine, Calif., 1976-81, Tribune Co. Syndicate, NYC, 1981—2002; contbg. corr. ABC News Nightline, from 1981; columnist Chgo. Tribune, 1978—2002. Lectr. fine arts U. Chgo. Contbg. editor: Esquire Mag., 1980—; books include We Didn't Have None of Them Fat Funky Angels on the Wall of Heartbreak Hotel and Other Reports from America, 1971; Running: A Nixon-McGovern Campaign Journal, 1973, Billion Dollar Baby, 1974, Johnny Deadline, Reporter: The Best of Bob Greene, 1976, (with Paul Galloway) Bagtime, 1977, American Beat, 1983, Good Morning, Merry Sunshine, 1984, Cheeseburgers, The Best of Bob Greene, 1985, Be True to Your School, 1987, Homecoming: When the Soldiers Returned From Vietnam, 1989, Hang Time: Days and Dreams With Michael Jordan, 1992, All Summer Long, 1993, Once Upon a Town: The Miracle of the North Platte Canteen, 2002, And You Know You Should Be Glad, 2006. Recipient at. Headliner award for best newspaper column in U.S., 1977, Peter Lisagor award, 1981

GREENE, TERRY J., legislative staff member; m. Tricia; children: Patrick, Brady, Douglas, Teddy. Student, Ariz. State U.; BA in Speech Comm., Drury Coll. Press sec. Congressman Thomas Ewing, Washington, 1991-95, dist. adminstr., 1995-96, chief of staff, chief advisor pub. policy, legis. matters, 1996—. Baseball scholar Ariz. State U. Office: 1808 Cypress Pointe Ct Mahomet IL 61853-3671

GREENER, RALPH BERTRAM, lawyer; b. Rahway, NJ, Sept. 23, 1940; s. Ralph Bertram and Mary Ellen (Esch) G.; m. Jean Elizabeth Wilson, Mar. 21, 1964; children: Eric Wilson, Erin Hope, Nicholas Christian. BA, Wheaton Coll., 1962; JD, Duke U., 1968. Bar: Minn. 1969. With Fredrikson & Byron P.A., Mpls., 1969—. Chmn. bd. Minn. Lawyers Mutual Ins. Co., Mpls. 1981—. 1st Lt. USMCR, 1962-65. Recipient award of profl. excellence Minn. State Bar Assn., 1993. Mem. Rotary Club (pres. Mpls. 2002-03). Office: Fredrikson & Byron PA 200 S 6th St Ste 4000 Minneapolis MN 55402-1425 Home: 1314 Marquette Ave #2402 Minneapolis MN 55403 E-mail: rgreener@fredlaw.com.

GREENFIELD, JOHN CHARLES, biochemist, professional society administrator; b. Dayton, Ohio, 1945; s. Ivan Ralph and Mildred Louise (House) Greenfield; m. Liga Miervaldis, Aug. 20, 1980; children: John Hollen, Mark Richard. BS cum laude, Ohio U., 1967; PhD, U. Ill., 1974. Instr. sci. area HS, Dayton, 1968-71; grad. rsch. asst. U. Ill., 1971-74; postdoctoral rsch. fellow Swiss Fed. Inst. Tech., Zurich, 1975-76; rsch. chemist infectious diseases rsch. Upjohn Co., Kalamazoo, 1976-82, sr. rsch. scientist drug metabolism rsch., 1982-93; sr. project mgr. Upjohn Labs., Kalamazoo, 1993-95, Pharmacia & Upjohn Inc., Kalamazoo, 1995-96; acquisitions review specialist, bus. devel. Pharmacia and Upjohn, Inc., Kalamazoo, 1996-98, clin. monitor, US market co. med. affairs, 1998-2000; dir. global med. svcs. Pharmacia Inc., Kalamazoo, 2000—03, Pfizer, Inc., Kalamazoo, 2003—04; v.p. bus. devel. Biomedical and Pharmaceutical Info. Solutions, Kalamazoo, 2004—07; exec. dir. Mich. Core Tech. Alliance, Grand Rapids, Mich., 2007—. Contbr. articles to profl. jours. Adult leader Boy Scouts Am. Am.-Swiss Found. Sci. Exch. fellow, 1975, NSF-NATO postdoctoral fellow, 1975—76. Mem.: AAAS, Drug Info. Assn., Am. Assn. Microbiology, Am. Assn. Pharm. Scientists, Am. Chem. Soc., Sigma Xi, Delta Tau Delta, Phi Lambda Upsilon, Blue Key, Phi Eta Sigma. Achievements include patents in field; identification, evaluation and management of worldwide research and development projects for new pharmaceutical agents. Home: 6695 E E Ave Richland MI 49083-9471 Office: Van Andel Inst 333 Bostwick Ave NE Grand Rapids MI 49503 Office Phone: 616-234-5516. Business E-Mail: john.greenfield@vai.org.

GREENFIELD, LAZAR JOHN, surgeon, educator; b. Houston, Dec. 14, 1934; s. Robert G. and Betty B. (Greenfield) Heath; m. Sharon Dee Bishkin, Aug. 29, 1956; children: John, Julie, Jeff. Student, Rice U., 1951-54; MD, Baylor U., 1958. Diplomate: Am. Bd. Surgery (dir. 1976-82), Am. Bd. Thoracic Surgery, cert. gen. vascular surgery, 1991. Intern Johns Hopkins Hosp., Balt., 1958-59, resident, 1961-66; chief surgery VA Hosp., Oklahoma City, 1966-74; prof. dept. surgery U. Okla. Med. Center, 1971-74; Stuart McGuire prof., chmn. dept. surgery Med. Coll. Va., Richmond, 1974-87; F.A. Coller prof., chmn. dept of surgery U. Mich., 1987—2002; CEO U. Mich. Health System, 2002—03; interim exec. v.p. med. affairs U. Mich. Med. Sch., 2002—03; sabbatical FDA, 2003—04. Mem. surgery A study sect. NIH. Author: Surgery in the Aged, 1975; editor-in-chief Surgery, Scientific Principles and Practice, 1993, 96, 3d edit., 2001, Surgery News, 2004-; editor Complications in Surgery and Trauma, 1983, 2d edit., 1990; contbr. to profl. publs. Served with USPHS, 1959-61. Recipient Disting. Alumni award Rice U., 1999; Thomas R. Franklin scholar, 1952, John and Mary Markle scholar in med. sci., 1968-73. Mem. Inst. of Medicine of NAS, Am. Surg. Assn., Am. Assn. Thoracic Surgery, Assn. Acad. Surgery, Soc. Univ. Surgeons, Johns Hopkins Soc. Scholars, Phi Delta Epsilon. Home: 505 E Huron St Ann Arbor MI 48104-1573 Office: UMMC Surgery 1327 Jones Dr # 201 Ann Arbor MI 48105 Home Phone: 734-668-7571; Office Phone: 734-936-6398. E-mail: lazarg@umich.edu.

GREENFIELD, LEE, state legislator; b. Bklyn., July 29, 1941; s. Solomen and Edith (Herschman) G.; m. Marcia Greenfield, Nov. 25, 1965. BS in Physics, Purdue U., West Lafayette, Ind., 1963; postgrad., U. Minn., 1963-73. Instr. applied math. U. Minn., Mpls., 1964-73; prin. asst. Hennepin County Bd. Commrs., Mpls., 1975-77; mgmt. analyst Office of Planning & Devel., Hennepin County, Mpls., 1977; rep. Minn. Ho. of Reps., St. Paul, 1979-2000; prin. adminstrv. asst. Hennepin County Dept. Human Svcs. and Pub. Health, 2001—. Mem. steering com. Reforming State Group, N.Y.C., 1993—, chmn., 1994-96. Bd. dirs. Twin City Cmty. Program for Affordable Health Care, Mpls., 1982-84, Arthritis Found., Mpls., 1988-90, Minn. Aids Project Mpls., 2002-, Minn. Vis. Nurse Agy., Mpls., 2003-, Ams. for Dem. Action, Mpls., 1979—, v.p., 1976-78. Recipient Dwight V. Dixon award Mental Health Assn. Minn., 1994. Mem. Mental Health Assn. Minn. (Disting. Svc. award 1987), Planned Parenthood of Minn. (Pub. Svc. award 1993). Dfl. Jewish. Office: Hennepin County Health Policy Ctr A-1702 Government Center Minneapolis MN 55487-0172 Home Phone: 612-724-7549; Office Phone: 612-348-3553. Business E-Mail: lee.greenfield@co.hennepin.mn.us.

GREENFIELD, NORMAN SAMUEL, psychologist, educator; b. NYC, June 2, 1923; s. Max and Dorothy (Hertz) G.; m. Marjorie Hanson Klein, May 17, 1969; children— Ellen Beth, Jennifer Ann, Susan Emery. BA, NYU, 1948; MA, U. Calif., Berkeley, 1951, PhD, 1953. Fellow med. psychology Langley Porter Clinic, U. Calif. Med. Center, 1949-50; VA Mental Health Clinic trainee San Francisco, 1950-53; instr. clin. psychology U. Oreg. Med. Sch., 1953-54; from asst. prof. to prof. psychiatry U. Wis. Med. Sch., Madison, 1954—2005, emeritus prof. psychiatry, 2006—; assoc. dir. Wis. Psychiat. Inst., U. Wis. Ctr. for Health Scis., 1961-74. Emeritus prof. psychiatry, 1991—. Co-editor: The New Hospital Psychiatry, Handbook of Psychophysiology, Psychoanalysis and Current Biological Thought; contbr. articles to profl. jours. Served with USAAF, 1943-46. Mem. AAUP, Am. Psychol. Assn., Soc. Psychophysiol. Rsch., Am. Psychosomatic Soc. Office: U Wis Psychiat Inst 6001 Research Park Blvd Madison WI 53719-1176 E-mail: ngreen5921@aol.com.

GREENFIELD, ROGER ALAN, restaurant company executive; b. Chgo., Oct. 14, 1951; s. Martin David and Helen Geneva (Solberg) G.; m. Elizabeth Mary Fritz, Mar. 15, 1986. BA, Occidental Coll. Owner American Grill, Glenview, Ill., The Diner, Glenview, Dixie Bar & Grill, Coyote Grill, Chgo., Jim McMahon's, Cucina Cucina!, Bar Louie, Chgo. Home: 3605 S Ocean Blvd Apt 107B Palm Beach FL 33480-5816 Office: Greenfield Restaurant Group 414 N Orleans Suite 310 Chicago IL 60610

GREENFIELD, SUSAN L., lawyer; m. Lawrence Abramson; children: Rebecca, Kate. BA, Wayne State U., 1970, JD, 1975. In house atty. Fruehoff Trailer Corp., Valeron Corp., 1977—87; staff atty. Guardian Industries Corp., 1987—94; with Palace Sports and Entertainment Inc., 1994—, v.p. & gen. counsel; v.p. -legal Detroit Pistons. Office: Palace Sports & Entertainment Inc 4 Championship Dr Auburn Hills MI 48326

GREENGUS, SAMUEL, academic administrator, theology studies educator; b. Chgo., Mar. 11, 1936; s. Eugene and Thelma (Romirowsky) G.; m. Lesha Bellows, Apr. 30, 1957; children: Deana, Rachel, Judith. Student, Hebrew Theol. Coll., Chgo., 1950-58; MA, U. Chgo., 1959, PhD, 1963. Prof. semitic langs. Hebrew Union Coll.-Jewish Inst. Religion, Cin., 1963-89, Julian Morgenstern prof. bible and near eastern lit., 1989—, dean rabbinic sch., 1979-84, dean Cin. campus, 1985-87, dean sch. grad. studies, 1985-90, dean faculty, 1987-98, v.p. for Acad. affairs, 1990-96. Vis. lectr. U. of Dayton, Ohio, 1964-69, Leo Baeck Coll., London, 1976-77; area supr. Tel Gezer Excavation, Israel, 1966-67; mem. bd. editors Hebrew Union Coll. Ann. Author: Old Babylonian Tablets from Ishchali and Vicinity, 1979, Studies in Ishchali Documents, 1986; mem. bd. editors Zeitschrift fur Altorientalische und Biblische Rechtsgeschichte; contbr. articles to profl. jours. Mem. Cin. Community Hebrew Schs. Bd., 1970-75; mem. vis. com. Sch. for Creative and Performing Arts, Cin., 1980-82; chmn. acad. officers, Greater Cin. Consortium Colls. and Univs., 1984-85, mem. exec. com., 1989-96. Am. Council Learned Socs. fellow, 1970-71, Am. Assn. Theol. Schs. fellow, 1976-77. Mem. Am. Oriental Soc., Assn. Jewish Studies, Soc. Bibl. Lit., Phi Beta Kappa. Jewish. Office: Hebrew Union Coll Jewish Inst Religion 3101 Clifton Ave Cincinnati OH 45220-2404 Home Phone: 513-281-4567; Office Phone: 513-221-1875. Business E-Mail: sgreengus@huc.edu.

GREENHILL, H. GAYLON, retired academic administrator; Chancellor U. Wis., Whitewater, 1991—99, chancellor emeritus, 1999—. Address: PO Box 507 Whitewater WI 53190-0507 E-mail: greenhig@mail.uww.edu.

GREENOUGH, WILLIAM TALLANT, psychobiologist, educator; b. Seattle, Oct. 11, 1944; s. Harrison and Maryon C. (Whitten) G.; 1 dau., Jennifer Anne. BA, U. Oreg., 1964; MA, UCLA, 1966, PhD, 1969. Instr. U. Ill., Urbana-Champaign, 1968-69, asst. prof., 1969-73, assoc. prof., 1973-77, chair neural and behavioral biology program, 1977-87, prof. psychology, psychiatry, cell and devel. biology, 1978—, dir. neurosci. program, 1999—2001, dir. Ctr. Advanced Study, 2000—; assoc. dir. Beckman Inst. for Advanced Sci. and Tech., 1987-91; prof. U. Ill. Ctr. Advanced Study, 1997—, Swanlund prof. psychology, psychiatry, cell and devel. biology, bioengineering, 1998—. Vis. prof. psychobiology U. Calif., Irvine, 1972; vis. prof. psychology U. Wash., 1975-76; program chmn. Winter Conf. on Brain Rsch., 1984-85, conf. chair, 1994-95; panel mem. integrative neural sys. NSF, 1987-91; dir. NSF Ctr. of Neurobiology of Learning and Memory, 1989-94; v.p., exec. com. Forum on Rsch. Mgmt., Fed. Behavioral, Psychol. and Cognitive Sci., 1991-93; mem. sci. adv. bd. Am. Psychol. Assn. Sci. Directorate; mem. NSF Biol. Sci. Directorate Adv. Com. Editor: (with R.N. Walsh) Environments as Therapy for Brain Dysfunction, 1976, (with J.M. Juraska) Developmental Neuropsychobiology, 1987; co-editor jour. Neurobiol. Learning and Memory, 1984-2004; contbr. numerous articles to profl. jour. Recipient William Rosen award for rsch. Nat. Fragile X Found., 1998; Cattell Found. fellow, 1975-76; USPHS and NSF grantee, 1969—; U. Ill. sr. scholar, 1985-88. Fellow AAAS (chair sect. I, Psychology 2001-02), Soc. for Rsch. into Child Devel. (disting. Sci. Contbn. award 2003, APA (Disting. Sci. Contbn. award 1999), Am. Psychol. Soc. (William James Fellow award 1998), Soc. Exptl. Psychology, Am. Acad. Arts & Sciences; mem. NAS, Soc. Neurosci. (councilor 1990-94, treas. 2003-05), Soc. Devel. Neurosci., Soc. Devel. Psychobiology (bd. dirs. 1977-80), Sigma Xi. Achievements include rsch. interests in morphological plasticity of cerebellum, experience and learning-based synapse formation, molecular mechanisms of mental retardation, and plasticity of glial cells. Office: U Ill Beckman Inst 405 N Mathews Ave Urbana IL 61801-2325 Office Phone: 217-333-4472. E-mail: wgreenou@uiuc.edu.

GREENSTEIN, JULIUS SYDNEY, zoology educator; b. Boston, July 13, 1927; s. Samuel and Helen (Shriber) G.; m. Joette Mason, Aug. 23, 1954; children: Gail Susan, Jodi Beth, Jay Mason, Blake Jeffrey, Joette Elise. BA, Clark U., 1948; MS, U. Ill., 1951, PhD, 1955; postgrad., Harvard U., 1966. Mem. faculty U. Mass., Amherst, 1954-59; faculty Duquesne U., Pitts., 1959-70, chmn. dept. biol. scis., 1961-70, prof., 1964-70; prof., chmn. dept. biology State SUNY, Fredonia, 1970-74, acting dean arts and scis., 1973-74; dean math. and natural scis. Shippensburg (Pa.) U., 1974-80; also dir. Ctr. for Sci. and the Citizen; pres. Ctrl. Ohio Tech. Coll., 1980-94, pres. emeritus, 1994—; dean, dir. Ohio State U., Newark, 1980-94, prof. zoology, 1980—. Vis. lectr. Am. Inst. Biol. Scis., 1966-76; disting. vis. prof. USAF Acad., 1994-95. Author: Contemporary Readings in Biology, 1971, Readings in Living Systems, 1972; spl. editor Internat. Jour. Fertility, 1958-69, Contraception, 1970-77; columnist Newark Advocate, 1981-93, Licking Countian, 1993-94; contbr. articles to profl. jours. Mem. Carnegie Civic Symphony Orch.; mem. sci. adv. bd. Human Life Found.; trustee Licking Meml. Hosp., Licking County Symphony Orch.; mem. campaign cabinet United Way Licking County; exec. bd. Cen. Ohio Rural Consortium and Pvt. Industry Coun.; mem. higher edn. panel Am. Coun. on Edn., labor com. Higher Edn. Coun. Ohio. Served in armored sch. AUS, World War II. Recipient Wisdom award honor, 197O Mem. AAAS, Am. Assn. Acad. Deans, Am. Assn. Univ. Adminstrs., Am. Assn. Anatomists, Am. Inst. Biol. Scis., Internat. Fertility Assn., Am. Soc. Zoologists, Am. Fertility Soc., Soc. Study Fertility (Eng.), Coun. Biol. Editors, Pa. Acad. Sci. (editorial bd. 1963-70), N.Y. State Acad. Sci., Soc. Study Devel. Biology, Ohio Assn. Regional Campuses (vice chair 1988-89, chair 1989-90, pres.), North Cen. Assn. Colls. and Schs. (cons., evaluator), Newark C. of C., Rotary, Sigma Xi. Achievements include contributions to understanding of causes and prevention of reproductive failure in mammals by studying early developmental stages of embryo, nature of male and female reproductive organs and endocrine glands; developed new techniques for staining specimens and smears; first to demonstrate that estradiol injections cause corpus luteum regression, hence early termination of pregnancy; investigated relationship of specific diseases to normal reproductive performance. Home: 1284 Howell Dr Newark OH 43055-1742 Office: Ohio State U at Newark University Dr Newark OH 43055-1797 E-mail: juliusg@peoplepc.com.

GREENSTREET, ROBERT CHARLES, architect, educator; b. London, June 8, 1952; s. Joseph Philip Henry and Joan (Dean) G.; m. Karen Eloise Holland, Sept. 6, 1975. Diploma in architecture, Oxford Brookes U., 1976, PhD in Architecture, 1983. Registered architect, Eng. Vis. asst. prof. Kans. State U., 1978-79; asst. prof. U. Kans., 1979-80; vis. prof. Ball State U., Muncie, 1980-81; prof. U. Wis., 1981—, asst. vice chancellor, 1985-86, chmn. dept. architecture, 1986-90, dean Sch. Architecture and Urban Planning Milw., 1990-2000, dep. chancellor for campus and urban design, 2000—, interim chancellor, 2003—04; dir. planning and design City of Milw., 2004—. Author, co-author 7 books; contbr. more than 150 articles to profl. jours. Fellow Royal Soc. Arts; mem. AIA (assoc.), Royal Inst. Brit. Architects, Wis. Soc. Architects, Chartered Inst. Arbitrators; mem. Am. Arbitration Assn., Assn. Collegiate Schs. of Architecture (pres. 1995-96). Anglican. Office: U Wis Dept Architecture PO Box 413 Milwaukee WI 53201-0413

GREENWOOD, DANN EDWARD, lawyer; b. Dickinson, ND, Sept. 21, 1952; s. Lawrence E. and Joyce E. (Henley) G.; m. Debra K. Ableidinger, June 15, 1975; children: Jay, Lindsey, Paige. BSBA magna cum laude, U. N.D., 1974, JD, 1977. Bar: N.D. 1977, U.S. Dist. Ct. N.D. 1980. Ptnr. Greenwood, Greenwood & Greenwood and predecessor firms, Dickinson, 1977-98, Greenwood & Ramsey PLLP, 1998—. Mem. N.D. Supreme Ct. Disciplinary Bd., 1983-89, Northern Lights Boy Scouts Council, Dickinson, 1985—; bd. dirs. Legal Assistance N.D., Bismarck, 1980-86. Mem. N.D. Bar Assn. (pres. 1998-99), Stark-Dunn County Bar Assn., N.D. Trial Lawyers Assn. (sec. 1983-84, treas.

1984-85, v.p. 1985-86, pres. 1987-88), Kiwanis, Masons, Shriners, Elks. Lutheran. Home: PO Box 688 Dickinson ND 58602-0688 E-mail: shadyln@ndsupernet.com, grlawdg@ndsupernet.com.

GREENWOOD, TIM, former state legislator, lawyer; m. Linda J. Greenwood; children: Kelly, Katharine. BA, Denison U., 1971; JD, U. Toledo, 1978. Bar: Ohio 1978. Ptnr. Spengler & Nathanson, Toledo, Spengler, Nathanson, Heyman, McCarthy & Durfee, Toledo; mem. Ohio Senate, Columbus, 1994-97, Ohio Turnpike Commn. Mem. Ho. Ho. of Reps., Columbus, 1989-92, 93-94; active United Way, Toledo-Northwestern Ohio Foodbank. Named Freshman Legislator of Yr., 1990. Mem. Ohio Bar Assn., Toledo Bar Assn., Toledo Jr. Bar Assn. (pres.), Sylvania C. of C., Legis. Exch. Coun. Republican. Home: 4325 Mockingbird Ln Toledo OH 43623-3218

GREER, CARL CRAWFORD, petroleum company executive; b. Pitts., June 12, 1940; s. Joseph Moss and Gene (Crawford) G.; m. Jerrine Ehlers, June 16, 1962 (div.); children: Caryn, Michael, Janet; m. Patricia Taylor, Feb. 4, 1989. BS, Lehigh U., 1962; PhD, Columbia U., 1966; PsyD, Ill. Sch. Profl. Psychology, Chgo., 1993. Lic. clin. psychologist and Jungian analyst. Assoc. in bus. Columbia U., 1964-66, asst. prof. banking and finance, 1966-67; retail mktg. mgr. Martin Oil Service Inc., Alsip, Ill., 1967-68, exec. v.p., 1968, pres., dir., 1968-76, chmn. bd., pres., 1976-85; pres., dir. Gen. Ptnrs. Martin Oil Mktg. Ltd., 1982—, Martin Exploration Mgmt. Co., 1985—. Mem. Beta Theta Pi, Tau Beta Pi, Beta Gamma Sigma, Omicron Delta Kappa. Presbyterian.

GREER, NORRIS E., lawyer; b. San Francisco, June 21, 1945; BA, U. Mo., Kansas City, 1967, JD, 1974. Bar: Mo. 1974. Atty. Shughart Thomson & Kilroy, Kansas City, Mo. Mem. ABA, Nat. Assn. Coll. and Univ. Attys., The Mo. Bar, Kansas City Met. Bar Assn., Lawyers Assn. Kansas City. Office: Shughart Thomson & Kilroy 12 Wyandotte Plz 120 W 12th St Ste 1500 Kansas City MO 64105-1929

GREER, RICHARD, radio personality; b. Syracuse, NY, July 11, 1950; children: Bill, Sarah. Radio host WNWV, Elyria, Ohio, 1990—. Avocations: singing, guitar, photography. Office: WNWV 538 W 2d St PO Box 4006 Elyria OH 44036

GREER, THOMAS H., newspaper executive; b. Nashville, July 24, 1942; s. Thomas H. and Eliza (Scruggs) G.; children: Kasey Lynn, Janna Whitney. BA in Polit. Sci., Dillard U., 1963. News/sports reporter Trenton (N.J.) Evening Times, 1965-73; news reporter The Plain Dealer, Cleve., 1973-75, sports editor, 1983-86, mng. editor, 1986-89, exec. editor, 1989-92, v.p., sr. editor, 1992-98; sr. v.p., 1998—; sports writer, columnist Phila. Daily News, 1977-80; sports columnist N.Y. Daily News, 1980-83. Judge Scripps-Howard Founds. Walker Stone/Editl. Writing award, 1993; nominating jury mem. Pulitzer Prize, 1989-90. Bd. dirs. Greater Cleve. Roundtable, Cleve., Bus. Volunteerism Coun., ARC, Cleve., Cuyahoga Plan, Plain Dealer Credit Union, Am. Cancer Soc. Named Paul Miller Disting. Journalism Lectr., Oklahoma State U., 1993. Mem. Am. Press Inst., Nat. Assn. Minority Media Execs. (bd. dirs.), Freedom Forum's Adv. Coun. for Sports Journalism, Am. Soc. Newspaper Editors, Nat. Assn. Black Journalists, AP Mng. Editors Assn., AP Sports Editors' Assn., Cleve. Zool. Soc., Cleve. Press Club, Omega Psi Phi. Office: The Plain Dealer 1801 Superior Ave E Cleveland OH 44114-2198

GREER, WILLIS ROSWELL, JR., finance educator; b. Memphis, Nov. 16, 1938; s. Willis Roswell and Myra Bell (Bridges) G.; m. Melinda S. Scott, June 28, 1963; children: Howard Willis, Catherine Irene Grubbs, Charles Walker. BS, Cornell U., 1961, MBA with distinction, 1966; PhD in Acctg., U. Mich., 1971. Cert. Mgmt. Acct., Cert. Bus. Appraiser. Lectr. acctg. and stats. U. West Indies, Trinidad, 1966-67; teaching asst., Paton fellow U. Mich., 1967-71; asst. prof. acctg. U. Oreg., 1971-75, assoc. prof., 1975-76; vis. prof. acctg. Dartmouth Coll., Amos Tuck Sch., 1976-77, assoc. prof., 1976-82; vis. scholar Manchester (Eng.) Bus. Sch., 1981; prof. acctg. Naval Postgrad. Sch., 1982-88, acad. assoc. fin. mgmt., 1983-84, chmn. dept. adminstrv. scis., 1984-87; prof. acctg. U. Iowa, Iowa City, 1988-96, assoc. dean grad. programs, 1989-92, head dept. acctg., 1992-95; lectr. acctg. and fin. analysis Tohoku U., Japan, 1993-94; dean Coll. Bus. Adminstrn. U. No. Iowa, Cedar Falls, 1996—2001. Cons. U.S. Small Bus. Adminstrn. Minority Bus. Devel. Program, several large firms in various mfg. and svc. industries; presenter numerous seminars and workshops. Co-author: (with Paul Wasserman) Consultants and Consulting Organizations, 1966, (with J. Peter Williamson) Interim Inventory Estimation Error, 1979, (with Shu Liao) Cost Analysis for Dual Source Weapon Procurement, 1983, Cost Analysis for Competitive Major Weapon Systems Procurement: Further Refinement and Extension, 1984; author: A Method for Estimating and Controlling the Cost of Extending Technology, 1988; editor: (with Dan Nussbaum) Cost Analysis and Estimating: Tools and Techniques, 1990; contbr. articles to profl. jours. Treas. Oaknoll Retirement Cmty., 1993—. Mem. Inst. Mgmt. Accts. (dir. Cedar Rapids chpt. 1990—), Am. Acctg. Assn., Decision Scis. Inst., Inst. Bus. Appraisers, Inc. Republican. Achievements include research on conditions under which dual source procurement of major weapon systems is beneficial to government; building an accurate model for forecasting research and development costs for specified technology advancement. Home: PO Box 224 Rollins MT 59931-0224

GREGERSON, LINDA KAREN, poet, language educator, critic; b. Elgin, Ill., Aug. 5, 1950; d. Olaf Thorbjorn and Karen Mildred Gregerson; m. Steven Mullaney, 1980; children: Emma Mullaney, Megan Mullaney. BA, Oberlin Coll., 1971; MA, Northwestern U., 1972; MFA, U. Iowa, 1977; PhD, Stanford U., 1987. Actress Kraken Theater Co., 1972—75; asst. poetry editor The Atlantic Monthly Press, 1982—86; staff editor Atlantic Monthly, Boston, 1982—87; asst. prof. Dept. English U. Mich., 1987—91, William Wilhartz asst. prof. English, 1991—94, assoc. prof. Dept. English, 1994—2001, prof. Dept. English, 2001—03, Frederick G. L. Huetwell prof., prof. English, 2003—, dir. MFA program in creative writing, 1997—2000. Mem. usage panel Am. Heritage Dictionary, 1987—; vis. asst. prof. creative writing program Dept. English Boston U., 1985—86; instr. lit. MIT, 1985—87; asst. editor Mich. Quarterly Rev., 1987—; editl. cons. Cambridge Univ. Press, 1989—, Harvard Univ. Press, 1989—, Oxford Univ. Press, 1989—, Wesleyan Univ. Press, 1989—, Ind. Univ. Press, 1989—, Bedford Books, 1989—, Univ. Mich. Press, 1989—, Wayne State Univ. Press, 1989—. Author: Fire in the Conservatory, 1982, The Reformation of the Subject: Spenser, Milton, and the English Protestant Epic, 1995, The Woman Who Died in Her Sleep, 1996, Negative Capability: Contemporary American Poetry, 2001, Waterborne, 2002, Magnetic orth, 2007. Recipient Levinson Prize award Poetry, 1991, Consuelo Ford award, Poetry Soc. Am., 1992, Isabel MacCaffrey award, Spenser Soc. Am., 1992, Pushcart prize, 1994, 2004, Acad. award in Lit., Am. Acad. Arts and Letters, 2002; fellow, Nat. Endowment Arts, 1985, 1992, Mellon, Nat. Humanities Ctr., 1991—92, Guggenheim, 2000; grantee Arts Found., Mich., 1994; Ingram Merrill grant, 1982—84. Mem.: MLA, Inst. Advanced Study (vis. mem. 1993—94), Milton Soc., Internat. Spenser Soc. (Isabel MacCaffrey award 1992), Renaissance Soc.Am., Shakespeare Assn. Am. Office: U Mich Dept English Lang and Lit 3147 Angell Hall Ann Arbor MI 48109-1045

GREGG, JOHN RICHARD, lawyer; b. Sandborn, Ind., Sept. 6, 1954; s. Donald Richard and Beverly June (Blackwood) G.; m. Sherry L. Biddinger, Nov. 18, 1989; children: John Blackwood, Hunter W. AS, Vincennes U., 1974; AB, Ind. U., 1976, JD, 1984; MPA, Ind. State U., 1978. Real estate agt. Peabody Coal, Jasonville, Ind., 1978-79; govt. affairs agt. Amax Coal, Evansville, Indpls., Ind., 1979-85; ptnr. Gregg & Brock, Vincennes, Ind., 1985—2002; mem. Ind. Gen. Assembly, 1986—2002; house majority leader, 1990-94, minority leader, 1994-96, spkr., 1996—2002; ptnr. Sommer, Barnard, Ackerson, Attys., 2002—. Adj. prof. Vincennes (Ind.) U., 1985—. Active United Meth. Ch.; del. Nat. Dem. Conv., 1992, 96, 2000. Mem. Wabash Valley Human Svcs. (bd. dirs. 1982-85), Knox County Bar Assn. (pres. 1993), Columbia Club, Indpls. Press Club, Torpedo Club, Knights of Pythias, Masons (33 deg., past master 1979), Sigma Pi. Democrat. Home: PO Box 301 Sandborn IN 47578-0301

GREGG, LAUREN, women's soccer coach; b. Rochester, Minn., July 20, 1960; BS in Psychology, U. N.C.; MS in Counseling and Consulting Psychology, Harvard U. Asst. soccer coach U. N.C., 1983; asst. coach Harvard U., Cambridge, Mass.; head coach U. Va., 1987-95; asst. coach U.S. Women's Nat. Soccer Team, 1996—. amed Coach of Yr. Nat. Soccer Coaches Assn. Am., 1990; recipient Gold medal Atlanta Olympics, 1996; Marie Jane postgrad. scholar. Office: US Soccer Fedn US Soccer House 1801 S Prairie Ave Chicago IL 60616-1319

GREGG, ROBERT LEE, retired pharmacist; b. White River, SD, Mar. 2, 1932; s. C.W. and Margaret (Maguire) G.; m. Julie D. Tyler, June 7, 1956; children: Allen, Mark, Susan. BS, S.D. State U., 1958. Registered pharmacist, S.D. Owner, mgr., pharmacist Kennebec (S.D.) Drug, 1958—79, Gregg Drug, Chamberlain, SD, 1978—2003; ret., 2003. Adv. coun. Coll. Pharmacy, S.D. State U., Brookings, 1985-98; pres. S.D. Bd. Pharmacy, Pierre, 1992-93. Past sec. Indsl. Devel. Corp., Kennebec; pres. Lake Francis Case Devel. Corp., Chamberlain, 1984-85, Brule County unit Am. Cancer Soc., 1992-2003. With Med. Svc. Corps. US Army, 1953—55, Republic of Korea. Named S.D. Horseperson of Yr., S.D. Horse Coun., 1999. Mem. S.D. Pharm. Assn. (pres. 1985-86, Bowl of Hygeia award 1992, S.D. Pharmacist of Yr. 1996), Nat. Assn. Retail Druggists, Chamberlain C. of C., NRA (life), VFW (life, quartermaster Kennebec 1965-76, Outstanding Post Quartermaster award 1965), Am. Legion (life), Am. Quarter Horse Assn., S.D. Trail Riders (bd. dirs. 1986-97), KC (4th degree). Republican. Roman Catholic. Avocations: equestrian activities, trail riding, big game hunting. Personal E-mail: rjgregg@midstatesd.net.

GREGOR, CLUNIE BRYAN, geology educator; b. Edinburgh, Mar. 5, 1929; came to U.S., 1968; s. David Clunie Gregor and Barbara Mary Moller-Beilby; m. Suzanne Assir, Apr. 24, 1955 (div. Apr. 1969); 1 child, Andrew James; m. Anna Bramanti, Apr. 15, 1969 (dec. Oct. 1993); children: Thomas James, Matthew James. BA, Cambridge U., Eng., 1951, MA, 1954; DSc, U. Utrecht, The Netherlands, 1967. Instr. Am. U. Beirut, 1958-64; rsch. asst. Delft (The Netherlands) Inst. Tech., 1964-65, dir. Crystallographic Lab., 1965-67; vis. prof. Case Western Res. U., Cleve., 1968-69; prof. West Ga. Coll., Carrollton, 1969-72, Wright State U., Dayton, Ohio, 1972—. Chmn. USA work group on geochem. cycles, 1972-88, vice chmn. panel on geochem. cycles NAS, 1988-90. Author: (monograph) Geochemical Behaviour of Sodium, 1967, The Evolving Earth, 1997; editor: Chemical Cycles in the Evolution of the Earth, 1988. Grantee, NSF, 1977—82, Sicily, 1978—80. Fellow Geol. Soc. (London); mem. Geol. Soc. Am., Am. Geophys. Union, Geochem. Soc. (sec. 1983-89). Home: 136 W North College St Yellow Springs OH 45387-1563 Office: Wright State U Dept Earth and Environmental Sciences Dayton OH 45435 Office Phone: 937-775-3442 3455, 937-775-3445.

GREGORY, STEPHANIE ANN, hematologist, educator; b. Vineland, NJ, June 23, 1940; d. Andonetta Gregory; m. Sheldon Chertow; children: Elizabeth Chertow, Jennifer Chertow, Daniel Chertow, Erica Chertow. BS cum laude, Boston Coll., 1961; MD cum laude, Med. Coll. Pa., 1965. Diplomate in internal medicine and hematology Am. Bd. Internal Medicine. Internal medicine intern Presbyn.-St. Luke's Hosp., Chgo., 1965-66, resident in internal medicine, 1966-68, fellow in hematology, 1969—72; chief resident in internal medicine Presbyn.-St. Lukes Hosp., Chgo., 1968-69; chief spl. morphology lab. sect. hematology Rush-Presbyn.-St. Luke's Med. Ctr., Chgo., 1972-76, dir. sect. hematology divsn. hematology/oncology, 1994—, Elodia Kehm prof. medicine, dir. hematology and stem cell transplantation, 1995—; from asst. prof. medicine to assoc. prof. medicine Rush Med. Coll., Chgo., 1972-86, prof. medicine, 1986—; adminstr., dir. Consultants in Hematology Rush U. Med. Ctr., Chgo., 1985—, sr. attending physician, 1982—, dir. sect. hematology, 2004—. Coord. continuing edn. sect. hematology Rush-Presbyn.-St. Luke's Med. Ctr., Chgo., 1970-76, dir. transfusion therapy svc. sect. hematology, 1972-76, asst. chmn. dept. medicine, 1972-77, clin. dir. Sheridan Rd. Pavilion, 1976-77, acting dir. sect. clin. hematology, 1980-81, assoc. dir. sect. hematology, 1993-94, asst. chair dept. medicine, 1993-94; co-dir. Lymphoma Ctr., Rush Univ Medical Ctr., Chgo., 1992—; mem. UN Security Coun. Commn. Experts, 1994; mem. med. adv. bd. Leukemia Rsch. Found., 1996—, Leukemia/Lymphoma Soc. Am., Lymphoma Rsch. Found.; chair B-cell Edn. Malignancies program, 2005-. Mentor Lean on Me support group for young adults with cancer Rush Univ. Medical Ctr., Chgo., 1992—. Recipient award Am. Women's Med. Assn., 1965, William B. Peck Sci. award for rsch. in hematopoietic stem cell studies Sci. Assembly of Interstate Postgrad. Med. Assn., 1973, Outstanding Alumni award MCP-Hahneman Med. Sch., 1998, Excellence in Medicine award Rush U. Med. Ctr., 2006; grantee Schweppe Found. Rsch., 1969-72, NIH tng. grantee Nat. Heart, Lung and Blood Inst., 1974-79; Schweppe fellow, 1969-72. Fellow ACP (mem. Ill. coun. 1994—, mentor physician mems. for advancement to fellowship designation ann. meeting 1996, Ill. Laureate award 1996); mem. AMA, Internat. Soc. Hematology (Inter-Am. divsn.), Internat. Soc. Exptl. Hematology (charter), Leukemia Soc. Am. (bd. trustees Ill. chpt. 1987—, chmn. patient aid com. Ill. chpt. 1988-90, treas. Ill. chpt. 1992-93, chairperson patient fin. aid com. Ill. chpt. 1992—, v.p. Ill. chpt. 1991-94, mem. med. adv. bd. Ill. chpt. 1996—), Am. Soc. Clin. Oncology, Am. Soc. Hematology (co-editor, 2005-), Cell Proliferation Soc., Ea. Coop. Oncology Group, Inst. Medicine Chgo., Chgo. Soc. Internal Medicine (exec. com. 1992—, sec.-treas. 1992-93, v.p. 1993-94, pres. 1994-95), Aplastic Anemia Found. Am. (hon. bd. trustees 1988—), Mark H. Lepper M.D. Soc. Tchrs. (elected), Alpha Omega Alpha, Sigma Xi. Office: Rush Univ Medical Ctr 1725 W Harrison St Ste 834 Chicago IL 60612-3861 Office Phone: 312-942-5982. Business E-Mail: stephanie_gregory@rush.edu.

GREGORY, VALISKA, writer; b. Chgo., Nov. 3, 1940; d. Andrej and Stephania (Lascik) Valiska; m. Marshall W. Gregory, Aug. 18, 1962; children: Melissa, Holly. BA cum laude, Ind. Ctrl. Coll., 1962; MA, Univ. Chgo., 1966; postgrad., Vassar Inst. Pub. Writing, 1984, Simmons Coll., 1986. Music and drama tchr. White Oak Elem. Sch., Whiting, Ind., 1962-64; tchr. Oak Lawn (Ill.) Meml. H.S., 1965-68; lectr. English U. Wis., Milw., 1968-74; adj. prof. English U. Indpls., 1974-83, Butler U., Indpls., 1983-85, writer-in-residence, 1993—; fellow Butler Writer's Studio, 1989-92. Founding dir. Butler U. Midwinter Children's Litf. Conf., 1989—; spkr., workshop leader schs., libr., confs., 1993—. Author: Sunny Side Up, 1986 (Chickadee Mag. Book of Month award 1986), Terribly Wonderful, 1986 (Grandparent's Mag. Best Book award 1986), The Oatmeal Cookie, 1987 (Best of Best Book list Chgo. Sun-Times), Riddle Soup, 1987 (Best of Best Book list Chgo. Sun-Times), Through the Mickle Woods (named Pick of List Am. Booksellers Assn. 1992, Parent's Choice award, 1992; State Ind. Read Aloud-List 1993), Happy Burpday, Maggie McDougal!, 1992 (State Ind. Read-aloud List 1993), Babysitting for Benjamin (Parent's Choice Honor award 1993), Kate's Giants, 1995, Loooking for Angels, 1996, (named Picked of the List Am. Book Sellers Assn., 1996), When Stories Fell Like Shooting Stars, 1996, (Family Circle Mag. Critics Choice, 1996), A Valentine for Norman Noggs, 1999, Shirley's Wonderful Baby, 2002. Recipient Ill. Wesleyan U. Poetry award, 1982, hon. mention Billee Murray Denny Nat. Poetry Award Bilee Murray Denny Poetry Found., 1982, Hudelson award Children's Fiction Work-In-Progress, 1982, Artistic Excellence and Achievement award State Art Treasure Arts Ind., 1989; Individual Artist Master fellow Ind. Arts Commn. and Nat. Endowment for Arts, 1986. Mem. AAUW (Creative Writer's pres. 1984-86), Author's Guild, Authors League Am., Soc. Children's Book Writers and Illustrators, Nat. Book Critic's Circle, Children's Reading Round Table, Soc. Midland Authors. Democrat. Office: Butler U 4600 Sunset Ave Indianapolis IN 46208-3487

GREILING, MINDY, state legislator; b. Feb. 1948; m. Roger Greiling; 2 children. BA, Gustavus Adolphis Coll.; MEd, U. Minn. State rep. Minn. Ho. Reps., Dist. 54B, 1993—. Office: 100 Constitution Ave Saint Paul MN 55155-1232

GREISINGER, JAMES, food products executive; With Dean Foods, Chgo., 1962—, v.p. food plants, 1985—91, v.p. Green Bay Food Co., 1992—96, v.p. specialty foods group Chgo., 1996—2000, pres., gen. mgr. specialty foods group, 2000—01, pres. specialty foods group, 2001—. Office: Specialty Food Group 3600 River Rd Franklin Park IL 60131

GREMILLION, ROBERT, publishing executive; b. New Orleans; Student, Loyola U., New Orleans. Station mgr. WGNO-TV Tribune, New Orleans, 1985-90; v.p., gen. mgr. CLTV ews and Tribune Regional Programming, 1990-97; CEO, pub. Sun-Sentinel, Ft. Lauderdale, Fla., 1997—2007; gen. mgr. WBZL-TV, 2002; exec. v.p. Tribune Publishing, Chgo., 2007—. Bd. dir. The Cardiology Coun. Broward. Office: Tribune Publishing 435 N Michigan Ave Chicago IL 60611 Office Phone: 312-222-9100.

GRENDELL, DIANE V., state legislator, nurse; m. Tim Grendell; children: James, Kate. Grad. in nursing, St. John's Coll.; JD, Cleve. Marshall Coll. Law; postgrad., Baldwin Wallace Coll. Bar: Ohio; RN, Ohio. Mem. Ohio Ho. of Reps., Columbus, 1993—. Recipient Seven Seals award, Wilson achievement award. Mem. Ohio Bar Assn., Ohio Nurses Assn., Chester C. of C., Chester and Geauga County Hist. Soc., Farm Bur. (chmn.), Sierra Club. Republican. Home: 7413 Tattersall St Chesterland OH 44026-2036

GRENDELL, TIMOTHY JOSEPH, lawyer; b. Cleve., Apr. 17, 1953; s. Edward J. and Josephine B. (Wawrzyniak) G.; m. Kiane Grendell; children: Katherine Mary, James Edward. BA magna cum laude, John Carroll U., 1975; JD, Case Western Res. U., 1978; LLM, U. Va., 1983. Bar: Ohio 1978, U.S. Ct. Mil. Appeals 1982, U.S. Dist. Ct. (no. dist.) Ohio 1984, U.S. Supreme Ct. 1987. Assoc. Taft, Stettinius & Hollister, Cin., 1983-84, Jones, Day, Reavis & Pogue, Cleve., 1984-88, ptnr., 1988—; atty. Ohio Senate, Columbus. Cons. U.S. Dept. Def., Washington, 1981-83. Contbr. articles to profl. jours. Co-chmn. assocs. cabinet United Way, Cleve, 1989—; mem. Highland Heights (Ohio) Assessment Rev. Bd., 1987; bd. dirs. Boy's Hope Northeastern Onio, 1987—. served to capt. JAGC, U.S. Army, 1978-83. Decorated Meritorious Svc. medal with oak leaf cluster; Singer scholar, 1978, named Who's Who in Am. Law (2nd edit.), Outstanding Young Men Am.,1980. Mem. ABA, Ohio Bar Assn., Cleve. Bar Assn., Cleve. Bldg. Industry Assn. (chmn. legal adv. com. 1988—), Order of Coif. Republican. Rsch. editor Case Western Res. U. Law Rev. 1977-78; contbg. rsch. editor U.S.-Can. Law Jour., 1978. Office: Ohio Senate Rm 034 Ground Fl Columbus OH 43215 Office Phone: 614-644-7718.

GREPPIN, JOHN AIRD COUTTS, philologist, editor, educator; b. Rochester, NY, Apr. 2, 1937; s. Ernest Haquette and Edna Barbara (Kill) G.; m. Mary Elizabeth Cleland Hannan, Sept. 30, 1961; children: Sarah Cleland Coutts, Carl Hannan Haquette. AB in Greek, U. Rochester, NYC, 1961; MA in Classics, U. Wash., 1966; PhD in Indo-European Studies, UCLA, 1972; postdoctoral student, Yerevan State U., USSR, 1974-75. Tchr. Greek, Latin Stowe (Vt.) Prep. Sch., 1961-62; tchr. Woodstock (Vt.) Country Sch., 1962-65, admissions dir., 1968-69; interim asst. prof. U. Fla., Gainesville, 1971-72; tchr. Isidore Newman Sch., New Orleans, 1972-74; from asst. to assoc. to prof. linguistics Cleve. State U., 1975—, dir. program in linguistics, 1979-83, 99—. Vis. prof. linguistics Philipps U., Marburg, Germany, 1993. Author: Initial Vowel and Aspiration in Classical Armenian, 1973, Classical Armenian Nominal Suffixes, 1975, Classical and Middle Armenian Bird Names: A Taxonomic and Mythological Study, 1978, An Etymological Dictionary of the Indo-European Components of Classical Armenian, 1984, Bark Galianosi: The Greek Armenian Dictionary to Galen, 1985, A Handbook of Armenian Dialectology, 1986, An Arabic-Armenian Pharmaceutical Dictionary, 1997, The Diffusion of Greco-Roman Medicine into the Middle East and the Caucasus, 1999; editor: Proc. of 1st Internat. Conf. on Armenian Linguistics, Phila., 1979, (with others) Interrogativity: A Colloquium of the Grammar, Typology and Pragmatics of Questions in Seven Diverse Languages, 1984, When Worlds Collide: The Indo-Europeans and the Pre-Indo-Europeans: The Bellagio Papers, 1990, Studies in Classical Armenian Literature, 1994, Studies in Honor of Jaan Puhvel, Part One: Ancient Languages and Philology, 1997, Part Two: Mythology and Religion, 1997; founding editor Ann. Armenian Linguistics, 1980-2002, Armenian and Anatolian Studies, 1979—, Proc. 4th Internat. Conf. on Armenian Linguistics, 1992, Classical Armenian Literature: Studies in Early Armenian Authors; mng. editor Raft, A Jour. of Armenian Poetry and Criticism, 1987-2000; editor Jour. Soc. Armenian Studies, 2002-2007; contbr. over 210 articles to Am., European and Soviet jours., over 267 revs. to London Times Lit. Supplement, N.Y. Times Book Rev., Boston Book Rev., others. Recipient Silver medal Congregazione Mekhitarista, Venice, Italy, 1979, Medal of David the Invincible award Armenian Philos. Acad., 2003; fellow Am. Coun. Learned Socs., 1965, NEH, 1978-79, NIH, 1984, Internat. Rsch. and Exchs. Bd., 1974-75, grantee, 1979-81, 84-87, 89, 92, 94, 98; grantee AGBU Manoogian Fund, 1977, 79-06, Gulbenkian Found., 1982, 85, 96, Rockefeller Found., 1987, Am. Coun. Learned Socs., 1987. Mem. Assn. Internat. des Études Arméniennes, Soc. for Study of the Caucasus, Am. Philol. Soc., Soc. Armenian Studies (exec. bd. 1982-86, 02-, sec. 1983-85), Am. Oriental Soc., Soc. Caucasologia Europaea, Cleve. Skating Club, Union club of Cleve. Avocations: piano, chamber music, birdwatching. Home: 3349 Fairmount Blvd Cleveland OH 44118-4262 Office: Cleve State U Dept Linguistics Cleveland OH 44115 Office Phone: 216-687-3967. Business E-Mail: j.greppin@csuohio.edu.

GREVE, JOHN HENRY, veterinary parasitologist, educator; b. Pitts., Aug. 11, 1934; s. John Welch and Edna Viola (Thuenen) G.; m. Sally Jeanette Doane, June 21, 1956; children— John Haven, Suzanne Carol, Pamela Jean BS, Mich. State U., East Lansing, 1956, D.V.M., 1958, MS, 1959; PhD, Purdue U., West Lafayette, Ind., 1963. Assoc. instr. Mich. State U., East Lansing, 1958-59; instr. Purdue U., West Lafayette, 1959-63; asst. prof. Iowa State U., Ames, 1963-64, assoc. prof., 1964-68, prof. dept. vet. pathology, 1968-99, interim chair dept. vet. pathology, 1992-95, counselor acad. and student affairs, 1991-92. Cons. to dean on alumni affairs Coll. Vet. Medicine; cons. in field. Mem. editl. bd. Lab. Animal Sci., 1971-83, Vet. Rsch. Comm., 1977-84, Vet. Parasitology, 1984-98; contbr. articles to sci. jours., chpts. to books. Dist. chmn. Broken Arrow dist. Boy Scouts Am., Ames, Iowa, 1975-77; devel. bd. Octagon Ctr. for the Arts, Ames, 2004-07. Named Disting. Tchr. Norden Labs., 1965, 99, Outstanding Tchr. Amoco Oil, Iowa State U., 1972, Faculty Mem. of Yr., Coll. Vet. Medicine, 1999; recipient Faculty Citation Iowa State U. Alumni Assn., 1978. Mem. AVMA (mem. editl. bd. jour. 1975-98, Excellence in Teaching award student chpt. 1990), Iowa Vet. Med. Assn., Am. Soc. Parasitologists, Midwestern Conf. Parasitologists (sec.-treas. 1967-75, presiding officer 1975-76), Am. Assn. Vet. Parasitologists (pres. 1968-70), Helminthological Soc. Washington, World Assn. for Advancement Vet. Parasitology, Am. Assn. Vet. Med. Colls., Izaak Walton League (bd. dirs. Iowa 1968-70), Honor Soc. Cardinal Key, Gamma Sigma Delta, Phi Eta Sigma, Phi Kappa Phi, Phi Zeta. Lodges: Kiwanis (Town and Country-Ames pres. 1967, 2006, Nebr.-Iowa lt. gov. 1972-73). Republican. Avocations: stamp collecting/philately, camping, gardening. Office: Iowa State U Coll Vet Med Found Ames IA 50011-1250 Office Phone: 515-294-0867. Business E-Mail: sdgreve@earthlink.net.

GREW, PRISCILLA CROSWELL, academic administrator, geologist, educator, museum director; b. Glens Falls, NY, Oct. 26, 1940; d. James Croswell and Evangeline Pearl (Beougher) Perkins; m. Edward Sturgis Grew, June 14, 1975. BA magna cum laude, Bryn Mawr Coll., 1962; PhD, U. Calif., Berkeley, 1967. Instr. dept. geology Boston Coll., 1967-68, asst. prof., 1968-72; asst. rsch. geologist UCLA, 1972-77, adj. asst. prof. environ. sci. and engring., 1975-76; dir. Calif. Dept. Conservation, 1977-81; commr. Calif. Pub. Utilities Commn., San Francisco, 1981-86; dir. Minn. Geol. Survey, St. Paul, 1986-93; prof. dept. geology U. Minn., Mpls., 1986-93; vice chancellor for rsch. U. Nebr., Lincoln, 1993-99, prof. dept. geoscis., 1993—, prof. conservation/survey divsn. Inst. Agr., 1993—, dir. U. Nebr. State Mus., 2003—, fellow Ctr. for Great Plains Studies, 2003—; coord. Native Am. Graves Protection and Repatriation Act, 1998—. Vis. asst. prof. geology U. Calif., Davis, 1973-74; chmn. Calif. State Mining and Geology Bd., Sacramento, 1976-77; exec. sec., editor Lake Powell Rsch. Project, 1971-77; cons., vis. staff Los Alamos (N.Mex.) Nat. Lab., 1972-77; com. on minority participation in earth sci. and mineral engring. Dept. Interior, 1972-75; chmn. Calif. Geothermal Resource Task Force, 1977, Calif. Geothermal Resources Bd., 1977-81; earthquake studies adv. panel US Geol. Survey, 1979-83, adv. com., 1982-86; adv. coun. Gas Rsch. Inst., 1982-86, rsch. coord. coun., 1987-98, vice-chmn., 1994-96, chmn., 1996-98, sci. and tech. coun., 1998-2001; bd. on global change rsch. NAS, 1995-99, subcom. on earthquake rsch., 1985-88, bd. on earth scis. and resources, 1986-91, bd. on mineral and energy resources, 1982-88, bd. on internat. sci. orgns., 2006—; mem. Minn. Minerals Coord. Com., 1986-93, US nat. com. for internat. union of geol. scis. (IUGS), 1985-93, US nat. com. for the internat. union of geodesy and geophysics 2001—, chmn., 2003—; mem. US Nat. Com. on Diversitas, 2000—07, vice chmn., 2004—07; adv. bd. Stanford U. Sch. Earth Scis., 1989—, Sec. of Energy Adv. Bd., 1995-97; com. on equal opportunities in sci. and tech. NSF, 1985-86, adv. com. on earth scis., 1987-91, adv. com. on sci. and tech. ctrs. devel., 1987-91, adv. com. on sci. and tech. ctrs., 1996, adv. com. on geoscis., 1994-97; mem. State-Fed. Tech. Partnership Task Force, 1995-99, Fed. Coun. for Continental Sci. Drilling, 1992-98, Gt. Plains Partnership Coun., 1995-99; trustee Am. Geol. Inst. Found., 1988— (Ian Campbell medalist 1999). Contbr. articles to profl. jours. Trustee 1st Plymouth Congl. Ch., Lincoln, 1997—2000; mem. edn. and outreach steering com. EarthScope, 2005—, chair edn. and outreach steering com., 2007—; bd. dirs. Abendmusik:Lincoln, 1995—97. Fellow NSF, 1962—66. Fellow AAAS (chmn. electorate nominating com. sect. E 1980-84, mem.-at-large 1987-91, chmn.-elect 1994, chmn. 1995, coun. del. 1997-98), Geol. Soc. Am. (nominations com. 1974, chmn. com. on geology and pub. policy 1981-84, audit com. 1988-90, chair 1990, com. on coms. 1986-87, 91-92, chmn. com. on coms. 1995, chair Day medal com. 1990, councilor 1987-91), Mineral. Soc. Am. (mem. Roebling medal com. 1999-2003), Geol. Assn. Can., Ctr. Great Plains Studies; mem. Am. Geophys. Union (chmn. com. pub. affairs 1984-89, chair Waldo Smith medal com. 2006-), Soc. Mayflower Descs., Nat. Parks and Conservation Assn. (trustee 1982-86), Nat. Assn. Regulatory Utility Commrs. (com. on gas 1982-86, exec. com. 1984-86, com. on energy conservation 1983-84), Nat. Sci. Collections Alliance (bd. dirs. 2006—),

Am. Assn. Petroleum Geologists (chair global climate change com. 2007-), Interstate Oil and Gas Compact Commn. (mem. Petroleum Profls. Task Force, 2001-03), Cosmos Club, Rotary, Country Club of Lincoln, Sigma Xi (pres. U. Minn. chpt. 1990-91). Congregationalist. Office: U Nebr State Mus 307 Morrill Hall Lincoln NE 68588-0338 Office Phone: 402-472-3779. Business E-Mail: pgrew1@unl.edu.

GREWCOCK, WILLIAM L., mining company executive; b. 1925; married BCE, U. Nebr., 1950. With Peter Kiewit Sons, Inc., Omaha, 1950—, mgr. Grand Island dist., 1960-65, v.p., 1965-82, sr. v.p., 1982-86, vice chmn., 1986—, also bd. dirs.; pres. Kiewit Mining Group, Inc. subs. Peter Kiewit Sons, Inc., Omaha, now chmn.; sr. v.p. Kiewit U.S. Co. subs. Peter Kiewit Sons, Inc., Omaha, 1982—, also bd. dirs. Office: Kiewit Constrn Group Inc 1000 Kiewit Plz Omaha NE 68131

GRIEMAN, JOHN JOSEPH, communications executive; b. St. Paul, Minn., Sept. 7, 1944; s. Roy and Agnes (Thell) G.; m. Joan Schultz, Sept. 12, 1964; children: Nancy, Amy, Angie, Ginette. BS in Acctg., Coll. of St. Thomas, St. Paul, 1966. Supr. Coopers & Lybrand, Mpls., 1966-72; treas. 1st Midwest Corp., Mpls., 1972-75; pvt. practice fin. cons. Mpls., 1975-76; dir. corp. planning and systems, asst. controller constrn. equipment, group mgr. corp. acctg. Am. Hoist & Derrick Co., St. Paul, 1976-82; controller Cowles Media Co., Mpls., 1982, v.p., 1983; controller Mpls. Star and Tribune Co., 1983-96; v.p., CFO Mpls. Star and Tribune, 1983-96; cons. bus. improvement New Brighton, Minn., 1996—. Bd. dirs. Jr. Achievement Upper Midwest, 1987—, Project for Pride in Living, Mpls., 1994—, Lifetrack Resources, 1999—, Mpls. Pub. Sch. Found., 2000—. Mem. Am. Inst. CPA's (chmn. mems. in industry com. 1979-81), Minn. Soc. CPA's (bd. dirs., treas. 1980-81, mem. of month 1977). Home and Office: 1410 18th St NW New Brighton MN 55112-5407

GRIESHEIMER, JOHN ELMER, state representative; b. St. Clair, Mo., July 19, 1952; s. Elmer Augustus and Mary (Middleton) G.; m. Rita Ann Maune, June 15, 1974; children: Sean, Aaron, Michelle. Cert. auto mechanics, East Cen. Coll., Union, Mo., 1971, AAS, 1973. Councilman ward II City of Washington, Mo., 1982-88; county commr. Franklin County, Union, Mo., 1989-92; state rep. State of Mo., Jefferson City, 1993—2002, sen., 2003—. Chmn. Solid Waste com., 1984-88, com. econ. devel., tourism and local govt., Mo. Senate; vice chmn. East Ctrl. Solid Waste Task Force Waste com., 1990-92. Adv. bd. dirs. 4 Rivers Vo-Tech. Sch., Washington, Mo. Mem. KC (4th degree), Lions Club. Republican. Roman Catholic. Home: 33 Oxford Dr Washington MO 63090-4609 Office: State of Mo State Capitol Building # PO Jefferson City MO 65101-1556

GRIEVESON, KOREN, chef; b. South Africa; Grad., Culinary Inst. America, 1996. Chef Aqua, San Francisco; sous chef Blackbird, Chgo., 1998—2003; chef de cuisine Avec, Chgo., 2003—. Solider US Army. Named one of America's Best New Chefs, Food & Wine Mag., 2008. Office: Avec 615 W Randolph St Chicago IL 60606*

GRIFFEY, KEN, JR., (GEORGE KENNETH GRIFFEY JR.), professional baseball player; b. Donora, Pa., Nov. 21, 1969; s. Ken and Bertie Griffey; m. Melissa Griffey; 1 adopted child, Tevin Kendall children: George Kenneth III, Taryn Kennedy. Outfielder Seattle Mariners, 1989—99, Cin. Reds, 2000—. Mem. US Team World Baseball Classic, 2006. Named All-Star Game MVP, 1992, Am. League MVP, 1997, Maj. League Player of Yr., 1997, Nat. League Comeback Player of Yr., 2005; named to Am. League All-Star Team, 1990—99, MLB All-Century Team, 1999, Nat. League All-Star Team, 2000, 2004, 2007, All-Time Rawlings Gold Glove Team, 2007; recipient Gold Glove award, 1990—99, Silver Slugger award, 1991, 1993—94, 1996—99. Achievements include led the Am. League in home runs, 1994 (40), 1997 (56), 1998 (56), 1999 (48), runs scored, 1997 (125), and runs batted in, 1997 (147); hit his 500th career home run on June 22, 2004; 6th all-time on career home run list. Office: Cin Reds 100 Main St Cincinnati OH 45202*

GRIFFIN, HENRY CLAUDE, retired chemistry professor; b. Greenville, SC, Feb. 14, 1937; s. Arthur Gwynn and Christa Lou (Wilson) G.; m. Barbara Jean Pierson, Sept. 3, 1960; children: Gwen Griffin Van Ark, Lyle Griffin Warshauer. BS, Davidson Coll., 1958; PhD, MIT, 1962. Instr. math. New Prep. Sch., Cambridge, Mass., 1960-61; rsch. assoc. Argonne Nat. Lab., Lemont, Ill., 1962-64, guest scientist, 1964-70; asst. prof. chemistry U. Mich., Ann Arbor, 1964-70, assoc. prof., 1970-89, prof., 1989—2005, prof. emeritus, 2005. Vis. scientist Swiss Fed. Reactor Inst., Wurenlingen, 1971-72; vis. rsch. engr. U. Calif., Berkeley, 1978-79; chairperson senate assembly U. Mich., 1993-94; dir. nuc. studies Environ. Rsch. Group, Ann Arbor, 1980-81. Inventor process for separation of Na-22. Mem. AAAS, Am. Chem. Soc. (chairperson steering com. Ctrl. region 1994-95), Am. Phys. Soc. Home: 1410 Harbrooke Ave Ann Arbor MI 48103-3618 Office: Univ Mich Dept Chemistry 930 N University Ave Ann Arbor MI 48109-1055 Home Phone: 734-994-3499. Business E-Mail: hcg@umich.edu.

GRIFFIN, J. TIMOTHY, air transportation executive; Grad., Fla. Atlantic U.; M, U. Wash. With Am. Airlines; sr. v.p. schedules and pricing Continental Airlines; sr. v.p. market planning and systems NW Airlines Corp., Minn., 1993—99, exec. v.p. mktg. & distbn., 1999—. Office: NW Airlines Corp 2700 Lone Oak Pky Eagan MN 55121 Office Phone: 612-726-2111.

GRIFFIN, JAMES ANTHONY, bishop, academic administrator; b. Fairview Park, Ohio, June 13, 1934; s. Thomas Anthony and Margaret Mary (Hanousek) Griffin. BA, Borromeo Coll., 1956; JCL magna cum laude, Pontifical Lateran U., Rome, 1963; JD summa cum laude, Cleve. State U., 1972; DHL (hon.), Ohio Dominican Coll., 1994; DD (hon.), Ohio No. U., 2007. Priest Roman Cath. Ch., 1960. Ordained priest Diocese of Cleve., 1960; assoc. pastor St. Jerome Ch., Cleve., 1960—61; sec.-notary Cleve. Diocesan Tribunal, 1963—65; asst. chancellor Diocese of Cleve., 1965—68, vice chancellor, 1968—73, chancellor, 1973—78, vicar gen., 1978—79; pastor St. William Ch., Euclid, Ohio, 1978—79; ordained bishop, 1979; aux. bishop Diocese of Cleve., vicar of western region Lorain, Ohio, 1979—83; bishop Diocese of Columbus, Ohio, 1983—2004, bishop emeritus, 2004—; disting. prof. theology Ohio Dominican U., 2005—07, interim pres., 2007—08. Mem clergy rels. bd. Diocese Cleve., 1972—75, mem clergy retirement bd., 1973—78, mem clergy pers. bd., 1979—83; disting. prof. theology Ohio Dominican U., 2005—07; Griffin chair in canon law Pontifical Coll. Josephinium, 2005. Author (with A. J. Quinn): (book) Thoughts for Our Times, 1969, Thoughts for Sowing, 1970; author: (with others) Ashes from the Cathedral, 1974, Sackcloth and Ashes, 1976, The Priestly Heart, 1983, Reflections on the Law of Love, 1991, Summary of the New Catholic Catechism, 1994, A Lenten Walk, 1998; author: They Were There, 2004, Easter Joy, 2007, Christmas Joy, 2007. Chmn. bd. govs. N. Am. Coll., Rome, 1984—88; co-chair Columbus Comty. Rels. Comn., 1992—95; mem Am's Promise, Columbus, 1997—2001, Columbus Coalition Domestic Violence, 2001—04; mem. adv. coun. Cmty. Shelter Bd., 2001—04; mem. adv. team Cmtys. in Sch., 2002—04; chmn. Mayor's Coun Youth, 1986—90; trustee St Mary Sem. 1976—78; bd. dirs., mem pension comt Cath Cemeteries Assn., 1978—83; vice-chancellor Pontifical Col. Josephinum, 1983—2004; treas. Cath. Relief Svc. Bd., 1988—91, pres., 1991—96; bd. dirs. Holy Family Cancer Home, 1973—78, Meals on Wheels, Euclid, 1978—79, Franklin County United Way, 1984—90. Decorated Knight of the Holy Sepulchre; recipient Human Rights award, Anti-Defamation League B'nai B'rith, 1987, Jessing award, Pontifical Coll., 1993, Gov's award, State of Ohio, 1994, Don Bosco medal, 1997, NG Minuteman award, 1999, Cmty. Svc. award, Columbus Urban League, 1999, Bronze Pelican award, Cath. Boy Scouts, 2002, Charity Newsies award, 2002, St. Thomas More award, 2004, Croiser award, Cath. Found. Columbus, 2005. Mem.: Columbus Bar Assn. (chmn. jud. advt. com. 1987—91, Liberty Bell award 1989), Am. Canon Law. Soc. Roman Catholic. Achievements include Griffin chair in canon law established Pontifical College Josephinum 2005. Office: Ohio Dominican U 1216 Sunbury Rd Columbus OH 43219

GRIFFIN, JEAN LATZ, political strategist, writer, publisher; b. Joliet, Ill., Mar. 6, 1943; d. Carl Joseph and Helene Monica (Bradshaw) Latz; m. Dennis Joseph Griffin, Sept. 16, 1967; children: Joseph, Timothy, Peter. BS in Chemistry, Coll. St. Francis, Joliet, 1965; MS in Journalism, U. Wis., 1967. Clin. investigation coord. Baxter Labs., 1967-68; reporter Joliet Herald News, 1968-70, Raleigh (N.C.) Times, 1974-75, Suburban Trib, Hinsdale, Ill., 1976-78, regional edn. reporter, 1978-82; gen. assignment reporter Chgo. Tribune, 1982-84, edn. writer, 1984-88, pub. health writer, 1988-94, govt., politics, and pub. policy reporter, 1994-97, econ. devel. reporter, 1997; strategist The Strategy Group, Chgo., 1998—; owner CyberINK, 1998—. Adj. journalism instr. Roosevelt U., Chgo., 2001—; facilitator U. Phoenix, 2004—. Author: One Spirit, 2006, In The Same Breath, 2006, (DVD) One Spirit, 2007. Bd. dirs. Residents for Emergency Shelter, Chgo., 1978-82, Genesis House, Chgo., 1995-98, vol. cook, 1994-98; devel. com. mem. Hope Now, Inc., 1998-00; membership chair Arlington Hts. C. of C., 2001-02; vol. Taoist Tai Chi instr., 2001-; pres. Taoist Tai Chi Soc.-Midwest, 2005-. Recipient Writing award Am. Dental Assn., 1969, Alumna Profl. Achievement award Coll. St. Francis, Joliet, 1985, First Prize in ednl. writing Edn. Writers Am., 1986, Grand prize, 1988, Benjamin Fine award Nat. Assn. Secondary Sch. Prins., 1988, Edward Scott Beck award for reporting Chgo. Tribune, 1988, Peter Lisagor award for pub. svc. Soc. Profl. Journalists, Chgo. chpt., 1988, Mark of Excellence Chgo. Assn. Black Journalists, 1992, Cushing award for Journalistic Excellence, Chgo. Dental Soc., 1992, Human First award Horizon Cmty. Svcs., Chgo., 1993, Robert F. Kennedy Grand Prize in Journalism, 1994, Editl. Excellence award Ill. Merchandising Coun., 1994; finalist Pulitzer Prize, 1994. Mem. Taoist Tai Chi Soc. USA-Ill. (pres. 2003-05). Office: CyberINK 621 N Belmont Ave Arlington Heights IL 60004 Office Phone: 847-506-4214. Personal E-mail: jlgrif@earthlink.net.

GRIFFIN, KENNETH C., investment company executive; b. Boca Raton, Fl., 1968; m. Anne Dias; 1 child. BA in Economics, Harvard U., 1989. With Glenwood Investment Corp.; founder, pres, CEO Citadel Investment Group, 1990—. Bd. trustees Chgo. Museum Contemporary Art, Art Inst. Chgo.; bd. dirs. Chgo. Public Education Fund, 2003—, Chgo. Public Library Found. Named one of Forbes' Richest Americans, 2006; named to Top 200 Collectors, ARTnews mag., 2004, 2006. Avocation: Collector of Imprssionism and Post-Impressionism Art. Office: Citadel Investment Group LLC 131 S Dearborn St Chicago IL 60603 Office Phone: 312-395-2100. Office Fax: 312-368-1348.

GRIFFIN, MARK W., paper company executive; BS, U. Memphis, 1972. CEO, pres. RIS Paper Co., Inc., Florence, Ky. Office: RIS Paper Co Inc 9435 Waterstone Blvd Ste 360 Cincinnati OH 45249-8227

GRIFFIN, MICHAEL J., former state legislator; b. Jackson, Miss., May 12, 1933; m. Janet Stark; children: Margaret, John, Martin, Michael, Robert, Gerald, Maureen. BA, Jackson C.C., 1959. City commr., Jackson, 1967-73; rep. Mich. Dist. 50, 1972-92, Mich. Dist. 64, 1993-98. Alt. chmn. joint com. on adminstrv. rules Mich. Ho. Reps., legis. coun., corps. & fin. com., tourism, fisheries, and wildlife com.; product mgr. Rhemm Mfg. Home: 1616 Cascade Ct Jackson MI 49203-3808

GRIFFITH, DENNISON W., academic administrator, artist, educator; BFA, Ohio Wesleyan U.; MFA, Ohio State U. Individual artists program coord. Ohio Arts Coun., 1978—83; exec. dir. Ohio Found. Arts; dep. dir. Columbus Mus. Arts, 1988—98; pres. Columbus Coll. Art & Design, 1998—, prof. painting, 1998—. Trustee Ross Art Mus., Delaware, Ohio, 2004—. Mem.: Nat. Assn. Schs. Art and Design (chair ethics com.), Higher Edn. Coun. Columbus (chmn.), Assn. Ind. Coll. Art & Design (exec. com.), Greater Columbus C. of C. (co-chmn. creative svcs. com., bd. mem.). Office: Office of President Columbus College Art & Design 107 N Ninth St Columbus OH 43215 Office Phone: 614-222-3220. Business E-Mail: dgriffith@ccad.edu.

GRIFFITH, DONALD KENDALL, lawyer; b. Aurora, Ill., Feb. 4, 1933; s. Walter George and Mary Elizabeth G.; m. Susan Smykal, Aug. 4, 1962; children: Kay, Kendall. Grad. in history with honors, Culver Mil. Acad., 1951; BA, U. Ill., 1955, JD, 1958. Bar: Ill. 1958, U.S. Supreme Ct. 1973. Assoc. Hinshaw & Culbertson, Chgo., 1959-65, ptnr., 1965-98, of counsel, 1999—. Spl. asst. atty. gen. Ill., 1970-72; lectr. Ill. Inst. Continuing Legal Edn., 1970-90. Mem. editl. bd. Ill. Civil Practice After Trial, 1970; co-editor The Brief, 1975-83; contbg. author Civil Practice After Trial, 1984, 89; contbr. articles to profl. jours. Trustee Lawrence Hall Youth Svcs., 1967-2000, v.p. for program, 1969-74; bd. dirs. Child Care Assn. Ill., 1970-73; bd. edn. Lake Forest HS, 1983-84; 2d lt. USAF, 1956. Fellow Am. Acad. Appellate Lawyers; mem. ABA (chmn. appellate advocacy com., tort and ins. practice sect. 1983-84), Ill. Bar Assn., Appellate Lawyers Assn. Ill. (pres. 1973-74), Univ. Club Chgo., Knollwood Club, Alpha Chi Rho (chpt. pres.), Phi Delta Phi. Office: Hinshaw & Culbertson 222 N LaSalle St Ste 300 Chicago IL 60601-1081 Office Phone: 312-704-3460. E-mail: dkg5558@earthlink.net.

GRIFFITH, JAMES W., manufacturing executive; B in Indsl. Engring, MBA, Stanford U. Formerly with Homestake Mining Co., Bunker Hill Co., Martin Marietta; with The Timken Co., Canton, Ohio, 1984—, head rail bus., 1996—98, pres., COO, bd. dirs., 1999—2002, pres., CEO, 2002—. Bd. dirs. Goodrich Corp. Trustee United Way of Ctrl. Stark County. Mem.: Mfrs. Alliance/MAPI (exec. com., trustee). Office: The Timken Co 1835 Dueber Ave SW Canton OH 44706-2798

GRIFFITH, JOHN FRANCIS, pediatrician, administrator, educator; b. Humboldt, Sask., Can., Feb. 14, 1934; came to U.S., 1963; s. J. Stuart and Grayce M. (Reid) G.; m. Shirley Shaw, Sept 2, 1961; children: Kathleen Ann, Karen Elizabeth, Kristine M., James Stuart. BA, U. Sask., 1956, MD, 1958. Diplomate Am. Bd. Pediatrics (chmn. bd. 1989—). Intern Montreal (Can.) Gen. Hosp., 1958-59, resident, 1959-60, gen. practice medicine, 1960-61; pediatric resident Montreal Children's Hosp., 1961-63, Case Western Res. U., Cleve., 1963-64, Mass. Gen. Hosp., Boston, 1964-67; research fellow neurology Harvard U. Med. Sch., Boston, 1964-66, research fellow neuropathology, 1966-67, teaching fellow neurology, 1967-69; research infectious diseases Children's Hosp. Med. Ctr., Boston, 1967-69; asst. prof. pediatrics Duke U. Med. Ctr., Durham, N.C., 1969-71, assoc. prof., 1971-76, assoc. prof. medicine, 1975-76; prof., chmn. dept. pediatrics U. Tenn., Memphis, 1976-86; prof. pediatrics and neurology Georgetown U., Washington, 1986-96. Emeritus prof. pediat. and neurology Georgetown U., Washington, 1996—; examiner, mem. written exam com. Am. Bd. Pediat., Chapel Hill, NC, 1979—83, mem. task force on recert., 1979—80, bd. dirs., 1985—89, exec. com. of bd. dirs., 1986, chair program dir. liaion com. and new directions com., 1985—86, chair rsch. and rev. com. and chair guidelines for combined tng. program, 1987—88, sec.-treas., 1986—87; mem. residency rev. com. Accreditation Coun., Chgo., 1982—86, chmn. evaluation com. on pediat. scientist tng. program, 1982—86; sr. v.p. univ. and acad. affairs Health Alliance Greater Cin.; assoc. dean U. Cin. Coll. Medicine. Contbr. articles to profl. jours. Howard Hughes Found., 1971-74; Multiple Sclerosis grantee, 1969-71; Benjamen Miler Meml. grantee, 1971-74; FDA grantee, 1978-80 Mem. Assn. Am. Med. Colls. (com. on AIDS 1987), Irish-Am. Pediatrics Soc., Soc. Pediatrics Rsch., Am. Pediatric Soc., AOA, Am. Acad. Pediatrics, Assn. Med. Sch. Pediatrics Dept. Chmn., Royal Coll. Physicians and Surgeons, Am. Bd. Pediatrics (chmn., bd. dirs. 1989-90), Sigma Chi. Office: Health Alliance 3200 Burnet Ave Cincinnati OH 45229-3099

GRIFFITH, JOHN RANDALL, health facility administrator, educator; b. Balt., Mar. 22, 1934; s. Richard Robinson and Eleanor (Bond) G.; m. Helen Klenner, Sept. 17, 1955; children: Julia, Alison, Richard. BS Indsl. Engring., The Johns Hopkins U., 1955; MBA Hospital Adminstrn., U. Chgo., 1957. From asst. prof. to prof. U. Mich. Sch. Pub. Health Dept. Health Mgmt. Policy, Ann Arbor, 1960—, interim dept. chair, 1987-88, dept. chair, 1988-91, Andrew Pattullo Collegiate prof. Hosp. Adminstrn., 1982—; dir. program, chmn. dept. Bur. Hosp. Adminstrn., Ann Arbor, Mich., 1970-82. Examiner Baldridge Nat. Quality Award, 1997—98. Author: Quantitative Techniques for Hospital Planning and Control, 1972, Measuring Hospital Performance, 1978, The Well Managed Community Hospital, 1987 (award, 1988), Moral Challenges of Health Care Management, The Well-Managed Health Care Organization, 1995 (award, 1999, 2000), 6th edit., 2006, Designing 21st Century Healthcare: Leadership in Hospitals and Health Systems, 1998; author: (with others) Thinking Forward: Six Strategies for Highly Successful Organizations, 2003. Bd. dirs., pres., Assn. Univ. Programs Health Adminstrn., 1974-75, Pattullo lectr., 1999; bd. dirs. Accredation Commn., 1977-83, Nat. Ctr. Healthcare Leadership, 2002-. Recipient Filerman Prize for Ednl. Leadership, Assn. Univ. Programs in Health Adminstrn., 2002. Fellow Am. Coll. Health Care Execs. (gold medal 1992, James A. Hamilton award), Tau Beta Pi, Omicron Delta Kappa. Home: 333 Rock Creek Ct Ann Arbor MI 48104-1857 Office: U Mich SPH II 109 Observatory St Ann Arbor MI 48109-2029 Home Phone: 734-769-0689; Office Phone: 734-936-1304. Business E-Mail: jrg@umich.edu.

GRIFFITH, MARY H., bank executive; b. Ky. m. Robert Griffith; 2 children. BA in English, Centre Coll., Danville, Ky. Sr. v.p., dir. pub. rels. First Ky. Nat. Corp.; v.p., dir. corp. comm. Nat. City Corp., Cleve., 1990, sr. v.p. mktg. comm., 1992, vice chmn. Ky., sr. v.p., 2001—. Bd. trustees Centre Coll.; bd. trustees, chair investment com., mem. exec. com. Bellarmine U., Louisville; chmn. bd. dirs. Louisville Free Pub. Libr. Found., Downtown Devel. Corp., Ky. Ctr. for Arts Endowment, Kentuckiana Works; bd. dirs. Shakertown at Pleasant Hill, Ky., Inc., Teach Ky. Recipient Disting. Alumni award Centre Coll., 1991. Office: Nat City Corp 101 S Fifth St Louisville KY 40202 Office Phone: 502-581-6424.

GRIFFITH, OWEN WENDELL, biochemistry professor; b. Oakland, Calif., June 19, 1946; s. Charles H. and Gladys C. (Farrar) G. BA, U. Calif., Berkeley, 1968; PhD, Rockefeller U., 1975. Asst. prof. Cornell U. Med. Coll., NYC, 1978-81, assoc. prof., 1981-87, prof., 1987-92; prof., chmn. biochemistry Med. Coll. Wis., Milw., 1992—2001, prof. biochemistry, 2001—, dean sch. biomed. scis., 2007—; sci. founder ArgiNOx Therapeutics, LLC, Milw., 2000—. Mem., chmn. med. biochemistry study sect. NIH, Bethesda, Md., 1988-92; founder ArgiNox Pharm., Inc., Redwood City, Calif., 2000-07, bd. dirs. Contbr. more than 160 articles to profl. jours. Grantee NIH. Mem. Am. Chem. Soc., Am. Soc. Biochemistry and Molecular Biology, Am. Soc. Pharmacology and Exptl. Therapeutics. Achievements include more than 40 patents and patent applications in biomedical research. Office: Med Coll Wis Dept Biochemistry 8701 W Watertown Plank Rd Milwaukee WI 53226-3548 Business E-Mail: griffith@mcw.edu.

GRIFFITH, ROGER, professional sports team executive; m. Jean Griffith; 1 child. Grad. Magna cum laude, Augsburg Coll., 1984; MBA in Gen. Mgmt., U. Minn., 1988. Dir. internal audit Northwest Airlines; divsn. mgr. ad specialty direct mail divsn. Taymark, a Taylor Corp. co.; exec. pres., CFO Minn. Timberwolves & Lynx, Mpls., 1994—, COO. Office: 600 1st Ave N Minneapolis MN 55403

GRIFFITH, SIMA LYNN, investment banker, consultant; b. NYC, Sept. 7, 1960; d. Morris Benjamin and Mary (Buberoglü) Nahum; m. Clark Calvin Griffith, Sept. 13, 1987. BA in English, Amherst Coll., 1982. Account exec. D.F. King & Co., Inc., NYC, 1982-84, asst. v.p., 1984-86, v.p., 1986-88, Wells & Miller, Mpls., 1988; pres. Griffith, Levi Capital, Inc, Mpls., 1988—96; prin. Aethlon, Capital LLC, Mpls., 1996—, mng. prin. Co-chmn. PRSA, IR seminars, 1987; bd. adv. Pacer, Inc. Bd. dirs. Children's Hosps. and Clinics, 2004—, Mpls. Found.; bd. govs. Children's Theater Co., 1999—2005; bd. adv. PACER; co-chair Women-to-Women. amed Not for Profit Dir. of Yr., Women on Boards, 2005; named one of Twin Cities Women to Watch, The Bus. Jour., 2002, Top Women in Fin., Fin. and Commerce newspaper, 2003; recipient Vision award, Nat. Assn. Women Bus. Owners, 2003. Mem.: Pub. Rels. Soc. Am. (bod. govs., investor rels. sec. 1987—89), Assn. Bus. Communicators (bd. govs. 1987—88). Office: Aethlon Capital LLC 4920 IDS Ctr 80 South 8th St Minneapolis MN 55402-2100 Office Phone: 612-338-0934, 612-338-6065. E-mail: sgriffith@aethlon.com.

GRIFFITHS, DAVID NEAL, utilities executive; b. Oxford, Ind., Sept. 11, 1935; s. David Scifres and Lorene Francis Griffiths; m. Alice Anne Goodpasture, Aug. 9, 1959 (div. 1972); children— Beth Anne, David Douglas; m. Barbette Suzanne Goetsch, June 7, 1975; children— Michael, Megan BS in Indsl. Econs., Purdue U., 1957. Various positions Delco Remy div. Gen. Motors Corp., Anderson, Ind., 1957-69; dep. commr. revenue State of Ind., Indpls., 1969-71, adminstrv. asst. to gov., 1971-72; exec. dir. Environ. Quality Control, Inc., Indpls., 1972-75; project mgr. EDP Corp., Sarasota, Fla., 1975-76, v.p. adminstrn., 1977-78; asst. to pres. Citizens Gas and Coke Utility, Indpls., 1978-80, v.p. pub. affairs, 1980-82, sr. v.p. adminstrn., 1982-92, exec. v.p., 1995-98, exec. v.p., COO, 1998—, pres., CEO, 1999—. Mem. ind. Energy Devel. Bd., Indpls., 1980-92, Midwest Govs.' Energy Task Force, 1972-75; chmn. Fed. Home Loan Bank of Indpls., 1990-93; trustee Mfrs. Alliance; bd. dirs. Ind. Farmers Mut. Ins. Co., Am. Gas Assn., Meth. Med. Group. Author: Implementing Quality with a Customer Focus, Management in a Quality Environment. Pres. Indsl. Mgmt. Club, Anderson and Madison County, Inc., 1961; Cen. Coun. Indsl. Mgmt. Clubs 1966; bd. dirs., chmn. Environ. Quality Conrol, Inc., Indpls., 1983-98, Life/Ledership Devel., Inc.; bd.dirs. Greater Indpls. Progress Com., Goodwill Industries Found., Life/Leadership Devel., Inc., Indy Partnership. Recipient Exchange Industrialist with USSR award YMCA, 1963; named Sagamore of Wabash, Gov. of Ind., 1971, 75. Mem. Govtl. Affairs Soc. Ind. (past pres.), Ind. Gas Assn. (bd. dirs.), Greater Indpls. C. of C. (bd. dirs., vice chair), Columbia Club (Indpls.). Republican. Methodist. Avocations: golf, swimming. Home: 8158 Brent Ave Indianapolis IN 46240-2725 Office: Citizens Gas & Coke Utility 2020 N Meridian St Indianapolis IN 46202-1393

GRIFFITHS, ROBERT PENNELL, banker; b. Chgo., May 6, 1949; s. George Findley and Marion E. (Winterrowd) G.; m. Susan Hillman, Jan. 31, 1976 (div. 2002); m. Janet Bauer, March, 22, 2003. BA, Amherst Coll., 1972; MS in Mgmt., Northwestern U., 1974. From comml. banking officer to v.p. No. Trust Co., Chgo., 1978—85; sr. v.p. comml. lending UnibancTrust Co., Chgo., 1985-88; pres., CEO Old Kent Bank of Naperville, Ill., 1988—90; sr. v.p. Old Kent Bank, Chgo., 1991—92; pres., CEO Uptown Nat. Bank Chgo., 1993—2001; mng. dir. Pvt. Bank and Trust Co., Chgo., 2002—. Mem.: Univ. Club (Chgo.), Onwentsia Club. Home: 2726 Aspen Ct Glenview IL 60026 Office: Pvt Bank and Trust Co 5260 Old Orchard Rd Skokie IL 60077

GRIGGS, LEONARD LEROY, JR., air transportation executive, consultant; b. Norfolk, Va., Oct. 13, 1931; s. Leonard LeRoy and Mary (Blair) G.; m. Denise Ziegler, Mar. 18, 1977; children: Margaret Rosalyn, Virginia Lorraine Williams, Julia Blair Havey, Deborah Branham Taylor. BS, US Mil. Acad., 1954; MS in Aero. Engring., Air Force Inst. Tech., 1960; MS in Internat. Affairs, George Wash. U., Washington, DC, 1967; disting. grad., Naval War Coll., 1967, Army War Coll., 1971. Registered profl. engr., Mo. Commd. 2d lt. U.S. Army, 1954; advanced through grades to col. USAF, 1970; served in Vietnam; ret., 1977; dir. Lambert St. Louis Internat. Airport, 1977-87; v.p. Ross & Baruzzini, Inc., 1987-89, Bangert Bros. Constrn. Co., St. Louis and Denver, 1989—; asst. adminstr. for airports FAA, Washington, 1990-93; airport dir. St. Louis Internat. Airport, 1993—2004; aviation cons., 2005—. Adj. prof. St. Louis U.; apptd. to Nat. Civil Aviation Rev. Commn., 1997. Bd. dirs. USO, St. Louis/Lambert, Airports Coun. Internat., 1997-98. Decorated Silver Star, D.F.C. with 4 oak leaf clusters, Bronze Star, Meritorious Svc. medal, Air medal with 22 oak leaf clusters, Purple Heart, Air Force Commendation medal with 2 oak leaf clusters, Army Commendation medal; Medal of Honor; Medal of Gallantry (Vietnam); recipient Aviation Engring. Safety award FAA, 1979. Mem. Airport Operators Coun. Internat., Am. Assn. Airport Execs., Profl. Engring. Soc. St. Louis, Order of Dadelians, St. Louis Air Force Assn., Engr. Club, Mo. Athletic Club, Army avy Club, Univ. Club, Order DeMolay. Home: 1609 Tradd Ct Chesterfield MO 63017-5627 Office: La Chateau Village 10411 Clayton Rd Ste307 Saint Louis MO 63131 Home Phone: 636-532-4313; Office Phone: 314-692-0044. Personal E-mail: col.griggs@sbcglobal.net.

GRIMES, DAVID LYNN, communications executive; b. Oklahoma City, June 9, 1947; s. Glenn Ross and Kathleen Sue G.; m. Sandra Kay Belt, Mar. 6, 1970; children: David Edwin, Emily Kathleen. BBA in Mktg., Ctrl. State U., Edmond, Okla., 1978; grad. internat. sr. mgrs. program, Harvard U., 1988. With Southwestern Bell Tel., 1970-83, rates and tariff Oklahoma City, 1975-77, industry mgr., 1977-79, dist. mgr. sales ops. St. Louis, 1979-80, mktg. mgr. Kansas City, Mo., 1980-82, Houston, 1982-83; divsn. mgr. Am. Bell, Houston, 1983-84; br. mgr. nat. accts. AT&T, Houston, 1984-85, v.p. sales Dallas, 1986-98; COO Sharetech, Parsippny, NJ, 1985-86; pres., COO Sykes Enterprises, 1998-2000, pres., CEO, 2000; sr. v.p. Tropic Networks, Dallas, 2001—04, pres., 2004—06, Sybaritic, Inc., 2007—. Mem. Nat. Bd. of Visitors Tex. Christian U., 1990-96; mem. adv. coun. Sch. Nat. Sci., U. Tex., Austin, 1988-93; bd. dirs. Tex. Bus. Hall of Fame Found., Dallas, 1988-93. Mem. Dallas C. of C. (mem. exec. com. econ. devel. 1991-93), Harvard Bus. Club Dallas, Univ. Club (Dallas), Avila Country Club, Brookhaven Country Club, Pinnacle Country Club, Tampa C. of C. (bd. dirs. 2000-01). Republican. Methodist. Avocations: golf, tennis, fishing, hunting. Home: 5510 Merrimac Ave Dallas TX 75206 Office: Sybaritic Inc 9220 James Ave S Minneapolis MN 55431 Office Phone: 952-746-0311. Personal E-mail: dlgrimes@sbcglobal.net. Business E-Mail: dgrimes@sybaritic.com.*

GRIMES, SALLY, marketing professional; m. Steve Grimes; 2 children. Grad., U. Chgo. Grad. Sch. Bus., 1997. With Kraft Foods, Inc., 1997—, brand mgr. e-commerce, dir. integrated mktg. North Am. grocery sector, 2005—. Named one of Top 40 Under 40, Crain's Chgo. Bus., 2006. Office: Kraft Foods Inc Three Lakes Dr Northfield IL 60093

GRIMES, STEVEN P., corporate financial executive; m. Sally Grimes; 2 children. With Deloitte & Touche LLP, 1994; prin. fin. officer Inland Western Retail Real Estate Trust, Inc. Named one of Top 40 Under 40, Crain's Chgo. Bus., 2006. Office: Inland Grp Inc 2901 Butterfield Rd Oak Brook IL 60523

GRIMLEY, JEFFREY MICHAEL, dentist; b. Alton, Ill., Feb. 3, 1957; s. John Richard and Joyce Imogene (Mallin) G.; m. Julie Ellen Gardner, Aug. 2, 1980; children: Joel Michael, Christopher Mark, Benjamin Jeffrey. BS, U. Iowa, 1979, DDS, 1983; cert., Miami Valley Hosp., Dayton, Ohio, 1984. Gen. practice dentistry, aperville, Ill., 1984—. Mem. ADA, Acad. Gen. Dentistry, Ill. Dental Soc., Chgo. Dental Soc. Methodist. Avocations: sports, photography. Office: Ste 112 1980 Three Farms Ave Naperville IL 60540-5365 Home Phone: 630-416-9583; Office Phone: 630-369-6980. Personal E-mail: grimleydds1@aol.com.

GRIMM, LOUIS JOHN, mathematician, educator; b. St. Louis, Nov. 30, 1933; s. Louis and Florence Agnes (Hammond) G.; m. Barbara Ann Mitko, May 6, 1967; children: Thomas, Mary. BS, St. Louis U., 1954; MS, Ga. Inst. Tech., 1960; PhD, U. Minn., 1965. Chemist USPHS, Savannah, Ga., 1958-61; asst. prof. U. Utah, Salt Lake City, 1965-69; assoc. prof. Mo. U. Sci. Tech., Rolla, 1969-74; prof. U. Mo., Rolla, 1974—, chmn. dept. math. and stats., 1981-87, dir. Inst. Applied Math., 1983-87. Vis. asst. prof. U. Minn., Mpls., 1966; vis. prof. U. Nebr., Lincoln, 1978-79, U. So. Calif., L.A., 1987-88; exch. scientist Polish Acad. Scis., Warsaw, 1981. Contbr. articles to profl. jours. With Med. Svc. Corps, AUS, 1956-58. Jefferson Smurfit fellow Univ. Coll. Dublin (Ireland), 1984; SF rsch. grantee. Mem. AAUP, SAR, Soc. for Indsl. and Applied Math., Polish Math. Soc., Gesellschaft für angewandte Mathematik und Mechanik, Math. Assn. Am. (Disting. Tchg. award 2001), Sigma Xi. Office: MO Univ Sci and Tech Dept Math & Stats Rolla MO 65409-0001

GRIMM, TERRY M., lawyer; b. Bloomington, Ill., Apr. 3, 1942; BA, Ind. U., 1964, JD cum laude, 1967. Bar: Ill. 1967, US Dist. Ct. (no., ctrl. & so. dists. Calif.), US Dist. Ct. (no. & ctrl. dists. Ill.), US Dist. Ct. (no. dist. Ind.), US Dist. Ct. (so. dist. NY), US Dist. Ct. (dist. Wyo.). Assoc. to ptnr. Winston & Strawn, LLP, Chgo., 1968—, mem. exec. com.; spl. prosecutor DuPage County Prosecutor's Office, Ill., 1975-76. Fellow Am. Coll. Trial Lawyers; mem. Ill. State Bar Assn., Order of the Coif. Office: Winston & Strawn 35 W Wacker Dr Ste 4200 Chicago IL 60601-9703 Office Phone: 312-558-5782. Office Fax: 312-558-5700. E-mail: tgrimm@winston.com.

GRIMSHAW, LYNN ALAN, lawyer; b. Portsmouth, Ohio, Sept. 14, 1949; s. Vaughn Edwin and Margaret (Jordan) G.; m. Beverly Gay Moore, Oct. 21, 1978; children: Jordan, Stuart. BS in Indsl. Mgmt., Purdue U., 1971; JD, U. Cin., 1975. Bar: Ohio 1978. Atty. Gerlach & Grimshaw, Portsmouth, 1975-76; pros. atty. Scioto County, Portsmouth, 1977—. Mem. Gov.'s Organized Crime Cons. Com., Ohio, 1984. Chmn. Scioto County Dem. Party, 1980-81. Mem. Ohio Pros. Atty. Assn. (pres. 1985), at. Dist. Atty.'s Assn. (bd. dirs. 1987), Scioto County Bar Assn. (pres. 1997), Kiwanis. Democrat. Methodist. Office: Scioto County Courthouse 6th and Courts Sts Portsmouth OH 45662

GRINDBERG, TONY, state legislator; m. Vanessa Grindberg; 1 child. Student, N.D. State Coll. Sci., Wahpeton, Moorehead State U. Dir. Interstate Bus. Coll.; mem. .D. Senate from 41st dist., Bismark, 1993—. Vice chmn. edn. com.; mem. govt. and vet. affairs com. N.D. State Senate. Mem. Midwestern Bus. Coll. Assn. (pres.), Rotary. Republican. Home: 2832 39 1/2 Ave S Fargo ND 58104-7014

GRISKO, JEROME P., JR., diversified financial services company executive; Ptnr. Baker & Hostetler, LLP, 1987-98; sr. v.p. mergers and acquisitions and legal affairs Century Bus. Sys., Cleve., 1998—, interim pres., 2000—. Office: Century Business Service 6050 Oak Tree Blvd #500 Cleveland OH 44131-6951

GRISSOM, MARQUIS DEON, professional baseball player; b. Atlanta, Apr. 17, 1967; Student, Fla. A & M. Outfielder Montreal Expos, 1988—94; with Atlanta Braves, 1994—97, Milw. Brewers, 1997—2000, L.A. Dodgers, 2001—02, San Francisco Giants, 2002—. Named to All-Star Team, Nat. League, 1993, 1994; recipient Golden Glove award, 1993—96. Achievements include leading the Nat. League in stolen bases, 1991-92.

GRISWELL, J. BARRY, insurance company executive; b. Ga. Bachelor's, Berry Coll., 1971; master's, Stetson U., 1972. Pres., CEO MetLife Mktg. Corp. (subs. MetLife Ins. Co.); agy. v.p. Principal Fin. Group, Des Moines, 1986-91, sr. v.p. individual ins. dept., 1991-96, exec. v.p., 1996-98, pres., 1998—2000, pres. and CEO, 2000—02, chmn., pres., CEO, 2002—06, chmn., CEO, 2006—. Past chair LIMRA Internat.; past chair bd. trustees Life Underwriting Tng. Coun.; bd. mem. Bus. Roundtable, Am. Coun. Capital Formation; bd. dir. Herman Miller Inc.; trustee S.S. Huebner Found. for Ins. Edn. Dir. Bus. Com. for Arts; trustee United Way Am.; past chmn. United Way Am. Nat. Tocqueville Council; trustee Central Coll., Berry Coll., Ga. Recipient Disting. American award, Horatio Alger Assn., 2003. Fellow: LIMRA Leadership Inst. Office: Principal Fin Group 711 High St Des Moines IA 50392*

GRISWOLD, TOM, radio personality; b. Cleve., 1953; Grad., Univ. Sch., Chagrin Fall, OH, 1971, Columbia U. Radio host WFBQ-FM, Indpls., 1983—; nat. syndicated radio host Premiere Radio Networks, 1995—. Co-host The Bob & Tom Show, 1983—. Co-recipient Radio Personality of Yr. award, Billboard mag., 1991—98, Marconi Radio award, Nat. Assn. Broadcasters, 1993, 1995, 1997, 1999, Marconi Radio award for Network Syndicated Personality of Yr., 2006, The Sagamore of the Wabash, 1994, Nat. Chmn.'s Citation award, Leukemia Soc. Am., 1996. Office: WFBQ 6161 Fall Creek Rd Indianapolis IN 46220

GROBSCHMIDT, RICHARD A., school system administrator; b. Milw., May 3, 1948; married; 1 child. BS, U. Wis., Oshkosh, 1972; MS, U. Wis., Milw., 1980. Polit. sci. tchr. South Milwaukee H.S., 1972-85; mem. from dist. 21 Wis. State Assembly, Madison, 1984-95; mem. from dist. 7 Wis. Senate, Madison, 1995—2003, chmn. edn. com.; asst. state supt. divsn. for librs., tech. and cmty. learning Dept. Pub. Instrn., State of Wis., Madison, 2003—. Home: 912 Lake Dr South Milwaukee WI 53172-1736 Office: 125 S Webster St PO Box 7841 Madison WI 53707 E-mail: richard.grobschmidt@dpi.state.wi.us.

GROETHE, REED, lawyer; b. Indpls., Mar. 21, 1952; s. Alfred Philip and Kathryn (Skerik) G.; m. Nancy Jayne Radefeld, June 2, 1974; children: Jacob Peter, Eric Alfred. BA, St. Olaf Coll., 1974; JD, U. Chgo., 1977. Bar: Wis. 1977. Law clk. to judge U.S. Ct. Appeals (5th cir.), Montgomery, Ala., 1977-78; assoc. Foley & Lardner, Milw., 1978-86, ptnr., 1986—. Pres. Bay Shore Luth. Ch., Whitefish Bay, Wis., 1985-89. Mem. ABA (tax sect.), Nat. Asn. Bond Lawyers, Wis. Bar Assn. Lutheran. Office: Foley & Lardner 777 E Wisconsin Ave Ste 3800 Milwaukee WI 53202-5367

GROETZINGER, JON, JR., lawyer, pharmaceutical executive, educator; b. NYC, Feb. 12, 1949; s. Jon M. and Elinor Groetzinger; m. Carol Marie O'Connor, Jan. 24, 1981; 3 children. AB magna cum laude, Middlebury Coll., 1971; JD in Internat. Legal Affairs, Cornell U., 1974. Bar: N.H. 1974, N.Y. 1980, Mass. 1980, Fla. 1982, Md. 1985, Ohio 1991, U.S. Supreme Ct. 1980. Assoc. McLane, Graf, Greene, Raulerson and Middleton, P.A., Manchester, NH, 1974-76; pvt. practice NH, Boston, 1977-81; chief internat. counsel Martin Marietta Corp., Bethesda, Md., 1981-88; pres., exec. v.p. Martin Marietta Overseas Corp., Bethesda, 1984-88; sr. v.p., gen. counsel, corp. sec. Am. Greetings Corp., Cleve., 1988—2003; CEO, pres. LifePill, Cleve., 2004—; vis. prof. law Case Western Reserve Sch. Law, Cleve., 2007—. Atty. John A. Gray Law Offices, Boston, 1978-81; chmn. internat. adv. bd. Case Western Res. U. Law Sch., 1995-; bd. mem. Can.-US Law Inst., 1995-. Contbr. articles to profl. pubs. Trustee Middlebury (Vt.) Coll., 1974—76, bd. overseers, 1977—; bd. dirs. Cleve. Coun. on World Affairs, 1992—98, 2000—, vice chmn., 2002—06, chmn. strategic planning com., 2000—02, exec. com., 2000—05, trustee, 1992—96, 1998—2005; bd. dirs. Can.-U.S. Law Inst., 1990—, The Conf. Bds. Coun. Chief Legal Officers, 1996—2003, membership chmn., 1997—98, program chair, 1999—2000, coun. chmn., 2000—02; chmn., pres. Greater Cleve. Gen. Counsel Assn., 2001—04; bd. dirs. Lake Erie Coll., 2002—, vice chmn., 2005—06, chmn. bd., 2006—07. Mem. ABA, N.H. Bar Assn., Fla. Bar Assn., Ohio Bar Assn., Cleve. Bar Assn., Md. Bar Assn., Am. Soc. Corp. Secs. (sec. Ohio chpt. 1995—, v.p. 1996-97, pres. 1997-98, adv. com. 1998-2006), Soc. of Benchers, Phi Beta Kappa. Office: LifePill 37455 Miles Rd Moreland Hills OH 44022 Home Phone: 440-247-8287. Personal E-mail: jgroetzi@yahoo.com.

GRONEMUS, BARBARA, state legislator; b. Nov. 21, 1931; d. Erwin J. and Irene (Resch) Barry; m. Lambert N. Gronemus, 1949; children: Michelle (Mrs. Jerome J. Carroll), Jacqueline (Mrs. Eric Baken), Margaret Susan (Mrs. David Williams). Former dir. nursing home activity; mem. from dist. 91 Wis. State Assembly, Madison, 1982—, mem. state affairs, small bus. coms., 1993, mem. agr. com., 1983—, vice chmn., 1985, chmn. subcom. on swing psuedorabies, 1985, vice chmn. commerce and consumer affairs, 1983, mem. excise/fees, tourism, recreation & forest productivity, 1985, mem. Minn.-Wis. boundary commn. legis. adv. com., 1983—, chmn. agr., forestry and rural affairs coms. Chmn. Trempealeau County Dem. Com., 1981-82, 3d Congl. Dist. Dem. Com., 1982-83. Mem. Am. Legion, Farmers Union, Whitehall Women's Club, Whitehall Rod and Gun Club, Trempealeau County Homemakers Club. Home: PO Box 676 36301 West St Whitehall WI 54773-8512 Office: Wis House of Reps Office Of House Mems Madison WI 53702-0001

GRONSTAL, MICHAEL E., state legislator; b. Council Bluffs, Iowa, Jan. 29, 1950; m. Connie Meisenbach. BA, Antioch Coll.; student, Loyola U. With Dem. Party State Ctrl. Com. 5th Dist.; chair Pottawattamie County Dem. Party, 1986-88; mem. Iowa Senate from 42nd dist., Des Moines, 1984—; asst. majority leader 71st, 72d Gen. Assemblies; majority whip 73rd Gen. Assembly; pres. of the senate 74th Gen. Assembly; minority leader 77th and 78th Gen. Assembly. Former mem. Govs. Drug Treatment Lic. Bd.; bd. dirs. River Bluffs Cmty. Mental Health Ctr., Chem. Dependency Agy. Democrat. Home: 220 Bennett Ave Council Bluffs IA 51503-5205 Office: State Capitol Dist 42 Des Moines IA 50319-0001 E-mail: mgronst@legis.state.ia.us.

GRONSTAL, THOMAS B., state agency administrator; b. Carroll, Iowa, June 14, 1951; m. Joan Gronstal; 2 children. Grad., Benedictine Coll., Atchison, Kans., 1973. With Ctrl. Nat. Bank, Des Moines, 1973—75, Iowa Divsn. Banking, 1975—78, supt., 2002—; positions including chmn. Carroll County State Bank, Iowa, 1978—2002. Mem. Iowa Workforce Devel. Regional Adv. Bd., Carroll Area Devel. Corp. Treas. Iowa Bankers Assn., 1987—89, pres., 1990, Carroll C. of C., 1989; mayor City of Carroll, 1994—99; mem. Gov.'s Strategic Planning Coun., 1999—2000, Carroll Area Devel. Corp., 1999—2001. Named to Iowa Vol. Hall of Fame, 1994. Office: Iowa Divsn Banking 200 E Grand Ave Ste 300 Des Moines IA 50309-1827 Office Phone: 515-281-4014. Office Fax: 515-281-4862.

GROSE, CHARLES FREDERICK, pediatrician, epidemiologist; b. Faribault, Minn., Apr. 15, 1942; s. Frederick G. and Marie A. (Swelland) G. BA, Beloit Coll., 1963; MD, U. Chgo., 1967. Bd. cert. in pediatric infectious disease. Resident Albert Einstein Coll. Medicine, Bronx, NY, 1967-68, fellow, 1970—75, U. Calif., San Francisco, 1975-76; asst. prof. Health Sci. Ctr. U. Tex., San Antonio, 1976-84; prof. pediatrics U. Iowa Hosp., Iowa City, 1985—. Cons. NIH, Bethesda, Md., 1988—. Editor Pediat. Infectious Disease Jour., 2003—; mem. editl. bd. Virology Jour.; contbr. articles to profl. and sci. jours. Capt. U.S. Army Med. Corps., Vietnam, 1968-70. Grantee NIH, 1978—. Fellow Infectious Disease Soc. Am., Pediatric Infectious Disease Soc., Am. Acad. Pediatrics, Am. Soc. Virology. Achievements include research on diagnosis and treatment of chickenpox and shingles, and on the etiologic agent which is varicella virus. Office: U Iowa Hosp Pediatrics 200 Hawkins Dr Iowa City IA 52242-1009 Business E-Mail: charles-grose@uiowa.edu.

GROSFELD, JAY LAZAR, surgeon, educator; b. NYC, May 30, 1935; m. Margie Faulkner; children: Lisa, Denise, Janice, Jeffrey, Mark. AB cum laude, NYU, 1957, MD, 1961. Diplomate Am. Bd. Surgery (spl. qualification Pediatric Surgery). Gen. surgery intern Bellevue and Univ Hosps. NYU, NYC, 1961—62; resident in gen. surgery Bellevue and Univ. Hosps. NYU, NYC, 1962—66; resident in pediatric surgery Ohio State U. Coll. Medicine, Children's Hosp., 1968—70; instr. surgery Ohio State U. Coll. Medicine, 1968—70; clin. instr. surgery NYU Sch. Medicine, NYC, 1965—66, asst. prof. surgery and pediatrics, 1970—72; prof., dir. pediatric surgery Ind. U. Sch. Medicine, Indpls., 1972—2005, chmn. dept. surgery, 1985—2003, Lafayette F. Page prof., 1981—2005, Lafayette F. Page prof. emeritus, 2005—; surgeon-in-chief James Whitcomb Riley Hosp. Children, 1972—2005; Lafayette Page prof. surgery, chmn. emeritus Ind. U. Sch. Medicine, Indpls., 2005—. Author: Common Problems in Pediatric Surgery, 1991, Central Surgical Association: The First 50 Years, 1991, Progress in Pediatric Trauma, 1992, Essentials of Pediatric Surgery, 1995, Pediatric Surgery, 6th edit., 2006, The Surgery of Childhood Tumors, 1999, Principles of Pediatric Surgery, 2003; editor-in-chief: Jour. Pediat. Surgery, 1994—; editor: Seminars in Pediat. Surgery; contbr. over 600 papers, reports, book chpts., articles for med. jours. Capt. M.C. US Army, 1966—68. Decorated Commendation medal; named Sagamore of the Wabash, 2002; recipient numerous fellowships, grants, teaching awards. Fellow: ACS (bd. govs. 1985—91), Am. Acad. Pediat. (exec. com. surg. sect. 1989—95, chmn. surg. sect. 1994—95, sec. surg. sect., William E. Ladd medal 2002—), Royal Coll. Physicians and Surgeons Glasgow (hon.), Royal Coll. Surgeons of Eng. (hon.); mem.: AMA, Halsted Soc. (v.p. 1995—96, pres. 1996—97), Accreditation Coun. Grad. Med. Edn. (surg. residency rev. com. 1996—2001, vice chair 2000—01), Am. Bd. Med. Specialities, World Fedn. Assns. Pediat. Surgeons (pres. 1998—2001, v.p.), Am. Bd. Surgery (bd. dirs. 1989—97, vice chair 1995, chmn. 1996—97, chmn.-elect), Am. Pediatric Surg. Assn. Found. (chmn. bd. dirs.), Internat. Soc. Surgery (sec., treas. Internat. Soc. Surgery Found. 2001—), Western Surg. Assn. (pres. 1997—98), Soc. Surg. Oncology, Brit. Assn. Pediat. Surgeons (exec. coun. 1990—93, Denis Browne Gold medal 1998), Ctrl. Surg. Assn. (sec. 1987—, pres.-elect 1988, pres. 1990), Soc. Surgery Alimentary Tract, Am. Trauma Soc., Ind. State Med. Assn., Marion County Med. Soc., Soc. Univ. Surgeons, Am. Surg. Assn. (first v.p. 2005—, pres. 2006—), British Assn. Pediat. Surgeons (hon.), Am. Pediat. Surg. Assn. (pres. 1994—95, bd. govs., pres.-elect), N.Y. Cancer Soc., Assn. Acad. Surgery, Pediat. Surgery Biology Club, Alpha Omega Alpha, Phi Beta Kappa. Office: J W Riley Childrens Hosp 702 Barnhill Dr Rm 2500 Indianapolis IN 46202-5128 Office Phone: 317-274-5716. Business E-Mail: jgrosfel@iupui.edu.

GROS LOUIS, KENNETH RICHARD RUSSELL, humanities educator; b. Nashua, NH, Dec. 18, 1936; s. Albert W. and Jeannette Evelyn (Richards) Gros L.; m. Dolores K. Winandy, Aug. 28, 1965; children: Amy Katherine, Julie Jeannette. BA, Columbia U., 1959, MA, 1960; PhD (Knapp fellow), U. Wis., 1964. Asst. prof. Ind. U., Bloomington, 1964—67, assoc. prof. English and comparative lit., 1967—73, prof., 1973—, assoc. chmn. comparative lit. dept., 1967—69, assoc. dean arts and scis., 1970—73, chmn. dept. English, 1973—78, dean arts and scis., 1978—80, v.p., 1980—88, chancellor, 1988—2001, v.p. acad. affairs, 1994—2001, trustee prof., 2001—. Bd. dirs. Anthem, Inc.; exec. coun. acad. affairs Nat. Assn. Univ. and Land Grant Colls., 1986-97, bd. dirs. Bd. dirs. Editor Yearbook of Comparative and Gen. Lit., 1968—, Vol. I: Literary Interpretations of Biblical Narratives, 1974, Vol. II, 1982; contbr. articles to profl. jours. Bd. dirs. Assoc. Group, 1983-95, Anthem Blue Cross and Blue Shield, 1995—; mem. Ind. Com. Humanities, chmn., 1980-81; chmn. Com. on Instnl. Coop., 1986-2000; mem. Nat. Commn. on Libr. Preservation and Access, 1986-93; vice chmn., bd. dirs. Ctr. for Rsch. Librs., 1986—, chmn. bd. dirs., 1987-88. Recipient Disting. Teaching award Ind. U., 1970 Mem. MLA, Nat. Coun. Tchrs. English, AAUP, Phi Beta Kappa. Home: 4965 E Heritage Woods Rd Bloomington IN 47401-9313 Office: Ind U Wylie Hall Bloomington IN 47405 E-mail: grosloui@indiana.edu.

GROSS, CHARLES ROBERT, county official, former state senator, former bank executive; b. St. Charles, Mo., Aug. 20, 1958; s. Jack Robert and Margaret Ellen (Stumberg) G.; m. Leslie Ann Goralczyk, May 27, 1984; children: Megan Marie, Madelynn Ann. BS in Pub. Adminstrn., U. Mo., 1981, MPA, 1982. Pers. mgr. Army and Air Force Exch. Svc., various cities, 1983-89; pers., safety dir. Ever-Green Lawns Corp., St. Charles, 1989-92; state rep. Mo. Legislature, Jefferson City, 1993—2000; real estate appraiser, 1994—2001; v.p. UMB Bank, 2001—07; state senator Mo. Legislature, Jefferson City, 2001—07; dir. adminstrn. St. Charles County Govt., Mo., 2007—. Pres. St. Charles County Young Reps., 1990-92; active Youth in Need, Bridgeway Counseling. Mem. St. Charles DARE, Kiwanis, Pacaderms, Alpha Kappa Psi (life). Lutheran. Avocations: golf, scuba diving, ice hockey. Home: 3019 Westborough Ct Saint Charles MO 63301-4550 Home Phone: 636-949-7520. E-mail: chuckgross58@hotmail.com.

GROSS, DAVID J.F., lawyer; b. St. Paul, 1963; BA, U. Minn., 1985; JD, Harvard U., 1989. Bar: Minn. 1990, admitted to: US Ct. of Appeals, Fed. Cir., US Ct. of Appeals, Eighth Cir., US Dist. Ct., Dist. Minn. Clerk US Ct. of Appeals, First Cir., 1989—90; trail atty. US Dept. Justice, Washington; litigator Covington & Burling, Skadden, Arps, Slate, Meagher & Flom; ptnr. Faegre & Benson LLP, Mpls.; adj. prof., Patent Litig. and Strategy U. Minn. Law Sch. Lectr. U. Minn. Career Guidance Programs. Co-author: The Power Trial Method. Named a Super Lawyer, Minn. Law and Politics; named one of 15 Attorneys of Yr., Minn. Lawyer, Top Ten IP Litigators of Yr., Chambers USA, Litigation's Rising Stars, The Am. Lawyer, 2007. Mem.: U. Minn. Coll. Liberal Arts Alumni Soc. Office: Faegre & Benson LLP 2200 Wells Fargo Ctr 90 S 7th St Minneapolis MN 55402-3901 Office Phone: 612-766-7000. Office Fax: 612-766-1600.

GROSS, DAVID LEE, geologist; b. Springfield, Ill., Nov. 20, 1943; s. Carl David and Shirley Marie (Northcutt) G.; m. Claudia Cole, June 11, 1966; children: Oliver David, Alexander Lee AB, Knox Coll., 1965; MS, U. Ill., 1967, PhD, 1969. Registered profl. geologist, Ill., Calif. Asst. geologist Ill. State Geol. Survey, Champaign, 1969-73, assoc. geologist, 1973-80, geologist, 1980—, coord. environ. geology, 1979-84, head environ. studies, 1984-89, asst. chief, 1991-99, sr. geologist emeritus, 1999—. Exec. dir. Gov.'s Sci. Adv. Com., Chgo., 1989-91; bd. dirs. First State Bank, Beardstown, Ill., chmn. 2001—. Contbr. numerous articles to profl. jours. Bd. govs. Channing-Murray Found., 1973-76, pres., 1976; trustee Unitarian Universalist Ch., Urbana, 1977-80, 99-02, chmn., 1977-79, 99-01; bd. dirs. Vol. Action Ctr., 1981-85, chmn., 1984-85; bd. dirs. United Way Champaign County, 1984-89, exec. com., 1984-85, chmn. United Way Campaign, U. Ill., 1986, chair Youth Vision Coun., 2003-05; bd. dirs. Vol. Ctr., 1994-97; mem. Gov.'s Sci. Adv. Com., 1989-97; vol. summer camp counselor for teenage youth, 1984-07; bd. dirs. Ill. Prairie chpt. ARC, 1997-03. NDEA fellow, 1969 Fellow Geol. Soc. Am., AAAS; mem. Internat. Union Quaternary Rsch., Am. Quaternary Assn., Am. Inst. Profl. Geologists (pres. Ill.-Ind. sect. 1980), Ill. State Acad. Sci., Rotary (pres. Urbana, Ill. chpt. 1986-87), Columbia (Chgo.) Yacht Club, Sigma Xi. Home: 3 Flora Ct Champaign IL 61821-3216 Office: Ill State Geol Survey 615 E Peabody Dr Champaign IL 61820-6918 E-mail: DLGgeology@aol.com.

GROSS, JAMES HOWARD, lawyer; b. Springfield, Ohio, Sept. 21, 1941; s. Cyril James and Virginia (Stieg) G.; m. Gail Sue Helmick, July 13, 1968; children: Karin G. Cramer, David James. BA, Ohio State U., 1963; LLB, Harvard U., 1966. Bar: Ohio 1966, D.C. 1975. Assoc. Vorys, Sater, Seymour and Pease, Columbus, Ohio, 1966-75, resident ptnr. Washington, 1975-77; ptnr. Vorys, Sater, Seymour and Pease LLP, Columbus, 1975—. White House fellow, spl. asst. to sec. HUD, Washington, 1972-73; city atty. City of Bexley, Ohio, 1985-07. Mem. Franklin County Rep. Cen. Com., 1973-75, Bexley City Coun., 1981-85. Lt. comdr. USNR, 1968-74. Mem. ABA, Ohio Bar Assn. (corp. law com.), Columbus Bar Assn., D.C. Bar Assn. Lutheran. Home: 5 Sessions Dr Bexley OH 43209-1440 Office: Vorys Sater Seymour and Pease LLP 52 E Gay St PO Box 1008 Columbus OH 43216-1008 Office Phone: 614-464-6231. Business E-Mail: jhgross@vssp.com.

GROSS, MICHAEL J., lawyer; b. Hays, Kans., 1964; BSME cum laude, Kans. State U., 1987; JD, U. Tex., 1990. Bar: Tex. 1990, DC 1992, Mo. 1994, Kans. 1995, US Patent and Trademark Office. Ptnr. Shook, Hardy & Bacon LLP, Kansas City, Mo. Mem.: DC Bar, State Bar Tex., Pi Tau Sigma, Tau Beta Pi. Office: Shook, Hardy & Bacon LLP 2555 Grand Blvd Kansas City MO 64108 Office Phone: 816-559-2224. Office Fax: 816-421-5547. E-mail: mgross@shb.com.

GROSS, MICHAEL LAWRENCE, chemistry professor; b. St. Cloud, Minn., Nov. 6, 1940; s. Ralph J. and Margaret T. (Iten) Gross; m. Kathleen M. Trammer, June 13, 1966 (div. 1981); m. Judith L. Stewart, 1994 (dec. 2003). BA, St. John's U., St. Cloud, 1962; PhD, U. Minn., 1966. Postdoctoral fellow U. Pa., Phila., 1966-67, Purdue U., Lafayette, Ind., 1967-68; asst. prof. chemistry U. Nebr., Lincoln, 1968-72, assoc. prof., 1972-78, prof., 1978-83, 3M alumni prof., 1983-88, C. Petrus Peterson prof., 1988-94; dir. Midwest Ctr. for Mass Spectrometry, Lincoln, 1978-94; prof. chemistry, immunology, and medicine Washington U., St. Louis, 1994—. Mem. metallobiochemistry study sect. NIH, Washington, 1985-88; mem. bd. on chem. scis. and tech. NRC, 1986-91; vis. prof. Internat. Grad. Sch., U. Amsterdam, The Netherlands, 1990, U. Warwick, Eng., 1988. Editor: High Performance Mass Spectrometry, 1978, Biological Mass Spectrometry: A Tutorial, 1991, Biological Mass Spectrometry: Present and Future, 1994, Practical Electrospray Ionization Mass Spectrometry, 2001, Mass Spectrometry Revs., 1982—90, Jour. Am. Soc. Mass Spectrometry, 1990—, Ency. Mass Spectrometry, 2003—; contbr. 460 chpts. to books, numerous articles to profl. jours. Mem. instnl. rev. bd. St. Elizabeth, Lincoln Gen. and Bryan Meml. hosps., 1982-90. Recipient award for disting. tchg. U. Nebr., 1978, Pioneer award Commonwealth of Mass., 1987, Outstanding Mentor award Washington U., 2001, Sommer award U. Nebr., 2004, J.J. Thomson medal, 2006; identified as one of Top 50 Cited Chemists in World, 1984-91. Mem.: Union Concerned Scientists, Am. Soc. Mass Spectrometry, Am. Chem. Soc. (Field and Franklin award 1999, Midwest award 2002, J.J. Thomson medal for disting. contbns. to internat. mass spectrometry 2006), Phi Lambda Upsilon, Sigma Xi. Democrat. Roman Catholic. Home: 6958 Waterman Ave Saint Louis MO 63130-4332 Office: Washington U Dept Chemistry Saint Louis MO 63130 Office Phone: 314-863-2221. E-mail: mgross@wustl.edu.

GROSS, RICHARD M., chemicals executive; Mem. staff hydrocarbons and energy rsch. divsn. Dow Chem. Co., Midland, Mich., 1974—79, mem. staff coal gasification rsch. La. divsn., 1979, tech. dir. consumer products rsch. applied sci. and tech. labs., dir. R&D and tech. svc. and devel. for chems. and metals, R&D dir. .Am. chems. and metals/hydrocarbons R&D, 1992—95, global v.p. core techs. R&D, 1995—98, v.p., dir. Mich. ops., 1997—98, corp. v.p. R&D, 1998—. 1st vice chmn. chem. engring. bd. Worcester Poly. Inst.; mem. adv. bd. Nat. Sci. Resources Ctr., Coll. Chemistry, U. Calif., Berkeley; mem. adv. bd. on chem. scis. and tech. NRC; bd. dirs. Mich. Molecular Inst. Mem.: AIChE, Coun. Chem. Rsch. (mem. governing bd. exec. com.), Indsl. Rsch. Inst., Am. Chem. Soc. Office: Dow Chem Co 47 Building Midland MI 48067

GROSS, THEODORE LAWRENCE, university administrator, author; b. Bklyn., Dec. 4, 1930; s. David and Anna (Weisbrod) G.; m. Selma Bell, Aug. 27, 1955 (dec. 1991); children: Donna, Jonathan; m. Joellen Gross, 2001. BA, U. Maine, 1952; MA, Columbia U., NYC, 1957, PhD, 1960. Prof. English CCNY, 1958—78, chmn. dept., 1970—72, assoc. dean and dean humanities, 1972—78, v.p. instl. advancement, 1976—77; provost Capitol Campus, Pa. State U., Middletown, 1979—83; dean Sch. Letters and Sci. SUNY Coll., Purchase, 1983—88; chmn. SUNY-Purchase Westchester Sch. Partnership, 1984—88; pres. Roosevelt U., Chgo., 1988—2002, chancellor, 2002—03. Vis. prof., Fulbright scholar, Nancy, France, 1964-65, 68-69, Dept. State lectr., Nigeria, Israel, Japan, Austria. Author: Albion W. Tourgée, 1964, Thomas Nelson Page, 1967, Hawthorne, Melville, Crane: A Critical Biography, 1971, The Heroic Ideal in American Literature, 1971, Academic Turmoil: The Reality and Promise of Open Education, 1980, Partners in Education: How Colleges Can Work with Schools to Improve Teaching and Learning, 1988, Roosevelt University: From Vision to Reality, 2002, The Rise of Roosevelt University: Presidential Reflections, 2005; editor: Fiction, 1967, Dark Symphony: Negro Literature in America, 1968, Representative Men, 1969, A Nation of Nations, 1971, The Literature of American Jews, 1973; gen. editor: Studies in Language and Literature, 1974, America in Literature, 1978; contbr. also essays, revs. With AUS, 1952-54. Grantee, Rockefeller Found., 1976-77, Am. Coun. Learned Socs. Mem. MLA, PEN, Nat. Coun. Tchrs. of English (chmn. lit. com.), Century Assn., Univ. Club, Chgo. Club. Home: 1100 N Lake Shore Dr Chicago IL 60611-1070 Office Phone: 312-341-2397. Personal E-mail: ted.gross@gmail.com. Business E-Mail: tgross@rcn.com.

GROSSBERG, GEORGE THOMAS, psychiatrist, educator; b. Hungary, Aug. 20, 1948; came to the U.S., 1957; s. Henry and Barbara (Rothman) G.; m. Darla Jean Brown, June 13, 1976; children: Jonathan, Anna-Leah, Aviva, Aliza Rebecca, Jeremy. BA, Yeshiva U., 1971; MD, St. Louis U., 1975. Diplomate Am. Bd. Psychiatry and eurology in Psychiatry and Geriatric Psychiatry. Chief resident in psychiatry St. Louis U., 1978-79, instr., 1979-81, asst. prof., 1982-86, assoc. prof., 1986-90, prof., 1990-98, Samuel W. Fordyce prof. and chmn. dept. psychiatry, 1995-98, Samuel w. Fordyce prof., dir. divsn. geriat. psychiatry, 1998—. Cons. on aging U.S. VA Hosps. Assn., Washington, 1990—. Contbr. articles to profl. jours. Adv. bd. St. Louis Alzheimers Assn., 1983-, St. Louis Sr. Olympics, 1998-; bd. dir. St. Louis Jewish Cmty. Ctr., 2000-. Recipient Pub. Svc. award, St. Louis Alzheimers Assn., 1989, Donovan-Sheer award, St. Louis Mental Health Assn., 1999, Fleischman-Hilliard award, Jewish Ctr. for Aged, 2000, Physician of Year award, Mo. Adult Daycare Assn., 2001. Mem. Am. Assn. Geriat. Psychiatry (pres. 1989-90), Am. Psychiat. Assn. (cons. on aging

1990—, Falk fellow 1977-79), Am. Geriat. Soc., Gerontol. Soc. Am., Internat. Psychogeriat. Assn. (treas. 1997—, pres. 2003-05). Avocations: antique collectibles, art, skiing. Office: Saint Louis U Sch Medicine 1438 S Grand Saint Louis MO 63104-1016 Office Phone: 314-977-4850. Business E-Mail: grossbgt@slu.edu.

GROSSBERG, MICHAEL LEE, theater critic, writer; b. Houston, Sept. 7, 1952; s. Fred Samuel and Esther R. (Rosenstein) G. BA, U. Tex., 1979, BS in Journalism, 1983. Film, theater critic, reporter Victor Valley Daily News, Victorville, Calif., 1983-85; film, theater critic Columbus (Ohio) Dispatch, 1985-87, theater critic, 1987—. Co-founder Free Press Assn., Mencken awards for outstanding journalism, dir., 1981-94. Contbr. Otis Guernsey/Burns Mantle Theater Yearbook: Best Plays, 1993-02; regional columnist Backstage, 1997—. Recipient First Place, Best Arts Reporting, Ohio SPJ Awards, 2002, 2003, Cleve. Press Club, 2003. Mem. Outer Critics Cir., Am. Theatre Critics Assn. (chmn. awards new plays com. 1993-99, exec. com. 1996-2002, vice chmn. 2001-04, chmn. conf. coms. 2007-), Libertarian Futurist Soc. (chmn. Prometheus award judges com. 1997-, pres. bd. 1999-2002, bd. sec. 2003-). Avocations: reading, travel, meditation, public speaking. Home: 3164 Plymouth Pl Columbus OH 43213-4236 Office: Columbus Dispatch 34 S 3rd St Columbus OH 43215-4241 Office Phone: 614-461-5266. Personal E-mail: mikegrossb@aol.com. Business E-Mail: mgrossberg@dispatch.com.

GROSSMAN, JEFFREY W., utilities company professional; BSBA, Drexel U. CPA. Various positions including auditor, mgr. gen. audit Columbia Gas, Svc. Corp., Columbia Gulf's Treasury Dept., Houston, Wilmington, Del., 1979-92; asst. controller Columbia Energy Group, Herndon, Va., 1992-96, v.p., controller, 1996—. Office: Columbia Energy Group 200 Civic Center Dr Columbus OH 43215-4157

GROSSMAN, JOEL B(ARRY), political science educator; b. NYC, June 19, 1936; s. Joseph and Selma G.; m. Mary Hengstenberg, Aug. 23, 1964; children: Alison, Joanna, Daniel. BA, Queens Coll., 1957; MA, U. Iowa, 1960, PhD, 1963. Faculty dept. polit. sci. U. Wis., Madison, 1963-96, prof., 1971-96, chmn. dept., 1975-78; prof. Johns Hopkins U., 1996—. Fellow in law and polit. sci. Harvard Law Sch., Cambridge, Mass., 1965-66; Fulbright lectr. U. Strathclyde, Glasgow, 1968-69; vis. prof. law U. Stockholm, 1973, John Hopkins U., 1995-96. Editor: Law and Soc. Review, 1978-82; author: Lawyers and Judges, 1965, Frontiers of Judicial Research, 1969, Law and Change in Modern America, 1971, Constitutional Law and Judicial Policy Making, 1972, 80, 88; contbr. articles to profl. jours. Chmn. Wis. Jud. Commn. 1985-87. Served with USAR, 1960-66. Mem. Wis. Civil Liberties Union (vice chmn. 1970-72), Am. Polit. Sci. Assn., Midwest Polit. Sci. Assn. (v.p. 1988-90), So. Polit. Sci. Assn., Law and Soc. Assn. Democrat. Home: 6606 Walnutwood Cir Baltimore MD 21212-1213 Office: Johns Hopkins U Rm 239 Mergenthaler Hall 3400 N Charles St Baltimore MD 21218 E-mail: jbgrossm@jhu.edu.

GROSSMAN, LISA ROBBIN, clinical psychologist, lawyer; b. Jan. 22, 1952; d. Samuel R. and Sarah (Kruger) G. BA with highest distinction & honors, Northwestern U., 1974, JD cum laude, 1979, PhD, 1982. Bar: Ill. 1981; registered psychologist, Ill. Jud. intern U.S. Supreme Ct., Washington, 1975; pre-doctoral psychology intern Michael Reese Hosp. and Med. Ctr., Chgo., 1979-80; therapist Homes for Children, Chgo., 1980-83; psychologist Psychiat. Inst. Cir. Ct. Cook County, Chgo., 1981-87; pvt. practice Chgo., 1984—. Invited participant workshop HHS, Rockville, Md., 1981. Contbr. articles to profl. jours. Mem.: APA (com. on legal issues 1992—95, state leadership organizing com. 1996—98, com. on profl. practice and stds. 1996—99, chair 1998, coun. reps. 2000—05, bd. profl. affairs 2001—03, chair exec. com. caucus of state and provincial reps. 2002, chair 2002, exec. com. women's caucus 2002—03, chmn. 2003, policy and planning bd. 2004—05, bd. dirs. 2006—08), ABA, Forensic Forum (pres. 2003), Soc. Personality Assessment, Chgo. Bar Assn., Ill. State Bar Assn., Chgo. Assn. for Psychoanalytic Psychologists (parliamentarian 1982), Ill. Psychol. Assn. (pres. 1995—96), Alpha Lambda Delta, Shi-Ai, Phi Beta Kappa, Mortar Bd. Office: 500 N Michigan Ave Ste 1520 Chicago IL 60611-3758 Office Phone: 312-245-5222. Personal E-mail: LRGrossman@aol.com.

GROSSMAN, MARY MARGARET, retired elementary school educator; b. East Cleveland, Ohio, Sept. 26, 1946; d. Frank Anthony and Margaret Mary (Buda) G. Student, Kent State U., 1965—67; BS in Elem. Edn. cum laude, Cleve. State U., 1971, postgrad., 1985, Lake Erie Coll., 1974—77, John Carroll U., 1978, postgrad., 1981—83, postgrad., 1985. Cert. elem. sch. tchr. grades 1 to 8 Ohio, cert. data processing Ohio. Tchr. Cleve. Catholic Diocese, 1971-72, Willoughby-Eastlake Sch. Dist., Ohio, 1972—2007; ret., 2007. Participant Nat. Econ. Edn. Conf., Richmond, Va., 1995. Eucharistic min. St. Christine's Ch., Euclid, 1988—, mem. parish pastoral coun., 1995—2000. Recipient Samuel H. Elliott Econ. Leadership award, 1986-87, Consumer Educator award NE Ohio Region, 1986, 1st pl. excellence in tchg. award Tchrs. in Am. Enterprise, 1984-85, 89-90; Martha Holden Jennings scholar, 1984-85. Mem. NEA, Ohio Edn. Assn. (human rels. award 1986-87, cert. merit 1987-88), NE Ohio Edn. Assn. (Positive Tchr. Image award 1988). Roman Catholic. Avocations: tai chi, softball, walking, tennis, bicycling. Home: 944 E 225th St Cleveland OH 44123-3308

GROSSMAN, REX, professional football player; b. Bloomington, Indiana, Aug. 23, 1980; s. Daniel and Maureen Grossman; m. Alison Miska, 2005. Student, U. Fla, 1999—2003. Quarterback Chgo. Bears, 2003—. Recipient Ed Block Courage award, 2006. Achievements include first freshman ever named MVP Southeast Conf. Championship Game, 2000. Office: Chicago Bears Football Club 1000 Football Dr Lake Forest IL 60045*

GROSSMAN, ROBERT D., lawyer; BA cum laude, Tulane U., 1974; JD with distinction, U. Mo., Kansas City, 1977; LLM in taxation, NYU, 1978. Bar: Mo. 1977, US Tax Ct. 1982, Kans. 1987. Mem. employee benefits group Lathrop & Gage LC, Kansas City, Mo. Mem.: ESOP Assn., Heart of Am. Tax Inst. Office: Lathrop & Gage LC 2345 Grand Blvd Ste 2800 Kansas City MO 64108 Office Phone: 816-292-2000. Business E-Mail: rgrossman@lathropgage.com.

GROSSMAN, THEODORE MARTIN, lawyer; b. NYC, Dec. 31, 1949; s. Albert and Sylvia Pia (Greenstein) G.; m. Linda Gail Steinbook, Dec. 5, 1976; children: Andrew Scott, Michael Steven. AB, Cornell U., 1971, JD, 1974. Bar: N.Y. 1975, U.S. Ct. Appeals (D.C. cir.) 1981, U.S. Ct. Appeals (2nd cir.) 1982, U.S. Ct. Appeals (5th cir.) 1984, U.S. Dist. Ct. (no. dist.) Ohio 1986, Ohio 1987, U.S. Dist. Ct. (so. dist.) N.Y. 1988, U.S. Dist. Ct. (ea. dist.) N.Y. 1988, U.S. Ct. Appeals (6th cir.) 1988, U.S. Supreme Ct., 2004. Assoc. Debevoise, Plimpton, Lyons & Gates, NYC, 1974-77, Rosenman Colin Freund Lewis & Cohen, NYC, 1977-80; trial and appellate counsel fed. programs br. of civil div. U.S. Dept. Justice, Washington, 1980-84; assoc. Jones Day, Cleve., 1984-86, ptnr., 1987—. Lectr. on cross-examination, deposition techniques, oral advocacy, trial tactics, and product liability law in ABA presentations and other seminars.; guest lectr. on internat. trade litig. Georgetown U. Law Ctr.; guest lectr. expert witnesses Case U. Law Sch.; counsel on behalf of the Lawyers' Com. for Civil Rights. Editor Cornell U. Law Rev., 1974. Trustee Cleve. Ctr. for Contemporary Art, 1992-96, treas., 1992-94. Named one of Top 10 Litigators, Nat. Law Jour., 2003. Fellow: Am. Coll. Trial Lawyers; mem.: ABA, Am. Law Inst. Home: 2979 Broxton Rd Shaker Heights OH 44120 Office: Jones Day 901 Lakeside Ave E Cleveland OH 44114-1190 Home Phone: 216-751-6486; Office Phone: 216-586-3939, 216-586-7268. E-mail: tgrossman@jonesday.com.

GROTHMAN, GLENN, state legislator; b. July 3, 1955; BA, U. Wis. Tax & estate planning atty.; assemblyman Wis. State Dist. 59, 1993—. Active Washington County Vol. Ctr. Mem. Washington County Bar Assn., Kiwanis, Moose. Address: 111 S 6th Ave West Bend WI 53095-3308

GROTZINGER, LAUREL ANN, librarian, educator; b. Truman, Minn., Apr. 15, 1935; d. Edward F. and Marian Gertrude (Greeley) G. BA cum laude, Carleton Coll., 1957; MS, U. Ill., 1958, PhD, 1964. Instr., asst. libr. Ill. State U., 1958-62; asst. prof. Western Mich. U., Kalamazoo, 1964-66, assoc. prof., 1966-68, prof., 1968—, asst. dir. Sch. Librarianship, 1965-72, chief rsch. officer, 1979-86, interim dir. Sch. Libr. and Info. Sci., 1982-86, dean grad. coll., 1979-92, prof. univ. libr., 1993—. Author: The Power and the Dignity, 1966, Perspectives: A Library School's First Quarter Century, 1970, Women's Work: Vision and Changes in Librarianship, 1994; mem. editl. bd. Jour. Edn. for Librarianship, 1973-77, Dictionary Am. Libr. Biography, 1975-77, Mich. Academician, 1990—; contbr. chpts. to books; contbr. articles to profl. jours., books; contbr. book revs. Trustee Kalamazoo Pub. Libr., 1991-93, v.p., 1991-92, pres., 1992-93; pres. Kalamazoo Bach Festival, 1996-97, bd. dirs. 1992-98, exec. com. 1996-98. Recipient Alumna award, U. Ill., Tchg. citation, We. Mich. U. Mem. ALA (sec.-treas. Libr. History Round Table 1973-74, vice chmn., chmn-elect 1983-84, chmn. 1984-85, mem.-at-large 1991-93), Spl. Librs. Assn., Assn. Libr. Info. Sci. Edn., Mich. acad. Sci., Arts and Letters (mem.-at-large, exec. com. 1980-86, pres. 1983-85, exec. com. 1990-94, pres. 1991-93, vice chmn. libr./info. scis. 1996-97, chair 1997-98), Internat. Assn. Torch Clubs (v.p. Kalamazoo chpt. 1992-93, pres. 1993-94, exec. com. 1989-95), Soc. Collegiate Journalists, Goldne Key, Phi Beta Kappa (pres. S.W. Mich. chpt. 1977-78, sec. 1994-97, pres. 1997-99), Beta Phi Mu, Alpha Beta Alpha, Delta Kappa Gamma (pres. Alpha Psi chpt. 1988-92), Phi Kappa Phi. Home: 2729 Mockingbird Dr Kalamazoo MI 49008-1626 Home Phone: 269-381-1865; Office Phone: 269-387-5418. Business E-Mail: laurel.grotzinger@wmich.edu.

GROVE, JANET E., retail executive; BS in Mktg., Calif. State U., Hayward, 1973. Exec. trainee Macy's West, San Francisco, 1973—74, from asst. buyer to gen. merchandise mgr., 1974—92; from sr. v.p. to exec. v.p. Broadway, Inc., 1992—96; sr. v.p. center core merchandising Federated Merchandising Group, Cin., 1996—97, exec. v.p. ready-to-wear and center core, 1997—98, exec. v.p. center core, cosmetics and home merchandising, 1998, CEO, exec. v.p. center core, cosmetics and home merchandising, 1999—; vice chair Macy's Inc. (formerly Federated Dept. Stores Inc.), Cin., 2003—. Recipient Humanitarian award, Nat. Jewish Med. and Rsch. Ctr., Denver, 2000, HUG award, Intimate Apparel Square Club, 2002. Office: Macy's Inc 7 W Seventh St Cincinnati OH 45202

GROVER, CHARLES W., insurance company executive; BS, Thomas Coll.; A in Bus. and Fin., U. Maine. With Union Central Life Ins., Cin., Manulife Fin. Toronto, Ontario, Canada, State Mutual Life Ins. Co.; exec. v.p. ePlanning, Inc., San Francisco; pres., CEO Clarica U.S., Inc., Fargo, ND, 2001—02.

GROWCOCK, TERRY D., manufacturing executive; b. 1945; BS Business Management, U. of St. Francis. Exec. King-Seeley Corp., United Technologies, Universal Nolin, Paragon Electric; v.p., gen. mgr Robertshaw Automotive; exec. v.p., gen. mgr. Manitowoc Ice, 1994—95; pres. Manitowoc Foodservice Group, 1995—98, The Manitowoc Co., Inc., 1998—2002, CEO, 1998—2007, chmn., 2002—. Bd. dir. Harris Corp., 2005—. Office: The Manitowoc Co Inc 2400 S 44th St Manitowoc WI 54221

GROWE, JOAN ANDERSON, former state official; b. Mpls., Sept. 28, 1935; d. Lucille M. (Brown) Johnson; children: Michael, Colleen, David, Patrick. BS, St. Cloud State U., 1956; cert. in spl. edn., U. Minn., 1964; exec. mgmt. program State and local govt., Harvard U., 1979. Tchr. elem. pub. schs., Bloomington, Minn., 1956-58; tchr. for exceptional children elem. pub. schs. St. Paul, 1964-65; spl. edn. tchr. St. Anthony Pub. Schs., Minn., 1965-66; mem. Minn. Ho. of Reps., 1973-74; sec. of state State of Minn., St. Paul, 1975-98. Mem. exec. coun. Minn. State Bd. Investment. Mem. Women Execs. in State Govt., Women's Polit. Caucus, Minn. Women's Econ. Roundtable; candidate U.S. Senate, 1984; bd. dirs. Minn. Internat. Ctr.; mem. Nat. Commn. for the Renewal of Am. Democracy (Project Democracy); bd. dirs. Nat. Dem. Inst. for Internat. Affairs; mem. adv. bd. Hubert H. Humphrey Inst. for Pub. Affairs; bd. dirs. Mpls. Found. Recipient Minn. Sch. Bell award, 1977, YMCA Outstanding Achievement award, 1978, Disting. Alumni award St. Cloud State U., 1979, Charlotte Striebel Long Distance Runner award Minn. NOW, 1985, The Woman Who Makes a Difference award Internat. Women's Forum, 1991, Esther V. Crosby Leadership award Greater Mpls. Girl Scout Coun., 1992, Pathfinder award for Innovative Solutions, Ctr. for Policy Alternatives, 1996, Breaking the Glass Ceiling award Women Execs. in State Govt., 1998. Mem. Nat. Assn. Secs. of State (pres. 1979-80), Internat. Womens Forum. Roman Catholic.

GROWNEY, ROBERT L., former communications company professional, venture capitalist; BSME, Ill. Inst. Tech., Chgo., 1974, MBA, 1982. Various mgr. positions to gen. mgr. Fixed Products Divsn. Motorola, Inc., Schaumburg, Ill., 1966-89, sr. v.p., gen. mgr. Radio Technologies Group, 1989-91, sr. v.p., gen. mgr. Paging and Telepoint Systems Group, 1991-92, exec. v.p., gen. mgr. Paging and Wireless Data Group, 1992-94, pres., gen. mgr. Messaging, Info. and Media Sector, 1994-97, pres., COO, 1997—2001, bd. dirs., 1997—2002, vice chmn., 2001—02; ptnr. Edgewater Funds, Chgo., 2002—. Exec. com. mem. bd. trustees Ill. Inst. Tech., chmn. oversight bd. Stuart Grad. Sch. Bus. Office: Edgewater Funds 900 N Mich Ave Ste 1800 Chicago IL 60611

GRUBB, FLOYD DALE, state legislator; b. June 26, 1949; BS, Purdue U., 1985. Agrl. economist; cash grain commodity broker; rep. Dist. 42 Ind. Ho. of Reps., mem. agr. com., chmn. Fin. Inst.; vice chmn. pub. health com. Farmer. Precinct committeeman, 1968—; chmn. Dem. Caucus, Ind. Named Outstanding Freshman House Dem., 1988. Mem. Am. Legion (adj. and comdr.), Nat. Fedn. Ind. Bus., Purdue U. Alumni Assn., Harry Truman Club, Ferguson Club. Home: PO Box 9 Covington IN 47932-0009

GRUBB, ROBERT L., JR., neurosurgeon; b. Charlotte, NC, May 9, 1940; MD, U. N.C., 1965. Intern Barnes Hosp., St. Louis, 1965-66, resident in gen. surgery, 1966-67, resident in neurosurgery, 1969-73; fellow NIH, Bethesda, Md., 1968-69; mem. staff Barnes-Jewish Hosp., St. Louis, St. Louis Children's Hosp.; prof. neurosurgery Washington U., St. Louis. Fellow ACS; mem. Am. Acad. Neurol. Surgery, AANS, CNS, SNS. Office: Washington U Sch Medicine 660 S Euclid Ave Box 8057 Saint Louis MO 63110-1093 Home Phone: 314-965-1330; Office Phone: 314-362-3567. Business E-Mail: grubbr@nsurg.wustl.edu.

GRUBBS, J. PERRY, church administrator; Pres. Ch. Extension of the Ch. of God, Anderson, Ind., 1987—. Office: Church of God PO Box 2069 Anderson IN 46018-2069

GRUBBS, ROBERT W., computer services company executive; Grad., U. Mo. Joined Anixter Internat. Inc., 1978; pres. Anixter U.S.A.; pres., CEO, Anixter Inc. subs. Anixter Internat. Inc., 1994—98; pres., CEO Anixter Internat. Inc., 1998—, bd. dirs., 1997—. Former dir. A. M. Castle & Co., 2000. Office: Anixter Internat Inc 2301 Patriot Blvd Glenview IL 60025-8020

GRUBER, JOHN EDWARD, editor, historian, photographer; b. Chgo., May 18, 1936; s. Edward David and Leah Elizabeth (Diehl) G.; m. Bonnie Jean Barstow, May 12, 1962; children: Richard J., Timothy J. BA in Journalism, U. Wis., 1959, postgrad., 1981-84. Editor, writer U. Wis., Madison, 1960-95; editor Vintage Rails, Waukesha, Wis., 1995-99. Author: Focus on Rails, 1989, (pamphlet) Madison's Pioneer Buildings, 1987; co-author: Caboose, 2001, (posters) Travel by Train, 2002, Railway Photography, 2003, Milwaukee Road's Hiawathas, 2006; acting editor Rail News, 1999; also articles; contbr. photographs to Trains mag., 1960—; contbg. editor: Classic Trains, 2000—; coord. Representatives of Railroad Work 2003-06. Dir. Historic Madison, Inc., 1981-89. Recipient Nat. Award in R.R. History for photography Rwy. and Locomotive Hist. Soc., 1994; James J. Hill Rsch. grant Hill Reference Libr., 1986. Mem. Mid-Continent Railway Hist. Soc. (bd. dirs. 1984-97, pres. 1988-89, sec. 1990-95, v.p. 1995-97, editor Mid-Continent Railway Gazette 1982-99), Ctr. for R.R. Photography and Art (pres. 1997—). Home: 1430 Drake St Madison WI 53711-2211 Office Phone: 608-251-5785. E-mail: jgruber@execpc.com.

GRUBERG, MARTIN, political science professor; b. NYC, Jan. 28, 1935; s. Benjamin and Mollie (Stolnitz) G.; m. Rosaline Kurfirst, Mar. 25, 1967 (dec. 1980); m. Humaira Sayeed, Aug. 15, 1983 (div. 1996); m. Vivian Foss, Feb. 14, 2007. BA, CCNY, 1955; PhD, Columbia U., NYC, 1963. Agt.-adjudicator Passport Agy., Dept. State, NYC, 1960-61; tchr. social studies Pelham (N.Y.) High Sch., 1961-62; instr. polit. sci. CUNY-Hunter Coll., 1961-62; tchr. social studies James Monroe and Seward Park High Schs., NYC, 1962-63; asst. prof. polit. sci. U. Wis., Oshkosh, 1963-66, assoc. prof., 1966-69, prof., chmn. dept., 1969-72, dir. pre-law program, 1966-69, 83—, coord. criminal justice program, 1983-87. Author: Women in American Politics, 1968, A Case Study in U.S. Urban Leadership: The Incumbency of Milwaukee Mayor Henry Maier, 1996, A History of Winnebago County Government, 1998, Introduction to Law, 2003; newspaper column: Women: Our Largest Minority, The Paper for Ctrl. Wiso., 1970-71, Spotlight on Women for Oshkosh Northwestern, 1971-73; Broadcast 16 weeks Civil Rights Revolution, Wis. State FM Network, 1974; editor: Wis. Polit. Scientist, 1986-91; contbr. articles to encys., profl. jours. Pres. Oshkosh Human Rights Coun., 1966-68; v.p. Winnebago chpt. NOW, 1970-71, sec. Oshkosh chpt., 1980-81, pres., 1981-83; pres. Women's Caucus of Midwest Polit. Scientists, 1980-81; pres. Fox Valley ACLU, 1985—. Recipient Am. Legion Aux. Americanism award, 1949, Buckvar award, 1955, Steigman award, 1955; .Y. State scholar, 1952; Columbia grantee, 1961, 62, Wis. Regents' rsch. grantee, 1964-70, 73-75. Mem. AAUP (state sec. 1975-81, pres.-elect 1981-82, 91-92, pres. 1982-83, 92-93), Am. Polit. Sci. Assn., Midwest Polit. Sci. Assn., Wis. Polit. Sci. Assn. (pres. 1974-75), Law and Soc. Assn., Acad. Criminal Justice Scis., Candlelight Club, Optimists. Home: 2121 Oregon St Oshkosh WI 54902-7058 Office: U Wis Clow Hall Oshkosh WI 54901 Office Phone: 920-424-0146. Business E-Mail: gruberg@uwosh.edu.

GRUEBELE, MARTIN, chemistry and biophysicist professor; b. Stuttgart, Germany, Jan. 10, 1964; arrived in US, 1980, naturalized, 2004; s. Helmut and Edith Victoria (Berner) Gruebele; m. Nancy Makri, July 10, 1992; 2 children. BS in Chemistry, U. Calif., Berkeley, 1984, PhD in Chemistry, 1988. Rsch. fellow Calif. Inst. Tech., Pasadena, 1989-92; from asst. prof. to assoc. prof. dept. chemistry U. Ill., Urbana, 1992—99, prof. chemistry and biophysics, 1999—2000, prof. chemistry, physics, and biophysics, 2000—01, Alumni Scholar prof. chemistry, prof. physics, biophysics and computational biology, 2002—05, Lycan prof. chemistry, physics, biophysics and computational biology, 2006—. Baker symposium lectr. Cornell U., 2004. Sr. editor: Jour. Phys. Chemistry, 1998—2005; mem. editl. bd. Jour. Chem. Physics, Chem. Phys. Lett., Ann. Rev. Phys. Chem., Chem. Physics. Recipient New Faculty award, Dreyfus Found., 1992, Nat. Young Investigator award, NSF, 1994, Coblentz award, 2000, Wilhelm Friedrich Bessel prize, Von Humboldt Soc., 2005; fellow, IBM, 1986—87, Dow Chem. Co., 1987—88, David and Lucile Packard Found., 1994; Sloan fellow, 1997, Alfred P. Sloan fellow, 1998, Cottrell scholar, 1995, Camille and Henry Dreyfus scholar, 1998, Univ. scholar, U. Ill., 1998. Fellow: Biophys. Soc., Am. Phys. Soc.; mem.: Am. Chem. Soc., Sigma Xi. Achievements include research in theoretical and experimental studies of novel transiet molecular species; studies in laser-control of chemical reactions and molecular vibrational relaxation; fast time-rsolved protein folding dynamics; laser-assisted scanning tunneling microscopy. Office: U Ill Dept Chemistry Box 5-6 600 S Mathews Ave Urbana IL 61801-3602

GRUEN, GERALD ELMER, psychologist, educator; b. Granite City, Ill., July 19, 1937; s. Elmer George and Velma Pearl G.; m. Karol Jane Selvidge, Mar. 20, 1960; children— Tami Jane, Christy Lynn. BA, So. Ill. U., 1959; MA, U. Ill., 1963, PhD, 1964. Postdoctoral fellow Heinz Werner Inst. Devel. Psychology, Clark U. and Worcester (Mass.) State Hosp., 1964-66; asst. prof. dept. psychol. scis. Purdue U., West Lafayette, Ind., 1966-69, assoc. prof., 1969-74, prof., 1974—2005, head dept. psychol. scis., 1987-97, prof. emeritus, 2005—. Author: (with T. Wachs) Early Experience and Human Development; contbr. chpt. to The Structuring of Experience, 1977; contbr. articles to profl. jours. Deacon Calvary Baptist Ch., West Lafayette. Recipient USPHS rsch. awards, 1968-71, Nat. Rsch. Svc. award NIMH, 1976-80, Research award Nat. Insts. Child Health and Human Devel., 1981—; recipient Ind. Psychol. Assn. Gordon Barrows award for disting. career contbns., 2000. Fellow APA, Am. Psychol. Soc. (charter mem.); mem. Midwestern Psychol. Assn., Soc. for Rsch. in Child Devel., Sigma Xi. Home: 3738 Westlake Ct West Lafayette IN 47906 Office: Purdue U Psychology Dept West Lafayette IN 47907 Personal E-mail: jjgruen@insightbb.com. Business E-Mail: gruen@psych.purdue.edu.

GRUENDER, RAYMOND W., federal judge, former prosecutor; b. St. Louis, July 5, 1963; BA, Washington U., 1984, MBA, JD, Washington U., 1987. Assoc. Lewis, Rice and Fingersh, 1987—90; ptnr. Thompson Coburn LLP, 1994—2000; asst. US atty., (ea. dist.) Mo. US Dept. State, St. Louis, 1990—94, 2000—01, US atty. (ea. dist) Mo, 2001—04; judge US Ct. Appeals, (8th cir.), 2004—. Office: US Courthouse 111 S Tenth St Saint Louis MO 63102

GRUMBO, HOWARD, state legislator; m. Joyce Helgeson; 3 children. BS, U. N.D., 1958; MA, Long Beach State U., 1972. Tchr. Lidgerwood (N.D.) Pub. Sch., 1958-90; ret., 1990; state rep. dist. 27, 1991—. Mem. industry, bus. and labor com., transp. com. N.D. Ho. Reps., 1993-95, polit. subcom. and judiciary, 1991, edn. com. and transp. com., 1995-97, 99-2001. Mem. Pk. Bd. Commn.; chmn. Cmty. Devel. Corp. Mem. Lions (pres.). Democrat. Home: PO Box 435 Lidgerwood ND 58053-0435

GRUNDBERG, BETTY, state legislator, property manager; b. Woden, Iowa, Feb. 16, 1938; d. Edwin and Eva Ruth Meyer; m. Arnie Grundberg, Dec. 31, 1960; children: Christine, Julie, Michael, Susan. BA, Wartburg Coll., 1959; MA, U. Iowa, 1969; postgrad., Drake U. Cert. tchr. Property mgr. and renovator, Des Moines, 1973—; with Des Moines Sch. Bd., 1975-90; legis. State of Iowa, Des Moines, 1993—. Chmn. edn. com.; mem. human resources com., labor com. Active LWV, Des Moines, 1972—. Republican. Home and Office: 224 Foster Dr Des Moines IA 50312-2540

GRUNDER, HERMANN A., science administrator, director, research scientist; b. Basel, Switzerland; MS in Mech. Engring., KarlsruheU.; PhD in Exptl. Nuc. Physics, U. Basel; doctorate (hon.), U. Frankfurt, 2000. Dep. dir. gen. sci. Lawrence Berkeley Nat. Lab., Calif.; dir. Thomas Jefferson Nat. Accelerator Facility, 1985—2000, Argonne Nat. Lab., 2000—05; ret., 2005. Lab. rep. to lab. ops. bd. Sec. Engery Adv. Bd. (SEAB); chair Nat. Ignition Facility Program Rev.; bd. dirs. vis. com. U. Chgo. Divsn. Physical Scis.; bd. dirs. Ill. Coalition; mem. steering com. U.S. Particle Accelerator Sch.; mem. adv. com. physics Los Alamos AOT Divsn. Named Scientist of Yr., Commonwealth Va., 1998; recipient U.S. Sr. Scientist award, Alexander von Humboldt Found., Germany, 1979, Disting. Assoc. award, U.S. Dept. Energy, 1996, Sec. of Energy Gold award, 2004. Fellow: AAAS, Am. Physical Soc.; mem.: Swiss Physical Soc., European Physical Soc. Business E-Mail: tmo@blackberry.net.

GRUNDHOFER, JOHN F., bank executive; b. LA, 1939; Student, Loyola U., 1960, U. So. Calif., 1964. Formerly with Wells Fargo & Co., San Francisco, also vice chmn.; now chmn., pres., CEO U.S. Bancorp (formerly First Bank System, Inc.), Mpls., 1990—2001, chmn., 2001—, also dir. Office: Us Bank 800 Nicollet Mall Ste 1500 Minneapolis MN 55402-7014

GRUNDY, KENNETH WILLIAM, political science professor; b. Phila., Aug. 6, 1936; s. William and Alma (Hahn) G.; m. Martha Jonet Paxson, June 25, 1960; children: William MacIntyre, Thomas Paxson, Anne Edmunds. BA with honors, Ursinus Coll., 1958; MA, Pa. State U., 1961, PhD, 1963. Asst. prof. polit. sci. San Fernando Valley State Coll., Northridge, Calif., 1963-66; assoc. prof. Case Western Res. U., Cleve., 1966-74, prof., 1974-88, Marcus A. Hanna prof., 1988—2005, prof. emeritus, 2005—, chmn. dept. polit. sci., 1974-76, dir. Ctr. for Policy Studies, 1998-2000. Vis. sr. lectr. Makerere U. Coll., Kampala, Uganda, 1967-68; vis. scholar Inst. Social Studies, The Hague, The Netherlands, 1972-73, U. Pretoria, 1998; vis. Fulbright prof. U. Zambia, Lusaka, 1977, Nat. U. Ireland, Galway, 1979-80; vis. adj. prof. Cleve. State U., 1992—; editl. adv. bd. Ctr. Internat. Race Rels., 1968—. Author: Conflicting Images of the Military in Africa, 1968, Guerrilla Struggle in Africa, 1971, Confrontation and Accommodation in Southern Africa, 1973, (with Weinstein) The Ideologies of Violence, 1974, We're Against Apartheid, But, 1974, Defense Legislation and Communal Politics, 1978, (with V. McHale and B. Hughes) Evaluating Transnational Programs in Government and Business, 1980, Soldiers Without Politics, 1983, The Militarization of South African Politics, 1986, rev. edit., 1988, South Africa: Domestic Crisis and Global Challenge, 1991, The Politics of the National Arts Festival, 1993; also articles; book rev. editor Internat. Jour. Comparative Sociology, 1973-83; assoc. editor Jour. African Policy Studies, 1991—; contbg. editor Current History, 1982-2003; mem. editl. adv. bd. African Affairs, 1983-93; mem. editl. bd. Jour. Third World Studies, 1988—, South African Jour. Internat. Affairs, 1993-98. Fellow NDEA, 1959-62, Rhodes U., Grahamstown, South Africa, 1989-90, Ctr. Internat. Race Rels., 1969-70; 1st Bradlow fellow South African Inst. Internat. Rels., 1982; grantee Rockefeller Found., 1967-68, Social Sci. Rsch. Coun., 1972, 79-80, Earhart Found, 1979. Mem. African Studies Assn. (mem. exec. coun.), Inter-Univ. Seminar on Armed Forces and Soc., Internat. Studies Assn. Home: 2602 Exeter Rd Cleveland OH 44118-4246 Office: Case Western Res U Dept Polit Sci Cleveland OH 44106 Business E-Mail: kwg@case.edu.

GRUNSFELD, ERNEST ALTON, III, architect; b. Chgo., June 5, 1929; s. Ernest Alton Jr. and Mary Jane (Loeb) G.; m. Sally Riblett, July 10, 1954 (dec. 1999); children: Marcia Grunsfeld, John Mace; m. Alice B. Kurland, Mar. 4 2006. Student, Inst. Design, Chgo., 1945, Art Inst. Chgo., 1946; BArch, MIT,

1952. Registered architect, Ill., Conn., Ind., Mich., N.C., Ohio, Mo., Wis. Ptnr. Yerkes & Grunsfeld, Chgo., 1956-65; owner Grunsfeld & Assocs., Architects, Chgo., 1965-75, sr. ptnr., 1975-84, owner, 1984—2001; prin. Grunsfeld Shafer Architects, LLC, 2001—. Corp. mem. Woodlawn Hosp., Chgo., 1968-70; mem. Highland Park (Ill.) Planning Commn., 1969-75; pres. Grunsfeld Meml. Fund, Chgo., 1970—. Contbr. articles to profl. jours. Bd. dirs. Urban Gateways, Chgo., 1968-89, mem. adv. bd., 1989—; life mem. Field Mus. Natural History, Chgo., 1970—, Chgo. Symphony Orch. Assn., 1975—, governing mem., 1995—; mem. exec. com. Coun. for Arts MIT, Cambridge, 1977-89, bd. dirs., 1977—; hon. life mem. Chgo. Hort. Soc., 1995—, governing mem., 2001—; benefactor, hon. governing mem. Art Inst. Chgo., 1980—. Recipient 1st Honor award Burlington Mills, 1968. Fellow AIA (corp. mem. Chgo. chpt., Honor award 1962, citation of merit 1969); mem. Lake Shore Country Club, Arts Club of Chgo. Office: Grunsfeld Schafer Architects LLC 939 Chicago Ave Evanston IL 60202 Office Phone: 847-424-1800 ext. 1.

GRUPPEN, LARRY DALE, psychologist, educational researcher; b. Zeeland, Mich., Jan. 27, 1955; s. Howard Melvin and Gertrude Jean (Huizenga) G.; m. Mary Louise Shell, May 27, 1978; children: Timothy Andrew, Matthew Scott. MA, U. Mich., 1984, PhD, 1987. Rsch. investigator U. Mich. Med. Sch., Ann Arbor, 1987-88, asst. rsch. scientist, 1988—. Contbr. articles to Jour. AMA, Acad. Medicine, other profl. publs. Grantee Agy. Health Care Policy and Rsch., 1991—, Mich. Alzheimer's Disease Rsch. Ctr., 1992—, NIH, 1993—. Mem. APA, Am. Ednl. Rsch. Assn., Soc. Med. Decision Making, Soc. Judgement and Decision Making. Achievements include investigation of foundation and development of medical expertise, clinical reasoning and expert judgment, development of computer-based educational methods in medical education, exploration of process of innovation dissemination. Office: U Mich Med Sch G1211 Towsley Ln Ann Arbor MI 48105-9573

GRUVER, NANCY, publishing executive; Founder, pub. New Moon Pub., Duluth, Minn., 1992—. Author: How To Say It To Girls, 2004; prodr. (mag.) New Moon: The Magazine for Girls and Their Dreams, 1992—. Office: New Moon Publishing 2 W 1st St Ste 101 Duluth MN 55802-2062 Home Phone: 218-728-4814; Office Phone: 218-728-5507. Business E-Mail: nancyg@newmom.org.

GRZESIAK, KATHERINE ANN, primary school educator; BS, Ctrl. Mich. U., 1968; MA in Tchg., Saginaw Valley State U., 1975; postgrad., various univs., 1975—. 6th grade tchr. Buena Vista Sch. Dist., Saginaw, Mich., 1968-69, 70-71; tchr. Carrollton Pub. Schs., Saginaw, 1972-80, St. Peter and Paul Elem. Sch., Saginaw, 1981-84, Sch. Dist. of City of Saginaw, 1984-90; instr. Ctr. for Innovation in Edn., Saratoga, Calif., 1989—; tchr. Midland (Mich.) Pub. Schs., 1991—; 5th grade tchr. Eastlawn Elem., Midland. Adj. faculty Saginaw Valley State U., University Center, Mich., 1976-80, 88-90; presenter in field. Contbr. articles to profl. jours. Recipient Presdl. award for Excellence in Sci. and Math. Tchg., 1994, Top Tchr. in Mich. Met. Woman mag., 1997, Nat. Educator award Milken Family Found., 1998; named Mich. Tchr. of Yr., 1998. Home: 3115 McGill St Midland MI 48642-3928 Office: Eastlawn Elem Sch 115 Eastlawn Dr Midland MI 48640-5561 Office Phone: 989-923-7112. E-mail: grzesiakka@mps.k12.mi.us.

GRZYWINSKI, RON, bank executive; b. Chgo., 1936; m. Audrey Grzywinski; 3 children. D (hon.), Northern Mich. U., 2001. Pres. First Nat. Bank, Lockport, Ill., Hyde Park Bank and Trust Co., Chgo.; co-founder, chmn., CEO ShoreBank Corp., Chgo.; chmn. bd. South Shore Bank, Chgo., 1973—. Mgmt. com. ShoreBank Corp.; charter mem. adv. com. econ. inclusion FDIC; bd. mem. Southern Devel. Bancorp., Ark., Grameen Bank, Bangladesh, Bangladesh Rural Advancement Com., XacBank, Mongolia, Aga Khan Found., Pakistan. Mem. Hyde Park-Kenwood Cmty. Ctr. Co-recipient Citizen Activist award, Gleitsman Found., 2006; named one of America's Best Leaders, US News & World Report, 2007; recipient Medal Entrepreneurial Excellence, Yale Sch. Mgmt., 1988, John W. Gardner award, Ind. Sector, 2005, Ethics award, Western Ill. U., 2006. Achievements include co-founder of the first and largest community development bank in the US. Avocation: gardening. Office: South Shore Banking Ctr 7054 S Jeffery Blvd Chicago IL 60649*

GSCHNEIDNER, KARL ALBERT, JR., metallurgist, educator, editor, consultant; b. Detroit, Nov. 16, 1930; s. Karl and Eugenie (Zehetmair) Gschneidner; m. Melba E. Pickenpaugh, ov. 4, 1957; children: Thomas, David, Edward, Kathryn. BS, U. Detroit, 1952; PhD, Iowa State U., 1957. Mem. staff Los Alamos Sci. Lab., 1957-62, sect. chief, 1961-62; vis. asst. prof. U. Ill., Urbana, 1962-63; assoc. prof. materials sci. and engring. Iowa State U., Ames, 1963-67, dir. Rare-earth Info. Ctr., 1966-96, prof., 1967-79, disting. prof., 1979—85, Anson Marston disting. prof., 1986—; vis. prof. U. Calif.-San Diego, La Jolla, 1979-80; cons. Los Alamos Nat. Lab., 1981-86, Teltech, 1987-2000. Author: Rare Earth Alloys, 1961, Scandium, 1975, others; editor: (38 vol. book) Handbook on the Physics and Chemistry of Rare Earths, 1978—, Industrial Applications of Rare Earth Elements, 1981; contbr. numerous chpts. in books and articles to profl. publs. Recipient William Hume-Rothery award AIME, Warrendale, Pa., 1978, Burlington No. award for Excellence in Rsch., Iowa State U., 1989, Significant Implication for Energy Related Techs. in Metallurgy and Ceramics award Dept. Energy, 1997; co-recipient Outstanding Sci. Accomplishment in Metallurgy and Ceramics award Dept. Energy, Washington, 1982, Frank H. Spedding award Rare Earth Rsch. Confs., 1991, Russell B. Scott Meml. award Cryogenic Engr. Conf., 1995, David R. Boyland Eminent Faculty award in Rsch. Coll. Engring., Iowa State U., 1997, Acta Materials Gold medal, 2008; named Sci. Alumnus of 2000, U. Detroit-Mercy. Fellow Minerals, Metals and Materials Soc., Am. Soc. Materials Internat., Am. Phys. Soc.; mem. AAAS, NAE, Am. Chem. Soc., Am. Crystallographic Assn., Materials Rsch. Soc., Iowa Acad. Sci., Materials Rsch. Soc. India (hon.), Cryogenic Soc. Am., Japan Inst. Metals (hon.). Roman Catholic. Achievements include patents in field. Office: Materials Sci and Engring Iowa State Univ 255 Spedding Hall Ames IA 50011-3020 Office Phone: 515-294-7931. Office Fax: 515-294-9579. E-mail: cagey@ameslab.gov.

GUAN, KUN-LIANG, biochemist, educator; b. Tongxian, China, Apr. 28, 1963; s. Xian Xiu and Mei Wen (Zhang) G.; m. Yuli Wang, Apr. 25, 1986; children: Jean, Eric. BS, Hangzheu U., 1982; PhD, Purdue U., 1989. Rsch. asst., postdoctoral fellow Purdue U., West Lafayette, Ind., 1983-91; lectr., asst. prof. U. Mich., Ann Arbor, 1991—, asst. rsch. scientist, 1992—, assoc. prof., 1996—. Patentee in field; contbr. articles to profl. jours. Grantee Am. Cancer Soc., 1993, NIH, 1994; McArthur fellow, 1998. Achievements include DNA encoding in 18 kd CDK6 inhibiting protein, discovering the essential disease gene in bulbonic plague is an tyrosine phosphatase, discovering the dual specific phosphatase class, determining the mechanism of MAP Kinase kinase activation. Office: Dept Biol Chemistry Univ Mich Ann Arbor MI 48109

GUARASCIO, PHILIP, advertising executive; b. NYC, June 28, 1941; s. Frank and Charlotte (Cohen) G.; m. Ruth Agness Hornick, Sept. 7, 1963, children: Lisa Marie, David Evan BA, Marietta Coll. Sr. v.p., dir. media mgmt. Benton & Bowles, Inc., NYC, bd. dirs.; exec. dir. advt. svcs. Gen. Motors, Detroit, 1985—90, exec. dir. mktg. programs and advt., 1990—91, exec.-in-charge corp. mktg. and advt., 1991—92, gen. mgr. mktg. and advt. N. Am. Ops., 1992—94, v.p./gen. mgr. mktg. and advt. No. Am. Ops., 1994—2000; ind. advisor NFL, 2000—04, lead exec. mktg. and sales, 2004—. Trustee Marietta Coll., Ohio, 1981-83. Served USAR, 1963—70. Mem. Nat. Cable TV Assn., Internat. Radio & TV Found., Am. Assn. Advt. Agys., Radio Advt. Bur., Nissequogue Country Club, St. James, N.Y. Avocations: golfing, tennis.

GUARIGILA, DALE A., lawyer; B, U. Kan., 1985; JD, U. Mo., Kansas City, 1985. Bar: Mo. 1985, US Dist. Ct. (ea. and we. dists.) Mo. Ptnr., group dep. Environ. Bryan Cave LLP, St. Louis. Office: Bryan Cave LLP One Metropolitan Sq 211 N Broadway, Ste 3600 Saint Louis MO 63102 Office Phone: 314-259-2606. E-mail: daguarigila@bryancave.com.

GUBOW, DAVID M., state legislator; AB in Urban Studies, U. Mich., 1971; JD, U. Detroit, 1974. Assoc. Zeff & Zeff, Detroit, 1975-76; ptnr. Gubow & Sirlin, Southfield, Mich., 1977-80, May, Gowing & Simpson, P.C., Bloomfield Hills, Mich., 1980-89; of counsel May, Simpson & Strote, P.C., Bloomfield Hills, 1989-91, Reosti, James & Sirlin, P.C., Detroit, 1991—; mem. dist. 35 Mich. Ho. of Reps., Lansing, 1985-98, asst. clerk, 1999—. Majority whip Mich. Ho. of Reps., 1985-94, former chmn. ins. and mental health com., vice chair judiciary com., mem. health policy, pub. utilities, tax policy, corrections and sr. citizens and retirement coms., chair spl. ad-hoc physician licensure com., adoption sub-com.; lectr. Inst. Continuing Legal Edn., Mich., Mich. Orgn. Diabetes Educators, Am. Soc. Indsl. Security, Mich. Pub. adminstr. Oakland County Mich., 1977-81; vice-chair, sec.-treas. Oakland County Bldg. Authority, Pontiac, Mich., 1976-80. Mem. State Bar Mich., Oakland County Bar Assn. (past chmn.), Judicial Conf. of 6th Cir. (life), Jewish Cmty. Coun., Jewish Welfare Fedn. Home: 26728 York Rd Huntington Woods MI 48070-1358 Address: Capitol Bldg Lansing MI 48909

GUDEMAN, STEPHEN FREDERICK, anthropology educator; b. Chgo, Ill, June 29, 1939; s. Edward and Frances (Alschuler) G.; m. Roxane Harvey, Sept. 20, 1965; children: Rebecca, Elise, Keren AB, Harvard U., 1961, MBA, 1965; MA, Cambridge U., Eng., 1963, PhD, 1970. Asst. prof. anthropology U. Minn.-Mpls., Minn., 1969-74, assoc. prof. anthropology Minn., 1974-78, prof. anthropology Minn., 1978—, chmn. dept. Minn., 1984-89, 96-97, 98-2001; mem. Inst. Advanced Study, Princeton, NJ, 1978-79; fellow Ctr. for Advanced Study, Palo Alto, Calif., 1995-96, Swedish Collegium for Advanced Study in the Social Sci., 2002—03. Sr. fellowship NEH, 1983-84; mem. selection com. Marshall Scholarships, 1983-86; Benedict Disting. vis. prof. Carleton Coll., 1981; Hardy Chair lecture Hartwick Coll., 1985 Author: Relationships, Residence and the Individual, 1976, Demise of a Rural Economy, 1978, Econ. As Culture, 1986, Conversations in Colombia, 1990; The Anthrop. of Econ., 2001; editor Cambridge Studies in Anthropology, 1989-96; contbr. numerous articles to profl. jour. Marshall scholar, 1961-63. Fellow Am. Anthropol. Assn. (bd. dir. 1987-91), Am. Ethnological Soc. (pres. 1989-91, bd. dir. 1987-91, assoc. editor 1981-84), Royal Anthropol. Inst. (sec., chmn. N.Am. com. 1983-88, Curl Bequest Essay prize 1971), Soc. Econ. Anthropology Avocations: tennis, jogging, music. Home: 1650 Dupont Ave S Minneapolis MN 55403-1101

GUELICH, ROBERT VERNON, retired management consultant; b. Dayton, Ohio, Oct. 30, 1917; m. Jane E. Schory, Dec. 6, 1941; children: Susan MacKenzie, Robert V. Jr., Helen Jane. BA, Ohio Wesleyan U., 1938; MBA, Harvard U., 1940. Reporter Dayton Jour., 1935-37; overseas corr., staff editor Air Force mag., 1942-46; asst. dir. public relations Firestone Co., Akron, Ohio, 1946-57; sr. v.p. pub. relations Montgomery Ward & Co., Chgo., 1957-81; sr. mgmt. cons. Hill & Knowlton, Chgo., 1981-83; asst. to chmn. Nat. Fitness Found., 1981-90; pres. Robert V. Guelich & Assocs., Inc., 1981—; pub. rels. cons. Exec. Svc. Corp. of Chgo., 1983-89. Chmn. Nat. Pub. Rels. Seminar, 1981. Bd. dirs. Nat. 4-H Coun., 1972-81; pres. bd. edn. New Trier Twp. High Sch., 1965-70. Maj. USAF, 1941-46. Recipient George Washington Honor medal Freedoms Found., 1977 Mem. Pub. Rels. Soc. Am. (bd. dirs. 1976-79, 3 Silver Anvil awards, 4 Presdl. Citations 1976, Outstanding Film award 1977), Chgo. Yacht Club, Mich. Shores Club, Phi Beta Kappa, Phi Gamma Delta, Sigma Delta Chi. Presbyterian. Home and Office: 380 Sterling Rd Kenilworth IL 60043-1048

GUENO, BARBARA, radio personality; Radio host Sta. WGCI-FM, Chgo. Office: Wgci Radio 233 N Michigan Ave Ste 2800 Chicago IL 60601-5704

GUEQUIERRE, JOHN PHILLIP, manufacturing executive; b. Milw., Sept. 10, 1946; s. Gerald Herbert and Louise Ann (Fenske) G.; m. Mary Rowlands Speer, Aug. 17, 1968; children: William Edward, Robert John, Elizabeth Louise. BA, U. Wis., 1968; MBA, U. Chgo., 1972. Systems analyst Inland Steel Co., East Chgo., Ind., 1968-72; analyst inventory INRYCO, Milw., 1972-73, supr. material planning, 1973-74, mgr. contract adminstrn., 1974-76; mgr. fin. Inland Steel Devel. Corp., Washington, 1976-78; mgr. fin. analysis Inland Steel Urban Devel. Corp., Chgo., 1978-80; v.p. adminstrn. Scholz Homes Inc., Tol., 1980-83; sr. v.p. adminstrn., dir. Schult Homes Corp., Middlebury, Ind., 1983-92, sr. v.p. ops., dir., 1992-95, pres. manufactured housing group, 1995-99; sr. v.p. mfg. Oakwood Homes, Middlebury, 1999-2000; chmn., CEO Pleasant St. Homes, LLC, 2000—. Chmn. budget subcom. United Way, Elkhart, Ind., 1983-89, bd. dirs. 1989-2000, treas., 1990-92, chmn. 1992; adult leader 4H, Elkhart County, 1983—; bd. dirs. Elkhart Chamber Found., 1993-98; bd. dirs. Ind. Assn. United Ways, 1993-2000, vice chmn., 1995-97, chmn., 1997. Mem.: Beta Gamma Sigma, Phi Kappa Phi, Phi Beta Kappa. Republican. Presbyterian. Office: Pleasant St Homes LLC 51700 Lovejoy Dr Middlebury IN 46540 Business E-Mail: johng@indianabuildingsystems.com.

GUERIN, D. MICHAEL, lawyer; b. La Crosse, Wis., Dec. 15, 1940; BS, Marquette U., 1970, JD, 1974. Bar: Wis. 1974, U.S. Dist. Ct. Wis.(Ea. and We. dist.) 1974, U.S. Ct. Appeals (7th cir.) 1974, U.S. Supreme Ct. 1995. Spl. agt. Dept. Justice, 1969—71; ptnr. Gimbel, Reilly, Guerin & Brown, Milw., 1971—. Lectr. at law, trial practice Marquette U., 1979—81, adj. prof. evidence, 1975—; bd. dirs., past pres. Marquette U. Law Alumni Assn., 1995—96. Mem. bd. ethics City of Milw., former police officer. Mem.: ABA, Wis. Bar Assn. (pres. 2005—06), Wis. Acad. Trial Lawyers, Assn. Trial Lawyers Am., State Bar Wis. (pres. 2005—06, 2005—06, mem. bd. govs.), Milw. Bar. Assn. (pres. 2000—01), Tau Epsilon Rho, Alpha Sigma Nu. Office: Gimbel Reilly Guerin & Brown Two Plaza East Ste 1170 330 E Kilbourn Ave Milwaukee WI 53202 Office Phone: 414-271-1440. Office Fax: 414-271-7680. E-mail: dmguerin@grgblaw.com.

GUERRI, WILLIAM GRANT, lawyer; b. Higbee, Mo., Mar. 30, 1921; s. Grant and Pearl (Zambelli) G.; m. Millicent K. Branding; children: Paula Ann Guerri Baker, Glenda Kay, William Grant. AB, Central Meth. U., 1943; LLB, Columbia, 1946. Bar: NY 1946, Mo. 1947. Ptnr. Thompson Coburn LLP, St. Louis, 1956—. Mem. bd. editors: Columbia Law Rev, 1945-46. Hon. mem. bd. dirs. St. Louis Heart Assn., chmn., 1972-73; bd. dirs. United Way Greater St. Louis, 1976-94; curator Ctrl. Meth. U., 1981-97. Fellow The Fellows of Am. Bar; mem. ABA, Mo. Bar Assn. (trustee 1984-92), Bar Assn. Met. St. Louis, Assn. of Bar of City of N.Y., Am. Law Inst., Am. Judicature Soc., Noonday Club, Round Table Club, Phi Delta Phi. Home: Apt 308 14300 Conway Meadows Ct E Chesterfield MO 63017-9612 Office: Thompson Coburn LLP Ste 3500 1 US Bank Plz Saint Louis MO 63101-1643 Office Phone: 314-552-6000. Business E-Mail: wguerri@thompsoncoburn.com.

GUFFEY, EDITH ANN, religious organization administrator; Asst. to dir. student records U. Kans., 1984-90, assoc. dir. admissions, 1990-91; sec. United Ch. of Christ, Cleve., 1991—. Office: United Ch of Christ 700 Prospect Ave E Cleveland OH 44115-1131

GUILLEN, ALITA (ALITA HAYTAYAN), newscaster; BA in English, U. N.H., 1992; MA in Broadcast Journalism, U. Miami, 1995. Anchor, prodr., reporter and host Dynamic Cable, Miami, Fla.; reporter and anchor WABU-TV, Boston, 1995—96; reporter and substitute anchor WTSP-TV, Tampa, Fla., 1997—99; morning news anchor and reporter WFOR-TV, Miami, 1999—2002; co-anchor weekend news and reporter WBBM-TV, Chgo., 2002—. Office: WBBM-TV 630 N McClurg Ct Chicago IL 60601

GUILLEN, OZZIE (OSWALDO JOSE BARRIOS GUILLEN), professional baseball manager; b. Ocumare del Tuy, Miranda, Venezuela, Jan. 20, 1964; m. Ibis Guillen; children: Oswaldo Jr., Oney, Ozney. Player San Diego Padres, 1980-84, Chgo. White Sox, 1984—97, Balt. Orioles, 1998, Atlanta Braves, 1998—2000, Tampa Bay Devil Rays, 2000; third base coach Montreal Expos, 2001—02, Fla. Marlins, 2002—03; mgr. Chgo. White Sox, 2003—. Named Rookie of the Yr. Baseball Writers' Assn. Am., 1985, The Sporting News, 1985; named to Am. League All-Star team, 1988, 90, 91; recipient Gold Glove award, 1990; named Am. League Mgr. Yr., Major League Baseball Writer Assn., 2005 mgr. World Series Champions, 2005, winning AL All-Star Team, 2006. Office: Chgo White Sox Comiskey Park 333 W 35th St Chicago IL 60616-3651

GUILLERY, RAINER WALTER, anatomy educator; b. Greifswald, Germany, Aug. 28, 1929; came to U.S., 1964; s. Hermann and Eva (Hackel) G.; m. Margot Cunningham Pepper, Dec. 21, 1954, (div. 2000); children: Peter, Edward, Philip, Jane. BSc in Anatomy, U. Coll., London, 1951, PhD, 1954. Asst. lectr. Univ. Coll., London, 1953-57, lectr., 1957-63, reader, 1963-64; assoc. prof. U. Wis., 1964-68, prof. anatomy, 1968-77; prof. dept. pharm. and physiol. Scis. U. Chgo., 1977-84; Dr. Lee's prof. anatomy Oxford U., England, 1984-96; vis. prof. anatomy U. Wis., 1996—2002, emeritus prof. anatomy, 2002—; hon. prof. Chinese U., Hong Kong, 2005. Author: (with M.S. Sherman) Exploring the Thalamus, 2001, 2d edit., 2006; mem. editl. bd. Jour. Comparative Neurology, 1971-2002, Jour. eurocytology, 1972-76, Jour. Neurophysiology, 1975-81, Neurosci., 1979-2005, Jour. Neurosci., 1980-90; editor-in-chief European Jour. Neurosci., 1987-92, mem. editl. bd., 1987—. Fellow U. Coll. London, 1987. Fellow Royal Soc.; mem. Soc. Neurosci., Anatomical Soc. G.B., Ireland (pres. 1994-96). Achievements include research on central nervous system, synapses, degeneration, developmental visual pathways. Office: U Wis Dept Anatomy Sch Medicine 1300 University Ave Madison WI 53706-1510 Office Phone: 608-263-4763. Business E-Mail: rguiller@wisc.edu.

GUILLILAND, MARTHA W., academic administrator; b. Pa. BS in Geology and Math., Catawba Coll., 1966; MS in Geophysics, Rice U., 1968; PhD in environ. engring./sys. ecology, U. Fla., 1973. Rsch. fellow sci. and pub. policy U. Mo., Kan. City, Mo., 1974—77; asst. prof. civil engring. and environment sci. U. Okla., 1975—77; exec. dir. Energy Policy Studies, Inc., El Paso, Tex., 1977—82; assoc. prof. civil engring. U. Nebr., Lincoln, 1988—90, dir. Ctr. Infrastructure Rsch., 1988—99; dean grad. sch. and asst. v.p. rsch. U. Ariz., 1990—93, vice provost academic affairs, 1993—95, academic v.p. info. and human resources, 1995—97, prof. hydrology and water resources, 1995—97; provost Tulane U., New Orleans, 1997—2000; pres. U. Mo., Kans. City, 2000—. Appointee Rsch. and Adv. Panel of Gen. Acctg. Office, Energy Engring. Bd. of Nat. Rsch. Coun., NAS Com. on Strategic Assessment of Dept. of Energy Coal Program, Nat. Inst. Global Change, Pres.'s Coun. of Advisors on Sci. and Tech., 2001. Author: (book) Energy Analysis: A New Public Policy Tool, co-author books; contbr. articles to profl. jours. Recipient Hubert H. Humphrey award, Policy Studies Orgn., 2002, Gov.'s award Excellence Total Qualty Efforts, Ariz.; fellow, W.K. Kellogg Found., 1985—88. Office: U Mo 5100 Rockhill Rd Kansas City MO 64110

GUISEWITE, CATHY LEE, cartoonist; b. Dayton, Ohio, Sept. 5, 1950; d. William Lee and Anne (Duly) G. BA in English, U. Mich., 1972; LHD (hon.), R.I. Coll., 1979, Eastern Mich. U., 1981. Writer Campbell-Ewald Advt., Detroit, 1972-73; writer Norman Prady, Ltd., Detroit, 1973-74, W.B. Doner & Co., Advt., Southfield, Mich., 1974-75, group supr., 1975-76, v.p., 1976-77; creator, writer, artist Cathy comic strip Universal Press Syndicate, Mission, Kans., 1976—. Author, artist: The Cathy Chronicles, 1978, What Do You Mean, I Still Don't Have Equal Rights??!!, 1980, What's a Nice Single Girl Doing with a Double Bed??!, 1981, I Think I'm Having a Relationship with a Blueberry Pie!, 1981, It Must Be Love, My Face Is Breaking Out, 1982, Another Saturday Night of Wild and Reckless Abandon, 1982, Cathy's Valentine's Day Survival Book, How to Live through Another February 14, 1982, How to Get Rich, Fall in Love, Lose Weight, and Solve all Your Problems by Saying "NO", 1983, Eat Your Way to a Better Relationship, 1983, A Mouthful of Breath Mints and No One to Kiss, 1983, Climb Every Mountain, Bounce Every Check, 1983, Men Should Come with Instruction Booklets, 1984, Wake Me Up When I'm a Size 5, 1985, Thin Thighs in Thirty Years, 1986, A Hand to Hold, An Opinion to Reject, 1987, Why Do the Right Words Always Come Out of the Wrong Mouth?, 1988, My Granddaughter Has Fleas, 1989, $14 in the Bank and a $200 Face in My Purse, 1990, Reflections (A Fifteenth Anniversary Collection), 1991, Only Love can Break a Heart, but a Shoe Sale Can Come Close, 1992, Revelations From a 45-Pound Purse, 1993; TV work includes 3 animated Cathy spls. (Emmy award 1987). Recipient Reuben award Nat. Cartoonists Soc., 1992. Office: Universal Press Syndicate 4520 Main St Ste 700 Kansas City MO 64111-7701

GULLESON, PAM, state legislator; Home: PO Box 215 Rutland ND 58067-0215 Office: ND Ho of Reps State Capitol Bismarck ND 58505

GULLICKSON, GLENN, JR., physician, educator; b. Mpls., July 9, 1919; s. Glenn and Grace (Stellwagen) G.; m. Glenna A. Swore, May 18, 1957; children: Mary, Glenn III. BA, U. Minn., 1942, MD, 1945, PhD, 1961. Diplomate: Am. Bd. Phys. Medicine and Rehab. Intern Gallinger Municipal Hosp., Washington, 1944-45; faculty U. Minn. Med. Sch., Mpls., 1946—, assoc. prof. phys. medicine and rehab., 1961-66, prof. phys. medicine and rehab., 1966-86, prof. emeritus, 1986—, acting head dept., 1974-75, interim head, 1982-85, asst. dir. Rehab. Center, 1954-61, dir. Rehab. Center, 1961-86. Exec. dir. Am. Congress Phys. Medicine and Rehab., 1960-66; mem. exam. com. phys. therapists Minn. Bd. Med. Examiners, 1961-71, pres., 1968-71; mem. med. adv. com. Minn. Soc. for Crippled Children and Adults, 1967-72; fellow stroke council Am. Heart Assn., mem. exec. com., 1971-74; mem. neurol. scis. research tng. com. Nat. Inst. Neurol. Diseases and Blindness, 1965-69; exec. com. Joint Com. Stroke Facilities, 1969-78. Served to lt. (s.g.), M.C. USNR, 1945-46, 53-54. Mem. AMA (prin. rep. intersplty. com. 1968-72, mem. residency review com. phys. medicine, rehab. 1971-79), AAUP, Minn. Med. Soc., Hennepin County Med. Soc., Minn. Med. Found., Am. Acad. Phys. Medicine and Rehab. (gov., v.p. 1968-69, pres. 1970-71), Am. Bd. Phys. Medicine and Rehab. (chmn. 1976-81, asst. to exec. dir. 1987-90), Am. Congress Rehab. Medicine (v.p. 1978-84, pres. 1984-85), Assn. Acad. Physiatrists, Sigma Xi.

GULLIKSON, ROSEMARY, lawyer; b. Chgo., Dec. 9, 1952; BS summa cum laude, No. Ill. U., 1974; JD cum laude, Northwestern U., 1994. Bar: Ill. 1994; RN Ill., 1974. Ptnr. Sonnenschein Nath & Rosenthal LLP, Chgo. Dir., pres. Tim & Tom Gullikson Found. Office: Sonnenschein Nath & Rosenthal LLP Sears Tower, Ste 8000 233 South Wacker Dr Chicago IL 60606 Office Phone: 312-876-8963. E-mail: rgullikson@sonnenschein.com.

GUMBLETON, THOMAS JOHN, bishop emeritus; b. Detroit, Jan. 26, 1930; Student, St. John Provincial Sem., Mich., Pontifical Lateran U., Rome. Ordained priest Archdiocese of Detroit, 1956; pastor St. Leo Ch.; ordained bishop, 1968; aux. bishop Archdiocese of Detroit, 1968—2006, aux. bishop emeritus, 2006—. Roman Catholic. Office: 4800 Graand Rive Ave Detroit MI 48208 Office Phone: 313-898-3328. Office Fax: 313-897-2980.*

GUND, GORDON, venture capitalist, investment company executive; b. Cleve., Oct. 15, 1939; s. George and Jessica (Roesler) G.; m. Llura Liggett; children: Grant Ambler, Gordon Zachary. BA, Harvard U., 1961; DPubSvc (hon.), U. Maryland, 1980; DHL, Whittier Coll., 1993; LLD (hon.), U. Vt., 1994; PhD (hon.), Goteburg U., Sweden, 1997. Chmn., CEO Gund Investment Corp., Princeton, NJ, 1968—. Bd. dirs. Kellogg Co., Corning Inc. Co-founder The Found. Fighting Blindness, 1971; mem. Nat. Adv. Eye Coun., 1980—84, U.S. Olympic Com., 2000—03. Mem.: Phi Beta Kappa (hon.; chair, bd. govs. 1996—99). Office: Gund Investment Corp PO Box 449 14 Nassau St Princeton NJ 08542-4523

GUNDERSON, SCOTT LEE, state legislator; b. Oct. 24, 1956; m. Lisa Gunderson, Oct. 17, 1981; children: Joshua, Hannah, Rebecca. Grad. H.S., Waterford, Wis. Former supr. Town of Waterford, Wis.; assemblyman Wis. State Dist. 83, 1994—. Owner Gundy's Sport. Mem. Racine County Fair Bd., Wis. State Fair Park Bd. Mem. Wind Lake C. of C. (past pres.), Waterford Lions, Wings Over Wis., Ducks Unlimited (com. chair). Address: State Capitol Rm 7W PO Box 8952 Madison WI 53708 E-mail: rep.gunderson@legis.state.wi.us.

GUNDRUM, MARK, state representative; b. Mar. 20, 1970; married. BA, U. Wis., 1988, JD, 1994. Bar: Wis. Atty.; state assembly mem. Wis. State Asssembly, Madison, 1998—; chair, judiciary com. mem. Com. on Campaigns and Elections, Madison, Com. on Corrections and the Cts., Madison, Com. on Criminal Justice and Homeland Security, Com. on Assembly Organization, Com. on Rules. Mem. Waukesha County (Wis.) Criminal Justice Task Force. Mem.: State Bar Assn. Wis. Republican. Office: State Capitol Rm 119 W PO Box 8952 Madison WI 53708-8952

GUNDRY, STANLEY N., publishing company executive; b. July 12, 1937; m. Patricia Smith, Aug. 3, 1958; 4 children. BA summa cum laude, L.A. Bapt. Coll., 1959; BD summa cum laude, Talbot Theol. Sem., 1963; STM, Union Coll., U. B.C., 1968; STD, Luth. Sch. Theology, 1975. Ordained to ministry Bapt. Ch., 1963. Pastor ooksack Valley Bapt. Ch., Everson, Wash., 1963-68; prof. theology Moody Bible Inst., 1968-79; sr. v.p., editor-in-chief Zondervan Pub., Grand Rapids, Mich., 1980—. Adj. prof. theology Trinity Evang. Divinity Sch., 1975-80. Pub. Wycliffe Bible Encyclopaedia, 1975, Love Them In: The Life and Theology of D.L. Moody, 1982; pub., co-editor: Tensions in Contemporary Theology, 1983, Perspectives on Evangelical Theology, 1979; co-author: NAS Harmony of the Gospels, 1986, NIV Harmony of the Gospels: A Revision of A.T. Robertson's Harmony, 1988. Mem. Am. Theol. Soc., Am. Soc. Ch. History, Evang. Theol. Soc. (pres. 1978), Inst. Biblical Rsch. (conf. faith and history). Home: 4142 Burton St SE Grand Rapids MI 49546-6119 Office: Zondervan Pub House 5300 Patterson Ave SE Grand Rapids MI 49530 Office Phone: 616-698-3475.

GUNN, ALAN, retired law educator; b. Syracuse, NY, Apr. 8, 1940; s. Albert Dale and Helen Sherwood (Whitnall) G.; m. Bertha Ann Buchwald, 1975; 1 child, William BS, Rensselaer Poly. Inst., 1961; JD, Cornell U., 1970. Bar: D.C. 1970. Assoc. Hogan & Hartson, Washington, 1970-72; asst. prof. law Washington U., St. Louis, 1972-75, assoc. prof., 1975-76; assoc. prof. law Cornell U., Ithaca, NY, 1977-79, prof., 1979-84, J. duPratt White prof., 1984-89; prof. law U. Notre Dame, Ind., 1989-96, John N. Matthews prof. Ind., 1996—2005, prof. emeritus Ind., 2005—. Apptd. spl. advocate St. Joseph County Probate Ct., 2001—. Author: (with James R. Repetti) Partnership Income Taxation, 1991, 4th edit., 2005; (with Larry D. Ward) Cases, Text and Problems on Federal Income Taxation, 5th edit., 2002; (with Vincent R. Johnson) Studies in American Tort Law, 1994, 3rd edit., 2005. Methodist. Office: U Notre Dame Law Sch Notre Dame IN 46556

GUNN, JAMES EDWIN, language educator; b. Kansas City, Mo., July 12, 1923; s. J. Wayne and Elsie M. (Hutchison) G.; m. Jane Frances Anderson, Feb. 6, 1947; children: Christopher Wayne, Kevin Robert. BS, U. Kans., Lawrence, 1947, MA, 1951. Editor Western Printing and Litho, Racine, Wis., 1951-52; asst. dir. Civil Def., Kansas City, Mo., 1953; instr. U. Kans., Lawrence, 1955, mng. editor Alumni Assn., 1956-58, adminstrv. asst. to the chancellor for univ. rels., 1958-70, lectr. English, 1970-74, prof., 1974-93, emeritus prof., 1993—. Cons. Easton Press, Norwalk, Conn., 1985-98; lectr. in field. Author: over 25 books including Station in Space, 1958, The Immortals, 1962, The End of Dreams, 1975, Alternate Worlds: The Illustrated History of Science Fiction (World Sci. Fiction Conv. Spl. award, 1976, Pilgrim award Sci. Fiction Rsch. Assn., 1976), The Listeners, 1972, The Dreamers, 1980, Isaac Asimov: The Foundations of Science Fiction, 1982 (Hugo award World Sci. Fiction Conv., 1983), The Science of Science-Fiction Writing, 2000, The Millennium Blues, 2001, Human Voices, 2002, Gift From The Stars, 2005, numerous plays, screenplays, radio scripts; editor: The Road to Science Fictions, 6 vols., 1977—2002; editor: (with Matthew Candelarie) Speculations on Speculations: Theories of Science Fiction, 2004;: Inside Science Fiction, 2006, 8 other books; contbr. 100 stories to mags.; contbr. articles. Dir. Ctr. for Study Sci. Fiction, Lawrence, 1984—. Lt. (j.g.) USN, 1943-46, PTO. Recipient Eaton award Eaton Conf., 1992, Hugo award, 1983, Grand Master award, Sci. Fiction Writers Am., 2007; Alumni Distinguished Achievement award, 2008; Mellon fellow U. Kans., 1981, 84. Mem. Author's Guild, Sci. Fiction and Fantasy Writers Am. (pres. 1971-72; Grand Master award 2007), Sci. Fiction Rsch. Assn. (pres. 1981-82, Pilgrim award 1976). Avocation: bridge. Home: 2215 Orchard Ln Lawrence KS 66049-2707 Office: U Kans English Dept 3116 Wescoe Hall Lawrence KS 66045-7590 Office Phone: 785-864-3380. Business E-Mail: jgunn@ku.edu.

GUNN, MARY ELIZABETH, retired language educator; b. Great Bend, Kans., July 21, 1914; d. Ernest E. and Elisabeth (Wesley) Eppstein; m. Charles Leonard Gunn, Sept. 13, 1936 (dec. Apr. 1985); 1 child, Charles Douglas. AB, Ft. Hays State U., Kans., 1935; BS in Edn., Ft. Hays State U., 1936, MA, 1967. Tchr. English Unified Sch. Dist. 428, Great Bend, 1963-80, Barton County CC, Great Bend, 1977-84, tchr. adult edn., 1985-87, tchr. ESL, 1988-94; ret., 1994. Recipient Nat. Cmty. Svc. award, DAR, 1996; Conf. Am. Studies fellow, De Pauw U., 1969. Mem.: AAUW (outstanding mem. 1991), NEA, Bus. and Profl. Women (Woman of Yr. 1974), Kans. Adult Edn. Assn. (Master Adult Educator 1986), Kans. Assn. Tchrs. English, PEO, Delta Kappa Gamma, Alpha Sigma Alpha. Democrat. Mem. United Ch. Of Christ. Avocations: travel, driving, needlepoint, crossword puzzles, reading. Home: 3820 Broadway Ste 8 Great Bend KS 67530

GUNN, MICHAEL PETER, lawyer; b. St. Louis, Oct. 18, 1944; s. Donald and Loretto Agnes (Hennelly) G.; m. Carolyn Ormsby Ritter, Nov. 27, 1969; children: Mark Thomas, Christopher Michael, John Ritter, Elizabeth Jane. JD, St. Louis U., 1968. Bar: Mo. 1968, U.S. Dist. Ct. (ea and we. dists.) Mo. 1968, U.S. Tax Ct. 1972. Assoc. Gunn & Gunn, St. Louis, 1968-81; ptnr. Gunn & Lane, St. Louis, 1981-86; pvt. practice Ballwin, Mo., 1986—. Rep. ea. dist. Mo. Ct. Appeals. Sgt. U.S. Army, 1969-75. Mem. ABA (ho. of dels. 1988—), St. Louis Bar Assn., The Mo. Bar (bd. govs. 1990-2001, exec. com. 1993-94, pres.-elect 1998-99, pres. 1999-2000), Lawyers Assn. St. Louis (pres. 1981-82), St. Louis Bar Found. (pres. 1988-89), Bar Assn. Met. St. Louis (pres. 1987-88), Nat. Conf. Bar Founds. (trustee 1990-95, pres. 1993-94). Roman Catholic. Home: 2232 Centeroyal Dr Saint Louis MO 63131-1910 Office: The Gunn Law Firm PC Ste 240 1714 Deer Tracks Trail Saint Louis MO 63131

GUNNING, TOM, art educator; BA, NYU, 1970, MA in Cinema Studies, 1974, PhD, 1986; PhD (hon.), in philosophy, 1998. Prof. dept. art history U. Chgo. Author: D.W. Griffith and the Origins of American Narrative Film: The Early Years, 1991, An Invention of the Devil? Religion and Early Cinema, 1992, The Films of Fritz Lang: Allegories of Vision and Modernity, 2000; contbr. articles to profl. jours. Guggenheim fellow, 1998. Office: Dept Art History U Chgo 5540 S Greenwood Ave Chicago IL 60637-1506 E-mail: tgunning@midway.uchicago.edu.

GUNSETT, DANIEL J., lawyer; b. Van Wert, Ohio, Oct. 8, 1948; BS in Chemical Engring., U. Mich., 1971; JD, U. N.C., 1974. Bar: Ohio 1974, US Dist. Ct., So. Dist. of Ohio, 1975, No. Dist., 1979, US Ct. of Appeals, Fifth Circuit, 1998. Ptnr. Baker & Hostetler, Columbus, Ohio, head, energy and environment practice, managing ptnr. Mem.: ABA (nat. resources, energy and environmental law section), Columbus Bar Assn. (environmental and real estate comt.), Ohio State Bar Assn. (environmental law com.), Electrical Cooperative Bar Assn. Office: Baker & Hostetler Capital Sq 65 E State St Ste 2100 Columbus OH 43215-4260 Office Phone: 614-462-2642. Office Fax: 614-462-2616. Business E-Mail: dgunsett@bakerlaw.com.

GUNTER, G. JANE, state legislator; 3 children. Grad. high sch. Rep. Dist. 7 N.D. Ho. of Reps., mem. human svcs. and polit. subdivsn. coms. Mem. Gov.'s Coun. Human Resources, Com. Children and Youth. Home: 6520 Willow Rd Towner ND 58788-9503

GUPPY, JOHN, professional sports team executive; b. Eng. m. Carla Guppy; 3 children. BSBA, New Hampshire Coll., 1990; M in Sports Mgmt., U. Mass., Amherst, 1992. Player Southampton Football Club, England; with API Soccer (formerly Soccer USA Ptnrs.), 1992—98; grp. dir. Octagon Mktg., Conn.; v.p. mktg. & sales Y/NJ MetroStars (Maj. League Soccer), 2000—02, exec. v.p., 2002—05; pres., CEO Chgo. Fire (Maj. League Soccer), 2005—. Office: Chgo Fire Toyota Pk 7000 S Harlem Ave Bridgeview IL 60455

GUPTA, KRISHNA CHANDRA, mechanical engineering educator; b. 1948; m. Karuna Gupta; 1 child, Anupama. B of Tech. with distinction, Indian Inst. Tech., 1969; MS in Mech. Engring., Case Inst. Tech., 1971; PhD in Mech. Engring., Stanford U., 1974. Grad. asst. Case Inst. Tech., Cleve., 1969-71; rsch. asst. Stanford (Calif.) U., 1971-74; from asst. prof. to prof. emeritus mech. engring. U. Ill., Chgo., 1974—2005, prof. emeritus, 2005—, assoc. dean, 2002—05. Mem. editl. adv. bd. Jour. Applied Mechanisms and Robotics 1993-2000; assoc. editor Mechanism and Machine Theory 1998-2004; contbr. articles to profl. jours. Recipient award of merit Procter & Gamble Co., 1978, South Pointing Chariot award, 1989, AM&R G.N. Sandor award, 1997; grantee in field. Fellow ASME (assoc. editor Jour. Mech. Design 1981-82, mem. editl. adv. bd. Applied Mechanics Rev. 1985-93, chmn. mechanisms com. 1989-90, gen chmn. 1990 design tech. conf., chmn. 1990 mechanisms conf., mem. design divsn. exec. com. 2001-2007, chair design divsn., 2005-06, immediate past chmn., 2006-2007, adv. com. design divsn., 2007—, editor newsletter divsn. design engring., best paper computers in engring. conf. 1991, Henry Hess award 1979, Design Divsn. Mechanisms and Robotics award 2002). Avocations: investments, speed reading. Office: Univ Ill Dept Mech and Indsl Engring MC 251 842 W Taylor St Chicago IL 60607 E-mail: kcgupta@uic.edu.

GUPTA, MAHENDRA R., dean; m. Sunita Gupta; children: Vivek, Sumi. BS in Statistics and Economics, Bombay U., 1978; MS in Indsl. Adminstrn., Carnegie Mellon U., Pitts., 1981; PhD, Stanford U., 1990. Joined Wash. U. Olin Sch. Bus., St. Louis, 1990, Geraldine J. and Robert L. Virgil prof. acctg. and mgmt., 2004—, sr. assoc. dean, dean, 2005—. Avocations: reading, cooking, movies. Office: Wash U Olin Sch Bus Campus Box 1133 One Brookings Dr Saint Louis MO 63130 Office Phone: 314-935-6344. E-mail: guptam@olin.wustl.edu.

GUPTA, SURAJ NARAYAN, physicist, researcher; b. Haryana, India, Dec. 1, 1924; came to U.S., 1953, naturalized, 1963; s. Lakshmi N. and Devi (Goyal) G.; m. (Letty) J. R. Paine, July 14, 1948; children: Paul, Ranee. MS, St. Stephen's Coll., India, 1946; PhD, U. Cambridge, Eng., 1951. Imperial Chem. Industries fellow U. Manchester, Eng., 1951-53; vis. prof. physics Purdue U., 1953-56; prof. physics Wayne State U., Detroit, 1956-61, disting. prof. physics, 1961-99, disting. prof. emeritus physics, 1999—. Author: Quantum Electrodynamics, 1977. Fellow Am. Phys. Soc., Nat. Acad. Scis. of India. Achievements include research in high energy physics, nuclear physics, relativity and gravitation, quantum theory with negative probability and quantization of the electromagnetic field; flat-space interpretation of Einstein's theory of gravitation and quantization of the gravitational field; regularization and renormalization of elementary particle interactions; phenomena at supercollider energies; development of the theory of bound states in quantum electrodynamics and quantum chromodynamics; mass matrix formulation of quark mixing and CP violation in weak interactions. Office: Wayne State U Dept Physics Detroit MI 48202 Home: 5515 Westwood Ln Bloomfield Hills MI 48301 Business E-Mail: doctorgupta@ameritech.net.

GUPTA, SURENDRA KUMAR, chemicals executive; b. Delhi, India, Apr. 5, 1938; arrived in US, 1963, naturalized, 1971; s. Bishan Chand and Devki Gupta; m. Karen Patricia Clarke, Oct. 12, 1968; children: Jay, Amanda. BSc with honors, Delhi U., 1959, MSc, 1961; MTech, Indian Inst. Tech., Bombay, 1963; PhD, Wayne State U., 1968. Rsch. assoc. Western Mich. U., Kalamazoo, 1968—73; indsl. fellow Starks Assocs., Buffalo, 1973—74; group leader New Eng. Nuc. Co., Boston, 1974—80, Pathfinder Labs., St. Louis, 1981—83; chmn. bd., chemist Am. Radiolabeled Chem., Inc., St. Louis, 1983—; owner Precision Biochem., Inc., Vancouver, BC, Canada, 2003—. Contbr. articles to profl. jours. Mem.: Am. Chem. Soc. (chmn. pub. rels. com. 1970—73). Hindu. Avocations: ping pong/table tennis, stamp collecting/philately, travel. Home: 22 Muirfield Ln Saint Louis MO 63141-7380 Office: Am Radiolabeled Chems Inc 101 ARC Dr Saint Louis MO 63146-3506 Office Phone: 314-991-4545. Business E-Mail: drgupta@arc-inc.com.

GUPTA, VINOD, business lists company executive; b. New Delhi, July 4, 1946; came to U.S., 1967; BTech., I.I.T., Kharagpur, India, 1967; MS, U. Nebr., 1969, MBA, 1971. Chief exec. officer Am. Bus. Lists Inc., Ralston, Nebr. Office: Info USA Inc 5711 S 86th Cir Omaha NE 68127-4146

GURALNICK, SIDNEY AARON, engineering educator; b. Phila., Apr. 25, 1929; s. Philip and Kenia (Dudnik) G.; m. Eleanor Alban, Mar. 10, 1951; children: Sara Dian, Jeremy. BSc, Drexel Inst. Tech., Phila., 1952; MS, Cornell U., 1955, PhD, 1958. Registered profl. engr., Pa.; lic. structural engr., Ill. Instr., then asst. prof. Cornell U., 1952-58, mgr. structural research lab., 1956-58; mem. faculty Ill. Inst. Tech., Chgo., 1958—, prof. civil engring., 1967—, Perlstein disting. prof. engring., now prof. emeritus, 1982—, dir. structural engring. labs., 1968-71, dean Grad. Sch., 1971-75, exec. v.p., provost, 1975-82, trustee, 1976-82, dir. Advanced Bldg. Materials and Sys. Ctr., 1987—. Devel. engr. Portland Cement Assn., Skokie, Ill., 1959-61; participant internat. confs.; cons. to govt. and industry. Author numerous papers in field. Trustee Inst. Gas Tech., 1976-81, Rsch. Inst. of Ill. Inst. Tech., 1976-82; commr.-at-large orth Ctrl. Assn. Schs. and Colls., 1985-89, cons., evaluator, 1989-93. With C.E., U.S. Army, 1950-51. McGraw fellow, 1952-53; Faculty Rsch. fellow Ill. Inst. Tech., 1960; European travel grantee, 1961 Fellow: ASCE (Collingwood prize 1961, Lifetime Achievement award Ill. sect. 1997, Civil Engr. of Yr. award Ill. sect. 1998); mem.: Ill. Univs. Transp. Rsch. Consortium (adminstrv. com. 1983—93), Transp. Rsch. Bd., Structural Engrs. Assn. Ill. (bd. dirs., pres.-elect 1989—90, pres. 1990—91, John F. Parmer award 1993), Soc. Exptl. Mechanics, Am. Concrete Inst., Chi Epsilon, Tau Beta Pi, Phi Kappa Phi, Sigma Xi. Office: Ill Inst Tech 3300 S Federal St Chicago IL 60616-3793 Business E-Mail: guralnick@iit.edu.

GURNETT, DONALD ALFRED, physics professor; b. Cedar Rapids, Iowa, Apr. 11, 1940; s. Alfred Foley and Velma (Trachta) G.; m. Marie Barbara Schmitz, Oct. 10, 1964; children: Suzanne, Christina. BS in Elec. Engring., U. Iowa, Iowa City, 1962, MS in Physics, 1963, PhD in Physics, 1965. Prof. physics and astronomy U. Iowa, Iowa City, 1965-75, 76-79, 80—; rsch. scientist Max-Planck Inst., Garching, Fed. Republic Germany, 1975-76; vis. prof. UCLA, 1979-80; mem. space physics com. Nat. Acad. Sci., Washington, 1975-78, mem. com. on solar terrestrial research, 1976-79, mem. com. on planetary and lunar exploration, 1982-85. Recipient Alexander von Humboldt Found. award, 1975, Disting. Sci. Achievement award NASA, 1981, Space Act award NASA, 1986, Sci. Achievement medal Gov. of Iowa, 1987, Disting. Iowa Scientist award Iowa Acad. Sci., 1989, Marion L. Huit award U. Iowa, 1990, Iowa Bd. Regents award for faculty excellence, 1994, Alfven medal European Geoscis. Union, 2006. Fellow Am. Geophys. Union (assoc. editor Jour. Geophys. Rsch. 1974-77), Am. Acad. Arts and Sci., Fleming medal 1989, Am. Phys. Soc. (award for excellence in plasma physics 1989); mem. Internat. Union Radio Sci. (Dellinger gold medal 1978), Soaring Soc. Am. (Iowa State gov. 1983-86), Nat. Acad. of Sci. Home: 4664 Canterbury Ct Iowa City IA 52245 Office: U Iowa Dept Physics and Astronomy 715 Van Allen Hall Iowa City IA 52242-1403 Business E-Mail: donald-garnett@uiowa.edu.

GUSEWELLE, CHARLES WESLEY, journalist, writer; b. Kansas City, July 22, 1933; s. Hugh L. and Dorothy (Middleton) G.; m. Katie Jane Ingels, Apr. 17, 1966; children— Anne Elizabeth, Jennifer Sue. BA in English, Westminster Coll., 1955; LHD (hon.), Park Coll., 1990. Reporter Kansas City (Mo.) Star, 1955-66, editorial writer of fgn. affairs, 1966-76, fgn. editor, 1976-79, asso. editor, columnist, 1979—. Author: A Paris Notebook, 1985, An Africa Notebook, 1986, Quick as Shadows Passing, 1988, Far from Any Coast, 1989, A Great Current Running, 1995, The Rufus Chronicle, 1996, A Buick in the Kitchen, 2000, On the Way to Other Country, 2001, Another Cat at the Door, 2004, A Little Christmas Music, 2006, A Gift of Wings, 2007; contbr. short stories to Brit., Am. lit. quars.; writer, narrator, host: A Great Current Running, 1995, This Place Called Home (Regional Emmy 1998), Water and Fire: A Story of the Ozarks, 2000, Stories Under the Stone, 2005. 1st lt. AUS, 1956-58. Recipient Aga Khan prize for fiction, 1977, Thorpe Menn Lit. award, 1989; inducted Writers Hall of Fame, 2000, Mo. Press Assn. Newspaper Hall of Fame, 2007. Home: 1245 Stratford Rd Kansas City MO 64113-1325 Office: 1729 Grand Ave Kansas City MO 64108-1413 Office Phone: 816-333-0994.

GUSTAFSON, COLE RICHARD, agricultural economics educator; b. St. Croix Falls, Wis., Nov. 21, 1955; s. Richard A. and Darelyne (Peroff) G.; m. Nancy J. Anderson, Mar. 17, 1979; children: Ana, Kelsey. BS, U. Minn., St. Paul, 1978, MS, 1980; PhD, U. Ill., 1986. Rsch. asst. U. Minn., St. Paul, 1978-80; agrl. economist Dept. Agriculture, Washington, 1980-86; assoc. prof. agrl. econs. N.D. State U., Fargo, 1986-98, asst. dean rsch., 1998—. Mem. Am. Agrl. Econs. Assn., So. Agrl. Econs. Assn., Western Agrl. Econs. Assn., Am. Econs. Assn., Phi Kappa Phi, Gamma Sigma Delta, Sigma Xi. Lutheran. Avocations: woodworking, constrn., farming. Office: ND State U Dept Agrl Experiment Sta Fargo ND 58105-5435

GUSTAFSON, DAN, state legislator; State rep. Dist. 67 Mich. Ho. of Reps., 1993-98; chief of staff Lt. Gov. Dick Posthumus, Lansing, Mich., 1998—. Home: 5537 Wild Iris Ln Haslett MI 48840-8685 Office: Lt Govs Office 505 Romney Bldg Lansing MI 48909

GUSTAFSON, DAVID HAROLD, industrial engineering and preventive medicine educator; b. Kane, Pa., Sept. 11, 1940; s. Harold Edward and Olive Albertina (McKalip) G.; m. Rea Corina Anagnos, June 23, 1962; children: Laura Lynn, Michelle Elaine, David Harold BS in Indsl. Engring., U. Mich., 1962, MS in Indsl. Engring, 1963, PhD, 1966. Dir. hosp. div. Community Systems Found., Ann Arbor, Mich., 1961-64; asst. prof. indsl. engring. U. Wis.-Madison, 1966-70, assoc. prof., 1970-74, prof., 1974—, Robert A. Ratner prof. indsl. engring. $D, 2000—, dir., founder Ctr. for Health Systems and Analysis, 1974—, chmn. dept. indsl. engring., 1984-88, adminstrv. com. Grad. Sch., 1995-98, mem. athletic bd., 2000—; sr. analyst Dec. and Designs Inc., McLean, Va., 1974. Dir. rsch. Govt. Health Policy Task Force, State of Wis., 1969-71; prin. cons. Medicaid Mgmt. Study Team, 1977-78; prin. investigator Nursing Home Quality Assurance System, 1979, Computer System for Adolscent Health Promotion, 1983, Computer System to Support Breast Cancer and People with AIDS, 1993; vis. prof. London Sch. Econs., 1983, Harvard U., 1999; developer computer-based support to measure and improve health care quality; chair Fed. Sci. Panel on Interactive Comms. in Health; dir. TECC Ctr. for Excellence in Cancer Comms., 2004, Network for Improvement of Addiction Treatment. Author: Group Techniques, 1975, Health Policy Analysis, 1992, Sustainability, 2005; contbr. articles to profl. jours. Adviser conflict resolution Luth. Ch., 1973-79; active numerous civic orgns. Recipient numerous grants, 1968—, Ragnar Onstad award for cmty. svc., 1990. Fellow Assn. for Health Svcs. Rsch., Inst. for Health Care Improvement (bd. dirs. 1990—), Am. Med. Informatics Assn.; mem. Inst. Indsl. Engring., Ops. Rsch. Soc., Med. Decision Making Avocations: jogging, guitar, water sports, cross country skiing, parenting. Office: U Wis Ctr Health Systems 610 Walnut St Madison WI 53705-2336

GUSTAFSON, WINTHROP ADOLPH, retired engineering educator; b. Moline, Ill., Oct. 14, 1928; s. Gustav A. and Katherine (Wenger) G.; m. Sarah Elizabeth Garner, Aug. 3, 1957; children: Charles Lee, Stanley Scott, John Winthrop, Richard Neil. BS, U. Ill., 1950, MS, 1954, PhD, 1956. Rsch. scientist Lockheed Missiles & Space Co., Palo Alto, Calif., 1956—60; assoc. prof. Sch. Aero. and Astronautics Purdue U., Lafayette, Ind., 1960—66, prof. Sch. Aero. and Astronautics, 1966—98, assoc. head Sch. Aero. and Astronautics, 1980—98, acting head Sch. Aero. and Astronautics, 1984—85, 1993, prof. emeritus Sch. Aero. and Astronautics, 1998—. Vis. prof. U. Calif. San Diego, 1968; rsch. engr. Allison divsn. GM., Indpls., summer 1962; mem. tech. staff Bell Telephone Labs., Whippany, N.J., summer 1966, NASA-Dryden Flight Rsch. Ctr., summer 1976; cons. Goodyear Aerospace Corp., Akron, Ohio, 1964, Los Alamos Sci. Lab., 1977, U.S. Army, 1986-87. Contbr. articles to profl. jours. Served to 1st lt. USAF, 1951-53. Mem. AIAA. Home: 209 Lindberg Ave West Lafayette IN 47906-2109 Office: Purdue U Sch Aeros & Astronautics Lafayette IN 47907

GUTH, SHERMAN LEON (S. LEE), psychologist, educator; b. NYC; s. Arthur and Caroline (Laub) G.; children from previous marriage: Melissa, Victoria; m. Ling Zhao; 1 child, Lillian. BS, Purdue U., 1959; MA, U. Ill., 1961, PhD, 1963. Lectr. dept. psychology Ind. U., Bloomington, 1962-63, instr., 1963-64, asst. prof., 1964-67, assoc. prof., 1967-70, prof., 1970—; dir. research and grad. devel. Sch. Optometry, 1980-88, chmn. dept. visual scis., 1982-85. Vis. assoc. prof. psychology Mich. State U., 1968-69; NIH spl. research fellow in psychology U. Calif., Berkeley, 1971-72; NSF program dir. for sensory physiology and perception, 1977-78 NIH research grantee, 1964—70, NSF research grantee, 1963—86. Fellow Optical Soc. Am. Achievements include being the creator of the ATD model for visual adaption and color perception. Office: Ind U Dept Psychology Bloomington IN 47405 Business E-Mail: guth@indiana.edu.

GUTHERY, JOHN M., lawyer; b. Broken Bow, Nebr., Nov. 22, 1946; s. John M. and Kay G.; m. Diane Messineo, May 26, 1972; 1 child, Lisa. BS, U. Nebr., 1969, JD, 1972. Bar: Nebr. 1972. Pres. Perry, Guthery, Haase & Gessford, P.C., L.L.O., Lincoln, Nebr., 1972—. Bd. govs. Nebr. Wesleyan U. Mem. AAJ, ABA (mem. litigation sect.), Nebr. Bank Attys. Assn. (past pres., 1985-86), Nebr. Assn. Trial Attys., Nebr. State Bar Assn. (pres. 1998-99, mem. Nebr.State Bar Found. mem. ho. dels. 1979-83, 87-95, exec. coun. 1988-94 pres. 1998-99, chair Nebr. bankruptcy sect.), Lincoln Bar Assn. (trustee 1985-88, pres. 1990-91). Office: Perry Guthery Haase & Gessford PC LLO 233 S 13th St Ste 1400 Lincoln NE 68508-2003 Office Phone: 402-476-9200. Business E-Mail: jguthery@perrylawfirm.com.

GUTHMAN, JACK, lawyer; b. Cologne, Germany, Apr. 19, 1938; came to U.S., 1939, naturalized, 1945; s. Albert and Selma (Cahn) G.; m. Sandra Polk, Nov. 26, 1967. BA, Northwestern U., 1960; LLB, Yale U., 1963. Bar: Ill. bar 1963. Law clk. to dist. judge U.S. Dist. Ct. No. Ill., 1963-65; since practiced in Chgo.; ptnr. Sidley & Austin, 1970-94, Shefsky & Froelich Ltd., Chgo., 1995—. Mem. City Chgo. Zoning Bd. Appeals, 1970-75, chmn., 1975-87. Democrat. Jewish. Office: Shefsky & Froelich Ltd 111 E Wacker Dr Ste 2800 Chicago IL 60601 Office Phone: 312-836-4034.

GUTHRIE, CARLTON L., automotive manufacturing company executive; b. Atlanta; m. Danielle Guthrie; children: Carille, Adam. BA with honors in Econs., Harvard U., 1974, MBA in Gen. Mgmt., 1978. With Phila. Nat. Bank, Procter & Gamble; mgmt. cons. Jewel Cos., Chgo.; sr. cons. consumer group McKinsey & Co., Chgo.; exec. v.p., COO James H. Lowry & Assocs., Chgo.; co-owner, pres., CEO, chmn. bd. Trumark, Inc., Lansing, Mich. Bd. dirs. Shorebank Corp., Chgo. and Detroit. Founder, chmn. bd. Single Parent Family Inst., Lansing, Mich.; corp. sponsor YMCA's Y Achievers Program, Lansing; bd. dirs. Joyce Found., Chgo., Ctrs. for New Horizons, Chgo.; adv. bd. Governor's State U. Sch. Bus., University Park, Ill.; nat. bd. dirs. Initiative for a Competitive Inner City, Boston; adv. com. mem. Joint Ctr. for Polit. and Econ. Studies, Washington. Recipient Chivas Regal Extrapreneur of the Yr. award, 1989. Mem. Nat. Assn. Black Automotive Suppliers (v.p., bd. dirs.), Runners' Club Chgo. (co-founder). Office: Trumark Inc 6501 Lynch Rd Detroit MI 48234-4140 Fax: 517-482-0795.

GUTHRIE, DIANA FERN, nursing educator; b. NYC, May 7, 1934; d. Floyd George and A. May (Moler) Worthington; m. Richard Alan Guthrie, Aug. 18, 1957; children: Laura, Joyce, Tammy. AA, Graceland Coll., 1953; RN, Independence Sanitarium, Mo., 1956; BS in Nursing, U. Mo., 1957, MS in Pub. Health, 1969; EdS, Wichita State U., Kans., 1982; PhD, Walden U., 1985. Cert. diabetes educator, bd. cert. advanced diabetes mgmt.; RN Mo., Kans., cert. holistic nursing, RN advanced practitioner; lic. profl. counselor Kans., cert. stress mgmt. edn., clin. hypnosis, healing touch, lic. marriage and family therapist. Instr. red cross U.S. Naval Sta., Sangley Point, Philippines, 1961-63; acting head nurse newborn nursery U. Mo., Columbia, 1963-64, birth defect nurse dept. pediat., 1964-65, nursing dir. clin. research ctr., 1965-67, research asst., 1967-73; diabetes nurse specialist Sch. Medicine U. Kans., Wichita, 1973—, asst. then assoc. prof. Sch. Medicine, 1974-85, prof. dept. pediat. and psychiatry Sch. Medicine, 1985-99, prof. emeritus, 2000; prof. dept. nursing Kans. U. Med. Ctr., Wichita, 1985-99, ret., 1999. Nurse cons. diabetes Mo. Regional Med. Program, Columbia, 1970-73; nat. advisor Human Diabetes Ctr. for Excellence, Lexington, Ky., 1982-90, Phoenix, 1983-92, Charlottesville, Ky., 1990-95; adj. prof. Sch. Nursing Wichita State U., 1985—. Author: Nursing Management of Diabetes, 1977, 5th edit., 2002, The Diabetes Source Book, 1990, 5th edit., 2003, Alternative and Complementary Diabetes Case, 2000; contbr. articles to profl. jours. Health adv. bd. Mid-Am. All Indian Ctr., Wichita, 1978-80; bd. dirs. Wichita Urban Indian Health Clinic, 1980-82; bd. trustees Graceland U., Lamoni, Iowa, 1996-2001, bd. trustees emeritus, 2002—. Named Kans. Counselor of Yr., Kans. Counseling Assn., 2006; recipient Disting. Hon. Nursing Alumnus award, Wichita State U. Sch. Nursing/Nursing Alumni Soc., 2007. Fellow: Am. Acad. Nursing; mem.: APHA, ANA, Am. Assn. Med. Psychotherapists (profl. adv. bd. 1985—), Am. Assn. Diabetes Educators (Kans. area Disting. Svc. award 1999), Am. Diabetes Assn. (Kans. area prof. edn. and youth com. 1988—, affiliate bd. dirs. 1979—83, pres. Kans. affiliate 1980—81, 1990—91, Outstanding Educator award 1979, Regional Outstanding Svc. award 1984, South Ctrl. Kans. Counselor of Yr. 2006, Kans. Counselor of Yr. 2006), Sigma Theta Tau (Exemplary Recognition award Epsilon Gamma chpt. 1996). Democrat. Mem. Cmty. Of Christ Ch. Avocations: harp, piano, painting, crafts, reading. Office: 200 S Hillside Wichita KS 67211-2127 Office Phone: 316-687-3100. Business E-Mail: dguthrie@kumc.edu.

GUTHRIE, RICHARD ALAN, physician; b. Pleasant Hill, Ill., Nov. 13, 1935; s. Merle Pruitt and Cleona Marie (Weaver) G.; m. Diana Fern Worthington, Aug. 18, 1957; children: Laura, Joyce, Tamara. AA, Graceland Coll., 1955; MD, U. Mo., 1960. Diplomate Am. Bd. Pediatrics, Am. Bd. Pediatric Endocrinology; cert. Nat. Bd. for Diabetes Educators. Intern US Naval Hosp., Camp Pendleton, Calif., 1960-61, dir. dependent svcs. Sangley Point, Philippines, 1961-63; asst. instr., resident in pediatrics U. Mo., 1963-65, NIH fellow in endocrinology and metabolism, 1965-68, asst. prof., dir. newborn svcs., 1968-71, assoc. prof. pediat., 1971-73; prof., chmn. dept. pediatrics U. Kans. Med. Sch., Wichita, 1973-82; exec. dir. Kans. Regional Diabetes Ctr., Wichita, 1982-84; pres. Mid-Am. Diabetes Assocs., Wichita, 1984—. Dir. Robert L. Jackson Diabetes Treatment, Edn. and Rsch. Ctr., 1985—. Author: Nursing Management in Diabetes Mellitus, 1976, 1997, 2003, The Child with Diabetes, 1970, Physiologic Management of Diabetes in Children, 1986, Diabetes Source Book, 1990, 2003; mem. editl. bd.: Practical Diabetology, 1982—92, Diabetes Self-Management, 1984—97, Diabetes Educator, 1985—89, assoc. editor: Diabetes Spectrum, 2000—05; contbr. articles to profl. jours. Mem. health ministries bd. Reorganized Ch. Jesus Christ Latter-day Saints; mem. adv. bd. Kans. Action for Children, 1978—, Kans. State Diabetes, 1988-93, 95—. With USN, 1960-63. Recipient grants NIH, 1968—, Outstanding Faculty award Wichita State U., 1976, 2000, Disting. alumnus award Graceland Coll., 1984, Humanitarian award Wesley Med. Found., 1997, award for outstanding cmty. svc. Am. Diabetes

Assn., 2001; Dr. McIver Furman Disting. lectureship in health scis. Del Mar Coll., Corpus Christi, Tex., 1986. Fellow Am. Acad. Pediatrics, Am. Coll. Endocrinology; mem. AMA, Am. Diabetes Assn. (bd. dirs. 1972-77, Outstanding Contbn. to Camping award 1992, Outstanding award for Reaching People 2003, Outstanding Physician Clinician award 2003), Kans. Diabetes Assn. (pres. 1974, chmn. bd. 1974-77, 85-87), Kans. State Med. Soc., Sedgewick County Med. Soc., Am. Pediat. Soc., Soc. Pediat. Rsch., Wichita Pediat. Soc. (bd. dirs. 1988, pres. 1990-92), Lawson Wilkins Pediat. Endocrinology Soc., Midwest Soc. Pediat. Rsch., Internat. Soc. for Pediat. and Adolescent Diabetes (edn. com. 1995—), Am. Assn. Diabetes Educators (bd. dirs. 1994-97), Am. Assn. Clin. Endocrinology 1992—), Endocrine Soc., Sigma Xi, Alpha Omega Alpha. Office: Mid-Am Diabetes Assocs 200 S Hillside St Wichita KS 67211-2127 Home: 2300 N Tyler Rd Apt 108 Andover KS 67205 Office Phone: 316-687-3100. Personal E-mail: rag33@hotmail.com.

GUTHRIE, ROY A., financial company executive; B Econs., Hanover Coll.; MBA, Drake U. CPA, Tex. Planning analyst consumer fin. operation Assoc. First Capital Corp., Irving, Tex., 1977-78, exec. v.p. subs. Assoc. Ins. Group, 1988-95, exec. v.p. subs. Assoc. Real Estate Fin. Svcs. Co., 1988-95, sr. v.p., comptr., 1988-95, sr. v.p. prin. domestic subs. Assoc. Corp. N.Am., 1988-95, exec. v.p., 1995-96, CFO, sr. exec. v.p., 1996—2001; pres., CEO, CitiCapital Citigroup, Inc., 2001, pres., CEO, CitiFinancial Internat., 2001; exec. v.p., CFO Discover Fin. Services div., Morgan Stanley. Bd. dirs. Dallas Zool. Soc., United Way Met. Dallas. Office: Discover Fin Services 2500 Lake Cook Rd Riverwoods IL 60015

GUTIERREZ, LUIS V., congressman, elementary education educator; b. Chgo., Dec. 10, 1953; m. Soraida Aracho; children: Omaira, Jessica. BA magna cum laude in English, Northeastern Ill. U., 1975. Social worker Ill. Dept. Children and Family Svcs.; adminstrv. asst. Mayor's Subcom. on Infrastructure, 1984-85; alderman for 26th ward Chgo. City Coun., 1986-93, pres. pro tempore, 1992; mem. U.S. Congress from 4th Ill. Dist., 1993—; mem. banking and fin. svcs. com., vet. affair com. Chmn. Housing, Land Acquisition and Disposition com., 1989—93. Democrat. Office: US Ho Reps 2367 Rayburn House Off Bldg Washington DC 20515-1304

GUTKNECHT, GIL (GILBERT WILLIAM GUTKNECHT JR), former congressman, former state legislator; b. Cedar Falls, Iowa, Mar. 20, 1951; s. Gilbert William Sr. and Joan (Kerns) G.; m. Mary Catherine Keefe, June 3, 1972; children: Margaret, Paul, Emily. BA, U. No. Iowa, 1973. Sales rep. J. S. Latta, Cedar Falls, 1973-78, Valley Sch. Supplies, Appleton, Wis., 1978-81; auctioneer Rochester, Minn., 1978-95; mem. Minn. Ho. Reps. from Dist. 30A, Rochester, 1982-95, floor leader, 1990—94; mem. US Congress from 1st Minn. dist., 1995—2007, mem. sci. com., budget com., agriculture com., standards com., human resources com., govt. reform com., 1997—, chmn. dairy nutrition & forestry com. Chair Minn. Presdl. Campaign of Rep. Jack F. Kemp, 1988. Named Guardian of Small Bus., Nat. Fedn. Independence Bus., 2002; recipient Friend of the Farm Bur. award, Minn. Farm Bur. Fedn., 2002, Taxpayers Friend award, Nat. Taxpayers Union, 2003. Republican. Roman Catholic. Avocations: fishing, boating, baseball.

GUTMANN, DAVID LEO, psychology professor; b. NYC, Sept. 17, 1925; s. Isaac and Masha (Agronsky) G.; m. Joanna Redfield, Aug. 18, 1951; children: Stephanie, Ethan. MA, U. Chgo., 1956, PhD, 1958. Lectr. psychology Harvard U., Cambridge, Mass., 1960-62; prof. U. Mich., Ann Arbor, 1962-76, Northwestern U., Chgo., 1976-97, prof. emeritus, 1998—, chief of psychology, 1976-81, dir. older adult program, 1978-95. Vis. emeritus prof. Hebrew U., Jerusalem, 1997. Author: Reclaimed Powers: Toward a New Psychology of Men and Women in Later Life, 1987, Reclaimed Powers: Men and Women in Later Life, 1994, The Human Elder in ature, Culture, and Society, 1997; co-author: (with Bardwick, Douvan and Horner) Feminine Personality and Conflict, 1979. With U.S. Mcht. Marine, 1943-46. Recipient Career Devel. award, NIMH, 1964—74. Fellow Gerontol. Soc. Am.; mem. Am. Vets. of Israel, Nat. Assn. Scholars. Jewish. Home: 277 W Hill Rd Wallingford VT 05773-9479 Home Phone: 802-446-2923. Personal E-mail: dgutmann2004@yahoo.com.

GUTOWICZ, MATTHEW FRANCIS, JR., radiologist; b. Camden, NJ, Feb. 23, 1945; s. Matthew F. and A. Patricia (Walczak) G.; m. Alice Mary Bell, June 27, 1977; 1 child, Melissa. BA, Temple U., 1968; DO, Phila. Coll. Osteo. Medicine, 1972. Diplomate Am. Bd. Radiology, Am. Bd. Nuclear Medicine. Intern Mercy Hosp., Denver, 1972-73; resident in diagnostic radiology Hosp. of U. Pa., Phila., 1973-76, fellow in nuclear medicine, 1976-77; chief dept. radiology and nuclear medicine Fisher Titus Med. Ctr., Norwalk, Ohio, 1977—; pres. Firelands Radiology, Inc., Norwalk, 1977—. Ptnr. Pacifica Seafood Restaurant, Palm Desert, Calif. Republican. Roman Catholic. Avocations: photography, tennis, scuba diving. Home: 23 Patrician Dr Norwalk OH 44857-2463 Office Phone: 419-668-8101 x 6205. Personal E-mail: matthewg@neo.rr.com.

GUTTAU, MICHAEL K., state agency administrator, banker; b. Council Bluffs, Iowa, Nov. 8, 1946; s. Detlef Hugo and Ethel Evelyn (Schmidt) G.; m. Judith Ann Frazier, June 28, 1968; children: Heidi Ann, Joshua Michael. BS in Farm Operation, Iowa State U., 1969; postgrad., U. Nebr., Omaha, 1975. Adminstrv. asst. to dean students, asst. instr. sociology Iowa State U., Ames, 1969; trainee, asst. cashier, cashier Treynor (Iowa) State Bank, 1972-78, pres., chmn., CEO, 1978—. Appt. Iowa Supt. Banking, 1995; bd. dirs. Mercy Midlands Corp., Omaha; advisor N.Y. Fed. Res. Bank, Russian Am. Bankers Forum Acad. for Advanced Studies in Banking and Fin.; presenter Internat. Russian Banking Conf. 1992-93, mem. steering com., 1992-93; mem. U.S. Dept. State-U.S./Slovakian Counterpart Team Agr. Fin. and Credit. Chmn. steering com. Pottawattamie County Riverbend Indsl. Site, Western Iowa Devel. Assn., Mercy Hosp., Council Bluffs, Treynor Cmty. Devel. Com.; bd. dirs. Deaf Missions Worldwide Christian Ministry for Deaf; mem. youth com. Pottawattamie County 4-H; founder, pres., bd. dirs. Treynor Devel. Found. Corp.; deacon, moderator, adult and H.S. Sunday sch. tchr. Zion Congl. Ch., Treynor. With U.S. Army, 1969-72, Vietnam; with Nebr. Army NG, 1972-80. Decorated DFC with oak leaf cluster, Bronze Star, Air medal with V device, 28 Air medals; Recipient Outstanding Citizen award Treynor Town and Country Club, Swords to Plowshares award Bus.-Banks Exch. Newspaper, Moscow, 1992. Mem. Am. Bankers Assn. (chmn. future of cmty. banking study, cmty. bankers adv. bd. and coun., dir. edn. coun., mem. adminstrv. com. govt. rels. com.), Iowa Bankers Assn. (pres.-elect 1994-95, chmn. legis. com., bd. dirs.), S.W. Iowa Bank Adminstrn. Inst. (pres.), Treynor Bus. Assn. (founder, past pres., bd. dirs.), Scabbard and Blade, Gamma Gamma, Theta Delta Chi. Republican. Avocation: aviation.

GUTTENBERG, ALBERT ZISKIND, planning educator; b. Chelsea, Mass., Nov. 6, 1921; s. Harry and Edith (Bernstein) G.; m. Mariella Mascardi, June 29, 1964. AB in Social Rels., Harvard U., 1948; postgrad. in sociology, U. Chgo., 1949-51; postgrad. in city planning, U. Pa., 1958-59. Planning asst. Planning Bd., City of Portland, Maine, 1954-56; planning analyst Planning Commn., City of Phila., 1956-60; chief gen. plans and programming sect. Comprehensive Planning div., 1960-61; sr. planner Nat. Capital Downtown Com., Washington, 1962-63; assoc. prof. urban planning U. Ill., 1964-69, prof. urban and regional planning, 1969-89; chair in urban and regional renewal Dept. Geodesy, Delft U. Tech., The Netherlands, 1977-78. Cons. in field. Author: (with others) Explorations into Urban Structure, 1964, New Directions in Land use Classification, 1965, (with others) Human Ecology, 1975, The Language of Planning, 1993, The Land Utilization Movement of the 1920s; editor Planning and Public Policy, 1974-89; contbr. articles on land use planning to profl. pubs. Served with U.S. Army, 1942-46. Guggenheim fellow, 1970-71; Brookings Inst. guest scholar, 1970-71; Gelderman Fund grantee Delft U. Tech., 1977; German Marshall Fund Travel grantee, Holland, 1979; recipient Fulbright Travel award Italy, 1986. Mem. Am. Planning Assn., Am. Inst. Cert. Planners (coll. fellows), Soc. Am. City and Regional Planning History, Fulbright Alumni Assn. Home: 711 Hamilton Dr Champaign IL 61820-6811 Office: 111 Temple Hoyne Buell Hall 611 E Lorado Taft Dr Champaign IL 61820-6921

GUTWEIN, ERIC A., state representative; Pres., CEO Fred Gutwein & Sons, Francesville, Ind.; pres. Flora (Ind.) Seeds, FG&S Trucking, Francesville; state rep. dist. 16 Ind. Ho. of Reps., Indpls., 2002—, mem. labor and employment, and human affairs coms. Republican. Office: Ind Ho of Reps 200 W Washington St Indianapolis IN 46202-2786

GUY, RALPH B., JR., federal judge; b. Detroit, Aug. 30, 1929; s. Ralph B. and Shirley (Skladd) G. AB, U. Mich., 1951, JD, 1953. Bar: Mich. 1953. Sole practice, Dearborn, Mich., 1954—55; asst. corp. counsel City of Dearborn, 1955—58, corp. counsel, 1958—69; chief asst. US Atty.'s Office (ea. dist.), Detroit and Mich., 1968—70, U.S. Atty., 1970—76; judge US Dist. Ct. (ea. dist.) Mich., Ann Arbor, 1976—85, US Ct. Appeals (6th cir.), Ann Arbor, 1985—94, sr. judge, 1994—. Treas. Detroit-Wayne County Bldg. Authority, 1966—73; chmn. sch. study com. Dearborn Bd. Edn., 1973; mem. Fed. Exec. Bd., 1970—, bd. dirs., 1971—73. Recipient Civic Achievement award, Dearborn Rotary, 1971, Distinguished Alumni award, U. Mich., 1972. Mem.: FBA (pres. 1974—75), ABA (state chmn. sect. local govt. 1965—70), Cin. Bar Assn., Out-County Suprs. Assn. (pres. 1965), Mich. Municipal League, Mich. Assn. Municipal Attys. (pres. 1962—64), at. Inst. Municipal Law Officers (chmn. Mich. chpt. 1964—69), Am. Judicature Soc., Dearborn Bar Assn. (pres. 1959—60), Detroit Bar Assn., State Bar Mich. (commr. 1975—), U. Mich. Alumni Club (local pres. Dearborn 1961—62), Rotary (local pres. 1973—74), Lambda Chi Alpha, Phi Alpha Delta. Office: US Ct Appeals 200 E Liberty St Rm 226 Ann Arbor MI 48104 also: Potter Stewart US Courthouse 100 E 5th St Cincinnati OH 45202-3988

GUY, WILLIAM LEWIS, retired energy consultant, former governor; b. Devils Lake, ND, Sept. 30, 1919; s. William L. and Mable (Leet) G.; m. Jean Mason, Jan. 30, 1943; children: William III, James, Debby, Holly, Nancy. BS in Agrl. Econs., N.D. Agrl. Coll., 1941; MS in Agrl. Econs., U. Minn., 1946; PhD (hon.), N.D. State U., 1968, Concordia Coll., Moorhead, Minn., 1972. Asst. county agt. Agr. Extension Svc., Fargo, N.D., 1947; farmer Amenia, N.D., 1947-60; gov. State of .D., Bismarck, 1961-73; staff dir. Western Gov. Energy Office, Denver, 1975-77; exec. dir. N.D. Community Found., Casselton, N.D., 1978-79; energy cons. Basin Electric Coop., Bismarck, 1980-85; ret., 1985. Bd. dirs. Dakota Gasification Co., Bismarck. Mem. N.D. Ho. of Reps., Bismarck, 1958-59; chmn. Nat. Gov. Conf., 1967; chmn. Midwest Gov.'s Assn., 1962-63; mem. nat. bd. dirs. Common Cause, 1985-91; bd. dirs. Platte River Whooping Crane Trust, 1982-85. Lt. (s.g.) USN, 1943-45. Recipient Sioux award U. N.D., 1970, Alumni Achievement award N.D. State U., 1970, N.D. Leadership award N.D. State Legis., 1972, Silver Antelope award Boy Scouts Am., 1968. Mem. Toastmasters (pres. 1955-56, winner regional speech contest 1957), Farmer Union, Farm Bur., Elks. Democrat. Presbyterian. Avocations: sailing, golf.*

GUYURON, BAHMAN, plastic surgeon, educator; b. Tabriz, Iran, Mar. 24, 1946; MD, U. Tehran Med. Sch., 1971. Cert. Am. Bd. Surgery, Am. Bd. Plastic Surgery. Intern, craniofacial surgery Flushing Hosp., NY, 1973—74; resident, gen. surgery Boston U., 1974—78; resident, plastic surgery Cleve. Clinic Found., Ohio, 1978—80, dir., sect. craniofacial surgery Ohio, 1981—83; fellow, craniofacial surgery Toronto U. Hosp. for Sick Children, 1980—81; staff mem. Cleve. Clinic Hillcrest Hosp.; chief, divsn. plastic surgery Mt. Sinai Med. Ctr., 1986—93; med. dir. Zeeba Surgery Ctr., Lyndhurst, Ohio, 1997—; clin. prof., surgery Case Western Reserve U., Ohio; divsn. chief, plastic and reconstructive surgery U. Hosps. Cleve., Ohio, 2005—; pres. Bahman Guyuron MD, Inc., 1982—. Bd. dirs. Noteworthy Med. Sys., Inc.; independent dir., mem. stock option com. Morgan's Food Inc., Cleve., 2003—; presenter in field. Contbr. several articles to peer-reviewed jours., chapters to books; pub. two textbooks, sr. editor Aesthetic Surgery Jour. Mem.: Aesthetic Surgery Edn. and Rsch. Found. (pres.-elect), Am. Assn. Plastic Surgeons (trustee), Plastic Surgery Endowment Fund (trustee), Plastic Surgery Edn. Found. (trustee), Am. Soc. Plastic Surgery (trustee), Northeast Ohio Soc. for Plastic and Reconstructive Surgery (pres.), Ohio Soc. for Plastic and Reconstructive Surgeons, Rhinoplasty Soc., Am. Soc. Maxillofacial Surgeons (past pres.), Am. Bd. Plastic Surgery (dir.). Achievements include being one of the leaders in the investigation and surgical treatment of migraine headaches; invention of multiple medical and non-medical devices. Office: 29017 Cedar Rd Lyndhurst OH 44124 Office Phone: 440-461-7999. Office Fax: 440-461-4713.*

GYSBERS, NORMAN CHARLES, counselor, educator; b. Waupun, Wis., Sept. 29, 1932; s. George S. and Mabel (Landaal) Gysbers; m. Mary Lou Ziegler, June 23, 1954 (dec. July 1997); children: David(dec.), Debra, Daniel; m. Barbara K. Townsend, May 12, 2001. AB, Hope Coll., 1954; MA, U. Mich., 1959, PhD, 1963. Tchr. Elem. and Jr. H.S., Muskegon Heights, Mich., 1954-56; lectr. edn. U. Mich., 1962-63; prof. counseling psychology U. Mo., Columbia, 1963—, now curators' prof. Cons. U.S. Office Edn.; mem. nat. adv. coms. ERIC Clearinghouses in Career Edn. and Counseling and Pers. Svcs.; rsch. and devel. com. for CEEB, Am. Insts. for Rsch. Project on Career Decision Making, Comprehensive Career Edn. Model, TV Career Awareness Project KCET-TV, L.A.; dir. 10 nat. rsch. projects and state projects in career devel.-guidance; Francqui prof. Universite Libre de Bruxelles. Editor: Vocat. Guidance Quar. 1962-70; (with L. Sunny Hansen) spl. issue Personnel and Guidance Jour., May 1975, Jour. Career Devel., 1979-, (with E. Moore and W. Miller) Developing Careers in the Elementary School, 1973, (with E. Moore and H. Drier) Career Guidance: Practices and Perspectives, 1973; author: (with E. Moore) Improving Guidance Programs, 1981, Designing Careers, 1984, (with E. Moore) Career Counseling, 1987, (with P. Henderson) Developing and Managing Your School Guidance Program, 1988, 4th edit., 2006, (with C. McDaniels) Counseling for Career Development, 1992, (with P. Henderson) Guidance Programs that Work, 1997, (with M. Heppner and J. Johnston) Career Counseling, 1998, 2d edit., 2003 (translated into Italian, Japanese, Korean and Chinese), (with P. Henderson) Leading and Managing Your School Guidance Program Staff, 1998, (with P. Henderson) Implementing Comprehensive School Guidance Programs, 2002; contbr. articles to profl. jours. and chpts. to textbooks. Elder Presbyn. Ch. Served with arty. U.S. Army, 1956-58. Recipient Am. Spirit award, USAF, 1987, Pillar of Excellence Ten Yr. award, Coll. Edn. U. Mo., 2003, Excellence in Tchg. award, Gov., 2004; William T. Kemper Excellence in Tchg. fellow, U. Mo., 2002. Mem.: ACA (pres. 1977—78, disting. profl. svc. award 1983), Internat. Assn. Ednl. and Vocat. Guidance, Mo. Guidance Assn. (outstanding svc. award 1978), Am. Vocat. Assn. (v.p. 1979—82, merit award guidance divsn. 1978), Am. Sch. Counselor Assn. (post-secondary sch. counselor of yr. 2001, Mary Geheke Lifetime Achievement award 2004), Assn. for Counselor Edn. and Supervision, Nat. Career Devel. Assn. (pres. 1972—73, nat. merit award 1981, Eminent Career award 1989). Home: 4 Bingham Rd Columbia MO 65203 Office: U Mo 201 G Student Success Ctr Columbia MO 65211-6060 Office Phone: 573-882-6386. E-mail: gysbersn@missouri.edu.

HAAN, PHILIP C., air transportation executive; married; 2 children. BA in Biology and Chemistry, Calvin Coll., Grand Rapids, Mich.; MS in Indsl. Adminstrn., Purdue U., West Lafayette, Ind. Various positions Ford Motor Co., Am. Airlines; with NW Airlines Corp., 1991-95, v.p. revenue mgmt., v.p. inventory sales and systems, v.p. pricing and area mktg., sr. v.p., internat., 1995-99, exec. v.p. internat., sales and info. svcs., 1999—2004, exec. v.p. internat., alliances and info. tech., chmn. NW Cargo, 2004—. Co-chair alliance steering com. KLM Royal Dutch Airlines; pres. Narita Radisson Hotel. Mem. internat. adv. bd. U. Minn. Carlson Sch. Mgmt. Office: NW Airlines Corp 2700 Lone Oak Pky Eagan MN 55121 Office Phone: 612-726-2111.

HAAS, BILL, state legislator; b. June 25, 1949; m. Joenie Haas; 2 children. AA, U. Minn., 1969. Employee benefits broker, 1971—; rep. Dist. 48A Minn. Ho. of Reps., 1994—, vice chair ways and means com.; mem. commerce, health and human svcs. coms.; mem. environment and natural resources com.

HAAS, HOWARD GREEN, retired bedding manufacturing company executive; b. Chgo., Apr. 14, 1924; s. Adolph and Marie (Green) H.; m. Carolyn Werbner, June 4, 1949; children: Jody, Jonathan Student, U. Chgo., 1942; BBA, U. Mich., 1948. Promotion dir. Esquire, Inc., Chgo., 1949—50; advt. mgr. Mitchell Mfg. Co., Chgo., 1950—52, v.p. advt., 1952—56, v.p. sales, 1956—58; sales mgr. Sealy, Inc., Chgo., 1959—60, v.p. mktg., 1960—65, exec. v.p., 1965—67, pres., treas., 1967—86, 1987. Bd. dirs. Brogden Tool & Die Co., Aurora Custom Machinery, Inc.; adj. prof. strategic mgmt. U. Chgo. Grad. Sch. Bus., 1989—. Author: The Leader Within, 1993 Past mem. nominating com. Glencoe Sch. Bd.; mem. print and drawing com. Art Inst. Chgo.; past chmn. parent's com. Washington U., St. Louis; past bd. dirs. Jewish Children's Bur.; mem. vis. com. Oriental Inst., U. Chgo.; past pres. Orch. of Ill. (Chgo. Philharm). 1st lt. USAAF, 1943-45, ETO Decorated Air medal with 3 oak leaf clusters; recipient Brotherhood award NCCJ, 1970, Human Rels. award Am. Jewish Com., 1977 Mem. Nat. Assn. Bedding Mfrs. (past vice chmn., trustee), Birchwood Tennis Club (Highland Park, Ill.), Masons Jewish. Personal E-mail: hghhaas@aol.com.

HAASE, ASHLEY THOMSON, microbiology professor, researcher; b. Chgo., Dec. 8, 1939; s. Milton Conrad and Mary Elizabeth Minter (Thomson) H.; m. Ann DeLong, 1962; children: Elizabeth, Stephanie, Harris. BA, Lawrence Coll., 1961; MD, Columbia U., 1965. Intern Johns Hopkins Hosp., Balt., 1965—67; clin. assoc. Nat. Inst. Allergy and Infectious Disease, Bethesda, Md., 1967—70; vis. scientist Nat. Inst. Med. Rsch., London, 1970—71; chief infectious disease sect. VA Med. Ctr., San Francisco, 1971—84, med. investigator, 1978—83; prof. microbiology U. Minn., Mpls., 1984—99, head dept., 1984—, Regents' prof., 1999—. Mem. fellowship screening com. Am. Cancer Soc., San Francisco, 1978-81; mem. UNESCO Internat. Cell Rsch. Orgn., India, 1978; mem. nat. adv. coun. Nat. Inst. Allergy and Infectious Diseases, 1986-91, mem. task force on microbiology and infectious diseases, 1991, Method to Extend Rsch. in Time investigator, 1989—, chair AIDS rsch. adv. com., 1993-96, chmn. vaccine subcom.; Javits neurosci. investigator Nat. Inst. Neurol. and Communicative Disorders and Stroke, 1988-95; chmn. panel on AIDS, 1988-95, U.S.-Japan Coop. Med. Sci. Program, 1988-95, chair US Delegation, 2005-; mem. OAR AIDS Rsch. Evaluation Working Group, 1995-96; mem. adv. com. for career awards in biomed. scis. Burroughs-Wellcome Fund, 1995-2000; trustee Lawrence U., 1997-2000; adv. coun. IH Office AIDS Rsch., 2002—05, Inst. Medicine, 2003—. Editor: Microbial Pathogenesis, 1988-94; contbr. articles on AIDS pathogenesis and other topics in neurovirology to profl. jours. Recipient Lucia R. Briggs Disting. Achievement award Lawrence Coll., 1990. Mem. AAAS (coun. del. sect.on med. scis. 2006—), Am. Soc. Microbiology, Assn. Am. Physicians, Am. Soc. Clin. Investigation, Am. Soc. Virology, Assn. Med. Schs. Microbiology Chmn., Infectious Diseases Soc. Am., Nat. Multiple Sclerosis Soc. (adv. com. 1978-84), Am. Assn. Immunologists, Phi Beta Kappa, Alpha Omega Alpha Democrat. Home: 14 Buffalo Rd Saint Paul MN 55127-2136 Office: U Minn Dept Microbiology 420 Delaware St SE Minneapolis MN 55455-0374 Business E-Mail: haase001@umn.edu.

HABECKER, EUGENE BRUBAKER, academic administrator; b. Hershey, Pa., June 17, 1946; s. Walter Eugene and Frances (Miller) H.; m. Marylou Napolitano, July 27, 1968; children: David, Matthew, Marybeth. AB, Taylor U., 1968; MA, Ball State U., 1969; JD, Temple U., 1974; PhD, U. Mich., 1981. Bar: Pa. 1974. Asst. dean Ea. Univ., St. Davids, Pa., 1970-74; dean students, asst. prof. polit. sci. George Fox U., Newberg, Oreg., 1974-78; exec. v.p. Huntington (Ind.) Coll., 1979-81, pres., 1981-91; pres, CEO Am. Bible Soc., NYC, 1991—2005; pres. Taylor U., 2005—. Evaluation cons. North Ctrl. Assn., Chgo., 1982-91; dir. Christian Colls. and Univs., Washington, 1982-88; bd. dirs. Christianity Today Internat., United Bible Socs. internat. exec. com., 1992-2001, LeTourneau U.; pres. Taylor U., 2005. Author: Affirmative Action in Independent College, 1977, The Other Side of Leadership, 1987, Leading With a Follower's Heart, 1990, Rediscovering the Soul of Leadership, 1996; contbr. articles to profl. jours. Recipient Christian Mgmt. award Christian Mgmt. Assn., 1989. Mem. Nat. Assn. Intercollegiate Athletes (coun. of pres.' 1985-90), Nat. Assn. Evangs. (bd. dirs. 1985-90), Christian Mgmt. Assn. Republican. Presbyterian.*

HABEL, CHRISTOPHER S., lawyer; b. Cin., Oct. 14, 1969; BS in Civil and Environ. Engring., U. Cin., 1992; JD, Ohio State U., 1995. Bar: Ohio 1995, US Dist. Ct. (no. dist.) Ohio 1999, US Dist. Ct. (so. dist.) Ohio 1999, US Ct. of Appeals (6th cir.). Ptnr. Frost Brown Todd LLC, Cin. Bd. dirs., pres. Valley View Found.; mem. Hamilton County Earthworks Appeals Bd.; mem. steering com. Met. Sewer Dist., Cin. Named Leading Lawyer in Environ. Law, Chambers USA, 2006; named one of Best Lawyers in Am., 2005, 2006, Ohio's Rising Stars, Super Lawyers, 2005, 2006. Mem.: ABA, Cin. Acad. Leadership for Lawyers, Cin. Bar Assn. (chair environ. law com. 2004—05), Ohio State Bar Assn. (mem. environ. law com.), Chi Epsilon. Office: Frost Brown Todd LLC 2200 PNC Ctr 201 E Fifth St Cincinnati OH 45202-4182 Office Phone: 513-651-6993. Office Fax: 513-651-6981. E-mail: chabel@fbtlaw.com.

HABEN, MARY KAY, candy company executive; b. Chgo., Apr. 12, 1956; d. Mitchell and Helen (Wrobleuski) Kretch; m. Edward Raymond Haben, Dec. 18, 1982; 1 child, Michael William. BSBA, U. Ill., 1977; MBA, U. Mich., 1979. Mktg. rsch asst. Kraft Foods Inc., Glenview, Ill., 1979-80, assoc. br. mgr., 1980-82, br. mgr., 1982-84, category mgr., 1984-88, exec. v.p., pres. Kraft Cheese divsn., 1998—2000, group v.p., pres. Kraft Cheese Mex. & Puerto Rico, 2000—01, group v.p., pres. cheese, enhancers & meals, 2001—04, sr. v.p. global convenience meals grocery & snacks sector, 2004—06; group v.p., mng. dir N. Am. The William Wrigley Jr. Co., Chgo., 2007—. Bd. dirs. Liz Claiborne, Inc., 2004—. Named one of 100 Best and Brighest Women in Advtg. Advertising Age Mag., 1988, 100 Best Mgrs. in the U.S. Bus. Month Mag., 1989, 40 Women Under AO Savvy Mag., 40 Under 40 to Watch Crain's Chgo. Bus., 1990. Avocations: sports, reading, travel. Office: The William Wrigley Jr & Co 410 N Michigan Ave Chicago IL 60611

HABERMAN, F. WILLIAM, lawyer; b. Princeton, NJ, Apr. 20, 1940; s. Frederick William and Louise (Power) H.; m. Carmen Marie Duffy, June 15, 1963; children: Frederick, Sarah. BA, U. Wis., 1962; LLB, Harvard Law Sch., 1965. Bar: Wis. 1965, Fla. 1993, U.S. Dist. Ct. (ea. dist.) Wis. 1966, U.S. Dist. Ct. (we. dist.) Wis. 1967. Ptnr. Michael, Best & Friedrich, Milw., 1965—. Bd. dirs. U. Wis. Milw. Found., 2003—. Co-author: Marital Property Law in Wisconsin, 1986. Trustee Pub. Policy Forum, Milw., 1998—; bd. dirs. Ctrl. YMCA, Milw., 1988-93, Richard and Ethel Herzfeld Found., Milw., 1985—, Wis. affiliate Am. Heart Assn., 1993-97; mem. Greater Milw. Com., 2000—; mem. adv. bd. Milw. Fair Housing Coun., 1989-90; mem. deferred giving adv. bd. Milw. Sch. Engring., 1989-93; bd. dirs. Milw. Children's Hosp. Found., 1994-98, Milw. Repertory Theater, 1997-2002. Fellow Am. Coll. Trust & Estate Counsel; mem. ABA, Wis. Bar Assn., Phi Beta Kappa. Home: 2727 E Shorewood Blvd Milwaukee WI 53211-2459 Office: Michael Best & Friedrich 100 E Wisconsin Ave Ste 3300 Milwaukee WI 53202-4108 Office Phone: 414-271-6560.

HABERMAN, JEREMY, music venue executive; b. 1972; Pres. Haberman Productions Inc., Ferndale, Mich.; co-founder The Magic Bag, The Bosco. Named one of 40 Under 40, Crain's Detroit Bus., 2006. Office: The Magic Bag 22920 Woodward Ave Ferndale MI 48220

HACHEY, GUY C., electronics executive; b. Charlemagne, Que., Can. Student, St. Jean Mil. Coll., Can., 1973—76; B in Commerce, McGill U., 1978; MBA, Concordia U., Montreal, 1984; grad. Tuck Exec. Devel. Program, Dartmouth Coll., 1994. Various pos., including supr., gen. supr. prodn., area mgr. trim assembly, dir. mfg. engring., gen. supt. mfg. GM, Therese, Que., Canada, 1978—89, plant mgr. Oshawa fabrication plant to prodn. mgr. car assembly plants, 1989—92; dir. mfg. ops. for heating, ventilating and air conditioning/heat exchangers bus. unit Delphi Thermal Systems, Lockport, NY, 1992—94, dir. mfg. ops. Pontiac, Mich., 1994—95; mfg. mgr. worldwide ops. Delphi Interior Syhstems, Pontiac, Mich., 1995—98; gen. mgr. Delphi Chassis Systems, Pontiac, Mich., 1998; pres. Delphi Energy & Chassis Systems, Troy, Mich., 1998—; v.p. Delphi Corp., Troy, Mich., 1998—. Office: World Hdqrs Delphi Corp 5725 Delphi Dr Troy MI 48098-2815 also: Delphi Energy & Chassis Systems 5725 Delphi Dr Bldg D Troy MI 48098

HACHTEN, RICHARD ARTHUR, II, healthcare system executive; b. LA, Mar. 24, 1945; s. Richard A. and Dorothy Margaret (Shipley) H.; m. Jeanine Hachten, Dec. 12, 1970; children: Kristianne, Karin. BS in Econs., U. Calif., Santa Barbara, 1967; MBA, UCLA, 1969. Mgmt. intern TRW Systems Group, Redondo Beach, Calif., 1969-72; adminstrv. asst. Meth. Hosp., Arcadia, Calif., 1972-73, asst. adminstr., 1973-74, assoc. adminstr., 1974-76, v.p. adminstrn., 1976-80; exec. v.p., adminstr., 1980-81; pres., adminstr., 1981-84; CEO Tri-City Hosp. Dist., Oceanside, 1984-91; pres. Bergan Mercy Health Sys., Omaha, 1991-95, Algent Health, Omaha, 1996—. Instr. health care mgmt. Pasadena (Calif.) City Coll. Bd. dirs., pres. Hospice of Pasadena, Inc.; bd. dirs. ARC, Arcadia, Mercy Housing Midwest, Omaha, Metropolitan Cmty. Coll. Found.; bd. governing mems. Omaha Symphony. Fellow Am. Coll. Healthcare Execs.; mem. Hosp. Coun. San Diego and Imperial Counties (chmn., bd. dirs.), Nebr. Hosp. Assn. (chmn. bd. dirs., chmn. dist. 1), Calif. Assn. Hosps. and Health Sys. (bd. dirs.), Am. Hosp. Assn. (policy bd. mem.), Rotary, Beta Gamma Sigma. Republican. Methodist. Office: Algent Health Ste 200 1010 N 96th St Omaha NE 68114-2595 Home: 1910 S 183rd Cir Omaha NE 68130-2769 Home Phone: 402-393-6988; Office Phone: 402-343-4420. Business E-Mail: rhachten@alegent.org.

HACKBARTH, TOM, former state legislator; b. Dec. 28, 1951; m. Mary Hackbarth; 3 children. Student, North Hennepin C.C. Rep. Dist. 50A Minn. Ho. of reps., 1994-96, 98—. Vice chair environment and natural resources fin. com.; mem. environment and natural resources policy com., jobs econ. devel. policy com. Office: 100 Constitution Ave Saint Paul MN 55155-1232

HACKEL, EMANUEL, science educator; b. Bklyn., June 17, 1925; s. Henry N. and Esther (Herbstman) H.; m. Elisabeth Mackie, June 24, 1950 (dec. Apr. 1978); children: Lisa M., Meredith Anne, Janet M.; m. Rachel A. Fisher, Oct. 18, 1981; stepchildren: Daniel E., Tabitha A., and Jessica K. Harrison. Student, .Y. U., 1941—42; BS, U. Mich., 1948, MS, 1949; PhD, Mich. State U., 1953. Fisheries biologist Mich. Dept. Conservation, 1949; mem. faculty Mich. State U., East Lansing, 1949—, prof. natural sci., 1962-74, chmn. dept. natural sci., 1963-74, prof. medicine, 1974-95, prof. emeritus, 1995—, prof. zoology, 1974-95, prof. emeritus, 1995—. Asst. dean coll. 1958-63; rsch. fellow Galton Lab., U. Coll., London, 1970-71, 77-78; vis. investigator blood group rsch. unit Lister Inst., London, 1956-57; cons. Mpls. War Meml. Blood Bank, 1983-95. Author: Guide to Laboratory Studies in Biological Science, 1951, Studies in atural Science, 1953, Natural Science, 1955, Vols. 1, 2, 3, 1952-63. Editor: The Search for Explanation-Studies in Natural Science, Vols. 1, 2, 3, 1967-68, Laboratory Manual for Natural Science, Vol. 1, 2, 3, 1967-68, Human Genetics, 1974, Theoretical Aspects of HLA, 1982, Bone Marrow Transplantation, 1983, HLA Techniques for Blood Bankers, 1984, Human Genetics 1984: A Look at the Last Ten Years and the Next Ten, Transfusion Management of Some Common Heritable Blood Disorders, 1992, Advances in Transplantation, 1993, HLA Typing Section, Clinical Laboratory Medicine, 1994, Human Genetics '94: A Revolution in Full Swing, 1994; contbr. articles on genetics, human blood group immunology and chem. nature of blood group antigens, human biochem. genetics, tissue typing, human histocompatability antigens to sci. jours. Served to lt. (j.g.) USNR, 1943-47; now lt. comdr. USNR Ret. Recipient Cooley Meml. award Am. Assn. Blood Banks, 1969, Elliott Meml. award Am. Assn. Blood Banks, 1987, alumni disting. faculty award Coll. Natural Sci. Mich. State U., 1995. Mem. Assn. Gen. and Liberal Studies (sec.-treas. 1962-65), AAUP, AAAS, Genetics Soc. Am., Am. Soc. Human Genetics, Am. Assn. Blood Banks (dir. 1983-84, chmn. sci. sect. 1983-84), Mich. Assn. Blood Banks (v.p. 1970, pres. 1975-77), Am. Inst. Biol. Sci., Biometric Soc., Transplantation Soc. Mich. (dir. 1975-84), Am. Assn. for Clin. Histocompatability Testing, N.Y. Acad. Scis., Sigma Xi, Phi Kappa Phi. Home: 244 Oakland Dr East Lansing MI 48823-4747

HACKENAST, SHERRI, race track owner, former race car driver; b. Frankfort, Ill., Jan. 17, 1975; d. Frank and Michelle. Owner, promoter Kentucky Lake Speedway, Calvert City; promoter Kankakee Speedway, Ill.; CEO A-Reliable Auto Parts. Named one of 40 Under 40, Crain's Chgo. Bus., 2005. Avocations: camping, racing. Mailing: Sherri Hackenast Racing 2247 West 139th St Blue Island IL 60406 Office Phone: 708-641-9999. Office Fax: 708-824-9128. E-mail: raceteam99@aol.com, sherriheckenast@aol.com.

HACKER, DOUGLAS A., air transportation executive; BS, Princeton Univ.; MBA, Harvard Univ. Exec. v.p., CFO UAL Corp., Chgo., 1999—2001, exec. v.p., pres. UAL Loyalty Svc., 2001—02, exec. v.p., strategy, 2002—. Bd. mem. Steppenwolf Theatre Co.; Columbia Mgmt. Group. Office: UAL Corp 1200 E Algonquin Rd Elk Grove Village IL 60007

HACKETT, EARL RANDOLPH, neurologist; b. Moulmein, Burma, Feb. 16, 1932; s. Paul Richmond and Martha Jane (Lewis) H.; m. Shirley Jane Kanehl, May 25, 1953; children: ancy, Raymond, Susan, Lynn, Laurie, Richard, Alicia. BS, Drury Coll., Springfield, Mo., 1953; MD, Western Res. U., 1957. Diplomate Am. Bd. Psychiatry and eurology, Am. Bd. Electrodiagnostic Medicine. Intern, then resident in neurology Charity Hosp., New Orleans, 1957-62; resident in internal medicine VA Hosp., New Orleans, 1958-59; mem. faculty La. State U. Med. Sch., New Orleans, 1962—, prof. neurology, 1973-88, head dept., 1977-88; clin. prof. neurology U. Mo., Columbia, 1988—. Mem. med. adv. bd. Myasthenia Gravis Found. Fellow Am. Acad. Neurology; mem. Am. Assn. Electrodiagnostic Medicine, Soc. Clin. eurologists, Mo. Med. Assn., Greene County Med. Soc., AOA. Methodist. Home: 2517 S Brentwood Blvd Springfield MO 65804-3201 Office: 1965 S Fremont Ave Ste 2800 Springfield MO 65804-2258

HACKETT, JAMES P., manufacturing executive; b. Columbus, Ohio, Apr. 22, 1955; BA, U. Mich., 1977. With Proctor and Gamble Co., 1977-81; joined Steelcase Inc., Grand Rapids, Mich., 1981—, sr. v.p. sales and mktg., 1990—93, pres. Turnstone, 1993, exec. v.p. Steelcase Ventures, 1994; exec. v.p., CEO Steelcase N. Am., 1994, pres., CEO, 1994, Steelcase Inc., 1994—. Bd. dir. Northwestern Mutual Life, Fifth Third Bancorp. Mem., past pres. bd. overseers Inst. Design, Ill. Inst. Tech. Office: Steelcase Inc 901 44th St SE Grand Rapids MI 49508

HACKETT, JOHN THOMAS, retired economist and financial executive; b. Ft. Wayne, Ind., Oct. 10, 1932; s. Harry H. and Ruth (Greer) H.; m. Ann E. Thompson, July 24, 1954; children: Jane, David, Sarah, Peter. BS, Ind. U., 1954, MBA, 1958; PhD, Ohio State U., 1961. Instr. Ohio State U., 1958-61; asst. v.p., economist Fed. Res. Bank, Cleve., 1961-64; dir. planning Cummins Engine Co., Columbus, Ind., 1964-66, v.p. finance, 1966-71, exec. v.p., 1971-88, also dir.; v.p. fin. and adminstrn. Ind. U., Bloomington, 1988-91; mng. gen. ptnr. CID Equity Ptnrs., L.P., Indpls., 1991—2002, ret., 2002. Former chmn. bd. dirs. Wabash at. Corp.; bd. dirs. Intertnhen Arts Acad., New Hampsh Pub. Raglen. 1st lt. AUS, 1954-56. Mem.: Ind. Acad., Beta Gamma Sigma. Home: PO Box 466 Keene NH 03431 also: PO Box 100 Glen Arbor MI 49736

HACKETT, ROGER FLEMING, historian, educator; b. Kobe, Japan, Oct. 23, 1922; s. Harold Wallace and Anna Luena (Powell) H.; m. Caroline Betty Gray, Aug. 24, 1946; children: Anne Marilyn, David Gray, Brian Vance. BA, Carleton Coll., 1947; MA, Harvard U., 1949, PhD, 1955. Prof. history Northwestern U., Evanston, Ill., 1953-61; prof. history U. Mich., Ann Arbor, 1961-93, prof. emeritus, 1993—, chmn. dept., 1975-77; dir. Ctr. for Japanese Studies, 1968-71, 78, 79. Cons. Office of Edn., HEW; mem. sub-com., joint com. Social Sci. Rsch. Coun. Author: Yamagata Aritomo in the Rise of Modern Japan 1838-1922, 1971; Editor: Jour. Asian Studies, 1959-62; contbr. articles and chpts to profl. jours. and books. Served with USMC, 1942-46. Social Sci. Rsch. Coun. fellow; Japan Found. fellow; Fulbright-Hays fellow; fellow St. Antony's Coll. Oxford U. Mem. Japan Soc., Assn. Asian Studies (exec. com., bd. dirs. 1966-69), Internat. House of Japan, Ann Arbor Racquet Club, Phi Beta Kappa. Home: 2122 Dorset Rd Ann Arbor MI 48104-2604 Office: U Mich Dept History Ann Arbor MI 48109 Business E-Mail: fhackett@umich.edu.

HACKETT, WESLEY PHELPS, JR., lawyer; b. Detroit, Jan. 3, 1939; s. Wesley P. and Helen (Decker) H.; children: Kelly D. Hackett Pell, Robin C. Hackett Story. BA, Mich. State U., 1960; JD, Wayne State U., 1968. Bar: Mich. 1968, U.S. Dist. Ct. (we. dist.) Mich. 1971, U.S. Ct. Appeals (6th cir.) 1972, U.S. Dist. Ct. (ea. dist.) Mich. 1972, U.S. Supreme Ct. 1972, U.S. Ct. Mil. Appeals 1991. Law clk. Mich. Supreme Ct., Lansing, 1968-70; ptnr. Brown & Hackett, Lansing, 1971-73; pvt. practice Lansing, 1973-84; ptnr. Starr, Bissell & Hackett, Lansing, 1984-87; pvt. practice East Lansing, Mich., 1987-98, Saranac, Mich., 1998—. Adj. prof. Thomas M. Cooley Law Sch., Lansing, 1973—; instr. Lansing C.C., 1981-99. Author: Evidence: A Trial Manual for Michigan Lawyers, 1981, Hackett's Evidence: Michigan and Federal, 2d edit., 1995, Michigan Lawyers Manual Part L, 1994, revised, 2002; co-author: Hiring Legal Staff, 1990. Mem. City of East Lansing Planning Commn., 1969-72; mem. Village of Saranac Planning Commn., 2000—; bd. dirs. St. Vincent Home for Children, Lansing, 1974-82; vestry St. John's Episcopal Ch., Ionia, Mich., 2004-08, sr. warden, 2004-08, 1st lt. USAF, 1961-65. Fellow Coll. Law Practice Mgmt.; mem. State Bar Mich. (chair legal econs. sect. 1990-91). Home Phone: 616-642-9094; Office Phone: 616-642-6074.

HACKL, DONALD JOHN, architect; b. Chgo., May 11, 1934; s. John Frank and Frieda Marie Hackl; m. Bernadine Marie Becker, Sept. 29, 1962; children: Jeffrey Scott, Craig Michael, Cristina Lynn. BArch., U. Ill., 1957, MS in Architecture, 1958. With Loebl Schlossman & Hackl Architects, Chgo., 1963—, assoc., 1967-74, exec. v.p., dir., 1974, pres., dir., 1975—. Prof. architecture Internat. Acad. Architecture, Sofia, Bulgaria; mem. Nat. Coun. Archtl. Registration Bds., 1980—; bd. dirs. Chgo. Bldg. Congress, 1983-94, v.p., 1985-94; design juries include: Reynolds Metals, Western Mont. Regional Design, Am. Inst. Steel Constrn., Precast Concrete Inst., Okla. Soc. Architects, UIA Gold Medal (6), UIA Celebration of Cities (2), Seoul, Korea, 2004, Sewaen Dist. 4 Internat. Design Competition, 2004; chmn. Ariz. Soc. Architects, Midwest Design Conf., 1983; design critic dept. arch. U. Ill., 1975-76, 81; vis. critic sch. architecture U. Notre Dame, 1977-78, 80, 82; adj. prof. Kent Coll. Law, Ill. Inst. Tech., 1983—; adj. faculty Shenzhen U., China, 1998-; guest lectr. Tongi U., Shanghai, 2004; cons. Pub. Svcs. Adminstrn., Washington, 1974-76; cons. in field. Prin. works include Water Tower Place, Chgo., 1976, King Faisel Specialist Hosp. and Rsch. Ctr., Riyadh, Saudi Arabia, 1978, Household Internat. Hdqrs., Prospect Heights, Ill., 1978, Shriners Hosp. for Children, Chgo., 1979, Square D Co. Hdqrs., Palatine, Ill., 1979, West Suburban Hosp., Oak Park, Ill., 1981, Allstate Pla. West, Northbrook, Ill., 1990, Sears Roebuck & Co. stores of future concept, 1985-89, Ford City Shopping Ctr. Redevel., Chgo., 1989, Commerce Clearing House, Riverwoods, Ill., 1986, Physicians' Pavilion Greater Balt. Med. Ctr., 1987, Two Prudential Plaza, Chgo., 1990, City Place with Omni Hotel, Chgo., 1990, 350 N. LaSalle, Chgo., 1990, Infinitec, Assistive Tech. Application Ctr. for United Cerebral Palsy Assn., Chgo., 1992, Shenzhen AVIC Plaza Bldg., Shenzhen, China, 1993, Ill. State U. Biol. and Chemistry Scis. Lab. Bldg., Normal, 1995, Old Orchard Shopping Ctr. Redevel., Skokie, Ill., 1994, Sun Comml. City, Changchun, China, 1993, Shekou Harbor Bldg., Shenzhen, 1995, East Shanghai Film and TV Ctr., 1995, Luo-Hu Comml. Ctr., Shenzhen, 1994, Shenzhen Internat. Exch. Plz., 1996, Jin Hui Plz., Shanghai, 1996, Shenzhen Cultural Ctr., 1997, Changchun Sun Housing Estates, China, 1999, Hdqrs. for Almacenes Paris LTDA, Santiago, Chile, 1999, John H. Stroger, Jr. Hosp. of Cook Cty., 2002, Grand Pier Ctr., Chgo., 2004 Computer/Engring. Bldg. U. Ill., 1999—, Bank of Mauritius, Port Louis, 2006, Olympic Swimming Facility-Design Study, Tianjin, China, 2006, North Ctrl. Coll. Performing Arts Ctr., 2006, Riva de Lago: Lake of the Ozarks, 2007. Mem. Met. Am. Cancer Crusade, 1973; life trustee West Suburban Hosp., 1983—, mem. exec. com., 1986-87; vice chmn. North Ctrl. Coll., 1990-2005, life trustee, 2006—; mem. Pres.'s Coun. U. Ill. Found.; mem. curricula adv. com. Dept. Architecture, U. Ill.; bd. dirs. World Trade Ctr., Chgo., 1995—; dir. Chgo. Loop Alliance, 2006, Resurrection Healthcare Found., 2007. With Ill. Air Nat. Guard, 1957—63. Fellow AIA (treas. Chgo. chpt. 1977-78, exec. com. 1978-81, v.p. 1981, pres. 1981, bd. dirs. Chgo. AIA Found. 1981-83, nat. v.p. 1985, 1st v.p. 1986, nat. pres. 1987, chmn. design com. 1985, exec. com. 1985-87, bd. dirs. 1981-87, documents com. 1974-79, chmn. 1980, exec. com. AIA Svc. Corp. 1983-84, chmn. internat. com. 1987-91, exec. com. 2006, sec. exec. com. AIA Coll. Fellows 2006), Nat. Coun. Archtl. Registration Bds., Royal Archtl. Inst. Can. (hon.), Colegios Architectos Mexicanos (hon.), Internat. Acad. Architecture (hon., prof.), Korean Inst. Archs. (hon.); mem. Internat. Union Archs. (bd. dirs., del. 1987—, 1st v.p. 1990-93, coun. 1993-96, v.p. region III 1996-99, treas. 2000—), Union Bulgarian Archs. (hon.), Soc. Cuban Archs., Japan Inst. Archs. (hon.), Colegio Arquitectos Cochabamba (Bolivia), Colegios Arquitectos Espana (hon.), Instituto do Arquitectos do Brazil (hon.), Tavern Clubs, Carlton Club, Econ. Club, Lake Zurich Club. Office: Loebl Schlossman and Hackl Inc 233 N Michigan Ave ste 3000 Chicago IL 60601-5708 Office Phone: 312-565-4500. Business E-Mail: dhackl@lshchicago.com.

HACKMAN, LARRY J., program director, consulant; m. Sandra McFarland, 1966; children: Alex, Kate. LHD (hon.), U. Mo., 1998. Former archivist State of N.Y., John F. Kennedy Libr., others; asst. commr. of edn. for archives and records adminstrn. N.Y. State; dir. Harry S. Truman Presdl. Libr., Independence, Mo., 1995-2000; retired, 2000; cons, 2000—. Lectr. in field; Mellon fellow in Modern Archives, U. Mich., Littauer fellow Sch. of Govt. at Harvard; past mem. governing bd. Rockefeller Archives Ctr.; pres. Truman Libr. Inst., 1998-2000. Recipient Disting. Pub. Svc. award Rockefeller Coll. of Pub. Affairs, SUNY, Albany, Disting. Svc. award Nat. Hist. Publs. and Records Commn., 1999. Office: Harry S Truman Libr 500 W Us Highway 24 Independence MO 64050-2481

HADDAD, ABRAHAM HERZL, electrical engineering educator, researcher; b. Baghdad, Iraq, Jan. 16, 1938; came to U.S., 1963; s. Moshe M. and Masuda (Cohen) H.; m. Carolyn Ann Kushner, Sept. 9, 1966; children: Benjamin, Judith, Jonathan. BSEE, Technion-Israel Inst. Tech., Haifa, 1960, MSEE, 1963; MA in Elec. Engring., Princeton U., 1964, PhD in Elec. Engring., 1966. Asst. prof. elec. engring. U. Ill., Urbana, 1966-70, assoc prof., 1970-75, prof., 1975-81; sr. staff cons. Dynamics Research Corp., Wilmington, Mass., 1979; program dir. NSF, Washington, 1979-83; prof. Ga. Inst. Tech., Atlanta, 1983-88; prof., chmn. Dept. Elec. Engring and Computer Sci. Northwestern U., 1988-98, prof. Dept. Elec. Engring and Computer Sci., 1996—, interim chmn. Dept. Elec. Engring and Computer Sci., 2001—02, 2004—, dir. master info. and tech., 1998—. Dir. Computer Integrated Mfg. Sys. Program, 1987—88; adv. U.S. Army Missle Command, Huntsville, Ala., 1969—79; vis. assoc. prof. Tel Aviv U., Israel, 1972—73; cons. Lockheed-Ga. Co., 1984—88; gen chmn. Am. Control Conf., 1993; sec. Am. Automatic Control Coun., 1990—2003; chmn. policy com. Internat. Fedn. Automatic Control, 1996—2002, chmn. awards com., 2002—05, mem. coun., 2005—. Editor: on-linear Systems, 1975; assoc. editor Control Engring. Practice, 1999—. Fellow AAAS, IEEE (editor Trans. on Automatic Control 1983-89, Centennial medal 1984, mem. awards bd. 1997-99, third millenium medal 2000); mem. Control Systems Soc. of IEEE (gen. chair 1984 Conf. on Decision and Control, Disting. mem. award 1985, v.p. fin. affairs 1989-90, pres.-elect 1991, pres. 1992, assoc. editor at large Trans. Automatic Control 1998-2003, chair Axelby award com. 2002-05). Jewish. Office: Northwestern U Dept EECS Evanston IL 60208-3118 Home Phone: 847-432-3638; Office Phone: 847-491-8175. Business E-Mail: ahaddad@ece.northwestern.edu.

HADDAD, GEORGE ILYAS, engineering educator, director; b. Aindara, Lebanon, Apr. 7, 1935; came to U.S., 1952, naturalized, 1961; s. Elias Ferris and Fahima (Haddad) H.; m. Mary Louella Nixon, June 28, 1958; children: Theodore N., Susan Anne. BS in Elec. Engring, U. Mich., 1956, MS, 1958, PhD, 1963. Mem. faculty U. Mich., Ann Arbor, 1963—, assoc. prof., 1965-69, prof. elec. engring., 1968—, Robert J. Hiller prof., 1991—, dir. electron physics lab., 1968-75, chmn. dept. elec. engring. and computer sci., 1975-87, 91-97, dir. ctr. for high-frequency microelectronics, 1987—. Cons. to industry. Contbr. articles to profl. jours. Recipient Curtis W. McGraw research award Am. Soc. Engring, Edn., 1970, Excellence in Research award Coll. Engring., U. Mich., 1985, Disting. Faculty Achievement award U. Mich., 1985-86, S.S. Attwood award, 1991, MTT-S Disting. Educator award, 1996. Fellow IEEE (editor proc. and trans.); mem. NAE, Am. Soc. Engring. Edn., Am. Phys. Soc., Acad. Engring., Sigma Xi, Phi Kappa Phi, Eta Kappa Nu, Tau Beta Pi. Office: U Mich Dept Elec Engring & Computer Sci 2309 EECS 1301 Beal Ave Ann Arbor MI 48109-2122 E-mail: jih@umich.edu.

HADLEY, ROBERT JAMES, lawyer; b. Wilmington, Ohio, Oct. 27, 1938; s. Robert Edwin and Ethel Edith (Slade) H.; m. Judith Ellen Gilbert, Aug. 11, 1962; children: Scott, Laura, Stephen. BA in History cum laude, Ohio State U., 1960; LLB, Harvard U., 1963. Bar: Ohio 1963. Assoc. Smith & Schnacke, Dayton, 1963-69, ptnr., 1970-89, Thompson Hine LLP, Dayton, 1989—2003. Pres. Man-to-Man Assocs., 1978-84, Dayton Habitat for Humanity, 1988; v.p. COPE Halfway House, Dayton, 1982-85; dir., sec. Friendship Village of Dayton, 1985-2006; loaned exec. United Way, 1980-82, cabinet 2001-02; active Kettering Civic Band, 1968—; bd. dirs. Parish Resource Ctr., 1995-2005, pres., 1999-2000; bd. dirs. South Cmty. YMCA, 1996-98, Greater Dayton Youth for Christ, 1980-86; bd. dirs., sec. Ministry of Money, 1992—. Named Kettering Man of the Yr., 1986; Rotary Found. grantee, Israel, 1974. Mem. Dayton Bar Assn., Dayton Racquet Club, Rotary (pres. Kettering 1986-87, dist. gov., group rep. Dist. 6670 1989-90, dist. gov. 1993-94), Phi Beta Kappa. Methodist. Avocations: music, travel, sports. Home: 4848 Glenmina Dr Dayton OH 45440-2002 Personal E-mail: rjh4848@earthlink.net.

HADLEY, STANTON THOMAS, manufacturing executive, director, lawyer; b. Beloit, Kans., July 3, 1936; s. Robert Campbell and Helen (Schroeder) H.; m. Charlotte June Holmes, June 9, 1962; children: Gayle Elizabeth, Robert Edward, Stanton Thomas, Steven Holmes. BS in Metall. Engring., Colo. Sch. Mines, 1958; LLB, U. Colo., 1962. Bar: Colo. 1962, U.S. Dist. Ct. 1962, U.S. Patent Office 1963. Metallurgist ASARCO, Leadville, Colo., 1957; tng. engr. Allis-Chalmers Co., West Allis, Wis., 1958—61; adminstrv. engr. Ball Corp., Boulder, Colo., 1961—62, atty., 1962—65; patent counsel Scott Paper Co., Phila., 1965—71, USG Corp., Chgo., 1971—76, gen. mgr. metals div., 1976—79, group v.p. indsl. group, 1979—84, sr. v.p. adminstrn., sec., 1984, sec., 1984—87, sr. v.p. staff services, 1987—89; pres. Ansco Photo-Optical Products Corp., Chgo., 1989—93, Visador Co., Marion, Va., 1994—98. Bd. dirs. Masonite Corp., WJE Assocs. Inc., USG Found. Bd. dirs. Ill. Safety Council, North Suburban YMCA, Northbrook Symphony Orch.; former mem. founders' council Field Mus.; mem. Chgo. United, Chgo. Assn. Commerce and Industry. Served with U.S. Army, 1959. Mem. Am. Soc. Metals, Licensing Execs. Soc., Assn. Corp. Patent Counsel. Clubs: Union League, Sunset Ridge Country, Executives. Republican. Home: 555 Valley Way Northfield IL 60093-1067 Office: STH Cons 555 Valley Way Northfield IL 60093-1067

HAECK, JAMES F., manufacturing executive; m. Carolyn Haeck; 1 child, Jessica. BA in Economics, U. Pitts. Joined The LTV Corp., 1968, v.p., gen. mgr. Tubular Prods. Co., 1991—93, v.p., gen. mgr. Cleveland Works, 1993—94, sr. v.p. flat rolled opers., 1994, sr. v.p. comml., 1995—98, exec. v.p. Cleve., 1998—2001; v.p. sales mktg. Universal Steel Co. Bd. dirs. Bayou Steel Corp., 2004—. Office: Universal Steel 6600 Grant Ave Cleveland OH 44105

HAENICKE, DIETHER HANS, academic administrator emeritus, educator; b. Hagen, Germany, May 19, 1935; came to U.S., 1963, naturalized, 1972; s. Erwin Otto and Helene (Wildfang) H.; m. Carol Ann Colditz, Sept. 29, 1962; children: Jennifer Ruth, Kurt Robert. Student, U. Gottingen, 1955-56, U. Marburg, 1957-59; PhD magna cum laude in German Lit. and Philology, U. Munich, 1962; DHL (hon.), Cen. Mich. U., 1986; DHL, We. Mich. U., 1998. Asst. prof. Wayne State U., Detroit, 1963-68, assoc. prof., 1968-72, prof. German, 1972-78, resident dir. Jr. Year in Freiburg (Ger.), 1965-66, 69-70, dir. Jr. Year Abroad programs, 1970-75, chmn. dept. Romance and Germanic langs. and lits., 1971-72, assoc. dean Coll. Liberal Arts, 1972-75, provost, 1975-77, v.p., provost, 1977-78; dean Coll. Humanities Ohio State U., 1978-82, v.p. acad. affairs, provost, 1982-85; pres. Western Mich. U., Kalamazoo, 1985-98, interim pres., 2006. Asst. prof. Colby Coll. Summer Sch. of Langs., 1964-65; lectr. Internationale Ferienkurse, U. Freiburg, summers 1961, 66, 67 Author: (with Horst S. Daemmrich) The Challenge of German Literature, 1971, Untersuchungen zum Versepos des 20. Jahrhunderts, 1962; editor: Liebesgeschichte der schonen Magelone, 1969, Der blonde Eckbert und andere Novellen, 1969, Franz Sternbalds Wanderungen, 1970, Wednesdays with Diether, 2003, University Governance and Humanistic Scholarship (Festschrift), 2002; contbr. articles to acad. and lit. jours. Mem. Mich. State Atty. Discipline Bd. Fulbright scholar, 1963-65 Mem. MLA, AAUP, Am. Assn. Tchrs. of German, Mich. Acad. Arts and Scis., Mich. Coun. for Arts and Cultural Affairs, Phi Beta Kappa. Office: Western Mich U Office of Pres Kalamazoo MI 49008-5202 Home Phone: 269-353-0942; Office Phone: 269-387-2351. Business E-Mail: diether.haenicke@wmich.edu.

HAERING, EDWIN RAYMOND, chemical engineering educator, consultant; b. Columbus, Ohio, Dec. 8, 1932; s. Edwin Jacob and Mary Mildred (Kunst) H.; m. Suzanne Rowe, June 9, 1956; children: Cynthia, David Arthur, Elizabeth. BChemE, MS, Ohio State U., 1956, PhD, 1966. Mem. faculty Ohio State U., Columbus, 1959-91, assoc. prof., 1973-82, prof. chem. engring., 1982-91, prof. emeritus, 1991—, vice chmn. dept., 1974-76, chmn. dept., 1977-78. Cons. in field. Author: Laboratory Manual for Unit Operations Laboratory, 1980; contbr. articles to profl. jours. Disaster svcs. vol. ARC, 1997—2005. Lt. (j.g.) USNR, 1956—59. NROTC scholar, 1951-56, Dow Chem. Co. scholar, 1956; Koppers tchg. fellow, 1962. Mem. AIChE (treas. Cen. Ohio sect. 1974-79), Am. Chem. Soc., Port Clinton Power Squadron (exec. com. 2003), Ohio State U. Faculty Club (pres. 1988-89), Sandusky Yacht Club, Lake Erie South Shore Hunter Sailing Assn. (treas. 1997-99), Sigma Xi, Tau Beta Pi. Avocations: golf, gardening, sailing. Home: 701 Stoutenberg Dr Lakeside Marblehead OH 43440-2049 Office: Ohio State U Dept Chem Engring 701 Stoutenberg Dr Lakeside Marblehead OH 43440-2049

HAEUSER, MICHAEL JOHN, library administrator; b. LaCrosse, Wis., July 5, 1943; s. Loyal Eldon and Kamilla (Brenengen) H.; m. Linda Kay Johnsrud, Aug. 31, 1968 (div. 1981); 1 child, Britton; m. Irene Jeanette Morris, June 20, 1987. BS in History, U. Wis., 1970, MA in History, 1972, MLS, 1973, cert., 1986. Readers svcs. libr. Knox Coll., Galesburg, Ill., 1973-74, head readers svcs., 1974-76; head libr. Linfield Coll., McMinnville, Oreg., 1976-81; dir. learning resources, head libr. Gustavus Adolphus Coll., St. Peter, Minn., 1981-97, coll. archivist, 1997—. Co-instr. Mil. History WWII, 1979; presenter in field. Author: With Grace, Elegance and Flair: The First 25 Years of Library Associates, 2002; cons. to editor books for coll. librs., Choice mag.; contbr. articles to profl. jours. Chmn. Core Curriculum Rev. Task Force, Linfield Coll., 1977-7; mem. coll. libr. com. Nat. Commn. Preservation and Access, 1989, team Bibliographic Instrn., 1982—; bd. dirs. Minn. Humanities Commn., 1990-97. With U.S. Army, 1963-66. NEH fellow, 1978; grantee, 1980, 83; grantee: Japan Found., 1978, U.S. Office Edn., 1979, 80, Murdock Trust, 1979, Hearst Found., 1980, Collins Found., 1980, Nat. Archives and Records Svc., 1983, Presser Found., 1983; recipient John Cotton Dana Libr. pub. rels. award 1983, 94. Mem. ALA (selected vol. pres.' program Chgo. chpt. 1985, sec. coll. libr. sect. 1990, Outstanding Pub. Rels. 1983), Assn. Coll. And Rsch. Librs., Assn. Coll. and Resource Librs. (nat. adv. coun. libr. sect. 1985), Am. Hist. Assn., Minn. Libr. Assn. (pres. 1988-90), Minn. Assn. Libr. Friends (bd. dirs. 1990), Minn. Humanities Commn. (bd. dirs. 1991-97). Lutheran. Avocations: skiing, outdoor work, reading, travel, association activities. Office: Gustavus Adolphus Coll Folke Bernadotte Meml Libr 800 W College Ave Saint Peter MN 56082-1485 Office Phone: 507-933-7572. Business E-Mail: haeuser@gac.edu.

HAFFNER, CHARLES CHRISTIAN, III, retired printing company executive; b. Chgo., May 27, 1928; s. Charles Christian and Clarissa (Donnelley) Haffner; m. Anne P. Clark, June 19, 1970. BA, Yale U., 1950. With R.R. Donnelley & Sons Co., Chgo., 1951—62, treas., 1962-68, v.p., treas., 1968-83, vice-chmn., treas., 1983-84, vice-chmn., 1984-90; ret., 1990. Chmn. Morton Arboretum, 1975—2001, Sprague Found., 1996—2000, Newberry Libr., 1986—2000, trustee; life trustee Sprague Found.; bd. govs. Nature Conservancy, 1973—84, chmn. Ill. chpt., 1984—87, life trustee, 1987—; mem. Chgo. Plan Commn., 1986—91; trustee Art Inst., Chgo., Latin Sch., Chgo., 1974—84, Ill. Cancer Coun., 1984—92, Chgo. City Day Sch., Lincoln Pk. Zool. Soc., Brooks Sch., 1987—95. 1st lt. USAF, 1952—54. Mem.: Casino Club, Caxton Club, Racquet Club, Commonwealth Club, Comml. Club, Chgo. Club. Home: 1530 N State Pkwy Chicago IL 60610-1610 Office: 35 E Wacker Dr Ste 1078 Chicago IL 60601-2398

HAFFNER, DAVID S., manufacturing executive; BS, U. Missouri-Columbia, 1974, MBA, 1980. Joined Leggett & Platt, Inc., Carthage, Mo., 1983, exec. v.p., 1995—2002, bd. dir., 1995—, COO, 1999—2002, pres., COO, 2002—06, pres., CEO, 2006—. Bd. dirs. Bemis Co. Inc., 2004—. Office: Leggett & Platt Inc PO Box 757 1 Leggett Rd Carthage MO 64836-9649

HAGAN, JOHN CHARLES, III, ophthalmologist; b. Mexico, Mo., Oct. 7, 1943; s. John Charles Hagan II and Cleta L. (Book) Neely; m. Rebecca Jane Chapman, July 15, 1967; children: Carol Ann, Catherine Elizabeth. BA, U. Mo., 1965; MD, Loyola U., Chgo., 1969. Diplomate Am. Bd. Ophthalmology. Intern Med. Coll. Wis., Milw., 1969-70; resident in ophthalmology Emory U., Atlanta, 1972-75; practice medicine, Kansas City, Mo., 1975—. Cons. Am. Running and Phys. Fitness Assn., Washington, 1973—. Editor: Mo. Medicine: The Jour. of the Mo. State Med. Assn.; contbr. over 120 articles to profl. jours Capt. M.C., USAF, 1970-72. Fellow ACS; mem. AMA, Am. Soc. Cataract and Refractive Surgery, Mo. Soc. Eye Physicians and Surgeons (pres. 1998), Kansas City Soc. Ophthalmology. Office: Discover Vision Ctrs 9401 N Oak Trafficway Kansas City MO 64155 Office Phone: 816-478-1230.

HAGAN, JOHN P., state representative; b. Alliance, Ohio, Apr. 11, 1955; married; 4 children. Attended Sch. Arch., Kent State U. Self-employed heating and plumbing contractor; state rep. dist. 50 Ohio Ho. of Reps., Columbus, 2000—, vice chair pub. utilities com., 2000—04, chair pub. utilities and energy com., 2004—, mem. econ. devel. and tech., homeland security engring. and archtl. design, and human svcs. and aging coms., mem. ways and means com. Trustee Marlboro Twp., 1990—2000; past commr. Stark County Regional Planning Commn.; past alt. North East Four County Regional Planning Commn., Tuscarawas County Solid Waste Dist. Bd. Mem.: Nat. Fedn. Ind. Bus., Air Conditioning Contractors Am., Stark County Twp. Assn., Stark County Farm Bur., Promise Keepers of Stark County, Marlboro Twp. Hist. Soc., NRA, Lexington Grange, Alliance Area C. of C., Massillon Rep. Club, Alliance Area Rep. Club (past pres.), Marlboro Ruritans, Lions (past pres. Marlboro chpt., Lion of Yr. 1996). Republican. Methodist. Office: 77 S High St 11th fl Columbus OH 43215-6111

HAGAN, MICHAEL CHARLES, transporation executive; Bachelor's, Brescia Coll., 1970. Mgmt. trainee Am. Comml. Barge Line Am. Comml. Lines, Jeffersonville, Ind., 1970-87, exec. v.p., 1989-90, pres., 1990, pres., CEO, 1992—; v.p. rail unit CSX, 1989-90. Office: Am Comml Lines 1701 Utica Pike Jeffersonville IN 47130-4747

HAGAN, ROBERT F., state legislator; b. Youngstown, Ohio, Mar. 31, 1949; m. Michele Hagan; children: Jennifer, Kristen, Thomas, James, Natalia. Engr. locomotive CSX Transp.; state rep. Dist. 53 Ohio Ho. of Reps., 1987-97; mem. Ohio Senate from 33rd dist., Columbus, 1997—. Vice chmn. Transp. and Urban Affairs com.; mem. commerce com., labor com., health and retirement com., human resources com. Trustee Northside Citizens Coalition. Named Pub. Ofcl. of Yr. Nat. Assn. Steel Workers Ohio, 1990, Ohioan of Yr. OCSEA, 1990, Legislators of Yr. Ohio Counseling Assn., 1991; recipient Legis. Leadership award Ohio Coalition for Edn. Handicapped Children, 1990, Legis. award Assn. Ohio Health Commrs., 1992. Mem. Nat. Fedn. Blind (chmn.), Steelworkers Oldtimers Club, Citizens League, United Transp. Union Local 604, Sierra Club. Office: Ohio Senate State Capitol Bldg Columbus OH 43215

HAGAN, SHEILA B., corporate lawyer; b. 1961; BA, Coll. St. Thomas; JD, U. Minn. Bar: 1987. V.p., gen. counsel IBP, Inc., Dakota Dunes, S.D. Office: IBP Inc 800 Stevens Port Dr Ste 836 Dakota Dunes SD 57049-5005

HAGAN-HARRELL, MARY M., state legislator; b. Cape Girardeau, Mo. m. Stan Harrell. BS in Elem. Edn. and Fine Arts, Southeast Mo. State U.; MLS, George Peabody Coll. Tchr., libr. Riverview Gardens (Mo.) Sch. Dist., 1960-86; committeewoman Ferguson Twp., 1972-89; state rep. Dist. 75 Mo. Ho. of Reps., 1986—. Chmn. retirement com., state employees com.; mem. appropriations, edn. and pub. safety com., govt. ogrn. com., higher edn. com., elem. and secondary edn. com., labor com., joint coms. pub. employees retirement, workers compensation and employment security com., health care contbns. for state employees com.; sec. St. Louis County Dem. Ctrl. Com., 1976-89. Mem. NEA, Nat. Orgn. Women Legislators, Women Polit. Caucus, Mo. Orgn. Women Legislators, Mo. Sch. Librs. Assn., Downettes Charitable Club. E-mail: mhaganha@services.state.mo.us.

HAGEDORN, JAMES, landscape company executive; Grad. AMP program, Harvard Bus. Sch. Sr. mgmt. roles Miracle-Gro; with The Scotts Co., 1995—, pres. N.Am. ops., pres., COO, 2000—03, chmn., CEO, 2003—. Exec. v.p. Scotts' U.S. Bus. Groups. Officer USAF. Office: c/o Scotts Co 14111 Scottslawn Rd Marysville OH 43041

HAGEL, CHUCK (CHARLES TIMOTHY HAGEL), senator; b. North Platte, Nebr., Oct. 4, 1946; s. Charles Dean and Betty (Dunn) Hagel; m. Lilibet Ziller, 1985; children: Allyn, Ziller. Student, Brown Inst. Radio & TV, Minn., 1966; BA, U. Nebr., 1971. Adminstrv. asst. to Rep. John Y. McCollister US Congress, 1971—77; vice chmn. Reagan-Bush Presdl. Inaugural Com., 1981; adminstr. US Vets. Adminstrn., 1981-82; co-founder, dir., & pres. Collins, Hagel and Clarke, Inc., 1982—85; co-founder, dir., & exec. v.p. Vanguard Cellular Systems, 1985—87; founding chmn. Comm. Corp. Internat. Ltd.; pres., CEO World USO, 1987-90; pres. McCarthy & Co. Investment Banking Firm, 1991-96; US Senator from Nebr., 1997—. Select com. intelligence US Senate, Congressional-Exec. Commn. China, com. rules and adminstrn., fgn. relations, com. banking, housing and urban affairs; mem. Bus.-Govt. Relations Coun., Washington, Coun. Excellence in Govt., Coun. Fgn. Relations. Bd. trustees Am. Red Cross (Heartland Chpt.), Bellevue U., Nebr., Constl. Heritage Inst., Eisenhower World Affairs Inst., Free Enterprise Coun., Fund for Democracy and Develop., German-Am. Bus. Assn., Hastings Coll., Nebr., Manville Personal Injury Settlement Trust, Nat. D-Day Mus., Nat. Fedn. Independent Bus. Found.; adv. bd. Friends of Vietnam Veterans' Meml.; chmn. bd. dirs. Am. Info. Systems, Inc., No Greater Love; bd. dirs. Eureka Bank, San Francisco, MTT Corp., Hungary, Omaha C. of C., Arlington Nat. Cemetery Hist. Soc.; chmn. Agent Orange Settlement Fund Payment Program, Vietnam Veterans' Meml. Tenth Anniversary; chmn. Great Plains Chpt. Paralyzed Veterans of Am.; v.p. Desert Storm Homecoming Found.; bd. govs. United Svc. Orgn. World. Served to sergeant 2nd bn., 47th inf., ninth inf. divsn. US Army, 1967—68, South Vietnam. Decorated Combat Infantryman Badge, Purple Heart with Oak Leaf Cluster, Vietnamese Cross of Gallantry; recipient Legis. of Yr., Vietnam Veterans Assn. Am., 2000, George W. Norris Disting. Lectr. award, U. Nebr., Kearney, 2002, Edmund S. Muskie Disting. Public Svc. award, Ctr. Nat. Policy, 2004, Disting. Internat. Leadership award, Atlantic Coun., 2004. Mem.: Internat. Republican Inst., Disabled Am. Veterans, Veterans of Fgn. Wars, Am. Legion. Republican. Episcopalian. Office: US Senate 248 Russell Office Bldg Washington DC 20510-0001 also: District Office 294 Federal Bldg 100 Centennial Mall North Lincoln NE 68508 Office Phone: 202-224-4224, 402-476-1400. Office Fax: 202-224-5213, 402-476-0605. E-mail: chuck_hagel@hagel.senate.gov.

HAGELIN, JOHN SAMUEL, political organization administrator, theoretical physicist; b. Pitts., June 9, 1954; s. Carl William and Mary Lee (Stephenson) Hagelin; m. Margaret Hagelin (div.). AB in physics summa cum laude, Dartmouth Coll., 1975; MA in quantum physics, Harvard U., 1976, PhD in quantum physics, 1981. Sci. assoc. European Lab. for Particle Physics (CERN), Geneva, 1981-82; rsch. assoc. Stanford Linear Accelerator Ctr. (SLAC), Calif., 1982-83; assoc. prof. physics Maharishi U. Mgmt., Fairfield, Iowa, 1983-84, prof. physics, 1984—, dir. Inst. Sci., Tech. and Pub. Policy, 1992—; co-founder Enlightened Audio Designs Group, 1991—; minister of sci. & tech. Global Country of World Peace; founder, pres. US Peace Govt., 2003—. Natural Law Party candidate US Presdl. Election, 1992, 96, 2000. Author: Manual for a Perfect Government, 1998; contbr. numerous articles to sci. journals. Recipient Kilby Young Innovator Award, 1992; Tyndall Fellow, Harvard U., 1979. Mem. Iowa Acad. Sciences Office: Maharishi U Mgmt Inst Sci Tech & Pub Policy 1000 N 4th St Fairfield IA 52557 also: US Peace Govt 2000 Capital Blvd Fairfield IA 52556

HAGEN, DANIEL C., lawyer; b. Cleve., 1954; BA summa cum laude, Baldwin-Wallace Coll., 1977; JD, Univ. Va., Charlottesville, 1980. Bar: Ohio 1980. Ptnr., chair, employee benefits practice Jones Day, Cleve. Mem.: ABA, Midwest Pension and Benefits Conf., Order of Coif. Office: Jones Day North Point 901 Lakeside Ave Cleveland OH 44114-1190 Office Phone: 216-586-7159. Office Fax: 216-579-0212. Business E-Mail: dchagen@jonesday.com.

HAGEN, JOHN WILLIAM, psychology professor; b. Mpls., May 11, 1940; s. Wayne Sigvart and Elfie Marie (Erickson) H.; adopted children— Darus Gene, Lonny John, Frederick F. BA, U. Minn., 1962; PhD, Stanford U., 1965. Asst. prof. psychology U. Mich., Ann Arbor, 1965-69, assoc. prof., 1969-73, prof., 1973—, chmn. developmental program, 1971-83, dir. Ctr. Human Growth and Devel., 1982-93. Mem. Mich. Gov.'s Spl. Commn. on Age of Majority, 1970-71; dir. Reading and Learning Skills Ctr., 1985—1996; exec. officer Soc. for Rsch. in Child Devel., 1989—; adv. coun. Mich. Dept. Edn., 1972-74; chmn. Univ. Com. on Internat. Year of Child, 1979-80; rsch. rev. com. Nat. Inst. Child Health and Human Devel., 1980—. Co-author: Perspectives on the Development of Memory and Cognition, 1977; cons. editor Merrill Palmer Quar, 1968-80, Child Devel, 1972—; contbr. articles to profl. jours. Bd. dirs. Guild House Campus Ministry, Ann Arbor, 1972-83; bd. dirs. Humane Soc. Huron Valley, 1991-2000; profl. adv. bd. Nat. Assn. Learning Disabilities, 2001-. Recipient Standard Oil Found. award, 1967; USPHS trainee, 1963-65; Woodrow Wilson fellow, 1962-63; James Neubacher Award, 1997. Fellow Am. Psychol. Assn., Internat. Acad. for Rsch. in Learning Disabilities (exec. com. 2001-), Am. Psychol. Soc.; mem. Am. Edn. Rsch. Assn., Midwestern Psychol. Assn., Soc. Research in Child Devel. (chmn. program com. 1981-83), Internat. Soc. Study of Behavioral Devel., Phi Beta Kappa. Clubs: Univ. (Ann Arbor), Alumni (Ann Arbor). Unitarian Universalist. Home: 3421 Burbank Dr Ann Arbor MI 48105-1518 Office: Soc Rsch in Child Devel 3131 S State St #302 Ann Arbor MI 48108 Office Phone: 734-998-6565. Business E-Mail: jwhagen@umich.edu.

HAGEN, LAWRENCE JACOB, agricultural engineer; b. Rugby, ND, Mar. 6, 1940; s. Lars and Alice (Hannem) H. BS, N.D. State U., 1962, MS, 1967; PhD, Kans. State U., 1980. Agrl. engr. USDA, Manhattan, Kans., 1967—. Contbr. tech. articles to profl. publs. Capt. USAF, 1963-69. Mem. Am. Soc. Agrl. Engrs., Soil & Water Conservation Soc. Am. Office: 1515 College Ave Manhattan KS 66502 Office Phone: 785-537-5545. E-mail: hagen@weru.ksu.edu.

HAGEN, RICHARD E. (DICK), state legislator; b. Pine Ridge, SD, Aug. 16, 1937; m. Mona Hagen; children: Shagne, Winona. Mem. S.D. Ho. of Reps., 1982-92, 93-2000, mem. health and human svc. com. and local govt. com.; painter, carpenter; mem. S.D. Senate from 27th dist., Pierre, 2001—. Mem. local govt. com., transportation com. S.D. House of Reps. Mem. Shannon County Sch. Bd. Democrat. Home: PO Box 3 Pine Ridge SD 57770-0003

HAGENLOCKER, EDWARD E., retired automobile company executive; b. 1939; married. BS, MS, Ohio State U., 1962, PhD, 1964; MBA, Mich. State U., 1982. With Ford Motor Co., 1964-98, chief engr., 1973—77, gen. mgr., 1978—80, dir., v.p. ops. Brazil, 1984-85, dir., pres., 1985-86, v.p., gen. mgr. truck ops. Dearborn, Mich., 1986-92, exec. v.p. N.Am. automotive ops., 1992-94, pres. Ford automotive ops., 1994-96, vice chmn., 1996-98.

HAGER, LOWELL PAUL, biochemistry educator; b. Girard, Kans., Aug. 30, 1926; s. Paul William and Christine (Selle) H.; m. Frances Erea, Jan. 22, 1949; children: Paul, Steven, JoAnn. AB, Valparaiso U., 1947; MA, U. Kans., 1950; PhD, U. Ill., 1953. Postdoctoral fellow Mass. Gen. Hosp., Boston, 1953-55; asst. prof. biochemistry Harvard U., Cambridge, Mass., 1955-60; mem. faculty U. Ill., Urbana, 1960—, prof. biochemistry, 1965—, head biochem. div., 1967-89, dir. Biotech. Ctr., 1987—. Chmn. physiol. chemistry study sect. NIH, 1965—; vis. scientist Imperial Cancer Rsch. Fund, 1964; cons. NSF, 1976. Editor life scis. Archives Biochemistry and Biophysics, 1966—; assoc. editor Biochemistry, 1973—; mem. editorial bd. Jour. Biol. Chemistry, 1874—. With USAAF, 1945. Guggenheim fellow U. Oxford, Eng., 1959-60, Max Planck Inst. Zellchemie, 1959-60. Mem. NAS (elected), Am. Chem. Soc., Am. Soc. Biol. Chemists, Am. Soc. Microbiology (chmn. physiology divsn. 1967). Achievements include rsch. in enzyme mechanisms, intermediary metabolism, tumor virus. Home: 5 Fields East Champaign IL 61822 Office Phone: 217-333-9686. Business E-Mail: l-hager@uiuc.edu.

HAGERMAN, DOUGLAS M., consumer products company executive, lawyer; b. South Bend, Ind., Dec. 1960; m. Jane Elizabeth Tadych; children: Caroline, Nora. BA summa cum laude, Drake U., Des Moines, Iowa, 1983; JD cum laude, Harvard U., 1986. CPA; bar: 1986. Assoc. Foley & Lardner LLP, Milw., 1986—95, ptnr., 1995—98, Chgo., 1998—2004; sr. v.p., gen. counsel, sec. Rockwell Automation Inc., Milw., 2004—. Office: Rockwell Automation Inc 1201 S 2Nd St Milwaukee WI 53204-2498 E-mail: dmhagerman@ra.rockwell.com.

HAGERTY, ROBERT E., academic administrator; b. Detroit, Mar. 16, 1937; s. Arthur E. and Paula (Buntrock) H.; m. Barbara Ann Anderson, Aug. 16, 1959; children: Scott Robertson, Mark David. AB, Western Mich. U., 1959; MA, Wayne State U., 1961, EdD, 1971. Tchr. Hazel Park (Mich.) Cmty. Schs., 1959-68, bldg. adminstr., 1968-74, dir. spl. edn., 1974-79, dir. evaluation and pupil svcs., 1979-83; supt. Kokomo (Ind.) N.W. Sch. Corp., 1983-85, Ionia (Mich.) Pub. Schs., 1985-93; head, dept. of edn. leadership Grand Valley State U., Grand Rapids, Mich., 1993—2003, dean, sch. of edn., 1999—2003; pres. William Tyndale Coll., Farmington Hills, Mich., 2004—. Author: Making Special Education Work, 1978, The Crisis of Confidence in American Education, 1994. Bd. dirs. Royal Oak (Mich.) YMCA, 1976-83, Met. YMCA, Ionia, 1989-93, Boys and Girls Clubs of Oakland, Hazel Park, 1974-83; chair High Hopes Com., Ionia, 1985-87; exec. bd. Hazel Park Youth Protection Com., 1959-83, Hazel Park Youth Aid Found., 1961-83. Recipient Disting. Svc. award Bd. Edn. Ionia, 1993, Disting. Award of Honor, Outstanding Man of Yr., Hazel Park Jaycees, 1970. Mem. Mich. Assn. Profs. of Edn. (past pres., Disting. Leadership award 1993), Am. Assn. Sch. Adminstrs. (Supt. of the Yr. 1989, 90), Nat. Sch. Pub. Rels. Assn. (Award of Honor 1987, Disting. Achievement award 1989), Ionia C. of C. (bd. dirs. 1985-93, exec. bd. 1987-92). Home: 6530 Balsam Dr # D Hudsonville MI 49426-9267 Office: William Tyndale College PO Box 2297 Farmington Hills MI 48333-2297

HAGEVIK, BRUCE, radio personality; b. Ortonvile, Minn. m. Marvette Hagevik. Grad. Psychology, Moorhead State Coll. Announcer, Ortonville, Minn.; news dir. Faribault, Minn.; radio host, news anchor Sta. WCCO Radio, Mpls., 1973—. Recipient award, AP, Northwest Broadcast News Assn., Radio and TV News Dirs. Assn. Office: WCCO 625 2nd Ave S Minneapolis MN 55402

HAGG, REXFORD A., lawyer, former state legislator; b. Sioux Falls, SD, May 10, 1957; m. Cindy Hagg; 1 child. Student, Nebr. U., S.D. State U. City atty. City of Box Elder, S.D., 1984—; mem. S.D. Ho. of Reps., 1988—98, vice chmn. judiciary com., mem. legis. procedure and taxation coms., speaker, 1997-98; atty. Whiting, Hagg & Hagg, Rapid City, S.D. Home: 1721 West Blvd Rapid City SD 57701-4555 Office: Whiting Hagg & Hagg 601 West Boulevard PO Box 8008 Rapid City SD 57709

HAGGERTY, JOSEPH K., lawyer, insurance company executive; b. 1946; AB, Wheeling Jesuit U., 1968; JD, U. Pitts., 1973. Bar: Iowa 1997, Ky. 1994, Pa. 1973. Sr. v.p., dep. gen. counsel ICH Corp.; sr. v.p., gen. counsel AmerUs Group Co., Des Moines, 1994—. Spkr. in field. Office: AmerUs Group Co 699 Walnut PO Box 1555 Des Moines IA 50306 Office Phone: 515-362-3600. Office Fax: 515-362-3652. E-mail: joe.haggerty@amerus.com.

HAGY, JAMES C., lawyer; b. Cleve., 1955; BA, Case Western Reserve U., 1975, JD, 1978. Bar: Ohio 1978, Ill. 1988. Ptnr., co-chair, real estate practice worldwide Jones Day, Chgo., 1992—2006; mng. dir. Rooftops Group LLC, Glenview, Ill., 2007—. Faculty mem. CoreNet Learning (formerly Inst. of Corp. Real Estate); adj. prof. Case Western Res. U. Sch. Law, Real Estate Ctr. John Marshall Law Sch. Editor: Law Rev., 1978; founding mem. (editorial bd.) Journ of Corp. Real Estate, Henry Stewart Publications, London; author: numerous articles in profl. publications. Named one of World's Leading Real Estate Lawyers, Euromoney mag. Mem.: Am. Coll. Real Estate Lawyers, Phi Beta Kappa, Order of Coif. Mailing: PO Box 716 Glenview IL 60025-0716 Office Phone: 312-269-4152. Business E-Mail: jchagy@jonesday.com, rooftopsgroup@comcast.net.

HAHM, DAVID EDGAR, classics educator; b. Milw., Sept. 30, 1938; s. Edgar David and Loraine Emily (Stebnitz) H.; m. Donna Lorraine Seifert, Aug. 8, 1964; children: Melanie Davida, Christopher David, Geoffrey Kenneth, Martha Maria. BA, Northwestern Coll., 1960; student, Wis. Luth. Sem., 1960-61; MA, U. Wis., 1962, PhD, 1966. Asst. prof. U. Mo., Columbia, 1966-69; asst. prof. classics Ohio State U., Columbus, 1969-72, assoc. prof., 1972-78, prof., 1978—, chmn., 1999—2006. Vis. fellow Corpus Christi Coll., Cambridge, Eng., 1990-91. Author: The Origins of Stoic Cosmology, 1977; contbr. articles to jours., chpts. to books. Trustee Dublin Hist. Soc., 1974-79, pres., 1974-76; active Archtl. Rev. Bd., Dublin, Ohio, 1976-83, chmn., 1980-82; mem. exec. bd. Worthington Hist. Soc., 1981-89, 93—; trustee Old Dublin Assn., 1996—, treas., 1997—. Fellow Ctr. Hellenic Studies; mem. AAUP, Am. Philol. Assn., Am. Philos. Assn., Classical Assn., Mid. West and South, History of Sci. Soc., Soc. Ancient Greek Philosophy. Lutheran. Office: Ohio State U Dept Greek and Latin 230 N Oval Mall Columbus OH 43210-1335 Office Phone: 614-292-7810. E-mail: hahm.1@osu.edu.

HAHN, ARTHUR W., lawyer; b. Chgo., July 30, 1944; s. Bernard and Ruth (Fireman) H.; m. Kathy Miller, June 20, 1969; children: Noah, Samuel. Student, London Sch. Econs., 1964—65; BA, Miami U., Oxford, Ohio, 1966; JD, Northwestern U., 1969. Law clk. to presiding judge U.S. Dist. Ct. Ill., Chgo., 1969—71; assoc., then ptnr. Pope, Ballard, Shepard & Fowle, Chgo., 1971—79; ptnr. Katten, Muchin, Pearl & Galler, Chgo., 1979—80; dir. Mercantile House Holdings, Chgo., 1980—84; pres., CEO N.Am. Futures divsn., Chgo., 1980—84; ptnr. Katten Muchin Zavis Rosenman, Chgo., 1984—. Faculty chmn. Ill. Inst. Tech. Chgo. Kent Coll. Law Grad. Sch. Fin. Svcs. Law, 1987-99; mem. Ill. Task Force on Fin. Svcs., Springfield, 1987, Mem. chmn. subcom. on internat. bankruptcy of CFTC. Editl. bd. mem. Oxford Press, Capitol Markets Law Jour.; contbr. articles on corp. and commodities law to profl. jours. Mem. Dem. Senatorial Campaign Com., Washington, 1988—. Mem. ABA (vice chair fin. products and svcs. com.), Chgo. Bar Assn. (founding chmn. commodities law com.), Futures Industry Assn. (bd. dirs. 1983-84), Inst. Fin. Mkts. (exec. com., trustee 1989—, chmn. internat. divsn.), Econ. Club, Std. Club, Legal Club, Wigmore Club. Office: Katten Muchin Rosenman LLC 525 W Monroe St Ste 1600 Chicago IL 60661-3693 Office Fax: 312-577-8892. Business E-Mail: arthur.hahn@kattenlaw.com.

HAHN, DAVID BENNETT, health facility administrator, consultant, marketing professional; b. Louisville, Ohio, June 5, 1945; s. Bennett E. and Betty J. (McGaughey) H.; m. Elizabeth Burdine, Oct. 4, 1975; children: Stephen, Sarah, Scott. BS in Agrl. Econs., Ohio State U., 1967; MBA, U. Toledo, 1977. Social worker, supr. Franklin County Welfare, Columbus, Ohio, 1968-71, pers. asst., 1971-73; pers. dir. Mansfield (Ohio) Gen. Hosp., 1973-76; adminstr. Kettering Hosp., Loudonville, Ohio, 1978-81; v.p. Marietta (Ohio) Hosp., 1981-92; CEO City Hosp., Bellaire, 1992-94, mktg. dir. med. integrated svcs., 1995—98; pres. Advanced Practice Systems, 1996—; v.p. Tech Risk Mat. Group, 1998—2002. Coach St. Clairsville H.S. Soccer. Mem. East Muskingham Civic Assn. Bd., 1982-92; bd. dirs., recreation coord. Marietta Soccer League; v.p. Mid-Ohio Mktg. Assn., 1992; soccer coach boys team St. Clairsville HS, 1996—; Bd. dirs. Belmont County Salvation Army, 1992—; mem. session and choir Presbyh. ch. Fellow Am. Coll. Health Care Execs.; mem. Assn. MBA Execs., Am. Mktg. Assn. (local chpt. bd. dirs.), Ohio Hosp. Assn. Com., Ohio Hosp. Soc. for Planning and Mktg., Loudonville C. of C. (pres. bd. dirs. 1981), Bellaire C. of C. (bd. devel. com. 1992-93), Wheeling Soccer Assn. (coach), St. Clairsville Area Soccer Assn. (bd. pres.), Pioneer Alumni Ohio State U. (bd. dirs., pres.), Rotary (bd. dirs. Loudonville club 1978-81), Lions (1st v.p.), Masons. Mem. Calvary Presbyterian. Avocations: soccer, reading, gardening, running. Office: PO Box 575 Saint Clairsville OH 43950 E-mail: dbhahn45@aol.com.

HAHN, EUGENE HERMAN, state legislator; b. Milw., July 21, 1929; s. L. Herman and Julia (Senft) H.; m. Lorraine Closs, 1949; children: Jeffrey, Robert, Eugene Jr., Andrew. Student, U. Wis., 1947-48. Town assessor Town of Cambria, Wis., 1957-61; county supr., 1972-91; mem. from dist. 47 Wis. State Assembly, Madison, 1991—. Chair consumer affairs com. Wis. Assembly, co-chair joint survey com. on tax exemptions, mem. agr., edn., transp. and correction and cts. coms.; dir. Fed. Land Bank, Sauk, Columbia, Dane, Adams, Juneau, Marquette, Green Lake, Wis., 1973-88. Committeeman Farmers Home Adminstrn., Columbia and Marquette Counties, 1969-72; chmn. county bd., Cambria, 1986-88. Mem. Wis. Farm Bur., Masons (past master, pardee), Wis. Corn Growers. Home: W3198 Old B Rd Cambria WI 53923-9757 Office: PO Box 8952 Madison WI 53708-8952

HAHN, FREDERIC LOUIS, lawyer; b. Chgo., Apr. 28, 1941; s. Max and Margery Ruth (Goodman) H.; m. Susan Firestone, Mar. 26, 1967; 1 child, Frederic Firestone. AB with highest distinction, Cornell U., 1962, MBA with highest distinction, 1963; JD magna cum laude, Harvard U., 1966. Bar: Ill. 1966; CPA, Ill. Assoc. Hopkins & Sutter, Chgo., 1966-72, ptnr., 1973-94, Mayer, Brown & Platt (now Mayer, Brown, Rowe & Maw), Chgo., 1994—. Bd. dirs. Lyric Opera of Chgo., 1988—. Recipient Gold medal (CPA exam) State of Ill., 1963. Mem. Phi Beta Kappa. Home: 1377 Scott Ave Winnetka IL 60093-1444 Office: Mayer Brown Rowe & Maw 71 South Wacker Dr Chicago IL 60606-4637 E-mail: fhahn@mayerbrownrowe.com.

HAHN, GEORGE LEROY, agricultural engineer, biometeorologist; b. Muncie, Kans., Nov. 12, 1934; s. Vernon Leslie and Marguerite Alberta (Breeden) H.; m. Clovice Elaine Christensen, Dec. 3, 1955; children— Valerie, Cecile, Steven, Melanie. BS, U. Mo., Columbia, 1957, PhD, 1971; MS, U. Calif., Davis, 1961. Agrl. engr., project leader and tech. advisor Agrl. Rsch. Svc., US Dept. Agr., Columbia, Mo., 1957, Davis, Calif., 1958-61, Columbia, 1961-78, Clay Center, ebr., 1978—. Contbr. articles to profl. jours. and books on impact of climatic and other environ. factors on livestock prodn., efficiency, and well-being, evaluation of methods of reducing impact and techniques for measuring dynamic responses and characterizing stress in meat animals. Recipient award Am. Soc. Agrl. Engrs.-Metal Bldgs. Mfrs. Assn., 1976 Fellow Am. Soc. Agrl. Engrs. (dir. prof. coun. 1991-93); mem. Am. Meteorol. Soc. (award for outstanding achievement in bioclimatology 1976), Internat. Soc. Biometeorology (treas. 1999-06), Am. Soc. Animal Sci. Office: US Meat Animal Rsch Ctr PO Box 166 Clay Center NE 68933-0166 Office Phone: 402-762-4271. Business E-Mail: leroy.hahn@ars.usda.gov.

HAHN, JAMES, state official; b. Muscatine, Iowa, Oct. 25, 1935; 4 children. Grad. h.s., Muscatine. Mem. agr. and natural resources com.; chair environ. protection appropriations com.; mem. local govt. com.; mem. natural resources com.; businessperson sand and gravel ready mix family bus.; businessperson fruits and vegetables family bus.; farmer, hog operation owner, 1964—90; ins. adjuster, 1990; real estate salesperson, 1989—; state rep. Iowa, 1991—. Mem.: Iowa Soybean Assn., Iowa Corn Growers, Farm Bur., Masons, Elks. Republican. Methodist. Office: State Capitol E 12th and Grand Des Moines IA 50319

HAHN, KENNETH P., manufacturing executive; b. 1958; Grad., U. Wis., Milw. CPA. Audit mgr. Price Waterhouse; corp. contr. Gehl Co., West Bend, Wis., 1988—, officer, 1994, v.p. fin., treas., 1997—. Office: Gehl Co PO Box 179 143 Water St West Bend WI 53095-3400 Fax: 262-334-6603.

HAIDOSTIAN, ALICE BERBERIAN, concert pianist, volunteer, not-for-profit fundraiser; b. Highland Park, Mich., Sept. 21, 1925; d. Harry M. and Siroun Vartabedian Berberian; m. Berj H. Haidostian, Oct. 1, 1949; children: Cynthia Esther Haidostian Wilbanks, Christine Rebecca Haidostian Garry, Dicran Berj. MusB, U. Mich., 1946, MusM, 1949. Pvt. piano tchr., 1946-48; tchr. music Detroit Pub. Sch., 1953; dir. vocal trio The Haidostians, 1959—71; dir. youth choral group Cultural Soc. Armenians from Istanbul, 1965—72. Chmn. adv. coun. Armenian Studies Program, U. Mich., 1984-99. Initiator (Operas) Anoush, Mich. Opera Theatre, 1981—82, 2001—02, Transparent Anatomical Manikin exhibit, Detroit Sci. Ctr., 1976. Initiated Centennial Celebration U. Mich. Sch. Music, Detroit, 1980; mem. Armenian Gen. Benevolent Union Alex Manoogian Sch., 1981—91, Detroit chpt. core group com., 1992—; chmn. Marie Manoogian group Armenian Gen. Benevolent Union Alex Manoogian Sch, 1993—; active Detroit Women's Symphony Orch, Mich. Opera; bd. trustees Mich. Opera Theatre, 1982—; active Oakway Symphony Orch.; mem. Save Orch. Hall women's divsn.Project HOPE, 1964—, pres., 1995—96, Detroit Armenian Women's Club, 1957—; active women's chpt. Armenian Gen. Benevolent Union, Detroit, 1944—93; bd. dirs. Childhelp USA Greater Detroit Aux., 1998—; active Detroit Sci. Ctr., 1976—, bd. trustees, 1999—; organist, choir dir. Armenian Congl. Ch., Detroit, 1946—48; mem. Chancel Choir Westminster Ch. Detroit, 1965—80; bd. dirs. Detroit Symphony Orch., 1986—88. Recipient Spirit of Detroit award, 1980, Heart of Gold award United Found. City Detroit, 1981, Nat. Svc. citation U. Mich. Alumnae Coun., 1980, Disting. Alumni Svc. award U. Mich., 1981, Leadership plaque Detroit Symphony Orch., 1988, Magic Flute award Internat. Found. Mozarteum, Salzburg, Austria, 1989, Lifetime Achievement award Outstanding Woman Mich. Project HOPE, 1998, Cmty. Svc. award Wayne County Med. Soc. Alliance, 2000; named Armenian Mother of Yr., Internat. Inst. Detroit, 1981. Mem. AAUW, Detroit Assn. Univ. Mich. Women (pres. 1969-71), Mich. Fedn. Music Clubs, Mich. State Med. Soc. Alliance, Wayne County Med. Soc. Aux. (pres. 1975-76), Pro Mozart Soc. Greater Detroit (pres. 1982-02, pres. emeritus 2002-, Cert. Appreciation 2002), Pro Musica Detroit (sec. 1969-90, 1st v.p. 1990—), Tuesday Musicale Detroit (pres. 1970-72), Univ. Mich. Alumni Assn. (chmn. alumnae coun. 1977-79), Univ. Mich. Sch. Music Alumni Soc., Women's Assn. Detroit Symphony Orch. (pres. 1986-88, vol. coun. Detroit Symphony Orch.), U. Mich. Alumni Assn. (bd. dirs.), U. Mich. Emeritus Club (pres. 1997-98). Avocation: piano. Home: 6838 Valley Spring Dr Bloomfield Hills MI 48301-2845

HAIG, SUSAN, conductor; BA in Music Theory and Composition, Princeton U.; DMA in Orchestral Conducting, MM in Orchestral Conducting, MM in Piano, State U. .Y., Stony Brook; PhD in Humanities (hon.), U. Windsor, 1998. Coaching/conducting fellow Juilliard Am. Opera Centre, 1981—83; assistant conductor Minnesota Opera, 1983—84, New York City Opera, 1984—86, Santa Fe Opera, 1986; resident coach and conducting assistant Canadian Opera Co., 1986—88; resident staff conductor Calgary Philharmonic Orch., 1988—91; artistic dir. and principal conductor Windsor Symphony Orch., 1991—2001; music dir. S.D. Symphony Orch., 2001—02; assoc. conductor Fla. Orch., Tampa, 2003—. Recipient Heinz Unger Conducting award, 1992, Mayor's award for excellence in the performing arts, 1999. Mailing: c/o Michael Gerard Mgmt Group 192 Catherine St E PO Box 22 Callander ON P0H 1H0 Canada

HAILE, H. G., German language and literature educator; b. Brownwood, Tex., July 31, 1931; s. Frank and Nell (Goodson) H.; m. Mary Elizabeth Huff, Sept. 1, 1952; children: Jonathan, Christian, Constance Haile Hunsaker. BA, U. Ark., 1952, MA, 1954; student, U. Cologne, Germany, 1955-56; PhD, U. Ill., 1957. Instr. U. Pa., 1956-57; asst. prof., then asso. prof. U. Houston, 1957-63; mem. faculty U. Ill., Urbana, 1963—, prof. German, 1965—, head dept., 1964-73; asso. mem. U. Ill. (Center for Advanced Study), 1969—. Vis. prof. U. Mich., U. Ga. Author: Das Faustbuch nach der Wolfenbuttler Handschrift, 1963, 95, The History of Doctor Johann Faustus, 1965, 1996, Artist in Chrysalis: A Biographical Study of Goethe in Italy, 1973, Invitation to Goethe's Faust, 1978, Luther: An Experiment in Biography, 1983, We Are All Sonsabitches Now, 2000; contbr. numerous articles to profl. and popular jours. Fulbright fellow, 1955; fellow Am.

Coun. Learned Socs., 1961-62. Office: U Ill 707 S Mathews 3072 Foreign Languages Urbana IL 61801 Home Phone: 217-649-1255. Personal E-mail: harryhaile@lettersfromthedustbowl.com. E-mail: harryhaile@aol.com.

HAILEY, V. ANN, retail executive; Sr. v.p., CFO Pillsbury Co., 1994—97; exec. v.p., CFO Limited Brands Inc., Columbus, Ohio, 1997—, bd. dir., 2001—. Bd. dir. Fed Reserve Bank of Cleveland, 2004—. Office: Limited Brands Inc 3 Limited Pkwy Columbus OH 43230-1467

HAIMAN, IRWIN SANFORD, lawyer; b. Cleve., Mar. 19, 1916; s. Alfred W. and Stella H. (Weiss) H.; m. Jeanne D. Jaffee, Mar. 8, 1942; children: Karen H. Schenkel, Susan L. Bensoussan. BA, Western Res. U., 1937; LL.B., Cleve. Marshall Law Sch., 1941; JD, Cleve. State U., 1969. Bar: Ohio 1941, U.S. Ct. Appeals (6th cir.) 1961, U.S. Supreme Ct. 1961. Asst. to pres. Tremco Mfg. Co., Cleve., 1936-42; house counsel William Edwards Co., Cleve., 1947-48; pvt. practice Cleve., 1948-68; ptnr. firm Garber, Simon, Haiman, Gutfeld, Friedman & Jacobs, 1968-80; ptnr. McCarthy, Lebit, Crystal & Haiman, 1981—. Lectr. in speech Western Res. U., 1948-70; dir. Washington Fed. Savs. and Loan Assn.; asst. law dir., prosecutor City of Lyndhurst, Ohio, 1965-79, law dir., 1979-84. Trustee Montefiore Home, Cleve., 1974-88 (life trustee 1988—)—, East End Neighborhood House, 1962-68; councilman City of South Euclid, 1948-54, pres., 1952-54; pres. Young People's Congregation, Fairmount Temple, 1951-52; sec., trustee Surburban Temple, 1962-65, trustee, 1983—, pres., 1984-87; chmn. speakers div., bd. dirs. Cleve. chpt. ARC, 1959-62; chmn. speaker and film div. Cleve. United Appeal, 1961-62; chmn. speakers div. Jewish Welfare Fund Cleve., 1973-79. Served as 1st lt. AUS, 1943-47. Mem. Ohio, Cleve. bar assns., Assn. Trial Lawyers Am., Zeta Beta Tau. Clubs: Oakwood Country, Lake Forest Country (pres. 1971-72, 75-79). Home: 20201 N Park Blvd Cleveland OH 44118-5000 Office Phone: 216-696-1422.

HAINES, JAMES S., JR., retired energy executive; JD, U. Mo. Columbia Law Sch., 1975. Asst. atty. gen. State of Mo.; atty. Mo. Pub. Svc. Commn.; staff atty. through v.p. regulatory affairs KGE, 1980—85, group v.p., 1985—92; exec. v.p., chief adminstrv. officer Westar Energy, 1992—95, exec. v.p., COO, 1995—96; pres., CEO El Paso Electric Co., 1996—2001, Westar Energy, Inc., Topeka, 2002—06, CEO, 2006—07. Adj. prof., Skov Prof. Bus. Ethics Coll. Bus. Adminstrn. Univ. Tex., El Paso.

HAINES, JOSEPH E., state legislator; b. Greene County, Ohio, Sept. 30, 1923; m. Joy Haines; children: Thomas, Thaddeus, Jonathan, Barbara. BS, Ohio State U., 1949. Chmn. then commr. Greene County, 1968-76; state rep. Dist. 75 Ohio State Congress, 1981-92; state rep. Dist. 74 Ohio Ho. of Reps., 1993-99; dep. dir. Ohio Dept. Agriculture, 2000—. Farmer; mem. agr. and natural resources com., fin. and appropriations com., energy and environ. com., fin. inst. com., rules com., hwy. and hwy. safety com., reference com. Mem. Nat. Assn. County Commrs. (chmn.), SW Dist. County Commr. Assn. (chmn.), Ohio Shorthorn Breeders (past pres.), Farm Bur., Kiwanis (past pres.), YMCA (bd. dirs.).

HAINES, STEPHEN JOHN, neurosurgeon; b. Burlington, Vt., Sept. 4, 1949; s. Gerald Leon and Frances Mary (Whitcomb) H.; m. Jennifer Lea Plombon; children: Christopher, Jeremy. AB, Dartmouth Coll., 1971; MD, U. Vt., 1975. Diplomate Am. Bd. Neurol. Surgery; diplomate Nat. Bd. Med. Examiners. Intern U. Minn., Mpls., 1975—76; resident neurol. surgery U. Pitts., 1976—81; from asst. prof. to prof. U. Minn., Mpls., 1982—93, prof. neurosurgery, otolaryngology and pediatr., 1993—97, head divsn. pediat. neurosurgery, 1985—97, chmn. and head dept. neurosurgery, 2003—; prof. neurosurg., Lyle A. French chair, head dept. neurosurg. U. Minn. Med. Sch., 2003—; prof. neurol. surgery, otolaryngology and pediats., chmn. dept. neurol. surgery Med. U. S.C., 1997—2003. Adv. panel FDA Neurologic Devices, 2002—05, chair, 2005; mem. Com. Postmarket Surveillance Pediat Med. Devices, Inst. Medicine, 2004—05. Contbr. articles to profl. jours. Fellow ACS; mem. AMA, Am. Assn. Neurol. Surgeons (Van Wagenen fellow 1981), Congress Neurol. Surgeons (pres. 1996), Soc. Clin. Trials, Neurosurg. Soc. Am., Am. Acad. Neurol. Surgery, Soc. Neurol. Surgeons. Office: Dept Neurosurgery MMC 96 420 Delaware St SE Minneapolis MN 55455 Office Phone: 612-626-5767. Business E-Mail: shaines@umn.edu, headneurosurg@umn.edu.

HAINJE, DICK G., FEMA administrator, former fire fighter; b. Sioux Falls, SD, Aug. 11, 1956; m. Becky Jones; 3 children. AA, S.D. State U., 1995. Fire fighter, asst. fire chief Sioux Falls Fire Rescue Dept., 1977—2001; EMT, 1978—; mem. dist. 11 S.D. Senate, Pierre, 1996—2001; region VII adminstr. FEMA, 2001—. Chair United Way City of Sioux Falls Employees; chair Fire Fighter Pension Fund, 1989—. Mem. S.D. EMT Assn., S.D. Fire Fighters Assn. Republican. Lutheran. Office: FEMA Region VII 9221 Ward Parkway Ste 300 Kansas City MO 64114-3372

HAIRSTON, GEORGE W., lawyer; b. Ironton, Ohio, Aug. 1, 1942; BBA, So. Meth. U., 1965; JD cum laude, Ohio State U., 1968. Bar: Ohio 1968, US Dist. Ct., So. Dist. of Ohio, 1970, US Ct. of Appeals, Sixth Circuit, 1973. Mng. ptnr. Baker & Hostetler, Columbus, Ohio, 1979—, mem. Operating Group & Policy Com. Bd. dirs. Central Benefits Mutual Insurance Co., Dennison Health Providers Assurance Co. Trustee Recreation Unlimited; mem. nat. council Ohio State U. Coll. of Law; bd. dirs. Osteopathic Heritage Found. Mem.: ABA, Columbus Bar Assn., Ohio State Bar Assn. Office: Baker & Hostetler Capitol Sq 65 E State St Ste 2100 Columbus OH 43215-4260 Office Phone: 614-462-2638. Office Fax: 614-462-2616. Business E-Mail: ghairston@bakerlaw.com.

HAJEK, BRUCE E., electrical engineer, educator; PhD, U. Calif., Berkeley, 1979. Prof. dept. elec. and computer enging. U. Ill., Urbana. Mem. NAE. Office: U Ill CSL 1308 W Main St Urbana IL 61801 E-mail: b_hajek@uiuc.edu.

HAKE, RALPH F., former appliance manufacturing executive; b. Cin., Jan. 25, 1949; m. Robin Hake; 1 child, Mark. BBA, U. Cin., 1971; MBA, U. Chgo., 1975. V.p. adminstrn.l. Mead Corp., Escababa, Mich., 1980-84, dir. corp. devel. Dayton, Ohio, 1984-87; various fin. and ops. positions including corp. v.p., contr. Whirlpool Corp., Benton Harbor, Mich., from 1987, pres. Bauknecht appliance group, exec. v.p. N.Am. appliance group, sr. exec. v.p. ops., until 1997, sr. exec. v.p., CFO, 1997-1999; exec. v.p., CFO Fluor Corp., Aliso Viejo, Calif., 1999—2001; chmn., CEO Maytag Corp., 2001—06. Bd. dirs. ITT Industries, 2002—. Served in U.S. Army, 1971-73. Mem. NAM (bd. dirs.). Avocations: woodworking, reading.

HAKEL, MILTON DANIEL, JR., psychologist, educator, writer, consultant; b. Hutchinson, Minn., Aug. 1, 1941; s. Milton Daniel and Emily Ann (Kovar) H.; m. Lee Ellen Pervier, Sept. 1, 1962; children: Lane, Jennifer BA, U. Minn., 1963, PhD, 1966. Diplomate in Indsl. and Orgnl. Psychology Am. Bd. Profl. Psychology. Prof. psychology Ohio State U., Columbus, 1968-85, U. Houston, 1985-91, chmn. dept., 1987-91; pres. Orgnl. Rsch. and Devel., 1977—2006; ptnr. Applied Rsch. Group, 1984-87; Ohio Bd. Regents eminent scholar, prof. Bowling Green State U., 1991—. Trustee Am. Bd. Profl. Psychology, 1987-90; mem. US nat. com. Internat. Union Psychol. Sci., 1997-01, mem. com. on assessment and tchr. quality NRC, 1999-00, mem. bd. testing and assessment, 1999-05, evaluate advanced tchr. cert., Ohio Bd. Regents, 2005—, chair com. higher learning accountability and productivity, 2005—. Co-author (sr.): Making It Happen: Doing Research with Implementation in Mind, 1982; author: Beyond Multiple Choice: Evaluating Alternatives to Traditional Testing, 1998; editor Current Directions in Psychol. Sci., 1998-99, Personnel Psychology, 1973-84, pub., 1984-2004; co-editor: Applying the Science of Learning to University Teaching and Beyond, 2002; contbr. 40 articles to profl. jours. Chair Human Capital Initiative Coordinating Com., 1991-99, co-chair Applying Sci. Learning to U. Edu. conf. steering com. Recipient James McKeen Cattell award, 1965; Fulbright-Hays Sr. scholar, 1978; NSF grantee, 1966-73; Disting. Svc. Contbrs. award, 1995. Fellow Assn. for. Psychol. Sci. (founding bd. dirs., co-chair Lifelong Learning at Work and at Home 2006—), Soc. Indsl. and Orgnl. Psychology (pres. 1984), Am. Assn. Adv. Sci., Internat. Assn. Applied Psychology (bd. dirs. 2004-), Summit Conf.; mem. Ohio Bd. Regents Com. Higher Learning Accountability and Productivity (chair 2006). Presbyterian. Home: 1435 Cedar Ln Bowling Green OH 43402-1476 Office: Bowling Green State U Dept Psychology Bowling Green OH 43403-0001 Office Phone: 419-372-8144. Business E-Mail: mhakel@bgsu.edu.

HALBERSTAM, HEINI, mathematics professor; b. Most, Czechoslovakia, Sept. 11, 1926; came to Eng., 1939, naturalized, 1998. s. Michael and Judith (Honig) H.; m. Heather M. Peacock, Mar. 11, 1950 (dec. 1971); children: Naomi Deborah, Judith Marion, Lucy Rebecca, Michael Welsford; m. Doreen Bramley, Sept. 28, 1972. BS with honours, Univ. Coll., London U., 1946, MS, 1948, PhD, 1952. Lectr. math. U. Exeter, 1949-57; reader Royal Holloway Coll., London U., 1957-62; Erasmus Smith prof. Trinity Coll., Dublin, Ireland, 1962-64; prof. Nottingham U., England, 1964-80; prof. math. U. Ill., Urbana-Champaign, 1980-96, prof. emeritus, 1996—. Vis. lectr. Brown U., 1955-56; vis. prof. U. Mich., 1966, U. Tel Aviv, 1973, U. Paris-South, 1972 Co-author: Sequences, 1966, 2d edit., 1983, Sieve Methods, 1975; co-editor math. papers of, W.R. Hamilton, H. Davenport, J.E. Littlewod, L.K. Hua; contbr. articles to profl. jours. Mem. London Math. Soc. (v.p. 1962-63, 74-77), Am. Math Soc. E-mail: heini@math.uiuc.edu.

HALBREICH, KATHY, museum director; b. NYC, Apr. 24, 1949; d. Irwin and Betty Ann (Stoll) H.; m. John Kohring; 1 child, Henry. BA, Bennington Coll., 1971; postgrad., Skowhegan Sch. Painting and Sculpture, Maine, 1965, Am. U., Mexico City, 1966. Adminstr. spl. programs Bennington Coll., Vt., 1975-766; dir. teaching seminar Assn. Collegiate Schs. Architecture, Washington, 1977; v.p. programs, trustee Artist Found., Boston, 1979-84; dir. com. on visual arts Hayden Gellery, List Visual Arts Ctr., MIT, Cambridge, Mass., 1976-86; ind. curatorial cons., 1986-88; curator contemporary art Mus. Fine Arts, Boston, 1988-90; dir. Walker Art Ctr., Mpls., 1991—2007; assoc. dir. Mus. Modern Art, NYC, 2007—. Cons. St. Louis Art Mus., Artists Space, N.Y.C., Capp St. Project, San Francisco, Mus. Modern Art, N.Y.C., Seattle Arts Commn., Southeastern Ctr. for Contemporary Art, Louis Comfort Tiffany Found., Beacon Cos., Frito-Lay Inc., New Eng. Gen. Svcs. Adminstrn. Art-in-Architecture Program, Nat. Endowment for Arts, VA Art-in-Architecture Program; trustee MA Coun. on the arts and Humanities; advisor Pub. Art Policy Project and Publ., Nat. Endowment for Arts, 1987; mem. nat. com. P!ub. Art in Am. Conf., Phila., 1987. Trustee Twin Cities Pub. TV, 1992. Mem. Assn. Art Mus. Dirs., Andy Warhol Found. for Visual Arts Inc. (bd. dirs. 1992), Mpls. Club. Named to Centennial Honor Roll, Am. Assn. Museums, 2006. Office: Mus Mod Art 11 W 53rd St New York NY 10019

HALE, DAVID CLOVIS, former state representative; b. Sacramento, Aug. 14, 1964; s. Clovis Ray and Judy Garland (Lee) H.; m. Shannon Lynn Ruyle, June 19, 1993. BA in Social Sci., Cedarville Coll., 1986; M in internat. bus., St. Louis U., 1995. Asst. mgr. Assocs. Fin. Corp., Fairborn, Ohio, 1986-87; br. fin. rep. Am. Family Fin. Svc., St. Louis, 1987-88; state rep. State of Mo., Jefferson City, 1989-94; mgr. external affairs AT&T Wireless Svcs., St. Louis, 1995-97, mgr. corp. comm. and pub. affairs, 1998—. Mem. Am. Legis. Exch. Coun. Health Care Task Force, 1989-93, Trade, Travel and Tourism Task Force, 1993-94, Missourians First Task Force, 1992-94; allocator United Way, 1990-93; active First Evang. Free Ch., St. Louis. Mem. World Affairs Coun. (bd. dirs.), St. Louis World Trade Club St. Louis. Office: AT&T Wireless Svcs 400 S Woods Mill Rd Chesterfield MO 63017-3429 Home: 2004 Chapel Wood Rd Columbia MO 65203-5720 E-mail: david-hale@attws.com.

HALE, JAMES THOMAS, retail executive, lawyer; b. Mpls., May 14, 1940; s. Thomas Taylor and Alice Louise (Mc Connon) H.; m. Sharon Sue Johnson, Aug. 27, 1960; children: David Scott, Eric James, Kristin Lynn. BA, Dartmouth Coll., 1962; LLB, U. Minn., 1965. Bar: Minn. Law clk. Chief Justice Earl Warren, U.S. Supreme Ct., 1965-66; asso. firm Faegre & Benson, Mpls., 1966-73, ptnr., 1973-79; v.p., dir. corp. growth Gen. Mills, Inc., 1979-80, v.p. fin. and control consumer non-foods, 1981; sr. v.p., gen. counsel, corp. sec. Dayton-Hudson Corp., Mpls., 1981-2000; exec. v.p., gen. counsel, corp. sec. Target Corp., 2000—04, cons., 2004—. Adj. prof. U. Minn., 1967-73; bd. dirs. Tennant Co., 2001-Mem. exec. com. Fund Legal Aid Soc., others. Mem. Order of Coif, Phi Beta Kappa. Office: Target Corp 1000 Nicollet Mall Minneapolis MN 55403-2467

HALES, DANIEL B., lawyer; b. Oak Park, Ill., Sept. 29, 1941; s. Burton W. and Marion (Jones) Hales; m. Deborah J. Dorr, June 4, 1966 (dec. Nov. 2002); children: Daniel R. J., Marion P., George B. BA in Econs., U. Mich., 1963; JD, Northwestern U., 1966. Bar: Ill. 1966, U.S. Dist. Ct. (no. dist.) Ill. 1967, U.S. Ct. Appeals (7th cir.) 1968, U.S. Supreme Ct. 1977. Gen. counsel Philadelphia Soc., Chgo. Dir. Chgo. Crime Commn.; pres., dir. Ams. for Effective Law Enforcement, Inc., Chgo.; chmn. Ill. Lawyers for Reagan and Bush, 1980; gen. counsel New Trier Rep. Orgn.; mem. bd. govs., v.p., treas. United Rep. Fund Ill. Mem.: Chgo. Bar Assn. (mem. trust law com. 1975—), Commonwealth Club, Law Club, Federalist Soc. (advisor). Office: 711 Oak St # 102 Winnetka IL 60093 Home Phone: 847-446-6474; Office Phone: 847-446-6474.

HALES, RALEIGH STANTON, JR., retired mathematics professor, academic administrator; b. Pasadena, Calif., Mar. 16, 1942; s. Raleigh Stanton and Gwendolen (Washington) Hales; m. Diane Cecilia Moore, July 8, 1967; children: Karen Gwen, Christopher Stanton. BA, Pomona Coll., 1964; MA, Harvard U., 1965, PhD, 1970. Tchg. fellow Harvard U., Cambridge, Mass., 1965—67; instr. math. Pomona Coll., Claremont, Calif., 1967—70, asst. prof., 1970—74, assoc. prof., 1974—85, prof., 1985—90, assoc. dean. coll., 1973—90; pres. Claremont Computations, 1983—90; prof. math. scis., v.p. acad. affairs Coll. Wooster, Ohio, 1990, pres., 1995—2007, pres. emeritus, 2007—; sr. cons. Academic Search, Inc., 2007—. Cons. Calif. Divsn. Savs. and Loan, 1968—70, Econs. Rsch. Assocs., LA, 1969, Devel. Econs., LA, 1971, Fed. Home Loan Bank Bd., Washington, 1971—72. Author: computer software; contbr. articles to profl. jours.; patentee calculator. Trustee Polytech. Sch., Pasadena, Calif., 1973—79, Foothill Country Day Sch., Claremont, 1985—90, chmn., 1989—90; coun. Internat. Badminton Fedn., 1989—99; bd. dirs. U.S. Badminton Assn., 1967—73, 1978—89, pres., 1985—88; mem. exec. bd. U.S. Olympic Com., 1989—90. Named Wig Disting. prof., Pomona Coll., 1971. Mem.: Wooster Country Club, Math. Assn. Am., Am. Math. Soc., Pasadena Badminton Club (pres. 1978—85). Republican. Episcopalian. Home: 1573 Willoughby Dr Wooster OH 44691 Office Phone: 330-264-4442. E-mail: shales@wooster.edu.

HALEY, DAVID, state legislator; b. Kansas City, 1958; m. Michelle Haley. Mem. Kans. Ho. of Reps. from 34th dist., Topeka, 1994-2000, Kans. Senate from 4th dist., Topeka, 2001—. Pub. affairs cons. Address: 936 Cleveland Ave Kansas City KS 66101-1226

HALEY, DAVID ALAN, healthcare executive; b. St. Louis, Aug. 29, 1943; s. John David and Helen Ermyl (Richardson) H.; children: Trisha Lynn, Jason Alan, Eric athan. BA, So. Ill. U., Edwardsville, 1966; MPH magna cum laude, UCLA, 1971. Adminstrv. asst. Kaiser Found. Hosp., Panorama City, Calif., 1971; assoc. adminstr. Our Lady of Lourdes Hosp., Pasco, Wash., 1971-74, Garfield Hosp., Monterey Park, Calif., 1974-75; assoc. exec. dir. Gen. Hosp., Ft. Walton Beach, Fla., 1976-79; v.p. ops. Our Lady of the Lake Regional Med. Ctr., Baton Rouge, 1979-88; pres. Phoenix Connection, Baton Rouge, 1988-89; CEO Gibson Gen. Hosp., Princeton, Ind., 1989-93; pres., CEO Four States Physicians Assn., Joplin, Mo., 1993-94; exec. dir. MedQuest Health Resources, Inc., 1995-96; pres., CEO The Haley Group, Frankfort, Ill., 1996—2004; CEO St. Anthony's Hospice, Henderson, Ky., 2004—06; v.p., COO Ctr, for Hospice and Palliative Care, South Bend, Ind., 2006—. Mem. Four Rivers Comprehensive Health Planning Agy., Richland, Wash., 1972-74; treas. S.E. Wash. State Hosp. Coun., Pasco, 1973, v.p. 1974; corp. mem. Mid La. Health Systems Agy., Baton Rouge, 1979-82; gubernatorial appointee La. Statewide Health Coord. Coun., Baton Rouge, 1984; gubernatorial appointee, Healthcare Facility Adminstrn. Bd., Indpls., 1991-93; sec.-treas. S.W. Ind. Hosp. Coun., Evansville, 1992-93. Served with USNR, 1967-69. USPHS fellow, 1969-71. Fellow Am. Coll. Healthcare Execs.; mem. Healthcare Fin. Mgmt. Assn., La. Hosp. Assn. (council on planning, 1984-87), Ind. Hosp. Assn. (mem. coun. pub. rels. 1992-93), Vis. Nurse Assn. Southwestern Ind. (bd. dirs. 1992-93), La. Assn. Bus. and Industry (health care council 1987); Kiwanis, Rotary. Republican. Home and Office: The Haley Group 3628 Raleigh Ct Mishawaka IN 46545

HALEY, GEORGE, Romance languages educator; b. Lorain, Ohio, Oct. 19, 1929; s. George and Mary (Haley). AB, Oberlin Coll., 1948; MA, Brown U., 1951, PhD (Pres.'s fellow), 1956. Prof. U. Chgo., 1968—, chmn. dept. Romance langs., 1970-74. Author: Vicente Espinel and Marcos de Obregón, 1959, The Narrator in Don Quixote, 1965, Diario de un Estudiante de Salamanca, 1977, El Quijote de Cervantes, 1984, Vicente Espinel y Marcos de Obregon: Biografia, Autobiografia y Novela, 1994, Indagaciones, 2005; mem. editl. bd. Modern Philology, 1967-95, Canente, 2004— Guggenheim fellow, 1962-63 Mem. Hispanic Soc. Am., MLA, Phi Beta Kappa. Home: 901 S Plymouth Ct Chicago IL 60605-2059 Office: 1050 E 59th St Chicago IL 60637-1559

HALEY, PAT, state legislator; m. Irene Haley; 3 children. Student, U. Minn., St. John's U. Mem. S.D. Ho. of Reps., 1993-2000, mem. commerce and state affairs com. Writer and pub. Home: 766 Utah Ave SE Huron SD 57350-2906

HALEY, THOMAS WILLIAM, manufacturing executive; b. Bird Island, Minn., Oct. 23, 1936; s. Mildred (Driscoll) H.; m. Carolyn Marie Peterson, June 16, 1962; children: Sheila, Marie. BS in Bus., U. Minn., 1964. Rsch. technician Honeywell, Inc., Mpls., 1960-64; rsch. analyst J.M. Dain & Co., Mpls., 1964-67; v.p. fin. Pawnee Corp., Pipestone, Minn., 1967-70; chmn., chief exec. officer Innovex, Inc., Hopkins, Minn., 1972—. Chmn. bd. Mag-Head Enging., Mpls., 1987—; bd. dirs. Precision Coatings, Mpls. Sgt. USMC, 1954-57. Mem. Phi Beta Kappa, Beta Gamma Sigma. Republican. Avocations: running, cooking, reading, golf. Office: Innovex Inc 5540 Pioneer Creek Dr Maple Plain MN 55359-9007

HALL, CURTIS E., lawyer; b. 1956; BA, U. Va., 1978; JD, Yale U., 1981. Bar: NY 1981, DC 1984, Mich. 1989. Asst. dist. atty. Manhattan, NYC; asst. US atty. Washington; atty. Miller, Canfield, Paddock & Stone, Kalamazoo, ptnr., 1992—94; gen. counsel Stryker Corp., Kalamazoo, 1994—, v.p., 2004—. Office: Stryker Corp 2725 Fairfield Rd Kalamazoo MI 49002

HALL, DAVID CHARLES, retired zoological park administrator, veterinarian; b. St. Paul, Aug. 12, 1944; s. Wilhelm Frank and Estelle Elizabeth H.; m. Sandra Jean Prink, Oct. 2, 1945; children: Jason Wilhelm, Jeremy Marvin. BME, U. Minn., 1966, DVM, 1976. Sr. mktg. engr. Rosemount Engring. Co., Eden Prairie, Minn., 1966-75; ptnr. Oregon (Wis.) Vet. Med. Clinic, 1976-86; dir. Henry Vilas Zool. Pk., Madison, Wis., 1986-2000; ret., 2000. Advisor Food divsn. Wis. Dept. Agrl. Trade and Consumer Protection, Madison, 1985-86, Exam. sect. Wis. Dept. Regulation and Licensing, Madison, 1981-82. Recipient Caleb Dorr acad. award, U. Minn., 1972-76. Mem. AVMA, Am. Assn. Zoo Vets., Am. Assn. Zool. Pks. and Aquariums, Phi Kappa Phi, Phi Zeta. Lodges: Optimists (pres. 1980). Luth. Avocations: skiing, swimming, hiking, hunting, other outdoor sports. Home: N3369 Koepp Rd Merrimac WI 53561

HALL, DONALD JOYCE, SR., greeting card company executive; b. Kansas City, Mo., July 9, 1928; s. Joyce Clyde and Elizabeth Ann (Dilday) H.; m. Adele Coryell, Nov. 28, 1953; children: Donald Joyce, Margaret Elizabeth, David Earl. AB, Dartmouth, 1950; LL.D., William Jewell Coll., Denver U., 1977. With Hallmark Cards, Inc., Kansas City, Mo., 1953—, adminstrv. v.p., 1958-66, pres., chief exec. officer, 1966-83, chief exec. officer, 1983-86, chmn. bd. only, 1983—. Dir. United Telecommunications, Inc., Dayton-Hudson Corp., William E. Coutts Co., Ltd.; past dir. Fed. Res. Bank Kansas City, Mut. Benefit Life Ins. Co., Business Men's Assurance Co., Commerce Bank Kansas City, 1st Nat. Bank Lawrence. Pres. Civic Council Greater Kansas City; past chmn. bd. Kansas City Assn. Trusts and Founds.; Bd. dirs. Am. Royal Assn., Friends of Art, Eisenhower Found.; bd. dirs. Kansas City Minority Suppliers Devel. Council, Kans. City Minority Suppliers Devel. Council,Kansas City Symphony; past pres. Pembroke Country Day Sch., Civic Council of Greater Kansas City; trustee, past chmn. exec. com. Midwest Research Inst.; trustee Nelson-Atkins Museum of Art. Served to 1st lt. AUS, 1950-53. Recipient Eisenhower Medallion award, 1973; Parsons Sch. Design award, 1977; 3d Ann. Civic Service award Hebrew Acad. Kansas City, 1976; Chancellor's medal U. Mo., Kansas City, 1977; Disting. Service citation U. Kans., 1980; named one of Forbes' Richest Americans, 2006 Mem. Kansas City C. of C. (named Mr. Kansas City 1972, dir.), AIA (hon.) Office: Hallmark Cards Inc Office Chmn Bd 2501 Mcgee St Kansas City MO 64108-2600

HALL, ELLIOTT SAWYER, lawyer; b. Detroit, May 1, 1938; s. Otis and Ethel (Burton) H.; m. Shirley Robinson, Oct. 3, 1976; children by previous marriage— Frederick, Lannis; 1 child by present marriage, Tiffany. B.A. in Polit. Sci., Wayne State U., 1962, J.D., 1965; LL.D., Shaw Coll., 1983. Bar: Mich. 1966. Pvt. practice law, Detroit, 1967-74, 75-83; corp. counsel City of Detroit, 1974; chief asst. pros. atty. Wayne County Prosecutor's Office, Detroit, 1983-85, ptnr. Dykenz, Gossett, 1985-87, 2002—, v.p. dealer develop., Ford Motor Co., 1989-2001, v.p. civic and external affairs, 1993-2001. Bd. dirs. Music Hall, Detroit, 1984—, Orch. Hall, Detroit, 1984—, Family Service of Detroit and Wayne County, 1984—, Ford Motor Co., 1987, NC Mutual Life Insurance Co.; mem. pub. safety and justice com. New Detroit, Inc., 1984—, Emergency Transitional Edn. Bd. DC, Detroit/Wayne County Port Authority, Detroit Symphony Orchestra, Mercy Coll. of Detroit, Nat. Rehabilitation Hosp., Marymount Coll., Shakesphere Theatre, Wolf Trap Found., Georgetown U., Clark Atlanta U., Congressional Black Caucus Found.; industry adv. bd., Kennedy Inst.; v.p. Econ. Club Wash., Federal City Coun.; bd. chmn. Joint Ctr. for Polit. and Econ. Studies, Wash., DC, Mt. Carmel Mercy Hosp., Howard U. Hosp., Wash., DC, Wash. Performing Arts Soc.; founding mem. Com. on Pub. Edn.; co-chmn. DC Com. on Pub. Edn.; trustee Wash. Opera, WETA-FM and WETA-TV, Founder's Soc. of Detroit Inst. of Arts, Com. Found. SE Mich., US Capital Hist. Soc., Wash. DC; treas. Children's Charities Found.; former pres. NAACP, Detroit Branch. Recipient Human Relations Inst. Civic Achievement award, Am. Jewish Com., Disting. Alumni award, Wayne State U. Law Sch., President's award, Nat. Bar Assn., OBA Achievement award, Wayne State U., 1994 Mem. Detroit Bar Assn. (pres-elect), Wolverine Bar Assn. (pres. 1981-82, President's award), Econ. Club Washington (v.p.). Democrat. Office: Dykema Gossett Ste 3800 400 Renaissance Ctr Detroit MI 48243

HALL, FRANKLIN R., entomology researcher, educator; b. Boston, Oct. 30, 1934; BS, Univ. Mass., 1956; MS, Syracuse Univ., 1961; PhD, Purdue Univ., 1967. Field rep. entomology Niagara Chemical Co., 1960-63; fruit crop specialist Chevron Chemical Co., Standard Oil Co. Calif., 1967-70; prof. devel. rep. agril. Chemagro Corp., 1970; head lab. pest control Applications Tech. Ohio State U., 1981—. Asst. prof. Ohio Agrl. Rsch. & Devel. Ctr. Ohio State Univ., 1970-73, assoc. prof., 1973-78, prof. entomology, 1978-2000, prof. emeritus, 2001. Mem. Entomology Soc. Am. Office: Ohio State U Lab Pest Control Application Tech Agrl R&D Ctr Wooster OH 44691

HALL, GLENN ALLEN, lawyer, state representative; b. Pekin, Ill., Oct. 22, 1955; s. Gerald Eugene and Vinetta Bell Hall; m. Mary Melodie Hall, Dec. 30, 1978; children: Kimberly, Jaired, Ellie, Chava, Justice. BS in Edn., U. Mo., 1980; JD, Regent U., 1989. Bar: Mo. 1989. Atty. Glenn Allen Hall, Atty. at law, Kansas City, Mo., 1989—2001; state rep. State of Mo., 1993-99; owner The Almond Branch, Salem, Mo., 2001—; atty. Glenn Allen Hall, Atty. at Law, Salem, Mo., 2001—. Author: No Justice in the Land, 1993, The Separation, 1999, When We Awake, 2003. Home: 5382 Maize Dr Virginia Beach VA 23464-6160 Fax: 573-729-2344. E-mail: salemjustice@earthlink.net.

HALL, HANSEL CRIMIEL, communications executive; b. Gary, Ind., Mar. 12, 1929; s. Alfred McKenzie and Grace Elizabeth (Crimiel) Hall. BS, Ind. U., 1953; LLB, Blackstone Sch. Law, 1982. Officer IRS, 1959-64; gasoline svc. sta. operator, then realtor Chgo., 1964-69; program specialist HUD, Chgo., 1969-73; dir. equal opportunity St. Paul, 1973-75; dir. fair housing Indpls., from 1975; human resource officer U.S. Fish and Wildlife Svc., Twin Cities, Minn. Cons. in civil rights; pres. bd. dirs. Riverview Towers Cooperative Assn., Inc., 1984-87; pres., CEO Crimiel Comms., Inc., 1988-; pres. West Bank Cmty. Coalition, Inc., 2002-03; CFO, treas. Korean War Vets. Edn. Grant Corp., 1996-2001; del. U.S. parliamentarian to Russia and Czechoslovakia, 1992, to Cuba, 1999; bd. dirs. Nat. Korean War Vets. Assn., 1992. With USAF, 1951-53, Korea. Recipient Amb. for Peace cert. Korean Vets. Assn., 1991, Korean Svc. medal Rep. of Korea, 1991. Mem. Res. Officers Assn. (life), Am. Inst. Parliamentarians, Nat. Assn. Parliamentarians, Minn. State Assn. Parliamentarians (pres. 1997-99), Toastmasters DTM, Ind. U. Alumni Assn., Omega Psi Phi, Phi Alpha Delta. Personal E-mail: crimielhh@hotmail.com.

HALL, HOWARD ERNEST, lawyer; b. Cleve., Oct. 4, 1945; s. Howard Leland and Edna Mae (Geiss) H.; m. Jamie L. Sundheimer, Sept. 21, 1968 (div.); children— Matthew Reed, Jennifer Kathleen, Michael John; m. Michelle M. Forne-Karotka, Oct. 22, 1994; stepchildren: Kyle D. Karotko, Desiree N. Karotko. BS, Bowling Green State U., Ohio, 1967; JD, U. Toledo, 1970. Bar: Ohio 1970; U.S. Dist. Ct. (no. dist.) Ohio 1972; U.S. Dist. Ct. (so. dist.) Ohio 1978. Sole practice, Parma, Ohio, 1970-72; assoc. Thomas E. Ray Law Office,

Cardington, Ohio, 1972-74; ptnr. Ray & Hall, Cardington, 1974-80, Howard E. Hall Law Office, Cardington, 1980-84, Hall & Elkin, Cardington, 1985—99; asst. prosecutor Morrow County, Ohio, 1977-82, prosecutor, 1985—99; judge Morrow County Common Pleas Ct., 1999—; solicitor Village of Cardington, 1974-77, 83-85. Trustee Morrow County chpt. ARC, Mt. Gilead, Ohio, 1981—; pres. trustees Morrow County Coun. on Alcohol and Drugs, Inc., Mt. Gilead, 1982—. Mem. ATLA, ABA, Ohio State Bar Assn., Ohio Acad. Trial Lawyers, Morrow County Bar Assn. (pres. 1983-85), Rotary, Masons (master 1984-85). Republican. Methodist. Avocations: jogging, sports. Home: 2807 Township Road 167 Cardington OH 43315-9715 Office: Hall & Elkin Law Office Hall Elkin Law Ofc 126 E Cardington OH 43338 Office Phone: 419-947-4515. E-mail: judgehall@rrohio.com.

HALL, JEFFREY A., lawyer; b. Junction City, Kans., Sept. 4, 1960; BS in Economics, U. Pa. Wharton Sch., 1982; JD magna cum laude, U. Mich., 1988. Bar: Ill. 1989. CPA Price Waterhouse, 1982—85; law clk. to Hon. James L. Ryan US Ct. of Appeals, 6th cir., 1988—89; ptnr. Bartlit, Beck, Herman, Palenchar & Scott LLP, 1993—. Lectr. law, trial advocacy, and tech. U. Chgo. Law Sch. Articles editor: U. Mich. Law Review. Named to The Am. Lawyer's Top 45 Under 45, 2003. Mem.: Order of the Coif. Office: Bartlit Beck Herman Palenchar & Scott Courthouse Place 54 W Hubbard St Chicago IL 60610 Office Phone: 312-494-4400.

HALL, JOAN M., lawyer; b. Inman, Nebr., Apr. 13, 1939; d. Warren J. and Delia E. (Allyn) McClurg; m. George J. Cotsirilos, Dec. 4, 1988; children: Colin Michael, Justin Allyn BA, Nebr. Wesleyan U., 1961; JD, Yale U., 1965. Bar: Ill. 1965, U.S. Dist. Ct. (no. dist.) Ill. 1965, U.S. Ct. Appeals (7th cir.) 1965. Assoc. Jenner & Block, Chgo., 1965-71, sr. ptnr., 1971—. Chmn. character and fitness Ill. Supreme Ct., 1988-89; mem. dist. admissions com. U.S. Dist. Ct. (no. dist.) Ill. Mem. exec. com. Yale Law Sch. Assn., 1976-86, treas., 1982-85; bd. dirs. Yale Law Sch. FUnd, 1978—, chmn., 1984-86; bd. dirs. Chgo. Lawyer's Com. Civil Rights Under the Law, 1978—, chmn., 1983-84; bd. dirs. Legal Assistance Found. Chgo., 1979-82; trustee Rush-Presbyn. St. Luke's Hosp., 1984—; mem. Gannon-Proctor Commn., 1982-84; trustee, bd. govs. Nebr. Wesleyan U., 1983—; bd. dirs. Goodman Theatre, Ill. Sports Facility Authority, 1986-96; mem. vis. com. Northwestern U. Sch. Law, 1987-92; mem. adv. coun. De Paul U. Sch. Law, 1987-94; bd. govs. Chgo. Lighthouse for the Blind. Fellow Am. Coll. Trial Lawyers; mem. ABA (chmn. litig. sect. 1982-83, fed. judiciary com. 1985-91, resource devel. coun. 1984-85, Ho. of Dels. 1991-93), Comml. Club (sec. 1995—), Econ. Club (Chgo., dir.). Office: Jenner & Block 1 E Ibm Plz Fl 4000 Chicago IL 60611-7603

HALL, KATHY L., orchestra executive; b. Donnellson, Iowa; Prin. bassoonist Cedar Rapids (Iowa) Symphony Orch., exec. dir., 1992. Office: Cedar Rapids Symphony 119 3rd Ave Se Cedar Rapids IA 52401-1403

HALL, TERRY, accountant; b. Champaign, Ill., Dec. 10, 1949; d. Albert L. and Catherine A. (Comstock) Hall; m. Thomas F. Johnston, Sept. 27, 1971 (div. Jan. 1979); 1 child, Daniel K. Johnston. BA, Barat Coll., Lake Forest, Ill., 1984. CPA Ill. Acct. Terry Hall, CPA, PC, Gurnee, Ill., 1985—. Bd. dirs. Lake Forest Profl. Women's Round Table, Ill. Bd. dirs. YWCA Lake County, Waukegan, Ill., 1987-89, Women in Dir.'s Chair, Chgo., 1989-96, Stage Two Theater Co., 1991-2003, Sch. Dist. 50, Ill., 2007—; found. bd., Ctr. for Women, 2006-; alumni coun. Lake Forest Acad., 1986-98; mem. Dist. 50 Ill. (Woodland) Sch. Bd., 2007—. Mem. AICPA, ABA (assoc.), Nat. Assn. Tax Preparers, Nat. Soc. Tax Profls., Ill. Soc. CPAs (mem. faculty, mem. state litigation com. 1988-95), Wis. Inst. CPAs (state litigation com. 1989-92), Chgo. Soc. Women CPAs, Lake County Estate Planning Coun., CPAs for the Pub. Interest (Outstanding Vol. 1991). Avocation: travel. Office: 5250 Grand Ave Ste 14 Gurnee IL 60031

HALL, TOM T., retired country singer, songwriter; b. Olive Hill, Ky., May 25, 1936; s. Virgil Hall; m. Dixie Dean. Student, Roanoke Coll. Founder pub. co. Hallnote Music. With group Tom Hall and the Kentucky Travelers, disc jockey, Sta. WMOR, Morehead, Ky., songwriter with, Newkeys Music, Inc., rec. artist with Mercury Records until 1977, with RCA, Mercury, Polygram records, 1977-2003; performed with band, The Storytellers, Carnegie Hall, N.Y.C., 1973; performed at Smithsonian Instn., 1979, White House, 1980; albums include Magnificent Music Machine, Natural Dreams, 1984, Homecoming, I Witness Life, The Storyteller, Songs of Fox Hollow, Country Classics, Ol' T's in Town, Places I've Done Time, Everything From Jesus to Jack Daniels, many others; songs include Harper Valley P.T.A.; author: Songwriter's Handbook, Laughing Man of Woodmont Coves, Acts of Life, Christmas and the Old House, The Storyteller's ashville, What a Book! Served in U.S. Army, 1957-61.

HALL, WILLIAM JOEL, retired civil engineer, educator; b. Berkeley, Calif., Apr. 13, 1926; s. Eugene Raymond and Mary (Harkey) H.; m. Elaine Frances Thalman, Dec. 18, 1948; children: Martha Jane, James Frederick, Carolyn Marie. Student, U. Calif., Berkeley, 1943-44, Kings Point, 1944-45; BSCE, U. Kans., Lawrence, 1948; MS, U. Ill., Urbana, 1951, PhD, 1954. Teaching asst. U. Kans., 1947-48; engr. Sohio Pipe Line Co., 1948-49; mem. faculty U. Ill., Urbana, 1954—93, prof. civil engring., 1959-93, head dept. civil engring., 1984-91; prof. emeritus, 1993—. Cons. in structural dynamics, seismic, materials to govts. and industrial orgns. Author books, articles, revs., book chpts. Recipient A. Epstein Meml. award, U. Ill., 1958, Halliburton Engring. Edn. Leadership award, 1980, Disting. Engring. Svc. award, U. Kans., 1985; Univ. scholar, U. Ill., 1986—89. Fellow AAAS; mem. ASCE (pres. Ctrl. Ill. sect. 1967-68, chmn. structural divsn. exec. com. 1973-77, chmn. tech. coun. on lifeline earthquake engring. exec. com. 1982-85, Kans. sect. award 1948, Walter L. Huber award 1963, Howard award 1984, Newmark medal 1984, C. Martin Duke award 1990, Norman medal 1992), Nat. Acad. Engring., Am. Concrete Inst., Am. Welding Soc. (Adams Meml. membership award 1967), Earthquake Engring. Rsch. Inst. (Housner medal 1998), Seismol. Soc. Am., Structural Engrs. Assn. Ill. (John Parmer award 1990), Sigma Xi, Tau Beta Pi (Daniel C. Drucker eminent faculty award 1993), Sigma Tau, Chi Epsilon (nat. honor mem. 1998), Phi Kappa Phi. Office: U Ill Civil Engring 3103 Newmark Lab 205 N Mathews Ave Urbana IL 61801-2350 Home: 101 W Windsor Rd #4308 Urbana IL 61802-6661 Office Phone: 217-333-3927. Personal E-mail: wj-efhall@insightbb.com. Business E-Mail: w-hall3@uiuc.edu.

HALLAUER, ARNEL ROY, geneticist; b. Netawaka, Kans., May 4, 1932; s. Roy Virgil and Mabel Fern (Bohnenkemper) H.; m. Janet Yvonne Goodmanson, Aug. 29, 1964; children: Elizabeth, Paul BS, Kans. State U., 1954; MS, Iowa State U., 1958, PhD, 1960. Rsch. agronomist USDA, Ames, Iowa, 1958-60, geneticist Raleigh, C, 1961-62, rsch. geneticist Ames, 1963-89; prof. Iowa State U., 1990—2002, C.F. Curtiss Disting. prof. agr. emeritus, 2003—. Author: (with J.B. Miranda) Quantitative Genetics in Maize Breeding, 1981, 2d edit., 1988; editor: Specialty Corns, 1994, 1st edit., 2000. 2d lt. US Army, 1954-56. Recipient Applied Rsch. and Ext. award 1981, Henry A. Wallace award for disting.svc. to agr., 1992, Disting. Alumni Achievement citation, 1996, Iowa State U., Genetics and Plant Breeding award Nat. Coun. Plant Breeding, 1984, Gov.'s Sci. medal State of Iowa, 1990, Burlington No. Career Rsch. Achievement award Iowa State Found., 1991, Centennial medal Phi Kappa Phi, 1997, Verdent Plant Genetics award Verdent Ptnrs., Chgo., 2001; named to USDA/Agrl. Rsch. Sci. Hall of Fame, 1992; named one of 150 Visionaries Iowa State U., 2007; honored Inter-Am. Inst. Coop. Agr. significant contbns. to agr., Washington, 2003, Arnel R. Hallauer Internat. Symposium plant breeding, Mexico City, 2003; USDA grantee, 1982, 85, 87, 90. Fellow Am. Soc. Agronomy (Agronomic Achievement award for crops 1989, Agronomic Rsch. award 1992), Crop Sci. Soc. (Dekalb Pfizer Crop Sci. award 1981, Pres.'s award 2002), Iowa Acad. Sci. (disting. fellow 1985); mem. NAS, 1988, Nat. Agri-Mktg. Assn. (nat. award for excellence in rsch. 1993), Am. Genetic Assn., Am. Statis. Assn., Kans. State U. Alumni Assn. (alumni fellow 1997), Iowa State Alumni Assn. (faculty citation 1987, Disting. Achievement Citation 1995), Gamma Sigma Delta (Disting. Svc. to Agr. award 1990, Rsch. Award of Merit 1999). Republican. Lutheran. Home: 516 Luther Dr Ames IA 50010-4735 Office: Iowa State U 1505 Dept Agronomy Ames IA 50010 Office Phone: 515-294-7823. Business E-Mail: hallauer@iastate.edu.

HALLENBECK, LINDA S., elementary school educator; m. Theodore R. Hallenbeck; 2 children. BS, Kent State U., 1974, MEd, 1976, postgrad. Cert. tchr. K-3, K-8, computer sci., math., Ohio Ohio, Nat. bd. cert. Grad. asst. Kent State U., Ohio, 1974—76; tchr. 3d grade Hudson Elem. Sch., Ohio, 1976—77; tchr. 1st grade Evamere Sch., Hudson, 1977—86; tchr. 5th grade J.P. McDowell Elem. Sch., Hudson, 1986—92, East Woods Sch., Hudson, 1992—2001; tchr. Hudson Mid. Sch., 2001—03; rsch. assoc. NSF, 2002—03, Mich. State U., 2003—04. Cons. NSF, Washington, 1989-95, tchr. in residence Office of Gov. Bob Taft, 1999-2001; tchr. Presdl. Acad. for Excellence in Tchg. Math. at Princeton and Northwestern U., Middle Sch. Math. State Trainer, Math Acad., 2001—; mem. exec. bd. Ohio Math./Sci. Coalition. Recipient Presdl. award for excellence in teaching sci. and math. NSF, 1993, Govs. Edn. leadership award, 1998, Ohio Pioneer in Edn award, 2000. Mem. Nat. Coun. Tchrs. Math., Ohio Coun. Tchrs. Math. (pres. 2004—), Ohio Math. Edn. Leadership Coun. Avocations: skiing, gardening, sewing, decorating. Home: 7615 Oxgate Ct Hudson OH 44236-1877 Office Phone: 330-650-4912.

HALLEY, JAMES WOODS, physics professor; b. Chgo., Nov. 16, 1938; m. Merile Hobbs (dec. 2001); 2 children. BS, MIT, 1961; PhD, U. Calif., Berkeley, 1965. NSF predoctoral fellow U. Calif., Berkeley, 1963-65; NSF postdoctoral fellow Faculte des Scis., Orsay, France, 1965-66; asst. prof. U. Calif., Berkeley, 1966-68; assoc. prof. U. Minn., Mpls., 1968-77, prof. physics, 1977—, fellow Supercomputing Inst., grad. faculty materials sci., 1989—. Vis. prof. Oxford U., 1973, Harwell AERE, 1973, U. Oreg., 1975, Yale U., 1976, Brookhaven N.L., 1976, 79, Harvard U., 1979, Mich. State U., 1980, Argonne, 1981—, Inst. Theoretical Physics, Santa Barbara, Calif., 1983, Santa Barbara, 97, Santa Barbara, 98, U. Calif., Santa Barbara, 1984, Berkeley, 93, IBM Almaden Rsch. Ctr., 1987, Australian Nat. U., 1988; cons. 3M, 1985—89, UNESCO, 1986, GM Corp., 1989—90, Ednl. Testing Svc., 1989, mem. GRE bd. examiners, 1991—96; cons. at. Renewable Energy Lab., 1992—97; physics bd. dirs. US Com. Sci. Coop. with Vietnam, 1985—. Author: Physics of Human Motion, 1981, Statistical Mechanics, 2006; editor: 7 books; contbr. articles to profl. jours. Recipient George Taylor Tchg. award, 1979, McMillan professorship, 1979; grantee, NSF, 1972—79, 1995—. Rsch. Corp., 1970—72, Corrosion Ctr., 1980—92, Ednl. Devel. Program, 1973, 1979, 3M, 1982, 2002—05, IBM Advanced Edn. Project, 1985, Dept. Edn., 1986, IBM, 1988—90, Electric Power Rsch. Inst., 1988—90, Dept. Energy, 1990—, Sumitomo Metal Industries, 1992—93, NASA, 1992—95; Bush fellow, 1983—84. Fellow: Am. Phys. Soc.; mem.: AAAS, Materials Rsch. Soc., Am. Chem. Soc. Achievements include research in theory of disorder in condensed matter; statistics and dynamics of polymers; physics of the fluid-solid interface; high temperature superconductivity; condensate fraction in bose superfluids. Office: Univ Minn Sch Physics and Astronomy Minneapolis MN 55455 Office Phone: 612-624-0395. E-mail: woods@woods1.spa.umn.edu.

HALLINAN, JOSEPH THOMAS, journalist; b. Barberton, Ohio, Sept. 3, 1960; s. Neil Patrick and Judith Ann (Tonovitz) H.; m. Pamela L. Taylor, Sept. 10, 2000; children: Jack, Katherine, Anne. BS magna cum laude, Boston U., 1984. Reporter The Indpls. Star, 1984-91; nat. corr. Newhouse News Svc., Washington, 1991-99; reporter Chgo. Tribune, 1999-2000; staff reporter The Wall St. Jour., 2000—07. Vis. prof. Vanderbilt U., 2006. Author: Going Up The River: Travels in a Prison Nation, 2001. Recipient Pulitzer Prize for investigative reporting, 1991; named Disting. Alumni, Boston U., 1992; Nieman fellow Harvard U., 1997-98. Roman Catholic. Avocations: fishing, travel. Home: 3750 Lake Shore Dr Chicago IL 60613

HALLINAN, MAUREEN THERESA, sociologist, educator; BA, Marymount Coll., 1961; MS, U. Notre Dame, 1968; PhD, U. Chgo., 1972. Prof. U. Wis., Madison, 1980-84; with U. Notre Dame, Ind., 1984—, William P. and Hazel B. White prof. arts and letters dept. sociology, dir. Ctr. Rsch. Ednl. Opportunity. Author: The Structure of Positive Sentiment, 1974; editor: Sociology of Edn., 1981—86, The Social Context of Instruction: Group Organization and Group Processes, 1983, The Social Organization of Schools: New Conceptualizations of the Learning Process, 1987, Change in Societal Institutions, 1990, Restructuring Schools: Promising Practices and Policies, 1995, Handbook of the Sociology of Education, 2000, Handbook of the Sociology of Education, Chinese edit., 2004, Handbook of the Sociology of Education, paperback edit., 2006; co-editor: Stability and Change in American Education: Structure, Process and Outcomes, 2003, School Sector and Student Outcomes, 2006; assoc. editor: Social Forces, 1977—80, 1998—2001, Sociology of Edn., 1979—81, 1991—2001; contbr. articles to profl. jours. Recipient U. Notre Dame Rsch. Achievement award, 2003. Mem.: Nat. Acad. Edn. (v.p. fellows 2001—05), Sociol. Rsch. Assn. (sec.-treas. 1999—2000, pres. 2000—01), Am. Sociol. Assn. (session organizer 1980, 1984, sec.-treas. 1988—90, session organizer 1989, chmn. sociology edn. sect. 1991—92, session organizer 1992, pres. 1995—96, session organizer 1996—2001, Willard Waller award 2004), Kappa Delta Phi (laureate chpt. 2007), Phi Beta Kappa. Office: U otre Dame Dept Sociology Notre Dame IN 46556 Business E-Mail: pauley.1@nd.edu.

HALLMAN, GARY L., photographer, educator; b. St. Paul, Aug. 7, 1940; s. Jack J. and Helen A. Hallman; 1 child, Peter J. BA, U. Minn., 1966, MFA, 1971. Mem. faculty dept. studio arts U. Minn., Mpls., 1970—, assoc. prof. photography, 1976—. Vis. adj. prof. R.I. Sch. Design, 1977-78; vis. exchange prof. U. .Mex., 1984-85; vis. assoc. prof. The Colo. Coll., Colorado Springs, 1990; mem. visual arts adv. bd. Minn. State Arts Coun., 1973-76; bd. dirs. Minn. Artists Exhbn. Program, 1989-91. Exhbns. include Internat. Mus. Photography, George Eastman House, 1974, Light Gallery, N.Y.C., 1975, Balt. Mus., 1975, Mus. Modern Art, N.Y.C., 1978, Mpls. Inst. Arts, 1996, B. Gray Gallery East Carolina U., Greenville, N.C., 1997, Nat. Mus. of Am., Washington, 1984, Frederick R. Weisman Art Mus., Mpls., 1998; Mississippi/Neva curator The State Russian Mus., St. Petersburg, 1998; Barg Gallery/Teheran Mus. Contemporary Art, 2001, Risk/Revisit: The Photography of Gary Hallman, PARTs Gallery, Mpls., 2002, McKnight Found. Open Spaces Project, 2002; co-curator Persian Silver, Tehran Mus. Contemporary Art, 2004, (solo) Mus. of Non-Conformist Art, St. Petersburg, Russa, 2005; represented in permanent collections Mus. Modern Art, N.Y.C., Internat. Mus. Photography, Rochester, N.Y., Nat. Gallery Can., Fogg Art Mus., Harvard U., Princeton U. Art Mus., Nat. Mus. Am. Art, Smithsonian Instn., Washington., Mus. Non-conformist Art, St. Petersburg, 2005, Gallery 13, Mpls., 2005. Served with USN, 1958-61. Nat. Endowment Arts fellow, 1975-76; Bush Found. fellow, 1976-77; McKnight Found. fellow, 1982, 90, Artist Assistance fellowship grant, 1996. Mem. Soc. Photog. Edn., Coll. Art Assn. Am. Office: U Minn Dept Studio Arts Minneapolis MN 55455 Office Phone: 612-625-8096. Business E-Mail: hallm001@umn.edu.

HALLMARK, DONALD PARKER, museum director, educator; b. McPherson, Kans., Feb. 16, 1945; s. Daniel Clell and Esther Ione (Hart) H.; m. Linda Lorraine Lego, June 10, 1967; m. Monica Lynn, Amy Kristen. BFA, U. Ill., 1967; MA, U. Iowa, 1970; PhD, St. Louis U., 1980. From asst. prof. to prof. Greenville (Ill.) Coll., 1970-81, chmn. art dept., 1976-81; dir. Richard W. Bock Sculpture Collection, Greenville, 1975-81, Frank Lloyd Wright's Dana-Thomas House Hist. Site, Springfield, Ill., 1981—. Founding bd. mem. Frank Lloyd Wright Bldg Conservancy, Chgo., 1988-96; adj. prof. Sangamon State U., Springfield, 1986-90; lectr. FLW Bldg. Conservancy, Hollyhock House, L.A., The Gamble House, Pasadena, Calif., The High Mus., Atlanta, Decorative Arts Soc. SAH, Chgo., Indpls. Pub. Libr., The atural Pattern of Structure Herberger Lectrs., Ariz. State U., Tempe, Art Inst. Chgo., FLW Bldg. Conservancy, Unity Temple, Oak Park, Ill,. FLW Home and Studio Lectrs., Oak Park Pub. Libr., Mus. of Our Nat. Heritage, Lexington, Mass., The Chgo. Arch. Found., Santa Fe Bldg., Chgo., Nat. Bldg. Mus., Washington, Ctrl. Ill. AIA, Decatur. Author: (booklet) The Dana-Thomas House: Its History, Acquisition and Preservation, 1992, (catalogue) Paul Ashbrook, 1990, (illustrated book) Springfield's Lawrence School Memorial Library, 1993, The Natural Pattern of Structure, 1995; TV interview appearances Bob Vila's Guide to Historic Homes, The Dana-Thomas House, 1996, interview Frank Lloyd Wright and the Prairie School, Films for Humanities and Scis., 1999, Home and Garden TV, 2000; editor newsletter Guidelines for the Conservation of Frank Lloyd Wright Decorative Arts, 1996. Cons., sponsor Ill. Govt. Intern Program, Springfield, 1985—; libr. cons., vol. Michael Victor II Libr. Springfield Art Assn., 1988-93. Faculty grantee Shell Found., 1975; Grad. fellow St. Louis U., 1976. Mem.: Nat. Trust for Historic Preservation, The Frank Lloyd Wright Bldg. Conservancy. Presbyterian. Avocations: slide library collecting, antiques, travel, gardening. Home: 605 W Sheridan Rd Petersburg IL 62675-1359 Office: Ill Hist Preservation Agy 301 E Lawrence Ave Springfield IL 62703-2232 Office Phone: 217-782-6776.

HALLORAN, KATHLEEN L., retired gas industry executive, accountant; b. Sandwich, Ill., July 19, 1952; d. Oscar L. and Gertrude L. Huber. BA in Acctg., Lewis U., 1974; MBA, No. Ill. U., 1979. CPA Ill. With NICOR, Inc., Naperville, 1974-84; asst. sec. No. Ill. Gas subs. NICOR, Inc., Naperville, 1983-84, asst. contr., 1984; sec., treas. NICOR Inc., Naperville, 1984-87; sec., contr. NICOR, Inc., Naperville, 1987-89, v.p., sec., contr., 1989-92, v.p. info. svcs. and gen. acctg., 1992-94; v.p. info. svcs. and rates No. Ill. Gas, Aurora, 1994-95, v.p. info. svcs., rates and human resources, 1995-96, sr. v.p. info. svcs., rates and human resources, 1996-98, sr. v.p. adminstrn., 1998-99, exec. v.p. fin. and adminstrn., 1999—2004; ret., 2004. Bd. dirs. Ctrl. DuPage Health, Voices Am.'s Children, Ill. Children's Healthcare Found.; mem. com. dirs. Voices Ill. Children; trustee Lewis U. Mem.: Chgo. Network. E-mail: khallor@nicor.com.

HALLWAS, JOHN EDWARD, retired English language educator; b. Waukegan, Ill., May 24, 1945; s. Emil Ferdinand and Ruth Edna (Wells) H.; m. Garnette Verna Stockstad, Jan. 3, 1966; children: John Darrin, Evan Bradley. BS in Edn., Western Ill. U., Macomb, 1967, MA, 1968; PhD, U. Fla., 1972. Grad. asst. Western Ill. U., Macomb, 1967-68, prof. English dept., 1970—2004; ret. Author: Western Illinois Heritage, 1983, Illinois Literature: The 19th Century, 1986, Macomb: A Pictorial History, 1990, Spoon River Anthology: An Annotated Edition, 1992, The Bootlegger: A Story of Small-Town America, 1998, others; editor Western Ill. Regional Studies, 1978-92; co-editor: Tales From Two Rivers book series, 1981—, Prairie State Books, 1987—; columnist Macomb Jour., 1981-84, Jacksonville (Ill.) Jour. Courier, 1984-85, 87-88. NDEA fellow U. Fla., Gainesville, 1968-70; recipient Faculty Svc. award Nat. U. Continuing Edn. Assn., 1981, Alumni Achievement award Western Ill. U., Macomb, 1983, MidAm. award, Soc. for Study of Midwestern Lit., 1994; named faculty lectr. Western Ill. U., Macomb, 1983, Disting. prof., 1992; Ann. John Hallwas Liberal Arts Lecture named in his honor, 2003—. Mem.: Soc. for Study Midwestern Lit., Ill. State Hist. Soc. (adv. bd. 1990—96), McDonough County Hist. Soc. (pres. 1981—83), Phi Beta Kappa, Phi Kappa Phi. Avocations: nature study, fitness walking, bicycling. Home: 31 Shorewood Dr Macomb IL 61455-9746 Office Phone: 309-298-2718. Business E-Mail: je-hallwas@wiu.edu.

HALPERIN, ERROL R., lawyer; b. Jan. 3, 1941; BS, De Paul U., 1964, JD, 1967; LLM in Taxation, NYU, 1968. Bar: Ill. 1968; U.S. Tax Ct. 1972. Asst. branch chief, legis. and regulations divsn. IRS, 1968-72; legis. atty., joint com. on taxation U.S. Congress, 1977-79; sr. ptnr., Corp. & Securities practices, mem. exec. com. DLA Piper Rudnick Gray Cary, Chgo. Mem.: Nat. Assn. Real Estate Investment Trusts, Nat. Assn. Bond Lawyers, Ill. State Bar Assn., Chgo. Bar Assn. Office: DLA Piper Rudnick Gray Cary Suite 1900 203 N La Salle St Chicago IL 60601-1293 Office Phone: 312-368-4033. Office Fax: 312-236-7516. Business E-Mail: errol.halperin@dlapiper.com.

HALPERN, JACK, chemist, educator; b. Poland, Jan. 19, 1925; came to U.S., 1962, naturalized; s. Philip and Anna (Sass) H.; m. Helen Peritz, June 30, 1949; children: Janice Henry, Nina Phyllis. BS, McGill U., 1946, PhD, 1949, DSc (hon.), 1997, U. B.C., 1986. NRC postdoc. overseas fellow U. Manchester, England, 1949-50; instr. chemistry U. B.C., 1950, prof., 1961-62; Nuffield Found. traveling fellow Cambridge (Eng.) U., 1959-60; prof. chemistry U. Chgo., 1962-71, Louis Block prof. chemistry, 1971-83, Louis Block Disting. Svc. prof., 1983—. Vis. prof. U. Minn., 1962, Harvard, 1966-67, Calif. Inst. Tech., 1968-69, Princeton U., 1970-71, Max. Planck Institut, Mulheim, Fed. Republic Germany, 1983—, U. Copenhagen, 1978; Sherman Fairchild Disting. scholar Calif. Inst. Tech., 1979; guest scholar Kyoto U., 1981; Firth vis. prof. U. Sheffield, 1982, Phi Beta Kappa vis. scholar, 1990; R.B. Woodward vis. prof. Harvard U., 1991; numerous guest lectureships; cons. editor Macmillan Co., 1963-65, Oxford U. Press; cons. Am. Oil Co., Monsanto Co., Argonne Nat. Lab., IBM, Air Products Co., Enimont, Rohm and Haas; mem. adv. panel on chemistry NSF, 1967-70; mem. adv. bd. Am. Chem. Soc. Petroleum Rsch. Fund, 1972-74, Trans Atlantic Sci. and Humanities Program, 2001--; mem. medicinal chemistry sect. NIH, 1975-78, chmn., 1976-78; mem. chemistry adv. coun. Princeton U., 1982—; mem. univ. adv. com. Ency. Brit., 1985—; mem. chemistry vis. com. Calif. Inst. Tech., 1991—; chmn. German-Am. Acad. Coun., 1993-96, chmn. bd. trustees, 1996—. Assoc. editor: Inorganica Chimica Acta, Jour. Am. Chem. Soc.; co-editor: Collected Accounts of Transition Metal Chemistry, vol. 1, 1973, vol. 2, 1977; assoc. editor Procs. NAS; mem. editl. adv. bd. Oxford Univ. Press, Internat. Series Monographs on Chemistry; mem. editl. bd. Jour. Organometallic Chemistry, Accounts Chem. Rsch., Catalysis Revs., Jour. Catalysis, Jour. Molecular Catalysis, Jour. Coord. Chemistry, Gazzetta Chimica Italiana, Organometallics, Catalysis Letters, Kinetics and Catalysis Letters; contbr. articles to Ency. Britannica, rsch. jours. Trustee Gordon Rsch. Confs., 1968-70; bd. govs. David and Arthur Smart Mus., U. Chgo., 1988—; bd. dirs. Ct. Theatre. Recipient Young Author's prize Electrochem. Soc., 1953, award in catalysis Noble Metals Chem. Soc., London, 1976, Humboldt award, 1977, Richard Kokes award Johns Hopkins U., 1978, Willard Gibbs medal, 1986, Bailar medal U. Ill., 1986, Wilhelm von Hoffman medal German Chem. Soc., 1988, Chem. Pioneer's award Am. Inst. Chemists, 1991, Paracelsus prize Swiss Chem. Soc., 1992, Basolo Medal, Northwestern U., 1993, Robert A. Welch award, 1994, Henry J. Albert award Internat. Precious Metals Inst., 1995, award in Organometallic Chem. Am. Chem. Soc., 1995, Order of Merit Federal Republic of Germany, 1996. Fellow AAAS, Royal Soc. London, Royal Soc. Can., Am. Acad. Arts and Scis., Chem. Inst. Can., Royal Soc. Chemistry London (hon.), N.Y. Acad. Scis., Japan Soc. for Promotion Sci.; mem. NAS (fgn. assoc. 1984-85, mem. coun. 1990—, chmn. chemistry sect. 1991-93, v.p. 1993—, assoc. editor Proceedings NAS), Am. Chem. Soc. (editl. bd. Advances in Chemistry series 1963-65, 78-81, chmn. inorganic chemistry 1985, award in inorganic chemistry 1968, award for disting. svc. in advancement of inorganic chemistry 1985, award in organometallic chemistry 1995), Max Planck Soc. (sci. mem. 1983—), Art Inst. Chgo., Renaissance Soc. (bd. dirs.), New Swiss Chem. Soc. (Paracelsus prize 1992), Am. Friends of the Royal Soc. (bd. dirs.), Sigma Xi. Home: 5801 S Dorchester Ave Apt 4A Chicago IL 60637 Office: U Chgo Dept Chemistry Chicago IL 60637 Office Phone: 773-702-7095. Business E-Mail: jhjh@uchicago.edu.

HALPIN, DANIEL WILLIAM, engineering educator, consultant; b. Covington, Ky., Sept. 29, 1938; s. Jordan W. and Gladys E. (Moore) H.; m. Maria Kirchner, Feb. 8, 1963; 1 child, Rainer. BS, U.S. Mil. Acad., 1961; MSCE, U. Ill., 1969, PhD, 1973. Research analyst Constrn. Engring. Research Lab., Champaign, Ill., 1970-72; faculty U. Ill., Urbana, 1972-73; mem. faculty Ga. Inst. Tech., Atlanta, 1973-85, prof., 1981-85; A.J. Clark prof., dir. Constrn. Engring. and Mgmt. U. Md., 1985-87; dir. divsn. Constrn. Engring. and Mgmt. Purdue U., West Lafayette, Ind., 1987—2006, interim head Sch. Civil Engring., 2000—01, Bowen engring head of constrn. engring. and mgmt., 2006—06, Bowen engring. head emeritus, 2006—. Cons. constrn. mgmt.; vis. assoc. prof. U. Sydney, Australia, 1981; vis. prof. Swiss Fed. Inst. Tech., 1985, U. Karlsruhe, Germany, 1998; vis. scholar Tech. U., Munich, 1979; vis. lectr. Ctr. Cybernetics in Constrn., Bucharest, Romania, 1973; cons. office tech. assessment U.S. Congress, 1986-87; mem. JTEC Team to evaluate constrn. tech., Japan, 1990; juror emeritus Constrn. Innovation Forum, 1994. Author: Design of Construction and Process Operations, 1976, Construction Management, 1980, 3d edit., 2005, Planung und Kontrolle von Bauproduktionsprozessen, 1979, Constructo -A Heuristic Game for Construction Management, 1973, Financial and Cost Control Concepts for Construction Management, 1985, Planning and Analysis of Construction Operations, 1992. Served with C.E., U.S. Army, 1961-67. Decorated Bronze Star; recipient Lifetime Achievement award INFORMS Constrn. sect., Coll. Simulation, 2004; grantee NSF, Dept. Energy, NIOSH. Mem. ASCE (hon.; past sect. pres. 1981-82, chmn. constrn. rsch. coun. 1985-86, Walter L. Huber prize 1979, Peurifoy Constrn. Rsch. award 1992, named disting. mem., 2006), Am. Soc. Engring. Edn., Nat. Acad. Constrn. (elected 2003), Constrn. Industry Inst. (rsch. com. 1996-2005, Carroll H. Dunn award 2006), Constrn. Innovation Forum (juror emeritus), Sigma Xi. Methodist. Business E-Mail: halpin@purdue.edu.

HALSTEAD, DAVID E., aeronautical engineer; s. Helen and George H. BS, MS, MS, Iowa State U. Lead engr. GE Aircraft Engines, Cin. Mem. ASME (Melville award 1998). Achievements include discovery (with others) that fluid flow through a gas turbine is orderly and predictable instead of turbulent as was onced believed. Office: GE Aircraft Engines One Neumann Way Cincinnati OH 45215-6301

HALTER, JEFFREY BRIAN, internal medicine educator, geriatrician; b. Mpls., Aug. 25, 1945; s. Cyril Joel and Marcella (Medoff) H.; m. Ellen Laura Kuper, June 25, 1972; children: Alexander, Loren, Ethan, Amy. BA magna cum laude, U. Minn., 1966, BS, MD, 1969. Diplomate Am. Bd. Internal Medicine (test com. on geriatrics 1986-88), Am. Bd. Endocrinology and Metabolism. Intern, then resident in internal medicine Harbor Gen. Hosp., Torrance, Calif., 1969-71; resident U. Wash. Sch. Medicine, Seattle, 1973-74, fellow div. metabolism, endocrinology and gerontology, 1975-77, acting instr., asst. prof., then assoc. prof. dept. medicine, 1974-84; staff physician VA Med. Ctr., Seattle,

1974-75, assoc. dir. Geriatric Rsch., Edn. and Clin. Ctr., 1978-84; prof. internal medicine, chief div. geriatric medicine U. Mich. Med. Sch., Ann Arbor, 1984—, rsch. scientist, med. dir. Inst. Gerontology, 1984—, dir. Geriatrics Ctr., 1988—. Chief geriatric sect. Ann Arbor VA Med. Ctr., 1984-92, dir. Geriatric Rsch., Edn. and Clin. Ctr., 1988-99; participant, presenter numerous congresses, symposia, confs., workshops in field; vis. prof. numerous univs., including Karolinska Inst., Stockholm, 1983, U. Copenhagen, 1983, Johns Hopkins U., 1985, 91, U. So. Calif., 1985, Harvard Med. Sch., 1987, 89, UCLA, 1991, U. Chgo., 1991, U. Melbourne, 1991, U. Adelaide, 1991, McGill U., 1991, U. Md., 1994; cons. Nat. Inst. on Aging; numerous others. Mem. editl. bd. Jour. Clin. Endocrinology and Metabolism, 1984-88, Am. Jour. Physiology: Endocrinology and Mebabolism, 1985-91, Diabetes, 1986-88, Yr. Book Endocrinology, 1986-91, Jour. Gerontology: Med. Scis., 1988-92; mem. editl. bd. Jour. Am. Geriatrics Soc., 1990-93, assoc. editor, 1993-97; guest editor Supplement on Diabetes in Elderly, Diabetes Care, 1990; contbr. over 300 articles and abstracts to med. jours., chpts. to books. With USPHS, 1971-73. AMA Goldberger fellow U. Geneva Inst. Clin. Biochemistry, 1969; grantee VA, 1978—, Nat. Inst. on Aging, 1985—, Nat. Inst. Diabetes, Digestive and Kidney Diseases, John A. Hartford Found., 1988-94, Am. Fedn. for Aging Rsch., 1994-95, Univers Found., 1991—. Fellow AAAS; mem. Am. Diabetes Assn. (chmn. com. on rsch. rev. 1989-90), Endocrine Soc., Am. Fedn. Clin. Rsch., Western Soc. Clin. Investigation, Am. Soc. Clin. Investigation, Gerontol. Soc. Am. (rsch., edn.-practice com. 1984-87, chmn. rsch. com. clin. medicine sect. 1986-87, chmn. clin. medicine sect., v.p. 1992-93), Am. Geriatrics Soc. (bd. dirs. 1990—, pub. policy com. 1993-97, chmn. long range planning com. 1995-97, pres. elect 1997-98, pres. 1998-99), Ctrl. Soc. Clin. Rsch. (chmn. endocrinology coun. 1993-94, chmn. geriatrics coun. 1995-96), Am. Physiol. Soc., Phi Beta Kappa, Alpha Omega Alpha. Avocations: running, swimming, skiing. Office: U Mich Geriatrics Ctr CCGCB Room 1111 1500 E Medical Center Dr Ann Arbor MI 48109-0005

HALVORSON, DEBBIE DEFRANCESCO, state legislator; b. Steger, Ill., Mar. 1, 1958; d. Richard Lavern and Joyce Winifred DeFrancesco; children: Stephanie, Matthew. Degree, Robert Morris Coll., Prairie State Coll.; postgrad., U. Va., 1997, Harvard U., 1999. Twp. clk. Crete (Ill.) Twp., 1993-96; rep. 40th dist. Ill. State Senate, 1996—. Mem. appropriations commn., local govt. commn., minority spokesman commerce and industry com. Dem. Whip Ill. State Senate. Named Edn. Hero, Ill. Edn. Assn., 1997, Freshman Legislator of Yr., Ill. Health Care Assn., 1997, Statesman of Yr., Ill., 1998. Mem.: LWV (Homewood-Flossmoor chpt.), Nat. Orgn. Women Legislators (bd. dirs.), Profl. Womens Network, Chgo. Heights Bus. and Profl. Women, Chgo. Southland C. of C., Crete Womens Club, Altrusa. Office: 417 Capitol Bldg Springfield IL 62706-0001 Address: 241 W Joe Orr Rd Chicago Heights IL 60411-1744

HALVORSON, GEORGE CHARLES, healthcare insurance company executive; b. Fargo, ND, Jan. 28, 1947; s. George Charles and Barbara Theone (Johnson) H.; m. Mary Elizabeth Probst, June 27, 1986; children: Jonathan Dale, Seth Gregory, George Charles IV, Michael Thomas. BA, Concordia Coll., Moorhead, Minn., 1968. Cert. health cons., 1981. Successively mgr. market rsch., mgr. corp. planning, dir. planning and budget, v.p. planning and budget, sr. v.p. Blue Cross & Blue Shield, St. Paul, 1968-76; exec. dir. HMO Minn., St. Paul, 1976-83; pres. Sr. Health Plan, St. Paul, 1983-86, Health Accord, Inc., Mpls., 1983-86, Group Health, Inc., Mpls., 1986—2002; chmn., CEO Kaiser Permanente, 2002—. Ops. dir. HMO/Jamaica, Kingston, 1985-86; cons. AIG/Am. Internat. Health, Washington, 1987-88; lectr. in field. Author: How to Cut Your Company's Health Care Costs, 1987; contbr. articles to profl. jours. Chmn. Boy Scout Food Drive, St. Paul, 1988; fund raiser United Way, Mpls., 1987-88. Recipient Internship award Wall St. Jour. Newspaper Fund, 1968. Mem. Nat. Coop. Bus. Assn. (bd. dirs.), Minn. Bus. Partnership (bd. dirs.), Group Health Assn. Am., Minn. Council HMO's (bd. dirs.), Decathlon Club (Bloomington, Minn.), Mpls. Club. Avocations: writing, hunting, chess. Address: Kaiser Permanente Oakland 1 Kaiser Plaza Oakland CA 94612 Office Phone: 510-271-5910.

HAM, ARLENE H., state legislator; b. Belle Fourche, SD, Aug. 1, 1936; widowed; 2 children. Owner, broker Real Estate bus.; chmn. S.D. Rep. Party, 1985-87; with Rep. Nat. Com., 1988-96; mem. S.D. Senate from 32nd dist., Pierre, 1996—. Bd. dirs. Luth. Social Svcs., U.S. West. Mem. 4-H Found., Wellspring. Mem. Nat. Realtors Assn., State Realtors Assn., Rapid City Realtors Assn. (bd. dirs.), Zonta Mental Health Assn., Vet. Bd. Examiners, S.D. Lottery Commn., S.D. Racing Commn., Rapid City C. of C. (Aethena award), Toastmistress. Republican. Lutheran. Office: State Capitol Bldg Dist 32 500 E Capitol Ave Pierre SD 57501-5070 Home: 2503 Golden Eagle Dr Rapid City SD 57701-8926

HAMANN, DERYL FREDERICK, lawyer, bank executive; b. Lehigh, Iowa, Dec. 8, 1932; s. Frederick Carl Hamann and Ada Ellen (Hollingsworth) Hamann Geis; m. Carrie Svea Rosen, Aug. 23, 1954 (dec. 1985); children: Karl E., Daniel A., Esther Hamann Brabec, Julie Hamann Hodgson; m. Eleanor Ramona Nelson Curtis, June 20, 1987. AA, Ft. Dodge Jr. Coll., Iowa, 1953; BS in Law, U. Nebr., 1956, JD cum laude, 1958. Bar: Nebr. 1958, U.S. Dist. Ct. Nebr. 1958, U.S. Ct. Appeals (8th cir.) 1958. Law clk. U.S. Dist. Ct. for Nebr., Lincoln, 1958-59; ptnr. Baird, Holm, McEachen, Pedersen, Hamann & Strasheim, Omaha, 1959—2003, sr. counsel, 2003—. Chmn. adv. com. Supreme Ct. Nebr., Omaha, 1986-95; chmn. bd. Great Western Bancorporation, Inc. Past pres. Omaha Estate Planning Coun. Mem. Nebr. Bar Found. (pres. 1981-86), Nebr. Assn. Bank Attys. (pres. 1985-86). Republican. Lutheran. Avocations: boating, reading. Office: Baird Holm McEachen Pedersen Hamann & Strasheim 1500 Woodmen Tower Omaha NE 68102 Business E-Mail: dhamann@bairdholm.com.

HAMBRICK, ERNESTINE, retired colon and rectal surgeon; b. Griffin, Ga., Mar. 31, 1941; d. Jack Daniel Hambrick and Nanni (Harper) Hambrick Rubens. BS, U. Md., 1963; MD, U. Ill., 1967. Diplomate Am. Bd. Colon and Rectal Surgery, Am. Bd. Surgery. Intern in surgery Cook County Hosp., Chgo., 1967-68, resident in gen. surgery, 1968-72, fellow colon and rectal surgery, 1972-73, attending surgeon, 1973-74, part-time attending surgeon, 1974-80; pvt. practice colon and rectal surgery Chgo., 1974-97; pres. med. staff Michael Reese Hosp., Chgo., 1990-92, chief surgery, 1993-95; founder, chmn. STOP Colon/Rectal Cancer Found., 1997—. Mem. Nat. Colorectal Cancer Round Table, 1997—, mem. steering com., 2000—. Contbr. articles to profl. jours. Trustee Rsch. and Edn. Found. Michael Reese Med. Staff, Chgo., 1994—98, treas., 1994—98. Fellow: ACS, Am. Coll. Gastroenterology, Am. Soc. Colon and Rectal Surgeons (v.p. 1992—93, trustee Rsch. Found. 1992—98). Avocations: travel, photography, scuba diving, flying, writing. Office: PMB 133 47 W Division St Chicago IL 60610 Personal E-mail: ehcrsone@aol.com.

HAMBRICK, JAMES L., chemicals executive; BS in Chem. Engring., Tex. A&M U. Mgmt. & mktg. positions Lubrizol Corp., Wickliffe, Ohio, 1978—98, global mgr. engine oil additives, 1998—2000, v.p. Asia-Pacific, 2000—03, pres., 2003—04, chmn., pres., CEO, 2004—. Bd. mem. Hospice of Western Reserve, Univ. Health Sys., Greater Cleve. Partnership, NE Ohio Council Higher Edn. Mem.: Am. Chemistry Council (bd. mem.), Am. Inst. Chem. Engineers. Office: Lubrizol Corp 29400 Lakeland Blvd Wickliffe OH 44092

HAMBURG, MARC D., investment company executive; V.p., CFO Berkshire Hathaway Inc., Omaha. Office: Berkshire Hathaway Inc 1440 Kiewit Plz Omaha NE 68131 Office Phone: 402-346-1400.

HAMEL, MARK EDWIN, lawyer; b. Ontonagon, Mich., Apr. 9, 1953; s. Peter C. and Marian E. (Peterson) H.; m. Pamela Kay Jenkins, May 31, 1975; children: Nathan, Gregory. BA, Carroll Coll., 1975; JD, Harvard U., 1978. Bar: Minn. 1979, U.S. Dist. Ct. Minn. 1979. Law clk. to presiding justice Minn. Supreme Ct., St. Paul, 1978-79; assoc. Dorsey & Whitney LLP, Mpls., 1979-85, ptnr., 1985—, chmn., real estate and land use practice group. Chmn. bd. dirs. Accessible Space, Inc., bd. dirs. Downtown Coun., Mpls., Minn. Mem. Minn. Bar Assn. (cert. real property law specialist), Hennepin County Bar Assn (real property sect.), Mpls. Lifetime Athletic Club. Presbyterian. Office: Dorsey & Whitney LLP Ste 1500 50 S 6th St Minneapolis MN 55402-1498 Office Phone: 612-340-8716. Office Fax: 612-340-2868. Business E-Mail: hamel.mark@dorsey.com.

HAMEL, WILLIAM JOHN, church administrator, minister; b. Marquette, Mich., July 30, 1947; s. John Peter and Jayne B. (Berklund) H.; m. Karen Margaret Holleen, Aug. 10, 1968; children: Krista Joy, Kari Elise. BS, Wheaton Coll., 1969; MDiv, Trinity Evang. Div. Sch., Deerfield, Ill., 1972; DD, Trinity Internat. U., 1998; DCM, Trinity Western U., 1998. Ordained minister Evang. Free Ch. Am., 1978. Pastor West Bloomington (Minn.) Evang. Free Ch., 1972-86; dist. supt. Midwest Dist. Evang. Free Ch. Am., Kearney, Nebr., 1986-90; exec. v.p. Evang. Free Ch. Am., Mpls., 1990-97, pres., 1997—. Mem. Evangelist Free Ch. Am. Office: Evang Free Ch Am 901 E 78th St Minneapolis MN 55420-1334 Office Phone: 952-854-1300. Business E-Mail: president@efca.org.

HAMEROW, THEODORE STEPHEN, historian, educator; b. Warsaw, Aug. 24, 1920; arrived in U.S.A., 1930, naturalized, 1930; s. Haim Schneyer and Bella (Rubinlicht) H.; m. Margarete Lotter, Aug. 16, 1954 (div. Dec. 27, 1996); children: Judith Margarete, Helena Francisca; m. Diane Franzen, Oct. 4, 1997. BA, CUNY, 1942; MA, Columbia U., 1947; PhD, Yale U., 1951. Instr. Wellesley Coll., 1950-51, U. Md., 1951-52; instr., asst. prof., then asso. prof. U. Ill, 1952-58; mem. faculty U. Wis., 1958-91, prof. history, 1961-91, G. P. Gooch prof. history, 1978-91, chmn. dept. history, 1973-76. Cons. editor Dorsey Press, 1961-71; mem. coun. Internat. Exch. Scholars, 1983-85, Nat. Coun. on Humanities, 1992-2000. Author: Restoration, Revolution, Reaction, 1958, Otto von Bismarck: A Historical Assessment, 1962, The Social Foundations of German Unification 1858-1871, 2 vols, 1969-72, The Birth of a New Europe: State and Society in the ineteenth Century, 1983, Reflections on History and Historians, 1987, From the Finland Station: The Graying of Revolution in the Twentieth Century, 1990, On the Road to the Wolf's Lair: German Resistance to Hitler, 1997, Remembering a Vanished World: A Jewish Childhood in Interwar Poland, 2001; co-author: History of the World, 1960, A History of the Western World, 1969; editor: Otto von Bismarck, Reflections and Reminiscences, 1962, The Age of Bismarck, 1973; editorial bd.: Jour. Modern History, 1967-70, Central European History, 1968-72, Revs. in European History, 1974-78. Served with inf. AUS, 1943—46. Mem. Am. Hist. Assn., Conf. Group Central European History (sec.-treas. 1960-62, chmn. 1976), Wis. Assn. of Scholars (pres. 1989-91). Home: 885 Terry Pl Madison WI 53711-1956 Office: U Wisc Dept History Madison WI 53711 Business E-Mail: dkhamerow@facstaff.wisc.edu.

HAMERS, ROBERT J., chemistry educator, researcher; BS, U. Wis., Madison, 1980; PhD, Cornell U., 1985. Prof. chemistry U. Wis., Madison, Evan P. Helfaer chair, 1996—, Irving Shain chair, 2004—, dept. chair chemistry, 2007—. Recipient IBM Corp. Outstanding Innovation award for Scientific Accomplishments with Scanning Tunneling Spectroscopy, 1987, IBM Rsch. Divsn. award for STM Studies of Surface Reactions on Semiconductors, 1989, Camille and Henry Dreyfus New Faculty award, 1990-1995, Vilas Associates award, 1998, IBM Corp. Faculty award, 2002, Arthur W. Adamson award for Disting. Svc. in the Advancement of Surface Chemistry, Am. Chem. Soc., 2005; NSF Presdl. Faculty fellow, 1992-97, John Simon Guggenheim Found. fellow, 2000, S.C. Johnson Co. Disting. fellow, 2000-03. Fellow: AAAS, Am. Vacuum Soc. (Peter Mark Meml. award 1993). Office: U Wisconsin 3345a Chemistry 1101 University Ave Madison WI 53706-1322 Home Phone: 608-829-3744; Office Phone: 608-262-6371. Fax: 608-262-0453. Business E-Mail: rjhamers@wisc.edu.

HAMIEL, JEFF, airport executive; Lic. comml. pilot. With Met. Airports Commn., Mpls., 1977—, exec. dir., 1985—. Lt. col. USAFR. Office: Met Airports Commn 6040 28th Ave S Minneapolis MN 55450-2701

HAMILTON, DAVID F., judge; b. 1957; BA magna cum laude, Haverford Coll., 1979; JD, Yale U., 1983. Law clk. to Hon. Richard D. Cudahy U.S. Ct. Appeals (7th cir.), 1983-84; atty. Barnes & Thornburg, Indpls., 1984-88, 91-94; judge U.S. Dist. Ct. (so. dist.) Ind., Indpls., 1994—. Counsel to Gov. of Ind., 1989-91; chair Ind. State Ethics Commn., 1991-94. V.p. for litigation, bd. dirs. Ind. Civil Liberties Union, 1987-88. Fulbright scholar, 1979-80; recipient Sagamore of the Wabash, Gov. Evan Bayh, 1991. Mem.: Am. Inns of Ct. (pres. chpt. 2001—03). Office: US Dist Ct So Dist Ind 46 E Ohio St Rm 330 Indianapolis IN 46204-1921

HAMILTON, J. RICHARD, lawyer; b. Wadsworth, Ohio, June 21, 1929; BSc, Ohio U., 1951; JD, Ohio State U., 1956. Bar: Ohio 1956. Ptnr. Baker & Hostetler, Cleve. Editor-in-chief Ohio State Law Jour. Mem. ABA (mem. antitrust law and internat. law sects.), Ohio State Bar Assn., Cleve. Bar Assn. Office: Baker & Hostetler 3200 National City Ctr 1900 E 9th St Ste 3200 Cleveland OH 44114-3475

HAMILTON, JEAN CONSTANCE, judge; b. St. Louis, Nov. 12, 1945; AB, Wellesley Coll., 1968; JD, Washington U., St. Louis, 1971; LLM, Yale U., 1982. Atty. Dept. of Justice, Washington, 1971-73, asst. U.S. atty. St. Louis, 1973-78; atty. Southwestern Bell Telephone Co., St. Louis, 1978—81; judge 22d Jud. Circuit State of Mo., St. Louis, 1982-88; judge Mo. Ct. Appeals (ea. dist.), 1988-90, U.S. Dist. Ct. (ea. dist.) Mo., 1990—, chief judge, 1995—2002. Office: US Courthouse 111 S 10th St Saint Louis MO 63102

HAMILTON, PETER BANNERMAN, retired manufacturing executive, lawyer; b. Phila., Oct. 22, 1946; s. William George Jr. and Elizabeth Jane (McCullough) H.; m. Elizabeth Anne Arthur, May 8, 1982; children— Peter Bannerman, Jr., Brian Arthur. AB, Princeton U., 1968; JD, Yale U., 1971. Bar: D.C. 1972, Pa. 1972, Ind. 1985. Mem. staff Office Asst. Sec. Def. for Systems Analysis and Office Gen. Counsel, Dept. Def., Washington, 1971-74; mem. firm Williams & Connolly, Washington, 1974-77; gen. counsel Dept. Air Force, Washington, 1977-78; dep. gen. counsel HEW, Washington, 1979, exec. asst. to sec., 1979; spl. asst. to Sec. and Dep. Sec. Def., Washington, 1979-80; ptnr. Califano, Ross & Heineman, Washington, 1980-82; v.p., gen. counsel, sec. Cummins Inc., 1983-86, v.p. law and treasury, 1987-88, v.p., CFO, 1988-95; sr. v.p., CFO, Brunswick Corp., Lake Forest, Ill., 1996-98, exec. v.p., CFO, 1998-99; vice chmn., pres. Brunswick Bowling and Billiards, 2000—04; vice chmn., pres Life Fitness, 2005, Brunswick Boat Group, 2006. Bd. dirs. Spectra Energy Corp. Articles editor: Yale Law Jour, 1970-71. Served to lt. USN, 1971-74. Home: 970 E Deerpath Lake Forest IL 60045-2212

HAMILTON, RICHARD CLAY, professional basketball player; b. Coatesville, Pa., Feb. 14, 1978; Student, U. Conn. Profl. basketball player Washington Wizards, 1999—2002, Detroit Pistons, 2002—. Named one of Top Good Guys in Sports, Sporting News, 2004; named to USA Basketball Sr. Men's Nat. Team, 1999, Ea. Conf. All-Star Team, NBA, 2006, 2007, 2008. Achievements include winning the NBA Championship, 2004. Office: Detroit Pistons 4 Championship Dr Auburn Hills MI 48326*

HAMILTON, ROBERT APPLEBY, JR., insurance company executive; b. Boston, Feb. 20, 1940; s. Robert A. and Alice Margaret (Dowdall) H.; m. Ellen Kuhlen, Aug. 13, 1966; children: Jennifer, Robert Appleby III, Elizabeth. Student, Miami U., Ohio, 1958-62. CLU; chartered fin. cons. With Travelers Ins. Co., various locations, 1962-65, ew Eng. Mut. Life Ins. Co., various locations, 1965-90, regional pension rep. Boston, 1968-71, regional mgr. Chgo., 1972-83, sr. pension cons., 1983-90; mktg. and fin. cons. Snowbeck Enterprises, Inc., Geneva, Ill., 1990-97, ret., 1997. Producer Sta. WCTV; mem. Rep. Town Com., Wenham, Mass., 1970-72, Milton Twp., Ill., 1973-75; mem. Wenham Water Commn., 1970-72. Mem. Midwest Pension Conf. (chmn. 1989-90), Am. Soc. Pension Actuaries (assoc.), Am. Soc. CLUs, Am. Assn. Fin. Planners, Profit Sharing Coun. Am., Chgo. Coun. Fgn. Rels., Port Clyde Sailing Club, Alpha Epsilon Rho. Republican. Home: 110 Hamilton Ln Wheaton IL 60187-1807 also: 90 Shumaker Lane Tenants Harbor ME 04860-9709 Personal E-mail: erisabob@aol.com.

HAMILTON, ROBERT OTTE, lawyer; b. Marysville, Ohio, July 27, 1927; s. George Robinson and Annette (Otte) H.; m. Phyllis Eileen Clark, Dec. 16, 1962; children: Nathan Clark, Scott Robert. AB, Miami U., Oxford, Ohio, 1950; JD, U. Mich., 1953. Bar: Ohio 1953, U.S. Supreme Ct. 1960. Sole practice, Marysville, 1953—; pros. atty. Union County, Ohio, 1957-65; city atty. City of Marysville, 1956-81. Mem. Union, Morrow and Del. Mental Health Bd.,d 1957-72; pres. Marysville Jaycees, 1954; mem. Union County Rep. Exec. Com., 1955-65, sec., 1955-60. Served with USN, 1945-46, to lt. (j.g.) USNR, 1946-66. Mem. ABA, Ohio State Bar Assn. (chmn. jr. bar sect. 1961, ho. of dels. 1976-86, exec. com. 1983-86), Ohio State Bar Found. (pres. 1996), Union County Bar Assn. (pres. 1960), Ohio Acad. Trial Lawyers, Masons. Home: 432 W 6th St Marysville OH 43040-1464 Office: 116 S Court St Marysville OH 43040-1545 Office Phone: 937-642-5877.

HAMILTON BROWN, TERRI, bank executive; BS in Econ., U. Chgo.; MS in City Planning, MIT. Former devel. officer Enterprise Found., Cleve.; former dir., dept. of cmty. devel. City of Cleve.; former exec. dir. Cuyahoga Metropolitan Housing Authority; pres. University Circle, Inc., 2003—05; sr. v.p., corp. diversity Nat. City Bank, 2005—. Trustee ShoreBank-Cleve. Trustee United Way Services, Cleve. Found., Greater Cleve. Partnership, Conv. and Visitors Bureau of Greater Cleve., Gilmour Acad. Office: Nat City Bank Nat City Ctr 1900 E Ninth St Cleveland OH 44114

HAMM, MIA (MARIEL MARGARET HAMM), retired professional soccer player; b. Selma, Ala., Mar. 17, 1972; m. Christian Corry, 1994 (div. 2001); m. Nomar Garciaparra, Nov. 22, 2003; 2 children. BS in Polit. Sci., U. NC, 1994. Forward U.S. Women's Nat. Soccer Team, 1987—2004; profl. soccer player Washington Freedom, 2001—03. Mem. US Women's Soccer Team, Athens Olympic Games, 2004. Author: Go for the Goal: A Champions Guide to Winning in Soccer and Life, 1999. Founder Mia Found., 1999. amed US Soccer Female Athlete of Yr., 1994—98, MVP, US Women's Cup, 1995, Best Female Athlete of Yr., ESPY, 1998, 2000, Women's World Player of Yr., FIFA, 2001, 2002; named to Pele's 100 greatest living soccer players list, U.S. Nat. Soccer Hall of Fame, 2007; recipient Soccer Player of Yr. Award, ESPY, 2000, 2001, Best Female Soccer Player, 2004. Achievements include being a member of U. NC NCAA National Championship teams, 1989-93; having number retired, U. NC, 1994; being a member of US Women's Soccer Gold Medal Team, Atlanta Olympics, 1996, Athens Olympic games, 2004; being a member of US Women's Soccer World Cup Championship Team, 1999; being a member of US Women's Soccer Silver Medal Team, Sydney Olympics, 2000; being the all-time leading international goal scorer for men and women. Office: US Soccer Fedn US Soccer House 1801 S Prairie Ave Chicago IL 60616-1319

HAMM, RICHARD L., church administrator; b. Crawfordsville, Ind., Dec. 21, 1947; m. Melinda Ann Fishbaugh; children: David Lee, Laura Ann. Student, St. Petersburg Jr. Coll., 1966-67; BA in Religion, Butler U., 1970; D of Ministry, Christian Theol. Sem., 1974. Pastor Abington (Ind.) Christian Ch., 1968, Little Eagle Creek Christian Ch., Westfield, Ind., 1970; assoc. pastor Ctrl. Christian ch., Kansas City, Kans., 1974; founding pastor North Oak Christian ch., Kansas City, Mo., 1975-82; sr. pastor 1st Christian Ch., Ft. Wayne, Ind., 1982-90; regional min. Christian Ch. (Disciples of Christ) Tenn., 1990-93; gen. min., pres. Christian Ch. (Disciples of Christ) U.S. and Can., 1993—2003; interim sr. pastor West St. Christian Ch., Tipton, Ind., 2003—. Bd. dirs. mid-Am. region Christian Ch. (Disciples of Christ), 1977-81, bd. dirs. Kans. region, 1980-81, bd. dirs. Ind. region, 1983-90, chair area new ch. com. Ind. region, 1984-87, 89, mem. commn. ministry Ind. region, 1985-87, 89, mem. gen. bd., 1986-90, bd. dirs. divsn. overseas ministries, 1991—, commn. on ministry, 1991—; moderator, Christian Ch. Greater Kansas City, 1980-81; v.p. Nat. Coun. Chs., 1996; mem. ctrl. com. World Coun. Chs., 1998—. Author: From Mainline to Front Line, 1997, 2020 Vision for the Christian Church (Disciples of Christ), 2001. Mem. Mayor's Task Force Domestic Violence, 1990. Recipient Recognition award North Kansas City Edn. Assn., 1979, Recognition award Ft. Wayne, Ind., Edn. Assn. and Ft. Wayne Community Schs., 1984, Ind. Region's Model Ministry award, 1990; named Ecumenist of Yr. of Tenn., 1993. Mem. Tenn. Assn. Chs. (pres.-elect 1992), Clergy United Action (pres. 1984-86), Associated Chs. Ft. Wayne and Allen County (bd. dirs., officer 1982-90), Rotary. Mem. Christian Ch. Office: Christian Church (Disciples of Christ) PO Box 1986 Indianapolis IN 46206-1986

HAMMER, DAVID LINDLEY, lawyer, writer, investor; b. Newton, Iowa, June 6, 1929; s. Neal Paul and Agnes Marilyn (Reece) H.; m. Audrey Lowe, June 20, 1953; children: Julie, Lisa, David. BA, Grinnell Coll., 1951; JD, U. Iowa, 1956. Bar: Iowa 1956, U.S. Dist. Ct. (no. dist.) Iowa 1959, U.S. Dist. Ct. (so. dist.) Iowa 1969, U.S. Ct. Appeals (8th cir.) 1996, U.S. Supreme Ct. 1977. Ptnr. Hammer Simon & Jensen, Dubuque, Iowa, Galena, Ill.; mem. grievance commn. Iowa Supreme Ct., 1973—85, mem. adv. rules com., 1986—92. Author: Poems from the Ledge, 1980, The Game is Afoot, 1983, For the Sake of the Game, 1986, To Play the Game, 1986, The 22nd Man, 1989, The Quest, 1993, My Dear Watson, 1994, The Before Breakfast Pipe, 1995, A Dangerous Game, 1997, The Vital Essence, 1999, A Talent for Murder, 2000, Yonder in the Gaslight, 2000, Straight Up with a Twist, 2001, A Deep Game, 2001, The Game is Underfoot, 2002, You Heard What Jesse Said, 2003, O College Fairest of Our Dreams, 2004, A Distinct Touch Watson, 2004, Heaven Will Protect the Working Girl, 2005, Cases of Identity, 2006, You know my mentions watson, 2007. Bd. dirs. Linwood Cemetery Assn., 1973—, pres., 1983-84; bd. dirs. Dubuque Mus. Art, 1998-2001, hon. dir., 2001—; bd. dirs., past pres., 1973-74, Finley Hosp., 1966-85, hon. dir.; bd. dirs. Finley Found., 1988-95; past campaign chmn., past pres. United Way; past bd. dirs. Carnegie Stout Pub. Libr. With U.S. Army, 1951-53. Named to, Finley Hosp. Hall of Fame, 2004. Fellow Am. Coll. Trial Lawyers; mem. ABA, Young Lawyers Iowa (past pres.), Iowa Def. Counsel Assn. (pres. 1991-92, del. to Def. Rsch. Inst. 1992-93), Assn. Def. Trial Attys. (exec. coun. 1983-86, past chmn. Iowa chpt.), Iowa State Bar Assn. (past chmn. continuing legal edn. com.), Iowa Acad. Trial Lawyers, Dubuque County Bar Assn. (past pres.), Baker St. Irregulars. Republican. Congregationalist. Mailing: PO Box 1808 Dubuque IA 52004-1808 Office Phone: 563-583-4010.

HAMMER, WILLIAM ROY, paleontologist, educator; b. Detroit, Nov. 15, 1949; BS, Wayne State U., 1971, MS, 1973, PhD, 1979. Asst. prof. geology Wayne State U., Detroit, 1980-81, Augustana Coll., Rock Island, Ill., 1981-87, assoc. prof., 1987-94, prof., chair dept. geology, dir. Fryxell Geology Mus., 1988—, Fritiof Fryxell endowed chair, 1998—. Rsch. assoc. Field Mus. Natural History, Chgo., 1993—; prin. investigator grants for Antarctic Rsch. NSF, Washington, 1981—; Am. Assn. Petroleum Geologists Disting. lectr., 1996-97. Contbr. articles to profl. jours.; contbg. author to 14 books and 3 field guidebooks. Mem. AAAS (mem.-at-large com. on geology and geography 1998—), Soc. Vertebrate Paleontology (chair Skinner prize com. 1998—), Paleontological Soc. (chair N/C sect. 1989-90), Soc. Econ. Paleontologists and Mineralogists (v.p. Great Lakes sect. 1985-86). Achievements include discovery of many new fossil reptiles and amphibians from Antarctica, including the first Jurassic dinosaurs from that continent. Office: Augustana Coll Dept Geology Rock Island IL 61201

HAMMERMAN, MARC RANDALL, nephrologist, educator; b. St. Louis, Sept. 29, 1947; s. Elmer and Lillian Hammerman; m. Nancy Tutt, Aug. 9, 1974; children: Seth, Megan. AB, Washington U., St. Louis, 1969, MD, 1972. Intern Barnes Hosp., St. Louis, 1972-73, resident, 1973-74, Mass. Gen. Hosp., Boston, 1976-77; instr. Washington U., St. Louis, 1977-78, asst. prof., 1979-84, assoc. prof., 1984-89, prof., 1989—, dir. renal div. Sch. Medicine, 1991—. Mem. study sect. NIH, 1990-95; investigator Am. Heart Assn., 1984; dir. Wash. U. O'Brien Ctr., 2007—. Contbr. over 100 sci. articles, revs. to profl. publs., chpts. to books. Lt. comdr. USPHS, 1974-76. NIH grantee, 1980—. Mem. Am. Fedn. for Clin. Rsch., Am. Soc. Clin. Investigation, Assn. Am. Physicians. Achievements include research in xenotransplantation of animal organs to treat kidney failure and diabetes in humans; the use of embryonic animal cells to prevent the rejection of transplanted organs by the human immune system; first to cure diabetic rats through the transplantion of embryonic pig pancreatic cells. Avocations: writing short stories, jewelry-making. Office: Washington U Sch Medicine Renal Div Box 8126 660 S Euclid Ave Saint Louis MO 63110-1010 E-mail: mhammerm@im.wustl.edu.

HAMMERSTROM, BEVERLY SWOISH, state legislator; b. Mineral Wells, Tex., Mar. 28, 1944; d. William Graham and Marjorie Wirth (Lillis) Swoish; m. Don Preston Hammerstrom, June 25, 1966 (div. Oct. 1976); children: Todd Preston, Rory Scott. BA, Adrian Coll., 1966; MPA, U. Toledo, 1994. Cert. mcpl. clk. Tchr. Geneva (N.Y.) Pub. Schs., 1966-69; substitute tchr. Darien (Wis.) Pub. Schs., 1970-71; tchr. Bedford Coop. Nursery Sch., Lambertville, Mich., 1975; retail mgr., buyer Gallerie, Toledo, 1975-78, Personal Touch, Toledo, 1978-80; clk. Bedford Township, Temperance, Mich., 1980-92; mem. Mich. Ho. of Reps., Lansing, 1993-98, Mich. Senate from 17th dist., Lansing, 1999—, majority fl. leader, 2003—. Bd. dirs. Family Med. Ctr., Temperance; emergency mgmt. bd. Washtenaw County, Ypsilanti, Mich., 1993-98, Monroe (Mich.) County, 1993-98; mem. health policy com. Nat. Coun. State Legis. Mem. Internat. Inst. Mcpl. Clks. (bd. dirs. Found. 1996), Mich. Assn. Clks. (life, pres. 1990-91), Am. Legis. Exch. Coun. (mem. health policy task force), Coun. State Govt. (health policies com., del. 1995—), Women in Govt. (state dir. 1999-2004, chmn. bd. 2004-06). Republican. Roman Catholic. Home: 1183 Oakmont Dr Temperance MI 48182-9563 Office: Mich Senate PO Box 30036 Lansing MI 48909-7536

HAMMES, JEFFREY C., lawyer; BBA, U. Wis., 1980; JD, Northwestern U. Scho. Law, 1985. CPA; bar: Ill. 1985, Calif. 2003. Atty. Arthur Andersen & Co., 1980—82, Kirkland & Ellis LLP, 1985—91, ptnr., mem. firm com., 1991—. Named one of World's Leading Lawyers Corp. M & A, Chambers Global, 2001—. Office: Kirkland & Ellis LLP 200 E Randolph Dr Chicago IL 60601 Office Phone: 312-861-2476. Office Fax: 312-861-2200. Business E-Mail: jhammes@kirkland.com.

HAMMOND, CELESTE M., law educator; BS cum laude, Loyola U.; JD, U. Chgo. Practicing atty., Chgo.; mem. faculty to prof., dir. real estate law prog. John Marshall Law Sch., Chgo., 1976—. Contbr. articles to profl. jours., chapters to books. Mem.: Chgo. Bar Assn. (chair real property law com. 2002), ABA, Chgo. Real Estate Exec. Women, Lambda Alpha Internat. Land Econs. Soc., Am. Coll. Real Estate Lawyers. Office: Ctr Real Estate John Marshall Law Sch 315 S Plymouth Ct Chicago IL 60604 Office Phone: 312-987-2366. E-mail: 7hammond@jmls.edu.

HAMMOND, DENNIS CLYDE, plastic surgeon, educator; b. Saginaw, Mich., May 2, 1959; BS with honors in Biology, U. Mich., Ann Arbor, 1981; MD with Distinction, U. Mich. Med. Sch., Ann Arbor, 1985. Cert. Am. Bd. Plastic Surgery, lic. Mich., 1986, Tenn., 1990, Wis., 1991, diplomate Nat. Bds., 1986. Intern and resident, gen. surgery Blodgett Meml. Med. Ctr., St. Mary's Health Svcs., Grand Rapids, Mich., 1985—88; resident, plastic and reconstructive surgery Grand Rapids Area Med. Edn. Ctr., Grand Rapids, Mich., 1988—90; fellow, aesthetic and reconstructive breast surgery and cosmetic surgery Inst. for Aesthetic and Reconstructive Surgery, Baptist Hosp., Nashville, 1990—91; fellow, hand and microvascular surgery Med. Coll. Wis., Milw., 1991—92; pvt. practice Ctr. Breast Body Contouring, Grand Rapids, Mich.; asst. clin. prof., dept. surgery Mich. State U., East Lansing. Invited visiting professorships; presenter in field. Contbr. several articles to profl. jours., chapters to books. Named one of America's Top Plastic Surgeons, MORE Mag., Country's Top Breast Surgeons, America's Top Doctors; recipient Best Paper award, Pharmacological Manipulation of Rat Flaps: Fact or Friction, Ann. Plastic Surgery Senior Residents Conf., NY, 1990, First prize President's award, Am. Roentgen Ray Soc., 1991, Clifford C. Snyder award, Computerized Morphologic Analysis of Tissue Expander Shape Using a Biomechanical Model, best paper, Ann. Mtg. Plastic Surgery Rsch. Coun., Charlottesville, Va., 1991, Doran Scholar award for rsch. project and publication, Endoscopic Tattooing of the Colon: Clinical Experience, 1992. Mem.: Am. Assn. Plastic Surgeons, Am. Cancer Soc. (bd. dirs.), Mich. Acad. Plastic Surgeons (First prize clin. award 1994, First prize basic sci. award 1988), Mich. State Med. Soc., Kent County Med. Soc., Midwest Assn. Plastic Surgeons (First prize clin. award 1988, First prize clin. award for Latissimus Dorsi Musculocutaneous Flaps and Tissue Expanders/Implants Immediate Breast Reconstruction 1995), Am. Soc. for Aesthetic Plastic Surgery, Am. Soc. Plastic and Reconstructive Surgeons, ACS, Gilda's Club of Grand Rapids (mem. adv. bd.). Achievements include invention of revolutionary SPAIR technique. Office: Ctr Breast Body Contouring 4070 Lake Dr SE Ste 202 Grand Rapids MI 49546 Office Phone: 616-464-4420. Office Fax: 616-464-4354.*

HAMMOND, EDWARD H., university president; b. McAllen, Tex., May 4, 1944; s. Will J. and Bergit A. (Lund) H.; m. Vivian hammeke, Aug. 26, 1967; children: Kelly Edvidge, Lance Edward, Julie Marie. BS in Speech, Kans. State Tchrs. Coll., 1966, MS, 1967; PhD, U. MO., 1971. Asst. dir. of field svcs. Kans. State Tchrs. Coll., Emporia, 1966-67; dir. student affairs Purdue U. North Cen. campus, Westville, Ind., 1967-68; counselor housing office U. Mo., Columbia, 1969-70; asst. dean of students So. Ill. U., Carbondale, 1970, asst. to pres. for student rels., 1970-73; v.p. student affairs Seton Hall U., S. Orange, J., 1973-76, U. Louisville, 1976-87; pres. Fort Hays State U., Hays, Kans., 1987—. Chair bd. trustees Boost Alcohol Consciousness Concerning the Health of U. Students of the U.S. Inc., 1987-93; trustee The Lincoln Found., 1979-87; mem. Inter-Assn. Task Force on Coll. Alcohol Abuse and Misuse, 1984—; vis. faculty mem. Ind. U., Bloomington, 1972-83; cons. in field. Contbr. articles to profl. jours. NDEA fellow U. Mo., 1968-70; named to Mid-Am. Edn. Hall of Fame, 1997. Mem. Am. Coun. on Edn., Am. Assn. State Colls. and Univs., Am. Assn. Univ. Adminstrs., Nat. Assn. Student Pers. Adminstrs. (nat. pres. 1983, John Jones award 1986), Kans. C. of C. and Industry (bd. dirs. 1990—), Pi Kappa Delta, Sigma Phi Epsilon. Avocations: golf, racquetball, water sports, tennis. Office: Fort Hays State U 600 Park St Bldg 1 Hays KS 67601-4099 E-mail: ehammond@fhsu.edu.

HAMMOND, HAROLD LOGAN, oral and maxillofacial pathologist, retired educator; b. Hillsboro, Ill., Mar. 18, 1934; s. Harold Thomas and Lillian (Carlson) H.; m. Sharon Bunton, Aug. 1, 1954 (dec. 1974); 1 child, Connie; m. Pat J. Palmer, June 3, 1986. Student Millikin U., 1953-57, Roosevelt U., Chgo., 1957-58; DDS, Loyola U., Chgo., 1962; MS, U. Chgo., 1967. Diplomate Am. Bd. Oral and Maxillofacial Pathology. Intern, U. Chgo. Hosps., Chgo., 1962-63, resident, 1963-66, chief resident in oral pathology, 1966-67; asst. prof. oral pathology U. Iowa, Iowa City, 1967-72, assoc. prof., 1972-80, assoc. prof., dir. surg. oral pathology, 1980-83, prof., dir., 1983-2004, prof. emeritus oral pathology, radiology and medicine, 2004-, dir. emeritus, Surg. Oral Pathology Lab., 2004-; cons. pathologist Hosp. Gen. de Managua, Nicaragua, 1970-90, VA Hosp., Iowa City, 1977-2004. Cons. editor: Revista de la Assn. Nicaragua, 1970-71, Revista de la Federacion Odontologica de Centroamerica y Panama, 1971-77. Contbr. articles to profl. jours. Mosby Pub. Co. scholar, 1962. Fellow AAAS, AAUP, Am. Acad. Oral and Maxillofacial Pathology; mem. Am. Men and Women of Sci., NY Acad. Scis., Internat. Assn. Oral Pathologists, Internat. Assn. Dental Rsch., N.Am. Soc. Head and Neck Pathologists, Am. Dental Assn., Am. Assn. Dental Rsch. Avocations: collecting antique clocks, collecting gambling paraphernalia, collecting toys. Home: 1732 Brown Deer Rd Coralville IA 52241-1157 Office: U Iowa Dental Sci Bldg Iowa City IA 52242-1001

HAMMOND, JOHN R., professional sports team executive; b. Zion, Ill., July 19, 1954; m. Marsha Hammond; 1 child, Lauryn Shay. BA, Greenville Coll., Ill., 1976; MS in Physical Edn., U. Nebr., 1981. Coach U. Nebr., Lincoln, 1979—81, Houston Baptist U., 1981—83, S.W. Mo. State U., 1983—89; asst. coach, scout Minn. Timberwolves, 1989—90; asst. coach LA Clippers, 1990—93, 2000—01; scouting dir. Detroit Pistons, 1994—99, asst. coach, 1997—99, dir. player pers., 2001—02, v.p. basketball ops., 2002—08; gen. mgr. Milw. Bucks, 2008—. Office: Milw Bucks 1001 N Fourth St Milwaukee WI 53203*

HAMMOND, JOHNIE, state legislator; b. Europa, Miss., Aug. 22, 1932; m. Earl Hammond. Student, U. Tex.; BA in Social Work, U. Minn., 1953; BBA in Bus. Mgmt., Iowa State U., 1981. With Story County Bd. of Suprs., 1975-79; mem. Iowa Ho. of Reps., 1982-94, Iowa Senate from 31st dist., 1994—. Mem. nat. adv. com. State Health Care Reform; bd. dirs. ICLU. Mem. First Bapt. Ch., Ames, Moingona Girl Scout Coun., Story County Battered Women's Shelter; bd. dirs. Caring Found. for Children. Mem. LWV, Nat. Coun. State Legislators, Iowa Women's Polit. Caucus, Ams. United for Separation of Ch. and State (mem. nat. adv. com.). Democrat. Home: 3431 Ross Rd Ames IA 50014-3961 E-mail: johnie_hammond@legis.state.ia.us.

HAMMONS, BRIAN KENT, lawyer; b. Wurzburg, Germany, Mar. 6, 1958; arrived in U.S., 1958; s. R. Dwain and Donna G. (Carender) H.; m. Kimberly M. Pflumm, July 26, 1980; children: April Michelle, David Dwain, Adam Carender. BS summa cum laude, Mo. State U., Springfield, 1980; JD cum laude, So. Meth. U., Dallas, 1985. Bar: Mo. 1985. Exec., treas., v.p. Hammons Products Co., Stockton, Mo., 1980-86, exec. v.p., sec., 1987-96, pres., COO, CEO, 1997—; assoc. Stinson, Mag & Fizzell, Kansas City, Mo., 1986-87. Bd. govs. Mo. State U., 2006—. Mem. Stockton Airport Bd., 1987—89, Stockton City Coun., 1989—91, Leadership Mo., 1990, Ozark Empire Fair Bd., 2004—07; pres. Stockton Cmty. Found., 2002—08, Stockton Cmty. Devel. Bd., 2003—; former cub scout leader Boy Scouts Am.; former soccer coach; Sunday sch. and Bible study tchr.; chair United Meth. Mo. Conf. Fin. and Adminstrn., 2004—. Mem.: Mo. Chamber Commerce and Industry (bd. dirs. 2003—), Springfield Area C. of C. (bd. dirs. 2003—05), Mo. Bar Assn., Young Presidents Orgn., Lions (pres. 1990—91), Masons (sec. 1980—81), Phi Delta Phi. Republican. Methodist. Avocations: running, flying, tennis, golf, hunting. Office: Hammons Products Co 105 Hammons Dr PO Box 140 Stockton MO 65785

HAMMONS, JOHN Q., hotel executive; Chmn., CEO John Q. Hammons Hotels, Inc. and Cos., Springfield, Mo. Office: John Q Hammons Hotels Inc & Cos #900 300 John Q Hammons Pkwy Springfield MO 65806

HAMNER, LANCE DALTON, prosecutor; b. Fukuoka, Japan, Sept. 18, 1955; parents Am. citizens; s. Louie D. and Mary Louise (Sloan) H.; m. Karla Jean Cleverly, Sept. 22, 1980; children: Lance Dalton Jr., Nicholas James, Louie Alexander, Samuel Sean, Victoria Jean. BS summa cum laude, Weber State Coll., 1984; JD magna cum laude, Ind. U., 1987. Bar: Ind., US Dist. Ct. (no., so. dist.) Ind. 1988. Atty. Barnes & Thornburg, Indpls., 1988-89; dep. prosecuting atty. Marion County Prosecutor's Office, Indpls., 1989-90; pros. atty. Johnson County, Franklin, Ind., 1991—. Legal corr. WGGR Radio News, Indpls., 1995; adj. prof. law Sch. Law Ind. U., Indpls., 1995—96, Bloomington, 1996—98; frequent spkr. on legal topics including search and seizure and interrogation law; lectr. Ind. Continuing Legal Edn. Forum, Indpls., 1992; mem. faculty Newly-Elected Pros. Sch. Ind. Pros. Attys. Coun., 1999; mem. faculty Indpls. Police Acad., 1999, Ind. Police Corps, 2000—05; adj. prof. law and pub. policy Franklin Coll., 2005—07. Author: Indiana Search & Seizure Courtroom Manual, 2001, 2002, 2004; editor: Ind. Law Jour., 1987. Scoutmaster Boy Scouts Am., Franklin, Ind., 1999-2003. Mem. Nat. Dist. Attys. Assn., Assn. Govt. Attys. in Capital Litigation, Ind. Prosecuting Atty.'s Coun., Nat. Eagle Scout Assn., Order of the Coif. Republican. Mem. Lds Ch. Avocations: fitness, writing. Office: Prosecutor's Office Courthouse Annex N 80 S Jackson St Franklin IN 46131-2353 Office Phone: 317-736-3750. Personal E-mail: lhamner@aol.com.

HAMP, STEVEN K., automotive executive; b. 1948; m. Sheila Ford. BA in Am. Hist., Butler U.; MA in Folklore/Folkife, Ind. U.; MMP, U. Mich., HDL (hon.), 2002. With Smithsonian Inst., Univ. Mich. Mus Art, Ind. Univ. Mus, History, Folklore, Anthropolgy, Henry Ford Historical Inst., 1978—2005, dir. ednl. programs, dir. programming, chmn. collections, pres., 1996—2005; v.p. chief of staff Ford Motor Co., 2005—06. Bd. dirs. Visteon Corp., 2001—. Chmn. bd. Henry Ford Acad., Henry Ford Learning Inst., Mich. Travel Commn.; mem. bd. Mich. Chapter Nature Conservancy, Detroit Metro Conv., Greenhills School, Kresge Found., Detroit Super Bowl XL Host Comm. Named Michiginian of the Yr., Detroit News, 1999; recipient Helen and William Milliken Disting. Svc. award, Mich. Environ. Coun., 2000. Mem.: SE Mich. Cultural Coalitiom.

HAMPER, ANIETRA, news anchor; BA in Comm. and Polit. Sci., Heidelberg Coll., 1995. Programming asst. Sta. WSYX-TV, Columbus, Ohio; anchor, reporter, prodr. Sta. WHEI-TV, Tiffin; prodn. asst. The McLaughlin Group, Washington; news asst. Sta. KARK-TV, Little Rock; anchor, reporter, dir. cmty. affairs Sta. WTTE-TV, Columbus; reporter Sta. WSYX-WTTE-TV, 1996—98, WKEF-TV, Dayton, 1998—99; anchor, reporter Sta. WRGT-TV, 1998—99; reporter Sta. WCMH-TV, Columbus, 1999—2001, anchor, 2001—. Recipient YWCA Women of Achievement award, U.S. Congrl. award, JC Penny Golden Rule award, Jefferson award. Mem.: Nat. Assn. Television Arts and Scis. Office: WCMH-TV 3165 Olentangy River Rd Columbus OH 43202 Office Phone: 614-261-4497. E-mail: anietra.hamper@nbc.com.

HAMPTON, PHILIP MICHAEL, consulting engineering company executive; b. Asheville, NC, Sept. 5, 1932; s. Boyd Walker and Helen Reba (Smith) H.; m. Wilma Christine Gross, July 7, 1951; children: Philip Michael, Deborah Lynn, Gregg Ashley. AB in Geology, Berea Coll., Ky., 1954. Draftsman-designer Johnson & Anderson, Inc., Pontiac, Mich., 1955-57, designer, also project mgr., 1957-59, dir. bus. devel., 1962-76, v.p., 1966-74, exec. v.p., 1974-76; v.p. Spalding G. DeDecker & Assos., Inc., Madison Heights, Mich., 1976-84; founder, pres. Hampton Engring. Assocs., Inc., 1985—; pres. HMA Consultants Inc., 1977—, Geo Internat., Inc., 1978—. V.p. JAVLEN Internat., 1971-73, Micuda-Hampton Assocs., Inc., 1985-86; co-founder, owner My World Shops and Hampton Galleries, Ltd., 1976-90; co-owner Hampton-Tyedten Galleries Ltd., 1979-81; mem. public adv. panel GSA, 1977-78; chmn. task force of com. fed. procurement of architect/engr. svcs. ABA, 1977-79. Editor: Total Scope, 1963-71. Pres. Waterford Bd. Edn., 1969-71; mem. state resolution com. Democratic Conv., 1972; exec. com. Oakland County Dem. Com., 1973-74; precinct del., 1972-76, 80—; trustee Environ. Research Assocs., sec.-treas., 1969-71, pres., 1971-73; chmn. Waterford Cable Communications Commn., 1981-88; mem. Cultural Council Pontiac, 1987-90; bd. dirs. Oakland C. of C., 1972-74, Readings for the Blind, Inc., 2002-; chmn. utilities com. Oakland Bus. Roundtable, 1993—; vice chmn. Pontiac Urban League, 1996—. Named to Honorable Order Ky. Colonels. Fellow Am. Cons. Engrs. Coun. (internat. engring. com. 1971-76, vice chmn. pub. rels. com. 1970-72, chmn. publs. com. 1972-74, chmn. ABA model procurement code com. 1977-79, nat. dir. 1986-89, mem. com. fellows 1988—, Pres. award 1990); mem. ASCE, AAAS, Nat. Water Well Assn. (chmn. tech. div. 1969-71), Cons. Engrs. Coun. Mich. (awards com. 1970-74), Am. Arbitration Assn. (comml. panel 1977—), Pontiac C. of C. (co-founder 1989), Oakland Bus. Roundtable (charter). Clubs: Pontiac Exchange, Pontiac-Detroit Lions Quarterback Club (co-founder, Am. Coun. Engring. Cons. Vernon B. Spalding Leadership award 2007). Presbyterian. Home and Office: 2440 Ostrum St Waterford MI 48328-1829 Office: 35 W Huron St Ste 801 Pontiac MI 48342-2128 Office Phone: 248-332-4332. Personal E-mail: heainc35@aol.com.

HAMPTON, TRENTON D., lawyer; b. Hamburg, Iowa, Aug. 31, 1960; BS, Northwest Mo. State U., 1982; JD, Creighton U., 1985. Bar: Iowa 1985, Nebr. 1987. Gen. counsel Ferrellgas, Inc., Liberty, Mo. Office: Farrellgas, Inc One Liberty Plaza Liberty MO 64068 Office Phone: 816-792-1600.

HAMPTON, VERNE CHURCHILL, II, lawyer; b. Pontiac, Mich., Jan. 5, 1934; s. Verne Churchill and Mildred (Peck) H.; m. Stephanie Hall, Oct. 5, 1973; children: J. Howard, Timothy H., Julia C. Thibodeau. BA, Mich. State U., 1955; LLB, U. Va., 1958. Bar: Mich. 1958. Since practiced in, Detroit; ptnr. firm Dickinson Wright, 1967—. Bd. dirs., sec. Carhartt, Inc., R & R Radio Corp. Former mem. Mich. Rep. Fin. Com.; bd. dirs. Detroit Bus./Edn. Alliance; corp. mem. Boys' Clubs Met. Detroit. Mem. ABA, State Bar Mich. (chmn. bus. law sect. 1980-84), Detroit Athletic Club, Country Club Detroit, Yondotega Club, Moorings Club (Fla.), Sigma Alpha Epsilon, Phi Alpha Delta. Republican. Episcopalian. Home: 360 Provencal Rd Grosse Pointe Farms MI 48236-2959 Office: Dickinson Wright PLLC 500 Woodward Ave Ste 4000 Detroit MI 48226-3416 Business E-Mail: vhampton@dickinsonwright.com.

HAMRICK, LINDA L., secondary school educator; b. Fort Wayne, Ind., Feb. 14, 1954; BS in Edn., Ball State U., 1977, EdD in Ednl. Leadership, 1991; MS in Edn., Ind. U., 1980. Cert. tchr., sch. adminstr., supt. Ind. Tchr. Fort Wayne (Ind.) Cmty. Schs., 1978—; adminstrv. intern Ft. Wayne (Ind.) Cmty. Schs., 1997—; educator-YIC Whitley County Probation, Columbia City, Ind., 1997—. Assoc. faculty Ind. U., 1987, 88; sch. supt. internship N.W. Allen County Schs., Fort Wayne, 1990-91. Site dir. youth basketball Ft. Wayne YMCA, 1982-86; site supr. Ft. Wayne Park Dept., 1980-85. Mem. AAPHERD, Ind. Middle Level Educators Assn., Internat. Reading Assn., Am. Endurance Ride Conf., Internat. Arabian Horse Assn., Upper Midwest Endurance Ride Conf. Avocations: horse riding endurance, snowmobiling, downhill skiing, boating, water-skiing. Office: South Side HS 3601 S Calhoun St Fort Wayne IN 46807-2006 Office Phone: 260-467-2600. Business E-Mail: linda.hamrick@fwcs.k12.in.us.

HANAWAY, CATHERINE LUCILLE, prosecutor; b. Schuyler, Nebr., Nov. 8, 1963; m. Christopher; children: Lucy, Jack. BA, Creighton U., 1987; JD, The Catholic U. of Am., 1990. Owner, atty. Hanamore Solutions, LLC; atty. Peper, Martin, St. Louis, 1990—93; campaign mgr. Bredemeier for Atty. Gen., 1996; dist. dir. Senator Kit Bond, 1993—96, 1996—98; polit. advisor Missourians for Kit Bond, 1998; mem. Mo. State Ho. of Reps., 1998—2004, spkr., 2002—04; exec. dir. Mo. Bush/Cheney, 2002; US atty. (ea. dist.) Mo. US Dept. Justice, St. Louis, 2005—. Mem. Housing Adv. Bd.; bd. dirs. Hope House, Foster and Adoptive Care Coalition. Mem.: Mo. Bar Assn., St. Louis Junior League, St. Louis Jaycees (past pres.). Republican. Roman Catholic. Office: US Attys Office 111 S 10th St 20th Fl Saint Louis MO 63102 Office Phone: 314-539-2200.

HANCOCK, JAMES BEATY, interior designer; b. Hartford, Ky. s. James Winfield Scott and Hettie Frances (Meadows) H. BA, Hardin-Simmons U., 1948, MA, 1952. Head interior design dept. Thornton's, Abilene, Tex., 1945-54; interior designer The Halle Bros. Co., Cleve., 1954-55; v.p. Olympic Products, Cleve., 1955-56; mgr., interior designer Bell Drapery Shops of Ohio, Inc., Shaker Heights, 1957-78, v.p., 1979—. Lectr. interior design; works include 6 original murals Broadway Theater, Abilene, 1940, mural Skyline Outdoor Theatre, Abilene, 1950, cover designs for Isotopics mag., 1958-60. With AUS, 1942-46. Recipient 2nd place award of oil painting West Tex. Expn., 1940, honorable mention, 1940, Diploma for being an Am. vet. of WWII who liberated France, Govt. of France; decorated Bronze Star for Svc. in France an Occupied Germany during WWII, 2007. Mem. Abilene Mus. Fine Arts (charter), Western Res. Hist. Soc., Cleve. Cir. of the Decorative Arts Trust (charter), Trideca Soc. Cleve Mus. Art, English Speaking Union. Home and Office: 1 Bratenahl Pl Apt 103 Cleveland OH 44108-1152

HANCOCK, MEL, former congressman; b. Cape Fair, Mo., Sept. 14, 1929; BS, S.W. Mo. State Coll., 1951. Chmn. bd. dirs. Fed. Protection Inc.; with Internat. Harvester Co.; mem. 101st-104th Congresses from 7th Mo. Dist., 1989-96; mem. ways and means com. Chmn. Taxpayer's Survival Assn. With USAF, USAFR. Mem. at. Rifle Assn. (life), Farm Bur., Am. Legion. Republican. Mem. Ch. of Christ. Office: 6220 W Farm Rd #140 Springfield MO 65802

HAND, ROGER, physician, educator; b. Bklyn., Sept. 25, 1938; s. Morton and Angela (Belvedere) H.; m. Susan Hand; children: Christopher, Jessica. BS, NYU, 1959, MD, 1962. Intern, then resident in internal medicine NYU Med. Ctr., 1962-68; postdoctoral fellow, asst. prof. Rockefeller U., NYC, 1968-73; clin. asst. prof. medicine Cornell U. Med. Coll., NYC, 1970-73; asst. prof., then assoc. prof. medicine McGill U., Montreal, Que., Canada, 1973-80; prof. medicine, dir. McGill Cancer Ctr., 1980-84; sr. physician Royal Victoria Hosp., Montreal, 1980-84; chmn. internal medicine Ill. Masonic Ctr., Chgo., 1984-88; prof. medicine U. Ill., Chgo., 1984—, chief sect. gen. internal medicine, 1988-95, prof. health policy and adminstrn. Sch. Pub. Health, 1995—2002. Prin. clin. coord. Ill. Found. Quality Health Care, Chgo., 1996-00; physician advisor OLR Med. Ctr., Chgo., 2000-01, ret., 2001-. Contbr. articles to profl. jours. Brig. gen. USAR, 1963-71, 85-03, ret.; diaster relief-search-and-rescue pilot auxs. USCG, USAF; vol. disaster relief programs ARC, FEMA. Decorated Air medal, Meritorious Svc. medal, Army Commendation medal, Legion of Merit; med. rsch. grantee. Fellow ACP, Royal Coll. Physicians and Surgeons, Am. Coll. Med. Quality; mem. Am. Soc. Clin. Investigation, Am. Soc. Biol. Chemists, Am. Assn. Cancer Research, Am. Soc. Clin. Oncology, Infectious Disease Soc., Can. Soc. Clin. Investigation, Cen. Soc. Clin. Rsch., Am. Cancer Soc.(bd. dirs. Ill. div.), Am. Health Quality Assn. Office Phone: 847-926-8229. E-mail: buckgeneral@ameritech.net.

HANDEL, DAVID JONATHAN, health facility administrator; b. NYC, Jan. 2, 1946; s. Milton M. and Ruth (Stamer) H.; m. Julia Elizabeth Noll, June 26, 1971; chldren: Daniel, Jennifer. BS, Cornell U., 1966; MBA, U. Chgo., 1968. Assoc. planning coordinator for health scis. Northwestern U., Chgo., 1970-73, adminstr. Northwestern U. Med. Clinics and Med. Assocs., 1973-76; dir. planning and implementation Mid-Ohio Health Planning Fedn., Columbus, Ohio, 1976-79; assoc. hosp. adminstr. Vanderbilt U. Hosps., Nashville, 1979-82, assoc. dir. ops., 1982-85; dir. Ind. U. Hosps., Indpls., 1985-96; exec. v.p., COO Clarian Health Ptnrs., Inc., Indpls., 1997—2004; dir. MHA program Ind. U., 2004—. V.p. United Hosp. Svcs., Indpls., 1986-88, pres., 1989-90, Bedford Reg. Med. Ctr., 1997-2004, La Porte Regional Health Sys., Inc., 1998-2004; chmn. Rehab. Hosp. Ind., 2002-07; with Goshen Health Sys., 2000-2004; bd. dirs. Ruth Lilly Health Edn. Ctr., Indpls; sr. v.p. bus. devel. and strategy Sisters of St. Francis Health Svc., Inc., 2007-; dir. MHA program Ind. U., 2004-07, exec. in residence, 2007-. Contbr. articles to profl. jours. Sr. asst. health svcs. officer USPHS, 1968-70. Fellow Am. Coll. Health Care Execs.; mem. Ind. Hosp. Assn. (bd. dirs. 1994-97). Office: Ind U BS4085 801 W Michigan St Indianapolis IN 46202 Business E-Mail: dhandel@iupui.edu.

HANDELMAN, HOWARD, political scientist, educator; b. NYC, Apr. 29, 1943; s. Victor and Ruth (Goodman) H.; m. Nancy Rae Forster, Sept. 22, 1967 (div.); 1 child, Michael Jesse. Student, London Sch. Econs., 1963-64; BA, U. Pa., 1965; MA in polit. sci., U. Wis., 1967; PhD in polit. sci., U.Wis., 1971. Instr. Ctr. for Latin Am., U. Milw., 1970-71, asst. prof., 1971-76, assoc. prof., 1976-81, prof., 1981—. Faculty assoc. Am. Universities Field Staff, Hanover, N.H., 1978-80. Author: Struggle in the Andes, 1974, Military Rule and the Road to Democracy in South America, 1981, The Politics of Rural Change in Asia and Latin America, 1981; co-author, editor: Paying the Costs of Austerity in South America, 1989; co-author: Politics in a Changing World, 1993, 2d edit., 1998, The Challenge of Third World Development, 1996, Mexican Politics, 1997. Mem. Latin Am. Studies Assn. Jewish. Avocations: jogging, music, raquetball. Office: U Wis-Milw Polit Sci Dept PO Box 413 Milwaukee WI 53201-0413

HANDELSMAN, JO, plant pathologist, educator; BS in agronomy, Cornell Univ., Ithaca, NY; PhD in molecular biology, U. Wis.-Madison. Asst. prof. to prof. U. Wis.-Madison, 1985—, dir. Inst. Pest & Pathogen Mgmt., 1997—99, Clark Lectr. Soil Biology, 2002—. Co-author: Biology Brought to Life, 1997. Grantee professorship, Howard Hughes Med. Inst., 2002—. Achievements include establishing Women in Sci. & Engring. Leadership Inst. Office: Dept Plant Pathology U Wisconsin-Madison 1630 Linden Dr Madison WI 53706 Office Phone: 608-263-8783. Office Fax: 608-265-5289.

HANDRICK, JOSEPH W., state legislator; b. Nov. 2, 1965; BA, U. Wis. Assemblyman Wis. State Dist. 34, 1994—, mem. census and redistricting com., 1999—, chair assembly com., 1999—. Mem. Oneida County, Wis. Mem. Wis. Equal Rights Coun. Mem. Minocqua Lakes Improvement Assn. (bd. dirs.). Address: PO Box 604 Minocqua WI 54548-0604

HANDY, JOHN W., shipping company executive, retired military officer; b. Raleigh, NC, Apr. 29, 1944; BS in History, Meth. Coll., 1966; Diploma, Squadron Officer Sch., 1972, Air Command and Staff Coll., 1979; MS in Systems Mgmt., U. So. Calif., 1979; Diploma, Air War Coll., 1982, Nat. War Coll., 1984; postgrad., Harvard U., 1993. Commd. 2d lt. USAF, 1967, advanced through ranks to gen., 2000; various assignments to dir. of programs and evaluations Hdqtrs. USAF, Washington, 1995-97; comdr. 21st Air Force, McGuire AFB, N.J., 1997-98; dep. chief of staff for installations and logistics Hdqtrs. USAF/The Pentagon, Washington, 1998-2000; vice chief of staff USAF/The Pentagon, Washington, 2000—01; comdr. U.S. Transp. Command, Scott AFB, Ill., 2001—05; exec. v.p. Horizon Lines, LLC, Charlotte, NC, 2005—. Bd. dir. Alien Tech., 2006—, American Roll-On Roll-off Carrier, Am. Auto Logistics; bd. trustee Methodist Coll., Fayetteville, NC, St. Louis Sci. Ctr. Decorated Def. Disting. Svc. medal, Disting. Svc. medal, Legion of Merit with oak leaf cluster, Meritorious Svc. medal with three oak leaf clusters, Air medal with oak leaf cluster, Antarctica Svc. medal, Vietnam Svc. medal with three svc. stars, Republic of Vietnam Gallery Cross with Palm, Order of Sword, 2005, others. Office: Horizon Lines Inc 4064 Colony Rd Ste 200 Charlotte NC 28211

HANDY, RICHARD LINCOLN, civil engineer, educator; b. Chariton, Iowa, Feb. 12, 1929; s. Walter Newton and Florence Elizabeth (Shoemaker) H.; married, Apr. 18, 1964 (div. 1980); 1 child, Beth Susan.; m. Kathryn Etona Claussen, Feb. 13, 1982. BS in Geology, Iowa State U., 1951, MS, 1953, PhD in Soil Engring. and Geology, 1956. Asst. prof. civil engring. Iowa State U., Ames, 1956-59, assoc. prof., 1959-63, prof., 1963-87, disting. prof., 1987-91, disting. prof. emeritus, 1991—; prof.-in-charge Spangler Geotech. Lab., 1963-91; cons. in soil engring., soil and rock testing, landslide stabilization; v.p. research W.N. Handy Co., 1958-91, chmn. bd., 1986-90; pres. Handy Geotech. Instruments, Inc., 1980-93, 1999—, chmn. bd. dirs., 1993—; mem., chmn. bd. dirs. Geopier Found. Co., L.C., 1993-95. Author: The Day the House Fell, 1995; co-author: (with M.G. Spangler) Soil Engineering 3rd edit., 1972, 4th edit. 1983, Geotechnical Engineering, 5th edit., 2007; contbr. articles to profl. jours. Recipient faculty citation Iowa State U., 1976; named Anson Marston Disting. Prof. Engring., Iowa State U., 1987. Fellow AAAS, Geol. Soc. Am., Iowa Acad. Sci.; mem. ASCE (Thomas A. Middlebrooks award 1986), Soil Sci. Soc. Am., Internat. Soc. Soil Mech. and Found. Engrs. Achievements include patents for soils and rock testing instruments. Home and Office: 1502 270th St Madrid IA 50156-7522 Home Phone: 515-795-3355; Office Phone: 515-795-3355. Business E-Mail: rlhandy@iowatelecom.net.

HANEY, TRACY, radio personality; b. Little Rock, Jan. 6, 1963; m. Lisa Haney; 1 child. Radio host of Midday Connection Sta. WMBI Radio, Chgo. Office: WMBI 820 N LaSalle Blvd Chicago IL 60610

HANKET, MARK JOHN, lawyer; b. Jan. 28, 1943; s. Laddie W. and Florence J. (Kubat) H.; m. Carole A. Dalpiaz, Sept. 14, 1968; children: Gregory, Jennifer, Sarah. AB magna cum laude, John Carroll U., 1965; JD cum laude, Ohio State U., 1968; MBA, Xavier U., 1977. Bar: Ohio 1968, Mich. 1993. Atty. Chemed Corp., Cin., 1973-77, asst. sec., 1977-82, sec., 1982-84, v.p., sec., 1984-86; v.p., gen counsel DuBois Chems. Divsn., 1986-87; v.p., sec. gen. counsel DuBois Chems., Inc., 1987-91; sec. gen. counsel Diversey Corp., 1991-94, v.p., sec. gen.

counsel, 1994-96; v.p. law and people excellence, sec. Americlean Sys., Inc., 1996-99; asst. gen. counsel Diversey Lever, Inc., 1999—2002; sr. counsel JohnsonDiversey, Inc., Southfield, Mich., 2002—06; pvt. practice, 2006—. Capt. US Army, 1968—73. Decorated Meritorious Svc. medal, Army Commendation medal with oak leaf cluster. Mem. ABA, Mich. Bar Assn., Am. Corp. Counsel Assn., Ohio Bar Assn. Office Phone: 248-514-0353. Personal E-mail: mjhanket@aol.com.

HANKS, ALAN R., retired chemistry professor; b. Balt., Nov. 30, 1939; s. Raymond Hanks and Lillian (Simon) Miller; m. Beverly Jean Henson, Jan. 17, 1961; children: Craig, Denise, Leta. BS in Physics, West Tex. State U., 1962; MS in Biophys. Chemistry, N. Mex. Highlands U., 1964; PhD in Biophysics, Pa. State U., 1967. Nuclear med. sci. officer Armed Forces Inst. Pathology, Washington, 1967-69; from asst. to prof. biochemistry, biophysics Tex. A&M U., Coll. Sta., Tex., 1969-82; state chemist, seed commnr., prof. Purdue U., West Lafayette, Ind., 1982—2005, prof. emeritus, 2005. Corr. mem., liaison Collaborative Internat. Pesticide Analytical Coun., 1988—2006; mem. FAO panel on pesticides UN, 1991—2006, mem. WHO panel on pesticides, 2001—06. Contbr. articles to profl. jours. Recipient World Food Day Bronze medal, FAO, 2006, Commrs. Citation Honor award, FDA, 2007. Fellow Assn. Ofcl. Analytical Chemists (chmn. methods bd. 1986-89, bd. dirs. 1990-96, sec.-treas. 1992-93, pres.-elect 1993-94, pres. 1994-95, chmn. liaison com. 1997-2001); mem. Assn. Am. Feed Control Ofcls. (chmn. minerals com. 1985-96, pres. 1999-2000, lab. methods and svc. com. 1988-93, bd. dirs. 1996-2001, codex observer mem. to codex com. on methods of analysis and sampling 2000-2005), Assn. Am. Plant Food Control Ofcls. (chmn. Magruder check sample com. 1988-90, bd. dirs. 1989-94, chmn. environ. affairs com. 1990-99, pres.-elect 1991-92, pres. 1992-93). Avocations: fishing, gardening, sports, travel, reading. Personal E-mail: abhanks@netscape.com.

HANKS, ROBIN, rehabilitation nurse; b. 1968; PhD from Dept. Psych., Wayne State U., 1996. Postdoctoral fellow U. Washington Sch. of Medicine; project dir. Southeastern Mich. Traumatic Brain Injury System; dir., Tng. predoctoral and postdoctoral tng. prog., Clinical Psych.; assoc. prof., Phys. Medicine and Rehab. Wayne State U. Sch. of Medicine; adj. prof., Psych. Wayne State U. Sch. of Sci.; chief of Rehab Psych. & Neuropsychology Rehab. Inst. Mich., 1999—. amed one of 40 Under 40, Crain's Detroit Bus., 2006. Office: Rehabilitation Institute of Michigan 261 Mack Ave Detroit MI 48201 Office Phone: 313-745-1203.

HANN, DANIEL P., former medical products executive, lawyer; BA, Calif. State U., 1977; MS, U. Ill., 1979; JD, Ind. U., 1984. Bar: Ind. 1984. Prof. econs. Franklin Coll., 1979—84; atty. Ice Miller Donadio & Ryan, 1984—89; sr. v.p., gen. counsel Biomet Inc., Warsaw, Ind., 1989—2006, interim pres., CEO, 2006—07, exec. v.p. adminstrn., 2007. Mem. listing & hearing rev. council NASDAQ. Mem.: Indpls. Bar Assn. (chmn. legis. com. 1988).

HANNA, MARSHA L., artistic director; b. Tiffin, Ohio, Nov. 27, 1951; d. Willis Leondadis and Frances Lucille (Neeley) H. BS, Bowling Green State U., 1980. Drama specialist City of Dayton, Ohio, 1975-80; gen. mgr. Illumination Theatre, 1978-85; product analyst Lexis/Nexis, 1980—86; instr. Sinclair C.C., 1986—; freelance stage dir., 1986—; resident dir. Human Race Theatre Co., 1986—, artistic dir., 1990—. Dir.: Equus, 1981, Beyond Therapy, 1983, The Diviners, 1984, Amadeus, 1985,Getting Out, 1987, Orphans, 1988, Fool for Love, 1989, A Shayna Maidel, 1990, A Christmas Carol, 1991, Closer Than Ever, 1993, The Good Times Are Killing Me, 1994, Cloud Nine, 1995, Three Tall Women, 1996, The Cherry Orchard, 1996, Quilters, 1997, Taking Sides, Stonewall Jackson's House, 1998, On Golden Pond, 1999, Three Days of Rain, 1999, Art, 2000, Resident Alien, 2001, I Hate Hamlet, 2002, The Dazzle, 2003, Odd Couple, 2004, Every Good Boy Deserves Favour (with Dayton Philharmonic), Johnny Appleseed, Copenhagen, 2005, The Elephant Man, Moonlight and Magnolias, 2006. Office: The Human Race Theatre Co 126 N Main St Ste 300 Dayton OH 45402-1766 E-mail: Marsha@humanracetheatre.org.

HANNA, MARTIN SHAD, lawyer; b. Bowling Green, Ohio, Aug. 4, 1940; s. Martin Lester and Julia Loyal (Moor) H.; m. Ann I. Amos; children: Jennifer Lynn, Jonathan Moor, Katharine Anne. Student, Bowling Green State U.; BS, Purdue U., 1962; JD, Am. U., 1965. Bar: Ohio 1965, D.C. 1967, U.S. Supreme Ct. 1969. Ptnr. Hanna, Middleton & Roebke, 1965-70; ptnr. Hanna & Hanna, Bowling Green, 1971—. Spl. counsel for atty. gen. Ohio, 1969-71, 82-85, Ohio Bd. Regents, 1974; instr. Bowling Green State U., 1970, Ohio Div. Vocat. Edn., 1970—, Ohio Peace Officer Tng. Council, 1968; legal adviser NW Ohio Vol. Firemen's Assn., 1970— Contbr. articles to profl. publs. Elder, lay minister Presbyn. Ch.; state chmn. Ohio League Young Republican Clubs, 1972-73; nat. vice chmn. Young Rep. Nat. Fedn., 1973-75, counselor to chmn., 1975-77; cive chmn. Wood County Rep. Exec. Com., Ohio, 1972-80, precinct committeeman, 1968-80; trustee Bowling Green State U., 1976-86; mem. Ohio State Fire Commn., 1979-87; mem. Ohio Rural Fire coun., 1993—. Recipient George Washington honor medal award Freedoms Found. at Valley Forge, 1969, award of merit Ohio Legal Ctr. Inst., 1973, Robert A. Taft Disting. Service award, 1974, James A. Rhodes Leadership award, 1975; named one of 10 Outstanding Young Men, Ohio Jaycees, 1968. Mem. ABA, D.C. Bar Assn., Ohio Bar Assn., Northwest Ohio Bar Assn., Wood County Bar Assn., Toledo Bar Assn., Am. Trauma Soc. (trauma and law com.), Phi Delta Phi, Pi Kappa Delta, Omicron Delta Kappa Office: Hanna & Hanna 700 N Main St Bowling Green OH 43402-1815 Home: PO Box 25 Bowling Green OH 43402-0025

HANNA, MILFORD A., agricultural engineering educator; b. West Middlesex, Pa., Feb. 26, 1947; s. Clayton S. and Clara (Burrows) H.; m. Lenora J. Uhrmacher, May 13, 1978; children: Michelle L., Charles C., Susan R., Andrew A. BS, Pa. State U., 1969, MS, 1971, PhD, 1973. Asst. prof. Calif. Poly. State U., San Luis Obispo, Calif., 1973-75, U. Nebr., Lincoln, 1975-79, assoc. prof., 1979-85, prof., 1985—, prof. food engring., 1990—, dir. Indsl. Agrl. Products Ctr., 1991—. Contbr. more than 70 articles to profl. jours. Recipient Rsch. award of Merit, Gamma Sigma Delta, 1991. Fellow Am. Soc. Agrl. Engrs. (chmn. Food Processing Engring. Inst. 1991-92, Engr. of Yr. Nebr. sect. 1991), Am. Assn. Cereal Chemists, Coun. for Agrl. Sci. and Tech., Kiwanis (gov. Nebr.-Iowa dist. 1992-93) dist. chmn. Worldwide Srvs. Project, 1994. Achievements include patent pending on starch-based plastic foams. Office: U Nebr 211 L W Chase Hall W Lincoln NE 68583-0730

HANNA, NESSIM, marketing educator; b. Assiut, Egypt, Apr. 30, 1938; came to U.S., 1961, naturalized, 1973; s. Yanni and Lulu Shehata (Oweda) H.; m. Dana Lascu, Aug. 28, 1987 (div. 1988); m. Margaret Ann Curzan, 1996. BS in Commerce, Cairo U., 1958; MS in Mktg., U. Ill., 1964, PhD in Mktg, 1969. Asst. prof., chmn. dept. mktg. W.Va. Inst. Tech., Montgomery, 1968-69; asso. prof. bus. adminstrn. Mid. Tenn. State U., Murfreesboro, 1969-70; prof. mktg. No. Ill. U., De Kalb, 1970—98; mktg. cons. Arab Rsch. and Adminstrn. Ctr., 1975-77, Investments Cons. Internat., 1974-77; with Roosevelt U., Schaumburg, Ill., 2001—. Vis. prof. mktg. U. Petroleum and Minirals, Dharan, Saudi Arabia, 1980-81, Norwegian Sch. Mgmt., Oslo, 1988; chmn. dept. mktg., dir. research inst. King Saud U., Kassim, Saudi Arabia, 1983-84; vis. scholar Hong Kong Bapt. U., fall 1991. Author: Marketing Opportunities in Egypt: A Business Guide, 1977, Principles of Marketing, 1985, Pricing Policies and Procedures, 1995, Winning Strategies, 1991, Consumer Behavior: An Applied Approach, 2001, 2d edit., 2005; contbr. articles to profl. jours. Named Outstanding Citizen Citizenship Council Met. Chgo., 1974 Mem. Southwestern Social Sci. Assn., Am. Mktg. Assn., Midwest Bus. Adminstrn. Assn., Assn. Egyptian-Am. Scholars (treas.), Acad. Mktg. Sci., Am. Inst. Decision Scis., Phi Beta Lambda, Beta Gamma Sigma, Phi Kappa Phi, Alpha Mu Alpha. Republican. Christian Orthodox. Avocation: overseas travel. Home: Ste 2219 1900 Lincoln Vill Cr Larkspur CA 94939 Home Phone: 415-785-7937. Personal E-mail: nessimh@aol.com.

HANNAH, WAYNE ROBERTSON, JR., lawyer; b. Freeport, Ill., Aug. 18, 1931; s. Wayne Robertson and Edith (Biene) H.; m. Patricia Anne Matthews, June 1, 1957; children— Tamara Lee, Wendy, Wayne Robertson III BA, Ill. Coll., 1953; JD, NYU, 1957. Bar: Ill. 1957, U.S. Dist. Ct. (no. dist.) Ill., U.S. Supreme Ct. Ptnr. Sonnenschein, ath & Rosenthal, Chgo., 1965—. Dir. Checker Motors Corp., N.Y.C. and Kalamazoo, 1982-86; lectr. Ill. Inst. Continuing Edn. Sec. 7th cir. Root-Tilden Scholarship Program NYU, 1967-94; chmn. Root-Tilden-Kern scholarship com., 1981-86, trustee law ctr., 1985—; pres. bd. Firman Cmty. Svcs, Chgo., 1972-75; trustee, pres., chmn. bd. Chgo. City Ballet, 1982-86. 2d lt. USMC, 1951-54. Fulbright scholar, 1953—54, Root-Tilden scholar, NYU, 1954—57. Mem. ABA (real estate com.), Chgo. Bar Assn. (chmn. condominium subcom. real estate com. 1977-78, sec., dir. condominium assn. 1991—), Ill. Bar Assn. (real estate com.), Econ. Club (Chgo.), Skokie Country Club (Glencoe, Ill.). Presbyterian. Avocations: tennis, golf. Office: Sonnenschein Nath and Rosenthal 233 S Wacker Dr Ste 8000 Chicago IL 60606-6491 Home Phone: 847-446-7409; Office Phone: 312-876-8045. Business E-Mail: whannah@sonnenschein.com.

HANNAY, WILLIAM MOUAT, III, lawyer; b. Kansas City, Mo., Dec. 3, 1944; s. William Mouat and Gladys (Capron) H.; m. Donna Jean Harkins, Sept. 30, 1978; children: Capron Grace, Blaike Ann, William Mouat IV. BA, Yale U., New Haven, Conn., 1966; JD, Georgetown U., Washington, DC, 1973. Bar: Mo. 1973, DC 1974, NY 1975, Ill. 1980. Law clk. to Judge Myron Bright US Ct. Appeals, 8th Cir., St. Louis, 1973-74; law clk. to Justice Tom Clark US Supreme Ct., Washington, 1974-75; assoc. Weil Gotshal & Manges, NYC, 1975-77; asst. dist. atty. NY County Dist. Atty.'s Office, NYC, 1977-79; ptnr. Schiff Hardin LLP, Chgo., 1979. Adj. prof. IIT/Chgo.-Kent Law Sch., 1983—. Author: International Trade: Avoiding Criminal Risks, 1994, Designing an Effective Antitrust Compliance Program, rev. 2006, Tying Arrangements, rev. 2006, International Antitrust Enforcement, rev. 2006; contbr. articles to profl. jours. Chmn. bd. dirs. Gilbert and Sullivan Soc. Chgo., 1984-87, Served with US Army, 1967-68, Vietnam. Mem. ABA (chmn. sect. internat. law and practice 1998-99, chmn. Africa law initiative coun. 2000-02, mem. ho. of dels. 2001-06, co-chair NCCUSL-ABA joint editl. bd. internat. law, 2007—), Chgo Bar Assn. (chmn. antitrust com. 1986-87), Yale Club (pres. 1987-89), Chgo. Yacht Club, Union League Club (Chgo.), Am. Law Inst. Democrat. Episcopalian. Home: 591 Plum Tree Rd Barrington IL 60010-2329 Office: Schiff Hardin LLP 7200 Sears Tower Chicago IL 60606 Home Phone: 847-381-8464; Office Phone: 312-258-5617. Business E-Mail: whannay@schiffhardin.com.

HANNEMANN, TIMOTHY W., aerospace transportation executive; BSEE, Ill. Inst. Tech., 1964, MSEE, 1966; completed exec. program, U. S.C., 1981. Various positions in mgmt. and devel. advanced sys. TRW Inc., Cleve., 1969, mgr. electronic devel. opers. comms. divsn., mgr. def. comms. divsn., 1986, v.p., gen. mgr. electronic sys. gorup, 1989-91, exec. v.p., gen. mgr. space and def. sector, 1991-95, exec. v.p., gen. mgr. space and electronics group, 1995—.

HANNER, JOHN, retail executive; Exec. v.p., COO Clark Retail Group, Oakbrook, Ill., 2000—. Office: Clark Retail Group Inc 3003 Butterfield Rd Oak Brook IL 60523

HANNIG, GARY L., state representative; b. Litchfield, Ill., July 22, 1952; m. Elizabeth Hannig. BS, U. Ill., Champaign, 1974. CPA. Mem. Ill. Ho. of Reps., 1978—, asst. majority leader, 1997—2005, dep. majority leader, 2005—. Mem. Holy Family Cath. Ch. Mem.: NRA, Wolfpack Antique Car Club, Macoupin County Hist. Soc., K. of C., Benld Croation Lodge. Democrat. Office: 300 Capitol Bldg Springfield IL 62706 Address: 218 S Macoupin St PO Box 8 Gillespie IL 62033

HANNON, BRUCE MICHAEL, engineering educator; b. Champaign, Ill., Aug. 14, 1934; s. Walter Leo and Kathleen Rose (Phalen) H.; m. Patricia Claire Coffey, Aug. 11, 1956; children: Claire, Laura, Brian. BSCE, U. Ill., 1956, MS in Engring. Mechanics, 1966, PhD in Engring. Mechanics, 1970. Engr. with chem. industry, 1957-66; instr. U. Ill., Urbana, 1966-71, assoc. prof. energy rsch., 1974-83, prof. regional sci., 1983—, Jubilee prof. liberal arts and scis., 1991—. Vis. prof. at. Ctr. for Supercomputing Applications; cons. NSF, NAS, NAE, chem. industry, various fed. energy agys; patentee in field. Contbr. articles to profl. jours. 1st lt. C.E. AUS, 1956-57. Named Engring. Tchr. of Yr., U. Ill., 1970, Man of Yr., Sierra Club, 1971; recipient 1st prize Mitchell Award Club of Rome, 1975. Home: 1208 W Union St Champaign IL 61821-3229 Office: U Ill 220 Daven Hall Urbana IL 61801 Office Phone: 217-333-0348. Business E-Mail: bhannon@uiuc.edu.

HANNUM, TERENCE J., artist, director, art critic; Attended projects in Painting, NYU, 2000; BA in Religion/Philosophy & studio Art, Fla. Southern Coll., Lakeland, Fla., 2001; post-baccalaureate cert. in Painting and Drawing, Sch. of Art Inst. Chgo., 2002, MFA in Painting and Drawing, 2004. Graphic designer Steppendwarf Theatre Comp., Lakeland, Fla., 2000; gallery asst. Harmon-Meeks Gallery, Naples, Fla., 2001; painting and drawing instr. The VonLiebig Art Ctr., Naples, Fla., 2002; tchr. asst. for Anatomy II, painting and drawing dept. Sch. of Art Inst. Chgo., 2003, office asst., painting and drawing dept., 2003; dir. Panel-House.com, Chgo. Writer (articles) Regulator, F News, Bridge Online, (art reviews) panel-house.com; one-man shows include New Work, Small Gallery, Lakeland, Fla., 2000, New Paintings, Liquid, Naples, Fla., 2001, exhibitions include Valentine's Day Peep Show, Hyde Park Fine Arts, Tampa, Fla., 2000, Sr. Thesis Exhbn., Melvin Gallery, Fla. So. Coll., Lakeland, Fla., 2001, Identities and Autobiographies, VonLiebig Art Ctr., Naples, Fla., 2002, The Pick-Up, 1926, Chgo., Ill., 2002, Faculty Biennial, VonLiebig Art Ctr., Naples, Fla., 2002, MFA Post-Baccalaureate Exhbn., G2, Chgo., Ill., 2002, Brilliant, Zolla/Lieberman Gallery, 2003, Song Lyrics, So-and-So Gallery, 2003, ArtHotel 2003, Embassy Suites, 2003, Stray Show, Zeek & Neen/Municipal, 2003, Modest Contemporary Art Projects. Mem.: Chgo. Art Critics Assn. Office: Panel-House c/o Terence Hannum PO Box 220651 Chicago IL 60622 Home: PO Box 220651 Chicago IL 60622-0651 Business E-Mail: terence@panel-house.com. E-mail: thannu@artic.edu.

HANRATH, LINDA CAROL, librarian, archivist; b. Chgo., Aug. 22, 1949; d. John Stanley and Victoria (Fraint) Grzesiakowski; m. Richard Alan Hanrath, Nov. 1, 1980; 1 child, Emily BA History, Rosary Coll., 1971, MLS, 1974. Tchr. social studies Notre Dame HS, Chgo., 1971—75; outreach libr. Indian Trails Pub. Libr., Wheeling, Ill., 1975—76, Arlington Heights Meml. Libr., Ill., 1976—78; corp. libr. William Wrigley Jr. Co., Chgo., 1978—. Mem. Spl. Librs. Assn. (chmn. libr. jobline com. 1981-83, 86-87, food agrl. and nutrition divsn. 1988-89, sec. Ill. chpt. 1984-86, pres.-elect 1993-94, pres. Ill. chpt. 1994-95, conf. bd. info. svcs. adv. coun. 1990—, winner Outstanding Achievement award 1997), Assn. Records Mgrs. and Adminstrs., Soc. Am. Archivists, Midwest Archives Conf., Beta Phi Mu Avocations: needlecrafts, skiing, reading, gourmet cooking, tap dancing. Home: 715 E Devon Ave Roselle IL 60172-1461 Office: William Wrigley Jr Co 410 N Michigan Ave Chicago IL 60611-4213 E-mail: lhanrath@wrigley.com.

HANRATTY, THOMAS JOSEPH, chemical engineer, educator; b. Phila., Nov. 9, 1926; s. John Joseph and Elizabeth Marie (O'Connor) H.; m. Joan L. Hertel, Aug. 25, 1956; children: John, Vincent, Maria, Michael, Peter. BS Chem. Engring., Villanova U., 1947; MS, Ohio State U., 1950; PhD, Princeton U., 1953; doctorate (hon.), 1979, Polytechnic INst. Toulouse, 1999, Tolouse Poly. Inst., 1999. Engr. Fischer & Porter, 1947-48; research engr. Battelle Meml. Inst., 1948-50; engr. Rohm & Haas, Phila., summer 1951; research engr. Shell Devel. Co., Emeryville, Calif., 1954; faculty U. Ill., Urbana, 1953—, assoc. prof., 1958-63, prof. chem. engring., 1963—, James W. Westwater prof. chem. engring., 1989-97. Cons. in field; vis. assoc. prof. Brown U., 1962-63 Contbr. articles to profl. jours. NSF sr. postdoctoral fellow, 1962; recipient Curtis W. McGraw award Am. Soc. Engring. Edn., 1963, Sr. Research award, 1979; Disting. Engring. Alumnus award Ohio State U., 1984; Shell Disting. prof., 1981-86; 1st winner Internat. prize for rsch. in multiphase flow, 1998; Sr. Univ. Scholar, U. Ill., 1987, Lamme award Ohio State Univ., 1997. Fellow Am. Phys. Soc.; mem. NAE, Am. Acad. Arts and Scis., NAS. AIChE (Colburn award 1957, Walker award 1964, Profl. Progress award 1967, Ernest Thiele award Chgo. sect. 1986), Serra Internat. Club. Roman Catholic. Home: 1019 W Charles St Champaign IL 61821-4525 Office: U Ill 205 Roger Adams Lab 600 S Mathews Ave Urbana IL 61801-3602 E-mail: hanratty@scs.uiuc.edu.

HANREDDY, JOSEPH, stage director; b. LA, Oct. 18, 1947; s. Harvey Joseph and Geraldine (Powers) H. BA, San Jose State U., 1969, MA, 1970. Artistic dir. Ensemble Theatre Project, Santa Barbara, Calif., 1979-85, Madison Repertory Theatre, 1987-1993, Milw. Repertory Theater, 1993—. Dir. San Diego Repertory Theatre, 1986, Cider Mill Playhouse, Binghamton, N.Y., 1985—, Santa Barbara Repertory Theatre, 1985. Office: Milwaukee Repertory Theatre 108 E Wells St Milwaukee WI 53202-3504

HANSELL, EDGAR FRANK, lawyer; b. Leon, Iowa, Oct. 12, 1937; s. Edgar Noble and Celestia Delphine (Skinner) H.; m. Phyllis Wray Silvey, June 24, 1961; children: John Joseph, Jordan Burke. AA, Graceland Coll., 1957; BBA, U. Iowa, 1959, JD with distinction, 1961. Bar: Iowa 1961, US Dist. Ct. (no. dist. 1966, so. dist. 1967), US Supreme Ct. 1999. Assoc. Nyemaster, Goode, West, Hansell & O'Brien, P.C., Des Moines, 1964—. Bd. dirs. The Vernon Co., Des Moines Internat. Airport, vice chair; mem. adv. com. to bd. dirs. The Lauridson Group, Inc.; adj. prof. law Drake U., Des Moines, 1990—95. Mem. editorial adv. bd. Jour. Corp. Law, 1985—. Bd. dirs. Des Moines Child Guidance Ctr., 1972-78, 81-87, pres., 1977-78; trustee Iowa Law Sch. Found., 1975-90, pres., 1983-87; bd. dirs. Iowa Natural Heritage Found., 1988-93, Iowa Sports Found., 1986-97; bd. dirs. Iowa State Bar Found., 1991-2000, pres., 1996-98. With USAF, 1961-64. amed Am. Best Lawyers for Bus., Chambers USA, 2003—; named one of The Best Lawyers in Am., 1983—. Mem. ABA, Iowa Bar Assn. (pres. young lawyers sect. 1971-72, bd. govs. 1971-72, 85-87, mem. grievance commn. 1973-78, Merit award young lawyers sect. 1977, 98, chmn. corp. and bus. law com. 1979-85, pres. 1989-90), Polk County Bar Assn., Des Moines Club (pres. 1979-80). Home: 139-37th Des Moines IA 50312-4303 Office: Nyemaster Goode West Hansell & O'Brien PC 700 Walnut St Ste 1600 Des Moines IA 50309-3800 Office Phone: 515-283-3150. Business E-Mail: efh@nyemaster.com.

HANSELL, RICHARD STANLEY, obstetrician, gynecologist, educator; b. Indpls., Nov. 18, 1950; s. Robert Mathey and Jewell (Martin) H.; m. Cathy C., Oct. 7, 1995; children: Elizabeth, Victoria. BA, DePauw U., 1972; MD, Ind. U., 1976. Cert. Am. Bd. Obstetrics and Gynecology. Practice medicine specializing in ob-gyn. Cedarwood Med. Ctr., St. Joseph, Mich., 1980-86; asst. prof. ob-gyn. Ind. U., Indpls., 1986-93, assoc. prof., 1993—2002, prof., 2002—. Instr. Western Mich. U., Kalamazoo, 1980-86; med. bd. Planned Parenthood, Benton Harbor, Mich., 1980-86; med. dir. Planned Parenthood of Ctrl. Ind., 1991-95; examiner Am. Bd. Ob-gyn., 1994—. Mem. AMA, Am. Coll. Ob-gyn., Assn. of Profs. of Gynecology and Obstetrics, Ind. State Med. Soc., Ctrl. Assn. Ob-gyn., Indpls. Med. Soc. Presbyterian. Avocations: golf, fishing. Office: Ind U Med Sch Dept Ob-Gyn 1001 W 10th St Indianapolis IN 46202-2859 Home Phone: 317-823-4235; Office Phone: 317-630-6594. Business E-Mail: rhansell@iupui.edu.

HANSEN, CARL R., management consultant; b. Chgo., May 2, 1926; s. Carl M. and Anna C. (Roge) Hansen; m. Christia Marie Loeser, Dec. 31, 1952; 1 child, Lothar. MBA, U. Chgo., 1954. Dir. mkt. rsch. Kitchens of Sara Lee, Deerfield, Ill., Earle Ludgin & Co., Chgo.; svc. v.p. Mkt. Rsch. Corp. Am., 1956—67; pres. Chgo. Assoc., Inc., 1967—. Chmn. Ill. adv. coun. SBA, 1973—74; exec. com. Ill. Gov.'s Adv. Coun., 1969—72; resident officer U.S. High Commn., Germany, 1949—52; chmn. Viking Ship Restoration Com.; mem. Cook County Bd. Commrs., 1970, 1974—, chmn. legis. com., adminstrn. com.; active Am. Scandinavian Found.; vice chmn. Rep. Ctrl. Com. Cook County; chmn. Cook County Young Reps., 1957—58, 12th Congl. Dist. Rep. Orgn., 1971—74, 1978—82, Suburban Rep. Orgn., 1974—78, 1982—86; del. Rep. Nat. Conv., 1968, 1984, 1992; chmn. Legis. Dist. Ill., 1964—; del. Rep. State Conv., 1962—96; committeeman Elk Grove Twp. Rep., 1962—2002; pres. John Ericsson Rep. League of Ill., 1975—76; Rep. presdl. elector State of Ill., 1972; bd. dir. Nat. Assn. Counties. 1st lt. US Army, 1948, maj. USAR. Mem.: VFW, Planning Forum, Nat. Assn. Counties, Am. Statis. Assn., Am. Mktg. Assn., Swedish Am. Hist. Soc., Dania Soc., Chgo. Hist. Soc., Lions, Am. Legion, Res. Officers Assn., Shriners, Masons, Sons of Norway. Home: 110 S Edward St Mount Prospect IL 60056-3414 Office: 118 N Clark St Chicago IL 60602-1304

HANSEN, CHARLES, lawyer; b. Jersey City, May 23, 1926; s. Charles Henry and Katherine (Bensch) H.; m. Carolyn P. Smith, Sept. 26, 1953; children: Mark, Melissa. BS, U. Mich., 1946; JD, Mich. Law Sch., 1950. Bar: N.Y. 1951, Wis. 1961, Mo. 1980. Engr. Westinghouse Electric Co., 1946; assoc. Mudge, Stern, Williams & Tucker, 1950-53; chief labor counsel, div. counsel Sylvania Electric Products, 1953-61; sec., gen. counsel Trane Co., La Crosse, Wis., 1961-69, exec. v.p., 1968-73; pres. Cutler-Hammer World Trade, Inc., 1973-77; v.p. Cutler-Hammer, Inc., 1973-77, exec. v.p., 1977-79; sr. v.p. law Emerson Electric Co., 1979-84, sr. v.p., sec., gen. counsel, 1984-89; ptnr. Bryan Cave, 1989-95, of counsel, 1995—. Adj. prof. Sch. Law St. Louis U., 1987—99. Served to lt. (j.g.) USNR, 1943-46. Mem. ABA, Wis., Mo. bar assns., Am. Law Inst., Order of Coif, Tau Beta Pi. Home: 8 Wydown Ter Saint Louis MO 63105-2217 Office: 211 Broadway 1 Metropolitan Sq Ste 3600 Saint Louis MO 63102-2750 Office Phone: 314-259-2676. Personal E-mail: hansenc1h@aol.com. Business E-Mail: chansen@bryancave.com.

HANSEN, CLAIRE V., financial executive; b. Thornton, Iowa, June 3, 1925; s. Charles F. and Grace B. (Miller) H.; m. Renee C. Hansen, Aug. 17, 1946; children: Charles James, Christopher David, Peter Chrissis. BSc, U. Notre Dame, 1947; MBA, Harvard U., 1948. Chartered fin. analyst. With Salk, Ward & Salk, Inc.; v.p. Salk Inst. Agency, 1954-59; with Duff, Anderson & Clark, Chgo., 1959-67, v.p., dir., 1967-71; dir. Duff and Phelps, Inc., 1972-88; exec. v.p. Duff & Phelps, 1973-75, pres., chief exec. officer, 1975-84, chmn. and CEO, 1984—87; chmn. bd. dir. Duff & Phelps Utilities Income, Inc., Chgo., 1987—2001, CEO, 2000—01; chmn. bd. dir. DNP Select Income Fund, Inc., 2002—05. Bd. dir. Chgo. Lung Assn., 1962-80, pres. 1973-75; bd. dir. Am. Lung Assn., 1971-83, Ctr. Religion and Psychotherapy in Chgo., 1979-83; trustee Glenwood Sch., 1974-95, chmn., 1983-87; bd. dirs. Auditorium Theatre Coun., 1983-88, treas., 1987-88; bd. dir. Schwab Rehab. Hosp., 1978-82, pres., 1980-82; bd. dir. Pelican Bay Found. Inc., 1993-99, treas., 1993-96, pres., 1996-97. Mem. Inst. Chartered Fin. Analysts, Univ. Club, Chgo. (Ill.) Club, Olympia Fields Country Club, Club Pelican Bay, Hole-in-the-Wall Golf Club. Republican. Episcopalian. Home: 5601 Turtle Bay Dr Apt 2001 Naples FL 34108-2703 Office: 5601 Turtle Bay Dr # 2001-02 Naples FL 34108 Personal E-mail: verdelle@msn.com.

HANSEN, DAVE, state senator; b. Green Bay, Wis., Dec. 18, 1947; married; 3 children. BS, U. Wis., Green Bay, 1971. Former tchr.; former truck driver; state sen. Wis. State Senate, 2000—, mem. joint com. for rev. adminstrv. rules, mem. environ. resources, human svcs. and aging, law revision, and univs., housing and govt. ops. coms., chair, labor and agr. com., mem. unemployment ins. adv. coun., mem. transp. projects commn. Mem. Brown Co. Human Svcs. bd.; mem. N.E.W. Zoo adv. bd. Democrat. Office: State Capitol Rm 19 S PO Box 7882 Madison WI 53707-7882 also: Dist Address 920 Coppens Rd Green Bay WI 54303 E-mail: Sen.Hansen@legis.state.wi.us.

HANSEN, DAVID RASMUSSEN, federal judge; b. Exira, Iowa, 1938; BA, N.W. Mo. State U., 1960; JD, George Washington U., 1963. Asst. clk. to minority House Appropriations Com. Ho. of Reps., 1960—61; adminstrv. aide 7th Dist. Iowa, 1962—63; law clerk, assoc. atty. Jones, Cambridge & Carl, Atlantic, Iowa, 1963—64; capt., judge advocate General's Corps US Army, 1964—68; pvt. practice Barker, Hansen & McNeal, Iowa Falls, Iowa, 1968—76; ptnr. Win-Gin Farms, Iowa Falls, 1971—; judge Police Ct., Iowa, 1969—73, 2d Jud. Dist. Ct., Iowa, 1976—86, US Dist. Ct. (no. dist.), Cedar Rapids, Iowa, 1986—91, US Ct. Appeals (8th cir.), Cedar Rapids, 1991—2002, chief judge, 2002—03, sr. judge, 2003—. Chmn. Hardin County Rep. Central Com., 1975—76; mem. Jud. Conf. of US, 2002—03, US Jud. Panel on Multidistrict Litig., 2004—. Mem.: Dean Mason Ladd Inn of Ct., Iowa State Bar Assn. Office: US Courthouse Rm 304 101 1st St SE Cedar Rapids IA 52401-1202

HANSEN, ERIK FREDERICK, lawyer; b. Wadena, Minn., Oct. 12, 1974; BA with honors, U. Minn., Morris, 1997; JD, U. Minn., Mpls., 2000. Bar: Minn. 2000, US Dist Ct. (dist. Minn.) 2000, US Ct. Appeals (8th cir.). Assoc. Hellmuth & Johnson, P.L.L.C., Eden Prairie, Minn. Named a Rising Star, Minn. Super Lawyers mag., 2006; named an Up and Coming Atty., 2006. Mem.: Minn. State Bar Assn. (chair membership com. 2004—06, mem. publs. com.). Office: Hellmuth & Johnson PLLC 10400 Viking Dr Ste 500 Eden Prairie MN 55344 Office Phone: 952-941-4005. E-mail: ehansen@hjlawfirm.com.

HANSEN, H. JACK, management consultant; b. Chgo., Mar. 28, 1922; s. Herbert Christian John and Laura Elizabeth (Osterman) Hansen; m. Joan Dorothy Norum, Nov. 28, 1980; children: Marilyn Joan, Gail Jean(dec.), Mark John, Jacquelyn Lee. BSME, Ill. Inst. Tech. Armour Coll. Engring., 1944; grad. student in personnel and acctg., U. Chgo., 1947—48; student in computer scis., Oakton CC, Des Plaines, Ill., 1977—78. Cert. mgmt. cons. Mech. and indsl. engr. Harper Wyman Co., Chgo., 1944-51; chief indsl. engr. Shakeproof divsn. Ill. Tool Works, Des Plaines, 1951-53; cons., prin. A.T. Kearney & Co., Chgo. and NYC, 1953-71; pres. H.J. Hansen Co., Elburn, Ill., 1971—2000. Acting mfg. engring. mgr. European Ops., Hobart Corp., 1974—78; owner, mgmt. cons. Hansen Mgmt. Search Co., Mt. Prospect, Ill., 1980—93; active turnaround cons., 1992—2000; apptd. by Kane County States Atty. Second Chance Panel, 2001—; apptd. to Kane County Chronicle's Readers adv. bd., 2002—04; guest lectr. U. Mich., U. Detroit, Iowa State U. Mem. Planning Commn. Village of Elburn, 1995—97, trustee, 1997—2001, chmn. Pers. Commn., mem. Fin. Commn., mem. Pub. Works Commn.; pres. Men's Club, 1987—90; mem. Friends of the Town and Country Libr., 2003—; amb. Elburn C. of C., 2007—; citizens adv. com. Kaneland Sch. Dist. 302, 2007—; pres. Good Shepherd Luth. Ch., Des Plaines, Ill., 1988—90; active mem. mcpl. legis. com. DuKane Valley Coun., 1997—2001; v.p., bd. dirs. Elburn and Countryside Cmty. Ctr., 2006—. With US Army, 1945—46. Named to Tilden Tech. Alumni Assn. Hall of Fame, 2000. Mem. Inst. Mgmt. Cons. (founding), Methods-Time Measurement Assn. (bd. dirs. 1964-70, pres. 1967-68), Am. Arbitartion Assn., Soc. Advancement Mgmt. (past bd. dirs.), coun. for Internat. Progress in Mgmt. (past bd. dirs.), Found. Internat. Progress in Mgmt. (past bd. dirs.), Econ. Devel. Com. (tech. com., membership com.), Elburn C. of C. Lutheran. Achievements include research in shingles prevention. Avocations: woodcarving, gardening, computers. Office: H J Hansen Co 317 Prairie Valley St Elburn IL 60119-8977

HANSEN, JAMES ALLEN, state agency administrator; b. West Point, Nebr., Jan. 10, 1939; s. Walter J. and Dorothy (Kay) H.; m. Janice A. Wenke, June 27, 1964 (div. 1975); m. Rebecca A. Bayer, Nov. 28, 1975. BA, Wayne State Coll., 1965. Pres. Farmers State Bank, Lexington, Nebr., 1972-80, No. Bank, Omaha, 1980-86, 1st at. Bank, Fremont, Nebr., 1986-87; regional v.p. Am. First Co., Omaha, 1987-90; mng. agt. FDIC/RTC, Burnsville, Minn., 1990; dir. Nebr. Dept. Banking & Fin., Lincoln, 1991-98; chmn., CEO Centennial Bank, Omaha, 1999—. Chmn. Conf. State Bank Suprs., Washington, 1992-97, vice-chmn. adv. bd., 2002—. Group study exch. team to Australia, Rotary Internat., 1970. 1st lt. U.S. Army N.G., 1960-66. Home: 18109 Mayberry St Omaha NE 68022 Office: Centennial Bank 9003 S 145th St Omaha NE 68138-3636

HANSEN, JO-IDA CHARLOTTE, psychology professor, researcher; d. Gordon Henry and Charlotte Lorraine (Helgeson) Hansen; m. John Paul Campbell. BA, U. Minn., 1969, MA, 1971, PhD, 1974. Asst. prof. psychology U. Minn., Mpls., 1974-78, assoc. prof., 1978-84, prof., 1984—, dir. Ctr. for Interest Measurement Rsch., 1974—, dir. counseling psychology program, 1987—, dir. Vocat. Assessment Clinic, 1997—, prof. human resources and indsl. rels., 1997—, assoc. dean for grad. studies Coll. Liberal Arts, 2005—. Author: User's Guide for the SII, 1984, 2d edit., 1992, Manual for the SII, 1985 2d edit. 1994; editor: Measurement and Evaluation in Counseling and Development, 1993-2000; editor Jour. Counseling Psychology, 1999-2005; contbr. over 150 articles to profl. jours., chpts. to books. Recipient early career award U. Minn., 1982, E.K. Strong, Jr. gold medal, 1984, Leona Tyler award, Am. Counseling Assn. Extended Rsch. award. Fellow APA (coun. reps. 1990-93, 97-99, pres. divsn. counseling psychology 1993-94, chmn. joint com. testing practices 1989-93, com. to revise APA/Am. Ednl. Rsch. Assn. nat. coun. measurement evalation testing stds. 1993-99, exam. com. Assn. State Provincial Psychology Bds. 1996-99, bd. sci. affairs, 2003-05, chair coun. of editors 2003-04; Leona Tyler award for rsch. and profl. svc. 1996); mem. ACA (extended rsch. award 1990, disting. rsch. award 1996), Assn. for Measurement and Evaluation (pres. 1988-89, Exemplary Practice award 1987, 90). Avocations: golf, theater, music, water and downhill skiing, spectator sports. Office: U Minn Dept Psychology Ctr Interest Measurement 75 E River Rd Minneapolis MN 55455-0280 Office Phone: 612-626-9062. Business E-Mail: hanse004@umn.edu.

HANSEN, OLE VIGGO, chemical engineer; b. Detroit, May 6, 1934; s. Oluf Viggo and Carrie Alma (Wary) H.; m. Shirley Elizabeth Ford, Dec. 29, 1966; 1 child, Victoria Louisa. BSChemE, Wayne State U., 1956; equivalent of BS in Meteorology, Tex. A & M Univ., 1958. Registered profl. engr., Mich. Engr. tech. svcs. 3M Co., Detroit, 1956-57; chem. engr. Fisher Body div. Gen. Motors, Detroit, 1960-64; mgr. mktg. Monsanto Co., St. Louis and Australia, 1964-76; dir. tech. mktg. Beltran Assocs., Inc., NYC, 1976-78; leader mist eliminator profit ctr. Koch -Glitsch, Inc., Wichita, Kans., 1978-99; ret. Bd. dirs. Divmesh of Canada, Ltd., Calgary, Alta., 1984-85. Contbr. articles to profl. jours.; patentee in field. Served to capt. USAF, 1956-60. Mem. Am. Inst. Chem. Engrs. (session chmn. nat. meeting 1980), Am. Meteorol. Soc., Soc. Automotive Engrs. Australasia. Avocations: 19th century history, classical music, travel. Home: 7800 Killarney Pl Wichita KS 67206-1633

HANSEN, ROBYN L., lawyer; b. Terre Haute, Ind., Dec. 2, 1949; d. Robert Louis and Shirley (Nagel) Wieman; m. Gary Hansen, Aug. 21, 1971 (div. 1985); children: athan Ross Hansen, Brian Michael Hansen; m. John Marley Clarey, Jan. 1, 1986; 1 child, John Zender Clarey. BA, Gustavus Adolphus, 1971; JD cum laude, William Mitchell Coll. Law, 1977. Bar: Minn. 1977, U.S. Dist. Ct. Minn. 1977. Atty. Briggs and Morgan P.A., St. Paul, 1977-93, Leonard, Street and Deinard, Mpls., 1993—. Trustee Actors Theatre, St. Paul, 1980—88, Minn. Mus. Am. Art, 1994—97; active Minn. Inst. Pub. Fin., 1987—93, bd. dirs., 1993—95, pres., 1995; bd. dirs. St. Paul Downtown Coun., 1985—93, St. Paul Area Conv. and Vis. Bur., 1995—2005, chair, 1999—2001; trustee Met. State U. Found., 1993—2005, chair, 2000—02; bd. dirs. Capital City Partnership, 1997—, St. Paul Found., 2005—07, Pk. Sq. Theatre, 2003—, chair, 2007—; mem. River Ctr. Conv. and Visitors Authority, 2005—06, The Amherst H. Wilder Found., 2006—, Minn. State Fair Found., 2005—, vice chair, 2007—. Mem. ABA, Minn. Bar Assn., Ramsey County Bar Assn., Nat. Assn. Bond Lawyers, St. Paul Area C. of C. (bd. dirs., exec. com. 1997-99). Office: Leonard Street and Deinard 150 S Fifth St Minneapolis MN 55402 Office Phone: 612-335-1987. Business E-Mail: robyn.hansen@leonard.com.

HANSEN, STEVEN D., state legislator; b. Sioux City, Iowa, Feb. 5, 1955; m. Glenda DenHerder. Student, Briar Cliff Coll.; BA, Morningside Coll., 1977; MA, U. S.D., 1988. Dir. Woodbury County Juvenile Detention Ctr., 1980-87; pvt. practice; mem. Iowa Senate from 1st dist., Des Moines, 1982—. Mem. Iowa Jaycees (past pres.), Sierra Club, Siouxland Ski Club. Democrat. Home: 3669 Lindenwood St Sioux City IA 51104-2255 E-mail: steven_hansen@legis.state.ia.us.

HANSEN, THOMAS J., engineering executive; BS in Mktg., No. Ill. U., DeKalb, 1971; MA in Bus. Adminstrn., Govs. State U., Univ. Park, Ill., 1978. Zone sales mgr. GE; various positions including regional sales mgr. and plant mgr. Singer Controls; sales and mktg. mgr. Shakeproof Indsl. Products businesses Ill. Tool Works (ITW), Glenview, 1980—83, gen. mgr. Shakeproof Indsl. Products divsn., 1983—86, v.p., gen. mgr. North Am. Indsl. Metal Fastener and Buckle divsns., 1986—90, pres. North Am. Indsl. and Automotive Fastener businesses, 1990—93, pres. Metal Fasteners and Components businesses, 1993, exec. v.p., 1998—2006, vice chmn., 2006—. Mem. adv. bd. Century Moving and Storage. Active United Way, Jr. Achievement. Mem. GM Supplier Coun., Indsl. Fastener Inst., Elgin Country Club. Office: Ill Tool Works 3600 W Lake Ave Glenview IL 60026-1215 Office Phone: 847-724-7500. Office Fax: 847-657-4572.

HANSEN, THOMAS NANASTAD, hospital administrator, pediatrician; b. Neenah, Wis., Oct. 11, 1947; m. Cheryl Bailey, June 9, 1979; children: Elaine Christ, William Thomas. BS in Physics summa cum laude, Tex. Christian U., 1970; MD, Baylor Coll. Medicine, 1973. Diplomate Am. Bd. Pediatrics. Intern in pediatrics Baylor Coll. Medicine, Houston, 1973-74, resident in pediatrics, 1974-76, postdoctoral fellow in neonatal perinatal medicine, 1976-78; postdoctoral fellow in pediatric pulmonary disease U. Calif., San Francisco, 1978-81; asst. prof. pediatrics Baylor Coll. Medicine, 1978-84, assoc. prof. pediatrics, 1984-89; prof. pediatrics and cell biology Tex. Children's Hosp. Found., Houston, 1989-95; head sect. on neonatology Baylor Coll. of Medicine, 1987-95, vice-chmn. rsch. dept. pediatrics, 1994-95, dir. child health rsch. ctr., 1994-95, co-dir. ctr. for tng. in molecular medicine, 1994-95; chmn. pediat., CEO Children's Hosp., Columbus, Ohio, 1995—2005; pres., CEO Children's Hosp. and Regional Med. Ctr., Seattle, 2005—. Mem. exam com. Am. Bd. Pediatrics, 1982—, sub-bd. neonatal-perinatal medicine, 1992—, chmn. credentials com., 1993—, chmn.-elect sub-bd. neonatal perinatal medicine, 1994. Contbr. numerous articles to profl. jours. Trustee Tex. Women's Hosp., 1988-91. Mem. Western Soc. for Pediatric Rsch., So. Soc. for Pediaatric Rsch., Soc. for Pediatric Rsch. (sec.-treas. 1986-91, chmn. student rsch. com. 1990—, trustee internat. chpt. 1992—), Am. Physiol. Soc., Am. Pediatric Soc., Am. Fedn. for Clin. Rsch., Am. Thoracic Soc., Am. Acad. of Pediatrics, N.Y. Acad. of Scis., Am. Soc. for Cell Biology, Assn. of Med. Sch. Pediatric Dept. Chmn., Sigma Xi. Office: Children's Hosp and Regional Med Ctr PO Box 5371 Seattle WA 98105-0371

HANSEN, W. LEE, economics professor; b. Racine, Wis., Nov. 8, 1928; s. William R. and Gertrude M. H.; m. Sally Ann Porch, Dec. 26, 1955; children—Ellen J., Martha L. BA, U. Wis., Madison, 1950, MA, 1955; PhD, Johns Hopkins U., 1958. Asst. prof. econs. UCLA, from 1958, assoc. prof., to 1965; assoc. prof. econs. U. Wis., Madison, from 1965, prof., prof. emeritus, 1996—. Sr. staff economist Pres.'s Coun. Econ. Advisers, Washington, 1964-65; trustee Nat. Coun. on Econ. Edn., N.Y.C., 1976-2000, sec., 1996-2000; mem. bd. founders NCEE, 2000—. Author: Benefits, Costs, and Finance of Public Higher Education, 1969, Education, Income, and Human Capital, 1970, The Labor Market for Scientists and Engineers, 1973, Perspectives on Economic Education, 1977, A Framework for Teaching Basic Economic Concepts, 1984, The End of Mandatory Retirement, 1989, Unemployment Insurance: The Second Half-Century, 1990, Academic Freedom on Trial: 100 Years of Sifting and Winnowing at the University of Wisconsin, 1998, Discussing Economics, 2005; contbr. articles to profl. jours. Sgt. US Army, 1951—53. Recipient Amoco Disting. Tchg. award U. Wis., 1982, Hilldale award, 1988, Disting. Svc. award Nat. Coun. on Econs. Edn., 1991, Marvin Bower award, 1994,, Henry H. Villard Rsch. award, 2000, Tchr. Acad. U. Wis., 1994, Outstanding Postsecondary Educator award nat. Fedn. Ind. Bus. Found., 1992, Leavey award for excellence in pvt. enterprise edn. Freedoms Found., 1996; Guggenheim fellow, 1969-70; Fulbright sr. scholar, Australia, 1988. Mem. AAUP (chair com. on the econ. status of the profession 1979-86, mem. nat. coun. 1980-82, retirement com. 1985-95), Am. Econ. Assn. (chmn. com. on econ. edn. 1983-88, exec. sec. commn. grad. edn. econs. 1988-91), Indsl. Rels. Rsch. Assn., Midwest Econs. Assn. (pres. 1987), Phi Beta Kappa. Unitarian Universalist. Office: U Wis Dept Econs 1180 Observatory Dr Madison WI 53706-1320 Business E-Mail: wlhansen@wisc.edu.

HANSER, FREDERICK OTTO, professional sports team executive; b. St. Louis, Apr. 13, 1942; s. S. Albert Hanser and Olive D. Mullen; m. Katharine Thompson; children: Tim, Kara. BA in Econs., Yale U., 1963; JD, Washington U., St. Louis, 1966. Assoc. Fordyce & Mayne, 1966-78; ptnr. Armstrong & Teasdale, LLP, St. Louis, 1978-96; pres., dir. Gateway Group Inc., 1996—; chmn. St. Louis Cardinals, 1996—. Mem. exec. com., bd. dirs. Miss. Valley Bancshares Inc. Mem. exec. bd. Greater St. Louis area coun. Boy Scouts Am.; bd. dirs. St. Louis Children's Hosp., mem. devel. bd.; bd. dirs. St. Louis Country Day Sch., Easter Seal Soc. Office: St Louis Cardinals 250 Stadium Plz Saint Louis MO 63102-1722

HANSMAN, ROBERT G., artist, educator; BFA, U. Kans., 1970. Asst. prof. Washington U., St. Louis. Instr. dept. parts and recreation Project Artspark, 1993, Arts Connection/City Faces, 1994—; instr. juvenile detention program Children's Art Ctr., 1995; established Jermaine Lamond Roberts Meml. Art Studio, clinton-Peabody Pub. Housing, 1997. One-man shows include St. Louis C.C. at Forest Park, 1988, MJF Arts Studio Gallery, 1990, University City Pub. Libr., 1992, 1995, Bonsack Gallery, 1995. Mem. pub. housing revitalization focus group Darst-Webbe, 1995. Named Reader's Poll Best Local Artist, The Riverfront Times, 1995; recipient First Pl. award/Best of Show, St. Louis Artists Guild, 1988, 1992, Componere Gallery, 1990, Not Just An Art Dirs. Club, 1990, The Gallery Connection, 1991, Art St. Louis Gallery, 1991, World of Difference award City Faces, 1996, Mo. Arts award, Mo. Arts Coun., 1997, Excellence in Tchg. award, Emerson Electric, 2000, Disting. Faculty award, 2001, honoree, Colin Powell's Am. Promise, 1999, Mo. Ho. of Reps., 1997; grantee, Bi-State Arts in Transit Project, 1995, 1996, 1999. Office: Washington U Sch Arch Campus Box 1079 One Brookings Dr Saint Louis MO 63130 E-mail: hansman@architecture.wustl.edu.

HANSON, ARTHUR STUART, physician, consultant; b. Mpls., Mar. 10, 1937; s. Arthur Emanuel and Frances Elenor (Larson) H.; m. Gail Joan Taylor, June 16, 1963; children: Marta Eileen, Peter Arthur. BA, Dartmouth Coll., 1959; MD, U. Minn., 1963. Diplomate Am. Bd. Internal Medicine, Am. Bd. Pulmonary Disease. Intern Hennipen County Med. Ctr., 1963-64; resident in internal medicine U. Minn., 1964-65, 68-70, fellow pulmonary disease, 1970-71; cons. in pulmonary and critical care medicine Park Nicollet Clinic, Mpls., 1971—, med. dir., 1975-82, v.p. legis. and cmty. affairs, 1982-86; dir. med. edn. Park Nicollet Med. Found., Mpls., 1982-86; pres., CEO Park Nicollet Inst., Mpls., 1986—2002. Bd. dirs. Minn. Health Data Inst., 1993-03. Pres., bd. chair Minn. Smoke Free Coalition, 1985-88, 96-98, 2005-07; vice chair Minn. Partnership for Action Against Tobacco, 1998-2003; chmn. bd. Smoke Free Generation Minn., 1984-90. Recipient Cmty. Leadership award, Am. Lung Assn. Hennepin County, 1987, Harvey H. Rogers Meml. award, Minn. Pub. Health Assn., 1988, award for excellence in health promotion, Minn. Health Commr., 1989, Physician of Excellence award, Park Nicollet Health Svcs., 2000, Lynn Smith 25-Yr. award, Am. Cancer Soc., 2001, Harold S. Diehl Lifetime Achievement award, U. Minn. Med. Found., 2007, Young Physician of Excellence award, Park Nicollet Methodist Hosp, 2000. Fellow ACP, AMA (del., chmn.), Am. Coll. Chest Physicians; mem. Minn. Med. Assn. (pres. 1992-93, Stop the Violence award 1994, Disting. Svc. award 1998), Minn. Healthcare Coalition on Violence, Hennepin Med. Soc. (pres. 1990-91, Charles Bolles Bolles-Rogers award 1998, Shotwell award 2007). Unitarian Universalist. Avocations: birding, gardening, physical fitness, reading, travel. Office: Park Nicollet Clinic Ste 300 6490 Excelsior Blvd Minneapolis MN 55426 Home Phone: 612-676-1591; Office Phone: 952-993-3242. Business E-Mail: hansoa@parknicollet.com.

HANSON, DALE S., retired bank executive; b. Milw., Nov. 11, 1938; s. Yngve Holger and Evelyn (Johnson) H.; m. Joan Benton, July 15, 1961; children—Thomas S., Tim B. BA in Econs., Carlton Coll., 1960; postgrad. Exec. Program, Credit and Fin. Mgmt. Stanford U., 1966-67. Asst. cashier First Bank, St. Paul, 1964-66, asst. v.p., 1966-68, v.p., 1968-82, sr. v.p., 1982-83, exec. v.p., 1983-84, pres., 1984-88; pres., mng. ptnr. FBS Mcht. Banking Group, 1987-90; mng. ptnr. Matrix Leasing Internat., 1989-90; exec. v.p. 1st Bank System, Mpls., 1984-91; v.p., treas., chief fin. officer C.H. Robinson Co., Mpls., 1991-98, also bd. dirs.; ret., 1998. Bd. dirs. W.A. Lang Co., Edwards Mfg. Co. Mem. Corp. Health One, Inc.; bd. dirs. St. Paul Chamber Orch., Twin City Pub. TV, St. Paul Riverfront Devel. Corp., 1985-91. 1st lt. USNG, 1961-67. Mem. Robert Morris Assocs. (pres. 1982-83), Fin. Execs. Inst. (bd. dirs. Twin Cities chpt.), Somerset Golf Club, Mpls. Club, Minn. Club (St. Paul). Republican. Presbyterian. Avocations: skiing, sailing, golf, photography. Office: care C H Robinson Co 8100 Mitchell Rd Ste 200 Eden Prairie MN 55344-2178

HANSON, DAVID JAMES, lawyer; b. Neenah, Wis., July 20, 1943; s. Vernon James and Dorothy O. Hanson; m. Diana G. Severson, Aug. 25, 1965 (div. Sept. 1982); children: Matthew Vernon, Maja Kirsten, Brian Edward; m. Linda Hughes Bochert, May 28, 1983; children: Scott Charles, Sarah Katherine. BS, U. Wis., 1965, JD, 1968. Bar: Wis. 1968, U.S. Dist. Ct. (we. dist.) Wis. 1968, U.S. Dist. Ct. (ea. dist.) Wis. 1969, U.S. Ct. Appeals (7th cir.) 1970, U.S. Supreme Ct. 1971. Asst. atty. gen. State of Wis. Dept. of Justice, Madison, 1968-71, dep. atty. gen., 1976-81; asst. chancellor, chief legal counsel U. Wis., Madison, 1971-76; ptnr. Michael, Best & Friedrich LLP, Madison, 1981—. Lectr. Law Sch., U. Wis., Madison, 1972-75; bd. dirs., chair govt. law sect. State Bar Wis., Madison, 1979-88. Contbr. articles to profl. jours. Bd. dirs. Sand County Found., Madison, 1988—, Wis. Ctr. for Academically Talented Youth, Madison, 1991-94, Access Cmty. Health Ctrs., 2004—, Wis. Law Alumni Assn., 2000—, chair 2004—, trustee Edgewood Coll., Madison, 1997—, chair 2003-05, Great Lakes Higher Edn. Corp. and affiliates, 2000—. Mem. ABA, Madison Club, Blackhawk Country Club. Democrat. Unitarian Universalist. Avocations: canoeing, skiing, golf, bicycling, hunting. Office: Michael Best & Friedrich PO Box 1806 Madison WI 53701-1806 Office Phone: 603-257-3501. E-mail: djhanson@michaelbest.com.

HANSON, DELL, state representative, farmer; b. Benton County, Iowa, Mar. 17, 1935; Grad., Vinton, Iowa. Farmer; operator implement bus.; state rep. dist. 39 Iowa Ho. of Reps., 2003—; mem. econ. growth com.; mem. environ. protection com.; mem. local govt. com.; vice chair justice sys. Benton County supr., Iowa. Mem. Am. Heart Assn., Benton County Habitat for Humanity, Benton County Devel. Bd.; mem. property com. Bethlehem Luth. Ch.; fundraiser Luth. Lakeside Camp. Republican.

HANSON, FLOYD BLISS, mathematician; b. Bklyn., Mar. 9, 1939; s. Charles Keld and Violet Ellen (Bliss) Hanson; m. Ethel Louisa Hutchins, July 27, 1962; 1 child, Lisa Kirsten. BS, Antioch Coll., Yellow Springs, Ohio, 1962; MS, Brown U., Providence, 1964, PhD, 1968. Space technician Convair Astronautics, San Diego, 1961; applied mathematician Arthur D. Little, Inc., Cambridge, Mass., 1961; physicist Wright-Patterson AFB, Dayton, Ohio, 1962; assoc. rsch. scientist Courant Inst., NYC, 1967-68; asst. prof. U. Ill., Chgo., 1969-75, assoc. prof., 1975-83, prof., 1983—2005, assoc. dir. Lab. for Advanced Computing, 1990—2005, assoc. dir. Lab. for Control & Info., 1993—2005, prof. emeritus, 2005—. Faculty rsch. participant Argonne Nat. Lab., Ill., 1985-87, faculty rsch. leave, 1987-88, rsch. assoc., 1988—; vis. prof. divsn. applied math. Brown U., 1994; vis. faculty Sch. Civil and Environ. Engring., Cornell U., 1995; vis. prof. stochastics Indian Inst. Sci, Bangalore, India, 2007. Assoc. editor-in-chief Applied and Computational Control Signals and Circuits, 1996-2005; author Applied Stochastic Processes and Control for Jump-Diffusions, 2007; contbr. articles in field to profl. jours., chpts. to books. Recipient Tchr. Recognition award, UIC CETL, 1999, Excellence in Tchg. award, Premier UIC, 2001—02; grantee, NSF, 1970—83, 1988—2006, 1973, Nat. Ctr. Supercomputer Applications, 1986—2004, Los. Alamos Nat. Lab., 1990—97, Cornell Theory Ctr., 1993—96, Pitts. Supercomputer Ctr., 1993—98, 2003—04, San Diego Supercomputer Ctr., 1998—2002. Mem. IEEE (tech. com. on control edn. appt. 2002-), Soc. Indsl. and Applied Math., Computer Soc. of IEEE, Control Sys. Soc. of IEEE, Resource Modeling Assn. Home: 5435 S East View Park Chicago IL 60615-5915 Office: U Ill Dept Math Stats and Computer Sci M/C 249 851 S Morgan St Rm 322 Chicago IL 60607-7042 Business E-Mail: hanson@uic.edu.

HANSON, GAIL G., physicist, researcher; b. Dayton, Ohio, Feb. 22, 1947; married 1968 (div. 1998); 2 children. BS in Physics, MIT, 1968, PhD in Exptl. High Energy Physics, 1973. Rsch. assoc. Stanford Linear Accelerator Ctr., 1973-76, physicist, continuing staff mem., 1976-84, physicist, permanent staff mem., 1984-89; prof. physics Ind. U., Bloomington, 1989-97, disting. prof., 1997—. Mem. subpanel High Energy Physics Adv. Panel, 1989-90; mem. physics adv. com. Univs. Rsch. Assn. Fermilab, 1990-94, mem. bd. overseers, 1991-97, dir. rev. panel, 1993-94, mem. vis. com., 1995-97; mem. com. examiners GRE Physics Test, 1992-2000; mem. collaboration exec. com. U.S. ATLAS, 1994-95. Guggenheim fellow, 1995. Fellow AAAS (mem. electorate nominating com. physics sect. 1996—), Am. Phys. Soc. (W.K.H. Panofsky prize 1996). Office: Ind U Dept Physics Bloomington IN 47405 E-mail: gail@indiana.edu.

HANSON, HEIDI ELIZABETH, lawyer; b. Portsmouth, Ohio, Nov. 13, 1954; BS, U. Ill., 1975, JD, 1978. Bar: Ill. 1978, U.S. Dist. Ct. (no. dist.) Ill., U.S. Ct. Appeals (7th cir.). Atty. water, air and land pollution divs. Ill. EPA, Springfield, Ill., 1978-85, atty. water pollution div. Maywood, Ill., 1985-86; assoc. Ross & Hardies, Chgo., 1987-89, ptnr., 1990-94; founder H.E. Hanson Law Offices, Western Springs, Ill., 1994—. Named hon. Ky. Col., 2000. Mem.: Indsl. Water, Waste and Sewer Group, Air and Waste Mgmt. Assn., Chgo. Bar Assn., Chicagoland C. of C. Avocation: gardening. Office: 4721 Franklin Ave Ste 1500 Western Springs IL 60558-1720 Personal E-mail: heh70@hotmail.com.

HANSON, JOHN NILS, industrial high technology manufacturing company executive; b. Berwyn, Ill., Jan. 22, 1942; s. Robert and Stephanie Ann (Kazluskas) H.; m. Stephanie Morgan, June 5, 1965; children: Laurel, Mark Nils. BS in Chem. Engring., MIT, 1964, MS in Nuclear Engring., 1965; PhD in Nuclear Sci. and Engring., Carnegie-Mellon U., 1969. Sr. scientist Bettis Atomic Power Labs., Westinghouse Electric Corp., West Mifflin, Pa., 1965-70; fellow White House, Washington, 1970-71; exec. asst. to U.S. Sec. Labor, Washington, 1971; asst. to gen. mgr. advanced test core Bettis Atomic Power Labs., Westinghouse Electric Corp., West Mifflin, Pa., 1971-73; asst. to pres. Gould Inc., Rolling Meadows, Ill., 1973-74, pres., gen. mgr. electric motor div. St. Louis, 1974-78, group v.p. elec. products Rolling Meadows, 1978-80; pres. Solar Turbines Internat., San Diego, 1980; v.p. Internat. Harvester, 1980-81, Caterpillar Tractor Co., Peoria, Ill., 1981—90; pres., COO Joy Technologies, 1990—94; pres. Joy Mining Machinery unit Harnischfeger Industries (renamed Joy Global Inc.), 1994—95; exec. v.p., COO Joy Global Inc., Milw., 1995—96, pres., COO, 1996—98, pres., CEO, 1998—2006, chmn., 2000—. Contbr. articles on indsl. tech. to profl. jours. Vice chmn. Friends of Scouting Fundraising-Boy Scouts Am., San Diego council, 1983—; mem. Judge Wallace Longrange planning com., 1983—, vice chmn. fin. adv. com., 1983—; mem. cabinet fund drive United Way, San Diego County Chpt., 1982—; mem. exec. fin. com. Pete Wilson for Senate campaign, San Diego, 1982; vice chmn. Children's Hosp. Research Ctr., 1983—; mem. vis. com. sponsored research MIT, Cambridge, 1978—; mem. Pvt. Industry Council, 1983. Mem. White House Fellows Assn., Greater San Diego C. of C. (bd. dirs.) Office: Joy Global PO Box 554 Milwaukee WI 53201

HANSON, LYLE, state legislator; m. Betty; two children. BS, U. N.D.; MS, Moorehead State U. N.D. State rep. Dist. 48, 1979—; substitute tchr. Mem. edn. and natural resources coms.; Dem. caucus leader. Recipient Legis. Conservationist of Yr. award N.D. Wildlife Fedn., 1981, Jamestown United Sportsman of Yr., 1994; named to Ofcls. Hall of Fame. Mem. United Sportsman, Elks, Eagles, Safari Club Internat., N.D. Wildlife Fedn., Found. for N.Am. Wild Sheep. Home: 337 15th Ave NE Jamestown ND 58401-3830

HANSON, MARK S., bishop; b. Mpls., Dec. 2, 1946; m. Ione Agrimson; children: Aaron Hanson, Alyssa, Rachel, Ezra, Isaac, Elizabeth. Grad., Minnehaha Acad., 1964; B Sociology, Augsburg Coll., 1968; Rockefeller fellow, Union Theol. Sem., 1969, MDiv, 1972; student, Luther Sem., 1973—74; Merrill fellow, Harvard U., 1979; D (hon.), Augsburg Coll., Capital U., Lenoir-Rhyne Coll., Wartburg Theological Sem., Acad. Ecumenical Indian Theology and Church Admin. Ordained 1974. Pastor Prince of Glory Luth. Ch., Mpls., 1973—79, Edina Cmty. Luth. Ch., Edina, Minn., 1979—88, U. Luth. Ch., Hope, Mpls., 1988—95; bishop St. Paul Area Synod Evang. Luth. Ch. Am., 1995; dir. social work Minn. St. Paul Children's Hosp., 1995—2001; presiding bishop Evang. Luth. Ch. Am., 2001—. Pres. Minn. Coun. Chs., 1998—2000, Lutheran World Federation, 2003—. Author: Faithful Yet Changing: The Church in Challenging Times, Faithful and Courageous, Christians in Unsettling Times. Office: Evang Luth Ch Am Office of Bishop 8765 W Higgins Rd Chicago IL 60631 E-mail: bishop@elca.org.

HANSON, PAULA E., state legislator; b. Jan. 21, 1944; m. Jim Hanson; 3 children. Mem. Minn. State Senate, 1992—, mem. various coms. Democrat. Home: 2428 Bunker Lake Blvd NE Andover MN 55304-7129

HANSON, RICHARD WINFIELD, biochemist, educator; b. Oxford, NY, Nov. 10, 1935; s. John Vincent and Agatha Helen H.; m. Gloria M. Lucchesi, June 10, 1961; children: Paul, Benjamin, Daria. BS, Northeastern U., 1959; MS, Brown U., 1961, PhD, 1963. Asst. prof to prof. biochemistry Temple U. Sch. Medicine, Phila., 1965-78; prof., chmn. dept. biochemistry Case Western U. Sch. Medicine, Cleve., 1978-99, Leonard and Jean Sheggs prof. biochemistry, 1993—. Cons. USPHS, FDA. Assoc. editor Jour. Biol. Chemistry; contbr. articles to profl. jours. Served to capt. Med. Service Corps, U.S. Army, 1963-65. Recipient Mead-Johnson award, 1971, Kaiser Permenante award, 1982, Maurice Saltzman award, 1991, Osborne Mendel award, 1995, William C. Rose award, 1999, Havorka prize, 2001; named 250th Anniversary Disting. Tchg. Prof., Princeton U., 2001-02; named to Cleve. Med. Hall of Fame, 2002. Mem. AAAS, Inst. Medicine NAS, Am. Soc. Biochemistry and Molecular Biology (pres. 1999-2000). Office: Case Western Res U Dept Biochemistry Rm W414 10900 Euclid Ave Cleveland OH 44106

HANSON, ROBERT ARTHUR, retired agricultural equipment executive; b. Moline, Ill., Dec. 13, 1924; s. Nels A. and Margaret I. (Chapman) H.; m. Patricia Ann Klinger, June 25, 1955. BA, Augustana Coll., Rock Island, Ill., 1948. Various positions Deere & Co., Moline, 1950-62, gen. mgr. Mexico, 1962-64, Spain, 1964-66, dir. mktg. overseas, 1966-70, v.p. overseas ops., 1972, sr. v.p. overseas div., 1973, dir., 1974—, exec. v.p., 1975-78, pres., 1978-85, chief oper. officer, 1979-82, chief exec. officer, 1982-89, chmn., 1982-90. With USMCR, 1943-46. Mem. Bus. Coun. Home: 2200 29th Avenue Court Dr Moline IL 61265-6926 Office: Deere & Co One John Deere Pl Moline IL 61265-8098

HANSON, ROBERT DUANE, engineering educator; b. Albert Lea, Minn., July 27, 1935; s. James Edwin and Gertie Hanson; m. Kaye Lynn Nielsen, June 7, 1959; children: Craig Robert, Eric Neil. Student, St. Olaf Coll., Northfield, Minn., 1953-54; BSE, U. Minn., 1957, MS in Civil Engring., 1958; PhD, Calif. Inst. Tech., Pasadena, 1965. Registered profl. engr., Mich., N.D. Design engr. Pitts.-Des Moines Stel, Des Moines, 1958-59; asst. prof. U. N.D., Grand Forks, 1959-61; rsch. engr. Calif. Inst. Tech., 1965; asst. prof. U. Calif.-Davis, 1965-66; from asst. prof. to prof. civil engring. U. Mich., Ann Arbor, 1966—2001, prof. emeritus, 2001—, chmn. dept. civil engring., 1976-84; sr. earthquake engr. Fed. Emergency Mgmt. Agy., 1994-2000. Vis. prof., dir. Earthquake Engring. Rsch.

Ctr., U. Calif., Berkeley, 1991; dir. BCS divsn. NSF, Washington, 1989-90; cons. NSF, 1979-88, 92-94; cons. Bechtel Corp., Ann Arbor, 1976-87, Sensei Engrs., Ann Arbor, 1977-90, Bldg. Seismic Safety Coun., 1988-94, Fed. Emergency Mgmt. Agy., 1992-94, 2000-05, applied tech. coun., 2005—. Contbr. articles to profl. jours. Recipient Reese Rsch. award ASCE, 1980; recipient Disting. Svc. award U. Mich., 1969; tchg. award Chi Epsilon, 1985, Attwood Engr. Excellence award, 1986. Fellow ASCE (life; com. chmn. 1975-94); mem. NAE, Earthquake Engring. Rsch. Inst. (hon., v.p. 1977-79, bd. dirs. 1976-79, 88-92, pres.-elect 1988, pres. 1989-91, past pres. 1991-92). Lutheran. Home: 2926 Saklan Indian Dr Walnut Creek CA 94595-3911 Home Phone: 925-946-9463. Personal E-mail: rdhanson2@aol.com.

HANSON, RONALD WILLIAM, lawyer; b. Aug. 3, 1950; s. Orlin Eugene and Irene Agnes Hanson; m. Sandra Kay Cook, Aug. 21, 1971; children: Alec Evan, Corinn Michele. BA summa cum laude, St. Olaf Coll., 1972; JD cum laude, U. Chgo., 1975. Bar: Ill. 1975, U.S. Dist. Ct. (no. dist.) Ill. 1975, U.S. Ct. Appeals (7th cir.) 1978, U.S. Ct. Appeals (10th cir.) 1989. Assoc. Sidley & Austin, Chgo., 1975-83, ptnr., 1983-88, Latham & Watkins, Chgo., 1988—, chmn. audit com., 1998—2005. Ofcl. advisor to Nat. Conf. of Commrs. on Uniform State Laws; lectr. Ill. Inst. Continuing Legal Edn., Springfield, Am. Bankruptcy Inst., Washington, Banking Law Inst., Practicing Law Inst., Am. Law Inst. Contbr. articles to profl. jours. Mem. ABA, Ill. Bar Assn., Chgo. Bar Assn., Order of Coif, Met. Club, Phi Beta Kappa. Republican. Lutheran. Home: 664 W 58th St Hinsdale IL 60521-5104 Office: Latham & Watkins Sears Tower Ste 5800 Chicago IL 60606-6306 Office Phone: 312-876-7700. Business E-Mail: ronald.hanson@lw.com.

HANSON, SAMUEL LEE, state supreme court justice; b. Mankato, Minn., Aug. 26, 1939; s. Lester Kenneth and Margaret Dorothy (Brockmeyer) H.; m. Beret Elizabeth Brown, July 28, 1962 (div. Apr. 1976); children: Greta E., Chrystina E., Benjamin D.; m. Mirja Pirkko Karikosky, Sept. 23, 1977; children: Leif O., Luke A., Jai . BA, St. Olaf Coll., 1961; LLB, William Mitchell Coll. Law, 1965. Bar: Minn. 1965, U.S. Dist. Ct. Minn. 1966, U.S. Ct. Appeals (8th cir.) 1966, U.S. Supreme Ct. 1971. Law clk. to hon. Douglas K. Amdahl Hennepin County Dist. Ct., Mpls., 1965; law clk. to hon. Robert J. Sheran Minn. Supreme Ct., St. Paul, 1966; assoc., shareholder Briggs and Morgan, St. Paul, Mpls., 1966—2000, pres., 1988-93; appt. Ct. of Appeals, Minn., 2000—02; justice Minn. Supreme Ct., Minn., 2002—. Mem. adv. com. Minn. Supreme Ct., St. Paul, 1984-86; adj. prof. William Mitchell Coll. Law, St. Paul, 1966-71; co-chair Minn. Legal Services State Planning Commn., 2002-; chair supreme ct. Gender Fairness Implementation Com., 2002-; liaison supreme ct. advisory com. gen. rules of practice, 2002-, supreme ct. Bd. of Legal Certification, 2002-; liaison supreme ct. adv. com. on rules of civil procedure, 2005-. Contbr. articles to profl. jours. Bd. dirs. Rural Ventures Inc., Mpls., 1981-87, Rural Tech. Partnership, St. Paul, 1987—, Global Vols., St. Paul, 1984—. Fellow Am. Coll. Trial Lawyers (chair Minn. chpt. 1991), Am. Bd. Trial Advocates, Crossroads, Inc. Avocations: rural development, organizational development. Home: 5510 Edgewater Blvd Minneapolis MN 55417-2605 Office: Minn Supreme Ct 305 Minn Jud Ctr 25 Rev Martin Luther King Jr Blvd Saint Paul MN 55155 Office Phone: 651-297-7676. Business E-Mail: sam.hanson@courts.state.mn.us.

HANSON, TOM, state official; b. Mahnomen, Minn., Aug. 7, 1963; m. Kris Hanson; 1 child. BA in History, magna cum laude, Concordia Coll., 1985; JD, George Mason Univ., 1993. Bar: Minn. Dep. chief of staff, dir. legis., cabinet affairs Gov. Minn.; commr. fin. State of Minn., 2006—. Office: Dept Fin 400 Centennial Office Bldg 658 Cedar St Saint Paul MN 55155 Office Phone: 651-202-8000. Office Fax: 651-296-8685. Business E-Mail: tom.j.hanson@state.mn.us.

HANSSON, DAVID HEINEMEIER, application developer; b. Denmark, 1979; arrived in Chgo., 2005; B in Bus. Adminstrn. and Computer Sci., Copenhagen Bus. Sch. Freelance programmer 37Signals LLC, 2001, ptnr. Co-author: Agile Web Devel. with Rails, 2005. Named one of 50 Who Matter Now, CNNMoney.com Bus. 2.0, 2006, Top 40 Under 40, Crain's Chgo. Bus., 2006; recipient Open Source award, Best Hacker, Google and O'Reilly, 2005, Jolt award, 2006. Achievements include producing Ruby on Rails, an open-source tool that makes it easier to use the Ruby programming language. Office: 37Signals LLC 400 N May St #301 Chicago IL 60622 E-mail: david@loudthinking.com.

HANUS, JEROME GEORGE, archbishop; b. Brainard, N.E., May 26, 1940; Student, Conception Sem., Mo., St. Anselm U., Rome, Princeton Theol. Sem., Princeton U. Joined Order of St. Benedict, 1961, ordained priest, 1966; abbot Conception Benedictine Abbey, 1977—87; pres. Swiss Am. Benedictine Congregation, 1984—87; ordained bishop, 1987; bishop Diocese of St. Cloud, Minn., 1987—94; co-adjutor archbishop Archdiocese of Dubuque, Iowa, 1994—95, archbishop Iowa, 1995—. Office: Archdiocese of Dubuque 1229 Mt Loretta Ave Dubuque IA 52004*

HANZLIK, PAUL F., lawyer; b. Oak Park, Ill., Aug. 23, 1942; BA cum laude, Wesleyan U., Middletown, Conn., 1964; LLB, Columbia U., 1967. Bar: Ill. 1971, U.S. Dist. Ct. (no. dist.) Ill. 1971, U.S. Supreme Ct. 1978, U.S. Ct. Appeals (7th cir.) 1978. With Foley & Lardner LLP, Chgo., mem. mgmt. com., chmn. energy regulation practice group. Contbr. articles to profl. jours. 1st Lt. U.S. Army, 1968-71. Mem. ABA, Chgo. Bar Assn. Office: Foley & Lardner LLP 321 N Clark St Ste 2800 Chicago IL 60610-4764 Office Phone: 312-832-4901. Business E-Mail: phanzlik@foley.com.

HARDEN, OLETA ELIZABETH, literature educator, academic administrator; b. Jamestown, Ky., Nov. 22, 1935; d. Stanley Virgil and Myrtie Alice (Stearns) McWhorter; m. Dennis Clarence Harden, July 23, 1966. BA, Western Ky. U., 1956; MA in English, U. Ark., 1958, PhD, 1965. Teaching asst. U. Ark., Fayetteville, 1956-57, 58-59, 61-63; instr. S.W. Mo. State Coll., Springfield, 1957-58, Murray (Ky.) U., 1959-61; asst. prof. English Northeastern State Coll., Tahlequah, Okla., 1963-65; asst. prof. Wichita (Kans.) State U., 1965-66; asst. prof. English Wright State U., Dayton, Ohio, 1966-68, assoc. prof., 1968-72, prof., 1972-93, asst. chmn. English dept., 1967-70, asst. dean, 1971-73, assoc. dean, 1973-74, exec. dir. gen. univ. services, 1974-76, pres. of faculty, 1984-85, prof. emerita, 1993—, coord. Irish studies, 2006—07. Author: Maria Edgeworth's Art of Prose Fiction, 1971, Maria Edgeworth, 1984; editor: The Extension, 1999—. Grantee, Ford Found., 1971. Mem. MLA, AARP (impact alliance leader Ohio, 2001—), AAUP, Coll. English Assn., Women's Caucus for Modern Langs., Am. Conf. for Irish Studies (presenter 1989, 91, 94, 95), Wright State U. Retiree Assn. (pres. 1995-96), Elizabeth McWhorter Harden Forensics Alumni Assn. (founder, pres. We. Ky. U. chpt. 2004—). Office: Wright State U Dept English 7751 Colonel Glenn Hwy Dayton OH 45431-1674 Home: 2618 Big Woods Trl Dayton OH 45431-8704 Office Phone: 937-775-2777. Personal E-mail: oharden@aol.com.

HARDEN, VAN, radio personality; Radio host morning show Sta. WHO-AM, Des Moines. Office: WHO Radio 1801 Grand Ave Des Moines IA 50309

HARDENBURGER, JANICE, state legislator; m. William Hardenburger. Kans. state senator Dist. 21, 1993—; farm ptnr., 1996—. Home: 562 25th Rd Haddam KS 66944-9037

HARDER, ELAINE RENE, state legislator; b. Windom, Minn., Dec. 27, 1947; d. Russell Jacob and Eunice Rupp; m. Ronald Dale Harder, 1970; children: Graydon, Nicole. BS in Secondary Edn., Mankato State U., 1970. Tchr. secondary sch.; owner sml. bus.; sales rep.; rep. Dist. 22B Minn. Ho. of Reps., 1995—. Chair ethics com. Minn. Ho. of Reps., mem. agriculture policy com., agriculture and rural devel. finance com., taxes com., property tax divsn. com.; life and heatlh ins. profl. 4-H youth devel. agt. U. Minn. Ext. Svc. AAUW, Minn. Assn. Life Underwriters, Minn. Home Econ. Assn., Jackson C. of C., Kiwanis, Phi Upsilon Omicron, Delta Clovia. Office: 487 State Office Bldg Saint Paul MN 55155 Home: 96 Becky Dr Jackson MN 56143-1155 E-mail: rep.Elaine.Harder@house.leg.state.mn.us.

HARDER, ROBERT CLARENCE, state official; b. Horton, Kans., June 4, 1929; s. Clarence L. and Olympia E. (Kubik) H.; m. Dorothy Lou Welty, July 31, 1953; children: Anne, James David. AB, Baker U., Baldwin, Kans., 1951; MTh, So. Meth. U., 1954; ThD in Social Ethics, Boston U., 1958; LHD (hon.), Baker U., 1983, Ottawa U., 1991. Ordained to ministry Meth. Ch., 1959; pastor East Topeka Meth. Ch., 1958-64; mem. Kans. Ho. of Reps., 1961-67; rsch. assoc. Menninger Found., Topeka, 1964-65; instr. Washburn U., Topeka, 1964, 68, 69; dir. Topeka Office of Econ. Opportunity, 1965-67; tech. asst. coordinator Office of Gov. of Kans., 1967-68; dir. community resources devel. League of Kans. Municipalities, 1968-69; dir. Kans. Dept. Social Welfare, Topeka, 1969-73, sec., 1973-87; projects adminstr. Topeka State Hosp., 1987-89. Adj. prof. pub. adminstrn. Kans. U., 1987-95, instr. Sch. Social Welfare, 1971-87; cons. Menninger Topeka, 1991-92; sec. Kans. Dept. Health and Environment, 1992-95. Contbr. articles to profl. jours. Recipient Disting. Svc. award East Topeka Civic Assn., 1963, Romana Hood award, 1965, Cert. of Recognition, State of Kans., 1979, 87, Spl. Commendation award Kans. Senate, 1987, Spl. Commendation, Kans. Ho. of Reps., 1987, Outstanding Alumnus award Perkins Sch. Theology, So. Meth. U., 1994, M. L. King Jr. Living the Dream Humanitarian award, 1997, Disting. Svc. award Kans. Children's Svc. League, 1998, Grant award for Exceptional Volunteerism, 1999, Advocacy award Disability Caucus, 2003, cert. appreciation Scott Sch., 2003, award of excellence Friends Edn. Award, 2004, Cmty. Leader award Topeka Pub. Schs., 2004, others; named Outstanding Pub. Ofcl. of the Yr., 1987. Mem. Am. Soc. Public Adminstrs. (Public Adminstr. of Yr. Kans. chpt. 1980), Am. Public Welfare Assn., Kans. Health Care Commn., Kans. Conf. Social Welfare (Outstanding Person of Yr. 1987). Democrat.

HARDGROVE, JAMES ALAN, lawyer; b. Chgo., Feb. 20, 1945; s. Albert John and Ruth (Noonen) H.; m. Kathleen M. Peterson, June 15, 1968; children: Jennifer Anne, Amy Kristine, Michael Sheridan. BA, U. Notre Dame, 1967; cert. English law, U. Coll. Law, 1969; JD, U. Notre Dame, 1970. Bar: Ill. 1970, U.S. Ct. Appeals (7th cir.) 1970, U.S. Dist. Ct. (no. dist.) Ill. 1970, U.S. Dist. Ct. (cen. dist.) Ill. 1978, U.S. Supreme Ct. 1980. Law clk. to presiding justice U.S. Ct. Appeals (7th cir.), Chgo., 1970-71; assoc. Sidley Austin Brown & Wood LLP, Chgo., 1971-76, ptnr., 1977—. Mem. ABA, Ill. Bar Assn., Chgo. Bar Assn., Legal Club. Home: 948 Ridge Ave Evanston IL 60202-1720 Office: Sidley Austin LLP One S Dearborn St Chicago IL 60603-2000 Home Phone: 847-475-5570; Office Phone: 312-853-7464. E-mail: jhardgrove@sidley.com.

HARDIN, CHRISTOPHER DEMAREST, medical educator; b. Syracuse, NY, July 31, 1961; BS in Biology, Cornell U., 1983; MS in Physiology, U. Rochester, 1986; PhD in Physiology and Biophysics, U. Cin., 1989. Sr. fellow Dept. Radiology U. Wash., Seattle, 1989-91, rsch. asst. prof. dept. radiology, 1991—93; asst. prof. physiology U. Mo., Columbia, 1993—99, assoc. prof. physiology, 1999—. Tutor, mentor, spkr. and cons. in field. Mem. internat. adv. bd. Physiological Research, 1997-; reviewer numerous jours.; guest reviewer 29 jours. in field; contbr. articles to profl. jours; contbr. chpts. to books. Albert J. Ryan fellow, 1986-89, Tng. Grant fellow U. Cin.,. 1985-86, Univ. Grad. fellow U. Rochester, 1983-85; recipient Jeffrey D. Doane Meml. award, 1987, Nat. Rsch. Svc. award, 1989-92, Dorsett L. Spurgeon Disting. Med. Rsch. award, 1999, other numerous awards and grants. Mem. AAAS, Internat. Soc. Heart Rsch. (N.Am. sect), Am. Physiol. Soc. (Harold Lamport award outstanding young investigator 1995), Biophysical Soc., Am. Physiological Soc. (elected fellow 2002, awards com. 2005-), Metabolomics Soc., Biophys. Soc., Am. Assn. Advancement Sci., Am. Heart Assn. (mem. sci. coun. basic sci. 1995-). Home: 4480 Roemer Rd Columbia MO 65202-7060 Office: Univ Mo Dept Physiology MA415 Med Sci Bldg Columbia MO 65212-0001 Business E-Mail: harding@missouri.edu.

HARDIN, LOWELL STEWART, retired economics professor; b. nr. Knightstown, Ind., Nov. 16, 1917; s. J. Fred and Mildred (Stewart) H.; m. Mary J. Cooley, Sept. 21, 1940; children: Thomas Stewart, Joyce Ann, Peter Lowell. BS, Purdue U., 1939, DAgr (hon.), 1990; PhD, Cornell U., 1943. Grad. asst., instr. Cornell U., 1939-43; instr., asst. and assoc. prof., prof. Purdue U., 1943-65, adj. prof. agrl. econs., 1965-66, prof., 1981-84, emeritus prof., asst. dir. internat. programs, 1984—, acting head dept. agrl. econs., 1954-57, head dept., 1957-65; also dir. Purdue Work Simplification Lab. Program adviser agr. Ford Found., 1965-66, program officer agr., 1966-81; former trustee Internat. Food Policy Rsch. Inst., Washington, Internat. Ctr. for Agrl. Rsch. in Dry Areas, Aleppo, Syria, Internat. Svc. for Nat. Agrl. Rsch., The Hague, The Netherlands, Winrock Internat. Inst. for Agrl. Devel., Little Rock, Ark. Author: (with L.M. Vaughan) Farm Work Simplification, 1949. Fellow AAAS, Am. Agrl. Econ. Assn. (pres. 1963-64); mem. Internat. Assn. Agrl. Economists, Sigma Xi, Alpha Gamma Rho, Phi Kappa Phi, Alpha Zeta, Sigma Delta Chi. Federated Church. Home: 2628 Calvin Ct W Lafayette IN 47906-1402 Office Phone: 765-494-8460.

HARDIN, TERRENCE ARMSTRONG, former radio broadcasting manager; b. Cin., Sept. 10, 1961; s. Oliver Wendell and Carol Lockwood H.; m. Dayna Lynn Glasson, Oct. 8, 1994. BFA in Radio, TV Comms., So. Meth. U., 1985. Cert. radio mktg. cons. Nat. sales mgr. Sta. WBAP and Sta. KSCS-FM, Dallas, 1986-88; gen. sales mgr. Sta. WMJI-FM, Cleve., 1988-90, Stas. KCBQ-AM-FM and Sta. KIHI-FM, Denver and San Diego, 1990-92, Sta. WPNT-FM, Chgo., 1992-95; v.p., gen. mgr. Stas. KYOT-FM, KZON-FM, KOY and KISO, Phoenix, 1995-99; gen. mgr. WLIT, 1999—. Guest speaker Ariz. State U., Tempe, 1995; advisor Glaser Capital, Cin., 1990—. Mem. awards com. Medallion of Merit Scholarship Found., Ariz. State U., Tempe, 1995-96; fund raiser Children's Cancer Ctr., Phoenix, 1995-96; exec. coun. Boys and Girls Club of Met. Phoenix. Mem. Am. Diabetes Assn. Avocations: travel, golf, mountain biking. Office: Wlit Fm Radio 233 N Michigan Ave Ste 2800 Chicago IL 60601-5704

HARDIS, STEPHEN ROGER, retired manufacturing company executive; b. NYC, July 13, 1935; s. Abraham I. and Ethel (Krinsky) H; m. Sondra Joyce Rolbin, Sept. 15, 1957; children: Julia Faye, Andrew Martin, Joanna Halley. BA with distinction, Cornell U., 1956; M.P.A. in Econs., Woodrow Wilson Sch. of Pub. and Internat. Affairs Princeton U., 1960. Asst. to controller Gen. Dynamics, 1960-61; fin. analyst Pfaudler Permutit Inc., 1961-64; staff asst. to controller, 1964; mgr. corp. long-range planning Ritter Pfaudler Corp., 1965-68, dir. corporate planning, 1968; treas. Sybron Corp., Rochester, NY, 1969—, v.p. fin., 1970-77, exec. v.p. fin. and planning, 1977-79; vice chmn., chief fin. and adminstrv. officer Eaton Corp., Cleve., 1979—, vice chmn., CEO, 1995, chmn., CEO, 1996-2000; ret., 2000; dir. Axcelis Techs., 2000—. Bd. dirs. Progressive, Nordson Corp., Lexmark Corp., Marsh & McLennan, Steeris, Am. Greetings. Past mem. Gov.'s Task Force on High Tech. Industry; past mem. bd. dirs. Rochester Area Hosp. Corp., Rochester Area Ednl. TV Sta., Genesee Hosp.; trustee Cleve. Clinic, Inc. With USNR, 1956-58. Mem. Phi Beta Kappa.

HARDY, DEBORAH LEWIS, dean, educator, dental hygienist; b. Nov. 11, 1963; Student, Christopher Newport Coll., 1982-84; BS in Dental Hygiene, Old Dominion U., 1989, cert. in gerontol. studies, 1991, MS in Dental Hygiene, 1991; postgrad., U. Tex., Dallas, 1993. Cert. ADA Joint Commn. on Nat. Dental Exam.; lic. S.E. Regional Va., Tex., Va.; cert. in cardiopulmonary resuscitation. Assoc. prof. Caruth Sch. Dental Hygiene Baylor Coll., Dallas, 1991-95; assoc. dean health occupations-dental N.E. Wis. Tech. Coll., Green Bay, 1995-97, assoc. dean health and cmty. svc., 1997—. Dental asst. Dr. William Griffin, Newport News, Va., 1989; dental asst., dental hygienist Dental Power, Inc., Newport News, 1988-90; dental hygienist Dr. John Caudill, Virginia Beach, 1990-91, Drs. Cash and Weisburg, Norfolk, Va., 1990-91; dental hygienist, educator Riverside Regional Convalescent Ctr., Newport News, 1991; part-time dental hygienist East Dallas Clinic, 1992-95, Nelson-Tebedo Dental Clinic, Dallas, 1995, Oneida (Wis.) Dental Clinic, 1997; cons., educator Skilled Nursing Facility, Collins Hosp., Baylor U. Med. Ctr., Dallas, 1992; lectr. and spkr. in field. Author: (book) Preventive Oral Health Services Provided by Nurses' Aides to Nursing Home Residents, 1991, (book chpt.) Oral Health and the Older Adult, 1995; editor: (newsletter) Oral Examiner, 1993-95; mem. editl. bd. Profl. Devel. Quar. PDQ, 1994-95; contbr. numerous articles and abstracts to profl. jours. Dental hygienist, educator Operation Smile Internat., Ghana Med. Mission, Accra, 1989; vol. Ea. Va. Med. Sch.-Ea. Shore, 1988, Girls Inc., Dallas, 1992; coord. Spirit of Christmas Program, Caruth Sch. Dental Hygiene, 1991, Sr. Student Oral Health Edn., St. Philip's Episcopal Sch. and Comty. Ctr., Dallas, 1993, Health Fair, Dallas Marriott Quorum Hotel, 1993. Recipient Acad. Dentistry for the Handicapped award, 1989, award for phenomenal achievement and leadership Women Dentists' Awards Luncheon, 1993; fellow Old Dominion U., 1990; also numerous rsch. grants in field. Mem. Am. Vocat. Assn., Nat. Dental Hygienists' Assn., Am. Dental Hygienists' Assn., Am. Assn. Dental Schs., Student Nat. Dental Assn. (faculty facilitator 1992-95), N.E. Wis. African Am. Assn. (membership chair 1997), Dallas Dental Hygienists' Soc. (Mem. of Month 1993, 95), Sigma Phi Alpha. Office: NE Wis Tech Coll PO Box 19042 2740 W Mason St Green Bay WI 54303-4966

HARDY, MICHAEL LYNN, lawyer; b. St. Louis, Aug. 28, 1947; s. William Frost and Ruth (Shea) H.; m. Martha Bond, Sept. 2, 1972; children: Brian M., Kevin S. AB, John Carroll U., 1969; JD, U. Mich., 1972. Bar: Ohio 1972. Assoc. Guren, Merritt, et al, Cleve., 1972-77, ptnr., 1977-84, Thompson Hine LLP and predecessor, Cleve., 1984—, ptnr.-in-charge Cleve. office, 2003—. Editor-in-chief Ohio Environ. Monthly, 1989-94, Ohio Environ. Law, 1992; bd. advisors Harvard Environ. Law Rev., 1976-78, The Environ. Counselor, 1988—. Trustee Nature Ctr. at Shaker Lakes, 2001—; bd. dirs. Nat. Club Assn., 2002—. Capt. US Army, 1969—74. Mem. ABA (nat. resources sect.), Ohio State Bar Assn. (sec. environ. law com. 1983-84, vice-chmn. 1984-86, chmn. 1987-91), Def. Rsch. Inst. (chmn. industrywide litig. com. 1989-91), Canterbury Golf Club. Home: 30649 Summit Ln Cleveland OH 44124-5836 Office: Thompson Hine LLP 3900 Key Ctr 127 Public Sq Cleveland OH 44114-1216 Office Phone: 216-566-5840. Business E-Mail: mike.hardy@thompsonhine.com.

HARDY, RICHARD ALLEN, mechanical engineer, engineering executive; b. Cleve., Sept. 16, 1928; s. Harry and Mae Hardy; m. Lois L. Fawcett, May 16, 1953 (dec. Dec. 1990); children: Pamela, Richard, James, Thomas. BSME, Case Inst. Tech., 1952. Founder, CEO Fluid Mechanics Inc., Cleve., 1957—. Cpl. U.S. Army, 1946-48. Recipient Weatherhead 100 award Cleve., 1989. Mem. Assn. of Diesel Specialists (various coms. 1960—). Roman Catholic. Achievements include helped design and build largest dynamic fuel-injection pump test stand in Western hemisphere. Avocations: racquetball, scuba. Home: 26875 Hilliard Blvd Cleveland OH 44145-3213

HARDY, SARALYN REECE, museum director; m. Randall Hardy; children: Stephen, Thomas, William. BA, U. Kans., 1976, MA in Am. studies, 1994. Project coord. Helen Foresman Spencer Mus. Art, U. Kans., Lawrence, 1977—79, dir., 2005—, Salina Art Ctr., Kans., 1986—2002; dir. mus. and visual arts Nat. Endowment for Arts, Washington, DC, 1999—2002. Recipient Women of Achievement award, Salina YWCA, Kansas Gov.'s Art Award, 1995. Mem.: Inst. Mus. and Libr. Svcs., Mus. Trustee Assn., Am. Assn. Mus., Am. Fedn. of Arts Mus. Dirs., Getty Leadership Inst. Office: Spencer Mus Art U Kans 1301 Mississippi St Lawrence KS 66045-7500 Office Phone: 785-864-4710. E-mail: srh@ku.edu.

HARDY, THOMAS CRESSON, insurance company executive; b. Hoisington, Kans., 1942; s. C.C. and Delia Hardy; children: Jay C., Glenn W. BA, U. Kans., 1963; MBA, Wharton Sch., U. Pa., 1965. CLU, CPCU, FLMI. With Exxon Corp., NYC, 1965-69; treas. Keene Corp., NYC, 1969-73; exec. v.p. fin. Fidelity Union Life Ins. Co. (co. acquired by Allianz of Am.), Dallas, 1973-79; v.p. Allianz of Am.; pres. Allianz Investment Corp., Dallas, 1979-82; pres., CEO Gt. Am. Res. Ins. Co., 1983-88; exec. v.p., COO Provident Life & Accident Ins. Co., Chattanooga, 1988-94; pres., CEO, bd. dirs. Loewen Life Ins. Group, 1997—2000, Mayflower Nat. Life Ins. Co., 1997—2000, Unity Fin. Life Ins. Co., 2001—. Chmn. bd. dirs. Security Instnl. Co., 1997-2000; pres., CEO, bd. dirs. Nat. Capitol Life, 1997-2000. Bd. dirs., pres. Chattanooga Symphony & Opera Assn., 1989-97, La. Philharm. Orch., 1999-2001; pres. Cin. Fire Mus., 2006; bd. dirs. exec. com. Chattanooga Allied Arts, 1992-97; mem. adv. bd. U. Kans. Bus. Sch., bd. dirs. 1994—; bd. visitors Berry Coll., 1992-99; trustee Huebner Found., 2005-, trustee, Cincinnati Symphony Orgns., 2007-. Mem. Fin. Execs. Inst. (chpt. pres., nat. bd. dirs.). Office: Unity Financial Life Ins Co 11311 Cornell Park Dr Ste 200 Cincinnati OH 45242 Office Phone: 513-247-0711. Business E-Mail: thardy@uflife.com.

HARDY, WILLIAM ROBINSON, lawyer; b. Cin., June 14, 1934; s. William B. and Chastine M. (Sprague) H.; children: Anita Christina, William Robinson Jr. AB magna cum laude, Princeton U., 1956; JD, Harvard U., 1963. Bar: Ohio 1963, U.S. Supreme Ct. 1975. Life underwriter New Eng. Mut. Life Ins. Co., 1956-63; assoc. Graydon, Head & Ritchey, Cin., 1963-68, ptnr., 1968-98. Mem. panel comml. and constrn. industry arbitrators Am. Arbitration Assn., 1972—, mem. panel large complex case program, 1993—, comml. arbitrator tng. faculty, 1998—; reporter joint com. for revision of rules of US Dist. Ct. for So. Dist. Ohio, 1975, 80, 83, mem., 1990—2003. Bd. dirs. Cin. Union Bethel, 1968-82, pres., 1977-82, emeritus, 1982—; bd. dirs. Ohio Valley Goodwill Industries Rehab. Ctr., Cin., 1970—, pres., 1981-92; mem. Cin. Bd. Bldg. Appeals, 1976-2001, vice chmn., 1983, chmn., 1983-2001; pres. Hamilton County (Ohio) Alcohol and Drug Addiction Svcs. Bd., 1990-92; trustee Substance Abuse Mgmt. and Devel. Inc., 1998-99. Capt. USAR, 1956-68; maj. gen. Ohio Mil. Res., comdr., 1996-2001. Recipient award of merit Ohio Legal Ctr. Inst., 1975, 76, Ohio Commendation medal, 1999. Mem. ABA, AAAS, AAJ, Ohio Bar Assn., Cin. Bar Assn., Ohio Acad. Trial Lawyers, Am. Arbitration Assn., Assn. for Conflict Resolution, 6th Cir. Jud. Conf. (life), Soc. Lees Va., Assn. Former Intelligence Officers, Diplomatic and Consular Officers Ret., Ohio Soc. Colonial Wars (gov. 1979), Princeton (NYC) Club, Bankers Club (Cin.), Phi Beta Kappa. Mem. Ch. Of Redeemer. Office: 432 Walnut St Ste 206 Cincinnati OH 45202-3909 Office Phone: 513-621-4220. Personal E-mail: wmrhardy@earthlink.net.

HARDYMON, DAVID WAYNE, lawyer; b. Columbus, Ohio, Aug. 22, 1949; s. Philip Barbour and Margaret Evelyn (Bowers) H.; m. Monica Ella Sleep, Mar. 13, 1982; children: Philip Garnet, Teresa Jeanette. BA in History, Bowling Green State U., 1971; JD, Capital U., Columbus, Ohio, 1976. Bar: Ohio 1976, U.S. Dist. Ct. (so. dist.) Ohio 1976; U.S. Supreme Ct. 1980, U.S. Ct. Appeals (6th cir.) 1982, Ky. 1999, U.S. Dist. Ct. (no. dist.) Ohio 1999, W.Va. 2000, U.S. Dist. Ct. (so. dist.) W.Va. 2000. Asst. prosecuting atty. Franklin County Prosecuter's Office, Columbus, Ohio, 1976-81; assoc. Vorys, Sater, Seymour & Pease, Columbus, 1981-86, ptnr., 1987—. Mem. Chmn's. Club Franklin Country Rep. Orgn., 1983. Fellow Columbus Bar Found.; mem. Ohio State Bar Assn., Columbus Bar Assn. Avocations: sailing, archery. Office: Vorys Sater Seymour & Pease LLP PO Box 1008 52 E Gay St Columbus OH 43215-3161 Office Phone: 614-464-5651.

HARE, PHIL (PHILIP G. HARE), congressman; b. Galesburg, Ill., Feb. 21, 1949; m. Rebecca Hare; children: Amy, Louis. Attended, Black Hawk C.C., 1967—68. Laborer Seaford Clothing Factory, Rock Island, SC, 1969—82; staff mem. to Rep. Lane Evans US Congress, 1983—2006; mem. US Congress from 17th dist., 2007—; mem. edn. & labor com., vets affairs com., congl. progressive caucus. Former pres. UNITE HERE Local 617. Served in USAR, 1969—75. Democrat. Roman Catholic. Office: 1118 Longworth House Office Bldg Washington DC 20515 also: 1535 47th Ave #5 Moline IL 61265

HARE, ROBERT YATES, musicologist, educator; b. McGrann, Pa., June 14, 1921; s. Robert Deemar and Beulah (Yates) H.; m. Constance King Rutherford, Mar. 31, 1948; children: Stephen, Beverly, Madeleine. MusB, U. Detroit, 1948; MA, Wayne State U., 1950; PhD, U. Iowa, 1959. Instr. Marietta (Ohio) Coll., 1949-51, Del Mar Coll., Corpus Christi, Tex., 1951-55; adj. instr. U. Tex., 1953—55; prof., chmn. grad. studies San Jose (Calif.) State U., 1956-65; prof., dean Eastern Ill. U. Music, 1965-74; prof. music history and lit. Ohio State U., Columbus, 1974-86, prof. emeritus, 1986—, dir. Sch. Music, 1974-78, dir. audio-rec. engring., 1979-82, arts adminstr. rsch. and faculty devel., 1982-86. Cons., lectr. in field; mem. coun. music edn. in higher edn. Ill. Music Educators Assn., 1969-74. Condr. coll. symphony band, 1956-63, San Jose Youth Symphony, 1957-59, univ. symphony, 1968-74, Ea. Ill. U. Symphony, 1968-74; French horn recitals, Carnegie Music Hall, Pitts., 1940, 42; French hornist, Pitts. Symphony Orch., 1941-44, Buffalo Philharm., 1943-44, Cin. Summer Opera Co., 1945, Indpls. Symphony Orch., 1945-46, San Antonio Symphony Orch., 1947-49; orchestrator, San Antonio Symphony Orch., 1947-49; recs. include Pitts. Symphony Orch., Indpls. Symphony Orch. (as French hornist), San Jose State U. Symphonic Band (as condr.); contbr. articles to profl. jours. Mem. com. grad. and profl. edn. in arts and humanities Ill. Bd. Higher Edn., 1969-70; mem. performing arts commn. Ill. Sesquicentennial, 1967; mem. exec. bd. Greater Columbus Arts Coun., 1974-76, Ohio Alliance for Arts in Edn., 1974-76; trustee Columbus Symphony Orch., 1975-79. Profl. Promise scholar Carnegie-Mellon U., 1939. Mem. Music Educators Nat. Conf. (publs. planning com. 1970-76), Am. Musicol. Soc., Coll. Music Soc., Masons, Shriners, Phi Mu Alpha, Sinfonia (hon.), Pi Kappa Lambda (hon.), Delta Omicron (hon.). Office: Ohio State U Coll Arts 305 Mershon Auditorium Columbus OH 43210 E-mail: rhare4@cox.net.

HARGRAVE, MARK WILLIAM, lawyer; b. Centerville, Iowa, Aug. 26, 1962; s. John George and Ruth Marie (Marvin) H.; m. Teresa Ann Baughman, May 26, 1984; children: Heather icole, Dylan Alexander. BSBA, Drake U., 1984, JD, 1987. Bar: Iowa 1987, Mo. 1991. Assoc. Nyemaster, Goode,

McLaughlin et al., Des Moines, 1987-90, Shook, Hardy & Bacon, LLP, Kansas City, Mo., 1990, ptnr. Co-author: Truth in Savings: Legal Analysis and Compliance Strategies, 1993. Mem. ABA, Mo. Bar Assn., Iowa Bar Assn. (Grad. Sr. award 1987), Order of the Coif, Order of Barristers. Office: Shook Hardy & Bacon LLP 2555 Grand Blvd Kansas City MO 64108 Office Phone: 816-474-6550. Office Fax: 816-241-5547. E-mail: mhargrave@shb.com.

HARGROVE, MIKE (DUDLEY MICHAEL HARGROVE), former professional baseball team manager; b. Perryton, Tex., Oct. 26, 1949; m. Sharon Rupprecht, Dec. 12, 1970; children: Kimberly Denise, Melissa Kathryn, Pamela Christine, Andrew Michael, Cynthia Michelle. BS in Phys. Edn. and Social Scis., Northwestern Okla. State U. First baseman Tex. Rangers, 1974-78, San Diego Padres, 1979, Cleve. Indians, 1979-85, coach minor league team, 1986, mgr. minor league team, 1987-89, coach, 1990-91, mgr., 1991-99; mgr., coach Balt. Orioles, 1999—2003; sr. adv., baseball ops. dept. Cleve. Indians, 2003—05; mgr. Seattle Mariners, 2005—07. Named Am. League Rookie of Yr. Baseball Writers' Assn. Am., 1974, Am. League Rookie Player of Yr. Sporting News, 1974; named to Am. League All-Star team, 1975, Am. League Mgr. of Yr. Sporting News, 1995.

HARKIN, THOMAS RICHARD, senator; b. Cumming, Iowa, Nov. 19, 1939; s. Patrick and Frances H.; m. Ruth Raduenz, 1968; children: Amy, Jenny. BS in Govt. and Economics, Iowa State U., 1962; JD, Cath. U. Am., 1972. Bar: Iowa 1972. Mem. staff Ho. of Reps. Select Com. U.S. Involvement in S.E. Asia, 1970; mem. 94th-98th Congresses from 5th Iowa Dist., mem. sci. and tech. com., mem. agr., nutrition and forestry coms.; US Senator from Iowa, 1985—; atty. Polk County Legal Aid Soc., 1973—74. Prin. author Americans with Disabilities Act; mem. com. agr., nutrition and forestry US Senate, com. appropriations, com. health, edn., labor and pensions, com. small bus. and entrepreneurship. Co-author: (with C.E. Thomas) Five Minutes to Midnight: Why the Nuclear Threat is Growing Faster than Ever, 1990. Dem. candidate for Presidency of U.S., 1992. Served with USN, 1962—67, served with USNR, 1968—74. Named Outstanding Young Alumnus Iowa State U. Alumni Assn., 1974; recipient Excellence in Public Svc. award Am. Acad. Pediatrics, 1991, Disting. Public Svc. award Med. Libr. Assn., 1995, William Steiger Meml. award Am. Conf. Govtl. Indsl. Hygienists, 1996, President's award Nat. Corn Grower's Assn., 2001, Richard and Barbara Hensen Leadership award and Disting. Lectureship U. Iowa Coll. Public Health, 2001, Friend of Seniors award Nat. Com. to Preserve Social Security and Medicare, 2002, Morris K. Udall award public svc. Parkinson's Action Network, 2002, Chronicles of Courage award VSA Arts, 2002, Spl. Recognition award AHA, 2003, Capitol Dome award Am. Cancer Soc., 2003, Disting. Cmty. Health Champion Nat. Assn. Cmty. Health Centers, 2005, Fred Rogers Integrity award Campaign for Commercial-Free Childhood, 2005, Nathan Davis award for Outstanding Govt. Svc., Am. Med. Assn., 2008. Mem.: Am. Legion. Democrat. Roman Catholic. Office: US Senate 731 Hart Senate Bldg Washington DC 20510-0001 also: Federal Bldg Ste 733 210 Walnut St Des Moines IA 50309-2106 Office Phone: 202-224-3254, 515-284-4574. Office Fax: 202-224-9369, 515-284-4937. E-mail: tom_harkin@harkin.senate.gov.*

HARKNA, ERIC, advertising executive; b. Tallinn, Estonia, June 24, 1940; came to U.S., 1947; s. Erich K. Harkna and Adelaide Mender; children: Britt, Kristiana, Christian Erik; m. Tonise Paul. BA, Colgate U., 1962; MBA, Columbia U., 1964. Account exec. Benton & Bowles, NYC, 1965-68; v.p., account supr. Kenyon & Eckhart, NYC, 1969-71, BBDO, Inc., NYC, 1973-74, v.p., mgmt. supr., 1974-76, sr. v.p., dir., 1977-82; exec. v.p., dir., 1979-82; pres., dir. BBDO, Inc., Chgo., 1982-84, pres., chief exec. officer, 1984-93; sr. v.p. BBDO Worldwide, Chgo., 1993—. Chmn. ann. awards dinner Advt. Age, 1987; chmn. Media Subcom., Chgo.; guest lectr. Chgo. Coun. Fgn. Rels., World Econ. Forum. Bd. dirs. United Cerebral Palsy Found., Chgo., 1982-94, Friends of Prentice Hosp.; v.p. nat. fund raising exec. com. Juvenile Diabetes Found. Internat., 1987-95, bd. dirs., 1990-96, internat. long range planning com. 1995-98; bd. dirs. Chgo. Coun. Profl. Psychology, 1991-96, Mus. Broadcast Commn., 1992—, U.S. Baltic Found., 1996—, Del. Place Bank. Colgate U. Norwegian Study grantee, 1961; recipient Internat. Bus. award Columbia U., 1964 Mem. Am. Assn. Advt. Agys. (regional bd. govs. 1994), Am. Mktg. Assn., Chgo. Coun. Fgn. Rels., Chgo. Advt. Club, Chgo. Econs. Club, Lake Shore Soc. Clubs, Execs. Club Chgo., N.Y. Athletic Club (N.Y.C.), N.Y. A.C. Yacht Club (Pelham), Chgo. Estonia House, Chgo. Yacht Club, 410 Club (founder, chmn., bd. dirs., bd. govs.). Office: BBDO Worldwide Inc 410 N Michigan Ave Ste 8 Chicago IL 60611-4273

HARL, NEIL EUGENE, economist, educator, lawyer, writer; b. Appanoose County, Iowa, Oct. 9, 1933; s. Herbert Peter and Bertha Catherine (Bonner) H.; m. Darlene Ramona Harris, Sept. 7, 1952; children: James Brent, Rodney Scott. BS, Iowa State U., 1955, PhD, 1965; JD, U. Iowa, 1961. Bar: Iowa 1961. Field editor Wallace's Farmer, 1957-58; research assoc. U.S. Dept. Agr., Iowa City and Ames, Iowa, 1958-64; from assoc. prof. to prof. Iowa State U., Ames, 1964—2004, Charles F. Curtiss dist. prof., 1976—, prof. emeritus, 2005—, dir. Ctr. Internat. Agrl. Fin., 1990—2004. Mem. adv. group to commr. IRS, 1979-80; mem. adv. com. Heckerling Inst. on Estate Planning, Miami, Fla., 1983-96; mem. adv. com. Office Tech. Assessment, U.S. Congress, 1988-95, vice chair, 1992-93, chair, 1993-94; mem. exec. bd. U.S. West Comms., Iowa, 1989-90; mem. adv. com. on agrl. biotech. USDA, 2000-02; mem. Fed. Commn. on Payment Limitations in Agr., 2002-03; lectr. in field. Author: Farm Estate and Business Planning, 1973, 15th edit., 2001, Legal and Tax Guide for Agricultural Lenders, 1984, supplement, 1987, Agricultural Law, 15 vols., 1980—81, Agricultural Law Manual, 1985;: rev. edit., 2006, The Farm Debt Crisis of the 1980s, 1990, Arrogance and Power: The Saga of WOI-TV, 2001, Farm Income Tax Manual, 2007; co-author: Farmland, 1982, Principles of Agricultural Law, 1997, Taxation of Cooperatives, 1999, Reporting Farm Income, 2000;: rev. edit., 2006, Family Owned Business Deduction, 2001, The Law of the Land, 2002; contbr. articles to profl. jours. Trustee Iowa State U. Agrl. Found., 1969-85; bd. dirs. Henry A. Wallace Birthplace Found., 2007-. 1st lt. AUS, 1955—57. Recipient Outstanding Tchr. award Iowa State U., 1973, Disting Svc. to Agr. award Am. Soc. Farm Mgrs. and Rural Appraisers, 1977, Iowa sect. 1996, Faculty Svc. award Nat. Univ. Ext. Assn., 1980, Disting. Svc. award Am. Agrl. Editors Assn., 1984, Disting. Achievement citation Iowa State U., 1985, Disting. Svc. to State Govt. award Nat. Gov.'s Assn., 1986, Disting. Svc. award Iowa State U., 1986, Farm Leader of Yr. award Des Moines Register, 1986, Henry A. Wallace award, 1987, Superior Svc. award USDA, 1987, Disting. Svc. to Iowa Agr. award Iowa Farm Bur., 1992, Faculty Excellence award, Iowa Bd. Regents, 1993, Charles A. Black award Coun. Agrl. Sci. Tech., 1997, Excellence in Internat. Agr. award Iowa State U., 1999, Disting. Svc. to Agr. award Chgo. Farmers Club, 1999, Exceptional Svc. to Agr. award Iowa Master Farmers, Wallaces Farmer, 2000, Pres.'s award disting. svc. Iowa State U., 2002, Lifetime Achievement award Iowa Farmers Union, 2003, Svc. to Am. and World Agr., Nat. Assn. County Agrl. Agts., 2006; named Seminar Leader of Yr. Nat. Assn. Accts., 2000. Fellow: Iowa State Bar Found., ABA Rsch. Found., Am. Coll. Trusts and Estates Counsel, Am. Agrl. Econs. Assn. (exec. bd. 1979—85, pres. 1983—84, Am. Agrl. Econs. Found. pres. 1993—94, Outstanding Ext. Program award 1970, Excellence in Communicating Rsch. Results award 1975, Disting. Undergrad. Tchr. award 1976); mem.: ABA, Iowa Barn Found. (bd. dirs. 1997—2005, v.p. 1999—2001), Am. Agrl. Law Assn. (pres. 1980—81, Disting. Svc. award 1984), Iowa Bar Assn. (Pres. award 1991), Golden Key. Home: 2821 Duff Ave Ames IA 50010 Home (Winter): 78-261 Manukai St # 3001 Kailua Kona HI 96740 Office: Iowa State U Dept Econs 381 Heady Hall Ames IA 50011-1070 Office Phone: 515-294-6354. Business E-Mail: harl@iastate.edu.

HARLAN, BYRON, newscaster; BA in Polit. Sci., U. Calif., San Diego; MA in Journalism, U. So. Calif.; MBA, U. Calif., Irvine. Reporter KMFB Radio, San Diego, KGTV, San Diego; instr. broadcast journalism San Diego State U.; corr. CBS Newspath CBS Network News Bur., Chgo.; weekend anchor and reporter WFLD-TV, Chgo., 1997—. Office: WFLD-TV 205 N Mich Ave Chicago IL 60601

HARLAN, CARMEN, television journalist; b. Detroit; married; 2 children. BA in Speech, U. Mich., 1975. Anchor, reporter, pub. affairs dir. Sta. WWWW-FM, 1975—78; gen. assignment reporter, noon anchor Sta. WDIV-TV, Detroit, 1978—81, evening newscaster, 1981—. Named Best Anchor, Hour Mag.; named one of Top 2 Anchorwomen in Country, Ladies Home Jour., 1991, Detroit's 100 Most Influential Women, Crain's Detroit Bus., 2002; recipient Emmy nominee, Child Advocacy award, Starr Commonwealth, Media award, So. Christian Leadership Conf. Office: WDIV-TV 550 W Lafayette Blvd Detroit MI 48226

HARLAN, KOHR, newscaster; BS in Journalism, U. Oreg. Anchor, reporter, Eureka, Calif., 1987; primary anchor Sta. KMTR-TV, Eugene, Oreg.; with Sta. KOIN-TV, Portland, Sta. KSAZ-TV, Phoenix; anchor, reporter KLAS-TV, Las Vegas, Sta. WTVD-TV, Raleigh/Durhan, NC, 1997—2000; anchor Sta. WISH-TV, Indpls., 2001—. Office: WISH-TV 1950 N Meridian St Indianapolis IN 46207

HARLAN, MARY ANN, lawyer; BA, Skidmore Coll.; JD, Case Western Reserve U. Ptnr. Calfee, Halter & Griswold LLP; asst. gen. counsel J.M. Smucker Co., gen. counsel, asst. sec., 2002—, v.p., gen. counsel, sec., 2005—. Office: JM Smucker Co 1 Strawberry Lane Orrville OH 44667

HARLAN, NORMAN RALPH, construction executive; b. Dayton, Ohio, Dec. 21, 1914; s. Joseph and Anna (Kaplan) H.; m. Thelma Katz, Sept. 4, 1955; children: Leslie, Todd. Indsl. Engring. degree, U. Cin., 1937. Chmn. Am. Constrn. Corp., Dayton, 1949, Harlan, Inc., realtors. Mem. Dayton Real Estate Bd., Ohio Real Estate Assn., Nat. Assn. Real Estate Bds., C. of C., Pi Lambda Phi. Home: 303 Glenridge Rd Kettering OH 45429-1631 Office: Am Constrn Corp 2451 S Dixie Dr Dayton OH 45409-1861

HARLAN, ROBERT ERNEST, retired professional football team executive; b. Des Moines, Sept. 9, 1936; m. Madeline Harlan; children: Kevin, Bryan, Michael. BJ, Marquette U., 1958. Former gen. reporter UPI, Milw.; sports info. dir. Marquette U., Milw., 1959; dir. cmty. rels. St. Louis Cardinals, 1966-68, dir. pub. rels., 1968-71; asst. gen. mgr. Green Bay Packers, Wis., 1971-75, corp. gen. mgr., 1975-81, corp. asst. to pres., 1981-88, exec. v.p. adminstrn., 1988-89, pres., CEO, 1989—2006, chmn., CEO, 2006—07; ret., 2007. Bd. dirs. Firstar Bank, Green Bay. Mem. exec. bd. Packer 65 Roses Sports Club. Served with U.S. Army. Mem. bd. of trustees, St. Norbert Coll., Wis. Avocation: golf.

HARLAN, TIMOTHY, state legislator; b. Boonville, Mo., Mar. 15, 1949; m. Linda Harlan; children: Reed, Brook. Degree in history, Westminster Coll.; degree in law, U. Mo., Columbia. Mem. Mo. Ho. of Reps., Jefferson City, 1994—. Mem. budget com., ethics com., joint rules com., fiscal rev. com., tobacco com., appropriations com., accounts, ops. and fin. com.; vice chmn. judiciary com.; chmn. critical issues com. Active Presbyn. Ch. Recognized as outstanding legislator by Mo. Assn. Osteopathic Physicians, LWV, Mo. State Med. Soc., Mo. Pharmacy Assn., Mo. Psychol. Assn., Mo. Coalition of Alliances for the Mentally Ill, Nat. Alliance for the Mentally Ill, St. Louis 2004, Jud. Conf. Mo., Mo. Bar, Mo. Optometric Assn., Mo. Nurses Assn., Mo. Perfusion Soc., Mo. Assisted Living Assn., Mo. Assn. Homes for the Aging. Democrat. Office: Mo House of Reps Rm 400CC 201 W Capitol Ave Jefferson City MO 65101 Fax: 573 526 1088. E-mail: tharlan@services.state.mo.us.

HARLESS, KATHERINE J., telecommunications industry executive; m. Skip Harless; children: Skip Jr., Ely, Bill. B in Acctg., U. Tex., 1972. With GTE, 1973—, regional pres. telephone ops. Tex. and Mexico, 1994-96, pres. airfone, 1996—2000; pres. info. services Verizon Communications, 2000—06; pres., CEO Idearc Inc., Dallas, 2006—. Vice chmn. Yellow Pages Assn., 2005—06, chmn., 2002, 2006—; bd. dir. Toro Co. Mem. adv. bd. McCombs Sch. Bus. Univ. Tex. Mem. Com. of 200 (trs. com. 200 found. bd.), Chgo. Network, Internat. Women's Forum, Execs. Club Chgo., Barbara Bush Found. (mem. celebration of reading com.), Leadership Am. Office: Idearc Inc 2200 W Airfield Dr Dallas TX 75261

HARMAN, JOHN ROYDEN, retired lawyer; b. Elkhart, Ind., June 30, 1921; s. James Lewis and Bessie Bell (Mountjoy) H.; m. Elizabeth Rae Crosier, Dec. 12, 1943 (dec. May 1995); 1 child, James Richard. BS, U. Ill., 1943; JD, Ind. U., 1949. Bar: Ind. 1949. Assoc. Proctor & Proctor, Elkhart, 1949-51; pvt. practice, Elkhart, 1952-60; ptnr. Cawley & Harman, 1960-65, Thornburg, McGill, Deahl, Harman, Carey & Murray, 1965-82, Barnes & Thornburg, Elkhart, 1982-89; ret., 1989. Atty. City of Elkhart, 1952-60. State del. Ind. Republican Com., 1962-70; pres., bd. dirs. Crippled Childrens Soc.; bd. dirs. United Community Services Elkhart County. 1st lt., F.A.,AUS, 1943-46, PTO. Fellow Ind. Bar Found; mem. ABA, Ind. Bar Assn., Elkhart County Bar Assn. (pres. 1977), Elkhart City Bar Assn. (pres. 1970), Elkhart C. of C. (pres. 1977, bd. dirs. 1972-75), Elcona Country Club (bd. dirs.), Phi Kappa Psi, Alpha Kappa Psi, Phi Delta Phi. Republican. Presbyterian. Avocation: golf. Office: NBD Bank Bldg 121 W Franklin St Ste 200 Elkhart IN 46516-3200

HARMAN, MIKE, real estate broker, small business owner; b. Troy, Kans., Aug. 27, 1952; m. Sue Harman; 2 children. Libertarian candidate for U.S. House 7th Dist., Mo., 1996. Office: 675 E 380th Rd Dunnegan MO 65640-9622

HARMEL, PAUL, photography company executive; Chmn, CEO Lifetouch, Eden Prairie, Minn. Office: Lifetouch 11000 Viking Dr Eden Prairie MN 55344-7257

HARMON, BUD GENE, animal sciences educator, consultant; b. Camden, Ind., July 2, 1931; s. Orvie M. and Margaret (Cooke) H.; m. Mary Lynne Jones, June 7, 1953; children: Brad Lee, Beth Ann, Jana Renee. BS, Purdue U., 1958; PhD, Mich. State U., 1962. Rsch. tchr. U. Ill., Urbana, 1962-75; rsch. dir. Ralston Purina, St. Louis, 1975-86; head dept. animal sci. Purdue U., West Lafayette, 1986-97, now prof. Mem. sci. adv. bd. Fats and Protein Found. Rsch. Bd., 1997—. With USN, 1951-55. Mem. Am. Soc. Animal Sci. (pres. 1994). Office: Purdue U Dept Animal Scis West Lafayette IN 47907

HARMON, CLARENCE, former mayor, law educator; m. Janet Kelley; 4 children. BS, Northeast Mo. State U.; MA in Criminal Justice Administrn. and Pub. Administrn., Webster U.; past postgrad., Harvard U. Past chief of police City of St. Louis; with St. Louis Police Dept., 1969-95, chief, 1991-95; dir. bus. devel., dir. dept. mkt. rsch. and analysis United Van Lines, Inc., 1995-97; mayor City of St. Louis, 1997—2001; tchr. So. Ill. U., Carbondale. Bd. dirs. United Way, St. Louis, St. Louis Symphony, Mo. Bot. Garden, Fair St. Louis; trustee Webster U., St. Louis Sci. Ctr. Danforth Found. fellow; recipient Reach Out award St. Vincent Home, 1992, Dr. Martin Luther King, Jr. Life and Legacy award, 1992; named Mo. Police Chief of Year Mo. Police Chiefs' Assn., 1995. Mem. Am. Assn. Indsl. Mgmt. (bd. dirs.). Address: 1920 Virginia Ave Saint Louis MO 63104-1523

HARMON, PATRICK, historian, retired editor, commentator; b. St. Louis, Sept. 2, 1916; s. Jack and Laura (Duchesne) H.; m. Anne M. Worland, Aug. 31, 1940; children— Michael, Timothy, Kathleen, Daniel, John, Sheila, Peggy, Brigid, Kevin, Teresa, Christopher. AB, U. Ill., Urbana, 1939. Sports editor ews-Gazette, Champaign, Ill., 1942-47, Gazette, Cedar Rapids, Iowa, 1947-51, Post, Cin., 1951-85; ret., 1985; sports commentator Sta. WCPO-TV, 1953-56, Sta. WKRC, 1958, Sta. WLW-TV, 1958-68; curator, historian Coll. Football Hall of Fame, Kings Island, Ohio, 1986-95; historian Nat. Football Found., Morristown, NJ, 1994—2005; ret., 2005. Contbg. sports editor: World Book, 1959—2004. Recipient Fred Hutchinson Meml. award for community service, 1969; named Internat. Churchmen's Sports Writer of Year, 1973 Mem. Sigma Chi. Home and Office: 608 Maple Trace Cincinnati OH 45246 Home Phone: 513-782-6457.

HARMON, ROBERT GERALD, public health executive; b. Barnsdall, Okla., Mar. 20, 1944; s. Thomas Frederick and Eleandor Virginia (Colley) H.; m. Carol Louise Kalnitsky, Aug. 22, 1971; children: Rex, Susan. BA in Zoology, Washington U., 1966, MD, 1970; MPH, Johns Hopkins U., 1977. Diplomate Am. Bd. Preventive Medicine. Intern, then resident U. Colo. Med. Ctr., Denver, 1970-73; asst. prof. health svcs. and internal medicine U. Wash., Seattle, 1977-80; chmn. dept. community medicine Maricopa Med. Ctr., Phoenix, 1980-85; dep. dir. Maricopa County Divsn. Pub. Health, Phoenix, 1980-82, dir., 1983-85; dir. Dept. Health State of Mo., Jefferson City, 1986-90; clin. prof. U. Mo. Sch. Medicine, Columbia, 1986-90; adminstr. Health Resources Svcs. Adminstrn. USPHS/HHS, Rockville, Md., 1990-93; sr. v.p. MetraHealth Ctr. for Corp. Health Inc., Oakton, Va., 1994-95; v.p., nat. med. dir. Optum divsn. UnitedHealth Group, McLean, Va., 1996—2004; dir., chief med. officer Ctr. for Health Care Policy and Evaluation Ingenix/United Health Group, Eden Prairie, Minn., 2004—05; dir. Duval County Health Dept., Jacksonville, 2006—. Adj. assoc. prof. Sch. Medicine, U. Ariz., Tucson, 1981-85; adj. prof., Sch. Pub. Health, U. Minn., 2005-. Contbr. over 50 articles to profl. jours. Bd. dirs. Partnership for Prevention, DC, 1996-2005, Nat. Bd. Pub. Health Examiners, DC, 2005-; with commd. corps USPHS, 1974-75, 90-93. Decorated Meritorious Svc. medal USPHS. Fellow Am. Coll. Preventive Medicine (pres. 2003-05); mem. Nat. Assn. County Health Ofcls. (pres. 1982-85), Am. Pub. Health Assn. (gov. councilor 1984-88), Assn. State and Territorial Health Ofcls. (exec. com. 1987-90), Ariz. County Health Ofcls. Assn. (founder, pres. 1984-85), Omicron Delta Kappa, Delta Omega. Republican. Methodist. Avocation: sports. Office: Duval County Health Dept 515 W 6th St Jacksonville FL 32225 Home Phone: 904-221-9416; Office Phone: 904-630-3220. E-mail: robert_harmon@doh.state.fl.us.

HARMON, ROBERT WAYNE, electrical engineering executive; b. Winchester, Ind., Oct. 22, 1929; s. Wayne and Theresa (Bishop) H.; m. Mary Louise Cobb; children: Wayne Charles, Keith Robert, Arthur Dean, Frederic Bruce. BSEE with highest distinction, Purdue U, 1951, MSEE, 1955. Engr. Aro, Inc., Tullahoma, Tenn., 1951-54; devel. engr. Ohio Brass Co., Barberton, Ohio, 1955-63, dir. new product devel., 1963-68; chief engr. A.B. Chance Co., Centralia, Mo., 1968-95. Cons. and legal tech. expert witness in field. Holder 30 patents in insulation, elect. apparatus. Fellow IEEE (life); mem. ASTM, Nat. Elec. Mfgrs. Assn. Avocations: geology, archaelogy, whitewater canoeing. Home: 342 Woodmere Dr Saint Charles MO 63303-0709 E-mail: robermon@aol.com.

HARMON, TERESA WILTON, lawyer; b. 1968; BS, U. Ala., 1990, MBA, 1991; JD, U. Chgo., 1994. Bar: Ill. 1994. Clk. for Hon. Phyllis Kravitch, U.S. Ct. Appeals (11th cir.), 1994; with Sidley Austin LLP, Chgo., 1995—, ptnr., 2003—. Adj. prof. U. Ill. Coll. Law. Mem.: ABA (sect. bus. law and uniform comml. code com.), Am. Law Inst., Chgo. Bar Assn. (co-chair comml. fin. and transactions com.). Office: Sidley Austin LLP Bank One Plz One S Dearborn St Chicago IL 60603

HARMONY, MARLIN DALE, chemistry professor; b. Lincoln, Nebr., Mar. 2, 1936; s. Philip and Helen Irene (Michal) H. AA, Kansas City Jr. Coll., Mo., 1956; BS in Chem. Engring., U. Kans., 1958; PhD in Chemistry, U. Calif.-Berkeley, 1961. Asst. prof. U. Kans., Lawrence, 1962-67, assoc. prof., 1967-71, prof., 1971-98, chmn., 1980-88, prof. emeritus, 1998—. Panel mem. NRC-Nat. Bur. Standards., 1969-78; mem. review panel NSF, 1977, 92. Author: Introduction to Molecular Energies and Spectra, 1972; contbg. editor: Physics Vade Mecum, 1981; mem. editorial bd. Structural Chemistry, 1989-98; contbr. articles to profl. jours.; patentee in field. Postdoctoral fellow NSF Harvard U., 1961-62. Fellow AAAS; mem. Am. Chem. Soc., Am. Phys. Soc., Sigma Xi, Alpha Chi Sigma, Phi Lambda Upsilon, Tau Beta Pi Democrat. Home: 1033 Avalon Rd Lawrence KS 66044-2505 Office: U Kans Dept Chemistry Lawrence KS 66045-0001 Business E-Mail: harmony@ku.edu.

HARMS, NANCY ANN, nursing educator; d. Orval M. and Ruth Marie (Nelson) H.; m. Gerhart J. Wehrbein. Diploma, Bryan Meml. Hosp., 1971; BS in Natural Sci., Nebr. Wesleyan U., 1971; BSN, U. Nebr., 1975, MSN, 1977, PhD, 1988. RN, Nebr. Staff nurse, asst. supr., ins. coord. Brewster Hosp., Holdrege, Nebr., 1971-72; instr. Immanuel Sch. Nursing, Omaha, 1972-75; coord. nursing care plan devel. Hosp. Info. Sys. U. Nebr. Med. Ctr., Omaha, 1975; asst. chair dept. Coll. St. Mary, Omaha, 1975-80; curriculum coord. Midland Luth. Coll., Fremont, Nebr., 1980-88, chair nursing divsn., 1988—2007, prof. Mem. ANA (mem. Ho. of Dels.), Nebr. Nurses' Assn. (Nurse Excellence award, Excellence in Writing award jour., adv. Nebr. Student Nurses Assn., mem. various coms.), Nat. League ursing, Sigma Theta Tau (theta omega, gamma pi chpts.).

HARPER, DONALD VICTOR, retired transportation and logistics educator, consultant; b. Chgo., Mar. 27, 1927; s. Victor Rudolph and Mildred Victoria (Safbom) H.; children: Christine Ann, Diane Elizabeth, David Victor. Student, Wright Jr. Coll., 1945, 46-47; BS in Journalism, U. Ill., Urbana, 1950, PhD in Econs., 1957. Instr. Coll. Commerce and Bus. adminstrn. U. Ill., Urbana, 1953-56; lectr. Carlson Sch. Mgmt. U. Minn., Mpls., 1956, asst. prof. Carlson Sch. Mgmt., 1956-59, assoc. prof., 1959-65, prof. transp. and logistics, 1965-97, chmn. dept. mgmt. and transp., 1967-70, dir. MBA and PhD programs, 1970-79, dir. PhD program, 1979-80, chmn. dept. mktg. and logistics mgmt., 1991-96; prof. emeritus, 1997—; cons. to bus. and govt. agys. Author: Economic Regulation of the Motor Trucking Industry by the States, 1959, Price Policy and Procedure, 1966, Transportation in America: Users, Carriers, Government, 2d edit, 1982; contbr. articles to profl. jours. Served with USN, 1945-46. Mem. Am. Econ. Assn. (Disting. Mem. award transp. and pub. utilities group 1988), Am. Mktg. Assn., Transp. Research Forum, Am. Soc. Transp. and Logistics, Transp. Club Mpls. and St. Paul, Assn. Transp. Law, Logistics and Policy. Home: 2451 Sheldon St Saint Paul MN 55113-3138 Office: U Minn Carlson Sch Mgmt 321 19th Ave S Minneapolis MN 55455-0438 Office Phone: 612-624-5833. Business E-Mail: dharper@csom.umn.edu.

HARPER, PATRICIA NELSEN, psychiatrist; b. Omaha, July 25, 1944; d. Eddie R. and Marjorie L. (Williams) Nelsen. BS, Antioch Coll., Yellow Springs, Ohio, 1966; MD, U. ebr., 1975; grad., Topeka Inst. Psychoanalysis, 1997. Cert. psychiatrist. Psychiatric residency Karl Menninger Sch. of Psychiatry, Topeka, 1975-78; staff psychiatrist The Menninger Clinic, Topeka, 1978-98; chmn. dept. mental health Park Nicollet Clinic, 2004—. Faculty mem. Karl Menninger Sch. of Psychiatry, Topeka, 1982-98. Program dir. Addictions Recovery Program C.F. Menninger Meml. Hosp., Topeka, 1987-98. Mem. Am. Psychiatric Assn., Am. Med Women Assn., Am. Psychoanalytic Assn. Office: Pk Nicollet Clinic 3800 Park Nicollet Blvd Minneapolis MN 55416-2527 Home Phone: 952-922-3099; Office Phone: 952-993-3307.

HARPER, STEVEN JAMES, lawyer; b. Mpls., Apr. 25, 1954; s. James Henry and Mary Margaret H.; m. Kathy Joseph Loeb, Aug. 21, 1976; children: Benjamin James, Peter William, Emma Suzanne. BA with distinction, MA in Econs., Northwestern U., 1976; JD magna cum laude, Harvard U., 1979. Bar: Ill. 1979, U.S. Dist. Ct. (no. dist.) Ill. 1979, U.S. Dist. Ct. (we. dist.) Wisc. 1988, U.S. Ct. Appeals (10th Cir.) 1989, U.S. Dist. Ct. (ea. dist.) Mich. 1997, U.S. Ct. Appeals (5th Cir.) 2001, U.S. Ct. Appeals (3rd Cir.) 2002, U.S. Ct. Appeals (7th Cir.) 2002. Assoc. Kirkland & Ellis LLP, Chgo., 1979-85, ptnr., 1985—; adj. prof. of law Northwestern U., Evanston, Ill., 1997—. Mem. ABA, Bd. of Visitors Northwestern U. 1999-; fellow Am. Coll. of Trial Lawyers 1999-. Office: Kirkland & Ellis LLP 200 E Randolph Dr Fl 54 Chicago IL 60601-6636

HARPER, TERRANCE G., journalism organization administrator; Exec. dir. Phi Kappa Psi Frat., 1990—99; fin. advisor UBS PaineWebber Inc., 1999—2001; dir. fundraising Kiwanis Internat. Found., Indpls., 2001—02; exec. dir. Soc. Profl. Journalists & Sigma Delta Chi Found., Indpls., 2002—. Office: Soc Profl Journalists Eugene S Pulliam Nat Journalism Ctr 3909 N Meridian St Indianapolis IN 46208 Office Phone: 317-927-8000 ext. 220. E-mail: tharper@spj.org.

HARPER, W(ALTER) JOSEPH, financial consultant; b. Columbus, Ohio, Apr. 6, 1947; s. Joseph and Patricia A. (Whetzle) Harper; m. J. Lynn Rutherford, Aug. 1, 1970; children: Tracy, Kelly, Brett. BS in Edn., Ohio State U., 1970. CFP, registered investment advisor Ohio. Tchr., coach Lake Wales (Fla.) Schs., 1970-71, Westerville (Ohio) Pub. Schs., 1971-74; securities salesman, fin. planner Investors Diversified Svcs., Columbus, 1974-83; fin. planner, investment mgr. Harper Assocs., Columbus, 1983—. Mem. golf team Ohio State U., 1966—69. Mem.: Inst. Cert. Fin. Planners (bd. dirs., pres. Ctrl. Ohio Soc.), Internat. Assn. Fin. Planning, Nat. Assn. Personal Fin. Advisors, Scioto Country Club, Rotary. Republican. Avocations: sports, children's activities, duck hunting. E-mail: harps@jadeinc.com.

HARPER, WILLIAM WAYNE, broadcast executive; b. Peoria, Ill., 1943; BA, Sanamon State U., 1985; MSA, Ctrl. Mich. U., 1991. Dir. Sta. WAND-TV, Decatur, Ill., 1962-70; account exec. Sta. WTWD-TV, Terre Haute, Ill., 1970-74, Sta. WFIE-TV, Evansville, Ind., 1974-77, Sta. WAND-TV, Decatur, 1977-80; gen. sales mgr. Sta. WRSP-TV, Springfield, Ill., 1980-83; v.p., gen. mgr. Sta. WVFT-TV, Roanoke, Va., 1983-84, Sta. WSMH-TV, Flint, Mich., 1984-90, Sta. WBRE-TV, Wilkes-Barre, Pa., 1990-94; gen. mgr. Sta. WBBJ-TV, Jackson, Tenn., 1994-95, Sta. WRSP/WCCU-TV, Springfield, 1997—. Office: Sta WRSP/WCCO-TV 3003 Old Rochester Rd Springfield IL 62703-5664

HARR, LUCY LORAINE, public relations executive; b. Sparta, Wis., Dec. 2, 1951; d. Ernest Donald Harr and Dorothy Catherine (Heintz) Harr Vetter BS, U. Wis., Madison, 1976, MS, 1978. Lectr. U. Wis., Madison, 1977-82; from asst.

editor to editor Everybody's Money Everybody's Money Credit Union Nat. Assn., Madison, 1979-84, mgr. ann. report, 1984-92, v.p. pub. rels., 1984-93, sr. v.p. credit union devel., 1993-96, sr. v.p. consumer rels. and corp. responsibility, 1996-97; owner Providing Solutions, Stoughton, Wis., 1997—; ptnr. Fourth Lake Comm., LLP. Dir. consumer appeals bd. Ford Motor Co., Milw., 1983-87. Author: Credit Union Basic Guide to Retirement Planning, 1998. Bd. dirs. Madison Area Crimestoppers, 1982-84; Midwest coord. of ofcls. USA Triathlon, 2003. Recipient Clarion award, 1982. Mem. Women in Comm. (pres. Madison profl. chpt. 1982-83, nat. v.p. programs 1986-87, vice-chair/sec. nat. interim bd. 1996-97, chair nat. bd. dirs. 1997-2001), Internat. Assn. Bus. Communicators (program chair dist. meeting 1981), Am. Soc. Assn. Execs. (Gold Circle award 1984) Avocations: bicycling, reading. E-mail: lharr@providing-solutions.com.

HARR, MILTON EDWARD, engineering educator, consultant; b. Chelsea, Mass., Oct. 19, 1925; s. Hyman and Ann (Kristal) H.; m. Florence Solomon, May 19, 1945; children: Faith, Karen, Robert. BS, Northeastern U., Boston, 1949; MS, Rutgers U., 1955; PhD, Purdue U., 1958; Docteur Honoris Causa, U. Brussels, 1987. Engr. Bureau of Reclamation, Provo, Utah, 1949, State Hwy. Dept., Beverly, Mass., 1949-53; asst. instr. Rutgers U., New Brunswick, N.J., 1953-55; instr. Purdue U., West Lafayette, Ind., 1955-58, asst. prof., 1958-60, assoc. prof., 1960-72, prof., 1972—. Jubilee prof. Chalmers Tech. Inst., Gothenburg, Sweden, 1996-97; cons. Bendix Corp., South Bend, Ind., Bougainville Copper Ltd., New Guinea, Brown and Root, Houston, Sandia Nat. Labs, Albuquerque, and many others; lectr. at many numerous colls. and univs. Author: Groundwater & Seepage, 1962, Foundations of Theoretical Soil Mechanics, 1966, Mechanics of Particulate Media, 1977, Reliability in Civil Engineering, 1987; editorial bd. Applied Ocean Research, 1978—, Internat. Jour. for Numerical and Analytical Methods in Geomechanics, 1978—; contbr. articles to profl. jours.; patentee in field. Bd. dirs. Ind. Joint Hwy. Research Project, 1969-72; adv. panel Am. Assn. State Hwy. Ofcls.; mem. Hwy. Research Bd. Com. on Stresses in Earth Masses, NASA Aeronautics Adv. Com., 1977-81, Task Force on Railway Maintenance Com., Transp. Research Bd., 1978-82, U.S. Com. on Large Dams; chmn. Track Structure Systems Design Com., 1976-79, Pavement Design Divsn. of HRB, 1964-70. Served with USN, 1943, ETO, with USMC, 1944-45, PTO. Recipient U.S. Sr. Scientist award Alexander von Humbolt Orgn., Bonn, Germany, 1983, Bechtel award Bechtel Engring. Co., Houston, 1983, G. Ernest Brooks award ASCE-Cleve. sect., Cleve., 1987; named Shaw Lectr., N.C. State U., 1984. Fellow ASCE; mem. at. Acad. Engrs., Ind. Acad. Sci., Third Marine Div. Assn., Elks, Sigma Xi, Chi Epsilon. Avocations: music, art. Home: 4440 Exeter Dr Unit N204 Longboat Key FL 34228-2228 Office: Purdue U 1284 Civil Engineering West Lafayette IN 47907-1284

HARRE, ALAN FREDERICK, academic administrator; b. Nashville, Ill., June 12, 1940; s. Adolph Henry and Hilda (Vogt) Harre; m. Diane Carole Mack, Aug. 9, 1964; children: Andrea Lyn, Jennifer Leigh, Eric Stephen. BA, Concordia Sr. Coll., 1962; MDiv, Concordia Sem., St. Louis, 1966; MA, Presbyn. Sch. Christian Edn., Richmond, Va., 1967; PhD, Wayne State U., 1976. Ordained to ministry Luth. Ch. Asst. pastor St. James Luth. Ch. Grosse Pointe, Grosse Pointe Farms, Mich., 1967-73; asst. prof. theology Concordia U., Seward, Nebr., 1973-78, assoc. prof., 1978-84, asst. to pres., 1981, dean student affairs, 1982-84, acting pres., 1984, pres. St. Paul, 1984-88, Valparaiso U., Ind., 1988—. Author: (book) Close the Back Door, 1984. Bd. dirs. Associated New Am. Colls., Cmty. Found. N.W. Ind., Inc., N.W. Ind. Forum, Ind. Campus Compact, Independent Coll. Ind. Found., Luth. Ednl. Conf. Am., Christmas in April, Porter County Cmty. Foun., Quality Life Coun.; mem. adv. bd. YMCA; mem. Pres.'s Coun. Mid-Continent Conf. Recipient Disting. Cmty. Leader award, 1998, Sam Walton Bus. Leader award, 1999, Crystal Globe award, 1999, Seeds of Hope award, 2006, Chief Exec. Leadership award. Mem.: Ind. Soc. Chgo., Ind. Conf. Higher Edn., Am. Assn. Higher Edn., Union League Club Chgo. Home: 3900 Hemlock Dr Valparaiso IN 46383-1814 Office: Valparaiso U Office of the President Valparaiso IN 46383-9978 E-mail: alan.harre@valpo.edu.

HARRIMAN, GERALD EUGENE, retired business administrator, economics professor; b. Dell Rapids, SD, May 30, 1924; s. Roy L. and Margaret (Schrantz) H.; m. Eileen Bernadine Bensman, June 10, 1950; children— G. Peter, Mary K., Margaret C., Elizabeth A. BS, U. Notre Dame, 1947; A.M., U. S.D., 1949; PhD, U. Cin., 1957. Expediter Minn. Mining & Mfg. Co., 1947-48; from instr. to asst. dean, chmn. dept. bus. adminstrn. and finance Xavier U., 1949-66; prof. bus. adminstrn., chmn. div. bus. and econs. Ind. U., South Bend, 1966-75, prof. bus. adminstrn. and econs., 1975-89, prof. emeritus, 1989—, dean faculties, 1975-87, acting chancellor, 1979, vice chancellor acad. affairs, 1987-89; ret., 1989. Vis. prof. fin. U. S.D., 1962; chmn. acad. deans Ind. Conf. Higher Edn., 1981-82; cons. in field. Mem. citizens adv. coun. long range fin. planning Coun. of City of Cin., 1963; mem. Community Edn. Roundtable, 1984—; mem. Scholarship Found. of St. Joseph County, Inc., 1992. Served with USNR, 1942-45. Mem.: Am. Econs. Assn., Am. Fin. Assn., Beta Gamma Sigma. Home: 16600 Gerald St Granger IN 46530-9579 Office: 1700 Mishawaka Ave South Bend IN 46615-1408

HARRINGTON, BERNARD JOSEPH, bishop; b. Detroit, Sept. 6, 1933; s. John and Norah Harrington. BS, Sacred Heart Seminary; M.Div., St. John's Provincial, 1982; MEd, U. Detroit, 1983. Ordained priest Archdiocese of Detroit, 1959, asst. supt. schs., pastor Holy Name Parish, pastor St. Rene Goupil Parish, aux. bishop, 1994-98; ordained bishop, 1994; bishop Diocese of Winona, Minn., 1998—. Roman Catholic. Office: Diocese of Winona PO Box 588 55 W Sanborn St Winona MN 55987-3655 Office Phone: 507-454-4643. Office Fax: 507-454-8106.*

HARRINGTON, BEVERLY, museum director; BS, Carnegie Mellon U., 1959; BAE, U. Wis., Oshkosh, 1967, MST, 1971; MSA, U. Wis., Milw., 1977. With art dept. U. Wis., Oshkosh, 1977-87; curator collections and exhibitions at arboretum Paine Art Ctr., Oshkosh, 1983-90; dir. Hearthstone Mus., Appleton, Wis., 1991—2004.

HARRINGTON, CAROL A., lawyer; b. Geneva, Ill., Feb. 13, 1953; d. Eugene P. and M. Ruth (Bowersox) Kloubec; m. Warren J. Harrington, Aug. 19, 1972; children: Jennifer Ruth, Carrie Anne. BS summa cum laude, U. Ill., 1974, JD magna cum laude, 1977. Bar: Ill. 1977, U.S. Dist. Ct. (no. dist.) Ill. 1977, U.S. Tax Ct. 1979. Assoc. Winston & Strawn, Chgo., 1977—84, ptnr., 1984—88, McDermott, Will & Emery, Chgo., 1988—, pvt. client dept. chair, 2006—. Adv. com. Heckerling Inst. Estate Planning; speaker in field. Co-author: Generation-Skipping Tax, 1996, Generation-Skipping Transfer Tax, Warren, Gorham & Lamont, 2000. Fellow Am. Coll. Trusts and Estate Coun. (bd. regents 1999-2005); mem. ABA (chmn. B-1 generation skipping transfer com. 1987-92, coun. real property, probate and trust law sect. 1992-98), Ill. State Bar Assn., Chgo. Bar Assn., Chgo. Estate Planning Coun. Office: McDermott Will & Emery 227 W Monroe St Ste 3100 Chicago IL 60606-5096 Office Phone: 312-984-7794.

HARRINGTON, JAMES TIMOTHY, lawyer; b. Chgo., Sept. 4, 1942; s. John Paul and Margaret Rita (Cunneen) H.; m. Roseanne Strupeck, Sept. 4, 1965; children: James Timothy, Roseanne, Maris Zajdela. BA, U. Notre Dame, 1964, JD, 1967. Bar: Ill. 1967, Ind. 1968, U.S. Dist. Ct. (no. dist.) Ill. 1967, U.S. Dist. Ct. (no. and so. dists.) Ind. 1968, U.S. Ct. Appeals (7th cir.) 1969, U.S. Ct. Appeals (4th cir.) 1977, U.S. Ct. Appeals (8th cir.) 1979, U.S. Ct. Appeals (3d cir.) 1981, U.S. Supreme Ct. 1979, U.S. Ct. Appeals (D.C. cir.) 1993. Law clk. U.S. Dist. Ct. (no. dist.) Ind., 1967—69; assoc. Rooks, Pitts & Poust, Chgo., 1969—75, ptnr., 1976—87, Ross & Hardies, Chgo., 1987—2003, McGuire-Woods, LLP, 2003—07. Adj. prof. environ. mgmt. Ill. Inst. Tech., 2004—, Stuart Grad. Sch. Bus.; lectr. environ. law and mgmt., fed. procedures, adminstrv. law, 1960—. Vice chmn. Mid Am. Legal Found., 1998—; past chmn., bd. dirs. Ill. Safety Coun., 2002-05; chmn., bd. adv. masters in environ. mgmt. program Ill. Inst. Tech. Sch. Bus. Fellow Am. Bar Found.; mem. Ill. Bar Assn., Ind. Bar Assn., Chgo. Bar Assn. (environ. law com.), Indsl. Water Waste and Sewer Group (past chmn.), Air and Waste Mgmt. Assn. (sec. Lake Mich. sect.), Assn. Environ. Law Inst., Lawyers Club Chgo., Union League Club Chgo. Roman Catholic. Home: 746 Foxdale Ave Winnetka IL 60093-1908 Office: McGuire-Woods LLP 77 W Wacker Dr Ste 4400 Chicago IL 60601 Office Phone: 312-849-8252. Business E-Mail: jharrington@mcguirewoods.com.

HARRINGTON, JEREMY THOMAS, priest, publishing executive; b. Lafayette, Ind., Oct. 7, 1932; s. William and Ellen (Cain) H. BA, Duns Scotus Coll., 1955; postgrad., U. Detroit, 1955, Marquette U., 1961; MA, Xavier U., Cin., 1965; MS in Journalism, Northwestern U., 1967; LHD (hon.), St. Bonaventure U., 1999. Ordained priest Roman Cath. Ch., 1959. Joined Order Friars Minor, 1950; tchr. Roger Bacon High Sch., Cin., 1960-64; assoc. editor St. Anthony Messenger, Cin., 1964-66, editor, 1966-81, pub., 1975-81, pub., CEO, 1991—2007; mem. bd. Franciscan Province Cin., 1969-72, 75-81, chief exec. bd., 1981-90; ret., 2007; commissary Holyland and Franciscan Monustery, Washington, 2007—. Author: Your Wedding: Planning Your Own Ceremony, 1974; editor: Conscience in Today's World, 1970, Jesus: Superstar or Savior?, 1972. Mem. Catholic Press Assn. (pres. 1975-77, dir.), Kappa Tau Alpha. Home: 1615 Vine St Cincinnati OH 45202 Office: St Anthony Messenger 28 W Liberty St Cincinnati OH 45202 Office Phone: 202-529-6800. Business E-Mail: jeremyh@myfranciscan.com.

HARRINGTON, JOHN TIMOTHY, retired lawyer; b. Madison, Wis., May 26, 1921; s. Cornelius Louis and Emily (Chisholm) H.; m. Deborah Reynolds, May 23, 1948; children— Elizabeth Chisholm, Samuel Parker, Hannah Quincy, Jane McRae BS, Harvard U., 1942, LL.B., 1948. Bar: Wis. 1949. Assoc. Quarles & Brady and predecessor firms, Milw., 1948-58, ptnr., 1958-91; ret., 1991—. Served to lt. comdr. USNR, 1942-46, PTO Home: 924 E Juneau Ave Milwaukee WI 53202-2748 Office: Quarles & Brady 411 E Wisconsin Ave Ste 2550 Milwaukee WI 53202-4497 Home Phone: 414-291-8885. Personal E-mail: jtharrington_4@sbcglobal.net.

HARRINGTON, MICHAEL FRANCIS, paper and packaging company executive; b. Butte, Mont., Aug. 6, 1940; s. Bernard Michael and Ruth Ann (Mullane) H.; m. Beverly Elaine Oswood, Dec. 30, 1967; children: Michael, Moria, Kevin. BS, Gonzaga U., Spokane, 1964, MBA, 1971; postgrad., Stanford U., 1985. Indsl. rels. rep. Kaiser Aluminum, Spokane, 1965-69; region indsl. rels. rep. Gen. Inst. Corp., Post Falls, Idaho, 1969-72; region employee rels.mgr. Boise Cascade Corp., Medford, Oreg., 1972-75, div. employee rels. mgr. Boise, Idaho, 1975-81, corp. dir. labor rels., 1981-91; v.p. human resources Smurfit Stone Container Corp. (formerly Jefferson Smurfit Corp.), St. Louis, 1991—. Mem. adv. bd. Gonzaga U. Sch. Bus., 1990—. Bd. dirs. Laumeier Sculpture Garden, St. Louis, 1995—, St. Joseph Sch. for Deaf, St. Louis, 1994—. Mem. Labor Policy Assn., Am. Forest and Paper Assn. (bd. dirs., chmn. employee rels. com. 1988—). Republican. Roman Catholic. Office: Jefferson Smurfit Corp 8182 Maryland Ave Saint Louis MO 63105-3769

HARRINGTON, NANCEY, state senator; m. Rex Harrington. Mem. Kans. State Senate Dist. 26, 1995—; vice chair fed. and state affairs com.; mem. judiciary com., transp. and tourism com. Home: PO Box 771017 Wichita KS 67277-1017

HARRIS, BILL, state legislator; b. Fork Mountain, Tenn., Sept. 1, 1934; m. Mary C. Harris; children: Billy M. Jr., Lonny E., Scott, Sherry. Student, U. Ariz. Auto dealer, bus. owner, Ashland, Ohio; mem. Ohio State Ho. Reps., Columbus, 1995-2000, Ohio Senate from 19th dist., Columbus, 2000—. Vice chmn. Buick at. Dealers' Coun. Trustee Samaritan Hosp., Ashland. Mem. Ohio Automobile Dealers Assn. (trustee), Ashland Area C. of C.

HARRIS, BOB, radio personality; Radio host Sta. KFGO-AM, Fargo, ND. Office: KFGO 1020 25th St S Fargo ND 58103

HARRIS, CHARLES ELMER, retired lawyer; b. Williamsburg, Iowa, Nov. 26, 1922; s. Charles Elmer and Loretto (Judge) H.; m. Marjorie Clark, Jul. 9, 1949 (div. June. 1969); m. Linda Rae Slaymaker, Nov. 25, 1992; children: Martha Ann, Julie Ann, Charles Elmer III. Student, St. Ambrose Coll., 1940-42; BSc, U. Iowa, 1946, JD, 1949. Bar: Iowa 1949. Mem. firm Brody, Parker, Roberts, Thoma & Harris, Des Moines, 1949-66, Herrick, Langdon, Belin Harris, Langdon & Helmick, Des Moines, 1966-78, Belin Harris Helmick, P.C., Des Moines, 1978-91, Belin, Harris, Lamson, McCormick, P.C., Des Moines, 1991-96; pvt. practice, Des Moines, 1997-99; ret., 1999. Lectr. tax schs., meetings, 1951, 55, 67, 69, 77-84, 90, 91. Comments editor: Iowa Law Rev., 1948-49. Bd. dirs. NCCJ, 1964-67, Iowa Bar Found., 1977-92, Iowa Law Sch. Found., 1977-90, United Way Found., 1981-89. Lt. (j.g.) USNR, 1943-46. Fellow Am. Coll. Trust and Estate Counsel; mem. ABA, Iowa Bar Assn. (bd. govs. 1973-80, Merit award 1980), Polk County Bar Assn. (pres. 1972-73), Polk County Jr. Bar Assn. (pres. 1952-53), Order of Coif, Sigma Chi, Delta Theta Phi. Roman Catholic. Home: 5141 Robertson Dr Des Moines IA 50312-2170 Personal E-mail: harris5141@aol.com.

HARRIS, CHARLIE J., JR., lawyer; b. Fayetteville, NC, July 25, 1956; BA, Tarkio Coll., 1978; JD, U. Mo., Kans. City, 1995. Bar: Mo. 1995, Kans. 1996, US Dist. Ct. (We. Dist. Mo.) 1995, US Dist. Ct. (Ea. Dist. Mo.), US Dist. Ct. (Dist. Kans.), US Dist. Ct. (No. Dist. Ill.), US Ct. Appeals (8th Cir.). Law clk. to Hon. Fernando J. Gaitan Jr. US Dist. Ct. (We. Dist. Mo.), 1995—97; atty. Shook, Hardy & Bacon LLP, Kans. City, Mo.; ptnr. Berkowitz Oliver Williams Shaw & Eisenbrandt LLP, Kans. City, Mo., 1999—. Recipient Pat Kelly Disting. Alumni award, U. Mo. at Kans. City Law Sch., 2005. Mem.: Mo. State Bar (pres.-elect 2006—07, pres. 2007—), Jackson County Bar, ABA. Office: Berkowitz Oliver Williams Shaw & Eisenbrandt LLP Ste 1200 2600 Grand Blvd Kansas City MO 64108 Office Phone: 816-627-0223. Office Fax: 816-561-1888. E-mail: charris@bowse-law.com.

HARRIS, CHRISTINE, dance company executive; b. Milw. Mktg. dir. Milw. Symphony Orch., 1984-90, head Arts in Cmty. Edn. program, 1990-95; with Inst. Music, Health and Edn., Mpls., 1996-97; exec. dir. Milw. Ballet, 1997—2002; pres. United Performing Arts Fund, 2002—. Office: United Performing Arts Fund 929 N Water St Milwaukee WI 53202

HARRIS, DONALD RAY, lawyer; b. Lake Preston, SD, Apr. 21, 1938; s. Raymond H. and Nona (Trousdale) H.; children: Beverly, Scott, Bradley, Lindi; m. Sharon K. Brown, Sept. 4, 1982. BA, State U. Iowa, 1959; JD, U. Iowa, 1961. Bar: Ill. 1963, U.S. Dist. Ct. (no. dist.) Ill. 1963, U.S. Ct. Appeals (3d, 4th, 6th, 7th, 9th and fed. cirs.) 1966-95, U.S. Dist. Ct. (we. dist.) Tex. 1989, U.S. Supreme Ct. 1977, U.S. Ct. Fed. Claims 1995, U.S. Dist. Ct. (ea. dist.) Wis. 1997. Assoc. Jenner & Block, Chgo., 1963-70, ptnr., 1970—. Lt. inf. U.S. Army, 1961-63. Mem. ABA, Ill. Bar Assn., Chgo. Bar Assn., Bar Assn. 7th Cir., Chgo. Coun. Lawyers, Am. Coll. Trial Lawyers, ITC Trail Lawyers Assn., Lawyers Club of Chgo. Office: Jenner & Block 330 N Wabash Chicago IL 60611-3586 Business E-Mail: dharris@jenner.com.

HARRIS, EARL L., state legislator; m. Donna J. Harris. Student, Purdue U., Ill. Inst. Tech. With Ky Package Store; rep. Dist. 12 Ind. Ho. of Reps., 1981-91, rep. Dist. 2, 1991—, mem. commerce com., govt. affairs com., aged and aging com., mem. ins. com., corp. and small bus. com.; chmn. ways and means com. Mem. AACP; past pres. Chgo. Black Coalition, Chgo. Homeowners Assn., Sunnyside Homeowners Assn.; chmn. African-Am. Leadership Forum; mem. N.W. Urban League. Home: 4114 Butternut St East Chicago IN 46312-2943

HARRIS, GENE T., school system administrator; m. Stanley E. Harris; 1 child, Wade Thomas. BA, Univ. Notre Dame; MA, Ohio State Univ.; PhD, Ohio Univ. Teacher Columbus Pub. Schools, prin., asst. supt., Ohio Dept. Edn.; dep. supt. Columbus Pub. Schools, 2000—01, supt., 2001—. Recipient Ingram award for outstanding leadership as a prin., Woman of Achievement, YWCA, 1991, African Am. Role Model Award, Phi Beta Sigma Frat., 2002, Cmty. Impact award, CMACAO, 2003, Outstading Accomplishments Award, The Cavaliers Club, Personal Achievement and Devoted Svc. Award, Nat. Coun. 100 Black Women-Columbus Chapter. Baptist. Office: Columbus Public Schools Office of Superintendent 270 E State St Columbus OH 43215 Office Phone: 614-365-5000.

HARRIS, GREGORY SCOTT, state representative; b. Denver, June 5, 1955; s. Herbert E. and Marcia Jean (Raabe) H. BS in Journalism with honors, U. Colo., 1977. Dir. public relations IMPACT Internat., Inc., Chgo., 1977-78; dir. edn. Nat. Home Furnishings Assn. (NHFA), Chgo., 1978-79, v.p. industry affairs, 1981-87, exec. v.p., chief operating officer, 1987-88; exec. dir. Interior Design Soc., Chgo., 1979-82; sec. NHFA Service Corp., 1986-87, v.p., 1986-87, pres., 1987-91, also bd. dirs.; pres. Open Hand: Chgo. Found., 1988-91; chief of staff Chgo. City Coun., 1992—2006; mem. Ill. Gen. Assembly, 2006—. Mem. Devel. Adv. Coun. City of Chgo., 1990-92; bd. dirs. Nonprofit Fin. Ctr.; mem. advocacy and pub. policy com. AFC, Ctr. Halsted Fin. com., 2003—. Trustee Design Found., Chgo., 1980-88; chmn. bd. dirs. AIDS Walk Found., 1990-91; bd. dirs. AIDS Legal Coun., 1992-94, Heartland Alliance for Human Needs and Human Rights; fin. dir. Simpson for Congress Com., 1991-92; mem. adv. bd. The Neofuturists, 2000. Recipient Leadership in Mktg. award Newspaper Pubs. Assn., 1983, Outstanding Young Chicagoan award Chgo. Jaycees, 1992, Outstanding Svc. to Immigrant and Refugee Cmty. award, 1996, Uptown C. of C. Ann. award, 1996, Voice of People Cmty. award, 1994, Equality award Human Rights Campaign, 1997, W. Clement Stone award, 1998, Biggest Heart award Hearts Found., 1999, Food For Life award, Florence Bezazian Citizenship award, 1999, Greater Chgo. Com. Humanitarian Efforts award, 2000, Inst. Cultural Affairs USA cert. of appreciation, 2000, Svc. award Cambodian Buddhist Assn., 2002, Chgo. House Pub. Svc. award, 2002, Hopeful Spirit award Names Project, 2005; named to City of Chgo. Hall of Fame, 1996. Office: 1967 W Montrose Chicago IL 60613 Office Phone: 773-348-3434. Business E-Mail: greg@gregharris.org.

HARRIS, IRVING, lawyer; b. Cin., May 23, 1927; s. Albert and Sadye H.; m. Selma Schottenstein, June 18, 1950; children: Jeffrey Philip, Jonathan Lindley (dec.), Lisa Ann Hollister. Undergrad. degree, U. Cin., 1948, LLB, 1951. Bar: Ohio 1951, US Dist. Ct. Ohio 1952, US Ct. Appeals (6th cir.) 1952, US Supreme Ct. 1960. Ptnr. Cors, Hair & Hartsock, 1954-81, Hartsock, Harris & Schneider, Cin., 1981-82, Porter, Wright, Morris & Arthur, Cin., 1982-89; ptnr. firm Harris, Harris, Field Schacter & Bardach Ltd., Cin., 1989-2000. Mem. Ohio Trade Mission to Orient, 1973, to Eng. and Germany, 1974; spl. counsel to Atty. Gen. Ohio, 1963-71; life mem. 6th Cir. Jud. Conf.; lectr. Advising, Oper. and Rebuilding the Financially Distressed Co., 1991; sponsor Disting. Visitor Series of Lectures, U. Cin. Coll. Law; bd. dirs. HRC Ltd. Partnership Hyatt Regency Cin. Mem. Ohio Devel. Financing Commn., 1974—84, vice-chmn., 1978—79; spl. counsel Ohio Atty. Gen.'s Office for the Police and Firemen's Disability and Pension Fund, 1994—97; trustee Skidmore Coll., 1976—90, trustee emeritus, 1991—, Big Bros.; trustee Cin. Symphony Orch., 1989—96; bd. overseers U. Cin. Law Sch., 1998—; arbitrator Ct. of Common Pleas of Hamilton County, 2001—; mediator US Dist. Ct. (so. dist.) Ohio Western divsn., 1999—2000. Mem. ABA (Sherman act com., sect. on antitrust and bus. law 1969-2000, subcoms. on derivative actions, bankruptcy, litigation of bus. and corp. litigation 1992-2000), Ohio Bar Assn., Cin. Bar Assn., Am. Judicature Soc., Potter Stewart Inn of Ct. (master of the bench), Queen City Club, Univ. Club, Cin. Tennis Club, Roaring Fork Country Club, Ocean Reef Club. Home: 18 Grandin Ln Cincinnati OH 45208-3365 Office: 3801 Carew Tower 441 Vine St Cincinnati OH 45202-2806

HARRIS, JOHN EDWARD, lawyer; b. Mpls., Nov. 16, 1936; s. John Law and Harriet Comilla (Hunt) H.; m. Ruth Wilder Esty, Aug. 26, 1958; children— Jeffrey Langdon, Stowe John Wilder, Benjamin Wood BA summa cum laude, Lawrence Coll., 1959; JD, Harvard U., 1962. Bar: Minn. 1962, U.S. Dist. Ct. Minn. 1962, U.S. Tax Ct. 1963. Assoc. Faegre & Benson, Mpls., 1962-69, ptnr., 1970-2000, head, trusts, estates and found. group, 1974-97. Trustee Ucross Found., Wyo., 1981-93, 97— Contbr. articles to Notre Dame Planning Inst., 1976, 78 Bd. dirs. Meth. Health Care Minn., 1986-93; chmn. Meth. Hosp., St. Louis Park, Minn., 1979-81, bd. dirs., 1993-94; pres. West Met. Hosp. trustee Coun., Mpls., 1980-81; chmn. Minn. Coun. on Founds., Mpls., 1985-88; bd. dirs. Twin Cities RISE!, 1995—. Mem. ABA (chmn. com. on charitable trusts, real property and trust law sect. 1973-77, exempt orgns. com., tax section 1991—), Minn. Bar Assn. (chmn. probate and trust law sect. 1979-80, mem. study com. Minn. Nonprofit Corps. 1986-91, mem. nonprofit corps. com. 1998—), Phi Beta Kappa Home: 713 Coventry Ln Minneapolis MN 55435-5653 Office: Faegre & Benson 2200 Wells Fargo Ctr 90 S 7th St Ste 2200 Minneapolis MN 55402-3901 E-mail: jharris@faegre.com, jharris331@excite.com.

HARRIS, JOSEPH MCALLISTER, retired chemist; b. Pontiac, Ill., July 27, 1929; s. Fred Gilbert and Catherine Marguerite (McAllister) H.; m. Margot Jeanette L'Hommedieu, Feb. 17, 1952; children: Timothy, Kaye, Paula, Bruce, Anne, Martha, Rebecca. BA, Blackburn Coll., Carlinville, Ill., 1952; postgrad., So. Ill. U., 1953-54, U. Ill., 1956-61. Technician Olin Ind., Inc., Energy, Ill., 1953-54; quality control staff Union Starch and Refining Co., Granite City, Ill., 1954; rsch. asst. Ill. State Geol. Survey, Urbana, 1954-61; chemist II Water Pollution Control Bd., Annapolis, Md., 1961-63; phys. chemist Ball Bros. Rsch., Inc., Muncie, Ind., 1963-66; engr. Radio Corp. Am., Marion, Ind., 1966-70; chemist OA Labs., Inc., Indpls., 1973-86, OA Labs. & Rsch., Inc., Indpls., 1986-93, cons., 1993—. Bd. dirs. Tri-County Hearing Assn. for Children, Muncie, 1967-70. Mem. Am. Chem. Soc., AAAS, Soc. Applied Spectroscopy. Republican. Presbyterian. Avocations: gardening, camping. Home: 800 E Washington St Muncie IN 47305-2533 Personal E-mail: berrijoe@aol.com.

HARRIS, JULES ELI, medical educator, physician, clinical scientist, administrator; b. Toronto, Ont., Can., Oct. 12, 1934; came to U.S., 1978; s. George Joseph and Ida Harris; m. Josephine Leikin; children: Leah, Daniel, Adam, Sheira, Robin, Naomi. MD, U. Toronto, 1959. Intern, then resident Toronto (Can.) Gen. Hsp., 1959-65; asst. prof. medicine M.D. Anderson Hosp. Med. Ctr., Houston, 1966-69; prof. medicine U. Ottawa (Ont.), 1969-78; prof. medicine, prof. immunology Rush Med. Coll., Rush U., Chgo., 1978—; dir. Rush Cancer Ctr., 1986-92; dir. Rush sect. med. oncology, 1978-93. Mem. gov.'s adv. bd. for cancer control State of Ill., 1988—; chmn. bd. trustees Ill. Cancer Coun., Chgo., 1987-88; chmn. immunology devices panel FDA, 1995—. Author: Immunology of Malignant Disease, 1975; editor Prostaglandin Inhibitors in Tumor Immunology and Immunotherapy, 1994. Mem. internat. bd. govs. Ben Gurion U. of Negev, Beer-Sheva, Israel, 1986-95; pres. bd., chmn. sci. adv. com. Israel Cancer Rsch. Fund, Chgo. Fellow ACP, Royal Coll. Physicians Can. (cert. in internal medicine); mem. Am. Soc. Clin. Oncology (chmn. pub. rels. com. 1987-89), Univ. Club, Alpha Omega Alpha. Jewish. Office: Rush-Presbyn-St Luke's Med Ctr 1725 W Congress Pkwy Chicago IL 60612-3809

HARRIS, K. DAVID, senior state supreme court justice; b. Jefferson, Iowa, July 29, 1927; s. Orville William and Jessie Heloise (Smart) H.; m. Madonna Theresa Coyne, Sept. 4, 1948; children: Jane, Julia, Frederick. BA, U. Iowa, 1949, JD, 1951. Bar: Iowa 1951, U.S. Dist Ct (so. dist.) Iowa, 1958. Sole practice Harris & Harris, Jefferson, 1951-62; dist. judge 16th Judicial Dist., Iowa, 1962-72; justice Iowa Supreme Ct., Des Moines, 1972-99, sr. justice, 1999—; ret., 2005. Served with U.S. Army, 1944-46, PTO. Mem. VFW, Am. Legion, Rotary. Roman Catholic. Avocation: poetry. Office: Iowa Supreme Ct State Capitol Bldg Des Moines IA 50319-0001 Office Phone: 515-386-4321.

HARRIS, LARRY, professional sports team executive; s. Del Harris; children: Zachary, Janaya. Grad. in Math., Eastern N.Mex. U. Actuary Wyatt Corp., Dallas; scout/video coord. Milw. Bucks, 1988—96, dir. scouting, 1996—98, dir. player pers., 1998—2001, asst. gen. mgr., 2001—03, gen. mgr., 2003—08.*

HARRIS, NEIL, historian, educator; b. Bklyn., 1938; s. Harold and Irene Harris. AB, Columbia U., NYC, 1958; BA, Cambridge U., Eng., 1960; PhD, Harvard U., 1965. From instr. to asst. prof. history Harvard U., Cambridge, Mass., 1965-69; assoc. prof. U. Chgo., 1969-72, prof., 1972-90, Preston and Sterling Morton prof. of history, 1990—, dir. Nat. Humanities Inst., 1975-77, chmn. dept. history, 1985-88. Mem. adv. bd. Temple Hoyne Buell Ctr., Columbia, 1984-89; mem. adv. com. dept. architecture Art Inst. Chgo., 1982—; mem. Smithsonian Council, 1978-84, chmn. 1984-92; visiting prof. Yale U., 1974; dir. d'etudes Ecole des Hautes Etudes en Sci. Sociales, Paris, 1985. Author: Artist in American Society, 1966, Humbug: The Art of P.T. Barnum, 1970, Cultural Excursions, 1990, Building Lives, 1999, Chicago Apartments, 2004; editor: Land of Contrasts, 1970, the WPA Guide to Illinois, 1983; bd. editors New Eng. Quar., 1982—, Winterthur Portfolio, 1978-80, 85-88, Frederick Law Olmsted Papers, 1973, Am. Scholar, 1994-2000; mem. editorial adv. bd. History Today, 1978-86. Trustee H.F. DuPont Winterthur (Del.) Mus., 1978-87, Newberry Libr.; mem. Nat. Mus. Svcs. Bd., Washington, 1977-84; vis. com. J. Paul Getty Mus., 1995—; bd. dirs. Nat. Mus. Am. History, 1997-2000, Terra Found. for Arts, 2002—. Am. Coun. Learned Socs. fellow, 1972-73, NEH fellow, 1980-81, Guggenheim fellow, 1999-2000; Getty scholar, 1991, Nat. Mus. Am. Art scholar, 1995-96; Boucher lectr. Johns Hopkins U., 1971, Cardozo lectr. Yale U., 1974, Tandy lectr. Whitney Mus. Am. Art, 1982, Kemper lectr. Pitzer Coll., 1980, Buell lectr. Columbia U., 1993; recipient Joseph Henry medal Smithsonian Instn., 1991. Fellow Am. Acad. Arts and Scis.; mem. Am. Antiquarian Soc., Am. Coun. Learned Socs. (vice chmn. N.Y. 1978-89, chmn. 1989-93), Phi Beta Kappa (senator united chpts. 1985-97, vis. lectr. 1985-86). Home: 4950 S Chicago Beach Dr Chicago IL 60615-3207 Office: U Chgo Dept History 1126 E 59th St Chicago IL 60637-1580 Office Phone: 773-702-8380. Business E-Mail: nh16@uchicago.edu.

HARRIS, PATTI B., telecommunications executive; Pres., CEO Harris-McBurney Co., Jackson, Mich. Office: Harris McBurney Co PO Box 267 Jackson MI 49204-0267 Fax: 517-787-6809. E-mail: info@hmcb.com.

HARRIS, PAUL N., lawyer; BA, U. Chgo., 1980; JD, Stanford Law Sch., 1983. Assoc. to ptnr.-in-charge Thompson Hine, LLP, Cleve., 1983—88, with, 1997—2003; sr. counsel Revco DS Inc. (now CVS), 1988—97; exec. v.p., sec., gen. counsel, mem. mgmt. com., mem. exec. coun. Keycorp, Cleve., 2003—. Trustee, past pres. bd. trustees Friends of Cleve. Sch. of the Arts; trustee Hawken Sch., Cuyahoga Cmty. Coll. Found., City Club Cleve.; mem. vis. com. Cleve.-Marshall Coll. Law. Mem.: Cleve. Bar Assn., Soc. Corp. Secs. and Governance Profls. Office: Keycorp 127 Public Sq Cleveland OH 44114-1306 Office Fax: 216-689-0840.

HARRIS, PHILLIP H., lawyer; BS, Ind. U.; JD, Georgetown U. Solicitor US Catholic Conf.; assoc. counsel Evangelical Lutheran Church Am., Chgo., 1995—96, gen. counsel, 1996—, chmn. elections com. Mem.: Md. Bar Assn., DC Bar Assn. Office: Evangelical Lutheran Church 8765 W Higgins Rd Chicago IL 60631 E-mail: phil.harris@elca.org.

HARRIS, SUSAN V., lawyer; b. 1961; BA, Oberlin Coll., 1983; JD, U. Chgo., 1992. Bar: Ill. 1992. With Sidley Austin Brown & Wood, Chgo., ptnr., 2000—. Mem.: ABA. Office: Sidley Austin Brown and Wood Bank One Plz 10 S Dearborn St Chicago IL 60603

HARRIS, THOMAS L., public relations executive; b. Dayton, Ohio, Apr. 18, 1931; s. James and Leona (Blum) H.; m. JoAnn K. Karch, Apr. 14, 1957; children: James Harris, Theodore Harris. BA, U. Mich., 1953; MA, U. Chgo., 1956. Exec. v.p. Daniel J. Edelman Inc., Chgo., 1957-67; v.p. pub. rels. Neddham Harper & Steers, Chgo., 1967-72; pres. Foote Cone & Belding Pub. Rels., Chgo., 1973-78, Golin-Harris Communications Inc., Chgo., 1978-89, also vice chmn.; adj. prof. Medill Sch. Journalism, Northwestern U., Evanston, Ill., 1987—2002; mng. ptnr. Thomas L. Harris & Co., Highland Pk., Ill., 1992—. Served with U.S. Army, 1953-55. Mem. Public Relations Soc. Am. (Gold Anvil award 2000). Office: Thomas L Harris & Co 600 Central Ave Highland Park IL 60035-3211 Office Phone: 847-266-1020. E-mail: ttlhco@aol.com.

HARRIS, YOLANDA, newscaster; b. Columbus, Ohio; married. BS in Broadcast Journalism, Bowling Green U. Reporter Call & Post Newspaper, Columbus, Ohio; with promotions, Kids Club dept. Sta. WSYX/WTTE-TV, reporter, 1996—99, weekend anchor, 1999—2002, main anchor, 2002—. Office: WSYX/WTTE-TV 1261 Dublin Rd Columbus OH 43215 E-mail: yharris@sbgnet.com.

HARRIS, ZELEMA M., academic administrator; b. Newton County, Tex., Jan. 12, 1940; d. James Robert and Gertrude Violet (Swearingen) Marshall; m. Manuel Holloway. BS, Prairie View A&M, 1961; MEd, U. Kans., 1972, EdD, 1976. U. Asst. dir. urban affairs U. Kans., Lawrence, 1970-72, asst. dir. Centennial Coll., 1970-72, dir. supportive edn. svcs., 1970-72; coord. curriculum evaluation Met. Community Coll., Kansas City, Mo., 1976-77, dir. curriculum evaluation, 1977-78, dir. edn. opportunity ctr., 1978-80, dir. dist. svcs., 1980; pres. Pioneer Community Coll., Kansas City, 1980-87, Pen Valley Community Coll., Kansas City, 1987-90, Parkland Coll., Champaign, Ill., 1990—. Co-author: Evaluation and Program Planning, 1978. Recipient Protestant award Kansas City Coun., 1987, Kansas City Spirit award Gillis Ctr. of Kansas City and Kansas City Star, 1987; named one of Women of Conscience, Panel of Am. Women, 1987. Mem. Nat. Inst. for Leadership Devel. Am. Assn. Women in Community Colls. (adv. bd.), Am. Assn. Community and Jr. Colls. (bd. dirs., Coun. on Black Am. Affairs), Black Women in Higher Edn., N. Cen. Assn. Colls. and Schs. (bd. dirs. N. Cen. region). Home: 7 Briar Hill Cir Champaign IL 61822-6137 Office: Parkland Coll Office of the President 2400 W Bradley Ave Champaign IL 61821-1806

HARRISON, DAVID D., corporate financial executive; BA, Marietta Coll., Ohio; MBA in Fin. Mgmt., Ohio U., Athens. CMA. With Borg-Warner, Gen. Elec.; CFO Coltec Industries, Pentair, Inc., 1994—96, exec. v.p. and CFO, 1996—. Office: Pentair Inc Ste 800 5500 Wayzata Blvd Golden Valley MN 55416

HARRISON, DONALD CAREY, academic administrator, cardiologist, educator; b. Blount County, Ala., Feb. 24, 1934; s. Walter Carey and Sovola (Thompson) H.; m. Laura Jane McAnnally, July 24, 1955; children: Douglas, Elizabeth, Donna Marie. BS in Chemistry, Birmingham So. Coll., 1954; MD, U. Ala., 1958. Diplomate Am. Bd. Internal Medicine (cardiovascular disease). Intern, asst. resident Peter Bent Brigham Hosp., 1958-60; fellow in cardiology Harvard U., 1961, NIH, 1961-63; mem. faculty Stanford U. Med. Sch., 1963-86, chief div. cardiology, 1967-86, prof. medicine, 1971-86; chief cardiology Stanford U. Hosp., 1967-86, William G. Irwin prof. cardiology, 1972-86; sr. v.p., provost for health affairs U. Cin. Med. Ctr., 1986—2003; sr. v.p., provost for health affairs, emeritis U. Cin. Med. Ctr.; prof. medicine, cardiology U. Cin. Coll. Medicine; CEO U. Cin. Med. Ctr., 1987—2003. Cons. to local hosps., industry and govt.; mng. dir. Charter Life Sci. Venture Fund; bd. dir. Med. Edn. and Consultation, AtriCure Med., Uterine Muscle Dysfunction, Inc., Kendle Industries, Entero Medics, Inc., Am. Heart Assn., U. Cin. Physicians. Mem. editorial bd. Internat. Jour. Clin. Practice, 1993—; mem. editorial bd. Drugs, 1980—, Am. Jour. Cardiology, 1984—; contbr. articles to med. jours., chpts. to books. Served with USPHS, 1961-63. Fellow Interam. Soc. Cardiology (v.p. 1980-86), Am. Coll. Cardiology (mem. chmn., v.p. 1972-73, sec. 1969-70, trustee 1972-78), Am. Heart Assn. (fellow coun. circulation, clin. cardiology and basic sci., chmn. program com. 1972-76, nat. chmn. publs. com. 1976-81, pres.-elect 1980-81, pres. 1982-83); mem. ACP, Am. Soc. Clin. Investigation, Am. Fedn. Clin. Rsch., Am. Assn. Physicians, Assn. U. Cardiologists, Am. Clin. and Climatol Assn., Brit. Cardiac Soc., Acad. Medicine Cin., Assn. Acad. Health Ctrs. (past chmn.). Home: 9250 Old Indian Hill Rd Cincinnati OH 45243-3438 Office: U Cin Med Ctr ML 0669 3130 Highland Ave Cincinnati OH 45267-0669 Office Phone: 513-558-6397. Business E-Mail: don.harrison@uc.edu, don@clsvc.com.

HARRISON, HOLLY A., lawyer; b. 1958; BA, U. Denver, 1981; JD, Boston U., 1984. Bar: Mass. 1984, Ill. 1985. Law clk. to Hon. Raymond J. Pettine, U.S. Dist. Judge Dist. R.I., 1984—85; with Sidley Austin Brown & Wood, Chgo., 1985—, ptnr., 1992—. Office: Sidley Austin Brown & Wood Ste 900 1 S Dearborn St Chicago IL 60603-2310

HARRISON, JEREMY THOMAS, dean, law educator; b. San Francisco, Dec. 23, 1935; s. James Gregory and Agnes Johanna (Patrick) H.; m. Roseanne E. Thomas, Dec. 29, 1962 (dec. Oct. 1983); children: James, Amelia, Roseanne, Jeremy, Alexandra, Nadya, Rachel; m. Laura Ellen Marrack, Apr. 28, 1990; children: Robert, Peter, Paul, Philip, John. BS, U. San Francisco, 1957, JD, 1960; LLM, Harvard U., 1962. Bar: Calif. 1961, Hawaii 1987. Assoc. Brobeck, Phleger & Harrison, San Francisco, 1960-61; law clk. to assoc. justice U.S. Ct. Claims, Washington, 1962-63; lectr. law U. Ghana, Accra, 1963-64, U. Ife, Ibadan, Nigeria, 1964-66; prof. law U. San. Francisco, 1966-85; dean Sch. Law U. Hawaii, Honolulu, 1985-94; dean Mich. State U. Coll. Law, East Lansing, 1996-98, prof. law, 1998—. Vis. prof. law Haile Sellassie I U., Addis Ababa, Ethiopia, 1971-74, U. Hawaii, 1977-79; Elips Disting. prof. law Gadjah Mada U., Yogyakarta, Indonesia, 1995-96. Author: Cases and Materials on Evidence, Africa, 1967, Cases and Materials on Ethiopian Civil Procedure, 1974. Counsel citizen's panel Hawaii's Jud. Adminstrn., Honolulu, 1985-86; bd. dirs. Straub Found., Honolulu; pres. Pacific Health Rsch. Inst., Honolulu, 1993-95. Mem. ABA, Am. Bar Found., Calif Bar Assn., Hawaii Bar Assn. Office: Mich State U Coll Law 465 Law College Bldg East Lansing MI 48824-1300 Business E-Mail: jharriso@law.msu.edu.

HARRISON, JOSEPH HORATIO, JR., lawyer; b. Evanston, Ill., Dec. 27, 1950; s. Joseph Horatio Sr. and Grace (Cobean) H.; m. Josephine Anne Mineo, Aug. 25, 1973; children: Joseph Horatio III, Marc E.M., Eleanor Grace, Theresa Maria, Thomas Andrew. AB, Princeton Univ., 1973; MA, Northwestern Univ., 1976, JD cum laude, 1979. Tchr. English York High Sch., Elmhurst, Ill., 1973-76; assoc. Sidley Austin Brown & Wood LLP, Chgo., 1979-82, ptnr., fin. practice, 1987—. Founding v.p., sec. & gen. counsel Nat. Futures Assn., 1982—87. Mem. ABA, Ill. State Bar Assn., Chgo. Bar Assn. (chmn. futures com. 1987-88), Futures Industry Assn. (assoc., dir. 1988-90), Univ. Club. Office: Sidley Austin LLP One S Dearborn St Chicago IL 60603 Office Phone: 312-853-7043. Office Fax: 312-853-7036. Business E-Mail: jharrison@sidley.com.

HARRISON, JOSEPH WILLIAM, state legislator; b. Chgo., Sept. 10, 1931; s. Roy J. and Gladys V. (Greenman) H.; m. Ann Hovey Gillespie, June 9, 1956; children: Holly Ann, Tracy Jeanne, Thomas Joseph, Amy Beth, Kitty Lynne, Christy Jayne. BS, U.S. Naval Acad., 1956; postgrad., Ind. U. Law Sch., 1968-70. Asst. to pres. Harrison Steel Castings Co., Attica, Ind., 1960-64, sales rsch. engr., 1964-66, asst. sec., 1966-69, sec., 1969-71, v.p., 1971-84, dir., 1968-74; mem. Ind. Senate, 1966—, majority leader, 1980—. Mem. Attica Consol. Sch. Bd., 1964-66, pres., 1966-67. Served with USN, 1956-60. Mem. Am. Legion, Sigma Chi. Lodges: Elks, Eagles. Republican. Methodist. Home: 504 E Pike St Attica IN 47918-1524 Office: PO Box 409 Attica IN 47918-0409 also: State Senate State Capitol 200 W Washington St Indianapolis IN 46204-2728

HARRISON, LOUIS S., lawyer; b. Evanston, Ill., 1959; BA magna cum laude in Math., Colgate U., 1981; MBA with honors in Fin., U. Chgo., 2002; JD with high honors, Duke U., 1984. Bar: Ill. 1984. Ptnr.-in-charge Lord, Bissell & Brook Wealth Preservation Grp.; ptnr. Harrison & Held, LLP, Chgo. Adj. prof. law DePaul U. Law Sch., Ill. Kent Sch. Law, Northwestern U. Contbr. articles to profl. publs.; sr. editor: Duke-Alaska Law Rev., 1983—84; co-author: Sorting Out Life's Complexities: What You Really Need to Know about Taxes, Wills, Trusts, Powers of Attys. and Health Care Decisions, 1992, Ill. Estate Planning Forms and Commentary. Named one of Top 100 Attys., Worth mag., 2005. Fellow: Am. Coll. Trust and Estate Counsel; mem.: Chgo. Estate Planning Coun., ABA, Ill. State Bar Assn., Chgo. Bar Assn. (mem. fed. taxation com., past chair estate and gift tax divsn., mem. trust law com.). Office: Harrison & Held LLP 333 W Wacker Dr Chicago IL 60606-1218 Office Phone: 312-332-5440. Office Fax: 866-456-8494. E-mail: lharrison@harrisonheld.com.

HARRISON, MARVIN, professional football player; b. Phila., Aug. 25, 1972; s. Linda Harrison; 1 child, Marvin Jr. BS in Retailing, Syracuse U., NY, 1995. Wide receiver Indpls. Colts, 1996—. Named to Am. Football Conf. Pro Bowl Team, 1999—2006, NFL All-Pro Team, 1999—2007. Achievements include holding NFL record for most receptions in one season (143), 2002; leading NFL in receptions, 2000, 2002, recieving yards, 1999, 2002; being the only player in NFL history to have four consecutive 100 or more reception seasons. Office: Indpls Colts 7001 W 56th St Indianapolis IN 46254

HARRISON, MICHAEL GREGORY, judge; b. Lansing, Mich., Aug. 4, 1941; s. Gus and Jean D. (Fuller) H.; m. Deborah L. Dunn, June 17, 1972; children: Abigail Ann, Adam Christopher, Andrew Stephen. AB, Albion Coll., Mich., 1963; JD, U. Mich., 1966; postgrad., Hague Acad. of Internat. Law, George Washington U. Bar: Mich. 1966, U.S. Dist. Ct. (ea. and we. dists.) Mich. 1967, U.S. Ct. Appeals (6th cir.). Asst. pros. atty. County of Ingham, Lansing, 1968-70, corp. counsel, 1970-76; judge 30th Jud. Cir. State of Mich., Lansing, 1976-2000; chief judge 30th Jud. Cir. State of Mich., Lansing, 1980-91; judge Ct. of Claims, 1979-2000; of counsel Foster, Swift, Collins and Smith, Lansing, 2000—. Counsel Capital Region Airport Authority, Lansing, 1970-76, Ingham Med. Ctr., Lansing, 1970-76; chmn. Ingham County Bldg. Authority, Mason, Mich., 1971-76; adj. prof. Thomas M. Cooley Law Sch., Lansing, 1976—. Editor Litigation Control, 1996; contbr. chpt. to Michigan Municipal Law, Actions of Governing Bodies, 1980; contbr. articles to profl. jours. Mem. shared vision steering com. United Way-C. of C.; mem. adv. bd. Hospice of Lansing; pres. Greater Lansing Urban League, 1974-76, Lansing Symphony Assn., 1974-76; chmn. Mid. Mich. chpt. ARC, Lansing, 1984-86; bd. dirs., sec. St. Lawrence Hosp., Lansing, 1980-88; bd. dirs. ARC Gt. Lakes Regional Blood Svcs., 1991-95, Lansing 2000, 1987-2000, Greater Lansing Symphony, 2002-, Mich. Supreme Ct. Hist. Soc.; mem. exec. bd. Chief Okemos coun. Boy Scouts Am., pres., 2003-05; mem. criminal justice adv. com. Olivet Coll.; hon. bd. dirs. Lansing Area Safety Coun.; mem. State Bar Bd. Commrs., 1993-96; chair State Bar Rep. Assembly; mem. felony sentencing guidelines steering com., chmn. caseflow mgmt. coordinating com., mem. juror use and mgmt. task force Mich. Supreme Ct.; mem. Mich. Supreme Ct. Hist. Soc.; mem. Mayor's Lansing Metro Regional Initiative. Recipient Disting. Citizens award Boy Scouts Am., Disting. Vol. award Ingham County Bar Assn., award of judicial excellence ABA, Disting. Alumni award Albion Coll., Mich. Super Lawters; named to Best Lawyers in Am., fellow, Nat. Conf. State Trial Judges. Fellow: Mich. Bar Found., Am. Bar Found.; mem.: ABA (Fund for Justice and Edn. coun. 2003—06, coun. mem. judicial divsn., coun. mem. tort and ins. practice sect., award of jud. excellence), Mich. State Bar Found. (pres. 1991—2000), Nat. Conf. State Trial Judges (exec. com. 1991—94, vice chmn. 1995—96, chmn. 1997—98), Mich. Judges Assn. (treas. 1991, sec. 1992, 2d v.p. 1993, 1st v.p. 1994, pres. 1995), Mich. State U. Am. Inn of Ct. (pres. 2001—03, master), Am. Judicature Soc. (bd. dirs. 1996—2002), Rotary Club, Lansing (pres. 2001—02), Country Club, Lansing. Avocations: skiing, golf, tennis, travel, photography. Office: 313 S Washington Sq Lansing MI 48933-2193 Office Phone: 517-371-8162. Business E-Mail: mharrison@fosterswift.com.

HARRISON, MICHAEL JAY, physicist, researcher; b. Chgo., Aug. 20, 1932; s. Nathan J. and Mae (Nathan) H.; m. Ann Tukey, Sept. 1, 1970. AB, Harvard, 1954; MS, U. Chgo., 1956, PhD, 1960. Fulbright fellow and H. Van Loon fellow in theoretical physics U. Leiden, Netherlands, 1954-55; NSF fellow U. Chgo., 1957-59; research fellow math. physics U. Birmingham, Eng., 1959-61; asst. prof. Mich. State U., East Lansing, 1961-63, assoc. prof., 1963-68, prof., 1968—, faculty grievance officer, 1972-73, dean Lyman Briggs Coll., 1973-81, adj. prof. epidemiology, 1993—, adj. prof. pediatrics and human devel., 2004—. Vis. research physicist Inst. Theoretical Physics, U. Calif., Santa Barbara, 1980-81; with Air Force Cambridge Research Center, summer 1953, M.I.T. Lincoln Lab., summer 1954, RCA Sarnoff Lab., summers 1961-63; physicist Westinghouse Labs., summer 1956; cons. RCA Lab., 1961-64, United Aircraft Co., 1964-66, U.K. Atomic Energy Authority, Harwell Lab., summer 1960, Thailand project in Bangkok, Mich. State U.-AID, summer 1968; vis. research affiliate theoretical biology and biophysics, Los Alamos Nat. Lab., 1987-88. Contbr. articles to U.S., fgn. profl. jours. Am. Council on Edn. fellow U. Calif., Los Angeles, 1970-71. Fellow Am. Phys. Soc.; mem. AAUP (chpt. treas. 1966-67), N.Y. Acad. Scis., Harvard Club of Ctrl. Mich. (pres. 1988-93), Rotary, B'nai B'rith, Phi Beta Kappa, Sigma Xi. Jewish. Avocations: hiking, travel, photography. Home: 277 Maplewood Dr East Lansing MI 48823-4746 Office: Mich State U Physics Dept East Lansing MI 48824 Home Phone: 517-337-7007; Office Phone: 517-355-9200 2205. E-mail: harrison@pa.msu.edu.

HARRISON, MOSES W., II, state supreme court chief justice; b. Collinsville, Ill., Mar. 30, 1932; m. Sharon Harrison; children: Luke, Clarence. BA, Colo. Coll.; LLB, Washington U., St. Louis. Bar: Ill. 1958, Mo. 1958. Pvt. practice, 1958-73; judge 3d Jud. Cir., Ill., 1973-79, 5th Dist. Appellate Ct., Ill., 1979-92; chief justice Ill. Supreme Ct., 1992—2003. Mem. ABA, Am. Judicature Soc., Ill. State Bar Assn. (former bd. govs.), Madison County Bar Assn. (former pres.), Tri-City Bar Assn., Met. St. Louis Bar Assn., Justinian Soc.

HARRISON, PATRICK WOODS, lawyer; b. St. Louis, July 14, 1946; s. Charles William and Carolyn (Woods) Harrison; m. Rebecca Tout, Dec. 23, 1967; children: Heather Ann, Heath Aaron. BS, Ind. U., 1968, JD, 1972. Bar: Ind. 1973, U.S. Dist. Ct. (so. dist.) Ind. 1973, U.S. Supreme Ct. 1977, U.S. Dist. Ct. Nebr. 1982. Assoc. Goltra, Cline, King & Beck, Columbus, Ind., 1972-73; ptnr. Goltra & Harrison, Columbus, 1973-78; pvt. practice Columbus, 1979-80; ptnr. Cline, King, Beck and Harrison, Columbus, 1980-85, Beck Harrison (formerly Beck, Harrison & Dalmbert), Columbus, 1985—. Ind. Nominating Commn. nominee Ind. Supreme Ct., 1984. With US Army, 1968—70. Fellow: Ind. Trial Lawyers Assn. (bd. dirs. 1984, emertitus dir. 1999, Co-Trial Lawyer of the Yr. 1999); mem.: Am. Trial Lawyers Assn. Republican. Baptist. Avocation: golf. Home: 14250 W Mount Healthy Rd Columbus IN 47201-9309 Office: Beck Harrison 320 Franklin St Columbus IN 47201-6732 Office Phone: 812-372-8858. Personal E-mail: pharrison@hughes.net. Business E-Mail: woodyh@beckharrison.com.

HARROLD, BERNARD, lawyer; b. Wells County, Ind., Feb. 5, 1925; s. James Delmer and Marie (Mounsey) H.; m. Kathleen Walker, Nov. 26, 1952; children— Bernard James, Camilla Ruth, Renata Jane. Student, Biarritz Am. U., 1945; AB, Ind. U., 1949, LLB, 1951. Bar: Ill. 1951. Since practiced in, Chgo.; assoc., then mem. firm Kirkland, Ellis, Hodson, Chaffetz & Masters, 1951-67; sr. ptnr. Wildman, Harrold, Allen & Dixon, 1967—. Note editor: Ind. Law Jour, 1950-51; contbr. articles to profl. jours. Served with AUS, 1944-46, ETO. Fellow Am. Coll. Trial Lawyers, Acad. Law Alumni Fellows Ind. U. Sch. Law; mem. ABA, Ill. Bar Assn. (chmn. evidence program 1970), Chgo. Bar Assn, Lawyers Club, Univ. Club, Order of Coif, Phi Beta Kappa, Phi Eta Sigma. Home: 809 Locust St Winnetka IL 60093-1821 Office: Wildman Harrold Allen & Dixon 225 W Wacker Dr Fl 30 Chicago IL 60606-1229

HARSDORF, SHEILA ELOISE, state legislator, farmer; b. St. Paul, July 25, 1956; d. Ervin Albert and Eloise Vivian (Sodergren) H.; m. Vernon Clark Bailey, Nov. 18, 1989. BS in Animal Sci., U. Minn., 1978; grad., Wis. Rural Leadership Program, 1986. Loan officer Prodn. Credit Assn. River Falls, Wis., 1978-80; dairy farmer, Beldenville, Wis., 1980-88; mem. Wis. Assembly from 30th dist., Madison, 1988-98, Wis. Senate from 10th dist., Madison, 2001—. Part-time dairy farmer; mem. adv. coun. for small bus., agrl. and labor Fed. Res. Bank Minn., Mpls., 1988; mem. Wis. Agrl. Stblzn. and Conservation svc. Com., 1987-88. Mem., chairwoman Pierce County Dairy Promotion Com., 1986; mem. Congressman's Adv. Coun. on Agr., 1988—, First Covenant Ch., River Falls. Mem. Wis. Farm Bur. (co-treas. 1982-85, Discussion Meet winner 1986), Wis. Holstein Assn., Dairy Shrine. Republican. Home: N6627 County Rd E River Falls WI 54022-4036

HARSHMAN, RICHARD R., manufacturing executive; b. Apr. 22, 1947; BS, Fordham U, Bronx, NY. Lucy Ellen/F & F Labs.; v.p. sales, mktg. Tootsie Roll; CEO, pres. Storck USA, Storck North America, 1985-98; CEO Favorite Brands Internat., Lincolnshire, Ill., 1998—.

HART, CARL KISER, JR., lawyer; b. Madison, Wis., Oct. 30, 1955; s. Carl Kiser Sr. and Eleanor Katie (Pauls) H.; m. Barbara Ann Brooks, May 28, 1980; children: Elizabeth Ann, Daniel Keith. BA, U. Wis., 1977; JD, U. Tulsa, 1981. Bar: Okla. 1981, Nebr. 1989, Wis. 1991. Asst. dist. atty. Okla.'s 16th Dist., Poteau, 1981-82, Okla.'s 26th Dist., Woodward, 1983-87, 1st asst. dist. atty., 1987-90; dep. county atty. Seward County, Nebr., 1991—98, Butler County, 1991—95, atty., 1996—2006; dep. county atty. Colfax County, Nebr., 2000—06, Platte County, Columbus, Nebr., 2007—. Trustee Woodward County Law Libr., 1987-90; bd. mem. Butler County Arts Coun., 1994-96, Butler County Cmty. Coalition, 1999—, Ctr. for Survivors, 1999-2005; trumpeter Columbus Jazz Orch., Seward Mcpl. Band, Concordia U. Cmty. Band. Mem. Okla. Bar Assn., Nebr. Bar Assn., Wis. Bar Assn., Rotary, Masons. Methodist. Avocation: trumpet playing. Home: 1209 N 4th St David City NE 68632-1105 Office: Platte County Attys Office Platte County Courthouse Columbus NE 68601 Office Phone: 402-563-4903.

HART, DANIEL, orchestra executive; Bassist Peoria (Ill.) Symphony Orch., Colo. Springs (Colo.) Symphony, Baton Rouge Symphony Orch.; exec. dir. Va. Symphony Orch., Norfolk, 1994-98, Columbus (Ohio) Symphony Orch., 1998—. Office: Columbus Symphony Orch 55 E State St Columbus OH 43215-4203

HART, GEORGE ZAVEN, state legislator; b. Detroit, May 13, 1927; AA, Henry Ford C.C.; BA, Wayne State U., 1952. City councilman, Dearborn, Mich., 1957-71; county commr. Wayne County, Mich., 1972-78; mem. from dist. 10 Mich. Senate, Lansing, 1978-82, 87-94, mem. from dist. 6, 1995—. Chmn. Com. on Transp. & Tourism, Spl. Com. on Sports Violence Mich. State Senate; mem. Mcpl. & Election Com., Consumer Affairs Com., State Affairs, Transp. & Tourism Com., Local Govt. & Vet. Com., Energy Com., Farming Agribus. and Food Sys. Com., Families, Mental Health and Human Svcs. com. Mich. State Senate; mem. joint commn. Adminstrv. Rules. Recipient Steering Wheel award Automobile Clubh, 1981. Mem. Am. Legion, Mason, Moose, Kiwanis, Goodfellows, Pulaski Civic Orgn. Address: 4200 Roemer St Dearborn MI 48126-3421 Office: 1015 Farnum Bldg PO Box 30036 Lansing MI 48909-7536

HART, JAMES WARREN, retired athletic administrator, professional football player; b. Evanston, Ill., Apr. 29, 1944; s. George Ezrie and Marjorie Helen (Karsten) H.; m. Mary Elizabeth Mueller, June 17, 1967; children: Bradley James and Suzanne Elizabeth (twins), Kathryn Anne BS, So. Ill. U., 1967. Quarterback St. Louis Cardinals Profl. Football Team, 1966—83, Washington Redskins Profl. Football Team, 1984; radio sports personality Sta. KMOX, 1975—84, Sta. KXOK, 1985—86; sports analyst Sta. WGN Radio, Chgo., 1985—89; athletics dir. So. Ill. U., Carbondale, 1988—99, assoc. chancellor for external affairs, 1999—2000; head coach So. Ill. Spl. Olympics, 1973—90, Mo. Spl. Olympics, 1976—78; co-owner Dierdorf & Hart's Steak House (2 locations), St. Louis; spl. asst. to vice chancellor for instnl. devel. So. Ill. U., 1999—2002. Co-author: The Jim Hart Story, 1977. Gen. campaign chmn. St. Louis Heart Assn., 1974-88; hon. chmn. St. Louis Sr. Olympics, 1986-88 Named Most Valuable Player in Nat. Football Conf., 1974, Most Valuable Player with St. Louis Cardinals, 1973, 1975, 1978, Man of Yr., St. Louis Dodge Dealers, 1975—76, Miller High Life, 1980; named to So. Ill. U. Sports Hall of Fame, 1978, Mo. Sports Hall of Fame, 1998, Mo. Valley Conf. Hall of Fame, 2001, Chicagoland Sports Hall of Fame, 2003; recipient Brian Piccolo Nat. YMCA award for most civic minded profl. athlete, 1980. Mem.: AFTRA, NFL Players Assn. (Byron Whizzer White award 1976), Fellowship Christian Athletes. Republican.

HART, JOHN FRASER, geography educator; b. Staunton, Va., Apr. 5, 1924; s. Freeman H. and Jean. B. (Fraser) H.; m. Meredith A. Davis, Feb. 5, 1949; children: Richard L., Meredith A. AB, Emory U., 1943; MA, Northwestern U., 1949, PhD, 1950. Asst., then assoc. prof. U. Ga., 1949-55; from asst. prof. to prof. Ind. U., 1955-67; exec. sec. Assn. Am. Geographers, 1965-66; prof. geography U. Minn., Mpls., 1967—; vis. prof. Clansfield State Coll., 1976-77; Disting. vis. prof. East Carolina U., 1977. Fulbright lectr. U. Lille (France), Durham U., 1960 Mem. editorial adv. bd. Geog. Rev., 1976-2004, Jour. Geography, 1985-88, Focus, 1988—; contbr. articles to profl. publs. With USNR, 1943-46. Recipient medaille de l'Université de Liège, 1960, Platinum Plow U. Minn. geography students, 1971; named Friend of S.D. Geography, 1979, Chevalier du Ordre du Bleuet D'Or, Chicoutimi, Que., Can., 1989. Fellow Am. Geog. Soc. (Vouras medal, 2002), Royal Geog. Soc., Royal Scottish Geog. Soc.; mem. Assn. Am. Geographers (editor annals 1970-75, citation for meritorious contbns. 1969, councilor West Lakes divsn. 1976-79, pres. 1979-80, hon. life mem. Southeastern divsn., Lifetime Achievement award 1987, 2005, J.B. Jackson prize 1991), Can. Assn. Geographers (councillor 1974-77), Inst. Brit. Geographers, Nat. Coun. Geog. Edn. (award for teaching geography 1971). Office: U Minn 414 Social Sciences 267 -19th Ave S Minneapolis MN 55455

HART, KATHERINE MILLER, college dean; b. Hinsdale, Ill., Jan. 31, 1943; d. Donald William and Katherine (Hiatt) H. BA, DePauw U., 1965; MPH, U. Ill., 1976. Mem. staff 1st Nat. Bank Chgo., 1965-68; dir. phys. placement svcs. AMA, Chgo., 1968-75; from staff assoc. to assoc. dean U. Ill., Chgo., 1975-90, assoc. dean, 1990—. Mem. Chgo. Ill. Union bd., 1986-88. Mem. Assoc. Am. Med. Colls. (planning com. faculty affairs profl. dev. conference, 1998), U. ECOS Bus. Team.

HART, RUSSELL HOLIDAY, retired lawyer; b. Chgo., May 1, 1928; s. Russell Holiday and Allegra (Prince) H.; m. Mary Gehres, June 16, 1951; children: Holiday Hart McKiernan, Robert Russell, Andrew Richard. AB, DePauw U., 1950; JD, Ind. U., 1956. Bar: Ind. 1956, U.S. Dist. Ct. (no. and so. dists.) Ind. 1956, U.S. Ct. Appeals (7th cir.) 1965, U.S. Supreme Ct. 1973. Assoc. Stuart & Branigin, Lafayette, Ind., 1956-61, ptnr., 1961-99; ret., 1999. Lectr. Ind. Continuing Legal Edn. Forum; tchr. trial lawyers Nat. Inst. for Trial Advocacy. Served with U.S. Army, 1951-53. Fellow: Acad. Law Alumni Ind. U. Sch. Law;, Ind. Bar Found. (sec., v.p. 1985), Internat. Acad. Trial Lawyers, Am. Coll. Trial Lawyers, Am. Bar Found., Internat. Soc. Barristers; mem.: ABA (del.), Nat. Assn. Railroad Trial Counsel (past pres.), Def. Trial Counsel of Ind. (past pres.), Ind. Def. Trial Counsel (diplomate), Tippecanoe County Bar Assn. (past pres.), Ind. Bar Assn. (pres.-elect 1986—87, pres. 1987—88, bd. mgrs., former treas., chmn. trial lawyers sect.). Office: Stuart & Branigin PO Box 1010 Lafayette IN 47902-1010 Home Phone: 765-463-1238; Office Phone: 765-423-1561.

HART, WILLIAM THOMAS, federal judge; b. Joliet, Ill., Feb. 4, 1929; s. William Michael and Geraldine (Archambeault) H.; m. Catherine Motta, Nov. 27, 1954; children: Catherine Hart Maher, Susan Hart DaMario, Julie Hart Boesen, Sally Hart Collins, Nancy Hart McLaughlin. JD, Loyola U., Chgo., 1951. Bar: Ill. 1951, U.S. Dist. Ct. 1951, U.S. Ct. Appeals (7th cir.) 1954, U.S.

Ct. Appeals (D.C. cir.) 1977. Asst. U.S. atty. U.S. Dist. Ct. (no. dist.) Ill., Chgo., 1954-56; assoc. Defrees & Fiske, 1956-59; spl. asst. atty. gen. State of Ill., 1957-58; assoc. then ptnr. Schiff, Hardin & Waite, 1959-82; spl. asst. state's atty. Cook County, Ill., 1960; judge U.S. Dist. Ct. Ill., 1982—; now sr. judge. Mem. exec. com. U.S. Dist. Ct. (no. dist.) Ill., 1988-92; visiting judge U.S. count appeal 9th cir 2007, mem. com. on adminstrn. fed. magistrates sys., Jud. Conf. U.S., 1987-92, 7th cir. Jud. Coun., 1990-92; mem. edn. com. Fed. Jud. Ctr., 1994-99; chair No. Dist. Ill. Ct. Hist. Assoc., 1998—. Pres. adv. bd. Mercy Med. Ctr., Aurora, Ill., 1980-81; v.p. Aurora Blood Bank, 1972-77; trustee Rosary H.S., 1981-82, 93-98; bd. dirs. Chgo. Legal Asst. Found., 1974-76. Served with U.S. Army, 1951-53. Decorated Bronze Star; named to Joliet/Will County Hall of Pride, 1992; recipient Disting. Jurist award Loyola U., Chgo., 2005. Mem. 7th Cir. Bar Assn., Law Club, Legal Club, Soc. Trial Lawyers, Union League Club of Aurora, Ill. (hon.), Inn of Ct., Serra Club of Aurora (v.p. 2000). Office: US Dist Ct No Dist Ill US Courthouse Rm 2246 219 S Dearborn St Chicago IL 60604-1702

HARTE, CHRISTOPHER M., publishing executive, investment manager; BA, Stanford U.; MBA, U. Tex. Pub. Centre Daily Times, State Coll., Pa., 1986—89, Akron Beacon Jour., Ohio, 1989—92; pres. Portland Press Herald/Maine Sunday Telegram, 1992—94; chmn. Star Tribune, Mpls., 2007—, interim pub., 2007—. Mem. exec. adv. bd. Avista Capital Partners; bd. dirs. Geokinetics, Harte-Hanks, Inc., Crown Resources Corp., Mincron Software. Mem.: Tex. Audubon Soc. (adv. bd.), Nat. Audubon Soc. (bd. dirs., asst. sec. & chair Governance Com.). Office: Star Tribune 425 Portland Ave Minneapolis MN 55488 Office Phone: 612-673-1714. E-mail: charte@startribune.com.*

HARTEN, ANN M., relocation services executive; married; 1 child. BA in Indsl. Psychology, Indiana U. of Pa. With Boise Cascade, 1987—2000, dir. integrated supply, 1999—2000; v.p., chief info. officer US ops. SIRVA, Westmont, Ill., 2000—. Office: SIRVA 700 Oakmont Ln Westmont IL 60559

HARTKE, CHARLES A., state legislator; b. Effingham, Ill., May 7, 1944; m. Kathy Hartke; 2 children. Farmer; mem. from 108th dist. Ill. Ho. of Reps., 1985—. Vice chmn. agr. com.; chmn. counties and twps. com.; mem. appropriations com., elem. and secondary edn. com., transp. and motor vehicles com., children com., econ. devel. and legis. info. system com., pub. safety and infrastructure appropriations coms., vets. affairs com. Address: 22021 E 1500th Avenue Teutopolis IL 62467

HARTLEY, DAVID, state legislator, lawyer; b. Dec. 16, 1942; m. Vicki Mayes. BA, U. Louisville, 1967, postgrad.; JD, Capital U., 1983. State rep. Dist. 62 Ohio Ho. of Reps., 1973-92, state rep. Dist. 73, 1993—. Minority leader commerce and labor, mem. pub. utilities com., agriculture and natural resources com.; mem. Clark County Dem. exec. com. Mem. exec. com. Interfaith Hospitality Network. Named Legislator of Yr., Children for the Enforcement of Support, 1987, Top Legislator, Ohio Union of Patrolmen Assn., 1990, Ohio's Most Effective Legislator for the Environment, Ohio Environ. Coun., 1993; recipient Outstanding Achievement award Sierra Club, 1990, Spl. award of merit Ohio Acad. Trial Lawyers, 1992, Dir.'s award Ohio Victims of Crime Program, 1993, Disting. Svc. award Ohio State Bar Assn., 1993. Mem. UAW. Office: Riffe Ctr 77 S High St Fl 10 Columbus OH 43266-0603 Fax: 614 644 9494.

HARTNETT, D. PAUL, state legislator; b. Sioux City, Iowa, Sept. 29, 1927; m. Marjorie Sheehan, 1951; children: Debbie (Mrs. Burchard), Cindy (Mrs. Spagnola), Marcy (Mrs. Closner), Joan, Michael. BA, Wayne State Coll., 1951, MS, 1958; PhD, U. Nebr., 1966. H.S. tchr., coach, adminstr., Nebr.; coll. prof.; mem. Nebr. Legislature from 45th dist., Lincoln, 1984—; chmn. urban affairs com. Nebr. Legislature, Lincoln, mem. gen. affairs com., natural resources com., mem. edn. com. of the states, mem. exec. bd. Past mem. Bellevue Sch. Bd. Mem. C. of C., Eagles, KC, Phi Delta Kappa. Office: 407 Greenbriar Ct Bellevue NE 68005-4714 also: State Capitol 1445 K St Lincoln NE 68508-2731

HARTNETT, JAMES PATRICK, engineering educator; b. Lynn, Mass., Mar. 19, 1924; s. James Patrick and Anna Elizabeth (Ryan) H.; m. Shirley Germaine Carlson, July 14, 1945 (div. 1969); children: James, David, Paul, Carla, Dennis; m. Edith Zubrin, Sept. 10, 1971. BS in Mech. Engring, Ill. Inst. Tech., 1947; MS, MIT, 1948; PhD, U. Calif., Berkeley, 1954. Engr. gas turbine div. Gen. Electric Co., 1948-49; rsch. engr. U. Calif., Berkeley, 1949-54; asst. prof. to prof. mech. engring. U. Minn., 1954-61; Guggenheim fellow, vis. prof. U. Tokyo, Japan, 1960; cons. ICA, Seoul, Korea, 1960; Fulbright lectr., cons. mech. engring. U. Alexandria, Egypt, 1961; H. Fletcher Brown prof. mech. engring., chmn. dept. U. Del., 1961-65; engring. cons., 1954-74; prof., head dept. energy engring. U. Ill., Chgo., 1965-74; dir. Energy Resources Ctr., 1974-98. Sci. exch. visitor, Romania, 1969; vis. prof. Israel Inst. Tech., 1971; cons. Asian Inst. Tech., Bangkok 1977; 1st Dr. Arcot Ramachandran prof. heat transfer Indian Inst. Tech., Madras, 1995-96. Editor: Recent Advances in Heat and Mass Transfer, 1961; co-editor: Internat. Jour. Heat and Mass Transfer, 1960—, (with T.F. Irvine, Jr.) Advances in Heat Transfer, 1963—, Heat Transfer-Japanese Research, Soviet Research, 1971, Fluid Mechanics-Soviet Research, 1971; contbr. articles on heat transfer, fluid mechanics, energy to tech. jours. Mem. organizing com. and sci. coun. Internat. Centre Heat and Mass Transfer, Ankara, Turkey, 1969—; mem., sec. Ill. Energy Resources Commn., 1974-85; mem. sci. coun. Regional Center for Energy, Heat and Mass Transfer for Asia and Pacific, 1976—; sec. Midwest Univs. Energy Consortium, 1980—. Recipient Profl. Achievement award Ill. Inst. Tech. Alumni Assn., 1977; recipient Luikov medal Internat. Ctr. Heat and Mass Transfer, 1981; Japan Soc. for Promotion of Sci. fellow, 1987. Fellow ASME (Meml. award heat transfer divsn. 1969, 40th Anniversary award 1989, AIChE-ASME Max Jakob Meml. award 1989), Indian Nat. Acad. Engring., Japanese Soc. Mech. Engrs. (hon.); mem. Internat. Higher Edn. Acad. of Scis./Moscow (Disting. prof. 1997), Sigma Xi, Tau Beta Pi, Pi Tau Sigma. Address: Univ of Ill 1919 W Taylor St Chicago IL 60612-7246

HARTNETT, WILLIAM J., state representative; b. Beaver Falls, Ohio; married; 5 children. BS in Edn., Kent State U.; MA in Edn., W.Va. U.; EdS, Kent State U.; civilian attendee, U.S. Army War Coll. Supt. Mansfield-Madison Sys. Sch., Ohio, 1974—84; v.p., interim pres. North Ctrl. Tech., 1994—98; state rep. dist. 73 Ohio Ho. of Reps., Columbus, 1998—, ranking minority mem. edn. com., mem. fin. and appropriates, pub. utilities, and ways and means coms., mem. fed. grant rev. and edn. oversight, and primary and secondary edn. subcoms. Mem. Richland County Bd. Mental Health, Ohio; chair, trustee Richland County Tech. Coll. Found.; campaign chair, pres. Richland County United Way; mem. Employee Participation Coun. North Ctrl. Ohio; adv. bd. Mansfield Correctional Instn.; bd. dirs. Mohican Inst. Mem.: Mansfield-Richland Area C. of C. (pres. 1984—94, chmn.'s award). Democrat. Office: 77 S High St 10th fl Columbus OH 43215-6111

HARTOG, JOHN, II, theology educator, librarian; b. Orange City, Iowa, Nov. 15, 1936; s. John and Gertrude Marie (Hofland) H.; m. Martha Griselda Nuñez, July 30, 1964; children: John III, Paul Anthony. AA, Northwestern Coll., 1956; student, Moody Bible Inst., 1956-57, Middle Coll. Langs., Middlebury, Vt., 1959; BA, Wheaton Coll., Ill., 1959; ThM, Dallas Theol. Sem., 1964; MSLS, East Tex. State U., 1970; ThD, Grace Theol. Sem., 1978; D in Ministry, Cen. Bapt. Theol. Sem., 1988. Ordained to ministry Gen. Assn. Regular Bapt. Chs., 1969. Min. religious lit. Immanuel Tract Soc., Dallas, 1964-66; pastor Lipscomb (Tex.) Community Ch., 1966-67; instr. libr. Mont. Inst. Bible, Billings, 1967-68, acad. dean Lewistown, 1973-77; prof., head libr. Calvary Bible Coll., Kansas City, Mo., 1984-89, acad. dean, 1987-89; prof., libr. Faith Bapt. Bible Coll., Ankeny, Iowa, 1968-70, 77-84, 89—; founding pastor Maranatha Bapt. Ch., Grimes, Iowa, 1995—. Author: The Fall of a Kingdom, 1983, Enduring to the End, 1987, When the Church Was Young and Bold, 1988, Abounding Grace, 1991, The Biblical Qualifications of a Pastor, 1992, Alive in Christ, 1993. Mem. Pi Gamma Mu, Phi Theta Kappa. Republican. Avocation: gardening. Office: Faith Bapt Theol Sem 1900 NW 4th St Ankeny IA 50021-2152

HARTSFIELD, JAMES KENNEDY, JR., orthodontist, geneticist; b. Decatur, Ala., Feb. 12, 1955; s. James Kennedy and Shirley Joann (Bridwell) H.; m. Karen Lee Whitaker, May 8, 1977; 1 child, Kennedy Whitaker. BS, U. SC, 1977; DMD, Med. U. SC, 1981; MS, Ind. U., 1983; M in Med. Sci., Harvard U., 1987; PhD, U. South Fla., 1993. Diplomate Am. Bd. Med. Genetics., Am. Bd. Orthodontics. Intern Hillsborough Dental Rsch. Clinic, Tampa, Fla., 1981-82; clin. fellow Ind. U., Indpls., 1982-83; rsch. fellow Harvard U., Boston, 1983-86, Mass. Gen. Hosp., Boston, 1984-86; clin. fellow U. South Fla., Tampa, 1986-87, asst. prof., 1987-93; assoc. prof. Sch. Dentistry and Sch. Medicine, Ind. U., Indpls., 1993—99, prof. Sch. Dentistry and Sch. Medicine, 1999—. Dir. Teratogen Info. Svc., U. South Fla., 1987-93; dir. oral facial genetics divsn. Sch. Dentistry Ind. U., 1993-, acting chmn. oral facial devel., 1998-99, chmn., 1999-2002, interim chmn. orthodontics and oral facial genetics, 2007—; pres. Meridian Orthodontics, PC, 2003-. Mem. editl. bd. Jour. Dental Rsch., 2007-; rev. bd. mem. Internat. Jour. Oral Maxillofacial Implants; contbr. articles to profl. jours. Med. adv. coun. Osteogenesis Imperfecta Found., 2007—. Recipient Physician-Scientist award NIH, 1989, 1st Ind. Rsch. Support and Transition award, 1996, B.F. Dewell Meml. Biomed. Rsch. award Am. Assn. Orthodontists Found., 2001, Disting. Faculty award Ind. U. Sch. Dentistry Alumni Assn., 2003; named Outstanding Faculty of Yr., Ind. Dental Assn., 2004 Fellow Am. Coll. Med. Genetics (founding), Am. Coll. Dentists, Coll. of Diplomates of Am. Bd. Orthodontics; mem. ADA, Am. Soc. Human Genetics, Am. Assn. for Dental Rsch., Internat. Assn. Dental Rsch. (v.p. craniofacial biology group 2003-04, pres. 2005-06), Internat. Coll. Dentists, Soc. Craniofacial Genetics (pres. 1989-90), Am. Dental Edn. Assn., Am. Cleft Palate Assn., Am. Assn. Orthodontists, Harvard Soc. for Advancement of Orthodontics (v.p. 2006-07, mem. bd. dirs. for Confs. on Orthodontic Advances in Sci. and Tech. 2006-, pres. 2007—). Presbyterian. Avocations: music, boating. Home: 8095 Sunfish Ct Indianapolis IN 46236-8887 Office: Ind U Schs Dentistry and Medicine 1121 W Michigan St Indianapolis IN 46202-5186: 13590 B North Meridian Ste 205 Carmel IN 46032 Home Phone: 317-823-9254; Office Phone: 317-278-1148.

HARTUNG, JAMES H., airport authority executive; Pres. Toledo-Lucas County Port Authority. Office: Toledo Lucas County Port Authority 1 Maritime Plz Toledo OH 43604

HARTZ, MICHAEL O., lawyer; b. Flint, Mich., July 24, 1953; BA, Kalamazoo Coll, 1975; JD, U. Detroit, 1978; LLM in Taxation, U. Fla., 1979. Bar: Mich. 1978, Fla. 1979, Ill. 1980. Ptnr. estate planning Katten Muchin Rosenman LLP, Chgo. Fellow: Am. Coll. of Trusts and Estates Counsel. Office: Katten Muchin Rosenman LLP 525 W Monroe St Ste 1900 Chicago IL 60661 Office Phone: 312-902-5279. Office Fax: 312-577-8789. E-mail: michael.hartz@kattenlaw.com.

HARTZLER, ED, state legislator; State rep. Dist. 123 Mo. Ho. of Reps., 1993—. Mem. appropriations com., banks and fin. instns. com., state rels. and vets. affairs com., govtl. orgn. and rev. com., ins. com., urban affairs com. Office: Mo House of Reps Rm 115D 201 W Capitol Ave Jefferson City MO 65101 Home: 1041 Trevino Rd Clinton MO 64735-9067 Office Fax: 573 526 1313; Home Fax: 816 331 0171. E-mail: ehartzle@services.state.mo.us.

HARTZLER, VICKY J., state legislator; Mem. Mo. Ho. of Reps., Jefferson City, 1994-2000. Address: 22804 E 299th St Harrisonville MO 64701-6320

HARVEY, DAVID R., chemical company executive; With Sigma-Aldrich Corp., St. Louis, 1981—; v.p. Europe Aldrich Chem. Co.; COO Sigma Aldrich Corp., S. Louis, Mo., 1986—99; pres., CEO Sigma-Aldrich Corp., St. Louis, 2000—05, chmn., 1999—. Bd. dir. CF Industries. Trustee St. Louis Sci. Ctr. Office: Sigma-Aldrich Corp 3050 Spruce St Saint Louis MO 63103

HARVEY, JACK K., holding company executive; b. 1943; With Douglas County Bank & Trust Co., Omaha, 1960—; chmn. bd., exec. v.p. State Bank Holding Co. (now Great Western Bank), Omaha. Office: Great Western Bank 14545 W Center Rd Omaha NE 68144-3276

HARVEY, JEFFREY A., physics professor; b. San Antonio, Texas, Feb. 15, 1955; BS in Physics, U. Minnesota, 1977; PhD in Physics, Calif. Inst. Tech., 1981. Rsch. assoc. Princeton U., Princeton, NJ, 1981—83, asst. prof., 1983—87, assoc. prof., 1987—90, prof., 1990—91, U. Chicago, 1991—. Mem. Aspen Ctr. for Physics, 1986—97; editorial bd. mem. Physical Review, 1989—91; dir. Theoretical Advanced Study Inst., 1992, 99; mem. ITP Advisory Bd., 1993—97, chair, 1995—96; mem. TASI Advisory Bd., 1997—2003; chair UCSB Physics External Review Com., 1997—98; editorial bd. mem. Classical & Quantum Gravity, 1998—; mem. physics advisory council Princeton U., 1998—2002. Recipient Presidential Young Investigator award, NSF, 1987; grantee Earl C. Anthony Fellowship, 1977—78, A. P. Sloan Fellowship, 1986—90. Fellow: Am. Acad. Arts & Sciences, Am. Physical Soc. Office: Enrico Fermi Inst U Chicago 5640 Ellis Ave Chicago IL 60637

HARVEY, PATRICIA A., school system administrator; BS in elem. edn., Lincoln U.; MA in sch. admin., Roosevelt U. Prin. Hefferan Elem. Sch., Chgo., Idaho; exec. asst. to gen. supt. Chgo. Schs., 1994—95, chief accountability officer, 1995—97; sr. fellow dir. urban edn. Nat. Ctr. Edn. and Econ., Wash., DC, 1997—99; supt. Saint Paul Pub. Schs., Saint Paul, Minn., 1999—. Office: Saint Paul Pub Sch 360 Colborne St Saint Paul MN 55102

HARVEY, PAUL, commentator, writer, columnist; b. Tulsa, Sept. 4, 1918; s. Harry Harrison and Anna Dagmar (Christensen) Aurandt; m. Lynne Cooper, June 4, 1940; 1 child, Paul Harvey. LittD (hon.), Culver-Stockton Coll., 1952, St. Bonaventure U., 1953; LLD, John Brown U., Ark., 1959, Mont. Sch. Mines, 1961, Trinity Coll. Fla., 1963, Parsons Coll., 1968; HHD, Wayland Bapt. Coll., 1960, Union Coll., 1962, Samford U., 1970, Howard Payne U., Tex., 1978, Sterling Coll., 1982; Degree (hon.), Rosary Coll., 1996; LHD (hon.), Hillsdale Coll., Mich., 2000. Announcer radio sta. KVOO, Tulsa; sta. mgr. Salina, Kans.; spl. events dir. radio sta. KXOK, St. Louis; program dir. radio sta. WKZO, Kalamazoo, 1941-43; dir. news and information OWI, Mich., Ind., 1941-43; news commentator, analyst ABC, 1944—; syndicated columnist Los Angeles Times Syndicate (formerly Gen. Features Corp.), 1954—; TV commentator, 1968. Author: Remember These Things, 1952, Autumn of Liberty, 1954, The Rest of the Story, 1956, You Said It, Paul Harvey, 1969, Our Lives, Our Fortunes, Our Sacred Honor; Album rec. Yesterday's Voices, 1959, Testing Time, 1960, Uncommon Man, 1962. Bd. dirs. John D. and Catherine T. MacArthur Found.; mem. bd. govs. Orchestral Assn. Chgo. Symphony Orch. Recipient citation DAV, 1949, 11 Freedoms Found. awards, 1952-76, radio award Am. Legion, 1952, citation of merit, 1955, 57, Cert. of merit VFW, 1953, Bronze Christopher's award, 1953, award of honor Sumter Guards, 1955, nat. pub. welfare services trophy Colo. Am. Legion, 1957,Great Am. KSEL award, 1962, Spl. ABC award, 1973, Ill. Broadcaster award, 1974, John Peter Zenger Freedom award Eagles, 1975, Am. of Year award Lions Internat., 1975, Outstanding Broadcast Journalism award, 1980, Gen. Omar N. Bradley Spirit of Independence trophy, 1980, Man of Yr. award Chgo. Broadcast Advt. Club, 1981, Golden Radio award Nat. Radio Broadcasters Assn., 1982, Best Speaking Voice award Am. Speech, Lang. and Hearing Assn., 1982, Horatio Alger award, 1983, Outstanding Broadcast Personality award Advt. Club Balt., 1984, Meritorius Svc. award Am. Acad. Family Physicians, 1984, Cert. of Appreciation Humane Soc. of U.S., 1985, Genesis award The Fund for Animals, 1986, Okla. Assn. Broadcasters award, 1987, Henry G. Bennett Disting. Svc. award Okla. State U., 1987, James Herriot award Humane Soc. U.S., 1987, Lowell Thomas award, 1989, Gold medal Internat. Radio & TV Soc., 1989, Others award Salvation Army, 1989, Journalism award Internat. Radio Festival, 1989, 5 Marconi awards Network Personality of Yr., 1989, 91, 96, 98, 2002, Dante award, 1990, William Booth award Salvation Army, 1990, Journalism award Chgo. Hall of Fame, 1990, Bd. of Dirs. award Nat. Religious Broadcasters, 1991, Great Am. Race Legend's award Interstate, 1991, Good Guy award Am. Legion, 1992, Outstanding Pub. Spkr. award Toastmasters Internat., 1992, Paul White award Radio T.V. ews Dirs., 1992, Peabody award 1993, 94, Spirit of Broadcasting award NAB, 1994, Silver award Am. Advertising Fedn., 1994, Hall of Fame award Broadcasting & Cable Mag., 1995, Am. Spirit award USAF, 1996, Lifetime Achievement award Radio Mercury, 1997, Lifetime Achievement award Gold Angel, 1998, Lifetime Achievement award Radio Mercury, 1997, Tex McCrary award Journalism from Congl. Medal Honor Soc., 2000, Lifetime Achievement award A.I.R. award Radio Broadcasters Chgo., 2001, R&R News/Talk Radio Lifetime Achievement award, 2003, NY Festivals World Gold Medal award best personality network/syndicated, 2004; Presdl. Medal of Freedom, The White House, 2005; elected to Okla. Hall of Fame, 1955, Nat. Assn. Broadcasters Hall of Fame, 1979; named Top Commentator of Yr. Radio-TV Daily, 1962, Father of Yr. Father's Day Coun., 1980, Laureate Lincoln Acad. of Ill., 1987 (Ill. highest honor); to Emerson Radio Hall of Fame, 1990; one of The Men of the Century Broadcast and Cable Mag., 1999; among 20th Century's Most Significant Americans George Mag., 1998. Mem. Washington Radio and Television Corrs. Assn., Aircraft Owners and Pilots Assn. Clubs: Chicago Press. Achievements include having broadcasts and columns reprinted in Congressional Record 102 times. Office: 333 N Michigan Ave Ste 1600 Chicago IL 60601-4005 Office Phone: 312-899-4085.

HARVEY, RAYMOND CURTIS, conductor; b. NYC, Dec. 9, 1950; s. Shirley Nathaniel and Doris Louise (Walwin) H. BMus, MMus, Oberlin Coll., 1973; M. in Musical Arts, Yale U., 1978, D in Musical Arts, 1984. Choral dir. Northfield (Mass.) Mt. Hermon Sch., 1973-76; asst. conductor Des Moines Metro Opera, Indianola, Iowa, 1977-80; music dir. Tex. Opera Theater, Houston, 1978-80; Exxon/arts endowment conductor Indpls. Symphony, 1980-83; assoc. conductor Buffalo Philharmonic, 1983-86; music dir. Marion (Ind.) Philharmonic, 1982-86, Springfield (Mass.) Symphony, 1986-94, Fresno Philharm. Orch., 1993-99, El Paso (Tex.) Opera, 1995—, Kalamazoo Symphony Orch., 1999—. Guest conductor Minn. Orch., 1991, 92, Detroit Symphony, 1990, 92, N.Y. Philharmonic, 1987, Atlanta Symphony, 1992, Louisville Orch., 1990, 93, Utah Symphony, 1993, Phila. Orch., 2001, Detroit Symphony, 1992, 2001. Democrat. Methodist. Avocations: running, exercise. Office: Kalamazoo Symphony Orch 359 S Burdick St Ste 100 Kalamazoo MI 49007

HARVEY, RONALD GILBERT, research chemist; b. Ottawa, Ont., Can., Sept. 9, 1927; arrived in U.S., 1948; s. Gilbert and Adeline (LeClair) H.; m. Helene H. Szpara, May 18, 1952; 1 child, Ronald Edward. BS in Biology, UCLA, 1952; MS in Chemistry, U. Chgo., 1956, PhD in Chemistry, 1960. Project leader Sinclair Rsch. Labs., Harvey, Ill., 1956-58; instr. U. Chgo., 1960-63, asst.prof., 1964-68, assoc. prof., 1968-75, prof., 1975-97, prof. emeritus, 1997—; postdoctoral fellow Imperial Coll., London, Eng., 1963-64. Cons. Nat. Cancer Inst., Washington, Farmacon Corp., Oakbrook, Ill., CIDAC, Palo Alto, Calif., 1978-80; OMNI Research Mayaguex, P.R., 1973-74, Nat. Inst. Environ. Health Sci., Washington, Am. Cancer Soc., Atlanta, U.S.-Israel Binational Sci. Found. Author: Polycyclic Aromatic Hydrocarbons Chemistry and Carcinogenesis, 1991, Polycyclic Aromatic Hydrocarbons, 1997; editor: Polycyclic Hydrocarbons and Carcinogenesis; mem. editl. bd. Polycyclic Aromatic Compounds (1990-), Mini Reviews in Organic Chemistry (2003-); contbr. more than 460 articles to profl. jours. Recipient ISPAC award for rsch. in polycyclic hydrocarbon chemistry, 1995, Ochsner award Am. Coll. Chest Physicians, 2006. Fellow Royal Chem. Soc., Am. Inst. Chemists; mem. AAAS, Am. Chem. Soc., Am. Assn. Cancer Rsch., Sigma Xi. Achievements include patents for synthesis of alpha-olefins, anti-androgen compounds. Home: 10550 Golf Rd Orland Park IL 60462-7420 Office: U Chgo Ben May Inst for Cancer Rsch 929 E 57th St Chicago IL 60637 Business E-Mail: rharvey@huggins.bsd.uchicago.edu.

HARVEY, WILLIAM D., utilities executive, lawyer; BA in Econs., U. Wis., Madison, 1971, JD, 1974. Solo practice, 1974—76; prin. Wheeler, Van Sickle, Anderson, Norman & Harvey, S.C., 1976—86; v.p. and assoc. gen. counsel Wis. Power & Light (now Alliant Energy Corp.), 1986—89, v.p. and gen. counsel, 1989—92, v.p. natural gas and gen. counsel, 1992—93, sr. v.p., 1993—98; exec. v.p. generation Alliant Energy-Wis. Power & Light Co. (now Alliant Energy Corp.), 1998—2004; pres. and COO Alliant Energy Corp., Madison, Wis., 2004—05, pres., CEO, 2005—06, chmn., pres., CEO, 2006—. Bd. dir. Am. Transmission Co.; chair bd. dir. Wis. Utilities Assn. Bd. dir. United Way of Dane County, 1993—2001, campaign chair, 2001, mem. cmty. bldg. com., 1996—2000; bd. dir. Greater Madison C. of C., 1993—, Madison Symphony Orch., 1998—2001; exec. com. Dane County Econ. Summit Coun.; bd. dir. Wis. Botechnology Assn., 1998—2001, Riverlands Conservancy, Inc. Office: Alliant Energy Corp 4902 N Biltmore Ln Madison WI 53718

HARVIE, CRAWFORD THOMAS, lawyer; b. NYC, Mar. 28, 1943; s. William Mead and Barbara Adele (Johnson) H.; m. Iris Ruth Alofsin, June 10, 1972; children: Katherine, Edward. AB, Stanford U., 1965; LLB, Yale U., 1968; cert. advanced mgmt. prog., Harvard U., 1992. Bar: NY 1969. Assoc. Debevoise & Plimpton, NYC, 1971-75; counsel TRW, Inc., Cleve., 1976-77, sr. counsel, 1978-79, asst. gen. counsel, v.p., 1980-83; v.p. law TRW Automotive, Cleve., 1983-90; v.p., assoc. gen. counsel TRW, Inc., 1990-95; sr. v.p., gen. counsel, sec. Goodyear Tire and Rubber Co., Akron, Ohio, 1995—. Trustee Cleve. Inst. of Music, 1989—; bd. overseers Blossom Music Ctr. Mem. Am. Corp. Counsel Assn., Assn. Gen. Counsel, Chief Legal Officer Roundtable-US. Home: 6537 Thornbrook Cir Hudson OH 44236-3552 Office: Goodyear Tire and Rubber Co 1144 E Market St Akron OH 44316-0001 Office Phone: 330-796-2408.

HARWICK, DENNIS PATRICK, insurance association administrator, lawyer; b. May 27, 1949; s. T. Dale and Lois L. (Patrick) H. BA, U. Idaho, 1971, JD, 1974. Bar: Idaho 1974, U.S. Dist. Ct. Idaho 1974. Legal officer Idaho Bank & Trust, Pocatello, 1974-79, v.p. legal Boise, 1979-85; exec. dir. Idaho State Bar and Idaho Law Found., Inc., 1985-90, CEO Washington State Bar Assn., 1990-97, Kans. Bar Assn./Kans. Bar Found., Topeka, 1998—2003; pres. Captive Ins. Cos. Assn., 2005—. Spokesman, 1983-85; mem. adv. coun. U. Idaho Coll. Letters and Sci., 1986-90; pres. Kans. Lawyers Svc. Corp., 1998-2003. Editor Corp. Newsletter, 1983-85. Bd. dirs. Boise Philharm., 1984-89, v.p. adminstrn., 1985-87; chmn. Idaho Commn. U.S. Constl. Bicentennial, 1986-88; chmn. Idaho Bus. Week Program, 1984; treas. Idaho State Dem. Conv., 1980. Mem. ABA, Nat. Assn. Bar Execs. (mem. exec. com., pres. 1996-97), Nat. Conf. Bar Founds. (trustee), Idaho State Bar (examiner/grader 1975-90), Idaho Bankers Assn. (spokesman), Am. Inst. Banking (state chmn. 1982-83), Idaho Assn. Commerce and Industry (chmn. coms.), Boise Bar Assn., Bar Assn. Adminstrn., Topeka Tennis Assn. (bd. dirs. 2000-05), Phi Beta Kappa. Clubs: Boise Racquet and Swim (bd. dirs. 1988-90, pres. 1990). Democrat.

HARWOOD, JULIUS J., metallurgist, educator; b. NYC, Dec. 3, 1918; m. Naomi Beitner, 1983; children: Dane L., Gail A., Caren L., Rochelle. BS, CCNY, 1939; MS, U. Md., 1953; D of Engring. (hon.), Mich. Tech. U., 1986. Materials engr. U.S. Naval Gun Factory, 1940-46; metall. Off Naval Rsch., 1946-60; mgr. metall. sci. lab. Ford Motor Co., Dearborn, Mich., 1960-69, mgr. rsch. planning engring. and rsch. staff, 1969—71, dir. Material Sci. Lab, engring. and rsch. staff, 1971—83; prof. engring. Wayne State U., Detroit, 1984; pres. Ovonic Synthetic Material Co., Troy, 1984—87, Harwood Cons., West Bloomfield, 1987—. Adj. prof. Wayne State U., Detroit, 1975. Editor 5 books on materials; contbr. articles to profl. jours. Fellow AAAS, TMS, Metall. Soc. (pres. 1973), Am. Soc. Metals (John H. Shoemaker award 1977, Distinction award), Engring. Soc. of Detroit (Gold Medal award 1983); mem. Am. Inst. Mining, Metall. and Petroleum Engrs. (hon., pres. 1976), Am. Ceramic Soc. (Orton lectr. 1978), Nat. Acad. Engrs. (life). Office: 5023 Pheasant Cv West Bloomfield MI 48323-2093 Office Phone: 248-681-6747.

HARWOOD, SANDRA STABILE, lawyer, state representative; b. June 25, 1950; BBA, Kent State U., 1988; JD, Univ. Akon Sch. of Law, 1991. State rep. dist. 65 Ohio Ho. of Reps., Columbus, 2002—, mem. judiciary, ranking minority mem. civil and comml. law, econ. devel. and environ, health. Democrat. Office: 77 S High St Columbus OH 43215-6111 Office Phone: 614-466-3488.

HASARA, KAREN A., mayor; b. Springfield, Ill., Oct. 17, 1940; m. Jerry Gott; 4 children. BA, Sangamon State U. Mem. Ill. Ho. of Reps., Springfield, 1986-91, 92-94, mem. appropriations I, elem. and sec. edn., counties and twps., agrl., children, aging, small bus., coal devel., mkt., fin. inst. and human svc. coms.; former spokesman on mental health Springfield; former vicespokesman on state govt. adminstrn.; mayor City of Springfield, 1995—. Office: City of Springfield 800 E Monroe St Ste 300 Springfield IL 62701-1699

HASE, DAVID JOHN, lawyer; b. Milw., Feb. 27, 1940; s. John Henry and Catherine Charlotte (Leekley) H.; m. Penelope Sue Pritchard, Sept. 2, 1964; children: Jeffrey David, Jennifer Anne, John Paul. AB, Dartmouth Coll., 1962; LLB, U. Wis., 1965. Bar: Wis. 1965, U.S. Dist. Ct. (ea. dist.) Wis. 1965, U.S. Ct. Appeals (7th cir.) 1971, U.S. Ct. Appeals (D.C. cir.) 1975, U.S. Ct. Appeals (9th cir.) 1989, U.S. Supreme Ct. 1975. Assoc. Grootemaat, Cook & Franke, Milw., 1965-67, ptnr., shareholder, 1968-70; shareholder Cook & Franke S.C., Milw., 1970-73; legal counsel to gov. Wis., Madison, 1973-74; dep. atty. gen. State of Wis., Madison, 1974-76; assoc. Foley & Lardner, Milw., 1976-77, ptnr., 1977-94; shareholder Cook & Franke S.C., Milw., 1994—. Mem. Sch. Bd., Mequon, Wis., 1971-94, treas., 1973-75, pres., 1975-94' trustee Frank L. Weyenberg Libr., 2004—. Mem. ABA. Democrat. Home: 2108 W Raleigh Ct Mequon WI 53092-5416 Office: Cook & Franke SC 660 E Mason St Ste 401 Milwaukee WI 53202-3877 Office Phone: 414-227-1281. E-mail: hase@cf-law.com.

HASEGAWA, PAUL M., horticulturist, educator; b. LA, Calif., June 25, 1948; BS, U. Calif., Riverside, 1970, MS, 1972, PhD, 1976. From asst. prof. to assoc. prof. dept. horticulture Purdue U., West Lafayette, Ind., 1981—85, prof. dept. horticulture Ctr. for Plant Environ. Stress Physiology, 1985—. Recipient Nat. Canners Assn. award, Am. Soc. for Horticultural Sci., 1974, Wilson J. Popenow award, 1980. Mem.: In Vitro Plant Biology, Internat. Assn. Plant Tissue Culture, Am. Soc. Plant Physiologists. Achievements include research in cellular and molecular determinants of plant osmotic tolerance and defense against insects. Office: Purdue U Dept Horticulture and Landscape Arch 1165 Horticulture Bldg Lafayette IN 47907-0391

HASELKORN, ROBERT, virology educator; b. Bklyn., Nov. 7, 1934; s. Barney and Mildred (Seplowin) H.; m. Margot Block, June 23, 1957; children: Deborah, David. AB, Princeton U., 1956; PhD, Harvard U., 1959. Asst. prof. biophysics U. Chgo., 1961-64, assoc. prof., 1964-69, prof., chmn. dept., 1969-84, F.L. Pritzker Disting. Service prof. dept. molecular genetics and cell biology, 1984—; dir. Ctr. for Photochemistry and Photobiology, 1987—; pres. Integrated Genomics, Inc., 2000—01. Chmn. bd. dirs. Integrated Genomics, Inc., Chgo., 1997—; cons. virology and rickettsiology study sect. USPHS, 1969-73; mem. sci. adv. bd. Sloan-Kettering Inst., 1978-79; mem. nitrogen fixation panel U.S. Dept. Agr., 1978-79; mem. panel sci. advs. UNIDO Internat. Ctr. for Genetic Engring. and Biotech., 1984-94, 97—; mem. recombinant DNA adv. com. NIH, 1991-95; adj. scientist Woods Hole Oceanographic Instn., 1994—. Editor: Virology, 1973-2000; mem. editl. bd. Molecular Microbiology; contbr. articles to profl. jours. Trustee Marine Biol. Lab., Woods Hole, Mass., 2003—. Recipient USPHS Rsch. Career Devel. award, 1963-69, Interstate Postgrad. Med. Assn. Rsch. award, 1967, Darbaker prize Bot. Soc. Am., 1982, Gregor Mendel medal in biol. scis. Acad. Scis. Czech Republic, 1996, Buzatti-Traverso lectr., CNR, Rome, 1997; Am. Cancer Soc. postdoctoral rsch. fellow ARC Virus Rsch. Unit, Cambridge, Eng., 1959-61, Guggenheim fellow Institut Pasteur, Paris, 1975, Sackler fellow Tel Aviv U., 1987. Fellow AAAS, Am. Acad. Arts and Scis. (chmn., midwest coun., v.p. 1993-99), Am. Acad. Microbiology; mem. NAS, Internat. Soc. Plant Molecular Biology (pres. 1987-89). Home: 5834 S Stony Island Ave Chicago IL 60637-2060 Office: U Chgo 920 E 58th St Chicago IL 60637 E-mail: rh01@uchicago.edu.

HASELWOOD, ELDON LAVERNE, retired education educator; b. Barnard, Mo., July 19, 1933; m. Joan Haselwood; children: Ann, Karen, Polly, Amy. BS in Edn., U. Omaha, 1960; MA in Libr. Sci., U. Denver, 1963; PhD, U. Nebr., 1972. Libr. Omaha Pub. Schs., 1960-61, Lewis Cen. Community Schs., Council Bluffs, Iowa, 1961-63; documents libr. U. Omaha, 1963-66; prof. dept. tchr. edn. U. Nebr., Omaha, 1966—99, coord. ednl. tech. Coll. Edn., 1993—2002, ret., 2002. Cons. Nat. Park Svc., Omaha, 1978—. Commr. Nebr. Libr. Commn., 1981—86; bd. dirs. U. Nebr. at Omaha Libr. Friends, 1980—. Cpl. US Army, 1953—55. Mem.: ALA (councilor 1988—91, excellence in tchg. award 1987), Nebr. Ednl. Media Assn. (disting. svc. award 1993), Nebr. Libr. Assn. (pres. 1981, meritorious svc. award 1983, Mad Hatter award 1998), Mountain Plains Libr. Assn. (rep. 1999—2001), Am. Assn. Sch. Librs. Home: 615 S 122nd St Omaha NE 68154-3015 Home Phone: 402-397-7918. Personal E-mail: hasel@alltel.net.

HASENOHRL, DONALD W., state legislator; b. Marshfield, Wis., Nov. 25, 1935; m. Kathleen Hasenohrl; children: Dena, Charles, Donald. Former farmer; mem. from dist. 70 Wis. State Assembly, Madison, 1974—, mem. hwy. com., 1979—, mem. excise and fees com., 1983—, chmn. transp. com., 1983—, mem. transp. project coms., mem. energy and commerce com., 1991—, mem. hwys., transp., excise and fees com., 1993, mem. consumer affairs, rural affairs & hwys. & transp. coms., 1995, mem. hwy. and transp., consumer affairs, rural affairs com., 1997. Chmn. Wood County Dem. Com., 1963-64; mem. Marshfield City Planning Com., 1966-67; bd. dirs. Ctrl. Wis. State Fair Assn. Named Outstanding Legislator of Yr., Wis. Mfr. Housing Assn., 1983. Mem. KC, Eagles, United Comml. Travelers, Marshfield Elks, Knights of Columbus, Lions Club, Bus. and Profl. Women's Club, Ctrl. Wis. Sportsmen's Club, Eau Pleine Boat Club. Roman Catholic. Office: PO Box 8952 Madison WI 53708-8952 Fax: 608-266-7038. E-mail: rep.hasenohrl@legis.state.wi.us.

HASER, WILLIAM H., automotive executive; BS in chem. engring., Cornell U.; grad., Northwestern U., Kellogg Sch. Mgmt. Bus. analyst Tenneco Automotive, 1983; asst. to CEO Tenneco Packaging; prod. mfg. mgr. Tenneco Specialty Packaging; plant gen. mgr., molded fiber Tenneco Automotive, contr., paperboard; v.p., chief info. officer Tenneco Packaging, 1995—98, Tenneco Automotive, Am. Bus., 1998—2002, Tenneco Automotive, Lake Forest, Ill., 2002—. Office: Tenneco Automotive 500 N Field Dr Lake Forest IL 60045

HASHIMOTO, KEN, dermatologist, educator; b. Niigata City, Japan, June 19, 1931; came to U.S., 1956; m. Noriko Sakai, Oct. 3, 1961; children: Naomi, Martha, Eugene, Amy. MD, Niigata U., 1955. Cert. Am. Bd. Dermatology, 1968, Dermatopathology, 1972. Asst. prof. dermatology Tufts U. Sch. Medicine, Boston, 1965-68; assoc. prof. medicine, anatomy U. Tenn., Memphis, 1968-70, prof. medicine, assoc. prof. anatomy, 1970-77, dir., dermatopathology, prof., 1975-77; prof., dir. dermatology, prof. anatomy Wright State U., Dayton, Ohio, 1977-80; chief, dermatology sect., dir. elec. microscopy lab. VA Med. Ctr., Dayton, 1977-80; dermatologist in chief Detroit Med. Ctr., 1987—; prof., chmn. dermatology Wayne State U., Detroit, 1980-99, prof. emeritus, 1999—. Mem. dermatol. drugs adv. com. FDA. Fulbright scholar, 1956-59; participant med. investigatorship career devel. program VA, 1969-77. Mem. Am. Soc. Dermatopathology (pres. 1986-87), Nat. Bd. Med. Examiners, Japanese Soc. Investigative Dermatology (hon.), Memphis Dermatological Soc. (pres. 1973-74), Soc. Investigative Dermatology (v.p. 1980-81, chmn. program com. 1985-86), Soc. Francaise de Dermatologie et de Syphilographie (corr. 1989), Japanese Assn. Dermatology (hon.). Office: Wayne State U Sch Medicine Dept Dermatology 540 E Canfield St Detroit MI 48201-1928

HASHMI, SAJJAD AHMAD, finance educator, dean; b. India, Dec. 20, 1933; m. Monica Ruggiero; children: Serena, Jason, Shawn, Michelle. BA, U. Karachi, 1953, MA, 1956; PhD in Ins., U. Pa., 1962. Lectr. Ohio State U., Columbus, 1962-64; asst. prof. Roosevelt U., Chgo., 1964-66; prof. Ball State U., Muncie, Ind., 1966-83, chmn. dept. fin., 1973-83; Jones disting. prof., dean emeritus Sch. Bus. Emporia (Kans.) State U., 1983—. Tech. advisor Ind. Arts Commn.; vice chmn. bd. trustees Kans. Ins. Edn. Found.; appeared on TV and radio programs, testified before NY, Kans. and Ind. legis. coms.; cons., spkr. in field. Author: Insurance is a Funny Business, 1972, Automobile Insurance, 1973, Contemporary Personal Finance, 1985, Make Every Second Count, 1989, Strategies for The Future, 1990; contbr. articles to profl. jours. Named Prof. of Yr., Ball State U. Students, 1971, Outstanding Tchr. of Yr., Ball State U., 1970. Mem. Am. Risk and Ins. Assn., Midwest Fin. Assn., Fin. Mgmt. Assn., Emporia C. of C., Emporia Country Club, Rotary, Beta Gamma Sigma, Sigma Iota Epsilon, Alpha Kappa Psi, Gamma Iota Epsilon, Phi Kappa Phi. Home: 7187 Boca Grove Pl # 204 Bradenton FL 34202 Personal E-mail: shashmi1@tampabay.rr.com.

HASLANGER, PHILIP CHARLES, journalist; b. Menominee, Mich., May 11, 1949; s. Harry LeRoy and Agnes Gertrude (Seidl) H.; m. Rosemary Ann Raasch Carta, May 27, 1972 (div.); children: Brian David, Sarah Marie; m. Ellen Jean Reuter, Apr. 9, 1983; children: Michael Kenneth, Julia Jane. BA in Sociology, U. Wis., 1971, MA in Journalism, 1973. With The Capital Times, Madison, Wis., 1973—, mng. editor, 1998—2006, contbg. editor, 2006—. Author: Stories of Call, 1998. Authorized lay pastor United Ch. of Christ, 2004—07; assoc. pastor Memorial United Ch. of Christ, Pitts., Wis.; ordained pastor United Ch. of Christ, 2007. Mem. Nat. Conf. Editl. Writers (bd. dirs. 1993, 94, 97, 2003, officer 1999-2002), New Media Fedn. Avocations: reading, music, hiking, theology. Home: 5409 Vicar Ln Madison WI 53714-3443 Office: The Capital Times 1901 Fish Hatchery Rd Madison WI 53713-1248 E-mail: phaslanger@madison.com.

HASLER, BRIAN K., state representative; b. Terre Haute, Ind., Oct. 28, 1958; m. Maggie McShaw; 2 children. BS, Ind. State U., 1980. Ombudsman Ind. Dept. Commerce, 1989—90; cons. Strategic Devel. Group, 1995—96, Brian Hasler Group, 1996—; state rep. dist. 77 Ind. Ho. of Reps., Indpls., 1996—, chair, tech., R & D com., mem. fin. instns., interstate and internat. cooperatoin, and pub. health coms., mem. health fin. commn., regulatory flexibility com., juvenile crime and restorative justice commn, Ind. Energy and Recycling devel. bd.; mem. Hoosier Millennium Task Force; gov.'s rep. Evansville Urban Enterprise Assn. Bd. Chair Workforce Devel. Commn.; mem. bus. com. Center City Corp.; econ. devel. dir. Office of Congressman Frank McCloskey, Ind. 8th Dist., 1985—89; vice mgr. Office of Congressman Bill Patman, Tex., 14th Dist., 1982—85; caseworker Office of Congressman Lee Hamilton, Ind., 9th Dist., 1981—82; staff asst. Ind. State Senate, 1980—81; co-chair, I-69 Legis. Coalition; bd. dirs. Timmy Found., Preservation Alliance. Named Legis. of Yr., Aviation Assn. Ind., 1997; recipient David and Goliath award, 1999, Key award, Ind. Coalition for Housing and Homeless Issues, 1999. Mem.: Evansville Number One Toastmasters Club (past pres.). Democrat. Roman Catholic. Office: Ind Ho of Reps 200 W Washington St Indianapolis IN 46204-2786

HASLETT, JIM, professional football coach; b. Pittsburgh, Pa., Dec. 9, 1955; BA in Elem. Edn., Ind. U. of Pa., 1978. Profl. football player Buffalo Bills and Y Nets, 1979-87; asst. football coach U. Buffalo, 1988-89; asst. coach Los Angeles Raiders, 1993-94, Pittsburgh Steelers, 1996-99; head coach New Orleans Saints, 2000—05; defensive coord. St. Louis Rams, 2006—. Named NFL Coach of the Yr., 2000; named to Coll. Football Hall of Fame, 2001. Office: c/o St Louis Rams 1 Rams Way Saint Louis MO 63045

HASSEBROOK, CHUCK, not-for-profit developer; m. Kate Borchman, Dec. 31, 1991; 2 children. BA, U. Nebr. Exec. dir. Ctr. for Rural Affairs, Walthill, Nebr. Mem. USDA Commn. on Small Farms, 1997—99, Nebr. Network 21 Food Sys. Com., 1993—97; former co-chmn. north ctrl. region tech. com. USDA Low Input Sustainable Agr. Rsch. Program; mem. agrl. sci. and tech. rev. bd. USDA, 1991—96. Mem. bd. regents U. Nebr., 1994—, vice chmn., 1999, chmn., 2000; mem. external adv. com. on bioethics Iowa State U., 1987—90; mem. Keystone Ctr. Structure of Agr. Group; bd. dirs. Bread for the World, 1988—94. Mem.: Agr. Builders Nebr. Mailing: 250 N 3d St Lyons NE 68038

HASSELBACHER, DARLENE M., human resources executive; b. Ill. Grad., Marycrest Coll., 1983; MBA, St. Ambrose U., 1985. Sr. v.p. Sears Mfg. Co., 1984-86; dir. human resources Lee Enterprises, Inc., 1986-97; v.p. human resources Aid Assn. for Luths., Appleton, Wis., 1997—. Vol. Emergency Shelter Bd.; mem. First English Luth. Ch.; bd. dirs. AAL Employee Credit Union. Mem. Media Human Resources Assn. (past pres.), Soc. for Human Resources Mgmt. Office: Aid Assn for Lutherans 4231 N Ballard Rd Appleton WI 54919-0001

HASSELL, STEPHEN C., information technology executive; BS, US Naval Acad., Annapolis, 1988; MBA, Kellogg Sch., Northwestern, Chgo., 1995. Mgr. Newport News Shipbuilding, 1995—98, dir., process innovation, CIO, 1998, v.p., 2000; pres. & CEO Naptheon Inc. (subs. Newport News); chief info. officer Invensys; v.p. & chief info. officer Emerson Elec. Co., St. Louis, 2004—. Decorated Navy Commendation medal; recipient CIO 100 award, CIO Mag. Office: Emerson Elec Co 8000 W Florissant Ave PO Box 4100 Saint Louis MO 63136-850

HASSERT, BRENT, state legislator; Owner Hassert Landscaping; mem. from 83d dist. Ill. Ho. of Reps., 1993—. Formerly mem. Will County Bd. Commrs.; formerly chmn., exec. Pub. Works and Natural Resources Coms., Will County; formerly commr. Will County Forest Preserve; formerly mem. Ill. Task Force for Solid Waste Legislation. Home: Brent Hassert State Representitive 1408 Joliet Rd Ste 102 Romeoville IL 60446-4405

HASSKAMP, KRIS, state legislator; b. Apr. 5, 1951; AA, Brainerd C.C.; BS, Bemidji State U. State rep. Dist. 12A, Minn., 1988—. Mem. com. edn. judiciary & local govt. coms., vice chmn. energy com., com. & econ. devel.-tourism & small bus. divsn. com., mem. environ. & natural resources-fin. divsn. gen. legis., vet. affairs & elec. coms., tax com., property tax divsn. com., commerce, tourism, consumer affairs, ins. and banking coms. Minn. Ho. of Reps. Lead Dem. local govt. and met. affairs. Home: 405 Superior Ave Crosby MN 56441-1264 Office: 100 Constitution Ave Saint Paul MN 55155-1232

HAST, ADELE, historian, editor, writer; b. NYC, Dec. 6, 1931; d. Louis and Kate (Miller) Krongelb; m. Malcolm Howard Hast, Feb. 1, 1953; children: David Jay, Howard Arthur. BA magna cum laude, Bklyn. Coll., 1953; MA, U. Iowa, 1969, PhD, 1979. Rsch. assoc. Atlas Early Am. History Project, Newberry Library, Chgo., 1971-75; assoc. dir. Atlas Great Lakes Indian History Project, 1976-79, Hist. Boundary Data File Project, 1979-81; editor in chief Marquis Who's Who, Inc., Chgo., 1981—86; survey dir. Nat. Opinion Rsch. Ctr., U. Chgo., 1986-89; rsch. fellow Newberry Libr., Chgo., 1989-95, scholar in residence, 1995—; exec. editor St. James Press, Chgo., 1990-92; mng. editor Hist. Ency. of Chgo. Women U. Ill., Chgo., 1991-93, dir., editor Hist. Ency. of Chgo. Women project, 1993-2001, sr. rsch. assoc. Ctr. for Rsch. on Women and Gender, 1999—2002. Mem. faculty Newberry Libr. Summer Inst. Cartography, 1980; cons. NEH planning grant Addams' Hull-House Mus., 2006. Author: Loyalism in Revolutionary Virginia, 1982, American Leaders Past and Present: The View from Who's Who in America, 1985, Hyman Libbie Henrietta (1988-1969) in Jewish Women in America: An Historical Encyclopedia, 1998; compiler: Iowa, Missouri, vol. 4 of Historical Atlas and Chronology of County Boundaries, 1788-1980, 1984, Libbie Hyman in Jewish Women: A Comprehensive Historical Encyclopedia, 2006; editor: International Directory of Company Histories, vols. 3-5, 1991-92, Women Building Chicago 1790-1990: A Biographical Dictionary, 2001; assoc. editor: Atlas of Great Lakes Indian History, 1987; curator exhibit on Chgo. history Spertus Inst. of Jewish Studies, 2002-03; contbr. articles to profl. jours. Treas., bd. dirs. Chgo. Map Soc., 1980-81, 93-95; mem. New Trier Twp. H.S. Bd. Caucus, 1972-74; mem. acad. coun. Am. Jewish Hist. Soc., 1985—; pres. Chgo. Jewish Hist. Soc., 1980-81, bd. dirs., 1977—. Recipient Alumna of Yr. award Bklyn. Coll., 1984, Colonial Williamsburg Found. grantee-in-aid, 1975, Brit. Acad. rsch. fellow, 1979; Am. Coun. Learned Socs. grantee-in-aid, 1980; NEH rsch. grantee, 1985, 87, 93-95, 97-98, fellow Jewish Women's Archive, 2003-04. Fellow Royal Hist. Soc., Phi Beta Kappa, Kappa Delta Pi; mem. Am. Hist. Assn., Orgn. Am. Historians, Chgo. Area Women's History Coun. (sec., treas. 1994-2004, bd. dirs. 1990—), Caxton Club (coun. 1990-93, 2003—, v.p. 2005—). Office: Newberry Library 60 W Walton St Chicago IL 60610-3380

HAST, MALCOLM HOWARD, biomedical scientist, educator; b. NYC, May 28, 1931; s. Irving William and Rose Lillian (Berlin) H.; m. Adele Krongelb, Feb. 1, 1953; children: David Jay, Howard Arthur. BA, Bklyn. Coll., 1953; postgrad., U. So. Calif., LA, 1955—57; MA, Ohio State U., Columbus, 1958; PhD (NIH fellow), Ohio State U., 1961; CBiol, FIBiol, Gt. Britain, 1991. Instr. U. Iowa, 1961-63; NIH spl. fellow U. Iowa Coll. Medicine, 1963-65, asst. prof., 1965-69; assoc. prof. otolaryngology-head and neck surgery Northwestern U. Feinberg Sch. Medicine, Chgo., 1969—74, prof., 1974—; dir. research otolaryngology Northwestern U. Med. Sch., Chgo., 1969-93, prof. cell and molecular biology (anatomy), 1977—2001; prof. basic and behavioral scis. Northwestern U. Dental Sch., 1989-2001; assoc. med. staff Northwestern Meml. Hosp., 1969-90, health profl., 1990-93; rsch. assoc. zoology Field Mus. Natural History, 1995—; assoc. editor Clinical Anatomy, 1995—. Mem. faculty appeals panel Northwesten U., 1974-83, chmn., 1999-2001, med. sch. appt. promotion and tenure com., 1986-91, gen. faculty benefits com., 2004—; mem. exec. com. of med. admissions com. Feinberg Sch. Medicine, 1991-, chmn., 1998-2003; mem. task force on new materials Am. Bd. Otolaryngology, 1969-72; dir. Ill. Soc. Med. Rsch., 1973-77; guest scientist Max Planck Inst. für Psychiatrie, 1976, Zoologisches Forchungsinstitut und Mus. A. Koenig, 1988; mem. Internat. Anat. Nomenclature Com., 1983-91; mem. exec. admissions com. Med. Scientist Tng. Program, 2002-; Brodel meml. lectr. Assn. Med. Illustrators, 1995; mem. Chgo. Clin. Ethics Programs; vis. prof. Royal Coll. Surgeons Eng., 1980-86, U. Edinburgh, 1987. Editor Annotated Translation of Vesalius' Fabrica, 1995-, elec. edit., 2003; contbr. articles to profl. jours., chpts. to books. Mem. adv. bd. Ctr. Deafness, 1977-80; bd. dirs. Cliff Dwellers Arts Found., 1979-82; trustee Wilmette Libr. Bd., 1982-83, Wilmette Bd. Health, 1999-2007. Served with US Army, 1953-55. NATO sr. fellow in sci. Oxford U., Eng., 1978; NIH rsch. grantee, 1964-84, 95—2004, NSF rsch. grantee, 1975-77, NEH grantee, 1995-2002; recipient Gould Internat. award, 1971, Disting. Alumnus award of Honor, Bklyn. Coll., 1977, Alumnus of Yr. award, 1984; Arnott demonstrator Royal Coll. Surgeons Eng., 1985. Fellow AAAS, Linnean Soc. London, Inst. Biology, Am. Speech-Hearing Assn., Royal Soc. Medicine; mem. AMA, AAUP (chpt. pres. 1977-82), Am. Physiol. Soc. (animal care and experimentation com. 1976-82), Am. Assn. Clin. Anatomists, Chgo. Laryngol. and Otol. Soc. (coun. 1988-89), Am. Soc. Mammalogists, Anat. Soc. Gt. Britain and Ireland, Am. Assn. History Medicine, Soc. Med. History Chgo., Amnesty Internat. (coord. Chgo. Health profls. group 1986-87), Am. Assn. Anatomists, Nat. Eagle Scout Assn., Sigma Xi (chpt. pres. 1971-72), Sigma Alpha Eta. Achievements include research on neuromuscular physiology, embryology and comparative anatomy of the larynx, history of medicine. Office: 303 E Chicago Ave Chicago IL 60611-3008

HASTAD, DOUGLAS NOEL, academic administrator, physical education educator; b. Fargo, ND, Dec. 18, 1949; s. Harold Noel and Olive Adelaide (Nugent) H.; m. Nancy Jo Seljevold, June 11, 1972; children: Jacob Noel, Rebekah Josie. BA, Concordia Coll., 1971; MS, Wash. State U., 1972; EdD, Ariz. State U., 1980; postgrad., Harvard U., 1992. Elem. phys. edn. specialist Moorhead Pub. Schs., Minn., 1972-76; instr. Concordia Coll., Moorhead, 1976-78; grad. assoc. Ariz. State U., Tempe, 1976-79; asst. prof. No. Ill. U., DeKalb, 1979-84; dept. chmn., assoc. prof. Tex. Christian U., Ft. Worth, 1984-89, interim dean, 1987-89; prof., dean dept. health, phys. edn. and recreation U. Wis., La Crosse, 1989—98, dean, human devel. programs, coll. health, phys. edn. and recreation, 1997—98, interim provost, vice chancellor academic affairs, 1998—99, provost, vice chancellor academic affairs, 1999—2000, interim chancellor, 2000—01, chancellor, 2001—06; acting pres. Carroll Coll., Waukesha, Wis., 2006—07, pres., 2007—. Coordinator statewide fitness evaluation project for youth, DeKalb, 1980-84; cons. U. Tex. Med. Br., Galveston, 1985-86. Author: Fitness in the Elementary School, 1986, 2d edit., 1989, Measurement and Evaluation in Physical Education and Exercise Science, 1989, 2d edit., 1994; editl. bd.: The Physical Educator, 1984—; contbr. articles to profl. jours. Vol. Spl. Olympics/Sr. Olympics, DeKalb, 1982-84; vice chmn. program com. Am. Heart Assn. Tex. br., Ft. Worth, 1985-86; dir. conf. on future directions for fitness Tarrant County Med. Soc., Ft. Worth, 1985, pub. sch. adv. bd., 1984-86; bd. dirs. Rotary Internat. Fellow Bush Foundation (hon.); mem. Am. Alliance for Health, Phys. Edn., Recreation and Dance, Golden Key Honor Soc. Home: N2166 Valley Rd La Crosse WI 54601-7118 Office: Carroll Coll Office of Pres 100 N East Ave Waukesha WI 53186

HASTEN, JOSEPH ERWIN, bank executive; b. Feb. 25, 1952; m. Jane Hasten, 1977; 3 children. B, Fairfield U., 1974; MBA, Northwestern U., 1978. Head, Midwest ops. Std. Chartered Bank, 1984—91; CEO Std. Chartered's South Korean and Indonesian Bus., 1991—95; pres., St. Louis bank Mercantile Bancorp, 1995—99; vice chmn. Firstar, now U.S. Bancorp, 1995—2001; vice chmn., corp. banking US Bancorp, St. Louis, 2001—05; pres., CEO ShoreBank Corp., Chgo., 2007—. Office: ShoreBank Corp 7054 S Jeffery Blvd Chicago IL 60649

HASTERT, DENNIS (JOHN DENNIS HASTERT), retired congressman; b. Aurora, Ill., Jan. 2, 1942; m. Thelma Jean Kahl, 1973; children: Joshua John, Ethan Allen. BA in Econ., Wheaton Coll., 1964; MS in Philosophy of Edn., No. Ill. U., 1967. Tchr., coach Yorkville (Ill.) High Sch., 1964—80; mem. Ill. House Reps., Springfield, 1980-86, US Congress from 14th Ill. dist., 1987—2007, chief dep. majority whip, 1994-99, spkr. of the House, 1999—2007, mem. commerce com., govt. reform and oversight com. Permanent chair Rep. Nat. Conv., 2000; mem. bd. dirs. Aurora Family Support Ctr. Author: Speaker: Lessons from Forty Years of Coaching and Politics, 2004. Named Ill. Coach of the Year, 1976, Guardian of the Seniors Rights, 60 Plus Assn., 1999; named an Outstanding Am., Nat. Wrestling Hall of Fame, 2000; named one of The 20 Top Legislators, Chgo. Sun Times, 1985; recipient Build Life award, Nat. Coalition for Athletic Equity, 1999, Taxpayer Hero award, Americans for Tax Reform, 1999, Disting. Citizen award, Three Fires Coun. (St. Charles, Ill.) Boy Scouts of Am., 2000, Alumnus of the Year award for Disting. Svc. to Society, Wheaton Coll., 2002, Golden Plate award, Acad. Achievement, 2004. Mem.: US Wrestling Assn., IL Wrestling Coaches Assn. (pres. 1977—78), US Olympic Com., US Olympic Movement, Farm Bureau, Lions (Yorkville). Republican. Protestant.

HASTINGS, BARRY G., trust company executive; Pres. No. Trust Corp., Chgo., 1993—. Office: No Trust Co 50 S Lasalle St Chicago IL 60675-0001

HASTINGS, JOYCE R., editor; Editor Wis. Lawyer, Madison. Office: State Bar Wis PO Box 7158 Madison WI 53707-7158

HASTINGS, KERRY P., lawyer; b. Cin., Oct. 27, 1971; BA, U. Mich., 1993; JD, Harvard U., 1996. Bar: Ohio 1996. Ptnr. Taft, Stettinius & Hollister LLP, Cin. Named one of Ohio's Rising Stars, Super Lawyers, 2005, 2006. Mem.: Cin. Acad. Leadership for Lawyers (class of 2006), Harvard Law Sch. Assn., ABA (mem., Labor and Employment Law Sect.), Cin. Bar Assn. (mem., Unauthorized Practice of Law Com.), Harvard Club Cin. Office: Taft Stettinius & Hollister LLP 425 Walnut St Ste 1800 Cincinnati OH 45202-3957 Office Phone: 513-381-2838. Office Fax: 513-381-0205.

HASTINGS, SUSAN C., lawyer; b. Mpls., 1959; BA, U. Iowa, 1980, JD with distinction, 1985. Bar: Ohio 1985, registered: US Dist. Ct. (No. Dist.) Ohio, US Ct. Appeals (6th cir.). Ptnr. Squire, Sanders & Dempsey LLP, Cleve., chmn., Labor & Employment Practice Group. Mem.: ABA (Labor & Employment Law Sect.), Ohio State Bar Assn. (Labor & Employment Law Sect.), Nat. Sch. Bd. Assn., Ohio Coun. of Sch. Bd. Attys. Office: Squire Sanders & Dempsey LLP 4900 Key Tower 127 Public Sq Cleveland OH 44114-1304 Office Phone: 216-479-8723. Office Fax: 216-479-8780. Business E-Mail: shastings@ssd.com.

HASTINGS, WILLIAM CHARLES, retired state supreme court chief justice; b. Newman Grove, Nebr., Jan. 31, 1921; s. William C. and Margaret (Hansen) H.; m. Julie Ann Simonson, Dec. 29, 1946; children— Pamela, Charles, Steven. B.Sc., U. Nebr., 1942, JD, 1948; LHD (hon.), Hastings Coll., 1991. Bar: Nebr. 1948. With FBI, 1942-43; mem. firm Chambers, Holland, Dudgeon & Hastings, Lincoln, 1948-65; judge 3d jud. dist. Nebr., Lincoln, 1965-79, Supreme Ct. Nebr., Lincoln, 1979-88, chief justice, 1988-95; ret., 1995. Bd. dir. Nat. Conf. Chief Justices, 1989-91. Pres. Child Guidance Ctr., Lincoln, 1962, 63; v.p. Lincoln Community Coun., 1968, 69; vice chmn. Antelope Valley coun. Boy Scouts Am., 1968, 69; pres. 1st Presbyn. Ch. Found., 1968—; mem. Lincoln Parks and Recreation Adv. Bd., Govs. task force correctional dept. medical svcs., 2000; mem. Nebr. Pub. Employees Retirement Bd. With US Army, 1943—46. Named to Nebr. Jaycee Hall of Fame, 1998, U. Nebr. Lincoln-Greek Hall of Fame, 2005; recipient Merit award, Acacia Nat. Frat., 2004. Mem. ABA, Nebr. Bar Assn. (George H. Turner award 1991, Pioneer award 1992), Am. Jud. Soc., Lincoln Bar Assn., Nebr. Dist. Judges Assn. (past pres.), Nat. Conf. Chief Justices (past bd. dirs.), Am. Judicature Soc. (Herbert Harley award 1997), Phi Delta Phi. Republican. Presbyterian (deacon, elder, trustee). Club: East Hills Country (pres. 1959-60). Home: 1544 S 58th St Lincoln NE 68506-1407 Personal E-mail: hwchastings@aol.com.

HATCH, MICHAEL WARD, lawyer; b. Pittsfield, Mass., Nov. 19, 1949; s. Ward Sterling and Elizabeth (Hubbard) H.; m. Lisa Schilling, June 8, 1974; children: Stuart, Andrew, Gillian. AB in Econs., St. Lawrence U., 1971; JD, Yale U., 1974. Bar: Wis. 1974, N.Y. 1980. Ptnr. Foley & Lardner LLP, Milw., 1974—, chmn. real estate practice group. Mem. ABA, N.Y. State Bar Assn., Wis. Bar Assn., Milw. Bar Assn., Am. Coll. Real Estate Lawyers, Urban Land Inst., Nat. Multi Housing Coun., Mortgage Bankers Assn. Wis., Bldg. Owners and Mgrs. Assn., Local Initiatives Support Corp., Milw. Athletic Club, Town Club. Avocations: architecture, historic preservation. Office: Foley & Lardner LLP 777 E Wisconsin Ave Ste 3800 Milwaukee WI 53202-5367 Office Phone: 414-297-5706. Office Fax: 414-297-4900. Business E-Mail: mhatch@foley.com.

HATCH, MIKE, former state attorney general; m. Patti Hatch; 3 children. BS in Polit. Sci. with honors, U. Minn., Duluth, 1970; JD, U. Minn., 1973. Commr. of commerce State of. Minn., 1983—89; pvt. practice law; atty. gen. State of Minn., 1999—2007. Democrat. Mailing: 320 E 135th St Burnsville MN 55337

HATFIELD, JERRY LEE, plant physiologist, agricultural meteorologist; b. Wamego, Kans., May 1, 1949; s. Virgil H. and Elsie L. (Fischer) H.; m. Patricia JoAnne Reigle, Sept. 1, 1968; children: Mark E., Andrew J. BS, Kans. State U., 1971; MS, U. Ky., 1972; PhD, Iowa State U., 1975. Biometeorologist U. Calif., Davis, 1975-83; plant physiologist USDA-Agrl. Rsch. Svc., Lubbock, Tex., 1983-89; lab. dir. Nat. Soil Tilth Lab., USDA-Agr. Rsch. Svc., Ames, Iowa, 1989—. Scientific quality review officer Agrl. Rsch. Svc., 2005—06. Editor: Biometerology and Integrated Pest Management, 1982, Limitations to Plant Root Growth, vol. 19, Advances in Soil Science, 1992, Soil Biology: Impacts on Soil Quality, Advances in Soil Science, 1993, Crops Residue Management, Advances in Soil Science, 1994, Utilization of Manure as a Soil Resource, Advances in Soil Science, 1998, Innovative Weed and Soil Management,

Advances in Soil Science, itrogen in the Environment, 2001, 2nd edit., Micrometeorogy in Agricultural Systems, 2005, The Farmers Decision: Balancing Economic Successful Agriculture Production with Environmental Quality, 2005; contbr. over 340 articles to profl. jours. Recipient Arthur S. Flemming award for outstanding svc. to fed. govt., 1997, Disting. Svc. award in agr., Kans. State U., 2002. Fellow Soil Sci. Soc. Am., Am. Soc. Agronomy (editor jour. 1989-95, editor-in-chief 1996-2002, pres.-elect 2006, pres. 2006-07, Agronomic Svc. award 1999), Crop Sci. Soc. Am.; mem. Am. Geophys. Union, Am. Meteorol. Soc. (chair agrl./forest com. 1980-81, agrl. and forest meteorology com. 1999-2002), Indian Agrometeorol. Soc. (hon.), Soil and Water Conservation Soc. (program chair 1997-98, bd. dirs. 2005-08, Pres. Leadership award 1998, 2005, 2008, Presdl. Rank award 2005, 2008), Phi Kappa Phi, Gamma Sigma Delta (Outstanding Alumni award 2005). Republican. Avocations: golf, reading, photography, landscaping. Office: USDA Agrl Rsch Svc Nat Soil Tilth Lab 2150 Pammel Dr Ames IA 50011-0001 Home Phone: 515-232-1963; Office Phone: 515-294-5723. Business E-Mail: jerry.hatfield@ars.usda.gov.

HATLEN, ROE HAROLD, restaurant executive; b. Libby, Mont., Nov. 6, 1943; s. Knute Harold and Hilda Elizabeth Halten; m. Beverly Joan Thompson, June 18, 1966; children: Kari, Erick, Lars. BBA, Pacific Lutheran U., 1965; MBA, U. Oreg., 1967. Auditor Kohnen & Larson, Eugene, Oreg., 1966—67, Herzinger, Porter, Addison & Blind, Eugene, Oreg., 1967—73; contr. Internat. King's Table, Inc., Eugene, Oreg., 1976—76, v.p. fin., treas., 1976—. Pres. bd. dirs. Ctrl. Luth. Found. Bd., 1979—82; mem. alumni bd. Pacific Luth. U., Tacoma, 1982—. With USAR, 1967—73. Mem.: Nat. Restaurant Assn., Oreg. Soc. C.P.A.s, Portland Cash Mgrs. Assn., Am. Inst. C.P.A.s (bd. accountancy). Home: 782 Kristen Ct Eugene OR 97401-2346 Office: Buffets Inc 1460 Buffet Way Eagan MN 55121-1133

HATLER, PATRICIA RUTH, lawyer; b. Las Vegas, Nev., Aug. 4, 1954; d. Houston Eugene and Laurie (Danforth) Hatler; m. Howard A. Coffin II; children: Sloan H. D. Coffin, Laurie H. M. Coffin. BS magna cum laude in Cognitive Psych., Duke U., 1976; JD, U. Va., 1980. Bar: Pa. 1980, Ohio 2002. Assoc. Dechert, Price & Rhoads, Phila., 1980-83; assoc. counsel Independence Blue Cross, Phila., 1983-86, sr. v.p., gen. counsel, corp. sec., 1987-99; exec. v.p., chief legal, governance officer Nationwide, Columbus, Ohio, 1999—. Office: Nationwide One Nationwide Plz Columbus OH 43215-2220 Office Phone: 614-677-8754. E-mail: hatlerp@nationwide.com.

HATTEBERG, LARRY MERLE, photojournalist; b. Winfield, Kans., June 30, 1944; s. Merle Lawrence and Mary Dorothy (Early) H.; m. Judy Beth Keller, June 6, 1965; children: Sherry Renee, Susan Michelle. Student, Kans. State Tchrs. Coll., 1962-63, Emporia-Wichita State U., 1963-66. Photographer Sta. KAKE-TV, Wichita, Kans., 1963, photojournalist, 1966-67, chief photographer, 1967-81, assoc. news dir., 1981-87, exec. news dir., 1987-88, co-anchor 5 p.m. newscast, 1988-92; co-anchor Evening News broadcasts KAKE-TV, Wichita, Kans., 1992—. Faculty Nat. Press Photographers TV Workshop, U. Okla., 1975—. Author: Larry Hatteberg's Kansas People,1991; developed Hatteberg's People series for TV, 1974. Served with USAR, 1966-72. Regional semi-finalist NASA Journalist-in-Spece Program; recipient Brotherhood award Kans. region NCCJ, 1995, regional lifetime Emmy award TV segment Hatteberg's People, Regional Emmy, 2000, 04. Life mem. Nat. Press Photographers Assn. (Nat. TV News Photographer of Yr. award 1975, 77, Joseph Sprague award 1983, Joseph Costa award 1991). Office: 1500 N West St Wichita KS 67203-1323

HATTERY, ROBERT RALPH, radiologist, educator; b. Phoenix, Dec. 15, 1939; s. Robert Ralph and Goldie M. H.; m. D. Diane Sittler, June 18, 1961; children: Angela, Michael. BA, Ind. U., Bloomington, 1961; MD, Ind. U., Indpls., 1964; cert. in diagnostic radiology, U. Minn. Mayo Grad. Sch. Medicine, Rochester, 1971. Diplomate Am. Bd. Radiology. Intern Parkland Meml. Hosp.-Southwestern Med. Sch., Dallas, 1964-65; fellow Mayo Clinic, Rochester, Minn., 1967-70, cons., 1970-81, chmn. dept. diagnostic radiology, 1981-86; instr. radiology Mayo Med. Sch., 1973-75, asst. prof. radiology, 1975-78, assoc. prof. radiology, 1978-82, prof. radiology, 1982—. Chair Mayo Group Practice Bd., 1991-93; chmn. bd. govs Mayo Clinic, Rochester, 1994-98; trustee Mayo Found., 1992-2002; trustee Am. Bd. Radiology. Author numerous jour. articles and abstracts, book chpts. Capt. USAF, 1965-67, Willford Hall Hosp., San Antonio. Fellow Am. Coll. Radiology; mem. Radiol. Soc. N.Am. (bd. dirs. 1999—), Am. Roentgen Ray Soc., Soc. Computed Body Tomography (pres. 1982-83), Soc. Genitourinary Radiography (pres. 1986-88), Am. Bd. Radiology (exec. dir.). Office: American Bd Radiology 5441 E Williams Blvd Tucson AZ 85711 Home Phone: 520-219-8599. Business E-Mail: rhattery@theabr.org.

HATTIN, DONALD EDWARD, geologist, educator; b. Cohasset, Mass., Nov. 16, 1928; s. Edward Arthur and Una Vestella (Whipple) H.; m. Marjorie Elizabeth Macy, July 15, 1950; children: Sandra Jane, Ronald Scott, Donna Jean. BS, U. Mass., 1950; MS, U. Kans., 1952, PhD (Shell fellow), 1954. Asst. instr. geology U. Kans., 1950-52, instr., 1953-54; asst. prof. geology Ind. U., Bloomington, 1954-60, assoc. prof., 1960-67, prof., 1967-95, prof. emeritus, 1995—; asst. geologist Kans. Geol. Survey, 1952, research assoc., 1959-68, 70-74, 77-82, 86-87. Vis. prof. Ernst-Moritz-Arndt U., Greifswald, German Dem. Republic, 1985; geologist Ind. Geol. Survey, 1957-58; cons. in field; mem. N.Am. Commn. on Stratigraphic Nomenclature, 1987-94; vis. disting. prof. U. Kans., 1991. Author: Stratigraphy of the Wreford Limestone, 1957, Stratigraphy of the Carlile Shale, 1962, Stratigraphy of the Graneros Shale in Central Kansas, 1965, Stratigraphy and Depositional Environment of Greenhorn Limestone of Kansas, 1975, Upper Cretaceous Stratigraphy and Depositional Environments of Western Kansas, 1978, Stratigraphy and Depositional Environment of Smoky Hill Chalk, Niobrara Chalk, Western Kansas, 1982, W. Ferdinand Macy, 1852-1901: Painter of New England Landscapes, 2004, Tales of a New England Boyhood: Scituate, Massachusetts, 1931-1946, 2006. Trainman, steam locomotive restoration specialist Ind. Railway Mus., French Lick. Capt. reserves USAF, 1950—60, lt. USAF, 1955—57. Recipient Erasmus Haworth Disting. Alumni honors in geology U. Kans., 1976, Alumni Disting. Tchg. award Coll. Arts and Scis. Ind. U., 1988, Disting. Tchg. and Mentoring award Grad. Sch. Ind. U., 1995; NSF grantee, 1975-77, 88-90, Am. Chem. Soc. grantee, 1978-80, 84-86; NSF fellow, 1969. Fellow: Geol. Soc. Am. (grantee 1975); mem.: Paleontol. Soc., Soc. Econ. Paleontologists Mineralogists, Am. Assn. Petroleum Geologists (Outstanding Educator award Ea. sect. 1993), Ind. Soc. Mayflower Descendants (chmn. scholarship com.). Office: Ind U Dept Geol Scis Bloomington IN 47405 Personal E-mail: hattin@indiana.edu.

HATTON, JANIE R. HILL, principal; Formerly prin. Milw. Trade and Tech. H.S.; cmty. supt. Milw. Pub. Schs., 1989-91; dir. Dept. Leadership Svcs., 1996-97; dep. supt. Leadership Svcs., Milw., 1997-99; prin. Pulaski H.S., Milw., 1999—2001, N. Div. H.S., Milw., 2001—. Recipient Milw. Prin. Yr. award Alexander Hamilton H.S., 1986, Nat. Principal of the Year award Nat. Assn. Secondary Sch. Principals and Met. Life Ins. Co., 1993, It Takes a Whole Village Leadership award, 1999. Mem. Milw. Links Inc., Delta Sigma Theta. Office: 1011 W Center St Milwaukee WI 53206-3299

HAUBIEL, CHARLES W., II, lawyer; b. July 1965; m. Michele R. Haubiel. B, Purdue U.; JD, Ohio State U. Bar: 1992. Atty. Vorys, Sater, Seymour & Pease; sr. staff counsel Big Lots Inc. (previously Consolidated Stores Corp.), Columbus, Ohio, 1997—99, dir., corp. counsel, asst sec., 1999—2000, v.p., gen. counsel, corp. sec., 2000—04, sr. v.p., gen. counsel, corp. sec., 2004—. Office: Big Lots Inc 300 Phillipi Rd Columbus OH 43228

HAUFLER, CHRISTOPHER HARDIN, botany educator; b. Niskayuna, NY, Apr. 20, 1950; s. J. Hervie and Patricia (DeLearie) Haufler. BA, Hiram Coll., 1972; MA, Ind. U., 1974, PhD, 1977. Assoc. instr. Ind. U., 1972—76, asst. prof, 1977; postdoctoral fellow Gray Herbarium, Harvard U., 1977-78; NEA postdoctoral fellow Mo. Bot. Garden, St. Louis, 1978-79; asst. prof. U. Kans., Lawrence, 1979-84, assoc. prof., 1984-90, chmn. dept. botany, 1985, prof., 1990—. Faculty sponsor undergraduate biology club, 1980—, search com., 1980—, field facilities com., 1980-92, curriculum com., 1980—, greenhouse com., 1980—, chair, 1984-88, honors and awards com., 1980-87, space com., 1980-86, chair departmental admissions and awards com., 1981-84, biology core rev. com., 1983-85, biol. scis. resource ctr., 1984-87, biol. scis. exec. com., 1985—, stewart Evolutionists, 1985, sec., 1986; mem. panel systematic biology NSF, 1987-93. Reviewer Index to Plant Chromosome Numbers, 1979-89; presenter papers in field. William R. Ogg Departmental fellow, 1976-77; Rsch. fellow Gray Herbarium, 1977-78. Mem. Bot. Soc. Am. (mem. nominating com. for officers pteridological sect. 1981, 82, sec.-treas. 1983-89, prog. organizer 1985, 87, 89, chair 1991-93, symposium organizer 1984, 85, 87, editor Ann. Bibliography Am. Pteridology 1978-82, assoc. editor Am. Jour. Botany 1994—, sec. 1991—, pres. 2006-, Best Paper award 1979, 80, 82, 83, 84, 92, 93), Am. Fern Soc. (mem. nominating com. for officers 1980, 83, assoc. editor Am. Fern Jour. 1986—), Am. Inst. Biol. Scis., Am. Soc. Plant Taxonomists (rsch. awards com. 1989-91, prog. dir. 1990-93, editl. bd. Systematic Botany 1985-87, assoc. editor 1994—), Nat. Geog. Soc., Soc. Systematic Biologists (editl. bd. 1992—), Internat. Assn. Pteridologists (sec. 1987—, compiler Internat. Report Pteridological Rsch. 1984-88), Brit. Pteridological Soc., Soc. for Study Evolution, Sigma Xi. Office: U Kans Dept Ecology and Evolutionary Biology 2041 Haworth Hall 1200 Sunnyside Ave Lawrence KS 66045 Office Phone: 785-864-3255. Office Fax: 785-864-5294. E-mail: vulgare@ku.edu.

HAUGELAND, JOHN, philosophy educator; b. Mar. 13, 1945; married. BS in Physics, Harvey Mudd Coll., 1966; PhD, U. Calif., Berkeley, 1976. Vis. instr. Pomona Coll., 1974, U. Calif., Berkekey, 1976; instr. U. Pitts., 1974—76, asst. prof., 1976—81, 1976—81, prof., 1986—99; prof. philosophy U. Chgo., 1999—, chair philosophy dept., 2004—. Author, Artificial Intelligence: The Very Idea, 1986, Having Thought, 1998; editor: Mind Design, 1981, 2nd edit., 1997; co-editor: The Road Since Structure, 2000. Fellow, John Simon Guggenheim Meml. Found., 2003. Office: U Chgo Dept Philosophy 1010 E 59th St Chicago IL 60637

HAUGLAND, ERLING, political organization executive; b. Crosby, ND; BA, U. N.D. Pres. Recreation Supply Co. Inc., Inpls., 1980—. Chmn. N.D. State Reps., Bismark, 1999—. Office: PO Box 1473 Bismarck ND 58502-1473

HAUPT, ROGER A., advertising executive; Joined Leo Burnett (became Leo Group), Chgo., 1984—2000; exec. v.p. Leo Group, 1989—97, 1999—2000, pres., CEO, 2000, COO, 1999; CAO Leo Group (became BCom3), 1997—99; chmn., CEO BCom3 (became Publicis Groupe SA), 2000—02; pres., COO Publicis Groupe SA, Chgo, 2002—04; chmn. Publicis Groupe Media.

HAURY, DAVID LEROY, science education specialist; b. Salem, Oreg., Sept. 17, 1947; s. Hubert Oscar and Anna Lorane (Davis) H.; m. Arlene H. Friesen, Dec. 26, 1968. BA in Biology, U. Oreg., 1974, MA in Biology, 1978; PhD in Sci. Edn., U. Wash., 1983. Cert. tchr., Oreg., S. Australia. Sci. tchr. Grant High Sch., Mt. Gambier, S. Australia, 1974-77; teaching assoc. U. Wash., Seattle, 1979-82; asst. prof. biology Judson Bapt. Coll., The Dalles, Oreg., 1982-84; asst. prof. sci. edn. Tufts U., Medford, Mass., 1984-90; assoc. prof. sci. edn. U. Lowell (Mass.), 1990-91, Ohio State U., Columbus, 1991—, dir.Eric Clearinghouse for Sci., Math. and Environ. Edn., 1991—. Cons. in field; dir. Sci. Edn. Programs and Leadership, Lowell, 1988-91. Editor Jour. of Sci. Tchr. Edn., 1988-94. Mem. adv. bd. Project Learning Tree, Mass., 1986-91, Tsongas Indsl. History Ctr., Lowell, 1989-91. Sgt. U.S. Army, 1968-72. Mem. Assn. for Edn. Tchrs. of Sci., ASCD, Nat. Assn. Rsch. in Sci. Teaching, Nat. Sci. Assn., Nat. Sci. Tchrs. Assn., Phi Beta Kappa, Phi Delta Kappa. Avocations: photography, nature study, bicycling, hiking. Office: Ohio State U 249 Arps Hall 1945 N High St Columbus OH 43210-1120 also: Ohio State U Eric Clearinghouse for Sci 1929 Kenny Rd Columbus OH 43210-1015

HAUSER, ELLOYD, finance company executive; Founder and CEO United Check Clearing Corp., 1984—98; pres., CEO Solutran Customized Payment Solutions (formerly United Check Clearing Corp), 1998—2001; chmn. Solutran, 1998—. Office: Solutran 3600 Holly Ln N Ste 60 Plymouth MN 55447-1286

HAUSER, STEPHEN CRANE, gastroenterologist; b. Oak Park, Ill., Oct. 6, 1951; s. Crane C. and Mary C. Hauser; m. Eleanor C. Blasi; 2 children. BA, Franklin & Marshall Coll., 1973; MD, U. Chgo., 1977. Fellow in gastroenterology Brigham and Women's Hosp., Boston, 1980-83, physician, 1983-98; clin. gastroenterologist and hepatologist Mayo Clinic, Rochester, Minn., 1998—. Mem. Am. Assn. for Study of Liver Disease, Am. Gastroenterol. Assn., Phi Beta Kappa, Alpha Omega Alpha. Office: Mayo Clinic Dept Gastroenterology and Hepatology 200 1st St SW Rochester MN 55905-0002

HAUSERMAN, JACQUITA KNIGHT, management consultant; b. Donalsonville, Ga., Apr. 23, 1942; d. Lendon Bernard and Ressie Mae (Robinson) Knight; m. Mark Kenny Hauserman, July 8, 1978 (div. Mar. 1998). BS in Math., U. Montevallo, Ala., 1964; MA in Tchg. Math., Emory U., 1973; MBA in Fin., Ga. State U., 1978. Fin. analyst Cleve. Electric Illuminating Co., 1982-83, gen. supr. employment svc., 1983-85, sr. corp. planning advisor, 1985-86, dir. customer svc., 1986-88, v.p. adminstrn., 1988-90; v.p. customer svc. & cmty. affairs Centerior Energy Corp., Independence, Ohio, 1990-93, v.p. customer support, 1993-95, v.p. bus. svcs., 1995-97; v.p., chief devel. officer Summa Health Sys., Akron, Ohio, 1999-2000; prin. Arcadia Consulting, Pepper Pike, Ohio, 2000—. Home and Office: 2901 Greenflower Ct Bonita Springs FL 34134-4387 E-mail: jhauserman@johnrwood.com.

HAUSLER, WILLIAM JOHN, JR., microbiologist, educator, public health service officer; b. Kansas City, Kans., Aug. 31, 1926; s. William John and Clifton (McCambridge) H.; m. Mary Lois Rice, Apr. 19, 1949 (dec. 1999); children: Cheryl Kaye Johnson, Kenneth Randall, Eric Rice, Mark Clifton. AB in Microbiology, U. Kans., 1951, MA in Microbiology, 1953, PhD in Microbiology and Math., 1958. Diplomate Am. Bd. Med. Microbiology (chmn. 1979-82, Profl. Recognition award 1995). Asst. instr. U. Kans., Lawrence, 1951-56, rsch. asst., 1956-58; assoc. bacteriologist Iowa State Hygienic Lab., Iowa City, 1958-59, asst. dir., prin. bacteriologist, 1959-65, dir., 1965-95; dir. emeritus, 1995—; asst. prof. U. Iowa Coll. Medicine, Iowa City, 1959-66, assoc. prof., 1966-90, prof., 1990—95, emeritus prof., 1995—; assoc. prof. U. Iowa Coll. Dentistry, 1966-90, prof., 1990—95, emeritus prof., 1995—. Cons. to Iran WHO, 1969, U.S. EPA, 1970-72, CDC, 1965—, People's Republic China WHO, 1990, WHO Western Pacific Region, 1991, UNDP India, 1992; cons. to industry; mem. mil. infectious diseases rsch. program Am. Inst. Biol. Scis., 2002. Editor: Standard Methods for the Examination of Dairy Products, 1972, Manual Clinical Microbiology, 3d edit., 1980, 5th edit., 1991, Compendium of Methods for the Microbiological Examination of Foods, 1980, 2d edit., 1984, Diagnostic Procedures for Bacterial Mycotic and Parasitic Infections, 1981, Laboratory Diagnosis of Infections Diseases: Principles and Practice, 1988; co-editor: Topley & Wilson's Microbiology and Microbial Infections, 9th edit., 1997; mem. editl. bd. various profl. jours.; contbr. articles to profl. jours. Councilman City Govt., University Heights, Iowa, 1966-69; commr. Iowa Air Pollution Control Commn., 1967-74; mem. exec. com. Iowa Dept. Environ. Quality, 1974-80, Nat. Com. for Clin. Lab. Standards, bd. dirs., 1987-93. Lt. comdr. USNR, 1944-67. Recipient Henry Albert Meml. award Iowa Pub. Health Assn., 1974. Fellow APHA, Am. Acad. Microbiology (chmn. 1983-89, Profl. Recognition award 1995); mem. Am. Soc. Microbiology, Assn. State and Territorial Pub. Health Lab. Dirs. (pres. 1984-85, Lifetime Achievement award 1998), Sigma Phi Epsilon, Rotary (Paul Harris fellow). Avocations: photography, woodworking, wilderness backpacking. Home: 11 The Woods NE Iowa City IA 52240-7986 Office: U Iowa Hygienic Lab Oakdale Hall Iowa City IA 52242 Office Phone: 319-335-4500. Personal E-mail: iahausler@yahoo.com.

HAUSMAN, ALICE, state legislator; b. July 31, 1942; M. Robert Hausman; 2 children. BS in Edn., Concordia Coll., 1963, MA in Edn., 1965. State rep. Dist. 66B Minn. Ho. of Reps., Minn., 1989—. Mem. econ. devel. com., transportation fin. com., transportation policy com., vice chmn. environ. & natural resources com., edn. fin. divsn. & regulated indsl. & energy coms., Minn. Ho. of Reps. Home: 1447 Chelmsford St Saint Paul MN 55108-1404 Office: 245 State Office Bldg Saint Paul MN 55155 E-mail: rep.Alice.Hausman@house.leg.state.mn.us.

HAUTMAN, PETE (PETER MURRAY), writer; b. Berkeley, Calif., 1952; V.p. mktg. Crowd Caps Inc., Minneapolis, 1981—88; owner Hautman Mktg. Svcs., 1988—91; writer, 1991—. Author: Drawing Dead, 1993 (selected NY Times Book Review Notable Books), Short Money, 1995, Mortal Nuts, 1996 (selected NY Times Book Review Notable Books), Mr. Was, 1996 (nominated Edgar Allan Poe Award, 1997), Ring Game, 1997, Stone Cold, 1998, Mrs. Million, 1999, Rag Man, 2001, Hole in the Sky, 2001 (Wis. Libr. Assn. Award, 2002), Doohickey, 2002, Sweetblood, 2003 (Best Young Adult Book of Yr., Mich. Libr. Assn., 2004), Godless, 2004 (Nat. Book Award for Young People's Lit., 2004). E-mail: pete@petehautman.com.

HAVERKAMP, JUDSON, editor; AB in History, Earlham Coll., 1967; MEd, U. Mass., 1976, postgrad. With U.S. Peace Corps/Ministry of Pub. Helath, Bangkok, Thailand, 1967-70; asst. fgn. student advisor U. Mass., Amherst, 1971-75, publs. coord. Ctr. for Internat. Edn., 1975-79; dir. residence, acad. advisor Bradford (Mass.) Coll., 1979-81; freelance writer and editor Mpls., 1981-84; assoc. editor Minn. State Bar Assn., Mpls., 1984-85, dir. publs., editor, 1985—. Office: Minn State Bar Assn 600 Nicollet Ave Ste 380 Minneapolis MN 55402-1641

HAW, BILL, association executive; Pres. Nat. Farms Inc., Kansas City, Mo. Office: National Farms Inc T White Bass Co 201 Main St Ste 2600 Fort Worth TX 76102-3134

HAWKINS, BRETT WILLIAM, retired political science professor; b. Buffalo, Sept. 15, 1937; s. Ralph C. and Irma A. (Rowley) H.; m. Linda L. Knuth, Oct. 31, 1974; 1 child, Brett William. AB, U. Rochester, 1959; MA, Vanderbilt U., 1962, PhD, 1964. Instr. polit. sci. Vanderbilt U., 1963; instr. in polit. sci. Washington and Lee U., 1963-64, asst. prof., 1964-65, U. Ga., Athens, 1965-68, assoc. prof., 1968-70, U. Wis., Milw., 1970-71, prof., 1971-99, ret, 2000. Author: ashville Metro, 1964, The Ethnic Factor in American Politics, 1970, Politics in the Metropolis, 2d edit. 1971, Politics and Urban Policies, 1971, The Politics of Raising State and Local Revenue, 1978, Professional Associations and Municipal Innovation, 1981; contbr. articles to profl. jours., chpts. in edited vols. Mem. Phi Beta Kappa, Iota of N.Y. Home: 5318 N Kent Ave Whitefish Bay WI 53217-5109 Personal E-mail: bretthwk@yahoo.com.

HAWKINS, JOSEPH ELMER, JR., physiologist, educator; b. Waco, Tex., Mar. 4, 1914; s. Joseph Elmer and Maude Burke (Schlenker) H.; m. Jane Elizabeth Daddow, Aug. 24, 1939 (dec. Sept. 2002); children: Richard Spencer Daddow, Peter Douglas Huntington, James Marion Davis, William Alexander Parmley, Priscilla Ann (Mrs. Philip A. Leach). Student, Altes Realgymnasium, Munich, 1929-30; AB, Baylor U., 1933; postgrad., Brown U., 1933-34; BA in Physiology, U. Oxford, 1937, MA, 1966, DSc in Clin. Medicine, 1979; PhD in Med. Sci., Harvard U., 1941. Tchg. fellow in physiology Harvard Med. Sch., 1937-41, instr., 1941-45; asst. investigator Nat. Def. Rsch. Com.-Office Sci. Rsch. & Devel., Harvard U., 1941-43; spl. rsch. assoc. Harvard Psycho-Acoustic Lab., Cambridge, Mass., 1943-45; asst. prof. physiology Bowman Gray Sch. Medicine, Wake Forest Coll., Winston-Salem, NC, 1945-46; rsch. assoc. neurophysiology Merck Inst. for Therapeutic Rsch., Rahway, NJ, 1946-56; assoc. prof. otolaryngology NYU Sch. Medicine, 1956-63; prof. physiol. acoustics U. Mich., Ann Arbor, 1963-84, prof. otolaryngology emeritus, 1984—, chmn. grad. program in physiol. acoustics, 1969-81. Disting. vis. prof. biology Baylor U., Waco, Tex., 1985-93; mem. IH sensory diseases study sect., 1958-61, communicative disorders rsch. tng. com., 1965-69, communicative scis. study sect., 1975-79; mem. Nat. Libr. Medicine Communicative Disorders Task Force, 1977-79; lectr. Armed Forces Inst. Pathology, 1969-74; cons. various pharm. cos. Contbr. to: Ency. Brit., 1974, 86, 99, Ency. Neuroscience, 1987, 99, 2003; editor: (with M. Lawrence and W.P. Work) Otophysiology, 1973, (with S.A. Lerner and G.T. Matz) Aminoglycoside Ototoxicity, 1981; contbr. articles to profl. jours. Mem. Bd. Edn., Cranford, NJ, 1958—61. Rhodes scholar Tex. and Worcester Coll., U. Oxford, 1934-37; USPHS spl. fellow Öronkliniken, Sahlgrenska Sjukhuset U. Göteborg, Sweden, 1961-63; NAS exch. lectr. to Yugoslavia and Bulgaria, 1977; Chercheur étranger de l'INSERM, Lab. d'Audiologie Expérimentale, U. Bordeaux II, 1978; recipient Disting. Achievement award Baylor U., 1982, City of Pleven, Bulgaria medal, 1982, U. Bordeaux medal, 1983, Humboldt Rsch. award for sr. U.S. scientists U. Würzburg, 1991, Hon. Citizen award, Bordeaux, 1991, Disting. Alumnus award Baylor U., 1996. Fellow AAAS, Acoustical Soc. Am.; mem. Am. Physiol. Soc., Assn. for Rsch. in Otolaryngology (award of merit 1985, Presdl. citation 2004), Collegium Oto-rhino-laryngologicum Amicitiae Sacrum, Bárány Soc., European Workshop for Inner Ear Biology, Am. Assn. for History of Medicine, Am. Otol. Soc. (assoc.), Prosper Menière Soc. (hon., Gold medal for basic sci. 1998), Pacific Coast Oto-ophthalmol. Soc. (hon.), Connétablie de Guyenne (Bordeaux, assoc.), Phi Beta Kappa, Sigma Xi. Anglican. Democrat. Achievements include research in ototoxic, noise-induced, and presbyacusic hearing loss; history of otolaryngology; masking of speech by noise. Avocations: Germanic and Romance languages and literature, gardening. Home: Glacier Hills Apt 258 1200 Earhart Rd Ann Arbor MI 48105 Office: U Mich Med Sch Kresge Hearing Rsch Inst Ann Arbor MI 48109-0506 Office Phone: 734-764-0215. Business E-Mail: josehawk@umich.edu.

HAWKINS, RICHARD ALBERT, medical educator, administrator; b. Greenwich, Conn., Mar. 27, 1940; s. Albert Rice and Florence Marie Elizabeth (Hansen) H.; m. Enriqueta Elias, May 9, 1964; children: Richard Alfred, Paul Andrés. BSc magna cum laude, San Diego State U., 1963; PhD, Harvard U., 1969; LHD (hon.), U. Phoenix, 1994. Rsch. fellow Metabolic Rsch. Lab. Radcliffe Infirmary, Oxford (Eng.) U., 1969-71; staff fellow in neurochemistry St. Elizabeth Hosp., Washington, 1971-72, NIMH/NIAAA sr. staff fellow in neurochemistry, 1972-74; chief phys. sci. br. FDA, Rockville, Md., 1974-76; assoc. prof. neurosurgery and physiology NYU Med. Ctr., NYC, 1976-77; prof. anesthesia and physiology Pa. State U., Hershey (Pa.) Med. Ctr., 1977-88; prof., chmn. physiology and biophysics The Rosalind Franklin U. Medicine and Sci., North Chicago, Ill., 1988-93, prof., 1988—; exec. v.p. acad. affairs, chief academic officer Herman M. Finch U. Health Scis./Chgo. Med. Sch., North Chicago, Ill., 1993-98, provost, 1998, pres., CEO, 1999—2003. Hon. prof. U. Valencia, Spain, 1989—. Contbr. numerous articles to profl. jours. Recipient Meritorious Rsch. award Morris Parker Found., 1992. Fellow Am. Heart Assn.; mem. Am. Physiol. Soc., Am. Soc. Neurochemistry, Biochem. Soc., Soc. for Neurosci., Alpha Omega Alpha. Home: 950 N Michigan Ave Chicago IL 60611 Office: Rosalind Franklin U Med and Sci 3333 Green Bay Rd North Chicago IL 60064-3037 Home Phone: 847-615-1826; Office Phone: 847-578-3218. Business E-Mail: rah@post.harvard.edu.

HAWKINS, WILLIAM A., III, medical products executive; b. 1954; BS, Duke U., 1976; MBA, U. Va., 1982. Corp. v.p., pres. Sherwood Davis & Geck div. Am. Home Products Corp., 1997—98; pres., CEO Novoste Corp., 1998—2002; sr. v.p., pres. vascular Medtronic Inc., Mpls., 2002—04, pres., COO, 2004—07, pres., CEO, 2007—. Bd. dir. DeLuxe Corp. Mem. bd. vis. Engring. Sch., Duke Univ.; trustee Darden Sch. Found., Univ. Va.; bd. mem. Guthrie Theatre. Office: Medtronic Inc 710 Medtronic Pkwy Minneapolis MN 55432-5604

HAWKINS, WILLIAM H., II, lawyer; b. Cin., July 18, 1948; BS, U. Cin., 1970, MEd, 1974; JD, No. Ky. U., 1978. Bar: Ohio 1978, Ky. 1979. Atty. then ptnr. Frost & Jacobs (now Frost Brown Todd); assoc. gen. counsel, sec. Convergys Corp., Cincinnati, Ohio, 1999—2001, gen. counsel, sec., 2001—03, sr. v.p., gen. counsel, corp. sec., 2003—. Office: Convergys Corp PO Box 1638 Cincinnati OH 45201

HAWKINSON, CARL E., state legislator; b. Galesburg, Ill., Oct. 7, 1947; m. Karen Zeches; 3 chilren. BA, Park Coll.; JD, Harvard U. Law practice; mem. from 94th dist. Ill. Ho. of Reps., 1983-86; now mem. Ill. State Senate. also: 1577 N Prairie St Galesburg IL 61401-1857

HAWKINSON, GARY MICHAEL, financial services company executive; b. Chgo., Oct. 30, 1948; s. Roy G. and June M. (Miller) H.; m. Patricia Kaye Schlievert, Jan. 9, 1971; children: Kenneth, Christopher. BBA in Fin., U. Toledo, 1971; postgrad., U. Harvard, 1989. Various mgmt. and analytical positions Toledo Edison Co., 1972-79, asst. treas., asst. sec., 1979-86; treas. Centerior Energy Corp., Independence, Ohio, 1986-96, dir. govtl. affairs, 1996-98; dir. fin. and adminstrn. Parkwood Corp., Cleve., 1998-99; dir. treasury Univ. Hosps. Health Sys., Cleve., 1999—. Trustee Luth. Med. Ctr. Found. Served to 2d lt. U.S. Army, 1971-72. Mem. Cleve. Treas.'s Club (v.p. 1988-89, pres. 1989-90), Rotary. Avocations: skiing, sailing. Office: Univ Hosps Health Sys 11100 Euclid Ave Cleveland OH 44106-1736 Home: 2113 Hathaway Ct Avon OH 44011-1677

HAWLEY, ELLIS WAYNE, historian, educator; b. Cambridge, Kans., June 2, 1929; s. Pearl Washington and Gladys Laura (Logsdon) H.; m. Sofia Koltun, Sept. 2, 1953; children— Arnold Jay, Agnes Fay. BA, U. Wichita, 1950; MA, U. Kans., 1951; PhD (research fellow), U. Wis., 1959. Instr. to prof. history North Tex. State U., 1957-68; prof. history Ohio State U., 1968-69, U. Iowa, 1969-94, prof. emeritus, 1994—, chmn. dept. history, 1986-89. Hist. cons. Pub. Papers of the Presidents: Hoover, 1974-78. Author: The New Deal and the Problem of Monopoly, 1966, The Great War and the Search for a Modern Order, 1979, (with others) Herbert Hoover and the Crisis of American Capitalism, 1973, Herbert

Hoover as Secretary of Commerce, 1981, Federal Social Policy, 1988, Herbert Hoover and the Historians, 1989; contbr. articles to profl. jours., essays to books Investigator Project to Study Hist. in Iowa Pub. Schs., Iowa City, 1978-79; cons. Quad Cities hist. project Putnam Mus., Davenport, 1978-79. Served to 1st lt. inf. AUS, 1951-53 North Tex. State U. Faculty Devel. grantee, 1967-68, U. Iowa, 1975-76. Mem. Am. Hist. Assn., Orgn. Am. Historians, So. Hist. Assn., AAUP (mem. exec. coun. Iowa chapt. 1982-84), Iowa Hist. Soc. Democrat. Home: 2524 E Washington St Iowa City IA 52245-3724 Personal E-mail: ellis.hawley@mchsi.com.

HAWLEY, RAYMOND GLEN, pathologist; b. Cambridge, Kans., Jan. 13, 1939; s. Pearl Washington and Gladys Laura (Logsdon) H.; m. Phyllis Ann Williams, Aug. 25, 1963; children: Bradford, Anthony, Douglas. BS, Kans. State U., 1961; MD, U. Kans., 1965. Intern Wesley Med. Ctr., Wichita, 1965-66; pathology resident Riverside Meth. Hosp., Columbus, Ohio, 1966-70; pathologist St. Joseph Hosp., Concordia, Kans., 1973-75, St. Joseph Med. Ctr., Wichita, 1975—82, Via Christi Regional Med. Ctr., Wichita, 1983—2000; with Coffeyville (Kans.) Regional Med. Ctr., 2000—, chief of staff, 2004, 2005. Maj. U.S. Army, 1970-73. Fellow Am. Coll. Pathologists; mem. AMA, Am. Soc. Clin. Pathologists, Kans. Soc. Pathology (sec.-treas. 1989-99, pres. 2004—06). Home: 512 Spruce St Coffeyville KS 67337-4834 E-mail: rhawley@cox.net.

HAWORTH, DANIEL THOMAS, chemistry professor; b. Fond du Lac, Wis., June 27, 1928; s. Arthur Valentine and Mary Lena (Wattawa) H.; m. Mary Hormuth, Dec. 27, 1952; children: Daniel G., M. Judith, Steven T. BS, U. Wis., Oshkosh, 1950; MS, Marquette U., 1952; student, Oak Ridge Sch. Reactor Tech., 1952; PhD, St. Louis U., 1959. Nuclear chemist Bur. of Ships, Washington, 1952-53; rsch. chemist All-Chalmer Mfg. Co., Milw., 1958-60; instr. chemistry Marquette U., Milw., 1955, from asst. prof. to assoc. prof., 1960-68, prof., 1968—. Vis. prof. chemistry U. Wis.-Milw., 2001—02. Contbr. numerous articles to profl. jours.; patentee in field. Served as cpl. U.S. Army, 1953-55. Recipient Pere Marquette award for tchg. excellence Marquette U., 1971, Nicolos Salgo Outstanding Tchr. award, 1971, Milw. Sect. award, Am. Chem. Soc. Mem. Am. Chem. Soc. (emeritus), N.Y. Acad. Scis., Wis. Acad. Arts/Scis./Letters, Sigma Xi (emeritus). Roman Catholic. Avocation: stamp collecting/philately. Home: 3483 N Frederick Ave Milwaukee WI 53211-2902 Office: Marquette Univ Dept Chemistry PO Box 1881 Milwaukee WI 53201-1881 Home Phone: 414-332-3048; Office Phone: 414-288-3534. Business E-Mail: daniel.haworth@marquette.edu.

HAWORTH, JAMES CHILTON, pediatrics educator; b. Gosforth, Eng., May 29, 1923; emigrated to Can., 1957, naturalized, 1972; s. Walter Norman and Violet Chilton (Dobbile) H.; m. Eleanor Marian Bowser, Oct. 18, 1951; children— Elizabeth Marian, Peter Norman James, Margaret Jean, Anne Ruth. M.B., Ch.B, U. Birmingham, Eng., 1945, MD, 1960. House physician Birmingham Gen. and Children's Hosps., 1946-47; fellow Cin. Children's Hosp., 1949-50; house physician Hosp. for Sick Children, London, 1951; pediatric registrar Alder Hey Children's Hosp., Liverpool, Eng., 1951-52; sr. registrar Sheffield Children's Hosp., 1953-57; pediatrician Winnipeg (Man., Can.) Clinic, 1957-65; asst. prof. dept. pediat. U. Man., Winnipeg, 1965-67, assoc. prof., 1967-70, prof., 1970-94, head dept. pediat., 1979-85, senate mem., 1985-90, prof. human genetics, 1987-94, prof. emeritus, 1994—, sr. scholar dept. biochemistry and med. genetics, 1999—2005. Mem. active staff Health Scis. Centre-Children's, 1957-93; cons. staff St. Boniface Hosp., 1974-93; hon. staff Health Sci. Ctr., 1993—. Contbr. articles to profl. jours. Bd. dirs. Man. Med. Svc. found., 1988—, exec. dir., 1995-2004. Served with Royal Naval Vol. Res., 1947-49. Fellow Royal Coll. Physicians (Can., London), Can. Coll. Med. Geneticists (hon.); mem. Can. Soc. Clin. Investigation, Am. Pediatric Soc., Soc. Pediatric Rsch., Can. Pediatric Soc. Home: 301 Victoria Crescent Winnipeg MB Canada R2M 1X8 Office: Childrens Hosp Dept Pediatrics 678 William Ave Winnipeg MB Canada R3E 0W1

HAWORTH, RICHARD G. (DICK HAWORTH), office furniture manufacturer; b. 1942; With Haworth, Inc., Holland, Mich., chm. bd., 1975—. Office: Haworth Inc 1 Haworth Ctr Holland MI 49423-8820

HAWTHORNE, MARION FREDERICK, chemistry professor; b. Ft. Scott, Kans., Aug. 24, 1928; s. Fred Elmer and Colleen (Webb) Hawthorne; m. Beverly Dawn Rempe, Oct. 30, 1951 (div. 1976); m. Diana Baker Razzala, Aug. 14, 1977. BA, Pomona Coll., Claremont, Calif., 1949, DSc (hon.), 1974; PhD (AEC fellow), UCLA, 1953; PhD (hon.), Uppsala U., Sweden, 1992. Rsch. assoc. Iowa State Coll., 1953-54; rsch. chemist Rohm & Haas Co., Huntsville, Ala., 1954-56, group leader, 1956-60, lab. head Phila., 1961; prof. chemistry U. Calif., Riverside, 1962-68, UCLA, 1968—98, univ. prof. chemistry, 1998—2006; univ. prof. chemistry emeritus U. Mo., Columbia, 2006—, dir. Internat. Inst. Nano and Molecular Medicine, 2006—. Vis. lectr. Harvard U., 1960, vis. prof., 68; vis. lectr. Queen Mary Coll., U. London, 1963; vis. prof. U. Tex., Austin, 1974; mem. sci. adv. bd. USAF, 1980—86, NRC Bd. Army Sci. and Tech., 1986—90; disting. vis. prof. Ohio State U., 1990; 1st Anton Burg lectr. U. So. Calif., 2004; mem. dir.'s external adv. bd. divsn. M Los Alamos Nat. Lab., N.Mex., 1991—94; lectr. in field. Editor-in-chief: Inorganic Chemistry, 1969—2000, assoc. editor:, 1966—69. Decorated Meritorious Civilian Svc. medal USAF; named Sr. Scientist Alexander von Humboldt Found., Inst. Inorganic Chemistry U. Munich, 1990—96, Centenary lectr., Royal Soc. Chemistry, London, 1998, Lloyd B. Thomas lectr., U. Mo., Columbia, 2007; recipient Chancellors Rsch. award, 1968, Herbert Newby McCoy award, 1972, Am. Chem. Soc. award Inorganic Chemistry, 1973, Glenn T. Seaborg medal, 1997, Tolman Medal award, 1986, Nebr. sect. Am. Chem. Soc. award, 1979, Disting. Svc. Advancement of Inorganic Chemistry award, Am. Chem. Soc., 1988, Disting. Achievements in Boron Sci. award, 1988, Bailar medal, 1991, Polyhedron medal and prize, 1993, Chem. Pioneer award, Am. Inst. Chemists, 1994, Willard Gibbs medal, Am. Chem. Soc., 1994, Internat. award in Polyhedral Borane Chemistry, Internat. Com. on Boron Chemistry, 1996, Basolo medal, Am. Chem. Soc., 2001, King Faisal Internat. Sci. prize, 2003; fellow Sloan Found., 1963—65, Japan Soc. Promotion Sci., 1986, Disting. Vis. scholar, Chinese U. Hong Kong, 2001. Fellow: AAAS; mem.: Nat. Acad. Sci. Bd. Army Sci. and Tech., Internat. Soc. Neutron Capture Therapy for Cancer (mem. exec. com. 1992—2000, pres. 1996—98), Am. Acad. Arts and Scis., US Nat. Acad. Scis. (award in chem. scis. 1997), Göttingen Acad. Scis. (corr.), Aircraft Owners and Pilots Assn. (named Col. Confederate Air Force 1984), Cosmos Club, Sigma Nu, Alpha Chi Sigma, Sigma Xi (Monie A. Ferst award 2003). Home: 1616 Glenbrook Ct Columbia MO 65203-5203 Business E-Mail: hawthornem@health.missouri.edu.*

HAWTHORNE, TIMOTHY ROBERT, direct response advertising and communications company executive; b. Evanston, Ill., June 29, 1950; s. John and Marjie Phyllis (Horner) H.; 1 child, Jessica Hope. BA cum laude, Harvard U., 1973. Editor, prodr. Sta. WCCO-TV, Mpls., 1973-78; field prodr. Sta. KYW-TV, Phila., 1978-80; pres., founder Producer/Writer Network, Newtown, Pa., 1980-82; v.p. prodn. Teleimage, Inc., Phila., 1982-83; pres. Hawthorne Prodns., Phila., Los Angeles and Fairfield, Iowa, 1983—; co-founder, pres. Fairfield TV, 1984-86; founder, chmn. & pres. Hawthorne Comm., Inc., Fairfield, 1986—. Prodr., writer, dir.: (TV series) Real People, That's Incredible, Ripley's Believe It Or Not, Entertainment Tonight, 1979-85. Dir. Fairfield Cultural Soc., 1985-87; mem. Pres. Soc. Maharishi Internat. U., Fairfield, 1984—. Named Iowa/Nebr. Entrepreneur of Yr., 1996. Mem. Dirs. Guild Am., Nat. Info. Mktg. Assn. (founding mem., bd. dirs.), Direct Mktg. Assn., Fairfield C. of C. Avocations: travel, skiing. Home: 1825 Okra Blvd Fairfield IA 52556-8709 Office: Hawthorne Dir Inc 300 N 16th St Fairfield IA 52556-2604

HAYDEN, JEREMY A., lawyer; b. Henderson, Ky., Apr. 17, 1974; BA, Western Ky. U., 1996; MSBA in Taxation, U. Cin., 2002; JD, U. Ky., 2000. Bar: Ky. 2000, Ohio 2002. Sr. assoc. Frost Brown Todd LLC, Cin. Mem., Planning Com. Southwestern Ohio Tax Inst.; founding bd. mem., gen. counsel Cin. Real Estate Club; co-chair Roebling Murals Merchandising project, Legacy Grp. Mentor Williams Coll. Bus., Xavier U.; bd. mem., gen. counsel Southbank Fund, 2004—06; co-chair Opening Doors Event, 2005; mem., Fin. Com. Diocesan Children's Home; mem. Northern Ky. Chamber Exec. Roundtable; mem., Adv. Bd. NKU Family Bus. Ctr. Named one of Ohio's Rising Stars, Super Lawyers, 2005, 2006, 40 Under 40, Cin. Bus. Ctr., 2006. Mem.: ABA (Sect. on Taxation), Northern Ky. Bar Assn. (Bus. and Tax Sect.), Ky. Bar Assn., Ohio State Bar Assn., Cin. Bar Assn. (Sect. on Taxation), Phi Delta Phi. Office: Frost Brown Todd LLC 2200 PNC Ctr 201 E Fifth St Cincinnati OH 45202-4182 Office Phone: 513-651-6800. Office Fax: 513-651-6981.

HAYDEN, JOHN, radio director; b. Kansas City, Mo., May 1, 1962; m. Donna Hayden; children: Lindsey, Jeff, Tanner. Program dir. Sta. WMBI Radio, Chgo. Office: WMBI 820 N LaSalle Blvd Chicago IL 60610

HAYDEN, JOHN W., real estate company executive; BA, Northwe. U.; MBA, Miami U. With Midland Co., 1981, v.p., 1987-96, sr. exec. v.p. Am. Home Groups, 1987-96, pres. Am. Modern Ins. Group, 1994-98, sr. exec. v.p., 1996-98, pres., CEO, 1998—, also bd. dirs. Office: Midland Co 7000 Midland Blvd Amelia OH 45102-2608

HAYDEN, JOSEPH PAGE, JR., finance company executive; b. Cin., Oct. 8, 1929; s. Joseph Page and Amy Dorothy (Weber) H.; m. Lois Taylor, Dec. 29, 1951; children: Joseph Page III, William Taylor, John Weber, Thomas Richard. BS in Bus, Miami U., Oxford, Ohio, 1951; student, U. Cin. Law Sch., 1952; DL (hon.), Miami U., 1986. With mobile home div. Midland-Guardian Co., Cin., 1952-61, v.p., 1954-60; pres., chief exec. officer, dir. Midland Co., Cin., 1961-80, chmn. bd., CEO, dir., 1980-98, chmn. exec. com., bd. dirs., 1998—. Former bd. mem. Firstar Corp. (now U.S. Bank); former Cin. mem. bus. adv. com. Miami U., Oxford, Ohio; former mem. pres.'s council Xavier U., Cin.; former trustee Miami U. Found. Mem. Met. Club (Cin., Ohio), Comml. Club (Ohio), Boca Bay Pass Club (Fla.), Lemon Bay Golf (Fla.), Useppa Island Club (Fla.), Sigma Chi. Clubs: Queen City, Hyde Park Golf and Country, Cincinnati, Ohio. Office: 7000 Midland Blvd Amelia OH 45102-2608

HAYDEN, (JOHN) MICHAEL, state official, former governor; b. Colby, Kans., Mar. 16, 1944; s. Irven Wesley and Ruth (Kelley) H.; m. Patti Ann Rooney, Aug. 26, 1968; children: Chelsi, Anne. BS, Kans. State U., 1966; MS, Ft. Hays State U., 1974. Exec. mgr. Rawlins County Promotional Council, Atwood, Kans., 1973-77; agt. E.C. Mellick Agy., Atwood, 1977; mem. Kans. Ho. of Reps. from 120th Dist., 1973—87, spkr., 1983—87; gov. State of Kans., Topeka, 1987—91; asst. sec. fish, wildlife & parks US Dept. Interior, Washington, 1991—93; sec. Kans. Dept. Wildlife & Parks, Topeka, 2002—. Acting chmn. Migratory Bird Commn., 1991—93; mem. N. Am. Wetlands Conservation Coun., 1993—96; pres., CEO Am. Sportfishing Assn., 1993—2001. Del. Rep. Nat. Conv., 1984, 88; former mem. Rep. Nat. Exec. Com.; former pres. US Hwy. 36 Assn. Served to 1st lt. US Army, 1967—70, Vietnam. Decorated two bronze stars, medal for valor; named Kans. Conservationist of Yr., Kans. Wildlife Fedn., 1988; named to Army Officers Candidate Sch. Hall of Fame, 1989; recipient Civil Justice Achievement award, Am. Tort Reform Assn., 1989, Chevron-Times Mirror Conservation award, 1995, Hunting Heritage award, Nat. Wild Turkey Fedn., 1996, 2004. Mem. Rep. Govs. Assn. (chmn. 1988), League Conservation Voters (chmn. 1998), Am. Legion, VFW, Ducks Unltd., Rotary. Republican. Methodist. Office: Kans Dept Wildlife & Parks 512 SE 25th Ave Pratt KS 67124*

HAYDEN, ROBERT W., insurance company executive; V.p. Midland Co., Amelia, Ohio, 1988—. Office: Midland Co 7000 Midland Blvd Amelia OH 45102-2608

HAYDOCK, WALTER JAMES, banker; b. Chgo., Dec. 14, 1947; s. Joseph Albert and Lillian V. (Adeszko) H.; m. Bonnie Jean Thompson, Aug. 22, 1970; children: Nicole Lynn, Matthew Michael. At, Harvard Bus. Coll., 1969—71, Daily Coll., 1971—73; BS in Acctg., DePaul U., 1976. Computer operator, jr. programmer Pepper Constrn. Co., Chgo., 1972—73; input analyst Continental Bank, Chgo., 1973—76, data control supr., 1976—79, corp. fixed asset adminstr., 1979—83, properties sys. analyst, 1983—87, props. sr. sys. supr., 1987—91; unit chief conversions Fed. Deposit Ins. Corp., Chgo., 1992—93, info. security specialist, 1993—96; info. security officer U. Ill., Chgo., 1996—2001, info. sys. adminstr., 2001—. Pres. Wal-Bon., Inc.; distbr. Lic. Disney Character Mdse. Dir. Dawnwood Homeowner Assn. Mem. Southwest Suburban Bd. Realtors. Home: 13525 Marissa Ct Homer Glen IL 60491 Office: 809 S Marshield Ave m/c 694 Chicago IL 60612-7209 Office Phone: 312-996-3768. Business E-Mail: whaydock@uic.edu.

HAYES, DAVID JOHN ARTHUR, JR., legal association executive; b. Chgo., July 30, 1929; s. David J.A. and Lucille (Johnson) H.; m. Anne Huston, Feb. 20, 1963; children— David J.A. III, Cary AB, Harvard U., 1952, JD, 1961. Bar: Ill. Trust officer, asst. sec. First Nat. Bank of Evanston, Ill., 1961-63; gen. counsel Ill. State Bar Assn., Chgo., 1963-66; asst. dir. ABA, Chgo., 1966-68, div. dir., 1968-69, asst. exec. dir., 1969-87, v.p., 1987-88, assoc. exec. v.p., 1989-90, sr. assoc. exec. v.p., 1990, exec. dir., 1990-94, exec. dir. emeritus, 1994—; exec. dir. Naval Res. Lawyers Assn., 1971-75; asst. sec. gen. Internat. Bar Assn., 1978-80, 90—, Inter-ABA, 1984—. Contbr. articles to profl. jours. Capt. JAGC, USNR Fellow Am. Bar Found. (life); mem. Ill. State Bar Assn. (ho. of dels. 1972-76), Nat. Orgn. Bar Counsel (pres. 1967), Chgo. Bar Assn., Michigan Shores Club. Home: 908 Pontiac Rd Wilmette IL 60091-1349 Office: ABA 750 N Lake Shore Dr Chicago IL 60611-4403 E-mail: djahayes@aol.com.

HAYES, JOHN FRANCIS, lawyer; b. Salina, Kans., Dec. 11, 1919; s. John Francis and Helen (Dye) H.; m. Elizabeth Ann Ireton, Aug. 10, 1950; children: Carl Ireton, Ann Chandler. AB, Washburn Coll., 1941, LLB, 1946. Bar: Kans. 1946, Mo. 1987. Pvt. practice, Hutchinson, Kans., 1946—; dir. Gilliland & Hayes, P.A. (and predecessors), 1946—. Mem. Commn. Uniform State Laws, 1975—; bd. dirs. Cen. Bank and Trust Co., Hutchinson, Cen. Fin. Corp., Waddell & Reed Funds. Mem. Kans. Ho. of Reps., 1953-55, 67-79, majority leader, 1975-77. Served as capt. AUS, 1942-46. Fellow Am. Bar Found., Am. Coll. Trial Lawyers; mem. Hutchinson C. of C. (pres. 1961), Kans. Assn. Def. Counsel (pres. 1972-73), Internat. Assn. Def. Counsel. Republican. Office: 20 W 2nd Ave Fl 2 Hutchinson KS 67501 also: 1211 Penntower Bldg 3100 Broadway St Kansas City MO 64111-2406 also: Epic Ctr 301 N Main Ste 1300 Wichita KS 67202 also: 900 Massachusetts Ste 400 Lawrence KS 66044-2868 Home Phone: 620-662-7359; Office Phone: 620-662-0537. E-mail: johnh@gh-hutch.com.

HAYES, JOHN PATRICK, electrical engineering and computer science educator, consultant; b. Newbridge, Ireland, Mar. 3, 1944; s. Patrick Joseph and Christine (Duggan) H.; m. Joan Benson, June 7, 1969; children: Thomas, Michael. BE in Elec. Engring., Nat. U. Ireland, Dublin, 1965; MS in Elec. Engring., U. Ill., 1967, PhD in Elec. Engring., 1970. Systems engr. Royal Dutch Shell Co., The Hague, The Netherlands, 1970-72; asst. prof. elec. engring. and computer sci. U. So. Calif., LA, 1972-77, assoc. prof., 1977-82; prof. U. Mich., Ann Arbor, 1982—2002, Shannon prof. engring. sci., 2002—. Cons. in field. Author: Computer Architecture and Organization, 1978, 3d edit., 1998, Digital System Design and Microprocessors, 1984, Hierarchical Modeling for VLSI Circuit Testing, 1990, Layout Minimization for CMOS Cells, 1992, Introduction to Digital Logic Design, 1993; contbr. articles to profl. jours. Fellow: IEEE (assoc. editor jour. 1989—94), Assn. Computing Machinery (assoc. editor jour. 1978—81); mem.: Sigma Xi. Office: U Mich Dept Elec Engring & Computer Sci Ann Arbor MI 48109 Office Phone: 734-763-0386. Business E-Mail: jhayes@eecs.umich.edu.

HAYES, ROBERT E., former state legislator; b. Battle Creek, Mich., Oct. 18, 1933; m. to Marilyn Hayes; children: Eric, Jennifer. BS, N.E. Mo. U.; JD, Ind. U. Pvt. practice law; state rep. Dist. 59 Ind. Ho. of Reps., 1974-80, 82-97, asst. majority floor leader, mem. human affairs and edn. com., mem. judiciary com., cts. and criminal code com., mem. rules and legis. procedures com. Mem. Am. Legion, Kiwanis, Eagles, Phi Delta Phi. Home: 3221 Sherwood Pl Columbus IN 47203-2612

HAYES, SCOTT BIRCHARD, retired raw materials company executive; b. Washington, Apr. 2, 1926; s. Webb C. II Hayes and Martha Baker; m. Dorothy Walter, Oct. 27, 1951; children: Scott B. Jr., James W., Timothy W., Michael S. BS, Yale U., 1950. Sr. v.p. Pickands Mather & Co., Cleve., 1953-87, ret., 1987. Bd. dirs., v.p. Hayes Presdl. Ctr., Fremont, Ohio, 1965, pres., 1987—; trustee Ohio Hist. Soc., 1993-96. With USN, 1944-46. Mem. Kirtland Country Club. Avocations: golf, tennis, squash, fishing. Home: PO Box 1070 Boca Grande FL 33921-1070

HAYES, STEPHEN MATTHEW, librarian; b. Detroit, Sept. 30, 1950; s. Matthew Cleary and Evelyn Mary (Warren) H. BS in Psychology, Mich. State U., 1972; MLS, Western Mich. U., 1974; MS in Adminstrn., U. Notre Dame, 1979. Cons. Western Mich. U., Kalamazoo, 1974; libr. U. Notre Dame, Ind., 1974-76, ref. and pub. documents libr. Ind., 1976-94; libr. Bus. Svcs. Libr., 1994—. Adv. bd. Ebsco's Bus. Sch., 2003—. Author/contbr.: What is Written Remains: Historical Essays on the Libraries of Notre Dame, 1994; editor: Environmental Concerns, 1975; contbr.: Depository Library Use of Technology: A Practitioner's Perspective, 1993. Apptd. mem. Depository Libr. Coun. to Pub. Printer, 1994—97; citizen appointee, com. on info. and tech. South Bend City Coun., 2006. Recipient Rev. Paul J. Foik award, 1998. Mem. AAUP, ALA (govt. documents roundtable 1978—, chair 1987-88, chair pubs. com. 1989-91, coord. com. on access to info. 1989-90, 93-95, exec. bd. dirs. 1988-91, awards com. 1991-93, chair Godort orgn. com. 1991-93, Godort legis. com., 1999-2002, bus. ref. and svc. sect. 1994—, bus. & adult ref. roundtable 1995—, edn. com. 1996-98, resolution com. 1997-99, task force or restrictions on access to govt. info. 2002-03), Assn. Pub. Data Users (census com., steering com. 1987-96), Indigo (fed. rec. commn. chair 1992-93, provosts task force libr. 2004-2005). Roman Catholic. Avocations: horseback riding, quilting, gardening. Home: PO Box 6032 South Bend IN 46660-6032 Office: U Notre Dame L012 Mendoza Coll Of Business Notre Dame IN 46556-5646 Office Phone: 574-631-5268. Business E-Mail: shayes1@nd.edu.

HAYNES, CORNELL **See NELLY**

HAYNSWORTH, HARRY JAY, IV, law educator; b. Greensboro, NC, Apr. 9, 1938; s. Harry J. Jr. and Ruth (Eberhardt) H. AB, Duke U., 1961, JD, 1964; postgrad., U. Denver Law Center, 1972; MAR, Luth. Theol. So. Sem., 1989; LLD (hon.), William Mitchell Coll. Law, 2004. Bar: SC 1965, Minn. 2005, U.S. Supreme Ct. 2005. Assoc. Haynsworth, Perry, Bryant, Marion & Johnstone, Greenville, SC, 1964-69, ptnr., 69-71; assoc. prof. law U. SC, 1971-74, prof., 1974-90, assoc. dean, 1975-76, 85-86, acting dean, 1976-77; of counsel Nexson, Pruet, Jacobs & Pollard, Columbia, SC, 1986-90, Briggs & Morgan, Mpls., 2005—; dean, prof. law So. Ill. U., Carbondale, 1990-95; dean, pres. William Mitchell Coll. Law, St. Paul, 1995—2004; dean emeritus William Mitchell Coll. Law, 2004—. Vis. prof. U. Leeds, Eng., 1978-79; commr. Nat. Conf. Commrs. on Uniform State Laws, 1992—; mem. S.C. Legis. Consumer Law Com., 1975-80. Author: Comments, S.C. Consumer Protection Code, 1983, 2d edit. 1990, Organizing a Small Business Entity, 1986, Marketing and Legal Ethics: The Rules and Risks, 1990, others; contbr. articles to profl. jours.; mem. editorial bd.: Am. Bar Assn. Jour, 1977-83, chmn. editorial bd., 1982-83. Chmn. bd. S.C. Commn. for Blind, 1973-75; bd. dirs. Greenville County Housing Commn., S.C., 1970-71; v.p., dir. United Speech and Hearing Ctr., Greenville, 1970-71; trustee Heathwood Hall, 1976-86, Randolph-Macon Women's Coll., Lynchburg, Va., 1970-75, Minn. Zoo, 1999—; chair, 2006—; trustee Episc. Diocese Minn., 2006—. Mem. ABA (small bus. com., spl. cons. corp. laws com. 1978-82, coun. sect. bus. law 1988-92), S.C. Bar Assn. (vice chmn. consumer and comml. law com. 1975-78, sec., exec. com. 1972-75, exec. dir. 1971-72), Minn. State Bar Assn., Am. Law Inst., 4th Cir. Jud. Conf., S.C. Bar Assn. Office: Briggs and Morgan 2200 IDS Ctr Minneapolis MN 55402 Home Phone: 651-433-3312; Office Phone: 612-977-8298. Business E-Mail: hhaynsworth@briggs.com.

HAYS, RUTH, lawyer; b. Fukuoka, Japan, Sept. 20, 1950; d. George Howard and Helen Jincy (Mathis) H. AB, Grinnell Coll., 1972; JD, Washington U., 1978. Bar: Mo. 1978. Law clk. U.S. Ct. Appeals (8th cir.), St. Louis, 1978-80; assoc. Husch & Eppenberger, LLC, St. Louis, 1980-87, ptnr., 1987—. Articles editor Urban Law Annual, 1977-78. Bd. dirs. Childhaven, St. Louis, 1982-93, pres. 1987-88. Olin fellow Monticello Coll. Found., St. Louis, 1975-78; recipient Spl. Svc. award Legal Svs. Ea. Mo., 1993. Mem. ABA, Mo. Bar Assn., Bar Assn. Met. St. Louis, Employee Benefits Assn. (pres. 1995), Order of Coif, Phi Beta Kappa. Office: Husch & Eppenberger LLC 190 Carondelet Plz Ste 600 Saint Louis MO 63105

HAYS, THOMAS S., medical educator, researcher; b. Winter Haven, Fla., Dec. 20, 1954; married. BS in Zoology, U. N.C., 1976, PhD in Cell Biology, 1985. Rsch. asst. dept. zoology U. N.C., Chapel Hill, 1975—76; rsch. asst. dept. biol. scis. Duke U., Durham, NC, 1976—79; asst. instr. quantitative and analytical microscopy Marine Biol. Lab., Woods Hole, Mass., 1981—83; asst. instr. optical microscopy U. Calif., Santa Cruz, 1982; postdoctoral fellow dept. molecular, cellular and devel. biology U. Colo., Boulder, 1985—89; asst. prof. dept. genetics and cell biology U. Minn., St. Paul, 1989—95, assoc. prof. dept. genetics and cell biology, 1995—. External reviewer NSF, 1989—. Reviewer: Jour. Cell Biology, Jour. Biol. Chemistry, Molecular Biology of the Cell, Molecular Cell Biology, Proceedings Nat. Acad. Sci. USA, Cell Motility and the Cytoskeleton, Jour. Cell Sci., Genetics; contbr. articles to profl. jours. Recipient Basil O'Connor Scholar award, March of Dimes, 1993, Establishe Investigator award, Am. Heart Found., 1996; fellow H.V. Wilson, U. N.C., 1983, R.J. Reynolds, 1983, Postdoctoral, NIH, 1985—88; grantee Tng., 1991—95, 1995—, Rsch. Tng., NSF, 1991—95, March of Dimes, 1995—; scholar Founders, Marine Biol. Lab., 1980. Mem.: Genetics Soc. Am., Am. Soc. Cell Biology. Office: U Minn Dept Genetics Cell Biology & Devel 6-160 Jackson Hall 321 Church St SE Minneapolis MN 55455

HAYSE, RICHARD FRANKLIN, lawyer; b. Kansas City, Mo., Sept. 6, 1943; s. Lewie Frank and Elizabeth Bronson (Humfreville) H.; m. Linda Rae Fairchild, Aug. 8, 1964; children: Adrienne Jennifer, Thomas Bronson. BA in Speech, Kansas State U., 1964; JD, Washburn Law Sch., 1969. Bar: Kans. 1969, U.S. Dist. Ct. Kans. 1969, U.S. Ct. Appeals (10th cir.) 1969, U.S. Supreme Ct. 1990. Broadcast journalist WIBW-TV-AM-FM, Topeka, 1964-68; asst. atty. gen. State of Kansas, Topeka, 1969-70; fgn. svc. info. officer U.S. Info. Agy., Washington, 1971-75; lawyer Eidson, Lewis, Porter & Haynes, Topeka, Kans., 1975-89, Hayse Law Offices, Topeka, 1989-90; ptnr. Morris, Laing, Evans, Brock & Kennedy, Chartered, Topeka, 1991—. Editor in chief Washburn Law Jour., author, 1969, co-author, 1970; contbr. chpts. to books. Pres. Topeka Lions Club, 1983-84, Topeka Youth Project, 1990-91, Topeka Symphony Soc., 1993-94, Cornerstone of Topeka, Inc., 1998-99. Mem. ABA, Kans. Bar Assn. (pres. 2005-06), Topeka Bar Assn. (dir. 1986-91). Avocations: gardening, sailing. Home: 1724 SW Collins Ave Topeka KS 66604-3219 Office: Morris Laing Evans Brock & Kennedy Chartered 800 SW Jackson St Ste 1310 Topeka KS 66612-1216 Office Phone: 785-232-2662.

HAYTAYAN, ALITA **See GUILLEN, ALITA**

HAYWARD, EDWARD JOSEPH, lawyer; b. Springfield, Mo., Dec. 4, 1943; s. Joseph Hunter and Rosemary Hayward; m. Ellinor Duffey, Aug. 30, 1968; children: Jeffrey, Stephen, Susan. Student, U. d'Aix Marseille, Aix-en-Provence, France, 1963-64; AB, Stanford U., 1965; JD magna cum laude, Harvard U., 1971. Bar: N.Y. 1972, Minn. 1980. Assoc. Cleary, Gottlieb, Steen & Hamilton, NYC and Brussels, 1971-74, Oppenheimer Wolff & Donnelly, LLP, Brussels, 1975-79, ptnr. Mpls., 1978—. Pres. pres. Twin Cities Fgn. Trade Zone Inc., Mpls., 1983—84. Chmn. legis. com. Minn. World Trade Assn., Mpls., 1984—87. Served to capt. US Army, 1965—68. Mem.: ABA, Minn. Bar Assn. (councillor internat. law sect. 1983—, sec. 1986—88, vice chmn. 1988—89, chmn. 1989—90), Minn. Dist. Export Coun. (chmn. 1996—), German-Am. C. of C. (bd. dirs. 1994—99, 2000—), French-Am. C. of C. (bd. dirs. 1983—, pres. 1985—87, 1996—2001, nat. sec. 1988—). Republican. Presbyterian. Avocations: languages, sports. Home: 6625 W Shore Dr Minneapolis MN 55435-1528 Office: Oppenheimer Wolff & Donnelly LLP 45 S 7th St Ste 3300 Minneapolis MN 55402-1609 Office Phone: 612-607-7280. Business E-Mail: ehayward@oppenheimer.com.

HAYWARD, THOMAS ZANDER, JR., lawyer; b. Oct. 21, 1940; s. Thomas Z. and Wilhelmina (White) H.; m. Sally Madden, June 20, 1964; children: Thomas Z., Wallace M., Robert M. BA, orthwestern U., 1962, JD, 1965; MBA, U. Chgo., 1970. Bar: Ill. 1966, Ohio 1966, U.S. Dist. Ct. (no. dist.) Ill. 1966, U.S. Supreme Ct. 1970. Assoc. Defrees & Fiske, Chgo., 1965-69, ptnr., 1969-81, Boodell, Sears, Giambalvo & Crowley, Chgo., 1981-87, Bell, Boyd, Lloyd, Chgo., 1987—. Mem. mgmt. and exec. coms. Bell, Boyd, Lloyd. Trustee Northwestern U., 1980-84, 97—, vice-chmn., 2000—; bd. dirs. Ill. Continuing Legal Edn., 1987-92, Chgo. Area Found. for Legal Svcs., 1983—; bd. dirs. Nat. Cowboy and Western Heritage Mus., 2004—; pres. Sigma Alpha Epsilon Found., 2005—. Recipient Northwestern U. Alumni Svc. award, 1973. Mem. ABA (ho. of dels. 1984—, fed. jud. com. 1993-97, bd. govs., exec. com. 1998-2001, chmn. fin. com. 2000-01), ABA/Am. Law Inst. (pres. continuing profl. edn. 2005—), Fed. Judiciary Com. (chmn. 2003-05), Ill. State Bar Assn., Chgo. Bar Assn. (pres. 1983-84), Chgo. Bar Found. (bd. dirs., pres. 2007—), Chgo. Club, Casino Club, Barrington Hills Country Club (pres. 1985-87). Republican. Presbyterian. Home: 8 W County Line Rd Barrington IL 60010-2613 Office: Bell Boyd & Lloyd 3 1st Nat Plz 70 W Madison St Ste 3100 Chicago IL 60602-4284 Business E-Mail: thayward@bellboyd.com.

HAZELTINE, JOYCE, former state official; b. Pierre, SD; m. Dave Hazeltine; children: Derek, Tara, Kirk (dec.). Student, Huron Coll., SD, No. State Coll., Aberdeen, SD, Black Hills State Coll., Spearfish, SD. Former asst. chief clk. SD Ho. of Reps.; former sec. SD State Senate; sec. of state State of SD, Pierre, 1987—2003. Bd. dirs. S.D. Bankers Found.; chair SD Bankers Found., 2004—; bd. dirs. Chiesman Ctr. Democracy, Black Hills Playhouse. Adminstrv. asst. Pres. Ford Campaign, SD; Rep. county chmn. Hughes County SD; state co-chair Phil Gramm for Pres., 1996; mem. Custer Co. Rep. Women; chair bd. dirs. Black Hills Playhouse. Mem. Nat. Assn. Secs. of State (exec. bd., pres.), Women Execs. in State Govts. (bd. dirs.). Republican.

HAZLETON, RICHARD A., chemicals executive; b. 1941; Pres., ceo Dow Corning Corp, Midland, Mich., 1965—, chmn., CEO. Former pres. Midland Jr. Achievement, Midland Co. United Way; dir. Chemical Bank and Trust Co.; pres., CEO Charles J. Strosacker Found.

H'DOUBLER, FRANCIS TODD, JR., surgeon; b. Springfield, Mo., June 18, 1925; s. Francis Todd and Alice Louise (Bemis) H'D; m. Joan Louise Huber, Dec. 20, 1951 (dec. Dec. 1983); children: Julie H'Doubler Thomas and Sarah H'Doubler Muegge (twins), Kurt, Scott; m. Marie Ruth Duckworth, Jan. 18, 1986 Student, Washington U., St. Louis, 1943, Miami U., Oxford, Ohio, 1943-44; BS, U. Wis., 1946, MD, 1948. Intern Milw. Hosp., 1948-49; resident in surgery U.S. Naval Hosp., Oakland, Calif., 1950-51; practice medicine specializing in alternative medicine Springfield, Mo., 1952—; mem. courtesy staff St. John's Hosp., Springfield, L.E. Cox Hosp., Springfield. Bd. dirs. Union Planters Bank. Active Singing Doctors; chmn. fundraising drive YMCA, 1960-61, Sch. Bond and Tax Levy Com., 1958, Greene County Rep. Com., 1974-75; past bd. trustees Shriners Hosps., past chmn. spinal cord injury com., past chmn. rsch. com., past chmn. long range planning com., emeritus mem. rsch. com.; mem. Commn. to Reapportion Mo. Senate, 1971, Rep. State Fin. Com., 1972-75, steering com. Wilson's Creekl Battlefield Nat. Park, 1951-61, pres.'s adv. coun. Sch. Ozarks, Point Lookout, Mo., 1975-89; trustee Cottey Coll., Nevada, Mo., past bd. chmn.; bd. trustees Forest Inst. With USNR, 1943-46, 49-51. Decorated Bronze Star with V, Purple Heart with oak leaf cluster; recipient Disting. Service award Mo. Jaycees, 1959; Humanitarian award S.W. Mo. Drug Travelers Assn., 1971; named Young Man of Yr., City of Springfield, 1959 Fellow Am. Coll. Nuclear Medicine (founder's group); mem. AMA, Greene County Med. Assn., Mo. Med. Soc., Southwestern Surg. Congress, Mo. Surg. Assn., Soc. Nuclear Medicine, Am. Thyroid Assn., Springfield Jr. C. of C. (past pres.), Springfield C. of C., DAV, VFW, SAR, Am. Legion, Green Gang (co-founder), Sigma Nu (Outstanding Alumnus nat. award 1980), Nu Sigma Nu. Clubs: Hickory Hills Country. Lodges: Mason (33 deg.), Shriners (imperial potentate 1980-81), Red Cross of Constantine, Order DeMolay Legion Honor (hon.), Royal Order Scotland. Presbyterian.

HEADLEE, RAYMOND, retired psychotherapist; b. Shelby County, Ind., July 27, 1917; s. Ortis Verl and May Mae (Wright) H.; m. Eleanor Case Benton, Aug. 24, 1941; children: Sue, Mark, Ann. AB in Psychology, Ind. U., 1939, A.M. in Exptl. Psychology, 1941, MD, 1944; grad., Chgo. Inst. Psychoanalysis, 1959. Diplomate: Am. Bd. Psychiatry and Neurology (examiner 1964—). Intern St. Elizabeth's Hosp., Washington, 1944-45, resident in psychiatry, 1945-46, Milw. Psychiat. Hosp., 1947-48, pres. staff, 1965-70; practice medicine specializing in psychiatry and psychoanalysis Elm Grove, Wis., 1949—; clin. asst. prof. psychiatry Med. Coll. Wis., 1958-59, clin. asso. prof., 1959-62, clin. prof., 1962-2000, chmn. dept. psychiatry, 1963-70; prof. psychology Marquette U., 1966-76; Bd. dirs. Elm Brook (Wis.) Meml. Hosp., 1969-71; ret., 2000. Author: (with Bonnie Corey) Psychiatry in Nursing, 1949, I Think, Therefore I Know, 1996; contbr. numerous articles to profl. jours. 1st lt. Ft. Knox Armored Med. Rsch. Lab., AUS, 1945, to col. USPHS. Fellow Am. Psychiat. Assn. (life), Am. Coll. Psychiatry (emeritus); mem. State Med. Soc. Wis. (editorial dir. 1971-77), Wis. Psychiat. Assn. (pres. 1971-72), Milw. Club.

HEADLEY, RICHARD D., corporate financial executive; b. Columbus, Ohio; m. Diane Headley; 1 child, Michael. BS, Ohio State U.; MBA, Tex. Christian U. Chmn. CEO Bank One Services Corp., 1992—97; sr. v.p., chief info. tech. officer Nationwide, 1997—99, exec. v.p., 1999—2000, pres., mng. dir. Nationwide Global, internat. opers., 2000—. Bd. mem. InsWeb; bd. dirs. Internat. Cooperative and Mutual Ins. Fedn.; adj. prof. Franklin U. Bd. trustees Franklin U., Columbus, Ohio, Godman Guild; trustee Akron Gen. Med. Ctr.; pres. Summit County YMCA; with United Way. Mem.: Am. Coun. of Life Insurers (chmn., internat. life ins. com.). Office: Nationwide One Nationwide Pl Columbus OH 43215

HEADRICK, DANIEL RICHARD, history and social sciences educator; b. Bay Shore, NY, Aug. 2, 1941; s. William Cecil and Edith (Finkelstein) H.; m. Rita Koplowitz, June 20, 1965 (dec. 1988); children: Isabelle, Juliet, Matthew; m. Kate Ezra, Aug. 23, 1992. B, Lycée de Garçons, Metz, France, 1959; BA, Swarthmore Coll., 1962; MA, Johns Hopkins U., 1964; PhD, Princeton U., 1971. Instr. history Tuskegee (Ala.) Inst., 1968-71, asst. prof., 1971-73, assoc. prof., 1973-75; assoc. prof. social scis. Roosevelt U., Chgo., 1975-82, prof., 1982—. Vis. NEH scholar Hawaii Pacific U., 2000; lectr. in field. Author: Ejercito y Politica, 1981, The Tools of Empire, 1981, Tentacles of Progress, 1988, The Invisible Weapon, 1991, The Earth and Its Peoples, 1997, When Information Came of Age, 2000. Coll. Tchrs. fellow NEH, 1983-84, 88-89, Guggenheim fellow, 1994, Sloan fellow, 1998; recipient Faculty Achievement award Burlington No. Found., 1988, 92. Mem. Am. Hist. Assn., World History Assn. (exec. com. 1991—), Soc. for History Tech. (exec. com. 1992—). Home: 5483 S Hyde Park Blvd Chicago IL 60615-5827 Office: Roosevelt U Univ Coll 430 S Michigan Ave Chicago IL 60605-1394 E-mail: dan.headrick@att.net.

HEADRICK, MIKE, newscaster; m. Rachel Headrick. Grad., Brigham Young U., 1998. City desk editor Brigham Young U., Salt Lake City, 1998; anchor, reporter Sta. KWES-TV, Midland, Tex., 1999—2000; anchor Sta. WCMH-TV, Columbus, Ohio, 2000—. Nominee Emmy awards (2), 2002. Office: WCMH-TV 3165 Plentangy River Rd PO Box 4 Columbus OH 43202

HEAGY, THOMAS CHARLES, banker; b. Fresno, Calif., Jan. 4, 1945; s. Clarence H. and Ruth (Geer) H.; m. Regina Victoria Polk, Apr. 12, 1980 (dec. Oct. 1983); m. Linda Anne Hutton, Jan. 10, 1987. BA in Physics, U. Chgo., 1967, MBA with honors, 1970; MSc in Fin., London Sch. Econs., 1970. Dep. mgr. mgmt. scis. First Nat. Bank Chgo., 1970-75; chmn. bd., chief exec. officer South Shore Nat. Bank, Chgo., 1975-80; exec. v.p. Exchange Nat. Bank Chgo., 1980-90; vice chmn. LaSalle Nat. Bank, 1990—, LaSalle Nat. Corp., 1990—. Bd. dirs. Chgo. Symphony, 1995—, The Regina V. Polk Scholarship Fund, Chgo., 1983—, Mus. Contemporary Art, Chgo., 1994—, Chgo. Music and Dance Theater, 1994—, Lyric Opera Chgo., 1999—; vis. com. Oriental Inst., U. Chgo., 1988—, Renaissance Soc., 1989—; bd. govs. Am. Rsch. Ctr. Egypt, 1996—. Home: 4939 S Greenwood Ave Chicago IL 60615-2815 Office: LaSalle Nat Bank 135 S Lasalle St Ste 340 Chicago IL 60603-4402

HEALY, BRYCE, state agency administrator; b. Chamberlain, SD, Jan. 28, 1971; m. Mary Healy. BS in Agrl. Bus., SD State U. Owner farm/ranch operation; dep. commr. SD Office Sch. and Pub. Lands, Pierre, SD; dir. equalization Marshall County, Britton, SD; dir. field svcs. SD Farmers Union; dep. commr. SD Office Sch. and Pub. Lands, Pierre. Office: 500 E Capitol Ave Pierre SD 57501-5070

HEALY, SONDRA ANITA, consumer products company executive; b. 1939; married; 3 children. BFA, Goodman Sch. Drama, 1963; MA, Nat. Coll., 1964. Owner, chair Turtle Wax, Chgo., 1973—. Office: Turtle Wax 5655 S 73rd Ave Chicago IL 60638

HEALY, WILLIAM J., II, mayor, former state legislator; b. 1962; s. William J. and Barbara Healy; m. Dee Healy, 1997; 1 child, Austin. AS, Kent State U.; BA in Mktg. summa cum laude, Rowan U., Glassboro, NJ; MBA in Polit. & Govt., NYU. Strategic mktg. cons.; founder, pres. Austin Healy Group; mem. Ohio Ho. of Reps. from Dist. 52, 2004—08; mayor City of Canton, Ohio, 2008—. Mem. Greater Canton Regional C. of C.; dean's adv. bd. Kent State; hon. bd. Congl. Youth Leadership; exec. com. Stark County Dem. Party. Mem.: NAACP, VFW (hon.), Greater Stark County Urban League, Ohio Domestic Violence Network, Canton Negro Oldtimers Athletic Assn., Am. Legion, McKinley HS Alumni Assn. (life), Jefferson-Jackson Dem. Club Greater Canton. Democrat. Office: City Hall 218 Cleveland Ave SW 8th Fl Canton OH 44702 Office Phone: 330-489-3283. Office Fax: 330-489-3282. Business E-Mail: healy@ci.canton.oh.us.*

HEANEY, GERALD WILLIAM, retired federal judge; b. Goodhue, Minn., Jan. 29, 1918; s. William J. and Johanna (Ryan) H.; m. Eleanor R. Schmitt, Dec. 1, 1945; children: William M., Carol J. Student, St. Thomas Coll., 1935—37; BSL, U. Minn., 1939, LLB, 1941, LLD for Pub. Svc., 2001. Bar: Minn. 1941. Lawyer securities div. Dept. of Commerce Minn., 1941—42; mem. firm Lewis. Hammer, Heaney, Weyl & Halverson, Duluth, 1946—66; judge U.S. Ct. Appeals (8th cir.), 1966—88, sr. judge, 1988—2006. Bd. regents U. Minn., 1964—65; Mem. Dem. Nat. Com. from Minn., 1955. Capt. AUS, 1942—46. Mem.: ABA, Am. Judicature Soc., Minn. Bar Assn. Roman Catholic.

HEAPHY, JOHN MERRILL, lawyer; b. Escanaba, Mich., Apr. 27, 1927; s. John Merrill and Catherine R. (Feeney) H.; m. Martha Jean Knowles, Nov. 16, 1951; children— John Merrill III, Catherine Jean Heaphy DeThorne, Barbara H. Murphy. BA, U. Mich., 1950; JD, Wayne State U., 1953. Bar: Mich. 1954. Atty. office of gen. counsel HEW, Washington, 1954-57; ptnr. Vandeveer & Garzia, P.C. and predecessor firms, Detroit, 1958-86, pres. firm, 1986-92; ret. Served with USNR, 1945-46. Fellow Am. Coll. Trial Lawyers; mem. ABA, Internat. Assn. Def. Counsel, Mich. Bar Assn., Delta Theta Phi, Alpha Sigma Phi. Republican. Home: 312 Honors Dr Shorewood IL 60404 Personal E-mail: joma27@comcast.net.

HEARNE, GEORGE ARCHER, academic administrator; b. Tampa, Fla., Oct. 31, 1934; s. William Duncan and Marguerite Estelle (Archer) H.; m. Jean May Helmstadter, June 9, 1956; children: Diana Leslie, George Harrison. BA, Bethany Coll., 1955; MDiv, Yale U., 1958; MA, Ill. State U., 1968; HHD (hon.), Culver-Stockton Coll., 1986; LLD, Bethany Coll., 1997. Min. Arlington Christian Ch., Jacksonville, Fla., 1958-59; dir. admissions Eureka (Ill.) Coll., 1960-70, v.p. student devel., 1970-73, dean admissions and student devel., 1973-77, dean admissions and coll. rels., 1977-82, v.p. coll. rels., 1982-84, exec. v.p., 1984-85, pres., 1985—. Bd. dirs. Christian Ch., Ill., Wis. and Ind., 1985—, Higher Edn. divsn. Christian Ch., St. Louis, 1985—; pres. Eureka Bd. Edn., 1967-76; active various cmty. drives. Mem. Assoc. Colls. Ill. (bd. dirs. 1985—), Fedn. Ill. Ind. Colls. and Univs. (bd. dirs. 1985—, exec. com. 2000—), Coun. for Advancement and Support of Edn., Coun. Ind. Colls., Coun. of Pres. (higher edn. div.). Lodges: Rotary. Avocations: reading, music, golf. Office: Eureka Coll 300 E College Ave Eureka IL 61530-1562 E-mail: ghearne@eureka.edu.

HEATH, ROBERT F., lawyer; BA, Harvard U., 1969; JD, Georgetown U., 1975, MBA, 1982. Atty. Davison & Easton, Stowe, Vt.; various sr. legal positions U.S. Dept. Transp.; sr. counsel RCA Comm., 1981—84, GE Am. Com., 1984—88; assoc. gen. counsel GE Medical Systems, Milw., 1988—97; sr. v.p., gen. counsel Omnicare, 1997; gen. counsel Briggs & Stratton Corp., Milw., 1997—, asst. sec., v.p., 2001—, sec., 2002—. Office: Briggs & Stratton Corp 12301 W Wirth St PO Box 702 Wauwatosa WI 53222 Office Phone: 414-259-5333. Office Fax: 414-259-5773.

HEATON, DAVE, state official; b. Sigourney, Iowa, Feb. 2, 1941; m. Carmen Heaton. BA, Iowa Wesleyan Coll., 1964. State rep. Iowa State Ho. of Reps. Dist. 97, Iowa, 1995—; owner Iris Restaurant. Mem. appropriations com.; chair human svcs. appropriations com.; mem. transp. com. With USAR. Mem.: Mt. Pleasant C. of C. (former bd. dirs.), Henry County Pork Prodrs., Henry County Farm Bur., Iowa Restaurant Assn. (past pres.), Kiwanis. Republican. Office: State Capitol E 12th and Grand Des Moines IA 50319

HEATON, GERALD LEE, lawyer; b. Detroit, Feb. 28, 1952; s. Gerald and Bernice Johanna (Cromp) H.; m. Ilene Renee Mann, Oct. 25, 1975. AA, North Cen. Mich. Coll., 1972; BA, Albion Coll., 1974; JD, Ohio No. U., 1976. Bar: Ohio 1977, U.S. Dist. Ct. (so. dist.) Ohio 1977. Ptnr. Lile & Heaton, Bellefontaine, Ohio, 1977-79, MacGillivray & Heaton, Bellefontaine, 1979—. Asst. pros. atty. Logan County, Bellefontaine, 1977-84; soliciter Village of Belle Center, Ohio, 1982—, Village of De Graff, Ohio, 1982—. Pres. United Way, Bellefontaine, 1984, bd. dirs., 1982—. Mem. ABA, Ohio Bar Assn., Logan County Bar Assn., Assn. Trial Lawyers Am., Logan County C. of C. Lodges: Lions, Masons. Republican. Roman Catholic. Avocations: golf, tennis, crossword puzzles. Home: 2431 Carriage Hill Dr Bellefontaine OH 43311-9430

HEATON, RODGER A., prosecutor; b. July 20, 1959; BS, U. Ill., 1981; JD, Ind. U., 1985. Prosecutor US Atty.'s Office, Springfield, Ill., 1990—2000, chief, civil divsn., 2003—05; litig. ptnr. Kirkland & Ellis LLP, Chgo., 2001—03; US atty. (ctrl. dist.) Ill. US Dept. Justice, Springfield, Ill., 2006—; mem. Atty. Gen. Adv. Com., 2007—08. Former adj. prof. U. Ill. Coll. Law. Recipient Dir.'s award, Exec. Office of US Attys., 1998. Office: US Attys Office 318 S 6th St Springfield IL 62701

HEATWOLE, MARK M., lawyer, director; b. Pitts., Jan. 28, 1948; s. Marion Grove and Phyllis Adelle (Leiter) H.; m. Sarah Ann Collier, Dec. 30, 1970; children: Mary Phyllis, Elizabeth Collier, Anna Bell. BA, Washington and Lee U., 1969, JD, 1972. Bar: Ill. 1972, U.S. Dist. Ct. (no. dist.) Ill. 1972, U.S. Ct. Appeals (7th cir.) 1977, U.S. Supreme Ct. 1980, U.S. Tax Ct. 1987. Assoc. Chadwell & Kayser, Ltd., Chgo., 1972-79, ptnr., v.p., 1979-89; ptnr. Winston & Strawn LLP, Chgo., 1990—2006; exec. v.p., gen. counsel Priva Techs., Inc., Chgo., 2006—. Treas. Lyric Opera Chgo. Guild, 1980—81, v.p., 1980—81, chmn. fundraising, 1986; vice-chmn. Gorton Cmty. Ctr., 1986; chmn. bd. Gorton Cmty. Ctr. Found., 1986—89; trustee Barat Coll., 1982—85, The Admiral, Chgo., 1988—2001, Allendale Assn., 1991—2000; mem. Art Inst. of Chgo. Old Masters Soc., 1999—; Mem. 1st ward Rep. com. on candidates Lake Forest (Ill.) Caucus, 1985—88, chmn. 1st ward, 1987—88, vice-chmn., 1989—90, chmn., 1990—91; mem. session Lake Forest Presbyn. Ch., 1978—84, chmn. ch. and society com., 1980; bd. dirs. Lyric Opera Chgo. Guild, 1976—2005, Lake Forest Symphony, 1987—91, Rehab. Inst. Chgo. Enterprises, 1991—2001, Gorton Community Ctr., 1982—88. Mem.: ABA (continuing legal edn. com. 1978—79, mem. antitrust com. young lawyers sect. 1978—81, com. on civil practice and procedure antitrust sect. 1980, bus. law sect. 1986—, patent trademark and copyright sect. 1990—), Chgo. Bar Assn. (chmn. profl. responsibility com. young lawyers sect. 1977—78, mem. exec. com. 1978—79, bd. dirs.), Valley Club Montecito, Lawyers Club, Econ. Club Chgo., Shoreacres Club (bd. govs. 1996—2004, pres. 2002—04). Republican. Office: Priva Techs Inc 875 N Michigan Ave Ste 1404 Chicago IL 60611 Home Phone: 312-643-2184; Office Phone: 312-759-3535. Business E-Mail: mark.heatwole@priva-tech.com.

HEAVICAN, MICHAEL G., state supreme court justice; b. 1947; BA, JD, U. Nebr. From dep. county atty. yo chief dep. county atty. Lancaster County, Nebr., 1975—81, county atty. Nebr., 1981—91; chief of criminal div. US Atty.'s Office Nebr. US Dept. Justice, Nebr., 1991—2001, US atty. Nebr., 2001—06; chief justice ebr. Supreme Ct., 2006—. Office: State Capitol Rm 2214 Lincoln NE 68509 Office Phone: 402-471-3738. Office Fax: 402-471-2197.

HEBDA, LAWRENCE JOHN, data processing executive, consultant; b. East Chicago, Ind., Apr. 9, 1954; s. Walter Martin and Barbara (Matczynski) H.; m. Cynthia Ruta Aizkalns, June 17, 1978. BS, Purdue U., 1976; MBA, U. Iowa, 1983. Cert. data processor. Programmer Inland Steel Co., East Chicago, 1976-77; data analyst Deere & Co., Moline, Ill., 1977-82, systems analyst, 1982-83, project mgr., 1983-84, dealer systems cons., 1984-85, corp. planning analyst, 1985-87, systems edn. adminstr., 1987-88, telecommunications analyst, 1988; info. systems sr. cons. Hewitt Assocs., Lincolnshire, Ill., 1988-93, MIS bus. mgr., 1994-97, mgr. software distbn./oper. sys., 1997-2000, mgr. client/server application support, 2000—02, sr. application project mgr., 2002—07; sr. program mgr. Discover Fin. Svcs., Riverwoods, Ill., 2007—. Instr. computer sci. dept. Coll. Lake County Ill., 1996—, computer info. systems adv. bd., 1999—. Mem. at. Rep. Congl. Com., 1982-85; charter mem. Rep. Presdl. Task Force, 1980; chmn. pastoral coun. Roman Cath. Ch., 1994-95. Recipient Cert. Recognition, at. Rep. Congl. Com., 1982-85, Presdl. Achievement award Rep. Nat. Com., 1984; nominee Adj. Faculty of Yr., Coll. Lake County, 2007. Mem. Data Processing Mgmt. Assn., Am. Legion, Internat. Platform Assn., DAV Comdr.'s Club, King's Men Religious Orgn. (v.p. 1985, pres. 1986-87), Toastmasters Internat. (assoc. area gov. 1983-84), K.C. (3d degree coun. 8022, 2001, Dep. Grand Knight 2002-03, fin. sec., 2003-06). Roman Catholic. Home: 675 Sussex Cir Vernon Hills IL 60061-2123 Office: Discover Fin Svcs 2500 Lake Cook Rd Riverwoods IL 60015 Office Phone: 847-295-5000. Personal E-mail: lxhebda@aol.com. Business E-Mail: ljhebda@hewitt.com.

HEBENSTREIT, JAMES BRYANT, agricultural products executive, venture capitalist; b. Long Beach, Calif., Mar. 8, 1946; s. William Joseph and Jean (Stark) H.; m. Marilyn Bartlett, Aug. 23, 1986. AB, Harvard U., 1968, MBA, 1973. Pres. Terra-Light div. Butler Mfg. Co., Boston, 1980-82, Capital for Bus., Inc. (SB/C, venture capital affiliate Commerce Bancshares), St. Louis and Kansas City, Mo., 1982-87; sr. v.p. fin., CFO Commerce Bancshares, Inc., Kansas City, 1985-87, bd. dirs., 1987—; pres. Bartlett and Co., Kansas City, 1992—. Lt. USNR, 1968-71. Office: Bartlett & Co 4800 Main St Kansas City MO 64112-2510 Home: 5828 Pembroke Ct Mission Hills KS 66208-1148

HECHT, DARYL L., state supreme court justice; b. Sac City, Iowa, June 25, 1952; s. Eldon E. and Darlene E. (Rubendall) H.; m. Sandra Ellen Bubke, June 16, 1973; children: Erica M., Lindsay M. BA, Morningside Coll., 1974; JD magna cum laude, U. S.D., 1977; MA in Law, U. Va. Sch. of Law, 2004. Bar: U.S. Dist. Ct. Iowa 1977, U.S. Dist. Ct. S.D. 1977. Atty. Crary, Huff, Inkster, Hecht & Sheehan, Sioux City, Iowa, 1977—99; judge Iowa Ct. of Appeals, 1999—2006; justice Iowa Supreme Ct., 2006—. Bd. dirs. Boys & Girls Home and Family Svcs., Sioux City, 1982-89. Mem. Assn. Trial Lawyers Am., Iowa Trial Lawyers Assn. (pres. 1994-95). Avocations: reading, politics. Office: Iowa Supreme Ct 1111 E Ct Ave Des Moines IA 50319 Office Phone: 515-281-5174.

HECHT, LOUIS ALAN, lawyer; b. Chgo., July 20, 1944; s. Bernard T. and Dorthe E. (Callen) H.; m. Joanne Lebow, Aug. 16, 1967; children— Jonathan D., Peter A. BS, U. Ill., JD, 1969. Bar: Ill. bar 1969. Mem. Hofgren, Wegner, Allen, Stellman & McCord, Chgo., 1969-71, Coffee & Sweeney, Chgo., 1971-74; patent counsel Molex, Inc., Lisle, Ill., 1974—77, gen. counsel, sec., 1978—. Mem. Am. Bar Assn., Ill. State Bar Assn., Chgo. Bar Assn., Am. Patent Lawyers Assn., Patent Lawyers Assn. Chgo. Office: Molex Inc 2222 Wellington Ave Lisle IL 60532-3820

HECKEL, JOHN LOUIS (JACK HECKEL), aerospace management executive; b. Columbus, Ohio, July 12, 1931; s. Russel Criblez and Ruth Selma (Heid) H.; m. Jacqueline Ann Alexander, Nov. 21, 1959 (div. 1993); children: Heidi, Holly, John; m. Linda Holleran, Aug. 1, 1994. BS, U. Ill., 1954; PhD with honors, Nat. U. San Diego, 1984. Divsn. mgr. Aerojet Divsn., Azusa, Calif., 1956-70, Seattle and Washington, 1956-70; pres. Aerojet-Space Gen. Co., El Monte, Calif., 1970-72, Aerojet Liquid Rocket Co., Sacramento, 1972-77; group v.p. Aerojet Sacramento Cos., 1977-81; pres. Aerojet Gen., La Jolla, Calif., 1981-85, chmn., CEO, 1985-87; pres., COO GenCorp., Akron, 1987-94, also bd. dirs. Bd. dirs. WD-40 Corp., Petritech, Corp. Bd. dirs. San Diego Econ. Devel. Corp., 1983-86, Akron Regional Devel. Bd., Akron Gen. Hosp., Summit County United Way; pres. Summit Edn. Partnership Found., Akron. Recipient Disting. Alumni award U. Ill. Ann. Alumni Conv., 1979 Fellow AIAA (assoc.); mem. Aerospace Industries Assn. Am. (gov. 1981), Navy League U.S., Am. Def. Preparedness Assn., San Diego C. of C. (bd. dirs.)

HECKEL, RICHARD WAYNE, metallurgical engineering educator; b. Pitts., Jan. 25, 1934; s. Ralph Clyde and Esther Vera (Zoerb) H.; m. Peggy Ann Simmons, Jan. 3, 1959 (dec. Apr. 1998); children: Scott Alan, Laura Ann Rowe. BS in Metall. Engring., Carnegie Mellon, 1955, MS, 1958, PhD, 1959. Sr. rsch. metallurgist E.I. duPont de Nemours & Co., Wilmington, Del., 1959—63; prof. metall. engring. Drexel U., Phila., 1963—71; head dept. materials sci. and engring. Carnegie Mellon, Pitts., 1971—76; prof. materials sci. and engring. Mich. Tech. U., Houghton, 1976—96, prof. emeritus, 1996—; tech. dir., owner Engring. Trends, Houghton, 2000—. Commr. at large Engring. Workforce Commn., 1997—, founder, tech. dir. Engring. Trends (e-commerce). Contbr. articles to profl. jours. Served as 1st lt. Ordnance Corps, U.S. Army, 1959-60. Recipient Lindback Teaching award Drexel U., 1968; Research award Mich. Tech. U., 1985 Fellow ASM Internat. (life; Bradley Stoughton Young Tchr. of Metallurgy award 1969, Phila. Ednl. Achievement award 1967); mem. The Metals, Minerals and Materials Soc., Am. Welding Soc. (Adams Meml. mem. 1966), Am. Soc. Engring. Edn., Sigma Xi, Omicron Delta Kappa, Tau Beta Pi, Phi Kappa Phi, Alpha Sigma Mu. Address: Engring Trends 1281 Hickory Ln Houghton MI 49931-1609 Home Phone: 906-482-2208; Office Phone: 906-482-1523. Personal E-mail: rheckel@chartermi.net, engtrend@up.net.

HECKEMEYER, ANTHONY JOSEPH, circuit court judge; b. Cape Girardeau, Mo., Jan. 20, 1939; s. Paul Q. and Frances E. (Goetz) H.; m. Elizabeth Faye Littleton, Feb. 13, 1964; children: Anthony Joseph, Matthew Paul, Mary Elizabeth, Andrew William, Sarah Kathryn. BS, U. Mo., 1962, JD, 1972; grad., Nat. Judicial Coll., 1980, Juvenile Coll., 1984. Bar: Mo. Mem. Mo. Ho. Reps., Jefferson City, 1964-72; sole practice Sikeston, Mo., 1972-81; presiding cir. judge State of Mo., Scott and Mississippi Counties, 1981—. Chmn. alcohol and substance abuse com. Nat. Council of Juvenile and Family Ct. Judges, Reno, 1987-88, presenter at U. Reno; majority party whip, chmn., vice chmn. agr. com., higher edn. com. as a miscellaneous resolution com. Named Outstanding Conservation Legislator Sears, 1968, Found. Mo. Wildlife Fedn., 1968, Man of Yr., Sikeston C. of C., 1989. Mem. Mo. Trial Judges Assn. (pres. 1995). Office: Presiding Cir Judge PO Box 256 Benton MO 63736-0256

HECKMAN, CAROL A., biology educator; b. East Stroudsburg, Pa., Oct. 18, 1944; d. Wilbur Thomas and Doris (Betts) H. BA, Beloit Coll., Wis., 1966; PhD, U. Mass., Amherst, 1972. Rsch. assoc. Yale U. Sch. Medicine, New Haven, 1973-75; staff mem. Oak Ridge (Tenn.) Nat. Lab., 1975-82; adj. assoc. prof. U. Tenn.-Oak Ridge Biomed. Grad. Sch., 1980-82; assoc. prof. Bowling Green (Ohio) State U., 1982-86, prof. biology, 1986—. Cons. NSF, Washington, 1977-80, NIH, Rockville, Md., 1996-98; dir. EM facility Bowling Green State U., 1982—; NSF trainee, Amherst, 1967-70; vis. prof. Univ. Coll. London. Contbr. articles to profl. jours., chpts. to books. Internat. Cancer Rsch. Tech. fellow Internat. Union Against Cancer, 1980, Heritage Found. fellow, 1982, guest rsch. fellow, Uppsala, Sweden, 1989-90; grantee NSF, 1981-84, 90-92, NIH, 1987-88, 98-2001, Dept. of Def., 2000-02. Mem. Am. Assn. Cancer Rsch., Am. Soc. Cell Biology, Microscopy Soc. Am., N.W. Ohio Microscopy (sec.-treas. 1986-90, pres. 1990-94), Soc. In Vitro Biology, Mid-Am. Drug Devel. (pres. 1999), Ohio Acad. Sci., Sigma Xi. Episcopalian. Achievements include research evaluation and development of in vitro anticarcinogens. Office: Bowling Green State U Dept Biol Scis Bowling Green OH 43403-0001 Office Phone: 419-372-8218. Business E-Mail: heckman@bgnet.bgsu.edu.

HECKMAN, JAMES JOSEPH, economist, educator; b. Chgo., Apr. 19, 1944; s. John Jacob and Bernice Irene (Medley) H.; m. Lynne Pettler, 1979; children: Jonathan Jacob, Alma Rachel. AB in Math. summa cum laude (Woodrow Wilson fellow), Colo. Coll., 1965, D (hon.), 2001; MA in Econ., Princeton U., 1968, PhD in Econ. (Harold Willis Dodds fellow), 1971; MA (hon.), Yale U., 1989; D (hon.), U. Chile, 2002, Universidad Autonoma del Estados de Mex., Toluca, 2003, U. Montreal, 2004; DHL (hon.), Bard Coll., 2004. From lectr. to assoc. prof. Columbia U., 1970-74; assoc. prof. econs. U. Chgo., 1973-76, prof., 1976—, Henry Schultz prof. of econ., 1985-95, prof. econs. Harris Sch. Pub. Policy, 1990—, dir. Ctr. for Program Evaluation Harris Sch. Pub. Policy, 1991—, Henry Schultz Disting. Svc. prof., 1995—, dir. Econs. Rsch. Ctr. dept. econs., 1997—, Changjiang River Scholar prof., 2004—; A. Whitney Griswold prof. econs. Yale U., New Haven, 1988-90, Sterling prof., 1990, prof. dept. stats., 1990, dir. dept. econs. Econs. Rsch. Ctr., 1997—; disting. prof. microeconometrics Univ. Coll., London, 2004—, disting. chair microeconomics, 2004—, prof. sci. and society Dublin, 2005. Rsch. assoc. Nat. Bur. Econs. Rsch., 1970-77, sr. rsch. assoc., 1977-85, 87—; Irving Fisher prof. econs. Yale U., 1984; treas. Chgo. Econ. Rsch. Assocs.; rsch. assoc. Econs. Rsch. Ctr.-NORC, 1985—; cons. in field; cons. Chgo. Urban League, 1978-86; mem. status Black Ams. com. NRC; lectr. in field.; hon. prof. U. Tucuman, Argentina, 1998, Hangzhou U. Sci. and Tech., Wuhan, China, 2001, Wuhan U., 2003. Co-author: (with Alan Krueger) Income Inequality in America: What Role for Human Capital Policy, 2004; editor Jour. Polit. Economy, 1981-87; assoc. editor Jour. Econometrics, 1977-83, Jour. Labor Econs., 1983—, Econs. Revs., 1987—, Rev. of Econs. and Statistics, 1994-2002, Jour. Econ. Perspectives, 1989-96, Labor Econs., 1992—; editor: (with B. Singer), Longitudinal Analysis of Labor Market Data, 1985; (with E. Leamer) Handbook of Econometrics, Vol. 5, 2001, vol. 6, 2005, (with Carmen Pages) Law and Employment Lessons from the Latin America and The Caribbean, 2004; Am. editor Rev. Econ. Studies, 1982-85; contbr. articles to profl. jours. Founding faculty and curriculum com. U. Chgo. Harris Sch. Pub. Policy. Recipient John Bates Clark prize, 1983, Louis Benezet Alumni prize

Colo. Coll., 1985, Nobel Prize in Econs., 2000, Paul Harris award Internat. Rotary Assn., 2002, Jacob Mincer award, 2005, Ulysses medal U. Coll. Dublin, Aigner award, 2005; J.S. Guggenheim Found. fellow, 1978-79, Social Sci. Rsch. Coun. fellow, 1977-78, Ctr. for Advanced Study in Behavioral Scis. fellow, 1978-79; NDEA fellow; NIH fellow. Fellow Am. Bar Found. (sr. rsch. affiliate 1989-91, sr. rsch. fellow 1991-), Econometric Soc. (mem. coun. 2001—), Am. Acad. Arts and Scis., Am. Statis. Assn., Soc. Labor Econs.; mem. NAS, Am. Econ. Assn. (exec. com. 2000-03), Midwest Econs. Assn. (pres.-elect 1996-97, pres. 1997-98), Western Econ. Assn. (pres.-elect 2005-), Indsl. Rels. Rsch. Assn., Econ. Sci. Assn. (founder), Econometric Soc. (coun. 2000-06), Phi Beta Kappa. Office: U Chgo Dept Econs 1126 E 59th St Chicago IL 60637-1580 Home Phone: 773-268-4547; Office Phone: 773-702-0634. Business E-Mail: jjh@uchicago.edu.

HEDBERG, PAUL CLIFFORD, broadcast executive; b. Cokato, Minn., May 28, 1939; s. Clifford L. and Florence (Erenberg) Hedberg; m. Juliet Ann Schubert, Dec. 30, 1962; children: Mark, Ann. Student, Hamline U., 1959-60, U. Minn., 1960-62. Program dir. Sta. KRIB, Mason City, Iowa, 1957-58, Sta. WMIN, Mpls., 1959; staff announcer Time-Life broadcast Sta. WTCN-AM-TV, Mpls., 1959-61, Crowell Collier Sta. KDWB, St. Paul, 1961-62; founder, pres. Sta. KBEW, Minn., 1963-81; founder, owner Sta. KQAD and KLQL-FM, Luverne, Minn., 1971-88; co-founder Sta. KMRS-AM, KKOK-FM, Morris, Minn., 1956-94, pres., 1974-94; founder, pres. Courtney Clifford Inc., Mpls., 1977-79; founder, owner Market Quoters Inc., Blue Earth, Iowa, 1974-96; pres. Complete Commodity Options Inc., Blue Earth, 1977-91; pres., owner Sta. KEEZ-FM, Mankato, Minn., 1977-92; founder, pres. Sta. KUOO-FM, Spirit Lake, Iowa, 1984-99; owner Sta. KRIB and KLSS-FM, Mason City, 1984-97; owner, pres. Sta. KAYL-AM-FM, Storm Lake, Iowa, 1990-99; pres. KLGA AM-FM, Algona, Iowa, 1993-99; CEO Hedberg Broadcasting Group, Blue Earth, 1976-99; pres. KSOU AM-FM, Sioux Center, Iowa, 1996-99. Pres. Blue Earth Indsl. Svcs. Corp., 1970—76, bd. dirs., Minn. Good Rds., v.p., 1976—79, pres., 1979—81; bd. dirs. Spirit Lake Industries; mem. affiliates bd. NBC Radio Network, 1990—95, chmn., 1991—95; pres., CEO Arnolds Park (Iowa) Amusement Pk., 1990—95; founder Sta. KUQQ-FM, Spirit Lake-Milford, 1996—99, Sta. KIHK-FM, Rock Valley, Iowa, 1997—99. Mem. Iowa Gt. Lakes Airport Commn., 1986—92; bd. dirs. Pavek Mus. Wonderful Wireless, St. Louis Park, Minn., 1987—. Named to, Mus. Broadcasting Hall of Fame, 2002; recipient Disting. Svc. award, Blue Earth Jaycees, 1971. Mem.: Iowa Broadcasters Assn. (Broadcaster of the Yr. 1998), Minn. AP Broadcasters (pres. 1966, bd. dirs. 1976—78), Minn. Assn. Broadcasters (radio bd. dirs. 1975—86, v.p. 1980—81, pres. 1983—84), Nat. Assn. Broadcasters (bd. dirs. 1985—89, 1993—95), Antique and Classic Boating Soc. (bd. dirs. 2003—), Iowa Lakes C. of C. (bd. dirs. 1985—86), Blue Earth C. of C. (pres. 1967, Leadership Recognition award 1967), Shriners, Masons, Grebdeh L. C. (founder 1995—). Lutheran. Home Phone: 239-434-8261. E-mail: Grebdeh@aol.com.

HEDDENS, LISA, state official; b. Rochester, Minn., June 6, 1964; AS, Des Moines Area C.C.; BS, Iowa State U. Cons.; family support coord.; disability rights advocate; substitute tchr.; state rep. Iowa, 2003—. Mem. health and human svcs. appropriations subcom.; mem. pub. safety standing com.; mem. environ. protection standing com.; mem. human resources standing com. Leader Girl Scouts Am.; bd. dirs. Arc of Story County, Westory Vol. Fire Dept. Office: State Capitol E 12th and Grand Des Moines IA 50319

HEDEEN, RODNEY A., manufacturing executive; BS in Indsl. Tech., U. Wis.; MBA, U. Louisville. With GE, Louisville, Hillenbrand Industries, Batesville, Ind., Cummins Engine Co., Columbus, Ind.; from sr. v.p. mfg./distgn. to pres. bus. sys. divsn. Reynolds & Reynolds, Dayton, Ohio, 1987—97, pres. bus. sys. divsn., 1997—2000; pres., CEO The Relizon Co., Dayton, 2000—. Bd. dirs. Dayton Area C. of C., Downtown Dayton Partnership. Mem. Internat. Bus. Forms Inst. (bd. dirs. N.Am. and internat. bd., mem. found. bd.). Office: Relizon 220 E Monument Dayton OH 45402-1223

HEDGE, H. KAY, state senator; b. Rose Hill, Iowa, Apr. 2, 1928; m. Alleen Hedge. Student, U. Iowa. Farmer; U.S. senator from Iowa, 1988—. Mem. Fremont United Meth. Ch., Iowa. Mem. Iowa Soybean Assn., Iowa Corn Growers, Iowa Cattlemen's Assn., Mahaska County Pork Prodrs., Mahaska County Farm Bur., Oskaloosa C. of C., Am. Legion. Republican. Home: 3208 335th St Fremont IA 52561-9796 E-mail: kay_hedge@legis.state.ia.us.

HEDIEN, WAYNE EVANS, retired insurance company executive; b. Evanston, Ill., Feb. 15, 1934; s. George L. and Edith P. (Chalstrom) H.; m. Colette Johnston, Aug. 24, 1963; 3 children. BSME, Northwestern U., 1956, MBA, 1957. Engr. Cook Electric Co., Skokie, Ill., 1957-64; bus. mgr. Preston Sci., Inc., Anaheim, Calif., 1964-66; security analyst Allstate Ins. Co., Northbrook, Ill., 1966-70, portfolio mgr., 1970-73, asst. treas., 1973-78, v.p., treas., 1978-80, sr. v.p., treas., 1980-83, exec. v.p., chief fin. officer, 1983-85, vice chmn., chief fin. officer, 1986, pres., 1986-89, chmn., 1989-94, The Allstate Corp., 1993-94, also bd. dirs.; retired, 1994. Mem. adv. coun. Kellogg Grad. Sch. Mgmt., Northwestern U.; bd. dirs. The PMI Group, Inc., Field Mus. Natural History, Morgan Stanley Dean Witter Funds. Mem. Comml. Club Chgo. Office: WEH Assocs 5750 Old Orchard Rd Ste 530 Skokie IL 60077-1081

HEDLUND, RONALD, baritone; b. Mpls., May 12, 1934; s. Cyril and Mildred H.; m. Barbara Smith, Nov. 12, 1974; children: Eric, Alexander. BA, Hamline U.; MusM, Ind. U., Juilliard Sch. Mem. faculty dept. music U. Ill., 1970—74, 1983—2006; bass soloist, instr. classical music seminar Eisenstadt and Vienna, Austria; ret., 2006. Singing voice cons. Carle Clinic Speech Ctr., Urbana, 1994—. Appeared throughout U.S. including opera cos. of San Francisco, Chgo., Houston, Miami, Seattle, Dallas, Ft. Worth, Phila., Washington, Omaha, Santa Fe, Lake George, Boston, N.Y.C. Opera, Met. Opera Nat. Co., New Orleans, Spoleto Festival, Edinburgh Festival, Vancouver Opera, Conn. Opera, Aspen Festival, R.I. Opera, Chgo. Opera Theater, Opera Theatre St. Louis, Utah Opera, Opera Ill., Ill. Opera Theatre; soloist with numerous orchs., recitals throughout U.S. Served with USNR, 1958-63. Office: 1st Choice Music Svcs 505 Eliot Dr Urbana IL 61801-6727 Office Phone: 217-244-3339. Business E-Mail: rhedlund@uiuc.edu.

HEDREN, PAUL LESLIE, retired parks director, historian; b. New Ulm, Minn., Nov. 12, 1949; s. Thomas Harry and Muriel Mary (Kunz) H.; m. Janeen Margaret Wolcott, June 19, 1974 (div. 1997); children: Ethne Olivia, Whitney Elizabeth; m. Connie Joyce Burns, Sept. 10, 2005. BA, St. Cloud State Coll., 1972. Park ranger, historian Ft. Laramie (Wyo.) Nat. Hist. Site, 1971-76; historian Big Hole Nat. Battlefield, Wisdom, Mont., 1976-78; chief ranger, historian Golden Spike at. Hist. Site, Brigham City, Utah, 1978-84; supt. Fort Union Trading Post Nat. Hist. Site, Williston, ND, 1984-97, Niobrara Nat. Scenic River/Mo. Nat. Recreational River, O'Neill, Nebr., 1997—2007. Author: First Scalp for Custer, 1980, With Crook in to the Black Hills, 1985, Fort Laramie in 1876, 1988 (Best Book of 1988 Wyo. State Hist. Soc.), Campaigning with King, 1991 (Merit award State Hist. Soc. Wis. 1991), The Great Sioux War 1876-77, 1991, Traveler's Guide to the Great Sioux War, 1996, We Trailed the Sioux, 2003; contbr. articles to profl. jours. Bd. dirs. Conv. and Vis. Bur., Williston, 1984-96, pres., 1994-96. Named Supt. of Yr. for Nat. Resources Mgmt., NPS, 2004; recipient Vivian Paladin award, Mont. Hist. Soc., 2005. Mem. Western Writers Assn. (Spur award 2005), Western History Assn. (mem. coun. 1990-93). Avocations: writing, lecturing. Office: 4603 North 135 St Omaha NE 68164 Home Phone: 402-336-2073; Office Phone: 402-336-3970. Business E-Mail: paul_hedren@nps.gov.

HEDRICK, LARRY WILLIS, retired airport executive; b. Newton, Kans., Dec. 23, 1939; s. A.C. and Goldie (Kerns) H.; m. Nancy Cashin, July 21, 1962; children: Christina, Kathleen, Thomas. BL, U. LaSalle, Chgo., 1973. Lic. airport mgr., Mass, pilot and instrument technician. Airport mgr., dir. civil def. Newton City-County Airport, 1966-73; airport mgr. Barnes Mcpl. Airport, Mass., 1973-77, Niagara Falls Internat. Airport, 1977-81, Greater Buffalo (N.Y.) Internat. Airport, 1981-87; appointed airport adminstr. Pt. Columbus Internat. Airport, Columbus, Ohio, 1987-91; appointed exec. dir. Columbus Airport Authority, 1991-2000; ret., 2001. Founding bd. mem. Airline Passengers of Am., 1987; guest speaker various univs. and airport confs. Bd. dirs. Greater Columbus Conv. and Visitors Bur., 1992; past squadron commdr. CAP Kans. Wing. With USN, 1958-62. Mem. Am. Assn. Airport Execs. (accredited 1973, nat. sec. 1982, treas. bd. dirs. 1983, 1st v.p. 1985, 2d v.p. 1984, nat. pres. 1986-87, Disting. Svc. award 1994), Nat. Fire Protection Assn. (airport industry's only rep.), Mass. Airport Mgmt. Assn. (pres. 1975-76).

HEETER, JAMES A., lawyer; b. Monett, Mo., Oct. 28, 1948; AB with honors, U. Mo., Columbia, 1970; JD cum laude, Harvard U., 1973. Bar: Mo. 1973. Mem. Stinson, Mag & Fizzell PC, Kansas City, Mo., 1973—95; ptnr. Sonnenschein Nath & Rosenthal LLP, Kansas City, Mo., 1995—, mng. ptnr. Kansas City office, 2001—, mem. exec. com. Mem. City Coun., Kansas City, Mo., 1983—87. Mem. Civic Coun. of Greater Kansas City. Mem. ABA, Mo. Bar, Kansas City Met. Bar Assn. Office: Sonnenschein Nath & Rosenthal LLP Ste 1100 4520 Main St Kansas City MO 64111 Office Phone: 816-460-2452. Office Fax: 816-531-7545. Business E-Mail: jheeter@sonnenschein.com.

HEFFELFINGER, THOMAS BACKER, lawyer, former prosecutor; b. Mpls., Feb. 13, 1948; BA in History, Stanford U., 1970; JD, U. Minn., 1975. Bar: Minn. 1976, US Dist. Ct. Minn. 1977, US Ct. Appeals (8th cir.) 1983, US Dist. Ct. (ea. dist.) Wis., 1999, Forest County Potawatomi Community Tribal Ct., 1999, US Supreme Ct., 2000, US Ct. Fed. Claims, 2000. Law clk. Office of the Hennepin County Atty., 1974-76, asst. atty. juvenile divsn., 1976, asst. atty. criminal divsn. trial sect., 1977-82, asst. atty. major offender unit, 1978-81, supr. burglary unit, 1981-82; asst. US atty. criminal divsn. US Dept. Justice, Minn., 1982-88, atty. white collar crime sect., 1982-85, supr. narcotics and firemans sect., 1985-86, US atty. Dist. Minn., 1991-93, 2001—06; ptnr. Opperman Heins & Paquin, 1988-91, Bowman & Brooke, 1993—2000, Best & Flanagan LLP, Mpls., 2000—01, 2006—. Contbr. articles to profl. jours. Candidate Hennepin County Atty., 1986; bd. dirs. Mpls. Chpt. ARC, 1987-2001, chair, 1998-; mem. Hennepin County Task Force on Youth and Drugs, 1987-88, Minn. Ho. of Reps. Rep. Caucus Drug Task Force, 1989-90, Minn. Commn. on Violent Crime, 1991; chmn. Minn. Commn. on Jud. Selection, 1990-91; mem. Flying Cloud Airport Adv. Commn., 1996-, chair, 1998-; bd. mem., Minn. Campaign Fin. & Pub. Disclosure Bd., 1998-2000; lectr. in field. Mem. ABA, Fed. Bar Assn., Minn. Bar Assn., Hennepin County Bar Assn., Minn. Am. Indian Bar Assn., Ethics Officer Assn., 1994-2001, Nat. Assn. Criminal Def. Lawyers, 1997-2001, Nat. Assn. Former US Attys., 1993-2001, 2006-Office: Best & Flanagan LLP 225 S Sixth St Ste 4000 Minneapolis MN 55402 E-mail: heffelfinger@bestlaw.com.

HEFNER, CHRISTIE ANN, publishing executive; b. Chgo., Nov. 8, 1952; d. Hugh Marston and Mildred Marie (Williams) H. BA in English and Am. Lit., summa cum laude, Brandeis U., 1974. Freelance journalist, Boston, 1974-75; spl. asst. to chmn. Playboy Enterprises, Inc., Chgo., 1975-78, v.p., 1978-82, bd. dirs., 1979—, pres., 1982-88, COO, 1984-88, chmn., CEO, 1988—. Bd. dirs. Playboy Found., Mag. Pubs. Assn. Bd. dirs. Creative Coalition, Rush Med. Ctr., Canyon Ranch, Bus. Com. for the Arts. Named Advocate of Yr., AIDS Legal Coun., 1998, Friend for Life, Howard Brown Med. Ctr., 1998; named one of 100 Most Powerful Women in World, Forbes mag., 2005—07; named to Today's Chgo. (Ill.) Woman Hall Fame, 2002; recipient Agness Underwood award, LA chpt. Women in Comm., 1984, Founders award, Midwest Women's Ctr., 1986, Human Rights award, Am. Jewish Com., 1986, Harry Kalven Freedom of Expression award, ACLU, Ill., 1987, Spirit of Life award, City of Hope, 1988, Eleanor Roosevelt award, Internat. Platform Assn., 1990, Will Rogers Meml. award, Beverly Hills C. of C. and Civic Assn., 1993, Humanitarian award, Rainbow/PUSH Coalition, 1998, Corp. Leadership award, AIDS Pastoral Care Network, 1998, Exec. Leadership award, Nat. Soc. Fundraising Execs., 1998, Champion of Freedom award, ADL, 2000, Spirit of Hope award, John Wayne Cancer Ctr., 2001, Bettie B. Port Humanitarian award, Mt. Sinai, 2001, Christopher Reeve 1st Amendment award, Creative Coalition, 2001, Bette B. Port Humanitarian award, Sianai Health Sys., 2001, Vanguard award, at. Cable & Telecommunications Assn., 2002, Philanthropic Innovator Luminary award, Com. of 200, 2002, Family Bus. Coun. Leadership award, U. Ill., Chgo., 2003, Friends of Cmty. award, Diversity Healthcare, Inc., 2005, Lifetime Achievement award, 25-Yr. Club, 2005. Mem. Nat. Cable and Telecomm. Assn. (Vanguard award 2002, Interlochen's Path of Inspiration award 2003), Mus. of TV and Radio Media Ctr., Brandeis Nat. Women's Com. (life), Com. of 200, World Pres. Orgn., Chgo. Network, Sierra Club, Emilys List, Phi Beta Kappa. Democrat. Office: Playboy Enterprises Inc 680 N Lake Shore Dr Chicago IL 60611-4455

HEFNER, DAVID STUART, health facility administrator, consultant; b. Boston, Tex., July 20, 1954; s. John Hardin and E. Patricia (Schwartz) H.; div. 1984; children: Tonia Marie, Brandi Lynn. BBA, U. Tex., 1976; M in Personnel Adminstrn., Brigham Young U., 1982. Founder, CEO Cons. Concepts, Inc., Salt Lake City, 1978, mng. ptnr., 1978—94; hosp. adminstr. Crook County Hosp., Sundance, Wyo., 1978-80, Tooele Valley Hosp., Utah, 1980-82; program mgr. BSL Tech., Salt Lake City, 1982-85; sr. ptnr. CSC Global Health Solutions; acting exec. dir., COO Penn State Milton S. Hershey Med. Ctr., Hershey, 2003, exec. dir., COO, 2003—06; sr. ptnr. CSC Global Health Solutions, 2006; pres. Univ. Chgo. Med. Ctr., 2006—. Adv. bd. mem. Infinity Markets, Inc.; faculty and adv. bd. mem. Landmark Edn. Mem.: Am. Arbitration Assn. (panel arbitrator). Office: Univ Chgo Med Ctr 5841 S Maryland Ave Chicago IL 60637

HEFT, JAMES LEWIS, academic administrator, theology studies educator; b. Cleve., Feb. 20, 1943; s. Berl Ramsey and Hazel Mary (Miller) Heft. BA in Philosophy, U. Dayton, 1965, BS in Edn., 1966; MA in Theology, U. Toronto, 1971, PhD in Hist. Theology, 1977. Prof. theology U. Dayton, Ohio, chmn. religious studies dept., 1983—89, provost, 1989—96, prof. faith and culture, chancellor, 1996—. Lectr. in field. Author: John XXII (1316-1334) and Papal Teaching Authority, 1986; editor: Faith and the Intellectual Life, 1996, A Catholic Modernity?, 1999, Beyond Violence--Religious Sources for Social Transformation in Judaism, Christianity, and Islam, 2004; contbr. articles to profl. jours. Trustee U. Dayton, Ohio, 1970—77, St. Mary's U., San Antonio, 1995—2003; trustee Greater Dayton Pub. TV, 1995—97; bd. dirs. Nat. Conf., 1990—2003. Recipient Excellence in Tchg. award, U. Dayton, 1983, 1st pl., Cath. Press Assn., 1990; scholar, U. Toronto, 1969—77. Mem.: Collegium (bd. dirs. 1990—94), Mariological Soc. Am. Roman Cath., Coll. Theology Soc., Cath. Theol. Soc. Am., Assn. Cath. Colls. and Univs. (bd. dirs. 1993—95, vice-chmn. 1996—), Nat. Cath. Edn. Assn. (bd. dirs. 1994—95). Roman Catholic. Avocation: theater. Office: U Dayton 300 College Park Ave Dayton OH 45469-0001 Office Phone: 937-229-2105. Business E-Mail: heft@udayton.edu.

HEFTY, THOMAS R., insurance company executive; b. 1947; BA, U. Wis., 1968; MA, Johns Hopkins U., 1969; JD, U. Wis., 1973. Atty. Fed. Trade Commn., 1973-74, CMI Investment, 1974-76; asst. gen. counsel Sentry Ins., 1976-79; dep. commr. Wis. Ins. Commn., 1979-82; v.p., sec., gen. counsel Blue Cross Shield United of Wis., 1982-84, sr. v.p., 1984-87, pres., CEO, 1987—; pres. United Wis. Services. Office: Blue Cross Shield United of WI 401 W Michigan St Milwaukee WI 53203-2804

HEGARTY, MARY FRANCES, lawyer; b. Chgo., Dec. 19, 1950; d. James E. and Frances M. (King) H. BA, DePaul U., 1972, JD, 1975. Bar: Ill. 1975, U.S. Dist. Ct. (no. dist.) Ill. 1976, U.S. Supreme Ct. 1980. Ptnr. Lannon & Hegarty, Park Ridge, Ill., 1975-80; pvt. practice Park Ridge, 1980—. Dir. Legal Assistance Found. Chgo., 1983—. Mem. revenue study com. Chgo. City Coun. Fin. Com., 1983; mem. Sole Source Rev. Panel, City of Chgo., 1984; pres. Hist. Pullman Found., Inc., 1984-85; apptd. Park Ridge Zoning Bd., 1993-94. Mem. Ill. State Bar Assn. (real estate coun. 1980-84), Chgo. Bar Assn., Women's Bar Assn. Ill. (pres. 1983-84), N.W.Suburban Bar Assn., Women's Bar Found. (v.p. 2003), Park Ridge Women Entrepreneurs, Chgo. Athletic Assn. (pres. 1992-93), Park Ridge C. of C. (pres. 2002-). Democrat. Roman Catholic. Office: 301 W Touhy Ave Park Ridge IL 60068-4204 Personal E-mail: mfhegarty@sbcglobal.net.

HEGEL, CAROLYN MARIE, farm owner and organization executive; b. Lagro, Ind., Apr. 19, 1940; d. Ralph H. and Mary Lucile (Rudig) Lynn; m. Tom Lee Hegel, June 3, 1962. Student pub. schs., Columbia City, Ind. Bookkeeper Huntington County Farm Bur. Co-op, Inc., Ind., 1959-67, office mgr. Ind., 1967-70; twp. woman leader Wabash County (Ind.) Farm Bur., Inc., 1970-73, county woman leader, 1973-76; dist. woman leader Ind. Farm Bur., Inc., Indpls., 1976-80, 2d v.p., bd. dirs., 1980—2006, chmn. women's com., 1980—2006, exec. com., 1988—2006; agr. program coord. Ivytech State Coll., 2007—. Farmer Andrews, Ind., 1962—; dir. Farm Bur. Ins. Co., Indpls., 1980—2006, exec. com., 1988—2006, audit com., 2000—06, chmn. audit com., 2003—06; bd. dirs., spkr. in field, bd. mem. Country Way Ins., 2002—06. Women in the Field columnist Hoosier Farmer mag., 1980—2006. Mem. rural task force Gt. Lakes States Econ. Devel. Commn., 1987—88; mem. Ind. Farm Bur. Svc. Co., 1980—; active Leadership Am. Program, 1988; Sunday sch. tchr., bd. dirs. children's activities Bethel United Meth. Ch., 1965—; pres. Bethel United Meth. Women, Lagro, 1975—81; bd. dirs. Ind. Farm Bur. Found., Indpls., 1980—, Ind. Inst. Agr., Food and Nutrition, Indpls., 1982—, Ind. 4-H Found., Lafayette, 1983—86; mem. Ind. Rural Health Adv. Coun., 1993—96, Hoosier Homestead Award Cert. Com., Indpls., 1980—; organizer farm divsn. Wabash County Am. Cancer Soc. Fund Dr., 1974; bd. dirs. N.E. Ind. Kidney Found., 1984—, Nat. Kidney Found. of Ind., 1985—89. Named Big Sister of Yr., Wabash County, Ind., 2003; named one of Outstanding Farm Woman of Yr., Country Woman Mag., 1987; recipient State 4-H Home Econs. award, Ind. 4-H, 1960. Mem.: Am. Farm Bur. Fedn. (midwest rep. to women's com. 1986—93), Producers Mktg. Assn. (bd. dirs. 1980—94), Ind. Agrl. Mktg. Assn. (bd. dirs. 1980—94), Women in Comm., Inc. Republican. Home: 3330 N 650 E Andrews IN 46702-9616 Office: Ind Farm Bur Inc PO Box 1290 225 S East St Indianapolis IN 46202-4058 E-mail: chegel@omnicityusa.com.

HEGEMAN, DANIEL JAY, state legislator; b. Cosby, Mo., Mar. 4, 1963; s. Donald Jay and Margaret Joan (Kowitz) H.; m. Francine Marie Walker, 1990; children: Hannah Marie, Joseph Daniel, Heidi Joan. BSA, U. Mo. Columbia. State rep. Dist. 6 Mo. State Rep., 1991-92, state rep. Dist. 5, 1992—. Treas. Hegeman Farm, Inc., 1988—. Mem. NW Mo. Holstein Assn. (v.p. 1991-92, pres. 1993-94, bd. dirs. 1994-95), Mid-Am. Dairymen, Inc. Dist. 14 (v.p. 1991-92), Andrew County Ext. Coun. (pres. 1990), Andrew County Farm Bur., Buchanan & Andrew County Dairy Herd Improvement Assn. (treas.), Cosby Masonic Lodge 600 (Worshipful Master 1989-90); Alpha Zeta, Omicron Delta Kappa, Alpha Gamma Rho.

HEGENDERFER, JONITA SUSAN, public relations executive; b. Chgo., Mar. 18, 1944; d. Clifford Lincoln and Cornelia Anna (Larson) Hazzard; m. Gary William Hegenderfer, Mar. 12, 1971 (dec. 1978). BA, Purdue U., 1965; postgrad., Calif. State U., Long Beach, 1966-67, Northwestern U., 1969-70. Tchr. English, Long Beach (Calif.) Schs., 1965-68; editl. asst. Playboy Mag., Chgo., 1968-70; comms. specialist AMA, Chgo., 1970-72; v.p. Home Data, Hinsdale, Ill., 1972-75; mktg. mgr. Olympic Savs. & Loan, Berwyn, Ill., 1975-79; sr. v.p. Golin/Harris Comms., Chgo., 1979-89; pres. JSH & A, Chgo., 1989—. Bd. dirs. Chgo. Internat. Film Festival, 1989, 90, 2005, 06. Author: Slim Guide to Spas, 1984, (video) PR Guide for Chicago LSCs, 1991; editor: Financial Information National Directory, 1972; contbr. articles to profl. jours. Co-chmn. pub. rels. com. Am. Cancer Soc., Chgo., 1984; mem. com. March of Dimes, Chgo., 1986; mem. pub. rels. com. Girl Scouts Chgo., 1989-90, bd. dirs., 1994-95; bd. dirs. Greater DuPage Women's Bus. Coun., 1992-93, Girl Scouts U.S. DuPage County, 1994—; vol. ctr. adv. com. United Way, Chgo., 1990-93; mem. cmty. svc. com. Publicity Club Chgo., 1990—. Recipient 5 Golden Trumpet awards Publicity Club Chgo., 1983, 96, 94, Silver Trumpet awards, 1984, 86, 88, Spectra awards Internat. Assn. Bus. Communicators, 1984, 85, 87, Gold Quill aard, 1985, Bronze Anvil award Pub. Rels. Soc. Am., 1985, award Nat. Creativity in Pub. Rels. award, 1995; named Influential Woman in Bus., 1998. Mem. Am. Mktg. Assn., Publicity Club Chgo., Pub. Rels. Soc. Am., Chgo. Women in Pub., Nat. Assn. Women Bus. Owners, DuPage Area Assn. Bus. Tech. (bd. dirs. 1997), Coun. on Fgn. Rels., Met. Women's Forum, Cinema Chgo. (bd. dirs. 1988-89, 2005-). Avocations: travel, photography. Office: JSH & A Ltd 2 Transam Plaza Dr Ste 450 Oakbrook Terrace IL 60181-4290 Home Phone: 630-852-3600; Office Phone: 630-932-4242. Business E-Mail: jonni@jsha.com.

HEGER, MARTIN L., bank executive; With Nat. Bank Detroit, Detroit, 1969-78, Fed. Home Loan Bank of Indpls., 1979-92, pres., 1992—. Office: Federal Home Loan Bank 8250 Woodfield Crossing Blvd Ste 210 Indianapolis IN 46240-4348

HEGERTY, NANNETTE H., police chief; b. Milw. m. George Hegerty; stepchildren: Suzanne, Scott. BS in Edn., U. Wis., 1972; MS in Mgmt., Cardinal Stritch Coll., 1985; student, FBI Nat. Tng. Acad., 1988. From officer to chief police Milw. (Wis.) Police Dept., 1976—2003, chief of police, 2003—; head Ea. Dist. Office U.S. Marshals Svc., 1994—2002. Office: Milwaukee Police Adminstrn Bldg 749 W State St Milwaukee WI 53233

HEIBERG, ROBERT ALAN, lawyer; b. St. Cloud, Minn., June 29, 1943; s. Rasmus Adolph and Irene (Shaffer) H.; m. Sharon Ann Olson, Aug. 2, 1969; children—Eric Robert, Mark Alan, Maren Ann BA summa cum laude, U. Minn., 1965, JD summa cum laude, 1968. Bar: Minn. 1968. Law clk. to assoc. justice Minn. Supreme Ct., 1968-69; assoc. Dorsey & Whitney, Mpls., 1969-73, ptnr., 1974—2003, of counsel, 2004—; instr. Law Sch., U. Minn., 1968-72, instr. legal assts. program, 1972-77. Articles editor Minn. Law Rev., 1967-68 Mem. adv. com. U. Minn. Legal Assts. Program, 1977-84, bd. visitors Law Sch., 1991-96. Mem. ABA (sect. real property, probate and trust law), Minn. Bar Assn. (chmn. com. on legal assts. 1979), Hennepin County Bar Assn., Am. Rose Soc. (accredited judge 1996), Order of Coif, Phi Beta Kappa Republican. Lutheran. Home: 4510 Wooddale Ave Minneapolis MN 55424-1137 Office: Dorsey & Whitney 50 S 6th St Ste 1500 Minneapolis MN 55402-1498 Home Phone: 952-926-4762; Office Phone: 612-340-2751. Business E-Mail: heiberg.robert@dorsey.com.

HEICHEL, GARY HAROLD, agronomist, educator; b. Park Falls, Wis., Nov. 9, 1940; s. Harold H. and Bernice I. (Comp) Heichel; m. Iris Fehl Martin, Apr. 24, 1988. BS, Iowa State U., 1962; MS, Cornell U., 1964, PhD, 1968; D in Natural Scis. (hon.), Swiss Fed. Inst. Tech., Zurich, 1998. Asst. plant physiologist Conn. Agrl. Expt. Stats., New Haven, 1968-73, assoc. plant physiologist, 1973-76, plant physiologist, 1976, USDA Agrl. Rsch. Svc., St. Paul, 1976-90, acting rsch. leader, 1988-90; head agronomy dept. U. Ill., Urbana, 1990-95, interim head plant pathology dept., 1994-95, head crop scis. dept., 1995—2004, prof. emeritus, 2004—. Adj. prof. agronomy U. Minn., 1976—90; program mgr. USDA Competitive Rsch. Grants Office, 1981; bd. dirs. Coun. Agrl. Sci. and Tech., 2005—; pres. Whiting's Neck Farm Estates, Inc., 2005—07. Contbr. chapters to books, articles to profl. jours. Pres., mem. adminstrv. bd. Cheshire (Conn.) United Meth. Ch., 1973—76, v.p. Cheshire Land Trust, 1975—76. Named Civil Servant of the Yr., Twin Cities Fed. Exec. Bd., St. Paul, 1984; Paul Harris fellow, Rotary Internat., 2002. Fellow: AAAS (chair sect. O 1997—98); mem.: Coun. Agrl. Sci. & Tech., Am. Soc. Plant Physiologists (trustee 1988—90), Am. Soc. Agronomy (pres. North Ctrl. sect. 1991—93, pres. 1997—98, Svc. award 2001), Crop Sci. Soc. Am. (pres. 1991—92, Monsanto Crop Sci. Disting. Career award 2006), Urbana Rotary (bd. dirs. 1997—99). Avocations: classical music, reading, hiking, gardening. Office: U Ill Dept Crop Scis 1102 S Goodwin Ave AW-101 Urbana IL 61801-4730 Business E-Mail: gheichel@uiuc.edu.

HEIDELBERGER, KATHLEEN PATRICIA, physician; b. Bklyn., Apr. 13, 1939; d. William Cyprian and Margaret Bernadette (Hughes) H.; m. Charles William Davenport, Oct. 8, 1977. BS cum laude, Coll. Misericordia, 1961; MD cum laude, Woman's Med. Coll. Pa., 1965. Intern Mary Hitchcock Hosp., Hanover, N.H., 1965-66, resident in pathology, 1966-70; mem. faculty U. Mich., Ann Arbor, 1970—, assoc. prof. pathology, 1976-79, prof., 1979—2002; ret., 2002. Mem. Am. Soc. Clin. Pathologists, U.S.-Can. Acad. Pathology, Soc. for Pediatric Pathology, Coll. Am. Pathologists.

HEIDORN, ROBERT E., lawyer; b. 1963; married; 2 children. BA, Miami U.; JD, U. Wis.-Madison. Bar: 1988. Pvt. practice Barnes and Thornburg, Indpls.; with Indiana Gas, 1995—2002; v.p., gen. counsel Vectren Corp., Evansville, Ind., 2002—. Bd. dirs. Evansville Coalition for the Homeless, Inc. Office: Vectren Corp 20 W Fourth St PO Box 209 Evansville IN 47702-0209 Office Phone: 812-491-4000.

HEIGAARD, WILLIAM STEVEN, state senator; b. Gardar, ND, May 18, 1938; s. Oliver and Gaufey (Erickson) H.; m. Paula Geston, 1960; children: Jody, Rebecca, Sara. BA, U. .D., 1961, JD, 1967. Bar: N.D. 1967. Asst. atty. gen., Bismarck, N.D., 1970-75; mem. N.D. Ho. of Reps., 1980-81, N.D. State Senate, 1981-92, majority leader, 1987-92; chmn. N.D. State Dem. Party, 2000—01. 1st lt. U.S. Army, 1962-64. Mem. Am. Legion, Eagles, Elks, Phi Delta Phi. Democrat. Lutheran. Office: 1116 N 14th St Bismarck ND 58501-4201 also: ND Democratic Party 1902 E Divide Ave Bismarck ND 58501-2301

HEIKES, KEITH, science administrator; b. 1957; With Ralston Purina, Chilicothe, Mo., 1978—81, Kabsu, Inc., Manhattan, Kans., 1981—90, Noba Inc., Tiffin, Ohio, 1990—, now COO; v.p. internat. programs 21st Century Genetics; with Coop. Resources Internat., Shawano, Wis. Office: Coop Resources Internat 100 Mbc Dr Shawano WI 54166-6095

HEIL, MICHAEL LLOYD, military officer, academic administrator; BS in Engring. Scis., USAF Acad., Colo., 1975; MS in Flight Structures, Columbia U., 1976; PhD in Solid Mechanics, Air Force Inst. Tech., 1986; MS in Nat. Resource Strategy, Indsl. Coll. of Armed Forces, 1994. Registered profl. engr., Colo. Commd. 2d lt. USAF, 1975, advanced through grades to col., 1995, structural engr. F-15 Sys. Program Office Wright-Patterson AFB, 1976—79, asst. prof., exec. officer dept. engring. mechanics, 1979—83, chief C-17 Structures Divsn., C-17 Sys. Program Office Wright-Patterson AFB, Ohio, 1986—88, mgr. Advanced Cruise Missile Sys. Program Office, 1988—89, dep. dir. Astronautical Scis. Divsn., Astronautics Lab. Edwards AFB, Calif., 1989—90, dep. dir. Propulsion Directorate, Phillips Lab., 1990—93, asst. dir. countermeasures Ballistic Missile Def. Orgn., The Pentagon Washington, 1994—95, comdr. Air Force Phillips Lab. Kirtland AFB, N.Mex., 1995—97, insp. gen. HQ material comd. Wright-Patterson AFB, 1997—98, comdr. Arnold Engring. Devel. Ctr. Arnold AFB, Tenn., 1998—2001, comdt. Inst. Tech. Wright-Patterson AFB, 2001—03, dir. propulsion directorate Rsch. Lab., 2003—05, dir. Ctr. Space Studies Inst. Tech., 2005—07; pres. and CEO Ohio Aerospace Inst., 2007—. Decorated Legion of Merit with two oak leaf clusters, Air Force Commendation medal. Home: 115 Walden Ridge Dr Hinckley OH 44233 Office: Ohio Aerospace Inst 22800 Cedar Pt Rd Brookpark OH 44142 Home Phone: 330-278-2408; Office Phone: 440-962-3001. Personal E-mail: mlheil@aol.com.

HEIM, STEVEN, state representative; AA in Polit. Sci., Vincennes U., 1988; BS in Polit. and Environ. Sci., Taylor U., 1991. Former reporter, freelance writer Pilot-News, South Bend Tribune; pub. rels. staff The Culver Acads., 1994—2000; interim comm. dir. Ind. U., South Bend, 2000—; state rep. dist. 17 Ind. Ho. of Reps., Indianapolis, 2002—. Founding dir. Culver Farmers' Market, 1999—2001; fin. sec. Cornerstone Cmty. Fellowship Ch., 1996—99, sponsor, Spring Break in Missions Work Project, 1996—2002. Republican. Office: Ind Ho of Reps 200 W Washington St Indianapolis IN 46204-2786

HEIMAN, DAVID GILBERT, lawyer; b. Cin., Apr. 12, 1945; s. Marcus G. and Ardith S. H.; m. Lynn Greentree, July 12, 1969; children: Stacy, Alisa. BBA, U. Cin., 1967, JD, 1970. Bar: Ohio 1971, U.S. Dist. Ct. (no. dist.) Ohio 1971, U.S. Ct. Appeals (5th and 6th cirs.)., U.S. Dist. Ct. (no. dist.) Tex. Ptnr. Hahn, Loeser, Freidheim, Dean & Wellman, Cleve., 1970-84, Jones, Day, Reavis & Pogue, Cleve., 1984-95, corp. group coord., 1995; now ptnr., coord. firm-wide bus. practice group Jones Day, Cleve., and practice area leader, bus. restructuring and reorganization practice. Editor Lender Liability Law Reporter. Vice chmn. Am. Jewish Com., Cleve., 1978-88. With U.S. Army, 1969-75. Recipient Young Leadership award Am. Jewish Com., Cleve., 1978. Mem. ABA (past chmn. comml. fin. svcs.), Ohio State Bar Assn. (chmn. com. 1979-82), Cleve. Bar Assn. (chmn. com. 1975-76). Office: Jones Day North Point 901 Lakeside Ave E Cleveland OH 44114-1190

HEIMLICH, HENRY J., physician, surgeon, educator; b. Wilmington, Del., Feb. 3, 1920; s. Philip and Mary (Epstein) Heimlich; m. Jane Murray, June 3, 1951; children: Philip, Janet, Elisabeth. BA, Cornell U., 1941, MD, 1943; DSc (hon.), Wilmington Coll., 1981, Adelphi U., 1982, Rider Coll., 1983, Alfred U., 1993. Diplomate Am. Bd. Surgery, Am. Bd. Thoracic Surgery. Intern Boston City Hosp., 1944; resident VA Hosp., Bronx, 1946—47, Mt. Sinai Hosp., NYC, 1947—48, Bellevue Hosp., NYC, 1948—49, Triboro Hosp., Jamaica, NY, 1949—50; attending surgeon divsn. surgery Montefiore Hosp., NYC, 1950—69; dir. surgery Jewish Hosp., Cin., 1969—77; prof. advanced clin. scis. Xavier U., Cin., 1977—89; assoc. clin. prof. surgery U. Cin. Coll. Medicine, 1969—78. Pres. Heimlich Inst.; mem. Pres.'s Commn. on Heart Disease, Cancer and Stroke, 1965; pres. Nat. Cancer Found., 1963—68, bd. dirs., 1960—70; founder Heimlich Inst. Found. Author: Postoperative Care in Thoracic Surgery, 1962; author: (with M.O. Cantor, C.H. Lupton) Surgery of the Stomach, Duodenum and Diaphragm, Questions and Answers, 1965; contbr. chapters to books, articles to profl. jours.; prodr.(film): Esophageal Replacement with a Reversed Gastric Tube (Medaglione Di Bronzo Minerva, 1961), Reversed Gastric Tube Esophagoplasty Using Stapling Technique, How to Save a Choking Victim: The Heimlich Maneuver, 1976, 1982, How to Save a Drowning Victim: The Heimlich Maneuver, 1981, Stress Relief: The Heimlich Method, 1983, (video): Dr. Heimlich's Home First Aid Video, 1989 (Vira award, 1989); editl. bd. films Reporte's Medicos, 1962. Cmty. Devel. Found., 1967—70; Save the Chidlren FEdn., 1967—68; United Cancer Coun., 1967—70. Served to lt. (s.g.) USNR, 1944—46. Recipient Lasker award for Pub. Svc., Lasker Found., 1984, China-Burma-India Vets. Assn. Americanism award, 1988, 1st Heimlich Humanitarian award, Spirit of Am. Festival, 1994, Heimlich Inst. established in perpetuity by Deaconess Assns., Inc. Fellow: ACS (chpt. pres. 1964), Am. Coll. Gastroenterology, Am. Coll. Chest Physicians; mem.: AMA (cons. to jour.), Ctrl. Surg. Assn., Collegium INternat. Chirurgiae Digestive, Pan Am. Med. Assn., Am. Gastroent. Assn., Soc. Surgery Alimentary Tract, N.Y. Soc. Thoracic Surgery, Cin. Soc. Thoracic Surgery, Soc. Thoracic Surgeons (founding mem.). Achievements include development of Heimlich Operation (reversed gastric tube esophagoplasty) for replacement of esophagus; invention of Heimlich chest drain valve, Heimlich Micro-Trach (HMT) for COPD, emphysema and cystic fibrosis; development of Heimlich Maneuver to save lives of victims of food choking and drowning and prevents and overcomes asthma attacks (listed in Random House, Oxford Am. and Webster dictionaries); Computers for Peace, a program to maintain peace throughout world and A Caring World. Office: Heimlich Inst Found Inc 311 Straight St Cincinnati OH 45219 Personal E-mail: hjheimlich@fuse.net.

HEINEMAN, DAVID EUGENE, governor; b. Falls City, Nebr., May 12, 1948; s. Jean Trevers and Irene Larkin H.; m. Sally Ganem, 1977; 1 child, Sam. BS, U.S. Mil. Acad., 1970. Sales rep. Procter & Gamble, 1976-77; campaign mgr. Hal Daub for Congress, 1977-78; dep. dir. Policy Rsch. Office, Nebr., 1979; dir. Nebr. State Rep. Exec. Com., 1979-81; chief of staff to Congressman Hal Daub, 1983-88; office mgr. for Congressman Doug Bereuter, 1990-94; city councilman City of Fremont, Nebr., 1990-94; state treas. State of Nebr., 1994—2000, lt. gov., 2001—05, gov., 2005—. Served in US Army, 1970—75. Decorated Army Commendation medal; recipient Outstanding Rep. Vol. award Douglas County Rep. Party, 1976, Outstanding Young Am. award Jaycees, 1980. Mem. Nat. Assn. State Treas. (pres. 1999-2000), Nat. Electronic Commerce Coordinating Coun. (exec. com. 1998-2000). Republican. Office: Office of Governor PO Box 94848 Lincoln NE 68509 Office Phone: 402-471-2244. Office Fax: 402-471-6031. E-mail: dave.heineman@gov.state.ne.us.

HEINEMAN, PAUL LOWE, consulting civil engineer; b. Omaha, Oct. 24, 1924; s. Paul George and Annie L. (Lowe) H.; m. Gloria Nixon; children by previous marriage: Karen E., John F., Ellen F. Student, U. Omaha, 1942-43; BSC.E., Iowa State U., 1945, MS, 1948. Registered profl. engr. Mo., Calif., N.Y., Kans., 25 other states and Republic of Colombia. Instr. Iowa State U., 1946-48; designer, project mgr. Howard, Needles, Tammen & Bergendoff (Cons. Engrs.), Kansas City, Mo., 1948-64, ptnr., 1965-86; exec. v.p. Howard, Needles, Tammen & Bergendoff Internat., Inc., Kansas City, 1967-84, pres., v.p. subs., 1983-86. Bd. dirs., sec.-treas. emeritus The Road Info. Program. Served with C.E. Corp USNR, 1945-46. Fellow ASCE, Am. Cons. Engrs. Coun., Inst. Traffic Engrs.; mem. NSPE, Am. Ry. Engring. Assn., Am. Concrete Inst., Am. Arbitration Assn., Engrs. Club (Kansas City). Presbyterian (elder 1958—). Home and Office: 2 J St Lake Lotawana MO 64086-9749

HEINEMAN, WILLIAM RICHARD, chemistry professor; b. Lubbock, Tex., Oct. 15, 1942; s. Ellis Richard and Edna (Anderson) H.; m. Linda Margaret Harkins, Oct. 25, 1969; children: David William, John Richard. BS, Tex. Tech. U., 1964; PhD, U. N.C., 1968. Rsch. chemist Hercules, Inc., Wilmington, Del., 1968-70; rsch. assoc. Case Western Res. U., Cleve., 1970-71, The Ohio State U., Columbus, 1971-72; asst. prof. U. Cin., 1972-76, assoc. prof., 1976-80, prof., 1980-88, dist. rsch. prof., 1988—. Mem. adv. bd. Analytical Chemistry, Washington, 1984-86, The Analyst, Eng., 1987-95, Selective Electrode Revs., 1987-92, Fresenius Jour. Analytical Chemistry, 199 1-94, Analytical Chimica Acta, 1991-93, Applied Biochemistry and Biotechnology, 1991—, Quimica Analitica, 1993—; U.S. editor Biosensors and Bioelectronics, Eng., 1987—; coun. Gordon Rsch. Confs. Author: Experiments in Instrumental Methods, 1984, Chemical Instrumentation, 1989; editor: Laboratory Techniques in Electroanalytical Chemistry, 1984, Chemical Sensors and Microinstrumentation, 1989. Recipient Charles N. Reilley award in Electroanalytical Chemistry, 1995, Humboldt prize Humboldt Soc., 1989, Rieveschl award U. Cin., 1988, Japan Rsch. award, Japan, 1987, Award in Chem. Sensors 6th Internat. Meeting on Chem/ Sensors, 1996, Excellence in Teaching award ACS Divsn. of Analytical Chemistry, 1997, Torbern Bergman Medal in Analytical Chemistry, Swedish Chem. Soc., Analysdagarna, 1999; named Disting. Scientist Tech. Socs. Coun., 1984; fellow Japan Soc. for Promotion of Sci., 1981. Mem. Am. Chem. Soc. (treas. analytical chem. divsn. 1983-86, 96-97, councilor 1984-98, chair-elect 1996-97, chair 1997-98, named Chemist of Yr. 1983, divsn. analytical chemistry award for excellence in tchg. 1997), Soc. for Electroanalytical Chemistry (pres. 1984-85, bd. dirs. 1984-90). Office: U Cin Dept Chemistry PO Box 210172 Cincinnati OH 45221-0172

HEINEMANN, DAVID J., state legislator; b. West Point, Nebr., July 18, 1945; s. Lester Otto and Rita Charlotte (LaNoue) H.; m. Kristine Stroberg, 1972; children: Julie, Suzanne. BA cum laude, Augustana Coll., 1967; postgrad., U. Kans., 1967-68; JD, Washburn U., 1973. Rsch. asst. Govt. Rsch. Ctr. U. Kans., 1967-68; ptnr. Heinemann & Quint, 1973—; mem. Kans. Ho. of Reps., Topeka, 1968—, chmn. pension and investments, rules and jour., mem. juvenile matters com., vice-chmn. jud. com., mem. legis. post audit, assessment, mem. local govt., legis. and jud. reapportionment com., mem. social and rehab. svc. inst. spl. study com., mem. com. rev. plans for prison constrn., mem. joint com. handicapped accessibility, former chmn. energy and natural resources com., spkr. pro tem, 1985; gen. counsel Kans. Corp. Commn., Topeka, until 1995. Bd. dirs. S.W. Devel. Svc. Inc.; author legis., 1977-82, Kans. Bar Assn. Jour., 1977-82. Contbr. articles to profl. publs. Pres. Garden City Cmty. Day Care Ctr., 1975—, bd. dirs., 1969-72; alt. del. Rep. Nat. Conv., 1972; dep. county atty. Finney County, 1975—; judge pro-tem Garden City Mcpl.; del. Kans. State Rep. Conv., 1972-78, 82; coord., primary and gen. campaigns for Sec. State Jakc Brier, 1978, 82; mem. Nat. Conf. State Legislators Pension Com., 1981-82, mem. Energy Com., 1983—; mem. Gov. Com. State Investment Practices. Named one of Outstanding Young Men of Am., 1982, Outstanding State Legis., Eagleton Inst. Polit., Rutgers U. Mem. Kans. Bar Assn., Garden City C. of C., Lions. Home: 3826 SW Cambridge Ct Topeka KS 66610-1166

HEINEN, JAMES ALBIN, electrical engineering educator; b. Milw., June 23, 1943; s. Albin Jacob and Viola (DeBuhr) H. BEE, Marquette U., 1964, MS, 1967, PhD, 1969. Registered profl. engr., Wis. Data analyst Med. Sch. Marquette U., Milw., 1963, teaching asst. elec. engring. dept., 1964-65, 65-66, research asst., 1966, ASA trainee, 1966-69, asst. prof., 1969—71, research assoc. Provost's Office, 1970, asst. prof. and grad. adminstr., 1971-73, assoc. prof., chmn. elec. engring. dept., 1973-76, assoc. prof., 1976-80, prof. elec. engring. and computer sci., 1980-87, prof., dir. grad. studies elec. and computer engring., 1987-95, prof. elec. and computer engring., 1995—99, rsch. prof., 1999—2000, prof. emeritus, 2000—, dir. signal processing rsch. ctr., 1990-99, co-dir. ctr. intelligent syss., controls, and signal processing, 1999—2001. Cons. in field. Contbr. numerous articles and revs. on elec. engring. and computer sci. to profl. jours. Recipient Outstanding Engring. Tchr. award Marquette U., 1979, Teaching Excellence award Marquette U., 1985. Mem. IEEE (various coms., tech. reviewer Trans. Automatic Control 1969—, Trans. Circuits and Systems Soc. 1980—, Signal Processing Soc. 1980—, sr. mem., Meml. award Milw. sect. 1981, assoc. editor Trans. Circuits and Systems 1983-85, assoc. editor Trans. Indsl. Electronics 1996-2000), Am. Soc. Engring. Edn., Sigma Xi, Tau Beta Pi, Eta Kappa Nu (Most Oustanding Elec. Engring. Tchr. in U.S. award 1974), Pi Mu Epsilon, Alpha Sigma Nu. Home: 8200 W Menomonee River Pky Wauwatosa WI 53213-2537 Office: Marquette U Haggerty Hall Rm 211 PO Box 1881 Milwaukee WI 53201-1881 Home Phone: 414-476-6367; Office Phone: 414-288-3500. Business E-Mail: james.heinen@marquette.edu.

HEINLEN, DANIEL LEE, alumni organization administrator, consultant; b. Columbus, Ohio, Nov. 16, 1937; s. Calvin Xenophon and Charlotte Elizabeth (Lanman) H.; m. Roberta Bishop, Mar. 20, 1966 (div. 1975); m. Gelene Vogel Kozlowski, June 17, 1978; children: Stephanie Heinlen, Kate Kozlowski Isler, Amy Heinlen. BS in Social Work, Ohio State U., 1960. Youth program dir., ext. dir. YMCA, Pitts., 1960-65; field dir. Alumni Assn., Ohio State U., Columbus, 1965-67, assoc. dir., 1967-73, dir. alumni affairs, 1973-92; pres., CEO Ohio State U. Alumni Assn., Inc., 1992—2003, pres., CEO emeritus, 2004—; sec. Alumni Assn. Bd., 1973—2003; pub. mag. Alumni Assn., Ohio State U., 1973—2003; sr. consulting v.p. Grenzebach Glier and Assoc., Inc., Chgo., 2004—07; pres. DLH. LLC, Lewis Center, Ohio, 2004—. Ex-officio trustee Ohio State U. Found.; presdl. search com. Ohio State U., 1990, 97, 2002; trustee Coun. for Advancement and Support of Higher Edn., Washington, 1986-88, 90-94, chmn., 1992-93; chmn. 75th anniversary Colloquium, Columbus, 1988, chmn. ann. assembly alumni track, 1988, chmn. ann. assembly, 1990; chmn. Mgmt. Inst. for Alumni Assn. Execs., Chgo., 1996, pres., 1994-96, bd. dirs., 1988-96; founding bd. Coun. Alumni Assn. Execs. 1989-96, pres. 1992-93; chmn. Univ. ProNet, Inc., Palo Alto, Calif., 1996-99, chmn. alumni dirs. Big Ten, 1973, 84, 93; mem. Ohio State U. Pres.'s Coun., 1991-98; bd. dirs. River Road Hotel Corp.; founding chmn. Self-Governing Alumni Forum, 2000-2003; chmn. task force on alumni advocacy Inter Univ. Coun., 2002. Author chpts. in books. Mem. exec. com. N.W. Ordinance U.S. Constn. Bicentennial Commn., Ohio, 1986-88; bd. dirs. Non-profit Mailers Fedn., Wash., 1985-88; mem. OSU Com. on Student Fin. Aids, Columbus, 1973-99, exec. com. Acad. Disting. Tchg., 1995-2003, Newcomen Soc. N.Am., 1975-90, 93-2003. Med. specialist USAR, 1962—67, hon. discharge USAR, 1967. Recipient Ohio State U. Coll. of Social Work Disting. Svc. award, 1996, Disting. Svc. award CASE Dist. 5, 2003, Everett Reese medal Svc. in Philanthropy Ohio State U., 2003, Frank Ashmore award CASE Internat., 2004, Ohio State U. Disting. Svc. award, 2005; named Hon. Trustee Easter Seal Rehab. Ctr. of Ctrl. Ohio, Columbus, 1988-92; D.L. Heinlen award for univ. advocacy named in his honor Ohio Sate U. Alumni Assn., Inc., 1995. Mem. Rotary (bd. dirs. Columbus Club 1986, v.p. 1987-89, pres. 1989-90), U. Club (bd. dirs., 2nd v.p. 1985-88, 94-95, 1st v.p. 1996), Faculty Club (mem. bd. control 1978-80, pres.-elect 1999, pres. 2000-01), Kit Kat (exec. com. 1999-2002, sec. 2001-07), Golden Key Nat. Honor Soc. (hon.), Sphinx Coun. (convener, 1983-2003, hon. chair Sr. Hon. Centennial Celebration). Avocations: tennis, sporting clays, horseback riding. Home and Office: 2981 E Powell Rd Lewis Center OH 43035-9517 Business E-Mail: heinlen.4@osu.edu.

HEINLEN, RONALD EUGENE, lawyer; b. Delaware, Ohio, May 28, 1937; s. Carl Elwood and Evelyn Lucille (Scott) H.; m. Mary Pauline Turney, Dec. 28, 1955; children: James Michael, Deborah Lynn, Robert Christopher. AB, Harvard U., 1959, JD, 1962. Bar: Ohio 1962. Assoc. Frost & Jacobs, Cin., 1962-69, ptnr., 1969—. Lectr. Tax Inst. NYU. Contbr. articles to profl. jour. Trustee Cin. Nature Ctr., 1986-95. Fellow Am. Soc. Hosp. Attys.; mem. ABA, Ohio State Bar Assn., Cin. Bar Assn. (chmn. tax sect.), Cin. Country Club, University Club. Office: Frost & Jacobs 2500 PNC Ct 201 E 5th St Ste 2500 Cincinnati OH 45202-4182

HEINRICHS, APRIL, soccer coach; b. Charlottesville, Va., Feb. 27, 1964; BA in Radio, TV and Motion Pictures, U. N.C., 1986. Lic. U.S. Soccer Federation "A" coaching license. Player U.S. Nat. Team, 1986—91; profl. soccer player Prato, Italy, 1987—92; head coach Princeton U., 1990, U. Md., 1991—95, U. Va., 1996—99; full time asst. U.S. Women's Nat. Team, 1995—97; mem. coaching staff 1995 Women's World Cup, 1995, 1996 Olympic Women's Soccer Team, 1996; head coach U.S. U-16 Nat. Team, 1997—2000; head coach, tech. dir. U.S. Women's Nat. Team, 2000—. Mem. NCAA Championship Team, 1983, 84, 86. Recipient U.S. Soccer Female Athlete of Yr. award, 1986, 89; voted female player of the 1980s Soccer America Magazine; first female inducted into Nat. Soccer Hall of Fame, 1998; named First Team All-American U. N.C. (3 times); inaugural recipient NSCAA Women's Com. award of Excellence, 2000. Achievements include coached U.S. Women's Soccer Team to Silver Medal, Sydney Olympic Games, 2000. Office: US Soccer House 1801-1811 S Prairie Ave Chicago IL 60616

HEINZ, JOHN PETER, lawyer, educator; b. Carlinville, Ill., Aug. 6, 1936; s. William Henry and Margaret Louise (Denby) H.; m. Anne Murray, Jan. 14, 1967; children: Katherine Reynolds, Peter Lindley Murray. AB, Washington U., St. Louis, 1958; LLB, Yale U., 1962. Bar: D.C. 1962, Ill. 1966, U.S. Supreme Ct. 1967. Teaching asst. polit. sci. Washington U., St. Louis, 1958-59, instr., 1960; asst. prof. Northwestern U. Sch. Law, Chgo., 1965-68, assoc. prof., 1968-71, prof., 1971-88, Owen L. Coon prof., 1988—2007, Owen L. Coon prof. emeritus, 2007—, dir. program law and social scis., 1968-70, dir. rsch., 1973-74, prof. sociology, 1987—. Affiliated scholar Am. Bar Found., Chgo., 1974—, vis. scholar, 1975-76, exec. dir., 1982-86, disting. research fellow, 1987—. Author: (with A. Gordon) Public Access to Information, 1979, (with E. Laumann) Chicago Lawyers, 1982, rev. edit., 1994, (with E. Laumann, R. Nelson, R. Salisbury) The Hollow Core, 1993, (with R. Nelson, R. Sandefur and E. Laumann) Urban Lawyers, 2005; contbr. articles to profl. jours. Served to capt. USAF, 1962-65 Grantee NIMH, 1970-72, NSF, 1970, 78-81, 84-86, 94-97, CNA Found., 1972, Am. Bar Found., 1974—, Russell Sage Found., 1978-80. Fellow: Am. Bar Found.; mem.: ABA, Chgo. Coun. Lawyers, Law and Soc. Assn. (Harry Kalven prize for disting. rsch. 1987). Home: 525 Judson Ave Evanston IL 60202-3083 Office: orthwestern U Sch Law 357 E Chicago Ave Chicago IL 60611-3059 Business E-Mail: j-heinz@law.northwestern.edu.

HEINZ, WILLIAM DENBY, lawyer; b. Carlinville, Ill., Nov. 26, 1947; s. William Henry and Margaret (Denby) H.; children: Kimberly, Rebecca, Elizabeth; m. Catherine Lamb Heinz. BS, Millikin U., 1969; JD, U. Ill., 1973. Bar: Ill. 1973, U.S. Dist. Ct. (no. dist.) Ill. 1974, U.S. Ct. Appeals (3d cir.) 1982, U.S. Ct. Appeals (5th cir.) 1973, U.S. Ct. Appeals (7th cir.) 1976, U.S. Supreme Ct. 1979. Law clk. to judge U.S. Ct. Appeals (5th cir.), Tuscaloosa, Ala., 1973-74; assoc. Jenner & Block, Chgo., 1974-80, ptnr., 1980—; mem. faculty NITA, 1981—. Adj. prof. Northwestern U. Sch. Law, 1995—; mem. bd. dir. The North Am. Co. for Life and Health Ins., 2002—; bd. visitors U. Ill. Coll. Law, 1990-93, pres.'s coun. U. Ill.; bd. dirs., chair Legal Aid Bur., Chgo.; bd. dirs. exec. com. Met. Family Svcs. Chgo; mem, bd. dirs. Ptnrs Fin. Holdings, Inc., 2003—. Recipient Disting. Grad. award U. Ill. Coll. Law, 1995. Fellow Am. Coll. Trial Lawyers; mem. ABA, Ill. Bar Assn. (civil practice and procedure sect. coun., com. on liaison with Ill. ARDC, task force on multi-disciplinary practice), Chgo. Bar Assn. (jud. evaluation com. 1990-93), ARDC Ill. Profl. Responsibility Inst., Cribbett Soc., U. Ill. Coll. Law, Legal Club (bd. dirs. 1998-2000), Westmoreland Country Club. Home: 437 Sheridan Rd Kenilworth IL 60043-1220 Office: Jenner & Block 1 E Ibm Plz Fl 46 Chicago IL 60611-3586 Office Phone: 312-923-2763. E-mail: wheinz@jenner.com.

HEIPLE, JAMES DEE, retired state supreme court justice; b. Peoria, Ill., Sept. 13, 1933; s. Rae Crane and Harriet (Birkett) Heiple; m. Virginia Kerswill, July 28, 1956 (dec. Apr. 16, 1995); children: Jeremy Hans, Jonathon James, Rachel Duffield. BS, Bradley U., 1955; JD, U. Louisville, 1957; cert. in Internat. Law, City London Coll., 1967; grad., Nat. Jud. Coll., 1971; LLM, U. Va., 1988. Bar: Ill. 1957, Ky. 1958, US Supreme Ct. 1962. Ptnr. Heiple and Heiple, Pekin, Ill., 1957—70; cir. judge 10th Cir. Ill., 1970—80; justice Ill. Appellate Ct., 1980—90, Ill. Supreme Ct., 1990—2000; ret., 2000. Dir. Gridley State Bank, 1958—59; v.p., dir. Washington State Bank, Ill., 1959—66; pub. adminstr. Tazewell County, 1959—61, asst. pub. defender, 1967—70; village atty., Tremont, 1961—66, Mackinaw, 1961—66; jud. clk. Ill. Appellate Ct., 1968—70; mem. Ill. Supreme Ct. Com. on Profl. Responsibilty, 1978—86. Chmn. Tazewell County Heart Fund., 1960; mem. Pekin Sch. Bd., 1970; sec. Tazewell County Rep. Ctrl. Com., 1966—70. Named Disting. Alumnus, U. Louisville, 1992; recipient Cert., Freedoms Found., 1975, George Washington Honor medal, 1976, Bradley Centurion award, Bradley U., 1995. Fellow: ABA (life), Ky. Bar Found., Ill. Bar Found. (life); mem.: SAR, Ill. Judges Assn. (pres. 1978—79), Tazewell County Bar Assn. (pres. 1967—68), Ky., Ill. (chmn. legal edn. com. 1972—74, chmn. jud. sect. 1976—77, chmn. Bench and Bar Coun. 1984—85), Sons of Union Vets, War of 1812, Pa. Hist. Soc., Ill. Hist. Soc., Ky. Hist. Soc., Peoria Country Club, Filson Club, Union League Chgo., Masons (33 degree), Pi Kappa Delta, Sigma Nu, Delta Theta Phi. Methodist. Office: PO Box 10495 Peoria IL 61612-0495 Office Phone: 309-682-7242. Business E-Mail: jamesdheiple@insightbb.com.

HEISE, MARILYN BEARDSLEY, public relations and publishing company executive; b. Cedar Rapids, Iowa, Feb. 26, 1935; d. Lee Roy and Angeline Myrtle Beardsley; m. John W. Heise, July 9, 1960; children: William Earnshaw, Steven James, Kathryn Kay Benninghoff. BA, Drake U., 1957. Prodn. mgr. Vend Mag., 1958—59; account exec. The Beveridge Orgn., Chgo., 1959—62; editor, pub. The Working Craftsman mag., Northbrook, Ill., 1971-78; columnist Chgo. Sun-Times, 1973-78; pres. Craft Books, Inc., Northbrook, 1978-84; v.p. Sheila King Pub. Rels., Chgo., 1984-87, Aaron D. Cushman, Inc., Chgo., 1987-88; pres. Creative Cons. Assocs., Inc., Glencoe, Ill., 1989—91, Heartfelt Charity Cards, 1991—2003. Mem. adv. panel Nat. Crafts Project, Ft. Collins, Colo., 1977; mem. adv. panel and com. Nat. Endowment for Arts, Washington, 1977; mem. editl. adv. bd. The Crafts Report, Seattle, 1978-86. Recipient achievement award Women in Mgmt., 1978. Mem. Pub. Rels. Soc. Am. (accredited).

HEISLER, QUENTIN GEORGE, JR., lawyer; b. Jefferson City, Mo., 1943; m. Susan D.; children: Sarah, Thomas, Margaret. AB magna cum laude, Harvard U., 1965, JD, 1968. Bar: Ill. 1968, U.S. Dist. Ct. (no. dist.) Ill. 1969, Fla. 1977. Assoc. McDermott, Will & Emery, Chgo., 1968-69, 70-75, ptnr., 1975—, chmn. firm pvt. client dept., 1998—2006, ptnr. in charge, 2006—. Co-author: Working With Family Businesses, 1995; gen. editor: Trust Administration in Illinois, 1979. Chmn. Winnetka Caucus, Ill., 1983; mem. Winnetka Bd. Edn., 1985-89; trustee Shedd Aquarium, 2002—, mem. exec. com., 2004—, chmn. planned giving com., 2006—; chmn. gift planning adv. com. Art Inst. Chgo., 2005—, Hadley Sch. for the Blind, 1998-2002; bd govs. Winnetka Cmty. House, 1998-99; mem. planned giving com. Ravinia Festival, 2006—. Named one of Best Lawyers in Am. 2006, nation's top 100 estate planning Lawyers by Worth mag.; named to Chambers USA: Am. Leading Bus. Lawyers, 2006,2007; named one of named an Ill. Super Lawyer in the area of estate planning and probate by Law & Politics. Fellow Am. Coll. Trust and Estates Counsel; mem. Chgo. Coun. Estate Planning, Chgo. Bar Assocs., Univ. Club (Chgo.), Harvard Club (bd. dirs. Chgo. chpt. 1984-95, pres. bd. 1989-91), Skokie Country Club (Glencoe, Ill.), Racquet Club (Chgo.), Sanctuary Country Club (Sanibel, Fla.). Office: McDermott Will & Emery LLP 227 W Monroe St Ste 4700 Chicago IL 60606-5096 Home Phone: 312-335-8294; Office Phone: 312-984-7606. Business E-Mail: qheisler@mwe.com.

HEISLEY, MICHAEL E., SR., manufacturing executive, professional sports team owner; b. Washington; m. Agnes Heisley; 5 children. BA, Georgetown U., 1960. With Robertson-Ceco Corp., Toms Foods, Inc., WorldPort Comm. Inc., Pettibone Corp.; chmn., CEO Heico Cos. LLC, St. Charles, Ill., 1979—; owner Memphis Grizzlies (formerly Vancouver Grizzlies), 2000—. Chmn. Davis Wire Corp., Toms Foods, Inc. Mem. St. Patrick's Cath. Ch. Named one of 400 Richest Ams., Forbes mag., 2006. Mem. Turnaround Mgmt. Assn., Union League Club, Chgo. Club. Office: Heico Cos LLC 70 W Madison St Ste 5600 Chicago IL 60602

HEISS, RICHARD WALTER, retired bank executive, consultant, lawyer; b. Monroe, Mich., July 8, 1930; s. Walter and Lillian (Harpst) H.; m. Nancy J. Blum, June 21, 1952; children: Kurt Frederick, Karl Richard. BA, Mich. State U., 1952; LLB, Detroit Coll., 1963, LLD (hon.), 1982; LLM, Wayne State U., 1969; cert., Stanford U. Exec. Program, 1979. Bar: Mich. 1963, U.S. Dist. Ct. (federal dist.) Mich. 1963. Asst. trust officer Mfrs. Nat. Bank of Detroit, 1960-62, trust officer, 1962-66; v.p., trust officer Mfrs. Nat. Bank Detroit, 1966-68, v.p., sr. trust officer, 1968-75, 1st v.p., sr. trust officer, 1975-77, sr. v.p., 1977-89, exec. v.p., 1989-92; dir. Detroit Coll. Law Found., 1995—, vice chair, 2001—07. Pres., CEO, Mfrs. Nat. Trust Co. Fla., 1984-88, chmn. bd., 1988-92; lectr. Inst. Continuing Legal Edn., Procknow Grad. Sch. Banking, U. Wis., Southwestern Grad. Sch. Bank, Am. Bankers Assn., Banking Sch. South; chmn. mem. exec. com. Trust Mgmt. Seminar, 1980; expert witness fiduciary law, 1993-2003. Mem. Legal-Fin. Network, Cmty. Found. S.E. Mich.; bd. dirs. Hist. Trinity, Inc., 1992—; trustee Mich. State U. Coll. Law, 1972-2007, pres., 1983-94; pres. Mich. State U. Bus. Sch. Alumni Bd., 1983; mem. allocation and evaluation com. United Way S.E. Mich., 1989-92. 1st lt. AUS, 1952-57. Fellow State Bar Mich. Found.; emeritus mem. Mich. Bar Assn., Am. Bankers Assn. (pres. 1981, exec. com. trust divsn., pvt. banking com. 1984-89, investment adv. com. 1984-89), Mich. Bankers Assn. (chmn. trust divsn. exec. com. 1975), Detroit Golf Club (bd. dirs., pres. 1983), Mich. Srs. Golf Assn. (bd. govs. 1994-), Club at Seabrook Island (golf and green com.), Delta Chi, Sigma Nu Phi. Republican. Lutheran. Home (Summer): 30684 Sudbury Ct Farmington Hills MI 48331-1368

HEISTAD, DONALD DEAN, cardiologist; b. Chgo., Apr. 2, 1940; m. Patricia Westmoreland; children: Wendy, Dean. BS, U. Ill., 1959; MD, U. Chgo., 1963. Asst. prof. medicine U. Iowa Coll. Medicine, Iowa City, 1970-73, assoc. prof. medicine, 1973-76, prof. medicine, 1976—, prof. pharmacology, 1987—, prof. cardiology, dir. cardiovascular divsn., 1995—2003, Zahn prof. cardiology, 1999—. Bd. dirs. Iowa Ctr. on Aging. Editor: Cerebral Blood Flow: Effects of Nerves, 1982; assoc. editor: Hypertension, 1989-93, Circulation Rsch., 1980-85, consulting editor; editor-in-chief: Arteriosclerosis, Thrombosis, and Vascular Biology, 1999-2007; contbr. almost 500 papers to profl. jours. and chpts to books. Pres. U. Iowa Faculty Senate, Iowa City, 1980-81; vice-chair coun. on circulation Am. Heart Assn., 1994-96, chair, 1996-98. Capt. U.S. Army, 1967-70. Recipient Irving S. Wright award Stroke Coun., 1976, Harry Goldblatt award Coun. for High Blood Pressure Rsch., 1980, Merit award, 1987, Disting.

Lecture award Coun. on Thrombosis, George E. Brown Meml. Lectr., Am. Heart Assn., 1999, Rsch. Achievement award, 2001; Disting. Alumni award U. Chgo., 1991, Novartis award Coun. High Blood Pressure Rsch., 1997; Landis award, Microcirculation Soc., 2001; George L. Duff Meml. Lecture, Am. Heart Assoc., 2005; Disting. Achievement award, Am. Heart Assoc. ATUB Coun., 2007. Fellow Coun. for High Blood Pressure Rsch., Am. Soc. for Clin. Investigation, Assn. Am. Physicians, Assn. Univ. Cardiologists (sec.-treas. 1998-2001, pres. 2002-03), Am. Physiol. Soc. (chair cardiovascular sect. 1995-96, Wiggers award 1999); mem. Internat. Soc. and Fedn. Cardiologists. Democrat. Office: U Iowa Coll Medicine Dept Medicine Iowa City IA 52242 E-mail: donald-heistad@uiowa.edu.

HEITKAMP, JOEL C., state legislator; b. Breckinridge, ND, Nov. 2, 1961; m. Susan Heitkamp; 2 children. Student, U. N.D. Mem. N.D. Senate from 27th dist., Bismark, 1994—; mem. fin., taxation and natural resources coms. N.D. Senate. Recipient Operator's award N.D. State Health Dept. Mem. Richland County Pheasants, Hankinson Dollars for Scholars, Mantador Fire Dept. and Cmty. Club. Home: 16543 94 1/2 St SE Hankinson ND 58041-9538

HELDER, BRUCE ALAN, metal products executive; b. Grand Rapids, Mich., July 1, 1953; s. Harry Martin and Margaret (Ditmar) Helder; m. Arlene Faye Docter, May 29, 1975; children: Amanda Joy, David Ryan, Joel Brent, Jonathan Bruce, Brandon Michael. Student, Calvin Coll., Grand Rapids, Mich., 1972-73, Grand Valley State Coll., Allendale, Mich., 1974. Lic. realtor assoc.; cert. media specialist. Indsl. sales rep. Newman Comm., Inc., Grand Rapids, 1971-81; v.p. sales and mktg. Best Metal Products Co., Grand Rapids, 1981—2001; pres. Bara Techs., Inc., Venture Property Mgmt. Co., 2001—. Mem. Real Estate Bd. Grand Rapids. Republican. Mem. Christian Reformed Ch. Home: PO Box 88153 Grand Rapids MI 49518-0153 Office: Bara Technologies Inc 3714 Jefferson Ave SE Grand Rapids MI 49548 Home Phone: 616-243-8626; Office Phone: 616-247-1800. Personal E-mail: bhelder@aol.com.

HELDMAN, JAMES GARDNER, lawyer; b. Cin., Mar. 7, 1949; s. James Norvin and Jane Marie (Gardner) H.; m. Wendy Maureen Saunders, Sept. 3, 1978; children: Dustin A., Courtney B. AB cum laude, Harvard U., 1971; JD with honors, George Washington U., 1974. Bar: D.C. 1975, U.S. Dist. Ct. (D.C. dist.) 1975, U.S. Ct. Appeals (D.C. cir.) 1975, U.S. Supreme Ct. 1980, Ohio 1981. Assoc. Perazich & Kolker, Washington, 1974-79, Wyman, Bautzer, Kuchel & Silbert, Washington, 1979-81, Strauss & Troy, Cin., 1981-83, ptnr., 1984—. Mem. ABA, Ohio State Bar Assn., Cin. Bar Assn. Avocations: tennis, platform tennis, biking. Office: Strauss & Troy The Fed Res Bldg 150 E Fourth St Cincinnati OH 45202-4018 Home Phone: 513-531-7221; Office Phone: 513-621-2120. Business E-Mail: jgheldman@strausstroy.com.

HELDMAN, PAUL W., lawyer, food service executive; BS, Boston U., 1973; JD, U. Cin., 1977. Bar: Ohio 1977. Assoc. Beckman, Lavercombe & Well, 1977-82; atty. The Kroger Co., Cin., 1982-86; sr. atty. Kroger Co., Cin., 1986-87, sr. counsel, 1987-89, v.p., gen. counsel, 1989-92, v.p., sec., gen. counsel, 1992-97, sr. v.p., sec., gen. counsel, 1997—2006, exec. v.p., sec., gen. counsel, 2006—. Office: The Kroger Co 1014 Vine St Ste 1000 Cincinnati OH 45202-1100

HELGERSON, HENRY, state legislator; b. Jan. 12, 1952; m. Nickoli A. Flynn. Grad., Rockhurst U. Kans. state rep. Dist. 86, 1983—. Dir. Children's Mus. Home: 12 E Peach Tree Ln Eastborough KS 67207-1059

HELGESON, JOHN PAUL, plant pathology and botany educator; b. Barberton, Ohio, July 25, 1935; s. Earl Adrian and Marguerite (Dutcher) H.; m. Sarah Frances Slater, June 10, 1957; children: Daniel, Susan, James. AB, Oberlin Coll., 1957; PhD, U. Wis., 1964. NSF postdoctoral fellow dept. chemistry U. Ill., Urbana, 1964-66; from asst. to prof. botany and plant pathology U. Wis., Madison, 1996—2002, prof. emeritus, 2003—. Plant physiologist USDA Argl. Rsch. Svc. plant disease resistance unit, Madison, 1966-90, rsch. leader, 1990-2003; program dir. USDA, Washington, 1982-83; vis. scientist Lab. of Cell Biology, Versailles, France, 1985-86. Lt. USAF, 1957-60. Mem. Am. Phytopathol. Soc., Am. Soc. Plant Physiologists. Achievements include development of tissue culture procedures for studying interactions of plants and fungi, of somatic hybridizations to obtain new disease resistances in plants, isolation of a gene for potato late blight resistance. Business E-Mail: jphelges@wisc.edu.

HELLAND, MARK DUANE, small business owner; b. Eldora, Iowa, May 19, 1949; s. Duane J. and Mary Carolyn (Bloomberg) H.; m. Lois Ann Lebakken, Aug. 15, 1970; children: Alissa, Jonathan. BA, Luther Coll., 1971; JD, U. Minn., 1974; postgrad., Harvard U., 1985-88. Bar: Minn. 1974, Wis. 1980. Assoc. Berg Law Offices, Stewartville, Minn., 1974-77; v.p. Legal Systems, Inc., Eau Claire, Wis., 1977-78; sr. editor Lawyers Coop. Pub. Co., Rochester, N.Y., 1978-80; exec. dir. Profl. Edn. Systems, Inc., Eau Claire, 1980-81, chief exec. officer, 1981-88, pub., 1988-91, Wiley Law Publs., Colorado Springs, Colo., 1991-93; pres. PESI, Eau Claire, 1993—, PESI Law Publ., LLC, Eau Claire, 2001—. Author: Minnesota Probate System, 1980, Wisconsin Rules of the Road, 1985. Mem. Greater Eau Claire C. of C. Office: PESI 200 Spring St Eau Claire WI 54703-3225 Home Phone: 715-831-8315; Office Phone: 715-833-5205. Business E-Mail: mark@pesi.com.

HELLER, ABRAHAM, psychiatrist, educator; b. Claremont, NH, Mar. 17, 1917; s. David and Rose Heller; m. Lora S. Levy, June 16, 1957; 1 child, Judith Rose. BA, Brandeis U., 1953; MD, Boston U., 1957. Diplomate Am. Bd. Med. Examiners, Am. Bd. Psychiatry and Neurology. Resident in psychiatry U. Colo., Denver, 1958-61; chief in-patient psychiatry Denver Gen. Hosp., 1961-65, asst. dir. psychiat. services, 1965-70, assoc. dir. psychiat. services, 1970-73, dir., community mental health services, 1970-72; chief psychiatry, dir. community mental health ctr. Newport (R.I.) Hosp., 1973-77; clin. assoc. prof. psychiatry Brown U., Providence, 1973-77; prof. psychiatry, community health Wright State U., Dayton, Ohio, 1977-91, vice chmn. dept., 1980-91, prof. emeritus, 1991—. Fellow Am. Psychiat. Assn. (disting. sr.), Am. Orthopsychiat. Assn., Am. Assn. for Social Psychiatry. Jewish. Home: 1400 Runnymede Rd Dayton OH 45419-2924 Office: Wright State U Sch Medicine Dept Psychiatry PO Box 927 Dayton OH 45401-0927 Office Phone: 937-223-8840. E-mail: abraham.heller@wright.edu.

HELLER, DAVID S., lawyer; BA, Northwestern U., 1974; JD, Georgetown U., 1978. Bar: Ill. 1978. Ptnr. fin. and real estate dept., co-chmn. insolvency and restructuring group Latham & Watkins LLP, Chgo. Spkr. in field. Named one of Top 10 Bankruptcy Attorneys in Country, Turnarounds & Workouts, 1997, Top 12 Outstanding Bankruptcy Lawyers of Yr., 2000. Office: Latham & Watkins LLP Sears Tower Ste 5800 233 S Wacker Dr Chicago IL 60606 Office Phone: 312-876-7670. Office Fax: 312-993-9767. E-mail: david.heller@lw.com.

HELLER, FRANCIS HOWARD, retired law and political science educator; b. Vienna, Aug. 24, 1917; came to U.S., 1938, naturalized, 1943; s. Charles A. and Lily (Grunwald) H.; m. Donna Munn, Sept. 3, 1949 (dec. Dec. 1990); 1 child, Denis Wayne. Student in Law, U. Vienna, 1935—37; JD, MA, U. Va., 1941, PhD, 1948; DHL (hon.), Benedictine Coll., 1988. Asst. prof. govt. Coll. William and Mary, 1947; asst. prof. polit. sci. U. Kans., Lawrence, 1948-51, assoc. prof., 1951-56, prof., 1956-72, Roy A. Roberts prof. law and polit. sci., 1972-88, prof. emeritus Lawrence, 1988—, assoc. dean Coll. Liberal Arts and Scis., 1957-66, assoc. dean of faculties, 1966-67, dean, 1967-70, vice chancellor for acad. affairs, 1970-72, acting provost, 1967—68, 1969—70. Vis. prof. Inst. Advanced Studies, Vienna, 1965, U. Vienna Law Sch., 1985, 97, Trinity U., Tex., 1992. Author: Introduction to American Constitutional Law, 1952, The Presidency: A Modern Perspective, 1960, The Korean War: A 25-Year Perspective, 1977, The Truman White House, 1980, Economics and the Truman Administration, 1982, USA: Verfassung und Politik, 1987, NATO: The Founding of the Alliance and the Integration of Europe, 1992, The Kansas State Constitution: A Reference Guide, 1992, The United States and the Integration of Europe, 1996. Mem. Kans. Commn. on Constl. Revision, 1957-61, Lawrence City Planning Commn., 1957-63, ednl. adv. commn. U.S. Army Command and Gen. Staff Coll., 1969-72; bd. dirs. Harry S. Truman Libr. Inst., 1958-96, v.p., 1962-96; bd. dirs. Benedictine Coll., chmn., 1971-79; mem. nat. adv. coun. Ctr. for Study of Presidency, 1991-97. Pvt. to 1st lt. arty. AUS, 1942-47, capt. 1951-52, maj. USAR, ret. Decorated Silver Star, Bronze Star with cluster; recipient Career Teaching award Chancellor's Club, 1986, Silver Angel award Kans. Cath. Conf., 1987, Disting. Svc. citation U. Kans., 1998; Austrian Cross of Honor for Sci. and Art 1st class, 2004. Mem. Am. Polit. Sci. Assn. (exec. council 1958-60), Order of Coif, Phi Beta Kappa, Pi Sigma Alpha (mem. nat. council 1958-60) Home: 1510 St Andrews Dr Lawrence KS 66047-1634

HELLER, LOIS JANE, physiologist, educator, researcher; b. Detroit, Jan. 4, 1942; d. John and Lona Elizabeth (Stockmeyer) Skagerberg; m. Robert Eugene Heller, May 21, 1966; children: John Robert, Suzanne Elizabeth. BA, Albion Coll., 1964; MS, U. Mich., 1966; PhD, U. Ill., Chgo., 1970. Instr. med ctr. U. Ill., Chgo., 1969-70, asst. prof., 1970-71, U. Minn., Duluth, 1972-77, assoc. prof., 1977-89, prof., 1989—. Author: Cardiovascular Physiology, 5th edit., 2003; contbr. numerous articles to profl. jours. Mem. Am. Physiol. Soc., Am. Heart Assn., Soc. Exptl. Biology and Medicine, Internat. Soc. Heart Rsch., Sigma Xi. Avocation: birding. Home: 9129 Congdon Blvd Duluth MN 55804-0005 Office: Univ Minn Sch of Medicine Duluth MN 55812

HELLER, REINHOLD AUGUST, art educator, consultant; b. Fulda, Hesse, Germany, July 22, 1940; came to U.S., 1949; s. Friedrich Leonhard and Brigitte Hermine (Schuler) H.; m. Vivian Faye Hall, June 11, 1966; children: Frederik Andreas, Erik Reinhold. Student, George Washington U., 1958-59; BS, St. Joseph's Coll., 1963; MA, Ind. U., 1966, PhD, 1968. Asst. prof., prof. U. Pitts., 1968-78; prof. U. Chgo., 1978—. Acting dir. Smart Gallery, U. Chgo., 1983-86; cons., guest curator at. Gallery of Art, Washington, 1972,78 Author: Edvard Munch: The Scream, 1973, Munch: His Life and Work, 1984, Hildegard Auer: Ein Verlangen Nach Kunst, 1987, Am. edit., 1989, Toulouse-Lautrec: Painter of Montmartre, 1997; (catalogue) The Art of Wilhelm Lehmbruck, 1973, The Earthly Chimera and the Femme Fatale, 1981, Brücke: German Expressionist Prints from the Granvil and Marcia Specks Collection, 1988, Art in Germany from 1909 to 1936: From Expressionism to Resistance: The Marvin and Janet Fishman collection, 1990, Lyonel Feininger: Awareness, Recollection and Nostalgia, 1992, Stark Impressions: Graphic Prodns. in Germany, 1919-1933, 1994, Gabrielle Münter: The Years of Expressionism, 1905-1920, 1997. Am. Coun. Learned Socs. and Social Sci. Rsch. Coun. fellow, 1966-68, Fulbright fellow, 1966, Guggenheim fellow, 1975-76; Eisenmann Found. rsch. grantee, 1988-89. Mem. MLA, Coll. Art Assn., German Studies Assn., Historians of German and Ctrl. European Art. Office: U Chgo Dept Art Hist 5540 S Greenwood Ave Chicago IL 60637-1506 E-mail: rheller@midway.uchicago.edu.

HELLER, STANLEY J., lawyer, physician, educator; b. Phila., May 10, 1941; s. Albert Curtis and Bianche (Solton) Heller; m. Martha Wright (div. 1975); children: Stephanie Gail, Michael Lawrence, Deborah Arlene; m. Brenda Anita West, Dec. 29, 1990. BA, Johns Hopkins U., Balt., 1962, MD, 1965; JD, Northwestern U., Evanston, Ill., 1988. Bar: Ill. 1988, Ga. 1996; diplomate Am. Bd. Internal Medicine, Am. Bd. Cardiovascular Diseases. Resident physician, medicine Rush-Presbyn. St. Lukes Hosp., Chgo., 1965-68; instr. U. Ill. Coll. Medicine, Chgo., 1968-70; asst. prof. Rush Med. Coll., Chgo., 1970-71; assoc. prof. Loyola Stritch Coll. Medicine, Chgo., 1971-79; clin. assoc. prof. Northwestern U. Med. Sch., Chgo., 1980—95; ptnr. Cirignani, Heller, Harman, and Lynch LLP, Chgo., 1988—. Dir. cardiac diagnostic lab. St. Joseph Hosp., Chgo., 1971—84, attending physician, 1971—85; pres. Northside Cardiology Group, Ltd., Chgo., 1973—84; attending physician Grant Hosp., Chgo., 1972—85, Augustana Hosp., Chgo., 1973—86; cons. physician Columbus Hosp., Chgo., 1980—84. Fellow, Am. Coll. Legal Med., 2002—; Cardiology fellow, USPHS, Chgo., 1968—70. Fellow: ACP (emeritus), Am. Heart Assn. (coun. clin. cardiology, emeritus), Am. Coll. Cardiology (emeritus); mem.: ATLA, ABA, Chgo. Bar Assn., Ga. Trial Lawyers Assn., Ill. Trial Lawyer Assn., Ill. Bar Assn. Avocations: skiing, hiking, reading. Office: Cirignani Heller and Harman LLP 150 S Wacker Dr Ste 2600 Chicago IL 60606-3417 Office Phone: 312-346-8700. Business E-Mail: sjh@cirignani.com.

HELLIE, RICHARD, historian, educator; b. Waterloo, Iowa, May 8, 1937; s. Ole Ingeman and Mary Elizabeth (Larsen) H.; children: Benjamin, Michael; m. Shujie Yu, Feb. 26, 1998. BA, U. Chgo., 1958, MA, 1960, PhD, 1965; postgrad., Ind. U., Bloomington, 1963, U. Moscow, 1963—64. Vis. asst. prof. Rutgers U., 1965—66; asst. prof. Russian history U. Chgo., 1966—71, assoc. prof., 1971—80, prof., 1980—2001, Thomas E. Donnelley prof., 2001—. Presenter in field; chmn. Coll. Russian Civilization course U. Chgo., 1967—, chmn. undergrad. studies in Russian Civilization, 1970—, chmn. Ea. European NDEA Title VI Area Com., 1974—78, coord. Coll. History, 1971—73, mem. Coun. U. Senate, 1976—79, mem. coll. com. academic standing, 1984—87, co-coord. Moscow exchange program, 1990—96, co-coord. Russian and Soviet studies workshop, sole coord. Russian and Soviet studies workshop, 1993—94, dir. Nat. Resource Ctr. Slavic, East European/Russian and Eurasian studies, 1997—2004, mem. faculty oversight com. on computing, 1999—2002, dir. Ctr. for East European, Russian and Eurasian studies, 1997—2004. Author: Muscovite Society, 1967, 1970, Enserfment and Military Change in Muscovy, 1971 (Am. Hist. Assn. Adams prize 1972), Slavery in Russia 1450-1725, 1982 (Laing prize U. Chgo. Press 1985, Russian translation with new post-Soviet foreword Kholopstvo v Rossii, 1450-1725, 1998), 1982, The Russian Law Code (Ulozhenie) of 1649, 1988, The Economy and Material Culture of Russia 1600-1725, 1999; editor: The Plow, the Hammer and the Knout: An Economic History of Eighteenth Century Russia, 1985, Ivan the Terrible: A Quarcentenary Celebration of His Death, 1987, The Frontier in Russian History, 1995, The Economy and Material Culture of Russia, 1999, The Soviet Global Impact 1945-1991, 2002; editor quar. jour. Russian History, 1988; translation editor: Kholopstvo v Rossii 1450-1725, 1998; contbr. numerous articles to profl. jours, presenter in field. Fgn. area tng. fellow Ford Found., 1962-65, Inter-Univ. Com. on Travel Grants award, 1963-64, Quantrell grant for Improvement of Tchg., 1969, Social Sci. Divsional Rsch. grants U. Chgo., 1970-88, 1991-94, 1996-97, 1998-99, Guggenheim fellow, 1973-74, fellow NEH, 1978-79; grantee NEH, 1982-83, summer, 1988, NSF, 1988-90, Bradley Found., 1988-91. Mem. PEN, Nat. Hist. Soc. (founding mem., bd. govs.), Am. Soc. Legal History (program com. ann. meetings 1976), Am. Assn. Advancement Slavic Studies (editl. bd. Slavic Rev. 1979-81), Econ. History Assn., Assn. Comparative Econ. Studies, Nat. Assn. Scholars, Jean Bodin Soc. Comparative Instl. History, Chgo. Consortium Slavic and East European Studies (pres. 1990-92), Nat. Hist. Soc. (founder, bd. govs. 1999-2002), Chgo. Com. Chgo. Coun. on Fgn. Rels. Office: U Chgo Dept History 1126 E 59th St Box 78 Chicago IL 60637-1580 Home: 5811 S Dorchester Ave Apt 2G Chicago IL 60637-1775 Office Phone: 773-702-8377. Business E-Mail: hell@midway.uchicago.edu.

HELLMAN, PETER STUART, technical manufacturing executive; b. Cleve., Oct. 16, 1949; s. Arthur Cerf and Joan (Alburn) H.; m. Alyson Dulin Ware, Sept. 18, 1976; children: Whitney Ware, Garrettson Stuart. BA, Hobart Coll., 1972; MBA, Case Western Res. U., 1984. V.p. Irving Trust Co., NYC, 1972-79; fin. planning assoc. Std. Oil Co., Cleve., 1979-82, mgr. fin. planning, 1982-84, dir. ops. analysis, 1984-85, asst. treas., 1985-86, treas., 1986-87, gen. mgr. crude oil supply and trading, 1987-89; v.p., treas. TRW Inc., Cleve., 1989-91, exec. v.p., CFO, 1991-94, asst. pres., 1994-95, pres., COO, bd. dirs., 1995-99; exec. v.p., CFO, chief adminstrv. officer Nordson Corp., Westlake, Ohio, 2000—04, pres., 2004—. Bd. dirs. Nordson Corp., QWest Comm. Internat. Inc., Baxter Internat. Trustee Case Western Res. U., Lorain C.C. Office: Nordson Corp 28601 Clemens Rd Westlake OH 44145-1119

HELLMAN, SAMUEL, radiologist, educator; b. NYC, July 23, 1934; s. Henry Sidney and Anna (Egar) Hellman; m. Marcia Sherman, June 30, 1957; children: Jeffrey, Richard, Deborah Susan. BS magna cum laude, Allegheny Coll., 1955, DSc (hon.), 1984; MD cum laude, SUNY, Syracuse, 1959, DSc (hon.), 1993; MS (hon.), Harvard U., 1968. Med. intern Beth Israel Hosp., Boston, 1959—60; asst. resident radiology Yale Sch. Medicine and Grace-New Haven Hosp., 1960—62, postdoctoral fellow radiotherapy and cancer research, 1962—64; postdoctoral fellow Inst. Cancer Research and Royal Marsden Hosp., London, 1965—66; asst. prof. radiology Yale Sch. Medicine, 1966—68; assoc. prof. radiology Harvard Med. Sch., 1968—70; dir. Joint Center for Radiation Therapy, 1968—83, assoc. prof., chmn. dept. radiation therapy, 1971, prof., chmn. dept., 1971—83, also Alvan T. and Viola D. Fuller-Am. Cancer Soc. prof.; physician-in-chief Meml. Sloan Kettering Cancer Ctr., 1983—88, Benno Schmidt chair in clin. oncology, 1983—88; dean div. biol. sci. and Pritzker Sch. Medicine, v.p. for Med. Ctr. U. Chgo., 1988—93, Pritzker prof., 1988—93, Pritzker disting. svc. prof., 1993—2006, Pritzker disting. svc. prof. emeritus, 2006—. Chmn. bd. sci. counselors divsn. cancer treatment Nat. Cancer Inst., 1980—84; bd. govs. Argonne Nat. Lab., 1990—93; trustee Brookings Inst., 1992—; bd. dirs. Varian Med. Systems Inc., Insightec; mem. sci. adv. bd. Ludwig Inst. for Cancer Rsch. Contbr. numerous articles to med. jours. Trustee Allegheny Coll., 1979—98, chmn. bd. trustees, 1987—93. Recipient Rosenthal award for cancer rsch., 1980, medal, City of Paris, 1986, award for Outstanding Contbns. to Cancer Care, Assn. Cmty. Cancer Ctrs., 1993. Fellow: AAAS; mem.: N.Y. Acad. Scis., Soc. Chmn. Acad. Radiology Depts., Inst. Medicine NAS, Assn. Am. Physicians, Am. Cancer Soc., Am. Soc. Hematology, Am. Assn. Cancer Rsch., Am. Soc. Clin. Oncology (pres. 1986, David A. Karnovsky lectr. 1994), Assn. Univ. Radiologists, Am. Coll. Radiology (gold medal 2003), Am. Soc. Therapeutic Radiologists (pres. 1983, Gold medal 1991), Am. Radium Soc., Alpha Omega Alpha, Sigma Xi, Phi Beta Kappa. Home: 1122 N Dearborn St Apt 25H Chicago IL 60610 Office: U Chgo Divsn Biol Scis 5841 S Maryland Ave Chicago IL 60637-1463 Office Phone: 773-702-4346. Business E-Mail: s-hellman@uchicago.edu.

HELLMERS, NORMAN DONALD, retired historic site director; b. New Orleans, Feb. 3, 1944; s. Leonard H. and Meta J.C. (Wegener) H.; m. Patricia I. O'Brien, May 29, 1966; children: Jennifer I., Jeffrey N. BA, Concordia U., River Forest, Ill., 1966; postgrad., U. Iowa, 1966-67, La. State U., 1968. Writer, photographer Nebr. Game and Pks. Commn., Lincoln, 1969-71; ranger nat. pks. various locations, 1972-73; dist. naturalist Shenandoah Nat. Pk., Luray, Va., 1973-76; chief interpretation Grand Portage (Minn.) Nat. Monument, 1976-81; supt. Lincoln Boyhood Nat. Meml., Lincoln City, Ind., 1981-90, Lincoln Home Nat. Hist. Site, Springfield, Ill., 1990—2003; ret., 2003. Lutheran. Avocations: photography, genealogy.

HELLMUTH, THEODORE HENNING, lawyer; b. Detroit, Mar. 28, 1949; s. George F. and Mildred Hellmuth; m. Laurie Hellmuth, May 29, 1970; children: Elizabeth Ann, Theodore Henning, Sara Marie. BA, U. Pa., 1970; JD cum laude, U. Mo.-Columbia, 1974. Bar: Mo. 1974, U.S. Dist. Ct. (ea. dist.) Mo. 1974, U.S. Ct. Appeals (8th cir.) 1978. Assoc., then ptnr. Armstrong Teasdale LLP, St. Louis, 1974—2002. Author: Missouri Real Estate, 1985, 2d edit., 1998, Lease Audits: The Essential Guide, 1994; editor Distressed Real Estate Law Alert, 1987-88, Litigated Commercial Real Estate Document Reports, 1987-95. Mem.: ABA, Am. Coll. Real Estate Lawyers, Order of Coif. Office: Armstrong Teasdale LLP 1 Metropolitan Sq Ste 2600 Saint Louis MO 63102-2740 E-mail: thellmuth@armstrongteasdale.com.

HELMAN, ROBERT ALAN, lawyer; b. Chgo., Jan. 27, 1934; s. Nathan W. and Esther (Weiss) H.; m. Janet R. Williams, Sept. 13, 1958; children: Marcus E., Adam J., Sarah E. Student, U. Ill., 1951—53; BSL, Northwestern U., 1954, LLB, 1956. Bar: Ill. 1956. Asso. firm Isham, Lincoln & Beale, Chgo., 1956-64, ptnr., 1965-66; ptnr. firm Mayer Brown, Rowe & Maw LLC, Chgo., 1967—. Bd. dirs. No. Trust Corp., 1986-2006; lectr. U. Chgo. Law Sch., 1974. Co-author: Commentaries on 1970 Illinois Constitution, 1971; assoc. editor Northwestern U. Law Rev., 1955-56; contbr. articles to profl. jours. Chmn. Citizens' Com. on Juvenile Ct., Cook County, 1969-81; pres. Legal Assistance Found., Chgo., 1973-76; chmn. vis. com. Northwestern U. Law Sch., 1989-92; bd. dirs. United Charities Chgo., 1967-73; hon. trustee Brookings Instn., trustee Aspen Inst., 1986-92. Mem. ABA, Chgo. Bar Assn., Am. Law Inst., Chgo. Coun. Lawyers, Lawyers Club Chgo., Comml. Club, Chgo. Club, Econ. Club, Order of Coif. Home: 4950 S Chicago Beach Dr Chicago IL 60615-3207 Office: Mayer Brown Rowe & Maw 71 S Wacker Dr Chicago IL 60606 Office Phone: 312-701-7020. Business E-Mail: rhelman@mayerbrown.com.

HELMERS, STEVEN J., lawyer, energy executive; m. Wanda Helmers; 4 children. BA magna cum laude, SD State U., 1978; JD cum laude, U. SD, 1981. Law clerk We. Div., U.S. Dist. Ct., 1981—83; atty. Lynn, Jackson, Shultz & Lebrun, P.C, 1983—87, Truhe, Beardsley, Jensen, Helmers & VonWald; gen. counsel, corp. sec. Black Hills Corp., Rapid City, SD, 2001—. Mem. Black Hills Area Boy Scout Coun., Rapid City Arts Coun., Black Hills Red Cross, Calvary Luth. Ch. Coun. Mem.: ABA, Rocky Mountain Mineral Law Found., Pennington County Bar Assn (pres. 1999), State Bar SD (Bar Commr. 1995—98). Office: Black Hills Corp 625 9th St Rapid City SD 57701 Office Phone: 605-721-2300. E-mail: shelmers@blackhillscorp.com.

HELMHOLZ, R(ICHARD) H(ENRY), law educator; b. Pasadena, Calif., July 1, 1940; s. Lindsay and Alice (Bean) H.; m. Marilyn P. Helmholz. AB, Princeton U., 1962; JD, Harvard U., 1965; PhD, U. Calif., Berkeley, 1970; LLD, Trinity Coll., Dublin, 1992. Bar: Mo. 1965. Asst. prof. history to prof. law & history Washington U., St. Louis, 1970-81; prof. law U. Chgo. Law Sch., 1981—84, Ruth Wyatt Rosenson prof. law, 1984—99, Ruth Wyatt Rosenson disting. svc. prof. law, 2000—. Maitland lectr. Cambridge U., 1987; Goodhart prof. Cambridge U., 2000-01. Author: Marriage Litigation, 1975, Select Cases on Defamation, 1985, Canon Law and the Law of England, 1987, Roman Canon Law in Reformation England, 1990, Spirit of Classical Canon Law, 1996, The Ius Commune in England: Four Studies, 2001, Oxford History of the Laws of England, Vol. 1, 2004. Guggenheim fellow, 1986; recipient Von Humboldt rsch. prize, 1992. Fellow Brit. Acad. (corr.), Am. Acad. Arts and Scis., Am. Law Inst., Medieval Acad. Am.; mem. ABA, Am. Soc. Legal History (pres. 1992-94), Selden Soc. (v.p. 1984-87), Univ. Club, Reform Club. Home: 5757 S Kimbark Ave Chicago IL 60637-1614 Office: U Chgo Law Sch 1111 E 60th St Chicago IL 60637-2776 Office Phone: 773-702-9580. Business E-Mail: dick_helmholz@law.uchicago.edu.

HELMKE, PAUL (WALTER PAUL HELMKE JR.), lawyer, former mayor; b. Bloomington, Ind., Nov. 24, 1948; s. Walter P. and Rowene Mary (Crabill) H.; m. Deborah Jane Andrews, Aug. 23, 1969; children: Laura Andrews, Kathryn Elizabeth. BA with highest honors, Ind. U., 1970; JD, Yale U., 1973. Bar: Ind. 1973, Fla. 1982. Atty. Helmke Beams LLP, Ft. Wayne, Ind., 1973-87, 2003—, Barnes & Thornburg LLP, Ft. Wayne, 2000—02; dir. govt. rels. Sentry Points LLP, 2004—06; mayor City of Ft. Wayne, 1988-2000. Asst. county atty. Allen County, Ft. Wayne, 1974-87; pres. Nat. Rep. Mayors and Local Ofcls. Orgn., 1993; pres. US Conf. of Mayors, 1997-98, pres., CEO Brady Campaign to Prevent Gun Violence, 2006-Chmn. Allen-Wells chpt. ARC, Ft. Wayne, 1985-87; candidate for Rep. nomination 4th U.S. Congl. Dist.-Ind., 1980; Rep. nominee for U.S. Senate, Ind., 1998; bd. dirs. Nat. League of Cities, 1995-97, chair pub. safety and crime prevention com., 1995; candidate for Rep. nomination 3d U.S. Congl. Dist. Ind., 2002. Recipient J.C. Gallagher prize Law Sch. Yale U., New Haven, Conn., 1972. Mem. Ind. Assn. Cities and Towns (pres. 1996-97). Republican. Lutheran. Office: Helmke Beams LLP 202 W Berry St Ste 300 Fort Wayne IN 46802-2216 also: Brady Ctr/Campaign to Prevent Gun Violence 1225 Eye St NW Ste 1100 Washington DC 20005 Office Phone: 260-422-7422, 202-289-7319. Personal E-mail: paulhelmke@aol.com. Business E-Mail: paulhelmke@helmkebeams.com, phelmke@bradymail.org.

HELQUIST, PAUL M., chemistry educator, researcher; b. Duluth, Minn., Mar. 5, 1947; s. Paul O. and Marie E. (Parent) H.; m. Christie M. Wick, June 11, 1970; children: Sandra Ann, Kristina Ann. BSc, U. Minn., Duluth, 1969; MSc, PhD, Cornell U., 1971; PhD honoris causa, U. Uppsala, Sweden, 1988. Postdoctoral fellow Harvard U., Cambridge, Mass., 1973-74; asst. prof. SUNY, Stony Brook, 1974-80, assoc. prof., 1980-84, prof., 1984-86, U. Notre Dame, Ind., 1986—, chmn. dept. chemistry and biochemistry Ind., 1988-93. Mem. exam. bd. Ednl. Testing Svc., Princeton, N.J., 1989-98; cons. Proctor and Gamble Pharms., 1990—, Circagen, 1999-2002; head Walther Cancer Rsch. Ctr. Drug Devel., 1998—; dir. NSF workshops for coll. organic chemistry tchrs., 1999—. Author: Synthetic Organic Chemistry: Modern Methods and Strategy, 1989. Recipient Catacosinos Cancer Rsch. award, 1979, Walther Cancer Inst. award, 2001; grantee IH, 1977—, NSF, 1979—; Am.-Scandinavian Found. fellow, 1982. Mem. Am. Chem. Soc. (instr. 1981—, Exceptional Achievement award 1991), U. Minn.-Duluth Acad. Sci. and Engring. (Walter Cancer Inst. Rsch. prize award 2004). Avocations: foreign languages, classical music, model building, amateur astronomy. Office: U Notre Dame Dept Chemistry & Biochemistry Notre Dame IN 46556 E-mail: helquist.1@nd.edu.

HELSENE, AMY L., lawyer; b. Austin, Minn., June 21, 1973; BA cum laude, U. Minn., Mpls., 1995; JD, U. Minn. Law Sch., Mpls., 1998. Bar: Minn. 1998. Clk. to Hon. James T. Swenson Hennepin County Dist. Ct.; assoc. Larkin, Hoffman, Daly & Lindgren, Ltd., Mpls. Contbr. articles to profl. jours. Named a Rising Star, Minn. Super Lawyers mag., 2006. Mem.: Vol. Lawyers Network, Douglas K. Amdahl Inns of Ct., Minn. Women Lawyers, ABA, Minn. State Bar Assn., Hennepin County Bar Assn., Phi Beta Kappa. Office: Larkin Hoffman Daly & Lindgren Ltd 1500 Wells Fargo Plz 7900 Xerxes Ave S Minneapolis MN 55431 Office Phone: 952-896-3326. E-mail: ahelsene@larkinhoffman.com.

HELTNE, PAUL GREGORY, researcher, museum director; b. Lake Mills, Iowa, July 4, 1941; s. Palmer Tilford and Grace Katherine (Hanson) H.;

children— Lisa, Christian. BA, Luther Coll., Decorah, Iowa, 1962; PhD, U. Chgo., 1970. Asst. prof. Johns Hopkins U. Sch. Medicine, Balt., 1970-82; dir. Chgo. Acad. Scis., 1982-91, pres., 1991—99, pres. emeritus, 1999—; co-dir. Nature Polis and Ethics Project, 1994—2002; dir. Ctr. for Humans and Nature, 2003—. Cons. WHO, Am. Petroleum Inst. Author, editor: Neotropical Primates: Status and Conservation, 1976, Lion-Tailed Macaque, 1985, Science Learning in the Informal Setting, 1988, Understanding Chimpanzees, 1989, Chimpanzee Cultures, 1994. Trustee Balt. Zool. Soc., 1972-82. Mem. Am. Assn. Mus. (edn. task force, accreditation site visitor), Assn. Sci. Mus. Dirs. (sec.-treas. 1986-96), Internat. Primatology Soc., Soc. Integrative and Comparative Biology, Soc. for Study Evolution, Systematic Zoology Soc. Office: Ctr for Humans and Nature 2430 N Cannon Dr Chicago IL 60614 Office Phone: 773-404-8276. Business E-Mail: paulheltne@humansandnature.org.

HELTON, SANDRA LYNN, telecommunications industry executive; b. Paintsville, Ky., Dec. 9, 1949; d. Paul Edward and Ella Rae (Van Hoose) H.; m. Norman M. Edelson, Apr. 15, 1978. BS, U. Ky., 1971; MBA, MIT, 1977. Capital budget adminstr. Corning (N.Y.) Glass Works, 1978-79, fixed assets mgr., 1979-80, contr. electronics divsn., 1980-82, mgr. customer fin. svcs., 1982-84, dir. fin. svcs., 1984-86, asst. treas., 1986-91, v.p., treas., 1991-94, sr. v.p., treas., 1994—97; exec. v.p. fin., CFO TDS Telecom, Chgo., 1998—2000, exec. v.p., CFO, 2001—. Bd. dirs. U.S. Cellular Corp., The Prin. Fin. Group. Vol. Mass. Gen. Hosp., Boston, 1976; treas. Corning Mus. of Glass; treas pres. bd. dirs. Chemung Valley Arts Coun., Corning, 1981-87; bd. dirs. Corning Summer Theatre, 1987-91, Arnot Hosp. Found., 1988—; mem. fin. com. Clemens Performing Arts Ctr., Elmira, N.Y., 1985-92; mem. adv. bd. Chase Lincoln, 1988-91; mem. bus. com. Met. Mus. Art, 1992—; pres. bd. dirs. Rockwell Mus., 1992—; mem. Regional Cultural Adv. Com., 1992—; mem. FEI com. on Corp. Fin., 1995—; bd. dirs. Arnot Ogden Meml. Med. Ctr., Arts of the So. Finger Lakes. Mem. Nat. Assn. Corp. Treass., Fin. Women's Assn., Soc. Internat. Treas., Fin. Execs. Inst. Avocations: music, tennis.

HELVESTON, EUGENE MCGILLIS, pediatric ophthalmologist, educator; b. Detroit, Dec. 28, 1934; d. Eugene McGillis and Ann (Fay) H.; m. Barbara Hiss, June 15, 1959; children: Martha Hiss, Lisa Hiss. BA, U. Mich., 1956, MD, 1960. Intern St. Joseph Hosp., Ann Arbor, Mich., 1960-61; resident Ind. U. Hosps., Indpls., 1961-66; dir. pediatric opthalmology Ind. U. Sch. Medicine, Indpls., 1967—, asst. prof., 1967-72, assoc. prof., 1972-76, prof., 1976—, chmn., 1981-83, dir. sect. pediatric ophthalmology, 1967—. Fellow in opthalmology Wilmer Inst., Balt., 1966-67 Author: Pediatric Ophthalmology Practice, 1973, Atlas of Strabismus Surgery, 4th edit., 1993, Strabismus: A Decision Making Approach, 1994; chief editor; Am. Orthoptic Jour., 1976-82; contbr. articles to profl. jours. Mem. med. adv. bd. Project Orbis, 1989—. Kellogg scholar, 1959; grantee Heed scholar Heed Found., Chgo., 1966; recipient Outstanding Heed Fellow award, 1975 Fellow ACS, Am. Acad. Ophthalmology, Am. Orthoptic Coun. (pres. 1976-80), Am. Assn. Pediat. Ophthalmology and Strabismus (pres. 1990), Internat. Strabismus Assn. (sec.-treas.). Office: Ind U Sch Medicine 702 Rotary Cir Indianapolis IN 46202-5133

HELVEY, WILLIAM CHARLES, JR., communications specialist; b. Springfield, Mo., Sept. 4, 1942; s. William C. Sr. and Alice (Essary) H.; m. Julia Faye Howard, June 16, 1962; children: Howard, Harold. BS in Art Edn., S.W. Mo. State U., 1965; MA in Art, U. Mo., 1970. Tchr. art Marshfield (Mo.) H.S., 1965-67; med. illustrator, program emphasis mgr. Mo. Regional Med. Program, Columbia, 1968-80; dir. instrl. media Ctrl. Meth. Coll., Fayette, Mo.; comm. cons., Columbia, 1981-83; state comm. sys. specialist Univ. Ext., Lincoln U., Jefferson City, Mo., 1983—2005; ind. film prodr. Helvey Prodns. Profl. artist, photographer, presenter in field; juror for art and photography; adj. prof. art Stephens Coll. One-man shows (83), in art and photography, group shows (over 100) in arts, including, Arts Ctr. of the Ozarks, Boone County Hist. Mus., Columbia, Mo., Arrow Rock State Hist. Site, Rozier Gallery, Jefferson City, Mo., Columbia Art League, U.S. Social Security Adminstrn., Nat. 4-H Ctr., Silver Springs, Md.; contbr. numerous articles to profl. jours. Project leader Boone County 4-H Clubs, Columbia, 1977-2002. Recipient Unsung Hero award U.S. Dept. Agr., 1988, Mo. Specialist award Mo. State Extension, 1990, 93, numerous awards in art, photography, film and video prodn. Mem.: Columbia Art League (chmn. Boone County art show 1975—, Lifetime Achievement award in art), Aircraft Owners and Pilots Assn. Avocations: nature, aviation, screenplay writing, fine art photography. Home: 908 Shepard Ct Columbia MO 65201-6135 E-mail: bhelvey@aol.com.

HEMANN, PATRICIA ALICE, federal judge; b. Chgo., June 28, 1942; d. George Carlyle and Nanon Amanda (DuBois) Wood; m. John Henry Hemann, June 19, 1965; children: John Jr., David, Michael. BA, U. Ill., 1964; JD, Cleveland-Marshall Coll. Law, 1980. Bar: Ohio 1980, U.S. Dist. Ct. (no. dist.) OH 1981, U.S. Ct. Appeals (6th cir.) 1985, U.S. Supreme Ct. Law clk. to Hon. William K. Thomas US Dist. Ct (no. dist.) OH, Cleve., 1980-82; assoc. Hahn, Loeser & Parks, Cleve., 1982-87, ptnr., 1987-93; magistrate judge US Dist. Ct. (no. dist.) OH, Cleve., 1993—. Instr. Cleve.-Marshall Coll. Law, vis. com., 1992—. Mem. ABA, Nat. Assn. Women Judges (dist. dir.), Fed. Bar Assn., Ohio Women's Bar Assn., Cleve. Bar Assn. Avocations: reading, travel. Office: US Courthouse 201 Superior Ave E Ste 414 Cleveland OH 44114-1201

HEMENWAY, ROBERT E., academic administrator, language educator; b. Sioux City, Iowa, Aug. 10, 1941; s. Myrle Emery and Katharine Leone (Cook) H.; m. Marilyn Wickstrom, June 16, 1962 (div. 1970); children: Gina, Jeremy; m. Mattie Fenter, May 12, 1972 (div. 1980); children: Robin, Karintha, Matthew, Langston; m. Leah Renee Hattemer, Dec. 19, 1981; children: Zachary, Arna. BA, U. Nebr., Omaha, 1963; PhD, Kent State U., Ohio, 1966. Asst. prof. English U. Ky., Lexington, 1966-68; assoc. prof. Am. studies U. Wyo., Laramie, 1968-73; prof. U. Ky., Lexington, 1973-86; dean arts and scis. U. Okla., Norman, 1986-89; chancellor U. Ky., Lexington, 1989-95, U. Kans., Lawrence, 1995—. Dean Gov.'s Scholar's Program, Ky., 1984-86; bd. dir., Am. Coun. on Edn. Author: Zora eale Hurston, 1977 (Best Biography of 1977 award Soc. Midland Authors 1978, Rembert Patrick prize Fla. Hist. Soc. 1978). Mem. Gov.'s Task Force on Literacy, Okla., 1987-89; bd. dirs. Okla. HS Sci. and Math., Oklahoma City, 1985-86, Coun. Colls. Arts and Scis., 1987-89. NEH fellow, 1974-75. Mem. MLA, Am. Studies Assn. (nat. coun.), South Atlantic Assn. Depts. English (pres. 1984-85). Lutheran. Avocation: bridge. Office: Univ Kansas Office of the Chancellor 230 Strong Hall Lawrence KS 66045-7501 Office Phone: 785-864-3131. Office Fax: 785-864-4120. E-mail: chancellor@ku.edu.

HEMKE, FREDERICK L., music educator; b. July 11, 1935; s. Fred L. and May H. (Rowell) H.; m. Junita Borg, Dec. 26, 1959; children: Elizabeth Hemke Shapiro, Frederic John Borg. Premiere prix, Cons. Nat. de Musique, Paris, 1956; BS in Music Edn., U. Wis., Milw., 1958; MusM in Music Edn., Eastman Sch. of Music, Rochester, NY, 1962; DMA in Musical Arts, U. Wis., 1975. Chmn. dept. preparatory wind and percussion Sch. of Music Northwestern U., Evanston, Ill., 1962-75, chmn. dept. music performance and studies, 1962-94, prof. of music (saxophone), 1963—, sr. assoc. dean, 1994—2003, acting dean, 2002, Louis and Elsie Snydacker Eckstein prof. music, 2003—, Charles Deering McCormick prof. tchg. exellence, 2004—. Faculty athletics rep. Northwestern U., Big 10 Conf., CAA 1982-2003; cons. Rico Internat., Frederick Hemke Saxophone Reeds, So. Music Co., San Antonio, Hemke Saxophone Series, Conn-Selmer Co., Elkhart, Ind. Instrumental soloist (recordings) The American Saxophone, Music for Tenor Saxophone, Allan Pettersson, Symphony No. 15 (with Stockholm Philharmonic); Quintet for String Quarter & Saxo-Warren Benson, Concerto-Ross Lee Finney, Simple Gifts for saxophone and organ; author: The Early History of the Saxophone, Hemke Saxophone Series, So. Music Co. Recipient Excellence in Teaching award Northwestern U. Alumni Assn., Music Alumni Achievement award, U. Wis., Milw.; grantee: Nat. Endowment for the Arts. Mem. Ill. Music Educators Assn., Pi Kappa Lambda, Kappa Kappa Psi, Phi Mu Alpha Sinfonia (past province gov.) Office: Northwestern U Sch of Music 1965 S Campus Dr Evanston IL 60208-0874 Business E-Mail: f-hemke@northwestern.edu.

HEMMER, J. MICHAEL, lawyer, rail transportation executive; b. Stillwater, Okla., May 28, 1949; BA with honors, Stanford U., Calif., 1971; JD with honors, U. Calif., Berkeley, 1976. Atty. Covington & Burling, Washington, 1976—2002, ptnr., 1984—2002; v.p. law Union Pacific RR Union Pacific Corp., Omaha, 2002—04, sr. v.p. law, gen. counsel, 2004—. Office: Union Pacific Corp 1400 Douglas St Omaha NE 68179 Office Phone: 402-544-5000.

HEMMER, JAMES PAUL, lawyer; b. Oshkosh, Wis., Mar. 28, 1942; s. Joseph John and Margaret Louise (Nuernberg) H.; m. Francine M. Chamallas, June 4, 1967; children— James, Christopher, Sarah. A.B. summa cum laude, Marquette U., 1964; LL.B., Harvard U., 1967. Bar: Ill. 1967. Assoc. Bell, Boyd & Lloyd, Chgo., 1967-74, ptnr., 1975—, mng. ptnr., 1990-93; adj. prof. law Marquette U., 1985-86, Chgo. Kent Coll. Law, 1991-93; lectr. Ill. Inst. Continuing Legal Edn.; bd. dirs. Sanford Corp., Constrn. Projects Mgmt. Inc., Holco Corp. Mem. Kenilworth (Ill.) Sch. Dist. 38 Bd. Edn., v.p. 1985-87, pres. 1987-89, Kenilworth Citizens Adv. Caucus; bd. dirs. Joseph Sears Sch. Devel. Fund. Wickersham fellow; Fulbright scholar. Mem. ABA, Ill. Bar Assn. (editor banking and comml. law newsletter), Alpha Sigma Nu, Phi Theta Psi, Phi Sigma Tau, Sigma Tau Delta. Clubs: University, Law, Legal (Chgo.); Kenilworth. Contbr. articles to legal jours.

HEMMER, PAUL EDWARD, musician, communications executive, composer; b. Dubuque, Iowa, Oct. 12, 1944; s. Andrew Charles and Elizabeth Marie (Goerdt) H.; m. Janet T. Demmer, Feb. 7, 1970; children: Michelle, Steven. BS in Music Edn., U. Wis., Platteville, 1966. Program dir. Sta. WDBQ-AM, Dubuque, Iowa, 1967-93; leader Paul Hemmer Orch., Dubuque, 1967-96; pres. Hemmer Broadcasting, Dubuque, Iowa, 1994—2000; v.p. Radio DBQ, Inc., Dubuque, 2000—. Composer: (musical comedies) Get the Lead Out, 1976, Joe Sent Me!, 1978, Key City Komedy Company, 1981, Steamboat Comin', 1991, Here's to Dubuque, 1998, Sketches from a Drawing Room, 1996; appeared in film Field of Dreams, 1989. Named Citizen of Yr., Dubuque Telegraph-Herald, 1976, Disting. alumni, U. Wis, Platteville, 1999. Mem. Internat. Radio Broadcasters Idea Bank, Rotary. Roman Catholic. Home: 2375 Simpson St Dubuque IA 52003-7720 Office: Radio DBQ 8th Bluff Dubuque IA 52001 Home Phone: 563-582-8825; Office Phone: 563-690-0830. Personal E-mail: dbqpaul@mchsi.com.

HEMSLEY, STEPHEN J., healthcare company executive; BS, Fordham U., 1974. Mng. ptnr. strategy and planning Arthur Andersen and Co.; sr. exec. v.p. UnitedHealth Group, Detroit, 1997-99, COO, 1998—2006, pres., 1999—, bd. dir., 2000—, CEO, 2006—. Trustee Minn. Pub. Radio, 2002—. Office: UnitedHealth Grp PO Box 1459 Minneapolis MN 55440-1459*

HENDEE, WILLIAM RICHARD, medical physics educator, academic administrator, radiologist; b. Owosso, Mich., Jan. 1, 1938; s. C.L. and Alvina M. H.; m. Jeannie Wesley, June 16, 1960; children: Mikal, Shonn, Eric, Gareth and Gregory (twins), Lara and Karel (twins). BS, Millsaps Coll., Jackson, Miss., 1959; PhD, U. Tex., 1962; DSc (hon.), Millsaps Coll., Jackson, Miss., 1988. Diplomate Am. Bd. Radiology, Am. Bd. Health Physics. AEC fellow Nat. Reactor Testing Sta., Idaho Falls, Idaho, 1960; asst. prof., then assoc. prof. physics Millsaps Coll., 1962-65, chmn. dept., 1964-65; instr. Miss. State U. (extension), 1963; asst. prof., then assoc. prof. radiology (med. physics) U. Colo. Med. Center, 1965-73, prof., 1974-85, chmn. dept., 1978-85; mem. staff VA Hosp., Denver, 1970-85, Mercy Hosp., 1971-85, Denver Gen. Hosp., 1971-85, Beth Israel Hosp., 1974-85; v.p. sci. and tech. AMA, Chgo., 1985-1991; prof. radiology, biophysics, radiation oncology, bioethics Med. Coll. Wis., Milw., 1991—2006, clin. prof. radiology and biophysics, 1985-91, sr. assoc. dean, v.p., 1991—2005, dean grad. sch., 1995—2006, pres. rsch. found., 2005—06, disting. prof. radiation oncology, biophysics, cmty. and public health, 2006—. Prof. bioengring. Marquette U., 1993—; vis. lectr. Oak Ridge Assoc. Univs., 1964; adj. prof. radiology Northwestern U. Sch. Medicine, 1986-91; adj. prof. elec. engring. U. Wis.-Milw., 2003-. Editor Med. Phys., 2005—; contbr. 375 articles to profl. jours., author/editor 24 books. Served with USMC, 1957-62. Recipient Disting. Alumnus award Millsaps Coll., 1967, Disting. Svc. award Nat. Wildlife Fedn., 1990, Wright Langham Meml. award U. Ky., 1991, Gold medal Am. Roentgen Ray Soc., 2005, Med. Coll. Sic. Disting. Svc. award, 2005; Gilbert X-ray fellow, 1960-62, summer fellow NSF, AEC; campus assoc. Danforth Found., gold medal Am. Roentgen Ray Soc., 2005; Disting. Svc. award, Med. Coll. Wis., 2005. Fellow Am. Coll. Radiology, Am. Inst. Med. and Biol. Engring. (pres. 1998-99); mem. AAAS, Health Physics Soc. (chmn. coms., Elda E. Anderson award 1972), Am. Assn. Physicists in Medicine (pres. 1976-77, Robert S. Landauer Meml. award 1977, William D. Coolidge award 1989), Nat. Wildlife Fedn. (Disting. Svc. award 1990), Soc. Biomed. Engring., (sr. mem.), Soc. Nuclear Medicine (pres. 1980-81, Benedict Cassen Meml. award 1984), Am. Acad. Home Care Physicians (Disting. Svc. award 1991), Am. Bd. Radiology (trustee 1995-05, pres. 2002-04), Omicron Delta Kappa, Theta Nu Sigma. Office: PO Box 170970 Whitefish Bay WI 53217-8087 Office Phone: 414-351-6527. Business E-Mail: whendee@mcw.edu.

HENDERSON, ANGELO B., journalist; m. Felecia Henderson; 1 child, Grant. BA in Journalism, U. Ky., 1985. Journalist Wall Street Jour., Detroit; sr. spl. writer Page One The Wall Street Jour. Deacon Hartford Meml. Bapt. Ch., Detroit. Recipient Journalism award Detroit Press Club Found., 1993, Unity award for excellence in minority reporting for pub. affairs/social issues, 1993, Best of Gannett award for bus. and consumer affairs reporting, 1996, Pulitzer prize for Feature Writing, 1999. Mem. Nat. Assn. Black Journalists (former pres. Detroit chpt., award for outstanding coverage of the black condition 1992). Office: c/o Wall Street Jour Det Bur 500 Woodward Ave Ste 1950 Detroit MI 48226-5497

HENDERSON, BRODERICK, state legislator; Parking control officer; mem. from dist. 35 Kans. State Ho. of Reps., Topeka. Address: 2710 N 8th St Kansas City KS 66101-1108

HENDERSON, DONALD L., agricultural products executive, landscape company executive; Gen. mgr. Deere & Co., Moline, Ill. Fellow Am. Soc. Agrl. Engrs. Office: Deer & Co 1 John Deere Pl Moline IL 61265-8098

HENDERSON, FRITZ A. (FREDERICK A. HENDERSON), automotive executive; b. Nov. 29, 1958; m. Karen Henderson; 2 children. BBA with high distinction, U. Mich., 1980; MBA with high distinction, Harvard U., 1984. From sr. analyst to dir. GM Corp., NY, 1984—87; from dir. to v.p. mortgage banking GMAC, 1987—90, from v.p. fin. to group v.p. fin. Detroit, 1991—92; exec. in charge of ops. automotive compontents group GM Corp., Pontiac, Mich., 1993, v.p., gen. mgr. Delphi Saginaw steering sys. Saginaw, Mich., 1996, v.p., mng. dir. Brazil Sao Paulo, Brazil, 1997—2000, group v.p., 2000—02; pres. Latin Am., Africa and Middle East region GM Corp, 2000—02; pres. GM Asia Pacific GM Corp., 2002—04, chmn. GM Europe, 2004—05, vice chmn., CFO, 2006—08, pres., COO, 2008—. Mem. GM Automotive Strategy Bd. GM Corp.; chmn. bd. dirs. Shanghai GM Co., Ltd., 2002; vice-chmn., bd. dirs. Pan Asia Tech. Automotive Ctr.; bd. dirs. Fuji Heavy Industries Ltd.; chmn. bd. dirs. GM Daewoo Auto & Tech. Co. George F. Baker scholar, 1984. Mem.: Conf. Bd. Fin. Execs. Internat., Japan Automobile Mfrs. Assn. (bd. dirs. 2002). Office: GM Corp 300 Renaissance Ctr Detroit MI 48265 Mailing: GM Corp PO Box 33170 Detroit MI 48232-5170*

HENDERSON, JANET E. E., lawyer; b. 1956; BA, U. Okla., 1978; JD, Columbia U., 1982. Bar: Okla. 1982, U.S. Dist. Ct. (no. dist.) Okla. 1982, Ill. 1986, U.S. Dist. Ct. (no. dist.) Ill. 1986. With Sidley & Austin, Chgo., 1985—, ptnr., 1990—. Lectr. on lender liability issues and bankruptcy to legal orgns., including Midwest Assn. Secured Lenders. Harlan Fiske Stone scholar Columbia U., 1982. Mem. ABA, Chgo. Bar Assn., Am. Bankruptcy Inst., Phi Beta Kappa. Office: Sidley & Austin Bank One Plz 10 S Dearborn St Chicago IL 60603 Fax: 312-853-7036.

HENDERSON, JEFFREY W., health products executive; BSEE, Kettering U., Flint, Mich.; MBA, Harvard Grad. Sch. Bus. Adminstrn. With GM; v.p., corp. treas. Eli Lilly & Co., 1998, v.p., corp. contr.; pres., gen. mgr. Eli Lilly Can., Inc.; exec. v.p., CFO Cardinal Health Inc., Dublin, Ohio, 2005—. Office: Cardinal Health Inc 7000 Cardinal Pl Dublin OH 43017

HENDERSON, JOHN L., academic administrator; Sr. asst. to pres. instl. devel. Cin. Tech. Coll., until 1987, v.p. instl. devel., 1987-88; pres. Wilberforce U., Ohio, 1988—. Mailing: PO Box 1001 Wilberforce OH 45384-1001

HENDERSON, RONALD, police chief; b. St. Louis, Dec. 24, 1947; A in Criminal Justice, Florissant Valley CC, Mo.; grad. exec. strategic mgmt. program, Sr. Mgmt. Inst. for Police, Boston, 1992; student, Dignitary Protection Sch., Washington, 1994. appointee Mo. Emergency Response Commn.; program dir. St. Louis Met. Police Dept. Intern Program; initiated New Year's Eve safety campaign. Several divsns. including vice-narcotics, internal affairs St. Louis Police Dept., patrolman, sgt., lt. col., comdr. bur. of patrol support, 1970-92, chief, 1995—. Bd. dirs. St. Louis Cath. Charities. Recipient Robert Lamb Jr. Humanitarian award Nat. Orgn. of Black Law Enfocement Officers, 1997. Office: Met Police Dept 1200 Clark Ave Saint Louis MO 63103-2801

HENDERSON, WILLIAM J., former postmaster general; b. June 16, 1947; 2 children. Grad., U. N.C. With U.S. Postal Svc., postmaster, divsn. gen. mgr. Greensboro, N.C., v.p. employee rels., chief mktg. officer, sr. v.p., chief operating officer, 1994-98, postmaster gen., CEO, 1998—2001. Mem. bd. dirs. comScore Networks, Inc., 2001—, Acxiom Corp., 2001—, Quad/Graphics Inc., 2001—. With U.S. Army. Recipient Roger W. Jones award for Exec. Leadership Am. U., 1998, John Wanamaker award U.S. Postal Svc., 1997 Office: comScore Networks Inc 500 W Madison St # 2980 Chicago IL 60661

HENDRICKSON, BRUCE CARL, life insurance company executive; b. Holdrege, Nebr., Apr. 4, 1930; s. Carl R. and Ruth E. (Bosserman) H.; m. Carol Schepman, June 12, 1952; children: Julie, Mark Bruce. BA, U. Nebr., 1952. C.L.U., chartered fin. cons. Sr. agt. Prin. Life Ins. Co., Holdrege, 1950—. Bd. govs. Central Nebr. Tech. C.C.; mem. Nebr. Edn. Commn. of States, Nat. Hwy. Safety Advisors Com.; elder First Presbyterian Ch., Holdrege; pres. Holdrege City Council, 1979-86; pres. Phelps County Cmty. Found.; trustee U. Nebr. Found.; moderator Cen. Nebr. Presbytery, Presbyn. Ch. USA, 1986-88, Gen. Assembly Coun., 1998-2004; dir. Mus. Nebr. Art, 1996-2002; mem. pres. club U. Nebr., mem. chancellors club. Served with USNR, 1953-56. Bruce Hendrickson Week declared by Gov. of ebr., 1975; recipient Distinguished Alumni Achievement award U. Nebr., 1977, Disting. Svc. award Nebr. State Assn. Life Underwriters, 1998. Mem. Nat. Assn. Life Underwriters (pres. 1975-76), Assn. Advanced Life Underwriting, Am. Soc. C.L.U.s., Life Underwriters Polit. Action Com. (chmn. 1989), Life Underwriters Tng. Coun. (trustee 1979-82), Million Dollar Round Table, Phi Kappa Psi. Clubs: Rotary (pres. 1960-61), Holdrege Country (Holdrege); Am. Legion, Elks. Republican. Office: Prin Fin Group PO Box 735 Holdrege NE 68949-0735

HENDRICKSON, CARL H., state legislator; Mem. Mo. Ho. of Reps., Jefferson City. Republican.

HENDRICKSON, JOHN P., lawyer; b. Oct. 7, 1955; m. Lisa A. Hendrickson. BS, S.D. State U., 1977; JD, U. Notre Dame, 1980. Ptnr., chmn. firm employee benefits dept. McDermott Will & Emery LLP, Chgo. Named one of top employee benefits lawyers in U.S., Nat. Law Jour. Office: McDermott Will & Emery LLP 227 W Monroe St Chicago IL 60606-5055 Home: 721 Taft Rd Hinsdale IL 60521-4934 Office Phone: 312-984-7645. Office Fax: 312-984-7700. Business E-Mail: jhendrickson@mwe.com.

HENDRIX, JON RICHARD, biology professor; b. Passaic, NJ, May 4, 1938; s. William Louis and Velma Lucile (Coleman) H.; m. Janis Ruth Rouhselange, Nov. 24, 1962; children— Margaret Susan, Joann Ruth, Amy Therese BS, Ind. State U., 1960, MS, 1963; Ed.D., Ball State U., Muncie, Ind., 1974. Sci. supr. Sch. Town of Highland, Ind., 1960-71; instr. Ind. U., Gary, 1968-69; assoc. prof. biology Ball State U., Muncie, 1972-80, prof., 1980-98, prof. emeritus, 1998—. Cons. Ind. Dept. Pub. Instrn., 1967-71, Ctr. for Values and Meaning, 1971—; mem. Ind. Sci. Edn. Adv. Bd., Dept. Pub. Instrn., 1967-71 Author: The Wonder of Somehow, 1974, The Wonder of Someplace, 1974, The Wonder of Sometime, 1974, Becomings: A Parent Guidebook for In-Home Experiences with Nine to Eleven Year Olds, 1974, Becomings: A Clergy Guidebook for Experiences with Nine to Eleven Year Olds and Their Parents, 1974; contbr. articles to profl. jours. Recipient Outstanding Young Educator award Highland Jr. C. of C., 1968, Outstanding Faculty award in edn. Ind. U. N.W. Campus, 1970, Outstanding Teaching Faculty award Ball State U., 1982, Ball State U. fellowship, 1971-73, Hon. Mem. award Nat. Assn. Biology Tchrs., 1992, Outstanding Undergrad. Sci. Tchr. in Nation, Soc. of Coll. Sci. Tchrs./Kendall Mgmt., 1997; named Ind. Prof. of Yr., Coun. for Advancement and Support of Edn./Carneige, 1997. Fellow Ind. Acad. Sci.; mem. Nat. Sci. Suprs. Assn. (dir. 1969-71), Ind. Sci. Suprs. Assn. (pres. 1968-69), AAUP, Assn. Suprs. and Curriculum Devel., Nat. Biology Tchrs. Assn. (bd. dirs. 1986, 91—), Nat. Sci. Tchrs. Assn. (life), Nat. Soc. Coll. Sci. Tchrs. (undergrad. tchg. award 1997), Central Assn. Coll. Biology Tchrs., Hoosier Assn. Sci. Tchrs. Inc. (bd. dirs. 1968-71, Disting. Svc. award 1997), Ind. Assn. Tchr. Educators, Ind. Assn. Suprs. and Curriculum Devel., Ind. Biology Tchrs. Assn., Kappa Delta Pi, Phi Delta Kappa, Sigma Xi. Home: 8800 W Eucalyptus Ave Muncie IN 47304-9365 Personal E-mail: jonh49@comcast.net.

HENDRIXSON, PETER S., lawyer; b. Wilmington, Del., Apr. 9, 1947; s. Philip Roe and Betty Jane (Schillo) H.; m. Carolyn Hodge Ford, June 14, 1969; children: Julie Elise, Bradley Scott. BA, Northwestern U., 1969; JD magna cum laude, Harvard U., 1972. Bar: Minn. 1973, U.S. Dist. Ct. Minn. 1973, U.S. Supreme Ct. 1978. Law clerk U.S. Ct. Appeals, Boston, 1972-73; assoc., ptnr. trial dept. Dorsey & Whitney, Mpls., 1973—, chair trial dept., 1989-93, chair trial and adminstrv. group, 1994—, mng. ptnr., 2000—04, trail ptnr., 2007, Of counsel, 2008. Editor, officer Harvard Law Review, 1970-72. Treas. Fraser for Mayor Com., Mpls., 1983-95; bd. govs. Children's Theatre, Mpls., 1987-92; various positions Mayflower Congl. Ch.; bd. dirs. La Creche Early Childhood Ctrs., Mpls., 1990-98, Children's Home Soc., St. Paul, 1990—, Guthrie Theater, 1995-00; pres. Children's Law Ctr.; mem. bd. Walker Art Ctr. Mem. Minn State Bar (chair anti-trust law sect. 1992-93), Phi Beta Kappa. Democrat. Congregationalist. Office: Dorsey & Whitney LLP 50 S 6th St Ste 1500 Minneapolis MN 55402 Office Phone: 612-340-2917. Office Fax: 612-340-2868. Business E-Mail: hendrixson.peter@dorsey.com.

HENDRY, JOHN V., retired state supreme court justice; b. Omaha, Aug. 23, 1948; BS, U. Nebr., 1970, JD, 1974. Pvt. practice, Licoln, 1974-1995; county ct. judge 3d Jud. Dist., 1995-98; chief justice Nebr. Supreme Ct., 1998—2006. Fellow: Nebr. State Bar Found.; mem.: Nebr. State Bar Assn. Office: Nebr Supreme Ct Rm 2214 State Capitol Lincoln NE 68509

HENG, STANLEY MARK, national guard officer; b. Nebraska City, Nebr., Nov. 4, 1937; s. Robert Joseph Sr. and Margaret Ann (Volkmer) H.; m. Sharon E. Barrett, Oct. 10, 1959; children: Mark, Nick, Lisa. Grad., Command and Gen. Staff Coll., 1969; student, Nat. Def. U., 1979; BA, Doane Coll., 1987. Commd. adj. Nebr. .G., 1966, advanced through grade to maj. gen., 1966-87; adj. Nebr. Mil. Dept., Lincoln, 1966-77, adminstrv. asst., 1978-86; adj. gen., dir. emergency mgmt. State of Nebr., Lincoln, 1987—2000. Mem. N.G. Assn. U.S., N.G. Assn. Nebr. (exec. sec. 1967-71, Svc. award 1970), Adj. Gens. Assn., Am. Legion. Democrat. Avocations: softball, basketball, running.

HENIKOFF, LEO M., JR., academic administrator, medical educator; b. Chgo., May 9, 1939; m. Carole A. Travis; children from previous marriage: Leo M. III, Jamie Sue. MD with highest honors, U. Ill., Chgo., 1963. Diplomate Am. Bd. Pediat., Am. Bd. Pediat. Cardiology. Intern Presbyn.-St. Luke's Hosp., Chgo., 1963-64, resident, 1964-66, fellow in pediatric cardiology, 1968-69; clin. instr. U. Ill. Coll. Medicine, Chgo., 1964-66; clin. instr. pediatrics Georgetown U. Med. Sch., Washington, 1966-68, clin. asst. prof., 1968; asst. prof. U. Ill. Coll. Medicine, Chgo., 1968-71; asst. prof. pediat. Rush Med. Coll., Chgo., 1971-74, assoc. prof., 1974-79, asst. dean admissions, 1971-74, assoc. dean student affairs, 1974-76, assoc. dean med. scis. and svcs., 1976-79, acting dean v.p. med. affairs, 1976-78, prof. pediatrics, prof. medicine, 1984—; v.p. inter-instl. affairs Rush-Presbyn.-St. Luke's Med. Ctr., Chgo., 1978-79, pres., 1984—2002; pres., CEO; trustee Rush-Presbyn.-St. Luke's Med. Ctr., Chgo., 1984—; dean and v.p. med. affairs Temple U. Sch. Medicine, Phila., 1979-84, prof. pediat. and medicine, 1979-84; pres. Rush U., Chgo., 1984—2002. Adj. attending Presbyn.-St. Luke's Hosp., 1969, asst., 1970-72, assoc., 1973-76, sr. attending, 1977-79, 84—; staff Temple U. Hosp., 1979-84; assoc. staff St. Christopher's Hosp. for Children, 1979-84; mem. Ill. Coun. of Deans, 1977-79; vice chmn. Chgo. Tech. Pk., 1984-85, 86-87, chmn., 1985-86, 87-88; chmn. bd. dirs. Mid-Am. Health Programs, Inc., 1985—, Rush North Shore Health Svcs., 1988-2002, Rush/Copley Health Care Sys. Inc., 1988-2002; bd. dirs. Harris Trust and Savs. Bank, Harris Bankcorp. Inc., Harris Fin. Corp., 1986—, Option Care, Inc., 2002—. Contbr. chpts. to books, articles to profl. jours. Bd. dirs. Fishbein Found., 1975-79, Chgo. Regional Blood Program, 1977-79, Sch. Dist. 69, 1974-75, Johnston R. Bowman Health Ctr. for Elderly, 1984-2002, Chgo. Chamber Musicians, 1998—; bd. mgrs. St. Christopher's Hosp. for Children, 1979-84; bd. govs. Temple U. Hosp., 1979-84, Heart Assn. S.E. Pa., 1979-84; trustee Episc. Hosp., 1983-84, Otho S.A. Sprague Meml. Inst., 1984-2002; adv. bd. Univ. Village Assn., 1984-2002; exec. com. Gov.'s Build Ill. Com.,

1985-2002. Lt. comdr. USPHS, 1964-68, Res. 1968—. Recipient Roche Med. award, 1962, Mosby award, 1963, Raymond B. Allen Instructorship award U. Ill. Coll. Medicine, 1966, also Med. Alumni award, 1988, Phoenix award Rush Med. Coll., 1977. Fellow Am. Acad. Pediat., Inst. Medicine Chgo., Coll. Physicians Phila., Am. Coll. Physicians Execs.; mem. Assn. Am. Med. Colls. (chmn. nominating com. 1980, mem. coun. deans 1977-84, mem. audit com. 1984), Coun. Tchg. Hosps. (adminstrv. bd. 1987-90), Pa. Med. Sch. Deans Com., AMA (mem. coun. on ethical and jud. affairs 1984-88), Pa. Med. Soc., Philadelphia County Med. Soc., Assn. Acad. Health Ctrs. (bd. dirs. 1988-94, chmn.-elect 1991-92, chmn. 1992-93), Alpha Omega Alpha (chmn. nat. nominating com. 1981-90, nat. dir. 1979-90, pres. 1989-90), Omega Beta Pi, Phi Eta Sigma, Phi Kappa Phi.

HENKE, JANICE CARINE, educational software developer, marketing professional; b. Hunter, ND, Jan. 28, 1938; d. John Leonard and Adeline (Hagen) Hanson; children: Toni L., Tom L., Tracy L. BS, U. Minn., 1965; postgrad., misc. schs., 1969—. Cert. elem. tchr., Minn., Iowa. Tchr. dance, 1953-56; tchr. kindergarten Des Moines Pub. Schs., 1964-65; tchr. elem. Ind. Sch. Dist. 284, Wayzata, Minn., 1969-93; pvt. bus. history Wayzata, 1978—; marketer, promoter health enhancement Jeri Jacobus Cosmetics Aloe Pro, Am. Choice Nutrition, Multiway, KM Matol, Wayzata, 1978—; developer ednl. software, marketer of software Computer Aided Teaching Concepts, Excelsior, Minn., 1983—; Edn. Minn. authorized rep. with Midwest Benefit Advisers, Excelsior, 1993—. Developer, author drug edn. curriculum, Wayzata, 1970-71; mem. programs com. Health and Wellness, Wayzata, 1988-93; chmn. Wayzata Edn. Assn. Ins. Com., 1991-93; mem. Staff Devel. Adv. Bd., Wayzata, 1988-93; coach Odyssey of the Mind, 1989-93. Author, developer computer software; contbr. articles to newspapers. Fundraiser Ind. Reps. Wayzata, 1976-79; mem. pub. rels. com. Lake Minnetonka (Minn.) Dist. Ind. Reps., 1979-81, fundraising chmn., 1981-82; chmn. Wayzata Ind. Reps., 1981-82; sec. PTO, Wayzata, 1981-82. Mem. NEA, Minn. Edn. Assn., Wayzata Edn. Assn. (bd. mem., ins. chairperson). Lutheran. Avocations: swimming, skiing, travel, reading, learning. Office: Henke Services Inc 20380 Excelsior Blvd Excelsior MN 55331-8733

HENKIN, ROBERT ELLIOTT, nuclear medicine physician; b. Pitts., June 7, 1942; s. Hyman and Nettie (Jaffee) H.; m. Denise Dulberg, June 26, 1966 (dec. 1985); children: Gregory, Joshua, Steven; m. Renae Marley, Nov. 27, 1988 (dec. Nov. 2006). Student, Cornell U., 1960-62; BA, NYU, 1965, MD, 1969. Diplomate Am. Bd. Nuclear Medicine, Nat. Bd. Med. Examiners. Internship gen. surgery Bellevue Med. Ctr., NYU, NYC, 1969—70; resident in diagnostic radiology Northwestern U., Chgo., 1970—72, resident in nuc. medicine, 1972—74, asst. prof. radiology, 1974—76; from asst. prof. to assoc. prof. radiology Loyola U., Maywood, Ill., 1976—80, dir. nuc. medicine, 1976—98, prof. radiology, 1980—2005, acting chair dept. radiology, 2000—02, dir. nuc. medicine, 2002—05, vice chair dept. radiology, 2002—05, prof. emeritus radiology, 2006—. Fellow Am. Coll. Radiology, Am. Coll. Nuc. Physicians (pres. 1990); mem. AMA, Am. Coll. Physician Execs., Soc. uc. Medicine (bd. dirs., trustee 1983-89, 2000-04, v.p. 1995-96, ho. dels. 1998-2004). Home: 875 E 22d St Ste 202 Lombard IL 60148-5025 Home Phone: 630-627-0072. Personal E-mail: unm@mindspring.com.

HENLEY, DOUGLAS E., medical association administrator; b. Hope Mills, NC, Jan. 1, 1951; m. Mary Henley. MD, U. NC Sch. Medicine, Chapel Hill, 1977. Diplomate Am. Bd. Family Practice. Resident NC Memorial Hospital, Chapel Hill, NC, 1977—80; pvt. practice Hope Mills, NC; exec. v.p. Am. Acad. Family Physicians; assoc. clinical instructor U. NC Sch. of Medicine. Mem. editl. bd. Family Practice News, Jour. Family Practice. Mem. N.C. Cervical Cancer Task Force, U.S. Congress' Office of Tech. Assessment Adv. Panel; bd. dirs. Am. Acad. Family Physicians Found. Office: Am Acad Family Physicians PO Box 11210 Shawnee Mission KS 66207-1210

HENNESSY, SEAN P., corporate financial executive; From mem. staff to sr. v.p. fin., CFO Sherwin-Williams, Cleve., 1984—2001, sr. v.p., CFO, 2001—. Office: Sherwin Williams 101 Prospect Ave NW Cleveland OH 44115-1075

HENNESSY, WILLIAM JOSEPH, prosecutor; b. St. Paul, May 18, 1942; s. William E. and Julia R. (Luger) H.; m. Sandra Hennessy, July 3, 1965 (div. Jan. 7, 1977); m. Sally Ann Kroiss, Dec. 31, 1996; 1 child, Patricia Lee. BA, St. Thomas U., 1964; LLB, JD, William Mitchell U., 1968. Bar: Minn. 1968, U.S. Supreme Ct. 1975. Sr. ptnr. Hennessy & Richardson, St. Paul, 1970—93; chief prosecutor Cook County, Grand Marais, Minn., 1995—. Mem. adv. com. on the Criminal Rules, Minn. Supreme Ct., 1997-99. Mem. Minn. County Attys. Assn. (bd. dirs. 1996-2001). Avocation: commercial and instrument airplane pilot. Office: Cook County 411 W 2nd St Grand Marais MN 55604-2307 Office Phone: 218-387-3670. Business E-Mail: county.attorney@co.cook.mn.us.

HENNING, GEORGE THOMAS, JR., retired steel company executive; b. West Reading, Pa., Sept. 26, 1941; s. George Thomas and Helen Virginia (Spangler) H.; m. Susan Young, July 21, 1962; children: George Thomas III, Michael Kevin. Mgr. econ. analysis Eastern Gas & Fuel, Boston, 1967; mgr. gen. acctg. Ohio River Co., Cin., 1968; asst. to contr. Eastern Gas & Fuel Assos., Boston, 1969; dir. corp. planning Boston Gas Co., 1970; contr. Eastern Assoc. Coal Corp., Pitts., 1971-74; v.p., contr. Lykes Resources, Inc., 1974-78; asst. contr. Jones & Laughlin Steel Corp., 1979-85; gen. mgr. coal mine ops. and raw materials sales LTV Steel Co., Cleve., 1986, gen. mgr. asset mgmt., 1986-89; v.p., chief fin. officer Pioneer Chlor Alkali Co., Inc., Houston, 1988-95; v.p., CFO Pioneer Cos., Inc., 1995; v.p., contr. The LTV Corp., Cleve., 1995-99, v.p., CFO, 1999—2001, ret., 2001; bus. cons., 2002—. Bd. dirs., v.p. Schlow Ctr. Region Libr.; bd. trustees Pa. State U., University Park. Mem. Pa. State Alumni Assn. (bd. dirs. Centre County chpt.), Lion's Paw Alumni Assn. (bd. dirs.), Omicron Delta Kappa. Methodist. Business E-Mail: ghenning63@psualum.com.

HENNING, JOEL FRANK, lawyer, writer; b. Chgo., Sept. 15, 1939; s. Alexander M. and Henrietta (Frank) H.; m. Grace Weiner, May 24, 1964 (div. July 1987); children: Justine, Sarah-Anne, Dara; m. Rosemary Nadolsky, June 21, 1992 (div. July 2007); 1 child, Alexandra. AB, Harvard U., 1961, JD, 1964. Bar: Ill. 1965. Assoc. Sonnenschein, Levinson, Carlin, Nath & Rosenthal, Chgo., 1965-70; fellow, dir. program Adlai Stevenson Inst. Internat. Affairs, Chgo., 1970-73; nat. dir. Youth Edn. for Citizenship, 1972-75; dir. profl. edn. Am. Bar Assn., Chgo., 1975-78; asst. exec. dir. comm. and edn. ABA, 1978-80; ptnr. Joel Henning & Assocs., 1980-87; sr. v.p., gen. counsel, mem. exec. com. Hildebrandt, Internat., Inc., 1987—; pres., pub. LawLetters, Inc., 1980-89; pub. Lawyer Hiring and Tng. Report, 1980-89; Chgo. theater critic Wall St. Jour., 1989—; pub. Almanac of Fed. Judiciary, 1984-89; editor Bus. Lawyer Update, 1980-87. Mem. faculty Inst. on Law and Ethics, Council Philos. Studies; chmn. Fund for Justice, Chgo., 1979-85 Author: Law-Related Education in America: Guidelines for the Future, 1975, Holistic Running: Beyond the Threshhold of Fitness, 1978, Mandate for Change: The Impact of Law on Educational Innovation, 1979, Improving Lawyer Productivity: How to Train, Manage and Supervise Your Lawyers, 1985, Law Practice and Management Desk Book, 1987, Lawyers Guide to Managing and Training Lawyers, 1988, Maximizing Law Firm Profitability: Hiring, Training and Developing Productive Lawyers, 1991-98, also articles. Chmn. Gov.'s Commn. on Financing Arts in Ill., 1970-71; bd. dirs. Ill. Arts Council, 1971-81, Columbia Coll., Chgo.; bd. dirs., v.p., pub. edn. exec. com. ACLU of Ill.; trustee S.E. Chgo. Commn.; mem. Joseph Jefferson Theatrical Awards Com. Fellow Am. Bar Found. (life); mem. Am. Law Inst., ABA (ho. of dels.), Chgo. Bar Assn., Chgo. Council Lawyers (co-founder), Social Sci. Edn. Consortium. Office: 150 N Michigan Ave Ste 3600 Chicago IL 60601-7572 Office Phone: 312-578-0663. E-mail: jfhenning@hildebrandt.com, jfhenning28@comcast.net.

HENNINGSEN, PETER, JR., manufacturing executive; b. Mpls., Oct. 6, 1926; s. Peter and Anna O. (Kjelstrup) H.; m. Donna J. Buresh, June 19, 1948; children— Deborah, Pamela, James. BBA, U. Minn., Mpls., 1950. Packaging engr. govt. and aero. products div. Honeywell, Inc., Mpls., 1950-72; mgr. packaging Internat. Tel. & Tel., NYC, 1972-80; v.p. Raymond Eisenhardt & Son, Inc., 1980-90; pvt. practice Eden Prairie, Minn., 1990—. Sr. assoc. Adalis Corp., 2004—; cons. in field. With USNR, 1944-46. Elected to Packaging Hall of Fame, Packaging Edn. Forum, 1995. Fellow Inst. Packaging Profls. (pres., 1970-71, chmn. bd., 1972-73, named Man of Yr., 1968); mem. ASTM, Aerospace Industries Assn. (chmn. packaging com. 1967), Masons, Shriners Methodist. Home and Office: 7610 Smetana Ln # 211 Eden Prairie MN 55344 Business E-Mail: peterhen@comcast.net.

HENRICK, MICHAEL FRANCIS, lawyer; b. Chgo., Feb. 29, 1948; s. John L. and A. Madeline (Hafner) H.; m. Cissi F. Henrick, Aug. 9, 1980; children: Michael Francis Jr., Derry Patricia. BA, Loyola U., 1971; JD with honors, John Marshall Law Sch., 1974. Bar: Ill. 1974, U.S. Dist. Ct. (no. dist.) Ill. 1974, U.S. Supreme Ct. 1979, Wis. 1985, U.S. Dist. Ct. (ea. dist.) Wis. 1985. Ptnr. Hinshaw & Culbertson, Chgo., Waukegan, Ill., 1974—. Named Ill. Super Lawyer Chgo. Mag., Leading Lawyer, 2005-07; recipient Corpus Juris Secundum award West Publ. Co., 1974. Fellow Am. Coll. Trial Lawyers; mem. ABA, Def. Rsch. Inst., Ill. Bar Assn., Lake County Bar Assn., Ill. Hosp. Attys. Assn., Internat. Assn. of Def. Counsel, Ill. Def. Attys. Assn., Soc. Trial Lawyers Def. Rsch. Inst., Am. Inns of Ct. Office: Hinshaw & Culbertson 110 N West St Waukegan IL 60085-4330 Business E-Mail: mhenrick@hinshawlaw.com.

HENRICKSON, BONNIE, women's college basketball coach; BS in Phys. Edn., St. Cloud State U., Minn., 1986; MS in Phys. Edn., Western Ill. U., 1988. Asst. coach U. Ia., 1995-97, Big 10 regular season conf. champions, 1995-96, Big 10 tournament conf. champions, 1996-97; asst. coach Va. Poly. U. Hokies, Blacksburg, Va., 1988-95, head coach, 1997—2005, Atlantic 10 tournament champions, 1997-98; head coach U. Kans., Lawrence, 2005—. Office: Athletic Dept U Kans 1502 Iowa St Lawrence KS 66045

HENRY, BARBARA ANN, publishing executive; b. Oshkosh, Wis., July 23, 1952; d. Robert Edward and Barbara Frances (Aylesworth) Henry BJ, U. Nev., 1974. With Gannett Co., 1974—; reporter Reno Gazette-Jour., 1974—78, city editor, 1978-80, mng. editor, 1980-82; asst. nat. editor USA Today, Washington, 1982-83; exec. editor Reno Gazette-Jour., 1981-86; editor, dir. Rochester Dem. & Chronicle and Times-Union, NY, 1986—91; pub. Great Falls Tribune, Mont., 1992-96; pres., pub. Des Moines Register, 1996—2000, The Indianapolis Star, 2000—; pres. Ind. Newspaper Group, 2002—; sr. group pres. Interstate Newspaper Group, 2005—. Recipient Publisher of the Year, Gannett Newspaper Group, 2001, Touchstone award, Girls Inc. of Indpls., 2007. Mem. Soc. Profl. Journalists, Associated Press Mng. Editors, Am. Soc. Newspaper Editors Avocation: skiing. Mailing: Indianapolis Star PO Box 145 Indianapolis IN 46206-0145 Office Phone: 317-444-8131. E-mail: barbara.henry@indystar.com.*

HENRY, BRIAN C., telephone company executive; V.p., CFO Mentor Graphics Corp., Oreg.; exec. v.p., CFO, Cin. Bell Inc., 1998; COO info. mgmt. group Convergys Corp., Cin., 1998-99; exec. v.p., CFO, Lante Corp, Chgo., 1999—. Office: Lante Corp # 400 600 W Fulton St Chicago IL 60661-1259

HENRY, COLLEEN, reporter; Student, Georgetown U., Northwestern U. Reporter WISN 12, Milw. Office: WISN PO Box 402 Milwaukee WI 53201-0402

HENRY, FREDERICK EDWARD, lawyer; b. St. Louis, Aug. 28, 1947; s. Frederick E. and Dorothy Jean (McCulley) H.; m. Vallie Catherine Jones, June 7, 1969; children: Christine Roberta, Charles Frederick. AB, Duke U., 1969, JD with honors, 1972. Bar: Ill. 1972, U.S. Dist. Ct. (no. dist.) Ill. 1972, Calif. 1982. Assoc. Baker & McKenzie, Chgo., 1972-79, ptnr., 1979—. Elder, session mem. Fourth Presbyn. Ch., Chgo., 2000—02; bd. dirs. Lincoln Park Conservation Assn., 1983—85, Old Town Triangle Assn., Chgo., 1980—83, pres., 1984. Recipient Willis Smith award, Duke U. Law Sch., 1972. Mem.: ABA, Calif. State Bar, Chgo. Bar Assn., Order of Coif. Office: Baker & McKenzie 1 Prudential Plz 130 E Randolph St Ste 3700 Chicago IL 60601-6342 Home: 230 W Division Apt 1508 Chicago IL 60610 E-mail: frederick.e.henry@bakernet.com.

HENRY, GERALD T., state legislator; m. Linda M. Becker. Mem. from dist. 48 Kans. State Ho. of Reps., Topeka. Exec. dir. Achievement Svc. Address: 215 N 5th PO Box 186 Atchison KS 66002-0186 Also: 3515 Neosho Rd Cummings KS 66016-9032

HENRY, JOHN THOMAS, retired newspaper executive; b. St. Paul, May 30, 1933; s. Harlan A. and Roxane (Thomas) H.; m. Carla Joyce Lechthaler, Jan. 2, 1982; children: Alexandra, Elizabeth, J. Thomas, Catherine. BBA, U. Minn., 1955. With St. Paul Pioneer Press Dispatch, 1955—, asst. to publisher, then bus. mgr., 1971-76, gen. mgr., chmn., pub., 1985-92; ret., 1992. V.p. St. Paul Jr. C. of C., 1965-66; bd. dirs., chmn. St. Paul Jr. Achievement; bd. dirs. Better Bus. Bur. of Minn., Boy Scouts Am., Minn. Coop. Office, Minn. Mus. Art; chmn. St. Paul Chamber Orch.; bd. dirs. St. Paul Downtown Coun., United Hosps., Minn. Sci. Mus., St. Paul United Way. With USAF, 1956-59. Recipient Disting. Service award Classified Advt. Mgrs. Assn., 1971 Mem. St. Paul C. of C. (chmn. bd. dirs. 1987). Lodges: Rotary. Home: 4436 Oakmede Ln Saint Paul MN 55110-7603 Office: NW Publs Inc 345 Cedar St Saint Paul MN 55101-1004

HENRY, MICHAEL E., computer company executive; m. Cynthia Henry; children: Reese, Reagan, Winsley. Grad. H.S. Programmer, installer Jack Henry & Assocs., Monett, Mo., 1973, mgr. R&D, 1983, chmn., CEO, 1994—, also bd. dirs. Office: Jack Henry & Assocs Inc 663 Hwy 60 PO Box 807 Monett MO 65708-8215

HENRY, PHYLLISS JEANETTE, marshal; AA in Law Enforcement, Des Moines Area C.C., 1972; B Gen. Studies, U. Iowa, 1984, MA in Comm. Studies, 1986, PhD in Comm. Rsch., 1988. Police officer Des Moines (Iowa) Police Dept., 1972-82; state adminstrv. dir. Roxanne Conlin for Gov. campaign, Iowa, 1982; intern Police Found., Washington, 1984; comm. rsch. analyst Starr and Assocs., 1985; mgr. support svcs. Dept. Pub. Safety Iowa State U., 1990-94; U.S. marshal so. dist. Iowa, apptd. by Pres. Clinton U.S. Dept. Justice, 1994—. Adv. com. Dirs. Marshals, 1995-97. Named Woman of Yr., Metro. Woman's Network, 1991, Officer of Yr. Internat. Assn. of Women, 1991. Mem. Iowa Assn. Women Police (co-founder, Officer of Yr. 1991), Fed. Exec. Coun. Policy Com., Nat. Ctr. for Women and Policing (adv. bd.). Office: Office US Marshal US Courthouse 123 E Walnut St Rm 343A Des Moines IA 50309-2035 E-mail: Phylliss.Henry@usdoj.gov.

HENRY, RICK, broadcast executive; Degree in engring., Ripon Coll., Wis. Pres., gen. mgr. Sta. WISN-TV, Milw., 1997—. Office: Sta WISN-TV 759 N 19th St Milwaukee WI 53233-2126

HENRY, ROBERT JOHN, lawyer; b. Chgo., Aug. 1, 1950; s. John P. and Margaret P. (Froelich) Henry; m. Sara Mikuta; children: Cherylyn, Deanna, Laurin, Joseph Mikuta, icholas Mikuta. BA cum laude, Loyola U., Chgo., 1973, JD cum laude, 1975. Bar: Ill 1975, U.S. Dist. Ct. (no. dist.) Ill. 1975. Atty. Continental Ill. at. Bank, Chgo., 1975-77, Allied Van Lines, Inc., Chgo., 1977-81, assoc. gen. counsel, 1981-88, gen. counsel, 1988-90, v.p. adminstrn., gen. counsel, 1990-93, v.p. gen. counsel, 1993-99; v.p., assoc. gen. counsel SIRVA, Inc., Chgo., 1999—2005; ptnr. Scopelitis, Garvin, Light & Hanson, Chgo., 2005—. Gen. counsel NFC N.Am., 1996-99. Bd. dirs. Naperville C. of C., 1999—2002. Alt. scholar Weymouth Kirkland Found., 1971. Mem. Chgo. Bar Assn. Office Phone: 312-422-1200. Business E-Mail: rhenry@scopelitis.com.

HENRY, WILLIAM LOCKWOOD, information technology executive; b. Pasadena, Calif., July 2, 1948; s. Edward Lockwood and Jane (Post) Henry; m. Pamela Ann Henry; children: Thomas Edward, Michael Lockwood. BS, UCLA, 1971, MS, 1973. Fin. exec. Ford Motor Co., Dearborn, Mich., 1973-81; dir. fin. Stroh Brewery Co., Detroit, 1981-82, v.p., fin. planner, 1982-84, v.p., sales, mktg. adminstr., 1985-1986, v.p. mktg. and planning, 1987-89; exec. v.p. Stroh Brewery Co, Detroit, 1989-91; pres., CEO Stroh Brewery Co., Detroit, 1991-99; pres. Budco, Highland Park, Mich., 1999—. Bd. dirs. Met. Affairs Corp., Century Coun. Mem.: Detroit Athletic Club. Office: Budco 13700 Oakland Ave Highland Park MI 48203

HENSEL, PAUL H., lawyer; b. Hinsdale, Ill., Apr. 11, 1948; BS in Fin. with high honors, U. Ill., 1969; JD cum laude, U. Mich., 1972. Bar: Ill. 1972. Assoc. to ptnr., chief administrative ptnr. Winston & Strawn, Chgo., 1972—, chmn. assoc. programs, chmn. bldg. com. Bd. dirs. B.F. Shaw Printing Co. Bd. trustees ALP Found. Rsch. and Edn.; mem. auxiliary bd. Art Inst. Chgo. Mem. ABA, Chgo. Bar Assn., Ill. State Bar Assn. Office: Winston & Strawn LLP 35 W Wacker Dr Ste 4200 Chicago IL 60601-9703 Office Phone: 312-558-5750. Office Fax: 312-558-5700. E-mail: phensel@winston.com.

HENSLEY, ANTHONY M., state legislator; b. Topeka, Sept. 2, 1953; s. Harland Leroy and Georgina (Haydon) H.; m. Deborah Hensley; 1 child, Kathleen. BS, Washburn U., 1975; MS, Kans. State U., 1985. Mem. from dist. 58 Kans. State Senate, 1977-92, mem. from dist. 19, 1992—, minority leader, 1997; spl. edn. tchr., 1975—. Chmn. Washburn U. Young Dems., 1972-73, Shawnee County Dem. Ctrl. Com., 1981-86, 2d Dist. Dem. Com., 1991-93; committeeman 8th precinct 4th Ward Dem. Com., Topeka, 1976—; mem. Breakthrough House. Named one of Outstanding Young Men in Am., 1978, 82. Mem. Optimists. Home: 2226 SE Virginia Ave Topeka KS 66605-1357

HENSON, C. WARD, mathematician, educator; b. Worcester, Mass., Sept. 25, 1940; s. Charles W. and Daryl May (Hoyt) H.; m. Faith deMena Travis, August 31, 1963; children: Julia Rebecca, Suzanne Amy, Claire Victoria. AB, Harvard U., 1962; PhD, MIT, 1967. Asst. prof. Duke U., Durham, NC, 1967-74, N.Mex. State U., Las Cruces, 1974-75, U. Ill., Urbana, 1975-77, assoc. prof., 1977-81, prof., 1981—, chmn. dept. math., 1988-92. Vis. assoc. prof. U. Wis., Madison, 1979-80; vis. prof. RWTH Aachen, Fed. Republic Germany, 1985-86, Univ. Tübingen, Fed. Republic Germany, 1992-93. Mem. Assn. for Symbolic Logic (sec.-treas. 1982-2000, pub. 1999-2004), Am. Math. Soc. Office: U Ill Dept Math 1409 W Green St Urbana IL 61801-2943 Office Phone: 217-333-2768. E-mail: henson@math.uiuc.edu.

HENSON, ROBERT FRANK, retired lawyer; b. Jenny Lind, Ark., Apr. 10, 1925; s. Newton and Nell Edith (Kessinger) H.; m. Jean Peterson Henson, Sept. 14, 1946 (dec. Apr. 8, 2006); children: Robert F., Sandra Henson Curfman, Laura, Thomas, David, Steven. BS, U. Minn., Mpls., 1948, JD, 1950. Bar: Minn. 1950, U.S. Supreme Ct. 1972. Atty. Soo Line R.R., 1950-52; ptnr. Cant, Haverstock, Beardsley, Gray & Plant, Mpls., 1952-66; sr. ptnr. Henson & Efron, Mpls., 1966-94, of counsel, 1995—2004; ret., 2004. Chmn. Minn. Lawyers Profl. Responsibility Bd., 1981-86; co-chmn. Supreme Ct. Study Com. on Lawyer Discipline, 1992-94. Trustee Mpls. Found., 1974-85, Emma Howe Found, 1986-90; chmn. Hennepin County Mental Health and Mental Retardation Bd., 1968-70. Served with USN, 1943-46. Fellow Am. Bar Found.; mem. ABA, Hennepin County Bar Assn. (pres. 1968-69), Minn. Bar Assn., Order of Coif. Unitarian Universalist. Personal E-mail: rhenson41025@comcast.net.

HENZLIK, RAYMOND EUGENE, zoophysiologist, educator; b. Casper, Wyo., Dec. 26, 1926; s. William H. Henzlik and Adeline Adele (Brown) Wolff; m. Wilma Louise Bartels, Oct. 1, 1950; children: Randall Eugene, Nancy Jo. BS, U. Nebr., Lincoln, 1948, MS, 1952, PhD, 1960; postgrad., Cornell U., Ithaca, NY, 1961-62. Tchr. biology and chemistry York (Nebr.) High Sch., 1948-50; sci. edn. supr. Tchrs. Coll., U. Nebr., Lincoln, 1951-53; tchr. biology Omaha North High Sch., 1953-56; instr. biology Nebr. Wesleyan U., Lincoln, 1957-59; asst. prof. zoology and biology U. Nebr., Lincoln, 1959-61; asst. prof. biology Ball State U., Muncie, Ind., 1962-67, assoc. prof. physiology, 1967-69, prof. physiology, 1970—. Adj. vis. prof. vet. physiology Tex. A&M U., College Station, 1984-85; anatomy cons. Nat. Prescription Footwear Applicators Assn., Muncie, 1962—; lectr. Pedorthics Tech. Program, Muncie, 1977—; cons. ednl. affairs Argonne (Ill.) Nat. Lab., 1970-76; dir. ednl. program Am. Diabetes Assn., Muncie, 1979-83; vis. prof. health sci. USAF European Ctr., Ramstein and Rhein Main, Germany, 1977-78; lectr. Ind. Health Care Assn., 1985-91. Author: Human Physiology Lab Manual, 1976-92; contbr. articles to profl. jours. Pres. Muncie Tech. Soc., 1975—80; mem. bd. Am. Diabetes Assn. Delaware County, Muncie, 1979—85. Radiation biology fellow NSF/AEC, U. Mich., 1960, Radiobiology fellow AEC/NSF, Cornell U., 1961-62, Radiation Biology Rsch. fellow U.S. Radiobiology Lab N.C. State U., 1965, P.R. Nuclear Ctr., 1967. Mem. AAAS, Nutrition Today Soc., Ind. Acad. Sci., Muncie Tech. Soc., Mensa, Sigma Xi, Phi Delta Kappa. Avocations: reading, book collecting. Home: 5009 N Somerset Dr Muncie IN 47304-6501

HEPNER, JAMES O., medical school director; BA, PhD, U. Iowa; MHA, Wash. U., St. Louis. Dir., 1967—; hosp. adminstr. Jewish Hosp., St. Louis; grant reviewer Dept. of Health and Human Svc.; dir. Interagy. Inst. for Fed. Healthcare Execs. Cons. Air Force Surgeon Gen. Co-editor-in-chief Best Practices and Benchmarking in Healthcare: A Practical Jour. for Client and Mgmt. Applications. Recipient Gold Medal for Excellence and Leadership Med. Svc. Corp., Outstanding Healthcare award Hosp. Assn. of Met. St. Louis. Mem. Assn. of Univ. Programs in Health Adminstrn. (past bd. chmn.), Am. Coll. of Healthcare Execs. (bd. chmn., Silver Medal award of excellence

HEPPNER, GLORIA HILL, health facility administrator, educator; b. Gt. Falls, Mont., May 30, 1940; d. Eugene Merrill and Georgia M. (Swanson) Hill; m. Frank Henry Heppner, June 6, 1964 (div. 1975); 1 child, Michael Berkeley. BA, U. Calif., Berkeley, 1962, MA, 1964, PhD, 1967. Damon Runyon postdoctoral fellow U. Wash., Seattle, 1967—68; asst. and assoc. prof. Brown U., Providence, 1969-79, Herbert Fanger meml. lectr., 1988; chmn. dept. immunology, dir. labs., sr. v.p. Mich. Cancer Found., Detroit, 1979-91; dir. breast cancer program Karmanos Cancer Inst., 1991—2003, dep. dir., 1994—2003; assoc. chair for rsch. dept. internal medicine Wayne State U. Sch. Medicine, Detroit, 1991—2001, asst. dean cancer program, 2002—03, spl. asst. to dean, Karmanos Cancer Inst., 2003, assoc. v.p. rsch., 2003—, interim v.p. rsch., 2006—. Mem. external adv. com. basic sci. program M.D. Anderson Hosp. and Tumor Clinic, Houston, 1984-94; mem. external adv. com. Case Western Res. U. Cancer Ctr., Cleve., 1988—, Roswell Park Meml. Inst., Buffalo, 1991-98; Sarah Stewart meml. lectr. Georgetown U., Washington, 1988; bd. sci. counselors Nat. Inst. Dental Rsch., 1993-97. Editor: Macrophages and Cancer, 1988; mem. editl. bd. Cancer Rsch., 1989-93, Jour. Nat. Cancer Inst., 1988, Sci., 1988-92; contbr. over 200 articles to sci. jours. Bd. dirs. Lyric Chamber Ensemble, 1996-99, Detroit Symphony Orch., 2005-. Recipient Mich. Sci. Trail-Blazer award State of Mich., 1987; fellow Damon Runyon-Walter Winchell Found., 1967-69. Mem. AAAS, Am. Assn. for Cancer Rsch. (bd. dirs. 1983-86, chmn. long-range planning com. 1989-91), Am. Assn. Immunologists, Metastasis Rsch. Soc. (bd. dirs. 1985-89), Women in Cancer Rsch. (nat. pres.), Internat. Differentiation Soc. (v.p. 1990-92, pres. 1992-94), LWV (bd. dirs. Grosse Pointe, Mich. 1989-95). Democrat. Avocations: music, theater. Office: 5057 Woodward Detroit MI 48201 Home Phone: 313-831-9038; Office Phone: 313-577-8848. E-mail: heppnerg@wayne.edu.

HERALD, J. PATRICK, lawyer; b. Latrobe, Pa., Sept. 27, 1947; s. John P. and Doris Faye (Galvin) H.; m. Bridget Grace Tobin, Aug. 17, 1973; children: Brian Michael, Matthew Patrick, Molly Bridget, John Francis. AB in History, John Carroll U., 1969; JD, U. Notre Dame Law Sch., 1972. Bar: Ill. 1972, U.S. Dist. Ct. (no. dist.) Ill. 1972, U.S. Ct. Appeals (7th cir.) 1975, U.S. Supreme Ct. 1978. Assoc. Baker & McKenzie, Chgo., 1972-79, ptnr., 1979—. Fellow Am. Coll. Trial Lawyers, Internat. Acad. Trial Lawyers; mem. ABA, Ill. Bar Assn., Chgo. Bar Assn., 7th Cir. Bar Assn., Soc. Trial Lawyers (bd. dirs. 1987-89), Internat. Assn. Def. Counsel, Chgo. Trial Lawyers Club (pres. 1982-83). Roman Catholic. Office: Baker & McKenzie 1 Prudential Plz 130 E Randolph St Fl 3500 Chicago IL 60601-6213 Home: 14 Sheffield Ln Oak Brook IL 60523 Office Phone: 312-861-2830. Business E-Mail: j.patrick.herald@bakernet.com.

HERB, MARVIN J., food products executive; b. 1937; BS, U. Buffalo, 1959; MBA, U. Toledo, 1964. Mgmt. trainee Kroger Co., Toledo, 1960-65; with Pepsi-Cola Co., Inc., 1965-72; various positions including pres. Pepsi-Cola Bottling Co. Indpls, Inc.; with Borden, Inc., NYC, 1972-76, v.p. dairy and svc. divsn., 1976-77, pres. dairy and svc. divsn., 1977-78, corp. v.p., pres. dairy and svc. divsn., 1978-81; chmn. bd. Hondo, Inc., Niles, Ill., 1981—. Trustee Loyola U., Chgo. Named one of Forbes' Richest Americans, 2006. Office: Hondo Inc 7400 N Oak Park Ave Niles IL 60714-3818

HERBERT, ADAM WILLIAM, JR., former academic administrator, educator; b. Muskogee, Okla., Dec. 1, 1943; s. Addie Herbert; m. Karen Y. Lofty, Apr. 1980. BA, U. So. Calif., 1966, MPA, 1967; PhD, U. Pitts., 1971. Instr., asst. prof., coord. acad. programs Ctr. Urban Affairs Sch. Pub. Adminstrn., U. So. Calif., LA, 1969-72; assoc. prof., chmn. urban affairs program div. environ. and urban systems Va. Poly. Inst. State U., Blacksburg, 1972-75, prof., dir. North Va. programs, Ctr. for Pub. Adminstrn. and Policy, 1978-79; White House fellow, spl. asst. sec. HEW, Washington, 1974-75; spl. asst. to under sec. HUD, Washington, 1975-77; prof., dean Fla. Internat. U., Miami, 1979-87, assoc. v.p. for acad. affairs, chief acad. officer North Miami campus, 1985-88, v.p., chief adminstrv. officer, 1987-88; pres. U. North Fla., Jacksonville, 1989—98; chancellor State Univ. Sys. of Fla., 1998—2001; Regents prof., exec. dir. Fla. Ctr. for Pub. Policy and Leadership U. North Fla., Jacksonville, Fla.; pres. Ind. Univ. Sys., Bloomington, 2003—07.

HERBERT, WILLIAM CARLISLE, lawyer; b. Gainesville, Fla., Aug. 25, 1947; s. Thomas Walter and Jean Elizabeth (Linton) H.; m. Mary Lee Dedinsky. AB, Princeton U., 1969; MSJ, orthwestern U., 1970, JD cum laude, 1976. Bar: Ill. 1976, US Ct. Appeals (7th cir.) 1977, Fla. 1978, US Dist. Ct. (no. dist.) Ill. 1978, US Supreme Ct. 1980, US Tax Ct. 1982. Law clk. to Hon. Latham Castle US Ct. Appeals (7th cir.), 1976-77; ptnr. Foley & Lardner, Chgo. Exec. editor Northwestern U. Law Rev., 1976. Mem. ABA, Ill. State Bar Assn., Fla. Bar, Chgo. Bar Assn., Legal Club Chgo., U. Club Chgo. Presbyterian. Office: Foley and Lardner 321 N Clark St 2700 Chicago IL 60610 Home Phone: 773-327-1092; Office Phone: 312-832-4551. E-mail: wcherbert@aol.com.

HERBRUCKS, STEPHEN, food products executive; b. 1950; m. Harry Herbrucks. Pres. Herbruck Poultry Ranch Inc., Saranac, Mich., Poultry Mgmt. Systems, Saranac, Mich., 1980—. Office: Herbruck Poultry Ranch Inc 6425 W Grand River Ave Saranac MI 48881-9669

HERBST, ARTHUR LEE, obstetrician, gynecologist; b. NYC, Sept. 14, 1931; s. Jerome Richard and Blanche (Vatz) H.; m. Lee Ginsburg, Aug. 10, 1958. AB magna cum laude, Harvard Coll., 1953, MD cum laude, 1959; DSc (hon.), N.E. Ohio U., 2001. Diplomate Am. Bd. Ob-gyn. (bd. dirs. 1985-93, dir. div. gynecol. oncology 1989-91). Intern Mass. Gen. Hosp., Boston, 1959—60, resident, 1960—62; resident in ob-gyn. Boston Hosp. for Women, 1962—65; instr., assoc. prof. ob-gyn. Mass. Gen. Hosp. and Harvard U. Med. Sch., Boston, 1965—76; Joseph B. DeLee prof. ob-gyn. U. Chgo., 1976—84, Joseph B. DeLee Disting. Service prof., 1984—2005, disting. prof. emeritus, 2005—; chmn. dept. ob-gyn. Chgo. Lying In Hosp., 1976—2001; chmn. exec. com. U. Chgo. Hosps. and Clinics, 1980. Chmn. dean's adv. bd. U. Ariz. Coll. Sci., 2006—. Contbr. articles to profl. jours. Nat. adv. coun. Wis. Alumni Rsch. Found., 2007—. Fellow Royal Coll. Obstetricians and Gynecologists (hon.), Inst. Med., Nat. Acad. Scis.; mem. AMA, ACS, ACOG, Am. Gynecol. and Obstet. Soc. (pres. 1997-98), Am. Assn. Profs. Ob-Gyn., Ctrl. Assn. Obstetricians and Gynecologists, Chgo. Gynecologic Soc., Soc. Pelvic Surgeons, Endocrine Soc., Infertility Soc., Soc. Gynecologic Oncologists. Home: 1234 N State Pkwy Chicago IL 60610-2219 Office: U Chgo Med Ctr 5841 S Maryland Ave MC2050 Chicago IL 60637-1463 Office Phone: 773-702-6671.

HERBST, ERIC, physicist, astronomer, chemist; b. NYC, Jan. 15, 1946; s. Stuart Karl and Dorothy (Polakoff) H.; m. Judith Strassman, Oct. 15, 1972; children: Elisabeth, Andrea, Seth. AB, U. Rochester, 1966; MA, Harvard U., 1969, PhD, 1972. Asst. prof. chemistry Coll. of William and Mary, Williamsburg, Va., 1974-79, assoc. prof.chemistry, 1979-80; assoc. prof. physics Duke U., Durham, NC, 1980-86, prof. physics, 1986-91, Univ. zu Köln, Cologne, Germany, 1988-89, Ohio State U., Columbus, 1991—, prof. astronomy, 1992—, prof. chemistry, 2003—. Cons. NASA, Washington, 1985-90, NSF, Washington, 1989-92. Contbr. over 290 articles and 25 revs. to profl. jours. Recipient Humboldt award Humboldt Found., 1988, Max Planck prize Max Planck Soc., 1993. Fellow Am. Phys. Soc., Royal Soc. Chem. (Centenary medal 2004); mem. Am. Astron. Soc., Am. Chem. Soc., Inst. Physics, Internat. Astron. Union. Achievements include theory of how organic molecules are formed in space; theory of floppy molecules. Office: Ohio State U Dept Physics 191 W Woodruff Ave Columbus OH 43210-1106 Home Phone: 614-292-6951; Office Phone: 614-292-6951. Business E-Mail: herbst@mps.ohio-state.edu.

HERBST, JAN FRANCIS, physicist, researcher; b. Tucson, May 1, 1947; s. Alva and Frances Theresa (Feler) H.; m. Margaret Mae Priest, July 24, 1982; children: Helen, John, Mary. BA in Physics, U. Pa., 1968, MS, 1968; PhD, Cornell U., 1974. Postdoctoral rsch. assoc. Nat. Bur. Standards, Gaithersburg, Md., 1974-76; asst. physicist Brookhaven Nat. Lab., Upton, NY, 1976-77; assoc. sr. rsch. physicist GM Rsch. Labs., Warren, Mich., 1977-81, staff rsch. scientist, 1981-85, mgr. magnetic materials sect., 1984—2002, sr. staff rsch. scientist, 1985-93, prin. rsch. scientist, 1993—, mgr. solid state materials for energy storage and conversion group, 2002—. Mem. basic energy scis. adv. com. Dept. Energy, 1996-2000, panel chair workshop on devel. of secure energy future, 2002; mem. panel for physics Nat. Rsch. Coun. bd. assessment NIST Programs, 2000—03. Contbr. articles over 100 to profl. jours. Recipient Campbell award GM Rsch. Labs., 1983, McCuen award GM Rsch. Labs., 1987, Kettering award GM Corp., 1987. Fellow Am. Phys. Soc. (sec.-treas. div. condensed matter physics 1985-90, nominating com. 1996-98, Internat. prize for new materials 1986). Achievements include patents in field. Avocations: reading, numismatics. Office: GM R&D Ctr MC 480-106-224 30500 Mound Rd Warren MI 48090-9055 Business E-Mail: jan.f.herbst@gm.com.

HERINGTON, LEIGH ELLSWORTH, state legislator, lawyer; b. Rochester, NY, Aug. 8, 1945; s. Donald G. and Ethel (Buck) H.; m. Anita Dixon, Dec. 12, 1970; children: Laurie, Tanya. AAS, Alfred State Coll., 1965; BBA, Kent State U., 1967, MBA, 1971; JD, U. Akron, 1976. Bar: Ohio 1976. Asst. sports info. dir. Kent State U., Ohio, 1969-70, asst. coord. internal comm., 1970-71, asst. dir. alumni rels., 1971-72; dir. pub. rels. Walsh Coll., Canton, Ohio, 1972-73; dir. comm. Hiram Coll., Ohio, 1973-77; sole practice Aurora, Ohio, 1977-78; mem. Ohio Senate from 28th dist., Columbus, 1994—; ptnr. Christley, Herington & Pierce, Aurora, Ohio, 1978—. Instr. law Hiram Coll., 1978—. Pres. Crestwood Bd. Edn., Portage County, Ohio, 1981; pres. Portage County United Way, 1984; chmn. crusade Am. Cancer Soc., served U.S. Army, 1968-69; v.p. Robinson Memorial Hos. Found.; chair Cancer Soc. Recipient Pres.'s award Portage County United Way, 1983; named Alumnus of Yr., Kent State U. Bus. Coll., 1984; Vol. of Yr., Portage County, 1986. Mem. ABA, Ohio State Bar Assn., Portage County Bar Assn., bd. attys. Ohio Coun. Sch., Pub. Rels. Soc. Am., Aurora-Streetsboro Club (charter), Rotary Club. Democrat. Office: Christley Herington & Pierce 215 W Garfield Rd Aurora OH 44202-8849 Address: 4039 Hardin Rd Ravenna OH 44266-9313 Office Phone: 330-562-3156. Office Fax: 330-562-9540. Business E-Mail: leh@chpohiolaw.com.

HERMAN, RICHARD H., academic administrator; m. Susan Herman. BA cum laude, Stevens Inst. Tech., 1963; PhD in Math., U. Md. Various positions UCLA, 1968—72, Pa. State U., 1972—90; dean Coll. Computer, Math. and Phys. Scis. U. Md., College Park, 1990—98; provost, vice chancellor acad. affairs U. Ill., Urbana-Champaign, 1998—, interim chancellor, 2004—05, chancellor, 2005—. Chmn. adv. com. for directorate math. and phys. sci. NSF; chair Joint Policy Bd. for Math.; mem. adv. bd. Mellon Coll. Sci. Contbr. articles to profl. jours. Bd. dirs. United Way, Champaign County C. of C. Fellow, Alexander von Humboldt Found. Mem.: Assn. Univs. for Rsch. in Astronomy, Inc. (mem. obs. coun.), Sigma Xi, Tau Beta Pi. Office: Office of Chancellor 204 Swanlund Adminstrn Bldg 601 E John St Champaign IL 61820

HERMAN, SARAH ANDREWS, lawyer; b. Fargo, ND, June 20, 1952; BA magna cum laude, U. N.D., 1974; JD, U. Mich., 1977. Bar: N.D. 1977, U.S. Dist. Ct. N.D. 1978. With illes, Hansen & Davies, Ltd., Fargo, ND, 1977—94, bd. dirs.; ptnr., trial and labor and employment practice groups Dorsey & Whitney LLP, ptnr. in charge Fargo office, 1997—, co-head labor employment group, 1996—2000, mgmt. com. mem., group head for firm-wide regulatory group: Labor and Employment, Energy, Environ., Legislative, Indian, and Gaming, 2000—05. Mem. Fed. Practice Com., 8th Cir. Gender Task Force. Co-chair N.D. Gender Fairness, 1993-94. Mem. ND State Bar Assn. (pres. 2000), Cass County Bar Assn. Office: Dorsey & Whitney LLP Ste 402 Dakota Ctr 51 N Broadway Fargo ND 58102 Office Phone: 701-235-6000. Office Fax: 701-235-9969. Business E-Mail: herman.sarah@dorsey.com.

HERMAN, SIDNEY N., lawyer; b. Chgo., May 14, 1953; s. Leonard M. and Suzanne (Nierman) H.; m. Meg Dobies. BA, Haverford Coll., 1975; JD, Northwestern U., 1978. Bar: Ill. 1978, U.S. Dist. Ct. (no. dist.) Ill. 1978, U.S. Ct. Appeals (7th cir.) 1982, U.S. Supreme Ct. 1983. Assoc. Kirkland & Ellis, Chgo., 1978-84, equity ptnr., 1984-93; founding ptnr. Bartlit Beck Herman Palenchar & Scott, Chgo., 1993—. Bd. dirs. Todd Shipyards Corp., Sigmatron, Inc., Chgo., Global Material Techs., Chgo. Lawyers' Com. for Civil Rights Under Law, Inc.; mem. law bd. Northwestern U. Sch. Law. Articles editor Northwestern U. Law Rev. Trustee Francis W. Parker Sch.; bd. mem. Chgo. Lawyers' com. for Civil Rights Under Law. Mem. ABA, Ill. Bar Assn. Jewish. Office: Bartlit Beck Et Al Courthouse Pl 54 W Hubbard St Ste 300 Chicago IL 60610-4668 Office Phone: 312-494-4400. Business E-Mail: skip.herman@bartlit-beck.com.

HERMANN, ROBERT JOSEPH, bishop; b. Weingarten, Mo., Aug. 12, 1934; BA in Philosophy, Cardinal Glennon Coll., St. Louis, 1959; attended, Kenrick Sem., St. Louis, 1963; MA in English, St. Louis U., 1966. Ordained priest Archdiocese of St. Louis, 1963; asst. pastor Our Lady Help of Christians Parish, Weingarten, 1963, St. Catherine of Siena, Pagedale, Mo., 1963—64, St. Cronan Parish, St. Louis, 1964—68; assoc. pastor Holy Ghost Parish, Berkeley, Mo., 1968—72, Holy Cross Parish, Baden, Mo., 1972—76, Most Holy Trinity Parish, St. Louis, 1976—79, St. Pius X Parish, Glasgow Village, Mo., 1979—82; pastor St. Andrew Parish, Lemay, Mo., 1982—88, Incarnate Word Parish, Chesterfield, Mo., 1988—2002; ordained bishop, 2002; aux. bishop Archdiocese of St. Louis, 2002—. Tchr. DeAndreas HS, St. Louis, 1966—67, St. Louis Prep. Sem. North, 1967—69; supr., acolyte internship program Kenrick Sem., 1982—2001. Roman Catholic. Office: Archdiocese of St Louis 4445 Lindell Blvd Saint Louis MO 63108 Office Phone: 314-633-2282. Office Fax: 314-633-2305. Business E-Mail: rhermann@archstl.org.*

HERMELING, CAROLINE L., lawyer; b. St. Louis, 1961; BA in Econs., U. Notre Dame, 1983; JD cum laude, St. Louis U., 1986. Bar: Mo. 1986, Ill. 1987, US Dist. Ct. (ea. dist. Mo.). Mng. ptnr. to bd. ptnr. Husch Blackwell Sanders LLP. Recipient Vol. Lawyer award, Legal Svcs. of Ea. Mo. Vol. Lawyers Prog., 2001, Justice award, St. Louis Daily Record, 2007. Mem.: Ill. State Bar Assn., Comml. Real Estate Women. Office: Husch & Eppenberger LLC Ste 600 190 Carondelet Plz Saint Louis MO 63105-3441 Office Phone: 314-480-1922. Office Fax: 314-480-1505. E-mail: carrie.l.hermeling@husch.com.

HERMES, MARJORY RUTH, machine embroidery and arts educator; b. Caldwell, Kans., June 28, 1931; d. Truman Homer and Olive Ruth (Ridings) Brown; m. Ogden S. Jones, Jr., Dec. 17, 1949 (div. Aug. 1956); m. Richard Lawrence Hermes, July 18, 1963 (dec. Feb. 5, 2005); children: Penelope, Peter, Deborah, Patricia, Pamela, Kristin. Student, U. Kans., 1949-50, Arkansas City Jr. Coll., 1953-54. Sec. Maurer-Neuer Corp., Arkansas City, Kans., 1954-56, Lesh, Bradley & Barrand, Lawrence, Kans., 1959-60; exec. sec. Houston Corp., Wichita, Kans., 1956-57; mgr. Ind. Ins. Co., Landstuhl, Fed. Republic Germany, 1960-62; sec. U. Kans., Lawrence, 1962-63; photograph restorer Herb's Studio, Lawrence, 1977-78; ptnr., agt. Hayes-Richardson-Santee Inc., Lawrence, 1978-83; instr. sewing and machine embroidery Self & Bob's Bernina, Lawrence, 1985-95. Mem. Lawrence Ins. Bd., 1980-83. Bd. dirs. United Way, Lawrence, 1981-83; host Am. Indian Athletic Hall of Fame, 1980-82; treas. local polit. campaigns, 1984, 88; leader Therapeutic Horse Riding Instrn., Lawrence, 1992-95; vol. Lawrence Sr. Ctr., 1999-2001. Mem. Nat. Machine Embroidery Instrs. Assn. (bd. dirs. for N.D., S.D., Nebr., Iowa, Mo., Minn. and Kans. 1987-90), Am. Sewing Guild, Am. Bus. Women's Assn. (v.p. Lawrence 1980-81, pres. 1981-82, Inner Circle award 1982, Woman of Yr. award 1984), Lawrence C. of C. (envoy 1978-83). Republican. Avocations: horsemanship, travel, sailing. Home: 2513 W 24th Ter Lawrence KS 66047-2818

HERNANDEZ, RAMON ROBERT, retired minister, school librarian; b. Chgo., Feb. 23, 1936; s. Eleazar Dario and Marie Helen Hernandez; m. Fern Ellen Muschinske, Aug. 11, 1962; children: Robert Frank, Maria Marta. BA, Elmhurst Coll., Ill., 1957; BD, Eden Theol. Sem., St. Louis, 1962; MA, U. Wis., 1970. Co-pastor St. Stephen United Ch. Christ, Merrill, Wis., 1960-64; dir. youth work Wis. Conf. United Ch. Christ, Madison, 1964-70; dir. T.B. Scott Free Library, Merrill, 1970-75, McMillan Meml. Library, Wisconsin Rapids, Wis., 1975-83, Ann Arbor (Mich.) Pub. Library, 1983-94; pastor Comty. Congl. Ch., Pinckney, Mich., 1994-98. Seminar leader on pub. libr. long-range planning, budgeting and handling problem patrons. Editl. com. mem. Songs of Many Nations Songbook, 1970; contbr. articles to profl. jours. Treas. Ann Arbor Homeless Coalition, 1985-88; bd. dirs., sec., v.p. Riverview Hosp. Assn., Wisconsin Rapids, 1977-83; bd. dirs. Hist. Soc. Mich., 1988-90, Ind. Living, Inc., Dane County, Wis., 2001-03; trustee Madison Pub. Libr, Wis., 2000-06 Mem. ALA, Wis. Libr. Assn. (Leadership award 1980, pres. 1980), Rotary (pres. Merrill chpt. 1974-75, Community Svc. award 1975, pres. Ann Arbor chpt. 1990-91, Paul Harris fellow 1994).

HERNANDEZ, ROBERTO, professional baseball player; b. Santurce, PR, Nov. 11, 1964; Student, U. S.C. Pitcher Chgo. White Sox, 1991-97, San Francisco Giants, 1997, Tampa Bay Devil Rays, 1998—2000, Kansas City Royals, 2001—02, Atlanta Braves, 2003, Phila. Phillies, 2004, NY Mets, 2005. Office: NY Mets 126 St and Roosevelt Ave Flushing NY 11368

HERPE, DAVID A., lawyer; b. Chgo., May 2, 1953; s. Richard S. and Beverly H.; m. Tina Demsetz, Aug. 21, 1977; children: Lauren E., Stacy P. BA in Econs., U. Ill., 1975; JD, U. Chgo., 1978. Bar: Ill. 1978, U.S. Dist. Ct. (no. dist.) Ill. 1979, U.S. Tax Ct. 1991. Assoc. then ptnr. Schiff, Hardin & Waite, Chgo., 1978-1996; ptnr. McDermott, Will & Emery, Chgo., 1996—. Co-author: Illinois Estate Planning, Will Drafting and Estate Administration Forms-Practice, 2nd edit., 1994; contbr. articles to legal jours. Mem. and dir. Chgo. Estate Planning Coun. (pres. 2000-01). Fellow Am. Coll. of Trust and Estate Counsel; mem. ABA. Office: McDermott Will & Emery 227 W Monroe St Ste 3100 Chicago IL 60606-5096

HERR, DAVID FULTON, lawyer, educator; b. St. Paul, July 13, 1950; s. Robert and Janet H.; m. Mary Kay Strand, Oct. 25, 1986; children: Ehrland A. Truitt, Alec F. BA, U. Colo., 1972, MBA, 1977; JD cum laude, William Mitchell Coll. Law, 1978. Bar: Minn. 1978, U.S. Dist. Ct. Minn. 1978, U.S. Ct. Appeals (8th cir.) 1978, U.S. Ct. Appeals (3rd cir.) 1983, U.S. Claims Ct. 1986, U.S. Supreme Ct., 1989. Assoc. Robins, Davis & Lyons, Mpls., 1978-81; from assoc. to ptnr., appleate litig. Maslon Edelman Borman & Brand, Mpls., 1981—. Adj. prof. William Mitchell Coll. Law, St. Paul, 1978—. Author: Multidistrict Litigation, 1986, (with others) Motion Practice, 1986, 3d edit., 1998, Discovery Practice, 1982, 4th edit., 2005, Minnesota Practice, 1986, 4th edit., 2005, Annotated Manual for Complex Litig. Manual, 2005, Multidistrict Litig., 2005, and other works. Fellow Am. Acad. Appellate Lawyers (pres. 2004-05); mem. Am. Law Inst., Minn. State Bar (chmn. litigation sect. 1985-86, task force on complex litigation 1990—, Advocate's award 1999), Hennepin County Bar Assn., Ramsey County Bar Assn., Lawyers-Pilots Bar Assn. Office: Maslon Edelman Borman & Brand LLP 3300 Wells Fargo Ctr 90 S 7th St Minneapolis MN 55402 Office Phone: 612-672-8350. Office Fax: 612-642-8350. Business E-Mail: david.herr@maslon.com.

HERRELL, RON, state representative; b. Rochester, Ind., Dec. 1, 1948; married. Assoc. degree, Ind. U., 1980. Ret. inspector Kokomo Fire Dept.; state rep. dist. 30 Ind. Ho. of Reps., Indpls., 1998—, mem. environ. affairs, ins., corps. and small bus., and ways and means coms. Former med. corpsman US Army. Mem.: Farm Bur., VFW 1152. Democrat. Office: Ind Ho of Reps 200 W Washington St Indianapolis IN 46204-2786

HERRERA, ALBERTO, JR., librarian; b. Bogotá, Colombia, Feb. 24, 1947; s. Alberto Herrera Salazár and Ada Emma (Miller) H.; m. Susan Louise Poorman, Aug. 21, 1971 (div. Dec. 1979). BS in Polit. Sci., U. Wis., 1968, MA in LS, 1982; MA in History, U. Oreg., 1973, postgrad., 1974-79. Grad. teaching fellow in history U. Oreg., Eugene, 1970-71, 74-78; claims rep. Social Security Adminstrn., Santa Ana, Riverside, Eureka, Calif., 1971-73; freelance hist. rschr., Eugene, 1978; job svc. rep. Oreg. Employment Div., Eugene, 1979-81; intern Libr. of Congress, 1982-83; reference libr. Congl. Rsch. Svc. Libr. of Congress, Washington, 1983-84; Am. history specialist Libr. of Congress, Washington, 1984-87; history reference and outreach libr. Golda Meir Libr., U. Wis., Milw., 1987-93; head of ref., 1993—; adj. instr. Sch. Libr. and Info. U. Wis., Milw., 1990, 91. Mem. Hispanic Coun. U. Wis., 1988—. Scholar Nat. Hispanic Scholarship Fund, 1978; Lyman Copeland Draper fellow, 1981. Mem. ALA, Assn. of Coll. and Rsch. Librs., Wis. Libr. Assn., Wis. Assn. Acad. Librs., Orgn. Am. Historians (contbg. editor for microforms Jour. Am. History 1988—), Western History Assn., State Hist. Soc. Wis. Avocations: photography, drawing, nature. Office: U Wis Golda Meir Libr PO Box 604 Milwaukee WI 53201-0604

HERRICK, TODD W., manufacturing executive; b. Tecumseh, Mich., 1942; Grad., U. Notre Dame, 1967. Dir. Tecumseh (Mich.) Products Co., 1973—, pres., COO, 1984—, CEO, 1987—2007, chmn. bd., 2003—07; chmn. emeritus Tecumseh (Mich.) Products Ct., 2007. Bd. trustees Howe Mil. Sch. Bd. mem. US C. of C. Capt. US Army. Office: Tecumseh Products Co 100 E Patterson St Tecumseh MI 49286-2087 Office Fax: 517-423-8760.

HERRIFORD, ROBERT LEVI, SR., retired military officer; b. Lewistown, Ill., May 4, 1931; s. John and Lola (Braden) H.; m. Muriel Jean Davis, July 10, 1949; children: Robert Levi, Thomas Merle, David William, Deborah S., Traci Ann. BS, U. Ariz., 1966, MBA, 1968. Enlisted U.S. Army, 1948, commd. 2d lt., 1952, advanced through grades to maj. gen., 1979; service in Vietnam, 1966-67; comdr. 269th Ordnance Group Ft. Bragg, NC, 1969-71; chief spl. items mgmt. Tank Automotive Command Detroit, 1971-72; comdr. Korean Procurement Agy. Seoul, 1973-74; dir. procurement Armaments Command Rock Island, Ill., 1974-76; comdr. Def. Contracts Region NY, 1976-78; asst. dep. chief of staff logistics Pentagon, 1978-80; dir. procurement and prodn. Devel. and Readiness Command Alexandria, Va., 1980-83; assoc. chief ops. officer, dir. support svcs. Argonne Nat. Lab., Ill., 1983—95; ret., 1995. Chmn. Minority Bus. Opportunity Council, N.Y.C., 1976-78. Decorated Legion of Merit, D.S.M., Def. Superior Service medal, Bronze Star, Airmedal, numerous others. Mem. Am. Def. Preparedness Assn., Assn. U.S. Army, Am. Legion, Nat. Contracts Mgmt. Assn. (chpt. pres. 1975-76) Office Phone: 217-793-1049. Personal E-mail: RobLHerr@insightbb.com.

HERRIN, MORELAND, retired engineering educator; b. Morris, Okla., Nov. 14, 1922; s. Birney D. and Lucille (Moreland) H.; m. Nancy M. Jameson, Dec. 24, 1946; children— Jeannie N., Stanley M., Gwen M. BSCE, Okla. State U., 1947, MS, 1949; PhD, Purdue U., 1954. Instr. Okla. State U., 1947-49, assoc. prof., 1954-58; prof. civil engring. U. Ill., Urbana, 1958—; ret. Dir. Ill. Coop. Transp. Program; design engr. Hudgins, Thompson & Ball (engrs.), Oklahoma City, 1949-50; materials engr. Garnett, Fleming, Cordray and Carpenter, Belvidere, Ill., 1957; asst. materials engr., road test Am. Assn. State Hwy. Ofcls., Ottawa, Ill., 1958; cons. hwy. materials, pavement design, 1955— Contbr. articles to profl. jours. Served to capt. USAAF, 1943-46. Recipient Epstein award U. Ill., 1962 Mem. Transp. Research Bd., Assn. Asphalt Paving Technology (pres. 1978), ASCE, Am. Soc. Engring. Edn., ASTM, Chi Epsilon, Tau Beta Pi. Mem. Christian Ch. (Disciples Of Christ). Home: 1414 W William St Champaign IL 61821-4407 Office: 1208 NCEL 205 N Mathews Ave Urbana IL 61801-2350

HERRMANN, DAN, food products executive; CFO Schwan's Sales Ent., Marshall, Minn.; v.p., CFO home svcs. Schwan's, 2002—. Office: Schwan's Sales Enterprises 115 W College Dr Marshall MN 56258 Office Fax: (507) 537-8450.

HERRON, DAVID A., stock exchange executive; Grad., U. Calif., Berkeley, 1976. Floor reporter Pacific Stock Exch., mem. and specialist, Boston Stock Exch., 1982—84; various positions Fidelity Investments, 1984—98; v.p. listed equities Charles Schwab & Co., Inc., 1998; CEO Chgo. Stock Exch. (CHX), 2002—, CHX Holdings, Inc. Gov. Boston Stock Exch., 1991; trustee Cin. Stock Exch., 1996—2001; ofcl. Am. Stock Exch. Bd. mem. Ill. Coun. Edn., Midwest Regional Bd. of Operation Hope. Mem.: Security Traders Assn. Chgo. (bd. mem.). Office: Chgo Stock Exch One Financial Pl 440 S LaSalle St Chicago IL 60605

HERRON, ORLEY R., college president; b. Olive Hill, Ky., Nov. 16, 1933; s. Orley R. and Hyllie W. (Weaver) H.; m. Donna Jean Morgan, Aug. 24, 1956; children: Jill Donette, Morgan Niles, Mark Weaver. BA, Wheaton Coll., 1955; MA, Mich. State U., 1959, PhD, 1965; LittD (hon.), Houghton Coll., 1972; LHD (hon.), Lesley Coll., 1983. Dean of students Westmont Coll., Santa Barbara, Calif., 1961-67; dir. doctoral program/student pers. U. Miss., 1967-68; asst. to pres. Ind. State U., 1968-70; pres. Greenville (Ill.) Coll., 1970-77, Nat Louis U. (formerly Nat. Coll. Edn.), Evanston, Ill., 1977-97; chmn., pres. ORH group eBooks Interactive, 1998—; founder AutoeDirect.com, Inc., 2000—; chmn., CEO Herron Multimedia, 2001—, BOT-Best of Thrift Travel, 2003—; chmn. Significant Living, 2003—; chmn., CEO Premier Entertainment, 2005—. Mem. Ill. Commn. for Improvement Elem. and Secondary Edn., 1983-1985; chmn. bd. Harris Bank, Wilmette, Ill., 1991—, also bd. dirs.; bd. dirs. Corp. Cmty. Schs. Am., 1989—. Author: Role of the Trustee, 1969, Input-Output, 1970, New Dimensions in Stude Personnel Administration, 1970, A Christian Executive in a Secular World, 1979, Who Controls Your Child?, 1980, Words to Live By, 1997, Notes for the New Millennium, 2000, Song of Blessing, 2004; (cassette) Governing Higher Education in the 70's, 1970; exec. prodr., composer, songwriter (CD) I Love You My Dearest Darling, 2001, (featuring Orley Herron and The Crew Cuts) Until We Meet Again, 2005. Rep. of Pres. U.S. 25th Anniversary UNESCO, 1971; adv. bd. Expt. on Internat. Living, Santa Barbara, 1961-67; mem. Gov.'s Task Force on Encouraging Citizen Involvement in Edn., 1986-87; nat. dir. educators for reelection of Pres., 1972; bd. dirs. Ch. Centered Evangelism; mem. Chgo. Sun. Evening Club, 1987-97; founder Santa Barbara Industries. Lt. comdr. U.S. aval Res., 1973-77. Recipient Crusader Christian Contbn. award Wheaton Coll., 1955, 74, Outstanding Citizen award Greenville Jaycees, 1971, Outstanding Educator award Religious Heritage of Am., 1987, Disting. Alumnus award Wheaton Coll., Outstanding Alumnus award New Philadelphia H.S., Amicus Polonae award, 1996. Mem. AAUP, SAG, Am. Assn. Higher Edn., Coun. Inter-Instnl. Cooperation (pres.), Coun. Advancement Small Colls. (sec.), Christian Coll. Consortium (exec. com.), Fedn. Ind. Ill. Colls. (exec. bd. 1971-97), Assn. Free Meth. Ednl. Instns. (pres. 1973-75), Rotary, Kiwanis. Office Phone: 847-295-4221.

HERRUP, KARL, neurobiologist; b. Pitts., July 16, 1948; s. J. Lester and Florence Bernice Herrup; m. Claire Morse, Aug. 20, 1972 (div. Jan. 1989); children: Rachael, Adam, Alex; m. Leslie Reinherz, Mar. 1, 1992; 1 adopted child, Leah. BA in Biology magna cum laude, Brandeis U., 1970; PhD in Neuro-and Behavioral Sci., Stanford U., 1974. Postdoctoral fellow in neurogenetics Harvard Med. Sch./Children's Hosp., Boston, 1974-77; postdoctoral fellow in pharmacology Biozentrum, Basel, Switzerland, 1978; asst. prof., then assoc. prof. human genetics Sch. Medicine Yale U., New Haven, 1978-84, assoc. prof. biology, 1986-88; assoc. prof. neurology Mass. Gen. Hosp., Boston, 1988-92; assoc. prof. neurosci. Harvard Med. Sch., Boston, 1988-92; dir. div. devel. neurobiology Eunice Kennedy Shriver Ctr. for Mental Retardation, Waltham, Mass., 1988-92; prof. Alzheimer Rsch. Ctr. Case Western Sch. Medicine, Cleve., 1992—, dir. Univ. Alzheimer Ctr., 1997—. Mem. staff Yale Comprehensive Cancer Ctr., New Haven, 1987-88. Contbr. articles to profl. publs.; mem. editorial bd. Jour. of Comprehensive Neurology, Neurobiology of Aging, Jour. of Neurosci. Fellow NSF, 1978, Med. Found., 1976, Jane Coffin Childs Meml. Rsch. Fund, 1974; recipient faculty award Andrew W. Mellon Found., 1982. Mem. Soc. for Neurosci. (mem. social issues com. 1987-90, program com. 1989-92, edn. com. 1992—, sec. Conn. chpt. 1982-84, v.p. 1987-88), Soc. for Devel. Biology, Sigma Xi. Office: Case Western Res Med Sch Alzheimer Rsch Lab 10900 Euclid Ave Cleveland OH 44106-1712

HERSETH, ADOLPH SYLVESTER (BUD HERSETH), classical musician; b. Lake Park, Minn., July 25, 1921; Student, New England Conservatory, Boston. Prin. trumpet player Chgo. Symphony Orch., 1948—. With U.S. Army, World War II. Named Instrumentalist of Yr., Musical Am., 1996. Office: care Chgo Symphony Orch Orchestra Hall 220 S Michigan Ave Chicago IL 60604-2596

HERSHER, RICHARD DONALD, management consultant; b. Atlantic City, May 24, 1942; s. Mayo Lawrence and Adele (Dahlman) H.; m. Betsy R. Schnitz, Mar. 15, 1970 (div. June 1983); children: Erin, Laura; m. Roza Khazina, Sept. 4, 1993. BS, U. Cin., 1966; MBA, U. Chgo., 1973. Indsl. engr. U.S. Steel Corp., Chgo., 1966-68; mfg. engr. Westinghouse Electric Corp., Chgo., 1968-73; sr. indsl. engr. Abbott Labs., North Chicago, Ill., 1973-76; plant mgr. DeMert & Dougherty, Chgo., 1976-79; pres. Hersher Assocs., Deerfield, Ill., 1979-83; exec. cons. Inst. Mgmt. Resources, Westlake Village, Calif., 1983-87; v.p. ops. Rex Precision Products, Gardena, Calif., 1987; sr. cons. Morris Anderson & Assocs., Rosemont, Ill., 1987-92; pres. Hersher Cons., Glenview, Ill., 1992—2003; sr. cons. Focus Mgmt. Group, 2003—. Mem. Inst. Indsl. Engrs., Am. Prodn. Inventory Control Soc. Personal E-mail: rhersher1@sbcglobal.net.

HERSTEIN, CARL WILLIAM, lawyer; b. Plainfield, NJ, Jan. 8, 1953; s. Robert L. and Marie (Burke) H.; m. Charlene Ruth Mosher, Aug. 16, 1975; children: Janette, Matthew, Diana, Jennifer. BA in Polit. Sci. with high distinction, highest honors, U. Mich., 1973; JD, Yale U., 1976. Bar: Mich. 1976. Congl. intern to Congressman Clarence Long Washington, 1972; acting divsnl. paymaster Parts Divsn. GM, Flint, Mich., 1973; law clk. Benton Hicks Beltz Behm & Nikola, Flint, 1974; ptnr. Honigman Miller Schwartz and Cohn LLP, Detroit, 1976—. Mem. fin. instns. adv. bd. U. Detroit-Mercy, 1985-95. Editor Yale Law Jour., 1975-76. Trustee John and Marnee Divine Found., Detroit, 1985—90; treas. Cath. Soc. Svcs. of Washtenaw County, Mich., 1990—92, chair, 1992—93; bd. dirs. St. Francis Parish, Ann Arbor, 1985—91, edn. commn, rep, 1990—91. Recipient William Jennings Bryan prize, 1973; James B. Angell scholar, 1973. Fellow Mich. State Bar Found.; mem. State Bar Mich., U. Mich. Pres. Club, U. Mich. Victors Club, U. Mich. Alumni Assn., Yale U. Alumni

Assn., KC, Otsego Ski Club, Ann Arbor Golf & Outing Country Club, Huron Valley Swim Club, Phi Beta Kappa, Mich. Supreme Ct. Hist. Soc. (bd.dirs., 2000—), U. Musical Soc. (vice chair, 2002—). Republican. Roman Catholic. Avocations: reading, skiing, golf, travel, drawing. Office: Honigman Miller Schwartz & Cohn LLP 2290 1st National Bldg 660 Woodward Detroit MI 48226

HERZBERG, THOMAS, artist, educator, illustrator; b. Chgo., Feb. 3, 1954; s. Carroll Alexander and Victoria Herzberg; m. Rosemary Ann Morrissey, Aug. 11, 1979; 1 child, Kyli Rose. BA, Northeastern U., 1975; MFA, No. Ill. U., 1979. Instr. Am. Acad. Art, Chgo., 2000—, fine art dept. chair, 2005—. Illustrations appeared in Chgo. mag., Advertising Age, Playboy mag., World Book, Chgo. Tribune, Washington Post, Art Inst. Chgo., Goodman Theatre, Chg. Exhibited Art Inst. Chgo., 1978, 84, De Cordova Mus., Lincoln., Mass., 1978-79, 83, Silvermine Guild Artists, New Canaan, Conn., 1980, Met. Mus. and Art Ctr., Coral Gables, Fla., 1980, 82, Hunterdon Art Ctr., Clinton, NJ, 1982, U. Dallas, 1983, 10th, 12th and 13th Ann. Soc. Newpaper Design, Am. Soc. Illustrators 28th, 39th and 41st Ann. Exhbns., 141st Am. Watercolour Soc., 2007, Ill. Watercolour Soc., 24th Show, 2008; represented in permanent collections USAF, De Cordova Mus., Terrance Gallery, Palenville, NY, Met. Mus. and Art Ctr., Silvermine Guild Artists, Carnegie Inst., Art Inst. Chgo., Lincoln Park Zoo, Chgo. Symphony Orch.; over 1900 illustrations in newspapers, mags., books, mus. graphics, 1981—. Mem. Air Force Art Program, 1998—, governing bd., 2004. Named Best of Show 3 Ann. Ill. Regional Print Show, 1980; recipient Award of Excellence New Horizons in Art North Shore Art League, 1980-82, Weston Press and Gallery award 8th Internat. Miniature Print Exhbn. Pratt Graphic Ctr., 1981, Cert. of Design Excellence Print's Regional Design Ann., 1994-97, also numerous awards Art Direction mag. creativity show, 1992-93, Soc. Newspaper Design, Cert. of Merit Soc. Illustrators. Office Phone: 312-461-0600. Personal E-mail: therzb@earthlink.net.

HERZENBERG, CAROLINE STUART LITTLEJOHN, physicist; b. East Orange, NJ, Mar. 25, 1932; d. Charles Frederick and Caroline Dorothea (Schulze) Littlejohn; m. Leonardo Herzenberg, July 29, 1961; children: Karen Ann, Catherine Stuart. SB, MIT, 1953; SM, U. Chgo., 1955, PhD, 1958; DSc (hon.), SUNY, Plattsburgh, 1991. Asst. prof. Ill. Inst. Tech., Chgo., 1961-66, research physicist ITT Research Inst., 1967-70, sr. physicist, 1970-71; lectr. Calif. State U., Fresno, 1975-76; physicist Argonne (Ill.) Nat. Lab., Ill., 1977-2001. Prin. investigator NASA Apollo Returned Lunar Sample Analysis Program, 1967—71; disting. vis. prof. SUNY, Plattsburgh, 1991; mem. final selection com. Bower award and prize for Achievement in Sci., 1993—94, bd. adv.; mem. nat. panel advisors PBS TV Bill Nye the Sci. Guy, 1991—95; mem. steering com. Midwest Consortium Internat. Security Studies, 1994—95. Prodr., host (TV series) Camera on Science; author: Women Scientists from Antiquity to the Present: An Index, 1986; author: (with R. H. Howes) Their Day in the Sun: Women of the Manhattan Project, 1999; contbr. articles to profl. jours. Past chmn. NOW chpt., Freeport, Ill.; candidate for alderman Freeport, 1975. Finalist Am. Phys. Soc. Congl. Scientist Fellowship, 1976—77; recipient award in sci., Chgo. Women's Hall of Fame, 1989. Fellow: AAAS, Assnq. Women in Sci. (nat. sec. 1982—84, pres. 1988—90), Am. Phys. Soc. (past chmn. com., past sec.-treas. Forum Physics and Soc., chair elect, past exec. bd. Forum History Physics, mem. panel pub. affairs); mem.: Sigma Xi. Home and Office: 1700 E 56th St Apt 2707 Chicago IL 60637-5092 E-mail: carol@herzenberg.net.

HERZIG, DAVID JACOB, retired pharmaceutical company executive, consultant; b. Cleve., Dec. 13, 1936; s. Marvin Laurence and Lillian Gertrude (Blaine) H.; m. Phyllis Glicksberg, Sept. 2, 1962; children: Michael, Pamela, Roberta, Karen. BA, Oberlin Coll., 1958; PhD in Chemistry, U. Cin., 1963. Vis. scientist NIH, Bethesda, Md., 1963-65, staff fellow, 1965-67; sr. rsch. assoc. NYU Sch. Medicine, NYC, 1967-68, Warner Lambert, Parke-Davis Co., Ann Arbor, Mich., 1968-77, dir. immunopharmacology, 1977-81, dir. sci. devel., 1981—91, v.p. drug devel. and sci. devel., 1991—99. Contbr. articles to profl. jours. Bd. dirs. Mich. Ctr. High Tech., 1992-95. Fellow Damon Runyon Meml. Fund. Mem. Licensing Exec. Soc., Mich. Biotech. Assn. (bd. dirs. 1993-96, pres. 1994-96), .Y. Acad. Scis., N.Y. Fencers Club (bd. dirs. 1970-77), Sigma Xi. Avocations: squash, fencing, furniture building. Home and Office: 3540 Windemere Dr Ann Arbor MI 48105-2842 E-mail: davidjhherzig@world.oberlin.edu, dherzig01@yahoo.com.

HESBURGH, THEODORE MARTIN, clergyman, former university president; b. Syracuse, NY, May 25, 1917; s. Theodore Bernard and Anne Marie (Murphy) H. Student, U. Notre Dame, 1934-37; PhB, Gregorian U., 1939; postgrad., Holy Cross Coll., Washington, 1940-43; STD, Cath. U. Am., 1945; 124 hon. degrees awarded between 1954-92. Joined Order of Congregation of Holy Cross, 1934, ordained priest Roman Cath. Ch., 1943. Chaplain Nat. Tng. Sch. for Boys, Washington, 1943-44; vets. chaplain U. Notre Dame, 1945-47, 138 hon. degrees awarded between 1954-98, 1948-49, exec. v.p., 1949-52, pres., 1952-87, pres. emeritus, 1987—, instr., asst. prof. religion, 1945-48, chmn. dept. religion, 1948-49. Fellow Am. Acad. Arts and Scis.; mem. Internat. Fedn. Cath. Univs., Commn. on Humanities, Inst. Internat. Edn. (pres., dir.), Cath. Theol. Soc., Chief Execs. Forum, Am. Philos. Soc., Nat. Acad. Edn., Coun. on Fgn. Rels. (trustee), Nat. Acad. Scis. (hon.), U.S. Inst. Peace (bd. dirs.). Author: Theology of Catholic Action, 1945, God and the World of Man, 1950, Patterns for Educational Growth, 1958, Thoughts for Our Times, 1962, More Thoughts for Our Times, 1965, Still More Thoughts for Our Times, 1966, Thoughts IV, 1968, Thoughts V, 1969, The Humane Imperative: A Challenge for the Year 2000, 1974, The Hesburgh Papers: Higher Values in Higher Education, 1979, God, Country, Notre Dame, 1990, Travels with Ted and Ned, 1992. Former dir. Woodrow Wilson Nat. Fellowship Corp.; mem. Civil Rights Commn., 1957-72; mem. of Carnegie Commn. on Future of Higher Edn.; chmn. U.S. Commn. on Civil Rights, 1969-72; mem. Commn. on an All-Volunteer Armed Force, 1970; chmn. with rank of ambassador U.S. delegation UN Conf. Sci. and Tech. for Devel., 1977-79; Bd. dirs. Am. Council Edn., Freedoms Found. Valley Forge, Adlai Stevenson Inst. Internat. Affairs; past trustee, chmn. Rockefeller Found.; trustee Carnegie Found. for Advancement Teaching, Woodrow Wilson Nat. Fellowship Found., Inst. Internat. Edn., utrition Found., United Negro Coll. Fund, others; chmn. Overseas Devel. Council; chmn. acad. council Ecumenical Inst. for Advanced Theol. Studies, Jerusalem. Decorated comdr. L'ordre des Arts et des Lettres. Recipient U.S. Navy's Disting. Pub. Service award, 1959; Presdl. Medal of Freedom, 1964, Gold medal Nat. Inst. Social Scis., 1969, Cardinal Gibbons medal Cath. U. Am., 1969, Bellarmine medal Bellarmine-Ursuline Coll., 1970; Meiklejohn award AAUP, 1970, Charles Evans Hughes award Nat. Conf. Christians and Jews, 1970; Merit award Nat. Cath. Ednl. Assn., 1971, Pres.' Cabinet award U. Detroit, 1971; Am. Liberties medallion Am. Jewish Com., 1971; Liberty Bell award Ind. State Bar Assn., 1971; Laetare medal Univ. Notre Dame, 1987, Pub. Welfare medal NAS, 1984; Pub. Svc. award Common Cause, 1984, Disting. Svc. award Assn. Cath. Colls. and Univs., 1982, Jefferson award Coun. Advancement and Support of Edn., 1982, Congl. Gold medal, 2000. Fellow Am. Acad. Arts and Scis.; mem. NAS (hon.), Internat. Fedn. Cath. Univs., Commn. on Humanities, Inst. Internat. Edn (pres., bd. dirs.), Cath. Theol. Soc., Chief Execs. Forum, Am. Philos. Soc., Nat. Acad. Edn., Coun. on Fgn. Rels. (trustee). Office: U Notre Dame 1315 Hesburgh Libr Notre Dame IN 46556

HESCHEL, MICHAEL SHANE, retail food products executive; b. June 18, 1941; m. Judi Heschel; 2 children. BS in Indsl. Engring., Ohio State U., 1964, MBA, 1965, MS in Indsl. Engring., 1967; PhD in Indsl. Engring., Ariz. State U., 1970. Former sr. mgmt. systems analyst Boeing Aircraft Co.; former corp. mgr. ops. rsch. FMC Corp.; former corp. v.p. info. svcs. Am. Hosp. Supply Corp.; former corp. v.p. info. resources Baxter Internat. Inc.; former chmn., CEO Security Pacific Automation Co.; group v.p. info. systems The Kroger Co., Cin., 1991-94, sr. v.p., 1994-95, exec. v.p., chief info. officer, 1995—. Office: The Kroger Co 1014 Vine St Cincinnati OH 45202-1100 Home Phone: 513-233-9490; Office Phone: 513-762-4374.

HESS, ASHLEY W., lawyer; b. May 25, 1973; BA, U. Va., 1995; JD, Washington and Lee U. Sch. of Law, 1998. Bar: Ky. 1998, Ohio 2003. Staffwriter Environ. Law Digest, 1996—97. Named one of 40 Under 40, Cin. Bus. Courier, 2005, Ohio's Rising Stars, Super Lawyers, 2005, 2006. Mem.: Young Professionals Assn. Louisville (founding mem. 1999, bd. dir. 1999—2001, chmn., workforce devel. com. 1999—2001), Bacchanalian Soc., Inc. (founding mem. 2002—), Ky. Bar Assn., Ohio State Bar Assn., ABA, U. Va. Alumni Assn., Lee Alumni Assn., Assn. for Corp. Growth, Cin. Bar Assn. (co-chair, Bus. Law Sect. 2003—06), U. Club Cin. (membership com. 2003—05, house & fin. com. 2004—). Office: Greenebaum Doll & McDonald PLLC 2800 Chemed Ctr 255 E 5th St Cincinnati OH 45202-4728 Office Phone: 513-455-7600. Office Fax: 513-455-8500.

HESS, EVELYN VICTORINE, medical educator; b. Dublin, Nov. 8, 1926; arrived in U.S., 1960, naturalized, 1965; d. Ernest Joseph and Mary (Hawkins) H.; m. Michael Howett, Apr. 27, 1954. MB, B.Ch, BAO, U. Coll., Dublin, 1949; MD, Univ. Coll., Dublin, 1980. Intern West Middlesex Hosp., London, Eng., 1950; resident Clare Hall Hosp., London, 1951-53, Royal Free Hosp. and Med. Sch., London, 1954-57; rsch. fellow in epidemiology of Tb Royal Free Med. Sch., London, 1955; fellow U. Tex. Southwestern Med. Sch., Dallas, 1958—59, asst. prof. internal medicine, 1960-64; assoc. prof. dept. medicine U. Cin. Coll. Medicine, 1964-69, McDonald prof. medicine, 1969—, dir. div. immunology, 1964-95. Sr. investigator Arthritis and Rheumatism Found., 1963-68; attending physician Univ. Hosp., VA Hosp.; cons. Children's Hosp., Cin., 1967—, Jewish Hosp., Cin., 1968—; mem. various coms., mem. nat. adv. coun. NIH; mem. various coms. FDA, Cin. Bd. Health. Contbr. articles to profl. jours., chapters to books. Active Nat. Pks. Assn., Smithsonian Instn., others. Recipient award Arthritis Found., 1973, 78, 83, Am. Lupus Soc., 1979, Am. Acad. Family Practice, 1980, State of Ohio, 1989, Spirit of Am. Women, 1989, Daniel Drake medal U. Cin., 2001, Gold medal Lupus Found., 2004, Lifetime Hess Rsch. award Lupus Found., 2005; fellow Royal Free Med. Sch., Scandinavia, 1956; Empire Rheumatism Coun. travelling fellow, 1958-59. Master ACP (gov. Ohio chpt. 1999-2003, Master Tchr. award 1995); fellow AAAS, Am. Acad. Allergy, Royal Soc. Medicine, ACR (master, Disting. Rheumatologist award 1996); mem. Heberden Soc., Am. Coll. Rheumatology, Pan-Am. League Assns. for Rheumatology (Gold medal 2003), Ctrl. Soc. Clin. Rsch., Am. Fedn. Clin. Rsch., Am. Assn. Immunologists, Am. Soc. Nephrology, Am. Med. Womens Assn. (Local Hero award 2004), Am. Soc. Clin. Pharmacology and Therapeutics, N.Y. Acad. Scis., Soc. Exptl. Biology and Medicine, Rheumatological Soc. Colombia (hon.), Rheumatological Soc. Peru (hon.), Rheumatological Soc. Italy (hon.), Clin. Immunol. Soc. Japan (hon.), Cuban Soc. Rheumatology (hon.), Alpha Omega Alpha. Achievements include research in immunology, rheumatic diseases. Home: 2916 Grandin Rd Cincinnati OH 45208-3418 Office: U Cin Med Ctr ML 563 ML 563 MSB Cincinnati OH 45267-0001 Office Phone: 513-558-4701. Business E-Mail: hessev@email.uc.edu.

HESS, FREDERICK J., lawyer; b. Highland, Ill., Sept. 22, 1941; s. Fred and Matilda (Maiden) H.; m. Mary V. Menkhus, Nov. 13, 1976; children: Frederick, M. Elizabeth. BS in Polit. Sci. and History, St. Louis U., 1963; JD, Washburn Sch. Law, Topeka, 1971. Bar: Kans. 1971, Ill. 1975, U.S. Supreme Ct. 1975, D.C. 1977, U.S. Tax Ct. 1977. Asst. U.S. atty. Dept. Justice, East St. Louis, Ill., 1971-73, 1st asst. U.S. atty., 1973-76; ct. appt. U.S. Atty. E. Dist. of Ill., 1977; ptnr. Stiehl & Hess, Belleville, Ill., 1977-82; U.S. atty. U.S. Dist. Ct. (so. dist.) Ill., East St. Louis, 1982-93; pvt. practice Lewis Rice & Fingersh, Belleville, 1993—. Bd. dirs., past pres. Nat. Assn. Former U.S. Attys., 1996; judge Ill. Ct. of Claims, 1997-2003; commr. Ill. Exec. Ethics Commn., 2004—. Served to capt. USAF, 1964-68. Fellow ABA Found., ISBA Found., Ill. Bar Assn.; mem. Kans. Bar Assn., D.C. Bar Assn., Tamarack Golf Club, Stone Wolf Golf Club. Republican. Office: Lewis Rice & Fingersh 325 S High St Belleville IL 62220-2116 Office Phone: 618-234-8636.

HESS, KARL, engineering and science educator; b. Trumau, Austria, June 20, 1945; arrived in US, 1977, naturalized, 1988; s. Karl Joseph and Gertrude (Resch) Hess; m. Sylvia Horvath, Sept. 1967; children: Ursula, Karl. PhD, U. Vienna, Austria, 1970; DSc (hon.), ETH, Zurich, Switzerland, 2003. Rsch. asst. U. Vienna, 1969-71, asst. prof., 1971-77, lectr., 1977; vis. assoc. prof. U. Ill., Urbana, 1977-80, prof. elec. and computer engring., 1988—, adj. prof. supercomputing applications, 1990—, prof. physics, Swanlund Endowed chair, 1996—, advanced study prof., 1997—2006, advanced study prof. emeritus, 2006—. Mem. Nat. Sci. Bd, 2006—. Contbr. articles to profl. jours. Scholar, U. Ill., 1982—83; Fulbright scholar, 1973—74. Fellow: NAE, NAS, IEEE (J. J. Ebers award 1994, David Sarnoff Field award 1995, H. Welker Meml. medal 2001), AAAS, Am. Acad. Arts and Scis., Am. Phys. Soc. Achievements include patents in field. Avocations: classical music, chess. Office: U Ill Beckman Inst 405 N Mathews Ave Urbana IL 61801-2325 Home: 75348 Melelina Pl Kailua Kona HI 96740 Office Phone: 217-333-6362. Business E-Mail: k-hess@uiuc.edu.

HESS, MARGARET JOHNSTON, religious writer, educator; b. Ames, Iowa, Feb. 22, 1915; d. Howard Wright and Jane Edith (Stevenson) Johnston; m. Bartlett Leonard Hess, July 31, 1937; children: Daniel, Deborah, John, Janet. BA, Coe Coll., 1937. Bible tchr. Cmty. Bible Classes, Ward Presbyn. Ch., Livonia, Mich., 1959-96, Christ Ch. Cranbrook (Episcopalian), Bloomfield Hills, Mich., 1980-93, Luth. Ch. of the Redeemer, Birmingham, Mich., 1993-99. Co-author (with B.L. Hess): How to Have a Giving Church, 1974, The Power of a Loving Church, 1977, How Does Your Marriage Grow?, 1983, Never Say Old, 1984; author: Love Knows No Barriers, 1979, Esther: Courage in Crisis, 1980, Unconventional Women, 1981, The Triumph of Love, 1987, Lessons from Life's Journey, 2003; contbr. articles to profl. jours. Home: 15191 Ford Rd Apt 302 Dearborn MI 48126-4696

HESS, SIDNEY J., JR., lawyer; b. Chgo., June 26, 1910; s. Sidney J. and Alma (Katz) Hess; m. Jacqueline Engelhardt, Aug. 28, 1948; children: Karen E. Hess Freeman, Lori Hess Pleiss. PhB, U. Chgo., 1930, JD, 1932. Bar: Ill. 1932. Practiced in, Chgo., 1932—; mem. firm Aaron, Aaron, Schimberg & Hess, 1933—84, D'Ancona & Pflaum, 1985—2003, Seyarth Shaw L.L.P., 2003—. Bd. dirs., legal counsel Jewish Fedn. of Met. Chgo., 1968-75, v.p., 1972-74, pres., 1974-76; dir., legal counsel Jewish United Fund Met. Chgo., 1971-75, pres., 1974-76; legal counsel Jewish Welfare Fund Met. Chgo., 1969-73; bd. dirs. S. Silberman & Sons, Chgo. Metallic Products, Inc., Vienna Sausage Mfg. Co. Mem. exec. com. Anti-Defamation League, 1954-57, HIAS, 1974-90; mem. nat. devel. coun., aims com., citizens bd. U. Chgo.; bd. dirs. Schwab Rehab. Hosp., 1957-65, pres., 1959-64; trustee Michael Reese Health Trust, 1991—, vice-chair, 2006—. Recipient Judge Learned Hand Human Rels. award Am. Jewish Com., 1979, Julius Rosenwald Meml. award Jewish Fedn. Met. Chgo., 1994, Army Commendation Medal (USAF); elected to Jewish Cmty. Ctrs. Hall of Fame, 1985, City of Chgo. Sr. Citizens Hall of Fame, 1987. Fellow Ill. Bar Found. (charter mem.); mem. ABA, Ill. State Bar Assn., Chgo. Bar Assn., Am. Judicature Soc., U. Chgo. Law Sch. Assn. (dir.), Standard Club (past pres., dir.), Mid-Day Club (Chgo.), Northmoor Country Club (Highland Park, Ill.), Tamarisk Country Club (Rancho Mirage, Calif.), Phi Beta Kappa, Pi Lambda Phi. Home: 1040 N Lake Shore Dr Chicago IL 60611-1165 Office: Ste 2400 131 S Dearborn St Chicago IL 60603-5577 Office Phone: 312-460-5624. Office Fax: 312-460-7624. Business E-Mail: shess@seyfarth.com.

HESSE, CAROLYN SUE, lawyer; b. Belleville, Ill., Jan. 12, 1949; d. Ralph H. Hesse and Marilyn J. (Midgley) Hesse Dierkes; m. William H. Hallenbeck. BS, U. Ill., 1971; MS, U. Ill., Chgo., 1977; JD, DePaul U., 1983. Bar: Ill. 1983, U.S. Dist. Ct. (no. dist.) Ill. 1983. Rsch. assoc. U. Ill., Chgo., 1974—77; tech. adviser Ill. Pollution Control Bd., Chgo., 1977—80; environ. scientist U.S. EPA, Chgo., 1980—84; assoc. Pretzel & Stouffer, Chartered, Chgo., 1984—87, Coffield Ungaretti Harris & Slavin, Chgo., 1987—88; ptnr. McDermott, Will & Emery, 1988—99; pvt. practice Chgo., 1999—2001; ptnr. Barnes & Thornburg, 2001—. Spkr. in field. Contbr. articles on environ. sci. to profl. jours. Mem. ABA, Chgo. Bar Assn. Office: Barnes and Thornburg 1 N Wacker DR # 4400 Chicago IL 60606-2807 Business E-Mail: chesse@btlaw.com.

HESSLER, DAVID WILLIAM, information and multimedia systems educator; b. Oak Park, Ill., May 9, 1932; s. William Wigney and Gwendolyn Eileen (Butler) H.; m. Helen Montgomery, Aug. 27, 1955; children: Leslie Susan McCormick, Laura Lynne. BA, U. Mich., 1955, MA, 1961; PhD, Mich. State U., 1972. Comml. photographer Oscar & Assocs., Chgo., 1950; equipment engr. Western Electric Co., Chgo., 1958-59; dir. librs. and media Ann Arbor (Mich.) Pub. Schs., 1966-67; asst. prof. edn. Western Mich. U., 1967-72, assoc. prof., 1974-77; dir. instrnl. svcs., dir. broadcasting, prof. edn. U. S.C., 1973-74; cons., asst. dir. Audio-Visual Edn. Ctr. U. Mich., Ann Arbor, 1960-66, prof. Sch. Info., 1977-98, prof. emeritus, 1998—, dir. instrnl. strategy svcs. for schs. of edn., libr. sci., 1979-81, pres. Ann Arbor sys. and tech., 1987—, exec. dir. for info. svcs. Info-Span, 1991-92; exec. v.p. Infotronix, Ann Arbor, 1993-97. Cons. Presdl. Commn. on World Hunger; cons. media and tech.; instrnl. designer and evaluator; bd. dirs. Kirsch Techs.; vis. prof., cons. dept. biblioteconomia U. Brazil, 1981. Author: (with J. Smith) Student Production Guide, 1975, Technology for Communication and Instruction, 1983; producer/dir. numerous films, filmstrips, TV programs and sound/slide programs for various ednl. levels. Lt. USAF, 1955-58; capt. Res. ret. Decorated Air Force Commendation medal; named Mich. Most Valuable Tchr. Chrysler Corp., 1965; Ednl. Profl. Devel. Act fellow, 1968-69. Mem. ALA, ASTD, Assn. Image and Info. Mgmt., M Club, Phi Kappa Phi. Home: 24 Southwick Ct Ann Arbor MI 48105-1410 Office: U Mich Sch Info West Hall 550 E University Ave Ann Arbor MI 48109-1092 Business E-Mail: dwh@umich.edu.

HESTER, DONALD DENISON, economics professor; b. Cleve., Nov. 6, 1935; s. Donald Miller and Catherine (Denison) H.; m. Karen Ann Helm, Oct. 24, 1959; children: Douglas Christopher, Karl Jonathan. BA, Yale U., 1957, MA, 1958, PhD, 1961. Asst. prof., assoc. prof. Yale U., New Haven, Conn., 1961-68; jr. vis. prof. Bombay Univ., India, 1962-63; econs. prof. U. Wis., Madison, 1968-2000, dept. chmn., 1990-93. Cons. Fed. Res., 1969-84; vis. prof. People's U. China, Beijing, 1987. Author: Indian Banks: Their Portfolios, Profits and Policy, 1964; co-author: Bank Management and Portfolio Behavior, 1975, Banking Changes in the European Monetary Union: An Italian Perspective, 2002; co-editor: Risk Aversion and Portfolio Choice, 1967; contbr. numerous articles to profl. jours. Mem. Wis. Coun. Econ. Affairs, 1983-87. Guggenheim fellow 1972, Econometric Soc. fellow, 1977, Faculty fellow Ford Found., 1967, others. Avocations: classical music, art, hiking, travel. Home: 2111 Kendall Ave Madison WI 53726-3915 Office: U Wis Dept Econs 1180 Observatory Dr Madison WI 53706-1320 Business E-Mail: ddhester@wisc.edu.

HESTER, THOMAS PATRICK, lawyer; b. Tulsa, Okla., Nov. 20, 1937; s. E.P. and Mary J. (Layton) H; m. Nancy B. Scofield, Aug. 20, 1960; children: Thomas P. Jr., Ann S., John L. BA, Okla. U., 1961, LLB, 1963. Bar: Okla. 1963, Mo. 1967, N.Y. 1970, D.C. 1973, Ill. 1975. Atty. McAfee & Taft, Okla. City, 1963-66, Southwestern Bell Telephone Co., Okla. City, St. Louis, 1966-72, AT&T, NYC, Washington, 1972-75; gen. atty. Ill. Bell Telephone Co., Springfield, 1975-77, gen. solicitor Chgo., 1977-83, v.p., gen. counsel, 1983-87; sr. v.p., gen. counsel Ameritech, Chgo., 1987-91, exec. v.p., gen. counsel, 1991-97; ptnr. Mayer, Brown & Platt, Chgo., 1997—; sr. v.p., gen. counsel, sec. Sears, Roebuck and Co., 1998-99, FMC Corp., 2000. Corp. counsel ctr. adv. bd. Northwestern U., 1987-97. Mem. Taxpayers Fedn. Ill., Springfield, 1987-97, chmn. bd. trustees 1987-88; mem. adv. bd. Ill. Dept. Natural Resources, 1991-2000—, chmn., 1993-98; trustee Art Inst. Chgo., 1995-2000. Fellow Am. Bar Found.; mem. Am. Law Inst.

HETLAND, JAMES LYMAN, JR., banker, lawyer, educator; b. Mpls., June 9, 1925; s. James L. and Evelyn E. (Lundgren) Hetland; m. Barbara Anne Taylor, Sept. 10, 1949; children: Janice E., James E., Nancy L., Steven T. BSL., U. Minn., 1948, JD, 1950. Bar: Minn. 1950. Law clk. Minn. Supreme Ct., 1949—50; assoc. firm Mackall, Crounse, Moore, Helmey & Palmer, Mpls., 1950—56; prof. U. Minn. Coll. Law, 1956—71; v.p. urban devel. First Nat. Bank Mpls., 1971—75, sr. v.p. law and urban devel., 1975—82, sr. v.p., gen. counsel, sec., 1982—88; sr. v.p. First Bank Sys., 1987—88; counsel to bd. and sec. First Bank, N.A., 1986—90; of counsel Rasmussen & Assocs., Ltd., 1990—99, Leighton, Hetland & Stein, PLLP, Mpls., 2002—. Adj. prof. Hubert Humphrey Inst., U. Minn., 1976—90, regents adv. com., 1982—90; adj. prof. Bus. Coll. ext., 1975—81, Coll. Law, 1980—90; labor arbitrator, 1967—; chmn. Minn. Citizens Coun. Crime and Delinquency, 1978—83; chmn. adv. coms. Minn. Supreme Ct., 1958—90; chmn. Telecommuters, Inc., 1992—96. Co-author: Minnesota Jury Instruction Guides, 1963, 2d edit., 1974, Minnesota Practice, 3 vols., 1970. Nat. v.p., mem. exec. com. Nat. Mcpl. League, 1979—82, pres., 1982—85, chmn. bd. dirs., 1985—87; bd. dirs. Mpls. Citizens League, 1953—67, chmn., 1963—64, Mpls. Charter Commn., 1963—70, Met. Coun. Twin Cities, St. Paul, 1967—71; bd. dirs. Mpls. Downtown Coun., 1971—, vice chmn., 1978—82, chmn., 1982—83; chmn. bd. Minn. Zool. Garden, 1978—83; vice chmn. Minn. Press Coun., 1973—81; vice chmn. bd. dirs. Minn. Health Care Cost Coalition, 1980, bd. dirs. interstudy, 1972—79, chmn., 1974; mem. Bus. Urban Issues Coun., Conf. Bd., 1980—89; bd. dirs. Freshwater Biol. Rsch. Found., 1971—85, adv. bd., 1985—; bd. dirs. Mpls. CC Found., 1978—83, Minn. Exptl. City, 1972—75, Minn. Campfire Girls, 1974—79, Mpls. YMCA, 1957—76, Ctr. Policy Studies, 1983—, Twin Cities Habitat for Humanity, 1988—95, Health Ctrl., Inc., 1973—87, mem. exec. com., 1977—87; bd. dirs. Citizen Coun. Crime and Justice, 1977—, chmn., 1979—82; mem. exec. com. Partnership Dataline USA, 1983; bd. dirs., mem. exec. com. Heatlh One, 1987—93; trustee Mpls. United Way, 1988—99; chmn. Mpls. Urban Tennis, 1987—94; trustee Metro State U., 1989—98. With US Army, 1943—46. Mem.: ABA, Hennepin County Bar Assn., Minn. Bar Assn., Rotary. Republican. Lutheran. Personal E-mail: heiland@q.com.

HETSKO, CYRIL MICHAEL, physician; b. Montclair, N.J., May 25, 1942; s. Cyril Francis and Josephine (Stein) H.; m. Theresa Hottenroth, Jan. 2, 1988; 1 child, Michael Dimitri; B.A., Amherst Coll., 1964; M.D., U. Rochester, 1968. Intern, U. Wis. Hosps., Madison, 1968-69, resident in internal medicine, 1969-72, clin. assoc. prof. medicine U. Wis., 1975-95, prof. 1995—; practice internal medicine, infectious diseases Dean Med. Ctr., Madison, 1975—, dir. Dean Care HMO, Inc., 1983-94; chmn. dept. medicine St. Mary's Hosp. Med. Ctr., Madison, 1985-87; dir. Physicians Ins. Co. Wis., Madison, 1990-93; trustee Internal Medicine Ctr. To Advance Rsch. and Edn., Washington, 1991—; mem. White House Health Profls. Outreach Group, Washington, 1993-94; dir. Nat. Commn. Office Lab. Accreditation, 1994—; pres. N. Ctrl. Med. Conf., 1995-96. Trustee Internat. Childrens Alliance, Washington, 1995—. Mem. Editorial Adv. Bd. Internal Medicine News, 1993—; cons. Health Ministry, Ekaterinburg, Russia, 1996—. Served to maj. M.C., AUS, 1972-75. Diplomate Nat. Bd. Med. Examiners, Am. Bd. Internal Medicine. Mem. AMA (alt. del. 1983-93, del. 1994—, mem. nat. coun. on med. svc. 1995—, bd. trustees, 2003-), Am. Soc. Internal Medicine (del. 1987-91, trustee 1991—), Am. Soc. Microbiology, Assn. Mil. Surgeons U.S., State Med. Soc. Wis. (Councillor 1979-81, dir. 1981-88, vice speaker Ho. of Dels. 1988-90, chmn. task force on AIDS 1987—, pres. 1991-92, Meritorious Svc. award 1988), Dane County Med. Soc. (chmn. com. on prepaid health plans 1977-82, trustee 1993—, Pres.'s award 1981), Wis. Soc. Internal Medicine (councillor 1981-87, pres. 1987-88, Outstanding Wis. Internist 1990), Orgn. State Med. Assn. Presidents, N.Y. Acad. Scis., New Eng. Soc. in City N.Y., Nat. Found. for Infectious Disease, Madison Acad. Medicine. Club: Madison. Office: Dean Med Ctr 1313 Fish Hatchery Rd Madison WI 53715-1911

HEUER, ARTHUR HAROLD, ceramics engineer, educator; b. NYC, Apr. 29, 1936; s. William Jacob and Hannah (Kaye) H.; m. Roberta Feinstein, Dec. 22, 1956 (div. 1974); children: Howard, Michael, James; m. Joan McKnee Hulburt, May 8, 1976. BS, CCNY, 1956; PhD, U. Leeds, Eng., 1965, DSc, 1977. Rsch. chemist Ind. Gen. Corp., Keasbey, N.J., 1956-60; rsch. engr. Electron Tube Div. Bendix Co., Eatontown, N.J., 1960-61; staff scientist AVCO Space Systems Div., Lowell, Mass., 1965-67; asst. prof. ceramics div. metall. and materials Case Western Res. U., Cleve., 1967-70, assoc. prof., 1970-74, prof., 1974—, dir. materials rsch. lab. Case Inst. Tech., 1974-80, Kyocera Prof. Ceramics, 1985—. External sci. mem. Max-Planck Inst. fur Metalforschung, Germany, 1990—. Editor: Zirconia I, Zirconia II; contbr. over 420 articles to profl. jours. Recipient Alexander von Humboldt award Max-Planck Inst., 1983, Gold Medal award ASM. Fellow Am. Ceramic Soc. (chmn. basic sci. com., Sosman Meml. lectr. 1986, editor jour. 1988-90, John Jeppson award 1990, Orton lectr. 1991, Disting. Life mem. 1996), U.K. Inst. Physics; mem. AAAS, NAE, ASM (Gold medal). Achievements include research in transformation toughening in Zirconia, electron microscopy in ceramics, dislocations in ceramics, phase transformations in ceramics, biomimetic processing of materials, materials science aspects of MEMS, rapid prototyping technology/solid freeform fabrication of engineering materials, mechanical properties of hard and soft tissue and surface hardening of stainless steels and titanium alloys; co-founding of CAM-LEM Inc. Home: 12526 Cedar Rd Ste 2 Cleveland OH 44106 Office: Case Western Res U Materials Sci and Engring 10900 Euclid Ave Cleveland OH 44106-7204 E-mail: heuer@cwru.edu.

HEUER, GERALD ARTHUR, mathematician, educator; b. Bertha, Minn., Aug. 31, 1930; s. William C. F. and Selma C. (Rosenberg) Heuer; m. Jeanette Mary Knedel, Sept. 5, 1954; children: Paul, Karl, Ruth, Otto. BA, Concordia Coll., 1951; MA, U. Nebr., 1953; PhD, U. Minn., 1958. Math. instr. Hamline U., 1955-56, Concordia Coll., Moorhead, Minn., 1956-57, asst. prof., 1957-58, assoc. prof., 1958-62, prof., 1962-95, Sigurd and Pauline Prestegaard Mundhjeld prof., 1988-95, chmn. dept., 1963-70, research prof., 1970-71, prof. emeritus, mathematician-in-residence, 1995—; mathematician Remington Rand Univac, summer 1958. Vis. prof. U. Nebr., Lincoln, 1960—61, Wash. State U., Pullman,

1980—81; mathematician Control Data Corp., 1960—62, cons., 1960—63; vis. lectr. Math. Assn. Am., 1964—66; cons. NSF-AID, India, 1968—69; guest spkr. Minn. sect. Math. Assn. Am., 1956, Nebr. sect. Math. Assn. Am., 1961, No. Ctrl. sect. Math. Assn. Am., 1974; vis. prof., scholar Math. Inst. Cologne (Germany) U., 1973—74; vis. prof., scholar Inst. Stats., Econs. and Ops. Rsch. Graz U., Austria, 1987—88, rsch. prof., Austria, 1990, vis. prof., Austria, 94, Austria, 97; dir. U.S. Math. Olympiad Tng. Session; leader U.S. team Internat. Math. Olympiad, 1988—90; invited plenary spkr. Internat. Symposium Ops. Rsch., Passau, Germany, 1995. Author (with Ulrike Leopold-Wildburger): (book) Balanced Silverman Games on General Discrete Sets, 1991, Silverman's Game, 1995; contbr. articles to profl. jours.; reviewer: Zentralblatt für Mathematik, 1967—, Math. Revs., 1978—. Grantee Rsch., NSF, 1963, 1964, 1966; scholar Bush Rsch., Concordia Coll., 1983—84, Centennial Rsch., 1992, 1993, 1994, 1995; Faculty fellow, NSF, Univ. Calif. Berkeley, 1966—67. Mem.: Österreichische Math. Gesellschaft (Vienna), Deutsche Math.-Vereinigung e.v. (Berlin), Nat. Geographic Soc., Am. Math. Soc., Math. Assn. Am. (pres. Minn. sect. 1959—60, nat. bd. govs. 1971—73, com. Putnam prize 1987—90, com. Am. math. competitions 1988—, problem books editl. bd. 1999—, cert. meritorious svc. 1994), Sigma Xi. Lutheran. Home: 1216 Elm St S Moorhead MN 56560-4049 Office: Concordia Coll Dept Math Moorhead MN 56562-0001 Office Phone: 218-299-3348. Business E-Mail: heuer@cord.edu.

HEWES, PHILIP A., computer company executive; BA, Colo. State U., 1974; JD, John Marshall Law Sch., 1977. Bar: Ill. Asst. corp. counsel Comdisco, Inc., Rosemont, Ill., 1977-92, sr. v.p. legal, sec., 1992—.

HEWITT, CHRISTOPHER J., lawyer; b. Oswego, NY; BBA, U. Toledo, 1990; MBA, JD, Georgetown U., 1994. Bar: NY 1995, Ohio 1998. Ptnr. Jones Day, Cleve. Named one of Top 40 Lawyers Under 40, Nat. Law Jour., 2005. Office: Jones Day North Point 901 Lakeside Ave Cleveland OH 44114-1190 Office Phone: 216-586-7254. Office Fax: 216-579-0212. E-mail: cjhewitt@jonesday.com.

HEWITT, PAMELA S., human resources specialist; b. 1953; Sr. v.p. human resources The Quaker Oats Co., Chgo., 1998—. Office: TheQuaker Oats Co 555 W Monroe St Chicago IL 60661-3716

HEYMAN, RALPH EDMOND, lawyer; b. Cin., Mar. 14, 1931; s. Ralph and Florence (Kahn) H.; m. Sylvia Lee Schottenstein, Jan. 2, 1984; children: Michael Cary, Cynthia Ann Heyman Eeg, Ginger Florence. AB magna cum laude (Rufus Choat scholar), Dartmouth Coll., 1953; LLB cum laude, Harvard U., 1956; LLM, U. Cin., 1957. Bar: Ohio 1956, Ill. 1957. Pvt. practice, Cin., 1956-58, Dayton, 1958—; assoc. Freiden & Wolf, 1956-58; from assoc. to ptnr. Smith & Schnacke, 1958-88; ptnr. Chernesky, Heyman & Kress, Dayton, Ohio, 1988—. Lectr. estate planning U. Cin., 1958-61; lectr. participant Southwestern Ohio Tax Inst., 1957-65; lectr., moderator Dayton Bar Assn. Tax Insts., 1975-79, 94; lectr. continuing edn. program U. Dayton, 1989; lectr. estate planning Dayton Area Tax Profls., 1993; lectr. on venture capital Miami Valley Venture Assn., 1998; dir., gen. counsel Towne Properties, Ltd., Hills Developers LLC, Aristocrat Products, Inc., K.K. Motorcycle Supply, Inc. Mem. Bd. Rural Zoning Commn. Montgomery County, 1969-71; bd. dirs., pres. Jewish Fedn. Dayton, 1993-97; nat. trustee NCCJ; past pres. Temple Israel; pres. Temple Israel Found., 1999-2001; bd. dirs. United Way Greater Dayton Area, 1999-2002. Recipient Humanitarian award NCCJ, 1997, Robert A. Shapiro Vol. award Jewish Fedn., 1998; named Ohio Super Lawyer, Law and Politics Mag., Cin. Mem. ABA, Ohio Bar Assn., Dayton Bar Assn. (past chmn. tax com.), Cin. Bar Assn., Lawyers Club, Bicycle Club, Meadowbrook Country Club, Dayton City Club (past pres.), B'nai Brith, Phi Beta Kappa Office: Chernesky Heyman & Kress PLL PO Box 3808 1100 Courthouse Plz SW Dayton OH 45401-3808 Office Phone: 937-449-2820. E-mail: reh@chklaw.com.

HEYMAN, WILLIAM HERBERT, financial services executive; b. NYC, Apr. 20, 1948; s. George Harrison and Edythe Jane (Forman) H., Jr.; m. Katherine Elizabeth Dietze, May 7, 2007. AB magna cum laude, Princeton U., 1970; JD cum laude, Harvard U., 1973. Bar: NY 1974, DC 1991. Assoc. Cravath, Swaine & Moore, NYC, 1975-78, White & Case, NYC, 1973-75, Stroock & Stroock & Lavan, NYC, 1978-79; gen. ptnr., COO Mercury Securities, NYC, 1979-88; mng. dir. Smith Barney, Harris Upham & Co., Inc., NYC, 1989-91; dir. divsn. market regulation SEC, Washington, 1991-93; mng. dir. Salomon Bros. Inc., Washington, 1993-95; exec. v.p. Citigroup Investments, Inc., NYC, 1995—2000, chmn., 2001—02; CEO Tribecca Investments LLC, NYC, 1996—2002; exec. v.p., chief investment officer Travelers Cos., 2002—, vice chmn., 2005—. Bd. dirs. Max Re Capital Holdings Ltd., Max Re Ltd.; bd. govs. Nat. Assn. Securities Dealers. Trustee Mt. Sinai-NYU Med. Ctr., 1994-99, Hosp. for Joint Diseases, 1994-98; mem. NY area firms adv. com. NY Stock Exch., 1996-2002; mem. adv. bd. fin. math. Courant Inst. Math. Scis. YU; bd. dirs. Student/Sponsor Partnership of NY, 1989-91, 93-2003, mem. adv. bd., 2004-; bd. dirs. 92d St. YM&YWHA, NYC, 1979-90, hon. bd. dirs., 1991-; coun. overseers United Jewish Appeal-Fedn. NY, 1986-88; mem. fin. com. NY State Reps., 1986-90, v.p. NY County Reps. Com., 1987-90; mem. nat. fin. com. George Bush for Pres., 1987-88; hon. chmn. Bicentennial Presdl. Inaugural, 1989; pub. mem. Adminstrv. Conf. of the U.S., 1989-90; mem. NY regional panel for selection of White House Fellows, 1989, 2002-05; mem. fin. products adv. com. Commodity Futures Trading Commn., 1992-93. Mem. Securities Industry Assn. (chmn. adv. coun.), Coun. on Fgn. Rels., Harvard Law Sch. Assn. (nat. coun. 1986-90), Econ. Club NY, Century Country Club (Purchase, NY), Army and avy Club (Washington), Univ. Club (NY), Nassau Club (Princeton, NJ), Mid Ocean Club (Bermuda), Doonbeg Golf Club (County Clare, Ireland), Phi Beta Kappa. Jewish. Office: St Paul Travelers Cos 385 Washington St Saint Paul MN 55102-1396 Home Phone: 212-517-4084. Business E-Mail: william.h.heyman@travelers.com.

HEYMANN, S. RICHARD, lawyer; b. Chgo., Sept. 18, 1944; s. Samuel R. and Ann (Menning) H.; m. Jane Ann Gebhart, June 14, 1980; children: Elizabeth Jane, Catherine Claire. BS, U. Wis., 1966; JD, U. Mich., 1969. Bar: Mo. 1969, Wis. 1988. Law clk. Minn. Supreme Ct., St. Paul, 1970-72; assoc. Bryan, Cave, McPheeters & McRoberts, St. Louis, 1972-79, ptnr., 1980-87, Foley & Lardner, Madison, Wis., 1987-99; dir. Inst. for Environ. Studies U. Wis., Madison, 1996—. Adj. prof. U. Wis. Law Sch.; fellow U. Wis. Bus. Ctr.Urban Land Econs. Rsch. Fellow, Ctr. for Urban Land Econs. Mem. U. Wis. Found., Wis. Alumni Assn. (bd. dirs. 1985-87), Madison Club, Maple Bluff Country Club. Office: U Wis Law Sch 801 Magdeline Rd Madison WI 53704 E-mail: srheymann@wisc.edu.

HIBBS, JOHN STANLEY, lawyer; b. Des Moines, Sept. 19, 1934; s. Ray E. Hibbs and Jean Waller (Lackey) Gravender; m. John S. II, Kari S. Hibbs Carroll, Jennifer R. Hibbs-Kraus. BBA, U. Minn., 1956, JD cum laude, 1960. Bar: Minn. 1960, U.S. Dist. Ct. Minn. 1960, U.S. Ct. Appeals (8th cir.) 1963, U.S. Tax Ct. 1965, U.S. Supreme Ct. 1970. Ptnr. Dorsey and Whitney, Mpls., 1960—, Health Practice Group. Chmn. Adv. Task Force on Minn. Corp. Law, Mpls., 1979-82, tax policy study group of Minn. Bus. Climate Task Force, Mpls., 1978-80; coun. Med. Group Practice Attys. Author: Minnesota Nonprofit Corporations-A Corporate and Tax Guide, 1979; contbr. over 150 profl. papers to publs. Served to capt. USAR, 1956-66. Fellow Am. Coll. Tax Counsel; mem. ABA (cons. com. on corp. laws 1981-82), Nat. Health Lawyers Assn., Am. Acad. Healthcare Attys., Coun. Med. Group Practice Attys., Minn. Bar Assn., Hennepin County Bar Assn. Republican. Lutheran. Avocations: sports, reading, travel, gardening. Office: Dorsey & Whitney LLP 50 S 6th St Ste 1500 Minneapolis MN 55402-1553

HICKEY, DAMON DOUGLAS, library director; b. Houston, Oct. 30, 1942; s. Thomas Earl and Ethel Elizabeth (Place) Hickey; m. Mary Lyons Temple, May 27, 1967; 1 child, Doralyn Temple Hickey Rossmann. BA, Rice U., 1965; MDiv, Princeton Sem., NJ, 1968; cert. in clin. pastoral care, Inst. of Religion, Houston, 1969; MSLS, U. N.C., 1975; MA, U. N.C., Greensboro, 1982; PhD, U. S.C., 1989. Assoc. pastor First Presbyn. Ch., Irving, Tex., 1969-71, Southminster Presbyn. Ch., Oklahoma City, 1971-72; pastor First Presbyn. Ch., Moore, Okla., 1971—72; catalog libr. U. N.C., Chapel Hill, 1972-73; acting curator rare books Duke U., Durham, NC, 1973-74; assoc. libr. dir. Guilford Coll., Greensboro, 1975-91, curator Friends Hist. Collection, 1980-91; dir. libr. Coll. Wooster, Ohio, 1991—. Adj. asst. prof. history Guilford Coll., 1990—91. Author: Sojourners No More: The Quakers in the New South, 1865-1920, 1997, When Chage is Set in Store: An Analysis of Seven Academic Libraries, 2001, Learn Library Management, 2003; editor: (jour.) The Southern Friend, 1983—91; contbr. chapters to books, articles and book revs. to profl. jours. Recipient Twiford Religious History Book award N.C. Soc. of Historians, Inc., 1998. Mem.: ALA, Assn. Coll. and Rsch. Librs. (chair coll. librs. sect. 2004—), Hist. Soc. N.C. (elect), Friends Hist. Assn., So. Hist. Assn., Orgn. Am. Historians, N.C. Friends Hist. Soc. (bd. dirs. 1977—91), Beta Phi Mu, Phi Alpha Theta. Democrat. Episcopalian. Avocations: church work, baseball. Office: Coll of Wooster Libraries Wooster OH 44691-2364 Office Phone: 330-263-2483. E-mail: dhickey@wooster.edu.

HICKEY, JOHN JOSEPH, state legislator; b. St. Louis, Feb. 23, 1965; State rep. Dist. 80 Mo. State Legislature, 1993—2002. Journeyman pipefitter. Mem. Northwest Twp. Airport Twp. and North County Young Dems., Pipefitters Local 562, North County Labor Club, Woodson Terr. Lions Club Internat.

HICKEY, JOHN THOMAS, JR., lawyer; b. Evanston, Ill., July 9, 1952; s. John Thomas and Joanne (Keating) H.; m. Candis Bailey, July 7, 1979; children: Alison, Jack, Patrick, Claire, Matthew. AB magna cum laude, phi beta kappa, Georgetown U., 1974; JD, U. Chgo., 1977. Bar: Ill. 1977, U.S. Dist. Ct. (no. dist.) Ill. 1977, U.S. Ct. Appeals (7th cir.) 1977, U.S. Ct. Appeals (10th cir.) 1987. Assoc. Kirkland & Ellis, Chgo., 1977-83, ptnr., mem. firm mgmt. com., 1983—. Mem. adv. bd. Leading Lawyers Network. Fellow Am. Coll. Trial Lawyers. Office: Kirkland & Ellis 200 E Randolph St Fl 59 Chicago IL 60601-6609 Office Phone: 312-861-2348. Office Fax: 312-861-2200. Business E-Mail: jhickey@kirkland.com.

HICKMAN, FREDERIC W., retired lawyer; b. Sioux City, Iowa, June 30, 1927; s. Simeon M. and Esther (Nixon) Hickman; m. Katherine Heald, July 15, 1964; children: Mary Sanders, Sara Ridder. AB, Harvard U., 1948, LLB magna cum laude, 1951. Bar: Ill. 1951. Assoc. Sidley & Austin, Chgo., 1951-55; ptnr. Hopkins & Sutter, Chgo., 1956-71, 75-92, sr. counsel, 1993-2001. Asst. sec. tax policy Dept. Treasury, Washington, 1972—75; draftsman Ill. Income Tax, 1969; author, lectr. taxation. Pres. Nat. Tax Assn., 1989—90; mem. Ill. Humanities Coun., 1977—82, Citizens Commn. Pub. Sch. Fin., 1977—78; chmn. bd. trustees Am. Conservatory Music, 1980—90. With USN, 1945—46. Mem.: ABA, Am. Coll. Tax Counsel (regent 1989—92), Internat. Fiscal Assn. (dir. 1973—77), Chikaming Country Club (Lakeside, Mich.), Legal Club (pres. Chgo. 1980—81), Union League Club (Chgo.), Comm. Club (Chgo.). Republican. Methodist. Home: 360 Green Bay Rd # 4E Winnetka IL 60093-4032

HICKS, CADMUS METCALF, JR., financial analyst; b. Hagerstown, Md., Dec. 21, 1952; s. Cadmus Metcalf Sr. and Marie Elizabeth (Keefauver) H.; m. Elizabeth Ann Dressel, May 31, 1980; children: Liza, Alethea, Cadmus III. BA, Wheaton Coll., Ill., 1974; MA, U. Chgo., 1976; PhD, Northwestern U., Evanston, Ill., 1980. Chartered fin. analyst. Rsch. analyst John Nuveen & Co. Inc., Chgo., 1980-85, asst. v.p., 1985-90, v.p., 1990—, asst. mgr. rsch. dept., 1993-96, mgr. rsch. dept., 1996-99, market strategist, 1999—, mng. dir., 2006—. Author: (with others) The Municipal Bond Handbook, 1983, Bond Credit Analysis: Framework and Case Studies, 2001, Readings in Fixed Income Performance Attribution, 2007, Handbook of Municipal Bands, 2008; contbr. articles to profl. jours. Mem. Nat. Fedn. of Mcpl. Analysts (bd. govs. 1991-93), Chgo. Mcpl. Analysts Soc. (pres. 1991-92), Investment Analysts Soc. of Chgo., Assn. for Investment Mgmt. and Rsch. Republican. Office: 333 W Wacker Dr Chicago IL 60606-1220 Office Phone: 312-917-7865. Business E-Mail: cadmus.hicks@nuveen.com.

HICKS, DREW M., lawyer; b. Dayton, Ohio, Sept. 11, 1976; BA, Duke U., 1999; JD, U. Cin. Coll. Law, 2003. Bar: Ohio 2003. Assoc. Keating, Muething & Klekamp PLL, Cin. Named one of Ohio's Rising Stars, Super Lawyers, 2005, 2006. Mem.: Cin. Bar Assn., Cin. Bar Assn. Office: Keating Muething & Klekamp PLL One E Fourth St Ste 1400 Cincinnati OH 45202 Office Phone: 513-579-6565. Office Fax: 513-579-6457.

HICKS, IRLE RAYMOND, food service executive; b. Welch, W.Va., Dec. 21, 1928; s. Irle Raymond and Mary Louise (Day) H. BA, U. Va., 1950. Bus. mgr. Hicks Ford, Covington, Ky., 1952-58; acct. Firestone Plantations Co., Harbel, Liberia, 1958-60; auditor Kroger Co., Cin., 1960-66, gen. auditor, 1966-68, asst. treas., 1968-72, treas., 1972—. Bd. dirs. Old Masons' Home Ky. Served with AUS, 1950-52. Mem. Fin. Execs. Inst., Bankers Club, Alpha Kappa Psi, Phi Kappa Psi. Clubs: Mason, Cincinnati. Episcopalian. Home: 454 Oliver Rd Cincinnati OH 45215-2507 Office: 1014 Vine St Cincinnati OH 45202-1141

HICKS, JUDITH EILEEN, nursing administrator; b. Chgo., Jan. 1, 1947; d. John Patrick and Mary Ann (Clifford) Rohan; m. Laurence Joseph Hicks, Nov. 22, 1969; children: Colleen Driscoll, Patrick Kevin. BSN, St. Xavier Coll., Chgo., 1969; MSN, U. Ill., Chgo., 1971. Staff nurse Mercy Hosp., Chgo., 1969-70, nursing supr., 1970-73; cons. continuing edn. Ill. Nurses Assn., Chgo., 1974-75; dir. ob-gyn. nursing Northwestern Meml. Hosp., Chgo., 1975-81; v.p. nursing Children's Meml. Hosp., Chgo., 1981-86; pres. Children's Meml. Home Health, Inc., 1986—2001, Children's Meml. Nursing Svcs., 1986—2001. Pres. Allied & Children's Home Health and Nursing Svcs., 1988, CM Healthcare Resources, Inc., 1988—2001, The Pediat. Pl., Inc., 1994—2001, Focused Health Solutions, Inc., 2000—; dir. Near North Health Corp., Chgo., 1982—85; pres. Pediat. Excellence Program Svc.; bd. dirs. Infant Welfare Soc. Chgo., Nat. Breast Cancer Assn., Children's Meml. Med. Ctr., 1985—2007. Mem. bd. trustees St. Xavier U., Chgo., 2005—. Recipient Jonas Salk Leadership award March of Dimes, 1998, Ernst and Young Outstanding Ill. Nurse Leader award, 1999, Entrepreneur of Yr. award Ernst and Young Midwest Region, 2006, Nursing Alumni of Yr. award, St. Xavier U., 2007; finalist Entrepreneur of Yr. award Ernst and Young, 2004. Mem. Am. Soc. Nursing Adminstrs., Women's Health Exec. Network (1984-85), Ill. Hosp. Assn. (chmn. coun. on nursing 1982-83), Inst. Medicine, Econ. Club of Chgo. Home: 2206 Beechwood Ave Wilmette IL 60091-1508 Office: Focused Health Solutions 1650 Lake Cook Rd Deerfield IL 60015 Personal E-mail: judithhicks@mac.com.

HICKS, KEN CARLYLE, retail executive; b. Tulsa, Jan. 6, 1953; s. Harold I. and Patricia Ann (Carlyle) H.; m. Lucile Catherine Boland, June 22, 1974. BS, U.S. Mil. Acad., 1974; MBA, Harvard U., 1982. Commd. 2d lt. U.S. Army, 1974, advanced through grades to capt., resigned, 1980; assoc. McKinsey & Co., Dallas, 1982-83; v.p., chief operating officer All-Flow, Inc., Buffalo, 1984; sr. engagement mgr. McKinsey Co., Dallas, 1984-87; sr. v.p. May Dept. Stores Co., St. Louis, 1987-90, GMM Home Furnishings, May Merchandising Co., NYC; sr.v.p. GMM Foley's Department Stores, Houston; exec. v.p. Home Shopping Network, FL; pres. and dir. Payless ShoeSource, Topeka, 1999—. Class agt. Harvard Bus. Sch., 1982—; co. exec. United Way, St. Louis, 1988. Mem. Harvard Club (N.Y.C.). Avocations: horseback riding, jogging. Home: 224 Fall Creek Rd Lawrence KS 66049-9066 Office: Payless ShoeSource Inc 3231 SE 6th Ave Topeka KS 66607-2260

HICKS, SARAH ELLINGTON, lawyer; b. Lexington, Ky., Oct. 29, 1977; BA, U. Miami, 2000; JD, U. Cin., 2003. Bar: Ohio 2003, US Dist. Ct. Southern Dist. Ohio. Law clerk Wood & Lamping L.L.P., Cin., assoc., 2003—. Named one of Ohio's Rising Stars, Super Lawyers, 2005, 2006. Mem.: Internat. Found. Employee Benefits, Ohio State Bar Assn., Cin. Bar Assn. Office: Wood & Lamping LLP 600 Vine St Ste 2500 Cincinnati OH 45202-2491 Office Phone: 513-852-6000. Office Fax: 513-852-6087.

HIER, DANIEL BARNET, neurologist; b. Chgo., Mar. 23, 1947; BA, Harvard U., 1969, MD, 1973. Medical intern Bronx Mcpl. Hosp., NYC, 1973-74; neurology resident Mass. Gen. Hosp., Boston, 1974-77, neurology fellow, 1977-79; neurologist Michael Reese Hosp., Chgo., 1979-89, chmn. neurology, 1987-89; head neurology U. Ill., Chgo., 1989—2003, assoc. prof. neurology, 1989-91, prof., 1991—. Fellow Am. Acad. Neurology, Am. Heart Assn. (stroke council). Home: 1206 Manor Dr Wilmette IL 60091-1029 Office Phone: 312-996-1759. E-mail: dbhier@gmail.com.

HIER, MARSHALL DAVID, lawyer; b. Bay City, Mich., Aug. 24, 1945; s. Marshall George and Helen May (Copeland) H.; m. Nancy Speed Brown, June 26, 1970; children: John, Susan, Ann. BA, Mich. State U., 1966; JD, U. Mich., 1969. Bar: Mo. 1969. Assoc. Peper, Martin, Jensen, Maichel and Hetlage, St. Louis, 1969-76, ptnr., 1976-95; prin. Bertram, Peper and Hier, P.C., St. Louis, 1996—. Bd. dirs. Gateway Ctr. Met. St. Louis, Mercantile Libr. Assn., St. Louis Soc. Blind and Visually Impaired. Contbr. articles to profl. jours. Mem. St. Louis Bar Assn. (editor jour. 1988—), St. Louis Civil Round Table (former pres.). Baptist. Home: 17141 Chaise Ridge Rd Chesterfield MO 63005-4457 Office Phone: 314-621-1988. Business E-Mail: hier@bphstl.com.

HIGBY, GREGORY JAMES, historical association administrator, historian; s. Warren James and Gertrude H.; m. Marian Fredal, June 2, 1979. BS in Pharmacy, U. Mich., 1977; MS in Pharmacy, U. Wis., 1980, PhD in Pharmacy, 1984. Staff pharmacist Higby's Pharmacy, Bad Axe, Mich., 1977-78; asst. to dir. Am. Inst. of the History of Pharmacy, Madison, Wis., 1981-84, asst. dir., 1984-86, assoc. dir., 1986, acting dir., 1986-88, dir., 1988—; rsch. assoc. U. Wis., Madison, 1984-86. Adj. asst. prof. U. Wis., Madison, 1984-94, adj. assoc. prof., 1994-2000, adj. prof., 2000—; cons. Smithsonian Instn., Washington, 1987, Am. Soc. Hosp. Pharmacists, Bethesda, Md., 1990, U.S. Pharmacopeial Conv., 1992-95, Am. Assn. Colls. Pharmacy, 1993-99; adv. com. Fed. Drug Law Inst., Washington, 1989-90. Author: In Service to American Pharmacy: The Professional Life of William Procter, Jr., U. Ala. Press, 1992; co-author: The Spirit of Voluntarism.The United States Pharmacopeia 1820-1995, 1995; editor: One Hundred Years of the National Formulary, 1989, Pill Peddlers: Essays on the History of the Pharmaceutical Industry, 1990, Historical Hobbies for the Pharmacist, 1994, The History of Pharmacy, A Selected Annotated Bibliography, 1995, The Inside Story of Medicines, 1997, Apothecaries and the Drug Trade, 2001, 150 Years of Caring: A Pictorial History of the APHA, 2002, Drugstore Memories: American Pharmacists Recall Life Behind the Counter, 2002, American Pharmacy: A Collection of Historical Essays, 2005; author poetry; editor: Pharmacy in History Jour., 1986—; contbr. articles to profl. jours. Recipient Edward Kremers award 1995. Mem. Am. Pharm. Assn., Am. Assn. Coll. Pharm., Am. Assn. for History of Medicine, Hist. Sci. Soc., Soc. for History of Tech., Internat. Acad. History of Pharmacy. Avocations: bird watching, bicycling, musician. Office: Am Inst of the History of Pharmacy 777 Highland Ave Madison WI 53705-2222 E-mail: greghigby@aihp.org.

HIGGINBOTHAM, EDITH ARLEANE, radiologist, researcher; b. New Orleans, Sept. 14, 1946; d. Luther Aldrich and Ruby (Clark) H.; m. Terry Lawrence Andrews (div. 1979); m. Donald Temple Ford (div. 1989). BS, Howard U., 1967, MS, 1970, MD, 1974. Diplomate Am. Bd. Radiology, Am. Bd. Nuclear Medicine. Intern St. Vincent's Hosp., NYC, 1974-75, resident in diagnostic radiology, 1975-78, resident in nuclear radiology, 1978-79; asst. prof. radiology, chief nuclear medicine Howard U., Howard U. Hosp., Washington, 1979-82; assoc. prof. clin. radiology, dir. nuclear medicine U. Medicine and Dentistry N.J., Newark, 1982-90; locum tenems radiologist Sterling Med., Cin., 1991-94, Med. Nat., San Antonio, 1990-91; diagnostic radiologist Diagnostic Health Imaging Systems, Lanham, Md., 1994-95; locum tenens radiologist, 1995-97; radiologist, dir. radiology N.E. Wash. Med. Group, Colville, Wash., 1997—99; radiologist Mount Carmel Hosp., Colville, 1997-99, Barstow (Calif.) Cmty. Hosp., 1999, Queen of Peace Hosp., Mitchell, SD, 1999—2002, New Ulm Med Ctr., Minn., 2002—03, dir. radiology, 2003; radiologist Naeve Hosp., Albert Lea (Minn.) Med. Ctr., Mayo Health Sys., 2003—. Cons. Biotech. Rsch. Inst., Rockville, Md., 1989-94; profl. assoc. Ctr. for Molecular Medicine and Immunology, Newark, 1984-90; asst. prof. radiology George Washington U., Washington, 1990; counselor Am. Coll. Radiology, SD, 2001; presenter in field. Contbr. articles to profl. jours. Named Outstanding Working Woman, Glamour mag., 1981, Hon. Dep. Atty. Gen., State of La., 1982. Mem.: SD Med. Assn. (continuing med. edn. com. 2001), Freeborn County Med. Soc. (pres. 2005), Minn. Med. Assn. (continuing med. edn. com. 2005), Soc. uclear Medicine, Radiol. Soc. N.Am., Am. Coll. Radiology, Phi Delta Epsilon, Sigma Xi. Roman Catholic. Avocations: aerobics, reading, music, travel. E-mail: ehigginbothammd@charter.net.

HIGGINS, HAROLD K., retired publishing executive; b. Walton, NY, Apr. 6, 1950; m. Sandra Higgins. AA, Tompkins -Cortland C.C., Groton, NY, 1970; BS in Journalism, S.D. State U., 1972. Reporter Rapid City (S.D.) Jour., 1972-74, AP, Mpls., 1974-76; sports editor, bus. editor, city editor St. Paul (Minn.) Pioneer Press, 1976-86; v.p., editor Aberdeen (S.D.) Am. News, 1986-89, pres., pub., 1989-92, Boulder (Colo.) Pub., Inc., 1992—98; pub. San Luis Obispo (Calif.) Tribune, 1998—2001; pres., pub. St. Paul (Minn.) Pioneer Press, 2001—07; ret., 2007. Office: St Paul Pioneer Press 345 Cedar St Saint Paul MN 55101

HIGGINS, JACK, editorial cartoonist; b. Chgo., Aug. 19, 1954; s. Maurice James and Helen Marie (Egan) Higgins; m. Mary Elizabeth Irving, Apr. 26, 1997; children: Thomas Patrick, Brigid Kathleen, Rose Perpetua. BA in Econs., Coll. Holy Cross, 1976. Editorial cartoonist The Daily Northwestern, Evanston, Ill., 1978—81; freelance editorial cartoonist Chgo. Sun-Times, 1980—84, editorial cartoonist, 1984—. Vol. Jesuit Vol. Corps, Washington, 1976—77. Finalist Pulitzer prize, 1986, Scripps-Howard Award, 2000; nominee Robert F. Kennedy Journalism award, 1993, 1994, others; named Ill. Journalist of Yr., 1996; recipient Peter Lisagor award, Chgo. Soc. Profl. Journalists, 1984, 1987, 1991, 1994, 1996, 1997, 1998, 1999, 2000, 2001, 1st prize, Internat. Salon Cartoons, Montreal, Que., Can., 1988, Pulitzer prize for editl. cartooning, 1989, Disting. Svc. award, Sigma Delta Chi, 1988, 1998, John Fischetti editl. cartooning award, 1998, Media Svc. award, Chgo. Lung Assn., 1993, Herman Kogan Media awards, Chgo. Bar Assn., 1993, 1995, Alumni Medal, St. Ignatius Coll. Prep. Sch., Chgo., 1992. Roman Catholic. Avocations: painting, bicycling. Office: Chicago Sun Times 350 N Orleans St Ste 1270 Chicago IL 60654-2148

HIGGINS, JAMES JACOB, statistics educator; b. Canton, Ill., Oct. 31, 1943; married, 1967; 2 children. BS, U. Ill., 1965; MS, Ill. State U., 1967; PhD in Stats., U. Mo., 1970. Asst. prof. math. U. Mo., Rolla, 1970-74; from asst. prof. to assoc. prof. math. U. South Fla., 1974-80; prof. stats. Kans. State U., Manhattan, 1980—; dept. head, 1990-95. Co-author (with Sallie Keller-McNulty): An Introduction to Probability and Stochastic Modeling, 1995; author: An Introduction to Modern Nonparametric Statistics, 2004, A SAS Companion for Nonparametric Statistics, 2005. Fellow Am. Statis. Assn.; mem. Inst. Math. Stats. Achievements include research in reliability theory; classical and Bayesian estimation theory; statistical modelling; experimental design; textbook author. Office: Kans State U Stats Lab Dickens Hall Manhattan KS 66506 E-mail: jhiggins@ksu.edu.

HIGGINS, LINDA I., state legislator; b. Mpls., Nov. 11, 1950; AA, Iowa Lakes C.C.; BS, Mankato State Coll. Mem. Minn. Senate from 58th dist., St. Paul, 1996—. Home: 1715 Emerson Ave N Minneapolis MN 55411-3226 Office: 226 Capitol 75 Constitution Ave Saint Paul MN 55155-1601

HIGGINS, RUTH ELLEN, theatre producer; b. Streator, Ill., Jan. 23, 1945; d. Thomas Francis and Mary Madeline (Ahearn) H.; m. Byron L. Schaffer, Oct. 17, 1975 (dec. May 1990); 1 child, Kareth Madeline Schaffer. BS in Edn. and Theater, No. Ill. U., 1967; MA in Theater Arts, U. Nebr., 1968; postgrad., No. Ill. U., 1970-74. Instr. Glenbrook North H.S., Northbrook, Ill., 1968-69; dir. theatre Highland C.C., Freeport, Ill., 1969-73; co-prodr. Dinglefest Theatre Co., Chgo., 1972-77; arts cons. Chgo. Cmty. Trust, 1973-74; exec. dir., founder Chgo. Alliance for the Performing Arts, 1974-79; prodr. New Tuners Theatre, Chgo.; exec. dir., co-founder Chgo. Coalition for Arts in Edn., 1979-83; gen. mgr. Theatre Bldg., Chgo., 1981-97, North Shore Ctr. Performing Arts, Skokie, Ill., 1997-99; dir. MBA arts mgmt. Roosevelt U., Chgo., 1999—. Cons. Office Cook County Assessor, Chgo., 1980, Donors Forum, Chgo., 1981, Paramount Fine Arts Ctr., Aurora, Ill., 1979-81, North Park Village, Chgo., 1982; mem. theatre adv. panel Ill. Arts Coun., 1992; bd. dirs. Nat. Alliance Mus. Theatre.; mem. theatre creation and presentation panel Nat. Endowment for Arts, 1992, 97; bd. mem. Nat. Alliance for Mus. Theatre, 1996-2000; co-chair New Works Panel 2000, Commn.'s Com., 1998-2000. Co-prodr. over 90 world premieres, plays and musicals, 1972—; host (TV program) Arts & The Community, NBC's Knowledge, 1978. Mem. Chgo. Coun. on Fine Arts, 1976-79; panel mem. Dance Adv. Panel/Ill. Arts Coun., Chgo., 1979; mem. Ill. Arts Coun. theatre adv. panel 1992; mem. Nat. Endowment for the Arts, Opera Musical Theatre New Am. Works Panel, 1993; bd. dirs. Community TV Network, Chgo., 1980-84, Performance Community, Chgo., 1974-2000; mem. adv. bd. Gospel Arts Workshop, Chgo., 1979-85. Recipient Svc. to Arts & Edn. award Ill. Alliance for Arts in Edn., Chgo., 1984, 1st place award for direction Readers Theatre Nat. Competition Jr. Colls. Avocation: sailing. Office: New Tuners Theatre Theatre Bldg 1225 W Belmont Ave Chicago IL 60657-3205

HIGGINSON, BOBBY, professional baseball player; b. Phila., Aug. 18, 1970; Baseball player Detroit Tigers, 1995—. Office: Detroit Tigers 2100 Woodward Detroit MI 48201

HIGHLEN, LARRY WADE, music educator, piano rebuilder, tuner; b. Warren, Ind., Oct. 31, 1936; s. Lawrence Wade and Anna Belle (Dungan) H.; m. Camille Pence (div. 1975); children: Laurel, Wade, Jennifer, Tanna. Student, Niles Bryant Coll., 1967, Ivy Tech. Coll., Kokomo, Ind., 1975-76, Ivy Tech. Coll., Ft. Wayne, Ind., 1983-84. Pvt. piano tchr., Kokomo, 1967-85; piano tchr. Barbara Martin Piano Svc., Indpls., 1985-88, 1990—, Van Wezel Performing Arts Hall, Sarasota, Fla., 1988-90. Author: Piano Abstract, 1981. Fellow Ancient and Mystical Order Rosae Crucis. Avocation: building experimental musical instruments. Home and Office: 1912 W Defenbaugh St Kokomo IN 46902-6032 Home Phone: 765-452-3103; Office Phone: 765-452-3103.

HIGHTMAN, CARRIE J., telecommunications industry executive, lawyer; b. Ill., 1957; m. Harry Hightman; 2 children. BA, Univ. Ill.; JD, Fla. State Univ. Assoc. counsel Fla. Office of Public Counsel, 1983—86; staff counsel Fla. Public Svc. Commn., 1983—86; ptnr., energy, telecom., public utilities practice group Schiff, Hardin & Waite, Chgo., 1986—2001; pres. SBC Ill., Chgo., 2001—. Trustee Chgo. Symphony Orch., DePaul Univ.; mem. Ill. Bus. Roundtable; bd. dir. Lyric Opera, Chgo., 2001—, Chgo. Urban League, 2003—, Abraham Lincoln Presdl. Libr. Found., Chicagoland C. of C. Named one of 100 Most Influential Women, Crain's Chgo. Bus., 2004; recipient Women of Achievement award, Anti-Defamation League, 2004. Mem.: Chgo. Bar Found. (bd. dir.). Office: SBC Illinois 225 W Randolph Chicago IL 60606

HIGI, WILLIAM LEO, bishop; b. Anderson, Ind., Aug. 29, 1933; Student, Mt. St. Mary of the West Sem.; MS, Xavier U., 1959. Ordained priest Diocese of Lafayette, Ind., 1959, bishop, 1984—; ordained bishop, 1984. Roman Catholic. Home: 610 Lingle Ave Lafayette IN 47901-1740 Office: Diocese of Lafayette PO Box 260 610 Lingle Ave Lafayette IN 47902-0260 Office Phone: 765-742-0275. Office Fax: 765-742-7513.*

HILDEBRAND, DANIEL WALTER, lawyer; b. Oshkosh, Wis., May 1, 1940; s. Dan M. and Rose Marie (Baranowski) H.; m. Dawn E. Erickson; children: Daniel G., Douglas P., Elizabeth A., Rachel E., Jacob E., Catherine E. BS, U. Wis., 1962, LLB, 1964. Bar: Wis. 1964, US Dist. Ct. (we. dist.) Wis. 1964, NY 1965, US Dist. Ct. (so. and ea. dists.) NY 1967, US Ct. Appeals (2d cir.) 1968, US Dist. Ct. (ea. dist.) Wis. 1970, US Ct. Appeals (7th cir.) 1970, US Supreme Ct. 1970, US Tax Ct. 1986, US Ct. Appeals (8th cir.) 1988, US Ct. Appeals (DC cir.) 1991, US Dist. Ct. (no. dist.) Ill. 2005. Assoc. Willkie, Farr & Gallagher, NYC, 1964-68; from assoc. to ptnr. DeWitt Ross & Stevens S.C., Madison, Wis., 1968—. Lectr. U. Wis. Law Sch., Madison, 1972-2000; mem. Joint Survey Com. on Tax Ememptions Wis; chair Code of Profl. Responsibility Rev. Com., 1985-87, chair Wis. Ethics 2000 Com., 2003-06. Editor: U. Wis. Law Rev., 1963-64. Pres. Wis. Law Fou., 1993-95, Wis. Jud. Commn., 1992-98, chmn., 1997-98. Fellow Am. Bar Found. (life), Wis. Bar Found. (life); mem. ABA (com. pub. fin. judicial campaigns 2001-02, trial practice com. litigation sect., ho. of dels. 1992-2006, standing com. on ethics 1997-03, Wis. state del. 1995-2003, bd. govs. 2003-06, exec. com. 2005-06, Amicus Briefs com., 2006-), Wis. Bar Assn. (bd. govs. 1981-93, exec. com. 1987-93, chmn. 1988-89, pres. 1991-92), Dane County Bar Assn. (pres. 1980-81), 7th Cir. Bar Assn., Am. Law Inst., Am. Acad. Appellate Lawyers, James E. Doyle Inn of Ct. Roman Catholic. Office: 2 E Mifflin St Ste 600 Madison WI 53703-2890 Office Phone: 608-283-5610. Business E-Mail: dwh@dewittross.com.

HILDEBRAND, ROGER HENRY, astrophysicist, physicist; b. Berkeley, Calif., May 1, 1922; s. Joel Henry and Emily (Alexander) H.; m. Jane Roby Beedle, May 28, 1944; children: Peter Henry, Alice Louise, Kathryn Jane, Daniel Milton. AB in Chemistry, U. Calif., Berkeley, 1947, PhD in Physics, 1951. Physicist, U. Calif., 1942-51; physicist Tenn. Eastman Corp., Oak Ridge Nat. Lab., 1945; asst. prof. dept. physics Enrico Fermi Inst., U. Chgo., 1952-55, asso. prof., 1955-60, prof., 1960—, prof. dept. astronomy and astrophysics, 1978—, Samuel K. Allison Disting. Service prof., 1985—, chmn. dept. astronomy and astrophysics, 1984-88; dir. Enrico Fermi Inst., 1965-68, dean coll., 1969-73. Assoc. lab. dir. for high energy physics Argonne (Ill.) Nat. Lab., 1958-64; chmn. sci. policy com. Stanford (Calif.) Linear Accelerator Ctr., 1962-66; mem. physics adv. com. Nat. Accelerator Lab., 1967-69; mem. sci. and ednl. adv. com. Lawrence Berkeley Lab., 1972-80; chmn. com. to rev. U.S. medium energy sci. AEC and NSF, 1974; chmn. airborne obs. users group NASA, 1983-84; chmn. sci. cons. group Stratopheric Obs. for Infrared Astronomy (SOFIA), NASA, 1985-89, mem. sci. working group, 1995-97, sci. coun., 1997—; mem. space astronomy and astrophysics Space Sci. Bd., 1987-90; mem. coun. Columbus Project, 1987-88; mem. sci. and tech. adv. panel for the submillimeter array Harvard/Smithsonian Ctr. for Astrophysics, 1989-95; mem. astronomy and astrophysics survey com. NAS Panel for Infrared Astronomy, 1989-90; chmn. Dannie Helneman prize com. Am. Inst. Physics, 1990; mem. sci. and tech. adv. group Large Millimeter Telescope, 1995—; mem. obs. vis. com. Assn. Univs. for Rsch. in Astronomy, 1993-96, chmn. Stratospheric Obs. Infrared Astronomy sci. coun., 1997—; mem. NASA review panel for Small Explorer (SMEX) Proposals, 2000; mem. NASA/JPL bd. for Planck High Frequency Instrument Detectors, 2000-02; mem. faculty Canary Islands Winter Sch. Astrophysics, 2000. Guggenheim fellow, 1968-69, Alfred P. Sloan Found. fellow, 1975. Fellow Am. Phys. Soc., Am. Acad. Arts and Scis.; mem. Am. Astron. Soc., Internat. Astron. Union, Midwestern Univs. Rsch. Assn. (dir. 19956-58, 62-68), Kavli Inst. for Comological Physics (chair adv. com. 2001-2003, assoc. mem. 2003-),Phi beta Kappa, Sigma Xi. Office: U Chgo Enrico Fermi Inst 5640 S Ellis Ave Chicago IL 60637-1433

HILDING, JEREL LEE, music and dance educator, retired dancer; b. New Orleans, Sept. 24, 1949; s. Oscar William and Loeta Dana (Boldra) H.; m. Krystyna Zofia Jurkowski, July 1, 1978; children: Dennis Jozef, Kristopher Jay. BA, La. State U., New Orleans, 1971. Prin. dancer Joffrey Ballet, NYC, 1975-89; dir. arts in edn. N.J. Ballet, 1989-90; assoc. prof., dir. dance U. Kans., 1990—. Avocations: piano, sports. Office: U of Kansas Dept Music and Dance 460 Murphy Hall 1530 Naismith Dr Lawrence KS 66045-0001

HILER, JOHN PATRICK, former government official, former congressman, business executive; b. Chgo., Apr. 24, 1953; s. Robert J. and Margaret F. Hiler; m. Catherine Sands BA, Williams Coll., 1975; MBA, U. Chgo., 1977. Mktg. dir. Charles O. Hiler and Son, Inc., Walkerton, Ind., 1977-80, Accurate Castings Co., La Porte, 1977-80; mem. 97th-101st congresses from 3d Ind. Dist., 1981-90; dep. adminstr. GSA, Washington, 1991-93; exec. Accurate Castings, Inc., La Porte, Ind., 1993—. Del. Ind. Rep. Conv., 1978, 90, 94, Rep. Nat. Conv., 1984, 88, White House Conf. on Small Bus., 1980; trustee Meml. Hosp. Mem. Ind. Mfrs. Assn., orth Ctrl. Ind. Med. Edn. Found. Roman Catholic. Office: Accurate Castings Inc PO Box 639 La Porte IN 46352-0639

HILES, BRADLEY STEPHEN, lawyer; b. Granite City, Ill., Nov. 11, 1955; s. Joseph J. and Betty Lou (Goodman) H.; m. Toni Jonine Failoni, Aug. 12, 1977; children: Eric Stephen, Nina Catherine, Emily Christine. BA cum laude, Furman U., 1977; JD cum laude, St. Louis U., 1980. Bar: Mo. 1980, U.S. Dist. Ct. (ea. dist.) Mo., 1980, Ill. 1981. From assoc. to ptnr. Blackwell Sanders Peper Martin, St. Louis, 1980—. V.p., sec., gen. counsel Miss. Lime Co., 1992. Editor-in-chief St. Louis Univ. Law Jour., 1979-80; contbr. articles to profl. jours. Mem. Bar Assn. of Met. St. Louis (chmn. environ. and conservation law com. 1993-94). Republican. Baptist. Avocations: gospel singing, bicycling. Home: 34 Meditation Way Ct Florissant MO 63031-6535 Office: Blackwell Sanders Peper Martin 720 Olive St Fl 24 Saint Louis MO 63101-2338 Home Phone: 314-921-1777; Office Phone: 314-345-6489. E-mail: bhiles@blackwellsanders.com.

HILGERT, JOHN A., state legislator; b. Omaha, Jan. 8, 1964; m. Cara Linden, Aug. 12, 1995; 1 child, John Linden Hilgert. BSBA, U. Nebr., 1986; grad., Creighton U., 1989; grad. officer basic course, U.S. Army Judge Adv. Gen. Sch., 1989, grad. trial advocacy course, 1990. V.p. instnl. advancement Cath. Charities, Omaha; mem. Nebr. Legislature from 7th dist., Lincoln, 1995—. Mem. Mandan Pk. Renovation Com., Dahlman Area Rehab. Effort, St. Frances Cabrini Cath. Ch.; former rep. Archdiocesan Pastoral Coun. With U.S. Army, 1989-92, Ops. Desert Storm. Decorated Bronze Star. Mem. ABA, Nebr. State Bar Assn., Omaha Bar Assn., Hanscom Pk. Neighborhood Assn., Columbus Pk. Neighborhood Assn., Nebr. Human Svcs. Assn., Spring Lake Pk. Neighborhood Assn., Deer Pk. Neighborhood Assn., S. Omaha Bus. Assn., Q St. Merchants Assn., VFW, Am. Legion, Sons of Italy, La Soc. Des 40 Hommes Et 8 Chevaux, KC, S. Omaha Optimists Internat., Christoforo Colombo Lodge, Fraternal Order Eagles.

HILKER, LYLE J., financial services organization executive; b. New London, Wis. BBA, U. Wis., Oshkosh, 1992. With Aid Assn. for Luths., Appleton, Wis., 1973—, dir. managerial acctg., 1985-88, asst. v.p. Expense Info. Svcs., 1988-92, 2d v.p. Expense Info. Svcs., 1992-93, 2d v.p. fin. and managerial reporting, 1993-95, 2d v.p. bus. process assurance and enhancement, 1995-97, v.p. bus. process assurance and enhancement, 1997; now also v.p. product svcs. Thrivent Finl. for Luths. (formerly known as Aid Assn. for Luths.), Appleton, Wis. Past pres. Bethlehem Luth. Ch., Hortonville, Wis.; also past pres. local chpt. Aid Assn. for Luths., Hortonville; past mem. Fox Valley Tech. Coll. Acctg. Adv. Com.; bd. dirs. Fox Valley Symphony. Office: Thrivent Finl for Luths 4321 Ballard Rd Appleton WI 54919-0001

HILL, BARON PAUL, congressman; b. Seymour, Ind., June 23, 1953; s. Edwin Merrill and Edith Goen Hill; m. Betty Jean Schepman, 1972; children: Jennifer, Cara, Elizabeth. BS in History, Furman U., 1975. Fin. analyst Merrill Lynch; mem. Ind. State Ho. Reps, 1982—90, US Congress from 9th Ind. dist., 1999—2005, 2007—, mem. energy & commerce com., sci. & tech. com. Exec. dir. State Student Assistance Commn., 1992; involved with Am.Red Cross, Seymour Chamber Commerce, Seymour Jaycees. Mem.: Elks Club. Democrat. Methodist. Office: 223 Cannon House Office Bldg Washington DC 20515 also: 320 W 8th St Ste 114 Bloomington IN 47404 Office Fax: 812-523-1474.

HILL, CHARLES, newspaper editor; Bur. chief AP, Detroit, 1991—. Office: 300 River Place Dr Ste 2400 Detroit MI 48207-5064

HILL, CHARLES GRAHAM, JR., chemical engineering educator; b. Elmira, NY, July 28, 1937; s. Charles Graham and Ethel Mayburn (Pfleegor) H.; m. Katharine Mertice Koon, July 11, 1964; children: Elizabeth, Deborah, Cynthia. BS, MIT, 1959, MS, 1960, ScD, 1964. Asst. prof. MIT, Cambridge, 1964-65, U. Wis., Madison, 1967-71, assoc. prof., 1971-76, prof. chem. engring., 1976—, John T. and Magdalen L. Sobota prof. chem. engring., 1995—, prof. food sci., 1989—, chmn. dept. chem. engring., 1989-92. Cons. A.D. Little, Cambridge, 1964-65, Joseph Schlitz Brewing Co., Milw., 1973-76, Nat. Bur. Stds., 1979-95. Author: Introduction to Chemical Engineering Kinetics and Reactor Design, 1977; contbr. articles to profl. jours. Capt. U.S. Army, 1965-67. Gen. Motors Nat. scholar, 1955-59; NSF fellow, 1959-62, Ford Found. fellow, 1964-65, Fulbright Sr. fellow, 2000. Fellow AIChE; mem. Am. Chem. Soc., Inst. Food Technologists, Am. Oil Chemists Soc., Soc. Biological Engring, Sigma Xi, Tau Beta Pi, Phi Lambda Upsilon. Republican. Presbyterian. Office: U Wis Dept Chem Engring 1415 Engineering Dr Madison WI 53706-1607 Office Phone: 608-263-4593. Business E-Mail: hill@engr.wisc.edu.

HILL, DARLENE, newscaster; b. Cleve. m. Bernard Murray, 1996; 2 children. B, Ohio State U. Gen. assignment reporter CBS affiliate, Monterey, Calif.; anchor and reporter KJRH-TV, Tulsa, Okla., WFLD-TV, Chgo., 1994—. TV Journalist The Expt. in Black and White, 2002 (Nat. Emmy award cmty. svc., regional Emmy award, AP award, Edward R. Murrow award, Scripps Howard Found. award, Nat. Assn. Black Journalists award, Soc. Profl. Journalists award). Mem.: Chgo. Assn. of Black Journalists, Nat. Assn. of Black Journalists, Alpha Kappa Alpha. Office: WFLD-TV 205 N Mich Ave Chicago IL 60601

HILL, DAVID K., JR., construction executive; Chmn., CEO Kimball Hill Homes, Rolling Meadows, Ill., 1990—. Office: 5999 New Wilke Rd Bldg 5 Rolling Meadows IL 60008-4506

HILL, EMITA BRADY, academic administrator, consultant; b. Balt., Jan. 31, 1936; d. Leo and Lucy McCormick (Jewett) Brady; children: Julie Beck, Christopher, Madeleine Vedel. BA, Cornell U., 1957; MA, Middlebury Coll., 1958; PhD, Harvard U., 1967. Instr. Harvard U., 1961-63; asst. prof. Western Reserve U., 1967-69; from asst. prof. to v.p. Lehman Coll. CUNY, Bronx, NY, 1970-91; chancellor, grad. faculty Ind. U., Kokomo, Ind., 1991-99, chancellor emerita, 1999—. Vis. advisor Salzburg Seminar Univs. Project; cons. in field. Trustee Am. U. in Central Asia; mem. Women's Forum of NY. Mem.: Internat. Assn. Univ. Pres., Phi Beta Kappa. Avocations: music, scuba diving, tennis.

HILL, GARY, video artist; b. Santa Monica, Calif., Apr. 4, 1951; Student, Art Students League, Woodstock, 1969. Founder, dir. Open Studio Video, Tarrytown, .Y., 1977-78; artist-in-residence Exptl. TV Ctr., Binghamton, N.Y., 1975-77, Portable Channel, Rochester, N.Y., 1978, Sony Corp., Hon. Atsugi, Japan, 1985, Chgo. Art Inst., 1986, Calif. Inst. Arts, Valencia, 1987, Hopital Ephémère, Paris, 1991; vis. assoc. prof. Ctr. Media, SUNY, Buffalo, 1979-80; vis. prof. art Bard Coll., Annandale-on-Hudson, N.Y., 1983; art faculty Cornish Coll. Arts, Seattle, 1985-92. One person shows include Mus. Modern Art, N.Y.C., 1980, 90, Whitney Mus. Am. Art, N.Y.C., 1983, Galerie des Archives, Paris, 1990, 91, Galerie Huset-Glyptotek Mus. Mus., Copenhagen & YYZ Artist's Outlet, Toronto, 1990, OCO Espace d'art contemporain, Paris, 1991, Watari Mus. Contemporary Art, Tokyo, 1992, Mus. Modern Art, Oxford, Eng., 1993, Mus. Contemporary Art, L.A., 1994, Mus. Contemporary Art, Chgo., 1994, Fundaicó La Caixa, Barcelona, Spain, Busch-Reisinger Mus., Harvard U. Art Mus, Cambridge, Mass., 1995, Moderna Museet, Stockholm, 1995, Inst. Contemporary Art, Phila., 1996, Kunst-und Ausstellungshalle der Bundesrepublik Deutschland (Forum), Bonn, Germany, 1996, Centro Cultural Banco do Brazil, Rio de Janeiro, 1997, Musée d'Art Contemporain de Montréal, Can., 1998, Donald Young Gallery, Seattle, 1998, Museu d'Art Contemporani, Barcelona, Spain, 1998, others; exhibited in group shows Am. Ctr., Paris, 1983, Whitney Mus. Am. Art, .Y., 1986, St. Gervais, Geneva, 2d Seminar on Internat. Video, 1987, ELAC Art Contemporain, Lyon, France, 1988, Biennial Exhbn., Whitney Mus. Am. Art, 1991, 93, Performing Objects, Inst. Contemporary Art, Boston, 1992, Cocido y Crudo, Centro Reina Sofia, Madrid, 1994, Light Into Art, Contemporary Arts Ctr., Cin., 1994, Facts and Figures, Lannan Found., L.A., 1994, Multiplas Dimensoes, Centro Cultural de Belem, Lisbon, Portugal, 1994, Beeld, Mus van Hedendaagse Kunst, Ghent, Belgium, 1994, Crossings, Kunsthalle Wien, Austria, 1998, Voices, Witte de with Rotterdam, The Netherlands, 1998; author: Primarily Speaking, 1981-83, Whitney Mus. Am. Art, 1983, Primarily Speaking Communications, 1988, And if the Right Hand did not Know What the Left Hand is Doing, Illuminating Video, 1990, Unspeakable Images, Camera Obscura, 1991, Finnish Nat. Gallery, Helsinki, Finland, 1995, Mus. Modern Art, N.Y.C., 1995, Albert Knox Gallery, Buffalo, 1996, World Wide Video Festival, Amsterdam, The Netherlands, 1997. Recipient prize ARTEC 91 Internat. Biennale, Nagoya, Japan, 1991; Rockefeller Intercult Media Arts fellow, 1989-90, Guggenheim fellow, 1990; recipient JOhn D. and Catherine T. MacArthur grant. Office: Donald Young Gallery 933 W Washington Blvd Chicago IL 60607-2218

HILL, LANCE, meteorologist; BS, Marquette U.; postgrad., Lyndon State Coll. Meteorologist KMEG-TV, Sioux City, Iowa, WANE-TV, Ft. Wayne, Ind., WISN, Milw. Recipient seal, Nat. Weather Assn. Mem.: Am. Meteorol. Soc. Avocations: mountain biking, hiking, camping, storm chasing. Office: WISN PO Box 402 Milwaukee WI 53201-0402

HILL, LLOYD LESTER, food service executive; b. Nacagdoches, Tex., Jan. 8, 1944; s. Lloyd Lester and Ruby (Murchison) Hill; m. Carol Ann London, Dec. 20, 1964; children: Ronald Lloyd, Brandt Lloyd; m. Sue Ann Staggs, June 25, 1978; 1 child, Joshua Lloyd. Student psychology, N. Tex. State U., 1962—65; student, U. Tex., 1965—67, Columbia U., 1980; MBA, Rockhurst Coll., 1985. Dist. sales mgr. Marion Health and Safety div. Marion Labs., Dallas and Los Angeles, 1969—74, regional sales mgr. Chgo., 1974—76, mgr. new bus. devel. Kansas City, 1976—77, dir. sales, 1977—79; regional mgr. Norton SPD, Cranston, RI, 1979—80; sr. v.p. Kimberly Services Inc., Kansas City, 1980—88, dir., 1982—88; exec. v.p., bd. dirs. Kimberly Quality Care, 1988—91, pres., 1991-94; exec. v.p., COO Applebee's Internat. Inc., Overland Pk., Kans., 1994, co-CEO, 1997, CEO, 1998—2006, chmn., 2000—, also bd. dirs., 1989—. Named one of America's Best CEOs, Institutional Investor mag., 2005. Republican. Methodist. Office: Applebees Internat Inc 4551 W 107th St Ste 100 Overland Park KS 66207-4037 Fax: 913-341-1694.

HILL, LOWELL DEAN, agricultural marketing educator; b. Delta, Iowa, Apr. 27, 1930; s. Frederick Carl and Harriet Jane (Atwood) H.; m. Betty Elaine Carpenter, Dec. 9, 1951; children: Rebecca Elaine, Brent Howard. BS in Agrl. Edn., Iowa State U., 1951; MS in Agrl. Econs., Mich. State U., 1961, PhD in Agrl. Econs., 1963. Asst. prof., then assoc. prof. dept. agrl. econs. U. Ill., Urbana, 1963-72, prof., 1972-77, L.J. Norton prof. agrl. mktg., 1977-98, L.J. Norton prof. emeritus, 1998—. Cons. Office Tech. Assessment, Washington, 1986-88, South Am. and Europe, 1995, FAO, Rome, 1978-80, U.S. AID, 1983, World Bank, Washington, 1989-90, 92-93, Argentina, Colombia, Chile, 1989-94, U.S. Feed Grains Coun., Venezuela, Japan, Korea, 1990-93, USDA, Russia, 1993-96; mem. adv. com. Fed. Grain Inspection Svc., USDA, 2000-2003. Author: Grain Grades and Standards: Historical Issues, 1990; editor: Role of Government in a Market Economy, 1982, Corn Quality in World Markets, 1985. Cpl. U.S. Army, 1952-54. Fellow East West Ctr.; recipient Quality of Comm. award, 1980, 88, Disting. Policy Contbr. award 1988, Extension Programs award, 1989, Disting. Svc. award USDA, 1989, Internat. Mktg. Support award Am. Soybean Assn., 1989, Faculty award for rsch. excellence, 1991; Univ. scholar, 1992. Fellow: Am. Agrl. Econ. Assn.; mem.: Coun. Agrl. Sci. and Tech. (chmn. 1989—90). E-mail: l-hill3@uiuc.edu.

HILL, LUTHER LYONS, JR., lawyer; b. Des Moines, Aug. 21, 1922; s. Luther Lyons and Mary (Hippee) H.; m. Sara S. Carpenter, Aug. 12, 1950; children— Luther Lyons III, Mark Lyons. BA, Williams Coll., 1947; LLB, Harvard U., 1950; LLD (hon.), Simpson Coll., 1979. Bar: Iowa 1951. Law clk. to Justice Hugo L. Black U.S. Supreme Ct., 1950-51; assoc., ptnr. Henry & Henry, Des Moines, 1951-69; mem. legal staff Equitable Life Ins. Co. of Iowa, 1952-87, exec. v.p., 1969-87, gen. counsel, 1970-87; of counsel Nyemaster, Goode, McLaughlin, Voigts, Wiest, Hansell O'Brien, Des Moines, 1992—. Counsel, adminstr. Iowa Life and Health Ins. Guaranty Assn. Bd. dirs., past pres. United Comty. Svcs. Greater Des Moines; past trustee, past chmn. Simpson Coll., Indianola, Iowa. Capt. M.I., AUS, WWII, ETO. Mem. ABA, Iowa Bar Assn., Polk County Bar Assn., Assn. Life Ins. Counsel, Des Moines Club, Wakonda Club. Republican. Avocation: mountain climbing. Office: Ste 1600 700 Walnut St Des Moines IA 50309-3800

HILL, RICHARD A., advertising executive; b. Detroit; Student, Mich. State U.; MS in Mktg., Wayne State U. With J. Walter Thompson, Young & Rubicam; media supr. Buick/GMC Truck divsn., assoc. media dir. McCann-Erickson, Troy, Mich., 1970-75, sr. account exec. Buick account, 1975-77, v.p. media, mktg. dir. Detroit, 1977-79, account supr. multi-products group, 1979-81, account supr. Buick, 1981-86, sr. v.p., mgmt. rep., 1986-91, dep. mgr., chmn. mgmt. bd., 1991-93, exec. v.p., gen. mgr., 1993-97, dir. profl. devel., 1997—, also exec. v.p., 1993—. Avocation: golf. Office: Mccann Erickson 360 W Maple Rd Birmingham MI 48009-3346

HILL, STEPHEN L., JR., lawyer, former prosecutor; m. Marianne Matteson; 2 children. BS in Polit. Sci., Southwest Mo. State U., 1981; JD, U. Mo., 1986; postgrad., London U. Staff U.S. Congressman Ike Skelton, 4th dist Mo., 1982; trial atty. Smith, Gill, Fisher & Butts, Kansas City, 1986-94; U.S. atty. Western Dist. Mo., Kansas City, 1993—2001; partner Blackwell Sanders Peper Martin, LLP, Kansas City, Mo., 2001—. Office: Blackwell Sanders Peper Martin Llp 4801 Main St Ste 1000 Kansas City MO 64112-2551 E-mail: shill@bspmlaw.com.

HILL, TERRI, diversified financial services company executive; BA in Orgnl. Comm., Ariz. State U.; cert. in human resources, Cornell U. With Am. Express, 1984—96, Nationwide Mutual Ins. Co., 1996—, sr. v.p. human resources and ops. Scottsdale Ins. Co., exec. v.p., chief adminstrv. officer, 2003—. Office: ationwide Mutual Ins Co One Nationwide Plaza Columbus OH 43215-2220

HILL, TESSA, non profit environmental group executive; BA in Edn., Park Recreation Adminstrn., U. Minn., 1968. Tchr. elem. schs., 1970; founder Kids For Saving Earth Worldwide, Mpls., 1989—. Adv. com. U.S. Environ. Protection Agy., Dept. Health Human Svcs. Agy. Toxic Substances Disease Registry. Editor CHEC Report, Kids for Saving Earth News/Programs. Bd. dirs. Children's Health Environ. Coalition, Nat. Coalition Against Misuse Pesticides. Home and Office: Kids for Saving Earth Worldwide 5425 Pineview Ln N Minneapolis MN 55442-1704 Business E-Mail: KSEWW@aol.com.

HILL, THOMAS CLARK, lawyer; b. Prestonsburg, Ky., July 17, 1946; s. Lon Clay and Corinne (Allen) H.; m. Barbarie Friedly, June 13, 1968; children: Jason L., Duncan L. BA, Case Western Reserve U., 1968; JD, U. Chgo., 1973. Bar: Ohio 1973, U.S. Supreme Ct. 1976. Assoc. atty. Taft, Stettinius & Hollister LLP, Cin., 1973-81, ptnr., 1981—. Author: Monthly Meetings in North America: A Quaker Index, 4th edit., 1998. Trustee, treas. Wilmington Coll., Ohio, 1982-94, 99—, sec., 2002-06, vice chair, 2006-; treas. Ams. sect. Friends World Commn. for Consultation, 1990-95, presiding clk., 1995-99, ctrl. exec. com., presiding clk., London, 2000-; trustee Wilmington Yearly Meeting of Friends (Quakers), 1986-98, Friends United Meeting, 1999-2004, presiding clk. trustees, 2002-04. Mem. ABA, Friends Hist. Assn. (bd. dirs. 1994-95). Republican. Mem. Soc. Of Friends. Avocation: Quaker history. Office: 425 Walnut St Ste 1800 Cincinnati OH 45202-3948 Office Phone: 513-357-9334. Business E-Mail: hill@taftlaw.com.

HILL, TYRONE, professional basketball player; b. Cin., Mar. 19, 1968; BA in Comm. Arts, Xavier U., 1986-90. Forward Golden State Warriors, San Francisco, 1990-93, Cleve. Cavaliers, 1993-97, Milw. Bucks, 1997-99, Philadelphia 76ers, 1999—2001, Cleveland Cavaliers, 2001—. Active NBA Stay In Sch. Program. All-time leading rebounder, scorer Xavier U.; leader Cleve. Cavaliers field-goal percentage, 1993-94; named to NBA All-Star Game Eastern Conf., 1995. Avocation: music. Office: Cleveland Cavaliers Gund Arena One Center Court Cleveland OH 44115

HILL, WILLIAM A(LEXANDER), judge; b. Carmel, Calif., Aug. 21, 1946; s. R. William and Ruth M. (McDonald) H.; m. Diane K. Hartman, Apr. 25, 1981; children: Erin, Georgia. BS, U. N.D., 1968, JD, 1971; cert., Hastings Coll. Law Coll. Advocacy, 1977; grad. in fed. evidence, U. Mich. Law Sch., 1981. Bar: N.D. 1971, Minn. 1974, U.S. Dist. Ct. N.D. 1971, U.S. Tax Ct. 1973, U.S. Ct. Appeals (8th cir.) 1973. Dep. sec. of state State of N.D., 1971-72; law clk. to judge U.S. Dist. Ct. .D., 1972-74; ptnr. Pancratz Law Firm, Fargo, N.D., 1974-83; magistrate U.S. Dist. Ct., N.D., 1975-83; judge U.S. Bankruptcy Ct., 1983—. Mem. 8th cir. bankruptcy appellate panel, 1996—2003; part-time magistrate U.S. Dist. Ct. N.D., 1975-83; active N.D. Supreme Ct. Joint Procedures Com. Commr., 1978-83. Mem. exec. bd. dirs. No. Lights coun. Boy Scouts Am., 1993-98; bd. dirs. Fargo Moorhead Symphony, 1995-2001, Heritage Hjemkomst Ctr., Moorhead, Minn.; chmn. Gethemane Episcopal Found., Fargo, 1981-83; pres. Plains Art Mus., Moorhead, 1982. Office: US Bankruptcy Ct Quentin N Burdick US Courthouse 655 1st Ave N Ste 350 Fargo ND 58102-4952 E-mail: william_hill@ndb.uscourts.gov.

HILLARD, TERRY G., retired protective services official; b. South Fulton, Tenn. BS in Corrections, MS in Corrections, Chgo. State U. Police officer Chgo. Police Dept., Ill., 1968—, comdr. Gresham dist. patrol divsn., 1991—93, dep. chief of patrol area 2, 1993—95, supt. of police, 1998—2003. With USMC, 63. Office: Chgo Police Dept Office of Supt 3510 S Michigan Ave Chicago IL 60653

HILLEGONDS, PAUL, former state legislator; b. Holland, Mich., Mar. 4, 1949; s. William C. and Elizabeth (Romaine) H.; m. Nancy; 1 child, Sarah. BA, U. Mich., 1971; JD, Coolegy Law Sch., 1986. Legis. asst. U.S. Rep. Philip Ruppe, Mich., 1971-74, adminstrv. asst., 1974-78; mgr. Ruppe's Congl. Campaign, 1974, 76; state rep. Dist. 54 Mich. Ho. of Reps., 1978-94, state rep. Dist. 88, 1995-96; pres., CEO Detroit Renaissance, 1997—2000. Asst. minority leader, 1983-85, minority leader, 1986-93; mem. Workers Compensation & Unemployment Ins. Subcoms., Mich. Ho. of Reps.; chmn. Rep. Campaign Com., leader Rep. Policy Com., Mich. Ho. of Reps. Trustee Kresge Found.; bd. mem. Grand Valley State U.; trustee Mich. Strategic Fund, Mich. Nature Conservancy. Recipient Disting. Svc. award Holland Jaycees, 198, Disting. Svc. award Assn. Ind. Colls., 1985; named One of Ten Outstanding Legislators of Yr., Nat. Rep. Legislators Assn., 1988. Mem. Ripon Soc., Assn. Pub. Justice, Holland Jaycees, Common Cause, Kiwanis. Office: Kresge Found 3215 W Big Beaver Rd Troy MI 48084

HILLER, STEVE, radio personality; b. Des Moines, Dec. 22, 1973; m. Natasha Hiller; 1 child, Darien. Radio music host Sta. WMBI Radio, Chgo.; now sr. creative services prodr. Moody Radio Network. Avocations: golf, football, water sports, Superman, road trips. Office: Moody Broadcasting Network 820 N La Salle Blvd Chicago IL 60610

HILLERT, GLORIA BONNIN, anatomist, educator; b. Brownton, Minn., Jan. 25, 1930; d. Edward Henry and Lydia Magdalene (Luebker) Bonnin; m. Richard Hillert, Aug. 20, 1960; children: Kathryn, Virginia, Jonathan. BS, Valparaiso U., Ind., 1953; MA, U. Mich., 1958. Instr. Springfield (Ill.) Jr. Coll., 1953-57; teaching asst. U. Mich., Ann Arbor, 1957-58; instr., dept. head St. John's Coll., Winfield, Kans., 1958-59; asst. prof. Concordia Coll., River Forest, Ill., 1959-63; vis. instr. Wright Jr. Coll., Chgo., 1974-76, Ill. Benedictine Coll., Lisle, 1977-78, Rosary Coll., River Forest, 1976-81; prof. anatomy and physiology Triton Coll., River Grove, 1982-92, prof. emeritus, 1992—; vis. asst. prof. Concordia U., 1993—. Vis. instr. Wheaton (Ill.) Coll., 1988; advisor Springfield Jr. Coll. Sci. Club, 1953-57, Concordia Coll. Cultural Group, 1959-62; program dir. Triton Coll. Sci. Lectr. Series, 1983-87; participant Internat. Educators Workshop in Amazonia, 1993. Dem. campaign asst., Maywood, Ill., 1972, 88; vol. Mental Health Orgn., Chgo., 1969-73, Earthwatch, St. Croix, 1987, Costa Rica, 1989, Internat. Med. Care Team, Guatemala, 1995, Earthwatch End of Dinosaurs, 1997. Mem. AAUW, Ill. Assn. Community Coll. Biol. Tchrs., Nat. Assn. Biol. Tchrs. Lutheran. Avocation: travel. Home: 1620 Clay Ct Melrose Park IL 60160-2419 Office: Triton Coll 2000 N 5th Ave River Grove IL 60171-1907

HILLIARD, ROBERT GLENN, insurance company executive, lawyer; b. Anderson, SC, Jan. 18, 1943; s. Baz Robert and Louise (Holcombe) H.; m. Heather Ann Prevost, Apr. 1, 1966; children: Kathryn Louise Stuart, Nancy Ann, Mary Elizabeth Glenn. BA, Clemson U., 1965; JD, George Washington U., 1968. Bar: S.C. 1969. Gen. counsel Liberty Life Ins. Co., Greenville, SC, 1965-82, 1975-82; v.p., gen. counsel, sec. Liberty Life Ins. Co., Greenville, SC, 1975-82; pres., chief exec. officer Liberty Life; pres. Liberty Life Ins. Co., Greenville, SC, 1982-88, chmn. bd., 1988-89; dir. Liberty Corp., 1982-89; pres., CEO, Security Life of Denver ING Americas, Atlanta, 1989—92, pres., CEO ING America Life, 1992—93, CEO, pres., chmn., 1993—2003; non-exec. chmn. Conseco, Carmel, Ind., 2003—04, chmn., 2004—. Bd. dirs. Carolina First Corp., Security Life; founder, chmn. emeritus Foothills Trail Conf.; chmn. Netherlands Ins. Co., ING Can., N.Am. Investment Centre, NN Fin. Bd. dir. Piedmont Hosp., Atlanta; vice chmn., fin., High Mus.; chmn. investment com., Clemson Univ. Found.; former chmn. bd. dirs. S.C. Gov.'s Sch. for Arts, Perception, Inc. Recipient Jim Kern award Am. Hiking Soc. Mem. ABA, S.C. Bar Assn., Am. Coun. Life Ins., Assn. Life Ins. Counsel, INternat. Ins. Soc., Org. for Internat. Investment, Internat. Bus. Fellows, Bare Minimum Track Club (co-founder, bd. dirs.), Greenville Country Club, Poinsett Club (S.C.), Colo. Concern, Colo. Forum, Denver Athletic Club, Univ. Club. Presbyterian. Office: Conseco 1355 Peachtree St Ste 640 Atlanta GA 30309 Office Phone: 404-745-9770. E-mail: rglennhilliard@aol.com.

HILLIKER, DONALD BECKSTETT, lawyer; b. Dixon, Ill., Jan. 6, 1944; s. Donald Herschel and Bernadette (Welch) H.; m. Carolyn Ann Beckstett, Dec. 16, 1972; children: Carrie Ford, Sarah Dillon. BS, Loyola U., Chgo., 1966; JD, Northwestern U., 1969. Bar: Ill. 1969, U.S. Dist. Ct. (no. dist.) Ill. 1969, U.S. Ct. Appeals (7th cir.) 1971, U.S. Ct. Appeals (6th cir.) 1988, U.S. Supreme Ct. 1978. Lawyer, legal aid bur. United Charities Chgo., 1969—70; assoc. Isham, Lincoln & Beale, Chgo., 1970—74, ptnr., 1976—79, Coin, Crowley, Nord & Hilliker, Chgo., 1979—81, Phelan, Pope & John, Ltd., Chgo., 1981—90, Pope & John, Ltd., Chgo., 1990—95; ptnr., chmn. pro bono com. McDermott, Will & Emery, Chgo., 1995—. Vis. asst. prof. law, asst. dean Sch. Law, Northwestern U., Chgo., 1975-76; mem. com. on profl. responsibility Ill. Supreme Ct., 1978-95; bd. dirs. Legal Assistance Found., pres., 2002-2004; adj. prof. law Northwestern U., Chgo., 1993—. Co-author: Law Journal Seminars Press, 1980, 84; contbr. articles to numerous legal jours.; editorial bd. Northwestern U. Law Rev., 1969-70. Pres. sch. bd. St. Clement Sch., Chgo., 1984-87; nat. chmn. ann. fund drive Northwestern U. Sch. Law, 1986-88, mem. visitors com., 1988-94. Reginald Heber Smith fellow, 1969-70. Fellow Am. Bar Found.; mem. ABA (co-chair ethics beyond the rules task force 1994-98, co-chair comml. and banking litig. com. 1997-98, standing com. ethics and profl. responsibility 1997-03, chair 2001-03, chair coord. coun. Ctr. Profl. Responsibility 2005—, litig. sect. coun. 1998-01, chair sect./divsn. com. on ethics and professionalism, co-chair pro bono and pub. interest com. 2003-06, commn. to evaluate model code jud. conduct 2003—07), Chgo. Bar Assn. (chair large law firm com. 1998-2000, profl. responsibility com.), Chgo. Coun. Lawyers (legal counsel 1981-83), Am. Law Inst., Ctr. Ethics and Corp. Policy (bd. dirs. 1991-94), Order of Coif. Democrat. Roman Catholic. Office: McDermott Will & Emery LLP 227 W Monroe St Ste 5200 Chicago IL 60606-5096 Office Phone: 312-984-7610. Office Fax: 312-984-7700. Business E-Mail: dhilliker@mwe.com.

HILLMAN, JORDAN JAY, law educator; b. 1924. M.A. in Polit Sci., U. Chgo., 1947, JD, 1950; SJD, Northwestern U., 1965. Bar: Ill. 1950. Mem. legal staff Ill. Commerce Commn., 1950-53; with Chgo. and Northwestern Ry., 1954-67, gen. counsel, 1963-67, v.p. law, 1966-67; prof. emeritus law Northwestern U., 1967-89, prof., rsch. counsel, prof. transp. ctr., 1989-91; sr. legal cons., gen. counsel U.S. Ry. Assn., 1974-76, spl. counsel, 1976-79; legal cons. Amtrak, 1978. Mem. Constn. Study Comm., State of Ill., 1963-67; mem. Zoning Amendment Com., Evanston, Ill., 1963-68; mem. Bd. Edn., Dist. 202, Evanston Twp. H.S., 1968-71; mem. Chgo. Transit Authority Bd., 1981-87. Mem. Phi Beta Kappa. Author: Competition and Railroad Price Discrimination, 1968; The Parliamentary Structuring of British Road-Rail Freight Coordination, 1973; The Export-Import Bank at Work; Promotional Financing in the Public Sector, 1982; Price Level Regulation for Diversified Public Utilities, 1989. Office: Northwestern U Sch Law 317 E Chicago Ave Chicago IL 60611-3008

HILLMAN, RICHARD EPHRAIM, pediatrician, educator; b. Pawtucket, RI, Oct. 6, 1940; s. Harold S. and Anne (Chernick) H.; m. Laura S. Smith, June 14, 1970; children: Helena, Stuart, Noah, Paul, Andrew, Anne. AB, Brown U., 1962; MD, Yale U., 1965. Diplomate: Am. Bd. Med. Examiners, Am. Bd. Pediatrics, Am. Bd. Human Genetics. Intern Grace-New Haven Hosp., 1965-66, resident, 1966-67; asst. prof. pediatrics Washington U., St. Louis, 1971-75, assoc. prof., 1975-78, prof. pediatrics, 1981-87, assoc. prof. genetics, 1977-81, prof. genetics, 1981-87; prof. biochemistry and child health U. Mo., Columbia, 1987—2000, prof. emeritus, dir. metabolic genetics rsch., 2000—. Chmn. mental retardation research com. Nat. Inst. Child Health and Human Devel., Bethesda, Md., 1983-87, assoc. chmn., 1995—. Lt. comdr. USN, 1969-71. Fellow Am. Acad. Pediatrics; mem. Soc. Pediatric Research (council), Am. Pediatric Soc., Am. Soc. Clin. Investigation, Soc. for Inherited Metabolic Disorders (pres.) Office: School of Medicine U Mo Columbia MO 65212

HILLS, ALAN, performing company executive; Grad., Wright State U. Arranger, handling co. tours rock Ballet Blue Suede Shoes; bus. mgr. Lord of the Dance prodn. at Beau Rivage Resort and Casino, Biloxi, Miss.; former gen. mgr. Cleve./San Jose Ballet; exec. dir. Cin. Ballet, 2001—. Office: Cin Ballet 1555 Central Pkwy Cincinnati OH 45214

HILLS, ARTHUR W., architectural firm executive; BS in Horticulture, Mich. State U., 1953; student, U. Toledo, 1957-58; B of Landscape Architecture, U. Mich., 1961. Registered architect, Mich., Ohio, Fla. Prin. Arthur Hills, Landscape Architect, 1960-66, Arthur Hills and Assocs., Toledo, 1966—. Prin. works include (golf courses) Golf Club Ga. (Best New Pvt. Course Golf Digest 1992), Harbour Pointe (Best New Pub. Course Golf Digest 1991), The Champions, Lexington, Ky., Bighorn Golf Club, Palm Desert, Calif., Dunes West, Charleston, S.C., Arthur Hills Course at Palmetto Dunes and Palmetto Hall Plantation, Hilton Head Island, Bonita Bay's Marsh Course, Bonita Springs, Fla. (one of Top 100 Courses in U.S. Golf Digest 1988—), TPC at Eagle Trace, Coral Springs, Fla. (one of Top 100 Courses in U.S. Golf Digest), Egypt Valley Country Club, Grand Rapids, Mich., Wingpointe, Salt Lake City, River Islands Golf Club, Knoxville, Tenn., Walking Stick, Pueblo, Colo., Windsor Parke, Jacksonville, Fla., The Legacy at Green Valley, Las Vegas, Nev., others. With U.S. Armed Svcs., 1952-54. Mem. Am. Soc. Golf Course Architects (officer, trustee), Am. Soc. Landscape Architects, Golf Course Supt.'s Assn. Am., Nat. Golf Found., at. Recreation and Pks. Assn., Ohio Pks. and Recreation Assn., Ohio Turfgrass Found., Urban Land Inst. Office: Arthur Hills & Assoc 7351 W Bancroft St Toledo OH 43615-3014

HILTON, JAMES L., university librarian; m. Molly Hilton; children: Michael, Meghan. BA in psychology, Univ. Tex., 1981; MA in psychology, Princeton Univ., 1983, PhD in social psychology, 1985. With U. Mich. Ann Arbor, 1985—2006, Arthur F. Thurnau prof. psychology, 1997—2000, assoc. provost for Academic, Info., and Instrnl. Tech., interim univ. libr., 2005; v.p., chief info. officer U. Va., Charlottesville, 2006—. Fellow, Sweetland Writing Ctr., CIC Academic Leadership Program. Office: Libr Adminstrn U Mich 818 Hatcher S Ann Arbor MI 48109-1205 Office Phone: 734-764-9356. Fax: 734-763-5080.

HILTON, THOMAS SCOTT, coal company executive; b. Biloxi, Miss., Aug. 28, 1952; s. Kenneth Leonard and Viola Elenor (Oline) H.; m. Claudia Anne List, Aug. 28, 1976; children: Sabrina Beth, Marshall Scott, Ramsey Mitchell. BS in Acctg., Kansas U., 1974. CPA, Kans., Mo., Ariz. Staff acct. Arthur Andersen & Co., Kansas City, Mo., 1974-76, sr. auditor, 1976-79, mgr., 1979-80; acctg. mgr. Ariz. div. Peabody Coal Co., Flagstaff, 1980, div. controller Ariz. div., 1980-83, div. controller Eastern div. Henderson, Ky., 1983-86, v.p., controller, 1986-88; sr. v.p. mktg. Peabody Devel. Co., St. Louis, 1988-92; v.p., contr. Peabody Holding Co. Inc., St. Louis, 1992—. Pres. Audubon coun. Boy Scouts Am., 1987-88, bd. dirs. St. Louis area coun., 1989—; treas. United Way Henderson County, Ky., 1986-88. Mem. AICPA. Avocations: golf, basketball. Office: Peabody Holding Co 701 Market St Ste 700 Saint Louis MO 63101-1895

HILTZ, KENNETH A., corporate financial executive; BBA, Xavier Univ.; MBA, Univ. Detroit. CPA, cert. mgmt. acct. Mng. dir. AlixPartners LLC; sr. v.p., CFO Harnischfeger Ind. (now Joy Global Inc.), 1999—2001; CFO, chief restructuring officer Hayes Lemmerz Internat. Inc., 2001—03; CFO Foster Wheeler Ltd., 2003—04, Dana Corp., Toledo, 2006—. Mem. adv. bd. Sch. Bus. Adminstrn., Oakland Univ. Office: Dana Corp 4500 Dorr St Toledo OH 43615

HIMES, JOHN HARTER, medical researcher, educator; b. Salt Lake City, July 25, 1947; s. Ellvert Hiram and Mildred Anna (Harter) H.; children: Rachel Anne, Matthew Hiram, Sarah Elizabeth; m. LaVell Gold. BS, Ariz. State U., 1971; PhD, U. Tex., 1975; MPH, Harvard U., 1982. Rsch., sr. scientist Fels Rsch. Inst., Yellow Springs, Ohio, 1976-79; Fels asst. prof. Wright State U. Sch. Medicine, Dayton, Ohio, 1977-79; sr. analyist, project dir. Abt Assocs., Cambridge, Mass., 1979-82; assoc. prof. CUNY, Bklyn., 1982-87; from assoc. prof. to prof. U. Minn. Sch. Pub. Health, Mpls., 1992—, dir. nutrition coord. ctr., 1995—. Expert com physical status WHO, Geneva, Switzerland, 1991-94, expert adv. panel nutrition, 1994—; mem. tech. working groups Ctrs. for Disease Control, Washington and Atlanta, 1988-97. Author: Parent-specific Adjustment for Assessment of Recumbent Length & Stature, 1981, Anthropometric Assessment of Nutritional Status, 1991; contbr. articles to profl. jours. Recipient Nathalie Masse Meml. prize Internat. Children's Ctr., Paris, 1979. Fellow Human Biology Coun.; mem. APHA, N.Am. Assn. Study Obesity, Internat. Assn. Human Auxology, Pan Am. Health Orgn. (tech. adv. nutrition 1994—2000, Nat. Ctr. Health Stats. (tech. working group 1994-97), Am. Soc. Nutritional Scis., Soc. for Study Human Biology, Sigma Xi, Phi Kappa Phi, Delta Omega. Home Phone: 952-920-1075. Business E-Mail: himes@epi.umn.edu.

HIMMELBERG, CHARLES JOHN, III, mathematics professor, researcher; b. North Kansas City, Mo., Nov. 12, 1931; s. Charles John and Magdalene Caroline (Batliner) H.; m. Mary Patricia Hennessy, Jan. 27, 1962; children: Charles, Ann, Mary, Joseph, Patrick. BS, Rockhurst Coll., 1952; MS, U. Notre Dame, 1954, PhD, 1957. Assoc. analyst Midwest Rsch. Inst., Kansas City, Mo., 1957-59; asst. prof. math. U. Kans., Lawrence, 1959-65, assoc. prof., 1965-68, prof., 1968—2005, emeritus prof., 2005—, chmn. dept. math., 1978-99. Mem. editorial bd. Rocky Mountain Jour. Math, 1972-88; contbr. articles to profl. jours. Mem. Am. Math. Soc., Math. Assn. Am. Roman Catholic. Office: U Kans Dept Math Lawrence KS 66045-7523 Business E-Mail: himmelberg@ku.edu.

HIMPSEL, FRANZ JOSEF, physicist, researcher; b. Rosenheim, Germany, 1949; arrived in US, 1977; Diploma in Physics, U. Munich, 1973, PhD in Physics, 1977. With IBM Rsch., Yorktown Heights, NY, 1977-95, 1st level mgr., 1982-85, 2nd level mgr., 1985-95; prof. physics U. Wis., Madison, 1995—, co-dir. sci. Synchrotron Radiation Ctr., 1997—2002, Ednor M. Rowe prof. physics, 2000—. Contbr. articles to sci. jours. Recipient Humboldt Rsch. Prize, 2005. Fellow: Am. Vacuum Soc. (Peter Mark award 1985), Am. Phys. Soc. (Davisson-Germer prize in Atomic or Surface Physics 2007); mem.: German Phys. Soc., NY Acad. Sciences. Office: U Wis Dept Physics 1150 University Ave Madison WI 53706-1390 Office Fax: 608-265-2334. E-mail: fhimpsel@wisc.edu.

HINDERAKER, JOHN HADLEY, lawyer, political blogger; b. Watertown, SD, Sept. 19, 1950; s. Irving Alden and Eula Mae (Jertson) H.; m. Shannon Faye Smith, Jan. 3, 1981 (div. 1993); children: Eric, Laura, Alison, Kathryn; m. Loree Kay Miner, June 4, 1994. AB magna cum laude, Dartmouth Coll., 1971; JD cum laude, Harvard U., 1974. Bar: Minn. 1974; admitted to practice US Ct. of Appeals, 8th Cir., 9th Cir., US Dist. Ct. Dist. Minn. Assoc. Faegre & Benson LLP, Mpls., 1974-81, ptnr., 1981—. Chmn. practice standards com., Faegre & Benson, 1986; fellow Claremont Inst.; lectr. in field. Contbr. articles to profl. jours. including Nat. Rev., Am. Enterprise, Am. Experiment Quarterly and newspapers from Fla. to Calif.; guest appearances Fox News; co-founder, blog writer: powerlineblog.com, 2002-. Bd. dirs. Ctr. of the Am. Experiment, 1996. Named Super Lawyer of the Yr., Jour. Law and Politics, 2005; named one of Minn. Top Commercial Litigators, Minn. Jour. of Law and Politics, Top 25 Web Celebs, Forbes mag., 2007, 50 Most Important People on the Web, PC World, 2007. Fellow Claremont Inst.; mem. ABA, Minn. State Bar Assn. (mem. ethics com. 1979-85), Hennepin County Bar Assn. Republican. Lutheran. Avocations: authoring commentaries on polit. and econ. issues, weightlifting. Office: Faegre & Benson 2200 Wells Fargo Ctr 90 S 7th St Minneapolis MN 55402-3901 Office Phone: 612-766-8430. Office Fax: 612-766-1600. Business E-Mail: JHinderaker@faegre.com. E-mail: powerlinefeedback@gmail.com.

HINDMAN, LARRIE C., lawyer; b. Meservey, Iowa, Mar. 30, 1937; s. Marvin C. and Fredona E. (Lemke) H.; m. Jeannie Carol Richey, June 18, 1961; children: Bryant C., Derek Cory. BS, Iowa State U., 1959; JD, U. Iowa, 1962. Bar: Mo. 1963, Kans. 1975. Ptnr. Stinson Morrison & Hecker LLP, Kansas City, Mo., 1962-2000. Contbr. legal articles to profl. jours. Mem.: Am. Land Title Assn. (lender counsel), Am. Coll. Real Estate Lawyers, Club at Porto Cima. Office: Stinson Morrison & Hecker LLP 1201 Walnut Ste 2800 Kansas City MO 64106-2150 Home: 1186 Grand Cove Rd Sunrise Beach MO 65079 Office Phone: 816-842-8600.

HINDMAN, LESLIE SUSAN, auction company executive; b. Hinsdale, Ill., Dec. 1, 1954; d. Don J. and Patricia (de Forest) H. Student, Pine Manor Coll., 1972-74, U. Paris, 1974-75, Ind. U., 1975-76. Mgr. Sotheby Parke Bernet, Chgo., 1978—82; pres. Leslie Hindman Auctioneers, Chgo., 1982—97, Salvage One Archtl. Artifacts, Chgo., 1986—2002; former co-owner Chgo. Antiques Ctr.; pres. Sotheby's, Chgo., 1997—99; chmn. Leslie Hindman Enterprises, 1999—; founder, pres. Eppraisals.com, 1999—2001, Leslie Hindman Auctioneers, Chgo., 2003—, AntiquesChicago, 2003—. Bd. mem. MB Fin. Bank. Host HGTV's At the Auction and The Appraisal Fair, 1995—2003; author: Adventures at the Auction, 2001; columnist: What's It Worth?, 1999—2003. Bd. mem. Children's Meml. Hosp., The Goodman Theatre, Chgo. Pub. Libr. Found., The Arts Club Chgo. Mem. Com. of 200, Internat. Women's Forum, Young Pres's. Orgn., Arts Club Chgo. Clubs: Women's Athletic (Chgo.) (bd. dirs. 1988—). Office: 122 N Aberdeen Chicago IL 60607 Office Phone: 312-280-1212. Business E-Mail: leslie@lesliehindman.com.

HINEGARDNER, LAURA A., lawyer; BA, U. Ky., 1993; JD, U. Cin., 1996. Bar: Ky. 1996, Ohio 1997. Atty. Katz, Teller, Brant & Hild, Cin. Former mem. Class VIII, Cin. Acad. Leadership for Lawyers; bd. mem. Fort Thomas Edn. Found. Mem. Charities Guild of Northern Ky. Named one of Ohio's Rising Stars, Super Lawyers, 2006. Avocations: sports, pilates. Office: Katz Teller Brant & Hild 255 E 5th St Ste 2400 Cincinnati OH 45202-4724 Office Phone: 513-977-3484. Office Fax: 513-762-0084.

HINES, J. A., state official; b. West Salem, Ohio, May 1, 1927; m. Pam Hines; children: Ruth, Steve, Sally, Norman, Amy. DVM, Ohio State U., 1953. State assemblyman, Wis., 2001—; mem. Westfield Sch. Bd., 1969—81; owner vet. practice, 1953—95; pres. Adams-Marquette Vet Svc., 1979—95; vet. surgeon Adams-Marquette Vet. Svc., 1995—. Mem. agr. com.; mem. edn. com.; mem. pub. health and longterm care; mem. tourism com. Mem.: Wis. Vet. Med. Assn., Nat. Inst. for Animal Agr., Am. Vet. Med. Assn., Am. Assn. Bovine Practitioners (Wis. Vet. of Yr. 1995). Republican. Office: State Capitol Rm 10 W PO Box 8952 Madison WI 53708-8952

HINES, MARSHALL, construction engineering company executive; b. Chgo., Dec. 29, 1923; s. Herbert Waldo and Helen (Gartside) H.; m. Janet Young, July 28, 1945; children: Karen Lynn, Keith Douglas, Dori Hines Alton. BCE, Mich. State U., 1947, MCE, 1948. Registered profl. engr., Mich. Project engr. The Christman Co., Lansing, Mich., 1948-55, supt., 1955-70, gen. supt., 1971-83, exec. v.p., 1983—96, ret. cons., 1996—. With U.S. Army, 1943-45. Mem. NSPE, Mich. Soc. Profl. Engrs. (bd. dirs. 1986, Constrn. Engr. Yr. 1990, Engr. of Yr. award 1994), Builders Exch. of Lansing (pres. 1988), Rotary (bd. dirs. Lansing club 1986-87). Republican. Methodist. Home: 1137 Rebecca Rd East Lansing MI 48823-5210 Office: The Christman Co 408 Kalamazoo Plz Lansing MI 48933-1990

HINES, NORMAN WILLIAM, law educator, retired dean; b. 1936; AB, Baker U., 1958; LLB, U. Kans., 1961; LLD, Baker U., 1999. Bar: Kans. 1961, Iowa 1965. Law clk. US Ct. Appeals 10th cir., 1961-62; tchg. fellow Harvard U., 1961-62; asst. prof. law U. Iowa, 1962-65, assoc. prof., 1965-67, prof., 1967-73, J.F. Rosenfield disting. prof., 1973—, dean, 1976—2004, dean emeritus, Joseph F. Rosenfield Prof., 2004—. Vis. prof. Stanford U., 1974—75. Editor (notes and comments): Kans. Law Rev. Founder, pres. Johnson County Heritage Trust. Fellow, Harvard U., 1961—62. Fellow: Am. Law Inst., Iowa State Bar Found., ABA Found.; mem.: Assn. Am. Law Schs. (exec. com. 2004—, pres. 2005), Order of Coif, Environ. Law Inst. (assoc.). Office: U Iowa Coll Law Iowa City IA 52242-0001 Office Phone: 319-335-9236. Business E-Mail: n-hines@uiowa.edu.

HINKELMAN, RUTH AMIDON, insurance company executive; b. Streator, Ill., June 4, 1949; d. Olin Arthur and Marjorie Annabeth (Wright) Amidon; m. Allen Joseph Hinkelman, Jr., Oct. 28, 1972; children: Anne Elizabeth, Allen Joseph III. AB in Econs., U. Ill., 1971. Underwriter Kemper Ins. Group, Chgo., 1971-75; acct. exec. ear North Ins. Agy., Chgo., 1975-76; underwriter Gen. Reinsurance Corp., Chgo., 1976-78, asst. sec., 1978-79, asst. v.p., 1979-83, 2nd v.p., 1983-87, v.p., 1987—. Home: 133 Linden Ave Wilmette IL 60091-2838 Office: Gen Reinsurance Corp 1 N Wacker Dr Ste 1700 Chicago IL 60606 Office Phone: 312-207-5332. Business E-Mail: rhinkelm@genre.com.

HINKENS, KAY L., social services association executive; Student, U. Wis., Oshkosh. With Aid Assn. for Luths., Appleton, Wis., 1971—, with employee credit union, 1971-85, co-founder, mgr. lending and mktg., Member Credit Union, 1986-91, v.p. Member Credit Union, 1991-94, pres. Member Credit Union, 1994—. Past tchr. Sunday sch. Mem. Mktg. Coun., Luth. Missionary Soc. (past pres.), Fox Cities Chpt. Credit Unions (past pres., treas.), Credit Union Exec. Soc. Office: Aid Assn for Lutherans 4321 N Ballard Rd Appleton WI 54919-0001

HINKLE, PHILLIP D., state representative; b. Peru, Ind., Dec. 25, 1946; married; 2 children. BS. MS, Ind. State U. Tchr. Ben Davis H.S., Wayne Twp., Ind., 1973—76; rsch. dir. Indpls. City-County Coun., 1976—79; Wayne Twp. Assessor Marion County, Ind., 1979—91; real estate assoc. F.C. Tucker Co., 1991—; councilman Indpls. City County Coun., 1991—2000; state rep. dist. 92 Ind. Ho. of Reps., Indpls., 2000—, mem. local govt. and ways and means coms. Former bd. dirs. Greater Indpls. YMCA; pres. Wayne Twp. Edn. Found.; campaign mgr. 6th Congl. Dist., 1978; pres. Marion County Twp. Assessors Assn., 1983—87, State Assessors Assn., 1988—89. Sp5 US Army, 1971—72, Ft. Gordon, Ga. Mem.: Ben Davis Youth Sports Assn. (adv. bd.), Suburban West Optimist Club. Republican. Office: Ind Ho of Reps 200 W Washington St Indianapolis IN 46204-2786

HINKLEY, GERRY, newspaper editor; Dep. mng. editor Milw. Jour. Sentinel, 1995—. Office: Milw Sentinel 333 W State St PO Box 661 Milwaukee WI 53201-0661

HINOJOSA, RAUL, physician, ear pathology researcher, educator; b. Tampico, Tamulipas, Mexico, June 18, 1928; came to U.S., 1962, naturalized, 1968; s. Raul Hinojosa-Flores and Melida (Prieto) Hinojosa; m. Berta Ojeda, Sept. 25, 1953; children—Berta Elena, Raul Andres, Jorge Alberto, María de Lourdes BS in Biology, Inst. Sci. and Tech., Tampico, 1946; MD, Nat. Autonomous U. Mexico, Mexico City, 1954. Asst. prof. U. Chgo, 1962-68, assoc. prof., 1968-97, assoc. prof. emeritus, 1998—, dir. temporal bone program for ear rsch., 1962—, rsch. assoc., 1968-88. Rsch. fellow biophysics Harvard U., Boston, 1963; rsch. assoc. in neuropathology, Harvard U., 1964, rsch. fellow in anatomy, 1965. Editor temporal bone histopathology update Am. Jour. of Otolaryngology, 1989-94. Recipient Rsch. Career Devel. award NIH, 1962-65, rsch. grantee, 1962—, hearing rsch. study sect. grantee, 1988-92. Mem. AAAS, Internat. Otopathology Soc., Microscopy Soc. Am., Midwest Soc. Electron Microscopists, Assn. Rsch. in Otolaryngology, Am. Otological Soc., N.Y. Acad. Scis. Office: U Chgo 5841 S Maryland Ave Chicago IL 60637-1463

HINRICHS, CHARLES A., paper company executive; b. St. Louis, Dec. 3, 1953; s. John H. and Anne B. (Beasley) Hinrichs; m. Linda J. Miller, Aug. 6, 1977; children: Christopher J., Jonathan C. BS in Acctg., U. Mo., 1976; MBA, St. Louis U., 1981. Asst. treas. United Mo. Bank of Kirkwood, St. Louis, 1976-79; asst. v.p. Commerce Bank of St. Louis, 1979-81; sr. v.p. Boatmen's Nat. Bank of St. Louis, 1981—; v.p. & treas. Smurfit-Stone Container Corp., 1998—2002, v.p. & CFO, 2002—05, sr. v.p. & CFO, 2005—. Bd. dir., mem. exec. com. Downtown St. Louis, Inc., 1990. Mem.: Forest Hills Country Club, Mo. Athletic Club. Office: Smurfit-Stone Container Corp 150 N Michigan Ave Chicago IL 60601

HINSHAW, ADA SUE, nursing educator, former dean; b. Arkansas City, Kans., May 20, 1939; d. Oscar A. and Georgia Ruth (Tucker) Cox; children: Cynthia Lynn, Scott Allen Lewis. BS, U. Kans., 1961; MSN, Yale U., 1963; MA, U. Ariz., 1973, PhD, 1975; DSc (hon.), U. Md., 1988, Med. Coll. of Ohio, 1988, Marquette U., 1990, U. Nebr., 1992, Mount Sinai Med. Ctr., NY, 1993, U. Medicine and Dentistry N.J., 1995, Grand Valley State U., 1995, U. Toronto, Can., 1996, St. Louis U., 1996, Georgetown U., 1998. Instr. Sch. Nursing U. Kans., 1963-66; asst. prof. U. Calif., San Francisco, 1966-71; prof. U. Ariz., Tucson, 1975-87; dir. nursing rsch. U. Med. Ctr., Tucson, 1975-87; dir. Nat. Inst. Nursing Rsch. Pub. Health Svc., Dept. Health and Human Svcs., NIH, Washington, 1987—94; prof. U. Mich. Sch. Nursing, Ann Arbor, 1994—, dean, 1994—2006, dean emeritus, 2006—. Contbd. articles to profl. jours. Recipient Kay Schilter award U. Kans., 1961, Lucille Petry Leone award Nat. League for Nursing, 1971, Wolanin Geriatric Nursing Rsch. award U. Ariz., 1978, Alumni of the Yr award Sch. Nursing U. Kans., 1981, Disting. Alumni award Sch. Nursing Yale U., 1981, Alumni Achievement award U. Ariz., 1990, Disting. citation Kans. Alumni Assn., 1992, Health Leader of the Yr. award Pub. Health Svc., 1993, Centennial award Columbia Sch. Nursing, 1993, Presdl. Meritorious Exec. Rank award, 1994. Mem. ANA (Nurse Scientist of Yr. Award 1985, Salute to Nurses award 1994), Coun. Nurse Rschrs. (Nurse Scientist of Yr. Award 1985), Md. urses Assn., Western Soc. for Rsch. in Nursing, Am. Acad. Nursing, Inst. Medicine (mem. 1989-, coun. mem. 1999-04, mem. com. 1995-99, Walsh McDermott medal, 2005), Sigma Xi, Sigma Theta Tau (Beta Mu Chpt. award of Excellence in Nursing Edn., 1980, Elizabeth McWilliams Miller Excellence in Rsch. Award, 1987), Alpha Chi Omega. Avocations: hiking, camping, bicycling. Office: U Mich Sch Nursing 400 N Ingalls St Rm 4221 Ann Arbor MI 48109-2003 E-mail: ahinshaw@umich.edu.

HINSHAW, JUANITA, electric distributor executive; CFO Graybar Elec., St. Louis, 2000—, sr. v.p., 2000—, bd. dir., 2000—. Bd. dir. Ipsco Inc., Insituform Technologies, Inc, Commerce Bank, 2002—; bd. mem. KETC/Channel 9, Grand Center, Md. U., United Way. Office: Graybar Electric PO Box 7231 Saint Louis MO 63177

HINTZ, CHAD JASON, lawyer; b. Minot, ND, July 3, 1974; m. Michelle Hintz. BA in Architecture, U. Minn., 1996; JD, William Mitchell Coll. Law, 2001. Bar: Minn. 2001, US Dist. Ct. (dist. Minn.) 2004, US Ct. Appeals (8th cir.) 2004. Assoc. Burke & Thomas, P.L.L.P., St. Paul, 2002—. Adj. prof. appellate advocacy William Mitchell Coll. Law, 2005—. Contbr. articles to profl. publs. Named a Rising Star, Minn. Super Lawyers mag., 2006—08. Mem.: Def. Rsch. Inst., Minn. Def. Lawyers Assn., Minn. State Bar Assn., Ramsey County Bar Assn. Office: Burke & Thomas PLLP 3900 Northwoods Dr Ste 200 Saint Paul MN 55112 Office Phone: 651-490-1808. E-mail: hintz@burkeandthomas.com.

HIPPEE, WILLIAM H., JR., lawyer; b. Des Moines, 1946; BS, U. Pa., 1968; JD, Stanford U., 1972. Bar: Minn. 1972. Ptnr. Dorsey & Whitney LLP, Mpls., 1972—. Office: 40 H Endrlives Inl Ste 2300 120 S 6th Ave Minneapolis MN 55402

HIRSCH, DAVID L., lawyer; BA, Pomona Coll., 1959; JD, U. Calif., Berkeley, 1962. Bar: Calif. 1963. Dir. real estate, constrn. and property mgmt. svcs. and risk mgmt. coun. Metaldyne/NI Industries, Inc., Taylor, Mich., 1966—; pres. NI Industries Inc., Taylor, Mich., 2004—. V.p. mem. commn. on Govt. Procurement for U.S. Congress, 1971. Mem. editl. bd. Bur. Nat. Affairs' Fed. Contracts Report. Fellow Am. Bar Found.; mem. ABA (life fellow of fellows, chair emerging issues com. sect. pub. contract law, sec. pub. contract law sect. 1977-78, mem. council 1978-80, chmn. 1981-82), Calif. Bar (bd. advisors pub. law sect.), Los Angeles County Bar Assn., Fed. Bar Assn., Nat. Contract Mgmt. Assn. (nat. bd. advisors), Fin. Exec. Inst. (legal advisor com. on govt. bus.). Office: Masco Tech Corp/NI Industries Inc 21001 Van Born Rd Taylor MI 48180-1340

HIRSCH, JOACHIM V. (JAKE), aeronautics company executive; Diploma, U. Reutlingen, Germany. Various mgmt. positions TRW Inc., v.p., mgr. dir. Occupant Restraint Sys. Group Europe; exec. v.p., COO Magna Europe AG; pres., COO Kautex Textron, Germany; chmn., pres., CEO Textron Fastening Sys., Troy, Mich. Office: 840 W Long Lake Rd Ste 450 Troy MI 48098-6372

HIRSCH, LAWRENCE LEONARD, physician, retired educator; b. Chgo., Aug. 20, 1922; m. Donna Lee Sturm; children: Robert, Edward, Sharon. BS, U. Ill., 1943; MD, U. Ill., Chgo., 1950. Diplomate: Am. Bd. Family Medicine. Intern. Ill. Masonic Med. Ctr., Chgo., 1950-51; practice medicine specializing in family medicine Chgo., 1951-70; dir. ambulatory care Ill. Masonic Med. Ctr., Chgo., 1970-71, dir. family practice residency program, 1971-75; prof., chmn. dept. family medicine Chgo. Med. Sch., 1975-89, prof. emeritus, 1989—. Mem. med. licensing bd. State of Ill., 1982-94, chmn., 1988-94, hosp. licensing bd., 1994-2004; bd. dirs. Ill. Coun. for continuing Med. Edn., 1981-85, pres., 1986-87; cons. recombinant DNA Abbott Labs., 1980-87; lectr. in field; staff pres. Ill. Masonic Med. Ctr., 1970. Book rev. editor: Soc. of Tchrs. Family Medicine, 1979-89; book reviewer: Jour. AMA, 1969-; contbr. articles to profl. jours. Bd. dirs. Mid-Am. chpt. ARC, Chgo., 1978-88; nat. pres. Alpha Phi Omega, Kansas City, Mo., 1974-78; exec. com. Chgo. Found. Med. Care and PSRO, 1977-84, Ill. State Inter-Ins. Exchange, 1975-2006; bd. dirs. Crescent Counties Found. for Med. Care, 1985-91; commr. Northbrook (Ill.) Park Dist., 1987-91, pres., 1990—; mem. Village of Northbrook Planning Commn., 1987-89. With US Army, 1943—46. Recipient Silver Beaver award Boy Scouts Am., 1963; recipient Silver Antelope award Boy Scouts Am., 1967, Disting. Eagle award Boy Scouts Am., 1969, Brotherhood award Lakeview Interfaith Council, 1968, Physician Speaker award AMA, 1981; inducted into City of Chgo. Sr. Citizens Hall of Fame, 1991. Fellow AAAS, Am. Acad. Family Physicians (mem. congress of dels.); mem. Chgo. Med. Soc. (pres. 1979, Pub. Svc. award 1990), Ill. Acad. Family Physicians (pres. 1977), Assn. Depts. Family Medicine (exec. com.), Masons, Shriners, Kiwanis (dir. local club). Democrat. Unitarian Universalist.

HIRSCH, RAYMOND ROBERT, chemicals executive, lawyer; b. St. Louis, Mar. 20, 1936; s. Raymond Winton and Olive Frances (Gordon) H.; m. Joanne Therese Dennis, Jan. 30, 1960; children: Amy Elizabeth, Thomas Christopher, Timothy Joseph, Mary Patricia. LL.B., St. Louis U., 1959. Bar: Mo. 1959. With Treasury Dept., 1960-62, Petrolite Corp., St. Louis, 1962—, sec., 1971—, v.p., gen. counsel, 1973-82, sr. v.p., gen. counsel, 1982-92; of counsel Guilfoil, Petzall & Shoemake, St. Louis, 1992-2000. Mem. Pub. Defender Commn., Mo. Mcpl. judge City of Bridgeton, Mo., 1970-73; mem. City of Des Peres Planning and Zoning Commn., 1974-78; mem. bd. edn. Spl. Sch. Dist. St. Louis County, 1981-83; mem. Mo. Air N.G., 1959-60; trustee Childhaven. Mem. ABA, Am. Soc. Corp. Secs., Mo. Bar Assn., Bar Assn. St. Louis, Mo. Athletic Club. Roman Catholic. Office: Guilfoil Petzall & Shoemake 100 S 4th St Saint Louis MO 63102-1800 Home: 28500 Altessa Way Bonita Springs FL 34135 Office Phone: 314-241-6890. Personal E-mail: rrhirsch@comcast.net.

HIRSCH, STEVEN W., lawyer; b. Concordia, Kans., Jan. 14, 1962; s. Frederick J. and Dora Lee (Cooper) H.; m. Anita J. Richardson, Dec. 13, 1987. BA cum laude, Kans. State U., 1983; JD with honors, Washburn U., 1986. Bar: Kans. 1986, U.S. Dist. Ct. Kans. 1986. Adminstrv. asst. Kans. Dept. of Treasury, Topeka, 1985-87; ptnr. Morgan & Hirsch, Kans., 1987—. Author: Simpson-T6 1st Century, 1982. Vol. fireman Oberlin City Fire Dept., 1987—; chmn. Decatur County Dem. Com., 1987—; Oberlin Conv. and Vis. Bur., 1988—; treas. United Ch. Oberlin, 1987—. Mem. Kans. Bar Assn., Kans. Trial Lawyers Assn., NE Kans. Bar Assn. Clubs: Bohemian. Lodges: Masons. Democrat. Baptist. Avocation: bike riding. Office: 124 S Penn Ave Oberlin KS 67749-2243

HIRSCHFIELD, BRADLEY, rabbi; BA, U. Chgo.; MA, MPhil, Jewish Theological Seminary. Cert. ordained Rabbi Metivta. Pres. Nat. Jewish Ctr. for Learning and Leadership (CLAL). Former prof. Dept. Talmud and Rabbinics Metivta; cons. communal inst. and found.; spkr. in field of religion and philosophy Aspen Inst., Wash. at. Cathedral; key panelist Parliament of the World's Religions, Barcelona, 2004. Author: (religion books) Embracing Life and Facing Death: A Jewish Guide to Palliative Care, 2003, Remember for Life: Holocaust Stories of Faith and Hope, 2007, You Don't Have to be Wrong for me to be Right: Finding Faith Without Fanaticism, 2008; Appeared in Documentary: Freaks Like Me; co-prodr.: (films) When Good Gods Go Bad, 2007; Radio and TV appearances incl. ABC-Nightline UpClose (the only rabbi ever featured), CNN, CBS, PBS-Frontline: Faith and Doubt at Ground Zero & Religion & Ethics Newsweekly, NPR, commentator WWSB-TV, Sarasota, Fla.; contbr. articles. Named one of The Top 50 Rabbis in America, Newsweek Mag., 2007. Jewish. Office: c/o CLAL 440 Park Ave S New York NY 10016-8012 Office Phone: 212-779-3300. Office Fax: 212-779-1009.

HIRSCHHORN, AUSTIN, lawyer; b. Detroit, Feb. 20, 1936; s. Herman and Dena Grace (Ufberg) H.; m. Susan Carol Goldstein, June 30, 1963; children: Laura Elsie, Carol Helen, Paula Gail. BA with honors, Mich. State U., 1957; JD, Wayne State U., 1960. Bar: Mich. 1961. Assoc. Arnold M. Gold Law Offices, Detroit, 1960-63; ptnr. Gold & Hirschhorn, Detroit, 1963-65; pvt. practice Detroit, 1965-68; ptnr. Boigon, Hirschhorn & Winston, Detroit, 1968-69, Boigon & Hirschhorn, Detroit and Southfield, 1969-78; pvt. practice Southfield, 1979-80; ptnr. Zemke & Hirschhorn (P.C.), Southfield, Mich., 1980-83, Austin Hirschhorn, P.C., Southfield, 1983-91; of counsel Rubenstein, Isaacs, Haroutunian & Sobel, P.C., Southfield, 1991-92; pvt. practice Austin Hirschhorn, P.C., Birmingham, Mich., 1992-96, Troy, Mich., 1996—. Lectr. Inst. Continuing Legal Edn., Mich. Trustee The Internat. Sch., Farmington Hills, Mich. With AUS, 1960-62. Mem. ABA, Fed. Bar Assn., Mich. Bar Assn., Oakland County Bar Assn., Am. Bankruptcy Inst., Comml. Law League Am. Jewish. Home: 26903 York Rd Huntington Woods MI 48070-1361 Office: 101 W Big Beaver Rd #1050 Troy MI 48084-5299 Home Phone: 248-399-2828; Office Phone: 248-680-1660. E-mail: austinh@ix.netcom.com.

HIRST, RICHARD B., air transportation executive, lawyer; b. 1944; BA, Harvard Coll., 1969; JD, Harvard Law Sch., 1972. Sr. v.p., gen. counsel Northwest Airlines, Inc., 1990-94, sr. v.p. corp. affairs, 1994—99, sr. v.p. corp. affairs & adminstrn., 2007—08, sr. v.p. corp. affairs, gen. counsel, 2008—. Office: orthwest Airlines Inc 2700 Lone Oak Pkwy Eagan MN 55121*

HIRT, JANE, editor; B in Journalism, U. Nebr., Lincoln. With Chgo. Tribune, 1990—2002, sports copy editor, fgn. and nat. desk copy editor, fgn. and nat. news editor; founding co-editor RedEye, 2002—05, editor, 2005—. Named one of Top 40 Under 40, Crain's Chgo. Bus., 2006. Office: RedEye Tribune Tower 435 N Michigan Ave Chicago IL 60611 E-mail: jhirt@tribune.com.

HISS, ROLAND GRAHAM, retired internist, educator; b. Newark, 1932; s. George Crosby and Adrianne (Graham) H.; m. Margaret Barringer McGrath, Aug. 23, 1957; children: John Barringer, Meredith Graham Brown. BS, U. Mich., 1955, MD, 1957. Diplomate Am. Bd. Internal Medicine. Intern in medicine Phila. Gen. Hosp., 1957-58; resident in medicine U. Mich. Hosp., Ann Arbor, 1961-64; fellow hematology Simpson Meml. Inst., Ann Arbor, 1964-66; faculty medicine U. Mich. Med. Sch., Ann Arbor, 1966—2003, chmn. dept. med. edn., 1982—2002; coordinator edn. Mich. Diabetes Research and Tng. Ctr., Ann Arbor, 1977—2003; ret., 2003. Contbr. 60 articles to profl. jours. Served to capt. USAF, 1958-61. Recipient Teaching award Kaiser Permanente Found. and U. Mich., 1976. Fellow ACP; mem. Am. Diabetes Assn., AMA, Mich. State Med. Soc. Home: 3551 Chatham Way Ann Arbor MI 48105-2827 E-mail: redhiss@umich.edu.

HITCH, ELIZABETH, academic administrator; Dir. higher edn. Ctrl. Mich. U., assoc. dean Sch. Edn., Health and Human Svcs., prof. dept. human environ. studies; mgr. instrn. design Sch. Medicine U. Mich., Ann Arbor; dean Coll. Edn. and Profl. Studies Ea. Ill. U., Charleston, Ill.; provost, vice chancellor U. Wis., LaCrosse, 2002—. Office: U Wis LaCrosse 145 Main Hall 1725 State St La Crosse WI 54601

HITCHCOCK, KEN, professional hockey coach; b. Edmonton, Alta., Can., Dec. 17, 1951; m. Nancy; children: Emily, Alex, Noah. Student, U. Alta., Edmonton, Can. Head coach Kamloops Blazers, 1984-90; asst. coach Phila. Flyers, 1990-93; head coach Kalamazoo Wings, 1993-94; coach All-Star Games IHL, 1993-94, 94-95; head coach Dallas Stars, 1996—2002, Phila. Flyers, 2002—06, pro scout, 2006; head coach Columbus Blue Jackets, 2006—. Named Coach of Yr. Minor Hockey, 1982-83, Alta. Minor Hockey Assn., 1983-84, WHL, 1986-87, 89-90, top coach Canadian Major Jr. Hockey, 1989-90. Achievements include being the head coach of Stanley Cup Champion Dallas Stars, 1999. Office: Columbus Blue Jackets Nationwide Arena 200 W Nationwide Blvd, Ste Level Columbus OH 43215

HITES, RONALD ATLEE, chemist, educator; b. Jackson, Mich., Sept. 19, 1942; s. Wilbert T. and Evelyn J.H.; m. Bonnie Rae Carlson, Dec. 26, 1964; children: Veronica, Karin, David. BA in Chemistry, Oakland U., Rochester, Mich., 1964; PhD in Analytical Chemistry, MIT, Cambridge, Mass., 1968. NAS fellow Agrl. Rsch., Peoria, Ill., 1968-69; mem. rsch. staff, dept. chemistry MIT, Cambridge, 1969-72, asst. prof. chem. engring., 1972-76, assoc. prof., 1976-79; prof. Ind. U., Bloomington, 1979-89, Disting. prof. pub. and environ. affairs and chemistry, 1989—, dir. Environ. Sci. Rsch. Ctr., 2001—. Cons. EPA, 1974—. Assoc. editor Environ. Sci. Tech., 1990—; mem. editorial bd. Chemosphere, 1979-99; contbr. articles to profl. jours. Grantee NSF, 1974—, EPA, 1974—, Dept. Energy, 1977-95. Fellow AAAS; mem. Am. Chem. Soc. (award in environ. sci. 1991), Am. Soc. for Mass Spectrometry (pres. 1988-90, mem. editl. bd. 1990-96), Soc. Environ. Toxicol. Chemistry (bd. dirs. 1997-2000, Founders award 1993), Internat. Assn. Great Lakes Rsch. (pres. 2008-, bd. dirs. 2006—), Sigma Xi. Office: Ind U Sch Pub and Environ Affairs 410H Bloomington IN 47405 Office Phone: 812-855-0193. Business E-Mail: hitesr@indiana.edu.

HITSELBERGER, CAROL A., lawyer; b. Washington, Jan. 7, 1964; AB magna cum laude, Bryn Mawr Coll., 1986; JD cum laude, Univ. Pa., 1989. Bar: Ill. 1989. Assoc. Mayer Brown Rowe & Maw, Chgo., 1989—98, ptnr., fin. & securitization, 1998—. Author (contbg.): Securitization of Financial Assets, 2001. Mem.: ABA. Office: Mayer Brown Rowe Maw Llp 230 S La Salle St Ste 400 Chicago IL 60604-1407 Office Phone: 312-701-7740. Office Fax: 312-706-8151. Business E-Mail: chitselberger@mayerbrownrowe.com.

HLAVACEK, ROY GEORGE, publishing executive; b. Chgo., Sept. 17, 1937; s. George Louis and Lillian Barbara H.; m. Nancy Elaine Wroblaski, Aug. 3, 1963; children: Carrie Lee Felix, Alexander Michael BS, U. Ill., 1960; MBA, U. Chgo., 1969. Project engr. R&D Ctr., Swift & Co., Chgo., 1960-65; v.p., editor, pub. Food Processing mag., Foods of Tomorrow mag. Food Publs. div. Putman Pub. Co., Chgo., 1965-92; v.p., group pub. Food Group, Delta Comms. Inc., Chgo., 1992-2001; v.p. comms. Inst. Food Technologists, 2001—. Adv. com. dept. food sci. U. Ill., Urbana-Champaign, 1988-93 Patentee in field Commr. Oak Park (Ill.) Landmarks Commn., 1972-79, chmn., 1976-79; treas. Oak Park Bicentennial Commn., 1973-76, Ernest Hemingway Found. of Oak Park, 1983-2000 Mem. ASME, Food Processing Machinery and Supplies Assn. (dir. 1987-91), Inst. Food Technologists (councilor 1975-81, chmn. Chgo. sect.), Pi Tau Sigma, Sigma Tau Home: 904 Forest Ave Oak Park IL 60302-1310 Office: Inst Food Technologists 525 W Van Buren Chicago IL 60607 Business E-Mail: rghlavacek@ift.org.

HO, DAVID KIM HONG, education educator; b. Honolulu, Mar. 5, 1948; s. Raymond T.Y. and Ellen T.Y. (Fong) Ho; m. Joan Yee, July 6, 1968 (div. Apr. 1982); 1 child, Michael J.; m. Patricia Ann McAndrews, June 25, 1983. BS in Indsl. Engring., U. So. Calif., LA, 1970; MBA, Butler U., Indpls., 1976; MS in Acctg., U. Wis., Whitewater, 1981. Cert. fellow in prodn. and inventory mgmt., supply chain profl. Indsl. engr. FMC Corp., LA, 1970-73, mgr. prodn. planning and inventory control Indpls., 1973-77; materials mgr. Butler Mfg. Co., Ft. Atkinson, Wis., 1977-81, systems mgr. Kansas City, Mo., 1981-82; dir. materials and systems Behlen Mfg. Co., Columbus, Nebr., 1982-84, v.p. operations, bd. dirs., 1984-86; mgr. corp. materials Lozier Corp., Omaha, 1986-90, plant mgr., 1990-91; v.p. mfg. Heatilator Inc., Mt. Pleasant, Iowa, 1991-93; prof. profl. studies Bellevue U., Nebr., 1993—. Instr. Met. C.C., Omaha, 1989—, Iowa Wesleyan Coll., Mt. Pleasant, 1991—92; evaluator Assn. of Collegiate Bus. Sch. Programs, Overland Pk., Kans., pres., 2006—07, bd. dirs. Cons., evaluator, team chmn. Higher Learning Commn. of the North Ctrl. Assn., Chgo., 2001—, bd. trustees, 2007—. Mem.: Assn. Ops. Mgmt., Inst. Supply Mgmt. Home: 11729 Fisher House Rd Bellevue NE 68123-1112 Office: Met CC PO 3777-Soc 121 Omaha NE 68103-0777 Office Phone: 402-738-4637. Business E-Mail: dho@mccneb.edu.

HOAGLIN, THOMAS E., savings and loan association executive; b. Charleston, W.Va., May 4, 1949; BA in Econs., Denison U., 1971; MBA, Stanford U., 1973. Chmn., CEO Banc One Services Corp., 1997—98; exec. v.p., pvt. banking Bank One Corp., 1998—99; vice chmn. AmSouth Bancorporation, 2000; chmn., pres., CEO Huntington Bancshares Inc., Columbus, Ohio, 2001—07, chmn., CEO, 2007—. Pres., chmn., CEO Huntington Nat. Bank, Columbus; bd. dir. Denison U., The Columbus (Ohio) Partnership, Columbus (Ohio) Downtown Devel. Corp., Columbus (Ohio) Coll. Art and Design, Ohio Ctr. Sci. and Industry, Capital South Corp., The Gorman-Rupp Co., Mansfield, Ohio, Am. Elec. Power Corp., 2007—; bd. trustees Ohio Health. Bd. dir. Greater Columbus (Ohio) C. of C., Ohio Bus. Roundtable. Mem.: The Fin. Svcs. Roundtable, World Pres. Org. Office: Huntington Bancshares Inc Huntington Ctr 41 South High St Columbus OH 43287

HOARD, HEIDI MARIE, lawyer; b. Mt. Clemons, Mich., Feb. 8, 1951; d. Duane Jay and Elizabeth Hoard; m. John B. Lunseth II, Jan. 11, 1980; children: John B. III, Steven J. BA, Macalester Coll., 1972; JD cum laude, U. Minn., 1976. Bar: Minn. 1976, U.S. Dist. Ct. Minn. 1976. Assoc. Faegre & Benson, Mpls., 1976-83, ptnr., 1984-93; sr. legal counsel Medtronic, Inc., 1993-95; v.p., gen. counsel, corp. sec. The Musicland Group, Minnetonka, 1995—. Mem. State Bd. Women in the Legal Profession Task Force, State Bd. Legal Cert., 1986-88, pres. Tel-Law, Bar Assn. Com., Mpls., 1978-80; bd. dirs. Fund for Legal Aid Soc. Mem. Minn. Region G, Law Enforcement Assistance Assn. Com., 1971-72; vol. aide U.S. Senate Nursing Home Investigation and Hearing, Mpls., 1971-72; student dir. Legal Aid Clinic, U. Minn., Mpls., 1975-76. Mem. Am. Soc. Corp. Secs. (bd. dirs. Minn. sect.), Am. Corp. Counsel Assn., Minn. Bar Assn., Phi Beta Kappa. Democrat. Office: Musicland Group 10400 Yellow Circle Dr Hopkins MN 55343

HOARD, LEROY, professional football player; b. New Orleans, May 15, 1968; Student, U. Mich. Running back Cleve. Browns, Minnesota Vikings, 1996—. Named to NFL Pro Bowl Team, 1994. Office: Minnesota Vikings 9520 Viking Dr Eden Prairie MN 55344-3898

HOBBINS, ROBERT LEO, lawyer; b. Des Moines, June 5, 1948; s. Leo Michael and Margaret Ellen Hobbins; m. Carmela Theresa Tursi, Dec. 27, 1974; children: Brian, Patrick, Edward. BA magna cum laude, Creighton U., 1970; JD, NYU, 1973. Bar: Minn. 1973. Assoc. Dorsey & Whitney, Mpls., 1973-78; ptnr., labor, employment law practice Dorsey & Whitney LLP, Mpls., 1979. Adj. faculty U. St. Thomas Sch. Law, 2002—. Root-Tilden scholar; Named a Super Lawyer, Minn. Law & Politics and Mpls. St. Paul Mag. Mem. ABA (labor sect., EEO law com.), Minn. State Bar Assn., Hennepin County Bar Assn., Creighton U. Alumni Assn. (v.p. 1994). Office: Dorsey & Whitney 50 S 6th St Ste 1500 Minneapolis MN 55402-4502 Office Phone: 612-340-2919. Office Fax: 612-340-2868. E-mail: hobbins.robert@dorseylaw.com.

HOBBS, LEWIS MANKIN, astronomer; b. Upper Darby, Pa., May 16, 1937; s. Lewis Samuel and Evangeline Elizabeth (Goss) H.; m. Jo Ann Faith Hagele, June 16, 1962; children: John, Michael, Dara. B of Engring. Physics, Cornell U., 1960; MS, U. Wis., 1962, PhD in Physics, 1966. Jr. astronomer Lick Obs., U. Calif., Santa Cruz, 1965-66; faculty U. Chgo., 1966—, prof. astronomy and astrophysics, 1976—2003, prof. emeritus, 2003; dir. Yerkes Obs. Williams Bay, Wis., 1974-82. Bd. dirs. Assn. Univs. for Rsch. in Astronomy, Washington, 1974-85; mem. Space Telescope Inst. Coun., 1982-87; astronomy com. of bd. trustees Univs. Rsch. Assn., Inc., Washington, 1979-83, chmn., 1979-81; bd. govs. Astrophys. Rsch. Consortium, Inc., Seattle, 1984-91; mem. Users Com. for Hubble Space Telescope, NASA, 1990-94; mem. telescope allocation com. Nat. Optical Astronomy Obs., 1998-2000. Contbr. articles to profl. jours. Bd. dirs. Mil. Symphony Assn. of Walworth County, 1972-88. Alfred P. Sloan scholar, 1955-60. Mem.: Internat. Astron. Union, Am. Phys. Soc., Am. Astron. Soc. Office: U Chgo Yerkes Observatory Williams Bay WI 53191 Office Phone: 262-245-5555.

HOBSON, DAVID LEE, congressman, lawyer; b. Cin., Oct. 17, 1936; m. Carolyn Alexander; children: Susan Marie, Lynn Martha, Douglas Lee. BA, Ohio Wesleyan U., 1958; JD, Ohio State U. Coll. Law, 1963; degree (hon.), Ctrl. State U., Wittenberg U. Resident counsel Kissell Co., Springfield, Ohio; atty. Union Ctrl. Life Ins. Co., Cin.; mem. Ohio State Senate, 1982-90, majority whip, 1986-88, pres. pro tem, 1988-90; mem. US Congress from 7th Ohio dist., 1991—, mem. appropriations com., ranking mem. energy and water devel. subcommittee. Trustee Ohio Wesleyan U. Mem. 121st TAC Fighter Wing Ohio Air Nat. Guard, 1958—63. amed Pub. Ofcl. of Yr., Dayton Chpt. NASW, 1991; recipient Nathan Davis award, AMA, 1990, Spirit of Enterprise award, US C. of C., 1992, Ground Water Protector award, Nat. Ground Water Assn., 2001, Healthcare Leadership award, Am. Assn Nurse Anesthetists, 2002, Pub. Svc. award, AIAA, 2007. Mem. ABA, AMVETS, Ky. Bar Assn., Ohio Bar Assn., Springfield Bd. Realtors, Springfield Area C. of C., Non-Commissioned Officers Assn., Masons (32 degrees), Am. Legion, VFW, Moose, Elks, Rotary, Shrine Club. Republican. Methodist. Office: PO Box 269 Springfield OH 45501-0269 also: US Ho Reps 2346 Rayburn Ho Office Bldg Washington DC 20515-3507 Office Phone: 202-225-4324, 937-325-0474. Office Fax: 937-325-9188.

HOBSON, MELLODY, investment company executive; b. Chgo., Apr. 3, 1969; BA, Woodrow Wilson Sch. Internat. Rels., Princeton U., 1991. Joined mktg. team Ariel Capital Mgmt., Inc., 1991—94, sr. v.p., dir. mktg., 1994—2000, pres., 2000—. Bd. mem. Tellabs, Inc., 2002—; fin. corr. ABC's Good Morning Am. Bd. dir. Chgo. Pub. Edn. Fund, Chgo. Pub. Libr., Field Mus.; bd. trustees Princeton U. Named a Global Leader Tomorrow, World Econ. Forum, Davos, Switzerland, 2001; named one of 30 Leaders of Future, Ebony, 40 under 40, Crain's Chgo. Bus. Office: Ariel Capital Mgmt LLC 200 E Randolph Dr Ste 2900 Chicago IL 60601 Office Phone: 312-726-0140. Office Fax: 312-612-2702.

HOCHBERG, KEVIN J., lawyer; b. 1954; BA, Univ. Md., 1977; MA, Univ. Chgo., 1978, JD, 1984. Bar: Ill. 1984. Ptnr. banking & comml. fin. Sidley Austin Brown & Wood LLP, Chgo., 1986—. Mem.: ABA, Am. Coll. Comml. Fin. Lawyers, Chgo. Bar Assn., Order of the Coif. Office: Sidley Austin Brown & Wood LLP Bank One Plz 10 S Dearborn St Chicago IL 60603 Office Phone: 312-853-2085. Office Fax: 312-853-7036. Business E-Mail: khochberg@sidley.com.

HOCHMAN, KENNETH GEORGE, lawyer; b. Mt. Vernon, NY, Nov. 12, 1947; s. Benjamin S. and Lillian (Gilbert) H.; m. Carol K. Hochman, Apr. 8, 1979; children: Brian Paul, Lisa Erin. BA, SUNY, Buffalo, 1969; JD, Columbia U., 1972. Bar: Ohio 1973, Fla. 1977, N.Y. 1979. Assoc. Jones Day, Cleve., 1972-79, ptnr., 1980—, chmn. wealth mgmt., 1989—. Trustee Katharine Kenyon Lippitt Found., Cleve., 1988, Kenridge Fund, Cleve., 1989, Bolton Found., Cleve., 1990, Elisha-Bolton Found., Cleve., 1993, Montefiore Found., Cleve., 2005. Trustee United Way of Cleve., Cleve., 2002—; pres. Temple Tifereth-Israel, Cleve., 2006—. Harlan Fiske Stone scholar Columbia U., 1971, 72. Fellow Am. Coll. Trusts and Estate Counsel; mem. Phi Beta Kappa. Office: Jones Day North Point 901 Lakeside Ave E Cleveland OH 44114-1190 Business E-Mail: kghochman@jonesday.com.

HOCHSCHILD, ROGER C., finance company executive; BA, Georgetown U.; MBA, Amos Tuck Sch. Bus. Sr. exec. MBNA Am. Bank, 1994—98; exec. v.p. diversified fin. services Morgan Stanley, 1988—2001, exec. v.p., chief adminstrv. officer, chief strategic officer, 2001—04, pres., COO, Discover Financial Services, 2004—. Office: Morgan Stanley 2500 Lake Cook Rd Riverwoods IL 60015 Office Phone: 224-405-0900. Office Fax: 224-405-2009.

HOCHSTER, MELVIN, mathematician, educator; b. Bklyn., Aug. 2, 1943; s. Lothar and Rose (Gruber) H.; m. Anita Klitzner, Aug. 29, 1965 (div. Feb. 1983); 1 child, Michael Adam; m. Margie Ruth Morris, Dec. 20, 1987; children: Hallie Margaret Hochster Morris, Sophie Elinor Hochster Morris, Louis Jacob, Daniel Craig Morris. BA, Harvard U., 1964; MA, Princeton U., 1966, PhD, 1967. Asst. prof. math. U. Minn., Mpls., 1967-70, assoc. prof., 1970-73; prof. math. Purdue U., West Lafayette, Ind., 1973-77; from prof. math. to disting. prof. math U. Mich., Ann Arbor, 1977—2004, Jack E. McLaughlin Disting. Univ. prof. math., 2004—. Guest prof. Math. Inst. Aarhus, Denmark, 1973-74; trustee Math. Sci. Rsch. Inst., Berkeley, Calif., 1985-87, mem. sci. adv. coun., 1989-93; bd. govs. Inst. for Math. and its Application, Mpls., 1985-87. Chmn. editorial com. Math. Revs., 1984-89. Guggenheim fellow, 1982 Fellow Am. Acad. Arts and Scis.; mem. Am. Math. Soc. (Frank Nelson Cole prize 1980), Math. Assn. Am., Nat. Acad. Sci. Office: U Mich Math Dept East Hall 530 Church St Ann Arbor MI 48109-1043

HOCKENBERG, HARLAN DAVID, lawyer; b. Des Moines, July 1, 1927; s. Leonard C. and Estyre M. (Zalk) H.; m. Dorothy A. Arkin, June 3, 1953; children: Marni Lynn, Thomas Leonard, Edward Arkin. BA, U. Iowa, 1949, JD, 1952. Bar: Iowa 1952. Assoc. Abramson & Myers, Des Moines, 1952-58, Abramson, Myers & Hockenberg, Des Moines, 1958-64; sr. ptnr. Davis, Hockenberg, Wine, Brown, Koehn & Shors, Des Moines, 1964-95; shareholder, dir. Sullivan & Ward, P.C., Des Moines, 1995—2007, Coppola, McConville, Coppola, Hockenberg & Scalise, PC, 2007—. Bd. dirs. West Des Moines State Bank, Rep. Jewish Coalition, Smoother Sailing Found. Mem. bd. editors U. Iowa Law Review. Mem. Citizens Ind. Cts., Internat. Rels. and Nat. Security Adv. Coun., Rep. Nat. Com., 1978; chmn. Coun. Jewish Fedns., Small Cities Com., 1970-71; mem. exec. com. Am. Israel Pub. Affairs Com.; pres. Wilkie House, Inc., Des Moines, 1965-66, Des Moines Jewish Welfare Fedn., 1973-74; mem. Presdl. Commn. on White House Fellowships, 1988-92; mem. Holocaust Meml. Coun., 2003-06. With USNR, 1945-46. Mem. Iowa State Bar Assn. (past chair professionalism com.), Des Moines C. of C. (pres. 1986, chmn. bur. econ. devel. 1979, 80, bd. dirs. 1986), Des Moines Club, Pioneer Club, Delta Sigma Rho, Omicron Delta Kappa, Phi Epsilon Pi Office: Coppola McConville Coppola et al 2100 Westown Pkwy Ste 210 West Des Moines IA 50265 Office Phone: 515-453-1055. Business E-Mail: hdhockenberg@csmclaw.com.

HODAPP, DON JOSEPH, food company executive; b. Madelia, Minn., Dec. 24, 1937; s. Philip Henry and Katherine Lillian (Quinn) H.; m. Dorothy Ann Berg, Sept. 7, 1959; children: Don Jr., Jennifer, Paul, Patrick, Laurie. BA in Math., St. John's U., Collegeville, Minn., 1959. Adv. mktg. rep. IBM Corp., Mpls., 1959-66; dir. data processing Geo. A. Hormel & Co., Austin, Minn., 1966-69, asst. controller, 1969-81, gen. mgr. Fremont, Nebr., 1981-85, v.p. strategic planning Austin, 1985-86, group v.p., 1986-92, exec. v.p., CFO, 1992—, also bd. dirs., 1986—. Bd. dirs., treasl. Hormel Found. Bd. regents St. John's U., Collegeville, Minn., 1990-99; bd. dirs. Ctr. for Rural Policy and Devel. Mem.: Rotary. Republican. Roman Catholic. Office: Hormel Foods Corp 1 Hormel Pl Austin MN 55912-3680

HODES, SCOTT, lawyer; b. Chgo., Aug. 14, 1937; s. Barnet and Eleanor (Cramer) H.; m. Maria Bechily, 1982; children— Brian Kenneth, Valery Jane, Anthony Scott. AB, U. Chgo., 1956; JD, U. Mich., 1959; LLM, Northwestern U., 1962. Bar: Ill. 1959, D.C. 1962, N.Y. 1981. Assoc. Arvey, Hodes, Costello & Burman, Chgo., 1959-61, ptnr., 1965-91, Ross & Hardies, Chgo., 1992—2003, Bryan Cave LLP, Chgo., 2004—. Bd. dirs. First Investors Life Ins. Co. NY, Richardson Electronics, Ltd.; dir. State Ill. Savs. and Loan Bd. Author: The Law of Art and Antiques, 1966, What Every Artist and Collector Should Know About the Law, 1974; Assoc. news editor: Fed. Bar News, 1963-70; co-editor: Conf. Mut. Funds, 1966, Legal Rights in the Art and Collectors' World, 1986; Contbr. articles to profl. jours. Chmn. Philippine Exch. Nurses award com., 1966; nat. chmn. Lawbooks USA, 1962-73; chmn. Mut. Funds and Investment Mgmt. Conf., 1966-75; co-chmn. Chgo. World Friendship Day, 1967; mem. Ill. Arts Coun., 1973-75; Committeeman Ill. 9th Dist. Dem. Com., 1970-82; bd. dirs. Michael Reese Hosp. Rsch. Inst., 1965-73, United Cerebral Palsy Chgo., 1976-84; governing bd. Chgo. Symphony Soc., 1978-1999; governing mem. Art Inst. Chgo., 1980—; com. on internat. investment and tech. Dept. State, 1980-83; bd. dirs. Chgo. Neighborhood Theatre Found., 1980-92, Harold Washington Found., 1988-2000; exec. com. Anti Defamation League, 1990-98; chmn. Mayor's Task Force on Neighborhood Land Use, 1986-88; chmn. Navy Pier Devel. Authority, 1988-89; mem. Ill. Atty. Gen. adv. com., 1991-95; spl. counsel Art in Embassies Program, Dept. State, 1992-94; co-chmn. Private Enterprise Rev. and Adv. Bd., Ill., 1992-94; pres. Lawyers Creative Arts, 2000-04; mem. exec. com. Mex. Fine Arts Ctr. Mus., 2003—. Capt. JAGC, AUS, 1962-64. Decorated Army Commendation medal; named one of Chicago's ten outstanding young men Jr. Assn. Commerce and Industry, 1968, Chgo. Artist's award for Support of Visual Arts, 1996, Disting. Svc. award Lawyer's Creative Arts, 1997, also Leavens award, 2006, Civic award Weizmann Inst. Sci., 2005. Mem. FBA. (chmn. coun. financing 1966-71, chmn. younger lawyers div. 1963-64, nat. coun. 1965—, hon. trustee found. 1994—, Disting. Svc. award 1971, 75, 86, Earl Kintner Outstanding Svc. award, 1998), Ill. Bar Assn., Chgo. Bar Assn., Chgo. Bar Found. (dir. 2007—), Chgo. Art Inst. (life), Chgo. Hist. Soc. (life), Judge Adv. Gens. Assn. (life), Masons (32 deg.), Chicagoland C. of C. (dir. 2006—), Standard Club, Mid-Day Club, Econ. Club Chgo., Zeta Beta Tau, Tau Epsilon Rho. Jewish. Home: 1540 N Lake Shore Dr Chicago IL 60610-6684 Office: Bryan Cave 161 N Clark St Ste 4300 Chicago IL 60601-7567 Business E-Mail: scott.hodes@bryancave.com.

HODGE, BOBBY LYNN, mechanical engineer, manufacturing executive; b. Yadkinville, NC, Oct. 14, 1956; s. Robert Henry and Betty Jean (Martin) H.; m. Robin Mayhue Renegar, June 8, 1979; children: Andrew, Adam. AAS with honors, Forsyth Tech. Inst., Winston-Salem, NC, 1976; BS in Engring. Tech., U. NC, Charlotte, 1978. Design engr. Clark/Gravely Corp., Clemmons, NC, 1978-79, project engr., 1979-80; design engr. Ingersoll-Rand, Davidson, NC, 1980-83, devel. engr., 1983-85; sr. applications engr. INA Bearing Co., Ft. Mill, SC, 1985-87, mgr. automotive driveline engring. group, 1987-88, mgr. automotive applications engring., 1988-89, dir. automotive applications engring., 1989-96, dir. automotive engring., 1996-99; v.p. engring./product devel. The Setco Group, Cin., 1999—2002, v.p. engring/quality, 2002—. Internat. spkr. on design and application of rolling element bearings and machine tool spindles. Contbr. articles to profl. jours. Mem. adv. coun. U. NC-Charlotte Coll. Engring. Mem. ASME, SAE, Soc. Mfg. Engrs., Soc. Tribologists and Lubrication Engrs., Am. Soc. Metals. Republican. Baptist. Achievements include 10 patents in field. Avocations: golf, hunting, woodworking. Home: 1518 Jolee Dr Hebron KY 41048-9514 Office: The Setco Group 5880 Hillside Ave Cincinnati OH 45233-1599 Home Phone: 859-689-2642. Personal E-mail: hodge1518@aol.com. Business E-Mail: bhodge@setcousa.com.

HODGE, DAVID CHARLES, academic administrator, geography professor; b. Stewartville, Minn., Sept. 27, 1948; BA magna cum laude, Macalester Coll., 1970; MS in Geography, Pa. State U., 1973, PhD, 1975. Rsch. asst. Pa. Transp. Inst. Pa. State U., 1973; asst. prof. geography McMaster U., 1974—75; rsch. assoc. Urban Transp. Program U. Wash., 1975—78, asst. prof., 1975—81, assoc. prof., 1981—92, assoc. chair geography, 1981—85, academic coord. Ctr. Social Sci. Computation and Rsch., 1982—91, cons. Academic Computer Svcs., 1986, 1987, undergraduate coord. geography, 1991—93, prof., 1992—2006, chair Dept. Geography, 1995—97, div. dean computing, rsch., and facilities Coll. Arts and Scis., 1996—98, adj. prof. Dept. Civil Engring., 1996—2006, acting dean Coll. Arts and Scis., 1998—99, dean, 1999—2006; pres. Miami U., Oxford, Ohio, 2006—, prof., 2006—. Program dir. Geography and Regional Sci. Program NSF, 1993—94. Editor: The Professional Geographer, 1994—97; contbr. articles to profl. jours. Named to Macalester Coll. Athletic Hall of Fame, 1996; recipient Outstanding Performance Award, NSF, 1994, Charles L. Hosler Alumni Scholar Medal, Pa State U. Coll. Earth and Mineral Scis., 2003; grantee Pa. State U. Centennial Fellow, 1996. Office: Miami U Office of Pres 213 Roudebush Hall Oxford OH 45056 Office Phone: 513-529-2345. Home Fax: 515-529-9596. E-mail: hodgedc@muohio.edu.

HODGE, RALPH J., communications executive; BS, BBA, MBA, East Tenn. State U. CPA. Various staff acctg. pos. Sprint United Telephone-Southeast, 1981—86; treas./info. sys. dir. United of Ind., 1986—88; controller, then treas. United-Midwest, 1988—92; dir.-earnings analysis and external reporting to asst. controller Sprint Corp. Local Telephone Divsn., 1992—96, v.p.-ops. and analysis, 1996—99, pres.-carrier markets, 1999—2001, pres.-bus. and wholesale markets, 2001—. Office: 6200 Sprint Pkwy Overland Park KS 66251

HODGE, ROBERT JOSEPH, retail executive; b. St. Louis, July 5, 1937; s. Joseph Edward and Alberta Marie (Oehler) H.; m. Carmen Maria Villalobos, Sept. 1, 1960; children: Ralph, Robert, Carmen. BS in Indsl. Relations, St. Louis U., 1959. Meat dept. merchandiser Kroger Co., Cleve., 1972-74, corp. v.p. deli/bakery Cin., 1981-83, v.p. Atlanta div., 1983-85, meat merchandiser St. Louis, 1977-80, v.p. gateway region, 1985-87; v.p. meat ops. Ralph's Grocery Co., Los Angeles, 1974-77; gen. mgr. Super X Drug, Melbourne, Fla., 1980-81; sr. v.p. Dillon Co., Hutchinson, Kans., 1987-89; sr. v.p. merchandising, manufacturing Kroger Co., Cin., 1989-92, pres. Cin./Dayton mktg. area, 1992—. Sgt. U.S. Army, res., 1959-66. Avocations: golf, skiing. Home: 614 Watchcove Ct Cincinnati OH 45230-3777 Office: Kroger Co 150 Tri County Pkwy Cincinnati OH 45246-3246

HODGES, MICHELE, chamber of commerce executive; b. 1967; 2 children. Pres. Troy Chamber of Commerce, Oakland Chamber Network, Mich. Named one of 40 Under 40, Crain's Detroit Bus., 2006. Office: Troy Chamber of Commerce 4555 Investment Dr 3rd Fl Ste 300 Troy MI 48098 Office Phone: 248-641-0197.

HODGES, RICHARD, former state legislator; b. Oct. 12, 1963; BA with honors, Oberlin Coll., 1986; MPA, U. Toledo, 1991. Ind. fin. cons., 1986-89; treas. Fulton County, Ohio, 1987-92; state rep. 82d Dist., Ohio, 1993-98. Co-regional coord. Voinovich for Gov., 1990; mem. Ohio adv. com. Bush for Pres., 1988; mem. Fulton County Republican Ctrl. and Exec. coms., 1986-90; mgr. Tom Van Meter for State Senator, 1986. Mem. Fulton County Farm Bur., Fulton and Defiance County Township Trustees Assn., Defiance County Pheasants Forever, Rotary. Republican. Home: 2101 S Aida Ave Tucson AZ 85710-8063

HODGMAN, DAVID RENWICK, lawyer; b. Boston, Sept. 22, 1947; s. Donald Renwick and Naomi (Meyer) H.; m. Liane Mary Blum, July 23, 1977; children: Daniel, Thomas, Jessica. BA, Grinnell Coll., 1969; JD, Yale U., 1974. Bar: Ill. 1974, US Tax Ct. 1981, US Dist. Ct. (no. dist. Ill.) 1975, US Ct. Appeals (7th cir.) 1987. Assoc. D'Ancona & Pflaum, Chgo., 1974-79, Schiff, Hardin & Waite, Chgo., 1979-82, ptnr., 1992; ptnr., mem. exec. com. Schiff Hardin, LLP, Chgo. Contbr. articles to profl. law jours. Named a Leading Lawyer, Ill. Leading Lawyer Network; named an Ill. Super Lawyer; named one of Top 100 Attys., Worth mag., 2006, Best Lawyers In Am. Fellow Am. Coll. Trust & Estate Counsel; mem. ABA, Ill. Bar Assn., Chgo. Bar Assn. (chair probate practice com. 1990-91), Chgo. Estate Planning Coun. Avocations: sports, family and minor home repairs. Office: Schiff Hardin 6600 Sears Tower Chicago IL 60606-6473 Office Phone: 312-258-5500. Office Fax: 312-258-5600. E-mail: dhodgman@schiffhardin.com.

HODGSON, PAUL EDMUND, surgeon, department chairman; b. Milw., Dec. 14, 1921; s. Howard Edmund and Ethel Marie (Niemi) H.; m. Barbara Jean Osborne, Apr. 22, 1945; children: Ann, Paul. BS summa cum laude, Beloit Coll., 1943; MD cum laude, U. Mich., 1945. Diplomate: Am. Bd. Surgery. Intern U. Mich. Hosp., 1945-46, resident in surgery, 1948-52; mem. faculty dept. surgery U. Mich., 1952-62, assoc. prof., 1956-62; prof. surgery U. Nebr. Coll. Medicine, Omaha, 1962-88, prof. emeritus, 1988—, asst. dean for curriculum, 1966-72, chmn. dept. surgery, 1972-84. Trustee Beloit Coll., 1977-80 Served to capt. M.C. U.S. Army, 1946-48. Mem. A.C.S., Frederick A. Coller Surg. Soc., Soc. Univ. Surgeons, Central Surg. Assn., Soc. Surgery Alimentary Tract, Am. Assn. Surgery Trauma, Western Surg. Assn., Am. Surg. Assn. Presbyterian. Office: Dept Surgery Med Ctr 983280 Nebraska Medical Center Omaha NE 68198-3280

HODNIK, DAVID F., retail company executive; b. 1947; Grad., Western Ill. U., 1970. Sr. auditor Paul Pettengill & Co., 1969-72; with Ace Hardware Corp., Hinsdale, Ill., 1972—, acct., 1972-74, mgr. acctg., 1974-76, controller, 1976-80, v.p., treas., 1980-82; v.p. fin., treas. ACE Hardware Corp., Oak Brook, Ill., 1982-88, sr. v.p., 1988-90, exec. v.p., 1990-93, exec. v.p., COO, 1993-95, pres., COO, 1995-96, pres., CEO, 1996—. Office: ACE Hardware Corp 2200 Kensington Ct Oak Brook IL 60523-2100 E-mail: hodnik@acehardware.com.

HOECKER, DAVID, engineering executive; b. Cin., July 7, 1948; s. Vernon and Ruth (Schnake) H.; m. Susan Ameling, Aug. 15, 1970; children: Sarah, Paul. BS, Rose Poly. Inst., Terre Haute, Ind., 1969; MSI.A., Purdue U., 1970; grad. program for execs., Carnegie-Mellon U., 1991. Cert. quality engr.; cert. quality mgr. Project mgr. Timken Co., Canton, Ohio, 1970-73, gen. supr., 1973-78, chief quality control engring. Lincolnton, N.C., 1978-82, chief engr. engring. services. Canton, Ohio, 1982-84, mgr. European Rsch. Northampton, Eng., 1984-89, gen. mgr. product engring. Canton, Ohio, 1989-93; gen. mgr. Timken Tooling Bus., Canton, 1993-95, gen. mgr. quality & tech., 1996—; v.p. The Wilderness Ctr. Inc., 1995-97, pres., 1997—2002. V.p. Canton Jaycees, 1973-74, Trinity United Ch. of Christ, 1983-84, 91-92, pres., 1993, chmn. endowment com., 1996, Brit. Timken Sports Club, 1986-89; dir. Young Life, Canton, 1975-78. Named Spoke of Yr. Canton Jaycees, 1972; named Key Man Canton Jaycees, 1974 Mem. ASME, Am. Soc. Quality Control (sr. mem., sec. Charlotte sect. 1980-81, treas. 1981), Canton Club. Republican. Office: Timken Co Mail Drop BON-07 PO Box 6929 Canton OH 44706-0929

HOEFT, ROBERT GENE, agricultural studies educator; b. David City, Nebr., May 21, 1944; s. Otto O. Hoeft and Lula (Barlean) Pleskac; m. Nancy A. Bussen, Sept. 1, 1990; children: Jeffrey, Angela. BS, U. Nebr., 1965, MS, 1967; PhD, U. Wis., 1972. Asst. prof. S.D. State U., Rapid City, 1972-73, U. Ill., Urbana, 1973-77, assoc. prof., 1977-81, prof., 1981—, head dept. crop scis., 2005—. Author: Modern Corn Production, 1986, Modern Corn & Soybean Production, 2000; editor Jour. Prodn. Agr., 1986-92. Recipient Funk award U. Ill., 1990, Robert E. Wagner award Potash and Phosphate Inst., 1998. Fellow Soil Sci. Soc. Am., Am. Soc. Agronomy (pres. 2002-03, CIBA-Geigy award 1978, Agronomic Extension award, grantee 1988, Agronomic Achievement award-soils 1995, Werner Nelson award for diagnosis of yield limiting factors 1996); mem. Coun. for Sci. and Tech. Office: U Ill 1102 S Goodwin Ave Urbana IL 61801-4730 Business E-Mail: rhoeft@uiuc.edu.

HOEG, DONALD FRANCIS, chemist, consultant, research and development company executive; b. Bklyn., Aug. 2, 1931; s. Harry Herman and Charlotte (Bourke) H.; m. Patricia Catherine Fogarty, Aug. 30, 1952; children— Thomas Edward, Robert Francis, Donald John, Mary Beth, Susan Catherine. BS in Chemistry summa cum laude, St. John's U., NYC, 1953; PhD in Chemistry, Ill. Inst. Tech., 1957. Fellow in chemistry and chem. engring. Armour Research Found., 1953-54; grad. research asst. Ill. Inst. Tech., 1954-56; research chemist W.R. Grace & Co., 1956-58, sr. research chemist, 1958-61; group leader addition polymer chemistry Roy C. Ingersoll Research Center, Borg-Warner Corp., Des Plaines, Ill., 1961-64, mgr. polymer chemistry, 1964-66, assoc. dir., head chem. research dept., 1966-75, dir., 1975-88; pres. DFH Assocs., 1988—. Former mem. solid state scis. adv. bd. NAS; bd. overseers Lewis Coll. Scis. and Letters of Ill. Inst. Tech., 1980-91; bd. dirs. Ill. Inst. Tech. Alumni, 1979-82, Mt. Prospect Combined Appeal, 1963-65 Bd. editors: Research Mgmt. Mag, 1979-82; contbr. numerous articles tech. publs., chpts. in books; patentee in field. TaPing Lin scholar, 1955-56; AEC asst., 1954; Armour Research Found. fellow, 1953-54; Ill. Inst. Tech. Achievement award, 1983 Mem. Am. Chem. Soc., AAAS, N.Y. Acad. Scis., Dirs. Indsl. Research, Am. Mgmt. Assn. (v.p. council 1984-88), Research Dirs. Assn. Chgo. (pres. 1977-78), Indsl. Research Inst. (bd. dirs. 1986-88), Sigma Xi. Office Phone: 847-577-5951. Personal E-mail: dfh1931@aol.com.

HOEKEMA, DAVID ANDREW, philosophy educator, academic administrator; b. Paterson, NJ, June 10, 1950; s. Anthony Andrew and Ruth Alberta (Brink) H.; m. Susan Alice Bosma, Jan. 2, 1972; children: Janna Elizabeth, Nicolas John. AB in Philosophy, Calvin Coll., 1972; PhD in Polit. Philosophy, Princeton U., 1982. Freelance photographer, 1967—; copy editor and writer Eerdsman Pub. Co., 1969—72; asst. instr. Princeton (N.J.) U., 1973-74; asst. prof. philosophy, tutor in Paracoll. St. Olaf Coll., Northfield, Minn., 1977-84, coord. Self-Resprct and Sex Roles Conf., 1981, field supr. St. Olaf Term in Far East, 1981-82; assoc. prof. U. Del., Newark, 1984-92; acad. dean Calvin Coll., Grand Rapids, Mich., 1992—98, prof. philosophy, 1998—. Vis. fellow Calvin Ctr. for Christian Scholarship, 1982-83; fellow Coolidge Rsch. Colloquium, 1991; dir. study in Ghana, 2004-05. Author: Rights and Wrongs: Coercion, Punishment and the State, 1986, Handbook for Adminstration of Learned Societies, 1990, In Place of In Loco Parentis: Campus Rules and Moral Community, 1994; publ. Christian Scholars' Rev.; contbr. articles to Christian Century, Commonweal, others; amateur musician voice, autoharp, piano; composer 3 pub. hymns. Fellow Soc. for Values in Higher Edn. (bd. dirs.); mem. Am. Philos. Assn. (exec. dir. 1984-92), Soc. Christian Philosophers, Am. Soc. for Aesthetics, Internat. Soc. Polit. and Legal Philosophy, Concerned Philosophers for Peace. Avocations: high fidelity recordings, bicycling. Home: 601 Kent Hills Rd NE Grand Rapids MI 49505-5110 Office: Calvin College Grand Rapids MI 49546 Office Phone: 616-526-6750. E-mail: dhoekema@calvin.edu.

HOEKSTRA, PETER, congressman, manufacturing executive; b. Groningen, The Netherlands, Oct. 30, 1953; arrived in US, 1957; m. Diane M. Johnson; children: Erin, Allison, Bryan. BA in Polit. Sci., Hope Coll., 1975; MBA, U. Mich., 1977. Furniture exec. Herman Miller, Inc., 1977-92, project mgr., product mgr., dir. product mgmt., dir. dealer mktg., v.p. dealer mktg., 1988-92, v.p. product mgmt., 1992-93; mem. US Congress from 2d Mich. dist., 1993—, chmn. select edn. subcom. edn. and the workforce com., 2001, mem. com. on transp. and infrastructure, mem. permanent select com. on intelligence, 2001—, chmn., 2004—07. Contbr. to project devel. Equa Chair, recognized as outstanding product of 1980s by Time Mag. Recipient Deficit Hawk award, Concord Coalition, 1996, Disting. Alumni award, Hope Coll. Alumni Assn., 2001, Pub. Policy award, Volunteer Ctr. Nat. Network Coun., 2003, Pub. Svc. award, Friends of Libraries USA and American Libraries Assn., 2003, Hero of Taxpayer, Americans for Tax Reform, 2004, Navigator award, Potomac Inst. Policy Studies, 2005. Republican. Christian Reformed Ch. Office: US Ho Reps 2234 Rayburn House Office Bldg Washington DC 20515-2202 E-mail: tellhoek@mail.house.gov.

HOEKWATER, JAMES WARREN, treasurer; b. Grand Rapids, Mich., Nov. 4, 1946; s. William Harold and Sena (Hoeksema) H.; m. Roberta Joyce Paczala, July 12, 1975; children: William Paczala, Elizabeth Veronica. BA, Mich. State U., 1970. CPA, Mich. With Touche Ross & Co., Detroit, 1970-77; v.p., controller Great Lakes div. Nat. Steel Corp., Detroit, 1977-83; treas. Nat. Steel Corp., Pitts., 1983-89, v.p., 1987-89; corp. contr. ITT Rayonier Inc., Stamford, Conn., 1989-94; treas. Acme Metals Inc., Riverdale, Ill., 1994—2002; cons., 2002—. Mem. AICPA. Republican. Episcopalian. Home: 6420 Lane Ct Hinsdale IL 60521-5354 Office: Acme Metals Inc PO Box 278630 Riverdale IL 60827-8630

HOENIG, JONATHAN, financial analyst, investment company executive, television personality; b. Chgo., Sept. 20, 1975; s. David and Ann Hoenig. B of Comm. Arts, orthwestern U., 1997. Former floor trader Chicago Board of Trade; commentator "Marketplace" NPR, Chgo., 1992; film critic, Sneak Previews PBS, Chgo., 1991-93; freelance prodr. WTTW-TV, Chgo., 1991-95; talk show host WNUR-FM, Evanston, Ill., 1995—; commentator FOX News; now mng. mem. Capitalistpig, LLC. Creator (radio show) Capitalist Pig, 1996. Named one of Thirty Under Thirty, Chicago Sun Times, 2006, Forty Under Forty, Crain's, 2006. Mem. NATAS, Nat. Assn. Radio Talk Show Hosts. Office: Capitalistpig LLC 531 S Plymouth Ct Chicago IL 60605

HOENIG, THOMAS M., bank executive; b. Ft. Madison, Iowa, Sept. 6, 1946; BA in Econs., St. Benedict's Coll., 1968; MA, PhD, Iowa State U. of Sci. & Tech., Ames, 1974. Economist banking supervision area Fed. Res. Bank Kans. City, 1973—81, v.p., 1981—86, sr. v.p., 1986—91, pres., CEO, 1991—. Mem. Free Open Market Com.; bd. dirs., mem. banking adv. bd. U. Mo., Kansas City; mem. banking adv. bd. U. Mo., Columbia. Trustee Benedictine Coll., Atchison, Kans., Midwest Rsch. Inst. Office: Fed Res Bank of Kans City 925 Grand Blvd Kansas City MO 64198 Office Phone: 816-881-2874.

HOESSLE, CHARLES HERMAN, zoological park administrator, director; b. St. Louis, Mar. 20, 1931; m. Marilyn Mueller, Jan. 5, 1952; children: Maureen, Kirk, Tracy, Bradley. AA, Harris Tchrs. Coll., 1951; student, Am. Assn. Zool. Parks and Aquariums Zoo Mgmt. Sch., 1976-77; LLD (hon.), Maryville Coll., 1986, St. Louis U., 1990, U. Mo., St. Louis, 1994. Reptile keeper St. Louis Zoo, 1963, asst. curator, 1964, curator reptiles and curator edn., 1968-69, gen. curator and dep. dir., 1969-82, dir., 1982—2002, dir. emeritus, 2002—. Adj. prof. dept. biology St. Louis U., 1973-74, 81-82, 83; owner, operator Exotic Pet Shop, St. Louis; host St. Louis Zoo Show, 1968-78 Chmn. Reptile Study Merit Badge counselors, St. Louis; mem. adv. bd. Mo. Coalition for Environment, 1997; state chmn. UN Day, 1982; mem. St. Louis County Counts; bd. dirs. Harris-Stowe State Coll. Found., City Mus.; mem. Bd. Regents Harris-Stowe State Coll. Recipient Disting. Alumnus award Harris-Stowe State Coll., 1987. Mem. Internat. Union Dirs. Zool. Gardens, Am. Zoo and Aquarium Assn. (bd. dirs. 1977-79, 85-87, v.p. 1988, pres. 1990-91, past pres. 1991-92, rep. to species survival commn. Internat. Union for Conservation Nature and Natural Resources), St. Louis Naturalists Club, St. Louis Ctr. for Internat. Rels. (bd. dirs. 1993—), St. Louis Mus. Collaborative (pres. 1993), Animal Protective Assn. (bd. dirs.), Internat. Friendship Alliance St. Louis County (chmn. cultural com.), Explorers, St. Louis Herpetological Society, Hawthorne Soc., St. Louis Rotary Club, St Louis Ambassadors Club (bd. dir.). Home: 10814 Forest Circle Dr Saint Louis MO 63128-2007

HOEVEN, JOHN, governor; b. Bismarck, ND, Mar. 13, 1957; m. Mical (Mikey); children: Marcela, Jack. B in history and econ., Dartmouth Coll., 1979; MBA, J.L. Kelloge Grad. Sch. Mngmt., Northwestern U., 1981. Exec. v.p. First Western Bank, Minot, N.D., 1986-93; pres., CEO Bank of ND (BND), 1993-2000; gov. State of ND, Bismarck, 2000—. Econ. adv. N.D. Univ.; trustee Bismarck State Coll.; regent Minot State U, chmn, Midwestern Gov. Conf. Cmty. chair Mo. Slope Areawide Campaign, 1998; chair Minot Chamber Commerce AFB Retention com., Minot Area Devel. Corp.; dir. Minot Kiwanis Club, Souris Valley Humane Soc, State Fair Adv. com.; mem. bd. dirs. First Western Bank and Trust, N.D. Bankers Assn., State Bank Bd., N.D. Small Bus. Investment Co., Prairie Pub. Broadcasting, N.D. Econ. Devel. Assn., Bismarck YMCA, Harold Schafer Leadership Ctr. Republican. Roman Catholic. Office: Gov Office Dept 101 600 E Blvd Ave Bismarck ND 58505-0001 Office Phone: 701-328-2200. Office Fax: 701-328-2205.

HOFER, ROY ELLIS, lawyer; b. Cin., Oct. 10, 1935; s. Eric Walter and Elsie Katherine (Ellis) H.; m. Suzanne Elizabeth Sturtz, June 6, 1956 (div. 1974); m. Cynthia Ann Corson, June 5, 1981; children: Kimberly, Tracy, Eric. BChemE, Purdue U., 1957; JD, Georgetown U., Washington, DC, 1961. Patent examiner US Patent & Trademark Office, Washington, 1957-59; patent agt. Exxon Corp., Washington, 1959-61; ptnr. Brinks Hofer Gilson & Lione, Chgo., 1961—, pres., 1995-99. Adv. com. No. Dist. Ill., 1991-95. Contbr. articles to profl. jours. Bd. dirs. Chgo. Lung Assn., 1982-83, Ctr. for Conflict Resolution, 1983-88, 90-91, pres., 1991-97; bd. dirs. Union League Club Chgo., 1984-88, Boys and Girls Club, Chgo., 1985-89, Ill. Inst. CLE, Chgo., 1986-88, Ill. chpt. Crohn's and Colitis Found. Am., 2001-06. Mem. ABA (dir. litigation sect. 1982-87), Fed. Cir. Bar Assn. (pres. 1993-94), Chgo. Bar Assn. (pres. 1988-89), Intellectual Property Law Assn. Chgo., Am. Intellectual Property Law Assn., Legal Club Chgo., Phi Eta Sigma, Tau Beta Pi, Omega Chi Epsilon. Republican. Office: Brinks Hofer Gilson & Lione Ste 3600 455 N Cityfront Plaza Dr Chicago IL 60611-5599 Office Phone: 312-321-4204. Business E-Mail: rhofer@usebrinks.com.

HOFER, THOMAS W., landscape company executive; Pres. Spring Green Lawn Care Corp., Plainfield, Ill. Office: Spring Green Lawn Care Corp 11909 S Spaulding School Dr Plainfield IL 60544-9501

HOFF, JOHN SCOTT, lawyer; b. Des Moines, Jan. 2, 1946; s. John Richard and Valetta R. (Scott) H.; m. Susan Murial Felver, June 21, 1972 (div. 1975); m. Shirley Jo Ward, June 21, 1975 (separated 1996); children: Jennifer Jo, John Baron. BSBA, Drake U., 1967; MBA, Calif. State U., Fullerton, 1971; postgrad., Oxford U., Eng., 1973; JD, Southwestern U., LA, 1975; MA in Mil. History, Am. Mil. U., 1995. Bar: Iowa 1976, Ill. 1977, Calif. 1980, Nebr. 1983, D.C. 1983, Wis. 1984, Mich., 1991, N.Y. 1995, Minn. 1996, U.S. Ct. Claims 1976, U.S. Ct. Customs and Patent Appeals 1976, U.S. Ct. Mil. Appeals 1976, U.S. Dist. Ct. (no. dist.) Ill. 1977, U.S. Ct. Appeals (7th cir.) 1979, U.S. Supreme Ct. 1982, U.S. Dist. Ct. (so. dist.) Iowa 1987, U.S. Ct. Appeals (9th and 10th cirs.) 1988, U.S. Dist. Ct. Ariz. 1990, U.S. Ct. Appeals (6th cir.) 1990, Mich. 1991, U.S. Ct. Appeals (8th cir.) 1991, U.S. Dist. Ct. (cen. dist.) Ill. 1996; CPCU; chartered cost analyst; FAA comml. pilot; cert. flight instr., instrument and mult-eng ratings. Staff atty. FAA Hdqrs., Washington, 1975-76; assoc. Lord, Bissell & Brook, Chgo., 1976-81; ptnr. Lapin, Hoff, Slaw & Laffey, Chgo., 1981-92, John Scott Hoff & Assocs., P.C., Chgo., 1992—; adj. prof. aviation law John Marshall Law Sch., Chgo., 1993—. Real estate broker Ill. Dept. Profl. Regulation, Springfield, 1980— Contbr. articles to profl. jours. Bd. dirs. USO of Ill., 1996—. Col. USAF, 1967—98. Decorated Legion of Merit. Mem. ABA, Aviation Ins. Assn. (dir. 1988-1990, v.p. 1990-92, pres. 1992-94), Air Force Assn. (v.p., pres. 1980-93), Internat. Soc. Air Safety Investigation (v.p.), Nat. Aero. Assn., Gen. Aviation Pilots' Assn., Res. Officers Assn., Mil. Officers Assn., Chgo. Bar Assn., Lawyers-Pilots Bar Assn., NTSB Bar Assn., Aircraft Owners and Pilots Assn., Exptl. Aircraft Assn., Nat. Assn. Flight Instrs., Aero. Club Chgo. Republican. Presbyterian. Avocations: flying, military history. Office: Hoff & Collins 20 S Clark St Ste 2210 Chicago IL 60603-1816 Office Phone: 312-346-8111. Business E-Mail: jsh@aviationattorney.com.

HOFFER, ALMA JEANNE, nursing educator; b. Dalhart, Tex., Sept. 15, 1932; d. James A. and Mildred (Zimlich) Koehler; m. John L. Hoffer, Oct. 7, 1954; children: John Jr., James Leo, Joseph V., Jerome P. BS, Bradley U., 1970; MA, W. Va. Coll. Grad. Study Inst., 1975; EdD, Ball State U., 1981, MA, 1986. Reg. Nurse. Staff nurse St Joseph Hosp., South Bend, Ind., 1958-59, Holy Cross Cen. Sch., St Joseph Hosp., South Bend, 1959-63; sch. nurse South Bend Sch. Corp., 1970-72; faculty staff Morris Harvey Coll., Charleston, W.Va., W.Va. Inst. Tech., Montgomery, 1975-76; asst. prof. Ball State U., Ind., 1976-77, Ind. U.-Purdue U., Ft. Wayne, 1977-81; assoc. prof. U. Akron, Ohio, 1981-83, 91-95, asst. dean, grad. edn. Ohio, 1983-90, assoc. prof. Ohio, 1991-93; prof., chair Dept. of ursing St. Francis Coll., Fort Wayne, Ind., 1993-95; prin. investigator rsch. project Well Begun is Well Done Children's Med. Ctr. Women's Bd. Akron, 1995-96; coord. parish nurse St. Hilary Ch., 2001—. Trustee Akron Child Guidance, 1983-88, 89-95, chair planning com., 1988; nursing Block Clin., Akron, 1988; educator, coord. parish nurses Internat. Parish Nurse Resource Ctr., 2003—; rsch. cons. St. Joseph Hosp., Ohio, 1989; cons. Health Sense, 1996-98; online faculty U. Phoenix, 2005—; rschr., presenter in field. Contbg. author: Family Health Promotion Theories and Assessment, 1989, Nursing Connections, 1992. Task force mem. Gov. Celeste's Employee Assistance Program for State U. Campuses, Ohio, 1983-84, del. People to People Citizen Amb. Program to Europe, 1988; mem. health and wellness com., coord. St. Hilary Parish; parish nurse educator Internat. Parish Nurse Resource Ctr., St. Louis, 2004—. Mem. ANA, Nat. League for Nursing, Midwest Nursing Rsch. Soc., Transcultural Nursing Soc. (chair certification and recertification com. 2000—, Leininger Leadership award 2002, 05), Cleve. Country Club, Sigma Theta Tau. Republican. Roman Catholic. Avocations: tennis, golf, skiing. Office: PO Box 794 Bath OH 44210-0794 Personal E-mail: ajhoffer@earthlink.net. Business E-Mail: ajh1@uakron.edu.

HOFFMAN, BARRY PAUL, lawyer; b. Phila., May 29, 1941; s. Samuel and Hilda (Cohn) H.; m. Mary Ann Schrock, May 18, 1978; children: Elizabeth Barron, Hayley Rebecca. BA, Pa. State U., 1963; JD, George Washington U., 1968. Bar: Pa. 1972, Mich. 1983. Asst. U.S. Senator Wayne Morse, Oreg., Washington; spl. agt. FBI, Washington; asst. dist. atty. Phila. Dist. Atty.'s Office; exec. v.p., gen. counsel Valassis Communications, Inc., Livonia, Mich., also bd. dirs. 1st lt. U.S. Army, 1963-65, Korea. Home: 49933 Standish Ct Plymouth MI 48170-2882 Office: Valassis Communications Inc 19975 Victor Pkwy Livonia MI 48152-7001 E-mail: hoffmanb@valassis.com.

HOFFMAN, BRIDGET C., lawyer; b. Cin., Feb. 22, 1977; BA in Polit. Sci., Xavier U., 1998; JD, U. Cin., 2002. Bar: Ohio 2002. Assoc. Taft, Stettinius & Hollister LLP, Cin., mem., Women's Resource Grp. Named one of Ohio's Rising Stars, Super Lawyers, 2005, 2006. Office: Taft Stettinius & Hollister LLP 425 Walnut St Ste 1800 Cincinnati OH 45202-1800 Office Phone: 513-381-2838. Office Fax: 513-381-0205.

HOFFMAN, CLARENCE, state representative; b. 1933; married; 2 children. Grad., S.D. State U., 1959. Former tchr.; owner, mgr. The Hoffman Ins. Agy., 1963—; mem. Iowa Ho. Reps., DesMoines, 1999—, mem. various coms.

including econ. devel., appropriations, labor and indsl. rels., ways and means, vice chair commerce and regulation com. Republican. Lutheran. Office: State Capitol East 12th and Grand Des Moines IA 50319 also: 869 S Fifth St Charter Oak IA 51439

HOFFMAN, DAVID H., city manager; BA, Yale U.; LLD, U. Chgo., 2005. Clk. to Supreme Ct. Justice Rehnquist; asst. US atty. US Atty.'s Office, Chgo., 1998—2005, dep. chief Narcotics & Gangs sect., 2002—05; inspector gen. City Hall, Chgo., 2005—. Dir. Project Safe Neighborhoods, Chgo., 2003—. Named one of 40 Under 40, Crain's Chgo. Bus., 2006. Office: Office of Inspector Gen City of Chgo PO Box 2996 Chicago IL 60654-2996 Office Phone: 773-478-7799. Office Fax: 773-478-3949.

HOFFMAN, ELIZABETH, academic administrator, economics professor; BA in History, Smith Coll., 1968; MA in History, U. Pa., 1969, PhD in History, 1972; PhD in Econs., Calif. Inst. Tech., 1979. Academic and adminstrv. positions U. Fla., Northwestern U., Purdue U., U. Wyo., U. Ariz., Iowa State U.; prof. econs., history, polit. sci., psychology U. Ill., Chgo., 1997—2000, prof. Inst. of Govt. and Pub. Affairs, 1997—2000, provost and vice chancellor, 1997—2000; pres. U. Colo. Sys., Boulder, Colo., 2000—05; prof. Grad. Sch. Pub. Affairs U. Colo., Denver, 2005—06; exec. v.p., provost Iowa State U., 2007—. Mem. bd. dir. Nat. Sci. Bd., 2002—. Author books; contbr. articles to profl. jours. Named one of 100 women making a difference, Today's Chgo. Woman, 1999, 25 Most Powerful People, Colo. Biz Mag., 2004; recipient Ronald H. Coase prize, Electronic Intelligence citation, ANBAR. Office: Iowa State U Provost Office 1550 Bdshr Ames IA 50011-2021

HOFFMAN, GENE D., food company executive, consultant; b. East St. Louis, Ill., July 29, 1927; s. Edmund H. and Bee (Hood) H.; m. Nancy P. Claney, Oct. 27, 1951; children: Kim Elizabeth, Keith Murdock. B.J. in Advt, U. Mo., 1948. Asst. advt. mgr. Montgomery Ward Co., 1948; copywriter, asst. mgr. advt. promotion Chgo. Tribune, 1949-50; mgr. promotion Phila. Bull., 1951-56; with The Kroger Co., 1956-77, gen. mgr. St. Louis div., 1956-61; dir. mktg. processed foods div., Cin., 1961-63, v.p., gen. mgr., 1964-66; corp. v.p. St. Louis, 1966; v.p. food mfg. divs., 1966-69; pres. Kroger Food Processing Co., 1969-72, Kroger Brands Co., 1972-74; sr. corp. v.p. parent co., 1974-75; corp. pres., bd. dirs. parent co., 1975-77; with Super Valu Stores, Inc., Mpls., 1977-88; pres. Super Valu Wholesale Food Cos., 1977-87, chmn., 1985-88; sr. corp. v.p. Super Valu Stores Inc.; chmn., chief exec. officer Food Giant, Inc.; pres., chief exec. officer Corp. Strategies Internat., Mpls., 1987—; pres. Mktg. Assocs., Inc., Mpls., 1987—; pres., chief exec. officer LeaderShape, Inc., Champaign, Ill., 1987—. Chmn., bd. dirs. Quality Containers Internat., Inc., 1989—; bd. dirs. Novate Enterprise, Inc., Americana Mag., Rural Ventures, Inc., Lewis Grocer Co., Vital Resources, Inc., WestCoast Grocery Co., Paragon Trade Brands, Inc. Chmn. Leader Shape Inst.; chmn., bd. govs. ATO Found. Served with AC USNR, 1945-46. Mem. Am. Mgmt. Assn., Food Mktg. Inst., Greater Cin. C. of C. (v.p., dir.), AIM, Alpha Delta Sigma, Alpha Tau Omega. Clubs: Interlachen Country (Mpls.), Comml., Cin., Hyde Park Golf and Country, Queen City, Bankers (Cin.); Tonka Racquets, Camargo Racquet. Episcopalian. Office: Corp Strategies Internat 2859 Gale Rd Wayzata MN 55391-2623

HOFFMAN, GILBERT L., information technology executive; Sr. v.p. & chief info. officer Maritz, Inc., St. Louis. Named a Premier 100 IT Leader, Computerworld mag., 2001. Office: SVP & CIO Maritz Inc 1375 N Hwy Dr Fenton MO 63099

HOFFMAN, JAY C., state legislator; b. Nov. 6, 1961; m. Laurie Hoffman; children: Emily, Katelyn. Grad., Ill. State U., 1983; JD, St. Louis U., 1986. Bar: Ill. 1986. Mem. from Dist. 112, Ill. Ho. of Reps., Dem. floor leader. Mem. exec. fin. inst., jud. criminal com., welfare reform task force Ill. H. of Reps. Dem Cand. for U.S. House, 20th district, I.L., 1996 Named Outstanding Legislator of Yr., Ill. State Atty. Assn., 1994. Address: 7 Driftwood Ln Collinsville IL 62234-5279 Also: 2099 M Stratton Bldg Springfield IL 62706-0001

HOFFMAN, JERRY IRWIN, retired dental educator; b. Chgo., Nov. 20, 1935; s. Irwin and Luba Hoffman; m. Sharon Lynn Seaman, Aug. 25, 1963; children: Steven Abram, Rachel Irene. Student, DePaul U., 1953-56; BS in Biology and Chemistry, Roosevelt U., 1956; DDS, Loyola U., Chgo., 1960; M of Health Care Adminstrn., Baylor U., 1972. Certificate, General Practice Residency, U.S. Army, 1978. Commd. officer U.S. Army, 1960 (served to 1962, returned 1964), advanced through grades to col., 1978, hdqrs. rep. local dental tng. confs. Europe Garmisch, Fed. Republic Germany, 1965-67; cons. to Comdg. Gen. U.S. Army Med. Research and Devel. Command, Washington, 1972-76; cons. Office of Surgeon Gen. U.S. Army, Washington, 1972-76, liaison rep. to Nat. Adv. Council and Oral Biology and Medicine Study Sessions of the Nat. Inst. Dental Research and NIH, 1973-76, resident in Gen. Practice Residency, 1976-78; comdg. officer U.S. Army Dental Activity, Fort Monmouth, NJ, 1979-82; ret., 1982; pvt. practice dentistry Chgo., 1962-64; assoc. prof. operative dentistry Loyola U. Sch. Dentistry, Maywood, Ill., 1982-93, dir. gen. practice residency, 1982-85, coordinator extramural dental resources, 1983-85, assoc. dean for clin. affairs, 1985-93; dir. sci. programs Chgo. Dental Soc., 1993—2002, ret., 2002. Staff dentist Silas B. Hayes Army Hosp., Fort Ord, Calif., 1976-79, Patterson Army Hosp., Ft. Monmouth, 1979-82; lectr., presenter seminars in field. Contbr. articles to profl. jours. Decorated Legion of Merit, Meritorious Svc. Medal with oak leaf cluster. Fellow: Am. Coll. Dentists, Internat. Coll. Dentists, Odontographic Soc.; master: Acad. Gen. Dentistry; mem. ADA, Ill. Dental Soc., Chgo. Dental Soc., Am. Assn. Dental Schs., Am. Soc. Assn. Execs., Assn. Healthcare Execs., Profl. Conv. Mgmt. Assn., Omicron Kappa Upsilon. Personal E-mail: ddscds@aol.com.

HOFFMAN, JOEL HARVEY, composer, educator; b. Vancouver, BC, Canada, Sept. 27, 1953; came to U.S., 1964; s Irwin and Esther Beatrice (Glazer) H.; m. Dorotea Vittoria Vismara, Dec. 30, 1988. MusB summa cum laude, U. Wales, Cardiff, 1974; MusM, Juilliard Sch. Music, 1976, D of Mus. Arts, 1978. Prof. composition Coll./Conservatory Music U. Cin., 1978—. Mem. faculty U. Cin.; artistic dir. Music 03 festival; resident composer MacDowell Colony Yaddo, Rockefeller Found., Camargo Found., Hindemith Found.; new music advisor Buffalo Philharm., 1991-92; composer-in-residence Nat. Chamber Orch., 1993-94. Composer: Sonata for Cello and Piano, 1982, Chamber Symphony, 1983, Double Concerto, 1984, Duo for viola and piano, 1984, Between Ten, 1985, Violin Concerto, 1986, The Hancock Trio, 1987, Fantasia Fiorentina for violin and piano, 1988, Crossing Points for string orch., 1990, Partenze for violin solo, 1990, Cubist Blues for piano trio, 1991, Music in Blue in Green for orch., 1991, Each for Himself/90? for piano solo, 1991, Metasmo for percussion trio, 1992, String Quartet No. 2, 1993, Self-Portrait with Mozart, 1994, Music for chamber orch., 1994, ChiaSsO for orch., 1995, L'Immensita dell'Attimo for voice and piano, 1995, The Music Within the Words, Part I for flute, oboe, cello and piano, 1996, Part II for viola, cello, harp and piano, 1996, Portogruaro Sextet for clarinet, horn, string trio, piano, 1996, l'Chaim Chantata, 1996, Stone Soup for violin and narrator, 1996, Millennium Dances for Orchestra, 1997, Self-Portrait with Gebirtig, 1998, Krakow Variations for viola sola, 1999, Reyzele, A Portrait for chamber ensemble, 1999, The Smile for orch., 2001, Gebirtig Speaks, for clarinet, string trio and piano, 2001, Round Midnight variation for piano, 2001, Self-Portrait with JS for string trio, 2001, The Memory Game, opera in three acts 2002, to listen, to hear, 2003, coast to coast, 2003; (recs.) Duo for Viola and Piano, CRI, 1991, Partenze for violin solo, Koch Internat., 1992, Music for Two Oboes, Centaur, 1995, Fantasy Pieces, Gasparo, 1996, Tum-Balalayke EMA Records, 1996;Cubist Blues, Gasparo, 2002; pianist in various recitals and solo concerts, Italy, France, Great Britain, US; pianist and arranger Trio Gebirtig. Artistic dir. Music 03 Festival. Recipient award Am. Acad.-Inst. Arts and Letters, 1987, commn. Nat. Endowment for the Arts, 1986, 91, Fromm Found., 1980, 82, Am. Harp Soc., 1982, Am. Music Ctr., 1991, Cin. Symphony Orch., 1993, Shanghai String Quartet, 1993, Nat. Chamber Orch., 1993; Ohio Arts Coun. fellow, 1983, 87, 91, 94, 96. Mem. ASCAP, Am. Music Ctr., Gruppo Aperto Musica Oggi, Coll. Music Soc., Composers Forum, Cin. Chamber Music Soc., U. Cin. Faculty Jewish Coun. (past pres.). Avocations: chinese, italian cooking. Office: U Cin Coll Conservatory Music Cincinnati OH 45221-0001 Fax: 513 556-0202. E-mail: joel.hoffman@uc.edu.

HOFFMAN, LAWRENCE A., rabbi; PhD, Hebrew Union Coll.-Jewish Inst. Religion, 1972. Cert. ordained Rabbi 1969. Co-founder, dir. Synagogue 2000; Barbara and Stephen Friedman Chair in Liturgy, Worship, and Ritual Hebrew Union Coll.-Jewish Inst. Religion, 2006—. Editor: Minhag Ami: My People's Prayer Book; co-editor: Two Liturgical Traditions; author (religion books): What is a Jew?, Israel: A Spiritual Travel Guide. Named one of The Top 50 Rabbis in America, Newsweek Mag., 2007. Office: Hebrew Union Coll-Jewis Inst Religion 3101 Clifton Avenue Cincinnati OH 45220-2448

HOFFMAN, MICHAEL J., manufacturing executive; BA in Mktg. Mgmt., U. St. Thomas, St. Paul; MBA, U. Minn. Sales, svc., mktg. positions Toro Co., Mpls., 1977—89, various mgmt. positions, 1989—97, v.p., gen. mgr., comml. bus., 1997—2000, v.p., gen. mgr. consumer bus., 2000—01, group v.p., consumer and landscape contractor bus., 2001—02, group v.p., consumer, landscape contractor, internat. businesses, 2002—04, COO, 2004—05, pres., 2004—, CEO, 2005—, chmn. bd., 2006—. Office: Toro Co 8111 Lyndale Ave S Minneapolis MN 55420 Office Phone: 952-888-8801.

HOFFMAN, NATHANIEL A., lawyer; b. Cin., Mar. 4, 1949; s. Ralph H. and Betty (Goldfarb) H.; m. Sara Naomi Fishman, Aug. 3, 1980; children: Joshua, Rebecca, Esther, David. BA, Yale U., 1971; JD, U. Mich., 1975. Bar: Calif. 1975, Wis. 1983. Assoc. McDonough, Holland & Allen, Sacramento, 1975—78, Herz, Levin, Teper, Sumner & Croysdale, Milw., 1982—85; ptnr. Michael, Best & Friedrich, Milw., 1985—2004, Whyte Hirschboeck Dudek SC, Milw., 2005—. Atty. N.Y.C. Pub. Devel. Corp., 1980-82. Mem. ABA, State Bar Wis., Milw. Bar Assn., State Bar Calif. Home: 3258 N 51st Blvd Milwaukee WI 53216-3236 Office: Whyte Hirschboeck Dudek SC 555 E Wells St Ste 1900 Milwaukee WI 53202 Home Phone: 414-444-5733; Office Phone: 414-978-5634. Business E-Mail: nhoffman@whdlaw.com.

HOFFMAN, PHILIP EDWARD, legislative consultant; b. Jackson, Mich., Nov. 10, 1951; s. Ralph Jacob Jr. and Nancy Joan (Vanantwerp) H.; m. Dennise Fitzgerald, Jan. 29, 1977; children: R. Jacob, Benjamin, Philip. BS, Ferris State U., 1974; postgrad. in edn., Mich. State U., 1975. Undercover narcotics investigator Region II Metro Squad, 1974-77; deputy sheriff Jackson County Sheriff's Dept., Jackson, 1974-82; mem. Mich. Ho. of Reps., Lansing, 1982-93, Mich. Senate from 19th dist., Lansing, 1993—2002; v.p. pro tempore Mich. Senate, Lansing; founder, prin. Hoffman Legis. Cons. LLC, 2003—. Treas., bd. dirs. Am. 1st Fed. Credit Union, Jackson, Mich., 1996—; treas., bd. trustees Jackson CC, 2004—. Pres. Great Sauk Trail coun. Boy Scouts Am., 1995-96, v.p. 1992-95; past pres. Land O'Lakes Coun., 1992-94; bd. dir. Port St. James, Beaver, Mich., 2002-, vice chmn. Beaver Island Boat Co., Mich., 2006-. Named Outstanding Legislator of Yr., Mich. Assn. Chiefs Police, 1993, Legis. Conservationist of Yr., Mich. United Conservation Clubs, 1994, Guardian of Small Bus., Nat. Fedn. Ind. Bus., 1996, Legis. of Yr., Mich. Sheriff's Assn., 1997; Federalism Summit, 1995; Toll fellow, 1995; Fleming fellow, 1994, 95, fellow Coun. State Govts., Ctr. for Policy Alternatives; recipient Silver Beaver award Boy Scouts Am., 1997, Advocate of Yr. award Mich. Mfrs. Assn., 1998, Flame Leadership award Ferris State U., 1998, Star award Dep. Sheriff's Assn. Mich., 1999, Legis. Leadership award Mich. Soft Drink Assn., 1999, Disting. Svc. award Ind. Colls. and Univs. of Mich. Assn., 2000; Am. Legion Legislative award, 2000, Disting. Svc. medal Mich Dept. Mil. and Vets Affairs, 2001, Legis. Leadership award Internat. Brotherhood Elec. Workers and Mich. Chpt. Nat. Elec. Contractors Assn., 2001, Disting. Citizen of Yr. award, Boy Scouts Am., 2001, Legislator of Yr. award, Police Officers Assn. Mich., 2001, Adjutant Gen. Patriot award Mich. Dept. Mil. and Vets. Affairs, 2001, Presdl. Citation award Mich. Sheriff's Assn., 2002, others. Mem. NAACP (life), Am. Legis. Exch. Coun. (Outstanding Legis. Mem. of Yr. 1992, chmn. telecom. task force, 1992-95, bd. dirs. 1996), Jackson C.C. Alumni Assn. (Disting. Svc. award 1987), Ferris State U. Alumni Assn. (Disting. Alumnus 1990), Mich. Jaycees (1 of 10 Outstanding Young People in Mich. 1985). Republican. Roman Catholic. Office: 721 N Capitol Ave Ste 3 Lansing MI 48906 Home Phone: 517-688-4580; Office Phone: 517-371-3333. Office Fax: 517-487-3505.

HOFFMAN, RICHARD BRUCE, lawyer; b. Columbus, Ohio, June 8, 1947; s. Marion Keith and Ruth Eileen (McLear) Hoffman; m. Sandra Kay Schenkel, July 26, 1975; children: Kipp Hunter, Tyler Blake. BS in Gen. Engring., U. Ill., 1970; JD, DePaul U., 1973; LLM, John Marshall Sch. of Law, 1981. Bar: Ill. 1973, U.S. Dist. Ct. (no. dist.) Ill. 1973, U.S. Patent and Trademark Office 1973, U.S. Ct. Appeals (7th cir.) 1979, U.S. Ct. Appeals (fed. and 9th cirs.) 1982. Assoc. McCaleb, Lucas & Brugman, Chgo., 1973-76, ptnr., 1976-84, Tilton, Fallon, Lungmus & Chestnut, Chgo., 1984-2001, Marshall, Gerstein & Borun LLP, Chgo., 2001—. Mem.: ABA, Intellectual Property Law Assn. Chgo., Internat. Trademark Assn., Am. Intellectual Property Law Assn., Chgo. Bar Assn., Ill. Bar Assn., Union League Club of Chgo., Lawyers Club Chgo. Office: Marshall Gerstein & Borun LLP 6300 Sears Tower 233 S Wacker Dr Chicago IL 60606-6357 Office Phone: 312-474-6300. Business E-Mail: rhoffman@marshallip.com.

HOFFMAN, RICHARD GEORGE, psychologist; b. Benton Harbor, Mich., Oct. 6, 1949; s. Robert Fredrick and Kathleen Elyce (Watts) Hoffman; m. Julia Ann May, Dec. 18, 1970; children: Leslie Margarete, Michael Charles, Angela Lynn, Jennifer Elizabeth. BS with honors, Mich. State U., East Lansing, 1971; MA in Psychology, LI U., 1974, PhD in Clin. Psychology, 1980. Lic. con. psychologst. Instr. pediat. U. Va., Charlottesville, 1977—80; asst. prof. pediat. and family medicine U. Kans., Wichita, 1980—84; asst. prof. behavioral sci. U. Minn., Duluth, 1984—90, dir. neuropsychology lab., 1986—, co-dir. hypothermia and water safety lab., 1987, assoc. prof. behavioral sci., 1990—, co-dir. neurobehavioral toxicology lab., 1990—, asst. dean for med. edn. and curriculum, 1997—2002; assoc. dean for med. edn. and curriculum U. Minn., Duluth, 2002—; vis. sr. fellow in human clin. neuropsychology U. Okla. Health Scis. Ctr., 1995—96. Assoc. dir. Child Evaluation Ctr., Wichita, 1981-82; dir. adminstrn. Comprehensive Epilepsy Clinic, Wichita, 1983-84; cons. psychologist U. Assocs., P.A., Duluth, 1984—. Contbr. articles to profl. jour. Pres. Home and Sch. Assn., St. Michael's Sch., Duluth, 1986. Grantee Rsch. grantee, NIH, 1985, USCG, 1986, Sch. Medicine U. Kans., 1984, U. Minn., 1984, US Army Med. Rsch. Command, 1988—, Naval Med. Rsch. Command, 1988, Gt. Lakes Protection Fund, 1991—93, Agy. for Toxic Substances and Disease Registry, 1992—95, 1995—. Fellow Am. Psychol. Soc., Am. Assn. Applied and Preventive Psychology; mem. APA, Nat. Acad. europsychologists. Democrat. Roman Catholic. Avocations: bicycling, hiking. Home: 219 Occidental Blvd Duluth MN 55804-1365 Office: U Minn Dept Behavioral Scis Duluth MN 55812 Office Phone: 218-726-8874. Business E-Mail: rhoffman@d.umn.edu.

HOFFMAN, ROBERT A., state representative; BS, MS, Ind. State U. Ret. vocat. dir. Connersville Area Vocat. Sch., Ind.; state rep. dist. 55 Ind. Ho. of Reps., Indpls., 1996—, mem. agr., natural resources and rural devel., edn., and fin. instns. coms. Pres. Leadership Fayette County; adv. bd. Purdue U. East; mem. Connersville Econ. Devel. Com.; mem. County Ext. Bd.; mem. labor/mgmt. com.; chmn. Bethany Christian Ch.; past pres. Fayette Meml. Hosp. Bd. Mem.: Ind. Coun. Vocat. Dirs., Ind. Assn. Area Vocat. Sch. Dists. Republican. Office: Ind Ho of Reps 200 W Washington St Indianapolis IN 46204-2786

HOFFMAN, SHARON LYNN, adult education educator; b. Chgo. d. David P. and Florence Seaman; m. Jerry Irwin Hoffman, Aug. 25, 1963; children: Steven Abram, Rachel Irene. BA, Ind. U., 1961; M Adult Edn., Nat.-Louis Univ., 1992. High sch. English tchr. Chgo. Pub. Schs., 1961-64; tchr. Dept. of Def. Schs., Braconne, France, 1964-66; tchr. ESL Russian Inst., Garmisch, Fed. Republic Germany, 1966, 67; tchr. adult edn. Monterey Peninsula Unified Schs., Ft. Ord, Calif., 1977-79; tchr. ESL MAECOM, Monmouth County, NJ, 1979-80; lectr., tchr. adult edn. Truman Coll./Temple Shalom, Chgo.; tchr. homebound Fairfax County Pub. Schs., Fairfax, Va., 1976; entry operator Standard Rate & Data, Wilmette, Ill., 1986-87; rsch. editor, spl. projects editor Marquis Who's Who, Wilmette, 1987-92; mem. adj. faculty Nat.-Louis U., Evanston and Wheeling, Ill., 1993-99, tutor coord., then coord. learning specialist, 1993-99; pres. Cultural Transitions, Pebble Beach, Calif., 1992—. Mem.: TESOL, ASTD, Nat. Coun. Tchrs. English. Personal E-mail: culturaltrans1@aol.com.

HOFFMAN, SUE ELLEN, retired elementary school educator; b. Dayton, Ohio, Aug. 23, 1945; d. Cyril Vernon and Sarah Ellen (Sherer) Stephan; m. Lawrence Wayne Hoffman, Oct. 28, 1967. BS in Edn., U. Dayton, 1967; postgrad., Loyola Coll., 1977, Ea. Mich. U., 1980; MEd, Wright State U., 1988. Cert. reading specialist and elem. tchr., Ohio. 5th grade tchr. St. Anthony Sch., Dayton, Ohio, 1967-68, West Huntsville (Ala.) Elem. Sch., 1968-71; 6th grade tchr. Ranchland Hills Pub. Sch., El Paso, Tex., 1973-74; 3rd grade tchr. Emerson Pub. Sch., Westerville, Ohio, 1976, St. Joan of Arc Sch., Aberdeen, Md., 1976-78, Our Lady of Good Counsel, Plymouth, Mich., 1979-80; 5th grade tchr. St. Helen Sch., Dayton, 1980—2002; ret., 2002. Selected for membership Kappa Delta Pi, 1988. Mem. Internat. Reading Assn., Ohio Internat. Reading Assn., Dayton Area Internat. Reading Assn., Nat. Cath. Edn. Assn. Roman Catholic. Home: 2174 Green Springs Dr Kettering OH 45440-1120 Personal E-mail: l-shoffman@msn.com.

HOFFMANN, CHARLES WESLEY, retired foreign language educator; b. Sioux City, Iowa, Nov. 25, 1929; s. John Wesley and Gertrude J. (Giessen) H.; m. Barbara Brandel Frank, Aug. 11, 1954; children: Eric Gregory, Karla Jennifer. BA, Oberlin Coll., 1951; MA, U. Ill., 1952, PhD, 1956. Fulbright fellow U. Munich, Germany, 1953-55; Instr. German UCLA, 1956-58, asst. prof., 1958-64; assoc. prof. Ohio State U., 1964-66, prof., 1966—92, chmn. dept. German, 1969-77, 86-87. Author: Opposition Poetry in Nazi Germany, 1962, Survey of Research Tool Needs in German Language and Literature, 1978; also: articles on 20th Century German lit; adv. editor: Dimension, 1968-74. Recipient Disting. Teaching award UCLA, 1962, Lou Nemzer award for def. acad. freedom, 1982, Exemplary Faculty award Ohio State U., 1991; Fulbright grantee Germany, 1953-55, 1981. Mem. MLA, Am. Assn. Tchrs. German, ACLU, AAUP (pres. Ohio State U. 1984-86). Home: 291 Mccoy Ave Worthington OH 43085-3748 Office: Dieter Cunz Hall Columbus OH 43210

HOFFMANN, THOMAS RUSSELL, business management educator; b. Milw., Sept. 10, 1933; s. Alfred C. and Florence M. (Morlock) H.; m. Lorna G. Gruenzel, Aug. 31, 1957; 1 child, Timothy Jay. BS, U. Wis., 1955, MS, 1956, PhD, 1959. Cert. in prodn. and inventory mgmt., 1976, in integrated resource mgmt., Am. Prodn. and Inventory Control Soc., 1982. Engring. trainee Allis-Chalmers Mfg. Co., 1956-59; asst. prof. U. Wis. Sch. Commerce, 1959-63; mem. faculty U. Minn. Sch. Mgmt., Mpls., 1963-99, prof., 1965-99, chmn. dept. mgmt. scis., 1969-78; dir. West Bank Computer Center, 1971-87. Cons. to industry. Author: Production Management and Manufacturing Systems, 2 edit., 1967-71, (with others) Fortran 77: A Structured, Disciplined Style, 1978, 83, 88, Production and Inventory Management, 1983, 2d edit., 1991, Production and Operations Management, 1989; editor-in-chief Jour. Ops. Mgmt., 1993-95; contbr. articles to profl. jours. Chmn. long range planning com. Luth. Ch., 1971, pres., 1974, 89, treas., 1977-82, 93-98; pres. Ctrl. Lutheran Ch. Found., 1996. Mem. Am. Prodn. and Inventory Control Soc. (pres. Twin Cities chpt., 1970-71, internat. pres. 1998). Home: 4501 Sedum Ln Edina MN 55435-4051 Office: U Minn Carlson Sch Mgmt Minneapolis MN 55455 Business E-Mail: tomhoff@umn.edu.

HOFFMEISTER, DONALD FREDERICK, zoologist, educator; b. San Bernardino, Calif., Mar. 21, 1916; s. Percival George and Julia Bell (Hillgartner) H.; m. Helen E. Kaatz, Aug. 11, 1938; m. 2d Florence Williamson, Aug. 15, 1995; children: James Ronald, Robert George. AB, U. Calif.-Berkeley, 1938, MA, 1940, PhD, 1944; ScD (hon.), MacMurray Coll., Jacksonville, Ill., 2000. Research, curatorial asst. Museum Vertebrate Zoology, U. Calif.-Berkeley, 1941-44, teaching asst. zoology, 1943-44; assoc. curator modern vertebrates Mus. Natural History, U. Kans., 1944-46, asst. prof. zoology, 1944-46; dir. Mus. Natural History, U. Ill., 1946-84, dir. emeritus, 1984—, mem. faculty univ., 1946—, prof. zoology, 1959-84, prof. emeritus, 1984—; research assoc. Mus. No. Ariz., 1969—. Author: Mammals, 1955, 1963, Fieldbook of Illinois Mammals, 1957, Zoo Animals, 1967, Mammals of Grand Canyon, 1971, Mammals of Ariz., 1986, Mammals of Illinois, 1989; also articles, reports. Fellow Ariz.-Nev. Acad. Sci.; mem. Am. Soc. Mammalogists (hon., sec. 1946-52, v.p. 1961-64, pres. 1964-66, Hartley H.T. Jackson award 1987), Midwest Mus. Conf. (hon., exec. v.p. 1962-63, pres. 1963-64), Am. Assn. Mus. (coun. 1973-76), Assn. Sci. Mus. Dirs. Home: Apt 215 401 Burwash Ave Savoy IL 61874-9574

HOFFSIS, GLEN F., dean; B in Animal sci., Ohio State U., 1962, DVM, 1966, M in Internal Medicine, 1969. Bd. cert. Am. Coll. Vet. Internal Medicine. Intern vet. medicine Colo. State U., 1967; dir. Ohio State U.'s Vet. Hosp., Columbus, 1991; mem. faculty Ohio State U., Columbus, 1970—, head sect. food animal medicine and surgery dept. vet. clin. scis., 1970—91; dean Ohio State U. Coll. Vet. Medicine, Columbus, 1995—2004. Food cons. FDA; past chmn. FDA Ctr. for Vet. Medicine Adv. Com. Authored and co-authored (100 sci. articles), animal editor Compendium on Continuing Edu. Mem.: Ohio Vet. Med. Assn. (mem. biologics and pharm. com., past v.p.), Am. Assn. Bovine Practitioners (past pres., Award of Excellence), Nat. Milk Prodrs. Fedn., Am. Vet. Med. Assn. (joint liaison com., reviewer).

HOFMAN, LEONARD JOHN, minister; b. Kent County, Mich., Jan. 31, 1928; s. Bert and Dora (Miedema) H.; m. H. Elaine (Ryskamp) H., Aug. 19, 1949; children: Laurie, Janice, Kathleen, Joel. BA, Calvin Coll., 1948; BTh, Calvin Sem., 1951, MDiv, 1981. Pastor Wright Christian Reformed Ch., Kanawha, Iowa, 1951-54, Kenosha Christian Reformed Ch., Kenosha, Wis., 1954-59, North St. Christian Reformed Ch., Zeeland, Mich., 1959-65, Ridgewood Christian Reformed Ch., Jenison, Mich., 1965-77, Bethany Christian Reformed Ch., Holland, Mich.; pres. bd. trustees Christian Reformed Ch., Grand Rapids, Mich., 1977-82; gen. sec. Christian Reformed Ch. in N.Am., Grand Rapids, Mich., 1982-94, adminstrv. sec. for interchurch rels., 1995—. Sec. bd. trustees Calvin Coll., Grand Rapids, 1970-76. Recipient Oustanding Service award Calvin Alumni Assn., 1978. Mem. Nat. Assn. Evangelicals (bd. dirs. 1986-98, exec. com. bd. dirs. 1990-98, 2d vice chmn., bd. dirs. 1993-94, 1st vice chmn., bd. dirs. 1995-96, chmn. bd. dirs. 1997-98). Home and Office: 2237 Radcliff Cir SE Grand Rapids MI 49546-7725

HOFSOMMER, DONOVAN LOWELL, history professor; b. Ft. Dodge, Iowa, Apr. 10, 1938; s. Vernie George and Helma J. (Schager) H.; m. Sandra Louise Rusch, June 13, 1965; children: Kathryn Anne, Kristine Beret, Knute Lars. BA, U. Northern Iowa, 1960, MA, 1966; PhD, Okla. State U., 1973. Tchr. Fairfield (Iowa) High Sch., 1961-65; instr. U. Northern Iowa, Cedar Falls, 1965-66, Lea Coll., Albert Lea, Minn., 1966-70; teaching asst. Okla. State U., Stillwater, 1970-73; assoc. prof. and dept. head Wayland Coll., Plainview, Tex., 1973-81; corp. historian So. Pacific Co., San Francisco, 1981-85; hist. cons. Burlington No. Inc., Seattle, 1985-87; vis. prof. U. Mont., Missula, 1986-87; exec. dir. ctr. Western studies Augustana Coll., Sioux Falls, SD, 1987-89; prof. history St. Cloud (Minn.) State U., 1989—. Cons. Dyanelectron and Dynarail, Pueblo, Colo., 1979-81, Grand Trunk Corp., Detroit, 1988-95; mem. editl. bd. annals of Iowa, Iowa City, 1975-94, R.R. history, Akron, Ohio, 1975—. Author: Prairie Oasis, 1975, Katy Northwest, 1976, Southern Pacific 1901-1985, 1986; co-author: History of Great Northern Railway, 1988, Quanah Route, 1991, Grand Trunk Corp., 1995, The Tootin' Louie, 2004, History of Minneapolis & Saint Louis, 2004, Steel Trails of Hawkeye Land, 2005, Minneapolis and the Age of Railways, 2005, HIstory of Iowa Central Railway, 2005; editor: Lexington Group Transport History, 1975—; mem. editl. bd. Annals of Iowa, Iowa City, 1975-92, R.R. History, Akron, Ohio, 1975—. With U.S. Army, 1960-66. Mem. Okla. Hist. Soc. (Wright Heritage award 1979), Ry. and Locomotive Hist. Soc. (Book award 1988, Sr. Achievement award 1995), Western History Assn., Orgn. Am. Historians, State Hist. Soc. Iowa, Am. Assn. for State and Local History (Leadership History award 2006). Episcopalian. Home: 1803 13th Ave SE Saint Cloud MN 56304-2231 Office: St Cloud State U Dept History Saint Cloud MN 56301 Office Phone: 320-308-4906.

HOFSTADTER, DOUGLAS RICHARD, cognitive scientist, educator, writer; b. NYC, Feb. 15, 1945; s. Robert and Nancy (Givan) H.; m. Carol Ann Brush, 1985; children: Daniel Frederic, Monica Marie. BS in Math. with distinction, Stanford U., 1965; MS, U. Oreg., 1972, PhD in Physics, 1975. Asst. prof. computer sci. Ind. U., Bloomington, 1977-80, assoc. prof., 1980-84; Walgreen prof. Cognitive Sci. U. Mich., Ann Arbor, 1984-88; prof. cognitive sci., computer sci. Ind. U., Bloomington, 1988—. Adj. prof. psychology, philosophy, history and philosophy of sci., comparative lit., dir. Ctr. for Rsch. on Concepts and Cognition, Ind. U. Author: Gödel, Escher, Bach: an Eternal Golden Braid, 1979, Metamagical Themas, 1985, Ambigrammi, 1987, Fluid Concepts and Creative Analogies, 1995, Rhapsody on a Theme by Clément Marot, 1996, Le Ton beau de Marot, 1997; editor: (with Daniel C. Dennett) The Mind's I, 1981; columnist: Metamagical Themas in Sci. Am., 1981-83. Recipient Pulitzer prize for gen. nonfiction, 1980; Am. Book award, 1980; Guggenheim fellow, 1980-81 Mem. Cognitive Sci. Soc., Am. Assn. Artificial Intelligence, Am. Lit. Translators Assn. Office: Ctr Rsch Concepts & Cognition 510 N Fess St Bloomington IN 47408-3822

HOGAN, BRIAN JOSEPH, editor; b. Aberdeen, SD, Apr. 11, 1943; s. Arthur James and Magdalena (Frison) H.; m. Jamie Isabelle Schwingel, June 21, 1987. BS in Aerospace and Mech. Engring., U. Ariz., 1965, BS in Geophysics-

Geochemistry, 1968; MS in Journalism, U. Utah, 1972. Rsch. asst. U. Va. Rsch. Labs for Engring. Scis., Charlottesville, 1965-66; exploration geophysicist Anaconda Co., Tucson, 1968-71; assoc. editor Benwill Pub. Co., Brookline, Mass., 1973-74; asst. editor Design News, Boston, 1974-75, midwest editor Chgo., 1975-87, sr. editor Newton, Mass., 1987-89, mng. editor, 1989-97; chief editor Mfg. Engring.-Soc. Mfg. Engrs., Dearborn, Mich. Author stage plays The Young O'Neil, 1983, Awakening, 1984. Precinct worker Cook County Rep. Com., Oak Park, Ill., 1986-87; interpreter Frank Lloyd Wright Home and Studio Found., Oak Park, 1981-87. Recipient numerous awards Am. Soc. Bus. Press Editors, Soc. Tech. Communication, Aviation Space Writers Assn. Mem. Am. Hist. Print Collectors Soc. Republican. Roman Catholic. Avocations: photography, print collecting, bicycling, hiking. Office: Mfg Engring 1 SME Dr PO Box 930 Dearborn MI 48121-0930 Office Phone: 313-425-3252. Business E-Mail: bhogan@sme.org.

HOGAN, JOSEPH M., health products executive; b. Mar. 7, 1957; m. Lisa Hogan; children: Tyler, Jason, Nicolas. BS in Bus. Adminstrn., Geneva Coll.; MBA, Robert Morris U., 1984. Sales, mktg. in plastics G.E., 1985—98; pres., CEO G.E. Fanuc Automation N. Am., 1998—2000; exec. v.p., COO G.E. Med. Sys., 2000; pres., CEO G.E. Healthcare Technologies, 2000—05; sr. v.p. G.E., 2005—; pres., CEO G.E. Healthcare, 2005—. Bd. mem. NY Acad. Med., Multiple Myeloma Rsch. Found.; mem. adv. bd. Ctr. Disease Control. Office: GE Healthcare 3000 N Grandview Blvd Waukesha WI 53188

HOGAN, MICHAEL J., academic administrator; m. Virginia Hogan; children: Christopher, David, Joe, AnnElizabeth. BA, U. No. Iowa; MA, U. Iowa, PhD in History. Vis. prof. SUNY, Stony Brook, 1974—75, U. Tex., Austin, 1976—77; from asst. prof. to assoc. prof. to prof. Miami U., Oxford, Ohio, 1977—86; prof. Ohio State U., 1986—2004, univ. disting. scholar, 1990—2004, chair dept. history, 1993—99, dean Coll. Humanities, 1999—2003, exec. dean Colls. Arts and Scis., 2001—04; exec. v.p., provost U. Iowa, Iowa City, 2004—07, Wendell Miller prof. history, 2004—06; pres. U. Conn., Storrs, 2007—. Louis Martin Sears disting. prof. history Purdue U.; cons. in field. Author: Informal Entente: The Private Structure of Cooperation in Anglo-America Economic Diplomacy, 1918-1928, 1977, The Marshall Plan: America, Britain, and the Reconstruction of Western Europe, 1947-1952, 1987 (Stuart L. Bernath Book Award, Soc. Historians of Am. Fgn. Rels., George Louis Beer Prize, Am. Hist. Assn., Quincy Wright Prize, Internat. Studies Assn.), A Cross of Iron: Harry S. Truman and the Origins of the National Security State, 1945-1954, 1998; editor: Paths to Power: The Historiography of American Foreign Relations to 1941, 2000; contbr. articles to profl. jours. Recipient Bernath Lecture prize, Soc. Historians of Am. Fgn. Rels., 1984; fellow, Harry S. Truman Libr. Inst., Woodrow Wilson Internat. Ctr. for Scholars. Mem.: Soc. Historians of Am. Fgn. Rels. (v.p. 2002, pres. 2003). Office: U Conn Office of Pres 352 Mansfield Rd, Unit 2048 Storrs Mansfield CT 06269-2048 Office Fax: 860-486-2048. E-mail: president@uconn.edu, mike.hogan@uconn.edu.

HOGAN, MICHAEL RAY, life science executive; b. Newark, Ohio, Apr. 21, 1953; s. Raymond Carl and Mary Adele (Whalen) H.; m. Martha Ann Gorman, July 24, 1976; children: Colleen Michael, Patrick Gorman, Mary Kate, Andrei Sean. BA, Loyola U., Chgo., 1978; M in Mgmt. with distinction, Northwestern U., 1980. Cert. FLMI, HIA. Assoc. McKinsey & Co., Inc., Chgo., 1980-81, engagement mgr., 1982-83; sr. v.p., treas. FBS Ins. Co., Mpls., 1984-85; group v.p., gen. mgr. Gen. Am. Life Ins. Co., St. Louis, 1986, v.p., 1987-89, exec. v.p., 1990-95; pres., CEO Cova Corp., St. Louis, 1995-96; corp. v.p., controller Monsanto Co., St. Louis, 1996-99; v.p., CFO, CAO Sigma-Aldrich Corp., 1999—. Cons. Swedish Trade Commn., Chgo., 1978, Lee Wards Creative Crafts Co., Elgin, Ill., 1979; chmn. Consultec, Inc., Atlanta, 1990-95, Cova Fin. Life Ins. Co., Oakbrook Terrace, 1995; chmn., CEO Genelco, Inc., St. Louis, 1990-95; adv. bd. Integrated Health Svcs. Managed Care, Owings Mills, Md., 1994-2002; pres. GenCare Health Sys., Inc., 1990-95. Contb. articles to profl. jours. Adv. bd. Washington U. Olin Sch. Nat. Coun., 2002—; active Experience St. Louis, 1986, Leadership Ctr. of Greater St. Louis, 1987—95, bd. dirs., 1988—95, v.p. comm., 1989—90, pres., 1991—92; bd. dirs. Focus St. Louis, Inc., 1996—2002, treas., 1996—98; bd. dirs. Combined Health Appeal of Greater St. Louis, 1992—97, v.p. programs, 1992—94, pres., 1995—96; corp. chmn. Juvenile Diabetes Rsch. Found. Walk, 2005; bd. dirs. St. Louis Coll. Pharmacy, 1995—2000, Wyman Ctr., 1997—2000, Combined Health Appeal of Am., 1997—98, United Way of Greater St. Louis, 1997—, vice-chmn., 1997—99; bd. dirs. Small World Adoption Found., 1998—2006, pres., 2000—06; bd. dirs. Pulaski Fin. Corp., 2006—; adv. bd. World Trade Ctr., St. Louis, 2007—. Scholar F.C. Austin Found., 1978-80, Phi Gamma Nu, 1980; recipient Nat. Vol. of Yr. award Combined Health Appeal of Am., 1996, Person of Yr. award Juvenile Diabetes Assn. St. Louis chpt., 1998, Gala Honoree, 1998, Health Citizen of Yr. award Combined Health Appeal Greater St. Louis, 1998, Corp. Leadership Divsn. award United Way Gtr. St. Louis, 1993, 95, Employee Divsn. award, 1997, 98, Michael R. Hogan Humanitarian award named in his honor Small World Adoption Found., 2004. Mem. Beta Gamma Sigma, Greenbriar Hills Country Club. Roman Catholic. Avocations: reading, golf, travel. Home: 9368 Robyn Hills Dr Saint Louis MO 63127-1316 Office Phone: 314-286-8003. Business E-Mail: mhogan@sial.com.

HOGAN, RANDALL J., manufacturing and electronics executive; BS in Civil Engring., MIT; MBA, U. Tex. Cons. McKinsey & Co.; with Gen. Electric; with Pratt & Whitney divsn. United Techs., pres. carrier transicold divsn.; exec. v.p. and pres. of elec. and elec. enclosures group Pentair, Inc., Golden Valley, Minn., 1998—99, pres. and COO, 1999—2000, pres. and CEO, 2001—02, chmn. and CEO, 2002—. Office: Pentair Inc Ste 800 5500 Wayzata Blvd Golden Valley MN 55416

HOGENKAMP, HENRICUS PETRUS CORNELIS, biochemistry researcher, educator; b. Doesburg, Gelderland, The Netherlands, Dec. 20, 1925; came to U.S., 1958; s. Johannes Hermanus and Maria Margaretha J. (Abeln) H.; m. Lieke Ter Haar, Apr. 25, 1953; children: Harry Peter, Derk John, Margaret Angelina. BSA, U. B.C., Vancouver, 1957, MSc, 1958; PhD, U. Calif., Berkeley, 1961. Rsch. biochemist U. Calif., Berkeley, 1961—62; assoc. scientist Fisheries Rsch. Bd. Can., Vancouver, B.C., 1962—63; asst. prof. U. Iowa, Iowa City, 1963—67, assoc. prof., 1967—71, prof., 1971—76; prof., head dept. biochemistry U. Minn., Mpls., 1976—92, prof. dept. biochemistry, 1992—2002, prof. emeritus, 2002. Vis. prof. Australian Nat. U., Canberra, Australia, 1966-67, Philipps U., Marburg, Fed. Republic of Germany, 1986-87, 1988, 1990; guest scientist U. Calif. Los Alamos (N.Mex) Sci. Lab., 1974-75. Sgt. Royal Netherlands Army, 1946-50, Indonesia. Recipient Alexander von Humboldt-Stiftung award Philipps U.-Fachbereich Microbiology, Marburg, Fed. Republic of Germany, 1986-87; named to Minn. Acad. Medicine,Mpls., 1980--; Guggenheim fellow U. Iowa, Iowa City, 1974-75. Mem. Am. Chem. Soc., Am. Soc. Biochemistry and Molecular Biology (mem. pub. affairs com. 1986-91), Assn. Med. Sch. Depts. Biochemistry, Internat. Union Biochemists (chmn. U.S. nominating com. 1988). Home: 2211 Marion Rd Saint Paul MN 55113-3805 Office: U Minn BMBB Dept Ste 6-155 321 Church St SE Minneapolis MN 55455 Office Phone: 612-625-4471.

HOGG, ROBERT, state representative; b. Iowa City, 1967; s. Bob and Carolyn Ladd Hogg; m. Kathryn Stoff; children: Robert, Dorothy, Isabel. Degree in history, U. Iowa, 1988; M in Energy Policy, 1991. Clk. Judge Donald Lay U.S. Ct. Appeals (8th cir.), St. Paul; with Leonard, Street and Deinard, St. Paul and Mpls.; clk. Judge Michael Melloy U.S. Dist. Ct., Cedar Rapids, Iowa, 1998; with Elderkin & Pirnie, PLC, Cedar Rapids; state rep. Iowa, 2003—. Mem. econ. devel. appropriations subcom.; mem. environ. protection standing com.; mem. pub. safety standing com.; mem. ways and means standing com. Mem.: Indian Creek Nature Ctr., Sierra Club (chair local Cedar-Wapsie Group 2001—02), Linn Law Club (former v.p.). Democrat. Episcopalian. Office: State Capitol E 12th and Grand Des Moines IA 50319

HOGG, ROBERT VINCENT, JR., mathematical statistician, educator; b. Hannibal, Mo., Nov. 8, 1924; s. Robert Vincent and Isabelle Frances (Storrs) H.; m. Carolyn Joan Ladd, June 23, 1956 (dec. June 1990); children: Mary Carolyn, Barbara Jean, Allen Ladd, Robert Mason; m. Ann Burke, Oct. 15, 1994. BA, U. Ill., 1947; MS, U. Iowa, 1948, PhD, 1950. Asst. prof. math. U. Iowa, Iowa City, 1950-56, assoc. prof., 1956-62, prof., 1962-65, chmn. dept. stats., prof. stats., 1965-83, 92-93, Hanson prof. mfg. productivity, 1993-95, prof. emeritus, 2001—. Co-author: Introduction to Mathematical Statistics, 1959, 6th edit., 2005, Finite Mathematics and Calculus, 1974, Probability and Statistical Inference, 1977, 7th edit., 2005, Applied Statistics for Engineers and Physical Scientists, 1987, 2d edit., 1992, A Brief Course in Mathematical Statistics, 2007; assoc. editor Am. Stats., 1971-74; contbr. articles to profl. jours. Vestryman local Episc. ch., 1958-60, 66-68, 91-92, 2001-03. With USNR, 1943-46. Grantee NIH, 1966-68, 75-78, NSF, 1969-74; Disting. Alumni Award, U. Iowa, 2003. Fellow Inst. Math. Stats. (program sec., bd. 1968-74, Carver medal 2006), Am. Statis. Assn. (pres. Iowa sect. 1962-63, coun. 1965-66, 73-74, vis. lectr. 1965-68, 77-85, chmn. tng. sect. 1973, assoc. editor jour. 1978-80, pres.-elect 1987, pres. 1988, past pres. 1989, Founders award 1991, Noether award 2001); mem. Math. Assn. Am. (pres. Iowa sect. 1964-65, 95-96, bd. govs. 1971-74, visa. lectr. 1976-81, Outstanding Tchg. award 1993), Internat. Statis. Inst., Rotary (pres. Iowa City 1984-85), Sigma Xi (pres. Iowa dist. chpt. 1970-71), Pi Kappa Alpha. Home: 30130 Trails End Buena Vista CO 81211 Office: U Iowa Dept Statis Acturial Sci Iowa City IA 52242 E-mail: rvh24@mccoymail.net.

HOGIKYAN, NORMAN DERTAD, otolaryngologist; b. Detroit, Apr. 3, 1961; BS magna cum laude, U. Mich., 1982, MD cum laude, 1988. Am. Bd. Otolaryngology-Head and Neck Surgery, Nat. Bd. Med. Examiners; lic. medicine and surgery, Mich. Intern, otolaryngology William Beaumont Hosp., Royal Oak, Mich., 1988-89; resident, otolaryngology Washington U. Med. Ctr., St. Louis, 1989-94; fellow, otolaryngology Loyola U., Maywood, Ill., 1994-95; mem. staff U. Mich Hosp., Ann Arbor, 1995—; cons. physician Ann Arbor VA Med. Ctr., 1995—; asst. prof. otolaryngology U. Mich., Ann Arbor, Mich., 1995—2002, assoc. prof. otolaryngology, 2002—, med. dir. speech and lang. pathology program, 1996—, assoc. prof., music, sch. music. Dir. U. Mich. Vocal Health Ctr., Livonia, 1996—. Expert analyst, reviewer Otolaryngology Jour. Club Jour., 1996—; contbr. articles to profl. jours., chpts. to books. Grantee U. Mich., Office of V.P. for Rsch., 1996; recipient 1st prize Joseph Agura Resident Rsch. Competition, 1991, 92, award for excellence in resident tchg. Washington U. Dept. Otolaryngology, St. Louis, 1994. Fellow ACS, Am. Acad. Otolaryngology-Head and Neck Surgery; mem. AMA, Mich. Otolaryn. Soc., Walter P. Work Soc., Alpha Omega Alpha, Phi Beta Kappa. Office: U Mich A Alfred Taubman Health Care Ctr 1500 E Medical Ctr Dr Rm 1904 Ann Arbor MI 48109-0312 Mailing: Vocal Health Ctr Ctr for Specialty Care 1900 Haggerty Rd Ste 103 Livonia MI 48152 Office Phone: 734-936-9598. Office Fax: 734-936-9625.*

HOGLE, WALTER S., career officer; BA in Psychology, Hartwick Coll., 1966; Diploma, Squadron Officer Sch., 1970; MS in Counseling, Troy State U., 1975; Diploma, Armed Forces Staff Coll., 1980, Nat. War Coll., 1986. Commd. 2d lt. USAF, 1967, advanced through ranks to lt. gen., 1998; various assignments tocomdr. 437th Airlift Wing, Charleston AFB, S.C., 1994-95; dir. of plans Hdqtrs. Air Mobility Command, Scott AFB, Ill., 1995-98; vice-comdr. Air Mobility Command, Scott AFB, Ill., 1998—. Decorated Disting. Svc. medal, Legion of Merit with oak leaf cluster, Disting. Flying Cross, Bronze Star, Meritorious Svc. medal with two oak leaf clusters, Air medal with five oak leaf clusters, Air Force Commendation medal with oak leaf cluster, Republic of Vietnam Gallantry Cross with Palm, others. Office: AMC/CV 402 Scott Dr Unit 3ec Scott Air Force Base IL 62225-5300

HOGSETT, JOSEPH H., political organization worker, former state official; b. Nov. 2, 1956; Law clk. Judge James H. Dixon Monroe Cir. Ct.; atty. Bingham, Summers, Welsh & Spillman, 1981—87; dep. sec. state Ind., 1987—88; sec. state State of Ind., 1989—94; chmn. Ind. Dem. Party, Indpls., 2003—. Candidate U.S. Senator, Ind., 1992, U.S. Ho. Reps. 2d dist., Ind., 1994.

HOGUET, DAVID DILWORTH, rental furniture executive; b. Sharon, Conn., Aug. 16, 1951; s. Joseph Lynch Hoguet and Diana Wood (Dilworth) Wantz; m. Karen Meisel, Oct. 9, 1983; children: Jennifer Leigh, Laura Beth. BA in History, U. Pa., 1973; MBA in Fin., NYU, 1975. With W.R. Grace, NYC, 1975-1980; treas. Chemed Corp., Cin., 1981-1983, v.p. fin., treas., 1984-86; pres. Globe Funriture Rentals, Cin., 1986-89, chmn., 1989—. Fundraiser Brooks Sch., North Andover, Mass., 1978—. Mem. Funriture Rental Assn. Am. (pres. 1991—), Young Pres. Orgn., Losantiville Club, Racquet Club. Avocation: squash. Home: 740 Crevelings Ln Cincinnati OH 45226-1713

HOGUET, KAREN M., retail executive; m. David Hoguet; 2 children. Grad., Brown U.; MBA, Harvard U., 1980. With Boston Cons. Group, Chgo.; sr. cons. mktg. and long-range planning Macy's Inc. (formerly Federated Dept. Stores, Inc.), Cin., 1982-85; dir. capital and bus. planning Macy's Inc., Cin., 1985-87, operating v.p. planning and fin. analysis, 1987-88, corp. v.p., 1988-91, sr. v.p. planning, 1991—97, treas., 1992—97, sr. v.p., CFO, 1997—2005, exec. v.p., CFO, 2005—. Mem.: Phi Beta Kappa. Office: Macy's Inc 7 W 7th St Cincinnati OH 45202-2424 Fax: 513-579-7555.

HOHULIN, MARTIN, state legislator; b. Ft. Scott, Kans., May 1, 1964; m. Marilyn Hohulin; 1 child, William. State rep. Dist. 126 Mo. State Congress, 1991—. Mem. agr.-bus. consumer protection com., ranking rep. appropriations and labor com.; farm owner and operator. Mem. Cattlemens Assn., Barton County Farm Bur., Lamar Metro Club.

HOITINK, HENRICUS A., plant pathology educator; PhD in Phytobacteriology, U. Wis. Prof. plant pathology and environ. grad. studies program Ohio State U., Wooster. Recipient Ruth Allen award Am. Phytopathol. Soc., 1998. Achievements include development of principles for conversion of solid wastes into products beneficial to society, to determine how beneficial microorganisms in composts provide biological control of plant diseases. Office: OARDC Plant Pathology 211 Selby Hall 1680 Madison Ave Wooster OH 44691-4096 E-mail: hoitink.1@osu.edu.

HOKENSTAD, MERL CLIFFORD, JR., social work educator; b. Norfolk, Nebr., July 21, 1936; s. Merl Clifford and Flora Diane (Christian) H.; m. Dorothy Jean Tarrell, June 24, 1962; children: Alene Ann, Laura Rae, Marta Lynn. BA summa cum laude, Augustana Coll., 1958; Rotary Found. fellow, Durham U., Eng., 1958-59; MSW., Columbia U., 1962; PhD, Brandeis U., 1969, Inst. Ednl. Mgmt., Harvard U., 1977. With Lower East Side Neighborhood Assn., NYC, 1962-64; community planning assoc. United Community Services, Sioux Falls, SD, 1964-66; instr. Augustana Coll., Sioux Falls, 1964-66; research assoc. Ford Found. Project on Community Planning for Elderly, Brandeis U., Waltham, Mass., 1966-67; prof., dir. Sch. Social Work, Western Mich. U., Kalamazoo, 1968-74; prof., dean Sch. Applied Social Scis., Case Western Res. U., Cleve., 1974-83, Ralph and Dorothy Schmitt prof., 1983—, chmn. PhD program, 1990-94; prof. internat. health Sch. of Medicine, 1994—. Vis. prof. Inst. Sociology, Stockholm U., 1978, Fulbright lectr., 1980; vis. prof. Nat. Inst. Social Work, London, 1981, Sch. Social Work, Stockholm U., 1982-86, Eotvos Lorand U., Budapest, Hungary, 1992, 95-96, London Sch. Econs., 1994; Fulbright rsch. scholar Inst. Applied Social Rsch., Oslo, 1989; fellow U. Canterbury, Christchurch, New Zealand, 1994; tech. com. UN World Assembly on Aging, 2000-02, US delegation, 2002. Author: Participation in Teaching and Learning: An Idea Book for Social Work Educators; editor: Meeting Human Needs: An International Annual, Vol. V, Linking Health Care and Social Services: International Perspectives; editor-in-chief Internat. Social Work Jour., 1985-87; co-editor: Profiles in Internat. Social Work, 1992, Issues in International Social Work, 1997, Models of International Exchange, 2003, Lessons from Abroad: International Social Welfare Innovations, 2004; (internat. issue) Jour. Gerontol. Social Work, 1988, Jour. Sociology and Social Welfare, 1990, Jour. Social Policy and Administration, 1993, Jour. Aging Internat., 1994, Jour. Applied Social Scis., 1996; contbr. articles to profl. jours., chpts. to books. Mem. alcohol tng. rev. com. Nat. Inst. Alcoholism and Alcohol Abuse, 1974-78; workshop leader Am. Assn. State Colls. and Univs., 1974; chmn. U.S. com. XVIII Internat. Congress Schs. Social Work, 1976; chmn. Kalamazoo County Cmty. Mental Health Svcs. Bd., 1971, vice chmn., 1972; mem. edn. and tng. task force Mich. Office Drug Abuse and Alcoholism, 1972-73; mem. Mich. Assn. Mental Health Bds., 1972; bd. dirs. Cleve. United Way Svcs., 1982-84, del. assembly, 1974-82, mem. periodic rev. oversight com., 1982, mem. leadership devel. com., 1978, cmty. resources com., 1988—; bd. dirs. Kalamazoo United Way, 1968-72; trustee Cleve. Internat. Program for Youth Workers and Social Workers, chmn. program com., 1985-87; mem. program devel. com. Cleve. Center on Alcoholism, 1976; trustee Alcoholism Services Cleve., Inc., 1977-86, v.p., 1982-85; trustee Cmty. Info./Vol. Action Ctr., 1982-88, chmn. leadership devel. com., 1984-86, chmn. unmet needs com., 1986-88, exec. com., 1985-88, v.p., 1986-88; exec. com. Western Reserve Geriatric Edn. Ctr., 1995-2006; mem. adv. com. Coun. for Internat. Exch. Scholars, 1991-93, Ctr. for Cmty. Solutions Coun. on Older Persons, 1991—, vice chmn., 2005-06, chmn. 2006—, chmn. caregiver support program initiative, 1995-96; mem. adv. coun. Cuyahoga County Dept. Sr. and Adult Svcs., 1998—2003, chair, 2001—03; bd. dirs. Western Res. Area Agy. on Aging, 2004—; mem. task force of social transition in Soviet Union, US State Dept. Bur. Human Rights and Humanitarian Affairs; mem. UN NGO Com. on Aging, 1996—; co-chmn. US Com. for Internat. Yr. of Older Persons, 1999. Named Outstanding Alumnus, Augustana Coll., 1980, Ohio Soc. Worker of the Yr., 1992, Columbia U. Sch. Social Work Hall of Fame, 2006; Fulbright Research fellow; NIMH trainee, 1960-62; Vocat. Rehab. trainee, 1966; Gerontology trainee, 1967; Rotary Found. fellow, 1958-59; recipient Golden Achievement Award, Golden Age Ctr., 2003. Mem. NASW (internat. com. 1989-93, chmn. 1992-93, found. pioneer 2003—, Internat. Rhoda G. Sarnat award 2006), Acad. Cert. Social Workers, Internat. Assn. Schs. Social Work (exec. bd. 1978-92, 98—, treas. 1978-86, v.p. N.Am. 1988-92, membership sec. 1996-00, Katherine Kendall award 2004), Internat. Coun. on Social Welfare (dir. U.S. com. 1982-92), Coun. on Social Work Edn. (del. 1972-75, 77-83, chmn. ann. program meeting 1973, chmn. com. on nat. legis. and adminstrv. policy 1975-79, nominating com. 1978-81, internat. com. 1980-86, 96-2006, chmn. com. 1982-84, dir. 1979-82, exec. com. 1986-89, pres. 1986-89, Lifetime Achievement award 2002), Nat. Conf. on Social Welfare (bd. dirs. 1978-80, chmn. sect. V program com. 1977-78), World Future Soc. (area coord. 1972-74), Fulbright Assn. (v.p. N.E. Ohio chpt. 1990-91), Nat. Coun. on Aging (bd. dirs. 1991-97, internat. com. 1991-97, pub. policy com. 1992-97). Democrat. Episcopalian. Home: 2917 Weymouth Rd Cleveland OH 44120-2234 Office: Case Western Res U 10900 Euclid Ave Cleveland OH 44106-1764 Office Phone: 216-368-2323. Business E-Mail: mch2@cwru.edu.

HOKIN, LOWELL EDWARD, biochemist, educator; b. Chgo., Sept. 20, 1924; s. Oscar E. and Helen (Manfield) H.; m. Mabel Neaverson, Dec. 1, 1952 (dec. Aug. 2003); children: Linda Ann, Catherine Esther (dec.), Samuel Arthur; m. Barbara M. Gallagher, Mar. 23, 1978 (div. July 1998); 1 child, Ian Oscar; m. Vivian Littlefield-Moore, Aug. 6, 2006. Student, U. Chgo., 1942-43, Dartmouth Coll., 1943-44, U. Louisville Sch. Medicine, 1944-46, U. Ill. Sch. Medicine, 1946-47; MD, U. Louisville, 1948; PhD, U. Sheffield, Eng., 1952. Postdoctoral fellow dept. biochemistry McGill U., 1952-54, faculty, 1954-57, asst. prof., 1955-57; mem. faculty U. Wis., Madison, 1957—, prof. physiol. chemistry, 1961-68, prof. pharmacology, 1968-99, prof., chmn. pharmacology, 1968-93, prof. emeritus, 1999—. Contbr. numerous articles to tech. jours., chpts. to numerous books on phosphoinositides, biol. transport, the pancreas, the brain and lithium in manic-depression. With USNR, 1943—45. Mem.: AAAS, N.Y. Acad. Scis., Am. Soc. Pharmacology and Exptl. Therapeutics, Biochem. Soc. (U.K.), Am. Soc. Biochemistry and Molecular Biology. Achievements include discovery of phosphoinositide signaling system. Home: 4021C Monona Dr Monona WI 53716 Office: U Wis Med Sch Dept Pharm 1300 University Ave Madison WI 53706-1510 Office Phone: 608-224-2190. Business E-Mail: lehokin@wisc.edu.

HOLABIRD, JOHN AUGUR, JR., retired architect; b. Chgo., May 9, 1920; s. John Augur and Dorothy (Hackett) H.; m. Donna Katharine Smith, Nov. 25, 1942 (div. 1969); children: Jean, Katharine, Polly, Lisa (dec.); m. Marcia Stefanie Fergestad, June 28, 1969 (dec. Mar. 1994); children: Ann, Lynn; m. Janet Nothhelfer Connor, May 7, 1996. BA, Harvard U., 1942, MArch, 1948. Archtl. designer Holabird & Root, Chgo., 1948-49, 55-64, assoc. firm, 1964-70, ptnr., 1970-87. Tchr. drama Francis Parker Sch., Chgo., 1949-55; stage designer NBC-TV, 1955 Major: archtl. works include Francis Parker Sch, Chgo., Ravinia Stage and Restaurant, Highland Park, Ill., 1970, Bell Telephone Labs, Naperville, Ill., 1975, Canal Bldg, Chgo., 1974. Pres. Park West Community Assn., 1962; dir. Lincoln Park Conservation Assn., 1960-64, Corlands, 1979-85; mem. Chgo. Commn. on Historic and Archtl. Landmarks, 1981-85; bd. dirs. Lincoln Park Community Conservation, 1964; trustee Francis Parker Sch., Ravinia Festival Assn., Ill. Inst. Tech., 1980-86. Served with U.S. Army, 1942-45. Decorated Silver Star, Bronze Star; Fourragère (Belgium); Order of William (The Netherlands). Fellow AIA (pres. Chgo. chpt. 1977-78, Lifetime Achievement award, Chgo. chpt. 2007); mem. Tavern Club, Harvard Club (dir. 1974-78), Phi Beta Kappa. Democrat. Home: 200 E Pearson St Apt 3W Chicago IL 60611-2352 Office: Holabird & Root 140 S Dearborn St Chicago IL 60603

HOLBROOK, JOHN SCOTT, JR., lawyer; b. Milw., Oct. 27, 1939; s. John Scott Holbrook and Francesca Marie (Eschweiler) Davidson; m. Mary Lynn Lorenz, June 13, 1980. BA, StanfordU., Palo Alto, Calif., 1961; JD, U. Mich., 1964. Bar: Wis. 1964. Ptnr. Quarles & Brady, Madison, Wis., 1964—. Mem. ABA, State Bar of Wis., Nat. Assn. of Bond Lawyers, Am. Coll. Bond Counsel. Office: Quarles & Brady 1 S Pinckney St Madison WI 53703-2892

HOLBROOK, KAREN ANN, retired academic administrator, biologist; b. Des Moines, Nov. 6, 1942; married, 1973; 1 child. BS, U. Wis., 1963, MS, 1966; PhD in Biol. Structure, U. Wash., 1972. From instr. to assoc. prof. U. Wash. Sch. of Medicine, Seattle, 1971-79, vice chmn. dept. biol. structure, 1981—93, prof., 1984—93, assoc. dean sci. affairs, 1985—93; sr. v.p. & prof. U. Ga., Athens, Ga., 1993—98; pres. Ohio State U., Columbus, Ohio, 2002—07. Instr. biology Ripon Coll., 1966-69; NIH trainee, 1969-72, trainee, sr. fellow dermatology, 1976-78, mem. study sect. gen. medicine; adj. assoc. prof. med. dermatology, U. Wash., 1979-84; mem. spl. study sect. Nat. Inst. Arthritis & Metabollic Diseases, Nat. Inst. Arthritis, Diabetes & Digestive Kidney Diseases, 1985-88; adj. prof. med. dermatology, 1984-93. Named Disting. Woman Physician/Scientist, 1996; recipient Kung Sun Oh Mem prize, 34th Annual Mation Spencer Fay Nat. Bd. award, Disting. Contribn. to Rsch. Admin. award. Mem. AAAS, Am. Assn. Anatomists, Am. Soc. Cell Biology, Soc. Invest Dermatology, Soc. Pediat. Dermatology, Am. Assn. Of Univ., Nat. Assn of State Univ & Land Grant Coll., Assn of Am. Med. Coll. Commn on Higher Edn.; bd. dir. ACT, Am. Coun. On Edn., Nat. Merit Scholarship Corp, Nat. Coun. For Sci. and Environment, Huntington Bancshares, Reservoir Venture Ptnrs., Columbus Tech. Coun., Columbus Ptnrshp., Ctr. of Sci. & Industry, Columbus Downtown Dev. Corp., Ctrl. Ohio United Negro Coll. Fund, United Way of Ctrl. Ohio, Greater Columbus Area C. of C., CEOs for Cities, Columbus Sch. For Girls; Sigma Xi; trustee, Cap. So. Urban Redev. Corp. Achievements include research in fine structural & biochemical analysis of human skin including development of the human epidermis and dermis in vivo prenatal diagnosis of inherited skin diseases, structural abnormalities of the dermis in individuals with inherited disorders of connective tissue metabolism, epidermis in inherited disorders of keratinization.

HOLBROOK, THOMAS ALDREDGE, state legislator; b. St. Louis, Nov. 23, 1949; Ill. state rep. Dist. 113, 1995—. Office: 9200 W Main St Ste 4 Belleville IL 62223-1710

HOLDEN, BETSY D., former food products company executive; b. Lubbock, Tex., 1956; BA, Duke U.; MA in edn., Northwestern U., MBA, 1982. Asst. product mgr. desserts Gen. Foods Corp., 1982—84; brand mgr., venture div. Kraft Foods Inc., 1984—85, brand mgr., Miracle Whip Northfield, Ill., 1985—87, group brand mgr., confections & snacks, 1987—90, v.p. new product devel. and strategy Northfield, Ill., 1990—91, v.p., mktg., dinners, & enhancers, 1991—93, pres. Tombstone Pizza Northfield, Ill., 1993—95, exec. v.p., gen. mgr. cheese divsn., 1995—97, pres. cheese divsn., 1997—98, exec. v.p., ops., procurement, research & devel., consumer insights and E-commerce, 1998—2000; pres., CEO Kraft Foods North America, 2000—01; co-CEO Kraft Foods Inc., 2001—03, pres., global mktg. & category devel., 2004—05. Bd. dir. Kraft Foods, Tribune Co., Tupperware Corp., Western Union, 2006—. Pres. Chicago's Off the Street Club; mem., bd. Grocery Manufacturers of Amer., Evanston Northwestern Healthcare.

HOLDEN, ROBERT (BOB HOLDEN), political science professor, former governor; b. Kansas City, Mo., Aug. 24, 1949; s. Lee Holden and Wanda Laird; m. Lori Hauser, 1983; children: Robert, John D. BS in Polit. Sci., Southwest Mo. State, 1973; Degree Kennedy Sch. Govt. for Public Execs. and Flemming Fellow Leadership Inst., Harvard U. Asst. to state treas. State of Mo., 1976—83; mem. Mo. Ho. of Reps., 1983-89; adminstrv. asst./liaison to U.S. Rep. Richard Gephardt US Ho. Reps., St. Louis, 1989—91; state treas. State of Mo., Jefferson City, 1993—2000, gov., 2001—05; vis. prof. public policy and leadership Webster U., 2006—; head Gov. Bob Holden Public Policy Forum @Webster U., 2006—. Past chmn. gen. approations com.; co-sponsor Excellence in Edn. Act; mem. Bd. Fund Commrs., Mo. State Employees Retirement System, Mo. Bus. Coun., Mo. Rural Opportunities Coun.; past chmn. Mo. Housing Devel. Commn.; chmn. The Holden Group LLC Dean Am. Legion Mo. Boy's State Legislative Sch.; mem. Holden Scholarship Fund, Leadership St. Louis; former mem. Confluence's Edn. Implementation, Tower Grove Hgts. Neighborhood

Assn., Save the Children's Program; mem. Mo. Coun. Econ. Edn., Coun. State Govts.; vice-chair Mo. Cultural Trust.; chmn. Midwest U.S.-China Assn. Mem. Nat. Assn. State Treas. (legis. chair). Democrat. Office: Webster Univ 470 E Lockwood Ave Saint Louis MO 63119 Office Phone: 314-968-7423. E-mail: bh1obf@webster.edu.*

HOLDEN, ROBERT WATSON, radiologist, educator, dean; b. Brazil, Ind., Mar. 31, 1936; s. John William and Naomi Ellen (Watson) H.; m. Miriam Ann Bognanno, June 20, 1964; children: Anne, Robert II, Jennifer. BS in Pharmacy, Purdue U., 1958; MD, Ind. U., 1963. Diplomate Am. Bd. Radiology. Intern L.A. County Gen. Hosp., 1963-64; resident radiology Vanderbilt U., Nashville, 1970-73; asst. prof. Ind. U. Sch. Medicine, Indpls., 1973-77, assoc. prof., 1977-82, prof., 1982—, prof., chmn. dept. radiology, 1991-95, dean, 1996—2000; ret., 2000. Chief vascular and interventional radiology Wishard Meml. Hosp., Indpls., 1973-79, chief radiology, 1977-91; counselor NIH, 1990-94. Contbr. over 100 articles to profl. jours. Chmn. bldg. com. 1st United Meth. Ch., Mooresville, 1988-95. Capt. U.S. Army, 1964-66. Recipient Gold medal Assn. Univ. Radiologists, 1999, Gold medal Am. Roentgen Ray Soc., 2000; named Disting. Alumnus, Purdue U. Sch. Phharmacy, 1992. Fellow Soc. Cardiovascular and Interventional Radiology, Am. Coll. Radiology (counselor, Gold medal 2005), Radiologic Soc. N.Am. (counselor), Ind. Roentgen Soc. (past pres.). Republican. Avocations: forestry, agriculture, tennis. Office: Ind U Sch Medicine fH 302 1120 South Dr Rm 302 Indianapolis IN 46202-5135 Home: 7800 Eagle Creek Overlook Dr Indianapolis IN 46254-9799 Home Phone: 317-216-1864; Office Phone: 317-274-7109. Business E-Mail: rholden@iupui.edu.

HOLDEN, SUSAN M., lawyer; BA magna cum laude, St. Cloud State Univ., 1984; JD cum laude, William Mitchell Coll. of Law, 1988. Cert.: civil trial specialist. Law clerk Sieben, Grose, Von Holtum & Carey, Mpls., 1985—88, atty., 1988—93, ptnr., bd. dir., 1993—. Bd. dirs. Minn. Continuing Legal Edn.; mem. Commn. on Judicial Selection Minn. Supreme Ct., 1995—99. Named a Woman to Watch Minn., Bus. Jour., 2005; named one of Leading Am. Atty., Top 50 Women Super Lawyers, Top 40 Personal Injury Lawyers, Super Lawyer, 15 Attorneys of Yr., Minn. Lawyer, 2005. Fellow: Am. Bar Found.; mem.: ABA, Douglas K. Amdahl Inn of Ct., Acad. Cert. Trial Lawyers Minn., Nat. Conf. of Bar Presidents, Assn. of Trial Lawyers of Am., Minn. Trial Lawyers Assn., Minn. Women Lawyers (mem. adv. bd.), Hennepin County Bar Assn. (pres. 1999—2000, bd. dirs.), Minn. State Bar Assn. (treas. 2003, pres.-elect 2004, pres. 2005—06), Phi Alpha Delta. Office: Sieben Grose Von Holtum & Carey Ste 900 800 Marquette Ave Minneapolis MN 55402

HOLDERMAN, JAMES F., JR., federal judge; b. 1946; BS, U. Ill., 1968, JD, 1971. Judge U.S. Dist. Ct. (no. dist.) Ill., Chgo., 1985—; asst. U.S. atty. City of Chgo., 1972-78; ptnr. Sonnenschein, Carlin et al, Chgo., 1978-85. Lectr. law U. Chgo., 1983—. Office: US Dist Ct US Courthouse 219 S Dearborn St Ste 2146 Chicago IL 60604-1801

HOLIHEN, JENNIFER A., real estate development company executive; CFO, treas., sec. Crossman Cmtys., Inc., Indpls., 1996—. Office: Crossman Cmtys Inc 9202 N Meridian St Ste 300 Indianapolis IN 46260-1833

HOLLAND, CHARLES JOSEPH, lawyer; b. Ottumwa, Iowa, 1949; m. Nancy Jo Daniels; children: Tyler, Emily, Clare. BA, U. Iowa, 1971, JD (with high honors), 1977. Bar: Iowa 1977, U.S. Dist. Ct. (so. dist., no. dist.) Iowa 1977. Assoc. Hayek, Hayek & Hayek, Iowa City, 1977-81; ptnr. Hayek, Hayek, Holland & Brown, Iowa City, 1981—92; pvt. practice, 1992—2000; ptnr. Holland & Anderson LLP, 2000—. Mem. exec. coun. Nat. Conf. Bar Pres., 2003—06. Dir. Iowa City Downtown Assn., 1988-92. Mem. Iowa Coun. Sch. Bd. Attys. (chair 2004), ABA, Iowa Bar Assn. (pres. 2001-02), Johnson County Bar Assn., Johnson County Land Use Plan Com. (chair 2007-08). Office: 300 Brewery Sq 123 N Linn St PO Box 2820 Iowa City IA 52244-2820 Office Phone: 319-354-0331.

HOLLAND, EDWARD J., ophthalmologist, surgeon; b. Chgo., Ill., June 23, 1956; Grad., Drake U.; MD, Loyola-Stritch Sch. Medicine, Maywood, Chgo., 1981. Cert. Am. Bd. Ophthalmology, 1986. Intern Henry Ford Hosp., Detroit; resident U. Minn., Mpls., 1982—85, dir., Cornea and Refractive Surgery Svc., 1987, asst. prof. to prof., Elias Potter Lyon chair, ophthalmology; fellow, cornea and external disease U. Iowa, Iowa City, 1985—86; fellow, ocular immunology Nat. Eye Inst., IH, Bethesda, Md., 1986—87; dir. cornea services Cin. Eye Inst.; prof. ophthalmology U. Cin. Dir. Am. Acad. Ophthalmology Skills Transfer Courses; mem. med. scientific adv. bd. OCuSoFT, Inc., 2007—; invited lectr. nationally and internationally. Contbr. articles to peer-reviewed jours.; edited (textbook) Cornea, co-edited Ocular Surface Disease: Medical and Surgical Management, guest appearance Miracle Workers (ABC), 2006. Named to Best Doctors in America. Mem.: Am. Soc. Cataract and Refractive Surgeons (chair cornea clin. com.), Min. Acad. Ophthalmology (past pres.), Am. Acad. Ophthalmology (bd. trustee 2005—, secretariat ann. mtg., sr. achievement award, honor award), Cornea Soc. (immediate past pres.), Eye Bank Assn. Am. (former chmn., med. adv. bd., chair-elect, Paton Soc. award 2002). Office: Cin Eye Laser Ctr 10700 Montgomery Rd Cincinnati OH 45242 also: Northern Kentucky Eye Laser 580 S Loop Rd Ste 200 Edgewood KY 41017 also: Cin Eye Inst 1945 Cincinnati Eye Institute Dr Cincinnati OH 45242 Office Phone: 877-984-2020, 513-984-5133. Office Fax: 513-469-2089.*

HOLLAND, JOHN MADISON, retired family practice physician; b. Holden, W.Va., Oct. 7, 1927; s. Ophia I. and Lou V. (Elliott) H.; m. Mary Louise Bourne, Sept. 2, 1950; children— David, Stephen, Nancy BS, Eastern Ky. State U., Richmond, 1949; MD, U. Louisville, 1952. Diplomate Am. Bd. Family Practice, Am. Bd. Hospice and Palliative Medicine. Intern St. Joseph Infirmary, Louisville, 1952-53; gen. practice family medicine Physicians Group, Springfield, Ill., 1955-80; med. dir. St. John's Hosp., Springfield, 1971-94, St. John's Hospice, 1995—; clin. prof. family practice So. Ill. U., Springfield, 1978—. Served to capt. USAF, 1953-55 Mem. Am. Acad. Family Physicians, Am. Acad. Hospice/Palliative Medicine. Baptist. Home: 2131 Lindsay Rd Springfield IL 62704-3242

HOLLAND, KEN, professional sports team executive; b. Vernon, BC, Can., Nov. 10, 1955; m. Cindi Holland; children: Brad, Julie, Rachel, Greg. Goalie Medicine Hat Tigers, 1974—76, Binghamton Dusters, 1976—79, Springfield Indians, 1979—80, Binghamton Whalers, 1980—83, Hartford Whalers, Adirondack Red Wings, 1983—84, Detroit Red Wings, amateur scouting dir., asst. gen. mgr., v.p., gen. mgr., 1987—2007, exec. v.p., gen. mgr., 2007—, also alt. gov. Named to Binghamton Hall of Fame, 1998. Achievements include being the general manager of Stanley Cup Champion Detroit Red Wings, 1997, 1998, 2002. Avocation: golf. Office: c/o Detroit Red Wings 600 Civic Center Dr Detroit MI 48226-4408

HOLLE, REGINALD HENRY, retired bishop; b. Burton, Tex., Nov. 21, 1925; s. Alfred W. and Lena (Nolte) H.; m. Marla Christianson, June 16, 1949; children: Todd, Joan. BA, Capital U., 1946, DD (hon.), 1979; MDiv, Trinity Luth. Sem., 1949; D of Ministry, Ohio Consortium Religious Stdy, 1977; DD (hon.), Wittenberg U., 1989. Ordained minister Evang. Luth. Ch. Am., then bishop. Assoc. pastor Zion Luth. Ch., Sandusky, Ohio, 1949-51; sr. pastor Salem Meml. Luth. Ch., Detroit, 1951-72, Parma Luth. Ch., Cleve., 1973-78; bishop Mich. dist. Am. Luth. Ch., Detroit, 1978-87; bishop NW Lower Mich. Synod Evang. Luth. Ch., Lansing, 1988-95. Bd. dirs. Aubsburg Fortress Pub. House, Wittenberg U. Author: Planning for Funerals, 1978; contbr. to Augsburg Sermon Series. Bd. dirs. Ronald McDonald House Ctrl. Mich., 1995-05, Planned Giving Luth. Social Svcs. Mich., 1995-06. Recipient Pub. Svc. citation Harper Woods City Coun., 1976, Recognition for Community Svc., Detroit Pub. Schs., 1974. Personal E-mail: rholle@juno.com.

HOLLENBAUGH, H(ENRY) RITCHEY, lawyer; b. Shelby, Ohio, Nov. 12, 1947; m. Diane Robinson Nov. 21, 1973 (div. 1989); children: Chad Ritchey, Katie Paige; m. Rebecca U., Aug. 8, 1995. BA, Kent State U., 1969; JD, Capital U., 1973. Bar: Ohio 1973, U.S. Dist. Ct. (so. dist.) Ohio 1974, U.S. Ct. Appeals (6th cir.) 1976, U.S. Supreme Ct. 1978. Investigator Ohio Civil Rights Com., Columbus, Ohio, 1969-72; legal intern City Atty.'s Office, Columbus, Ohio, 1972-73, asst. city prosecutor, 1973-75, sr. asst. city atty., 1975-76; ptnr. Hunter, Hollenbaugh & Theodotou, Columbus, Ohio, 1976-85, Delligatti, Hollenbaugh, Briscoe & Milless, Columbus, Ohio, 1985-91, Climaco Seminatore Delligatti & Hollenbaugh, Columbus, 1991-93, Delligatti, Hollenbaugh & Briscoe, Columbus, 1993-95, Draper, Hollenbaugh, Briscoe, Yashko & Carmany, 1996-99, Carlile Patchen & Murphy LLC, Columbus, 1999—, chmn. Litig. Dept., 1999—. Mem. Ohio Pub. Defender Commn., 1988-94; chmn. Franklin County Pub. Defender Commn., 1986-92. Treas. The Gov's. Com., 1987-96, Friends With Celeste, Friends of Gov's. Residence, 1987-92, Participation 2000, 1987-91, Ohio Legal Assistance Found., 1998—. Fellow ABA Found. (chair commn. on advt. 1993-97, ho. of dels. 1993—, chair nat. conf. lawyers and reps. of media 2000-04); mem. ABA (bd. govs. 2007—), Ohio State Bar Assn. (bd. govs. 1989-94, pres. 1992-93), Columbus Bar Assn. (pres. 1987-88), Nat. Conf. Bar Pres., Nat. Assn. Criminal Def. Lawyers, Brookside Golf and Country Club. Democrat. Methodist. Avocations: golf, politics. Home: 8549 Glenalmond Ct Dublin OH 43017-9737 Office: Carlile Patchen & Murphy LLC 336 E Broad St Columbus OH 43215-3202 Home Phone: 614-799-1031; Office Phone: 614-228-6135. Business E-Mail: hrh@cpmlaw.com.

HOLLENBERG, PAUL FREDERICK, pharmacology educator; b. Phila., Sept. 18, 1942; s. Frederick Henry and Catherine (Dentzer) H.; m. Emily Elizabeth Vanootighem, May 6, 1967; children: Kathryn Mary, David Paul. BS in Chemistry, Wittenberg U., 1964; MS in Biochemistry, U. Mich., 1966, PhD in Biochemistry, 1969. Postdoctoral fellow U. Mich., Ann Arbor, 1969, U. Ill., Urbana, 1969-72; asst. prof. Northwestern U., Chgo., 1972-81, assoc. prof., 1981-84, prof. pathology and molecular biology, 1984-87; prof. pharmacology, chmn. dept. Wayne State U. Sch. Medicine, Detroit, 1987-94, U. Mich. Med. Sch., Ann Arbor, 1994—. Pharmacology test com. Nat. Bd. Med. Examiners; mem. Chem. Pathology Study Sect. NIH, 1987-91. Co-founder, assoc. editor Chem. Rsch. in Toxicology, 1988—; assoc. editor Jour. Pharmacology and Exptl. Therapeutics; mem. editl. bd. Drug Metabolism and Disposition, British Jour. Pharmacology. Schweppe Found. research fellow, 1974-77; NIH research grantee, 1974—. Mem. Am. Chem. Soc., Am. Soc. Biochemists and Molecular Biologists, Am. Soc. Pharmacology and Exptl. Therapeutics (sec./treas. 1998-99, pres.-elect 2001-02, pres. 2002-03), Am. Assn. for Cancer Rsch., Soc. Toxicology, Internat. Soc. for Study of Xenobiotics. Avocations: reading, running, golf. Home: 1968 Woodlily Ct Ann Arbor MI 48103-9728 Office: Univ Mich 2301 MSRB III Sch Medicine 1150 W Medical Center Dr Ann Arbor MI 48109-0632 Office Phone: 734-764-8166. Business E-Mail: phollen@umich.edu.

HOLLIMAN, W. G. (MICKEY), JR., furniture manufacturing executive; Founder, pres., CEO Action Industries subs. Furniture Brands Internat., 1970-96; pres., chmn., CEO, Furniture Brands Internat., St. Louis, 1996—. Office: Furniture Brands Internat Ste 1900 101 S Hanley Rd Saint Louis MO 63105-3493

HOLLINGSWORTH, HOLLY, newscaster; BA in Radio/Television Studies, Ashland U. Asst. prodr. Sta. WKYC-TV, Cleve., 1991; reporter, anchor, prodr. Sta. WEWS-TV; anchor Sta. WTVG-TV, Toledo, 1994—96; gen. assignment reporter Sta. WCMH-TV, Columbus, 1996—97, anchor, 1997—. Nominee Emmy award, 1999, 2000, 2001; recipient Media CrimeStopper of Yr. award, Ctrl. Ohio CrimeStoppers, 2001, Broadcast Media award, Ohio Pharmacists Assn., 2002, Media Vol. of Yr. award, March of Dimes, Ohio, 2002. Office: WCMH-TV 3165 Olentangy River Rd PO Box 4 Columbus OH 43202

HOLLINGSWORTH, LAURA L., publishing executive; b. Chgo., 1967; m. John Hollingsworth; 3 children. Advt. exec., Green Bay, Wis., Olympia, Wash., Rockford, Ill., Lansing, Mich.; v.p. advt. Des Moines Register, 2002—05, gen. mgr., 2005—07, pres. & pub., 2007—. Mem. bd. Variety -The Children's Charity, Character Counts!, Iowa; mem. cmty. devel. bd. Greater Des Moines Partnership. Recipient Pres.'s Ring for Excellence in Advt., Gannett Co., Inc., 2000—04. Office: Des Moines Register PO Box 957 Des Moines IA 50306-0957 Office Phone: 515-284-8471. E-mail: lholling@dmreg.com.*

HOLLINGSWORTH, PIERCE, publishing executive; Pub. Real Estate Bus., Wheaton, Ill., Real Estate Profiles, Wheaton, 1998—. Office: PO Box 300 Wheaton IL 60189-0300

HOLLINGTON, RICHARD RINGS, JR., lawyer; b. Findlay, Ohio, Nov. 12, 1932; s. Richard Rings and Annett (Kirk) H.; m. Sally Stecher, Apr. 4, 1959; children: Florence A., Julie A., Richard R. III. Peter S. BA, Williams Coll., 1954; JD, Harvard U., 1957. Bar: Ohio 1957. Ptnr. Marshman, Hornbeck & Hollington, Cleve., 1958-67, McDonald, Hopkins, Hardy & Hollington, Cleve., 1967-69; law dir. City of Cleve., 1971-72; sr. ptnr. Baker & Hostetler, Cleve., 1969-71, 73—. Vice chair Sky Fin. Group, 1998-2004, lead dir., 1999-2003; dir. The Ohio Bank, 1958-2001; mem. adv. com. on banking policy FDIC, 2002-2006; mem. Ohio Banking Commn., 2001—, fin. dir. Hunting Valley, 2004—. Mem. Ohio Gen. Assembly, 1967-70, Cuyahoga County Rep. Ctrl. Com., 1962-66; exec. com. Ohio Rep. Fin. Com., 1971-98, Cuyahoga County Rep. Orgn., 1968-98, Geauga County Rep. Orgn., 1998—; trustee Cleve. State U., 1970-73, Greater Cleve. Hosp. Assn., 1976-82, Cleve. Mus. atural History, 1969-81, Cleve. Zool. Soc., 1970-99, N. E. Ohio Regional Sewer Dist., 1972-73, Cuyahoga County Hosp. Found., 1968-73, Cleve. 500 Found., 1990-95, U. Findlay, 1991—, City Club Forum Found., 2005—; mem. bds. commrs. grievance and discipline Ohio Supreme Ct., 1993-95, mem. unauthorized practice of law com., 2005—. Mem. ABA, Ohio Bar Assn., Greater Cleve. Bar Assn., Sixth Cir. Jud. Conf. (life), Eighth Dist. Ohio Jud. Conf. (life), Ct. isi Prius, Union Club (Cleve.), The Country Club (Pepper Pike), Pepper Pike Club, Roaring Gap (N.C.) Club, Rolling Rock (Pa.) Club. Home: 13792 County Line Rd Chagrin Falls OH 44022-4008 Office: Baker & Hostetler 3200 National City Ctr 1900 E 9th St Ste 3200 Cleveland OH 44114-3475 Home Phone: 440-423-1246; Office Phone: 216-861-7623.

HOLLINGWORTH, ROBERT MICHAEL, toxicology researcher; b. Yorkshire, England, Oct. 4, 1939; married; 1961; 2 children. BSc, Univ. Reading, 1962; PhD, Univ. Calif., 1966. Asst. prof. to prof. insect toxicology Purdue Univ., West Lafayette, Ind., 1966-87; dir. Pesticide Rsch. Ctr., prof. entomology Mich. State Univ., 1987—; dir. at. Food Safety Toxicol. Ctr., 1991-99. Vis. prof. Stauffer Chem. Co., 1974-75. Mem. Toxicology Study Sect, NIH, 1976-80; Environ. Protection Agy., sci. adv. panel, Fifra, 1982-84; chmn. Divsn. Pesticide Chem. Am. Chem. Soc., 1984. Fellow AAAS, Am. Chem. Soc., Soc. Toxicology, Am. Coun. Sci. Health; mem. Soc. Risk Analysis. Achievements include research on metabolism and mode of action of insecticides and related chemicals. Office: Mich State U 106 Ctr for Integrated Planet Systems East Lansing MI 48824-1302

HOLLINS, MITCHELL LESLIE, lawyer; b. NYC, Mar. 11, 1947; s. Milton and Alma (Bell) H.; m. Nancy Kirchheimer, Mar. 27, 1977 (div. 1999); m. Jan C. Philipsborn, Oct. 24, 1999; children: Herbert K. II, Dorothy Ann, Betsy Ann Mizell. BA, Case Western Res. U., 1967; JD, NYU, 1971. Bar: Ill. 1971, U.S. Dist. Ct. (no. dist.) Ill. 1971. Editor NYU Jour. Internat. Law and Politics, 1970—71; assoc. Sonnenschein Nath & Rosenthal, Chgo., 1971—78, ptnr., 1978—2000, Piper Rudnick, Chgo., 2000—02; COO, gen. counsel Meadow Ptnrs. LLC, Chgo., 2003—04; v.p. Oak Brook (Ill.) Bank, 2004—05, chief legal officer, 2004—, sec., 2004—, sr. v.p., 2005—. Asst. sec., asst. gen. counsel Jr. Achievement Chgo., 1980-2004, dir. 1980—; bd. dirs. Young Men's Jewish Coun., 1973-75; bd. dirs. young people's divsn. Jewish United Fund Met. Chgo., 1972-76; bd. dirs. Med. Rsch. Inst. Coun., mem. exec. com., 1979-92, sec., 1981-82, gen. counsel, 1983-86, vice chmn., 1987-92, chmn. jr. bd., 1978-79. Mem. ABA, Lake Shore Country Club (mem. bd. govs. 1984-92, sec. 1985-92), Lawyers Club. Republican. Home: 265 Wentworth Ave Glencoe IL 60022-1931 Office: Oak Brook Bank 1400 16th St Oak Brook IL 60523 Office Phone: 630-990-2265 ext. 252. Business E-Mail: mhollin@obb.com.

HOLLIS, DONALD ROGER, management consultant; b. Warren, Ohio, Mar. 4, 1936; s. Louis and Lena (Succo) Hollis; m. Marilyn G. Morganti, Aug. 23, 1958; children: Roger, Russel Kirk, Gregory, Heather. BS, Kent State U., 1959. Regional mgr. Glidden Corp., San Francisco, 1959-65, dir. mgmt. info. svcs. Cleve., 1965-68; dir. mgmt. info. services SCM Corp., NYC, 1968-71; v.p. Chase Manhattan Bank, NYC, 1971-81; sr. v.p. First Chgo. Corp., 1981-85, exec. v.p., 1986-95, head sys., data processing, cash mgmt. and security products and quality programs, 1986-95; pres., CEO DRH Strategic Cons., Chgo., 1995—. Bd. dirs. Exss, Wausau Fin. Sys.; Life Trustee III Inst. Tech. Office: c/o Diamond 875 N Michigan Ave Ste 2300 Chicago IL 60611

HOLLIS-ALLBRITTON, CHERYL DAWN, retail paper supply store executive; b. Elgin, Ill., Feb. 15, 1959; d. L.T. and Florence (Elder) Saylors; stepparent Bobby D. Hollis; m. Thomas Allbritton, Aug. 10, 1985. BS in Phys. Edn., Brigham Young U., 1981; cosmetologist, 1981. Retail sales clk. Bee Discount, North Riverside, Ill., 1981-82, retail store mgr., Downers Grove, Ill., 1982, Oaklawn, Ill., 1982-83, St. Louis, 1983; retail tng. mgr. Arvey Paper & Office Products (divsn. Internat. Paper), Chgo., 1984, retail store mgr., Columbus, Ohio, 1984—. Republican. Mem. LDS Ch. Avocations: writing, reading, travel. Office: Arvey Paper & Office Products 431 E Livingston Ave Columbus OH 43215-5586 Home Phone: 614-751-9336; Office Phone: 614-221-0153.

HOLLISTER, NANCY, state legislator; Lt. gov. State of Ohio, 1995-98, rep. Ho. of Reps., 1999—. Office: State House 77 S High St Columbus OH 43266-0001

HOLLISTER, WINSTON NED, pathologist; b. Milw., Mar. 23, 1942; s. Harold Arthur and Jeannette Clara (Gastrav) H.; m. Carol Jean Potter, Dec. 7, 1963 (div. May 1978); children: Timothy Carl, David Andrew; m. Margaret Ravenel Papen, Oct. 29, 1988; children: Charles Davis, Margaret Ravenel. BS in Physics, U. Wis., 1964; MD, Med. Coll. Wis., 1971. Diplomate Am. Bd. Internal Medicine, Am. Bd. Pathology. Staff pathologist St. Joseph's Hosp., Milw., 1976—; pres., CEO Franciscan Shared Lab, Wauwatosa, Wis., 1988-90; med. dir., chmn. bd. dirs. Med. Sci. Labs., Wauwatosa, 1989—2003. Cons. in field. Contbr. articles to profl. jours. Vestry mem. St. Paul's Episcopal Ch., Milw., 1978-83. Lt. USN, 1964-67. Recipient Houghton & Houghton award Med. Soc. Wis., 1971. Fellow Coll. Am. Pathologists (clin. practice com. 1984-87); mem. ACP, Am. Pathology Found. (pres. 1994-96), Oconomowoc Lake Club, Pine Lake Yacht Club. Republican. Episcopalian. Avocations: sailing, skiing, tennis, travel, music. Home: 4940 N Maple Lane Nashotah WI 53058 Office: 4940 N Maple Ln Nashotah WI 53058

HOLLORAN, THOMAS EDWARD, business educator; b. Mpls., Sept. 27, 1929; s. Edward Francis and Florence G. (Loftus) H.; m. Patricia M. Holloran, June 26, 1954; children: Mary Patricia Harley, Anne Florence. BS, U. Minn., 1951, JD, 1955. Bar: Minn. 1955, Fed. 1955. Ptnr. Wheeler and Fredrikson, Mpls., 1955-67; exec. v.p. Medtronic, Inc., Mpls., 1967-73, pres., 1973-75; chmn., chief exec. officer Inter-Regional Fin. Group, Inc. (renamed Dain Rauscher Corp), Mpls., 1976-85; prof. mgmt. U. St. Thomas, St. Paul, 1986—2001, prof. emeritus Coll. Bus., 2001—, sr. disting. fellow Sch. Law, 2001—. Bd. dirs. Flexsteel Industries, Inc., Dubuque, Iowa; dir. emeritus Medtronic, Inc. Spl. judge Mcpl. Ct. of Shorewood, Excelsior, Tonka Bay, Greenwood and Deephaven, Minn., 1961-65; Mayor, City of Shorewood, 1971-74; chmn. Urban Coalition, Mpls., 1977-78, City of Mpls. Task Force on Tech., 1983-84; mem. Mpls.-St. Paul Met. Airports Commn., 1974-82, vice chmn., 1976-82, chmn., 1989-91; bd. trustees Coll. St. Scholastica, 1971-81, chmn., 1979-81; trustee Coll. St. Thomas, 1979-88, U. Minn. Found., 1983-85, Bush Found., 1982—2000, chmn. 1991-96; trustee Mpls. Art Inst., 1986-93, Mpls. Children's Health Ctr., 1983-84; pres. Upper M.W. Coun., Mpls., 1978-80; bd. dirs. InterStudy, Excelsior., 1975-85, Minn. Press Coun., 1982-87, mem. corp. bd. Cath. Archdiocese Mpls. and St. Paul, 1990-2007, mem. bd. St. Paul's Cath. Seminary, 2006-. With USN, 1952-54, Korea. Mem. ABA, Minn. State Bar Assn. Roman Catholic. Office Phone: 651-962-4243.

HOLLOWELL, MELVIN J, JR., lawyer; b. Honolulu, Hawaii, 1959; m. Desiree Hollowell; children: Melvin, Desiree. BA, Albion Coll., 1981; JD, Univ. Va. Law Sch., 1984. Bar: Mich. 1984. Asst. county corp. counsel Wayne County, Mich., 1985—86, purchasing dir. Mich., 1987—88, asst. exec. Mich., 1988—91; shareholder Butzel Long, Detroit. Bd. dirs., chmn. NAACP Freedom Fund Dinner, Detroit, 1995; gen. counsel Dem. Nat. Com. Voting Rights Inst. Mich. Democrat. Office: Mich State Dem Party Chair 606 Townsend St Lansing MI 48933

HOLMAN, JAMES LEWIS, financial consultant, management consultant; b. Chgo., Oct. 27, 1926; s. James Louis and Lillian Marie (Walton) Holman; m. Elizabeth Ann Owens, June 18, 1948 (div. 1982); children: Craig Stewart, Tracy Lynn, Mark Andrew, Bonnie Gwen(dec.); m. Geraldine Ann Wilson, Dec. 26, 1982. BS in Econs. and Mgmt., U. Ill., 1950, postgrad., 1950, Northwestern U., 1954—55. Traveling auditor, then statistician, asst. contr. parent buying dept. Sears, Roebuck & Co., Chgo., 1951—54; asst. to sec.-treas. Hanover Securities Co., 1954—65; asst. to controller chem. ops. divsn. Montgomery Ward & Co., Inc., 1966—68; controller Henrotin Hosp., 1968; bus. mgr. Julian, Dye, Javid, Hunter & Najafi Associated, 1969—81, cons., 1981—84. Vol. cons., adminstrv. asst. Fiji Sch. Medicine, Suva, 1984—86, cons., 1987—89; vol. bus. cons. U.S. Peace Corps, Honduras, 1989, cons., 1989—; cons., dir., sec.-treas Comprehensive Resources Ltd., Glenview, Ill., 1982, Wheaton, 82, Walnut Creek, Calif., 82; sec.-treas. Medtran, Inc., 1980—83; sec. James C. Valenta, P.C., 1979—82; sponsored project adminstr. Northwestern U., Evanston, Ill., 1984. Sec. B.R. Ryall YMCA, Glen Ellyn, Ill., 1974—76; treas. DuPage Symphony, 1955—58; trustee Gary Meml. United Meth. Ch., Wheaton, 1961—69, 1974—77; bd. dirs. B.R. Ryall YMCA, 1968—78, DuPage Symphony, 1954—58, Goodwill Industries, Chgo., 1978—79. With USN, 1944—46. Mem.: Kiwanis (bd. dirs. Chgo. 1956—60, bd. dirs. youth found. 1957—60, pres. 1958—60). Baha'I. Home and Office: 60 N Nicoll Ave #408 Glen Ellyn IL 60137

HOLMAN, MAUREEN, lawyer; b. Mpls., Jan. 30, 1952; BA, U. Nebr., 1973; JD, U. N.D., 1983. Bar: N.D. 1983, Minn. 1983. Atty. Serkland Law Firm, Fargo, ND. Mem.: ABA, Order of Coif, State Bar Assn. N.D. (bd. govs. 1995—97, joint task force on family law 1995—, disciplinary bd. Supreme Ct. 1997—), Cass County Bar Assn., Minn. State Bar Assn. (pres.-elect 2002—03), Phi Delta Phi, Phi Beta Kappa. Office: Serkland Law Firm PO Box 6017 10 Roberts St Fargo ND 58108-6017

HOLMAN, RALPH THEODORE, retired biochemistry professor, nutritionist; b. Mpls., Mar. 4, 1918; s. Alfred Theodore and May Carlia Anna (Nilson) Holman; m. Karla Calais, Mar. 26, 1943; 1 child, Nils Teodore. AA, Bethel Jr. Coll., 1937; BS, U. Minn., 1939; MS, Rutgers U., 1941; PhD, U. Minn., 1944. Instr., div. of biochemistry U. Minn., Mpls., 1944-46; NRC-Nat. Acad. Scis. fellow Med. Nobel Inst., Stockholm, Sweden, 1946-47; Am. Scandinavian Found. fellow U. Uppsala, Sweden, 1947; assoc. prof. biochemistry and nutrition Tex. A&M U., College Station, 1948-51; assoc. prof. biochemistry Hormel Inst., U. Minn., Austin, 1951-56, prof., 1956-88, exec. dir., 1975-85, emeritus prof., 1988—; also adj. prof. of biochemistry Mayo Med. Sch., Rochester, Minn., 1977—. Mem. nutrition study sect. NIH, 1959-63; pres., organizer Golden Jubilee Internat. Congress on Essential Fatty Acids and Prostaglandins, 1980; mem. adv. bd. Deul. Conf. on Lipids, 1960-86; Sinclair Meml. lectr. Third Internat. Congress on Essential Fatty Acids and Eicasanoids, Adelaide, 1992. Founding editor Progress in Lipid Research, 1951—; editor Lipids, 1974-85; mem. editl. bd. Jour. Nutrition, 1962-66; contbr. 400 publs. on nutritional biochemistry of lipids; initiated omega 3 and omega 6 nomenclature for essential fatty acids, 1963; current rsch. on essentiality of omega 3 fatty acids. Pres. Mower County Coun. Churches., Austin, 1953-57; mem. Hormel Found., Austin, 1979-86. Recipient Fachini award Italian Oil Chemists, Milan; named Disting. Alumnus Bethel U., 1998. Fellow Am. Inst. Nutrition (Borden award 1966); mem. NAS, Am. Chem. Soc., Am. Oil Chemists Soc. (pres. 1974-75, Lipid Chemistry award 1979, Baldwin Disting. Svc. award 2001), Am. Soc. Biol. Chemists, Am. Orchid Soc. (rsch. com. 1980-85), Am. Heart Assn. (bd. dirs. Minn. affiliate 1991-93). Democrat. Congregationalist. Achievements include original research on essential nature of omega 3 polyunsaturated fatty acids. Home: 1403 2nd Ave SW Austin MN 55912-1609 Office: U Minn Hormel Inst 801 16th Ave NE Austin MN 55912-3679

HOLMES, ARTHUR S., manufacturing executive; m. Christy Holmes. BS, MS, Pa. State U.; MBA, Northwestern U. Founder, chmn., CEO Chart Industries, Inc., Cleve., 1989—; chmn. ALTEC Internat. Ltd. Partnership. Bd. dirs. 1st Bank Milw. Mem. bd. advisors Biterbo Coll.; mem. La Crosse Area Devel. Com.; mem. sch. adv. bd. U. Wis. Named Pa. State Disting. Engring. Alumnus, 1993; recipient Pope John XXIII award Viterbo Coll., 1999. Office: Chart Industries Inc 1 Infinity Corporate Centre Dr Ste 300 Cleveland OH 44125-5370 Fax: 440-753-1491.

HOLMES, CARL DEAN, state representative, landsman; b. Dodge City, Kans., Oct. 19, 1940; s. Haskell Amos and Gertrude May (Swander) H.; m. Willynda Coley, Nov. 29, 1986; 1 child from previous marriage, Randall; 1 stepson, Bret Carpenter. Student, Kans. U., 1958-60; BBA, Colo. State U., Ft. Collins, 1962.

Mgr. Holmes Motor Co., Plains, Kans., 1962-65; v.p. Holmes Chevrolet, Inc., Meade, Kans., 1962-78; owner Holmes Sales Co., Plains, 1965-80; land mgr. Holmes Farms, Plains, 1962—; mem. Kans. Ho. of Reps., Topeka. Chmn. Greater S.W. Regional Planning Commn., Garden City, Kans., 1980-82; del. Rep. Dist. Conv., Great Bend, Kans., 1984, Rep. State Conf., Great Bend, Kans., 1984, Rep. State Conv., Topeka, 1984, Rep. Dist. Conv., Russell, Kans., 1988, Rep. State Conv., Topeka, 1988; City of Plains Councilman, 1977-82, Coun. pres., 1979-82, mayor, 1982-89; mem. 125 dist. Kans. Ho. Reps., Topeka, 1985—; precinct committeeman Meade County Reps., 1986-89; pres. Kans. Mayors Assn., 1984-85; pres. League Kans. Municipalities, 1987-88; chmn. Kans. Ho. of Reps. Energy & atural Resources com., 1993-96, Kans. flood task force, 1993, Kans. Electric Utility Restructuring Task Force, 1996-97, Kans. Ho. of Reps. Fiscal Oversight Com., 1997—2002, Kans. Ho. of Reps. Utilities Com., 1999—, Kans. Joint Com. Administrative Rules and Regulations, 1991-, chmn. 2003, vice chmn. 2004; mem. tax partnership task force Nat. Conf. State Legislatures, 2001, chmn., 1998; mem. energy and transp. fed. assembly, 2001—02; mem. energy and electric utilities com. nat. conf. state legislature, 2002-, vice chmn., 2003-; mem. Ho. select com. on security, 2003-; mem. adv. com. energy, 2001-, vice chmn. 2002-; mem. nat. council electric policy, 2003-; mem. energy standing com. Nat. Conf. State Legislatures State and Fed. Assembly, 1989-94, Kans. Ho. of Reps. Appropriations Com., 1997-98; mem. environ standing com. NCSL-SFA, 1995-2001; mem. Am. Legis. Exch. Coun., Nat. Task Force on Energy, Environ. and Natural Resources, Kans. Environ. Leadership Program, 1999. Recipient Fox award Kans. Water Office, 1998, Intergovtl. Leadership award League of Kans. Municipalities, 1994; Fred Diehl award Kans. Municipal Utilities, 2003. Mem. Liberal C. of C., Lions, Masons (past master), Scottish Rite, R.A.M., K.T., S.A.R., U. Kans. Alumni Assn., Nat. Eagle Scout Assn. Methodist. Avocations: flying, photography, genealogy. Home: PO Box 2288 Liberal KS 67905-2288 Office: Kansas House Reps State House Topeka KS 66612

HOLMES, NANCY ELIZABETH, pediatrician; b. St. Louis, Aug. 3, 1950; d. David Reed and Phyllis Anne (Hunger) Holmes; m. Arthur Erwin Kramer, May 15, 1976; children: Melanie Elizabeth Kramer, Carl Edward Kramer. BA in Psychology, U. Kans., 1972; MD, U. Mo., 1976. Diplomate Am. Acad. Pediatrics. Intern., resident in pediatrics St. Louis Children's Hosp., Washington U., St. Louis, 1976-81; pediatrician Ctrl. Pediatrics, St. Louis, 1981—. Sch. physician Sch. Dist. Clayton, Mo., 1985—92; asst. prof. clin. pediats. Washington U., St. Louis, 1993—2000, assoc. prof., 2000—, prof. clin. pediat.; cons. 1st Congregational Preschool, Clayton, 1984—86, Jewish Hosp. Daycare Ctr., St. Louis, 1993—97, Flynn Park EArly Edn. Ctr., University City, Mo., 1994—; cmty. outpatient experience Preceptor Hosp., St. Louis Children's Hosp., 1991—93, 1994—; mem. med. exec. com. St. Louis Children's Hosp., 1992—94. Vol. reading tutor Flynn Park Sch., University City, 1992—98, cub scout leader, 1993—98; mem. com. Troop 493 Boy Scouts Am., 2000—; elder Trinity Presbyn. Ch., University City, 1989—92, 1996—2001, Webster Groves Presbyn. Ch., 2006—; bd. dirs. Children's Hosp. Care Group. Fellow Am. Acad. Pediatrics; mem. AMA, Mo. State Med. Assn., St. Louis Metro. Med. Soc, St. Louis Pediatric Soc. Presbyterian. Avocations: reading, gardening, photography, travel. Office: Ctrl Pediatrics Inc 8888 Ladue Rd Ste 130 Saint Louis MO 63124-2056 Office Phone: 314-862-4002.

HOLNESS, GORDON VICTOR RIX, engineering executive, mechanical engineer; b. London, Sept. 6, 1939; arrived in US, 1969, naturalized, 1989; s. Ernest Arthur and Ivy A. (Rix) H.; m. Susan F. Sage (dec.); m. Audrey A. Bezz, Apr. 18, 1984. Cert., Croydon Tech. Coll., Surrey, Eng., 1962; diploma in environ. engring., Nat. Coll., London, 1964. Registered profl. engr. Mich., Minn., Tex., Conn., Calif., Kans., Colo., Fla., Ariz., NY, DC, Ala., NC, Ky., Ohio, Mo., Tenn., Ill., Ont., Can. Design engr. West Sussex County Coun., Chichester, Sussex, Eng., 1956-59, C. McKechnie Jarvis & Ptnrs., London, 1959-64, Barlow Leslie & Ptnrs., Croydon, 1964; sr. engr. R. J. Tamblyn & Ptnrs., Toronto, Ont., Canada, 1964-66; asst. chief engr. Giffels Assocs., Windsor, Ont., Canada, 1966-69; from asst. chief engr. to chmn. and CEO, bd. dirs. Albert Kahn Assocs. Inc., Detroit, 1969—2001, also bd. dirs.; ret. chmn. emeritus, 2001. Contbr. articles to profl. jours. Bd. dirs. YMCA, Mt. Clemens, Mich., 1980-82; commr. Grosse Pointe Shores Planning Commn.; trustee Grosse Pointe Shores Improvement Found. Fellow ASHRAE (chmn. energy mgmt. com. 1987, chmn. govt. affairs com. 1989, chmn. bd. policy com., bd. dirs. 2002-04, v.p. 2004-06, treas. 2007-08); mem. SPE, Am. Cons. Engrs. Coun., Chartered Inst. Bldg. Svcs. of Eng., Engring. Soc. Detroit, Mich. Soc. Profl. Engrs. (v.p. 1986, fellow 1998), Detroit Econ. Club (bd. dirs.). Republican. Presbyterian. Avocations: golf, tennis, chess, sailing. Home: 55 S Edgewood Dr Grosse Pointe Shores MI 48236-1226 Personal E-mail: gholness@comcast.net.

HOLONYAK, NICK, JR., electrical engineering educator; b. Zeigler, Ill., Nov. 3, 1928; s. Nick and Anna (Rosoha) Holonyak. BS, U. Ill., 1950, MS, 1951, PhD (Tex. Instruments fellow), 1954; DSc (hon.), Northwestern U., 1992; DEng. (hon.), Notre Dame U., 1994. Tech. staff Bell Telephone Labs., Murray Hill, NJ, 1954—55; physicist, unit mgr., mgr. advanced semiconductor lab. GE Co., Syracuse, NY, 1957—63; prof. elec. engring. and materials research lab. U. Ill., Urbana, 1963—, John Bardeen chair prof. elec. & computer engring. & physics, 1993—; mem. Center Advanced Study, 1977—. Author (with others): Semiconductor Controlled Rectifiers, 1964, Physical Properties of Semiconductors, 1989. With US Army, 1955—57. Named to, Consumer Electronics Hall of Fame, 2006; recipient Cordiner award GE, 1962, John Scott medal, City of Phila., 1975, GaAs Conf. award with Welker medal, 1976, Monie A. Ferst award, Sigma Xi, 1988, at. Medal Sci., NSF, 1990, Indsl. Application Sci., NAS, 1993, Centennial medal, ASEE, 1993, 50th Ann. award, Am. Elec. Assn, 1993, Japan prize, 1995, at. Medal of Tech. award, 2002, Internat. Global Energy prize, 2003, Lemelson-MIT prize, 2004, MRS Von Hippel award, 2004. Fellow: AAAS, IEEE (life Morris Liebmann award 1973, Jack A. Morton award 1981, Edison medal 1989, medal of honor 2003, Third Millennium medal), Internat. Engring. Consortium, Am. Phys. Soc., Am. Acad. Arts and Scis., Am. Phys. Soc., Optical Soc. Am. (Charles H. Townes award 1992, Frederic Ives medal 2001); mem.: NAS (Indsl. Application of Sci. award 1993), NAE, Lincoln Acad. Ill. (laureate 2005), We. Soc. Engrs. (Washington award 2004), Ioffe Inst. (hon.), Math. Assn. Am., Russian Acad. Scis. (fgn. mem.), Minerals, Metals and Materials Soc. (John Bardeen award 1995), Math. Assn. Am., Electrochem. Soc. (Solid State Sci. and Tech. award 1983), Tau Beta Pi (Outstanding Alumnus award 1999), Eta Kappa Nu (eminent mem. 1998, Karapetoff Eminent Mems. award 1994, eminent mem. 1998). Office: U Ill Dept Elec/Computer Engring 1406 W Green St Urbana IL 61801-2918 Home: 101 Windsor Rd 2103 Urbana IL 61802

HOLOVATY, ADRIAN, editor, web site designer; BA journalism, U. of Mo., Columbia, Mo., 2001. Online intern CopleyNet, Joliet, Ill., 2000; reporter The Columbia Missourian, 2000, columnist, 2000—01, copy editor, 2001, infographic artist, 2001; online editor The Maneater, 1999—2001; weekend producer Washington Post, Newsweek Interactive, 2001; product developer, asst. database editor The Atlanta Journal Constitution, 2002; lead developer World Online, 2002—05; editor, editorial innovations Washington Post, Newsweek Interactive, 2005—. Speaker in field. Co-recipient Web Savvy Award, U-Wire, 2000; named one of 40 Under 40, Crain's Chicago Business, 2005; recipient Online Pacemaker, Associate Collegiate Press, 2000, Batten Award for Innovations in Journalism, 2005. Achievements include design of chicagocrime.org database; holovaty.com; development of Trodo, 2002; cowroting Django open-source high-level Python Web framework. Office: c/o Washthington Post PO Box 17370 Arlington VA 22216

HOLSCHER, ROBERT F., airport terminal executive; With Kenton County Airport Bd, Hebron, Ky., 1961—; dir. avaiation Cincinnati-N. Kentucky Internat. Airport, 1975—. Office: Kenton County Airport Bd PO Box 752000 Cincinnati OH 45275-2000

HOLSCHUH, JOHN DAVID, federal judge; b. Ironton, Ohio, Oct. 12, 1926; s. Edward A. and Helen (Ebert) H.; m. Carol Eloise Stouder, May 25, 1952; 1 child, John David Jr. BA, Miami U., 1948; JD, U. Cin., 1951. Bar: Ohio 1951, U.S. Dist. Ct. (so. dist.) Ohio 1952, U.S. Ct. Appeals (6th cir.) 1953, U.S. Supreme Ct. 1956. Atty. McNamara & McNamara, Columbus, Ohio, 1951-52, 54; law clk. to Hon. Mell. G. Underwood U.S. Dist. Ct., Columbus, 1952-54; ptnr. Alexander, Ebinger, Holschuh, Fisher & McAlister, Columbus, Ohio, 1954-80; judge U.S. Dist. Ct. (so. dist.) Ohio, 1980—, chief judge, 1990-96. Adj. prof. law Ohio State U. Coll. Law, 1970; mem. com. on codes of conduct Jud. Conf. U.S., 1985-90. Pres. bd. dirs. Neighborhood House, Columbus, 1969-70; active United Way of Franklin County, Columbus. Fellow Am. Coll. Trial Lawyers; mem. Order of Coif, Phi Beta Kappa, Omicron Delta Kappa. Home and Office: US Dist Ct 109 US Courthouse 85 Marconi Blvd Rm 109 Columbus OH 43215-2823 Office Phone: 614-719-3310.

HOLSTEIN, JOHN CHARLES, former state supreme court judge; b. Springfield, Mo., Jan. 10, 1945; s. Clyde E. Jr. and Wanda R. (Polson) H.; m. Mary Frances Brummell, Mar. 26, 1967; children: Robin Diane Camacho, Mary Katherine Link, Erin Elizabeth Lary. BA, S.W. Mo. State Coll., 1967; JD, U. Mo., 1970; LLM, U. Va., 1995. Bar: Mo. 1970. Atty. Moore & Brill, West Plains, Mo., 1970-75; probate judge Howell County, West Plains, 1975-78, assoc. cir. judge, 1978-82; cir. judge 37th Jud. Cir., West Plains, 1982-87; judge so. dist. Mo. Ct. Appeals, Springfield, 1987-88, chief judge so. dist., 1988-89; judge Supreme Ct. Mo., Jefferson City, 1989—2002, chief justice, 1995-97; shareholder Thomson & Kilroy, P.C., Springfield, 2002—. Instr. bus. law S.W. Mo. State Coll., 1976-77, pub. sch. law S.W. Bapt. U., 1999-2000. Lt. col. USAR, 1969-87. Office: Shugart Thomson & Kilroy PC 901 St Louis St Ste 1200 Springfield MO 65806

HOLSTEN, MARK, state legislator; b. Sept. 5, 1965; m. Lisa; 1 child. BA, U. Minn. State rep. Minn. Ho. Reps., Dist. 56A, Minn., 1993—. Tchr. U. St. Thomas. Home: 7790 Minar Ln N Stillwater MN 55082-9363

HOLT, DONALD A., agronomist, consultant, researcher, retired academic administrator; b. Minooka, Ill., Jan. 29, 1932; s. Cecil Bell and Helen (Eickoff) H.; m. Marilyn Louise Jones, Sept. 6, 1953; children: Kathryn A. Holt Stichnoth, Steven Paul, Jeffrey David, William Edwin. Grad., Joliet Jr. Coll., 1952; BS in Agrl. Sci., MS in Agronomy, U. Ill.; PhD in Agronomy, Purdue U. Farmer, Minooka, Ill., 1956-63; instr., asst. prof., assoc. prof. then prof. agronomy Purdue U., West Lafayette, Ind., 1964-82; prof., head dept. agronomy U. Ill., Urbana-Champaign, Ill., 1982-83, dir. Ill. Agr. Expt. Sta., assoc. dean Coll. Agr., 1983-96, sr. assoc. dean Coll. Agr., cons. environ. sci., 1996-2002, ret., 2002, prof. emeritus, 2003—; interim dir. Nat. Soybean Rsch. Lab., 2003—03. Cons. Deere and Co., Ottumwa, Iowa, 1978, NASA, Houston, 1979, Control Data Corp., Mpls., 1978-79, EPA, Corvallis, Oreg., 1981-90. Town Bd. commr., Otterbein, Ind., 1972-76. Fellow AAAS, Am. Soc. Agronomy (pres. 1988), Crop Sci. Soc. Am.; mem. Agrl. Rsch. Inst. (pres. 1991), Am. Forage and Grassland Coun., Ill. Forage and Grassland Coun., Gamma Sigma Delta (internat. pres. 1974-76). Republican. United Methodist. Office: U Ill 170 N5RC 1101 W Peabody Dr Urbana IL 61801-4723 Home: 3879 E Forest Lodge Loop Monticello IN 47960 Home Phone: 217-356-1668. Business E-Mail: d-holt@uiuc.edu.

HOLT, GLEN EDWARD, editor; b. Abilene, Kans., Sept. 14, 1939; s. John Wesley and Helen Laverne (Schrader) H.; m. Leslie Edmonds, Jan. 29, 1994; children from previous marriage: Kris, Karen, Gordon. BA, Baker U., 1960; MA, U. Chgo., 1965, PhD, 1975. From instr. to asst. prof. Wash. U., St. Louis, 1968-82; dir. honors div. Coll. Liberal Arts, U. Minn., 1982-87; exec. dir. St. Louis Pub. Libr., 1987—2004; editor Pub. Libr. Quar., 2004—; nonprofit planning and policy cons. Cons. Chgo. Hist. Soc., 1976-79, Mo. Hist. Soc., St. Louis, 1979-87, Buffalo-Erie County Pub. Libr., 1997-98; mem. Online Computer Libr. Ctr. Pub. Libr. Adv. Com., 1991-95. Co-editor: St. Louis, 1975; co-author: Chicago, A Guide to the Neighborhoods, 1979, Measuring Your Library's Value to the Community, 2006, Library Success Stories, 2006. Recipient Cmty. Svc. award Commerce Bank, 2001; named Woodrow Wilson Found. fellow, 1963-64, Danforth fellow, 1963-68. Mem. ALA, Pub. Libr. Assn. (Charlie Robinson award 2001). Avocation: photography. Home: 4954 Lindell Blvd Apt 4W Saint Louis MO 63108-1520 E-mail: leholt@aol.com.

HOLT, LESLIE EDMONDS, librarian; b. Mpls. d. Peter Robert and Elizabeth Knox (Donovan) Edmonds; m. Glen Edward Holt, Jan. 29, 1994. BA, Cornell Coll., 1971; MA, U. Chgo., 1975; PhD, Loyola U., Chgo., 1984. Asst. children's libr. Indian Trails Libr. Dist., Wheeling, Ill., 1972-73; libr. Erikson Inst. for Early Edn., Chgo., 1973-75; youth svcs. libr. Rolling Meadows (Ill.) Libr., 1975-82; libr. multicultural head start resource ctr. Chgo. Pub. Libr., 1982-84; asst. prof. grad. sch. libr. and info. sci. U. Ill., Urbana, 1984-90, assoc. dean, 1988-89; dir. youth svcs. and family literacy St. Louis Pub. Libr., 1990—. Pre-sch. advisor Rolling Meadows (Ill.) Park Dist., 1978-85; cons. to reading program The Latin Sch., Chgo., 1980-82; vis. lectr. Loyola U. of Chgo., 1980-84, U. Ill. Extension, Belleville, 1992; product mgr. Mister Anderson's Co., McHenry, Ill., 1981-84; instr. Nat. Coll. Edn., Evanston, Ill., 1982-84, Webster U., Webster Groves, Mo., 1991; cons. for libr. devel. Ill. Math. and Sci. Acad., Aurora, Ill., 1986-90; peer reviewer, advisor U.S. Dept. Edn. Office Edn. Rsch. and Improvement, 1987-89; libr. cons. Reading Rainbow Resources Guide, Sta. WNET-TV, N.Y.C., 1987, 88; adj. instr. U. Mo., Columbia, 1991, 92, 93; literary advisor Grace Hill Neighborhood Svcs., 1991-95; cons. Paschen-Tishman-Jahn, 1988; presenter in field. Author: An Investigation of the Effectiveness of an On-Line Catalog in Providing Bibliographic Acccess to Children in a Public Library Setting, 1989, Family Liracy Programs in Public Libraries, 1990; contbr. articles to profl. jours. Mem. Success by Six Com., United Way of Met. St. Louis, 1993—. Grantee in field. Mem. ALA (mem. Carroll Preston Baber award jury 1992-94, World Book award 1986), Nat. Assn. Edn. Young Children, Internat. Reading Assn., Mo. Libr. Assn. (mem. summer reading program com. 1991, mem. Mark Twain award com. 1992), USA Toy Libr. Assn. (charter mem.), Assn. Libr. Svc. to Children (mem. toys, games and realia evaluation com. 1983-85, chair local arrangements 1984-85, chair rsch. com. 1985-88, mem. Randolph Caldecott com. 1987, mem. software evaluation 1988-89, mem. svc. to children with spl. needs 1989-91, chair Charlemae Rollins pres. program 1990-91, active, 1991, chair edn. com. 1991-93, 93—, bd. dirs. 1993-96, v.p., pres.-elect 1997-98, pres. 1998-99, past pres. 1999-2000), Children's Reading Round Table (mem. spl. award com. 1987-88). Office: St Louis Pub Lib 1301 Olive St Saint Louis MO 63103-2325

HOLT, ROBERT THEODORE, political science professor, educator, dean; b. Caledonia, Minn., July 26, 1928; s. Oscar Martin and Olga Linnea (Mattson) H.; m. Shirley J. Russell, Dec. 14, 1957; children: Susan Jane, Ann Carol, Sharon Linnea. AB magna cum laude, Hamline U., 1950; MPA, Princeton U., 1952, PhD, 1957. Instr. dept. polit. sci. U. Minn., Mpls., 1956-57, asst. prof., 1957-60, assoc. prof., 1960-64, prof., 1964-2001, prof. emeritus, 2001—, chmn. dept., 1978-81, dir. Ctr. for Comparative Studies in Tech. Devel. and Social Change, 1967-80, dir. rsch. devel. Coll. Liberal Arts, 1975-78, dean Grad. Sch., 1982-91, chair rsch. exec. coun., 1988-91, interim dean Coll. Liberal Arts, 1996, prof. emeritus, 2001. Bd. dirs. Coun. Grad. Schs., 1984-90, chair, 1989-90; mem. Assembly Social and Behavioral Scis., NAS, 1972-75. Author: Radio Free Europe, 1958, (with F.W. Van de Velde) Strategic Psychological Operations, 1960, The Soviet Union: Paradox and Change, 1962, (with J.E. Turner) The Political Basis of Economic Development, 1966, The Methodology of Comparative Research, 1970, Political Parties in Action, 1971, (with Turner and Chase) American Government in Comparative Perspective, 1979 With U.S. Army, 1953-55. Fellow Ctr. for Advanced Studies in Behavioral Scis., 1961-62. Mem. Am. Polit. Sci. Assn., Internat. Studies Assn., Mid West Polit Sci. Assn., Assn of Grad. Schs. (exec. com. 1985-88, chair grad. student fin. assistance com. 1986-91), 39er's Club. Episcopalian. Office: U Minn Polict Sci Dept 1414 Social Sci Tower 267 19th Ave S Minneapolis MN 55455-0499 Business E-Mail: holt@umn.edu.

HOLT, RONALD LEE, lawyer; b. Reading, Pa., Dec. 23, 1952; s. Carl John and Mary Catherine (Rossi) H.; m. Sharon Louella Nelsen, June 2, 1973; children: Angela, Valerie, Jeremy. BS in Speech summa cum laude, Evang. Coll., Springfield, Mo., 1975; JD with highest honors, Rutgers U., 1979. Bar: Mo. 1980, U.S. Dist. Ct. (we. dist.) Mo. 1980, U.S. Ct. Appeals (5th and 10th cirs.) 1988, U.S. Ct. Appeals (8th cir.) 1992. Law clk. to presiding judge U.S. Dist. Ct. (we. dist.) Mo., Kansas City, 1979-81; assoc. Stinson, Mag & Fizzell, Kansas City, 1981-86, ptnr., 1986-88, Bryan Cave and predecessor firm Bryan, Cave, McPheeters & McRoberts, Kansas City, 1988—. Mng. editor Rutgers U. Law Rev., 1978-79. Bd. dirs. Christian Conciliation Svc. of Kansas City, 1986-95, pres., 1989-91); bd. dirs. Christian Legal Soc. (bd. dirs. 1991-95, pres. Kansas City chpt. 1990, Mo. state membership dir., 1991-93). Mem. Kansas City Met. Bar Assn., Christian Legal Soc. Office: Bryan Cave 1200 Main St 3500 One Kansas City Pl Kansas City MO 64105-2100

HOLTSCHNEIDER, DENNIS H., academic administrator, priest; b. Detroit, Jan. 14, 1962; BA, Niagara U., 1984; MDiv, ThM, Mary Immaculate Sem., Northampton, Pa., 1989; EdD, Harvard U., 1997. Ordained priest Roman Cath. Ch., 1989. Assoc. dean, asst. prof. St. John's U., NYC, 1996-99; exec. v.p., COO, Niagara U., Niagara Falls, Y, 2000—04; pres. DePaul U., Chicago, Ill., 2004—. Mem. N.Y. Acad. Pub. Edn. (life). Office: DePaul U 1 E Jackson Chicago IL 60604

HOLTZ, MICHAEL P., hotel executive; Pres., CEO Amerihost Properties, Inc., Arlington Heights, Ill. Office: Amerihost Properties Inc Ste 400 2355 S Arlington Heights Rd Arlington Heights IL 60005-4500

HOLTZMAN, DAVID MICHAEL, neurologist; b. St. Louis, July 31, 1961; BS in Med. Edn., Northwestern U., 1983, MD, 1985. Bd. cert. neurology. Intern/resident U. Calif., San Francisco, 1985—89, postdoctoral rsch. tng. William C. Mobley Lab., 1989—94; lab. dir. Washington U., 1994, Charlotte and Paul Hagemann assoc. prof. neurology, 2001—, prof. molecular biology and pharmacology, 2002—; Andrew and Gretchen Jones chmn. dept. neurology Washington U. Sch. Medicine, St. Louis, 2003—. Asst. prof. U. Calif., San Francisco, 1991—94. Recipient Paul Beeson Physician Faculty Scholar award in aging rsch., MetLife award for rsch. on Alzheimer's disease, 2007, Potamkin prize, Am. Acad. Neurology, 2003. Office: Washington Univ Sch Medicine Dept Neurology 660 S Euclid Ave Saint Louis MO 63110

HOLTZMAN, ROBERTA LEE, French and Spanish language educator; b. Detroit, Nov. 24, 1938; d. Paul John and Sophia (Marcus) H. AB cum laude, Wayne State U., Detroit, Mich., 1959, MA, 1973, U. Mich., Ann Arbor, 1961. Fgn. lang. tchr. Birmingham (Mich.) Sch. Dist., 1959—60, Cass Tech. H.S., Detroit, 1961-64; from instr. to prof. French and Spanish, Schoolcraft Coll., Livonia, 1964—84, chmn. French and Spanish depts., 1984—2004, adj. prof. French, 2004—05, prof. emerita French and Spanish, 2005—. Trustee Cranbrook Music Guild, Ednl. Community, Bloomfield Hills, Mich., 1976-78. Fulbright-Hays fellow, Brazil, 1964. Mem. AAUW, NEA, MLA, Nat. Mus. Women in Arts (co-founder 1992), Nat. Trust, Am. Assn. Tchrs. Spanish and Portuguese, Am. Assn. Tchrs. French, Mich. Edn. Assn., U. Mich. Alumnae Club of Birmingham. Avocations: swimming, book collecting, photography, travel. Office: Schoolcraft Coll 18600 Haggerty Rd Livonia MI 45152-2696 Business E-Mail: rholtzma@schoolcraft.edu.

HOLZBACH, RAYMOND THOMAS, gastroenterologist, educator, writer; b. Salem, Ohio, Aug. 19, 1929; s. Raymond T. and Nelle A. (Conroy) H.; m. Lorraine E. Cozza, May 26, 1956; children: Ellen, Mark, James. BS, Georgetown U., 1951; MD, Case Western Res. U., 1955. Diplomate Nat. Bd. Med. Examiners, Am. Bd. Internal Medicine. Intern, asst. resident U. Ill. Research and Edn. Hosps., Chgo., 1955-56; sr. asst. resident medicine Cleve. Met. Gen. Hosp., 1959-60; asst. chief gastroenterology Case Western Res U., 1961-63; physician Gastroenterology Unit U. Hosps. of Cleve., 1961-63; instr. medicine Case Western Res. U. Sch. Medicine, Cleve., 1961-64, clin. instr. medicine, 1964-71; head gastrointestinal research unit, assoc. physician div. medicine St. Luke's Hosp., Cleve., 1967-73, dir. div. gastroenterology, 1970-73; head gastrointestinal research unit dept. medicine Cleve. Clinic Found., 1973—. Vis. prof. numerous instns. including Mayo Med. Sch., 1974, U. Calif., San Diego, 1977, U. Heidelberg, 1978, U. Pa., 1979, U. Zurich, 1980, U. Munich, 1982, U. Minn. Med. Ctr., 1985, med. ctrs., numerous Japanese univs., 1985, 92, Karolinska Inst., 1986, Royal Soc. London, 1987, Pa. State U. Sch. Med., U. Helsinki, RWTH-Aachen, Düsseldorf, Fed. Republic of Germany, U. Groningen, Utrecht, U. Amsterdam, The Netherlands, 1989, U. Perugia, Italy, Va. Commonwealth U.-Med. Coll. Va., Richmond, Christ Ch. Sch. Medicine, U. Otago, New Zealand, SUNY, Buffalo Sch. Medicine, 1990, Pontifical/Cath. U. Chile Sch. Medicine, 1991, Hiroshima U. Sch. Medicine, 1992, Kyoto U. Sch. Medicine, 1992, Sch. Medicine U. Jikei, Tokyo, 1992, Tel Aviv U., Israel Sch. Medicine, 1995, U. Leipzig, Germany, 1996, U. Heidelberg, Germany, 1996; lectr. in field. Mem. editl. bd. Gastroenterology jour., 1984-89; contbr. revs. and articles to med. jours. Served to capt. USAF, 1957-59. Recipient Alexander von Humboldt Found. Spl. Program award, 1978, 82. Fellow ACP; mem. ABA, Am. Gastroent. Assn. (rsch. com. 1976-79), Ctrl. Soc. Clin. Rsch., Am. Assn. for Study of Liver Diseases, AAAS, Am. Soc. Biol. Chemists, Am. Physiol. Assn., Biophys. Soc., Internat. Assn. Study of Liver, Am. Fedn. Clin. Rsch., Midwest Gut Club, Am. Soc. Clin. Nutrition, Ohio State Med. Assn., Sigma Xi. Unitarian Universalist. Office: Cleve Clin Found 9500 Euclid Ave Cleveland OH 44195-0001 Personal E-mail: tomholzbach@adelphia.net.

HOLZER, EDWIN, advertising executive; b. June 22, 1933; MusB, Yale U., 1954, MusM, 1955; postgrad., Ind. U., 1956. Acct. exec. Benton & Bowles Inc., NYC, 1959-62; account supr. William Esty Co., NYC, 1962-66, Grey Advt. Inc., NYC, 1966-68, mgmt. supr., 1968-70; exec. v.p. Grey Inc., NYC, 1970-73; pres., CEO, COO Grey-North Inc., Chgo., 1973-85; chmn., CEO, Grey Chgo. (name changed to LOIS/GGK 1988), 1988; chmn., CEO LOIS/EJL (formerly Lois/USA), Chgo., from 1988; chief marketing officer CornerDrugstore.com, 2000—.

HOMBURGER, THOMAS CHARLES, lawyer; b. Buffalo, Sept. 16, 1941; s. Adolf and Charolotte E. (Stern) Homburger; m. Louise Paula Shemin, June 6, 1965; children: Jennifer Anne, Richard Ephraim, Kathryn Lee. BA, Columbia U., NYC, 1963, JD, 1966. Bar: Ill. 1966, US Dist. Ct. (no. dist.) Ill. 1966. Assoc., ptnr. Sonnenschein, Carlin, Nath & Rosenthal, Chgo., 1966—86, Bell, Boyd & Lloyd LLP, Chgo., 1986—2002, chmn. real estate, 2002—. Adj. prof. John Marshall Law Sch., 1989—. Contbr. articles to profl. jours. Chmn. nat. exec. com. Anti-Defamation League, 2000—03; chmn. Chgo. regional bd. Anti-Defamation League, B'nai Brith, 1986—88; mem. Glencoe Bd. Edn., Ill., 1984—89; pres. Anti-Defamation League, 2003—06, vice chmn., 2006—. Mem.: ABA (real property divsn., probate & trust law sect., fin. subcom.), Chgo. Mortgage Attys. Assn. (pres. 1975—77), Am. Coll. Real Estate Lawyers (bd. govs. 2000—03), Chgo. Bar Assn. (chmn. real property law com. 1984—85), Ill. Bar Assn. (real property sect.), Std. Club, Law Club Chgo., Lambda Alpha Internat. Home: 20 East Cedar St Apt 2F Chicago IL 60611-1149 Office: Bell Boyd & Lloyd LLP 70 W Madison St Ste 3100 Chicago IL 60602-4284 Office Phone: 312-807-4267. Personal E-mail: tc@homburger.cnchost.com. Business E-Mail: thomburger@bellboyd.com.

HONG, ELLEE PAI, newscaster; b. Republic of Korea; B, EWHA Women's U., Seoul, Republic of Korea; M, Northwestern U. Former anchor WIFR-TV, Rockford, Ill., WAND-TV, Decatur, Ill.; weekday morning anchor WFSB-TV, Hartford, 2001—03; morning news anchor WMAQ-TV (NBC Chgo.), 2003—. Office: WMAQ-TV NBC Tower 454 N Columbus Dr Chicago IL 60611-5555 Business E-Mail: ellee.paihong@nbc.com.

HONG, HOWARD VINCENT, library administrator, philosophy educator, editor, translator; b. Wolford, ND, Oct. 19, 1912; BA, St. Olaf Coll., 1934; postgrad., Wash. State Coll., 1934—35; PhD, U. Minn., 1938; postgrad., U. Copenhagen, 1938—39; DLitt (hon.), McGill U., Montreal, 1977; DD (hon.), Trinity Sem., Columbus, Ohio, 1983; DHL (hon.), Carleton Coll., 1987; ThD (hon.), U. Copenhagen, 1992. With English dept. Wash. State Coll., 1934-35; with Brit. Mus., 1937; mem. faculty dept. philosophy St. Olaf Coll., Northfield, Minn., 1938-78, asst. prof. philosophy, 1940-42, assoc. prof., 1942-47, prof., 1947-78, chmn. Ford Found. self-study com., 1955-56, dir. Kierkegaard Library, 1972-84. Vis. lectr. U. Minn., 1955; mem. Nat. Lutheran Coun. Scholarship and Grant Rev. Bd., 1958-66; lectr. Holden Village, Washington, 1963-70; mem. Minn. Colls. Grant Rev. Bd., 1970 Author, editor, contbr.: Integration in the Christian Liberal Arts College, 1956, This World and the Church, 1955; editor, contbg. author: Christian Faith and the Liberal Arts, 1960; co-editor, translator: (with Edna H. Hong) works by Gregor Malantschuk, numerous works by Soren Kierkegaard, Soren Kierkegaard's Journals and Papers, Vol. I, 1968 (Nat. Book award for transl. 1968), Søren Kierkegaard's Journals and Papers, Vol. II, 1970, Søren Kierkegaard's Journals and Papers, Vol. III-IV, 1975, Søren Kierkegaard's Journals and Papers, V-VII, 1978, The Controversial Kierkegaard (Gregor Malantschuk), 1980, Two Ages (Søren Kierkegaard), 1978, The Sickness unto Death (Søren Kierkegaard), 1980, The Corsaair Affair (Søren Kierkegaard), 1981, Fear and Trembling-Repetition, 1983, Philosophical Fragments-Johannes Climacus, 1985, Either/Or, 1987, Stages on Life's Way, 1988, The Concept of Irony, 1989, For Self-Examination and Judge for Yourself!, 1990, Eighteen Upbuilding Discourses, 1990, Practice in Christianity, 1991, Concluding Unscientific Postscript, 1992, Three Discourses on Imagined Occasions, 1993, Upbuilding Discourses in Various Spirits, 1993, Works of Love, 1995, Without Authority, 1997, Point of View, 1998, The Moment and Late Writings, 1998, The Book on Adler, 1998, The Essential Kierkegaard, 2000, Kierkegaard's Concept of Existence (Gregor Malantschuk), 2003; gen. editor Kierkegaard's Writings,

1972—. Field sec. War Prisoners Aid, U.S., Scandinavia, and Germany, 1943-46; sr. rep. Service to Refugees, Luth. World Fedn., Germany and Austria, 1947-49; sr. field officer refugee div. World Council Chs., Germany, 1947-48; curator Kierkegaard House Found., 1999—. Decorated Order of Dannebrog (Denmark), Order of the Three Stars (Latvia); recipient award Minn. Humanities Comm., 1983, Minn. Forest Stewardship award DNR, 2002, 03; fellow Am.-Scandinavian Found.-Denmark, 1938-39, Am. Council Learned Socs., 1952-53, Rockefeller Found., 1959, sr. rsch. fellow Fulbright Commn., 1959-60, 64, sr. fellow NEH, 1970-71; grantee NEH, 1972-73; publ. grantee Carlsberg Found., 1974, 86, 88, editing-translating grantee NEH, 1978-90, 95-98. Home: 5174 E 90 Old Dutch Rd orthfield MN 55057 Office: St Olaf Coll Kierkegaard Libr Northfield MN 55057

HONG, MEI, chemistry professor; BA, Mt. Holyoke Coll., 1992; PhD, U. Calif. Berkeley, 1996. NIH postdoctoral fellow Mass. Inst. Tech., Cambridge; rsch. prof. U. Mass., Amherst; assoc. prof. chemistry Iowa State U., Ames, Iowa, 1999—. Mem. editl. bd.: Jour. Magnetic Resonance. Recipient Beckman Young Investigator award, 1999, Rsch. Corp. Innovation award, 2000, Career award, NSF, 2001, Pure Chemistry award, Am. Chem. Soc., 2003; Alfred P. Sloan Fellow, 2002. Achievements include development and application of solid-state NMR spectroscopy to investigate the structure and dynamics of membrane and insoluable fibrous proteins. Office: Dept Chemistry 1605 Gilman Hall Iowa State Univ Ames IA 50011-3111 Office Phone: 515-294-3521. E-mail: mhong@iastate.edu.

HONHART, FREDERICK LEWIS, III, academic director; b. San Diego, Oct. 29, 1943; s. Frederick Lewis Jr. and Rossiter (Hyde) H.; m. Barbara Ann Baker, Aug. 27, 1966; children: David Frederick, Stephen Charles. BA, Wayne State U., 1966; MA, Case-Western Res. U., 1968, PhD, 1972. Cert. archivist. Field rep. Ohio Hist. Soc., Columbus, 1972-73; asst. dir. univ. archives & hist. collections Mich. State U., East Lansing, 1974-79, dir., 1979—. Mem. adv. bd. Mich. Nat. Hist. Publs. & Records Commn., Lansing, 1979—; cons. in field. Creator: (microcomputer sys.), MicroMARC:amc, 1986 (Coker prize 1988), Micro-MARC for Integrated Format, 1995; contbr. articles to profl. jours. Fellow Soc. Am. Archivists; mem. Internat. Coun. Archives (steering com. univ. archives sect. 2000-04, pres. univ. archives sect. 2004-06), Mich. Archival Assn. (pres. 1984-86), Midwest Archives Conf. (chair program com. 1982, 94, chair Author Awards com. 2001), Olds Forge Flying Club (pres. 2005—). Avocations: reading, sports, flying. Office: Mich State U 101 Conrad Hall East Lansing MI 48824-1327 Office Phone: 517-355-2330.

HONIG, GEORGE RAYMOND, pediatrician; b. Chgo., May 5, 1936; s. Joseph C. and Raymonde S. (Moses) Honig; m. Karen R. Jacobson, Dec. 18, 1960 (dec.); children: Sharon, Debra, Robert; m. Olga M. Weiss, May 24, 1998. BS in Liberal Arts and Sci., U. Ill., 1959, MD, 1961, MS in Pharmacology, 1961; PhD in Biochemistry, George Washington U., 1966. Diplomate Am. Bd. Pediatrics, Nat. Bd. Med. Examiners. Intern Johns Hopkins Hosp., Balt., 1961-62, fellow in pediatrics, 1961-63, asst. resident in pediatrics, 1962-63; rsch. assoc. Nat. Cancer Inst. NIH, 1963-66; fellow in pediatric hematology U. Ill., Chgo., 1966-68, from asst. prof. to assoc. prof. pediat., 1968—74, prof., 1974-75, 1984—2003, prof. emeritus, 2004—, attending physician, 1968-75, dir. pediatric hematology svc., 1972-75, head dept. pediat. Coll. Medicine, 1984—2003. Attending physician, dir. divsn. hematology Children's Meml. Hosp., Chgo., 1975—83; prof. emeritus U. Ill. Coll. Medicine, 2004—. Contbr. articles to profl. jours. Mem.: AAUP, Soc. Pediatric Rsch., Am. Pediatric Soc., Am. Soc. Hematology, Am. Soc. Biochemistry and Molecular Biology, Am. Assn. Cancer Rsch., Am. Acad. Pediat., Alpha Omega Alpha. Office: U Ill Coll Medicine 840 S Wood St Chicago IL 60612-7317 Home Phone: 312-664-3769; Office Phone: 312-996-1788. Business E-Mail: ghonig@uic.edu.

HONOLD, LINDA KAYE, human resources development executive; b. Lansing, Mich., Aug. 16, 1956; d. Ervin Charles and Patricia Kathleen (Couzzins) Gaulke; m. Reynolds Keith Honold, dec. 5, 1987; 1 child, Samatha Kaye. BA in Polit. Sci., U. Wis., Eau Claire, 1980; MS in Indsl. Rels., U. Wis., Madison, 1987; PhD in Human and Orgnl. Sys., Fielding Grad. Inst., Santa Barbara, Calif., 1999. Editorial asst. Lake Pub. Co., Libertyville, Ill., 1980-81; econ. devel. rep. Projects With Industry, Menomonie, Wis., 1981-83; exec. dir. Am. Cancer Soc., Eau Claire, 1983-85; career counselor Hmong Assn., Sheboygan, Wis., 1985-87; mem. resource team personal devel. Johnsonville Foods, Sheboygan Falls, Wis., 1987—90; orgnl. devel. cons., 1990—. Author: Developing Employees Who Love to Learn, 2001; co-author: Organizational DNA, 2003; contbr. articles to profl. jours. Sec. Civil Svc. Commn., Sheboygan, 1986-95; del. Dem. Party, San Francisco, 1984, LA, 2000; chair Wis. State Dem. Party, 2001-06. Mem. Am. Soc. Personnel Adminstrs., Am. Soc. Tng. and Devel., Sheboygan County S. of C. (chmn. edn. coun.), Mortar Bd., Altrusa (sec. 1987-90), Sheboygan Svc. Club. Lutheran. Avocations: jogging, reading, sailing. Home: 3055 E Newport Ct Milwaukee WI 53211-2910

HOOD, ANTOINETTE FOOTE, dermatologist; b. Honolulu, 1941; MD, Vanderbilt U., 1967. Cert. dermatology. Intern Vanderbilt Affiliated Hosps, 1967-68; fellow dermatology Harvard U., 1973-75, resident dermatology, 1975-76; resident dermatology-pathology Mass. Gen. Hosp., Boston, 1976-78; faculty Johns Hopkins School of Med., 1980—93; Dir. Dermatopathology Indiana Univ. School of Med., 1993—2002; exec. dir. American Board of Dermatology, Detroit, 2001—; Dir. Dermatopathology Ea. Va. School of Med, 2002—. Office: Pariser Dermatology Specialists Ltd 601 Medical Tower Norfolk VA 23507

HOOD, DENISE PAGE, federal judge; b. 1952; BA, Yale Univ., 1974; JD, Columbia Sch. of Law, 1977. Asst. corp. counsel City of Detroit, Law Dept., 1977-82; judge 36th Dist. Ct., 1983-89, Recorder's Ct. for the City of Detroit, 1989-92, Wayne County Circuit Ct., 1993-94; district judge U.S. Dist. Ct. (Mich. ea. dist.), 6th circuit, 1994—. Recipient Judicial Service award Black Women Lawyers Assn., 1994. Mem. Am. Bar Assn., State Bar of Mich., Detroit Bar Assn. (Chmn. of Yr. award 1988), Assn. of Black Judges of Mich., Mich. Dist. Judges Assn., Am. Inns of Ct., Wolverine Bar Assn. (bd. of dirs.), Women Lawyers Assn. of Mich., Fed. Bar Assn., Nat. Assn. of Women Judges, Nat. Bar Assn. Judicial Coun., Mich. Judicial Inst. Office: US Courthouse 231 W Lafayette Blvd Rm 251 Detroit MI 48226-2789

HOOK, JOHN BURNEY, investment company executive; b. Franklin, Ind., Sept. 6, 1928; s. Burney S. and Elsie C. (Hubbard) H.; m. Georgia Delis, Feb. 8, 1958; children— David, Deborah. BS, Ind. U., 1956, MBA, 1957. CPA, Ohio.; cert. fin. analyst. Store mgr. Goodman-Jester, Inc., Franklin, Ind., 1949-50; auditor Ernst & Ernst, Indpls., 1953-56; financial analyst Eli Lilly & Co., Indpls., 1957-59; gen. ptnr. Ball, Burge & Kraus, Cleve., 1966-72; pres., dir. Cuyahoga Mgmt. Corp., 1966-81; mng. ptnr. Hook Ptnrs., Cleve., 1984—96. Mem. AICPA, Am. Inst. CFAs, Union Club (Cleve.), Westwood Country Club, Ironwood Country Club (Palm Desert, Calif.). Republican. Methodist. Home: 435 Bates Dr Bay Village OH 44140 also: 73233 Ribbonwood Palm Desert CA 92260

HOOPS, H. RAY, college president; BA, Eastern Ill. U.; MA in Audiology, Speech Scis., PhD in Audiology, Speech Scis., Purdue U.; MBA, Moorhead State U. Vice chancellor academic affairs U. Miss., 1988-94; pres. U. Southern Ind., Evansville, 1994—. Contbr. articles to profl. jours. Founder Project '95 State of Miss. (Nat. Council State Govt. Assn. award). Recipient two Nat. Service awards U.S. Dept. Health, Edn. Welfare; Sr. Fulbright-Hayes Rsch. scholar U. Philippines. Fellow Am. Speech Hearing Assn. (Nat. Rsch. award). Office: Univ Southern Indiana Office of the President 8600 University Blvd Evansville IN 47712-3590

HOOPS, JAMES M., state representative; b. Bowling Green, Ohio, Mar. 9, 1959; married; 1 child. BS in Bus. and Compuer Engring., Northwest State of La. Coll. State rep. dist. 75 Ohio Ho. of Reps., Columbus, 1998—, vice chair, fin. and appropriations com., mem. edn., health, and transp. and pub. safety coms., mem. fed. grant rev. and edn. oversight, and children's healthcare and family svcs. subcoms. Past mem. Athletes in Action Basketball Team; former auditor Henry County, Ohio; former pres. Filling Home of Mercy Bd. Mem.: Putnam County Twp. Assn., Henry County Bus. Adv. Coun., Van Wert Twp. Assn., Paulding County Twp. Assn., Napoleon/Henry County C. of C., Henry County United Way, Henry County Farm Bur., Henry County Right to Life, Fort to Port Imp Orgn., Henry County Gideons, Napoleon Optimist Club, Deshler Lions Club. Republican. Office: 77 S High St 13th fl Columbus OH 43215-6111

HOOVER, PAUL, poet; b. Harrisonburg, Va., Apr. 30, 1946; s. Robert and Opal (Shinaberry) H.; m. Maxine Chernoff, 1974; children: Koren, Philip, Julian. BA cum laude, Manchester Coll., 1968; MA, U. Ill., 1973. Asst. editor U. Ill. Press, Champaign, 1973-74; prof. English, Columbia Coll., Chgo., 1974—. Co-founder Poetry Ctr., Sch. of Art Inst. of Chgo., 1974, bd. mem. 1974-87, pres. 1975-78; editor OINK!, 1971-85; co-founder, editor New Am. Writing, 1986. Author: Letter to Einstein Beginning Dear Albert, 1979, Somebody Talks a Lot, 1983, Nervous Songs, 1986, Idea, 1987 (Carl Sandburg award Friends of Chgo. Pub. Libr. 1987), Saigon, Illinois, 1988, The Novel: A Poem, 1990; editor: Postmodern American Poetry, 1994, Viridian, 1997 (Georgia prize 1997), Totem and Shadow: New and Selected Poems, 1999, Rehearsal in Black, 2001, Winter (Mirror), 2002, Fables of Representation: Essays, 2003; contbr. to various periodicals including New Yorker, Partisan Rev., New Directions, Sulfur, Chgo. Rev., Triquarterly, Am. Poetry Rev., New Republic; author: (screenplay) Viridian, 1994. Nat. Endowment for Arts fellow, 1980; Ill. Arts Coun. fellow, 1983, 84, 86; recipient Gen. Electric Found. award for Younger Writers, 1984, Jerome J. Shestack award, 2003. Mem. MLA. Office: Columbia Coll Dept of English 600 S Michigan Ave Chicago IL 60605-1900 Home: 369 Molino Ave Mill Valley CA 94941-2767

HOOVER, WILLIAM LEICHLITER, forestry and natural resources educator, financial consultant; b. Brownsville, Pa., July 29, 1944; s. Aaron Jones and Edith (Leichliter) H.; m. Peggy Jo Spangler, Aug. 30, 1976; children: Jennifer Mary, Monica Susan, Samuel Spangler. BS, Pa. State U., 1966, MS, 1971; PhD, Iowa State U., 1977. Rsch. asst. Pa. State U., Iowa State U., 1970-74; asst. prof. Purdue U., West Lafayette, Ind., 1974-79, assoc. prof. dept. forestry & natural resources, 1980-85, prof., 1986—, asst. dept. head & extension coord. Dir. Nat. Timber Tax website. Author: A Guide to Federal Income Tax for Timber Owners, Timber Tax Management; contbg. editor taxes Tree Farmer Mag. Mem. Boy Scouts Am., Silver Beaver. 1st lt. C.E., u.S. Army, 1967-69. Decorated Bronze Star. Mem. Internat. Soc. Ecol. Econs., Forest Products Soc., Soc. Am. Foresters, Soc. Range Mgmt. Republican. Presbyterian. Home: 206 Connolly St West Lafayette IN 47906-2724 Office: Purdue U Dept Forestry West Lafayette IN 47907 E-mail: billh@fnr.purdue.edu.

HOPEN, HERBERT JOHN, horticulture educator; b. Madison, Wis., Jan. 7, 1934; s. Alfred and Amelia (Sveum) H.; m. Joanne C. Emmel, Sept. 12, 1959; children: Timothy, Rachel. BS, U. Wis., 1956, MS, 1959; PhD, Mich. State U., 1962. Asst. prof. U. Minn., Duluth, 1962-64; prof. U. Ill., Urbana, 1965-85, prof., acting head, 1983-85; prof. horticulture U. Wis., Madison, 1985-97, prof. emeritus, 1997, chmn. dept. horticulture, 1985-91. Mem. Am. Soc. Hort. Sci., Weed Sci. Soc. Am., North Ctrl. Weed Sci. Soc., Ygdrasil, Torske Klubben, Sigma Xi. Avocations: reading, gardening. Office: U Wis Dept Hort 1575 Linden Dr Madison WI 53706-1514 Office Phone: 608-262-1490. Business E-Mail: hjhopen@wisc.edu.

HOPKINS, JEFFERY P., federal judge; b. 1960; JD, Ohio State U., 1985. Bar: Ohio 1985, U.S. Dist. Ct. (so dist.) Ohio 1986, 1986 (Fed.). Law clk. to Hon. Alan E. orris U.S. Ct. Appeals (6th cir.), 1985-87; assoc. Squire, Sanders & Dempsey, 1987-90; asst. U.S. atty. So. Dist. Ohio, 1990-96; bankruptcy judge U.S. Dist. Ct. (so. dist.) Ohio, Cin., 1996—. Bd. dir. Fed. Judicial Ctr., mem. edn. com.; adj. prof. Coll. Law U. Cin. Mem.: Nat. Conf. Bankruptcy Judges, Am. Law Inst. of ABA (faculty bankruptcy law course), Sigma Pi Phi. Office: US Bankr Ct So Dist Ohio 221 E 4th Ste 800 Cincinnati OH 45202-4124

HOPKINS, LEWIS DEAN, architecture educator; b. Lakewood, Ohio, Feb. 20, 1946; s. W. Dean and Harriet (Painter) H.; m. Susan Brewster Cocker, Aug. 24, 1968; children: Joshua, Nathaniel. BA, U. Pa., 1968, postgrad., 1968-69, M of Regional Planning, 1970, PhD, 1975. Asst. prof. landscape arch. Inst. Environ. Studies/U. Ill., Urbana-Champaign, 1972-79, assoc. prof. landscape arch., urban and regional planning, 1979-84, prof., head dept. urban and regional planning, 1984-97, prof. landscape arch., 1984—. Vis. lectr. dept. town and regional planning U. Sheffield, Eng., 1980; coord. grad. program in landscape arch. U. Ill., 1976-79, chair search com. for head dept. landscape arch., 1985, chair com. to evaluate dir. Inst. Environ. Studies, 1990, com. pub. adminstrn. program, 1990, campus budget strategies com., 1991-94, chancellors strategic planning com., 1993-95, campus senate, 1976-79, 82-84, chair ednl. policy com. 1978-79, senate coun. 1978-79, 82-83, budget com. 1984-86; project dir. Ill. Streams Info. sys., 1981-90; fellow Com. Instnl. Coop. Acad. Leadership Program, 1989-90; external site visit team dept. landscape arch. and environ. planning, Ariz. State U., 1990; rsch. adv. com. Ill.-Ind. Sea Grant Program, 1991—; exec. com. Office of Solid Waste Rsch., 1992-95; Fulbright sr. scholar to Nepal, 1997-98. Co-editor: (with Gill-Chin Lim) Jour. Planning Edn. and Rsch., 1987-91; mem. editl. bd. Jour. Planning Lit., Computers, Environment and Urban sys., Urban and Regional Info. Sys. Assn. Jour., Jour. Planning Edn. and Rsch., others; reviewer: European Jour. Ops. Rsch., Geographical Analysis, Internat. Regional Sci. Rev., Landscape Jour., Mgmt. Sci., Transp. Rsch., others; contbr. articles to profl. jours. Fellow Am. Inst. Cert. Planners; mem. AAUP (pres. campus chpt. 1983-84), Am. Planning Assn. (chair nominating com. Ill. chpt. 1988), Assn. Collegiate Schs. of Planning (regional rep. to exec. bd. 1989-91), Inst. Mgmt. Scis., Regional Sci. Assn., Urban and Regional Inf. Sys. Assn. for Planning Accreditation Bd. (chair site visit teams 1988, 92, 94, team mem. 1995, com. on dual degree programs 1992-93), Planning Accreditation Bd. (chair 1997—). Achievements include research in human and computer problem solving processes for incompletely defined spatial problems; land and water resources management, information, and decision support systems; comprehensive planning processes and institutions. Office: U Ill Urbana-Champaign Dept Urban/Regional Plan 611 E Taft Dr Champaign IL 61820-6921

HOPLAMAZIAN, MARK SAMUEL, hotel executive; b. Bryn Mawr, Pa., Nov. 27, 1963; s. Harry Joseph and Victoria (Sarkisian) Hoplamazian; m. Rachel DeYoung Kohler, Sept. 28, 1991; 3 children. BA, Harvard U., 1985; MBA, U. Chgo., 1989. Fin. analyst The First Boston Corp., NYC, 1985-87; mcht. banker Pritzker & Pritzker, Chgo., 1989—, sr. v.p., exec. v.p. to pres. Pritzker Org. LLC; interim pres. Global Hyatt Corp., 2006, pres., CEO, 2006—. Mem. Discovery Class of the Henry Crown Fellowship Aspen Inst., 2003—; bd. trustees Latin Sch. Chgo.; advisory bd. Facing History and Ourselves. Mem.: Beta Gamma Sigma. Avocations: japanese art, squash, golf. Office: Global Hyatt Corp 71 S Wacker St Chicago IL 60606

HOPP, ANTHONY JAMES, advertising agency executive; b. Detroit, Jan. 31, 1945; s. William J. and Beverly (Gildea) H.; m. Nancy Jane Dunckel, Nov. 11, 1969; children: Beth, Michael. BA in Advt./Mktg., Mich. State U., 1967, MA in Advt./Psychology, 1968. Asst. account exec. Campbell-Ewald Adv., Warren, Mich., 1968-70; account exec. Lintas Campbell-Ewald, Warren, Mich., 1970-74, account supr., 1974-75, v.p., account supr., 1975-79, sr. v.p., mgmt. supr., 1979-85, group sr. v.p., group mgmt. supr., 1985-88, exec. v.p., account dir., 1988-93, pres., 1993-95, vice chmn., 1995—97, also bd. dirs.; chmn. & CEO Lintas Campbell-Ewald (now Campbell-Ewald), Warren, Mich., 1997—. Bd. dirs. C-E Comm., Warren, Lintas Ams. Recipient Robert E. Healy award Interpublic Group of Cos., 1989. Mem. Adcraft, Hunters Creek, Bloomfield Hills Country Club, Pine Lake Country Club. Avocations: golf, hunting, boating. Office: Lintas-Campbell-Ewald 30400 Van Dyke Ave Warren MI 48093-2368

HOPP, DANIEL FREDERICK, lawyer, manufacturing company executive; b. Ann Arbor, Mich., Apr. 14, 1947; s. Clayton A. and Monica E. (Williams) H.; m. Maria G. Lopez, Dec. 20, 1968; children: Emily, Daniel, Melissa. BA in English, U. Mich., 1969; JD summa cum laude, Wayne State U., 1973. Bar: Ill. 1974, Mich. 1980. Atty. Mayer, Brown and Platt, Chgo., 1973-79, Whirlpool Corp., Benton Harbor, Mich., 1979-84, asst. sec., 1984-85, sec., asst. gen. counsel, 1985-89, v.p., gen. counsel, sec., 1989-98, sr. v.p. corp. affairs, gen. counsel sec., 1998—. Bd. dirs. Horizon Bank, Mich. City, Ind., Lakeland Regional Health Sys., St. Joseph, Mich., Coun. World Class Communities, Benton Harbor, Mich.; mem. City of St. Joseph Planning Commn. Served in US Army, 1969—71. Mem.: Berrien County Bar Assn., Mich. Bar Assn. Republican. Mem. Ch. Of Christ. Avocation: golf. Office: Whirlpool Corp Adminstrv Ctr 2000 N M-63 Benton Harbor MI 49022-2692

HOPP, NANCY SMITH, marketing executive; b. Aurora, Ill., Nov. 1, 1943; d. C. Dudley and Margaret (McWethy) Smith; m. Edward Thompson Reid, July 19, 1963 (div. Feb. 1966); 1 child, Edward Thompson Jr.; m. James C. Hopp, Feb. 4, 1978. Cert., Chgo. Sch. Interior Design, 1965; BA in Social Scis., Aurora U., 1968, MS in Bus. Mgmt., 1982. Dir. pub. rels. Sta. WLXT-TV, Aurora, 1969-70; bookstore mgr. Waubonsee Coll., Sugar Grove, Ill., 1970-79, dir. purchasing, 1979-85, dir. pub. rels., 1984-85; dir. devel. Assn. for Individual Devel., Aurora, 1985-87; dir. pub. rels. Provena Mercy Ctr., Aurora, 1988-95; dir. mktg. Dreyer Med. Clinic, Aurora, 1995—. Ninety for the 90s com. Ill. Dept. Aging, 1989. Editor: Volunteers Make the Difference, 1982; author Pigeon Woods Cookbook; producer (film) Caring Counts; contbr. articles to profl. jours. Bd. dirs. Family Support Ctr., Aurora, 1984-90, Aurora Area United Way, 1990-96, Corridor Group, 1993-94, Assn. Individual Devel., 1996—2005, Suicide Prevention Svcs., 1998-2000; adv. coun. Mercy Ctr. Health Care, Aurora, 1985-87; moderator New Eng. Congl. Ch., Aurora, 1983; charter mem. bd. dirs. Aurora Cmty. Coordinating Coun., 1985-86; mem. Block Grant Working Com., Aurora, 1987-2000, Kane County Womens Health Coalition, 1999—; bd. dirs., sec. Cities in Schs./Aurora 2000, Inc., 1993-94, Paramount Arts Ctr. Endowment Bd., 1999-2005, Fox Valley Arts Hall of Fame, 2001-04, 06—. Recipient citation U.S. Dept. HEW, 1969, Christian Svc. award, 1996, Lyle Oncken Cmty. Svc. award Mental Health and Mental Retardation Svcs., Inc., 2004; named Woman of the Day, Sta. WAIT-AM, Chgo., 1974, Optimist of Yr. for Cmty. Svc., 1987, Woman of Distinction, YWCA, 1990. Mem. Women in Mgmt. (Nat. Charlotte Danstrom Woman of Achievement award 1984), Nat. Soc. Fund Raising Execs. (ethics com. Chgo. chpt. 1987), Ill. Assn. Coll. Stores (pres. 1976), Nat. Assn. Ednl. Buyers (com. 1984)), Exch. Club. Republican. Avocations: art, music, water sports. Home: 175 S Western Ave Aurora IL 60506-4617 Office: Dreyer Med Clinic 1877 W Downer Pl Aurora IL 60506-7334

HOPPE, MARK A., bank executive; b. 1954; BBA in Fin., U. Wis.-Madison, 1976, MBA in Fin., 1977. Credit analyst First Wis. Bank, Madison, 1977; credit analyst, loan officer Old Kent Bank & Trust Co., 1978—81; joined LaSalle Bank, 1981, exec. v.p.; vice chmn. LaSalle Nat. Leasing Corp., 1996; mgr. comml. banking dept. Standard Fed. Bank, Troy, Mich., 2000—05, CEO, 2005—07; pres., CEO Cole Taylor Bank, Rosemont, 2008—; pres. Taylor Cap. Group Inc., Rosemont, 2008—. Mem. bd. dirs. YMCA Met. Detroit, Detroit Symphony Orchestra. Mem.: Econ. Club Chgo., Econ. Club Detroit. Office: Cole Taylor Corp 9550 West Higgins Rd Rosemont IL 60018*

HOPPE, THOMAS J., state legislator; b. Evanston, Ill., Mar. 21, 1957; BA, Benedictine Coll., 1979. State rep. Dist. 46 Mo. State Congress, 1991—. Mem. edn., fees and salaries com., local govt. and related matters com., urban affairs com.; mktg. cons. Mem. KC, Grandview, Belton & Kansas City C. of C.

HOPPER, DAVID HENRY, theologian, educator; b. Cranford, NJ, July 31, 1927; s. Orion Cornelius and Julia Margaret (Weitzel) H.; m. Nancy Ann Nelson, June 10, 1967 (div. June 1984); children: Sarah Elizabeth, Kathryn Ann, Rachel Suzanne. BA, Yale U., 1950; BD, ThM, Princeton Theol. Sem., 1953, ThD, 1959. Ordained Presbyn. minister, 1961. Asst. prof. Macalester Coll., St. Paul, 1959-67, assoc. prof., 1967-73, James Wallace prof. of religion, 1973—2001, prof. emeritus, 2001—. Author: Tillich: A Theological Portrait, 1967 (N.J. Authors award 1968), A Dissent on Bonhoeffer, 1975, Technology, Theology, and the Idea of Progress, 1991. With USN, 1945-46. Recipient Newberry ACM Faculty fellow, 1992-93, Templeton Found. Sci./Religion Course award, 1996. Mem. Internat. Bonhoeffer Soc., Hist. of Sci. Soc., Kierkegaard Soc. Home: 1757 Lincoln Ave Saint Paul MN 55105-1954 E-mail: dhhopper@earthlink.net.

HOPPER, STEPHEN RODGER, hospital administrator; b. Chgo., Aug. 28, 1949; s. Rodger Patterson and Dorothy Ann (Newberg) H.; m. Janet Sue Waddill, June 10, 1972; children: Nathan John, Amanda Sue. BA, Ill. Coll., 1971; MHA, U. Minn., 1974. Adminstrv. resident Rochester (Minn.) Meth. Hosp., 1973-74; dir. support svcs. Jennie Edmundson Hosp., Council Bluffs, Iowa, 1974-78; asst. adminstr. Trinity Meml. Hosp., Cudahy, Wis., 1978-83, sr. v.p. med. svcs., 1983-84; pres., chief exec. officer McDonough Dist. Hosp., Macomb, Ill., 1985—. Bd. dirs. Midamerica Nat. Bank, Canton, Ill., chmn bd., 2004-06; bd. dirs. VHA MidAm., 2007-. Bd. dirs. Macomb Area Indsl. Devel., 1985—, Wesley Village, 2007—. Fellow Am. Coll. Healthcare Execs.; mem. Ill. Hosp. Assn. (past pres. region 1-B, bd. dirs. 1992-95, mem. venture corp. bd. 1999—), Macomb C. of C. (bd. dirs. 1990-94), Rotary (pres.-elect Macomb 1995-96, pres. 1996-97, asst. dist. gov. 2000-03). Avocations: golf, reading, computers, travel. Home: 112 W Totem Trl Macomb IL 61455-1272 Office: McDonough Dist Hosp 525 E Grant St Macomb IL 61455-3318 Office Phone: 309-836-1675. Business E-Mail: srhopper@mdh.org.

HOPSON, JAMES WARREN, publishing executive; b. St. Louis, May 24, 1946; s. David Warren and Ruth L. (Dierkes) H.; m. Julie Ann Eastlack, Dec. 21, 1968; children: John, Benjamin, Gillian. BJ, U. Mo., 1968; MBA, Harvard U., 1973. Project mgr. Des Moines Register & Tribune, 1973-76, dir. ops., 1976-78, circulation dir., 1978-79; gen. mgr. Corpus Christi (Tex.) Caller Times, 1979-82; pub. Middlesex News, Framingham, Mass., 1982-88; pres. N.E. Group-Harte-Hanks Comms., Framingham, 1984-88; pub. The Press of Atlantic City, N.J., 1989-94; pres. Community Newspaper Co., Boston, 1994-95, Thomson Ctrl. Ohio, Newark, 1995-2000; pub. Wis. State Jour., Madison, Wis., 2000—; v.p. publishing Lee Enterprises, Madison, 2000—. Pres. Vol. Ctr. Atlantic County, 1992—; treas. DeCordova Mus., Lincoln, Mass., 1983-89, dir., 1983-89; sec. Family Health Svc. Ctrl. Ohio, 1997—, treas.; bd. dirs. Audit Bur. of Circulations, 1999—; bd, dirs. Madison Art Ctr., United Way of Dane County. 1st lt. U.S. Army, 1968-73, Vietnam. Mem. New Eng. Newspaper Assn. (chmn. circulation com. 1986-88), Mass. Newspaper Pub. Assn. (dir. 1984-88), Metrowest C. of C. (chmn. 1987-88, dir. audit bur. of circulations 1999—), Greater Madison C. of C. (bd. dirs.) Office: 1901 Fish Hatchery Rd Madison WI 53713-1248

HORBACH, LANCE, state official; b. Grundy Center, Iowa, Feb. 14, 1958; m. Jody Horbach; 4 children. Degree in arch., Iowa State U., 1980. Owner Horbach Furniture, 1984—99; commr. Tama County Zoning, 1996—98; indsl. liaison C.C., 1999; ins. salesperson, 2000. Mem. appropriations com.; mem. econ. devel. com.; chair mem. justice sys. appropriations com.; mem. labor and indsl. rels. com. Mem.: Farm Bur., Lions, Eagles. Republican. Roman Catholic. Office: State Capitol E 12th and Grand Des Moines IA 50319

HORISBERGER, DON HANS, conductor, musician; b. Millersburg, Ohio, Mar. 2, 1951; s. Hans and Jeannette (Grossniklaus) H. MusB, Capital U., Columbus, Ohio, 1973; MusM, orthwestern U., Evanston, Ill., 1974, MusD, 1985. Dir. music 1st Presbyn. Ch., Waukegan, Ill., 1976-88; with Chgo. Symphony Chorus, 1977—, sect. leader, 1984-91, asst. condr., 1990-98, assoc. conductor, 1998—; dir. Waukegan Concert Chorus, 1979-97; organist/choirmaster Ch. of the Holy Spirit, Lake Forest, Ill., 1988—. Lectr. in music Capital U., Columbus, Ohio, 1974-75; asst. to lang. coach Chgo. Symphony Chorus, 1978—. Fulbright-Hayes grantee 1975. Mem. Am. Choral Dirs. Assn. (chair cmty. choruses cen. div. spl. interest 1988-91), Assn. Profl. Vocal Ensembles (chorus Am.). E-mail: DHorisberger@chslf.org.

HORISZNY, LAURENE HELEN, lawyer; b. Lansing, Mich., Oct. 14, 1955; d. Walter and Jennie Ann (Pellpshen) H.; m. Richard C. Stavoe Jr., June 25, 1983; children: Andrea Kristen, Charles Ross. BA, Mich. State U., 1977; JD, Ohio State U., 1980. Bar: Mich. 1980, U.S. Dist. Ct. (ea. and we. dists.) Mich. 1980. Lawyer Consumers Power Co., Jackson, Mich., 1980-85; corp. counsel Ex-Cell-O Corp., Troy, Mich., 1985-86; sr. lawyer, asst. sec. BorgWarner Inc., Auburn Hills, Mich., 1986, v.p., gen. counsel, sec., 1993—2007, chief compliance officer, 2007—. Exec. bd. Land 'O Lakes coun. Boy Scouts Am., 1984-85. Mem. ABA, Mich. Bar Assn., Nature Conservancy. Avocations: scuba diving, cross country skiing, down-hill skiing, tennis. Office: Borg Warner 3800 Automation Ave Ste 500 Auburn Hills MI 48326-1786

HORN, CHARLES F., state senator, lawyer, electrical engineer; b. Bellefontaine, Ohio, July 20, 1924; s. Huber H. and Mary C. Horn; m. Shirley E. Horn, Aug. 1, 1953; children: Holly E., Charles J., Heidi E. BSEE, Purdue U., 1949; LLB, Cleve. State U., 1954. Application engr. Westinghouse Electric, Cleve., 1949-51; engr. Hertner Electric Co., Cleve., 1951-53; owner, engr. Lease Equipment Engring., Cleve., 1953-61; owner, ptnr. IRBATCO, Cleve., 1953-61; atty. Dayton, Ohio, 1961—; city coun. mem. City of Kettering, Ohio, 1963-69, mayor Ohio, 1969-80; county commr. Montgomery County, Ohio, 1980-84; mem. Ohio State Senate, Columbus, 1985—. Adv. panel Office of Sci. and Tech.; chair Econ. Devel., Tech. and Aerospace Com.; senate rep. Thomas Edison Tech. Bd., Devel. Financing Policy Bd., Ohio Indsl. Tng. Program Bd.; 3-term chair Fed. Labs Consortium Adv. Bd., 1980-83; cons. NSF; participant U.S. Conf. Mayors.; chair Ohio Econ. Study, 1997, 98, 99. Organizer Miami Valley Coun. Govts., Montgomery County; trustee Nat. Aviation Hall of Fame, Cox Arboretum, Cmty. Devel. Corp.; past trustee Grandview Hosp., Kettering C. of C.,

Dayton Area Sr. Citizens, Kidney Soc., Leukemia Soc., Pub. Opinion Ctr.; founder, chmn. Camp for Kids Who Can't; past adv. bd. Kettering Meml. Hosp.; past chmn. mcpl. sect. United Way Campaign; promoter formation of Wright Tech. Network; founder and past chair of Regional Econ. Strategies Forum. Served with U.S. Army Air Corps, 1942-45, CBI Theatre. Recipient numerous awards including Michael A. DeNunzio award U.S. Conf. of Mayors, 1980, Citizen award Pub. Children Svc. Assn. Ohio, 1988, Legislator of Yr. award Nat. Assn. Social Workers, 1989, Tech. award Dayton Area Tech. Network, 1989, Disting. Legis. Svc. award Ohio Human Svcs. Dirs. Assn., 1989, Pub. Svc. award Quality Dayton, 1990, Tom Bradley Regional Leadership award Nat. Assn. Regional Coun., 1989, Vol. of Yr. award Camp Kern YWCA, Pub. Svc. award Ohio Computer Tech. Ctr., 1990, Topcat Tech. award State of Ohio, 1997, Guardian of Small Bus. award Nat. Fedn. of Ind. Bus., 1998. Mem. Eta Kappa Nu, Tau Beta Pi. Republican. Avocations: tennis, golf, bicycling, horticulture. Office: Horn Coen & Rife 2323 W Schantz Kettering OH 45409 also: State Senate Ohio Senate Bldg Ste 222 Statehouse Columbus OH 43215

HORN, DAVID C., lawyer; b. Cin., Jan. 4, 1952; BA, Yale U., 1974; JD, Vanderbilt U., 1977. Bar: Ohio 1977. Ptnr. Frost & Jacobs (now Frost Brown Todd), Cin.; asst. gen. counsel AK Steel Holdings Corp., Middletown, Ohio, 2000—01, v.p., gen. counsel, 2001—05, sec., 2003—, head human resources, 2003—04, sr. v.p., gen. counsel, 2005—. Trustee Vol. Lawyers for the Poor Found. Mem.: Butler County Bar Assn., Ohio Bar Assn., Fed. Bar Assn., ABA, Order of the Coif. Office: AK Steel Holding Corp 703 Curtis St Middletown OH 45043

HORN, JOAN KELLY, political research and consulting firm executive; b. St. Louis, Oct. 18, 1936; M. E. Terrence Jones; 6 children from previous marriage. BA, U. Mo., St. Louis, 1973, MA, 1975. Pre-sch., elem. sch. Montessori tchr.; founder pre-schs. St. Louis and St. Joseph, Mo.; adj. faculty dept. polit. sci. U. Mo., St. Louis, 1982-86; with St. Louis County Office Community Devel., 1977-80, St. Louis Housing Authority, 1980-82; pres. Community Cons. Inc., 1975-90; elected to 102nd Congress from 2nd dist. Mo., 1990, mem., 1991-92; dir. community devel. agy. City of St. Louis. Author articles on pub. policy issues. Mem. Dem. State Com.; Dem. candidate for U.S. House, 1992, 96. Mem. U. Mo. Alumni Alliance, U. Mo.-St. Louis Alumni Assn. (bd. dirs.). Roman Catholic. Office: 1015 Locust Ste 1200pt 2 Saint Louis MO 63101

HORN, WALLY E., state legislator; b. Bloomfield, Iowa, Nov. 28, 1933; m. Phyllis Peterson. BS, Northeastern Mo. State, 1958, MA, 1962; postgrad., Tex. A&M U., U. Iowa. Tchr., coach Jefferson Sr. High, Cedar Rapids, Iowa; facilitator info. office Cedar Rapids Cmty. Sch. Dist.; mem. Iowa Ho. of Reps., Des Moines, 1972-82, Iowa Senate from 27th dist., Des Moines, 1982—; majority leader Iowa Senate, 1992-97. Mem. Christian Ch.; former bd. dirs. Linn County Hist. and Mus. Assn.; bd. dirs. Cedar Rapids Kids League Baseball, Iowa. With U.S. Army, 1953-55. Mem. Cedar Rapids Edn. Assn., Am. Legion, Kiwanis (past pres.). Democrat. Home: 101 Stoney Point Rd SW Cedar Rapids IA 52404-1069 Office: State Capitol Dist 27 E 9th And Grand Des Moines IA 50319-0001 E-mail: wally_horn@legis.state.ia.us.

HORNBACH, DANIEL J., biologist, educator; BS in Biology magna cum laude, U. Dayton, 1974, MS in Biology, 1976; PhD in Zoology, Miami U., Ohio, 1980. Asst. prof. dept. biology U. Va., Va., 1980—84, Macalester Coll., St. Paul, 1984—87, assoc. prof. dept. biology, 1987—93, prof. dept. biology, 1993—97, DeWitt Wallace prof. dept. biology, 1998—, chair dept. biology, 1996—99, provost, 1993—95, 1999—2005, dean, 1999—2005. Mem. faculty Mountain Lake Biol. Sta. U. Va., 1981, 82, 84; team mem. Higginsi Eye Pearly Mussel Endangered Species Recover Team U.S. Fish and Wildlife Svc., 1995—; adj. prof. grad. faculty divsn. water quality dept. fisheries and wildlife U. Minn., 1996—. Assoc. editor: Am. Midland Naturalist, 1995—2001. Recipient Alumni Spl. Achievement award, U. Dayton, 1994; grantee, NSF, 1987, 1988, U.S. Army Corps of Engrs., 1987—90, 1996, Pew Charitable Trusts, 1990, Blandin Found., 1990—91, Minn. Dept. atural Resources, 1990—91, 1992—93, US EPA, 1991, 1992—96, Wis. Dept. Natural Resources, 1992, 1997—98, U.S. Nat. Pk. Svc., 1993—96, 1997, 1998, 2000—02, 2001—04, 2004—, U.S. Fish and Wildlife Svc., 1994—95, Legis. Commn. on Minn. Resources, 1997—98, 1999—2001. Mem.: N.Am. Benthological Soc., Malacological Soc. London (Sir Charles Maurice Yonge award 2002), Coun. on Undergrad. Rsch., Am. Malacological Union. Office: Macalester College 1600 Grand Ave Saint Paul MN 55105

HORNBAKER, ALICE JOY, writer; b. Cin., Feb. 3, 1927; children: Christopher Albert, Holly Jo, Joseph Bernard III. BA cum laude and honors in Journalism, San Jose State U., Calif., 1949. Asst. woman's editor San Jose Mercury-News, 1949-55; columnist Life After 50, Cin. Post newspaper, 1993—2002; freelance writer Cin., 1995—; writer, broadcaster The Alice Hornbaker Show www.wmkvfm.org and 89.3 FM Cin., 1996; freelance feature writer www.grandparentworld.com; broadcaster www.wmkvm.com. Owner, mgr. Frisch's Big Boy Restaurant, Cin., 1955—68; dir. pub. rels. Children's Home Soc. Calif., Santa Clara, 1968—71; asst. dir. pub. rels. United Fund Calif., Santa Clara, 1971—; editor Tristate Sunday Enquirer mag., 1986—89, columnist Generations, 1976—93; editl. dir. Writers Digest Sch., Cin., 1971—75; columnist, critic, mag. writer, reporter, copy editor Tempo sect. Cin. Enquirer, 1975—93, book editor, critic, columnist on aging, feature writer Tempo sect.; reporter news segments on aging Sta. WKRC-TV, 1983—86; commentator on aging Sta. WMLX-AM, 1991—93; broadcaster, writer Sta. WMKV-FM, 1995—; tchr. adult edn. Forest Hills Sch. Dist., Thomas More Coll., 1973—. Author: (Book) Preventive Care: Easy Exercise Against Aging, 1974; columnist: internet 3 times weekly Life After 50; contbr. articles to various publs. including: People, Modern Maturity, St. Anthony Messenger, N.Y. Times Sun mag., Ohio Heitage mag.others., fiction to Enquirer mag. Recipient Bronze award in Am. health journalism, Am. Chiropractic Assn., 1977, 1978, Golden Image award, Assn. Ohio Philanthropic Homes, 1989, 1st pl. for feature writing, Cin. Editors Assn., 1983, 1st and 3rd pl. feature writing awards, Ohio Profl. Writers, Inc., 1992, Journalist of Yr. award, Ohio chpt. Am. Coll. Health Care Adminstrs., 1993, Journalism award, Greater Cin. Joint Coun. on Geriat. Care, 1993, Bronze award, Nat. Mature Media, 2003, 2005. Mem. Blue Pencil of Ohio State U. (pres. 1981-82), Women in Comm., Ohio Newspaper Women's Assn. (v.p. 1981-83, 1st pl. human interest story 1977-85, 2d pl. column award 1979, Tops in Ohio award 1982, M.M. McMullen 2d pl. award, 1982, Recognition award 1985, 4th pl. on aging Nat. Legacies contest 1994), Soc. Profl. Journalists (treas. 1981-82), Ohio Press Women, Inc. (1st and 3d pl. awards for feature writing 1992). E-mail: ajhornbaker@yahoo.com.

HORNE, JOHN R., farm equipment company executive; b. Gary, Ind., 1938; Grad., Purdue U., 1960, Bradley U., 1964. Group v.p., gen. mgr. Navistar Internat. Transp. Corp.; pres., COO, now CEO Navistar Internat. Corp., 1995—, also bd. dirs., 1995—; pres., CEO Navistar Internat. Corp. and Internat. Truck & Engine Corp., 1995—; also chmn. bd. dirs. Navistar Internat. Corp. Mem.Soc. Automotive Engrs. (chmn. fin. com.). Office: Internatl Truck & Engine Corp PO Box 1488 Warrenville IL 60555-7488

HORNING, DANIEL D., underwriter; B Gen. Studies, U. Mich., 1982. Ptnr. Grand Haven (Mich.) group Northwestern Mut. Fin. Network. Bd. regents U. Mich., Ann Arbor, 1994—. Mem.: U. Mich. Alumni Club (past pres.), Pres.' Club, Victors Club, Mich. M Club. Republican. Office: 16964 Robbins Rd Ste 100 Grand Haven MI 49417

HOROWITZ, JACK, biochemistry educator; b. Vienna, Nov. 25, 1931; came to U.S., 1938; s. Joseph and Florence (Gutterman) H.; m. Carole Anne Sager, June 11, 1961; children— Michael Joseph, Jeffrey Frederick. BS, CCNY, 1952; PhD, Ind. U., 1957. Rsch. assoc. Columbia U., NYC, 1957-61; asst. prof. biochemistry Iowa State U., Ames, 1961-65, assoc. prof. biochemistry, 1965-71, prof. biochemistry, 1971-95, Univ. prof., 1995-2000, Univ. prof. emeritus, 2000—, chmn. dept. biochemistry, 1971-74, chmn. molecular, cellular and devel. biology program, 1977-80. Vis. scholar Rockefeller U., N.Y.C., 1968; vis. prof. Yale U., 1974-75; vis. scientist MIT, 1990-91; program dir. biophysics and biochemistry NSF, 1993-94. Contbr. articles to profl. jours. NSF fellow, 1952-54, 57-59; IH and NSF grantee, 1961—; recipient faculty citation Iowa State U., 1989. Mem. RNA Soc., Am. Soc. Biochemistry and Molecular Biology, AAAS, Phi Beta Kappa, Sigma Xi, Phi Kappa Phi Jewish. Home: 2014 Country Club Blvd Ames IA 50014-7013 Office: Iowa State U Dept Biochemistry Biophys Ames IA 50011-0001 Business E-Mail: jhoro@iastate.edu.

HOROWITZ, SAMUEL BORIS, biomedical researcher, educational consultant; b. Perth Amboy, NJ, Aug. 26, 1927; s. Sol and Lillian (Levine) H.; m. Joan Hughes, June 15, 1956 (div. 1971); m. Marian Sylvia Herman, May 23, 1973 (div. 1986); 1 child, Ann Julia AB, Hunter Coll., NYC, 1951; PhD, U. Chgo., 1956. Research assoc. Eastern Pa. Psychiat. Inst., Phila., 1958-62; vis. investigator Inst. Physiol. and Med. Biophysics U. Uppsala, Sweden, 1962-63; head lab. A. Einstein Med. Ctr., Phila., 1963-72; chief cellular physiology lab. Mich. Cancer Found., Detroit, 1972-93, chmn. dept. biology, 1975-78, chmn. dept. physiology and biophysics, 1981-93. Contbr. articles to profl. jours. Served with U.S. Army, 1946-47 Fellow AAAS; mem. Am. Assn. Cancer Research, Am. Soc. Cell Biology, Sigma Xi. Home and Office: 4159 Woodland Dr Ann Arbor MI 48103-9775 Home Phone: 734-426-2403; Office Phone: 734-426-2403. E-mail: sbg3210@aol.com.

HORR, WILLIAM HENRY, retired lawyer; b. Portsmouth, Ohio, Sept. 23, 1914; s. Charles Chick and Effie (Amberg) H.; m. Marjorie Bell Marshall, Aug. 31, 1940; children— Robert W., Thomas M., Catherine, James C., Elizabeth; m. 2d Wilma Crawford, Mar. 12, 1988. AB, Ohio Wesleyan U., 1936; JD, U. Cin., 1939. Bar: Ohio 1939. Practice in, Portsmouth, 1939-42, 45-99; atty. Skelton, Kahl, Horr, Marshall & Burton, 1939-42, 45-78; spl. agt. FBI, Louisville, Indpls., Newark, 1942-45; substitute judge Mcpl. Ct., Portsmouth, 1955-80; gen. counsel Ohio Wesleyan U., 1966-70. Mem. Portsmouth Bd. Edn., 1947-60; pres. Portsmouth YMCA.; trustee Ohio U. Portsmouth Br., Shawnee State C.C., 1975-80, Ohio Wesleyan U., 1953-68; chmn. bd. Hill View Retirement Ctr., 1973-85. Recipient Disting. Svc. award Portsmouth Jr. C. of C., 1947. Mem. Ohio Bar Assn. (past mem. exec. com.), Portsmouth Bar Assn. (past pres.), Phi Delta Phi, Phi Kappa Psi, Omicron Delta Kappa, Rotary (past pres.). Republican. Methodist. Home: 1610 28Th #3329 Portsmouth OH 45662-2641

HORRELL, KAREN HOLLEY, insurance company executive, lawyer; b. Augusta, Ga., July 10, 1952; d. Dudley Cornelius and Eleanor (Shouppe) Holley; m. Jack E. Horrell, Aug. 14, 1976. BS, Berry Coll., 1974; JD, Emory U., 1976. Bar: Ohio 1977. Counsel Am. Fin. Corp., 1980-81; sec., asst. sec. numerous other fin. and ins. cos.; gen. counsel numerous subsidiaries Great Am. Ins. Co., corp. counsel Cin., 1977-80, v.p., gen. counsel, sec., 1981-85, sr. v.p., gen. counsel, sec., bd. dirs., 1985—; pres. corp. svcs. Great Am. Ins. Property & Casualty Group, 1999—. Bd. dirs. Tri-Health, Inc., Bethesda, Inc, spkr. in field, 2005. Trustee Cmty. Chest, 1987—91, Seven Hills Sch., 1991—2000, v.p., 1995—99; mem. cabinet United Appeal, 1984; bd. dirs. YWCA, 1984—90, v.p. fin., 1986—89; mem. Hamilton County Blue Ribbon Task Force on Child Abuse and Neglect Svcs., 1989—91; trustee Ohio Ins. Inst., 1994—2000, chair, 1996—99, Bethesda Hosp. Inc.; chair Ohio Joint Underwriting Assn., 1992—97; trustee Berry Coll., 1999—; mem. Hamilton County Hosp. Commn., 1999—, vice chair, 2002—; bd. dirs. Children's Home, 2001—. Mem. ABA, Cin. Bar Assn. (admissions com. 1978-91, nominating com. 1987-90). Democrat. Office: Great Am Ins Co 580 Walnut St Cincinnati OH 45202-3110 Home: 11817 Quarterhorse Ct Cincinnati OH 45249-1279

HORSAGER, KENT R., former grain exchange executive; BS in agrl. econ., U. Minn.; MS in agrl. econ., U. Calif., Davis. Pres. Horsager Trading Co., 1987—2000; bd. dirs. Mpls. Grain Exch., 1991—, bd. chmn., 1996—99, CEO and pres., 2000—05. Oilseed and product mcht. Cargill, Inc., Internat. Oilseed Processing Group; econ. lectr. U. Mainz, Germersheim, Germany; mktg. cons. Superior Farming Co., Germersheim, Germany.

HORSCH, LAWRENCE LEONARD, venture capitalist, corporate financial executive; b. Mpls., Dec. 2, 1934; s. Leonard Charles and Cecilia May (Chamberlain) H.; m. Kathleen Joanne Simmer, Aug. 25, 1956; children: Daniel Lawrence, Timothy John, Christopher Girard, Catherine Jessica, Sarah Elisabeth. BA with honors, Coll. St. Thomas, 1957; MBA, Northwestern U., 1958. Investment banker Paine Webber Jackson & Curtis, Mpls., 1961-67; v.p. N.Am. Fin. Corp., Mpls., 1967-71; pres. Eagle Investment Corp., Mpls., 1971-87; chmn., CEO Munsingwear Inc., Mpls., 1987—90; chmn. bd. Eagle Mgmt. & Fin. Corp., Mpls., 1990—. Chmn. bd. dirs. Sci. Med. Life Sys., Maple Grove, Minn., 1971-94, Leuthold Funds, Inc.; bd. dirs. Boston Scientific Corp., 1995-2003, Med. C.V. Inc., 2003-05. 1st lt. USAF, 1959-61. Mem. Fin. Analysts Fedn., Mpls. Rotary, Minikahda Country Club. Home: 1404 Hilltop Rdg Saint Joseph WI 54082-2013 Office: Eagle Mgmt & Fin Corp PO Box 235 Stillwater MN 55082-0235 Office Phone: 715-549-5294.

HORSCH, ROBERT B., biotechnologist; b. Pitts. m. Linda Horsch; children: Elsa, Laura, Michael. BS in Biology, U. Calif., Riverside, 1974, PhD in Genetics, 1979. V.p. product and technology cooperation Monsanto, Middleton, Wis. Postdoctoral fellow plant physiology U. Sask, 1979—81. Recipient Nat. Medal Tech, 1998, Disting. Alumnus award, Univ. Calif. Riverside, 2001. Achievements include being on team that devel. world's first practical sys. to introduce improved genes into crop plants and gene transfer capability to most important crops including soybean, corn, wheat, cotton. Avocations: backpacking, bike riding, cross country skiing, pottery, tinkering with cars. Office: Monsanto Co 8520 University Green Middleton WI 53562 E-mail: robert.b.horsch@monsanto.com.

HORST, DEENA LOUISE, state legislator; b. Sacramento, Feb. 14, 1944; s. Orlo John and Louise Helena (Schultze) Poovey; m. Gordon Lee Horst, 1966; children: Randall, Rebecca. BSE, Emporia State U., 1966, MA, 1972; postgrad., Kans. State U., 1993—. Elem. tchr. Peabody Sch., 1966-68; mid. sch. art tchr., dept. chmn. South Mid. Sch., Unified Sch. Dist. # 305, 1968—; mem. from dist. 69 Kans. State Ho. of Reps., 1995—. Vice chmn. Kans. 2000 com., K-12 edn. com.; chmn. e-govt. com., vice chmn. higher edn. com., chmn. arts and cultural resources joint com. Kans. House of Reps.; chmn. Kans. Commemorative Coin Commn. State and nat. ofcl. U.S. Jaycee Women, 1968-84; sec. Saline County Rep. Ctrl. Com., Kans., 1992-95; mem. adv. bd. Consumer Credit Counseling, Hertzler Health Found. Named Outstanding State Pres., U.S. Jaycee Women, 1979-80; co-recipient Master Tchr. award State of Kans., 1991. Mem. C. of C., Phi Alpha, Alpha Theta Rho, Phi Delta Kappa, Epsilon Sigma Alpha (Zone Outstanding Sister award 1990), Edn. Budget Com., Legis. Edn. Planning Com., Delta Kappa Gamma. Republican. Address: 920 S 9th St Salina KS 67401-4806 Office Phone: 785-296-7501. Personal E-mail: deena@worldlinc.net.

HORST, J. ROBERT, lawyer; b. 1943; BA, Case Western Reserve U., 1965; JD, Boston U. Law, 1971. Assoc. gen. counsel Eaton Corp., Cleve., 1991—98, dep. gen. counsel, 1998—99, v.p., gen. counsel, 2000—05. Office: Eaton Corp Eaton Ctr 1111 Superior Ave NE Cleveland OH 44114-2584

HORSTMANN, JAMES DOUGLAS, retired academic administrator; b. Davenport, Iowa, Oct. 2, 1933; s. Leonard A. and Agnes A. (Erhke) H.; m. Carol H. Griffiths, Sept. 8, 1956; children: Kent, Karen, Diane. BA, Augustana Coll., 1955. C.P.A., Ill., Wis. Staff acct., auditor Arthur Andersen & Co., Chgo., 1955-61; v.p., controller Harry S. Manchester, Inc., Madison, Wis., 1961-65; sr. v.p. fin., treas. H. C. Prange Co., Sheboygan, Wis., 1965-83, also dir.; dir. planned giving Augustana Coll., Rock Island, Ill., 1983-85, v.p. for devel., 1985-93, v.p. planned giving, 1993-98, v.p. emeritus, 1998—; pres. Schonstedt Instrument Co., 1993-95, ret., 1995—. Chmn. Wis. Mchts. Fedn.; bd. dirs. First Wis. Nat. Bank, Fond du Lac, 1975-83; cons. Score, 2004. Chmn. Sheboygan County (Wis.) Rep. Party, 1969-70; vice-chmn. Wis. 6th Congl. Dist., 1972-73, Rock Island County Reps., 2000-02; del. Nat. Rep. Conv., 1976; campaign chmn. Sheboygan United Way, 1977, treas., 1973-75, v.p., 1975-78, pres., 1978-79; bd. dirs. Public Expenditure Survey Wis., 1981-83, Rock Island YMCA, 1986-87, Franciscan Health Care Systems, 1988-92, Christ Luth. H.S. Found., 2000-03, Alternatives for the Older Adult, 2001—, v.p. 2003, pres., 2004-07, Marriage and Family Counseling, 2003—, Thrivent for Lutherans, 2003; v.p. Sheboygan Arts Found., 1973-75; v.p., bd. dirs. Sheboygan Retirement Home, 1977-83; bd. dirs. Franciscan Mental Health Ctr., 1984-94, pres., 1985-88; trustee Friendship Manor, 1993-2003, pres., 2000-02; trustee Coun. on Children at Risk, 1989-2001, Franciscan Med. Ctr., 1990-92, Cmty. Found. of the Great River Bend, 2002—, chmn., 2005-06; trustee Villa Montessori Sch., 1999-2005, pres. 2000-04; v.p. German Am. Heritage Ctr., 2000-05; treas. Trinity Vis. Nurse/Homecare Assn., 2001, vice chair, 2004, Trinity Regional Health Sys., trustee 2007; Pathway Hospice, 2001; bd. dirs. Augustana Hist. Soc., 2001—, Quad Cities Health Initiatives, 2005—. With USN, 1955-57. Named Outstanding Fund Raising Exec. Nat. Soc. Fund Raising Execs., 1992; recipient Outstanding Svc. award Augustana Coll., 1979, Jr. Achievement Free Enterprise Found., 2003; recipient award Modern Woodmen Am. Cmty. Svc., 2007. Mem. Am. Heart Assn. (bd. dirs. Quad City chpt. 1999—, pres. 2002-), Am. Cancer Soc. (bd. dirs. Rock Island unit 1992-2001), Wis. Inst. CPAs, Ill. Soc. CPAs, Sheboygan County Assn. CPAs, Fin. Execs. Inst. (dir.), Quad-City Estate Planning Coun., Augustana Hist. Soc. (bd. dirs. 1999—), Augustana Coll. Alumni Assn. (pres. 1970-71), Econ. Club Sheboygan (pres. 1976-77), Kiwanis. Lutheran. Home: 1245 36th Ave Rock Island IL 61201-6022

HORVITZ, MICHAEL JOHN, lawyer; b. Cleve., Feb. 15, 1950; s. Harry Richard and Lois Joy (Unger) H.; m. Jane Rosenthal, Aug. 25, 1979; children: Katherine R., Elizabeth R. BS in Econs., U. Pa., 1972; JD, U. Va., 1975; LLM in Taxation, NYU, 1980. Bar: Ohio 1975, Fla. 1976, NY 2007. Assoc. Hahn, Loeser, Freedheim, Dean & Wellman, Cleve., 1975-78; counsel Hollywood, Inc., Fla., 1978-79; assoc. Jones Day, Cleve., 1980-85, ptnr., 1985-2000, of counsel, 2001—. Adv. bd. Kirtland Capital Ptnrs., L.P., 1992-2007; chmn. Parkland Mgmt. Co., 1992—; vice chmn. Horvitz Newspapers, Inc., 1994—; pres. H.R.H. Family Found., 1992—; chmn. H.R.H. Family Trust, 1992-2003; corp. adv. IMG Worldwide, Inc., 1999-2004, chmn. bd. dirs., 2004. Trustee Jewish Cmty. Fedn. Cleve., 1993-99, 2002-2007, Case Western Res. U., 1992-2005, Musical Arts Assn., 1992—, Cleve. Ctr. Econ. Edn., 1992-95, Am. Cancer Soc., Cuyahoga County unit, 1989-95, Hathaway Brown Sch., Mt. Sinai Med. Ctr., Cleve. chpt. Am. Jewish Com., 1984-95, Montefiore Home for the Elderly, 1982-90, Health Hill Hosp. for Children, 1982-95, bd. pres., 1987-89; bd. dirs. Cleve. Mus. Art, 1991—, pres. bd., 1996-2001, chmn. bd., 2001—; bd. dirs. U. Va. Law Sch. Found., 1999—, pres., 2002-05, chmn. bd., 2005-; trustee Cleve. Clinic Found., 2006-. Office: Jones Day 901 Lakeside Ave E Cleveland OH 44114-1190 also: Parkland Mgmt Co 1001 Lakeside Ave E Ste 900 Cleveland OH 44114-1172

HORWICH, ALLAN, lawyer; b. Des Moines, Apr. 8, 1944; s. Joseph Maurice and Bernice (Davidson) Horwich; m. Carolyn Ruth Allen, Feb. 28, 1975; children: Benjamin, Diana, Eleanor, Flannery. AB, Princeton U., 1966; JD, U. Chgo., 1969. Bar: Ill. 1969, U.S. Dist. Ct. (no. dist.) Ill. 1969, U.S. Ct. Appeals (7th cir.) 1971, U.S. Supreme Ct. 1976, U.S. Ct. Appeals (10th cir.) 1983, U.S. Dist. Ct. (ctrl. dist.) Ill. 1990, U.S. Dist. Ct. (ea. dist.) Wis. 1995, U.S. Dist. Ct. (ea. dist.) Mich. 1995, U.S. Ct. Appeals (6th cir.) 1996. Assoc. Schiff Hardin LLP, Chgo., 1969-74, ptnr., 1975—, vice-chmn., 1989-95. Adj. prof. law orthwestern U. Sch. Law, 1999—2000, sr. lectr. law, 2000—; mem. adv. bd. Wall St. Lawyer. Contbr. articles to profl. jours. Fellow: Am. Bar Found. (life). Home: 216 W Concord Ln Chicago IL 60614-5743 Office: Schiff Hardin LLP 6600 Sears Tower Chicago IL 60606 Home Phone: 312-649-5618; Office Phone: 312-258-5618. Business E-Mail: ahorwich@schiffhardin.com.

HORWICH, GEORGE, economist, educator; b. Detroit, July 23, 1924; s. Charles and Rose (Katzman) H.; m. Geraldine Lessans, Dec. 27, 1953; children: Ellen Beth, Karen Louise, Robert Lloyd, Susan Jean. Student, Wayne State U., 1942-43, 46, Ind. U., 1943-44; AM, U. Chgo., 1951, PhD, 1954. Lectr. econs. Extension Ctrs. Ind. U., Gar and Calumet, 1949-52, instr. econs. Bloomington, 1952-55; rsch. assoc. Nat. Bur. Econ. Rsch., NYC, 1955-56; from asst. prof. to prof. econs. Purdue U., West Lafayette, Ind., 1956-99, chmn. econs. dept., 1974-78, Burton D. Morgan prof. for study pvt. enterprise, 1981-94, prof. emeritus, 1999—. Sr. rsch. assoc. Brookings Instn., Washington, 1958-62; sr. economist U.S. Dept. Energy, Washington, 1978-80; spl. asst. for contingency planning U.S. Dept. Energy, 1984; adj. scholar Am. Enterprise Inst., 1984—; collaborating scientist energy divsn. Oak Ridge Nat. Lab., 1988-94; mem. U.S. Treasury Cons. Group, Washington, 1969; cons. Fed. Res. Bank, Chgo., 1971; vis. prof. econs. U. Calif., San Diego, 1971-72, People's Univ. of China, Beijing, 1992, Kobe (Japan) U. Commerce, 1996-97; vis. scholar Victoria U., New Zealand, 1997; staff Ind. Coun. Econ. Edn., West Lafayette, 1974—, Ctr. Pub. Policy and Pub. Adminstrn., Purdue U., West Lafayette, 1977—; advisor Econ. Inst. Rsch. and Edn., Boulder, Colo., 1977—; cons. U.S. Dept. Energy, 1980-88, Fortune 500 cos., 1965—, U.S. Dept. State, Washington, 1982, 92, Hudson Inst., 1991; vis. prof. Yokohama (Japan) City U., 2000; lectr. Wabash Area Lifetime Learning Assn, 2003—. Author: Money, Capital and Prices, 1964; (with others) Costs and Benfits of a Protective Tariff on Refined Petroleum Products After Crude Oil Decontrol, 1980, Energy: An Economic Analysis, 1983; (with D.L. Weimer) Oil Price Shocks, Market Response and Contingency Planning, 1984; Responding to International Oil Crises, 1988; editor: Monetary Process and Policy, 1967, (with P.A. Samuelson) Trade, Stability, and Macroeconomics, 1974; (with J.P. Quirk) Essays in Contemporary Fields of Economics, 1981; (with E.J. Mitchell) Policies for Coping with Oil-Supply Disruptions, 1982, Energy Use in Transportation Contingency Planning, 1983; (with G.J. Lynch) Food, Policy and Politics, 1989; contbr. articles to profl. jours. With U.S. Army, 1943-46, ETO. NSF grantee; Fulbright rschr., 1996-97. Mem. Internat. Assn. Energy Econs., Am. Econ. Assn., Midwest Econs. Assn., Mont. Pelerin Soc., Nat. Assn. Scholars, Phila. Soc., Assn. Pub. Policy Analysis and Mgmt. Home: 120 Seminole Dr West Lafayette IN 47906-2116 Office: Purdue U Dept Econs 403 W State St West Lafayette IN 47907-2056

HORWITZ, IRWIN DANIEL, otolaryngologist, educator; b. Chgo., Mar. 31, 1920; s. Sol and Belle (Stern) H.; m. Isabel Morwitz, July 23, 1944; children— Steven, Judd, Clare. BS, U. Ill., 1941, MD, 1943. Intern Cook County Hosp., Chgo., 1944; resident Ill. Eye and Ear Infirmary, Chgo., 1946-48; practice otolaryngology Chgo., 1948—; clin. prof., head divsn. otolaryngology Chgo. Med. Sch., 1969; prof. Rush Med. Sch., 1976—; formerly chief divsn. otolaryngology Mt. Sinai Hosp., former pres. med. staff. Contbr. articles profl. jours. Served to capt., M.C. AUS, 1944-46. Fellow A.C.S.; mem. AMA, Chgo. Otol. and Laryngol. Assn., Am. Acad. Ophthalmology and Otolaryngology, Ill., Chgo. med. socs. Office: 9669 Kenton Ave Skokie IL 60076-1266

HORWITZ, RALPH IRVING, internist, epidemiologist, educator, dean; b. Phila., June 25, 1947; s. Sidney and Sara (Altus) H.; m. Sarah McCue, Aug. 5, 1970; 1 child, Rebecca Margaret Taylor. BS, Albright Coll., 1969; MD, Pa. State U., 1973. Diplomate Am. Bd. Internal Medicine. Intern McGill U., Royal Victoria Hosp., Montreal, Que., Canada, 1973-75; postdoctoral tng. in epidemiology, clin. scholars program Yale U. Sch. Medicine, New Haven, 1975; sr. resident Harvard U., Mass. Gen. Hosp., Boston, 1977-78; co-dir. clin. scholars program Yale U. Sch. Medicine, New Haven, 1978—2003, asst. prof. medicine, 1978-82, assoc. prof. medicine and epidemiology, 1982-88, prof., 1988—2003, chief gen. internal medicine, 1982-94, vice chmn. internal medicine, 1993-94, chmn. internal medicine, 1994—2003, Harold H. Hines Jr. Prof. Medicine and Epidemiology, 1991—2003; chief Beeson Med. Svc. Yale-New Haven Hosp., 1993—2003; v.p. med. affairs Case Western Res. U., Cleveland, Ohio, 2003—06, dean sch. medicine, 2003—06; dir. Case Rsch. Inst., 2003—06; Arthur Bloomfield prof. and chmn. dept. medicine Stanford U. Sch. Medicine, Calif., 2006—. Mem. nat. selection com. faculty scholar program Henry J. Kaiser Family Found., Menlo Park, Calif., 1987-90; mem. com. allocating resources in biomed. rsch. Inst. Medicine, Washington, 1988-89; mem. profl. standards rev. orgn., Woodbridge, Conn., 1980-82; editorial bd. The Lancet, 1991-96; past chmn. bd. dirs. Am. Bd. Internal Medicine. Contbr. over 200 articles to profl. jours. Trustee Am. Bd. Internal Medicine Found. Recipient Faculty Scholar award Kaiser Family Found., 1981-86 Fellow ACP, AAAS, Am. Coll. Epidemiology, Pa. State U. Alumni Assn.; mem. Am. Soc. Clin. Investigation, Assn. Am. Physicians, Am. Epidemiol. Soc., Inst. Medicine. Jewish. Office: Stanford Univ Sch Medicine 300 Pasteur Dr S-102 Stanford CA 94305 Office Phone: 650-736-1484. Business E-Mail: ralph.horwitz@stanford.edu.

HORWITZ, RONALD M., business administration educator; b. Detroit, June 25, 1938; s. Harry and Annette (Levine) H.; m. Carol Bransky, Mar. 30, 1961; children: Steven, Michael, David, Robert. BS, Wayne State U., 1959, MBA, 1961; PhD, Mich. State U., 1964. CPA, Mich. Prof. fin. U. Detroit, 1963-73, 75-79; healthcare cons., dir. personnel devel. Arthur Young & Co., Detroit, 1974-75; prof. fin., dean Sch. Bus. Adminstrn. Oakland U., Rochester, Mich., 1979-90, acting v.p. for acad. affairs, 1992-93, prof. fin., 1991—2002, prof. emeritus of fin., 2002—. Contbr. articles to profl. jours. Bd. trustees Providence Hosp. and Med. Ctr., 1995—, The Roeper Sch., 1996—; pub. mem. Greater Detroit Health Coun., 1980—; mem. fin. com. Ascension Health, St. Louis, 1998-2001, audit com., 2001—; audit com. Daus. of Charity Nat. Health System, 1988-93; mem. adv. bd. Providence Hosp., Southfield, 1980-95. Stonier fellow Am. Bankers Assn., 1963. Mem. Healthcare Fin. Mgmt. Assn. (bd. dirs. 1976-80), Mich. Assn. CPA's (grantee 1960), Fin. Mgmt. Assn., Acctg. Aid Soc. Detroit (founder), Mich. Bridge Assn. (pres. 1974-76). Avocation: bridge (life master). E-mail: horwitz@oakland.edu.

HORWOOD, RICHARD M., lawyer; b. East Cleveland, Ohio, Apr. 7, 1940; s. Manuel L. and Esther L. (Schwartz) H.; m. Janet Hershfield, June 30, 1968; children: Sarah Ann, Daniel Lewis. BA, Colgate U., 1962; LLB, U. Pa., 1965; MBA, Am. U., 1967; LLM in Taxation, George Washington U., 1969. Bar: Ill. 1970, US Dist. Ct. (no. dist. Ill.) 1970. Ptnr. Horwood, Marcus & Berk, Chartered, Chgo., 1983—. Adv. bd. US Tax Mgmt., Washington, 1980. Contbr. articles to profl. jours. Mem. Chgo. Fund on Aging and Disabilities, 1995; bd. dirs. Chgo. Estate Planning Coun.; mem. planned giving adv. bd. Art. Inst. Chgo., Shedd Aquarium; pres. Meals on Wheels Chgo. Named one of Top 100 Attys., Worth mag., 2005—06. Office: Horwood Marcus & Berk Chartered Ste 3700 180 N LaSalle Chicago IL 60601 Office Phone: 312-606-3230. E-mail: rhorwood@hmblaw.com.

HOSCH, JULIE, state senator; b. Delaware County, Iowa, Dec. 7, 1939; Attended, Kirkwood C.C., N.E. Iowa C.C. Mem. Iowa State Senate, Des Moines, 2003—, vice chair agr. com., mem. edn. com., human resources com., local govt. com. and ways and means com. Mem.: Iowa Cattlewomen's Assn., Am. Legion Aux. Republican. Address: 403 Hayes St SW Cascade IA 50233

HOSKINS, RICHARD JEROLD, lawyer; s. Walter Jerold and Gladys (Gaither) H.; children: Stephen Weston, Philip Richard. BA, U. Kans., 1967; JD, Northwestern U., 1970. Bar: Y 1971, Ill. 1976, US Supreme Ct. 1982. Assoc. Davis Polk & Wardwell, NYC, 1970-73; asst. US atty., So. Dist. NY, 1973-76; assoc. Schiff Hardin & Waite, Chgo., 1976-77, ptnr., 1978—. Adj. prof. U. Va. Law Sch., 1980-83, Northwestern U. Law Sch., 1992-98, sr. lectr., 1999—. Contbr. articles to profl. jours. Chancellor emeritus Episcopal Diocese of Chgo.; bd. visitors and govs. St. John's Coll. Named Hon. Canon, St. James Cathedral, Chgo.; recipient Childres Meml. award for Tchg. Excellence, Northwestern U. Sch. Law, 2007. Fellow Am. Coll. Trial Lawyers, Am. Bar Found.; mem. ABA, Ill. State Bar Assn., Chgo. Bar Assn., 7th Cir. Bar Assn., Assn. of Bar of City of NY, Chgo. Coun. Lawyers, Law Club Chgo., Met. Club (Chgo.). Episcopalian. Office: 6600 Sears Tower Chicago IL 60606 Office Phone: 312-258-5509. Business E-Mail: rhoskins@schiffhardin.com.

HOSMER, CRAIG WILLIAM, state legislator; b. Springfield, Mo., Mar. 16, 1959; BA, U. Mo. Columbia, 1982; JD, George Washington U., 1986. State rep. Dist. 138 Mo. State Congress, 1991—. Chmn. criminal law com., mem. higher edn. com., civil and adminstrv. law com., correctional insts. com., judiciary com. Office: State Capitol Rm 404 A Jefferson City MO 65101

HOSTETTLER, JOHN NATHAN, former congressman; b. Evansville, Ind., July 19, 1961; s. Earl Eugene and Esther Aline (Hollingsworth) H.; m. Elizabeth Ann Hamman, Nov. 12, 1983; children: Matthew, Amanda, Jaclyn, Jared BSME, Rose-Hulman Inst. Tech., 1983. Reg. profl. engr. Engr. So. Ind. Gas and Electric, Evansville, 1986-94; mem. US Congress from 8th Ind. dist., Washington, 1995—2007; mem. agrl. com., homeland security com., judiciary com. Vice chair House Armed Services Comm. Special Oversight Panel on Terrorism, 2001—07. Deacon 12th Avenue Gen. Baptist, 1986-1995. Republican. Baptist.

HOTCHKISS, EUGENE, III, retired academic administrator; b. Berwyn, Ill., Apr. 1, 1928; s. Eugene and Jeanette (Kennan) H.; m. Suzanne Ellen Troxell, Nov. 17, 1962; 1 dau., Ellen Sinclair. AB, Dartmouth Coll., 1950; PhD, Cornell U., 1960; LLD (hon.), Ill. Coll., 1976, Lake Forest Coll., 1993. Asst. to dean Dartmouth Coll., 1953-54, asst. dean, 1954-55, asso. dean, 1958-60; asst. dean Cornell U., Ithaca, N.Y., 1955-58; dean students, lectr. history Harvey Mudd Coll., Claremont, Calif., 1960-63, dean coll., 1962-68; exec. dean Chatham Coll., Pitts., 1968-70; pres. Lake Forest (Ill.) Coll., 1970-93, pres. emeritus, 1993—; interm pres. Eckerd Coll., 2000-01. Lt. (j.g.) USNR, 1950-53. Mem. Chgo. Coun. Fgn. Rels., Econ. Club, Chgo. Onnentsia Club, Caxton Club, Phi Beta Kappa, Phi Kappa Phi, Chi Phi.

HOTELLING, HAROLD, economics professor, lawyer; b. NYC, Dec. 26, 1945; s. Harold and Susanna Porter (Edmondson) H.; m. Barbara M. Anthony, May 4, 1974; children: Harold, George, James, Claire, Charles. AB, Columbia U., 1966; JD, U. N.C., 1972; MA, Duke U., 1975, PhD, 1982. Bar: N.C. 1973. Legal advisor U. N.C., Chapel Hill, 1972-73; instr. bus. law U. Ky., Lexington, 1977-79, asst. prof., 1980-84; asst. prof. dept. econs. Oakland U., Rochester, Mich., 1984-89; assoc. prof. econs. Lawrence Technol. U., Southfield, Mich., 1989—, chmn. dept. humanities social scis. and comm., 1994-99. Contbr. articles to profl. jours. Lt. j.g. USNR, 1968—70. Episcopalian. Home: 2112 Bretton Dr S Rochester Hills MI 48309-2952 Office: Lawrence Technol U Dept Humanities Southfield MI 48075 Office Phone: 248-204-3530. Business E-Mail: hotelling@ltu.edu.

HOTH, STEVEN SERGEY, lawyer, educator; b. Jan. 30, 1941; s. Donald Leroy and Ina Dorothy (Barr) H.; m. JoEllen Maly, July 29, 1967; children: Andrew Steven, Peter Lindsey. AB, Grinnell Coll., 1962; JD, U. Iowa, 1966; postgrad., U. Pa., 1968, Oxford U., Eng., 1973. Bar: U.S. Ct. Appeals (8th cir.) 1966, U.S. Tax Ct. 1967, U.S. Ct. Claims 1967, U.S. Dist. Ct. Iowa 1968, U.S. Dist. Ct. ND 1968, U.S. Dist. Ct. SD 1968, U.S. Supreme Ct. 1973, U.S. Ct. Appeals (7th cir.) 1982. Law clk. to chief justice U.S. Ct. Appeals (8th cir.), Fargo, ND, 1967-68; assoc. Hirsch, Adams, Hoth & Krekel, Burlington, Iowa, 1968-72, ptnr., 1972-91; pvt. practice Burlington, 1992—. Asst. atty. Des Moines County, Burlington, 1968-72, atty., 1972-83; alt. mcpl. judge, Burlington, 1968-69; lectr. criminal law Southeastern C.C., West Burlington, 1972-82; assoc. prof. polit. sci. Iowa Wesleyan Coll., Mt. Pleasant, 1981-82; Pres. of Amerail, Inc., Iowa Truck Rail, Amerail, Inc.; pres. Burlington Truck Rail, Burlington Short Line R.R. Inc., Iowa Internat. Investments, Burlington Storage and Transfer; sec. Burlington Loading Co. Contbr. numerous articles to profl. jours. Chmn. Des Moines County Civil Svc. Commn.; trustee Charles H. Rand Lecture Trust; mem. Des Moines County Conf. Com., Des Moines County Conf. Bd.; dir. Burlington Med. Ctr. Staff Found.; moderator 1st Congl. Ch., Burlington; bd. dir. UN Assn.; clk. Burlington North Bottoms Levy and Drainage Dist.; bd. mem., pres. Burlington Cmty. Sch. Dist. Bd. Edn., chmn. commn. on ministry, mem. exec. com. Nat. Assn. Congl. Christian Chs., moderator; treas. 1st dist. Dem. Com.; bd. dirs. Legal Aid Soc. Planned Parenthood Des Moines County. Recipient Chmn.'s award ARC, 1980; Reginald Heber Smith fellow in legal aid Cheyenne River Indian Reservation, Eagle Butte, SD, 1967-68; named Lord of Foleshill. Mem. Missionary Soc.-Nat. Assn. Congl. Christian Chs., ABA (internat. sect., tax sect.), Iowa State Bar Assn. (liaison to Iowa Med. Soc.), Des Moines County Bar Assn., Am. Judicature Soc., Agrl. Law Com., Iowa Def. Coun., Iowa Archaeol. Soc., Soc. for German Am. Studies, Manorial Soc. Gt. Britain, Grinnell Coll. Alumni Assn. (bd. dirs.), Malawi Soc., Burlington-West Burlington C. of C. (bd. dirs.), Nat. Assn. Congrl. Christian Ch., Burlington Golf Club, New Crystal Lake Club (pres.), Elks, Eagles, Masons, Rotary. Office: PO Box 982 Hoth Bldg 200 Jefferson St Burlington IA 52601 Office Phone: 319-754-5000. Business E-Mail: hothlaw@mchsi.com.

HOTTINGER, JAY, state legislator; b. Newark, Ohio, Dec. 1, 1969; m. Cheri Moss, May 21, 1994. BA, BS summa cum laude, Capital U., Columbus, Ohio, 1992. Mgr. Jay Co.; councilman City of Newark, Ohio, 1992-94; pres. pro tem Newark City Coun., 1994; rep. dist. 77 Ohio Ho. of Reps., Columbus, 1995-98; mem. Ohio Senator from 31st dist., Columbus, 1998—2006. Bd. dirs. East Mound Comty. Devel. Corp., Am. Cancer Soc. (Newark). Named Outstanding Young Man of Licking County, 1992. Mem. Police Athletic League, Newark Area C. of C.

HOTTINGER, JOHN CREIGHTON, state legislator, lawyer; b. Mankato, Minn., Sept. 18, 1945; s. Raymond Creighton and Hilda (Baker) H.; m. Miriam Jean Willging, Oct. 31, 1971; children: Julie, Creighton, Janna. BS, Coll. St. Thomas, St. Paul, 1967; JD, Georgetown U., 1971. Bar: Minn. 1972, U.S. Dist. Ct. Minn. 1977, U.S. Dist. Ct. (no. dist.) Ohio 1981, U.S. Ct. Appeals (5th cir.) 1991, U.S. Supreme Ct. 1992. Legis. asst. Hon. Donald M. Fraser, Washington, 1968-69, Dem. Study Group, Washington, 1969-73; ptnr. Farrish, Johnson, Maschka & Hottinger, Mankato, 1973-85; sr. ptnr. Hottinger Law Offices, Mankato, 1985-91; ptnr. Gislason, Dosland, Hunter & Malecki, Mankato, 1991-95; sr. ptnr. Hottinger Law Office, Mankato, 1995—; of counsel MacKenzie and Gustafson, St. Peter, 1997—; mem. Minn. Senate, 1991—, asst. majority whip, 1993-95, majority whip, 1996-2000, chair health and family security com., 1997-2000, asst. majority leader, 2001—. Chair Bd. of Govt. Innovation and Cooperation, 1995. Dem. candidated Minn. Senate, 1982, U.S. Ho. of Reps., 1994; chair Midwestern Legis. Conf., 2000—01; mem. exec. com. Coun. State Govts., 2000—, v.p., 2002. Mem. ABA, 5th Dist. Bar Assn., Minn. Bar Assn. Roman Catholic. Avocation: computer ops., writing. Office: Hottinger Law Office Box 3183 Mankato MN 56002-3183

HOUGHTON, MARY, bank executive; BA cum laude, Marquette U., Milw.; MA in Internat. Studies, Johns Hopkins U., Balt. Co-founder, pres. ShoreBank Corp., 1973—; sr. lender, sr. operating officer South Shore Bank; chair ShoreBank Internat., ShoreCap Internat. Short-term advisor Grameen Bank, Bangladesh, 1983—93, Bangladesh Rural Advancement Com., Aga Khan Rural Support Program, Pakistan; dir. K-REP Bank, Kenya, 1999—. Mem. World Bank policy adv. group Cities Alliance. Co-recipient Citizen Activist award, Gleitsman Found., 2006; named one of America's Best Leaders, US News & World Report, 2007; recipient Cmty. Banker the Yr. award, American Banker, 2004. Achievements include co-founder of the first and largest community development bank in the US. Office: South Shore Banking Ctr 7054 S Jeffery Blvd Chicago IL 60649*

HOUK, JAMES CHARLES, physiologist, educator; b. Northville, Mich., June 3, 1939; s. James Charles and Elowene (Tower) H.; m. Antoinette Iacuzio, Dec. 28, 1963; children: Philip, Nadia, Peter. BSEE, Mich. Tech. U., 1961; MSEE, MIT, 1963; PhD, Harvard U., 1966. Instr. Harvard U. Med. Sch., 1967-69, asst. prof., 1969-73; lectr. MIT, 1971-73; assoc. prof. Johns Hopkins U. Med. Sch., 1973-78; adj. assoc. prof. U. N.C., 1975; prof. physiology Northwestern U. Med. Sch., 1978—, chair dept. physiology, 1978—2001. Co-author: Medical Physiology 14th edit., 1980, Handbook of Physiology--The Nervous System II, 1981, Encyclopedia of Neuroscience, 1987, Models of Information Processing in the Basal Ganglia, 1995; contbr. chpts. to books. Recipient Javits award NIH, 1984-92. Mem. IEEE, AAAS, Soc. for Neurosci., Am. Physiol. Soc., European Neurosci. Assn., Assn. Chmn. Depts. Physiology, Internat. Neural Network Soc. Office: Northwestern U 303 E Chicago Ave Chicago IL 60611-3093 Office Phone: 312-503-8219.

HOUK, ROBERT SAMUEL, chemistry professor; b. New Castle, Pa., Nov. 23, 1952; s. Robert H. and Rose B. Houk; m. Linda Lembke, Oct. 3, 1981; children: Andrew, Mary. BS, Slippery Rock State Coll., 1974; PhD, Iowa State U., 1980. Asst. prof. chemistry Iowa State U., Ames, 1981-87, assoc. prof., 1987-91, prof., 1991—. Cons. Perkin Elmer Sciex, Norwalk, Conn., 1982—. Author: Handbook of ICP-MS, 1992; contbr. articles to profl. jours. Recipient M.F. Hasler award Spectroscopy Soc. Pitts., 1993, Wilkinson Teaching award Iowa State U., 1993. Mem. Am. Chem. Soc. (award in chem. instrumentation 1993), Soc. for Applied Spectroscopy (L.W. Strock award 1986, Maurice F. Hasler award 1993), Am. Soc. for Mass Spectrometry. Achievements include construction of first inductively coupled plasma-mass spectrometer for trace elemental analysis. Office: Iowa St Univ Ames Lab Ames IA 50011-0001

HOULTON, LISE, performing company executive; m. Michael Gilliland; children: Kaitlyn, Raina. Tchr. Minn. Dance Theatre, Mpls.; dancer Am. Ballet Theatre, NYC, Stuttgart Ballet, Germany, Minn. Dance Theatre. Office: Minn Dance Theatre 528 Hennepin Ave Sixth Fl Minneapolis MN 55403

HOUSE, GEORGE, radio personality; m. Diane House. Radio host WIBM, Jackson, Mich., WEAQ, Eau Claire, Wis., WAXX, Eau Claire, Wis., WAYY, Eau Claire, Wis. Avocations: golf, fishing, acting, movies. Office: WAXX PO Box 1 Eau Claire WI 54702

HOUSE, JAMES STEPHEN, social psychologist, educator; b. Phila., Jan. 27, 1944; s. James Jr. and Virginia Miller (Sturgis) H.; m. Wendy Fisher, May 13, 1967; children: Jeff, Erin. BA, Haverford Coll., 1965; PhD, U. Mich., 1972. From. instr. to assoc. prof. sociology Duke U., Durham, NC, 1970-78; assoc. prof. sociology/assoc. rsch. scientist Survey Rsch. U. Mich., Ann Arbor, 1978-82, assoc. chair dept. sociology, 1981-84, prof. sociology, 1982—2005, chair dept. sociology, 1986-90, dir. Survey Rsch. Ctr., Inst. Social Rsch., 1991-2001, Angus Campbell collegiate prof. sociology and survey rsch., rsch. prof. Survey Rsch. Ctr, 2005—. Author: Work Stress and Social Support, 1981; co-editor: Sociological Perspectives on Social Psychology, 1995, A Telescope on Society, 2004; Making Americans Healthier: Social and Economic Policy as Health Policy, 2008; assoc. editor Social Psychology Quar., 1988-91, Jour. Health & Social Behavior, 1997-2000, Internat. Ency. of the Social and Behavioral Scis., 2001; contbr. chpts. to books and articles to profl. jours. Guggenheim fellow, 1986-87, Ctr. for Advanced Study in the Behavioral Scis. fellow, 2005-06. Fellow: AAAS, Soc. Behavioral Medicine, Am. Acad. Arts and Scis.; mem.: NAS, Soc. for Epidemiol. Rsch., Soc. for Psychol. Study of Social Issues, Acad. Behavioral Medicine Rsch., Am. Sociol. Assn., Inst. Medicine of NAS. Office: Univ Mich Inst Social Rsch PO Box 1248 Ann Arbor MI 48106-1248 Office Phone: 734-764-6526. Business E-Mail: jimhouse@umich.edu.

HOUSE, TED C., state legislator; b. Kansas City, Mo., Aug. 22, 1959; s. Keith and Ilene House; m. Mardi House. BA, Meth. Coll., 1981; JD, U. Mo. Kansas City, 1984. Intern legis. U.S. Congressman Ike Skelton, 1979; state rep. Mo. State Congress, 1980; atty. gen. State of Mo., 1982-84; mem. Mo. Ho. of Reps. from 15th dist., Jefferson City, 1988-94, Mo. Senate from 2nd dist., 1995—. Mem. appropriations com., edn. and pub. safety com., transp. com., labor and indsl. rels. com., conservation, parks and tourism com., econ. devel. com. Francis Howell Sch. Dist.; vice chmn. civil and criminal law com., ins. and housing com.; EMT Howard County Ambulance Svc.; legal investigator Trade Offense Divsn. Office Miss. Atty. Gen.; assoc. Heggs, Pryor & House. Mem. St. Charles C. of C. (govt. concerns com.), Salvation Army (bd. dirs.), Teen Parent Day Care Ctr., Phi Mu Alpha. Home: 2361 Delaware Dr Saint Charles MO 63303-2944

HOUSER, DONALD RUSSELL, mechanical engineering educator, consultant; b. River Falls, Wis., Sept. 2, 1941; s. Elmont Ellsworth and Helen (Bunker) H.; m. Colleen Marie Collins, Dec. 30, 1967; children: Kelle, Kerri, Joshua. BS, U. Wis., 1964, MS, 1965, PhD, 1969. Instr. U. Wis., Madison, 1967-68; from asst. prof. to prof. Ohio State U., Columbus, 1968—2003, emeritus prof., 2003—, dir. Gear Dynamics and Gear Noise Rsch. Lab., 1979—2006, dir. Ctr. for Automotive Rsch., 1994-99. V.p. Gear Rsch. Inst., State Coll., Pa., 1990-99. Author: Gear Noise, 1991; contbg. editor Sound and Vibration mag., 1988-96; assoc. editor Jour. Mech. Design, 1993-94; mem. adv. bd. JSME Internat. Jour., 1996-2000; contbr. articles to profl. jours. Elder St. Andrews Presbyn. Ch., Columbus, 1972-75. Fellow ASME (legis. liaison Ohio coun. 1976-80, Century II medallion 1980, Darle Dudley award 2007); mem. Am. Gear Mfrs. Assn. (acad.), Soc. Automotive Engrs. Roman Catholic. Achievements include development of technology for measuring gear transmission error under load. Office: Ohio State U 201 W 19th Ave Columbus OH 43210 Office Phone: 614-292-5860. Business E-Mail: houser.4@osu.edu.

HOUSER, HUBERT, state representative; b. Pottawattamie County, Iowa, Oct. 9, 1942; m. Paula Ackerman. Student, Carson Macedonia Cmty. Sch., Iowa State U. Mem. Iowa Senate, DesMoines, 2001—, chair natural resources and environment com., mem. various coms. including agr., appropriations, local govt. and transp. Active Pottawattomie County Bd. Suprs., 1979—93, Carson-Macedonia Sch. Bd., Macedonia Meth. Ch. Mem.: Farm Bur., Cattlemen's Assn. Republican. Office: State Capitol Bldg East 12th and Grand Des Moines IA 50319 Home: 34697 Beechnut Rd Carson IA 51525-4069

HOUSER, THOMAS J., lawyer; b. Belmond, Iowa, 1964; m. Susan Houser; 2 children. BA, Coll. St. Thomas, 1986; JD, U. Iowa, 1989. Bar: Iowa 1989. Sr. shareholder Davis, Brown, Koehn, Shors & Roberts, P.C., West Des Moines, Iowa. Bd. dirs. Iowa Lutheran Hosp. Found., 1993—98, Iowa Health Found., 1998—; pres., bd. dirs. Fin. Planning Assn. Iowa, 2000—01. Named one of Forty Under 40, Des Moines Bus. Record, 2003, Top 100 Attys., Worth mag., 2005—06. Fellow: Am. Coll. Trust and Estate Counsel; mem.: ABA, Iowa State Bar Assn. (mem. probate sect. coun. 2005—, mem. pres.'s task force for CLE (continuing legal edn.) reform 2005—), Polk County Bar Assn. Office: Davis Brown Koehn Shors & Roberts PC 4201 Westown Pky Ste 300 West Des Moines IA 50266 Office Phone: 515-246-7845. Office Fax: 515-243-0654.

HOUSTON, MICHAEL J., dean, management educator; BS in Commerce, U. Ill., 1968, PhD in Mktg., 1973. Joined Carlson Sch. Mgmt., U. Minn., Mpls., 1986, Ecolab-Pierson M. Grieve chair in internat. mktg., academic dir. Carlson Brand Enterprise, assoc. dean internat. programs, interim co-dean, 2005—06. Office: U Minn Carlson Sch Mgmt 321 Nineteenth Ave S, Ste 3-150 Minneapolis MN 55455 Office Phone: 612-625-2075. Office Fax: 612-624-6374. E-mail: mhouston@umn.edu.

HOVDA, THEODORE JAMES, lawyer; b. Forest City, Iowa, Oct. 15, 1951; s. Ernest J. and Doris (Goodnight) H.; m. Susan J. Miller, Feb. 24, 1973; children: Theodore James III, Lee Joseph, Margaux Ann. BS, Iowa State U., 1973; JD, U. Iowa, 1977. Asst. county atty. Hancock County, Garner, Iowa, 1977-78, county atty., 1979-98; mem. Riehm & Hovda, Garner, 1977-98, Hovda Law Office, 1998—. County chmn. Hancock County Rep. Ctrl. Com., 1979-98. Mem. Iowa Bar Assn., Hancock County Bar Assn., Dist. 2A Bar Assn., Rotary, Masons. Republican. Methodist. Home: 785 11th Street Pl Garner IA 50438-1848 Office: Hovda Law Office PO Box 9 395 State St Garner IA 50438-0009 Office Phone: 641-923-3108. Office Fax: 641-923-3108. Personal E-mail: tshovda@kalnetisp.net.

HOVEN, TIM, state legislator; b. Dec. 22, 1963; BA, U. Wis., Oshkosh. Assemblyman Wis. State Dist. 60, 1994—. Mem. Ozaukee County (Wis.) Bd., Port Washington (Wis.) Bd. Rev., Ozaukee County Econ. Devel. Corp. Mem. Ducks Unltd. Address: 204 S Webster St Port Washington WI 53074-2129

HOVER, GERALD R., state agency administrator; BA, Mich. U.; MS, PhD, Calif. State U., San Ann. Asst. state pk. Utah State Pk.; dir. Kans. Wildlife and Pk. Dept., Pratt, 1993—; sec., 1998—. Office: Kans Wildlife & Pk Dept 512 SE 25th Ave Pratt KS 67124-8174 Fax: 316-672-2972.

HOVERSON, ROBERT L., finance company executive; With Provident Fin. Group, Cin., 1985-92, sr. v.p., 1992-98, pres., CEO, 1998—. Office: Provident Fin Group Inc 1 E 4th St Cincinnati OH 45202-3717 Fax: 513-345-7185.

HOVLAND, JODY, theater director; MA in English, U. N.Dak.; MFA in Acting, U. Iowa, 1981. Co-artistic dir. Riverside Theatre, Iowa City, 1981—. Artist-in-residence Dept. Theater and Comms. Studies Cornell U., 2004—. Named Best Actor, Iowa City (Iowa) News and Entertainment Weekly, 1997; recipient Svc. to Arts in Our Region award, Iowa City Area C. of C., 1999. Office: Riverside Theatre 213 N Gilbert St Iowa City IA 52245

HOWARD, CLARK, radio personality; Owner travel agy. chain; radio host The Clark Howard Show WTMK radio, Milw., 1987—. Office: WTMJ 720 E Capital Dr Milwaukee WI 53212

HOWARD, GLENN L., state legislator; b. Aug. 25, 1939; m. Florence Howard. Student, Ala. State U., U. Indpls. Mem. Ind. Senate from 33d dist. Mem. Judiciary, Planning & Pub. Svc., Transp., Health & Environ. Affairs, Pub. Policy and Internat. Cooperation Coms. Ind. State Senate. Mem. Indpls. City County Coun.; active Cmty. Affairs & News Media Rels., pub. affairs Indpls. Power & Light Co., Ind. State Black Expo and Urban League; bd. dirs. Noble Ctrs.; mem. Father Kelly's Youth Club; bd. dirs. Meals on Wheels, Indpls. Housing Strategy, Indpls. Campaign for Healthy Babies. Democrat. Home: 1005 W 36th St Indianapolis IN 46208-4129

HOWARD, JAMES JOSEPH, III, utility company executive; b. Pitts., July 1, 1935; s. James Joseph Jr. and Flossie (Wenzel) H.; m. Donna J. Fowler; children: James J. IV, Catherine A., Christine A., William F. BBA, U. Pitts., 1957; MS, MIT, 1970. With Bell Telephone of Pa., Pitts., 1957-78, v.p., gen. mgr., 1976-78; v.p. ops. Wis. Telephone Co., Milw., 1978-79, exec. v.p., chief operating officer, 1979-81, pres., chief exec. officer, 1981-83, chmn., chief exec. officer, 1983; pres., chief operating officer Ameritech, Chgo., 1983-87, dir.; pres., chief exec. officer No. States Power Co., Mpls., 1987—, chmn., 1988—, Xcel Energy, 2000-2001, chmn. emeritus. Bd. dirs. Walgreen Co., Deerfield, Ill., No. States Power Co., Mpls., Honeywell, Mpls., Fed. Res. Bank of Mpls., Ecolab, St. Paul, ReliaStar Fin., Mpls., Edison Electric Inst., Electric Power Rsch. Inst., chmn. Nuclear Energy Inst. Trustee U. St. Thomas, St. Paul. Sloan fellow MIT, 1969. Mem. Conf. Bd. N.Y.

HOWARD, JANET C., former state legislator; m. Allen Howard; children: Shirle, Raymond, George. Student, Ea. Ky. U., U. Cin. Councilwoman City of Forest Park, Ohio; senator Ohio State Senate, Columbus. Mem. Nat. Fedn. Rep. Women; bd. dirs. Hamilton County Rep. Women's Club; mem. Beechwood PTA, Forest Park Commn. Forum, adv. coun. Winton Woods Sch., adv. bd. Hamilton County Human Svcs., task force Forest Park Quality of Life. Mem. Greenhills-Forest Park Kiwanis.

HOWARD, JERRY THOMAS, former state legislator; b. Oak Ridge, Mo., Mar. 28, 1936; s. John Thomas and Sylvia Ann (Brecheisen) H.; m. Shirla Jean Rathjen McFaddin, 1973; children: Eliza Jane, John Trevor, Erin Penney, Michael Penney, Bill McFaddin. BS, Southeast Mo. U., 1960. Mem. from Dist. 156, Mo. State Ho. of Reps., 1973-77, 87-90; mem. Mo. State Senate, 1990—2001; farmer, 2001—; prin. Rural Resources. Vice chmn. com. agr., conservation, parks and tourism; mem. com. fin. and govtl. orgn., com. judiciary, com. appropriations, com. adminstrv. rules; chmn. com. on aging, families and mental health, com. on wetlands, spl. com. on welfare reform, others. Mem. Elks, Am. Legion, Masons, Scottish Rite, Shriners.

HOWARD, JOHN LAWRENCE, lawyer; b. Danville, Ill., May 16, 1957; s. Charles R. and Kathryn (Tormohlen) H.; m. Julia Louise Steinfirst, Oct. 13, 1984. BS, Ind. U., 1979, JD, 1982; LLM, George Washington U., 1989. Bar: Ind., 1982, US Supreme Ct., 1986, Fed. Cir. Ct., 1987, US Ct. Appeals (4th cir.), 1989. Dep. prosecutor 30th Jud. Cir., Rensselaer, Ind., 1982-84; lawyer US Office Pers. Mgmt., Washington, 1984-85; spl. asst. to gen. counsel US Consumer Product Safety Commn., Washington, 1984-85; legal counsel to chmn. US Merit Sys. Protection Bd., Washington, 1986-88; assoc. dep. atty. gen. US Dept. Justice, Washington, 1988-90; dep. counsel to v.p. Office of V.P., Washington, 1990; counsel to v.p. Dan Quayle, 1991-93; various positions Tenneco, Inc., 1993—95, gen. counsel, 1998—99; sr. v.p., gen. counsel W.W. Grainger, Inc., 2000—. Contbr. articles to profl. jours. Mem. Fed. Bar Assn., Fed. Cir. Bar Assn., Army & Navy Club Washington. Republican. Office: WW Grainger 100 Grainger Pky Lake Forest IL 60045-5201 Office Phone: 847-535-1000. Office Fax: 847-535-9243. E-mail: john_howard@grainger.com.

HOWARD, JOHN MALONE, surgeon, educator; b. Autaugaville, Ala., Aug. 25, 1919; s. Fontaine Maury and Mary Lorena (O'Brien) H.; m. Nina Lyman Abernathy, Dec. 22, 1943; children: John Malone Jr., Robert Fontaine, Nina Louise, George Glenn, Susan Elaine, Laura Leigh. BS, Birmingham So., 1941; MD, U. Pa., 1944. Resident in surgery U. Pa., 1944-50; mem. faculty Baylor U., Houston, 1950-55; prof., chmn. Emory U., Atlanta, 1955-57; chair surgery Hahnemann Med. Coll., Phila., 1958-62; dir. emergency med. svcs. Med. Coll. Ohio, Toledo, Ohio, 1974-78, prof. surgery, 1974—, prof. emeritus; pvt. practice surgery Toledo, 1990—. Dir. U.S. army surg. rsch. team Korean War. Editor: Studies of Battle Casualties in Korea, vol. III, 1953, vol. I, 1955, vol. II, 1955, vol. IV, 1955 (with others) Surgical Diseases of the Pancreas, 1960, 3rd edit., 1997, The Chemistry of Trauma, 1963, Cardiovascular Surgery-Supplement to Circulation, 1963, Septic Shock. Clinical and Experimental Experiences, 1964, Studies of Ultraviolet Irradiation: Its Efficiency in Preventing Infections in Operative Wounds, 1964; contbr. chpts. to books, more than 400 articles to profl. jours. Capt. U.S. Army Med. Corps., 1951-53. Decorated Legion of Merit; recipient Distinction award Nat. Rsch. Coun., Disting. Achievement award Am. Trauma Soc. Mem. Royal Coll. Surgeons Edinburgh (hon.), Brazilian Coll. Surgeons (fgn.). Avocations: fishing, boating, history, gardening. Home: 11004 Winslow Rd Whitehouse OH 43571-9643 Office: Med Coll Ohio Dowling Hall 3065 Arlington Ave Toledo OH 43614-2570

HOWE, G. EDWIN, healthcare executive; m. Suzanne Howe. Degree in bus. adminstrn., U. Wis., 1962; MBA, U. Chgo. From adminstrv. asst. to asst. dir. Ohio State U. Hosps.; pres. St. Luke's Hosp., Milw., 1974—87, Aurora Health Care, Milw., 1987—. Office: Aurora Health Care PO Box 343910 Milwaukee WI 53234-3910

HOWE, JONATHAN THOMAS, lawyer; b. Evanston, Ill., Dec. 16, 1940; s. Frederick King and Rosalie Charlotte (Volz) H.; m. Lois Helene Braun, July 12, 1963; children: Heather C., Jonathan Thomas Jr., Sara E. BA with honors,

Northwestern U., 1963; JD with highest distinction, Duke U., 1966. Bar: Ill. 1966, U.S. Dist. Ct. (no. dist.) Ill. 1966, U.S. Ct. Appeals (7th cir.) 1967, U.S. Tax Ct. 1968, U.S. Supreme Ct. 1970, U.S. Ct. Appeals (D.C. cir.) 1976, U.S. Ct. Appeals (9th cir.) 1980, U.S. Ct. Appeals (4th, 5th, 11th cirs.) 1983, U.S. Claims Ct. 1990. Ptnr. Jenner & Block, Chgo., 1966—85, sr. ptnr. in charge assn. and adminstrv. law dept., 1978—85; founding and sr. ptnr., pres. Howe & Hutton, Chgo., Washington & St. Louis, 1985—. Exec. and adv. coms. to Ill. Sec. of State to revise the Ill. Not for Profit Act, 1983-86; dir. Pacific Mut. Realty Investors, Inc., 1985-86; dir. cable TV options for pub. Chgo. Access Corp., 1995-97, Bostrom Corp., 2001—. Contbg. editor Ill. Inst. for Continuing Legal Edn., 1973—, Sporting Goods Bus., 1977-91, Meeting News, 1978-88, Meetings Mgr., 1988—, Meetings and Convs., 1991—; contbr. articles to profl. jours.; legal editor Meetings and Convs., 1990—. Mem. Dist. 27 Bd. Edn., orthbrook, Ill., 1969-89, sec., 1969-72, pres., 1973-84; chmn. bd. trustees Sch. Employee Benefit Trust, 1979-85; founding bd. dirs., pres. Sch. Mgmt. Found. Ill., 1976-84; mem. exec. com. Northfield Twp. Rep. Orgn., 1967-71; bd. deacons Village Presbyn. Ch. Northbrook, 1975-78, trustee, 1981-83; mem. Arts and Music Forum, 4th Presbyn. Ch., Chgo., 1990-93; spl. advisor Pres.'s Coun. Phys. Fitness and Sports, 1983—, Duke U. Sch. of Law Bd. of Visitors (life mem.). Named Industry Leader of Yr., Meeting Industry, 1987, Sch. Bd. Mem. Yr. (twice), Ill. State Bd. Edn.; recipient Internat. Found. PaceSetters award Hospitality Sales Mktg. Assn., 1996. Fellow Internat. Forum of Travel and Tourism Advs., Am. Soc. Assn. Execs. (vice-chmn. legal com. 1983-86), Am. Bar Found. (life); mem. ABA (antitrust sect. Nat. Inst. com., trade assn. law com. corp. banking and bus. law sect., sect. on litig., adminstrv. law sect., internat. law com., continuing edn. com., tort and ins. practice, vice-chmn. com. sports law 1986—, task force on membership benefits for disabled lawyers, standing com. meetings and travel 1988-93, spl. advisor 1993—), Acad. Hospitality Industry (dir., pres. 1994—), Ill. Bar Assn. (antitrust sect., civil practice sect., sch. law sect., adminstrv. law sect., co-editor Antitrust Newsletter 1968-70), Chgo. Bar Assn. (def. of prisoners com. 1966-83, antitrust law com. 1971—, continuing edn. com. 1977—, chmn. assn. and non-profit soc. law com. 1984-86), Am. Soc. Assn. Execs. (vice-chmn. legal com., founder legal sect.), N.Y. Soc. Assn. Execs., Acad. Hospitality Industry Attys. (founder, bd. dir., pres. 2001—), Nat. Sch. Bds. Assn. (nat. bd. dir. 1979-89, exec. com. 1981-89, sec.-treas. 1983-85, 2d v.p. 1985-86, chmn. devel. com. 1982-87, pres. 1987-88), DC Bar Assn., Am. Judicature Soc., Ill. Assn. Sch. Bds. (pres. 1977-79, bd. dir. 1971-88), Chgo. Bar Found. (life), Assn. Forum Chicagoland (assoc.), Nat. Sch. Bds. Found. (pres./trustee 1995-2002), U.S. C. of C. (legal coun. 1998—), Greater Washington Soc. Assn. Execs., Legal Club, Law Club, Mid-Am. Club, Tower Club, Univ. Club Chgo., Order of Coif, Psi Upsilon. Home: 126 W Delaware Pl Chicago IL 60610-3252 Office: 20 N Wacker Dr Ste 4200 Chicago IL 60606-9833 Office Phone: 312-263-3001. Business E-Mail: jth@howehutton.com.

HOWE, STANLEY MERRILL, manufacturing executive; b. Muscatine, Iowa, Feb. 5, 1924; s. Merrill Y. and Thelma F. (Corriel) H.; m. Helen Jensen, Mar. 29, 1953; children: Thomas, Janet, Steven, James. BS, Iowa State U., 1946; MBA, Harvard U., 1948. Prodn. engr. HON Industries, Muscatine, Iowa, 1948-54, v.p. prodn., 1954-61, exec. v.p., 1961-64, pres., 1964-90, chmn., 1984-96, chief exec. officer, 1979-91. Trustee Iowa Wesleyan Coll. Gerard Swope fellow Harvard U., 1948. Mem. AM, Bus. Instl. Furniture Mfrs. Assn. Clubs: Rotary, Elks, 33. Methodist. Office: Hon Industries Inc 414 E 3d St PO Box 1109 Muscatine IA 52761-0071

HOWELL, ANDREW, state legislator; Law enforcement officer, Ft. Scott, Kans.; mem. from dist. 4 Kans. State Ho. of Reps., Topeka. Home: 194 W 110th St Carbondale KS 66414-9313

HOWELL, GEORGE BEDELL, investment company executive; b. Schenectady, Sept. 19, 1919; s. Jesse M. and Grace (Gerhaeusser) Howell; m. Mary Barbara Crohurst, July 10, 1944; children: Raymond Gary, Terry Barbara, Janice Patricia, Nancy Jo, George Bedell Jr. BS in Adminstrv. Engring., Cornell U., 1942. With GE, 1946-59; v.p. mfg. Leece Neville Co., Cleve., 1959-61, Royal Electric Co., Pawtucket, RI, 1961-62; dir. ops. packaging equipment and product devel. Acme Steel Co. (merged with Interlake Steel Corp. 1965), 1962-64; v.p. adminstrv. svc. Interlake Steel Corp., Chgo., 1964-66, v.p. internat. divsn., v.p. Acme Products divsn., 1966-70; CEO Golconda Corp., Chgo., 1970-72; v.p. devel. Internat. Minerals & Chems. Corp., 1972-73, sr. v.p., pres. industry group, 1974-77, exec. v.p., 1977-81; pres., CEO Wurlitzer Co., 1982-86, chmn., pres., CEO, 1986-87, vice chmn., 1987-88; prin. Mid West Ptnrs., Chgo., 1988-89; gen. ptnr. Pfingsten Ptnrs., Chgo., 1989-94, ptnr., 1994—, mem. adv. com., 2002—06; chmn. Hallcrest Holding Corp., 1992-97. Chmn. bd. trustees Village of Oak Brook, Ill., 1965—73, pres., 1973—79; mem. McGraw Wildlife Found.; trustee Christ Ch., Oak Brook, vice chmn., 1992—97, trustee emeritus, 1998; mem. univ. coun. Cornell U., 2001—. Recipient Foremost Benefactor award, Cornell U., 2006; N.Y. State and Univ. scholar, 1942. Mem.: Ocean Reef Club (Fla.), Medinah Country Club. Office: 520 Lake Cook Rd Ste 375 Deerfield IL 60015-5632 Office Phone: 847-374-9140. Business E-Mail: ghowell@pfingsten.com.

HOWELL, J. MARK, electronics company executive; Mgr. Ernst & Young LLP; corp. controller ADESA Corp., 1992-94; exec. v.p fin., CFO, treas., sec. Brightpoint, Inc., Indpls., 1994-96; COO, 1995—; pres., 1996—; also bd. dirs. Office: 501 Airtech Pkwy Plainfield IN 46168-7408

HOWELL, JOEL DUBOSE, internist, educator; b. Tex., May 11, 1953; s. Wilson and Nora (Levitas) Howell; m. Linda C. Samuelson, June 26, 1976; children: Jonathan Samuelson, Benjamin Samuelson. BS, Mich. State U., 1975; MD, U. Chgo., 1979; PhD in History and Sociology of Sci., U. Pa., 1987. Intern, resident in internal medicine U. Chgo., 1979-82; Robert Wood Johnson clin. scholar U. Pa., Phila., 1982-84; instr. U. Mich., Ann Arbor, 1984-86, asst. prof., 1986-90, assoc. prof., 1990-97, prof., 1997—, Victor Vaughan prof. history medicine, 2001—. Editor: (book) Technology and American Medicine Practice: 1880-1930, 1988, Medical Lives and Scientific Medicine at Michigan; author: Technology in the Hospital, 1995. Scholar Henry J. Kaiser Family Fedn. Faculty, 1989—92, Charles E. Culpeper Found. Med. Humanities, 1992—96. Fellow: ACP, Am. Osler Soc., Am. Assn. History Medicine. Office Phone: 734-647-4844. Business E-Mail: jhowell@umich.edu.

HOWELL, ROBERT EDWARD, hospital administrator; b. Marietta, Ohio, Jan. 19, 1949; married; 3 children. BS, Muskingham Coll., 1971; MS in Hosp. and Health Svcs. Adminstrn., Ohio State U., 1977. Assoc. dir. U. Minn. Hosps. and Clinics, Mpls., 1980-86; exec. dir. Med. Coll. Ga. Hosps. and Clinics, Augusta, 1986-94; dir., CEO, U. Iowa Hosps. and Clinics, Iowa City, 1994—. Mem. exec. com. Accreditation Coun. for Grad. Med. Edn. Mem. Coun. Tchg. Hosps. (past chmn.), Am. Assn. Med. Colls. (exec. com.), Am. Hosp. Assn. (coord. com. med. edn.), Univ. Health System Consortium (exec. com.). Office: U VA Med Ctr 3007 McKim Hall PO Box 800809 Charlottesville VA 22908-0809

HOWELL, R(OBERT) THOMAS, JR., lawyer, former food company executive; b. Racine, Wis., July 18, 1942; s. Robert T. and Margaret Paris (Billings) H.; m. Karen Wallace Corbett, May 11, 1968; children: Clarinda, Margaret, Robert. AB, Williams Coll., 1964; JD, U. Wis., 1967; postgrad., Harvard U., 1981. Bar: Wis. 1968, Ill. 1968, U.S. Dist. Ct. (no. dist.) Ill. 1968, U.S. Tax Ct. Assoc. Hopkins & Sutter, Chgo., 1967-71; atty. The Quaker Oats Co., Chgo., 1971-77, counsel, 1977-80, v.p., assoc. gen. corp. counsel, 1980-84, v.p., gen. corp. counsel, 1984-96, corp. sec., 1994-96; of counsel Seyfarth Shaw, Chgo., 1997—2007; gen. counsel Am. Bar Assn. Bd. dirs. Ill. Inst. of Continuing Legal Edn., Lawyers for Creative Arts. Editor (mags.) Barrister, 1975-77, Compleat Lawyer, 1983-87. Bd. dirs. Metro. Family Svcs.; bd. dirs. Chgo. Bar Found., 1987—, pres., 1991-93; trustee 4th Presbyn. Ch., Chgo., 1989-92, pres., 1994-96, 2007-; bd. dirs. Chgo. Equity Fund, 1992-96. Capt. USAR, 1966—72. Mem. ABA, Ill. Bar Assn., Wis. Bar Assn., Chgo. Bar Assn. (bd. mgrs. 1977-79, chmn. young lawyers sect. 1974-75), Lawyers Club Chgo. (pres. 2004-05), Econ. Club Chgo., Univ. Club Chgo. (bd. dirs. 1982-85, 87-88, v.p.). Presbyterian. Home: 853 W Chalmers Pl Chicago IL 60614-3233 Office: Gen Counsel Am Bar Assn 321 N Clark St Ste 2100 Chicago IL 60610 Office Phone: 312-988-5215. Business E-Mail: thowell@staff.aba.net.

HOWELL, THOMAS, history professor; b. Houston, Jan. 20, 1944; s. John Thomas and Hazel (Hall) H.; m. Donna Jo Walker, Aug. 14, 1971; children: Catherine Jewel, Judith Hazel. BA, La. Coll., Pineville, 1964; MA, La. State U., 1966, PhD, 1971. Instr. La. State U., Baton Rouge, 1967—68, La. Coll., Pineville, 1968—70, asst. prof., 1970—72, assoc. prof., 1972—77, prof., 1977, Crowell prof., 1984—2006, chmn. dept. history and polit. sci., 1975—95, chmn. divsn. social and behavioral scis., 1995—2000, chmn. divsn. history and polit. sci., 2000—06; prof., chmn. history dept. William Jewell Coll., Liberty, Mo., 2006—. Lectr. La. Endowment for Humanities, 1983, 86, 87, 1990—96, 2001—, project dir., 1989, 2000, 03. Mem. La. Elections Integrity Commn., 1980—86, vice-chmn., 1981; coord. La. Civitan Youth Citizenship Seminar, 1975—76; commr. Gulf Coast Athletic Conf., 1981—; mem. NAIA Nat. Eligibility Commn., 1983—, chmn., 1994—; mem. hearing com. disciplinary bd. La. Bar Assn., 1995—2001. Mellon summer fellow, 1981; Fulbright lectr. U. Iceland, 1986-87; inductee Nat. Assn. Intercollegiate Athletics Hall of Fame, 1999. Mem. La. Hist. Assn., So. Hist. Assn., SW Assn. Pre-Law Advisers, Orgn. Am. Historians, Alpha Chi, Phi Alpha Theta. Home: 917 Cambridge Cir Liberty MO 64068 Office Phone: 816-415-7617.

HOWERTON, JIM, state legislator; Mem. Mo. Ho. of Reps., Jefferson City. Republican.

HOWLAND, JOAN SIDNEY, law librarian, educator; b. Eureka, Calif., Apr. 9, 1951; d. Robert Sidney and Ruth Mary Howland. BA, U. Calif., Davis, 1971; MA, U. Tex., 1973; MLS, Calif. State U., San Jose, 1975; JD, Santa Clara U., Calif., 1983; MBA, U. Minn., 1997. Assoc. librarian for pub. svcs. Stanford U. Law Library, Calif., 1975-83, Harvard U. Law Library, Cambridge, Mass., 1983-86; dep. dir. U. Calif. Law Library, Berkeley, 1986-92; dir. law libr., Roger F. Noreen prof. law U. Minn. Sch. of Law, 1992—, assoc. dean info. tech., 2001—. Questions and answers column editor Law Libr. Jour., 1986-91; memt. column editor Trends in Law Libr. Mgmt. & Tech., 1987-94. Mem. ALA, ABA (com. on accreditation 2001—), Am. Assn. Law Librs., Am. Assn. Law Schs., Am. Indian Libr. Assn. (treas. 1992—), Am. Law Inst. Office: U Minn Law Sch 120/410 Walter F Mondale Hall 229 19th Ave S Minneapolis MN 55455-0400 Office Phone: 612-625-9036. E-mail: howla001@umn.edu.

HOWLAND, WILLARD J., radiologist, educator; b. Neosho, Mo., Aug. 28, 1927; s. Willard Jay and Grace Darlene (Murphy) H.; m. Kathleen V. Jones, July 28, 1945; children: Wyck, Candice, Charles, Thomas, Heather AB, U. Kans., 1948, MD, 1950; MA, U. Minn., 1958; DSc (hon.), Coll. Med. N.E. Ohio, 1990. Intern U.S. aval Hosp., Newport, RI, 1950-51; pvt. practice medicine Kans., 1951-55; resident Mayo Clinic, Rochester, Minn., 1955-58; radiologist Ohio Valley Gen. Hosp., Wheeling, W.Va., 1959-67; prof., dir. diagnostic radiology Med. Units U. Tenn., Memphis, 1967-68; dir., chmn. dept. radiology Aultman Hosp., Canton, Ohio, 1968-87, pres. med. staff, 1978; prof., chmn. radiology coun. Coll. Medicine N.E. Ohio U., Rootstown, 1976-87, program dir. integrated radiology residency, 1976-87. Author, co-author three books and rsch. papers in field. With U.S. Army, 1945-46, USN, 1950-51. Fellow Am. Coll. Radiology; mem. AMA, Radiol. Soc. N.Am., Am. Roentgen Ray Soc., Ohio State Radiol. Soc. (pres. 1980-81), Masons. Republican. Presbyterian. Home and Office: 4521 Bishops Gate Rd NW Canton OH 44708 Office Phone: 330-479-1046. Personal E-mail: whowland1@neo.rr.com.

HOWREY, EUGENE PHILIP, retired economics and statistics professor; b. Geneva, Ill., Dec. 1, 1937; s. Eugene Edgar and Ellen Pauline (Boord) H.; children: Patricia Marie, Richard Philip, Margaret Ellen, Mark McCall. AB, Drake U., Des Moines, Iowa, 1959; PhD, U. NC, Chapel Hill, 1964; MA (hon.), U. Pa., Phila., 1972. Asst. prof. econs. Princeton U., NJ, 1963-69; assoc. prof. econs. U. Pa., Phila., 1969-73; prof. econs. U. Mich., Ann Arbor, 1973—2005, prof. stats., 1978—2005. Cons. Mathematica, Inc., Princeton, 1965-75; guest lectr. Inst. Advanced Studies, Vienna, 1974, 76. Contbr. articles to profl. jours. Research grantee NSF, 1975, 79, 84 Mem. Ann Arbor Bicycle Touring Soc. (pres. 1979-80), Phi Beta Kappa. Roman Catholic. Avocation: bicycling. Personal E-mail: eph@umich.edu.

HOXIE, FREDERICK EUGENE, history professor; b. Hoolehua, Hawaii, Apr. 22, 1947; s. John Wadman and Catherine (Agee) H.; m. Elizabeth Anne Schroder, July 11, 1970 (dec. Dec. 1983); children: Silas, Charles; m. Holly Frances Hanscom, Jan. 3, 1986; stepchildren: Stephen Hoskins, Philip Hoskins. BA, Amherst Coll., 1969, PhD in Humane Letters (hon.), 1994; MA, Brandeis U., 1976, PhD, 1977; PhD in Humane Letters (hon.), L.I. U., 2000. Tchr. Phila. Pub. Schs., 1969-70; high sch. tchr. Punahou Sch., Honolulu, 1970-72; asst. prof. Antioch Coll., Yellow Springs, Ohio, 1977-82, assoc. prof., 1982-83; dir. D'Arcy McNickle Ctr. for Am. Indian History, Newberry Libr., Chgo., 1983-94, v.p. rsch. and edn., 1994-98; Swanlund prof. history U. Ill., Urbana, 1998—. Cons. Cheyenne River Sioux Tribe, Eagle Butte, S.D., 1977-78, U.S. Senate Com. on Indian Affairs, Washington, 1989-90, Little Big Horn Coll., Crow Agency, Mt., 1990-98, Nat. Park Svc., Denver Support Ctr., 1997-98, Dept. of Justice, 2000-01, 04—. Author: A Final Promise, 1984, 2d edit., 2001, Parading Through History, 1995; co-author: The People: A History of Native America, 2007; editor: Indians in American History, 1988, 2d edit., 1997, Ency. of North American Indians, 1996, Talking Back to Civilization, 2001, Lewis and Clark and the Indian Country, 2007. Bd. dirs. Ill. Humanities Coun., Chgo., 1997-2003; trustee Nat. Mus. Am. Indian, Smithsonian, 1990-95, 2007-2008, Amherst Coll., 2001—07. Humanities fellow Rockefeller Found., 1984-85, fellow NEH, 1990-91, 2007—, fellow Mellon Found., 2005. Mem. Am. Hist. Assn. (program chmn. 1992), Am. Soc. for Ethnohistory (pres. 1995-96), Orgn. Am. Historians (exec. bd. 1997-2000). Avocations: running, tennis. Office: U Ill Dept History 309 Gregory Hall 810 S Wright St Urbana IL 61801-3644 E-mail: hoxie@uicu.edu.

HOYE, DONALD J., hardware distribution company executive; b. 1949; Dealer acct. ServiStar, a predecessor of TruServ, from 1971, numerous positions, including v.p. sales, ops.-info. sys.; pres., CEO, Coast to Coast; pres., COO, TruServ Corp., Chgo., until 1999, pres., CEO, 1999—. Office: TruServ Corp 8600 W Bryn Mawr Ave Chicago IL 60631-3579

HOYT, JAMES LAWRENCE, journalism educator, writer; b. Wausau, Wis., July 18, 1943; s. Lawrence Beryl and Eleanor (Kischel) H.; m. Cheryl Johannes, July 23, 1966; children: Randall James, Rebecca Cheryl, Diane Caroline. BS, U. Wis., 1965, MS, 1967, PhD, 1970; postgrad., U. Pa., 1967-68. Reporter Sta. WTMJ-TV, Milw., 1965-67; prof. journalism Ind. U., Bloomington, 1970-73; writer, editor NBC News, Washington, 1972; prof. journalism U. Wis., Madison, 1973—; dir. U. Wis. Sch. Journalism, Madison, 1981-91. Chmn. athletic bd., faculty rep. NACC Big Ten Conf. Western Collegiate Hockey Assn., U. Wis., Madison, 1991-2001. Author: Mass Media in Perspective, 1984, Writing News for Broadcast, 1994; contbr. articles to profl. jours. Named to Wis. Broadcasters Hall of Fame, 2007; recipient Carol Brewer award, Wis. AP, 1996. Mem. Assn. for Edn. in Journalism and Mass Comm. (Disting. Broadcast Educator 2002), Radio-TV News Dirs. Assn., Broadcast Edn. Assn., Internat. Radio-TV Soc. (Frank Stanton fellow 2001). Methodist. Avocation: tuba. Office: U Wis Sch Journalism 821 University Ave Madison WI 53706-1412 Home: 3415 Conservancy Middleton WI 53562-1161 Office Phone: 608-238-1389. Business E-Mail: jlhoyt@wisc.edu.

HOYT, KENNETH BOYD, education educator, writer; b. Cherokee, Iowa, July 13, 1924; s. Paul Fuller and Mary Helen (Tinker) H.; m. Phyllis June Howland, May 25, 1946; children: Andrew Paul, Roger Alan, Elinore Jane. BS, U. Md., 1948; MA, George Wash. U., Washington, DC, 1950; PhD, U. Minn., 1954; EdD (hon.), Crete Coll., 1981. Tchr., counselor Northeast H.S., Md., 1948-49; dir. guidance Westminster H.S., Md., 1949-50; tchg. asst. U. Minn., 1950-51, instr. ednl. psychology, 1951-54; asst. prof. U. Iowa, Iowa City, 1954-57, assoc. prof., 1957-60, prof. edn., 1961-69; dir. Splty. Oriented Student Research Program, prof. edn. U. Md., Silver Spring, 1969-74; dir. office career edn. US Office Edn., 1974-82; disting. vis. scholar Embry Riddle Aero. U., 1982-84; disting. prof. edn. Kans. State U., 1984—2003, dir. counseling high skills vocat. tech. career options program, 1993-98, prof. emeritus, 2003—. Cons. Ordnance Civilian Personnel Agy., 1954-60, Iowa Dept. Pub. Instrn., 1954-69, U.S. Dept. Labor, 1956-68, 65—, U.S. Office Edn., 1958—, Nat. Inst. Edn., 1973—. Author: (with L.A. Van Dyke) The Drop-Out Problem in Iowa High Schools, 1958, (with C.P. Froehlich) Guidance Testing, 1960, Selecting Employees for Developmental Opportunites and Guidance Services; Suggested Policies for Iowa Schools, 1963, Career Education: Contributions to an Evolving Concept, 1976, Career Education: Where It Is and Where It Is Going, 1981, Career Education: History and Future, 2005; co-author: Career Education: What It Is and How To Do It, 1972, Career Education and the Elementary School Teacher, 1973, Career Education in the Middle Junior High School, 1973, Career Education for Gifted and Talented Students, 1974, Career Education in the High School, 1977, Counseling for High Skills, 2001, Career Education: History and Future, 2005; Editor: Counselor Education and Supervision, 1961-65; mem. editl. bd.: Personnel and Guidance Jour, 1960-63; Contbr. articles to profl. jours. With AUS, 1943—46. Fellow APA (divsn. 17); mem. Am. Counseling Assn. (pres. 1966-67, Arthur Hitchcock Outstanding Disting. Profl. Svc. award, 1994), Am. Vocat. Assn. (Outstanding Svc. award 1972), Assn. Counselor Edn. and Supervision (Disting. Svc. award 1965, Outstanding Career award 1990), Nat. Career Devel. Assn. (Eminent Career award 1981, pres. elect 1991-92, pres. 1992-93), Am. Sch. Counselors Assn., Am. Ednl. Rsch. Assn., Nat. Assn. for Industry Edn. Cooperation (vice-chmn. 1992—), Phi Delta Kappa. Address: 13816 Sheradan Ave Urbandale IA 50323 E-mail: kbhoyt@mchsi.com.

HRIBAL, C. J., language educator; b. Chgo. m. Krystyna Hribal; children: Tosh, Roman, Hania. BA, St. Norbert Coll.; MA in Creative Writing, Syracuse U., 1982. Instr. MFA program U. Memphis; mem. fiction faculty MFA program for writers Warren Wilson Coll., Asheville, NC, 1989—; prof. English Marquette U., Milw., 1990—, dir. undergraduate studies. Author: Matty's Heart (selected for New Voices award), American Beauty, 1987, (introduction) The Boundaries of Twilight: Czecho-Slovak Writing from the New World, 1991; editor, 1991; author: (short stories) The Clouds in Memphis, 2000 (Assoc. Writing Programs award in short fiction, 1999), And That's the Name of That Tune (Sternig award for short fiction). Recipient award for short fiction, AWP; fellow, NEA, Bush Found., Loft-Mentor fellow, fellow, John Simon Guggenheim Meml. Found., 2003. Office: Marquette U English Dept Coughlin Hall, 261 PO Box 1881 Milwaukee WI 53201-1881 E-mail: cj.hribal@mu.edu, cjhribal@hribal.com.

HRUBETZ, JOAN, retired dean, nursing educator; b. Collinsville, Ill., June 1, 1935; d. Frederick and Josephine (Nepute) H. RN, St. John's Hosp., St. Louis, 1956; BSN, St. Louis U., 1960, MA, 1970, PhD in Edn. and Counseling, 1975. Staff nurse St. John's Hosp., St. Louis, 1956-59; instr. med./surg. nursing St. Louis Mcpl. Sch. Nursing, 1960-63; asst. dir. nursing svc. Barnes Hosp., St. Louis, 1963-65, asst. dir. sch. nursing, 1965-68, ednl. cons., 1968-70, dir. sch. nursing, 1970-74; dir. undergrad. mprog. nursing St. Louis U., 1975-82, asst. to assoc. prof. nursing, 1975—, assoc. prof. pastoral health care, 1986—, dean Sch. Nursing, 1982. Lectr. in field. Contbr. articles to profl. jours. Bd. dirs. Paraquad, Inc., Ctr. Independent Living, 1985-87, hon. mem., 1987—; bd. dirs. Kenrick-Glennon Seminar, 1988, sec. bd., 1989-90; mem. adv. com. project on Clin. Edn. in Care of Elderly, 1989. Group Health Found. grantee, 1987-88, 88-89, St. Louise U. Hosps. grantee, 1980-83, others. Mem. Mo. Assn. Adminstrs. of Baccalaureate and Higher Deg. Progs. in Nursing, St. Louis Assn. Deans and Dirs. of Schs. Nursing, Am. Assn. Colls. of Nursing (adv. com. to baccalaureate data project), Am. Nurses Assn., Mo. Nurses Assn., 3rd Dist. Mo. Nurses Assn., Nat. League Nursing, Mo. League for Nursing, St. Louis Reg. League for Nursing, Midwest Alliance in Nursing (governing bd. 1985-87, chair 1986-87, resolutions com. 1987-89), Conf. Jesuit Schs. Nursing, St. Louis Met. Hosp. Assn. Office: St Louis U Sch Nursing 3525 Caroline St Rm 222 Saint Louis MO 63104-1007

HSU, JUDY, newscaster; b. Taipei, Taiwan; U.S. married; 1 child. BA in Broadcast Journalism, U. Ill., Champaign, 1992. With WPGU-FM, Champaign-Urbana, Ill., 1993—94, WCIA-TV, Champaign-Urbana, Ill., 1993—94; reporter KFMB-TV, San Diego, 1994—95, weekend anchor, 1995—96, anchor 4pm news, 1996—2001; anchor afternoon news updates KFMB-AM, San Diego, 1996—2001; co-anchor News This Morning and reporter WLS-TV, Chgo., 2001—, host All About Kids. Named one of San Diego Women Who Mean Bus., San Diego Bus. Jour.; recipient Best One-Hour Newscast Emmy, Outstanding Achievement Splty. Reporting Emmy, Best News Story, San Diego Press Club, Best Series, Best Show. Mem.: NATAS, Asian Am. Journalists Assn. Office: WLS-TV 190 N State St Chicago IL 60601

HU, HOWARD, occupational medicine physician, educator; b. NYC, June 12, 1956; s. Henry Hung-Yuan and Mabel (Liang) H.; m. Sudha Kotha Hu, June 30, 1993; 1 child, Krishna. BSc in Biology, Brown U., 1976; MD, Albert Einstein Coll. Medicine, 1982; MPH, Harvard Sch. Pub. Health, 1982, MS in Epidemiology, 1986, DSc in Epidemiology, 1990. Lic. Mass., 1984, Mich., 2006, diplomate Am. Bd. Internal Medicine, 1985, Am. Bd. Preventive Medicine, Occupl. Medicine, 1987. Intern in medicine Boston City Hosp., 1982-83, jr. asst. resident, internal medicine, 1983—84, sr. asst resident internal medicine, 1984—85; resident, occupl. medicine Harvard Sch. Pub. Health, 1985-87, occupl. health rsch. fellow dept. environ. health, 1987-88, asst. prof. occupl. medicine, dept. environ. health, 1990-94, assoc. prof. occupl. medicine, dept. environ. health, 1994—2002, prof. occupl. and environ. medicine, dept. environ. health, 2002—06, adj. prof. occupl. and environ. medicine, dept. environ. health, 2006—, dir. residency program in occupl. and environ. medicine, 1996—2006, dir., occupl. and environ. medicine core, Nat. Inst. for Occupl. Safety and Health Ednl. Resource Ctr., 1996—2006; instr. in medicine, dept. medicine Harvard Med. Sch., 1988-92, asst. prof. medicine, dept. medicine, 1992—97, assoc. prof. medicine, dept. medicine, 1997—2006; attending physician, emergency dept. Whidden Meml. Hosp., 1985-87; attending physician occpl. medicine Mass. Respiratory Hosp., 1985—; attending physician occupl. health program U. Hosp./Boston U. Med. Ctr., 1987; assoc. physician (clin. and rsch.), Channing Lab., Dept. Medicine Brigham and Women's Hosp., 1988—2006, rsch. assoc. physician, Channing Lab., dept. medicine, 2006—; occpl./environ. medicine cons. Brigham and Women's Hosp. Employee Health Svcs., 1990-95; chair, dept. environ. health scis. U. Mich. Sch. Pub. Health, 2006—, prof. environ. health scis., dept. environ. health scis., 2006—, NSF Internat. Endowed Chair environ. health scis., 2007—, prof. epidemiology, 2007—; prof. medicine U. Mich. Sch. Medicine, 2007—. Asst. vis. physician, dept. medicine, Boston City Hosp., 1985-88; vis. physician South Cove Health Ctr., Boston, 1987-90; assoc., Ctr. for Health and the Global Environ., Harvard Med. Sch., 1996-2006; Alice Hamilton vis. prof., divsn. occupl. and environ. medicine, dept. medicine, U. Calif. San Francisco, 1997; dir., metals epidemiology rsch. group, Channing Lab., dept. medicine, Brigham and Women's Hosp., Harvard Med. Sch., and dept. environ. health, Harvard Sch. Pub. Health, 1991-2006; dir., Commn. to Investigate the Health and Environ. Effects of Nuclear Weapons Production, Internat. Physicians for the Prevention of Nuclear War, 1992-95; assoc. dir. and dir. metals core, Harvard Nat. Inst. Environ. Health Scis., Environ. Scis. Ctr., Harvard Sch. Pub. Health, 2000-06; prin. investigator, dir., Harvard Ctr. for Children's Environ. Health and Disease Prevention Rsch., 2004-; co-dir., Mich./Harvard-Harvard/Mich. Metals Epidemiology Rsch. Group., 2006-; cons. in occupl. and environ. medicine, Ctr. for Occupl. and Environ. Medicine, Northeast Specialty, 1985-2006; cons. in field; vis. scientist, Sri Ramachandra Med. Coll. and Rsch. Inst., Chennai, India, 2000-, vis. prof. 2000-01; vis. prof., dept. environ. medicine, U. Rochester, 2004; mem. numerous task forces in field; guest lectr. in field. Editl. bd. Einstein Comm. Health Newsletter, 1977-82, Jour. of Health and Human Rights, 1993-, Environ. Health Perspective, 1998-, Am. Jour. Insdl. Medicine, 2004-, Harvard Jour. of Minority Pub. Health, 1995—; book rev. co-editor: sect. on occupl. safety and health, Am. Pub. Health Assn., 1988-92; med. editor, Environ. Health Perspectives, 1998-2004; contbr. articles to profl. jours. and publs.; contbr. chpts. to books; peer-reviewer for several profl. jours. Recipient Nat. Health Svc. Corp. scholarship, 1978-82, Nat. Rsch. Svc. award 1985-88, Agy. for Toxic Substances and Disease Registry Clin. Environ. Medicine award 1990-92, Will Solimene award of excellence Am. Med. Writers Assn., 1994, Nat. Inst. for Environ. Health Scis. Progress and Achievement of the Yr. award, 1998-99, Harriett Hardy award, New England Coll. Occupl. and Environ. Medicine, 2006; Sr. Fulbright Scholar in India, 2000-01; grantee in field. Mem. APHA(program com., occupl. safety and health sect. 1981-82, mem. program com., Asian-Am. caucus, 1987-88), ACP, Mass. Coalition for Occupl. Safety and Health, Physicians for Social Responsibility, Physicians for Human Rights, Internat. Soc. for Environ. Epidemiology(mem. com. 1992-98), AAAS, Assn. Occupl. and Environ. Clinics (mem. quality assurance com. 1995-98), Soc. for Occupl. and Environ. Health, Am. Coll. Occupl. and Environ. Medicine, Sigma Xi. Office: Dept Environ Health Scis Bldg 1 Rm 6667 U Mich Sch Pub Health 109 S Observatory St Ann Arbor MI 48109-2029 Office Phone: 734-764-3188. Office Fax: 734-936-7283. Business E-Mail: howardhu@umich.edu.*

HUANG, THOMAS SHI-TAO, electrical engineering educator, researcher; b. Shanghai, June 26, 1936; came to U.S., 1958; s. Chien Liang and Allen (Chien) H.; m. Margaret Y. ee, Apr. 4, 1959; children: Caroline B., Marjorie A., Thomas T., Gregory T. BS, Nat. Taiwan U., Taipei, 1956; MS, MIT, 1960, ScD, 1963. Asst. prof. MIT, Cambridge, Mass., 1963-67, assoc. prof., 1967-73; prof. Purdue U., West Lafayette, Ind., 1973-80, U. Ill., Urbana, 1980—, 1996—. Vis. prof. Swiss Inst. Tech., Zurich, U. Hannover, Federal Republic of Germany, U. Que., Can., others; cons. IBM, AT&T Bell Labs., MIT Lincoln Lab., Kodak, others.

Author 6 books; editor 15 books; contbr. more than 500 articles to tech. jours. Recipient A. V. Humboldt U.S. Sr. Scientist award Alexander V. Humboldt Found., 1976-77; Honda Lifetime Achievement award, 2000, Okawa prize for info. and telecomm., 2005; Guggenheim fellow, 1971-72; fellow Japan Assn. for Promotion of Sci., 1986. Fellow IEEE (Signal Processing Soc. Tech. Achievement award 1987, Soc. award 1991, Third Millennium medal 2000, Jack S. Kilby medal 2001), Optical Soc. Am., Internat. Assn. for Pattern Recognition (King-Sun Fu Prize, 2002), Internat. Optical Engring. Soc. (Electronic Imaging Scientist of Yr. award 2006); mem. NAE, Chinese Acad. Engring. (fgn.), Chinese Acad. Scis. (fgn.). Office: Univ Ill Beckman Inst 405 N Mathews Ave Urbana IL 61801-2325 Office Phone: 217-244-1638.

HUANG, VICTOR TSANGMIN, food scientist, researcher; b. Republic of China, Dec. 12, 1951; came to U.S., 1975; s. Shen Tan and Yeh Gee (Lai) H.; m. Jean Fong Chen, June 9, 1978; children: Hank Su, Andrea Su. BS, Hsing-Hua U., Hsin-Chu, Republic of China, 1973; MS, U. Chgo., 1977; PhD, Ohio State U., 1981. Teaching asst. U. Chgo., 1975-77; rsch. assoc. Ohio State U., Columbus, 1977-81; food scientist Pillsbury Co., Mpls., 1981—. Presenter dairy, baby and bakery product formulation field, 1977-94. Contbr. articles to profl. jours.; patentee frozen desserts and microwave food formulation fields in U.S. and Europe. Vice pres. Minn. Taiwanese Assn., Mpls., 1985. 2d lt. Taiwan Army, 1973-75. Mem. Am. Dairy Sci. Assn., Inst. Food Technologists, Am. Assn. Cereal Chemists, Am. Chem. Soc., Toastmasters (pres. Mpls. 1988). Office: General Mills 330 University Ave SE Minneapolis MN 55414-1779 Personal E-mail: huang3813@netzero.net.

HUBBARD, DEAN LEON, academic administrator; b. Nyssa, Oreg., June 17, 1939; s. Gaileon and Rhodene (Barton) H.; m. Aleta Ann Thornton, July 12, 1959; children: Melody Ann, Dean Paul John, Joy Marie BA, Andrews U., 1961, MA, 1962; diploma in Korean Lang., Yunsei U., Seoul, Korea, 1968; PhD, Stanford U., 1979. Dir. English Lang. Schs., Seoul, 1966-71; asst. to pres. Loma Linda U., Calif., 1974-76; acad. dean Union Coll., Lincoln, Nebr., 1976-80, pres., 1980-84, NW Mo. State U., Maryville, 1984—. Chair Acad. Quality Consortium, 1993-96; examiner Malcolm Baldridge Nat. Quality Award, 1993-96; judges panel Mo. Quality Award, 1994-96; adv. coun. edn. statistics U.S. Dept. Edn., 1997-99. Mem. ACE Leadership Devel. Coun., 1996-98. Avocation: classical music. Office: NW Mo State U Office of President AD143 800 University Dr Maryville MO 64468-6001

HUBBARD, LINCOLN BEALS, medical physicist, consultant; b. Hawkesbury, Ontario, Sept. 8, 1940; arrived in U.S., 1957; s. Carroll Chauncey and Mary Lunn (Beals) Hubbard; m. Nancy Ann Krieger, Apr. 3, 1961; children: Jill, Katrina. BS in Physics, U. NH, 1961; PhD, MIT, 1967. Diplomate Am. Bd. Radiology, cert. health physicist Am. Bd. Health Physics. Postdoctoral appointee Argonne Nat. Lab., 1966—68; asst. prof. math. and physics Knoxville (Tenn.) Coll., 1968—70; asst. prof. physics Furman U., Greenville, SC, 1970—74; chief physicist Mt. Sinai Hosp., Chgo., 1974—75, 1979—2002, Cook County Hosp., Chgo., 1975—88; prof. med. physics Rush U., 1986—; ptnr. Fields, Griffith, Hubbard & Assoc., Ltd., 1978—93; pres. Hubbard, Broadbent & Assoc., Ltd., 1993—. Author (with S.S. Stefani): Mathematics for Technologists, 1979; author: (with G.B. Greenfield) Computers in Radiology, 1984. Fellow: Am. Coll. Radiology, Am. Assn. Physicists in Medicine. Home and Office: 4113 W End Rd Downers Grove IL 60515-2307 Home Phone: 630-963-2913; Office Phone: 630-963-2913.

HUBBARD, STANLEY STUB, broadcast executive; b. St. Paul, May 28, 1933; s. Stanley Eugene and Didrikke A. (Stub) H.; m. Karen Elizabeth Holmen, June 13, 1959; children: Kathryn Elizabeth Hubbard Rominski, Stanley Eugene II, Virginia Anne Hubbard Morris, Robert Winston, Julia Didrikke Coyte. BA, U. Minn., 1955; PhD (hon.), Hamline U., 1995, U. Minn., 2004. With Hubbard Broadcasting, St. Paul, 1951—, pres., 1967—, chmn., CEO, 1983—; past chmn. US Satellite Broadcasting Co., Inc., 1981—99. Mem. broadcast adv. com. on comm. subcom. Ho. of Reps., 1977—79; mem. adv. com. on advanced TV, FCC, 1988—95; mem. US Nat. Inf. Infastructure Adv. Coun., 1994—96. Contbr. articles to profl. jours. Chmn. St. Croix Valley Youth Ctr., 1968—; trustee Hubbard Broadcasting Found.; mem. bd. dirs. U. Minn. Found., Mpls., Assn. Maximum Svc. TV, U. St. Thomas, Minn. Bus. Partnership, Heart Rhythm Found.; past advisor Gov.'s Crime Commn., Ramsey County Ice Arena Com.; past bd. dirs. The Guthrie Theater, The Psychoanalytic Found. of Minn., Sci. Mus. of Minn., Am. Friends of Jamaica; past mem. Hazelden adv. com. Met. Airports Pub. Found. Adv. Bd.; bd. visitors U. Minn. Med. Sch., 2004; steering com. Salvation Army Twin Cities; chmn. pres. coun. Twin Cities Pub. TV, 2004. Recipient Ellis Island Medal of Honor, 2004, Mitchell Charnley award Northwest Broadcast News Assn., 1991, Internat. Humanitarian award Am. Friends of Jamaica, 1989, Arthur C. Clarke award Satellite Broadcasting and Comm. Assn., 1994, DreamMaker award Children's Cancer Rsch. Fund, 1994, Disting. Svc. award Nat. Assn. Broadcasters, 1995, Spurgeon award Boy Scouts Am., 1985, Avatar award Broadcast Cable and Fin. Mgmt., 1995, Human Rights award Am. Jewish Com., 1995, Cmty. Leadership award Mpls./St. Paul chpt. Alzheimer's Assn., 1995, Most Innovative Product award Minn. High Tech. Coun., 1995, Journalism Innovator award U. Nebr., 1996, Minn. Family Bus. award U. St. Thomas, 1996, Disting. Alumnus award Breck Sch., 1996, Minn. and Dakotas Entrepreneur of Yr. award, 1996, Heritage award US Hockey Hall of Fame, 1996, U. Minn. M Club Hall of Fame Lifetime Achievement award, 1996, Broadcasters' Found. Golden Mike award, 1997, Acad. of Achievement's Golden Plate award, 1997; named to Broadcasting and Cable Hall of Fame, 1991, Soc. Satellite Profl. Internat. Space Hall of Fame, 1992, Acad. Achievement's Golden Plate award, 1997, Broadcast Pioneer award Minn. Broadcasters Assn., 1998, John Hogan Disting. Svc. award Radio & TV News Dir. Assn., 2000, Promax TV Century award, 2003; inductee St. Croix Valley Athletics Hall of Fame, 2000, Pavek Mus. of Broadcasting Hall of Fame, 2001, ProMax TV Cent. Award, 2003, Minn. Bus. Hall Fame, 2006; named one of First Fifty Giants of Broadcasting Libr. Am. Broadcasting, 2003, Forbes' Richest Americans, 2006. Mem. Nat. Acad. TV Arts and Scis. (past chmn. bd. trustees, found. pres. 2003—, Minn. chpt. Silver Cir. award 2001, Golden Cir. award 2004), Broadcast Pioneers, Internat. Radio and TV Soc. Avocations: sailing and boating, reading, photography. Office: Hubbard Broadcasting Inc 3415 University Ave W Saint Paul MN 55114-2099 Home Phone: 651-642-4206; Office Phone: 651-642-4200. Business E-Mail: jmahoney@hbi.com.

HUBER, CHARLES G., JR., lawyer; BA, U. Mo., St. Louis; JD, Washington U. Joined Ralston Purina, 1989; v.p., asst. gen. counsel Ralcorp Holdings, Inc., corp. v.p., gen. counsel, 2003—. Office: Ralcorp Holdings, Inc PO Box 618 Saint Louis MO 63188-0618 Office Phone: 341-877-7000.

HUBER, DAVID LAWRENCE, physicist, researcher; b. New Brunswick, NJ, July 31, 1937; s. Howard Frederick and Katherine Teresa (Smith) H.; m. Virginia Hullinger, Sept. 8, 1962; children: Laura Theresa, Johanna Jean, Amy Louise, William Hullinger. BA, Princeton U., 1959; MA, Harvard U., 1960, PhD, 1964. Instr. U. Wis., Madison, 1964-65, asst. prof., 1965-67, assoc. prof., 1967-69, prof., 1969—. Dir. Synchrotron Radiation Ctr., 1985-97, Phys. Scis. Lab, Stoughton, Wis., 1992—; disting. vis. prof. U. Mo., Kansas City, 1988. A.P. Sloan fellow, 1965-67, Guggenheim fellow, 1972-73, Nat. Assn. State Univs. and Land Grant Colls. fellow Office of Sci. and Tech. Policy, 1990-91. Fellow Am. Phys. Soc.; mem. AAAS, Sigma Xi. Office: Univ Wis Phys Scis Lab 3725 Schneider Dr Stoughton WI 53589-3034 also: U Wis Dept Physics 1150 University Ave Madison WI 53706-1302

HUBER, DENNIS G., communications executive; B in Mktg. and Mgmt., Rockhurst U., MBA in Mgmt. Mgr. new product systems to group mgr. product devel. US Sprint, 1987—88, dir. voice card tech., 1988—90, dir. invoicing products and svcs., 1990—94, v.p.-bus. integration tech. solutions, 1994—2000; sr. v.p.-network/IT Sprint PCS Divsn., 2000—02; pres. Sprint North Supply, New Century, Kans., 2002—. Office: Sprint North Supply 600 New Century Pkwy New Century KS 66031

HUBER, GREGORY B., state legislator; b. Jan. 25, 1956; MD, U. Wis., 1981. Asst. dist. atty. Marathon County Dist. Atty.'s Office; mem. from dist. 85 Wis. State Assembly, Madison, 1985, 88—. Pres. Rib Mountain State Park. Mem. Wausau Jaycees (past bd. dirs.), Wis. Alumni Club (bd. dirs.). Office: 406 S 9th Ave Wausau WI 54401-4541

HUBER, JOAN ALTHAUS, sociology educator; b. Bluffton, Ohio, Oct. 17, 1925; d. Lawrence Lester and Hallie (Althaus) H.;; m. William Form, Feb. 5, 1971; children: ancy Rytina, Steven Rytina. BA, Pa. State U., 1945; MA, Western Mich. U., 1963; PhD, Mich. State U., 1967. Asst. prof. sociology U. Notre Dame, Ind., 1967-71; asst. prof. sociology U. Ill., Urbana-Champaign, 1971-73, assoc. prof., 1973-78, prof., 1978-83, head dept., 1979-83; dean Coll. Social and Behavioral Sci., Ohio State U., Columbus, 1984-92; coordinating dean Coll. Arts and Sciences, Ohio State University, Columbus, 1987-92, provost, 1992-93; sr. v.p., provost emeritus prof. Sociology emeritus, 1994. Author: (with William Form) Income and Ideology, 1973, (with Glenna Spitze) Sex Stratification, 1983, On the Origins of Gender Inequality -Baulder and Paradigm, 2007; Editor: Changing Women in a Changing Society, 1973, (with Paul Chalfant) The Sociology of Poverty, 1974, Macro-Micro Linkages in Sociology, 1991. NSF research awardee, 1978-81 Mem. Am. Sociol. Assn. (v.p. 1981-83, pres. 1987-90), Midwest Sociol. Soc. (pres. 1979-80). Office: Ohio State U Dept Sociology 300 Bricker Hall 190 N Oval Mall Columbus OH 43210-1321 Home: Apt 34 1864 Riverside Dr Columbus OH 43212 Office Phone: 614-292-8872. Business E-Mail: huber.3@osu.edu.

HUBER, SCOTT, transportation services executive; b. St. Louis, 1964; BSBA, U. Mo., St. Louis, 1985, BS in Fin., 1986; JD, St. Louis U., 1989. Bar: Mo. 1989, Ill. 1990, US Ct. Appeals 8th Cir. 1990, US Dist. Ct. Ea. Dist. Mo. 1990. Sr. staff atty. Unigroup, Inc., Fenton, Mo. Mem.: Bar Assn. Met. St. Louis, ABA, Mo. Bar. Office: Unigroup Inc 1 Premier Dr Fenton MO 63026

HUBERS, DAVID RAY, financial services company executive; b. Milaca, Minn., Jan. 28, 1943; s. Herman and Marie (Timmer) Hubers; m. Shirley A. Erickson, June 12, 1964; children: Stephanie, Lisa, Christa. BS in Acctg., U. Minn.-Mpls., 1965; MBA, U. Minn-Mpls., 1970. Adminstrv. asst. investments IDS, Inc., Mpls., 1969—71, analyst-fin. group, 1971—74, analyst-sr. securites, 1974—76, dir. investment rsch., 1976—80, v.p. corp. strategy, 1980—82; sr. v.p. fin.,CFO Am Express Fin. Advisors, Inc., Mpls., 1982—93, also dir., pres., 1993—. Mem.: Inst. Chartered Fin. Analysts (chartered fin. analyst), N.Am. Soc. Corp. Planning, Assn. for Corp. Growth, Nat. Assn. Accts., Fin. Execs. Inst., N.Y. Bank and Fin. Analysts Soc., Twin Cities Soc. Security Analysts. Republican. Home: 15 Lake Ct North Oaks MN 55127-6209 Office: American Express Financial Corp IDS Tower # 10 Minneapolis MN 55440

HUBLER, MARY, state legislator; b. Milw., July 31, 1952; BS, U. Wis., Superior, 1973; JD, U. Wis., Madison, 1980. Former tchr., coach; atty.; mem. from dist. 75 Wis. State Assembly, Madison, 1984—, vice chairwoman tourism, recreation and forest product coms., 1985-98, mem. joint fin. com., until 1996; rural affairs & forestry State of Wis. Mem. Wis. Bar Assn. Office: PO Box 544 Rice Lake WI 54868-0544 also: Wis State Assembly State Capitol Madison WI 53702-0001

HUCAL, MICHELLE, editor; b. 1978; Degree in Journalism, Mich. State U., 2000. Assoc. editor Home Décor Buyer, Chgo.; editor Environ. Design + Constrn. mag., Troy, Mich., 2002—. Bd. dirs. US Green Bldg. Coun. Named one of 40 Under 40, Crain's Detroit Bus., 2006. Mem.: Am. Soc. Bus. Publ. Editors (Editorial Excellence award 2005). Office: Environmental Design + Contruction 2401 W Big Beaver RD Ste 700 Troy MI 48084 Office Phone: 248-244-1280. Office Fax: 248-362-5103. Business E-Mail: hucalm@bnpmedia.com.

HUCLES, ANGELA KHALIA, professional soccer player; b. Va. Beach, July 5, 1978; BA in anthropology, U. Va., 2000. Soccer player, midfielder U.S. Women's Nat. Team, 2001; mem. Boston Breakers, WUSA, 2001—03, San Diego Spirit, 2003—. Columnist women's sports Boston Metro, 2002. Named First Team All-ACC, 1996, 1997, 1998, 1999, Mid Atlantic All-Star, 1996, 1997, 1998, 1999. Office: US Soccer Fedn 1801 S Prairie Ave Chicago IL 60616

HUDDLESTON, MARK WAYNE, academic administrator, political scientist, educator; b. Syracuse, NY, Dec. 31, 1950; s. Charles Proctor Huddleston and Joan Elaine Veldran; m. Melanie Kay Sharp, Nov. 19, 1983 (div. Jan. 1987); 1 child, Andrew Charles; m. Emma Elizabeth Bricker, Oct. 6, 1990; children: Katherine Anne, Giles Martin. BA in Polit. Sci., SUNY, Buffalo, 1972; MA in Polit. Sci., U. Wis., 1973, PhD in Polit. Sci., 1978. Lectr. U. Wis., Madison, 1976-77; asst. prof. SUNY, Buffalo, 1977-80, U. Del., Newark, 1980-83, assoc. prof., 1983-94, prof. polit. sci., 1994—2004, chmn. polit. sci., 1999-2000, assoc. provost, 2000—01, dean Coll. Arts and Scis., 2001—04; pres. Ohio Wesleyan U., 2004—07, U. NH, 2007—. Cons. Internat. City/County Mgmt. Assn., Bosnia-Herzegovina, 1996-2000, Kazakhstan, 1998-2000. Author: The Government's Managers, 1987, The Higher Civil Service in the U.S., 1996 (Choice award 1996), The Public Administration Workbook, 4th edit., 2000. Mem. ASPA, Am. Polit. Sci. Assn. Avocations: aviation, photography, hunting. Office: Office of Pres / U NH Thompson Hall 105 Main St Durham NH 03824 Office Phone: 740-368-3001. E-mail: mwh@owu.edu.

HUDKINS, CAROL L., state legislator; b. North Platte, Nebr., Feb. 21, 1945; m. Larry Hudkins; children: Janet, Kathy. Mem. Nebr. Legislature from 21st dist, Lincoln, 1992—; mem. agr. gen. affairs com.; mem. judiciary com. Mem. agr. gen. affairs com., judiciary com., rules com. (chair), natural resources com., transp. and comm. com, exec. bd., reference com. Mem. Saunders County Hist. Soc., Ned. Cattlemen, Saunders County Livestock Feeders; Neb. Cattlewomen. Republican. Methodist.

HUDNUT, ROBERT KILBORNE, clergyman, writer; b. Cin., Jan. 7, 1934; s. William Herbert and Elizabeth (Kilborne) H.; m. Mary Lou Lundell; children by previous marriage: Heidi, Robert Kilborne, Heather, Matthew. BA with highest honors, Princeton, 1956; M.Div., Union Theol. Sem., NYC, 1959. Ordained to ministry Presbyn. Ch., 1959; asst. minister Westminster Presbyn. Ch., Albany, NY, 1959-62; minister St. Luke Presbyn. Ch., Wayzata, Minn., 1962-73, Winnetka (Ill.) Presbyn. Ch., 1975-94. Exec. dir. Minn. Pub. Interest Research Group, 1973-75; Co-chmn. Minn. Joint Religious Legis. Coalition, 1970-75. Author: Surprised by God, 1967, A Sensitive Man and the Christ, 1971, A Thinking Man and the Christ, 1971, The Sleeping Giant: Arousing Church Power in America, 1971, An Active Man and the Christ, 1972, Arousing the Sleeping Giant: How to Organize Your Church for Action, 1973, Church Growth Is Not the Point, 1975, The Bootstrap Fallacy: What The Self-Help Books Don't Tell You, 1978, This People-This Parish, 1986, Meeting God in the Darkness, 1989, Emerson's Aesthetic, 1996, Call Waiting, 1999. Pres. Greater Met. Fedn. Twin Cities, 1970—72; chmn. Citizens Adv. Com. on Interstate 394, 1971—75; mem. planning commn. City of Cottage Grove, Minn., 2001—04; chmn. Dem. Party 33d Senatorial Dist. Minn., 1970—72, Minnetonka Dem. Party, 1970—72; fusion candidate for mayor City of Albany, 1961; chmn. Philbrook for Gov. Campaign, 2004—05; nat. chmn. Presbyns. Ch. Renewal, 1971; bd. dir. Minn. Coun. Chs., 1964—70; trustee Princeton U., 1972—76, Asheville (N.C.) Sch., 1979—2003. Rockefeller fellow, 1956; named Outstanding Young Man Minnetonka, 1967; recipient Distinguished Service award Minnetonka Tchrs. Assn., 1969 Mem.: Phi Beta Kappa.

HUDSON, CHERYL L., communications executive; Pres. Intouch Comm. Group GlobalHue, Inc., Southfield, Mich. Recipient Outstanding Women in Mktg. and Comms. award, Ebony Mag., 2001. Office: GlobalHue Inc 26555 Evergreen Rd Ste 1700 Southfield MI 48076-4206

HUDSON, KATHERINE MARY, manufacturing executive; b. Rochester, NY, Jan. 19, 1947; d. Edward Klock and Helen Mary (Rubacha) Nellis; m. Robert Orneal Hudson, Sept. 13, 1980; 1 child, Robert Klock. Student, Oberlin coll., 1964-66; BS in Mgmt., Ind. U., 1968; postgrad., Cornell U., 1968-69. Various postitions in fin., investor rels., communications, gen. mgr. instant photography Eastman Kodak Co., Rochester, 1970-87, chief info. officer, 1988-91, v.p., gen. mgr. printing and pub. imaging, 1991-93; pres., CEO Brady Corp., Milw., 1994—2003, chmn. bd., 2003. Bd. dirs. CNH Global N.V., Charming Shoppes, Inc. Trustee Alverno Coll., 1994—; bd. dirs. Med. Coll. Wis., 1995—. Recipient Chief of the Yr. award Info. Week Mag., 1990, Athena award Rochester C. of C., 1992, WESG Breaking Glass Ceiling award, 1993, Sacajewea award, 1995; Lehman fellow N.Y. State, 1968; named Wis. Bus. Leader of Yr., 1995. Republican. Avocations: golf, fishing, creative writing. E-mail: knh53092@yahoo.com.

HUDSON, ROBERT PAUL, medical educator; b. Kansas City, Kans., Feb. 23, 1926; s. Chester Lloyd and Jean (Emerson) H.; m. Olive Jean Grimes, Aug. 1, 1948 (div. 1963); children: Robert E., Donald K., Timothy M.; m. Martha Isabelle Holter, July 10, 1965; children: Stephen, Laurel. BA, U. Kans., 1949, MD, 1952; MA, Johns Hopkins U., 1966. Instr. U. Kans., Kansas City, 1958-59, assoc. in medicine, 1959-63, asst. prof., 1964-69, assoc. prof., 1969—, prof., chmn. history of medicine, 1969-95, ret. Author: Disease and Its Control, 1983; mem. editl. bd. Bull. History of Medicine, Balt., 1981-94; contbr. articles to profl. jours. 1st lt. U.S. Army, 1953-55. Master ACP; mem. Am. Assn. for History of Medicine (pres. 1984-86), Am. Osler Soc. (bd. govs., pres. 1987-88). Home: 12925 S Frontier Rd Olathe KS 66061-8647 Office: Kans U Med Ctr 39th And Rainbow Blvd Kansas City KS 66160-0001 E-mail: lastroma@earthlink.net.

HUDSON, STEVEN DANIEL, lawyer, judge; b. Trenton, Mo., Sept. 7, 1961; s. Jerry Daniel and Dorothy Louise (Wilhite) H.; m. Lora Sue Barnett, Dec. 21, 1986; children: Samantha Sue, Tanner Glen. BS in Bus. Adminstrn., William Jewell Coll., Liberty, Mo., 1983; JD, U. Mo., Kansas City, 1986. Bar: Mo. 1986, U.S. Dist. Ct. (we. dist.) Mo. 1986. Pvt. practice, Trenton, Mo., 1986—; pros. atty. Grundy County, 1995-99; assoc. cir. judge Grandy County Cir. Ct., 1999—. Mem. Trenton R-9 Vocat. Agr. Adv. Bd., 1990—; mem. North Ctrl. Mo. Coll. Office Occupations Adv. Bd., Trenton, 1991-93. Past pres., v.p. North Ctrl. Mo. Fair Bd., Trenton, 1987—; mem. Miss Trenton Scholarship Pageant Bd., 1988-95. Mem. Mo. Bar Assn., 9th Jud. Cir. Bar Assn. (pres. 1995), 3rd Jud. Cir. Bar Assn., Trenton Area C. of C. (mem. bd. 1988-90). Republican. Methodist. Avocation: sports. Office: 1013 Main St Trenton MO 64683-1839

HUEBSCH, MICHAEL D., state legislator; b. July 19, 1964; Grad., Oral Roberts U. Assemblyman Wis. State Dist. 94, 1994—. Mem. LaCrosse County Bd., Wis., LaCrosse Area Devel. Corp. Mem. Rotary. Address: 419 W Franklin St West Salem WI 54669-1531

HUELSKAMP, TIM, state legislator; b. Fowler, Kans., Nov. 11, 1968; m. Angela Huelskamp; adopted children: Natasha, Rebecca, Athan. BA, Coll. Santa Fe, 1991; PhD, Am. U., 1995. Mem. Kans. Senate, Topeka, 1996—, mem. elections and local govt. com., mem. energy and natural resources com., mem. transp. and tourism com., mem. joint com. on children and families. Named Top Friend of the Taxpayer, Kans. Taxpayers Network; recipient Daniel Award for Courageous Leadership, Kansans for Life, Ronald Reagan Outstanding Leadership Award, Kans. Rep. Assembly. Republican. Office: Rm 128-S State Capitol Bldg Topeka KS 66612-1504 also: PO Box 379 Fowler KS 67844-0410 Fax: 810-821-2712. E-mail: thuelska@ink.org.

HUELSMAN, JOANNE B., state legislator; b. Mar. 21, 1938; married. JD, Marquette U., 1980. Attorney, realtor, businesswoman; former mem. Wis. Assembly from 31st dist.; mem. Wis. Senate from 11th dist., Madison, 1990—. Republican. Home: 235 W Broadway Ste 210 Waukesha WI 53186-4826

HUETHER, ROBERT, state legislator; m. Karen; four children. Student, N.D. State U. N.D. State rep. Dist. 27, 1989—; dir. Cass County Elec./Minnkota Power; farmer. Mem. state and fed. govt. appropriations/human resources divsn., edn. and transp. coms. Democrat. Mailing: PO Box 679 Lisbon ND 58054-0679

HUFF, JOHN DAVID, church administrator; b. Muskegon, Mich., Nov. 20, 1952; s. Lucius Barthol and Marian (Brainard) H.; m. Diane Lynn Church, May 17, 1975; children: Joshua, Jason, Jessica. B in Religious Edn., Reformed Bible Coll., 1977; MA in Sch. Adminstrn., Calvin Coll., 1983; postgrad., Western Mich. U., 1984-93. Cert. ch. educator. Dir. edn. 1st Christian Reformed Ch., Visalia, Calif., 1977—79, Bethany Reformed Ch., Grand Rapids, Mich., 1979—83, Haven Reformed Ch., Kalamazoo, 1983—90, exec. dir. ops., 1990—93; exec. dir. Manitoqua Ministries, Frankfort, Ill., 1993—; pastor preaching and adminstrn. First Reformed Ch., DeMotte, Ind., 2002—. Cons. David C. Cook Pubs., 1988-90, Office Evangelism Reformed Ch. in Am., 1987-91; tchr. trainer, mem. renewal forum Synod of Mich. Reformed Ch. in Am., 1987-90; regional evangelism trainer Synod of Mid-Am., 1995-2002; bd. dirs. Chgo. Christian Counseling Ctr., 1995-2000, bd. officer, 1996-2000; v.p. Illiana Classis Reformed Ch. in Am., 1999, pres., 2000; Denominational "Refocus Leaders" facilitator Classis Illiana, 1998-2000, Classis Chgo., 1999-2001; mem. adj. faculty Trinity Christian Coll., 1996; adj. prof. Reformed Bible Coll., 2000. Author: Effective Decision Making for Church Leaders, 1988, Leader's Guide for Out of the Saltshaker and into the World, 1988. Vice-chmn. Youth Com. Bill Glass Crusade, Visalia, 1978, chmn. Cen. Valley Ch. Workers Conf., Visalia, 1978; mem. Youth Com. City-Wide Easter Svcs., Visalia, 1979; trustee Reformed Bible Coll., Grand Rapids, 1984-91, exec. com., 1985-91, asst. sec. bd. dirs., 1986-87, sec. bd. dirs., 1987-90; chmn. S.W. Mich. Christian Discipleship Com., 1984-85. Recipient DeVos award Reformed Bible Coll., 1977; Mich. State scholar, 1970. Mem. Bibl. Archeol. Soc., Christian Educators-Reformed ch. Am., Inst. for Am. Ch. Growth (cons. 1986-93), Christian Mgmt. Assn. Cen. Valley Youth Ministers (sec. 1978-79), Alban Inst., Am. Camping Assn. (bd. dirs. Ill. chpt. 1995-98), Christian Camping Internat., Delta Epsilon Chi. Republican. Avocations: reading, civil war information. Home and Office: 9991 W 1200 N Demotte IN 46310 Personal E-mail: johnhuff@netnitco.net.

HUFF, MARSHA ELKINS, lawyer; b. Tulsa, Apr. 11, 1946; BA with honors, U. Tulsa, 1968, MA, 1970; JD cum laude, Loyola U. of Chgo., 1974. Bar: Wis. Ptnr. Foley & Lardner, Milw. Mem. editorial bd. Loyola U. Law Jour., 1973-74. Mem. ABA (mem. sect. taxation). Office: Foley & Lardner 777 E Wisconsin Ave Ste 3800 Milwaukee WI 53202-5367

HUFFMAN, FORDHAM E., lawyer; b. Hilliard, Ohio, 1954; BA, Ohio State Univ., 1977, JD, 1980. Bar: Ga. 1980, Ohio 1984. Law clk. Judge Max Rosenn, US Ct. of Appeals, Third Cir., 1980; now ptnr.-in-charge Columbus office Jones Day, Ohio. Editor-in-chief Law Rev., 1980. Mem.: Columbus (Ohio) Bar Assn., Ohio State Bar Assn., State Bar of Ga. Office: Jones Day 325 John H McConnel Blvd Ste 600 PO Box 165017 Columbus OH 43216-5017 Office Phone: 614-469-3934. Office Fax: 614-461-4198. Business E-Mail: fehuffman@jonesday.com.

HUGGINS, LOIS M., human resources specialist, consumer products company executive; BA, Franklin and Marshall Coll. Various positions Sara Lee Corp., Chgo., 1987—97; divisional v.p. human resources Sara Lee Intimate Apparel, 1997—2000; leader orgn. devel. and diversity initiative Sara Lee Corp., 2000—03, v.p. human resources, 2003—04, sr. v.p. global human resources, 2004—05, sr. v.p., chief people officer, 2005—. Co-chair global human resources steering com. Sara Lee Corp., Chgo., bd. dirs. Office: Sara Lee Corp 3 First National Plz Chicago IL 60602-4260 Office Phone: 312-726-2600. Office Fax: 312-726-3712.

HUGHES, CLYDE MATTHEW, religious denomination executive; b. Huntington, W.Va., Dec. 7, 1948; s. Donald Lee and Audrey Arlene (Stevers) H.; m. Linda May Daniels, June 10, 1972; children: Crystal, Dustin, Tina, Wesley, Timothy, Penny, Heidi, Robin. Diploma, Amb. Bible Inst., London, Ohio, 1972; BA, Cedarville Coll., Ohio, 1974; MA, Meth. Theol. Sch. in Ohio, 1980; DD, Heritage Bible Coll., Dunn, NC, 1994. Ordained to ministry Internat. Pentecostal Ch. of Christ, 1974. Pastor Internat. Pentecostal Ch. of Christ, Hillsboro, Ohio, 1981-82, nat. dir. Sunday sch. London, 1976-82, dir. ch. ministries, 1982-84, asst. gen. overseer, 1984-90, gen. overseer, chmn. gen. bd., 1990—. Mem. nat. com. Mission Am., 1997—; bd. dirs. Beulah Heights Bible Coll., Atlanta, 1982—, chmn. bd. 1990-96. Editor-in-chief The Pentecostal Leader; contbr. articles to religious publs. Chmn. bd. dirs. Locust Grove Rest Home, 1990-98. Mem. Nat. Assn. Evangs. (bd. dirs. 1990—2001), Madison County Evang. Assn. (bd. dirs. 1990-2001), London Ministerial Assn., Chs. United with Israel (bd. gov. 2002-), Mission Am. (nat. com. 1997-), Pentecostal/Charismatic Chs. N.Am. (bd. dirs. 1994—, exec. com. 2001), Internat. Pentecostal Press Assn. (N.Am. chpt. exec. com., 2001—, second v.p.). Mem. Internat. Pentecostal Ch. Of Christ. Home: 7040 Danville Rd London OH 43140-9766

HUGHES, EDWARD F. X., healthcare educator, preventive medicine physician; b. Boston, Jan. 10, 1942; s. Joseph Daniel and Elizabeth (Dempsey) Hughes; m. Susan Lane Mooney, Feb. 11, 1967; children: Edward, John, Dempsey. BA in Philosophy, Amherst Coll., Mass., 1962; MD, Harvard U., Cambridge, Mass., 1966; MPH, Columbia U., NYC, 1969. Intern, resident surg. Columbia-Presbyn. Med. Ctr., NYC, 1966-68; instr. to assoc. prof. Mt. Sinai Sch. Medicine, NYC, 1969-77; rsch. assoc. Nat. Bur. Econ. Rsch., NYC, 1970-77; prof. prevention medicine Northwestern U. Med. Sch., Chgo., 1977—, founder, dir. ctr. health svc. policy rsch., 1977-94; prof. health industry mgmt. and mgmt. & strategy J. L. Kellogg Grad. Sch. Mgmt., Northwestern U.,

Evanston, Ill., 1977—, dir. health industry mgmt. program, 1980—83, co-dir. biotech. program, 2001—. Cons. Nat. Ctr. Health Svcs. Rsch., Rockville, Md., 1975-82, AMA, Chgo., 1981-83, Midwest Bus. Group on Health, Chgo., 1983-85; expert witness for providers, health Plans and pharm. firms, 1993—. Editor: Hospital Cost Containment: A Policy Analysis, 1979, A Perspective on Quality in American health Care, 1988 (Bradley award 1962, Health Career Scientist award 1973-75); mem. editl. bd. Managed Care Interface (Latiolias Honor medal 1999, Beta Gamma Sigma award), Jour. Clin. Outcomes, Group Health News, Counseline; contbr. articles to profl. jours. Health Care Financing Adminstrn. grantee, Washington, 1978-84, Ford Found., 1983-86, Robert Wood Johnson Found, 1978-82, NIH, 1983-95, Pew Charitable Trusts, 1990-92, Baxter Found., 1991-96. Fellow N.Y. Acad. Medicine, Am. Coll. Physician Execs.; mem. APHA, Americas Health Ins. Plans (acad. dir. exec. leadership program), Assn. Health Svcs. Rsch. (co-founder, v.p. 1981-83, bd. dirs. 1981-84), Assn. Tchrs. Preventive Medicine (bd. dirs. 1973-76), Med. Adminstrs. Conf., Nat. Assn. Managed Care Physicians (med. adv. bd.), Boston Latin Sch. Chgo. Club (bd. dirs. 1983-86), Chapoquoit Yacht Club (West Famouth, Mass.) Home: 810 Lincoln St Evanston IL 60201-2405 Office: Kellogg Sch Mgmt 2001 Sheridan Rd Evanston IL 60208-0814 Office Phone: 847-491-8384. Business E-Mail: efx-hughes@kellogg.northwestern.com.

HUGHES, JIM, state representative; b. Columbus, Ohio, Sept. 17, 1964; married; 1 child. BS in Transp. and Linguistics, Ohio State U., BSBA; JD, Capital U. Asst. city prosecutor City of Columbus Prosecutor's Office; asst. county prosecutor Franklin County Prosecutor's Office; atty. Wiles Boyle Burkholder & Bringardner Co., LPA; state rep. dist. 22 Ohio Ho. of Reps., Columbus, 1999—, chair, higher edn. subcom., mem. banking pensions and securities, fin. and appropriations, ins., rules and reference, and state govt. coms., mem. ethics and elections subcom. Deacon Ascension Luth. Ch., Ohio. Mem.: Tourette Syndrome Assn. Ohio (profl. adv. bd.), Charity Newsies, Faith Am., Ohio State U. Alumni Assn., Shamrock Club of Ohio, Agonis Club of Columbus, Alladin Temple Shrine (mem. reception unit), Phi Gamma Deltga. Republican. Office: 77 S High St 13th fl Columbus OH 43215-6111

HUGHES, JOHN, chemical company executive; b. St. David's, Wales, Apr. 10, 1943; came to U.S., 1964; s. Essex James and Mary Ann Hughes; m. Linda Kay Petersen; children: Stacey Ann, Bradford James. BS in Chemistry, U. Wales, 1964; MBA, U. Chgo., 1968. With AMCOL Internat., Arlington Heights, Ill., 1965—, now chmn. Office: AMCOL Internat 1500 W Shure Dr Arlington Heights IL 60004-1443

HUGHES, JOHN RUSSELL, neurologist, educator; b. DuBois, Pa., Dec. 19, 1928; s. John Henry and Alice (Cooper) H.; m. Mary Ann Dick, June 14, 1958; children: John Russell Jr. (dec.), Christopher Alan, Thomas Gregory, Cheryl Ann. AB summa cum laude, Franklin and Marshall Coll., 1950; BA with honors, Oxford U., Eng., 1952, MA with honors, 1955, DM (hon.), 1976; PhD, Harvard U., 1954; MD, Northwestern U., 1975. Neurophysiologist NIH, 1954-56; dir. electroencephalography dept. Meyer Hosp., SUNY, 1956-63; dir. div. lab. scis., including electroencephalography Northwestern U. Med. Center, 1963-77, prof. neurology, 1968—; dir. EEG and Epilepsy Clinic, U. Ill. Med. Center, 1977—; staff U. Ill. Hosp., Community Hosp., Geneva, Delnor Hosp., St. Charles; dir.neurophysiology Humana-Michael-Reese Med. Ctr., 1992—. Cons. Chgo. VA Westside Hosp., Mercyville and Copley Meml. Hosp., Aurora, Ill., others; participant debate on brain death BBC-TV; bd. dirs. Am. Bd. EEG and Neurophysiology; participant Am. Med. EEG Assn.; rep. Internat. Fedn. EEG and Clin. Neurophysiology lectr. tour of Africa, 1989; keynote speaker Internat. Course of Neurophysiology, Oxford U., 1993, invited speaker, 1996, 99, 02, 05; invited spkr. Damascus Med. Sch., Syria, 1998, Royal Soc. of Medicine, London, 2003; found. lectr. Cleveland Clinic, 2007; lectr. in field. Author: Functional Organization of the Diencephalon, 1957, Atlas on Cerebral Death and Coma, 1976, Chinese Translation, 1997, Japanese Translation, 1998, EEG in Clinical Practice, 1982, 2d edit., 1994, EEG Evoked Potentials in Psychiatry and Behavioral Neurology, 1983, JFK and Sam, 2005; contbr. articles to profl. jours. Command Surgeon, USAR, 1986-90, with Army Med. R & D Command, 1990—, mobilization replacement for maj. gen., comdr. Recipient Alumni award Franklin and Marshall Coll., 1978, Lifetime Achievement award Am. EEG and Clin. Neurophysiol. Soc., 2000. Mem. Am. Electroencephalography Soc. (treas. 1965-68), Eastern Electroencephalography Soc. (sec.-treas. 1961-64), Ctrl. Electroencephalography Soc., Am. Med. EEG Assn. (bd. dirs.), Am. Bd. EEG and Neurophysiology (bd. dirs.), Internat. EEG and Clin. Neurophysiology (bd. dirs.), Am. Acad. EEG (bd. dirs.), Brit. Soc. of neurophysiology (hon.), Chgo. Acad. Medicine, Am. Epilepsy Soc., Am. Physiol. Soc., Soc. Neuroscis., Am. Acad. Neurology, Phi Beta Kappa, Sigma Xi (lectr. 1960—) Achievements include research on coding in central nervous system, new theory on neural mechanisms in olfaction, electro-clin. correlations in different types of epilepsy, organic aspects in juvenile delinquency. Home: 720 Roslyn Ter Evanston IL 60201-1722 Office: U Ill Consultation Clinic Epilepsy 912 S Wood St Chicago IL 60612-7325 E-mail: JHughes@uic.edu.

HUGHES, LOUIS RALPH, information technology executive; b. Cleve., Feb. 10, 1949; s. Louis R. and Anna E. (Holland) H.; m. Candice A. Baranchik, May 20, 1972; children: Brian W., Brittany K. B of Mech. Engring., GM Inst., 1971; MBA, Harvard U., 1973. V.p. fin. GM Can., 1985-86, GM Europe, Switzerland, 1987-89; chmn., mng. dir. Adam. Opel, Germany, 1989-92; pres. GM Europe, 1992-94; exec.v.p. GM Corp., 1992—2000; pres. GM Internat., Switzerland, 1994-98; exec. v.p. new bus. strategies Gen. Motors Corp., Detroit, 1998—2000; pres., COO Lockheed Martin Corp., 2000; chmn. Maxager Technology, San Rafael, Calif., 2001—; chief of staff Afghanistan Reconstruction Group, 2004. Bd. dir. BT Group, ABB, Sulzer; mem. supervisory bd. Deutsche Bank AG, 1993—2000. Avocations: skiing, mountain climbing, antiques. Office: Maxager Technology Bd Directors 2173 E San Francisco Blvd San Rafael CA 94901

HUGHES, T. LEE, newspaper editor; Bur. chief AP, Milw., 1993—. Office: 918 N 4th St Milwaukee WI 53203-1506

HUGHES, THOMAS A., lawyer, utilities executive; BS, Mo. Valley Coll.; JD, Univ. Mo. Gen. counsel Mo. Pub. Svc. Commn.; staff atty. Detroit Edison, Mich. Consol. Gas Co., 1978—83, regulatory atty. supr., 1983—88, gen. atty., regulatory affairs, 1988—93, assoc. gen. counsel, mgr., 1993—98, asst. v.p., mgr., assoc. gen. counsel, 1998—2001, v.p. gen. counsel, 2001—; and chief compliance officer DTE Energy, 2005—. With US Army, 1963—65, artillery. Mem.: Met. Detroit Bar Assn. Found., Am. Corp. Counsel Assn. (Mich. chpt.), Mich. Bar Assn. Office: DTE Energy Co 2000 2nd Ave Detroit MI 48226-1279

HUGI, ROBERT F., lawyer; b. Kansas City, Mo., Mar. 2, 1958; BS with highest distinction, Northwestern Univ., 1980; JD cum laude, Univ. Chgo., 1986. Bar: Ill. 1986. Assoc. Mayer Brown Rowe & Maw, Chgo. & London, 1986—95, ptnr., fin. & securitization, 1995—. Contbr. articles to profl. jours. Office: Mayer Brown Rowe Maw Llp 230 S La Salle St Ste 400 Chicago IL 60604-1407 Office Phone: 312-701-7121. Office Fax: 312-706-8153. Business E-Mail: rhugi@mayerbrownrowe.com.

HUGOSON, GENE, state legislator, farmer; b. Sept. 1945; m. Patricia Hugoson; one child. BA, Augsburg Coll.; postgrad., Mankato State U. Farmer; Dist. 26A rep. Minn. Ho. of Reps., St. Paul, 1986-95; commr. Agr. Dept., 1995—. Former mem. econ. devel., internat. trade and redistricting coms., Minn. Ho. of Reps.; mem. Agr., rules and legis. adminstrn., transp. and transit, and taxes coms.; asst. minority leader. Office: State of Minn Dept of Agr 90 Plato Blvd W Saint Paul MN 55107-2004

HUHEEY, MARILYN JANE, ophthalmologist, educator; b. Cin., Aug. 31, 1935; d. George Mercer and Mary Jane (Weaver) Huheey. BS in Math., Ohio U., Athens, 1958; MS in Physiology, U. Okla., 1966; MD, U. Ky., 1970. Diplomate Am. Bd. Ophthalmology. Tchr. math. James Ford Rhodes H.S., Cleve., 1956-58; biostatistician Nat. Jewish Hosp., Denver, 1958-60; life sci. engr. Stanley Aviation Corp., Denver, 1960-63, N.Am. Aviation Co., LA, 1963-67; intern U. Ky. Hosp., 1970-71; emergency room physician Jewish Hosp., Mercy Hosp., Bethesda Hosp., Cin., 1971-72; ship's doctor, 1972; resident in ophthalmology Ohio State U. Hosp., Columbus, 1972-75; practice medicine specializing in ophthalmology Columbus, 1975—. Mem. staff Univ. Hosp., Grant Hosp., St. Anthony Hosp., 1975—79; clin. asst. prof. Ohio State U. Med. Sch., 1976—, dir. course ophthalmologic receptionist/aides, 1976; mem. Peer Rev. Sys. Bd., 1986—92, mem. exec. com., 1988—92; mem. Ohio Optical Dispensers Bd., 1986—91; bd. dirs. Ctrl. Ohio Radio Reading Svc., 1997—2003; mem. Ohio Bd. Cosmetology, 1999—. Mem. United Way, mem. planning com., 1992—93; Dem. candidate Ohio Senate, 1982. Fellow: Am. Acad. Ophthalmology; mem.: LWV, AAUP, Herb Soc., Grandview Area Bus. Assn., Columbus Coun. World Affairs, Life Care Alliance (pres. sustaining bd. 1987—88), Am. Coun. the Blind (bd. dirs. 1995—96), Columbus EENT Soc., Ohio State Med. Assn. (dr.-nurse liaison com. 1983—87), Ohio Soc. Prevent Blindness (chmn. med. adv. bd. 1978—80), Franklin County Acad. Medicine (mem. profl. rels. com. 1979—82, mem. legis. com. 1981—89, mem. edn. and program com. 1981—88, chmn. 1982—85, chmn. cmty. rels. com. 1987—90, chmn. resolution com. 1987—92, mem. fin. com. 1988—92), Ohio Ophthalmol. Soc. (bd. govs. 1984—89, del. to Ohio State Med. Assn. 1984—88), Am. Assn. Ophtalmologists, Columbus Area Women's Polit. Caucus, Federated Dem. Women Ohio, Columbus C. of C., Mercedes Benz Club (bd. dirs. 1981—83), Wicked Investment Club (pres. 1999—2004, treas. 2005—), Columbus Met. Club (mem. forum com. 1982—85, mem. fundraising com. 1983—84, chmn. 10th anniversary com. 1986), Colubmus Bus. and Profl. Women's Club, Zonta (mem. program com. 1984—86, chmn. internat. com. 1983), Phi Mu. Home: 2396 Northwest Blvd Columbus OH 43221-3829 Office: 1335 Dublin Rd Ste 25A Columbus OH 43215-1000 Office Phone: 614-488-8836. E-mail: mhuheey1@yahoo.com.

HULBERT, SAMUEL FOSTER, college president; b. Adams Center, NY, Apr. 12, 1936; s. Foster David and Wilma May (Speakman) H.; m. Joy Elinor Husband, Sept. 3, 1960; children: Gregory, Samantha, Jeffrey. BS in Ceramic Engring., Alfred U., 1958, PhD, 1964. Registered profl. engr., La, S.C. Asst. varsity and freshman football coach Alfred U. (N.Y.), 1959—61; lab. instr. N.Y. State Coll. Ceramics, Alfred, 1958—59; instr. math and physics Alfred U., 1960—64; asst. prof. ceramic and metall. engring. Clemson U. (S.C.), 1964—68, head divsn. interdisciplinary studies, assoc. prof. materials and bioengring., 1968—71; assoc. dean engring research and interdisciplinary studies, prof. materials engring. and bioengring., dir. materials engring. and bioengring., 1970—73; prof. bioengring., dean Sch. Engring. Tulane U., New Orleans, 1973—76; pres.-designate spl. asst. to pres. Rose-Hulman Inst. Tech., Terre Haute, Ind., 1976, pres., 1976—. Bd. dirs. Ind. Bus. Modernization & Tech. Corp., Thomas & Skinner, Inc., Old Nat. Bank, Interactive Intelligence, Inc., Centerfield Capital Ptnrs. Mem. editorial bd. Jour. Biomed. Materials Rsch., 1970—, Interactive Intelligence, 2001-; contbr. articles in field of biomaterials and artificial organ design to profl. jours. Recipient medal Italian Soc. Orthopaedics, 1973, Delitala medal Instituto Ortopedico Rizzoli, 1973, Clemson award for outstanding contbns. to biomaterials, 1973, George Winters award European Soc. Biomaterials, 1982, Founder's award Soc. Biomaterials, 2001, Lifetime Achievement award Ind. Health Industry Forum, 1996, Ernst & Young Supporter of Indiana Entrepreneurship award, 1998, Chapman S. Root award Hospice of the Wabash Valley, 2000. Fellow Am. Inst. for Med. and Biol. Engring., Am. Biomaterials Scis. and Engring., Internat. Acad. Ceramics; mem. Am. Soc. Artificial Internal Organs, Biomed. Engring. Soc., Soc. Biomaterials (dir. 1974—, pres. 1975-76, founder's award 2001, William C. Hall award 2001), Am. Ceramic Soc., at. Inst. Ceramics Engrs., Am. Soc. Engring. Edn., Ind. Colls. and Univ. Assn., Ind. Colls. of Ind., Ind. Conf. Higher Edn., Assn. Ind. Tech. Univs. (sec., treas. 1977-78, pres. 1987-90), Presidents of Ind. Colls. and Univs., Vigo County Hist. Soc. (dir. 1979—, pres. 1995—), Keramos, Blue Key, Ind. Acad., Internat. Acad. Ceramics, Rotary, Sigma Xi. Republican.

HULL, ELIZABETH ANNE, retired English language educator; b. Upper Darby, Pa., Jan. 10, 1937; d. Frederick Bossart and Elizabeth (Schmik) H.; m. Dean Carlyle Beery, Feb. 5, 1955 (div. 1962); children: Catherine Doria Beery Pizarro, Barbara Phyllis Beery Wintczak; m. Frederik Pohl, July 1984. Student, Ill. State U., 1954-55; AA, Wilbur Wright Jr. Coll., Chgo., 1965; B in Philosophy, Northwestern U., 1968; MA, Loyola U., Chgo., 1970, PhD, 1975. Teaching asst. Loyola U., Chgo., 1968-71; prof. English, coord. honors program William Rainey Harper Coll., Palatine, Ill., 1971-2001; ret., 2001; theater critic Lerner ewspapers/Pioneer Press, Lincolnwood, Ill., 2004—05. Judge nat. writing competition Nat. Coun. Tchrs. of English, 1975-2004, John W. Campbell award, 1986—. Co-editor: (with F. Pohl) Tales from the Planet Earth; contbr. articles to profl. jours. Pres. Lexington Green Condominium Assn., Schaumburg, Ill., 1982-84; bd. dirs. Hunting Ridge Homeowner's Assn., Palatine, 1984-86; Dem. candidate for U.S. Ho. of Reps. for 8th Congl. Dist. Ill., 1996; bd. dirs. .W. Cmty. Hosp. Aux., 2001-03; mem. steering com. Constituency on Vols. Ill. Hosp. Assn., 2001-03; pres. Honors Coun.-Ill. Region, 1992-93. Recipient orthwestern U. Alumni award for Merit, 1995, Thomas Clareson award Sci. Fictin Rsch. Assn., 1998, Excellence award Nat. Inst. for Staff and Orgnl. Devel., 1998. Mem. MLA, Midwest MLA, Popular Culture Assn., Sci. Fiction Rsch. Assn. (editor 1981-84, sec. 1987-88, pres. 1989-90), Ill. Coll. English Assn. (pres. 1975-77), World Sci. Fiction Assn. (N.Am. sec. 1978—), Palatine Area LWV (bd. dirs. 1991—, v.p. 1995-96, pres. 1998-2000), Am. Assn. for Women in C.C. (v.p. comm., bd. dirs. Harper Coll. chpt. 1993-96). Home: 855 Harvard Dr Palatine IL 60067-7026 E-mail: citylife@lernernews.com.

HULSEMAN, ROBERT L., manufacturing executive; b. Apr. 5, 1932; Pres. Solo Cup Co., Highland Park, Ill., 1953-90, pres., CEO, 1990—2004, chmn., CEO, 2004—06, chmn., 2006, chmn. emeritus, 2006. Office: Solo Cup Co 1700 Old Deerfield Rd Highland Park IL 60035-3792

HULSHOF, KENNY CHARLES, congressman; b. Sikeston, Mo., May 22, 1958; m. Renee Lynn Howell; 1 child. BS in Agr. Econs., U. Mo., Columbia, 1980; JD, U. Miss. Sch. Law, 1983. Bar: Mo. 1983, Miss. 1983. Asst. pub. defender 32nd Mo. Jud. Circuit, 1983—86; asst. pros. atty. Cape Girardeau County, Mo., 1986—89; spl. prosecutor Mo. Atty. Gen. Office, 1989—96; mem. US Congress from 9th Mo. dist., 1997—, mem. ways and means com., mem. budget com., mem. health subcommittee, mem. social security subcommittee. Rep. candidate for Boone County Prosecutor, 1992, US Congress, 1994, 96; mem. MU Farm Ho. Found. Named Statesman of Month, Jefferson City, Mo. News Tribune, 1993; recipient Lon O. Hocker award, Trial Advocacy, Mo. Bar Assn., 1992, Nat. Energy Leadership award, Nat. Biodiesel Bd., 2004. Mem.: Boone County, Mo. Farm Bur., NRA, Nat. Dist. Atty. Assoc., Mo. Bar Assn., Miss. Bar Assn., Ducks Unlimited. Republican. Roman Catholic. Office: US House Reps 409 Cannon House Office Bldg Washington DC 20515 Office Phone: 202-225-2956. Office Fax: 202-225-5712.

HULTGREN, SCOTT J., microbiologist educator; PhD, Northwestern U., 1988. Postdoc. Umea U., Sweden; assoc. prof. Dept. Molecular Microbiology Wash. U. Sch. Medicine, St. Louis. Recipient Eli Lilly and Co. Rsch. award, Am. Soc. Microbiology, 1998. Office: Dept Molecular Microbio Wash U Sch Medicine 660 S Euclid Ave # 8230 Saint Louis MO 63110-1010

HUME, LINDEL O., state legislator; b. Winslow, Ind., June 7, 1942; m. Judith Hume. BS, Oakland city Coll.; postgrad., U. Evansville. Mgr. internal auditing Potter & Brumfield; mem. Ind. Ho. of Reps., 1974-82, Ind. Senate from 48th dist., 1982—; minority whip; mem. agr. and small bus. com.; mem. ethics, interstate coop and transp. com.; ranking mem. elec. com.; mem. rules and legis. procedure com.; ranking minority mem. govt. and regulatory affairs com. Mem. adv. bd. Gibson County Salvation Army. Mem. Inst. Internal Auditors (past pres.), Kiwanis (past pres.). Home: 1797 Concord Dr Princeton IN 47670-9762 Office: State Senate State Capitol Indianapolis IN 46204

HUMERICKHOUSE, JOE D., state legislator; m. Thelma Humerickhouse. Ind. fee appraiser, Osage City, Kans.; mem. from dist. 59 Kans. State Ho. of Reps., Topeka. Address: 912 S 5th Osage City KS 66523 Also: 712 S 5th St Osage City KS 66523-1512

HUMKE, RAMON LYLE, utilities executive; b. Quincy, Ill., Nov. 19, 1932; s. E.G. and Florence K. (Koch) H.; m. Carolyn Jacobs Humke, Nov. 20, 1955; 1 child, Steven K. Student, Quincy Coll., 1952-53, Springfield Coll., Ill., 1956-58, Carleton Coll., 1968; LLD, U. Indpls., 1988. Various mgmt. positions Ill. Bell Telephone Co., 1951-73; dir. forecasting and productivity AT&T, NYC, 1974-75; v.p. pers. Ill. Bell Tel. Co., Chgo., 1978-82; v.p. corp. affairs Ameritech, Chgo., 1982-83; pres., CEO Ind. Bell Telephone Co. Inc., Indpls., 1983-89, Ameritech Svcs., Chgo., 1989-90; pres., COO Indpls. Power & Light Co., 1990—, also bd. dirs.; vice chmn. Ipalco Enterprises, Inc. Indpls., Indpls., 1991—; also bd. dirs. Ipalco Enterprises, Inc., Indpls. Chmn. bd. Meridian Ins. Group, Meridian Mut. Ins. Co.; bd. dirs. LDI Mgmt. Chmn. Infrastructure Commn., 1990, Indpls.; bd. dirs. Indpls. Downtown, Inc., 1992—; adv. bd. Crossroads of Am. chpt. Boy Scouts Am. With U.S. Army, 1953-56, ETO. Named Ky. Col., 1983, Ark. Traveler, 1985, Sagamore of the Wabash, 1987, 89; recipient medal of merit U.S. Treasury Dept., 1984, 85, Charles Whistler award, 1989, Benjamin Harrison medallion award, 1990, Americanism award, 1991, Good Scout award Boy Scouts Am., 1993, Hoosier Heritage award, 1993, Ind. Acad., 1996. Mem. Indpls. C. of C. (chmn. 1997-98, dir.), Columbia Club, Crooked Stick Golf Club, Indpls. Athletic Club, Meridian Hills Country Club, Skyline Club (bd. govs.), Twin Lakes Golf Club. Avocations: golf, hiking.

HUML, DONALD SCOTT, manufacturing executive; b. Lake Geneva, Wis., May 8, 1946; s. Robert Francis and Shirley (Roberts) H.; m. Joyce Cora Featherstone, Oct. 2, 1965; children: Tiffany Lynn, Alison Michelle, Andrew Scott. BBA, Marquette U., 1969; MBA, Temple U., 1980. Mgr. treasury ops. Allis-Chalmers Corp., West Allis, Wis., 1970-73; dir. fin. services CertainTeed Corp., Valley Forge, Pa., 1973-75, asst. treas., 1975-78, v.p., treas., 1978-81, v.p., comptroller, 1981-83, v.p., div. pres., 1983-86, v.p., group pres., 1986-89, v.p., chief fin. officer, 1989-90; v.p., CFO Saint-Gobain Corp., Valley Forge, Pa., 1990-94; sr. v.p., CFO Snap-on Inc., Kenosha, Wis., 1994—2002; exec. v.p., CFO Greif, Inc., Delaware, Ohio, 2002—. Mem. adv. bd. Marquette U. Sch. Bus. Adminstrn. Mem. Am. Mgmt. Assn., Fin. Execs. Inst., Conf. Bd. CFO Coun., Leading CFOs, Beta Gamma Sigma. Republican. Roman Catholic. Avocations: tennis, running, reading. Office: Greif Inc 425 Winter Rd Delaware OH 43015 Home: PO Box 346 Boca Grande FL 33921 Office Phone: 740-549-6137. Business E-Mail: don.huml@greif.com.

HUMMEL, GREGORY WILLIAM, lawyer; b. Sterling, Ill., Feb. 25, 1949; s. Osborne William and Vivian LaVera (Guess) H.; m. Teresa Lynn Beveroth, June 20, 1970; children: Andrea Lynn, Brandon Gregory. BA, MacMurray Coll., 1971; JD, Northwestern U., 1974. Bar: Ill. 1974, U.S. Dist. Ct. (no. dist.) Ill. 1974. Assoc. Rusnak, Deutsch & Gilbert, Chgo., 1974-78; ptnr. Rudnick & Wolfe, Chgo., 1978-97; mem. Bell, Boyd & Lloyd LLP, Chgo., 1997—. Mem. vis. com. dept. music U. Chgo. Editor Jour. Criminal Law & Criminology Northwestern U., 1973-74; co-author: Illinois Real Estate Forms, 1989; contbr. articles to law jours. Mem. gov. coun. Luth. Gen. Hosp. Advocate Health Care Sys., 1998-2007; trustee Mac Murray Coll., Jacksonville, Ill., 1986-2001; trustee, sec.-treas. Homes for Children Found; bd. advisors Chgo. area coun. Boy Scouts Am., ChildServ; trustee Nat. Inst. Constrn. Law and Practice; mem. steering com. Increment Fin. Coalition Coun. Devel. Fin. Authorities. Mem. Internat. Bar Assn. (past co-chmn. com. internat. constrn. projects), Am. Coll. Constrn. Lawyers (past pres.), Urban Land Inst. (trustee), Urban Land Inst. Found. (gov.), Chgo. Dist. Coun. (past chmn.), Lambda Alpha Internat. (Ely chpt. past pres.), Econ. Club (Chgo.). Office: Bell Boyd & Lloyd LLP 3 1st Nat Plaza 70 W Madison St Ste 3300 Chicago IL 60602-4207 Office Phone: 312-807-4253. E-mail: ghummel@bellboyd.com.

HUMPHREY, KAREN ANN, college director; d. Martin and Eleanor (Schwartau) Annexstad; m. Charles W. Humphrey; children: Karna, Kirk. BA in Am. Studies, U. Minn. Cmty. affairs editor KRBI Radio, St. Peter, Minn., 1976-77; assoc. editor Dassel Cokato Enterprise and Dispatch, Dassel, Minn., 1979-89; legis. asst. to U.S. Sen. Dave Durenberger, 1989-95; comms. cons. Karen Humphrey and Co., Watertown, Minn., 1995-98; cmty. rels. mgr. Barnes & Noble, Minnetonka, Minn.; pres. Minn. Hist. Soc., St. Paul, 1996-98; dir. planned giving Bethany Coll., Lindsborg, Kans., 1998—2002, coord. Disting. Professorship in Swedish Studies, 2000, v.p. instnl. advancement, 2002—, dir. planned giving. Mem. hon. com. for Vandringer Conf.: Norwegians in the Am. Mosaic, 2000. Active Bethany Luth. Ch., Bethany Coll. Symphonic Band, Lindsborg Cmty. Orch. Mem. Assn. Luth. Devel. Execs., U. Minn. Alumni Assn., Norwegian-Am. Hist. Assn. (bd. dirs.), Minn. Pub. Radio, Dassel Leikarring, Oral History Assn., Kans. State Hist. Soc. (bd. dirs.). Office: Bethany Coll 421 N 1st St Lindsborg KS 67456-1897 E-mail: khumphrey@ks-usa.net.

HUMPHREYS, KATIE, health agency administrator; b. South Bend, Ind. BS, Western Mich. U.; MS, Ind. U., South Bend; MBA, U. Notre Dame. Dir. health care policy Gov. Evan Bayh's adminstrn.; interim gen. mgr. Ind. Toll Rd.; commr. Ind. State Dept. Adminstrn.; dep. dir. Ind. State Budget Agy.; city contr., dir. adminstrn. and fin. City of South Bend; dep. commr. Ind. State Dept. Health, 1997—. With St. Joseph's Med. Ctr. South Bend, No. Ind. Health Sys. Agy., Logan Ctr. South Bend, No. Ind. State Hosp.; tchr. South Bend Cmty. Schs. Office: Ind State Dept of Health 2 N Meridian St Indianapolis IN 46204-3003

HUNDERT, EDWARD M., former academic administrator, educator; b. Woodbridge, NJ; m. Mary Hundert; 3 children. BS in Math. and History of Sci. and Medicine, summa cum laude, Yale U., 1978; MA in Philosophy, Politics and Econs., first class honors, Oxford U., 1980; MD, Harvard U., 1984. Diplomate Am. Bd. Neurology and Psychiatry. Med. intern Mount Auburn Hosp., Cambridge, Mass., 1984—85; resident in adult psychiatry, rsch. fellow, Labs. for Psychiatric Rsch. McLean Hosp., Belmont, Mass., 1985—88, chief resident, 1987—88; clin. fellow in psychiatry Harvard Med. Sch., Boston, 1984—88, instr. psychiatry, 1988—90, asst. prof. psychiatry, 1990—93, asst. prof. med. ethics, 1990—97, assoc. dean for student affairs, 1990—97, assoc. master, William B. Castle Soc., 1992—97, assoc. prof. psychiatry, 1994—97, faculty fellow, Harvard U. Mind/Brain/Behavior Initiative, 1996—99; prof. psychiatry U. Rochester Sch. Medicine and Dentistry, 1997—2002, prof. med. humanities NY, 1997—2002, sr. assoc. dean for med. edn., 1997—2000, dean, 2000—02; pres. Case Western Res. U., Cleve., 2002—06, prof. biomed. ethics, 2002—. Asst. psychiatrist McLean Hosp., Belmont, 1988—94, hosp. ethicist, 1988—97, assoc. psychiatrist, 1995—97; psychiatrist Strong Meml. Hosp., Rochester, NY, 1997—2002. Author: Philosophy, Psychiatry and Neuroscience: Three Approaches to the Mind, 1989, Lessons from an Optical Illusion: On Nature and Nurture, Knowledge and Values, 1995. Mem.: Phi Beta Kappa. Office: Case Western Res U Adelbert Hall 216 10900 Euclid Ave Cleveland OH 44106-7001

HUNDERTMARK, JEAN L., state representative; b. Feb. 25, 1954; married; 2 children. Grad., Bryant and Stratton Coll., Milw., 1973. Restaurant owner; state assembly mem. Wis. State Assembly, Madison, 1998—, chair, labor and workforce devel. com., mem. aging and long-term care, edn., tax and spending limitations, and vets. adn mil. affairs coms. Office: State Capitol Rm 13W PO Box 8952 Madison WI 53708-8952

HUNDLEY, ELAINE E., retired nursing education administrator; b. Mandan, ND, Apr. 11, 1933; d. Valentine and Constantina Elisabeth (Braun) Helbling; m. James B. Hundley, Sept. 7, 1954; children: Mary Jo, Leslie, Jamie, John, Rachel. RN Diploma, Sisters of St. Joseph Sch. of Nursing of N.D., 1954; Coronary Care Cert., Parkland Coll., 1971; BA in Nursing, Sangamon State U., 1975; MA in Nursing Adminstrn./Edn., Columbia Pacific U., 1984. Cert. continuing edn. and staff devel., ANCC; cert. CNA instr. Clinic staff nurse Grand Forks (N.D.) Clinic, 1954-55; staff nurse med.-surg. units, house supr., nurse asst. instr. St. Michael's Hosp., Grand Forks, 1955-68; sch. nurse St. Michael's Sch., Grand Forks, 1960-64; coronary care staff nurse Burnham Hosp., Champaign, Ill., 1972-73; mem. ICU staff St. John's Hosp., Springfield, Ill., 1975; dir. staff devel. Springfield Humana Hosp., 1977-80, ICU staff nurse, staff nurse recovery rm., med.-surg. units, emergency rm., 1975-77; dir. continuing edn. nursing/allied health Lincoln Land C.C., Springfield, 1981-97, ret., 1997. Mem. profl. edn. bd. Am. Cancer Soc., Am. Heart Assn. Active planning bd. Sangamon County Health Dept., Ill. Mem. ANA, Ill. Nurses Assn. (pres., program chair, bd. dirs. 9th dist. 1975—, chair commn. continuing edn. 1993-97, Staff Devel./Continuing Edn. award 1999), State Nurses Active in Politics in Ill., Health Svcs. Area Region Ill. Coun. Continuing Edn. (pres., v.p., sec., treas. 1978—). Roman Catholic. Avocations: music, reading, gardening, quilting, photography. Home: RR 1 Rochester IL 62563-9801 Office: Lincoln Land CC Shepherd Rd Springfield IL 62794

HUNHOFF, BERNIE P., state legislator; b. Yankton, SD, Sept. 5, 1951; s. Bernard P. Sr. and Margaret (Modde) H.; m. Myrna Mulloy, 1974; children: Katie, Chris. BA, Mt. Marty Coll., 1974. Legis. aide U.S. Rep. Frank Denholm, 1974; chmn. Yankton County Dem. Party, 1984-86; mem. S.D. Senate, 1993—, mem. appropriations com.; pub. rels. dir. U. S.D. Sch.Medicine, 1977-79; editor, pub. The Observer, Yankton, S.D., 1979-85, S.D. Mag., Yankton, 1985—. Co-author: Uniquely S.D., 1989—. Home: PO Box 175 Yankton SD 57078-0175

HUNIA, EDWARD MARK, foundation executive; b. Sharon, Pa., Jan. 8, 1946; s. Edward and Estelle (Maleski) H.; m. Mary Sue Marburger, Sept. 25, 1976; children: Stephen, Adam. BSME, Carnegie Mellon U., 1967, MSME, 1968; MBA, U. Pitts., 1971. CFA. Sr. systems analyst Pitts. Plate Glass Industries, 1968-73; asst. to treas. Carnegie Mellon U., Pitts., 1973-76, dir. internal audit, 1976-78, asst. controller, dir. fin. systems, 1978-81, treas., 1981-90; v.p. for finance, treas. U. Pitts., 1990-92; sr. v.p., treas. The Kresge Found., Troy, Mich.,

1992—. Mem. Assn. for Investment Mgmt. and Rsch., Fin. Analysts Soc. Detroit. Avocations: tennis, golf, running, books. Home: 4393 Barchester Dr Bloomfield Hills MI 48302-2116 Office: The Kresge Foundation 2701 Troy Center Dr Ste 150 Troy MI 48084-4755

HUNKE, DAVID L., publishing executive; b. Houston; m. Janet Hunke; children: Evan, Jenna. BS, U. Kans., Lawrence, 1974. With Kansas City Star; dir. advt. Miami Herald; with Gannett Co. Inc., 1992—, exec. v.p. for mktg. Cin. Enquirer and Cin. Post Ohio, 1997-99, pub., pres. digital edits. Rochester Dem. and Chronicle NY, 1999—2005; pres., pub. Detroit Free Press, Gannett Co. Inc., Mich., 2005—; CEO Detroit Newspaper Partnership, Mich., 2006—. Recipient Lifetime Humanitarian award, Lifetime Assistance Found., 2004. Office: Detroit Free Press 600 West Fort St Detroit MI 48226 E-mail: dhunke@dnps.com.*

HUNT, EFFIE NEVA, retired dean, literature educator; b. Waverly, Ill., June 19, 1922; d. Abraham Luther and Fannie Ethel (Ritter) H. AB, MacMurray Coll. for Women, 1944; MA, U. Ill., 1945, PhD, 1950; postgrad., Columbia U., 1953, Univ. Coll., U. London, 1949-50. Key-punch operator U.S. Treasury, 1945; spl. librarian Harvard U., 1947, U. Pa., 1948; Instr. English U. Ill., 1950-51; librarian Library of Congress, Washington, 1951-52; asst. prof. English Mankato State Coll., 1952-59; prof. Radford Coll., 1959-63, chmn. dept. English, 1961-63; prof. Ind. State U., 1963-86; dean Ind. State U. (Coll. Arts and Scis.), 1974-86, dean and prof. emerita, 1987—. Author articles in field. Fulbright grantee, 1949-50 Mem. AAUP, MLA, Nat. Council Tchrs. English, Am. Assn. Higher Edn., Audubon Soc. Home: 3365 Wabash Ave Apt 4 Terre Haute IN 47803-1655 Office: Ind State U Root Hall Eng Dept Terre Haute IN 47809-0001

HUNT, HOLLY, small business owner; b. San Angelo, Tex., Nov. 19, 1942; d. Cagle O. and Zelma (Richardson) H.; m. Rowland Tackbary, Dec. 14, 1974 (div. 1987); children: Hunt Tackbary, Jett Tackberry, Trent Tackberry. BA in Eng. Lit., Tex. Tech., Lubbock, 1965. Buyer Foley's Dept. Store, Houston, 1965-68; designer Tempo, NYC, 1969-73; owner, designer Holly Hunt Inc., NYC, 1973-83; owner, exec. v.p. Availco Equity Availco Syatems, Chgo.; owner, pres. Holly Hunt, Ltd., Chgo., 1983--, 1986. Mem., art collector, Mus. Contrary art Chgo., 1978--. Mem. ASN, ISID. Republican. Presbyterian. Avocations: tennis, skiing, reading, art. Office: Holly Hunt Ltd 1728 Merchandise Mart Chicago IL 60654

HUNT, KEVIN J., food products executive; BA, Dartmouth Coll.; MBA, Columbia Univ., 1976. With Ralcorp Holdings, Inc., St. Louis, 1985—, corp. v.p., 1995—2003, pres., co-CEO, 2003—, bd. dirs., 2004—05; CEO Bremner, Inc., 1995—, Nutcracker Brands, Inc., 2003—. Office: Ralcorp Holdings Inc ste 2900 800 MarketSt Saint Louis MO 63101 Office Phone: 314-877-7000. Office Fax: 314-877-7666.

HUNT, LAWRENCE HALLEY, JR., lawyer; b. July 15, 1943; s. Lawrence Halley Sr. and Mary Hamilton (Johnson) H.; m. Katherine Collins; children: Caroline Smith, Laura Hamilton, Darwin Halley. AB, Dartmouth Coll., 1965; cert., Inst. d'Etudes Politiques, Paris, 1966; JD, U. Chgo., 1969. Bar: N.Y. 1970, Ill. 1971, U.S. Ct. Appeals (9th cir.) 1980, U.S. Ct. Appeals (2d cir.) 1981, U.S. Supreme Ct. 1981. Assoc. Davis Polk & Wardwell, NYC, 1969-70, Sidley & Austin, Chgo., 1970-75; ptnr. Sidley Austin LLP and predecessor firms, Chgo., 1975—; mem. exec. com. Sidley Austin, Chgo., 1985—2002. Mem. securities adv. com. Ill. Sec. of State, Springfield, Ill., 1977—87; prof. grad. program fin. svcs. law Ill. Inst. Tech.-Chgo.-Kent Coll. Law, 1987—99; dir. Melanoma Rsch. Found., 2006—. Mng. editor U. Chgo. Law Review, 1968-69; contbr. aticles to profl. jours. James B. Reynolds scholar Dartmouth Coll., 1965-66. Fellow: Am. Bar Found., Ill. Bar Assn.; mem.: ABA (com. on commodity regulation, past chmn. subcom. on futures commn. merchants, past mem. exec. coun.), Internat. Bar Assn. (past chmn. bus. law com. sub-com. futures and options), Indian Hill Club, Mid-Day Club. Avocations: hockey, golf. Office: Sidley Austin LLP One South Dearborn St Chicago IL 60603 Office Phone: 312-853-7000. Business E-Mail: lhunt@sidley.com.

HUNT, MICHAEL O'LEARY, wood science and engineering educator; b. Louisville, Dec. 9, 1935; s. George Henry and Tressie (Truax) H.; children: Elizabeth H. Schwartz, Lynne T. Lattimer, Michael O. Jr. BS, U. Ky., 1957; M.Forestry, Duke U., 1958; PhD, N.C. State U., 1970. Product engr. Wood Products div. Singer Co., Pickens, SC, 1959-60; asst. prof. wood sci. Purdue U., West Lafayette, Ind., 1960-70, assoc. prof., 1970-79, prof., 1979—, dir. Wood Rsch. Lab., 1979—2002. Contbr. articles over 80 articles to profl. jours. Chmn. campus preservation com. Wabash Valley Trust for Historic Preservation, Lafayette. Recipient Servaas Meml. award Hist. Landmarks Found. of Ind., 1994, H. Fannon award Lafayette Neighborhood Housing Svcs., 1998, Downie Meml. award Wabash Valley Trust, 2002. Mem. Forest Products Soc. (pres. 1990-91, Fred Gottschalk Meml. award 1984), Soc. of Wood Sci. and Tech., Assn. Preservation Tech., Rotary. Achievements include patent for lightweight, high-performance structural particleboard. Office: Purdue Univ Wood Rsch Lab West Lafayette IN 47907-2033 Business E-Mail: huntm@purdue.edu.

HUNT, ROBERT CHESTER, construction company executive; b. Dayton, Ohio, 1923; Grad., Case Inst. Tech., 1942. With Huber Hunt & Nichols Inc., Indpls., 1947—, sec., 1950-51, gen. mgr., 1951-52, v.p., 1952-56, vice chmn., CEO, from 1956; chmn. bd. dirs. Hunt Constrn. Group, Inc., Indpls., 2000—. Dir. Bank One Indpls., .A., formerly Am. Fletcher Nat. Bank, Citizens Gas & Coke Utility, Indianapolis, Past pres. Indianapolis Athletic Club. Office: Hunt Constrn Group Inc 2450 S Tibbs Ave Indianapolis IN 46241-4821

HUNT, ROBERT G., construction company executive; b. Feb. 15, 1948; BS in bus., Ball State U.; MS in Engring., Purdue U. Joined Huber, Hunt & Nichols Inc., Indpls., 1974, from field engr. to divsn. mgr., pres. Phoenix and Tampa, CEO Indpls., 1999—; pres. The Hunt Corp., Indpls.; CEO, chmn. Hunt Constrn. Corp. Office: Hunt Construction Group 2450 S Tibbs Ave Indianapolis IN 46241

HUNT, ROGER SCHERMERHORN, healthcare administrator; b. White Plains, NY, Mar. 7, 1943; s. Charles Howland and Mildred Russell (Schermerhorn) H.; m. Mary Adams Libby, June 19, 1965; children: Christina Markle, David. BA, DePauw U., 1965; MBA, George Washington U., 1968. Adminstrv. resident Lankenau Hosp., Phila., 1966-68; asst. adminstr. Hahnemann Med. Coll. and Hosp., Phila., 1968-71, hosp. dir., 1971-74, assoc. v.p., hosp. adminstr., 1974-77; dir. Ind. U. Hosp., Indpls., 1977-84; pres. Luth. Gen. Hosp., Pk. Ridge, Ill., 1984-90; pres., CEO Fontbonne Health Sys., Toronto, Canada, 1990-92; sr. v.p. Northwestern Healthcare etwork, Chgo., 1993-96; pres., CEO ViaHealth, Rochester, NY, 1996-99; prin. Hunt Healthcare, Deerfield, Ill., 1999—2002; CEO, BroMenn Healthcare Sys., Bloomington, Ill., 2002—. Chmn. Alliance of Indpls. Hosp., 1981; pres. United Hosp. Services, 1979-81; assoc. prof. hosp. adminstrn. Ind. U. Sch. Medicine, 1977-84; vice chmn. Pa. Emergency Health Services Council, 1975-77; pres. Chester County Emergency Med. Service Council, 1971-77. Pres. Wayne Area Jr. C. of C., 1970-71, state dir., 1971-72; bd. dir. Rochester Philharm. Orch., 1998-99. Fellow Am. Coll. Healthcare Exec. (regent for Ind. 1984, Ill. 1988-90, Postgrad. tng. award 1968); mem. Am. Hosp. Assn., Hosp. Assn. of NY State (bd. dir. 1998-99), Ind. Hosp. Assn. (bd. dir. 1982-84), Met. Chgo. Healthcare Coun. (bd. dirs. 1986-95), DePauw U. Alumni Assn. (bd. dir. 1988-94), Greater Rochester Metro C. of C. (bd. dir. 1998-99), Comm. Cancer Ctr. (bd. dir. 2002—, chmn. 2004—), Ill. Symphony Orch. (bd. dir. 2003—), McLean C. of C. (bd. dirs. 2005—). Office: BroMenn Healthcare PO Box 2850 Bloomington IL 61702-2850 Office Phone: 309-454-0700. Business E-Mail: rhunt@bromenn.org.

HUNT, V. WILLIAM (BILL), automotive supplier executive; b. Washington D.C., Sept. 26, 1944; BA, Ind. U., 1966, JD, 1969. Labor counsel TRW Automotive Worldwide; counsel Arvin, Inc., Columbus, Indiana, 1976-80, v.p. adminstrn. Troy, Mich., 1980-82, sec., 1982-90, exec. v.p., 1990-96, pres., 1996-98, CEO, 1998-2000, also bd. dirs.; vice chmn., pres. ArvinMeritor, Inc., Troy, 2000—. Chmn. Pres.'s Coun.; mem. dean's adv. coun. Ind. U. Sch. Bus., Ind. U. Well House Soc.; bd. dirs. Ind. U. Found.; co-chmn. Ctrl. Ind. Corp. Partnership. Mem. Mfrs. Alliance (trustee), Motor and Equipment Mfrs. Assn. (bd. dirs.).

HUNTER, BRUCE, state representative, customer service administrator; b. June 1955; m. Betty Brim-Hunter. Customer svc. mgr. Citi Group; state rep. dist. 62 Iowa Ho. of Reps., 2003—; mem. human resources com.; mem. pub. safety com.; mem. transp. com.; mem. adminstrn. and regulation subcom. Democrat. Office: State Capitol East 12th and Grand Des Moines IA 50319

HUNTER, BUDDY D., holding company executive; b. Wilsontown, Mo., Feb. 28, 1930; s. Harold H. and Marie (Miller) H.; (div.); children— Bruce, Beverly, Brenda, Brett BS, Northeast Mo. State U., 1950. Pres. S.P. Wright & Co., Springfield, Ill., 1956-69; chmn. bd., pres., chief exec. officer AMEDCO Inc., St. Louis, 1969-86; chmn. Huntco Inc., Chesterfield, Mo., 1986—. Bd. dirs. Mark Twain BancShares, St. Louis, Svc. Corp. Internat., Houston, Cash Am. Investments, Ft. Worth, numerous other cos. Bd. dirs. Meml. Med. Ctr.; exec. adv. council Breech Sch. Bus., Drury Coll., Springfield, Mo. Capt. USAF, 1951-56 Mem. Masons, Shriners. Avocations: tennis, skiing, jogging.

HUNTER, HARLEN CHARLES, orthopedic surgeon; b. Estherville, Iowa, Sept. 23, 1940; s. Roy Harold and Helen Iola (King) H.; m. JoAnn Wilson, June 30, 1962; children: Harlen Todd, Juliann Kristin. BA, Drake U., 1962; DO, Coll. Osteo. Med. and Surgery, Des Moines, 1967. Diplomate Am. Osteo. Bd. Orthop. Surgery, Am. Osteo. Acad. Sports Medicine. Intern Normandy Osteo. Hosp., St. Louis, 1967-68, resident in orthops., 1968-72, chmn. dept. orthops., 1976-77; founder Orthopedics and Sports Medicine, PC, Bedford, Ind.; chmn. dept. surgery Bedford Regional Med. Ctr., 2002—04. Founder, orthop. surgeon Mid-States Orthop. Sports Medicine Clinics of Am., Ltd. Sports Med. Ctrs., Chesterfield, Mo., Fairview Heights, Ill., Jerseyville, Ill., Herman, Mo., 1977-99, Hunter Trauma Team, 1988-92; founder, pres. Life Style Health Systems, 1992; assoc. prof. orthop. Kansas City Coll. Osteopathy, 1993, Pikeville Coll. Osteopathic Medicine, 2005—; adj. prof. Lake Erie Coll. Osteo. Medicine, 1995—; staff Normandy Osteopathic, 1972-90, Outpatient Surgery Ctr., St. Louis, 1990-99, Luth. Med. Ctr., 1989-99, St. Joe's of Kirkwood, 1990-99, Bedford Med. Ctr., Dunn Meml.; clin. instr. Kirksville Coll. Osteo. Medicine; orthop. cons., team physician to high schs.; pres. Health Specialists, Inc.; program dir. sports medicine Family Physicians, 1993-94; host weekly TV program Raceology Weekly Spl. on Motorsports; med. adv. bd. Mo. Athletic Activities Assn.; cons. sports medicine Sports St. Louis newspaper; founder Ann. Sports Medicine Clinic for Trainers and Coaches, 1 yr. fellowship in sports medicine; adj. clin. assoc. prof. Coll. Osteo. Surgery, Des Moines; orthop. surgeon Iowa State Boys Basketball Tournament, 1966-85; founder Mobile Sports Medicine Semi Truck, 1988, Hunter Sports Medicine Clinic, Belleville, Ill.; sponsor U.S. Biathalon Assn., 1989; staff photographer Ind. Motor Speedway, 1973—, Daytona Internat. Speedway, 1979-96, ARCA, 2000—, USAC, 2005—; adv. bd. Motorsport Rsch. Group Human Performance Internat., Daytona Beach, Fla., 1990—; mem. Sports Medicine Commn. Ind. State Med. Assn.; lectr. in field Co-author: Motorsports Medicine, 1992; host daily radio program Making a Difference, For Your Health; radio host Racing USA with Dr. Hunter, 2006; contbr. articles to profl. jours. Pres. adv. bd. Bedford Salvation Army; candidate Lawrence County Commr., 2004. Recipient Clinic Spkr. award Iowa H.S. Baseball Coaches Assn., 1982, 83, Hall of Fame award Mo. Athletic Trainers Assn., 1987, Sibley Medallion award for outstanding svc. Lindenwood U., Ann. Outstanding Soccer Player of Yr. award Mo. Athletic Club, Hunter 100 Stock Car Race, Peveley, Mo., Bob Scott Photography award Indpls. Motor Speedway, 2002; named Businessman of Yr., Nat. Rep. Congl. Com., 2003; Harlen C. Hunter Sports Complex named in his honor Lindenwood U., St. Charles, Mo., 1988. Fellow Am. Coll. Osteo. Surgeons, Am. Osteo Acad. Orthops. (past chmn. com. on athletic injuries), Am. Osteo. Acad. Sports Medicine; mem. Am. Osteo. Assn., Mo. Assn. Osteo. Physicians and Surgeons (Medallion award 1990), Am. Coll. Sports Medicine, Am. Orthop. Soc. Sports Medicine (del. sports medicine exch. program to China 1985), AMA, Am. Coll. Occupl. Medicine, Ind. Med. Assn. (sports medicine com. 1999—), Ind. Osteo. Assn. (bd. trustees 2003-), St. Louis Met. Med. Assn., Sports Car Club Am. (med. dir. pro racing 1989-91), World Congress Motorsport Scis., St. Louis Auto Racing Club (Amb. award 1989, 91), 500 Old Timers Club, The Butler Soc., Elks, Lions, Masons, Shriners. Republican. Methodist. Home: 604 Heltonville Rd E Bedford IN 47421-9250 Home Phone: 812-278-8130; Office Phone: 812-275-1234. Business E-Mail: drsptmed@insightbb.com.

HUNTER, JAMES GALBRAITH, JR., lawyer; b. Phila., Jan. 6, 1942; s. James Galbraith and Emma Margaret (Jehl) H.; m. Pamela Ann Trott, July 18, 1969 (div.); children: James Nicholas, Catherine Selene; m. Nancy Grace Scheurwater, June 21, 1992. B.S. in Engring. Sci., Case Inst. Tech., 1965; J.D., U. Chgo., 1967. Bar: Ill. 1967, U.S. Dist. Ct. (no. dist.) Ill. 1967, U.S. Ct. Appeals (7th cir.) 1967, U.S. Ct. Claims, 1976, U.S. Ct. Appeals (4th and 9th cirs.) 1978, U.S. Supreme Ct. 1979, U.S. Dist. Ct. (cen. dist.) Ill. 1980, Calif. 1980, U.S. Dist. Ct. (cen. and so. dists.) Calif. 1980, U.S. Ct. Appeals (5th cir.) 1982, U.S. Ct. Appeals (fed. cir.) 1982. Assoc. Kirkland & Ellis, Chgo., 1967-68, 70-73, ptnr., 1973-76; ptnr. Hedlund, Hunter & Lynch, Chgo., 1976-82, Los Angeles, 1979-82; ptnr. Latham & Watkins, Hedlund, Hunter & Lynch, Chgo. and Los Angeles, 1982—. Served to lt. JAGC, USN, 1968-70. Mem. ABA, State Bar Calif., Los Angeles County Bar Assn., Chgo. Bar Assn. Clubs: Metropolitan (Chgo.), Chgo. Athletic Assn., Los Angeles Athletic. Exec. editor U. Chgo. Law Rev., 1966-67. Office: Latham & Watkins Sears Tower Ste 5800 Chicago IL 60606-6306 also: 633 W 5th St Los Angeles CA 90071-2005

HUNTER, J(AMES) PAUL, literature and language professor, literary critic; b. Jamestown, NY, June 29, 1934; s. Paul W. and Florence I. (Walmer) H.; children: Debra, Lisa, Paul III, Anne, Ellen Harris. AB, Ind. Central Coll., 1955; MA, Miami U., Oxford, Ohio, 1957; PhD, Rice U., 1963. Instr., U. Fla., Gainesville, 1957-59, Williams Coll., Williamstown, Mass., 1962-64; asst. prof. U. Calif., Riverside, 1964-66; assoc. prof. English Emory U., Atlanta, 1966-68, prof., 1968-80, chmn. dept., 1973-79; prof. English, dean Coll. Arts and Sci., U. Rochester, NY, 1981-86; prof. English U. Chgo., 1987—, Chester D. Tripp prof. humanities, 1990-96, Barbara E. and Richard J. Franke prof. humanities, 1996—2001; dir. Franke Inst. for the Humanities, 1996—2001, Franke prof. emeritus, 2001—; prof. of English U. of Va., 2001—. Gen. editor Bedford Cultural Edits., 1994—. Author: The Reluctant Pilgrim, 1966, Occasional Form, 1975, Norton Introduction to Poetry, 9th edit., 2007, Norton Introduction to Literature, 9th edit., 2005, New Worlds of Literature, 2d edit., 1994, Before Novels, 1990; co-editor: Rhetorics of Order/Ordering Rhetorics, 1989; editor: Norton Critical Edition of Mary Shelley's Frankenstein, 1996. Sr. advisor Andrew W. Mellon Found., 1999—. Guggenheim fellow, 1976-77, NEH fellow, 1985-86, Nat. Humanities Ctr. fellow, 1986, 95-96. Mem. MLA, Am. Soc. 18th Century Studies (2d v.p. 1994-95, 1st v.p. 1995-96, pres. 1996-97, Louis Gottschalk prize 1991), Southeastern Am. Soc. 18th Century Studies (pres. 1977-78), Soc. Atlantic MLA (pres. 1992-93), N.E. Am. Soc. 18th Century Studies (pres. 1982-83), Ill. Humanities Coun. (chair 2000-04), Fedn. State Humanities Couns (chmn. bd. 2005—). Home Phone: 773-536-4691; Office Phone: 312-458-9978. Business E-Mail: jph7f@virginia.edu.

HUNTER, MATTIE, human services executive; b. Chgo., June 1, 1954; d. Lucious and Flabe (Davis) H. BA, Monmouth Coll., Ill., 1976; MA, Jackson State U., Miss., 1982. Summer counselor Chgo. Housing Authority, 1972-76; asst. mgr. Whitney's Fashions, Chgo., 1976; tng. specialist City Colls. of Chgo., 1977-81; youth service worker Dept. Human Services City of Chgo., 1977-81; program dir. Human Services Devel. Inst. Chgo., 1982-85, exec. asst. to pres., 1985—. Conf. planner, community liaison, and mktg. Bakeman & Assocs., Chgo., 1986—. Author: (newsletter) Nat. Elk Alcoholism Commn., 1982. Mem. Community Devel. Adv. Council City of Chgo., 1986; mem. steering com. Cook County Democratic Women, Chgo., 1985—; staff asst. Polit. Action Conf. of Ill., Chgo., 1984—; vol. Warren county Rep. Orgn., Monmouth, 1975; fundraiser Nat. Polit. Congress of Black Women, Chgo., 1985—; vol. coordinator Hands Across Am., Chgo., 1986, March of Dimes Telethon, Chgo., 1979-81, Muscular Distrophy, Chgo., 1980, 81, 85, local adv. council Chgo. Housing Authority, 1968-76; precinct coordinator congl. dist. race, Chgo., 1980, 1976, 3rd Ward Regular Democratic Orgn., Chgo., 1970-72; asst. ward coordinator Washington for Mayor City of Chgo., 1983; surveyor Joint Ctr. for Polit. Studies, Washington, 1973; ambassador of mercy United Way, Chgo.; vice chmn. adv. council Chgo. Intervention etwork Dept. of Human Services, 1985—, convocations com. Monmouth Coll., 1973-74, cultural affairs com., 1975-76; bd. dirs. Black Leadership Roundtable of Ill., Chgo., 1986—. Named one of Outstanding Young Women Am., 1985; recipient award of Appreciation, Dept. Human Services City of Chgo., 1981, award of Gratitude, Human Resources Devel. Inst. Chgo., 1984. Mem. Notaries Assn. of Ill., Inc., Nat. Black Alcoholism Council (chmn. Orgn. Devel. Com., award of Appreciation), Nat. Forum Black Pub. Adminstrs., Nat. Assn. for Female Execs. Democrat. Baptist. Avocations: volleyball, softball, bowling. Home: 5604 S Prairie Ave Apt 3 Chicago IL 60637-5306

HUNTER, ROBERT TYLER, investment management company executive; b. Peoria, Ill., Jan. 14, 1943; s. Thomas Oakford and Joan (Sargent) H.; m. Mary Michelle Tyrrell, June 12, 1965. A.B., Harvard U., 1965. Pres. First Union Trust Co., Kansas City, Mo., 1973-81; sr. v.p., trust div. mgr. Centerre Bank, Kansas City, 1981-84; v.p., mgr. client services and mktg. DST Systems, Inc., Kansas City, 1984-85; sr. v.p. mktg. Waddell & Read Asset Mgmt. Co., Kansas City, 1985— Treas. M.S. Soc., Mission, Kans.; bd. dirs. Boys and Girls Club, Kansas City; trustee Menorah Hosp. Found., Kansas City; bd. govs. Kansas City Philharmonic Assn.; bd. dirs., com. chmn. Kansas City Youth Symphony. Fellow Fin. Analyst Fedn.; mem. Fin. Analyst Soc. Kansas City, Corp. Fiduciaries Soc. of Kansas City (past pres.), Estate Planning Assn. Republican. Roman Catholic. Clubs: Harvard/Radcliffe (pres. 1983-85); Kansas City Rcquet (Merriam, Kans.). Avocations: tennis; swimming; reading; coaching. Home: 8326 Mullen Rd Lenexa KS 66215-6019

HUNTER, TORII KEDAR, professional baseball player; b. Pine Bluff, Ark., July 18, 1975; m. Katrina Hall; children: Torii Jr., Monshadrik. Outfielder Minn. Twins, 1997—2007, LA Angels of Anaheim, 2008—. Mem. South squad Jr. Olympics, 1992. Named Gatorade Ark. Player of Yr., 1993; named to Am. League All-Star Team, 2002, 2007; recipient Gold Glove award, 2001—07, Carl R. Pohlad award, 2004. Mailing: c/o LA Angels of Anaheim Angel Stadium 2000 Gene Autry Way Anaheim CA 92806

HUNTER, VICTOR LEE, marketing executive, consultant; b. Garrett, Ind., Mar. 1, 1947; s. John Joseph and Martha May (Brown) H.; m. Linda Ann Loudermilk, Dec. 19, 1969; children: Jed, Andrew, Matthew, Holly. BS, Purdue U., 1969; MBA, Harvard U., 1971. Dir. mktg. Kreuger, Inc., Green Bay, Wis., 1971-75; pres. B&I Furniture, Milw., 1975-81, Hunter Bus. Group, LLC, Milw., 1981—. Bd. dirs. Wm. K. Walthers Co., Milw. Author: Business-to-Business Marketing: Creating a Community of Customers, 1997. Lay leader United Meth. Ch., Whitefish Bay, Wis., 1985; mem. exec. com. Greater Milw. Conv. and Visitors Bur. Mem. Direct Mktg. Assn., Wis. Pres.' Orgn., Strategic Accounts Mgmt. Assn. (bd. dirs.), Dean's Leadership Coun. Prudue U. Coll. Sci. Office: Hunter Business Group PO Box 12970 Milwaukee WI 53212-0970 Office Phone: 414-203-8066. Business E-Mail: vhunter@hunterbusiness.com.

HUNTINGTON, CURTIS EDWARD, actuary; b. Worcester, Mass., July 30, 1942; s. Everett Curtis and Margaret (Schwenzfeger) H. BA with distinction, U. Mich., 1964, M.Actuarial Sci., 1965; JD cum laude, Suffolk U., 1976. With New Eng. Mut. Life Ins. Co., Boston, 1965-93, v.p., auditor, 1980-84, corp. actuary, 1984-93; prof. math., dir. actuarial program U. Mich., Ann Arbor, 1993—, also assoc. chmn. math dept. Treas. Actuarial Edn. and Rsch. Fund, 1986-89, chmn., 1989-92, dir. 1985—, exec. dir., 1994—, mem. editl. bd. numerous profl. jours. Trustee The Actuarial Found., 1998—. Served with USPHS, 1965-67. Mem. Soc. Actuaries (gen. chmn. edn. and exam. com. 1985-87, bd. govs. 1986-89, v.p. 1989-91), Am. Acad. Actuaries (bd. dirs. 1997-2000), Am. Soc. Pension Actuaries (dir. 1996—, quality control chmn., 2005-), Am. Coll. Life Underwriters, Internat. Actuarial Assn. (sec., nat. corr. U.S.), New Zealand Soc. Actuaries, American Acad. Actuaries (dir., 2005), Casualty Actuarial Soc. Office: U Mich Dept of Math 2864 East Hall Ann Arbor MI 48109-1109

HUNTLEY, ROBERT STEPHEN, newspaper editor; b. Winston-Salem, NC, Mar. 6, 1943; m. Linda Fabry; children: Kristine Elizabeth, Katherine Vallie. BA in Journalism, U. N.C., 1965. Reporter UPI, various locations, 1965-69, writer, editor broadcast and gen. news depts. Chgo., 1969-77, exec. editor nat. broadcast dept., 1977-78; bur. chief Commodity News Svc., Chgo., 1978-79, U.S. News & World Report, Chgo., 1979-82, assoc. editor Washington, 1982-85, sr. editor, 1985-86; reporter, rewrite specialist Chgo. Sun Times, 1986-90, met. editor, 1990-91, asst. mng. editor/metro, 1991-97; editl. page editor, 1997—. Bd. dirs. City ews Bur., Chgo, 1993-97, pres., 1996; media fellow Hoover Instit. Stanford U., 2001. Author (with Truman K. Gibson): Knocking Down Barriers: My Fight for Black America, 2005. V.p. Ill. Freedom of Info. Coun., 1994. Recipient Stick-O-Type award for feature writing Chgo. Newspaper Guild, 1987, Appreciation cert. for outstanding contbns. to freedom of info. Nat. Ctr. Freedom of Info. Studies at Loyola U.-Chgo., 1993. Office: Chgo Sun-Times 350 N Orleans Chicago IL 60654 Office Phone: 312-321-2535. Business E-Mail: shuntley@suntimes.com.

HUNTLEY, THOMAS, state legislator, science educator; b. Feb. 1938; m. Gail Huntley; two children. BS, U. Minn.; PhD in Biochemistry, Iowa State U. Assoc. prof. biochemistry U. Minn., Duluth; Dist. 6B rep. Minn. Ho. of Reps., St. Paul, 1993—. Home: 1924 Wallace Ave Duluth MN 55803-2461

HUNTRESS, BETTY ANN, retired small business owner, secondary school educator; d. Emmett Slater and Catherine V. Brundage; m. Arnold Ray Huntress, June 26, 1954; children: Catherine, Michale, Carol, Alan. BA, Cornell U., Ithaca, NY, 1954. Tchr. h.s., Bordentown, NJ, 1954-55; tchr. Midland Pub. Schs., Mich., 1968—98; ret., 1998. Asst. to prof. Delta Coll., Northwood Inst., Midland; tchr. Midland Pub. Schs., 1998—2000; owner, mgr. The Music Stand, Midland, 1979—82. Bd. dirs. Midland Ctr. for Arts, 1978-86, v.p., 1980-84, Friends of the Ctr., 1985—; charter bd. mgrs. Matrix Midland Ann. Arts and Sci. Festival, 1977-80; cons. Girl Scouts US, 1964-76; bd. dirs. Literacy Coun. Midland County, 1986-94, sec., 1987-91; active Mich. Internat. Coun., 1975-76, Midland Hist. Soc., 1990—, Dow Chem. Centennial Com., 1996-98; mem. Presbyn. ch. choir, 1963—. Named Midland Musician of Yr., 1977. Mem. AAUW (dir. 1962-73, pres. 1971-73, mem. Mich. state divsn. 1983-85, bd. dirs. 1993-95, Outstanding Woman as Agt. of Change award 1977, fellowship grant named in her honor 1976), LWV (bd. dirs. 1986-90, com. charter schs. 1995-99), Music Soc. Midland Ctr. for arts (dir. 1971-86, chmn. 1976-79), Midland Symphony League Soc. (2d v.p. 1995-99), Cmty. Concert Soc., Woman's Study Club of Midland (pres. 1995-96), Friends of Libr., Kappa Delta Epsilon, Pi Lambda Theta, Alpha Xi Delta. Presbyterian.

HUPE, PALLAS, announcer; b. Ankara, Turkey; married; 2 children. M in Politics, Philosophy and Econs., Oxford U., Eng. Host children's TV show, Saudi Arabia; from asst. prodr. to prodr., reporter, anchor various stas. in Tallahassee, Fla. and Wilmington, N.C.; main anchor WPBN/WTOM, Traverse City, Mich.; freelancer WJBK-TV, Detroit; co-anchor, med. reporter weekend 10 pm WKBD-TV, Detroit, 2002—03; co-anchor noon, weathercaster, spl. projects reporter WJBK-TV, Detroit, 2003—. Recipient Best Spot News coverage award in N.C., RTNDAC, Best Pub. Affairs coverage award in Fla., AP. Office: WJBK Fox 2 PO Box 2000 Southfield MI 48037-2000

HURAS, WILLIAM DAVID, retired bishop; b. Kitchener, Ont., Can., Sept. 22, 1932; s. William Adam and Frieda Dorothea (Rose) H.; m. Barbara Elizabeth Lotz, Oct. 5, 1957; children— David, Matthew, Andrea. BA, Waterloo Coll., Ont., 1954; BD, Waterloo Sem., Ont., 1963; MTh, Knox Coll., Toronto, Ont., 1968; MDiv, Waterloo Luth. U., 1973; DD (hon.), Wilfred Laurier U., Waterloo, 1980, Huron Coll., London, Ont., 1989. Ordained to ministry Luth. Ch. in Am., 1957. Pastor St. James Luth. Ch., Refrew, Ont., 1957-62, Advent Luth. Ch., North York, 1962-78; bishop Eastern Can. Synod Luth. Ch. in Am., Kitchener, 1978-85, Eastern Synod Evangel. Luth. Ch. in Can., 1986-98; ret., 1998. Exec. com. Can. sect. of Luth. Ch. in Am., 1969-79, Luth. Merger Commn., Can., 1978-85; pres. Luth. Coun. Can., 1985-88; chmn. Group Svcs. Inc., Evangelical Luth. Ch. in Can., 1993—2001; mem. Anglican-Luth. Jt. Working Group, 1995-2001. Bd. govs. Waterloo Luth. U., 1966-75, Waterloo Luth. Sem., 1973-75, 78-2004. Mem. Order of St. Lazarus of Jerusalem (Ecclesiastical Grand cross 1985). Lutheran.

HURD, HEIDI M., dean, humanities and law educator; b. Laramie, Wyo., Oct. 19, 1960; d. Carroll Parsons and Jeanne Marie H.; children: Gillian K.J. and Aidan A. (twins). BA with honors, Queen's U., Kingston, Ont., Can., 1982; MA, Dalhousie U., Halifax, NS, Can., 1984; JD, U. So. Calif., LA, 1988, PhD, 1992. Asst. prof. U. Pa. Law Sch., Phila., 1989-94, prof. law and philosophy, 1994—2002, assoc. dean, 1994-96, co-dir. Inst. Law and Philosophy, 1998—2000; Herzog rsch. prof. law U. San Diego, 2000—02; dean, prof. philosophy, David Baum prof. law U. of Ill. Coll. Law, 2002—. Vis. asst. prof. dept. philosophy U. Iowa, Iowa City, 1991-92; vis. prof. law U. Va. Law Sch.,

Charlottesville, 1997-98. Author: Moral Combat, 1999; contbr. articles to profl. jours. Office: U Illinois College Law Dean Office 504 E Pennsylvania Ave Champaign IL 61820-6909 Office Phone: 217-333-9857. E-mail: hhurd@law.uiuc.edu.

HURD, RICHARD NELSON, pharmaceutical executive; b. Evanston, Ill., Feb. 25, 1926; s. Charles DeWitt and Mary Ormsby (Nelson) H.; m. Jocelyn Fillmore Martin, Dec. 22, 1950; children: Melanie Gray, Suzanne Dewitt. BS, U. Mich., 1946; PhD U. Minn., 1956. Chemist Gen. Electric Co., Schenectady, NY, 1948-49; R&D group leader Koppers Co., Pitts., 1956-57; rsch. chemist Mallinckrodt Chem. Works, St. Louis, 1957-63, group leader, 1963-66, Comml. Solvents Corp., Terre Haute, Ind., 1966-68, sect. head, 1968-71; mgr. sci. affairs G. D. Searle Internat. Co., Skokie, Ill., 1972-73, dir. mfg. and tech. affairs, 1973-77; rep. to internat. tech com. Pharm. Mfrs. Assn., Skokie, Ill., 1973-77; v.p. tech. affairs Elder Pharms., Bryan, Ohio, 1977-81; v.p. rsch. & devel. U.S. Proprietary Drugs & Toiletries div. Schering-Plough Corp., Memphis, 1981-83; v.p. sci affairs Moleculon, Inc., Cambridge, Mass., 1984-88; v.p. regulatory affairs Pharmaco-LSR, Inc., Austin, Tex., 1989-94; prin. Hurd & Assocs., Inc., Evanston, Ill., 1994—. Contbr. articles to profl. jours.; patentee in field. Mem. Ferguson-Florissant (Mo.) Sch. Bd., 1964-66; bd. dirs. United Fund of Wabash Valley (Ind.), 1969-71. With USN, 1943-46, 53-55. E.I. DuPont de emours & Co., Inc. fellow, 1956. Fellow AAAS; mem. Am. Acad. Dermatology (life), Am. Soc. Photobiology, Am. Chem. Soc., N.Y. Acad. Sci., Am. Pharm. Assn., Am. Assn. Pharm. Scientists, Food and Drug Law Inst., Drug Info. Assn., Sigma XI, Mich. Shores Club (Wilmette, Ill.). Presbyterian. Achievements include codevelopment of Ralgro and Oxsoralen; research in thioamides as a class of organic compounds; development of macrocyclic synthetic routes for natural products; development of psoralens for photochemotherapy of dermatologic disorders. Home Phone: 847-864-9773. Personal E-mail: hurdreg@earthlink.net.

HURLEY, SAMUEL CLAY, III, investment management company executive; b. Peoria, Ill., Jan. 25, 1936; s. Samuel Clay Jr. and Wilmina Marie (Loveless) H.; m. Dorothy Jane Atkinson, Aug. 19, 1967; children: Samuel C. IV, Bruce Hilliard. AB in Econs., Brown U., 1958; MBA in Fin., Northwestern U., 1960; postgrad., Harvard U., 1984—. Portfolio mgr. Continental Ill. Nat. Bank, Chgo., 1960-62; mgr. bank rels. Internat. Harvester Co. (later Navistar), Chgo., 1962-71; asst. treas. Internat. Harvester Credit Corp., Chgo., 1962-71, Anchor Hocking Corp. (now owned by Newell Corp.), Lancaster, Ohio, 1971-74, treas., 1975—, v.p., 1983-87; gen. ptnr. Steele and Co. Ltd., Columbus, Ohio, 1988-90; pres. Hurley Investment Counsel Ltd., Lancaster, 1990—. Trustee Lancaster-Fairfield Cmty. Hosp., 1984-91, Fairfield County Hospice, Fairfield County Found.; mem. Fairfield County Bd. Mental Retardation and Devel. Disabilities, Lancaster, 1981-95. Mem. Lancaster Country Club, Rotary, Capitol Club (Columbus). Republican. Episcopalian. Home: 148 E Wheeling St Lancaster OH 43130-3705 Office: 109 N Broad St Ste 350 Lancaster OH 43130-3785 E-mail: hicl@hotmail.com.

HURLEY, WALTER ALLISON, bishop; b. Fredericton, Can., May 30, 1937; BA, Sacred Heart Sem.; MDiv, St. John's Sem.; grad studies in Edn., U. Detroit; JCL, Cath. U. of Am., 1984. Ordained priest, 1965; assoc. pastor St. Dorothy, Warren, Mich., 1965—69; vicar Warren-Centerline, 1969—72; pastor St. Cyprian, Riverview, 1972—76, Sacred Heart, Roseville, 1976—79, St. Lucy, St. Clair Shores, 1979—82, Our Lady of Sorrows Parish, Farmington, 1990—2003; judicial vicar Met. Tribune Archdiocese of Detroit, 1984—89, Moderator of the Curia, 1986—90; ordained bishop, 2003; aux. bishop Archdiocese of Detroit, 2003—05; bishop Diocese of Grand Rapids, 2005—. Cardinal's del. and project mgr. for construction of Pope John Paul II Cultural Ctr., Washington, 1995—2001; del. of Cardinal Maida for matters relating to issues of sexual abuse by clergy and religious, 1988—95, 2002—. Roman Catholic. Office: Diocese of Grand Rapids 660 Burton St SE Grand Rapids MI 49507 Office Phone: 616-243-0491. Office Fax: 616-243-4910. E-mail: bwhurley@dioceseofgrandrapids.org.*

HURST, DAN, radio personality; b. Ft. Worth; BA in Broadcast Journalism, Palm Beach Atlantic U., 1981. With KCMO-AM, Kansas City, Mo., KLSI-FM, Mix 93; radio host KUDL, Kansas City, Mo., 1987—. Office: 4935 Belinder Westwood KS 66205

HURTER, ARTHUR PATRICK, economist, educator; b. Chgo., Jan. 29; s. Arthur P. and Lillian T. (Thums) Hurter; m. Florence Evalyn Kays; children: Patricia Lyn, Arthur Earl. BSChemE, MSChemE, Northwestern U., MA in Econs., PhD in Econs., Northwestern U. Chem. engr. Zonlite Rsch. Lab., Evanston, Ill., 1957-58; assoc. dir. Rsch. Transp. Ctr., Northwestern U., Evanston, 1963-65; asst. prof. dept. Indsl. Engring. and Mgmt. Scis. Tech. Inst., Northwestern U., 1962-66, prof., 1970—; prof. of transp., 1992—; chmn. dept. Northwestern U., 1969-89, assoc. prof. fin. Grad. Sch. Mgmt., 1969-70, prof., 1970—. Faculty mem. Newspaper Mgmt. Ctr., Transp. Ctr., 1989—; cons. U. Chgo., ESCOR, Sears Roebuck & Co., Standard Oil of Ind., Ill.; bd. dirs. Ill. Environ. Health Rsch. Ctr., 1972-77; mem. com. Sci. Tech. Adv., Ill. Inst. Natural Resources, 1980-84. Author: The Economics of Private Truck Transportation, 1965, Facility Location and the Theory of Production, 1989; contbr. articles to profl. jours. Pres. Coun. St. Scholastical H.S., 1972-80; elder Granville Ave. Presbyn. Ch., 1976-89; deacon 1st Presbyn. Ch., Evanston, trustee, 2003-06. Grantee Resources for the Future, 1964, Office of Naval Research, 1965, NSF, Social Sci. Research Council dissertation fellow Mem. Am. Econ. Assn., Regional Sci. Assn., Ops. Research Soc. Am., Inst. Mgmt. Scis., Inst. Indsl. Engrs., Sigma Xi, Phi Lambda Upsilon, Tau Beta Pi, Alpha Pi Mu (Disting. Engr. award). Home: 1505 W Norwood St Chicago IL 60660-2414 Office: Dept Indsl Engring Mgmt Sci Technological Inst Northwestern U Evanston IL 60208-0001 Office Phone: 847-491-3414. Business E-Mail: hurter@iems.northwestern.edu.

HURWICZ, LEONID, economist, educator; b. Moscow, Aug. 21, 1917; arrived in U.S., 1940; m. Evelyn Hurwicz; children: Sarah, Michael, Ruth, Maxim. LLM, U. Warsaw, Poland, 1938; DSc, Northwestern U., Evanston, Ill., 1980; D honoris causa (hon.), U. Autónoma de Barcelona, Spain, 1989; D of Econs. honoris causa (hon.), Keio U., Tokyo, 1993; LLD (hon.), U. Chgo., 1993; D honoris causa (hon.), Warsaw Sch. Econs., Poland, 1994; Dr.rer.pol honoris causa (hon.), U. Bielefeld, 2004. Rsch. assoc. Cowles Commn. U. Chgo., 1944—46; from assoc. prof. to prof. Iowa State U., Ames, 1946—49; prof. econ., math. and stats. U. Ill., 1949—51, U. Minn., Mpls., 1951—99, Regents' prof., 1969—88, Regent's prof. emeritus, 1988—, Carlson prof. econs., 1989—92, prof. econs., 1992—. Vis. prof. econs. Stanford U., Calif., 1955—56, 1958—59, Harvard U., Cambridge, Mass., 1969—71, U. Calif., Berkeley, 1976—77, Northwestern U., Evanston, Ill., 1988—89, U. Calif., Santa Barbara, 1998, Calif. Inst. Tech., 1999, U. Mich., Ann Arbor, 2002; Fisher lectr. U. Copenhagen, 1963; hon. prof. Ctrl. China U. Sci. and Tech., Wuhan, 1984; vis. lectr. People's U., Beijing, 1986, Tokyo U., 1982, Hebrew U., Jerusalem, 1993, Australian Econometric Mtgs., Melbourne, 1997; vis. Fulbright lectr. Bangalore U., India, 1965—66; vis. disting. prof. econs. U. Ill., 2001; invited lectr. Chuo U., Keio U., UN U., Inst. Adv. Studies (symposium participation), Tokyo, 1999, Symposium Devel. Western China, Chongqing, 2000, Pub. Econ. Theory Conf. Warwick U., England, 2000; cons. Econ. Design, Istanbul, 2000, Ctr. China U. Sci. and Tech., Wuhan, 2000, Peking U., 2000. Co-author (co-editor (with K.J. Arrow): Studies in Resource Allocation Processes, 1977; co-author: (co-editor (with K.J. Arrow and J. Uzawa) Studies in Linear and Non-Linear Programming, 1958; co-author: (co-editor (with J.S. Chipman) Prefences, Utility and Demand, 1971; co-author: (co-editor (with D. Schmeidler and H. Sonnenschein) Social Goals and Social Organization, 1985; editor: Econ. Design, 1993, Review of Econ. Design, 1997, Jour. of pub. Econ. Theory, 1999, Advances in Mathematical Economics, 1999, Econs. Bull., 2001; mem. adv. bd.: Jour. of Math. Econs.; co-editor (with Thomas Marschak): Econ. Theory, 2003; contbr. articles to profl. jours. Co-recipient Nobel Memorial Prize in Econ. Scis., 2007; recipient Nat. medal Sci., 1990; fellow, Ctr. Advances Studies in Behavioral Scis., 1955—56; scholar Sherman Fairchild Disting. scholar, Calif. Inst. Tech., 1984—85. Fellow: Am. Econ. Assn. (disting., lectr. 1972), Econometric Soc. (pres. 1969); mem.: NAS, Am. Acad. Arts and Scis. Office: Univ Minn Dept Econs 271 19th Ave S Minneapolis MN 55455-0430 Home Phone: 612-728-0388. E-mail: hurwicz@umn.edu.

HUSAR, RUDOLF BERTALAN, mechanical engineering educator; b. Martonos, Yugoslavia, Oct. 29, 1941; came to U.S., 1966; s. Ga'bor and Ilona Huszar; m. Janja Djukic, Oct. 8, 1967; children: Maja, Attila. Degree in mech. engring., U. Zagreb, Croatia, 1962; diploma in mech. engring., Tech. U., Germany, 1966; PhDME, U. Minn., 1971. Design technician W. Hofer, Krefeld, Germany, 1962-63; rsch. asst. Tech. U., Berlin, 1963-66; from rsch. asst. to assoc. U. Minn., Mpls., 1966-71; rsch. fellow Calif. Inst. Tech., Pasadena, 1971-73; prof. Washington U., St. Louis, 1973—. Vis. prof. U. Stockholm, 1976; co-chmn. Interagy. Com. Health and Environ. Effects of Advanced Energy Tech., 1978; coop. program mem. Devel. and Appin. Space Tech. Air Pollution, EPA/NASA, 1978; dir. Ctr. for Air Pollution Impact and Trend Analysis (CAPITA), St. Louis, 1979—; mem. com. on atmospheric-biospheric interactions NAS, 1979-81. Editor: Atmospheric Environment, 1980, Indojaras, 1980; mem. adv. bd. Environ. Sci. Tech., 1980; contbr. chpt. to: Air Quality Criteria for Particulate Matter, EPA, 1995. Rsch. fellow U. Glasgow, Scotland, 1965, U. Minn., 1966-71; grantee, EPA, 1973—, NOAA, 1991—, U.S. Dept. Def., 1989-92. Mem. Air & Waste Mgmt. Assoc., Ges. Aerosolforschung. Office: Wash U CAPITA PO Box 1124 Saint Louis MO 63188-1124

HUSARIK, ERNEST ALFRED, educational administrator; b. Gary, Ind., July 2, 1941; m. Elizabeth Ann Bonnette; children: Jennifer, Amy. BA in History, Olivet Nazarene U., 1963; MS in Ednl. Adminstrn., No. Ill. U., 1966; PhD in Ednl. Adminstrn. and Curriculum Devel., Ohio State U., 1973. Supt. Ontario (Ohio) Pub. Schs., 1973—75, Euclid (Ohio) Pub. Schs., 1975—86, Westerville (Ohio) Pub. Schs., 1986—2000, Carmel Clay Sch. Corp., 2000—01; ednl. specialist MS Cons., Inc. Past pres. Sch. Study Coun. Ohio; gd. govs. Westerville Fund; mem. adv. and distbn. com. Martha Holden Jennings Found.; pres. Westerville chpt. Am. Heart Assn.; past chmn. Franklin County Ednl. Coun.; past mem. alumni adv. coun. Ohio State U.; past pres. Euclid C. of C., Ohio. Named Ohio Supr. of Yr., 1994; named one of top 100 Edn. Adminstrs. N.Am., Exec. Educator, 1993. Mem.: ASCD, Hamilton-Boone County Ednl. Svc. Ctr. (chmn.), Franklin County Area Supt.'s Assn. (exec. com.), Ind. Assn. Pub. Sch. Supts., Ohio Assn. Supervision and Curriculum Devel., Ohio State U. Edliners (pres.), Sci. amd Math. Achievement Required for Tomorrow, Ohio Math. and Sci. Coalition (exec. bd.), Buckeye Assn. Sch. Adminstrs. (bd. dirs., pres., Disting. Svc. award 2001), Am. Assn. Sch. Adminstrs., Olivet Nazarene U. Alumni Assn. (past mem. alumni bd. dirs.), Carmel C. of C., Westerville Area C. of C. (bd. dirs.), Rotary (pres. Westerville, Rotarian of Yr.), Sigma Tau Delta, Phi Delta Kappa (past chpt. pres.). Office: 1029 Wood Glen Rd Westerville OH 43081-3240 E-mail: edwardH568@aol.com.

HUSBY, DONALD EVANS, engineering company executive; b. Mpls., Nov. 30, 1927; s. Olaf and Elsie Louise (Hagen) H.; m. Beverly June Tilbury, Sept. 24, 1949. BS, S.D. State U., 1952. Student engr., jr. asst., sr. engr., mgr. new products Westinghouse Electric Corp., Cleve., 1952-72; engring. mgr., v.p. engring. lighting div. Harvey Hubbell, Inc., Christiansburg, Va., 1972-76; pres. Elliptipar Inc., West Haven, Conn., 1976-78; fellow engr., mgr. engring. sect. Westinghouse Electric Corp., Vicksburg, Miss., 1978-82; engring. mgr. new products devel. Cooper Industries Crouse-Hinds LTG Products div., 1982-84; utility sales mgr. central region Cooper Lighting, Mpls., 1985-89; chief exec. officer Husby & Husby Inc., Madison, Minn., 1990—2008. Mem. indsl. adv. counsel Underwriters Labs.; provider ednl. seminars in lighting, tech. expert for NVLAP, NIST, U.S. Dept. Commerce. Contbr. articles to profl. jours.; patentee in field. With USN, 1945—47. Fellow Illuminating Engrs. Soc. (chmn., sec., dir., Disting. Service award 1989); mem. Internat. Municipal Signal Assn., Soc. Plastics Engrs., Nat. Elec. Mfrs. Assn., Am. Nat. Standards Inst., Am. Soc. Quality Control, Am. Soc. Engring. Physicists, Miss. Engring. Soc., D.C. Soc. Profl. Engrs., Designers Lighting Forum., Mensa Internat., Toastmasters Internat. Mem. Christian Ch. Home and Office: 705 5th Ave PO Box 66 Madison MN 56256-0066 Home Phone: 320-598-7786; Office Phone: 320-598-7786.

HUSEBOE, ARTHUR ROBERT, American literature educator; b. Sioux Falls, SD, Oct. 6, 1931; s. Carl and Lillian Ruth (Auby) H.; m. Doris Louise Eggers, May 27, 1953. BA, Augustana Coll., 1953; MA, U. S.D., 1956; PhD, Ind. U., 1963; LHD (hon.), Dana Coll., 1984. Teaching assoc. Ind. U., Bloomington, 1959-60; instr. U. S.D., Vermillion, 1960-61; prof. Augustana Coll., Sioux Falls, SD, 1961—. Pres. S.D. Humanities Found., Sioux Falls, 1994-96, Fedn. of State Humanities Couns., Washington, 1988-91; exec. dir. Nordland Heritage Found., Sioux Falls, 1980-, Ctr. Western Studies, Augustana, 1989—; NEH regional heritage chair, 1989-06. Author: An Illustrated History of the Arts in South Dakota, 1989, Sir George Etherege, 1987, Herbert Krause, 1985, Sir John Vanbrugh, 1976; Co-Author: A New South Dakota History, 2005. Bd. dirs. S.D. Symphony, Sioux Falls, 1966-2005; mem. Nordland Fest Assn., Sioux Falls, 1975-. With U.S. Army, 1953-55. Recipient Gov.'s award in the Arts State of S.D., 1989; NEH grantee, 1975-77, 79-83, 92-94; named to S.D. Hall of Fame, 2001. Mem. MLA, We. Lit. Assn. (pres. 1976-77), Norwegian-Am. Hist. Assn., S.D. State Hist. Soc. Lutheran. Avocations: travel, theater, classical music. Home: 813 E 38th St Sioux Falls SD 57105-5939 Office: Ctr for Western Studies Box 727 Augustana Coll Sioux Falls SD 57197-0001 Business E-Mail: arthur.huseboe@augie.edu.

HUSEMAN, DAN, state official; b. Cherokee, Iowa, June 28, 1952; m. Barbara Huseman; 3 children. BA, Buena Vista Coll., 1974. Farmer, 1974—; state rep. Iowa, 1995—. Mem. agr. com.; chair environ. protection ethics; mem. natural resources com.; mem. transp., infrastucture, and capitals appropriations com.; mem. ASCS Com.; former mem. Cherokee Chamber Agr. Com.; former officer Cherokee County Farm Bur.; former pres. Little League Pork Prodrs. Precinct worker various campaigns; mem. Internat. Luth. Laymen's League. Mem.: St. Paul Luth. Ch. Soybean Assn. Republican. Lutheran. Office: State Capitol E 12th and Grand Des Moines IA 50319

HUSER, GERI D., state official; b. Des Moines, Iowa, July 14, 1963; m. Dan Huser. BA, Briar Cliff Coll., 1985; MBA, Drake U., 2003, JD, 2004. Social worker Polk County Gen. Relief, 1986—90; program mgr. Polk County Family Enrichment Ctr., 1990—96; mem. Met. Planning Orgn., 1990—, Altoona City Coun., 1991—; planning specialist Polk County Social Svcs., 1996—; state rep. Iowa, 1997—. Mem. adminstrv. and rules com.; mem. local govt. com.; mem. transp. com.; mem. ways and means com. Mem. Child Abuse Prevention Coun., 1993—95, Greater Des Moines Housing Partnership, 1995—97; chmn. Met. Planning Orgn., 1996—. Mem.: East Polk Interagy. Assn., Mitchellville C. of C., Pleasant Hill C. of C., S.E. Polk Booster Club. Democrat. Office: State Capitol E 12th and Grand Des Moines IA 50319

HUSHEN, JOHN WALLACE, manufacturing executive; b. Detroit, July 28, 1935; s. J. Wallace and Hilda Carol (Jean) H.; m. Margaret Corinne Aho, Apr. 25, 1959 (div. May 1978); children: Susan Lisa, Jane Louise, Peter Matthew; m. Lane Gay Johnston, Feb. 8, 1985 (div. May 2002); 1 child, John Case. BA, Wayne State U., 1958. Reporter The Detroit News, 1959-66; campaign press sec. Griffin for Senate, Mich., 1966; press sec. U.S. Senator Robert P. Griffin, Washington, 1967-70; dir. pub. info. U.S. Dept. Justice, Washington, 1970-74; dep. press sec. Pres. Gerald R. Ford, Washington, 1974-76; dir. govt. relations Eaton Corp., Washington, 1976-79, dir. pub. affairs Cleve., 1979-81, v.p. govt. rels. Washington, 1981-91, v.p. corp. affairs Cleve., 1991-99. Trustee Citizens League Rsch. Inst., Cleve., pres., 1998-2000; trustee YMCA, Cleve. Mem.: Senate Press Secs. Assn. (pres. 1969—70), Former Senate Aides, St. Andrews South Golf Club, Capitol Hill Club.

HUSMAN, CATHERINE BIGOT, retired insurance company executive, consultant; b. Des Moines, Feb. 10, 1943; d. Edward George and Ruth Margaret (Cumming) Bigot; m. Charles Erwin Husman, Aug. 5, 1967; 1 child, Matthew Edward. BA with highest distinction, U. Iowa, 1965; MA, Ball State U., 1970. Actuarial asst. Am. United Life Ins. Co., Indpls., 1965—68, assoc. actuary, 1971—74, group actuary, 1974—84, v.p., corp. actuary, 1984—97, v.p., chief actuary, 1997—2002; cons., 2002—04. Mem. group tech. com. Mut. Life Ins. Co., 1986-98; mem. profitability studies com. Life Office Mgmt. Assn. Inc., 1991-99. Mem. women's adv. com. United Way Ctrl. Ind., 1991—93; mem. Exec. Svc. Corps, 2002—, asst. treas., 2005—06; docent Pres. Benjamin Harrison Home, 2002—; vol. Indpls. Mus. Art, 2002—05, Clowes Meml. Hall, 2002—06, Indpls. Civic Theater, 2002—, Ronald McDonald House, 2004—; bd. dirs., mem. fin. com. St. Elizabeth's Home, 1991—99, sec., 1994, mem. exec. com., treas., 1995; bd. dirs., mem. adminstrv. svcs., mem. exec. com. Heritage Place, 1993—99, treas., 1995—99. Fellow Soc. Actuaries; mem. Am. Acad. Actuaries, Actuaries Club Ind., Ky. and Ohio, Actuarial Club Indpls. (pres. 1979-80), Phi Beta Kappa. Republican. Roman Catholic. Avocations: reading, tennis. Home: 13530 Belford Ct Carmel IN 46032-8209 Personal E-mail: cbhusman@earthlink.net.

HUSSEY, DAVID HOLBERT, physician; b. Savanna, Ill., 1937; MD, Washington U., St. Louis, 1964. Intern MD Anderson Hosp., Houston, 1964-65, resident, 1965-68; physician U. Iowa Hosps. Office: U Iowa Hosps Rm W189-Z GH Iowa City IA 52242

HUSTED, JON, state representative; b. Royal Oak, Mich., Aug. 25, 1967; married; 1 child. BS, MA, U. Dayton. Dir., Edn. and Pub. Improvement Found. Dayton (Ohio) C. of C.; state rep. dist. 37 Ohio Ho. of Reps., Columbus, 2000—, chair primary and secondary edn. subcom., mem. fin. and appropriations, and pub. utilities coms. Bd. dirs. Tech Prep Consortium; bd. mem. Kettering Enterprise Zone Rev. Bd. Named Montgomery County Rep. of Yr., 1996; named one of Dayton Area Top 40 Bus. Leaders Under 40, Bus. News. Republican. Office: 77 S High St 13th fl Columbus OH 43215-6111

HUSTED, RUSSELL FOREST, research scientist; b. Lafayette, Ind., Apr. 4, 1950; s. Robert Forest and Miriam Ruth (Jackson) H.; m. Nancy Lee Driscoll, Oct. 25, 1969 (div. Feb. 1986); children: Jacqueline Marie, Randall Forest; m. Ruth Elaine Hurlburt, Nov. 12, 1988. BS in Chemistry with highest distinction, Colo. State U., 1972; PhD in Pharmacology, U. Utah, 1976. Post-doctoral fellow dept. medicine U. Iowa, Iowa City, 1976-79, rsch. scientist dept. medicine, 1979-81, 1982—; asst. prof. U. Conn. Sch. Medicine, Farmington, 1981-82. Contbr. articles to profl. jours. Mem. Parks and Recreation Com., North Liberty, 1997—. Mallinckrodt scholar Colo. State U., 1968. Mem. AAAS, Am. Soc. Nephrology, Am. Physiol. Soc., Soc. Gen. Physiology, N.Y. Acad. Sci., Sigma Xi. Democrat. Methodist. Office: Univ Iowa 3180 Medical Labs Iowa City IA 52242 Home Phone: 319-626-6354; Office Phone: 319-335-7618. Business E-Mail: russell-husted@uiowa.edu.

HUSTING, PETER MARDEN, advertising consultant; b. Bronxville, NY, Mar. 28, 1935; s. Charles Ottomar and Jane Alice (Marden) H.; m. Carolyn Riddle, Mar. 26, 1960; children: Jennifer, Gretchen, Charles Ottomar; m. Myrna Diaz, May 11, 1996. BS, U. Wis., 1957; grad., Advanced Mgmt. Program, Harvard U., 1974. Sales rep. Crown Zellerbach Corp., San Francisco, 1958-59; media analyst Leo Burnett Co., Chgo., 1959-61, time buyer, 1961-62, asst. account exec., 1962-63, account exec., 1963-68, v.p., account supr., 1968-72, sr. v.p., account dir., 1972-79, group exec., 1979-86, exec. v.p., 1979-92, dir. human relations internat., 1986-92, also bd. dirs., ret., 1992; pres. Husting Enterprises, Chgo., 1993—. Dir. Columbian Mutual Life Ins. Co., Harley-Davidson Customer Funding Corp. Trustee Shedd Aquarium Soc., Chgo., 1980-94, hon. life trustee, 1995—; bd. dirs. Chgo. Better Govt. Assn., 1976-92, Leadership Coun. Met. Open Cmtys., Chgo., 1980-86, Lyric Opera Guild, 1971-78, Chgo. Forum, 1969-76. Served with AUS, 1958. Mem.: Indian Hill (Winnetka) (bd. govs. 1975-79), The Valley Club (Montecito, Calif.), Coral Casino Club (Santa Barbara). Avocations: flying, swimming, hunting, trekking, golf. Office: Husting Enterprises 150 S Wacker Dr Ste 3100 Chicago IL 60606-4103

HUSTON, KATHLEEN MARIE, library administrator; b. Sparta, Wis., Jan. 7, 1944; BA, Edgewood Coll., 1966; MLS, U. Wis., Madison, 1969. Libr. Milw. Pub. Libr., 1969-90; city libr. Milw. Pub. Libr. System, 1991—. Office: Milwaukee Pub Libr 814 W Wisconsin Ave Milwaukee WI 53233-2309

HUSTON, MICHAEL JOE, lawyer; b. Logansport, Ind., Dec. 21, 1942; s. Harry Hobart and Dorothie Ann (Chew) H.; m. Joan Frances Jernigan, June 12, 1965; children: Scott Howard, Todd Michael, Julie Ann. BS, U.S. Military Acad., 1965; JD, Ind. U., 1972. Bar: Ind. 1972, U.S. Dist. Ct. (so. dist.) Ind. 1972, U.S. Dist. Ct. (no. dist.) Ind. 1975, U.S. Ct. Appeals (D.C. cir.) 1980. Commd. 2nd lt. U.S. Army, 1965, advanced through grades to capt., 1967, resigned, 1970; assoc. Baker & Daniels, Indpls., 1972-78, ptnr., 1979—. Contbr. articles to profl. jours. Bd. dirs., pres. Woodland Springs Homeowners Assn., Carmel, Ind., 1976-82; trustee Carmel United Meth. Ch., 1982-84. Fellow Ind. Bar Found. (master fellow 1991); mem. ABA, Ind. State Bar Assn., Indpls. Bar Assn., West Point Soc. Ind. (pres. 1996-98), Geist Sertoma Club (pres. 1996-97). Office: Baker & Daniels 300 N Meridian St Ste 2700 Indianapolis IN 46204-1782

HUSTON, STEVEN CRAIG, lawyer; b. Morris, Ill., June 3, 1954; s. Raymond P. and Evelyn M. (Bass) Huston; m. Nina Huston. BA, Ill. Coll., 1977; JD, John Marshall Law Sch., 1980; MBA, Northwestern U., 1989. Bar: Ill. 1980, U.S. Dist. Ct. (no. dist.) Ill. 1980, U.S. Ct. Appeals (7th cir.) 1980. Assoc. Siegel, Denberg et al, Chgo., 1980-83; staff atty. William Wrigley Jr. Co., Chgo., 1983-84, asst. sec. legal, 1984-94, asst. v.p. legal, 1994-96, counsel North Am., 1996—2001; v.p., gen. counsel Symons Corp., 2002—03; v.p., gen. counsel, sec. Dayton Superior Corp., 2003—. Bd. dirs. SOS Am. Mem.: ABA, Am. Corp. Counsel Assn., Chgo. Bar Assn.

HUTCHINS, BECKY J., state legislator; m. Joel R. Hutchins. Mem. from dist. 50 Kans. State Ho. of Reps., Topeka. Address: 700 Wyoming Ave Holton KS 66436-1180

HUTCHINS, ROBERT AYER, architectural consultant; b. NYC, Oct. 19, 1940; s. Robert Senger and Evelyn Reed (Brooks) Hutchins; m. Saran Niel Morgan, Jan. 4, 1964; children: Amey, Elisabeth, Margaret. BA, Harvard U., 1962, MArch, 1965; MDiv, McCormick Theol. Sem., 1992. Cert. Nat. Coun. Archtl. Registration Bds., 1976; lic. architect, Ill. Architect Skidmore, Owings & Merrill, Chgo., 1966—89, ptnr., 1980—89. Pres. Chgo. Architecture Found., 1983—86, v.p., 1986—89. Housing adv. Protestants for the Common Good, 2000—02; bd. dirs. Lincoln Park Zool. Soc., Chgo., 1976—91; bd. govs. Met. Planning Coun., Chgo., 1977—2004; bd. trustees McCormick Theol. Sem., 1990—91. Mem.: AIA (corp.), Chgo. Presbytery Property Ministries, Chgo. Cultural Affairs Adv. Bd. (vice chmn. 1984—90).

HUTCHINSON, DENNIS, radio director; m. Joy Hutchinson, 1994; children: Kelly, Ben. News dir. WUGN, Midland, Mich., 1998—. Coach ch. softball team; dir. Christian edn. local ch. Office: WUGN 510 E Isabella Rd Midland MI 48640

HUTCHISON, DAVE, state legislator; b. July 26, 1943; BA, St. Norbert Coll. Assemblyman Wis. State Dist. 1; chmn. info. policy com. Producer Touring All Canada Touring Show. Mem. Rotary, YMCA, Luxemburg C. of C. Address: N8915 State Highway 57 Luxemburg WI 54217-9600

HUTMACHER, JAMES K., state legislator, water drilling contractor; b. Chamberlain, SD, Sept. 24, 1953; Water drilling contractor, Chamberlain, S.D.; mem. S.D. Senate from 25th dist., Pierre, 1994—; mem. agr., natural resources, edn. and taxation coms. S.D. Senate, Pierre. Democrat.

HUTTER, JOE, state representative, retired protective services official; b. Dubuque, Iowa, Aug. 31, 1937; BA, We. Ill. U. Police officer, Bettendorf, Iowa; pk. commr.; state rep. dist. 82 Iowa Ho. of Reps., 2003—; mem. human resources com.; mem. judiciary com.; mem. state govt. com.; mem. health and human svcs. subcom. Coord. srs. and law enforcement together program Scott County Sheriff's Office; mem. Scott County Ext. Coun. With USN. Mem.: AARP, Bettendorf Jaycees. Republican. Office: State Capitol East 12th and Grand Des Moines IA 50319

HUTTNER, SIDNEY FREDERICK, librarian; b. Portal, ND, Feb. 18, 1941; s. Frederick W. and Fern May (Nolting) H.; m. Elizabeth Ann Stege, Oct. 24, 1981; 1 child, Erica Marie. BA in Tutorial Studies, U. Chgo., 1963, MA in Philosophy, 1969. Asst. head spl. collections U. Chgo. Libr., 1970-80; head George Arents Rsch. Libr. Syracuse (N.Y.) Libr., 1980-84; curator spl. collections U. Tulsa Libr., 1984-98; head spl. collections U. Iowa Librs., 1999—. Author: A Register of Artists, Engravers, Booksellers, Bookbinders, Printers and Publishers in New York City, 1821-1842, 1993, The Lucile Project website. Fellow Woodrow Wilson Found., 1963-64. Avocation: bookbinding. Home: 5 Glendale Cir Iowa City IA 52245-3208 Office: Spl Collections U Iowa Librs Iowa City IA 52240-1420 Office Phone: 319-335-5922. Business E-Mail: sid-huttner@uiowa.edu.

HUTTON, EDWARD LUKE, retired medical products executive; b. Bedford, Ind., May 5, 1919; s. Fred and Margaret (Drehobl) H.; m. Kathryn Jane Alexander; children Edward Alexander, Thomas Charles, Jennie Hutton Jacoby. BS with distinction, Ind. U., 1940, MS with distinction, 1941; LLD (hon.), Ind. U., Cumberland Coll., 1992. Dep. dir. Joint Export Import Agy. (USUK), Berlin,

1946-48; v.p. World Commerce Corp., 1948-51; asst. v.p. W.R. Grace & Co., 1951-53, cons., 1960-65, exec. v.p., gen. mgr. Dubois Chems. div., 1965-66, group exec. Specialty Products Group and v.p., 1966-68, exec. v.p., 1968-71; cons. internat. trade and fin., 1953-58; fin. v.p., exec. v.p. Ward Industries, 1958-59; pres., CEO Chemed Corp., Cin., 1970—93, chmn., 1993—2004, non-exec. chmn., 2004—; chmn. Omnicare, Inc., Cin., 1981—2003, non-exec. chmn., 2003—08, chmn. emeritus, 2008—. Chmn. bd. dirs. Nat. San. Supply Co., 1983-97; E. Hutton Internat. scholarship program establisher, Ind. U., 2003; bldg. funder, Hutton Sch. Bus., Cumberland Coll., Williamsburg, Ky., 2004. Co-chmn. Pres.'s Pvt. Sector Survey on Cost Control, exec. com., subcom.; former trustee Millikin U., 1973-84. 1st lt., U.S. Army, 1945-47. Recipient Disting. Alumni Svc. award Ind. U., 1987. Mem. AAUP (governing bd. dirs. 1958—), Econ. Club, Princeton Club, Univ. Club, Queen City Club, Bankers Club. Home: 6680 Miralake Ln Cincinnati OH 45243-2722 Office: Chemed Corp 255 E 5th St Ste 2600 Cincinnati OH 45202-4700 Business E-Mail: edward.hutton@chemed.com.

HUTTON, JOHN JAMES, medical researcher, educator, retired dean; b. Ashland, Ky., July 24, 1936; s. John James and Alice (Virgin) H.; m. Mary Ellyn Labach, June 13, 1964; children: Becky, John, Elizabeth. AB, Harvard U., 1958, MD, 1964. Diplomate Am. Bd. Internal Medicine. Sect. chief Roche Inst., Nutley, N.J., 1968-71; prof. medicine U. Ky., Lexington, 1971-79, U. Tex., San Antonio, 1980-84; prof. pediatrics U. Cin., 1984—, dean Coll. Medicine, 1987—2002. Editor Internal Medicine, 1983-2000; contbr. articles to profl. jours. Mem. Am. Soc. Hematology, Assn. Am. Physicians, Am. Soc. Clin. Investigation. Office: Univ Cincinnati 6913 Fox Hill Ln Cincinnati OH 45236-4905 also: Childrens Hosp MLC 7024 Cincinnati OH 45229-3039 Home Phone: 513-793-9249; Office Phone: 513-636-0265. E-mail: john.hutton@cchmc.org.

HUVAERE, JASON, production company executive; b. 1974; Attended, Northwood U., 1993. Pres., dir. ops. Paxahau Promotions Grp., L.L.C., Ferndale, Mich., 1998—. Prodr.: Movement 2006, Detroit's Electronic Music Festival. Named one of 40 Under 40, Crain's Detroit Bus., 2006. Office: Paxahau Promotions Group LLC 326 Hilton Ferndale MI 48220

HWANG, JENNIE S., electronics executive, writer; married; children: Raymond, Rosalind. BA, Cheng-Kung U., Taiwan; MS, Kent State U.; MA, Columbia U.; PhD, Case Western Res. U. Dir. rsch. Lockheed Martin Corp., Cleve., 1976—81; dept. head Sherwin Williams Co., Cleve., 1981—82; dir. SCM Corp., Cleve., 1982—89; pres., chief exec. officer IEM-Fusion, Inc., Cleve., 1990—; pres. and CEO H-Technologies Group, Cleveland, OH. Invited lectr. worldwide; U.S. rep. Internat. Electrotech. Commn.; bd. dirs. various profl. orgns. Author: 5 books; contbg. author to three high tech. books.; patentee in field. Named to Women in Tech. Internat. Hall of Fame, 2000; recipient Disting. Alumni award, 1997, 1999. Mem. Am. Chem. Soc., Am. Ceramic Soc., Am. Welding Soc., Am. Soc. Metals, Internat. Hybrid Microelectronics Soc., Inst. Packaging and Interconnecting Cirs., Sinfare Mount Tech. Assn, NAE, 1998—. Office: H-Technologies Group 26001 Miles Rd Ste 1 Cleveland OH 44128 E-mail: jslhwang@aol.com.

HYDER, ANTHONY K., academic administrator, science educator; BS in Physics, U. Notre Dame, 1964; MS in Space Physics, Air Force Inst. Tech., 1964, PhD in Nuclear Physics, 1971. With Air Force Office of Sci. Rsch.; sci. advisor Office of Under Sec. of Def. Rsch. and Advanced Tech., 1989—90; dir. Space Power Inst., assoc. v.p. rsch. Auburn U., 1982—91, rsch. fellow Space Power Inst., 1991—95; assoc. v.p. grad. studies and rsch., prof. physics and aerospace engring. Univ. of Notre Dame, 1993—. Mem. Air Force Sci. Adv. Bd., 1990—96; sci. adv. bd. Def. Intelligence Agy., 1990—95. Co-author (with D. Flood): Spacecraft Power Systems, 1998; co-author: Defense Conversion Strategies, 1996, The Behavior of Systems in the Space Environment; contbr. articles to profl. jours. Recipient R&D award, USAF; fellow Doctoral fellow, Air Force Inst. Tech. Mem.: AIAA, IEEE, Omicron Delta Kappa, Sigma Pi Sigma, Tau Beta Pi. Achievements include research in in the interaction of spacecraft with the space environment. Office: Univ of Notre Dame 501a Main Bldg 225 Nieuwland Science Bldg otre Dame IN 46556-5670

HYERS, THOMAS MORGAN, physician, biomedical researcher; b. Jacksonville, Fla., June 16, 1943; s. John and Joan (Clemens) H.; m. Elizabeth Mclean, June 12, 1965; children: Justin, Adam. BS, Duke U., 1964, MD, 1968. Diplomate Am. Bd. Internal Medicine, Am. Bd. Pulmonary Diseases. Intern in medicine Cleve. Met. Gen. Hosp., 1968-69; asst. chief Nat. Blood Resource Br., Nat. Heart, Lung and Blood Inst., NIH, 1971-72, pulmonary disease adv. com., 1983-86; resident in medicine U. Wash., Seattle, 1972-74; chief resident, instr. medicine, 1974-75; fellow in pulmonary diseases U. Colo. Health Scis. Ctr., Denver, 1975-76, research fellow Cardiovascular Pulmonary Research Lab., 1976-77, asst. prof. medicine, staff physician respiratory care, assoc. investigator, 1977-82; research assoc. Denver VA Med. Ctr., 1979-82; assoc. prof. medicine, dir. div. pulmonary diseases St. Louis U. Med. Ctr., 1982-85, prof. medicine, divsn. dir., 1985-98; dir. NIH Specialized Ctr. Research in Adult Respiratory Failure, 1983-93. Contbr. articles to profl. jours. Served to comdr. USPHS, 1969-71. Named hon. Ky. col. grantee NIH, Nat. Heart, Lung and Blood Inst. Fellow ACP, Am. Coll. Chest Physicians; mem. Am. Heart Assn. (mem. councils on thrombosis and cardiopulmonary disease), Internat. Soc. Thrombosis and Haemostasis, Am. Lung Assn. (Eastern Mo. chpt.), Am. Fedn. Clin. Research, Am. Physiol. Soc., Western Soc. Clin. Investigation, Am. Thoracic Soc., Phi Beta Kappa. Office: CARE Clin Rsch 533 Couch Ave Ste 140 Saint Louis MO 63122-5561 Office Phone: 314-909-9779. E-mail: studies@careinternet.com.

HYLANDER, JESSICA S., lawyer; BA, Miami U., 1999; JD, U. Mich., 2003. Bar: Ohio 2003, Ct. of Appeals Sixth Cir., US Dist. Ct. Southern Dist. Ohio. Assoc. Dinsmore & Shohl LLP, Cin. Named one of Ohio's Rising Stars, Super Lawyers, 2006. Mem.: Ohio State Bar Assn., Cin. Bar Assn. Office: Dinsmore & Shohl LLP 255 E Fifth St Ste 1900 Cincinnati OH 45202-4700 Office Phone: 513-977-8200. Office Fax: 513-977-8141.

HYMAN, MICHAEL BRUCE, judge; b. Elgin, Ill., July 26, 1952; s. Robert I. and Ruth Hyman; m. Leslie Bland, Aug. 14, 1977; children: Rachel Joy, David Adam. BSJ with honors, Northwestern U., 1974, JD, 1977. Bar: Ill. 1977, U.S. Supreme Ct. 1989. Asst. atty. gen. Antitrust divsn. State of Ill., Chgo., 1977—79; trial atty. Much Shelist Freed Denenberg Ament & Rubenstein, Chgo., 1979—85, ptnr., 1985—2006; judge Cir. Ct. of Cook County, Ill., 2006—. Chmn. panelist various continuing legal edn. seminars. Columnist Editor's Briefcase, CBA Record, 1988-90, 93—2004, The Red Pencil, 1986-89; contbr. chpt. to book, articles to profl. jours.; host (cable TV program) You and the Law, 1995-2004. Trustee North Shore Congregation Israel, Glencoe, 1980-89, 95-2001, v.p., 1987-89. Mem.: ABA (assoc. editor 1985—89, sect. litig., chmn. antitrust litig. com. 1987—90, mng. editor 1989—90, editor-in-chief Litig. News 1990—92, task force on civil justice reform 1991—93, chmn. monographs and unpub. papers com. 1992—95, editor-in-chief Litig. Docket 1995—2001, Tips From the Trenches 2001—02, co-jud. divsn. mem. chair 2002—04, chmn. consumer and personal rights litig. com. 2002—05, exec. com. lawyer's conf. 2002—, jud. divsn. ann. meeting. co-chair 2004—05, atty.-client taskforce 2005—, sec. 2005—06), Chgo. Bar Found. (bd. dirs.), Decalogue Soc. Lawyers (co-chair CLE programs 2001—04, trustee 2001—, fin. sec. 2002—03, rec. sec. 2003—04, pres. 2004—05), Am. Soc. Writers on Legal Subjects (chair book award com. 1997—, bd. dirs., treas. 2005—), Ill. Bar Assn. (antitrust coun. 1981—87, vice chair, sec., co-editor newsletter 1982—85, chmn. coun. 1985—86, rep. on assembly 1986—92, chmn. bench and bar sect. coun. 1990—91, professionalism com. 1992—95, chair 1993—94, rep. on assembly 1994—99, vice chair ARDC com. 1995—96, cable TV com. 1995—2005, chair ARDC com. 1996—97, chair 1997—99, bench and bar sect. coun. 1998—2003, rep. on assembly 2001—04), Chgo. Bar Assn. (editor-in-chief CBA record 1988—90, 1992—94, CBA News 1994—98, vice-chair class action com. 1999—2000, chair 2000—01, bd. mgrs. 2003—04, 2d v.p. 2003—04, editor-in-chief CBA record 2003—, 1st v.p. 2004—05, pres. 2005—06). Jewish. Avocations: writing, Abraham Lincoln.

HYMOWITZ, THEODORE, plant geneticist, educator; b. NYC, Feb. 16, 1934; s. Bernard and Ethel (Rose) H.; m. Ann Einhorn, Dec. 25, 1960 (div. 1985); children: Madeleine, Sara, Jessica; m. Barbara E. Bohen, June 11, 1989 (div. 1998). BS, Cornell U., 1955; MS, U. Ariz., 1957; PhD, Okla. State U., 1963. Agronomist IRI Rsch. Inst., Campinas, Brazil, 1964-66; from asst. to assoc. prof. U. Ill., Urbana, 1967-75, prof., 1975—2005, prof. emeritus, 2005—. With U.S. Army, 1957-59. Recipient Rsch. award Land of Lincoln Soybean Assn., 1990, Funk award, 1991; scholar Loeb Found., Stillwater, Okla., 1961-62, Fulbright scholar, 1962-63. Fellow AAAS, Linnean Soc. London, Am. Soc. Agronomy, Crop Sci. Soc. Am. (Frank N. Meyer medal 1988). Achievements include research in the establishment of chromosomal map of the soybean, inheritance of the absence of seed lectin in soybeans, elucidation of genomic relationships among species in the genus Glycine, development of soybean cultivar lacking the Kunitz trypsin inhibitor, history of the introduction of the soybean to N.Am. Office: U Ill Dept Crop Sci 1102 S Goodwin Ave Urbana IL 61801-4730

HYSLOP, DAVID JOHNSON, retired arts administrator; b. Schenectady, June 27, 1942; s. Moses McDickens Hyslop; m. Sally Fefercorn, Aug. 12, 1995; 1 child, Alexander. BS in Music Edn., Ithaca Coll., 1965. Elem. sch. vocal music supr., Elmira Heights, N.Y., 1965-66; mgr. Elmira Symphony Choral Soc., 1966; asst. mng. dir. Minn. Orch., Mpls., 1969-72; gen. mgr. Oreg. Symphony Orch., Portland, 1972-78; exec. dir. St. Louis Symphony Soc., 1978-89, pres., 1989-91, Minn. Orch., 1991—; ret. Bd. dirs. Am. Symphony Orch. League, 1988-96, chmn., 1994, mem. exec. and nominating coms., 1990-93; bd. dirs. Minn. Citizens for Arts, Mpls. Downtown Coun., 1992-97, Mpls. Visitors and Conf. Bur., 1996-98; mem., co-chmn. arts edn. task for Mo. Arts Coun., 1989-90; mem. rec. panel Nat Endowment for Arts, 1986-88, mem. challenge grant panel, 1987-88, mem. music overview panel, 1987-88, mem. music creation and presentation panel, 1999; chmn. music and performing arts com. Regional Commerce and Growth Assn., St. Louis, 1987-89; bd. dirs. Minn. State Fair Found., 2002--. Martha Baird Rockefeller grantee, 1966. Mem. Am. Symphony Orch. League (chmn. major mgrs. and policy com. 1985-87, orch. mgmt. fellowship program 1979-88, orch. assessment program 1988), Regional Orch. Mgrs. Assn. (founder), Minn. Orchestral Assn., Mpls. Club, Arena Club. Avocations: basketball, travel, reading, study of German. Home: 2019 Irving Ave S Minneapolis MN 55405-2521 Office: Minn Orch 1111 Nicollet Mall Minneapolis MN 55403-2477 E-mail: dhyslop@mnorch.org.

IAMMARTINO, NICHOLAS R., corporate communications executive; m. Eileen Iammartino. B in Chem. Engring., Cooper Union; M in Chem. Engring., NYU; MBA in Fin., Adelphi U. Process engr. Esso Rsch. and Engring. Co., 1969-71; bus. and tech. news writer Chem. Engring. mag. McGraw-Hill, 1971-76; chem. industry securities analyst Merrill Lynch, 1976-78; from sr. writer to bus. pubs. mgr. dept. corp. comm. Celanese Corp., 1979-85; corp. mgr. fin. comm. and adminstrn. Philip Morris, Inc., 1985; dir. fin. comm. Borden, Inc., N.Y., 1986-89, dir. external comm. N.Y., 1989, dir. pub. affairs N.Y., 1994-95, v.p. pub. affairs Columbus, Ohio, 1995—. Bd. dirs. Borden Found., Inc.; mem. assn. bd. Columbus Zool. Pk. Assn. Office: Borden Inc 180 E Broad St Columbus OH 43215-3799

IANNOTTI, JOSEPH PATRICK, orthopedic surgeon; b. NYC, Dec. 16, 1954; s. Frank Thomas and Victoria (Artuso) I.; 1 child, Matthew; m. Karen Bloomberg, July 26, 2003. BS, Fordham U., 1975; MD, Northwestern U., 1979; PhD in Cell Biology, U. Pa., 1987. Diplomate Am. Bd. Orthopaedic Surgery. Resident in orthopedic surgery U. Pa., Phila., 1979-83, chief resident, 1983-84, asst. prof. orthopedic surgery, 1984-93, assoc. prof., 1993-97, prof., 1997-2000; chief of shoulder svc. Hosp. of U. Pa., Phila., 1988-2000; chmn. dept. orthopedic surgery Cleve. Clinic Found., 2000—; prof. Cleve. Clinic Lerner Sch. Medicine. Author, editor: Rotator Cuff Disorders, 1992; editor: Basic Science Orthopaedics, 1994, The Shoulder Evaluation and Management, 1999, 2006, Complex and Revision Problems in Shoulder Surgery, 1998, 2005; contbr. over 200 articles to profl. jours. NIH postdoctoral fellow U. Pa., 1980-81; recipient career devel. award NIH, 1984-89, DeForest Willard award U. Pa., 1984; N.Am. travel fellow Am. Orthopaedic Assn., 1985, Am. Brit. Can. fellow, 1993. Fellow Am. Acad. Orthopaedic Surgeons; mem. Orthopaedic Rsch. Soc., Am. Shoulder and Elbow Surgeons (pres. 2005-06), Acad. Orthopaedic Soc., Pa. Orthopaedic Soc. Office: Cleve Clinic Found 9500 Euclid Ave # A-41 Cleveland OH 44195-0001 Office Phone: 216-445-5151. Business E-Mail: iannotj@ccf.org.

IATRIDIS, PANAYOTIS GEORGE, medical educator; b. Alexandria, Egypt, Dec. 10, 1926; naturalized citizen, 1975; m. Catherine Iatridis; children: Yanna, Mary. MD, U. Athens, Greece, 1951, DSc with honors in Physiology, 1968. Lic. physician Greece, Egypt, N.C., Ind., Ill. Resident Univ. Med. Clinic, Athens, 1951-53, Greek Hosp., Alexandria, Egypt, 1953-55, asst. dir. dept. medicine, 1959-62; rsch. assoc. dept. physiology U. N.C., Chapel Hill, 1963-66, asst. prof. physiology, 1969-72, faculty grad. sch., 1969-72; vis. rsch. scientist Protein Found./Harvard Sch. Pub. Health, Boston, 1966; rsch. scientist dept. physiology U. Athens, 1967-69; faculty Ind. U., prof. physiology, biophysics and medicine, asst. dean Gary, dir. N.W. Ctr. for Med. Edn. Mem. search and screen com. Exec. Dir. of Lake County Med. Ctr. Devel. Agy., 1984; pres., CEO N.W. Ctr. Med. Svcs. Corp., 1985—; bd. dirs. Lake Shore Health Sys. of Ancilla Sys. Corp., 1986—, mem. quality assurance com., 1986—; lectr. in field; lectr. in field. Contbr. numerous articles and abstracts to profl. jours.; editl. bd. Ind. Medicine, 1992—. Mem. coun. St. Iakovos Greek Orthodox Ch., 1985; bd. dirs. World Affairs Coun. of N.W. Ind., 1985—; mem. ad hoc com. on AIDS Gary Cmty. Sch. Corp., 1985; bd. visitors Modern Greek Studies, Ind. U., Bloomington, 1985; mem. N.W. Ind. Forum Found., 1987—; chmn. Porter Starke Infection Control Com., 1988—; bd. dirs. N.W. Ind. Symphony, 1988-89; mem. N.W. Ind. Forum legis. Subcom., 1988, edn. com., 1992—; bd. dirs. N.W. Ind. chpt. Am. Lung Assn., 1977-84, exec. com., 1979-84; bd. dirs. Am. Cancer Soc., 1978-83, mem. med. edn. com., 1978-83; mem. coun. SS Constantine and Helen, Greek Orthodox Cathedral, Merrillville, Ind., 1979-81; vice chmn. Cmty. Health Assn., Lake County, 1979-81, chmn. med. adv. com., 1979-81, chmn. editl. bd., 1980-81; mem. rsch. com. Ind. affiliate Am. Heart Assn., 1982-84, vice chmn., 1983-84; mem. City of Gary Econ. Devel. Commn., 1984; group leader People to People Med. Edn. Delegation to People's Republic of China, 1984; founder, 1st pres. Greek Orthodox Ch. of Porter County, 1980-81. Recipient medal of St. Paul Greek Orthodox Archdiocese of North and South Am.; grantee Dept. HEW/NIH/USPHS, 1973-76, Lake County Med. Ctr. Devel. Agy., 1975-82, 82-85, 85, 85-86, 86-87, 86, 87, 88, 89, 90, 91, 92, Ind. State Bd. Health, Divsn. Maternal and Child Health, 1985, 858-86, 86-87, 87-89, Innkeepers Tax for Med. Edn., 1993, 94. Fellow ACP; mem. Acad. Athens (corr.), Ind. State Med. Soc. (commn. on med. edn. 1986—, vice chmn. commn. on conv. arrangements 1988), Porter County Med. Soc. (care of indigent com. 1986), Lake County Med. Soc. (care of indigent com. 1986), Rotary (chmn. membership devel. com. 1987-88). Office: Ind U NW Ctr for Med Edn 3400 Broadway Gary IN 46408-1101

IBEN, ICKO, JR., astrophysicist, educator; b. Champaign, Ill., June 27, 1931; s. Icko and Kathryn (Tomlin) I.; m. Miriam Genevieve Fett, Jan. 28, 1956; children: Christine, Timothy, Benjamin, Thomas. BA, Harvard U., 1953; MS, U. Ill., 1954, PhD, 1958. Asst. prof. physics Williams Coll., 1958-61; sr. rsch. fellow in physics Calif. Inst. Tech., Pasadena, 1961—64; assoc. prof. physics MIT, Cambridge, 1964-68, prof., 1968-72; prof. astronomy and physics, head dept. astronomy U. Ill., Champaign-Urbana, 1972-84, prof. astronomy and physics, 1972-89, disting. prof. astronomy and physics Urbana, 1989—99, disting. prof. emeritus, 2000; holder of Eberly family chair in astronomy Pa. State U., 1989-90. Vis. prof. astronomy Harvard U., 1966, 68, 70; vis. fellow Joint Inst. for Lab. Astrophysics U. Colo., 1971—72; vis. prof. astronomy and astrophysics U. Calif., Santa Cruz, 1972; vis. prof. physics and astronomy Inst. for Astronomy U. Hawaii, 1977; adv. panel astronomy sect. NSF, 1972—75; vis. com. Aura Observatories, 1979—82; vis. scientist astronomical coun. Union Soviet Socialist Rep. Acad. Sci., 1985; sr. vis. fellow Australian Nat. U., 1986; vis. prof. U. Bologna, Italy, 1986, Hokkaido U. Grad. Sch. Sci., 2001; sr. rsch. fellow U. Sussex, England, 1986; George Darwin lectr. Royal Astronomical Soc., London, 1984; McMillin lectr. Ohio State U., 1987; vis. eminent scholar U. Ctr. Ga., 1988; guest prof. Christian Albrechts U. Kiel, 1990; sr. fellow Nicolaus Copernicus Astron. Ctr., Warsaw, 2002. Contbr. articles to profl. jours. John Simon Guggenheim Meml. fellow, 1985—86, Japan Soc. for Promotion of Sci. fellow, U. Tokyo, 1985, Niigata U., 1990, vis. Japan Soc. for Promotion of Sci. Eminent Scientist, Hokkaido U., 2003—04. Fellow Royal Astron. Soc. (Eddington medal 1990); mem. Am. Astron. Soc. (councilor 1974-77, Henry Norris Russell lectr. 1989), U.S. Nat. Acad. of Scis., Internat. Astronom. Union. Home: 3910 Clubhouse Dr Champaign IL 61822-9280 Office: U Ill Dept of Astronomy 1002 W Green St Urbana IL 61801-3074

IBERS, JAMES ARTHUR, chemist, educator; b. LA, Calif., June 9, 1930; s. Max Charles and Esther (Imerman) I.; m. Joyce Audrey Henderson, June 10, 1951; children: Jill Tina, Arthur Alan. BS, Calif. Inst. Tech., 1951, PhD, 1954. NSF post-doctoral fellow, Melbourne, Australia, 1954-55; chemist Shell Devel. Co., 1955-61, Brookhaven Nat. Lab., 1961-64; mem. faculty Northwestern U., 1964—, prof. chemistry, 1964-85, Charles E. and Emma H. Morrison prof. chemistry, 1986—. Recipient Disting. alumni award Calif. Inst. Tech., 1997. Mem. NAS, Am. Acad. Arts and Sci., Am. Chem. Soc. (inorganic chemistry award 1979, Disting. Svc. in the Advancement of Inorganic Chemistry award 1992, Linus Pauling award 1994), Am. Crystallographic Assn. (Buerger award 2002). Office: Northwestern U Dept Chemistry Evanston IL 60208-3113 Home: 990 N Lake Shore Dr 17C Chicago IL 60611-1366 Business E-Mail: ibers@chem.northwestern.edu.

IBRAHIM, IBRAHIM NAMO, bishop; b. Telkaif, Mosul, Iraq, Oct. 1, 1937; arrived in US, 1978; s. Namo Ibrahim and Rammo Yono. Grad., Mosul Sem., Iraq, 1951, St. Sulpice Sem., Paris, 1962; STD, Rome, 1975. Ordained priest, 1962; dir. sem. Baghdad, Iraq, 1964-68; assoc. pastor St. Joseph Ch., Baghdad, 1975-78; pastor Chaldean Ch., LA, 1979-82; vicar apostolic USA, Faithful of the Oriental Rite (Chaldean), 1982; ordained bishop, 1982; bishop Eparchy of St. Thomas the Apostle of Detroit, Southfield, Mich., 1985—. Chaldean Catholic. Office: Eparchy of St Thomas the Apostle 25603 Berg Rd Southfield MI 48034-2556 Office Phone: 248-351-0440. Office Fax: 248-351-0443.*

ICHINO, YOKO, ballerina; b. Los Angeles, Cali. m. David Nixon. Studied with Mia Slavenska, LA. Mem. Joffrey II, NYC, Joffrey Ballet, NYC, Stuttgart Ballet, Fed. Republic Germany; tchr. ballet, 1976; soloist Am. Ballet Theatre, 1977-81; guest appearances, 1981-82; prin. Nat. Ballet Can., Toronto, Ont., 1982-90. Various guest appearances including World Ballet Festival, Tokyo, 1979, 85, Tokyo Ballet, 1980, with Alexander Godunov and Stars, summer, 1982, Sydney Ballet, Australia, N.Z. Ballet, summer 1984, Ballet de Marseille, 1985-87, Deutsche Opera Ballet Berlin, 1985-90, Munich Opera Ballet, 1987-90, Australian Ballet, 1987, 89, Staatsoper Berlin, 1989, 90, Komische Opera, Berlin, 1991-93, David Nixon's Dance Theater, Berlin, 1990, 91, Birmingham Royal Ballet, 1990-93, Deutsche Opera Ballet, Berlin, 1994-95; tchr. Australian Ballet, 1989, Birmingham Royal Ballet, 1991, 93, Nat. Ballet of Can., 1993, Cullberg Ballet, Sweden, 1994, Nat. Ballet Sch., 1994, 95, Ballet de Monte-Carlo, 1994, Geneva Ballet, 1995-98, Nederlands Dance Theater, 1995, Rambert Dance, 1995, Royal Winnipeg Ballet, 1999; tchr. numerous ballet workshops; dir. profl. program Ballet Met, 1995-2003; guest master tchr., coach No. Ballet Theatre, 2002—. First Am. trained woman recipient medal Third Internat. Ballet Competition, Moscow, 1977. Office: No Ballet Theatre West Park Centre Spen Ln Leeds LS16 5BE England

ICHIYAMA, DENNIS YOSHIHIDE, art educator, educational association administrator; b. Aiea, Hawaii, May 28, 1944; s. Edwin Kiyotada and Florence Fusae (Inoshita) I. BFA, U. Hawaii, 1966; MFA, Yale U., 1968; postgrad., Allgemeine Gewerbeschule, Basel, Switzerland, 1975-77. Instr. U. Bridgeport, Conn., 1968-70; sr. graphic designer Graphic Communications Ltd., Hong Kong, 1970-71; instr. Carnegie-Mellon U., Pitts., 1971-74; asst. prof. Cornell U., Ithaca, NY, 1974-75; assoc. prof. Ind. U., Bloomington, 1977-78; asst. prof. U. Ill., Chgo., 1978-79; assoc. prof. Wichita (Kans.) State U., 1979-81; prof., chmn. divsn. art and design Purdue U., West Lafayette, Ind., 1985-92, head dept. visual and performing arts, 1993—. Design cons. US Postal Svc., Washington, 1986, Purdue U. Press, West Lafayette, 1989—, Interior Design Educators Coun., Ithaca, 1985-87; vis. scholar U. Iowa Ctr. for Book, 1990; fellow Ctr. for Artistic Endeavor Purdue U., Sch. Liberal Arts, 1992, 2003-; artist-in-residence Hamilton Wood Type & Printing Mus., Wis., 1999-2000, Ctr. for Book and Paper Arts, Columbia Coll., Chgo., 2005, Minn. Ctr. Book Arts, Mpls., 2006; bd. dir. Coll. Art Assn., 2002-, v.p. coms., 2006-, chair nominating com., 2006-, chair profl. devel. fellowships in art history and visual arts, 2006-, mem. exec. com, 2006-, mem. conf. com., 2006-, mem. budget and fin. com., 2006-, chair task force, 2006-. Design work exhbns. in Can., US, Germany, Finland, France, Czechoslovakia; exhibited in shows at Centre Georges Pompidou, 1985, Poster Biennale, Warsaw, 1982, Biennale of Graphic Design, Brno, Czechoslovakia, 1982, 92, Columbia U. Rare Book and Manuscript Libr., Ctr. Book and Paper Arts, Columbia Coll., Chgo., 2006; represented in collection of the Plakatsammlung of Kunstgewerbemuseum, Zurich, Rochester Inst. Tech. Libr., NY, Lahti Art Mus., Finland, Stern Book Arts and Spl. Collections Ctr., San Francisco Pub. Libr., Purdue U. Librs., Ruth and Marvin Sackner Archive of Concrete and Visual Poetry; author essays in Contemporary Designers, 1985, T Y P O G R A M S, Pure Type Forms, 2000, The Hamilton Type Specimen Sheets Portfolio, 2001, book revs.; book reviewer Choice (ALA, Assn. Coll./Rsch. Librs.). Recipient Typographic Excellence award Type Dirs. Club, 2006; grantee Nat. Endowment for Humanities, 1984; IAC master fellow Ind. Arts Commn., 1985, 2001; grantee Nat. Endowment for Arts, 1989, Individual Artist program Indian Art Commn., 2001-03, 05-06; fellow Prix du Rome, Am. Acad. Rome, 2006-07. Fellow Soc. Fellows, Am. Acad., Rome (2006-); mem. Am. Ctr. for Design, Am. Inst. Graphic Arts, Graphic Design Educators Assn., Alliance Typographique Internat., Internat. Soc. Typographic Designers, Soc. Typographic Arts, Nat. Coun. Art Adminstrs. (nat. bd. dirs. 1998—), Internat. Coun. Fine Arts Deans, Coll. Art Assn. Am. (nat. bd. dirs. 2002—), Arts Ind. (state coun. 1993-99), Hui na opio o Hawaii (advisor 1986-93), Greater Lafayette Mus. Art. Buddhist. Avocations: swiss posters, artists books, Chinese and Japanese seals, printing history, hand bookbinding and letterpress printing. Office: Purdue U Dept Visual and Performing Arts Bldg 552 W Wood St West Lafayette IN 47907-2002 Home Phone: 765-743-0440; Office Phone: 765-494-3071. E-mail: diad@purdue.edu.

IDOL, ANNA CATHERINE, magazine editor; b. Chgo., July 8, 1941; d. Melvin Oliver and Louise Hildegard (Bullington) Lokensgard; m. William Ross Idol, Oct. 25, 1959 (div. Mar. 1962); 1 child, Laura Jeanne; m. Michael Wataru Sugano, Jan. 28, 1990. BS, Lake Forest Coll., Ill., 1980; MBA, Northwestern U., Evanston, Ill., 1982. treas. Chgo. Women in Pub., Chgo., 1970-71. Editor Rand McNally Co., Chgo., 1968-78, product mgr. adult reference, 1983-84; founder, pres. Bullington Laird, Inc., Chgo., 1986—; mng. editor Elks Mag., Chgo., 1997—. Pub.: Center Within, 1988 (award Heartsong Rev. 1989); writer, concept advt. alert, 1990 (Harvey Comm. award). Pres. Am. Buddhist Assn., 1985-93; mem. bd. Buddhist Temple Chgo., 1985-93; v.p. Buddhist Coun. Midwest, 1985-89. Democrat. Buddhist. Avocations: wilderness adventure, travel, reading. Office: Elks Mag 425 W Diversey Pkwy Chicago IL 60614-6196 Office Phone: 773-755-4894. Business E-Mail: annai@elks.org.

IGLAUER, BRUCE, record company executive; Educated, Lawrence U. Shipping clk. Delmark Records, 1970; founder, pres. Alligator Records, Chgo., 1971. Produced recording of Hound Dog Taylor and the Houserockers, 1971; producer for artists including Big Walter Horton, Son Seals and Fenton Robinson. Office: Alligator Records PO Box 60234 Chicago IL 60660-0234

IGNOFFO, CARLO MICHAEL, insect pathologist-virologist; b. Chicago Heights, Ill., Aug. 24, 1928; s. Joseph and Lucy (Sardo) I.; m. Florence F. Mielcarek, Sept. 3, 1949. BS, No. Ill. U., 1950; MS, U. Minn., 1954, PhD, 1957. Asst. prof. Iowa Wesleyan Coll., Mt. Pleasant, 1957-59; insect pathologist U.S. Dept. Agr., Brownsville, Tex., 1959-65; dir. entomology Internat. Minerals & Chems. Corp., Wasco, Calif. and Libertyville, Ill., 1965-71; lab. dir. U.S. Dept. Agr., Columbia, Mo., 1971-91; prof. dept. entomology U. Mo., 1974—. Served with Chem. Corps U.S. Army, 1954-56. Mem. AAAS, Internat. Orgn. Biol. Control (pres. 1974), Am. Inst. Biol. Scis., Soc. Invertebrate Pathology (editorial bd. 1965-68, assoc. editor 1992—, treas. 1968-70), Entomol. Soc. Am. Achievements include isolating, commercializing 1st viral pesticide; patentee in field. Office: Research Park 1503 S Providence Rd Columbia MO 65203-3535 E-mail: ignoffoc@missouri.edu.

IHLENFELD, JAY V., manufacturing executive; BS, Purdue U., 1974. Bus. dir., engring. fluids and sys. 3M Co., St. Paul, gen. mgr., performance materials divsn., 1999, v.p., performance materials divsn., 1999—2001; exec. v.p. Sumitomo 3M Ltd., Tokyo, 2001—02; sr. v.p., rsch. and devel. 3M Co., St. Paul, 2002—. Mem. Internat. Adv. Bd., Alliance for Global Sustainability. Office: 3M Co 3M Ctr Saint Paul MN 55144

IKENBERRY, STANLEY OLIVER, education educator, director, former university president; b. Lamar, Colo., Mar. 3, 1935; s. Oliver Samuel and Margaret (Moulton) Ikenberry; m. Judith Ellen Life, Aug. 24, 1958; children: David Lawrence, Steven Oliver, John Paul. BA, Shepherd Coll., 1956; MA, Mich. State U., 1957, PhD, 1960, LHD (hon.); LLD (hon.), Millikin U.; LHD (hon.), Millkin U., Ill. Coll., Rush U., W.Va. U., Towson State U., U. Nebr., Bridgewater Coll., Va., Bradley U., Shepherd Coll., Roosevelt U., Juniatta Coll., Pa., 2003, Northeastern U. Instr. office evaluation svc. Mich. State U., 1958—60, instr. instl. rsch. office, 1960—62; asst. to provost for instl. rsch., asst. prof. edn. W.Va. U., 1962—65, dean coll. human resources and edn., assoc. prof. edn., 1965—69; prof., assoc. dir. ctr. study higher edn. Pa. State U., 1969—71, sr. v.p., 1971—79; pres. U. Ill., Urbana, 1979—95, pres. emeritus, Regent prof., 1995—; pres. Am. Coun. on Edn., Washington, 1996—2001. Bd. dirs. Aquila Inc., Kans. City; pres. bd. overseers Tchrs. Ins. and Annutiy Assn./Coll. Retirement Equities Fund. Named hon. alumnus, Pa. State U. Fellow: Am. Acad. Arts and Scis.; mem.: Cosmos Club (Washington), Comml. Club Chgo. Office: U Ill 347 Education 1310 S 6th St Champaign IL 61820

ILGAUSKAS, ZYDRUNAS, professional basketball player; b. Kaunas, Lithuania, June 5, 1975; m. Jennifer Ilgauskas, 2004. Profl. basketball player Atletas Basketball Club, Kaunas, 1994—95; draft pick Cleve. Cavaliers, 1996, ctr., 1997—. Named to All-Rookie First Team, NBA, 1998, Ea. Conf. All-Star Team, 2003, 2005. Achievements include leading the NBA in offensive rebounds (299), 2004-05. Avocations: soccer, fishing. Office: Cleve Cavaliers Quicken Loans Arena One Center Ct Cleveland OH 44115-4001

ILGEN, DANIEL RICHARD, psychology professor; b. Freeport, Ill., Mar. 16, 1943; s. Paul Maurice and Marjorie V. (Glasser) I.; m. Barbara Geiser, Dec. 26, 1965; children: Elizabeth Ann, Mark Andrew. BS in Psychology, Iowa State U., 1965; MA, U. Ill., 1968, PhD in Indsl.-Orgnl. Psychology, 1969. Asst. prof. dept. psychology U. Ill., Urbana, 1969-70; instr. Dutchess County C.C., Poughkeepsie, NY, 1971-72; from asst. prof. to prof. dept. psychol. scis. Purdue U., West Lafayette, Ind., 1972-83, area head indsl.-orgnl. psychology, 1978-83; Hannah prof. organizational behavior depts. mgmt. and psychology Mich. State U., East Lansing, 1983—. Vis. assoc. prof. dept. mgmt. and orgn. U. Wash., Seattle, 1978-79; vis. prof. dept. mgmt. U. Western Australia, 1991, 2000. Co-author (with J.C. Naylor and R.D. Pritchard): A Theory of Behavior in Organizations, 1980; co-author: (with E.J. McCormick) Industrial Psychology, 1985; co-editor (with E. Pulakos): The Changing Nature of Performance, 1999; co-editor: (with C. Hulin) Computational Modeling of Behavior in Organizations, 2000; co-editor: (with W. Borman and R. Klimoski) Industrial and Organizational Psychology, The Comprehensive Handbook of Psychology, vol. 12, 2002; contbr. chpts. to books and artilces to profl. jours.; editor: Organizational Behavior and Human Decision Processes, 1998—2001. Capt. M.I., U.S. Army, 1970-72. Grantee Purdue U. Found., 81-82, U.S. Army Rsch. Inst., 1974-82, Office Naval Rsch., 1982-86, 90—. Fellow Am. Psychol. Assn. (edn. tng. com., coun. reps. 1985-87), Soc. Indsl. and Organizational Psychology of Am. Psychol. Assn. (pres. 1987-88, Disting. Sci. Contbn. award 2001), Am. Psychol. Soc., Acad. Mgmt. (Herbert Heneman Jr. Disting. Lifetime Contbn. award 2002); mem. Soc. Orgnl. Behavior, Sigma Xi. Office: Mich State U Depts Mgmt And Psychol East Lansing MI 48824-1117 E-mail: Ilgen@msu.edu.

ILGEN, DOROTHY L., arts foundation executive; Asst. dir. Mo. Arts Coun.; exec. dir. Kans. Arts Commn., Ind. Arts Commn., Indpls., 1995—. Active numerous coms. and commns. various local, state, regional, and nat. orgns.; bd. dirs. Mid-Am. Arts Alliance, Arts Midwest, mem. program planning com.; bd. dirs., mem. planning and budget com., nominating com. Nat. Assembly of State Arts Agys.; panelist arts design panel NEA, Nat. Access Task Force. Office: Indiana Arts Commission 150 W Market St Ste 618 Indianapolis IN 46204

ILITCH, DENISE, food services executive; Pres. Bright Lites Inc., Detroit; vice chair Little Caesar Enterprises Inc., 1997—; pres. Olympia Devel. LLC, 1996—; exec. v.p. Ilitch Holdings, Detroit, 1999—. Bd. dirs. Detroit br. Fed. Res. Bank of Chgo. Office: Ilitch Holdings Inc 2211 Woodward Ave Detroit MI 48201-3467

ILITCH, MARIAN, professional hockey team and food service executive; m. Michael Ilitch; children: Denise Ilitch Lites, Ron, Mike Jr., Lisa Ilitch Murray, Atanas, Christopher, Carole. Co-owner, sec.-treas. Little Caesar Internat., 1959—, Detroit Red Wings, 1982—; sec.-treas. Olympia Arenas, Inc. (Olympia Entertainment Inc.), 1982—; co-owner, sec.-treas. Fox Theatre, 1987—, Detroit Tigers, 1992—. Little Foxes Fine Gifts, 1992—, The Second City, 1993—, Olympia Devel. LLC, 1996—, Hockeytown Cafe, 1999—, Blue Line Distributing, Uptown Entertainment, Champion Foods; co-founder, vice-chmn. Ilitch Holdings, Inc., 1999—. Recipient Pacesetter Award, Roundtable for Women in Foodservice, 1988, Nat. Preservation Honor Award, 1990. Office: Ilitch Holdings Inc Fox Office Ctr 2211 Woodward Ave Detroit MI 48201-3400

ILITCH, MICHAEL, professional hockey team and food products executive; b. July 20, 1929; m. Marian Ilitch; children: Denise Ilitch Lites, Ron, Mike Jr., Lisa, Atanas, Christopher, Carole. Founder, owner Little Caesars Restaurant, 1959—; owner, pres. Detroit Red Wings Hockey Team, 1982—; founder Blue Line Distbg., Am.'s Pizza Cafe; owner Olympia Arenas, Inc. (formerly Olympia Stadium Corp.), 1983—, Adirondack Red Wings Hockey Team, Detroit Dir. of Arena Football League; owner, chmn., former pres. Detroit Tigers Baseball Team; chmn. Ilitch Holdings, Inc. Little Caesars Love Kitchen program, 1985—. With USMC, 4 yrs. Named one of 400 Richest Americans, Forbes mag.; named to Hockey Hall of Fame, 2003; recipient Lester Patrick trophy, 1991, Bus. Statesman award, Harvard Bus. Sch. Club Detroit, 1990, Joe Louis award, Sports Illustrated Mag. and Detroit Inst. Arts, Humanitarian of Yr. award, March of Dimes, Sec. award, US Dept. Vets. Affairs, 2007. Office: Detroit Red Wings 600 Civic Center Dr Detroit MI 48226-4419 also: Detroit Tigers Tiger Stadium 2100 Woodward Ave Detroit MI 48201-3470 also: Little Caesars Enterprizes 2211 Woodward Ave Detroit MI 48201-3467

ILTIS, HUGH HELLMUT, botanist, educator, environmental advocate; b. Brno, Czechoslovakia, Apr. 7, 1925; arrived in US, 1939, naturalized, 1944; s. Hugo and Anne (Liebscher) I.; m. Grace Schaffel, Dec. 20, 1951 (div. Mar. 1958); children: Frank S., Michael George; m. Carolyn Merchant, Aug. 4, 1961 (div. June 1970); children: David Hugh, John Paul; m. Sharyn Wisniewski Nov. 3, 2006. BA, U. Tenn., 1948; MA, Washington U., St. Louis and Mo. Bot. Garden, 1950, PhD, 1952; PhD (hon.), U. Guadalajara, Mex., 2007. Rsch. asst. Mo. Bot. Garden, 1948-52; asst. prof. botany U. Ark., 1952-55; asst. prof. U. Wis.-Madison, 1955-60, assoc. prof., 1960-67, prof., 1967-93, prof. emeritus, 1993—, curator herbarium, 1955-67, dir. univ. herbarium, 1967-93, dir. emeritus, 1993—. Vis. prof. U. Va., Biol. Sta., 1959; expdns. to Costa Rica, 1949, 89, Peru, 1962-63, Mex., 1960, 71-72, 77-79, 81-82, 84, 87-88, 90, 93-96, Guatemala, 1976, Ecuador, 1977, St. Eustatius, P.R., 1989, USSR, 1975, 79, Nicaragua-Honduras, 1991, Venezuela, 1991, Hawaii, 1967; adv. bd. Flora N.Am., 1970-73, Gov. Wis. Commn. State Forests, 1972-73; rsch. assoc. Mo. Bot. Garden, Bot. Rsch. Inst. Tex.; co-instigator Reserva Biosfera Sierra de Manantlán, Jalisco, Mex.; lectr. in field. Co-author: Flora de Manantlan, Jalisco, Mexico, 1995, SIDA, vol. 13, 1995, Atlas of the Wisconsin Prairie and Savana Flora, 2000; co-author: (with T.S.Cochrane) Checklist of the Vascular Plants of Wis., 2001; editor: Extinction or Preservation: What Biological Future for the South American Tropics?, 1978; contbr. articles to profl. jours. With US Army, 1944—46, ETO. Recipient Biologia award, U. Tenn., 1948, Presdl. Merit cert., Mex., 1987, Feinstone Environ. award, SUNY, Syracuse, 1990, Conservation award, Conservation Coun. Hawaii, 1990, Nat. Wildlife Fedn. Spl. Achievement award, 1992, Puga medal, U. de Guadalajara, Mex., 1994, Disting. Alumnus award, Mo. Bot. Garden, 1999. Fellow AAAS, Linnean Soc. (London); mem. Am. Inst. Biol. Scis., Bot. Soc. Am. (Merit award 1996, Centennial award 2006), Soc. Econ. Botany (Econ. Botanist of Yr. award 1998), Am. Soc. Plant Taxonomists (Asa Gray award 1994), Internat. Assn. Plant Taxonomy, Soc. Bot. Mex., Soc. Study Evolution, Ecol. Soc. Am., Wis. Acad. Arts, Sci. and Letters, Forum for Corr.-Internat. Ctr. Integrative Studies, Nature Conservancy (cofounder and trustee emeritus Wis. chpt., Nat. Oakleaf award 1963), Wilderness Soc., Sierra Club, Nat. Parks Assn., Citizens Natural Resources Assn. Wis., Natural Resource Def. Coun., Environ. Def. Fund, Friends of Earth, Population Connection, Negative Population Growth, Soc. Conservation Biology (Disting. Achievement award 1994), Natural Areas Assn., Sigma Xi, Phi Kappa Phi. Achievements include co-discovery of Zea diploperennis, Z. nicaraguensis (wild species of the maize genus) and Lycopersicon chmielewskii (high sugar-content wild tomatoes). Home: 2784 Marshall Pky Madison WI 53713-1023 Office: U Wis Dept Botany 430 Lincoln Dr Madison WI 53706-1313 Home Phone: 608-256-7247; Office Phone: 608-262-2792. Office Fax: 608-262-7509. Personal E-mail: swis@charter.net.

IMESCH, JOSEPH LEOPOLD, bishop emeritus; b. Grosse Pointe Farms, Mich., June 21, 1931; s. Dionys and Margaret (Margelisch) I. BS, Sacred Heart Sem., 1953; student, .Am. Coll., Rome, 1953-57; STL, Gregorian U., Rome, 1957. Ordained priest Archdiocese of Detroit, Mich., 1956; sec. to Cardinal Dearden, 1959—71; pastor Our Lady of Sorrows Ch., Farmington, Mich., 1971—77; ordained bishop, 1973; aux. bishop Archdiocese of Detroit, 1973—79; bishop Diocese of Joliet, Ill., 1979—2006, bishop emeritus, 2006—. Roman Catholic. Office: Chancery Office 425 Summit St Joliet IL 60435-7155 Office Phone: 815-722-6606. Office Fax: 815-722-6602.*

IMMELT, MARK W., bank executive; With Cen. Nat. Bank Cleve. (KeyCorp predecessor); exec. v.p. No. Ind. Key Bank; sr. v.p., sr. trust officer 1st Fin. Bancorp, 1996, sr. v.p.; pres., CEO 1st Nat. Bank Southwestern Ohio, Hamilton, 1999—. Office: 300 High St Hamilton OH 45011-6078

IMRAY, THOMAS JOHN, radiologist, educator; b. Milw., Nov. 11, 1939; s. George William and Genevieve (Bresnehan) I.; m. Carla Marie Rake, Aug. 17, 1963; children: John Scott, Jean Ann, Jeff William. BA, Marquette U., 1961, MD, 1965. Diplomate Nat. Bd. Med. Examiners, Am. Bd. Radiology (guest examiner 1975-76, 79, 85-2002). Intern St. Mary's Hosp., San Francisco, 1965-66; resident in radiology U. Minn., Mpls., 1966-70, instr., 1969-70; asst. prof. Med. Coll. of Wis., Milw., 1973-77, assoc. prof., 1977-80, U. Calif., Irvine, 1980-82; prof. and chmn. dept. radiology U. Nebr. Med. Ctr., Omaha, 1982-96, prof. dept. radiology, 1996—2005, prof. emeritus radiology, 2005—. Vis. prof. Vanderbilt U., Nashville, 1976, 82, U. Wis., Madison, 1978, SUNY Downstate Med. Ctr., Bklyn., 1978, Harvard Med. Sch., Boston, 1980, Loyola U. Sch. Medicine, Maywood, Ill., 1980, UCLA-Wadsworth VA Hosp., 1981, UCLA, 1982 Northwestern U. Sch. Medicine, Chgo., 1984, Meth. Hosp., Indpls., 1984, U. Mo., Kans. City, 1985, U. Iowa, Iowa City, 1986, U. Ark., Little Rock, 1987, Keio U. Sch. Medicine, Tokyo, 1989, Mich. State U., 1993. Contbr. articles to profl. jours. Mem. Tech. Task Force on Diagnostic Radiology Nebr. Dept. Health, 1983-84; Major U.S. Army M.C., 1970-73. Co-recipient Magna Cum Laude in Sci. Exhibits award Am. Soc. Neuroradiology, 1987; GE grantee, 1985-87. Fellow Am. Coll. Radiology; mem. AMA (rep. to radiology residency rev. com., 1987), Radiol. Soc. N. Am. (award 1981, 82), Am. Coll. Radiology (com. on satellite communications 1981-83), Am. Roentgen Ray Soc. (award 1986), Assn. Univ. Radiologists, Soc. Chmn. Acad. Radiology Depts., Am. Soc. Uroradiology, Nebr. State Radiol. Soc., Nebr. State Med. Assn., Omaha Metro Med. Soc., Omaha Mid-West Clin. Soc. (hosp. and svc. exhibits com. 1984, award 1986), Omaha C. of C. (task force on edn. 1983-85, edn. coun. steering com. 1984, edn. coun. 1985), Rotary Internat. (program com. 1986), Marquette U. Club (bd. dirs. Omaha chpt., 1987), Alpha Omega Alpha (alumni and faculty mems. com., 1986). Roman Catholic. Avocation: swimming. Office: Nebr Health Sys Dept Radiology 981045 ebr Med Ctr Omaha NE 68198-1045

INCROPERA, FRANK PAUL, mechanical engineering educator; b. Lawrence, Mass., May 12, 1939; s. James Frank and Ann Laura (Leone) I.; m. Andrea Jeanne Eastman, Sept. 2, 1960; children: Terri Ann, Donna Renee, Shaunna Jeanne. BSME, MIT, 1961; MS, Stanford U., 1962, PhD, 1966. Jr. engr. Barry Controls Corp., Watertown, Mass., 1959; thermodynamics engr. Aerojet Gen. Corp., Azusa, Calif., 1961; heat transfer specialist Lockheed Missiles and Space Co., Sunnyvale, Calif., 1962-64; mem. faculty Purdue U., 1966-98, prof. mech. engring., 1973-98, head dept., 1989-98; dean of engring. U. Notre Dame, Ind., 1998—2006, Clifford and Evelyn Brosey prof. mech. engring., 1998—. Cons. in field. Author: Introduction to Molecular Structure and Thermodynamics, 1974, Fundamentals of Heat Transfer, 1985, 90, 96, 2001, 06; Fundamentals of Heat and Mass Transfer, 1981, 85, 90, 96, 2001, 06, Liquid Cooling of Electronic Devices by Single-Phase Convection, 1999; also articles. Recipient Solberg Teaching award Purdue U., 1973, 77, 86, Potter Teaching award, 1973, Von Humboldt sr. scientist award Fed. Republic Germany, 1988; named One of the 100 most frequently cited engrs. in the world Inst. for Sci. Info., 2000. Fellow AAAS, ASME (Melville medal 1988, Heat Transfer Meml. award 1988, Worcester Reed Warner award 1995); mem. Am. Soc. Engring. Edn. (Ralph C. Roe award 1982, George Westinghouse award 1983), Nat. Acad. Engring. Achievements include invention of bloodless surg. scalpel. Office: U Notre Dame Coll Engring 257 Fitzpatrick Hall Notre Dame IN 46556 Business E-Mail: fpi@nd.edu.

INGALLS, MARIE CECELIE, former state legislator, retail executive; b. Faith, SD, Mar. 31, 1936; d. Jens P. and Ida B. (Hegre) Jensen; m. Dale D. Ingalls, June 20, 1955; children: Duane (dec.), Delane. BS, Black Hills State Coll., 1973, MS, 1978. Elem. tchr. Meade County Schs., Sturgis, SD, 1957-72, Faith Sch. Dist. 46-2, 1973-76; elem. prin. Meade Sch. Dist. 46-1, Sturgis, 1976-81; owner, operator Ingalls, Sturgis, 1978-99; mem., asst. majority whip S.D. House Reps., Pierre, 1986-92; lobbyist S.D. Legislature. Bd. dirs. S.D. Retailers Assn., 1990—98, treas., 1992—93. Former sec. S.D. Rep. Orgn; Rep. nominee S.D. Commr. Sch. and Pub. Lands, 1998. Recipient Woman of Achievement award City of Sturgis, 1986, Retail Bus. of Yr. 1998. Mem. S.D. Cattlewomen, S.D. Stockgrowers (edn. chair), S.D. Farm Bur. (bd. dirs. dist. V 1993-2001, 03—, dist. dir. women's com. 2003-05 women's chair 2005-07), Meade County Farm Bur., Faith C. of C. (pres. 1989), Sturgis C. of C. (past bd. dirs.), Key City Investment Club. Republican. Lutheran. Avocations: knitting, crocheting, piano, reading, golf. Home: 17054 Opal Rd Mud Butte SD 57758 Personal E-mail: mcingalls@gwtc.net.

INGBAR, DAVID H., physician, researcher; b. Boston, Aug. 1, 1953; s. Sidney H. and Mary Lee Ingbar; m. Mary E. Meighan, Oct. 14, 1991. BA, Reed Coll., 1974; MD, Harvard Med. Coll., 1978. Diplomate Am. Bd. Internal Medicine. Intern then resident U. Wash., Seattle, chief resident; pulmonary fellow Yale U., New Haven, 1982-85, asst. prof. medicine, 1985-91; assoc. prof. medicine U. Minn., Mpls., 1991-98, prof. medicine, physiology and pediat., 1998—, dir. pulmonary, allergy and critical care divsn., 2001—. Dir. med. ICU and respiratory care Yale New Haven Hosp., 1986-91, U. Minn., 1991—; pres. Assn. Pulmonary and Crit. Care Medicine Program Dir., 2003-04. Mem.: Am. Thoracic Soc. (pres. 2007—). Office: U MN Pulmonary & Critical Care Dept Medicine MMC 276 UMMC 420 Delaware St SE Minneapolis MN 55455-0374 Office Phone: 612-624-0999. Business E-Mail: ingba001@umn.edu.

INGERSOLL, ROBERT STEPHEN, former diplomat, federal agency administrator; b. Galesburg, Ill., Jan. 28, 1914; s. Roy Claire and Lulu May (Hinchliff) I.; m. Coralyn Eleanor Reid, Sept. 17, 1938 (dec.); children: Coralyn Eleanor, Nancy, Joan (dec.), Gail, Elizabeth. Grad., Phillips Acad., 1933; BS, Yale U., 1937. With Armco Steel Corp., 1937-39, Ingersoll Steel & Disc div. (later Ingersoll Products div.), 1939-41, 42-54; pres. Ingersoll Products div., 1950-54; adminstrv. v.p. Borg-Warner Corp., 1953-56, pres., 1956-61, chmn., 1961-72, CEO, 1958-72, also dir.; with Cen. Rsch. Lab., 1941-42; U.S. amb. to Japan, 1972-73; asst. sec. state for East Asian Affairs U.S. Dept. State, Washington, 1974, dep. sec. state, 1974-76. Ptnr., past bd. dirs. First Chgo. Capital Mkts. Asia Ltd.; former chmn. Panasonic Found.; former mem. Bus. Coun. Pres. Winnetka (Ill.) Sch. Bd., 1957-63; dep. chmn., life bd. trustees U. Chgo.; trustee Smith Coll., 1966-71, Aspen Inst. Humanistic Studies, Calif. Inst. Tech.; past bd. dirs. Johnson Found., Trilateral Commn. N.Am.; past mem. coun. Yale U.; past mem. adv. coun. Caterpillar Asia Pacific; past vice-chmn. Pacific adv. coun. United Techs. Nat. Park Found. Mem. Japan Soc. (chmn. N.Y.C. chpt. 1978-85), Chgo. Coun. Fgn. Rels., Coun. Fgn. Rels. N.Y.C., Indian Hill Club, Chgo. Club, Econ. Club (Chgo.), Comml. Club. Home and Office: One Arbor Ln Apt 202 Evanston IL 60201

INGHAM, NORMAN WILLIAM, literature educator, genealogist; b. Holyoke, Mass., Dec. 31, 1934; s. Earl Morris and Gladys May (Rust) I. AB in German and Russian cum laude, Middlebury Coll., 1957; postgrad. Slavic philology, Free U. Berlin, 1957—58; MA in Russian lang. and lit., U. Mich., 1959; postgrad. in Russian lang. and lit., Leningrad State U., 1961—62; PhD in Slavic langs. and lit., Harvard U., 1963. Cert. genealogist. Postdoctoral rschr. Czechoslovak Acad. Scis., Prague, 1963—64; asst. prof. dept Slavic langs. and lits. Ind. U., Bloomington, 1964—65; asst. prof. Harvard U., Cambridge, Mass., 1965—70, lectr., 1970—71; assoc. prof. U. Chgo., 1971—82, prof., 1982—2006, chmn. dept., 1977—83, dir. Ea. Europe and USSR lang. and area ctr., 1978—91, prof. emeritus, 2006—. Mem. Am. Com. Slavists, 1977-83; mem. com. Slavic and Ea. European studies U. Chgo., 1979-91, chmn., 1982-91, also other coms.; dir. Ctr. for East European and Russian/Eurasian Studies, 1991-96; cert. genealogist, 1994—. Author: E.T.A. Hoffman's Reception in Russia, 1974; editor: Church and Culture in Old Russia, 1991; co-editor: (with Joachim T. Baer) Mnemozina: Studia litteraria russica in honorem Vsevolod Setchkarev; mem. editorial bd. Slavic and East European Jour., 1978-87, adv. bd., 1987-89; assoc. editor Byzantine Studies, 1973-81; contbg. editor The Am. Genealogist, 1995—; contbr. and translator articles and book revs. Fulbright fellow, 1957-58, vis. fellow Dumbarton Oaks Ctr. for Byzantine Studies, 1972-73. Mem. Am. Assn. Advancement Slavic Studies (rep. coun. on mem. instns. 1985-96, area rep. nat. adv. com. for Ea. European lang. programs 1985-96), Am. Assn. Tchrs. Slavic and East European Langs., Early Slavic Studies Assn. (v.p. 1993-95, pres. 1995-97), Chgo. Consortium for Slavic and East European Studies (v.p. 1982-84, 98, pres. 1984-86, 98-2000, exec. coun. 1992-94), Phi Beta Kappa. Home: 128 Pleasant St Granby MA 01033-9551

INGRAHAM, JAMES H., diversified financial services company executive; BBA, JD, U. Kans. Atty. Breyfogle, Gardner, Davis & Kreamer, Olathe, Kans.; legal dept. H&R Block, 1980, sec., 1990—2002; asst. v.p., corp. counsel sec. H&R Block Tax Svcs., 1993—96; v.p. legal sec. H&R Block, 1996—99, v.p., gen. counsel, 1999—2001; sr. v.p., gen. counsel sec. H&R Block Inc., Kans. City, Mo., 2001—. Office: H&R Block Inc 4400 Main St Kansas City MO 64111

INGRAM, WILLIAM THOMAS, III, mathematics professor; s. William Thomas and Virginia I.; m. Barbara Lee Gordon, June 6, 1958; children: William Robert, Kathie Ann, Mark Thomas. BA, Bethel Coll., 1959; MS, La. State U., 1961; PhD, Auburn U., 1964. Instr. Auburn U., Ala., 1961-63; instr. math. U. Houston, 1964-65, asst. prof., 1965-68, assoc. prof., 1968-75, prof., 1975-89, U. Mo., Rolla, 1989—2003, prof. emeritus, 2003—, chmn., 1989-98. Contbr. articles to profl. jours. Mem. Am. Math. Soc., Math. Assn. Am. (Disting. Tchg. award 2003). Presbyterian. Avocation: photography. Home: 284 Windmill Mountain Rd Spring Branch TX 78070 Office: Univ Mo Rolla Dept Math and Statistics Rolla MO 65409-0020

INKLEY, JOHN JAMES, JR., lawyer; b. St. Louis, Nov. 7, 1945; s. John James Sr. and Morjorie Jane (Kenna) I.; m. Catherine Ann Mattingly, Apr. 13, 1971; children: Caroline Marie, John James III. BSIE, St. Louis U., 1967, JD, 1970; LLM in Taxation, Washington U., St. Louis, 1976. Bar: Mo. 1970, U.S. Dist. Ct. (we. dist.) Mo. 1970, U.S. Dist. Ct. (ea. dist.) Mo. 1975, U.S. Tax Ct. 1975, U.S. Supreme Ct. 1975. Assoc. Padberg, Raack, McSweeney & Slater, St. Louis, 1970-73; ptnr. Summer, Hanlon, Summer, MacDonald & Nouss, St. Louis, 1973-81; city atty. City of Town and Country, Mo., 1979-84, spl. counsel Mo., 1984-88; ptnr. Hanlon, Nouss, Inkley & Coughlin, St. Louis, 1981-83; ptnr., chmn. banking and real estate dept. Suelthaus & Kaplan, St. Louis, 1983-91; ptnr. Armstrong Teasdale LLP (and predecessor firm), St. Louis, 1991—; co-chmn. bus. svcs. group, 1993-2000; exec. com. St. Louis, 1994—. Mem. ABA, Mo. Bar Assn., Bar Assn. Met. St. Louis. Roman Catholic. Home: 35 Muirfield Ln Saint Louis MO 63141-7382 Office: Armstrong Teasdale LLP 1 Metropolitan Sq Ste 2600 Saint Louis MO 63102-2740

INMAN, LORINDA K., nursing administrator; Exec. dir. Iowa Bd. Nursing, Des Moines. Office: Iowa Bd Nursing State Capitol Complex 1223 E Court Ave Des Moines IA 50309-5622

INMAN, MARIANNE ELIZABETH, academic administrator; b. Berwyn, Ill., Jan. 9, 1943; d. Miles V. and Bessee M. (Hejtmanek) Plzak; m. David P. Inman; Aug 1, 1964. BA, Purdue U., 1964; AM, Ind. U., 1967; PhD, U. Tex., 1978. Dir. Comml. Div. World Instruction and Translation, Inc., Arlington, Va., 1969-71; program staff mem. Ctr. for Applied Linguistics, Arlington, 1972-73; lectr. in French No. Va. Community Coll., Bailey's Crossroads, 1973; faculty mem., linguistic researcher Tehran (Iran) U., 1973-75; intern mgmt. edn. rsch. & devel. S.W Ednl. Devel. Lab., Austin, Tex., 1977-78; asst. prof., program dir. Southwestern U., Georgetown, Tex., 1978; dir. English lang. inst. Alaska Pacific U., Anchorage, 1980-87, chairperson all-U. requirements, 1984-88, assoc. dean acad. affairs, 1988-90; v.p. dean of coll. Northland Coll., Ashland, Wis., 1990-95; pres. Ctrl. Meth. Univ., Fayette, Mo., 1995—. Contbr. Pres. Commn. Foreign Lang. and Internat. Studies, Washington, 1978-79; manuscript evaluator The Modern Lang. Jour., Columbus, Ohio, 1979-84; cons. Anchorage Sch. Dist., 1984-90; cons., evaluator The Higher Learning Commn. of N. Cen. Assn. Colls. and Schs., Chgo., 1990—; mem. dean's task force Coun. of Ind. Colls., 1993-95; pres. Ind. Colls. and Univs. Mo., 1996-00. Co-author: English for Medical Students, 1976; co-author and editor: English for Science and Engineering Students, 1977; contbr. articles to profl. jours. Treas. Alaska Humanities Forum, Anchorage, 1982-87; mem. Anchorage Matanuska-Susitna Borough Pvt. Industry Coun., 1983-86, Sister Cities Commn., Anchorage, 1984-90; mem. Multicultural Edn. Adv. Bd., Anchorage, 1987-90; with speakers bur. Wis. Humanities Com., 1992-95, Mcpl. Libr. Bd., 1993-95; active Mo. Humanities Coun., 1997-03, 04—, vice chmn., 2005—07, chmn., 2007-; bd. dirs. Mo. Colls. Fund, Ind. Colls. and Univs. of Mo.; mem. bd. Great Rivers Coun. Boy Scouts Am., 1996—; mem. presdl. adv. com. Mo. Coordinating Bd. for Higher Edn. Named Fellow of Grad. Sch., U. Tex. Austin, 1977-78, Nat. Teaching Fellow, Alaska Pacific U., Anchorage, 1980-81; recipient Pub. Svc. award Sister Cities Commn., Anchorage, 1987, Kellogg Found. Nat. fellowship, Battle Creek, Mich., 1988-91. Mem. LWV, Nat. Assn. Women Edn., Nat. Assn. Ind. Colls. and Univs. (bd. dirs. 2005-, chair policy and pub. rels. com. 2007-), Am. Assn. Higher Edn., Am. Coun Tchg. Fgn. Langs., Nat. Assn. Schs. and Colls. of United Meth. Ch. (bd. dirs.), Tchrs. English to Speakers Other Langs., Nat. Coun. Tchrs. English, Gold Peppers, Mortar Board, Alpha Chi, Alpha Lambda Delta, Delta Rho Kappa, Kappa Delta Pi, Omicron Delta Kappa, Phi Kappa Phi, Pi Delta Phi, Pi Lambda Theta, Sigma Delta Pi, Sigma Epsilon Pi, Sigma Kappa. Avocations: community theater, hiking, camping, fishing. Office: Ctrl Methodist Univ 411 Ctrl Methodist Sq Fayette MO 65248-1198 Business E-Mail: minman@centralmethodist.edu.

INUI, THOMAS SPENCER, physician, educator; b. Balt., July 10, 1943; s. Frank Kazuo and Beulah Mae (Sheetz) Inui; m. Nancy Stowe, June 14, 1969; 1 child, Tazo Stowe. BA, Haverford Coll., 1965; MD, Johns Hopkins U., 1969, ScM, 1973. Diplomate Am. Bd. Internal Medicine. Intern Johns Hopkins Hosp., Balt., 1969—70, resident in internal medicine, 1970—73; clin. scholar Johns Hopkins U., Balt., 1971—73, chief resident, instr., 1973—74; chief of medicine USPHS Indian Hosp., Albuquerque, 1974—76; chief gen. medicine, dir. health svc. rsch. Seattle VA Med. Ctr., 1976—86; dir. Robert Wood Johnson clin. scholars program U. Wash., Seattle, 1977—92, prof. dept. medicine and health svcs., 1985—92, head div. gen. internal medicine, 1986—92; prof., chmn. of dept. ambulatory care and prevention Harvard Med. Sch. and Harvard Pilgrim Health Care, Boston, 1992—2000; pres., CEO Fetzer Inst., 2000—01, Regenstrief Inst., Indianapolis, 2002—. Scholar-in-residence Assn. Am. Med. Coll., 2002. Contbr. articles to profl. publs. Surgeon USPHS, 1974—76. Fellow: ACP; mem.: APHA (mem. coun. 1988—90), Inst. Medicine, Soc. Tchrs. Family Medicine, Assn. Health Svcs. Rsch., Am. Fedn. Med. Rsch., Soc. Gen. Internal Medicine (pres. 1988—89, mem. coun. 1983—89), Alpha Omega Alpha, Phi Beta Kappa. Office: Regenstrief Institute 1050 Wishard Blvd RG-6 Indianapolis IN 46202 E-mail: tinui@iupui.edu.

IQBAL, ZAFAR MOHD, biochemist, molecular biologist, pharmacologist, cancer researcher, toxicologist, consultant; b. Hyderabad, India, Dec. 12, 1938; came to U.S., 1965, naturalized, 1973; s. M.A. and Haleemunissa (Begum) Rahim. BSc, Osmania U., 1958, MSc, 1962; PhD, U. Md., 1970. Diplomate Am. Bd. Forensic Medicine, Am. Bd. Forensic Examiners. Fellow in molecular pharmacology Nat. Cancer Inst./NIH, Bethesda, Md., 1971-74; asst. prof. pharmacology Case Western Res. U., Cleve., 1974-76; assoc. dir. ERC programs in occupational toxicology U. Ill. Med. Ctr., Chgo., 1980-81, assoc. prof. microbiology, 1977-80, assoc. prof. occupational medicine and environ. health, 1976-93, assoc. prof. preventive medicine, 1982-93; faculty grad. coll. U. Ill., Chgo., 1977-93, dir. Carcinogenesis Labs., 1983-93, chair recombinant DNA instnl. com., 1982-93; chair HIV hazards in rsch. com. U. Ill. Grad. Coll. Faculty, Chgo., 1976-93; dir. Toxicology-Cancer, Chgo., 1987—; affiliate Lurie Cancer Ctr. Northwestern U., Chgo., 1996—. Cons. in field to OSHA, 1980-81, Clements Assocs., 1976-79, Expert Resources, 1982—, Ill. Cancer Coun., 1981-82, Toxicology Cancer, 1987—; lectr. continuing edn.; grant reviewer study sects. NIH; program project reviewer Nat. Cancer Inst., 2000; merit grant reviewer VA, 1981-82; mem. tech. bd. panel Gt. Lakes Protection Fund, 1989—; participant profl. confs.; NSF-Coun. Sci. and Indsl. Rsch. exch. scientist, 1981; sponsor, trainer India-U.S. exch. scientists NSF, 1985-86; peer reviewer: (jours.) Sci., Cancer Rsch., Jour. Biochem., Toxicology, Carcinogenesis, others, also books and films; spl. advisor RRL (India) Dirs., 1980-86; mem. U.S. AID's-Asia Environ. Partnership and Environ Tech. Network Asia, 1994—, Environ. and Tech. Network Asia-Latin Am. Program, 1996—; chair recombinant DNA com. U. Ill., Chgo., 1983-93; contbr. WHO Internat. Agy. for Rsch. Cancer, Tallinn,

1975, Budapest, 1979, Tokyo, 1981, Banff, 1983; mem. exec. bd. sci. and tech. advs. Am. Bd. Forensic Exams., 1997—. Author, editor: Molecular Mechanisms of Toxic Response; Pancreatic Carcinogenesis Mechanisms; editor Jour. Molecular Toxicology and Carcinogenesis; mem. editl. adv. bd. Forensic Examiner, 1995—, editl. bd. 2002—; exec. bd. sci. and tech. advisors Am. Bd. Forensic Examiners, 1996—; contbr. more than 100 articles to profl. jours. NSF-CSIR exch. scientist, 1981; sponsor, trainer India-U.S. Exch. Scientists, NSF, 1985-86; spl. advisor RRL (India) Dirs., 1980—; pres. Rahim Meml. Found., 1995—. Fellow Coun. Sci. and Indsl. Rsch., India, 1963-65; Fogarty Internat. fellow Nat. Cancer Inst., NIH, 1970-71, staff fellow, 1971-74; grantee Nat. Cancer Inst./NIH, Nat. Inst. Occupational Safety and Health, EPA, State of Ill., 1974-93. Fellow Am. Coll. Forensic Examiners (life, diplomate, bd. cert. forensic medicine, editl. bd. advisors 1995—); mem. AAAS, Am. Assn. Cancer Rsch., Am. Pancreatic Assn., N.Y. Acad. Scis., Am. Chem. Soc., Soc. Toxicology, Am. Coll. Toxicology, Nat. Registry of Forensic Examiners, B.E.S.T. N.Am., Registry Global World Leaders, Soc. Toxicology (molecular biology, carcinogenesis and mechanism splty. sects.), NIHAA, Sigma Xi. Office: Toxicology-Cancer PO Box 60267 Chicago IL 60660-0267 Personal E-mail: toxicancer@yahoo.com.

IRBE, ARTURS, professional hockey player; b. Riga, Latvia, Feb. 2, 1967; Goaltender Sharks, 1991-96, Stars, 1996-97, Canucks, 1997-98, Carolina Hurricanes, 1998—2004, Columbus Blue Jackets, 2004—. Goaltender Latvia Nat. Team, World Championships, 1996—2002. Named to NHL All-Star Game, 1994, 1999. Office: Carolina Hurricanes 1400 Edwards Mill Rd Raleigh NC 27607-3624

IRELAND, EMORY, lawyer; b. San Diego, Oct. 15, 1944; BA, Yale U., 1966; JD, Stanford U., 1969. Bar: Wis. 1969. Ptnr. Foley & Lardner LLP, Milw. Recipient Pres. Award, State Bar Wis. Mem: State Bar Wis., State Bar Ill. Office: Foley & Lardner LLP 777 E Wisconsin Ave Ste 3800 Milwaukee WI 53202-5367 Office Phone: 414-297-5624. Office Fax: 414-297-4900. Business E-Mail: eireland@foley.com.

IRICK, LARRY D., lawyer, energy executive; b. 1956; BS, Emporia State U.; JD, Duke U. Bar: 1982. With Westar Energy, Inc., Topeka, 1999—, v.p., gen. counsel, corp. sec. Office: Westar Energy Inc 818 S Kansas Ave PO Box 889 Topeka KS 66601-0889 Office Phone: 785-575-1625.

IRONS, WILLIAM GEORGE, anthropology educator; b. Garrett, Ind., Dec. 25, 1933; s. George Randall and Eva Aileen (Veazey) I.; m. Marjorie Sue Rogasner, Nov. 4, 1972; children: Julia Rogasner, Marybeth Rogasner. BA, U. Mich., 1960, MA, 1963, PhD, 1969; postgrad., London Sch. Econs., 1964—65. With Army C.E., 1956-58; asst. prof. social rels. Johns Hopkins U., 1969-74; asst. prof. anthropology Pa. State U., 1974-78; assoc. prof. anthropology Northwestern U., Evanston, Ill., 1978-83, prof., 1983—. Cons. Nat. Geog. Soc., NSF, AAAS, Social Sci. Rsch. Coun., Time-Life Books, U. Wash. Press, Random House, Worth Pubs., Rutgers U. Press, U. Tex. Press, Pelenum Press, Oxford U. Press, Cornell U. Press. Author: Perspectives on Nomadism, 1972, The Yomut Turkmen, 1975, Evolutionary Biology and Human Social Behavior, 1979, Adaptation and Human Behavior, 2000; mem. bd. editors Evolution and Human Behavior. With AUS, 1954-56. Recipient Lifetime Achievement award Commn. on Nomadic Peoples, Internat. Union Anthrop. and Ethnol. Scis.; grantee NSF, 1973, 76, 83, 85, 86, Ford Found., 1974, Harry Frank Guggenheim Found., 1976. Fellow AAAS, Am. Anthrop. Assn.; mem. Assocs. in Current Anthropology, Human Behavior and Evolution Soc. (pres. 2001-03), Internat. Soc. Human Ethology, Internat. Soc. for Behavioral Ecology, Ctr. for Advanced Studies in Religion and Sci., Inst. for Religion in an Age of Sci., Evolutionary Anthropology Soc. (pres. 2004—), Phi Kappa Phi. Achievements include research on Turkmen of Iran, human behavioral ecology, evolutionary ethics. Home: 2604 Payne St Evanston IL 60201-2133 Office: Northwestern U Dept Anthropology 1810 Hinman Ave Evanston IL 60208-0809 Business E-Mail: w-irons@northwestern.edu.

IRSAY, JAMES STEVEN, professional football team owner; b. Lincolnwood, Ill., June 13, 1959; s. Robert Irsay and Harriet Pogerzelski; m. Margaret Mary Coyle, Aug. 2, 1980; children: Carlie Margaret, Casey Coyle, Kalen. B in Broadcast Journalism, So. Meth. U., 1982. With Balt. Colts., from early 1970's; owner, CEO Indpls. Colts, 1997—. Bd. dirs. Noble Ind. Composer, performer single Hoosier Heartland, 1985, single and video Go Colts, 1985, Colors, 1990. Bd. dirs. United Way Ctrl. Ind.; dir. Greater Indpls. Progress Com. Named World Champions, Super Bowl XLI. Achievements include purchased in auction Jack Kerouac's orignial scroll of On the Road, 2001. Avocations: weightlifting, guitar, song writing. Office: Indpls Colts 7001 W 56th St Indianapolis IN 46254-9725 also: Indianapolis Colts PO Box 535000 Indianapolis IN 46253

IRVINE, PHYLLIS ELEANOR, nursing educator, administrator; b. Germantown, Ohio, July 14, 1940; m. Richard James Irvine, Feb. 15, 1964; children: Mark, Rick. BSN, Ohio State U., 1962, MSN, 1979, PhD, 1981; MS, Miami U., Oxford, Ohio, 1966. Staff nurse VA Ctr., Dayton, Ohio, 1962-66; mem. nursing faculty Miami Valley Hosp. Sch. Nursing, Dayton, 1968-78; teaching asst., lectr. Ohio State U., Columbus, 1979-82; assoc. prof. Ohio U., Athens, 1982-83; prof., dir. N.E. La. U., Monroe, 1984-88; prof., dir. sch. nursing Ball State U., Muncie, Ind., 1988—. Reviewer Health Edn. Jour., Reston, Va., 1987; contbr. articles to profl. jours. Mem. Mayor's Commn. on Needs of Women, La., 1984-88; 1st v.p., bd. dirs. United Way of Ouachita, La., 1986-88. Mem. ANA, Ind. Nurses Assn., Ind. Coun. Deans and Dirs. of Nursing Edn. (pres. 1992-98), Internat. Coun. Women's Health Issues (bd. dirs. 1986-92, 98-2000), Assn. for the Advancement Health Edn., Sigma Theta Tau. Office: Ball State U Cn418 Nursing Muncie IN 47306-0001

IRVING, LEE G., bank executive; Chief acctg. officer, exec. v.p. KeyCorp, Cleve. Office: KeyCorp 127 Public Square Cleveland OH 44114-1306

IRWIN, GERALD PORT, physician; b. Muncie, Ind., July 11, 1945; s. Francis Inlow and Helen Marcella I.; m. Martha Sue Vincent, Mar. 10, 1946; 1 child, Tamara Suzette. AB in Biol. Sci., Ind. U., 1968; MD, Ind. U., Indpls., 1972. Diplomate Am. Bd. Family Physicians. Intern and resident Ball Meml. Hosp., Muncie, Ind., 1972-73; pvt. practice Alexandria, Ind., 1973—. Med. dir. Richland Twp. Fire Dept., Anderson. Mem. AMA (Physician Recognition award 1992-95, 98-2001, 2007—), Am. Acad. Family Physicians,Ind. State Med. Assn., Ind. Assn. Family Physicians, Lions, Elks. Methodist. Avocations: computers, backpacking. Office: PO Box 124 Alexandria IN 46001-0124 Home Phone: 765-724-6252; Office Phone: 765-724-7711.

IRWIN, GLENN WARD, JR., medical educator, physician, academic administrator; b. Roachdale, Ind., July 18, 1920; s. Glenn Ward and Elsie (Browning) I.; m. Marianna Ashby; children: Ann Graybill Irwin Warden, William Browning, Elizabeth Ashby Irwin Schiffli. BS, Ind. U., Bloomington, 1942; MD, Ind. U., Indpls., 1944; LLD (hon.), Ind. U., 1986, Marian Coll., 1987. Diplomate: Am. Bd. Internal Medicine. Intern Meth. Hosp., Indpls., 1944-45; resident in internal medicine Ind. U. Med. Ctr., Indpls., 1945-46, 48-50; mem. faculty Ind. U., Indpls., 1950—, instr., asst. prof. then assoc. prof., 1950-61, prof. medicine, 1961-86, prof. emeritus, 1986, dean Sch. Medicine, 1965-73, dean emeritus, 1986, v.p., 1974-86; chancellor Ind. U.-Purdue U., Indpls., 1973-74, chancellor emeritus, 1989. Sr. assoc. Ind. U. Found. Bd. dirs. Goodwill Industries of Ctrl. Ind., Indpls., Greater Indpls. Progress Com., Greater Indpls. YMCA, Walther Med. Rsch. Inst., Walther Oncology Ctr., Indpls. Health Inst., Eiteljorg Mus. Western Art and the Am. Indian; elder 2d Presbyn. Ch. Served to capt. M.C. U.S. Army, 1946-48. Recipient Disting. Alumnus award Ind. U. Sch. Medicine, 1972, Otis R. Bowen Physician County Service award, Benjamin Harrison award, Ind. Acad. award; named Sagamore of the Wabash, Gov. of Ind., 1961, 79, 86. Fellow ACP (gov. for Ind. 1964-70); mem. AMA, Ind. State Med. Assn., Marion County Med. Soc., Ind. Soc. of Chgo., 500 Festival Assn., James Whitcomb Riley Meml. Assn. (bd. govs. 1986—), Newcomen Soc., Sigma Xi, Alpha Omega Alpha, Beta Gamma Sigma, Sigma Theta Tau. Clubs: Columbia (Indpls.), Contemporary (Indpls.), Meridian Hills Country, Skyline (bd. dirs.). Lodges: Masons (33 degree), Rotary. Home: 8025 N Illinois St Indianapolis IN 46260-2938 Office: Ind U-Purdue U at Indpls 1120 South Dr Indianapolis IN 46202-5135 Home Phone: 317-255-7445; Office Phone: 317-274-5160. E-mail: drglenni@aol.com.

ISAACS, ROGER DAVID, public relations executive; b. Boston, Oct. 23, 1925; s. Raphael and Agnes (Wolfstein) I.; m. Joyce R. Wexler, Oct. 23, 1949; children: Gillian, Jan. Student, U. Wis., 1943; AB, Bard Coll., 1949. With Pub. Rels. Bd., Inc., Chgo., 1948—, account supr., 1948-51, ptnr., 1951-60, exec. v.p., 1960-66, pres., 1966-75, chmn., pres., 1975-86; chmn. PRB, a Needham Porter Novelli Co., Chgo.; exec. v.p., gen. mgr. Doremus Porter Novelli, Chgo., 1986-89; sr. counselor Porter/Novelli, Chgo., 1989-91, The Fin. Rels. Bd., Inc., Chgo., 1991—. Bd. dirs. North Bank, Chgo. Past bd. dirs. Anti-Defamation League Chgo., Jewish Family and Cmty. Svc., Sr. ctrs. Met. Chgo., Highland Park Hosp., Met. Crusade of Mercy, Suburban Fine Arts Ctr., Asthma and Allergy Found., Spertus Coll.; cmty. adv. bd. Sta. WBEZ; bd. dirs. Chgo. Crime Commn.; libr. vis. com. Spertus Inst.; life bd. dirs. Evanston Northwestern Healthcare Found. With AUS, 1943-45. Decorated Purple Heart. Mem. Pub. Rels. Soc. Am. (accredited), Met. Club, Publicity Club Chgo., Birchwood Club Home: 1045 Hillcrest Rd Glencoe IL 60022-1215 Personal E-mail: joroisaacs@aol.com.

ISAACSON, DEAN LEROY, statistician; b. St. Cloud, Minn., Apr. 10, 1941; married. BS, Macalester Coll., 1963; MS, U. Minn., 1966, PhD, 1968. Asst. prof. math. and stats. Iowa State U., Ames, 1968, assoc. prof. math. and stats., 1972, prof. math. and stats., 1976—84, prof. stats., 1984—, acting dir. statis. lab, head of stats., 1984-86, dir. statis. lab., head stats., 1986—2002. Author book on Markov Chains; contbr. numerous articles to profl. jours. Fellow Am. Statis. Assn.; mem. Inst. of Math. Stats. Office: Iowa State U Sci and Tech Statis Lab 102 Snedecor Hl Ames IA 50011-0001 E-mail: dli@iastate.edu.

ISAACSON, MILTON STANLEY (JIM), research and development company executive, engineer; b. Dayton, Ohio, Apr. 23, 1932; s. Max and Sylvia Mariam (Kirsin) I.; m. Joan Sue Koor, Sept. 4, 1955; children: Julie Fay, Jill Ellen, Jan Lynn. BSEE, Ohio State U., 1955. Registered profl. engr., Ohio. Design engr., mgr. quality control, divsn. mgr., dir. R & D Globe Industries, Dayton, 1957—70; pres. Nu-Tech Industries, Inc., Trotwood, Ohio, 1970—. Officer, bd. dirs. Food Svcs., Dayton, 1970-95. Bd. dirs. Grace House Sexual Abuse Resource Ctr., Dayton, 1985—, pres., 1985-89; bd. dirs. Temple Israel Found., 1987-90, pres., 1990; v.p. Jewish Fedn. Greater Dayton, 1984—; bd. dirs. Big Bros./Big Sisters of Greater Dayton, 1965-95, pres., 1978-79; bd. dirs. Old Time Newsies, 1969—, pres., 1991-92. 1st lt. USAF, 1955-57. Recipient Dr. Alan F. Wasserman Leadership award Jewish Fedn. Dayton, 1972, Boss of the Yr. award Nat. Trail chpt. Am. Bus. Womens Assn., 1975, Outstanding Pub. Svc. award Sta. WKEF, Dayton, 1979, Outstanding Svc. award Big Bros./Big Sisters of Greater Dayton, 1977, 88, 304 Cmty. svc. award, 2002, Hon. Judge Carl D. Kessler Meml. award The Grace House, 1991. Mem. IEEE, Rotary (pres. Trotwood club 1989, sec. 1993—), Eta Kappa Nu. Achievements include patents for brushless DC motors and medical devices. Avocations: fishing, travel. Office: Nu-Tech Industries Inc 5905 Wolf Creek Pike Dayton OH 45426-2439 Office Phone: 937-298-6636.

ISAACSON, SAMUEL B., lawyer; b. Johnstown, Pa., June 28, 1957; BA magna cum laude, Dickinson Coll., 1979; JD, Pa. State Univ., 1982. Bar: Pa. 1982, Ill. 1983, DC 1985. Ptnr., head of Chgo. Litigation group DLA Piper Rudnick Gray Cary, Chgo. Mem.: ABA, Ill. State Bar Assn., Chgo. Bar Assn., Def. Rsch. Inst., Lawyers Club Chgo., Fedn. of Insurance & Corp. Counsel, Phi Beta Kappa. Office: DLA Piper Rudnick Gray Cary Suite 1900 203 N LaSalle St Chicago IL 60601-1293 Office Phone: 312-368-2163. Office Fax: 312-251-5827. Business E-Mail: samuel.isaacson@dlapiper.com.

ISAAK, LARRY A., educational association administrator; m. Ruth Isaak; children: David, Corey. BSBA in Acctg., U. N.D., 1973, MBA, 1996. CPA. Asst. legis. budget analyst and auditor N.D. Legis. Coun., 1974-81; with Office of Mgmt. and Budget, 1981-84, state's exec. budget analyst; vice chancellor for adminstrv. and student affairs N.D. Univ. Sys., 1984-94, co-interim chancellor, 1994, chancellor, 1994—2003; pres. Midwestern Higher Edn. Compact, 2003—. Student affairs and liaison Student Affairs Coun., N.D. Student Assn.; dir. higher edn. computer network. Mem. AICPA, State Higher Edn. Exec. Officers Assn., N.W. Acad. Computing Consortium (past v.p., bd. dirs.), Nat. Assn. of State Higher Edn. Fin. Officers (chair 1994), State Soc. of Cert. Pub. Accts. (chair, mem. govtl. acctg. com.). Office: MHEC Ste 130 1300 S Second St Minneapolis MN 55454-1079 Office Phone: 612-626-8292. E-mail: larryj@mhec.org.

ISEMINGER, GARY HUDSON, philosophy educator; b. Middleboro, Mass., Mar. 3, 1937; s. Boyd Austin and Harriet Herring (Hudson); m. Andrea Louise Grove, Dec. 18, 1965; children: Andrew, Ellen. BA, Wesleyan U., 1958; MA, Yale U., 1960, PhD, 1961. Instr. philosophy Yale U., 1961-62, Carleton Coll., Northfield, Minn., 1962-63, asst. prof., 1963-68, assoc. prof., 1968-73, prof., 1973-94, William H. Laird prof. philosophy and liberal arts, 1994—2002, Stephen R. Lewis, Jr. prof. philosophy and liberal learning, 2002—04, emeritus, 2004—. Vis. fellow Kings Coll., London, 1966, U. Lancaster, 1991; chair student-faculty adminstrn. com. Carleton Coll., 1970-71, dept. philosophy, 1972-75, 86-89, 98—, ednl. policy com., 1973-74, English dept. rev. com., 1973-74, com. Lucas Lectrs. in Arts, 1977-81, presdl. inauguration, 1987, edn. dept. rev. task force, 1988, Am. studies program rev. com., 1992, mem. tenure and devel. rev. com., 1985-87, Coll. Coun., 1987, Coll. Marshall, 2001-04; acad. vis. London Sch. Econs., 1971; vis. prof. philosophy U. Minn., 1979, Mayo Med. Sch., 1986, 87, U. Lancaster, 1994, Trinity Coll. Dublin, 2000, Lingnan U., Hong Kong, 2003; Belgum meml. lectr. St. Olaf Coll., 1997; vis. lectr. Uppsala (Sweden) U., 2005; panelist divsn. fellowships NEH, 1980, 91; commentator Minn. Pub. Radio, 1981; dir. London arts program Associated Colls. Midwest, 1982; cons. Harvard U. Press, Univ. Calif. Press, Prentice-Hall, Cornell U. Press, Holt, Rinehart and Winston, Vanderbilt U. Press, Jour. Aesthetics and Art Criticism, Dialogue, Notre Dame Jour. Formal Logic, Jour. of Philosophy and Phenomenological Rsch., Inquiry; external reviewer, evaluator various philosophy depts.; presenter in field. Author: An Introduction to Deductive Logic, 1968, Logic and Philosophy: Selected Readings, 1968, 2d edit., 1980, Knowledge and Argument, 1984, Intention and Interpretation, 1992, The Aesthetic Function of Art, 2004; mem. editl. bd. Am. Philos. Quar., 1989-92, Jour. of Aesthetics and Art Criticism, 1993—; contbr. articles, revs. to profl. jours. Mem. Minn. Humanities Commn., 1984-90, chair 1988-89 Grantee NSF Coun. Philos. Studies, 1968, Bush Found., 1983, Sloan Found. 1984, Faculty Devel. Endowment, 1989, 94, 2000, NEH, 1990, 91; recipient summer stipend NEH, 1971, 78, Disting. Alumnus award Wesleyan U., 1993; Woodrow Wilson fellow, 1958, fellow Univ. Coll., London, 1975, 78, Inst. Adv. Studies in the Humanities, U. Edinburgh, 1985; vis. scholar Cambridge U., 1996, York U., 2002. Mem. AAUP (pres. Carleton chpt. 1967-68), Am. Philos. Assn. (program com. western divsn. 1982, task force on the philosophy major 1989-90, program com. ctrl. divsn. 1991, chmn. com. on tchg. philosophy 1993-96, com. to award Matchette prize in philosophy 1993-95, bd. officers 1993-96), Am. Soc. Aesthetics (trustee 1996-99), Minn. Philos. Soc. (pres. 1978-79), Phi Beta Kappa (pres. Carleton chpt. 1968-69). Avocations: timpani, jazz vibraphone, choral singing. Office: Carleton College One North College St Northfield MN 55057-4002 E-mail: giseming@carleton.edu.

ISENBERG, HOWARD LEE, manufacturing executive; b. Chgo., Dec. 21, 1936; children: Suzanne, Marc, Alan. BS, U. Pa., 1958. CPA, Ill. V.p. Conley Electronics, Chgo., 1960-63, Barr Co. div. Pittway Corp., Niles, Ill., 1963-68, pres. Barr Co. div., 1969-92; v.p. Pittway Corp., Niles, Ill., 1970-92, CCL Custom Mfg. (acquired Barr Co. in 1992), 1992—. Vice chmn., trustee Lake Forest (Ill.) Acad., 1986-98; trustee Providence-St. Mel H.S., Chgo., 1994—, Nat. Def. U. Found., 2003—; chmn. The Barr Fund, 1993—. Office: CCL Custom Mfg 6133 N River Rd Ste 800 Rosemont IL 60018-5175 Office Phone: 847-825-0060 x 102. Business E-Mail: hisenberg@cclcustom.com.

ISENSTEIN, LAURA, library director; b. Toledo; BA in History, U. Mich., 1971, MA in Libr. Sci., 1972. Libr. Baltimore County Pub. Libr., 1972-81, area branch mgr., 1981-85, coord. info. svcs., 1985-94; founder, prin. LIA Assocs., Tng. Consultancy, 1988-95; dir. Pub. Libr. Des Moines, 1995-00. Mem. OCLC Adv. Coun. for Pub. Librs.; spkr. in field. Mem. editl. bd. Jewish Press; contbr. articles to profl. jours. Mem. cmty. edn. advt. coun. Des Moines Pub. Schs.; mem. Mayors' Select Com. Shared Svcs. Focus Group. Mem. ALA, Pub. Libr. Assn. (chmn., mem. various coms.), Urban Librs. Couns., Iowa Libr. Assn., Rotary Internat., Greater Des Moines Leadership Inst. Avocations: gourmet cooking, travel, reading mysteries. Office: Pub Libr Des Moines 100 Locust St Des Moines IA 50309-1767

ISMAIL, TAREK, lawyer; b. Alexandria, Egypt, Sept. 22, 1969; BA in Economics, Carleton Coll., Northfield, Minn., 1991; JD, U. Ill. Coll. Law, 1994. Bar: orthern Dist. Ill. 1994, US Dist. Ct., Fed. Cir. 1995. Clerk US Dist. Ct., Northern Dist. Ill., 1994—95; assoc. Mayer, Brown & Platt, 1995—2000; ptnr. Bartlit Beck Herman Palenchar & Scott LLP, Chgo., 2000—. Named one of Litigation's Rising Stars, The Am. Lawyer, 2007. Office: Bartlit Beck Herman Palenchar & Scott LLP Courthouse Pl 54 W Hubbard St Chicago IL 60610 Office Phone: 312-494-4400. Office Fax: 312-494-4440.

ISON, CHRISTOPHER JOHN, investigative reporter; b. Crandon, Wis., Aug. 20, 1957; s. Luther Arnold Jr. and Penny (Koyn) I.; m. Nancy Cassutt, Aug. 1, 1988. BA, U. Minn., 1983. Editor in chief Minn. Daily, Mpls., 1982-83; reporter News-Tribune & Herald, Duluth, Minn., 1983-86, Star Tribune, Mpls., 1986—. Recipient Pulitzer prize for investigative reporting, 1990. Mem. Investigative Reporters and Editors. Office: Star Tribune 425 Portland Ave Minneapolis MN 55488-0002

ISRAEL, MARTIN HENRY, astrophysicist, educator, academic administrator; b. Chgo., Jan. 12, 1941; s. Herman and Anna Catherine Israel; m. Margaret Ellen Mitouer, June 20, 1965; children: Elisa, Samuel. SB, U. Chgo., 1962; PhD, Calif. Inst. Tech., Pasadena, 1969. Asst. prof. physics Washington U., St. Louis, 1968-72, assoc. prof., 1972-75, prof., 1975—, assoc. dir. McDonnell Ctr. for Space Scis., 1982-87, acting dean faculty arts and scis., 1987-88, dean faculty, 1988-94, vice chancellor, 1994-95, vice chancellor acad. planning, 1995-97. Com. on space astronomy and astrophysics NRC, 1976-79; high energy astrophysics mgmt. ops. working group NASA, 1976-84, co-chair Cosmic Ray Program Working Group, 1980-87, space and earth scis. adv. com., 1985-88, chair Particle Astrophysics Magnet Facility Definition Team, 1985-87, astrophysics coun., 1986-87, prin. investigator Heavy Nuclei Expt. High Energy Astronomy Obs., 1971-89, structure and evolution of the universe subcom., 1996-99, chair ACCESS steering com., 1998-2000, mem. Space Sta. Utilization adv. subcom., 1998-2002, mem. GSFC Space Sci. vis. com., 1997-2001, chair, 2000-01, chair sci. ballooning roadmap team, 2004-08; mem. GSFC Ctr. Dir.'s Vis. Com., 2000-01; chair Space Sci. Working Group, Assn. Am. Univs., 1983-85; chair nat. organizing com. 19th Internat. Cosmic Ray Conf., 1985, 1982-85. Contbr. articles on cosmic ray astrophysics and observation of elemental and isotopic composition of cosmic rays to profl. jours. Sloan Found. fellow, 1970; recipient Exceptional Sci. Achievement award NASA, 1980. Fellow Am. Phys. Soc. (chair astrophysics divsn. 1980-81); mem. Am. Astron. Soc. (mem. exec. com. high energy astrophysics divsn. 1982-84), AAUP, AAAS. Home: 2 Valley View Pl Saint Louis MO 63124-1810 Office: Washington U Campus Box 1105 1 Brookings Dr Saint Louis MO 63130-4899 Office Phone: 314-935-6263. Business E-Mail: mhi@wuphys.wustl.edu.

ISRAELOV, RHODA, financial planner, entrepreneur; b. Pitts., May 20, 1940; d. Joseph and Fannie (Friedman) Kreinen; divorced; children: Jerome, Arthur, Russ. BS in Hebrew Edn., Herzlia Hebrew Tchrs. Coll., NYC, 1961; BA in English Lang. and Lit., U. Mo., Kansas City, 1965; MS, Coll. Fin. Planning, 1991. CFP, CLU. Hebrew tchr. various schs., 1961-79; ins. agt. Conn. Mut. Life, Indpls., 1979-81; fin. planner, 1st v.p. investments Smith Barney, Inc., Indpls., 1981—. Instr. for mut. fund licensing exams. Pathfinder Securities Sch., Indpls., 1983-87; cons. channel 6 News, 1984-85; guest Radio Sta. WTUX Contbr. columns in newspapers Indpls. Bus. Jour., 1982, Jewish Post & Opinion, 1982—86, Beacon, 1985, Indianapolis Star. Named Bus. Woman of Yr., Network of Women in Bus., 1986; recipient Gold Medal award, Personal Selling Power, 1987. Mem. Fin. Planning Assn., Nat. Assn. Life Underwriters, Women's Life Underwriters Conf. (founder), Soc. Fin. Svc. Profls., Nat. Coun. Jewish Women, Nat. Assn. Profl. Saleswomen, Nat. Spkrs. Assn. (pres. Ind. chpt. 1986-87, treas. 1984), Registry Fin. Planning Practitioners, Toastmasters (chpt. ednl. v.p. 1985-86), Soroptimists (bd. dirs.), Ctrl. Ind. Mensa. Avocations: piano, folk, square, folk and ballroom dancing, theater. Office: Smith Barney Bank One Center Tower 111 Monument Cir Ste 3100 Indianapolis IN 46204-5193 Home Phone: 317-844-6167. Personal E-mail: israelov@yahoo.com. Business E-Mail: rhoda.israelov@smithbarney.com.

ISTOCK, VERNE GEORGE, retired bank executive; b. Sept. 20, 1940; BA in Econs., U. Mich., 1962, MBA in Fin., 1963. Credit analyst trainee NBD Bancorp. Inc., Detroit, 1963—66, group head, 1971-77, head U.S. divsn., 1977-82, sr. v.p., 1979-82, exec. v.p., 1982-85, vice chmn., dir., 1985-93, chmn., CEO, 1994-95, also bd. dirs.; chmn. NBD Bank; pres., CEO First Chgo. NBD Corp., Chgo., 1995-98, chmn., 1996-98; chmn. bd. Bank One Corp., Chgo., 1999—2000, pres., 2000; ret., 2000. Bd. dirs. Kelly Svcs. Inc., Masco Corp., Rockwell Automation, Inc. Bd. dirs. Chgo. Coun. Fgn. Rels., Chgo. Crime Commn. Mem. U. Mich. Alumni Assn. (past pres., lifetime dir.), Bankers Roundtable (past dir.)., Econ. Club Chgo. (past dir.), Mich. Bus. Roundtable (past bd. dirs.), Comml. Club of Chgo., Econ. Club Detroit (past dir.), Ill. Bus. Roundtable (past dir.).

IVERS, MIKE, radio personality; Radio host WMJI, Cleve. Office: 6200 Oak Tree Blvd 4th Fl Cleveland OH 44131

IVERSON, STEWART E., JR., state legislator, political organization administrator; b. Iowa Falls, Iowa, July 16, 1950; m. Vicki Bortell Iverson; 4 children. AA, Ellsworth C.C., Iowa Falls, Iowa, 1970; BA, Buena Vista Coll., 1987. Mem. Iowa Ho. of Reps., Des Moines, 1988-94, Iowa Senate from 5th dist., Des Moines, 1994—; senate majority leader, 1996—; chmn. Iowa Rep. Party, 2008—. Mem. First Luth. Ch.; former mem. Dows Cmty. Sch. Bd. With USMC, 1971-73. Mem. Soybean Assn., Pork Prodrs., Corn Growers, Farm Bur., Am. Legion, Elks. Republican. Office: State Capitol 5th Dist 3 9th And Grand Des Moines IA 50319-0001 Home: 1944 Sandy Beach Rd Clarion IA 50525-7608 Office: Iowa Rep Party 621 E Ninth St Des Moines IA 50309 Business E-Mail: siverson@iowagop.org. E-mail: stewart_iverson@legis.state.ia.us.*

IVES, ANTHONY RAGNAR, ecologist; b. Ottawa, Ontario, Canada, Mar. 11, 1961; BA in Biology, BA in Math., U. Rochester, 1983; MA in Biology, Princeton U., NJ, 1985, PhD in Biology, 1988. Life scis. rsch. fellowship U. Wash., 1988—90; asst. prof. to assoc. prof. to prof., zoology U. Wis., Madison, 1990—, Vilas assoc., 1999—2000. Invited spkr. in field. Co-editor (with M.E. Hochberg): Parasitoid Population Biology, 2000; contbr. articles to profl. jours., chapters to books. Office: Dept Zoology U Wis-Madson 459 Birge Hall Madison WI 53706 Office Phone: 608-262-1519. Office Fax: 608-262-9226. Business E-Mail: arives@wisc.edu.*

IZZO, THOMAS, college basketball coach; b. Iron Mountain, Mich., Jan. 30, 1955; m. Lupe Izzo; 1 child, Raquel. Grad., No. Mich. U., 1977. Head coach Ishpeming (Mich.) H.S., 1977-79; asst. coach No. Mich. U., 1979-83; with Mich. State U., East Lansing, 1983—, head coach, 1995—. Asst. coach Goodwill Games, 2001; head coach USA Pan Am. Games, 2003. Named to No. Mich. U. Hall of Fame, 1990, Upper Peninsula Hall of Fame, 1998; Divn. I Nat. Coach of Year by Nat. Assn of Basketball Coaches, 2001. Office: Mich State U Athletic Dept 222 Breslin Ctr Jensen Fieldhouse East Lansing MI 48824

JABERG, EUGENE CARL, theology educator, administrator; b. Linton, Ind., Mar. 27, 1927; s. Elmer Charles and Hilda Carolyn (Stuckmann) J.; m. Miriam Marie Priebe; children: Scott Christian, Beth Amy, David Edward. BA, Lakeland Coll., 1948; BD, Mission House Theol. Sem., 1954; MA, U. Wis., 1959, PhD, 1968. Ordained to ministry, United Ch. of Christ, 1959. U.S. army corr., 1949—50; staff announcer WKOW-TV, Madison, Wis., 1955-58, 67-68, WHBL, Sheboygan, 1943—56, WHA, Wis. U. Sta., 1957—58, KTCA=TV, Mpls., 1968—80; minister Pilgrim Congl. Ch., Madison, 1956-57; assoc. prof. speech Mission House Theol. Sem., Plymouth, Wis., 1958-62; asst. prof. communications United Theol. Sem., New Brighton, Minn., 1962-76, prof. communications, 1976-91, dir. admissions, 1984-87, dir. MDiv program, 1988-90, prof. emeritus, 1991—, acting dir. Masters programs, 1997-99. Bus. ptnr. Dimension 3 Media Svcs., Mpls., 1988-90; coord. spl. projects CTV North Suburbs Cable Access, 1991-2002; vis. scholar Cambridge U., Eng. Author: A History of Lakeland-Mission House, 1962; author: The Video Pencil, 1980; contbr. articles, revs. to various publs.; producer films, videotapes. Artistic dir. Interfaith Players, Mpls., 1965-73; TV prodr., moderator Town Meeting of Twin Cities, Mpls., 1967-70; prodr., writer, host various radio and TV series, Mpls., 1970-89; mem. Ctr. Urban Encounter, Mpls., 1972-74, New Brighton Human Rights Commn., 1975-77; bd. mem. office comm. United Ch. Christ, N.Y.C., 1975-81; mem. North Suburban Sys. Cable Access Commn., 1986-91. Kaltenborn Radio scholar, 1957; grantee Assn. Theol. Sems., 1983; recipient Minn. Community

TV award, 1993, Judges Choice award Alliance of Cmty. Media, 1999; named into Gallery of Distinction Lakeland Coll., 1996—; named to Sta. CTV-15 Hall of Fame, Roseville, Minn., 1998. Mem. Religious Speech Communication Assn. (co-chmn. 1972-74), World Assn. Christian Communication. Democrat. Avocations: travel, hiking, spectator sports, films. Home: 1601 Innsbruck Dr Minneapolis MN 55432-6046 Office: United Theol Sem 3000 5th St NW Saint Paul MN 55112-2507 Personal E-mail: ecjaberg@aol.com.

JACHE, ALBERT WILLIAM, retired chemistry professor, academic administrator, research scientist; b. Manchester, NH, Nov. 5, 1924; s. William Frederick and Esther (Ruemely) J.; m. Lucy Ellen Hauslein, June 14, 1948; children: Ann Gail, Ellen Ruth, Philip William, Heidi Verena. BS, U. N.H., 1948, MS, 1950; PhD, U. Wash., 1952. Sr. chemist Air Reduction Co., Murray Hill, NJ, 1952-53; rsch. assoc. dept. physics Duke U., 1953-55; asst. prof. dept. chemistry Tex. A&M U., College Station, 1955-58, assoc. prof., 1958-61; cons. Ozark Mahoning Co., Tulsa, 1960-61, assoc. rsch. dir., 1961-64; sr. rsch. assoc. Olin Mathieson Chem. Corp. (now Olin Corp.), New Haven, 1964-67, sect. mgr., 1965-67, cons., 1967-75; prof. chemistry Marquette U., Milw., 1967-90, prof. emeritus, 1990—, chmn. chem. dept., 1967-72, dean Grad. Sch., 1972-77, assoc. acad. v.p. for health scis., 1974-77, assoc. v.p.-acad. affairs, 1977-85; scientist-in-residence Argonne (Ill.) Nat. Lab., 1985-86, scientist, 1991-96, temporary appointment, 1991-96; with ChemLab, 2000—. Program coordination com. Med. Center S.E. Wis.; lectr. U. Tulsa, 1963-64, New Haven Coll., 1967; cons. Allied Chem. Corp., 1977-78, 2000-; salt panel com. remediation buried and tank wastes NAS/NRC, 1996-97. Trustee Milw. Sci. Ednl. Found.; pres. Milw. Sci. Ednl. Trust, 1973—; trustee Argonne Univs. Assn., 1977-80; chmn. Assn. Grad. Schs. in Cath. Univs., 1973-75; mem. AUA nuclear engring. edn. com. U. Chgo, 1977-89, chmn., 1984, sec., 1989; double bass player River Cities Symphony Orch., 1997-2001, Evergreen Comty. Orch., 1994—, Evergreen String Ensemble, 1994-2000, Marietta Chamber Orch., 1994-97. With AUS, 1942-46. Fellow AAAS (Sr. Scientists and Engrs. Am.), Am. Inst. Chemists; mem. Am. Chem. Soc. (chmn.-elect, program chmn. div. fluorine chemistry 1981, chmn. div. fluorine chemistry 1982), Sigma Xi, Omicron Kappa Upsilon, Alpha Sigma Nu. Achievements include research and numerous patents in the area of inorganic fluorine chemistry with emphasis on anhydrous hydrogen fluoride as a solvent or reaction medium and Hypofluorite chemistry. Home and Office: 301 Ohio St Marietta OH 45750-3139 Personal E-mail: albert@jache.com.

JACHNA, JOSEPH DAVID, photographer, educator; b. Chgo., Sept. 12, 1935; m. Virginia Kemper, 1962; children: Timothy, Heidi, Jody. BS in Art Edn., Inst. Design, Ill. Inst. Tech., 1958, MS in Photography, 1961. Part-time photographic asst. Derwin Studio Darkroom, Chgo., 1953-54; photo-technician Eastman Kodak Labs., Chgo., 1954; photographer's asst. DeSort Studio, Chgo., 1956-58; free-lance photographer Chgo., 1961—; instr. photography Inst. Design, Ill. Inst. Tech., Chgo., 1961—69; assoc. prof. U. Ill., Chgo., 1969—75, prof., 1976—2001, prof. emeritus, 2001—. One-man shows include Art Inst. Chgo., 1961, St. Mary's Coll., Notre Dame, Ind., 1963, U. Ill., Chgo., 1965, 77, Lightfall Gallery Art Ctr., Evanston, Ill., 1970, U. Wis., Milw., 1970, Ctr. for Photog. Studies, Louisville, 1974, Nikon Photog. Salon, Tokyo, 1974, Afterimage Gallery, Dallas, 1975, Visual Studies Workshop Gallery, Rochester, N.Y., 1979, Chgo. Ctr. for Contemporary Photography, 1980, Focus Gallery, San Francisco, 1981, Photogenesis, Albuquerque, 1983, Andover (Mass.) Gallery, 1984, Chgo. State U., 1985, Tweed Mus. Art, Duluth, Minn., 1986, Gallery 954, Chgo., 1993, State of Ill. Galleries, Chgo., Lockport and Springfield, 1994, Fermilab, Batavia, Ill., 1995, Stephen Daiter Gallery, Chgo., 2000, Bruce Silverstein Gallery, N.Y.C., 2003, City Gallery Photography, Chgo., 2007; exhibited in group shows at Art Inst. Chgo, 1963, 83, MIT, Cambridge, 1968, Walker Art Ctr., Mpls., 1973, 89, Renaissance Soc. Gallery U. Chgo., 1975, Mus. Contemporary Art, Chgo., 1977, 96—, Mus. Art RISD, Providence, 1978, Carpenter Ctr. Visual Arts, Harvard U., Cambridge, 1981, Nexus, Atlanta, 1983, Nat. Mus. Art., Washington, 1984, San Francisco Mus. Modern Art, 1985, Internat. Ctr. Photography, Tucson, 1992, Gallery 312, Chgo., 1996, Stockholm Subway, Sweden, 1999, Hyde Park Art Ctr., Chgo., 2001, Stephen Daiter Gallery, Chgo., 2002, 2003, Taken by Design: Photography at the Inst. of Design, 1937-1971, Art Inst. Chgo., 2002; represented in permanent collections, Mus. Modern Art, N.Y.C., Internat. Mus. Photography, George Eastman House, Rochester, N.Y., MIT, San Francisco Mus. Modern Art, Mpls. Inst. Arts, Art Inst. Chgo., Ctr. Photog. Studies, Louisville, Ctr. for Creative Photography, U. Ariz., Tucson. Ferguson Found. grantee, 1973, Nat. Endowment for Arts grantee, 1976, Ill. Arts Council, 1979; Guggenheim fellow, 1980. Home and Studio: 5707 W 89 Pl Oak Lawn IL 60453-1225 Personal E-mail: jjachna@sbcglobal.net.

JACKELS, MICHAEL OWEN, bishop; b. Rapid City, SD, Apr. 13, 1954; Student, U. Nebr., 1972—74; BA in philosophy, St. Pius X Sem., Erlanger, Ky., 1977; MA in theology (scripture), Mt. St. Mary Sem., Emmitsburg, Md., 1981; STD in spiritual theology, Angelicum U., Rome, 1989. Ordained deacon Diocese of Lincoln, Nebr., 1980, ordained priest Nebr., 1981, asst. pastor Cathedral Risen Christ Nebr., 1981—82, religion tchr. Pius X HS Nebr., 1981—85, asst. pastor St. Thomas Aquinas Ch., U. Nebr. Nebr., 1982—85, diocesan dir. religious edn. Nebr., diocesan master of ceremonies Nebr., named chaplain Sch. Sisters of Christ the King Nebr., 1992, named co-vicar for religious Nebr., 1994; named monsignor, 1994; served Congregation for the Doctrine of the Faith, Vatican, 1997—2005; ordained bishop, 2005; bishop Diocese of Wichita, Kans., 2005. Roman Catholic. Office: Diocese Wichita 424 N Broadway Wichita KS 67202 Office Phone: 316-269-3900. Office Fax: 316-269-3936. E-mail: jackelsm@cdowk.org.*

JACKLEY, MARTIN J. (MARTY JACKLEY), prosecutor; b. 1970; BS in Electrical Engring., SD Sch. Mines & Tech., 1992; JD, U. SD, 1995. Bar: SD 1995, Minn. 1997, US Dist. Ct. SD 1997, US Ct. Appeals (8th cir.) 1998, US Supreme Ct. 1999. Law clk. to Hon. Richard Battey US Dist. Ct. SD, Rapid City, 1995—97; spl. asst. atty. gen. State of SD, 2001—05; ptnr. Gunderson, Palmer, Goodsell & Nelson LLP, Rapid City, 2002—06; US atty. dist. SD US Dept. Justice, Sioux Falls, SD, 2006—. Office: US Attys Office PO Box 3303 Sioux Falls SD 57101 Home Phone: 605-271-4414; Office Phone: 605-330-4400, 605-357-2330. Business E-Mail: marty.j.jackley@usdoj.gov.

JACKMAN, ROBERT N., state legislator, veterinarian; b. Rushville, Ind., Feb. 7, 1943; m. Karen Jackman; 2 children. DVM, Purdue U., 1967. Vet., prin. Jackman Animal Clinic, Milroy, Ind.; mem. Ind. Senate from 42nd dist., Indpls., 1996—; mem. agrl. and small bus. com. Ind. Senate, Indpls., mem. govtl. and regulatory affairs com., mem. transp. and interstate coop. com., mem. natural resources com. Mem. Milroy United Meth. Ch.; past pres. Milroy Econ. Devel. Com.; pres. Anderson Twp. Regional Sewer Dist.; mem. Rushville County Sch. Bldg. Coop. Mem. AVMA, Ind. Vet. Med. Assn., Am. Assn. Bovine Practitioners, Am. Assn. Swine Practitioners, Milroy Cmty. Club (Citizen of Yr. 1983, 91), Milroy Coyote Club (Man of Yr. 1981), Masons (past master # 139 club). Republican. Office: 200 W Washington St Indianapolis IN 46204-2728

JACKSON, DARREN RICHARD, automotive parts company executive; b. Detroit, Nov. 13, 1964; s. Richard Dennis and Connie May (Ellis) J.; m. Terry Ann Hall, May 28, 1988; children: Ryan David, Bridget Caffrey. BS in Acctg., Marquette U., 1986. CPA, Wis. Supr. KPMG Peat Marwick, Milw., 1985-89; dir. fin. reporting Carson, Pirie, Scott & Co., Milw., 1989-90, dir. treasury svcs., 1990-91, v.p., treas., CFO, 1992-1998; CFO, Full-line Store Div. Nordstrom, Inc.; sen. v.p. fin. & treas. Best Buy Co., Inc., Mpls., 2000-2001, sr. v.p., CFO, 2001—02, exec. v.p., CFO, 2002—07; exec. v.p. customer operating groups Best But Co., Inc., Mpls., 2007—08; pres., CEO Advance Auto Parts, Inc., Roanoke, Va., 2008—. Bd. dirs. Advance Auto Parts, Inc., 2004—. Bd. trustees Marquette U.; bd. dirs. Cristo Rey Network Schools. Office: Advance Auto Parts Inc 5008 Airport Rd Roanoke VA 24012

JACKSON, DAVID D., state legislator; b. Topeka, Nov. 7, 1946; m. Annette Sorber; children: Chad, Traci. BS cum laude, Kans. State U., 1968. Housing mgmt. specialist HUD, 1971-83; v.p. Midwest Mgmt., Inc., 1983-85; pres. Jackson's Greenhouse & Garden Ctr., Inc., 1985—; mem. Kans. State Senate, 2000—. Adv. bd. Cmty. Nat. Bank, 2003—. Bd. dirs. Seaman Unified Sch. Dist. 345 Sch. Bd., 1983-95, Kona Billfisher Owners Assn., 2002—; pres. Sunrise Optimist Club orth Topeka, 1985-86, North Topeka on the Move, Inc., 1997—; comdr. Sons Am. Legion Post 400, 1985-86; clk. Soldier Twp. Bd., 1994—; v.p. North Topeka Bus. Alliance, 1998-2000; active Neighborhood Element Adv. Com. to the Topeka Shawnee County Consol. Plan for 2025, 1999, Capitol Area Planning Coun., 2003. Mem.: Greater Topeka C. of C. (bd. dirs. 2003—). Republican. Lutheran. Home: 2815 NE Rockaway Trail Topeka KS 66617 Office: State Capitol Rm 5135-B Topeka KS 66612 E-mail: hort68@netzero.net.

JACKSON, DON, radio personality; Radio host WMJI, Independence, Ohio. Office: WMKI 6200 Oak Tree Blvd 4th Fl Cleveland OH 44131

JACKSON, EDGAR B., JR., medical educator; b. Rison, Ark., May 30, 1935; m. Thelma Jackson, 1957; children: Gary, David, Michael, Laura. BA, Case Western Res. U., 1962, MD, 1966. Intern Cleve. Met. Gen. Hosps., Cleve., 1966—67, chief resident medicine, 1969—70; from sr. instr. medicine to asst. prof. to asst. clin. prof. Case Western Res. U., Cleve., 1970—83, assoc. clin. prof., 1983—86, clin. prof. medicine, 1986—, asst. dean, 1971—74, asst. prof. cmty. medicine, 1974—79; chief of staff, sr. v.p. for clin. affairs Univ. Hosps. of Cleve.; asst. prof. cmty. health Case Western Res. U., Cleve., 1977—88. Contbr. numerous articles to profl. jours. With US Army, 1959—61. Named Carnegie Common Wealth Clin. scholar, 1970—72. Mem.: APHA, Am. Sickle Cell Anemia Assn. Inc. Office: Univ Hosp 11100 Euclid Ave Cleveland OH 44106-1736

JACKSON, EDWIN ATLEE, retired physicist, educator; b. Lyons, NY, Apr. 18, 1931; s. Frederick Wolcott and Helen Jean (Carroll) J.; m. Cynthia Ann Gregg; children: Eric Hugh, Mark Wolcott. BS in Physics, Syracuse U., NY, 1953, MS in Physics, 1955, PhD in Physics, 1958. Asst. lectr. Brandeis U., Waltham, Mass., 1957—58; postdoctoral Airforce Cambridge Rsch. Ctr., Bedford, Mass., 1958—59; rsch. staff Princeton U., NJ, 1959—61; asst. prof. U. Ill., Urbana, 1961—64, assoc. prof., 1964—77, physics prof., 1977—98, prof. emeritus, 1998—. Dir. ctr. for complex systems rsch. Beckman Inst. U. Ill., Urbana, 1989-98; vis. faculty FOM-Inst. Voor Plasma Fysica, Jutphaas, The Netherlands, 1967-68; vis. staff Los Alamos Sci. Lab., N.Mex., 1971; vis. prof. Chalmers U., Göteberg, Sweden, 1984; JIFT prof. Nagoya U., Japan, 1984; core rschr. Santa Fe Inst., 1992-98. Author: Equilibrium Statistical Mechanics, 1968, Perspectives of Nonlinear Dynamics, vol. 1, 1989, vol. 2, 1990, Japanese transl., 1994, Exploring Nature's Dynamics, 2001; contbr. more than 80 articles to profl. jours. Fellow Am. Phys. Soc. Business E-Mail: eaj@uiuc.edu.

JACKSON, ERIC C., Internet company executive; Pres., CEO Internet, Inc., Milford, Ohio, 1999—. Office: Integrated Technologies ITE 424 Wards Corner Rd Loveland OH 45140-6950

JACKSON, G. JAMES, protective services official; b. Columbus, Ohio; Student, Harvard U., Ohio State U., Northwestern U., FBI Acad. Patrolman Columbus Divsn. Police, 1958-67, sgt., 1967-71, lt., 1971-74, capt., 1974-77, dep. chief, 1977-90, chief, 1990—. With USMC. Office: Office Chief Police 120 Marconi Blvd Columbus OH 43215-2376

JACKSON, GREGORY WAYNE, orthodontist; b. Chgo., Sept. 4, 1950; s. Wayne Eldon and Marilyn Frances (Anderson) J.; m. Nora Ann Echtner, Mar. 17, 1973; children: Eric, David. Student, U. Ill., 1968-70; DDS with honors, U. Ill., Chgo., 1974; MSD, U. Wash., 1978. Practice dentistry specializing in orthodontics, Chgo., 1978—. Instr. orthodontic dept. U. Ill. Coll. Dentistry, Chgo., 1978-81. Coach Little League Baseball, Oak Brook, Ill., 1986-89. Served to lt. USN, 1974-76. Mem. ADA, Ill. State Dental Soc., Chgo. Dental Soc., Am. Assn. Orthodontists, Midwestern Soc. Orthodontists, Ill. Soc. Orthodontists, Omicron Kappa Upsilon. Evangelical. Avocations: golf, tennis, skiing. Office: 6435 S Pulaski Rd Chicago IL 60629-5148

JACKSON, J. DAVID, lawyer; b. York, Pa., 1949; BA magna cum laude, St. Olaf Coll., 1971; JD summa cum laude, Washington U., 1974. Bar: Minn. 1974. Law clerk 8th cir. U.S. Ct. Appeals, 1974-75; ptnr., trial practice group Dorsey & Whitney, Mpls. Mem. Order of Coif. Office: Dorsey & Whitney Ste 1500 50 S 6th St Minneapolis MN 55402-1498 Office Phone: 612-340-2760. Office Fax: 612-340-2807. Business E-Mail: jackson.j@dorsey.com.

JACKSON, JAMES G., police chief; m. Mary Jackson; children: James, Jason, Michelle. Student, Harvard U., FBI Nat. Exec. Inst., Northwestern U. Joined Columbus (Ohio) Police Dept., 1958, patrolman, sgt., 1967—71, lt., 1971—74, capt., 1974—77, dep. chief, 1977—90, chief of police, 1990—. Mem.: Nat. Orgn. Black Law Enforcement Execs., Internat. Assn. Chiefs Police, Major City Chiefs Assn. Office: Columbus Police Dept 120 Marconi Blvd Columbus OH 43215-0009

JACKSON, JAMES SIDNEY, psychologist, educator; b. Detroit, July 30, 1944; s. Pete James and Johnnie Mae (Wilson) J. BS, Mich. State U., 1966; MA, U. Toledo, 1970; PhD, Wayne State U., 1972. Probation counselor Lucas County Juvenile Ct., Toledo, 1967-68; tchg. and rsch. asst. Wayne State U., Detroit, 1968-71; from asst. prof. to prof. psychology U. Mich., Ann Arbor, 1971—, faculty assoc. Rsch. Ctr. Group Dynamics, 1971—86, dir. Rsch. Ctr. Group Dynamics, 1996—2005, faculty assoc. Inst. Gerontology, 1976—, dir. program rsch. on Black Ams., 1976—2005, faculty assoc. Ctr. Afro-Am. and African Studies, 1982—, rsch. prof., 1986—, assoc. dean Rackham Sch. Grad. Studies, 1987-92, prof. pub. health, 1990—, Daniel Katz Collegiate prof., 1994-95, Daniel Katz Disting. Univ. prof. psychology, 1995—; Hill Disting. vis. prof. U. Minn., Ann Arbor, 1995; dir. Ctr. Afro-Am. and African Studies U. Mich., Ann Arbor, 1998—2005, dir. Inst. Social Rsch., 2005—. Chair sociol. psychology tng. program U. Mich., 1980-86, 93-96; cons. Emergency Sch. Aid Project, 1973-74, Commn. on Equal Opportunity in Psychology, 1970, Project to Provide Psychol. Svcs. to Head Start Programs, 1973-74, European Econ. Commn. Project on Racism, Xenophobia and Immigration, 1989—; mem. com. on aging and com. on status of Black Ams., panel on race, ethnicity and health in later life, Nat. Acad. of Scis.; mem. com. on African Am. Population Year 2000 and 2010 U.S. Census Bur.; mem. nat. adv. com. Boston Mus. Sci., 1998-2002; mem. Nat. Adv. Coun. on Aging, NIH, 1996-99; mem. bd. sci. counselors, Nat. Inst. Aging; invited rschr. Ecole des Hautes Etudes en Scis. Sociales, Paris, 1992-2004; disting. lectr. gerontology UCLA, 1992; mem. steering com. Nat. Acad. Aging Soc., 1995—. Author: The Black American Elderly: Research on Physical and Psychosocial Health, 1988, African American Elderly, 2d edit., 1997, (with Gurin P., Hatchett S.) Hope and Independence: Blacks Response to Electoral and Party Politics, 1989, Life in Black America, 1991, (with Chatters L., Taylor R.) Aging in Black America, 1993, (with H. Neighbors) Mental Health in Black America, 1996, (with R. Taylor and L. Clatters) Family Life in Black America, 1997; editor: New Directions: African Americans in a Diversifying Nation, 2000; editl. cons. Jour. Behavioral and Social Scientists; editl. bd. Jour. Gerontology, Applied Social Psychology Ann., Psychol. Bull., Jour. Social Issues; cons. editor Psychology and Aging; contbr. articles to profl. jours. Bd. dirs. Pub. Commn. on Mental Health, Ronald McDonald House, Ann Arbor, 1993—; bd. trustees Greenhills Sch., Ann Arbor, 1997-2003, v.p., 2002-03. Recipient Disting. Faculty Svc. award U. Mich., 1976, Harold R. Johnson Diversity Svc. award U. Mich., 2000, Orgn. Black Alumni Achievement award Wayne State U., 2005, James McKeen Cattell Fellow award Assn. for Psychol. Sci., 2005; Urban Studies fellow Wayne State U., 1969-70; NSF fellow, 1969; Sr. Postdoctoral fellow Groupe d'Études et de Recherches sur la Science, École des Hautes Études en Sciences Sociales, 1986-87; Sr. Ford Found. Minority Postdoctoral fellow, 1986-87; Fogarty Sr. Internat. fellow, 1993-94; Robert W. Kleemeier award for rsch., Gerontol. Soc. Am. Fellow APA (divs. 9-20, policy and planning bd., fin. com. 1984-86, award for early contbns. 1983, Tenth Anniversary Peace and Social Justice award Soc. for the Study of Peace, Conflict and Violence, Peace Psychology divsn. 2000, com. on internat. rels., 1999-02, chair 2001-02, Disting. Career Contbns. ro Rsch. award Divsn. 45, 2001), AAAS (past chmn. sect. social, econ. and polit. scis.), Am. Psychol. Soc., Gerontol. Soc. Am. (task force on minority issues in gerontology, chmn. 1988-92, ann. sci. conv. program com., Minority Task Force Mentoring award 2003, Disting. Mentorship in Gerontology award behavioral and social sci. sect. 2004); mem. Assn. Advancement of Psychology (trustee 1973-89, chmn. 1978-80), Inst. of Medicine, at. Acad. Scis., Black Students Psychol. Assn. (nat. chmn. 1970-71), Assn. Black Psychologists (nat. chmn. 1972-73), Soc. Psychol. Study of Social Issues, World Future Soc., Assn. Behavioral and Social Scientists, Gerontol. Soc. Am. (chair behavioral and social scis. sect. 1997-98), Internat. Platform Assn., NIMH (nat. mental health coun. 1989-93, panel on equal access com. on instl. cooperation 1989-92), Psi Chi, Alpha Phi Alpha. Home: 340 Orchard Hills Dr Ann Arbor MI 48104-1832 Office: U Mich 5110 Inst Social Rsch 426 Thompson St Ann Arbor MI 48104-2321 Home Phone: 734-623-7783; Office Phone: 734-763-2491. Business E-Mail: jamessj@umich.edu.

JACKSON, JANET ELIZABETH, city attorney, association executive; b. Randolph, Va. d. Robert and Joan (Morton) J.; 1 child, Harrison Michael Sewell. BA, Wittenberg U., 1975; JD, George Washington U., 1978. Bar: Ohio 1978, U.S. Dist. Ct. (so. dist.) Ohio 1979, U.S. Dist. Ct. (no. dist.) Ohio 1983. Asst. atty. gen. Office Ohio Atty. Gen., Columbus, 1978-80, chief crime victims compensation sect., 1980-82, chief workers compensation and civil rights sects., 1983-87; with Sindell, Sindell & Rubenstein, Cleve., 1982-83; judge Franklin County Mcpl. Ct., Columbus, 1987-97; city atty. City of Columbus, 1997—. Atty. gen.'s ethics and profl. responsibility adv. coun.; joint task force gender bias Ohio Supreme Ct. and Ohio State Bar Assn.; mem. com. to study impact of substance abuse on cts., Supreme Ct., 1989-90. Chair bd. trustees YWCA, 1988-95; vice-chair bd. trustees, mem. exec. com. United Way Franklin County; chair Right from the Start Community Forum; bd. dirs. Met. Women's Ctr., 1980-86, S.E. Community Mental Health Ctr., 1987, Columbus Urban League, 1987-90, Maryhaven, 1987-89, Riverside Meth. Hosp.; trustee Wittenberg U.; chair task force child care City of Columbus; vol. Columbus Pub. Schs.; past mem., chairperson Minority Task force on AIDS; mem. AIDS community adv. coalition, 1987-90, task force domestic violence, 1988; mem. svc. team Explorer Divsn. Boy Scouts Am.; trustee Franklin U. Recipient Sharon Wilkin award Met. Women's Ctr., Dr. Martin Luther King Jr. Humanitarian award Love Acad., 1987, Polit. Leadership award 29th Dist. Citizens' Caucus, 1987, Citizenship award Omega Psi Phi, 1987, Outstanding Accomplishments award Franklin County Dem. Women, 1988, Community Svc. award Met. Dem. Women's Club, 1989, Warren Jennings award Franklin County Mental Health Bd., 1989, Martin Luther King Jr. Humanitarian award Columbus Edn. Assn., 1991, Women of Achievement award YWCA, 1992, Citizen's award Columbus Assn. Edn. Young Children, 1993, Citations award Pi Lambda Theta, 1993, Blue Chip award Social Svcs., 1994, Peacemaker award Choices, David D. White award Black Alumni Assn. Capitol Law Sch., Cmty. Svc. award Columbus-Franklin County AFL-CIO. Mem. Internat. Mcpl. Lawyers Assn. (state chmn., mem. steering com. legislation and pub. policy and mgmt.), at. Conf. Black Lawyers (Disting. Barrister award 1988, John Mercer Langston award 1994), Ohio State Bar Assn. (coun. dels. 1993—, commn. racial and ethnic fairness, bd. govs. women in the profession sect.), Columbus Bar Assn., Women Lawyers Franklin County, The Links, Inc. (pres. Twin Rivers chpt. 1992-94), Columbus Mortar Bd. Alumni Club, Golden Key Nat. Honor Soc. (hon.). Office: Columbus City Atty City Hall 90 W Broad St Rm 200 Columbus OH 43215-9013

JACKSON, JESSE LOUIS, civil rights activist, clergyman; b. Greenville, SC, Oct. 8, 1941; s. Noah Robinson, Charles Henry (Stepfather) and Helen Burns Jackson; m. Jacqueline Lavinia Brown, 1963; children: Santita, Jesse Louis Jr., Jonathan Luther, Yusef DuBois, Jacqueline Lavinia. Student, U. Ill., 1959-60; BA in Sociology and Economics, NC AT State U., 1964; student, Chgo. Theol. Sem., 1964—66, MDiv, 2000; degree (hon.), NC AT State U., Pepperdine U., Oberlin U., Oral Roberts U., U. RI, Howard U., Georgetown U. Ordained to ministry Baptist Ch., 1968; Chgo. dir. Operation Breadbasket project, So. Christian Leadership Conf., Chgo., 1966—67, nat. dir., 1967-71; founder, exec. dir. Operation PUSH (People United to Serve Humanity), Chgo., 1971—96; founder PUSH-Excel and PUSH for Econ. Justice, 1977—96; founder, nat. pres. Nat. Rainbow Coalition Inc., Chgo., 1984—96; shadow senator from DC US Senate, Washington, 1991—96; founder, nat. pres. Rainbow/Push Coalition, Inc., Chgo., 1996—; spl. envoy of the President & Sec. State for the Promotion of Democracy in Africa US Dept. State, Washington, 1997—2000; founder The Wall St. Project, 1997—, Citizenship Edn. Fund, 1984. Candidate for Dem. nomination US Presdl. Election, 1983—84, 1987—88; lectr. for high schs., colls., prof. audiences in Am., Europe. Host, Both Sides with Jesse Jackson, CNN, 1992-2000; Author: Straight From the Heart, 1987, Keep Hope Alive, 1989; co-author: (with Jesse L. Jackson, Jr.) Legal Lynching: Racism, Injustice, and the Death Penalty, 1996, It's About the Money: How You Can Get Out of Debt, Build Wealth, and Achieve Your Financial Dreams!, 1999. Active Black Coalition for United Cmty. Action, 1969. Recipient Presdl. Award Nat. Med. Assn., 1969, Humanitarian Father of Year Award Nat. Father's Day Com., 1971, Presdl. Medal of Freedom, 2000; named Third Most Admired Man in Am. Gallup Poll, 1985, one of six new leaders on the rise US News World Report, 100 Most Influential Black Americans, Ebony mag., 2006. Address: Rainbow PUSH Coalition 930 E 50th St Chicago IL 60615-2702 E-mail: jjackson@rainbowpush.com.

JACKSON, JESSE LOUIS, JR., congressman; b. Greenville, SC, Mar. 11, 1965; m. Sandra Jackson; children: Jessica Donatella, Jesse L. III. BS in Bus. Mgmt., NC A&T U., 1987; MA in Theology, Chgo. Theol. Sem., 1990; JD, U. Ill., 1993. Natl. field dir. The Rainbow Coalition, 1993—95; mem. US Congress from 2d Ill. dist., Washington, 1995—, mem. house appropriations com., 1997—. Co-chair, comm. group Dem. Policy Com.; mem. Congressional Black Caucus, Congressional Steel Caucus. Author: Legal Lynching: Racism, Injustice and the Death Penalty, 1996, It's About the Money, 1999, A More Perfect Union: Advancing New American Rights, 2001. Named one of 100 Most Influential Black Americans, Ebony mag., 2006. Democrat. Baptist. Office: US Ho Reps 2419 Rayburn Ho Office Bldg Washington DC 20515-1302 Office Phone: 202-225-0773. Office Fax: 202-225-0899. E-mail: webmaster@jessejacksonjr.org.

JACKSON, JOHN CHARLES, retired secondary school educator, writer; b. Columbus, Ohio, Mar. 12, 1939; s. John Franklin and Mari Jane (Lusch) J.; m. Carol Nancy Tiggelbeck, June 24, 1990. Tchr. social studies Buckeye Local Sch., West Mansfield, Ohio, 1961-62, Grandview Heights (Ohio) City Schs., 1962-91; ret., 1991. Cooperating tchr. Project Bus. program Jr. Achievement, Grandview, 1984—91. Recipient Career Tchr. award Ohio State U. Coll. Edn. Alumni Soc., 1995; Martha Holden Jennings Found. scholar, 1968-69. Mem. Ohio Ret. Tchrs. Assn. (life), Franklin County Ret. Tchrs. Assn. (life), Ohio State U. Alumni Assn. (life), Am. Mensa Ltd. Republican. Methodist. Avocations: reading, tennis, college football. Home: 5741 Aspendale Dr Columbus OH 43235-7506

JACKSON, KORY A., lawyer; b. Oxford, Ohio; BA in Eng. Lit., U. Cin., 1997, JD, 2000. Bar: Ohio 2000, US Dist. Ct. Southern Dist. Ohio 2001, US Dist. Ct. Southern Dist. Ind. 2005, US Ct. of Appeals Sixth Cir. 2005. Assoc. Vorys, Sater, Seymour and Pease LLP, Cin. Mem., Conf. Com. Greater Cin. Minority Counsel Prog.; vol. legal cons. Sch. Creative and Performing Arts. Named one of Ohio's Rising Stars, Super Lawyers, 2006. Mem.: ABA, Ohio State Bar Assn., Cin. Bar Assn. Office: Vorys Sater Seymour and Pease LLP Atrium Two Ste 2000 221 E Fourth St PO Box 0236 Cincinnati OH 45201-0236 Office Phone: 513-723-4602. Office Fax: 513-852-7847.

JACKSON, MARCUS, electric power industry executive; Engr. Kansas City Power and Light Co., 1974-80, with, 1983—, asst. dir. power supply, sr. dir. power supply, v.p. power prodn., sr. v.p. power supply, exec. v.p., COO, 1996-99, exec. v.p., CFO, 1999—; project engr. Provo Arabia Ltd., Saudi Arabia, 1980-83. Pres., chmn. bd. KLT Power, Inc. Office: Kansas City Power & Light Co PO Box 418679 Kansas City MO 67201-8679

JACKSON, MICHAEL B., service company executive; Pres., CEO Specialized Svcs. Inc., Southfield, Mich., 1988—. Office: Specialized Svcs Inc 23077 Greenfield Rd Ste 470 Southfield MI 48075-3736 Fax: 248-557-0755.

JACKSON, MIKE, newscaster; m. Dawn Jackson; children: Nicole, Courtney. AA in Mass Comm., W.Va. State Coll. Ops. mgr., announcer Sta. WBES-FM, Charleston, W.Va.; news dir., anchor, prodr. Sta. WOAY-TV, Oak Hill; anchor Sta. WJLA-TV, Springfield, Va., WWHO-TV, Columbus, Ohio, Sta. WCMH-TV, 1994—. Nominee Emmy awards (2), 1985, 2002; recipient 1st pl. Reporting award, Nat. Assn. Black Journalists, Washington, 1993. Office: WCMH-TV 3165 Plentangy River Rd PO Box 4 Columbus OH 43202

JACKSON, MONICA DENEE, purchasing agent; b. Detroit, Aug. 18, 1966; d. Arthur James and Nossie Lucille Jackson. BS in Mktg., Bus. Logistics, Wayne State U., Detroit, 1999. Credit supr. 1st of Am. Bank, S.E. Mich., Detroit, 1990—93; fin. clk. County of Wayne, Detroit, 1995—2000, purchasing agt., 2000—. Vol. Meals on Wheels, Detroit. Mem.: Nat. Assn. Purchasing Mgrs. Baptist. Avocation: bowling. E-mail: jacksonmdj@hotmail.com.

JACKSON, REBECCA R., lawyer; b. Ark., 1942; BA magna cum laude, St. Louis U., 1975, JD, 1978. Bar: Mo. 1978, Ill. 1979. Ptnr. Bryan Cave, St. Louis. Mem. ABA. Office: Bryan Cave One Met Sq 211 N Broadway Saint Louis MO 63102-2733

JACKSON, REGINALD W., lawyer; b. Phila., Aug. 24, 1955; BA, Cornell U., 1977; JD, U. Pa., 1980. Bar: OH 1980, US Dist. Ct. (no. and so. dists.), US Ct. Appeals (6th cir.). Mem. Vorys, Sater, Seymour and Pease, Columbus, Ohio; pres. Am. Bankruptcy Inst., 2007—. Exec. editor ABI Jour.; contbr. articles to profl. jours. amed one of Am.'s Top Black Lawyers, Black Enterprise Mag., 2003. Mem. ABA (bus. law com.), Columbus Bar Assn. (chmn. bankruptcy law com. 1990-92), Am. Bankruptcy Inst. (bd. trustees, exec. com. bd., chair environ. subcommittee), Am. Coll. Bankruptcy, OH State Bar Found. (pres. 2001), OH State Bar Assn. (dist. 7 rep., bd. govs., coun. dels. 2002-04). Office: Vorys Sater Seymour and Pease PO Box 1008 52 E Gay St Columbus OH 43215-3161

JACKSON, ROGER A., human resources specialist, automotive executive; Various positions Rockwell Internat., 1977—95; v.p. human resources Allen Bradley (subsidiary of Rockwell Internat.), 1991—95; sr. v.p. human resources Lear Corp., Southfield, Mich., 1995—. Office: Lear Corp 21557 Telegraph Rd Southfield MI 48086-5008 Office Phone: 248-447-1500.

JACKSON, VALERIE PASCUZZI, radiologist, educator; b. Oakland, Calif., Aug. 25, 1952; d. Chris A. Pascuzzi and Janice (Mayne) Pacuzzi; 1 child, Price Arthur III. AB, Ind. U., 1974, MD, 1978. Diplomate Am. Bd. Radiology. Intern, resident in diagnostic radiology Ind. U. Med. Ctr., 1978-82; from asst. prof. radiology to prof. radiology Ind. U. Sch. Medicine, Indpls., 1982-94, John A. Campbell prof. radiology, 1994—. Dir. residency program in radiology Ind. U. Sch. Medicine, 1994—2003, chair dept. radiology, 2004—; trustee Am. Bd. Radiology. Contbr. over 80 articles to profl. jours., chapters to books. Fellow: Soc. Breast Imaging (pres. 1990—92), Am. Coll. Radiology (bd. chancellors, chair 3 coms., pres. 2002—03); mem.: AMA, Radiol. Soc. N.Am., Am. Roentgen Ray Soc., Am. Inst. Ultrasound in Medicine, Alpha Omega Alpha. Office: Indiana U Sch Med Dept Rad 550 N Univ Blvd Rm 0663 Indianapolis IN 46202-2859

JACKSON, WILLIAM VERNON, Latin American studies and library science educator; b. Chgo., May 26, 1926; s. William Olof and Lillian (Scharenberg) J. BA summa cum laude, orthwestern U., Evanston, Ill., 1945; MA, Harvard U., Cambridge, Mass., 1948, PhD, 1952; MLS, U. Ill., 1951; Diploma (hon.), U. Ctrl. Venezuela, 1968. Tchr. York Cmty. HS, Elmhurst, Ill., 1946—47; tchg. fellow Harvard U., 1948—50; spl. recruit Libr. of Congress, 1951—52; libr., asst. prof. libr. sci. U. Ill., Urbana, 1952—58, assoc. prof., 1958—62, U. Wis., Madison, 1963—65, faculty rsch. fellow, summer, 1963, 1964; prof. libr. sci., dir. internat. libr. info. ctr. U. Pitts., 1966—70; prof. libr. sci. George Peabody Coll. for Tchrs., 1970—76; prof. Spanish and Portuguese Vanderbilt U., Nashville, 1970—76; prof. libr. sci. U. Tex. Austin, 1976—86, assoc. Inst. Latin Am. Studies, 1976—, prof. emeritus, 1986—. Vis. lectr. U. Minn. Libr. Sch., summers 1954-56, Columbia U. Sch. Libr. Svc., summers 1960, 90, Syracuse U. Sch. Libr. Sci., summer 1962, Simmons Coll. Sch. Libr. Sci., summer, 1974, 75, Coll. Librarianship, Aberystwyth, Wales, summer 1977, U. Zulia, Maracaibo, Venezuela, summer 1980, Dominican U. Libr. Sci., summers 1981-84, 86, 89-98, 2000, 02-05, Pratt Inst. Sch. Info. and Libr. Sci., summers 1995-98, Coll. St. Catherine, summer 1999, 2001, LI U. Palmer Sch. Libr. and Info. Sci., summer 2001, U. South Fla. 2005; vis. prof. Inter-Am. Libr. Sch., U. Antioquia, Medellín, Colombia, 1960, 68, adviser internat. exec. coun., 1961-63; cons. State Dept., 1956, 59, 61, 62, 67, 77, 2002, 03, 04; Regional AID Office for Ctrl. Am. and Panama, 1965-66, AID Mission to Brazil, 1967-72, AID Mission to Colombia, 1970-71, USIA, 1979-80, 85, 87, 89-92, 94-2000, OAS, 1970-71; Coun. Rectors Brazilian Univs., 1972; cons. rsch. libs. NY Pub. Libr., 1965-70, Hispanic Found., Libr. Congress, Washington, 1964-65; Fulbright rsch. scholar, France, 1956-57; Fulbright lectr. U. Córdoba (Argentina), 1958, adviser, 1970; adviser U. San Marcos, Peru, 1962, 75; external examiner U. West Indies, Jamaica, 1974-78; cons. Bibliothèque Nationale, France, 1979, 81-87; ofcl. rep. 350th anniversary Harvard U., 1986, Libr. of Congress Bicentennial, 2000; sr. fellow Dominican U., 1989—; vis. prof. faculty philosophy and letters U. Buenos Aires, 1991; dir. various activities on the Quin centennial and librs. in Latin Am., 1992; adv. U. Francisco Marroquín, Guatemala, 1992-2005; U. del Norte, Barranquilla, Colombia, 1993, various univs. and librs. in El Salvador, 1994-2003, Nat. Libr. and Archives Sch., Mexico City, 1995; advisor Francisco Marroquin Found., 2002-06, Am. U. Paris, 2005; pres. Coun. Books and Librs. in L.Am., 1993—; adviser Nat. Pedagogical U., Honduras, 2006; lectr. in field Author: Basic Library Techniques, 1955, A Handbook of American Library Resources, 1955, 2d edit., 1962, Studies in Library Resources, 1958, The Foundation Grants Program, 1959, The Libraries of the Associated Colleges of the Midwest, 1960, Aspects of Librarianship in Latin America, 1962, second series, 1992, Library Guide for Brazilian Studies, 1964, The National Textbook Program and Libraries in Brazil, 1967, Resources of Research Libraries, 1969, Steps Toward the Future Development of a National Plan for Library Services in Colombia, 1971, Catalog of Brazilian Acquisitions of Library of Congress, 1964-74, 1977, Resources for Brazilian Studies at the Bibliothèque Nationale, 1980, Library Resources of Harvard University, 1986, Las Megabibliotecas, una Bibliografía Comentada, 1993, Resources of Research Libraries: A Bibliographical Guide to Printed Material, 1998, Nueve Bibliotecarios Distinguidos, 2004; (video) A Conversation with Dr. William V. Jackson, 2008; editor: U. Ill. Library Sch. Assn. News Letter, 1954-56, Assn. Coll. Research Libraries Monographs, 1961-66, Latin Am. Collections, 1974, Reference Publications in Latin American Studies, 1977-92, Library and Information Science Education in the Americas: Present and Future, 1981, Library and Information Science in France: A 1983 Overview, 1984, Doce Bibliotecarios Latinoamericanos, 1992; mem. editorial staff Libr. Trends, 1958-62, Ency. Libr. and Info. Sci., 1971-90, Jour. Libr. History, 1976-88, Internat. Jour. Revs. in Libr. and Info. Sci., 1985-88; assoc. editor World Librs., 1990-99, consulting editor, 2000-; contbr. articles to profl. jours. and encys. Mem. ALA (chmn. internat. rels. round table 1965-66, trustee endowment funds 1977-86), Ill. Libr. Assn., Assn. Libr. and Info. Sci. Edn., Bibliog. Soc. Am., Assn. Coll. and Rsch. Libraries, MLA, Am. Assn. Tchrs. Spanish and Portuguese, Theatre Libr. Assn., Conf. on Latin Am. History, Latin Am. Studies Assn., Sem. on Acquisition Latin Am. Library Materials (pres. 1977-78), Assn. Caribbean U. and Rsch. Libraries, Asociación Paceña de Bibliotecarios (hon.; La Paz, Bolivia), Henry Wade Rogers Soc., John Harvard Soc., Phi Beta Kappa, Beta Phi Mu (pres. 1955-56), Phi Sigma Iota, Sigma Delta Pi (hon.), Phi Lambda Beta (hon.) Clubs: Harvard (Chgo.), Caxton (Chgo.). Home: 196 W Kathleen Dr Park Ridge IL 60068-2618 Office: Dominican U 7900 W Division St River Forest IL 60305

JACKWIG, LEE M., federal judge; b. 1950; BA, Loyola U. of Chgo., 1972; JD, DePaul U., 1975. Asst. atty. gen. State of Iowa, 1976-79, dep. indsl. commr., 1979-83; asst. U.S. atty. S.D. Iowa, Dept. Justice, 1983-86; bankruptcy judge U.S. Bankruptcy Ct. (so. dist.) Iowa, Des Moines, 1986—. Office: US Courthouse Annex 110 E Court Ave Ste 443 Des Moines IA 50309-2044

JACOB, BERNARD MICHEL, architect; b. Paris; arrived in U.S., 1950, naturalized; s. Paul and Therese (Abase) J.; m. Rosamond Gale Tryon; children: Clara, Paul. Diploma in architecture, Cooper Union; BArch, U. Minn. Registered architect, Minn. Sr. designer Ellerbe Assocs., St. Paul; head design Grover Dimond & Assocs., St. Paul; co-founder Team 70 Architects, St. Paul, 1970—, pres., 1977—83, Bernard Jacob Architects Ltd., Mpls., 1983—. Mem. constrn. panel Am. Arbitration Assn., 1973—; lectr. Sch. Architecture, U. Minn., Mpls., 1982— Editor: Architecture Minn. Mag., Minn. Soc. Architects, 1970-80; archtl. criticism columnist: Mpls. Star and Tribune, 1980-83, Corp. Report Mag., 1983; reviewer: (archtl. books) Choice Mag.; co-author: Skyway Typology/Mpls., Pocket Architecture/A Walking Guide to the Architecture Downtown Mpls. and St. Paul, 2d. rev. edit., 1988, Letters to Palladio, 1999. Founding chmn. Heritage Preservation Commn., St. Paul; past mem. St. Paul Planning Bd.; apptd. mem. Minn. State Designer Selection Bd., 1987-90; bd. dirs. Winslow House, 1995-97; chmn. archtl. subcom. Minn. Gov.'s Residence Coun., 1996-99. Fellow: AIA. Office: 825 Nicollet Mall Ste 1447 Minneapolis MN 55402-2703 Office Phone: 612-332-5517. Business E-Mail: palladio@skypoint.com.

JACOB, JOHN EDWARD, corporate executive, communications executive; b. Trout, La., Dec. 16, 1934; s. Emory and Claudia (Sadler) J.; m. Barbara Singleton, Mar. 28, 1959; 1 child, Sheryl Renee. BA, Howard U., 1957, MSW, 1963; LHD (hon.), Old Dominion U., 1983, Fisk U., 1984; LLD (hon.), LaFayette Coll., 1985, Tuskegee U., 1986, Cen. State U., 1986, Fla. Internat. U., 1988, Dominican Coll., 1988, Howard U., 1990, Am. U., 1993; LHD (hon.), Morris Brown U., 1991, So. Ill. U., Boston Coll., LHD (hon.), 1992. Caseworker, then child welfare casework supr. Balt. Dept. Public Welfare, 1960-65; mem. staff Washington Urban League, 1965-70, acting exec. dir., 1968-70; dir. community orgn.-tng. Eastern region Nat. Urban League, 1970; exec. dir. San Diego Urban League, 1970-75; pres. Washington Urban League, 1975-79; exec. v.p. Nat. Urban League, NYC, 1979-81, pres., CEO, 1982—94; various exec. positions Anheuser-Busch Co., St. Louis, 1994—2002, exec. v.p., global comm., 2002—, dir., 1990—. Field work instr, Howard U. Sch. Social Work, 1963-65, lectr., 1967-69, chmn. bd.; cons., lectr. in field; bd. dirs. Local Initiative Support Corp., Bennett Coll., Nat. Westminster Banco, Anheuser Busch Co., 2001-, Nat. Park Found., NY Tel. Co., Coca-Cola Enterprises Inc., Morgan Stanley.; exec. v.p. Nat. Urban League, NYC, 1979-81, pres. and CEO, 1982-2004. Author weekly column To Be Equal, 1982. Vice chmn. bd. trustees Howard U., 1971-78, chmn. 1988-91, chmn. emeritus 1991—; mem. jud. nominating commn. US Dist. Ct. and US Cir. Ct., Washington, 1978; bd. overseers U. Calif., San Diego, 1974-75; bd. dirs. NCCJ, 1983-88, Eisenhower Found., 1984-86, Ind. Sector, 1984-89, Jr. Achievement, 1985-91, Legal Aid Soc., Drucker Found., Nat. Conference, Econ. Policy Inst., Nat. Parks Found., Local Initiatives Support Corp., The Muny at Forest Park, University of Missouri-St. Louis Chancellor's Coun., Fair St. Louis, St. Louis 2004., St/ Louis Club; chmn. Citizens' Commn. on AIDS for NYC and No. NJ, 1985. Capt. USAR, 1957—65. Recipient Whitney M. Young Meml. award Washington Urban League, 1979, United Way Am. profl. leadership award, Public Service award United Black Fund Washington, 1979, Achievement award Eastern province Kappa Alpha Psi, 1976, Outstanding Community Service award Howard U. Sch. Social Work Alumni Assn., 1979, Spl. Citation Atlanta Club, Howard U. Alumni Assn., 1980, Hudson L. Lavell Social Action award, Phi Beta Sigma, 1982, Exemplary Service award, Alumni Club L.I. Howard U., 1983, Achievement award, Zeta Phi Beta, 1984, Blackbook's Bus. & Profl. award, Dollars and Sense mag., 1985, Nat. Kappaman Achievement award Durham Alumni Chpt., Kappa Alpha Psi, 1984, Bayard Rustin Humanitarian award, 1989, Lifetime Achievement award St. Louis chpt. NAACP, 1991, Equal Justice award Nat. Bar Assn., 1991, Alumni Achievement award, Howard U., 2002; decorated Airborne Parachutist badge, 1958. Mem.: St. Louis Club. Democrat. Episcopalian. Office: 1 Busch Pl Saint Louis MO 63118-1849

JACOB, KEN, state legislator; b. St. Louis, Jan. 23, 1949; BS, U. Mo. Columbia. State rep. Dist. 25 Mo. Ho. of Reps., Jefferson City, 1983-96; mem. Mo. Senate from 19th dist., Jefferson City, 1996—. Social worker.

JACOBI, FREDRICK THOMAS, newspaper publisher; b. Neenah, Wis., July 10, 1953; s. H. Paul and Patricia Mary (Steele) J.; m. Kim Lee Muenchow, Aug. 23, 1980; children: James Paul, Steven Thomas. AA in Bus., U. South Fla., 1973; BBA in Fin., Mktg., U. Wis., 1976; MBA in Mktg., U. Wis., Whitewater, 1980. Cert. newspaper circulation. City dist. mgr. Madison (Wis.) Newspapers Inc., 1977-79, city circulation mgr., 1979-80, circulation mgr., 1980-81, mktg. mgr., 1981-82, circulation dir., 1982-85, Gannett Co., Inc., Reno, Nev., 1985-88, regional circulation dir. Arlington, Va., 1988-90; pub., pres. Wausau (Wis.) Daily Herald, Gannett Co., Inc., 1990-92, Springfield (Mo.) News-Leader, 1993-96; v.p. Midwest region Gannett Co., Inc., 1993-96; pub., pres. Ft. Myers (Fla.) ews-Press, 1996-2000, Rockford (Ill.) Register-Star, 2000—. Bd. dir. Coun. of 100, Rockford Coll., Inland Press Found.; com. chmn. Sales and Mktg. Exec., Madison, Ill., 1985. Editor: Circulation-Central States, 1985. Program chmn. Jr. Achievement of Nev., Reno, 1987—88; pres. Springfield Bus. and Devel. Corp., 1996; bd. dir. Ozarks Press Assn., Make A Wish Mo., Horizon Econ. Devel., 1997—2000, Lee County Pub. Schs. Found., 1997—2000. Mem.: Newspaper Assn. Am., Inland Press Assn., Ill. Press Assn., Young Pres.'s Orgn., The Exec. Com., Rotary. Republican. Roman Catholic. Avocations: micro-computers, running, gardening. Office: Rockford Register Star 99 E State St Rockford IL 61104 Office Phone: 815-987-1451. E-mail: fjacobi@rrstar.com.

JACOBI, PETER PAUL, journalism educator, writer; b. Berlin, Mar. 15, 1930; came to U.S., 1938, naturalized, 1944; s. Paul A. and Liesbeth (Kron) J.; m. Harriet Ackley, Dec. 8, 1956 (div. 1979); children: Keith Peter, John Wyn. BS in Journalism, Northwestern U., 1952, MS, 1953. Mem. journalism faculty Northwestern U., Evanston, Ill., 1955-81, profl. lectr., 1955-63, asst. prof., 1963-66, assoc. prof., 1966-69, prof. journalism, 1969-81, assoc. dean, 1966-74; communications cons. and workshop leader NYC, 1980-84; communications cons. Bloomington, Ind., 1985—; prof. journalism Ind. U., Bloomington, 1985-99, prof. emeritus, 1999—. News assignment editor, newscaster, theatre and music reporter NBC, Chgo., 1955-61; news editor ABC, Chgo., 1951-53; radio commentator on music and opera, 1958-65; theatre and film critic Sta. WTTW, Chgo., 1964-74, arts critic, 1975-77; theatre and film critic Hollister ewspapers Suburban Chgo., 1963-70; music columnist Chicagoan mag., 1973-74; script cons. Goodman Theater, Chgo., 1973-75; syndicated commentator on arts and media N.Am. Radio Alliance, 1978-80; arts corr. Christian Sci. Monitor, 1956-81; music critic, columnist Bloomington (Ind.) Herald-Times, 1985—; columnist Arts Indiana, 1987-2001, Editors Only, 1994—, Editor's Workshop, 1995-98. Author: Writing with Style, The News Story and the Feature, 1982, The Messiah Book-The Life and Times of G.F. Handel's Greatest Hit, 1982, (with Jack Hilton) Straight Talk about Videoconferencing, 1986, The Magazine Article: How to Think It, Plan It, Write It, 1991, (with others) From Budapest to Bloomington, Janos Starker and the Hungarian Cello Tradition, 1999; contbg. essayist Lyric Opera Companion, 1991; editor Chgo. Lyric Opera News, 1958-61, Music Mag./Musical Courier, Chgo., 1961-62; contbr. articles on writing to Folio, Ragan Report, other mags., articles on arts to Sat. Rev., Chgo. Daily News, N.Y. Times, Highlights for Children, World Book, others. Mem. AAUP, ATAS, Assn. Edn. in Journalism, Soc. Profl. Journalists, Ind. Arts Commn. (chmn. 1990-93), Arts Midwest, Bloomington Cmty. Arts Commn. Home: 3003 N Browncliff Ln Bloomington IN 47408-1317 Office: Ind U Sch Journalism Bloomington IN 47405 Office Phone: 812-334-0063.

JACOBS, ALEXIS A., automobile company executive; With Columbus (Ohio) Fair Auto Auction, now owner, CEO, pres. Amb. Charity Newsies; mem. athletic dept. steering com. Ohio State U., Columbus;, also sponsor 3 athletic scholarships; bd. dirs. Salesian Boys and Girls Club, also former chmn. fundraising com.; formerly active Recreation Unltd., Dave Thomas Adoption Found. Three-Tour Challenge. Mem. Nat. Auto Auction Assn. (pres.). Office: Columbus Fair Auto Auction 4700 Groveport Rd Columbus OH 43207-5217 Fax: 614-497-1132.

JACOBS, ANDREW, JR., former congressman, educator; b. Indpls., Feb. 24, 1932; s. Andrew and Joyce Taylor (Wellborn) J.; m. Kim Hood; children: H.B. James Andrew, B.N. Steven Michael. BS, Ind. U., 1955, LL.B., 1958. Bar: Ind. Practiced in Indpls., 1958-65, 73-74; mem. Ind. Ho. of Reps., 1958-60, 89th-92d congresses from 11th Dist., 1965-73, 94th-97th congresses from 11th Dist. Ind., 1975-83, 98th-103rd Congresses from 10th Dist. Ind., 1983-96. Ranking minority mem. ways & means subcom. on social security; adj. prof. Ind. U., 1996—. Author: The 1600 Killers: A Wake-Up Call for Congress, 1999. Served with USMC, 1950-52. Mem. Indpls. Bar Assn., Am. Legion. Democrat. Roman Catholic. Address: 1201 W 64th St Indianapolis IN 46260-4409

JACOBS, BRUCE EDWARD, management consultant; b. St. Louis, Mar. 27, 1952; s. Robert A. and Sara Lee (Brown) J.; m. Linda C. Schneider, May 26, 1973; children— Robert R., Nicholas C., Luke E., B.S., Washington U., 1976. Indsl. engr. Granite City Steel Co. (Ill.), 1974-75; project engr. Emerson Electric Co., St. Louis, 1976-77, sr. project engr., 1977-78; dir. mfg. Schlueter Mfg. Co., St. Louis, 1978-79; prin. White Haven Cons. Group, St. Louis, 1979-83; supr. cons. Fox & Co., St. Louis, 1983—; pres, CEO Grede Foundries, Milw., 1987—; cons. St. Louis Zoo, 1975-76, Mo. Goodwill Industries, 1976-79; lectr. in field. Patentee in field. Mem. Inst. Mgmt. Cons., Am. Inst. Indsl. Engrs. (Region XI dir., pres. 1980, 1st place award in community affairs 1980, chpt. award of excellence 1980). Republican. Roman Catholic. Home: 6909 Dartmouth Ave Saint Louis MO 63130-3133 Office: Grede Foundries 9898 W Bluemound Rd Milwaukee WI 53226-4365 E-mail: bjacobs@grede.com.

JACOBS, CARYN LESLIE, lawyer, former prosecutor; b. Chgo., Mar. 3, 1958; d. Edward Jesse and Ann Marie (Paun) J.; m. Daniel Goldman Cedarbaum, Sept. 6, 1987; children: Jacob Jesse, Samuel Goldman. AB with distinction, Stanford U., 1980; JD cum laude, Harvard U., 1983. Bar: Ill., US Dist. Ct. (no. dist. Ill.) 1984, US Ct. Appeals (8th cir.) 1986, US Ct. Appeals (7th cir.) 1987. Law clk. to Hon. Susan Getzendanner US Dist. Ct. (no. dist. Ill.), Chgo., 1983-85; assoc. Mayer, Brown & Platt, Chgo., 1985-88; asst. US atty. Chgo., 1988-93; ptnr. Mayer, Brown, Rowe & Maw, Chgo., 1993—. Mem. ABA, Phi Beta Kappa. Office: Mayer Brown Rowe & Maw 71 S Wacker Dr Chicago IL 60606 Office Phone: 312-701-7621. Office Fax: 312-706-8645. E-mail: cjacobs@mayerbrown.com.

JACOBS, DANNY O., surgeon, medical educator; MD, PhD. Arnold K. Lempke Disting. Prof. Surgery Creighton U. Sch. of Medicine, Omaha, 1997—, chair dept. surgery, 2000—. Mem.: Acad Scis. Inst. Medicine.

JACOBS, DENNY, state legislator; b. Moline, Ill., Nov. 8, 1937; s. Oral G. and Caroline Harroun (Pinkerton) J.; m. Mary Ellen Duffy, June 10, 1955; children: Patricia, Denise, Elizabeth, Michael, J.P., Tory. BA, Augustana Coll., 1959. Co-owner J & J Music, 1966-82; mktg. dir. Group W Cable, 1985-86; mayor East Moline, Ill., 1973—; mem. Ill. State Senate, 1986—. Vice chmn. transp. com., mem. agr., conservation, energy and environment com., chmn. citizens coun. econ. devel., chmn. intergovt. com. Ill. State Senate. Mem. Moose, Elks (Disting. Citizen award 1986), Eagles, KC. Address: 3511 8th St East Moline IL 61244-3521 Also: 606 19th St Moline IL 61265-2142

JACOBS, DONALD P., finance educator; b. Chgo., June 22, 1927; s. David and Bertha (Nevod) J.; children: Elizabeth, Ann, David; m. Dinah Nemeroff, May 28, 1978. BA, Roosevelt Coll., 1949; MA, Columbia U., 1951, PhD, 1956. Mem. research staff Nat. Bur. Econ. Research, 1952-57; instr. Coll. City N.Y., 1955-57; mem. faculty to Morrison prof. fin. Northwestern U. Sch. Mgmt., 1970—75, chmn. dept., 1969-75, dean, 1975—2001, Gaylord Freeman Disting. prof. banking, 1978—. Chmn. bd. AMTRAK, 1975-79; bd. dirs. CDW Corp., Prologis Corp., Terex Corp.; co-dir. staff Presdl. Commn. Structure and Regulation, 1970-71; sr. economist banking and currency com. U.S. Ho. of Reps. Contbr. articles to profl. jours. Served with USNR, 1945-46. Ford Found. fellow, 1959-60, 63-64 Mem. Am. Econ. Assn., Am. Statis. Assn., Am. Fin. Assn., Econometrics Soc., Inst. Mgmt. Sci. Office: Northwestern Univ J L Kellogg Sch Mgmt 2001 Sheridan Rd Evanston IL 60208-0814 Office Phone: 847-491-2838.

JACOBS, DOUGLAS C., professional sports team executive; m. Georgia Jacobs; 3 children. BS, Miami U., Ohio; MBA, Case Western Res. U. CPA. Mng. ptnr. Arthur Andersen LLP, Cleve.; exec. v.p. Gucci Timepieces; exec. v.p. fin. The Cleve. Browns. Pres. Jr. Achievement Greater Cleve., Inc.; councilman Kirkland; chmn. Pacific Legan Found., Calif.; pres. Big Bros./Big Sisters Orange County; vice chmn. Orange County Performing Arts Ctr.; treas. Bowers Mus. Found. With USN. Office: The Cleveland Browns 76 Lou Groza Blvd Berea OH 44017

JACOBS, FRANCIS ALBIN, biochemist, educator; b. Mpls., Feb. 23, 1918; s. Anthony and Agnes Ann (Stejskal) J.; m. Dorothy Caldwell, June 5, 1953; children: Christopher, Gregory, Paula, Margaret, John. BS, Regis Coll., Denver, 1939; postgrad, U. Denver, 1939-41; Fellow in Biochemistry, St. Louis U., 1941-49, PhD, 1949. Postdoctoral fellow Nat. Cancer Inst., Bethesda, Md., 1949-51; instr. physiol. chemistry U. Pitts. Sch. Medicine, 1951-52, asst. prof., 1952-54; asst. prof. biochemistry U. N.D. Sch. Medicine, Grand Forks, 1954-56, asso. prof., 1956-64, prof., 1964-87, prof. emeritus, 1987—. Dir., research supr. Nat. Sci. Research Participation Program in Biochemistry, 1959-63; advisor directorate for sci. edn. NSF. Contbr. articles to profl. jours. Mem. bishop's pastoral council Diocese of Fargo, N.D., 1979-86. Fellow AAAS, N.D. Acad. Sci. (editor 1967, 68); mem. Am. Soc. for Biochemistry and Molecular Biology, Am. Soc. for Nutritional Scis., Soc. Exptl. Biology and Medicine, Am. Chem. Soc. (chmn. Red River valley sect. 1971), AAAS, AMA, Sigma Xi (pres. chpt. 1965-66, Faculty award for Outstanding Sci. Resch. U. N.D. chpt. 1982, cert. of recognition 1987), Alpha Sigma Nu, Phi Lambda Upsilon, Phi Rho Sigma. Home: 1525 Robertson Ct Grand Forks ND 58201-7303 E-mail: fjacobs@medicine.nodak.edu.

JACOBS, IRWIN LAWRENCE, diversified corporate executive; b. Mpls., July 15, 1941; s. Samuel and Rose H. Jacobs; m. Alexandra Light, Aug. 26, 1962; children: Mark, Sheila, Melinda, Randi, Trisha. Student pub. schs. Chmn. Watkins Inc., Winona, Minn., 1978—; pres., CEO Minstar, 1982—94; chmn. Genmar Holdings, Inc., Mpls., 1982—; chmn. bd. Genmar Industries, Inc., Mpls.; chmn. Jacobs Trading Co., Mpls.; pres., CEO Jacobs Investors, Inc., Mpls.; pres. Jacobs Realty II, Inc., Mpls., 1993—, Jacobs Mgmt. Corp., 1983—, Gateway S/B, Inc., 1993—; chmn. FLW Outdoors (formerly Operation Bass, Inc.), Gilbersville, Ky., 1996—. Mem.: Mpls., Lafayette Country, Oakridge Country. Office: Genmar Holdings Inc 2900 IDS Ctr 80 S 8th St Minneapolis MN 55402-2100

JACOBS, JOEL, former state legislator, municipal official; m. Carol Jacobs; six children. BS, Moorhead State U.; postgrad., St. Cloud State U. Bus. instr.; Dist. 49B rep. Minn. Ho. of Reps., St. Paul, 1972-95; commr. of pub. utilities St. Paul, 1995—. Chmn. regulated industries and energy com., vice chmn. ways and means com., mem. rules and legis. adminstrn. and taxes coms., Minn. Ho. of Reps. Office: 121 7th Pl E Ste 350 Saint Paul MN 55101-2163

JACOBS, JOHN PATRICK, lawyer; b. Chgo., Oct. 27, 1945; s. Anthony N. and Bessie (Montgomery) J.; m. Linda I. Grams, Oct. 6, 1973; 1 child, Christine Margaret. BA cum laude, U. Detroit, 1967, JD magna cum laude, 1970. Bar: Mich. 1970, US Dist. Ct. (ea. dist.), Mich. 1970, US Dist. Ct. (we. dist.), Mich. 2004, US Ct. Appeals (6th cir.) 1974, US Ct. Appeals (DC cir.) 1988, US Ct. Appeals (4th cir.) 2001, US Supreme Ct. 1978, US Ct. Appeals (7th cir.) 2005, US Dist. Ct. (no. dist.), Ind. 2005. Law clk. to chief judge Mich. Ct. Appeals, Detroit, 1970-71; assoc., then ptnr. Plunkett & Cooney PC, Detroit, 1972-92, also bd. dirs.; founding ptnr., prin. mem. O'Leary, O'Leary, Jacobs, Mattson, Perry & Mason PC, Southfield, Mich., 1992-99; prin., owner John P. Jacobs, PC, 1999—. Investigator Atty. Grievance Com., Detroit, 1975-84; mem. hearing panel Atty. Discipline Bd., Detroit, 1984-87, 94—; adj. prof. law Sch. Law, U. Detroit, 1983-84, faculty advisor, 1984-89, Pres.'s Cabinet, 1982—; elected rep. State Bar Rep. Assembly, Lansing, Mich., 1980-82, 91-92, 93-96; fellow Mich. State Bar Found., 1990-2005; pres., treas., mem. steering com. Mich. Bench-Bar Appellate Conf. Com., 1994—; apptd. mem. Mich. Supreme Ct. Com. on Appellate Fees, 1990, on Delay Docket Reduction, 2003-05; spl. mediator appellate negotiation program Mich. Ct. Appeals, 1995—; mem. exec. com. Mich. Appellate Bench-Bar Conf. Found., 1996—; appellate counsel to State Bar of Mich., mem. profl. ethics com., 1998, mem. multi-disciplinary practice com., 1999. Bd. editors Mich. Lawyers Weekly. Bd. dirs. Holy Cross Childrens Svcs. Mich., Clinton, 1988-95, 99—, chmn. pub. policy com., 1993-95, pub. policy liaison, 1999—; apptd. mem. State Bar Mich. Blue Ribbon Com. Improving Def. Counsel-Insurer Rels., 1998-99, Appellate Delay Reduction Task Force, 2003-05, Supreme Ct. Com. Regarding Case Mgmt., 2003-06. Named Lawyer of Yr., Mich. Lawyers Weekly, 2004, Mgsr. Malloy Cath. Lawyer of Yr., Archdiocese of Detroit, 2001, Lawyer of Yr. Excellence in Def. award, Mich. Def. Trial Counsel, 2004, Mich.'s Best Appellate Lawyer, Super Lawyers, Detroit News, 2006, 2007, 2008, Best Lawyers in Detroit, DBus. Mag., 2007; named one of 100 Most Influential Lawyers in Mich., Super Lawyers, Detroit News, 2006, 2007, 2008; recipient Robert E. Dice Med. Malpractice Def. Atty. award, Mich. Physicians, 1986, Lawyer of Yr. and Lifetime Achievement award, Mich. Def. Trial Counsel, 2004, Lawyer of Yr.; fellow Reginald Heber Smith fellow, 1971—72. Fellow Am. Acad. Appellate Lawyers, Mich. Std. Jury Instn. (subcom. employment law 1984-87); mem. ABA (litigation sect., appellate subcom., torts and ins. practice), Internat. Assn. Def. Counsel (v.p., amicus curiae com., med. and legal malpractice coms., product liability com.), Fedn. Ins. and Corp. Counsel, Mich. Def. Trial Counsel (chmn. amicus curiae com. 1986-88, chmn. future planning com., bd. dirs. 1989—, treas. 1993-94, sec. 1994-95, v.p. 1995-96, program chair 1990, 94, 95, pres., 1996-97), Def. Rsch. Inst. (state rep. 1997-98, Outstanding Performance Citation 1997, nat. appellate com. steering com. 1997—), Cath. Lawyers Soc. (bd. dirs. 1988-98, emeritus dir. 1998—, pres. 1994-95), Supreme Ct. US Hist. Soc., Supreme Ct. Mich. Hist. Soc., Am. Constitutional Soc. (bd. dirs. 2005), Detroit Athletic Club. Democrat. Roman Catholic. Avocations: collecting antique law books, films.

JACOBS, LEONARD J., state legislator; m. Carol Jacobs; five children. Farmer and rancher; county commr., 1991—; rep. N.D. State Ho. Reps. Dist. 35, 1993—, mem. indsl., bus. and labor coms. Treas. S.W. Water Authority. Mem. Assn. Counties, N.D. Water Users, Adams County Social Svc., Lions, K.C.

JACOBS, LESLIE WILLIAM, lawyer; b. Akron, Ohio, Dec. 5, 1944; s. Leslie Wilson and Louise Francis (Walker) J.; m. Laurie Hutchinson, July 12, 1962; children— Leslie James, Andrew Wilson, Walker Fulton. Student, Denison U., 1962-63; BS, Northwestern U., 1965; JD, Harvard U., 1968. Bar: Ohio 1968, D.C. 1980, U.S. Supreme Ct. 1971, Brussels 1996. Law clk. to Chief Justice Kingsley A. Taft Ohio Supreme Ct., 1968-69; assoc. Thompson, Hine and Flory, Cleve., 1969-76, ptnr., 1976—, chmn. antitrust, internat. and regulatory area, 1988-99; chmn. bus. regulation and trade dept. Thompson Hine LLP and predecessor, Cleve., 1999—. Lectr. conf. bd. Ohio Legal Ctr. Insts., Ohio State Bar Assn. Antitrust and Corp. Counsel Insts., Fed. Bar Assn., ABA, Canadian Inst., Internat. Assn. Young Lawyers, others; mem. Ohio Bd. Bar Examiners, 1990-94. Contbr. articles to profl. jours. Chmn. EconomicsAmerica, 1990-93; mem. vis. com. Case Western Res. U. Sch. Law, 1985-91; dir., mem. exec. com., chair audit com. The Holden Arboretum; mem. Leadership Cleve., 1988; mem. exec. bd. Greater Cleve. Coun. Boy Scouts Am. Lt. comdr. USNR, 1967—79. Fellow Am. Bar Found. (life), Ohio State Bar Found. (life, trustee 1985-87, Ritter award 1997); mem. ABA (ho. dels. 1986-2004, antitrust law sect. coun. 1985-88, officer 1991-97, state del. 1995-2001, nominating com. 1995-2001, bd. gov. 2001-2004, task force on corp. responsibility), Ohio State Bar Assn. (pres. 1987, Ohio Bar medal 1990), Cleve. Bar Assn. (chmn. jud. selection com. 1982, chmn. jud. election monitoring comm. 2004—, trustee 1983-85), Am. Law Inst., 6th Cir. Jud. Conf. (life), Nat. Conf. Bar Pres., Harvard Club (N.Y.C.), Chagrin Valley Hunt Club, Union Club (Cleve.), Castalia Trout Club. Republican. Presbyterian. Office: Thompson Hine LLP 3900 Key Ctr 127 Public Sq Cleveland OH 44114-1291 Home Phone: 440-423-0400; Office Phone: 216-566-5675. Business E-Mail: les.jacobs@thompsonhine.com.

JACOBS, LIBBY SWANSON, state official; b. Lincoln, Nebr., Oct. 1, 1956; m. Steven G. Jacobs. BA, U. Nebr.; MPA, Drake U. Dir. pub. rels. Am. Lung Assn., 1983—86; dir. comms. IA Bankers Assn., 1986—88; mgr., ops. mgr. disability income svcs. Prin. Fin. Group, 1989—96, asst dir., 1996—2002, dir. cmty. rels., 2002—; majority whip Iowa Ho. of Reps., 1999—2006, mem. Iowa, 1994—. Mem. adminstrn. and rules com.; mem. appropriations com.; mem. commerce and regulation com.; mem. state govt. com.; mem. judiciary com., 1994. Bd. mem. Drake Univ., Blank Children's Hosp.; co-chair Downtown Cmty. Alliance; past chair Midwestern Legis. Conf.; bd. mem. Choose Des Moines Cmtys., Greater Des Moines Partnership, Greater Des Moines Convenient Vis. Bur. Mem.: PEO. Republican. Office: State Capitol E 12th and Grand Des Moines IA 50319

JACOBS, LLOYD A., vascular surgeon; b. Holland, Mich., 1940; MD, Johns Hopkins U., 1968. Diplomate Am. Bd. Surgery. Intern Johns Hopkins Hosp., Balt., 1969-70, resident, 1970-71, U. Calif., San Diego, 1971-72, Wayne State U., Detroit, 1972-74; prof. surgery U. Mich. Sch. Medicine, Ann Arbor, 1974—2003, sr. assoc. dean, 1996—2003; COO U. Mich. Health Sys., Ann Arbor, 1997—; pres. Med. Coll. Ohio, 2003—. Hosp. appts.: VA Hosp., Ann Arbor, Mich., U. Mich. Hosp., Ann Arbor, chief of staff, VAH Med. Ctr., 1989-96. Fellow ACS; mem. AMA, Internat. Soc. Cardio Vascular Surgeons, Midwest Surgeons Assn. Office: 3045 Arlington Ave ML-213 Toledo OH 43614

JACOBS, NORMAN JOSEPH, publishing executive; b. Chgo., Oct. 28, 1932; s. Herman and Tillie (Chapman) J.; m. Jeri Kolber Rose, Jan. 2, 1977; 1 son, Barry Herman; children by previous marriage: Carey, Murray, Dale. BS in Mktg, U. Ill., 1954. Display salesman Chgo. Daily News, 1954-57; dist. mgr. Davidson Pub. Co., Chgo., 1957-62; v.p. Press-Tech, Inc., Evanston, Ill., 1962-69; pres. Century Pub. Co., Evanston, 1969—. Bd. dirs. Chgo. Bulls. With USNR, 1951—59. Mem. B'nai B'rith, Birchwood Tennis Club, Alpha Delta Sigma, Tau Epsilon Phi. Jewish. Office: Century Pub Co 990 Grove St 3rd Fl Evanston IL 60201-6510 Home Phone: 847-831-0738; Office Phone: 847-491-6440. Business E-Mail: njacobs@centurysports.net.

JACOBS, RICHARD E., real estate company executive, sports team owner; 3 children from previous marriage. Ptnr. Jacobs, Visconsi & Jacobs; former chmn., chief exec. officer Cleve. Indians. Office: Richard E Jacobs Group 25425 Center Ridge Rd Cleveland OH 44145-4122

JACOBSON, CARRIE ISABELLE, lawyer; BA with distinction, U. Wis., Madison, 1995; JD magna cum laude, Hamline U. Sch. Law, 2000. Bar: Minn. 2000, US Dist. Ct. (dist. Minn.) 2001. Atty. adult prosecution divsn. Hennepin County Atty.'s Office, 1998—2000; assoc. atty. workers' compensation def., underinsured and uninsured motorist def., no-fault arbitrations and personal injury def. litig. Hansen, Dordell, Bradt, Odlaug & Bradt, 2000—02; assoc. atty. workers' compensation def., no-fault arbitrations and personal injury def. litig. Brown & Carlson, P.A., Mpls., 2002—. Primary editor, assoc.: Hamline Jour. Pub. Law and Policy. Named a Rising Star, Minn. Super Lawyers mag., 2006. Mem.: Minn. Women Lawyers, ABA, Minn. State Bar Assn., Minn. Def. Lawyers Assn. Office: Brown & Carlson PA 5411 Circle Down Ave Ste 100 Minneapolis MN 55416 Office Phone: 763-591-9950.

JACOBSON, HOWARD, classics educator; b. Bronx, NY, Aug. 21, 1940; s. David and Jeannette (Signer) J.; m. Elaine Z. Finkelstein, June 10, 1965; children: Michael oam, Daniel Benjamin, Joel Avram, David Moses. BA, Columbia U., 1962, PhD, 1967; MA, U. Chgo., 1963. Instr. Greek and Latin Columbia U., 1966-68; asst. prof. classics U. Ill., 1968-73, assoc. prof., 1973-80, prof., 1980—; Lady Davis vis. prof. Hebrew U., Jerusalem, winter 1983. Mem. Inst. for Advanced Study, Princeton, N.J., 1993-94. Author: Ovid's Heroides, 1974, The Exagoge of Ezekiel, 1983, A Commentary on Pseudo-Philo's Liber Antiquitatum Biblicarum (2 vols.), 1996; editor for Latin studies: Illinois Classical Studies Supplements. Nat. Endowment for Humanities fellow, 1971-72, 89; assoc. Ctr. for Advanced Study, U. Ill., 1983-84, spring 1994. Mem. Am. Philol. Assn. (Charles J. Goodwin Merit award 1985), Corr. assoc. Forum on Israel Studies CUNY; Phi Beta Kappa. Jewish. Office: Dept Classics 4090 Foreign Languages Bldg 707 S Mathews Ave Urbana IL 61801-3625 Home Phone: 217-359-1947; Office Phone: 217-333-7573.

JACOBSON, JEFF, state legislator; BA, Yale U., 1983; JD summa cum laude, Dayton Law Sch., 1988. Mem. Ohio Ho. of Reps. from 40th dist., Columbus, 1990-2000, Ohio Senate from 6th dist., Columbus, 2001—. Precinct capt. Montgomery County Reps., chmn.; exec. v.p. Ohioans for Fair Representation; lawyer. Mem. Antioch Temple Shrine, Mason (32d degree).

JACOBSON, MARIAN SLUTZ, lawyer; b. Cin., Nov. 10, 1945; d. Leonard Doering and Emily Dana (Wells) Slutz; m. Fruman Jacobson, Sept. 21, 1975; 1 child, Lisa Wells. BA cum laude, Ohio Wesleyan U., 1967; JD, U. Chgo., 1972. Bar: Ill. 1972, U.S. Dist. Ct. (no. dist.) Ill. 1972, U.S. Ct. Appeals (7th cir.) 1973. Assoc. Sonnenschein Nath & Rosenthal, Chgo., 1972-79, ptnr., 1979—. Mem. vis. com. U. Chgo. Law Sch., 1992-94, 05-. Mem. ABA, Chgo. Coun. Lawyers, Met. Club Chgo. (bd. govs. 1998—), Hyde Park Neighborhood Club (bd. dirs. 2003-). Office: Sonnenschein Nath & Rosenthal 7800 Sears Tower Chicago IL 60606-6491 Office Phone: 312-876-8167. Business E-Mail: mjacobson@sonnenschein.com.

JACOBSON, MICHAEL F., lawyer; b. 1967; Grad., U. Colo., 1989; JD, Detroit Coll. Law., 1992. Bar: Mich. 1992, Fla. Ptnr. Hertz Schram & Saretsky P.C., Bloomfield Hills, Mich., 1999—2005; atty. Jaffe Raitt Heuer & Weiss P.C., Southfield, Mich., 2005—06, ptnr., 2006—. Named one of 40 Under 40, Crain's Detroit Bus., 2006. Office: Jaffe Raitt Heuer & Weiss PC 27777 Franklin Rd Ste 2500 Southfield MI 48034-8214 Office Phone: 248-351-3000. Business E-Mail: mjacobson@jaffelaw.com.

JACOBSON, NORMAN L., retired agricultural educator, researcher; b. Eau Claire, Wis., Sept. 11, 1918; s. Frank R. and Elma E. (Baker) J.; m. Gertrude A. Neff, Aug. 24, 1943; children: Gary, Judy. BS, U. Wis., 1940; MS, Iowa State U., 1941, PhD, 1947. Asst. prof. animal sci. Iowa State U., Ames, 1947-49, assoc. prof., 1949-53, prof., 1953, Disting. prof. agr., 1963-89, assoc. dean Grad. Coll., 1973-88, assoc. v.p. rsch., 1979-88, assoc. provost, 1988-89, dean Grad. Coll. Ames, 1988-89, emeritus disting. prof. agr., 1989—, interim chair dept. food sci. and human nutrition, 1990-92. Contbr. articles to profl. jours., chpts. to books. Served to lt. USN, 1942-46, ETO, PTO. Fellow AAAS, Am. Soc. for Nutritional Scis., Am. Soc. Animal Sci. (Morrison award 1970), Am. Dairy Sci. Assn. (pres. 1972-73, Am. Feed Mfrs. Assn. award 1955, Borden award 1960, award of honor 1978, Disting. Svc. award 1989). Presbyterian. Personal E-mail: nljacob@iastate.edu.

JACOBSON, RICHARD JOSEPH, lawyer; b. Ft. Benning, Ga., July 12, 1943; s. Harold Gordon and Ruth Fern (Enenstein) J.; m. Judy Josephine Dunbar, Sept. 17, 1966; 1 child, David Dunbar. AB, Harvard U., 1965, PhD, 1970; JD, U. Va., 1977. Bar: Ill. 1977, Va. 1977, D.C. 1979, U.S. Dist. Ct. (no. dist.) 1977, U.S. Ct. Appeals (7th cir.) 1991. Asst. prof. English U. Va., Charlottesville, 1970-74; assoc. Keck, Mahin & Cate, Chgo., 1977-83, ptnr., 1984-96; prin. Flaherty, Jacobson & Youngerman, P.C., Chgo., 1996—. Adj. prof. Sch. Law Northwestern U., Chgo., 1999—. Author: Hawthorne's Conception of the Creative Process, 1965; contbr. articles to profl. jours. Pres. North Park Condominium assn., Chgo., 1978-80. Woodrow Wilson Nat. fellow, 1965. Fellow Am. Bar Found.; mem. Va. State Bar Assn., DC Bar Assn., Chgo. Bar Assn. (chmn. com. preventing atty. malpractice 2000-01), Assn. Profl. Responsibility Lawyers, Cliff Dwellers Club, Lawyers Club Chgo., Chgo. Lit. Club. Home: 850 W Adams St Apt 3D Chicago IL 60607-3088 Office: Flaherty Jacobson & Youngerman PC 134 N Lasalle St Ste 1600 Chicago IL 60602-1108 Personal E-mail: rjacobson@fjylaw.com.

JACOBSON, ROBERT ANDREW, chemistry professor; b. Waterbury, Conn., Feb. 16, 1932; s. Carl Andrew and Mary Catherine (O'Donnell) J.; m. Margaret Ann McMahan, May 26, 1962; children: Robert Edward, Cheryl Ann BA, U. Conn., 1954; PhD, U. Minn., 1959. Instr. Princeton U., NJ, 1959-62, asst. prof. NJ, 1962-64; assoc. prof. Iowa State U., Ames, 1964-69, full prof., 1969-99, asst. dean Scis. and Humanities, 1982-85, prof. emeritus, 1999—. Chemist Ames Lab, Iowa, 1964-69, sr. chemist, 1969-99. Contbr. articles to profl. jours. Recipient Wilkinson Teaching award Iowa State U., Ames, 1974, 91. Mem. Am. Chem. Soc., Am. Crystallographic Assn. (chmn. apparatus and standards com. 1982-83) Avocations: gardening, painting. Home: 2732 Thompson Dr Ames IA 50010-4759 Office: Iowa State U 1271 Gilman Ames IA 50011-3111 Office Phone: 515-294-1144. E-mail: raj@ameslab.gov.

JACOBSON, SHELDON HOWARD, engineering educator; b. Montreal, Sept. 9, 1960; BSc, McGill U., 1981, MSc, 1983; PhD, Cornell U., 1988. Asst. prof. Case We. Res. U., Cleve., 1988—93; assoc. prof. Va. Tech., Blacksburg, 1993—99, U. Ill., Urbana, 1999—2002, prof., 2002—, assoc. Ctr. for Advanced Study, 2002—03. Sci. adv. bd. BioPop Inc., Charlotte, NC, 2000—02. Recipient Best Application award, Inst. Indsl. Engring. Ops. Rsch. Divsn., 1998, Aviation Security Rsch. award, Aviation Security Internat., 2002; Willett Faculty scholar, U. Ill., 2002—08, Guggenheim fellow, 2003. Office: Univ Illinois 201 N Goodwin Ave MC-258 Urbana IL 61801-2302

JACOBSON, WALTER (SKIPPY JACOBSON), newscaster, journalist; b. Chgo. m. Susie Jacobson; 2 children; 2 children from previous marriage. BA in Polit. Sci., Grinnell Coll., Iowa; MA in Journalism, Columbia U., NYC. Reporter Chgo. Daily News, Chgo. Am., UPI, City News Bur., Time mag.; news writer WBBM-TV, Chgo., 1963—70; reporter and commentator WMAQ-TV, Chgo., 1971—72; investigative reporter WBBM-TV, 1973—76, co-anchor 10pm news, 1973—89, anchor 5pm news, 1976—86; co-anchor Fox News at Nine WFLD-TV, 1993—. TV journalist: Walter Jaconson's Perspective (Peabody award, Peter Lisagor awards, Du-Pont Columbia judges award), Walter Jacobson's Jour.: China (Emmy award), Studebaker: Less Than They Promised (Peabody award). Co-recipient Best Local Election Coverage in the U.S., Du-Pont Columbia judges; named Best Local Anchor in U.S., Wash. Journalism Rev. Poll, 1985; recipient Emmy awards, NATAS (Chgo. chapt.), Peter Lisagor awards, Soc. Profl. Journalists. Office: WFLD-TV 205 N Mich Ave Chicago IL 60601

JACOVER, JEROLD ALAN, lawyer; b. Chgo., Mar. 20, 1945; s. David Louis and Beverly (Funk) J.; m. Judith Lee Greenwald, June 28, 1970; children: Aric Seth, Evan Michael, Brian Ethan. BSEE, U. Wis., 1967; JD, Georgetown U., 1972. Bar: Ohio 1972, Ill. 1973, U.S. Ct. Appeals (7th cir.) 1974, U.S. Ct. Appeals (Fed. cir.) 1983. Atty. Ralph Nader, Columbus, Ohio, 1972-73, Brinks Hofer, Gilson & Lione, Chgo., 1973—, shareholder, 1977—, pres., 2000—06. Mem. ABA, Am. Intellectual Property Law Assn. (bd. dirs. 1994-98), Decalogue Soc. Lawyers, Intellectual Property Law Assn. Chgo. (bd. dirs. 1993-94, 98-99, pres. 2000), Intellectual Property Law Assn. Chgo. Ednl. Found. (pres. 1990-93), Am. Techion Soc. (pres. 1994-97). Office: Brinks Hofer Gilson & Lione Ste 3600 455 N Cityfront Plaza Dr Chicago IL 60611-5599 E-mail: jjacover@brinkshofer.com.

JACOVIDES, LINOS JACOVOU, electrical engineer, researcher; b. Paphos, Cyprus, May 10, 1940; s. Jacovos and Zoe (Evangelides) Jacovides; m. Katie McNamee; children: James, Michael, Christina, Julia. BS, U. Glasgow, Scotland, 1961, MS, 1962; PhD, U. London, 1965. Sr. rsch. engr. Def. Rsch. Labs. GM, Calif., 1965-67; sr. rsch. engr. elec. engring. GM Rsch. Labs., Warren, Mich., 1967-76, dept. rsch. engr. elec. engring. dept., 1975-85, asst. dept. head elec. engring. dept., 1985-87, prin. rsch. engr., 1987-88, head elec. and electronics dept., 1988-98; dir. Delphi Rsch. Labs., Warren, 1999—, Shelby Township, Mich., 1999—. Editor: Electric Vehicles, 1981; contbr. articles to profl. jours. Fellow: IEEE; mem.: Soc. Automotive Engrs., Industry Applications Soc. of IEEE (pres. 1990). Home: 154 Touraine Rd Grosse Pointe Farms MI 48236-3322 Office: M/C 483 478 103 51786 Shelby Pky Shelby Township MI 48315-1786 E-mail: linos@aol.com, linos.jacovides@delphi.com.

JACOX, ADA KATHRYN, nurse, educator; b. Centreville, Mich. d. Leo H. and Lilian (Gilbert) Jacox. BS in Nursing Edn., Columbia U., 1959; MS in Child Psychiat. ursing, Wayne State U., 1965; PhD in Sociology, Case Western Res. U., 1969. RN. Dir. nursing Children's Hosp.-Northville State Hosp., Mich., 1961—63; assoc. prof., then prof. Coll. Nursing Univ. Iowa, Iowa City, 1969—76; prof., assoc. dean Sch. Nursing U. Colo., Denver, 1976—80; prof., dir. rsch. ctr. sch. nursing U. Md., Balt., 1980—90, dir. ctr. for health policy rsch., 1988—90; prof. sch. nursing, Independence Found. chair health policy Johns Hopkins U., Balt., 1990—95; prof., assoc. dean for rsch. Coll. Nursing Wayne State, Detroit, 1996. Co-chmn. panels to develop clin. guidelines for pain mgmt. U.S. Agy. for Health Care Policy and Rsch., 1990—94; chair AIDS study sect. NIH, 1990—92. Co-author: Organizing for Independent Nursing Practice, 1977 (named Book of Yr., Am. Jour. Nursing), A Process Measure for Primary Care: The Nurse Practitioner Rating Form, 1981 (named Book of Yr., Am. Jour. Nursing); editor: Pain: A Sourcebook for Nurses, 1977 (named Book of Yr., Am. Jour. Nursing). Recipient Disting. Achievement in Nursing Rsch. and Scholarship, Alumni Assn., Columbia U. Tchrs. Coll., 1975, Disting. award for spl. achievement, Nat. Coalition for Cancer Survivorship, 1994, Cameo award for rsch. excellence, Sigma Theta Tau, 1996, Rozella Schlotfeldt Leadership award, MAIN, 1997; fellow Carver fellow, U. Iowa, 1972. Fellow: Am. Acad. Nursing; mem.: Wayne State U. Alumni Assn. (Disting. Alumni award 1994), Inst. of Medicine, NAS (com. on nat. needs for biomed. and rsch. pers. 1984—87), Am. Acad. ursing, Am. Health Quality Assn. (bd. dirs. 1998—2001), Am. Pain Soc. (chair clin. practice guidelines com. 1995—2000, bd. dirs. 1999—2001), Am. Nurses Found. (pres. 1982—85), AMA (mem. health policy agenda work group 1983—86), ANA (dir. 1978—82, 1st v.p. 1982—84). Office: Wayne State U Coll Nursing 5557 Cass Ave Detroit MI 48202-3615

JAEGER, AL (ALVIN A. JAEGER), state official; b. Beulah, ND, Dec. 10, 1943; m. Naomi Berg, 1969 (dec. 1979), m. Kathy Grangaard Anderson, 1986; children: Todd, Stacy, Heidi. AA, Bismarck State Coll., 1963; BS, Dickinson State U., 1966; postgraduate studies, U. ND, 1968, Mont. State U., 1970. Tchr. Killdeer HS, 1966-69, Kenmare HS, 1969-71; mktg. analyst Mobil Oil Corp., 1971-73; real estate broker, 1973-93; sec. state State of ND, 1993—. Active Charity Luth. Ch., 1966-72. Served in ND Army Nat. Guard, 1980. Named Realtor of Yr. Mem. Nat. Assn. Secs. State (exec. com., com. chmn.), Fargo-Moorhead Area Assn. Realtors (mem. coms. edn., profl. stds., bylaws, multiple listing svc.), ND Assn. Realtors (past chairperson state bylaws), Bismarck Kiwanis Club. Republican. Lutheran. Office: Office Sec of State Dept 108 600 E Boulevard Ave Bismarck ND 58505-0500 Office Phone: 701-328-2900. Business E-Mail: sos@nd.gov.

JAEGER, JEFF TODD, professional football player; b. Tacoma, Wash., Nov. 26, 1964; Student, Wash. Coll. With Cleve. Browns, 1987; kicker L.A. Raiders, 1989-96, Chgo. Bears, 1996—. Achievements inlude playing in Pro Bowl, 1991; shares single season record for most field goals made (35), 1993. Office: Chgo Bears 1000 Football Dr Lake Forest IL 60045-4829

JAFFE, HOWARD ALLEN, financial company executive; b. Chgo., June 17, 1953; s. Richard Lee Jaffe and Bette Carol (Steinberg) Whitehead; m. Beverly Ann Geisel, June 22, 1975; children: Victoria, Katharine. BS, No. Ill. U., 1974; MBA, Loyola U., Chgo., 1978. Various positions to sr. v.p. NBD Ill. Banks, Highland Park, Ill., 1975-90; exec. v.p., chief fin. officer No. States Fin. Corp., Waukegan, Ill., 1990-95; exec. v.p. and chief fin. officer Avondale Fed. Savings Bank, Chgo., 1995—; v.p. and chief fin. officer Avondale Fin. Corp., Chgo., 1995—. Contbr. articles to profl. publs. Mem. Sch. Dist. 70 Bd. Edn., Libertyville, Ill., 1991-95; bd. dirs., treas. healthreach clinic for medically underserved, Waukegan, 1991—. Alumni scholar No. Ill. U., 1973-74. Mem. Rotary (pres.). Avocations: golf, computers. Home: 1129 Virginia Ave Libertyville IL 60048-4439 Office: Avondale Fed Savings Bank 20 N Clark St Chicago IL 60602-4109

JAGER, MELVIN FRANCIS, lawyer; b. Joliet, Ill., Mar. 23, 1937; s. Melvin Van Zandt and Lucille Marie (Callahan) J.; m. Virginia Sue Maitland, Aug. 15, 1959; children: Lori, Jennifer, Scott, Christy. BSME, JD, U. Ill., 1962. Bar: Ill. 1962, D.C. 1962. Assoc. Iron, Birch, Swindler & McKie, Washington, 1962-65; ptnr. Hume, Clement, Brinks, Willian & Olds Ltd., Chgo., 1965-80, Lee, Smith & Jager, Chgo., 1981-83, Niro, Jager & Scavone, Chgo., 1984-85, Brinks, Hofer, Gilson & Lione Ltd., Chgo., 1985—2004, Ocean Tomo LLC, 2004—06. Editor U. Ill. Law Rev., 1961-62; adj. prof. law No. Ill. U. Sch. Law, 1979-80, John Marshall Law Sch., 1992, U. Ill. Coll. Law, Champaign, 1992-2003; chmn. Practicing Law Inst. Trade Secret Protection Symposium, 1986, 89. Author: Trade Secrets Law, 1984, Licensing Law Handbook, 2005; editor: Worldwide Trade Secrets Law, 2005; contbg. author: Sorting Out the Ownership Rights in Intellectual Property: A Practical Guide to Practical Counseling and Legal Representation, 1980. Mem. bd. edn. Glen Ellyn, Ill., 1974-80; chmn. Civic Betterment Party Nominating Com., Glen Ellyn, 1982-88; chmn. Glen Ellyn Environ. Protection Com., 1971-72; chmn. budget rev. com. Glen Ellyn United Fund, 1972, Glen Ellyn Ednl. Loan Fund trust, 1973. Mem. ABA (chmn. litigation sect. intellectual properties and patents com. 1984-88), Ill. State Bar Assn. (chmn. patent, trademark and copyright, coun. 1982-83, editor newsletter 1979-82), Chgo. Bar Assn., Am. Patent Law Assn., Intellectual Property Law Assn. of Chgo. (pres. 1997), Lic. Execs. Soc. (pres. U.S.A./Can. 1993-94, lic. found. pres., 2001-04, pres., 2003-04), Am. Law Inst., Glen Ellyn Jaycees (life mem., pres. 1972, trustee), Chgo. Law Club, Union League Club, Phi Gamma Delta, Phi Delta Phi. Republican. Roman Catholic. Home: 2302 Walfert Rd Sanibel FL 33957 Office: Ocean Tomo LLC 200 W Adams Chicago IL 60606 Home Phone: 239-472-5706; Office Phone: 312-327-4419. E-mail: mfjager@msn.com.

JAHN, HELMUT, architect; b. Nurnberg, Germany, Jan. 4, 1940; came to U.S., 1966; s. Wilhelm Anton and Karolina (Wirth) J.; m. Deborah Ann Lampe, Dec. 31, 1970; 1 child, Evan Dipl. Ing.-Architect, Technische Hochschule, Munich, 1965; postgrad., Ill. Inst. Tech., 1966-67; D.F.A. (hon.), St. Mary's Coll., otre Dame, Ind., 1980. Registered architect, Ill., Calif., Colo., Fla., Ind., Minn., N.Y., Tex., Va., Nat. Coun. Archtl. Registration Bds. Germany. With P.C. von Seidlein, Munich, 1965-66; with C.F. Murphy Assocs., Chgo., 1967-81, asst. to Gene Summers, 1967-73, exec. v.p., dir. planning and design, 1973-81; prin. Murphy/Jahn, Chgo., 1981-92, pres., 1982—, chief exec. officer, 1983—. Mem. design studio faculty U. Ill., Chgo., 1981; Elliot Noyes prof. archtl. design Harvard U., Cambridge, Mass., 1981; Davenport vis. prof. archtl. design Yale U., New Haven, 1983; thesis prof. IIT, Chgo., 1989-92. Prin. works include Kemper Arena, Kansas City, Mo., 1974 (Nat. AIA honor award, Am. Inst. Steel Constrn. award), Auraria Library, Denver, 1975, John Marshall Cts. Bldg., Richmond, Va. 1976, H. Roe Bartle Exhbn. Hall, Kansas City, Mo., 1976, Fourth Dist. Cts. Bldg., Maywood, Ill., 1976, Monroe Garage, Chgo., 1977, Michigan City (Ind.) Library, 1977 (AIA Ill. Council honor award, AIA-ALA First honor award, Am. Inst., Steel Constrn. award), St. Mary's Coll. Athletic Facility, South Bend, Ind., 1977 (AIA Ill. Council Honor award, AIA Nat. honor award, Am. Inst. Steel Constrn. award), Springfield Garage, Ill., 1977, Glenbrook Profl. Bldg., Northbrook, Ill., 1978, Rust-Oleum Corp. Hdqrs., Vernon Hills, Ill., 1978 (Am. Steel Constrn. award), La Lumiere Gymnasium, La Porte, Ind., 1978, Prairie Capital Convention Ctr.-Parking Garage, Springfield, Ill., 1979, W.W. Grainger Corp. Hdqrs., Skokie, Ill., 1979, Xerox Centre, Chgo., 1980, De La Garza Career Ctr., East Chicago, Ind., 1981 (ASHRAE Energy award), Area 2 Police Hdqrs., Chgo., 1981, Oak Brook (Ill.) Post Office, 1981, Commonwealth Edison Dist. Hdqrs., Downers Grove, Ill., 1981 (ASHRAE Energy award), First Source Ctr., South Bend, Ind., 1982, Argonne (Ill.) Program Support Facility, 1982 (Owens-Corning Fiberglass Energy Conservation award), One South Wacker Office Bldg., Chgo., 1982, Addition to Chgo. Bd. of Trade, 1982 (Reliance Devel. Group Inc. award for Disting. Arch., Am. Inst. Steel Constrn. award, Structural Engring. Assn. Ill. award), Mercy Hosp. Addition, Chgo., 1983, 11 Diagonal St., Johannesburg, Republic of South Africa, 1983, U. Ill. Agrl. Engring. Sci. Bldg., Champaign, 1984, Learning Resources Ctr., Coll. of DuPage, Glen Ellyn, Ill., 1984, Plaza East, Milw., 1984 (Disting. Architect award Milw. Art Commn.), Shand Morahan Corp. Hdqrs., Evanston, Ill., 1984, 701 Fourth Ave. S., Mpls., 1984, O'Hare Rapid Transit Sta., Chgo., 1984 (Nat. Honor award), State of Ill. Ctr., Chgo., 1985 (Structural Engring. Assn. Ill. award, AIA Chgo. chpt. award 1986), Parktown Stands, Johannesburg, 1986, Two Energy Ctr., Naperville, Ill., 1986, Hawthorne Ctr. Office Bldg., Vernon Hills, Ill., 1986, Park Ave. Tower, N.Y.C., 1986, 300 E. 85th St. Apts., N.Y.C., Northwestern Terminal, Chgo., 1987 (Structural Engring. Assn. of Ill. award 1987), United Airlines Terminal, 1987 (Structural Engring. Assn. of Ill. award, Nat. AIA Honor award, R.J. Reynolds Meml. award, 1988, AIA Chgo. chpt. award), One Liberty Place, Phila., 1987, Oakbrook (Ill.) Terr. Tower, 1987, O'Hare Internat. Airport, 1988 (AIA Chgo. chpt. award), Merchandise Mart Bridge, Chgo., 1988, Wilshire/Westwood Office Bldg., L.A., 1988, 425 Lexington Ave, N.Y.C., 1989, 750 Lexington Ave., 1989, Cityspire, N.Y.C., 1989, Messe Frankfurt Convention Ctr., Germany, 1989, Barnett Ctr., Jacksonville, Fla., 1990, Messe Frankfurt Tower, Germany, 1991 (AIA Chgo. chpt. award 1992), Livingston Plaza, Bklyn. Hgts., N.Y., 1991, Two Liberty Place, Phila., 1991 (AIA Chgo. chpt. award 1992), 120 LaSalle, Chgo., 1992 (AIA Chgo. chpt. award 1992), One Am. Plz., Trolley Sta., San Diego, 1992 (AIA Chgo. chpt. award 1992), Mannheim (Germany) Ins. Bldg., 1992 (AIA Chgo. chpt. award 1992), Hyatt Roisy, Paris, 1992, Munich (Germany) Order Ctr., 1993 (AIA Chgo. Chpt. award, Nat. AIA Honor award), Hitachi Tower, Singapore, 1993, Caltex House, Singapore, 1993, Kempinski Hotel, Munich, 1994, (AIA Chgo. Chpt. award), Pallas, Stuttgart, Germany, 1994, 70 KU Damn, Berlin, 1994, (AIA Chgo. Chpt. award, Nat. AIA Honor award), Second Internat. Bangkok Airport, Charlemagne, Brussels, Century 21, Shanghai, China, FKB Airport, Köln, Germany; contbr. to numerous group and solo exhbns. of archtl. drawings and design. Recipient citation Progressive Architecture, 1977, award for Chgo. cen. area plan, 1985, Dean of Architecture award Chgo. design awards, 1991; Arnold W. Brunner meml. prize in architecture, 1982; Chgo. chpt. award AIA, 1975-79, 81-83, 86-88, nat. honor award, 1979, 87, N.Y. State award, 1986; lst honor award ALA, 1978, energy award ASHRAE, 1981, Presdl. Desirn award Nat. Endowment Arts, 1988, R.S. Reynolds Meml. award, 1988; numerous others. Fellow AIA, Architecture Soc./Art Inst. Chgo., Chgo. Archtl. Club; mem. AIA (numerous Chgo. chpt. awards 1975—). Clubs: Comml. of Chgo., Economic of Chgo., Saddle & Cycle. Roman Catholic. Office: Murphy/Jahn 35 E Wacker Dr Ste 300 Chicago IL 60601-2157

JAHNS, JEFFREY, lawyer; b. Chgo., July 6, 1946; s. Maxim G. and Josephine Barbara (Czernek) J.; m. Jill Metcoff, Sept. 8, 1973; children: Anna Hope, Claire Martine, Elizabeth Grace. AB, Villanova U., 1968; JD, U. Chgo., 1971. Bar: Ill. 1971, U.S. Dist. Ct. (no. dist.) Ill. 1971, U.S. Ct. Appeals (7th cir.) 1973, U.S. Supreme Ct. 1974. Assoc. Roan & Grossman, Chgo., 1971-77, ptnr., 1977-81, Seyfarth Shaw LLP, Chgo., 1981—. Mem. tax mgmt. adv. bd. Bur. Nat. Affairs, Washington, 1981—. Co-author: Corporate Acquisition Debt Interest Deduction, 1973; contbr. numerous articles to legal publs., chpts. to books. Trustee, sec. Chgo. Architecture Found., 1982—; bd. dirs. Prairie Ave. House Mus., 1995-98; trustee, treas. Graham Found., 1998—; bd. dir., treas. Am. Friends of Coubertin Inc., 2007. Ctr. for Urban Studies fellow U. Chgo., 1969-71. Mem. ABA, Chgo. Bar Assn. (chmn. various coms.), Internat. Coun. Shopping Ctrs., Union League Club, Econ. Club Chgo., Lambda Alpha. Office: Seyfarth Shaw LLP 131 S Dearborn St Ste 2400 Chicago IL 60603-5577 Home Phone: 773-728-0994; Office Phone: 312-460-5819. Business E-Mail: jjahns@seyfarth.com.

JAHR, ARMIN N., II, clergy member, church administrator; Exec. dir. Luth. Brethren Home Missions, Fergus Falls, Minn. Office: Luth Brethren Home Missions PO Box 655 Fergus Falls MN 56538-0655

JAIN, DIPAK CHAND, dean, marketing educator, consultant; b. Tezpur, India, June 9, 1957; came to U.S., 1983; s. Jagdish C. and Sumitra (Jain) J.; m. Sushant Jain, Dec. 12, 1989; children: Dhwani, Kalash, Muskaan. BS in math. and stats., Gauhati U., Assam, India, 1976, MS in math. stats., 1978; MS in mgmt. sci., U. Tex., Dallas, 1986, PhD in mktg., 1987. Asst. prof. Gauhati U., 1979-83; teaching and rsch. asst. U. Tex., Dallas, 1983-86; asst. prof. mktg. Kellogg Sch. Mgmt., Northwestern U., Evanston, Ill., 1986-89, assoc. prof., 1990-93, prof. mktg., 1993—, Sandy and Morton Goldman prof. entrepreneurial studies, 1994—, assoc. dean for acad. affairs, 1996—2001, dean, 2001—. Vis. prof. mktg., Sasin Grad. Inst. Bus. Adminstrn., Chulalongkorn U., Bangkok, 1989-; mktg. dept. editor, Management Science; bd. dirs. Deere & Co., Hartmarx Corp., Peoples Energy Corp., UAL Corp., No. Trust Corp., 2004-; cons. to pharm. and telecom. firms, consumer goods co. Recipient Outstanding Educator Award, State of Assam, India, 1982, Sidney Levy Award for Excellence in Tchg., Kellogg Sch. Mgmt., 1994—95, Alumni Prof. of Yr. Award, 2002, Pravasi Bharatiya Samman Award, govt. India, 2004. Office: Northwestern U 2001 Sheridan Rd Evanston IL 60208-0814 Office Phone: 847-491-2728. E-mail: d-jain@kellogg.northwestern.edu.

JAKUBAUSKAS, EDWARD BENEDICT, college president; b. Waterbury, Conn., Apr. 14, 1930; s. Constantine and Barbara (Narstis) J.; m. Ruth Friz, Aug. 29, 1959; children— Carol, Marilyn, Mark, Eric. BA, U. Conn., 1952, MA, 1954; PhD, U. Wis., 1961. Economist FPC, 1956, Dept. Labor, 1956-58; instr. U. Wis., 1961-62, asst. prof. econs., 1962-63; asst. prof. Iowa State U., 1963-65, assoc. prof., 1965-66, prof., 1966-71; dean U. Wyo., 1971-76, prof. econs., 1971-79, v.p. acad. affairs, 1976-79; pres. SUNY, Geneseo, 1979-88, Cen. Mich. U., Mt. Pleasant, 1988-92; cons. in higher edn., 1992—. Author: Manpower Economics, 1971. Served with U.S. Army, 1954-56. Mem. Am. Assn. State Univs. and Colls. Mem. United Chs. of Christ.

JAKUBOWSKI, THADDEUS JOSEPH, bishop emeritus; b. Chgo., Apr. 5, 1924; STB, STL, St. Mary of the Lake Sem., Mundelein, Ill.; MA in Classics, Loyola U., Chgo. Ordained priest Archdiocese of Chgo., 1950, aux. bishop, 1988—2003, aux. bishop emeritus, 2003—; assoc. pastor St. Ann, St. Bartholmew; pastor St. Robert Bellarmine; ordained bishop, 1988. Exec. dir. Cath. League for Religious Assistance to Poland; co-vicar for senior priests Archdiocese of Chgo. Roman Catholic. Office: 6002 W Berteau Ave Chicago IL 60634-1630*

JALLINGS, JESSICA, reporter, newscaster; b. Wis. BA in Journalism, U. Wis. With WISC-TV, Madison, Wis.; reporter WGBA-TV, Green Bay, Wis., WGLV-TV, Jacksonville, Fla.; reporter, anchor WISN, Milw., 2001—. Office: WISN PO Box 402 Milwaukee WI 53201-0402

JAMBOR, ROBERT VERNON, lawyer; b. Chgo., Aug. 29, 1936; s. Vernon C. and Anne M. Jambor; m. Arlene M. Gale, Nov. 9, 1957 (dec. Aug. 1993); children: Robyn, Cheryl, Steven; m. Terri J. Skyrme, Jan. 11, 1995. BME, Kettering U., 1958; JD, John Marshall Law Sch., Chgo., 1963. Bar: Ill. 1963, U.S. Dist. Ct. Ill. 1963, U.S. Ct. Appeals (7th cir.) 1974, U.S. Ct. Appeals (fed. cir.) 1982, U.S. Supreme Ct. 1983. Product engr. product devel. Electro-Motive div. Gen. Motors Corp., La Grange, Ill., 1958-63; asso. firm Marks & Clerk, Chgo., 1961-63; patent atty. Borg-Warner Corp., Chgo., 1964-69; ptnr. Haight, Hofeldt, Davis & Jambor, Chgo., 1970-87, Dorn, McEachran, Jambor & Keating, Chgo., 1987—2000; counsel Jenner & Block LLP, Chgo., 2001—05, Leydig Voit & Mayer, LTD, Chgo., 2005—. Mem. ABA, Ill. Bar Assn., Fed. Cir. Bar Assn., Am. Intellectual Property Law Assn., Intellectual Property Law Assn. Chgo. Home Phone: 262-245-9209; Office Phone: 815-963-7661. Business E-Mail: rjambor@leydig.com.

JAMES, CHARLES FRANKLIN, JR., retired engineering educator; b. Des Arc, Mo., July 16, 1931; s. Charles Franklin and Beulah Frances (Kyte) J.; m. Mollie Keeler, May 18, 1974; children: Thomas Elisha, Matthew Jeremiah. BS, Purdue U., 1958, MS, 1960, PhD, 1963. Registered profl. engr., Wis. Sr. indsl. engr. McDonnel Aircraft Co., 1963; asst. prof. U. RI, Kingston, 1963—66, prof., chmn. dept. indsl. engring., 1967—82, co-founder, mem Robotics Rsch. Ctr., 1980—83; assoc. prof. U. Mass., Amherst, 1966—67; C. Paul Stocker prof. engring. Ohio U., Athens, 1982-83; dean Coll. Engring. and Applied Sci., U. Wis., Milw., 1984—95; academic v.p. Milw. Sch. Engring., 1995—2000; ret., 2000. Cons. Asian Productivity Orgn.; arbitrator Fed. Mediation and Conciliation Svc., Am. Arbitration Assn.; bd. dirs. Badger Meter Co., Milw., 1986-2002; vis. prof. Massey U., New Zealand, 1978-79. Contbr. articles to profl. jours. Bd. dir., v.p. Clay County Water Dist. No. 7, Mo. 2004—; mem. corp. bd. Milw. Sch. Engring., 2000—. With USAF, 1951-55. Recipient Silver medal Tech. U. Budapest, Hungary, 1989. Mem. NSPE, ASME, Wis. Soc. Profl. Engrs. (pres. Milw. chpt. 1993-94, Outstanding Profl. Engr. in Edn. 1993, state-wide treas. 1994-96), Inst. Indsl. Engrs., Am. Soc. Engring. Edn., Soc. Mfg. Engrs., Am. Foundrymen's Soc., Engrs. and Scis. of Milw. (bd. dir. 1988-95, v.p. 1991-93, pres.-elect 1993-94, pres. 1994-95). Office Phone: 816-750-4615. Personal E-mail: cfjames@earthlink.net.

JAMES, DONNA A., diversified financial services company executive; m. Larry James; children: Christopher, Justin. B in Acctg., NC Agrl. & Tech. State U. CPA. Auditor Coopers and Lybrand; with Nationwide Mutual Ins. Co., 1981—, v.p., asst. to chmn. and CEO, 1996, v.p. human resources, 1996—97, sr. v.p. human resources, 1997—99, sr. v.p., chief human resources officer, 1999—2000, exec. v.p., chief adminstrv. officer, 2000—03, dir. life ins. and life and annuity ins., 2001—02, pres. strategic investments, 2003—. Bd. dirs. Ltd. Brands, Inc. Bd. govs. United Way; bd. advisors sch. bus. NC Agrl. Tech. Sate U.; trusussutee Bennett Coll. Recipient Spirit of Advocacy award, 2001, Outstanding African-Am. Woman in Fin. Svcs. award, Mark D. Philmore Urban Bankers, Ohio Women of Courage award. Office: Nationwide Mutual Ins Co One Nationwide Plaza Columbus OH 43215-2220

JAMES, ELIZABETH JOAN PLOGSTED, pediatrician, educator; b. Jefferson City, Mo., Jan. 15, 1939; d. Joseph Matthew Plogsted and Maxie Pearl (Manford) Plogsted Acuff; m. Ronald Carney James, Aug. 25, 1962; children: Susan Elizabeth, Jason Michael. BS in Chemistry, Lincoln U., 1960; MD, U. Mo., 1965. Diplomate Am. Bd. Pediat., Am. Bd. Neonatal-Perinatal Medicine. Resident in pediat. U. Mo. Hosps. & Clinics, Columbia, 1965-68, fellow in neonatology, 1968-69, dir. neonatal-perinatal medicine Children's Hosp., 1971—2007; fellow in neonatal-perinatal medicine U. Colo. Hosps., Denver, 1969-71; from asst. to assoc. prof. pediatrics and obstetrics sch. medicine U. Mo., 1971-83, prof. child health and obstetrics, 1983—. Dir. pediatric edn. program dept. child health sch. medicine U. Mo., Columbia, 1989-98. Mem. editl. bd. Mo. Medicine, 1983—; contbr. chpts. to books and articles to profl. jours. Fellow Am. Acad. Pediat. (sect. neonatal-perinatal medicine); mem. Mo. State Med. Assn., Boone County Med. Soc., Alpha Omega Alpha. Roman Catholic. Avocations: classical music, bicycling, gardening. Office: U Mo Hosps & Clinics Childrens Hosp 1 Hospital Dr Columbia MO 65201-5276 Office Phone: 573-882-7919. Business E-Mail: jamese@health.missouri.edu.

JAMES, FRANCIS EDWARD, JR., investment advisor; b. Woodville, Miss., Jan. 5, 1931; s. Francis Edwin and Ruth (Phillips) J.; m. Iris Senn, Nov. 3, 1952; children: Francis III, Barry, David. BS, La. State U., 1951; MS, Rensselaer Poly. Inst., 1966, PhD, 1967. Commd. 2d lt. USAF, 1950, advanced through grades to col., 1972; prof. mgmt. and statistics, chmn. dept quantitative studies Air Force Inst. Tech., Wright Patterson AFB, 1967-71, dir. grad. edn. div. mgmt. programs, 1972-74; ret. USAF, 1974; chmn. James Investment Rsch., Inc., Alpha, Ohio, 1972—. Cons. math. modeling. Author: A Matrix Solution for the General Linear Regression Model; contbr. articles to profl. jours. Bd. dirs. James Capital Alliance, Inc. Decorated Legion of Merit, D.F.C., Air medal, Joint Services Commendation medal, Meritorious Service medal; recipient Outstanding Acad. Achievement award Rensselaer Poly. Inst., 1965, first Alumni Fellow appointment Rensselaer Poly. Inst. Mem. Am. Statis. Assn., Mil. Ops. Research Soc., Am. Fin. Assn., Investment Counsel Assn. Am., Mktg. Technicians Assn., Soc. Logistics Engring. (Eckles award 1973, tech. chmn.), Sigma Iota Epsilon, Epsilon Delta Sigma. Lodges: Masons; Rotary. Home: 2604 Lantz Rd Dayton OH 45434-6627 Office: James Investment Rsch Inc PO Box 8 Alpha OH 45301-0008 Personal E-mail: drfrankejames@yahoo.com.

JAMES, GEORGE BARKER, II, financial executive; b. Haverhill, Mass., May 25, 1937; s. Paul Withington and Ruth (Burns) J.; m. Beverly A. Burch, Sept. 22, 1962; children: Alexander, Christopher, Geoffrey, Matthew. AB, Harvard U., 1959; MBA, Stanford U., 1962. Fiscal dir. E.G. & G. Inc., Bedford, Mass., 1963-67; fin. exec. Am. Brands Inc., NYC, 1967-69; v.p. Pepsico, Inc., NYC, 1969-72; sr. v.p., chief fin. officer Arcata Corp., Menlo Park, Calif., 1972-82; exec. v.p. Crown Zellerbach Corp., San Francisco, 1982-85; sr. v.p., chief fin. officer Levi Strauss & Co., San Francisco, 1985-98; sr. ptnr. Pacific States Investors Group LLC, 2002—. Bd. dirs. Pacific States Industries, Inc., Sharper Image, Inc., Callious Software Inc. Author: Industrial Development in the Ohio Valley, 1962. Mem. Andover Town Com., Mass., 1965-67; mem. Select Congl. Com. on World Hunger; mem. adv. coun. Calif. State Employees Pension Fund; chmn. bd. dirs. Towle Trust Fund; trustee Nat. Corp. Fund for the Dance, chmn. Cate Sch., Levi Strauss Found., Stern Grove Festival Assn., Zellerbach Family Fund, San Francisco Ballet Assn., Com. for Econ. Devel.; bd. dirs. Stanford U. Hosp., Calif. Pacific Med. Ctr.; dir. KQED Pub. Broadcasting; chmn. World Affairs Coun.; mem. San Francisco Com. on Fgn. Rels.; overseer Hoover Instn., Standford U.; trustee Grace Cathedral, San Francisco. With US Army, 1960-61. Mem. Pacific Union Club, Bohemian Club, Menlo Circus Club, Harvard Club, N.Y. Athletic Club. Home: 207 Walnut St San Francisco CA 94118-2012

JAMES, J. BRADFORD, financial officer; BS in Acctg., Kent State U., 1969; MBA, Case Western Res. U., 1988. CPA. Acct. Arthur Andersen & Co., 1969-73; from corp. contr. to CFO Donn Corp., Westlake, Ohio, 1973-86; v.p. fin. USG Interiors, Inc., 1987-89, sr. v.p., CFO, 1991-94, group v.p. world wide ceilings, 1994-95, exec. v.p., 1995-98; sr. v.p., CFO IMC Global, Northbrook, Ill., 1998—. Office: Imc Global 3033 Campus Dr Ste E490 Minneapolis MN 55441-2655

JAMES, JEFFERSON ANN, performing company executive, choreographer; b. July 12, 1943; d. Robert Mitchell and Dorothea Jefferson (Lewis) Miller; m. Martin Edward James, June 16, 1964; 1 child, Rachel Eleanor. Student, Juilliard Sch. Music, NYC, 1961—63; BFA, Coll. Conservatory Music, U. Cin., 1970. Vis. prof. Western Coll., Oxford, Ohio, 1970—72; artistic dir. Dance '70, Cin., 1970, Contemporary Dance Theater, Cin., 1972—. Bd. dirs. Cin. Commn. on Arts, 1981—87, OhioDance Assn., Cleve., 1984—92, Cleve., 2000—. Choreographer Corbett Awards Finalist, 1975, artist category, 1995; dir.: Corbett Awards (Arts Orgn. 1982, finalist 1990, 95). Mem. presenting/touring panel Ohio Arts Coun., 1993—96; active Cin. Arts Allocation Com., 1994—2000, chmn., 1996—97; cmty. arts coord. for grand opening celebration Aronoff Ctr. for Arts, 1995; mem. steering com. Regional Cultural Planning Com. (Ohio, Ky., Ind.), 1996—98. Recipient Ohio Gov.'s award for the Arts, 1998, Ohio Dance award for contbns. to field, 1999. Office: Contemporary Dance Theater Inc 1805 Larch Ave Cincinnati OH 45224-2928 Home Phone: 513-591-2557; Office Phone: 513-591-2557. Personal E-mail: Jfrsonj@aol.com.

JAMES, LEBRON RAYMONE, professional basketball player; b. Akron, Ohio, Dec. 30, 1984; s. Gloria James and McClelland Anthony; children: LeBron Jr., Bryce Maximus. Forward Cleve. Cavaliers, 2003—. Mem. US Olympic Men's Basketball Team, Athens, 2004, US Men's Basketball Nat. Team, 2006—08. Co-host: ESPY Awards show, 2007; guest host: (TV series) Saturday Night Live, 2007; featured on cover Vogue, 2008. Named Nat. HS Player of Yr., USA Today, 2003, NBA Rookie of Yr., 2004, NBA All-Star Game MVP, 2006, 2008; named one of 100 Most Influential People, Time Mag., 2005, Most Influential People in the World of Sports, Bus. Week, 2007; named to NBA All-Rookie First Team, 2004, Ea. Conf. All-Star Team, NBA, 2005, 2006, 2007, 2008, All-NBA 1st Team, 2006; recipient Bronze medal, Olympic Games, 2004, Espy award for best breakthrough, 2004, Best Male Athlete award, Black Entertainment TV (BET), 2006—07, Espy award for best BA player, 2007. Achievements include being picked number 1 in the 2003 NBA Draft; member of the Bronze Medal-winning 2004 US Olympic Team; youngest player in NBA history to record a triple-double, Jan. 19, 2005; youngest player in NBA history to score 50 points in one game, March 20, 2005; youngest player in NBA history to score 4,000 career points, Nov. 12, 2005; youngest player in NBA history to score 5,000 career points, Jan. 21, 2006; youngest player in NBA history to score 10,000 career points Feb. 27, 2008. Office: Cleveland Cavaliers 1 Center Ct Cleveland OH 44115-4001*

JAMES, MARION RAY, retired publishing executive, editor; b. Bellmont, Ill., Dec. 6, 1940; s. Francis Miller and Lorraine A. (Wylie) James; m. Janet Sue Tennis, June 16, 1960; children: Jeffrey Glenn, David Ray, Daniel Scott, Cheryl Lynne. BS, Oakland City Coll., Ind., 1964; MS, St. Francis Coll., Fort Wayne, Ind., 1978. Sports and city editor Daily Clarion, Princeton, Ind., 1963-65; English tchr. Jac-Cen-Del HS, Osgood, Ind., 1965-66; indsl. editor Whirlpool Corp., Evansville and LaPorte, Ind., 1966-68, Magnavox Govt. and Indsl. Electronics Co., Ft. Wayne, Ind., 1968-79; editor, pub., founder Bowhunter mag., Ft. Wayne, 1971-88, editor-in-chief Kalispell, Mont., 1989-2001, editor emeritus, 2001—06. Instr. Purdue U., Ft. Wayne, 1980—88. Author: Bowhunting for Whitetail and Mule Deer, 1975, Successful Bowhunting, 1985, My Place, 1991, The Bowhunter's Handbook, 1997, Of Blind Pigs and Big Bucks, 2002, Unforgettable Bowhunters, 2007; editor: Pope and Young Book of Bowhunting Records, 1975, 1993, 1999, Bowhunting Adventures, 1977. Named Alumnus of the Yr., Oakland City Coll., 1982; named to Hall of Fame, Mt. Carmel HS, Ill., 1983, Archery Hall of Fame, 2003; recipient Best Editl. award, United Cmty. Svc. Publs., 1970—72. Mem.: Ft. Wayne Assn. Bus. Editors (pres. 1975—76, Ft. Wayne Bus. Editor of the Yr. award 1969), Outdoor Writers Assn. Am. (Excellence in Craft Lifetime Achievement award 1999), Toastmasters (Able Toastmaster award), Pope and Young Club (pres. 2006—), Mu Tau Kappa, Alpha Psi Omega, Alpha Phi Gamma. Home: 11631 Blue Grass Rd Evansville IN 47725 Mailing: PO Box 55 Inglefield IN 47618 Personal E-mail: mrjames12640@aol.com.*

JAMES, PHYLLIS A., lawyer; b. L.I., NY, Mar. 23, 1952; BA magna cum laude in Am. hist. and lit., Harvard U., 1974, JD, 1977. Bar: Calif. 1978, Mich., Fed. Dist. Ct. Calif., US Ct. Appeals (9th cir.). Jud. law clerk Hon. Theodore R. Newman Jr. DC Ct. Appeals, 1977—78; mem. Pillsbury Madison & Sutro, San Francisco, 1979—94; corp. counsel City of Detroit Law Dept., 1994—2001; sr. v.p. and sr. counsel MGM Mirage, Las Vegas, Nev., 2001—. Pursuant State Mich. Trial Ct. Assessment Commn., 1997—98. Recipient Capt. Jonathan Fay prize. Mem.: Mich. Bar Assn., Calif. Bar Assn., Phi Bet Kappa. Office: MGM Mirage 3600 Las Vegas Blvd S Las Vegas NV 89109 Office Phone: 702-693-7590. Office Fax: 702-693-7591. Business E-Mail: phyllis_james@mgmmirage.com.

JAMES, SHERMAN ATHONIA, epidemiologist, educator; b. Hartsville, SC, Oct. 25, 1943; s. Jerome and Helen Genese (Bachus) J.; m. Vera Lucia Moura; children: Sherman Alexander, Scott Anthony. AB, Talladega Coll., 1964; PhD, Washington U., 1973. Prof. epidemiology U. N.C., Chapel Hill, 1973-89, U. Mich., Ann Arbor, 1989—2003, assoc. dean acad. affairs Sch. Pub. Health; prof. pub. policy Duke U., Durham, NC, 2003—. Cons. NIMH, NIH, Bethesda, Md., 1979-83, Nat. Heart, Lung and Blood Inst., 1985—, Nat. Inst. Environ. Health Sci., 1990—; cons. NAS, Washington, 1994—. Contbr. articles to profl. jours. Capt. USAF, 1964-69. Fellow Soc. of Fellows, U. Mich., 1993—. Fellow Am. Heart Assn., Acad. Behavioral Medicine Rsch., Soc. Behavioral Medicine, Am. Coll. Epidemiology; mem. Am. Men and Women of Sci. Inst. Medicine. Avocations: travel, photography, tennis, nature walks. Office: Duke Univ 213 Sanford Inst 90245 Durham NC 27708

JAMES, SHERYL TERESA, journalist; b. Detroit, Oct. 7, 1951; d. Reese Louis and Dava Helen (Bryant) J.; m. Eric Torgeir Vigmostad, June 15, 1974; children: Teresa, Kelsey. BS in English, Ea. Mich. U., 1973. Staff writer, editor Lansing (Mich.) Mag., 1979-82; staff writer Greensboro (N.C.) News & Record, 1982-86, St. Petersburg (Fla.) Times, 1986-91, Detroit Free Press, 1991—. Cons. Poynter Inst., St. Petersburg, 1989—; cons. to high sch. newspapers, St. Petersburg, 1989—. Recipient Penney Missouri Awd. U. Missouri/J.C. Penney, 1985, 1st Pl. Feature Writing Awd. Fla. Soc. Newspaper Editors, 1991, Pulitzer Prize, Feature Writing, 1991, finalist, 1992, Alumna Achievement Awd. Eastern Michigan U., 1992. Democrat. Roman Catholic.

JAMES, TROY LEE, state legislator; b. Texarkana, Tex. s. Samuel and Anniebell James; m. Betty Jean Winslow; 1 child, Laura. Student, Bethany Coll., Case We. Res. U., Fenton Coll. State rep. Dist. 12 Ohio Ho. of Reps., 1967-92, state rep. Dist. 10, 1993—. Chmn. environ. and natural resources com., econ. devel. and small bus. com.; mem. rules, aging and housing com., labor, hwys. and pub. safety com., select com. on Deinstitutionalization, select com. to investigate problems of maintaining basic utility rates; precinct committeeman Ward 11 Dem. Orgn., pres. Mem. Black Elected Dems. Ohio exec. com. Nat. Conf. State Legislatures, Common Fed. Taxation, Trade and Econ. Devel.; mem. Dem. Exec. Coun.; self-employed businessman; with Ohio Crankshaft; bd. dirs. Fedn. Cmty. Planning; mem. Citizen's League, Consumer Protection Agy. Cleve. Recipient Nat. award Nat. Soc. State Legislators, 1974, ENA award Nat. Assn. Career Women, 1978; named Legislator of Yr. Communicative Disorders Commn., 1988. Mem. NAACP, Nat. Soc. Social Workers, Ohio Soc. State Legislators, Phyllis Wheatly Assn. (bd. dirs.), Boy Scouts Am., 40th and 43d St. Neighborhood Block Club, 11th Ward Dem. Club. Fax: 614 644 9494.

JAMES, WILLIAM MORGAN, bishop; Bishop Ch. of God in Christ, Toledo. Office: St James Holiness Ch of God in Christ 3758 Chippendale Ct Toledo OH 43615-1111

JAMES, WILLIAM RAMSAY, broadcast executive; b. South Bend, Ind., Oct. 6, 1933; s. William Stubbs and Rose (Ramsay) James; m. Jane Mehrer, Dec. 29, 1955; children: William Harold, Martha Courtney Quay. BS in Mech. Engring., Princeton U., 1955; MBA, Harvard U., 1960. CPA Mich. Plant mgr. N. A. Woodworth Co., Ferndale, Mich., 1960-62; ptnr. Touche Ross & Co., Detroit, 1962-69; v.p., gen. mgr. Sta. WJR, Detroit, 1969-80; exec. v.p. Capital Cities Comm., NYC, 1980-86, pres. Cable TV div. Bloomfield Hills, Mich., 1980-86; pres. James Comm. Inc., 1986-87; mng. ptnr. James Comm. Ptnrs., Bloomfield Hills, 1988—. Trustee, treas. William Beaumont Hosp., Royal Oak, Mich. 1st lt. USAF, 1956—58. Mem.: AICPA, Mich. Assn. CPAs, Everglades Club (Palm Beach, Fla.), Orchard Lake (Mich.) Country Club, Country Club (Bloomfield Hills). Republican. Episcopalian. Office: James Communications Ptnrs 6150 Highland Rd Waterford MI 48327 Office Phone: 248-886-0337. Personal E-mail: wrj@michigan-aviation.com.

JAMES, WILLIAM W., financial consultant; b. Oct. 12, 1931; s. Will and Clyde (Cowdrey) James; m. Carol Ann Muenter, June 17, 1967; children: Sarah James Banks, David William. AB, Harvard U., 1953. Cert. trust and fin. advisor. Asst. to dir. overseas divsn. Becton Dickinson & Co., Rutherford, NJ, 1956-59; stockbroker Merrill Lynch, Pierce, Fenner & Smith, Inc., St. Louis, 1959-62; with trust divsn. Boatmen's Nat. Bank, St. Louis, 1962-90, v.p. in charge estate planning, sr. v.p., 1972-90; sr. v.p. Boatmen's Trust Co., St. Louis, 1989-96, fin., trust mktg. cons., 1996—. Mem. gift and bequest coun. Barnes Hosp., St. Louis, 1963—67, St. Louis U., 1972—78; dir. Mark Twain Summer Inst., St. Louis, 1987—92. With US Army, 1953—55. Mem.: Am. Inst. Banking, Mo. Bankers Assn., Estate Planning Coun. St. Louis, Harvard Alumni Assn. (bd. dirs. 1987—90), Noonday Club (St. Louis), Mo. Athletic Club, Harvard Faculty Club (Cambridge, Mass.), Harvard Club St. Louis (pres. 1972—73). Republican. Home: 1415 Michele Dr Saint Louis MO 63122-1404

JAMESON, J(AMES) LARRY, chemical company executive; b. Elizabethtown, Ky., 1937; s. William Kendrick and Ruth Helen (Krause) J.; m. Mary Louise Wojcik, June 26, 1965; children: Renee, Jennifer, Julie. BA in Math., Bellarmine Coll., 1959; BS in Chem. Engring., U. Detroit, 1963, MBA, 1970. Tech. mgr. automotive products Rinshed Mason et Cie, Paris, 1965-69; ops. mgr. vinyl coated fabrics Inmont Corp., Toledo, 1969-75, v.p., gen. mgr. European ops. London, 1975-79, v.p., gen. mgr. automotive finishes products Detroit, 1979-83, sr. v.p. worldwide automotive, 1983-86; pres. Coatings & Colorants div. BASF, Clifton, N.J., 1986-93; pres., CEO Pirelli Cable Corp., Florham Park, N.J., 1993-96; v.p. Ferro Chem. Corp., Cleve., 1996—. Mem. Soc. Automotive Engrs., Orchard Lake Country Club, The Country Club. Avocations: golf, tennis, skiing, hunting. Office: Ferro Corp 1000 Lakeside Ave E Cleveland OH 44114-1147

JAMESON, JAMES LARRY, medical educator, endocrinologist, internist; b. Fort Benning, Georgia, June 21, 1954; MD, U. North Carolina, Chapel Hill, 1981. Cert. NBME, 1982, Am. Bd. Internal Medicine, 1985, Endocrinology & Metabolism, 1987. Intern Mass. Gen. Hospital, Boston, 1981—82, resident, 1982—83, fellow, 1983—85; rsch. assoc. Howard Hughes Medical Inst., Boston, 1985—87; asst. physician Mass. Gen. Hospital, Boston, 1987—92, chief thyroid unit, 1987—93; asst. prof. Harvard Medical Sch., Boston, 1987—92, assoc. prof., 1992—93; dir. molecular biology Mass. Gen. Hospital, Boston, 1991—93, assoc. physician, 1992—93; dir. endocrinology & metabolism Northwestern U., 1993, Irving S. Cutter prof. medicine div. endocrinology, metabolism, & molecular medicine, 1993—, chmn. medicine, 1993—. Fellow: Am. Acad. Arts & Sciences; mem.: Inst. Medicine. Office: Northwestern U Galter Pavilion Ste 3-150 251 E Huron St Chicago IL 60611

JAMESON, JENNIFER A., lawyer; BA, U. Minn., 1996, JD cum laude, 1999. Bar: Minn. 1999. Law clk. to Hon. Gary Larson Hennepin County Dist. Ct., 2000; assoc. McGrann, Shea, Anderson, Carnival, Straughn & Lamb, Chartered, Mpls. Vol. Chrysalis Legal Progs., 2001—. Named a Rising Star, Minn. Super Lawyers mag., 2006. Mem.: Minn. Women Lawyers, Minn. State Bar Assn., Collaborative Law Inst. Office: McGrann Shea Anderson Carnival Straughn & Lamb Chartered 2600 US Bancorp Ctr 800 Nicollet Mall Minneapolis MN 55402 Office Phone: 612-338-2525. E-mail: jaj@mcgrannshea.com.

JAMPEL, ROBERT STEVEN, ophthalmologist, educator; b. NYC, Nov. 3, 1926; s. Carl Edward and Frances (Hirschman) J.; m. Joan I. Myers, Oct. 2, 1952; children— Henry, Delia, James, Emily. AB, Columbia U., NYC, 1946, MD, 1950; MS, U. Mich., Ann Arbor, 1957, PhD, 1958. Assoc. in ophthalmology Columbia U., NYC, 1962-69, asst. prof. ophthalmology, 1969-70; prof., chmn. ophthalmology Wayne State U., Detroit, 1970—, dir. Kresge Eye Inst., 1970—. Served to lt. USN, 1952-54 Mem. Am. Acad. Ophthalmology, Assn. Research in Vision, Assn. Univ. Profs. Ophthalmology, Acad. Neurology. Home: 4363 Barchester Dr Bloomfield Hills MI 48302-2116 Office: Hutzel Hosp 4717 St Antoine St Detroit MI 48201-1423

JANAK, PETER HAROLD, retired automotive company executive; b. Detroit; BS in Aerospace Engring., Miss. State U., 1963; grad. exec. program, Stanford U., 1994. Rsch. fluid amplifiers dept. aerospace engring. Miss. State U., State College, 1962—63; propulsion engr. space disvn. Chrysler Corp., New Orleans, 1963—65; from sr. engr. to chief performance analysis sect. Teledyne-Brown Engring., Hunstville, Ala., 1965—68; head propulsion tech. sect. TRW Def. and Space Sys. Group, Houston, 1968—71, mgr. surveillance sys. engring. McLean, Va., 1972—78, mgr. signal processing sys. dept., 1978—79, mgr. SURTASS engring., 1979—80, mgr. undersea surveillance projects and combat sys., 1980—83, mgr. def. sys. ops. Fairfax, Va., 1987—90, mgr. tax modernization program, 1990—92, dep. gen. mgr. divsn. info svcs., 1992—94, v.p., gen. mgr. divsn. info. svcs., 1994—95; mgr. propulsion sys. dept. Technologieforschung, GmbH, Stuttgart, Germany, 1971—72; v.p., dep. gen. mgr. ea. divsn. PRC Sys. Svcs., McLean, 1983—84, pres., gen. mgr. divsn. sys. engring. and analysis, 1984—87; v.p., chief info. officer TRW Inc., Cleve., 1995—98; chief info. officer Delphi Automotive Sys., Troy, Mich., 1998—99; v.p., chief info. officer Delphi Corp., Troy, 1999—2003. Mem. external rsch. adv. bd. Miss. State U. Mem.: IEEE, Conf. Bd., Working Coun. Chief Info. Officers, Soc. Automotive Engrs., Soc. Mfg. Engrs.

JANEZICH, JERRY R., state legislator, small business owner; b. Mar. 16, 1950; m. Patricia Janezich; three children. BS, St. Cloud State U. Small bus. owner; former Dist. 5B rep. Minn. Ho. of Reps., St. Paul, 1992—; now senator Minn. State Senate. Vice chmn. judiciary, local govt. and met. affairs com., mem. commerce, regulated industries and taxes coms., Minn. Ho. of Reps. Home: 12991 Rudstrom Rd Side Lake MN 55781-8462

JANICAK, PHILIP GREGORY, psychiatrist, educator; b. Chgo., Aug. 2, 1946; s. Edward and Josephine (Raskauskas) J.; m. Mary Judith Cray, Oct. 16, 1976; 1 child, Matthew Cray. BS in Psychology with honors, Loyola U., Chgo., 1969, MD, 1973. Diplomate Am. Bd. Psychiatry and Neurology. Asst. clin. prof. dept. psychiatry Loyola U., Maywood, Ill., 1976-78; rsch. assoc. U. Chgo., 1979-81; asst. prof. U. Ill., Chgo., 1982-85, assoc. prof., 1986-92, prof., 1992—2004, Rush U., 2004—. Chief rsch. unit Ill. State Psychiat. Inst., Chgo., 1984-96; med. dir. psychiat. clin. rsch. ctr. U. Ill., 1996-2004, Rush U., 2004-. First author: Principles and Practice of Psychopharmacotherapy, 1993, 4th edit., 2006. NIMH grant co-investigator, 1986, 91, 93; NIMH grant prin. investigator, 1990; IH grant assoc. program dir. 2000-2004. Fellow Am. Psychiat. Assn. (disting. fellow). Roman Catholic. Business E-Mail: pjanicak@rush.edu.

JANICK, JULES, horticultural scientist, educator; b. NYC, Mar. 16, 1931; s. Henry Spinner and Frieda (Tullman) Janick; m. Shirley Reisner, June 15, 1952; children: Peter Aaron, Robin Helen Janick Weinberger. BS, Cornell U., 1951; MS, Purdue U., 1952, PhD, 1954; DS in Agr. (hon.), U. Bologna, Italy, 1990; Doctor (hon.), Tech. U., Lisbon, Portugal, 1994. Instr. Purdue U., West Lafayette, 1954-56, asst. prof., 1956-59, assoc. prof., 1959-63, prof., 1963-88, James Troop Disting. prof. in horticulture, 1988—; dir. Purdue Ctr. for New Crops and Plant Products, 1990—. Cons. Food and Agrl. Orgn., Rome, Italy, 1988. Author: Horticultural Science, 4th edit., 1986, Classical Papers in Horticultural Science, 1989; co-author: Plant Science: An Introduction to World Crops, 3d edit., 1981; co-editor: Advances in Fruit Breeding, 1975, Methods in Fruit Breeding, 1983, Advances in New Crops, 1990, New Crops, 1993, Fruit Breeding (3 vols.), 1996; editor: Hort. Revs., Plant Breeding Revs., Progress in New Crops, 1996, Perspectives on New Crops and New Uses, 1999, Trends in ew Crops and New Uses, 2002. Fellow AAAS, Portuguese Hort. Assn., Am. Soc. Hort. Sci. (pres. 1986-87), Internat. Soc. Hort. Sci. Jewish. Avocation: drawing.

Home: 420 Forest Hill Dr West Lafayette IN 47906-2316 Office: Dept Horticulture and Landscape Architecture Purdue U 625 Agriculture Mall Dr West Lafayette IN 47907-2010 Home Phone: 765-463-5411. E-mail: janick@purdue.edu.

JANIS, F. TIMOTHY, technology company executive; b. Chgo., Apr. 11, 1940; s. Fabian M. and Phyllis (Underwood) Janiszewski; m. Kathryn Dickey; children: Mark David, Paul Joseph, Melissa Ann. BS in Chemistry, Wichita State U., 1962, MS in Chemistry, 1963; PhD in Chemistry, Ill. Inst. Tech., 1968. Asst., then assoc. prof. chemistry Ill. Benedictine Coll., Lisle, Ill., 1969-74; asst. acad. dean Franklin (Ind.) Coll., 1974-77; divn. dir. Indpls. Ctr. for Advanced Rsch., 1977-92; founder and pres. ARAC, Inc., Franklin, Ind., 1992—. Cons. Argonne (Ill.) Nat. Lab., 1968-74, Office Pers. Mgmt., Denver, 1988-94; mem. adv. bd. R&D Enterprise Asia Pacific, 1999. Co-author: Moving R&D to Marketplace, 1993, rev. edit., 1995, 25 publs. on tech. transfer; internat. editor Tech. Bus. Mag., 1998-2000. Mem. Lisle Cmty. High Sch. Bd., 1970-72; bd. dirs. Near North Devel. Corp., Indpls., 1990-94. Named Sagamore of the Wabash, Gov. of State of Ind., 1990. Mem. Tech. Transfer Soc. (treas., pres. 1990-92, exec. dir. 1993-96). Roman Catholic. Avocations: golf, reading, sightseeing. Office: 604 Davis Dr Franklin IN 46131-7682 Home Phone: 317-736-8218. Office Fax: 317-738-3980. Business E-Mail: tjanis@aracinc.com.

JANKE, RONALD ROBERT, lawyer; b. Milw., Mar. 2, 1947; s. Robert Erwin and Elaine Patricia (Wilken) J.; m. Mary Ann Burg, July 3, 1971; children—Jennifer, William, Emily. B.A. cum laude, Wittenberg U., 1969; J.D. with distinction, Duke U., 1974. Bar: Ohio 1974. Assoc. Jones Day, Cleve., 1974-83, ptnr., 1984—. Served with U.S. Army, 1970-71, Vietnam. Mem. ABA (chmn. environ. control com. 1980-83), Ohio Bar Assn., Greater Cleve. Bar Assn., Environ. Law Inst. Office: Jones Day N Point 901 Lakeside Ave E Cleveland OH 44114-1190 Office Phone: 216-586-7279. Business E-Mail: rrjanke@jonesday.com.

JANOS, JAMES See VENTURA, JESSE

JANSEN, JAMES STEVEN, lawyer; b. Marshalltown, Iowa, Mar. 16, 1948; s. Virgil Charles and Virginia Rae (Hiatt) J.; m. Patricia Jean Beard, Nov. 24, 1984; children: Katherine, Emily, Ashley, Kristen. BS in Edn., U. Nebr., 1970; JD, Creighton U., 1973. Bar: Nebr. 1974, U.S. Dist. Ct. Nebr. 1974. Dep. county atty. County of Douglas, Omaha, 1974-78, county atty., 1991—2003; assoc. Naviaux, Kinney, Jansen and Dosek, Omaha, 1979-83; from assoc. to ptnr. Stave, Coffey, Swenson, Jansen and Schatz, Omaha, 1984—90; assoc. atty. McGrath, North, Mullin and Kratz PC LLO, Omaha, 2003—05, ptnr., 2005—. Bd. dirs. Domestic Violence Coord. Coun. Greater Omaha, 1996-2003, co-chair, 1996-97, chmn., 1997-98; bd. dirs. Omaha Cmty. Partnership, 1991-2003, chmn., 2000-01; mem. ebr. Drug and Violent Crime Policy Bd., Lincoln, 1991-98, bd. dirs. Project Harmony Child Protection Ctr., 1996—, chmn., 1998. Mem. Nebr. State Bar Assn., Omaha Bar Assn., Nebr. County Atty.'s Assn. (bd. dirs. 1991—98, pres. 1997-98). Democrat. Roman Catholic. Avocations: golf, reading. Office: McGrath North Mullin and Kratz PC LLD 3700 First National Tower 1601 Dodge St Omaha NE 68102 Office Phone: 402-341-3070. Business E-Mail: jjansen@mcgrathnorth.com.

JANSSEN, RAMON E., state legislator; b. Hooper, Nebr., July 5, 1937; m. Nancy Janssen; children: Nick, Michael, Nola. Owner City Meat Market, Hooper, Nebr., ickerson Meat Market; mem. Nebr. legislature from 15th dist., Lincoln, 1992—; mem. bldg. maintenance, edn., agrl. Nebr. Legislature, Lincoln, mem. govt., mil., and vet. affairs coms., chmn. gen. affairs com. Bd. dirs. Farmer's Home Ins. Co. Mem. Hooper Comml. Club, Elkhorn Valley Golf Club (past pres.), Lions Club. Address: Nebr State Senate State Capitol Rm 1015 Lincoln NE 68509 Also: PO Box 159 Nickerson NE 68044-0159

JANTZ, KENNETH M., construction executive; b. Boise, Idaho; m. Linda Rae Bennett. Assoc. in Sci., Boise Jr. Coll., 1964; BS, Idaho State Univ., 1966. V.p., treas. Peter Kiewit Sons, Omaha, 1992—2000; mgmt. Morrison Knudsen. Recipient Profl. Achievement award, Idaho State Univ. Coll. Bus., 2004.

JANZEN, PETER S., lawyer, food products executive; b. Chgo., Apr. 2, 1959; BA in Polit. Sci., Hamline U., 1981, JD, 1984. Bar: Minn. 1984. With law dept. Land O' Lakes Inc., 1983—, v.p., gen. counsel, 2003—. Mem.: US Trademark Assn., ABA, Minn. State Bar Assn. Office: Land O Lakes Inc 4001 Lexington Ave N Saint Paul MN 55126 Office Phone: 651-481-2222. Office Fax: 651-481-2832.

JAQUA, RICHARD ALLEN, pathologist; b. Fort Dodge, Iowa, Apr. 15, 1938; s. John Franklin and Esther J.; m. Mary Joanne Stewart, Dec. 29, 1969 BA magna cum laude, Yale U., 1960; MD, Harvard U., 1965. Diplomate: Am. Bd. Pathology, Am. Bd. Nuclear Medicine. Teaching fellow pathology Harvard Med. Sch., 1965-67; resident clin. pathology NIH, 1967-69; intern pathology Mass. Gen. Hosp., Boston, 1965-66; fellow tumor pathology Meml.-Sloane Kettering Cancer Center, NYC, 1969-70; asst. prof. pathology U. S.D. Sch. Medicine, Vermillion, 1970-73, asso. prof., 1973-74, asso. prof., acting chmn. dept. lab. medicine, 1974-77, prof., chmn. dept. lab. medicine, 1977—2002, dir. Electron Microscopy Lab. and Clin. Virology Lab., 1979—2002; pathologist VA Hosp., Sioux Falls, SD, 1978—2002; physician Lab. Clin. Medicine, Sioux Falls, 1970—2002. Part-time prof. pathology Sch. Medicine U. S.D., 2003—; prof. emeritus U. S.D. Sch. Medicine. Served with USPHS, 1967-69. Recipient Outstanding Prof. awards U. SD Med. Students, 1971, 75, 77, U. SD Faculty Recogition award, 1986, U. SD Sci. Faculty award, Student Am. Med. Assn., 1992, Lifetime Achievement award, 2002, U. SD Centennial Tchg. award, 2007; VA grantee, 1980-82. Fellow Coll. Am. Pathologists, Am. Soc. Clin. Pathologists; mem. AAAS, Sigma Xi, Alpha Omega Alpha. Home: 27546 483rd Ave Canton SD 57013-5511 Office: USD Health Sci Ctr 1400 W 22nd St Sioux Falls SD 57105-1505 Business E-Mail: rjaqua@usd.edu.

JAQUES, DAMIEN PAUL, theater critic; b. Oak Park, Ill., Nov. 3, 1946; s. Norman Sands and Marion Esther (Werle) J.; m. Patricia A. Mehigan, July 7, 1976 (div. May 1989). BA, Marquette U., 1968. Field organizer, transp. aide Robert Kennedy Presdl. Campaign, Wis., Ind., Calif., 1968; campaign mgr. Carol Bauman Candidate for Congress, Milw., 1968; reporter Sheboygan (Wis.) Press, 1968-69, Evening Press, Binghamton, N.Y., 1969-72; reporter, music critic Milw. Jour., 1972-77, entertainment copy editor, 1977-80, theater critic, 1980—; corr. Back Stage, 1994—; host weekly radio prgm. Milwaukee Presents WHAD. Mem. Am. Theatre Critics Assn. (jurist Outstanding New Play award 1983-93, exec. bd., 1985-88, 1994-97, dir. Found., 1994-97). Avocations: travel, reading, cooking, fishing. Office: The Milwaukee Journal Sentinel PO Box 371 Milwaukee WI 53201-0371

JARBOE, MARK ALAN, lawyer; b. Flint, Mich., Aug. 19, 1951; s. Lloyd Aloysius and Helen Elizabeth (Frey) J.; m. Patricia Kovel, Aug. 20, 1971; 1 child, Alexander. Student, No. Mich. U., 1968-69; AB with high distinction, U. Mich., 1972; JD magna cum laude, Harvard U., 1975. Bar: Minn. 1975, U.S. Dist. Ct. Minn. 1975, U.S. Ct. Appeals (8th cir.) 1975, U.S. Ct. Appeals (7th cir.) 1993. Law clk. to presiding justice Minn. State Ct., St. Paul, 1975-76; from assoc. to ptnr. Dorsey & Whitney LLP, Mpls., 1976-81, ptnr., 1982—, and chmn., Indian law practice group and Indian & gaming practice group, mem. policy com., 1991, 2005—. Lectr. U. Minn. Law Sch., Hamline U. Sch. Law. Contbr. articles to profl. jours. Pres. parish coun. Ch. of Christ the King, Mpls., 1981-83. Mem. Minn. Am. Indian Bar Assn., Mensa, Phi Beta Kappa. Republican. Roman Catholic. Office: Dorsey & Whitney LLP 50 S 6th St Ste 1500 Minneapolis MN 55402-1498 Office Phone: 612-340-2686. Office Fax: 612-340-2868. Personal E-mail: jarboe.mark@gmail.com. Business E-Mail: jarboe.mark@dorsey.com.

JAROS, MIKE, state legislator, administrative assistant; b. Apr. 12, 1944; m. Annette Nordine; three children. BA, U. Minn. Exec. asst. U. Minn., Duluth; Dist. 7B rep. Minn. Ho. of Reps., St. Paul, 1973-80, 85—. Former chmn. higher edn. divsn. edn. com., Minn. Ho. of Reps., former mem. labor-mgmt. rels. com.; chmn. commerce and econ. devel.-internat. trade, technology and econ. devel. divsn. coms., mem. taxes com. Recipient Nat. Scholastic Press award, at. Latin Testing award. Office: 559 State Office Bldg Saint Paul MN 55155-0001

JARRETT, CHARLES ELWOOD, lawyer, insurance company executive; b. Abilene, Tex., Apr. 11, 1957; s. Jerry Vernon and Martha (McCabe) J.; m. Stephanie J. Baker, Apr. 16, 1988; 1 child, Megan McCabe. AB, Dartmouth Coll., 1980; JD, U. Mich., 1983. Bar: Mass. 1984, US Dist. Ct. (dist. Mass.) 1984, Ohio 1986, US Dist. Ct. (no. dist. Ohio) 1986, US Ct. Appeals (6th cir.) 1987, US Supreme Ct. 1988. Assoc. Choate, Hall & Stewart, Boston, 1984-86, Baker & Hostetler, Cleve., 1986-90, ptnr., 1990—2000; chief legal officer The Progressive Corp., Ohio, 2000—, sec., v.p. Ohio, 2001—. Office: Progressive Corp 6300 Wilson Mills Rd Mayfield OH 44143

JARRETT, VALERIE BOWMAN, real estate company executive, former stock exchange executive; b. Shiraz, Iran, Nov. 14, 1956; d. James Edward and Barbara (Taylor) B.; 1 child, Laura Allison. BA, Stanford U., 1978; JD, U. Mich., 1981. Bar: Ill. 1981, U.S. Dist. Ct. (no. dist.) Ill. 1981. Assoc. Pope, Ballard, Shepard & Fowle Ltd., Chgo., 1981-84, Sonnenschein, Carlin, Nath & Rosenthal, Chgo., 1984—87; dep. corp. counsel for fin. and devel. City of Chgo., 1987—91, dep. chief of staff for Mayor Richard Daley, 1991—95, commr., dept. planning and devel.; chmn. Chgo. Transit Authority, 1995—2003; exec. v.p., mng. dir. The Habitat Co., Chgo., 1995—2007, CEO, 2007—. Bd. dirs. USG Corp., 1998—, Joyce Found., Met. Planning Coun., Chgo. Stock Exch. Inc., 2000—07, chmn., 2004—07, Local Initiative Support Corp.; exec. counsel Chgo. Metropolis 2020. Dir. RREEF Am. II, Navigant Cons., Inc.; pres. Southeast Chgo. Commn., Chicago-land C. of C.; trustee Mus. Sci. and Industry, Windows to the World Comm., U. Chgo.; vice chmn. U. Chgo. Hosps. Leadership Greater Chgo. fellow, 1985-86; recipient Govt. Support award, Women's Bus. Devel. Ctr., 1992 Mem. Econ. Club, Comml. Club. Democrat. Avocation: travel. Office: The Habitat Co 350 West Hubbard St Chicago IL 60610 Office Phone: 312-527-5400.

JARTZ, JOHN G., food company executive; b. 1953; With Quaker Oats Co., Chgo., 1980—, sr. v.p. bus. devel., corp. sec., gen. counsel, 1997—. Office: The Quaker Oats Co 555 W Monroe St Chicago IL 60661-3716

JARVEY, JOHN ALFRED, federal judge; b. Mpls., 1956; BS, U. Akron, 1978; JD, Drake U., 1981. Law clk. to Hon. Donald E. O'Brien U.S. Dist. Ct. (no. dist.) Iowa, Cedar Rapids, 1981-83; trial atty. US Dept. Justice, Washington, 1983-87; chief magistrate judge US Dist. Ct. (no. dist.) Iowa, Cedar Rapids, 1987—2007; dist. judge US Dist. Ct. (so. dist.) Iowa, 2007—. Office: US Dist Ct 123 E Walnut St Rm 300 PO Box 9344 Des Moines IA 50306

JÄRVI, NEEME, conductor, music director; b. Tallinn, Estonia, June 7, 1937; arrived in U.S., 1980; s. August and Elss Jarvi; m. Liilia Jarvi, Sept. 2, 1961; children: Paavo Jarvi, Kristjan Jarvi, Maarika Jarvi. Diploma in Music and Conducting, St. Petersburg State Conservatorium, USSR, 1960; doctorate (hon.), U. Aberdeen, Scotland, Music Conservatory Tallinn, Estonia, Gothenberg U., Sweden, U. Mich. Condr. Estonian Radio Symphony Orch., 1960-63, chief condr., 1963-76, Estonian State Opera, 1963-76, Estonian State Symphony, 1976-80; prin. condr. Gothenburg (Sweden) Symphony Orch., 1982—; prin. condr., music dir., condr. laureate Royal Scottish Orch., Glasgow, 1984-88; music dir. Detroit Symphony Orch., 1990—2005, music dir. emeritus, 2005—. Prin. guest condr. Birmingham Symphony Orch., England, 1980—83; guest condr. N.Y. Philharm. Orch., Boston Symphony Orch., Phila. Orch., Chgo. Symphony, Royal Concertgebow, Amsterdam, Philharmonia London, London Symphony, Scandinavian Orch., Met. Opera House, NYC. Rec. artist music of Ellington, Barber, Beach and Ives with DSO, rec. artist Sibelius Symphony, Stenhammar Symphony, Berwald Symphony, Dvorak Symphony, Gade Symphony, Svendsen Symphony, Brahms Symphony, R. Strauss Symphony, Glasounov Symphony, Eduard Tubin Schostakovitch Symphony, Prokoffiev Symphony, Rimski-Korsakov Symphony, Part Symphony. Decorated Knight Comdr. orth Star Order Sweden; recipient 1st prize in conducting, Accademia Nazionale di Santa Cecilia, 1971.

JARVI, PAAVO, conductor, music director; b. Tallinn, Estonia, 1963; U.S., 1980, arrived in US, 1980, naturalized; Studied at, Curtis Inst. of Music, Los Angeles Philharm. Inst. Prin. guest condr. Royal Stockholm Philharm., City of Birmingham, Eng.; music dir., condr. Cin. Symphony Orch., 2001—. Condr. UBS Verbier Youth Orch. (summer series); artistic adv. Estonian Nat. Symphony Orch., 2002—; guest condr. London Symphony, London Philharm., Orch. of the Age of Enlightenment, BBC Philharm., Atlanta Symphony Orch., Boston Symphony Orch., Cleveland Symphony Orch., Chgo. Symphony Orch., Dallas Symphony Orch., Detroit Symphony Orch., Houston Symphony Orch., LA Symphony Orch., Montreal Symphony Orch., Phila. Symphony Orch., Pitts. Symphony Orch., San Francisco Symphony Orch., Toronto Symphony Orch. Named Editor's Choice, Feb. 2003 edit. of Gramophone; recipient Kultuurkapital award, Estonian Min. of Culture, Spirit of Cin. Queen City Adv. award, 2004. Office: CSO Administrative Offices Music Hall 1241 Elm St Cincinnati OH 45202

JARVIS, GILBERT ANDREW, humanities educator, writer; b. Chelsea, Mass., Feb. 13, 1941; s. Vernon Owen and Angeline M. (Burkard) J.; m. Carol Jean Ganter, Jan. 26, 1963; children: Vicki Lynn, Mark Christopher. BA, St. Norbert Coll., De Pere, Wis., 1963; MA, Purdue U., 1965, PhD, 1970. Prof. Ohio State U., Columbus, 1970-95, chmn. humanities edn., 1980-83, assoc. chmn. dept. ednl. theory and practice, 1983-87, chmn. dept. ednl. studies, 1987-95, dir. ESL programs, 1994-2000, chmn. prof. emeritus, 1995—. Cons. Internat. Edn. Program, U.S. Dept. Edn., Washington, 1977-84, others. Author: Et Vous?, 1983, 3d edit., 1989; Invitation, 1979, 4th edit., 1993, Y tu?, 1986, 2d edit., 1988, Connaître et se connaître, 3d edit., 1986, Invitation Essentials, 1991, 2d edit., 1995, Invitation au monde francophone, 2000, 2d edit., 2005; editor: The Challenge for Excellence, 1984; mem. editl. bd. Modern Lang. Jour., 1979-86; adv. bd. Can. Modern lang. Rev., 1982-2006. Mem. Am. Coun. Tchg. Fgn. Langs. (editor Rev. Fgn. Lang. Edn. 1974, 75, 76, 77), Phi Delta Kappa. Avocations: travel, photography. Home: 8337 Evangeline Dr Columbus OH 43235-1136

JARVIS, LINDA MARIE, music director, educator; b. Minneapolis, Minn., Oct. 17, 1954; d. Lyle Dayton and Edna Walker Bergseth; children: Kathryn, Paul. BA Music Edn., Augsburg Coll., 1976. Organist/choir dir. Mt. Olivet Luth. Ch., Minneapolis, Minn., 1977—87; music tchr. Hopkins Pub. Schools, Minnetonka, Minn., 1992—; dir. of music ministry St. Philip the Deacon Luth. Ch., Plymouth, Minn., 1996—; freelance performer and instr. Minneapolis, Minn. Repertoire and stds. chmn. Am. Choral Dirs. Assn. of Minn., Eden Prairie, Minn., 2000—. Singer: (choral workshop) Carnegie Hall, 2000. Mem.: Am. Guild Organists, Am. Choral Dirs. Assn. Lutheran. Avocations: hiking, skiing, travel. Office: Hopkins N Jr HS 10700 Cedar Lake Rd Minnetonka MN 55305 Home: 309 Sunset Dr S Hopkins MN 55305-1149

JASIEK, JERRY, professional sports team executive; m. Tammy Jasiek. BS in Acctg., U. Ill., 1982. Sr. v.p., hockey adminstr. St. Loius Blues Hockey Club, 1997—. Office: Savvis Ctr 1401 Clark Ave Saint Louis MO 63103-2709

JASPAN, STANLEY S., lawyer; b. NYC, Apr. 13, 1946; BS, Cornell U., 1968; JD, Yale U., 1971. Bar: Wis. 1971. Mng. ptnr. Foley & Lardner LLP, Milw., 1999—. Lectr. in law, adj. assoc. prof. Marquette U. Law Sch., 1978-88. Mng. editor: Yale Law Jour., 1970-71. Mem. ABA, State Bar Wis., N.Y. State Bar Assn., Milw. Bar Assn. Office: Foley & Lardner LLP Firstar Ctr 777 E Wisconsin Ave Ste 3800 Milwaukee WI 53202-5367 Office Phone: 414-297-5814. Business E-Mail: sjaspan@foley.com.

JAST, RAYMOND JOSEPH, lawyer; b. Joliet, Ill., July 14, 1947; s. Francis Anthony and Mary Gertrude (Wilhemi) J.; m. Susan Ann Hoffstein (div. 1976); m. Mary Elizabeth Etzel, May 30, 1981; 1 child, Alyson Mary. BA, MacMurray coll., 1969; JD, U. Mich., 1972. Bar: Ill. 1972, DC 1973, US Dist. Ct. (no. and ctrl. dist.) Ill., US Ct. Appeals (7th and 10th cir.). Asst. to dir. bureau of consumer protection FTC, Washington, 1972-75; ptnr. Peterson & Ross, Chgo., 1975-95, Wilson Elser Moskowitz Edelman & Dicker, Chgo., 1995—. Mem. ABA (mem. Torts adn Insurance Practice Sect.), Profl. Liablity Underwriting Soc. (adv. bd.), Dirs. and Officers Liability Reporter. Roman Catholic. Avocations: deer hunting, jogging. Home: 567 Oak St Winnetka IL 60093-2649 Office: Wilson Elser et al 120 N La Salle St Chicago IL 60602-2424 Office Phone: 312-704-0550 143. Office Fax: 312-701-1522. Business E-Mail: raymond.jastr@wilsonelser.com.

JAUDES, RICHARD EDWARD, lawyer; b. St. Louis, Feb. 22, 1943; s. Leo August, Jr. and Dorothy Catherine (Schmidt) Jaudes; m. Mary Kay Tansey, Sept. 22, 1967; children: Michele, Pamela. BS, St. Louis U., 1965, JD, 1968. Bar: Mo. 1968, U.S. Dist. Ct. (ea. dist.) Mo. 1973, U.S. Ct. Appeals (8th cir.) 1973, U.S. Supreme Ct. 1990. With Peper, Martin, Jensen, Maichel & Hetlage, St. Louis, 1973-97, mng. ptnr., 1990-93; ptnr., chair labor and employment practice group Thompson Coburn LLP, St. Louis, 1997—, mem. mgmt. com., 1997—2000. Bd. dirs. Baldor Electric Co. Vol. counsel St. Louis chpt. MS Soc., 1990—. Lt. USN, 1968—73, comdr. USNR. Office: Thompson Coburn LLP One US Bank Plz Saint Louis MO 63101-1693 Home Phone: 314-821-2659; Office Phone: 314-552-6431. E-mail: rjaudes@thompsoncoburn.com.

JAVOSKY, RUDOLPH V., retail executive; b. Toronto; m. Carole Javosky; 3 children. Grad, McGill U. Sr. design ptnr. Bregman + Hamann Architectural and Engring. Firm, Toronto; exec. v.p. design and constrn. Campeau Corp., 1987—88; sr. v.p., store design and constrn. Federated Dept. Stores, 1988—. Mem.: AIA, Inst. Store Planners, Royal Archtl. Inst. Canada, Nat. Assn. Store Fixture Manufacturers. Office: Federated Dept Stores Inc 7 West 7th St Cincinnati OH 45202

JAY, BURTON DEAN, insurance actuary; b. Sparta, Ill., Jan. 16, 1937; m. Eva May Eudy, Aug. 10, 1958; children— Cynthia Ann, Sylvia Ruth Putnam, Jon Russell. BA in Math, Ripon Coll., 1959. Actuarial student Northwestern Nat. Life Ins. Co., Mpls., summers 1957-59; various actuarial positions United of Omaha Life Ins. Co., Omaha, 1962-67, exec. v.p., chief actuary, 1967-91; sen., v.p. actuary Mut. of Omaha Ins. Co., 1991—. Bd. dirs. Omaha Ballet, 1986-95, exec. com., 1988-89, v.p. fin., 1988-89. 1st lt. AUS, 1959-62. Fellow Soc. Actuaries (part VI com. 1967-73, chmn. 1969-73, program com. 1975-80, chmn. 1980, planning com. 1986-88, task force on long term care valuation methods 1991-95, bd. govs. 1982-86, 88-90, v.p. 1985-86, 88-90, chmn. com. on health fin. issues 1993-98); mem. Am. Acad. Actuaries (com. on life ins. fin. reporting principles 1975-82, chmn. 1980-82, bd. dirs. 1981-88, treas. 1983-86, v.p. 1986-88, state health com. 1997—, chmn. 1997—, chmn. health orgn. risk based capital task force 1997-99, valuation task force 1997—), Life Ins. Mktg. Rsch. Assn. (fin. mgmt. rsch. com. 1974-78, chmn. 1977-78), Am. Coun. Life Ins. (actuarial com. 1983). Methodist (adminstrv. bd.). Home: 3056 Armbrust Dr Omaha NE 68124-2723 Office: Mutual of Omaha Ins Co Mutual Of Omaha Plz Omaha NE 68175-0001

JAYABALAN, VEMBLASERRY, nuclear medicine physician, radiologist; b. India, Apr. 3, 1937; came to U.S., 1970; s. Parameswaran and Janakay (Amma) Menon; m. Vijayam Jayabalan, May 2, 1963; children: Kishore, Suresh. B.Sc., Madras Christian Coll., India, 1955; M.B., BS, U. Madras, 1961; Diploma in Med. Radioagnosis, U. Liverpool, Eng., 1967. Diplomate: Am. Bd. Radiology, Am. Bd. Nuclear Medicine. Intern Jipmer Hosp., Pondicherry, India, 1961-62; resident in cariology K.E.M. Hosp., Bombay, 1962-63; resident in radiology Mt. Sinai Hosp., Chgo., 1970—72; fellow in nuclear medicine Michael Reese Hosp., Chgo., 1972-73; dir. nuclear medicine Hurley Med. Ctr., Flint, Mich., 1973—. Assoc. clin. prof. radiology Mich. State U. Fellow Internat. Coll. Physicians; mem. Genesee County Med. Soc., Mich. Med. Soc., Radiol. Soc. N.Am., Am. Coll. Nuclear Physicians, Soc. Nuclear Medicine, Am. Coll. Internat. Physicians. Home: 6286 W Cimarron Trl Flint MI 48532-2018 Office: Hurley Med Ctr Flint MI 48503 Office Phone: 810-257-9194.

JAYE, DAVE, state legislator; b. Feb. 2, 1958; BA with hons., U. Mich., 1981, MA with hons., 1982. Mem. Mich. Ho. of Reps from 26th dist., Lansing, 1988-94, Mich. Ho. of Reps. from 32nd dist., Lansing, 1994-97; real estate broker, 1996—; mem. Mich. Senate from 12th dist., Lansing, 1998—. Mem. Liquor Control, Corps. & Fins. Coms. Mich. Ho. of Reps. Named Man of Yr., State Young Reps., 1985. Mem. Macomb County Taxpayers, Kiwanis, KC. Home: 8303 Waschull Dr Washington MI 48094-2333 Address: PO Box 30036 Lansing MI 48909-7536

JAYNE, THOMAS R., lawyer; m. Patti Jayne; 4 children. BA, Westminster Coll., 1973; JD, U. Mo., 1976. Bar: Mo. 1976, Ill. 1979, Tex. 1995. Ptnr. Thompson Coburn LLP, St. Louis. Pres. bd. mgrs. Ctrl. Inst. for the Deaf; mem. Knowles Found. Bd.; bd. govs. Truman State U., Kirksville, Mo., 2000—. Office: Thompson Coburn LLP One US Bank Plz Saint Louis MO 63101 Office Phone: 314-552-6000.

JEAN, KENNETH, conductor; b. NYC; Studied violin, San Francisco State U.; studied conducting with Jean Morel, Juilliard Sch. Music. Conducting debut Carnegie Hall with Youth Symphony Orch. N.Y.; European debut with Internat. Festival Youth Orchs., Aberdeen, Scotland, 1980; music dir. Youth Symphony Orch. N.Y.; conducting asst. Cleve. Orch.; resident condr. Detroit Symphony Orch., 1978-85; prin. guest condr. Hong Kong Philharm.; music dir. Fla. Symphony Orch.; assoc. condr. Chgo. Symphony Orch., 1986—; music dir. Tulsa Philharm. Orch; has appeared with numerous other U.S. orchs., Scottish Chamber Orch., Orch. Swiss Radio, Park Theater Orch., Stockholm, Belgrade Strings, S.W. German Radio Orch. (Donaueschinger Festival); has recorded works of Chinese composers, also Brahms Hungarian Dances with Hong Kong Philharm. Recipient Leopold Stokowski Conducting award Am. Symphony Orch., 1984, Seaver/Nat. Endowment Arts Condr. award, 1990. Office: Chgo Symphony Orch 220 S Michigan Ave Chicago IL 60604-2596 also: Fla Symphony Orch 1900 N Mills Ave Ste 3 Orlando FL 32803-1444

JEANNE, ROBERT LAWRENCE, entomologist, educator; b. NYC, Jan. 14, 1942; s. Armand Lucien and Ruth (Stuber) Jeanne; m. Louise Grenville Bluhm, Sept. 18, 1976; children: Thomas Lucien, James McClure. BS in Biology, Denison U., 1964; postgrad., Justus-Liebig U., Giessen, Fed. Republic Germany, 1964-65; MA, Harvard U., 1968, PhD in Biology, 1971. Instr. biology U. Va., Charlottesville, 1970-71; asst. prof. biology Boston U., 1971-76; asst. prof. entomology U. Wis., Madison, 1976-79, assoc. prof., 1979-83, prof., 1983—. Rschr.: numerous publs. on social insects. Fellow Rotary Found., 1964—65, Guggenheim Meml., 1986—87. Fellow: AAAS; mem.: Wis. Acad. Scis., Arts and Letters, Animal Behavior Soc., Internat. Union Study Social Insects (chmn. protempore, sec.-treas. 1979—80, pres. western hemisphere sect. 1981, assoc. editor Insectes Sociaux 1986—2002), Assn. Tropical Biology, Phi Beta Kappa, Sigma Xi. Achievements include numerous discoveries relating to nest construction, nest architecture, commmunication, defense, caste polymorphism, polyethism, social organization, and life histories in social wasps. Office: U Wis Dept Entomology 1630 Linden Dr Madison WI 53706-1520 Home Phone: 608-271-9481; Office Phone: 608-262-0899. Business E-Mail: jeanne@entomology.wisc.edu.

JEAVONS, NORMAN STONE, lawyer; b. Cleve., Apr. 18, 1930; s. William Norman and Mildred (Stone) J.; m. Kathleen Taze, Oct. 18, 1936; children: Kathleen Stone, Ann Lindsey. BA, Dartmouth Coll., 1952; LL.B., Case Western Res. U., 1958. Bar: Ohio 1958. Atty. firm Baker & Hostetler, Cleve., 1958—, sr. ptnr., 1968—. Mem. policy com., trustee Laurel Sch., Shaker Hts., Ohio, 1980-99, Beech Brook, Cleve., 1972—, Storm King Sch., Cornwall-on-Hudson, N.Y. Served to lt. j.g. USCG, 1952-55. Mem. ABA, Ohio Bar Assn., Cleve. Bar Assn., Order of Coif, Ct. of Nisi Prius. Clubs: Univ. (Cleveland); Cleveland Racquet (Pepper Pike). Republican. Home: 32555 Creekside Dr Pepper Pike OH 44124-5223 Office: Baker & Hostetler 3200 National City Ctr 1900 E 9th St Ste 3200 Cleveland OH 44114-3475

JEBSEN, HARRY ALFRED ARTHUR, JR., history educator; b. Chgo., Apr. 8, 1943; s. Harry Alfred Arthur Jebsen; m. Elaine Claire Melchert, Sept. 5, 1964; children— Timothy Paul, Christopher Warren. B.A., Wartburg Coll., Waverly, Iowa, 1965; M.A., U. Cin., 1966, Ph.D., 1971. Prof. history Texas Tech U., Lubbock, 1969-81, dir. urban studies, 1972-81, assoc. dean arts and scis., 1980-81; dean Coll. of Arts and Scis., Capital U., Columbus, Ohio, 1981-88, provost, 1988-95, prof. history, 1995—. Author: History of Dallas, Texas Park System, 1971. Contbr. articles to profl. jours. Bd. dirs. Luth. Coun. for Cmty. Action, Lubbock, 1970-78, U. Ministries of Lubbock, 1971-81, Luth. Social Services of Central Ohio, Columbus, 1984-92. Recipient Fish and Loaves award Luth. Coun. for Cmty. Action, Lubbock, 1977; NDEA fellow, Cin., 1966-69. Mem. Am. Assn. Higher Edn., N.Am. Soc. Sport Historians. Democrat. Avocations: golf, reading. Home: 1397 Goldsmith Dr Westerville OH 43081-4526 Office: Capital U 2199 E Main St Columbus OH 43209-2394 Office Phone: 614-236-6191. Business E-Mail: hjebsen@capital.edu.

JECKLIN, LOIS UNDERWOOD, art corporation executive, consultant; b. Manning, Iowa, Oct. 5, 1934; d. J.R. and Ruth O. (Austin) Underwood; m. Dirk C. Jecklin, June 24, 1955; children: Jennifer Anne, Ivan Peter. BA, U. Iowa, 1992. Residency coord. Quad City Arts Coun., Rock Island, Ill., 1973-78; field rep. Affiliate Artists Inc., NYC, 1975-77; mgr., artist in residence Deere & Co., Moline, Ill., 1977-80; dir. Vis. Artist Series, Davenport, Iowa, 1978-81; pres. Vis. Artists Inc., Davenport, 1981-88; pres., owner Jecklin Assocs., Davenport, 1988—2004; personal mgr. to composer Bright Sheng, 2005—. Asst. to exec. dir. Walter W. Naumburg Found., N.Y.C., 1990-2004; personal mgr., composer Bright Sheng, 2005—; cons. writer's program St. Ambrose Coll., Davenport, 1981, 83, 85; mem. com. Iowa Arts Coun., Des Moines, 1983-84; panelist Chamber Music Am., N.Y.C., 1984, Pub. Art Conf., Cedar Rapids, Iowa, 1984; panelist, mem. com. Lt. Gov.'s Conf. on Iowa's Future, Des Moines, 1984. Trustee Davenport Mus. Art, 1975-98, hon. trustee, 1998-2003; mem. nat. adv. coun. Figge Art Mus., Davenport, 2005; trustee Nature Conservancy Iowa, 1987-88; steering com. Iowa Citizens for Arts, Des Moines, 1970-71; bd. dirs. Tri-City Symphony Orch. Assn., Davenport, 1968-83; founding mem. Urban Design Coun., HOME, City of Davenport Beautification Com., 1970-72; bd. dirs. Mus. Arts and Design, YC, 1995—; devel. coun. U. Iowa Mus. Art, 1996-2002; mem. Washington chpt. Arttable, 2005—. Recipient numerous awards Izaak Walton League, Davenport Art Gallery, Assn. for Retarded Citizens, Am. Heart Assn., Ill. Bur. Corrections, many others; LaVernes Noyes scholar, 1953-55. Republican. Episcopalian. Home and Office: 1232-27th St NW Washington DC 20007

JEDDA, JOHN, meteorologist; BS in Meteorology, St. Cloud State U. Morning and weekend meteorologist, Duluth, Minn.; morning weatherman KWWL-TV, Waterloo, Iowa; weekend weatherman KMSP-TV, Mpls.; weekend meteorologist, prodr., anchor NewsCenter 13 WEAU-TV. Recipient Seal of Approval for TV weathercasting, Am. Meteorology Assn. Avocations: golf, music, basketball. Office: WEAU-TV PO Box 47 Eau Claire WI 54702

JEEVANANDAM, VALLUVAN, surgeon, educator; b. Tuticorin, Tamil Nadu, India, Aug. 20, 1960; s. Malayappa and Chellam Jeevanandam; m. Sheela Jambukesan, June 30, 1985; children: Veena, Vinesh. AB in BioChemistry, Columbia U., MD summa cum laude, 1984. Bd. cert. cardiothoracic surgery Am. Bd. Thoracic Surgery, 1993, bd. cert. surgery Am. Bd. Surgery, 1990. Intern, resident Columbia U., Presbyn. Hosp., NYC, 1984—89, CT fellow, 1989—91; assoc. prof. surgery Temple U., Phila., 1995—98, U. Chgo., 1998—2002, prof. surgery, 2002—. Dir. heart failure and transplantation Temple U., Phila., 1992—98; chief cardiothoracic surgery U. Chgo., 1998—, dir. heart transplantation and mech. devices, 1998—. Contbr. articles to profl. jours. John Jay scholar, Columbia U., 1977—80. Mem.: Soc. Heart Transplantation, Soc. Thoracic Surgeons, Am. Assn. Thoracic Surgery, Alpha Omega Alpha, Phi Beta Kappa. Independent. Hindu. Achievements include patents for laser heart revascularization. Avocations: tennis, photography. Office: Univ Chicago 5841 S Maryland Ave Chicago IL 60637 Office Phone: 773-834-3244. Personal E-mail: jeevan@uchicago.edu.

JEFF, KEVIN IEGA, choreographer, performing company executive; Grad., Julliard Sch. Founder JUBILATION! Dance Co., NYC, 1982; former artistic dir. Joseph Holmes Chgo. Dance Thearer; founder, artistic dir. Deeply Rooted Dance Theatre, Chgo.; artist-in-residence Howard U. dance major prog.; artist-in-residence, choreographer Jahari Dance Troupe, Purdue U. Choreographed for Alvin Ailey Am. Dance Theatre Ensemble, Berkeley, Calif., Cleo Parker Robinson Dance Ensemble, Denver, Williams/Henry Dance Theatre, Kans. City, Dallas Black Dance Theater. Choreographer (films) She's Gotta Have It, Beauty and the Beast, (productions) The Wiz, Porgy and Bess, Deeply Rooted. Named one of 100 Outstanding Alumni, Julliard Sch., 2005; recipient Best Choreography, Black Theater Alliance, 1996, merit award, Nat. Coun. for Culture and Arts, Internat. Conf. of Blacks in Dance; fellow Nat. Endowment for Arts. Office: Deeply Rooted Dance Theater 3712 N Broadway Ste 148 Chicago IL 60613 Office Phone: 312-913-9773. Office Fax: 312-913-9774.

JEFFERSON, JAMES WALTER, psychiatrist, educator; b. Mineola, NY, Aug. 14, 1937; s. Thomas Hutton and Alice (Withers) J.; m. Susan Mary Cole, June 25, 1965; children: Lara, Shawn, James C. BS, Bucknell U., Lewisburg, Pa., 1958; MD, U. Wis., 1964. Diplomate Am. Bd. Psychiatry and Neurology, Am. Bd. Internal Medicine. Asst. prof. psychiatry U. Wis. Med. Sch., Madison, 1974-78, assoc. prof., 1978-81, prof., 1981-92; disting. sr. scientist Dean Found. for Health, Rsch. and Edn., Madison, 1992-98; clin. prof. psychiatry U. Wis. Med. Sch., Madison, 1992—; disting. sr. scientist Madison Inst. Medicine, 1998—. Pres. Healthcare Tech. Sys., Madison, 1998-2005; co-dir. Lithium Info. Ctr., Madison, 1975—, Obsessive Compulsive Info. Ctr., Madison, 1990—; dir. Ctr. Affective Disorders, Madison, 1983-92. Co-author: Neuropsychiatric Features of Medical Disorders, 1981, Lithium Encyclopedia for Clinical Practice, 1983, 2nd edit., 1987, Depression and Its Treatment, 1984, 2d edit., 1992, Anxiety and Its Treatment, 1986, Handbook of Medical Psychiatry, 1996. Served to maj. US Army, 1968-71. Fellow ACP, Am. Psychiat. Assn.; mem. Collegium Internat. Neuropsychopharmacologium, Am. Soc. Clin. Psychopharmacology (nat. bd. trustees 1996—). Avocations: bicycling, travel. Office: Madison Inst Medicine 7617 Mineral Point Rd Madison WI 53717-1623 Office Phone: 608-827-2451. Business E-Mail: jjefferson@healthtechsys.com.

JEFFREY, JUDY, school system administrator; BA, U. of No. Iowa, 1963; MA, Creighton U., 1981. With Council Bluffs Cmty. Sch. Dist.; adminstr. Early Childhood, Elementary and Secondary Edn. div. Iowa Dept. Edn., 1996—, dir. edn., 2004—. Tchr. Cedar Falls and Goldfield dists., Iowa; instr. Creighton U.; pres. Coun. of Chief State Sch. Officers Dep. Commn., 2001—03, bd. dirs., co-chair, Task Force on Math and Sci. Edn.; serves on Reauthorization Task Force Elementary and Secondary Edn. Act. Office: Iowa Dept Edn Grimes State Office Bldg 400 E 14th and Grand Des Moines IA 50319-0146 Office Phone: 515-281-3436. Office Fax: 515-281-4122. Business E-Mail: judy.jeffrey@iowa.gov.

JEFFRIES, KIM, radio personality; b. Tex. m. Bruce Jeffries; 4 children. In Theater and Speech, Northwestern U.; grad. Broadcasting, Brown Inst. Host Sta. WJON-Radio, St. Cloud; host Sta. KS95; reporter Sta. WCCO-TV, Mpls.; host Morning Show Sta. WCCO Radio, Mpls., 1998, radio host midday live. Contbr. articles to profl. jours. Vol. Charis prison ministry, numerous other orgns. Avocations: church activities, sports, travel. Office: WCCO 625 2nd Ave S Minneapolis MN 55402

JEFFRIES, MICHAEL S. (MIKE JEFFRIES), apparel executive; b. Elk City, Okla., July 13, 1944; m. Susan Jeffries; 1 child, Andrew. BA in Econs., Claremont McKenna Coll., 1966; MBA, Columbia U., 1968. With Abraham and Straus, 1968; exec. v.p. merchandising Bullock's, 1980-83; pres., CEO Alcott & Andrews, 1983-89; exec. v.p. merchandising Paul Harris, 1990-92; pres., CEO Abercrombie & Fitch Co., New Albany, Ohio, 1992—98, chmn., CEO, 1998—. Office: Abercrombie & Fitch Co 6301 Fitch Path New Albany OH 43054

JEFFRIES, TELVIN, retail executive; With Best Products, 1987—93; various human resources positions including sr. v.p. Kohl's Corp., Menomonee Falls, Wis., 1993—2003, exec. v.p., 2003—. Com. chmn. Holy Redeemer Instl. Ch. of God in Christ Ednl. complex project. Named one of Rising Stars: 40 Under 40, Chain Store Age, 2004. Office: Kohls Corp N56 W17000 Ridgewood Dr Menomonee Falls WI 53051-5660 Home: 3435 N Lake DR Milwaukee WI 53211-2919 Office Phone: 262-703-7000. E-mail: telvin.jeffries@kohls.com.

JEFFS, THOMAS HAMILTON, II, retired bank executive; b. Grosse Pointe Farms, Mich., July 11, 1938; s. Thomas Raymond and Geraldine (Bogan) J.; m. Patricia Lucas, June 20, 1964; children: Leslie, Laura, Caroline BBA in Gen. Bus., U. Mich., 1960, MBA, 1961. With NBD Bank, 1962-99, pres., COO, until 1999; vice chmn., bd. dirs. First Chgo. NBD Corp., 1995-98. Bd. dirs. MCN Energy Group, Inc., Detroit, Intermet Corp., Local Initiatives Support Corp. Bd. dirs. Detroit Symphony, Econ. Club Detroit; chmn. New Detroit, Inc.; dir. Detroit Renaissance, Inc. With U.S. Army, 1960-62. Mem. Bankers Roundtable, Detroit Athletic Club, Detroit Club (pres. 1982), Detroit Country Club, Yondotega Club, Grosse Pointe Club. Republican. Episcopalian. Office: NBD Bank 611 Woodward Ave Detroit MI 48226-3408 Home: PO Box 675 Boca Grande FL 33921-0675

JEGEN, SISTER CAROL FRANCES, religious studies educator; b. Chgo., Oct. 11, 1925; d. Julian Aloysius and Evelyn W. (Bostelmann) J. BS in History, St. Louis U., 1951; MA in Theology, Marquette U., 1958, PhD in Religious Studies, 1968; degree (hon.), St. Mary of the Woods, Terra Haute, Ind., 1977. Elem. tchr. St. Francis Xavier Sch., St. Louis, 1947-51; secondary tchr. Holy Angels Sch., Milw., 1951-57; coll. tchr. Mundelein Coll., Chgo., 1957-91; prof. pastoral studies Loyola U., Chgo., 1991—. Adv. coun. U.S. Cath. Bishops, Washington, 1969-74; trustees Cath. Theol. Union, Chgo., 1974-84. Author: Jesus the Peace Maker, 1986, Restoring Our Friendship with God, 1989, Transformed by the Trinity, 2008; co-author: (with Byron Sherwin) Thank God, 1989; editor: Mary According to Women, 1985. Participant Nat. Farm Worker Ministry, Fresno, Calif., 1977—; mem. Pax Christi, U.S.A., 1979—, Jane Addams Conf., Chgo., 1989. Recipient Loyola Civic award Loyola U., Chgo., 1981, Chgo. medallion for Excellence in Catechesis, 1996, Sor Juana award Hispanic Ministry, 2000; named one of 100 Women to Watch Today's Chgo. Woman, 1989. Mem. Cath. Theol. Soc. Am., Coll. Theology Soc., Cath.-Jewish Scholars Dialog, Liturgical Conf. Democrat. Roman Catholic. Avocations: music, gardening. Home: Wright Hall 6364 N Sheridan Rd Chicago IL 60660-1700

JEGEN, LAWRENCE A., III, law educator; b. Chgo., Nov. 16, 1934; s. Lawrence A. and Katherine M. Jegen; children: Christine M., David L. BA, Beloit Coll., Wis., 1956; JD, U. Mich., 1959, MBA, 1960; LLM, NYU, 1963. Bar: Ill. 1959, US Dist. Ct. (no. dist.) Ill. 1959, US Dist. Ct. (so. dist.) Ind. 1962, Ind. 1966, US Tax Ct. 1966, US Ct. Appeals (7th cir.) 1980, US Supreme Ct. 1980. Tax cons. Coopers & Lybrand, NYC, 1960-62; asst. prof. law Ind. U., Indpls., 1962-64, assoc. prof., 1964-66, prof., 1966—, Thomas F. Sheehan prof. tax law and policy, 1982—, prof. philanthropic studies Ctr. Philanthropy, 1992—, external tax counsel, 1997—. Ind. U. rep. to Nat. Assn. Coll. and Univ. Attys., 1994—; co-founder, co-dir. Ann. Tax Inst. for Colls. and Univs., 1994—; bar rev. lectr., vis. prof. in field; spl. counsel Ind. Dept. Revenue, 1963-65, Gov.'s Commn. on Med. Edn., 1970-72; mem. commr.'s adv. com. IRS, 1981-82; advisor otre Dame Estate Planning Inst.; mem. Ind. Corp. Law Survey Commn.; State Tax Notes corr. for Tax Analysts; contbg. editor Inst. Bus. Planning's Tax Planning Svc.; bd. dirs., officer Ind. Continuing Legal Edn. Forum; 1st chmn. bd. dirs. Baccalaureate Edn. Sys. Trust of Ind.; mem. Ind. Gen. Assembly Study Commn.-Ind. Gen. Corp. Act; mem. Ind. Corps. Survey Commn., 1965—; commr. Nat. Conf. Uniform State Laws, 1981-91; dir. N.Am. Wildlife Assn., 1981-90. Author: Indiana Will and Trust Manual, 1967-95; Lifetime and Estate, Personal and Business Planning, 1987; Estate Planning and Administration in Indiana, 1979, numerous other books, articles, chpts. Chmn. bd. dirs. Ind. Bar Ednl. Sys. Tchrs., 1988-89; mem. adv. bd. Ind. U. Ctr. on Philanthropy. amed hon. sec. of state, State of Ind., 1967, 1980, hon. dep. atty. gen., 1968, hon. state treas., 1969, Ford fellow, 1963; recipient Spl Alumni Tch. award, Ind. U. Alumni Assn., 1970, 1976, 1980, 1985, Excellence in Taxation award for improvement tax adminstrn., State of Ind. Quality for Ind. Taxpayers, Inc., 1990, The Thomas Hart Benton Mural medallion, 1993, The Thomas Hart Benton Mural medallion, 1994, 3 Sagamore of the Wabash awards, State Ind., Internat. award, Assn. Continuing Legal Administrators for Excellence in Continuing Legal Edn., Ind. U. Most Outstanding Law Prof. award 6 times, Pres.'s Cir. Commemorative medallion, Ind. U. Disting. Tchg. award, Tchr. of Significance, Ind. U. Fellow Am. Bar Found. (life), Am. Coll. Probate Counsel, Am. Coll. Tax Counsel; mem. ABA, FBA, Mid-West Inst. Estate and Tax Planning (adv. bd.), Ind. Bar Assn. (chmn. taxation sect. 1969-70, presdl. citation 1971), Indpls. Bar Assn. (Dr. Morton Finney Jr. Excellence in Legal Edn. award), Ind. Trial Lawyers Assn. (corp. taxation, estate taxation, state and local taxation). Achievements include having a law professorship created at Indiana University in his honor in 2006. Office: Indiana Univ Sch Law 530 W New York St Indianapolis IN 46202-3225 Office Phone: 317-251-5300. Personal E-mail: profjegen@aol.com.

JELLEMA, JON, state legislator, educator; b. Bloomington, Ind., Dec. 7, 1943; s. William Harry and Frances (Peters) J.; m. Betsy Zevalkink; children: Frances, Kate, Jon R., Elizabeth. BA, Calvin Coll., 1966; MA, Mich. State U., 1972. Prof. Grand Valley State U., Allendale, Mich., 1972-94; asst. dean William James Coll., Grand Valley State U., Allendale, 1986-87; dir. liberal studies program Grand Valley State U., Allendale, 1988-89, chmn. English dept., 1989-91, prof. English dept., 1991-94; mem. Mich. Ho. of Reps., Lansing, 1994-2000; dean Arts and Humanities divsn. Grand Valley State U., Allendale, 2001—04, assoc. v.p. academic affairs, 2004—. Vice-chmn. appropriations com., vice chmn. subcom. on transp., chmn. joint capital outlay comm., chmn. policy comm., mem. edn. commn. states, mem. urban caucus. Pres. Grand Haven (Mich.) Pub. Sch. Bd., 1972-84; founder North Ottawa Cmty. Coalition; active Grand Rapids Mus. Mem. Greater Grand Rapids Coun. for Arts (bd. dirs.), World Affairs Coun. (bd. dirs.), Phi Kappa Phi. Avocations: sailing, skiing. Home: 510 Park Ave Grand Haven MI 49417-2107 Office: 290 LSH-GVSU Allendale MI 49401 Office Phone: 616-331-2400. E-mail: jellemaj@gvsu.edu.

JEMIELITY, THOMAS JOHN, language educator; b. Cleve., Dec. 17, 1933; s. Joseph Henry and Margaret Anne (Wielgus) Jemielity; m. Barbara Gray, Aug. 7, 1965; children: David Christopher, Samuel Andrew, Sarah Margaret. MA, John Carroll U., Cleve., 1958; PhD, Cornell U., 1965. Lectr. English Carleton U., Ottawa, Ont., Canada, 1962-63; instr. U. Notre Dame, Ind., 1963-65, asst. prof. English Ind., 1965-70, assoc. prof. Ind., 1970-90, prof. Ind., 1990—2003, prof. emeritus Ind., 2003—. Vis. lectr. Lancaster (Eng.) U. Author: Satire and the Hebrew Prophets, 1992, Ancient Biblical Satire, 2007; contbr. articles to profl. jours. including online mags., NY Observer. Summer fellow, Ind. Com. Humanities, 1988. Mem.: Johnson Soc. Ctrl. Region (pres. 1985), Johnson Soc. London, Johnson Soc. (Lichfield, Eng.), Jane Austen Soc. N.Am., Am. Soc. 18th Century Studies. Home: 20408 Kern Rd South Bend IN 46614-5046 Office: U Notre Dame Dept English Notre Dame IN 46556 Business E-Mail: thomas.j.jemielity.1@nd.edu.

JEN, ENOCH, electro-optical technology products executive; b. Phila., 1952; B in Math., Mich. State U., 1973, MBA in Acctg., 1974. CPA, Mich. With Ernst & Young, Grand Rapids, Mich.; contr., treas. Hi-Ram, Inc.; CFO Porter-Hadley Co., Am. Lumber Sales Corp.; sr. contr. The Hager Group Cos.; CFO Hope Rehab. etwork, Inc.; contr. Gentex Corp., Zeeland, Mich., 1990; v.p. fin., treas. Gentex, Zeeland, 1991—. Mem. AICPA, Mich. Assn. CPA. Office: Gentex Corp 600 N Centennial St Zeeland MI 49464-1318 Office Fax: 616-772-7348. E-mail: publicrelations.ir@gentex.com.

JENEFSKY, JACK, wholesale company executive; b. Oct. 27, 1919; s. David and Anna (Saeks) Jenefsky; m. Beverly J. Mueller, Feb. 23, 1962; 1 child, Anna Elizabeth 1 stepchild, Cathryn Jean Mueller. BSBA, Ohio State U., 1941; postgrad., Harvard Bus. Sch., 1943; MA in Econs., U. Dayton, 1948. Surplus broker, Dayton, 1946—48; sales rep. Remington Rand-Univac, Dayton, 1949—56, mgr. AF acct., 1957—59, br. mgr. Dayton, 1960—61, regional mktg. cons. Midwest region, 1962—63; pres. Bowman Supply Co., Dayton, 1963—. Selection adv. bd. Air Force Acad., 3d congl. dist. chmn., 1974—82; chmn. 3d dist. screening bds. Mil. Acad., 1976—82; coord. Great Lakes region, res. assistance program CAP, 1970—73. From pvt. to capt. USAAF, 1942—46, CBI, maj. USAF, 1951—53, col. Res. Mem.: Miami Valley Mil. Affairs Assn. (trustee 1985—, pres. bd. trustees 1987—88), Nat. Sojourners (pres. Dayton 1961—62), Ohio State U. Alumni Assn. (pres. Montgomery County, Ohio 1959—60), Dayton Area C. of C. (chmn. spl. events com. 1970—72, chmn. rsch. com. on mil. affairs 1983—87), Air Force Assn. (comdr. Ohio wing 1957—59), Res. Officers Assn. (pres. Ohio dept. 1956—57, nat. coun. 1957—58, chmn. R&D com. 1961—62), Harvard Bus. Sch. Club Dayton (pres. 1961—62, chmn. selection com., Fed. Govt. Employee of Yr. 1991, 1992), Lions. Jewish. Home: 136 Briar Heath Cir Dayton OH 45415-2601 Office: Bowman Supply Co PO Box 1404 Dayton OH 45401-1404 Office Phone: 937-254-6241. Business E-Mail: bowman.supply@att.net.

JENKINS, DARRELL LEE, librarian; b. Roswell, N.Mex., Aug. 12, 1949; s. Lindon C. and Joyce (King) J.; m. Susan Jenkins. BA, Ea. N.Mex. U., 1971; MLS, U. Okla., 1972; MA, N.Mex. State U., 1976. Asst. edn., psychology, gift libr. N.Mex. State U., Las Cruces, 1972—73, edn. psychology libr., 1973—74, asst. reference libr., 1974—75, asst. catalog libr., 1975—76, asst. serials libr., 1976—77, acting head reference dept., 1977; adminstrv. svcs. libr. So. Ill. U., Carbondale, 1977—82, dir. libr. svcs., 1982—91, head social scis. divsn., 1992—2001. Cons. U.S. Naval Base, So. Ill. U., Groton, Conn., 1985-91; chmn. bd. dirs. CEC Comm., Inc., 1997-99. Author: Specialty Positions in ARL Libraries, 1982; co-author: Library Development and Fund Raising Capabilities, 1988; contbr. articles to profl. jours. Mem. ALA (chmn. libr. orgn. mgmt. sect. 1985-86), Am. Soc Info. Sci., Assn. Christian Librs., Ill. Libr. Computer System Orgn. (pres. 1985-86), Phi Kappa Phi, Beta Phi Mu, Phi Alpha Theta (Outstanding Libr. award 2002). Republican. Mem. Ch. Assembly God. Avocations: tennis, swimming, bicycling. E-mail: dj779@hotmail.com.

JENKINS, G. WILLARD, state representative; b. Bolckow, Mo., Aug. 26, 1937; m. Kay Jenkins; children: Mike, Julie, Ross, Dave. BS in Mech. Engring., U. Mo., Rolla, 1959; MBA, U. Iowa, 1968. Staff engring./product planning Deere & Co., 1958—93; tech./fin. planning cons., 1993—96; mem. Iowa Ho. Reps., DesMoines, Iowa, 1997—, chair internat. rels. com., chair commerce; mem. various coms. including appropriations, econ. devel. Mem.: Soc. Automotive Engring., Am. Soc. Agrl. Engrs., Aircraft Owners, Pilots Assn., Rotary. Republican. Presbyterian. Office: State Capitol Bldg East 12th and Grand Des Moines IA 50319 also: 6 Winter Ridge Rd Waterloo IA 50701

JENKINS, GEORGE L., lawyer, entrepreneur; b. Wheeling, W.Va., Jan. 30, 1940; s. George Addison and Mildred Irene (Liggett) J. AB magna cum laude, Kent State U., 1963; JD with honors, U. Mich., 1966. Bar: Ohio 1966. Assoc. Vorys, Sater, Seymour & Pease, Columbus, Ohio, 1966-71, ptnr., 1975—; 1st asst. atty. gen. State of Ohio, Columbus, 1971-75. Bd. dirs. Fleagane Enterprises, Inc., JMHS, Inc., Impex Logistics, Inc., Nat. Am. Logistics, Inc., ECNext, Inc., CP Techs., Inc. Mem. ABA, Ohio Bar Assn., Columbus Bar Assn. (chmn. various coms. 1966—), Columbus Athletic Club, Muirfield Country Club, Desert Mountain Club, others. Democrat. Methodist. Avocations: tennis, jogging, travel, reading, golf. Office: Vorys Sater Seymour & Pease PO Box 1008 52 E Gay St Columbus OH 43215-3161 E-mail: gljenkins@vssp.com.

JENKINS, JAMES ROBERT, lawyer, manufacturing executive; b. Waukegan, Ill., June 10, 1945; s. William Ivy and Louise Elnora (Lampkins) J.; m. Anita Louise Horne, June 29, 1968; children: James R. II, Andrea Louise. AB in Philos., U. Mich., 1967, JD, 1973. Bar: Mich. 1973, Ill. 1974. Law clk. to assoc. Koster & Bullard, Ann Arbor, Mich., 1971-73; law clk. to Justice Seidenfeld Ill. Ct. Appeals (2nd dist.), Waukegan, 1973-74; asst. defender State of Mich. Appellate Defender Office, Detroit, 1974-75; dep. defender Fed. Defender Office, Detroit, 1975-76; v.p., sec., gen. counsel, counsel sec. to corp. bd. dirs., counsel to exec. com., mem. fin. com. Dow Corning Corp., Midland, Mich., 1976—2000; sr. v.p., gen. counsel Deere & Co., Moline, Ill., 2000—. Trustee Alma Coll., 1985—. 1st lt. US Army, 1967—70, Vietnam. Decorated Bronze Star. Fellow Mich. State Bar Found.; mem. Mich. State Bar Assn., Am. Law Inst., Am. Arbtration Assn. (bd. dirs.), Assn. Corp. Counsel (chmn, 2005-, vice chmn. bd. dirs.). Office: Deere Co 1 John Deere Pl Moline IL 61265-8098

JENKINS, JOHN ANTHONY, lawyer; b. Cin., Apr. 11, 1926; s. John A. and Norma S. (Snyder) J.; m. Margery N. Jenkins, May 24, 1997; children: Julie Anne, John Anthony III. BEE, Ohio State U., 1951, JD, 1953. Bar: Ohio, 1954, U.S. Supreme Ct. 1963. Assoc. Knepper White Richards & Miller, Columbus, Ohio, 1954-58, ptnr., 1958-78, Arter & Hadden, Columbus, 1978-94, of counsel, 1995—, mem. mgmt. com. Cleve., 1984-89. Dir. Gen. Exploration Co., Dallas, 1972-80; gen. ptnr. Columbus Lasher P/S, Columbus, Ohio, 1976—, Indian Bend Ltd. P/S, Phoenix, 1978—; pres. Mummy Mountain Devel., Phoenix, 1978-89. Author: Ohio Public Contract law, 1989, 3d edit., 1994; contbr. articles to profl. jours. Trustee Citizens Rsch., Inc., Columbus, 1960-72; pres. Columbus Kiwanis Found., 1973-76; pres. Beta Theta Pi Bldg. Assn., Columbus, 1972-76. With U.S. Army, 1944-46. Fellow Am. Bar Found.; mem. ABA (chmn. com.), Ohio Bar Assn. (chmn. com.), Columbus Bar Assn. (chmn. com.), Capital Club, Muirfield Village Golf Club, Scioto Country Club, Golf Club (Gahanna, Ohio), Desert Mountain Club (Scottsdale, Ariz.) Masons, Shriners. Republican. Avocation: golf. Home: 10692 EHoney Mesquite Dr Scottsdale AZ 85262 Office: Arter & Hadden 10 W Broad St Ste 2100 Columbus OH 43215-3422

JENKINS, JOHN I., academic administrator; BA, U. Notre Dame, 1976, MPhil, 1978; PhB, Oxford U., 1987, PhD, 1989; MDiv, Jesuit Sch. Theology, Berkeley, 1988; licentiate in Sacred Theology, Jesuit Sch. Theology, Berekeley, 1988. Ordained a priest Basilica of the Sacred Heart, Notre Dame U., 1983. Mem. faculty U. otre Dame, 1990—, prof. ancient philosophy, medieval philosophy, philosophy of the religion, adj. prof. London program, 1988—89, religious superior of Holy Cross priests, fellow, trustee, 1997—2000, v.p. and assoc. provost, 2001—05, pres., 2005—; dir. Old Coll. program for Notre Dame undergraduate candidates for Congregation of Holy Cross, 1991—93. Author: Knowledge and Faith in Thomas Aquinas, 1997, (articles published in) The Jour. Philosophy, Medieval Philosophy and Theology, The Jour. of Religious Ethics; spkr. Ann. Aquinas Lecture, U. Dallas, 2000. Recipient Lilly Teaching Fellowship, Notre Dame U., 1991—92. Office: Office of the President U Notre Dame 400 Main Bldg Notre Dame IN 46556

JENKINS, LYNN M., state official, former state legislator; b. Topeka, June 10, 1963; m. Scott M. Jenkins; children: Hayley, Hayden. AA, Kans. State U., 1984; BS, Weber State Coll., 1985. CPA. CPA, 1985—; rep. Kans. State Ho. Reps., 1998—2000; mem. Kans. State Senate, 2000—03, mem. gen. govt. budget com., ins. com., post audit com., govt. orgn. and elections com., taxation com.; treas. State of Kans., 2003—. Mem. Pooled Money Investment Bd., Coll. Savings Plan etwork. Mem. adv. bd. Ct. Apptd. Spl. Advocate; bd. dirs. YMCA Metro, Family Svc. and Guidance Ctr., Kans. Children's Svc. League; treas., bd. dirs. Prince of Peace Presch.; active Jay Snideler PTO, Susanna Wesley United Meth. Ch.; mem. Kans. Pub. Employee's Retirement Sys., Aspen Inst. Rodel Fellowship in Pub. Leadership Program, Am. Coun. Young Polit. Leaders; mem. hon. bd. gov. Dwight D. Eisenhower Excellence in Pub. Svc.;mem. adv. coun. Kans. State U. Acctg. Dept.; mem. found. bd. Auburn-Washburn Pub. Sch. Mem. Kans. Soc. CPAs, Nat. Assn. Unclaimed Property Adminstr., Nat. Assn. State Treasurers (sr. v.p.) Republican. Methodist. Office: 900 SW Jackson St Ste 201 Topeka KS 66612-1235 Office Phone: 785-296-3171.

JENKINS, MELVIN LEMUEL, lawyer; b. Halifax, NC, Oct. 15, 1947; s. Solomon Green and Minerva (Long) Jenkins; m. Wanda Joyce Holly, May 20, 1972; children: Dawn, Shelley, Melvin, Holly Rae-Ann. BS, NC Agrl. and State U., 1969; JD, U. Kans., 1972. Bar: Nebr. 1973, US. Dist. Ct. Nebr. 1973. Atty. Legal Aid Soc., Kansas City, Mo., 1972, HUD, Kansas City, Mo., 1972—73; regional atty. U.S. Commn. on Civil Rights, Kansas City, Mo., 1973—79, regional dir., 1979—2002; atty. Stennis and Assocs., Omaha, 2002—. Chmn. A.M. Roundtable, Kansas City, 1981—83; mem. Kansas City Human Relations Commn., 1980. Mem. Mo. Black Adoption Adv. Bd., Kansas City, 1981—; bd. dirs. Joan Davis Spl. Sch. Mem.: ACLU, ABA, Fed. Bar Assn., Nat. Bar Assn., Nebr. Bar Assn., Urban League, Masons (master mason for civil rights 1979). Mem. Ame Ch. Home: 8015 Sunset Cir Grandview MO 64030-1461 Office: 300 S 19th St Ste 216 Omaha NE 68102 Office Phone: 402-342-4093.

JENKS, CARL M., lawyer; b. Cleve., 1945; BA, Carleton Coll., 1967; MA, Duke Univ., 1973, PhD, 1979; JD, Harvard Univ., 1980. Bar: Ohio 1982. Law clk. Judge Walter R. Mansfield, US Ct. of Appeals, Second Cir., 1980—81; ptnr., chair, general tax practice Jones Day, Cleve. and NYC. Author (numerous articles): profl. publications. Named to Best Lawyers in America. Fellow: Am. Coll. of Bankruptcy, Am. Coll. of Tax Coun.; mem.: Am. Law Inst. Fluent in Portuguese. Office: Jones Day North Point 901 Lakeside Ave Cleveland OH 44114-1190 also: Jones Day 222 E 41st St New York NY 10017-6702 Office Phone: 216-586-7173, 212-326-8321. Office Fax: 216-579-0212, 212-755-7306. Business E-Mail: cmjenks@jonesday.com.

JENKS, THOMAS EDWARD, lawyer; b. Dayton, Ohio, May 31, 1929; s. Wilbur L. and Anastasia A. (Ahern); m. Marianna Fischer, Nov. 10, 1961; children: Pamela (dec.), William, David, Christine, Daniel, Douglas Student, Miami U., Oxford, Ohio, 1947-50; JD cum laude, Ohio State U., Columbus, 1953; grad. with honors, US aval Sch. Justice, Newport, RI, 1953. Bar: Ohio 1953, U.S. Dist. Ct. (so. dist.) Ohio 1961, U.S. Supreme Ct. 1971, U.S. Ct. Appeals (6th cir.) 1984. Pvt. practice, Dayton, 1955—; atty. Jenks, Pyper & Oxley, Dayton. Lectr. in med. malpractice law; mediator. Served to 1st lt. USMC, 1953-55 Named, Ohio Super Lawyer. Fellow Am. Coll. Trial Lawyers, Ohio Bar Found.; mem. ABA (ho. of dels. 1985-88), Am. Bar Found. (life), Dayton Bar Assn. (life, pres. 1978-79), Ohio Bar Assn. (life, bd. govs. litig. sect., 1990-98), Internat. Assn. Def. Counsel, Ohio Assn. Civil Trial Attys., Am. Bd. Trial Advs. (adv.), Kettering C. of C. (past pres.), Kettering Holiday at Home Found. (past pres.), Order of Coif, Dayton Lawyers Club (pres. 1999-2002),

Optimist Club (past pres. Oakwood chpt.), Phi Delta Phi, Sigma Chi. Republican. Roman Catholic. Office: Jenks Pyper & Oxley Courthouse Plz SW 10 N Ludlow St Dayton OH 45402 Office Phone: 937-223-3001. Business E-Mail: tjenks@jpolawyers.com.

JENNESS, JAMES M., food products executive; b. Chgo., May 15, 1946; m. Sharon Jenness; 3 children. B in Mktg., DePaul U., Chgo., M in Bus. Adminstrn. Vice chmn., COO Leo Burnett Co., mem. exec. com., bd. dirs.; CEO Integrated Merchandising Sys. LLC; chmn., CEO Kellogg Co., Battle Creek, Mich., 2005—06, chmn., 2006—. Co-trustee W.K. Kellogg Found. Trust; bd. dirs. Kellogg Co., 2000—, Grocery Mfrs. Am., Schwarz Paper Co.; guest lectr. DePaul U., Chgo. Bd. dirs. exec. com. mem., chair mktg. com. Children's Meml. Hosp.; bd dirs. Mercy Home for Boys and Girls; bd. trustees DePaul U., Chgo., chmn. coll. commerce advisory coun. Mem.: Econs. Club Chgo. Office: Kellogg Co 1 Kellogg Sq Battle Creek MI 49016-3599

JENNINGS, LOREN G., state legislator, business owner; b. June 1951; m. Bonnie Jennings. Student, Vocat.-Tech. Sch. Bus. owner; Dist. 18B rep. Minn. Ho. of Reps., St. Paul, 1984—. Former vice chmn. appropriations com., Minn. Ho. of Reps., former mem. environ. and natural resources, housing and regulated industries coms.; vice chmn. health and human svcs.-human svcs. fin. divsn., mem. fin. instns. and ins. and regulated industries and energy coms. Address: PO Box 27 Rush City MN 55069-0027 Also: 3340 465th St Harris MN 55032-3701

JENNINGS, STEPHEN GRANT, academic administrator; b. Indpls., Dec. 6, 1946; s. Grant Orville and Helen Zura (MacDonald) J.; m. Sarah Ferguson, Apr. 26, 1969; children: Amy Jennings Bishop, Meredith Jennings Poole. BA, Trinity U., 1968; MS, Miami U., Oxford, Ohio, 1970; PhD, U. Ga., 1976; diploma in ednl. mgmt., Harvard U., 1982; LLD, Coll. Ozarks, Point Lookout, Mo., 1997; LHD, Simpson Coll., 1998. Asst. dean for resident life So. Meth. U., Dallas, 1970-73; asst. dir. housing U. Ga., Athens, 1973-76; assoc. dean students Tulane U., New Orleans, 1976-80; v.p. student svcs. Furman U., Greenville, SC, 1980-83; pres. Coll. of Ozarks, Point Lookout, Mo., 1983-87, Simpson Coll., Indianola, Iowa, 1987-98, Oklahoma City U., 1998-2001, U. Evansville, Ind., 2001—. Instnl. cons. Am. Coll. in London, 1995; bd. dirs. Old Nat. Bank, Nat. Pub. Radio and TV (WNIN). Mem. Coun. Ind. Colls., Nat. Assn. Schs., Colls. and Univs. (bd. dirs. 1993—), Nat. Assn. Intercollegiate Athletics (coun. of pres. 1983-87), So. Assn. Colls. and Schs. (vis. teams 1982—), North Cen. Assn. Colls. and Schs. (vis. teams 1989—), So. Assn. Coll. Student Pers. (pres. 1983), Harvard U. Alumni Assn. (class rep.), Rotary, Evansville Club, Sigma Alpha Epsilon. Avocations: sports, golf, reading. Office: U Evansville Office of President 1800 Lincoln Ave Evansville IN 47722-0001

JENNISON, ROBIN L., former state legislator, lobbyist; s. Denise Jennison. Grad., Fort Hayes State U. Kans. state rep. Dist. 117, 1990—; spkr. Kans. House of Rep., 1999—2001; farmer, stockman; lobbyist Ruffin Properties, 2002—. Mem. Kans. Farm Bur., Kans. Livestock Assn., Kans. Wheat Growers Assn. Office: Ruffin Properties PO Box 17087 Wichita KS 67217

JENSEN, BAIBA, school system administrator; Former prin. Hawkins Elem. Sch., Brighton, Mich.; prin. Scranton Middle Sch., 2004—05; dir. instructional support Brighton Sch. Dist., 2001—04, 2005—. Recipient Elem. Sch. Recognition awards U.S. Dept. Edn., 1989-90. Office: Brighton Sch Dist 125 S Church St Brighton MI 48116

JENSEN, DICK LEROY, lawyer; b. Audubon, Iowa, Oct. 25, 1930; s. A.B. and Bernice (Fancher) J.; m. Nancy Wilson, June 30, 1956; children: Charles F., Sarah R. (dec.). LL.B., U. Iowa, 1954. Bar: Iowa 1954. Practice in, Audubon, Iowa, 1958-60; gen. counsel, sec. Walnut Grove Products, Co., Atlantic, Iowa, 1960-64; legal staff W.R. Grace & Co., Atlantic, 1964-66; gen. counsel, v.p., sec. Spencer Foods, Inc., Iowa, 1966-72, dir., 1968-72; mem. Dreher, Simpson and Jensen, Des Moines, 1972—. Notes and legis. editor Iowa Law Rev., 1953—54. Pres. S.W. Iowa Mental Health Inst., 1964-66. Served to lt. USNR, 1955-58. Mem.: Masons, Phi Delta Phi, Sigma Nu. Republican. Presbyterian. Home: 4823 Cedar Dr West Des Moines IA 50266 Office: Dreher Simpson & Jensen The Equitable Bldg Ste 222 Des Moines IA 50309-3723 Office Phone: 515-288-5000. Business E-Mail: djensen@dreherlaw.com.

JENSEN, ELWOOD VERNON, biochemist; b. Fargo, ND, Jan. 13, 1920; s. Eli A. and Vera (Morris) J.; m. Mary Welmoth Collette, June 17, 1941 (dec. Nov. 1982); children: Karen Collette, Thomas Eli; m. Hiltrud Herborg, Dec. 21, 1983 AB, Wittenberg U., 1940, DSc (hon.), 1963; PhD, U. Chgo., 1944; DSc (hon.), Acadia U., 1976, Med. Coll. Ohio, 1991; MD (hon.), U. Hamburg, 1994, U. Athens, 2005. Faculty U. Chgo., 1947-90, assoc. prof. biochemistry Ben May Inst. Cancer Rsch., 1954-60, prof., 1960-63, Am. Cancer Soc. rsch. prof. physiology, 1963-69, dir. Ben May Inst., 1969-82, dir. Biomed. Ctr. Population Research, 1972-75, prof. physiology, 1969-73, 77-84, prof. biophysics, 1973-84, prof. biochemistry, 1980-90, Charles B. Huggins disting. svc. prof., 1981-90, emeritus prof., 1990—; rsch. dir. Ludwig Inst. for Cancer Rsch., 1983-87; scholar-in-residence Fogarty Internat. Ctr. NIH, 1988, Cornell U. Med. Coll., 1990—91; prof. Inst. for Hormone and Fertility Rsch. U. Hamburg, Germany, 1992—97. Adv. coun., GM Cancer Rsch. Found.; Nobel vis. prof. Karolinska Inst., Huddinge, Sweden, 1998, STINT vis. scientist, 1998-99, prof. emeritus, 1999-2001; John and Gladys Strauss chair for cancer rsch. U. Cin., 2002-03, George and Elizabeth Wile chair in cancer rsch. and disting. prof., 2004—; vis. scientist NICHD/NIH, 2001; vis. prof. Max-Planck-Inst. for Biochemie, Munich, 1958; chemotherapy rev. bd. Nat. Cancer Inst., 1960-62, bd. sci. counselors, 1969-72; mem. Nat. Adv. Coun. Child Health and Human Devel., 1976-80; adv. com. biochemistry and chem. carcinogenesis Am. Cancer Soc., 1968-72, coun. for rsch. and clin. investigation, 1974-77; mem. assembly life scis. NRC, 1975-78; com. on sci., engring. and pub. policy Nat. Acad. Scis., 1981-82; rsch. adv. bd. Clin. Rsch. Inst. of Montreal, 1987-96, Klinik for Tumor Biologie, Freiburg, 1993-2002, Strang Cancer Prevention Ctr., 1994-98; cons. Rockefeller U. Hosp., 1990-92; internat. adv. bd. Fondazione Giovanni Lorenzini, Milan, 2001—. Mem. editl. bd. Perspectives in Biology and Medicine, 1966—, Archives of Biochemistry and Biophysics, 1979-84, Biochemistry, 1969-72, Life Scis., 1973-78, Breast Cancer Rsch. and Treatment, 1980—, Endocrine-Related Cancer, 1994-2004, Jour. Biol. Markers, 1998—, Internat. Jour. Oncology, 2004-; assoc. editor: Jour. Steroid Biochemistry, 1974-94; contbr. articles to profl. jours. Recipient D.R. Edwards medal, 1970, La Madonnina prize, 1973, Pap award, 1975, prix Roussel, 1976, Nat. award Am. Cancer Soc., 1976, Gregory Pincus Meml. award, 1978, Gairdner Found. award, 1979, Lucy Wortham James award, 1980, Charles F. Kettering prize, 1980, Golden Plate award, 1980, Nat. Acad. Clin. Biochemistry award, 1981, Scientist of Yr. award Achievement Rewards for Coll. Scientists Found., 1981, Pharmacia award, 1982, Hubert H. Humphrey award, 1983, Rolf Luft medal, 1983, Renzo Grattarola medal, 1984, Fred C. Koch award, 1984, Axel Munthe award, 1985, Humboldt Sr. Rsch. prize, 1992, Joseph Bolivar DeLee award Chgo. Lying-In Hosp., 1995, Brinker Internat. award for breast cancer rsch. Susan G. Komen Found., 2002, Albert Lasker award for Basic Med. Rsch., Albert and Mary Lasker Found., 2004; Thomson Sci. laureate in physiology/medicine, 2006; citations: Ohio State Senate and Ho. Reps., 2004; Guggenheim fellow, 1946-47. Mem. NAS (coun. 1981-84), AAAS (Amory prize 1977), Am. Soc. Biochemistry and Molecular Biology, Am. Chem. Soc., Am. Assn. Cancer Rsch. (G.H.A. Clowes award 1975, Dorothy P. Landon prize 2002), Endocrine Soc. (pres. 1980-81), Am. Gyn/Ob Soc. (hon.), St. Paul Surg. Soc. (hon.), EORTC Receptor and Biomarker Group (hon.), Honorable Order Ky. Cols. Office: U Cin Dept Cell Biology Vontz Ctr Molecular Studies 3125 Eden Ave Cincinnati OH 45267-0521 Office Phone: 513-558-5750. Business E-Mail: elwood.jensen@uc.edu.

JENSEN, ERIK HUGO, pharmaceutical quality control consultant; b. Fredericia, Denmark, June 27, 1924; came to U.S. 1950; s. Alfred Marinus and Clara Krista (Sorensen) J.; m. Alice Emy Olesen, Oct. 8, 1949; children: Ian Peter, Lisa Joan, Linda Anne. BS, Royal Danish Sch. Pharmacy, Copenhagen, 1945, MS, 1948, PhD, 1954. Head product development AB Ferrosan, Malmo, Sweden, 1955-57; research scientist Upjohn Co., Kalamazoo, Mich., 1957-62, head quality control, 1962-63, mgr. quality control, 1963-66, asst. dir. quality control, 1966-81, dir. quality control, 1981-85, exec. dir. control devel. and adminstrn., 1985-86; pres., cons. Jensen Enterprises, 1986—. Author: A Study on Sodium Borohydride, 1954; contbr. articles to profl. jours.; patentee in field. Bd. dirs. Kalamazoo Inst. Arts, 1971-73, treas., 1973-74, pres., 1974-75. Mem. Pharm. Mfr.'s Assn. (quality control sect. recorder 1971-78, vice chmn. 1978-80, chmn. 1980-83), Acad. Pharm. Scis. (vice chmn. 1968-69, chmn. 1971-72) Lodge: Kiwanis (treas. 1962-65). Avocations: painting, sculpting, photography.

JENSEN, HAROLD LEROY, medical liability insurance administrator, physician; b. Mpls., Aug. 17, 1926; s. Harold Hans and Nell Irene (Cameron) Jensen; m. Nancy Elizabeth Scharff, Sept. 9, 1950 (div. 1976); children: Eric Richard, Kris Ann, Beth Susan; m. Sandra Lee Steinel, Oct. 18, 1976. BS, U. Ill., 1950, MD, 1955. Intern Ill. Ctrl. Hosp., Chgo., 1955-56, resident, 1956-57; pvt. practice in internal medicine Ill., 1957—87; mem. staff Ingalls Meml. Hosp., Harvey, Ill., dir. continuing med. edn., 1979-87, v.p. med. affairs, 1987-2000, cons. med. affairs, 2000—. Asst. clin. prof. medicine U. Ill.; guest lectr. Gov.'s State U., University Park, Ill.; bd. gov. ISMIE Mut. Ins. Co., 1986—. Mem. editl. bd.: Chgo. Healthcare, 1990—93; contbr. articles to profl. jours. Chmn. Med. Polit. Action Com., 1990—92; pres. bd. dirs. Homewood (Ill.) Pub. Libr., 1970—76; mem. policy bd. Cook County Healthcare Summit, 1990; chmn. Met. Chgo. Health Info. Network, 1995—2000. With US Army, 1944—46. Mem.: AMA (del. 1983—95), Ill. Med. Physicians' Svc. Orgn. (bd. dirs. 1995—96), Am. Coll. Utilization Rev. Physicians (bd. dirs. 1985—89, cert.), ACP Execs., Chgo. Health Econ. Coun. (vice chmn. 1981—85), Ill. Med. Soc. (trustee 1983—86, sec., treas. 1986, chmn. bd. trustees 1988—90, treas. 1988—96), Chgo. Med. Soc. (pres. 1985—86), Flossmoor Country Club (pres. 1972—73). Republican. Office: ISMIE Mutual Ins Co 20 N Michigan Ave Chicago IL 60602-4811

JENSEN, JIM, state legislator; b. Omaha, Jan. 17, 1934; m. Joan Vecera, 1959; children: Jon, Jeff, Jill, Jay, Joel. Student, Omaha U. Contractor pvt. practice, Omaha, 1959—; mem. Nebr. Legislature, Lincoln, 1994—. Chmn. Omaha Zoning Bd. Appeals, 1987—; vice chmn. Papio/Mo. River Natural Resources Bd., 1990—. Mem. Pride Omaha (bd. dirs. 1989—), Met. Omaha Builders Assn. (bd. dirs. 1960—), Rotary Club.

JENSEN, JOHN W., state legislator; b. York, Nebr., Mar. 28, 1926; m. Myrtle L. Shipp; 5 children. Farmer, 1947—; mem. Iowa Senate from 11th dist., Des Moines, 1978—. Bd. dirs. Iowa Plastics Tech. Ctr. Mem. Bapt. Ch. With USMC, WWII. Mem. Corn Growers Assn., Cattlemen's Assn., Bremer County Farm Bur. Republican. Home: 1339 120th St Plainfield IA 50666-9646 E-mail: john_jensen@legis.state.ia.us.

JENSEN, KATHRYN PATRICIA (KIT), broadcast executive; b. Fairbanks, Alaska, June 20, 1950; d. Edward Leroy and Doris Patricia (Fee) Bigelow; 1 child, Alexander Morgan. BA, U. Alaska, 1974. Sta. mgr., program dir. Sta. KUAC-FM, U. Alaska, Fairbanks, 1976-82; gen. mgr. Sta. KUAC-FM-TV, U. Alaska, Fairbanks, 1982-87; pres., gen. mgr. Sta. WCPN-FM, 1987—2001; COO Stas. WVIZ/PBS and 90.3 WCPN Ideastream, Cleve., 2001—. Founding mem. Alaska Pub. Radio Network, 1978-85; bd. dirs. Nat. Pub. Radio, 1983-89, Pub. Radio Internat., 1997—; mentor Civic Innovation Lab, 2007; bd. dirs. Parkworks, 2007. Bd. dirs. United Way, Cleve., 2001—04. Recipient Elaine B. Mitchell award Alaska Pub. Radio Network, 1988, Oebie award, 1992, 95, William H. Kling Innovation and Entrepreneurship award Pub. Radio Internat., 1995, Leadership in Non-profit Mgmt. award Case We. Res. U., Mandel Ctr. Non-Profit Orgns., 1999, No. Ohio Live Rainmakers award, 2002, Cleve. Preservation award, 2006, Arts Prize Cleve. award, 2006; named Pub. Radio Gen. Mgr. of Yr., DEI/PRADO, 1999. Episcopalian. Avocations: reading, gardening. Office: Stas WVIZ & WCPN Ideastream 1375 Euclid Ave Cleveland OH 44115 Office Phone: 216-916-6100.

JENSEN, KENNETH R., data processing executive; BA in Econs., Princeton U.; MBA in Acctg. and Econs., PhD in Acctg. and Econs., U. Chgo. Exec. v.p. Fiserv, Inc., Brookfield, Wis., 1984—86, CFO, sec., treas., dir., 1984—, sr. exec. v.p., 1986—. Office: Fiserv Inc 255 Fiserv Dr Brookfield WI 53045

JENSEN, LYNN EDWARD, retired medical association administrator, economist; b. Rock Springs, Wyo., May 27, 1945; s. Glen and Helen (Anderson) J.; m. Carol Jean Lombard, June 10, 1967 (dec. Dec. 2001); children: Chelsea, Kara; m. Janet Gayle Clash, Jan 24, 2004. BA, Idaho State U., 1967; PhD, U. Utah, 1979. Rsch. assoc. Dept. Commerce, Washington, 1967, U. Utah, 1971-74, Utah State Planning Office, 1971-74; economist AMA Rsch. Ctr., Chgo., 1974-75, dir., 1975-85; v.p. health policy AMA, Chgo., 1985-96, group v.p. strategic mgmt. and devel., 1996-97, COO, 1997-2000, interim exec. v.p., 1998, ret., 2000. Mem. Robert Wood Johnson Found. Adv. Com., Princeton, N.J., 1983-84, Johnson & Johnson Cmty. Health Program, 1985-88; health adv. com. GAO. Editor-in-chief Intermountain Econ. Rev., 1972-73; assoc. editor Jour. Bus. and Econ. Stats., 1981-85; contbr. articles to profl. jours. With U.S. Army, 1968-70. Mem. AMA, Assn. Am. Med. Soc. Execs., Am. Soc. Assn. Execs., Am. Econ. Assn., Nat. Assn. Bus. Economists. Presbyterian. Avocations: reading, computers, swimming, photography, bicycling. Home: 1310 W Francis Dr Arlington Heights IL 60005-2210 Personal E-mail: lejensen@comcast.net.

JENSEN, RICHARD JORG, biologist, educator; b. Sandusky, Ohio, Jan. 17, 1947; s. Aksel Carl and Margaret (Wolfe) Jensen; m. Faye Robertson, May 30, 1970. BS, Austin Peay State U., 1970, MS, 1972; PhD, Miami U., 1975. Asst. prof. Wright State U., 1975-79; prof. St. Mary's Coll., 1979—. Guest prof. U. Notre Dame, Ind., 1981—, dir. Greene-Nieuwland Hebarium, 1988—; sr. rsch. fellow Ctr. field Biology, Austin Peay State U., 1986—88; vis. scholar dept. botany Miami U., 1987; panelist systematic biology program NSF, 1983—87; exec. com. Am. Midland Maturalist, 1990—. Assoc. editor: Am. Midland Naturalist, 1989—2004; mem. editl. bd. Plant Systematics and Evolution, 1990—96; assoc. editor: Systematic Botany, 1996—2000. Named to Acad. Hall of Fame, Austin Peay State U., 1998; grantee, NSF, 1973, 1979, 1985, 1987, 1995, Rsch. Corp., 1984, Eli Lilly, 1990. Fellow: Ind. Acad. Sci. (co-chair program com. 1988, fellow com., biol. survey com., publ. com., grantee 1983, 1991); mem.: Internat. Oak Soc. (bd. dirs. 1997—, membership chair 1997—, webmaster 2000—06, Spl. Svc. award 2006), Soc. Systematic Biology, Internat. Assn. Plant Taxonomy, Bot. Soc. Am., Am. Soc. Plant Taxonomists (rsch. com. 1987—90, chmn. 1989—90, treas. 1991—96, honors and awards com. 2000—02, coun. mem. at large 2000—03, chair 2001, pres.-elect 2004, pres. 2005, past pres. 2006, Disting. Svc. award 1996), Sigma Xi (grantee 1974). Democrat. Avocations: reading, computing, genealogy. Home: 2044 Carrbridge Ct South Bend IN 46614-3514 Office: St Mary's Coll Dept Biology Notre Dame IN 46556 Also: Greene-Nieuwland Herbarium Univ of Notre Dame Dept Biol Scis Notre Dame IN 46556 Office Phone: 574-284-4674. Business E-Mail: rjensen@saintmarys.edu.

JENSEN, SAM, lawyer; b. Blair, Nebr., Oct. 30, 1935; s. Soren K. and Frances (Beck) J.; m. Marilyn Heck, June 28, 1959 (div. Jan. 1987); children: Soren R., Eric, Dana; m. Carmen Patton, Apr. 7, 1990. BA, U. Nebr., 1957, JD, 1961. Bar: Nebr. 1961. With Smith Bros., Lexington, Nebr., 1961-63, Swarr, May, Smith and Andersen, Omaha, 1963-83, Erickson & Sederstrom, P.C., Omaha, 1983—2005, Berens and Tate, P.C., L.L.O., Omaha, 2005—. Chmn. bd. dirs., v.p. bd. dirs. Omaha Public Power Dist., 1979-81; chmn. Nebr. Coordinating Commn. for Postsecondary Edn., 1976-78. Del. Nat. Rep. Conv., 1960, mem. Nebr. Rep. Ctrl. Com., 1968-70; mem. Regents Commn. Urban U., U. Nebr., Omaha, chmn. Task Force on Higher Edn.; mem. Hwy Commn. State of Nebr., 1989-95; vice chmn. Opera Omaha, 1992-95, v.p., 1994-96. Recipient Disting. Service award U. Nebr., 1981 Mem. Omaha Bar Assn. (past exec. com.), Nebr. Bar Assn. (chmn. com. public relations 1973-76), Am. Bar Assn., U. Nebr. Alumni Assn. (pres. 1976-78), Rotary Club, Omaha Club, Beta Theta Pi, Phi Delta Phi. Clubs: Rotary, Omaha, Racquet. Office: Berens and Tate PC LLO 10050 Regency Cir Ste 400 Omaha NE 68114 Home Phone: 402-963-9715; Office Phone: 402-391-1991. Personal E-mail: samjensen@cox.net. Business E-Mail: samj@berenstate.com.

JENSON, JON EBERDT, metal products executive; b. Madison, Wis., Aug. 1934; s. Theodore Joel and Gertrude Beatrice (Eberdt) J.; m. Jeannette Marie Hasman, May 1, 1976; children: James, Peter. BS, U. Wis., 1956; postgrad., Goethe U., Frankfort, Germany, 1956; diploma, U. Cologne, West Germany, 1957. From staff rep. to dir. mktg. and tech. svcs. Forging Industry Assn., Cleve., 1959-75; exec. v.p., sec. Am. Metal Stamping Assn., Cleve., 1975-80; pres. Precision Metalforming Assn., Independence, Ohio, 1980-2000, pres. emeritus, 2000—; interim dir. Precision Machined Products Assn., Brecksville, Ohio, 2001—02. Exec. dir., sec. Forging Industry Ednl. and Rsch. Found., Cleve., 1967-75; lectr. NYU, 1973-75; Ohio bd. advisors Liberty Mut. Ins. Co. Author: Forging Industry Handbook, 1966; editor: Metal Forming mag, 1975-90, pub. 1990-2000. Bd. regents Insts. Orgn. Mgmt., U.S. C. of C., 1977-83, vice chmn., 1982, chmn., 1983; mem. bd. regents Marycrest Sch., Independence, Ohio, 1979-86; bd. dirs. Cleve. Conv. and Visitors Bur., 1988; chmn. Consuming Industries Trade Action Coalition, 1999-; mem. U.S. adv. trade com. With USNR, 1958-59. Rotary Internat. fellow, 1956 Mem. Am. Soc. Assn. Execs. (cert. assn. exec.), Cleve. Soc. Assn. Execs., Rockwell Springs Trout Club. Home: 5700 Brookside Rd Cleveland OH 44131-6013 E-mail: jjenson@pma.org.

JERGER, EDWARD WILLIAM, engineering educator, dean; b. Milw., Mar. 13, 1922; s. Nickolaus and Ann (Huber) J.; m. Dorothy Marie Post, Aug. 2, 1944 (dec. 1981); children: Betty Ann Murphy, Barbara Lee Smyth; m. Elizabeth Cordiner Sweitzer, Mar. 27, 1982. BS in Mech. Engring, Marquette U., 1946; MS, U. Wis., 1948; PhD, Iowa State U., 1951. Registered profl. engr., Iowa, Ind. Process engr. Wis. Malting Co., Manitowoc, 1946-47; asst. prof. mech. engring. Iowa State U., 1948-55; asso. prof. mech. engring. U. Notre Dame, 1955-61, prof., head mech. engring., 1961-68, asso. dean, 1968-82, prof. mech. engring., 1982-97, prof. emeritus, 1989—. Cons. U. Madre De Maestra Santiago, Dominican Republic, 1965-71 Bd. dirs. Beaufort County Schoolbook Found. Served with USAAF, 1943-46. Mem. ASME, Am. Soc. Engring. Edn., Nat. Soc. Profl. Engrs., Nat. Fire Protection Assn., Sigma Xi, Phi Kappa Phi, Pi Tau Sigma (nat. v.p. 1969-74, pres. 1974-78), Tau Beta Pi. Home: 4 Coburn Ct Bluffton SC 29909-4560 Personal E-mail: profjerger@davtv.com.

JERNSTEDT, RICHARD DON, public relations executive; b. McMinnville, Oreg., Feb. 26, 1947; s. Don and Catherine (Anderson) Jernstedt; m. Jean Diane Woods, Dec. 28, 1969; children: Ty Parker, Tiffin Kay. BS, U. Oreg., 1969. Mgr. mktg. com. Container Corp. Am., Chgo., 1976—78; exec. v.p. Golin/Harris, Chgo., 1983—85, pres., 1988—91; CEO Golin/Harris Comm., Chgo., 1991—. Bd. dirs. Off the St. Club of Chgo., 1984; bd. govs. 410 Club, 1991—. Lt. (j.g.) USNR, 1968—72. Named Outstanding Jr., U. Oreg., 1968; recipient Golden Trumpet award, Publicity Club of Chgo. Mem.: Arthur Page Soc., Corp. Voice (bd. dirs.), Coun. Pub. Rels. Firms (bd. dirs., vice chmn.), Internat. Pub. Rels. Assn., Pub. Rels. Soc. Am. (Silver Anvil award 1986), Internat. Assn. Bus. Communicators. Republican. Presbyterian. Avocations: sports, music, photography, travel.

JEROME, JERROLD V., retired insurance company executive; BS, Linfield Coll., 1952; MBA, Stanford U., 1959. V.p. Teledyne, Inc., LA, 1962-90; pres., CEO Unitrin, Inc., Chgo., 1990-92, vice chmn., 1992-94, chmn., 1994-99; ret., 1999. Office: Unitrin Inc 1 E Wacker Dr Chicago IL 60601-1802

JEROME, JOSEPH WALTER, mathematics professor; b. Phila., June 7, 1939; s. Joseph Walter and Hermena Josephine (Ostertag) J.; m. Sara Tobin, July 2, 1999. BS in Physics, St. Joseph's U., 1961; MS, Purdue U., 1963, PhD, 1966. Vis. asst. prof. U. Wis., Madison, 1966-68; asst. prof. Case Western Res. U., Cleve., 1968-70; faculty Northwestern U., Evanston, Ill., 1970—, assoc. prof., 1972, prof. math., 1976—. Vis. fellow Oxford (Eng.) U., 1974—75; vis. prof. U. Tex., Austin, 1978—79, Rush Med. Coll., Chgo., 1994—97; cons. Bell Labs., NJ, 1981—87; vis. scientist, 1982—83; vis. scholar U. Chgo.1, 1985; mem. adv. panel Internat. Workshops on Computational Electronics, 1990—; reviewer in field. Author (with S. Fisher): Springer Lecture Series Math. 479, 1975, Approximation of Nonlinear Evolution Systems, 1983, Analysis of Charge Transport, 1995; editor: Modelling and Computation for Applications, 1998; editor: (with G.Q. Chen and G. Gasper) Nonlinear Partial Differential Equations, 2005; mem. editl. bd.: Jour. Nonlinear Analysis, Jour. Computational Electronics; contbr. more than 120 articles to profl. jours. Br. Sci. Coun. Sr. Vis. fellow Oxford, 1974-75; NSF Rsch. grantee, 1970—, Office Naval Rsch. Rsch. grantee, 2005—; recipient Disting. Alumnus award Purdue U. Sch. Sci., 1996. Mem. Am. Math. Soc., Soc. for Indsl. and Applied Math. Roman Catholic. Office: orthwestern U 2033 Sheridan Rd Evanston IL 60208-0830 Office Phone: 847-491-5575. Business E-Mail: jwj@math.northwestern.edu.

JEROME, KATHLEEN A., writer, retired publishing executive; b. Biloxi, Miss., May 14, 1955; d. Clarence and Marianne M. Boehm; children: Lindsay, Eric. BS in Biology Edn., Miami U., Oxford, Ohio, 1977. High sch. biology tchr., Ill., 1978-79; home tutor Fed. Homebound Program, Ill., 1980; from sci. editor to pres. Scott Foresman & Co., Glenview, Ill., 1981—95; pvt. practice Daniel Island, SC, 1996—. Mem. Nat. Sci. Tchrs. Assn., Internat. Reading Assn., Trident Literacy Assn. (bd. dirs. 2003—). Office Phone: 843-856-3532. E-mail: kjerome@verticalconnectpress.com.

JEROME, NORGE WINIFRED, nutritionist, anthropologist, educator; b. Grenada, Nov. 3, 1930; arrived in U.S.A., 1956, naturalized, 1973; d. McManus Israel and Evelyn Mary (Grant) Jerome. BS magna cum laude (hon.), Howard U., 1960; MS, U. Wis., 1962, PhD, 1967. Cert. nutrition splty.; fellow Am. Coll. Nutrition. Asst. prof. U. Kans. Med. Sch., Kans. City, 1967—72, assoc. prof., 1972—78, prof., 1978—95, dir. cmty. nutrition divsn., 1981—95; dir. Office of Nutrition, AID, Washington, 1988—91; sr. rsch. fellow Univ. Ctr., AID, Washington, 1991—92; interim assoc. dean minority affairs U. Kans. Med. Sch., Kans. City, 1996—98, prof. emerita, 1996—. Tech. adv. group The Nat. Ctr. for Minority Health; dir. ednl. resource centers U. Kans. Med. Center, 1974-77, head cmty. nutrition lab., 1978-95; cons. Children's TV Workshop, 1974-77; chair adv. bd. Teenage Parents Ctr., 1971-75; planning and budget coun., children and family svc. United Cmty. Svc., 1971-80; panel on nutrition edn. White House Conf. on Food, Nutrition and Health, 1969; bd. dir., health care com. Prime Health, 1976-79; bd. dir. Coun. on Children, Media and Merchandising; consumer edn. task force Mid Am. Health Systems Agy., 1977-79; commr. N. Am. working group Commn. Anthropology Food and Food Habits, Internat. Union Anthrop. and Ethnol. Sci., 1979-80; chmn. com. nutritional anthropology Internat. Union utritional Sci., 1979-80; lipid metabolism adv. com. NIH, 1978-80; nat. adv. panel multi-media campaign to improve children's diet U.S. Dept. Agrl., 1979-81; bd. advisers Am. Coun. on Sci. and Health, 1985-88; cons. in field. Sr. author: Nutritional Anthropology, 1980; asso. editor: Jour. Nutrition Edn., 1971-77; adv. council, 1977-80; editor: Nutritional Anthropology Communicator, 1974-77; mem. editl. bd.: Med. Anthropology: Cross Cultural Studies in Health and Illness, 1976-88, Internat. Jour. Nutrition Planning, 1977-88, Nutrition and Cancer: An Internat. Jour, 1978-2000, Jour. Nutrition and Behavior, 1981-86; contbr. articles to profl. journals. Mem. com. man food sys. NRC, 1980-83; bd. dirs. Kans. City Urban League, 1969-77, Crittenton Ctr., Kans. City, Mo., 1979-80, Johnson County Kans. Libr. Found., 2004—, exec. com., 2005—; mem. awards com. in nutrition edn. Met. Life Found., 1983-85; pres. Assn. for Women in Devel., 1991-93; trustee U. Bridgeport, Conn., 1992—; trustee Child Health Found., 1992-2000, chmn. bd. dirs., 1996-98; v.p., bd. trustees U. Bridgeport, Conn., 1997—; bd. dirs. Black Health Care Coalition of Kansas City, 1993-2002, Solar Cookers Internat., 1992-2000, pres., 1998-2000, Johnson County, Kans. Found. on Aging, 2001-04, Health Care Found. Greater Kansas City, 2004-06; mem. Commn. on Aging, Johnson County, Kans., 1997-2007; bd. dirs., vice chair cmty. adv. com. Kansas City Health Care Found., 2004. Decorated Dau. Brit. Empire; recipient First Higuchi Irvin Youngberg Rsch. Achievement award U. Kans., 1982, Excellence in Academia award Inst. Caribbean Studies, 2002, Disting. Svc. award NAACP, 2005, Johnson County Trailblazer award, 2006. Fellow Am. Soc. for Nutritional Sci., Am. Anthrop. Assn. (chair com. nutritional anthropology 1974-77, founder com. nutritional anthropology 1974), Soc. Applied Anthropology, Am. Coll. Nutrition, Soc. Med. Anthropology, Am. Soc. Nutritional Sci., 1998; mem. Am. Public Health Assn. (food and nutrition coun. 1975-78, governing coun. 1982-85), Am. Inst. Nutrition (program com. 1983-86), Am. Soc. Clin. Nutrition, Am. Men and Women of Sci., Nat. Acad. Sci. (world food and nutrition study panel), N.Y. Acad. Sci., Inst. Food Technologists, Am. Dietetic Assn., Assn. for Women in Devel. (pres. 1991-93), Soc. Behavioral Medicine, Club of Rome (U.S. assoc.). Office: U Kans Med Ctr 3901 Rainbow Blvd Mail Stop 1008 Kansas City KS 66160 Office Phone: 913-588-2770. Business E-Mail: njerome@kumc.edu.

JERSE, EDWARD, state representative; b. Cleve., Apr. 8, 1958; married; 3 children. BA in Hist., Georgetown U., 1980; JD, Harvard U., 1983. Lawyer Arter & Hadden, Ohio; asst. atty. gen. Office Of Atty. Gen. Ohio; state rep. dist. 7 Ohio Ho. of Reps., Columbus, 1995, ranking minority mem. fin. and appropriations com., mem. criminal justice, health, judiciary, and ways and means coms., mem. transp. and justice subcom.; atty. Moscarino & Treu LLP, Cleveland, Ohio, 1983. Adj. faculty Case Western Res. U. Sch. Law, Cleve., 1990. Sr. assoc. Cleve. Tomorrow, 1984—85; councilman Euclid (Ohio) City Coun., 1989—93. Mem.: Phi Beta Kappa. Democrat. Office: Moscarino & Treu LLP 1422 Euclid Ave Ste 630 Cleveland OH 44115 Office Phone: 216-621-1000. Office Fax: 216-622-1556.

JESCHKE, THOMAS, gifted education educator; Dir. spl. edn. Des Moines Pub. Schs., 1975-93, exec. dir. student and family svcs., 1993—. Recipient Coun. of Admin. of Spec. Edn. Outstanding Admin. award, 1994. Office: Des Moines ISD Adminstrv Office 1801 16th St Des Moines IA 50314-1902

JESKE, MARC R., lawyer; b. 1952; m. Laura Jeske; 2 children. BA, U. Ill., Champaign, 1974; JD, MBA, Northwestern U., 1979. Bar: Ill. 1979. In-house counsel Chgo. and Northwestern Transp. Co., 1979—87, Inland Steel Industries, 1987—2001; gen. counsel & corp. sec. Ispat Inland Inc., 2001—. Avocation: running. Office: Ispat Inland Inc 3210 Watling St East Chicago IN 46312 Office Phone: 219-399-5528.

JESKEWITZ, SUZANNE E., state representative; b. Galesville, Wis., Feb. 21, 1942; m. James Jeskewitz; 2 children. BA, U. Wis., LaCrosse, 1964. Tchr., 1964—69; program dir. YMCA, 1978—87; assoc. dir. Menomonee Falls C. of C., 1987—91; pub. rels. rep.; cmty. banking coord.; real estate broker, 1990—95; state assembly mem. Wis. State Assembly, Madison, 1996—, chair, ways and means com., mem. children and families, colls. and univs., and criminal justice coms. Mem. planning commn., Menomonee Falls, Wis., 1992—96; mem. chamber amb. com., scholarshp bd., bd. leadership; bd. mgrs. YMCA. Republican. Office: State Capitol Rm 314 N PO Box 8952 Madison WI 53708-8952

JESSEN, LLOYD K., pharmacist, lawyer; BS in Pharmacy, S.D. State U., 1978; JD, Drake U., 1985. Lic. pharmacist, S.D., Minn., Iowa; bar: Iowa 1985. Staff phamacist K-Mart Corp., Mason City, Iowa, 1978-79; cmty. pharmacy mgr. People's Drug Stores, Inc., Spencer, Iowa, 1979-82; hosp. pharmacist Mercy Hosp. Med. Ctr., Des Moines, 1982-86; legal rschr. Drake Legal Rsch. Svc., Drake U., Des Moines, 1983-84; staff atty. Iowa Supreme Ct., Des Moines, 1986-87; chief investigator Iowa Bd. of Pharmacy Examiners, Des Moines, 1987-90, exec. sec., dir. and drug control program adminstr., 1990—. Pharmacy/drug law lectr. Drake U., Des Moines, 1988-99, U. Osteo. Medicine and Health Sci., Des Moines, 1989-94, U. Iowa Coll. of Pharmacy, Iowa City, 1989-99, U. Iowa Coll. of Medicine, 1990-94, Am. Inst. of Bus., Des Moines, 1988-90; presenter in field. Editor (newsletter) Iowa Bd. of Pharmacy Examiners, 1990-99. Grantee Bur. of Justice Assistance/U.S. Dept. Justice, 1990-91, 91-92, 92-93, 93-94. Mem. Am. Soc. for Pharmacy Law, Iowa Pharmacists Assn., Nat. Assn. of Bds. of Pharmacy, Nat. assn. of State Controlled Substance Authorities. Office: Iowa Bd of Pharmacy Examiners 400 SW 8th St Ste E Des Moines IA 50309-4688

JESSUP, PAUL FREDERICK, financial economist, educator; b. Evanston, Ill., Apr. 16, 1939; s. Paul S. and Gertrude (Strohmaier) J.; m. Johanna A.M. Friesen, June 27, 1970; children: Christine Marieke, Paul Charles Friesen. BS, Northwestern U., 1960, PhD, 1966; AM, Harvard U., 1963; BA, U. Oxford, Eng., 1963; MA, U. Oxford, 1983. Economist com. banking and currency U.S. Ho. of Reps., Washington, 1963-64; faculty U. Minn., Mpls., 1967-82, prof. fin., 1973-82; with Jessup & Co., Inc., St. Paul, 1982—; William Kahlert prof. mgmt. and econs. Hamline U., St. Paul, 1988—. Dir. Gerbill Inc.; Sabbatical prof. in residence Fed. Res. Bank, Mpls., 1973-74 Author: The Theory and Practice of Nonpar Banking, 1967, (with Roger B. Upson) Returns in Over-the-Counter Stock Markets, 1973, Competing for Stock Market Profits, 1974, Modern Bank Management: A Casebook, 1978, Modern Bank Management, 1980, Invest To Win: A Coach's Guide to Stocks, Bonds and Mutual Funds, 2001; editor: Innovations in Bank Management: Selected Readings, 1969; contbr. articles to profl. jours. Mem. Midwest Fin. Assn. (past pres.), Univ. Club. Home: 1979 Shryer Ave W Saint Paul MN 55113-5414 Office: Hamline U 1536 Hewitt Ave Saint Paul MN 55104-1284

JETT, ERNEST CARROLL, JR., paper company executive, lawyer; b. Liberty, Tex., July 10, 1945; m. Janene L. Jett. BA cum laude, Baylor U., 1967; MA, La. State U., 1969; JD, U. Tex., 1973. Bar: Tex. 1973, U.S. Dist. (so. dist.) Tex. 1979, U.S. Ct. Appeals (5th cir.) 1979, U.S. Supreme Ct. 1979, Mo. 1980. Mem. legal staff Cooper Industries, Inc., 1973-75, Tenneco, Inc., 1975-79; v.p., gen. counsel, sec. Leggett & Platt, Inc., Carthage, Mo., 1979—. Editor Tex. Internat. Law Jour. 1972-73. Mem. ABA, Am. Corp. Coun. Assn., Am. Soc. Corp. Secs., State Bar Tex., Mo. Bar Assn., Phi Alpha Theta, Alpha Chi, Phi Eta Sigma, Phi Delta Phi, Pi Gamma Mu. Office: Leggett & Platt Inc PO Box 757 1 Leggett Rd Carthage MO 64836-9649 Home: 4702 S Jackson Ave Joplin MO 64804-4837 Office Phone: 417-358-8131. E-mail: ernest.jett@leggett.com.

JETTKE, HARRY JEROME, retired government official; b. Detroit, Jan. 2, 1925; s. Harry H. and Eugenia M. (Dziatkiewicz) J.; m. Josefina Suarez-Garcia, Oct. 22, 1948; 1 child, Joan Lillian Clark. BA, Wayne State U., 1961; grad. Cert. drug specialist FDA. Owner, operator Farmacia Virreyes/Farmacias Regina, Toluca, Mexico, 1948-55; intern pharmacist Cunningham Drug Stores, Detroit, 1955-63; drug specialist, product safety specialist FDA, Detroit, 1963-73; acting dir. for Cleve., U.S Consumer Product Safety Commn., 1973-75, compliance officer, 1975-78, supr. investigations, 1978-82, regional compliance officer, 1982-83, sr. resident, 1983-90. Served with Fin. Dept., U.S. Army, 1942-43. Mem. Am. Soc. for Quality Control (chmn. Cleve. sect. 1977-78, cert. quality technician, cert quality engr.), Assn. Nat. Mexicana de Estadistica y Control de Calidad, Ohio Gun Collectors Assn., Cleve. Fed. Exec. Bd. (policy com.), Civilian Police Acad. Westlake Police Dept. Roman Catholic. Home: 25715 Yeoman Dr Cleveland OH 44145-4745

JETTON, GIRARD REUEL, JR., lawyer, retired oil industry executive; b. Washington, Feb. 19, 1924; s. Girard Reuel and Hallie (Grimes) J.; m. Mera Riddell, Sept. 4, 1948 (dec. Dec. 1997); children: Mera Elizabeth, Robert Girard, James Thomas. BS in Engring., George Washington U., 1945, BA, 1947; JD, Harvard U., 1950. Bar: D.C. 1951, Md. 1959, Ohio 1960. Elec. engr. in rsch., 1944-45; patent atty. Washington, 1950-51; atty. IRS, Washington, 1951-54; trial atty. Dept. Justice, Washington, 1954-55; atty. then ptnr. McClure & McClure, Washington, 1955-60; with Marathon Oil Co., Findlay, Ohio, 1960-85, asst. to chmn. bd., 1969-73, corp. sec., 1973-85; pvt. practice Findlay, 1985—. With USNR, 1945-46. Mem. Bar Assn. D.C., Findlay/Hancock County Bar Assn., Met. Club (Washington). Home and Office: PO Box 813 Leland MI 49654-0813

JEWELL, JOSEPH, entrepreneur; b. Stevensville, Mich., 1982; s. Stephen and Suzanne Jewell. BS, Calif. Inst. Tech., 2002; MSE, U. Mich., 2004. Co-founder & v.p. test preparation PrepMe.com, Chgo., 2005—. Co-author: Up Your Score: The Underground Guide to the SAT, 2001-2002 edit., 2000. Co-recipient 1st prize, Fortune Small Bus. Student Startup Competition, 2006; named one of Best Entrepreneurs Under 25, Bus. Week, 2006; recipient US Presdl. Scholar medallion, 2000; Rhodes scholar, Oxford U., 2004—06.

JEWETT, JOHN RHODES, real estate executive; b. Indpls., Nov. 24, 1922; s. Chester Aten and Grace (Rhodes) J.; m. Marybelle Bramhall, June 12, 1946; children: John R., Jane B. BA, DePauw U., 1944. Econ. research analyst Eli Lilly & Co., Indpls., 1946-48; with Pitman-Moore Co., Indpls., 1948-65, v.p., asst. to pres., 1959-65; with F.C. Tucker Co., Inc., Indpls., 1965—, v.p., 1978-98, Colliers Turley Martin Tucker, Indpls., 1998—. Pres. Market Sq. Arena, 1974-79, Ind. Pacers (profl. basketball team), 1977-79 Served with AUS, 1943-46. Mem. Met. Indpls. Bd. Realtors, Ind. Assn. Realtors, Nat. Assn. Realtors. Clubs: Meridian Hills Country, Kiwanis. Home: 8504 Bent Tree Ct Indianapolis IN 46260-2348 Office: 2500 One American Sq Indianapolis IN 46282

JEZEK, KENNETH CHARLES, geophysicist, educator, researcher; b. Chgo., May 17, 1951; s. Rudolph and June J.; m. Rosanne M. Graziano, Jan. 27, 1984. BSc in Physics with honors, U. Ill., 1973; MSc in Geophysics, U. Wis., 1977, PhD in Geophysics, 1980. Observer Bartol Rsch. Found. Cosmic Ray Lab., McMurdo Sta., Antarctica, 1973-74; postdoctoral fellow Inst. Polar Studies Ohio State U., Columbus, 1980-81; project assoc. Geophysical and Polar Rsch. Ctr. U. Wis., 1981-83; geophysicist U.S. Army Cold Regions Rsch. and Engring. Lab., Hanover, N.H., 1983-85, 87-89; mgr. polar oceans and ice sheets program NASA, Washington, 1985-87; rsch. asst. prof. Thayer Sch. Engring. Dartmouth Coll., Hanover, 1987-89; assoc. prof. geology Ohio State U., Columbus, 1989-95, prof. dept. geol. sci., 1995—, dir. Byrd Polar Rsch. Ctr., 1989-95, 97-99. Prin. investigator Greenland, 1982, 85, Greenland Sea, 1988, Greenland Ice Sheet, 1991, 92; geophysicist Ross Ice Shelf, Antarctica, 1974-75, Devon Island Ice Cap, 1975, Camp Century Greenland, 1977, Southern Greenland Ice Sheet, 1981, East Antarctica, 1981-82; field leader Ross Ice Shelf, 1976-77, Dome C East Antarctica, 1978-79; cons. Polar Ice Coring Office, Greenland, 1983; mem. ad hoc com. remote sensing polar regions Nat. Rsch. Coun., 1985-89, geophys. data com., 1987-94, glaciology com. polar rsch. bd., 1988-95, glaciology rep. SCAR, 1990—, earth studies com. NAS, 1991-95, mem. NAS sci. panel rev. NASA earth obs. sys. data info. sys., 1992-95, mem. NAS sci. panel rev. nat. space sci. data ctr., 1992; mem. numerous NASA coms.; mem. Environ. Task Force, 1992; lab. coord. Sea Ice Electromagnetic Accelerated Rsch. Initiative Office Naval Rsch., 1992. Assoc editor: Jour. Geophys. Rsch., 1991-94; contbr. articles, abstracts to profl. jours. NSF grantee, 1982-83, 83-84, 95-97, Office Naval Rsch. grantee, 1984-89, CRREL grntee, 1985-86, NASA grantee, 1985-87, 87-89, 88-92, 90, 91-93, 95-98, ONR grantee, others. Mem. Am. Geophys. Union (chmn. snow, ice and permafrost com. 1992-94), Soc. Exploration Geophysicists, Internat. Glaciol. Soc. (coun. 1991—), Sigma Xi. Office: Ohio State U Byrd Polar Rsch Ctr 1090 Carmack Rd Columbus OH 43210-1002

JEZUIT, LESLIE JAMES, manufacturing executive; b. Chgo., Nov. 4, 1945; s. Eugene and Tillie (Fleszewski) Jezuit; m. Janet Diane Bushlus, Oct. 12, 1968; children: Douglas Blake, Kevin Lane. BS in Mech. and Aerospace Engring., Ill. Inst. Tech., 1969, MBA, 1974. Mgr. engring. graphic systems group Rockwell Internat., Chgo., 1968-74, dir. comml. systems Cicero, Ill., 1974-75; v.p. mktg. and sales Mead Digital Sys., Dayton, Ohio, 1975-80; v.p. mktg. and sales Signal divsn. Fed. Signal Corp., University Park, Ill., 1980-81, pres. Signal divsn., 1981-85, v.p. corp. devel. Oak Brook, Ill., 1985-86; div. mgr. power distbn. div. Eaton Corp., Milw., 1986-87, gen. mgr. indsl. control and power distbn. div., 1987-88, v.p., 1988-91; pres., COO Robertshaw Controls Co., Richmond, Va., 1991-95; pres., CEO, chmn. bd dirs. Quixote Inc., Chgo., 1995—; chmn. Transp. Mgmt. Techs., LLC, Chgo., 1998-2001, Quixote Corp., 2001. Instr. Keller Sch. Mgmt., Chgo., 1982—83. Active United Way, Chgo., 1983—85; mem. Chgo. Crime Commn.; bd. dirs. Better Bus. Bur. Milw., 1986, United Performing Arts Found. Milw., 1986, Greater Milw. Com., 1991—92. Mem.: Gas Appliance Mfrs. Assn. (bd. dirs. 1994—96), Am. Hwy. Users Assn. (bd. dirs. 2001—, vice chmn. 2003), Monee C. of C., Will County Local Devel. Co. (v.p. 1984—85, Bus. Man of the Yr. award 1985), S. Surburban C. of C., Met. Club (Chgo.). Republican. Achievements include patents in field. Avocations: boating, fishing, cross country skiing, photography. Home: 26576 Countryside Lake Dr Mundelein IL 60060-3342 Office: Quixote Inc 35 E Wacker Dr Chicago IL 60601-2108 Office Phone: 312-467-6755. Personal E-mail: quixpres@msn.com.

JIBBEN, LAURA ANN, state agency administrator; b. Peoria, Ill., Oct. 1, 1949; d. Charles Otto and Dorothy Lee (Skaggs) Becker; m. Michael Eugene Hagan, July 7, 1967 (div. Apr. 1972); m. Louis C. Jibben, July 14, 1972. BA in Criminal Justice, Sangamon State U., 1984; MBA, Northwestern U., 1990. Asst. to chief of adminstrn. Ill. Dept. Corrections, Springfield, 1974-77, exec. asst. to dir., 1977-80, dep. dir., 1980-81; mgr. toll services Ill. Tollway Dept., Oak Brook, 1981-86; chief adminstrv. officer Regional Transp. Authority, Chgo., 1986-90, fund mgr. loss financing plan, 1987-90, also, chmn. pension trust, exec. dir., 1990-96; v.p., gen. mgr. MTA, Inc., Chgo., 1996-99; ptnr. Hanson Engrs., Inc., Oak Brook, Ill., 1999-2000; sr. project mgr., cons. mgmt. Alfred Benesch & Co., 2000—02, v.p., 2002—. Cons. labor studies Sangamon State U., Springfield, 1981; bd. dirs. Chgo. Found. for Women. Mem. surface tranps. adv. panel U. Ill., 1997—2000; apptd. mem. transp. adv. bd. City of Naperville, 1988—90; bd. dirs. Family Shelter Svcs., 1990—91; bd. dirs., chair devel. com. Govt. Assistance Program, 1997—2000, sec. bd., 1999; mem. nat. adv. bd. Women's Transp. Seminar, 1996—2004; mem. Peoria Women's Fund Grants Com., 2003—; mem. Midwest Traffic Conf. program com. Bradley U., 2002—; acting pres. Ctrl. Ill. chpt. WTS, 2004—, pres., 2004—05. Recipient Appreciation award VFW, Chgo., 1983, award Ill. State Toll Hwy. Authority, 1986; named Woman of Yr., Nat. Women's Transp. Seminar, 1991, AAUW, 1991. Mem. NAFE, Women's Transp. Seminar (Woman of Yr. award Chgo. chpt. 1991, Nat. Woman of Yr. 1991), Beta Sigma Phi (treas., v.p., corr. sec. Naperville and Easton, Ill. chpts.), Lambda Alpha. Avocations: reading, jogging, gardening, golf. Office: Alfred Benesch & Co 205 N Michigan Ave Ste 2400 Chicago IL 60601 Office Phone: 312-565-0450. Business E-Mail: ljibben@benesch.com.

JINDRA, CHRISTINE, editor; b. Cleve., Sept. 18, 1947; d. Lad Joseph and Ann Frances (Makar) J.; m. Peter J. Junkin, Aug. 1, 1970 (div. Dec. 1987); children: William Patrick, Michael Lad. BS in Journalsim, Ohio State U., 1969. City reporter Buffalo News, 1969-70; metro reporter Plain Dealer, Cleve., 1970-82, assignment editor, nat. reporter, 1982-84, state editor, 1984-86, metro editor, 1986-88, feature editor, 1988-92, asst. mng. editor, 1992-2001, Sunday editor, 2001—. Mem.: Women's Cmty. Found., Women's City Club. Avocations: skiing, gardening, travel, cooking. Office: Plain Dealer 1801 Superior Ave E Cleveland OH 44114-2198 Home Phone: 440-232-1460; Office Phone: 216-999-4839. E-mail: cjindra@plaind.com.

JISCHKE, MARTIN C., retired academic administrator; b. Chgo., Aug. 7, 1941; m. Patricia Fowler; 2 children. BS in Physics with honors, Ill. Inst. Tech., 1963, Doctoral Degree (hon.); MS in Aeronautics and Astronautics, MIT, 1964, PhD in Aeronautics and Astronautics, 1968; Doctoral Degree (hon.), Nat. Agrl. U. Ukraine. Engr. Rand Corp., Santa Monica, Calif., 1965; research engr. Battelle N.W. Lab., Richland, Washington, 1970; research fellow Donald W. Douglas Lab., Richland, 1971, Nat. Aeronautics and Space Adminstrn., Moffett Field, Calif., 1973; from asst. prof. to prof. aerospace, mech. and nuclear engring. U. Okla., 1968-75, prof., dir. Sch. Aerospace, Mech. and Nuclear Engring., 1977-81, interim pres., 1985, dean Coll. Engring., 1981-86, mem. various coms., 1985; White House fellow, spl. asst. to sec. of transp. U.S. Dept. Transp., Washington, 1975-76; chancellor U. Mo., Rolla, 1986-91; pres. Iowa State U., Ames, 1991-2000, Purdue U., 2000—07. Bd. dirs. Wabash Nat. Corp., 2002-, chmn. 2007-; bd. dirs. Kerr McGee Corp., Wabash Nat. Corp., Duke Realty Corp., Ctrl. Ind. Corp. Partnership, Assn. Am. Univs., NCAA, Nat. Assn. State Univs. and Land Grant Colls., Mo. Alliance for Sci., 1987-91, The Keystone Found., 1984-90, Mo. Corp. for Sci. and Tech., vice-chmn., 1990-91; participant Japanese Econ. Found. Vis. Leaders Program, 1983; mem. Gov.'s Coun. on Sci. and Tech. State of Okla., 1983-84, Gordon Rsch. Conf. on Geophysics; mem. planning com. for 80's Okla. State Regents for Higher Edn.; mem. organizing com. 14th Midwestern Mechanics Conf.; mem. adv. com. for engring. sci. NSF Engring. Directorate, 1985-88; mem. com. on statewide postsecondary telecomm. policy Mo. Coordinating Bd. for Higher Edn., 1987-91; chmn. Congrl. Aero. Adv. Com., 1987-89; sci. adviser to Gov. of Mo., 1990-91; mem. Am. Coun. on Edn. Com. on Math. and Sci., 1990-91; mem. coun. Nat. Acads. Govt. Univ. Industry Roundtable; chair Big Ten Conf. Coun. Presidents/Chancellors; mem. Pres.'s Coun. of Advisors on Sci. and Tech., 2006-. Contbr. articles and reports to profl. pubs. Civilian aide Sec. of Army, State of Mo. East, 1987-91; bd. dirs. Bankers Trust, 1995—, Iowa Spl. Olympics, Am. Coun. on Edn., 1996—, Nat. Merit Scholarship Corp., 1997—99; mem. Kellogg Commn. on the Future of State and Land-Grant U., 1995—2000; founding pres. Global Consortium of Higher Edn. and Rsch. for Agr., 1999. Decorated Ukraine medal of merit; recipient Ralph Teetor award Soc. Automotive Engrs., 1971, Brandon H. Griffith award U. Okla., U. Okla. Regents award for superior teaching, 1975, IIT Prof. Achievement award, 1992, Delta Tau Delta Achievement award, 1992, Engrs. Club St. Louis Achievement award, 1991, Dept. Army Outstanding Civilian Svc. medal, 1991, Justin Smith Morrill award USDA, 2004; NASA fellow, 1966; NSF fellow, 1965; AEC/NORCUS summer faculty fellow, 1970-71, NASA/ASEE fellow, 1973. Fellow AAAS, AIAA (assoc., sec.-treas. Okla. chpt., vice chmn., chmn.); mem. ASME, AAUP (v.p., pres. Okla. chpt.), NSPE, Am. Phys. Soc., Am. Soc. Engring. Edn. (Centennial Medallion 1993), Nat. Assn. State Univs. and Land Grant Colls. (bd. dirs., chair 1997-98), Assn. Big Twelve Univs. (pres. 1994-96), Mo. Soc. Profl. Engrs., Rotary, Phi Beta Kappa, Tau Beta Pi, Sigma Xi, Pi Tau Sigma, Sigma Gamma Tau, Sigma Pi Sigma, Phi Eta Sigma. Home: 500 McCormick Rd West Lafayette IN 47906 Office: Wabash Nat Corp PO Box 6129 Lafayette IN 47905

JOCHUM, PAM, state representative; b. Dubuque, Iowa, Sept. 26, 1954; AA, BA, Loras Coll. Pub. info. and mktg. dir. Loras Coll.; instr. N.E. Iowa C.C.; mem. Iowa Ho. Reps., Des Moines, 1993—, mem. various coms. including judiciary, mem. state govt. ways and means com. Chair Alzheimer Memory Walk, CROP Walk; del. Dem. Nat. Conv., 1980, floor whip, 1984; chair Dubuque County Dem. Ctrl. Com., 1982; statewide co-chair U.S. Senator Tom Harkin's Re-Election Com.; former bd. dirs. Dubuque County Assn. for Retarded Citizens, Dubuque County Compensation Bd., Loras Coll. Arts and Lectr. Series, Nat. Cath. Basketball Tournament, Sacred Heart Cath. Ch., Women's Recreation Assn., Mississippi Valley Promise, LWV. Democrat. Office: State Capitol East 12th and Grand Des Moines IA 50319 also: 2368 Jackson St Dubuque IA 52001 E-mail: pam.jochum@legis.state.ia.us.

JOCKETTY, WALT (WALTER J. JOCKETTY), professional baseball team manager, professional sports team executive; b. Mpls., Feb. 19, 1951; m. Sue Jocketty; children: Ashley, Joey. BBA, U. Minn., 1974. Dir. minor league ops. Oakland A's, 1980—83, dir. baseball adminstrn., farm dir., 1984—90; dir. baseball adminstrn., baseball ops. Oakland Athletics, 1991—93; asst. gen. mgr. Colo. Rockies, 1994; v.p., gen. mgr. St. Louis Cardinals, 1995—2007; spl. adv. to pres., CEO Cin. Reds, 2008, gen. mgr., 2008—. Named Maj. League Baseball's Exec. of Yr., Baseball Am., 2000, The Sporting News, 2000, 2004; recipient Rube Foster Legacy award, Negro Hall of Fame, 2004. Office: Cin Reds Great Am Ball Pk 100 Main St Cincinnati OH 45202*

JOCKUSCH, CARL GROOS, JR., mathematics professor; b. San Antonio, July 13, 1941; s. Carl Groos and Mary English (Dickson) J.; m. Elizabeth Ann Northrop, June 17, 1964; children: William, Elizabeth, Rebecca. Student, Vanderbilt U., 1959-60; BA with highest honors, Swarthmore Coll., 1963; PhD, M.I.T., 1966. Instr. ortheastern U., 1966-67; asst. prof. math. U. Ill., Urbana-Champaign, 1967-71, assoc. prof., 1971-75, prof., 1975—. Contbr. articles to profl. jours.; editor Jour. Symbolic Logic, 1974-75, Proc. Am. Math. Soc., 1997—. Mem. Assn. Symbolic Logic, Am. Math. Soc., Math. Assn. Am. Home: 704 E McHenry St Urbana IL 61801-6846 Office: Univ Ill Dept Math 1409 W Green St Urbana IL 61801-2943

JODARSKI, RICHARD R., social services association executive; m. Judith Jodarski; children: Jeremy, Jennifer. BS in Psychology, U. Wis., La Crosse, 1972. Account exec. Merrill, Lynch, Pierce, Fenner and Smith, 1975-78; bank trust officer, 1978-81; sr. trust officer First Nat. Bank of Manitowoc, Wis., 1981, v.p., sr. trust officer Wis., 1998; pres., CEO Aid Assn. for Lutherans Trust Co., Appleton, Wis., 1998—. Pres. Stangel Found.; bd. dirs. Manitowoc Mut. Ins. Co. Active Manitowoc YMCA Endowment Fund, Capitol Civic Centre, Manitowoc Symphony Orch. Office: Aid Assn for Lutherans 4321 N Ballard Rd Appleton WI 54919-0001

JODOCK, DARRELL HARLAND, minister, educator; b. Northwood, ND, Aug. 15, 1941; s. Harry N. and Grace H. (Hansen) J.; m. Janice Marie Swanson, July 8, 1972; children: Erik Thomas, Aren Kristofer. BA summa cum laude, St. Olaf Coll., 1962; BD with honors, Luther Theol. Sem., 1966; postgrad., Union Theol. Sem., NYC, 1966-67; PhD, Yale U., 1969. Ordained to ministry Am. Luth. Ch., 1973, Luth. Ch. in Am., 1978. Instr. Luther Theol. Sem., St. Paul, 1969-70, asst. prof., 1970-73, 75-78; asst. pastor Grace Luth. Ch., Washington, 1973-75; prof. dept. religion Muhlenberg Coll., Allentown, Pa., 1978-99, head dept. of religion, 1978-92, Class of 1932 rsch. prof., 1989; disting. prof. religion Gustavus Adolphus Coll., St. Peter, Minn., 1999—. Chmn. various coms. N.E. Pa. Synod Evang. Luth. Ch. in Am., 1979-99, del. to nat. assembly, 1995, 97, 99, 2005; adv. bd. Berman Ctr. for Jewish Studies, 1985-92; founder, chmn. bd. Inst. for Jewish-Christian Understanding, 1988-99; bd. Inst. for Ecumenical and Cultural Rsch., Collegeville, 1999—; chair Assn. Tchg. Theologians of the Evang. Luth. Ch. Am., 2002-06, Evang. Luth. Ch. Am. Consultative Panel Luth.-Jewish Rels., 2001—, chair, 2005—. Author: The Church's Bible: Its Contemporary Authority, 1989; translator: Luther and the Peasants' War (Hubert Kirchner), 1972; editor and co-author: Ritschl in Retrospect: History, Community and Science, 1995, Catholicism Contending with Modernity: Roman Catholic Modernism and Anti-Modernism in Historical Context, 1999, Covenantal Conversations: Christians in Dialogue with Jaws and Judaison, 2008; contbr. articles to profl. jours. Recipient Paul C. Empie Meml. award Muhlenberg Coll., 1987; Danforth Found. fellow 1962-69, Inst. for Ecumenical and Cultural Rsch. fellow, 1982-83, Covenant award Gustavus Adolphus Coll., 2007. Mem. Am. Acad. Religion (pres. 19th Century theology group 1981-86, 1997-2001), Am. Soc. Ch. History, Soc. for Values in Higher Edn., Internat. Schleiermacher Soc., Internat. Bonhoeffer Soc., Søren Kierkegaard Soc., Phi Beta Kappa, Omicron Delta Kappa (campus leadership 1985—). Office: Gustavus Adolphus Coll Dept Religion 800 W College Ave Saint Peter MN 56082-1485

JOEKEL, RONALD G., fraternal organization administrator; BA, Wesleyan U., Lincoln, Nebr., 1956; MEd, U. Nebr., 1959, EdD, 1966. Prin., tchr., DeWitt, Nebr., 1956-60; supt., 1960-63; supr., instr. Wesleyan U., Lincoln, Nebr., 1963-65, asst. dir., asst. prin., 1966-67, assoc. prof., 1970-72, assoc. dir., assoc. prof., 1971-72, assoc. dean, assoc. prof., 1972-88, assoc. dean, acting chair, 1988-89, chair, 1989-95; exec. dir. Phi Delta Kappa Internat., Bloomington, Ind., 1995—. Cons. Workers Compensation, Ohio, 1976-79. Dir. Ohio Dept. Highway Safety, Columbus, 1985-90, Dept. Pub. Svc., Cleve., 1990—; exec. dir. Ohio State Employment Rels. Bd., Columbus, 1984; asst. dir. Ohio Dept. Adminstrv. Svcs., Columbus, 1984-85, Ohio Dept. Natural Resources, Columbus, 1984-85; chmn. Nuclear Power Emergency Evaluation Com., Columbus, 1985-90; bd. dirs. Ohio Retirement Study Commn., 1983-84, North East Ohio Regional Sewer Dist., Cleve., 1991—. Office: Phi Delta Kappa International PO Box 789 Bloomington IN 47402-0789

JOERRES, JEFFREY A., employment services executive; BS, Marquette U., Milw., 1983. Various mgmt. positions IBM; v.p. sales and mktg. ARI Network Svcs.; v.p. mktg. Manpower, Inc., Milw., 1993, sr. v.p. European ops. and global account mgmt. and devel., pres., CEO, 1999—, chmn., 2001—. Bd. dirs. Artisan Funds, Johnson Controls, NAM; bd. trustees Comm. Econ. Devel. Bd. trustees Marquette U., 2000—; mem. Commn. Tech. & Adult Learning Nat. Gov. Assn. Mem.: Am. Soc. Tng. & Devel. Office: Manpower Inc 5301 N Ironwood Rd Milwaukee WI 53217-4982 Office Phone: 414-961-1000.

JOERSZ, FRAN WOODMANSEE, secondary school educator; b. Bismarck, ND, Apr. 29, 1954; d. Joe G. and Winnie (McGillic) Woodmansee; m. Jon D. Joersz; children: Brett, Ben, Courtney. Student, Bismarck State Coll., 1972; BA in Edn., U. Wyo., 1975. Tchr. 3rd grade Deer Trail (Colo.) Pub. Sch., 1975-76; tchr. 8th grade remedial reading Mandan (N.D.) Jr. High Sch., 1976-78; tchr. title I reading Saxvik St. Mary's Grade Sch., Bismarck, 1979; tchr. 8th grade devel. reading Wachter Jr. High Sch., Bismarck, 1979-81; tchr. 7th grade devel. reading written and oral communications Hughes Jr. High Sch., Bismarck, 1981—. Bd. dirs. Rape Victim Adv. Program; founding bd. dirs. Our Kids Need to Know; state bd. dirs. Make A Wish Found. Recipient Milken award, 1994; named Edn. alumna of Yr., U. Wyo., 2003. Mem. PEO, ND Edn. Assn. (Tchr. of Yr. 1991, Profl. Courage award 1994), Internat. Reading Assn., Nat. Assn. Student Activity Advisers. Avocations: walking, reading, volleyball, writing, travel. Home: 520 N Mandan St Bismarck ND 58501-3748 Office: Horizon Mid Sch 500 Ash Coulee Dr Bismarck D 58503 Office Phone: 701-221-3555. Business E-Mail: fran_joersz@educ8.org.

JOHANNES, ROBERT J., lawyer; b. Milwaukee, Wis., July 31, 1952; BA summa cum laude, Marquette U., 1974; JD, U. Chgo., 1977. Bar: Wis. 1977. Mem. Michael, Best & Friedrich LLP, Milw., 1977—. Mem. ABA, Wis. Bar Assn., Phi Beta Kappa. Office: Michael Best Friedrich LLP 100 E Wisconsin Ave Ste 3300 Milwaukee WI 53202-4108

JOHANNSEN, CHRIS JAKOB, agronomist, educator, administrator; b. Randolph, Nebr., July 24, 1937; s. Jakob J. and Marie J. (Lorenzsen) J.; m. Joanne B. Rockwell, Aug. 16, 1959; children: Eric C., Peter J. BS, U. Nebr., Lincoln, 1959, MS, 1961; PhD, Purdue U., 1969. Program leader lab. for applications of remote sensing Purdue U., West Lafayette, Ind., 1966—69, from asst. prof. to assoc. prof. agronomy, 1969—77, prof., 1985—2003, dir. ag data network, 1985—87, dir. lab. for applications of remote sensing, 1985—2003, dir. emeritus, prof. emeritus, 2003—; prof. U. Mo., Columbia, 1977-84, dir. geogrpahic resources ctr., 1981-84; dir. Ag Data Network, Purdue U., 1985-87, Nat. Resources Rsch. Inst., 1987-93, Environ. Scis. and Engring. Inst./Purdue U., West Lafayette, 1994-96. Vis. prof. U. Calif., Davis, 1980—81; cons. Lockheed Electronics, Houston, 1975—76, NOAA, Columbia, Mo., 1978—80, FAO UN, Nairobi, Kenya, 1983, 87, Rome, 87, U.S. Agy. Internat. Devel., Ea. Africa, 1983, USDA-Soil Conservation Svc., Washington, 1984—85, IBM, 1991, Ball Aerospace Corp., 1995, Space Imaging Inc., 1996—, Bayer CropSci. Inc., 1998—, RapidEye Corp., 2001—, Lanworth Inc., 2007—; pres. Ecologistics Ltd., 1996—2002, assoc., 2002—; vis. chief scientist Space Imaging Inc., 1996—97; adj. prof. Katholieke U. Leuven (Belgium), 2000—06. Pres. coun. St. Andrew's Luth. Ch., Columbia, 1975-77; asst. scoutmaster Boy Scouts Am., Gt. Rivers coun., Columbia, 1979-84, West Lafayette, 1985-91; pres. Purdue Luth. Ministry, 1989-95; apptd. mem. West Lafayette Redevel. Authority, 2001-2004;

ch. coun. Our Savior Lutheran Ch., West Lafayette, 2005-07. Recipient Tech. Innovation Rsch. award NASA, 1979, Disting. Svc. award Mo. Assn. Soil and Water Conservation Dists., 1982, Agr. Alumni Merit award U. Nebr., 1995, Career award Purdue Coop. Ext. Specialist Assn., 2003, Cert. of Achievement, Agr. Alumni Assn. of Purdue U., 2006. Fellow: Ind. Acad. Scis., Soil and Water Conservation Soc. (pres. 1982—83, HughHammond Burnett award 2005), Am. Soc. Agronomy, Soil Sci. Soc. Am., Am. Soc. Photogrammetry and Remote Sensing (Outstanding Svc. award 1992); mem.: Geosci. and Remote Sensing Soc. of IEEE, Internat. Union Soil Sci., World Assn. Soil and Water, Rotary (Lafayette chpt. bd. dirs. 1995—98), Epsilon Sigma Phi (Internat. award 2000, Global Awareness award 2004, Internat. award 1987). Home: 209 Cedar Hollow Ct West Lafayette IN 47906-1671 Office: Purdue Univ AGRY 915 W State St West Lafayette IN 47907-2054 Home Phone: 765-463-7641; Office Phone: 765-494-4773. Business E-Mail: johan@purdue.edu.

JOHANSSON, NILS A., information services executive; b. 1948; Grad., U. Uppsala, Sweden, 1972; MBA, U. Ill., 1975. With Am. Hosp. Supply Corp., 1973-81; group contr. Bell & Howell Co., Skokie, Ill., 1981-87, treas., 1987-88, treas., v.p., 1988-89, bd. dirs., 1990—, v.p. fin., CFO, 1989—, bd. dirs., 1990, sr. v.p. fin., CFO, 1992-94.

JOHN, GERALD WARREN, pharmacist, educator; b. Salem, Ohio, Feb. 16, 1947; s. Harold Elba and Ruth Springer (Pike) J.; m. Jean Ann Marie Orris, Nov. 5, 1977; children: Patrick Warren, Jeanette Lynn. BS in Pharmacy, Ohio No. U., 1970; MS, U. Md., 1974. Registered pharmacist, Ohio, S.C. Staff pharmacist North Columbiana County Cmty. Hosp., Salem, 1970-72; asst. resident in hosp. pharmacy U. Md. Hosp., Balt., 1972-73, sr. resident, 1973-74, chmn. patient care pharmacies, 1974-76; dir. pharmacy Ohio Valley Hosp., Steubenville, 1976-97; exec. dir. Tri-State Health Svcs., Inc., 1997—. Mem. adv. bd. Contemporary Pharmacy Practice, 1977-83; preceptor profl. externship program Ohio No. U. Sch. Pharmacy, 1977—; adj. clin. instr. practical experience program Duquesne U. Sch. Pharmacy, 1976—; dir. pharmacy Trinity Med. Ctr., Steubenville, 1997—. Columnist Weirton Daily Times, 1990-94. Trustee, v.p. Valley Hospice Inc., 1985-98, 2000-05. Named Hosp. Pharmacist of Yr., Md. Soc. Hosp. Pharmacists, 1976, Outstanding Young Man of Am., U.S. Jaycees, 1977. Fellow Am. Soc. Con. Pharmacists; mem. Am. Soc. Hosp. Pharmacists, Ohio Soc. Hosp. Pharmacists, Jefferson County Acad. Pharmacy, Southeastern Ohio Soc. Hosp. Pharmacists (pres. 1985-87), Rho Chi, Phi Eta Sigma. Methodist. Avocation: Karate (black belt). Office Phone: 740-264-8669. Personal E-mail: gwjohn47@yahoo.com. Business E-Mail: gjohn@trinityhealth.com.

JOHN, JAMES EDWARD ALBERT, mechanical engineer, educator; b. Montreal, PQ, Can., Nov. 6, 1933; s. Richard Rodda and Margaret Gwendolyn (Howard) J.; m. Constance Brandon Maxwell, Aug. 15, 1958; children—Elizabeth, James, Thomas, Constance. BS in Engring, Princeton U., 1955, MS in Engring, 1957; PhD in Mech. Engring, U. Md., 1963. Research engr. Airco, Murray Hill, N.J., 1956-59; instr. dept. mech. engring. U. Md., College Park, 1959-63, asst. prof., 1963-65, assoc. prof., 1965-69, prof., 1969-71; exec. dir. Com. on Motor Vehicle Emissions, Nat. Acad. Scis., Washington, 1971-72; prof., chmn. dept. mech. engring. U. Toledo, 1972-77, Ohio State U., Columbus, 1977-82; dean Coll. Engring. U. Mass., Amherst, 1983; pres. GMI Engring. and Mgmt. Inst., 1991—98, Kettering U. (formerly GMI Engring. and Mgmt. Inst.), 1998—. Author: Gas Dynamics, 1969, rev. edit., 1984; (with W. Haberman) Introduction toFluid Mechanics, 1971, rev. edits., 1980, 88, Engineering Thermodynamics, 1980, rev. edit., 1989. Mem. ASME, Soc. Automotive Engrs., Am. Soc. Engring. Edn. Office: GMI Engring & Mgmt Inst 1700 W 3rd Ave Flint MI 48504-4832

JOHNS, DIANA, secondary school educator; BS, Mich. State U.; MS, U. Mich. Jr. high school tchr. Crestwood Dist. Schools, Dearborn Heights, Mich., sr. high sch. tchr., sci. dept. chair. Outstanding Earth-Sci. Tchr. award, 1992, Tchr. of the Year award Crestwood Sch. Dist., Scholarship award Crestwood High Sch. Chpt. NHS. Mem. Nat. Assn. Geology Tchrs., Mich. Earth Sci. Tchrs. Assn. Office: Crestwood Sr High Sch 1501 N Beech Daly Rd Dearborn Heights MI 48127-3403

JOHNS, JANET SUSAN, physician; b. Chgo., July 18, 1941; d. Nicholas C. and Doris Ann (Douglas) J.; m. Harlan R. Bullard; children: George, Sam. AB, Ind. U., 1963, MD, 1966. Diplomate Am. Acad. Family Practice. Intern Meml. Hosp., South Bend, Ind. Office: Purdue U Student Health 1826 Push West Lafayette IN 47905 Home: 22526 N Hermosillo Dr Sun City West AZ 85375-3045

JOHNS, WILLIAMS DAVIS, JR., geologist, educator; b. Waynesburg, Pa., Nov. 2, 1925; s. William Davis and Beatrice (VanKirk) J.; m. Mariana Paull, Aug. 28, 1948 (dec. Apr. 1993); children: Sydney Ann (dec.), Susan Helen, David William, Amy Matilda; m. Carla Waal, Nov. 6, 1999. BA, Coll. Wooster, 1947; MA, U. Ill., 1951, PhD, 1952. Spl. rsch. asst. petrology Engring. Expt. Sta., U. Ill., 1949-52; rsch. asst., then asst. prof. geology U. Ill., 1952-55; mem. faculty Washington U., St. Louis, 1955-69, prof. earth scis., 1964-69, chmn. dept., 1962-69; with dept. geology U. Mo., Columbia, 1970-97, prof. emeritus, 1997—. Vis. prof. U. Pitts., 1990-91, U. Vienna, 1994. Recipient U.S.-German Scientist award U. Goettingen, 1976-77; Fulbright fellow U. Goettingen, 1959-60, U. Heidelberg, 1968-69, U. Vienna, 1983-84. Fellow Geol. Soc. Am., Mineral. Soc. Am.; mem. Mineral. Soc. Great Britain and Ireland, Mineral. Soc. Can., Deutsches Mineralogisches Gesellschaft, Geochem. Soc., Phi Beta Kappa. Presbyterian (elder). Home: 2200 Yuma Dr Columbia MO 65203-1452 Business E-Mail: wmjohns@centurytel.net.

JOHNSEN, DAVID C., dean, dental educator; BS, U. Mich., 1965, DDS, 1970; MS in Pediat. Dentistry, U. Iowa, 1973. Diplomate Am. Bd. Pediat. Dentistry. Pediat. dentistry instr. U. Iowa Coll. of Dentistry, Iowa City, 1972-73, prof. pediat. dentistry, dean, 1995—; from asst. to assoc. prof. W.Va. U. Hosp., 1974-80, Case Western Res. U., Cleve., 1980-95, interim dean, 1993-95, dir. pediat. dentistry residency program, 1990-95. Bd. mem. Am. Dental Edn. Assn. Coun. of Deans, 1998—2001. Contbr. articles to profl. jours. Mem. Head Start, World Vision, QualChoice Managed Health Care, Ctrs. for Disease Control, HHS Bur. Maternal and Child Health. Recipient numerous grants. Mem. Monongalia (Ohio) County Dental Soc., Iowa Pediat. Dentistry Alumni Assn., Am. Assn. for Dental Rsch., Am. Assn. Dental Schs., Am. Acad. Pediat. Dentistry (bd. of dirs. 1988-91), Am. Dental Education Assn. (pres. 2002-03). Office: U Iowa Coll Dentistry Rm 308 Iowa City IA 52242

JOHNSON, ALEX MOORE, dean, law educator; b. Portland, Oreg., Oct. 5, 1953; s. Alex M. and Margaret Johnson; m. Karen J. Anderson. BA, Claremont U., 1975; JD, UCLA, 1978. Bar: Calif. 1978, U.S. Dist. Ct. (cen. and so. dists.) Calif. 1978. Atty. Latham & Watkins, LA, 1978-80, 82-84; assoc. prof. law U. Minn., Mpls., 1980-82, William S. Pattee prof. law, dean, law sch. Mpls., 2002—; asst. prof. U. Va., Charlottesville, 1984—88, prof. law, 1989-93, Mary and Daniel Loughran prof. law, 1993—2002, vice provost for faculty, 1995—2002; chair Law Sch. Admissions Coun., 2001—03. Vis. prof. U. Tex., Austin, 1988-89, Stanford Law Sch., 1991. Contbr. articles to profl. jours. Mem. Law Sch. Admission Coun. (bd. trustees 1994, minority affairs com. 1989-94, chmn. 2001-2003), Assn. Am. Law Schs. (chair curriculum and rsch. com. 1993—), U. Va. Alumni Assn. (chmn. career counseling panel 1987—). Office: U Minn Sch Law Walter F Mondale Hall Rm 381 229-19th Ave S Minneapolis MN 55455 Office Phone: 612-625-4841. E-mail: alexjohn@umn.edu.

JOHNSON, ALICE M., state legislator; b. Apr. 1, 1941; 4 children. AA, Mpls. Cmty. Coll., 1986; BA, Concordia Coll., St. Paul, 1993. Dist. 48B rep. Minn. Ho. of Reps., St. Paul, 1986—. Chair K-13 education fin. divsn.; mem. labor mgmt. rels., Internat. Trade Com. Minn. Ho. Reps. Home: 801 Ballantyne Ln NE Minneapolis MN 55432-2054

JOHNSON, ARTHUR GILBERT, microbiology educator; b. Eveleth, Minn., Feb. 1, 1926; s. Arthur Gilbert and Selma (Niemi) J.; m. Mildred Louise Anderson, June 15, 1951; children: Susan, Sally, Gary, Peter. BA, U. Minn., 1950, M.Sc., 1951; PhD, U. Md., 1955. Biochemist Walter Reed Army Inst. Rsch., Washington, 1952-55; asst. prof. U. Mich., 1956-62, assoc. prof., 1962-66, prof. microbiology, 1966-78; prof., head dept. med. microbiology/immunology U. Minn. Sch. Medicine, Duluth, 1978-99, prof. emeritus, 1999—. Mem. pre, postdoctoral and spl. fellowships study sect. NIH, 1968-70; mem. nat. adv. dental rsch. coun. NIH, 1972-75; mem. Nat. Bd. Med. Examiners, 1980-84; mem. bacteriology and mycology study sect. NIH, 1983-87, chmn., 1986-87; cons. microbiology. Editor Infection and Immunity, 1977-86. Served with US Merchant Marine, 1943-46. Mem. Am. Assn. Immunologists, Am. Soc. Microbiology, Infectious Diseases Soc. Am., Soc. Biol. Therapy, Immunocomprised Host Soc., Internat. Endotoxin Soc., Assn. Med. Sch. Microbiology and Immunology Chairs (pres. 1991-92). Achievements include research on immunology. Home: 209 Rockridge Cir Duluth MN 55804-1857 Office: U Minn Sch Medicine Dept Microbiology/Immunology Duluth MN 55812 Office Phone: 218-726-7561.

JOHNSON, BRAD, professional football player; b. Marietta, Ga., Sept. 13, 1968; m. Nikkie Johnson. Postgrad in phys. edn., Fla. State Univ. Quarterback Tampa Bay Buccaneers, 2001—04, Wash. Redskins, 1999—2000, Minn. Vikings, 1992—98, 2005—. Involved Muscular Dystrophy Assn., Children's Miracle Net., Children's Hosp., Toys for Tots. Achievements include being a member of Super Bowl XXXVII Champion Tampa Bay Buccaneers, 2002. Office: 9520 Vikings Dr Eden Prairie MN 55344

JOHNSON, BRUCE E., former lieutenant governor, state legislator; b. Tripoli, Libya, May 25, 1960; m. Kelley Johnson; children Shane, Megan, Connor, Morgan Christine BS, Bowling Green State U., 1982; JD, Capital U., 1985. Mem. Ohio Senate from 3rd dist., Columbus, 1994—2001; chmn. Senate Judiciary Com.; chmn. Ways & Means Com.; mem. counsel Chester, Wilcox & Saxbe, Columbus; dir. OH Dept. Devel., Columbus, 2001—07; lt. gov. State of OH, Columbus, 2005—07. Recipient Watchdog of the Treasury, Crime Victims Witness Assn award for Outstanding Legis. Mem. Columbus Bar Assn., Ohio Bar Assn. Republican.

JOHNSON, BRUCE S., law librarian, educator; married; 3 children. BA, Amherst Coll., 1970; JD, NYU, 1973; MLS, Rutgers U., 1978. Bar: NJ 1973. Assoc. Young, Rose & Millspaugh, Newark, 1973—76; reference libr. Law Libr. Seton Hall U. Sch. Law, Newark, 1977—78; chief reference libr. U. Mich. Sch. Law, Ann Arbor, 1978—84; assoc. prof. law, head Coleman Karesh Law Libr. U. SC Sch. Law, Columbia, 1984—92; prof. law, dir. Law Libr. Moritz Coll. Law, Ohio State U., Columbus, 1992—97, assoc. dean info. svcs., prof. law, 1997—. Contbr. articles to profl. jours. Mem.: ABA, Ohio State Bar Assn., Am. Assn. Law Librs. Office: Ohio State U Moritz Coll Law Drinko Hall 274B 55 W 12th Ave Columbus OH 43210 Home: 1847 Suffolk Rd Columbus OH 43221 Office Phone: 614-292-6691. E-mail: johnson.726@osu.edu.

JOHNSON, C. NICHOLAS, dance company executive; b. Jan. 15, 1955; MFA in Dance/Drama, U. Ariz.; studied with, Stefan Niedzialkowski, Frank Hatchett, Richard Levi, De Marco, NYC. Assoc. artistic dir. Goldston & Johnson Sch. of Mimes; chief officer Mid-Am. Dance Theatre, Wichita, Kans.; asst. prof., dir. dance, modern dance, jazz, mime Coll. Fine Arts Wichita State U. Freelance tchr., dir., choreographer and performer various U.S. ballet schs. and univs. Performer Marcel Marceau World Ctr. Mime, Invisible People Mime Theatre, Internat. Children's Theatre Festival, Hong Kong. Kans. Arts Commn. fellow, 1999. Office: Wichita State U Sch Performing Arts-Dance PO Box 101 Wichita KS 67260-0001 Home Phone: 316-686-3640; Office Phone: 316-978-3645. Personal E-mail: alltheacreations@cox.net. Business E-Mail: nick.johnson@wichita.edu.

JOHNSON, C. TERRY, lawyer; b. Bridgeport, Conn., Sept. 24, 1937; s. Clifford Gustave and Evelyn Florence (Terry) J.; m. Suzanne Frances Chichy, Aug. 24, 1985; children: Laura Elizabeth, Melissa Lynne, Clifford Terry. AB, Trinity Coll., 1960; LLD, Columbia U., 1963. Bar: Ohio 1964, U.S. Ct. Appeals (6th cir.) 1966, U.S. Dist. Ct. (so. dist.) Ohio 1970. Legal dep. probate ct. Montgomery County, Dayton, Ohio, 1964-67; head probate dept. Coolidge Wall & Wood, Dayton, 1967-79, Smith & Schnacke, Dayton, 1979-89, Thompson, Hine and Flory, Dayton, 1989-92; head estate planning and probate group Dayton office Porter, Wright, Morris & Arthur, Dayton, 1992—. Frequent lectr. on estate planning to various profl. orgns. Contbr. articles to profl. jours. Fellow Am. Coll. Trust and Estate Counsel; mem. Ohio Bar Assn. (bd. govs. estate planning, trust and probate law sect., chmn. 1993-95), Dayton Bar Assn. (chmn. probate com. 1992-94), Ohio State Bar Found. (trustee 1995-2000), Ohio CLE Inst. (trustee 1995-99, chair 1998-99), Dayton Legal Secs. Assn. (hon.), Dayton Bicycle Club. Home: 8307 Rhine Way Centerville OH 45458-3017 Office: Porter Wright Morris & Arthur 1 S Main St Ste 1600 Dayton OH 45402-2028 Office Phone: 937-449-6701. E-mail: cjohnson@porterwright.com.

JOHNSON, CARL RANDOLPH, chemist, educator; b. Charlottesville, Va., Apr. 28, 1937; BS, Med. Coll. Va., 1958; PhD in Chemistry, U. Ill., 1962. NSF rsch. fellow chemistry Harvard U., 1962; from asst. to prof. chemistry Wayne State U., Detroit, 1962—90, Disting. prof., 1990—2001, chair dept. chemistry, 1997—2001, Disting. prof. emeritus, 2002—. Humboldt sr. scientist, 1991; bd. dirs. Organic Syntheses, Inc. Mem. adv. bd.: Jour. Organic Chemistry, 1976—81. Alfred P. Sloan fellow, 1965-68. Mem. Am. Chem. Soc. (assoc. editor jour. 1984-89, Harry and Carol Mosher award 1992, Arthur C. Cope Sr. Scholar award 2002). Achievements include research in organic sulfur chemistry, especially sulfoxides and sulfoximines, exploratory synthetic chemistry, synthesis of compounds of potential medicinal activity, organometallic chemistry, synthesis of natural products, enzymes in synthesis. Home: 118 Wilton Coves Dr Hartfield VA 23071 E-mail: crj@chem.wayne.edu.

JOHNSON, CHAD, professional football player; b. Miami, Fla., Jan. 9, 1978; Student, Langston U., Okla., 1996; grad. in Phys. Ed., Oreg. State U., 2000. Wide receiver Cin. Bengals, 2001—. Named to AFC Pro Bowl Team, 2003—06, All-AFC Team, Pro Football Weekly, 2004, All-Pro 2nd Team, Coll. & Pro Football Weekly, 2004, NFL All-Pro Team, 2005—06. Achievements include leading the AFC in receiving yards in all three seasons from 2003 to 2005; led NFL in receiving yards, 2006. Office: Cin Bengals 1 Paul Brown Stadium Dr Cincinnati OH 45202

JOHNSON, CHERYL (C.J. JOHNSON), newspaper columnist; Gossip columnist Mpls. Star Tribune. Office: Mpls Star Tribune 425 Portland Ave Minneapolis MN 55488-1511

JOHNSON, CURTIS J., state agency administrator; b. Platte, SD, Dec. 30, 1939; m. Mary Ellen Johnson; children: Kent, Craig. BS, U. SD; MS, SD State U. Sci. tchr., Huron, SD; prin. Dupree schs., SD; ins. agt. Huron; commr. SD Office Sch. and Pub. Lands, Pierre, 1990—. Mem.: NEA, Western States Land Commrs. Assn. (esec. bd.), Aircraft Owners and Pilots Assn., Beadle Club, Rotary Club, Shriners, Masons. Avocations: hunting, reading, flying. Office: 500 E Capitol Ave Pierre SD 57501-5070

JOHNSON, CURTIS LEE, publishing executive, editor, writer; b. Mpls., May 26, 1928; s. Hjalmar N. and Gladys (Goring) J.; m. Jo Ann Lekwa, June 30, 1950 (div. 1974); children: Mark Alan, Paula Catherine; m. Rochelle Miller Hickey, Jan. 11, 1975 (div. 1980); m. Betty Axelrod Fox, Aug. 28, 1982 (div. 1990). BA, U. Iowa, 1951, MA, 1952. Mag. and ency. editing and writing, Chgo., 1953-60; textbook and edni. editing and writing, 1960-66; editor, pub. December Press, 1962—, pres., 1985—; free-lance editing and writing, 1966-72, 78—; mng. editor Aldine Pub. Co., 1972-73; v.p. St. Clair Press, 1973-77; sr. writer Bradford Exchange, 1978-81; mng. editor Regnery Gateway, 1981-82. Author: (with George Uskali) How to Restore Antique and Classic Cars, 1954; Hobbledehoy's Hero, 1959, Nobody's Perfect, 1973, Lace and a Bobbitt, 1976, The Morning Light, 1977, Song for Three Voices, 1984; The Mafia Manager, 1991, (with R. Craig Sautter) Wicked City Chicago, 1994, Thanksgiving in Vegas, 1995, 500 Years of Obscene.and Counting, 1997; editor: (with Jarvis Thurston) Stories from the Literary Magazines, 1970, Best Little Magazine Fiction, 1970, (with Alvin Greenberg), 1971, (with Jack Conroy) Writers in Revolt, 1973, (with Diane Kruchkow) Green Isle in the Sea, 1986, Who's Who in Writers, Editors & Poets, 1985-96; essays The Forbidden Writings of Lee Wallek, 1978; (with R. Craig Sautter) 26 Martyrs, 2004, Little by Little, 2004, Salud: Selected Writings, 2007; contbr. articles to profl. jours.; cons. editor Panache mag, 1967-76. With USN, 1946—48, with USNR, 1948—53. Nat. Endowment Arts writing grantee, 1973, 81 Mem.: Nat. Writers Union, Club d'Ronde, Phi Beta Kappa. Office: 1097 Sandwick Ct Highland Park IL 60035 Home Phone: 847-940-4122; Office Phone: 847-940-4122.

JOHNSON, DALE, contractor equipment company executive; With Graco Inc., Mpls., 1977—, v.p. contractor equipment divsn., 1996-2000, pres., COO, 2000—. Office: Graco Inc PO Box 1441 Minneapolis MN 55440-1441

JOHNSON, DARRYL THOMAS, communications educator; BS in Edn., MS in Edn., NW Mo. State Univ. Cert. Nat. Bd. Tchg. Standards, 2002. Tchr. NE Nodaway County R-V High School, Ravenwood, Mo., 1992—93, Plattsburg (Mo.) H.S., 1993—95, Smithville (Mo.) H.S., 1995—, also chair, English Dept. Adj. instr. Maple Woods Comty. Coll., 2002—04; mem. NW Mo. State Univ. Adv. Coun. in Secondary English Methods. Named Smithville H.S. Tchr. of Yr. (eight times), Mo. Tchr. of Yr., 2007. Office: Smithville High Sch 645 S Commercial Smithville MO 64089 E-mail: djohnson39@kc.rr.com.

JOHNSON, DAVE, state legislator; b. Aug. 21, 1963; m. Tracy Johnson; 1 child. BA, Augsburg Coll.; JD, U. Minn. Bar: Minn. Mem. Minn. Senate from 40th dist., St. Paul, 1996—2002. Home: 5750 Marsh Pointe Dr Excelsior MN 55331-7100

JOHNSON, DAVID, state senator; b. West Branch, Iowa, Dec. 1950; BA in History, Beloit Coll., 1973. Mem. Iowa State Senate, DesMoines, 2003—, vice chair natural resources and environment com., mem. agr. com., bus. and labor rels. com., state govt. com., transp. com., vice chair health and human svs. subcom. Lector St. Mary's Cath. Ch., Ashton. Recipient Svc. award, Iowa Newspaper Assn., FFA, C. of C., Iowa H.S. Football Coaches Assn. Mem.: NRA, Iowa Newspaper Found., Pheasants Forever, Farm Bur., Iowa Cattlemen's Assn., Iowa Holstein Assn., Spencer Area Arts Coun., Iowa Nat. Heritage Found., Lakes Art Ctr., Parker Hist. Soc., Osceola County Hist. Soc., Ocheyedan Catfish Club, Osceola's Country Sportsmen's Club. Republican. Home: PO Box 279 Ocheyedan IA 51354-0279 Office: State Capitol Bldg East 12th and Grand Des Moines IA 50319

JOHNSON, DAVID ALLEN, vocalist, minister, lyricist, investment advisor; b. Indpls., Dec. 15, 1954; s. Eugene Robert and Vivian Claire (Moon) J. BA in English, Ind. U., 1977; cert., Columbia Sch. of Broadcasting, 1985. Ordained to ministry United Christian Ch., 1996. Founder, pres. Worldwide Assn. Disabled Entrepreneurs, Indpls., 1993—. Founder Global Access and Info. Network (GAIN), L.L.C., DAJ Consulting Co.; wealth mgmt. exec. Singer, songwriter gospel and love songs; contbr. poems and articles to various publs.; concert promoter in field. Named 2000 Poet of the Yr., Famous Poets Soc. Mem. Mensa, Internat.-Nat. Ctr. for Creativity, Toastmasters (pres. 2000-01—). Republican. Avocations: reading, writing, biblical research, basketball. Home and Office: 5958 Devington Rd Apt 1 Indianapolis IN 46226 E-mail: wealthmanagerxec@yahoo.com.

JOHNSON, DAVID CHESTER, academic administrator, sociologist, educator; b. Jan. 21, 1933; s. Chester Laven and Olga Henriett (Resnick) J.; m. Jean Ann Lunnis, Sept. 10, 1955 (dec. 1996); children: Stephen, Andrew, Jennifer. BA, Gustavus Adolphus Coll., 1954; MA, U. Iowa, 1956, PhD, 1959; LLD, Luther Coll., 1993. Instr. to prof. sociology Luther Coll., Decorah, Iowa, 1957-69; dean arts and scis. East Stroudsburg (Pa.) U., 1969-76; v.p. acad. affairs St. Cloud (Minn.) State U., 1976-83; dean Gustavus Adolphus Coll., St. Peter, Minn., 1983-90; chancellor U. Minn., Morris, 1990-98; cons. to Scandinavian univs., 1999—. Leader of numerous hiking groups to Norwegian and Transylvanian mountains. Bd. dirs. Swedish Inst.; bd. dirs., v.p. Osher Lifelong Learning Inst., U. Minn. NSF sci. faculty fellow Inst. Social Rsch., Oslo, 1965-66, adminstrv. fellow Am. Coun. Edn., Luther Coll., 1968-69, Summer Leadership fellow Bush Found., Inst. Edn. Mgmt., Harvard U., 1981; Kennedy Swedish Fund grantee, 1976. Mem. U. Minn. Retirees Assn. (pres.), Am. Swedish Inst. Democrat. Lutheran. Home: 1235 Yale Pl Apt 1705 Minneapolis MN 55403-1948

JOHNSON, DAVID LYNN, retired materials scientist, educator; b. Provo, Utah, Apr. 2, 1934; s. David Elmer and Lucile (Maughan) J.; m. Rolla LaRae Page, June 26, 1959; children: Jeannette, David Page, Brice Aaron, Jeffrey Lynn, Karyn Rae. BS, U. Utah, 1956, PhD, 1962. Mem. faculty dept. materials sci. and engring. orthwestern U., Evanston, Ill., 1962—2002, prof., 1971—2002, chmn. dept. materials scis. and engring., 1982-87, Walter D. Murphy Disting. prof., 1987—2002. Cons. in field. Contbr. articles to profl. jours. NSF grantee, 1971-77, 79— Fellow AAAS, Am. Ceramic Soc. (chmn. basic sci. div. 1978-79, trustee 1980-81, 1990-93); mem. Acad. Ceramics (charter), Metall. Soc., Materials Research Soc., Internat. Inst. for Sci. of Sintering, Am. Powder Metallurgy Inst., Sigma Xi, Alpha Sigma Mu, Phi Eta Sigma, Phi Kappa Phi, Tau Beta Pi. Mem. Lds Ch. Achievements include demonstration of ultra-rapid sintering of ceramics in high temperature gas plasmas; development of advanced sintering models; novel synthesis of nanophase powders. Office: orthwestern U Dept Materials Sci/Engring 2220 Campus Dr Evanston IL 60208-3108 E-mail: dl-johnson@northwestern.edu.

JOHNSON, DEAN ELTON, state legislator, Lutheran pastor; b. June 24, 1947; m. Avonelle Johnson. BA, Luther Coll.; MDiv, Luther Theol. Sem. Lutheran pastor; mem. Minn. Ho. of Reps., St. Paul, 1977-82, Minn. Senate from 15th dist., St. Paul, 1982—. Mem. elections and ethics, fin., gen. legis. and pub. gaming, transp., rules and adminstrn. and gaming regulation coms., Minn. State Senate; minority leader. Office: PO Box 996 605 E 4th St Willmar MN 56201

JOHNSON, DICK, newscaster; b. Cambridge, Mass. married; 3 children. B in Polit. sci., DePauw U., 1976. Former polit. reporter, weekend news anchor WTHR-TV, Indpls.; former weekday news anchor KDFW-TV, Dallas; top gen. assignment reporter, Sunday morning news anchor WLS-TV (ABC Chgo.), 1982—2002; anchor weekday morning news WMAQ-TV (NBC Chgo.), 2002—. Recipient Chgo. Emmy award, DuPont-Columbia award. Office: WMAQ-TV NBC Tower 454 N Columbus Dr Chicago IL 60611-5555

JOHNSON, DONALD CLAY, librarian, curator; b. Clintonville, Wis., Aug. 19, 1940; s. Everett Clay and Gertrude Edna Dorthea J. BA, U. Wis., 1962, PhD, 1980; MA, U. Chgo., 1967. Curator S.E. Asia Collection Yale U., New Haven, 1967-70; head reference libr. No. Ariz. U., Flagstaff, 1971-72; asst. libr. reader svcs. at. U. Malaysia, Kuala Lumpur, 1972-74; head reader svcs. Coll. William and Mary, Williamsburg, Va., 1980-87; curator Ames Libr. South Asia, U. Minn., Mpls., 1987—. Author: Southeast Asia: A Bibliography, 1970, Guide to Reference Materials on Southeast Asia, 1970, Index to Southeast Asian Journals, 1982, Agile Hands and Creative Minds, a Bibliography of Textile Traditions in Afghanistan, Bangladesh, Bhutan, India, Nepal, Pakistan, and Sri Lanka, 2000, Wedding Dress Across Cultures, 2003, Dress Sense: emotional and sensory experience the body and cloths, 2007. Ford Found. scholar, 1963-64; Rsch. grantee Am. Inst. Indian Studies, 1989-90, 94; Fulbright fellow, 2003-04. Mem. ALA (life), Assn. for Asian Studies (editor Resources for Scholarship series 1997-98). Avocation: textiles in South and Southeast Asia. Office: U Minn Ames Libr South Asia 309 19th Ave S Minneapolis MN 55455-0438 Office Phone: 612-624-5801. Business E-Mail: d-john4@umn.edu.

JOHNSON, DONALD LEE, retired agricultural materials processing company executive; b. Aurora, Ill., Mar. 9, 1935; s. Leonard F. and Fern J. (Johnson) J.; m. Virginia A. Wesoloski, Sept. 3, 1960; children: Joyce E., Janis M., Jolene G., Jay R. AS, Joliet Jr. Coll., 1959; BS, U. Ill., 1962; DSc, Washington U., 1966. Devel. engr. Petrolite Corp., Webster Groves, Mo., 1962-64; sr. devel. engr. A.E. Staley Co., Decatur, Ill., 1965-67, rsch. mgr. chem. div., 1967-75, dept. dir. rsch. div., 1975-87; v.p. product and process tech. Grain Processing Corp., Muscatine, Iowa, 1987-2000. Adv. coun. adult vocat. edn. State of Ill., Springfield, 1983—87; mem. organizing com. Ann. Symposium on Biotech. for Fuels and Chems., 1985—97; departmental vis. com. botany dept. U. Tex., Austin, 1986—99; mem. applied sci. adv. coun. Miami U., Oxford, Ohio, 1987—97; chmn. rev. com. Solar Energy Rsch. Inst., Golden, Colo., 1988—89; mem. sci. and Industry Adv. Bd., Nat. Renewable Energy Lab., Golden, Colo., 1993—99; mem. Bd. on Higher Edn. in the Workforce NRC, 2001—; mem. sci. adv. bd. Mascoma Corp., 2006—. Contbr. sci. papers to profl. jours.; patentee in field. Staff sgt. USAF, 1953-57. Mem. AAAS, AIChE, Am. Chem. Soc., Nat. Acad. Engring., Am. Legion, Rotary. Republican. Avocations: sailboat racing, running. Home: 106 Cape Fear Dr Hertford NC 27944-9239 Office Phone: 252-426-6499. Personal E-mail: virdon@mchsi.com, donaldljohnson5@mchsi.com.

JOHNSON, DOUGLAS J., state legislator, secondary education counselor; b. Aug. 17, 1942; AA, Va. Jr. Coll.; BS, U. Minn., Duluth; MEd, Wis. State U. H.s. counselor; mem. Minn. Ho. of Reps., St. Paul, 1970-74, Minn. Senate from 6th dist., St. Paul, 1976—. Chmn. tax laws and taxes com., Minn. State Senate, mem. elections and ethics, pub. utilities and energy, redistricting, rules and adminstrn., jobs, energy and cmty. devel. coms. Office: 1136 Lagoon Rd Tower MN 55790-8138 also: State Senate State Capitol Building Saint Paul MN 55155-0001

JOHNSON, E. PERRY, lawyer; b. Pa., 1943; BA, W.Va. U., 1965, JD, 1968. Bar: W. Va. 1968, D.C. 1981, Mo. 1983. Instr. Boston U. Sch. Law, 1973-74, asst. dir., 1977-79, bur. competition, exec. asst. to chmn., 1979, dep. dir., 1979-80, dir., 1980-81; ptnr. Bryan Cave LLP, St. Louis. Vis. asst. prof. W. Va. U., 1972-73; adj. prof. St. Louis U. Sch. Law, 1985-86. With USN, 1968-72. Mem. ABA. Office: Bryan Cave LLP One Metropolitan Square 211 N Broadway Ste 3600 Saint Louis MO 63102-2733 E-mail: epjohnson@bryancave.com.

JOHNSON, EUGENE LAURENCE, lawyer; b. Wisconsin Rapids, Wis., Nov. 30, 1936; s. Elmer Hilding and Claribel May Johnson; m. Barbara Dell Braley, June 18, 1960; children: Mark, Ben, Christopher. BSCE, U. Wis., Madison, 1959, JD, 1962. Bar: Minn. 1963, Calif. 1965, US Patent Office 1963. Atty. Pillsbury Co., Mpls., 1962-64; assoc. Mellin, Hanscom & Hursh, San Francisco, 1964-66; ptnr. Dorsey & Whitney, Mpls., 1966-98, Eugene L. Johnson, PA, Wayzata, Minn., 1998—. Program founder, adj. prof. intellectual property law William Mitchell Coll. Law, 1967-75. Capt. USAR. Mem. Minn. Bar Assn. (past bd. govs.), Am. Intellectual Property Law Assn., Minn. Intellectual Property Law Assn. (past pres.), Am. Swedish Inst. (bd. trustees), Mpls. Athletic Club. Republican.

JOHNSON, EUGENE M., neurologist, molecular biologist, pharmacologist, educator; b. Oct. 20, 1943; BSc in Pharmacy, U. Md., 1966, PhD in Medicinal Chemistry, 1970. Instr. Dept. Medicinal Chemistry U. Md., Balt., 1968—69; rsch. fellow NIH, Bethesda, Md., 1970—72; rsch. fellow Dept. Pharmacology Am. Heart Assn., Dallas, 1972—73; from rsch. fellow Dept. Pharmacology to prof. Washington State U. Sch. Medicine, St. Louis, 1972—83, prof., 1983—; asst. prof. Dept. Pharmacology Med. Coll. Pa., Phila., 1973—96. Assoc. dir. Alzheimer's Disease Rsch. Ctr. Washington U. Sch. Medicine, 1990—, dir. Neuropharmacology Tng. Program, 1991—, mem. adv. bd. Alzheimer Disease Assn. Scientist, 1992—, com. chmn., 1993—. Mem. editl. bd.: Synapse, 1988—91, Neuron, 1989—94, Jour. euroscience, 1989—, Neurobiology of Aging, 1990—, Jour. Neurotrauma, 1991—. Recipient Jacob Javits Neuroscience Investigator award, NINDS, 1987, Decade of the Brain medal, Am. Assn. Neurol. Surgeons, 1994, Merit award, Nat. Inst. Aging, 1995; fellow, Am. Heart Assn., 1978. Office: Dept Neurology Washington Univ Sch Medicine 4566 Scott Ave Campus Box 8103 Saint Louis MO 63110

JOHNSON, G. ROBERT, lawyer; b. Mpls., July 2, 1940; BA, U. Minn., 1965, JD, 1968. Bar: Minn. 1968. Spl. asst. atty. gen. Minn. Pollution Control Agy., 1968-71; past ptnr. Popham, Haik, Schnobrich & Kaufman Ltd., Mpls.; ptnr. Oppenheimer, Wolff & Donnelly LLP, Mpls., 1997—. Mem. ABA, Minn. Bar Assn. chmn. continuing legal edn. 1986-87), Nat. Coun. State Legislatures (liaison 1987—). Office: Oppenheimer Wolff & Donnelly LLP 3400 Plaza VII 45 S 7th St Ste 3400 Minneapolis MN 55402-1609

JOHNSON, GARRETT BRUCE, lawyer; b. Akron, Ohio, Sept. 15, 1946; s. Vincent Hadar and Elizabeth Irene (Garrett) J.; m. Barbara Peters Silver, May 31, 1969; children: Emily Peters, Adam Garrett. AB, Princeton U., 1968; JD, U. Mich., 1971. Bar: Ill. 1973, US Dist. Ct. (no. dist. Ill.) 1973, US Ct. Appeals (7th cir.) 1979, US Supreme Ct. 1990. Fellow Max Planck Inst. Fgn. and Internat. Criminal Law, Freiburg, Germany, 1971-72; assoc. Kirkland & Ellis, Chgo., 1973-78, ptnr., 1978—. Article and book rev. editor Mich. Law Rev. 1970-71. Humboldt scholar, 1971-72. Office: Kirkland & Ellis 200 E Randolph Dr Fl 58 Chicago IL 60601-6636 Office Phone: 312-861-2268. Office Fax: 312-861-2200. E-mail: gjohnson@kirkland.com.

JOHNSON, GARY L., publishing executive; b. Mpls., Aug. 19, 1938; s. Maurice Fred and Alta Elizabeth J.; m. Carol Ann Schlisler, Sept. 8, 1962. Diploma, Bethany Coll. of Missions, Mpls., 1959; student, Augsburg Coll., 1960-63. Mgr. Bethany Book Shop, Mpls., 1960-63, Bethany Printing Divsn., Mpls., 1963-76; pres. Bethany House Pubs., Mpls., 1963—. Avocation: songwriting. Office: Bethany House Pubs 11400 Hampshire Ave S Minneapolis MN 55438-2852

JOHNSON, GARY M., lawyer; b. 1947; BS, Gustavus Adolphus Coll., 1969; JD, NYU, 1973. Law clk. to justice U.S. Ct. Appeals (3d cir.), Phila., 1973-74; assoc. Dorsey & Whitney, Mpls., 1974-79, ptnr., 1980—. Fellow Am. Coll. Trust and Estate Counsel; mem. Minn. Bar Assn., Hennepin County Bar Assn., Order of Coif. Office: Dorsey & Whitney Ste 1500 50 South Sixth Street Minneapolis MN 55402-1498 Office Phone: 612-340-2774. Business E-Mail: johnson.gary@dorsey.com.

JOHNSON, GARY THOMAS, cultural organization administrator, museum administrator; b. Chgo., July 26, 1950; s. Thomas G., Jr. and Marcia Johnson; m. Susan Elizabeth Moore, May 28, 1978; children: Christopher Thomas, Timothy Henry, Anna Louisa. AB, Yale U., 1972; Hons. BA, Oxford U., 1974, MA, 1983; JD, Harvard U., 1977. Bar: Ill. 1977, US Dist. Ct. (no. dist.) Ill. 1977, US Ct. Appeals (7th cir.) 1985, US Supreme Ct. 1986, NY 1993, Supreme Ct. Eng. and Wales 2004. Assoc. Mayer, Brown & Platt, Chgo., 1977-84, ptnr., 1985-94, Jones Day, Chgo., 1994—2005; pres., CEO Chgo. History Mus., 2005—. Mem. spl. commn. adminstrn. justice Cook County Ill. Supreme Ct., 1984—88, 1992—94; v.p. Criminal Justice Project Cook County, 1987—91; trustee Lawyer's Com. Civil Rights Under Law, 1992—94, bd. dirs., 1994—, regional co-chair, 1996—2001, mem. exec. com., 1998—, co-chair, 2001—03. Bd. dirs. Chgo. Lawyers' Com. Civil Rights Under Law, 1981—90, Legal Assistance Found., Chgo., 1987—96, pres., 1994—96; bd. dirs. After Sch. Matters, Chgo. Metro History Fair Edn. Ctr. Rhodes scholar, Oxford U., 1972—74. Fellow: Ill. Bar Found. (life), Am. Bar Found. (life; state chair 2003—); mem.: ABA (ho. of dels. 1991—97), Law Soc. Eng. and Wales, Chgo. Coun. Lawyers (pres. 1981—83), Ill. State Bar Assn., Am. Judicature Soc. (bd. dirs. 1987—91), Am. Law Inst., Comml. Club Chgo. Office: Chgo Hist Museum 1601 N Clark St Chicago IL 60614-6071 Personal E-mail: gary.johnson.bk.72@aya.yale.edu. E-mail: gtjohnson@chicagohistory.org.

JOHNSON, H(ERBERT) FISK, manufacturing executive; AB, Cornell U., 1979, ME, 1980, MS, 1982, MBA, 1984, PhD, 1986. With S.C. Johnson & Son, Inc., Racine, Wis., 1987—, pres., gen. mgr. Canada, mng. dir. corp. new products and tech. Racine, Wis., vice chmn., 1999—2000, chmn., 2000—, CEO, 2004—. Mem. Pres. Adv. Com. Trade Policy and Negotiation, 2002—, World Bus. Coun. Sustainable Devel., 2002—; trustee emeritus Cornell U., 2002—; bd. dirs. Conservation Internat., mem. exec. bd. ctr. environ. leadership in bus.; former trustee nat edn. trust Phi Psi. Named one of Forbes' Richest Americans, 2006. Office: SC Johnson & Son Inc 1525 Howe St Racine WI 53403-2236 Office Phone: 262-260-2000. Office Fax: 262-260-6004.

JOHNSON, HOWARD PAUL, agricultural engineering educator; b. Odebolt, Iowa, Jan. 27, 1923; s. Gustaf Johan and Ruth Helen (Hanson) J.; m. Patricia Jean Larsen, June 15, 1952; children: Cynthia, Lynette, Malcolm. BS, Iowa State U., 1949, MS in Agrl. Engring., 1950; MS in Hydraulic Engring., U. Iowa, 1954; PhD, Iowa State U., 1959. Engr., Soil Conservation Service, Sioux City, Iowa, 1949; instr. Iowa State U., Ames, 1950-53, 54-59, asst. prof., 1959-60, assoc. prof., 1960-62, prof. agrl. engring., 1962-80, head dept., 1980-88, prof. emeritus; cons., 1960-80. Contbr. numerous articles, papers to profl. lit. Co-editor Hydrologic Modeling, 1981. Patentee flow meter. Pres., Sawyer Sch. PTA, Ames, 1965; precinct rep. Republican party, Ames, 1980. Served with AUS, 1943-46, ETO. Recipient Iowa State U. Gamma Sigma Delta Merit award, 1983; EPA grantee, 1975-80; Anson Marston Disting. Prof. Engring., 1986. Fellow AAAS, Am. Soc. Agrl. Engrs. (div. chmn. 1969-70, tech. coun. 1974-76, Engr. of Yr. Iowa sect. 1981, Mid-Central sect. 1982, John Deere medal 1994). Baptist. Lodge: Rotary. Avocations: reading, photography, fishing, writing.

JOHNSON, J. BRENT, insurance company executive; m. JoAnn Johnson; children: Steven, Jason, Justine. Degree in acctg., U. Wis., Milw. Auditor Wis. Pub. Svc. Commn.; budget dir. Am. Family Mutual Ins. Co., Madison, Wis., v.p., controller, 1987-98, exec. v.p. fin., treas., 1999—. Office: Am Family Ins Group 6000 American Pkwy Madison WI 53783-0001

JOHNSON, JAMES DAVID, concert pianist, organist, educator; b. Greenville, SC, Aug. 7, 1948; s. Theron David and Lucile (Pearson) J.; m. Karen Elizabeth Jacobson, Feb. 1, 1975. MusB, U. Ariz., 1970, MusM, 1972, D of Mus. Arts, 1976; MusM, Westminster Choir Coll., 1986. Concert pianist, organist Pianists Found. Am., Boston Pops Orch., Royal Philharm., Nat. Symphony Orch., Leningrad Philharmonic, Victoria Symphony, others, 1961—; organist, choirmaster St. Paul's Episcopal Ch., Tucson, 1968-74, First United Meth. Ch., Fairbanks, Alaska, 1974-89, All Saints Episc. Ch., Omaha, 1995—; prof. music U. Alaska, Fairbanks, 1974-96, chair music dept., 1991-94; Isaacson prof. of music U. Nebr., Omaha, 1994—2001, chair dept. music, 1999—2001, Robert M. Spire chair in music, 2002—. Recordings include Moszkowski Etudes, 1973, Works of Chaminade Dohnanyi, 1977, Mendelssohn Concerti, 1978, Beethoven First Concerto, 1980, Beethoven, Reinecke, Ireland Trios with Alaska Chamber Ensemble, 1988, Kabalevsky Third Concerto, Muczynski Concerto, Muczynski Suite, 1990, Beethoven Third Concerto, 1993 (2002). Recipient Record of Month award Mus. Heritage Soc., 1979, 80, Excellence in Tchg. award U. Nebr. at Omaha, 2001; named Tchr. of Yr., Nebr. Music Tchrs. Assn., 2005. Fellow Music Tchrs. Nat. Assn.; mem. Am. Guild Organists, Phi Kappa Phi, Pi Kappa Lambda, Omicron Delta Kappa. Episcopalian. Avocations: painting, woodworking, icon writing. Office: U Nebr Dept Music Omaha NE 68182-0001 Office Phone: 402-554-3353. Personal E-mail: jjpiano@cox.net. Business E-Mail: j.djohnson@mail.unomaha.edu.

JOHNSON, JAMES L., lawyer; b. 1948; BS, U. Minn., 1972; JD, William Mitchell Coll. Law, 1976. Bar: Minn. 1976. Asst. gen. counsel Control Data Corp., 1978—90; gen. counsel, sec. Norand Corp., 1990—97; v.p., gen. counsel, sec. HNI Corp., Muscatine, Iowa, 1997—, sec. bd. dirs. Bd. dirs. Assn. Bus. and Industry. Mem.: Assn. Corp. Counsel Iowa Chpt.

JOHNSON, JAMES J., lawyer; BA, Mich. State U., 1969; JD, Ohio State U., 1972. Bar: Ohio 1972. Atty, legal divsn. Procter & Gamble Co., Cin., 1973—76, counsel, legal divsn., 1976, asst. brand mgr, PS&D, 1976—79, sr. counsel, legal divsn., 1979—81, divsn. counsel, indsl. divsn., 1981—85, divsn. counsel, PS&D and BS&HCP divsn., 1985—88, assoc. gen. counsel, 1988—90, dep. gen. counsel, 1990—91, v.p., gen. counsel, 1991—92, sr. v.p., gen. counsel, 1992—99, chief legal officer, 1999—2004, chief legal officer, sec., 2004—. Mem.: Chief Legal Officer Roundtable (exec. com.), Ohio Legal Assistance Found. (bd. trustees), Nat. Legal Aid and Defender Assn. (corp. adv. com.), Civil Justice Reform Group (steering com.), Assn. of Gen. Counsel (exec. com.), Queen City Club, Camargo Club, Commonwealth Club. Office: Procter & Gamble Co 1 Procter And Gamble Plz Cincinnati OH 45202-3393 Office Phone: 513-983-1100.

JOHNSON, JAMES P., religious organization executive; Pres. Christian Ch. Found., Inc., Indpls. Mem. Christian Ch. Office: Christian Ch Found Inc 130 E Washington St PO Box 1986 Indianapolis IN 46206-1986

JOHNSON, JANET HELEN, literature educator; b. Everett, Wash., Dec. 24, 1944; d. Robert A. and Jane N. (Osborn) J.; m. Donald S. Whitcomb, Sept. 2, 1978; children: J.J., Felicia. BA, U. Chgo., 1967, PhD, 1972. Instr. Egyptology U. Chgo., 1971-72, asst. prof., 1972-79, assoc. prof., 1979-81, prof., 1981—; dir. Oriental Inst., 1983-89; research assoc. dept. anthropology Field Mus. of Natural History, 1980-84, 94-99, 2003—; Morton D. Hull disting. svc. prof. U. Chgo., 2003—. Author: Demotic Verbal System, 1977, Thus Wrote Onchsheshonqy, 1986, 3d revised edit., 2000, (with Donald Whitcomb) Quseir al-Qadim, 1978, 80; editor: (with E.F. Wente) Studies in Honor of G.R. Hughes, 1977, Life in a Multi-Cultural Society, 1992. Recipient Morton D. Hall disting. svc., 2003; grantee, Smithsonian Instn., 1977—83, NEH, 1978—81, 1981—85, Nat. Geog. Soc., 1978, 1980, 1982. Mem. Am. Rsch. Ctr. in Egypt (bd. govs. 1979—, exec. com. 1984-87, 90-96, v.p. 1990-93, pres. 1993-96). Office: U Chgo Oriental Inst 1155 E 58th St Chicago IL 60637-1540 Home Phone: 773-493-8685; Office Phone: 773-702-9530. Business E-Mail: j-johnson@uchicago.edu.

JOHNSON, JAY WITHINGTON, former congressman; b. Bessemer, Mich., Sept. 30, 1943; s. Ruben W. and Catherine W. (Withington) J.; m. Jane Sholtz (div.); m. Jo Lee Works, June 26, 1982; stepchildren: Christopher, Joanna AA, Gogebic Community Coll., 1963; BA, No. Mich. U., 1965; MA, Mich. State U., 1970. Disk jockey Sta. WFMK, Lansing, Mich., 1968-69; news anchorman Sta. WILX-TV, Lansing, 1969-70; radio news reporter Sta. WOWO, Ft. Wayne, Ind., 1970-73; news anchorman Sta. WPTV-TV, West Palm Beach, Fla., 1973-76; radio news reporter Sta. WVCG/WLVE-FM, Miami, Fla., 1976; TV producer Sta. WPLG-TV, Miami, 1976; news anchorman, mng. editor Sta. WPEC-TV, West Palm Beach, 1977-80; news anchorman Sta. WOTV-TV, Grand Rapids, Mich., 1980-81, Sta. WFRV-TV, Green Bay, Wis., 1981-87, Sta. WLUK-TV, Green Bay, 1987-96; mem. 105th Congress from 8th Wis dist., 1997-98, mem. agrl., transp. and infrastructure coms.; acting dep. asst. sec. congl. rels. USDA, 1999-2000; dir. U.S. Mint, Washington, 2000-2001. Vol. Big Bros./Big Sisters, Green Bay, 1982-87 (Vol. of Yr. 1985); pres., bd. dirs. Family Violence Ctr., Green Bay, 1982-87; v.p. communications United Way, Green Bay, 1987—; adv. bd. Libertas Alcohol Treatment Ctr., 1989—. With U.S. Army, 1966-68. Recipient Gov's award Gov. Tommy Thompson, 1988; named Citizen of Yr. Masons, 1987.

JOHNSON, JOEL W., food products executive; BA, Hamilton Coll.; MBA, Harvard Univ. With General Foods Corp., 1967—91; exec. v.p. sales and mktg. Hormel Foods Corp., Austin, Minn., 1991-92, pres., 1992—2004, CEO, 1993—2005, chmn., 2006—. Bd. mem., past chmn. Am. Meat Inst.; bd. mem. Grocery Mfr. Am.; bd. dirs. Ecolab Inc., Meredith Corp., US Bancorp. Bd. mem. Hormel Found.; mem. bd. overseers Carlson Sch. Mgmt., Univ. Minn.; trustee Hamilton Coll. Served through capt. US Army, Vietnam. Decorated Bronze Star. Office: Hormel Foods Corp 1 Hormel Pl Austin MN 55912-3680

JOHNSON, JOHN D., energy and food products executive; b. Rhame, ND, Sept. 24, 1949; m. Shirley Johnson; 3 children. BBA, Black Hills State U., Spearfish, SD, 1970. Feed cons. GTA feeds divsn. Harvest States, Inver Grove Heights, Minn., 1976, regional sales mgr., dir. sales and mktg., gen. mgr. GTA Feeds, group v.p. Farm Mktg. and Supply, 1992, pres., CEO, 1995; pres., gen. mgr. CHS Inc. (merger of Cenex and Harvest States), Inver Grove Heights, Minn., 1998—2000, pres., CEO, 2000—. Bd. dirs. Ventura Foods, LLC, Sparta Foods, Goldkist, Inc., CF Industries. Named CEO Communicator of Yr., Coop. Communicators Assn. Mem. Nat. Coop. Refinery Assn. (bd. dirs.), Nat. Coun. Farmer Coops. (bd. dirs.) Office: CHS Inc PO Box 64089 Saint Paul MN 55164-0089 Office Phone: 651-355-6000.

JOHNSON, JOHN FRANK, professional recruitment executive; b. Bklyn., Apr. 23, 1942; s. John Henry and Sirkka (Keto) J.; m. Martha Lear Fryer, Aug. 31, 1963 (div. Apr. 1988); children: Kristin Lin, Heather Alane; m. Virginia K. Yeaser, Nov. 16, 1989 BA in Econs., Tufts U., 1963; MBA in Indsl. Relations, Columbia U., 1964. Indsl. relations analyst Ford Motor Co., Dearborn and Livonia, Mich., 1964-67; various human resources positions Gen. Electric Co., Chgo. and Louisville, Ky., 1967-76; successively assoc., v.p., mng. dir., exec. v.p. and mng. dir. Lamalie Amrop Internat., Cleve., 1976-84; pres. LAI Ward Howell (formerly Lamalie Amrop Internat.), NYC and Cleve., 1984-95, pres., CEO Cleve., 1987-94, chmn., 1995-99; vice chmn. TMP Worldwide Exec. Search, Cleve., 1999—; sr. client ptnr. Korn/Ferry Internat., Cleve., 2003—. Mem. Human Resource Planning Soc., The Planning Forum, Assn. for Corp. Growth, Internat. Assn. Corp. and Profl. Recruiters, The Club (Cleve.), Union Club (Cleve.), Internat. Game Fishing Assn., Kirtland Country Club, Calusa Pines Golf Club. Avocations: big game fishing, golf, travel, wine collecting, thoroughbred racing. Office: Korn Ferry Internat 600 Superior Ave Ste 1300 Cleveland OH 44114 Home Phone: 216-226-8010; Office Phone: 216-479-6818.

JOHNSON, JOHN IRWIN, JR., neuroscientist; b. Salt Lake City, Aug. 18, 1931; s. John Irwin and Ann Josephine (Freeman) J. AB, U. Notre Dame, 1952; MS, Purdue U., 1955, PhD, 1957. Instr., then asst. prof. Marquette U., Milw., 1957-60; USPHS spl. research fellow U. Wis., Madison, 1960-63; Fulbright-Hays research scholar U. Sydney, Australia, 1964-65; asso. prof. biophysics, psychology and zoology Mich. State U., East Lansing, 1965-69, prof., 1969-81, chmn. dept. biophysics, 1973-78, prof. anatomy, 1981-99, prof. radiology and neurosci., 1999—. Vis. fellow psychology dept. Yale U., New Haven, 1975-76 Recipient Career Devel. award NIH, 1965-72, research grantee, 1966-79; research grantee NSF, 1969-71, 71-73, 73-76, 78-89, 91—; 3d hon. life mem. Anat. Assn. Australia and N.Z., 1973 Mem. Soc. Neurosci., Am. Assn. Anatomists, Soc. for Comparative and Integrative Biology, Am. Soc. Mammalogists, Animal Behavior Soc., AAUP, ACLU, Sigma Xi. Home: 2494 W Grand River Ave Okemos MI 48864-1447 Office: Mich State U Dept Radiology 519A E Fee Hall East Lansing MI 48824-1316 E-mail: johnij@aol.com, johnij4@yahoo.com.

JOHNSON, JOHN WARREN, retired professional society administrator; s. Walter E. and Eileen L. J.; m. Marion Louise Myrland; children: Daniel Warren, Karen Louise, ancy Marie. BA, U. Minn., Mpls., 1951. CEO Am. Collectors Assn., Inc., Mpls., 1955-96; ret., 1996. Bd. dirs. Western Nat. Ins. Group, Western Nat. Ins. Co., Mpls. and Seattle. Author: Political Christians, 1979, You Can Manage Your Money, 1981, 38 Days to Cape Town, 1981, Credit Guide for Collectors, 1984, The Pearls of Saigon, 1987, The Use of Humor in Public Speaking Is No Joke!, 1991, 53 Days to Beijing, 1991, The Strange Blood of East Africa, 1995. Mem. Mpls. City Coun., 1963-67; mem. Minn. State Ho. of Reps., 1967-74, asst. majority leader, 1972-74; Rep. candidate for Gov. of Minn., 1974-2007. With USNR, 1947-53. Mem. Am. Soc. Assn. Execs. (chmn. bd. 1986-87), U.S. C. of C. (chmn. bd. regents 1973, bd. dirs. 1990-92), Minn. Soc. Assn. Execs. (past pres.). Lutheran. Office: 5108 James Ave S Minneapolis MN 55419

JOHNSON, JOY ANN, diagnostic radiologist; b. New Richmond, Wis., Aug. 16, 1952; d. Howard James and Shirley Maxine (Eidem) J.que BA in Chemistry summa cum laude, U. No. Colo., 1974; D of Medicine, U. Colo., 1978. Diplomate Am. Bd. Radiology, Nat. Bd. Med. Examiners; cert. added qualification pediatric radiology. Resident in radiology U. Colo., 1978-81, fellow in pediat. radiology, 1981-82; asst. prof. diagnostic radiology and pediatrics, chief sect. pediatric radiology Clin. Radiology Found. U. Kans. Med. Ctr., Kansas City, 1982-87; radiologist Radiology Assocs. Ltd., Kansas City, Mo., 1987-92; mem. staff Bapt. Med. Ctr., Kansas City, Mo., 1987-92; radiologist Children's Mercy Hosp., Kansas City, 1992-95, Leavenworth-Kansas City Imaging, 1996—; assoc. prof. U. Mo., Kansas City, 1992—; chief of staff Cushing Mem. Hosp., 2002—04. Speaker Radiol. Soc. Republic of China, 1985, RSNA 2000 panel mem. Contbr. articles to med. jours. Nat. Cancer Inst. fellow, 1982. Mem. AMA, Am. Coll. Radiology, Radiol. Soc. N.Am., Am. Inst. Ultrasound in Medicine (mem. program com. Kansas City 1984), Soc. Pediatric Radiology (mem. com. for cmty. bsed pediat. radiologists 1998-2003), Am. Assn. Women in Radiology, Lambda Sigma Tau. Avocations: horseback riding, physical fitness, sports, reading. Office: Leavenworth-Kansas City Imaging 9201 Parallel Pkwy Kansas City KS 66112-1528

JOHNSON, JULIA F., bank executive; Sr. v.p. Banc One Corp, Columbus, Ohio, 1993—; with Bank One, Columbus, 1985—99, dir., office of info. and policy, 1999—2003. Office: Banc One Corp Dept OH-0152 100 E Broad St Dept Oh-152 Columbus OH 43215-3607

JOHNSON, JULIE MARIE, lawyer, lobbyist, judge; b. Aberdeen, SD, Aug. 7, 1953; d. Howard B. and Jerauldine (Dilly) J.; m. Bryan L. Hisel. BA in Govt., Comm., U. S.D., 1974, MA in Polit. Sci., 1976, JD, 1976. Bar: S.D. 1977, U.S. Dist. Ct. S.D. 1977. Assoc. Siegel, Barnett Law Firm, Aberdeen, 1977; law clk. Fifth Judicial Circuit Ct., Aberdeen, 1977-78; ptnr. Maloney, Kolker, Fritz, Hogan & Johnson, Aberdeen, 1978-84; dep. sec. SD Dept. Labor, Aberdeen, Pierre, 1983-84, sec. Gov.'s Cabinet, 1985-87, SD Dept. Revenue, Pierre, 1995; pres. Industry and Commerce Assn. SD, Pierre, 1987-95; exec. dir. SD Rural Devel. Coun., Pierre, 1995—2003; acting exec. dir. SD Math., Sci. and Tech. Coun., 2002—03; adminstrv. law judge SD, 2003—. Adj. faculty SD State U., 1996—; chair Gov.'s Red Tape Task Force, 2004—05; legal counsel SD Vietnam War Meml. Dedication Com., Inc., 2004—07. Treas. SD Cmty. Found., Pierre, 1987-95; mem. Pvt. Industry Coun., 1985-87, SD Coun. on Vocat. Edn., 1985-87; bd. dirs. Mo. Shores Women's Resource Ctr., Pierre, 1988-89; chmn. SD Main St. Adv. Coun., 1987-91; bd. dirs. United Way, 1988-96, chmn., 1991; mem. Shortgrass Arts Coun., 1987—, South Dakotans for Arts, 1981—, Solid Waste Mgmt. Plan Task Force, 1990, SD Citizens Adv. Coun. Hazardous Waste, 1991-92, gov.'s adv. coun. on health care reform, 1992-93, gov.'s Homestate Underground Lab adv. coun., 2002-04; bd. dirs. Hist. SD Found., 1996-99; founding mem., legal counsel Outdoor Women of SD, Inc., 1995—; bd. trustees USD Found., 1992—; trustee, mem. bus. affairs com., 1996—, com. on trustees, Kelley Ctr. for Entrepreneurship adv. bd., presdl. search com. Dakota Wesleyan U., 1999-2000; founding mem., treas. SD Discovery Ctr. and Aquarium, Inc., bd. dirs., 1988-92; mem. SD Water Congress, 1990-97, bd. dirs., 1987-95; bd. dirs. Nyoda Girl Scout Coun., 1997-99; mem. adv. bd. W.O. Farber Ctr. for Excellence in Civic Leadership, 1998—; bd. dirs. Farber Fund, 1987—; founding mem. SD Chambers and Econ. Devel. Coun., 1989—; mem. Network Mgmt. Team Nat. Rural Devel. Partnership, 1998-2001; course leader Leadership Ctrl. SD, 1996—; mem. Children's Care Hosp. and Sch. Found. Bd., 1997—, vice chair, 2005—, investment com., 1999—, joint exec. com., 2003—, devel. com., 2004—, chair governance com., 2005—; mem. Nat. Rural Devel. Partnership Presdl. Transition Team, 2000-01, Agr. and Econ. Devel. Task Force, 2001, SD Habitat for Humanity Bd., 2001—, vice chair, 2005—; bd. dirs. Historic SD Found., 1995-98, Genesis of Innovation, 2000-03; acting exec. dir. SD Math., Sci. and Tech. Coun., 2000-03; vol. chmn. SD WWII Meml. Dedication, 2001; vol. chair SD Korean War Meml. Dedication Com., 2003-04, seating/decorating co-chair, 2003-04; chmn. Govs. Red Tape Task Force, 2004-05, vice chair, 2005—07; bd. dirs. SD Habitat for Humanity, 2001—07, pro bono lobbyist, 2004-07, vice chair, 2005—07; founder, treas. Friends of Discovery Ctr., SD; trustee, mem. coms. Dakota Wesleyan U., Children's Care Hosp. Found., U. SD Found.; active SD Vietnam War Meml., 2005-06, chair dignitaries, 2005-06, legal counsel dedication com., 2005-06, mem. fundraising com., 2005-06. RJR Nabisco fellow Women Execs. in State Govt., Harvard, 1986; named Outstanding Young Citizen Jaycees, Aberdeen, 1982, S.D. Jaycees, 1983. Mem. S.D. Bar Assn. (chmn. adminstrv. law com. 2001-04, chair adminstrv. law sect., 2004-06, mem. CLE com., Worker's compensation com., chmn. ad law sect. 2004-06), Industry and Commerce Assn. S.D. (bd. dirs. 1985-87), U. S.D. Alumni Assn. (exec. com. 1987-96, pres. 1990-92), AAUW, Bus. and Profl. Women U.S.A. (nat. legis. chmn. 1987-88, 92-94, nat. chmn. issues mgmt. 1991-93, pres. S.D. 1984-85, Woman of Yr. award Aberdeen chpt. 1982), Women Execs. in State Govt. (bd. didrs. 1985-87), Coun. State Mfrs. Assn., S.D. Mining Assn. (bd. dirs. 1991-95, Gold PAC, 1995-), Nat. Indsl. Coun., Coun. State C.'s of C., Ducks Unltd., Rotary, WIG Investment Club, Rocky Mountain Elk Found. Republican. Lutheran. Address: 1100 E Church St Apt 352 Pierre SD 57501-2354 Office: 210 E 4th St Pierre SD 57501 Home: 1414 Sharpstone Dr Mitchell SD 57301-6250 Business E-Mail: juliem.johnson@absolutelyaberdeen.com.

JOHNSON, KENNETH HARVEY, veterinary pathologist; b. Hallock, Minn., Feb. 17, 1936; s. Clifford H. and Alma (Anderson) J.; Sept. 17, 1960; children: Jeffrey, Gregory, Sandra. BS, U. Minn., 1958, DVM, 1960, PhD, 1965. Jr. asst. health officer NIH, Bethesda, Md., 1958; practice vet. medicine Edina, Minn., 1960; USPHS-NIH non-service fellow U. Minn., St. Paul, 1960-65, asst. prof. dept. vet. pathology and parasitology, 1965-69, assoc. prof., 1969-73, prof., 1973-98, prof. emeritus dept. vet. pathobiology, 1998—, head, sect. pathology, dept. vet. biology, 1974-76, chmn. dept. vet. pathobiology Coll. Vet Medicine, 1976-83. Cons. Minn. Mining & Mfg. Co., Medtronic Inc., Natural-Y Surg. Specialties; principle and co-investigator several NIH grants, 1965-98. Mem. editl. bd. Amyloid, the Internat. Jour. of Exptl. and Clin. Investigation; contbr. chpts.: Veterinary Clinics of North America, 1971, Spontaneous Animal Models of Human Disease, 1979, Kirk's Current Veterinary Therapy; contbr. articles to sci. jours. Councilman Nativity Lutheran Ch., St. Anthony Village, Minn., 1972-75. Recipient Tchr. of Yr. award, 1968-69, Norden award for disting. tchr. in vet. medicine, 1970, Beecham award for rsch. excellence, 1989, Ralston Purina Small Animal Rsch. award, 1990, Phi Zeta faculty achievement award, 1992, Outstanding Achievement award Bd. of Regents of U. Minn., 2001. Mem.: Am. Coll. Vet. Pathologists (hon.). Home: 3510 Skycroft Dr Minneapolis MN 55418-1780 Business E-Mail: johns049@netzero.com.

JOHNSON, LAEL FREDERIC, lawyer; b. Yakima, Wash., Jan. 22, 1938; s. Andrew Cabot and Gudney M. (Fredrickson) Johnson; m. Eugenie Rae Call, June 9, 1960; children: Eva Marie, Inga Margaret. AB, Wheaton Coll., 1960; JD,

Northwestern U., 1963. Bar: Ill. 1963, U.S. Dist. Ct. (no. dist.) Ill. 1964, U.S. Ct. Appeals (7th cir.) 1966. V.p., gen. counsel Abbott Labs., Abbott Park, Ill., 1981-89, sr. v.p., sec., gen. counsel, 1989-94; of counsel Schiff Hardin LLP, Chgo., 1995—2005. Bd. trustees Santa Fe Art Inst.; mem., past chmn. Law Sch. bd. Northwestern U.; bd. dirs. Music Theater Workshop. Mem.: Assn. Gen. Counsel. Home Phone: 312-379-1938; Office Phone: 312-258-5536.

JOHNSON, LARRY (LARRY ALPHONSO JOHNSON JR.), professional football player; b. Pomfret, Md., Nov. 19, 1979; s. Larry Johnson, Sr and Christine Johnson. BA in Integrative Arts, Pa. State U., 2002. Running back Kans. City Chiefs, 2003—. Vol. coach Jr. Player Devel. Program, Kansas City, Mo.; founder L.J's Legacy and Growth Youth Found., 2005. amed to All-Pro 2nd Team, AP, 2005, All-AFC Team, Pro Football Weekly, 2005, AFC Pro Bowl Team, 2005, NFL All Pro Team, 2007; recipient Doak Walker award, 2002, Maxwell award, 2002, Walter Camp award, 2002, Derrick Thomas award, Kans. City Chiefs, 2005. Achievements include rushing for 1,351 yards after November 1st during the 2005 season, which is the highest mark in NFL history; ranked first in rushing in the AFC and third in the NFL, 2005, second in the NFL, 2006. Office: c/o Kansas City Chiefs 1 Arrowhead Dr Kansas City MO 64129

JOHNSON, LARRY WALTER, lawyer; b. Princeton, Minn., May 21, 1934; s. Alfred Herbert and Lillian Martha (Wetter) J.; m. Mary Ann Lindstrom, June 14, 1958; children: Lawrence W. II, Kristin Jane. BS in Law, U. Minn., 1957, LLB, 1959. Bar: Minn. 1959. Assoc. Dorsey & Whitney, Mpls., 1961-66, ptnr., 1967-95, of counsel, 1996—. Bd. dirs. Remmele Engring., Inc. Co-author, co-editor Minnesota Estate Administration, 1968. Bd. dirs. Minn. Bus. Found. Excellence in Edn., St. Paul. 1981-85, Walker Sponsor's Fund, Mpls., 1987; trustee Walker Meth. Residence and Health Services, Inc., Mpls., 1985-86. Served to 1st lt. U.S. Army, 1959-61. Mem. Minn. Bar Assn., Hennepin County Bar Assn., Mpls. Athletic Club. Republican. Congregationalist. Avocation: handball. Home: 5400 W Highwood Dr Minneapolis MN 55436-1225 Office: Dorsey and Whitney 50 S 6th St Ste 1500 Minneapolis MN 55402-1553

JOHNSON, LAWRENCE ALAN, cereal technologist, educator, administrator; b. Columbus, Ohio, Apr. 30, 1947; s. William and Wyoma (Swift) J.; m. Bernice Ann Miller, June 15, 1969; children: Bradley, David. BS, Ohio State U., 1969; MS, N.C. State U., 1971; PhD, Kans. State U., 1978; doctorate U. Gent (hon.), Belgium, 2007. Rsch. chemist Durkee Foods div. SCM Corp., Strongsville, Ohio, 1973-75; assoc. rsch. chemist Food Protein R&D Ctr. Tex. A&M U., College Station, 1978-85; dir. Ctr. for Crops Utilization Rsch. Iowa State U., Ames, 1991—. Mem. rsch. com. Am. Soybean Assn., St. Louis, 1987-91, Nat. Corn Grower's Assn., St. Louis, 1990-91. Author: (with others) Handbook of Cereals, 1991; editor: (book/procs.) Technologies for Value-Added Products from Proteins and Co-Products, 1989, Corn Chemistry and Technology; contbr. more than 150 articles to profl. jours. 1st lt. U.S. Army, 1971-73, Vietnam. Recipient Rsch. award Corn Refiners Assn., 1998. Mem. Am. Assn. Cereal Chemists (assoc. editor jour. 1982-85, dir. 2002-04), Am. Soc. Agrl. Engrs., Am. Oil Chemists Soc. (assoc. editor jour. 1989—, v.p. 2003-04, pres. 2004-05, Archer Daniels Midland Rsch. award 1986, 92, 99, 2001, 02), Royal Swedish Acad. Agr. and Forestry (fgn. mem. 1999), Inst. Food Techs. Republican. Lutheran. Achievements include 11 patents, 125 research publications. Home: 2226 Buchanan Dr Ames IA 50010-4368 Office: Ctr Crops Utilization Rsch Iowa State U Ames IA 50011-0001 Office Phone: 515-294-0160, 515-294-4365. Business E-Mail: ljohnson@iastate.edu.

JOHNSON, LAWRENCE EUGENE, lawyer; b. Morrison, Ill., Sept. 26, 1937; s. Frederick Eugene and Ruth Helen (Lorke) J.; m. Debby Karen McCaleb, June 17, 1961; children: Mark Lawrence, Eric Eugene, Lori Ann Johnson Purtzer. BS, No. Ill. U., 1960, MS, 1962; JD, U. Ill., 1965. Bar: Ill. 1965, U.S. Dist. Ct. (ctrl. dist.) Ill. 1965, U.S. Ct. Appeals (7th cir.) 1965; lic. pilot. Pvt. practice, 1965-68; states atty. County of Champaign, Ill., 1968-72; pvt. practice Champaign, 1972—. Spl. asst. atty. gen. litigation Ill. Dept. Revenue, 1982-86, Ill. Dept. Labor, 1982-86, Ill. Dept. Transp., 1986-90, Ill. Dept. Conservation, 1988-90, Ill. Dept. Nuclear Safety, 1989-90. Bd. mem. Ill. State Bd. Elections, 1990-95, vice chmn., 1993-95; chmn. Ill. Liquor Control Commn., 1972-73; hearing officer Ill. State Bd. Elections, 1988-90; mem. airport hazard zoning task force divsn. aeronautics Ill. Dept. Transp., 1987-88. With U.S. Army, 1955-57. Mem. U.S. Pilots Assn. (bd. dirs. 1989—), Ill. Pilots Assn. (pres. 1991-93, v.p., bd. dirs. 1989-91), Illini Area Pilots Assn. (pres. 1989-91), Ill. Trial Lawyers Assn., Champaign Urbana Kiwanis Early Risers, Champaign Urbana Ambucs, AMVETS (life). Office: Johnson & Assocs PO Box 1127 202 W Hill St Champaign IL 61824-1127 E-mail: lejai@shout.net.

JOHNSON, LESTER LARUE, JR., artist, educator; b. Detroit, Sept. 28, 1937; s. Lester L. and Haroldine M. (Stanley) J. BFA, MFA, U. Mich. Prof. Coll. for Creative Studies, Detroit. Exhibitions include Whitney Mus. Art, Nat. Acad. Design, N.Y.C., Kalamazoo Inst. Arts, Mich., Saginaw Art Mus., Detroit Inst. Arts, Univ. Mich. Mus. Art, Ann Arbor, Centro de Memoria e Cultura dos Correios, Salvador, Bahia, Brazil, Detroit Pretty City at G.R. N'Namdi Gallery and the Univ. Cultural Assn., 2003, Klemm Gallery, Siena Heights U., Adrian, 2004, Buckham Gallery, Flint, 2005, Represented in permanent collections Osaka U. Arts, Japan, Mus. Afro-Brasileiro at Fed. U. of Bahia, Salvador, Brazil, Fed. Reserve Bk. Chgo., Detroit, U. Mich. Mus. Art, Ann Arbor, U. Mich. Cardiovascular Ctr., Dana-Farber Cancer Inst., Boston, prin. works include Bishop Internat. Airport, Flint, U. Mich. Mus. Art, Ann Arbor. Recipient John S. Newberry Purchase prize, 54th Exhibit Mich. Artists, Detroit Inst. Arts, 1964, recognition award African-Am. Music Festival; grantee Andrew W. Mellon Found. Office: Coll for Creative Studies 201 E Kirby St Detroit MI 48202-4034 Office Phone: 313-664-7486. Business E-Mail: ljohnson@ccscad.edu.

JOHNSON, MARGARET ANN (PEGGY), library administrator; b. Atlanta, Aug. 11, 1948; d. Odell H. and Virginia (Mathiasen) Johnson; m. Lee J. English, Mar. 4, 1978; children: Carson J., Amelia J. BA, St. Olaf Coll., 1970; MA, U. Chgo., 1972; MBA, Met. State U., 1990. Music cataloger U. Iowa Librs., Iowa City, 1972-73; analyst Control Data Corp., Bloomington, Minn., 1973-75; br. libr. St. Paul Pub. Librs., 1975-77; head tech. svcs. St. Paul Campus Librs., U. Minn., 1977-86; collection devel. officer Univ. Librs., U. Minn., Mpls., 1987-90; asst. dir. St. Paul Campus Librs., U. Minn., 1987-95; planning officer U. Librs. U. Minn., Mpls., 1993-97, asst. univ. libr., 1997—2003, interim univ. libr., 2002, assoc. univ. libr., 2003—. Libr. cons. Mekerere U., Kampala, Uganda, 1990, U. Nat. Rwanda, 1990, Inst. Agr. and Vet. Hassan II, Rabat, Morocco, 1992—2000, Ecole Nat. Agr., Meknes, Morocco, 2000, China Agrl. U., Beijing, 2001—, Xi'an Eurasia U., Xi'an, China, 2005. Author: Automation and Organizational Change in Libraries, 1991, The Searchable Internet, 1996, Fundamentals of Collection Development and Management, 2004; editor: New Directions in Technical Services, 1997; editor Technicalities Jour., 2000—, Libr. Resources and Tech. Svcs., 2003—; editor Guide to Tech. Svcs. Resources, 1994, Recruiting, Educating and Tng. Librarians for Collection Devel., 1994, Collection Mgmt. and Devel., 1994, Virtually Yours, 1998; contbr. articles to profl. jours. Recipient Samuel Lazerow Rsch. fellowship Assn. Coll. and Rsch. Librs., Inst. for Sci. Info., 1987; Blackwell scholar Assn. for Libr. Collections and Tech. Svcs., 2005. Mem. ALA, Internat. Assn. Agrl. Librs. and Documentalists, U.S. Agrl. Info. Network, Assn. for Libr. Collections and Tech. Svcs. (pres. 1999-2000, 50th Ann. Presdl. citation 2007). Office: U of Minn Librs 499 Wilson Libr 309 19th Ave S Minneapolis MN 55455-0438 Office Phone: 612-624-2312. Business E-Mail: m-john@umn.edu.

JOHNSON, MARK ALAN, lawyer; b. Marysville, Ohio, June 5, 1960; s. Neil Raymond and Elizabeth Johnson; m. Deborah Anne Hillis, Sept. 21, 1984. BA, Otterbein Coll., 1982; JD, Ohio State U., 1985. Bar: Ohio 1985, U.S. Dist. Ct. (so. dist.) Ohio 1985, U.S. Ct. Appeals (6th cir.) 1987, U.S. Dist. Ct. (no. dist.) Ohio 1991, U.S. Ct. Appeals (5th cir.) 1998. Assoc. Baker and Hostetler LLP, Columbus, Ohio, 1985-92, ptnr., 1993—. Named one of Ohio's Super Lawyers, 2005, 2007, 2008. Mem. ABA (litigation sect., mem. bus. torts litigation com., coml. and banking litigation com.), Martindale-Hubbell AV rating Ohio Bar Assn., Columbus Bar Assn. Office: Baker & Hostetler LLP 65 E State St Ste 2100 Columbus OH 43215-4215 Office Phone: 614-228-1541. Business E-Mail: mjohnson@bakerlaw.com.

JOHNSON, MARK EUGENE, lawyer; b. Independence, Mo., Jan. 8, 1951; s. Russell Eugene and Reatha (Nixon) J.; m. Vicki Ja Lane, June 11, 1983. AB with honors, U. Mo., 1973, JD, 1976. Bar: Mo. 1976, U.S. Dist. Ct. (we. dist.) Mo. 1976, U.S. Ct. Appeals (8th cir.) 1984, U.S. Supreme Ct. 1993. Ptnr. Stinson Morrison Hecker LLP, Kansas City, Mo., 1976—. Editor Mo. Law Rev., 1974-76. Pres. Lido Villas Assn., Inc., Mission, Kans., 1979-81. Mem. ABA, Mo. Bar Assn., Kansas City Bar Assn., Lawyers Assn. Kansas City, Def. Rsch. Inst., Internat. Assn. Def. Counsel, Mo. Orgn. Def. Lawyers, Carriage Club, Order of Coif, Phi Beta Kappa, Phi Eta Sigma, Phi Kappa Phi, Omicron Delta Kappa. Republican. Presbyterian. Home: 4905 Somerset Dr Shawnee Mission KS 66207-2230 Office: Stinson Morrison Hecker LLP 1201 Walnut St Ste 2900 Kansas City MO 64106-2150 Office Phone: 816-691-2724. Office Fax: 816-412-1208. Business E-Mail: mjohnson@stinson.com.

JOHNSON, MARK P., lawyer; b. Billings, Mont., Aug. 14, 1955; BA cum laude, Yale U., 1977; JD, Harvard U., 1980. Bar: Mo. 1980, US Dist. Ct. We. Dist. Mo. 1980, US. Ct. Appeals 10th Cir. 1982, US Ct. Appeals 8th Cir. 1982, US Supreme Ct. 1985. Ptnr. Spencer Fane Britt & Browne, Kansas City, Mo., 1987—94, Sonnenschein Nath & Rosenthal LLP, Kansas City, Mo., 1994—. Counsel Am. Strokes Found. Mem.: ABA, Racial Justice Collaborative, Kansas City Met. Bar Assn., Mo. Bar, Assn. Yale Alumni. Office: Sonnenschein Nath & Rosenthal LLP Ste 1100 4520 Main St Kansas City MO 64111 Office Phone: 816-460-2424. Office Fax: 816-531-7545. Business E-Mail: mjohnson@sonnenschein.com.

JOHNSON, MARY ANN, vocational school owner; b. Chgo., June 26, 1956; d. Truly and Pearlie Mae (Bell) J.; children: Pamela Ann, Russell Alan Jr. AA, Joliet Jr. Coll., Ill., 1990; student mgmt. info. systems, Governor State U. Student intern Argonne (Ill.) Nat. Lab., 1972-79; owner, pres. Tech. Soft Svcs., Chgo., 1991—. Lectr., condr. seminars on running small bus. Author: Running a Small Business, 1996. Avocations: self-defense, computers. Office: Tech Soft Services Inc PO Box 101074 Chicago IL 60610-8901 Home Phone: 708-342-1727; Office Phone: 312-527-1200. Personal E-mail: tsschgo160@aol.com.

JOHNSON, MARYL RAE, cardiologist; b. Fort Dodge, Iowa, Apr. 15, 1951; d. Marvin George and Beryl Evelyn (White) Johnson. BS, Iowa State U., 1973; MD, U. Iowa, 1977. Diplomate Am. Bd. Internal Medicine, Am. Bd. Cardiovasc. Diseases. Intern U. Iowa Hosps., Iowa City, 1977-78, resident, 1978-81, fellow, 1979-82; assoc. in cardiology U. Iowa Hosps. and Clins., Iowa City, 1982-86, asst. prof. medicine cardiovasc. divsn., 1986-88; asst. prof. medicine Med. Ctr. Loyola U., 1988-92, assoc. prof., 1992-94, Rush. U., 1994-97, Northwestern U. Med. Sch., 1998—2002; prof. medicine U. Wis. Med. Sch., Madison, 2002—. Med. dir. cardiac transplantation U. Iowa Hosp., 1986—88; assoc. med. dir. cardiac transplantation Loyola U., 1988—94, assoc. med. dir. Rush Heart Failure and Cardiac Transplant Program, 1994—97; dir. heart failure cardiac transplant program Northwestern U. Med. Sch., 1998—2001, dir. heart failure program, 2001—02; med. dir. heart failure and transplantation U. Wis. Hosp. and Clinics, 2002—. Assoc. editor: Jour. Heart and Lung Transplantation, 1995—99, 2007—, mem. editl. bd.:, 2000—06. Mem. Nat. Heart Lung and Blood Adv. Coun., Bethesda, Md., 1979—83; mem. biomed. rsch. tech. rev. com. NIH, 1990—93, chairperson, 1992—93, chair biomed. rsch. tech. spl. emphasis panel, 1999—2002. Recipient Jane Leinfelder Meml. award, U. Iowa Coll. Medicine, 1977, Clin. Investigator award, NIH, 1981, New Investigator Rsch. award, 1981, 1986; Barry Freeman scholar, 1974. Mem.: ACP, AAAS, AMA, United Network Organ Sharing (thoracic organ com. 2005—, vice chair 2006—), Am. Soc. Transplantation (chair membership com. 2003—04, bd. dirs. 2004—06, sec.-treas. 2006—), Am. Coll. Cardiology (heart failure and cardiac transplant com. 2002—07, chair 2004—07), Am. Heart Assn., Ctrl. Soc. Clin. Rsch., Internat. Soc. Heart and Lung Transplantation (mem. program com. 2005), Order of Rose, Alpha Omega Alpha, Iota Sigma Pi, Phi Kappa Phi, Alpha Lambda Delta. Office: U Wis Madison E5/582D CSC 5710 600 Highland Ave Madison WI 53792 Office Phone: 608-263-0080. Business E-Mail: mrj@medicine.wisc.edu.

JOHNSON, MICHAEL O., window manufacturing executive; CFO, sr. v.p. corp. bus. svcs. Andersen Corp., Bayport, Minn. Office: Andersen Corp 100 4th Ave N Bayport MN 55003

JOHNSON, MILLARD WALLACE, JR., mathematics and engineering professor; b. Racine, Wis., Feb. 1, 1928; s. Millard Wallace and Marian Manilla (Rittman) J.; m. Ruth Pugh Gifford, Dec. 26, 1953; children: Millard Wallace III, Jeannette Marian Brooks, Charles Gifford, Peter Allen. BS in Applied Math. and Mechanics, U. Wis., Madison, 1952, MS, 1953; PhD in Math, MIT, Cambridge, 1957. Rsch. asst. MIT, 1953-57, lectr., 1957-58; mem. staff Math. Rsch. Ctr. U. Wis., Madison, 1958-94, prof. mechanics, 1958-63, prof. mechanics and math., 1964-94, mem. staff Rheology Rsch. Ctr., 1970—, mem. Engine Rsch. Ctr., 1985—, prof. emeritus math. and engring.-physics depts., 1994—. Contbr. articles to profl. jours. Adv. bd. Internat. Math. and Statis. Librs. (IMSL), 1971-92. With USN, 1946-48. Fellow ASME; mem. Soc. Rheology, Soc. Indsl. and Applied Math., Am. Acad. Mechanics, Brit. Soc. Rheology, Wis. Acad. Scis., Arts and Letters, Phi Beta Kappa. Home: 802 Blue Ridge Pkwy Madison WI 53705-1148 Office: U Wis Dept Eng Phys 1500 Engineering Dr Madison WI 53706-1609 Office Phone: 608-263-1646. Business E-Mail: mwjohns1@wisc.edu.

JOHNSON, NICHOLAS, writer, lawyer, educator; b. Iowa City, Sept. 23, 1934; s. Wendell A.L. and Edna (Bockwoldt) Johnson; m. Karen Mary Chapman, 1952 (div. 1972); children: Julie, Sherman, Gregory, Alexander; m. Mary Eleanor Vasey, 1991. BA, U. Tex., 1956, LL.B., 1958; L.H.D., Windham Coll., 1971. Bar: Tex. 1958, D.C. 1963, U.S. Supreme Ct. 1963, Iowa 1974; lic. radio amateur. Law clk. to judge John R. Brown, U.S. 5th Circuit Ct. Appeals, 1958-59; law clk. to U.S. Supreme Ct. Justice Hugo L. Black, 1959-60; acting assoc. prof. law U. Calif. at Berkeley, 1960-63; assoc. Covington & Burling, Washington, 1963-64; adminstr. Maritime Adminstrn., chmn. Maritime Subsidy Bd. U.S. Dept. Commerce, 1964-66; commr. FCC, 1966-73; adj. prof. law Georgetown U., 1971-73; Poynter fellow Yale U., 1971; vis. prof. U. Ill., Champaign-Urbana, 1976, U. Okla., Norman, 1978, Ill. State U., Normal, 1979, U. Wis., Madison, 1980, ewhouse Sch., Syracuse U., 1980, U. Iowa Coll. Law, 1981—; vis. prof. dept. communications studies U. Iowa. 1982-85; vis. prof. Western Behavioral Scis. Inst., U. Calif., San Diego, 1986-91. Vis. prof. Calif. State U., Los Angeles, 1986, New Sch. Soc. Resource ConnectEd, 1990, U. Iowa dept. theater arts, 1999; regents prof. U. Calif., San Diego, 2000; co-dir. U. Iowa Inst. for Health, Behavior and Environ. Policy, 1990-93; chmn., dir. Nat. Citizens Comm. Lobby, 1975—, Nat. Citizens Com. for Broadcasting, 1974-78; pub. access, 1975-77; commentator Nat. Pub. Radio, 1975-77, 83-86, Sta. WRC-AM, Washington, 1977, Sta. WSUI, Iowa City, 1982-87; presdl. advisor White House Conf. on Libraries and Info. Services, 1979; exec. com. World Acad. Art and Sci., 1993-97. Author: Cases and Materials on Oil and Gas Law, 1962, How to Talk Back to Your Television Set, 1970, Japanese transl., 1971, Life Before Death in the Corporate State, 1971, Test Pattern for Living, 1972, Broadcasting in America, 1973, Cases and Materials on Communications Law and Policy, 1981, 82, 83, 84, 85, 86, Readings for Law of Electronic Media, 1993-94, (with David Loundy) Law of Electronic Media in a Cyberspace Age, 1996; syndicated columnist: Gannett News Service, 1982-84, Register and Tribune Syndicate, 1984, Cowles Syndicate, 1985-86, King Features Syndicate, 1986, Iowa City Press Citizen, 1998-2001; contbr. to legal, gen., internat. publs.; contbg. editor, host PBS The New Tech Times, 1983-84. Dem. candidate for U.S. Ho. of Reps. from 3d Iowa Dist., 1974; bd. dirs. Ctr. for Study Commercialism, 1991-96, Citizens Ind. Pub. Broadcasting, 1999-2002, Common Cause, 1990-96, Internat. Soc. Gen. Semantics, 1960-2000, Iowa City Cmty. Sch. Dist., 1998-2001, Virtual Classroom Project, 1990-91, Vol. in Tech. Assistance, 1994-2000; mem. adv. bd. Ctr. Media Edn., 1993-, Cultural Environ., Movement, 1992-, Fairness and Accuracy in Reporting, 1996—, Inst. Pub. Accuracy, 1997-, Open Soc. Inst. Media Group, 1999-2000, Project Censored, 1976-, U. Iowa Info. Arcade, 1991-92, War and Peace Found., 1988-, Working Assets Long Distance, 1992-96; mem. Broadband and Telecom. Commn., Iowa City, 1981-87. Named One of 10 Outstanding Young Men in U.S., U.S. Jaycees, 1967, recipient New Republic Pub. Defender award, 1970, Civil Liberties Award Ga. ACLU, 1972, DeWitt Carter Reddick award U. Tex., 1977, George Stoney award Nat. Fedn. Local Cable Programmers, 1987; fellow World Acad. Art and Sci., 1991—. Mem. D.C., Iowa Bar Assn. (Citizenship award 1951), State Bar Tex., Golden Key, Order of Coif, Phi Beta Kappa, Phi Delta Phi, Phi Eta Sigma, Pi Sigma Alpha. Democrat. Unitarian Universalist. Home and Office: PO Box 1876 Iowa City IA 52244-1876 Office Phone: 319-337-5555. E-mail: nicholas@nicholasjohnson.org.

JOHNSON, NIEL MELVIN, archivist, historian; b. Galesburg, Ill., July 28, 1931; s. Clarence Herman and Frances Albertina (Nelson) J.; m. Verna Gail Applegate, May 1, 1952; children: Kristin, David. BA, Augustana Coll., 1953; MA, State U. Iowa, 1965, PhD, 1971. Tchr. Unit #115, Biggsville, Ill., 1954-57; asst. historian U.S. Army Weapons Command, Rock Island, Ill., 1957-60, chief historian, 1960-63; instr. Augustana Coll., Rock Island, Ill., 1967-69; asst. prof. Dana Coll., Blair, Nebr., 1969-74; vis. asst. prof. U. Nebr., Omaha, 1975-76; archivist, historian Harry S. Truman Libr., Independence, Mo., 1977-92. Pres. Portal to the Plains, Inc., Blair, Nebr., 1973-77, Am. Friends of Emigrant Inst. Sweden, East Moline, Ill., 1984-89. Author: George S. Viereck: German-American Propagandist, 1972, Portal to the Plains, 1974, Power, Money and Women: Words to the Wise from Harry S. Truman, 1999; co-author: Rockford Swedes: American Stories, 1993; contbr. articles in field to profl. jours., newspapers. Coord. New Sweden '88 com. of Greater Kansas City, Mo.; chmn. Historic Trails City Com., Independence, 1988-93. Recipient Commendation, Concordia Hist. Inst., St. Louis, 1977. Mem. Midwestern Archives Conf., Jackson County Hist. Soc., Scandinavian Assn. (pres. 1987-89). Democrat. Lutheran. Avocations: painting, writing, photography, golf, Truman impersonator. Home: 15804 Kiger Cir Independence MO 64055-3750

JOHNSON, OWEN C., food products executive; B in Quantitative and Labor Econs., U. Ill. V.p. bank mergers and acquisitions BankAmerica; sr. v.p. adminstrn. Lit-Am. Trading; v.p. human resources, purchasing, transp., corp. comm. and adminstrn. and pres. Greenfuels, Inc. Nisource, Inc., 1990—98; sr. v.p. human resources and adminstrn. ConAgra Foods, Inc., Omaha, 1998—2001, exec. v.p., chief adminstrv. officer, 2001—. Office: ConAgra Foods Inc One ConAgra Dr Omaha NE 68102-5001 Office Phone: 402-595-4000.

JOHNSON, OWEN VERNE, historian, educator; b. Madison, Wis., Feb. 22, 1946; s. Verner Lalander Johnson and Marianne Virginia (Halvorson) Muse; m. Marta Kucerova, July 17, 1969 (div. Jan. 26, 2001); children: Eva, Hana; m. Ann Coonradt Tryon, May 12, 2001. BA in History with distinction, Wash. State U., Pullman, 1968; MA in History, U. Mich., 1970, cert. in Russian Ea. European studies, 1978, PhD in History, 1978. Reporter Pullman Herald, Wash., 1961-67; reporter, announcer Sta. KWSU Radio-TV, Pullman, 1965-68; reporter, editor, producer Sta. WUOM, Ann Arbor, Mich., 1969-77; adminstrv. asst. Ctr. Russian and Ea. European Studies U. Mich., Ann Arbor, 1978-79; asst. prof. Sch. Journalism So. Ill. U., Carbondale, Ill., 1979-80; asst. prof. Ind. U., Bloomington, 1980-87, assoc. prof., 1987—, dir. grad. studies, 1990-91, acting dir. Polish studies, 1989-90, 2004—05, dir. Russian and Ea. European Inst., 1991-95, USA swimming and Big 10 swim announcer, 1993—; program host WFIU, Bloomington, 2007—. Mem. Modern Sweden Seminar, Uppsala, 1967; mem. Studia Academica Slovaca Comenius U., Bratislava, 1973; field advisor journalism Am. Coun. Tchrs. Russian, 1993—96; adj. prof. history Ind. U., Bloomington, 1996—. Author: Slovakia 1918-38: Education and the Making of a Nation, 1985; co-author: Eastern European Journalism Before, During and After Communism, 1999; contbr. articles to profl. jours.; mem. editl. bd. Slovakia, 1978—89, Journalism Monographs, 1986—88, Kosmas, 1996—, Media Rsch./Medijska istrazivanija, 2002—, Otázky zurnalistiky, 2007—; corr. editor: Journalism History, 1985—2000, cons. editor: Slavic Rev., 1985—91, corr.: Slovak Spectator, 2004—. Capt. USAR, 1971—79. Recipient Excellence in Journalism award, Sigma Delta Chi, 1966; grantee, Nat. Coun. Soviet and E. European Rsch., 1988—90, Am. Coun. Learned Socs./Social Sci. Rsch. Coun. Joint Com. Ea. Europe, 1983, Internat. Rsch. and Exchs. Bd., 1973—74, 1982, 1989, 2003—04. Mem.: Slovak Studies Assn. (pres. 1988—91), Orgn. Am. Historians, Czechoslovak Studies Assn. (editor newsletter 1980—84, mem. exec. com. 1988—92, Stanley Pech award 1987—88), Assn. Edn. Journalism and Mass Comm. (head history divsn. 1985—86), Am. Assn. Advancement Slavic Studies (mem. edn. com. 1988—90), Am. Hist. Assn. Democrat. Presbyterian. Office: Ind U Sch Journalism 200 Ernie Pyle Hall Bloomington IN 47405 Office Phone: 812-855-9247. Office Fax: 812-855-0901. Business E-Mail: johnsono@indiana.edu.

JOHNSON, PATSY, nursing association administrator; Exec. administr. Kans. State Bd. Nursing, Topeka. Office: Kansas Board Of Nursing 900 SW Jackson St Rm 1051 Topeka KS 66612-1232

JOHNSON, PAUL OREN, lawyer; b. Mpls., Feb. 2, 1937; s. Andrew Richard and LaVerne Delores (Slater) J.; children: Scott, Paula, Amy. BA, Carleton Coll., 1958; JD cum laude, U. Minn., 1961. Bar: Minn. 1961. Atty. Briggs & Morgan, St. Paul, 1961-62, Green Giant Co., Le Sueur, Minn., 1961-66, asst. sec., 1967-74, sec., 1975-79, v.p., gen. counsel, 1971-79, v.p. corporate rels., 1973-79, mem. mgmt. com., 1976-79; gen. counsel H.B. Fuller Co., St. Paul, 1979-84, sr. v.p., sec., 1980-90, mem. mgmt. com., 1981-90. Bd. dirs. The Fulcrum Group, chmn. bd. dirs. Bd. dirs. Boy Scouts Am.; bd. dirs. Rep. County Com., 1965; bd. dirs. Minn. State U., 1979-82, v.p., 1980-82; chmn. bd. dirs. Minn. Com. Serving Deaf and Hard of Hearing, 1992-98; bd. dirs. vice chair Minn. Acads.; bd. dirs., mem. exec. com., treas. Self Help for Hard of Hearing. Office: Lexington-Riverside 403-1077 Sibley Meml Hwy Saint Paul MN 55118-3680

JOHNSON, RICHARD ARNOLD, statistics educator, consultant; b. St. Paul, July 10, 1937; s. Arnold Verner and Florence Dorothy J.; m. Roberta Anne Weinard, Mar. 21, 1964; children— Erik Richard, Thomas Robert B.E.E., U. Minn., Mpls., 1960, MS in Math., 1963, PhD in Stats., 1966. Asst. prof. stats. U. Wis., Madison, 1966-70, assoc. prof., 1970-74, prof. stats, 1974—, chmn. dept. stats., 1981-84; head Greentree Statis. Consulting, Madison, Wis., 1978—. Cons. industry, Dept. Energy; cooperating scientist Dept. Agr.; lectr. in more than 22 countries. Co-author: Statistical Concepts and Methods, 1977, Applied Multivariate Statistical Analysis, 1982, 6th edit., 2007, Probability and Statistics for Engineers, 7th edit., 2005, Statistics-Principles and Methods, 1985, 5th edit., 2006, Business Statistics-Decision Making with Data, 1997, Statistical Reasoning and Methods, 1998; founding editor Stat. and Probability Letters, 1992—2007. Recipient Frank Wilcoxon prize, 1991; NATO sr. postdoctoral fellow, 1972; numerous grants NSA, NSF, ONR, Air Force, NASA. Fellow Inst. Math. Stats. (program sec. 1980-86, mem. of council 1980-86), Am. Statis. Assn. (sect. rep. to council 1980-82), Royal Statis. Soc.; mem. Internat. Statis. Inst. Lutheran. Avocations: fishing, cross country skiing. Office: Greentree Statis Cons 7122 Valhalla Trl Madison WI 53719-3039 E-mail: rich@stat.wisc.edu.

JOHNSON, RICHARD FRED, lawyer; b. July 12, 1944; s. Sylvester Hiram and Naomi Ruth (Jackson) Johnson; m. Sheila Conley, June 26, 1970; children: Brendon, Bridget, Timothy, Laura. BS, Miami U., Oxford, Ohio, 1966; JD cum laude, Northwestern U., 1969. Bar: Ill. 1969, Ind., 2004, U.S. Dist. Ct. (no. dist.) Ill. 1969), U.S. Dist. Ct. (ctrl. dist.) Ill. 2000, U.S. Dist. Ct. (no. dist.) Ind., 2006, U.S. Ct. Appeals (7th cir.) 1977, U.S. Ct. Appeals (2d cir.) 1980, U.S. Ct. Appeals (9th cir.) 1991, U.S. Ct. Appeals (5th cir.) 1993, U.S. Supreme Ct. 1978. Law clk. U.S. Dist. Ct. (no. dist.) Ill., Chgo., 1969-70; assoc. firm Lord, Bissell & Brook, Chgo., 1970-77, ptnr., 1977—2004, Hughes, Socol, Piers, Resnick and Dym, Ltd., Chgo., 2004—. Lectr. legal edn. Contbr. articles to profl. jours. Recipient Am. Jurisprudence award 1968. Mem. Chgo. Bar Assn., Union League. Home: 521 W Roscoe St Chicago IL 60657-3518 Office: Hughes Socol Piers Resnick & Dym Ltd 70 W Madison Chicago IL 60602 Office Phone: 312-604-2618. Business E-Mail: rjohnson@hsplegal.com.

JOHNSON, RICK, state official; m. Cindy Johnson. Former commr., bd. chmn. Osceola County; Spkr. of Ho. Mich. Ho. Reps., Dist. 102, 2001—. Mem. Pine River Sch. Bd. Edn.; dist. dir. Mich. Farm Bur. Mem.: Osceola County Republican Party (chmn.). Republican.

JOHNSON, ROB, newscaster; married. BA in Comm., DePauw U., Greencastle, Ind., 1990. Anchor and reporter KALB-TV, Alexandria, La., 1990—92, KLFY-TV, Lafayette, La., 1992—94; primary anchor KATV-TV, Little Rock, 1994—95; anchor 4 and 5pm news KRPC-TV, Houston, 1995—98; weekend anchor and reporter WLS-TV, Chgo., 1998—. TV journalist Hope in Honduras (Emmy award, 2000). Vol. Crohn's and Colitis Found.; bd. dirs. Voices of Ill. Children. Recipient Best Radio Documentary award, Soc. Profl. Journalists, 1989, Best Documentary award, AP, 1994, Best Newscast award, 1995, 1997, Best Election Coverage award, 1995, Houston Press Club award, 1996. Office: WLS-TV 190 N State St Chicago IL 60601

JOHNSON, ROBERT GRAHAM, surgeon, educator, researcher; b. Norman, Okla., July 28, 1953; s. William Froman Johnson and Mary Elizabeth Griffin Davison; m. Cindy Snodgrass, Aug. 2, 1975; children: Chase, Rainey. MD, U. Okla., 1978. Diplomate Am. Bd. Surgery, Am. Bd. Thoracic Surgery. Resident in gen. surgery U. Okla., Oklahoma City, 1978-83, resident in cardiothoracic surgery, 1983-85; fellow in cardiac surgery rsch. Mass. Gen. Hosp., Boston, 1980—81; mem. faculty Harvard U. Med. Sch., Boston, 1985—89, assoc. prof., 1989—99; prof., chair dept. surgery St. Louis U., 1999—. Fellow ACS, Am.

Coll. Cardiology, Am. Coll. Chest Physicians (pres. 2001); mem. AMA, Soc. Univ. Surgeons, Alpha Omega Alpha. Episcopalian. Office: St Louis U 3635 Vista at Grand Blvd Saint Louis MO 63110 Home Phone: 314-726-0189; Office Phone: 314-577-8352. E-mail: johnsorg@slu.edu.

JOHNSON, ROGER, state agency administrator; b. Turtle Lake, ND; m. Anita Johnson; 3 children. BA in Agricultural Economics, ND State U. Elected agrl. commr. ND Dept. Agrl., Bismarck, 1996—. Pres. Mid. Am. Internat. Agrl.-Trade Coun. Mem.: Interstate Pest Control Compact (chmn. 2005), Food Export Assn. Midwest (past pres.), Midwestern Assn. State Departments of Agriculture (past pres.). Democrat. Methodist. Office: ND Dept Agrl 600 E Blvd 6th Fl Bismarck ND 58505-0200

JOHNSON, S. CURTIS, chemicals executive; BA in Econ., Cornell U., 1977; MBA, Northwestern U., 1983. Mgmt. positions S.C. Johnson & Sons, 1983—89, dir. worldwide bus. develop., 1989—93, v.p., mng. dir. Mexican Johnson, 1993—95, v.p., mng. dir. bus. develop., 1995—96; pres. Comml. Markets Inc., 1996—2002; chmn. JohnsonDiversey Inc., Sturtevant, Wis., 2002—. Co-founder Wind Point Partners LP; mem. bd. dir. Cargill, Inc.; bd. dir. Johnson Fin. Group Inc. Named one of Forbes' Richest Americans, 2006. Office: Johnson Diversey PO Box 902 8310 16th St Sturtevant WI 53177-0902

JOHNSON, S.A. (TONY JOHNSON), automotive executive; Pres., CEO Onan Corp., 1981—85; CEO Pentair Inc., 1985—89; founder Hidden Creek Inustries, Mpls.; mng. ptnr. J2R Partners. Chmn., dir. Automotive Industries Holding, Inc., 1990—95, Tower Automotive, 1993—; dir. Dura Automotive Sys., Inc. Office: Tower Automotive 27175 Haggerty Rd Novi MI 48377-3626

JOHNSON, SANDRA HANNEKEN, law educator; b. St. Louis, Jan. 20, 1952; d. Clarence F. and Mary Rose (Uykosky) Hanneken; m. Robert G. Johnson, 1973; children: Emily, Kathleen. AB summa cum laude, St. Louis U., 1973; JD, NYU, 1976; LLM, Yale U., 1977. Bar: N.Y. 1978. Asst. prof. law N.Y. Law Sch., 1977-78, St. Louis U., 1978-81, assoc. prof. law, 1981-84, prof. of law, 1984—, Tenet prof. health care law & ethics, 2000—, assoc. dean, 1979—81, 1985—88, interim dean, 1991—92, provost, 1998—2002; vis. prof. Univ. Houston Law Ctr., 1991, Washington U. Sch. Law, 1995. Dir. Ctr. for Health Law Studies, St. Louis, 1982-85, 88-91; cons. Inst. of Medicine Project on Nursing Homes, N.Y., 1985; mem. Hastings Ctr. Project on Ethics in Nursing Homes, N.Y., 1988-91. Co-author: ursing Homes and the Law, 1985, Health Law, 1987, 2nd edit., 1991, Health Law Cases Materials & Problems, 4th edit.; mem. bd. editors Law, Medicine and Health Care, 1985—; contbr. articles to profl. jours. Participant St. Louis Leadership Devel. Program, 1980-81; bd. mem. Inst. for Peace & Justice, St. Louis, 1988-90; mem. Instl. Rev. Bd., St. Louis U., 1989-90. Grantee Nat. Inst. of Dispute Resolution, 1985, AARP, 1988; Edmund Pellegrino medal, 2003, HEAL Inst.; Woman of the Year 2002, St. Louis Daily Record; fellow, Hastings Ctr. Mem. ABA, Am. Soc. Law Medicine & Ethics (dir. Mayday Project on Legal & Regulatory Issues in Pain Relief, Disting. Health Law Tchr. award, William J. Curran award), Midwest Bioethics Roundtable, St. Louis Health Lawyers Assn. (chmn.), Phi Beta Kappa, Alpha Sigma Nu. Office: St Louis U Sch of Law 3700 Lindell Blvd Saint Louis MO 63108-3412

JOHNSON, SANKEY ANTON, manufacturing executive; b. Bremerton, Wash., May 14, 1940; s. Sankey Broyd and Alice Mildred (Norum) J.; m. Carolyn Lee Rogers, Nov. 30, 1968; children: Marni Lee, Ronald Anton. BS in M.E, U. Wash.; MBA, Stanford U. V.p., gen. mgr. Cummins Asia Pacific, Manila, Philippines, 1974-78; v.p. automotive Cummins Engine Co., Columbus, Ind., 1978-79; v.p. North Am. Bus., 1979-81; pres., chief exec. officer Onan Corp., Mpls., 1981-85; exec. v.p. Pentair Inc., St. Paul, from 1985, chief operating officer, 1985—, pres., 1986-89; chmn. Hidden Creek Industries, Mpls., 1989—2004; mng. ptnr. OG Ptnrs., Mpls., 2004—. Trustee Mfr.'s Alliance. Bd. advisors Stanford Grad. Sch. Bus. Mem. Lafayette Club. Home: 2310 Huntington Point Rd W Wayzata MN 55391-9743 Office: OG Partners 294 Grove Ln E Wayzata MN 55391 Office Phone: 952-404-4100.

JOHNSON, SHANNON, professional basketball player; b. Aug. 18, 1974; Grad., U.S.C., 1996. Mem. 2 ABL Champion Columbus Quest; profl. basketball player Valencia, Spain, Orlando Miracle (now Conn. Sun), 1999—2002, Conn. Sun, 2003, San Antonio Silver Stars, 2004—06, Detroit Shock, 2007—. Named All-WNBA 2nd Team, 1999, 2000, Inaugural WNBA All-Star Team, 1999, WNBA All-Star Team, 2000, 2002, 2003. Achievements include mem. US Women's Basketball Team, Athens Olympics, 2004. Mailing: Detroit Shock Palace Sports & Entertainment 5 Championship Dr Auburn Hills MI 48326

JOHNSON, SIDNEY B., state legislator; b. Sedalia, Mo., Aug. 19, 1942; m. Jean M. Turner; four children. BS, U. of Mo., Columbia. Farmer; county commr. Buchanan County, 1983-90; mem. Mo. Senate from 34th dist., Jefferson City, 1990—.

JOHNSON, STANLEY R., economist, educator; b. Burlington, Iowa, Aug. 26, 1938; married; 2 children. BA in Agrl. Econs., Western Ill. U., 1961; MS, Tex. Tech. U., 1962; PhD, Tex. A&M U., 1966. Asst. prof. dept. econs. U. Mo., Columbia, 1964-66, assoc. prof. depts. econs. and agrl. econs., 1967-70, prof., 1970-85, adj. prof., 1985—, chmn. dept. econs., 1972-74; assoc. prof. dept. agrl. econs. U. Conn., Storrs, 1966-67. Exec. dir. Food and Agrl. Policy Rsch. Inst., 1984-96; prof., dir. Ctr. Agrl. and Rural Devel. Iowa State U., Ames, 1985-97; vis. assoc. prof. agrl. econs. Purdue U., 1971-72; economist Agr. Can., Ottawa, 1975; vis. prof. econs. U. Ga., 1975-76, U. Calif., Berkeley, 1981; chmn. bd. Midwest Agribus. Trade Rsch. and Info. Ctr., 1987-96; vice provost Iowa State U., 1996—; hon. prof. Ukrainian State Agrl. U., 1994, Chinese Acad. Scis., 1996. Author: Advanced Econometric Methods, 1984, Demand Systems Estimation, 1984, Advvanced Econometric Methods, 1988, Industrial Policy for Agriculture in Global Economy, 1993, Agricultural Sector Models for U.S., 1993, Conservation of Great Plains Ecosystems: Current Scientific and Future Options, 1995; mem. internat. editl. bd. Advances in Agrl. Mgmt. and Econs., 1989; editor-in-chief: Agr. Econs., Jour. Internat. Assn. Agrl. Economists; mem editl. bd.: Internat. Review Econs. and Finance, 1997; contbr. chpts to books, articles to profl. jours. Chmn. bd. dirs. Inst. Policy Reform, 1990—; co-chair World Food Conf., 1988. Recipient Chancellor's award for outstanding rsch., 1980, Internat. Honor award Office of Internat. Cooperation and Devel./USDA, 1987, Charles F. Curtiss Disting. Professorship, 1990, Internat. Svc. award Wilton Park, 1993; named to Merlin Cole Meml. Professorship, 1994-97; numerous grants in econs. Fellow Am. Agrl. Econs. Assn.; mem. Am. Agrl. Econs. Assn. Found., V. I. All-Union Acad. Agrl. Scis. (fgn.), Ukrainian Acad. Agrl. Scis. (fgn. academician), Mo. Valley Econ. Assn. (bd. dirs. 1977-82, pres.-elect 1979-80, pres. 1980-81), Russian Acad. Agrl. Sci. (fgn. academician), Hungarian Acad. Sci. Office: Iowa State U 218 Beardshear Hl Ames IA 50011-0001

JOHNSON, STEVE, radio personality; Former news reporter AP Radio Network, UPI, USA News, CBS News, IMS Radio News; co-founder 30 station statewide radio network; announcer Sta. WUGN Radio, Midland, Mich. Office: WUGN 510 Isabella Rd Midland MI 48640

JOHNSON, STEVEN M., food service executive; CPA. With Ernst & Young LLP; contr. Fugate Enter., Inc., 1985—91; COO Coulter Enterprises, Inc., 1992—98; dir. Total Entertainment Restaurant Corp., 1998—, CEO, 1999—.

JOHNSON, STEVEN R., state legislator; b. June 15, 1947; m. Shannon Johnson. BS, MBA, Ind. U. Supr. chem. lab. Ind. U., Kokomo; owner Tuess Inc., pres.; rep. Ind. Ho. of Reps., 1980-82, 84-86; mem. Ind. Senate from 21st dist., 1986—; mem. legis. appointment and elec. com. State Legis., ranking mem. ethics com., mem. corrections, crime and civil procedures com., chmn. planning and pub. svc. com. Chmn. Howard County Reps., 1988-91; mem. Cmty. Assistance Found. Mem. Kokomo c. of C., Christian Businessman's Com., Elks, Rotary. Office: State Senate State Capitol Indianapolis IN 46204 Home: 108 E St Clair St Apt A Indianapolis IN 46204-1194

JOHNSON, THOMAS LEE, state legislator; b. Oakland, Calif., Apr. 30, 1945; s. WallaceJ.; m. Virginia Van Der Molen, 1968; children: Sorne, Derek, Kirk. BA, U. Mich., 1970; JD, DePaul U., 1974. Investigator State Atty.'s Office, DuPage County, Ill., 1970-74; assoc. Laraia, Solano, Berns & Kilander, Ltd., Wheaton, Ill., 1976-77; atty. Johnson, Westra, Broecker, Whittaker & Newitt, PC, Carol Stream, Ill., 1977—; mem. Ill. Ho. of Reps., 1993—, chmn. judiciary, criminal law, pub. utilities coms., also health care, human svcs., appropriations coms. Owner Buterfirld Hardware Store, Wheaton, 1977—. Past chmn. Winfield Twp. (Ill.) Rep. com.; past precinct committeeman Winfield Twp.; candidate U.S. Congress, 1984; del. Dole, 1988; campaign advisor Citizens to Elect Jim Ryan, 1990; mem. Sci. Tech. Mus., Wheaton Youth Outreach, Family Inst., Christian Legal Soc. Mem. ABA, Ill. Bar Assn., DuPage County Bar Assn., Am. Legion.

JOHNSON, TIMOTHY PATRICK, health and social researcher; b. Batavia, NY, July 14, 1954; s. Elmore Thomas and Sara (McKinsey) J.; m. LuEllen Doty, June 20, 1988; children: Sara Elizabeth, Elliott William. BA, Western Ky. U., 1977; MA, U. Wis., Milw., 1978; PhD, U. Ky., 1988. Rsch. analyst dept. medicine U. Ky., Lexington, 1980-82, rsch. coord. survey rsch. ctr., 1982-88; staff assoc. for psychometrics Am. Bd. Family Practice, Lexington, 1988-89; asst. rsch. prof. epidemiology and biostatistics sch. pub. health U. Ill., Chgo., 1991—2002, project coord. survey rsch. lab., 1989-91, asst. dir. survey rsch. lab., 1991-93, assoc. dir., 1993-96, acting dir., 1996-98, dir., 1998—, assoc. prof. pub. adminstrn., 1996—2003, prof. pub. adminstrn., 2003—, assoc. rsch. prof. pub. health, 2002—03, rsch. prof. public health, 2003—. Contbr. chpts. to books, articles to profl. jours. Mem. APHA, AAAS, Am. Sociol. Assn., Am. Assn. Pub. Opinion Rsch., Am. Statis. Assn., Am. Coll. Epidemiology, Am. Assn. for the Advancement of Sci. Roman Catholic. Office: U Ill Survey Rsch Lab 412 S Peoria St Chicago IL 60607-7063 Business E-Mail: timj@uic.edu.

JOHNSON, TIMOTHY PETER, senator; b. Canton, SD, Dec. 28, 1946; s. Vandal Charles and Ruth Jorinda (Ljostveit) J.; m. Barbara Brooks, June 6, 1969; children: Brooks Dwight, Brendan Vandal, Kelsey Marie. BA in Polit. Sci., U. SD, 1969, MA in Polit. Sci., 1970, JD, 1975; postgrad., Mich. State U., 1970-71. Bar: SD 1975, US Dist. Ct. SD 1976. Fiscal analyst Legis. Fiscal Agy., Lansing, Mich., 1971-72; pvt. practice Vermillion, SD, 1975-86; mem. SD Ho. of Reps., 1979—82, SD Senate, 1983—86, US Congress from SD, 1987-97; US Senator from SD, 1997—. Adj. inst. U. SD, Vermillion, 1974-83; mem. SD Code Commn., Pierre, 1982-86; mem. com. appropriations US Senate, com. banking, housing, and urban affairs, com. budget, com. energy and natural resources, com. Indian affairs, select com. ethics. Mem. Vermillion City Planning Commn., 1977-78; treas. Clay County Dem. Com., Vermillion, 1978; del. Dem. Nat. Conv., 1988, 92, 96. NSF grantee, 1969-70; recipient Outstanding Citizen award Vermillion, SD, 1983, Friend of Edn. award SD Edn. Assn., 1983, Billy Sutton award legis. achievement, 1984, Friends of NAFIS award Nat. Assn. Federally Impacted Schools, 1998, Arthur T. Matrix award Retired Officers Assn., 2001, Congressional Leadership award Nat. Telephone Coop. Assn., 2001, George Buck Gillispie Congressional award meritorious svc. Blinded Veterans Found., 2003. Mem. SD Bar Assn., Clay County Bar Assn., Phi Beta Kappa, Omicron Delta Kappa. Democrat. Lutheran. Office: US Senate 136 Hart Senate Ofc Bldg Washington DC 20510-0001 also: District Office Ste 103 320 S First St Aberdeen SD 57401-1554 Office Phone: 202-224-5842, 605-226-3440. Office Fax: 202-228-5765, 605-226-2439. E-mail: tim@johnson.senate.gov.

JOHNSON, TIMOTHY VINCENT, congressman, lawyer; b. Champaign, Ill., July 23, 1946; 9 children. Attended, US Military Academy, 1964; BA, U. Ill., 1969; JD, U. Ill. Coll. of Law, 1972. Alderman Urbana City Council, 1971—75; atty. priv. practice, 1972—; mem. from 104th Dist. Ill. Ho. of Reps, 1977—2000; mem. U.S. Congress from 15th Ill. dist., Washington, 2001—, mem. agr. com., sci. com., transp. and infrastructure com. Mem. Congressional Fire Services Caucus, Congressional Internet Caucus, Congressional Rural Caucus, Legislative Audit Commn. Mem. US Army, 1964—65. Recipient Order of the Coif. Mem.: Phi Beta Kappa (Bronze tablet). Republican. Assembly Of God. Office: US Ho of Reps 1229 Longworth Ho Office Bldg Washington DC 20515-1315

JOHNSON, TOM MILROY, dean, physician, educator; b. Northville, Mich., Jan. 16, 1935; s. Waldo Theodore and Ruth Jeanette (Christensen) J.; m. Emily Chapin Rhoads, June 13, 1959 (div. Aug. 1983); children— Glenn C., Heidi R.; m. Jane Susan Robb, June 10, 1987; 1 stepchild, Elizabeth K. BA in Psychology with honors, Coll. of Wooster, 1956; MD, Northwestern U., 1961; postgrad. in health systems mgmt., Harvard U., 1974. Rotating intern Detroit Receiving Hosp., 1961-62; resident in internal medicine U. Mich. Med. Ctr., Ann Arbor, 1962-65, fellow in pulmonary disease, 1967-68; asst. prof. internal medicine Mich. State U., East Lansing, 1968-71, assoc. prof., asst. dean Coll. of Medicine Grand Rapids, 1971-77; prof. medicine, dean Sch. of Medicine U. N.D., Grand Forks, 1977-88; prof., assoc. dean Coll. Human Medicine, Mich. State U., 1988-94; campus dean, CEO Kalamazoo Ctr. for Med. Studies Mich. State U., 1994-98, prof. emeritus medicine East Lansing, 1999—; cons. in med. edn. Fla. State U., 1999—2001. Bd. dirs. No. Mich. Regional Health Svcs., Petosky, 1991—2001. Contbr. articles to profl. jours. Capt. M.C., USAF, 1965-67. A. Blaine Brower Traveling scholar ACP, 1977; Tom M. Johnson lecture hall named in his honor Grand Rapids Med. Ctr., 1982; recipient Physician Leadership award Mich. Hosp. Assn., 1999, Disting. Alumni award Coll. of Wooster, 2003. Fellow ACP (Laureate award Mich. chpt.); mem. AMA, Mich. State Med. Soc., Studebaker Drivers Club, Antique Automobile Club of Am., Alpha Omega Alpha. Avocation: restoration of antique automobiles and older farm houses. Home and Office: 4815 Barton Rd Williamston MI 48895-9305 E-mail: tmilroyjohnson@yahoo.com.

JOHNSON, W. BRUCE, retail executive; BA, MBA, JD, Duke U. Mgmt. cons. Booz-Allen & Hamilton Inc., Arthur Andersen & Co.; v.p., tech. ops. and info. tech. Colgate-Palmolive Co.; dir., orgn. and sys. Carrefour SA; sr. v.p., supply chain and ops. Kmart Holding Corp., 2003—04; exec. v.p., supply chain and ops. Sears Holdings Corp., Hoffman Estates, Ill., 2004—08, interim pres., CEO, 2008—. Office: Sears Holdings Corp 3333 Beverly Rd Hoffman Estates IL 60179 Office Phone: 847-286-7197.*

JOHNSON, WALLACE STEPHEN, JR., Asian languages educator; b. Hampton, Va., Nov. 6, 1932; s. Wallace Stephen and Ellen Virginia (Weston) J.; m. Diantha Sibley Haviland, June 3, 1970; 1 child, Wallace Stephen III BA, Johns Hopkins U., 1957; PhD, U. Pa., 1968; postgrad., Harvard U. Law Sch., 1970-71. Prof. Asian langs. U. Kans., Lawrence, 1965—. Translator: The T'ang Code: General Principles, 1979; editor: A Concordance to the T'ang Code, 1965, An Index to the Pien-tzu lei-pien, 1967, A Concordance to the Kuan-tzu, 1970, A Concordance to the Han-fei tzu, 1975, A Reader in Chinese Literature, 1976, A Reader in Chinese Anthropology-Sociology, 1976, A Reader in Chinese International Relations, 1976, A Reader in Chinese Art History, 1976, (with Grace Wan) A Reader in Chinese History, 1972; editor Jour. Asian Legal History. Fellow Am. Council Leared Soc., 1970, Harvard U. Law Sch., 1970, Howard Found., 1972, Humboldt Found., 1972 Mem. Assn. for Asian Studies Home: 1633 Stratford Rd Lawrence KS 66044-2529 Office: U Kans Wescoe Hall Room 2116 1445 Jayhawk Blvd Lawrence KS 66045-0001 Office Phone: 785-864-9130. E-mail: wjohnson@ku.edu.

JOHNSON, WILBUR CORNEAL (JOE JOHNSON), wildlife biologist; b. Kalamazoo, Nov. 16, 1941; BS, Mich. State U., 1964, MS, 1967. Cert. wildlife biologist. Wildlife technician W.K. Kellogg Bird Sanctuary, Mich. State U., Augusta, 1964-85, chief wildlife biologist, bird sanctuary mgr., 1985—. Recipient Miles B. Pirnie Meml. award Mich. Duckhunters Assn., 1993. Mem. Wildlife Soc., Pheasants Forever (nat. bd. 1988-2001), Trumpeter Swan Soc. (nat. bd., 2003-), Miss. Flyway Coun. (tech. sect., chair swan com., mem. giant Can. goose com., rsch. com.). Office: WK Kellogg Bird Sanctuary Mich State Univ 12685 E C Ave Augusta MI 49012-9707

JOHNSON, WILLIAM HOWARD, retired agricultural engineer, educator; b. Sidney, Ohio, Sept. 3, 1922; s. Russell Earl and Dollie (Gamble) J.; m. Wyoma Jean Swift, Oct. 2, 1943; children: Lawrence Alan, Cheri Ellen, Dana Sue. BS, Ohio State U., 1948, MS, 1953; PhD, Mich. State U., 1960. Registered profl. engr. Mem. faculty Ohio Agrl. Expt. Sta., Wooster, 1948-64, Ohio Agrl. Rsch. and Devel. Ctr., Wooster, 1964-70, prof., assoc. chmn. dept. agrl. engring., 1959-70; part-time prof. Ohio State U., 1964-70; prof., head dept. agrl. engring. Kans. State U., Manhattan, 1970-81, dir. Engring. Expt. Sta., 1981-87; ret., 1987. Cons. farm equipment cos. Author: (with B.J. Lamp) Principles, Equipment and Systems for Corn Harvesting, 1966; also articles. Recipient Disting. Alumnus award Coll. Engring., Ohio State U., 1974; named to Coll. Engring. Kans. State U. Hall of Fame, 1992. Fellow Am. Soc. Agrl. Engrs. (pres. 1986-87, McCormick-Case Gold Medal award 1994), Kans. Engring. Soc. (pres. 1985-86), Sigma Xi, Tau Beta Pi. Achievements include research on soil-plant-machine relationships, harvesting, design for soiltillers, planters, harvesters. Home: 2121 Meadowlark Rd #131 Manhattan KS 66502 Office: Kans State U Dept Agrl Engring Seaton Hall Manhattan KS 66506 Business E-Mail: wjohnson@ksu.edu.

JOHNSON, WILLIAM S., transportation executive; Mem. corp. fin. group Amoco; v.p. venture devel. Amoco Chem. Asia Pacific, Hong Kong; v.p. global bus. mgmt. Amoco Polyers, Inc.; pres. Amoco Fabrics and Fibers Co.; exec. v.p., CFO Budget Group, Inc., 2000—.

JOHNSON-LEIPOLD, HELEN P., outdoor recreation company executive; b. Dec. 1956; d. Samuel Curtis and Imogene (Powers) Johnson; m. Craig L. Leipold; children: Kyle, Connor, Curtis, Bradford, Chris. BA in Psychology, Cornell U., 1978. With Foote, Cone & Belding, Chgo., 1979—85; v.p. consumer mktg. svcs. worldwide SC Johnson, 1992-95, exec. v.p. N.Am. businesses, 1995-97, v.p. personal and home care products, 1997-98, v.p. worldwide consumer products-mktg., 1998—99; chmn., CEO Johnson Outdoors Inc. (formerly Johnson Worldwide Assocs. Inc.), Racine, Wis., 1999—; chmn. Johnson Fin. Group, 2004—. Co-owner Nashville Predators, NHL, 1997—; bd. dirs. The Home Depot, 2006—, SC Johnson & Co., JohnsonDiversey, Inc.; founder, chmn. Next Generation Now. Named one of Forbes' Richest Americans, 2006. Office: Johnson Outdoors Inc 555 Main St Racine WI 53403 Office Fax: 262-631-6601.

JOHNSRUD, DUWAYNE, state legislator; b. Boscobel, Wis., Sept. 4, 1943; s. Gordon and Louise Johnsrud; m. Jacqueline Johnsrud, 1965; children: Jennifer, Jaret, Zachary. BS, U. Wis., La Crosse, 1970. Farmer, Eastman, Wis.; mem. from dist. 96 Wis. State Assembly, Madison, 1984—. Mem. Eastman Sch. Bd., 1982; mem. Crawford County Bd., 1982—; mem. Crawford County Farm Bur. Mem. Am. Legion, Prairie du Chien Lions Club, Eagles, Delta Sigma Pi. Office: RR 1 Box 91A Eastman WI 54626-9758

JOHNSTON, CYRUS CONRAD, JR., medical educator; b. Statesville, NC, July 16, 1929; m. Marjorie Tarkington, Feb. 20, 1960; 2 children. BA, Duke U., 1951, MD, 1955. Diplomate Am. Bd. Internal Medicine. Intern Duke Hosp., Durham, NC, 1955-56; resident in medicine Barnes Hosp., St. Louis, 1956-57; rsch. fellow in endocrinology and metabolism Ind. U., Indpls., 1959-61, instr. medicine, 1961-63, asst. prof., 1963-67, assoc. prof., 1967-69, prof. medicine, 1969-97, disting. prof. medicine, 1997—2002, disting. prof. emeritus, 2002—; assoc. dir. Gen. Clin. Rsch. Ctr. Ind. U. Med. Ctr., Indpls., 1962-67, program dir., 1967-72, prin. investigator, 1968-88, dir. divsn. endocrinology and metabolism, 1968-94. Mem. aging rev. com. Nat. Inst. Aging, 1982-85, chmn. geriatrics rev. com., 1985-86; mem. nursing sci. rev. com. NIH, 1988-89; mem. com. for protection of human subjects Ind. U.-Purdue U., Indpls., 1966—, chmn., 1978—; chmn. Nat. Osteoporosis Found. Sci. Adv. Bd., 1992-96; med. adv. panel Paget's Disease Found., 1989—; bd. trustees Nat. Osteoporosis Found., 1992—, pres., 1996-2001; mem. Nat. Adv. Coun. on Aging, 1992-95. Assoc. editor Bone and Mineral, 1985-94, Bone, 1995-2004; editl. bd. Jour. Bone and Mineral Rsch., Jour. Clin. Endocrinology and Metabolism, 1988-91. Capt. USAF, 1957-59. Recipient Career Rsch. Devel. award USPHS, 1963-68, Sandoz prize Internat. Assn. Gerontology, 1993, Experience Excellence Recognition award Glenn W. Irwin, Jr., MD, 2001. Mem. ACP, AAAS, AMA, Am. Assn. Clin. Endocrinologists (Yank D. Coble, Jr. M.D. Disting. Svc. award 1998), Am. Fedn. Clin. Rsch., Am. Soc. for Bone and Mineral Rsch. (Frederic C. Bartter award 1996), Am. Clin. and Climatological Soc., Ctrl. Soc. for Clin. Rsch., Endocrine Soc. Office: Indiana Univ Dept Medicine 541 N Clinical Dr CL 459 Indianapolis IN 46202-5124 E-mail: cjohnsto@iupui.edu.

JOHNSTON, GLADYS STYLES, university official; b. St. Petersburg, Fla., Dec. 23, 1942; d. John Edward and Rosa (Moses) Styles; m. Hubert Seward Johnston, July 30, 1966. BS in Social Sci., Cheney U., 1963; MEd in Ednl. Adminstrn., Temple U., 1969; PhD in Ednl. Adminstrn.-Orgnl. Theory, Cornell U., 1974. Tchr. Chester (Pa.) Sch. Dist., 1963-66, West Chester (Pa.) Sch. Dist., 1966-67, asst. prin., elem. prin., dir. Summer Sch., 1968-71; dir. Head Start Chester County Bd. Edn., West Chester, 1967-69; teaching asst., rsch. asst. Cornell U., Ithaca, N.Y., 1971-74; asst. prof. ednl. adminstr. and supervision Rutgers U., New Brunswick, N.J., 1974-79, assoc. prof., chmn. dept. Grad. Sch. Edn., 1979-83, chmn. dept. mgmt. Sch. Bus., 1983-85; dean, prof. Coll. Edn., Ariz. State U., Tempe, 1985-91; provost, v.p. for acad. affairs DePaul U., Chgo., 1991-93, chancellor, 1993—. Disting. Commonwealth vis. prof. Coll. William and Mary Sch. Edn., Williamsburg, Va., 1982-83; manuscript reviewer Jour. Higher Edn., Jour. Ednl. Leadership, Prentice Hall Pub. Co., Englewood Cliffs, N.J.; speaker and conf. presenter in field; cons. AT&T, Ednl. Testing Svc., Prentice-Hall Pub. Co.; cons. to coordinating bd. Tex. Coll. and Univ. System. Author: Research and Thought in Administration Theory, 1986; mem. editorial bd. Ednl. Evaluation and Policy Analysis, Ednl. Adminstrn. Quar., Ednl. and Psychol. Rsch. Jour.; contbr. articles and book revs. to profl. jours., chpts. to books. Bd. dirs. Edn. Law Ctr., 1979-86, Sta. KAET-TV, Phoenix, 1987—, Found. for Sr. Living, 1990-91; mem. adv. coun. to bd. trustees Cornell U., 1981-86; trustee Middlesex Gen. Univ. Hosp., 1983-86. Recipient Outstanding Alumni award Temple U.; Andrew D. White fellow Cornell U. Mem. ASCD, Am. Assn. Colls. for Tchr. Edn., Nat. Conf. Profs. Ednl. Adminstrn., Am. Ednl. Rsch. Assn. (proposal reviewer 1979—, chmn. task force for participation and membership 1981—, chmn. E.F. Linquist award com. 1985, mem. govt. rels. com. 1986—, publ. com. 1986—), Phi Kappa Phi, Phi Delta Kappa, Alpha Phi Sigma. Office: U of Nebraska at Kearney Office of Chancellor 905 W 25th St Kearney NE 68845-4238

JOHNSTON, JAMES ROBERT, library director; b. Wheaton, Ill., June 3, 1947; s. Robert W. and Elizabeth S. (Townsend) J.; m. Carol Ann Trezza, June 14, 1969; children: Steven J., Julie M. BA, U. Notre Dame, 1969; MLS, Fla. State U., 1973. Head librarian Grande Prairie Library Dist., Hazel Crest, Ill., 1973-76; chief librarian Joliet (Ill.) Pub. Library, 1976—; pres. bd. dirs. Ill. Library Employees Benefit Plan. Mem. automation com. Heritage Trail Libr. Sys., Shorewood, Ill.; pres. Ill. Libr. Employees Benefit Plan, Joliet; bldg. cons. Co-author: Illinois Library Trustees Association Booklet "Selecting Consultants", 1986; contbr. speeches and articles in field. V.p. Joliet/Will County Project Pride; mem. events com. C. of C. Mem. Ill. Libr. Assn. (pub. libr. sect. 1977-78, legis. devel. com. 1977-82, jr. mems. roundtable 1976-77, regional planning com. 1996, Title III rev. com. 1996—, interlibr. coop. subcom., intellectual freedom com.), Kiwanis, Beta Phi Mu. Avocations: model building, softball, bowling, golf. Home: 2208 Graystone Dr Joliet IL 60431-8785 Office: Joliet Pub Library 150 N Ottawa St Joliet IL 60432-4192 Home Phone: 815-436-6154; Office Phone: 815-740-2670. Business E-Mail: jrjohnston@joliet.lib.il.us.

JOHNSTON, JANIS L., law librarian, educator; MLS, U. Ill.; JD cum laude, Ind. U. Dir. Marion County Law Libr., Indpls.; rural devel. coord. Indian Inst. Cultural Affairs, Bombay; assoc. dir. Kresge Libr. Notre Dame Law Sch., lectr. legal rsch. & Am. legal sys., dir. London Law Ctr.; dir. Albert E. Jenner, Jr. Meml. Law Libr. U. Ill. Coll. Law, Champaign, 1999—, assoc. prof law, assoc. prof. libr. adminstrn., Richard W. and Marie L. Corman scholar in law. Contbr. articles to profl. jours. Office: U Ill Coll Law 504 E Pennsylvania Ave Champaign IL 61820 Office Phone: 217-333-2914.

JOHNSTON, JEFFERY W., publishing executive; b. Lockport, NY, Dec. 14, 1951; s. Sidney W. and Barbara (Jeffery) J.; m. Marcia Lynn Paca, Aug. 3, 1974; children: Paul W., Sarah E., David P. BA, Dartmouth Coll., 1974. Sales rep. John Hancock Ins., Boston, 1974-76; from sales rep. to editor edn., coll. textbooks Allyn Bacon Publ., Rochester, N.Y., 1976-85; from editor edn., coll. textbooks to exec. editor Merrill Publ., Columbus, Ohio, 1985-90; v.p., editor-in-chief Merrill Imprint-Macmillan Publ., Columbus, 1990-94; v.p., publisher Merrill Imprint-Prentice Hall, Columbus, 1994—. Republican. Avocations: running, reading. Office: Prentice Hall 445 Hutchinson Ave Columbus OH 43235-5677

JOHNSTON, LLOYD DOUGLAS, social sciences educator; b. Boston, Apr. 18, 1940; s. Leslie D. and Madeline B. (Irvin) Johnston; m. Janet Wilson, Nov. 13, 2004; 1 stepchild, Leah Wilson Brown; 1 child from previous marriage, Douglas Leslie. BA in Econs., Williams Coll., 1962; MBA, Harvard U., 1965, postgrad., 1965—66; MA in Social Psychology, U. Mich., 1971, PhD, 1973. Research asst. Grad. Sch. Bus. Adminstrn., Harvard U., Boston, 1965-66; asst. study dir. Inst. Social Research, U. Mich., Ann Arbor, 1966-73, asst. research scientist, 1973-75, assoc. rsch. scientist, 1975-78, sr. rsch. scientist and program dir., 1978-98; disting. sr. rsch. scientist, rsch. prof. Inst. Social Rsch., U. Mich., Ann Arbor, 1998—; chmn. exec. com. U. Mich. Substance Abuse Rsch. Ctr.

Excellence, 1990-95, acting dir., 1994-95. Prin. investigator Monitoring the Future: A Continuing Study of Lifestyles and Values of Am. Youth, 1975—, Youth, Education and Society, 1996—, also other nat. and internat. survey studies; cons. to WHO, UN, EEC, Coun. of Europe, Pan Am. Health Orgn., White House, U.S. Congress, various founds., numerous fgn. govts., fed. agys., univs., rsch. insts., TV networks, Nat. Partnership for Drug Free Am., 1978—; chmn. tech. planning group; mem. Resource Group for Goal Seven, Nat. Ednl. Goals Panel, 1991-2002; mem. extramural sci. adv. bd. Nat. Inst. on Drug Abuse, 1990-94; mem., also chmn. prevention subcom., Nat. Adv. Coun. on Drug Abuse, 1982-86, Presdl. appointee White House Conf. for a Drug-Free Am., 1987-88, Presdl. appointee Nat. Commn. for Drug Free Schs., 1989-90; chmn. drug epidemiology sect. Internat. Coun. on Alcohol and Addictions, 1982-2002; mem. Com. on Problems of Drug Dependence, 1982-86; mem. or chmn. various adv. coms. various univs., founds.; mem. various working groups NAS; mem. various coms. and adv. groups Nat. Inst. Drug Abuse, 1975—; mem. or chmn. 7 working groups WHO, 1975—; invited lectr. nat. and internat. confs. and convs.; testimony before Congress and fed. regulatory agys. Author: Drugs and American Youth, 1973, Student Drug Use in America, 1975-81, 82, Monitoring the Future Nat. Survey Results on Drug Use 1975-2006, vol. 1 and 2, 2007, over 60 other books and monographs on drug use and lifestyles of Am. secondary sch. students and young adults, 1972—, 31 reference vols.; editor: Conducting Follow Up Research on Drug Treatment Programs, 1977; contbr. more than 130 chpts. to books, articles to profl. jours. Recipient Nat. Pacesetter award in rsch. Nat. Inst. on Drug Abuse, 1982, 1st Sr. Rsch. Scientist award and lectureship U. Mich., 1987, Regents award for disting. pub. svc., 1998, Disting. Rsch. Scientist award, 1998. Fellow Coll. on Problems of Drug Dependence; mem. APA, Soc. for Psychol. Study Social Issues (sec.-treas. 1976-79), Am. Sociol. Assn., Am. Pub. Health Assn. Home: 5538 Lawrence Ct Pinckney MI 48169-9257 Office: U Mich Inst Social Rsch Ann Arbor MI 48109 Business E-Mail: lloydj@umich.edu.

JOHNSTON, MICHAEL FRANCIS, auto parts company executive; b. Concord, Mass., May 21, 1947; s. Harold William and Julia Theresa (May) J.; children: Scott, Evon, Meghan. BS, Lowell U., 1969; MBA, Mich. State U., Troy, 1987. Asst. mgr. ops. analysis Western Union, NYC, 1969-71; fin. analyst Microdot, Greenwich, Conn., 1971-72, asst. to gen. mgr. Detroit Diamond div. Wyandotte, Mich., 1972-73, asst. to gen. mgr. Wittek Mfg. div. La Grange Park, Ill., 1973-75, plant mgr. Detroit Diamond div. Wyandotte, 1976-78, v.p., gen. mgr. Internat. div. Mt. Clemens, Mich., 1978-87; v.p., gen. mgr. Kaynar div. Microdot, Fullerton, Calif., 1987-89; fin. analyst United Tech.-Otis, NYC, 1975-76; v.p., gen. mgr. SLI div. Johnson Controls Inc., Milw., 1989-93, v.p. and gen. mgr. battery group, 1993—96, pres., North America/Asia Pacific, 1997—99; pres., COO Visteon Corp., 2000—04, bd. dir., 2002—, CEO, 2004—05, chmn., CEO, 2005—. Mem. bd. dir. Flowserve Corp., Dallas, Whirlpool Corp., Mich. Office: Visteon Corp 17000 Rotunda Dr Dearborn MI 48120

JOHNSTON, RICHARD FOURNESS, biologist, educator; b. Oakland, Calif., July 27, 1925; s. Arthur Nathaniel and Marie (Johnson) J.; m. Lora Lee Bliler, Feb. 7, 1948; children: Regan, Janet, Cassandra. BA, U. Calif., Berkeley, 1950, MA, 1953, PhD, 1955. Asst. prof. dept. biology N.Mex. State U., 1956-58; mem. faculty depts. zoology and ecology U. Kans., Lawrence, 1958—, prof., 1968-92, prof. emeritus, 1992—, chmn., 1979-82, editor mus. publs., 1974-76, 86-91; program dir. systematic biology NSF, Washington, 1968-69; editor Ann. Rev. Ecology and Systematics, 1968-92, Current Ornithology, 1981-87. Mem. adv. panel biol. scis. Smithsonian Fgn. Currency Program, 1969-71 Served with AUS, 1943-46. Am. Acad. Arts and Scis. grantee, 1957; nat. Acad. Sci. grantee, 1959; NSF grantee, 1959-83. Fellow Am. Ornithol. Union (Coues award 1975), AAAS, mem. Ecol. Soc. Am., Soc. Systematic Zoology (editor jour. 1967-70, pres. 1977), Soc. Study Evolution. Home: 615 Louisiana St Lawrence KS 66044-2337 Business E-Mail: rfj@ku.edu.

JOHNSTONE, ROBERT PHILIP, retired lawyer; b. Bellefonte, Pa., Dec. 1, 1943; s. B. Kenneth and Helene (Hetzel) J.; m. Susan Alice Hardy, June 22, 1968; children: Natalie, ancy. BS with honors, Denison U., 1966; JD magna cum laude, U. Mich., 1969. Bar: Ind. 1969. Assoc. Barnes, Hickam, Pantzer & Boyd, Indpls., 1969-75, ptnr., 1976-82, Barnes & Thornburg, Indpls., 1982—2004; ret., 2004. Chmn. litigation dept. Barnes & Thornburg, 1988-89, mem. mgmt. com., 1988-89; bd. dirs. Protective Order Pro Bono Porject, 2004—; lectr., panelist legal seminars and trial advocacy programs. Sec.-treas. Contemporary Art Soc. of Indpls. Mus. Art, 1983—84; v.p., bd. dirs. Friends of Herron Gallery, Herron Sch. Art, 1981—85; bd. dirs. Eagle Creek Park Found., 2001—04. Fellow Am. Coll. Trial Lawyers (state com. 1992-97, state chair 1995-96); mem. Ind. Bar Assn., Order of the Coif, Woodstock Club (Indpls., bd. dirs. 1988-90, v.p. 1989, pres. 1990), Indpls. Art Ctr. (bd. dirs. 1991-97), Dramatic Club (Indpls.), Phi Beta Kappa, Omicron Delta Kappa. Home: 1065 W 52nd St Indianapolis IN 46228-2463 Office: Barnes & Thornburg 11 S Meridian St Indianapolis IN 46204-3535

JOHO, JEAN, chef; Student, Hotel Restaurant Sch., Strasbourg, France. Apprentice L'Auberge de L'Ill, Alsace, France; sous chef Michelin three star restaurant; chef Maxim's, Chgo., Brasserie Jo, Chgo., 1995; owner, chef Everest, Chgo.; co-founder Corner Bakery. Named Best Am. Chef: Midwest, James Beard Found., Best Chef of Yr., Bon Appetit; recipient Best New Restaurant award, James Beard Found., 1995, Culinary award of excellence, Robert Mondavi. Mem.: Maitre Cuisiniers de France, Le Grande Table Du Monde Traditions and Qualite. Office: Everest 440 La Salle St 40th Fl Chicago IL 60605

JOLEY, LISA ANNETTE, lawyer, brewery company executive; b. Centralia, Ill., Mar. 30, 1958; BS magna cum laude, Murray State U., Ky., 1980; JD magna cum laude, So. Ill. U., 1983. Bar: Ill. 1983, Mo. 1984. Sr. assoc. gen. counsel litig. Anheuser-Busch Cos. Inc., St. Louis, v.p., dep. gen. counsel litig., 2000—02, v.p., dep. gen. counsel, 2002—04, v.p., gen. counsel, 2004—. Mem.: Mo. Bar Assn., Ill. State Bar Assn., St. Clair County Bar Assn., Bar Assn. Met. St. Louis, ABA, Pi Sigma Alpha. Office: Anheuser-Busch Cos Inc One Busch Pl Saint Louis MO 63118 Office Phone: 314-577-2000.

JOLIVETTE, GREGORY, state representative; b. Hamilton, Ohio, 1951; married; 3 children. BS in History, Loyola U., Chgo. Former mayor, city councilman City of Hamilton, Ohio; small bus. owner; rep. dist. 54 Ohio Ho. of Reps., Columbus, 1997—, chair, health com., mem. mcpl. govt. and urban revitalization, pub. utilities, and transp. and pub. safety coms. Recipient Legis. Achievement award, LifeCenter of Cin., 2000. Mem.: Hamilton and Fairfield Cs. of C., Hamilton Elks, KC. Republican.

JOLY, HUBERT BERNARD, hotel and travel company executive; b. Laxou, France, Aug. 11, 1959; s. Jean-Louis and Denise (Grandjean) J.; m. Nathalie Christiane Motte, Sept. 19, 1981; children: Stanislas, Agathe. MBA, Ecole des Hautes Etudes Comml., Jouy-en-Josas, France, 1981; MPA, Inst. d'Etudes Politiques, Paris, 1983. Asst. to chmn. and CEO Sacilor, Paris, 1981-82; assoc. McKinsey & Co., Paris, 1983-84, San Francisco, 1984-85, mgr. Paris, 1985-89, prin., 1990-91, YC, 1992-93, Paris, 1993-96, co-leader European electronics practice, 1994-96; pres. EDS France, Paris, 1996-99; chmn. EDS Progical, 1996-99; v.p. EDS Europe, 1998-99; CEO Havas Interactive Inc., 1999—2000; sr. v.p. N.Am. integration Vivendi Universal, 2001—02, exec. v.p., corp. chief info. officer, 2002, exec. v.p. monitoring US assets, dep. CFO, 2002—04; pres., CEO Carlson Wagonlit Travel, 2004—08, Carlson Companies, Inc., Minnetonka, Minn., 2008—. Mem. World European Forum, Global Leaders for Tomorrow, 1996. Author: Excellence in Electronics, 1993, Wake Up Europe!, 1999; contbr. articles to profl. jours. Bd. mem. Am. C. of C. in France, 1998—. Mem. Ctr. d'Etude Prospective es Stratègique. Office: Carlson Companies Inc 701 Carlson Pkwu Minnetonka MN 55305*

JONAS, HARRY S., medical education consultant; b. Kirksville, Mo., Dec. 3, 1926; s. Harry S. and Sarah (Laird) J.; m. Connie Kirby, Aug. 6, 1949; children— Harry S., III, William Reed, Sarah Elizabeth. BA, Washington U., St. Louis, 1949, MD, 1952. Intern St. Luke's Hosp., St. Louis, 1952-53; resident Barnes Hosp., St. Louis, 1952-56; practiced medicine specializing in ob-gyn., Independence, Mo., 1956-74; prof. ob-gyn, chmn. dept. ob-gyn Truman Med. Center; asst. dean U. Mo-Kansas City Sch. Medicine, 1975-78, dean, 1978-87, med. edn. cons., 2000—, spl. cons. to the dean; asst. v.p. med. edn. AMA, Chgo., 1987-2000; sr. ptnr. DJW Assocs., LLC, 2003—. Mem. Independence City Council, 1964-68; mem. Jackson County (Mo.) Legislature, 1973-74. Mem. ACOG (pres. 1986-87), Ctrl. Assn. Obstetricians and Gynecologists, Assn. Profs. Gynecology and Obstetrics, Assn. Am. Med. Colls., A.C.S., AMA, Mo. Med. Assn., Jackson County Med. Soc., Kansas City Gynecol. Soc., Chgo. Gynecol. Soc. Home: 207 NW Spruce St Lees Summit MO 64064-1430 Office: U Mo-Kansas City Sch Medicine 2411 Holmes St Kansas City MO 64108-2741 also: 838 E High St Ste 261 Lexington KY 40502 Business E-Mail: jonash@umkc.edu. E-mail: hsj@djwassociates.com.

JONAS, JIRI, chemist, educator; b. Prague, Czechoslovakia, Apr. 1, 1932; arrived in US, 1963; s. Frantisek and Jirlna (Vondrak) Jonas; m. Ana M. Masiulis, June 1, 1968. BSc, Tech. U. Prague, 1956; PhD, Czechoslovak Acad Sci., 1960; D honoris causa (hon.), U. Rio de Janeiro, 2003. Research assoc. Inst. Organic Chemistry, Czechoslovak Acad. Sci., Prague, 1960-63; vis. scientist, dept. chemistry U. Ill., Urbana, 1963-65, from asst. to assoc. prof., 1966-72, prof., 1972—2001, prof. Ctr. for Advanced Study, 1996-2001, prof. emeritus, 2001—, sr. staff mem. Materials Research Lab., 1970-93, dir. sch. chem. scis., 1983-93, dir. Beckman Inst. Advanced Sci. and Tech., 1993—2001, dir. emeritus, 2001—. Mem. editl. bd. Jour. Magnetic Resonance, 1975—2000, Jour. Chem., 1980—83, Jour. Chem. Physics, 1986—89, Accts. Chem. Rsch., 1990—93, Ann. Rev. Phys. Chemistry, 1991—95; contbr. articles to profl. jours. Recipient U.S. Sr. Scientist award, Alexander von Humboldt Found., 1988; Alfred P. Sloan fellow, 1967—69, J. S. Guggenheim fellow, 1972—73, Sr. scholar, U. Ill., 1985—88. Fellow: AAAS, Am. Phys. Soc., Am. Acad. Arts and Scis.; mem.: NAS, Materials Rsch. Soc., Am. Chem. Soc. (assoc. editor. Jour. Am. Chem. Soc., Joel Henry Hildebrand award 1983), Am. Philos. Soc., NBTC Club (Naples, Fla.). Office: Univ of Ill 166 Roger Adams Lab 600 S Mathews Urbana IL 61801 Business E-Mail: j-jonas@uiuc.edu.

JONASON, WILLIAM A., lawyer; b. 1958; BA in Econ. with honors, St. Olaf Coll., 1980; JD with distinction, Univ. Iowa, 1983. Bar: Minn. 1983. Law clk., Chief Judge Donald Lay US Ct. of Appeals (8th cir.), 1983—84; ptnr., corp. group; co-chair, closely held businesses group Dorsey & Whitney LLP, Mpls., and mem., policy com. Adj. prof. law Hamline Law Sch., 1988—89, St. Thomas Law Sch., 2004. Sr. articles editor Iowa Law Rev., 1982—83. Bd. dir. Volunteer Connection, Rochester Pub. Libr. Found., Rochester Pub. Sch. Found., YMCA Camp Olson. Mem.: Minn. Bar Assn., Hennepin Co. Bar Assn. Office: Dorsey & Whitney LLP Ste 1500 50 S Sixth St Minneapolis MN 55402-1498 Office Phone: 612-340-2600, 612-492-6111. Office Fax: 612-340-7800. Business E-Mail: jonason.bill@dorsey.com.

JONCKHEERE, ALAN MATHEW, physicist; b. Howell, Mich., Feb. 12, 1947; s. August Peter and Elizabeth Gertrude (Nash) Jonckheere; m. Barbara Jean Minter, Aug. 16, 1969; children: Jessica Susan, Laura Jean and Amanda Jean (twins). BS, Mich. State U., 1969; MS, U. Wash., 1970, PhD, 1976. Instr. physics dept. Fermi Nat. Accelerator Lab., Batavia, Ill., 1976—78, staff physicist, 1978—, assoc. dept. head meson dept., 1981—83, assoc. dept. head exptl. areas, 1983—84, coord. Beams group, 1984—85, accelerator divsn. exptl. support dept., 1985—88, rschr. divsn. D0 dept., 1989—. Researcher elem. particle physics Stanford Linear Accelerator Ctr., Lawrence Berkeley Lab., Calif. Contbr. papers to physics publs. Office: Fermi Natl Accelerator Lab PO Box 500 Batavia IL 60510-0500 Business E-Mail: Jonckheere@fnal.gov.

JONDAHL, LYNN, foundation administrator; BA, Iowa State U., 1958; MDiv, Yale U., 1962. Ordained min. United Ch. of Christ, 62. Mem. ho. reps. State of Mich., Lansing, 1972—94, chmn. taxation com., mem. coll. and univ. consumers and judiciary coms., mem. juvenile justice subcom.; exec. dir. Mich. Prospect for Renewed Citizenship, Flint. Campus pastor Calif. State Coll., LA; co-dir. Christian Faith and Higher Edn. Inst. Mich. State U. Active Foster Grandparent Program, Student Advocat. Ctr., Ctr. Handicapped Affairs; corp. mem. United Ch. Bd. Nomeland Ministries. Named Legislator of Yr., Mich. Fedn. Pvt. Child and Family Agys., 1985, Mich. Twp. Assn., 1987, Citizens Alliance to Uphold Spl. Edn., 1990, Assn. Retarded Citizens Mich., 1990, Outstanding Legislator, AAUP, 1985, Outstanding Legislator of Yr., Mich. Assn. Deaf, Hearing and Speech Svcs., 1990; recipient Consumers Advocate award, Mich. Citizen's Lobby, 1974, Philip Hart award, Consumer Educators Mich., 1980. Mem.: ACLU, Mich. Women's Studies Assn., Mich. China Coun.

JONES, B. TODD, lawyer, former prosecutor; s. Paul and Sylvia Jones. Grad., Macalester Coll., 1979; JD, U. Minn., 1983. Mng. ptnr. Greene Espel, Mpls., 1996—97; asst. U.S. atty. for Minn., 1997—98; U.S. atty. Minn. dist. U.S. Dept. Justice, 1998—2001; ptnr. Robins, Kaplan, Miller & Ciresi, Mpls., 2001—. With USMC. Office: Robins Kaplan Miller & Ciresi 2800 LaSalle Plaza 800 LaSalle Ave Minneapolis MN 55402

JONES, BENJAMIN ANGUS, JR., retired agricultural engineering educator, science administrator; b. Mahomet, Ill., Apr. 16, 1926; s. Benjamin Angus and Grace Lucile (Morr) J.; m. Georgeann Hall, Sept. 11, 1949; children: Nancy Kay Jones-Kepple, Ruth Ann Jones-Sommers. BS, U. Ill., 1949, MS, 1950, PhD, 1958. Registered profl. engr., Ill. Asst. prof., asst. ext. engr. U. Vt., Burlington, 1950-52; instr., agrl. engr. U. Ill., Urbana, 1952-54, asst. prof., agrl. engr., 1954-58, assoc. prof., agrl. engr., 1958-64, prof., agrl. engr., 1964-92, prof. emeritus, 1992—, assoc. dir., agrl. exptl. sta., 1973-92; assoc. dir. emeritus, 1992—, U. Ill., Urbana, 1992. Cons. various Ill. Drainage Dists., 1958—. Co-author: (textbook) Engineering Application in Agriculture, 1973; contbr. articles to Jour. Soil & Water Conservation, Encyclopedia Britannica, Agrl. Engring., Transactions of ASAE, Proceedings of ASCE, Soil Sci. Soc. Am. Proceedings, Crops and Soils, Jour. Hydrology, Water Resources Bulletin. Merit badge examiner Boy Scouts Am., Burlington, 1950-52; lay mem. Cen. Ill. Con. United Meth. Ch., 1978-81. With USN, 1944-46. NSF fellow. Fellow Am. Soc. Agrl. Engrs. (bd. dirs., trustee); mem. Soil and Water Conservation Soc., Am. Soc. for Engring. Edn., Sigma Xi, Gamma Sigma Delta, Alpha Epsilon. Home: 2012B Eagle Ridge Ct Urbana IL 61802-8617

JONES, C. PAUL, lawyer, educator; b. Grand Forks, ND, Jan. 7, 1927; s. Walter M. and Sophie J. (Thorton) J.; m. Helen M. Fredel, Sept. 7, 1957; children: Katherine, Sara H. BBA, JD, U. Minn., 1950; LLM, William Mitchell Coll. of Law, 1955. Assoc. Lewis, Hammer, Heaney, Weyl & Halverson, Duluth, Minn., 1950-51; asst., chief dep. Hennepin County Atty., Mpls., 1952-58; asst. US atty. US Atty's. Office, St. Paul, 1959-60; assoc. Maun & Hazel, St. Paul, 1960-61; ptnr. Dorfman, Rudquist, Jones, & Ramstead, Mpls., 1961-65; state pub. defender Minn. State Pub. Defender's Office, Mpls., 1966-90. Adj. prof. law William Mitchell Coll. of Law, St. Paul, 1953-70, prof. law, 1970—2001, prof. emeritus, 2001-. assoc. dean for acad. affairs, 1991-95; adj. prof. U. Minn., Mpls., 1970-90; mem. adv. com. on rules of criminal procedure Minn. Supreme Ct., 1970—. Author: Criminal Procedure from Police Detention to Final Disposition, 1981; Jones on Minnesota Criminal Procedure, 1955, 64, 70, 75; Minnesota Police Law Manual, 1955, 67, 70, 76 Mem. Minn. Gov.'s Crime Commn., St. Paul, 1970s, Minn. Fair Trial-Free Press Assn., Mpls., 1970s, Citizens League, Mpls., 1955—, Mpls. Aquatennial Assn., Mpls., 1955-60, Minn. Coun. on Crime and Justice, 1991—. Recipient Reginald Heber Smith award Nat. Legal Aid and Defender Assn., 1969 Fellow Am. Coll. Trial Lawyers; mem. Am. Bd. Trial Advs., ABA, Minn. State Bar Assn., Hennepin County Bar Assn., Ramsey County Bar Assn., Nat. Legal Aid & Defender Assn. Clubs: Suburban Gyro of Mpls. Lodges: Rotary. Democrat. Lutheran. Avocations: fishing, hunting, golf, desert watching. Home: 5501 Dewey Hill Rd Edina MN 55439-1906 Office: William Mitchell Coll Law 875 Summit Ave Saint Paul MN 55105-3030

JONES, CAROLYN, dean, law educator; 1 child, Alison. BA, U. Iowa, 1976, JD, 1979; LLM, Yale U., 1982. Bar: Iowa. Asst. city atty. Sioux City, 1979—80; assoc. Klass, Whicher and Mishne, 1981—82; prof. St. Louis U. Sch. Law, 1982—90, U. Conn. Law Sch., 1990—2004, assoc. dean academic affairs; dean U. Iowa Coll Law, 2004—. Vis. prof. law U. Exeter, Washington U., U. Iowa, 1986—87, 1989, Moritz Coll. Law, Ohio State U., 2004. Recipient Sanxay Prize, Order of Coif. Office: U Iowa Coll Law 276 Boyd Law Building Iowa City IA 52242 E-mail: carolyn-jones@uiowa.edu.

JONES, CHARLES W., labor union executive; b. Gary, Ind., Apr. 29, 1923; s. Charles Browning and Inez (Teegarden) J.; m. Ursula M. Wilden, Aug. 25, 1950; children: Charles Alan, Newton Browning, Donna Ruth, Doris Ursula. Grad. high sch., Gary. Boilermaker various constrn. contractors; organizer, then staff rep., rsch. & edn. dir., internat. v.p. Internat. Brotherhood of Boilermakers, Iron Ship Builders, Blacksmiths, Forgers and Helpers, Kansas City, Kans., now internat. pres.; ret. Chmn. bd. dirs. BB&T Co.; v.p. bldg. constrn. trades dept., v.p. metal trade dept. AFL-CIO. Office: Internat Brotherhood Boilermaker Iron Ship Bldrs Blacksmiths 753 State Ave Ste 570 Kansas City KS 66101-2511

JONES, CLAYTON M., electronics company executive; b. Nashville, 1949; BS, U. Tenn., 1971; MS, George Washington U. Former fighter pilot USAF; various exec.-level positions aerospace industry; with Rockwell Collins Corp., Cedar Rapids, Iowa, 1995—, sr. v.p., 1999—2001, pres, CEO, 2001—, chmn., 2002—. Mem. AIAA (bd. dirs.), Gen. Aviation Mfrs. Assn. Office: Rockwell Internat Corp 400 Collin Rd NE Cedar Rapids IA 52498-0001

JONES, COBI, professional soccer player; b. Detroit, June 16, 1970; Student, UCLA. Midfielder Coventry City, 1994—95, Vasco da Gama, 1995—96, L.A. Galaxy, 1996—, U.S. Nat. Team, 1996—. With gold medal U.S. team Pan Am. Games, 1991; with U.S. Olympic Team, 1992, U.S. Nat. Team, 1992—95, including victory over Ivory Coast, 1992. Host (TV series) Megadose (MTV), guest appearance Beverly Hills 90210, 1994. Achievements include tied for all-time assist lead, with 11. Office: c/o US Soccer Fedn 1801-1811 S Prairie Ave Chicago IL 60616

JONES, DANIEL W., construction executive; Pres., cheif operating officer Zaring Nat. Corp., Cin., 1989—. Office: Zaring National Corp 625 Eden Park Dr #1250 Cincinnati OH 45202-6024

JONES, DAVID A., former consumer products company executive; Mgmt. positions GE; exec. v.p. Electrolux Corp., 1985—89; pres., CEO The Regina Co., 1989—94; chmn., CEO, COO Thermoscan, Inc., 1995—96; chmn., pres., CEO Spectrum Brands Inc., Atlanta, 1996—98, chmn., CEO, 1998—2007, chmn., 2007. Bd. dir. Pentair Inc., Simmons Bedding Co.

JONES, DAVID D., JR., marine engine equipment executive; BSME, MSME, N.C. State U., PhD in Mech. Engring. Various mgmt./exec. level positions, 1977—; v.p., gen. mgr. Force outboard Divsn. U.S. Marine; pres. Mercury Marine divsn. Brunswick Corp., 1989-97; CEO, pres. Outboard Marine, Waukegan, Ill., 1997—.

JONES, DENNIS C., state representative, lawyer; b. 1955; children: Rolley, Casey, Christopher, Spencer. BA, Washburn U., 1984; JD, Washburn U. Topeka. Del. 1st Dist. state com., 1994—; atty. County of Kearny, 1988—, City of Lakin and Deeerfield, 2003—; chmn. Republican Party, 2003—. Aide to campaign Hugoton's Don Concannon, 1974; chmn. Kearny County Republican Com., 1988—2003. Mem.: Dist. Atty.'s Assn. (pres.), Kans. County Assn. (pres.). Republican. Office: Kans Republican Party 2025 SW Gage Blvd Topeka KS 66604

JONES, EDWARD, retired pathologist; b. Wellington, Kans., Mar. 21, 1935; s. Thomas S. and Grace W. (Sydebotham) Imel; m. Barbara A. Blount, Aug. 30, 1956 (dec. April 20, 1998); children: Kimberly Riegel, Sheila, Matt, Tom; m. Debbie S. Clarke, Aug. 17, 2003. AB in Chemistry, U. Kans., 1957, MD, 1961. Diplomate Am. Bd. Pathology in Anat. and Clin. Pathology; cert. med. rev. officer. Intern St. Francis Hosp., Wichita, Kans., 1961-62; sr. asst. USPHS, Yuma, Ariz., 1962-64; gen. practice medicine Lawrence (Kans.) Meml. Hosp., 1964-65; resident in pathology St. Luke's Hosp., Kansas City, Mo., 1965-69; pathologist Ctrl. Kans. Med. Ctr., Gt. Bend, 1969-2001, dir., 1974-76, pres., 1976-78; ret., 2001. Physician cons. Hoisington Luth. Hosp., Kans., 1969-, St. Joseph's Meml. Hosp., Larned, Kans., 1969-, Edwards County Hosp., Kinsley, Kans., 1969-. Bd. dirs. Cedar Park Place, Gt. Bend, 1980-88; bd. dirs. Ctrl. Kans. Med. Ctr., 1999-, chmn., 2002. Fellow Coll. Am. Pathologists (del., foreman 1978-87), Am. Soc. Clin. Pathologists; mem. Kans. Soc. Pathologists (pres. 1980-81), Gt. Bend Cmty. Theater Club. Avocations: theater, musical theater. Personal E-mail: doctoto@msn.com.

JONES, EDWIN CHANNING, JR., retired electrical and computer engineering educator; b. Parkersburg, W.Va., June 27, 1934; s. Edwin Channing and Helen M. J.; m. Ruth Carol Miller, Aug. 14, 1960; children: Charles, Cathleen, Helene. BSEE, W.Va. U., 1955; Diploma, U. London, 1956; PhD, U. Ill., 1962. Engr. GE, Syracuse, NY and Bloomington, Ill., 1955, 62, Westinghouse Electric Co., Balt., 1959; asst. prof. elec. engring. U. Ill., Urbana, 1962-66; asst. prof. Iowa State U., Ames, 1966-67, assoc. prof., 1967-72, prof., 1972—2001, univ. prof., 1995—2001, assoc. chair dept., 1997—2001, univ. prof. emeritus, 2001—. Mem. Accreditation Bd. Engring. Tech., N.Y.C., 1984-87. Author handbook chpts. on electronic engring. Lt. US Army, 1956—58. Recipient Linton F. Grinter Disting. Svc. award, Accreditation Bd. Engring. Tech., 2001. Fellow AAAS, IEEE (pres. edn. soc. 1975-76, mem. ednl. activities bd. 1975-76, 78-81, 84-87, accreditation activity award), Am. Soc. Engring. Edn.; mem. Soc. History of Tech., Sigma Xi, Tau Beta Pi, Eta Kappa Nu, Phi Kappa Phi, Phi Beta Delta. Avocations: photography, slide rule collecting. Mailing: 5289 Nolan Pkwy Oak Park Heights MN 55082

JONES, EMIL, JR., state legislator; b. Chgo., Oct. 18, 1935; s. Emil Sr. and Marilla (Mims) J.; children: Debra, Renee, John, Emil III; m. Lorrie Stone, Nov. 19, 2005. A in Bus. Adminstrn., City Coll. Chgo., 1970. Mem. Ill. Ho. Reps., Springfield, 1972-82, Ill. Senate, Springfield, 1982—, Senate Dem. leader, 1992—2002, mem. exec. com., pres., 2002—05, senate pres., 2003—, bd. dirs. pres.' forum, 2004—. Active Task Force on Long Term Care, Morgan Pk. Civic League, Chgo. Named one of 100 Most Influential Black Americans, Ebony mag., 2006; named to Hall of Fame, Tilden Tech. Inst., 2004; recipient Legis. of the Yr. award, Keep Chgo. Beautiful, 2002, Outstanding Legis. award, Chgo. Prin. & Adminstr. Assn., 2003, Small Victories award, Chgo. Assn. for Retarded Citizens, 2003, Legis. of the Yr., Ill. Assn. of Minorities in Govt., 2003, Humanitarian of the Yr., Abraham Lincoln Ctr., 2003, Social Action award, Nat. Assn. of Black Social Workers, 2003, Dem. Legis. of the Yr., Ill. State Crime Commn., 2003, Champion Justice award, Ill. Equal Justice Coalition, 2003, at. Winn Newman Econ. Equity award, Svc. Employee Internat. Union, 2003, Person of the Yr. award, United Food & comml., 2003, Person of Yr., United Food & Comml. Workers, 2003, Mark Excellence award, Nat. Forum Black Pub. Adminstrs., 2004, LifeSaver award, Save-A-Life Found., 2004, Impact award, Chgo. Minority Bus. Devel. Coun., 2004, Paul Simon Pub. Svc. award, Ill. Hunger Coalition, 2004, Man of Yr. award, Best Buddies, 2005, Let Talent Shine award, Coll. Summit, Chgo., 2005, John R. Hammell award, Chgo. Chpt. ACLU, 2005, Friends of Africa award, Continental Africa C. of C., 2006, Dave Peteron award, Chgo. Tchr. Union, 2006, Lifeline award, Cmty. Mental Health Coun., 2006. Mem. Nat. Black Caucus State Legislators, Nat. Conf. State Legislators, Knights of St. Peter Claver, Shriners. Democrat. Roman Catholic. Home: 11357 S Lowe Ave Chicago IL 60628-4714 Office: 507 W 111th St Chicago IL 60628-4019 also: James R Thompson Ctr 100 W Randolph St Ste 16 600 Chicago IL 60601-3220 Office: 327 State Capitol Springfield IL 62706

JONES, FRANK N., chemist, researcher, educator, consultant; b. Columbia, Mo., Dec. 27, 1936; s. Frank Norton and Sara Bay (Neale) J.; m. Nancy H. Jones, Jan. 1960 (div. Aug. 8, 1982); 1 child, David S. AB, Oberlin Coll., 1958; PhD, Duke U., 1962. Instr. Duke U., Durham, N.C., 1961-62; postdoctoral fellow MIT, Cambridge, 1962-63; staff chemist, rsch. supr. Ctrl. Rsch. Fabrics and Finishes E.I. duPont de Nemours, Inc., Wilmington, Del., 1963-73; R&D mgr. Celanese, Louisville, 1973-79; rsch. mgr. Cargill, Inc., Mpls., 1979-83; prof., chair polymers and coatings N.D. State U., Fargo, 1983-90; prof. Ea. Mich. U., Ypsilanti, 1990—, dir. NSF Industry/Univ. Rsch. Ctr. in Coatings, 1990—2001. Cons. Exxon, 1984-98, Monsanto, 1983-92. Author: (with others) Organic Coatings: Science and Technology, Vol. I, 1992, Vol. II, 1994, 2d edit., 1999; editor: Proceedings of the American Chemical Society Division of Polymeric Materials: Science and Engineering, Vol. 73, 1995, Vol. 74, 1996; contbr. numerous articles to profl. jours. including Jour. Applied Polymer Sci., Macromolecules, Jour. Coatings Tech., among others. Recipient awards Roon Found., 1986, 87, 91; NSF fellow, 1960-61; grantee NSF, 1990-2001, Exxon Chem. Co., 1985-98, Ford Motor Co., 1995-98. Mem. Am. Chem. Soc. (divsn. polymeric materials sci. and engring. chmn. sec. 1993-94, vice chmn. 1995, chmn. elect 1996, chmn. 1997), Fed. Socs. for Coatings Tech. (Matiello lectr. 1995). Achievements include publications and patents in compounds with liquid crystalline properties and coating binders based thereon, polymeric vehicle for coatings, solventless liquid coatings, coatings with improved mar resistance, polymer nanoparticles., among others. Office: East Mich U Nat Sci Found Coatings Rsch 430 W Forest Ave Ypsilanti MI 48197-2453 Office Phone: 734-487-2203. E-mail: frankjones@comcast.net.

JONES, GEORGE HUMPHREY, retired healthcare executive, hospital facilities and communications consultant; b. Kansas City, Mo., July 10, 1923; s. George Humphrey and Mary R. (Marrs) J.; m. Peggy Jean Thompson, Nov. 23, 1943; children: Kenneth L., Daniel D., Kathleen Jones Smith, Carol R. Jones Johnson, Janet S. Jones Fitts. Student, U. Mo., Kansas City, 1940-43, Wis. State U., Oshkosh, 1943. Police officer Kansas City (Mo.) Police Dept., 1947-51; elec. contr. Paramount Elec. Svc., Kansas City, 1947-50; electrician Automatic Temp. Control Co., Kansas City, 1951-57; pres., chief ops. George H. Jones Co., Kansas City, 1957-65; sales mgr. Nycon Inc., Lee's Summit, Mo., 1965; design engr. Midland Wright Corp., Kansas City, 1966; dist. sales mgr. Comm. Electronics, Kansas City, 1967; plant ops. supr. Rsch. Med. Ctr., Coll. of Nursing and hdqrs. Health Midwest, Kansas City, 1968-77, dir. plant ops. and comm., 1977-90; hosp. facilities and comm. cons. Overland Park, Kans., 1990-99; ret. Guest lectr. Nat. U., San Diego, 1987. Vol. Salvation Army Emergency Svcs.; bd. dirs. Camellot Fine Arts Acad., 1974—76, v.p., bd. dirs., 1975—76; adv. dir. Rsch. Med. Ctr., 1990—; mem. Heart of Am. Wing Commemorative Air Force. With USAF, 1942—46, with US Army, 1950—51. Fellow Am. Soc. Hosp. Engring., Healthcare Info. and Mgmt. Systems Soc.; mem. Kansas City Area Hosp. Engrs. (pres. 1985, bd. dirs. 1985-89), Am. Legion, Alpha Phi Omega. Presbyterian. Avocations: fishing, photography. Home and Office: 9540 Rosewood 110 Overland Park KS 66207-3234 Personal E-mail: ghpj43@sbcglobal.net.

JONES, JAMES E., state legislator; b. Ashby, Nebr., Nov. 19, 1931; m. Patricia Ann McConnell, 1953; children: Gordon, Steven, Vernon, Gregg. Farmer, rancher, ebr.; mem. Nebr. Legislature from 43rd dist., Lincoln, 1992—; mem. banking, comml. and ins., natural resources coms. Nebr. Legislature, Lincoln. Also: HC 2 Box 79 Eddyville NE 68834-9410

JONES, JEFFREY A., lawyer; b. Shelbyville, Ind., Dec. 6, 1969; BS, Gustavus Adolphus Coll., St. Peter, Minn., 1992; JD, William Mitchell Coll. Law, 1995. Bar: Minn. 1995. Atty. Jeffrey A. Jones & Assocs., P.A., Mpls. Named a Rising Star, Minn. Super Lawyers mag., 2006. Mem.: Hennepin County Bar Assn., Minn. Trial Lawyers Assn., Am. Trial Lawyers Assn. Office: Jeffrey Jones & Assocs PA 33 S 6th St Ste 4530 Minneapolis MN 55402 Office Phone: 612-335-9975. E-mail: jeffjoneslaw@yahoo.com.

JONES, JEFFREY W., retail executive; Grad. summa cum laude, Mercyhurst Coll. CPA. Sr. acct. Arthur Anderson & Co., 1984-88; v.p., contr., treas. Dairy Mart Convenience Stores, Inc., 1988-94; v.p., contr., mktg. Clark Refining and Mktg. Inc., 1994-98; treas., CFO Lids Corp., Boston, 1998—99; exec. v.p., CFO Clark Retail Group, Inc., Oak Brook, Ill., 1999—2003; sr. v.p., CFO Vail Resorts Devel. Co., Colo., 2003, Vail Resorts Inc., Colo., 2003—. Office: Vail Resorts Inc PO Box 7 Vail CO 81658

JONES, JOHN, professional sports team executive; b. New Orleans, Feb. 6, 1952; m. Cindy Jones. Grad., Loyola U., New Orleans, 1973. Tchr., journalist; writer ew Orleans Times-Picayune; editor Packer Report, 1974—75; instr. journalism Loyola U., New Orleans, 1976—78; dir. pub. rels. NFL Mgmt. Coun., 1987—94; exec. v.p., COO Green Bay (Wis.) Packers, 1999—. Bd. dirs. Green Bay Packer Hall of Fame, Bellin Hosp., Green Bay, Green Bay Boys & Girls Club. Office: 1265 Lombardi Ave Green Bay WI 54307

JONES, JOHN BAILEY, federal judge; b. Mitchell, SD, Mar. 30, 1927; s. John B. and Grace M. (Bailey) J.; m. Rosemary Wermers; children: John, William, Mary Louise, David, Judith, Robert BSBA, U. S.D., 1951, LLB, 1953. Bar: S.D. 1953. Sole practice, Presho, S.D., 1953-67; judge Lyman County, Kennebec, S.D., 1953-56; mem. S.D. Ho. of Reps., Pierre, 1957-61; judge S.D. Cir. Ct., 1967-81, U.S. Dist. Ct. S.D., Sioux Falls, 1981—; now sr. judge. Mem. Am. Judicature Soc., S.D. Bar Assn., Fed. Judges Assn., VFW, Am. Legion Lodges: Elks, Lions. Methodist. Avocation: golf. Office: US Dist Ct 400 S Phillips Ave Rm 302 Sioux Falls SD 57104-6851

JONES, JOHN O., state legislator; Ill. state rep. Dist. 107, 1995—. Office: PO Drawer 1787 1116 Main St Mount Vernon IL 62864-3819

JONES, LAWRENCE WILLIAM, retired physicist; b. Evanston, Ill., Nov. 16, 1925; s. Charles Herbert and Fern (Storm) J.; m. Ruth Reavley Drummond, June 24, 1950; children: Douglas Warren, Carol Anne, Ellen Louise. BS, Northwestern U., 1948, MS, 1949; PhD, U. Calif. at Berkeley, 1952. Research asst. U. Calif. Radiation Lab., Berkeley, 1950-52; mem. faculty U. Mich., Ann Arbor, 1952—, prof. physics, 1963-98, chmn. dept. physics, 1982-87, prof. emeritus, 1998—. Physicist Midwestern U. Rsch. Assn., 1956-57; vis. physicist Lawrence Radiation Lab., Berkeley, 1959—, cons., 1964-66; vis. scientist CERN, Geneva, Switzerland, 1961-62, 65, 85—, assoc., 1988—; vis. physicist Brookhaven Nat. Lab., Upton, N.Y., 1963—, Fermi Nat. Accelerator Lab., Batavia, Ill., 1971—; vis. prof. Tata Inst. Fundamental Rsch., Bombay, India, 1979, U. Sydney Australia, 1991; elem. particle physics panel of physics survey com. NRC, 1984; cons. ctrl. design group Superconducting Super Collider Nat. Lab., 1985-87, vis. physicist, 1991-94; cons. NASA, 1974-81, 2002; trustee Univs. Rsch. Assn., 1982-87; disting. vis. scholar U. Adelaide, 1991; vis. scientist U. Auckland, 1991; co-chmn. sci. adv. com. Mich. Environ. Coun., 2000—; mem. internat. adv. com. Bolivian Obs. of Mt. Chacaltaya, 2001—. Mem. adv. panel for Cosmic Rays Jour. of Physics G., 1991-95. Guggenheim fellow, 1965; Sci. Rsch. Coun. fellow, 1977. Fellow Am. Phys. Soc. Home: 2666 Parkridge Dr Ann Arbor MI 48103-1731 Office: U Mich Dept Physics Ann Arbor MI 48109-1040 Business E-Mail: lwjones@umich.edu.

JONES, LEANDER CORBIN, history professor, media specialist; b. Vincent, Ark., July 16, 1934; s. Lander Corbin and Una Bell (Lewis) J.; A.B., U. Ark., Pine Bluff, 1956; M.S., U. Ill., 1968; Ph.D., Union Grad. Inst., 1973; m. Lethonee Angela Hendricks, June 30, 1962; children: Angela Lynne, Leander Corbin. Tchr. English pub. high schs., Chgo. Bd. Edn., 1956-68; vol. English-as-fgn. lang. tchr. Peace Corps, Mogadiscio, Somalia, 1964-66; TV producer City Colls. of Chgo., 1968-73; communications media specialist Meharry Med. Coll., 1973-75; assoc. prof. Black Americana studies Western Mich., U., 1975-89, prof., 1989—, chmn. African studies program, 1980-81, co-chmn. Black caucus, 1983-84; pres. Corbin 22 Ltd., 1986—; dir. 7 art workshop Am. Negro Emancipation Centennial Authority, Chgo., 1960-63. Mem. Mich. Commn. on Crime and Delinquency, 1981-83; mem. exec. com. DuSable Mus. African Am. History, 1970—; mem. Prisoners Progress Assn., 1977-82, South African Solidarity Orgn., 1978—, Dennis Brutus Def. Com., 1980-83; chmn. Kalamazoo Community Relations Bd., 1977-79; bd. dirs. Kalamazoo Civic Players, 1981-83; pres. Black Theater of Kalamazoo, 1978-85; dir., dramaturg Mich. Black Repertory Theatre, 1987-90; exec. prodr. Ransom Street Playhouse, Kalamazoo, 1993—. Served with U.S. Army, 1956-58. Faculty Enrichment grantee Govt. Can., 1992. Mem. Assn. Study African-Am. History, NAACP (exec. com. Kalamazoo br. 1978-82), Theatre Arts and Broadcasting Skills Ctr. (pres. 1972—), AAUP, Mich. Orgn. African Studies, Nat. Council Black Studies, Popular Culture Assn., 100 Men's Club, Kappa Alpha Psi. Dir. South Side Ctr. of Performing Arts, Chgo., 1968-69, Progressive Theatre Unltd., Nashville, 1974-75, Mich. Black Repertory Theatre, 1987-90; chmn. Tenn. Region N.AM. Zone of 2d World Festival Black and Artican Arts and Culture, 1975, Nat. Black Media Consortium, 1985; writer, producer, dir. TV drama: Roof Over my Head, Nashville 1975; designer program in theatre and TV for hard-to-educate; developer edn. programs in Ill. State Penitentiary, Pontiac, and Cook County Jail, Chgo., 1971-73. Writer, dir. 10 Score!, 1976, Super Summer, 1978; dir. Trouble in Mind, 1979, Day of Absence, 1981, 85, Happy Ending, 1981, Who's Got His Own, 1983, Take A Giant Step, 1985; producer For Colored Girls Who Have Considered Suicide When the Rainbow is Enuf, 1984; featured at Civic Theater, Kalamazoo, in Great White Hope, 1979, Dutchman, 1980, Moon On a Rainbow Shawl, 1980, Five on the Black Hand Side, 1982, Who's Got His Own, Guys and Dolls, Black Girl, Tambourines to Glory, 1983, Day of Absence, Take a Giant Step, 1985, Soldier's Play, 1986, Beef, No Chicken, 1989, Black Eagles, 1994; author: Roof Over My Head, 1975, Africa is for Reel, 1983, Journal of Black Studies, 1985; exec. producer and host TV series Fade to Black, 1986—. Home: PO Box 2404 Portage MI 49081-2404 Office Phone: 616-387-2662. E-mail: leander.jones@wmich.edu.

JONES, LEE BENNETT, chemistry professor, academic administrator; b. Memphis, Mar. 14, 1938; s. Harold S. and Martha B. J.; m. Vera Kramar, Feb. 8, 1964; children: David B., Michael B. BA magna cum laude, Wabash Coll, 1960; PhD, M.I.T., 1964; DSC (hon.), Wabash Coll., 1992. Faculty U. Ariz., Tucson, 1964-85, prof. chemistry, 1972-85, asst. head dept. chemistry, 1971-73, head dept., 1973-77, dean Grad. Coll., 1977-79, provost Grad. Studies and Health Scis., 1979-82, v.p. rsch., 1982-85; prof. chemistry, exec. v.p., provost U. Nebr., Lincoln, 1985—2002, exec. v.p., provost emeritus, 2002—. Chmn. bd. dirs. Coun. Grad. Schs., 1986; mem. Grad. Records Exam. Bd., 1986-91; mem. Midwest Higher Edn. Commn., 1995—. Mem. editl. bd. Jour. Chem. Edn, 1975-79; contbr. numreous articles to sci. jours. Mem. Nebr. R&D Authority, 1985—, Midwest Higher Edn. Commn.; vice chmn. Nebr. Ednl. Telecomm. Commn., 1987-88, 91-92. NSF fellow, 1961-63, 64— Mem. AAAS, AAUP, Am. Chem. Soc., Chem. Soc. (London), N.Y. Acad. Scis., Phi Beta Kappa. Office: U Nebr 106 Varner Hall 3835 Holdrege St Lincoln NE 68503-1435 Home: 5645 E Towner St Tucson AZ 85712 Personal E-mail: LBJones@nebraska.edu.

JONES, LINDA, communications educator; BA in English, U. Mich., 1972; MS in Journalism with distinction, Northwestern U., 1985. Reporter The Chelsea (Mich.) Standard, 1973-75; county govt., police reporter The Marshall (Mich.) Evening Chronicle, 1975-77; edn. reporter The Bay City (Mich.) Times, 1977--79, asst. met. editor, 1979-81, met. editor, 1981-86; vis. asst. prof. dept. journalism Roosevelt U., 1986-88; asst. prof. Medill Sch. Journalism Northwestern U., 1988-92, dir. tchg. newspaper program, 1992—; assoc. prof. journalism Roosevelt U., Chgo., 1992—, dir. Sch. Comm., 1995—. Acting dir. Multicultural Journalism Ctr., Urban Journalism Ctr.; tchr. workshop sessions Journalism Edn. Assn./Nat. Scholastic Press Assn. convs., 1992-96, chair Multicultural Scholarship Com., 1996. Contbr. articles to profl. jours.; judge and lectr. in field. Office: Roosevelt Univ 505 E Ctr for Profl Advancement 430 S Michigan Ave Chicago IL 60605-1394 E-mail: ljones@roosevelt.edu.

JONES, MARY LAURA, not-for-profit developer; b. Mpls., 1946; d. William Ray and Emily H. Jones; children: Donald Aaron, Justin David, Mark Joseph Bushman. BA in English, U. S.C., 1968; MA in History, Northwestern U., 2004. Vol. U.S. Peace Corps, 1968—71; assoc. dir. funding and devel. The Inst. of Cultural Affairs, Chgo., 1971-75, dir. Cleve. region, 1975-79, dir. Pacific and Oceania region Apia, Western Samoa, 1979-83, co-creator Cmty. Devel. Tng. Curriculum Chgo., 1984—85, dir. Uptown Cmty. Resource Ctr., 1987—2006; prin. Jones-Otto Neighborhood Devel. Co., Chgo., 2006—. Bd. dirs. Ebenezer Luth. Ch. Mem. Uptown C. of C. (bd. dirs.). Home: 4750 N Sheridan Rd Chicago IL 60640-5042 Office Phone: 773-636-2022. E-mail: mljones@rcn.com.

JONES, MAURICE D., lawyer; b. 1959; BS, Brigham Young U.; JD, U. Ill. Bar: 1988. Ptnr. Davis & Kuelthau, S.C.; legal counsel Banta Corp.; sec., gen. counsel Manitowoc Co., Manitowoc, Wis., 1999—2002, v.p., gen. counsel, sec., 2002—04, sr. v.p., gen. counsel, sec., 2004—. Office: Manitowoc Co Inc 2400 S 44th St Manitowoc WI 54221-0066 Office Phone: 920-652-1741. Office Fax: 920-652-9777. Business E-Mail: mjones@manitowoc.com.

JONES, NATHAN JEROME, farm machinery manufacturing company executive; b. Marion, Ind., 1957; BBA in Acctg., U. Wis., Eau Claire, 1979; MBA in Fin., Mktg., U. Chgo., 1983. From acct. to various fin. assignments Deere & Co., Moline, Ill., 1978-91, asst. treas., 1991-94, treas., 1994-98, v.p., 1996-98, sr. v.p., fin., acctg., CFO, 1998—. Office: Deere & Co 1 John Deere Pl Moline IL 61265-8098

JONES, NATHANIEL RAPHAEL, lawyer, retired federal judge; b. Youngstown, Ohio, May 13, 1926; s. Nathaniel B. and Lillian (Rafe) J.; m. Lillian Graham, Mar. 22, 1974; children: Stephanie Joyce, Pamela Haley stepchildren: William Hawthorne, Rickey Hawthorne, Marc Hawthorne. AB, Youngstown State U., 1951, LL.B., 1955, LL.D. (hon.), 1969, Syracuse U., 1972. Editor Buckeye Rev. newspaper, 1956; exec. dir. FEPC, Youngstown, 1956—59; pvt. practice, 1959—61; mem. firm Goldberg & Jones LLP, 1968—69; asst. U.S. atty. (no. dist.) Ohio US Dept. Justice, 1961—67; asst. gen. counsel Nat. Adv. Commn. on Civil Disorders, 1967—68; gen. counsel NAACP, 1969—79; judge US Ct. Appeals (6th Cir.), 1979—2002, sr. judge, 1995—2002; sr. counsel Blank Rome LLP, Cin., 2002—, chief diversity officer & inclusion officer, 2006—. Adj. prof. U. Cin. Coll. Law, 1983—, Cleve. State U. Sch. Law, Case We. Reserve Sch. Law; trial observer, South Africa, 1985; dir. Buckeye Rev. Pub. Co.; chmn. Con. on Adequate Def. and Incentives in Mil.; mem. Task Force-Vets. Benefits; lectr. South African Judges seminar, Johannesburg. Co-chmn. Nat. Underground Railroad Freedom Ctr., Cin. Roundtable; observer Soviet Union Behalf com. on Soviet Jewry; bd. dirs. Cin. Youth Collaborative, Knowledge Works Found., Am. Constitution Soc.; bd. trustees Legal Aid Soc. Greater Cin., So. African Legal Services Found.; mem. adv. com. Urban Morgan Internat. Human Rights Inst.; mem. diversity adv. bd. Toyota Motor Mfr. N. Am., Inc. With USAF, 1945—47. Named a Great Living Cincinnatian, The Great Cin. C of C, 1997; named one of The Fifty Most Influential Blacks in Cin. in the Last Half Century, Radio Station WCIN, 2003, Fifth Third Bank, 2003; named to The Nat. Bar Assn. Hall of Fame; recipient Thurgood Marshall award, Nat. Bar Assn. Jud. Coun., 2002, Young Lawyers Divsn. Fellows award, ABA, 2005, Metropolitan award, 2005, Trailblazer award, Just The Beginning Found., 2006, Lifetime Achievement award, The Am. Lawyer mag., 2007. Mem.: FBA, ABA (co-chmn. com. constl. rights criminal sect. 1971—73, chmn. Africa coun., chmn. jud. clerkship initiative 1999—2000, chmn. spl. advisor coun. on racial and ethnic justice 1994—97), Cin. Bar Assn., Nat. Conf. Black Lawyers, Urban League, Am. Arbitration Assn., Nat. Bar Assn., Mahoning County Bar Assn., Ohio State Bar Assn., Houston Law Club (Youngstown), Elks, Kappa Alpha Psi. Baptist. Office: Blank Rome LLP 201 E 5th St Ste 1700 Cincinnati OH 45202 E-mail: Jones-n@blankrome.com.

JONES, PATRICIA L., lawyer; BA, U. Minn.; JD, William Mitchell Coll. Law. Sr. v.p., chief accounting officer, gen. counsel, sec. H.B. Fuller Co., 2000—. Office: HB Fuller Co 1200 Willow Lake Blvd PO Box 64683 Saint Paul MN 55164-0683 Office Phone: 651-236-5900.

JONES, PETER D'ALROY, historian, writer, retired educator; b. Hull, England, June 9, 1931; arrived in U.S., 1959, naturalized, 1968; s. Alfred and Madge (Rutter) D'Alroy; m. Johanna Maria Hartinger, Feb. 20, 1987; 1 child, Heather Marie; children from previous marriage: Kathryn Beauchamp Fly Ebert, Barbara Collier Rosenberg. BA, Manchester U., Eng., 1952, MA, 1953; postgrad. rsch. in collective bargaining, Inst. Solvay U. Brussels, 1954; PhD, London U. Sch. Econ., 1963. Freelance editor, London, 1953-56; linguist RAF, 1956—57; lectr. U.S. history dept. Am. studies Manchester U., 1957-58; vis. asst. prof. econs. Tulane U., 1959-60; from asst. to full prof. Smith Coll., 1960-68; William R. Kenan Jr. prof. Am. instns. and values Trinity Coll., Hartford, 1980—81; prof. history U. Ill., Chgo., 1968-98, prof. emeritus, 1998—. Vis. prof. Columbia U., U. Mass., U. Hawaii, U. Düsseldorf, Fed. Republic Germany; Fulbright prof. U. Warsaw, Poland, UNAM, Mexico City, U. Salzburg, Austria; mem. com. examiners Grad. Record Exams. Ednl. Testing Svc., Princeton, N.J., 1966-70; mem. Am. studies com. Am. Coun. Learned Socs., 1973-75; adv. to publs. Author: Economic History of U.S.A. Since 1783, 1956, 2nd edit., 1965, The Story of the Saw, 1961, America's Wealth, 1963, The Consumer Society, 1965, 2d edit., 1967, The Christian Socialist Revival, 1968, The Robber Barons Revisited, 1968, Robert Hunter's Poverty: Social Conscience in the Progressive Era, 1965, La Sociedad Consumidora, 1968, Since Columbus: Poverty and Pluralism in the History of the Americas, 1975, The U.S.A.: A History of Its People and Society, 2 vols., 1976, Henry George and British Socialism, 1991; co-editor: Biographical Dictionary of American Mayors, 1820-1980, 1981, Ethnic Chicago, 1981, rev. and enlarged edit., 1984, 4th edit., 1995; contbr. several entries to Ency. World Biography, 1988, 94; contbr. numerous articles and book revs. to profl. jours., popular newspapers. R.W. Emerson prize com Phi Beta Kappa, 1991—94. Mem. London Sch. Econs. Soc. (life). Personal E-mail: verdi1901@aol.com.

JONES, ROBERT BROOKE, microbiologist and immunologist educator; b. Knoxville, Tenn., Sept 14, 1942; s. Robert Melvin and Evaleen (Brooke) J.; m. Barbara Burgess McLawhorn, Sept. 7, 1963; children— Julia Ashley, Jonathan Davis, Quinnette Brooke. A.B. in Chemistry, U. N.C., 1964, M.D., 1970, Ph.D. in Biochemistry, 1970. Diplomate Am. Bd. Internal Medicine. Intern U. Wash., Seattle, 1970-71; resident U. Wash., Seattle, 1974-76; fellow in infectious diseases, 1976-78; asst. prof. Ind. U. Sch. Medicine, Indpls., 1978-83, assoc. prof. medicine, microbiology and immunology, 1983-86, prof., 1986—, assoc. dean, 1997—, CEO, med. dir. Wishard Health Svcs., Indpls.; dir. Midwest Sexually Transmitted Diseases Research Ctr., Indpls., 1983—; mem. NIH bacteriology rev. group, 1987. Contbr. sci. articles to profl. jours. Served to lt. comdr. U.S. Navy, 1971-74. NIH grantee, 1983. Fellow ACP; mem. Am. Venereal Disease Assn. (bd. dirs. 1983—), Am. Soc. Microbiology, Infectious Disease Soc. Am., Am. Fedn. Clin. Research, Order Golden Fleece, Sigma Xi, Alpha Omega Alpha. Republican. Mem. Society of Friends. Office: Ind U Fisler # 302 Dept Medicine Indianapolis IN 46202-5114 also: Wishard Health Svcs 1001 W 10th St Indianapolis IN 46202-2859

JONES, ROBERT E., construction executive; m. Mary Jane Jones; 1 child, Tom. Student, Washington U. With The Jones Co., St. Louis, 1953—, pres., 1961—, chmn. bd. Bd. dir. St. John's Bank and Trust Co. Tech. advt. com. St. Louis County Planning Commn.; chmn. bd. Met. St. Louis Sewer Dist. Mem. Builders Assn. Greater St. Louis. (chmn. labor com.), Nat. Assn. Home Builders (life dir.). Office: Jones Company Ste 200 16640 Chesterfield Grove Ct Chesterfield MO 63005-1422

JONES, ROBERT GERARD, lawyer; b. Latrobe, Pa., Nov. 13, 1956; BSME, W. Va. U., 1979; JD, St. Louis U., 1987. Bar: Mo. 1987, DC 1988. Sr. engr. Exxon Coal U.S., 1979—84; assoc. Crowell & Moring, Washington, 1987—91; of counsel Arch Mineral Corp., 1991—94; sr. counsel Arch Coal, Inc., St. Louis, 1994—2000, v.p. law, gen. counsel, 2000—. Office: Arch Coal Inc One City Place Dr Ste 300 Saint Louis MO 63141 Office Phone: 314-994-2700.

JONES, SHIRLEY M., state legislator; b. Chgo., Nov. 9, 1939; 2 children. Student, George Williams Coll. Mem. from Dist. 6, Ill. Ho. of Reps., 1987—, vice chmn. aging com. Also mem. higher edn., housing, human svc. appropriations, pub. utilities, revenue and state adminstrn. coms. Home: 55 E 36th St Chicago IL 60653-1030

JONES, STEPHANIE J., federal agency administrator; BA in English Lit. & Afro-Am. Studies, Smith Coll.; JD, U. Cin. Bar: Ohio 1986, U.S. Dist. Ct. Appeals (6th cir.) 1989, U.S. Dist. Ct. (so. dist.) Ohio 1987. Assoc. Graydon, Head & Ritchey, Cin., 1986-90; law prof. Salmon P. Chase Coll. Law Northern Ky. U.; chief edn. rep., spokesperson Dept. Edn. Region V, 1994—. Adj. prof. law Northwestern U. Sch. Law, Chgo.; lectr. in field; investigative, gen. news, feature reporter Cin. Post, 1982-83; exec. asst. Lionel Richie and the Commodores. Mem. Ohio Atty. Gen.'s Coun. on Ethics and Profl. Responsibility, 6th Cir. Jud. Conf. (life). Office: 111 N Canal St Ste 1094 Chicago IL 60606-7204

JONES, STEPHANIE TUBBS, congresswoman, lawyer, prosecutor; b. Cleve., Sept. 10, 1949; m. Mervyn L. Jones, Sr. (dec.); 1 child. BA in Sociology, Case Western Res. U. Flora Mather Coll., 1971; JD, Case Western Res. U. Sch. Law, 1974; D (hon.), Myers U., Notre Dame Coll., Ctrl. State U. Bar: Ohio 1974, US Dist. Ct. (no. dist.) Ohio 1975, US Ct. Appeals (6th cir.) 1981, US Supreme Ct. 1981. Asst. gen. counsel, EEO adminstr. N.E. Ohio Regional Sewer Dist., 1974-76; asst. prosecutor Cuyahoga County Prosecutor's Office, 1976-79; trial atty. Cleve. dist. office EEO, 1979-81; judge Cleve. Mcpl. Ct., 1982-83, Cuyahoga County Ct. of Common Pleas, 1983-91; prosecutor Cuyahoga County, Cleve., 1991-98; mem. US Congress from 11th Ohio dist., 1999—, mem. small bus. com., 1999—2002, mem. banking and fin. svcs. com., 1999—2002, mem. ways and means com., 2003—, chairwoman stds. of official conduct com. Vis. com. bd. overseers Franklin Thomas Backus Sch. Law, Case Western Res. U. Bd. trustees Cmty. Re-entry Prog.; bd. trustees class of 1984 Leadership Cleve. Alumnae; mem. Task Force on Violent Crime, Substance Abuse Initiative; trustee Cleve. Police Hist. Soc.; bd. trustees Bethany Bapt. Ch. Recipient Outstanding Vol. Svcs. in Law and Justice award Urban League Greater Cleve., 1986, Women of Yr. award Cleve. chpt. Nat. Assn. Negro Bus. and Profl. Women's Clubs, Inc., 1987, award in recognition of outstanding svc. to judiciary and black cmty. Midwest region Nat. Black Am. Law Student Assn., 1988, Career Women of Achievement award YWCA, 1991, Disting. Svc. award Cleve. chpt. NAACP, 1997; named Black Profl. of Yr., Black Profl. Assn. Cleve., 1995, 1994; named one of Most Influential Black Americans, Ebony mag., 2006; Ohio Dem. of Yr., Ohio Dem. Party, 1995; inductee Collinwood HS Hall of Fame, 1994, Soc. Benchers of Case Western Res. U. Sch. Law, 1996. Mem. ABA, Nat. Black Prosecutor's Assn., Nat. Dist. Atty.'ş Assn. (met. prosecutor's com.), Nat. Coun. Negro Women, Nat. Coll. Dist. Attys. (bd. regents), Ohio State Bar Assn. (Nettie Cronise Lutes award 1997), Ohio Prosecuting Attys. Assn. (exec. com.), Cleve. Bar Assn. (trustee), orman S. Miner Bar Assn. (past treas.), Cuyahoga Women's Polit. Caucus, Delta Sigma Theta (Greater Cleve. Alumnae chpt., Althea Simmons award 1993). Democrat. Baptist. Office: US House Reps 1009 Longworth House Office Bldg Washington DC 20515-3511 Office Phone: 202-225-7032. Office Fax: 202-225-1339. E-mail: Stephanie.Tubbs.Jones@mail.house.gov.

JONES, SUSIE, radio personality; Grad. Speech Comms., U. Minn. With Sta. KSTP, Sta. KARE, Sta. WCCO-TV, Mpls.; radio host afternoon drive Sta. KCCO-AM, Mpls., 1996—, Saturday radio host. Office: WCCO 625 2nd Ave S Minneapolis MN 55402

JONES, THOMAS FRANKLIN, protective services official; b. Atlantic City, Dec. 19, 1940; BA, Southeastern U., 1968. From agent to spl. agent in charge FBI, Cleve., 1968-95; ret., 1995; chief of police Cleve. Clinic Found., 1997—. Office: Police Dept Cleve Clinic Found 9500 Euclid Ave Cleveland OH 44195-0001

JONES, THOMAS WALTER, astrophysics educator, researcher; b. Odessa, Tex., June 22, 1945; s. Theodore Sydney and LaVerne Gertrude (Neis) J.; m. Karen Gay Cronquist, June 15, 1968 (div.); 1 child, Walter Brian. BS in Physics, U. Tex., 1967; MS in Physics, U. Minn., 1969, PhD in Physics, 1972. Asst. physicist U. Calif., San Diego, 1972-75; asst. scientist Nat. Radio Astronomy Obs., Charlottesville, Va., 1975-77; asst. prof. dept. astronomy U. Minn., Mpls., 1977-80, assoc. prof., 1980-84, prof., 1984—, chmn. dept. astronomy, 1981-97. Contbr. articles to profl. jours. Mem. Am. Astron. Soc., Royal Astron. Soc., Internat. Astron. Union, Sigma Xi. Office: U Minn Dept Astronomy 116 Church St SE Minneapolis MN 55455-0149 Home: 1385 Eldridge Ave W Saint Paul MN 55113-5805

JONES, TONY, academic administrator; Dir. Glasgow Sch. Arts, 1980—86; pres. Sch. Art Inst. Chgo., 1986—92; dir. Royal Coll. Art, London, 1992—96; pres. & co-CEO Sch. Art Inst. Chgo., 1996—. Named Hon. Dir. Bd., Osaka U. Arts (Japan), 2000, Hon. Prof., U. Wales, 1995; recipient Scotland's Newbery Medal, 1986. Fellow: Royal Coll. Art (sr.); mem.: Am. Inst. Architects (hon.). Office: School of Art Institute of Chicago Office of the President 37 S Wabash Ave Ste 821 Chicago IL 60603 Office Phone: 312-899-5136. Office Fax: 312-263-5629. E-mail: tonyjones@saic.edu.

JONES, TREVOR OWEN, biomedical industry executive, management consultant; b. Maidstone, Kent, Eng., Nov. 3, 1930; came to U.S., 1957, naturalized, 1971; s. Richard Owen and Ruby Edith (Martin) J.; m. Jennie Lou Singleton, Sept. 12, 1959; children: Pembroke Robinson (dec.), Bronwyn Elizabeth. Higher Nat. Cert. in Elec. Engring., Aston Tech. Coll., Birmingham, Eng., 1952; Ordinary Nat. Cert. in Mech. Engring., Liverpool Tech. Coll., Eng., 1957; DSc (hon.), Cleve. State U., 2006. Registered profl. engr., Wis.; chartered engr., U.K. Student engr., elec. machine design engr. Brit. Gen. Electric Co., 1950-57; project engr., project mgr. Nuc. Ship Savannah, Allis-Chalmers Mfg. Co., 1957-59; with GM, 1959-78, staff engr. in charge Apollo computers, 1967, dir. electronic control sys., 1970-72, dir. advanced product engring., 1972-74; dir. GM Proving Grounds, 1974-78; v.p. engring., automotive worldwide TRW Inc., Cleve., 1978-80, v.p. transp. electronics group, 1980-87; chmn. bd. dirs. Libbey-Owens-Ford Inc., 1987-94; chmn., CEO Internat. Devel. Corp., 1987—; from vice chmn. to chmn. Echlin Inc., 1995-98, chmn. bd. dir., interim pres. and CEO, 1997; chmn., founder, CEO Biomec Inc., 1998—2007; chmn. Electrosonics Med., Inc., 2007—, CEO, 2007—. Chmn. emeritus Ohio Fuel Cell Coalition; vice chmn. Motor Vehicle Safety Adv. Coun., 1971; chmn. Nat. Hwy. Safety Adv. Com., 1976; assoc. NRC, 2002. Author, patentee automotive safety and electronics. Trustee Lawrence Inst. Tech., 1973-76; exec. bd. Clinton Valley coun. Boy Scouts Am., 1975; bd. govs. Cranbrook Inst. Sci., 1977; mem. Sec. of Def. Def. Sci. Bd. Task Force on Internat. Arms Devel. Cooperation, 1995-98; chmn. at. Rsch. Coun. Com. Partnership for a New Generation Vehicle, 1994-2001; vice chair bd. trustees Cleve. State U., 2001-06, mem., 2007; trustee Cleve. Orch., 2003—. Officer Brit. Army, 1955-57. Recipient Safety award, US Dept. Transp., 1978. Fellow Brit. Instn. Mechanical Engrs. (hon.), Brit. Instn. Elec. Engrs. (Hooper Mem. prize 1950), IEEE (life, exec. com. vehicle tech. soc. 1977-81), Royal Soc. of the Arts, Mfg. and Commerce, Soc. Automotive Engrs. (Arch T. Colwell paper award 1974-75, Vincent Bendix Automotive Electronics award 1976, Edward N. Cole award 1988), Engring. Soc. Detroit, Engring. Soc.

Cleve., Instn. Mech. Engrs. (hon.); mem. NAE, Union Club, Royal Poinciana Country Club (Naples, Fla.) Republican. Episcopalian. Home: Two Bratenahl Pl Ste 9EF Bratenahl OH 44108 also: Ste 2001 4151 Gulf Shore Blvd N Naples FL 34103 Home Phone: 216-681-5621; Office Phone: 216-357-3310 ext. 1003. Business E-Mail: tojones@elecsonmed.com.

JONES, WELLINGTON DOWNING, III, banker; b. Topeka, Feb. 16, 1945; s. Wellington Downing Jr. and Nancy (Neiswanger) J.; m. Andrea Loftus, May 2, 1970; children: Wellington Downing IV, Heather, Lindsey. BSBA, Northwestern U., 1967; postgrad., Grad. Sch. Banking, Madison, Wis., 1980, Harvard U., 1987. Mktg. rep. IBM, Chgo., 1969-76; v.p. data processing 1st Bank & Trust (name 1st Source Bank 1981), South Bend, Ind., 1976-79, v.p. retail banking, 1979-81; sr. v.p. 1st Source Bank, South Bend, 1981-88; pres. 1st Nat. Bank Mishawaka (acquired by 1st Source Bank 1983), Ind., 1983; exec. v.p. 1st Source Corp., South Bend, 1988—98, pres., 1998—. Bd. dirs. Trustcorp Mortgage, South Bend. Bd. dirs. Neighborhood Housing Svcs., South Bend, 1986—, Entertainment Dist. Bd., South Bend, 1991—, United Way St. Joseph County, South Bend, 1991—; chmn. South Bend Mayor's Housing Forum, 1991—; pres. No. Ind. Hist. Soc., South Bend, 1991—. Sgt. USMCR, 1967-73. Mem. Signal Point Club (Niles, Mich.), Morris Park Country Club. Presbyterian. Avocations: golf, platform tennis, reading, investments. Office: 1st Source Bank 100 N Michigan St South Bend IN 46601-1630

JONES, WENDELL E., state legislator; b. Nov. 4, 1937; m. Jane; 3 children. BS in Speech & Hearing Therapy, Ball State U. Speech therapist, dir. spl. edn. Dist. 15, Palatine, Ill.; mem. Ill. Senate, Springfield, 1998—. Rep. precinct capt.; pres. Village Palatine, 1973-77, trustee, 1967-73. Republican. Office: State Capitol 611 C Capitol Bldg Springfield IL 62706-0001 also: 110 W Northwest Hwy Palatine IL 60067-3558

JONES, WILLIAM AUGUSTUS, JR., retired bishop; b. Memphis, Jan. 24, 1927; s. William Augustus and Martha (Jones) J.; m. Margaret Loaring-Clark, Aug. 26, 1949; 4 children. BA, Southwestern at Memphis, 1948; B.D., Yale U., 1951. Ordained priest Episcopal Ch., 1952; priest in charge Messiah Ch., Pulaski, Tenn., 1952-57; curate Christ Ch., Nashville, 1957-58; rector St. Mark Ch., LaGrange, Ga., 1958-65; asso. rector St. Luke Ch., Mountainbrook, Ala., 1965-66; dir. research So. region Assn. Christian Tng. and Service, Memphis, 1966-67; exec. dir. Assn. Christian Tng. and Service, 1968-72; rector St. John's, Johnson City, Tenn., 1972-75; bishop of Mo. St. Louis, 1975-93. Adj. staff Christ Ch., Wilmington, Del., 2001. Episcopalian.

JONKER, BRUCE A., manufacturing executive; V.p., CFO Gradall Industries, Inc., New Philadelphia, Ohio. Office: Gradall Industries Inc 406 Mill Ave SW New Philadelphia OH 44663-3835

JOOS, DAVID W., energy executive; BS in Engring. Sci., Iowa State U., 1975, MS in Nuc. Engring., 1976. With CMS Energy Corp., 1976—; pres., CEO elec. Consumers Energy Corp., 1997—2000; exec. v.p., COO elec. CMS Energy Corp., 2000—01, pres. and COO, 2001—04, pres. and CEO, 2004—. Mem.: Assn. Edison Illuminating Co., Mich. Coll. Found., Mich. Mfg. Assn. Office: CMS Energy One Energy Plz Jackson MI 49201

JORDAN, JIM (JAMES D. JORDAN), congressman, former state legislator; b. Troy, Ohio, Feb. 17, 1964; m. Polly Jordan; children: Rachel, Benjamin, Jessie, Isaac. BS in Econ., U. Wis., 1986; MA in Edn., Ohio State U., 1991; JD, Capital U., 2001. Asst. wrestling coach Ohio State U., Columbus; mem. Ohio Ho. of Reps. from 85th dist., Columbus, 1995—2000, Ohio State Senate from 12th dist., Columbus, 2001—07, US Congress from 4th Ohio dist., 2007—, mem. judiciary com., small bus. com., oversight and govt. reform com. Mem. Champaign County Rep. Exec. Com., Mad River Valley Young Rep. Club, Citizens Against Govt. Waste, Right to Life Orgns. Big Ten and NCAA wrestling champion, 1985, 86; recipient: Outstanding Legis. award, 2004, "Defender of Life award Ohio Right to Life Soc., Leadership in Govt. award Ohio Roudtable & freedom Forum, 2001; named Watchdog of the Treasury, 1996, 2000, 2004, Friend of the Taxpayer, 1997, Pro-life Legis. of Yr. United Conservatives of Ohio, 1998 Republican. Evangelical. Office: US House Reps 515 Cannon House Office Bldg Washington DC 20515 also: 24 W Third St Rm 314 Mansfield OH 44902 Office Phone: 419-522-5757. Office Fax: 419-525-2805.

JORDAN, JOHN W., II, holding company executive; b. 1948; Grad., U. Notre Dame, 1969. With Carl Marks & Co., 1972—82, The Jordan Co., NYC, 1982—; CEO Jordan Industries, Inc., Deerfield, Ill., 1982—. Office: Jordan Industries 1751 Lake Cook Rd Ste 550 Deerfield IL 60015-5624 also: Jordan Industries Inc 875 N Michigan Ave Chicago IL 60611-1803

JORDAN, KAREN, newscaster; b. Nashville, Tenn. d. Robert Jordan; m. Christian Farr. BA in English, Spelman Coll., Atlanta, 1994; MA in Broadcast Journalism, Medill Sch. of Journalism, Evanston, Ill., 1995. Medill News Svc. reporter WMAQ-AM, Chgo., 1995; reporter WIFR-TV, Rockford, Ill., 1995—97; weekend anchor and reporter WKEF-TV, Dayton, Ohio, 1997—99; main anchor and reporter WRGT-TV, Dayton, Ohio, 1999—2000; anchor weekend news and reporter WPHL-TV, Phila., 2000—03; co-anchor weekend news WLS-TV, Chgo., 2003—. Office: WLS-TV 190 N State St Chicago IL 60601

JORDAN, MICHELLE DENISE, judge; b. Chgo., Oct. 29, 1954; d. John A. and Margaret (O'Dood) J. BA in Polit. Sci., Loyola U, Chgo., 1974; JD, U. Mich., 1977. Bar. Ill. 1977, U.S. Dist. Ct. (no. dist.) Ill. 1978. Asst. state's atty. State's Attys. Office, Chgo., 1977-82; pvt. practice Chgo., 1983-84; with Ill. Atty. Gen.'s Office, Chgo., 1984-90, chief environ. control div., 1988-90; ptnr. Hopkins & Sutter, Chgo., 1991-93; apptd. dep. regional adminstr. region 5 U.S. EPA, Chgo., 1994—. Active Operation Push, Chgo., 1971—. Recipient Kizzy Image Achievement and Svc. award, 1990, Suzanne E. Olive Nat. EEO award 1996, Rainbow-PUSH Seed Sower award, 2004; named in Am.'s Top 100 Bus. and Profl. Women, Dollars and SenseMag., Chgo., 1988. Mem. Ill. Bar Assn., Chgo. Bar Assn. (bd. mgrs., chmn. criminal law com. 1987-88, mem. hearing divsn., jud. evaluation com. 1987-88, exec. coun. 1987-88), Cook County Bar Assn., Nat. Bar Assn., Alpha Sigma Nu. Democrat. Baptist.

JORDAN, NICK M., state legislator, hotel recreational facility executive; b. Kansas City, Mo., Dec. 2, 1949; s. Dwight M. and Joveta M. (Mills) J.; m. Linda Joyce Jarred, May 28, 1971; 1 child, Shelly Reneé. Grad. high sch., Overland Park, Kans. Restaurant mgr., asst. mgr., dir. mktg. Glenwood Manor Hotel, Overland Park, 1964-74; asst. dir. mktg. Radisson Muehlebach Hotel, Kansas City, Mo., 1974-79; dir. mktg. Grand Am. Hotel Corp., Overland Park, 1979-81, Regency Park Resort, Overland Park, 1981-83; pres. Overland Park Conv. and Visitors Bur., 1983-93; mem. Kans. Senate from 10th dist., 1995—. Vice chmn. Kans. Travel and Tourism Commn., Topeka, 1990—; appointee Johnson County (Kans.) Transp. Coun., 1988-92. Bd. dirs. Lakeview Village K.C. Coun. Prison Fellowship. Recipient Gov.'s Tourism award Kans. Assn. Broadcasters, 1987. Mem. Travel Industry Assn. Kans. (past pres., bd. dirs., Disting. Svc. award 1991), Internat. Assn. Conv. and Visitors Burs. (chmn. continuing edn. com. 1992-93), Rotary (bd. dirs. 1987-89). Avocations: reading, tennis, travel. Home: 7013 Albervan St Shawnee Mission KS 66216-2333 Office: The Hospitality Group 7013 Albervan Shawnee KS 66216 Address: Kansas Senate State Capitol Rm 143-N Topeka KS 66612

JORDAN, THOMAS FREDRICK, physics professor; b. Duluth, Minn., June 4, 1936; s. Thomas Vincent and Mildred (Nystrom) J. BA, U. Minn., 1958; PhD, U. Rochester, 1962. Rsch. assoc. U. Rochester, 1961-62, instr., 1962-63; NSF postdoctoral fellow U. Bern, Switzerland, 1963-64; asst. prof. U. Pitts., 1964-67, assoc. prof., 1967-70; prof. U. Minn., Duluth, 1970—. Vis. prof., workshop participant U. Wis., 1965, Aspen (Colo.) Inst. for Humanistic Studies, 1966, Summer Inst. for Theoretical Physics, U. Colo., 1967, Internat. Ctr. for Theoretical Physics, Trieste, Italy, 1968, U. Rochester, 1976-77, Syracuse U., Nat. Inst. for uclear Rsch., Firenze, Italy, U. Geneva., U. Paris 1982, Internat. Ctr. for Theoretical Physics, Trieste, workshop on early universe, Erice, Italy, Geneva, U. Bern, 1986, U. Calif. at Santa Barbara, 1988, U. Tex., 1990, 94, 2003, 04, 05. Author: Linear Operators for Quantum Mechanics, 1969, Quantum Mechanics in Simple Matrix Form, 1985; contbr. numerous article to profl. jours. Rsch. fellow Alfred P. Sloan Found., 1965-67, Temple U., 1984, Bush Found. fellow U. Tex., 1994; Fulbright Rsch. grantee U. Göttingen, Fed. Republic of Germany, 1991-92, 2003.

JORDE, TERRY J., bank executive; b. 1958; married; 3 children. BA in Fin., U. Ill. Champaign-Urbana. Pres. Ind. Cmty. Banks of ND; pres., CEO CountryBank USA, Cando, ND. Mem. Fed. Reserve Bd. Consumer Adv. Coun., Nat. Adv. Coun., Fannie Mae; bd. mem. ND Dept. Fin. Institutions; chmn., Agr.-Rural Am. Com. Ind. Cmty. Bankers of Am., chmn., Securities Corp., chmn., Services Network, treasurer, vice chmn., chmn. Bd. mem. Towner County Econ. Devel. Corp., Towner County Med. Ctr., ND Devel. Fund. Named one of 25 Women to Watch, US Banker, 2006. Office: CountryBank USA PO Box 549 Cando ND 58324 Office Phone: 701-968-4421.

JORGENSON, MARY ANN, lawyer; b. Gallipolis, Ohio, 1941; BA, Agnes Scott Coll., 1963; MA, Harvard U., 1964; JD, Case Western Res. U., 1975. Bar: Ohio 1975, N.Y. 1982. Ptnr., chair firm's corp. practice Squire, Sanders & Dempsey LLP, Cleve., 1990—2004. Office: Squire Sanders & Dempsey LLP 127 Public Sq Ste 4900 Cleveland OH 44114-1284 Office Phone: 216-479-8654. Business E-Mail: mjorgenson@ssd.com.

JORNDT, LOUIS DANIEL, former retail drug store chain executive; b. Chgo., Aug. 24, 1941; s. Louis Carl and Margaret Estelle (Teel) J.; m. Patricia McDonnell, Aug. 1, 1964; children— Kristine, Michael, Kara BS in Pharmacy, Drake U., 1963; MBA, U. N.Mex., 1974. Various mgmt. positions Walgreen Co., Chgo., 1963-68, dist. mgr., 1968-75, regional dir. Deerfield, Ill., 1975-79, regional v.p., 1979-82, v.p., treas., 1982-85, sr. v.p., treas., 1985-89, pres., chief oper. officer, 1989-97, CEO, chmn., 1997—2003; ret., 2003. Bd. dirs. Better Bus. Bur. Chgo., 1982—, Chgo. Assn. Commerce and Industry; nat. chmn. Drake U. Pharmacy Alumni Fund. Mem. Nat. Assn. Corp. Treas., Fin. Execs. Inst. Clubs: Economic (Chgo.); Glen View (Ill.) Golf. Avocations: golf, swimming, reading.

JORNS, DAVID LEE, retired university president; b. Tulsa, Jan. 10, 1944; s. Victor Lee and Nancy Jane (Pollard) J.; m. Audrey Parkes; children: Molly, Ben. BS in Radio and TV, Okla. State U., 1966, MA in Speech and Drama, 1968; PhD in Theatre History and Criticism, UCLA, 1973. Teaching asst. UCLA, 1970-73; asst. prof. U. Mo., Columbia, 1973-77, assoc. prof., 1977-80, dir. of theatre, 1977-80; chmn. theatre arts Mankato (Minn.) State U., 1980-84; dean fine arts and humanities West Tex. State U., Canyon, 1984-88; v.p. acad. affairs and provost No. Ky. U., Highland Heights, 1988-92; pres. Eastern Ill. U., Charleston, 1992-99. Contbr. articles, revs. to profl. publs.; producer 25 plays; editor The Jour. Opinion for the Performing Arts, 1975. Lt. USN, 1967-70. Mem. Ky. Coun. of Chief Acad. Officers, Soc. for Coll. & Univ. Planning, Assn. for Gen. & Liberal Studies, Am. Assn. for Higher Edn. Democrat. Avocations: computers, painting, reading.

JOSCELYN, KENT BUCKLEY, lawyer; b. Binghamton, Dec. 18, 1936; s. Raymond Miles and Gwen Buckley (Smith) J.; children: Kathryn Anne, Jennifer Sheldon. BS, Union Coll., 1957; JD, Albany Law Sch., NY, 1960. Bar: N.Y. 1961, U.S. Ct. Mil. Appeals 1962, D.C., 1967, Mich. 1979. Atty. adviser hdqts. USAF, Washington, 1965-67; assoc. prof. forensic studies U. Ind., Bloomington, 1967-76; dir. Inst. Rsch. in Pub. Safety, 1970-75; head policy analysis divsn. Highway Safety Rsch. Inst. U. Mich., Ann Arbor, 1976-81; dir. transp. planning and policy Urban Tech. Environ. Planning Program, Ann Arbor, 1981-84; prin. Joscelyn and Treat P.C., Ann Arbor, 1981—93, Joscelyn, McNair & Jeffrey P.C., Ann Arbor, 1993-2001; pvt. practice Ann Arbor, 2001—. Cons. Law Enforcement Assistance Adminstrn., U.S. Dept. Justice, 1969-72; Gov.'s appointee as regional dir. Ind. Criminal Justice Planning Agy., 1969-72; vice chmn. Ind. Organized Crime Prevention Coun., 1969-72; commr. pub. safety City of Bloomington, Ind., 1974-76. Editor Internat. Jour. Criminal Justice, 1972-. Capt. Judge Advocate USAF, 1961—64. Mem. ABA, D.C. Bar Assn., NY State Bar Assn., Mich. State Bar Assn., Transp. Rsch. Bd. (chmn. motor vehicle and traffic law com. 1979-82), Am. Soc. Criminology (life), Assn. for Advancement Automotive Medicine (life), Acad. Criminal Justice Scis. (life), Assn. Chiefs Police (assoc.), Nat. Safety Coun., Assn. Former Intelligence Officers (life), Product Liability Adv. Coun., Sigma Xi, Theta Delta Chi Office: Kent B Joscelyn PC PO Box 130589 Ann Arbor MI 48113-0589 Office Phone: 734-662-7904. Business E-Mail: kbjpc@earthlink.net.

JOSEPH, BRIAN DANIEL, language educator; b. Nov. 22, 1951; AB cum laude, Yale U., 1973; AM, Harvard U., 1976, PhD, 1978. Asst. prof. Ohio State U., Columbus, 1979—85, assoc. prof., 1985—88, dept. chmn., 1987—97, prof. linguistics, 1988—; Kenneth E. Naylor prof. South Slavic languages and linguistics, 1997—. Session lectr. hist. linguistics U. Alberta, 1978—79; vis. prof. U. Aegean, 1989, U. Calif., Santa Cruz, 1991, U. Ill., 1999, Mich. State U., 2003; vis. tchg. fellow U. Canterbury, New Zealand, 1997; mem. cognitive sci. planning com. Ohio State U., 1989—91, mem. program rev. com. dept. Slavic languages and literatures, 1995—97, mem. eval. com. ctrl. adminstrn., 1997—98, mem. South Asia coord. com., 2001—02, mem. steering com. Ohio Tchg. Enhancement Program, 2000—01, mem. pres. and provost's adv. com., 2003—, numerous others; cons. various univs. Co-editor (with Johanna DeStefano, Neil Jacobs and Ilse Lehiste): When Languages Collide: Perspectives on Language Conflict, Language Competition, and Language Coexistence, 2003; contbr. articles to profl. jours., chapters to books. Recipient numerous fellowships and grants. Fellow: Am. Acad. Arts & Sciences; mem.: Bulgarian Studies Assn., Am. Assn. Advancement Slavic Studies, SE European Studies Assn., Am. Assn. Tchrs. Slavic and East European Languages, Modern Greek Studies Assn. (mem. exec. com. 1991—93, chmn. publications com. 1995—99, mem. symposium com. 2000—01), Linguistic Soc. Am. (mem. summer inst. fellowship com. 1995, mem. nom. com. 1996—97, chmn. nom. com. 1998, program com. cons. 1998—99, mem. ad hoc com. former inst. dirs. 1993—). Office: Dept Linguistics Ohio State Univ 222 Oxley Hall Columbus OH 43210-1298 Office Phone: 614-292-4981. Office Fax: 614-292-8833. E-mail: bjoseph@ling.ohio-state.edu.

JOSEPH, CHRIS, business services executive; BA, Miami U. Ohio; MBA, U. Chicago. Investment mgr. Wind Point Ptnrs., Chicago; co-founder, sr. v.p. ops. Integration Alliance Corp., 1994-98; CFO Parson Group, 1998—. Bd. dirs. Chicagoland C. of C., Boys & Girls Club Chgo. Recipient INC 500 Award, 2000.

JOSEPH, CURTIS SHAYNE, professional hockey player; b. Keswick, Ont., Can., Apr. 29, 1967; Student, U. Wis. Goaltender St. Louis Blues, 1989-92, Edmonton Oilers, 1992-98, Toronto Maple Leafs, 1998—2002, Detroit Red Wings, 2002—05, Phoenix Coyotes, 2005—07, Calgary Flames, 2008—. Mem. Team Can., Olympic Games, Salt Lake City, 2002. Named OHA Most Valuable Player, 1987, WCHA Most Valuable Player, 1989, WCHA Rookie of Yr., 1989; recipient King Clancy Meml. Trophy, 2000. Achievements include being a member of gold medal Canadian Hockey team, Salt Lake City Olympic Games, 2002. Office: Calgary Flames PO Box 1540 Stn M Calgary AB Canada T2P 3B9

JOSEPH, DANIEL DONALD, aeronautical engineer, educator; b. Chgo., Mar. 26, 1929; s. Samuel and Mary (Simon) J.; m. Ellen Broida, Dec. 18, 1949 (div. 1979); children: Karen, Michael, Charles; m. Kay Jaglo, Feb. 9, 1990. MA in Sociology, U. Chgo., 1950; BS in Mech. Engring, Ill. Inst. Tech., 1959, MS, 1960, PhD, 1963. Asst. prof. mech. engring. Ill. Inst. Tech., 1962-63; mem. faculty U. Minn., 1963—, assoc. prof. fluid mechanics, 1965-69, prof. aerospace engring. and mechanics, 1969-90, Russell J. Penrose prof. Mpls., 1990—. Author 4 books on stability and bifurcation theory and fluid dynamics; editor 3 books; editorial bd. SIAM Jour. Applied Math, Jour. Applied Mechanics, Jour. Non-Newtonian Fluid Mechanics, others; contbr. articles to sci. jours. Guggenheim fellow, 1969-70, Timoshenko medal Am. Soc. of Mechanical Engineers, 1995. Mem. NAS, ASME, NAE, Am. Phys. Soc., Am. Acad. Arts and Scis., Soc. Engring. Sci. (G.I. Taylor medal 1990, Bingham medal Soc. of Rheology). Achievements include contbns. to math. theory of hydrodynamic stability; rheology of viscoelastic fluids. Home: 1920 S 1st St Apt 2302 Minneapolis MN 55454-1279 Office: U Minn Dept Aerospace Engring 110 Union St SE Minneapolis MN 55455-0153 Office Phone: 612-625-0309. Business E-Mail: joseph@aem.umn.edu.

JOSEPH, JULES K., retired public relations executive; b. Cin., Jan. 18, 1927; s. Leslie Bloch and Ellen (Kaufman) J.; m. Elizabeth Levy, Sept. 9, 1948; children— Ellen Beth, Barbara Ann, John Charles. BA in Journalism, U. Wis., 1948. Mem. press relations staff Gimbels, Milw., 1948-52; bur. chief Fairchild Publs., Milw., 1952-60; co-founder, chmn. emeritus Zigman-Joseph-Stephenson Assocs. in Pub. Rels., Milw., 1960-94; ret., 1994. Pres. Friends of Art of Milw. Art Ctr., 1961-62; v.p. Milw. County Mental Health, 1967; bd. dirs. Milw. Repertory Theatre, Camp Webb, Milw. Pks. Bd., St. John's Home for the Aged, Milw., DePaul Hosp., Charles Allis Art Libr., Wis. Olympics Com.; bd. dirs. Frank Lloyd Wright Heritage Tourism Program; adv. bd. Salvation Army. Recipient Chancellor's award for outstanding contbn. to mass communication U. Wis., 1988. Mem. Pub. Rels. Soc. Am. (accredited, treas. Wis. 1970-71, bd. dirs. counselors sect. 1991-92), Soc. for Profl. Journalists, Phi Kappa Phi. Episcopalian. Home: 10610 N Magnolia Dr Mequon WI 53092-5054 Office: 735 W Wisconsin Ave Milwaukee WI 53233-2413 Personal E-mail: jjoseph8@wi.rr.com.

JOSEPH, MARILYN SUSAN, gynecologist; b. Aug. 18, 1946; BA, Smith Coll., 1968; MD cum laude, SUNY Downstate Med. Ctr., Bklyn., 1972. Diplomate Am. Bd. Ob-Gyn, Nat. Bd. Med. Examiners. Intern U. Minn. Hosps., 1972-73, resident in ob-gyn, 1972-76; med. fellow specialist U. Minn., 1972-76, asst. prof. ob-gyn, 1976—, dir. women's clinic, 1984—. Med. dir. Boynton Health Svc., 1993—. Author: Differential Diagnosis Obstetrics, 1978. Fellow Am. Coll. Ob-Gyn (best paper dist. VI meeting 1981); mem. Hennepin County Med. Soc., Minn. State Med. Assn., Minn. State Ob-Gyn Soc. Avocations: cooking, bird watching, travel. Office: Boynton Health Svc 410 Church St SE Minneapolis MN 55455-0346 E-mail: mjoseph@bhs.umn.edu.

JOSEPH, ROBERT THOMAS, lawyer; b. June 12, 1946; s. Joseph Alexander and Clara Barbara (Francis) J.; m. Sarah Granger, May 22, 1971; children: Paul, Timothy. AB, Xavier U., 1968; JD, U. Mich., 1971. Bar: Mich. 1971, Ill. 1976, US Dist. Ct. (no. dist.) Ill. 1976, US Ct. Appeals (7th cir.) 1983. Staff atty. FTC Bur. Competition, Washington, 1971-76, asst. to dir., 1972-74; atty. Sonnenschein Nath & Rosenthal, LLP, Chgo., 1976—, ptnr., 1978—. Trustee Northbrook Libr. Bd., Ill., 1979-89, pres., 1983-85. Recipient Disting. Svc. award FTC, 1976. Mem. ABA (chair franchising com. of antitrust law sect. 1984-87, chair videotapes com. 1987-90, chair publs. com. 1991-94, coun. 1994-97, program officer 1997-99, com. officer 1999-2000, vice-chair 2000-2001, chair 2002-03, mem. governing bd. forum on franchising 1997-2003), Met. Club. Roman Catholic. Office: Sonnenschein Nath Rosenthal LLP 233 S Wacker Dr Ste 7800 Chicago IL 60606-6491

JOST, LAWRENCE JOHN, lawyer; b. Alma, Wis., Oct. 9, 1944; s. Lester J. and Hazel L. (Johnson) J.; m. Anne E. Fisher, June 10, 1967; children— Peter, Katherine, Susan. BSCE, U. Wis., 1968, JD, 1969. Bar: Wis. 1969, U.S. Dist. Ct. (ea. dist.) Wis. 1969, U.S. Ct. Appeals (7th cir.) 1969, U.S. Supreme Ct. 1980. Law clk. to judge U.S. Dist. Ct., Milw., 1969-70; assoc. firm Brady, Tyrrell, Cotter & Cutler, 1970-74; assoc. Quarles & Brady, 1974-76, ptnr., 1976—, chair real estate group, 1985—, chair real property sect., 2002—. Vis. tchr. gen. practice Wis. Law Sch. Bd. dirs. Milw. Chamber Theatre, 1998-2001, Marcus Ctr. for the Performing Arts, 2003—; pres. Vis. Nurse Assn. Milw., 1982-85, VNA, Corp., 1982-86; bd. dirs. Wis. Heritage Inc., 1980-82, Vis. Nurse Found., 1986-95, pres., 1993-94; bd. dirs. Milw. Repertory Theater, 1987-95, 2001—, pres., 1990-92; bd. dirs. United Performing Arts Fund, 1989-93. Mem. ABA, Wis. Bar Assn. (lectr. seminars), Milw. Bar Assn., Am. Coll. Real Estate Lawyers, Am. Coll. Mortgage Attys. (state chair), Nat. Assn. Indsl. and Office Properties (bd. dirs. Wis. chpt. 2003—). Mem. Plymouth United Ch. of Christ Office: Quarles & Brady LLP 411 E Wisconsin Ave Ste 2550 Milwaukee WI 53202-4497 Office Phone: 414-277-5000. Business E-Mail: ljj@quarles.com.

JOYCE, JOSEPH M., lawyer, retail executive; b. Mpls., 1951; BSBA, U. Minn., 1973; JD, William Mitchell Coll. Law, 1977. Bar: Minn. 1977. Legal counsel Tonka Corp., Minnetonka, Minn., 1977-81, sec., gen. counsel, 1981-87, v.p., sec., gen. counsel, 1987—91; v.p. human resources, gen. counsel Best Buy Co. Inc., Mpls., 1991—97, v.p., gen. counsel, 1997—2000, sr. v.p., gen. counsel, sec., 2000—. Sec. bd. dir. Best Buy Children's Found. Office: Best Buy Co Inc PO Box 9312 Minneapolis MN 55440-9312

JOYCE, WILLIAM H., retired engineering company executive, chemical engineer; b. 1935; BS, Pa. State U., 1957; MBA, NYU, 1971, PhD, 1984. With Union Carbide Corp., Danbury, Conn., 1957—2001, past exec. v.p. ops., pres., COO, 1993—95, CEO, 1995; chmn., pres., CEO Union Carbide Corp. (merged with Dow Chemical Co.), Danbury, Conn., 1996—2001; vice chmn. bd. The Dow Chem. Co., Danbury, 2001; chmn., CEO Hercules, Inc., Willmington, Del., 2001—03, Nalco Co., Naperville, Ill., 2003—07. Bd. dirs. CVS Corp., El Paso. Trustee U. Rsch. Assn. Inc. Recipient Nat. medal of Tech., NSF, 1993, Industry Achievement award, Plastics Acad., 1994, Lifetime Achievement award, 1997, Perkin award, Soc. Chemical Industry, 2003. Mem.: NAE, NAS (co-chmn., Gov.-Univ.-Industry Rsch. Roundtable), Am. Plastics Coun. (bd. dirs.), Soc. Chem. Industry (treas., bd. dirs.). Office: Nalco Co 1601 W Diehl Rd Naperville IL 60563-1198 Office Phone: 877-813-3523. Office Fax: 630-305-2900.

JOYCE-HAYES, DEE LEIGH, lawyer; b. Lexington, Va., Aug. 29, 1946; d. Robert Newton and Dorothy Lucille (Markham) Joyce; m. Lester Stephen Vossmeyer, Dec. 28, 1971 (div. Apr. 1984); 1 child, Robert Stephen; m. Gary Lee Hayes, Aug. 29, 1986; 1 child, Elena. BA in Govt., Coll. William and Mary, 1968; JD, St. Louis U., 1980. Bar: Mo. 1980. Spl. asst. to dep. under sec. U.S. Dept. Transp., Washington, 1970-72; rsch. analyst Lee Creative Rsch., St. Louis, 1972-74; bank officer Mark Twain Banks, St. Louis, 1974-77; asst. cir. atty. Cir. Atty.'s Office St. Louis, 1981-92; cir. atty. Office of Cir. Atty., St. Louis, 1993—. Bd. dirs. Children's Advocacy Svcs. St. Louis, 1990—; bd. dirs. Backstoppers, St. Louis, 1994—; pres., 1996-97; gubernatorial appointee Mo. Sentencing Advs. Commn., 1995—; co-chmn. Operation Weed and Seed, St. Louis, 1994—; mem. disciplinary com. 22d Cir. Bar Com., St. Louis, 1992—; adj. prof. law Wash. U., 1997—. Bd. dirs. The Backstoppers, St. Louis, 1993—, pres. bd., 1996; mem. exec. com. Regional Violence Prevention Initiative, Mo. and Western Ill., 1994—; mem. nat. and St. Louis chpt. Women's Polit. Caucus; mem. com. on missions and social concerns Grace United Meth. Ch., St. Louis, 1988—. Mem. ACLU, at. Dist. Atty. Assn., Mo. Assn. Prosecuting Atty. (treas. 1996-97, v.p. 1997-98), Met. St. Louis Bar Assn., Mound City Bar Assn., Kappa Alpha Theta. Democrat. Avocations: gardening, travel, scuba diving, cooking, reading. Office: St Louis Cir Atty 1320 Market St Rm 330 Saint Louis MO 63103-2774

JOYNER, JOHN BROOKS, museum director; b. Balt., Nov. 24, 1944; s. Joseph Brooks and Majel Ethel (Sanichas) J.; m. Marcia Lee Perkins, Apr. 5, 1966 (div. 1979); 1 child, Shelly Lyn; m. Georgina Louise Davis, May 1, 1982; children: Jonathan Burgess, Isabel Clare. BA, U. Md., 1966, MA, 1969; postgrad., NYU, 1968-71. Teaching asst. U. Md., College Pk., 1966-68, mus. fellow, 1969-70; adj. lectr. Hunter Coll., CUNY, NYC, 1970-71; curator Towson State U. Art Gallery, Towson, MD., 1972-74; dir., curator Nickle Arts Mus./U. Calgary, Alta., Can., 1975-80; lect. U. Alta., Edmonton, Can., 1980-83; exec. dir. South Bend (Ind.) Art Ctr., 1983-87; dir. Montgomery (Ala.) Mus. Fine Arts, 1987-93, Vancouver Art Gallery, 1993-96, The Gilcrease Mus., Tulsa, Okla., 1996—2001, Joslyn Art Mus., Omaha, 2001—. Grants reviewer Inst. Mus. Svcs., Washington, 1988-89; project dir. George Rickey in South Bend, 1983-85; founder/dir. Brooks Joyner Art Cons. Ltd., Calgary, Alta., Can., 1980-83. Author: Marion Nicol R.C.A., 1979, (exbn. catalogue) The Drawings of Arshile Gorky, 1969; contbr. articles to art mags. Sec. Cottage Hill Found., Montgomery, 1989; adv. Jr. League of Montgomery, 1988-89. Recipient fellowship NYU, 1969, Smithsonian Instn., Washington, 1972. Mem. Assn. Art Mus. Dirs., Am. Assn. Museums (small mus. adminstrs. com., accreditation reviewer 1989), Can. Art Mus. Dirs. Orgn., Internat. Coun. Museums. Republican. Avocations: gardening, tennis, jack russell terriers. Office: Joslyn Art Mus 2200 Dodge St Omaha NE 68102-1292 Office Phone: 402-342-3300.

JUDD, WILLIAM ROBERT, engineering geologist, educator; b. Denver, Aug. 16, 1917; s. Samuel and Lillian (Israelske) J.; m. Rachel Elizabeth Douglas, Apr. 18, 1942; children: Stephanie (Mrs. Chris Wadley), Judith (Mrs. John Soden), Dayna (Mrs. Erick Grandmason), Pamela, Connie. AB, U. Colo., 1941, postgrad., 1941-50. Registered profl. engr., Colo., engring. geologist, Oreg. Engring. geologist Colo. Water Conservation Bd., 1941-42; supervisory engring. geologist Denver & Rio Grande Western R.R., Colo. and Utah, 1942-44; head geology sect. No. 1, acting dist. geologist-Alaska U.S. Bur. Reclamation, Office of Chief Engr., Denver, 1945-60; head basing tech. group RAND Corp., Santa Monica, Calif., 1960—66; prof. rock mechanics Purdue U., Lafayette, Ind., 1966-87, head geotech. engring., 1976-86; tech. dir. Purdue U. Underground Excavation and Rock Properties Info. Center, 1972-79, prof. emeritus civil engring., 1988—. Geotech. cons., U.S., Mexico, Cuba, Honduras, Greece, 1950-; geoscience editor Am. Elsevier Pub. Co., 1967-71; chmn. panel on ocean scis. Com. on Instl. Cooperation, 1971-85; founder and chmn. Nat. Acad. Sci. U.S. Nat. Com. on Rock Mechanics, 1963-69, co-chmn. panel on rsch.

requirements, 1977-81, chmn. panel on awards, 1972-82; mem. U.S. Army Adv. Bd. on Mountain and Arctic Warfare, 1956-62, USAF Sci. Adv. Bd. Geophysics Panel Study Group, 1964-67; com. on safety dams NRC, 1977-78, 82-83; Nat. dir. Nat. Ski Patrol System, Inc., 1956-62; Alex du Toit Meml. lectr., S.Africa and Rhodesia, 1967; owner Rayanbill Galleries, 1986—2007. Author: (with E.F. Taylor) Ski Patrol Manual, 1956, (with D. Krynine) Principles of Engineering Geology and Geotechnics, 1957, Sitzmarks or Safety, 1960; editor: Rock Mechanics Research, 1966, State of Stress in the Earth's Crust, 1964; co-editor: Physical Properties of Rocks and Minerals, 1981; editor-in-chief: Engring. Geology, 1972-92, hon. editor, 1996-2008. Recipient Merit award U.S. Bur. Reclamation, 1957, Spl. Rsch. award NRC, 1982; named to Colo. Ski Hall of Fame, 1983; named hon. life mem. Nat. Ski Patrol System, Inc., 1988. Fellow ASCE, Geol. Soc. Am. (Disting. Practice award engring. geology divsn. 1989), South African Inst. Mining and Metallurgy; mem. Assn. Engring. Geologists (hon.), Internat. Assn. Engring. Geologists (Hans Cloos medal 1994), India Soc. Engring. Geology (life), Ind. Acad. Scis., U.S. Com. on Large Dams (exec. coun. 1977-83, com. on earthquakes 1976-90), U.S. Ski Assn. (hon. life), U.S. Recreational Ski Assn. (hon. life). Home and Office: 1051 Cumberland Ave West Lafayette IN 47906 Office Phone: 765-464-2255. Personal E-mail: williamjudd@verizon.net.

JUDGE, BERNARD MARTIN, retired editor, publishing executive; b. Chgo., Jan. 6, 1940; s. Bernard A. and Catherine Elizabeth (Halloran) J.; m. Kimbeth A. Wehrli, July 9, 1966; children: Kelly, Bernard R., Jessica. Reporter City News Bur., Chgo., 1965-66, editor, gen. mgr., 1983-84; reporter Chgo. Tribune, 1966-70, city editor, 1974-79, asst. mng. editor met. news, 1979-83; assoc. editor Chgo. Sun-Times, 1984-88; from editor to pub. Chgo. Daily Law Bull., 1988—2007, editor emeritus, 2007—; v.p. Law Bull. Pub. Co., Chgo., 1988—2007; pub. Chgo. Lawyer, 1989—2007. Bd. dir. Constnl. Rights Found., Chgo., 1992—, chmn. bd. dir., 1995-97; trustee Fenwick Cath. Prep. HS, Oak Park, Ill., 1989—; bd. dir. Abraham Lincoln Presdl. Libr. and Mus., 2004-06, Illinois First Amendment Ctr. Bd., 2004, chmn., 2007-Named to Chgo. Journalism Hall of Fame, 2000. Mem. Sigma Delta Chi. Home: 360 E Randolph St Apt 1905 Chicago IL 60601-7335 Office: Law Bull Pub Co 415 N State St Chicago IL 60610-4631 Office Phone: 312-644-7006.

JUDGE, JOHN, state legislator; m. Patty Judge, 1969; 3 children: Douglas, William Joseph. Farmer, cattleman; mem. Iowa Senate, Des Moines, 1999—, mem. agr. com., mem. local govt. com., mem. small bus., econ. devel. and tourism com., mem. transp. com. With USMC, Vietnam. Democrat. E-mail: john_judge@legis.state.ia.us.

JUDGE, NANCY ELIZABETH, obstetrician, gynecologist; b. Holyoke, Mass., May 21, 1951; d. Martin P. and Barbara Judge; m. David B. Wood, Oct. 30, 1982; children: David, William, Elizabeth, Meredith. AB, Smith Coll., 1973; MD, U. Mass., 1977. Intern Case Western Res. U./MetroHealth Med. Ctr., Cleve., 1977-78, resident, 1978-81; staff physician MetroHealth Med. Ctr. Case Western Res. U. Hosps., Cleve., 1981-90; dir. reproductive imaging ctr. Case Western Res. U. Hosps., 1990—, maternal-fetal medicine cons., 1990—. Asst. prof. reproductive biology Case Western Res. U., 1981—. Contbr. articles to profl. jours. Active Cleve. Art Mus., Playhouse Sq. Assn., Cleve. Garden Ctr. Fellow ACOG; mem. Cleve. Ob.-Gyn. Soc. (pres.).

JUDGE, PATTY JEAN, lieutenant governor, nurse; b. Fort Madison, Iowa, Nov. 2, 1943; m. John Judge; 3 children. Attended, U. Iowa; RN, Iowa Meth. Sch. Nursing, 1965. Lic. Real Estate Broker. Mediator Iowa Farmer Creditor Mediation Svc.; mem. Iowa State Senate, 1992—98, majority leader, 1994—98; sec. agr. State of Iowa, 1998—2007, lt. gov., 2007—. Agr. sec. US Home Land Security, Agrl. Sector Govt. Coordinating Coun.; mem. Senate Natural Resources Com., Ways and Means Com., Appropriations Com., Small Bus. and Econ. Devel. Com., Human Services Com. Mem., bd. dirs. Albia Area Chamber of Commerce; leader 4-H; mem. PEO, Iowa State Fair Bd.; parliamentarian Dem. Nat. Conv., 2000. Mem.: Nat. Assn. State Departments of Agr. (sec., chair, standing com. on agrl. security), Future Farmers of Am. Democrat. Office: Lieutenant Governor State Capitol Rm 9 Des Moines IA 50319 Office Phone: 515-281-0225. Office Fax: 515-281-6611.

JUENEMANN, SISTER JEAN, hospital executive; b. St. Cloud, Minn., Nov. 19, 1936; d. Leo A. and Teresa M. (Oster) J. Diploma, St. Cloud Sch. Nursing, 1957; student, Coll. St. Benedict, 1957-59; BSN cum laude, Seattle U., 1967; MHA, U. Minn., 1977. Dir. nursing svc. Queen of Peace Hosp., New Prague, Minn., 1963-65, 67-77, asst. adminstr., 1967-77, CEO, 1977—. Mem. bd. Bush Med. Fellows Program; spkr. at confs. Chmn. Cmty. Com. Prevention Chem. Abuse, New Prague, 1975-80; bd. dirs. St. Cloud (Minn.) Hosp., St. Benedict's Coll., St. Joseph, Minn. Recipient Disting. Svc. award Minn. Hosp. & Health Assn., 1996; Bush Found. Summer fellow Cornell U., U. Calif., Berkeley, 1982. Fellow Am. Coll. Healthcare Execs.; mem. AAUW (past pres. New Prague chpt.), Am. Hosp. Assn. (CEO of Yr. 1989), Soc. Health Care Planning & Mktg., Cath. Hosp. Assn., Women's Health Leadership Trust, New Prague Opportunities, Rotary (pres. New Prague chpt. 1994-95, asst. gov. dist. 1998-99), Sigma Theta Tau. Fax: (612) 758-5009. E-mail: Sjean@qofp.org.

JUERGENS, GEORGE IVAR, history professor; b. Bklyn., Mar. 20, 1932; s. George Odegaard and Magnhild (Julin) J.; m. Bonnie Jeanne Brownlee; children: Steven Erik, Paul Magnus. BA, Columbia Coll., 1953; BA, MA, Oxford U., 1956; PhD, Columbia U., 1965. Instr. Dartmouth Coll., Hanover, NH, 1962-65; asst. prof. Amherst (Mass.) Coll., 1965-67; assoc. prof. Ind. U., Bloomington, 1967-80, prof. history, 1980—. Cons. Nat. Endowment Humanities, Washington, 1971— Author: Joseph Pulitzer and the New York World, 1966, News From The White House, 1981; assoc. editor: Jour. Am. History, 1968-69. With U.S. Army, 1956-58. Recipient Disting. Teaching award Amoco Found., 1982; Kellett fellow Columbia U., 1954-56; sr. faculty fellow Nat. Endowment Humanities, 1971-72; fellow Rockefeller Found., 1981-82 Mem. AAUP, Orgn. Am. Historians, Phi Beta Kappa Home: 2111 E Meadow Bluff Ct Bloomington IN 47401-6885 Office: Ind U Dept History Bloomington IN 47405 Business E-Mail: juergens@indiana.edu.

JUGENHEIMER, DONALD WAYNE, advertising executive, communications educator, academic administrator; b. Manhattan, Kans., Sept. 22, 1943; s. Robert William and Mabel Clara (Hobert) J.; m. Bonnie Jeanne Scamehorn, Aug. 30, 1970 (dec. 1983); 1 child, Beth Carrie; m. Kaleen B. Brown, July 25, 1987. BS in Advt., U. Ill.-Urbana, 1965, MS in Advt., 1968, PhD in Communications, 1972. Advt. copywriter Fillman & Assocs, Champaign, Ill., 1963-64, 66; media buyer Leo Burnett Co., Chgo., 1965-66; asst., assoc. prof. U. Kans., Lawrence, 1971-80, prof. journalism, dir. grad. studies and rsch., 1980-85; Manship prof. journalism La. State U., Baton Rouge, 1985-87; prof., chmn. dept. communications and speech Fairleigh Dickinson U., Teaneck, NJ, 1987-89, 92-95, dean coll. liberal arts, 1989-92; chair dept. English, lang. and philosphy, 1995; prof. Sch. Journalism So. Ill. U., Carbondale, 1995—2005; prof., chair dept. advt. Coll. Mass Comm. Tex. Tech U., 2005—. Dir. Sch. Journalism So. Ill. U., Carbondale, 1995-2002; adj. faculty Turku (Finland) Sch. Econs., 1999—; adv. cons. U.S. Army, Fort Sheridan, Ill., Pentagon, Washington, 1981-90, Am. Airlines, 1989-91, IBM Corp., 1989—, U.S. Dept. Def.; cons. editor Grid Publ., Columbus, Ohio, 1974-84; grad. and rsch. dir. U. Kans., 1978-84, adv. chmn., 1974-78; adj. prof. Turku (Finland) Sch. Econs. and Bus. Adminstrn., 1998—. Author: Advertising Media Sourcebook and Workbook, 1975, 3d edit., 1989, 4th edit. 1996, Strategic Advertising Decisions, 1976, Basic Advertising, 1979, 2d edit., 1991, Advertising Media, 1980, Problems and Practices in Advertising Research, 1982, Advertising Media: Strategy and Tactics, 1992, Advertising Media Planning: A Brand Management Approach, 2004,2008, Advertising Media Workbook and Sourcebook, 2005, 2008, Advertising Account Planning: A Practical Approach, 2006; bd. editors Jour. Advt., 1985-89, Jour. Interactive Advt., 2000—, Jour. Current Issues and Rsch. in Advt., 1990—. Subscription mgr. Jour. of Advt., 1971-74, bus. mgr., 1974-79; chmn. Univ. divsn. United Fund, Lawrence, 1971-72; pres. Sch.-Cmty. Rels. Coun., Lawrence, 1974-75. Recipient Hope Tchg. award U. Kans, 1977, 78, Kellogg Nat. fellow W.K. Kellogg Found., 1984-88; named Outstanding Young Men in Am. Nat. Jaycees, 1978. Mem. AAUP, Am. Acad. Advt. (pres. 1984-86, exec. dir. 2004-2008), Assn. Edn. in Journalism (head advt. divsn. 1977-78), Kappa Tau Alpha, Alpha Delta Sigma. Presbyterian. Avocations: skiing, sailing, writing, travel, reading. Office: Coll Mass Comm Tex Tech Univ Box 43082 Lubbock TX 79409-3082 Home: 4015 69t St Lubbock TX 79413 Home Phone: 806-788-0607; Office Phone: 806-742-3385 276. Business E-Mail: donald.jugenheimer@ttu.edu.

JUHL, DANIEL LEO, manufacturing and marketing firm executive; b. Sioux City, Iowa, Aug. 18, 1935; s. Burnett Andrew and Margret Anne (Osinger) J.; m. Colleen Ann Eagan, Dec. 20, 1958; children: Gregory, Michael, Jennifer. Student, U. S.D., 1956; BSME, UCLA, 1959; postgrad., Harvard U., 1976. Design engr. Edler Industries, Newport Beach, Calif., 1959-61; v.p. mfg. Raybestos-Manhattan Corp. (now Rayteck Corp.), Trumbull, Conn., Can. and Europe, 1961-80; v.p. ops. Easco/KD Tools, Lancaster, Pa., 1980-83; mgr. ops. S.K. Wellman Corp., Bedford Heights, Ohio, 1983-86; gen. mgr. N.Am. Systems, Bedford Heights, 1986; indsl. mgmt. cons., 1987; pres., chief exec. officer Stanhope Products Co., Brookville, Ohio, 1987-2000, Nat. Extrusions Co., Bellefontaine, Ohio, 1987—, athan Hale Furniture Co., 1987-2000; pres., CEO DJ Ventures Inc., Centerville, Ohio, 2000—. Contbr. numerous articles to trade jours.; patentee high temperature lightweight plastic insulation, molecular sieve used in auto air conditioning. Fund raiser United Way, 1980-2000. Mem. Soc. Automotive Engrs. (chmn. com. 1987), Soc. Plastics Industry, Elks. Avocations: travel, sports, woodworking.

JULIEN, CATHERINE, history professor; b. Palo Alto, Calif., May 19, 1950; d. Robert K. and Jean (Blaine) Julien; 1 child, Clara E.P. BA in Anthropology, U. Calif., Berkeley, 1971, MA in Anthropology, 1975, PhD in Anthropology, 1978. Dir. mus. programs Courthouse Mus., Merced, Calif.; lectr. and internat. study tour leader Smithsonian's Am. Mus. Natural History and Calif. Alumni Assn.; instr. Calif. State U., U. Bonn (Germany), U. Calif., Berkeley; assoc. prof. history We. Mich. U., Kalamazoo, 1996—. Author: Reading Inca History (Erminie Wheeler-Voegelin prize, 2000, Katherine Singer Kovacs prize MLA); contbr. articles to profl. jours. Fellow, John Simon Guggenheim Meml. Found., 2003. Mem.: Phi Beta Kappa. Office: We Mich U Dept History 4354 Friedmann Hall Kalamazoo MI 49008-5334 Office Phone: 269-387-4632. Office Fax: 269-387-4651. E-mail: catherine.julien@wmich.edu.

JULIEN, THOMAS THEODORE, religious denomination administrator; b. Arcanum, Ohio, June 27, 1931; s. Russel Ray and Clara (Cassel) J.; m. Doris Mardella Briner, Aug. 21, 1953; children: Becky Jean, Terry Lee, Jacqueline Sue. BA, Bob Jones U., 1953; MDiv, Grace Theol. Sem., Winona Lake, Ind., 1957, DD (hon.), 1996; cert. French lang., U. Grenoble, France, 1960. Ordained to ministry Fellowship of Grace Brethren Chs., 1956. Pastor Grace Brethren Ch., Ft. Wayne, Ind., 1955-58; missionary Grace Brethren Fgn. Missions, Grenoble, 1959-64, field supt. Macon, France, 1964-78, dir. for Europe, 1964-86; exec. dir. Grace Brethren Internat. Missions, Winona Lake, 1986-2000. Author: Handbook for Young Christians, 1959, Inherited Wealth, 1976, Spiritual Greatness, 1979, Seize the Moment, 2000, Antioch Revisited, 2006. Decorated chevalier de Republique (Ctrl. African Republic). Home: 545 S Circle Dr Warsaw IN 46580 Office: Grace Brethren Internat Missions PO Box 588 Winona Lake IN 46590-0588 Office Phone: 574-268-1888. Personal E-mail: tjulien@gbim.org.

JULIUS, STEVO, internist, physiologist, educator; b. Kovin, Yugoslavia, Apr. 15, 1929; came to U.S., 1965, naturalized, 1971; s. Dezider and Jelena (Engel) J.; m. Susan P. Durrant, Sept. 17, 1971; children: Nicholas, Natasha. MD, U. Zagreb, 1953, ScD, 1964; MD (hon.), U. Goteborg, Sweden, 1979. Intern, then resident in internal medicine Univ. Hosp., Zagreb, 1953-60, sr. instr. internal medicine, 1962-64; rsch. asst. U. Mich. Med. Sch., 1961-62, mem. faculty, 1965—, prof. internal medicine, 1974—, assoc. prof. physiology, 1980-83, prof. physiology, 1983-98, chief divsn. hypertension, 1974-99, Frederick G.L. Huetwell prof. hypertension, 1996—. Co-editor: The Nervous System in Arterial Hypertension, 1976; contbr. articles to med. jours. Fellow Am. Coll. Cardiology; mem. Internat. Soc. Hypertension (v.p., Astra award 1984, established Stevo Julius award, 2000), Am. Heart Assn. (couns. high blood pressure rsch. and epidemiology, life achievement award coun. for high blood pressure 1994), Am. Physiol. Soc. (adv. bd.), Am. Fedn. Clin. Rsch., Soc. Exptl. Biology and Medicine, Coun. for High Blood Pressure Rsch. (adv. bd.). Office: Univ Mich Med Sch Sect Hypertension 3918 Taubman Ctr Ann Arbor MI 48109-0356

JUNEWICZ, JAMES J., lawyer; b. Oct. 1, 1950; s. John and Genevieve J.; m. Virginia Bornyas. BS, Georgetown U., 1972; JD, Duquesne U., 1976; LLM, NYU, 1978. Bar: Pa. 1977, D.C. 1978, Ill. 1984. Asst. gen. counsel SEC, Washington, 1982—84; ptnr. Mayer, Brown, Rowe & Maw LLP, Chgo., 1987—2007, Winston & Strawn LLP, Chgo., 2007—. Office: Winston & Strawn LLP 35 W Wacker Dr Chicago IL 60601 Office Phone: 312-558-5600, 312-558-5257.

JUNG, HOWARD J., retail executive; Chmn. Ace Hardware Corp., Oak Brook, Ill. Office: Ace Hardware Corp 2200 Kensington Ct Oak Brook IL 60523

JUNGE, MICHAEL KEITH, lawyer; b. Fargo, ND, June 17, 1956; s. Herman Keith Jr. and Helen Beatrice (Perschke) J.; m. Ember Reighgott, Oct. 23, 1993. BA, St. Olaf Coll., 1978; JD, William Mitchell Coll., 1982. Bar: U.S. Dist. Ct. Minn. 1986. Asst. atty. McLeod County, Glencoe, Minn., 1982-87, county atty., 1987—. Instr. St. Olaf Coll., Northfield, Minn., 1993. Mem. Minn. County Atty. Assn. (treas. 1994-95), 8th Dist. Bar Assn. (pres. 1993-94). Office: McLeod County Atty 830 11th St E Ste 214 Glencoe MN 55336-2200

JURA, JAMES J., electric utility executive; b. Creston, Nebr., Dec. 9, 1942; s. Joseph James and Edna Helena (Mackenstadt) J.; m. Sylvia; children: Joseph, James, John, Fredericka. BA, U. Wash., Seattle, 1967; MBA, Seattle U., 1971; postgrad., Harvard U., 1985. With indsl. rels. staff Boeing Co., Seattle, 1968-71; with policy devel. staff OSHA, Washington, 1971-73; legis. and budget analyst Office Mgmt. and Budget, Washington, 1973-78; asst. adminstr. Bonneville Power Adminstrn., U.S. Dept. Energy, Washington, 1978-80, from exec. asst. adminstr. to adminstr. Portland, Oreg., 1980-91; CEO, gen. mgr. Assoc. Electric Coop. Inc., Springfield, Mo., 1991—. Bd. dirs. Assn. Mo. Elec. Coops., Mo. Employers Mut. Ins. Co. With US Army, 1963-65. Republican. Office: Associated Electric Coop PO Box 754 Springfield MO 65801-0754 Office Phone: 417-881-1204. Business E-Mail: jjura@aeci.org.

JURGENSEN, WILLIAM G., insurance company executive; BS in Fin., Creighton U., Omaha, Nebr., MBA. Exec. v.p. Norwest Corp.; corp. banking officer Norwest Investment Svcs., pres., CEO; mgmt. First Chicago NBD Corp.; exec. v.p. Bank One Corp.; CEO Nationwide Mutual Ins., 2000—, Nationwide Fin. Svcs., 2000—. Fin. Svcs. Roundtable; Ohio Bus. Roundtable; Columbus Downtown Develop. Corp.; Columbus Partnership; vice chmn., trustee Loyola U., Chgo.; trustee Newberry Libr.; bd. dir. Greater Columbus C. of C., Law Enforcement Found. Ohio, Columbus Children's Hosp.; chair Governor's Commn. on Teaching Success, 2001—03. Office: ationwide Ins 1 Nationwide Plz Columbus OH 43215

JURS, PETER B., lawyer; b. Toledo, Aug. 8, 1972; BA, Miami U., 1994; JD, U. Cin., 1997. Bar: Ohio 1997, US Ct. of Appeals Sixth Cir. 1998, US Dist. Ct. Southern Dist. Ohio 1999, Ky. 2000. Law clerk Hon. James G. Carr, US Dist. Judge, Western Divsn., Northern Dist. Ohio, 1997—98; assoc. Rendigs, Fry, Kiely & Dennis L.L.P, Cin. Named one of Ohio's Rising Stars, Super Lawyers, 2006. Mem.: Ohio Assn. Civil Trial Attorneys, Def. Rsch. Inst., Northern Ky. Bar Assn., ABA, Ky. Bar Assn., Ohio State Bar Assn., Cin. Bar Assn. Office: Rendigs Fry Kiely & Dennis LLP 1 W Fourth St Ste 900 Cincinnati OH 45202 Office Phone: 513-381-9369. Office Fax: 513-381-9206.

JUST, DAVID GLEN, savings and loan association executive; b. Oskaloosa, Iowa, Feb. 10, 1944; s. Alvin E. and Ada L. (Hasty) J.; m. Barbara Ann Mahan; children: Michelle M. Just Grady, David G., Heather L. Just Jenkins. Dipl., Am. Inst. of Bus., Des Moines, 1963. CPA, Iowa. Acct. Daniel Gardiner, CPA, Des Moines, 1967-70, Alexander Grant & Co., Des Moines, 1970-71; account mgr. Fed. Home Loan Bank, Des Moines, 1971-77; pres. The Cameron Savs. & Loan Assn., Cameron, Mo., 1977—; Pres & CEO Cameron Fin. and Cameron Savs. Cameron Fin. Corporation, Cameron, MO. V.p., dir. Del Lago Resort and Conf. Ctr., Montgomery, Tex., 1990—. Treas. Cameron Econ. Devel. Corp., 1990—, Com. to Promote Cameron, 1986-90. With USAF, 1963-67; bd. dirs. Cameron Community Hosp., 1983—; pres. Prince of Peace Luth. Ch., 1978-84, 1990—. Mem. Mo. League of Savs. Instns. (dir. 1988-90), Lions (pres., dir.). Democrat. Lutheran. Avocations: golf, hobby farming. Office: Cameron Fin Corp 1304 N Walnut St Cameron MO 64429-1327

JUSTEN, RALPH, museum director; b. Milw., Mar. 10, 1952; Exec. dir. Nat. R.R. Mus., Green Bay, Wis., 1997—. Office: Nat RR Mus 2285 S Broadway Green Bay WI 54304-4832 E-mail: rjjusten@nationalrrmuseum.org.

JUSTICE, BRADY RICHMOND, JR., medical services executive; b. Albertville, Ala., Dec. 26, 1930; s. Brady R. and Kate (McEachern) J.; m. Sandra Gearner, Dec. 29, 1956; children: David, Michael, Lori Blankenship, Kathryn Justice. BBA, Baylor U., 1953. CPA, Ind. Ptnr. Arthur Andersen & Co., Dallas, 1953-64, Indpls., 1964-72; exec. v.p. Basic Am. Industries, Inc., Indpls., 1972-83; pres. Basic Am. Med., Inc., Indpls., 1983-92; sr. v.p. Columbia Hosp. Corp., 1992-93; chmn. Heritage Capital Corp., Indpls., 1993—. Mem. Columbia Club, Lions (pres. Indpls. chpt.). Republican. Baptist. Office: Heritage Capital Corp 6900 Gray Rd Indianapolis IN 46237-3209

KABARA, JON JOSEPH, biochemical pharmacology educator; b. Chgo., Nov. 26, 1926; s. John Stanley and Mary Elizabeth (Wielgus) K.; m. Virginia Christie (dec. 1974); children: Christie Anne, Mary K., Sheila Jon, Pat Lee; m. Annette Elser Sproull (dec. 1986), children: Timothy, Steven; m. Betty Z. Tabor, 1992. BS, St. Mary's Coll., Minn., 1948; MS, U. Miami, 1950; PhD (Univ. scholar), U. Chgo., 1959. Prof. chemistry U. Detroit, 1957-68; prof., assoc. dean Mich. Coll. Osteo. Medicine, Pontiac, 1967-70; prof. assoc. dean pharmacology Mich. State U., E. Lansing, 1970-71, prof. biomechanics, 1971-89, prof. emeritus, 1989; dir. research and devel. Med.-Chem. Labs., Galena, Ill., 1950—, Kabe Realtor, 1986—; pres. div. research and devel. Galena's Kitchen Chemist, 1989—, Tech. Exch. Inc., 1989; co-owner, pres., dir. R&D Lil Gen. Miniature Golf Course, Galena, Ill., 1996—. Cons. in neurochemistry and microbiology. Contbr. over 200 articles to profl. jours.; editor: Cosmetic Preservation Preservative-Free Cosmetic & Drug Formulations and Korkies Cookbook, other books on lipid pharmacology; U.S. and fgn. patentee in field. Pres. Mich. NE PTA, 1959; active Little League, 1973-75. Damon Runyon Cancer fellow, 1949-50; Mt. Sinai fellow, 1949-51; Bishop Heffron awardee St. Mary's Coll., 1970; named Man of Year St. George High Sch. Alumni Club, 1970; recipient Disting. Alumni award 50th Anniversary, St. Mary's U., Minn., 1998. Fellow Am. Inst. Chemists; mem. Am. Oil Chem. Soc., N.Y. Acad. Sci., Detroit Physiology Soc., Assn. Analytical Chemists, AAAS, Am. Soc. Clin. Pathologists, Sigma Xi, other orgns.

KABAT, LINDA GEORGETTE, civic leader; b. Cleve., Nov. 26, 1951; d. Michael G. and Georgette (deVos) Paul; m. John Edward Kabat Jr., Apr. 23, 1977; 1 child, Susan Marie. Student, Cleve. Inst. Music, 1969-72. With sales dept. Higbee Co., Fairview Park, Ohio, 1972; customer svc. rep. Ashland Chem. Co., Cleve., 1972-74, Celanese Corp., Lakewood, Ohio, 1974-76; with sales dept. May Co., North Olmsted, Ohio, 1979; customer svc. rep. Diamond Shamrock Corp., Cleve., 1979-82; in sales May Co., North Olmsted, 1989-97; with Concepts Direct, Longmont, Colo., 1999—2004, Sopris West Ednl. Svcs., 2006—07. Chpt. pres. Cath. War Vets. Aux., Cleve., 1973-75, pres. Ohio, 1975-77, nat. sec., 1977-79, state sec., 1991-92. Mem. Mu Phi Epsilon (pres. 1971-72, historian 1970-71). Republican. Avocations: camping, travel, needlecrafts, music.

KACEK, DON J., management consultant; b. Berwyn, Ill., May 4, 1936; s. George J. and Rose (Krizik) K.m. Carolyn K. Hiner, July 22, 1961; children: Scott M., Stacey M. BSME, Ill. Inst. Tech., 1958. Engring. sect. mgr. Sunstrand Corp., Rockford, Ill., 1958-72; group v.p. Kysor Indsl. Corp., Cadillac, Mich., 1972-76; dir. product devel. Ransburg Corp., Indpls., 1976-77, pres., 1977-88, CEO, chmn. bd. dirs., 1978-88; mgmt. cons. Indpls., 1988—; owner, chmn. bd. dirs. Advanced Automation Techs., Inc., Indpls., 1989-2000. Bd. dirs. Arvin Meritor Industries, Inc., Troy, Mich. Inventor Burn Rate Control Valve, 1966. With AUS, 1960. Recipient Sagamore of the Wabash award Gov. Ind., 1985. Home: 5 Augusta Ct Lake In The Hills IL 60156-4494

KACZKA, JEFF, trucking and relocation services executive; CFO I-Net, 1995—96, Wang, 1996—98, Allied Worldwide, Naperville, Ill., 1999—2001; sr. v.p., CFO Owens & Minor, Inc., Richmond, Va., 2001—07.

KACZMARCZYK, JEFFREY ALLEN, journalist, music and dance critic; b. Patuxent River Naval Air Base, Md., Jan. 7, 1963; s. Frank Joseph and Diane Catherine Kaczmarczyk; m. Cynthia L. Shimmel, Aug. 13, 1988; children: Jessica, Michael, David. BA, Western Mich. U., 1986; postgrad., Calif. State U. Editor-in-chief Western Herald, Kalamazoo, Mich., 1986-87; staff writer, acting editor Albion (Mich.) Recorder, 1987; staff writer, columnist Hastings (Mich.) Banner, 1987-92; arts writer, classical music critic The Grand Rapids (Mich.) Press., 1992—. Freelance arts writer, critic Kalamazoo (Mich.) Gazette, 1990-93; editor The Weekender, Hastings, 1991-93. Dir., sec. Thornapple Arts Coun., Hastings, 1992-97; dir. Grand Rapids Area Coun. for Humanities, 1995-2001; vestryman Emmanuel Episcopal Ch., Hastings, 1997-99, sr. warden, 1999. Episcopalian. Office: The Grand Rapids Press 155 Michigan St NW Grand Rapids MI 49503-2353 Home: 819 E Grant St Hastings MI 49058-1323 Home Phone: 269-945-3871; Office Phone: 616-222-5585. Business E-Mail: jkaczmarczyk@grpress.com.

KADANOFF, LEO PHILIP, physicist, educator; b. NYC, Jan. 14, 1937; s. Abraham and Celia (Kibrick) Kadanoff; children: Marcia, Felice, Betsy. AB, Harvard U., 1957, MA, 1958, PhD, 1960. Fellow Neils Bohr Inst., Copenhagen, 1960—61; from asst. prof. to prof. physics U. Ill., Urbana, 1961—69; prof. physics and engring., univ. prof. Brown U., Providence, 1969—78; prof. physics U. Chgo., 1978—82, John D. MacArthur Disting. Service prof., 1982—2004, prof. emeritus, 2004—. Mem. tech. com. R.I. Planning Program, 1972—78, mem. human svcs. rev. com., 1977—78; pres. Urban Obs. R.I., 1972—78. Author: Electricity Magnetism and Heat, 1967; co-author: Quantum Statistical Mechanics, 1963; adv. bd. Sci. Year, 1975—79, editl. bd. Statis. Physics, 1972—79, Nuc. Physics, 1980—. Recipient Wolf prize in physics, Wolf Found., Israel, 1980, Boltzmann medal, Internat. Union Pure and Applied Physics, 1990, Grande Medaille d'Or, Acad. Scis. Inst. France, 1998, Nat. Medal Sci., 1999; fellow NSF, 1957—61, Sloan Found., 1963—67. Fellow: AAAS, Am. Acad. Arts and Scis., Am. Phys. Soc. (Buckley prize 1977, Onsager prize 1998); mem.: NAS, Am. Philosophical Soc. Home: 5421 S Cornell Ave Apt 15 Chicago IL 60615-5678 Office: U Chgo James Franck Inst 5640 S Ellis Ave Chicago IL 60637-1433

KAESBERG, PAUL JOSEPH, virology researcher; b. Engers, Germany, Sept. 26, 1923; came to U.S., 1926, naturalized, 1933; s. Peter Ernst and Gertrude (Mueller) K.; m. Marian Lavon Hanneman, June 13, 1953; children— Paul Richard, James Kevin, Peter Roy. BS in Engring, U. Wis., Madison, 1945, PhD in Physics, 1949; D. atural Scis. (hon.), U. Leiden, The Netherlands, 1975. Instr. biometry and physics U. Wis., 1949-51, asst. prof. biochemistry, 1956-58, assoc. prof., 1958-60, prof., 1960-63, prof. biophysics and biochemistry, 1963—, Beeman prof. biophysics and biochemistry, 1983-87, chmn. Biophysics Lab., 1970-88, Wis. Alumni Research Found. prof., 1981—, Beeman prof. molecular virology and biochemistry, 1987-90, prof. emeritus, 1990. Cons. in field. Contbr. chapts. to books and articles to profl. jours. Mem. NAS, Am. Soc. Virology (pres. 1987-88). Office: U Wis Inst Molecular Virology 1525 Linden Dr Madison WI 53706-1534 Home: 6205 Mineral Pt Rd Apt 803 Madison WI 53705-4581 Personal E-mail: pjkaes@aol.com.

KAFARSKI, MITCHELL I., chemical processing company executive; b. Detroit, Dec. 15, 1917; s. Ignacy A. and Anastasia (Drzazgowski) Kafarski; m. Zofia Drozdowska, July 11, 1967; children: Erik Michael, Konrad Christian. Student, U. Detroit, 1939-41, Shrivenham Am. U., Eng., 1946. Process engr. Packard Motor Car Co., Detroit, 1941-44; organizer, dir. Artist and Craftsman Sch., Esslingen, Germany, 1945-46; with Nat. Bank of Detroit, 1946-50; founder, pres. Chem. Processing Inc., Detroit, 1950-65, also bd. dirs.; chmn. bd., pres., treas. Aactron Inc., Madison Heights, Mich., 1965—; chmn. bd., pres. Imtech of Mich., Inc., 1988-92. Treas. Detroit Magnetic Insp. Co., 1960-65; also dir.; v.p. KMH Inc., Detroit, 1960-64; also dir.; treas. Packard Plating Inc., Detroit, 1962-67, also dir. Commr. Mich. State Fair, 1965-72; mem. com. devel. and planning to build Municipal Stadium State of Mich., 1965-88; benefactor, mem. Founders Soc., Detroit Inst. Arts, 1965—; trustee Founders' Soc., Detroit Inst. Arts, 1982-90; sponsor, host world celebrity for World Preview Mich., 1965-66; mem. dist. adv. council SBA, 1971-73; del. White House Conf. on Aging, 1971; organizer, treas. Mich. Reagan for Pres. Com., 1980; treas. Straith Meml. Hosp., Southfield, Mich., 1972—, chmn. bd., 1976; trustee Mich. Opera Theater, 1982—; bd. dirs. Gilbert and Sullivan Light Opera Soc., Palm Beach, Fla., 1985—; White House rep. to opening of first U.S. Trade Center, Warsaw, Poland, 1972; chmn. fund-raising Bloomfield Arts Assn., Birmingham, Mich., 1973-74; mem. Space Theatre Consortium, Inc., Seattle, 1981-83; bd. regents Orchard Lake (Mich.) Schs., 1981-83; Vice chmn. Republican State Nationalities Council Mich., 1969-73; bd. dirs. Bloomfield Arts Assn., 1973-84, Friends of Kresge Library, Oakland U., 1973-86; presdl. appointee bd. dirs. U.S.A. Pennsylvania Ave. Devel. Corp., Washington, 1973-81; chmn. bd. Straith Meml. Hosp., Detroit, 1971—, Detroit Sci. Center, 1972—, corp. dir.; mem. Internat. Soc. Palm Beach; trustee Greater Palm Beach Symphony, 1986; mem. Citizen's Commn. to Improve Mich. Cts., 1986-88; contbr. Kravis Ctr. for Performing Arts, West Palm Beach, 1989; mem. Bus. Com. for the Arts, Palm Beacvh, 1991—. Served with AUS, 1944-46, ETO. Recipient Nat. award for war prodn. invention War Prodn. Bd., 1943; decorated knight's Cross Order of Poland's Rebirth Restituta, 1975, chevalier Chaine des Rotisseurs, 1982, Knight of Malta Order of St. John. Mem. Nat. Assn. Metal Finishers, Mich. Assn. Metal Finishers (dir., chmn. bd. 1976), N.A.M., Am. Electroplaters Soc., Cranbrook Acad. Arts, Am.-Polish Action Coun. (chmn. 1971-76), Am. Assn. Mus. (treas. Detroit), Poinciana Club, Village Club. Clubs: Capitol Hill (Washington); Detroit Athletic. Home: 21 Kingsley Manor Ct Bloomfield Hills MI 48304-3520 Office: Aactron Inc 29306 Stephenson Hwy Madison Heights MI 48071-2394 Office Phone: 248-642-2730.

KAFFER, ROGER LOUIS, bishop emeritus; b. Joliet, Ill., Aug. 14, 1927; s. Earl Louis and Helen Ruth (McManus) K. BA, St. Mary of the Lake, Mundelein, Ill., 1950, STB, 1952, MA, 1953, licentiate in sacred theology, 1954; licentiate of canon law, Pontifical Gregorian U., Rome, 1958; D of Pastoral Ministry, St. Mary of the Lake, Mundelein, Ill., 1983; MEd, DePaul U., 1965; LHD (hon.), Felician Coll., 1986; DHL (hon.), Coll. St. Francis, 1990; doctorate (hon.), Lewis U., 1990. Ordained priest Diocese of Joliet, Ill., 1954, eccles. notary, 1954—56, asst. chancellor, 1958—65; ordained bishop, 1985; aux. bishop Diocese of Joliet, 1985—2002, aux. bishop emeritus, 2002—, vicar gen., vicar for clergy, 1985—2004; rector St. Charles Borromeo Sem., Lockport, Ill., 1965—70; prin. Providence HS, New Lenox, Ill., 1970—85; rector Cathedral of St. Raymond, Joliet, 1985. Past. mem. Marriage Tribunal, Diocesan Sem. Bd., Diocesan Bd. Religious Edn. Named Cleric of Yr., KC, 1973, Citizen of Yr., New Lenox Assn. Commerce, 1976, Man of Yr., Joliet Cath. High Alumni Assn., 1978, Citizen of Yr., UNICO, Joliet, 1996; recipient DeLa Salle medallion, Lewis U., 1984, Lifetime Achievement award, Joliet C. of C., 1999, award, Paluch Family Found., 2002. Mem.: Nat. Conf. Cath. Bishops Conf. Ill., KC (Ill. state chaplain 1993—). Roman Catholic. Avocations: youth work, retreat work. Office: 425 Summit St Joliet IL 60435-7155 Office Phone: 815-722-6606. Office Fax: 815-722-6602.*

KAFOURE, MICHAEL D., food products executive; married; 3 children. BS in Mgmt. and Adminstrn., Ind. U. Joined Campbell Taggart, 1967, pres., COO bakery ops., 1990; pres. Merico, Inc.; sr. v.p. Interstate Bakeries Corp., Kansas City, Mo., 1995, pres., COO, 1995—. Office: Interstate Bakeries Corp 12 E Armour Blvd Kansas City MO 64111

KAGAN, STUART MICHAEL, pediatrician; b. Milw., June 22, 1944; s. Harry and Bertha (Pittleman) K.; m. Gloria Jean Glass, Aug. 1, 1971; children: Jennifer Anne, Abigail Elizabeth. BS, U. Wis., 1966; MD, U. Utah, 1969; MPH, U. Kans., 1997. Diplomate Am. Bd. Pediat. Intern in pediats. Kans. U. Med. Ctr., Kansas City, 1969-70, resident in pediats., 1970-71, fellow in pediat. cardiology, 1971-73; pvt. practice Overland Park, Kans., 1975-88; occupational medicine physician Employer Health Svc., Kansas City, Mo., 1988—, med. rev. officer, 1994—, acting med. dir., 1994-99. Lt. comdr. USN, 1973-75. RecipientKans. Cardiology fellowship Kans. U. Med. ctr., 1972. Mem. Am. Coll. Occupational and Environ. Medicine, Am. Soc. Addiction Medicine, Great Plains Occupational and Environ. Medicine. Avocations: conservation, jogging, computers, astronomy. Office: Employer Health Services 9724 Legler Rd Lenexa KS 66219-1282

KAGEN, STEVEN L., congressman, physician; b. Appleton, Wis., Dec. 12, 1949; s. Marv Kagen; m. Gayle Kagen; 4 children. BS with honors in Molecular Biology, U. Wis., Madison, 1972, MD, 1976. Cert. Am. Bd. Internal Medicine, 1979, Am. Bd. Allergy & Immunology, 1981, diagnostic lab. immunology Am. Bd. Allergy & Immunology, 1988. Teamster Foremost Dairy; intern to resident internal medicine Northwestern U. Sch. Medicine, Chgo., 1976—79; fellow allergy/immunology Med. Coll. Wis., Milw., 1979—81; founder Kagen Allergy Clinics, Appleton, Wis., 1981—, Oshkosh, Wis., 1981—, Green Bay, Wis., 1986—, Fond du Lac, Wis., 1990—; consulting staff HCA Med. Ctr., Port St. Lucie, Fla., 1986—93; asst. clin. prof. allergy & clin. immunology dept. medicine Med. Coll. Wis., Milw.; active staff dept. medicine Mercy Med. Ctr., Oshkosh, Appleton Med. Ctr., Wis.; affiliate staff dept. medicine Bellin Hosp., Green Bay, Wis.; mem. US Congress from 8th Wis. dist., 2007—, mem. agr. com., transp. & infrastructure com. Bd. dirs. Joint Coun. Allergy, Asthma and Immunology 1988-1992, 1988—92; allergy cons. CNN, 1995—2002; dir. Nat. Pollen Network. Contbr. articles to med. jours. Named one of Best Drs. in Am., 1996—97; recipient Founder's award, Fox Cities Children's Mus., 1996, Children's Environ. Health Recognition award, EPA, 2005. Mem.: AMA, State Med. Soc. Wis., Wis. Allergy Soc., Am. Coll. Allergy, Asthma & Immunology, Am. Acad. Allergy, Asthma & Immunology (Pub. Outreach award 2004), Am. Meteorol. Soc. (assoc.). Democrat. Jewish. Achievements include patents in field. Office: 1232 Longworth House Office Bldg Washington DC 20515 also: 700 E Walnut St Green Bay WI 54301 Office Phone: 920-432-8800, 920-437-1954, 202-225-5665. Office Fax: 202-225-5729.

KAHALAS, HARVEY, business educator; b. Boston, Dec. 3, 1941; s. James and Betty (Bonfeld) K.; m. Dianne Barbara Levine, Sept. 2, 1963; children: Wendy Elizabeth, Stacy Michele. BS, Boston U., 1965; MBA, U. Mich., 1966; PhD, U. Mass., 1971. Data processing coord. Ford Motor Co., Wayne, Mich., 1963-66; lectr. Salem (Mass.) State Coll., 1966-68; asst. prof. bus. Worcester (Mass.) Poly. Inst., 1970-72; asst. prof. Va. Poly. Inst. and State U., Blacksburg, 1972-75, assoc. prof., 1975-77, SUNY, Albany, 1977-79, assoc. dean, 1979-81, dean, 1981-87, U. Mass., Lowell, 1989-94, Wayne State U., 1997—2005; prof. SUNY, Albany, 1979-89, U. Mass., Lowell, 1989-94, Wayne State U., 1997—; pres. HKE Inc., 1987-97; exec. dir. Ctr. Indsl. Competitiveness U. Mass., Lowell, 1990-94, Commonwealth disting. prof., 1994-97; dir. Ctr. for Bus. Rsch. and Competitiveness, U. Mass., Dartmouth, 1994-97; exec. dir. Inst. for Orgn. and Indsl. Competitiveness Wayne State U., 2001—. Program dir. Aspen Inst., 1994—97; exec. dir. Inst. Orgnl. and Indsl. Competitiveness Wayne State U., 2001—; bd. dirs. Lumigen Inc., Southfield, Mich.; cons. Aspen Inst./Fund for Corp. Initiatives, NYC, 1980—94, GE, Schenectady, NY, 1981—85, GM, Tarrytown, NY, 1987—89. Contbr. articles to profl. jours. Bd. dirs. Nat. Found. Ileitis and Colitis, Albany, NY, 1982—89, Fund for Corp. Initiatives, NYC, 1980—, Blue Cross Northeastern N.Y., Albany, 1983—89, Capital Dist. Bus. Rev., Albany, 1984—, Greater Detroit Area Health Coun., 1998—2001, Greater Detroit Conv. and Visitors Bur., 2001—. Named Disting. Alumni, U. Mass., 1982, Disting. Lectr. USIA, 1985, Am. Participant USIA, 1989; Fulbright scholar, 1987, 88, Aspen Inst. scholar, 1997. Mem. Fulbright Assn. (life), Acad. Mgmt. (treas. 1971-73, mem. exec. com.), Human Resource Planning Soc. (hon.), Human Resource Systems Profls. (hon.), Pers. Accreditation Inst. (life), Beta Gamma Sigma, Sigma Iota Epsilon, Delta Tau Kappa. Office: Wayne State Univ Sch Bus Adm 218 Prentis Bld 5201 Cass Ave Detroit MI 48202-3930

KAHAN, MITCHELL DOUGLAS, museum director; BA, U. Va., 1973; MA, Columbia U., 1975; M of Philosophy, CUNY, 1978, PhD, 1983. Mus. aide Nat. Mus. Am. Art, Washington, 1978; curator Montgomery Mus. Fine Art, Ala., 1978-82, N.C. Mus. Art, Raleigh, 1982-86; dir. Akron Art Mus., Ohio, 1986—. Cons. La. World's Exposition, New Orleans, 1983-84. Author: Art Inc.: American Paintings in Corporate Collections, 1979, Roger Brown, 1981, Minnie Evans, 1986, Art Since 1850-Akron Art Museum, 2001. Columbia U. fellow, 1973, Smithsonian Inst. fellow, 1976-78, CUNY grad. research fellow, 1978, Nat. Endowment for Arts fellow, 1987. Mem. Coll. Art Assn., Intermus Conservation Assn. (trustee 1986-95, pres. 1990-92, 95), Assn. Art Mus. Dirs. (trustee, 2004—), Akron Area Arts Alliance (pres. 2003-2004), Akron Roundtable (pres. 2001). Office: Akron Art Mus One South High Akron OH 44308 Office Phone: 330-376-9185 210. E-mail: hPine@akronartmuseum.org.

KAHAN, PAUL, chef; BS in Applied Math. and Computer Sci., No. Ill. U. Chef Metropolis, erwin, Frontera Grill/Topolobampo, Chgo.; owner, chef Blackbird, Chgo., 1997—. Named Best New Chef, Food & Wine, 1999. Office: Blackbird 619 W Randolph St Chicago IL 60606

KAHANA, EVA FROST, sociology educator; b. Budapest, Hungary, Mar. 21, 1941; came to U.S., 1957; d. Jacob and Sari Frost; m. Boaz Kahana, Apr. 15, 1962; children: Jeffrey, Michael. BA, Stern Coll., Yeshiva U., 1962; MA, CCNY, CUNY, 1965; PhD, U. Chgo., 1968; HLD (hon.), Yeshiva U., 1991. Nat. Inst. on Aging predoctoral fellow U. Chgo. Com. on Human Devel., 1963-66; postdoctoral fellow Midwest Council Social Research, 1968; with dept. sociology Washington U., St. Louis, 1967-71, successively research asst., research assoc., asst. prof.; with dept. sociology Wayne State U., Detroit, 1971-84, from assoc. prof. to prof., dir. Elderly Care Research Ctr., 1971-84; prof. Case Western Res. U., Cleve., 1984—, Armington Prof., 1989-90, chmn. dept. sociology, 1985—2005, dir. Elderly Care Research Ctr., 1984—, Pierce and Elizabeth Robson prof. humanities, 1990—. Cons. Nat. Inst. on Aging, Washington, 1976-80, NIMH, Washington, 1971-75. Co-author: (with E. Midlarsky) Altruism in Later Life, 1994, (with B. Kahous & L. Harel) Survivors of the Holocoust: Late Life Adaptation; editor: (with others) Family Caregiving Across the Lifespan, 1994; mem. editl. bd. Gerontologist, 1975-79, Psychology of Aging, 1984-90, Jour. Gerontology, 1990-94, Applied Behavioral Sci. Rev., 1992—, Annals Family Medicine, 2004-; contbr. articles to profl. jours., chpts. to books (recipient Pub.'s prize 1969). Bd. dirs. com. on aging Jewish Community Fedn., Cleve.; bd. dirs. Jewish Family and Children's Svc.; vol. cons. Alzheimer's Disease and Related Disorders Assn., Cleve. NIMH Career Devel. grantee, 1974-79, Nat. Inst. Aging Merit award grantee, 1989—; Mary E. Switzer Disting. fellow Nat. Inst. Rehab., 1992-93; recipient Arnold Heller award excellence in geriatrics and gerontology Menorah Park Ctr. for Aged, 1992, Diekhoff awrd for disting. grad. tchg., 2002; named Outstanding Gerontological Rschr. in Ohio, 1993, 2003, Outstanding Gerontol. Educator in Ohio, 2004. Fellow Assn. for Gerontology in Higher Edn., Gerontol. Soc. Am. (chair behavioral social sci. com. 1984-85, Disting. Mentorship award 1987, Polisher award 1997); mem. Am. Sociol. Assn. (coun. sect. on aging 1985-87, Disting. Scholar award sect. on aging and life course 1997, chair sect. on aging and life course, 2000-2001), Am. Social Assn., Soc. for Traumatic Stress, Wayne State U. Acad. Scholars (life), Sigma Xi. Avocations: reading, antiques, travel.

KAHLER, HERBERT FREDERICK, manufacturing executive; b. St. Augustine, Fla., Sept. 20, 1936; s. Herbert E. and Marie (Strieter) K.; m. Erika Rozsypal, May 16, 1964; children: Erik, Stephen, Christopher, Michael, Craig. AB, Johns Hopkins, 1958; LLB, Harvard U., 1961. Bar: N.Y. bar 1962. With Simpson, Thacher & Bartlett, NYC, 1961-65; sec., gen. counsel Insilco Corp., Meriden, Conn., 1965-70; pres., CEO W.H. Hutchinson & Son, Inc., Chgo., 1970-73, Miles Homes Co., Mpls., 1973-86; v.p., dir. Insilco Corp., 1979-88; pres. Kahler & Assocs., 1988—; pres., CEO Crown Fixtures, Inc., Plymouth, Minn., 1990—, Power Generation Svc., Inc., 1990—97, chmn., 1997—; pres., CEO Crown Tonka Calif., Inc., 2000—. Hon. consul Republic of Austria, 1998—. Bd. corporators Meriden Hosp., 1965-70, Harvard, 1970; bd. govs. Meriden/Wallingford Hosp., 1987; bd. dirs. St. Paul Chamber Orch., 1974-87, St. Paul Opera Assn., 1975-77, Minn. Opera Co., 1977-87. Lt., arty. AUS, 1962-64. Mem. ABA, Mpls. Club, Phi Beta Kappa. Office: Crown Fixtures Inc 10700 Highway 55 Ste 300 Plymouth MN 55441-6134 Office Phone: 763-541-1410.

KAHN, DOUGLAS ALLEN, law educator; b. Spartanburg, SC, Nov. 7, 1934; s. Max Leonard and Julia (Rich) K.; m. Judith Bleich, Sept. 24, 1959; m. Mary Briscoe, June 12, 1970; children— Margery Ellen, Jeffrey Hodges. BA, U. N.C., 1955; JD with honors, George Washington U., 1958. Bar: D.C. 1958, Mich. 1965, U.S. Ct. Appeals (D.C. cir.) 1958, U.S. Ct. Appeals (5th and 9th cirs.) 1959, U.S. Ct. Appeals (3d, 4th and 6th cirs.) 1960, U.S. Supreme Ct. 1963. Atty. Civil and Tax div. U.S. Dept. Justice, 1958-62; assoc. Sachs and Jacobs, Washington, 1962-64; prof. law U. Mich., Ann Arbor, 1964—, Paul G. Kauper Disting. prof., 1984—. Vis. prof. Stanford Law Sch., 1973, Duke Law Sch., 1977, Fordham Law Sch., 1980-81, U. Cambridge, 1996, Ave Maria Law Sch., 2008. Author: (with Gann) Corporate Taxation, 1989, (with Waggoner and Pennell) Federal Taxation of Gifts, Trusts and Estates, 1997, (with Lehman) Corporate Income Taxation, 2001, (with J. Kahn) Federal Income Tax, 2005, (with J. Kahn and T. Perris) Taxation of S Corporations, 2008; comment editor George Washington U. Law Rev., 1956-58; contbr. articles to profl. jours. Recipient Emil Brown Found. prize, 1969 Mem. ABA, Order of Coif. Republican. Jewish. Office: U Mich Law Sch 625 S State St Ann Arbor MI 48109-1215 Home Phone: 734-944-5546; Office Phone: 734-764-9341. Business E-Mail: dougkahn@umich.edu.

KAHN, EUGENE S., former department store chain executive; BA, CCNY, 1971. Asst. buyer Gimbels East, 1971-73, buyer, 1973-76; various merchandising positions Bamberger's, from 1976, sr. v.p., gen. mdse. mgr., 1984-88; group sr. v.p. Macy's Northeast, 1988-89, Macy's South/Bullock's, 1989-90; pres., CEO G. Fox divsn. May Dept. Stores, 1990-92, pres., CEO Filene's divsn., 1992-98, vice chmn. parent co. St. Louis, 1996-97, exec. vice chmn., 1997-98, pres., CEO, 1998-2001, chmn., CEO, 2001—05. Trustee Washington U., St. Louis; trustee, treas. Mary Inst./Country Day Sch., St. Louis.

KAHN, JAMES STEVEN, retired museum director; b. NYC, Oct. 14, 1931; 3 children. BS in Geology, CCNY, 1952; MS in Mineralogy, Pa. State U., 1954; PhD in Geol. Sci., U. Chgo., 1956. Instr. U. R.I., Kingston, 1957, asst. prof., 1958-60, research assoc. Narragansett Marine Lab., 1957-60; group leader U. Calif., Livermore, 1960-70; dept. head Physics Internat. Co., San Leandro, Calif., 1970-71; div. head geophysics U. Calif., Livermore, 1972—74, dep. assoc. dir. human resources, 1975-78, assoc. dir. nuclear testing, 1978-80, dep. dir. lab., 1980-87; pres., chief exec. officer, dir. Mus. Sci. and Industry, Chgo., 1987-97; retired, emeritus. Trustee Mus. Sci. and Industry; mem. math. scis. edn. bd. NAS, 1991-94; chmn. sci. adv. com. Gov. Ill., 1994-98; IMAX Corp. Co-author: Statistical Analysis in Geological Sciences, 1962; contbg. author: Microstructure, 1968; contbr. articles to sci. jours. Trustee Geol. Soc. Am. Found., 1997—, fellow Geol. Soc. Am.; bd. dirs. Franklin and Eleanor Roosevelt Inst., 1994-2001, Dubuque (Iowa) Art Inst., 1999-02, emeritus trustee Dubuque Mus. Art; rector sci. and medicine Lincoln Acad. Ill., 1994-2002; mem., vice-chmn. Bd. Natural Resources and Conservation, State of Ill. Centennial fellow Pa. State U. Coll. Earth and Mineral Scis., 1996. Mem.: Sigma Xi. Personal E-mail: jbkahn@mac.com.

KAHN, PHYLLIS, state legislator; b. Mar. 23, 1937; m. Don Kahn; two children. BA, Cornell U., 1957; PhD in Biophysics, Yale U., 1962; MPA, Harvard U., 1986. Dist. 59B rep. Minn. Ho. of Reps., St. Paul, 1972—. Former chmn. state dept. divsn. appropriations com., Minn. Ho. of Reps., former mem. econ. devel., agr., environ. and natural resources coms.; chmn. govt. op. com., state govt. fin. divsn. and edn.-higher edn. fin. divsn. coms. Home: 367 State Office Bldg Saint Paul MN 55155-0001 Office: Minn State Senate State Capitol Building Saint Paul MN 55155-0001

KAHRILAS, PETER JAMES, medical educator, researcher; b. Culver City, Calif., June 9, 1953; s. Peter Jerome and Leticia (Llorett) K.; m. Elyse Anne Lambiase, Mar. 30, 1984; children: Genevieve Anne, Ian James, Miranda Elyse. Student, Yale U., 1971-75, U. Rochester, NYC, 1975-79. Resident in medicine U. Hosp. of Cleve., 1979-82; fellow in gastroenterology Northwestern U., Chgo., 1982-84; rsch. fellow Med. Coll. of Wis., Milw., 1984-86; asst. prof. medicine Med. Coll. Wis., Milw., 1986—90, assoc. prof. medicine, 1990—95, prof. medicine, 1995—; chief gastroenterology Northwestrn U. Feinberg Sch. Medicine, Chgo., 1999—2006. Contbr. articles to profl. jours. NIH grantee, 1990—. Fellow ACP, Ctrl. Soc. for Clin. Rsch., Am. Coll. Gastroenterology; mem. Am. Gastroenterol. Assn., Am. Fedn. for Clin. Rsch., Am. Soc. for Clin. Investigation, Am. Motility Soc. Democrat. Home: 203 Columbia Ave Park Ridge IL 60068-4923 Office: Northwestern U 676 N St Clair Ste 1400 Chicago IL 60611 Home Phone: 847-823-4799; Office Phone: 312-695-4016. Business E-Mail: p-kahrilas@northwestern.edu.

KAHRL, ROBERT CONLEY, lawyer; b. Mt. Vernon, Ohio, June 2, 1946; s. K. Allin and Evelyn Sperry (Conley) K.; m. LaVonne Elaine Rutherford, July 12, 1969; children: Kurt Freeland, Eric Allin, Heidi Elizabeth. AB, Princeton U., 1968; MBA, JD, Ohio State U., 1975. Bar: Ohio 1975, U.S. Ct. Appeals (6th cir.) 1976, U.S. Dist. Ct. (no. dist.) Ohio 1977, U.S. Ct. Appeals (9th cir.) 1979, U.S. Ct. Appeals (fed. cir.) 1984, U.S. Ct. Appeals (D.C. cir.) 1986. Law clk. to presiding judge U.S. Ct. Appeals (6th cir.), Cleve., 1975—76; assoc. Jones, Day, Reavis & Pogue, Cleve., 1976—84, ptnr., 1985—; ptnr., practice leader intellectual property practice area Jones Day (formerly Jones, Day, Reavis & Pogue), Cleve., 1991—. Author: Patent Claim Construction, 2001—06. With USN, 1968—72. Mem. Ohio State Bar Assn. (chmn. emeritus intellectual property sect.), Am. Intellectual Property Law Assn., Order of Coif. Republican. Presbyterian. Home: 7624 Red Fox Trl Hudson OH 44236-1926 Office: Jones Day North Point 901 Lakeside Ave E Cleveland OH 44114-1190 Office Phone: 216-586-3939. E-mail: rckahrl@jonesday.com.

KAISER, ANN CHRISTINE, magazine editor; b. Milw., Apr. 7, 1947; d. Herbert Walter and Annette G. (Werych) Gohlke; m. Louis Dan Kaiser; children: Richard L., Michael D. BS in Journalism, Northwestern U., 1969. Reporter Waco (Tex.) Tribune-Herald, 1969-71; editor Country Woman, Greendale, Wis., 1971—, Taste of Home, Greendale, 1993—. Named among People of the Yr., Milw. Mag., 1998. Lutheran. Avocations: sailing, tennis, golf, travel. Office: Reiman Media Group 5400 S 60th St Greendale WI 53129-1404

KAISER, DANIEL HUGH, historian, educator; b. Phila., July 20, 1945; s. Walter Christian and Estelle Evelyn (Jaworsky) K.; m. Jonelle Marie Marwin, Aug. 10, 1968; children: Nina Marie, Andrew Eliot. AB, Wheaton Coll., 1967; AM, U. Chgo., 1970, PhD, 1977. Asst. prof. history U. Chgo., 1977-78, Grinnell (Iowa) Coll., 1979-84, assoc. prof., 1984-86, prof. history, 1986—, Joseph F. Rosenfield prof. social studies, 1984—, chair dept. history, 1988-90, 96-98. Mem. adv. bd. Soviet Studies in History, 1979-85; rsch. assoc. dept. Slavonic studies, vis. mem. Darwin Coll., Cambridge (Eng.) U., 1992-93; vis. prof. dept. Slavic langs. and lits. Ctr. for Medieval and Renaissance Studies, UCLA, 1996. Author: The Growth of the Law in Medieval Russia, 1980; editor: The Workers' Revolution in Russia, 1917, 1987; translator, editor: The Laws of Rus' Tenth to Fifteenth Centuries, 1992; co-editor: (with Gary Marker) Reinterpreting Russian History 860-1860s, 1994; editl. bd. Slavic Rev., 1996-2001; contbr. articles to profl. jours. Elder 1st Presbyn. Ch., Grinnell, 1985, 87-89. Fellow Ford Found., 1973-1974, Nat. Endowment Humanities, 1979, 92-93, 2000, John Simon Guggenheim Meml. Found., 1986, Fulbright-Hays Faculty Rsch. Abroad Found., 1986, Woodrow Wilson Internat. Ctr. Scholars, 1986, Internat. Rsch. Exchs. Bd. fellow to USSR/Russia, 1974-75, 78-79, 86, 93. Mem. Am. Assn. for Advancement Slavic Studies, Am. Hist. Assn., Early Slavic Studies Assn. (v.p. 1995-97, pres. 1997-99), Slavonic and East European Medieval Studies Group (U.K.), Study Group on 18th Century Russia (U.K.), 18th Century Russian Studies Assn, Early Slavic Studies Assn. (v.p. 1995-1997, pres. 1997-1999). Office: Grinnell Coll Dept History Grinnell IA 50112-1670 E-mail: kaiser@grinnell.edu.

KAISER, GORDON S., JR., lawyer; b. Lakewood, Ohio, 1948; BA, Baldwin-Wallace Coll., 1970; JD, Case Western Res. U., 1973. Bar: Ohio 1973, registered: US Dist. Ct. (No. Dist.) Ohio. Ptnr. Squire, Sanders & Dempsey, Cleve., chmn., Corp. Practice Group. Mem.: Order of Coif. Office: Squire Sanders & Dempsey 4900 Key Tower 127 Public Sq Ste 4900 Cleveland OH 44114-1304 Office Phone: 216-479-8681. Office Fax: 216-479-8780. Business E-Mail: gkaiser@ssd.com.

KAISER, MARTIN, editor-in-chief; b. Milw., Oct. 11, 1950; Sports editor Chicago Sun-Times; assoc. mng. editor Baltimore Sun; v.p. & mng. editor Milw. Journal Sentinel, 1994—97, sr. v.p. & editor, 1997—. Mem.: Am. Soc. Newspaper Editors (chmn. readership issues com. 2003—, treas. designate 2005—06, treas. 2006—07, bd. dir., sec. 2007—08). Office: Milwaukee Journal Sentinel PO Box 371 Milwaukee WI 53201-0371 Office Phone: 414-224-2345. E-mail: mkaiser@journalsentinel.com.*

KAKOS, GERARD STEPHEN, thoracic and cardiovascular surgeon; b. NYC, Mar. 15, 1943; s. Stephen George Kakos and Margaret Misouic; m. Diana Toon, Dec. 19, 1964; children: Stephanie Lynn, Anna Katherine, Kristin Margaret. BA, Ohio State U., 1963, MD, 1967. Bd. cert. Am. Bd. Surgery, Am. Bd. Thoracic Surgery; lic., Ohio. NIH rsch. fellow in cardiovasc. surgery Duke U. Med. Ctr., Durham, N.C., 1970-71; intern in surgery Coll. Medicine Ohio State U., Columbus, 1967-68, asst. resident in surgery Coll. Medicine, 1969-73, sr. resident in surgery Coll. Medicine, 1971-72, adminstrv. chief resident in surgery Coll. Medicine, 1971-72, chief resident thoracic & cardiovasc. surgery Coll. Medicine, 1972-73, from asst. prof. to assoc. prof. surgery Coll. Medicine, 1970-85, assoc. clin. prof. surgery Coll. Medicine, 1985—. Chief divsn. thoracic surgery dept. surgery Ohio State U., Columbus, 1984-86, assoc. dir. working party for therapy of lung cancer (Nat. Cancer Inst.), 1973-76. Contbr. numerous articles to med. jours. Bd. dirs. Franklin County chpt. Cen. Ohio Heart Assn., 1978, Columbus Sch. for Girls, 1993-95. Capt. U.S. Army, 1968-76. Fellow ACS; mem. AMA, Internat. Soc. for Surgery, Am. Assn. Thoracic Surgery, Soc. for Vascular Surgery, Soc. Thoracic Surgery, Assn. for Acad. Surgery, Ohio State Med. Assn., Ohio State U. Hosps. Med. Soc., Columbus Surg. Soc., Acad. Medicine of Columbus and Franklin County, R. M. Zollinger Club, Alpha Epsilon Delta, Alpha Omega Alpha, Sigma Xi (Ohio state chpt.). Republican. Roman Catholic. Avocations: hunting, scuba diving. Office: 85 McNaughten Rd #110 Columbus OH 43213-5111

KALAFUT, MARK A., lawyer; BA, U. Mich., 1974, JD, 1977. Bar: Iowa, Nebr., Ct. Appeals, Third and Ninth DC Cir. Gen. counsel Union Pacific Railroad Co.; v.p., assoc. gen. counsel Terra Industries, Inc., 1989—2001, v.p., gen. counsel, corp. sec., 2001—. Com. gen. counsels The Fertilizer Inst. Mem. bd. dirs. Coun. on Sexual Assault and Domestic Violence, Am. Soc. Corp. Secs.; former bd. mem. Sioux City Chamber of Commerce, Siouxland Initiative and Girls, Inc. Office: Terra Industries Inc 600 Fourth St PO Box 6000 Sioux City IA 51101

KALAI, EHUD, economist, researcher, educator; b. Tel Aviv, Dec. 7, 1942; arrived in U.S., 1963; s. Meir and Elisheva (Rabinovitch) Kalai; m. Marilyn Lott, Aug. 24, 1967; children: Kerren, Adam. AB with distinction, U. Calif., Berkeley, 1967; MS, Cornell U., 1971, PhD in Applied Math., 1972. Asst. prof. dept. stats. Tel Aviv U., 1972-75; vis. asst. prof. decision scis. J. L. Kellogg Grad. Sch. Mgmt. Northwestern U., Evanston, Ill., 1975-76, assoc. prof., 1976-78, prof. managerial econs. and decision scis., 1978-82, Charles E. Morrison Chair prof. decision scis., 1982-2001, prof. math., 1990—, James J. O'Connor disting. prof. decision and game scis., 2001—, IBM rsch. chair managerial econs., 1980-81, J. L. Kellogg rsch. chair in decision theory, 1981-82, chmn. meds. dept., 1983-85, dir. Ctr. Strategic Decision-Making, 1995—. Expert testimony in ct. cases, 1982—; Oskar Morgenstern rsch. prof. game theory YU, NYC, 1991; cons. Israeli Def. Forces, 1974—75, 1st Nat. Bank, Chgo., 1987, Arthur Anderson, 1990, Kaiser Permanente, 1995, Nath Sonnenschein and Rosenthal, 1999, Baxter Healthcare Corp., 1999—. Founder, editor Games and Econ. Behavior Jour., 1988—, mem. editl. bd. Math. Social Scis., 1980—90, Jour. Econ. Theory, 1980—88, Internat. Jour. Game Theory, 1984—; contbr. articles to profl. jours. Sgt. Israeli Def. Forces, 1960—63. Grantee, NSF, 1979—; Sherman Fairchild Disting. scholar, Calif. Inst. Tech., 1994—95. Fellow: Econometric Soc.; mem.: Game Theory Soc. (founder, exec. v.p. 1998—2003, pres. 2003—06), Pub. Choice Soc., Am. Math. Soc., Beta Gamma Sigma. Office: Kellogg Grad Sch of Mgmt Northwestern Univ Evanston IL 60208-0001 Home: 800 Elgin Rd 1003 Evanston IL 60201 Office Phone: 847-491-7017. Business E-Mail: kalai@kellogg.northwestern.edu.

KALAINOV, SAM CHARLES, insurance company executive; b. Steele, ND, May 11, 1930; s. George and Celia Mae (Makedonsky) K.; m. Delores L. Holm., Aug. 10, 1957; children: John Charles, David Mark. BS, N.D. State U., 1956. CLU. Life ins. agt. Am. Mut. Life Ins. Co., Fargo, N.D., 1956-60, supt. agys. Des Moines, 1960-70, sr. v.p. mktg., 1972-80, pres., chmn., CEO, 1980-95; v.p. agy. Western States Life Ins. Co., Fargo, 1970-72; chmn. bd. dirs. Am. Mut. Holding Corp., Amerus Life, 1995-2000. Bd. dirs. Am. Coun. Life Ins., Washington, Bankers Trust, Des Moines; past chmn. Des Moines Devel. Corp. Bd. dirs. Luth. Health Sys., Fargo, 1974-91, City Corp., Des Moines, 1981-95, Civic Ctr. Ct., 1981-95, Iowa Luth. Hosp., 1982-91; trustee Drake U.; past chmn. Des Moines Conv. and Visitors Bur.; civilian aide to Sec. Army at Large, 1991; past state dir. Selective Svc. Sys.; bd. mem. N.D. State U. Devel. Found. With inf. AUS, 1947-49, lt., 1952-55. Decorated Bronze Star; recipient Alumni Achievement award N.D. State U., 1983, Patrick Henry award Army Nat. Guard, 1998. Mem. Nat. Assn. Life Underwriters, Greater Des Moines C. of C. (past chmn., Nat. Leadership award 1978), Corp. for Internat. Trade (chmn.), Alexis de Tocqueville Soc., Am. Legion, Rotary (past pres. Des Moines chpt.), Grand Lodge Iowa, Royal Order of Jesters, Za-Ga-Zig Temple. Office: AmerUs Group 699 Walnut St Des Moines IA 50309-3929

KALBFLEISCH, JOHN DAVID, statistics educator; b. Grand Valley, Ont., Can., July 16, 1943; s. Claude Elwyn and Janet Marjorie (Agnew) Kalbfleisch; m. Catherine Sharon Allen; children: Michael Allen, Heidi Kathryn, Kirby Ann. BSc in Math. and Physics, U. Waterloo, 1966, M of Math in Stats., 1967, PhD in Stats., 1969. Rsch. assoc. dept. stats. Univ. Coll., London, 1969-70; asst. prof. dept. stats. SUNY, Buffalo, 1970-73; assoc. prof. dept. stats. U. Waterloo, 1973-79, prof. dept. stats. and actuarial sci., 1979—2002, chmn. dept. stats. and actuarial sci., 1984-90, dean faculty of math., 1990-98; prof., chair dept. biostats.

U. Mich., Ann Arbor, 2002—. Vis. prof. dept. biostats. U. Wash., 1979-80, dept. biostats. U. Mich., 1987, dept. epidemiology U. Calif., San Francisco, 1988, dept. statistics U. Auckland, 1998, Nat. U. Singapore, 1999. Author: (with R.L. Prentice) The Statistical Analysis of Failure Time Data, 1980, 2d edit., 2002; assoc. editor Can. Jour. Stats., 1981-89, 1998-2004, Annals of Stats., 1980-83, Biometrics, 2003—; contbr. articles to profl. jours. Recipient Gold medal, Statis. Soc. Can., 1994, COPSS Fisher award, 1999; fellow, Royal Soc. Can., 1994, Am. Statis. Assn., Inst. Math. Stats. Mem.: Internat. Statis. Inst., Royal Statis. Soc., Inst. Biomedical Soc., Statis. Soc. Canada, Internat. Statis. Inst. Office: U Mich Dept Biostatistics Ann Arbor MI 48109 Home Phone: 734-332-6082; Office Phone: 734-615-7067. Business E-Mail: jdkalbfl@umich.edu.

KALDHUSDAL, TERRY LEE, elementary school educator; b. Calif. m. Janet Kaldhusdal; 3 children. BA in journalism, Calif. State Polytechnic Univ., San Luis Obispo; MS in Tech. in Edn., Lesley Coll., Cambridge, Mass. Tchg. cert. Chapman Coll., Calif. Tchr. LA Sch. Sys., Calif., 1991—93, Wales Elem. Sch., 1993—99, Magee Elem. Sch., Genesee Depot, Wis., 1999—. Named Wis. Elem. Sch. Tchr. of Yr., 2006, Wis. Tchr. of Yr., 2007. Mem.: Internat. Reading Assn. Office: Magee Elem Sch PO Box 37 Genesee Depot WI 53127 Business E-Mail: kaldhust@kmsd.edu.

KALETA, PAUL J., lawyer, utilities executive; b. Queens, NY, Aug. 18, 1955; AB in Philosophy and English cum laude, Hamilton Coll., 1978; JD cum laude, Georgetown U., 1981. Bar: DC 1982, NY 1993, US Supreme Ct. 1987. Assoc. Skadden, Arps, Slate, Meagher & Flom, Washington, 1982—84; ptnr. Swidler & Berlin, Washington, 1985-91; v.p., gen. counsel Niagara Mohawk Power Corp., Syracuse, NY, 1991-98; v.p., gen. counsel, sec. Koch Industries, Inc., Wichita, Kans., 1998—2005; sr. v.p., gen. counsel, corp. sec. Sierra Pacific Resources, Reno, 2006—. Vice chmn. Utility Law Commn. Mem. ABA, NY State Bar Assn. Office: Sierra Pacific Resources 6100 Neil Rd Reno NV 89511

KALIL, CHARLES JAMES, lawyer, chemicals executive; b. 1951; BA, Mich. State U.; JD, Georgetown U. Law Ctr. Asst. US atty. US Dept. Justice (ea. dist. Mich.), 1976—80; atty. environ. law Dow Chem. Co., Midland, Mich., 1980—82; gen. counsel Petrokemyia (joint venture of Dow and SABIC), Rotterdam, Netherlands, 1982—83, regional counsel to Mid. East/Africa Geneva, 1983—86; various litig. and fin. roles Dow Chem. Co., Midland, Mich., 1986—92, gen. counsel and area dir. govt. and pub. affairs Dow L.Am., 1992—97, mgr. global litig. INSITE tech., 1997, asst. gen. counsel corp. fin. law Midland, Mich., 2000—03, assoc. gen. counsel, dir. corp. legal affairs, 2003—04, corp. v.p., gen. counsel, 2004—, corp. sec., mem. Office of the Chief Exec., 2005—. Office: Dow Chem Co 2030 Dow Ctr Midland MI 48674

KALINA, JOHN, auto parts company executive; Chief info. officer Walbro Corp., 1995—96; exec. info. tech. cons. IBM, 1997—99; c.p., chief info. officer BorgWarner Inc., Chgo., 1999—. Office: Borgwarner 3850 Hamlin Rd Auburn Hills MI 48326-2872

KALINSKY, ROBERT A., lawyer; b. Cedar Rapids, Iowa, Aug. 24, 1973; BS in Biomedical Engring., U. Iowa, 1996, JD with distinction, 2001. Bar: Minn. 2001, US Dist. Ct. (dist. Minn.) 2001, US Patent and Trademark Office 2001. Software engr. MCI Telecom.; assoc. Merchant & Gould, P.C., Mpls. Named a Rising Star, Minn. Super Lawyers mag., 2006. Mem.: Minn. Intellectual Property Law Assn., ABA, Minn. State Bar Assn. Office: Merchant & Gould PC 3200 IDS Ctr 80 S 8th St Minneapolis MN 55402 Office Phone: 612-336-4771. E-mail: rkalinsky@merchant-gould.com.

KALIS, HENRY J., state legislator, farmer; b. Mar. 2, 1937; m. Violet Kalis; four children. Farmer; Dist. 26B rep. Minn. Ho. of Reps., St. Paul, 1974—. Former chmn. transp. com., Minn. Ho. of Reps., former mem. agr., appropriations, health and human svcs. coms., former ex officio environ. and natural resources fin., health and housing, higher edn. human svcs., judiciary and state govt. divsn. coms.; chmn. capital investment com., mem. econ. devel., infrastructure and regulation fin., and ways and means coms. Address: RR 1 Box 55 Walters MN 56097-9601 Also: 10043 600th Ave Walters MN 56097-4703

KALISCH, BEATRICE JEAN, nursing educator, consultant; b. Tellahoma, Tenn., Oct. 15, 1943; d. Peter and Margaret Ruth Petersen; children— Philip P., Melanie J. BS, U. ebr., 1965; MS, U. Md., 1967, PhD, 1970. Pediatric staff nurse Centre County Hosp., Bellefonte, Pa., 1965-66; instr. nursing Philipsburg (Pa.) Gen. Hosp. Sch. Nursing, 1966; pediatric staff nurse Greater Balt. Med. Center, Towson, Md., 1967; asst. prof. maternal-child nursing Am. U., 1967-68; clin. nurse specialist N.W. Tex. Hosp., Amarillo, 1970; assoc. prof. maternal-child nursing, curriculum coordinator nursing Amarillo Coll., 1970-71; chmn. baccalaureate nursing program, asso. prof. nursing U. So. Miss., 1971-74; prof. nursing, chmn. dept. parent-child nursing U. Mich. Sch. Nursing, Ann Arbor, 1974-86, Shirley C. Titus Disting. prof., 1977—, Titus Disting. prof. nursing mgmt., 1989—, dir. nursing bus. and health sys. program, 2000—; prin., dir. nursing consultation svcs. Ernst & Young, Detroit, 1986-89. Prin. investigator USPH grant to study image of nurses in mass media and the informational quality nursing news, U. Mich., 1977-86, prin. investigator to study intrahosp. transport of critically ill patients, 1991—; prin. investigator to study use of HIA nurse in N.Y.C. labor market, U. Mich.; prin. investigator to study the impact of managed care on critical care, U. Mich.; vis. Disting. prof. U. Ala., 1979, U. Tex., 1981, Tex. Christian U., 1983. Author: Child Abuse and Neglect: An Annotated Bibliography, 1978; co-author: Nursing Involvement in Health Planning, 1978, Politics of Nursing, 1982, Images of Nurses on Television, 1983, The Advance of American Nursing, 1986, revised, 1994, The Changing Image of the Nurse, 1987; co-editor: Studies in Nursing Mgmt.; contbr. articles to profl. jours. Recipient Joseph L. Andrews Bibliog. award Am. Assn. Law Libraries, 1979; Book of Yr. award Am. Jour. Nursing, 1978, 83, 86, 87, Outstanding Achievement award U. Md., 1987, Distinguished Alumni award U. Nebr., 1985, Shaw medal Boston Coll., 1986; USPHS fellow. Fellow: Am. Acad. Nursing; mem.: ANA, APHA, Am. Coll. Healthcare Execs., Am. Orgn. Nurse Execs., Sigma Theta Tau, Phi Kappa Phi. Presbyterian. Office: U Mich Sch Nursing 400 N Ingalls St Ann Arbor MI 48109-0482 Business E-Mail: bkalisch@umich.edu.

KALLAS, HANI R., lawyer; b. Kettering, Ohio, Dec. 30, 1968; BS, Miami U., 1991; JD, U. Cin. Coll. Law, 1994. Bar: Ohio 1994. Ptnr. Vorys, Sater, Seymour and Pease LLP, Cin., 1994—. Named one of Ohio's Rising Star, Super Lawyers, 2006. Mem.: Order of Coif. Office: Vorys Sater Seymour and Pease LLP Atrium Two Ste 2000 221 E Fourth St PO Box 0236 Cincinnati OH 45201-0236 Office Phone: 513-723-4615. Office Fax: 513-852-7864.

KALLICK, DAVID A., lawyer; b. Chgo., Nov. 7, 1945; s. Joseph N. and Elizabeth A. (Just) K.; m. Arline E. Chizewer, Nov. 26, 1972; children: Michelle, Robert. AB in History, Princeton U., 1967; JD, Northwestern U., 1971. Bar: Ill. 1971, Calif. 1972. Law clk. to presiding justice Ill. Appellate Ct., Chgo., 1971-72; assoc. McCutchen, Doyle, Brown & Enersen, San Francisco, 1972-74; asst. dean U. So. Calif. Law Ctr., LA, 1974-76, Ill. Inst. Tech.-Kent Coll. Law, Chgo., 1976-79; ptnr. Hurley Kallick & Schiller, Ltd., Deerfield, Ill., 1979-92, Tishler & Wald, Ltd., Chgo., 1992—. Past bd. dirs. Congregation Solel, Highland Park, Ill., Birchwood Club, Highland Park; past bd. mem., pres. Sch. Dist. 107, Highland Park; former trustee Legacy 107 Edn. Found., Highland Park. With USAR, 1968-74. Mem. ABA, Calif. Bar Assn., Ill. Bar Assn., Chgo. Bar Assn., Princeton Univ. Club. Home: 1887 Spruce Ave Highland Park IL 60035-2150 Office: 200 S Wacker Dr Ste 3000 Chicago IL 60606-5807 Office Phone: 312-876-3800. Business E-Mail: dkallick@tishlerandwald.com.

KALLIK, CHIP, radio director; m. Sarah Kallik. BA Comm., Ohio State U. News anchor, reporter WEOL, Elyria, Ohio, WMJI, Cleve., 1991—94, dir. news ops., 1994—. Recipient Nat. Headline award Consistently Outstanding News Reporting, 1995. Avocations: golf, bowling, theater. Office: WMJI 6200 Oak Tree Blvd 4th Fl Cleveland OH 44131

KALMAN, ANDREW, manufacturing executive, director; b. Hungary, Aug. 14, 1919; came to U.S., 1922, naturalized, 1935; s. Louis and Julia (Bognar) K.; m. Violet Margaret Kish, June 11, 1949; children: Andrew Joseph, Richard Louis, Laurie Ann. With Detroit Engring. & Machine Co., 1947-66, exec. v.p., gen. mgr., 1952-66; exec. v.p. and dir. Indian Head, Inc., 1966-75, also dir. Dir. Acme Precision Products, 1959-80, Reef Energy Corp., 1980-84. Trustee emeritus Alma (Mich.) Coll.; bd. dirs. Am. Hungarian Found., New Brunswick, N.J.; mem. adv. coun., mem. exec. com., U. Mich. Ctr. for Communication Disorders. Home: 708 S Military St Dearborn MI 48124-2108 Office: The Buhl Bldg 535 Griswold Ste 1900 Detroit MI 48226 Office Phone: 313-965-4182.

KALMAN, MARC, radio station executive; b. Appleton, Wis. m. Gail Thoen; children: Robert, Todd, Stacie. Student, Am. U. Disc jockey Sta. WJPD, Ishpeming, Mich., 1967, Sta. WMBD, Peoria, Ill., 1967; account exec. Sta. WMIN, 1968, Sta. KRSI, 1968-69, Sta. WDGY, 1969-74, gen. sales mgr., 1974-81; v.p./gen. mgr. Blair Radio, 1981-88; gen. sales mgr. Sta. WCCO, 1988-92; v.p./gen. mgr. Sta. WLOL, Mpls. Bd. dirs. Variety Children's Hosp. Mem. Minn. Broadcasters Assn. (bd. dirs.). Avocation: spectator sports. Office: Clear Channel Radio 1600 Utica Ave S Ste 400 Saint Louis Park MN 55416-1480

KALT, DAVID, diversified financial services company executive; b. 1967; MS, DePaul U., 1995. Chief tech. officer TRAMS, Inc., 1998—2000; pres., founder Third Party Solutions, 1994—98; CEO OptionsXpress Holdings, Inc., Chgo., 2000—, also pres., chief tech. officer, 2000—. Named one of 40 Under Forty, Crain's Bus. Chgo., 2005. Avocation: collecting vintage Gibson guitars. Office: OptionsXpress Inc Ste 220 39 S LaSalle St Chicago IL 60690 Office Fax: 312-629-5256.

KALTER, ALAN, advertising agency executive; m. Chris Lezotte. With W.B. Doner & Co., Southfield, Mich., 1967—, exec. v.p., dir. retail divsn., 1990, vice chmn. account mgmt., 1990-92, pres., COO, 1992-95; CEO, chmn. W. B. Doner & Co. (dba Doner), Southfield, Mich., 1995—. Office: W B Doner & Co 25900 orthwestern Hwy Southfield MI 48075-1067

KALVER, GAIL ELLEN, dance company executive, musician; b. Chgo., Nov. 25, 1948; d. Nathan Eli and Alice Martha (Jaffe) K. BS in Music Edn., U. Ill., 1970; MA in Clarinet Chgo. Musical Coll., Roosevelt U., 1974. Profl. musician, Chgo., 1970-77; assoc. mgr. Ravinia Festival, Highland Park, Ill., 1977-83; exec. dir. Hubbard Street Dance Chgo., 1984—. Bd. dirs. Chicago Dancers United, Ill. Arts Alliance; mem. dance panel Ill; music consul., Nat. Radio Theatre. Arts Council, Chgo., 1983-85; mem. grants panels Chgo. Office Fine Arts, 1985; conf. mem., DanceUSA, 2005. Editor: Music Explorer (for music edn.), 1983-86. Mem. grants panels NEA, 1992-94; cons. music Nat. Radio Theatre, Chgo., 1983—; mem. adv. coun. Dance Initiative Chgo. Cmty. Trust, Dancers Responding to AIDS; mem. exec. com. Dance for Life, 2003. Recipient Arts Mgmt. Excellence award, ABBY award, 2003. Office: Hubbard St Dance Chgo 1147 W Jackson Blvd Chicago IL 60607-2905

KAMERICK, EILEEN ANN, corporate financial executive, lawyer; b. Ravenna, Ohio, July 22, 1958; d. John Joseph and Elaine Elizabeth (Lenney) K.; m. Victor J. Heckler, Sept. 1, 1990; 1 child, Connor Joseph Heckler. AB in English summa cum laude, Boston Coll., 1980; postgrad., Exeter Coll., Oxford, Eng., 1981; JD, U. Chgo., 1984, MBA in Finance and Internat. Bus. with honors, 1993. Bar: Ill. 1984, U.S. Dist. Ct. (no. dist.) Ill. 1985, Mass. 1986, U.S. Ct. Appeals (7th cir.) 1988, U.S. Supreme Ct. 1993. Assoc. Reuben & Proctor, Chgo., 1984—86, Skadden, Arps et al, Chgo., 1986—89; atty. internat. Amoco Corp., Chgo., 1989—93, sr. fin. mgr. corp. fin., 1993—96, dir. banking and fin. svcs., 1996—97, v.p., treas., 1998—99, Whirlpool Corp., Benton Harbor, Mich., 1997; v.p., gen. counsel GE Capital Auto Fin. Svcs., Barrington, Ill., 1997—98; v.p., CFO BP Am., 1998—2000; exec. v.p., CFO United Stationers Inc., Des Plaines, Ill., 2000—01, Bcom3, Chgo., 2001—03; exec v.p., CFO, chief adminstrv. officer Heidrick & Struggles Internat., Inc., Chgo., 2004—. Advisor fin. com. Am. Petroleum Inst., 1992; bd. dirs. Heartland Alliance, ServiceMaster, Westell Tech., Associated Banc-Corp. Vol. adv. 7th Cir. Bar Assn., Chgo., 1987—; bd. dirs. Boys & Girls Clubs of Chgo., Cove Sch. Mem. Phi Beta Kappa. Roman Catholic. Office: Heidrick & Struggles Internat Inc 233 S Wacker Dr Ste 4200 Chicago IL 60606 Office Phone: 312-496-1557. Personal E-mail: eakesq@aol.com.

KAMIN, BLAIR DOUGLASS, architecture critic; b. Red Bank, NJ, Aug. 6, 1957; s. Arthur Z. and Virginia P. Kamin. BA, Amherst Coll., 1979; M in Environ. Design, Yale U., 1984; HHD (hon.), Monmouth U., 2003. Reporter Des Moines Register, 1984-87; suburban reporter Chgo. Tribune, 1987—91; culture news reporter, 1992; architecture critic, 1992—. Nominating juror Pulitzer Prize, 2000, 02, Gabriel Prize, 2007; adj. prof. art North Ctrl. Coll., 2005—; instr. Graham Sch. Continuing Edn., U. Chgo., 2006. Author: Why Architecture Matters: Lessons from Chicago, 2001, contbr. articles to profl. jours. Recipient Nat. Edn. Reporting award Edn. Writers Assn., 1985, Edward Scott Beck award Chgo. Tribune, 1990, George Polk award for Criticism, 1996, Pulitzer Prize for Criticism, 1999, Inst. Honor for Collaborative Achievement, AIA, 1999, Peter Lisagor award for Exemplary Journalism, 1993-98, 2001, 03, 06, Engring. Journalism award Am. Assn. Engring. Socs. and Engring. Found., 1996, Richard Driehaus Found. Preservation award Landmarks Preservation Coun. Ill., 1997, Wright Spirit award Frank Lloyd Wright Bldg. Conservancy, 2001, Presdl. citation AIA, 2004; named to Chgo. Media Elite, Crains Chgo. Bus., 2005. Jewish. Office Phone: 312-222-4138. Business E-Mail: bkamin@tribune.com.

KAMIN, CHESTER THOMAS, lawyer; b. Chgo., July 30, 1940; s. Alfred and Sara (Liebenson) Kamin; m. Nancy Schaefer, Sept. 8, 1962; children: Stacey Allison, Scott Thomas. AB magna cum laude, Harvard Coll., 1962; JD, U. Chgo., 1965. Bar: Ill. 1965, U.S. Dist. Ct. (no. dist.) Ill. 1965, U.S. Dist. Ct. DC 1994, U.S. Ct. Appeals (fed. cir.) 1967, U.S. Ct. Appeals (7th cir.) 1970, U.S. Ct. Appeals (5th cir.) 1975, U.S. Ct. Appeals (2d cir.) 1987, U.S. Ct. Appeals (6th cir.) 1996, U.S. Supreme Ct. 1971. Law clk. Ill. Appellate Ct., 1965-66; assoc. Jenner & Block, Chgo., 1966-72, ptnr., 1975—; spl. counsel to Gov. State of Ill. Springfield, 1973-74. Mem. steering com. Com. Cts. and Justice, 1971—; mem. Ill. Law Enforcement Commn., 1975—77; adj. prof. U. Chgo. Law Sch. Contbr. articles to profl. jours. Fellow: Am. Coll. Trial Lawyers, Am. Bar Found.; mem.: ABA, Lawyers Club, Chgo. Coun. Lawyers, Chgo. Bar Assn., Ill. State Bar Assn., Quadrangle Club. Office: Jenner & Block 1 E Ibm Plz Fl 4700 Chicago IL 60611-3599 E-mail: ckamin@jenner.com.

KAMINS, JOHN MARK, lawyer; b. Chgo., Feb. 7, 1947; s. David and Beulah (Block) K.; m. Judith Joan Sperling, May 5, 1968; children: Robert, Heather. AB with high honors and distinction, U. Mich., 1968, JD, 1970. Bar: Mich. 1971, Fla. 1991. Assoc., Honigman Miller Schwartz and Cohn, Detroit, 1971-75, ptnr., 1976—; lectr. Inst. on Continuing Legal Edn. Pres. Mich. chpt. Leukemia and Lymphoma Soc., 1991-92, 93-96, nat. trustee, 1996—2004, nat. exec. com., 1997—, chmn. nat. bd. trustees, 2004—, chmn. nat bd. dirs., 2005-06; pres. Goodwill Industries of Greater Detroit Found., 2001-03; pres. Temple Beth El, Bloomfield Hills, Mich., 1994-96. Mem. Nat. Assn. Bond Lawyers (vice chmn. com. on opinions 1985-86), Mich. Bar Assn. (chairperson, pub. corp. law sect. 1992-93). Jewish. Home: 1315 Stuyvessant Rd Bloomfield Hills MI 48301-2144 Office: Honigman Miller Schwartz & Cohn llp 2290 First National Bldg Detroit MI 48226 Office Phone: 313-465-7436.

KAMINSKI, DONALD LEON, surgeon, gastroenterologist, educator; b. Elba, Nebr., Nov. 9, 1940; s. Edwin and Irene (Syntek) K.; m. Maureen M. Cudmore, Nov. 28, 1964; children: Christian, Julie, Jane, Kathryn. BS, Creighton U., 1962, MD, 1966. Diplomate: Am. Bd. Surgery. Intern. St. Louis U., 1966-67, resident in surgery, 1967-71; attending surgeon St. Louis U. Hosp., 1972—, dir. gen. surgery, 1982—. Mem. Soc. Univ. Surgeons, Am. Surg. Assn., Central Surg. Soc., Alpha Omega Alpha Republican. Roman Catholic. Home: 1025 Joanna Ave Saint Louis MO 63122-1821 Office: St Louis U 3635 Vista at Grand PO Box 15250 Saint Louis MO 63110-0250

KAMINSKY, MANFRED STEPHAN, physicist; b. Koenigsberg, Germany, June 4, 1929; came to U.S., 1958; s. Stephan and Kaethe (Gieger) K.; m. Elisabeth Moellering, May 1, 1957; children: Cornelia K.B., Mark-Peter. First diploma in physics, U. Rostock, Germany, 1951; PhD in Physics magna cum laude, U. Marburg, Germany, 1957. German Research Soc. fellow and grad. asst. in physics U. Rostock, 1950-52; lectr. Rostock Med. Tech. Sch., 1952; German Research Soc. fellow and research asst. Phys. Inst., U. Marburg, 1953-57, sr. asst., 1957-58; research asso. Argonne (Ill.) Nat. Lab., 1958-59, asst. physicist, 1959-62, assoc., 1962-70, sr. physicist, 1970-86, dir. Surface Sci. Center-CTR Program, 1974-80, dir. Tribology Program, 1984-86; sole propr. Surface Treatment Sci. Internat., Hinsdale, Ill., 1986—. Cons. Office Tech. Assessment U.S. Congress, 1986, NRC com. on tribology, 1986-88; guest prof. Inst. Energy, U. Que., Montreal-Varennes, 1976-82; E.W. Mueller lectr. U. Wis., Milw., 1978; symposium chmn. Internat. Conf. Metall. Coatings, 1985-93. Author: Atomic and Ionic Impact Phenomena on Metal Surfaces, 1965; contbr. articles to profl. jours.; editor: Radiation Effects on Solid Surfaces, 1976; co-editor: Surface Effects on Controlled Fusion, 1974, Surface Effects in Controlled Fusion Devices, 1976, Dictionary of Terms for Vacuum Science and Technology, 1980; patentee in field. Bd. dirs. Com. 100, Hinsdale, 1970-75, 90-92, pres., 1973-74; pres. St. Vincent de Paul Soc., Hinsdale, 1972-73. Named Outstanding New Citizen of Year Citizenship Council Chgo., 1968; Japanese Soc. Promotion of Sci. fellow, 1982. Fellow Am. Phys. Soc.; mem. Am. Chem. Soc., Scientific Research Soc., Research Soc. Am., AAAS, Union German Phys. Socs., Am. Vacuum Soc. (sr., trustee 1982-84, chmn. Midwest sect. 1967-68, co-founder Gt. Lakes chpt., dir. 1968-70, chmn. fusion tech. div. 1980-81, editorial bd. jour. 1978-83, hon. 1986), Internat. Union Vacuum Sci., Techs. and Applications (chmn. fusion div. 1984-86), Sigma Xi. also: 300 Galen Dr Apt 506 Key Biscayne FL 33149-2177 Office: 906 S Park Ave Hinsdale IL 60521-4519

KAMISAR, YALE, lawyer, educator; b. NYC, Aug. 29, 1929; s. Samuel and Mollie (Levine) K.; m. Esther Englander, Sept. 7, 1953 (div. Oct. 1973); children: David Graham, Gordon, Jonathan; m. Christine Keller, May 10, 1974 (dec. 1997); m. Joan Russell, Feb. 28, 1999. AB, NYU, 1950; LLB, Columbia U., 1954; LLD, CUNY, 1978. Bar: D.C. 1955. Rsch. assoc. Am. Law Inst., NYC, 1953; assoc. Covington & Burling, Washington, 1955-57; assoc. prof., then prof. law U. Minn., Mpls., 1957-64; prof. law U. Mich., Ann Arbor, 1965-92, Clarence Darrow disting. univ. prof., 1992—2004; prof. San Diego U., 2004—. Vis. prof. law Harvard U., 1964-65, San Diego U., 2000-02; disting. vis. prof. law Coll. William and Mary, 1988; cons. Nat. Adv. Commn. Civil Disorders, 1967-68, Nat. Commn. Causes and Prevention Violence, 1968-69; mem. adv. com. model code pre-arraignment procedure Am. Law Inst., 1965-75. Reporter-draftsman: Uniform Rules of Criminal Procedure, 1971-73; author: (with J.H. Choper, S. Shiffrin and R.H. Fallon), Constitutional Law: Cases, Comments and Questions, 10th edit., 2006; (with W. LaFave, J. Israel and N. King) Modern Criminal Procedure: Cases and Commentaries, 11th edit., 2005, Criminal Procedure and the Constitution: Leading Cases and Introductory Text, 2002; (with F. Inbau and T. Arnold) Criminal Justice in Our Time, 1965; (with J. Grano and J. Haddad) Sum and Substance of Criminal Procedure, 1977, Police Interrogation and Confessions: Essays in Law and Policy, 1980; contbr. articles to profl. jours. Served to 1st lt. AUS, 1951-52. Recipient Am. Bar Found. Rsch. award, 1996. Office: U Mich Law Sch 625 S State St Ann Arbor MI 48109-1215 Business E-Mail: ykamisar@umich.edu.

KAMMASH, TERRY, nuclear engineering educator; b. Sult, Jordan, Jan. 27, 1927; came to U.S., 1946; m. Sophie C. Kammash, Dec. 31, 1956; 1 child, Dean. BS, Pa. State U., 1952, MS, 1954; PhD, U. Mich., 1958. Instr. engring. mechs. Pa. State U., University Park, 1952-54, U. Mich., Ann Arbor, 1954-58, from asst. prof. to assoc. prof. nuclear engring., 1958-67, prof. nuclear engring., 1967—. Physicist Lawrence Livermore Lab., Livermore, Calif., 1961-62; rsch. scientist Los Alamos (N.Mex.) Nat. Lab., summer 1958; cons. Battelle N.W. Labs., Richland, Wash., 1975-78, Argonne (Ill.) Nat. Lab., 1972-77. Author: Fusion Reactor Physics, 1975; editor/author: Fusion Energy in Space Propulsion, 1995. Fellow AIAA (assoc., nuclear propulsion com. 1993)), Am. Nuclear Soc. (fusion tech. com. 1979), Arthur Holly Compton award 1977, Outstanding Achievement award 1977), Am. Phys. Soc. (plasma physics comm. 1977). Office: U Mich Dept Nuclear Engring and Radiol Scis Ann Arbor MI 48109

KAMPINE, JOHN P., anesthesiology and physiology educator; MD, Marquette U. Med. Sch., Milwaukee, WI, 1961, PhD in Physiology, 1965. Intern Med. Coll. of Wis., Milwaukee, 1961—62, Milw. Cty. Gen. Hosp.; fellow, neurosciences NIH, Bethesda, Md., 1965—67; US Pub. Health Svc. postdoctoral rsch. fellow Marquette Sch. Medicine; rsch. assoc. Nat. Inst. Neurological Diseases and Blindness Lab. of Neurochemistry; instr. physiology Med. Coll. of Wis., Milw., 1962—67, asst. prof. physiology and anesthesiology, 1967—71, assoc. prof., 1971—74, prof., chair dept. anesthesiology, 1979—2005, prof. physiology, 1979—2005, prof. anesthesiology and physiology, 1974—. Pres. Assn. for U. Anesthesiologists; mem., surgery, anesthesia, and trauma study sect. NIH. Mem.: Am. Physiological Soc. (chmn., circulation group), Soc. Academic Anesthesia (pres., chmn.), Inst. Medicine-NAS. Office: Froedtert Meml Hosp PO Box 26099 9200 W Wisconsin Ave Milwaukee WI 53226-3596

KAMPOURIS, EMMANUEL ANDREW, retired corporate executive; b. Alexandria, Egypt, Dec. 14, 1934; arrived in US, 1979; s. Andrew George and Euridice Ann (Caralli) Kampouris; m. Myrto Stellatos, July 4, 1959 (dec.); children: Andrew, Alexander. Student, King's Sch., Bruton, Somerset, UK, 1953; MA in Law, Oxford U., 1957; cert. in ceramic tech., North Staffordshire Coll. of Tech., UK, 1962. Plant mgr., dir. "KEREM", Athens, Greece, 1962-64; dir. "HELLENIT", Athens, Greece, 1962-65; mng. dir. Ideal Standard, Athens, 1966-79; v.p., group exec. internat. and export Am. Standard Inc., New Brunswick, NJ, 1979-84, sr. v.p. bldg. products, 1984-89; pres., chief exec. officer Am. Standard Inc., Am. Standard Cos. Inc., NYC, 1989-99, now chmn.; bd. dirs. Click Commerce Inc, Chgo., Horizon Blue Cross Blue Shields, Stanley Works, Alticor Inc. Bd. dirs. Ideal Refractories SAI, Athens; bd. dirs. Ideal Standard Mexico, Am. Standard Sanitaryware (Thailand) Ltd., INCESA, San Jose, Costa Rica, Hoxan Corp., Sapporo, Japan. Bd. dirs. Greek Mgmt. Assn., Athens, 1975—77, Fedn. of Greek Industries, Athens. Mem.: Young Pres. Orgn., Chief Execs. Orgn., Econ. Club of N.Y., Oxford Union, Oxford Law Soc., Am. Hellenic C. of C. (gen. sec. 1975—79), Spring Brook Country (Morristown, N.J.); Quogue Field, Quogue Beach (L.I., N.Y.), Chemists Club, Laurel Valley Golf Club. Greek Orthodox. Avocations: golf, tennis, classical music.

KAMPS, CHARLES Q., retired lawyer; b. Milw., Mar. 21, 1932; s. John G. and Mary (Quarles) K.; m. Mary B. Stehling, Sept. 28, 1963; children: Charles Jr., Louisa. LLB, Marquette U., 1959. Bar: Wis. 1959. Ptnr. Quarles & Brady, Milw., 1959—99. Pres. Preserve Our Parks, Inc. Mem. U.S. Sailing Assn; Milwaukee Yacht Club (past commodore, 1971-72). Office: Quarles & Brady 411 E Wisconsin Ave Ste 2040 Milwaukee WI 53202-4497 Office Phone: 414-277-5513. E-mail: cqk@quarles.com.

KAMSICKAS, JAMES, automotive executive; b. Saginaw, Mich., 1967; B in Prodn. and Ops. Mgmt., Mich. State U., 1989. V.p. Lear Corp., Southfield, Mich., 1999—2004, v.p., North Am. Ops., interior systems divsn., 2004—. Named one of 40 Under 40, Crain's Detroit Bus., 2006. Office: Lear Corporation Corporate Headquarters PO Box 5008 21557 Telegraph Rd Southfield MI 48086 Office Phone: 248-447-1500. Office Fax: 248-447-1722.

KAMYSZEW, CHRISTOPHER D., film executive, educator, curator; b. Warsaw, May 7, 1958; came to U.S., 1982; s. Mieczyslaw and Zofia K.; children: Oliver G., Samuel, Jacob. BA, U. Warsaw, 1982, MA in Polish Lit. and Lang., 1984. Freelance writer and translator, Poland, 1977-81; freelance theatre dir. Dearborn Theatre Co., Chgo., 1982-83, Ossetynski Actors Lab., LA, 1982-83; head lit. sect. Krag-Underground Publishers, Warsaw, 1980-83; head archives dept. Polish Mus. Am., Chgo., 1985-88, dir., curator, 1988-93; pres. Soc. for the Arts, Chgo., 1993—. Bd. dirs. Gallery 58, Chgo.; pres. Inst. Symbological Rsch., Chgo., 1986-95, Internat. Ind. Theatre Found., Washington, 1985-86; exec. dir. Polish TV-USA, 1994-97. Co-author, editor: Collective Works of L.-F Celine, 1983, Literary Essays by L. Tyrmand, 1983; curated more than 200 exhbns. in U.S. Dir., chmn., CEO Polish Film Festival, 1988—, Europe Film Festival, 1996—; founder, pres. Chgo. Internat. Documentary Festival, 2003-. Recipient Zycie Warszawy award, 1977, Audience award Edinburgh Theatre Festival, 1980, award for disting. translation Assn. Polish Translators, 1990, award Found. of Friends of Polish Mus., 1991, award Ministry Fgn. Affairs of Poland, 1993, Laterna Magica award disting. achievements in film, 1994, Copernican award, 2002, Warsaw Gold medal Acad. Fine Arts, 2004; Wiehmann Found. scholar, 1982, Golden Cross of Merit, 2001. Avocations: reading, classical music, map collecting, cross country skiing. Office: Society for Arts 1112 N Milwaukee Ave Chicago IL 60622-4017 Office Phone: 773-486-9612. Personal E-mail: christopherkamyszew@msn.com.

KANAVAS, THEODORE J., state senator; b. Apr. 29, 1961; BA, U. Wis., 1983; postgrad., Law Sch., Pepperdine U. Former dir. midwest ops., tech. co. co-founder software co.; state sen. Wis. State Senate, Madison, 2001—, mem. edn., human svcs. and aging, privacy, electronic commerce and fin. instns. coms. Mem. Elmbrook (Wis.) Sch. Bd., 2000—. Mem.: Elmbrook Hist. Soc., Order of Ahepa Chpt. 43. Republican. Greek Orthodox. Office: State Capitol Rm 22 S PO Box 7882 Madison WI 53707-7882

KANE, FRANCIS JOSEPH, bishop; b. Chgo., Oct. 30, 1942; BA, Niles Coll. Sem., Ill., 1963; STB, St. Mary of the Lake Sem., Mundelein, Ill., 1969. Ordained priest Archdiocese of Chgo., 1969; assoc. pastor St. John Fisher Parish, 1969—75; assoc. dir., Ctr. Pastoral Ministry Archdiocese of Chgo., 1973—83; assoc. pastor St. Nicholas of Tolentine Parish, 1975—79; dir., Office of Evangelization and Christian Life Archdiocese of Chicago, 1983—93; pastor St. Joseph Parish, Wilmette, Ill., 1993—2003; ordained bishop, 2003; aux. bishop Archdiocese of Chicago, 2003—. Episcopal liaison for ann. cath. appeal Archdiocese of Chgo., 2003—, Episcopal liaison, Office for Lay Ecclesial Ministry, 2003—; bd. dirs. St. Joseph Sem., 2004—07. Mem.: KC, Equestrian Knights of the Holy Sepulchre Jerusalem, US Conf. Cath. Bishops (mem. cath. campaign for human devel. com. 2004—, mem. social devel. and world peace com. 2004—), Rotary Club of Wilmette. Roman Catholic. Office: 1651 W Diversey Pkwy Chicago IL 60614 Office Phone: 773-388-8670. Office Fax: 773-388-8676.*

KANE, JOHN C., retired health care products company executive; b. 1939; married. BS, West Chester State Coll., Pa., 1961. With Merck Co., 1967-70; mgr. plant Schick Co., until 1974; gen. mgr. Lav Industries; ops. mgr. corp. procurement Abbott Labs., North Chicago, Ill., 1974-76, dir. corp. procurement, 1976-77, dir. ops., devel. corp. materials mgr., 1977-78, div., v.p. Puerto Rican site, 1978-79, dir. v.p. corp. materials mgmt., 1979-81, v.p. chem. and agrl. products, from 1981, exec. v.p. Ross Labs. divsn., COO, pres. Columbus, Ohio, 1989—93; pres., COO, dir. Cardinal Health Inc., Dublin, Ohio, 1993—2001, vice chmn., 2000—01; ret., 2001. Bd. dir. Tenet Healthcare Corp., 2003—, Connetics Corp., Greif Brothers Corp. Bd. vis. Savannah (Ga.) Coll. Art Design.

KANE, LUCILE M., retired archivist, historian; b. Maiden Rock, Wis., Mar. 17, 1920; d. Emery John and Ruth (Coty) Kane BS, River Falls State Tchrs. Coll., 1942; MA, U. Minn., 1946. Tchr. Osceola (Wis.) High Sch., 1942-44; asst. publicity dept. U. Minn. Press, Mpls., 1945-46; rsch. fellow, editor Forest Products History Found., St. Paul, 1946-48; curator manuscripts Minn. Hist. Soc., St. Paul, 1948-75, sr. rsch. fellow, 1979-85, sr. rsch. assoc., 1985—, mem. hon. coun., 1988—. State archivist, 1975—79. Author, compiler: A Guide to the Care and Administration of Manuscripts, 2d edit., 1966, (with Kathryn A. Johnson) Manuscripts Collections of the Minnesota Historical Society, Guide No.2, 1955, The Waterfall That Built a City, 1966 (updated edit. pub. as The Falls of St. Anthony, 1987), (with Alan Ominsky) Twin Cities: A Pictorial History of Saint Paul and Minneapolis, 1983; transl., editor, Military Life in Dakota, The Jour. of Philippe Regis de Trobriand, 1951; editor: (with others) The Northern Expeditions of Major Stephen H. Long, 1978; contbr. articles to profl. jours. Recipient award of Merit Western History Assn., 1982, Disting. Svc. award Minn. Humanities Commn., 1983, award of Distinction Am. Assn. State and Local History, 1987; co-recipient Theodore C. Blegen award Minn. Hist. Soc., 1996. Fellow: Soc. Am. Archivists. Home: 11377 180th Ave Bloomer WI 54724-4733

KANE, ROBERT LEWIS, public health service officer, educator; b. NYC, Jan. 18, 1940; m. Rosalie Smolkin, June 17, 1962; children: Miranda, Ingrid, Kate AB, Columbia Coll., NYC, 1961; MD, Harvard U., 1965. Acting coordinator sr. clerkship program dept. community medicine U. Ky., Lexington, 1968-69; svc. unit dir. USPHS Indian Hosp., Shiprock, N.Mex., 1969-70; spl. asst. to regional health dir. USPHS HEW Region VIII, Denver, 1970-71; from asst. to assoc. prof. family and community medicine U. Utah Sch. Medicine, Salt Lake City, 1970-77; sr. researcher The Rand Corp., Santa Monica, Calif., 1977-85; from assoc. prof. to prof. medicine UCLA Sch. Medicine, 1978-85; prof. Sch. Pub. Health UCLA, 1980-85, U. Minn., 1985—, dean, 1985-90; intern U. Ky. Med. Ctr., Lexington, 1965-66, resident in community medicine, 1966-69. Adj. prof. Leonard Davis Sch. Gerontology, U. So. Calif., 1982-85; mem. expert com. on aging WHO, 1986-2002; Minn. endowed chair in long-term care and aging, 1989—; mem. adv. com. on Alzheimer's Disease, Washington, 1988-96; mem. com. on quality Inst. Medicine, 1988-90. Co-author: A Will and A Way, 1985, Long-term Care: Principles, Programs, and Policies, 1987, Essentials of Clinical Geriatrics, 5th edit., 2004, Understanding Health Care Outcomes Research, 2nd edit., 2005, The Heart of Long Term Care, 1998, Assessing Older Persons, 2000, It Shouldn't Be This Way, 2005, Meeting the Challenge of Chronic Illness, 2005. With USPHS, 1969-70. Home: 2715 E Lake Of The Isles Pky Minneapolis MN 55408-1053 Office Phone: 612-624-1185. Business E-Mail: kanex001@umn.edu.

KANE, SCOTT A., lawyer; b. Carson City, Mich., 1969; BS, Western Mich. U., 1994; JD, U. Cin., 1997. Bar: Ohio 1997, US Dist. Ct. Southern Dist. Ohio 1997, US Ct. of Appeals Sixth Cir. 1999. Ptnr. Squire, Sanders & Dempsey L.L.P., Cin. Mem., former chmn. Common Pleas Ct. Com.; mem., Electronic Data Discovery Task Force Squire, Sanders & Dempsey L.L.P, Cin.; mem., Adv. Bd. LexisNexis Applied Discovery. Served in USAR, vet., Operation Desert Storm. Named one of Ohio's Rising Stars, Super Lawyers, 2005, 2006. Mem.: Ohio State Bar Assn., Potter Stewart Inn of Ct. (barrister), Cin. Bar Assn. (mem., bd. of Professionalism Com.), FBA (exec. com., Cin./Northern Ky. chpt.). Office: Squire Sanders & Dempsey LLP 312 Walnut St Ste 3500 Cincinnati OH 45202-4036 Office Phone: 513-361-1240. Office Fax: 513-361-1201.

KANFER, FREDERICK H., psychologist, educator; married; 2 children. Student, Cooper Union Sch. Tech., Sch. Engring., 1942-44; BS cum laude, L.I. U., 1948; MA, Ind. U., 1952, PhD, 1953. Lic. psychologist, Oreg. Rsch. asst. Ind. U., 1949-52; asst. Psychol. Clinic, 1952-53, tchg. fellow in abnormal psychology, 1953; trainee VA Hosp., Indpls., 1951-52; asst. prof. psychology, dir. Psychoednl. Clinic, Washington U., St. Louis, 1953-57; cons. and asso. E.H. Parsons, M.D. and Assocs., St. Louis, 1955-57; assoc. prof. Purdue U., 1957-62; vis. prof. med. psychology U. Oreg. Med. Sch., summers 1958, 60, prof. psychiatry, 1962-69; vis. prof. psychology U. Oreg., Eugene, summers and winters 1967, 79; prof. psychology U. Cin., 1969-73; prof. U. Ill., Champaign, 1973-95, prof. emeritus, 1995—; sr. fellow, prof. U. Minn., Mpls., 1995-98. Fulbright lectr. Ruhr U., Bochum, Germany, 1968; guest prof. U. Salzburg, Austria, 1987; cons., spkr. in field; lectr., vis. prof. including univs. Oxford, Madrid, Heidelberg, Amsterdam, Berlin, Oslo, Cologne, Munich, Graz, Rome, Verona, Munster, Marburg, Wurzburg, London, Nijmegen, Copenhagen, Basel, Stockholm, Trondheim, Salzburg, Fribourg, Bern, Athens, Budapest; organizer, supr. postdoctoral tng. program for European psychologists univs. Cin. and Ill., 1969-87; vis. lectr. Inst. Environ. Health, U. Cin. Med. Sch., 1970-73, vis. prof. psychiatry, 1973-79; Morton vis. prof. Ohio U., 1976; sr. lectr. U. Bern, 1980-92; Disting. vis. prof. Dept. Air Force, 1983; adv. bd. Cambridge Ctr. for behavioral Studies, 1982-98; bd. advisors Internat. Alliance Health Edn., Stockholm, 1983—; mem. interna t. adv. bd. Max-Planck Inst. Psychiatry, 1985-90. Author: (with J.S. Phillips) Learning Foundations of Behavior Therapy, 1970, (with others) Premier Symposium Sobre Apprendizaje y Modificacion de Conducta en Ambientes educativos, 1975, (with Bruce K. Schefft) Guiding the Therapeutic Change Process, 1988, (with H. Reinecker and D. Schmelzer) Selbstmanagement-Therapie, 1991, 3d rev. edit., 2000, (with D. Schmelzer) Wegweiser Verhaltenstherapie: Psychotherapie als chance, 2001; contbr. numerous articles to profl. publs.; editor: (with A.P. Goldstein) Helping People Change: A Textbook of Methods, 1975, 3d rev. edit., 1980, 4th rev. edit., 1991, Maximizing Treatment Gains: Transfer Enhancement in Psychotherapy, 1979, (with P. Karoly) The Psychology of Self-Management, 1982; (with S. Englund, C. Lenhoff and J. Rhodes) A Mentor Manual: For Adults Who Work With Pregnant and Parenting Teens, 1995; assoc. editor: Psychol. Reports, 1961-99, Jour. Addictive Behaviors, 1974-80; editl. bd. Behavior Therapy, 1969-74, Behavior Modification, 1975-84, Cognitive Therapy and Research, 1976-80, 83-92, Behavioral Assessment, 1979-81, Clin. Psychology Rev., 1980-85, 87-92, Revista de Psicologia Generaly Aplicada, 1980—, Jour. Social and Clin. Psychology, 1982-98, Jour. Clin. Psychology and Psychosomatics, 1982—; internat. editl. bd. Verhaltens Therapie (Behavior Therapy), study and editl. reviewer; adv. editor: Research Press, 1978-96. With U.S. Army, 1944-46. Recipient Alexander von Humboldt Sr. Scientist award, 1987-88; U. Ill. Rsch. Bd. grantee, 1973-78; U. Ill. Rsch. Bd. univ. scholar, 1990-93. Fellow Am. Psychol. Assn. (exec. council div. 12); mem. Midwestern Psychol. Assn., AAAS, Assn. Advancement Behavioral Therapies (dir. 1972-74), Am. Bd. Examiners Profl. Psychology (diplomate), Sigma Xi; hon. life mem. Italian Soc. Behavior Therapy, German Assn. Clin. Behavior Therapy, Orgn. Behavior Therapy Uruguay Office: U Ill Dept Psychology 603 E Daniel St Champaign IL 61820-6232 E-mail: fkanfer@s.psych.uiuc.edu.

KANG, EMIL J., orchestra executive; b. NY, 1969; BS in Econs., Rochester U., NY. Orch. mgr. Seattle Symphony Orch., 1996-99; v.p. ops. Detroit Symphony Orch., 1999-2000, pres., exec. dir., 2000—. Office: Detroit Symphony Orch 3663 Woodward Ave Ste 100 Detroit MI 48201-2444

KANNE, MARVIN GEORGE, newspaper publishing executive; b. St. Louis, 1937; Student, St. Louis U. V.p., dir. ops. St. Louis Post-Dispatch. Mem. Am. Assn. Indsl. Mgmt., Am. Mgmt. Assn., IRRA Indsl. Rels. Rsch. Assn. Office: Saint Louis Post-Dispatch 900 N Tucker Blvd Saint Louis MO 63101-1099

KANNE, MICHAEL STEPHEN, federal judge; b. Rensselaer, Ind., Dec. 21, 1938; s. Allen Raymond and Jane (Robinson) Kanne; m. Judith Ann Stevens, June 22, 1963; children: Anne, Katherine. Student, St. Joseph's Coll., Rensselaer, 1957—58; BS, Ind. U., 1962, JD, 1968; postgrad., Boston U., 1963, U. Birmingham, Eng., 1975. Bar: Ind. 1968. Assoc. Nesbitt and Fisher, Rensselaer, 1968—71; sole practice Rensselaer, 1971—72; atty. City of Rensselaer, 1972; judge 30th Jud. Cir. of Ind., 1972—82, US Dist. Ct. (no. dist.) Ind., Hammond, 1982—87, US Ct. Appeals (7th cir.), Chgo., 1987—, Moot Ct. Competitions, 1998—; chmn. US Cts. Design Guide, 1988—95. Lectr. law St. Joseph's Coll., 1976—89, St. Frances Coll., 1990—91; faculty Nat. Inst. for Trial Advocacy, South Bend, Ind., 1978—88; mem. Ad Hoc Com. on Law Clerk Hiring, 2004. Bd. visitors Ind. U. Sch. Law, 1987—, Ind. U. Sch. Pub. and Environ. Affairs, 1991—; trustee St. Joseph's Coll., 1984—. 1st lt. USAF, 1962—65. Named Outstanding Alumnus, Today's Cath. Tchr., 1991; recipient Disting. Svc. award, St. Joseph's Coll., 1973, Disting. Grad. award, Nat. Cath. Ednl. Assn. Mem.: FBA, Tippecanoe County Bar Assn., Jasper County Bar Assn. (pres. 1972—76), Ind. State Bar Assn. (bd. dirs. 1977—79, Presdl. citation 1979), Law Alumni Assn. Ind. U. (pres. 1980). Roman Catholic. Avocations: horseback riding, weightlifting. Office: Charles A Halleck Federal Bldg 2447H 4th and Ferry St Lafayette IN 47902-1340 also: US Ct Appeals 219 S Dearborn St Chicago IL 60604

KANTROWITZ, ADRIAN, surgeon, educator; b. NYC, Oct. 4, 1918; s. Bernard Abraham and Rose (Esserman) K.; m. Jean Rosensaft, Nov. 25, 1948; children: Niki, Lisa, Allen. AB, NYU, 1940; MD, L.I. Coll. Medicine, 1943; postgrad. physiology, Western Res. U., 1950. Diplomate: Am. Bd. Surgery, Am. Bd. Thoracic Surgery. Gen. rotating intern Jewish Hosp. Bklyn., 1944; asst. resident, then resident surgery Mt. Sinai Hosp., NYC, 1947; asst. resident Montefiore Hosp., NYC, 1948, asst. resident pathology, 1949, fellow cardiovascular rsch. group, 1949, chief resident surgery, 1950, adj. surg. svc., 1951-55; USPHS fellow cardiovascular rsch., dept. physiology Western Res. U., 1951-52; asst. prof. surgery SUNY Coll. Medicine, 1955-56, assoc. prof. surgery, 1957-64, prof., 1964-70; dir. cardiovascular surgery Maimonides Med. Ctr., Bklyn., 1955-64, dir. surgery, 1964-70; chmn. dept. surgery Sinai Hosp. Detroit, 1970-75, chmn. dept. cardiovascular surgery, 1975-85; prof. surgery Wayne State U. Sch. Medicine, 1970—. Contbr. articles profl. jours. 1st lt. to major M.C. AUS, 1944—46. Recipient H.L. Moses prize to Montefiore Alumnus for outstanding rsch. accomplishment, 1949; 1st prize sci. exhibit Conv. N.Y. State Med. Soc., 1952; Gold Plate award Am. Acad. Achievement, 1966; Max Berg award for outstanding achievement in prolonging human life, 1966; Theodore and Susan B. Cummings humanitarian award Am. Coll. Cardiology, 1967 Fellow ACS, N.Y. Acad. Sci.; mem. Internat. Soc. Angiology, Am. Soc. Artificial Internal Organs (pres. 1968-69, Barney Clark award 1993), N.Y. County Med. Soc., Harvey Soc., N.Y. Soc. Thoracic Surgery, N.Y. Soc. Cardiovascular Surgery, Am. Heart Assn., Am. Physiol. Soc., Am. Coll. Cardiology, Am. Coll. Chest Physicians, Bklyn. Thoracic Surgery Soc. (pres. 1967-68), Pan Am. Med. Assn., Soaring Soc. Am., Am. Ski Assn. Achievements include being pub. pioneer motion pictures taken inside living heart, 1950; contbr. to devel. pump-oxygenators for human heart surgey; pioneer devel. mech., artificial hearts; performed 1st permanent partial mech. heart surgery in humans, 1966; 1st use phase-shift intra-aortic balloon pump in patient in cardiogenic shock; 1st human heart transplant in U.S., Dec. 1967. Home: 70 Gallogly Rd Auburn Hills MI 48326-1227 Office: 300 River Place Dr Detroit MI 48207-4233 E-mail: adriank3ak@aol.com.

KANTROWITZ, JEAN, health products executive; b. Passaic, NJ, May 27, 1922; d. Nathan and Yetta (Applebaum) Rosensaft; m. Adrian Kantrowitz, Nov. 25, 1948; children: Niki, Lisa, Allen. BS, Rider Coll., 1942; MS, U. N.C., 1945; MPH, U. Mich., 1975. Adminstrv. asst. Maimonides Med. Ctr., Bklyn., 1961-70, Sinai Hosp., Detroit, 1970-78, '80-83; program coord., sr. clin. instr. child psyciatry divsn. Case Western Res. U. Sch. Medicine, Cleve., 1978-80; v.p. adminstrn. and bus. devel. L.VAD Tech., Inc., Detroit, 1983—. Mgmt. cons. NIH, Washington, 1974— Mem. Am. Soc. Artificial Internal Organs (co-chair project bionics, history, artificial organs work group). Home: 70 Gallogly Rd Auburn Hills MI 48326-1227 Office: LVAD Tech Inc 300 River Place Dr Ste 6850 Detroit MI 48207-5095 Office Phone: 313-446-2800.

KANZEG, DAVID GEORGE, radio station executive; b. Cleve., Apr. 9, 1948; s. George and Ida Marie Ada (Hienz) K. BA, Wooster Coll., Ohio, 1970; MS, Syracuse U., NY, 1971; postgrad., SUNY, 1972. Cert. ESL lang. instr. Instr. English Meyer Lang. Ctr., Bogota, Colombia, 1969; grad. teaching asst. Syracuse U., 1971; instr. speech State U. Coll. at Buffalo, N.Y., 1971-73; exec. producer Sta. WCMU-FM Cen. Mich. U., Mt. Pleasant, 1973-76; radio program mgr. Sta. WLRH/Madison County Pub. Libr., Huntsville, Ala., 1976-77; radio program dir. Sta. WOUB-AM-FM Ohio U. Telecommunications, Athens, 1977-83; mgr. programming Radio Sta. WNYC, NYC, 1983—86; sta. advisor Corp. for Pub. Broadcasting, Cleve., 1978-87; dir. programming Radio Sta. WCPN, Cleve., 1987—99, v.p. programming divsn., 1999—2002; cons. Corp. for Pub. Broadcasting Mgmt. Consulting Svc., 1993—; dir. programing for TV, radio and web Sta. WCPN, 2002—, Sta. WVIZ, 2002—. Participant seminars on future pub. radio, San Francisco and Washington, 1984-85; panel mem. Airlie IV Seminar on Art of Radio, .Y.C., 1983; radio organizer Nat. Assn. Ednl. Broadcasters, Washington, 1976-78; exec. producer Future Forward Nat. Radio Series, 1985. Author: Transit Revisions, 1988, Ever Young: Douglas Moore and the Persistence of Legend, 1993; contbr. articles to pubs; author, co-creator website. Mem. Isabella County sub-com. on transp., Mt. Pleasant, Mich., 1975; incorporator Mid-Mich. Opera Assn., Mt. Pleasant, 1975, Tenn. Valley Opera Assn., Hunstville, 1976; mem. media panel Ohio Arts Coun., Columbus, Ohio, 1979-80; active Airlie II Seminar on Art of Radio, 1979. Recipient Tech. Prodn. award Ohio Ednl. Broadcasting, 1980, Ohio State award, 1986. Mem. Ohio Pub. Radio Programming (group chmn. 1978-80), Assn. Inds. in Radio, Sigma Delta Pi. Avocations: roller coasters, opera, traction, bicycling, travel. Home: 16253 Shurmer Rd Cleveland OH 44136-6115 Office: Sta WCPN/Cleve Pub Radio 3100 Chester Ave Ste 300 Cleveland OH 44114-4604

KAO, MIN H., manufacturing executive; BS, Nat. Taiwan U.; MS in Elec. Engring., PhD in Elec. Engring., U. Tenn. With Magnavox Advanced Products; sys. analyst Teledyne Sys.; co-founder Garmin Corp., 1989, chmn., CEO; dir. Garmin Internat., Inc. Named one of Forbes' Richest Americans, 2006, 50 Who Matter Now, Business 2.0, 2007. Office: Garmin Internat Inc 1200 E 151st St Olathe KS 66062-3426

KAO, PAI CHIH, clinical chemist; b. Nanking, China, June 20, 1934; came to U.S., 1965, naturalized, 1976; s. Gung and Chuu Hui (Chang) K.; m. Joyce Kao; 1 child, Wayne LeRoy. PhD in Biochemistry, U. Louisville, 1971. Diplomate Am. Bd. Clin. Chemistry, Am. Bd. Clin. Biochemistry. Instr. dept. social medicine at. Def. Med. Ctr., Taipei, Taiwan, 1958-65; postdoctoral investigator Oak Ridge (Tenn.) Nat. Lab., 1971-73; head dept. new methods devel. and radioimmunoassay CBL Lab., Columbus, Ohio, 1973-75; prof. emeritus clin. chemistry, dept. lab. medicine and pathology Mayo Clinic, Rochester, Minn., 1975—. Cons. clin. chemistry sect., clin. chemistry and hematology devices panel FDA. Contbr. articles to profl. jours. Fellow Nat. Acad. Clin. Biochemistry, N.Y. Acad. Scis.; mem. Am. Bd. Clin. Chemistry, Assn. Clin. Scientists. Home: 1432 Ridge Cliff Ln NE Rochester MN 55906-8705 Office: Mayo Clinic 1014 Plummer Rochester MN 55905-0001 Home Phone: 507-288-5946; Office Phone: 507-284-2691.

KAPLAN, ARNOLD, health service organization executive; BS in Commerce, Engring., Drexel U., 1962; MS in Indsl. Adminstrn., Carnegie-Mellon U., 1964. Sr. v.p., CFO Air Products Chem., Inc.; CFO United Healthcare Corp., Mpls., 1998-2001. Past bd. dirs. Baum Sch. Art. Recipient Drexel 100 award, 1992. Mem. Fin. Execs. Rsch. Found. (bd. dirs.), Phi Kappa Phi.

KAPLAN, GEORGE A., medical educator; BA, Johns Hopkins U., Balt., 1964; PhD in Psychology, Cornell U., 1968. Asst. prof. Stanford U., Calif.; lectr. Calif. State U.; asst. prof. Lone Mountain Coll., San Francisco; postdoctoral fellow in health psychology U. Calif., San Francisco, 1978—80, postdoctoral fellow in epidemiology Berkeley, 1980; vis. scientist Inst. of Epidemiology and Behavioral Medicine, San Francisco, 1980—85; chief Human Population Lab. Calif. Dept. Health Svcs., 1981; lectr. dept. epidemiology U. Calif., Berkeley, 1986—97; prof., chair dept. epidemiology U. Mich., Ann Arbor, 1997—, rsch. affiliate, Population Studies Ctr., rsch. prof., Survey Rsch. Ctr. Assoc. Can. Inst. for Advanced Rsch., 1996—; docent Dept. Cmty. Health and Gen. Practice, U. Kuopio, Finland; sr. investigator Kuopio Ischemic Heart Disease Study; dir. Mich. Interdisciplinary Ctr. on Social Inequalities, Mind and Body. Contbr. over 130 articles to profl. jours., chpts. in books. Mem.: Inst. Medicine of NAS. Achievements include research in include studies of factors associated with athergenesis to the impact of macroeconomic phenomena on the health of populations. Office: Univ Mich Dept Epidemiology 109 Observatory St 1014 SPHI Ann Arbor MI 48109-2029 Office Phone: 734-764-5435. E-mail: gkaplan@umich.edu.

KAPLAN, HARVEY L., lawyer; b. Kansas City, Mo., Nov. 11, 1942; BS in Pharmacy, U. Mich., 1965; JD, U. Mo., 1968. Bar: Mo. 1968, U.S. Tax Ct. 1971, U.S. Supreme Ct. 1971, U.S. Ct. Appeals (5th, 6th, 8th, 9th and 10th cirs.). Ptnr. Shook, Hardy & Bacon LLP, Kansas City, chair Pharm. and Med. Device Litig. Div. Mem. bd. editors Mo. Law Rev., 1967-68. Named Best of Bar, Kans. City Bus. Jour.; named one of 500 Leading Lawyers in Am., Lawdragon, 500 Leading Litigators in Am., Top 10 Super Lawyers Mo., Top 10 Super Lawyers Kans., Ams. Leading Lawyers for Bus., Chambers USA, Best Lawyers in Am., The Legal 500 US. Fellow Internat. Acad. Trial Lawyers (bd. dirs. 1991-97, 98—, sec.-treas. 2001-02), Internat. Soc. Barristers, Am. Bar Found.; mem. Am. Soc. Pharmacy Law, Mo. Orgn. Def. Lawyers (bd. dirs. 1985-93), Internat. Assn. Def. Counsel (bd. dirs. 1991-94, def. counsel trial acad. 1989, dir.-elect 1992, dir. 1993, v.p., found. bd. dirs. 2001-03), Def. Rsch. Inst. (chmn. drug and med. device litigation com. 1991-94, bd. dirs. 1995-98), Phi Delta Phi. Office: Shook Hardy & Bacon LLP 2555 Grand Blvd 19th fl Kansas City MO 64108-2613 Office Phone: 816-474-6550. Business E-Mail: hkaplan@shb.com.

KAPLAN, JOEL H., lawyer; b. Bklyn., Jan. 10, 1946; BS, Cornell U., 1966; JD, U. Chgo., 1969. Bar: Ill. 1969, US Supreme Ct. 1978. Ptnr. Seyfarth Shaw LLP, Chgo., 1975—, chmn. Labor & Employment Practice Group, 1992—94, mem. exec. com. Bigelow teaching fellow, instr. criminal law & legal writing U. Chgo. Law Sch., 1969—70. Mem.: ABA (railway & airline labor law com.). Office: Seyfarth Shaw LLP 55 E Monroe St Ste 4200 Chicago IL 60603 Office Phone: 312-269-8821. Office Fax: 312-269-8869. Business E-Mail: jkaplan@seyfarth.com.

KAPLAN, JOSEPH, pediatrician; b. Boston, Mar. 7, 1941; Student, Dartmouth U., 1958-60; BA, NYU, 1962; MD, Johns Hopkins U., 1966. Intern, resident in pediatrics Johns Hopkins Hosp., Balt., 1969-72; mem. staff Children's Hosp. Mich., Detroit, 1972—; prof. pediat., medicine and immunology-microbiology Wayne State U. Sch. Medicine, Detroit, 1972—. Contbr. article to prof. publ. Maj. U.S. Army, 1969-72. Recipient Rsch. Career Devel. award NIH, 1975-80. Office: Children's Hosp 3901 Beaubien St Detroit MI 48201-2196 E-mail: jkaplan@med.wayne.edu.

KAPLAN, MANUEL E., physician, educator; b. NYC, Nov. 6, 1928; s. Morris Jacob and Sylvia (Schiff) K.; m. Rita Goldman, May 22, 1955; children— Anne J., Eve D., Joshua M. BSc. Diplomate Am. Bd. Internal Medicine, Am. Bd. Hematology. Intern Boston City Hosp., 1954-55, resident, 1955-56, 58-59; fellow in hematology Thorndike Lab., 1959-62; attending hematologist Mt. Sinai Hosp., NYC, 1962-65, asst. chief hematology, 1963-65; asst. prof. medicine Washington U. Sch. Medicine, St. Louis, 1965-69; asso. prof. medicine U. Minn. Sch. Medicine, Mpls., 1969-72, prof. medicine, 1972-97, prof. emeritus, 1997—. Chief hematology and oncology Mpls. VA Med Ctr., 1969-93; med. dir. physician asst. program Augsburg Coll., Mpls., 1995-2000. Contbr. numerous articles to profl. jours. Served with USPHS, 1956-58. Mem. Am. Fedn. Clin. Research, Am. Soc. Clin. Investigation, Am. Soc. Hematology, Am. Assn. Immunology, AAAS, others Jewish. Home: 2950 Dean Pky Apt 1201 Minneapolis MN 55416-4427 E-mail: mannykaplan@aol.com.

KAPLAN, MARK E., allergist; b. Highland Pk., Ill., May 26, 1958; MD, Chgo. Coll. Medicine, 1987; MPH, Northwestern U., 1984. Cert. allergy and immunology 1993, 2003, internal medicine 1991, 2001. Intern Northwestern U., Chgo., 1987—88, resident, internal medicine, 1988—90, fellowship, allergy immunology, 1991—92, Children's Meml. Hosp., Chgo., 1991—92; assoc. Highland Pk. (Ill) Hosp., 1993—, Lake Forest Hosp., Ill., 1993—; cons. Victory Meml. Hosp., Waukegan, Ill., 1994—; allergist Allergy and Asthma Cons. -Highland Pk.; clin. instr. Northwestern U., 1993—. Office: Allergy and Asthma Cons Highland Pk 1160 Pk Ave W Ste 3 S Highland Park IL 60035

KAPLAN, RANDY KAYE, podiatrist; b. Detroit, Sept. 18, 1954; s. Earl Gene and Renee Joy (Sheftel) K. D of Podiatric Medicine, Ohio Coll., Cleve., 1979. Diplomate Am. Bd. Podiatric Surgery. Resident Kern Hosp., Warren, Mich., 1979-80; pvt. practice specializing in podiatric medicine, surgery Detroit, 1980—. Clin. instr., mem. staff Kern Hosp., Warren, 1980—; adj. prof. Ohio Coll. Podiatric Medicine, 1986—, Pa. Coll. Podiatric Medicine, 1986—; mem. staff, mem. resident tng. com. Providence Hosp., 1995; lectr. in field. Contbr. articles to profl. jours. Co-founder The Great Lakes Conf., 1988. Recipient Earl G. Kaplan award for polit. action excellence, 1994; Inspector Gen's. Integrity award U.S. HHS, 1995. Fellow Am. Coll. Foot Surgeons; mem. Am. Diabetes Assn., Am. Podiatric Med. Assn. (continuing edn. com. 1988-94, labor rels. com. 1990-94, Meritorious Svc. award 2003), Mich. Podiatric Med. Assn. (bd. dirs. 1985—, 2d v.p. 1988-90, pres. 1990-93, Podiatrist of Yr. Southeastern divsn. 1987-88, Shining Star award 1992), Kern Hosp. Resident Alumni Assn., Mich. Pub. Health Assn., Phi Alpha Pi (Man of Yr. 1979). Jewish. Office: 25725 Coolidge Hwy Oak Park MI 48237-1307 E-mail: rklions@aol.com.

KAPLAN, SHELDON, lawyer, director; b. Mpls., Feb. 16, 1915; s. Max Julius and Harriet (Wolfson) K.; m. Helene Bamberger, Dec. 7, 1941; children— Jay Michael, Mary Jo, Jean Burton, Jeffrey Lee. BA summa cum laude, U. Minn., 1935; LLB, Columbia U., 1939. Bar: N.Y. 1940, Minn. 1946. Pvt. practice, NYC, 1940-42, Mpls., 1946—; mem. firm Lauterstein, Spiller, Bergerman & Dannett, NYC, 1939-42; ptnr. Maslon, Kaplan, Edelman, Borman, Brand & McNulty, Mpls., 1946-80. Chmn. Kaplan, Strangis and Kaplan, Mpls., 1980—; bd. dirs. Stewart Enterprises Inc., Creative Ventures Inc. Decisions editor Columbia Law Review, 1939. Served to capt. AUS, 1942-46. Mem. Minn. Bar Assn., Hazeltime Nat. Golf Club, Mpls. Club, Phi Beta Kappa. Home: 2950 Dean Pkwy Minneapolis MN 55416-4446 Office: Kaplan Strangis & Kaplan 5500 Wells Fargo Ctr Minneapolis MN 55402 Office Phone: 612-375-1138. Business E-Mail: sk@kskpa.com.

KAPLAN, SIDNEY MOUNTBATTEN, lawyer; b. Bombay, Jan. 31, 1939; s. Charles von Pickens Kaplan and Jennie (Churchill) Goldberg; m. Donna Darrow, Feb. 14, 1989; children: Gary, Michael, Rory Patel. BA cum laude, Roosevelt U., 1960; JD, Ill. Inst. Tech., 1964. Bar: Ill., 1964, Minn., 1977, Colo., 1982, U.S. Dist. Ct. Ill. (no. dist.) 1964. Ptnr. Hess & Kaplan, Chgo., 1975-89, Baker & McKenzie, Chgo., 1989—. Bd. dirs. Jerome Gerson Meml. Found.; advisor to Prince Faisl, U.S. Affairs Mem. Ill. Bar Assn., DuPage County Bar Assn., Cook County Bar Assn. Office: Baker & McKenzie 130 E Randolph Dr 1 Prudential Plz Chicago IL 60601

KAPLAN, THOMAS ABRAHAM, physicist, educator; b. Phila., Feb. 24, 1926; s. Michael Jay and Nellie (Cohan) K.; m. Patricia Ruth Roe, Nov. 24, 1956; children: Melissa Ann, Andrea Jean, Laurie Michelle. BSME, U. Pa., 1948, PhD in Physics, 1954. Rsch. assoc. Engring. Rsch. Inst., U. Mich., Willow Run, 1954-56; rsch. assoc. Brookhaven Nat. Lab., Upton, NY, 1956-58; staff mem. Lincoln Lab., MIT, Lexington, Mass., 1959-70; prof. physics Mich. State U., East Lansing, 1970-95, prof. emeritus, 1995—. Cons. Naval Rsch. Lab., Washington, summer 1979-80; vis. scientist Max-Planck Inst. für Festkörperforschung, Stuttgart, Fed. Republic Germany, 1981-82, 88-89, summer 1983-84, Inst. für Festkörperforschung der Nuclear Physics Rsch. Inst. Jülich, Fed. Republic Germany, 1982; disting. vis. prof. U. Tsukuba, Ibaraki, Japan, 1989. Contbr. numerous articles on theoretical condensed matter physics to profl. jours. Petty officer 2nd class USN, 1944-46. Recipient Sr. Scientist award Alexander von Humboldt Stiftung, 1981. Fellow Am. Phys. Soc.; mem. Sigma

Xi. Democrat. Jewish. Avocations: singing, playing piano and trumpet. Office: Mich State U Dept Physics Astronomy East Lansing MI 48824 Business E-Mail: kaplan@pa.msu.edu.

KAPNICK, RICHARD BRADSHAW, lawyer; b. Chgo., Aug. 21, 1955; s. Harvey E. and Jean (Bradshaw) Kapnick; m. Claudia Norris, Dec. 30, 1978; children: Sarah Bancroft, John orris. BA with distinction, Stanford U., 1977; MPhil in Internat. Rels., U. Oxford, 1980; JD with honors, U. Chgo., 1982. Bar: Ill. 1982, N.Y. 1993. Law clk. to justice Seymour Simon Ill. Supreme Ct., Chgo., 1982—84; law clk. to Justice John Paul Stevens U.S. Supreme Ct., Washington, 1984—85; assoc. Sidley Austin LLP, Chgo., 1985—89, ptnr., 1989—. Mng. editor: U. Chgo. Law Rev., 1981—82. Vestryman Christ Ch., Winnetka, Ill., 2000—03; trustee Chgo. Symphony Orch., 1995—, vice chmn., 2001—06; bd. dirs., chmn. Civic Orch. Chgo., 1999—2001; bd. dirs. Cabrini Green Legal Aid Clinic, 1990—94, chmn. bd., 1991—93, mem. adv. bd. dirs., 1995—2006, chmn., 2005—06; mem. bd. Stanford Inst. Econ. Policy Rsch., 1999—. Fellow, Leadership Greater Chgo., 1989—90; Marshall scholar, 1978—80. Mem.: Chgo. Club, Phi Beta Kappa, Order of the Coif. Republican. Episcopalian.

KAPP, C. TERRENCE, lawyer; b. Pine Bluff, Ark., Oct. 1, 1944; s. Robert Amos and Guenevere Patricia (DeVinne) Kapp; m. Betsy Langer, May 2, 1987. BA, Colgate U., 1966; JD, Cleve. State U., 1971; MA summa cum laude, Holy Apostles Coll., 1984. Bar: Ohio 1971, U.S. Dist. Ct. (no. dist.) Ohio 1973, U.S. Supreme Ct. 1980, U.S. Tax Ct. 1996. Ptnr. Kapp & Kapp, East Liverpool, Ohio, 1971-84; pvt. practice Cleve., 1984—; ptnr. Marshman, Snyder & Kapp, Cleve., 1991-93, Kapp Law Offices, Cleve., 1994—. Contbr. articles to profl. jours. Chair St. John's Cathedral Endowment Trust, Cleve., 1992—94; pres., bd. dirs. Lake Erie ature and Sci. Ctr., Bay Village, Ohio, 1991—92. Mem.: ABA (judge finals nat. appellate adv. competition 1987, taxation com. exec. 1988—, nat. chmn. divorce laws and procedures com. family law sect. 1989—93, vice-chmn. step families com. 1991—93, task force client edn. 1991—, commr. presdl. commn. non-lawyer practice 1992—96, chmn. alternative funding com. 1992—, chair nat. symposium image family law atty-fact or myth 1993, domestic rels. taxatoin problems com. exec. tax sect., lit. sect., cert. Outstanding Svc. 1988, 1989, 1993, 1995), Cuyahoga County Bar Assn. (bar admissions com. exec. 1986—, cert. grievance com. 1990—, chair family law sect. 1991—92, jud. selection com. 1991—, unauthorized practice law com. 1992—, cert. Outstanding Leadership 1992), Ohio State Bar Assn. (family law com. exec. 1987—, family law curriculum com. Ohio CLE Inst. 1992—), Bay Men's Club, Cleve. Athletic Club (pres., bd.dirs.). Roman Catholic. Avocations: sailing, handball, racquet sports, dog training. Office: Kapp Law Offices PO Box 40447 Bay Village OH 44140-0447 Office Phone: 440-870-7500. Business E-Mail: kapplawoffices@ameritech.net.

KAPRAL, FRANK ALBERT, microbiologist and immunology educator; b. Phila., Mar. 12, 1928; s. John and Erna Louise (Melching) K.; m. Marina Garay, Nov. 22, 1951; children: Frederick, Gloria, Robert; m. Esther McKenzie, May 10, 2003. BS, U. of the Scis. in Phila., 1952; PhD, U. Pa., 1956. With U. Pa., Phila., 1952-66, assoc. in microbiology, 1958-66; assoc. microbiologist Phila Gen. Hosp., 1962-64, chief microbiology research, 1964-66, chief microbiology, 1965-66; asst. chief microbiol. research VA Hosp., Phila, 1962-66; assoc. prof. med. microbiology Ohio State U., Columbus, 1966-69, prof. med. virology, immunology and med. genetics, 1969—95, prof. emeritus dept. molecular virology, immunology and med. genetics, 1995—. Cons. Ctr. Disease Control, Atlanta, 1980, Proctor and Gamble Co., 1981-87. Contbr. articles to profl. jours. Active Ctrl. Ohio Diabetes Assn., 1992-93. With AUS, 1946-47. Grantee, Ctrl. Ohio Diabetes Assn., 1992—93; Rsch. grant, NIH, 1959—95. Fellow Am. Acad. Microbiology, Infectious Diseases Soc. Am.; mem. AAAS, Am. Soc. for Microbiology, Am. Assn. for Immunologists, Sigma Xi. Democrat. Roman Catholic. Achievements include patents for implant chamber. Home: 873 Clubview Blvd S Columbus OH 43235-1771 Personal E-mail: elaureo2@yahoo.com.

KAPSNER, CAROL RONNING, state supreme court justice; b. Bismarck, ND, Nov. 25, 1947; m. John Kapsner; children: Mical, Caithlin. BA in English lit., Coll. of St. Catherine; postgrad., Oxford U.; MA in English lit., Ind. U.; JD, U. Colo., 1977. Atty. Kapsner and Kapsner, Bismarck, 1977-98; justice N.D. Supreme Ct., 1998—. Mem. N.D. Bar Assn. (past bd. govs.), N.D. Trial Lawyers Assn. (past bd. govs.), Burleigh County Bar Assn. (pres. 1980, mem. Jud. Conference 1988-96). Office: Supreme Ct State Capitol 600 E Boulevard Ave Dept 180 Bismarck ND 58505-0530 Fax: 701-328-4480. E-mail: ckapsner@ndcourts.com.

KAPTUR, MARCIA CAROLYN (MARCY KAPTUR), congresswoman; b. Toledo, June 17, 1946; BA in Hist., U. Wis., Madison, 1968; M in Urban Planning, U. Mich., Ann Arbor, 1974; postgraduate student, U. Manchester, Eng., 1974, MIT, 1981; LLD (hon.), U. Toledo, 1993. Urban planner Toledo-Lucas County Plan Commns., 1969—75; dir. planning Nat. Ctr. Urban Ethnic Affairs, 1975—77; asst. dir. urban affairs domestic policy staff Exec. Office of Pres., 1977-79; mem. US Congress from 9th Ohio dist., 1983—, mem. appropriations com., mem. budget com., co-chair Congl. Ukrainian Caucus. Author: Women in Congress. Adv. com. Gund Found.; exec. com. Lucas County Dem. Com.; mem. Dem. Women's Campaign Assn. Named Legislator of Yr., Nat. Mental Health Assn.; recipient Americanism award, VFW, 1999, Barbed Wire award, 1999, Director's award, Georgetown U. Edmund A. Walsh Sch. Fgn. Svc., Ellis Island Medal of Honor, 2002. Mem. Am. Planning Assn., Am. Inst. Cert. Planners, NAACP, Urban League, Polish Mus., U. Mich. Urban Planning Alumni Assn. (bd. dirs.), Polish Am. Hist. Assn., Lucas County Dem. Bus. and Profl. Women's Club, Fulton County Dem. Women's Club. Democrat. Roman Catholic. Office: Dlst Office One Maritime Plz 6th Fl Toledo OH 43604 Office Phone: 202-225-4146, 419-259-7500. Office Fax: 419-255-9623.

KAPUSTA, GEORGE, botany educator, agronomist, researcher; b. Max, ND, Nov. 20, 1932; m. 1958; 4 children. BS, N.D. State U., 1954; MS, U. Minn., 1957; PhD in Botany, So. Ill. U., 1975. Agronomist N.D. State U., 1958-64; assoc. prof. So. Ill. U., Carbondale, 1964-80, prof. agronomy, 1980—. Recipient Outstanding Rsch. & Exten award Land of Lincoln Soybean Assn., 1978. Fellow Weed Sci. Soc.; mem. Agronomy Soc. Am., Soil Sci. Soc. Am., Sigma Xi. Office: Southern Illinois Univ Plant & Soil Science Rsch Sta Mail Code 4415 Carbondale IL 62901-4415

KAPUT, JIM L., lawyer; b. Toms River, NJ, May 28, 1960; BS, U Pa., 1982; JD, Cornell U., 1986. Bar: Ill. 1987. Assoc. Sidley & Austin (now Sidley Austin Brown & Wood), Chgo., ptnr., 1994—2000; sr. v.p., gen. counsel The ServiceMaster Co., Downers Grove, Ill., 2000—. Avocation: running. Office: The ServiceMaster Co 3250 Lacey Rd Ste 600 Downers Grove IL 60515-1700

KARDOS, PAUL JAMES, insurance company executive; b. North Vandergrift, Pa., Mar. 20, 1937; s. Joseph and Mary K.; m. Paulette Laura Sobota, Oct. 29, 1966; children— Diane, Brian. BS in Math, Grove City Coll., 1962. With Life Ins. Co. of N. Am., until 1977, v.p., until 1977; sr. v.p. Horace Mann Educators, Springfield, Ill., 1977-78, exec. v.p., 1978-79, pres., 1979—; dir., pres., CEO INA Corp. subs.

KARIM, MUHAMMAD BAZLUL, political scientist, educator; b. Mymensingh, Bangladesh, Dec. 26, 1949; arrived in U.S., 1975; s. Abdul and Akika Khatoon Bari; m. Jean Ellickson, July 26, 1975. BA with honors, Dhaka U., Bangladesh, 1972, MA in Geography, 1973, Western Ill. U., 1978; cert. in computer programming, Strayer Coll., Washington, 1981; MA in Internat. Studies, U. Denver, 1984, cert. in devel. studies, 1985, PhD in Internat. Studies, 1991. Asst. dir. Integrated Rural Devel. Program, Dhaka, 1973-74; rsch. asst. Rajshahi (Bangladesh), 1974-75; rsch. assoc. Ethikos Rsch., Inc., Silver Spring, Md., 1980-81; rsch. asst. Internat. Food Policy Rsch. Inst., Washington, 1981; owner Asian Am. Net., 1996—; instr. Spoon River Coll., Macomb, 1991-95; asst. prof. Western Ill. U., Macomb, 1994—98; web content editor and rschr. Mayer, Brown, Rowe & Maw LLP, Chgo., 2000—. Cons. Ill. Dept. Human Rights, 1998-99; presenter in field. Author: A Farmer's Market in America, 1981, The Green Revolution: An International Bibliography, 1986, Structural Constraints to Participatory Development: An Examination of Social Stratification System in Rural Bangladesh, 1992, Participation, Development and Social Structure: An Empirical Study in a Developing Country, 1994; editor Who's Who of Asian Ams., 1998-; contbr. articles and rsch. reports to profl. jours. Vol. flood victims, Kampsville, Ill., 1993; election judge primary and gen. election Macomb City Precinct 7, McDonough County, Ill., 1990. Rsch. fellow Shell Cos. Found., 1987; grad. rsch. assistantship U. Denver, 1984-85, stipend and tuition scholar, 1983-84. Mem. Assn. Third World Studies (life, web master 1996—2000). Office Phone: 312-782-0600. Office Fax: 312-701-7711. Business E-Mail: info@asianamerican.net.

KARKHECK, JOHN PETER, physics professor, researcher; b. NYC, Apr. 26, 1945; s. John Henry and Dorothy Cecilia (Riebling) K.; m. Kathleen Mary Shiels, Nov. 8, 1969; children: Lorraine, Michelle, Eric. BS, LeMoyne Coll., 1966; MA, SUNY, Buffalo, 1972; PhD, SUNY, Stony Brook, 1978. Various positions Grumman Corp., Bethpage, NY, 1964-68; grad. asst. SUNY, Buffalo, 1968-70; tchr. secondary schs. Mattituck (N.Y.) Sch. Dist., 1970-71, Shelter Island (N.Y.) Sch. Dist., 1971-73; grad. asst. SUNY, Stony Brook, 1973-78, postdoctoral fellow, 1978-79, rsch. assoc., 1979-81; asst. prof. physics GMI Engring. and Mgmt. Inst., Flint, Mich., 1981-84, assoc. prof., 1984, prof., dir. physics, 1988-89, head. dept. sci. and math., 1989-93; prof., chmn. dept. physics Marquette U., Milw., 1993—2003, dir. physics for medicine program, 2003—, asst. vice provost for grad. studies, 2004—; dir. Marquette U., Bridging the Worlds: Physics Project for Lugazi Diocese, 2003—. Physics assoc. Brookhaven Nat. Lab., Upton, N.Y., 1975-79, cons., 1979-85, STS, Hauppauge, N.Y., 1983, BID Ctr., Flint, 1985-90; acad. assoc. Mich. State U., 1988, 90, vis. scholar, 1989, vis. scientist, 1991; reviewer Addison-Wesley Pub., 1990, 93; regional dir. Mich. Sci. Olympiad, 1991-92, 92-93; co-dir. NATO Advanced Study Inst., 1998, editor, 1999-2000. Contbr. numerous articles to profl. jours. Den leader Cub Scouts Am., Flint, 1987-91; leader Boy Scouts Am., 1991-98; bd. dirs. Flint Area Sci. Fair, 1991-93; mem. sci. curriculum adv. com. Milw. Acad. Sci., 2000-03; judge local sci. fairs. Dept. Energy rsch. grantee, 1977-79, NATO travel grantee, 1983-86, 89, NATO ASI grantee, 1998. Mem. Am. Phys. Soc., AAAS, AAPT, Sigma Xi (v.p. Marquette U. chpt. 1998-99, pres., 1999-2000). Roman Catholic. Avocations: swimming, reading, bicycling, travel, learning German. Home: 6592 N Bethmaur Ln Glendale WI 53209-3320 Office: Marquette Univ Dept Physics PO Box 1881 Milwaukee WI 53201-1881 Office Phone: 414-288-5321. Business E-Mail: john.karkheck@marquette.edu.

KARLEN, DOUGLAS LAWRENCE, soil scientist, researcher; b. Monroe, Wis., Aug. 28, 1951; s. Lawrence Herman and Marian Bertha (Trumpy) K.; m. Linda Sue Bender, June 9, 1973; children: Sarah Jean, Steven Douglas, Holly Lin. BS, U. Wis., 1973; MS, Mich. State U., 1975; PhD, Kans. State U., 1978. Rsch. soil scientist Coastal Plains Soil, Water Conservation Rsch. Ctr., USDA-ARS, Florence, SC, 1978-88, Nat. Soil Tilth Lab. USDA-ARS, Ames, Iowa, 1988—; supervisory soil scientist, rsch. leader Soil and Water Quality Unit, Nat. Soil Tilth Lab., USDA-ARS, Ames, 2005—. Team leader Leopold Ctr. for Sustainable Agr., Ames, 1989—94. Asst. scoutmaster, com. chmn. Boy Scouts Am., Ankeny, Iowa, 1991—2005. Fellow Am. Soc. Agronomy (bd. rep. Ag sys. 1997-99, Agronomic Rsch. award 2001, Werner L. elson award for diagnosis of Yeild limiting factors 2001), Crop Sci. Soc. Am. (assoc. editor 1988-93, tech. editor 1994-99), Soil Sci. Soc. Am. (bd. rep. divsn. S6, 2002-05, Agronomic Achievement award 1996), Applied Soil Sci. Rsch. award 2002); mem. Coun. Agrl. Sci. and Tech., Soil and Water Conservation Soc. Am., Internat. Soil Tillage Rsch. Orgn. (asst. sec. gen. 2003—). Episcopalian. Office: USDA-ARS-MWA-NSTL 2150 Pammel Ct Ames IA 50011-4420 Office Phone: 515-294-3336. Business E-Mail: karlen@nstl.gov.

KARLEN, GREG T., real estate executive; Pres. Madison Marquette Realty Svcs., Minnetonka, Minn., 1989—. Office: Madison Marquette Realty Svcs 11100 Wayzata Blvd Ste 601 Minnetonka MN 55305-5522

KARLIN, EDWARD J., lawyer; b. Chgo., Mar. 10, 1952; BA with distinction, Ind. U., 1974; JD cum laude, Northwestern U., 1977. Bar: Ill. 1977, US Ct. Appeals (7th cir.), US Dist. Ct. (no. dist.) Ill. Mem. Seyfarth, Shaw, Fairweather & Geraldson, Chgo.; ptnr. Seyfarth LLP, Chgo., mem. exec. com., head, Corp. Practice Area. Bd. mem. Physician Insurers Assn. Am. Mem.: Chgo. Bar Assn. (banking law sect.), ABA (bus. law sect.), Phi Beta Kappa. Office: Seyfarth Shaw LLP 55 E Monroe St Ste 4200 Chicago IL 60603 Office Phone: 312-460-5875. Office Fax: 312-460-7875. Business E-Mail: ekarlin@seyfarth.com.

KARLIN, JEROME B., retail executive; Grad., U. Ill. Coll. Pharmacy, 1965. Joined Walgreen Corp., Deerfield, Ill., 1963, store mgr., 1967-73, dist. mgr., 1973-79, dir. Health Svcs., 1979-82, western regional v.p., 1982-87, v.p. western store ops., 1987-98, exec. v.p. store ops., 1999. Office: Walgreen Corp 200 Wilmot Rd Deerfield IL 60015-4620

KARLL, JO ANN, retired judge, lawyer; b. St. Louis, Nov. 16, 1948; d. Joseph H. and Dorothy Olga (Pyle) K.; m. William Austin Hernlund, Sept. 9, 1990. BS magna cum laude, Maryville U.; JD, St. Louis U. Bar: Mo. 1993. Ins. claims adjuster, 1967-88; mem. Mo. Gen. Assembly dists. 104 and 105, 1991-93; dir. Mo. State Divsn. Workers' Compensation, Jefferson City, 1993-2000, adminstrv. law judge, 2000—03; pvt. practice High Ridge, Mo., 2003—. Founder, 1st pres. scholarship fund Mo. Kids' Chance, Inc., 1995-96, bd. dirs., 1995—2007, North Jefferson Ambulance Bd., 2004-06, pres. bd. dirs. 2005. Mem. Internat. Assn. Indsl. Accident Bds. and Commns. (past pres.). Office: Karll Law Ctr LLC 1682 Old Gravois Rd High Ridge MO 63049 Home Phone: 636-677-0757; Office Phone: 636-677-7000. E-mail: karll.law@sbcglobal.net.

KARLS, KEN, foundation executive, former political organization administrator; m. Karen Karls; 4 children. Exec. dir. Cystic Fibrosis Assn. of ND, 2003—. Served State Resolutions Com., ND. Vice chmn. ND Rep. Party, chmn., 2003—07; vice chair Bismarck Area Rep. Coun.; mem. Burleigh County Election Canvassing Bd. Republican. Avocations: golf, hunting, fishing, bicycling. Office: Cystic Fibrosis Assn ND 921 S 9th St Suite 115 Bismarck ND 58504 Office Phone: 701-222-3998. E-mail: cfa@btinet.net.*

KARMAN, JAMES ANTHONY, manufacturing executive; b. Grand Rapids, Mich., May 26, 1937; s. Anthony and Katherine D. Karman; m. Carolyn L. Hoehn, Aug. 29, 1959; children: Robb Thomas, Janet Ellen, Edward John, Christopher James. BS cum laude, Miami U., Oxford, Ohio, 1959; MBA, U. Wis., 1960. Instr. corp. fin. U. Wis., Madison, 1960-61; asst. mgr. investment dept. Union Bank & Trust Co., Grand Rapids, 1961-63; treas. RPM, Inc., Medina, Ohio, 1963-69, v.p., treas., 1969-72, v.p., sec.-treas., 1972-73, exec. v.p., sec.-treas., 1973-78, pres., 1978—, also bd. dirs., CFO, 1982-93, vice chmn., 1999—. Instr. Am. Inst. Banking, 1962; bd. dirs. Metro. Fin. Corp., Shiloh Industries, Inc., A. Schulman, Inc. Trustee Trinity Cathedral, Cleve., Western Res. Hist. Soc., Boys & Girls Club, Cleve., The Leelanau Sch., Glen Arbor, Mich.; past bd. trustees Cleve. Orch., Boys Hope, Cleve., Cleve. Playhouse; mem. adv. coun. Miami U. Sch. Bus. Adminstrn.; mem. bd. visitors U. Wis.; mem. corp. coun., fin. com. Cleve. Mus. Art.; mem. Bluecoats, Inc., Cleve. Mem. U.S. Power Squadron, Gt. Lakes Hist. Soc., Mayfield Country Club, Cleve. Playhouse Club, Pine Lake Trout Club, Union Club (Cleve.), St. Louis Club, Order of Artus, Phi Beta Kappa. Home: 110 Seaspray Ave Palm Beach FL 33480-4227

KARMEIER, DELBERT FRED, engineer, consultant, realtor; b. Okawville, Ill., Apr. 2, 1935; s. Wilbert and Ida (Harre) K.; m. Naomi Firnhaber, Oct. 18, 1958; children: Kenton Howard, Dianne Jill. BSCE, U. Ill., 1957, MS in Transp. Engring., 1959. Rsch. assoc. U. Ill., 1958-59; traffic engr. St. Louis County, Mo., 1959-65, traffic commr., 1965-69; dir. transp. City of Kansas City, Mo., 1969-74, dir. aviation and transp., 1974-90; dir. pub. works City of Hartford, Conn., 1990-92; assoc. exec. dir. Am. Pub. Works Assn., Chgo., 1992-94; cons. Torres Cons. Engrs., Kansas City, Mo., 1994-95; assoc. Reece & Nichols, Leawood, Kans., 1995—. Mem. Nat. Com. on Uniform Traffic Control Devices, 1971-85 Automotive Safety Found. fellow U. Ill., 1959. Mem. Inst. Transp. Engrs. (pres. Missouri Valley sect. 1965-66), Airport Operator's Coun. Internat., Am. Rd. and Transp. Builder's Assn. (dir. 1973-83, chmn. pub. transit adv. coun. 1980-83), Transp. Rsch. Bd., Am. Pub. Works Assn., U. Ill. Alumni Club Kansas City (pres. 1996—), Thrivent Fin. for Lutherans (v.p. West Jackson County chpt. 2003—06), Leawood Rotary Club, Beta Sigma Psi (nat. editor 1963-69, pres. Kansas City alumni 1981-82, Disting. Alumnus award 1971, nat pres. 1986-88, nat. treas. 1996-2004). Lutheran. Home: 12206 Avila Dr Kansas City MO 64145-1750 Office: Reece Nichols Realtor 12150 State Line Rd Leawood KS 66209-1255 Office Phone: 913-906-3722. Personal E-mail: delkarm@aol.com.

KARMEIER, LLOYD A., state supreme court justice; b. Washington County, Ill., Jan. 12, 1940; m. Mary Karmeier; 2 children. BS, JD, Univ. Ill. Bar: Ill. 1964, US Dist. Ct. (so. dist. Ill.), US Supreme Ct. Law clk. Justice Byron O. House, Ill. Supreme Ct., 1964—68; state's atty. Washington County, Ill., 1968—72; law clk. Judge James L. Foreman, US Dist Ct., Ill., 1972—73; atty. Hohlt, House, DeMoss & Johnson, 1964—86; resident cir. judge Washington County, Ill., 1986—2004; assoc. justice Ill. Supreme Ct., 2004—. Chmn. Com. on Pattern Jury Instructions Ill. Supreme Ct., 2003—04. Mem.: Ill. Judges Assn., Ill. State Bar Assn. (assembly mem. 1996—2002), Ea. St. Louis Bar Assn., St. Clair County Bar Assn., Washington County Bar Assn., So. Ill. Am. Inn of Ct. (pres. exec. com. 2003). Office: Illinois Supreme Court PO Box 266 Nashville IL 62263

KAROL, NATHANIEL H., lawyer, consultant; b. NYC, Feb. 16, 1929; s. Isidore and Lillian (Orlow) K.; m. Liliane Leser, July 20, 1967; children: David, Jordan. BS in Social Sci, CCNY, 1949; MA (fellow), Yale U., 1950; LL.B., N.Y. U., 1957, LL.M., 1959, JD, 1966. Bar: N.Y. 1957. Mgmt. trainee Curtiss Wright Corp., Wood-Ridge, NJ, 1956-57; practiced in NYC, 1957-58; contracting officer USAF, NYC, 1958-62; chief contract mgmt. survey and cost adminstrn. Office of Procurement, NASA, Washington, 1962-64; asst. dir. cost reduction, 1964-66; dep. asst. sec. Grants Adminstrn., HEW, Washington, 1966-69; univ. dean CUNY; exec. dir. Research Found., 1969-73; v.p. Hebrew Union Coll., Cin., 1973-75; partner, nat. chmn. cons. services for edn. Coopers & Lybrand (C.P.A.s), Chgo., 1975-81; pres. Nathaniel H. Karol & Assocs. Ltd., 1981—. Cons. to govt. agys. and ednl. instns. Author: Managing the Higher Education Enterprise. Served with U.S. Army, 1953-56. Recipient Outstanding Performance award HEW, 1968, Superior Performance award, 1969 Mem. N.Y. Bar, Nat. Assn. Coll. and Univ. Bus. Officers, Nat. Assn. Coll. and Univ. Attys. Home and Office: 1228 Cambridge Ct Highland Park IL 60035-1014

KARP, GARY, marketing and public relations executive; V.p. mktg. and pub. rels. Alliant Foodsvc., Deerfield, Ill., 1992-96, v.p. catagory mgmt., 1996—. Office: Alliant Food Service 9933 Woods Dr Skokie IL 60077-1057

KARPIEL, DORIS CATHERINE, state legislator; b. Chgo., Sept. 21, 1935; d. Nicholas and Mary (McStravick) Feinen; m. Harvey Karpiel, 1955 (div.); children: Sharon, Lynn, Laura, Barry. AA, Morton Jr. Coll., 1955; BA, No. Ill. U., 1976. Real estate sales assoc. Bundy-Morgan BHG; coordinator Bloomingdale Twp. Republican Presdl. Hdqrs., Ill., 1960, 64, 68; former pres. Bloomingdale Twp. Rep. Orgn.; mem. Twp. Ofcls. of Ill.; trustee Bloomingdale Twp., 1974-75, supr., 1975-80; precinct committeewoman Bloomingdale Twp. Rep. Central Com., 1972, chmn., 1978-80; mem. Ill. Ho. of Reps., 1979-82, Ill. State Senate from 25th Dist., 1984—. Mem. Am. Legislators Exchange Council, Rep. Orgn. Schaumberg Twp.; former sec. DuPage County Suprs. Assn.; former sec. DuPage County Twp. Ofcls.; mem. DuPage County Women's Rep. Orgn., Meml. Hosp. Guild, Am. Cancer Soc. Mem. LWV, DuPage Bd. Realtors, Pi Sigma Alpha. Clubs: Bloomingdale Roselle and Streamwood Country, University Women's, St. Walters Women's. Address: 400 Lake St Ste 220 Roselle IL 60172-3572

KARR, GERALD LEE, agricultural economist, state senator; b. Emporia, Kans., Oct. 15, 1936; s. Orren L. and Kathleen M. (Keller) K.; B.S., Kans. State U., 1959; M.S. in Agrl. Econs., So. Ill. U., 1962, Ph.D. in Econs., 1966; m. Sharon Kay Studer, Oct. 18, 1959; children: Kevin Lee, Kelly Jolleen. Livestock mgr. Eckert Orchards Inc., Belleville, Ill., 1959-64; grad. asst. So. Ill. U., Carbondale, 1960-64; asst. prof. econs. Central Mo. State U., Warrensburg, 1964-67; asst. prof. agrl. econs., head dept. Njala U., Sierra Leone, West Africa, 1967-70; asst. prof. agrl. econs. U. Ill., Urbana, 1970-72; asso. prof. agrl. econs., chmn. dept., mgr. coll. farms Wilmington (Ohio) Coll., 1972-76; farmer, Emporia, Kans., 1976—; mem. Kans. Senate, 1981-98, minority leader, 1991-96; rsch. advisor Bank of Sierra Leone, Freetown, summer 1967; agrl. sector cons. Econ. Mission to Sierra Leone, IBRD, 1973. Mem. Lyon County Farmer Union, Lyon County Livestock Assn., Omicron Delta Epsilon, Farm House. Contbr. articles to profl. jours. Democrat. Methodist. Club: Kiwanis.

KARRAKER, LOUIS RENDLEMAN, retired corporate executive; b. Jonesboro, Ill., Aug. 2, 1927; s. Ira Oliver and Helen Elsie (Rendleman) K.; m. Patricia Grace Stahlheber, June 20, 1952; children: Alan Louis, Sharon Elaine Cohen. BA, So. Ill. U., Carbondale, 1949, MA, 1952; postgrad., U. Wis., Madison, 1951—52, Washington U., St. Louis, 1954—56. V.p. pers. Am. Appraisal Assocs., Inc., Milw., 1969-73, v.p. adminstrn., 1973-74, group v.p., dir., 1974-77, exec. v.p., dir., 1977-79, pres., dir., 1979-82; bus. mgr. Concordia Coll., Ann Arbor, Mich., 1986-91; ret., 1991. Asst. to chmn. Parker Pen Co., Janesville, Wis., 1967-69, personnel mgr., 1964-67; asst. to pres. Augustana Coll., Sioux Falls, SD, 1962-64, acting chmn., dept. social scis., 1960-61, asst. prof. history, 1956-60; cons., spkr. in field Columnist The Jour. Times, Racine, Wis., 1993-99 Trustee Better Bus. Bur., Milw., 1979-82, Citizens Govtl. Rsch. Bur., Milw., 1979-82; speaker, canvasser Rep. Party, S.D., 1956-60. With USNR, 1952-53, Korea. Mem.: Hoover Presdl. Libr. Assn., Heritage Found., Am. Legion. Lutheran. Avocations: church activities, travel, fishing. Home: 217 S 7th St Apt 11 Waterford WI 53185-4500 Personal E-mail: karr217@webtv.net.

KARSKY, TIMOTHY J., state agency administrator; b. ND; m. Sharon Karsky; 2 children. BS in Mgmt./Mktg., No. State Coll., Aberdeen, SD, 1981. With FDIC, 1982—86; chief examiner ND Dept. Fin. Instns., 1986—89, asst. commr., 1989—97, 1999—2001, commr., 2001—; loan officer local bank, Bismarck, ND, 1997—99. Chmn. ND State Banking Bd., ND State Credit Union Bd. Mem.: Conf. State Bank Suprs. (treas. 2003, vice chmn. 2006—07). Office: ND Dept Fin Instns 2000 Schafer St Ste G Bismarck ND 58501-1204 Office Phone: 701-328-9933. Office Fax: 701-328-9955.

KARTER, ELIAS M., paper products company executive; b. 1940; married. BS, U. Maine, 1962, MS, 1963, PhD, 1967. Asst. mill mgr. Westvaco Corp., 1963-78; resident mgr. Boise So. Co., Deridder, La., 1978-80; with Ga. Kraft Co., Rome, from 1981, former pres., chmn., chief exec. officer, also bd. dirs.; now v.p. mfg. and tech. The Mead Corp., Dayton, Ohio, 1994-96, exec. v.p., 1996—. Served to capt. U.S. Army, 1968-70.

KASER, BOB, radio personality; Pub. rels. asst., radio color commentator IHI Flint Generals, IHL Saginaw (Mich.) Gears, 1982, Easter League Erie Glades, 1983—84, Western League Seattle Thunderbirgs, 1984—89; radio announcer for IHL Grand Rapids Griffins Wood 1300, Grand Rapids, Mich., 1991—. Office: Woodradio 1300 77 Monroe Ctr Ste 1000 Grand Rapids MI 49503

KASHANI, HAMID REZA, lawyer, computer consultant; b. Tehran, Iran, May 1, 1955; came to U.S., 1976; s. Javad K. BSEE with highest distinction, Purdue U., 1978, MSEE, 1979; JD, Ind. U., 1986. Bar: Ind. 1986, U.S. Dist. Ct. (so. and no. dists.) 1986, U.S. Ct. Appeals (7th cir.) 1986, U.S. Supreme Ct. 1994, U.S. Ct. Appeals (9th cir.) 1996. Rsch. asst. Purdue U., West Lafayette, Ind., 1978-79, 80-81; engr. Cummins Engine Co., Columbus, Ind., 1981-82; assoc. faculty Ind. U.-Purdue U., Indpls., 1983-84; sr. software engr. Engineered System Devel., Indpls., 1985-87; computer cons. Hamid R. Kashani, Indpls., 1986—; pvt. practice law Indpls., 1986—; cons. Good Techs., Indpls., 1987-90; pres. Virtual Media Techs., Inc., 1998—. Cons. Prism Imaging, Denver, 1990-93, Ind. Bar Assn., 1989-95. Editor: Computer Law Desktop Guide, 1995. Mem., bd. dirs. ACLU, 1997—, Ind. Civil Liberties Union, Indpls., 1987—, mem. legis. com., 1987—, mem. screening com., 1985—, del., 1989, 91, 93, 95, 97, 99, 2001, acting v.p. fundraising, 1995-96, v.p. edn., 1996—, chair long-range planning com., 1991-92, 96—, chmn. nominating com., 1997—, pres., 1999—; bd. dirs. ACLU, 1997—. Fellow Ind. U. Sch. Law, 1984; recipient Cert. of Appreciation Ind. Correctional Assn., 1988; named Cooperating Atty. of Yr. Ind. Civil Liberties Union, 1990, 95, 98. Mem. ABA (vice chmn. YLD computer law com. 1990-91, chmn. computer law exec. com. 1991-93, litigation exec. com. 1987-89, 90-93, YLD liaison standing com. on jud. selection, tenure and compensation 1992-94, 95-96, sci. and tech. co-chair first amendment rights in the digital age com. 1997—, vice chair com. on opportunities for minorities and women 1997-99, YLD liaison to ABA tech. coun. 1992-93, vice chmn. nat. info. infrastructure com. sect. sci. and tech. 1993-97, chair privacy info. and civil liberties ABA sect. of individual rights and responsibilities 1998-2002, co-chair technology com., mem. standing com. on jud. selection, tenure and compensation 1995-96, chair privacy info. and civil liberties sect. of individual rights and responsibilities 1998-2002), IEEE (Outstanding Contbns. award 1983), Indpls. Bar Assn. (chmn. articles and bylaws coms. 1994-95), Ind. State Bar Assn. (vice chair computer comms. com. 1995-98, chair computer comms. com. 1998—, chair computer comm. com. 1998—), Eta Kappa Nu, Tau Beta Pi, Phi Kappa Phi, Phi Eta Sigma. Office: 445 N Pennsylvania St Ste 600 Indianapolis IN 46204-1818 Office Phone: 317-632-1000. E-mail: hkashani@kashanilaw.com.

KASICH, JOHN R., former congressman; b. McKees Rocks, Pa., May 13, 1952; BA, Ohio State U., 1974. Administrv. asst. Ohio State Senate, 1975-77; mem. Ohio Legislature, 1979-82, 98th-106th Congressses from 12th Ohio dist., Washington, 1983-2001; mem. nat. security com., armed svc. com.; mem. house budget com., chmn.; chmn. New Century Project, Columbus, 2001—. Author: Stand for Something, 2006.

KASISCHKE, LOUIS WALTER, lawyer; b. Bay City, Mich., July 18, 1942; s. Emil Ernst and Gladys Ann (Stuady) K.; m. Sandra Ann Colosimo, Sept. 30, 1967; children: Douglas, Gregg. BA, Mich. State U., 1964, JD, 1967; LLM, Wayne State U., 1971. Bar: Mich. 1968, U.S. Dist. Ct. (southeastern dist.) Mich. 1968; CPA. Acct. Touche Ross & Co., Detroit, 1967-71; atty. Dykema Gossett, Detroit, 1971—; pres. Pella Window and Door Co., West Bloomfield, Mich., 1990-98. Bd. dirs. Barton Malow Co., Southfield. Author: Michigan Closely Held Corporations, 1986; contbr. articles to profl. jours. Mem. ABA, AICPA, State Bar Mich. (editor column Mich. Bar Jour. 1971-83), Mich. Assn. CPAs, Am. Coll. Tax Counsel Republican. Lutheran. Avocations: mountain climbing, skiing, running, squash, golf. Home: 3491 N Lakeshore Harbor Springs MI 49740 Office: Dykema Gossett 39577 Woodward Ave Ste 300 Bloomfield Hills MI 48304-5086

KASPROW, BARBARA ANNE, biomedical researcher, writer; b. Hartford, Conn., Apr. 23, 1936; d. Stephen G. and Anna M. Kasprow. AB cum laude, Albertus Magnus Coll., 1958; postgrad., Laval U., 1958, Yale U., 1958-61; PhD, Loyola U., Chgo., 1969. Staff microbiology dept. Conn. State Dept. Health, 1957; lab. asst. dept. microbiology Yale U., New Haven, 1958—59; tng. scholar USPHS, 1959—60; asst. rsch. and editl. dept. anatomy Yale U., New Haven, 1961; rsch. assoc. N.Y. Med. Coll., 1961—62; rsch. assoc. to sr. rsch. assoc. and adminstrv. assoc. Inst. for Study Human Reprodn. St. Ann Ob-Gyn. Hosp., Cleve., 1962—67, asst. to dir. grad. med. edn., asst. dir. adminstrn. grad. rsch. endocrinology, Inst. for Study Human Reprodn., 1962—67; sr. rsch. assoc. dept. anatomy Stritch Sch. Medicine, Chgo., Hines, Ill., 1967—69; asst. prof. anatomy Loyola U., Chgo., 1969—75; asst. to v.p. University Rsch. Sys., 1975-79; v.p. med. topics Univ. Rsch. Sys., 1979—; asst. to pres. Internat. Basic and Biol.-Biomed. Curricula, Lombard, Ill., 1979—. Lectr. in field; invited U.S. del. on reprodn. to Vatican, 1964; round table leader Brazil-Israel Congress on Fertility and Sterility, Brazil Soc. Human Reprodn., São Paulo, 1972. Editl. asst. vol. VIII/3 Handbuch der Histochemie, Gustav Fischer Verlag, 1963; prodn. aide ednl. med. film The Soft Anvil, 1965-66; co-editor: Biology of Reproduction, Basic and Clinical Studies, 1973; contbr. articles to profl. jours. Recipient Certificate of Outstanding Achievement and Scholarship award Am. Assn. German Tchrs. and New Britain German Assn., 1954; named Honorary Citizen São Paulo, 1972. Mem. AAAS (life), Am. Assn. Anatomists, Am. Soc. Zoologists-The Soc. Integrative and Comparative Biology, Pan Am. Assn. Anatomy (co-organizer symposium on reproduction New Orleans 1972), Midwest Anatomists Assn. (program officer ann. meeting Chgo. 1974), Sigma Xi (life). Roman Catholic. Achievements include biological elucidation of growth horizons in uterine development, growth, and maturity; perfection of a hormonal model-system in highly controlled (surgerized) animals to ascertain quantitative relationships of purified estradiol-17beta and progesterone required for promotion of and duplication of these uterine growth horizons; development of experimental paradigms for the biomorphological elucidation of hormonally stimulated growth responses in endocrine target organs, and cyto-and histochemical elucidation of growth stimulants. Office: 607 E Wilson Ave Lombard IL 60148-4062

KASS, LAWRENCE, hematologist, oncologist, educator; b. Toledo, Ohio, Sept. 30, 1938; AB magna cum laude, U. Mich., 1960; MD with hons., U. Chgo., 1964, MS Anatomy, 1964. Diplomate Nat. Bd. Med. Examiners, Am. Bd. Internal Medicine/Internal Medicine and Hematology, Med. Oncology, Am. Bd. Pathology/Hematology. Intern Peter Bent Brigham Hosp., Boston, 1964-65, asst. resident internal medicine, 1965-66; sr. asst. resident internal medicine U. Hosps. of Cleve., 1966-68; Elliott Hoyt fellow in hematology Univ. Hosps. of Cleve., 1967-68; various to rsch. assoc. U. Chgo., 1968-70; asst. prof. internal medicine U. Mich. Med. Sch., Ann Arbor, 1970-73, assoc. prof. internal medicine, 1973-78; prof. path., medicine Case Western Res. U. Sch. Medicine, Cleve., 1978—; head hematopathology MetroHealth Med. Ctr., Cleve., 1978—. Cons. in medicine, VA Hosp., Ann Arbor; editorial cons. Williams and Wilkins Pubs., Balt., 1974—, Archives of Pathology and Lab. Medicine Blood, The Jour. of Hematology, The Jour. of Histochemistry and Cytochemistry, Western Jour. of Medicine, Am. Jour. of Hematology, Biotechnic & Histochemistry, 1975—, Rsch. Career Selection Rev. Com., VA, Washington, 1976—; active numerous coms. in field. Contbr. articles to profl. jours. Maj. med corps. U.S. Army, 1968-70. Recipient Internat. Giovanni DiGuglielmo prize, Giovanni DiGuglielmo Found., Accademia Nazionale Die Lincei, Rome, 1976, Diamond Cover award Nat. Soc. Histotechnologists and Jour. of Histotechnology, 1988, C.V. Mosby award, 1964, Merck award 1964. Fellow Am. Coll. Phys., Coll. Am. Pathologists; mem. AAAS, Am. Soc. Hematology, Am. Fedn. Clin. Rsch., Am. Soc. Clin. Oncology, Soc. Exptl. Biology and Medicine, Cen. Soc. Clin. Rsch., Histochem. Soc., Biol. Stain Commn., Am. Soc. Clin. Path., Phi Eta Sigma, Phi Beta Kappa, Alpha Omega Alpha. Office: MetroHealth Med Ctr 2500 Metrohealth Dr Cleveland OH 44109-1900 Office Phone: 216-778-4945. Office Fax: 216-778-5701. Business E-Mail: lkass@metrohealth.org.

KASTEL, HOWARD L., lawyer, business executive; b. Chgo., June 11, 1932; s. William A. and Beatrice (Seltzer) K.; m. Joan Herron, Dec. 20, 1953; children: Mark Alan, Jeffrey Lawrence. BA, Harvard U., 1954; JD cum laude, Loyola U., Chgo., 1960. Bar: Ill. 1960, U.S. Dist. Ct. (no. dist.) Ill. 1960, U.S. Ct. Appeals (7th cir.) 1965, U.S. Ct. Appeals (2d, 3d, 4th, 5th, 8th and 9th cirs.), U.S. Supreme Ct. Assoc. Aaron, Aaron, Schimberg & Hess, Chgo., 1960-62; ptnr. Altheimer & Gray, Chgo., 1962-80, Kastel & Rutkoff, Chgo., 1980-83, Holleb & Coff, Chgo., 1983-84, McDermott, Will & Emery, Chgo., 1984-97, of counsel, 1997—; pres., CEO Wanger Asset Mgmt. Ltd., Chgo., 1998-99; ptnr. Wanger Asset Mgmt. LP, Chgo., 1998-99; prin. Fox, Hefter, Swibel, Levinei & Cadnole, 2000—. Mem. Fin. Acctg. Standards Bd. Task Force on Non-Bus. Orgns., 1981-83, mem. Labor Law Com., 1961-72, Civil Practice Com., 1971-88, Securities Law Com., 1981-88, Jud. Com., 1983—. Sgt. USMC, 1954-56. Mem. ABA (law and acctg. com. 1977—, chmn. subcom. internat. acctg., fed. regulations of securities subcom. on SEC practice and enforcement matters 1979—). Avocations: yacht racing, treking, cross country skiing, golf. Home: 1501 N State Pkwy Chicago IL 60610-1676 also: 10393 Holt Chapel Hill NC 27517-8542 Home Phone: 312-787-8827; Office Phone: 312-224-1224.

KASTELIC, DAVID ALLEN, lawyer, energy and food products executive; b. Ely, Minn., Apr. 19, 1955; m. Janice E Kastelic. BS cum laude, St. John's U., Collegeville, Minn., 1977; JD magna cum laude, U. Minn., Mpls., 1980. Bar: Minn. 1980, US Fed. Ct. 1980, US Ct. Appeals (8th cir.) 1985, US Supreme Ct. 1985, US Tax Ct. 1985. Sr. v.p. CHS Inc., Inver Grove Heights, Minn., gen. counsel, 2003—. Office: CHS Inc PO Box 64089 Saint Paul MN 55164-0089 Office Phone: 651-355-3712. Office Fax: 651-355-4554. E-mail: david.kastelic@chsinc.com.

KASTEN, G. FREDERICK, JR., investment company executive; Pres., CEO Robert W. Baird Co., Milw., 1979—98, chmn., CEO, 1998—2000, chmn., 2000—. Bd. dir. Regal Beloit Corp. Office: Robert W Baird Co 777 E Wisconsin Ave Milwaukee WI 53202-5300

KASTEN, MARY ALICE C., state legislator; b. Matthews, Mo., June 6, 1928; d. Clarence Alvin and Ruth (Hill) Critchlow; m. Melvin C. Kasten, 1949; children: Mark, Michael, Margaret. BS, Southeast Mo. State U., 1949; postgrad., U. Pitts. State rep. Mo. State Congress. Del. Nat. Conf. Edn. and Citizenship; mem. Cape Girardeau Sch. Bd., Nat. Joint Com. Representing Sch. Bd. Assn., Mo. State Bd. Edn., State Adv. Com. on Vocat. Edn. Bd. Regents mem. Southeast Mo. State U. Mem. Nat. Sch. Bd. Assn., Mo. Sch. Bd. Assn.

KASTNER, CHRISTINE KRIHA, newspaper correspondent; b. Cleve., Aug. 27, 1951; d. Joseph Calvin and Grace (Weber) Kriha; m. Donald William Kastner, June 30, 1979; 1 child, Paul Donald. Assoc., Lakeland C.C., 1976; BA in Comms., Cleve. State U., 1983. Asst. editor, comms. specialist TRW, Inc., Cleve., 1978-85; editor Kaiser Permanent, Cleve., 1985-87; dir. pub. rels. Northeastern Ohio chpt. Arthritis Found., Cleve., 1991-92; newspaper corr. The Plain Dealer, Cleve., 1992—. Contbg. author: Encyclopedia of Cleveland History, 1988. Recipient Gold Addy award Am. Advt. Fedn., 1986, Award of Excellence Women in Comms., Inc., 1987, Bronze Quill award Internat. Assn. Bus. Communicators, 1987. Mem. Soc. Profl. Journalists. Roman Catholic. Avocations: bicycling, reading. Home and Office: 5003 Clubside Rd Lyndhurst OH 44124-2540

KASTOR, FRANK SULLIVAN, language educator; b. Evanston, Ill., Aug. 19, 1933; s. Herman Walker and Rebecca (Sullivan) K.; m. Tina Bennett, Oct. 28, 1979; children: Dacaeber, Mark, Harlan, Kristina, Patrick, Liam, Mary Elisabeth, Caroline. BA, U. Ill., 1955, MA, 1956; PhD, U. Calif., Berkeley, 1963. Teaching asst. U. Ill., 1955-56, U. Calif., Berkeley, 1960-63; asst. prof. English U. So. Calif., 1963—66, 1967—68; assoc. prof. English No. Ill. U., 1968-69; prof. English Wichita State U., 1969—, chmn. dept., 1969-75, prof. emeritus, 1998. Contbr. to: The Milton Ency., The Dictionary of Literary Biography; author books, articles, revs., TV documentaries, C.S. Lewis study guides. Served with USAF, 1956-59. Rsch. grantee U. Calif., Berkeley, 1962, U. So. Calif., 1964, No. Ill. U., 1969, Wichita State U., 1970, 72, 73, 74, 84, 86, 92; Fulbright lectr., Spain, 1966-67; Kans. Com. for Humanities grantee, 1973, 74, 94; recipient NEH award, 1971, 84. Mem. MLA, AAUP, Milton Soc. Am., N.Y. C.S. Lewis Soc., C.S. Lewis Soc. of Kans. (a founder), Phi Kappa Phi. Christian Ch. E-mail: fskdr3@cox.net.

KASTORY, BERNARD H., finance educator, former food products executive; BSChemE, U. Ill.; MBA, Northwestern U. Joined N.Am. corn refining divsn. Corn Products Bestfoods, 1967—, plant mgr. Corpus Christi, Tex., project mgr. devel. Stockton, Calif., plant mgr. corn refining plant Argo, Ill., v.p. mfg. and engring. corn proudcts, v.p., gen. mgr. ops., v.p. tech. corn refining bus., 1989-92, pres. corn refining bus., 1992-95; chmn., CEO Bestfoods Baking Co., 1995-97; sr. v.p. fin. and adminstrn. Bestfoods, 1997-98, sr. v.p. Asia, Latin Am., Balkins, 1999—2000; dir. Corn Products Internat. Inc., 2001—; F. William Harder prof bus. adminstrn. Skidmore Coll., Saratoga Springs, NY, 2001—. Office: c/o Corn Products Westbrook Corporate Center Westchester IL 60154

KASULIS, THOMAS PATRICK, humanities educator; b. Bridgeport, Conn., Mar. 5, 1948; s. Joseph John and Albina Anna (Checkanouskas) K.; m. Ellen Elizabeth Sponheimer, June 5, 1970; children: Telemachus, Matthias, Benedict. BA, Yale U., 1970, MPh, 1972, PhD, 1975; MA, U. Hawaii, 1973. Asst. prof. philosophy U. Hawaii, Honolulu, 1975-80; from asst. prof. to prof. philosophy and religion Northland Coll., Ashland, Wis., 1981-91; prof. comparative studies The Ohio State U., Columbus, 1991—, chair East Asian langs. and lit., 1993-95, chair comparative studies, 1995-98. Mellon faculty fellow in humanities Harvard U., Cambridge, Mass., 1979-80; vis. facility rschr. Osaka (Japan) U., 1982-83; Numata vis. prof. U. Chgo., Ill., 1988. Author: Zen Action/Zen Person, 1981, Intimacy or Integrity: Philosophy and Cultural Difference, 2002, Shinto: The Way Home, 2004; editor, co-translator: The Body: Toward an Eastern Mind-Body Theory, 1987; co-editor: Self as Body in Asian Theory and Practice, 1993, Self as Person in Asian Theory and Practice, 1994; contbr. chpts. to books and articles to profl. jours. Fellow Japan Found., 1982-83, 2004; NEH fellow, 1986-87, 2000; Sr. Rsch. fellow East West Ctr., Honolulu, 1988. Mem. Soc. for Asian and Comparative Philosophy (pres. 1988-91), Am. Soc. for the Study of Religion (pres. 1999-2002). Home: 1465 Montcalm Rd Upper Arlington OH 43221-3450 Office: Ohio State Univ Comparative Studies 451 Hagerty Hall 1775 College Rd Columbus OH 43210-1340 Home Phone: 614-487-9756; Office Phone: 614-292-7892. Business E-Mail: kasulis.1@osu.edu.

KATCHER, RICHARD, lawyer; b. NYC, Dec. 17, 1918; s. Samuel and Gussie (Appelbaum) K.; m. Shirley Ruth Rifkin, Sept. 24, 1944; children: Douglas P., Robert A., Patti L. BA, U. Mich., 1941, JD, 1943. Bar: Mich. 1943, N.Y. 1944, Ohio 1946. Assoc. Noonan, Kaufman & Eagan, NYC, 1943-46; from assoc. to ptnr. Ulmer, Berne & Laronge, Cleve., 1946-72; ptnr. Baker & Hostetler, Cleve., 1972-95. Lectr. in fed. income taxation Case Western Res. U. Sch. Law, Cleve., 1953-69, 71-72; mem. adv. bd. on intercollegiate athletics, U. Mich., 2001-2004; chmn. Nat. Conf. Lawyers and CPAs, 1982-. Contbr. articles on fed. tax to profl. jours. Recipient Disting. Alumni Service award U. Mich., 1987, Leadership medal Pres.' Soc. of U. Mich., 1991. Fellow ABA (coun. sect. taxation 1973-76), Am. Coll. Tax Counsel (regent); mem. Am. Bar Retirement Assn. (bd. dirs., v.p. 1986-87, pres. 1987-88), U. Mich. Pres. Soc. (chmn. exec. com. 1987-90), at. Conf. Lawyers and CPAs (chmn. 1982-83), U. Mich. Cleve. Club (pres. 1959, Outstanding Alumnus award 1987), U. Mich. Alumni Assn. (dir. 1994-98, sec. 1997-98). Avocation: tennis. Home: 26150 Village Ln Apt 104 Beachwood OH 44122-7527 Office: Baker & Hostetler 3200 National City Ctr 1900 E 9th St Ste 3200 Cleveland OH 44114-3475 Office Phone: 216-861-7476. E-mail: RKatcher@bakerlaw.com.

KATEHI, LINDA P.B., engineering educator; b. Athens, Greece, Jan. 30, 1954; arrived in US, 1979; d. Vasilios and Georgia (Begni) K.; m. Spyros Tseregounis, July 10, 1980; children: Erik Tseregounis, Helena Tseregounis. BSEE, Nat. Tech. U., Athens, 1977; MSEE, UCLA, 1981, PhD in Elec. Engring., 1984. Teaching asst. at. Tech. U. Athens, 1977—78; rsch. engr. Dept. Def. Naval Rsch. Lab, GETEN, Athens, 1978—79; rsch. asst. UCLA, 1979-84; asst. prof. elec. engring. U. Mich., Ann Arbor, 1984—89, assoc. prof. elec. engring. and computer sci., 1989—94, prof. electrical engring. and computer sci., 1994—2001, coll. engring. assoc. dir. grad. program, 1994—95, mem. exec. com. Coll. Engring., 1995—98, assoc. dean grad. edn., 1998—99, sr. assoc. dean academic affairs, 1999—2001; John A. Edwardson dean engring. Purdue U., West Lafayette, Ind., 2001; prof. computer and elec. engring., provost and vice chancellor academic affairs The U. Ill., Urbana-Champaign, 2002—. Reviewer Army Rsch. Office, 1984—, NSF, 1984—, chair. adv. com. to Engring. Directorate, 2005—, mem. adv. com. to Directorate for Computer and Info. Sci. and Engring., 2002—; strategic directions com. U. Mich., 1999—, assoc. dean and assoc. provosts academic programs group, 1999—, chair, provost com. on faculty mentoring, 1999—; mem. adv. com. on electron devices Dept. Defense, 1999—; chair Pioneer Revolutionary Technologies Subcom., Aerospace Enterprise NASA, 2002—, mem. Aerospace Tech. Adv. Com., 2002—, mem. aeronautics technical adv. com.; mem. Army Rsch. Lab. adv com. on Sensors and Electrons Divsn. AUS, 2003—; mem. engring. adv. com. Iowa State U., 2003—; mem. nominating com. Nat. Medal Tech.; mem. Kauffman at. Panel for Entrepreneurship; mem. telecomm. bd. NRC, mem. Army Rsch. Lab adv. com. divsn. sensors and electonics; mem. DoD Adv. Group on Electron Devices. Contbr. articles to profl. jours. Recipient Rsch. Excellence Award, Elec. Engring. and Computer Sci. Dept., U. Mich. Ann Arbor, 1993, Humboldt Rsch. Award, 1994, Faculty Recognition Award, U. Mich. Ann Arbor, 1994. Fellow: AAAS (mem. bd.), IEEE (Antennas and Propagation Soc., Microwave Theory and Techniques Soc., Microwave Theory and Techniques Soc. 3d Millenium Medal 2000); mem.: NAE, Advanced Computational Electromagnetics Soc., Internat. Soc. Hybrid Microelectronics, Internat. Union Radio Sci. (Booker Young Scientist Award 1987), Union Radio Sci. Internat., Sigma Xi. Achievements include patents in field. Avocations: skiing, tennis, gardening. Office: U Ill Urbana Office Provost and Vice Chancellor Acad Affairs Swanland Adminstrn Bldg MC 304 601 E John St Champaign IL 61820

KATEN-BAHENSKY, DONNA, health facility administrator; BA in Anthropology, U. Mo., Columbia, 1980, MS in Pub. Health Adminstrn., 1982. COO, assoc. hosp. dir., acting hosp. dir. U. Nebr. Hosp., Omaha, 1991—98; vice chancellor bus. and fin. U. Nebr. Med. Ctr., Omaha, 1996—97; v.p. ambulatory care Nebr. Health Sys., Omaha, 1997—98; COO Med. Coll. Va. Hosps., Richmond, 1998—2000, exec. v.p., COO, 2000—02, Clinics of Va. Commonwealth U. Health Sys., Richmond, 2000—02; dir., CEO U. Iowa Hosps. and Cilinics, Iowa City, 2002—. Adj. faculty, preceptor grad. program in health adminstrn. Med. Coll. Va. Hosps.; mem. U. Health Sys. Consortium, Am. Coll. Healthcare Execs.; mem. adv. bd. Pfizer Health Solutions.

KATTEN, MELVIN L., lawyer; b. Chgo., Sept. 5, 1936; s. Bert and Jeanette (Shure) K.; m. Renee J. Kaufman, Dec. 21, 1958; children: Pamela, Bonnie, Mitchell, Betsy. BS in Acctg., U. Ill., 1958; JD, John Marshall Law Sch., 1963. Bar: U.S. Dist. Ct., U.S. Tax Ct. With IRS, Chgo., 1958-64; sr. ptnr. Katten Muchin & Zavis, Chgo., 1964—. Bd. dirs. Amserv, Inc., Reno, Wash. Sci., Wayzeta, Minn. Active Better Govt. Assn., Chgo., Anti Defamation League, Chgo., bd. dirs. Roosevelt U., Chgo., Auditorium Theatre Roosevelt U., Amalgamated Bank. Mem. Stanard Club. Office: Katten Muchin & Zavis 525 W Monroe St Ste 1600 Chicago IL 60661-3693

KATZ, ADRIAN IZHACK, medical educator, physician; b. Bucharest, Romania, Aug. 3, 1932; came to U.S., 1965, naturalized, 1976; s. Ferdinand and Helen (Lustig) K.; m. Miriam Lesser, Mar. 31, 1965; children— Ron, Iris. MD, Hebrew U., 1961. Research fellow Yale U., 1965-67, Harvard U., 1967-68; intern Belinson Med. Center, Israel, 1961, resident, 1962-65; practice medicine specializing in internal medicine and nephrology New Haven, 1966-67, Boston, 1967-68, Chgo., 1968—; attending physician U. Chgo. Hosps., 1968—2002, head nephrology sect., 1973-82; asst. prof. medicine U. Chgo., 1968-71, assoc. prof., 1971-74, prof., 1975—2002, prof. emeritus, 2002—. Fogarty sr. internat. fellow, vis. scientist Lab Cell Physiology, Coll. de France, Paris, 1977-78; vis. prof. cellular and molecular physiology Yale U., 1988; vis. scientist dept. molecular medicine Karolinska Inst., Stockholm, 1994—. Co-author: Kidney Function and Disease in Pregnancy; contbr. chpts. to books, articles to profl. jours. Fellow A.C.P.; mem. Am. Physiol. Soc., Am. Soc. Clin. Investigation, Assn. Am. Physicians, Am. Soc. Nephrology, Internat. Soc. Nephrology, Central Soc. Clin. Research, N.Y. Acad. Scis. Home: 1125 E 53rd St Chicago IL 60615-4410 Office: U Chgo 5841 S Maryland Ave Chicago IL 60637-1463 Business E-Mail: akatz@medicine.bsd.uchicago.edu.

KATZ, DAVID ALLAN, federal judge; b. Nov. 1, 1933; s. Samuel and Ruth (Adelman) K.; m. Joan G. Siegel, Sept. 4, 1955; children: Linda, Michael S., Debra. BBA, Ohio State U., 1955, JD summa cum laude, 1957. Bar: Ohio 1957. Ptnr. Spengler Nathanson, Attys., Toledo, 1957-86, mng. ptnr., 1986-93; judge U.S. Dist. Ct. (no. dist.) Ohio, Toledo, 1994—. Dir., corp. sec. Seaway Food Town, Inc., Maumee, Ohio, 1980-94; trustee St. Vincent Med. Ctr., 1987-96, sec., 1988-90, vice chmn.-treas., 1990-94, chmn., 1994-96, St. Vincent Med. Ctr. Found., chmn., 1990-92; trustee The Toledo Symphony; v.p. Jewish Edn. Service N.Am., 1985-91; trustee Mercy Health Sys. NW Ohio, 1996—. Pres. Temple B'nai Israel, Toledo, 1970-73, Jewish Welfare Fedn., Toledo, 1977-79, Toledo Bar Assn. Found., 1983-94; trustee Advocates for Victims and Justice, Inc.; bd. dirs. Toledo Zoo Found. Fellow Ohio Bar Found., Toledo Bar Found.; mem. ABA, Toledo Bar Assn. (sec., trustee 1972-78), Ohio State Bar Assn. Office: US Court House 1716 Spielbusch Ave Ste 210 Toledo OH 43624-1347 Home Phone: 419-536-5250; Office Phone: 416-213-5710.

KATZ, DONALD L., lawyer; b. Buffalo, 1965; BA in Comparative Lit., Hobart Coll., 1988; JD magna cum laude, Mich. State U. Coll. of Law, 2000. Bar: Mich. 2001. Securities broker A. G. Edwards & Sons, Inc., 1990—92; pres. Papa's Manhattan Pasta Co., NY, 1992—94; municipal bond broker Lebenthal & Co., 1994—95; portfolio mgr., investment advisor Katz & Co., Am. Investment Services, Inc., 1995—2001; tax assoc., vice chmn. aviation practice group Jaffe, Raitt, Heuer and Weiss, P.C., Detroit, 2001—03; sr. atty., deputy dir. aviation and transportation practice group Miller, Canfield, Paddock and Stone P.L.C., 2003—. Mem.: Mich. Bus. Aviation Assn., Nat. Bus. Aviation Assn., State Bar Mich., ABA. Office: 150 W Jefferson Ste 2500 Detroit MI 48226-4415 Business E-Mail: katz@millercanfield.com.

KATZ, JOSEPH JACOB, retired chemist, educator; b. Apr. 19, 1912; s. Abraham and Stella (Asnin) K.; m. Celia S. Weiner, Oct. 1, 1944; children: Anna, Elizabeth, Mary, Abram. BSc, Wayne U., 1932; PhD, U. Chgo., 1942. Research asso. chemistry U. Chgo., 1942-43, asso. chemist metall. lab., 1943-45; sr. chemist Argonne Nat. Lab., Ill., 1945—92, ret. Ill., 1992; Tech. adviser U.S. delegation UN Conf. on Peaceful Uses Atomic Energy, Geneva, 1955; chmn. AAAS Gordon Research Conf. on Inorganic Chemistry, 1953-54. Am. editor Jour. Inorganic and Nuclear Chemistry, 1955-82. Recipient Distinguished Alumnus award Wayne U., 1955, Profl. Achievement award U. Chgo. Alumni Assn., 1983, Rumford Premium Am. Acad. Arts & Scis., 1992; Guggenheim fellow, 1956-57 Mem. Am. Chem. Soc. (award for nuclear applications in chemistry 1961, sec.-treas. div. phys. chemistry 1966-76), Nat. Acad. Scis., Phi Beta Kappa, Sigma Xi. Office: Argonne at Lab 9700 Cass Ave Argonne IL 60439-4803 Home: 5550 S Shore Dr Apt 601 Chicago IL 60637-5032 E-mail: jjkatz@worldnet.att.net.

KATZ, LEWIS ROBERT, law educator; b. NYC, Nov. 15, 1938; s. Samuel and Rose (Turoff) K.; m. Jan Karen Daugherty, Jan. 14, 1964; children: Brett Elizabeth, Adam Kenneth, Tyler Jessica. AB, Queens Coll., 1959; JD, Ind. U., 1963. Bar: Ind 1963, Ohio 1971. Assoc. Snyder, Bunger, Cotner & Harrell, Bloomington, Ind., 1963-65; instr. U. Mich. Law Sch., Ann Arbor, 1965-66; asst. prof. Case Western Res. U. Law Sch., Cleve., 1966-68, assoc. prof., 1968-71, prof., 1971—, John C. Hutchins prof. law, 1973—. Dir. Ctr. for Criminal Justice, Case Western Res. U., 1973-91, dir. fgn. grad. studies, 1992—; cons. criminal justice agys. Author: Justice is the Crime, 1972, The Justice Imperative: Introduction to Criminal Justice, 1979, Ohio Arrest Search and Seizure, 2007; (with J. Shapiro) New York Suppression Manual, 1991, Know Your Rights, 1994; (with P.C. Giannelli, B. Blair, J. Lipton) Ohio Criminal Law, 2d edit., 2003; (with P.C. Giannelli) Ohio Criminal Justice, 2007; (with B.W. Griffin) Ohio Felony Sentencing Law, 2007, (with N.P. Cohen) Questions and Answers: Criminal Procedure, 2003. Mem. regional bd. Anti-Defamation League; trustee Women's Law Fund. Recipient Disting. Tchr. award Case West Res. U. Law Alumni Assn., Tchr. of Yr. award Case Western Res. U., 1999; Nat. Defender Project of Nat. Legal Aid and Defender Assn. fellow, 1968. Mem. ABA. Home: 29550 S Woodland Rd Pepper Pike OH 44124-5743 Office: Case Western Res U Law Sch Law Sch Cleveland OH 44106 Home Phone: 216-514-4744; Office Phone: 216-368-3287. Business E-Mail: lewis.katz@case.edu.

KATZ, REUVEN J., lawyer; b. Cin., 1924; m. Catherine S. Katz; children: Stewart, Sharon. BA, U. Cin., 1988, LHD (hon.), 2001; JD, Harvard Law Sch., 1950. Bar: Ohio 1950. Assoc. and ptnr. Paxton & Seasongood; pvt. practice Reuven J. Katz Co., L.P.A.; ptnr. Katz, Teller, Brant & Hild, 1980—. Pres. Big Brothers Assn. Cin., Coun. Aging Cmty. Chest; bd. mem. Johnny Bench Scholarship Fund, Greater Cin. Found., Jewish Vocat. Svc., Shetlering Oaks Hosp., U. Cinn. Coll. Medicine Cmty. Advisory Bd.; past chmn. bd. U. Cin. Found. Officer USAAF, World War II. Named one of Top 50 Lawyers Cin., Law and Politics Media, Inc., Top 100 Lawyers Ohio; recipient Lifetime Achievement award in Law, Cin. Bar Found., 1999, Chairman's award, U. Cin. Found., 1999. Mem.: Sports Lawyers Assn. (bd. mem.), Tournament Players Club Rivers Bend (bd. gov.), Palm Beach Polo and Country Club, Cin. Country Club, U. Club Cin. Avocations: golf, tennis, theater. Office: Katz Teller Brant & Hild 255 E Fifth St Ste 2400 Cincinnati OH 45202-4787 Office Phone: 513-721-4532. Business E-Mail: rkatz@katzteller.com.

KATZ, ROBERT L., lawyer; BCL magna cum laude, McGill U., Montreal, Can., LLB; student, NYU Sch. Law. Assoc. Milbank, Tweed, Hadley & McCloy, NYC and London, 1986—95; asst. gen. counsel GM AG, Zurich, Switzerland, 1996—98; gen. counsel, regional compliance officer Europe, Mid. East and Africa ops. Delphi Corp., Paris, 1999—2006; sr. v.p., gen. counsel, mem. strategy bd. Fed.-Mogul Corp., Southfield, Mich., 2007—. Office: Federal-Mogul Corp 26555 Northwestern Hwy Southfield MI 48033-2146

KATZ, ROBERT STEPHEN, rheumatologist, educator; b. Balt., July 31, 1944; s. Irving Gilbert and Shirley Ann (Feldman) K.; m. Carlen Jo Levin, Dec. 12, 1972; children: Jeremy, Alexandra, Gena. BA, Columbia U., 1966; MD, U. Md., 1970. Diplomate Am. Bd. Internal Medicine. Intern Barnes-Jewish Med. Ctr./Washington U. Med. Ctr., St. Louis, 1970—71, resident in internal medicine, 1971—72; fellow in rheumatology Johns Hopkins Hosp., Balt., 1974—76; assoc. prof. medicine Rush U. Med. Ctr., Chgo., 1976—. Mem., chmn. med. adv. bd. Lupus Found. Ill.; chmn. med. sci. com. No. Ill. chpt. Arthritis Found., 1985-87. Med. editor WBBM-TV, 1991-92, med. editor Fox TV WFLD, 1993—; chmn. Med. Adv. Bd. Chicago Sun-Times Medlife sect.; contbr. articles to profl. jours. Bd. dirs. Agers Found. Am. Lt. USN, 1970-72. Mem. AMA, Cen. Rheumatism Soc., Am. Coll. Rheumatology, Chgo. Med. Soc. Office: Dept Internal Medicine Rush Presbyn St Luke Med Ctr 1725 W Harrison St Ste 1039 Chicago IL 60612-3862 Home Phone: 773-472-9002; Office Phone: 312-226-8228. E-mail: rkatzrheum@aol.com.

KATZ, STUART CHARLES, lawyer, musician; b. Chgo., June 9, 1937; s. Jerome H. and Sylvia L. (Singer) K.; m. Penny Schatz, Jan. 23, 1959; children: Steven, Lauren. BA, Roosevelt U., Chgo., 1959; JD with distinction, John Marshall Law Sch., 1964. Bar: Ill. 1964, U.S. Dist. Ct. (no. dist.) Ill. 1965, U.S. Supreme Ct. 1967. Exec. v.p., gen. counsel Heitman LLC, Chgo., 1972—. Jazz pianist and vibraphonist, appeared in concerts with Benny Goodman, Gene Krupa, Bud Freeman. Mem.: ABA, Chgo. Bar Assn., Ill. Bar Assn. Office: 191 N Wacker Dr Ste 2500 Chicago IL 60606-1885 E-mail: skatz@heitman.com.

KATZENELLENBOGEN, JOHN ALBERT, chemistry professor; b. Poughkeepsie, NY, May 10, 1944; s. Adolph Edmund Max and Elisabeth (Holzheu) K.; m. Benita Schulman, June 11, 1967; children: Deborah Joyce, Rachel Adria. BA, Harvard U., 1967, PhD, 1969. Asst. prof. chemistry U. Ill., Urbana, 1969-75, assoc. prof. chemistry, 1975-79, prof. chemistry, 1979—, prof. Beckman Inst., 1988—, Roger Adams prof. chemistry, 1992-96, Swanlund prof. of chemistry, 1996—. Chmn. BNP study section NIH, 1987-91; adv. com. AUI Brookhaven, 1986-90. Mem. editorial Biochemistry, Jour. Med. Chem., Steroids; contbr. articles to profl. jours. Recipient Berson Yalow award Soc. Nuclear Medicine, 1988, Paul Aebersold award Soc. Nuc. Medicine, 1995; Camille and Henry Dreyfus tchr. scholar, 1974-79, Univ. scholar, 1987-90; Roy O. Greep Lecture award, Endocrine Soc., Aebersold award, Soc. Nuclear Medicine; fellow Alfred P. Sloan Found., 1974-76, Guggenheim fellow, 1977-78, Dreyfus Fellow. Fellow AAAS, Am. Acad. Arts and Scis.; mem. Am. Chem. Soc.(Arthur C. Cope scholar, 1999, E.B. Hershberg award for Important Discoveries in Medicinally Active Products, 2007), Chem. Soc. (London). Office: U Ill Dept Chemistry 461B Roger Adam Lab 600 S Mathews Ave Urbana IL 61801-3602 Business E-Mail: jkatzene@uiuc.edu.

KATZMAN, DAVID, investment company and professional sports team executive; BA in Acctg. and Fin., Mich. State U.; student, Detroit Coll. Law. Founder DeeKay Enterprises, Inc., 1987; pres. Home Depot S.O.C., 1997—2000; mng. ptnr. Camelot Ventures, 1999—; vice chmn. Cleve. Cavaliers, 2005—, Quicken Loans. Bd. dirs. 1-800-Contacts, 2003, RealAge.com, ePrize. Office: Camelot Ventures 20555 Victor Pky Ste 100 Livonia MI 48152 E-mail: dkatzman@camelotventures.com.

KATZMAN, RICHARD A., cardiologist, internist, consultant; b. Cleve., Mar. 22, 1931; s. Abraham N. and Anne Ruth (Kustin) K.; m. Roberta Brown, July 28, 1962; children: Audrey, Sharon, Naomi, Noah. BS, Case Western Reserve U., 1952; MD, U. Chgo., 1955. Diplomate Am. Bd. Internal Medicine. Prin. Richard A. Katzman M.D., Cleve., 1963—; dir. electrocardiography, dept. cardiology Metro Health Med. Ctr., 1992-97; staff cardiologist Mt. Sinai Hosp., Cleve., 1998-2000. Assoc. clin. prof. medicine Case Western Reserve U. V.p. Cleve. Coll. Jewish Studies, 1985-88. Capt. U.S. Army Med. Corps., 1956-58. Fellow Am. Coll. Physicians, Am. Coll. Chest Physicians. Home: 28950 Gates Mills Blvd Pepper Pike OH 44124-4744 Office: Parkway Med Bldg 24755 Chagrin Blvd Beachwood OH 44122

KAUFERT, DEAN R., state legislator; b. Neenah, Wis., May 23, 1957; Grad., Neenah H.S. Owner trophy and engraving shop, Neenah; mem. from dist. 55 Wis. State Assembly, Madison, 1990—. Bd. dirs. Neenah-Menasha Bowling Assn., Youth Go Bd. Mem. Optimists. Address: 1360 Alpine Ln Neenah WI 54956-4433

KAUFFMAN, ERLE GALEN, geologist, paleontologist; b. Washington, Feb. 9, 1933; s. Erle Benton and Paula Virginia (Graff) K.; children: Donald Erle, Robin Lyn, Erica Jean; m. Claudia C. Johnson, Sept. 1989. BS, U. Mich., 1955, MS, 1956, PhD, 1961; MSc (hon.), Oxford U., 1970; DHC, U. Göttingen, Germany, 1987. Teaching fellow, instr. U. Mich., Ann Arbor, 1956-60; from asst. to full curator dept. paleobiology Nat. Mus. Natural History Smithsonian Instn., Washington, 1960-80; prof. geology U. Colo., Boulder, 1980-96, chmn. dept. geol. scis., 1980-84, interim dir. Energy, Minerals Applied Rsch. Ctr., 1989-91; prof. geology Ind. U., 1996—2003, prof. emeritus, 2004—. Adj. prof. geology George Washington U., Washington, 1962-80; cons. geologist, Boulder, 1980-96. Author, editor: Cretaceous Facies, Faunas and Paleoenvironments Across the Cretaceous Western Interior Basin, 1977; contbg. editor: Concepts and Methods of Biostratigraphy, 1977, Fine-grained Deposits and Biofacies of The Cretaceous Western Interior Seaway, 1985, High Resolution Event Stratigraphy, 1988, Paleontology and Evolution: Extinction Events, 1988, Extinction Events in Earth History, 1990, Evolution of the Western Interior Basin, 1993; contbr. articles. to profl. jours. Recipient U.S. Govt. Spl. Svc. award, 1969, NSF Best Tchr. award U. Colo., 1985 named Disting. Lectr. Am. Geol. Inst., 1963-64, Am. Assn. Petroleum Geologists, 1984, 85, 91, 92; Fulbright fellow Australia, 1986. Fellow Geol. Soc. Am., AAAS; mem. Paleontol. Soc. (councilor under 40, pres. elect 1981, pres. 1982, past pres. 1983, chmn. 5 coms.); mem. NRC (rep.), Palaeontol. Assn., Internat. Paleontol. Assn. (v.p. 1982-88), Paleontol. Research Instn., Soc. Sedimentary Geology (com. mem., Spl. Svc. award 1985, Best Paper award 1985, Raymond C. Moore Paleontology medal 1991, William H. Twenhofel medal 1998), Rocky Mountain Assn. Geologists (project chief) (Scientist of Yr. 1977), Paleontol. Soc. Wash. (pres., sec., treas.), Geol. Soc. Wash. (councilor), Md. Acad. Scis. (hon. Paleontology sect.), Sigma Xi, Phi Kappa Phi, Sigma Gamma Epsilon. Democrat. Avocations: music, fishing, climbing, photography. Office: Dept Geol Sci Ind Univ 1001 E 10th St Bloomington IN 47405-1405 Business E-Mail: claudia@indiana.edu.

KAUFFMAN, PETER H., lawyer, energy executive; b. 1946; AB, U. Ill., JD, 1972. Bar: Ill. 1972. Joined Peoples Energy Corp., 1972, asst. gen. counsel, sec., 1998—, Peoples Gas and North Shore Gas (subsidiary of Peoples Energy Corp.), 1998—. Office: Peoples Energy Corp 130 E Randolph Dr Chicago IL 60601

KAUFFMAN, SANDRA DALEY, state legislator; b. Osceola, Nebr., Jan. 26, 1933; d. James Richard and Erma Grace (Heald) Daley; m. Larry Allen Kauffman, Sept. 4, 1955; children: Claudia Kauffman Boosman, Matthew Allen. BA, U. Nebr., 1954; postgrad., U. Kansas City, summer 1957. Tchr. Falls City (Nebr.) High Sch., 1954-55, Westport High Sch., Kansas City, Mo., 1955-59; sales rep. Manson Industries, Topeka, Kans., 1974-75; dir. pub. affairs Bishop Hogan High Sch., Kansas City, 1985-86; mem. Mo. Ho. of Reps., Jefferson City, 1987-98. Mem. Kansas City Citizens Assn., 1981—, Kansas City Consensus, 1985—; mem. women's coun. U. Mo., Kansas City, 1986—; mem. rsch. mental health bd., bd. govs. Carondelet Aging Svcs., 1992—. Recipient Friend of Edn. award Ctr. Edn. Assn., 1986, Disting. Legislator award Mo. C.C. Assn.; named Mem. of Yr., Mo. Congress Parents and Tchrs., 1979. Mem. Am. Legis. Exch. Coun., Nat. Conf. State Legislatures, Network Bd., Nat. PTA (hon. life), Nat. Order Women Legislators, Mo. PTA (hon. life), South Kansas City C. of C., Grandview C. of C., Women C. of C., Mo. Women's Coun., Women Legislators Mo. (pres.). Republican. Methodist. Home: 620 E 90th Ter Kansas City MO 64131-2918 Office: Mo Ho of Reps State Capitol Building Jefferson City MO 65101-1556

KAUFMAN, ANDREW MICHAEL, lawyer; b. Boston, Feb. 19, 1949; s. Earle Bertram and Miriam (Halpern) K.; m. Michele Moselle, Aug. 24, 1975; children: Peter Moselle, Melissa Lanes, Caroline Raney. BA cum laude, Yale U., 1971; JD, Vanderbilt U., 1974. Bar: Tex. 1974, Ga. 1976, Ill. 1993, U.S. Ct. Appeals (5th and 11th cirs.) 1981. Assoc. Vinson & Elkins, Houston, 1974-76, ptnr., 1982-83, Austin, 1983-92, Dallas, 1992; assoc. Sutherland, Asbill & Brennan, Atlanta, 1976-80, ptnr., 1980-81, Kirkland & Ellis LLP, Chgo., 1993—. Adj. prof. Vanderbilt Law Sch., 2005—. Editor in chief Vanderbilt U. Law Rev., 1973-74. Mem. nat. alumni bd. Vanderbilt U.Law Sch., 1994—2000; Alumni fund raiser Yale U., 1971—, mem. alumni schs. com., 1986—92, 2003—; mem. med. ethics coun. Seton Hosp., 1988—92; participant Leadership Austin, 1987—88; bd. dirs. KLRU-TV, 1989—93; mem. Austin (Tex.) Entrepreneurs Coun., 1991—92; mem. adv. bd. Dallas Bus. Com. Arts Leadership Inst., 1992—93; governing bd. mem. Chgo. Symphony Orch.; bd. dirs. United Way, Austin, Tex.; pub. TV Ballet Austin, Tex., 1986—92; mem. adv. bd. Austin Tech. Incubator, 1989—93. Mem. ABA (bus. law sect. 1978—, chmn. lease financing and secured transactions subcom. of com. devels. in bus. financing 1993-99, UCC com., legal opinions com., comml. fin. svcs. com.), Tex. Bar Assn., Yale U. Alumni Assn., Order of Coif, Headliners Club, Yale Club, N.Y.C. and Chgo., Knights of the Symphony Austin. Avocation: sailing. Office: Kirkland & Ellis LLP 200 E Randolph St Fl 54 Chicago IL 60601-6636 Office Phone: 312-861-2313. Business E-Mail: Andrew.Kaufman@chicago.kirkland.com.

KAUFMAN, BARRY D., retail executive; JD, St. Louis U.; B, U. Mo. Atty. Blumenfeld, Kaplan & Sandweiss, St. Louis; sr. real estate coun., sr. v.p. May Realty, Inc., 1976—93; v.p. real estate Sears Merchandise Group, 1993—97; pres., COO Richard E. Jacobs Group, 1998—99; pres., CEO Ltd. Property Svcs., Columbus, Ohio, 1999—. Office: Ltd Brands Inc Three Ltd Pkwy Columbus OH 43230

KAUFMAN, DONALD LEROY, building products executive; b. Erie, Pa., May 9, 1931; s. Isadore H. and Lena (Sandler) K.; m. Estelle Friedman, Aug. 15, 1954; children: Craig Ivan, Susan Beth, Carrie Ellen. BS in Bus. Adminstrn, Ohio State U., 1953, LL.B., 1955. Bar: Ohio 1955. Pres. Alside, Inc., Akron, Ohio, 1974—, chief exec. officer, 1982—. V.p., bd. dirs. Assoc. Materials Inc. Mem. adv. com. U. Akron; trustee Jewish Welfare Fund, Akron, 1958-65, young leaders div., 1961-65; trustee Akron City Hosp. Found., 1984-91, Menorah Park Home for Aged, Akron Children's Hosp. Found. Mem. Akron Bar Assn., Sigma Alpha Mu, Tau Epsilon Rho. Home: 2825 Roundhill Rd Akron OH 44333-2273 Office: PO Box 2010 Akron OH 44309-2010

KAUFMAN, DONALD WAYNE, research ecologist; b. Abilene, Tex., June 7, 1943; s. Leo Fred and Marcella Genevieve (Hobbie) Kaufman; m. Glennis Ann Schroeder, Aug. 5, 1967; 1 child, Dawn. BS, Ft. Hays Kans. State Coll., 1965, MS, 1967; PhD, U. Ga., Athens, 1972. Postdoctoral fellow U. Tex., Austin, 1971-73; asst. prof. U. Ark., Fayetteville, 1974-75, SUNY, Binghamton, 1975-77; assoc. program dir. Population Biology, NSF, Washington, 1977-80; asst. prof. biology Kans. State U., Manhattan, 1980-84, assoc. prof. biology, 1984-91, prof. biology, 1991—; adj. curator mammals Sternberg Mus. Nat. History Ft. Hays State U., Hays, Kans., 2000—. Adj. prof. biology U. N.Mex., 1998; vis. scientist Savannah River Ecology Lab., Aiken, SC, 1973-74; acting dir. Konza Prairie Rsch. Natural Area, 1986-87, coord., 1990-91; dir. Konza Prairie Long-Term Ecol. Rsch. Program, 1985-90; grant rev. panelist EPA, 1981-85, USDA, 1995-96; cons. NSF, 1984, Nat. Pk. Svc., 2000. Contbr. articles to profl. jours. Recipient Alumni Achievement award, Fort Hays State U., 2005; fellow NDEA, 1967—69. Mem. AAAS, Am. Soc. Mammalogists (award 1972, bd. dirs. 1989-92), Ecol. Soc. Am., Am. Inst. Biol. Scis., The Wildlife Soc. (pres. Kans. chpt. 2005-07), Soc. Conservation Biology, Ctrl. Plains Soc. Mammalogists (bd. govs. 2000-06), Sigma Xi. Office: Kans State U Div Biology Ackert Hall Manhattan KS 66506 Office Phone: 785-532-6622. Business E-Mail: dwkaufma@ksu.edu.

KAUFMAN, JEFFREY ALLEN, publisher; b. Mpls., May 28, 1952; s. Theodore and Jean Louise (Tiegs) K. Student, Mankato State U., 1970-71, Ariz. State U., 1971-72; BA, U. Minn., 1975. Pres. Creative Resources, Inc., Mpls., 1976-80; sr. v.p. Literary Resources, Inc., Phoenix, 1980-81; pres. Multi-Media, Phoenix, 1981-83, Where To Go, Inc., Excelsior, Minn., 1983-86; v.p. The Old Utica Co., Mpls., 1986-88; chmn. Actif, Inc., Wayzata, Minn., 1988-89; ptnr. S&K Group, Mpls., 1989-90; editor in chief Spl. Events Pub., Inc., Mpls., 1990-92; founder Electronic Claims Processing, Inc., Edina, Minn., 1992-96; co-owner BIO-Works, Inc., 1994—, Kaufman Capital Funding. Cons. Control Data Corp., Mpls., 1978—81; dir. Nexus Inc., Mpls., 1978—81; founder ECP Inc., 1992; chmn. Dr. Zen Diabetic Ctrs., Inc., 2002—. Author: (books) Where To Go in Minneapolis and Saint Paul, 1984, Where To Go in Los Angeles, 1985, (screenplay) Born To Be Chief, 1985. Avocations: golf, flying, equestrian. Home: P O Box 415 Rosemount MN 55068 E-mail: jeffrey_kaufman@msn.com.

KAUFMAN, PETER BISHOP, biological sciences educator; b. San Francisco, Feb. 25, 1928; s. Earle Francis and Gwendolyn Bishop (Morris) K.; m. Hazel Elizabeth Snyder, Apr. 5, 1958; children— Linda Myrl, Laura Irene BS, Cornell U., 1949; PhD in Botany, U. Calif.-Davis, 1954. Instr. botany U. Mich., Ann Arbor, 1956-58, asst. prof., 1958-62, assoc. prof., 1962-72, prof. botany, cellular and molecular biology and bioengring. program, 1972-97, emeritus prof. dept. biology, 1998—, 1st yr. seminar Residential Coll., 1997—2002, sr. rsch. scientist integrative medicine program. Cons. NASA Space Biology Program; vis. prof. U. Lund, Sweden, 1964-65, U. Colo., Boulder, 1973-74; mem. faculty agr. Nagoya U., Japan, 1981 Author: Laboratory Experiments in Plant Physiology, 1975, Plants, People and Environment, 1979, Botany Illustrated, 1983, 2d edit., 2005, Practical Botany, 1983, Plants: Their Biology and Importance, 1989; co-author: Handbook of Molecular and Cellular Methods in Biology and Medicine, 1995, 3d edit., 2008, Methods in Gene Biotechnology, 1997, 2d edit., 2006, atural Products from Plants, 1998, 2d edit., 2006, Creating a Sustainable Future Living in Harmony with the Earth, 2002, Botany Illustrated, 2nd edit., 2006.; Co-Author: Recent Advances in Plant Biotechnology Mem. Mich. Natural Areas Coun.; mem. exec. com. U. Mich. Program in Scholarly Rsch. for Urban Minority Students. Grantee NIH, NSF, NASA, Cherry Mktg. Inst. Mich. Fellow AAAS; mem. Am. Inst. Biol. Scis., Am. Soc. Plant Biologists, Am. Soc. Gravitational and Space Biology (sec.-treas., 1985-1993), Internat. Soc. Plant Molecular Biologists, Bot. Soc. Am., Mich. Bot. Club (pres. 1985-89), Sigma Xi. Democrat. Presbyterian. Office: U Mich B570E MSRB II West Medical Dr Ann Arbor MI 48109 Home: 7261 Hashley Rd Manchester MI 48158 Business E-Mail: pbk@umich.edu.

KAUFMAN, RAYMOND L., energy company executive; b. Cleve., Mar. 9, 1940; s. Eugene and Elizabeth T. Kaufman; m. Janet Spangler, Sept. 1, 1962; 1 child, Jason. Student, Kent State U., 1958. Personnel dir. NESCO, Cleve., 1965-71; founder Advancement Corp., Cleve., 1971. Pres., owner Art Healan. Served with U.S. Army, 1961-63. Mem. AIC, Cleve. C. of C. Lodges: Rotary.

KAUTZMANN, DWIGHT C. H., federal magistrate judge; b. Bismarck, ND, Dec. 30, 1945; m. Karen Ann Clausen, Aug. 19, 1972; children: Dreux, Don, DeAnn. BA, N.D. State U., 1968; JD, U. N.D., 1971. Bar: N.D. 1971, U.S. Ct. Appeals (8th cir.) 1974, U.S. Supreme Ct. 1977, U.S. Mil. Ct. Appeals 1994. Pvt. practice, Mandan, N.D., 1971-96; judge Mandan Mcpl. Ct., 1973-76; chmn. Legal Svcs. Com. N.D., 1976-79; magistrate judge U.S. Dist. Ct. N.D., Bismarck, 1978—. Mem. State Bar Assn. N.D. (pres. 1988), N.D. Trial Lawyers (pres. 1990-91), Bar Great Plains and Rocky Mountain States (chancellor 1992), Blue Key, Phi Alpha Delta. Office: US Courthouse PO Box 1578 220 E Rosser Ave Bismarck ND 58501-3867

KAWAOKA, YOSHIHIRO, virologist, educator; m. Yuko Kawaoka. BS in Vet. Medicine, Hokkaido U., Japan, 1978; DVM, Ministry of Agriculture and Fishery, Japan, 1978; MS, Hokkaido U., Japan, 1980, PhD, 1983. Postdoctoral rschr. St. Jude Children's Rsch. Hosp., Memphis; prof. virology dept. pathobiological scis. U. Wis., Madison; prof. U. Tokyo Inst. Med. Sci. Contbr. articles to sci. jours. Office: Dept Pathobiological Scis U Wis Sch Vet Medicine 2015 Linden Dr W Madison WI 53706-1102 Office Phone: 608-265-4925. Office Fax: 608-265-5622. E-mail: kawaokay@svm.vetmed.wisc.edu.

KAY, DICK, news correspondent; BS Speech Edn., Bradley U., 1962. With several radio and TV stas., Peoria, Ill.; news dir. Sta. KFRV-TV, Green Bay, Wis., 1965; news writer NBC 5, Chgo., 1968—70, reporter, 1970—, polit. editor, commentator. Named to Silver Cir. TV Acad., 2001; recipient Disting. Alumnus award, Bradley U., 1985, Regional Emmy award, 1996, George Foster Peabody medallion, 1984, award for Best Editl. or Commentary, AP, 1998—99, Peter Lisagor award, Soc. Profl. Journalists Chgo. chpt. The Chgo. Headline Club, 2000, Dante award, Joint Civic Com. Italian Ams., 1984, numerous others, 8 Chgo. Emmy awards. Office: NBC 454 N Columbus Dr Chicago IL 60611

KAYE, GORDON ISRAEL, pathologist, anatomist, educator; b. NYC, Aug. 13, 1935; s. Oscar Swarz and Rebecca (Schachman) K.; m. Nancy Elizabeth Weber, June 4, 1956; children: Jacqueline Elizabeth, Vivienne Rebecca. AB, Columbia U., 1955, AM, 1957, PhD, 1961. From rsch. asst. cytology to dir. Columbia U., NYC, 1953—63, dir. F. Higginson Cabot Lab. Electron Microscopy, 1963—76; rsch. and tchg. asst. cytology Rockefeller Inst., NYC, 1957-58; from Alden March prof. to prof. emeritus Albany (N.Y.) Med. Coll., 1976—99, prof. emeritus pathology, 1999—; prof. biomed. sci. SUNY Sch. Pub. Health, 1986-99; pres., CEO Waste Reduction by Waste Reduction, Inc., Troy, NY, 1993-98, chmn., 1998—2007, exec. v.p., 2002—06, acting CEO, 2006—07, waste mgmt. cons., em coniss., 2007—. Mem. seminar on creative process Wenner-Gren Found., 1964-65; cons. electron microscopy dept. pathology N.Y. VA Hosp., 1965—99; Raymond C. Truex Disting. lectr. Hahnemann U., 1987. Co-author: Key Facts in Histology, 1985, Histology: A Text and Atlas, 1995, 4th edit., 2003; co-author: (in German) Atlas der Histologie, 1995; co-author: Histology, nat. med. series rev. series, 1997; editor: Current Topics in Cellular Anatomy, 1981; assoc. editor The Anat. Reocrd, 1972—98, editl. reviewer Exptl. Eye Rsch., 1964, Cancer, 1972—, Investigative Ophthalmology, 1973—, Gastroenterology, 1969—, Jour. Morphology, 1999—. Trustee Palisades free Libr., 1965-71; mem. Citizens Adv. Com., Sparkill Palisades Fire Dist., 1968-69; pres. Palisades Free Libr., 1969-71; trustee Orangetown Pub. Libr., 1971-73, Friends of Chamber Music, Troy, N.Y., 1988—; mem. citizens adv. com. Title III Program, S. Orangetown Ctrl. Sch. Dist., 1972-75; chmn. N.Y. State Low Level Waste Group, 1986-95; trustee Rockland Country Day Sch., 1974-78. Recipient Charles Huebschman prize in zoology Columbia U., 1954, Career Scientist award Health Rsch. Coun. N.Y.C., 1963-72, Rsch. Career Devel. award Nat. Inst. Arthritis and Metabolic Diseases, NIH, USPHS, 1972-76, Tousimis prize in biology, 1984; Ford Found. scholar, 1951-55; NSF predoctoral fellow, 1955-56, Nat. Inst. Neurol. Diseases and Blindness predoctoral fellow, 1959-61 Mem.: Lab. Animal Mgmt. Assn., Am. Assn. Lab. Animal Scis., Am. Assn. Vet. Lab. Diagnosticians, N.Y. Soc. Electron Microscopists (dir. 1964—67), Internat. Soc. Eye Rsch., Assn. Career Scientists Health Rsch. Coun., Harvey Soc., Am. Soc. Cell Biology, Am. Assn. Anatomists, Assn. Am. Med. Colls. (rep. con. acad. socs. 1979—2002, mem. adminstrn. bd. CAS 1985—86), Assn. Anatomy Chmn. (pres. 1980—81), Arthur Purdy Stout Soc. Surg. Pathologists (hon.), Waquoit Bay Yacht Club, Sigma Xi. Achievements include research in disposal of radioactively labeled animal carcasses; patents for methods for treatment and disposal of regulated medical waste; patents in field. Home Phone: 518-273-0292; Office Phone: 518-369-6399. Personal E-mail: wr2kaye@aol.com.

KAYE, RICHARD WILLIAM, labor economist; b. Chgo., May 14, 1939; s. Albert Louis and Helen (Beckman) K.; m. Betty Ann Terry, Aug. 7, 1964; children: Ronald, William, Richard, Timothy. AB, Cornell U., 1960; MBA, Columbia U., 1962. Various fin. positions Inland Steel Co., Chgo., 1964-81; dir. info. svcs. No. Ind. Pub. Svc. Co., Hammond, 1981-86, dir. econ. analysis, 1986-88. Vis. dir. Purdue U., 1988; ct.-appointed receiver, 1989—92; mgmt. and fin. cons., 1993—97; labor market economist, 1998—. Advisor Calumet Coll., Whiting, Ind., 1985—; active Village Planning Commn., village trustee. Lt. (j.g.) USNR. Mem. Am. Mgmt. Assn., Cornell U. Alumni Assn., Columbia U. Alumni Assn., Rotary. Avocations: tennis, golf. Home: 2801 Cherrywood Ln Hazel Crest IL 60429-2126 Office: IDES 33 S State St Chicago IL 60603-1229 Home Phone: 708-799-3360; Office Phone: 312-793-6288. Business E-Mail: richard.kaye@illinois.gov.

KAYLOR, DAVE, newscaster; grad., postgrad., Ohio State U. Tchr. Brookhaven High Sch., Columbus, Ohio; with Sta. WNRE, Circleville; co-anchor, exec. prodr. evening news Sta. WTVG-TV, Nashville; anchor Sta. WBNS-TV, Columbus, 1980—. Named Best Male Anchor ofYr. Large Markets, Nat. Acad. Television Journalists, Washington; recipient Emmy award. Office: WBNS-TV 770 Twin Rivers Dr Columbus OH 43215

KAZA, GREG JOHN, economist, educator; b. Wyandotte, Mich., Nov. 11, 1960; s. John J. and Mary A. Kaza. BA in Econs., U. Detroit, 1989; MSF in Internat. Fin., Walsh Coll., Troy, Mich., 1998. V.p. policy rsch. The Mackinac Ctr., Midland, Mich., 1989-91; adj. prof. Northwood Inst. and Walsh Coll., Troy, Mich., 1998—2000; state rep. State of Mich., 1993-98; exec. dir. Citizen Legislators' Caucus Found., Washington, 1999-2000, Ark. Policy Found., Little Rock, 2001—. Author 9 state laws. Contbr. articles to profl. jours. Mem.: Highpointers Club. Republican. Roman Catholic. Office: Ark Policy Found Stephens Bldg 111 Center St Ste 1200 Little Rock AR 72201 Office Phone: 501-537-0825.

KAZANOWSKI, LARRY, engineer; Degree in engring., MIT; MBA, Stanford U. With Ford Motor Co.; v.p. bus. strategy Visteon Automotive Sys.; CEO, pres. Cambridge Industries, Madison Heights, Mich., 1999—. Office: Cambridge Industries 2068 Lansing Pl Syosset NY 11791-9610

KAZIMIERCZUK, MARIAN KAZIMIERCZUK, electrical engineer, educator; b. Smolugi, Poland, Mar. 3, 1948; came to U.S., 1984; s. Stanislaw and Stanislawa (Tomaszewska) K.; m. Alicja owowiejska, July 5, 1973; children: Andrzej, Anna. MS, Tech. U. of Warsaw, Poland, 1971, PhD, 1978, DSc, 1984. Instr. elec. engring. Tech. U. of Warsaw, Poland, 1972-78, assoc. prof., 1978-84; project engr. Design Automation, Inc., Lexington, Mass., 1984; vis. prof. Va. Poly. Inst., Blacksburg, 1984-85, Wright State U., Dayton, Ohio, 1985—. Author: Resonant Power Converters, 1995, Electronic Devices: A Design Approach, 2003; contbr. articles to profl. jours. Recipient Univ. Edn. and Tech. award Polish Ministry of Sci. award, 1981, 84, 85, Polish Acad. Sci. award, 1983. Fellow IEEE (Harrel V. Noble award 1990); mem. Assn. Polish Engrs., Polish Soc. Theoretical and Applied Elec. Scis. Roman Catholic. Home: 3620 Cypress Ct Dayton OH 45440-4515 Office: Wright State U Dept Elec Engring Dayton OH 45435 Office Phone: 937-775-5059. Business E-Mail: mkazim@cs.wright.edu, marian.kazimierczuk@wright.edu.

KEANE, JAMES P., manufacturing executive; Joined Steelcase, Grand Rapids, Mo., 1997; sr. v.p. corp. strategy rsch. devel. Steelcase Inc., sr. v.p. fin. CFO, 2001—. Mem.: Microfield (bd. dirs. 1998—). Office: Steelcase Inc 901 44th St Grand Rapids MI 49506

KEANE, JOHN B., lawyer, electric power industry executive; b. Beverly, Mass., Aug. 25, 1946; m. Katherine Keane; 2 children. BA in Econs., Brown U., 1968; JD, Harvard U., 1972. Bar: Mass. 1972, Ohio (corp.) 2004. With Hill & Barlow, Boston, 1972—80, N.E. Utilities, Berlin, Conn., 1980—2002, v.p., sec., gen. counsel corp., 1992—93, v.p., treas., 1993—98, v.p. adminstrn., 1998—2002; pres. Bainbridge Crossing Advs., West Hartford, Conn., 2003—04; sr. v.p., gen. counsel, sec. Am. Electric Power Co. Inc., Columbus, Ohio, 2004—. Bd. dirs. Columbus Mus. Art. Office: Am Electric Power Co Inc 1 Riverside Plz Columbus OH 43215-2372 Office Phone: 614-716-2929. Business E-Mail: jbkeane@aep.com.

KEANE, WILLIAM FRANCIS, nephrology educator, research foundation executive; b. NYC, Sept. 21, 1942; s. William F. and Theresa (Crotty) K.; m. Stephanie M. Gaherin, June 10, 1967; children: Alicia Anne, Elizabeth Gaherin. BS, Fordham U., 1964; MD, Yale U., 1968. Diplomate Am. Bd. Internal Medicine, Am. Bd. Nephrology. Intern Cornell N.Y. Hosp. Med. Ctr., 1968-69, resident, internal medicine, 1969-70, 72-73; fellow nephrology U. Minn. Hosps., Mpls., 1973-75; chmn. dept. Hennepin County Med. Ctr., Mpls., 1991—; asst. prof. medicine U. Minn., Mpls., 1976-82, assoc. prof., 1982-87, prof., 1987-89; pres. Minn. Med. Rsch. Found., Mpls., 1989-95; nephrologist Hennepin County Med. Ctr., Mpls., 1995. Chmn. dept. medicine Hennepin County Med. Ctr., 1992—. Mem. Am. Coll. Physicians, Am. Fedn. Clin. Rsch., Am. Soc. Clin. Pharmacology and Therapeutics, Am. Soc. Nephrology. Office: Hennepin County Med Ctr 701 Park Ave Minneapolis MN 55415-1623 Home: PO Box 665 Spring House PA 19477-0665

KEANEY, WILLIAM REGIS, engineering and construction services executive, consultant; b. Pitts., Nov. 2, 1937; s. William Regis Sr. and Emily Elizabeth (Campi) K.; m. Sharon Lee Robinson, Feb. 23, 1956; children: William R., James A., Robert E., Susan Elizabeth. BBA in Mktg. and Internat. Mktg., Ohio State U., 1961. Sales engr. Burdett Oxygen Co., Cleve., 1961-64, A.O. Smith Co., Milw., 1964-66; pres. W.R. Keaney & Co., Columbus, Ohio, 1966-71, Power Equipment Service Corp., Columbus, 1971-80, Gen. Assocs. Corp., Worthington, Ohio, 1980—. Cons. Mannesmann, Houston, 1984-85, TVA, Knoxville, 1984-86, Power Authority of .Y., White Plains, 1985-86, Utility Power Corp., Atlanta, 1985-86; mem. various task forces in the field. Vol. Cen. Ohio Lung Assn., Columbus, 1984-86. Mem. ASME (subgroups on nonferrous alloys, strenght/nonferrous alloys), ASTM (B2 com.), Am. Welding Soc., Welding Rsch. Coun., Worthington C. of C. (leadership program 1991-92), Mil. Vehicle Collectors Club, Masons. Democrat. Methodist. Avocations: antique cars, genealogy, camping, photography. Home: 1314 Oakview Dr Columbus OH 43235-1135 Office: Keaney & Co PO Box 762 Columbus OH 43085-0762 Personal E-mail: bkeaney@aol.com.

KEARFOTT, KIMBERLEE JANE, nuclear engineer, educator, health physicist; b. Oakland, Calif., Jan. 30, 1956; d. William Edward and Edith (Chamberlin) K. BSc, St. Mary's U., Halifax, NS, Can., 1975; ME in Nuclear Engring., U. Va., 1977; ScD, MIT, 1980. Coop. engr. Babcock & Wilcox Co., Lynchburg, Va., 1975-77; rsch. asst. Mass. Gen. Hosp., Boston, 1980; asst. prof. Cornell U. Med. Sch., NYC, 1980-84; rsch. assoc. Sloan-Kettering Cancer Ctr., NYC, 1980-84; from asst. to assoc. prof. Ariz. State U., Tempe, 1984-89; assoc. prof. Ga. Inst. Tech., Atlanta, 1989-93; assoc. prof. Med. Sch. Emory U., Atlanta, 1990-93; prof. U. Mich., Ann Arbor, 1993—, dir. faculty devel. Coll. Engring., 1994-97. Contbr. articles to profl. jours. including Jour. Health Physics, Jour. of Nuc. Medicine, Jour. Computer Assisted Tomography, Jour. Med. Physics. Mem. IEEE, AAUW, Am. Nuc. Soc. (bd. dirs. 1996-01, Women's Achievement award 1995), Soc. uc. Medicine (Tetalman award 1991), Assn. Women in Sci., Soc. Women Engrs., Health Physics Soc. (bd. dirs. 1992-95, Anderson award 1992), Order of Engr. Office: U Mich Dept Nuclear Engring and Radiol Sci Ann Arbor MI 48109-2104 Office Phone: 734-763-9117. Business E-Mail: kearfott@umich.edu.

KEARNEY, JOSEPH D., dean, law educator; b. Dec. 28, 1964; BA summa cum laude, Yale U., 1986; JD cum laude, Harvard U., 1989. Bar: Ill., Wis. Law clerk to Judge Diarmuid F. O'Scannlain U.S. Ct. Appeals, Ninth Cir., Portland, Oreg., 1989—90; to Justice Antonin Scalia U.S. Supreme Ct., Washington, DC, 1995—96; assoc. Sidley & Austin, Chgo., 1990—95, 1996—97; asst. prof. Marquette U. Law Sch., 1997—2001, assoc. prof., 2001—03, dean, prof. law, 2003—. Contbr. articles to law jours. Mem.: Am. Inns Ct. (mem. Thomas Fairchild Chap. 1999—), Federalist Soc., Milwaukee Lawyers' Chap. (mem. bd. dirs. 2000—), Wis. Bd. Bar Examiners, Wis. Bar Assn. (mem. bd. dirs. Ea. Dist. 2002—). Office: Marquette U Law Sch 1103 W Wisconsin Ave PO Box 1881 Milwaukee WI 53201 Office Phone: 414-288-1955. E-mail: joseph.kearney@marquette.edu.

KEARNS, JAMES CANNON, lawyer; b. Urbana, Ill., Nov. 8, 1944; s. John T. and Ruth (Cannon) K.; m. Anne Shapland, Feb. 12, 1983; children: Rose, John. BA, U. Notre Dame, 1966; JD, U. Ill., 1975. Bar: Ill. 1975, U.S. Dist. Ct. (cen. dist.) Ill. 1975, U.S. Ct. Appeals (7th cir.) 1976, U.S. Supreme Ct. 1992. Ptnr. Heyl, Royster, Voelker & Allen, Peoria, Ill., 1975-81, Urbana, 1981—. Mem. ABA, Nat. Assn. RR Trial Coun., Ill. Bar Assn., Champaign County Bar Assn., Def. Rsch. Inst., Ill. Assn. Def. Trial Counsel, Am. Bar Found., Nat. Assn. Coll. and Univ. Attys., Internat. Assn. Defense Coun. Roman Catholic. Avocations: reading, jogging. Office: Heyl Royster Voelker & Allen PO Box 129 102 E Main St Ste 300 Urbana IL 61801-2733 E-mail: jkearns@hrva.com.

KEARNS, MERLE GRACE, state agency administrator; b. Bellefonte, Pa., May 19, 1938; d. Robert John and Mary Katharine (Fitzgerald) Grace; m. Thomas Raymond Kearns, June 27, 1959; children: Thomas, Michael, Timothy, Matthew. BS, Ohio State U., 1960. Tchr. St. Raphael Elem. Sch., Springfield, Ohio, 1960-62; substitute tchr. Mad River Green Dist., Springfield, 1972-78; instr. Clark Tech. Coll., Springfield, 1978-80; commr. Clark County, Ohio, 1981-91; mem. Ohio Senate, Columbus, 1991-2000, majority whip, 1998—2000; mem. Ohio Ho. of Reps., Columbus, 2001—05, majority floor leader, 2005; dir. Ohio Dept. Aging, 2005—07; ret., 2007. Pres. Bd. County Commrs., 1982—83, 1987, 90. Sec. County Commrs. Assn. Ohio, 1988, 2d v.p., 1989—90, 1st v.p., 1990; mem. exec. com. Springfield Reps., 1984—2001; chair Ohio Children's Trust Fund, 1995—2000; past chair Legis. Office of Edn. Oversight; active NCSL Welfare Reform Task Force, 2001—05; vice-chair Policy Consensus Initiative Bd., 2002—; chair Head Start Plus Study Coun.; hon. chair Srs. 4 Kids, Ohio, 2007; senate pres. public position Ohio Commn. on Conflict Mgmt. and Dispute Resolution, 2007; bd. dirs. Springfield Symphony, 1980—86, Arts Coun., 1980—85; bd. dirs., mem. exec. bd. Nat. Conf. State Legislatures, 2000—03. Named Woman of the Yr., Springfield Pilot Club, 1981, Wittenburg Woman of Accomplishment, 1991, Watchdog of Treasury, 1991, 1996, 2000, Legislator of the Yr., Assn. Mental Health and Drug Addition Svcs. Bds., 1996, Pub. Childrens Svcs. Agys. Ohio, 1999, Ohio Cmty. Colls., 1997, Ohio Disting. Nurses, 2000, Advance Practice Nurse Assn., 2002, Legis. Co-Person of the Yr., Assn. Joint Vocat. Sch. Supts., 1996, Mental Health Adv. of the Yr., 2002, Outstanding Head Start Legislator of the Yr., Miami Valley, 2002, Legislator of Yr., Ohio Fedn. Tchrs., 2003, Advocate of Yr., Ohio County Alzheimer Assn., 2004, Alzheimer Legis. Advocate of Yr., 2004, Outstanding Citizen, Clark County Leadership Forum, 2006, One of Top Ten Women, Miami Valley, Dayton Daily News, 2007; recipient Pub. Policy Leadership award, 1997, Disting. Svc. Pub. Ofcls. award, Assn. Ohio Philanthropic Homes, 1999, 1st Ann. Jane Swart Disting. Svcs. to Nursing, 2000, Citizenship award, Ohio State U. Coll. Human Ecology, 2000, Legislator of Yr., Behavioral Health Authorities Assn., 2003, Ohio Better World award, Ohio Mediation Assn., 2004;, Ohio State U. scholar, 1957—59. Mem.: LWV (bd. dirs. 1964—78, pres. 1975—78), Ohio Nurses Assn. (Legislator of the Yr. 1995, 1999), Rotary, Omicron Nu. Roman Catholic. Avocation: reading.

KEATING, DANIEL LOUIS, law educator; b. Chgo., Oct. 14, 1961; s. Thomas Joseph and Joanne Clara (Shaughnessy) K.; m. Jane Marie Stevens, Aug. 2, 1986. BA, Monmouth Coll., 1983; JD, U. Chgo., 1986. Bar: Ill. 1986, U.S. Dist. Ct. (no. dist.) Ill. 1986. Lawyer 1st Nat. Bank Chgo., 1986-88; prof. law Washington U., St. Louis, 1988—, assoc. dean. Olin Found. John Olin Fellow, 1985. Mem. Order of Coif.

KEDZIE, NEAL J., state senator; b. Waukesha, Wis., Jan. 27, 1956; m. Kerrie Kedzie; children: Erika, Ryan, Sean. BS, grad. work, U. Wis., Whitewater, 1978. Facilities mgr. Girl Scouts Racine County, Wis., 1978—88; comml./indsl. coord. mktg. Wis. So. Gas Co., 1988—94; govt. rels. rep. Wis. Elec. Power Co., 1994—96; assembly mem. Wis. State Assembly, 1996—2002; state sen. Wis. State Senate, 2002—, mem. joint survey com. on tax exemptions, chair. environ. com., mem. aging and long-term care, fin. instns., and natural resources coms. Mem. Am. Legis. Exch. Coun.; Bowhay Inst. for Legis. Devel.; mem. state legis. wing Civil Air Patrol; former sec. Lauderdale-LaGrange Vol. Fire Dept.; former dir. govtl. affairs Menomonee Valley Bus. Assn.; former mem. Milwaukee County Local Emergency Planning Com.; town chair LaGrange Twp., Wis., 1988—98; chmn. LaGrange Twp. Planning and Zoning Commn., 1988—98; supr. LaGrange Town Bd., 1987—88; mem. Wis. Environ. Edn. Bd., 1998—. Mem.: Walworth County Local Emergency Planning Commn., Walworth County Towns Assn., Walworth County Farm Bur., Nat. Conf. State Legislators, Walworth County Hist. Soc., Walworth and Rock County Rep. Party, Nat. Assn. Sportsmen Legislators, Boy Scouts USA. Republican. Roman Catholic. Office: State Capitol Rm 307 N PO Box 8952 Madison WI 53707-7882 also: Dist Address N7661 Hwy 12 Elkhorn WI 53121

KEEFER, J(AMES) MICHAEL, lawyer; b. Ft. Wayne, Ind., July 16, 1947; s. James Martin and Helen Patricia (Smith) K.; m. Jan Elaine McDonald, June 3, 1972; children: Christopher, Sean, Alison. AB in Hist., U. Notre Dame, 1969, JD, 1972. Bar: Ind. 1972, U.S. Dist. Ct. (no. and so. dists.) Ind. 1972. With legal dept. Lincoln Nat. Corp., Ft. Wayne, Ind., 1972—2002; 2d v.p., assoc. gen. counsel Lincoln Nat. Corp. and Lincoln Nat. Life Ins. Co., 1982-88, v.p., assoc. gen. counsel, 1988—2002; v.p., gen. counsel and dir. Lincoln Investment Mgmt., Inc., Ft. Wayne, 1997-2000; v.p., dep. gen. counsel Lincoln Nat. Reassurance Co., 2001—02; of counsel Barnes & Thornburg, Ft. Wayne, 2002—03; sr. v.p., gen. counsel, sec. Security Benefit Group, Topeka, 2003—. Bd. dirs. Allen County unit Am. Cancer Soc., Ft. Wayne, 1975-82, Embassy Theatre Found., 1998-2003, The Lincoln Mus., 1996-2000, Ft. Wayne-Allen County Hist. Soc., pres., 1993-95, Ft. Wayne Mus. Art, 1999-2003; bd. dirs. Topeka Performing Arts Ctr., 2004—. Fellow: Ind. Bar Found., Am. Coll. Investment Counsel; mem.: Assn. Life Ins. Counsel (sec.-treas. 1994—2000, bd. govs. 2000—, pres.-elect 2003—), Am. Corp. Counsel Assn., Am. Coun. Life Ins. (various task forces), Allen County Bar Assn. (bd. dirs., pres. 1996—97), Ind. Bar Assn. Roman Catholic. Office: Security Benefit Group One Security Benefit Plaza Topeka KS 66636 Home: 5621 SW Urish RD Topeka KS 66610-9158 E-mail: michael.keefer@securitybenefit.com.

KEEGAN, DANIEL T., museum director; BA, U. Wis.; MFA, So. Ill. U. Dir. Kemper Mus. Contemporary Art, Kansas City, Mo., San Jose Mus. Art, 2000—08, Milw. Art Mus., 2008—. Tchr. W.Va. Wesleyan Coll., Avila Coll., Kansas City. Office: Milw Art Mus 700 N Art Mus Dr Milwaukee WI 53202 Office Phone: 408-291-5381. E-mail: dan.keegan@mam.org.*

KEEGAN, ROBERT J., manufacturing executive; b. NY, July 27, 1947; m. Lynn Keegan; 2 children. BS in Math., LeMoyne Coll.; MBA in Fin., U. Rochester, 1972. With Kodak, Rochester, NY, 1972—95; gen. mgr. Kodak New Zealand, 1986—87; dir. fin. photographic products group Kodak, Rochester, NY, 1987—90; gen. mgr. Kodak Spain, 1990—91; gen. mgr. consumer imaging Kodak European Middle Ea. African Region, 1991—93; exec. v.p., global strategy officer Avery Dennison Corp., Pasadena, Calif., 1995—97; pres. Kodak Profl., 1997; corp. v.p. Kodak, Rochester, 1997—2000, pres. consumer imaging, sr. v.p., 1997—2000, exec. v.p., 2000; pres., COO Goodyear Tire & Rubber Co., 2000—03, chmn., pres., CEO, 2003—. Office: Goodyear Tire & Rubber Co 1144 E Market St Akron OH 44316

KEEGSTRA, KENNETH G., plant biochemistry administrator; Dir. dept. energy Plant Rsch. Lab. Mich. State U., East Lansing. Office: Mich State Univ Plant Rsch Lab Dept Energy 106 Plant Biology Lab East Lansing MI 48824-1312

KEEHN, SILAS, retired bank executive; b. New Rochelle, NY, June 30, 1930; s. Grant and Marjorie (Burchard) K.; m. Marcia June Lindquist, Mar. 26, 1955; children: Elisabeth Keehn Lewis, Britta Keehn Scott, Peter. AB in Econs, Hamilton Coll., Clinton, NY, 1952; MBA in Fin, Harvard U., 1957. With Mellon Bank .A., Pitts., 1957-80, v.p., then sr. v.p., 1967-78, exec. v.p., 1978-79, vice-chmn., 1980; v.p. Mellon Nat. Corp., 1979-80, vice-chmn., 1980; chmn. bd. Pullman, Inc., Chgo., 1980; pres. Fed. Res. Bank Chgo., 1981-94; ret., 1994. Bd. dirs. Kewaunee Sci. Corp., Nat. Futures Assn. Trustee Rush U. Med. Ctr., Hamilton Coll., Clinton, N.Y. With USNR, 1953-56. Mem. Chgo. Club, Comml. Club Chgo., Econ. Club Chgo., Univ. Club, Links Club (N.Y.C.), Rolling Rock Club (Ligonier, Pa.), Indian Hill Club. Office: 707 Skokie Blvd Ste 600 Northbrook IL 60062-2841 Office Phone: 847-509-2757.

KEELEY, LARRY, innovation strategist; Co-founder, pres. Doblin Inc., Chgo., 1981—. Lectr. in field; adj. prof., graduate design strategy courses Inst. Design, Ill. Inst. Tech., bd. dir.; lectr. in innovation Northwestern U., Kellogg Sch. Mgmt., U. Chgo.; bd. dir. WBEZ-FM, Chgo. Named one of Magnificent Seven Gurus of Innovation, BusinessWeek, 2005.

KEELING, JOE KEITH, religious studies educator, retired dean; b. Muskogee, Okla., Apr. 21, 1936; s. William Lytle and Anna Madge (Watts) Keeling; m. Marjorie Ann Brotherton, 1957; children: Kara Kay, William Kent. BA in History, Northeastern State U., 1958; BD in Theology, So. Meth. U., 1962; MA in Theology, U. Chgo., 1967, PhD, 1974. Ordained to ministry United Meth. Ch., 1962. Dir. orientation, acad. advisor U. Chgo., 1964-68; asst. prof. religion Augustana Coll., Sioux Falls, SD, 1968-72; from asst. to assoc. prof. philosophy and religion Rockford (Ill.) Coll., 1972-86, dean of spl. acad. programming, assoc. dean of coll., 1981-86; adj. assoc. prof. dept. medicine U. Ill. Coll of Medicine at Rockford, 1984-86; provost, dean, prof. religion and philosophy Baker U., Baldwin City, Kans., 1986-96; v.p., dean Ctrl. Meth. U., Fayette, Mo., 1996—2002, prof. emeritus philosophy and religion, 2002—. Mem. bd. ordained ministry Kans. Eastern Conf. United Meth. Ch., 1987—96; cons., evaluator, mem. accreditation rev. coun. North Ctrl. Assn. Colls. and Schs. Higher Learning Commn., Am. Conf. Acad. Deans, Midwest Bioethics Ctr.; author, lectr. in field. Mem. Kansas City Regional Coun. Higher Edn., 1986—94; mem. instl. rev. com. Swedish-Am. Hosp., Rockford, 1981—86. Mem.: AAUP (Ill. state coun. mem. 1979—81), Archeol. Inst. Am. (bd. dirs. Rockford chpt. 1984—86), Am. Acad. Religions (v.p. Midwest region 1981—82, pres. 1982—83), Rockford C. of C. (bd. dirs. 1983—86), Fayette Round Table Club (pres. 2005—06), Rotary (pres. 2006—07). Democrat. Avocations: fishing, camping, canoeing. Home: PO Box 429 878 Highway 5 And 240 Fayette MO 65248-9509 Office: Ctrl Meth U Stedman 313 411 Central Methodist Sq Fayette MO 65248-1129 Home Phone: 660-248-2692; Office Phone: 660-248-6276. Business E-Mail: kkeeling@centralmethodist.edu.

KEENAN, BARBARA BYRD, professional society administrator; b. Martinsburg, W.Va., Aug. 31, 1952; d. James Leonard and Elizabeth (Somerfield) Byrd; m. Terrence James; 1 child, Marjorie Lynn. BS, Old Dominion U., 1973, MS, 1975; postgrad., U. Maryland, 1976. Cert. assn. exec. Instr. Old Dominion U., Norfolk, Va., 1972-75; asst. prof. U. Maryland, Balt., 1975-76; assoc. dir. Am. Dental Hygienists Assn., Chgo., 1976-79; dir. edn. Am. Coll. Preventive Medicine, Washington, 1979-81; dir. profl. affairs Tex. Pharm. Assn., Austin, 1981-83; dir. edn. and research Tex. Med. Assn., Austin, 1983-86; exec. v.p. Internat. Assn. Hospitality Accts., Austin, 1986-90; pres. Community Assn. Inst., Alexandria, Va., 1990—2002; exec. v.p. Inst. Food Technologists, Chgo., 2003—. Chair Assns. Advance Am. Com., 1994—; chair Internat. Food Info. Svc., 2003—; bd. mem. Partnership for Food Safety Edn., 2006—. Mem. editl. bd.: Jour. Assn. Leadership, 2003—, vice chmn.:, 2005—. Chair, Educational Bd., Journal Assoc. Leadership 2006-2007; bd. dirs. Nat. Bd. Cardiopulmonary Credentialing, Gaitersburg, N.D., 1981-82, mem. exec. com. 1982; bd. dirs. South Tex. Arthritis Found., San Antonio, 1987-89, Capital Area Arthritis Found., Austin, 1986-89; founding chmn. Travis County Adult Literacy Coun., Austin, 1984-90, chmn. emeritus 1990—; bd. dirs. Am. Hotel and Motel Assn. Research Found., 1988-90. Recipient award Internat. Assn. Bus. Communicators, 1988; named one of Outstanding Young Women Am., 1981, Top 10 Bus. Women of Yr., Am. Bus. Women's Assn., 1986, Disting. Alumni award Old Dominion U., 1999; inaugural recipient Barbara Bird Keenan award Nat. Bd. for Cert. of Comty. Assn. Mgrs. Fellow Am. Soc. Assn. Execs. (charter, vice chmn. 1991-92, planning com. 1985-88, 91-92, chair Assn. Advance Am. com. 1994, bd. dirs. 1985-86, 88—, chmn. ednl. sect. 1985-86, chmn. task force on social responsibility 1989—, chair fellows 1989-90, chair univ. com. 2002-, Excellence award 1985, 88, 94, CAE commr. 1991-93, sec.-treas. 1993-94, gov. task force 1992-93, chair rsch. com. 1996-97, Mgmt. Achievement award 1983, Key award 1996, award of excellence in edn. 1997); mem. Town Lake Bus. Women's Assn. (Woman of Yr. 1986), Tex. Soc. Assn. Execs. (com. chair 1981—), Greater Washington Soc. Assn. Execs. (CAE cert. com., instr. and tutor 1991-92, cmty. svc. com. 1996-97, bd. dirs. 1997—, chair 2001-2002, Monument award in edn. 1992), Leadership Austin, Leadership Tex. (bd. dirs., tng. group 1987—), Internat. Assn. Hosp. Accts. (hon. 1990), William Smith Assn. (mem. rsch. coun. 2003—), U.S. C. of C. (mem. Com. of 100). Home and Office: 1322 Isabella St Evanston IL 60201-1623 Office: Inst Food Technologists 525 W Van Buren St Chicago IL 60607 Office Phone: 312-782-8424. E-mail: bbkeenan@ift.org.

KEENAN, JAMES GEORGE, classics educator; b. NYC, Jan. 19, 1944; s. George F. and Cecilia Anna (Schmidt) K.; m. Laurie Haight; children: James, Kathleen, Kenneth, Mary, Lisa, Brian, Laura. AB, Holy Cross Coll., 1965; MA, Yale U., 1966, PhD, 1968. Asst. prof. Classics U. Calif., Berkeley, 1968-73; assoc. to full prof. Classics Loyola U. of Chgo., 1973—, chmn. classics, 1978-84, acting chmn., 1987-88. Cons. Petra Scrolls Conservation Project, 1995. Co-editor: Greek Papyri: The Tebtunis Papyri, vol. IV, 1976. Fellow Nat. Endowment for Humanities, 1973-74; travel grantee Am. Council Learned Socs., 1974, 83, 86; grant-in-aid Am. Philos. Soc., 1987. Mem. Am. Philol. Assn., Am. Soc. Papyrologists (pres. 1989-93), Chgo. Classical Club (pres. 1999-2001), Classical Assn. Midwest and South, Assn. Internat. des Papyrologues (mem. com. 1995-2004), Egypt Exploration Soc., Internat. Soc. Arabic Papyrology. Roman Catholic. Office: Loyola U Chgo Dept Classical Studies 6525 N Sheridan Rd Chicago IL 60626-5344 Home Phone: 773-761-9440; Office Phone: 773-508-3665. Business E-Mail: jkeenan@luc.edu.

KEER, LEON MORRIS, engineering educator; b. LA, Sept. 13, 1934; s. William and Sophia (Bookman) Keer; m. Barbara Sara Davis, Aug. 18, 1956; children: Patricia Renee, Jacqueline Saundra, Harold Neal, Michael Derek. BS, Calif. Inst. Tech., 1956, MS, 1958; PhD, U. Minn., 1962. Registered profl. engr., Calif. Mem. tech. staff Hughes Aircraft Co., Culver City, Calif., 1956-59; research fellow, instr. U. Minn., Mpls., 1959-62; asst. prof. Northwestern U., Evanston, Ill., 1964-66, assoc. prof., 1966-70, prof. engring., 1970—, Walter P. Murphy prof. mech. and civil engring., 1994—, assoc. dean research and grad. studies, 1985-92, chmn. dept. civil engring., 1992-97. Preceptor Columbia U., NYC, 1963—64; dir. Ctr. for Surface Engring. and Tribology, 1997—; dept. acad. advisor civil and structural engring. Hong Kong U., 1998—2002; Chau Wei-Yin meml. lectr. Hong Kong Poly. U., 2000; S.W. Mechanics lecture tour, 2003—04. Co-editor: (monograph) Solid Contact and Lubrication, 1980; mem. editl. bd.: Jour. Mechanics of Materials; contbr. articles to profl. jours. Fellow, NATO, 1962, Guggenheim Found., 1972, Japanese Soc. for the Promotion of Sci., 1986. Fellow: NAE (elected 1997), ASME (life; tech. editor Jour. Applied Mechanics 1988—92, Innovative Rsch. award tribology divsn. 2001, Daniel C. Drucker medal 2003), ASCE (life; chmn. engring. mech. divsn. 1992—93), Acoustical Soc. Am., Am. Acad. Mechanics (sec. 1981—88, pres.-elect 1987—88, pres. 1988—89); mem.: Tau Beta Pi, Sigma Xi. Home: 2601 Marian Ln Wilmette IL 60091-2207 Office: Northwestern U Dept Civil Engring 2145 Sheridan Rd Evanston IL 60208-0834 Business E-Mail: l-keer@northwestern.edu.

KEESE, JAN, elementary school educator; Tchr. Crocker Elem. Sch., Ankeny, Iowa. Instr. Grad. Sch. Edn., Viterbo U. Named Ankeny Educator of Yr., 2005, Iowa Tchr. of Yr., Iowa Dept. Edn., 2007. Mem.: Iowa Literacy Coun. Office: Crocker Elem Sch 2910 SW Applewood Ankeny IA 50023 Business E-Mail: jkeese@ankeny.k12.ia.us.

KEFAUVER, WELDON ADDISON, publishing executive; b. Canal Winchester, Ohio, Apr. 3, 1927; s. Ross Baker and Virginia Marie (Burtner) K. BA, Ohio State U., Columbus, 1950. Mem. faculty Columbus Acad., 1956-58; mng. editor Ohio State U. Press, 1958-64, dir., 1964-84, dir. emeritus, 1984—. Dir. Am. Univ. Press Svcs., Inc., 1971-72, 76-79; mem. US del. 2d Asian Pacific Conf. Publs., Taiwan, 1978 Author: Scholars and their Publishers, 1977; editl. adv. bd. Scholarly Publishing. Served with AUS, 1945-46. Recipient Centennial Svc. award Ohio State U., 1970; citation Ohioana Libr. Assn., 1974; Disting. Svc. award Ohio State U., 1986; recognized for svc. to Ohio State U. by Ohio Senate and Ohio Ho. of Reps., 1986. Mem. Assn. Am. Univ. Presses (v.p. 1971-72, dir. 1971-72, 76-79, pres. 1977-78), Soc. Scholarly Pub., Nathaniel Hawthorne Soc., AAUP, Phi Eta Sigma, Phi Kappa Phi Clubs: Torch (Columbus), Crichton (Columbus), Ohio State U. Faculty (Columbus). Home: 675 Eastmoor Blvd Columbus OH 43209-2252 Office: 1050 Carmack Rd Columbus OH 43210-1002

KEFFER, RICHARD, lawyer; BA in Bus. & Economics, Greenville Coll., 1977; JD, Wash. U. Sch. of Law, 1980. Assoc. Beckett and Steinkamp, 1980—84; assoc. gen. counsel Pet, Inc., Pillsbury Co., 1984—95; atty. Premcor Refining Group, Inc., 1995—2003; gen. counsel, sec., corp. compliance officer Aurora Foods, Inc., 2003—04; v.p., gen. counsel, sec. D&K Healthcare Resources, Inc., St. Louis, 2004—. Office: D&K Healthcare Resources Inc 8235 Forsyth Blvd Saint Louis MO 63105

KEGERREIS, ROBERT JAMES, management consultant, marketing professional, educator; b. Detroit, Apr. 2, 1921; s. I. G. and A. M. (Merry) K.; m. Katherine L. Falknor, Oct. 30, 1943; children: Merry, Duncan, Melissa. BA, BS, Ohio State U., 1943, MBA, 1946, PhD, 1968, U. Dayton, 1982, EdD (hon.), EdD (hon.), U. Dayton; LLD (hon.), U. Akron, Wilberforce U.; ScD (hon.), Cen. State U., Japan, 1992; EconD (hon.), Okayama U., Japan, 1992. Economist Fed. Res. Bank, Cleve., 1946-49; pres. KV Stores, Inc., Woodsfield, Ohio, 1949-69; v.p., sec. KBK Devel. Co., Inc., 1955-62; assoc. prof. Ohio U., Athens, 1967-69; dean Coll. Bus. and Adminstrn. Wright State U., Dayton, Ohio, 1969-71, v.p. adminstrn., 1971-73, pres., 1973-85; cons. RJK Co., Dayton, 1985—. Lt. (j.g.) USN, 1943—46. Mem. Moraine Country Club, Bicycle Club, Pelican Bay Country Club. Methodist. Avocations: flying, golf.

KEIDERLING, TIMOTHY ALLEN, chemistry educator, researcher; b. Waterloo, Iowa, June 22, 1947; s. Glenn Allen and Ethel V. (Kalainoff) K.; m. Candace Ruth Crawford, Sept. 4, 1976; 1 son, Michael Crawford. B.S., Loras Coll., 1969; MA, Princeton U., 1971, PhD, 1974. NSF fellow Princeton U., 1969-72; rsch. assoc. U. So. Calif., LA, 1973-76; asst. prof. U. Ill., Chgo., 1976-81, assoc. prof. chemistry, 1981-85, prof., 1985—, acting head, 1997-2000, assoc. dean arts and scis., 2003-04; guest prof. Max Planck Inst., Garching, Germany, 1984, U. Freiburg, 2004, U. Padova, Italy, 2005; sr. vis. Oxford U., 1994. Contbr. chpts. to books, more than 240 articles to profl. jours. Fellow Fulbright Found. 1984, Guggenheim Found. 2004-05; grantee NSF, NIH, DOD, Petroleum Rsch. Found., various times; sr. rsch. scholar U. Ill., 1991-94. Mem. Am. Chem. Soc., Am. Phys. Soc., Biophys. Soc., Soc. Applied Spectroscopy (nat. sec. 2007—). Achievements include the development of technique of vibrational circular dichroism, making of first such measurements of polypeptides, proteins and nucleic acids, and first magnetic applications to small molecules; research in protein folding and theoretical modelling of peptide structure and spectra. Office: U Ill Dept Chemistry 845 W Taylor St M/C 111 Chicago IL 60607-7061

KEIM, ROBERT BRUCE, lawyer; b. Nebraska City, Nebr., Jan. 10, 1946; s. Ernest Jacob and Ruby Rebecca (Mohr) K.; m. Barbara Ann Simmons, Aug. 10, 1968; 1 child, Robert Boyd. BS, U. Nebr., 1968; JD cum laude, Washburn U., 1974. Bar: Mo. 1974, Kans. 1985. Atty. Morris, Larson, King & Stamper, Kansas City, Mo., 1974-89, Shughart, Thomson & Kilroy, P.C., Overland Park, Kans., 1989-90, chmn. corp. fin. and transactional law dept., 1989-90; atty. Kutak Rock LLP, Kansas City, Mo., 1999—. Bd. dirs., mem. audit com. Osborn Labs., Olathe, Kans. Community advisor Jr. League of Johnson & Wyanadotte Counties, Overland Park, 1990—; active fin. com., deacon Rolling Hills Ch., Overland Park, 1990—, Econ. Devel. Coun. Overland Park, 1991—. Lt. U.S. Army, 1968-71. Avocations: running, golf, backpacking. Home: 10021 Juniper Ln Shawnee Mission KS 66207-3446

KEISER, GEORGE J., state legislator; m. Kathy Keiser; four children. Owner Quality Printing Svc.; former commr. Bismarck City, N.D.; rep. N.D. State Ho. of Reps. Dist. 47, 1993—, vice chmn. indsl., bus. and labor com., mem. transp. com.

KEISER, KENNETH E., food products executive; With Pepsi-Cola Metro. Bottling, 1976—90; sales, oper. Pepsi-Cola Bottling Group; pres. Pepsi-Cola Puerto Rico; pres., COO Delta Beverage Group, 1990—2000, PepsiAmericas (prior to merger with Whitman), 1998—2002; pres., COO worldwide PepsiAmericas, Mpls., 2002—. Office: Pepsi Americas 4000 Dain Rauscher Plaza 60 S Sixth St Minneapolis MN 55402

KEITH, DAMON JEROME, federal judge; b. Detroit, July 4, 1922; s. Perry A. and Annie L. (Williams) K.; m. Rachel Boone Keith, Oct. 18, 1953; children: Cecile Keith, Debbie, Gilda. BA, W.Va. State Coll., 1943; JD, Howard U., 1949; LLM, Wayne State U., 1956; PhD (hon.) (hon.), U. Mich., Howard U., Wayne State U., Mich. State U., NY Law Sch., Detroit Coll. Law, W.Va. State Coll., U. Detroit, Atlanta U., Lincoln U., Marygrove Coll., Detroit Inst. Tech., Shaw Coll., Ctrl. State U., Yale U., Loyola Law Sch., LA, Ea. Mich. U., Va. Union U., Ctrl. Mich. U., Morehouse Coll., Western Mich. U., Tuskegee U., Georgetown U., Hofstra U., DePaul U. Bar: Mich. 1949. Atty. Office Friend of Ct., Detroit, 1951—55; sr. ptnr. firm Keith, Conyers Anderson, Brown & Wahls, Detroit, 1964—67; mem. Wayne County Bd. Suprs., 1958—63; dist. judge US Dist. Ct. (ea. dist.) Mich., 1967—77, chief judge, 1975—77; judge US Ct. Appeals (6th cir.), Detroit, 1977—95, sr. judge, 1995—. Mem. Wayne County (Mich.) Bd. Suprs., 1958—63; chmn. Mich. Civil Rights Commn., 1964—67; pres. Detroit Housing Commn., 1958—67; commr. State Bar Mich., 1960—67; mem. Detroit Bar Assn., Mich. Com. Manpower Devel. and Vocat. Tng., 1964, Detroit Mayor's Health Adv. Com., 1969; rep. dist. judges 6th Cir. Jud. Conf., 1975—77; adv. com. on codes of conduct Jud. Conf. US, 1979—86; subcom. on supporting pers. Jud. Conf. Com. on Ct. Adminstrn., 1983—87; chmn. Com. on the Bicentennial of Constn. of Sixth Cir., 1985—; nat. chmn. Jud. Conf. Com. on the Bicentennial of Constn., 1987—; mem. Commn. on the Bicentennial of U.S. Constn., 1990; lectr. Howard U., 1972, Ohio State U. Law Sch., 1992, NY Law Sch., 1992; guest lectr. Howard U. Law Sch., 1981; Bicentennial of Constn. lectr. W.Va. State Coll., 1987; keynote speaker Black Law Students Assn., Harvard Law Sch., 1987. Contbr. articles to profl. jours. Trustee Med. Corp. Detroit, Interlochen Arts Acad., Cranbrook Sch., U. Detroit, Mich. chpt. Leukemia Soc. Am.; mem. Citizen's Adv. Com. Equal Ednl. Opportunity Detroit Bd. Edn.; gen. co-chmn. United Negro Coll. Fund Detroit; 1st v.p. emeritus Detroit chpt. NAACP; mem. com. mgmt. Detroit YMCA; mem. Detroit coun. Boy Scouts Am., Detroit Arts Commn.; vice chmn. Detroit Symphony Orch.; vis. com. Wayne State U. Law Sch.; adv. coun. U. Notre Dame Law Sch.; chmn. Citizen's Coun. for Mich. Pub. Univs.; deacon Tabernacle Missionary Bapt. Ch.; Deacon Bapt ch.; bd. dirs. Detroit Bd. Table, NCCJ. US Army, 1943—46. Named 1 of 100 Most Influential Black Ams., Ebony Mag., 1971—92, Damon J. Keith Elementary Sch. named in his honor, Detroit Bd. Edn., 1974, Damon J. Keith Ann. Civic and Humanitarian award established in his honor, Highland Park YMCA, 1984, 15th Mich. Legal Milestone The Uninvited Ear presented in honor of The Keith Decision, 1991; named one of The Century's Finest Michiganders, Mich. Chronicle, 1999; recipient Mich. Chronicle outstanding Citizen award, 1960, 1964, 1974, Alumni citation, Wayne State U., 1968, Ann. Jud. award, 1971, Citizen award, Mich. State U., Disting. Svc. award, Howard U., 1972, Jud. Independence award, 1973, Spingarn medal, NAACP, 1974, Fed. Judge of Yr. award, Black Law Students Assn., 1974, award for Outstanding Contbns. to Black Community, Nat. Assn. Black Social Workers, 1974, Judge of Yr. award, Nat. Conf. Black Lawyers, 1974, Bill of Rights award, Jewish Community Coun., 1977, A. Philip Randolph award, Detroit Coalition Black Trade Unionists, 1981, Human Rights Day award, B'nai B'rith Women's Coun. Met. Detroit, Robert L. Millender award, So. Christian Leadership Conf. Mich. chpt., 1982, Afro-Asian Inst. award, Histadrut in Israel, 1982, civil rights lectr. award, Creighton U. Ahmanson Law Ctr., 1983, Nat. Human Rels. award, Greater Detroit Roundtable of NCCJ, 1984, Knights of Charity award, Pontifical Inst. for Mission Extension, 1986, Disting. Pub. Svc. award, Mich. Anti-Defamation League of B'nai B'rith, 1987, Nat. Chpt. award, 1988, Black Achievement award, Equitable Fin. Cos., 1987, Menorah award, Afro-Asian Inst. Histadrut of Israel, 1988, Dr. George Derry award, Marygrove Coll. Detroit, One Nation award, The Patriots Found./GM, 1989, 1st Ann. Move Detroit Forward award, City of Detroit, 1990, Gov's. Minuteman award, Rotary Club Lansing, 1991, Disting. Warrior award, Detroit Urban League, 1998, Edward J. Devitt award for disting. svc. to justice, 1998, Pinnacle award, Turner Broadcasting Sys., 2000, Spirit of Excellence award, ABA, 2001. Mem.: ABA (coun. sect. legal edn. and admission to bar), Am. Judicature Soc., Nat. Lawyers Guild,

Detroit Bar Assn. (pres'. award), Mich. Bar Assn. (champion of justice award), Nat. Bar Assn. (William H. Hastie award Jud. Coun., 8th Ann. equal Justice award), Detroit Cotillion Club, Alpha Phi Alpha. Office: US Ct Appeals US Courthouse 231 W Lafayette Blvd Rm 240 Detroit MI 48226-2779 also: Potter Stewart US Courthouse 100 E 5th St Cincinnati OH 45202-3988

KEJR, JOSEPH, former state legislator; m. Geena Kejr. Kans. state rep. Dist. 67, until 1998; farmer. Home: 10143 W Stimmel Rd Brookville KS 67425-9719

KELCH, ROBERT PAUL, former dean, pediatric endocrinologist; b. Detroit, Dec. 3, 1942; s. Paul and Iona Bertha (Schmitt) Kelch; m. Jeri Anne Parker, Aug. 17, 1963; children: Randall Paul, Julie Marie. PhB, Wayne State U., Detroit, 1964; MD, U. Mich., Ann Arbor, 1967. Intern then Wyeth pediatric residency fellow U. Mich. Med. Center, 1967—70, research fellow, 1969—70, mem. faculty, 1972—94, prof. pediatrics, 1977—94, acting chmn. dept., 1979—80, chmn. dept., 1981—94; physician-in-chief C.S. Mott Children's Hosp. U. Mich., 1983—94; chief clin. affairs U. Mich. Hosps., 1989—92; NIH trainee pediatric endocrinology U. Calif. Med. Center, San Francisco, 1970—72; prof. pediat., dean U. Iowa Coll. Medicine, Iowa City, 1994—2003, v.p. statewide health svcs., 2001—02; exec. v.p., med. affairs, prof. pediatrics U. Michigan, Ann Arbor, 2003—. Co-author: A Practical Approach to Pediatric Endocrinology, 1975; contbr. articles to med. jours. With USNR. Fellow: Am. Acad. Pediat.; mem.: Midwest Soc. Pediat. Rsch. (pres. 1983—84), Lawson Wilkins Pediat. Endocrine Soc., Ctrl. Soc. Clin. Rsch., Assn. Med. Sch. Pediat. Dept. Chmn. (pres. 1989), Am. Soc. Clin. Investigation, Am. Fedn. Clin. Rsch., Endocrine Soc., Am. Bd. Pediat. (sec.-treas. 1992, chmn. 1995), Soc. Pediat. Rsch. (pres. 1988), Inst. Medicine NAS. Methodist. Office: U Michigan Health Sys M7324 Med Sci Bldg Box 0626 1500 E Med Ctr Dr Ann Arbor MI 48109 Office Phone: 734-647-9351, 734-647-9351. E-mail: rkelch@med.umich.edu.

KELEHER, JAMES P., archbishop emeritus; b. July 31, 1931; BA, St. Mary of the Lake Sem., Mundelein, Ill., 1954; DST, St. Mary of the Lake Sem., 1961, Licentiate in Sacred Theology, 1968; MA in Ednl. administrn., Loyola U., Chgo., 1967; PhD, Gregorian U., Rome. Ordained priest Archdiocese of Chgo., 1958; assoc. pastor St. Henry parish; tchr., athletic dir. Quigley Prep. Sem.; teaching positions St. Mary of the Lake Sem., Mundelein, Ill., Niles Coll., 1969—72; rector Quigley Prep. Sem., Chgo., 1976—78; pres., rector St. Mary of the Lake Sem., Mundelein, Ill., 1978—84; ordained bishop, 1984; bishop Diocese of Belleville, Ill., 1984—93; archbishop Archdiocese of Kansas City in Kans., 1993—2005, archbishop emeritus, 2005—. Mem. Papal Visitation Com. for Sems.; chmn. bishop's com. on priestly formation; mem. com. migration; mem. com. econ. concerns of the Holy See Nat. Conf. Cath. Bishops. Mem.: Midwest Assn. Theol. Schs., Nat. Cath. Edn. Assn. (sem. dept.). Roman Catholic. Office: Archdiocese of Kansas City Chancery Office 12615 Parallel Kansas City KS 66109*

KELLEHER, NEIL L., chemist, educator; b. Clinton, Md., Apr. 28, 1970; s. William J. and Ann C. Kelleher; m. Jennifer Kelleher, Aug. 12, 1992; children: Emily, Lauren. BS in Chemistry, Pacific Luth. U., 1992, BA in German, 1992; postgraduate studies, U. Konstanz, Germany, 1992—93; MS in Bioanalytical Chemistry, Cornell U., 1995, PhD in Bioanalytical Chemistry, 1997. Fulbright scholar U. Konstanz, Germany, 1992—93; rsch. asst. Cornell U., Ithaca, NY, 1993—97; postdoctoral asst. Harvard Med. Sch., 1997—99; asst. prof. to assoc. prof. chemistry U. Ill., Urbana-Champaign, 1999—. Contbr. articles to profl. jours. Recipient Burroughs Wellcome award in pharm. scis., 2000—03, NIH, 2000—02, Rsch. Corp. Innovation award, 2001, Career award, NSF, 2002—; grantee, NIH, 1993—96; Searle scholar, 2000—03, Cotrell scholar, 2002, Packard fellow, 2002—. Mem.: AAAS, Am. Soc. Mass Spectrometry (Rsch. award 2001), Am. Chem. Soc. Office: Univ Ill Dept Chemistry 53 Roger Adams Lab 47-5 600 S Mathews Ave Urbana IL 61801 Office Phone: 217-244-3927. Office Fax: 217-244-8068. E-mail: kelleher@scs.uiuc.edu.

KELLEHER, TIMOTHY JOHN, retired publishing company executive; b. Massillon, Ohio, Jan. 4, 1940; s. John Joseph and Catherine Isabelle (Quinlan) K.; m. Mary Gray Thornton, Aug. 27, 1966; children— Catherine, Joseph, Sarah BS in Polit. Sci., Xavier U., Cin., 1962; postgrad., Xavier U., 1965, Morehead State U., Ky., 1975-76. Mgr. labor rels. GM, Norwood, Ohio, 1964-73; pers. mgr. Rockwell Internat., Winchester, Ky., 1973-77, dir. labor rels. Troy, Mich., 1977-82; v.p. human resources Detroit Free Press, 1982-89; sr. v.p. labor rels. Detroit Newspaper Agy., 1989—2004; ret. Dir. Detroit Macomb Hosp. Corp. Bd. dirs. Greater Detroit Alliance of Bus., annually 1983-89, Winchester/Clark Hist. Soc., Ky., 1975, pres., 1976-77; bd. dirs. New Detroit Inc., annually 1983-89. Served to sgt. U.S. Army, 1962-64 Mem. Coop. Edn. Assn. Ky. (bd. dirs. 1975-77, Employer of Yr. award 1976), Indsl. Rels. Rsch. Assn., Xavier U. Alumni Assn. (pres. Detroit chpt. 1991-93), Forest Lake Country Club (bd. dirs. 1991-94, 2000-02, pres. 2002). Republican. Roman Catholic. Avocations: golf, fishing. E-mail: TKelleher@cinci.rr.com.

KELLER, DEBORAH KIM, former soccer player; b. Winfield, Ill., Mar. 24, 1975; Student in phys. edn., U. N.C. Mem. U.S. Nat. Women's Soccer Team, 1995—. Named Soccer Am. Player of Yr., 1996, Offensive Most Valuable Player, NCAA Tournament, 1996, U. N.C. Athlete of Yr., 1997. Achievements include 3d-place 1995 FIFA Women's World Cup, Sweden; mem. U-20 Nat. Team, Nordic Cup, Germany, 1994; mem. gold-medal North team, 1995 U.S. Olympic Festival, Denver; led U. N.C. to CAA Championship, 1996. Office: US Soccer Fedn 1801-1811 S Prairie Ave Chicago IL 60616

KELLER, DENNIS JAMES, management educator; b. July 6, 1941; s. Ralph and Dorothy (Barckman) K.; m. Constance Bassett Templeton, May 28, 1966; children: Jeffrey Breckenridge, David McDaniel, John Templeton. AB, Princeton U., 1963; MBA, U. Chgo., 1968. Account exec. Motorola Comm., Chgo., 1964-67; v.p. fin. Bell & Howell Comm., Waltham, Mass., 1968-70; v.p. mktg. Bell & Howell Schs., Chgo., 1970-73; pres. Keller Grad. Sch. Mgmt., Chgo., 1973-81, chmn., CEO, 1981—87. Chmn. bd., CEO DeVry Inc., 1987-04, chmn. bd. 2004-; cons., evaluator North Ctrl. Assn., Chgo., 1979-84; bd. dirs. Nicor Inc., 1994-, Ryerson Inc., Chgo., 2005-07. Trustee Glenwood Sch. for Boys, Ill., 1980-02, Chgo. Zool. Soc., Brookfield, Ill., 1979-, Princeton U., NJ, 1994-98, 2000-, Lake Forest Acad.-Ferry Hall, Ill., 1980-87, George M. Pullman Found., Chgo., 1987-02, Mpala Wildlife Found., Nairobi, Kenya, 2001—, African Wildlife Found., Washington, chmn. 2005—; bd. trustees U. Chgo., 1998-; bd. dirs. Great Books Found., Chgo., 1986-98; chmn. U. Chgo. Grad. Sch. Bus. Coun., 1994-02, Princeton U. Sch. Engring. and Applied Scis. Leadership Coun., 1992-; commr. North Cen. Assn.-Commn. on Instns. of Higher Edn., 1985-88. Nat. Merit scholar, 1959-63; U. Chgo. Grad. Sch. Bus. fellow, 1967-68. Mem. Hinsdale Golf Club, Econ. Club, Comml. Club Chgo., Chgo. Club, Nantucket Golf Club, Sankaty Head Golf Club. Republican. Mem. United Ch. of Christ. Office: DeVry Inc 1 Tower Ln Ste 2350 Oakbrook Terrace IL 60181 Business E-Mail: dkeller@devry.com.

KELLER, ELIOT AARON, broadcast executive; b. Davenport, Iowa, June 11, 1947; s. Norman Edward and Millie (Morris) Keller; m. Sandra Kay McGrew, July 3, 1970; 1 child, Nicole. BA, U. Iowa, 1970; MS, San Diego State U., 1976. Corr. Sta. WHO-AM-FM-TV, Des Moines, 1969-70; newsman Sta. WSUI-AM, Iowa City, 1968-70; newsman, corr. Sta. WHBF-AM-FM-TV, Rock Island, Ill., 1969; newsman Sta. WOC-AM-FM-TV, Davenport, Iowa, 1970; freelance newsman and photographer Iowa City, 1969-77; pres., bd. dirs. mem. KZIA, Inc. (formerly KRNA, Inc. and Communicators, Inc.), Cedar Rapids, 1971—, treas., 2003—; gen. mgr. Sta. KRNA FM, Iowa City, 1974-98, Sta. KQCR FM, Cedar Rapids, 1994-95, Sta. KXMX FM, 1995—98, Sta. KZIA-FM, 1998—, Sta. KGYM-AM, 2006—. Dir. KZIA, Inc. (formerly KRNA, Inc. and Communicators, Inc.), Cedar Rapids, Iowa; adj. instr. dept. comm. studies U. Iowa, Iowa City, 1983, 84; mem. adv. bd. dept. comm. arts Wartburg Coll., Waverly, 2001—; mem. prof. adv. bd. Sch. Journalism and Mass Comm. U. Iowa, 2002—. Named Broadcaster of Yr., Iowa Broadcasters Assn., 2001; named to Hall of Fame, Advt. Fedn. Cedar Rapids, Iowa, 2004. Mem.: Iowa City Area C. of C. (chmn. local govt. task force 1981, chmn. transp. subcom. 2000—05, vice chmn. 2004—05, chmn. legis. coun. 2005—, named Vol. of Yr. 2004), Iowa Assn. R.R. Passengers (chmn. excursion 1988—), R.R. Passenger Car Alliance, Mid-Continent Rlwy. Hist. Soc. (bd. dir. 2000—03). Jewish. Home: 1244 Devon Dr NE Iowa City IA 52240-9628 Office: Sta KZIA FM and KGYM AM 1110 26th Ave SW Cedar Rapids IA 52404-3430 Office Phone: 319-363-2061. Business E-Mail: eliot@kzia.com.

KELLER, JUAN DANE, retired lawyer; b. Cape Girardeau, Mo., Jan. 30, 1943; s. Irvin A. and Mercedes (Crippen) K.; m. Sandra Anne Solomon; children: Mary, John, Katharine, Robert, Michael, Cassandra. AB in History, U. Mo., 1965, JD, 1967; LLM, Georgetown U., 1971. Bar: Mo. Assoc. Bryan, Cave, St. Louis, 1971-78, ptnr., 1979—2004. Contbg. author: Missouri Bar Taxation Handbook, 1988-95. Capt. JAGC, U.S. Army, 1967-71. Mem. ABA, Mo. Bar (tax com. 1971—), Met. St. Louis Bar Assn., Order of Coif. Methodist. Home: 12512 Glencroft Dr Saint Louis MO 63128-2513 Personal E-mail: juandk@aol.com.

KELLER, MICHAEL C., diversified financial services company executive; m. Sue Keller; 4 children. BS in Math., U. Mich. Mktg. rep. IBM, 1982—87, indsl. sector program mgr., 1988, mktg. mgr., 1989—91, mgr., cons. svcs., 1992—93, bus. unit exec., 1993—94, automotive industry exec., 1995—96, dir., cons. & sys. integration, 1996—97; sr. v.p., bus. & ptnr. mgmt. Bank One Corp., Columbus, Ohio, 1989—99, chief tech. officer, corp. infrastructure, 1999—2001; exec. v.p., chief info. officer Nationwide, Columbus, Ohio, 2001—. Mem.: Columbus Tech. Leadership Coun. Office: Nationwide One Nationwide Pl Columbus OH 43215-2220

KELLER, MICHELLE R., science educator; b. Rolla, ND, Aug. 15, 1951; d. Raymond Charles Halone and Yvonne M. (Klier) Edwards; m. Fred F. Keller, June 30, 1973; 1 child, Brent F. BS in Foods and Nutrition, N.D. State U., 1973; cert. sci. edn., Minot State U., 1977; MEd in Secondary Sci. Edn., N.Dak. State U., 2001. Instr. sci. Bisbee (N.D.)-Egeland H.S., 1975—. Judge Seiko Youth Challenge, 1993, 94; ND tchr. portfolio trainer, assessor. Access Excellence fellow Genentech/NSF, 1994; recipient Presdl. award for excellence in sci. tchg., 1993, Edn.'s Unsung Hero award 1998; named Hon. Mention Tchr., Radio Shack/Tandy scholars program, 1998, 99. Mem. Am. Assn. Physics Tchrs. (pres. N.D. sect. 2001—), Nat. Sci. Tchrs. Assn., N.D. Sci. Tchrs. Assn., N.D. Orienteering Alliance, Nat. Edn. Assn., N.D. Edn. Assn. Democrat. Roman Catholic. Avocations: walking, reading, gardening. Home: PO Box 265 201 3rd Ave W Bisbee ND 58317-0265 Office: Bisbee-Egeland H S P O Box 217 204 3rd Ave W Bisbee ND 58317 Home Phone: 701-656-3435; Office Phone: 701-656-3536. E-mail: mkeller@ndsualumni.net.

KELLER, WILLIAM FRANCIS, publishing consultant; b. Meyersdale, Pa., May 22, 1922; s. Lloyd Francis and Dorothy Marie (Shultz) K.; m. Frances Jane Core, Mar. 31, 1944. AA, Potomac State Coll. of W.Va. U., 1941; BS, U. Md., 1943, MS, 1945. Ednl. rep. Blakiston Co., 1945-51, assoc. editor, 1951-54; editor coll. div. McGraw Hill Book Co., NYC, 1954-56; editor-in-chief Blakiston divsn. McGraw Hill Book Co., 1956-65, gen. mgr. div., 1965-68; pres. Year Book Med. Publs., Chgo., 1968-81, chmn. bd., 1968-82; pub. cons. Crystal Lake, Ill., 1982-95; administrv. sec. Am. Med. Pubs. Assn., 1985-91. Served with U.S. Army, 1945-46. Office: 7916 W Hillside Rd Crystal Lake IL 60012-2939

KELLERMEYER, ROBERT WILLIAM, physician, educator; b. Wheeling, W.Va., Sept. 4, 1929; s. William F. and Mabel I. (Keller) M.; m. Audrey L. Shanaberger, June 12, 1954; children: Suzanne, Scott, Mark. BA, Washington and Jefferson Coll., 1951; MD, Western Res. U., 1955. Diplomate Am. Bd. Internal Medicine, Am. Bd. Hematology, Am. Bd. Med. Oncology. Intern dept. medicine Univ. Hosps. Cleve., 1955-56, asst. resident, 1956-57, chief resident, 1962-63, co-dir. div. hematology and oncology, 1974-83; sr. instr. dept. medicine Univ. Hosps.-Case Western Res. U., 1963-66, asst. prof. medicine, 1965-68, assoc. prof., 1969-75, prof., 1975-96, emeritus prof., 1996—; David and Inez Myers prof. hematology Case Western Res. U., 1978-96; med. dir. Aultman Cancer Ctr. Aultman Hosp., Canton, Ohio, 1993—2000; prof. medicine N.E. Ohio Univs. Coll. Medicine, 1994—. Author: The Red Cell, 1970. With USPHS, 1957-59. Recipient Career Devel. award USPHS, 1966, Am. Cancer Soc. postdoctoral fellow, 1959-62; John and Mary R. Markle scholar, 1965. Mem. Am. Soc. Hematology, Cen. SOc. Clin. Rsch., Am. Fedn. Clin. Rsch., Am. Assn. Cancer Edn., Ea. Coop. Oncology Group, Am. Soc. Clin. Oncology. Office: Aultman Hosp 2600 6th St SW Canton OH 44710-1702

KELLEY, BRUCE GUNN, insurance company executive, lawyer; b. Phila., Mar. 17, 1954; s. Robb Beardsley and Winifred Elizabeth Gray (Murray) K.; m. Susan Aldrich Barnes, Oct. 1, 1983; children: Dashle Gunn, Barnes Gunn, Onnalee Kinkaid. AB, Dartmouth Coll., 1976; JD, U. Iowa, 1979. Bar: Iowa 1979; CPCU; CLU. Assoc. Bradshaw, Fowler, Proctor & Fairgrave, Des Moines, 1979-84, ptnr., 1984-85; gen. counsel Employers Mut. Casualty Co., Des Moines, 1985-89, exec. v.p., 1989-91, pres., 1991—, also bd. dirs. Trustee Am. Inst. for Chartered Property Casualty Underwriters/Ins. Inst. Am.; bd. dirs. Property Casualty Insurers Assn. of Am. Bd. dirs. Property Loss Rsch. Bur. Recipient Disting. Eagle Scout award, Boy Scouts Am. Mem. Polk County Bar Assn., Beta Gamma Sigma, Des Moines Club, Rotary, Masons. Republican. Mem. United Church of Christ. Home: 14 Glenview Dr Des Moines IA 50312-2546 Office: EMC Ins Cos PO Box 712 Des Moines IA 50306-0712

KELLEY, FRANK NICHOLAS, dean; b. Akron, Ohio, Jan. 19, 1935; s. John William Kelley and Rose (Hadinger) Bates; m. Judith Carol Lowe, Jan. 1, 1960; children: Katherine Rose Bruno, Frank Michael, Christopher Patrick. BS, U. Akron, 1958, MS, 1959, PhD, 1961. Br. chief propellant devel. Air Force Rocket Propulsion Lab., Edwards AFB, Calif., 1965-69, chief of plans, 1969-70, chief scientist, 1970-73, Air Force Materials Lab., Wright-Patterson AFB, Ohio, 1973-77, dir., 1977-78; dir. Inst. Polymer Sci. U. Akron, 1978-88, dean Coll. Polymer Sci. and Engring., 1988—. Bd. dirs. Premix, Inc., North Kingsville, Ohio; cons. USAF, Thiokol Corp., others. Editor: Polymers in Space Research, 1965; contbr. articles to profl. jours. Lt. USAF, 1961-64; capt. USAF Res., 1964. Named Outstanding Alumnus, Tau Kappa Epsilon, 1991. Mem. Am. Chem. Soc. Mem. Christian Ch. (Disciples Of Christ). Avocation: woodworking. Office: U Akron Coll Polymer Sci and Polymer Engring Akron OH 44325-0001

KELLEY, JAMES, automotive sales executive; b. Decatur, Ind., June 13, 1918; m. Lavon Kelley; children: Suzanne Horton, Barbara Kraegel, Tom Kelley. Grad., G.E. Apprentice Sch. Early career positions with GE; founder Jim Kelley Buick, 1952; now chmn., co-CEO Kelley Automotive Group. Owner, developer Sycamore Hills Golf Club, 1989. Bd. dirs. Ft. Wayne Jr. Achievement, Big Bros. and Big Sisters, Boys and Girls club of Ft. Wayne, YMCA, Hoosier Celebrity Golf Tournament, Arthritis Found., Ft. Wayne Aviation Mus. Mem. Ft. Wayne C. of C. 9bd. dirs.), Sycamore Hills Golf Club (bd. dirs.), Ind. Golf Assn. (bd. dirs.), Western Golf Assn. (bd. dirs.). Avocations: aviation, indy car racing, health and fitness.

KELLEY, JOHN JOSEPH, JR., lawyer; b. Cleve., June 17, 1936; s. John Joseph and Helen (Meier) K.; m. Gloria Hill, June 20, 1959; children: John Joseph III, Scott MacDonald, Christopher Taft, Megan Meredith. BS cum laude in Commerce, Ohio U., 1958; LL.B., Case Western Res. U., 1960. Bar: Ohio bar 1960. Clk. firm Walter & Haverfield, Cleve., 1957-60; assoc. Walter, Haverfield, Buescher & Chockley, Cleve., 1960-66, partner, 1967-72; chief exec. officer Fleischmann Enterprises, Cin., 1972-77; pvt. practice law Cin., 1977-87; ptnr. Kohnen & Patton, Cin., 1988—. Chmn. bd. Basic Packaging Systems, Inc., 1982-87; dir. Orgamac Leasing Ltd; pres. Naples Devel. Inc., 1974-87, Yankee Leasing Co. Mem. Lakewood (Ohio) City Council, 1965-72, pres., 1972; mem. exec. com. Cuyahoga County (Ohio) Republican Central Com., 1965-72; mem. Hamilton County (Ohio) Rep. Policy Com.; Ohio chmn. Robert Taft, Jr. Senate Campaign Com., 1970, 76; bd. govs. Case Western Res. U., 1961, 84-87. Mem. ABA, Assn. Ohio Commodores, Ohio State Bar Assn., Cin. Bar Assn., Cin. Country Club, Queen City Club (Cin.), Wendemer Country Club (Naples). Home: 5 Woodbrook Dr Cincinnati OH 45241-3255 Office: PNC Center 201 E Main St Ste 800 Cincinnati OH 45202 Office Phone: 513-381-0656. Business E-Mail: jkelley@kplaw.com.

KELLEY, LYDIA R.B., lawyer; b. Mar. 12, 1964; m. Stephen W. Kelley. BA, Wellesley Coll., 1986; JD, U. Mich., 1989. Ptnr., chmn. firm recruiting & devel. com. McDermott Will & Emery LLP. Mem.: U.S. Dist. Ct. N. Dist. Ill., Ill. Bar Assn., Fed. Tax Inst. Adv. Com. Office: McDermott Will & Emery 227 W Monroe St Chicago IL 60606 Office Phone: 312-984-6470. Office Fax: 312-984-7700. Business E-Mail: lkelley@mwe.com.

KELLEY, MARK ALBERT, physician, educator, health products executive; b. Boston, Oct. 31, 1947; s. Albert Joseph and Virginia Marie Kelley; m. Gail Riggs Kelley, Aug. 4, 1974; children: Christopher Riggs, Amy Morgan. AB, Harvard U., Cambridge, Mass., 1969; MD, Harvard U., Boston, 1973. Diplomate Am. Bd. Internal Medicine, Am. Bd. Pulmonary Disease, Am. Bd. Critical Care. Intern Hosp. U. Pa., Phila., 1973—74, resident, 1974—76, chief med. resident, 1977—78, fellow in pulmonary diseases, 1976—77; dir. pulmonary fellowship U. Pa., Phila., 1979—82, from asst. to assoc. prof. medicine, 1979—92, prof., 1992-2000; dir. pulmonary fellowship tng. program, 1979—82; vice chmn. med. U. Pa. Sch. Medicine, Phila., 1986—90; dir. pulmonary fellowship tng. program, 1979—82; assoc. chmn. clin. svcs., dir. med. residency tng. program, 1982—86; dir. faculty group practice, 1985—90; vice dean clin. affairs U. Pa. Sch. Medicine, Phila., 1990—99; chief of medicine Phla. VA Med. Ctr., 1999—2000; exec. v.p. Henry Ford Health Sys., Detroit, 2000—; CEO Henry Ford Med. Group, Detroit, 2000—; fellow in pulmonary disease Hosp. U. Pa., Phila., 1978—79. Spkr. in field. Mem. editl. bd. Annals Internal Medicine, 1990—93, Critical Care Medicine, 1992—98. Fellow: ACP, Am. Coll. Chest Physicians; mem.: Am. Bd. Med. Specialties, Soc. Critical Care Medicine, Am. Bd. Internal Medicine (critical care medicine test com. 1988—93, chmn. 1990—93, bd. govs. 1990—98, exec. com. 1993—98, sec.-treas. 1994—96, chmn. 1997—98, sec.-treas. found. bd. 1999—2003, chmn. 2003—06), Am. Thoracic Soc. (chmn. nat. manpower study 1996—2000, critical care work force project 2001—04), Alpha Omega Alpha. Office: 1 Ford Pl Detroit MI 48202-3450 Office Phone: 313-876-8701. Business E-Mail: mkelley1@hfhs.org.

KELLEY, PATRICK MICHAEL, minister, state legislator; b. Maryville, Mo., Oct. 27, 1948; s. Gilbert B. and Wilma M. K.; m. Nancy E. Schroeder, July 30, 1976; children: Ryan, Shane, Kristen. BS, William Jewell, 1970; MDiv, St. Paul, 1985. V.p. Kelley-Rickman Construction Col, 1970-72, pres., 1972-75; salesman Sequoia Supply Co., North Kansas City, Mo., 1975-77; owner, pres. Energy Expositions, North Kansas City, 1977-83; pastor United Meth. Chs., Bates County, Mo., 1983-87, Aldersgate United Meth. Ch., Lee's Summit, Mo., 1987-90, Glenwood Park United Meth. Ch., Independence, Mo., 1990—; Rep. caucus chmn. Mo. State Ho. Reps., 1991, 92, minority floor leader, 1993, 94. Chmn. Lee's Summit D.A.R.E. task force; adv. bd. Community Mental Health Svcs., Lee's Summit; bd. dirs. Community Svcs. League, Lee's Summit. Mem. Lee's Summit Rep. Club (treas., pres.). Home: 3924 SW Windsong Dr Lees Summit MO 64082-4051 Office: Mo Ho Reps Capitol Bldg Jefferson City MO 65101 E-mail: pkelley@services.state.mo.us.

KELLEY, PATRICK WAYNE, prosecutor; b. Woodriver, Ill., Aug. 21, 1958; s. Merle Wayne and Alice Marilyn (Walker) K.; m. Tammie Ann Klein, Oct. 15, 1988; children: Andrew, Michael. B in Liberal Arts and Scis., Bradley U., 1980; JD, Cornell U., 1983. Bar: Ill. 1983, U.S. Dist. Ct. (ctrl. dist.) Ill. 1986. Assoc. Reinhard, Boener, Van Deren, Norris & Rieselbach, Milw., 1983-85; asst. state's atty. Sangamon County State's Atty., Springfield, Ill., 1985-87; assoc. Ensel, Jones, Blanchard & LaBarre, Springfield, 1987-89; asst. U.S. atty. U.S. Atty. Ctrl. Dist. Ill., Springfield, 1989-92; first asst. state's atty. Sangamon County State's Atty., Springfield, 1992-94, state's atty., 1994—. Dir. Boys and Girls Club Springfield, 1992-97; treas., dir. Mental Health Ctr. Cen. Ill., Springfield, 1995—; mem. pattern jury instrns. com. Ill. Supreme Ct., Springfield, 1996—. Mem. Ill. State's Attys. Assn. (treas., legis. chmn. 1994—), Am. Bus. Club. Republican. Avocations: photography, running, bicycling, firearms. Office: Sangamon County States Atty 402 County Bldg Springfield IL 62701

KELLEY, STEVE, state legislator, lawyer; b. 1953; m. Sophie Kelley; two children. BA, Williams Coll.; JD, Columbia U. Lawyer; Dist. 44A rep. Minn. Ho. of Reps., St. Paul, 1992-96; mem. Minn. Senate from 44th dist., St. Paul, 1996—. Home: 121 Blake Rd S Hopkins MN 55343-2020 Office: 321 Capitol 75 Constitution Av Saint Paul MN 55155-0001

KELLEY, THOMAS WILLIAM, automotive sales executive; b. Ft. Wayne, Ind., Aug. 21, 1952; BS, Ind. U. Joined Jim Kelley Buick, 1974; various mgmt. and exec. level positions Kelley Automotive Group (formerly Jim Kelley Buick), Ft. Wayne, Ind., pres., co-CEO. Bd. dirs. Jr. Achievement, Big Bros. and Big Sisters, Boys and Girls Club of Ft. Wayne, YMCA. Mem. Ft. Wayne C. of C. (bd. dirs.). Avocations: golf, indy car racing.

KELLEY, WILLIAM G., retail stores executive; CEO, chmn. bd. dirs. Consolidated Stores Corp., Columbus, Ohio, until 2000, strategic advisor, 2000—. Office: Consolidated Stores Corp PO Box 28512 300 Phillipi Rd Columbus OH 43228-0072

KELLMAN, SANDRA Y., lawyer; b. Mar. 21, 1952; BA with high honors, Univ. Ill., Urbana-Champaign, 1973; JD cum laude, Northwestern Univ., 1977. Bar: Ill. 1977. Ptnr. co-chmn. Lodging & Timeshare practice group DLA Piper Rudnick Gray Cary, Chgo. Editor (note & comment): Jour. of Criminal Law & Criminology; contbr. articles to profl. jours. Office: DLA Piper Rudnick Gray Cary Suite 1900 203 N LaSalle St Chicago IL 60601-1293 Office Phone: 312-368-4082. Office Fax: 312-236-7516. Business E-Mail: sandra.kellman@dlapiper.com.

KELLOGG, WILLIAM S., retail executive; b. 1943; With Federated Dept. Stores, Inc., Cin., 1962-66, Kohl's Dept. Stores, Inc., Menomonee Falls, Wis., 1966-77, pres., 1977-82, chmn., 1982—. Named one of Forbes Richest Americans, 2006. Office: Kohl's Dept Stores N56 W 17000 Ridgewood Dr Menomonee Falls WI 53051-7026

KELLY, A. DAVID, lawyer; b. St. Paul, June 8, 1948; s. David and Katherine (Tappins) Kelly; m. Elizabeth Woehrle, Oct. 25, 1978; children: Charles, George. BA, Carleton Coll., 1970; JD, Harvard U., 1973. Bar: Minn. 1973. Ptnr. Faegre & Benson, Mpls., 1973-90, Oppenheimer, Wolff & Donnelly, Mpls., 1990-95, Kelly, Hannaford & Battles, Mpls., 1995—. Chmn. Voyageurs Nat. Pk. Assn., Mpls., 1984—90; pres. St. Paul Boys' and Girls' Club, 1992—95; trustee Union Gospel Mission, 1982—92, Carleton Coll., Northfield, Minn., 1972—76, Minn. Mus. Am. Art, 2003—08, chmn. Office: 900 Baker Bldg 706 Second Ave S Minneapolis MN 55402

KELLY, ARTHUR LLOYD, investment company executive; b. Chgo., Nov. 15, 1937; s. Thomas Lloyd and Mildred (Wetten) Kelly; m. Diane Rex Cain, Nov. 25, 1978; children: Mary Lucinda, Thomas Lloyd, Alison Williams. BS with honors, Yale U., 1959; MBA, U. Chgo., 1964. With A.T. Kearney, Inc., 1959-75, mng. dir. Dusseldorf, Germany, 1964-70, v.p. for Europe Brussels, 1970-73, internat. v.p. London, 1974-75, ptnr., dir., 1969-75, mem. exec. com., 1972-75; pres., COO, dir. LaSalle Steel Co., Chgo., 1975-81; pres., CEO, dir. Dalta Corp., Chgo., 1982—; mng. ptnr. KEL Enterprises L.P., Chgo., 1983—. Dir. BASF Aktiengesellschaft, Ludwigshafen, Germany, BMW A.G., Munich, DataCard Corp., Minnetonka, Minn., Deere & Co., Moline, Ill., No. Trust Corp., Chgo., Snap-On, Inc., Kenosha, Wis., Robert Bosch G.m.b.H., Stuttgart; trustee U. Chgo.; mem. adv. coun. Ditchley Found., Oxford, England; bd. dirs. Chgo. Coun. Fgn. Rels. Fellow: Royal Geog. Soc. London (life); mem.: Coun. Fgn. Rels. NYC, World Pres.' Orgn., Brook Club (NYC), Yale Club (NYC), Racquet Club, Econ. Club, Comml. Club, Casino Club, Everglades Club (Palm Beach), Chgo. Club, Beta Gamma Sigma. Office: 20 S Clark St Ste 2222 Chicago IL 60603-1805

KELLY, CHARLES ARTHUR, lawyer; b. Evanston, Ill., Mar. 2, 1932; s. Charles Scott and Bess (Loftis) K.; m. Frances Kates, Sept. 9, 1961 (div. 1979); children: Timothy, Elizabeth, Mary; m. Patricia Lynn Francis, June 28, 1979 (div. 1995); m. Jean E. Glazier, June 25, 2005. BA with honors, Amherst Coll., 1953; LLB, Harvard U., 1956. Bar: DC 1956, Ill. 1956. Assoc. Hubachek & Kelly, Chgo., 1956-64, ptnr., 1964-82, Chapman & Cutler, Chgo., 1982—2002, ptnr. of counsel, 2002—08. Sec. Speedfam Internat., Inc., 1992-99, gen. counsel, 1998-99. Bd. dirs. Gads Hill Ctr., Chgo., pres., 1977—82; bd. dirs. Quetico Superior Found., Mpls., v.p., 1964—; bd. dirs. Lakeland Found., Chgo., 1960—96, pres., 1970—85, Ernest C. Oberholtzer Found., Mpls., 1962—2002, v.p., treas., 1998—2002; bd. dirs. Chgo. Hearing Found., 1990—94, Wilderness Rsch. Found., Chgo. Recipient Legion of Merit, USAF, 1982. Fellow Am. Coll. Trust and Estate Counsel; Mem. ABA, Chgo. Bar Assn., Ill. Bar Assn., Fed. Bar Assn., Univ. Club, Mid-Am. Club, Mich. Shores Club (Wilmette, Ill.), Harvard Club (Boston). Republican. Presbyterian. Office: Chapman and Cutler 111 W Monroe St Ste 1800 Chicago IL 60603-4080 Office Phone: 312-845-3009. Business E-Mail: ckelly@chapman.com.

KELLY, CHARLES HAROLD, advertising executive; b. Omaha, Mar. 30, 1950; s. Kerwood Michael and Erma Lenore (Johnson) K.; m. Susan Marie Nielsen, Dec. 28, 1971; children: Matthew Michael, Laura Elizabeth. BA,

Hastings Coll., 1972; MS, Iowa State U., 1973. Account exec. Kerker & Assocs., Mpls., 1977-80, v.p., dir. client services, 1983—99; account exec. Foote, Cone & Belding, Chgo., 1980-82; account supr. Bozell, Jacobs, Kenyon & Eckhardt, Mpls., 1982-83; chmn, CEO Kerker, Mpls. Bd. dirs. YMCA of Greater Mpls.; bd. of visitors Penn State U., Coll. of Comm. Mem. Advt. Fedn. Mpls. (pres. 1987-88), Am. Assn. Advt. Agys. (past pres. Twin Cities). Republican. Lutheran. Avocations: jogging, golf, photography, music. Office: Kerker 7701 France Ave S Minneapolis MN 55435-5288 Office Phone: 952-897-9420.

KELLY, CHRISTOPHER M., lawyer; b. Buffalo, Apr. 27, 1961; BA summa cum laude, Canisius Coll., 1983; JD with honors, Duke Univ., 1986. Bar: New York 1988, Ohio 2001. Atty. Simpson Thacher & Bartlett, NYC; ptnr., chair capital markets practice Jones Day, NYC, Cleve., 2006—. Office: Jones Day 222 East 41st St New York NY 10017-6702 Office Phone: 212-326-3438. Business E-Mail: ckelly@jonesday.com.

KELLY, DANIEL P., cardiologist, molecular biologist; b. Oct. 6, 1955; m. Therese J. Michelau; 3 children. BS in Biology, U. Ill., 1978, MD, 1982. Diplomate Am. Bd. Internal Medicine, Am. Bd. Cardiovasc. Disease. Intern in medicine Barnes Hosp., St. Louis, 1982—83, asst. resident in medicine, 1983—85; chief med. resident John Cochran VA Hosp., Washington U. Svc., 1984—85; rsch. postdoctoral fellow cardiovascular divsn. and dept. biol. chemistry Washington U. Sch. of Medicine, St. Louis, 1985—87, fellow in clin. cardiology, 1987—89, instr. of medicine cardiovascular divsn., 1989—90, asst. prof. medicine cardiovascular divsn., 1990—95, asst. prof. molecular biology and pharmacology, 1993—95, co-dir. Ctr. Adults with Congenital Heart Disease, 1993—, assoc. prof. medicine and molecular biology & pharmacology, 1995—, dir. Ctr. for Cardiovascular Rsch., 1996—, prof. medicine and molecular biology & pharmacology, 1999—, prof. pediatrics, 2000—, co-dir., Cardiovascular Div., Dept. Medicine. Lectr. rsch. and clin. fellowship program Washington U. Sch. Medicine, 1989, lectr. pharmacology and pathophysiology, 94; attending physician medicine and cardiology svcs. Barnes and Jewish Hosps., St. Louis, 1989. Contbr. chapters to books, articles to profl. jours. Recipient Lucille P. Markey Scholar award, Markey Found., 1989, Basal O'Connor Scholar award, March of Dimes, 1991, Rsch. Tng. grantee, NHLBI, 1994—, 1996—. Fellow: Am. Coll. Cardiology; mem.: AAAS, Am. Soc. for Clin. Investigation, Internat. Soc. Adult Congenital Heart Disease, Internat. Soc. Heart Rsch., Am. Heart Assn. (basic sci. coun., Established Investigator award 1995), Am. Fedn. Clin. Rsch., Alpha Omega Alpha, Phi Beta Kappa. Office: Washington U Sch of Medicine Clinical Sciences Rsch Bldg North Addition Rm 810 Saint Louis MO 63110-1010 Office Phone: 314-362-8908, 314-362-8912. Office Fax: 314-362-0186. E-mail: dkelly@im.wustl.edu.

KELLY, DENNIS MICHAEL, lawyer; b. Cleve., May 6, 1943; s. Thomas Francis and Margaret (Murphy) K.; m. Marilyn Ann Divoky, Dec. 28, 1967; children: Alison, Meredith. BA, John Carroll U., 1961-65; JD, U. Notre Dame, 1968. Bar: Ohio 1968. Law clk. U.S. Ct. Appeals (8th cir.), Cleve., 1968-69; assoc. Jones, Day, Reavis & Pogue, Cleve., 1969-75, ptnr., 1975—. Mem. Ohio Bar Assn., Bar Assn. Greater Cleve. Office: Jones Day Reavis & Pogue North Point 901 Lakeside Ave E Cleveland OH 44114-1190 Office Phone: 216-586-7180. E-mail: dmkelly@jonesday.com.

KELLY, DONALD PHILIP, entrepreneur; b. Chgo., Feb. 24, 1922; s. Thomas Nicholas and Ethel M. (Healy) K.; m. Byrd M. Sullivan, Oct. 25, 1952; children: Patrick, Laura, Thomas. Student, Loyola U., Chgo., 1953-54, De Paul U., 1954-55, Harvard U., 1965. Mgr. tabulating United Ins. Co. Am., 1946-51; mgr. data processing A.B. Wrisley Co., 1951-53, Swift & Co., 1953-65, asst. controller, 1965-67, controller, 1967-68, v.p. corporate devel., controller, 1968-70, fin. v.p., dir., 1970-73, Esmark, Inc., Chgo., 1973, pres., COO, 1973-77, pres., CEO, 1977-82, chmn., pres., CEO, 1982-84; pres. Kelly, Briggs & Assocs., Inc., Chgo., 1984-86; chmn. Beatrice Co., Chgo., 1986-88; chmn., CEO E-II Holdings Inc., Chgo., 1987-88; pres., CEO D.P. Kelly & Assocs., L.P., Oak Brook, 1988—; chmn., pres., CEO Envirodyne Industries Inc., 1989-96. With USNR, 1942-46. Mem. Chgo. Club. Office: DP Kelly and Assocs LP 701 Harger Rd Ste 190 Oak Brook IL 60523-1490

KELLY, DOUGLAS LAIRD, lawyer, investment company executive; b. Pensacola, Fla., Mar. 4, 1949; s. John L. and Shirley (Perkins) K.; m. Cynthia Jane Benedict, Dec. 28, 1971; children: Laura Elizabeth, Michael Laird. BS in Fin., U. Colo., 1971; JD, Washington U., 1973. Bar: Mo. 1974. Assoc. Peper, Martin, Jensen, Maichel & Hetlage, St. Louis, 1974-78, ptnr., 1978—94; atty. A.G. Edwards, St. Louis, 1994—, exec. v.p., CFO, corp. sec., treas., dir. of law & compliance. Mem. ASD Nat. Adjudicatory Council. Mem. ABA, Mo. Bar Assn. Office: AG Edwards 1 N Jefferson Ave Saint Louis MO 63103

KELLY, GERALD F, JR., retail executive; BA in econ., U. of Ill. Mng. ptnr. Prof. Computer Resources, Inc., 1980—82; prin. Arthur Young & Co., 1982—84; v.p., mgmt. services Wilson Sporting Goods Co., 1984—86; sr. v.p. info. services Payless Shoesource, Inc., 1986—90, sr. v.p., CFO, 1990—96, sr. v.p. logistics, info. sys. and tech., 1986—2001; sr. v.p, chief info. officer Sears Roebuck and Co., 2002—.

KELLY, JAMES MICHAEL, plant and soil scientist; b. Knoxville, Feb. 2, 1944; s. Woodrow Wilson and Thelma Lucille (Miller) K.; m. Susan Kay Morris, Aug. 9, 1969; children: John Kip, Christopher Kenneth. BS, E. Tenn. State U., 1966; MS, U. Tenn., 1968, PhD, 1973. Cert. profl. soil scientist. Assoc. ecologist NUS Corp., Pitts., 1973-74; rsch. assoc. Forestry Dept. Purdue U., West Lafayette, Ind., 1975-76; program mgr. Tenn. Valley Authority, Oak Ridge, 1977-88, sr. rschr., 1990-94; sr. tech. specialist, team leader, 1994-95; prof., chair dept. forestry Iowa State U., Ames, 1995—2001, chair dept. natural resource ecology and mgmt., 2002—04; dean Coll. Natural Resources Va. Tech. U., Blacksburg, 2004—. Vis. prof. agronomy Purdue U., 1988-89; adj. prof. U. Tenn., Knoxville, 1980-95, forestry dept. Purdue U., 1985-95. Author: Carbon Forms and Functions in Forest Soils, 1995; assoc. editor Soil Sci. Soc. Am. Jour., 1989-95, Forest Sci., 1998-01; editl. bd. Forest Ecology and Management, 2001-05; contbr. more than 100 articles to profl. jours. Head referee Ayso Youth Soccer, Oak Ridge, 1985-88; troop com. Boy Scouts Am., Oak Ridge, 1989-95. Oak Ridge Assoc. Univ. fellow, 1970-72; Elec. Power Rsch. Inst. grantee, 1978, 82, 89, 91, 95, NSF grantee, 1995; recipient Rsch. Champion award Elec. Power Rsch. Inst., 2002. Fellow Soil Sci. Soc. Am. (chmn. divsn. S7 1986-87, bd. dirs. 1988-89, awards com. 1992-93, fellows com. 1997-99, profl. svc. com. 2000-02); mem. AAAS, Ecol. Soc. Am., Soc. Am. Foresters, Exptl. Aircraft Assn. (chpt. pres. 1991-93), Trees Forever (bd. dirs. 1995-05), Sigma Xi, Gamma Sigma Delta, Xi Sigma Pi. Achievements include research and application of environmental science. Office: Va Tech Univ Coll Natural Resources Blacksburg VA 24061 Office Phone: 540-231-5481. Business E-Mail: jmkelly@vt.edu.

KELLY, JANET LANGFORD, oil industry executive, lawyer; b. Kansas City, Mo., Nov. 27, 1957; m. John Kelly; children: Jack, Kate. BA, Grinnell Coll., 1979; JD, Yale U., 1983. Bar: NY 1985, Ill. 1989, Mich. 2004. Law clk. to Hon. James J. Hunter III US Ct. Appeals (3rd cir.), 1983-84; ptnr. Sidley & Austin LLP, Chgo., 1984-89; sr. v.p., sec., gen. counsel Sara Lee Corp., Chgo., 1995-99; exec. v.p. corp. devel., gen. counsel, sec. Kellogg Co., Battle Creek, Mich., 1999—2001, exec. v.p. corp. devel. & adminstrn., gen. counsel, sec., 2001—06; dep. gen. counsel ConocoPhillips Co., Houston, 2006—07, sr. v.p. legal, gen. counsel, sec., 2007—. Sr. editor Yale Law Jour., 1983. Bd. dirs. Am. Arbitration Assn., Constl. Rights Found.; mem. adv. bd. Chgo. Vol. Legal Svcs. Found. Mem.: ABA. Office: ConocoPhillips 600 N Dairy Ashford Rd Houston TX 77079 Office Phone: 281-293-1000. E-mail: janet.l.kelly@conocophillips.com.

KELLY, JEFFREY D., bank executive; b. Aug. 13, 1953; BS in bus. adminstrn., Ohio State U., 1977; MS in econ., U. Akron, 1979. Mgmt. asst., bank investment divsn. at. City Corp., sr. v.p., 1990—94, exec. v.p., chief funds mgmt. officer, 1994—97, chmn. asset-liability com., 1997—2000; chmn. Nat. City Mortgage Co., 1997—2000, Nat. City Equity Ptnrs., 1998—2000; CFO, exec. v.p. Nat. City Corp., Cleve., 2000—04, vice-chmn., CFO, 2004—. Bd. dirs. Progressive Ins. Corp., 2000—; adv. bd. FTVentures. Sec., trustee Great Lakes Sci. Ctr.; bd. trustees Cuyahoga Cmty. Coll.; mem. Fin. Svcs. Roundtable. Office: Nat City Corp 1900 E 9th St Cleveland OH 44114-3484 Office Phone: 216-575-2000, 800-738-3888. Office Fax: 216-575-2353.

KELLY, JOHN MARTIN, lawyer; b. Oshkosh, Wis., Dec. 13, 1948; s. Martin Paul and Ivy Cecile (James) Kelly; m. Teresa Jean Wendland, July 24, 1982. BA, U. Wis., Madison, 1971; JD, Georgetown U., 1974; postgrad. in bus., Harvard Bus. Sch., 1976-77. Bar: Wis. 1974, D.C. 1975. Atty. office chief counsel IRS, Washington, 1974—76; assoc. Dempsey, Magnusem, Williamson & Lampe, Oshkosh, 1977—82; ptnr. Dempsey, Williamson, Kelly & Hertel, LLP, Oshkosh, 1983—. Mem. ABA, Wis. Bar Assn., D.C. Bar Assn., Winnebago County Bar Assn. Office: Dempsey Williamson Kelly & Hertel LLP 1 Pearl Ave Oshkosh WI 54903-0886 Business E-Mail: jmkelly@dempseylaw.com.

KELLY, JOHN TERENCE, architect; b. Elyria, Ohio, Jan. 27, 1922; s. Thomas Alo and Coletta Margaret (Conrad) K. BArch, Carnegie Mellon U., 1949; MArch, Harvard U., 1951, M of Landscape Architecture, 1952. Prin. architect John Terence Kelly, Cleve., 1954—. Vis. critic, lectr. U. Mich., U. Cin., Case Western Res. U., McGill U. Bd. dirs. Nova. With inf. AUS, 1943-46. Recipient Cleve. Arts prize in Architecture, 1968, hist. Bldg. award Architects Soc. Ohio, 1986; Charles Eliot Norton fellow, 1952, Fulbright fellow, Munich, Germany, 1953. Mem. AIA (nat. com. design). Home: 2646 N Moreland Blvd Cleveland OH 44120-1461

KELLY, MARILYN, state supreme court justice; b. Apr. 15, 1938; m. Donald Newman. BA, Ea. Mich. U., 1960, JD (hon.); postgrad., U. Paris.; MA, Middlebury Coll., 1961; JD with honors, Wayne State U., 1971. Assoc. Dykema, Gossett, Spencer, Goodnow & Trigg, Detroit, 1973-78; ptnr. Dudley, Patterson, Maxwell, Smith & Kelly, Bloomfield Hills, Mich., 1978-80; owner Marilyn Kelly & Assocs., Bloomfield Hills, Birmingham, Mich., 1980-88; judge Mich. Ct. of Appeals, 1989-96; justice Mich. Supreme Ct., 1997—. Tchr. lang., lit. Grosse Pointe Pub. Schs., Albion Coll., Ea. Mich. U.; past mem. rep. assembly, comms. com., family law coun. Mich. State Bar; co-chair Open Justice Commn., 1999—; mem. governing bd. Nat. Consortium for Racial & Ethnic Fairness in Cts. Active Mich. Dem. Party, 1963—; former bd. dirs. Channel 56-Pub. TV, Detroit, Women's Survival Ctr., Pontiac; former mem. citizens advisory com. Detroit Public Schools, Wayne County Community Coll., Oakland County Community Coll. Recipient Disting Alumni award Ea. Mich. U., Disting. Svc. award Mich. Edn. Assn., Eleanor Roosevelt Humanities award State of Israel Bonds Atty. Div., 2003. Mem. Soc. Irish-Am. Lawyers, Women Lawyers Assn. (past pres.), Oakland County Bar Assn. (past chair family law com.), State Bar Mich. (Michael Franck award 2003); Fellow Mich. State Bar Found. Office: Mich Supreme Ct 3034 West Grand Blvd Detroit MI 48202

KELLY, PETER GALBRAITH, lawyer; b. Harford, Conn., June 30, 1937; s. John Patrick and Anna Matilda (Jensen) K.; m. Susan Ann Roach, Sept. 2, 1961; children: Bridget B., Peter G., Jr., Matthew J., Paula M. BS, Georgetown U., 1959; JD, Yale U., 1962. Assoc. Townley and Updike, NYC, 1962-65, Schatz and Schatz, Hartford, 1965-66; ptnr. Adinolfi, Kelly & Spellacy, Hartford, 1967-69; prin. Updike, Kelly & Spellacy, Hartford, 1970-2000; of counsel Wald, Harkrader & Ross, Washington, 1981-84; prin. Black, Manafort, Stone & Kelly Pub. Affairs Co., Alexandria, Va., 1985—. Bd. dirs. Richard Roberts Real Estate Growth Trust, Avon, Conn., Homestead Fin. Corp., Burlingame, Calif. Chmn. Ctr. for Democracy, 1985—, Compliance Review Commn. Dem. Nat. Conv., 1978-80, Harford Dem. Town Com., 1975-78, Hartford Civic Ctr. Com., 1975, Hartford Charter Revision Commn., 1967; active Dem. Nat. Com., 1976-84, 84— fin. chmn. and related com. corps., 1981-85, treas., 1979-81, exec. bd. The Democracy Program, treas., 1983-84; dir. and treas. Nat. Dem. Inst. Internat. Affairs, 1984; bd. trustees and corporator Inst. of Living, 1978; bd. of regents, Georgetown U., 1973-81, emeritus, 1981—. Office: Updike Kelly & Spellacy PC One State St Ste 2400 Hartford CT 06103

KELLY, RANDY C., former mayor St. Paul; b. Aug. 2, 1950; m. Kathy Kelly; two children. BA, U. Minn. Mem. Minn. Ho. of Reps., St. Paul, 1974-90, Minn. Senate from 67th dist., St. Paul, 1990—2001; mayor St. Paul, 2001—06. Vice chmn. fin. com., mem. crime prevention, fin. divsn. family svc., fin. state govt. divsn., and jobs, energy and cmty. devel. coms., Minn. State Senate.

KELLY, RAYMOND J., JR., lawyer; b. 1940; BA, U. Notre Dame, 1962; JD, DePaul U., 1967. Bar: Ill. 1967, US Supreme Ct., US Ct. Appeals (6th, 7th, 8th, 9th, 11th cir.), US Dist. Ct. (no. dist.) Ill., US Dist. Ct. (ctrl. dist.) Ill., US Dist. Ct. (no. dist.) Ind., US Dist. Ct. (ea. dist.) Mich., US Dist. Ct. (we. dist.) Mich., US Dist. Ct. (we. dist.) Tex. Ptnr. Seyfarth Shaw LLP, Chgo., chmn. pro bono com. Officer USN, 1962—64. Mem.: Defense Rsch. Inst. (ADR com., trial tactics & techniques com., product liability com.), Nat. Health Lawyers Assn., Fed. Bar Assn., Ill. Bar Assn. (civil practice & procedure sect.), ABA (litig. sect., torts & ins. sect., intellectual property sect.). Office: Seyfarth Shaw LLP 55 East Monroe St Ste 4200 Chicago IL 60603 Office Phone: 312-269-8822. Office Fax: 312-269-8869. Business E-Mail: rkelly@seyfarth.com.

KELLY, RICHARD C., energy executive; BS in Acctg., Regis U., MBA; postgrad., U. Colo., U. Mich. With auditing dept. Pub. Svc. Co. Colo., 1968-74, staff asst. to mgr. acctg., 1974-76, corp. reports mgr., 1976-83, mgr. acctg., asst. contr., 1983-86, treas., 1986-87, v.p. fin. svcs., 1987-90, sr. v.p. fin., 1990—97; exec. v.p., CFO New Century Energies, Denver, 1997—2000; pres. enterprises Xcel Energy Inc., Minneapolis, Minn., 2000—02, v.p., CFO, 2002—03, pres., 2003—, COO, 2003—03, CEO, chmn., 2005—. Past pres. Arvada Optimist Club; past dir. Ronald McDonald House, Denver Metro C. of Colo. Pub. Expenditures Coun., Mercy Housing; bd. dir. Minneapolis Downtown Coun.; mem. Regis Acctg. Adv. Com. Office: Xcel Energy Inc 414 Nicollet Mall Minneapolis MN 55401-1993

KELLY, ROBERT J., supermarket executive; Exec. v.p. retailing Vons Co., Calif.; chmn. bd. dirs., pres., CEO Eagle Food Ctrs., Inc., Milan, Ill., 1995—. Office: Eagle Food Ctrs Inc PO Box 6700 Milan IL 61264-6700

KELLY, THOMAS, advertising executive; V.p. media svcs. Hawthorne Direct, Fairfield, Iowa, pres., CEO. Office: Hawthorne Direct Inc PO Box 1366 300 N 16th St Fairfield IA 52556-2604

KELLY, TOM (JAY THOMAS KELLY), retired professional sports team manager; b. Graceville, Minn., Aug. 15, 1950; s. Joseph Thomas and Anna Grace (Heisenbottle) K.; children: Sharon Clare, Thomas John. Student, Mesa Jr. Coll., Ariz., 1968-69. Profl. baseball player Minn. Twins, Mpls., 1968-77, coach, 1982-86, mgr., 1987—2001, mgr. minor league team Toledo, 1978-82. Managed Minn. Twins team to World Series Championship, 1987, 91; named Am. League Mgr. of Yr. Sporting News, 1991. Mem. Assn. Profl. Baseball Players, U.S. Trotting Assn., Nat. Greyhound Assn. Avocation: harness racing. Office: Minn Twins Hubert H Humphrey Metrodome 34 Kirby Puckett Pl Minneapolis MN 55415-1596

KELLY, WILLIAM GARRETT, judge; b. Grand Rapids, Mich., Nov. 30, 1947; s. Joseph Francis and Gertrude Frances (Downes) K.; m. Sharon Ann Diroff, Aug. 11, 1979; children: Colleen, Joseph, Caitlin, Meaghan and Patricia. BA, U. Detroit, 1970, JD, 1975. Bar: Mich. 1975, U.S. Dist. Ct. (we. dist.) Mich. 1975. Tchr. Peace Corps, Ghana, Republic of West Africa, 1970-72; asst. prosecutor Kalamazoo (Mich.) Prosecutor's Office, 1975-77; atty. Office of Defender, Grand Rapids, 1977-78; judge 62d B Dist. Ct., Kentwood, 1979—. Faculty Mich. Jud. Inst., Lansing, 1985—, 2d Nat. Conf. on Ct. Tech., Denver, 1988, Nat. Jud. Coll., 2001--; chmn.-elect Jud. Conf. State Bar Mich., 1990-91, chmn., 1991-92. Bd. dirs. Nat. Ctr. for State Cts., 1994-2000; pres. Kentwood Jaycees, 1979-80. Named one of Five Outstanding Young Men of Mich., Mich. Jaycees, 1982. Mem. ABA (chmn. nat. conf. spl. ct. judges 1992-93, chmn. traffic ct. program 2002-), State Bar Mich., Grand Rapids Bar Assn., Cath. Lawyers Assn. Western Mich. (pres. 1987), Mich. Dist. Judges Assn. (pres. 1989). Roman Catholic. Office: 62d B Dist Ct 4740 Walma SE Kentwood MI 49512

KELSCH, RAEANN, state legislator; m. Thomas D. Kelsch; 3 children. BBA, U. N.D. Mem. N.D. Ho. of Reps.; vice chmn. judiciary com.; mem. govt. and vets. affairs com. Bd. dirs. United Way; active AID, Inc. Republican. Home: 611 Craig Dr Mandan ND 58554-2353 Office: ND Ho of Reps State Capitol Bismarck ND 58505

KELSH, JEROME, state legislator; b. Fullerton, ND, Oct. 25, 1940; s. George L. and Freda (Nelson) K.; m. Romona Keller; children: Scott, Jock, Steven. BS, U. .D., 1962. Mem. N.D. Senate from 26th dist., Bismark, 1985—; chmn. agr. com. N.D. Senate, Bismark, mem. edn. com., mem. transp. com. Agribusinessman. Mem. adv. bd. Ellenda Hosp.; past chmn. Fullerton Centennial Com.; past mem. Fullerton Sch. Bd.; mem. Fullerton Betterment Bd. Office: Rte 1 Box 27 Fullerton ND 58441 also: State Senate State Capitol Bismarck ND 58505

KELSO, BECKY, former state legislator; b. 1948; m. Michael Kelso; 2 children. BA in Comm., U. Minn. Mem. Minn. Ho. of Reps., 1986-98; mem. capital investment com.; mem. edn. com.; mem. regulated industries and energy com.; mem. transp. and transit com. Home: 60 S Shannon Dr Shakopee MN 55379-8025

KELSO, CAROL, state legislator; b. May 26, 1945; BA, Iowa State U. Assemblywoman Wis. State Dist. 88. Pres. Brown County Planning Commn.; mem. Brown County Harbor Commn., 2020 Hwy. Coalition. Address: 416 E Le Capitaine Cir Green Bay WI 54302-5153

KEMNITZ, JOSEPH WILLIAM, physiologist, researcher; b. Balt., Mar. 15, 1947; s. Harold Clarence and Alice Mae (Ziebarth) K.; m. Amanda Marye Tuttle, Jan. 5, 1991; children: Julia Ellen, Joseph Andrew. BA, U. Wis., 1969, PhD, 1976. Rsch. assoc. Wis. Nat. Primate Rsch. Ctr., Madison, 1976-79, asst. scientist, 1979-84, assoc. scientist, 1984-94, sr. scientist and assoc. dir., 1995-96, dir., 1996—; assoc. scientist dept. medicine U. Wis., Madison, 1991-94, sr. scientist dept. medicine, 1995-97, prof. dept. physiology. Cons. NIH, Bethesda, Md., 1981—; mem. Children's Diabetes Ctr., Madison, Wis., 1990—; steering com. Inst. on Aging, Madison, 1989—. Assoc. editor Hormones and Behavior, 1986-96; contbr. articles to profl. jours. Grantee (various) NIH, 1977—. Mem. Am. Physiol. Soc., Am. Inst. Nutrition, Am. Diabetes Assn., Am. Soc. Primatologists, Gerontol. Soc. Am., N.Am. Assn. Study of Obesity, Internat. Primatol. Soc. Office: Primate Rsch Ctr UW 1220 Capitol Ct Madison WI 53715-1237

KEMNITZ, RALPH A., lawyer; b. Aberdeen, SD, Sept. 2, 1942; s. Ralph L. and Delphia F. (Benscoter) K.; m. Julianne K. Ufen, Jan. 19, 1965; children: Ralph, Candice, Kimberly. BS, No. State, 1966; JD, U. S.D., 1969. Bar: S.D. 1969. Atty. S.D. Legal Services, Ft. Thompson, 1969-71; assoc. Kemnitz Law Office, Philip, S.D., 1971-82; ptnr. Kemnitz & Barnett, Philip, 1982—. States atty. Haakon County, Philip, 1971-85. Chmn. S.D. Racing Commn., Pierre, 1984—; chmn., state del. Haakon County Reps., Philip, 1974-76. Named one of Outstanding Young Men in Am. Jaycees, 1973. Mem. ABA, S.D. Bar Assn., S.D. Trial Lawyers Assn., Philip City C. of C. (pres. 1972). Republican. Methodist. Home: PO Box 245 Philip SD 57567-0245 Office: Kemnitz & Barnett PO Box 489 Philip SD 57567-0489

KEMPENICH, KEITH, state legislator; m. Melinda. Mem. N.D. Ho. of Reps., vice chmn. transp. com., mem. indsl., bus. and labor com. Rancher; crop adjuster. Mem. Lions, Farm Bur., Farmers Union, Aircraft Owners and Pilots Assn. Home: HC 4 Box 10 Bowman ND 58623-8810

KEMPER, ALEXANDER C., finance company executive; married Christine Kemper. BA in Am. History, Northwestern U. Credit analyst to pres. UMB Bank, n.a., Kansas City, Mo., 1987-94; pres. UMB Fin. Corp., Kansas City, Mo., 1995-96, pres., CEO, chmn. bd. dirs., 1996—. Bd. dirs. Greater Kans. C. of C., Pioneer Svc. Co., Kemper Realty Co., Stagecoach Inc., UMB Mortgage Co., UMB Bank South Banking Area, UMB Bank, n.a. -Metro Bank Area, UMB Fin. Corp., UMB Bank of Kansas City, UMB Bank of Colo. Mem. Am. Royal Assn. (bd. dirs.), Agr. Future of Am. (bd. dirs.). Office: UMB Fin Corp 1010 Grand Blvd Kansas City MO 64106-2225

KEMPER, DAVID WOODS, II, banker; b. Kansas City, Mo., Nov. 20, 1950; s. James Madison and Mildred (Lane) K.; m. Dorothy Ann Jannarone, Sept. 6, 1975; children: John W., Elizabeth C., Catherine B., William L. BA cum laude, Harvard U., 1972; MA in English Lit., Oxford, Worcester Coll., 1974; MBA, Stanford U., 1976. With Morgan Guaranty Trust Co., NYC, 1975-78; v.p. Commerce Bank of Kansas City, Mo., 1978-79, sr. v.p., 1980-81; pres. Commerce Bancshares, Inc., 1982-86, pres., ceo, 1986-91, chmn., pres., ceo, 1991—; also dir. Commerce Bancshares, Inc; chmn. Commerce Bank N.A., St. Louis, 1985—. Bd. dirs. Kansas City, Tower Properties, Kansas City, Ralcorp Holdings, Inc. Contbr. articles on banking to profl. jours. Trustee Mo. Bot. Garden, Washington U., Donald Danforth Plant Sci. Ctr. Mem. Acad. Arts and Scis., Fin. Svcs. Roundtable, Kansas City Country Club, River Club (Kansas City), St. Louis Club, St. Louis Country Club, Racquet Club, Old Warson Country Club (St. Louis). Office: Commerce Bancshares Inc 8000 Forsyth Blvd Clayton MO 63105

KEMPER, JAMES DEE, lawyer; b. Olney, Ill., Feb. 23, 1947; s. Jack O. and Vivian L. Kemper; m. Diana J. Deig, June 1, 1968; children: Judd, Jason. BS, Ind. U., Bloomington, 1969, JD summa cum laude, 1971. Bar: Ind. 1971. Law clk. U.S. Ct. Appeals (7th cir.), Chgo., 1971-72; ptnr. Ice Miller LLP, Indpls., 1972—, mng. ptnr., 1993—98. Note editor: Ind. U. Law Rev., 1970—71; contbr. articles to profl. jours. Past officer, bd. dirs. Marion County Assn. Retarded Citizens, Inc., Indpls.; past bd. dirs. Ctrl. Ind. Easter Seal Soc., Indpls., Crossroads Rehab. Ctr., Inc., Indpls.; pres., bd. govs. Orchard Country Day Sch., Indpls.; bd. dirs. Eiteljorg Mus. Native Ams., Butler U. Fellow: Ind. Bar Found.; mem.: ABA (mem. employee benefit com.), Gt. Lakes TE/GE Coun., Ind. Bar Assn., Stanley K. Lacy Leadership Alumni, U.S. C. of C. (mem. employee benefit com.), The Group, Inc. Office: Ice Miller LLP Ste 3100 1 American Sq Indianapolis IN 46282-0200

KEMPER, JONATHAN MCBRIDE, banker; b. Kansas City, Mo., July 23, 1953; s. James Madison Jr. and Mildred (Lane) K.; m. Nancy Lee Smith, Nov. 26, 1983; children: Charlotte Lee, Nicolas Thornton, David Benjamin Royce. AB, Harvard U., 1975, MBA, 1979. Asst. bank examiner Fed. Res. Bank, NYC, 1975-76; asst. treas. Second Dist. Securities, NYC, 1976-77; account officer Citicorp, Chgo., 1981-83; v.p. Commerce Bank of Kansas City, Mo., 1983-84, sr. v.p. Mo., 1984-85, pres. Mo., 1985—, chief exec. officer Mo., 1988—, also bd. dirs. Mo. Bd. dirs. Tower Properties, Gen. USA Life Reassurance Co.; vice-chmn. Commerce Bancshares, 1988—. Bd. dirs. Civic Coun. Kansas City, Downtown Coun., Kansas City Pub. Libr., Midwest Rsch. Inst.; vice chmn. Nat. Trust for Historic Preservation; co-chair Mo. Lewis and Clark Commn. Office: Commerce Bank of Kansas City 1000 Walnut St PO Box 419248 Kansas City MO 64141-6248

KEMPER, RUFUS CROSBY, JR., retired bank executive; b. Kansas City, Mo., Feb. 22, 1927; s. Rufus Crosby and Enid (Jackson) Kemper; m. Mary Barton Stripp; children: Rufus Crosby III, Pamela Warrick Gabrovsky, Sheila Kemper Dietrich, John Mariner, Mary Barton Wolf, Alexander Charles, Heather Christian. Grad., Phillips Acad., Andover, Mass., 1942; student, U. Mo.; LL.D. (hon.), William Jewel Coll., 1976; DFA (hon.), Westminster Coll., 1983. Joined City Nat. Bank & Trust Co. (now UMB Fin. Corp.), Kansas City, 1950; exec v.p. UMB Fin. Corp., 1957—59, pres., 1959—71, chmn. & CEO, 1971—2000; sr. chmn. UMB Fin. Corp. & UMB Bank, 2000—04; ret., 2004. Hon. trustee Thomas Jefferson Found.; mem. nat. com. Whitney Mus. Am. Art, NYC.; commr. Nat. Mus. Am. Art., Washington; founder, chmn. bd. trustees The Kemper Mus. Contemporary Art, Kansas City, 1994-; trustee Kemper family foundations; founder, mem. bd. dirs. The Agriculture Future of Am., 1996-. Served USNR, WWII. Recipient Key Man Kansas City Jr. C. of C., 1952, Disting. Svc., 1964, Man of Yr. Award Kansas City Press Club, 1974, Outstanding Kansas Citian Award Native Sons Kansas City, 1975, 82, 1st Advocacy Award Mid-Continent Small Bus. Assn., 1980, Banker Adv. of Yr. Award Small Bus. Adminstrn., 1981, Lester Milgram Humanitarian Award, 1982, Man of Yr. Award Downtown, Inc., 1982, Pirouette Award Kansas City Ballet Guild and Kansas City Tomorrow Alumni Assn., 1983, Faculty Alumni Award U. Mo. Columbia Alumni Assn., 1982, Mo. Arts Coun. Award, 1984, Kansas City Chancellor's Medal U. Mo., 1984, Disting. Svc. Award St. Paul Sch. Theology, 1987, Advocacy Award Mo. Citizens for the Arts, 1987, Outstanding Patron of Excellence in the Arts and Architecture Am. Inst. Architects -Kansas City, 1994, VIP Leadership Award Centurions Leadership Program Greater Kansas City C. of C., 1995; named Man of Yr. Kansas City Press Club, 1974, Kansas Citian of Yr., 1997; named one of Top 200 Collectors ARTnews mag., 2004. Mem. Am. Royal Assn. (v.p., bd. dirs.), Man of the Month Fraternity, Beta Theta Pi (Man of Yr. 1974) Clubs: River, Carriage, Kansas City Country, Kansas City, 1021, Mo, Chathan, Mass., Garden of the Gods, Cheyenne Mountain

Country (Colorado Springs, Colo.). Republican. Episcopalian. Avocations: Collector Old Masters, modern and contemporary art, farming, tennis, sailing, horseback riding, raising cattle. Office: Kemper Mus Contemporary Art 4220 Warwick Blvd Kansas City MO 64111

KEMPF, DONALD G., JR., retired lawyer; b. Chgo., July 4, 1937; s. Donald G. and Verginia (Jahnke) K.; m. Nancy Kempf, June 12, 1965; children: Donald G. III, Charles P., Stephen R. AB, Villanova U., 1959; LLB, Harvard U., 1965; MBA, U. Chgo., 1989. Bar: Ill. 1965, U.S. Supreme Ct. 1972, N.Y. 1986, Colo. 1992. Assoc. Kirkland & Ellis, Chgo., 1965-70, ptnr., 1971-2000; exec. v.p., chief legal officer, sec. Morgan Stanley, NYC, 2000—05; ret., 2005. Trustee Chgo. Symphony Orch., 1995—, Am. Inns of Ct., 1997-2006, v.p., 2002-06; bd. govs. Chgo. Zool. Soc., 1975—, Art Inst. Chgo., 1984—; bd. dirs. United Charities Chgo., 1985-2003, chmn. bd., 1991-93; trustee NYC Opera, 2002-05; commr. Antitrust Modernization Commn., 2004-07. Capt. USMC, 1959-62. Recipient Stephen E. Banner award, 2004. Fellow Am. Coll. Trial Lawyers; mem. Am. Econ. Assn., ABA, Chgo. Club, Econ. Club, U. Club, Mid-Am. Club, Saddle and Cycle Club (Chgo.), Snowmass (Colo.) Club, Roaring Fork Club, Country Club Fla., Quail Ridge (Fla.) Club, Westmoreland Club. Roman Catholic. Personal E-mail: dkempf@kempflaw.com.

KEMPF, JANE ELMIRA, marketing executive; b. Phila., Sept. 28, 1927; d. Albert Thomas and Alice (Gaston) Mullen; m. Peter Kempf, Sept. 4, 1948 (dec. Mar. 1985); children: Peter Albert, Jan Michael, Richard Allen, Jeffery Val. Grad. high sch., Yeadon, Pa. News dir. Sta. WIFF, Auburn, Ind., 1968-69; city editor The Evening Star, Auburn, 1969-76, columnist, 1969—2001; paralegal Warren Sunday Atty., Auburn, 1977-85; mktg. mgr. City Nat. Bank, Auburn, 1986-89; with communications mktg. Lincoln Fin. Corp., Ft. Wayne, Ind., 1989-90; prin. JK Communications Bus. Svcs., Auburn, Ind., 1990—, Auburn Pub. Co., 1997—. Prin. Auburn (Ind.) Pub. Author: Jane's Friends and Family Cookbook, vol. 1, 1997, vol. 2, 1999, Nutritional Nuggets, 2006. Mem. Auburn Network Enterprising Women, Ladies Literary Club, PEO Sisterhood (past pres., treas., rec. sec.), Auburn C. of C. (past sec., bd. dirs.). Presbyterian. Avocation: art. Home: 1117 Packard Pl Auburn IN 46706-1340 Office: Auburn Pub Co 1117 Packard Pl Auburn IN 46706-1340 Personal E-mail: jemkemph@sbcglobal.net.

KEMPSTON DARKES, V. MAUREEN, automotive executive; b. Toronto, Can. BA in History and Polit. Sci., U. Toronto, LLB; D in Commerce (hon.), St. Mary's U., Halifax, 1995; LLD (hon.), U. Toronto, 1996, U. Victoria, 1996, McMaster U., 1997. Bar: Ont. Mem. legal staff GM Can. Ltd., 1975-79, asst. counsel Detroit, 1979-80, head tax staff, 1980-84, mem. treas. office NYC, 1985-87, acting treas., gen. dir. pub. affairs, 1987-91, v.p. corp. affairs, 1991, bd. dirs., 1991, gen. counsel, sec., 1992, pres., gen. mgr., v.p. GM Oshawa, Ont., 1994—2001; group v.p. GM, Detroit, 2002—; and pres. GM LAAM, Detroit, 2002—. Appointed Free Trade Agreement Automotive Select Panel, 1989, Transp. Equipment Sectoral Adv. Group on Internat. Trade, 1994; bd. dirs. CAMI Automotive, CN Rail, Noranda Inc., Thomson Corp. Active Ont. Govt. Edn. Accountability Bd.; mem. arts and sci. adv. bd. U. Toronto; bd. govs. U. Waterloo; mem. adv. com. U. We. Ont.'s Richard Ivey Sch. Bus.; bd. dirs. Women's Coll. Hosp. Found., New Directions; chair major gifts fundraising campaign Women's Coll. Hosp.; mem. coun. adv. govs. YMCA Greater Toronto. Recipient Margaret Brent Women Lawyers of Achievement award, ABA, 1998, Disting. Svc. Citation, Automotive Hall of Fame, 1999, Order of Ont., 1997, Officer of Order of Can., 2000. Mem. Bus. Coun. on Nat. Issues, Can. Vehicle Mfrs. Assn., Natural Resources Can. Min. Adv. Coun. on Indsl. Energy Efficiency, Automotive Adv. Com. Office: GM Group VP & Pres LAAM 300 Renaissance Ctr Detroit MI 48265-3000

KENDALL, LEON THOMAS, finance and real estate educator, retired insurance company executive; b. Elizabeth, NJ, May 20, 1928; m. Nancy O'Donnell; 6 children. BS in Acctg. magna cum laude, St. Vincent Coll., 1949; MBA in Mktg., Ind. U., 1950, DBA in Econs., 1956; LLD (hon.), Cardinal Stritch Coll., 1988. Teaching asso. Ind. U. Sch. Bus., 1950-53; economist Fed. Res. Bd., Atlanta, 1956-58, U.S. Savs. and Loan League, Chgo., 1958-64; v.p., economist N.Y. Stock Exchange, 1964-67; pres. Assn. Stock Exchange Firms, 1967-72, Securities Industry Assn., 1972-74; chmn., dir. Mortgage Guaranty Ins. Corp., Milw., 1974-89; vice chmn. MGIC Investment Corp., 1980-89; Norman Strunk prof. fin. instns. Kellogg Sch. of Mgmt., Northwestern U., Evanston, Ill., 1988—. Bd. dirs. Anthracite Capital, Inc., CoreCar, Inc., CBOE; commr. N.J. Mortgage Study, 1971-72; mem. Wis. Expenditures Study Commn., 1985-86. Author: (with Miles Colean) Who Buys the Houses, 1958, The Savings and Loan Business: Its Purposes, Functions and Economic Justification, 1962, Anatomy of the Residential Mortgage, 1964, Readings in Financial Institutions, 1965, The Exchange Community in 1975, 1965; editor: Thrift and Home Ownership: Writings of Fred T. Greene, 1962; contbr.: chpt. to American Enterprise: The Next Ten Years, 1961, The World Capital Shortage, 1977, Securitization Primer, 1996. Mem. deans adv. council Ind. U. Sch. Bus.; mem. adv. bd. Fed. Home Loan Mortgage Corp; vis. com. divsn. social scis. U. Chgo. Served with USAF, 1954-56. Grad. fellow Ind. U., 1950-53; Found. for Econ. Edn. fellow Pitts. Plate Glass Co., 1952 Mem. Acad. Alumni Fellows Ind. U. Sch. Bus., Lambda Alpha, Delta Epsilon Sigma, Beta Gamma Sigma. Office: MGIC Investment Corp MGIC Pla Milwaukee WI 53201

KENISON, RAYMOND ROBERT, fraternal organization administrator; b. Mo., Sept. 23, 1932; s. Raymond Roy and Emma Oleta (Holder) Kenison; m. Marjorie White, Feb. 1, 1955; children: Debra Kenison Brown, Peggy Kenison Crim, Raymond Roger, Robert B. AA, Hannibal LaGrange Coll., 1953; BA, U. Mo., 1961; postgrad., Cen. Bapt. Sem., Kansas City, 1957, Midwestern Bapt. Sem., 1965; DivD, Hannibal LaGrange Coll., 1994. CFP; cert. instr. Pastor 1st Bapt.Ch., Bates City, Mo., 1954-56, Friendship Bapt. Ch., Mexico, Mo., 1956-62, Immanuel Bapt. Ch., Hannibal, Mo., 1962-77; dir. devel. Mo. Bapt. Children's Home, Bridgeton, 1977-80, exec. dir., 1980—, pres., 1992—. Pres. bd. trustees Hannibal-Lagrance Coll.; co-founder, pres. Viability R & D Group; pres. MBCH Found., 2001—; chmn. contract com. Spl. Care Homes of Mo., 2002—; pres. MBCH Properties, 2002—; pres., chmn. bd. MBCH Profl. Devel. Inst., 2003. Mem. Child Welfare League Am., Inc.; pres. Hannibal Coun. Alcohol and Drug Abuse; bd. dirs. Hannibal Cmty. Chest, 1974—79, Alliance Children and Families, Mo. Alliance Children and Families; pres. Hannibal Ministerial Alliance. Named Kenison Complex in his honor. Mem.: Viability R & D Group (co-founder, pres.), Inst. CFPs, S.W. Assn. Child Care Execs., Mo. Child Care Assn. (bd. dirs., pres. 1994—), So. Bapt. Child Care Execs. (pres.), Nat. Soc. Fund Raising Execs. (sec.), Nat. Assn. Homes Children, Nat. Foster Parents Assn., Hannibal Investment Club (pres. 1976—78, 1982—83). Home: 4 River Hills Hannibal MO 63401-6218 Office: Mo Bapt Children's Home 11300 Saint Charles Rock Rd Bridgeton MO 63044-2721

KENLEY, HOWARD, state legislator; b. Ft. Stockton, Tex., Mar. 28, 1945; s. Howard A. Jr. and Elvira (Hayten) K.; m. Sally Butler; children: John, Bill, Betsy. AB, Miami U., Oxford, Ohio, 1967; JD, Harvard U., 1972. Atty. Cadick, Burns, Duck & Neighbours, Indpls., 1972-73; pres., owner Kenley's Supermarkets, oblesville, Ind., 1974-93; owner Cambridge Investment Inc., 1998; judge Noblesville City Ct., 1974-89; senator Dist. 20 Ind. State Senate, 1992—, mem. fin., judiciary, edn., planning and pub. policy coms., mem. fin. com., judiciary com., planning/pub. svc. com., senator Indpls. Bd. dirs. Society Bank of Ind. Bd. dirs. Boys and Girls Club of Noblesville 1975, adv. bd. 1st United Meth. Ch., Key Bank Noblesville Edn. Found., mem. Noblesville Econ. Devel. Bd. 2000-. 1st lt. US Army, 1969—71. Deocrated Army Commendation medal; named Bd. Mem. of Yr. Noblesville Boys and Girls Club, 1984-85. Mem. Ind. State Bar Assn., Hamilton County Bar Assn., 50 Club of Hamilton County, Elks, Beta theta Pi, mem. ELKS Club, 1980-, mem. HAM County 50 Club 1976-, mem. Am. Legion, 2000-. Office: Indiana State Senate 200 W Washington St Indianapolis IN 46204-2785 Office Phone: 317-232-9400, 317-232-9453. Office Fax: 317-232-9660.

KENNEDY, CHARLES ALLEN, lawyer; b. Maysville, Ky., Dec. 11, 1940; s. Elmer Earl and Mary Frances Kennedy; m. Patricia Ann Louderback, Dec. 9, 1961; 1 child, Mimi Mignon. AB, Morehead State Coll., 1965, MA in Edn., 1968; JD, U. Akron, 1969; LLM, George Washington U., 1974. Bar: Ohio 1969. Asst. cashier Citizens Bank, Felicity, Ohio, 1961-63; tchr Triway Local Sch. Dist., Wooster, Ohio, 1965-67; with office of gen. counsel Fgn. Agr. and Spl. Programs Divsn. USDA, Washington, 1969-71; ptnr. Kauffman, Eberhart, Cicconetti & Kennedy Co., Wooster, 1972-86, Kennedy, Cicconetti, Knowlton & BuyTendyk, LPA, Wooster, 1986—. Mem.: ABA, Wayne County Bar Assn., Ohio Assn. Justice, Ohio State Bar Assn., Am. Coll. Barristers, Am. Assn. Justice, Fed. Bar Assn., Lions, Exch. Club, Elks, Phi Delta Kappa, Phi Alpha Delta. Republican. Home: 275 W Henrietta Wooster OH 44691 Office: Kennedy Cicconetti & Knowlton Law 558 N Market St Wooster OH 44691-3406 Office Phone: 330-262-7555. Personal E-mail: knndy558@netscape.net.

KENNEDY, CORNELIA GROEFSEMA, federal judge; b. Detroit, Aug. 4, 1923; d. Elmer H. and Mary Blanche (Gibbons) Groefsema; m. Charles S. Kennedy, Jr. (dec.); 1 son, Charles S. III. BA, U. Mich., 1945, JD with distinction, 1947; LL.D. (hon.), No. Mich. U., 1971, Eastern Mich. U., 1971, Western Mich. U., 1973, Detroit Coll. Law, 1980, U. Detroit, 1987. Bar: Mich. bar 1947. Law clk. to Chief Judge Harold M. Stephens, U.S. Ct. of Appeals, Washington, 1947-48; assoc. Elmer H. Groefsema, Detroit, 1948-52; partner Markle & Markle, Detroit, 1952-66; judge 3d Judicial Circuit Mich., 1967-70; dist. judge US Dist. Ct., Eastern Dist. Mich., Detroit, 1970-79, chief judge, 1977-79; circuit judge US Ct. Appeals, (6th cir.), 1979-99, sr. judge, 1999—. Mem. Commn. on the Bicentennial of the U.S. Constitution (presdl. appointment). Recipient Sesquicentennial award U. Mich. Fellow Am. Bar Found.; mem. ABA, Mich. Bar Assn. (past chmn. negligence law sect.), Detroit Bar Assn. (past dir.), Fed. Bar Assn., Am. Judicature Soc., Nat. Assn. Women Lawyers, Am. Trial Lawyers Assn., Nat. Conf. Fed. Trial Judges (past chmn.), Fed. Jud. Fellows Commn. (bd. dirs.), Fed. Jud. Ctr. (bd. dirs.), Phi Beta Kappa. Address: 744 Fed Ct House 231 1st Detroit MI 48226

KENNEDY, CRAIG, rental company executive; b. St. Louis; m. Mary Kennedy; 2 children. Programmer/analyst Enterprise Rent-a-Car, St. Louis, 1989—90, programming supr., 1990, founder Advanced Tech. Group, 1991—92, dir. software devel., 1992—93, asst. v.p., 1993—96, v.p. info. systems, 1996—2002, chief info. officer, 2002—, sr. v.p., 2003—. Office: Enterprise Rent-a-Car 600 Corporate Park Dr Saint Louis MO 63105-4211

KENNEDY, GEORGE DANNER, chemical company executive; b. Pitts., May 30, 1926; s. Thomas Reed and Lois (Smith) K.; m. Valerie Putis; children: Charles Reed, Jamey Kathleen, Susan Patton, Timothy Christian. BA, Williams Coll., 1948. With Scott Paper Co., 1947-52, Champion Paper Co., 1952-65; pres. Brown Co., 1965-71; exec. v.p. Internat. Minerals & Chem. Corp., Northbrook, Ill., 1971-78, pres., 1978-86; chmn. Mallinckrodt Group (formerly IMCERA), St. Louis, 1986—, CEO, 1983-91; also bd. dirs., chmn. exec. com. IMCERA (formerly Internat. Minerals & Chem. Corp.), Northbrook, Ill. Former chmn. nominting com. Kemper Nat.; former chmn. compensation com., bd. dirs. exec. com. Am. Nat. Can Co.; dir. Health Share, Acton, Mass; mng. ptnr. Berkshires Capital Investors, Willimstown, Mass. Bd. dirs. Children's Meml. Hosp. and Children's Meml. Med. Ctr., Inst. Internat. Edn., Sand County Found.; trustee Chgo. Symphony; gov. mem. Chgo. Orch. Assn.; dir. Lyric Opera Chgo., Ctr. for Workforce Preparation and Quality Edn.; regional trustee Boys and Girls Club of Am.; trustee Nat. Com. Against Drunk Driving. Mem. Indian Hill Club, Chgo. Club, Sleepy Hollow Country Club, Taconic Golf Club. Office: PO Box 559 Winnetka IL 60093-0559

KENNEDY, JOHN PATRICK, lawyer, corporate financial executive; b. Oct. 2, 1943; s. Arch R. and Kathryn R. (Delahunty) K.; children: Kathleen, Elizabeth, Christina, Patrick, Lindsay. BA in Econs., U. Kans., 1965, JD, 1967; MBA in Fin., U. Mo., 1972, LLM, 1973. Bar: Kans. 1967, Mo. 1968, Ohio 1973, Wis. 1985, U.S. Supreme Ct. 1972, U.S. Dist. Ct. (we. dist.) Mo. 1972, U.S. dist. Ct. Kans. 1967. Trial atty. Kodas, Gingerich & Stites, Kansas City, Mo., 1967-69; sr. atty. Mobay Chem. Co., Kansas City, Mo., 1969-73; gen. counsel Johnson Controls, Inc., Milw., 1984—2004, corp. sec., 1987—2004, sr. v.p., 2002—04, pres. Controls Group, 2004—. Small bus. advisor, venture capitalist. Contbr. articles to profl. jours. Served with USAR, 1967-73. Recipient Wall St. Jour. award, 1972, A. Jurisprudence awards, 1966-67. Mem. ABA, Ohio Bar Assn., Columbus Bar Assn., Wis. Bar Assn., Am. Corp. Counsel Assn. Democrat. Roman Catholic. Office: Johnson Controls Inc 5757 N Green Bay Ave PO Box 591 Milwaukee WI 53201 Office Phone: 414-228-1200.

KENNEDY, JOSEPH PAUL, chemist, researcher; b. Budapest, Hungary, May 18, 1928; arrived in U.S., 1956; s. Laszlo and Rosa (Farkas) Kennedy; m. Ingeborg G. Hausen, Feb. 10, 1956; children: Katherine, Cynthia, Julie. PhD, U. Vienna, Austria, 1954; MBA, Rutgers U., 1961; D (hon.), Kossuth U., Hungary, 1989. Rsch. fellow Sorbonne, U. Paris, 1955; rsch. assoc. McGill U., Montreal, Que., Canada, 1956; rsch. chemist Celanese Corp., Summit, NJ, 1957-59; sr. rsch. assoc. Esso Rsch. Engring. Co., Linden, NJ, 1959-70; prof. polymer sci. U. Akron, Ohio, 1970-80, disting. prof. polymer sci. and chemistry, 1980—. Cons. Akron Cationic Polymer Devel. Co., 1983—. Author: (book) Cationic Polymerization, 1975, Carbocationic Polymerization, 1982, Designed Polymers by Carbocationic Macromolecular Engineering: Theory and Practice, 1992. Named Outstanding Rschr., Alumni Assn. U. Akron, 1979; recipient Morley award and medal, Cleve. Am. Chem. Soc., 1982, award Disting. Svc. in Sci., Soc. Polymer Sci., Japan, 2000. Mem.: Am. Chem. Soc. (Polymer Chemistry award 1985, 1995, Applied Polymer Sci. award 1995, George Stafford Whitby award 1996, Goodyear medal 2008), Hungarian Acad. Scis. Avocation: Japanese art of the Meiji. Home: 510 Saint Andrews Dr Akron OH 44303-1228 Office: U Akron Inst Polymer Sci Akron OH 44325-0001 Home Phone: 330-972-7512; Office Phone: 330-972-7512. Business E-Mail: josep19@uakron.edu.

KENNEDY, LAWRENCE ALLAN, mechanical engineering educator; b. Detroit, May 31, 1937; s. Clifford Earl and Emma Josephine (Muller) K.; m. Valaree J. Lockhart, Aug. 3, 1958; children: Joanne E., Julie A., Janet A., Raymond L., Jill M., Brian G. BS, U. Detroit, 1960; MS, Northwestern U., 1962, PhD, 1964. Registered profl. engr., N.Y. Chmn. dept., prof. mech. and aero. engring. SUNY-Buffalo, 1964-83; chmn. dept. mech. engring., prof. Ohio State U., Columbus, 1983—94, Ralph W. Kurtz disting. prof., 1992-95; prof. mech. engring. and chem. engring. U. Ill., Chgo., 2004—, prof. emeritus mech. engring., 2004—, dean coll. engring., 1994—2004, dean emeritus, 2004—, Stanley Kaplan scholar, 2002—; prof. mech. engring. Ohio State U., Columbus, 2006—. Vis. assoc. prof. mech. and aero. engring. U. Calif.-San Diego, 1968-69, VonKarman Inst., Rhode-St. Genese, Belgium, 1971-72; Goebel vis. prof. mech. and aero. engring. U. Mich., Ann Arbor, 1980-81; vis. prof. mech. & aerospace engring. Princeton U., 1993-94; cons. Cornell Aero. Lab., Buffalo, 1968-72, Tech. Adv. Service, Fort Washington, Pa., 1969—, Ashland Chem. Corp., Dublin, Ohio, 1983-90, Mech. Engring. Sci. and Application, Buffalo, 1972-83, Columbia Gas, 1987-92; vis. faculty fellow mech. and aerospace engring. Princeton U., 1994. Contbr. numerous articles on engring. to profl. jours.; editor: Progress in Astronautics and Aeros., Vol. 58, 1978, Exptl. Thermal and Fluid Scis., 1987-95; editor in chief Jour. Thermal & Fluid Scis., 1997—; assoc. editor Applied Mechanics Revs., 1985-88, Jour. Propulsion & Power, 1992-98. Recipient Ralph R. Teetor award 1984, AT&T Found. award, 1987, Ralph Coats Roe award, 1993; NATO fellow, 1971-72, NSF fellow, 1968-69, W.P. Murphy fellow, 1960-63; Agard lectr., 1971-72. Fellow AIAA, ASME, AAAS, Am. Phys. Soc.; mem. Combustion Inst., Am. Soc. Engring. Edn., Soc. Automotive Engrs. Roman Catholic. Avocations: skiing, squash, hiking, music. Office: Ohio State Univ 201 W 19th Ave Columbus OH 43210 Office Phone: 614-292-2926. Personal E-mail: lkennedy@uic.edu.

KENNEDY, MARK RAYMOND, former congressman; b. Benson, Minn., Apr. 11, 1957; m. Debbie Kennedy; 4 children. BA in Acctg., St. John's U., Minn., 1979; MBA, U. Mich., 1983. CPA. Campaign worker for election of Rudy Boschwitz to US Senate, 1978; certified pub. acct. Arthur Andersen & Co., 1978—81; dir. corp. & internat. fin. The Pillsbury Co., 1983—87; sr. v.p., treas. Federated Dept. Stores Inc., Cin., 1987—92; CFO, sr. v.p. merchandising, ops. & advt. ShopKo Stores, Green Bay, Wis., 1992—94; CFO, v.p. adminstrn. Dept 56 Inc., Eden Prarie, Minn., 1995—2000; mem. US Congress from 6th Minn. dist. (formerly 2nd), 2001—07. Mem. agriculture com., transportation & infrastructure com.; subcom. gen. farm commodities, risk mngmt., conservation, credit, rural devel. and rsch., aviation, highways and transit (vice ch.), co-chmn., Minn. Rep. Party Platform Co., 1998 Founder Minn. Rough Riders Issues Forum. Recipient Friend of the Farm Bur. award, Minn. Farm Bur. Fedn., 2002. Mem.: Toastmasters, Lions. Republican. Roman Catholic.

KENNELLY, SISTER KAREN MARGARET, church administrator, nun, retired academic administrator; b. Graceville, Minn., Aug. 4, 1933; d. Walter John Kennelly and Clara Stella Eastman. BA, Coll. St. Catherine, St. Paul, 1956; MA, Cath. U. Am., 1958; PhD, U. Calif., Berkeley, 1962. Joined Sisters of St. Joseph of Carondelet, Roman Cath. Ch., 1954. Prof. history Coll. St. Catherine, 1962-71, acad. dean, 1971-79; exec. dir. Nat. Fedn. Carondelet Colls., 1979-82; province dir. Sisters of St. Joseph of Carondelet, St. Paul, 1982-88; pres. Mt. St. Mary's Coll., LA, 1989-2000, pres. emerita, 2000—; congl. dir. Sisters of St. Joseph of Carondelet, St. Louis, 2002—08. Cons. N. Ctrl. Accreditation Assn., Chgo., 1974—84, Ohio Bd. Regents, Columbus, 1983—89; trustee colls., hosps., Minn., Mo., Wis., Calif., 1972—; chmn. Sisters St. Joseph Coll. Consortium, 1979—82. Editor, co-author: Am. Cath. Women, 1989; author (with others): Women of Minnesota, 1977; author: Women Religious and the Intellectual Life: The North American Achievement, 1996; co-editor: Gender Identities in American Catholicism, 2001;: Cath. Coll. Women in Am., 2002. Bd. dirs. Am. Coun. on Edn., 1997—99, Nat. Assn. Ind. Colls. and Univs., 1997—2000, Assn. Cath. Colls. and Univs., 1996—2000, Western Region Nat. Holocaust Mus., 1997—2000; coord. History Homes Religious Nature, 1988—. Fellow Fulbright, 1964. Mem.: Western Assn. Schs. and Colls. (sr. commn. 1997—2000), Assn. Cath. Colls. and Univs. (exec. bd. 1996—2000), Am. Coun. Edn. (bd. dirs. 1997—99), Nat. Assn. Ind. Colls. and Univs. (bd. dirs. 1997—99), Am. Assn. Rsch. Historians Medieval Spain, Medieval Acad., Am. Cath. Hist. Assn. Avocations: skiing, cuisine. Office: 1880 Randolph Ave Saint Paul MN 55105 Home Phone: 314-961-6189; Office Phone: 314-966-4048. Personal E-mail: kkennelly33@hotmail.com.

KENNER, HOWARD A., state legislator; b. Chgo., Dec. 26, 1957; s. Tyrone and Emma (Payne) K. BS, U. Ill., 1980. CPA, Ill. Ill. state rep. Dist. 24. Mem. Appropriations, Gen. Svcs., Human Svcs., Health Care Availability and Access, Insurance Coms.; chmn. Com. on State Govt. Adminstr.; ptnr. Goodall, Kenner & Assoc. CPAs, Chgo.

KENNETT, CHRISTIE SHIH, lawyer; b. 1970; married; 2 children. BA, Univ. Ill.; JD, St. Louis Univ. Bar: 1995. Faculty fellow St. Louis Univ. Law Sch., 1995—2001; assoc., tax, real estate, corp. law Husch & Eppenberger, St. Louis, 2001—04; atty., securities law unit State Farm Ins., Bloomington, Ill., now dir., govt. affairs. Bd. mem. Zoning Bd. of Appeals, Bloomington, Ill.; bd. dir. McLean County YWCA, Parklands Found.; pres. Ctrl. Ill. Chapter, Orgn. of Chinese Americans. Named one of Best Lawyers Under 40, Nat. Asian Pacific Am. Bar Assn., 2004, Top Asian Am. Corp. Execs. under 45, Goldsea. Office: Govt Affairs State Farm Ins One State Farm Plz Bloomington IL 61710

KENNETT, ROBERT L., medical organization executive; V.p. pub. Jour. AMA, Chgo. Office: AMA 515 N State St Chicago IL 60610-4325

KENNEY, BRIAN A., financial services executive; BBA, U. Notre Dame, 1981; MBA in Fin., U. Mich., 1983. With Morton Internat., Inc., Peterson & Co., United Air Lines Corp.; mng. dir., corp. fin. & banking AMR Corp., 1990-95; treas. GATX Corp., Chgo., 1995-99, v.p., CFO, 1999—. Office: GATX Corp 500 W Monroe St Chicago IL 60661

KENNEY, COLLEEN M., lawyer; b. 1959; BS, No. Ill. U., 1981, MS, 1982; JD, U. Chgo., 1991. Bar: Ill. 1991. Ptnr. Sidley Austin Brown & Wood, Chgo., 2000—. Office: Sidley Austin Brown and Wood Bank One Plz 10 S Dearborn St Chicago IL 60603

KENNEY, CRANE H., lawyer; b. Quincy, Mass., Dec. 31, 1962; BA cum laude, U. Notre Dame, 1985; JD cum laude, U. Mich., 1988. Bar: Ill. 1988. Assoc. Schiff, Hardin & Waite; counsel Tribune Co., Chgo., 1994—95, sr. counsel, 1995—96, v.p., chief legal officer, 1996, v.p., gen. counsel, sec., 1996—2000, sr. v.p., gen. counsel, sec., 2000—. Office: Tribune Co 435 N Michigan Ave Ste 600 Chicago IL 60611-4001 Office Phone: 312-222-9100, 312-222-2491. Office Fax: 312-222-4206. E-mail: ckenney@tribune.com.

KENNEY, FRANK DEMING, lawyer; b. Chgo., Feb. 20, 1921; s. Joseph Aloysius and Mary Edith (Deming) K.; m. Virginia Stuart Banning, Feb. 12, 1944; children: Claudia Kenney Carpenter, Pamela Kenney Voetberg, Sarah Kenney Swanson, Stuart Deming Kenney AB, U. Chgo., 1948, JD, 1949. Bar: Ill. 1948, U.S. Dist. Ct. (no. dist.) Ill. 1949. Assoc. J.O. Brown, Chgo., 1948-49; assoc., ptnr. Winston & Strawn, and predecessors, Chgo., 1949-92, ret., 1992. 1st lt. AUS, 1942-46, CBI, PTO. Mem. ABA, Ill. Bar Assn., Chgo. Bar Assn. (chmn. real property law com. 1982-83), Lawyers Club Chgo., Fox River Valley Hunt Club, Quadrangle Club, Nat. Beagle Club Am. (bd. dirs. 1981-92), Spring Creek Basset Hunt Club (master 1977-93, chmn. bd., 1993-98, hon. chmn. bd. 1998-2002, hon. master 2002-), Kappa Sigma (nat. housing fin. commr. for U.S. and Can., 1959-91). Republican. Roman Catholic. Office: Winston & Strawn 35 W Wacker Dr Ste 3800 Chicago IL 60601-1695

KENNEY, WILLIAM PATRICK, state legislator; b. San Francisco, Jan. 20, 1955; s. Charles Frances and Barbara Clare Kenney; m. Sandra Louise Ehrlich, Dec. 28, 1979; children: Kristin Allison, William Charles, Carlton Patrick, Elizabeth Alexandria. AA, Saddleback Jr. Coll., 1976; BA, U. No. Colo., 1978. Player Kansas City Chiefs, 1978-89, Washington Redskins, 1989; broker, officer Bill Kenney and Assocs., Lee's Summit, Mo., 1992—; mem. Mo. Senate from 8th dist., Jefferson City, 1995—. Named Most Valuable Player Kansas City Chiefs, 1983; named to Pro Bowl Am. Football Conf. NFL, 1983. Home and Office: 2808 SW Arthur Dr Lees Summit MO 64082-4062

KENNON, ROZMOND HERRON, retired physical therapist; b. Birmingham, Ala., Dec. 12, 1935; m. Gloria Oliver; children: Shawn, Rozmond Jr. BA, Talldega Coll., 1956; cert., U. Colo., 1957. Asst. chief phys. therapist St. John's Hosp., St. Paul, 1957-58, Creigthon Meml. St. Joseph's Hosp., Omaha, 1958-61; asst. chief, phys. therapist Sister Kenny Inst., Mpls., 1962, chief phys. therapy, 1962-64; cons. in phys. therapy Mt. Sinai Hosp., Mpls., 1963-70; pvt. practice, 1964-98. Contbr. articles to profl. jours. Bd. dirs. Southdale YMCA, Edina Human Rights, Southside Med. Ctr., Mpls., Boy Scouts Am.; trustee Talladega (Ala.) Coll.; pres., CEO Daniel Kennon and Verna Herron Kennon Family Found.; pres. Talladega Bd. Trustees; exec. bd. dirs. Greater Ala. Coun. Boy Scouts Am. Mem. Am. Phys. Therapy Assn., Am. Registry Phys. Therapists, Ala. Phys. Therapy Assn. (mem. social-econ. com., past chmn. profl. practice com., bd. dirs., past sec.). Home: 5120 Lake Crest Cir Hoover AL 35226-5027

KENRICH, JOHN LEWIS, retired lawyer; b. Lima, Ohio, Oct. 17, 1929; s. Clarence E. and Rowena (Stroh) Katterheinrich; m. Betty Jane Roehll, May 26, 1951; children: John David, Mary Jane, Kathryn Ann, Thomas Roehll, Walter Clarence. BS, Miami U., Oxford, Ohio, 1951; LLB, U. Cin., 1953. Bar: Ohio 1953, Mass. 1969. Asst. counsel B.F. Goodrich Co., Akron, Ohio, 1956-65; asst. sec., counsel W.R. Grace & Co., Cin., 1965-68, v.p. Splty. Products Group divsn., 1970-71; corp. counsel, sec. Standex Internat. Corp., Andover, Mass., 1969-70; v.p., sec. Chemed Corp., Cin., 1971-82, sr. v.p., gen. counsel, 1982-86, exec. v.p., chief adminstrv. officer, 1986-91, ret., 1991. Trustee Better Bus. Bur., Cin., 1981-90; mem. bus. adv. coun. Miami U., 1986-88; mem. City Planning Commn., Akron, 1961-62; mem. bd. visitors Coll. Law U. Cin., 1988-92; mem. area coun. trustees Franciscan Sisters of Poor Found., Cin., 1989-93; bd. govs. Ohio River Valley chpt. Arthritis Found., 1992-95, 2000—04; mem. Com. on Reinvestment City of Cin., 1991-93. 1st lt. JAGC U.S. Army, 1954-56. Mem. Beta Theta Pi, Omicron Delta Kappa, Delta Sigma Pi, Phi Eta Sigma. Republican. Presbyterian.

KENT, DEBORAH, automotive executive; div.; children: Jessica, Jordan. BA in Psychology, So. Ill. U.; MA in Indsl. Psychology, Washington U., St. Louis. Quality control supr., reliability engr. Ford Motor Co. Assembly Plant, Dearborn, Mich., area mgr. Wixom, Mich., 1987-92, mfg. mgr. Chgo., 1992-94, plant mgr. Avon Lake, Ohio, 1994—. Office: Ford Motor Co 650 Miller Rd Avon Lake OH 44012-2398

KENT, JERALD L., communications company executive; BA (hons.), Washington U., MBA. CPA Mo. Tax mgr. Arthur Andersen & Co., 1979-83; from sr. v.p. to exec. v.p., CFO Cencom Cable Assocs., Inc., 1983-90, exec. v.p., CFO, 1990-93; prin., owner Charter Communications, St. Louis, 1993—2002; CEO AAT Communications, St. Louis, 2002—. Bd. dirs. CCA Acquisition Corp., CCT Holdings Corp., CCA Holdings Corp., The Magic House Children's Mus. Chmn. finance com. Incarnate Word Ch. Recipient 1997 Regional Entrepreneurs of Yr. in Telecomms. and Entertainment award Ernst & Young, USA Today, DASDAQ, Kauffman Found., 1997. Mem. Young Pres. Orgn., Alumni Assn. Exec. com. Washington U. Office: AAT Communications 12444 Powerscourt Dr Saint Louis MO 63131 Fax: (314) 965-5761.

KENTOR, PAUL MARTIN, allergist; b. Pitts., 1944; MD, U. Ill. Coll. Medicine, 1970. Cert. internal medicine 1973, allergy and immunology 1977.

Intern U. Ill. Hosp., Chgo., 1970—71, resident, 1971—73; fellow, allergy and immunology Grant Hosp., Chgo., 1975—77; allergist Evanston Hosp., Evanston, Ill.; assoc. prof. orthwestern U. Office: Evanston Hosp 636 Ch St Ste 610 Evanston IL 60201 also: 1215 Old McHenry Rd Buffalo Grove IL 60089 also: 580 Roger Williams Highland Park IL 60035

KEOUGH, MICHAEL J., paper manufacturing executive; b. 1952; With Internat. Paper, 1975-85, Crown Zellerbach, 1985; head multiwall and retail bag bus. Gaylord Container Corp., Deerfield, Ill., head corrugated container ops., 1993, v.p., gen. mgr. container ops., pres., COO, 2000—.

KEPLER, DAVID E., II, chemicals executive; BSChemE, U. Calif. With western divsn. computer and process systems grp. Dow Chem. Co., 1975, computer svcs. mgr. U.S.A. ea. divsn. Strongsville, Ohio, 1984—88, comml. dir. performance products Can., 1989—91, dir. info. systems pacific area, 1991—93, dir. chems. and plastics info. systems, 1993—94, dir. global info. systems applications, 1995, dir. global info. application, 1995—98, v.p., chief info. officer, 1998—2000, corp. v.p. eBusiness, 2000—04, corp. v.p. advanced electronic materials bus., global purchasing and supply chain, 2002—04, corp. v.p. shared services, 2004, chief info. officer, 2004—, sr. v.p. shared svcs., environment, health and safety, mem. Office of the Chief Exec., 2006—. Bd. dirs. Midland Cmty. Cancer Svcs., Alden B. Dow Mus. Sci. and Art; campaign chair United Way Midland County, 2004; bd. dirs. US C. of C. Mem.: AIChE, Am. Chem. Soc. Office: Dow Chem Co 2030 Dow Ctr Midland MI 48674

KERATA, JOSEPH J., secondary school educator; b. Cleve., Jan. 20, 1949; s. Joseph John and Lillian (Potocky) K.; m. Lynne E. Armington, July 20, 1990. BS in Edn., Ohio State U., 1971; MEd, Cleve. State U., 1978; postgrad., Ohio Wesleyan U., Princeton U. Tchr. sci. grades 7-8 Spellacy Jr. High Sch., Cleve., 1972-73; tchr. BSCS and gen. biology grades 10-12 Willoughby South High Sch., 1973-79; tchr. earth sci., physics, biology grades 10-12 Colegio Roosevelt, Lima, Peru, 1979-80; tchr. English adult edn. Academia Secretaria Y Typografia, Lima, 1980; tchr. gen. sci. grades 7-9 Eastlake Jr. High Sch., Willowick, Ohio, 1980-83; tchr. AP and honors biology Eastlake North High Sch., Willowick, 1983—, chair dept. sci., 1984—. Mem. North Ctrl. Evaluation Team, 1978, cirriculum devel. and revision com., 1978, 85; judge sci. fairs several sch. dists., 1977—. Recipient Krecker Outstanding Sci. Dept. award, 1976, Outstanding Educator award Edinboro U., 1984, Sci. Tchr. of Yr. award Lubrizol Corp., 1991, Gov.'s Ednl. Leadership award, 1992, Ohio Tchr. of Yr. award, 1993; Martha Holden Jennings scholar, 1990; Woodrow Wilson Nat. fellow, 1992. Mem. NEA, Nat. Sci. Tchrs. Assn., Nat. Assn. Biology Tchrs., Ohio Edn. Assn., Ohio Acad. Sci., Willoughby-Eastlake Tchrs. Assn. (grievance chmn. 1981—), Cleve. Regional Assn. Biologists (original). Office: Eastlake North High Sch 34041 Stevens Blvd Eastlake OH 44095-2905

KERBER, LINDA KAUFMAN, historian, educator; b. NYC, Jan. 23, 1940; d. Harry Hagman and Dorothy (Haber) Kaufman; m. Richard Kerber, June 5, 1960; children: Ross Jeremy, Justin Seth. AB cum laude, Barnard Coll., 1960; MA, NYU, 1961; PhD, Columbia U., 1968; DHL, Grinnell Coll., 1992; MA (hon.), Oxford U., 2006. Instr., asst. prof. history Stern Coll., Yeshiva U., NYC, 1963-68; asst. prof. history San Jose State Coll., Calif., 1969-70; vis. asst. prof. history Stanford U., Calif., 1970-71; asst. prof. history U. Iowa, Iowa City, 1971-75, prof., 1975-85, May Brodbeck prof., 1985—. Vis. prof. U. Chgo., 1991-92, Oxford U., England, 2006—. Author: Federalists in Dissent: Imagery and Ideology in Jeffersonian America, 1970, paperback edit., 1980, 97, Women of the Republic: Intellect and Ideology in Revolutionary America, 1980, paperback edit., 1986, Toward an Intellectual History of Women, 1997, No Constitutional Right to Be Ladies: Women and the Obligations of Citizenship, 1998, paperback edit., 1999 (Littleton-Griswold prize in legal history Am. Hist. Assn., Joan Kelley prize in womens history Am. Hist. Assn.); co-editor: Women's America: Refocusing the Past, 1982, 6th edit., 2004, U.S. History As Women's History, 1995; mem. editl. bd. Signs: Jour. Women in Culture and Society, Jour. Women's History; contbr. articles and book revs. to profl. jours. Fellow Danforth Found., EH, 1976, 83-84, 94, Am. Coun. Learned Socs., 1975, Nat. Humanities Ctr., 1990-91, Guggenheim Found., 1990-91, Radcliffe Inst. for Advanced Study, 2003. Mem. Orgn. Am. Historians (pres. 1996-97), Am. Hist. Assn. (pres. 2006), Am. Studies Assn. (pres. 1988), Am. Soc. for Legal History, Berkshire Conf. Women Historians, Soc. Am. Historians, Japan U.S. Friendship Commn., PEN Am. Ctr., Am. Acad. Arts and Scis., Am. Philos. Soc. Jewish. Office: U Iowa Dept History Iowa City IA 52242

KERBER, RICHARD E., cardiologist; b. NYC, May 10, 1939; s. Max and Pauline Kerber; m. Linda K. Kaufman; children: Ross, Justin. AB in Anthropology, Columbia U., 1960; MD, NYU, 1964. Diplomate Am. Bd. Internal Medicine, Am. Bd. Cardiology. Med. intern/resident Bellevue Hosp., NYC, 1964—66; med. resident Stanford (Calif.) U. Hosp., 1968—69, cardiology fellow, 1969—71; asst. prof. internal medicine U. Iowa, Iowa City, 1971—74, assoc. prof. internal medicine, 1974—78, prof. medicine, 1978—. Editor: Echocardiography in Coronary Artery Disease, 1988. Capt. US Army, 1966—68. Grantee RO1 grant, NHLBI, 1995—2008. Fellow: Am. Coll. Cardiology, Am. Heart Assn., Am. Heart Assn. (chmn. coun. on cardiopulmonary and critical care 1997—99, 1997—99, award of Meritorious Achievement 1996, Scientific Coun. Dist. Achievement award 2001), Am. Coll. Cardiology (gov. for Iowa 1976—79, 1976—79); mem.: Assn. Am. Physicians, Assn. Univ. Cardiologists, Am. Soc. for Clin. Investigation, Am. Soc. Echocardiology (sec. 1978—80, treas. 1993—95, v.p. 1995—97, pres. 1997—99, sec. 1978—80, treas. 1993—95, v.p. 1995—97, pres. 1997—99). Office: U Iowa Dept Medicine 200 Hawkins Dr Iowa City IA 52242-1009

KERBER, RONALD LEE, industrial corporation executive; b. Lafayette, Ind., July 2, 1943; s. John Andrew Kerber and Edith Helen (McMaster) Kerkhoff; children: John, Mark, Stephen, Jacqueline. BS, Purdue U., 1965; MS, Calif Inst. Tech., 1966, PhD, 1970. Registered profl. engr., Mich. Tech. staff Aerospace Corp., Los Angeles, 1971-72; prof. Mich. State U., E. Lansing, 1969-85, assoc. dean, 1984-85; program mgr. Defense Advanced Research Projects Agy., Arlington, Va., 1983-84; dep. undersec. U.S. Dept. Defense, Washington, 1985-88; v.p. advanced systems and tech. McDonnell Douglas Corp., St. Louis, 1988-89, v.p. tech. and bus. devel., 1989-91; exec. v.p., chief tech. officer Whirlpool Corp., Benton Harbor, 1991—2000; pres. SBDC Corp., Charlottesville, Va., 2000—. Contbr. articles to profl. jours. Mem. ASME, IEEE, Am. Phys. Soc.

KERBIS, GERTRUDE LEMPP, architect; m. Walter Peterhans (dec.); m. Donald Kerbis (div. 1972); children: Julian, Lisa, Kim. BS, U. Ill.; MA, Ill. Inst. Tech.; postgrad., Grad. Sch. Design, Harvard U., 1949-50. Archtl. designer Skidmore, Owings & Merrill, Chgo., 1954-59, C.F. Murphy Assocs., Chgo., 1959-62, 65-67; pvt. practice architecture Lempp Kerbis Assocs., Chgo., 1967—; lectr. U. Ill., 1969; prof. William Rainey Harper Coll., 1970—95, Washington U., St. Louis, 1977, 82, Ill. Inst. Tech., 1989-91. Archtl. cons. Dept. Urban Renewal, City of Chgo.; mem. Northeastern Ill. Planning Commn., Open Land Project, Mid-North Community Orgn., Chgo. Met. Housing and Planning Council, Chgo. Mayor's Commn. for Preservation Chgo.'s Hist. Architecture; bd. dirs. Chgo. Sch. Architecture Found., 1972-76; trustee Chgo. Archtl. Assistance Ctr., Glessner House Found., Inland Architect Mag.; lectr. Art Inst. Chgo., U. N.Mex., Ill. Inst. Tech., Washington U., St. Louis, Ball State U., Muncie, Ind., U. Utah, Salt Lake City. Prin. archtl. works include U.S. Air Force Acad. dining hall, Colo., 1957, Skokie (Ill.) Pub. Library, 1959, Meadows Club, Lake Meadows, Chgo., 1959, O'Hare Internat. Airport 7 Continents Bldg, 1963; prin. developer and architect: Tennis Club, Highland Park, Ill., 1968, Watervliet, Mich. Tennis Ranch, 1970, Greenhouse Condominium, Chgo., 1976, Webster-Clark Townhouses, Chgo., 1986, Chappell Sch., 1993; exhibited at Chgo. Hist. Soc., 1984, Chgo. Mus. Sci. and Industry, 1985, Paris Exhbn. Chgo. Architects, 1985, Spertus Mus.; represented in permanent archtl. drawings collection Art Inst. Chgo. Active Art Inst. Chgo. Recipient award for outstanding achievement in professions YWCA Met. Chgo., 1984 Fellow AIA (bd. dirs. Chgo. chpt. 1971-75, chpt. pres. 1980, nat. com. architecture, arts and recreation 1972-75, com. on design 1975-80, head subcom. inst. honors nomination); mem. Chgo. Women in Architecture (founder), Chgo. Network, Internat. Women's Forum, Arts Club Chgo., Cliff Dwellers (bd. dirs. 1987-88, pres. 1988, 89), Lambda Alpha. Office: Lempp Kerbis Assocs 172 W Burton Pl Chicago IL 60610-1310 Personal E-mail: lk172@aol.com.

KERIAN, JON ROBERT, retired judge; b. Grafton, ND, Oct. 23, 1927; s. Cyril Robert and Elizabeth Antoinette (Kadlec) K.; m. Sylvia Ann Larson, Dec. 28, 1959; children: John, Ann. PhB, U. N.D., 1955, LLB, 1957, JD, 1971. Bar: N.D. 1957, U.S. Dist. Ct. N.D. 1958, U.S. Ct. Appeals (8th cir.) 1971, U.S. Supreme Ct. 1963. Pvt. practice law, Grand Forks, N.D., 1958-61; asst. atty. gen. State of N.D., Bismarck, 1961-67; ptnr. Bosard, McCutcheon, Kerian, Schmidt, Minot, .D., 1967-80; dist. judge State of N.D., Minot, 1980—92, surrogate judge, 1993—, ret., 1992. History instr. Bismarck State Coll., 1965-67; asst. city atty. City of Minot, 1968-76; atty. Zoning & Planning Commn., Minot, 1969-76; lectr. in field. Contbr. articles to profl. jours.; editor ABA newsletter, The Judges News, 1990—-95. Mem. ABA (bd. editors Judges Jour. 1990-95), Western States Bar Conf. (pres. 1982-83), N.D. Bar Assn. (pres. 1979-80), Nat. Conf. State Trial Judges (exec. com. 1983-89). Home: 1800 8th St SW Minot ND 58701-6410 Office: PO Box 340 Minot ND 58702-0340 Personal E-mail: judex1@srt.com.

KERKMAN, SAMANTHA, state representative; b. Mar. 6, 1974; BA, U. Wis., Whitewater, 1996. Former legis. aide Wis. State Legis., Madison; state assembly mem. Wis. State Assembly, Madison, 2000—, mem. joint com. on audit, mem. audit, fin. instns., govt. ops., judiciary, urban and local affairs, and ways and means coms. Mem.: Randall Fire Dept. Aux., Twin Lakes Chamber and Area Bus. Assn., Powers Lake Sportsmen Club, Twin Lakes Am. Legion Aux. Post 544. Republican. Office: State Capitol Rm 109 W PO Box 8953 Madison WI 53708-8953

KERLEY, JAMES J., manufacturing executive; b. 1923; CFO Emmerson Electric Co., Inc., 1981-84, vice chmn., 1981-85, also bd. dirs.; acting chmn., CEO Rohr, Inc., Chula Vista, Calif., 1993, chmn., 1993—, also bd. dirs. Office: DT Industries Inc 907 W 5th St Dayton OH 45407-3306

KERN, DAVID GRAHAM, lawyer; b. Cin., Aug. 28, 1973; BA, U. South, 1996; JD, Ohio State U., 2000. Bar: Ohio 2000, US Dist. Ct. Southern Dist. Ohio 2001. Asst. atty. gen. Ohio, 2000—02, asst. solicitor; assoc. Kohnen & Patton LLP, Cin. Named one of Ohio's Rising Stars, Super Lawyers, 2006. Mem.: Federalist Soc. for Law and Pub. Policy Studies, Cin. Bar Assn. Office: Kohnen & Patton PNC Ctr Ste 800 201 E Fifth St Cincinnati OH 45202 Office Phone: 513-381-0656. Office Fax: 513-381-5823.

KERN, MICHAEL L., III, corporate financial executive; b. 1973; BS in Fin. and Bus. Economics, Wayne State U. Cert. CFA. Founder The Lawn Masters; analyst Shanker & Stout P.C., 1996; mng. dir., Valuation and Lit. Adv. Services Grp. Stout Risius Poss, Mich., mng. dir., Real Estate Valuation Grp. Farmington Hills, Mich., CFO, COO. Named one of 40 Under 40, Crain's Detroit Bus., 2006. Mem.: Assn. Mgmt. Consulting Firms, Investment Analysts Soc. of Detroit, CFA Inst. Office: Stout Risius Ross 32255 Northwestern Hwy Ste 201 Farmington Hills MI 48334 Office Phone: 248-432-1239. Office Fax: 248-208-8822. Business E-Mail: mkern@srr.com.

KERNS, BRIAN D., former congressman; b. Ind., May 22, 1957; s. Noel and Rosalie K.; m. Lori Myers. BA in polit. sci., Ind. State U., MPA. Dir. publs. and pub. rels. St. Joseph's Coll., Rensselaer, Ind.; pub. info. specialist State Ind. Dept. Natural Resources; reporter, photographer WTWO TV, Terre Haute, Ind.; former Chief of Staff, Deputy Chief of Staff, Spokesman Capitol Hill; mem. U.S. Congress from 7th Ind. dist., 2001—03. Mem. Congressional com. Transportation and Infrastructure, Internat. Rels., Policy; subcom. Highways and Transit, Water Resources and Environ., East Asia and Pacific, Nat. Security, Foreign Affairs, Retirement Security, Captial Markets, Tax Policy, Americas; Reg. Rep. for Ind., Ill. and Mich. Recipient Best Feature Story Yr., United Press Internat., Zorah Shrine Childrens Adv. award. Mem.: Eagles, Elks, Masons. Republican. Episcopalian.

KERNS, STEVE, geneticist; Pres. Universal Pig Genes, Eldora, Iowa. Office: Universal Pig Genes 30355 260th St Eldora IA 50627-8201

KERR, ALEXANDER DUNCAN, JR., lawyer; b. Pitts., May 6, 1943; s. Alexander Duncan Sr. and Nancy Greenleaf (Martin) K.; m. Judith Kathleen Mottl, May 25, 1969; children: Matthew Jonathan, Joshua Brandon. BS in Bus., Northwestern U., 1965, JD, 1968. Bar: Ill. 1968, Pa. 1969, US Dist. Ct. (ea. dist.) Pa. 1969, US Dist. Ct. (no. dist.) Ill. 1969, US Ct. Appeals (3rd cir.) 1969, US Ct. Appeals (7th cir.) 1975, US Supreme Ct. 1975. Assoc. Clark, Ladner, Fortenbaugh & Young, Phila., 1968-69, 73-74; asst. U.S. atty. U.S. Dept. Justice, Chgo., 1974-79; assoc., ptnr. Keck, Mahin & Cate, Chgo., Oak Brook, Ill., 1979-90; shareholder Tishler & Wald, Ltd., Chgo., 1990—. Staff atty. Park Dist. La Grange, Ill., 1985-2001; active Ill. St. Andrew Soc., North Riverside, 1982—, pres., 1995-97, chmn. bd., 2007-; vestryman, lay reader, chancellor, chalice bearer Emmanuel Episcopal Ch., 1980-99; mem. Pack 177, Troop 19, Order of the Arrow, Boy Scouts Am., La Grange, 1980-2000. With USN, 1969-75. Mem. Am. Legion, DuPage Club, Atlantis Divers. Home: 709 S Stone Ave La Grange IL 60525-2725 Office Phone: 312-876-3800. Office Fax: 312-876-3816. Business E-Mail: akerr@tishlerandwald.com.

KERR, DAVE, state official, marketing professional; m. Patty Kerr; children: Ryan, Dan. Degree in Biol. Sci., Psychology, Kans. State U., 1968; MBA, U. Kans., 1970. Leader com. on Econ. Devel., Edn.; mem. Kans. State Senate, 1984—2004, pres., 2000—04; chmn. Kans. Ethanol, LLC, 2007; pres. Hutchinson Reno County C. of C., 2007. Bd. dirs. Hutchinson Hosp. Corp., Reno County Mental Health Adv. Com.; with Hutchinson Hosp. Bd. Dirs., Bds. Leadership Hutchinson, Hutchinson C.of C., Healthy Families, Nickerson and Hutchinson HS booster clubs. Mem.: Kans. Tech. Enterprise Corp. (mem. bd. dirs. 1987—98), Republican Ctrl. Com. (sec. 1981—84), Kans. C. of C. and Industry, Kans. Farm Bur., Legis. Post Audit, Joint Pensions, Investments and Benefits (vice chmn.), Legis. Coordinating Coun. (chmn.), Interstate Coop. (chmn.), Ways and Means Com., Commerce Com., Calendar and Rules Com. (chmn.). Republican. Office: PO Box 2620 Hutchinson KS 67504

KERR, DAVID MILLS, state legislator; b. Pratt, Kans., May 4, 1945; s. Fred H. and Eleanor Mills (Barrett) K.; m. Mary Patricia O'Rourke, Aug. 24, 1979; children: Ryan, Daniel. BA, Kans. State U., 1968; MBA, U. Kans., 1970. Auditor Trans World Airlines, Kansas City, Mo., 1970-72, mgr. fin., 1972-76; pres. Agronomics Internat., Hutchinson, Kans., 1976-84; mem. Kans. State Senate, Topeka, 1984—2004, chmn. edn. com., 1992-95, chmn. ways and means com., chmn. joint budget com., 1996-2000, pres. state senate, 2001—04. Bd. dirs. Kans. Tech. Enterprises Corp., Health Care, Inc.; chmn. Senate econ. devel. com., 1988, edn. com., 1993, Senate ways and means com., 1995; chmn. com. on econ. devel. Nat. Conf. State Legislatures; mem. Gov.'s Criminal Justice Coordinating Coun., 1988. Mem. Advanced Tech. Commn., Topeka, 1985; chmn. Task Force on Capitol Markets and Tax, Topeka, 1986; bd. dirs. Hutchinson Hosp. Corp., 1993, Kansas, Inc. amed Kans. Exporter of Yr., Internat. Trade Inst., 1981. Mem. Kans. C. of C. (bd. dirs. 1983-86). Republican. Presbyterian. Avocations: travel, reading, golf, hunting, fishing. Home: 72 Willowbrook St Hutchinson KS 67502-8948 Office: PO Box 2620 Hutchinson KS 67504-2620 also: State Senate State Capital Topeka KS 66612

KERR, MICHAEL D., construction company executive; BSCE, Purdue U. With Huber, Hunt & Nichols Inc., Indpls., 1969—, from project engr., supt., project mgr., to exec. v.p., now pres., COO, 1999—. Mem. Associated Gen. Contractors, Indpls. Athletic Club.

KERR, SYLVIA JOANN, science educator; b. Detroit, June 19, 1941; d. Frederic Dilmus and Maud (Dirst) Pfeffer; widowed; children: David, Kathleen. BA, Carleton Coll., 1963; MS, U. Minn., 1966, PhD, 1968. Asst. prof. Augsburg Coll., Mpls., 1968-71; instr. Anoka Ramsey Community Coll., Coon Rapids, Minn., 1973-74; from asst. prof. to full prof. Hamline U., St. Paul, 1974—. Contbr. articles to profl. jour. NIH fellow U. Minn., 1972, 74-75. Office: Hamline U Dept Biology 1536 Hewitt Ave Saint Paul MN 55104-1205 E-mail: sKerr@piper.hamline.edu.

KERR, WILLIAM ANDREW, lawyer, educator; b. Harding, W.Va., Nov. 17, 1934; s. William James and Tocie Nyle (Morris) K.; m. Elizabeth Ann McMillin, Aug. 3, 1968 AB, W.Va. U., 1955, JD, 1957; LLM, Harvard U., 1958; BD, Duke U., 1968. Bar: W.Va. 1957, Pa. 1962, Ind. 1980. Assoc. McClintic, James, Wise and Robinson, Charleston, W.Va., 1958; assoc. Schnader, Harrison, Segal and Lewis, Phila., 1961-64; asst. prof. law Cleve. State U., 1966-67, assoc. prof. law, 1967—68; assoc. prof. law Ind. U., Indpls., 1968—69, 1972—74, prof., 1974—98, prof. emeritus, 1998—; contract atty. Indpls. Pub. Defender Agy., 1998—2007. Asst. U.S. atty. So. Dist. Ind., Indpls., 1969-72; exec. dir. Ind. Jud. Ctr., 1974-86; dir. research Ind. Pros. Attys. Council, 1972-74; mem. Ind. Criminal Law Study Commn., 1973-89, sec., 1973-83; reporter speedy trial com. U.S. Dist. Ct. (so. dist.) Ind., 1975-84; trustee Ind. Criminal Justice Inst., 1983-86; bd. dirs. Indpls. Lawyers Commn., 1975-77, Ind. Lawyers Commn., 1980-83; mem. records mgmt. com. Ind. Supreme Ct., 1983-86. Author: Indiana Criminal Procedure: Pretrial, 1991, Indiana Criminal Procedure: Trial, 2 vols., 1998. Bd. dirs. Ch. Fedn. Greater Indpls., 1979-87. Served to capt. JAGC, USAF, 1958-61. Decorated Air Force Commendation medal; Ford Found. fellow Harvard Law Sch., 1957-58; recipient Outstanding Prof. award Students Ind. U. Sch. Law, 1974, Disting. Service award Ind. Council Juvenile Ct. Judges, 1979, Outstanding Jud. Edn. Program award Nat. Council Juvenile and Family Ct. Judges, 1985. Mem. Ind. State Bar Assn., Indpls. Bar Assn., Phila. Bar Assn., W.Va. Bar Assn., Nat. Dist. Attys. Assn., Am. Judicature Soc., Fed. Bar Assn. (Outstanding Service award Indpls. chpt. 1975), Order of Coif, Phi Beta Kappa. Office: 55 Monument Cir Ste 1017 Indianapolis IN 46204-5901 Office Phone: 317-917-0608.

KERR, WILLIAM T., publishing and broadcast executive; b. Seattle, Apr. 17, 1941; m. Mary Lang, Oct. 15, 1966; 1 child, Susannah Gaskill Kerr Adler. BA, U. Wash., 1963, Oxford U., Eng., 1965; MA, Harvard U., 1967, MBA, 1969. V.p. Dillon Read & Co., NYC, London, 1969—73; cons. McKinsey & Co., NYC, 1973-79; v.p. New York Times Co., NYC, 1979-91; pres. New York Times Mag. Group, NYC, 1985-91; exec. v.p., pres. mag. group Meredith Corp., Des Moines, 1991-94, pres., chief oper. officer, bd. dirs., exec. com., 1994-96, pres., CEO, 1997-98, chmn., CEO, 1998—2006, chmn., 2006—. Bd. dirs. Prin. Fin. Group, Whirlpool Corp., Interpublic Group Cos., Arbitron, Inc.; trustee Oxford U. Press, Harvard Bus. Sch. Publs., Internat. Fedn. Periodical Press. Bd. dirs. Bus. Com. for Arts. Mem.: Lost Tree Club, Reform Club, Des Moines Club, Wakonda Club, Quogue Field Club, The Brook Club, Union Club, Century Assn. Roman Catholic. Office: Meredith Corp 1716 Locust St Des Moines IA 50309-3023

KERRIGAN, JOHN E., academic administrator; BA in Liberal Arts, Loras Coll., Iowa; BS in Civil Engring., U. Iowa, MA in Polit. Sci.; PhD in Polit. Sci., U. Colo.; HHD (hon.), U. City Manila, 1992; LLD (hon.), Loras Coll., 2004. Civil engr. Iowa City, 1958—61; asst. city mgr. City of Rock Island, Ill., 1961—64; city mgr. Aspen, Colo., 1964—66; program specialist, Nat. Ministry of Municipal and Rural Affairs The Ford Found., Amman, Jordan, 1966—68; adminstrv. rep. Beirut, 1966—68; asst. dir. Bur. Govtl. Affairs U. Colo., 1968—70; chmn., Pub. Affairs and Cmty. Svc. U. Oregon, 1970—75; dean, Coll. Pub. Affairs and Cmty. Svc. U. Nebr., Omaha, 1976—85; v.p acad. affairs U. Houston, Downtown, 1985—90; chancellor U. Wis., Oshkosh, 1990—2000; pres. Loras Coll., Dubuque, Iowa, 2002—04, pres. emeritus, 2004—. Contbr. Office Fax: 920-424-0853. Business E-Mail: kerrigan@uwosh.edu.

KERSEY, CLYDE R., state representative; b. Terre Haute, Ind., Nov. 4, 1937; married; 2 children. Grad., Ind. U., 1971, degree, 1974. Tchr. North Vigo (Ind.) H.S., 1972—; ret.; state rep. dist. 43 Ind. Ho. of Reps., Indpls., 1996—, chmn., sch. fin. subcom., chmn., ethics com., mem. edn., labor and employment, and ways and means coms. Served USAF and Air NG, 1960—68. Mem.: West Ctrl. Ind. Econ. Devel. Com., Vigo County Tchr. Assn., Ind. State Tchr. Assn., Leadership Terre Haute Class IX, Harry Truman Club. Democrat. Methodist. Office: Ind Ho of Reps 200 W Washington St Indianapolis IN 46204-2786

KERTÉSZ, IMRE, writer; b. Budapest, Hungary, Nov. 9, 1929; m. Magda Kertész. With Világosság, Budapest, Romania, 1948—51. Author: Sorstalanság, 1975, A nyomkereső: Két regény, 1977, A kudarc, 1988, Kaddis a meg nem született gyermekért, 1990, Az angol lobogó, 1991, Gályanapló, 1992, A holocaust mint kultúra: három előadás, 1993, Jegyzőkönyv, 1993, Valaki más: a változás krónikája, 1997, A gondolatnyi csend, amíg a kivégzőosztag újratölt, 1998, A száműzött nyelv, 2001; writer: (films) Fateless, 2005. Active Mil. Svc., 1951—53. Recipient Brandenburger Literaturpreis, 1995, Leipziger Buchpreis zur Europaischen Verstandigung, 1997, Herder-Preis, 2000, WELT-Literaturpreis, 2000, Ehrenpreis der Robert-Bosch-Stiftung, 2001, Hans Sahl-Preis, 2002, Nobel prize in Lit., 2002. Inmate: Auschwitz, Buchenwald, Zeitz 1944-45 Achievements include being first Hungarian to win Nobel Prize for Lit. Office: orthwestern U Press 625 Colfax St Evanston IL 60208-4210 Home: Berlin Germany also: Budapest Hungary

KESLER, JAY LEWIS, retired academic administrator; b. Barnes, Wis., Sept. 15, 1935; m. H. Jane Smith; children: Laura, Bruce, Terri. Student, Ball State U., 1953-54; BA, Taylor U., 1958, LHD (hon.), 1982; Dr. Divinity (hon.), Barrington Coll., 1977; DD (hon.), Asbury Theol. Sem., 1984, Anderson U., 1999; HHD (hon.), Huntington Coll., 1983; LHD, John Brown U., 1987; LLD (honoris causa), Gordon Coll., 1992; DD (hon.), Union U., 2000, Trinity Internat. U., 2001; LHD (honoris causa), So. Wesleyan U., 2002. Dir. Marion (Ind.) Youth for Christ, 1955-58, crusade staff evangelist, 1959-60, dir. Ill.-Ind. region, 1960-62, dir. coll. recruitment, 1962-63, v.p. pers., 1963-68, v.p. field coordination, 1968-73, pres., 1973-85, also bd. dirs.; pres. Taylor U., Upland, Ind., 1985-2000, chancellor, 2000—03, pres. emeritus, 2003—; tchg. pastor Upland Cmty. Ch., 2002—. Bd. dirs. Star Fin. Group, Christianity Today, Brotherhood Mut. Ins. Co., Nat. Ass. Evangs., Youth for Christ Internat., Youth for Christ U.S.A.; mem. bd. reference Christian Camps Inc.; mem. Council for Christian Colls. and Univs., bd. mem., 2001; chmn. United Christian Coll. Fund; mem. adv. bd. Christian Bible Soc.; co-pastor 1st Bapt. Ch., Geneva, 1972—85; mem. faculty Billy Graham Schs. Evangelism; lectr. Staley Disting. Christian Sch. Lecture Program; past gov.'s appointee Ind. Commn. on Youth; tchr. Upland Cmty. Ch., 2002—. Spkr. on Family Forum (daily radio show and radio program), 1973-98; mem. adv. com. Campus Life mag.; author: Let's Succeed With Our Teenagers, 1973, I Never Promised You a Disneyland, 1975, The Strong Weak People, 1976, Outside Disneyland, 1977, I Want a Home with No Problems, 1977, Growing Places, 1978, Too Big to Spank, 1978, Breakthrough, 1981, Parents & Teenagers, 1984 (Gold Medallion award), Family Forum, 1984, Making Life Make Sense, 1986, Parents and Children, 1986, Being Holy, Being Human, 1988, Ten Mistakes Parents Make With Teenagers (And How to Avoid Them), 1988, Is Your Marriage Really Worth Fighting For?, 1989, Energizing Your Teenagers' Faith, 1990, Raising Responsible Kids, 1991, Grandparenting: The Agony and the Ecstasy, 1993, Challenges for the College Bound, 1994, Emotionally Healthy Teenagers, 1998; contbr. articles to profl. jours. Bd. advisors Prison Fellowship Internat., Christian Camps Inc., Christian Educators Assn. Internat., Evangelicals for Social Action, Love and Action, Venture Middle East, Internat. Com. of Reference for New Life 2000. Named sr. fellow, Coun. Christian Coll., 2000, Sagamore of the Wabash, 2000; recipient Angel award, Religion in Media, 1985, Outstanding Youth Leadership award, Religious Heritage Am., 1989. Office: Taylor U Office Pres 236 W Reade Ave Upland IN 46989-1002

KESLER, STEPHEN EDWARD, geology educator; BS with honors, U. N.C., 1962; PhD, Stanford U., 1966. Asst. prof. econ. geology La. State U., Baton Rouge, 1966-70; assoc. prof. U. Toronto, Ont., Canada, 1970-77; prof. U. Mich., Ann Arbor, 1977—, assoc. chair, 1998—2007. Vis. scientist Nat. Inst. Geography, Guatemala, 1966-69, Consejo Recursos Minerales, Mexico City, 1974-75; with Dirección General Minas, Santo Domingo, 1983-84; cons. exploration for metallic and non-metallic mineral deposits. Author: Our Finite Mineral Resources, 1975; (with others) Economic Geology of Central Dominican Republic, 1984, Mineral Resources: Economics and the Environment, 1994; assoc. editor Econ. Geology, 1981-91, Ore Geology Revs., 1999-2005; mem. editl. bd. Jour. Geochem. Exploration, 1984-98. Pres. bd. trustees Lord of Light Luth. Ch., 1989-91. Fellow Geol. Soc. Am., Soc. Econ. Geologists (councillor 1983-86, internat. lectr. 1989-90, v.p. 1990-91, Thayer Lindsley lectr. 1994-95, pres. 1998-99, Penrose medal 2007); mem. Assn. Exploration Geochemists (councillor 1981-84), Soc. Mining Engrs. of AIME (program chmn. 1977). Lutheran. Office: U Mich Dept Geol Scis Ann Arbor MI 48109 Office Phone: 734-763-5057.

KESSEL, RICHARD GLEN, zoology educator; b. Fairfield, Iowa, July 19, 1931; BS in Chemistry summa cum laude, Parsons Coll., 1953; MS in Zoology and Physiology, U. Iowa, 1956, PhD in Zoology and Cytology, 1959; postgrad., Marine Biol. Lab., 1957. Trainee dept. anatomy Wake Forest U. Sch. Medicine, Winston-Salem, NC, 1959-60, Nat. Inst. Gen. Med. Sci. postdoctoral rsch. fellow, 1960-61, instr. anatomy, 1959-61, asst. prof., 1961; asst. prof. biology U. Iowa, Iowa City, 1961—64, assoc. prof., 1964-68, prof., 1968—97, prof.

emeritus, 1998—. Vis. investigator Hopkins Marine Sta., Pacific Grove, Calif., 1966; ind. investigator Marine Biol. Lab., Woods Hole, Mass., summers 1960, 62, 64. Author: (with C.Y. Shih) Scanning Electron Microscopy in Biology: A Students' Text-Atlas of Biological Organization, 1974, (with R.H. Kardon) Tissues and Organs: A Text-Atlas of Scanning Electron Microscopy, 1979, (with C.Y. Shih) Living Images, 1982, (with R. Roberts and H. Tung) Freeze Fracture Images of Cells and Tissues, 1991, Basic Medical Histology, 1998; assoc. editor Jour. Exptl. Zoology, 1978-82; mem. editorial bd. Jour. Submicroscopic Cytology, 1980—; mem. internat. bd. editors Scanning Electron Microscopy in Biology and Medicine; contbr. articles to profl. jours., chpts. to books Grantee USPHS, 1961-78, NSF, 1969-71, Whitehall Found., 1982-84; Bodine fellow; George Lincoln Seeley scholar; Nat Inst. Gen. Med. Sci.-USPHS, 1964-69; established endowed med. scholarship U. Iowa Coll. Medicine, established embryology course lecture Marine Biol. Lab., Woods Hole, Mass. Mem. AAAS, Am. Soc. Cell Biology, Am. Assn. Anatomists, Electron Micros. Soc. Am., Am. Physiol. Soc., Soc. Study of Reprodn., Am. Soc. Zoologists, Am. Inst. Biol. Sci., Soc. Devel. Biology, The 1847 Soc., Whitman Soc., Sigma Xi, Phi Kappa Phi, Beta Beta Beta. Office: Univ Iowa Dept Biol Scis Iowa City IA 52242

KESSINGER, MARGARET ANNE, medical educator; b. Beckley, W.Va., June 4, 1941; d. Clisby Theodore and Margaret Anne (Ellison) K.; m. Loyd Ernst Wegner, Nov. 27, 1971. MA, W.Va. U., 1963, MD, 1967. Diplomate Am. Bd. Internal Medicine and Med. Oncology. Internal medicine house officer U. Nebr. Med. Ctr., Omaha, 1967-70, fellow med. oncology, 1970-72, asst. prof. internal medicine, 1972-77, assoc. prof., 1977-90, prof., 1990—, assoc. chief oncology hematology sect., 1988-91, chief oncology hematology sect., 1991-99; assoc. dir. clin. rsch. U. Nebr. Med. Ctr./Eppley Cancer Ctr., Omaha, 1999—. Contbr. articles to profl. publs. Fellow ACP, Am. Assn. Cancer Edn.; mem. Am. Soc. Clin. Oncology, Am. Assn. Cancer Rsch., Internat. Soc. Exptl. Hematology, Am. Soc. Hematology, Sigma Xi, Alpha Omega Alpha. Republican. Methodist. Avocations: aviation, gardening, canning, skiing. Office: U Nebr Med Ctr 987680 Nebraska Med Ctr Omaha E 68198-0001 E-mail: makessin@unmc.edu.

KESSLER, JOAN F., judge, lawyer; b. June 25, 1943; m. Frederick P. Kessler, Sept. 1966; 2 children. BA, U. Kans., 1961-65; postgrad., U. Wis., 1965-66; JD cum laude, Marquette U., 1968. Law clk. Hon. John W. Reynolds U.S. Dist. Ct. (ea. dist.) Wis., Milw., 1968—69; assoc. Warschafsky, Rotter & Tarnoff, Milw., 1969-71; pvt. practice Milw., 1971-74; assoc. Cook & Franke, S.C., Milw., 1974-78; U.S. atty. Eastern Dist. Wis., Milw., 1978-81; ptnr. Foley & Lardner, Milw., 1981—2004; judge Ct. Appeals Wisc., Milw., 2004—. Lectr. profl. responsibility U. Wis. Law Sch., Marquette U. Law Sch., Milw., 1994-96; bd. govs. State Bar of Wis., 1985-95, chair, 1993, bd. dirs. family law sect., 1991-94; mem. Jud. Coun. Wis., Madison, 1989-92; mem. Milw. Bd. Attys. Profl. Responsibility, 1979-85. Bd. dirs. Legal Aid Soc., 1974-78, v.p., 1978, Urban League, 1980-82, Women's Bus. Initiative Corp., 1989-91, Girl Scouts U.S., Milw., 1994-96; bd. dirs., pres. Voters for Choice in Wis., 1989-93. Fellow Am. Matrimonial Lawyers (bd. govs. 1990-96, v.p. 1996-99), Am. Bar Found.; mem. ABA (chair sect. individual rights and responsibilities 2003-04, coun. mem. 1997-2004, editor Human Rights 1997-99), ACLU. Office: Judge Ct Appeals Wis 633 W Wisconsin Milwaukee WI 53203 Office Phone: 414-227-4684. E-mail: joan.kessler@wicourts.gov.

KESSLER, JOHN WHITAKER, real estate developer; b. Cin., Mar. 7, 1936; s. Charles Wilmont and Elisabeth (Whitaker) K.; m. Charlotte Hamilton Power, Aug. 8, 1964; children: Catherine, Elizabeth, Jane. BS, Ohio State U., 1958. Mem. sales dept. Armstrong Cork Co., Lancaster, Pa., 1958-59; mgr. spl. products div. M & R Dietetics Labs., Columbus, Ohio, 1959-62; co-founder, mng. partner Multicon, Columbus, 1962-70; pres. Multicon Communities div. Multicon Properties, Inc., 1970-72; prin. John W. Kessler Co., Columbus, 1972—; chmn. Marsh & McLennan Real Estate Advisors Inc., 1980—, New Albany Co., 1991—. Bd. dir. Bank One Corp., Abercrombie & Fitch. Office: New Albany Co PO Box 772 New Albany OH 43054-0772

KESSLER, PHILIP JOEL, lawyer; b. Detroit, Nov. 15, 1947; s. Herbert Jerome and Mary Rita (Bloomgarden) K.; m. Ruth Ann Kessler, Dec. 22, 1968 (div. 1981); children: Herbert Jeffrey, Jennifer Ann; m. Mary Ray Brophy, Jan. 29, 1988. AB in English with distinction, U. Mich., 1969; JD, U. Calif., Berkeley, 1972. Bar: Mich. 1972, U.S. Dist. Ct. (ea. dist.) Mich. 1972, U.S. Ct. Appeals (6th cir.) 1976, U.S. Dist. Ct. (no. dist.) Tex. 1990, U.S. Tax Ct. 1990. Assoc. Butzel Long Gust Klein & Van Zile, Detroit, 1972-79, ptnr., 1979-82; shareholder Butzel Long (and predecessor firms), 1982—, chmn., 2006—. Legal rsch. tchg. fellow Detroit Coll. Law, 1975-77; asst. prof. law 1977-85; lectr. in field; local rules adv. com. U.S. Dist. Ct. for Ea. Dist. Mich., mem. 1991-95, chair 1994-95; life mem. Jud. Conf. U.S. Ct. Appeals for 6th Cir.; bd. dirs. The Beaumont Found., 1995-96, THAW Fund, 1995—. Mem. Founders Soc. Detroit Inst. Arts, 1988—. Fellow Am. Bar Found., Am. Coll. Trial Lawyers, Internat. Soc. BarristersMich. Bar Found.; mem. Detroit Athletic Club, Franklin (Mich.) Hills Country Club. Avocation: golf. Office: Butzel Long 150 W Jefferson Ave Ste 100 Detroit MI 48226 Office Phone: 313-225-7018. Business E-Mail: kessler@butzel.com.

KESSLER, ROBERT W., municipal official; BA in Urban Studies, U. Minn., St. Paul, 1974; MPA in Housing, Comty. Devel., U. So. Calif., Washington, Pub. Affairs Ctr., 1981; postgrad. studies in Project Mgmt., Program Evaluation U. Minn., 1978-94. City planner Office of the Mayor, St. Paul, Minn., 1973-74; devel. grant asst., comty. devel. divsn. City of St. Paul, 1975-80; program analyst HUD, Washington, 1980-81; asst. to chief of staff Mayor's Office City of St. Paul, 1982; comty. devel. specialist City of St. Paul, 1982-83, econ. devel. specialist neighborhood divsn., 1983-86; dir. St. Paul 503 Devel. Co., 1986-87; asst. to mayor City of St. Paul, 1987-88, dir. Mayor's info. and complaint office, 1988-90, license and permit mgr., 1990-92, dir. Office Lic., Inspections and Environ. Protection, 1992—. With U.S. Army Med. Bn., Vietnam, 1969-70. Decorated Bronze Star, U.S. Army, 1970. Mem. Internat. City/County Mgmt. Assn. (affiliate). Home: 2190 Dahl Ave Saint Paul MN 55119-5877 Office: Lics Inspections & Environ Protection 350 Saint Peter St Ste 300 Saint Paul MN 55102-1510

KESSLER, WILLIAM EUGENE, healthcare executive; b. St. Louis, Dec. 15, 1944; s. Joseph John and Margaret Mary (Burns) K.; m. Patricia Christine Wilson, Nov. 9, 1968; children: Christina, William, John, Timothy, Jennifer, Catherine, Joseph, Daniel. BS in Commerce, St. Louis U., 1966, MHA, 1968. Various positions St. John's Hosp., St. Louis, 1963-67; adminstrv. resident St. Mary's Hosp., Grand Rapids, Mich., 1967-68; pres. St. Anthony's Health Ctr., Alton, Ill., 1971—. Chmn., prof. and tech. adv. com. Joint Commn. on Accreditation Healthcare Orgn., 1990-94; speaker profl. and community settings, 1972—; preceptor St. Louis U., 1980—, U. Mo., Columbia, 1991; bd. dir. Hosp. Assn. Met. St. Louis, 1975-85. Contbr. articles to profl. jour., 1972—. Admissions advisor US Mil. Acad., 1973-83; treas., bd. dir. Cath. Childrens' Home Alton, 1981-89; v.p. diocesan bd. edn. Diocese of Springfield, Ill., 1981-82, pres. 1982-84, mem. bd. edn. 1986-92; mem. diocesan fin. coun., 1987—; chmn. ARC, Alton, 1983-85; bd. dir. Am. Cancer Soc., Alton, 1984-90; pres. St. Louis Metropolitan Hosp. Coun., 1996. Served to capt. US Army, 1968-71. Decorated Army Commendation medal; recipient Alton Jaycees Disting. Svc. award, Alumni Merit award St. Louis U., 1994; named Knight of the Equestrian Order of the Holy Sepulchre, 1997; recipient Pro Ecclesia et Pontifice Cross Pope John Paul II, 2002, Mercy H.S., Alumni Merit award, 2002. Fellow: Am. Coll. Healthcare Execs. (regent's adv. coun. 1987—93, nominating com. 1991—94, regent 2002, chair ethics com., Regent's award, Sr. Healthcare Exec. of the Yr. award 1993); mem.: Southwestern Ill. Indsl. Assn. (exec. com. 1983—88, bd. dirs. 1989—, chmn. 1997), St. Louis U. Hosp. Administrn. Alumni Assn. (pres. 1978), Cath. Health Assn. U.S.A. (bd. dirs. 1987—, exec. com. 1989—92, chmn.-elect 1990—, chair 1991), Ill. Hosp. Assn. (exec. com. 1981—86, chmn. 1984—85), Am. Hosp. Assn. (Ho. of Dels. 1984—88), Stadium (St. Louis), Stadium Club (St. Louis), Rotary (pres. Alton chpt. 1981-82, Paul Harris fellow 1985), Rotary (pres. Alton chpt. 1981—82, Paul Harris fellow 1979, 1985). Avocations: photography, sports, family travel. Home: 1216 N Hanser Ln Godfrey IL 62035-1840 also: St Clare's Hosp 915 E 5th St Alton IL 62002-6434 Office: Saint Ambrose Parish 820 W Homer Adams Parkway Godfrey IL 62035

KESTELL, STEVEN G., state representative; b. Plymouth, Wis., June 15, 1955; m. LuAnne Kestell; children: Joshua, Benjamin, Travis. Grad., Plymouth H.S., 1973. Retail mgmt., 1976—97; sales mgr., 1997—98; state assembly mem. Wis. State Assembly, Madison, 1998—, chair, children and families com., mem. agr., edn., family law, and small bus. and consumer affairs coms., mem. child abuse and neglect prevention bd. Legis. mem. Commn. on Hwy. Safety, Madison, Wis. Bd. mem. Family Resource Ctr. Mem.: Wis. Farm Bur., Sheboygan County Hist. Soc., Plymouth Morning Kiwanis. Republican. Office: State Capitol Rm 17W PO Box 8952 Madison WI 53708-8952

KESTNER, ROBERT STEVEN, lawyer; b. St. Louis, Aug. 6, 1954; s. Robert Steven Sr. and Josephine Ann (LiPuma) K.; m. Denise Marie Dalhart, Apr. 25, 1981; children: Alexander, Jonathan, Joseph. BA in Mathematics & Economics, Ohio Wesleyan U., 1976; JD, Ohio State U., 1979. Bar: Ohio 1979, U.S. Dist. Ct. (no. dist.) Ohio 1979. Assoc. Baker & Hostetler, Cleve., 1979—88, ptnr., gen. bus. practice coord., 1988—2003, exec. ptnr., mem. policy com., 2003—. Mem. exec. campaign cabinet United Way; bd. dirs. Greater Cleve. Partnership. Mem. ABA, Ohio Bar Assn., Cleve. Bar Assn., Cleve. Mus. of Art (bd. regents), The Country Club, Pepper Pike. Office: Baker & Hostetler LLP 1900 E Ninth St Cleveland OH 44114-3485 Office Phone: 216-861-7558. Office Fax: 216-696-0740. Business E-Mail: skestner@bakerlaw.com.

KETEFIAN, SHAKÉ, nursing educator; d. Krikor and Zaghganoush (Soghomonian) K. BSN, Am. U. Beirut, 1963; MEd, Columbia U., 1968, EdD, 1972. From asst. prof. nursing to prof. NYU Sch. Edn., Health, Nursing and Arts Professions, NYC, 1972-84; dir. continuing edn. in nursing NYU, NYC; with U. Mich., 1984—; prof., assoc. dean for grad. studies, dir. doctoral and postdoctoral studies U. Mich. Sch. Nursing, Ann Arbor, 1984—91, dir. internat. affairs, 1996—, acting dean, 1991-92. Contbr. articles to profl. jours. Fellow AAUW, Am. Acad. Nursing (governing coun.); mem. ANA, Midwest Nursing Rsch. Soc. (chair sci. integrity task force 1994-96, 2001-03), NC Nurses Assn., Internat. Network for Doctoral Edn. in Nursing (co-founder, pres.), Sigma Theta Tau Internat. Office: U Mich Sch Nursing 400 N Ingalls Ann Arbor MI 48109 Home Phone: 734-665-0094; Office Phone: 734-763-6669. Business E-Mail: ketefian@umich.edu.

KETTELER, THOMAS R., retail executive; CPA, ptnr. Alexander Grant & Co.; v.p. fin. Schottenstein Stores Corp., 1981—2000, dir., 1985—2000, COO, 1995—2000; dir. Am. Eagle Outfitters, Columbus, Ohio, 1994—2003, exec. v.p. fin., treas., 2000—. Office: Schottenstein Stores Corp 1800 Moler Rd Columbus OH 43207-1680

KETTERING, STEVE, state senator; b. July 1943; Rep. Iowa State House, 1998—2002; mem. Iowa State Senate, DesMoines, 2003—, mem. bus. and labor rels. com., mem. commerce com., mem. judiciary com., mem. natural resources and environment com., mem. transp. com. Republican. Office: State Capitol Bldg East 12th and Grand Des Moines IA 50319 Home: 275 Crescent Park Dr Lake View IA 51450-0428

KETTERSON, ELLEN D., biologist, educator; b. Orange, NJ, Aug. 9, 1945; d. John B. and Lois (Meadows) K.; m. Val Nolan, Jr., Oct. 17, 1980. BA in Botany, Ind. U., 1966, MA in Botany, 1968, PhD in Zoology, 1974. NIH fellow Wash. State U., 1975-77; asst. prof. biol. scis. Bowling Green State U., 1975-77; vis. asst. prof. to asst. prof. biology Ind. U., Bloomington, 1977-84, from assoc. prof. to prof. biology, 1984—, co-dir. Ctr. for Integrative Study Animal Behavior, 1990—2002. Vis. scientist Purdue U., Lafayette, Ind., 1991, Rockefeller U., 1985, U. Va., 1984. Mem. editl. bd. Current Ornithology, 1989—, editor, 1994-98; mem. editl. bd. Animal Behaviour, 1997—, assoc. editor, 1991-94; mem. editl. bd. Evolution, 1994, editor, 1994-99; editor: Jour. Avian Biology, 1999—2004. NSF Rsch. grants, 1978—; Guggenheim fellow, 2004. Fellow Am. Ornithologists Union (v.p. 1995-96, coun. 1988-91, Elliot Coues award 1996), Animal Behavior Soc. (Exemplar award 2004), Royal Soc. London (sci. editor Proced 2005—); mem. AAAS, Internat. Ornithol. Com., Ecol. Soc. Am., Am. Soc. aturalists, Assn. Field Ornithologists, Cooper Ornithol. Soc., Soc. Conservation Biology, Soc. Study of Evolution, Soc. Integrative and Comparative Biology, Soc. Behavioral Neuroendocrinology, Wilson Ornithol. Soc. (Margaret M. Nice award 1998), Sigma Xi. Office: Indiana U Dept Biology Bloomington IN 47405 E-mail: ketterso@indiana.edu.

KEVOIAN, BOB, radio personality; b. 1950; Grad., Long Beach State U., 1973. Radio host WFBQ-FM, Indpls., 1983—; nat. syndicated host Premiere Radio Networks, 1995—. Co-host The Bob & Tom Show, 1983—. Co-recipient Radio Personality of Yr. award, Billboard, 1991—98, Marconi Radio award, Nat. Assn. Broadcasters, 1993, 1995, 1997, 1999, Marconi Radio award for Network Syndicated Personality of Yr., 2006. The Sagamore of the Wabash, 1994, Nat. Chmn.'s Citation award, Leukemia Soc. Am., 1996. Office: WFBQ 6161 Fall Creek Rd Indianapolis IN 46220

KEY, ANNIE L., state representative; b. Camden, Ala. 1 child, Stephanie. Degree, Cuyahoga C.C., Cleve. State U. Mem. econ. devel. and small bus. com. Ho. Reps., mem. bus. com., mem. retirement and aging com., mem. trans. and pub. safety com. Mem. adv. bd. Hough Neighborhood Empowerment Zone; mem. Nat. Coun. egro Women, Inc.; area v.p. St. Clair/Superior Coalition; mem. Sch. Cmty. Coun.; exec. bd. mem. Cuyahoga County Dem. Party; mem. Cuyahoga County Women's Polit. Caucus. Office: House of Representatives 77 South High St 10th Floor Columbus OH 43215-6111

KEY, JACK DAYTON, librarian; b. Enid, Okla., Feb. 24, 1934; s. Ernest Dayton and Janie (Haldeman) K.; m. Virgie Ruth Richardson, Aug. 12, 1956; children— Toni, Scot, Todd. BA, Phillips U., Enid, Okla., 1958; MA, U. N.Mex., 1960; MS, U. Ill., 1962. Staff supr. Grad. Library U. Ill., 1960-62; pharmacy librarian U. Iowa, 1962-64; med. librarian Lovelace Found. for Med. Edn. and Research, Albuquerque, 1965-70; dir. Mayo Med. Ctr. Librs., Rochester, Minn., 1970-94, dir. emeritus, 1994—; prof. emeritus biomed. comm. Mayo Med. Sch. Cons. in field; participant Naval War Coll. Conf., 1979; Alberta A. Brown lectr. Western Mich. U., 1979 Author: The Origin of the Vaccine Inoculation by Edward Jenner, 1977, William Alexander Hammond (1828-1900), 1979; editor: Library Automation: The Orient and South Pacific, 1975, Automated Activities in Health Sciences Libraries, 1975-78, Classics and Other Selected Readings in Medical Librarianship, 1980, Journal of a Quest for the Elusive Doctor Arthur Conan Doyle, 1982, Medical Vanities, 1982, William A. Hammond, M.D., 1828-1900: The Publications of an American Neurologist, 1983, Classics in Cardiology, Vol. 3, 1983, Vol. 4, 1989, Medical Casebook of Dr. Arthur Conan Doyle from Practitioner to Sherlock Holmes and Beyond, 1984, Medicine, Literature and Eponyms: An Encyclopedia of Medical Eponyms Derived from Literary Characters, 1989, Conan Doyle's Tales of Medical Humanism and Values, 1992; contbr. articles to profl. jours. Served with USN, 1952-55. U. N.Mex. fellow, 1958-59, N.Mex. Library Assn. Marion Dorroh Meml. scholar, 1960, Rotary Paul Harris fellow, 1979; recipient Outstanding Hist. Writing award Minn. Medicine, 1980, Spl. Svc. award Am. Acad. Dermatology, 1992, Farthing award Baker St. Jour., 1993; decorated knight Icelandic Order of Falcon, 1980; named to Phillips U. Hall Fame, 1988. Mem. Med. Library Assn., Am. Inst. History Pharmacy, Am. Assn. History Medicine, Am. Med. Writers Assn., Am. Osler Soc. (pres. 1990-91), Mystery Writers of Am., Alcuin Soc., Baker St. Irregulars, Ampersand Club, Sigma Xi (cert. of recognition 1982) Mem. Christian Ch. (Disciples Of Christ). Home: PO Box 231 54 Skyline Dr Sandia Park NM 87047-0231 Office: Mayo Clinic Rochester MN 55905-0001 Office Phone: 507-284-2691.

KEYES, JAMES HENRY, manufacturing executive; b. LaCrosse, Wis., Sept. 2, 1940; s. Donald M. and Mary M. (Nodolf) K.; m. Judith Ann Carney, Nov. 21, 1964; children: James Patrick, Kevin, Timothy. BS, Marquette U., 1962; MBA, Northwestern U., 1963. Instr. Marquette U., Milw., 1963-65; CPA Peat. Marwick & Mitchell, Milw., 1965-66; with Johnson Controls, Inc., Milw., 1967—, mgr. sys. dept., 1967-71, divsn. contr., 1971-73, corp. contr., treas., 1973-77, v.p., CFO, 1977-85, exec. v.p., 1985-86, pres., 1986-99, chief operating officer, 1986-88, chief exec. officer, 1988—2002, chmn. bd. dirs., 1993—. Bd. dirs. Baird Capital Devel. Fund. 1st Wis. Trust Co., LSI Logic, Inc., Universal Foods Corp. Active Milw. Symphony Orch., 1980—. Mem. Fin. Execs. Inst., Am. Inst. CPA's, Wis. Inst. CPA's., Machinery and Allied Products Inst. Office: Johnson Controls Inc 5757 N Green Bay Ave Milwaukee WI 53209-4408

KEYES, JEFFREY J., lawyer; BA magna cum laude, U. Notre Dame, 1968; JD cum laude, U. Mich., 1972. Bar: Minn. 1972. Shareholder Briggs and Morgan, P.A., Mpls.; fellow Am. Coll. Trial Lawyers, Mpls. Mem. Gov.'s Task Force on Tort Reform, 1986; chmn. fed. practice com. U.S. Dist. Ct. Minn., 1990-93, 2002—, chmn. adv. group on civil justice reform act, 1991-93; trainer U.S. Magistrate Judges Tng. Conf. on Settlement, Mpls., 1992; lectr. in field. Contbr. articles to law jours. Chmn. bd. dirs. The Playwright's Ctr. Mem. ABA (chmn. antitrust sect. franchise com. 1989-90, contbg. editor Antitrust Monograph 1987, co-editor Antitrust Sect. State Antitrust Law Handbook, Minn. chpt. 1990), Minn. State Bar Assn. (co-chair Women in the Legal Profn. task force 1996-97, chmn. civil litigation sect. 1985-86), Hennepin County Bar Assn. Office: Briggs & Morgan 80 S 8th St 2200 Minneapolis MN 55402-2157

KEYS, ARLANDER, federal judge; b. 1943; BA, DePaul U., 1972, JD, 1975. Trial atty. Nat. Labor Rels. Bd., 1975-80; regional atty. Fed. Labor Rels. Authority, Chgo., 1980-86; adminstrv. law judge SSA, Dept. of HHS, 1986-88, chief adminstrv. law judge, 1988-95; magistrate judge U.S. Dist. Ct. (no. dist.) Ill., 1995—, presiding magistrate judge, 1998—2004. With USMC, 1963—67. Mem. ABA, FBA (past pres. Chgo. chpt.), Ill. Jud. Coun., Chgo. Bar Assn., Cook County Bar Assn., 7th Cir. Bar Assn., Just the Beginning Found. Office: US Dist Ct 219 S Dearborn St Ste 2240 Chicago IL 60604-1802 Office Phone: 312-435-5630. Fax: 312-554-8546.

KEYSER, RICHARD LEE, distribution company executive; b. Harrisburg, Pa., Oct. 28, 1942; s. Harold L. and Mary J. K.; m. Mary Ellen Carter, June 20, 1964; children: Jeffrey, Jennifer. BS, U.S. Naval Acad., 1964; MBA, Harvard U., 1971. Commd. ensign USN, 1964, advanced through grades to lt., 1966; resigned, 1969; mktg.-analysis mgr. Fleetguard, Inc., Dallas, 1971-72, dir. logistics Cookeville, Tenn., 1973-77; gen. mgr. parts ops. Cummins Engine Co., Inc., Columbus, Ind., 1977-83, exec. dir. mktg. ops., 1983-84; pres. NL-Hycalog, Houston, 1984-86; v.p. ops. W.W. Grainger, Inc., Chgo., 1986-87, exec. v.p., 1988-90, pres., COO, 1991—95, pres., CEO, 1995—97, chmn., CEO, 1997—. Bd. dirs. Morton Internat. County chmn. blood program ARC, Cookeville, 1976-77; bd. dirs. Preserve To Enjoy, Inc., Columbus, 1983-84, Irene Josselyn Clinic, Northfield, Ill., 1989-92, Lake Forest Grad. Sch. Mgmt., 1992—, Evanston Hosp. Corp., 1996—. Former lt. comdr. USNR. Fellow Am. Prodn. and Inventory Control Soc. (cert.); mem. Chgo. Club, Harvard Bus. Sch. Club Chgo. (v.p. 1988-89, pres. 1989-90), Comml. Club Chgo. Office: WW Grainger Inc 100 Grainger Pkwy Lake Forest IL 60045-5201*

KHABIBULIN, NIKOLAI, professional hockey player; b. Sverdlovsk, Russia, Jan. 13, 1973; Goaltender Winnipeg Jets (now Phoenix Coyotes), 1994—96, Phoenix Coyotes, 1996—99, Long Beach Ice Dogs (IHL), 1999—2000, Tampa Bay Lightning, 2001—05, Chicago Blackhawks, 2005—. Goaltender Team Russia, World Cup of Hockey Tournament, 1996, Team Russia, Olympic Games, Salt Lake City, 2002. Co-recipient James Gatschene Memorial Trophy (MVP), IHL, 2000; named to NHL All-Star Game, 1998, 1999, 2002, 2003. Achievements include being a member of Stanley Cup Champion Tampa Bay Lightning, 2004. Office: c/o Chicago Blackhawks 1901 W Madison St Chicago IL 60612

KHANDEKAR, JANARDAN DINKAR, oncologist, educator; b. Indore, India, Feb. 1, 1944; came to U.S., 1971; s. Dinker and Sulaochan (Dawlae) K.; m. Amita Oomen, Aug. 28, 1971; children: Manoj, Melin. MD, MBBS, U. Indore, 1969; sabbatical, Northwestern U., Baylor U., 1992. Diplomate Am. Bd. Internal Medicine, Am. Bd. Med. Oncology. Intern M.Y. Hosp., Indore, 1967-70; resident in medicine Allegheny Gen. Hosp., Pitts., 1972-73; head divsn. med. oncology Evanston (Ill.) Hosp., 1975-98, from asst. attending physician to assoc. attending physician, 1975-79, sr. attending physician, 1979—; fellow Med. Rsch. Coun., Montréal, Que., Canada, 1970-71, Tufts U., Boston, 1973-75; asst. prof. medicine Northwestern U., Chgo., 1975-80, assoc. prof., 1980-86, prof. medicine, 1986—, Kellogg/Scanlon chair in oncology, 1991-98; dir. cancer control Northwestern U. Cancer Ctr., Chgo., 1991—; assoc. dir. Kellogg Cancer Care Ctr. Evanston Hosp., 1979-87, dir., 1987—; Louise Coon chmn. dept. medicine Evanston Northwestern Healthcare, 1998—. Active NIH Ad Hoc Com. on Nat. Prostate Cancer Program, NIH Team for Audit Clin. Trials at Yale U., Roswell Park Meml. Inst., Mayo Clinic, etc.; chmn. rsch. com. and adv. com. Searle Clin. Pharmacology Unit; sr. investigator Eastern Coop. Oncology Group, 1976-83, Community Clin. Oncology Program, 1983—; lectr. in field. Author (with others): (novels) Radiation-Associated Thyroid Carcinoma, 1977, Adjuvant Therapy of Cancer, 1977; editor: (Archives) of Internal Medicine, 2004; contbr. articles. Recipient cert. of merit Nat. Cancer Inst. Humanitarian award Cancer Wellness Ctr., 2003; grantee Ill. Cancer Coun., 1983-98, Duke U., 1983-90, Nat. Cancer Inst., 1983—, Women's Health Inst., 1993, Evanston Hosp., 1993—, NIH, 1988-91, 93—. Fellow ACP (laureate); mem. AAAS, Am. Soc. Clin. Oncology, Am. Fedn. Clin. Rsch., Am. Assn. Cancer Rsch., Inst. Medicine (Chgo.). Office: Evanston Hosp 2650 Ridge Ave Evanston IL 60201-1781

KHOURY, GEORGE GILBERT, printing company executive, sports association executive; b. St. Louis, July 30, 1923; s. George Michael and Dorothy (Smith) K.; m. Colleen E. Khoury Czerny, Apr. 3, 1948; children: Colleen Ann, George Gilbert. Grad., St. Louis U., 1946. V.p. Khoury Bros. Printing, St. Louis, 1946—; exec. dir. George Khoury Assn. Baseball Leagues, Inc., St. Louis, 1967—. Author: (novel) Brothers Baseball Bombshells, 2003. Served with U.S. Army, 1943-45, NATOUSA, MTO. Decorated Purple Heart with oak leaf cluster. Roman Catholic. Office: George Khoury Assn Baseball Leagues 5400 Meramec Bottom Rd Saint Louis MO 63128-4624 Personal E-mail: czernyce@msn.com.

KIBBIE, JOHN, state legislator; b. Palo Alto County, Iowa, July 14, 1929; m. Kathryn Kibbie; 6 children. Farmer; mem. Iowa Ho. of Reps., Des Moines, 1960-64, Iowa Senate, Des Moines, 1964-68, 88—; mem. nat. conv. platform com., 1968; mem. agr. com., mem. natural resources and environment com.; ranking mem. state govt. com.; mem. transp. com. Mem. Sacred Heart Ch.; trustee Kerber Milling Co.; bd. dirs. Benton Banks of Palo Alto County; bd. pres. Iowa Lake C.C.; former mediator Iowa Mediation Svc. With U.S. Army, Korea, 1951-53. Mem. VFW, Nat. Corn Growers, Farm Bur., Pork Prodrs., Iowa Soybean Assn., Pheasant Forever, Cattlemen's Assn., Farmer's Union, KC (dir. Ayrshire chpt.), Am. Legion, Moose. Democrat. Office: State Capitol 9th And Grand Ave Des Moines IA 50319-0001 E-mail: john_kibbie@legis.state.ia.us.

KIDDER, C. ROBERT, finance company executive; b. 1943; BSIE, U. Mich., 1966; MS, Iowa State U., 1968. With Ford Motor Co., Detroit, 1968-69, McKinsey & Co., NYC, 1972-78, Dart Industries, 1978-80, Duracell Europe, 1980-81, Duracell Internat. Inc., 1981-95, pres., CEO, 1988-95, past chmn., CEO; chmn., CEO Borden, Inc., Columbus, Ohio, 1995—2002, chmn., 2002—04; pres. Borden Capital Inc., 2001—03; prin. Stonehenge Partners Inc., 2004—06; chmn. CEO 3Stone Advisors LLC, Columbus, Ohio, 2006—. Dir. Morgan Stanley. Bd. trustees Ohio U., 2003—. With USN, 1969—72. Office: 3Stone Advisors LLC Ste 600 191 W Nationwide Blvd Columbus OH 43215

KIDDER, FRED DOCKSTATER, retired lawyer; b. Cleve., May 22, 1922; s. Howard Lorin and Virgina (Milligan) K.; m. Eleanor (Hap) Kidder; children— Fred D. III, Barbara Anne Donelson, Jeanne Louise Haffeman. BS with distinction, U. Akron, 1948; JD, Case Western Res. U., 1950. Bar: Ohio 1950, Tex. 1985, U.S. Dist. Ct. (no. dist.) Ohio 1950, U.S. Dist. Ct. (no. dist.) Tex. 1985. Assoc. Arter & Hadden and predecessors, Cleve., 1950-79, ptnr., 1960-79, Jones Day and predecessors, Cleve., 1980-89, regional mng. ptnr. Tex., 1985-86; gen. counsel Lubrizol Corp., Cleve., 1989-92, spl. counsel, 1993—2003; gen. counsel Lubrizol Found., 2003—. Gen. counsel The Lubrizol Found., 2003—; mem. Am. Soc. Corp. Secs. Contbr. articles to profl. jours. Trustee Ohio Found. Ind. Colls., 2004—; gen. coun. Lubrizol Found., 2003—; past pres. Estate Planning Coun.; past co-chmn. bd. trustees Lake Erie Coll.; past trustee, v.p., Alzheimer's Assn., Cleve.; trustee, sec. Cleve. Sight Ctr.; trustee Bus. Advisors Cleve.; past alumni coun. U. Akron; past. corp. coun. Dallas Mus. Art; past pres. Case Western Reserve U. Law Sch. Alumni Assn.; past chmn. Shaker Heights Recreation Bd. Mem. ABA, Tex. Bar Assn., Ohio State Bar Assn., Cleve. Bar Assn., Ohio Fedn. Ind. Colls. (trustee), Estate Planning Coun. (past pres.), Blue Coats, Soc. Benchers (past chmn.), The Country Club, Cleve. Skating Club, Tax Club Cleve. (past pres.), Order of Coif, Ct. of Nisi Prius (former judge), Pepper Pike Club (past sec.), Phi Eta Sigma, Beta Delta Psi, Phi Sigma Alpha, Phi Delta Theta, Phi Delta Phi. Office: Lubrizol Foundation Wickliffe OH 44092-2298

KIDDER, JOSEPH P., city service director; b. Akron, Ohio; m. Vicki Kidder; children: Raechel, Paul. Degree in acctg., U. Akron, 1980. Ward 6 councilman City of Akron, 1984-92, svc. dir., 1992—. Past chmn. budget and fin. com., Akron City Coun. Office: Office of Svc Dir Mcpl Bldg 166 S High St Rm 201 Akron OH 44308-1628

KIECOLT-GLASER, JANICE KAY, psychologist; b. Okla. City, Okla., June 30, 1951; d. Edward Harold and Vergie Mae (Lively) Kiecolt; m. Ronald Glaser, Jan. 18, 1980. BA in Psychology with honors, U. Okla., 1972; PhD in Clin. Psychology, U. Miami, 1976. Lic. psychologist, Ohio. Clin. psychology intern Baylor U. Coll. Medicine, Houston, 1974-75; postdoctoral fellow in adult clin. psychology U. Rochester, N.Y., 1976-78; asst. prof. psychiatry Ohio State U. Coll. Medicine, Columbus, 1978-84, assoc. prof. psychiatry and psychology, 1984-89, prof. psychiatry and psychology, 1989—, dir. divsn. health psychology, 1994—, active various coms. Mem. AIDS study sect. NIMH, 1988-91. Editl. bd. Brain, Behavior and Immunity jour., 1986—, Health Psychology jour., 1989—, Brit. Jour. Health Psychology, 1996—, Jour. Behavioral Medicine, 1994—, Psychosomatic Medicine, 1990—, Jour. Cons. and Clin. Psychology, 1992—, Jour. Gerontology, 1992—; reviewer Jour. Personality and Social Psychology, Psychiatry Rsch. jour.; author: Detecting Lies, 1997, Unconscious Truths, 1998, Handbook of Human Stress and Immunity, 1994; contbr. articles to profl. jours., chpts. to books. NIMH grantee, 1985—; recipient Merit award NIMH, 1993; Ohio State Disting. scholar, 1994, Devel. Health Psychology award, Divsn. Health Psychology and Adult Devel. and Aging, Norman Cousins award, Psychoneuroimmunology Rsch. Soc., 1998. Fellow Am. Psychol. Assn. (Outstanding Contbns. award 1988), Acad. Behavioral Medicine Rsch.; mem. Phi Beta Kappa, Inst. Medicine. Avocations: jogging, fiction writing. Office: Ohio State U Coll Medicine Dept Psychiatry 1670 Upham Dr Columbus OH 43210

KIEFER, GARY, newspaper editor; Mng. editor features Columbus (Ohio) Dispatch. Office: Columbus Dispatch 34 S 3rd St Columbus OH 43215-4241

KIEFFER, SUSAN WERNER, geologist, educator, media consultant; b. Warren, Pa., Nov. 17, 1942; BS in Physics and Math., Allegheny Coll., 1964; MS in Geol. Scis., Calif. Inst. Tech., 1967, PhD in Planetary Scis., 1971; DSc (hon.), Allegheny Coll., 1987. Rsch. physicist UCLA, 1971-73, asst. prof. geology, 1973-79; geologist U.S. Geol. Survey, Flagstaff, Ariz., 1979-90; prof. geology Ariz. State U., Tempe, 1988—, Regents prof., 1991-93; prof., head dept. geol. sci. U. B.C., Vancouver, Canada, 1993-95; co-founder Kieffer & Woo, Inc., Palgrave, Ont., Can., 1996-2000; founder Kieffer Inst. for Devel. of Sci. Based Edn., 1997-99; Walgreen chair, prof. geology U. Ill., Urbana, 2001—. W.H. Mendnhall lectr. U.S. Geol. Survey, 1980. Editor (with A. Navrotsky): Microscopic to Macroscopic: Atomic Environments to Mineral Thermodynamics, 1985. Recipient Disting. Alumnus award, Calif. Inst. Tech., 1982, Meritorious Svc. award, Dept. Interior, 1986, Spendiarov award, Soviet Acad. Scis., 1990; Alfred P. Sloan Found. fellow, 1977—79, MacArthur fellow, 1995—. Fellow: Mineral Soc. Am. (award 1980), Meteoritical Soc., Geol. Soc. Am. (Arthur L. Day medal 1992), Am. Geophys. Union, Am. Acad. Arts and Scis.; mem.: NAS. Avocations: athletics, music. Office: U Ill Dept Geology MC 102 1301 W Green St Urbana IL 61801 Business E-Mail: skieffer@uiuc.edu.

KIEL, SHELLEY, state senator; b. Galesburg, Ill., Aug. 16, 1950; m. Gary Kiel, Mar. 11, 1989; children: Darien, Brien, Joseph MS, U. Nebr., Omaha, 1977. V.p. mktg. and ednl. design Flat Worl, Inc.; tchr.; state senator State of Nebr., Lincoln. Chmn. Metropolitan Cmty. Coll. (bd. govs.); mem. Save our Llbrs. STeering Com. Mem. Dundee Mem. Pk. Assn. (pres.), Omaha Neighborhood Courage, PTA bds. Lewis and Clark, Kennedy, Dundee schls., Omaha Libr. bd., Women's Fund. Mem. Met. Cmty. Coll. Bd. Govs.,Pi Beta Phi House Corp. (pres.) Creighton U.; Leadership Omaha Alumni Assn. Congregationalist.

KIENBAUM, THOMAS GERD, lawyer; b. Berlin, Nov. 16, 1942; came to U.S., 1957; s. Gerd Wilhelm Kienbaum and Albertine Brigitte (Kramm) Kettler; m. Karen Smith, June 24, 1966 (div.); 1 child, Ursula; m. Elizabeth Hardy, Jan. 22, 1992. AB, U. Mich., 1965; JD magna cum laude, Wayne State U., 1968. Bar: Mich. 1968, Ill. 1991, U.S. Supreme Ct. 1983. Assoc. Dickinson, Wright, Moon, Van Dusen & Freeman, Detroit, 1968-76, ptnr., 1976-97; ptnr., founder Kienbaum Opperwall Hardy & Pelton, Detroit and Birmingham, 1997—. Adv. bd. Nat. Employment Law Inst.; bd. vis. Wayne State U. Law Sch., 1996—; mem. Atty. Discipline Bd., 2007—. Contbr. articles to profl. jours. Bd. dirs. Wayne County Neighborhood Legal Svc., 1972-76, 87-88, mem. Atty. Discipline Bd., 2007-. Fellow ABA, State Bar of Mich. Found.; mem. Am. Judicature Soc., Coll. Labor and Employment Lawyers, State Bar Mich. (pres. 1995-96), Detroit Bar Assn. (pres. 1985-86), Barristers Assn. (pres. 1978-79), Oakland County Bar Assn., Order of the Coif. Avocations: reading, skiing, squash, sailing. Office: Kienbaum Opperwall Hardy & Pelton 280 North Old Woodward Ave Ste 400 Birmingham MI 48009-6202 Home Phone: 248-594-8560; Office Phone: 248-645-0000. Business E-Mail: tkienbaum@kohp.com.

KIERLIN, BOB, state legislator; b. June 1, 1939; 2 children. BSME, MBA, U. Minn. Mem. Minn. Senatefrom 32nd dist., St. Paul, 1999—. Republican. Office: 127 State Office Bldg 100 Constitution Ave Saint Paul MN 55155-1232 Home: PO Box 302 Winona MN 55987-0302

KIESAU, JEAN, retail executive; Pres. Home of Economy, Grand Forks, N.D. Office: Home of Economy 1508 N Washington St Grand Forks ND 58203-1458

KIESCHNICK, GERALD B., religious organization administrator; b. Houston, Tex., Jan. 29, 1943; m. Terry Kieschnick; children: Andrew, Angela Keith. BS, Tex. A&M U., 1964; grad., Concordia Theological Seminary, Springfield, Ill., 1970; M.Div., Concordia Theological Seminary, Fort Wayne, In., 1977; LLD (hon.), Concordia U., Austin, Tex., 1996. Pastor Good Shepherd Luth. Ch., Biloxi, Miss., 1970—73, Redeemer Luth. Ch., Beaumont, Tex., 1973—81; dir. public relations, Tex. dist. Luth. Ch. -Mo. Synod, 1976—86, circuit counselor, Tex. dist., 1978—81; pastor Faith Luth. Ch., Georgetown, Tex., 1981—86; pres. Tex. dist. Luth. Ch. -Mo. Synod, 1991—2001, chair, commn. church and theology issues, 1998—2001, pres., 2001—. Office: Luthern Ch Missouri Synod 1333 S Kirkwood Rd Saint Louis MO 63122

KIESSLING, LAURA LEE, chemist, researcher; b. Milw., Sept. 21, 1960; d. William E. and LaVonne V. (Korth) K. SB, MIT, 1983; PhD, Yale U., 1989. Teaching asst. MIT, Cambridge, Mass., 1982-83, Yale U., New Haven, 1983-84, rsch. asst., 1984-89; rsch. fellow Calif. Tech. U., Pasadena, Calif., 1989-91; asst. prof. chemistry U. Wis., Madison, Wis., 1991-97, assoc. prof., 1997-99, prof. chemistry, prof. biochemistry, 1999—, dir., Keck Ctr. for Chem. Genomics, 2001—. Cons. Ophidian, Inc., 1997-99, Alfred P. Sloan Found. Chemistry Fellowships, 1997-, mem. selection com., 2003-; mem. bioorganic and natural products study sect. NIH, 1997-2000, chair bioorganic and natural products chemistry study sect., 2000-02; sci. adv. bd. Promega, Inc., 1999—; Dowd Lectr., Dept. Chemistry, U. Pitts., Pa., 1999; chair, organizer, NSF Workshop on Frontiers in Glycoscience, 2000; chair, spkr., Symposium on Chemical Biology, Am. Soc. for Cell Biology, San Francisco, Calif., 2000, Med. Glycobiology, Annual Soc. for Glycobiology Mtg., 2001; mem. vis. com. Lawrence Berkeley Lab., 2000; mem. Chancellor search com., U. Wis. Madison, 2000; mem. Com. on Summer Meeting, Am. Soc. for Cell Biology, 2001; reviewer, Dreyfus Found. Rsch. Grants, 2002. Mem. editl. bd. Chemistry and Biology, 1997-, Organic Reactions, 2000-; mem. editl. bd. Organic & Biomolecular Chemistry, 2002, Annual Reviews of Biochemistry, 2005-; selection com. for editor Jour. Organic Chemistry, 1999; reviewer, NIH and NSF; contbr. articles to profl. jour. Recipient Bausch and Lomb Sci. award, 1978, Dow Chems. New Faculty award, 1992, Shaw Scientist award, 1992-97, Procter and Gamble U. Exploratory Rsch. award, 1992-95, Shaw Scientist award, 1992-97, Nat. Young Investigator award NSF, 1994-99, Beckman Young Investigator award, 1994-96, Am. Cancer Soc. Jr. Faculty award, 1995-97, Zeneca Excellence in Chemistry award, 1996, Dreyfus Tchr.-Scholar award Dreyfus Found., 1996-2001, Lake Mills, Wis. Disting. Alumni, 1999, Carbohydrate Rsch. award for Creativity in Carbohydrate Chemistry, 2001, Tetrahedron Young Investigator award in Bioorganic or Medicinal Chemistry, 2005; Postdoctoral fellow Am. Cancer Soc., 1989-91, Alfred P. Sloan Found. fellow, 1997-99, MacArthur fellow John D. and Catherine MacArthur Found., 1999-2004. Fellow AAAS (repr., Divsn. Chemistry, 2001-04); mem. Am. Acad. Arts & Sciences, Am. Chem. Soc. (Arthur C. Cope scholar 1999, Horace Isbell award, Carbohydrate Divsn., 2000, Francis P. Garvan-John M. Olin medal, 2007, editor-in-chief, Chemical Biology, 2005-), Soc. Glycobiology, Am. Soc. for Biochemistry and Molecular Biology, NAS, Sigma Xi, Phi Lambda Upsilon. Avocations: canoeing, rowing, running. Office: U Wis Dept Chemistry 1101 University Ave Madison WI 53706-1322 also: U Wis Dept Chemistry Rm 471C 433 Babcock Dr Madison WI 53706-1544 Fax: 608-265-0764.

KIFFMEYER, MARY, former state official; b. Balta, ND, Dec. 29, 1946; m. Ralph Kiffmeyer, 1968; children: Christina, Patrick, James, John. RN, St. Gabriel's Sch. ursing, Little Falls, Minn. RN Minn. Sec. state State of Minn., St. Paul, 1999—2007. Mem. Minn. State Exec. Coun., Minn. State Bd. Investment. Mem. adv. bd. The Heartland Inst., Election Assistance Commn. Standards; bd. dirs. Hope for the City, Cradle of Hope, Close-up Found., Downtown Mpls. YMCA. Recipient Leadership award, Nat. Electronic Commerce Coordinating Coun., In the Arena award, Ctr. for Digital Govt., Commitment to Absentee Voting for the Military award, Fed. Voter Assistance, Outstanding Woman in Govt. award, Minn. Women of Today, 2003. Mem.: Nat. Assn. Secs. of State (past pres., chair com. bus. services, pres. 2003). Republican.

KIKOLER, STEPHEN PHILIP, lawyer; b. NYC, Apr. 24, 1945; s. Sigmund and Dorothy (Javna) K.; m. Ethel Lerner, June 18, 1967; children: Jeffrey Stuart, Shari Elaine. AB, U. Mich., 1966, JD cum laude, 1969. Bar: Ill. 1969, U.S. Dist. Ct. (no. dist.) Ill. 1969, U.S. Ct. Appeals (7th cir.) 1988, U.S. Ct. Appeals (11th cir.) 1994, U.S. Ct. Appeals for the Armed Forces 1970, U.S. Supreme Ct. 1994. Capt. Judge Advocate Gen.'s Corps U.S. Army, 1970-73; with Much, Shelist, Denenberg, Ament & Rubenstein PC, Chgo. Mem. ABA, Ill. State Bar Assn., Chgo. Bar. Assn. (real property law com., mechanics' liens subcom.), Soc. Ill. Constrn. Attys. Home: 2746 Norma Ct Glenview IL 60025-4661 Office: Much Shelist Denenberg Ament & Rubenstein PC 191 N Wacker Dr Chicago IL 60606-1615 Home Phone: 847-965-8323; Office Phone: 312-521-2495. Business E-Mail: skikoler@muchshelist.com.

KILBANE, CATHERINE M., lawyer; b. Cleve., Apr. 10, 1963; BA cum laude, Case Western Res. U., 1984, JD cum laude, 1987. Bar: Ohio 1987. Ptnr. Baker & Hostetler, Cleve., 1997—2003; sr. v.p., gen. counsel, sec. Am. Greetings Corp., Cleve., 2003—. Bd. dirs. The Andersons, Inc., 2007—. Bd. trustees United Way Greater Cleve., The Cleve. Leadership Ctr., Cuyahoga Community Coll. Found. Mem. Cleve Bar Assn., Assn. Corp. Counsel, Am. Soc. Corp. Secrtaries, Delta Theta Phi. Office: Am Greetings Corp One American Rd Cleveland OH 44144

KILBANE, SALLY CONWAY, economics professor; b. Cleve., Nov. 11, 1942; d. John J. and May (Carlin) Conway; m. Thomas Stanton Kilbane, June 4, 1966; children: Sarah, Thomas, Eamon, James, Carlin. BSN, St. John Coll., 1964; MSN, Case Western Res. U., 1971, MA, 1982, PhD, 1987. Pub. health nurse City of Cleve., 1964-65; instr. nursing St. John Hosp., Cleve., 1965-67, 68-69; instr. econs. Case Western Res. U., Cleve., 1988-93; adj. asst. prof. econs. Cleve. State U., 1988—. Congl. candidate Rep. Primary 10th Dist., 1992. Home: 20000 Lorain Rd Apt 607 Cleveland OH 44126-3460

KILBANE, THOMAS STANTON, lawyer; b. Cleve., Mar. 7, 1941; s. Thomas Joseph and Helen (Stanton) K.; m. Sally Conway Kilbane, June 4, 1966; children: Sarah, Thomas, Eamon, James, Carlin. BA magna cum laude, John Carroll U., 1963; JD, Northwestern U., 1966. Bar: Ohio 1966, US Dist. Ct. (no. dist.) Ohio 1969, US Supreme Ct. 1975, US Ct. Claims 1981, US Ct. Appeals (6th cir.) 1982, US Ct. Appeals (3d cir.) 1990, US Ct. Appeals (5th cir.) 1998, US Ct. Appeals (2d, 7th and 9th cirs.) 2002, US Ct. Appeals (4th cir.) 2003, US Ct. Appeals (1st cir.) 2004, US Ct. Appeals (8th cir.) 2005, US Ct. Appeals (10th cir.) 2005, US Ct. Appeals (11th cir.) 2005, US Ct. Appeals (DC cir.). Assoc. Squire, Sanders & Dempsey, Cleve., 1966-76, ptnr., 1976—, adminstrv. com., 1979-80, mgmt. com., 1981-83, 87-90, mng. ptnr. litigation practice area, 1991—2007. Fed. ct. panelist US Dist. Ct. (no. dist.) Ohio; mem. adv. bd. Inst. Transnat. Arbitration. Mem. editl. bd. Northwestern U. Law Rev., 1965-66. Active Rep. Presdl. Task Force; bd. dirs. United Way Svcs.; chmn. Supreme Ct. Hist. Soc., o. Ohio, 2003-. 1st lt. US Army, 1967—68, capt. US Army, 1968—69, Vietnam. Decorated Bronze Star; named Greater Cleve. Cath. Man of Yr., 1996. Fellow ABA, Am. Coll. Trial Lawyers, Internat. Acad. Trial Lawyers, Am. Bar Found., Master Bencher of John M. Manos Inn of Ct.; mem. Fed. Bar Assn., Am. Coll. Barristers, Ohio Bar Assn. (AAA corp. counsel com., ctr. for pub. resources constrn. com.), Greater Cleve. Bar Assn., Jud. Conf. 6th Cir., Jud. Conf. 8th Jud. Dist. Ohio (life), Union Club, The 50 Club, The Club, Alpha Sigma Nu. Republican. Roman Catholic. Office: Squire Sanders & Dempsey 4900 Key Tower 127 Public Sq Cleveland OH 44114-1304 Office Phone: 216-479-8564. Office Fax: 216-479-8780. Business E-Mail: tkilbane@ssd.com.

KILBRIDE, THOMAS L., state supreme court justice; b. LaSalle, Ill. married; 3 children. BA magna cum laude, St. Mary's Coll., 1978; JD, Antioch Sch. Law, 1981. Practicioner U.S. Dist. Ct., Ill., U.S. Seventh Cir. Ct. Appeals; justice Ill. Supreme Ct., 2000—. Former mem. bd. dirs., former v.p., former pres. Ill. Twp. Attys. Assn. Vol. legal adv. Cmty. Caring Conf., Quad City Harvest Inc.; charter chmn. Quad Cities Interfaith Sponsoring Com.; former mem. Rock Island Human Rels. Com.; former vol. lawyer, charter mem. Ill. Pro Bono Ctr. Mem.: Rock Island County Bar Assn., Ill. State Bar Assn. Office: Ill Supreme Ct State of Ill Bldg 160 N LaSalle St Chicago IL 60601

KILBURG, PAUL J., federal judge; b. 1945; Chief bankruptcy judge U.S. Bankruptcy Ct. (no. dist.) Iowa, Cedar Rapids, 1993—; judge State of Iowa, 1978-93. Served in USAF, 1963-68. Office: Bankruptcy Ct 425 2d St SE Cedar Rapids IA 52407 Fax: (319) 286-2290.

KILDEE, DALE EDWARD, congressman; b. Flint, Mich., Sept. 16, 1929; s. Timothy Leo and Norma Alicia (Ullmer) K.; m. Gayle Heyn, Feb. 27, 1965; children: David, Laura, Paul. BA, Sacred Heart Sem., 1952; tchr.'s cert., U. Detroit, 1954; MA, U. Mich., 1961; postgrad. (Rotary Found. fellow), U. Peshawar, Pakistan, 1958-59. Tchr. U. Detroit HS, 1954-56, Flint Central HS, 1956-64; mem. Mich. Ho. of Reps., 1964-74, Mich. Senate, 1975-76, US Congress from 7th Mich. dist., 1977-93, US Congress from 5th Mich. dist. (formerly 9th), 1993—; sr. mem. edn. and the workforce com., ranking minority mem. subcom. on early childhood, youth, & families; chair Congl. Auto Caucus, 1993—; co-chair Native Am. Caucus, 1997; mem. resources com.; mem. edn. and the workforce com. Recipient Excellence in Public Svc. awrad, Am. Acad. Pediatrics, 1988, Disting. Svc. award, Mich. Edn. Assn., 1993, Civitas award, 1999, Lifetime Achievement award, Ctr. Civic Edn., 2002, Friend of CACFP award, Child and Adult Care Food Program, 2002, NAICU award advocacy independent higher edn., Nat. Assn. Independent Colleges and Universities, 2003, Friend of Nat. Parks award, Nat. Parks Conservation Assn., 2005. Mem. NAACP (life), Am. Fedn. Tchrs., Urban League, Phi Delta Kappa. Lodges: K.C; Optimists. Democrat. Roman Catholic. Office: US Ho of Reps 2107 Rayburn House Bldg Washington DC 20515-2209 also: District Office 432 N Saginaw St Ste 410 Flint MI 48502-2018 Office Phone: 202-225-3611, 810-239-1437. Office Fax: 202-225-6393, 814-239-1439.

KILGARIN, KAREN, state official, public relations consultant; b. Omaha, Mar. 12, 1957; d. Bradford Michael and Verna Jane (Will) Kilgarin; 1 child, Celeste Mattson Torrence. BA, U. Nebr., Kearney, 1979. With Real Estate Assocs., Inc., Omaha, 1979—84; capital bur. chief Sta. KETV, Omaha, 1984—92; dir. comm. and publs. Nebr. Edn. Assn., Lincoln, 1995—98, 1999—; dep. chief staff to gov., dir. pub. rels. State of Nebr., Lincoln, 1992—95, dir. dept. adminstrv. svcs., 1998—99. Mem. Nebr. Senate, Omaha, 1980—84; judicial nominating com. Gubernatorial appointment, 2000; mem. Capital Environment Commn. Mayor appointment, 2000. Mem. exec. com. Nebr. Dem. Com., Lincoln, 1995—98; trustee U. Nebr.-Kearney Found., 1992—95, mem. chancellor's adv. coun., 1995—. Recipient Oustanding Alumni award U. Nebr.-Kearney, 1993, Omaha South H.S., 1995, Wings award LWV, Omaha, 1995, President's award Nebr. Broadcasters Assn., 1995. Mem. NEA (pub. rels. coun. of states), Soc. Profl. Journalists, State Edn. Editors. Presbyterian. Avocations: photography, collecting, politics. Office: NSEA 605 S 14th St Lincoln NE 68508-2726

KILLEEN, MICHAEL F., retail executive; Ptnr. Arthur Andersen LLP, 1978—99; bus. cons., 2000—01; sr. exec. v.p. fin. and corp. strategies OfficeMax, Shaker Heights, Ohio, 2001—02, CFO, 2002—. Office: OfficeMax PO Box 228070 Shaker Heights OH 44122-8070

KILLION, THEO, retail executive; m. Dana Killion; 4 children. BA, MEd, Tufts U. Sportswear buyer, exec. trainee, labor rels. mgr. R.H. Macy & Co., 1974—83, dir. human resources, 1984—94; sr. v.p. human resources divsn. Home Shopping Network, Inc., 1995—96; v.p. human resources Lane Bryant, 1997—99; v.p. human resources, store ops. Ltd. Brands, Inc., Columbus, Ohio, 1999—. Recipient Benjamin E. Mays award, A Better Chance, Inc., 2000. Office: Ltd Brands Three Ltd Pkwy Columbus OH 43230

KILMAN, JAMES WILLIAM, surgeon, educator; b. Terre Haute, Ind., Jan. 22, 1931; s. Arthur and Irene (Piker) K.; m. Priscilla Margaret Jackson, June 20, 1968; children: James William, Julia Anne, Jennifer Irene. BS, Ind. State U., 1956; MD, Ind. U., 1960. Intern Ind. U. Med. Ctr., Indpls., 1960-61, resident surgery, 1961-66, asst. prof., 1966-69, assoc. prof., 1969-73; prof. surgery Ohio State U. Coll. Medicine, 1973-91, prof. surgery emeritus, 1991—; chmn. dept. thoracic surgery Children's Hosp., 1975-91; attending surgeon Univ. Hosp., Columbus, Ohio; attending staff Children's Hosp., Columbus, pres. staff, 1978; attending staff Grant Hosp., Riverside Hosp. Cons. surgeon VA Hosp., Dayton; pres. Columbus Acad. Medicine, 1977. Contbr. articles to profl. jours. Trustee Central Ohio Heart Assn., Acad. Medicine Edn. Found., Children's Hosp., 1978—. Served with USNR, 1951-55. USPHS Cardiovascular fellow, 1963-64; recipient Alumni Achievement award, Ind. State U., 1989. Fellow ACS, Am. Coll. Cardiology, Am. Acad. Pediats., Coll. Chest Physicians; mem. Columbus Surg. Soc. (hon., pres. 1974), Columbus Acad. Medicine (coun. 1971-73), Am. Surg. Assn., Soc. Univ. Surgeons, Am. Assn. Thoracic Surgery, Cen. Surg. Assn., Western Surg. Assn., Soc. Vascular Surgery, Internat. Cardiovasc. Soc., Internat. Soc. Surgeons, Chest Club, Cardiovasc. Surgery Club, City Club, Palm Aire Country Club, Faculty Club, Capital Club, Columbus Athletic Club, Pickaway County Country Club, Am. Boxer Club (bd. dirs. 2000-03, pres. 2001-03, AKC del. 2002-05), Pinnacle Club (Grove City, Ohio), Sigma Xi, Alpha Omega Alpha. Achievements include research in infant cardiopulmonary bypass and surgery for congenital heart lesions. Home: 4231 Jackson Pike Grove City OH 43123 Personal E-mail: leoline@aol.com.

KILPATRICK, CAROLYN CHEEKS, congresswoman; b. Detroit, June 25, 1945; d. Marvell and Willa Mae (Henry) Cheeks; divorced; children: Kwame, Ayanna. AS, Ferris State Coll., Big Rapids, Mich., 1965; BS, Western Mich. U., 1972; MS in Edn., U. Mich., 1977. Tchr. Murray Wright High Sch., Detroit, 1972-78; mem. Mich. Ho. of Reps., Lansing, 1978-96, U.S. Congress from 13th Mich. dist. (formerly 15th), Washington, 1997—; mem. appropriations com. Del. Dem. Convs., 1980, 84, 88. Participant Mich. African Trade Mission, 1984, UN Internat. Women's Conf., 1986; del. participant Mich. Dept. Agr. to Nairobi (Kenya) Internat. Agr. Show, 1986. Recipient Anthony Wayne award Wayne State U., Disting. Legislator award U. Mich., Disting. Alumni award Ferris State U., Woman of Yr. award Gentlemen of Wall St., Inc., Burton-Abercrombie award 15th Dem. Congrl. dist.; named one of Most Influential Black Americans, Ebony mag., 2006. Mem. Nat. Orgn. 100 Black Women. Democrat. Office: House of Reps 1610 Longworth House Office Bldg Washington DC 20515-2215 also: Dist Office 1274 Library Ste 1B Detroit MI 48226 Office Phone: 202-225-2261, 313-965-9004. Office Fax: 202-225-5730, 313-965-9006.

KILPATRICK, KWAME MALIK, mayor; b. Detroit, June 8, 1970; s. Bernard Kilpatrick and Carolyn (Cheeks) Kikpatrick; m. Carlita Poles; children: Jelani, Jalil, Jonas. BS in Polit. Sci., Fla. A&M Univ.; JD, Detroit Coll. Law, 1999. Cert. teacher Florida A&M U. Mem. Mich. Ho. Reps., 1996—2001; mayor City of Detroit, 2002—. Designer Clean Mich. Initiative, 1998; former leader Democratic Caucus. Named an Most Influential Black Americans, Ebony mag., 2006. Democrat. Achievements include youngest elected mayor of any major US city. Office: Coleman A Young Municipal Ctr 2 Woodward Ave Rm 1126 Detroit MI 48226 Office Phone: 313-224-3400.

KILROY, JOHN MUIR, lawyer; b. Kansas City, Mo., Apr. 12, 1918; s. James L. and Jane Alice (Scurry) K.; m. Lorraine K. Butler, Jan. 26, 1946; children: John Muir, William Terence. Student, Kansas City Jr. Coll., 1935-37; AB, U. Kansas City, 1940; JD, U. Mo., 1942. Bar: Mo. 1942. Practice in, Kansas City, 1946—; ptnr. Shughart, Thomson & Kilroy, 1948—, pres., 1977-86, chmn. bd. dirs., 1980-88, chmn. emeritus, 1988—. Instr. med. jurisprudence U. Health Scis., 1973-93; panelist numerous med.-legal groups ACS, Mo. Med. Assn., Kans. U. Med. Sch., S.W. Clin. Soc. Contbr. articles to profl. jours. Chmn. bd. dirs. Kansas City Heart Assn.; mem. adv. bd. Midwest Christian Counseling Svc.; bd. dirs., pres. Della Lamb Cmty. Svc., 1991, chmn. bd. dirs., 1993; bd. dirs. Laubach Literacy Coun., 1998-2001, Kingswood Manor, 1992-94, Mo. Meth. Found., 1993-2002. Named Man of Yr., Sigma Chi, 1989. Fellow Am. Coll. Trial Lawyers; mem. ABA, Mo. Bar Assn. (chmn. med. legal com.), Kansas City Bar Assn. (Litigator Emeritus award 1990), Internat. Assn. Barristers, Internat. Assn. Def. Counsel, Am. Coll. Legal Medicine, Am. Bd. Profl. Liability Attys., Fedn. Ins. Counsel, Law Soc. U. Mo., Order Barristers U. Mo., Lawyers Assn., Kansas City (pres. 1968), Kansas City C. of C., Univ. Club (v.p. 1984, pres. 1985), Indian Hills Country Club, Kansas City Club. Office: Shughart Thomson & Kilroy 120 W 12th St Ste 1800 Kansas City MO 64105-1922 Home: 8101 Mission Rd Apt 411 Prairie Village KS 66208-5248

KILROY, WILLIAM TERRENCE, lawyer; b. Kansas City, Mo., May 24, 1950; s. John Muir and Katherine Lorraine (Butler) K.; m. Marianne Michelle Maurin, Sept. 8, 1984; children: Kyle E., Katherine A. BS, U. Kans., 1972, MA, 1974; JD, Washburn U., 1977. Bar: Mo. 1977. Assoc. Shughart, Thomson & Kilroy, Kansas City, Mo., 1977-81, mem., dir., 1981—. Contbr. articles to profl. publs. Mem. Kans. City Citizens Assn., 1980—; pres., bd. govs. Sch. Law Washburn, 1992-94; with Civic Coun. of Greater Kansas City, 1999—; legal coun. Heart of Am. Coun. Boy Scouts Am., 1988-92, mem. exec. com., 1988-95, Cmty. adv. Greater Kans. City Cmty. Found. and Affiliated Trusts, 1993-2000; bd. dirs. Kansas City Neighborhood Alliance, 1998-2004, Greater Kansas City Crime Commn., 1999—. Mem. Lawyers Assn. Kansas City, Kansas City Bar Assn. (chmn. civil rights com. 1984), Mo. Bar Assn., ABA (subcom. on arbitration, labor law sect. 1977—), Greater Kansas City C. of C., Kansas City Club, Kansas City Country Club. Office: Shughart Thomson & Kilroy 12 Wyandotte Plz 120 W 12th St Ste 1800 Kansas City MO 64105-1929 Office Phone: 816-374-0533. Business E-Mail: tkilroy@stklaw.com.

KILZER, RALPH, state legislator; b. Bently, SD, Aug. 30, 1935; m. Marcia; six children. BA, St. John U.; MD, Marquete U. Clin. prof. surgery UND Sch. Med.; mem. N.D. Ho. of Reps., Bismark, 1957, N.D. Senate from 47th dist., Bismark, 1996—. Founder Bone and Joint Ctr. Mem. Knight of the Holy Sepulchre; with U.S. ARmy. Recipient U. Mary McCarthy award. Mem. AMA, Am. Acad. Ortho. Surgeons, NFIB, Elks Club, Knights of Columbus; Legis. Chmn. N.D. Med. Assn. Republican; Roman Caholic. Office: 1982 Mesquite Loop Bismarck ND 58503-0198 E-mail: rkilzer@stae.nd.us.

KIM, BYUNG RO, environmental engineer; BSCE, Seoul Nat. U., 1971; MS in Environ. Engring., U. Ill., 1974, PhD in Environ. Engring., 1976. Registered profl. engr., Tenn. Environ. engr. Tenn. Valley Authority, Chattanooga, 1976-80; asst. prof. civil engring. Ga. Inst. Tech., Atlanta, 1980-85; staff rsch. engr. GM Rsch. Labs., Warren, Mich., 1985-90; staff tech., specialist Ford Rsch. Lab., Dearborn, Mich., 1990—. Adj. prof. environ. engring. Wayne State U., Detroit, 1994—. Contbr. articles to profl. jours. Office: PO Box 2053 Dearborn MI 48123-2087

KIM, CHIN-WOO, linguist, educator; b. Chungju, Korea, Mar. 22, 1936; came to U.S., 1961, naturalized, 1983; s. Hyong-gi and Kyong-ok K.; m. Beverly Jean Kircher, June 14, 1964 (div. June 1982); children: Joseph H., Daniel H; m. Kui-Soon Choe, Oct. 29, 1988. BA in English, Yonsei U., 1958, Wash. State U., 1962; MA, UCLA, 1964, PhD in Linguistics, 1966. Asst. prof. linguistics U. Ill., Urbana, 1967—69, assoc. prof. linguistics, East Asian langs., speech, and English as an internat. language, 1969—72, prof., 1972—, chmn. dept. linguistics, 1979—86, dir. Ill.-Tehran Rsch. Ctr., 1974—78, assoc. dir. Linguistic Inst., 1977, dir. Program in East Asian Studies, 1990—91; assoc. dir. Konan Internat. Exch. Ctr. Konan U., Kobe, Japan, 1993—94, 2004—05; head linguistics U. Ill., 1999—2004. Vis. prof. linguistics U. Hawaii, 1972-73, 86-87, adj. prof. U. Tehran, Iran, 1974-76, vis. prof. English Yonsei U., Korea, 1983-84, Konan U., Kobe, Japan, 1993-94, Korea U., Seoul, 1995-96, chair prof. in humanities Yonsei U., Seoul, 2007-. Author works in field. Bd. dirs. East Asian Language Inst. Ind. U., 1984-93; pres., bd. trustees Korean Language Sch., Urbana, Ill., 1988-92. Served with Korean Air Force, 1958-61. Am. Council Learned Socs. fellow, 1965-66; postdoctoral fellow MIT, 1966-67; Ctr. Advanced Study Fellow, U. Ill., 1984-85, Overseas Korean of the Year Award, Korean Broadcasting Soc., 2001. Mem. Linguistic Soc. Am., Linguistic Soc. Korea, Internat. Cir. Korean Linguistics (pres. 1978-80), Phonology-Morphology Cir. (adv. bd. 1995—), Internat. Soc. Korean Studies (pres. N.Am. br. 2005—), Internat. Assn. Humanistic Studies Lang. (pres. 2000—), Korean Assn. Speech Scis. (sr. advisor 1999—) Home: 1401 N Raintree Woods Urbana IL 61802-7749 Office: U Ill Dept Linguistics 707 S Mathews Ave Urbana IL 61801-3625 Office Phone: 217-244-2824. Business E-Mail: cwkim@illinois.edu, cwk1401@yonsei.ac.kr.

KIM, CHONG LIM, political science professor; b. Seoul, July 17, 1937; arrived in US, 1962; s. Soo Myung and Chung Hwa (Moon) K.; m. Eun Hwa Park, Aug. 21, 1963; children: Bohm S., Lahn S., Lynn S. BA, Seoul Nat. U., 1960; MA, U. Oreg., 1964, PhD, 1968. Instr. U. Oreg., Eugene, 1965-67; asst. prof. U. Iowa, Iowa City, 1968-70, assoc. prof., 1970-75, prof., 1975—. Author: Legislative Connection, 1984, Legislative Process in Korea, 1981, Patterns of Recruitment, 1974; editor: Legislative Systems, 1975, Political Participation in Korea, 1980; contbr. numerous articles to profl. jours. Mem. Am. Polit. Sci. Assn., Midwest Polit. Sci. Assn. Avocations: reading, travel. Office: U Iowa Dept Polit Sci Iowa City IA 52242 Home Phone: 319-337-7871. Business E-Mail: chong-kim@uiowa.edu.

KIM, E. HAN, financial economist, educator; b. Seoul, Republic of Korea, May 27, 1946; came to U.S., 1966; s. Chang Yoon and Young Ja (Chung) K.; m. Tack Han, June 14, 1969; children— Juliane H., Elaine H., Deborah H. BS, U. Rochester, 1969; MBA, Cornell U., 1971; PhD, SUNY-Buffalo, 1975. Asst. prof. Ohio State U., Columbus, 1975-77, assoc. prof., 1979-80; assoc. prof., then prof. fin. and bus. adminstrn. U. Mich., Ann Arbor, 1980-84, Fred M. Taylor Disting. prof., 1984—, chmn. dept. fin., 1988-91; dir. Mitsui Life Fin. Rsch. Ctr., 1990—. Vis. assoc. prof. U. Chgo., 1978-79; vis. rsch. fellow Korea Devel. Inst., 1986-87; econ. cons. Govt. of Korea, 1985-87, 98; Cycle and Carriage vis. prof. Nat. U. Singapore, 1989; Yamaichi prof. econs. U. Tokyo, 1990-91; cons. Bank of Korea, 1985, U.S. Dept. Treasury, IRS, 1988-94, World Bank, 1989-91, 93, Posco, 1995-98, Korea Stock Exch., 1997-98; co-chair Citizens for Econ. Freedom, 1997-99; bd. dirs. Posco, Hana Bank, Mut. Savs. Bank. Assoc. editor Jour. Fin., 1979-83, 88-92, Fin. Rev., 1982—2003, Internat. Jour. Fin., 1990—94, Internat. Rev. Fin. Analysis, 1990-92, Rev. No. Am. Jour. of Econs. and Fin., 1990—99, Rev. Quantitative Fin. and Acctg., 1990—, Pacific Basin Fin. Jour., 1991-96; editl. bd. Jour. Bus. Rsch., 1977—; adv. bd. Asia-Pacific Jour. Mgmt., 1990-96, Jour. Asian Bus., 1996—; contbr. articles to profl. jours. Mem. Korea-Am. Econ. Assn. (sec. gen. 1985, v.p. 1986, pres. 1996), Am. Econ. Assn., Am. Fin. Assn., Western Fin. Assn. Avocations: tennis, golf. Office: Univ Mich Ross Sch Bus Ann Arbor MI 48109

KIM, MI JA, dean, academic administrator; b. Seoul, Republic of Korea, Jan. 23, 1940; came to U.S., 1966; d. Si Hyung and Jung Kwon (Ahn) Lee; m. Heung Soo Kim, Jan. 14, 1964; children: Yoon Hi and Joseph. BS in Nursing, Yon Sei U., Seoul, 1962; PhD in Physiology, U. Ill., Chgo., 1975; JD (hon.), North Park Coll., 1995. Staff nurse Severance Hosp., Seoul, 1962-63; health nurse Am. Embassy, Seoul, 1963-66; asst. prof. Coll. Nursing/Univ. Ill., Chgo., 1975-79, assoc. prof., 1979-84, prof., 1984—, assoc. dean for rsch. dir. of grad. studies and assoc. dean acad. affairs, 1984-88, acting dean, 1988-89, dean, 1989-95, vice chancellor for rsch. and dean of grad. coll., 1995-99, dir. Acad. of Internat. Leadership Devel., 2001—. Cons. Nat. Ctr. Nursing Rsch., Bethesda, Md., 1987-91, Bd. Regents Higher Edn., Boston, 1989, WHO, Geneva, 2000, Nat. Inst. Gen. Med. Scis., NIH, 2000; mem. nat. adv. coun. Nat. Ins.; sci. and tech. rev. Nat. Ctr. Rsch. Resources, NIH, 2004—; treas., bd. trustees Commn. Grads. Fgn. Nursing Schs. Internat., 2004-; rschr. assessment exercise Higher Edn. Funding Agy., UK, 2005—. Mem. adv. bd. Health of the Pub., PEW Charitable Trust, Robert Wood Johnson found., 1992-96; adv. coun. Ctr. Bioethics and Human Dignity, 1994—. Named 100 Most Influential Women in Chgo., Chgo. Tribune, 1991, Univ. Scholar, U. Ill., 1985-88, Outstanding Nurse Educator, Korean Nurses Assn., Seoul, 1983; recipient Disting. Health and Edn. award Midwest Cmty. Coun. Chgo., 1994, Book of Yr. award Am. Jour. Nursing, 1984, Golden Apple award, students of Coll. Nursing, U. Ill., 1976, 78; Fulbright scholar Yon Sei U., Seoul, 2001. Fellow Am. Acad. Nursing; mem. North Am. Nursing Diagnosis (bd. dirs. 1985-92), Am. Thoracic Soc., Chgo. Lung Assn. (bd. dirs. 1977-97, Leadership Recognition award 1996), Chgo. Heart Assn. (bd. govs. 1980-88), Am. Physiol. Soc., Internat. Leadership Inst. (adv. coun. 1998-99), Sigma Theta Tau (Disting. lectr. 1987, Mary Tolle Wright award for Excellence in Leadership, 1997). Avocation: golf. Office: U Ill Chgo Rm 1156 Coll of Nursing Chicago IL 60612-7350 Business E-Mail: mjkuic@uic.edu.

KIM, MICHAEL CHARLES, lawyer; b. Honolulu, Mar. 9, 1950; s. Harold Dai You and Maria Adrienne K. Student, Gonzaga U., 1967—70; BA, U. Hawaii, 1971; JD, Northwestern U., 1976. Bar: Ill. 1977, U.S. Dist. Ct. (no. dist., gen. and trial law.) Ill. 1977, U.S. Ct. Appeals (7th cir.) 1981, U.S. Supreme Ct. 1986. Assoc. counsel Nat. Assn. Realtors, Chgo., 1977-78; assoc. Rudnick & Wolfe, Chgo., 1978-83, Rudd & Assocs., Hoffman Estates, Ill., 1983-85; ptnr. Rudd & Kim, Hoffman Estates and Chgo., 1985-87; prin. Michael C. Kim & Assocs., Chgo. and Schaumburg, Ill., 1987-88; ptnr. Martin, Craig, Chester & Sonnenschein, Chgo. and Schaumburg, 1988-91, Arnstein & Lehr LLP, Chgo., 1991—2004; prin. Michael C. Kim & Assocs., Chgo., 2004—. Gen. counsel Assn. Sheridan Condo-Coop Owners, Chgo., 1988—; adj. prof. John Marshall Law Sch., Chgo. Author column Apt. and Condo News, 1984-87; co-author Historical and Practice Notes; contbr. articles to profl. jours. Bd. dirs. Astor Villa Condo Assn., Chgo., 1987-91, 2002-05, treas., 1987-89, 2002-03, sec., 2002, pres., 2003-05. Mem. ABA (mem. real property and probate sect., mem. forum on constrn. industry), Chgo. Bar Assn. (chmn condominium law subcom. 1990-92, chmn. real property legis. subcom. 1995-97, vice chmn. real property law com., 1998-99, chmn. real proprty law com. 1999-2000), Ill. State Bar Assn. (real estate law sect. coun. 1990-94, corp. and securities law sect. coun. 1990-92), Asian Am. Bar Assn. Greater Chgo. Area (bd. dirs. 1987-88, 90-91), Cmty. Assns. Inst. Ill. (bd. dirs. 1990-92, pres. 1992), Coll. Cmty. Assn. Lawyers (bd. govs. 1994-98), Assn. Condominium, Townhouse and Homeowner Assns., Univ. Club (Chgo.). Avocations: squash, photography, travel. Office: Michael C Kim & Assocs 19 S LaSalle St Ste 303 Chicago IL 60603 Office Phone: 312-419-4000. Business E-Mail: mck@mkimlaw.com.

KIMBALL, CLYDE WILLIAM, physicist, researcher; b. Laurium, Mich., Apr. 20, 1928; s. Clyde D. and Gertrude M. K. BS in Engring. Physics, Mich. Coll. Mining and Tech., 1950, MS, 1952; PhD in Physics, St. Louis U., 1959. Staff scientist aeronutronic div. Ford Co., 1960-62; assoc. physicist Argonne Nat. Lab., Ill., 1962-64; prof. physics No. Ill. U., De Kalb, 1964—, Presdl. rsch. chair, 1982-86, rsch. prof., 1986-88, disting. prof., 1988—, advisor to pres. sci. and tech., 1982-88, dir. lab. for nanosci., engring. and tech., 2002—. Program dir. low temperature physics Materials Research Div., NSF, Washington, 1978-79; chair, bd. govs. Consortium for Advanced Radiation Sources, 1994—; exec. com. Basic Energy Sci. Synchrotron Rsch. Ctr., 1994—; exec. dir. Inst. for anosci., Engring. and Tech., No. Ill. U., 1992—; chair bd. No. Ill. Nanotech, 1994—. Contbr. articles to profl. jours. Served with U.S. Army, 1952-54 Fellow Am. Phys. Soc.; mem. AAAS, Am. Assn. Physics Tchrs., Sigma Xi. Home: PO Box 842 Dekalb IL 60115-0842 Office: No Ill U Dept Physics Faraday West 217 Dekalb IL 60115 Business E-Mail: ckimball@niu.edu.

KIMBLE, BERNIE, radio director; b. Rochester, NY; Program dir. WNWV, Elyria, Ohio. Office: WMWV 538 W Broad St PO Box 406 Elyria OH 44036

KIMBLE, JUDITH E., molecular biologist, cell biologist; b. Providence, Apr. 24, 1949; BA, U. Calif., Berkeley, 1971; PhD, U. Colo., 1978; postgrad., MRC, Cambridge, Eng., 1978-82. Asst. prof. to assoc. prof. U. Wis., 1983-92; prof. molecular biology, biochemistry U. Wisc., Madison, 1992—, prof. med. genetics, 1994—. Investigator Howard Hughes Med. Inst., Md., 1994—. Mem. NAS, Am. Acad. Arts and Sci., Am. Soc. Cell Biology, Am. Soc. Biochemistry and Molecular Biology, Genetic Soc. Office: HHMI/Dept Biochemistry U Wisc-Madison 433 Babcock Dr Madison WI 53706-1544

KIMMEY, JAMES RICHARD, JR., foundation administrator; b. Boscobel, Wis., Jan. 26, 1935; s. James Richard and Frances Dale (Parnell) Kimmey; m. Sarah Webster Eastman, June 21, 1958; children: Elisabeth Webster, James Richard III. BS, U. Wis., 1957, MS, 1959, MD, 1961; MPH, U. Calif., Berkeley, 1967. Diplomate Am. Bd. Preventive Medicine. Intern Univ. Hosps., Cleve., 1961-62; med. resident Univ. Hosp., Madison, 1962-63; served from surgeon to med. dir. USPHS, 1963-68, chief kidney disease br., 1964-66, regional health dir. NY, 1967-68; exec. dir. Cmty. Health Inc., NYC, 1968-70, Am. Pub. Health Assn., 1970-73; sec. Health Policy Coun. Wis., 1973-75; pres. James R. Kimmey Assos., Inc., 1975-85; dir. Midwest Ctr. Health Planning, 1976-79; exec. dir. Inst. Health Planning, 1979-87; prof. pub. health, dir. Ctr. for Health Svcs. Edn. Rsch. St. Louis U. Med. Ctr., 1987-91; dean sch. pub. health St. Louis U., 1991-93, v.p. health scis., 1993-98, exec. v.p., 1998-2000; dir. Inst. Urban Health Policy, 2000-2001; pres. Mo. Found. for Health, 2001—. Adj. prof. NYU, NYC, 1968—70; lectr. Johns Hopkins, 1971—73; clin. instr. U. Wis., 1974—87; pres. Inst. Health Planning, 1979—86; chair Task Force Accreditation Health Professions, 1997—99, St. Louis ConnectCare, 1998—2001; dir. Ctr. Engring. Tech., 1998—2001; vice chair St. Louis Access Health, 1999—2001. Editor: (book) The Nation's Health, 1972—73; mng. editor: Am. Jour. Pub. Health, 1970—73, mem. editl. adv. bd.: Health Cost Mgmt., 1983—87; contbr. articles to profl. jours. Pres. World Fedn. Pub. Health Assns., 1972—73; mem. sci. adv. bd. Gorgas Inst., 1970—73; bd. dirs. Internat. Union Health Edn., 1970—73. Decorated USPHS Commendation medal. Fellow: APHA (governing coun. 1978—81, chmn. cmty. health planning sect. 1979—80, governing coun. 1983—87, 1989—92), Am. Coll. Preventive Medicine; mem.: Prospective Payment Assessment Commn. (commr. 1991—97), Mo. Pub. Health Assn. (Mo. Communicator of the Yr. award 1994), Am. Coll. Health Adminstrs., Am. Health Planning Assn. (dir. 1974—75, 1977—78, corp. sec. 1977—78, pres. 1980—81, Richard H. Schlesinger award 1978, James R. Kimmey award 1994), Alpha Sigma Nu, Delta Omega, Alpha Omega Alpha, Phi Eta Sigma. Democrat. Episcopalian. Office: Grand Ctrl Bldg Ste 400 1000 St Louis Union Sta Saint Louis MO 63103 Home: 1805 Park Ave #2D Saint Louis MO 63104 Home Phone: 314-621-3424; Office Phone: 314-345-5500. Business E-Mail: jkimmey@mffh.org.

KIMPTON, JEFFREY S., academic administrator; b. 1950; m. Julie Kimpton; children: Meghan, Adam. Attended polit. sci. & pre-law, Augustana Coll., Rock Island, Ill., 1968—70; BS in music edn., cum laude, U. Ill., 1973, MS in music edn. & sch. adminstr., 1975; cert. in corp. financial mgmt. & acctg., Am. Mgmt. Assn., 1995. Cert. teaching & adminstr. Ill., N.Y., Minn., Kans. Various teaching & adminstr. positions Pub. Sch. Sys., Wichita, Kans., Apple Valley, Minn., Corinth, NY, 1973—88; dir. instl. edn. Yamaha Corp. Am., 1988—96; dir. pub. engagement Annenberg Inst. Brown U., 1996—99; dir. sch. music U. Minn., 1999—2003, prof. music edn., 1999—2003; pres. Interlochen Ctr. for Arts, 2003—. Mem. Rotary Club Traverse City; corp. bd. Munson Healthcare; bd. dir. Traverse Area Arts Coun., ArtServe Mich. Office: Office of the Pres Interlochen Ctr for Arts PO Box 199 Interlochen MI 49643

KINCAID, JOHN BRUCE, lawyer; b. Chgo., Aug. 25, 1938; s. Cecil Eldred and Marguerite (Donahue) K.; m. Sharon Louise Middleton, Jan. 8, 1966; children: Stacy, Sarah, Tara. BS, No. Ill. U., 1960; JD, Chgo. Kent Coll. Law, 1963. Bar: Ill. 1963, US Dist. Ct. (no. dist. Ill.) 1964, US Ct. Appeals (7th cir.) 1978, US Supreme Ct. 1973. Ptnr. Hinshaw-Culbertson, Chgo., 1963-70, mng. ptnr. Mirabella & Kincaid, Wheaton, Ill., 1970—. Pres. United Way, Wheaton, 1982-84; trustee, elder First Presbyn. Ch., Wheaton, 1981-83. Mem. Assn. Trial Lawyers Am., Ill. Trial Lawyers Assn., Ill. Bar Found. (pres 1996-98), Ill. State Bar (Ill. tort coun. 1983-85), DuPage Bar Assn. (bd. dirs. 1972-75, chmn. profl. responsibility com. 1980-85, pres. 1991-92). Republican. Office: Mirabella & Kincaid Ste 100 1737 S Naperville Rd Wheaton IL 60187 Office Phone: 630-665-7300. Office Fax: 630-665-7609. E-mail: mkpclaw@aol.com.

KINCAID, RICHARD D., real estate company executive; B, Wichita State U.; MBA, U. Tex. With First Nat. Bank Chgo., Barclays Bank PLC; sr. v.p. finance Equity Group Investments, Inc., 1990—95; exec. v.p., CFO Equity Office Properties Trust, exec. v.p., COO, 1997—2001, pres., CEO, 2001—. Mem.: Real Estate Capitol Adv. Com. Office: Equity Office Properties Trust Two N Riverside Plaza Chicago IL 60606

KIND, RONALD JAMES, congressman, lawyer; b. La Crosse, Wis., Mar. 16, 1963; s. Elroy and Greta Kind; m. Tawni Zappa; 2 children. BA with honors, Harvard U., 1985; MA, London Sch. Econs., 1986; JD, U. Minn., 1990. Atty. Quarles and Brady, Milw., 1990—92; district atty. La Crosse County, 1992—96; mem. US Congress from 3rd Wis. dist., 1997—, mem. edn. and the workforce com., mem. resources com., mem. budget com. Active Freshman Bipartisan Campaign Fin. Reform Task Force; co-founder Upper Miss. River Congl. Caucus. Active Boys' and Girls' Club, La Crosse YMCA; bd. dirs. Coulee Coun. Alcohol or Other Drug Abuse. Mem. New Dem. Network, La Crosse Optimists Club. Democrat. Lutheran. Office: US Ho Reps 1406 Longworth Ho Office Bldg Washington DC 20515-4903 Office Phone: 202-225-5506.

KINDER, PETER D., lieutenant governor, former state senator; b. Cape Girardeau, Mo., May 12, 1954; s. James A. and Mary Frances (Hunter) K. Attended, U. Mo. Columbia, SE Mo. State U.; JD, St. Mary U., 1979. Spl. asst. to Rep. Bill Emerson US Congress, Washington, 1981-82; mem. Mo. State Senate from 27th dist., Jefferson City, 1992—2005, pres. pro. tempore, 2000—05; lt. gov. State of Mo., Jefferson City, 2005—. Staff counsel, real estate rep., 1983-87; assoc. publ., S.E. Missourian Newspaper, 1987-2002, asst. to the pres., 1987-94. Mem. Mo. Bar Assn., Am. Cancer Soc., Mo. Farm Bur., Area Wide United Way, Lions Club. Republican. Methodist. Office: Office Lt Governor State Capitol Bldg Rm 121 Jefferson City MO 65101 Office Phone: 573-751-4727. Office Fax: 573-751-9422. E-mail: ltgov@mail.mo.gov.

KINDT, JOHN WARREN, lawyer, educator; b. Oak Park, Ill., May 24, 1950; s. Warren Frederick and Lois Jeannette (Woelffer) K.; m. Beth Talbot Busbee; children: John Warren Jr., James Roy Frederick. AB, Coll. William and Mary, 1972; JD, U. Ga., 1976, MBA, 1977; LLM, U. Va., 1978, SJD, 1981. Bar: D.C. 1976, Ga. 1976, Va. 1977. Advisor to gov. State of Va., Richmond, 1971-72; asst. to Congressman M. Caldwell Butler, U.S. Ho. of Reps., Washington, 1972-73; staff cons. White House, Washington, 1976-77; asst. prof. U. Ill., Champaign, 1978-81, assoc. prof., 1981-85, prof., 1985—. Cons. 3d UN Conf. on Law of Sea; lectr. exec. MBA program U. Ill. Author: Marine Pollution and the Law of the Sea, 4 vols., 1986, 2 vols., 1988, 92, 93, 2007, Economic Impacts of Legalized Gambling, 1994; contbr. articles to profl. jours. Caucus chmn., del. White House Conf. on Youth, 1970; co-chmn. Va. Gov.'s Adv. Coun. on Youth, 1971; mem. Athens (Ga.) Legal Aid Soc., 1975-76. Rotary fellow, 1979-80; Smithsonian ABA/ELI scholar, 1981; sr. fellow London Sch. Econs., 1985-86. Mem. Am. Soc. Internat. Law, D.C. Bar Assn., Va. Bar Assn., Ga. Bar Assn. Home: 801 Brookside Ln Mahomet IL 61853-9545 Office: U Ill 350 Wohlers Hall Champaign IL 61820 Office Phone: 217-333-6018.

KINDT, MONICA V., lawyer; b. San Juan, Nov. 21, 1974; BA, St. Olaf Coll., 1996; JD, Fla. Costal Sch. Law, 1999. Bar: Ohio 1999, US Dist. Ct. Southern Dist. Ohio 1999. Assoc. Cohen, Todd, Kite & Stanford, LLC, Cin., 2005. Named one of Ohio's Rising Stars, Super Lawyers, 2006, 2007, Best lawyers in Am., 2008. Mem.: at. Assn. Bankruptcy Trustees (trustee Cin. Chpt. 7 panel), Ohio State Bar Assn., Cin. Bar Assn. Achievements include fluency in French, Spanish, Portuguese. Office: Cohen Todd Kite & Stanford LLC 250 E Fifth St Ste 1200 Cincinnati OH 45202-4139 Office Phone: 513-421-4020. Office Fax: 513-241-4490.

KING, ALBERT I., engineering educator; b. Tokyo, June 12, 1934; U.S. citizen; married; 2 children. BSc, U. Hong Kong, 1955; MS, Wayne State U., 1960; PhD in Engring. Mechanics, 1966. Demonstrator civil engring., Hong Kong, 1955-58; asst., instr. engring. mechanics Wayne State U., 1958-60, from instr. to assoc. prof., 1960-76, assoc. neurosurgery Sch. Medicine, 1971—, prof. bioengring., 1976—, Disting. Prof. mech. engring., 1990—. Recipient NIH Career Devel. award, Volvo award, 1984, H.R. Lissner award ASME, 1996. Mem. NAE, Am. Soc. Engring. Edn., Am. Soc. Mech. Engrs. (Charles Russ Richards Meml. award 1980), Am. Acad. Orthopaedic Surgeons, Sigma Xi. Achievements include rsch. in human response to acceleration and vibration, automotive and aircraft safety, biomechanics of the spine, mathematical modelling of impact events, low back pain rsch. Office: Bioengring Ctr 818 W Hancock St Detroit MI 48201-3719 E-mail: king@rrb.eng.wayne.edu.

KING, ANDRE RICHARDSON, architectural graphic designer; b. Chgo., July 30, 1931; s. Earl James and Margie Verdetta (Doyle) K.; children: Jandra Maria, Andre Etienne; m. Sally M. Ryan, Sept. 19, 1980. Student, Chgo. Tech. Coll., 1956-57, U. Chgo., 1956-59; BAE., Art Inst. Chgo., 1959; grad., Gemological Inst. Am., 1992. ARK, Archtl. & Environ. Graphic Design Firm est., 1982—; With Skidmore, Owings & Merrill, Chgo., 1956-82; ind. designer, cons., 1982—. Mem. alumni bd. Chgo. Art Inst. Served with USAF, 1951-55. Recipient Design award Art Inst. Chgo., 1959, DESI award, 1982; Hon. consul of Barbados, W.I., 1971— Mem. AIA (assoc.), Am. Inst. Graphic Designers, Soc. Environ. Graphic Designers, Soc. Topographic Arts, Chgo. Soc. Communicating Arts, Art Dirs. Club of Chgo. (pres. 1979-80, 80-82), Art Inst. Chgo. Alumni (bd. dirs.), Arts Club of Chgo., Consular Corps of Chgo., Tavern Club of Chgo., Sigma Pi Phi, Beta Boule. Home: 6700 S Oglesby Ave Apt 1603 Chicago IL 60649-1301 Office Phone: 773-667-5963. Business E-Mail: arkdesign@sbcglobal.net.

KING, CHARLES ROSS, physician; b. Nevada, Iowa, Aug. 22, 1925; s. Carl Russell and Dorothy Sarah (Mills) K.; m. Frances Pamela Carter, Jan. 8, 1949; children— Deborah Diane, Carter Ross, Charles Conrad, Corbin Kent Student, Butler U., 1943; BS in Bus., Ind. U., 1948, MD, 1964. Diplomate Am. Bd. Family Practice. Dep. dir. Ind. Pub. Works and Supply, 1949-52; salesman Knox Coal Corp., 1952-59; rotating intern Marion County Gen. Hosp., Indpls., 1964-65; family practice medicine Anderson, Ind., 1965—. Sec.-treas. staff Cmty. Hosp., 1969-72, pres.-elect, dir., chief medicine, 1973—, bd. dirs., 1973-75; sec.-treas. St. John's Hosp., 1968-69, chief medicine, 1972-73, chief pediatrics, 1977—; bd. dirs. Rolling Hills Convalescnet Ctr., 1968-73; pres. Profl. Ctr. Lab., 1965—; vice chmn. Madison County Bd. Health, 1966-69, chmn., 1986—; chmn. bd. dirs. Star Fin. Bank, Anderson. Bd. dirs. Family Svc. Madison County, 1968-69, Madison County Assn. Mentally Retarded, 1972-76, Anderson Fine Arts Ctr., 1996—; trustee St. Johns Health System., 1898—; chmn. bd. dirs. Anderson Downtown Devel. Corp., 1980—; mem. Paramont Restoration Steering Com., 1994—; trustee, sec.-tread. St. John's Med. Ctr., 1989—; mem. exec. com. Madison United Way Fund, vice-chmn., 1995, chmn., 1996; mem. exec. com. Stop Teen Pregnancy Program, 1995—; exec. commr. Health Search Madison County, 1995—. With U.S. Army, 1944-46. Recipient Dr. James Macholtz award, Spl. Olympics, 1986, Sagamore of Wabash award, State of Ind. Gov., 2002. Fellow Royal Soc. Health, Am. Acad. Family Practice (charter); mem. AMA (numerous Physicians Recognition awards), Ind. Med. Assn., Pan Am. Med. Assn., Am. Acad. Gen. Practice, Madison County Med. Soc. (pres. 1970), 9th Dist. Med. Soc. (sec.-treas. 1968), Anderson C. of C. (bd. dirs. 1979-82), Indpls. Mus. Art (corp. mem.), Anderson Country Club (bd. dirs. 1976-79), Phi Delta Theta (pres. Alumni Assn. 1952), Phi Chi. Clubs: Anderson Country (bd. dirs. 1976-79). Methodist. Office: 2015 Jackson St Anderson IN 46016-4337 Personal E-mail: chardrkm@aol.com.

KING, D. KENT, school system administrator; b. Preston, Mo., 1943; m. Sandy King; 3 children. BA, Ctrl. Mo. State U., 1964; MA, Drury Coll., Springfield, 1967; PhD in Ednl. Adminstrn., Okla. State U., 1972. From tchr. to prin. Houston Sch. Dist., Tex. County, Mo., 1964—70; supt. Licking Sch. Dist., Mo., 1971—77, Rolla Sch. Dist., Mo., 1977—96; dir. Mo. Sch. Improvement Program, 1996—99; dep. commr. Mo. Dept. Edn., Jefferson City, Mo., 1999—2000, commr., 2000—. Office: Mo Dept Edn PO Box 480 Jefferson City MO 65102-0480 Office Phone: 573-751-4446. Office Fax: 573-751-1179.

KING, DONALD A., JR., real estate company executive; Prin. ptnr. The RREEF Funds, Chgo., 1979—. Office: 41st Fl 875 N Michigan Ave Fl 41 Chicago IL 60611-1803

KING, DOUGLAS WILLARD, lawyer; b. St. Louis, Oct. 19, 1959; s. M. Kenton and June Ellen (Greenfield) K. AB summa cum laude, Harvard U., 1981; JD with honors, U. Chgo., 1984. Bar: Mo. 1984, U.S. Dist. Ct. (ea. dist.) Mo. 1985, U.S. Ct. Appeals (8th cir.) 1988. Assoc. Bryan, Cave, McPheeters & McRoberts, St. Louis, 1984-92; ptnr. Bryan Cave LLP, St. Louis, 1993—. Mem. ABA, Bar Assn. Met. St. Louis. Republican. Presbyterian. Office: Bryan Cave LLP 1 Metropolitan Sq 211 N Broadway, Ste 3600 Saint Louis MO 63102-2733 E-mail: dwking@bryancave.com.

KING, EMERY CLARENCE, TV news correspondent; b. Gary, Ind., Mar. 30, 1948; s. Emery Howard and Natalie (Harridy) K.; m. Jacqueline K., Apr. 17, 1976 Student, Purdue U., Ind., Ind. U. Reporter Sta. WJOB-AM, Hammond, Ind., 1970-72; reporter Sta. WWCA-AM, Gary, Ind., 1972-73; reporter, anchor Sta. WBBM-AM-FM, Chgo., 1973-77; polit. reporter Sta. WBBM-TV, Chgo., 1977-80; White House correspondent NBC News, Washington, 1982—. Lectr. in field Recipient Emmy awards, Chgo., 1978, 80; 1st Place award Monte Carlo Internat. Film Festival, 1982 Mem. Radio-TV Correspondents Assn., White House Correspondents Assn. Office: BC News 4001 Nebraska Ave NW Washington DC 20016-2733

KING, G. ROGER, lawyer; b. Ashland, Ohio, Sept. 16, 1946; BS, Miami U., 1968; JD, Cornell U., 1971. Bar: Ohio 1971, D.C. 1972. Legis. asst. U.S. Senator Robert Taft Jr., Washington, 1971-73; profl. staff counsel Labor and Human Resources Com., U.S. Senate, Washington, 1973-74; ptnr. Jones Day, Columbus, Ohio. Office: Jones Day 41 S High St Columbus OH 43215-6103 E-mail: gking@jonesday.com.

KING, J. B., medical device company executive, lawyer; AB, Ind. U., 1951; LLB, Mich. U., 1954. Bar: Ind. 1954, Mich. 1954. Atty., ptnr. Baker & Daniels, 1954-87; v.p., gen. counsel Eli Lilly and Co., Indpls., 1987-95, Guidant Corp., Indpls., 1995—. Bd. dirs. Ind. Corp. Survey Commn., Bank One, Indpls. Indpls. Water Co.; conf. bd. Coun. Chief Legal Officers. Mem. bd. govs. Riley Meml. Assn. Fellow Ind. Bar Found.; mem. ABA, Ind. State Bar Assn., Indpls. Bar Assn., 7th Cir. Bar Assn., Nat. Tax Assn. (com. on multistate taxation), Assn. Gen. Counsel, Ind. Legal Found. (bd. dirs.), Ind. Fiscal Policy Inst. (bd. govs.), Ind. Corp.Survey Commn. Home: 5840 High Fall Rd Indianapolis IN 46226-1018 Office: Guidant Corp PO Box 44906 Indianapolis IN 46244-0906

KING, J. JOSEPH, electronics executive; Group v.p. internat. Molex, exec. v.p., pres., COO, 1999—, bd. dirs. Office: Molex Inc 2222 Wellington Ct Lisle IL 60532

KING, JAMES EDWARD, retired museum director, consultant; b. Escanaba, Mich., July 23, 1940; s. G. Willard and Grace (Magee) K. BS, Alma Coll., 1962, DSc (hon.), 2002; MS, U. N.Mex., 1964; PhD, U. Ariz., 1972. Lab asst. in biology Alma Coll., Mich., 1960-62; rsch. asst. dept. biology U. N.Mex., Albuquerque, 1962-64; teaching asst. dept. botany and plant pathology Mich. State U., East Lansing, 1964-66; plant industry inspector Mich. Dept. Agriculture, Lansing, 1966-68; rsch. asst. dept. geochronology U. Ariz., Tucson, 1968-71, rsch. assoc. dept. geoscis., 1971-72; assoc. curator paleobotany Ill. State Mus., Springfield, 1972-78, head sci. sects. and full curator, 1978-85, asst. dir. for sci., 1985-87; adj. assoc. prof. dept. geology U. Ill., Urbana, 1979-88; dir. Carnegie Mus. Natural History, Pitts., 1987-96, Cleve. Mus. Natural History, 1996—2001; mus. cons., 2001—. Adj. prof. biology Sangamon State U., Springfield, Ill., 1983-87; adj. rsch. scientist Hunt Inst. Bot. Documentation, Carnegie Mellon U., Pitts., 1988—; adj. prof. dept. geology and planetary sci., U. Pitts., 1988-96; vis. scientist in residence Alma (Mich.) Coll., 1985; mem. adv. bd. dept. geosci. U. Ariz., 2005—. Author sci. papers on topics related to geology and paleobotany; mem. editorial bd. Jour. Archaeol. Sci., 1980-87. Bd. dirs. Western Pa. Conservancy, 1996-97, Allegheny Land Trust, 1995-96; trustee Chagrin River Watershed Ptnrs., 1997-2001; mem. exec. com. Univ. Cir., Inc., 1996-2001. Fellow Ill. State Acad. Sci. (pres. 1981-82); mem. Am. Assn. Mus. (bd. dirs. 1994-97), Am. Quaternary Assn., (treas., exec. com. 1976-84), Am. Assn. Stratigraphic Palynologists, Assn. Sci. Mus. Dirs. (v.p. 1992-93, pres. 1993-96), Assn. Systematics Collections (v.p. 1989-91, pres. 1991-93), Sigma Xi (pres. Springfield chpt. 1985-86). Home and Office: Ste 326 6336 N Oracle Rd Tucson AZ 85704

KING, JAMES R., lawyer; b. Geneva, Ill., Oct. 24, 1946; BA, Miami U., 1968; JD, Ohio State U., 1974. Bar: Ohio 1974. Ptnr. Jones Day, Columbus. Office: Jones Day 325 John H Mc Cournel Blvd Ste 600 Columbus OH 43215-6103

KING, JENNIFER ELIZABETH, editor; b. Summit, NJ, July 15, 1970; d. Layton E. and Margery A. (Long) K. BS in Journalism, Northwestern U., Evanston, Ill., 1992. Asst. editor Giant Steps Media, Chgo., 1992-93, assoc. editor Corp. Legal Times, 1993-94, dir. confs., 1994-95, mng. editor Corp. Legal Times, 1995-2001, v.p. editl. Corp. Legal Times, 2001—; acting mng. editor Ill. Legal Times, 1996-97; mng. editor U.S. Bus. Litig., 1997. Office: Corporate Legal Times LLC 656 W Randolph St # 500-e Chicago IL 60661-2114

KING, LARRY, editor; b. Fonda, Iowa; Degree, U. Nebr. From reporter to exec. editor Omaha World-Herald, 1975—98, exec. editor, 1998—. Office: Omaha World-Herald World-Herald Sq 1334 Dodge St Omaha NE 68102-1138

KING, LAWRENCE EDMUND, lawyer; b. Fairbanks, Ark., Sept. 16, 1965; s. Robert Wendell and Helen Jane (Lamar) K.; m. Tamara Kay Biby, July 21, 1988; c. three. BA in Polit. Sci., U. ND, 1989, JD, 1992. Bar: ND 1992, US Dist. Ct. (Dist. ND) 1992, Minn. 1995, Sisseton Wahpeton Sioux Tribal Ct., Turtle Mountain Band Chippewa Indians Tribal Ct., Three Affiliated Tribes Tribal Ct., Spirit Lake Sioux Nation Tribal Ct., Standing Rock Sioux Nation Tribal Ct. Assoc. Zuger Kirmis & Smith, Bismarck, ND, 1992, ptnr. Chmn. fin. com.

McCabe United Meth. Ch., Bismarck, 1995. Recipient William Holland scholarship U. N.D., 1990, William Depuy scholarship, 1990. Mem. ABA (dist. rep. young lawyers divsn. 1994, pres ND young lawyers sect. 1993), ND Bar Assn. (pres. 2006-07), Big Muddy Bar Assn. (past pres.). Mailing: Zuger Kirmis & Smith PO Box 1695 Bismarck ND 58502 Office Phone: 701-223-2711. E-mail: lking@zkslaw.com.

KING, LYNDEL IRENE SAUNDERS, museum director; b. Enid, Okla., June 10, 1943; d. Leslie Jay and Jennie Irene (Duggan) Saunders; m. Blaine Larman King, June 12, 1965. BA, U. Kans., Lawrence, 1965; MA, U. Minn.-Mpls., 1971, PhD, 1982. Dir. Frederick R. Weisman Art Mus., U. Minn., Mpls., 1979—; dir. exhbns. and mus. programs Control Data Corp., 1979, 80-81; exhbn. coord. Nat. Gallery of Art, Washington, 1980. Recipient Cultural Contbn. of Yr. award Mpls. C. of C., 1978; Honor award Minn. Soc. Architects, 1979. Mem. Assn. Art Mus. Dirs. (chair art issues com. 1998-2000, chair tech. comm. com. 2000, bd. trustees 1998—), Art Mus. Assn. Am. (v.p. bd. dirs. 1984-89), Assn. Coll. and Univ. Mus. and Galleries (v.p. 1989-92), Am. Assn. Mus., Internat. Coun. Mus., Upper Midwest Conservation Assn. (pres. bd. dirs. 1980—), Minn. Assn. Mus. (steering com. 1982), Am. Fedn. Arts Bd. Home: 326 W 50th St Minneapolis MN 55419-1247 Office: Weisman Art Mus 333 E River Rd Minneapolis MN 55455-0367 E-mail: wamdir@umn.edu.

KING, MICHAEL HOWARD, lawyer; b. Chgo., Mar. 10, 1943; s. Warren and Betty (Fine) K.; m. Candice M. King, Aug. 18, 1968; children: Andrew, Julie. B.S. Washington U., St. Louis 1967, J.D. 1970. Bar: Ill. 1970, U.S. Dist. Ct. (no. dist.) Ill. 1970, U.S. Dist. Ct. (ea. dist.) Wis. 1972, U.S. Ct. Appeals (7th cir.) 1974, U.S. Ct. Appeals (5th cir.) 1979, U.S. Ct. Appeals (8th cir.) 2007, U.S. Supreme Ct. 1975, U.S. Ct. Appeals (3d cir.) 1983, U.S. Tax Ct. 1987, U.S. Ct. Appeals (10th cir.) 1987, U.S. Dist. Ct. (no. dist.) Calif. 1987, U.S. Dist. Ct. Nebr. 1988, U.S. Dist. Ct. (ctrl. dist.) Ill. 1992, U.S. Dist. Ct. (no. dist.) N.Y. 1992, U.S. Ct. Appeals (2nd cir.) 1994. Spl. atty. organized crime, racketeering sect. U.S. Dept. Justice, Washington, 1970-73; asst. U.S. atty. No. Dist. Ill., Chgo., 1973-75; assoc. Antonow & Fink, Chgo., 1976, ptnr., 1977-79; ptnr. Ross & Hardies, Chgo., 1979-2003, McGuire Woods LLP, 2003-05, LeBoeuf, Lamb, Greene and MacRae LLP, 2005—; chmn. Bd. Commr. Office of State Appellate Defender. Co-author Model Jury Instructions in Criminal Antitrust Cases, 1982, Handbook on Antitrust Grand Jury Investigations, 1988; contbr. articles to profl. jours. Bd. dirs. Chgo. Youth Ctrs., 1977-82; trustee Cove Sch., 1984-88, the Goodman Theatre, 1993. Mem. ABA (litigation sect., antitrust sect., criminal practice procedure com.), Ill. Bar Assn., Chgo. Bar Assn. (judiciary com., antitrust com.), Am. Judicature Soc., Fed. Bar Assn., Assn. Trial Lawyers Am., Mid-Am. Club (bd. govs.), Econ. Club, Chgo. Inn of Cts., Phi Delta Phi, Alpha Epsilon Pi.

KING, NORAH MCCANN, federal judge; b. Steubenville, Ohio, Aug. 13, 1949; d. Charles Bernard and Frances Marcella (Krumm) McCann; married; 4 children. BA cum laude, Rosary Coll. (now Dominican U.), 1971; JD summa cum laude, Ohio State U., 1975. Bar: Ohio 1975, So. Dist. of Ohio 1980. Law clerk U.S. Dist. Ct., Columbus, Ohio, 1975-79; counsel Frost, King, Freytag & Carpenter, Columbus, Ohio, 1979-82; asst. prof. Ohio State U., Columbus, 1980-82; U.S. magistrate judge U.S. Dist. Ct., Columbus, 1982—, chief magistrate judge, 2000—04. Recipient award of merit Columbus Bar Assn., 1990. Mem.: Fed. Bar Assn., Coun. U.S. Magistrate Judges. Office: US Dist Ct 85 Marconi Blvd Rm 235 Columbus OH 43215-2837 Office Phone: 614-719-3390.

KING, ORDIE HERBERT, JR., oral pathologist; b. Memphis, Aug. 11, 1933; s. Ordie Herbert and Hazel (Eaton) King; m. Violette Papagianis, Mar. 21, 1974; children: Catherine Ann, Alexander Carlos;children from previous marriage: Anna LaVelle, Ordie Herbert III. BS, Memphis State U., 1957; DDS, U. Tenn., 1959, PhD, 1965. Diplomate Am. Bd. Oral and Maxillofacial Pathology. USPHS postdoctoral fellow U. Tenn., 1960-62, rsch. assoc. dept. pathology, 1963-65, asst. prof. pathology, 1965, resident oral pathology City of Memphis Hosps., 1962-63; asst. prof. pathology Northwestern U., 1966; assoc. prof. oral pathology St. Louis U., 1967-69, prof., 1969-70, chmn. dept., 1967-70, chmn. dept. dentistry univ. hosps., 1967-70; acting chmn., vis. assoc. prof. oral pathology Washington U., St. Louis, 1969-70, clin. prof. pathology Sch. Dental Medicine, 1972-80; prof. oral pathology, assoc. prof. pathology W.Va. U., Morgantown, 1970-74, prof. pathology, 1974, dir. Cytopathology Lab., Med. Ctr., 1971-74; prof. pathology Sch. Dental Medicine So. Ill. U., Alton, 1974-97, chmn. dept. diagnostic specialties Sch. Dental Medicine, 1979-92. Dir. So. Ill. Pathology Lab., Ltd., Godfrey, 1977—; dental cons. to chief med. examiner State of Tenn., 1963—65; mem. exec. com. St. Louis U. Hosps., 1967—70; mem. med. staff W. Tenn. Cancer Clinic, 1962—65, W.Va. U. Hosp., 1970—74; mem. med./dental staff dept. pathology Alton Meml. Hosp., 1986—; cons. VA Hosp., Clarksville, W.Va., 1973—74; dental cons. St. Louis County Med. Examiner, 1968—70; cons. cancer control program Nat. Ctr. Chronic Disease Control, USPHS, 1967—70; mem. Mo. Bd. Dental Splty. Examiners, 1982—84. Fellow: Am. Acad. Oral Pathology; mem.: ADA, Am. Cancer Soc. (bd. dirs. W.Va. divsn. 1972—74), Am. Soc. Cytopathology, Ill. Walking Horse Assn. (bd. dirs. 2000—), Spotted Saddle Horse Assn. Ill. (v.p. 2001, 2005—07, pres. 2002—04), Tenn. Walking Horse Breeders and Exhibitors Assn., Spotted Saddle Horse Breeders and Exhibitors Assn., Omicron Kappa Upsilon, Phi Rho Sigma, Kappa Alpha Order, Delta Sigma Delta. Home: 6111 Vollmer Ln Godfrey IL 62035-1062 Office: So Ill Path Lab Ltd Godfrey IL 62035

KING, REATHA CLARK, community foundation executive; b. Ga. m. N. Judge King Jr.; children: N. Judge III, Scott. BS in Chemistry and Math., Clark Coll., 1958; PhD in Chemistry, U. Chgo., 1960; MBA, Columbia U., 1977; doctorate (hon.), Smith Coll., 1993, S.C. State U., 1995. Rsch. chemist Nat. Bur. Standards, Washington, 1963-68; mem. chemistry faculty York Coll. CUNY, Jamaica, 1968-77, assoc. dean divsn. natural scis. and math., 1970-74, assoc. dean acad. affairs, 1974-77; pres. Met. State U., St. Paul, Mpls., 1977-88; pres., exec. dir. Gen. Mills Found., Mpls., 1988—. Bd. dirs. Minn. Mut. Ins. Co., St. Paul, H.B. Fuller Co., St. Paul, N.W. Corp., Mpls.; cons., spkr. in field. Contbr. numerous articles to profl. jours. Bd. dirs. Coun. on Founds., Washington, Minn. Coun. on Found., H.B. Fuller Co. Found., St. Paul, Corp. Nat. and Cmty. Svc., vice-chair; chair corp. adv. coun. ARC; bd. overseers Clark Atlanta U.; mem. ministers and missionaries benefit bd. Am. Bapt. Ch., N.Y.C. Recipient Sisterhood award for disting. humanitarian svc. Nat. Conf. Christian and Jews, 1993, Woman of Distinction award St. Croix Valley Girl Scouts, 1995. Mem. NAACP (cmty. svc. award in edn. 1994), Delta Sigma Theta. Home: 110 Bank St SE Apt 2005 Minneapolis MN 55414-3905

KING, ROBERT CHARLES, biologist, educator; b. NYC, June 3, 1928; s. Charles James and Amanda (McCutchen) King. BS, Yale U., 1948, PhD, 1952. Scientist biology dept. Brookhaven Nat. Lab., 1951-55; mem. faculty Northwestern U., 1956—, prof. biology, 1964-99, prof. emeritus, 2000—. Chmn. 8th Brookhaven Symposium in Biology, 1955; vis. investigator, fellow Rockefeller U., 1959; NSF sr. postdoctoral fellow U. Edinburgh, Scotland, 1958, Commonwealth Sci. and Indsl. Research Orgn. Div. Entomology, Canberra, Australia, 1963, Sericultural Expt. Sta., Tokyo, Japan, 1970 Author: Genetics, 2d edit., 1965, A Dictionary of Genetics, 7th edit., 2006, (with W.D. Stansfield and P.K. Mulligan) Ovarian Development in Drosophila melanogaster, 1970, also numerous papers; editor: Handbook of Genetics Series, 5 vols., (with H. Akai) Insect Ultrastructure, 2 vols., 1982. Fellow AAAS; mem. Am. Soc. Zoologists, Histochem. Soc., Am. Soc. Cell Biology (treas. 1972-75), Electron Microscopy Soc. Am., Genetics Soc. Am., Am. Soc. Naturalists, Soc. Devel. Biology, Entomol. Soc. Am., Genetics Soc. Can., Genetics Soc. Korea, Sigma Xi (pres. Northwestern U. chpt. 1966-67) Home: 2890 Fredric Ct Northbrook IL 60062-7504 Business E-Mail: r-king@northwestern.edu.

KING, ROBERT HENRY, minister, religious organization administrator, former education educator; b. Sunny South, Ala., Apr. 1, 1922; s. Henry C. and Della S. (Bettis) K.; m. Edna Jean McCord, June 1, 1949; children: Jocelyn, Jann, Roger. BD, Immanuel Luth. Sem., Greensboro, NC, 1949; MEd, U. Pitts., 1956; MA, Ind. U., 1968, PhD, 1969. Ordained to ministry Luth. Ch.—Mo. Synod, 1949. Pastor Victory Luth. Ch., Youngstown, Ohio, 1949-57, St. Philip Luth. Ch., Chgo., 1957-65; asst. prof. Concordia Tchrs. Coll., River Forest, Ill., 1968-70; prof. edn. Lincoln U., Jefferson City, Mo., 1970-87; v.p. Luth. Ch.—Mo. Synod, St. Louis, 1986—. Pastor Pilgrim Luth. Ch., Freedom, Mo., 1977-97; dir. lay ministry Concordia Coll., Selma, Ala., 1987-90; vis. instr. Concordia Sem., St. Louis, 1989—; dir. workshop Obot Idim Sem., Nigeria, 1990. Contbr. articles to profl. jours. Mem. Jefferson City Sch. Bd., 1973-76. Lilly Found. fellow, 1965. Mem.: Mo. Assn. Adult Continuing Edn., Phi Delta Kappa. Lutheran. Office: 901 Roland Ct Jefferson City MO 65101-3576

KING, SHARON LOUISE, retired lawyer; AB, Mt. Holyoke Coll., 1954; JD with distinction, Valparaiso U., 1957; LLM in Taxation, Georgetown U., 1961. Bar: Ind. 1957, D.C. 1958, Ill. 1962. Trial atty. tax divsn. U.S. Dept. Justice, 1958—62; ptnr. Sidley Austin LLP, Chgo.; ret. Bd. dirs., past pres. Lawyer's Com. for Better Housing, Inc.; mem. North Shore Sr. Ctr., 2006—, bd. dirs., 2006—. Fellow Am. Coll. Tax Counsel; mem. ABA (chmn. com. closely-held corps. taxation sect. 1979-81, regulated pub. utilities com. taxation sect. 1982-83, coun. dir. taxation sect. 1983-86), Chgo. Bar Assn. (bd. mgrs. 1973-75, chmn. fed. tax com. 1983-84), Ill. State Bar Assn. (counsel dir. sect. fed. taxation 1989-91), Women's Bar Found. (bd. dirs., past pres.). Office: Sidley Austin LLP One S Dearborn St Chicago IL 60603

KING, STEVE, congressman; b. Storm Lake, Iowa, May 28, 1949; m. Marilyn King; 3 children. Student, N.W. Mo. State U., 1967-70. Mem. Iowa State Senate from 6th dist., Des Moines, 1996—2002; vice chair natural resources and environ. com.; mem. appropriations com., mem. bus. and labor rels. com.; mem. commerce com., mem. state govt. com.; mem. US Congress from 5th Iowa dist., 2003—; mem. Ho. Judiciary com. Mem. St. Martin's Cath. Ch.; bd. dirs. Odebolt Cmty. Housing. Mem. Iowa Cattleman's Assn., Land Improvement Contractors Am., U.S. C. of C., Odebolt C. of C., SAC County Farm Bur. Republican. Office: US Ho Reps 1432 Longworth Ho Office Bldg Washington DC 20515-1505

KING, TIM, charter school administrator; b. Chgo., 1967; BA, LLD, Georgetown U. Pres. Hales Franciscan HS, Chgo., 1994—2005; founder & CEO Urban Prep Charter Acad. for Young Men, Chgo., 2006—. Named one of 40 Under 40, Crain's Chgo. Bus., 2006. Office: Urban Prep Academies Ste 203 420 N Wabash Chicago IL 60611 also: Englewood Campus 6201 S Stewart Ave Chicago IL 60621 Office Phone: 312-276-0259. Office Fax: 312-755-1050.

KINGDON, JOHN WELLS, political science professor; b. Wisconsin Rapids, Wis., Oct. 28, 1940; s. Robert Wells and Catherine (McCune) K.; m. Kirsten Berg, June 16, 1965; children: James, Tor. BA, Oberlin Coll., 1962; MA, U. Wis., 1963, PhD, 1965. Asst. prof. polit. sci. U. Mich., Ann Arbor, 1965-70, assoc. prof., 1970-75, prof., 1975-98, prof. emeritus, 1998—, chmn. dept. polit. sci., 1982-87. Author: Candidates for Office, 1968, Congressmen's Voting Decisions, 1973, 3d rev. edit., 1989, Agendas, Alternatives and Public Policies, 1984, 2d edit., 1995, America the Unusual, 1998. NSF grantee, 1978-82, Soc. Sci. Research Council grantee, 1969-70; Guggenheim fellow, 1979-80, Ctr. for Advanced Study in Behaviorial Scis. fellow, 1987-88. Fellow Am. Acad. Arts and Scis.; mem. Midwest Polit. Sci. Assn. (pres. 1987-88). Office: U Mich Dept Polit Sci Ann Arbor MI 48109

KINGSLEY, JAMES GORDON, college administrator; b. Houston, Nov. 22, 1933; s. James Gordon and Blanche Sybil (Payne) K.; m. Martha Elizabeth Sasser, Aug. 24, 1956 (div. 1992); children: Gordon Alan, Craig Emerson; m. Suzanne H. Patterson, Oct. 30, 1993; 1 child, Aaron T. AB, Miss. Coll., 1955; MA, U. Mo., 1956; BD, ThD, ew Orleans Bapt. Theol. Sem., 1960-65; HHD (hon.), Mercer U., 1980; LittD (hon.), Seinan Gakuin U., Japan, 1989; postgrad., U. Louisville, 1968-69, Nat. U. Ireland, 1970, Harvard U., 1976. Asst. prof. Miss. Coll., 1956-58; instr. Tulane U., 1958-60; asst. prof. William Jewell Coll., Liberty, Mo., 1960-62; assoc. prof. Ky. So. Coll., Louisville, 1964-67, prof., 1967-69; prof. lit. and religion William Jewell Coll., 1969-93, dean, 1976-80, pres., 1980-93; v.p. Health Midwest, Kansas City, Mo., 1994—2002; dep. dir. Nelson-Atkins Mus. of Art, 1995-96; prin. Halaxton Coll., Grantham, England, 2003—. Vis. fellow Cambridge (Eng.) U., 1988. Author: A Time for Openness, 1973, Frontiers, 1983, Conversations with Leaders for a New Millenium, 1991, A Place Called Grace, 1993, Kansas City Sesquicentennial: A Celebration of the Heart, 2001; contbr. articles to profl. jours. Bd. dirs. Mo. Repertory Theatre, Episcopal Sem. S.W. LaRue fellow, 1976. Mem. English Speaking Union, Burren Conservancy, Cambridge Soc. Episcopalian. Home: Lakewood 402 NE Point Dr Lees Summit MO 64064-1561 Office: Harlaxton College Grantham LINCS NG32 1AG England

KINLIN, DONALD JAMES, lawyer; b. Boston, Nov. 29, 1938; s. Joseph Edward and Ruth Claire (Byrne) K.; m. Donna C. (McGrath), Nov. 29, 1959; children: Karen J., Donald J., Joseph P., and Kevin S. BS in acctg., Syracuse U., 1968, MBA, 1970; JD, U. Nebr., 1975. Bar: Nebr., 1976, Ohio, 1982, U.S. Supreme Ct., 1979, U.S. Claims Ct., 1982, U.S. Tax Ct., 1982, U.S. Ct. Appeals (5th and fed. cir.), 1982. Atty. USAF, Mather AFB, Calif., 1976-78; sr. trial atty. Air Force Contract Law Ctr., Wright Patterson AFB, Ohio, 1978-86, dep. dir., 1986-87; ptnr. Smith and Schnacke, Dayton, Ohio, 1987-89, Thompson and Hine LLP, Dayton, Ohio, 1989—. Mem. adv. bd. Fed. Publ. Inc., Govt. Contract Costs, Pricing & Acctg. Report. Contbr. articles to legal jours. Pres. Forest Ridge Assn., Dayton,Ohio, 1984-96; sec., gen. counsel U.S. Air and Trade Show, 1994-98, chmn., 1998—; bd. dir. Nat. Aviation Hall of Fame, 1998—. Mem. ABA (chmn. sect. pub. contract law 1993-94), sec., budget and fin. officer sect., coun. mem., chmn. fed. procurement divsn., vice chmn. acctg., cost and pricing com., truth in negotiations com., chmn. cost acctg. stas. sub com.), Fed. Bar Assn., Ohio Bar Assn., Nebr. Bar Assn., Contracts Appeals Bar Assn. (bd. govs. 1998-2001). Avocation: travel. Office: Thompson Hine LLP 10 W 2nd St Dayton OH 45402-1758

KINNEY, EARL ROBERT, mutual funds company executive; b. Burnham, Maine, Apr. 12, 1917; s. Harry E. and Ethel (Vose) K.; m. Margaret Velie Thatcher, Apr. 23, 1977; children: Jeanie Elizabeth, Earl Robert, Isabella Alice. AB, Bates Coll., 1939; postgrad., Harvard U. Grad. Sch., 1940. Founder, North Atlantic Pack Co., Bar Harbor, Maine, 1941, pres., 1941-42, treas., dir., 1941-64; with Gorton Corp. (became subs. Gen. Mills, Inc. 1968), 1954-68, pres., 1958-68; v.p. Gen. Mills, Inc., 1968-69, exec. v.p., 1969-73, chief fin. officer, 1970-73, pres., chief operating officer, 1973-77, chmn. bd., 1977-81; pres., chief exec. officer IDS Mut. Fund Group, Mpls., 1982-87. Bd. dirs. Idexx Labs., Inc. Trustee Bates Coll., also chmn. alumni drives, 1960-64. Office: 4900 IDS Ctr Minneapolis MN 55402 Office Phone: 612-332-1369.

KINNEY, ELEANOR DE ARMAN, law educator; b. Boston, Jan. 17, 1947; d. Thomas DeArman and Eleanor Shepard (Roberts) K.; m. Charles Malcolm Clark Jr., June 25, 1983; children: Janet Marie, Brian Alexander, Margaret Louise. AB, Duke U., 1969, JD, 1973; MA, U. Chgo., 1970; MPH, U. N.C., 1979. Bar: Ohio 1973, N.C. 1977, U.S. Dist. Ct. (no. dist.) Ohio 1974. Assoc. Squire, Sanders & Dempsey, Cleve., 1973-77; estate planning officer Duke U. Med. Ctr., Durham, N.C., 1977-79; program analyst HHS, Washington, 1979-82; asst. gen. counsel Am. Hosp. Assn., Chgo., 1982-84; vis. prof. Ind. U. Sch. Law, Indpls., 1984-85, asst. prof., 1985-88, found. dir. William S. & Christine S. Hall Ctr. for Law and Health, 1987—, assoc. prof., 1988-90, Hall Render prof. law & exec. dir. Latin Am. Law Program, 1990—; adj prof. Ind. U. Sch. Public & Environ. Affairs & Sch. Medicine. Cons. Adminstrv. Conf. U.S., Washington, 1985—91; mem. exec. bd. Ind. State Bd. of Health, 1989—99; Fulbright fellow Nat. Univ. LaPlata, Argentina, 1999—2000. Author: Protecting American Health Care Consumers, 2002. Ed., Guide to Medicare Coverage Decision-Making and Appeals, 2002. Contbr. articles to legal jours., also monographs, chpts. to books. Mem.: ABA (coun. sect. on adminstrv. law and regulatory practice 1997—, vice-chair 2003—04, chair-elect 2004—05), Am. Law Inst., Am. Assn. Law Schs. (bd. mem. sect. on on adminstrv. law law 1998—, vice chair 2003—04, chair-elect 2004—05, chair 2005—), Am. Pub. Health Assn. Office: Indiana U School of Law Inlow Hall Room 136F 530 W New York St Indianapolis IN 46202-3225 Office Phone: 317-274-1912, 317-274-4091. Business E-Mail: ekinney@iupui.edu.

KINNEY, JOHN FRANCIS, bishop; b. Oelwein, Iowa, June 11, 1937; s. John F. and Marie B. (McCarty) Kinney. Student, St. Paul Sem., 1957-63, N.Am. Coll., Rome, 1968-71; JCD, Pontifical Lateran U., 1971. Ordained priest Archdiocese of St. Paul and Mpls., Minn., 1963, vice chancellor, 1966-73, aux. bishop, 1976—82; assoc. pastor Ch. of St. Thomas, Mpls., 1963-66, Cathedral, St. Paul, 1971-74, chancellor, 1973; pastor Ch. of St. Leonard, St. Paul, 1974; ordained bishop, 1977; bishop Diocese of Bismark, ND, 1982—85, Diocese of St. Cloud, Minn., 1995—. Mem.: Canon Law Soc. Am. Roman Catholic. Office: Diocese of Saint Cloud 214 Third Ave PO Box 1248 Saint Cloud MN 56302-1248 Office Phone: 320-251-2340. Office Fax: 320-258-7618. E-mail: jkinney@gw.stcdio.org.*

KINNEY, THOMAS J. JOHN, adult education educator; b. Dansville, NY, Jan. 31, 1946; m. Linda G. Gates, Dec. 12, 1970; children: Matthew, Andrew. BA in Psychology, Syracuse U., 1968; MSW in Mgmt., SUNY, Albany, 1974. Case worker Livingston County Social Svc., Geneseo, NY, 1969—72; tng. specialist N.Y. State Dept. Social Svcs., Albany, 1974—76; dir. continuing edn. U. Albany, SUNY, 1976—82, dir. profl. development program, Nelson A. Rockefeller coll. pub. affairs and policy, 1983—99, spl. asst. to provost, 1997-99; chief learning officer, v.p. edn. Premier Health Alliance, Chgo., 1999—2001; CEO Kinney and Assoc., 2000—; faculty Keller Grad. Sch. Mgmt., 2002—, U. Phoenix Sch. Bus., 2001—. Bd. dirs. Synquest Technologies, Inc.; mem. Task Force N.Y. State Work Force 21st Century; mem. SUNY 2000 Task Group Social Svcs.; dir. Ctr. Profl. Devel. and Continuing Edn. Rsch., chmn. quality forum Rockefeller Coll. Press; prof. Russian Acad. Edn.; co-founder Russian-Am. Ctr. Adult and Continuing Edn., Moscow; mem. task force employee assistance programs N.Y. State Assembly; mem. implementation adv. com. WorkKeys project Am. Coll. Testing; presenter in field. Editor Jour. Continuing Social Work Edn. Named Continuing Educator of Yr., Continuing Edn. Assn. N.Y., 1988; named to Internat. Adult and Continuing Hall of Fame, 1996 Fellow N.Y. State Acad. Pub. Adminstrn.; mem. Am. Assn. Adult and Continuing Edn. (treas., past chair commn. continuing profl. edn., Outstanding Svc. medallion 1994, pres. 1998-2000), Nat. Univ. Continuing Edn. Assn. (chair divsn. continuing edn. professions, mem. fin. com., mem. task force displaced profls.). Avocation: wood carving. Office Phone: 630-667-8468. E-mail: thomaskinney@msn.com.

KINNISON, WILLIAM ANDREW, retired university president; b. Springfield, Ohio, Feb. 10, 1932; s. Errett Lowell and Audrey Muriel (Smith) K.; m. Lenore Belle Morris, June 11, 1960; children— William Errett, Linda Elise, Amy Elisabeth. AB, Wittenberg U., 1954, BS in Edn., 1955; MA, U. Wis., 1963; PhD (1st Flesher fellow), Ohio State U., 1967; postgrad., Harvard U. Inst. Ednl. Mgmt., 1970; LL.D., Calif. Luth. Coll., 1983; Th.D., John Carroll U., 1983; LLD, Lenoir-Rhyne Coll., 1987; LHD, Capital U., 1995. Asst. dean admissions Wittenberg U., Springfield, 1958-65, asst. to pres., 1967-70, v.p. for univ. affairs, 1970-73, v.p. adminstrn., 1973, pres., 1974-95, pres. emeritus, 1995—; pres., CEO Heritage Ctr. of Clark County, 1997—2002. Author: Samuel Shellabarger: Lawyer, Jurist, Legislator, 1969, Building Sullivant's Pyramid: An Administrative History of the Ohio State University, 1970, Concise History of Wittenberg University, 1976, An American Seminary, 1980, Springfield and Clark County: an Illustrated History, 1985, also articles. Asst. to dir. Sch. Edn. Ohio State U., Columbus, 1965-67; past chmn. Assn. Ind. Colls. and Univs. Ohio; trustee Ohio Found. Ind. Colls., 1974-95, chair bd. trustees, 1995; chmn. standing com. Luth. World Ministries, 1976-82; mem. exec. coun. Luth. Ch. in Am., 1978-86; mem., chmn. Commn. for a New Luth. Ch., 1982-86; bd. dirs. Am. Assn. Colls., 1982-84. With U.S. Army, 1956-58. Mem. Clark County Hist. Soc. (trustee 1963—), Orgn. Am. Historians, Blue Key, Phi Beta Kappa, Phi Delta Kappa, Kappa Phi Kappa, Pi Sigma Alpha, Tau Kappa Alpha, Delta Sigma Phi, Omicron Delta Kappa. Clubs: Cosmos, Rotary. Home: 1820 Timberline Dr Springfield OH 45504-1236

KINNOIN, MEYER D., state legislator; m. Diane; 4 children. Mem. N.D. Senate, 1989—; vice chmn. state and fed. govt. com. Past mem. agr. com., fin. and tax. com. .D. Senate; former mem. Mountrail County Park Commn., Housing Commn., U.S. Dept. Agr.; farmer Recipient Disting. Svc. Award Jaycees. Address: 6695 Clearlake Rd Palermo ND 58769-9314

KINS, JURIS, lawyer; b. Jelgava, Latvia, Apr. 24, 1942; came to US, 1949; s. Arnolds and Zenta (Dunis) K.; m. Olita Gita Kakis, Oct. 11, 1969; children: Aleksis A., Mikus N. BSChemE, U. Wis., 1964; MSChemE, U. Mich., 1965; JD, U. Wis., 1969. Bar: Wis. 1969, Ill. 1969. Assoc. ptnr. Chadwell & Kayser, Ltd., Chgo., 1969-90; ptnr. Vedder, Price, Kaufman & Kammholz, Chgo., 1990-93; Abramson & Fox, Chgo., 1993—. Pres. Latvian Peoples Support Group, Chgo., 1991—. Mem. ABA, Chgo. Bar Assn., Ill. Bar Assn., Wis. Bar Assn., Latvian Bar Assn. Avocations: tennis, skiing. Office: Abramson & Fox One E Wacker Dr Ste 3800 Chicago IL 60601 E-mail: juriskins@aol.com.

KINTNER, PHILIP L., history professor; b. Canton, Ohio, Jan. 23, 1926; s. William Wagner and Effie (Erwin) K.; m. Anne Genung, Dec. 27, 1951 (dec. June 2003); children: Karen, Judith, Jennifer. BA, Wooster Coll., 1950; MA, Yale U., 1952, PhD, 1958. Instr. Trinity Coll., Hartford, Conn., 1954-56, Reed Coll., Portland, Oreg., 1957-58, Trinity Coll., 1958-59, asst. prof., 1959-64; vis. assoc. prof. U. Iowa, Iowa City, 1964-65; assoc. prof. Grinnell (Iowa) Coll., 1964-69; coll. entrance bd. exam commissioner European History, Princeton, NJ, 1968-70; chief reader advanced placement European history, 1969-72; ACM prof. Florence (Italy) Program, 1989-90; prof. Grinnell Coll., 1970-96, Rosenthal prof. humanities, 1976-96; prof. emeritus, 1996—. With U.S. Army, 1944-46. Recipient numerous travel/study grants for rsch. and publ. in Germany. Mem. Sixteenth Century Studies Conf. Avocations: woodworking, cooking, mineral hunting. Home: 716 Broad St Grinnell IA 50112-2226 Office: Grinnell Coll PO Box 805 Grinnell IA 50112-0805 E-mail: kintner@grinnell.edu.

KIPNIS, DAVID MORRIS, physician, educator; b. Balt., May 23, 1927; s. Rubin and Anna (Mizen) Kipnis; m. Paula Jane Levin, Aug. 16, 1953; children: Lynne, Laura, Robert. AB, Johns Hopkins U., 1945, MA, 1949; MD, U. Md., 1951. Intern Johns Hopkins Hosp., 1951—52; resident Duke Hosp., Durham, NC, 1952—54, U. Md. Hosp., 1954—55; asst. prof. medicine Washington U. Sch. Medicine, St. Louis, 1958—63, assoc. prof., 1963—65, prof., 1965—, Busch prof., chmn. dept. medicine, 1972—92; disting. prof. medicine Washington U. Sch. of Medicine, St. Louis, 1992—; asst. physician Barnes Hosp., assoc. physician, 1963—72, physician-in-chief, 1972—93, disting. univ. prof., 1993—. Chmn. endocrine study sect. NIH, 1963—64, diabetes tng. program com., 1970—; chmn. Nat. Diabetes Adv. Bd. Editor: Diabetes, 1973; mem. editl. bd.: Am. Jour. Medicine, 1973, Am. Jour. Med. Scis.; contbr. articles to profl. jours. With US Army, 1945—46. amed Banting lectr., Brit. Diabetes Assn., 1972; scholar Markle scholar in med. scis., 1957—62. Mem.: NAS (coun. mem. 1997—2000), Nat. Acad. Scis., Inst. Medicine, Am. Acad. Arts and Scis., Am. Soc. Biol. Chemists, Endocrine Soc. (Oppenheimer award 1965), Am. Diabetes Assn. (Lilly award 1965, Banting medal 1977, Best medal 1981), Am. Fedn. Clin. Rsch., Assn. Am. Physicians (Kober medal 1994), Am. Soc. Clin. Investigation. Home: 7200 Wydown Blvd Saint Louis MO 63105-3023 Office: Barnes Hosp Dept Medicine PO Box 8212 660 S Euclid Ave Saint Louis MO 63110-1010

KIPPER, BARBARA LEVY, wholesale distribution executive; b. Chgo., July 16, 1942; d. Charles and Ruth (Doctoroff) Levy; m. David A. Kipper, Sept. 9, 1974; children: Talia Rose, Tamar Judith. BA, U. Mich., 1964. Reporter Chgo. Sun-Times, 1964-67; photo editor Cosmopolitan Mag., NYC, 1969-71; vice chmn. Chas Levy Co., Chgo., 1984-86, chmn., 1986—. Trustee Spertus Inst. Jewish Studies, Chgo. Hist. Mus., Golden Apple Ind., Joffrey Ballet of Chgo., Chgo. Zool. Soc. Recipient Deborah award Com. Women's Equality, Am. Jewish Congress, 1992, Shap Shapiro Human Rels. award The Anti-Defamation League of B'nai B'rith, Personal PAC's Leadership award, 1996, Disting. Cmty. Leadership award, ADL, Jewish Culture, 2004, Golden Sceptre award Nat. Found. Jewish Culture; named at. Soc. Fund Raising Execs. Disting. Philanthropist, 1995. Mem.: Chgo. Network, Com. of 200, Internat. Women's Forum, Econ. Club of Chgo., Chgo. etwork, The Standard Club. Jewish. Office Phone: 708-356-3601. Business E-Mail: bkipper@chaslevy.com.

KIPPERMAN, LAWRENCE I., lawyer; b. Chgo., Nov. 22, 1941; s. Solomon and Idelle (Goldman) Kipperman; m. Carol A. Kipperman, Jan. 29, 1967 (div. Sept. 1985); children: Anna, Lynne. BA, U. Ill., 1963, JD, 1966; LLM, George Washington U., 1968. Bar: Ill. 1966, U.S. Dist. Ct. (no. dist.) Ill. 1966, U.S. Supreme Ct. 1968, Ohio 1970, U.S. Ct. Appeals (7th cir.) 1973, U.S. Ct. Appeals (8th cir.) 1986. Atty. NLRB, Washington, 1966-70; assoc. Burke, Haber & Berick, Cleve., 1970-71, Sidley Austin Brown & Wood (now Sidley Austin LLP), Chgo., 1971—73, ptnr., 1973—2000; sr. counsel Sidley Austin LLP, Chgo., 2000—. Lectr. Ill. Inst. Continuing Legal Edn., 1985, Am. Arbitration Assn. Mem.: ABA, Ill. State Bar Assn., Chgo. Bar Assn., Legal Club Chgo. Jewish. Avocations: architecture, baseball, basketball, jazz. Office: Sidley Austin Brown & Wood Bank One Plz Chicago IL 60603-2000 Home Phone: 312-266-9348; Office Phone: 312-853-7471. Business E-Mail: lkipperman@sidley.com.

KIRBY, DOROTHY MANVILLE, social worker; b. Burke, SD, Oct. 23, 1917; d. Charles Vietz and Gail Lorena (Coonen) Manville; m. Sigmund Kirby, July 11, 1941 (div. 1969); children; Paul Howard, Robert Charles. BA, Wayne

State U., 1970, MSW, 1972. Cert. social worker, Mich.; lic. marriage and family therapist, Mich. Pvt. practice social work, Allen Park, Mich., 1973—. Instr. stress, personal effectiveness and comm. Pres. Allen Park Symphony Orch., 1990-92. Mem.: LWV (pres. Allen Park 1965—66), NASW (clin.), AAUW, Mich. Assn. Marriage and Family Therapy (sec. 1982), Nat. Assn. Marriage and Family Therapy. Presbyterian. Avocation: playing violin. Home and Office: 15720 Wick Rd Allen Park MI 48101-1535 Office Phone: 313-382-0623. E-mail: dmkirby@ameritech.net.

KIRBY, TERRY, professional football player; b. Hampton, Va., Jan. 20, 1970; B of Psychology, U. Va. Running back Miami (Fla.) Dolphins, 1993-95, San Francisco 49ers, 1996-98; NFC Championship Game, 1997; running back Cleve. Browns, 1999—. Office: c/o Cleve Browns 1085 W 3rd St Cleveland OH 44114

KIRCHER, JOHN JOSEPH, law educator; b. Milw., July 26, 1938; s. Joseph John and Martha Marie (Jach) K.; m. Marcia Susan Adamkiewicz, Aug. 26, 1961; children: Joseph John, Mary Kathryn. BA, Marquette U., 1960, JD, 1963. Bar: Wis. 1963, U.S. Dist. Ct. (ea. dist.) Wis. 1963, U.S. Ct. Appeals (7th cir.) 1992. Sole practice, Port Washington, Wis., 1963-66; with Def. Research Inst., Milw., 1966-80, research dir., 1972-80; with Marquette U., 1970—, prof. law, 1980—, assoc. dean acad. affairs, 1992-93. Chmn. Wis. Jud. Council, 1981-83. Author: (with J.D. Ghiardi) Punitive Damages: Law and Practice, 1981, 2d edit (with C.M. Wiseman), 2000; editor Federation of Defense and Corporate Counsel Quarterly; mem. editorial bd. Def. Law Jour.; contbr. articles to profl. jours. Recipient Teaching Excellence award Marquette U., 1986, Disting. Service award Def. Research Inst., 1980, Marquette Law Rev. Editors' award, 1988. Mem. ABA (Robert B. McKay Professor award 1993), Am. Law Inst., Wis. Bar Assn., Wis. Supreme Ct. Bd. of Bar Examiners (vice chair 1989-91, chair 1992), Am. Judicature Soc., Nat. Sports Law Inst. (adv. com. 1989—), Assn. Internationale de Droit des Assurances, Scribes. Roman Catholic. Office: PO Box 1881 Milwaukee WI 53201-1881 Home Phone: 414-351-5242; Office Phone: 414-288-7095. Business E-Mail: john.kircher@marquette.edu.

KIRCHHOEFER, GREGG G., lawyer; b. St. Louis, Mar. 27, 1950; s. Theodore Frank and Virginia May (Schumacher) K.; m. Mary Cunningham Fanning, Sept. 25, 1976; 1 child, John Cordes. BS in Commerce and Fin., St. Louis U., 1972, JD cum laude, 1982. Bar: Ill. Mgr. Burroughs, St. Louis, 1972-73; product mgr. Comshare, Chgo., 1975-79; cons. McCormick Baron, St. Louis, 1979-82; assoc. Bell, Boyd & Lloyd, Chgo., 1982-84, Kirkland & Ellis LLP, Chgo., 1984-88, ptnr., 1988—. Bd. dirs. Bell Flavors and Fragrances, Inc., Chgo., Boys Hope/Girls Hope, Chgo. Author: The Computer Law Association and Illinois Institute for Continuing Legal Edn., 1991, Proceedings of the SAE International Computer Conference, 1989; contbr.many articles to profl. jours. Mem. ABA (liaison, sci. and tech. sect.), Computer Law Assn., Internat. Bar Assn. Office: Kirkland & Ellis 200 E Randolph Dr Fl 54 Chicago IL 60601-6636 E-mail: gkirchhoefer@kirkland.com.

KIRCHICK, CALVIN B., lawyer; b. NYC, Apr. 6, 1946; s. Jean Kirchick; m. Judith Madian, Apr. 28, 1968; children: Ross, Lisa, Joelle. BA magna cum laude, U. Mich., 1968, JD magna cum laude, 1972. Assoc. Baker & Hostetler, Cleve., 1972-81, ptnr., 1982—. Contbr. articles to profl. jours. Endowment counsel Coun. Jewish Fedns., N.Y.C., 1976-90, Cleve., 1996—; rec. sec. Green Rd. Synagogue, Beachwood, Ohio, 1982-85, trustee, 1981-86; founding trustee, v.p. Internat. Coun. Dati Tzioni Schs., 1994—; founding trustee Solomon Schecter Day Sch. leve., 1978-85; trustee Jewish Nat. Fund Cleve., 1984-94; co-founder, trustee Fuchs Bet Sefer Mizrachi, Cleve., 1984—. Angell scholar U. Mich., 1966. Fellow Am. Coll. Trust and Estate Coun.; mem. ABA (generation skipping transfer tax com. legis. and regulations planning and drafting 1988—, charitable deduction com. legis. 1987—, GSST com. 1987—, estate and gift tax com. 1987—), Ohio State Bar Assn., Greater Cleve. Bar Assn. (probate and trust law sect. com. 1987—), Phi Beta Kappa, Phi Kappa Phi, Order of Coif; mem. ACTEC (com. on Charitable Giving, 1995—). Republican. Jewish. Avocations: bicycling, skiing, swimming, modern history, jewish religious studies. Office: Baker & Hostetler 3200 Nat City Ctr 1900 E 9th St Ste 3200 Cleveland OH 44114-3475

KIRILA, JILL S., lawyer; b. Sharon, Pa., 1972; BA, Ohio State U., 1994; JD, Georgetown U., 1997. Bar: Ohio 1997, US Ct. of Appeals Sixth Cir., US Dist. Ct. orthern Dist. Ohio, US Dist. Ct. Southern Dist. Ohio. Sr. assoc. Squire, Sanders & Dempsey L.L.P., Cin. Mem., Alumni Admissions Com. Georgetown U.; mem., Parenthesis and Human Resources Com. Ctr. Vocat. Alternatives. Named one of Ohio's Rising Stars, Super Lawyers, 2006. Office: Squire Sanders & Dempsey LLP 1300 Huntington Ctr 41 South High St Columbus OH 43215-6197 Office Phone: 614-365-2700. Office Fax: 614-365-2499.

KIRK, BALLARD HARRY THURSTON, architect; b. Williamsport, Pa., Apr. 1, 1929; s. Ballard and Ada May (DeLaney) K.; m. Vera Elizabeth Kitchener, Mar. 13, 1951; children: Lisa Lee, Kira Alexandria, Dayna Allison, Courtlandt Blaine. BArch, Ohio State U., 1959. Pres. Kirk Assocs., Architects, Columbus, Ohio, 1963—. Mem. Ohio Bd. Bldg. Standards, Columbus, 1973-78, 92-99; pres. Nat. Coun. Archtl. Registration Bds., Washington, 1983-84, Ohio Bd. Examiners Architects, Columbus, 1973-93; bd. dirs. Nat. Archtl. Accrediting Bd., Washington, 1986-89. Mem. AIA (bd. dirs. Columbus chpt. 1988-92), Coll. of Fellows. Republican. Mem. Brethern Ch. Home: 2557 Charing Rd Columbus OH 43221-3673 Office Phone: 614-284-5706. Personal E-mail: kirkarch@sbcglobal.net.

KIRK, CAROL, lawyer; b. Henry, Ill., Dec. 23, 1937; d. Howard P. and Mildred Root McQuilkin; m. Robert James Kirk, Aug. 20, 1961; children: Kathleen, Nancy, Sally. BS in Music Edn., U. Ill., 1960; JD, Ind. U., Indpls., 1989. Bar: Ind. 1989. Pvt. piano tchr., 1957-85; pub. sch. music tchr., 1960-62; dir. Ind. State Ethics Commn., Indpls., 1989-97; atty. and investigator Disciplinary Commn., Supreme Ct. Ind., Indpls., 1997—. Pres. Coun. on Govtl. Ethics Laws, (Internat.), 1993-94. Exec. editor Articles & Prodn. Ind. Law Rev., 1988-89. Mem. Met. Devel. Commn., Indpls., 1982-87; chairperson Pub. Radio Adv. Bd., Indpls., 1983-84, treas. Cmty. Svc. Coun., Indpls., 1988-91. Invitee to Nat. 4H Congress, Chgo., 1956; named 4H Family of Yr., Washington Twp., 4-H, Indpls., 1980, Vol. of Week, Voluntary Action Ctr., Indpls., 1980. Mem. LWV (pres. Indpls. 1979-83), Ind. Bar Assn., Indpls. Bar Assn., Phi Alpha Delta, Mu Phi Epsilon. Avocation: choir singing. Office: Discip Commn Supreme Ct Ind 1165 South Tower 115 W Washington St Indianapolis IN 46204-3420 E-mail: rkirk1937@aol.com.

KIRK, MARK STEVEN, congressman; b. Champaign, Ill., Sept. 15, 1959; s. Francis Gabriel and Judith Ann (Brady) Kirk; m. Kimberly Vertolli. BA, Cornell U., 1981; MS, London Sch. of Econs., 1982; JD, Georgetown U., 1992. Bar: Ill. 1992, D.C. 1993. Parliamentary aide Julian Critchley, London, 1982-83; chief of staff US Rep. John Porter, Washington, 1984-90; officer World Bank, Washington, 1990; spl. asst. to asst. sec. of state US Dept. State, Washington, 1991-93; atty. Baker & McKenzie, Washington, 1993-95; counsel Ho. Internat. Rels. Com., Washington, 1995-99; mem. US Congress from 10th Ill. dist., Washington, 2001—; mem. armed svcs. com., transp. and infrastructure com., budget com.; mem. Ho. appropriations com. Bd. dirs. Population Resource Ctr., Princeton, NJ. Contbr. articles to various newspapers. Organizer Bush/Quayle Campaign, No. Ill., 1988, Dole for Pres., 1988, various states; campaigner Porter for Congress, No. Ill., 1984-90. Lt. USNR, 1989—. Kellogg Fellow, Chgo., 1980, Radm James Fellow, Washington, 1984; recipient Coun. of Jewish Fedn. award Washington, 1988. Mem. Navy League, Naval Res. Assn., New Trier Rep. Orgn. Republican. Presbyterian. Avocations: backpacking, skydiving. Office: US House Reps 1531 Longworth House Office Bldg Washington DC 20515-1310 Home: 275 Whistler Rd Highland Park IL 60035-5947

KIRK, NANCY A., state legislator, nursing home administrator; m. Henry Kirk. BS, Ill. State U., 1964; MSW, U. Kans., 1976. Nursing home adminstr.; mem. from dist. 56 Kans. State Ho. of Reps., Topeka. Address: 932 SW Frazier Ave Topeka KS 66606-1948

KIRK, THOMAS GARRETT, JR., librarian; b. Phila., Aug. 2, 1943; s. Thomas Garrett and Bertha (C.) K.; m. Elizabeth B. Walter, Aug. 29, 1964; children: Jennifer E., Cynthia M., Kristen A. BA, Earlham Coll., Richmond, Ind., 1965; MA, Ind. U., 1969; postgrad., Drexel U., 1987-88. Sci. libr. Earlham Coll., 1965-79; libr. cons. Richmond, Ind., 1972—; acting dir. librs. U. Wis., Parkside, Kenosha, 1979-80; dir. libr. Berea (Ky.) Coll., 1980-94, Earlham (Ind.) Coll., 1994-2000, dir. librs., coord. info. svcs., 2001—. Vis. instr. Ind. U. Libr. Sch., summers 1977, 78; bd. dirs SOLINET, 1981-84, 85-86, treas., 1982-84; bd. dirs. Ky. Libr. Network, 1985-87, 91-93, OCLC Mems. Coun., 1986-92, 1999-2005, exec. com. 2001-02, mem. standing joint com. on membership, 2003-05, mem. fin. com., 2003—05; v.p. Pvt. Acad. Libr. Network Ind., 1995-96, pres., 1996-97, 2005-06, OCLC Strategic Directions and Governance Adv. Com., 2000-01; adv. bd. OCLC Coll. and Univ. Librs., 1995-98. Author: Library Research Guide to Biology, 1978, College Libraries in Encyclopedia Library of Information Science, 2003; editor: Course-related Library and Literature Instruction, 1979, Increasing the Teaching Role of Academic Libraries, 1984; editl. bd. Coll. and Rsch. Librs., 1996-2002, Internet Reference Svcs. Quar., 1996-2002. Bd. dirs. Coll. Libr. Dirs. Mentor Program, 2002—; mem. midwest adv. com. NITLE, 2002—; mem. exec. com. Acad. Librs. Ind., 2003—05; sr. advisor Coun. Ind. Colls., 2003—. Mem. ALA (coun. 1986-90), Assn. Coll. Rsch. Librs. (v.p., pres.-elect 1992-93, pres. 1993-94, exec. com. 1984-85, 86-90, 92-95, rep. to Coalition for Networked Info. 1990-95, info. literacy adv. com. 2000-2002, Miriam Dudley Bibliog. Instrn. Libr. of Yr. award 1984, Acad./Rsch. Libr. of Yr. 2004), Inst. for Info. Literacy (adv. com. 1998-2003, chair 2001-03), Ind. Libr. Fedn., Ind. Coop. Libr. Svcs. Authority (exec. com. 1999-2001), Ky. Libr. Assn. (Acad. Libr. of Yr. award 1984), Phi Kappa Phi. Mem. Soc. Of Friends. Office: Earlham Coll Lilly Libr Richmond IN 47374 Office Phone: 765-983-1360. Business E-Mail: kirkto@earlham.edu.

KIRKEGAARD, R. LAWRENCE, architect, acoustical engineer; b. Denver, Dec. 11, 1937; s. Raymond Lawrence and Frances Jean (Stocking) K.; m. Joslyn Ann Hills, Mar 23, 1959; children: Dana Lawrence, Jonathan Eric, Bradford Andrew. AB cum laude, Harvard U., 1960, MArch, 1964. Cons. archtl. acoustics Bolt, Beranek & Newman, Cambridge, Mass., 1962-64; supervisory cons., regional mgr. Chgo., 1964-75; pres., prin. cons. R. Lawrence Kirkegaard & Assocs., Inc., Chgo., Ill., 1976—. Frequent panelist for Nat. Endowment for Arts Design Arts Challenge Grant program. Prin. archtl. acoustics works: new projects include new Concert Hall for Tanglewood, Ordway Music Theatre, St. Paul, new performing arts cts. in Denver, Fort Lauderdale, Charlotte, N.C., Maui, Portand, Oreg., L.A., Greenville, S.C., Cin., New Concert Hall for Atlanta, Ga.; internat. projects include performing arts ctrs. in Taipei and Tainan, Taiwan, Bergamo, Italy, Edmonton, remodeling of the Tyl Theatre, Prague, Royal Philharmonic Hall, Liverpool, Eng., Barbican Concert Hall, London, Maison de Musique, Toulose, France; remodeling projects include Carnegie Hall (post-renovation), Orch. Hall, Chgo., Davies Symphony Hall, San Francisco, Heinz Hall, Pitts., Mahaffey Theatre, St. Petersburg, Fla., Guthrie Theatre, Oreg. Shakespeare Festival, Stratford Shakespeare Festival, Ont., Young Peoples' Theatre, Toronto; new schs. of music include Rice U., Northwestern U., U. Ala., Iowa State U., Pacific Luth. U., Red Deer Coll., Alta., Cin. Convervatory Mus., Luther Coll., .D. State U.; remodeling projects include U. Chgo., Carleton Coll., Oberlin Conservatory. Co-founder Chestnut Hill Mental Health Ctr., Greenville, S.C. Mem. AIA (hon., nat. com. on arts and recreation), Acoustical Soc. Am., Harvard Grad. Sch. Design Alumni Coun., U.S. Inst. Theatre Tech., Am. Symphony Orch. League, Harvard Club (Chgo.). Office: R Lawrence Kirkegaard & Assocs Inc 801 W Adams St Fl 8 Chicago IL 60607-3013 Home: 19 Patricia Ln Harwich Port MA 02646-2019 Home (Summer): 146 Kingsbridge Cir Naperville IL 60540

KIRKHAM, M. B., plant physiologist, educator; b. Cedar Rapids, Iowa; d. Don and Mary Elizabeth (Erwin) K. BA with honors, Wellesley Coll.; MS, PhD, U. Wis. Cert. profl. agronomist. Plant physiologist U.S. EPA, Cin., 1973-74; asst. prof. U. Mass., Amherst, 1974-76, Okla. State U., Stillwater, 1976-80; from assoc. prof. to prof. Kans. State U., Manhattan, 1980—. Guest lectr. Inst. Water Conservancy and Hydroelectric Power Rsch., Inst. Farm Irrigation Rsch., China, 1985, Inst. Exptl. Agronomy, Italy, 1989, Agrl. U. Wageningen, Inst. for Soil Fertility, Haren, Netherlands, 1991, Massey U., New Zealand, 1991, Lincoln U., New Zealand, 1998, Environ. and Risk Mgmt. Group Hort. Rsch., 1998, Palmerston North, New Zealand, 1998, U. Hannover, Germany, 2003; William A. Albrecht seminar spkr. U. Mo., 1994; vis. scholar Biol. Labs., Harvard U., 1990; vis. scientist environ. physics sect. dept. sci. and indsl. rsch. Palmerston North, 1991, The Hort. and Food Rsch. Inst. New Zealand, Ltd., Crown Rsch. Inst., Palmerston North, 1998, 2005, Landcare Rsch., Lincoln, New Zealand, 1998; mem. peer rev. panel USDA/Nat. Rsch. Initiative, Washington, 1994; mem. rev. panel USDA Office Sci. Quality Rev. Water Quality Nat. Program, 2001; apptd. mem. US Nat. Com. for Soil Sci. of NAS, 2001—04; participant confs. and symposia; spkr., presenter in field. Author: Principles of Soil and Plant Water Relations, 2005; editor: Water Use in Crop Production, 1999; co-editor (with I.K. Iskander): Trace Elements in Soil, 2001; cons. editor Plant and Soil Jour., 1979—2005, mem. editl. bd. BioCycle, 1978—82, Field Crops Rsch. Jour., 1983—91, Soil Sci., 1997—, Jour. Crop Improvement, 1996—, Jour. Environ. Quality, 2002—, Crop Sci., 2004—, mem. editl. adv. bd. Internat. Agrophysics, 2000—, Australia Jour. Soil Rsch., 2004—; contbr. more than 220 articles and papers to sci. jours. Recipient Best Reviewer award, Water Resources Engring. divsn. Jour. Irrigation and Drainage Engring., ASCE, 1996, grad. faculty tchg. award, Coll. of Agr., Kanas State Univ., 2001, Carl Sprengel Agronomic Rsch. award, Am. Social of Agronomy, 2007; grantee, NSF, USDA, US Dept. Energy, Kans. Ctr. Agrl. Resources and the Environ., Manhattan; NSF postdoctoral fellow, U. Wis., 1971—73, NDEA fellow, E.I. du Pont de emours and Co. summer faculty fellow, 1976. Fellow: AAAS, Crop Sci. Soc. Am. (editl. bd. 1980—84, 2004—, chair crop physiology and metabolism divsn. 2007), Royal Meteorol. Soc., Soil Sci. Soc. Am. (travel grantee to internat. congress Japan 1990), Am. Soc. Agronomy (editl. bd. 1985—90); mem.: Am. Chem. Soc., Am. Math. Assn., Am. Phys. Soc., Internat. Assn. Hydrol. Sci., Royal Soc. New Zealand, Internat. Water Resources Assn., Am. Geophys. Union, Internat. Assn. Vegetation Sci., Am. Phytopathol. Soc., Water Environment Fedn., Growth Regulator Soc. Am., Soc. Exptl. Biology (London), NY Acad. Sci., Scandinavian Soc. Plant Physiology, Japanese Soc. Plant Physiology, Soc. Francaise de Physiologie Végétale, Am. Meteorol. Soc., Bot. Soc. Am., Internat. Union Soil Sci. (1st vice chmn. commn. soil physics 1994—98, sec. commn. on soils, food security and human health 2002—), Internat. Soil Tillage Rsch. Orgn., Am. Soc. Hort. Sci., Am. Soc. Plant Physiology (editl. bd. 1982—87), Sigma Xi (sec. chpt. 1997—99, Outstanding Sr. Scientist award 2002), Gamma Sigma Delta (Disting. Faculty award Kan. State U. chpt. 2001), Phi Kappa Phi (scholar award 2000). Home: 1420 McCain Ln Apt 244 Manhattan KS 66502-4680 Office: Kans State U Dept Agronomy Throckmorton Hall Manhattan KS 66505-5501 Office Phone: 785-532-0422. Business E-Mail: mbk@ksu.edu.

KIRKPATRICK, ANNE SAUNDERS, systems analyst; b. Birmingham, Mich., July 4, 1938; d. Stanley Rathburn and Esther (Casteel) Saunders; children: Elizabeth, Martha, Robert, Sarah. Student, Wellesley Coll., 1956-57, Laval U., Quebec City, Can., 1958, U. Ariz., 1958-59; BA in Philosophy, U. Mich., 1961. Sys. engr. IBM, Chgo., 1962-64; sr. analyst Commonwealth Edison Co., Chgo., 1981-97. Treas. Taproot Reps., DuPage County, Ill., 1977—80; pres. Hinsdale (Ill.) Women's Rep. Club, 1978—81. Mem.: Wellesley Chgo. (bd. dirs. 1972—73). Home: 222 E Chestnut St Unit 8B Chicago IL 60611-2376 Personal E-mail: a.kirkpatrick@sbcglobal.net.

KIRKPATRICK, JOHN EVERETT, lawyer; b. Meadville, Pa., Aug. 20, 1929; s. Francis Earl and Marjorie Eloise (Roudebush) K.; m. Patricia Ann Benkert, Aug. 9, 1952 (div. June 1963); children: Amy Kirkpatrick Fidler, John Scot, Ann Kirkpatrick Mullen; m. Phyllis Jean Daeuble, Aug. 31, 1963. AB, Amherst Coll., 1951; JD, Harvard U., 1954. Bar: Ohio 1955, Ill. 1962. Assoc. Squire, Sanders & Dempsey, Cleve., 1954-61, Kirkland, Ellis, Hodson, Chaffetz & Masters, Chgo., 1962-64; sr. ptnr. Kirkland & Ellis, Chgo., 1965—95, of counsel, 1995—. Contbr. articles on tax and estate planning to profl. jours. Mem. Cen. DuPage Hosp. Devel. Commn., Winfield, Ill.; elder 1st Presbyn. Ch., Wheaton, Ill., 1983—. Mem. ABA, Ill. State Bar Assn., Chgo. Bar Assn., Chgo. Golf Club, Mid Am. Club. Republican. Avocation: golf. Office: Kirkland & Ellis 200 E Randolph St Fl 54 Chicago IL 60601-6636 Home Phone: 630-469-0605; Office Phone: 312-861-2060. E-mail: jkirkpatrick@kirkland.com.

KIRKPATRICK, LARRY, radio personality; m. Terri Kirkpatrick, 1977; children: Mark, Bill, Amy, Scott, Timotny. Min., 1976—82; staff announcer WUGN, Midland, Mich., 1982—89, 2000—; min. Bay City, 1989—2000. Office: WUGN 510 Isabella Rd Midland MI 48640

KIRKPATRICK, R(OBERT) JAMES, geologist, educator; b. Schenectady, NY, Dec. 31, 1946; s. Robert James and Audrey (Rech) K.; m. Susan A. Wilson, Sept. 4, 1968 (div. 1984); children: Gregory Robert, Geoffrey Stephen; m. Carol A. Hanna, Sept. 3, 1985. AB, Cornell U., 1968; PhD, U. Ill., 1972. Asst. U.S. Geol. Survey, Denver, 1968; rsch. and teaching asst. U. Ill., Urbana, 1968-72; sr. rsch. geologist prodn. rsch. div. Exxon, Houston, 1972-73; rsch. fellow in geophysics Harvard U., Cambridge, 1973-75; asst. rsch. geologist Scripps Instn. Oceanography, La Jolla, Calif., 1976-78; asst. prof. dept. geology U. Ill., Urbana, 1978-80, assoc. prof., 1980-83, prof., 1983-88, prof., head dept., 1988-97, exec. assoc. dean Coll. Liberal Arts & Scis., 1997—2007; dean. Coll. Natural Sci. Mich. State U., 2007—. Mem. ocean crust panel Joint Oceanographic Instns. for Deep Earth Studies, 1977-78, active margin panel, 1978, downhole measurements panel, 1977-78; chair, Cements Divsn., Am. Ceramic Soc., 2004-05, trustee, 2006-; R.E. Grim prof. U. Ill., Urbana, 2005-07, emeritus, 2007-; cons. various corps. Editor: Initial Reports of the Deep Sea Drilling Project, Vols. 46 and 55, 1979, 80; co-editor: Kinetics of Geochemical Processes, 1981; assoc. editor American Mineralogist, 1987-90; contbr. over 200 articles to profl. jours. Overseas fellow Churchill Coll., Eng., 1985-86; grantee NSF, 1977—, Dept. Energy, 2000—, various other orgns., 1978—. Fellow Geol. Soc. Am., Mineral. Soc. Am. (councillor 1990-93, Dana medal 2004), Am. Ceramic Soc.; mem. Am. Geophys. Union (VGP award com. 1985-88, chmn. 1986-88), Internat. Mineral. Assn. (alt. U.S. del. 1982, coord. com. 1986 meeting, chmn. program com. 1986, U.S. rep. Commn. on Crystal Growth, v.p. 1986-90, sec. Commn. on Mineral Physics 1986-91). Office: Mich State U Coll Natural Sci 103 Natural Sci Bldg East Lansing MI 48824 Office Phone: 517-355-4470.

KIRKPATRICK, SHARON MINTON, nursing educator, academic administrator; b. Independence, Mo., Aug. 31, 1943; d. Charles Russell and Minnetta (Brotherton) Minton; m. John P. Kirkpatrick; children: John Brent, Kraig Russell. Grad. in nursing, Ind. Sanitarium and Hosp., Independence, 1965; AA, Graceland Coll., Lamoni, Iowa, 1965; BSN, Calif. State U., Sacramento, 1976; M in Nursing, U. Kans., 1981, PhD in Nursing, 1988. RN, Mo., Iowa. Office coordinator Family Practice Physicians, Cupertino, Calif., 1965-67; head nurse Truman Med. Ctr. East, Kansas City, Mo., 1977-79; teaching asst. U. Kans. Med. Ctr., Kansas City, 1980; asst. prof. nursing Graceland Coll., 1980-86, chmn. div. nursing, 1986-94, prof., dean Independence Campus, 1990-94, v.p., dean. nursing, 1994—2002, v.p. instl. advancement, 2002—05, v.p. Independence campus, 2005—. Dir. cmty. health projects Haiti, Dominican Republic, Jamaica, Zambia, Malawi, Nepal, India, Congo. Contbr. articles to profl. jours. Trustee Independence Sanitarium and Hosp., 1977-86, Independence Regional Health Ctr., 2000—, Med. Ctr. of Ind., 2003—; mem. corp. body Truman Neurol. Ctr., Kansas City, 1979-86. Mem. ANA (coun. on cultural diversity), Mo. Nurses Assn. (bd. dirs., pres. 1991-93), Profl. Nurses Assn. (pres. 1982-84), Collegiate Nurse Educators Greater Kansas City (pres. (1991-92), Jr. Women's Club Cupertino (past pres.), Sigma Theta Tau. Mem. Reorganized Lds Ch. Avocations: travel, cultural studies, backpacking, boating, reading. Home: 5665 NE Northgate Xing Lees Summit MO 64064-1240 Office: Graceland Univ Lamoni IA 50140 Office Phone: 816-833-0524. Business E-Mail: kirkpat@graceland.edu.

KIRKSEY, AVANELLE, nutrition educator; b. Mulberry, Ark., Mar. 23, 1926; BS, U. Ark., Fayetteville, 1947; MS, U. Tenn., Knoxville, 1950; PhD, Pa. State U., University Park, 1961; postdoctoral, U. Calif., Davis, 1976; DSc honoris causa, Purdue U., Ind., 1997. Assoc. prof. Ark. Polytechnic U., Russellville, 1950—55; rsch. asst. Pa. State U., University Park, 1956—58, fellow Gen. Foods, 1958—60; assoc. prof. Purdue U., West Lafayette, Ind., 1961—69, prof. nutrition, 1970—85, disting. prof., 1985—96, disting. prof. emeritus, 1997. Prin. investigator nutrition project in rural Egypt; coord. nutrition program Indonesian Univs., 1987—91. Contbr. articles to profl. jours. Named Meredith Disting. Prof. Nutrition, Purdue U.; named to Nutrition Hall of Fame, 2007; recipient endowment, Kirksey Annual Lecture Series, 1997, Borden award, Am. Home Econs. Assn., 1980. Fellow Am. Inst. Nutrition (Lederle award 1994); mem. .Y. Acad. Scis., Phi Kappa Phi, Sigma Xi. Office: Purdue U Dept Food Nutrition West Lafayette IN 47907 Office Phone: 479-452-2340. Personal E-mail: akirksey01@cox.net.

KIRKWOOD, WILLIAM THOMAS, corporate professional; b. Marion, Ohio, Aug. 19, 1948; s. Hugh E. and Mildred M. (Schaeffer) K. Jr.; m. Deborah Hedges, Jan. 4, 1967 (div. Aug. 1980); children: Krista, Konni, Bobby; m. Beth C. Mitchell, May 30, 1981 (div. Aug. 1988). BS in Acctg., Franklin U., 1976. CPA. Acct. Worthington (Ohio) Foods, Inc., 1970-75, cost. supr., 1975-78, acctg. mgr., 1978-82, controller, 1982-86, asst. treas., 1986—; exec. v.p. and CFO Worthington Foods, Inc. Office: Worthington Foods Inc 900 Proprietors Rd Columbus OH 43085-3194

KIRSCH, WILLIAM S., former insurance company executive, lawyer; b. July 28, 1956; Grad., Northwestern U.; JD, Stanford U. With Kirkland & Ellis, 1981—2003, mng. ptnr., 1986—2003, mem. mgmt. com., co-chair, fin. com., mem. compensation com.; acting gen. counsel Conseco, Inc., Carmel, Ind., 2003, exec. v.p., gen. counsel, sect., 2003, pres., CEO, 2004—06, bd. dir., 2004—06.

KIRSCHNER, BARBARA STARRELS, gastroenterologist; b. Phila., Mar. 23, 1941; m. Robert H. Kirschner (dec.). MD, Women's Med. Coll. Pa., 1967. Diplomate Am. Bd. Pediatrics; cert. in pediatric gastroenterology and nutrition. Intern U. Chgo., 1967-68, resident, 1968-70; mem. staff U. Chgo. Children's Hosp., 1977-83, asst. prof. pediatrics, 1984-88, prof. pediatrics and medicine, 1988—, mem. com. on nutrition and nutritional biology. Contbr. articles to profl. jours. Pediatric Gastroenterology fellow U. Chgo., 1975-77; recipient Davidson award in Pediatric gastroenterology Acad. Pediatrics, 1993, Joseph Brenneman award Chgo. Pediat. Soc., 2001. Mem. Am. Gastroenterologic Assn., N.Am. Soc. Pediatric Gastroenterology, Soc. Pediatric Rsch., Alpha Omega Alpha. Office: U Chgo Med Ctr 5839 S Maryland Ave # MC 4065 Chicago IL 60637-5417 Home Phone: 773-288-2299; Office Phone: 773-702-6152.

KIRSCHNER, STANLEY, chemist; b. NYC, Dec. 17, 1927; s. Abraham and Rebecca K.; m. Esther Green, June 11, 1950; children— Susan Joyce, Daniel Ross. BS magna cum laude, Bklyn. Coll., 1950; AM, Harvard U., 1952; PhD, U. Ill., 1954. Research chemist Monsanto Chem. Co., Everett, Mass., 1951; teaching asst. in chemistry Harvard U., 1950-52, U. Ill., Urbana, 1952-54; mem. faculty dept. chemistry Wayne State U., Detroit, 1954—, prof., 1960—, prof. emeritus, 1992—. Vis. prof. U. London, 1963-64, U. Florence, Italy, 1976, U. Sao Paulo, Brazil, 1969, Tohoku U., Sendai, Japan, 1978, Tech. U. Lisbon, Portugal, 1984, U. Porto, Portugal, 1984 Author: Advances in the Chemistry of Coordination Compounds, 1961, Coordination Chemistry, 1969, Inorganic Syntheses, Vol. 23, 1985; contbr. articles to profl. jours. Served with USN, 1945-46. Recipient Pres.'s award for excellence in teaching Wayne State U., 1979, Gold award Engring. Soc. of Detroit, 1995, Heyrovsky medal Czechoslovak Acad. Scis., 1978, Catalyst award in chem. edn. Chem. Mfrs. Assn., 1984, Faculty Svc. award Wayne State U. Alumni Assn., 1986; fellow Fulbright Found., 1963-64, NSF, 1963-64, Ford Found., 1969-70. Fellow AAAS, Am. Inst. Chemists, N.Y. Acad. Scis.; mem. AAUP, Am. Chem. Soc. (chmn. divsn. edn., bd. dirs. 1985-93, Henry Hill award 1995, Brazilian Acad. Scis., Internat. Conf. Coordination Chemistry (permanent sec. 1966-89, emeritus 1990), Internat. Union Pure and Applied Chemistry (com. nomenclature of inorganic chemistry 1991-93), Chem. Soc. Chile (hon.), Chem. Soc. (London). Office: Dept Chemistry Wayne State Univ Detroit MI 48202

KIRSCHNER, WILLIAM STEVEN, lawyer; b. LA, Jan. 9, 1950; s. Robert and Ethel Ada (Bershad) K.; m. Sandy Bernstein, Aug. 31, 1976 (div. 1981); m. Laurie Kay Miller, Aug. 11, 1983; 1 child, Beryl Susan Elizabeth Miller. BA, Bklyn Coll., 1971; JD, Fordham U., 1976. Bar: N.D. 1980, Minn. 1981, Ga. 1977, N.Mex. 1995, U.S. Dist. Ct. N.D. 1981, U.S. Dist. Ct. Minn. 1985, U.S. Ct. Appeals (8th cir.) 1985. Assoc. Brian Nelson, Fargo, N.D., 1980-82; sole practice Fargo, 1982-84; ptnr. Kirschner & Baker Legal Clinic, Fargo, 1984-86; mng. atty. William Kirschner & Assocs., Fargo, 1986—2001; asst. county atty. Dona Ana County, N.Mex., 2001—02; city atty. City of Alamogordo, N.Mex., 2002—03; assoc. Holt & Babington, Las Cruces, N.Mex., 2003—04; exec. v.p., gen. counsel, sec. Conseco Inc., 2003—06. Bd. dirs. Alcohol Out Reach, Fargo, 1983-85, Youth Depot, Fargo, 1985, Temple Beth El, Fargo, 1986-88; sec. legal com. N.D. ACLU, 1986-95. Francis Kneller scholar Bklyn. Coll., 1969. Mem. Cass County Bar Assn., Nat. Lawyers Guild, N.D. Trial Lawyers Assn., Fargo Criminal Def. Lawyers Assn. (organizer), N.D. State Bar Assn. (ethics com. 1987-91). Office Phone: 317-817-6100. Office Fax: 317-817-2847.

KIRSNER, JOSEPH BARNETT, physician, educator; b. Boston, Sept. 21, 1909; s. Harris and Ida (Waiser) K.; m. Minnie Schneider, Jan. 6, 1934 (dec. Dec. 4, 1998); 1 son, Robert S. MD, Tufts U., 1933; PhD in Biol. Scis., U. Chgo., 1942; DSc (hon.), Tufts U., 1993. Intern Woodlawn Hosp., Chgo., 1933—34, resident in internal medicine, 1934—35; asst. in medicine U. Chgo., 1935—37, from asst. prof. to assoc. prof., 1937—51, prof., 1951—, Louis Block Disting. Service prof. medicine, 1968—, chief of staff, also dep. dean for med. affairs, 1971—76. Cons. NIH, 1956-69; hon. pres. Gastrointestinal Research Found., 1961-; Mem. drug efficacy adv. com. to NRC; chmn. adv. group Nat. Commn. on Digestive Diseases, 1978; chmn. emeritus sci. adv. com. Nat. Found. Ileitis and Colitis. Editor, author: Kirsner's Inflammatory Bowel Disease, 6th edit., 2004, The Growth of Gastroenterologic Knowledge During the 20th Century, 1994, Early Days of American Gastroenterology, 1996; contbr. more than 800 articles to profl. jours. Served with M.C. AUS, 1943-46, ETO, PTO. Recipient Julius Friedenwald medal disting. work gastroenterology, 1975, Horatio Alger award, 1979, hon. Gold Key for Disting. Service U. Chgo. Med. Alumni Assn., 1979, Alumni medal U. Chgo. Alumni Assn., 1989, Disting. Educator award Am. Gastroenterological Assn., 1999, Tufts U. Dean's medal, 2006; Joseph B. Kirsner award for excellence in rsch. in clin. gastroenterology established in his honor, Am. Gastroent. Assn., 1990; G. Brohée lectr. World Cong. Gastroenterology, 1994, Laureate award Lincoln Acad. Ill., Dean's medal Tufts U., 2006. Mem. Am. Assn. Physicians, ACP (master, John Phillips award), Am. Gastroent. Assn. (past pres., governing bd.), Am. Gastroscopic Soc. (past pres.), Am. Soc. Gastrointestinal Endoscopy (past pres., Rudolf Schindler award), Am. Soc. Clin. Investigation, Ctrl. Soc. Clin. Rsch., Chgo. Soc. Internal Medicine (past pres.), Inst. Medicine Chgo. (George H. Coleman medal, Lifetime Achievement award 2004) Achievements include research in gastrointestinal disorders, inflammatory disease of gastrointestinal tract. Home: 5805 S Dorchester Ave Top C Chicago IL 60637-1730 Office: U Chgo Med Ctr 5841 S Maryland Ave MC 2200 Chicago IL 60637-1470 Office Phone: 773-702-6101. Business E-Mail: jkirsner@medicine.bsd.uchicago.edu.

KIRWIN, KENNETH FRANCIS, law educator; b. Morris, Minn., May 10, 1941; s. Francis B. and Dorothy A. (McNally) K.; m. Phyllis J. Hills, June 2, 1962; children— David, Mark, Robert. BA, St. John's U., 1963; JD, U. Minn., 1966. Bar: Minn. 1966, U.S. Dist. Ct. Minn. 1968, U.S. Ct. Appeals (8th cir.) 1969. Law clk. to assoc. justice Supreme Ct., Minn., 1966-67; assoc. Lindquist & Vennum, Mpls., 1967-70; prof. law William Mitchell Coll. Law, St. Paul, 1970—2006, prof. emeritus, 2006—. Staff dir. Uniform Rules Criminal Procedure, 1971-74, reporter, 1982-87; reporter Uniform Victims of Crime Act, 1991-92; adj. prof. U. Minn. Law Sch., 1977, 80; active Minn. Lawyers Profl. Responsibility Bd., 1975-81, Minn. Bd. Continuing Legal Edn., 1975-83. Author: (with Maynard E. Pirsig) Cases and Materials on Professional Responsibility, 1984. Mem. Ramsey County Bar Assn., Minn. State Bar Assn. (chair rules of profl. conduct com., 2002-05, co-chair multi jurisdictional practice task force, 2005-06), ABA (mem. standing com. on discipline 1983-89), Am. Law Inst. Home: 1418 Brookshire Ct New Brighton MN 55112-6390 Office: William Mitchell Coll Law 875 Summit Ave Saint Paul MN 55105-3030 Home Phone: 651-633-7581; Office Phone: 651-290-6346. Business E-Mail: kenneth.kirwin@wmitchell.edu.

KISCADEN, SHEILA M., state legislator; b. St. Paul, Apr. 21, 1946; d. Harvey Richard and Bea Mae (Conway) Martineau; m. Richard Craig Kiscaden, Sept. 12, 1970; children: Michael, Karen. BS in Edn., U. Minn., 1969; MS in Pub. Adminstrn., U. So. Calif., LA, 1986; MA in Internat. Devel., U. Sussex, 2006. Tchr. So. St. Paul Secondary Schs., Minn., 1969-70, Jobs 70, Rochester, Minn., 1970-71; regional coord. Planned Parenthood, Rochester, Minn., 1971-76; vol. svc. coord. Olmsted County, Rochester, Minn., 1977-80, human svc. planner, 1980-82, legis. liaison, 1982-85; prin. Cons. Collaborator, Rochester, Minn., 1987—; mem. Minn Senate from 30th dist., St. Paul, 1992—. Bd. dirs. Ability Bldg. Ctr. Found. Bd., Rochester, Minn., 1989-94, Dyslexia Inst. Minn., Rochester, Minn., 1989-94, Hands for Humanity, 2004-05, Ctr. for Victims of Torture, 2005—; team leader Global Vols., 1989—; candidate for lt. gov. State of Minn., 2006. Fulbright scholar, 1970, Bosh fellow, 2004. Mem.: Phi Beta Kappa. Republican. Office: Minn State Senate 325 State Capitol Saint Paul MN 55155-0001

KISCHUK, RICHARD KARL, insurance company executive; b. Detroit, Mar. 14, 1949; s. Russell and Aubrey Ann (Artt) K.; m. Sandra Jean Dierkes, June 26, 1971; children: Robert Charles, Kirsten Grace, Erin Michelle, Danielle Laraine, Russell Olan, Erika Anne. BS, U. Mich., 1969, M in Actuarial Sci., 1971; MS in Bus. Adminstrn., Ind. U., 1979. Enrolled actuary. Actuarial trainee Lincoln Nat. Life, Ft. Wayne, Ind., 1971-72, actuarial asst., 1972-1973, asst. actuary, 1973-77, asst. v.p., 1977-80, 2d v.p., 1980-82; v.p. Lincoln Nat. Corp., Ft. Wayne, Ind., 1982-86; v.p., dir. Lincoln Nat. Health and Casualty Ins. Co., 1985-87, Lincoln Nat. Life Reins. Co., 1985-87, Lincoln Nat. Adminstrv. Service; chief operating officer, dir. Lincoln Intermediaries, Inc., 1985-87, Spl. Pooled Risk Adminstrs., Inc., 1985-87, Underwriters and Mgmt. Services, Inc., 1985-87; pres. Crown Point Mgmt. Cons., Inc., 1987—, Beneficient Solutions, Inc., 1998—. Mem. editorial adv. bd. CLU Jour., 1983-91; contbr. articles to profl. jours. Fellow Soc Actuaries (chmn. fin. reporting sect. 1982-85, bd. govs. 1986-89), mem. Am. Acad. Actuaries. Avocations: camping, backpacking, canoeing, photography. Office: Crown Point Mgmt Cons Inc PO Box 355 Pendleton IN 46064-0355 Office Phone: 765-778-4340. E-mail: rkischuk@umich.edu.

KISER, GERALD L., furniture company executive; Case goods divsn. mfg. mgr. Broyhill; v.p. ops. Kincaid Furniture Co. subs. La-Z-Boy Inc., Houston, La-Z-Boy Corp., Monroe, Mich., exec. v.p., COO, pres., COO. Mem. Am. Furniture Mfrs. Assn. Office: La-A-Boy Inc 1284 N Telegraph Rd Monroe MI 48162

KISHEL, GREGORY FRANCIS, federal judge; b. Virginia, Minn., Jan. 26, 1951; AB, Cornell U., 1973; JD, Boston Coll., 1977. Bar: Minn. 1978, U.S. Dist. Ct. Minn. 1978, U.S. Ct. Appeals (8th cir.) 1978, Wis. 1985, U.S. Dist. Ct. (we. dist.) Wis. 1985. Staff atty. Legal Aid Svc. of N.E. Minn., Duluth, 1978-81; pvt. practice Duluth, 1981-86; judge U.S. Bankruptcy Ct., St. Paul, 1986-2000, chief judge, 2000—. Judge U.S. Bankruptcy Ct., Duluth, 1984-86; pro tem mem. bankruptcy appellate panel 8th Cir. Ct., 1996—. Mem.: Am. Bankruptcy Inst., Minn. Bar Assn., Nat. Conf. Bankruptcy Judges (chair internat. law rels. com. 2004—06), Polish Geneal. Soc. Minn. (pres. 1996—2000). Office: Bankruptcy Court 300 S 4th St Ste 301 Minneapolis MN 55415

KISKA, TIMOTHY OLIN, communications educator, radio producer; b. Detroit, July 26, 1952; s. Edward Frederick and Mary Clare (Barnhart) K.; m. Patricia Irene Anstett, May 23, 1981; children: Caitlin, Amy, Eric. BA, Wayne State U., 1980, MA, 1995, PhD, 2003. Mem. staff Detroit Free Press, 1970-74, reporter, 1974-85, automotive writer, 1985-87; columnist Detroit News, 1987—2002. Asst. prof. comm. U. Mich., Dearborn, 2001-; mem. student newspaper publs. bd. Wayne State U., 1994-97, 99-2001; prodr. Sta. WWJ, 2004-. Author: Detroit's Powers and Personalities, 1989; From Soupy to Nuts! A History of Detroit TV, 2005. Mem.: Assn. Edn. in Journalism and Mass Communication. Home: 20050 Marford Ct Grosse Pointe Woods MI 48236-2324 Office: Univ Mich Dearborn 4901 Evergreen Rd Dearborn MI 48128 Home Phone: 313-886-2401; Office Phone: 313-583-6381. Business E-Mail: tkiska@umd.umich.edu.

KISKER, CARL THOMAS, pediatrician, educator; BA, Johns Hopkins U., 1958; MD, U. Cin. Coll. Medicine, 1962. Diplomate Am. Bd. Pediatrics, Am. Bd. Pediatric Hematology-Oncology. Lic. physician Ohio, Iowa. Intern U. Oreg. Coll. Medicine, 1962-63; sr. asst. surgeon NIH, 1963-65; jr. resident pediat. Children's Hosp., Cin., 1965-66, sr. resident pediat., 1966-67, fellow pediat. hematology, 1967-69, asst. attending pediatrician, 1968-69, attending pediatrician, 1969-73, dir. hemophilia project, 1971-73, dir. clin. hematology lab., 1972-73; asst. prof. pediat. U. Cin., 1969-72, assoc. prof. pediat., 1972-73, U. Iowa, Iowa City, 1973-79, dir. divsn. pediat. hematology-oncology, 1973-97, prof. pediat., 1979—. Med. lectr. various student and profl. groups; active mem. Pediat. Hematology-Oncology Group, Cin., Children's Cancer Study Group, L.A.; pres. Midwest Blood Club.; mem. adv. coun. Nat. Hemophilia Ctrs., 1979—.$D Mem. editl bd. Pediat. Today; contbr. numerous sci. papers to profl. jours. and chpts. in books. Mem. Iowa Found. Fund Raising Com. Lederle Med. Student Rsch. fellow, 1959; recipient state and fed. grants, Alumni of Yr. award U. Cin. Coll. Medicine, 2002. Mem. Am. Soc. Hematology, Mid-west Soc. for Pediat. RSch., Am. Fedn. for Clin. RSch., Am. Heart Assn., Internat. Soc. Thrombosis and Haemostasis (sub-com. on neonatal hemostasis), Ctrl. Soc. for Pediat. Rsch., Soc. Pediat. Rsch., Johnson County Med. Soc., Prairie Region Affiliated Blood Svcs., Am. Pediat. Soc.

KISOR, HENRY DU BOIS, retired editor, columnist, critic, writer; b. Ridgewood, NJ, Aug. 17, 1940; s. Manown and Judith (Du Bois) K.; m. Deborah L. Abbott, June 24, 1967; children: Colin, Conan. BA, Trinity Coll., 1962, LittD (hon.), 1991; MS in Journalism, Northwestern U., 1964. Copy editor Wilmington News-Jour. (Del.), 1964-65, Chgo. Daily News, 1965-73, book editor, 1973-78, Chgo. Sun-Times, 1978—2006; ret., 2006. Adj. prof. Medill Sch. Journalism Northwestern U., Evanston, Ill., 1979-82 Author: What's That Pig Outdoors?: A Memoir of Deafness, 1990, Zephyr: Tracking a Dream Across America, 1994, Flight of the Gin Fizz: Midlife at 4,500 Feet, 1997, Season's Revenge, 2003, A Venture into Murder, 2005, Cache of Corpses, 2007. Bd. dirs. Chgo. Hearing Soc., 1975-76. Recipient Stick-O-Type award Chgo. Newspaper Guild, 1981, 85, Outstanding Achievement award Ill. UPI, 1983, 85, 1st pl. award Ill. UPI columns divsn., 1985, James Friend Meml. Critic award Friends of Lit., 1988, Best Non-fiction award, 1991; finalist Pulitzer Prize nomination in criticism Columbia U., 1981; named to Chgo. Journalism Hall of Fame, 2001; NEH seminar fellow, 1978. Mem.: Deaf Pilots Assn. Avocations: photography, aviation. Personal E-mail: h.kisor@comcast.net.

KISSEL, EDWARD W., metal products executive; BS, Rennselaer Poly. Inst.; MS in Mgmt., MIT. Various positions including dir. ops. for Latin Am. region Goodyear Tire & Rubber Co., Akron, Ohio; v.p. mfg. and engring. Engelhard Corp., Iselin, N.J., 1987-90; exec. v.p., pres. passenger and light truck divsn. Continental-Gen. Tire, Inc.; CEO Kissel Group Ltd., 1993-99; pres., COO OM Group, Inc., 1999—. Office: 3500 Terminal Tower 50 Public Sq Cleveland OH 44113-2201

KISSEL, RICHARD JOHN, lawyer; b. Chgo., Nov. 27, 1936; s. John and Anne T. (Unichowski) K.; m. Donna Lou Heidersbach, Feb. 11, 1961; children: Roy Warren, David Todd, Audrey Anne. BA, Northwestern U., 1958; JD, Northwestern U., Chgo., 1961. Assoc. Peterson, Lowrey, Rall, Barber & Ross, Chgo., 1961-65; divsn. counsel Abbott Labs., North Chicago, Ill., 1965-70; mem. Pollution Control Bd., Chgo., 1970-72; adminstrv. asst. Gov.'s Staff, Chgo., 1972; ptnr. Martin, Craig, Chester & Sonnenschein, Chgo., 1973-88, Gardner, Carton & Douglas, Chgo., 1988—2000, chmn. mgmt. com., 1996-98, of counsel, 2000—. Adj. prof. U. Ill. Sch. Pub. Health, Chgo., 1973-76; instr. Kent. Sch. Law, Ill. Inst. Tech., Chgo., 1974-78; vis. com. Northwestern U. Law Sch., 1996-99. Recipient Ill. award IAWA, 1996; bd. dirs. Harbour Ridge Realty, Co. Contbr. articles to profl. jours. Mem. Lake Forest (Ill.) Sewer Adv. Com.; pres. Lake Forest Lake Bluff Sr. Citizens Found. Fellow Internat. Soc. Barristers; mem. Ill. State Bar Assn., Chgo. Bar Assn., Ill. State C. of C. (chmn. environ. affairs 1973-76), Com. on Cts. for 21st Century, Knollwood Club (Lake Forest; gov. 1976-82), Lake Forest/Lake Bluff Sr. Citizens Found (bd. dirs., pres.), 100 Club Lake County (bd. dirs.), Harbour Ridge Yacht & Country Club, Harbor Ridge Realty (bd. dirs.). Roman Catholic. Office: Drinker Biddle 191 N Wacker Dr Chicago IL 60606-1698 Home Phone: 847-295-4028; Office Phone: 312-569-1442. Business E-Mail: rkissel@gcd.com.

KISSELL, DON R., state legislator; Mem. dist. 17 Mo. Ho. of Reps. Office: 121 Courtfield Dr O Fallon MO 63366-4393

KISSINGER, JIM, communications executive; B in Indsl. Rels., Rockhurst Coll. Various human resource mgmt. pos. Pepsi Cola, TJ Lipton, and Beatrice Foods; human resources mgr. United Telephone, 1984—86, mgr. employee rels., 1986—87, dir. employee rels., 1987—89, dir. human resources, asst. v.p. human resources, Long Distance Divsn. info. svcs., network and mktg. units, 1989—91; asst. v.p. human resources ops. for Sprint Bus. Sprint Corp., 1991—94, v.p. human resources, Long Distance Divsn., 1994—2000, v.p. human resources, PCS Divsn., 2000—03, sr. v.p. human resources, 2003—. Mem. sch. bd. 2 area parochial schs., Kansas City; bd. dirs. Inroads, Kansas City. Office: Sprint Corp 6200 Sprint Pkwy Overland Park KS 66251

KISTENBROKER, DAVID H., lawyer; BA magna cum laude, U. Wis., 1975; MA, Marquette U., 1977, JD, 1980. Bar: Ill. 1980, Wis. 1980, US Ct. Appeals, 2nd, 6th and 7th Cir., US Dist. Ct., No. Dist. Ill., US Dist. Ct., We. Dist. Mich., US Supreme Ct. Ptnr., chmn. Securities Litig. Practice, co-chair Corp. Governance Practice, mem. exec. com. and bd. dirs. Katten Muchin Zavis Rosenman, Chgo. Office: Katten Muchin Zavis Rosenman 525 W Monroe St Chicago IL 60661 Office Phone: 312-902-5452. Office Fax: 312-577-4481. E-mail: david.kistenbroker@kmzr.com.

KITCH, FREDERICK DAVID, advertising executive; b. Chgo., Sept. 7, 1928; s. John Raymond and Mary Minerva (Wheeler) K.; m. Beverly Jane West, Nov. 24, 1976; children: William Mark, Stephen Neal, Michael Bruce Hile. BS in Journalism, Northwestern U., 1951. Mgmt. tng. Swift & Co., Chgo., 1954-55, dept. head Evansville, Ind., 1955-57; account exec. Keller-Crescent Co., Evansville, Ind., 1957-60, sr. account exec., 1960-65, v.p. account supervision, 1965-72, v.p. direct client services, 1972-80, exec. v.p. client services, 1980-86, exec. v.p. mktg. and sales, 1986-93, also bd. dirs., ret., 1993; founder, chmn. Kitch & Schreiber, Inc., Evansville, 1994—. Past pres. bd. dirs. Evansville Rescue Mission, 1981-97; pres. Welborn Hosp. Found., Evansville, 1984-91, Operation City Beautiful, Evansville, 1985-87; sec., treas. Vanderburgh County Redevel. Authority; v.p. Oak Meadow Homeowners Assn. Served to lt. U.S. Army, 1951-53. Recipient Silver Medal Tri State Advt. Club, 1980. Mem. Affiliated Advt. Internat. (sec.-treas.), 1980, Evansville Country Club (bd. dirs.). Republican. Episcopalian. Avocations: tennis, golf. Office: Kitch & Schreiber Inc 320 NW King Jr Blvd Evansville IN 47735

KITCH, PAUL R., lawyer; b. Southfield, Mich., 1966; BSEE summa cum laude, U. Mich., 1989, MBA with high distinction, 1993, JD, 1993. Bar: Ill. 1993, US Ct. Appeals Fed. Cir., US Dist. Ct. No. Dist. Ill., registered: US Patent & Trademark Office. Shareholder Jenkens & Gilchrist, P.C., Chgo., 2001—, firm co-leader intellectual property practice group. Mem.: ABA, Intellectual Property Law Assn. Chgo., Am. Intellectual Property Law Assn., Chgo. Bar Assn. Office: Jenkens & Gilchrist PC Ste 2600 225 W Washington St Chicago IL 60606-3418 Office Phone: 312-425-3900. Office Fax: 312-425-3909. Business E-Mail: pkitch@jenkens.com.

KITE, STEVEN B., lawyer; b. Chgo., May 30, 1949; s. Ben and Dolores (Braver) K.; m. Catherine Lapinski, Jan. 13, 1980; children: David, Julia. BA, U. Ill., 1971; JD, Harvard U., 1974. Bar: Ga. 1974, U.S. Dist. Ct. Ga. 1974, U.S. Ct. Appeals (5th and 11th cirs.) 1981, Ill. 1985, Fla. 1986. Ptnr. Kutak Rock, Atlanta, 1974—84, Gardner Carton & Douglas LLP, Chgo., 1984—2005, Sonnenschein Nath & Rosenthal LLP, Chgo., 2005—. Author, editor: Law For Elderly, 1978; author: Tax-Exempt Financing for Health Care Organizations, 1996; co-author: Bond Financing, 1994. Bd. dirs. Atlanta Legal Aid Soc., 1979-84; trustee Sr. Citizens Met. Atlanta, 1980-83. Mem. ABA, Ill. Bar Assn., State Bar Ga., Chgo. Bar Assn., Fla. Bar Assn., Nat. Assn. Bond Lawyers. Avocations: travel, sports, reading. Office: Sonnenschein Nath & Rosenthal LLP 233 S Wacker Dr Ste 7800 Chicago IL 60606 Office Phone: 312-876-8195. Business E-Mail: skite@sonnenschein.com.

KITNA, JON, professional football player; b. Tacoma, Washington, Sept. 21, 1972; m. Jennifer Kitna; children: Jordan, Jada, Jalen. Postgrad in math edn., Ctrl. Wash. Quarterback Seattle Seahawks, 1997—2000, Cin. Bengals, 2001—06, Detroit Lions, 2006—. Office: Detroit Lions 222 Republic Dr Allen Park MI 48101

KITTLE, JIM, JR., state representative, political party administrator; m. Sherry Kittle; children: Sawyer, Kenzie. Postgrad, Ind. Univ., Ind. Univ. Sch. law. Chmn., CEO Kittle's Furniture Group, 1979—; state chmn. Ind. Republican State Ctrl. Com., 2002—. Vice chair Bush for Pres. Team, 2000; delegate Three ational Conventions; fin. chmn. McIntosh Campaign, 2000. Chmn. Retail Divsn. United Way Ctrl. Ind.; bd.dirs. Human Soc. Indpls.; adv. bd. St. Vincent Hosp.; bd. dirs. Ind. Chamber Commerce, Better Bus. Bur., Nat. Retail Fedn. Republican. Office: Ind State Rep Party 47 S Meridian St 2nd Fl Indianapolis IN 46204

KITTO, JOHN BUCK, JR., mechanical engineer; b. Evanston, Ill., Dec. 22, 1952; s. John Buck and Marie (Comstock) K.; children: Christopher Daniel, Andrew Comstock. BSME, Lehigh U., 1975; MBA, U. Akron, 1980. Registered profl. engr., Ohio, Pa. Sr. engr. McDermott Tech. Inc. subs. Babcock & Wilcox Co., Alliance, Ohio, 1975-80, research engr., 1980-81, program mgr., 1981-94, bus. devel. specialist, 1995-99; bus. devel. mgr. The Babcock and Wilcox Co., Barberton, Ohio, 1999—. Editor: Heat Exchangers for Two Phase Flow, 1983, Two-Phase Heat Exchanger, 1985, Maldistribution of Flow, 1987, Steam: Its Generation and Use, 2005; author and patentee in field. Fellow ASME (chmn. chpt. 1983-84, chmn. exec. com. of heat transfer divsn. 1992-93, v.p. region V 1992-95, officer bd. comms. 1991-95, sr. v.p. 1995-98, mem. bd. govs. 1998-2002, Prime Movers award 1992, Dedicated Svc. award 1992, George Westinghouse Silver medal 1991); mem. Tau Beta Pi, Pi Tau Sigma, Beta Gamma Sigma, Sigma Iota Epsilon. Republican. Avocations: reading, hiking, board games, coaching soccer. Home: 1225 Arrowhead Dr SW Dellroy OH 44620 Office: Babcock & Wilcox Co PO Box 351 20 S Van Buren Ave Barberton OH 44203-0351 Home Phone: 330-735-2473; Office Phone: 330-860-2303. Office Fax: 330-860-1409.

KITZKE, EUGENE DAVID, research and development company executive; b. Milw., Sept. 2, 1923; s. Leo R. and Regina R. (Tomczyk) Kitzke; m. Lorraine Grace Shummon, Sept. 2, 1946; children: Mary Victoria, Paul Simon, Patrice Lynn, Jerome Peter. BS, Marquette U., 1945, MS, 1947; diploma in basic clin. sci., Med. Coll. Wis., 2002. Instr. microbiology St. Mary's Sch. Nursing, Grand Rapids, Mich., 1946-47; assoc. prof. Aquinas Coll., 1947-51; lab researcher S.C. Johnson & Son, Inc., Racine, Wis., 1951-57, research mgr., 1957-76, v.p. corp. R&D, 1976-81; pres. Oak Crete Block Corp., South Milwaukee, Wis., 1980—; developer Wind Crest Subdiv., Wind Lake, Wis., 1993. Adj. prof. dept. environ. medicine Med. Coll. Wis., Milw., 1973—81; owner Danel Enterprise, South Milwaukee; judge Marquette U. Sci. Fair; bd. dirs. Songcards, inc. Author: (book) For the Next Generation, 1986; contbr. articles to tech. jours., fiction and poetry to mags.; author pubs. in field. Mem. pres.' coun. Alverno Coll., 1979—87. Recipient H. F. Johnson Cmty. Svc. award, 1996; Disting. scholar, Marquette U., 1995. Mem.: AAAS, Hist. Sci. Soc., Palm Soc. (exec. bd., past pres.), Sigma Xi, Sigma Tau Delta, Phi Sigma. Roman Catholic. Achievements include patents in field. Home: 616 Aspen St South Milwaukee WI 53172-1702 Office: PO Box 413 South Milwaukee WI 53172-0413 also: 7101 S Pennsylvania Ave Oak Creek WI 53154-2439

KLAAS, PAUL BARRY, lawyer; b. St. Paul, Aug. 9, 1952; s. N. Paul and Ruth Elizabeth (Barry) K.; m. Barbara Ann Bockhaus, July 30, 1977; children: James, Ann, Brian. AB magna cum laude, Dartmouth Coll., 1974; JD cum laude, Harvard U., 1977. Bar: Minn. 1977, US Dist. Ct. Minn. 1977, US Ct. Appeals (8th cir.) 1979, US Ct. Appeals (10th cir.) 1980, US Supreme Ct. 1982, US Ct. Appeals (9th cir.) 1989, US Ct. Appeals (fed. cir.) 1994; solicitor Eng. and Wales 2006. Assoc. Dorsey & Whitney, Mpls., 1977-82, ptnr. trial group, 1983—, ptnr.-in-charge London, 2005—, ptnr.-in-charge (internat.), 2007—. Co-chair Internat. Arbitration and Litigation Practice Group, 1996—, chair, Trial Group, 2000-06; adj. prof. William Mitchell Coll Law, St. Paul, 1980-85. Bd. dirs. St. Paul Chamber Orchestra, City of London Sinfonia Orchestra. Fellow: Am. Coll. Trial Lawyers; mem.: Law Soc. Eng. and Wales, Phi Beta Kappa. Office: Dorsey & Whitney 50 S 6th St Ste 1500 Minneapolis MN 55402-1498 also: Dorsey & Whitney 21 Wilson St London EC2M 2TD England Office Phone: 612-340-2817, 44-020-7826-4567. Office Fax: 612-340-2868, 44-020-7588-0555. Business E-Mail: klaas.paul@dorsey.com.

KLAASSEN, CURTIS D., toxicologist, educator; b. Ft. Dodge, Iowa, Nov. 23, 1942; s. Henry Herman and Luwene Sophie (Nieman) K.; m. Cherry Klaassen, Sept. 30, 1968; children: Kimberly, Lisa. BS, Wartburg Coll., Waverly, Iowa, 1964; PhD, U. Iowa, 1968. Diplomate Am. Bd. Toxicology. Prof. toxicology U. Kans. Med. Ctr., Kansas City. Editor: Casarett & Douls Toxicology, 1991. Recipient USPHS Rsch. Career Devel. award, 1971-76, Achievement award, Soc. Toxicology, 1976, Burroughs Wellcome scholar, 1982-87. Mem. Soc. of Toxicology (pres. 1990-91). Lutheran. Office: Univ of Kans Med Ctr 39 Rainbow Kansas City KS 66103-2071

KLAHR, SAULO, nephrologist, educator; b. Santander, Colombia, June 8, 1935; came to U.S., 1961, naturalized, 1970; s. Herman and Raquel (Konigsberg) K.; m. Carol Declue, Dec. 29, 1965; children: James Herman, Robert David. BA, Colegio Santa Librada, Cali, Colombia, 1954; MD, U. Nat., Bogota, Colombia, 1959. Intern Hosp. San Juan de Dios, Bogota, 1958-59; resident U. Hosp., Cali, 1959-61; mem. faculty Washington U. Sch. Medicine, St. Louis, 1966—, prof. medicine, 1972-86, Joseph Friedman prof. renal disease, 1986-91, Simon prof. medicine, co-chmn. dept., 1991-97, dir. renal div., 1972-91; physician in chief Jewish Hosp., St. Louis, 1991-96; assoc. physician Barnes Hosp., 1972-75, physician, 1975-96, Barnes-Jewish Hosp., 1996—. Established investigator Am. Heart Assn., 1968-73; mem. adv. com. artificial kidney chronic uremia program USPHS, 1971—; bd. dirs. Eastern Mo. Kidney Found., 1973-75, chmn. med. adv. bd., 1973-74; rsch. com. Mo. Heart Assn., 1973-80, chmn., 1980-81; sci. adv. bd. Nat. Kidney Found., 1978, chmn., 1983-84, chmn. rsch. and fellowship com., 1979-81, v.p., 1986-88, pres., 1988-90; mem. gen. medicine B study sect. USPHS, 1979-83, chmn. gen. medicine B study sect., 1981-83; mem. cardiovascular and renal rev. group FDA, mem. VA Merit Rev. Bd. Nephrology, 1984-87, chmn., 1986-87; chmn. rsch. com. adv. bd. kidney, urology Nat. Inst. Diabetes and Digestive and Kidney Diseases, 1991-92, chmn. adv. bd., 1992-93; mem. adv. coun. Inst. Diabetes, Digestive Diseases and Kidney Diseases, 1995-98. Editor: Contemporary Nephrology, Chronic Renal Disease, Nutrition and the Kidney; editor in chief Am. Jour. Kidney Diseases, 1992-96; mem. editorial bd. Am. Jour. Nephrology, Am. Jour. Physiology and Renal and Electrolyte, Kidney and Body Fluids in Health and Disease, Internat. Jour. Pediatric Nephrology; assoc. editor Jour. Clin. Investigation; editor Kidney Internat., 1997-2005, sr. editor, 2005-; contbr. articles to profl. jours., book chpts. USPHS postdoctoral fellow, 1961-63; recipient David M. Hume award Nat. Kidney Found., 1992, Thomas Addis medal Internat. Soc. Nutrition and Renal Metabolism, 1996. Fellow ACP, AAAS, Royal Coll. Physicians (London), Australian, Chilean, Colombian, Spanish, Polish and Italian Socs. Nephrology (hon.); mem. Am. Soc. Nephrology (councillor 1980-81, sec.-treas. 1981-84, pres. 1985-86, John P. Peters award 1998), Am. Soc. Clin. Investigation, Am. Physiol. Soc., Biophys. Soc., N.Y. Acad. Scis., Am. Soc. Renal Biochemistry and Metabolism (pres. 1982-84), Ctrl. Soc. Clin. Rsch., Soc. Exptl. Biology and Medicine, Assn. Am. Physicians, Soc. Gen. Physiologists, Internat. Soc. Nephrology (councillor 1987-95, mem. mgmt. com. 1987-95, chmn. program com. Sydney meeting 1997, mem. exec. com. 1997—), Sigma Xi, Alpha Omega Alpha. Home: 11544 Ladue Rd Saint Louis MO 63141-8341 Office: Barnes-Jewish Hosp Washington U Med Ctr 216 S Kingshighway Blvd Saint Louis MO 63110-1092 Office Phone: 314-454-7107. Business E-Mail: sklahr@im.wush.edu.

KLAPPA, GALE E., energy executive; BA in mass communications, U. Wis.-Milw., 1972. Pres., CEO, SWEB; pres. N.Am. Group, Mirant; with So. Co., Atlanta, 1974—2003, chief mktg. officer, chief strategic officer, exec. v.p., CFO, treas.; pres., CEO, Wis. Energy Corp., 2003—, chmn., 2004—. Dir. Edison Electric Inst.; vice chmn. Nuclear Electric Ins. Ltd. Adv. coun. U Wis.-Milw. Sch. Bus.; bd. dir. United Way Greater Milw., Met. Milw. Assn. Commerce. Office: Wis Energy Corp 231 W Michigan St Milwaukee WI 53203

KLAPPERICH, FRANK LAWRENCE, JR., investment banker; b. Oak Park, Ill., Oct. 11, 1934; s. Frank Lawrence and Marjorie (Doan) K.; m. Margaret Monroe Touborg, Mar. 9, 1957; children: Margaret Friis, Susan Doane, Frank Lawrence III, Elizabeth Monroe. AB, Princeton U., 1956; MBA, Harvard U., 1961, postgrad., 1979. With Kidder, Peabody & Co., Inc., Chgo., 1961—, v.p., 1964—, dir., 1972-86, mng. dir., 1986-88, sr. v.p., 1988-90, ret., 1990; pres. Charter Capital Corp., 1991—. Governing mem. Orchestral Assn. Chgo. Symphony Orch., 1995—; vice chmn. governing mems., 1996-98; bd. dirs. Cmty. Found. Collier County, 2005— With USN, 1956—59, ret. LCDR USNR. Mem.: Inst. Chartered Fin. Analysts, Securities Industry Assn. (chmn. Ctrl. States dist. 1986—87), Investment Analysts Soc. Chgo., Harvard Bus. Sch. Alumni Assn. (bd. dirs. 2005—), Classic Chamber Concerts Inc. (bd. dirs. 2005—), Harvard Bus. Sch. Assn. Chgo., English Speaking Union (bd. dir-s.Naples chpt. 2005—), Hole-in-the-Wall Golf Club (Naples), Indian Hill Club (Winnetka, Ill.), Princeton Club SW Fla. (bd. dirs. 2003—, pres. 2007—), Harvard Club of Naples (Fla., pres. 2001—03), Forum Club SW Fla. (bd. dirs. 2002—05), Econ. Club, Bond Club (pres. 1983—84), Mid-Day Club (trustee 1987—90), Chgo. Club, Charter Club (governing bd. 1987—97), Princeton Club (Chgo., pres. 1970—71). Home: 345 Woodley Rd Winnetka IL 60093-3740 Office Phone: 312-984-0984.

KLARICH, DAVID JOHN, lobbyist, lawyer; b. Hamilton, Ohio, July 17, 1963; s. Victor Martin and Janet Dawn (Carlson) K.; m. Cheryl Ruth O'Donnell, June 18, 1988. BA in Biology and Chemistry, U. Mo., 1985; MA in Pub. Policy, Regent U., 1990, JD, 1990. Bar: Mo. 1990. Mem. Mo. Ho. of Reps. from 92nd & 94th dists., Jefferson City, 1990-94, Mo. Senate from 26th dist., Jefferson City, 1994—2002, Riezman and Berger, P.C., Clayton, Mo., 1995—2002; apptd. commr. Mo. Indsl. Rels., 2002—03; mng. mem. Citizens for Policy Reform, LLC. Chmn. judiciary com. Mo. State Senate, 2001—02. Chmn. judiciary com. Mo. State Senate, 2001—02; chmn. West County Rep. Orgn. Recipient Adminstrn. of Justice award Jud. Conf. Mo., 1991, 99, Mo. Bar award, 1993, 97, 2000, 01, Mo. Hosp. Assn. award, 1995, Jud. Conf. award, 2000, 02, Legal Svcs. award, 2000, award Mo. Assn. Probate and Assoc. Cir. Judges, 2001; named Mo. Bar Outstanding Legis. of Yr., 1996, Voice of Bus. award Assoc. Industries, 1998, Mo. Lawyers weekly v.p. and coming Lawyer Mem. Bar Assn. Met. St. Louis, Young Lawyers Assn., Vol. Lawyers Assn., St. Louis Lawyers Assn., Mo. Assn. Trial Attys., St. Louis Eagle Scout Assn., Nat. Eagle Scout Assn., Jaycees, Lions, Mo. C. of C. (Spirit of Enterprise award 1997), Theta Xi. Mem. Assembly of God Ch. Personal E-mail: dklarich@sbcglobal.net.

KLASSEN, LYNELL W., rheumatologist, transplant immunologist; b. Gossel, Kans., Jan. 24, 1947; married; 4 children. AB, Tabor Coll., 1969; MD, U. Kans., 1973. Resident in internal medicine U. Iowa Hosps. and Clins., 1973-75, chief resident internal medicine, 1977-78, asst. prof., 1978-82, assoc. prof. rheumatology & immunology, 1982-90; prof., vice chmn. internal medicine U. Nebr. Med. Ctr., 1990—; rsch. assoc. immunology Arthritis & Rheumatism Br., IH, 1975-77. Assoc. chief staff rsch., chief arthritis svc. rheumatology Omaha VA, 1982—; chmn. sci. rev. com. Nat. Inst. Alcohol Abuse, Alcoholism, 1989-95. Mem. Edn. Coun., Am. Coll. Rheumatology, Am. Coll. Physicians, Am. Assn. Immunology. Achievements include rsch. in mechanisms of hematopoietic allograft rejection, pathophysiology of graft-versus-host disease, use of cytotoxic therapy in non-malignant diseases. Office: Omaha Dept Vet Affairs Med Ctr 4101 Woolworth Ave Omaha NE 68105-1850

KLAUSER, JAMES ROLAND, lawyer; b. Milw., Feb. 16, 1939; s. Samuel and Ruth Shirley (Burmeister) K.; m. Shirley Krueger, Nov. 20, 1975; children: David James, James William. BS, U. Wis., 1961, JD, 1964, MA in Public Law, 1968. Bar: Wis. 1964. Atty. Chgo. Title & Trust Co., 1964-65; pvt. practice, Union Grove, Wis., 1965-68; counsel, staff atty. Wis. Legis. Coun., Madison, 1968-71, Senate Rep. Caucus, Madison, 1971-79; ptnr. DeWitt, Sundby, Huggett, Schumacher & Morgan SC, Madison, 1979-86; sec. Wis. Dept. Adminstrn., Madison, 1987-97; spl. counsel to gov. State of Wis., Madison, 1995-97; ptnr. DeWitt, Ross, Stevens, Madison, 1997—. Mem. Wis. State Investment Bd., Madison, 1987-97; chmn. Exec. Cabinet Quality Workforce, Madison, 1991-97. Een. chmn. Thompson for Wis., 1986—; mem. Gov.'s Commn. on Taliesin, Madison, 1988-92; bd. dirs. Wis. Housing and Econ. Devel. Authority, Madison, 1991-97. Recipient Disting. Svc. to State Govt. award Nat. Gov.'s Assn., 1991. Mem. Wis. Bar Assn. Republican. Lutheran. Avocations: reading, history, sailing, water sports. Office: DeWitt Ross & Stevens SC Two E Mifflin St Madison WI 53703

KLAUSNER, JEFFREY S., dean; m. Diane Klausner; children: Amy, Jenny. BS, U. Md., 1968; MS, U. Minn., 1977; DVM, U. Georgia, Athens, Ga., 1972. Clin. internship Angell Mem. Animal Hosp., Boston, 1972—73; graduate student and vet. medicine resident U. Minn. Coll. Vet. Medicine, St. Paul, 1974—77; asst. prof. U. Minn. Coll. Vet. Medicine, Small Animals Clin. Sciences, St. Paul, 1977—81, assoc. prof., 1981—90, prof., chair dept., 1990—; interim dean U. Minn. Coll. Vet. Medicine, St. Paul, 1998—2000, dean, 2000—. Contbr. articles to peer-reviewed jours. Named Veterinarian of Yr., Minn. Vet. Med. Assn., 2000. Mem.: Am. Assn. Cancer Rsch., Am. Med. Informatics Assn., Met. Animal Hosp. Assn., Vet. Cancer Soc., Am. Assn. Animal Technicians Educators, Am. Assn. Vet. Clinicians, Soc. Vet. Urology (pres. 1978), Minn. Vet. Med. Assn., Am. Animal Hosp. Assn., Am. Vet. Med. Assn., Am. Coll. Vet. Internal Medicine, Phi Kappa Phi, Soc. of Phi Zeta. Office: U Minn Coll Vet Medicine 1365 Gortner Ave Saint Paul MN 55108 Office Phone: 612-624-9227. E-mail: klaus001@tc.umn.edu.

KLAVITER, HELEN LOTHROP, magazine editor; b. Lima, Ohio, Mar. 5, 1944; d. Eugene H. and Jean (Walters) Lothrop; m. Douglas B. Klaviter, June 7, 1969 (div. 1982); 1 child, Elizabeth. BA, Cornell Coll., Mt. Vernon, Iowa, 1966. Communication specialist Coop. Extension Service, Urbana, Ill., 1969-71; mng. editor The Poetry Found. Poetry Mag., Chgo., 1973—. Editorial cons. Harper & Row, N.Y.C., 1983-87. Bd. dirs. Ill. Theatre Ctr., 1989—95, St. Clement's Open Pantry, 1990—, Episc. Diocese of Chgo. Hunger Commn., 1992—. Episcopalian. Office: Poetry Mag The Poetry Found 444 N Michigan Ave Ste 1850 Chicago IL 60611 Office Phone: 312-799-8004. Business E-Mail: hklaviter@poetrymagazine.org.

KLEBBA, RAYMOND ALLEN, property manager; b. Chgo., Apr. 16, 1934; s. Raymond Aloysius and Marie Cecelia (Tobin) K.; m. Barbara Ann Gurbal, Oct. 7, 1961; children: Anne, Daniel, Mary, Theresa. Student, Loyola U., Chgo., 1954-56; cert. property mgr., Inst. Real Estate Mgmt., 1970. Corr., rep. Western R.R. Assn., Chgo., 1956-61; pres. Midland Warehouses, Chgo., 1961-68; v.p., gen. mgr. Strobeck, Reiss Sch. Mgmt. Co., Chgo., 1968-70, real estate mgr., broker, 1970—83; v.p., dir. Mid-Am. Nat. Bank, Chgo., 1983-90; br. mgr. Bank of Highwood/Deerfield, Ill., 1990-94; v.p. sales First Colonial Mortgage Corp., Chgo., 1994-95; bus. mgr. St. Matthias Parish, Chgo., 1995-98; real estate broker Tempo Real Estate, Inc., Chgo., 1998—. Chicagoland individual casting champion 1999—. Mem. Chgo. Bd. Realtors (vice chmn. comml. and indsl. leasing and property mgmt. coun.), Inst. Real Estate Mgmt. (life; chmn. chpt. of yr. com. 1975-76), Rotary, Moose, KC. Avocations: bowling, golf, gardening, fishing. Home: 4933 N Leavitt St Chicago IL 60625-1308 Office Phone: 773-271-3200.

KLECZKA, GERALD DANIEL, former congressman; b. Milwaukee, Wis., Nov. 26, 1943; s Harry J. and Agnes P. (Dusza) Kleczka; m. Bonnie L. Scott, 1978. Student, U. Wis., Milw. Mem. Wis. Assembly, 1968-74; mem. Wis. Senate, 1974-84, U.S. Congress from 4th Wis. dist., Washington, 1984—2005. Mem. ways and means com., ways and means health subcom., house budget com. Mem. Wis. Dem. Com., Milwaukee County Dem. Com. With Air N.G., 1963-69. Mem. LaFarge Lifelong Learning Inst., Thomas More Found., Polish Nat. Alliance-Milw. Soc., Polish Am. Congress. Democrat.

KLEEFISCH, REBECCA, reporter; b. Waterville, Ohio; m. Joel Kleefisch. B Journalism, U. Wis. Anchor WIFR-TV, Rockford, Ill.; reporter, anchor WISN 12, Milw., 1999—. Office: WISN PO Box 0402 Milwaukee WI 53201-0402

KLEFFNER, GREGORY WILLIAM, retail executive, accountant; b. St. Louis, Nov. 21, 1954; s. Francis R. and Charlotte P. (Petersen) Kleffner; m. Renee A. Drake, June 10, 1993; children: Patricia Elaine, Laura Elizabeth, Michael Gregory. BSBA, Washington U., 1977. Staff Arthur Andersen & Co., St. Louis, 1977-79, sr. acct., 1979-81, mgr. to ptnr. and head audit dept., 1981—2002; v.p., controller Kellwood Co., St. Louis, 2002—, corp. officer and v.p. finance, 2005—. Bd. mem. Grand Center, Inc., St. Louis County Industrial Develop. Authority, St. Louis County Business Finance Co. Mem. Am. Inst. CPA's, Mo. Soc. CPA's, St. Louis County Econ. Devel. Assn. (loan rev. com. 1986-87), Am. Y-Flyer Yacht Racing Assn. (sec.-treas 1984—). Avocations: sailing, golf. Office: Kellwood Co 600 Kellwood Parkway Chesterfield MO 63017 Business E-Mail: gregkleffner@kellwood.com.

KLEIMAN, DAVID HAROLD, lawyer; b. Kendallville, Ind., Apr. 2, 1934; s. Isadore and Pearl (Wikoff) K.; m. Meta Dene Freeman, July 6, 1958; children: Gary, Andrew, Scott, Matthew. BS, Purdue U., 1956; JD, Northwestern U., 1959. Bar: Ind. 1959. Assoc. firm Bamberger & Feibleman, Indpls., 1959-61; ptnr. Bagal, Talesnick & Kleiman, Indpls., 1961-73, Dann Pecar Newman & Kleiman, Indpls., 1973—; dep. pros. atty., 1961-62; counsel Met. Devel. Commn., 1965-75; Ind. Heartland Coordinating Commn., 1975-81. Editor: Jour. of Air Law and Commerce, 1958-59. Chmn. Young Leadership Coun., 1967; v.p. Indpls. Hebrew Congregation, 1973, bd. dirs., 2003—; pres. Jewish Cmty. Ctr. Assn., 1972-75; pres. Jewish Welfare Fedn., 1981-84; v.p. United Way Ctrl. Ind., 1982-86, pres., 1986, chmn. bd. dirs., 1987; bd. dirs. Jewish Fedn., 1972—, Ind. Symphony Soc., 1991-96; bd. dirs. Ind. Repertory Theatre, 1986—, pres. 1991-94; trustee Indpls. Found., 2000—; bd. dirs. Ctrl. Ind. Cmty Found., 2000—, English Found., 2000—. Recipient Young Leadership award, 1968, Isadore Fiebleman Man of Yr. award, 1987, Mossler Cmty. Svc. award, 1988, Chalfie Cmty. Svc. award, 1998. Mem. ABA, Ind. State Bar Assn., Indpls. Bar Assn., Comml. Law League Am., Am. Coll. Bankruptcy, Columbia Club, Skyline Club (bd. dirs. 1993—), B'nai B'rith, Broadmoor Country Club. Office: Dann Pecar Newman & Kleiman One American Square PO Box 82008 Indianapolis IN 46282-2008

KLEIN, BARBARA A., information technology executive; b. Pitts., Apr. 22, 1954; m. Michael E. Klein. BS in Acctg. & Fin., Marquette U.; MBA, Loyola U., Chgo., 1977. CPA. With Sears, Roebuck & Co.; v.p. fin. bakeries & food service The Pillsbury Co., 1993—96, v.p., corp. contr., 1996, Ameritech Corp., 1996—2000; v.p. fin., CFO Dean Foods Co., 2000—02; sr. v.p., CFO CDW Computer Centers, Inc., Vernon Hills, Ill., 2002—. Bd. dirs. Corn Products Internat. Inc., 2004—, Cabot Microelectronics Corp., 2008—. Bd. mem. Tax Assistance Prog. Mem.: Chgo. Fin. Exchange, Fin. Executives Inst., Chgo. Network, Ill. Soc. CPAs, AICPA. Office: CDW Computer Centers Inc 200 N Milwaukee Ave Vernon Hills IL 60061*

KLEIN, GABRIELLA SONJA, retired communications executive; b. Chgo., Apr. 11, 1938; d. Frank E. Vosicky and Sonja (Kosner) Becvar; m. Donald J. Klein. BA in Comm. and Bus. Mgmt., Alverno Coll., 1983. Editor, owner Fox Lake (Wis.) Rep., 1962-65, McFarland (Wis.) Comty. Life and Monona Cmty. Herald, 1966-69; bur. reporter Waukesha (Wis.) Daily Freeman, 1969-71; cmty. rels. staff Waukesha County Tech. Coll., Pewaukee, Wis., 1971-73; pub. rels. specialist JI Case Co., Racine, Wis., 1973-75, corp. publs. editor, 1975-80; v.p., bd. dirs. publs. Image Mgmt. Valley View Ctr., Milw., 1980-82; pres. Comm. Concepts Unltd., Racine, 1983-98; ret., 1998. Past pres. Big Bros./Big Sisters Racine County; past v.p. devel. Girl Scouts Racine County, bd. dirs. Recipient award Wis. Press Assn., Nat. Fedn. Press Women, Silver medal Ad Club Racine, 1998, Outstanding Alumna award Alverno Coll., 1999, Edn. Cmty. Leader of Yr., Racine Area Mfrs. and Commerce, 2000, Thanks Badge award Girl Scouts of Racine County, 2000, Cmty. Trustee award Leadership Racine, 2004, Thanks Badge II award Girl Scouts Racine County, 2005, Oustanding Youth Adv. award Racine County Youth as Resources, 2006; named Wis. Woman Entrepreneur of Yr., 1985, Vol. of Yr. Racine Area United Way, 1994, Woman of Distinction Bus., Racine YWCA, 1995. Home: 3045 Chatham St Racine WI 53402-4001

KLEIN, JERRY, state legislator; b. Nov. 21, 1951; m. Bev.; 4 children. Bismarck Jr. Coll., Mary Coll. Pres. Fessenden Econ. Devel.; mem. N. D. Senate, Bismark, 1996—. Mem. Fessenden Vol. Fire Dept. Mem. N. D. Grocers Assn. (pres.); bd. dirs. CArrington Health Ctr. Office: Dist 14 PO Box 265 Fessenden ND 58438-0265 E-mail: jklein@state.nd.us.

KLEIN, KAREN K., federal judge; Magistrate judge U.S. Dist. Ct. N.D., Fargo. Office: 655 1st Ave N Ste 440 Fargo ND 58102-4952 Fax: 701-297-7075.

KLEIN, LLOYD WILLIAM, cardiologist, researcher; b. NYC, Sept. 29, 1952; s. Julian and Zali (Heimlich) K.; m. Barbara Joyce Visocan, Sept. 4, 1982; children: Laura, Jenny. AB cum laude with honors in Chemistry, Kenyon Coll., 1973; MD, U. Cin., 1977. Diplomate Am. Bd. Internal Medicine with subspecialty in cardiovascular disease, Nat. Bd. Med. Examiners; cert. Interventional Cardiology, 1997. Intern/resident Albert Einstein Coll. Medicine/Bronx Mcpl. Hosp. Ctr., 1977-80; clin. fellow in cardiology Mt. Sinai Med. Ctr./CCNY, NYC, 1980-82; attending physician emergency rm. Bronx Mcpl. Hosp. Ctr., 1980-83; assoc. dir. cardiac catheterization labs. Phila. Heart Inst./Presbyn.-U. Pa. Med. Ctr., 1983-88; dir. interventional cardiology, dir. rsch./edn. Cardiac Catheterization Labs., Northwestern Meml. Hosp., Chgo., 1988-90; dir. divsn. cardiology VA Lakeside Med. Ctr., Chgo., 1989-90; med. dir. Rush Heart Inst./Oak Park Hosp./Rush Sys. for Health, Oak Park, Ill., 1998—2001; dir. interventional cardiology Rush-Presbyn.-St. Luke's Med. Ctr., Chgo., 1990—2001, co-dir. Cardiac Catheterization Labs., 1990—2004, assoc. dir. cardiology sect., dir. clin. svcs., 2001—04; dir. rsch. Gottlieb Meml. Hosp., Melrose Pk., Ill., 2004—, dir. prof. devel., 2004—. Instr. medicine, clin. assoc. cardiology Mt. Sinai Sch. Medicine/CCNY, 1982-83; asst. prof. clin. medicine U. Pa., Phila., 1983-88; assoc. prof. medicine Northwestern U., Chgo., 1988-90, Rush U. Med. Sch., Chgo., 1990-97, prof., 1997—. Editor: Quick Reference to Internal Medicine, 1994, Coronary Stenosis Morphology: Analysis and Clinical Implication, 1997, Resource Utilization in cardiac Disease, 1998; contbr. numerous articles and abstracts to profl. jours., chpts. to books; editl. review cons. Annals of Internal Medicine, Circulation, Am. Heart Jour., Archives of Internal Medicine, Jour. of Heart and Lun Transplantation, Critical Care Medicine, Chest; editl. bd. Jour. Am. Coll. Cardiology, 1990-94, 95-98, 2000-04, Am. Jour. Cardiology, 1989—, Catheterization and Cardiovascular Diagnosis, 1994—, Cardiac Chronicle, 1990-94, Cardiovascular Therapeutics, 1997; contbg. editor: Year Book of Critical Care Medicine, 1990-94; assoc. editor Jour. Invasive Cardiology, 2001— Mem. Tobacco Free Ill. Named One of Best Cardiologists in Chgo., Chgo. Mag., 1995, 2004, 06; recipient award Am. Chem. Soc., AMA Physician's Recognition award; George Gund scholar; grantee N.Y. Heart Found., 1982-83, Am. Heart Assn. Southeastern Pa., 1984-85, ADAC Labs., Inc., 1985-87, Glaxo Inc. G.B., 1986-87, Philips, Inc., 1990-92, Boston Sci., Inc., 1990-92, Baxter, Inc., 1994-96, Rush U. Com. on Rsch., 1996-98, SmithKlein, 1997-2000, Robert Wood Johnson Found., 1994-98. Fellow ACP, Am. Coll. Cardiology (mem. database com., database devel. and outcomes assessment subcom. 1996—, Ill. chpt. bd. councilors 1997-2006, mem. program com. 1995-2005, rsch. presentation evaluation com. 1995-2004), Coun. on Clin. Cardiology of Am. Heart Assn., Soc. for Cardiac Angiography and Interventions (registry, program and interventional cardiology com. 1995—, chair 2000—), Coun. on Circulation of Am. Heart Assn.; mem. Am. Fedn. Clin. Rsch., Am. Heart Assn. of Met. Chgo. (chmn. tobacco issues com. 1993-96, pub. policy and gove. rels. com. 1991-2004, vice chair 1995-97), Am. Heart Assn. (West Suburban divsn. founding pres. 1998), Philander Chase Soc., Alpha Omega Alpha, Sigma Chi. Avocations: reading, skiing, chess, classical music. Office: Clinical Cardiology Assocs Gottlieb Meml Hosp Profl Bldg Room 314 701 North Ave Melrose Park IL 60160 Office Phone: 708-681-7878. Business E-Mail: iklein@rpslmc.edu. E-mail: lloydklein@comcast.net.

KLEIN, MATTHEW M., state legislator; m. Isabell; 6 children. Student, Ellendale Coll., Amarillo Jr. Coll., U. So. Calif., UCLA; BS, N.D. State U. Mem. N.D. Ho. of Reps., 1993—, mem. judiciary and industry, bus. and labor coms., mem. govt. and vet. affairs com.; chair govt. and vet. affairs com. Cons. in English. Recipient Worldwide Constrn. Mgr. of Yr. award. Mem. Am. Legion. Home: 1815 7th St NW Minot ND 58703-1314

KLEIN, MILES VINCENT, physics professor; b. Cleve., Mar. 9, 1933; s. Max Ralph and Isabelle (Benjamin) K.; m. Barbara Judith Pincus, Sept. 2, 1956; children: Cynthia Klein-Banai, Gail. BS, Northwestern U., 1954; PhD, Cornell U., 1961. NSF postdoctoral fellow Max Planck Inst., Stuttgart, Germany, 1961; prof. U. Ill., Urbana, 1962—. Co-author: Optics, 1986; contbr. articles to profl. jours. A.P. Sloan Found. fellow, 1963. Fellow AAAS, Am. Phys. Soc. (Frank Isakson prize 1990), Am. Acad. Arts and Scis.; mem. IEEE (Sr.), Nat. Acad. Scis. Office: Materials Rsch Lab 104 S Goodwin Ave Urbana IL 61801-2902 Business E-Mail: mvklein@uiuc.edu.

KLEIN, WARD M., consumer products company executive; With Ralston Purina Co., 1979, Energizer Holding, 1986—, vice-pres. mktg., 1992—94, vice-pres., gen. mgr. global lighting prods., 1994—96, v.p. Asia Pacific & Latin Am., 2000—02, pres., internat., 2002—04, pres., COO, 2004—05, CEO, 2005—. Chmn. various foreign divisions Energizer Holdings. Office: Energizer HQ 533 Marryville University Saint Louis MO 63141 Office Phone: 800-383-7323.

KLEINDORFER, DAWN OLSON, medical educator, neurologist; b. Dec. 8, 1970; BS in Biology (with high honors), Ind. U.; MD, Washington Univ. Sch. Medicine, 1997. Med. residency, dept. neurology U. Mich., 1998—2001; fellowship, cerebrovascular disease divsn., dept. neurology U. Cinn., Coll. Medicine, 2001—02; chief resident, dept. neurology U. Mich., 2000—01; asst. prof., neurology U. Cinn. Selected participant Early Career Women in Academic Medicine Profl. Develop. Seminar, 2004. Contbr. articles to profl. jours. Recipient Top Enrollment award, PROFESS study, Platinum Level, Outstanding Resident Rsch. award, Mich. eurological Assn., Am. Heart Assn. Health Initiatives Vol. award, 2004; Nat. Stroke Assn. Rsch. Fellowship award, 2002. Mem.: AMA, Am. Stroke Assn., Phi Beta Kappa. Recipient of the Hazel K. Goddess Scholar grant for stroke research in women, 2004-2006. In a two-year study running concurrently in Atlanta and Cincinnati, African American beauticians will be educated about the signs of a stroke, and they will then educate their clientele during their appointments. Office: Univ Neurology Inc 222 Piedmont Ave # 3200 Cincinnati OH 45219-4217 Office Phone: 513-475-8730, 513-558-5328. Office Fax: 513-475-8033. Business E-Mail: dawn.kleindorfer@uc.edu.

KLEINE, ROBERT J., state official; m. Judy Karandjeff. BA, We. Md. Coll.; MA, Mich. State U. Dir. office revenue and tax analysis Dept. Mgmt. and Budget, Mich.; editor Pub. Sector Reports Pub. Sector Consultants, Inc., sr. economist, v.p.; pres. Kleine Consulting; state treas. State of Mich., Lansing, 2006—. Office: Treasury Bldg 430 W Allegan St Lansing MI 48922 E-mail: mistatereasurer@michigan.gov.

KLEINFELD, ERWIN, mathematician, educator; b. Vienna, Apr. 19, 1927; came to U.S., 1940; s. Lazar and Gina (Schönbach) K.; m. Margaret Morgan, July 2, 1968; children— Barbara, David. BS, CCNY, 1948; MA, U. Pa., 1949; PhD, U. Wis., 1951. Instr. U. Chgo., 1951-53; asst. prof. Ohio State U., 1953-56, asso. prof., 1957-60, prof., 1960-62; prof. math. Syracuse U., 1962-67, U. Hawaii, 1967-68, U. Iowa, 1968—2002, prof. emeritus, 2002—. Vis. lectr. Yale, 1956-57; cons. at. Bur. Standards, 1953; rsch. specialist U. Conn., 1955; research mathematician Bowdoin Coll., 1957; rsch. asso. Cornell U., summer 1958, U. Calif., LA, 1959, Stanford, 1960, Inst. Def. Analysis, 1961-62, AID-India, 1964-65; vis. prof. Emory U., 1976-77; Cons. Edn. IX Project, World Bank, U. Indonesia, 1985-86, Mucia/Ind. U.-(ITM) Shah Alam, Malaysia Project, 1988-89. Editorial bd. Jour. Algebra-Academic Press; cons. editor, Merrill Pub. Co.-Div. Bell & Howell. Contbr. articles research jours. Served with AUS, 1945-46. Wis. Alumni Rsch. Found. fellow, 1949-51, vis. rsch. fellow U. New Eng., Australia, 1992; grantee U.S. Army Rsch. Office, 1955-70, NSF, 1970-75. Mem. Am. Math. Soc., Sigma Xi. Home: 1555 N Sierra 120 Reno NV 89503 Home Phone: 775-337-0196. Business E-Mail: mkleinfd@math.uiowa.edu.

KLEINGARTNER, LARRY, agricultural association executive; b. Kulm, ND, Mar. 14, 1945; s. William Fred and Elsie (Riebhagen) K.; m. Nancy Lee Brand, Sept. 2, 1978; children: Jessie Lee, Brita Paula, Anika Rae. AA, Bismarck Jr. Coll., 1965; BA, Jamestown Coll., 1967; MA, U. Hawaii, 1974. Vol. U.S. Peace Corps, Maharastra, India, 1968-71; dir. mktg. N.D. Dept. of Agr., Bismarck, N.D., 1975-79; exec. dir. Nat. Sunflower Assn., Bismarck, 1980—. Contbr. artilces on agr. to prof jours. V.p. New Horizons Fgn. Adoption Svcs., Bismarck, 1983—; bd. dirs. Bismarck Mandan Civic Chorus, 1980; Sunday sch. tchr. Lord of Life Luth. Ch., Bismarck, 1978—, coun. mem., 1984—. Nat. Def. Lang. fellow, 1972-74. Avocations: cross country skiing, horseback riding, music. Office: Nat Sunflower Assn 4023 State St Bismarck ND 58503-0620 Office Phone: 701-328-5103. Office Fax: 701-328-5101. Business E-Mail: klngrtnr@sunflowernsa.com.

KLEINHENZ, CHRISTOPHER, foreign language educator, researcher, director; b. Indpls., Dec. 29, 1941; m. Margaret Ellen Zechiel, Aug. 1, 1964; children: Steven Russell, Michael Thomas. BA, Ind. U., 1964, MA, 1966, PhD, 1969. Asst. prof., dir. Bologna program Ind. U., 1970-71; instr. U. Wis., Madison, 1968-69, asst. prof., 1969-70, asst. prof., dept. French and Italian, 1971-75, assoc. prof., 1975-80, chmn. medieval studies program, 1975—80, 1981—84, 1989—95, 1996—2003, prof., 1980—2007, chmn. dept., 1985-88, Carol Mason Kirk prof. Italian, 2000—07, dir. honors program, 2005—07. Dir. devel. grant NEH, Madison, 1976-79, co-dir. rsch. tools grant, 1980-84. Author: The Early Italian Sonnet, 1986, Movement and Meaning in the Divine Comedy, 2005; editor: Medieval Manuscripts and Textual Criticism, 1976, Medieval Studies in North America, 1982, Routledge Studies in Medieval Literature, 1996-2002, Dante Studies, 1988-2003, Medieval Italy: An Encyclopedia, 2004; co-editor: Saint Augustine the Bishop: A Book of Essays, 1994, Routledge Medieval Casebooks, 1991—, Fearful Hope: Approaching the New Millennium, 1999, Courtly Arts and the Art of Courtliness, 2006; assoc. editor: Dante Ency., 2000; chmn. editl. bd. Medieval Acad. Reprints for Teaching, 1981-93; bibliographer MLA, NYC, 1981-88, BIGLLI, Rome, 1994—, Dante Studies, 1984-2002, ICLS, 2002-2006; book rev. editor Italica, 1984-93; co-translator: Dante Alighieri, Il Fiore and the Detto d'Amore, 2000. Chmn. com. on ctrs. and regional assns. Medieval Acad., 1993-99. Recipient Chancellor's Disting. Tchg. award, 2004, Leonard Covello Lifetime Achievement award, 2005, Hilldale award, 2006, Disting. Svc. to the Profession award Assn. Depts. Fgn. Langs., 2006; Newberry Libr./NEH grantee, 1988-89. Mem. Medieval Assn. of Midwest (pres. 1984-85, 2003-04), Dante Soc. Am. (mem. coun. 1985-91), Am. Boccaccio Assn. (v.p. 1987-93, pres. 1993-97), Am. Assn. Tchrs. of Italian (v.p. 1993-98, pres. 1999-03, Disting. Svc. award 2006). Avocations: sports, stamp collecting/philately, photography, travel. Home: 2247 Fox Ave Madison WI 53711-1922 Office: U Wis Dept French and Italian 1220 Linden Dr Madison WI 53706-1525 Office Phone: 608-262-5816. Business E-Mail: ckleinhe@wisc.edu.

KLEINMAN, BURTON HOWARD, real estate investor; b. Chgo., Nov. 19, 1923; s. Eli I. and Pearl (Cohan) K.; m. Shirley A. Freyer, Sept. 6, 1950 (div. Oct. 1969); children: Kim, Lauri. BS in Engring., U.S. Naval Acad., 1948. Commd. ensign USN, 1948, resigned, 1949; v.p. C.F. Corp., Chgo., 1958-80, pres., 1980-85; owner B.H. Kleinman Co., Northfield, Ill., 1955—. Bd. dirs. United Way Northfield, 1970-72, North Shore Mental Health Assn., 1978-82. Mem. Northfield C. of C. (bd. dirs. 1976-81), Ridge & Valley Tennis Club. Libertarian. Unitarian Universalist. Avocations: tennis, scuba diving, sailing, flying. Home: 570 Happ Rd orthfield IL 60093-1112 Office: BH Kleinman Co 456 W Frontage Rd Northfield IL 60093-3034 Home Phone: 847-441-6456; Office Phone: 847-441-5544. E-mail: gonavy48@aol.com.

KLEINMAN, MICHAEL A., trust company executive; BA English, Rockhurst Coll.; JD, St. Louis U. Cert. fin. planner. With legal sect. estate and gift tax divsn. IRS; dir. pub. rels. Nat. Assn. Intercollegiate Athletics; with MidAm. Bank & Trust (now Firstar Bank), 1971, United Mo. Bank Kans. City; exec. v.p., mgr. employee benefit divsn. Midwest Trust, Overland Park, Kans. Chmn. planned giving com. Rockhurst U. Mem.: Internat. Assn. Fin. Planners, Estate Planning Soc. Kansas City, Mo. Bar Assn. Office: Midwest Trust Company 5901 College Blvd Ste 100 Leawood KS 66211-1834

KLEINWORTH, EDWARD J., agricultural company executive; Pres. St. Ansgar Mills, Inc. Office: St Ansgar Mills Inc PO Box 370 Saint Ansgar IA 50472-0370

KLEIS, DAVID, state legislator; Mem. Minn. Senate from 16th dist., St. Paul, 1995—. Office: Minnesota State Senate 151 State Office Bldg Saint Paul MN 55155-0001 Also: 45 20th Ave N Saint Cloud MN 56303-4436

KLEMENS, THOMAS LLOYD, editor; b. Pitts., Mar. 28, 1952; s. Robert F. and Ann E. (Lacy) K.; m. Norreen McLellan, Aug. 4, 1973; children: Jonathan, Zachary. BFA, Carnegie-Mellon U., 1974; BSCE, U. Pitts., 1983; postgrad., Roosevelt U., Chgo., 1990-91. Registered profl. engr., Ill. Choir dir., tchr. Wellsville (Ohio) H.S., 1975-76; asst. band dir., tchr. North Hills H.S., Ross Twp., Pa., 1976-79; field engr. S.J. Groves & Sons, Pitts., 1983; structural engr. Sargent & Lundy, Chgo., 1983-87; field engr. Structural Preservation Systems, Inc., Margate, NJ, 1987; project mgr. Northwest Group, Inc., West Chicago, Ill., 1987; engr., purchasing agt. L.J. Keefe Co., Mt. Prospect, Ill., 1987-89; from assoc. editor to editor Hwy. & Heavy Constrn. Cahners Pub., Des Plaines, Ill., 1989-91, editor Hwy. & Heavy Constrn. Products, 1991-93, sr. editor Consulting/Specifying Engr., 1993-94; co-owner Wordwright, Palatine, Ill., 1993—. Instr. Motorola U., 1996-98; com. on constrn. equipment Transp. Rsch. Bd., Washington, 1991-93 adj. faculty William Rainey Harper Coll., Palatine, 1997—. Author Hwy. and Heavy Constrn., 1989-91, editor, 1991-92; author, editor Infrastructure, 1992-93; sr. editor Cons./Specifying Engr., 1993-94; editor PM Engr., Bus. News Pub., 1994-96, Plumbing Engr., TMB Pub., 1996-2003; sr. editor enging. HanleyWood LLC, 2003—. Mem. ASCE, Am. Concrete Inst., Am. Soc. Testing and Materials. Office: Hanley Wood Bus Media 8725 W Higgins Rd Ste 600 Chicago IL 60631 Home Phone: 847-934-8298; Office Phone: 773-824-2511. Business E-Mail: tklemens@hanleywood.com.

KLEMM, RICHARD O., state legislator; b. Chgo., May 05; s. Oren E. and Edythe (Neilsen) K.; m. Nancy Klemm; 7 children. BS, Purdue U., 1954. Pres., mem. Crystal Lake Dist. 46 Bd. Edn., 1964-71; trustee Nunda Twp., 1964-72; chmn., mem. McHenry County Bd., 1972-80; Ill. state rep. Dist. 63, 1981-92; Ill. state sen. Dist. 23, 1993—. Vice-spokesman Exec. Com.; mem. Labor and Commerce Com.; former minority spokesman, mem. Constnl. Officers Com.,

Vets. Affairs Com.; former mem. Environ. and Energy Com. Ill. Ho. of Reps.; pres., bd. chmn. Food Warming Equipment Co., Inc., Crystal Lake, 1972—. Recipient numerous comty. svc. awards. Mem. Sigma Nu.

KLEMM, RON, radio producer; b. Hammond, Ind. married; 1 child. BA Music and Comm., Dordt Coll. Ops. mgr. Classic 99, St. Louis. Avocation: golf. Office: Classic 99 85 Founders Ln Saint Louis MO 63105

KLEMME, RALPH F., state representative; b. Plymouth County, Iowa, Nov. 17, 1939; m. Karen Oloff. Grad. H.S., LeMars, Iowa. Grain and livestock farmer, 1959—; mem. Iowa Ho. Reps., DesMoines, 2003—, mem. various coms. including adminstrn. and regulation, appropriations, agr., local govt. and transp. Active LeMars Cmty. Sch. Bd., pres.; bd. mem. St. John's Luth. Ch., Plymouth County Compensation Bd., Plymouth County Draft Bd. Mem. Iowa Army Nat. Guard. Mem.: Soybean Assn., Plymouth County Farm Bur. Pork Prodrs., Cattlemen's Assn. Home: 167 Edward Dr Se Le Mars IA 51031-2781

KLENK, JAMES ANDREW, lawyer; b. Evergreen Park, Ill., July 18, 1949; s. Paul Theodore and Joan (Launspach) K.; m. Carol Evans, Aug. 26, 1972; children: Paul Andrew, Matthew Evans. BA, Beloit Coll., 1971; JD, U. Wis., 1974. Bar: Ill. 1974, Wis. 1974, U.S. Supreme Ct. 1978. Law clk. to Judge Thomas E. Fairchild U.S. Ct. Appeals (7th cir.), Chgo., 1974-75; assoc. Kirkland & Ellis, Chgo., 1975-78; ptnr. Reuben & Proctor, Chgo., 1978-86, Isham, Lincoln & Beale, Chgo., 1986-88, Sonnenschein, Nath & Rosenthal, Chgo., 1988—. Articles editor Wis. Law Rev. Mem. ABA (litigation sect., torts and ins. practice sect., bus. law sect.), Ill. Bar Assn., Media Law Ctr., Order of Coif, Phi Beta Kappa. Office: Sonnenschein Nath & Rosenthal 8000 Sears Tower Chicago IL 60606 Office Phone: 312-876-8062. Business E-Mail: jklenk@sonnenschein.com.

KLENK, TIMOTHY CARVER, lawyer; b. Glen Cove, NY, Apr. 29, 1939; s. Horace I. and Laura (Dugan) K.; m. Ann Ruth Schuessler, 1961 (dec. 1966); 1 child, Carolyn; m. Margaret Jo Garrett, Aug. 30, 1969. AB, Wheaton Coll., 1961; JD, Northwestern U., 1967. Bar: Ill. 1967, U.S. Dist. Ct. (no. dist.) Ill. 1968, U.S. Dist. Ct. (cen. dist.) Wis. 1976, U.S. Dist. Ct. (cen. dist.) Ill. 1981, U.S. Ct. Appeals (7th cir.) 1979, U.S. Supreme Ct. 1980. Systems engr. IBM, NYC, 1961-62; assoc. Kirkland & Ellis, Chgo., 1967-70, Pope, Ballard, Shepard & Fowle Ltd., Chgo., 1970-74, ptnr., 1974-77, dir., 1977-94, mng. dir., 1993-94; ptnr. Ross & Hardies, Chgo., 1994—2003, McGuireWoods LLP, 2003—. Bd. dirs. Living Bibles Internat. U.S., Naperville, Ill., 1983-91, also v.p. 1st lt. U.S. Army, 1962-64. Mem. ABA, Ill. Bar Assn., 7th Cir. Bar Assn., Am. Judicature Soc., Christian Legal Soc. (bd. dirs. 1986—, pres. 1988-90), Am. Arbitration Assn. (arbitrator), Order of Coif. Republican. Avocations: flying, water sports, skiing. Office: Ross & Hardies 150 N Michigan Ave Ste 2500 Chicago IL 60601-7567 E-mail: tklenk@mcguirewoods.com.

KLENKE, DEBORAH ANN, band and choral director, department chairman; b. Oak Park, Ill., May 20, 1958; d. Myron and Rita Frances Joshel; children: S. Joel, Jeremy. BS, Elmhurst Coll., 1986. Dir. music, dept. chmn. Faith Christian Elem.-Jr. HS, Geneva, Ill., 1987—2003; dir. bands St. Peter Sch., Geneva, Ill., 1991—99. Prin. flutist West Suburban Symphony, Hinsdale, 1991—2003; freelance flutist. Mem.: Ill. Grade Sch. Music Assn., Ill. Music Educators Assn., Chgo. Flute Club. Office: Faith Christian Elem -Jr HS 1745 Kaneville Rd Geneva IL 60134 Personal E-mail: debklenke@yahoo.com.

KLEVEN, MARGUERITE, state legislator; Mem. S.D. Senate from 29th dist., Pierre, 1995—; mem. appropriations com., chmn. govt. ops. and audit com. S.D. Senate, Pierre. Republican.

KLIEBENSTEIN, DON, retired lawyer; b. Marshalltown, Iowa, May 3, 1936; s. Donald B. and Gertrude E. (Skeie) K.; m. Mary L. Delfs, June 11, 1960; 1 child, Julie Ann. Student, Grinnell Coll., 1953-55; BA, U. Iowa, 1957, JD, 1961. Bar: Iowa 1961, U.S. Dist. Ct. (no., so. dists.) Iowa 1961, U.S. Supreme Ct. 1971. Pvt. practice, Grundy Center, Iowa, 1961-67; ptnr. Kliebenstein & Heronimus, Grundy Center, 1967-77, Kliebenstein, Heronimus & Schmidt, Grundy Center, 1977-98, Kliebenstein Heronimus Schmidt and Harris, Grundy Center, 1999—2003; of counsel Kliebenstein, Heronimus, Schmidt and Harris, 2004—; ret., 2005. County atty. Grundy County, 1965-98. Mem. ABA, Iowa State Bar Assn., Grundy County Bar Assn. (pres. 1979-80), 1st Jud. Dist. Bar Assn. (pres. 1975-76). Republican. Methodist. Home: 701 9th St Grundy Center IA 50638-1238 Home Phone: 319-824-6180; Office Phone: 319-824-6951.

KLIEBHAN, SISTER M(ARY) CAMILLE, academic administrator; b. Milw., Apr. 4, 1923; d. Alfred Sebastian and Mae Eileen (McNamara) K. Student, Cardinal Stritch Coll., Milw., 1945-48; BA, Cath. Sisters Coll., Washington, 1949; MA, Cath. U. Am., 1951, PhD, 1955. Joined Sisters of St. Francis of Assisi, Roman Catholic Ch., 1945; legal sec. Spence and Hanley (attys.), Milw., 1941-45; instr. edn. Cardinal Stritch Coll., 1955-62, assoc. prof., 1962-68, prof., 1968—, head dept. edn., 1962-67, dean students, 1962-64, chmn. grad. div., 1964-69, v.p. for acad. and student affairs, 1969-74, pres., also bd. dirs., 1974-91, chancellor, 1991—. Mem. TEMPO, 1982—2001, bd. dirs., 1986—89; bd. govs. Wis. Policy Rsch. Inst., 1987—97; bd. dirs. Goals for Milw. 2000, 1980—83; treas. Wis. Found. Ind. Colls., 1974—79, 1987—90, v.p., 1979—81, pres., 1981—83; bd. dirs. DePaul Hosp., 1982—91, Sacred Heart Sch. Theology, 1983—2004, dir. emerita, 2004; bd. dirs. Viterbo Coll., 1990—98, Milw. Cath. Home, 1991—2001, St. Ann Ctr. for Intergenerational Care, 1991—99, Wis. Psychoanalytic Found., 1989—96, St. Coletta's of Mass., 1995—98, Internat. Inst. Wis., 1984—94, Milw. Achiever Program, Inc., 1983—2003, dir. emerita, 2004; bd. dirs. Franciscan Pilgrimage Programs, Inc., 1997—2007, Friends of Internat. Inst. Wis., 1994—, Mental Hea.th Assn. Milwaukee County, 1983—87, Pub. Policy Forum, 1987—90, Better Bus. Bur. of Wis., Inc., 1989—2001, YWCA Greater Milw., 1996—2001, St. Camillus Campus, 1996—2001, mem. adv. bd., 1989—96. Mem. Am. Psychol. Assn., Rotary Club of Milw. (v.p., pres. elect 1992-93, pres. 1993-94), St. Mary's Acad. Alumnae Assn., Phi Delta Kappa, Delta Epsilon Sigma, Psi Chi, Delta Kappa Gamma, Kappa Delta Pi. Business E-Mail: ckliebhan@stritch.edu.

KLIKA, CRISTINE M., state official; BS in Civil Engring., Purdue U. Registered profl. engr., Ind. With pvt. cons. firm designing rds. and bridges; county engr. Monroe County, Ind.; design engring. supr. Ind. Dept. Transp., cons. svcs. supr., design svcs. mgr. Design divsn., chief Tech. Svcs. divsn., mgr. Preliminary Engring. sect., to 1997, dep. commr. Office of Planning and Intermodal Transp., 1997—. Office: Ind Dept Transp 100 N Senate Ave Rm N755 Indianapolis IN 46204-2216

KLINCK, CYNTHIA ANNE, library director; b. Salamanaca, NY, Nov. 1, 1948; d. William James and Marjorie Irene (Woodruff) K.; m. Andrew Clavert Humphries, Nov. 26, 1983. BS, Ball State U., 1970; MLS, U. Ky., 1976. Reference/ young adult libr. Bartholomew County Libr., Columbus, Ind., 1970-74; dir. Paul Sawyier Pub. Libr., Frankfort, Ky., 1974-78, Washington-Centerville Pub. Libr., Dayton, Ohio, 1978—. Libr. bldg. cons.; libr. cons., trainer OPLIN Task Force. Contbr. articles to profl. jours. Bd. dirs. Bluegrass Comty. Action Agy., Frankfort, Ky., 1971-73; founder, bd. dirs. FACTS, Inc., Frankfort, 1972-74; co-founder, bd. dirs. Seniors, Inc., Dayton, Ohio, 1980-81, 91—; trustee, officer South Comty., Inc. Mental Health Ctr., Dayton, 1980-89; pres. Miami Valley Librs.; govt. affairs com., ann. conf. planning com., fin. resources task force conf. presenter Ohio Libr. Coun.; program presenter Ohio Libr. Coun. Confs.; del. to Am. Libr. Assn. Congress on Profl. Edn.; mem. Create-The-Vision Cmty. Planning Task Force, com. chair. Named one of Dayton's Top Ten Women, Dayton Daily News, 2005; recipient Vol. of Yr., So. Metro Regional C. of C. Mem. ALA, Am. Soc. for Info. Sci., Am. Soc. for Pers. Adminstrn., Ohio Libr. Assn. (chmn. legis. com.), South Metro Regional C. of C. (exec. com., bd. dirs., chmn. edn. com., chair), Rotary (bd. dirs.), Pub. Libr. Assn. Mng. for Results (trainer), Book of Kells Project(dir. 2007-08) Office: Washington-Centerville Pub Libr 111 W Spring Valley Rd Dayton OH 45458-3761 Office Phone: 937-435-7375.

KLINE, JAMES EDWARD, lawyer; b. Fremont, Ohio, Aug. 3, 1941; s. Walter J. and Sophia Kline; m. Mary Ann Bruening, Aug. 29, 1964; children: Laura Anne Kline, Matthew Thomas, Jennifer Sue. BS in Social Sci., John Carroll U., University Heights, Ohio, 1963; JD, Ohio State U., Columbus, 1966; postgrad., Stanford U., Calif., 1991. Bar: Ohio 1966, NC 1989, US Tax. Ct. 1983. Assoc. Eastman, Stichter, Smith & Bergman, Toledo, 1966-70; ptnr. Eastman, Stichter, Smith & Bergman (name now Eastman & Smith), Toledo, 1970-84, Shumaker, Loop & Kendrick, Toledo, 1984-88; v.p., gen. counsel Aeroquip-Vickers, Inc. (formerly Trinova Corp.), Toledo, 1989-99; exec. v.p. Cavista Corp., 2000—01; dir. devel. Toledo Mus. Art, 2002—03; v.p., gen. counsel, sec. Cooper Tire and Rubber Co., Findlay, Ohio, 2003—. Corp. sec. Sheller-Globe Corp., 1977—84; adj. prof. U. Toledo Coll. Law, 1988—94; bd. dirs. Plastic Techs., Inc.; trustee Promedica Health Edn. and Rsch. Corp., 2002—07; dir. Toledo Cmty. Bd. First Merit Bank. Author: (with Robert Seaver) Ohio Corporation Law, 1988. Trustee Kidney Found. of Northwestern Ohio, Inc., 1972-81, pres., 1979-80; bd. dirs. Toledo Botanical Garden (formerly Crosby Gardens), 1974-80, pres., 1977-79; bd. dirs. Toledo Zool. Soc., 1983-96, 99—2004, pres., 1991-93; bd. dirs. Toledo Area Regional Transit Authority, 1984-90, pres., 1987-88; bd. dirs. Home Away From Home, Inc. (Ronald McDonald House NW Ohio), 1983-88; trustee Toledo Symphony Orch., 1981—, St. John's H.S., 1988-91; trustee Lourdes Coll., 1988-96, chmn., 1994-96; trustee Ohio Found. Ind. Colls., 1991-2007, Pro-Medica Health Edn. and Rsch. Corp., 2002-07, Toledo Opera, 2003-2005, ProMedica Found., 2006-07. Fellow Ohio Bar Found.; mem. ABA, Nat. Assn. Corp. Dirs., Ohio Bar Assn. (corp. law com. 1977—, chmn. 1983-86), NC Bar Assn., Mfrs. Alliance (chair Law Coun. II 1997-99), Toledo Area C. of C. (trustee 1994—, chmn. 2000-01), Confrerie des Chevaliers du Tastevin, Inverness Club, Toledo Club (trustee 1990-97), Stone Oak Country Club, Ottawa Skeet Club, Fiddlers Creek Club, Answer Club, Rockwell Springs Trout Club. Roman Catholic. Home: 216 Treetop Pl Holland OH 43528-8451 Office: Cooper Tire & Rubber Co 701 Lima Ave Findlay OH 45840 Office Phone: 419-427-4757. Personal E-mail: jektreetop@sbcglobal.net. Business E-Mail: jekline@coopertire.com.

KLINE, JOHN, congressman; b. Allentown, Pa., Sept. 6, 1947; m. Vicky Kline; children: Kathy, Dan. BA in Biology, Rice U., 1969; MPA, Shippensburg U. Pa., 1988. Mem. US Congress from Minn. 2nd dist., 2003—. Military aide to Pres. Carter; military aide to Pres. Reagan. Active USMC, 1969—94, retired as Colonel USMC. Recipient Hero of the Taxpayer award, Small Bus. Adv. award, Spirit of Enterprise award, True Blue award, Family Rsch. Coun. Republican. Responsibilities while military aide to pres. included carrying "nuclear football" — package containing launch codes for nuclear attack. Office: US Ho Reps 1429 Longworth Ho Office Bldg Washington DC 20515-2302

KLINE, KENNETH ALAN, mechanical engineering educator; b. Chgo., July 11, 1939; s. George Lester and Beverly Gretchen (Hanson) K.; m. Nancy Ann Bixler, June 25, 1960; children: Lisa Suzanne, John Kenneth, Jeffery Eastbury, Gretchen Mary. BS, U. Minn., 1961, PhD, 1965. Rsch. asst. U. Minn., Mpls., 1961-62, rsch. fellow, 1962-65; sr. rsch. engr. Esso Prodn. Rsch. Co., Houston, 1965-66; assoc. prof. Wayne State U., Detroit, 1966-73, prof. mech. engring., 1973—, interim chair dept. mech. engring., 1986-87, chair, 1987-95, interim dean of engring., 1996—, chair mech. engring., 1997—. Cons. Ford Motor Co., Detroit, 1976—, vis. scientist, 1984-85; vis. prof. U. Munich, 1972-73. Editor Proc. 6th Internat. Conf. Vehicle Structures, 1986; contbr. articles to profl. jours. Patentee ops. in submarine wells, layng pipes in water. Rep. precinct del., Grosse Pointe Park, Mich., 1982-84; vol. Grosse Pointe Neighborhood Club, 1973-82. A.P. Sloan Found. nat. scholar, 1959-61; NSF fellow 1961-64, NASA fellow 1964-65; recipient Sr. U.S. Sci. award Alexander von Humboldt-Stiftung, Fed. Republic Germany, 1972; prin. investigator NSF Rsch. Experiences for Undergrad. Sites, 1995—. Fellow ASME (chair 1974-75, 89-91, program chair winter ann. meeting 1993, gen. chair internat. mech. engring. congress & expo. 1994, nat. nominating com. 1997—, chair nat. dept. heads com., 1998—, Dedicated Svc. award 1996), AIAA, Soc. Automotive Engrs. (chair 1984-86, Forest R. McFarland award 1993), Soc. Rheology, Engring. Soc. (vice chair Detroit 1988—). Avocations: birdwatching, tree farming, reading, swimming. Office: Wayne State U Engring Rm 2105 Detroit MI 48202 Home Phone: 231-547-4808. Business E-Mail: kline@eng.wayne.edu.

KLINE, PHILLIP D., prosecutor, former state attorney general; b. Kansas City, Kans., Dec. 31, 1959; s. James R. and Janet S. (Shirley) K.; m. Deborah Suzanne Shattuck, July 22, 1989; 1 child, Jacqueline Hillary. BS in Pub. Rels. and Polit. Sci., Cen. Mo. State U., 1982; JD, U. Kans., 1987. Bar: Kans. 1987, U.S. Ct. Appeals (10th cir.), U.S. Dist. Ct. Kans. News reporter WHB Radio, Kansas City, Mo., 1981-82; pub. rels. rep. Mid-America, Inc., Kansas City, Mo., 1982-84; assoc. Blackwell, Sanders, Matheny, Weary & Lombardi, Overland Park, Kans., 1987—95; legislator State of Kans., 1992—2000, atty. gen., 2003—06; dist. atty. Johnson County, Kans., 2006—. Nominee Kans. 2d Congl. Dist., 1986; former chmn. taxation com.; fin. chmn. Johnson County Reps., 1990-91; chmn. Shawnee Reps., 1991-92; chmn., co-chmn. Corp. Woods Charity Jazz Festival, Overland Park, 1991-95; bd. dirs. Shawnee Mission Edn. Found., 1994-95, Rep. Ho. Campaign Com. Mem. Johnson County Bar Assn., Kans. Bar Assn., Rotary (bd. dirs., v.p. 1991-93, pres. 1994-95, Disting. Svc. award 1991). Republican. Methodist. Avocations: history, reading, athletics. Office: Johnson County Dist Atty 100 N Kansas Olathe KS 66061

KLINEFELTER, SARAH STEPHENS, retired dean, broadcast executive; b. Des Moines, Jan. 30, 1938; d. Edward John and Mary Ethel (Adams) Stephens; m. Neil Klinefelter. BA, Drake U., Des Moines, 1958; MA, U. Iowa, Iowa City, 1968; postgrad., Harvard U., Cambridge, Mass., 1984, U. Wis., Madison, 1987, Vanderbilt U., Nashville, Tenn., 1991-92. Chmn. humanities dept. High Sch. Dist. 230, Orland Pk., Ill., 1958-68; chmn. communications and humanities div. Kirkwood Community Coll., Cedar Rapids, Iowa, 1968-78; prof. English Sch. of the Ozarks, Point Lookout, Mo., 1978-86; gen. mgr. Sta. KSOZ-FM, Point Lookout, 1986-90; dean div. of performing and profl. arts Coll. of the Ozarks, Point Lookout, 1989-2001. Commr. Skaggs Cmty. Hosp., Branson, Mo., 1986—; chmn. Branson Planning and Zoning Commn., 1983—2004; project dir. Mo. Humanities Bd.; commr., examiner North Ctrl. Assn. Higher Edn., 1978—85; commr. Iowa Humanities Bd., 1971—78; chair Taney County Planning and Zoning Commn., 1989—98, 2005—; pres. Branson Arts Coun., 1997—2002; co-chair Taney County Bd. Adjustment; FDA noro-virus grant coord. Branson City Health Dept., 2003—04; elderhostel instr. Ozark Adventures, 2001—. Democrat. Presbyterian. Home: 182 Hensley Rd Forsyth MO 65653-5137 Personal E-mail: klinefelter@centurytel.net.

KLING, WILLIAM HUGH, broadcast executive; b. St. Paul, Apr. 29, 1942; s. William Conrad and Helen A. (Leonard) Kling; m. Sarah Margaret Baldwin, Sept. 25, 1976. BA in Economics, St. John's U., 1964; MA in Comm., Boston U. Pres. Minn. Pub. Radio, Inc., St. Paul, 1966—; CEO Greenspring Co., 1986—, Am. Pub. Media Group, 1999—; founding dir. Nat. Pub. Radio, 1968-70, dir., 1977-80; chmn., founding pres. Pub. Radio Internat., 1982-86, vice chmn., 1986-93; regent St. John's U., 2005—. Co-founder, chmn. Gather.com, 2005—; bd. dirs. Wenger Corp., Irwin Fin.; mem. several fund bds. Capital Group Am. Funds, chmn. New Economy Fund, chmn. Small Cap World Fund. Bd. dirs. Minn. Orch., 1987—93; trustee J. L. Found., 1988—2006; bd. dirs., chmn. Fitzgerald Theater Corp., 1983—; James Madison coun. Libr. of Congress, 1992—94. Named Disting. Minnesotan, 1995; named one of 100 Disting. Minnesotans of the Century, Mpls. Star Tribune, 2000; named to Minn. Broadcasters Hall of Fame, 2004; recipient Edward R. Murrow award, 1981, award for Excellence, Channels Mag., 1987. Mem.: Woodhill Country Club, Mpls. Club. Office: Am Pub Media Group 480 Cedar St Saint Paul MN 55101-2274

KLINGER, STEVEN J., paper company executive; b. Atlanta, Mar. 5, 1959; BBA in Acctg., Ga. State U., 1982. Payroll acct. corp. acctg. Ga.-Pacific Corp., Atlanta, 1982—83, gen. acctg. mgr. distbn., 1983—87, sr. auditor internal audit dept., 1987—88, asst. to contr./ops. contrs. dept., 1988—90, mgmt. trainee softwood lumber, 1991—92, mgr. bus. planning forest resources, 1992—93, dir. acquisition and divestiture fin. dept., 1993—94, divsn. contr. pkg., 1994—95, divsn. contr. containerboard and pkg., 1995—96, regional mgr. J&J corrugated, 1996—98, regional mgr. S.E. pkg. ops., 1998—2000, v.p. pkg. ops., 2000—01, pres. packaging, 2001—03, exec. v.p. and pres. packaging, 2003—05; pres., COO Smurfit-Stone Container Corp., Chgo., 2006—. Past. chmn. Fibre Box Assn.; bd. mem. Internat. Corrugated Case Assn. Mem. bd. adv. Ga. State Univ.; bd. mem. Carr Alliance, Atlanta Acad. Office: Smurfit-Stone Container Corp 150 N Michigan Ave Chicago IL 60601

KLINGLER, GWENDOLYN WALBOLT, state representative; b. Toledo, May 28, 1944; d. L. Byron and Elizabeth (Brown) Walbolt; m. Walter Gerald Klingler, June 11, 1966; children: Kelly Michelle, Lance, Jeffrey. BA, Ohio Wesleyan U., 1966; MA, U. Mich., 1969; JD, George Washington U., 1981. Bar: Ill. Rsch. assoc. U. Mich., Ann Arbor, 1966-71; abstractor Year Book Med. Pub., Chgo., 1972-75; law clk. FDA, Rockville, Md., 1980; atty. Atty. Gen.'s Office State of Ill., Springfield, 1981-84, appellate prosecutor, 1984-92; ptnr. Boyle, Klingler & McClain, Springfield, 1992-95. Mem. Springfield Bd. of Edn., 1987-91, pres., 1988; alderman Springfield City Coun., 1991-95; Rep. Ill. Ho. of Reps., 100th Dist., 1995-2003. Recipient Woman of Achievement award in Govt., Women-in-Mgmt., 1994, Disting. Alumni award Leadership Springfield, 1996. Mem. AAUW, Cen. Ill. Women's Bar Assn. (chair membership com.), Sangamon County Bar Assn., Greater Springfield C. of C., Women-in-Mgmt. Republican. Presbyterian (elder). Home: 1600 Ruth Pl Springfield IL 62704-3362 E-mail: klingler@housegopmail.state.il.us.

KLINKER, SHEILA ANN J., state legislator, middle school educator; m. Victor Klinker; children: Kerri, Kevin, Kelly. BS in Edn., Purdue U., MS in Elem. Edn., MS in Adminstrn. and Supervision. Outreach liaison Purdue U. Sch. Edn., 1982—; state rep. Ind. Ho. of Reps., Indpls., 1982—. Mem. St. Mary's Cathedral Parish; 1st woman appointee Tippecanoe Area Plan Commn.; bd. dirs. Lafayette Symphony, Opera de Lafayette, Tippecanoe County Chld Care, Purdue Musical Orgn.; past chairwoman pub. svc. divsn. United Way. Recipient Outstanding Svc. award Ind. Advocates for Children, Legis. award Assn. of BPW's Outstanding Woman in Politics, Woman of Distinction award Sycamore Girl Scout Coun., Salute to Women in Politics award, Outstanding Svc. for Pub. Interest award Ind. Optometric Assn., Pres.'s Spl. Svc. award Ind. Soc. Profl. Land Surveyors, Spl. Recognition award Ind. Chpt. NASW, Legis. Efforts Recognition award Ind. Residential Facilities Assn., Ind. Assn. for Counseling and Devel., Tippecanoe Arts Fedn. award, Purdue U. Musical Orgn. Alumni award, Marriage and Family Therapists Svc. award, 1998, Social Workers Svc. award, 1998, Ind. Assn. for Gifted Leadership award, 1998. Mem. Bus. and Profl. Women's Assn., Lafayette C. of C. (edn. com.), Delta Kappa Gamma, Phi Delta Kappa, Kappa Alpha Theta (mem. adv. bd.). Democrat. Home: 633 Kossuth St Lafayette IN 47905-1444 Office: Ind Ho of Reps State House Third Fl Indianapolis IN 46204

KLIPHARDT, RAYMOND A., engineering educator; b. Chgo., Mar. 18, 1917; s. Adolph Lewis and Hortense Marietta (Brandt) K.; m. Rhoda Joan Anderson, May 5, 1945; children: Janis Kliphardt Emery, Judith Kliphardt Ecklund, Jill Kliphardt White, Joan Kliphardt Quinn, Jennifer Kliphardt Miller. BS, Ill. Inst. Tech., Chgo., 1938, MS, 1948. Instr. North Park Coll., Chgo., 1938-43; asst. prof. Northwestern U., Evanston, Ill., 1945-51, assoc. prof., 1952-63, prof. engring. scis., 1964-87, prof. emeritus, 1987—, dir. U. Khartoum project, 1964-68, dir. focus program, 1975-78, chmn. engring. scis. and applied maths. dept., 1978-87. Cons. applied maths. div. Argonne Nat. Lab., Lemont, Ill., 1962-63; cons. on patent litigation Kirkland and Ellis, Chgo., 1976-77. Author: Analytical Graphics, 1957; Program Design in Fortran IV, 1970. Mem. bd. edn. Morton Grove, Ill., 1952-55, Niles Twp., Ill., 1957-58. Served as ensign USNR, 1943-45. Recipient Western Electric Fund award for excellence in instrn. of engring. students, Am. Soc. Engring. Edn., 1967. Office: Northwestern U Technol Inst Evanston IL 60208-0001 Personal E-mail: rrklip1@aol.com.

KLOBASA, JOHN ANTHONY, lawyer; b. St. Louis, Feb. 15, 1951; s. Alan R. and Virginia (Yager) Klobasa. BA in Econs., Emory U., 1972; JD, Wash. U., 1975. Bar: Mo. 1975, U.S. Dist. Ct. (ea. dist.) Mo. 1975, U.S. Ct. Appeals (8th cir.) 1976, U.S. Supreme Ct. 1979, U.S. Tax Ct. 1981, U.S. Ct. Appeals (9th cir.) 1990, U.S. Ct. Appeals (10th cir.) 1993. Assoc. Kohn, Shands, Elbert, Gianoulakis & Giljum LLP, St. Louis, 1975—80, ptnr., 1981—. Spl. counsel City of Town and Country, Mo., 1987; spl. counsel City of Des Peres, Mo., 1987, alderman, 1989-91. Mem.: ABA, Met. St. Louis Bar Assn., Mo. Bar Assn., Order of Coif, Phi Beta Kappa. Republican. Office: Kohn Shands Elbert Gianoulakis & Giljum LLP One US Bank Plz Ste 2410 Saint Louis MO 63101-1643 Office Phone: 314-241-3963. Business E-Mail: jklobasa@ksegg.com.

KLOBUCHAR, AMY JEAN, senator, lawyer; b. Plymouth, Minn., May 25, 1960; d. Jim and Rose Klobuchar; m. John Bessler, 1993; 1 child, Abigail Bessler. BA, Yale U., 1982; JD, U. Chgo. Law Sch., 1985. Assoc. ptnr. Dorsey & Whitney LLP, 1985—93; ptnr. Gray Plant Mooty LLP, 1993—98; mem. Minn. Supreme Ct. Jury Task Force; atty. Hennepin County, 1999—2007; US Senator from Minn., 2007—. Named Super Lawyer, Minn. Law & Politics; named one of 10 Attorneys of Yr., Minn. Lawyer, 2001; recipient 40 Under 40 award, CityBusiness, 1996, Alumni of Yr. award, Wayzata High Sch., 1999, Leadership award, MADD, 2001, Achievement and Leadership award, Ann Bancroft, 2004. Mem.: Minn. County Attorneys Assn. (pres. 2002—03). Democrat. Avocation: cross-country bicycling. Office: 302 Hert Senate Office Bldg Washington DC 20510 Office Phone: 202-224-3244.

KLOEPPEL, DANIEL L., career officer; m. Debbie. BA in Econs., Northwestern U., 1970. Enlisted USN, 1970, advanced through grades to rear adm.; stationed at Naval Air Station, Cecil Field, Fla., 1973; stationed on USS Forestall; stationed at Naval Air Station, Kingsville, Tex., 1975-77, pilot New Orleans, 1977-79; various assignments VA-2082, New Orleans, 1979-89, VA-204, 1990-92; comdr. USS George Washington, Olathe, Kans., 1992; comdr. joint transportation reserve unit U.S. Transportation Command, Scott AFB, Ill., dir. plans and policy, 1998—; asst. dep. readiness Readiness Command Region 10, New Orleans; dep. commander Maritime Defense Zone Pacific, San Francisco, Naval Air Force Pacific Fleet, San Diego; comdr. Iceland Defense Force, 1998. Pilot Ozark Airlines, 1977-86, Trans World Airlines, 1986—. Decorated Legion of Merit, Meritorious Svc. medal with oak leaf cluster. Mem. Naval Reserve Assn., Reserve Officers Assn., Assn. Naval Aviation, Navy League, Phi Delta Theta Alumni Assn.

KLONGLAN, GERALD EDWARD, sociology educator; b. Nevada, Iowa, Apr. 1, 1936; s. Bernie R. and Willene Rebecca (Maland) K.; m. Donna Eileen Becvar, June 29, 1960; children: Jason, Suzanne. BS, Iowa State U., 1958, MS, 1962, PhD, 1963. Mem. faculty Iowa State U., Ames, 1963—2001, prof. sociology, 1972—2001, chmn. dept. sociology and anthropology, 1976-90, interim assoc. dean Coll. Sci. and Humanities, 1988-89; asst. dir. Iowa Agr. and Home Econ. Expt. Sta., 1990—2001; assoc. dean nat. programs Coll. Agr., 1995—2001; staff sociologist U.S. Dept. Agr., Coop. State Rsch. Svc., Washington, DC, 1991-93. Evaluation rschr. AID, Malawi, 1967, project cons., Ghana, 1976; ednl. cons. King Saud U., Saudi Arabia, 1981-83, Peking U., People's Republic of China, 1984-85; project implementor U. Zambia, Lusaka, 1982-83; family rsch., Norway, 1988, Czech Republic, 1995; project dir. mgmt. tng. Czech Republic and Slovak Republic, 1991-96; project dir. agr. rsch., Russia, Ukraine, other countries of former Soviet Union, 1992-99. Author: Social Indicators, 1972; (research monographs) Adoption Diffusion of Ideas, 1967; Creating Interorganizational Coordination, 1975, Communication Policy, 1983. Vol. scientist Am. Cancer Soc., 1969—; bd. dirs. Luth. Campus Ministry, Ames, 1972-78, chmn. bd., 1974-76; pres. Bethesda Luth. Ch., Ames, 1994-95. Recipient Wilton Park award Iowa State U., 1983 Mem. Rural Sociol. Soc. (coun. 1974-76, 91-92, v.p. 1977-78, pres. 1985-86), Am. Sociol. Assn. (com. on internat. sociology 1993-96), Midwest Sociol. Soc. (tng. com. 1975-78), Sigma Xi (pres. Iowa State U. chpt. 1983-84). Home: 1622 Maxwell Ave Ames IA 50010-5536 Office: Iowa State U Coll Agr 138 Curtiss Hl Ames IA 50011-0001 E-mail: klonglan@iastate.edu.

KLOPMAN, GILLES, chemistry professor; b. Brussels, Feb. 24, 1933; came to U.S., 1965; s. Alge and Brana Klopman; m. Malvina Pantiel, Sept. 5, 1957. BA, Athenee d'Ixelles, Belgium, 1952; lic. chemistry, U. Brussels, 1956, D in Chemistry, 1960. Rsch. scientist Cyanamid European Rsch. Inst., Geneva, 1960-67; postdoctoral fellow U. Tex., 1964-65; assoc. prof. Case Western Res. U., Cleve., 1967-69, prof. chemistry, 1969—, chmn. dept., 1981—86, interim dean sci. and math., 1986—88, C.F. Mabery prof. of rsch., chmn. dept., 1988—2003, C.F. Mabery prof. rsch. emeritus, 2003—, prof. environ. health scis., 2007—. V.p. Biofor, Ltd., PA, 1986-95; pres. Discovery Software Inc., 1991-93, Multicase, Inc., 1995—. Author: All Valence Electrons SCF Calculations, 1970, Chemical Reactivity and Reaction Paths, 1974; contbr. articles to profl. jours. Recipient Kahlbaum prize, Swiss Chem. Soc., 1971; grantee NSF, NIH, EPA, PRF, ONR. Mem. AAUP, Am. Chem. Soc. (Morley medal 1993, Patterson-Crane award, 2005), Brit. Chem. Soc., Belgium Chem. Soc., Sigma Xi. Office: Case Western Res U 10900 Euclid Ave Cleveland OH 44106-1712 E-mail: klopman@po.cwru.edu, klopman@multicase.com.

KLOSKA, RONALD FRANK, manufacturing executive; b. Grand Rapids, Mich., Oct. 24, 1933; s. Frank B. and Catherine (Hilaski) K.; m. Mary F. Minick, Sept. 7, 1957; children: Kathleen Ann, Elizabeth Marie, Ronald Francis, Mary Josephine, Carolyn Louise. Student, St. Joseph Sem., Grand Rapids, Mich.,

1947-53; PhB, U. Montreal, Que., Can., 1955; MBA, U. Mich., 1957. Staff acct. Coopers & Lybrand, Niles, Mich., 1957, staff to sr. acct., 1960—63; treas. Skyline Corp., Elkhart, Ind., 1963, v.p., treas., 1964—67, exec. v.p. fin., 1967—74, pres., 1974—85, pres., chief ops. officer, 1985—91, vice chmn., chief adminstrn. officer, 1991—94, vice chmn., chief adminstrn. officer, sec., 1994—95, vice chmn., dep. CEO, chief adminstrn. officer, 1995—98, vice chmn., CEO, chief adminstrn. officer, 1998—2001, dir., cons., 2001—. With US Army, 1957—60. Mem. Mich. Soc. CPAs, Ind. Soc. CPAs, South Bend Country Club. Roman Catholic. Home: 1329 E Woodside St South Bend IN 46614-1455 Office: Skyline Corp 2520 Bypass Rd Elkhart IN 46514-1584

KLOSS, LINDA L., medical association administrator; B, Coll. St. Scholastica, Minn., 1968. Former sr. mgr. MediQual Systems, Inc., Mass., InterQual, Inc., Chgo.; exec. v.p., CEO Am. Health Info. Mgmt. Assn., Chgo., 1995—. Bd. dirs. Am. Health Info. Mgmt. Assn., 1980—86, pres. bd. dirs., 1985; bd. dir. Nat. Alliance for Health Info. Tech., 2004—. Recipient Sr. Alice Lamb award for achievement, Coll. St. Scholastica, 1984. Office: Am Health Info Mgmt Assn 233 N Michigan Ave Ste 2150 Chicago IL 60601-5519 Business E-Mail: lkloss@ahima.org.

KLOSTER, CAROL GOOD, wholesale distribution executive; b. Richmond, Va., Aug. 18, 1948; d. David William and Lucy (McDowell) Good; m. John Kenneth Kloster III, Feb. 15, 1975; children: John Kenneth IV, Amanda Aileen. AB, Coll. William and Mary, 1970. Personnel supr. Charles Levy Circulating Co., Chgo., 1974-75, warehouse supr., 1976-77, warehouse mgr., 1978-80, dir. sales, 1980-83, asst. v.p., dir. mktg., 1984; v.p., gen. mgr. Video Trend of Chgo., 1985-86; v.p. gen. mgr. Levy Home Entertainment, 1986-92; pres., CEO Chas Levy Co., 1992—. Mem. bd., Family Focus Inc. Recipient Algernon Sidney Sullivan award Coll. William and Mary, 1970. Presbyterian. Home: 619 W North St Hinsdale IL 60521-3152 Office: Chas Levy Company 1930 George St Ste 1 Melrose Park IL 60160-1501

KLOSTERMAN, ALBERT LEONARD, technical development business executive, mechanical engineer; b. Cin., Oct. 22, 1942; s. Albert Clement and Mary J. Klosterman; m. Lynne Marie Gabelein, Jan. 4, 1964; children: Scott, Lance, Kimberly, Brad. BSMechE, U. Cin., 1965, MSMechE, 1968, PhD, 1971. Instr. U. Cin., 1966-70, adj. assoc. prof., 1974—; project mgr. Structural Dynamics Rsch. Corp., Milford, Ohio, 1970-72, mem. tech. staff, 1972-73, dir. tech. staff, 1973-78, v.p., gen. mgr., 1978-83, sr. v.p., chief tech. officer, gen. mgr., 1983-95; sr. v.p., chief scientist, 1995—. Mem. exec. steering com. Initial Graphics Exchange System/Product Data Exch. Specification of Nat. Standards Bd., Gaithersburg, Md., 1984—. Mem. editorial bd. Internat. Jour. Vehicle Design, 1979—. Recipient Disting. Alumnus award U. Cin., 1988. Mem. Assn. Computing Machinery, ASME (assoc.), Phi Kappa Theta. Republican. Roman Catholic. Home: 5444 Forest Ridge Cir Milford OH 45150-2821 Office: Structural Dynamics Rsch Corp 2000 Eastman Dr Milford OH 45150-2712

KLOTMAN, ROBERT HOWARD, retired music educator; b. Cleve., Nov. 22, 1918; s. Louis Klotman and Pearl (Warshawsky) Kaplan; m. Phyllis Helen Rauch, Apr. 4, 1943; children: Janet Lynn, Paul Evan. BS in Music Edn., Ohio No. U., 1940; MA in Music, Case-Western Res. U., 1950; EdD, Columbia U., 1956; MusD (hon)., Ohio o. U., 1984. Supr. music pub. schs., Dola, Ohio, 1940-42; tchr. instrumental, vocal music pub. schs. Euclid, Ohio, 1942, 46; tchr. instrumental music pub. schs. Cleveland Heights, Ohio, 1946-59; dir. music edn. pub. schs. Akron, Ohio, 1959-63; divisional dir. music edn. pub. schs. Detroit, 1963-69; prof., chmn. dept. music edn. Ind. U., Bloomington, 1969-83, prof. emeritus, 1987—2008. Vis. prof. Shanghai Conservatory of Music, 1985, U. Alta., Edmonton, Can., summer 1991; guest lectr. U. Bar-Ilan, Israel, 1984; ednl. dir. firm Scherl & Roth (string importers), Cleve., 1956-70; mem. adv. bd. Contemporary Music Project, Ford Found., 1964-65; ednl. cons. Summy-Birchard Co. (music pubs.); mem. bicentennial com. J. C. Penney Co., 1974-76. Condr.: Akron Youth Symphony Orch., 1959—63, Oak Park (Mich.) Symphony, 1967—69, Bloomington Youth Symphony Orch., 1969—75, Terre Haute Youth Symphony, 1992, Great Lake Music Camp Orch., 1982—96; author: Learning to Teach Through Playing: String Techniques and Pedagogy, 1971, The School Music Administrator and Supervisor: Catalysts for Change in Music Education, 1973, Teaching Strings, 1996; author: (with others) Humanities Through the Black Experience, Foundations of Music Education, 1983, 1988; co-author: Administrating and Supervising Music, 1991; contbg. author: Ency. of Edn., 1971; editor: Orch. ews, 1959—70; mem. editl. bd.: Music Educators Jour., 1962—64, Instrumentalist, 1974—91; editor (with others): Scheduling Music Classes, 1968; editor, contg. author: Music Performance Trust Funds Guide; composer: Action with Strings, 1962, Renaissance Suite, 1964, String Literature for Expanding Technique, 1973. Bd. dirs., sec. Ind. U. Credit Union, 1974-87; chmn. ednl. com. Chamber Music Am., 1993-95. With inf. AUS, 1942-46, ETO, PTO. Recipient citation Nat. Assn. Negro Musicians Inc., 1966, citation Black Music Caucas, 1978, Outstanding Hoosier Musician award, 1986, Disting. Service award Am. String Tchrs. Assn., 1987, Sagamore of the Wabash Govs. award, 1991, medal of honor Midwest Orch./Band Conf., 2003; named to MENC Hall of Fame, 2004; Lowell Mason fellow, 2005. Mem. Chamber Music Am. (chair edn. com. 1993-95), Am. String Tchrs. Assn. (pres. 1962-64, dir. pubs. 1985-94, chmn. past pres. coun. 1998-2000), Music Educators Nat. Conf. (chmn. commn. on tchr. edn. 1968-72, pres. 1976-78, Disting. Svc. award 1989, chmn. Hall of Fame com. 1996-2002, Hall of Fame 2004), Rotary, Phi Mu Alpha Sinfonia, Phi Delta Kappa. Democrat. Jewish. Avocations: tennis, swimming, reading.

KLOUCEK, FRANK JOHN, state legislator; b. Yankton, SD, Sept. 27, 1956; s. Robert R. and Rose M. (Stekly) K.; m. Joan Marie Novak, 1980; children: Jennifer, Michelle, Kimberlee. BS, S.D. State U., 1978. Mem. S.D. Ho. of Reps., 1991-93, S.D. Senate, 1993—, vice chair senate agrl. com., 1993, 94, mem. health and human svcs., local govt. coms.; farmer; pres., chmn. resolution com. S.D. Farmers Union, 1992—. Committeeman Bon Homme County Dem. Com., 1986-88, pres. 1989—; mem. St. Georges Cath. Ch., Scotland. Recipient Disting. Svc. award S.D. Pharm. Assn., 1995. Mem. S.D. Farmers Union (county pres. 1986, Action Officer award 1989, 90), S.D.Soybean Growers Assn. (state sec. 1987, recognition plaque 1987), Lions (Bon Homme), K.C., Block and Bridle, Animal Agriculture Orgn., Alpha Zeta, Alpha Epsilon. Roman Catholic. Home: 29966 423rd Ave Scotland SD 57059-5714

KLUENDER, KEITH R., psychology educator; BS, Carroll Coll., 1979; MA, Northeastern U., 1981; PhD, U. Tex., 1988. Lectr. in psychology Northeastern U., 1981-82; rsch. asst. U. Tex., Austin, 1982-88, asst. instr., 1988-93; asst. prof. U. Wis., Madison, 1988-93, assoc. prof. psychology, 1993—, affiliate prof. neurophysiology, 1996—. Vis. scientist IBM Watso Rsch., 1983; presenter in field. Cons. editor Jour. Speech and Hearing Rsch., Perception and Psychophysics; reviewer various jours. in field; contbr. articles to profl. jours. Vilas assoc. prof., 1995; grantee U. Wis. Grad. Sch., 1989-90, 90-91, 96—, NIH-NIDCD, 1989-94, 94-99, Biomed. Rsch. Support, 1989-91, NSF, 1992-97, IBM, 1993, NIH, 1994—, NIDCD, 1990—; recipient Young Investigator award NSF, 1992-96, Troland Rsch. award NAS, 1997. Mem. APA, AAAS, Acoustical Soc. Am. (mem. speech tech. com.), Assn. for Rsch. in Otolaryngology, Behavioral and Brain Scis. Assoc., Internat. Soc. for Ecol. Psychology, psychonomic Soc., Sigma Xi. Office: U Wis Dept Psychology 1202 W Johnson St Madison WI 53706-1611

KLUES, JACK, communications executive; Exec. v.p. worldwide media svcs. Leo Burnett Co., Inc., Chgo.; CEO StarCom Worldwide, Chgo., 1999—. Office: Leo Burnett Co Inc 35 W Wacker Dr Chicago IL 60601-1648

KLUG, SCOTT LEO, former congressman; b. Milwaukee, Wis., Jan. 16, 1953; s. Ralph William Klug and Josephine (Farrell) Weber; m. Tess Summers, Mar. 4, 1978; children: Keefe, Brett, Collin Phillip. BA, Lawrence U., 1975; MS in Journalism, Northwestern U., 1976; MBA, U. Wis., 1990. Reporter TV sta., Wausau, Wis., 1976-78; reporter Sta. KING-TV, Seattle, 1978-81; investigative reporter Sta. WJLA-TV, Washington, 1981-88; anchor, reporter Sta. WKOW-TV, Madison, Wis., 1988-90; v.p. pub. fin. dept. Blunt, Ellis & Loewi, Madison, 1990; mem. 102nd-105th U.S. Congress from 2d Wis. dist., Washington, D.C., 1991-98, mem. commerce com.; publ., CEO Trails Media Group Inc., Madison, 1999—; pub. affairs counsel Foley and Lardner, Washington, 1999—. Reporter, producer documentaries (Emmy awards 1989, 90). Named Nat. Humanitarian of Yr., Humane Soc., 1986; John McCloy fellow Columbia U. Sch. Journalism, 1987. Republican. Avocations: tennis, basketball, cooking. Office: Trails Media Group PO Box 317 Black Earth WI 53515 also: Foley and Lardner Verex Plaza 150 E Gilman St Madison WI 53703

KLUGMAN, STEPHAN CRAIG, newspaper editor; b. Fargo, ND, May 11, 1945; s. Ted and Charlotte (Olson) K.; m. Julie Sue Terpening, Sept. 18, 1971; children: Josh, Carrie. BA in Journalism, Ind. U., 1967. Copy editor Chgo. Sun-Times, 1967-68, asst. telegraph editor, 1968-72, telegraph editor, 1972-74, city editor, 1974-76, asst. mng. editor features, 1976-78; asst. prof. Medill Sch. Journalism, Northwestern U., Evanston, Ill., 1978-79, dir. undergrad. studies, 1979-82; editor Jour.-Gazette, Ft. Wayne, Ind., 1982—. Mem. Am. Soc. Newspaper Editors. Office: Jour-Gazette 600 W Main St Fort Wayne IN 46802-1408 Home Phone: 260-744-4396; Office Phone: 260-461-8853. Business E-Mail: cklugman@jg.net.

KLUSMAN, JUDITH ANDERSON, state legislator; b. Neenah, Wis., Dec. 14, 1956; m. Timothy A. Klusman; children: Charles, James. Student, Concordia Coll.; MDiv, Wartburg Theol. Sem., Dubuque, Iowa, 2004. Mem. from dist. 56 Wis. State Assembly, Madison, 1988—2000, asst. majority leader, co-chair joint survey com. retirement svc., mem. ways and means, assembly rules and orgn. coms. Mem. com. on agr. and internat. trade Nat. Conf. State Legislators; mem. task force on agr. and environ; mem. Legis. Coun. Spl. Com. on Child Custody, Support and Visitation Laws; mem. Legic. Coun. Spl. Com. on Remediation of Environ. Contamination. Mem. Outagamie County Local Emergency Planning Com.; mem. Wis. Rural Leadership Program; mem. World Dairy Ctr. Authority Bd. Recipient Key award 4-H, 1975, Outstanding Young Farm Couple award Winnebago County Farm Bur., 1983, Friend of Edn. award Neenah chpt. Wis. Edn. Assn., 1986-87, Friend of Agr. award Wis. Farm Bur. Fedn., 1990, 92, 94, Outstanding Alumni Winnebago County 4-H, 1992, Buardian of Small Bus. award Fedn. of Ind. Bus., 1992. Mem. Rotary Internat., Wis. Rural Leadership Alumni.

KMENTA, JAN, retired economics professor; b. Prague, Czechoslovakia, Jan. 3, 1928; came to U.S., 1963; m. Joan Helen Gaffney, Aug. 9, 1959; children: David, Steven. B in Econ. (hon.), Sydney U., 1955; MA, Stanford U., 1959, PhD, 1964; doctorate (hon.), U. Saarland, Germany, 1989. Lectr. U. N.S.W., Sydney, 1957-61; sr. lectr. Sydney U., 1961-63; asst. prof. U. Wis., Madison, 1963-65; prof. Mich. State U., East Lansing, 1965-73, U. Mich., Ann Arbor, 1973—2006; ret., 2006. Vis. prof. U. Bonn, Germany, 1971-72, 1979-80, U. Saarland, Saarbrucken, Germany, 1984, 85, 86. Author: Elements of Econometrics, 2d edit., 1986; editor: (with others) Evaluation of Econometric Models, 1980, Large-Scale Macro-Econometric Models, 1981; contbr. articles to profl. jours. Recipient U.S. Sr. Scientist Prize, Humboldt Found., Bonn, 1979; Fulbright scholar, 1957-59. Fellow Am. Statis. Assn., Econometric Soc.; mem. Am. Econ. Assn., Czechoslovak Soc. Arts and Scis. in Am. Home: PO Box 1107 Ann Arbor MI 48106-1107

KNABE, GEORGE WILLIAM, JR., pathologist, educator; b. Grand Rapids, Mich., June 29, 1924; s. George William and Dorothy Emma (Fischofer) K., m. Lorine Jeanette Moffit, Jan. 16, 1954; children: Katharine J., Elizabeth J., Ann C., Dorothy M. Student, Mich. State U., 1942-43, The Citadel, Charleston, SC, 1943-44, Johns Hopkins U., 1944-45; MD, U. Md., 1949. Diplomate Am. Bd. Pathology. Intern Balt. City Hosp., 1949-50; resident pathology Cleve. Clin. Found., 1950-51, Henry Ford Hosp., Detroit, 1953-54; chief lab. svc. VA Ctr., Dayton, Ohio, 1955-57; vis. prof. pathology U. El Salvador Sch. Medicine, 1957-59; asst. prof. pathology U. P.R. Sch. Medicine, 1959-60; prof., chmn. dept. pathology Sch. Medicine, U. S.D., 1960-68, dean., 1967-72; dir. med. edn. St. Luke's Hosp., Duluth, 1972-78; prof. pathology U. Minn.-Duluth Sch. Medicine, 1972—, assoc. dean clin. affairs., 1972-76; chief. dept. pathology Virginia (Minn.) Regional Med. Ctr., 1978-98; pres. Range Pathology, 1998—. Bd. dirs Health Sys. Agy. of Western Lake Superior, Duluth 1975-82, No. Lakes Health Care Consortium, 1984—, U. Minn. Health and Med. Sch. Adv. Groups 1972—. 1st lt. to capt. M.C., USAF, 1951-53; surgeon to capt., USPHS Res., 1957—. Mem. AMA, U.S. and Can. Acad. Pathology, Am. Soc. Clin. Pathologists, Coll. Am. Pathologists. Avocations: art, horticulture, photography. Home: 1008 S 7th Ave Virginia MN 55792-3151 Office: Range Pathology 1008 7th Ave S Virginia MN 55792-3151 Home Phone: 218-749-3341; Office Phone: 218-749-3341. Personal E-mail: knabejr@yahoo.com.

KNAPP, HOWARD RAYMOND, internist, clinical pharmacologist; b. Red Bank, NJ, Oct. 5, 1949; s. Howard Raymond and Jane Marie (Ray) K.; m. Brenda Louise Carr, 1984; 1 child, Matthew. AB in Biology, Washington U., St. Louis, 1971; MD, Vanderbilt U., 1977, PhD in Pharmacology, 1984. Diplomate Am. Bd. Internal Medicine, cert. clin. densitometrist. Asst. prof. medicine and pharmacology Vanderbilt U., Nashville, 1984-89, assoc. prof., 1990; assoc. prof. internal medicine and pharmacology U. Iowa, Iowa City, 1990-97, prof. internal medicine and pharmacology, 1997-2000, assoc. dir. NIH Clin. Rsch. Ctr., 1997-2000; exec. dir. Billings Clin. Res. Divsn., Mont., 2000—05, v.p. rsch. Mont., 2006—. Mem. NIH Nutrition Study Sect., Bethesda, Md., 1994—96; cons. pharm. firms, grant orgns. and govtl. entities; mem. applied pharmacol. task force Nat. Bd. Med. Examiners, 1997—2000; mem. expert panel on cardiovasc. and renal drugs U.S. Pharmacopeia, 2000—05. Editor-in-chief Lipids, 1995-2006; contbr. numerous articles to profl. jours., chpts. to books. Grantee NIH, Am. Heart Assn., others. Fellow ACP, Am. Heart Assn. (vascular biol. rsch. rev. com. 1993-95, arteriosclerosis coun.); mem. Ctrl. Soc. for Clin. Rsch. (chair clin. pharmacol. sect. 1992-95), Am. Soc. for Clin. Pharmacology and Therapeutics, Am. Oil chemists Soc. (gov. bd., 2002-04, v.p., 2005-06, pres., 2006-07), Am/ Diabetes Assn., NY Adad. Sci., Am. Chem. Soc. Achievements include first demonstration that calcium ionophores stimulate eicosanoid synthesis; first evidence that N-3 fatty acids reduce platelet activation and blood pressure in patients; first demonstration of the effects of 5-lipoxygenase inhibition in humans. Office: Billings Clinic Rsch Ctr 1045 N 30th St Billings MT 59101-0733 Office Phone: 406-255-8475. Business E-Mail: hknapp@billingsclinic.org.

KNAPP, JAMES IAN KEITH, judge; b. Bklyn., Apr. 6, 1943; s. Charles Townsend and Christine (Grange) K.; m. Joan Elizabeth Cunningham, June 10, 1967 (div. Mar. 1971); 1 child, Jennifer Elizabeth; m. Carol Jean Brown, July 14, 1981; children: Michelle Christine, David Michael Keith. AB cum laude, Harvard U., 1964; JD, U. Colo., 1967; M in Law in Taxation, Georgetown U., 1989. Bar: Colo. 1967, Calif. 1968, U.S. Supreme Ct. 1983, D.C. 1986, Ohio 1995. Dep. dist. atty. County of L.A., 1968-79; head dep. dist. atty. Pomona br. office, 1979-82; dep. asst. atty. gen. criminal divsn. U.S. Dept. Justice, Washington, 1982-86, dep. assoc. atty. gen., 1986-87, dep. asst. atty. gen. tax divsn., 1988-89, acting asst. atty. gen. tax divsn., 1989, acting dep. chief organized crime sect. criminal divsn., 1989-91, dep. dir., asset forfeiture office criminal divsn., 1991-94; adminstrv. law judge Social Security Adminstrn., 1994—. Editor: California Uniform Crime Charging Standards and Manual, 1975 Vice chmn. Young Reps. Nat. Fedn., 1973-75; pres. Calif. Young Reps., 1975-77; mem. exec. com. Rep. State Ctrl. Com., Calif., 1975-77; pres. Miami Valley Episc. Russian Network, 2004-06. Mem.: DC Bar Assn., Calif. Bar Assn. Episcopalian. Avocations: travel, reading. Office: Office of Disability Adjudication and Review 10 N Ludlow Ste 300 Dayton OH 45402

KNAPP, PAUL RAYMOND, think-tank executive; b. Long beach, Calif., Sept. 8, 1945; s. Franklin L. and Ella Jo (Andrews) K.; m. Shirley K. Wheeler, July 16, 1967 (div. 1987); children: Michele Ann, Erica Elizabeth, Matthew Gary; m. Nancy Jane Gift, May 1, 1988. BS, Calif. State U., Chico, 1970; MBA magna cum laude, U. Chgo., 1977. With Kemper Corp., various locations, 1969-77; sr. v.p., cFO Kemper Fin. Svcs., Inc., Chgo., 1977-87; pres., CEO Kessler Asher Group, Chgo., 1988-90; dir., chmn., pres., CEO, Catalyst Inst., Chgo., 1991—. Bd. dirs. Berger Mut. Funds, Denver, Futures Industry Inst., Washington, 1992—, Internat. Fedn. for Bus. Edn., Kansas City, Mo., 1993—. U.S. nat. com. for Pacific Econ. Cooperation, Washington, 1995—; bd. dirs. Allendale Assn., Lake Villa, Ill., 1988—. Home: 1410 N State Pkwy Chicago IL 60610-1512

KNAPP, THOMAS JOSEPH, lawyer; b. Chgo., Aug. 27, 1952; s. William Bernard and Jeannette Cecilia (Zarnowiecki) K.; m. Lee Ann Schiller, Sept. 27, 1980; children: Brian Thomas, Terrence Joseph, Christopher Ryan, Katharine Cannon. BA, U. Ill., 1974; JD, Loyola U., Chgo., 1977. Bar: Ill. 1977, Fla. 1979, D.C. 1979, Tex. 1987, U.S. Dist. Ct. (no. and cen. dists.) Ill., U.S. Ct. Appeals (5th, 7th, 8th and 9th cirs.), U.S. Supreme Ct. 1986. Law clk. to presiding justice Cir. Ct. Cook County, Chgo., 1977-78; asst. atty. gen. consumer protection div. Atty. Gen. Ill., Chgo., 1978-80; atty. Burlington No. R.R. Co., Chgo., 1980-83, asst. gen. solicitor, 1983-85, asst. gen. counsel Ft. Worth, 1985-86, assoc. gen. counsel, 1986-88, labor counsel, 1988-95; of counsel Paul, Hastings, Janofsky & Walker, L.L.P., Washington, 1996-98, 2000—02; asst. gen. counsel The Boeing Co., Seattle, 1998—2002; v.p., gen. counsel and sec. Northwestern Corp., Sioux Falls, SD, 2002—. Commr. Village of Wilmette, Ill., 1985; mem. cable TV adv. bd. City of Bedford, 1992-94. Mem. ABA, Assn. Trial Lawyers Am., at. Assn. R.R. Trial Counsel, Ill. Trial Lawyers Assn., Chgo. Council of Lawyers, Commn. of Airline R.R. Labor Lawyers. Clubs: Tavern (Chgo.), Union League of Chgo. Roman Catholic. Avocations: sailing, golf, photography. Home: 7116 Darby Rd Bethesda MD 20817-2914 Office: Northwestern Corp 3010 W 69th St Sioux Falls SD 57108 Office Phone: 605-978-2930. Business E-Mail: tom.knapp@northwestern.com.

KNAPPENBERGER, PAUL HENRY, JR., science museum director; b. Reading, Pa., Sept. 5, 1942; s. Paul Henry and Kathryn (Medrick) K.; m. Naomi Knappenberger; children— Paul Charles, Timothy Alan, Shannon Rose Lalor, Heidi Kathrin. AB in Math, Franklin and Marshall Coll., 1964; MA in Astronomy (NASA fellow), U. Va., 1966, PhD in Astronomy, 1968. Astronomer Fernbank Sci. Center, Atlanta, 1968-72; instr. Emory U. and Ga. State U., Atlanta, 1970-72; dir. Sci. Mus. of Va., Richmond, 1973-91; pres. The Adler Planetarium, Chgo., 1991—. Asst. prof. Va. Commonwealth U., U. Richmond, 1973-81; bd. dirs. Assn. Sci. and Tech. Centers, pres., 1985-87; instr. astronomy Yellowstone Inst.; former v.p. Midlothian Athletic Assn.; mem. council Nat. Mus. Act, 1984-86. Former mem. bd. dirs. Mus. Film etwork, Exhibit Research Collaborative; co-founder Planetarium Show Network; dir. Informal Sci. Instructional Services, Ltd. NSF Sci. Edn. grantee, 1971-72; grantee NEH, Inst. Mus. Services. Mem. Am. Astron. Soc., AAAS, Internat. Planetarium Soc., Va. Acad. Sci., Va. Assn. Museums (council 1979-91), Am. Assn. Museums, Great Lakes Planetarium Assn. Home: 6n488 Splitrail Ct Saint Charles IL 60175-6928 Office: Adler Planetarium 1300 S Lake Shore Dr Chicago IL 60605-2403

KNAPSTEIN, MICHAEL, advertising executive; BS in Comm./Advt. and Pub. Rels., U. Wis., Stevens Point, 1979. Copywriter TAM Advt., Wausau, Wis., creative dir.; copy/contact Waldbillig & Besteman, Inc., Madison, Wis., 1979, co-owner, 1988, CEO, 1993—. Represented in permanent collections Nikon, Eastman Kodak. Active Start Smart, United Way Dane County. Mem. Madison Advt. Fedn. (bd. dirs.), Am. Advt. Fedn. (bd. dirs., chair exec. com. ctrl. region). Home: 1528 Red Oak Ct Middleton WI 53562 Fax: 608-829-0901.

KNEBEL, DONALD EARL, lawyer; b. Logansport, Ind., May 26, 1946; s. Everett Earl and Ethel Josephine (Hultgren) K.; m. Joan Elizabeth Vest, June 5, 1976 (div. 1980); 1 child, Mary Elizabeth; m. Jennifer Colt Johnson, Sept. 25, 1999. BEE with highest distinction, Purdue U., 1968; JD magna cum laude, Harvard U., 1974. Bar: Ind. 1974, U.S. Ct. Appeals (7th cir.) 1980, U.S. Ct. Appeals (3rd cir.) 1986, U.S. Ct. Appeals (6th cir.) 1987, U.S. Ct. Appeals (fed. cir.) 1988, U.S. Ct. Appeals (4th cir.) 2005. Assoc. Barnes, Hickam, Pantzer & Boyd, Indpls., 1974—81; ptnr. Barnes & Thornburg LLP, Indpls., 1981—. Contbr. articles on intellectual property, antitrust and distbn. law to profl. publs. Trustee Indpls. Civic Theatre, 1986—95, chmn., 1988—91, hon. trustee, 1995—2002, trustee, 2002—, chmn., 2002—05; mem. campaign cabinet United Way, 2007—; chmn. United Way Tocqueville Soc., 2005—07. Fellow: Am. Coll. Trial Lawyers; mem.: ABA, TechPoint (dir.), TechLaw Group (v.p. 2002—03, pres. 2004—05), 7th Cir. Bar Assn., Indpls. Bar Assn., Ind. Bar Assn., Columbia Club, Kiwanis (pres. 1991—92). Presbyterian. Office: Barnes & Thornburg LLP 11 S Meridian St Indianapolis IN 46204-3535 Home Phone: 317-873-0335; Office Phone: 317-231-7214. Business E-Mail: dknebel@btlaw.com.

KNECHT, RICHARD ARDEN, family practitioner; b. Grand Rapids, Mar. 7, 1929; s. Fredrick William and Eva Rae (Blakley) K.; m. Joan Matson, Dec. 26, 1951 (div. 1975); children: Richard Arden, Karrie Jo, Jeffrey Paul; m. Patricia Irene Gilmore, Aug. 14, 1976; 1 child, Kimberly Kahler. BS, U. Mich., 1951, MD, 1955. Diplomate Am. Bd. Family Practice, Am. Bd. Geriatric Medicine; cert. med. dir. Intern St. Mary Hosp., Grand Rapids, Mich., 1955-56; pvt. practice, Fife Lake, Mich., 1956—. Fellow Am. Acad. Family Physicians, Am. Geriatric Soc., Royal Soc. Medicine; mem. Mich. Med. Soc. (com. on aging 1988—), Mich. Acad. Family Practice (chmn. com. on aging 1986-88, pub.'s award 1988), Mich. Med. Dirs. Assn. (pres. 1996-97). Avocations: archaeology, motorcycling, geology, hunting, fishing. Home and Office: PO Box 130 125 Morgan St Fife Lake MI 49633 Personal E-mail: r.knecht@charter.net.

KNEEN, JAMES RUSSELL, health care administrator; b. Kalamazoo, Dec. 16, 1955; s. Russell Packard and Joyce Elaine (Knapper) K.; m. Peggy Jo Howard, Aug. 4, 1979; children: Benjamin Russell, Katherine Elaine. BA, Alma Coll., 1978; MHA, U. Mo., 1982. Systems analyst Bronson Meth. Hosp., Kalamazoo, 1976-79; cons. U. Mo., Columbia, 1979-81; adminstrv. resident Meth. Hosp. Ind., Indpls., 1981-82; div. dir. psychiat. care svcs. Parkview Meml. Hosp., Ft. Wayne, Ind., 1982-88; exec. v.p. Meml. Hosp., Ocomonowoc, Wis., 1988-90; exec. dir. Meml. Hosp. Found., Oconomowoc, 1988-90; pres., CEO Fostoria (Ohio) Community Hosp., 1990-94; pres. United Health Partnership, Toledo, 1995—. Bd. dirs. Washington House Alcoholism Treatment Ctr., 1983-88; bd. dirs., sec.-treas. Parkview Regional Outreach, 1985-88; bd. dirs., pres. Seneca County chpt. Am. Cancer Soc. Fellow Am. Coll. Healthcare Execs.; mem. Am. Hosp. Assn., Wis. Hosp. Assn. (coun. on health care delivery systems), Regent's Adv. Coun. Wis. (bd. dirs.), Ohio Hosp. Assn. (various coms.), Rotary (bd. dirs. Fostoria chpt). Office: United Health Ptrn 2200 Jefferson Ave Toledo OH 43624-1120

KNEEZEL, RONALD D., lawyer; b. 1956; BA, U. Ill., 1978, MBA, 1982, JD. Bar: 1982. Atty. Foley & Lardner Attys. at Law, Milw., 1982—88; v.p., gen. counsel Banta Corp., Menasha, Wis., 1988—, sec., 1991—. Named one of 300 top-paid corporate gen. counsels, Corp. Counsel Mag., 2000. Mem.: ABA. Office: Banta Corp 225 Main St PO Box 8003 Menasha WI 54952-8003 Office Phone: 920-751-7708. Office Fax: 920-751-7790.

KNEPPER, GEORGE W., historian, educator; b. Akron, Ohio, Jan. 15, 1926; s. George W. and Grace (Darling) K.; m. Phyllis Watkins, Aug. 21, 1949; children: Susan Lynne, John Arthur. BA, U. Akron, 1948; MA, U. Mich., 1950, PhD, 1954. Mem. faculty U. Akron, 1948-49, 54-92, assoc. prof. history, head dept., 1959-62; dean U. Akron (Coll. Liberal Arts), 1962-67, prof. history, 1964-88, disting. prof. history, 1988-92. Author: New Lamps for Old, One Hundred Years of Urban Higher Education at the University of Akron, 1970, An Ohio Portrait, 1976, Akron: City at the Summit, 1981, Ohio and Its People, 1989, Summit's Glory: Sketches of Buchtel Coll. and the University of Akron, 1990, Ohio Lands Book, 2002; editor: Travels in the Southland; The Journal of Lucius Verus Bierce 1822-23, 1966. Served to ensign USNR, 1943-46. Fulbright fellow U. London, Eng., 1953-54 Mem. Am., So. hist. assns., Orgn. Am. Historians, Ohio Acad. History, Omicron Delta Kappa, Alpha Tau Omega, Phi Alpha Theta, Alpha Sigma Lambda. Office: Univ Akron Coll Liberal Arts Dept History Akron OH 44325-0001 Home: 1199 Inverness Ln Stow OH 44224

KNERLY, STEPHEN JOHN, JR., lawyer; b. Lakewood, Ohio, Dec. 15, 1949; s. Stephen John Sr. and Mary Louise (Johnson) K.; m. Catherine Arion de Bravura; 1 child, Alexandra M. C. AB summa cum laude, Bowdoin Coll., 1972; AM, Fletcher Sch. Law & Diplomacy, 1973; JD, Case Western Res. U., 1976. Bar: Ohio 1976. Law clk. Stephen J. Knerly and Assocs., Cleve., 1973-74, Hahn, Loeser, Freedheim, Dean et al, Cleve., 1975-76, assoc., 1976-83; ptnr. Hahn, Loeser & Parks, Cleve., 1984—; CEO, mng. ptnr. Hahn, Loeser & Parks, LLP, Cleve., 1993—. James Bowdoin scholar Bowdoin Coll., 1972; named Consul Honoraire de France, Cleve. Mem. French-Am. C. of C. (trustee), Am. Red Cross, Phi Beta Kappa. Home: 10390 Mitchells Mill Rd Chardon OH 44024-8613 Office: Hahn Loeser & Parks LLP 200 Public Sq Ste 3300 Cleveland OH 44114-2301

KNETTER, MICHAEL MARK, dean; b. Rhinelander, Wis., Apr. 8, 1960; s. Edmund David and Margaret Helen Knetter; m. Karen Joy Goedewaagen, July 31, 1988; children: Maxine, Lillian. BA in math and economics, U. Wis., Eau Claire, 1983; PhD, Stanford U., 1988. Asst. prof. economics Dartmouth Coll., Hanover, NH, 1988—94, assoc. prof., vice chair dept. economics, 1994—97; assoc. dean MBA program, prof. internat. economics Dartmouth Coll. Tuck Sch. Bus., 1997—2002; dean U. Wis. Sch. Bus., Madison, 2002—, prof. fin., investment, and banking, 2002—. Rsch assoc. Nat. Bur. Econ. Rsch., 1992-; trustee Lehman Bros./First Trust Income Opportunity Fund, Lehman Bros. Liquid Assets trust; former sr. staff economist Pres.' Coun. Econ. Advisors for

George H.W. Bush and Bill Clinton. Rsch. fellow German Marshall Fund, 1991; Pub. Policy grantee Lynde and Harry Bradley Found., 1991. Mem. Am. Econ. Assn. Office: Univ Wis School of Business 5110 Grainger Hall 975 University Ave Madison WI 53706 Office Phone: 608-262-1758. Office Fax: 608-265-3121. Business E-Mail: mknetter@bus.wisc.edu.

KNIFFEN, JAN ROGERS, finance executive; b. Herrin, Ill., Sept. 19, 1948; s. Paul Rogers and Evelyn Rose (Manering) K.; m. Janet Ann Rohn, Aug. 27, 1975; children: Julie Ann Meyer, Natalie Ann Meyer. Student, U. Ill., 1966-68; BS in Journalism, So. Ill. U., 1968-71; MBA in Fin., Lindenwood Coll., 1975-78; post-grad., St. Louis U., 1985—. Mgmt. trainee ACF Industries, St. Charles, Mo., 1972-73, order inquiry rep., 1973-75, sr. market analyst, 1975-77, sr. planner strategic planning, 1977-79, mgr. leasing, sales adminstrn. Earth City, Mo., 1979-81, dir. bus. planning, estimating, and scheduling, 1981-83, asst. treas., 1983-85, May Dept. Stores Co., St. Louis, 1985-86, v.p., treas., 1986-91, sr. v.p., treas., 1991—. Adj. prof. bus. adminstrn. Lindenwood Coll., 1978—; fin. advisor Job Network, St. Louis, 1987. Bd. mgrs. St. Charles (Mo.) County YMCA, 1981-86; bd. overseers Lindenwood Coll., 1986-93, bd. dirs., 1993—, alumni coun., 1983-86. Capt. USAF, 1970-75. Mem.: Noon Day (St. Louis). Republican. Presbyterian. Avocation: distance running. Office: May Dept Stores Co 611 Olive St Saint Louis MO 63101-1721

KNIGHT, CHARLIE, radio personality; Grad. high sch., Dallas. Radio host Oldies 95, Mission, Kans. Office: Oldies 95 FM 5800 Fatridge Dr 6th Fl Mission KS 66202

KNIGHT, CHRISTOPHER NICHOLS, lawyer; b. New Haven, Sept. 7, 1946; s. Douglas Maitland and Grace Wallace (Nichols) K.; m. Emily Byrn Turner, Oct. 20, 1979; children: Ethan Douglas, Benjamin Walker Lester, Christopher N. Jr. BA, Yale U., 1968; JD, Duke U., 1971. Bar: Wis. 1971, U.S. Dist. Ct. (ea. dist.) Wis. 1973, U.S. Ct. Appeals (7th cir.) 1977, N.C. 1979, U.S. Dist. Ct. (mid. dist.) N.C. 1979, Minn., 1980, U.S. Supreme Ct. 1980, U.S. Ct. Appeals (4th, 8th cirs.) 1980, U.S. Dist. Ct. Minn. 1980, Ill. 1982, N.Y., 1996. Assoc. Quarles & Brady, Milw., 1971-78, ptnr., 1978-79, Smith & Moore LLP, Greensboro, NC, 1979—80, Kutak Rock, Mpls., 1980-82, Isham Lincoln & Beale, Chgo., 1982-88, Hopkins & Sutter, Chgo., 1988-2001, Foley & Lardner LLP, Chgo., 2001—, mng. ptnr., 2003—04. Bd. dirs. Lyric Opera Chgo., 2003—06, Chgo. Humanities Festival, 2005—, vice chmn., 2006—; bd. trustees Writers' Theatre, 2004—, pres., 2006—. Mem. ABA, Ill. State Bar Assn., Minn. State Bar Assn., NY State Bar Assn., NC State Bar Assn., State Bar Wis., Am. Bar Found., Nat. Assn. Bond Lawyers, Chicagoland C. of C. (bd. dirs. 2004-07), Econ. Club of Chgo. Congregationalist. Office: Foley & Lardner LLP Ste 2800 321 N Clark St Chicago IL 60610-4764 Office Phone: 312-832-4515. E-mail: cknight@foley.com.

KNIGHT, JEFFREY ALAN, corporate financial executive; b. Bay City, Mich., Aug. 6, 1951; s. Dean Leroy and Mary Margaret (McLeod) K.; m. Ramona Margo Robins, Aug. 30, 1980; 1 child, Alexis. BBA in Acctg., Western Mich. U., 1973. CPA, Mich. Staff auditor Coopers & Lybrand, Detroit, 1973-75, supr., 1976-77; mgr. acctg. systems Guardian Industries Corp., Northville, Mich., 1978, asst. controller, 1979-80, corp. controller, 1981-83, v.p. fin., CFO, 1984—, now group v.p. fin., CFO. Mem. Fin. Execs. Inst., Am. Inst. CPA's, Mich. Assn. CPA's. Office: Guardian Industries Corp 2300 Harmon Rd Auburn Hills MI 48326

KNIGHT, JOHN ALLAN, clergyman, theology studies educator; b. Mineral Wells, Tex., Nov. 8, 1931; s. John Lee and Beulah Mae (Bounds) K.; m. Justine Anne Rushing, Aug. 22, 1958; children— John Allan, James Alden, Judith Anne. BA, Bethany Nazarene Coll., 1952; MA, Okla. U., 1954; B.D., Vanderbilt U., 1957, PhD, 1966. Ordained to ministry Ch. of Nazarene, 1954; pastor Tenn. Dist. Ch. of Nazarene, 1953-61, 71-72; prof., chmn. dept. philosophy and religion Trevecca azarene Coll., Nashville, 1957-69; chmn. dept. philosophy and religion Mt. Vernon (Ohio) Nazarene Coll., 1969-71, pres., 1972-75; pastor Grace Nazarene Ch., Nashville, 1971-72; pres. Bethany (Okla.) Nazarene Coll., 1976-85; gen. supt. Internat. Ch. of the Nazarene, 1985—2001, vice chair Bd. Gen. Supts., 1990-92, chair Bd. Gen. Supts., 1992-94; ret., 2001. Coordinator U.S. Govt. Project Studying Possible Coop. Ventures for Tenn. Colls. and Univs., 1969; mem. gen. bd. Internat. Ch. of Nazarene, 1980-85 Author: Commentary on Philippians, 1968, The Holiness Pilgrimage, 1971, In His Likeness, 1976, Beacon Bible Expositions, Vol. 9, 1985, What the Bible Says About Tongues -Speaking, 1988; co-author: Sanctify Them --That the World May Know, 1987; co-author: Go --Preach, The Preaching Event in the 90s; author: All Loves Excelling, 1995, Bridge to Our Tomorrows, 2000; editor-in-chief: Herald of Holiness, Kansas City, Mo., 1975-76. Pres. bd. govs. Okla. Ind. Coll. Found., 1979-81; trustee So. Nazarene U., Okla. Recipient Lily Found. Theology award Vanderbilt U., 1958-59; Carré fellow Vanderbilt U., 1960-62 Mem. Soc. Sci. Study Religion, Am. Acad. Religion, Wesley Theol. Soc. (pres. 1979), Evang. Theol. Assn. Clubs: Kiwanis Internat. Mem. Ch. Of Nazarene. Office: Internat Ch of the Nazarene 6401 Paseo Blvd Kansas City MO 64131-1213 E-mail: jkharlo@aol.com.

KNIGHT, ROBERT EDWARD, bank executive, educator; b. Alliance, Nebr., Nov. 27, 1941; s. Edward McKean and Ruth (McDuffee) K.; m. Eva Sophia Youngstom, Aug. 12, 1966. BA, Yale U., 1963; MA, Harvard U., 1965, PhD, 1968. Asst. prof. U.S. Naval Acad., Annapolis, Md., 1966—68; lectr. U. Md., 1967—68; fin. economist Fed. Res. Bank Kansas City, Mo., 1968—70, rsch. officer, economist, 1971—76, asst. v.p., sec., 1977, v.p., sec., 1978—79; pres. Alliance Nat. Bank, 1979—94, chmn., 1983—94; pres. Robert E. Knight & Assocs., banking and econ. cons., Cheyenne, Wyo., 1979—. Chmn., CEO Eldred Found., 1985—; vis. prof., chmn. banking and fin. East Tenn. State U., Johnson City, 1988; faculty Stonier Grad. Sch. Banking, 1972-2002, Colo. Grad. Sch. Banking, 1975-82, Am. Inst. Banking, U. Mo., Kansas City, 1971-79, Prochnow Grad. Sch. Banking, U. Wis., 1980-84; extended learning faculty Park Coll., 1996-2005; mem. Coun. for Excellence for Bur. Bus. Rsch. U. Nebr., Lincoln, 1991-94, mem. Grad. Sch. Arts and Scis. Coun. Harvard, 1994—; chmn. Taxable Mcpl. Bondholders Protective Com., 1991-94. Contbr. articles to profl. jours. Bd. dirs. Stonier Grad. Sch. Banking, 1979-82, Nebr. Com. for Humanities, 1986-90, People of Faith (Royal Oaks) Found., 2000-04; trustee Knox Presbyn. Ch., Overland Park, Kans., 1965-69; bd. regents Nat. Comml. Lending Sch., 1980-83; mem. Downtown Improvement Com., Alliance, 1981-94; trustee U. Nebr. Found., 1982-94; fin. com. United Meth. Ch. Alliance, 1982-85, trustee, 1990-93; mem. Box Butte County Indsl. Devel. Bd., 1987-94; bd. mem., treas. Sun City Homeowners Found., Sun City, Ariz., 2005-07; chmn., CEO, Knight Mus. Found., 1994—. Woodrow Wilson fellow, 1963—64. Mem. Am. Econ. Assn., Am. Fin. Assn., So. Econ. Assn., Nebr. Bankers Assn. (com. state legis. 1980-81, com. comml. loans and investments 1986-87), Am. Inst. Banking (state com. for Nebr. 1980-83), Am. Bankers Assn. (econ. adv. com. 1980-83, cmty. bank leadership coun.), Western Econ. Assn., Rotary, Masons. Home and Office: 429 W 5th Ave Cheyenne WY 82001-1249

KNIGHT, ROBERT G., mayor, investment banker; b. Wichita, Kans., July 31, 1941; s. Edwar G. and Melba (Barbour) K.; m. Jane Carol Benedick, Aug. 12, 1967; children— Jennifer, Amy, Kristin BA, Wichita State U. Rep. First Securities Co., Wichita, Kans., 1970-76, v.p., 1984—, Mid-Continent Mcpls., Wichita, Kans., 1977-82, Ranson & Co., Wichita, Kans., 1982-84; mayor City of Wichita, 1980-81, 84—. Trustee Salvation Army, Wichita, 1980—, Urban Ministeries, Wichita, 1980—, Southwestern Coll., Winfield, Kans., 1980—; bd. dirs. Kans. Water Authority, Topeka, 1983—; commr. City of Wichita, 1979—. Served with USMCR, 1962-66 Recipient award of honor Concerned Citizens for Community Standards, 1982 Mem. Nat. League Cities, Kans. League Municipalities Republican. Methodist. Avocation: sports. Office: Mayors Office City Hall 1st Fl 455 N Main St Wichita KS 67202-1600

KNOBEL, DALE THOMAS, historian, educator, university president; b. East Cleveland, Ohio, Sept. 14, 1949; s. Harry Spencer and Gwynne Ann K.; m. Tina Jamieson, June 19, 1971; children: Allison. BA, Yale U., 1971; PhD, Northwestern U., 1976. Asst. prof. history Northwestern U., Evanston, Ill., 1976-77, Tex. A&M U., College Station, 1977-84, assoc. prof. history, 1984-96, dir. univ. hons. prog., 1987-92, exec. dir. honors programs and acad. scholarships, 1992-95, assoc. provost for undergrad. programs, 1995-96; provost, dean of faculty, prof. history Southwestern U., Georgetown, Tex., 1996-98; pres., prof. history Denison U., Granville, Ohio, 1998—. Author: America for the Americans: The Nativist Movement in the United States, 1996, Paddy and the Republic: Ethnicity and Nationality in Antebellum America, 1985; co-author: Prejudice, 1982; contbr. Immigrant America, 1994, Fleeing the Famine, 2003, University Presidents as Moral Leaders, 2006; book rev. editor Jour. of Early Republic, 1987-89; contbr. articles to profl. jours. Chmn. Bryan Hist. Landmark Commn., 1987-93; trustee Bryan Tex. Pub. Libr., 1989-92, Brazos Valley Mus. Natural History, 1994-96, Inst. for Internat. Edn. Students, Chgo., 1999—2005, Newark Midland Theater Assn., 1999-, The Works: Ohio Ctr. for History, Art, and Tech.; pres. Denison Univ. Rsch. Found., 1998—, North Coast Athletic Conf., 2004-06, Five Colls. Ohio, Inc., 2004-06; vice chmn. Ohio Found. Ind. Colls., 2002-06; chmn. Ohio Campus Compact, 2001—, Great Lakes Coll. Assn., 2007-; sec. Assn. Ind. Colls. and Univs. Ohio, 2006-; chmn. Lakeside Chautauqua Found., 2006—; trustee Lakeside Assn., 2006—; pres. coun. NCAA, 2003-06. Am. Assn. State and Local History grantee, 1984; NEH grantee, 1978; NSF grantee, 1972-74; W.K. Kellogg Found. grantee, 1985-87. Mem. Nat. Collegiate Honors Coun., Orgn. Am. Historians, Immigration History Soc., Soc. for Hist. of the Early Am. Republic, Union Club Cleve., Univ. Club Chgo., Univ. Club NY, Rocky Fork Hunt and Country Club, Phi Beta Kappa, Phi Alpha Theta, Omicron Delta Kappa, Phi Kappa Phi, Phi Beta Delta. Methodist. Home: 204 Broadway W Granville OH 43023-1120

KNOEBEL, SUZANNE BUCKNER, cardiologist, educator; b. Ft. Wayne, Ind., Dec. 13, 1926; d. Doster and Marie (Lewis) Buckner. AB, Goucher Coll., 1948; MD, Ind. U.-Indpls., 1960. Diplomate: Am. Bd. Internal Medicine. Asst. prof. medicine Ind. U., Indpls., 1966-69, assoc. prof., 1969-72, prof., 1972-77, Krannert prof., 1977—. Asst. dean rsch. Ind. U., Indpls., 1975-85; assoc. dir. Krannert Inst. Cardiology, Indpls., 1974-90; asst. chief cardiology sect. Richard L. Roudebush VA Med. Ctr., Indpls., 1982-90; editor-in-chief ACC Current Jour. Rev., 1992-2000. Fellow Am. Coll. Cardiology (v.p. 1980-81, pres. 1982-83); mem. Am. Fedn. Clin. Research, Assn. Univ. Cardiologists Office: Krannert Inst 1701 N Senate Ave Indianapolis IN 46202 Home Phone: 317-841-9233; Office Phone: 317-962-0061. Business E-Mail: sknoebel@iupui.edu.

KNOKE, DAVID HARMON, sociology educator; b. Phila., Mar. 4, 1947; s. Donald Glenn and Frances Harriet (Dunn) Knoke; m. Joann Margaret Robar, Aug. 29, 1970; 1 child, Margaret Frances. BA, U. Mich., 1969, MSW, 1971, PhD, 1972; MA, U. Chgo., 1970. Asst. prof. sociology Ind. U., Bloomington, 1972-75, assoc. prof., 1975-81, prof., 1981-85, dir. Inst. Social Rsch. and Ctr. for Survey Rsch., 1982-84; prof. sociology U. Minn., Mpls., 1985—, chmn., 1989-92, undergrad. dir., 1995-98, grad. dir., 1998—2002. Mem. sociology program rev. panel NSF, 1981-83; mem. sociology rev. panel Fulbright Scholars, 1993-95; mem. sociology com. Grad. Records Exams., 1998-2000. Author: Change and Continuity in American Politics, 1976, (with Peter J. Burke) Log-Linear Models, 1980, (with James R. Wood) Organized for Action, 1981, (with George W. Bohrnstedt and Alisa Potter Mee) Statistics for Social Data Analysis, 1982, 4th edit., 2002, (with James H. Kuklinski) Network Analysis, 1982, (with Edward O. Laumann) The Organizational State, 1987, Organizing for Collective Action, 1990, Political Networks, 1990, (with George W. Bohrnstedt) Basic Social Statistics, 1991, (with Franz Pappi, Jeffrey Broadbent and Yutaka Tsujinaka) Comparing Policy Networks, 1996, (with Arne Kalleberg, Peter Marsden and Joe Spaeth) Organizations in America, 1996, (with Peter Capelli, Laurie Bassi, Harry Katz, Paul Osterman and Michael Useem) Change at Work, 1997, Changing Organizations, 2001, (with Song Yang) Social Network Analysis, 2007. Recipient NIMH Rsch. Scientist Devel. award, 1977-82, 14 rsch. grants NSF; Nat. Merit scholar, 1965-69, Fulbright Sr. Rsch. scholar, Germany, 1989, scholar, U. Minn. Coll. Liberal Arts, 1996-99; Ctr. Advanced Study Behavioral Scis. fellow, 1992-93. Mem. Am. Sociol. Assn. (chair orgns. and occupation sect. 1992-93), Sociol. Rsch. Assn., Acad. of Mgmt., Internat. Network for Social Network Analysis, European Group for Orgnl. Studies. Unitarian Universalist. Home: 7305 Wooddale Ave S Minneapolis MN 55435-4157 Office: U Minn Dept Sociology Minneapolis MN 55455 Office Phone: 612-624-4300. Business E-Mail: knoke@atlas.socsci.umn.edu.

KNOLL, GLENN FREDERICK, nuclear engineering educator; b. St. Joseph, Mich., Aug. 3, 1935; s. Oswald Herman and Clara Martha (Bernthal) K.; m. Gladys Hetzner, Sept. 7, 1957; children: Thomas, John, Peter. BS, Case Inst. Tech., 1957; MSChemE, Stanford U., 1959; PhD in Nuclear Engring., U. Mich., 1963. Asst. research physicist U. Mich., Ann Arbor, 1960-62, asst. prof. nuclear engring., 1962-67, assoc. prof., 1967-72, prof., 1972—2000, prof. emeritus, 2000—, chmn. dept. nuclear engring., 1979-90, interim dean engring., 1995-96, also mem. bioengring. faculty. Vis. scientist Institut für Angewandte Kernphysik, Kernforschungszentrum Karlsruhe, Fed. Republic Germany, 1965-66; sr. vis. fellow dept. physics U. Surrey, Guildford, Eng., 1973; summer cons. Electric Power Research Inst., Palo Alto, Calif., 1974; cons. in field. Author: Radiation Detection and Measurement, 1979, 3d edit., 2000, Principles of Engineering, 1982; editor-in-chief IEEE/Nuclear and Plasma Scis. Soc., 1995-99; editor Nuclear Instns. and Methods in Physics Rsch., 1995—. Recipient excellence in rsch. award Coll. Engring., U. Mich., 1984, Attwood award, 2000, Ann. Merit award IEEE/NPSS, 1996, Millennium medal, 2000; Fulbright travel grantee, 1965-66; NSF fellow, 1958-60, Sci. Rsch. Coun. sr. fellow, 1973; vis. fellow Japan Soc. Promotion of Sci., 1987. Fellow IEEE, Am. Inst. Med. and Biol. Engring., Am. Nuclear Soc. (bd. dirs. 1989-91, Arthur Holly Compton award 1991); mem. Am. Soc. Engring. Edn. (Glenn Murphy award 1979), Nat. Acad. Engring., Sigma Xi, Tau Beta Pi. Achievements include patents in field. Office: U Mich Dept Nuclear Engring 121 Cooley Bldg Ann Arbor MI 48109 E-mail: gknoll@umich.edu.

KNOLL, JAY B., lawyer; Asst. gen. counsel Visteon Corp.; gen. counsel, sec. Collins & Aikman Corp., Troy, Mich. Office: Collins & Aikman Corp 250 Stephenson Hwy Ste 100 Troy MI 48083

KNOLLENBERG, JOSEPH CASTL (JOE KNOLLENBERG), congressman; b. Mattoon, Ill., Nov. 28, 1933; m. Sandie (Moto) Knollenberg; children: Martin, Stephen. BS in Social Sci., Eastern Ill. U., 1955. CLU. Agent, owner ins. co., 1960-93; mem. US Congress from 9th Mich. Dist. (formerly 11th), 1993—, mem. budget com. appropriations, mem. stds. of offcl. conduct coms. Past chmn., Birmingham Cable TV Community Adv. Bd., 18th Dist. Rep. Com., Rep. Com. Oakland County, 1978-86; past pres. St. Bede's Parish Coun., Evergreen Sch. PTA (Birmingham Sch. Dist.), Bloomfield Glens Homeowner's Assn., Cranbrook Homeowner's Assn.; past coord. Southfield Ad Hoc Park and Recreation Devel. Com.; past mem. Southfield Mayor's Wage and Salary Com.; chmn. Candidate Assistance Com./State Com., Oakland County Campaign, 1978; former regional/vice chair 17th Dist. Com., 1975-77; mem. Rep. State Com; exec. com. mem. and fin. com. Rep. Com. Oakland County; founder, mem. Rep. Leadership Com. Oakland County, 1984—; mem. Allstate Ins. Co's P.A.C.; del. Rep. Nat. Conv., 1980; del. to every state convention since 1974. Served as CPL US Army, 1955—57. Recipient Baltic Freedom award, Baltic Am. Freedom League, 2000, Legis. of Yr., Am. Small Manufactures Coalition, 2004. Mem. Am. Soc. Chartered Life Underwriters, Detroit Assn. Life Underwriters, Oakland County Lincoln Rep. Club, Troy C. of C. (current vice chmn.). Republican. Roman Catholic. Office: US Congress 2349 Rayburn HOB Washington DC 20515-2211 also: District Office 30833 Northwestern Hwy Ste 100 Farmington Hills MI 48334 Office Phone: 202-225-5802, 248-851-1366. Office Fax: 202-226-2356.

KNOPF, MATTHEW J., lawyer; b. 1956; BA summa cum laude, SUNY, Stony Brook, 1981; JD, Univ. Chgo., 1986. Bar: Ill. 1986, Minn. 2000. Sr. v.p., gen. counsel County Seat Stores, Inc; atty. Skadden, Arps Law, NYC; ptnr., mergers, acquisitions corp. group Dorsey & Whitney LLP, Mpls., and co-chair, bus. restructuring practice group. Bd. dir. Minnetonka Ctr.Arts. Office: Dorsey & Whitney LLP Ste 1500 50 S Sixth St Minneapolis MN 55402-1498 Office Phone: 612-340-5603. Office Fax: 612-340-2868. Business E-Mail: knopf.matthew@dorsey.com.

KNOPMAN, DAVID S., neurologist; b. Phila., Oct. 6, 1950; AB, Dartmouth Coll., 1972; MD, U. Minn., 1975. Diplomate Am. Bd. Psychiatry and Neurology. Intern Hennepin County Med. Ctr., 1975-76; resident U. Minn., 1976-79, asst. prof. neurology Mpls., 1980-86, assoc. prof. neurology, 1986-98, prof., 1998—2000; cons. dept. neurology Mayo Clinic, Rochester, Minn., 2000—; prof. Mayo Clinic Coll. Medicine, Rochester, 2000—. Office: Mayo Clinic Dept Neurology Rochester MN 55905 Office Phone: 507-284-2511.

KNORR, JOHN CHRISTIAN, entertainment executive, bandleader, producer; b. Crissey, Ohio, May 24, 1921; s. Reinhold Alfred and Mary (Rieth) K.; m. Jane Lucy Hammer, Nov. 8, 1941; children: Gerald William, Janice Grace Knorr Wilcox. Student, Ohio No. U., 1940-41. Violin soloist with Helen O'Connell, 1934-35; reed sideman Jimmy Dorsey, Les Brown and Sonny Dunham orchs., 1939-48; mem. theater pit orchs. and club shows, Ohio, 1949-57; leader Johnny Knorr Orch., Toledo, 1958—. Mgr. Centennial Ter.; owner Johnny Knorr Entertainment Agy.; bandleader, show producer; mem. Royal Ct. of Jesters #21, 1987. Recs. include Live at Franklin Park Mall, 1973, Let's Go Dancing, 1979, encore, 1984, (TV spl.) An Era of Swing, 1973, Live at Centennial Terrace, 1986, Let's Dance, 1989, Oh Johnny, 1997, One More Time, 2000. Trustee Presbyn. Ch. Served to cpl. AUS, 1944-45. Recipient outstanding dance band citations, Chgo., 1966, Des Moines, 1968, Las Vegas, 1969, Nat. Ballroom Operators Assn., Omaha, 1970, Entertainment Operators Assn., 1973; named Grand Duke of Toledo, King of the Hoboes, 1975; named to First Libbey H.S. Hall of Fame, 1994; winner in instrumental category Peoples Choice Awards for Performing Arts, 1997; inducted into Lake Erie West People's Choice Awards Hall of Fame, 1999. Mem. Am. Fedn. Musicians, Am. Legion, Exch. Club, Circus Fans Am., Masons, Shriners, Ind. Order Foresters. Home and Office: 5709 Eagles Landing Dr Oregon OH 43616-1159

KNOTE, JOHN A., diagnostic radiologist; b. Marion, Ind., Aug. 4, 1938; m. Jan Knote; 3 children. MD, Ind. U., 1964. Diplomate Am. Bd. Nuclear Medicine, Am. Bd. Radiology. Intern Bapt. Meml. Hosp., Memphis, 1964-65; resident in radiology Ind. U., Indpls., 1965-68; diagnostic radiologist Arnett Clinic, Lafayeete, Ind.; dir. dept. radiology Purdue U. Student Hosp.; dir. radiology Lafayette Home Hosp., White County Meml. Hosp. Bd. dirs. YMCA, Boys Club; charter mem. Home Hosp. Found. Bd. Dirs. Fellow Am. Coll. Radiology (budget and fin. com., steering com., spkr. coun.), Am. Coll. of Nuclear Medicine; mem. AMA (vice spkr. ho. of dels. 1999, mem. coun. on med. svcs., chmn. subcom. on health care reform/fin., subcom. on managed care, del. from Ind.), Orgn. of State Med. Assn. Pres. (past pres.), Forum for Med. Affairs (past pres.), Ind. State Med. Assn. (trustee, chmn. bd., chmn. commn. on legislation, mem. future planning com.), Lafayette C. of C. (fed. govt. task force), Ind. Trotting and Pacing Horse Assn. (past pres.), Ind. Roentgen Soc. (past pres., Gold medal 1997). Office: AMA 515 N State St Chicago IL 60610-4325

KNOTT, JOHN RAY, JR., language educator; b. Memphis, July 9, 1937; s. John Ray and Wilma (Henshaw) K.; m. Anne Percy, Dec. 5, 1959; children: Catherine, Ellen, Walker, Anne. AB, Yale U., 1959, Carnegie fellow, 1960; PhD, Harvard U., 1965. Instr. Harvard U., 1965-67; mem. faculty U. Mich., Ann Arbor, 1967—2006, prof. English, 1976—2006, prof. emeritus English, 2006—, chmn. dept., 1982-87, assoc. dean Coll. Arts and Scis., 1977-80, acting dean Coll. Arts and Scis., 1980-81, interim dir. Inst. for Humanities, 1987-88, interim dir. Program in the Environment, 2001—02; ret., 2006. Dir. region IV Mellon Fellowship Selection Com., 1989-94. Author: Milton's Pastoral Vision, 1971, The Sword of the Spirit, 1980, Discourses of Martyrdom in English Literature, 1563-1694, 1993, Imagining Wild America, 2002; editor: The Triumph of Style, 1967, Mirrors: An Introduction to Literature, rev. edit., 1987, The Huron River: Voices From the Watershed, 2000, Reimagining Place, 2001; contbr. articles on Abbey, Berry, Browne, Bunyan, Fox, Foxe, Haines, Milton, and Spenser to scholarly jours. Woodrow Wilson fellow, 1960-61; NEH fellow, 1974 Mem.: MLA, Nature Conservancy. Office: Univ Mich Dept English Ann Arbor MI 48109

KNOTTS, FRANK BARRY, physician, surgeon; b. St. Louis, Jan. 27, 1948; s. Frank Louis and Anna Lee (Amerman) K.; m. Wendy Diane Lautz Horton (div.); children: Ryan Matthew, Kara Luan; m. Denise Marie Stern, Aug. 26, 1984. BA in Physics, Johns Hopkins U., 1969; PhD in Molecular Biology, UCLA, 1974, MD, 1975. Diplomate Am. Bd. Surgery with subspecialties in gen. surgery and surg. crit. care. Mem. Rotary. Avocations: flying, scuba, skiing, software devel. Home: 26029 Edinborough Cir Perrysburg OH 43551-9545 Office: St Vincent Mercy Med Ctr 2409 Cherry St MOB 303 Toledo OH 43608

KNOUS, PAMELA K., wholesale distribution executive; b. Minn. Student, Carleton Coll.; BA in Math., U. Ariz., BS in Bus. Adminstrn. Ptnr. KPMG Peat Marwick, LA, 1977—91; group v.p. finance The Vons Companies, Inc., 1991—94; sr. v.p., CFO The Vons. Companies, Inc., 1994; exec. v.p., CFO The Vons Companies, Inc., 1995—97, treas.; exec. v.p., CFO Supervalu Inc., Mpls., 1997—. Bd. dir. Tennant Co., Twin Cities Pub. Television. Office: Supervalu Inc 11840 Valley View Rd Eden Prairie MN 55344 Office Phone: 952-828-4000. Office Fax: 952-828-8998.

KNOWLES, RICHARD ALAN JOHN, language educator; b. Southbridge, Mass., May 17, 1935; s. Clarence Fay and Mildred Elizabeth (Branniff) K.; m. Jane Marie Boyle, Sept. 1, 1958; children: Jonathan Edwards, Katherine Mary. BA magna cum laude, Tufts U., 1956; MA, U. Pa., 1958, PhD, 1963. Physics asst. Tufts U., Medford, Mass., 1954-56; asst. instr. English U. Pa., Phila., 1956-60; from asst. prof. to prof. U. Wis., Madison, 1962-90, Dickson-Bascom prof. humanities, 1990—. Vis. lectr. U. Pa., 1967, George Washington U., Am. U., 1969, Cath. U., Washington, 1985; manuscript reader various univs., 1965—; cons. Am. Players Theater, Spring Green, Wis., 1980-83; poetry judge Brittingham Poetry Prize, Madison, 1986—, NEH referee, panelist, Washington, 1988—. Author: (with others) Shakespeare Variorum Handbook, 1971; author: Shakespeare Variorum Handbook, rev., 2003; editor: (with others) English Renaissance Drama, 1978; editor: New Variorum As You Like It, 1977; co-editor New Variorum Shakespeare, 1978—; mem. editl. bd. Shakespeare Notes, 1996—. Officer, prodr. Madison Savoyards, Wis., 1978—; pres. Friends U. Wis. Librs., Madison, 1982—84. Folger Libr. fellow, Washington, 1968, Guggenheim fellow, N.Y., 1976-77; NEH fellow 1983-87; Rsch. fellow Humanities Rsch. Inst., Madison, 1990. Mem. MLA, Shakespeare Assn. Am., Internat. Assn. Univ. Profs. English, Assn. Lit. Scholars and Critics, Nakoma Country Club. Democrat. Avocations: theater, chamber music, opera, gardening, carpentry. Home: 2226 Commonwealth Ave Madison WI 53726-5302 Office: U Wis Dept English 600 N Park St Madison WI 53706-1403 E-mail: rknowles@facstaff.wisc.edu.

KNOX, DEBBY, newscaster; m. Richard Triman; 2 children. Grad., U. Mich. With various stas., Elkhart, Ind., South Bend; anchor Sta. WISH-TV, Indpls., 1980—. Recipient Casper award, Ind. State Med. Journalism awards (3), Associated Press award, United Press Internat. award. Office: WISH-TV 1950 N Meridian St Indianapolis IN 46207

KNOX, JAMES EDWIN, lawyer; b. Evanston, Ill., July 2, 1937; s. James Edwin and Marjorie Eleanor (Williams) Knox; m. Rita Lucille Torres, June 30, 1973; children: James Edwin III, Kirsten M., Katherine E., Miranda G. BA in Polit. Sci., State U. Iowa, 1959; JD, Drake U., 1961. Bar: Iowa 1961, Ill. 1962, Tex. 1982. Law clk. to Hon. Tom C. Clark, U.S. Supreme Ct., Washington, 1961-62; assoc., then ptnr. Isham, Lincoln & Beale, Chgo., 1962-70; v.p. law N.W. Industries, Inc., Chgo., 1970-80; exec. v.p., gen. counsel Lone Star Steel Co., Dallas, 1980-86; sr. v.p. law Anixter Internat. Inc., Chgo., 1986—2002. Instr. contracts and labor law Chgo. Kent Coll. Law, 1964—69; arbitrator Nat. Rlwy. Adjustment Bd., 1967—68; ptnr. Mayer, Brown & Platt, Chgo., 1992—96; gen. counsel Arris Group, Inc., 1996—2002. Mem.: ABA, Ill. Bar Assn., Phi Beta Kappa, Order of Coif. Republican. Office: Anixter Internat Inc 2301 Patriot Blvd Glenview IL 60025-8020 Home Phone: 773-935-0425; Office Phone: 224-521-8796.

KNOX, LANCE LETHBRIDGE, venture capitalist; b. Hartford, Conn., Sept. 25, 1944; s. Robert Chester and Leonice Katherine (Merrels) K.; children: Michele Merrels, Elizabeth McVarish; m. Mary E. Lambert, 1981. BA, Williams Coll., 1966; MBA, NYU, 1970. Asst. cashier Citibank, N.C., NYC, 1968-70, asst. v.p., 1970-72, v.p., 1972-74, sr. credit officer, 1973-74; v.p. fin. GATX Corp., Chgo., 1974-77; pvt. investor venture capital, 1978—. Pres. Bistrot Zinc, Chgo.

KNOX, WILLIAM ARTHUR, judge; b. Fargo, ND, Jan. 8, 1945; BS, N.D. State U., 1966; JD, U. Minn., 1968. Law specialist USCG, Boston, 1968—69, Juneau, Alaska, 1970—72; prof. Law Sch., U. Mo., Columbia, 1972—85; magistrate judge U.S. Cts., Jefferson City, Mo., 1985—. Author: West's Federal Criminal Forms, 2002, West's Missouri Criminal Practice, 2005. Office: 131 W High St Jefferson City MO 65101-1557 Home Phone: 573-634-4952; Office Phone: 573-634-3418. Business E-Mail: william.knox@mow.uscourts.gov.

KNUE, PAUL FREDERICK, newspaper editor; b. Lawrenceburg, Ind., July 11, 1947; s. Paul F. and Neil (Beadel) K.; m. Elizabeth Wegner, Sept. 6, 1969; children: Amy, Katherine BS in Journalism and English, Murray State U., 1969. Mng. editor Evansville Press, Ind., 1975-79; editor Ky. Post, Covington,

1979-83, Cin. Post., 1983—. Trustee Scripps Howard Found. Mem. Am. Soc. Newspaper Editors, AP Mng. Editors Assn., AP Soc. Ohio (trustee). Office: E W Scripps Co 125 E Court St Cincinnati OH 45202-1212 Home: 321 Whispering Pines Dr Loveland OH 45140-8809

KNUTH, RUSS, histologist, radio personality; Grad. Atmospheric Scis., St. Cloud State U. With Digital Cyclone; meteorologist Sta. WCCO-Radio, Mpls. Office: WCCO 625 2nd Ave S Minneapolis MN 55402

KNUTSEN, ALAN PAUL, pediatrician, immunologist, allergist; b. Mpls., July 21, 1948; s. Donald Richard and Shirley Marie (Erickson) K.; m. Kim A.; children: Laura Joelle, Brian A., Benjamin C., Elizabeth G., Katherine M., Amy S., Summer A. BA in Biology, U. Calif., 1971; MD, St. Louis U., 1975. Resident pediatrics St. Louis U. Med. Ctr., 1975-78; fellow allergy Duke U. Med. Ctr., Durham, NC, 1978-80;, 1980-93; dir. dept. allergy and immunology St. Louis U. Med. Ctr., 1985—; prof. St. Louis U., 1993—, 1993—. Mem. credentials com. St. Louis U. Med. Ctr., 1980—, infectious disease com., 1980—; dir. pediatric immunology lab, 1983—; dir. pediatric allergy/immunology trng. program. Contbr. articles to profl. jours. Mem. Am. Acad. Allergy/Immunology, Clin. Immunology Soc., Phi Beta Kappa, Alpha Omega Alpha. Democrat. Lutheran. Office: St Louis U Pediatric Rsch Inst 1465 S Grand Blvd Saint Louis MO 63104-1003 Home: 44 S Gore Ave Saint Louis MO 63119-2910 Home Phone: 314-961-3179; Office Phone: 314-268-4014. Business E-Mail: knutsenm@slu.edu.

KNUTSON, DAVID LEE, state legislator, lawyer; b. Mpls., Nov. 24, 1959; s. Howard Arthur and Jerroldine Margo (Sundby) K.; m. Laurie Sjoquist, June 25, 1983; children: Ann Marie, Timothy David. BA, St. Olaf Coll., 1982; JD, William Mitchell Coll. Law, 1986. Bar: Minn. 1986, U.S. Dist. Ct. Minn. 1986, U.S. Ct. Appeals (8th cir.) 1987, U.S. Tax Ct. 1989. Pvt. practice, Apple Valley, Minn., 1986—; mem. Minn. State Senate from Dist. 37, 1993—, asst. minority leader, 1995—2002. Bd. dirs. Our Saviour's Shelter for Homeless, Mpls., 1988-90, City Task Force on Arts, Burnsville, 1988, Legal Assistance Dakota County, Ltd., 1994—, Dakota County Tech. Coll. Found., 1994—; bd. dirs. Minn. Valley YMCA, 1988-2000, chmn., 1991-93, 99-00; bd. dirs. Serve Minn., 2003-. amed one of Ten Outstanding Young Minnesotans, Minn. Jaycees, 1993, Legislator of the Biennium, Minn. Retailers Assn.; recipient Lake Conf. Disting. Alumni award, 1996, Pro Bono Publico award Legal Svcs. Coalition, 1998, YMCA Disting. Vol. award, 1999, Outstanding Achievement award Burnsville H.S., 2001. Mem. Minn. Bar Assn., Dakota County Bar Assn., Burnsville Jaycees (bd. dirs. 1988-90), Apple Valley C. of C., Burnsville C. of C. (bd. dirs. 1990-92), No. Dakota County C. of C., Burnsville Breakfast Rotary. Republican. Avocations: reading, travel, sports. Office: Severson Sheldon Dougherty & Molenda PA Ste 600 7300 W 147th St Apple Valley MN 55124 Home Phone: 952-431-6232; Office Phone: 952-432-3136. E-mail: knutsond@seversonsheldon.com.

KO, WEN-HSIUNG, electrical engineering educator; b. Shang-Hong, Fukien, China, Apr. 12, 1923; came to U.S., 1954, naturalized, 1963; s. Sing-Ming and Sou-Yu (Kao) K.; m. Christina Chen, Oct. 12, 1957; children: Kathleen, Janet, Linda, Alexander. BSEE, Nat. Amoy U., Fukien, China, 1946; MS, Case Inst. Tech., Cleve., 1956, PhD, 1959. Engr., then sr. engr. Taiwan Telecommunication Adminstrn., 1946-54; mem. faculty Case Inst. Tech., Cleve., 1956-93; prof. elec. and biomed. engring. Case Western Res. U., Cleve., 1967-93, prof. emeritus, 1994—, dir. engring. design center, 1970-82; pres., prin. Wen H. Ko & Assocs., Cleve., 1996—. Cons. NSF, N.Am. Mfg. Co., NIH, 1966-82; pres. Transducer Rsch. Found., 1986-2004; rschr. in med. implant electronics, telemetry and stimulation, microsensors and microactators, micro-electro-mech.-sys. Recipient career achievement award Transducer Internat. Conf., Chgo., 1997. Fellow IEEE, AIMBE; mem. Instrument Soc. Am., Bio-Med. Engring. Soc., Sigma Xi, Eta Kappa Nu. Home: 1356 Forest Hills Blvd Cleveland OH 44118-1359 Office: Case Western Res U EECS Dept Cleveland OH 44106 Business E-Mail: whk@cwru.edu.

KOBACH, KRIS WILLIAM, law educator, political organization administrator; b. Madison, Wis., Mar. 26, 1966; s. William Louis and Janice Mardell (Iverson) K. AB, Harvard Coll., 1988; M in Philosophy, Politics, Oxford U., Eng., 1990, PhD in Philosophy, Politics, 1992; JD, Yale U., 1995. Bar: Kans. 1995, US Dist. Ct. Kans. 1995, US Ct. Appeals (10th cir.) 1995. Adj. prof. Yale U., New Haven, 1994-95; judicial clk. J. Tacha US Ct. Appeals, 10th Cir., Lawrence, Kans., 1995-96; assoc. prof. Sch. of Law U. Mo., Kans., 1996; chmn. Kans. Rep. Party, 2007—. Author: (books) Political Capital, 1989, The Referendum: Direct Democracy in Switzerland, 1993; contbg. author: Referendums Around the World, 1994. Recipient Marshall Scholarship Brit. Govt., 1988; Tchg. Fellowship prize Yale U., New Haven, Conn., 1994. Mem. Federalist Soc., Overland Park Rotary Club. Republican. Lutheran. Avocations: skiin, rowing, squash, collecting antique maps. Office: Kans Rep Party 2025 SW Gage Blvd Topeka KS 66604 Office Phone: 785-234-3456. Business E-Mail: republicanparty@ksgop.org.*

KOBS, JAMES FRED, direct marketing consultant; b. Chgo., June 27, 1938; s. Fred Charles and Ann (Ganser) K.; m. Nadine Schumacher, May 18, 1963; children: Karen, Kathleen, Kenneth BS in Journalism, U. Ill., 1960. Copywriter Rylander Co., Chgo., 1960—62; mng. dir. Success Mag., Chgo., 1963—65; mail order mgr. Am. Peoples Press, Westmont, Ill., 1966—67; exec. v.p. Stone & Adler Advt., Chgo., 1967—78; chmn. Kobs & Brady Advt., Inc. (now Draft Fcb), Chgo., 1978—88, vice chmn., 1988; chmn. Kobs Gregory & Passavant, Chgo., 1989—2001; pres. Kobs Strategic Cons., Chgo., 2002—. Guest lectr. U. Wis., U. Ill., NYU; adj. prof. direct mktg. Northwestern U. Medill Sch. Journalism Grad. Program; instr. U. Chgo. Strategic Direct Mktg. Cert. Program; internat. lectr. in field Author: Profitable Direct Marketing, 2d edit., 1991, 24 Ways to Improve Your Direct Mail Results, 99 Proven Direct Response Offers; contbr. articles to periodicals Past chmn. Direct Mktg. Ednl. Found Recipient numerous local and nat. advt. awards; named to Direct Mktg. Hall of Fame Mem. Direct Mktg. Assn. (dir., sec., exec. com., recipient Silver and Gold Mailbox, Gold Medallion, Gold Echo, Ed Mayer award), Chgo. Assn. Direct Mktg. (past pres., Direct Marketer of Yr.), Boys and Girls Clubs of Chgo. (corp. bd.), Alpha Delta Sigma Office: Kobs Strategic Consulting 222 N Columbus Dr Ste 2202 Chicago IL 60601

KOCH, ALBERT ACHESON, music distribution company executive, management consultant; b. Atlanta, May 16, 1942; s. Albert H. and Harriet M. (Acheson) K.; m. Bonnie Royce, June 6, 1964; children: Bradford Allen, David Albert, Robert Acheson, Donald Leonard. BS cum laude, Elizabethtown Coll., 1964. With Ernst & Young, 1964-88, nat. dir. client svcs. nat. office Cleve., 1977-81, mng. ptnr. Detroit office, 1981-88; mng. ptnr. Equity Ptnrs. Am., Troy, Mich., 1988-94; vice chmn., mng. prin. Alix Ptnrs. LLC, Southfield, Mich., 1995—2001, chmn., 2002—; prin. mem., gen. ptnr. Questor Ptnrs., Southfield, Mich., 2002—; exec. v.p., CFO Kmart Corp., Troy, Mich., 2002—03; chmn., interim pres., CEO, Champion Enterprises, Inc., Auburn Hills, Mich., 2003—04; chmn., pres., CEO Polar Corp., Holdingford, Minn., 2004—; pres., CEO Handleman Co., Troy, Mich., 2007—. Bd. dirs. SPX Corp., Numatics, Inc., Highland, Mich., 1991—, Champion Enterprises, Inc., 2003-04, Tecumseh Products Co., Mich., 2004-07; mem. adv. com. on replacement cost implementation SEC, 1976. Co-author: SEC Replacement Cost Requirements and Implementation Manual, 1976. Bd. dirs. Detroit Med. Ctr., 1990-94, Harper-Grace Hosps., 1982-91, DMC Health Care Ctrs., 1984-94, New Detroit, 1986-87, Elizabethtown Coll., 1981-93, Met. Detroit YMCA, 1982-94, Mich. Colls. Found., 1981-96, Detroit Symphony Orch., 1983-88, Detroit Receiving Hosp. Univ. Clinic, 1988-94, Grace Hosp., 1991-92; trustee Bloomfield Hills Bd. Edn., 1992-2000. 1st lt. Fin. Corps, USAR, 1966-72. Recipient Educate for Svc. award Elizabethtown Coll., 1966. Fellow Am. Coll. Bankruptcy, Life Mgmt. Inst.; mem. AICPA (Elijah Watt Sells Gold medal award 1965), Am. Bankruptcy Inst., Mich. Assn. CPAs, Am. Inst. CPAs, Bloomfield Hills Country Club, Orchard Lake County, The Sanctuary Golf Club. Office: Handleman Co 500 Kirts Blvd Troy MI 48084 also: Alix Partners LLC 2000 Town Ctr Ste 2400 Southfield MI 48075-1463

KOCH, CHARLES DE GANAHL, industrial company executive; b. Wichita, Kans., Nov. 1, 1935; s. Fred Chase and Mary Clementine (Robinson) Koch; m. Liz Koch; 2 children. BS in Gen. Engring, MIT, 1957, MS in Mech. Engring., 1958, MSChemE, 1959; DSc (hon.), George Mason U.; JD (hon.), Babson Coll.; PhD in Commerce (hon.), Washburn U. Engr. Arthur D. Little, Inc., Cambridge, Mass., 1959-61; v.p. Koch Engring. Co., Inc., Wichita, 1961-63, pres., 63-71, chmn., 1967-78; pres. Koch Industries, Inc., Wichita, 1966-74, chmn., CEO, 1967—. Bd. dirs. Intrust Bank, N.A., Mercatus Ctr. Chmn. Inst. Humane Studies, Claude R. Lambe Charitable Found., Charles G. Koch Charitable Found. Named one of World's Richest People, Forbes mag., 1999—, Forbes Richest Ams., 2006; recipient Entrepreneurial Leadership award, Nat. Found. for Tchg. Entrepreneurship, Adam Smith award, Am. Legis. Exch. Coun., Brotherhood/Sisterhood award, Nat. Conf. Christians and Jews, Disting. Citizen award, Boy Scouts of Am., Free Enterprise award, Coun. Nat. Policy, Spirit of Justice award, Heritage Found., Dir.'s award for global vision in energy, NY Merc. Exch., 1999, Nat. Disting. Svc. award, Tax Found., 2000. Mem.: Flint Hills Nat., Mt. Pelerin Soc., The Vintage Club. Office: Koch Industries PO Box 2256 4111 E 37th St N Wichita KS 67220

KOCH, CHARLES JOHN, credit agency executive; Pres., COO, CEO Charter One Bank FSB, 1976—; pres. Charter One Fin. Inc., Cleve., First Fed. Savings Ball. Office: Charter One Fin Inc 1215 Superior Ave E Cleveland OH 44114-3249

KOCH, CHRISTOPHER A., school system administrator; Grad., So. Ill. U.; MA, PhD in Ednl. Policy and Leadership, George Washington U. Adminstr. Office of Vocational and Adult Edn. US Dept. Edn.; dir. spl. edn. Ill. State Bd. Edn. (ISBE), Springfield, 2001—06, chief edn. officer, 2002—03, interim state supt., 2006—07, state supt., 2007—. Mem.: Nat. Assn. of Dirs. of Spl. Edn. Office: Ill State Bd Edn 100 N 1st St Springfield IL 62777 Office Phone: 866-262-6663.

KOCH, DAVID HAMILTON, chemical company executive; b. Wichita, Kans., May 3, 1940; m. Julia Koch; children: David Jr., Mary Julia, John Mark. BSChemE, MIT, 1962, MSChemE, 1963. Rsch. engr. and process design engr. Amicon Corp., Cambridge, 1963-64, Arthur D. Little, Inc., Cambridge, Mass., 1964-67, Halcon Internat., Inc., NYC, 1967-70, Sci. Design Comp. (affiliate of Halcon Internat., Inc.), NYC; with Koch Industries, Inc., Wichita, Kans., 1970—, exec. v.p., 1981—, bd. dirs.; chmn. bd. dirs., CEO Chem. Tech. Grp., LLC (subs. Koch Industries, Inc.). Bd. dirs. Hosp. for Spl. Surgery, NYC. Bd. trustees Meml. Sloan Kettering, NYC (also mem. bd. overseers and managers), House Ear Inst., LA, Johns Hopkins U., Prostate Cancer Found., LA; gov. NY Presbyn. Hosp., NYC, Deerfield Acad., Mass.; bd. dirs. Am. Mus. Natural Hist., NYC, Aspen Inst., Colo., Inst. Human Origins, Phoenix, Ariz., Rockefeller U., NYC, MIT (life mem. of corp.), Reason Found., Santa Monica, Calif., CATO Inst., Washington, TV Sta. WNET, NYC; bd. overseers, tV Sta. WGBH, Boston; bd. visitor, M.D. Anderson Cancer Adv. Bd., Houston, Tex.; bd. assoc., Whitehead Inst., Cambridge, Mass.; bd. advs. John Hopkins Med. Ctr.; chmn.'s coun. Met. Mus. Art, YC; mem. Libertarian Party Candidate for V.P. US, 1980; vice-chmn., bd. dir Am. Ballet Theatremem; nat. dinner chmn. Rep. Gov.'s Assn., 1999; active Nat. Cancer Adv. Bd., James Madison Coun., Libr. Congress, Washington. Named a honoree, NY Acad. Medicine's 10th Ann. Gala, 2004; named in honor David H. Koch Bldg., MIT; named one of World's Richest People, Forbes mag., 2001—, Forbes Richest Ams., 2006; recipient Businessman of Yr., Manhattan Rep. Party, 2002, Corp. Citizenship award, Woodrow Wilson Internat. Ctr. Scholars, 2004, Entrepreneurial Leadership award, Nat. Found. for Tchg. Entrepreneurship, Award for Excellence in Corp. Leadership, Soc. Meml. Sloan-Kettering, 2005. Mem. River Club (NY), Racquet & Tennis Club (NY), Explorers Club (NY), numerous others. Avocations: skiing, tennis, golf. Office: Koch Industries, Inc 667 Madison Ave 22nd Fl New York NY 10021-8029 also: Koch Industries, Inc 4111 E 37th St N Wichita KS 67220 Office Phone: 212-319-1100, 316-828-5500. Business E-Mail: david.koch@kochchemtech.com.

KOCH, DAVID VICTOR, librarian, administrator; b. Highland, Ill., Feb. 19, 1937; s. Victor Hugo and Eunice Louise (Matter) K.; m. Noel Janet Wyandt, July 15, 1959 (div. 1968); 1 child, John David; m. Carolyn Melvin, Mar. 21, 1970 (div. 1979); 1 child, Victor Louis; m. Loretta Marie Peterson, Aug. 25, 1979; 1 child, Elizabeth Louise. BA in Lit., DePauw U., 1959; MA in English and Modern Lit., So. Ill. U., 1963, postgrad., U. Cin. Reporter, columnist Dayton (Ohio) Jour. Herald newspaper, 1959-61; instr. dept. English Wright State U., Dayton, 1964-69; asst. rare books libr. Morris Libr., So. Ill. U., Carbondale, 1961-64, rare books libr., 1970-80, curator spl. collections, univ. archivist, 1980-91, dir. spl. collections and devel., 1991-96, assoc. dean spl. collections and devel. svcs., 1997—. Mem. Midwest Archives Conf., 1980—; mem. Conf. of Editors of Learned Jours., 1974—; mem. univ. acad./student affairs com. So. Ill. U., Carbondale, 1984-86, univ. rsch. com., 1980-82, 97—, libr. affairs mgmt. com., 1991—, libr. affairs exec. com., 1991—, univ. libr. of the future com., 1992—; mem. adv. bd. Ill. State Archives, 1997—, Ill. State Hist. Records, 1997-99, internal rev. com., Internat. Edn. Assn., 1999—. Editor: (with Joseph Katz and Dick Allen) The Mad River Review, 1965-68, (with Alan Cohn and Kenneth Duckett) ICarbS; contbr. articles to profl. jours. Home: 2800 W Sunset Dr Carbondale IL 62901-2046 Office: So Ill U Spl Collections Morris Libr Carbondale IL 62901-6632

KOCH, DONALD LEROY, retired geologist, state agency administrator; b. Dubuque, Iowa, June 3, 1937; s. Gregory John and Josephine Elizabeth (Young) K.; m. Celia Jean Swede, July 5, 1962; children: Kyle Benjamin, Amy Suzanne, Nathan Gregory. BS, U. Iowa, 1959, MS in Geology, 1967, postgrad., 1971-73. Research geologist Iowa Geol. Survey, Iowa City, 1959-71, chief subsurface geology, 1971-75, asst. state geologist, 1975-80, state geologist and dir., 1980-86; state geologist and bur. chief Geol. Survey Bur., Iowa City, 1986—2002; ret., 2002—. Contbr. articles to profl. jours. Fellow Iowa Acad. Sci. (bd. dirs. 1986-89); mem. Geol. Soc. Iowa (pres. 1969), Iowa Groundwater Assn. (pres. 1986), Rotary, Sigma Xi. Avocations: bicycling, camping, chess, coin collecting/numismatics. Home: 1431 Prairie Du Chien Rd Iowa City IA 52245-5615 E-mail: statefossil@aol.com.

KOCH, ERIC ALLAN, state representative; b. 1964; BSBA, Georgetown U.; JD, Ind. U. Ptnr. Applegate McDonald & Koch, P.C.; state rep. dist. 65 Ind. Ho. of Reps., Indpls., 2003—, mem. agr. natural resources and rural devel., cts. and criminal code, and tech. R & D coms. Basketball coach Bedford Boys Club; chmn. bd. Dunn Meml. Hosp.; mem. PL221 Sch. Improvement com. Parkview Intermediate Sch.; past bd. mem. Ind. Heritage Arts. Mem.: Ind. Farm Bur., NRA, Brown County Art Guild (patron mem.), Brown County Art Gallery Found. Republican. Office: Ind Ho of Reps 200 W Washington S Indianapolis IN 46204-2786

KOCH, LORETTA PETERSON, librarian, educator; b. Anna, Ill., Mar. 5, 1951; d. Vance G. and Dorothy M. (Cline) Peterson; m. David Victor Koch, Aug. 25, 1979; 1 child, Elizabeth; stepchildren: John, Victor. AB in in English with high honors, U. Ill., 1973, MS in LS, 1974; postgrad., So. Ill. U., Carbondale, 1976. Adult svcs. libr. Carbondale Pub. Libr., 1974-81; owner, operator L. Koch-Words, editing and word processing, Carbondale, 1981-85; rsch. asst. So. Ill. U., 1973, asst. humanities libr., 1985-86, libr. tech. asst. III humanities div., 1986-89, asst. humanities libr., 1989-92, acting humanities libr., 1992-93, humanities libr., 1993—, asst. prof. libr. affairs, 1989-95, assoc. prof. libr. affairs Carbondale, 1995—, mem. faculty exec. bd., 1989-91. Participant confs. and workshops; presenter in field; field reader grant proposals Ill. Coop. Collection Mgmt. Coordinating Com., 1993. Contbr. articles to profl. publs. Divsn. coord. fund drive United Way, 1989, 90; room parent Lakeland Sch., 1993-94, Parrish Sch., 1994-95, 95-96, 96-97, Thomas Sch., 1998-99, 99-2000; asst. leader troop 813, Girl Scouts U.S.A., 1993-94. Mem. ALA (chmn. poster session abstracts booklet com. 1993-94), Assn. of Coll. and Rsch. Libr. (comm. com. women's studies sect. 1993-95), Libr. Adminstrn. and Mgmt. Assn. (using stats. for libr. evaluation com.), Reference and adult svcs. divsn. Ill. Libr. Assn. (nominations com. resources and tech. svcs. forum 1993-94), Margaret Atwood Soc., Midwest Assn. for Can. Studies, Assn. for Can. Studies in U.S., Beta Phi Mu. Home: 2800 W Sunset Dr Carbondale IL 62901-2046 Office: So Ill U Humanities Div Morris Libr Carbondale IL 62901 E-mail: lkoch@lib.siu.edu.

KOCH, ROBERT LOUIS, II, manufacturing company executive, mechanical engineer; b. Evansville, Ind., Jan. 6, 1939; s. Robert Louis and Mary L. (Bray) K.; m. Cynthia Ross, Oct. 17, 1964; children: David, Kevin, Kristen, Jennifer. BSME, U. Notre Dame, 1960; MBA, U. Pitts., 1962; D of Tech. (hon.), Vincennes U., 1992, Ivy Tech State Coll., 2002. Registered profl. engr., Ind. V.p. Ashdee Corp., Evansville, 1962-68, pres., 1968-82; ptnr. Fesk Partnership, Evansville, 1964—; chmn., CEO Gibbs Die Casting Corp., Henderson, Ky., 1976—; pres., CEO Koch Enterprises, Inc., Evansville, 1982—; chmn., dir. UNISEAL, Inc., Evansville, 1984—2005; v.p., dir. Brake Supply Co., Evansville, 1986—; chmn. bd. Marco Sales, Inc., St. Louis, 1997—. Exec. in residence U. So. Ind., Evansville, 1967; bd. dirs. Fifth-Third Bancorp, Cincinnati, Ohio, Bindley Western Industries, Indpls., So. Ind. Properties, Inc., Evansville, So. Ind. Minerals, Inc., N.Am. Green, Inc., Audubon Metals LLC, Ind. Econ. Devel. Corp.; lead dir. Vectren Corp.; chmn. bd. dirs. Uniseal Rubber Products, Inc., Arnold, Mo., 1988-95. Inventor, patentee water purifier, drying oven, powder coating booth, electro painting system. Contr., dep. mayor City of Evansville, 1976-80; active Gov.'s Fiscal Policy Adv. Com., Indpls., 1978-89, Pres. Adv. Coun. Indiana Univ., 1992—, Purdue U., 1992—, parents exec. com., West Lafayette, 1985-88, sch. bd. nominating com., 1987-89; vice-chmn. bd. trustees U. Evansville, 1985-92, chmn. bd. trustees, 1993-96; pres. Signature Sch. Found. Inc., Evansville, 1994—, pres. bd. dirs., 2001; vice-chmn. bd. trustees Evansville Mus. Arts and Scis., 1982-92; bd. dirs. SW Ind. Pub. Broadcasting, 1985-89, Pub. Edn. Found., Evansville, 1986-88, Hoosiers for Higher Edn., 1991-98, Commit, Inc., Cmty. Alliance Found., 1991—, Ind. Colls. Ind., 1992—, Found. for Ind. Higher Edn., 1996-2000, Project E, 2000-04; treas. Vanderburgh County Rep. Com., Evansville, 1984-88; pres. Cath. Edn. Found., Evansville, 1978-82; chmn. Ind. Econ. Devel. Coun., 1991-92, Ind. Humanities Coun. Bus. Forum, 1999, United Way of Southwestern Ind. Campaign, 1998; co-chmn. Ind. Bus. Higher Edn. Forum, 1991-96; pres. Cath. Found. Southwestern Ind., 1992—; v.p. Ind. Acad., Indpls., 1999--; pres. Evansville Regional Bus. Com., 2002--. 1st lt. USAR, 1961-67. Recipient Challenger award Nat. Assn. Woodworking Machinery Mfrs., Louisville, 1980, Boy Scout's Disting. Citizen's award, 1991, Rotary Club Citizenship award, 1991, Sagamore of the Wabash, 1999; named Exec. of Yr. Profl. Secs. Assn., 1984, Knight of the Order of the Holy Sepulchre, 1996, Entrepreneur of Yr., Ind. Mfg., 1998, Ind. Bus. Leader of Yr. Ind. C. of C., 2002, Evansville Bus. Hall of Fame, 2006. Mem. Metro Evansville C. of C. (bd. dirs. Met. 1983-96, named Bus. Person of Yr. 1998), Ind. C. of C. (bd. dirs., chmn. 1991—), Young Pres. Orgn., World Pres. Orgn., Evansville Country Club, Victoria Nat. Golf Club. Avocations: golf, tennis, skiing. Office: Koch Enterprises Inc 10 S 11th Ave Evansville IN 47744-0001

KOCH, STEVEN, lawyer, investment banker, finance company executive; b. Evanston, Ill., Feb. 9, 1956; s. David and Sylvia (Kurtzon) K.; m. Ellen Liebman, May 17, 1986 (dec. Dec. 2005). BA, Hampshire Coll., Amherst, Mass., 1977; MBA, JD, U. Chgo., 1982. Bar: Ill. 1982. Law clk. to judge U.S. Ct. Appeals (7th cir.), 1982—83; assoc. Lehman Bros. Kuhn Loeb, NYC, 1983—85; joined First Boston (now Credit Suisse), 1985, mng. dir., 1989—93, co-head mergers and acquisitions group, 1993—2000, co-chmn. mergers and acquisitions group, 2000—; vice chmn. Credit Suisse, 2000—. Bd. mem. Mount Sinai Hosp. Med. Ctr., Chgo., Greater Chgo. Food Depository. Office: Credit Suisse Securities USA LLC 227 W Monroe St Chicago IL 60606-5016 Office Phone: 312-750-3000. Business E-Mail: Steven.Koch@credit-suisse.com.

KOCHAR, MAHENDR SINGH, physician, health facility administrator, research scientist, educator, writer, consultant; b. Jabalpur, India, Nov. 30, 1943; arrived in U.S., 1967, naturalized, 1978; s. Harnam Singh and Chanan Kaur Kochar; m. Arvind Kaur, 1968; children: Baltej (Baj), Ajay (Jay). MB, BS, All India Inst. Med. Scis., New Delhi, 1965; MSc, Med. Coll. Wis., 1972; MBA, U. Wis., Milw., 1987. Diplomate Am. Bd. Internal Medicine, Nephrology and Geriat., Am. Bd. Family Practice, Am. Bd. Mgmt., Am. Bd. Clin. Pharmacology. Intern All India Inst. Med. Scis. Hosp., New Delhi, 1966—67, Passaic Gen. Hosp., NJ, 1967—68; resident medicine Allegheny Gen. Hosp., Pitts., 1968—70; fellow clin. pharmacology Milw. VA Med. Ctr., 1970—71, attending physician, 1973; fellow nephrology and hypertension Milw. County Gen. Hosp., 1971—73, attending physician, 1973—95, St. Michael Hosp., Milw., 1974—, dir. hemodialysis unit, 1975—80; clin. asst. prof. medicine and pharmacology and toxicology Med. Coll. Wis., Milw., 1973—75, asst. prof., 1975—78, assoc. prof., 1978—84, prof., 1984—, assoc. dean continuing med. edn., 1985—86, assoc. dean grad. med. edn., 1987—99, sr. assoc. dean acad. affairs, 1994—95, sr. assoc. dean grad. med. edn., 1999—. Attending physician St. Joseph's Hosp., Milw., 1975—; chmn. medicine Northpoint Med. Group, Milw., 1974-75; dir. Milw. Blood Pressure Program, 1975-78; dir. Hypertension Clinic, Milw. County Downtown Med. and Health Services, 1975-79; chief hypertension. VA Med. Ctr., Milw., 1978-2000, assoc. chief staff edn., 1979-2000; exec. dir. Med. Coll. Wis. Affiliated Hosps. Inc., Milw., 1987—; bd. dir. Accreditation Coun. Grad. Med. Edn., Milw. Author: Hypertension Control, 1978, 2nd rev. edit., 1985; editor: Textbook of General Medicine, 1983, Concise Textbook of Medicine, 2d edit., 1990, 3d edit. 1998, 4th edit., 2003. Recipient Grad. of Last Decade award U. Wis., Milw., 1998, Disting. Alumnus award, 2004, Disting. Svc. award Med. Coll. of Wis., 1998. Fellow ACP (pres., gov. Wis. chpt. 1994-98, bd. regents 1997-2003, chmn. bd. govs. 1998-99, Laureate award 2000, Key Contact award 2001, master 2004), Am. Coll. Cardiology (gov. dept. vets. affair, 1999-2000), Am. Coll. Clin. Pharmacology, Am. Heart Assn. (high blood pressure coun.), Royal Coll. Physicians (London), Am. Coll. Physician Execs.; mem. AMA (del. Wis., mem. coun. on med. edn. 2005—), Am. Assn. Physicians from India (pres. Wis. chpt. 1995-97, Most Disting. Physician award 2004), Am. Fedn. Med. Rsch., Milw. Acad. Medicine (pres. 1996-97, trustee 1997-2003, pres.'s award 1998), Milwaukee County Med. Soc. (bd. dirs. 2000-2002, pres. elect 2002-03, pres. 2003, Disting. Svc. award 2005), Wis. Med. Soc. (dels. AMA, bd. dirs., Disting. Svc. award 2001), Soc. Tchg. Scholars. Office: Med Coll Wis 8701 Watertown Plank Rd Milwaukee WI 53226

KOCHER, JUANITA FAY, retired auditor; b. Falmouth, Ky., Aug. 9, 1933; d. William Birgest and Lula (Gillespie) Vickroy; m. Donald Edward Kocher, Nov. 18, 1953. Grad. high sch., Bright, Ind. Cert. internal auditor and compliance officer. Bookkeeper Mchts. Bank and Trust Co., West Harrison, Ind., 1952-56, teller, asst. cashier, 1962-87, br. mgr., 1979-87, internal auditor, 1987-96, ret., 1996; bookkeeper Progressive Bank, New Orleans, 1956-58; with proof dept. 1st Nat. Bank, Cin., Ohio, 1958-59, teller Harrison, Ohio, 1959-62. Bookkeeper Donald E. Kocher Constrn., Harrison, 1981—. Mem. Am. Bankers Assn., Ind. Bankers Assn. Home: 11277 Biddinger Rd Harrison OH 45030

KOCORAS, CHARLES PETROS, federal judge; b. Chgo., Mar. 12, 1938; s. Petros K. and Constantina (Cordonis) K.; m. Grace L. Finlay, Sept. 22, 1968; children: Peter, John, Paul. Student, Wilson Jr. Coll., 1956-58; BS, DePaul U., 1961, JD, 1969. Bar: Ill. 1969. Various positions IRS, Chgo., 1962-69; assoc. Bishop & Crawford, 1969-71; 1st asst. US atty. (no. dist.) Ill. US Dept. Justice, Chgo., 1971-77; chmn. Ill. Commerce Commn., Chgo., 1977-79; ptnr. Stone, McGuire, Benjamin and Kocoras, Chgo., 1979-80; judge US Dist. Ct. (no. dist.) Ill., Chgo., 1980—2006, chief judge, 2002—06, sr. judge, 2006—. Adj. prof. trial practice, evening divsn. John Marshall Law Sch., 1975—. With Army N.G., 1961-67. With Ill. Nat. Guard USAR, 1961—67. Mem. Chgo. Bar Assn., Fed. Criminal Jury Instrn. Com. 7th Cir., Beta Alpha Psi. Greek Orthodox. Office: US Courthouse 2588 Dirksen Bldg 219 S Dearborn St Chicago IL 60604-1702

KOEBEL, SISTER CELESTIA, health care system executive; b. Chillicothe, Ohio, Jan. 12, 1928; BS, Coll. of Mount St. Joseph, 1958; MHA, St. Louis U., 1964; D, U. Albuquerque, 1976. Asst. dir. nursing svcs. Good Samaritan Hosp. & Health Ctr., Dayton, Ohio, 1961-62; adminstrv. resident Providence Med. Ctr., Seattle, 1963-64; pres. St. Joseph Healthcare Corp., Albuquerque, 1964-85, Sisters of Charity Health Care Systems, Cin., 1985-96; hon. offcl. Cath. Health Initiatives, Denver, 1996—. Mem. Am. Hosp. Assn. (adv. coun., 1987-88), N.Mex. Hosp. Assn. (treas. 1968-69, v.p. 1970, pres. 1972).

KOEHLER, JANE ELLEN, librarian; b. Belleville, Ill., Oct. 18, 1944; d. Edward William and Elizabeth Ellen (Sanford) Hindman; m. Robert Philip Koehler, Feb. 18, 1936; children: Clare Anne, Beth Ellen. BS, Eastern Ill. U., 1967; MS, U. Ill., 1970. Cert. edn. educator. Library asst. Belleville (Ill.) Pub. Library, 1964-65; tchr. librarian Sch. Dist. 72, Woodstock, Ill., 1966-73; dir. library services Sch. Dist. 200, Woodstock, 1969-73; dir. youth services Woodstock Pub. Library, 1980-89, asst. dir., 1989—. Author: (short story) Northwest Herald, 1980; columnist Woodstock Ind., 2001—. Bd. dir. Auxillary Mem. Hosp.; vol. Turning Point (Crisis Intervention), 1978-88; mem. Ill. Literary Heritage Com., 1984-85; chmn. Mem. Hosp. for Mem. Library Adminstr. Coun. of orthern Ill. (sec. 1990), Woodstock Fine Arts Assn. Republican. Roman Catholic. Avocations: writing, swimming, skiing, guilting, travel, theater. Home: 13171 Hickory Ln Woodstock IL 60098-3617 Office: Woodstock Pub Library 414 W Judd St Woodstock IL 60098-3131

KOEHLER, JIM, electronics executive; CFO Micro Electronics Inc., Columbus, Ohio. Office: Micro Electronics Inc PO Box 1143 Hilliard OH 43026-6143

KOELINER, LAURETTE, manufacturing executive, human resources specialist; b. Bklyn, Oct. 21, 1954; BA Bus. Mgmt., U. Ctrl. Fla.; MBA, Stetson U., Deland, Fla. From contract analyst to mgr. contracts and pricing for Missile Systems Co. McDonnell, Douglas, Titusville, Fla., 1978—88, bus. mgr. Tomahwk Cruise Missile Program, 1988—89, dir. strategic and bus planning Tomahawk, 1989—90, head internal support and service ops. Titusville, 1990—92, dir. structuring and managinoverhead budget St. Louis, 1992—94, dir. human resources, security, 1994—96; dir. internal audit, mgmt. control systems and exec. devel. McDonnell Douglas-Boeimg, St. Louis, 1996—99; v.p. corp. controller Boeing Co., Seattle, 1999—2002; exec. v.p., chief people and adminsrn. officer The Boeing Co., Chgo., 2002—. Bd, dirs. Sara Lee Corp. Mem. Adv. Coun. U. Portland (Oreg.)., New Leaders for New Schs., Chgo.; Intiman Theater Seattle. Named to Hall of Fame, U. Ctrl. Fla. Coll. Bus. Adminstrn., 2003. Mem.: Soc. for Human Resource Mgmt., Econ. Club Chgo., Chicagoland C. of C. (bd. dirs.), Nat. Contracts Mgmt. Assn. Office: The Boeing Co 100 N Riverside Pla Chicago IL 60606

KOELLNER, LAURETTE, aerospace transportation executive; b. Bklyn., Oct. 21, 1954; B in Bus. Mgmt., U. Ctrl. Fla.; MBA, Stetson U. Cert. contracts mgr. Nat. Contracts Mgmt. Assn. Analyst contracts, advanced to various positions McDonnell Douglas, 1978—86, mgr. contracts and pricing missle sys. co. Titusville, Fla., 1986—88, bus. mgr. Tomahawk Cruise Missle prog., 1988—89, dir. strategic and bus. planning, 1989—90, head internal support and svcs. ops. missle prodn. facility, 1990—92; budget mgr. McDonnell Douglas Aerospace, St. Louis, 1992—94, dir. human resources divisn., 1994—96, v.p., gen. auditor, 1996—97, Boeing Co. (formerly McDonnell Douglas), St. Louis, 1997—99, v.p., corp. controller, 1999—2004, exec. v.p., 2004—; pres. Connexion by Boeing, 2004—06, Boeing Internat., 2006—. Bd. dirs. Sara Lee Corp., Exostar, Chgo. Coun. Fgn. Rels., Chicagoland C. of C.; mem. bd. regents U. Portland; mem. dean's exec. coun. coll. bus. adminstrn. U. Ctrl. Fla. Named to Hall of Fame, U. Ctrl. Fla., 2003. Mem.: Economic Club Chgo. Office: Boeing World Hdqs 100 N Riverside Chicago IL 60606 Office Phone: 312-544-2000.

KOENEMANN, CARL F., retired electronics company executive; b. Chicago; CFO Motorola, Inc., Schaumburg, Ill., exec. v.p., CFO, 1991—2002.

KOENIG, JACK LEONARD, chemist, educator; b. Cody, Nebr., Feb. 12, 1933; s. John and Lucille (Ewart) K.; m. Jeanus Brosz, July 5, 1953; children: John, Robert, Stan, Lori. BS, Yankton Coll., 1955; MS, U. Nebr., 1957, PhD, 1959. Chemist E. I. DuPont, Wilmington, Del., 1959-63; prof. Case Western Res. U., Cleve., 1963—. Program officer NSF, Washington, 1972-74. Author: Chemical Microstructure of Polymer Chains, 1982, Spectroscopy of Polymers, 1992; co-author: Physical Chemistry of Polymers, 1985, Theory of Vibrational Spectroscopy of Polymers, 1987. With U.S. Army, 1953-55. Recipient Disting. Lectr. award BASF, 1990, Internat. Rsch. award Soc. Plastics Engrs., 1991, Disting. Svc. award Cleve. Tech. Socs. Coun., 1991, Pioneer in Polymer Sci. award Polymer New Mag., 1991, ACS award in applied polymer sci. Am. Chem. Soc., 1997. Fellow Am. Physics Soc.; mem. NAE, Am. Chem. Soc. (award in applied polymer sci. 1997), Soc. Applied Spectroscopy. Achievements include research in characterization of polymers by spectroscopic methods. Office: Case Western Res U 10900 Euclid Ave # 7202 Cleveland OH 44106-1712 Business E-Mail: Jack.Koenig@case.edu, jlkg@case.edu.

KOENIG, MICHAEL EDWARD DAVISON, information science educator; b. Rochester, NY, Nov. 1, 1941; s. Claremont Judson and Mary Fletcher (Davison) K.; m. Nancy Crane Packard, 1966 (div. 1976); children: Christopher Wells Bowen, Davison Packard; m. Luciana Marulli, Feb. 2, 1980. BA in Psychology, Yale U., 1963; MLS, U. Chgo., 1968, MBA, 1970; PhD in Information Sci., Drexel U., 1982. Info. svcs. mgr. Pfizer, Inc., Groton, Conn., 1970-74; info. ops. dir. Inst. Scientific Info., Phila., 1974-77, devel. dir., 1977-78; v.p. ops. Swets N.Am., Berwyn, Pa., 1978-80; assoc. prof. Columbia U., NYC, 1980-85; v.p. info. mgmt. Tradenet, Inc., NYC, 1985-88; prof., dean sch. libr. and info. sci. Dominican U., River Forest, Ill., 1988-96, prof., dean emeritus, 1996-99; dean Coll. Info. and Computer Sci. Long Island U., Brookville, NY, 1999—2005, prof. Coll. Info. and Computer Sci., 2005—. Chmn. editl. bd. Third World Librs., 1991-96. Contbr. more than 100 articles to profl. jours. Lt. USNR, 1963-65. Mem. ALA (councilor 1993-97, 01-05), Am. Soc. Info. Sci., Internat. Soc. Scientometrics and Informetrics (pres. 1995-97), Assn. Computing Machinery, Spl. Librs. Assn., Grolier Club, Caxton Club, Elizabethan Club. Home: 16 Buckwalter Farm Ln Phoenixville PA 19460-2317 Home Phone: 610-933-5039; Office Phone: 516-299-2176. E-mail: michael.koenig@liu.edu.

KOENIGSKNECHT, ROY A., dean; b. Fowler, Mich., Dec. 27, 1942; s. Joseph I. and Katherine (Zimmermann) K.; m. Marilie A. Dani, Aug. 20, 1966; children: John, Adam, Amanda. AB in Psychology, Central Mich. U., 1964; MA in Speech and Lang. Pathology, Northwestern U., 1965, PhD in Communicative Disorders, 1968. Head speech and lang. pathology Northwestern U., Evanston, Ill., 1973-78, prof. speech and lang. pathology, 1975-85, chair communicative disorders, 1978-81, assoc. dean Grad. Sch., 1981-85; prof. speech and hearing sci. Ohio State U, Columbus, 1985—; dean Grad. Sch. Ohio State U., Columbus, 1985-95; v.p. Ohio State U. Rsch. Found., Columbus, 1985-95. Mem. Grad. Record Exams. Bd., 1991-95, NIH adv. bd. on deafness and other communicative disorders, 1990-95; cons. evaluator Commn. on Instns. Higher Edn., 1996—. Author: Developmental Sentence Analysis, 1974; Interactive Language Development, 1975. Contbr. articles to profl. jours. Mem. adv. coun. on grad. study Ohio Bd. Regents, Columbus, 1985-95; bd. dirs. Friends of Evanston Pub. Libr., 1984, Evanston Pub. Libr., 1985. Recipient Disting. Alumni award Central Mich. U., 1977; Fulbright fellow, 1982. Fellow Am. Speech-Lang. Hearing Assn. (exec. bd. 1986-91, pres. 1990), AAU Assn. Grad. Schs.), Com. on Instnl. Cooperation Grad. Deans (chair 1985-86), Nat. Assn. State U. and Land Grant Colls.-Coun. Rsch. Pol. and Grad. Edn. (exec. com. 1995-96), Torch Club Columbus (pres. 2005-2006). Avocations: golf, skiing. Home: 720 Gatehouse Ln Columbus OH 43235-1732 Office: Ohio State U 105 Pressey Hall Columbus OH 43210-1335 Home Phone: 614-888-8339; Office Phone: 614-292-8118. Business E-Mail: koenigsknecht.1@oso.edu.

KOENKER, DIANE P., history professor; b. Chgo., July 29, 1947; m. Roger Koenker; 1 child. AB in History, Grinnell Coll., 1969; AM in Comparative Studies in History, U. Mich., 1971, PhD in History, 1976. From asst. prof. to assoc. prof. in history Temple U., Phila., 1976-83; asst. prof. history U. Ill., Urbana-Champaign, 1983-86, assoc. prof., 1986-88, prof. history, 1988—, dir. Russian and East European Ctr., 1990-96, editor Slavic Rev., 1996—2006. Vis. lectr. history U. Ill., Urbana-Champaign, 1975; vis. fellow Australian Nat. U., 1989, Fulbright-Hays Faculty Rsch. Abroad, 1993; lectr. in field. Author: Moscow Workers and the 1917 Revolution, 1981, paperback edit., 1986, (with William G. Rosenberg) Strikes and Revolution in Russia 1917, 1989, Republic of Labor: Russian Printers and Soviet Socialism, 1918-1930, 2005; editor: Third All-Russian Trade Union Conference 1917, 1982, (with William G. Rosenberg and Ronald Grigor Suny) Party, State and Society in the Russian Civil War: Explorations in Social History, 1989, (with Ronald D. Bachman) Revelations from the Russian Archives, 1997, (with Anne E. Gorsuch) Truizm: The Russian and East European Tourist under Capitalism and Socialism, 2006; editor, translator: (with S.A. Smith) Notes of a Red Guard, 1993; mem. editl. bd. Cambridge Soviet Paperbacks; mem. adv. bd. Soviet Studies in History, 1986-89; book reviewer to numerous jours.; contbr. articles to profl. jours. Fellow Temple U., 1977, 82, Russian Inst.-Columbia U., 1977-78, NEH, 1983-84, NEH, 1984-85, 94-95, MUCIA Exch. fellow Moscow State U., 1991, Guggenheim Found., 2006; grantee Am. Coun. Learned Socs.-Social Sci. Rsch. Coun., 1977-78, Temple U., 1979-81, 82-83, William and Flora Hewlett Internat. Rsch. grant, 1986, 91, Nat. Coun. for Soviet and East European Rsch., 1989, Arnold O. Beckman Rsch. Bd. grant, 1990-91, 2002—, IREX Travel grant, 1993, 2006, Nat. coun. Eurasian and East European Rsch. grant, 2007; recipient Fulbright-Hays Faculty Rsch. award for USSR, 1989. Mem. Am. Hist. Assn. (mem. membership com. 1996-98, European History sect. chair 2001, Chester Higby prize European sect. 2003), Am. Assn. Advancement Slavic Studies (bd. dirs. 1996—), Midwest Workshop of Russian and Soviet Historians, Assn. Women in Slavic Studies. also: U Ill Dept History 810 S Wright St Urbana IL 61801-3644

KOEPPEL, HOLLY KELLER, electric power industry executive; b. Pitts., May 17, 1958; married; 2 children. BS in Bus., Ohio State U., Columbus; MS in Bus., Ohio State U. From mgr. to v.p. Asia-Pacific Ops. Consolidated Natural Gas, Sydney, Australia, 1984—2000; v.p. new ventures for corp. devel. Am. Electric Power Co., Columbus, Ohio, 2000—02, exec. v.p. comml. ops., 2002—04, exec. v.p. AEP Utilities East, 2004—06, exec. v.p., CFO, 2006—. Office: Am Elec Power Co 1 Riverside Plz Columbus OH 43215-1000 Office Phone: 614-716-1000.

KOEPPEN, RAYMOND BRADLEY, lawyer; b. Valparaiso, Ind., July 9, 1954; s. Raymond Carl August and Thelma Gleda (Moore) K.; m. Debra Gail Ray, Dec. 21, 1985. BS, Ball State U., 1976; MA, Kent State U., Ohio, 1983; JD, Valparaiso U., 1983. Bar: Ind. 1984, Fla. 1984. Assoc. Sachs & Hess, P.C., Hammond, Ind., 1984-85, Lucas Holcomb Medrea, Merrillville, Ind., 1985; city atty. City of Valparaiso, 1985-88; ptnr. Clifford, Clauden, Alexa & Koeppen, Valparaiso, 1988-90; mng. ptnr. Douglas, Koeppen & Hurley, Valparaiso, 1991—. Mem. com. Valparaiso Popcorn Festival, 1985-97; mem. Valparaiso Econ. Devel. Corp., 1986, 87; mem. Valparaiso C. of C.; bd. dirs. Boys and Girls Club of Porter County, 1986—, chmn. bd. dirs., 1995-97. Greek Ministry of Culture and Sci. scholar, 1975; Fulbright scholar U.S. Ednl. Found., 1976. Mem. ABA, Ind. State Bar Assn., Porter County Bar Assn., Fla. Bar Assn., Phi Alpha Theta, Pi Gamma Mu, Beta Theta Pi. Presbyterian. Avocations: golf, basketball, reading, travel, community volunteering. Home: 2005 Beulah Vista Blvd Valparaiso IN 46383-2950 Office: Douglas Koeppen et al PO Box 209 14 Indiana Ave Valparaiso IN 46383-5634 Office Phone: 219-462-2126. Business E-Mail: bkoeppen@dkhlaw.org.

KOETZLE, GIL, state legislator, fire fighter, professional association administrator; b. Sioux Falls, SD, May 22, 1952; s. Donald John Sr. and Elizabeth Odilla (Lefebvre) K.; m. Debra Anne Phelps, Aug. 26, 1972; children: Jesse John, Stephanie Michael. Student, N.D. State Sch. Sci., 1970-72. Fire fighter, 1976-82; operator fire apparatus, 1982—; mem. S.D. Senate from 15th dist., Pierre, 1992—. Treas. Fire Fighters Local 814, Sioux Falls, 1980-81, sec., 1981-84, pres., 1984-85; state rep. Internat. Assn. Fire Fighters, 1985—; sec. Profl. Fire Fighters S.D., 1987-93, lobbyist, 1987-92. Ch. commentator and lector Roman Catholic Ch., mem. parish coun., leader parish youth group, head diocese social justice com. Named Outstanding Young Leader, S.d. Jaycees, 1992, Future Leader, Sioux Falls Argus Leader, 1990. Democrat. Avocations: golf, coaching sports, family, politics. Home: 705 N Prairie Ave Sioux Falls SD 57104-2220

KOFF, ROBERT HESS, academic administrator, adult education educator; b. Chgo., June 5, 1938; s. Arthur Karl and Dorothy (Hess) K. BA, U. Mich., 1961; MA, U. Chgo., 1962, PhD, 1966. Lic. psychologist, Calif. Instr., counselor S. Shankman Orthogenic Sch. U. Chgo., 1961—64; tchr. U. Chgo. Lab. Sch., 1963—64; instr. U. Ill., Champaign, 1964, U. Chgo., 1964—66; vis. scientist Lab. for Hypnosis Rsch., asst. prof. Stanford U., Calif., 1966—72; prof., dean Roosevelt U., Chgo., 1972—79; univ. dean SUNY, Albany, 1979—92; program dir., sr. v.p. Danforth Found., St. Louis, 1992—2003; prof., asst. vice chancellor Ctr. Advanced Learning Washington U., St. Louis, 2003—. Vis. scholar Oxford U., Eng., 1965; chmn. N.Y. State Ednl. Conf. Bd., Albany, 1981-92. Mem. Nat. Adv. Coun. on Edn. of Disadvantaged Children, Washington, 1979-82, Gov.'s Adv. Commn. on Children and Youth, Albany, 1981-92. Mem. APA (com. chmn.), Am. Ednl. Rsch. Assn., Nat. Register Health Svc. Providers in Psychology. Office: Ctr for Advanced Learning/Washington U Campus Box 1135 Saint Louis MO 63130 Office Phone: 314-935-5946.

KOGGE, PETER MICHAEL, computer scientist, educator; b. Washington, Dec. 3, 1946; s. Roy and Louise (McGrath) K.; m. Mary Ellen Clarke, June 12, 1971; children: Peter Michael, Mary Elizabeth, Timothy McGrath. BSEE, U. Notre Dame, 1968; MS in Systems Info. Scis., Syracuse U., 1970; PhDEE, Stanford U., 1973. Jr. engr. IBM, Owego, NY, 1968-72, staff engr., 1972-74, adv. engr., 1974-76, sr. engr., 1976-81, mem. sr. tech. staff, 1981-93; IBM fellow, 1993; McCourtney prof. computer sci. U. Notre Dame, Ind., 1994—, interim dept. chair computer sci. dept. Ind., 2000—01, prof. elec. engring., assoc. dean rsch. Coll. Engring Ind., 2001—. Adj. prof. computer scis. SUNY, Binghamton, 1977—94; past mem. rev. com. NSF Computing Divsn.; program chair 6th Symposium on Frontiers of Massively Parallel Computation, 1996; disting. vis. scientist NASA Jet Propulsion Lab., 1997; program com. Supercomputing, 1998, 99, 2000, 02, 03, 04, 05, Internat. Symposium on Computer Arch., 1999, Micro, 2005, Internat. Solid State Circuits Conf., 2003, 04, 05, 06, Internat. Conf. Supercomputing, 2003, 04, 05; program vice chair 7th Symposium on Frontiers of Massively Parallel Computation, 1999; program co-chmn. Great Lakes Conf. on VLSI, 2002. Author: Architecture of Pipelined Computers, 1980, Architecture of Symbolic Computers, 1991; editor conf. proc. Internat. Conf. on Parallel Processing, 1988. Recipient IBM Outstanding Innovation awards for Space Shuttle, IOP, 3838 Array Processor, AI Parallel Processor, Pres.'s award for patents, Daniel L. Slotnick award for most original paper Internat. Conf. Parallel Processing, 1994, Outstanding Computer Sci. and Engring. Dept. Instrn., 1999. Fellow IEEE; mem. Assn. for Computing Machinery, Am. Assn. Artificial Intelligence, IBM Acad. Tech. Roman Catholic. Office: U Notre Dame Dept Computer Sci and Engring 384 Fitzpatrick Hl Engrng Notre Dame IN 46556-5637 Business E-Mail: kogge@cse.nd.edu.

KOGUT, JOHN ANTHONY, wholesale distribution executive; b. Lackawanna, NY, Dec. 8, 1942; s. John J. and Rose J. (Gaj) K.; m. Deborah A. Hillman; children: David J., Robert J., Katherine A., Lindsey A., Kimberly M. BS in Pharmacy, U. Buffalo, 1965; MBA, Syracuse U., 1978. Pharmacist, mgr. Fay's Drug Co., Liverpool, NY, 1969-75, v.p., 1975-82, sr. v.p., 1982-89, pres., 1989-95; pres. Health Mart divsn., v.p. Franchise Svcs. FoxMeyer Corp., 1995-96; pres. Health Mart Divsn., v.p. mktg. McKesson Corp., 1996-99; pres. pharmac ops. Cmty. Health Svcs., Inc., Chgo., 1999—. Mem. N.Y. State Bd. Pharmacy, 1987-95. Served to capt. U.S. Army, 1966-69 Mem. Am. Pharm. Assn., Pharm. Soc. of State N.Y., Am. Mgmt. Assn., Nat. Assn. Chain Drug Stores (pharmacy affairs com. chmn. 1982-83), N.Y. State Bd. Pharmacy. Republican. Roman Catholic. Home Phone: 315-595-6670; Office Phone: 315-595-6170. Business E-Mail: jkogut@pharmacyaide.com.

KOHART, MARY BETH, real estate company executive; BS in Fin. and Real Estate, Ind. U., 1992, student in Spanish. Cert. comml. investment mem. Mem. staff valuation svcs. Sturges, Griffin, Trent & Co. (now CB Richard Ellis); with Hines; mem. staff to prin. office svcs., v.p. Colliers Turley Martin Tucker, Indpls., 1999. Bd. mem. Kappa Alpha Theta Alumni Assn. Mem.: Comml. Real Estate Women Network (pres. 2005), Soc. Indsl. and Office Realtors, Therapy Dogs Internat., Indpls. Jr. League. Office: Colliers Turley Martin Tucker 1 American Sq Ste 1300 Indianapolis IN 46282 Office Phone: 317-639-0487. Office Fax: 317-639-0504. E-mail: mkohart@ctmt.com.

KOHL, DAVID, dean, emeritus librarian; b. Grand Island, Nebr., July 31, 1942; s. D. Franklin and La Vern Harriet (De Long) K; m. Marilyn L. Kohl, Sept. 28, 1969 (div. 1986); 1 child: Nathaniel F. BA cum laude, Carleton Coll., 1965; ThM Divinity Sch., U. Chgo., 1967, DMn, 1969, MA, 1972. Asst. dir. Admission and Aid U. Chgo., 1969-72; Social Scis. reference librarian Washington State U., Pullman, 1972-77, head ctrl. circulation, 1977-80; undergrad librarian U. Ill., Urbana, 1980-86; asst. dir. Pub. Svcs. U. Colo., Boulder, 1986-91, head Norlin Libr., 1989-91; dean, univ. libr. U. Cin., 1991—2002, emeritus, 2002—; dir. U. Cin. Digital Press, 1996—. Assoc. prof. U. Ill. Urbana Libr. Sch., 1984-86, Emporia State U., 1991-92, Ind. U., Bloomington, 1992, U. Ky., 1994; cons. in field. Author: Handbooks for Library Management (6 vols.), 1984-86, 12 Years 'Til 2000, 1990; editor-in-chief Jour. Acad. Librarianship, 2003; rev. editor RQ Reference Tools, 1988—; contbr. articles to profl. jours. Relief houseparent for Learning Disabled Student Whitman County Mental Health, Pullman, Wash., 1973-75; Koinonia House Bd. (pres. 1979-80), Pullman, 1975-81; mem. bd. Mental Health Found., Boulder County, 1986-91. Rockefeller fellow Rockefeller Found., 1965-66; Disciples House scholar Disciples Divinity House, Chgo., 1965-69. Mem. ALA (v.p., pres. reference and adult svc. divsn. 1993—), Libr. Guild. Presbyterian. Avocation: jogging. Home: 2929 Courtropes Ln Cincinnati OH 45244-3807 E-mail: david.kohl@uc.edu.

KOHL, HERBERT H., senator, professional sports team owner; b. Milw., Feb. 7, 1935; BA, U. Wis., Madison, 1956; MBA, Harvard U., 1958. Pres. Kohl's Grocery and Dept. Stores, 1970—79, Herbert Kohl Investments; owner, pres. NBA Milw. Bucks, 1985—; US Senator from Wis., 1989—. State chmn. Dem. Party, Wis., 1975-77; ranking minority mem. jud. subcommittee on terrorism, tech. & govt. info.; mem. com. appropriations, com. judiciary, spl. com. aging. Served with USAR, 1958—64. Recipient Nat. Boys and Girls Club award, 2000, Honored Cooperator award, Nat. Cooperative Bus. Assn., 2001, Silvio O. Conte award, Pub. Awareness and Edn., Brain Injury Assn. Am., 2002, Disting. Svc. to Agr. award, Wis. Farm Bur. Fedn., 2002, Friend of Farm Bur., Am. Farm Bur., 2002, Friend of Public Power award, Mcpl. Electric Utilities of Wis., 2002, Disting. Svc. award, Food Rsch. and Action Ctr., 2003, Charles Dick Medal of Merit, at. Guard Assn. US, 2003, Nat. Leadership award, Coalition Juvenile Justice, 2004, Leadership award, Family Svcs. N.W. Wis., 2004, Children's Champion award, Nat. Child Support Enforcement Assn., 2004. Democrat. Jewish. Office: US Senate 330 Hart Senate Office Bldg Washington DC 20510-0001 also: US Senator Herb Kohl Ste 950 310 W Wisconsin Ave Milwaukee WI 53203-2205 Office Phone: 202-224-5653, 414-297-4451. Office Fax: 202-224-9787, 414-297-4455. E-mail: senator_kohl@kohl.senate.gov.

KOHLER, HERBERT VOLLRATH, JR., diversified manufacturing company executive; b. Sheboygan, Wis., Feb. 20, 1939; s. Herbert Vollrath and Ruth Miriam (DeYoung) Kohler; m. Natalie Black; children: Laura Elizabeth, Rachel DeYoung, Karger David. Grad., The Choate Sch., 1957; BS in Indsl. Adminstrn., Yale U., 1965. With Kohler Co., Wis., 1965—, gen. supr. warehouse div., 1965-67, factory systems mgr., 1967-68, v.p. operations, 1968-71, exec. v.p., 1971-72, chmn. bd., chief exec. officer, 1972—, pres., 1974—, dir., 1967. Ret. chmn. Kohler Found.; dir. emeritus Harnischfeger Corp.; dir. Nat. Assn. Manufacturers. Dir. Nat. Outward Bound, Inc.; trustee Lawrence U., Appleton, Wis.; dir. Friendship House, Sheboygan, Wis. With US Army, 1957—58. Named one of Forbes' Richest Americans, 2000—, World's Richest People, Forbes mag., 2002—; named to Nat. Kitchen and Bath Hall of Fame, 1989, Nat. Housing Hall of Fame, 1993, Morgan Horse Hall of Fame, 1996; recipient Ellis Island Medal of Honor, 1997. Mem.: Am. Morgan Horse Assn., Am. Horse Show Assn., Sheboygan Economic (pres. 1973—74). Republican. Episcopalian. Achievements include patents for over 200 design and utility innovations. Avocation: breeding Morgan show horses. Office: Kohler Co 444 Highland Dr Kohler WI 53044

KOHLER, KENNETH JAMES, lawyer; b. Redwood Falls, Minn., Sept. 18, 1956; s. James Claire and Blanche (Genevieve) K.; m. Gail Ann Buldhaupt, May 21, 1983; children: Benjamin Thomas, Rebecca Erin. BA, U. Minn., Morris; JD, Hamline U. Asst. Redwood County Atty., Redwood Falls, Minn., 1983-85, Nobles County Atty., Worthington, Minn., 1985—; ptnr. Mork, Darling, Hagemann & Kohler, Worthington, 1985—. Bd. dirs. S.W. Women's Shelter, Marshall, Minn., 1985—. Served to cpt. Minn. N.G., 1984—. Mem. ABA, Minn. Bar Assn., Assn. Trial Lawyers Am., County Atty.'s Assn., Dist. Attys.' Assn., Nobles County Child Protection Team. Lodges: Kiwanis. Lutheran. Office: Nobles County Attorneys Office PO Box 607 Worthington MN 56187-0607 Home: 5321 River Dr Fargo ND 58102-7003

KOHLER, LAURA E., human resources executive; married; 3 children. Grad., Duke U., 1984; MFA, Cath. U., 1987. Past tchr. Chgo. Pub. Schs.; past corp. team facilitator; past mgr. Nat. Players, Washington; past residence mgr. Olney (Md.) Theatre; founder Chgo.; past exec. dir. Kohler Found., Inc.; v.p. human resources Kohler Co., 1990—, past v.p. comm., 1994—99, sr. v.p. human resources, also bd. dirs. Office: Kohler Co 444 Highland Dr Kohler WI 53044-1500

KOHLHEPP, ROBERT J., apparel executive; BS, Thomas More Coll.; MBA, Xavier Univ., 1971. Mgmt. positions through v.p. fin. Cintas Corp., Cin., 1967—79, exec. v.p., 1979—84, bd. dir., 1979—, pres., COO, 1984—95, pres., CEO, 1995—97, CEO, 1997—2003, vice-chmn., 2003—. Bd. dir. Parker Hannifin Corp. Office: Cintas Corp 6800 Cintas Blvd Mason OH 45040 Mailing: Cintas Corp PO Box 625737 Cincinnati OH 45262-5737

KOHLMEYER, JASON C., lawyer; b. Moorhead, Minn., May 5, 1972; BA, Concordia Coll., 1995; JD, Hamline U., 2000. Bar: Minn. 2000, US Dist. Ct. (dist. Minn.) 2002, US Ct. Appeals (8th cir.) 2005, US Supreme Ct. 2006. Shareholder Manahan, Bluth & Kohlmeyer, Law Office, Mankato, Minn. Served in USAR, 1989—95. Named a Rising Star, Minn. Super Lawyers mag., 2006; named one of Top Ten Up and Coming Attys., Minn. Lawyer, 2002. Mem.: Amdahl Inn of Cts., Assn. Trial Lawyers of Am. (chair criminal law sect. 2006—07), Minn. Trial Lawyers Assn., 6th Dist. Bar Assn. (pres. 2004—05), ABA (chair family law com.-young lawyers divsn. 2003—05, YLD Family Law Fellow 2004—06), Minn. State Bar Assn. (chair new lawyers sect. 2004—05). Office: Manahan Bluth & Kohlmeyer Law Office 110 S Broad St PO Box 287 Mankato MN 56002 Office Phone: 507-387-5661. E-mail: Kohlmeyer@manahanbluth.com.

KOHLS, WILLIAM RICHARD, bank executive; b. St. Johns, Mich., Apr. 17, 1957; s. Richard William and Helen A. (Arndt) K.; m. Susan Marie Matbick, Mar. 12, 1983. BBA, orthwood Inst., 1979. Controller Pacesetter Bank and Trust, Owosso, Mich., 1979-82; asst. v.p., controller First Nat. Bank, Howell, Mich., 1982-85; v.p., sec. and treas. Ind. Bank Corp., Ionia, Mich., 1985—. Bd. dirs. IBC Services Corp., Belding, Mich., 1986—. Home: 600 Covered Vlg Belding MI 48809-1667 Office: Ind Bank Corp 230 W Main St PO Box 491 Ionia MI 48846

KOHLSTEDT, JAMES AUGUST, lawyer; b. Evanston, Ill., June 1, 1949; s. August Lewis and Deloris (Weichelt) K.; m. Patricia Ann Lang, Oct. 8, 1977; children: Katherine, Matthew, Lindsey, Kevin. BA, Northwestern U., 1971; JD, MBA, Ind. U., 1976. Bar: U.S. Dist. Ct. (no. dist.) Ill. 1976, U.S. Tax Ct. 1978. Tax specialist Peat Marwick, Mitchell & Co., Chgo., 1976-77; assoc. Bishop & Crawford Ltd., Oak Brook, Ill., 1977-83, 1984-85; ptnr. Arnstein, Gluck, Lehr & Milligan, Oak Brook, 1985-87, Keck, Mahin and Cate, Oak Brook, 1987-96, McBride Baker & Coles, 1996-2001, mem. mgmt. com., 1997; chair McBride Baker & Coles Trade and Profl. Assn. Practice Group; sr. ptnr. The Kohlstedt Law Firm LLC, 2001—. Bd. dir. Nat. Entrepreneurship Found., Bloomington, Ind., 1981-92, Camp New Hope Devel. Bd., Oak Brook, 1983; mem. sch. bd. Lyons Twp. H.S. Dist. 204, La Grange, Ill., 1985—, v.p., 2005—; mem. Hinsdale (Ill.) Cmty. House Coun., 1991-94; mem. area leadership com. Superconducting Super Collider, 1987-88; mem. citizens adv. com. on edn. to U.S. Congressman Harris Fawell, 1986-93; bd. dir. Ill. Corridor Partnership for Excellence in Edn., 1988-94, DuPage Conv. and Visitors Bur., 1997-2001; mem. exec. bd. Visit Ill., 1997-2003; mem. planned giving com. Elmhurst Coll., 1986—; mem. citizens adv. panel U.S. Army ROTC Cadet Command, 1991-94; bd. dir. Ill. Math and Sci. Acad. Alliance, 1989-95; del. White House Conf. Travel and Tourism, 1995; mem. allied adv. bd. midwest chpt. Am. Soc. Travel Agents, 1995; Collegiate Edn. adv. com. Dept. Def., 1995. Recipient Outstanding Young Citizen of Chgo. award 1987, award of excellence Nat. Sch. Pub. Rels., 2005. Mem. ABA, Ill. Travel and Tourism Assn., Ill. Bar Assn., DuPage Estate Planning Coun., Oak Brook Jaycees (pres. 1984—, chmn. bd. 1985, trustee 1985-86), Beta Gamma Sigma. Republican. Lutheran. Office Phone: 630-571-0793. Business E-Mail: jim@ktlawpro.com.

KOHLSTEDT, SALLY GREGORY, historian, educator; b. Ypsilanti, Mich., Jan. 30, 1943; BA, Valparaiso U., 1965; MA, Mich. State U., 1966; PhD, U. Ill., 1972. Asst. prof. Simmons Coll., Boston, 1971-75; assoc. prof. to prof. Syracuse (N.Y.) U., 1975-89; prof. history of sci. U. Minn., Mpls., 1989—; dir. Ctr. for Advanced Feminist Studies, 1997-98. Vis. prof. history of sci. Cornell U., 1989, Amerika Inst. U. Munich, 1997; vis. assoc. Calif. Inst. Tech., 2004, lectr. in field. Author: The Formation American Scientific Community: AAAS, 1848-1860, 1976; editor: (with Margaret Rossiter) Historical Writing on American Science, Osiris, 2d Series, 1, 1985, (with R.W. Home) International Science and National Scientific Identity: Australia between Britain and America, 1991, The Origins of Natural Science in the United States: The Essays of George Brown Goode, 1991, (with Barbara Haslett et al.) Gender and Scientific Authority, 1996, (with Helen Lonino) The Women, Gender, and Science Question, 1997, The History of Women in Science: An Isis Reader, 1999, (with Bruce Leavenstein and Michael Sokal) The Establishment of Science in America: The American Association for the Advancement of Science, 1999; contbr. articles to profl. jours.; mem. editl. bd. Signs, 1980-88, 90-93, Sci., 1980-81, News and Views: History of Am. Sci. Newsletter, 1980-86, Sci., Tech. and Human Values, 1983-90, Syracuse Scholar, 1985-88, chair, 1988, Minerva, 2000—, Isis, 2002—; assoc. editor Am. Nat. Biography, 2d edit., 1988-98, consulting edit., 1993-99; Gryphon Press Reprints in the History of Science, 1993-98; reviewer books, articles, proposals for NSF, NEH, U. Chgo. Press, others; editor sci. biography series Cambridge U., 1997-2003. Grantee NSF, 1969, 78-79, 84, 93-95, 2002, 06, Smithsonian Instn. predoctoral fellow, 1970-71, Danforth Assoc., 1975-82, Syracuse U. grantee, 1976, 82, Am. Philos. Soc. rsch. grantee, 1977, Haven fellow Am. Antiquarian Soc., 1982, Fulbright Sr. fellow U. Melbourne, Australia, 1983, Woodrow Wilson Ctr. fellow, 1986, Smithsonian Instn. Sr. fellow, 1987. Fellow AAAS (nominating com. 1980-83, 96-98, sect. chair 1986, bd. dirs. 1998-2002, chair divsn. on sci., ethics and religion 2003—, coun. 2004—), Am. Hist. Assn. (profl. com. 1974-76, rep. U.S. Nat. Archives Adv. Coun. 1974-76), Berkshire Conf. Women Historians (program com. 1974), Forum on the History Sci. in Am. (coord. com. 1980-86, chair 1985, 86), History of Sci. Soc. (sec. 1978-81, coun. 1982-84, 89-91, 94-96, com. on pubis. 1982-87, chair nominating com. 1985, 99, women's com. 1972-74, vis. lectr. 1988-89, chair edn. com. 1989, pres. 1992, 93, Pfizer prize com. 2006—), Internat. Congress for History of Sci. (U.S. del. 1977, 81, vice chair 1985) Orgn. Am. Historians (chair com. on status of women 1983-85, endowment fund drive, auction subcom. 1990-91). Lutheran. Home: 108 Pillsbury Run SE Minneapolis MN 55455 Business E-Mail: sgk@umn.edu.

KOHN, SHALOM L., lawyer; b. Nov. 18, 1949; s. Pincus and Helen (Roth) K.; m. Barbara Segal, June 30, 1974; children: David, Jeremy, Daniel. BS in Acctg. summa cum laude, CUNY, 1970; JD magna cum laude, Harvard U., 1974, MBA, 1974. Bar: Ill. 1975, U.S. Dist. Ct. (no. dist.) Ill. 1975, U.S. Ct. Appeals (7th cir.) 1976, U.S. Supreme Ct. 1980, N.Y. 1988, U.S. Dist. Ct. (so. dist.) N.Y. 1988, others. Law clk. to chief judge US Ct. Appeals (2d cir.), NYC, 1974-75; assoc. Sidley Austin LLP, Chgo., 1975-80, ptnr., 1980—. Exec. com. Adv. Coun. Religious Rights in Eastern Europe and Soviet Union, Washington, 1984-86; bd. dirs. Brisk Rabbinical Coll., Chgo. Contbr. articles to profl. jours. Mem. ABA, Chgo. Bar Assn. also: 787 Seventh Ave New York NY 10019 Office: Sidley Austin LLP One South Dearborn Chicago IL 60603 Home Phone: 847-933-9223; Office Phone: 312-853-7756, 212-839-5440. Business E-Mail: skohn@sidley.com.

KOHN, WILLIAM IRWIN, lawyer; b. Bronx, NY, June 27, 1951; s. Arthur Oscar and Frances (Hoffman) K.; m. Karen Mindlin, Aug. 29, 1974; children: Shira, Kinneret, Asher. Student, U. Del., 1969—71; BA with honors, U. Cin., 1973; JD, Ohio State U., 1976. Bar: Ohio 1976, US Dist. Ct. (no. and so. dists.) Ohio 1976, Ind. 1982, US Dist. Ct. (no. and so. dists.) Ind. 1982, DC 1992, US Supreme Ct., 1992, Ill. 1994, US Dist. Ct. (no., ctrl., and so. dists.) Ill., NY 2006, US Dist. Ct. (so. dist.) NY 2007; cert. Bus. Bankruptcy Law Am. Bankruptcy Bd. Cert. Ptnr. Krugliak, Wilkins, Griffith & Dougherty, Canton, Ohio, 1976-82, Barnes & Thornburg, Chgo., 1982—2001, Sachnoff & Weaver Ltd., Chgo., 2002, Schiff Harden LLP, Chgo., 2002—06, Benesch Friedlander Coplan & Aronoff, LLP, Cleve., 2006—. Adj. prof. law U. Notre Dame, Ind., 1984—90; bd. dirs. Ctr. for Disability and Elder Law, 2006. Author: West's Indiana Business Forms, West's Indiana Uniform Commercial Code Forms; contbr. articles to profl. jours. Bd. dirs. Family Svcs., South Bend, 1985—94, Jewish Fedn., Highland Park United Way, Jewish Family and Cmty. Svcs., 2000—05. Named Vol. of Yr., Ctr. for Disability and Elder Law, 2006; recipient Excellence in Pub. Interest Svc. award, US Dist. Ct. (no. dist.) Ill. and Fed. Bar Assn., 2006. Mem. ABA (bus. bankruptcy subcom.), Am. Bankruptcy Inst. (insolvency sect.), Ill. Bar Assn., Chgo. Bar Assn., Comml. Law League, Am. Bd. Certification (treas.). Office: Benesch Friedlander Coplan & Aronoff LLP 2300 BP Tower 200 Public Sq Cleveland OH 44114-2378 Office Phone: 216-363-4182. Business E-Mail: wkohn@bfca.com.

KOHRMAN, ARTHUR FISHER, pediatrics educator; b. Cleve., Dec. 19, 1934; s. Benjamin Myron and Leah (Fisher) K.; m. Claire Hoffenberg, Nov. 10, 1955; children: Deborah, Benjamin, Ellen, Rachel. BA, BS, U. Chgo., 1955; MD, Western Res. U., 1959. Diplomate Am. Bd. Pediatrics. Lic. Ill., Ind. Intern Cleve. Met. Gen. Hosp., 1959-60; resident in pediatrics Case Western Res. U., Cleve., 1960—62; post doctoral fellow Stanford U., Palo Alto, Calif., 1965-68; from asst. prof. to prof. Mich. State U., East Lansing, 1968—81, assoc. chmn. dept. human devel., 1968—78, assoc. dean Coll. Human Medicine, 1977—81; prof., assoc. chmn. dept. pediatrics U. Chgo., 1981-96; pres. La Rabida Children's Hosp. and Research Ctr., Chgo., 1981-96; prof. pediatrics, assoc. chmn. Northwestern U. Sch. Medicine and Children's Meml. Hosp., Chgo., 1997—2002; prof. preventive medicine Sch. Medicine, Northwestern U., Chgo., 2000—02, prof. emeritus pediatrics and preventive medicine, 2003—. Congl. fellow Office Tech. Assessment, U.S. Congress, 1980-81; pres. Children's Hospice Internat., 1983-86; chmn. instl. rev. bd. U. Chgo., 1986-96. Contbr. numerous scholarly articles to profl. jours. Served to capt. USAF, 1962-65. Recipient Outstanding Service award Am. Diabetes Assn. Mich. chpt., 1977. Fellow Am. Acad. Pediatrics (chmn. com. on bioethics 1990-94); mem. Am. Pediatric Soc., Ambulatory Pediatric Assn., Soc. Pediatric Rsch., Lawson Wilkins Pediatric Endocrine Soc., Alpha Omega Alpha.

KOHRT, CARL FREDRICK, research and development company executive; b. Normal, Ill., Dec. 18, 1943; s. Carl Fred and Catherine Elizabeth (Traughber) K.; m. Margaret Lynne McCartney; children: Kristopher Alan, Brian Douglas, Jason Ivor. BS, Furman U., 1965; PhD, U. Chgo., 1971; MS, MIT, 1991. Postdoctoral fellow James Franck Inst., U. Chgo., 1970—71; sr. scientist rsch. labs. Eastman Kodak, Rochester, NY, 1971-76, rsch. lab. head, 1977-79, asst. div. dir. rsch. labs., 1979-84, asst. to vice chmn. Kodak office, 1984-85, div. dir. electronic rsch. labs., 1985-87, dir. rsch. photographic rsch. labs., 1987-90; Kodak's mem. of Sloan fellow program MIT, Cambridge, 1990—91, gen. mgr. health scis. divsn., 1991-95, exec. v.p., asst. COO, 1995-98, exec. v.p., asst. COO, chief tech. officer, 1998-2000; pres., CEO Battelle Meml. Inst., Columbus, Ohio, 2001—. Vice chmn., bd. dirs. Battelle Energy Alliance LLC, Brookhaven Sci. Assocs.; chair bd. trustees COSI Columbus; bd. trustees Furman U.; bd. dirs. Pharos LLC, Battelle Energy Alliance, LLC; chair bd. govs. UT-Battelle LLC, mem. coun. competitiveness. Contbr. articles to profl. jours.; patentee in field. Chmn. sustaining membership Boy Scouts Am., Rochester, 1988, scoutmaster, Pittsford, NY, 1976-88, mem. exec. bd. Otetiana coun., 1997; chair Cmty. Needs Study, Greece, NY, 1973; bd. dirs. Greater Columbus C. of C; trustee Ohio Bus. Roundtable. Woodrow Wilson fellow (hon.), 1965, NSF Grad. fellow, 1965—70. Mem.: Indsl. Rsch. Inst. (alt. rep.). Presbyterian. Avocations: backpacking, whitewater canoeing, music. Office: Battelle Meml Inst 505 King Ave Columbus OH 43201

KOIVISTO, DON, state legislator; married. BS, Ctrl. Mich. U., 1971. Mem. Mich. Ho. of Reps. from 110th dist., Lansing, 1980-86; chmn. Agrl. & Forestry Com.; mem. Conservation, Tourism, Econ. Devel., Mil. & Vets. Affairs Com., Mich. Senate from 38th dist., Lansing, 1990—; mem. appropriations com.; mem. agr. com., higher edn. com., natural resources com.; mem. joint capital outlay com.; mem. gaming and casino oversight com. Mem. Agriculture and Forestry, Health Policy, Joint Adminstrv. Rules & Natural Resources & Environ. coms. Mich. State Senate. Also: PO Box 30036 Lansing MI 48909-7536 Home: 515 E Vaughn St Apt 227 Ironwood MI 49938-2275

KOIVO, ANTTI JAAKKO, electrical engineering educator, researcher; b. Ilmajoki, Finland, Apr. 9, 1932; s. Niilo J. and Elma S. (Lahti) Koivuniemi; m. Anne Pihlak, Apr. 19, 1969 (div.); children: Lilli S., Allan T. Diploma engring., Finland Inst. Tech., 1956; PhD in Elec. Engring., Cornell U., 1963. From asst. to full prof. Purdue U., Lafayette, Ind., 1965—. Vis. rschr. Finnish Acad. Sci., AIST, Ministry Internat. Trade and Industry of Japan, Armstrong Lab. of Wright-Patterson AFB, Wright Lab. of Tyndall AFB, U. Hannover, Germany, Helsinki U. Tech. Contbr. articles on to profl. jours.; numerous conf. presentations. Office: Purdue U Sch Elec/Computer Engring West Lafayette IN 47907 Home Phone: 765-497-3170; Office Phone: 765-494-3436. E-mail: koivo@ecn.purdue.edu, aneurin04@yahoo.com.

KOKONAS, NICK J., restaurant owner; b. 1968; m. Dagmara Cepuritis; 2 children. BA, Colgate U., 1990. Derivatives trader Chgo. Merc. Exch., 1990—94; founder Third Moment Trading LLC, Chgo., 1996—2002; co-founder & ptnr. Alinea, Chgo., 2005—; mng. ptnr. Achatz LLC, Chgo. Named one of 40 Under 40, Crain's Chgo. Bus., 2006. Office: Alinea 1723 N Halsted Chicago IL 60614 Office Phone: 312-867-0110. E-mail: info@alinearestaurant.com.

KOLA, ARTHUR ANTHONY, lawyer; b. New Brunswick, NJ, Feb. 16, 1939; s. Arthur Aloysius and Blanche (Raym) K.; m. Jacquelin Lou Draper, Sept. 3, 1960; children— Jill, Jean, Jennifer; m. Anna Molnar, Apr. 15, 1977 AB, Dartmouth Coll., 1961; LLB, Duke U., 1964. Bar: Ohio 1964, U.S. Dist. Ct. (no. dist.) Ohio 1969, U.S. Ct. Appeals (6th cir.) 1971, U.S. Supreme Ct. 1972. Assoc. Squire, Sanders & Dempsey, Cleve., 1964-65, assoc., 1968-74, ptnr., 1974-94; pvt. practice Kola Law Office, Cleve., 1994—. Asst. prof. law Ind. U., Bloomington, 1967-68; instr. labor law Case Western Res. U., Cleve., 1976 Bd. visitors Duke U. Sch. Law, 1985—. Served to capt. U.S. Army, 1965-67 Mem. Ohio Bar Assn., Cleve. Bar Assn. (chmn. labor and employment law sect. 1993-94), Am. Arbitration Assn. (bd. dirs. 1991-97). Office: Kola Law Office 6100 Oak Tree Blvd Ste 200 Independence OH 44131-6914 Office Phone: 216-328-2009.

KOLAKOWSKI, DIANA JEAN, economic development director; b. Detroit, Aug. 28, 1943; d. Leo and Genevieve (Bosh) Zyskowski; m. William Francis Kolakowski, Jr., Oct. 22, 1966; children: Wiliam Francis III, John. BS, U. Detroit, Mich., 1965. Lab. asst. chemistry dept. U. Detroit, 1961-65; rsch. chemist Detroit Inst. Cancer Rsch., Mich. Cancer Found., 1965-70; substitute tchr. Warren (Mich.) Consol. Schs., 1979-81; Commr. Macomb County, Mt. Clemens, Mich., 1983—2006; vice chmn. Macomb County Bd. Commrs., Mt. Clemens, 1993-95, chmn., 1995-97; econ. devel. dir. City of Warren, 2006—. Dir. S.E. Mich. Transp. Authority, Detroit, 1983—85; trustee Macomb County Ret. System, Mt. Clemens, 1988—91, 1992—95, 2003—06; del. S.E. Mich. Coun. Govts., Detroit, 1987—2006, vice chmn., 1995—99, chmn., 1999—2000, Regional Transit Coord. Coun., 1995—97; bd. dirs. Creating a Healthier Macomb, 1996—2001, Macomb Bar Found., 1996—2006. Contbr. articles to sci. jours. Trustee Myasthenia Gravis Found., Southfield, Mich., 1964-71; dir. Otsikita coun. Girl Scouts Am., 1995-96; mem., sec. Sterling Heights (Mich.) Bd. Zoning Appeals, 1978-83; mem. Macomb County Dem. Exec. Com., Mt. Clemens, 1982—, 10th and 12th Dem. Congl. Dist. Exec. Com., Warren, 1982—, del. 1996 Dem. Nat. Conv.; mem. behavioral medicine adv. coun. St. Joseph Hosp., Warren Cmty. Chorus Named Woman of Distinction, Macomb County Girl Scouts U.S.A., 1996, Woman of Yr., Am. Fedn. State, County and Mcpl. Employees 411, 2004; recipient Leadership award, Cath. Social Svcs. Macomb, 1997, Polish Pride award, Polish Am. Citizens for Equity, 1997, Excellence in County Govt. award, 1997, Regional Ambassador award, S.E. Mich. Coun. Govt., 2005; GM scholar, U. Detroit, 1961—65. Mem.: Warren Hist. Soc., Polish Am. Congress, Alpha Sigma Nu. Roman Catholic. Avocations: singing, piano, crossword and jigsaw puzzles. Home: 33488 Breckenridge Dr Sterling Heights MI 48310-6082 Office: Mayor's Office City of Warren One City Sq Ste 215 Warren MI 48093 Office Phone: 586-574-4519.

KOLATA, DAVID, advocate; b. 1969; BA, U. Notre Dame, 1991; MA in polit. sci., U. Toronto, 1993; PhD in polit. sci., Vanderbilt U., 2002. Policy analyst Environ. Law & Policy Ctr., Chgo.; sr. policy analyst & exec. dir. Citizens Utility Bd., Chgo., 2001—; columnist Daily Southtown, Chgo., 2005—. Named one of 40 Under 40, Crain's Chgo. Bus., 2006. Office: Citizens Utility Bd Ste 1760 208 S LaSalle St Chicago IL 60604 Office Phone: 800-669-5556, 312-263-4282. Office Fax: 312-263-4329. E-mail: dkolata@CitizensUtilityBoard.org.

KOLB, DAVID ALLEN, psychologist, educator; b. Moline, Ill., Dec. 12, 1939; s. John August and Ethel May (Petherbridge) K.; m. Alice Yoko; 1 son, Jonathan Demian. AB cum laude, Knox Coll., 1961; PhD, Harvard U., 1967; ScD (h.c.), U. N.H., 1984; PhD (h.c.), Internat. Mgmt. Ctr., Buckingham, 1988; LittD (h.c.), Franklin U., 1994; DHL (h.c.), SUNY, 1996. Asst. prof. organizational psychology MIT, Cambridge, 1965-70, assoc. prof., 1970-75; prof. organizational behavior and mgmt. Case Western Res. U., Cleve., 1976—, deWindt Prof. Leadership and Enterprise Devel. Weatherhead Sch. Mgmt., 1992-97, chmn. dept., 1984-90. Vis. prof. mgmt. London Grad. Sch. Bus., 1971; dir. Devel. Research Assos., 1966-80; mgmt. cons., U.S., Australia, N.Z., Indonesia, Singapore, Malaysia, Thailand, Japan. Author: Experiential Learning: Experience as the source of learning and development, 1984, Kolb Learning Style Inventory 3.1, 2005; co-author: Organizational Behavior: An Experiential Approach, 8th edit, 2007, Organizational Behavior: A Book of Readings, 8th edit, 2007, Changing Human Behavior: Principles of Planned Intervention, 1974, Innovation in Professional Education: Steps on Journey from Teaching to Learning, 1995, Conversational Learning: An Experiential Approach to Knowledge Creation, 2002. Woodrow Wilson fellow, 1962. Mem. Internat. Assn. Applied Social Scientists (charter), Soc. Intercultural Edn., Tng. and Rsch. (charter), Coun.l Advancement of Experiential Learning (Research Excellence award 1984, Morris T. Keaton Adult and Experiential Learning award 1991, Case Weatherhead Rsch. Recognition award 2002-03). Office: Case Western Res U Dept of Orgn Behavior Cleveland OH 44106 Office Phone: 216-368-2050. E-mail: dak5@msn.com.

KOLB, VERA M., chemist, educator; b. Belgrade, Yugoslavia, Feb. 5, 1948; arrived in U.S., 1973; d. Martin A. and Dobrila (Lopicic) Kolb; m. Cal Y. Meyers, 1976 (div. 1986); m. Michael S. Gregory, 1997 (div. 1999). BS, Belgrade U., 1971, MS, 1973; PhD, So. Ill. U., 1976. Fellow So. Ill. U., Carbondale, 1977-78, vis. faculty lctr., 1978-85; assoc. prof. chemistry U. Wis., Parkside, 1985-90, prof. chemistry, 1990—, dept. chair, 1995-97. Vis. scientist Salk Inst. Biol. Studies U. Calif., San Diego, 1992—94; instr. San Francisco State U., 1997; vis. scholar Northwestern U., 2002—03. Editor: (book) Teratogens, Chemicals which Cause Birth Defects, 2nd edit., 1993, 1988; contbr. articles to profl. jours.; musician (violinist): Racine Symphony Orch., Parkside Cmty Orch., 2002—05. Assoc. dir. higher edn. Wis. Space Grant Consortium, 1995—97, assoc. dir. for special initiatives, 2002—05; violinist Racine (Wis.) Symphony Orch., Parkside Cmty. Orch. Recipient Rsch. and Higher Edn. awards, Wis. Space Grant Consortium, 1999—, Hall of Fame, Southeastern Wis. Educators, 2002; grantee, NIH, 1984—87, Am. Soc. Biochemistry and Molecular Biology, 1988; Fulbright grantee, 1973—76, NASA fellow, 1992—94. Mem.: Am. Chem. Soc. (task force occupl. safety and health 1980—94). Achievements include patents in field. Office: Univ Wis Parkside Dept Chemistry PO Box 2000 Kenosha WI 53141-2000 Office Phone: 262-595-2133.

KOLEHMAINEN, JAN WALDROY, professional association administrator; b. Virginia, Minn., July 8, 1940; s. John Ilmari and Astrid Irene (Petrell) K.; m. Katherine Lorene MacDanel, June 18, 1966; children: Lynn Kristine, Mark Daven. BA, Heidelberg Coll., 1962; MA, Bowling Green U., 1965. Asst. dir. admissions Syracuse U., .Y., 1965-68; dir. admissions St. Xavier Coll., Chgo., 1968-72; dir. med. soc. rels. AMA, Chgo., 1972-80; dir. interspity. affairs Minn. Med. Assn., Mpls., 1980-82; exec. dir. Am. Acad. Neurology, Mpls., 1982-99; ret., 1999. Mem. Am. Soc. Assn. Execs., Minn. Soc. Assn. Execs. (bd. dirs. 1989-93, sec.-treas. 1991-93), Am. Assn. Med. Soc. Execs. (bd. dirs. 1984-88), Profl. Conv. Mgrs. Assn. (bd. dirs. 1992-93). Avocations: tennis; fishing; reading. Office: Am Acad Neurology 1080 Montreal Ave Saint Paul MN 55116-2386

KOLEK, ROBERT EDWARD, lawyer; b. Chgo., June 1, 1943; s. Joseph and Mary Kolek; m. Linda L. Bernicchi, Aug. 27, 1966; children: Kimberley M. Szalkus, Robert E. Jr. BBA, Loyola U., Chgo., 1965, JD, 1968. Bar: Ill. 1968. Law clk. to Hon. Thomas Kluczynski, Ill. Supreme Ct., Chgo., 1968-70. Mem. ABA, Chgo. Bar Assn. Roman Catholic. Avocation: photography. Office: Schiff Hardin LLP 6600 Sears Tower Chicago IL 60606 Office Phone: 312-258-5500. E-mail: rKolek@schiffhardin.com.

KOLESON, DONALD RALPH, retired college dean, educator; b. Eldon, Mo., June 30, 1935; s. Ralph A. and Fern M. (Beanland) Koleson; children: Anne, David, Janet. BS in Edn., Ctrl. Mo. State U., 1959; MEd, So. Ill. U., 1973. Mem. faculty So. Ill. U., Carbondale, 1968—73; dean tech. edn. Belleville Area Coll., Ill., 1982—93; ret., 1993. Mem.: Nat. Assn. Two-Yr. Schs. of Constrn. (pres. 1984—85), Am. Welding Assn., Am. Vocat. Edn. Assn., Jesters, Shriners, Masons. Office Phone: 618-235-2700 ext. 6720. Personal E-mail: donkole@aol.com.

KOLK, FRITZ D., retail executive; CFO Meijer Inc., Grand Rapids, Mich. Office: Meijer Inc 2629 Walker Ave NW Grand Rapids MI 49544-1305

KOLKER, ALLAN ERWIN, ophthalmologist; b. St. Louis, Nov. 2, 1933; s. Paul P. and Jean Kolker; m. Jacquelyn Krupin, Dec. 8, 1957; children: Robin, Marci, David, Scott. AB, Washington U., St. Louis, 1953, MD, 1957. Diplomate Am. Bd. Ophthalmology (dir. 1994-98). Intern St. Louis Children's Hosp., 1957-58; resident in ophthalmology Washington U./Barnes Hosp., St. Louis, 1960-65; glaucoma fellow Washington U., St. Louis, 1963—64, staff, faculty, 1964—, prof. ophthalmology, 1974-96, clin. prof. ophthalmology, 1996—. Med. dir. The Glaucoma Inst., pvt. practice; mem. glaucoma com. Prevent Blindness Am. Author: (with J. Hetherington) Becker and Shaffer's Diagnosis and Therapy of the Glaucomas, 3d, 4th, 5th edit., 1983, (with T. Krupin) Complications in Ophthalmic Surgery, 1999; contbr. numerous articles to profl. jours., chpts. to books. Served with USPHS, 1958-60. NIH spl. fellow, 1963-65; grantee, 1969-80; 1st Disting. Eye Alumni award Washington U., 1990, Alumni/Faculty award Washington U. Sch. Medicine, 2002. Mem. AMA, Assn. Rsch. in Vision and Ophthalmology, Am. Acad. Ophthalmology (mem. coun. 1986-92, trustee 1994-98, Life Achievement award 2002), Am. Bd. Ophthalmology (dir. 1994-98), Am. Ophthal. Soc., Am. Glaucoma Soc. (founding mem., pres. 1992-94, Spl. Honor award 2002), Mo. Ophthal. Soc. (pres. 1986-87), St. Louis Med. Soc. Home: 176 Plantation Dr Saint Louis MO 63141-8352 Office: Glaucoma Cons Midwest 12601 Olive Blvd Saint Louis MO 63141-6313 Office Phone: 314-878-7962.

KOLKEY, ERIC SAMUEL, customer communications specialist; b. Chgo., Sept. 30, 1960; s. Eugene Louis and Gilda P. (Cowan) K. Student, Columbia Coll., 1979-82. Booking agt. C.O.D. Club, Chgo., 1979—83; mgr. Video Plus, Chgo., 1984—90; freelance screenwriter, 1991—96; customer comm. specialist AVI Midwest, Bensenville, Ill., 1997—2004, Rentacrate, 2004—06; with bus. devel. Rothschild Investments, 2006—. Lectr. Northwestern U., Evanston, Ill., 1982. Contbr. articles to profl. jours. Active Presdl. Trust, Washington, 1992, Nat. Rep. Senatorial Com., Washington, 1992, Rep. Party Platform Planning Com., Washington, 1992. Recipient Cert. of Recognition Rep. Nat. Com., 1991, Cert. of Award Rep. Presdl. Adv. Com., 1992. Avocation: weightlifting. Home: 750 N Dearborn St Apt 2302 Chicago IL 60610-5379 Office: AVI Midwest 621 Busse Hwy Bensenville IL Office Phone: 847-233-9944 ext. 223, 812-983-8915. Business E-Mail: eric.kolkey@midwest.com, ekolkey@rothschildinv.com.

KOLKEY, GILDA, artist; b. Chgo. d. David and Evelyn (Jacobson) Cowan; m. Gene Kolkey (dec.); children: Daniel, Sandor, Eric. BA in Painting, U. Ill., Champaign; student, Art Inst. Chgo., 1950, student, 1978—79. Art tchr. Highland Park (Ill.) Recreational Ctr., 1976. Exhibited in group shows at Thompson Ctr., Chgo., 1998—99, ArtLink Gallery, Ft. Wayne, Ind., 1998, Art House, 2001, Mars Gallery, 2001, Jettsett Gallery, 2002, Chgo. Anthenaeum, Shaumburg, Ill., 2002, Art Inst. Chgo. and Vicinity Shows, Andersen Mus., Kenosha, Wis., 2003, Later Impressions, 2003, San Juried Show, 2006, Scott Jackson's Halloween Shows, 2002—; featured in Chgo. Art Rev., 1989; Ency. of Living Artists, 1997, Chicago Open, 2003; featured in Chgo. Soc. Artists Calendar, 2005, 2006, 2007, 2008, Art Buzz Coffee Table Book, 2008. Recipient award of Excellence, North Shore Art League, 1965—66, Painting award, New Horizons in Painting, 1959, Scan Members Show, 1992, San Juried Show, 1992—2000, Hon. Mention, Women's Club Evanston, 1972. Mem.: Chgo. Artists Coalition, Chgo. Soc. Artists, Arts Club Chgo., Mid-Am. Club. Home: 1100 N Lake Shore Dr Apt 21B Chicago IL 60611-1088

KOLLER, DON, state legislator; b. Granite City, Ill., Dec. 3, 1942; Mo. state rep. Dist. 153, 1985—. Owner grocery store. Home: PO Box 135 Summersville MO 65571-0135 Office: 201 W Capitol Ave Jefferson City MO 65101-1556

KOLODZIEJ, EDWARD ALBERT, political scientist, educator; b. Chgo., Jan. 4, 1935; s. Albert Stanley and Anna Caroline (Chudzik) K.; m. Antje Heberle, Aug. 15, 1959; children: Peter, Andrew, Matthew, Daniel. BS summa cum laude, Loyola U., Chgo., 1956; MA, U. Chgo., 1957, PhD, 1961. Analyst nat. security fgn. affairs div. Congl. Research Service, Library of Congress, Washington, 1960-62; asst. prof. polit. sci. U. Va., Charlottesville, 1962-67, assoc. prof., 1967-73, chmn. dept. govt. and fgn. affairs, 1967-69, prof. polit. sci., 1973-83; head dept. U. Ill., Urbana, 1973-77, dir. Office Arms Control, Disarmament and Internat. Security, 1983-86, research prof. polit. sci., 1983—2001, elected univ. scholar, 1988; dir. Ctr. Global Studies, 2001—. Vis. prof. LaTrobe, Melbourne, 1999, Senshu U., Tokyo, 2001; cons. in field Author: The Uncommon Defense and Congress, 1966, French International Policy under de Gaulle and Pompidou: The Politics of Grandeur, 1974, Making and Marketing Arms: The French Experience and Its Implications for the International System, 1987; editor: American Security Policy, 1979, Security Policies of Developing States, 1981, Limits of Soviet Power in the Developing World, 1987, Security and Arms Control: Guide to National and International Policy-Making, 2 vols., 1989, Cold War as Cooperation, 1991, Coping with Conflict After the Cold War, 1996, Power, Politics and Promise of Human Rights, 2003, International Relations and Security, 2005; mem. editl. bd. Internat. Studies Quar., Defence and Peace Econs., Contemporary Security Policy, European Security; contbr. articles on fgn. and security policy and decision-making to profl. jours., U.S., Europe; also contbg. author books. Mershon Postdoctoral fellow nat. security Ohio State U., 1964-65, Rockefeller Postdoctoral fellow in internat. rels., Paris, 1965-66, Ford Found. fellow in social sci., 1969-71, Fulbright Rsch. fellow, 1986; NSF grantee, 1971, Deutscher Akademischer Austauschdienst grantee, 1975, Ford Found. Internat. Arms Control Competition grantee, 1976, Ctr. for Advanced Study, U. Ill., 1979, 95—, Rockefeller Found. grantee, 1980, grantee NEH, 1981, Woodrow Wilson Ctr., 1987, U.S. Inst. Peace grantee, 1987, 91, grantee Ford Found., 1993; recipient Burlington award for outstanding tchg. and scholarship, 1985. Mem. Internat. Inst. Strategic Studies London, Council Fgn. Relations N.Y., Am., Midwest internat. polit. sci. assns., Internat. Studies Assn. Home: 711 W University Ave Champaign IL 61820-3919 Office: U Ill Dept Polit Sci Urbana IL 61801 Business E-Mail: edkoloj@uiuc.edu.

KOMIVES, PAUL J., federal judge; b. 1932; AB, U. Detroit, 1954; JD, U. Mich., 1958. Bar: Mich. 1958, D.C. 1958, U.S. Ct. Appeals (6th cir.) 1961, U.S. Ct. Appeals (D.C. cir.) 1961, U.S. Supreme Ct. 1963. Asst. U.S. atty. U.S. Dist. Ct. (ea. dist.) Mich., 1961-66; spl. prosecutor Mich. Cir. Ct., Detroit, 1966-67; pvt. practice, 1967-71; magistrate judge U.S. Dist. Ct. (ea. dist.) Mich., Detroit, 1971—. Adj. prof. Detroit Coll. Law, 1972-2000; adj. prof. Wayne State U. Law Sch., Detroit, 1998—. Office: US Dist Ct Ea Dist Mich 629 US Courthouse 231 W Lafayette Blvd Detroit MI 48226-2700 Fax: 313-234-5497.

KOMMEDAHL, THOR, plant pathology educator; b. Mpls., Apr. 1, 1920; s. Thorbjørn and Martha (Blegen) K.; m. Faye Lillian Jensen, June 2, 1924; children: Kris Alan, Siri Lynn, Lori Anne. BS, U. Minn., 1945, MS, 1947, PhD, 1951. Instr. U. Minn., St. Paul, 1946-51, asst. prof. plant pathology, 1953-57, assoc. prof., 1957-63, prof., 1963-90, prof. emeritus, 1990—; asst. prof. plant pathology Ohio Agrl. Research and Devel. Ctr., Wooster, 1951-53, Ohio State U., Columbus, 1951-53; prof. Univ. Coll., U. Minn., St. Paul, 1990—. Cons. botanist and taxonomist Minn. Dept. Agr., 1954-60, Sci. Mus. Minn., 1990—; 7th A.W. Dimock lectr. Cornell U., 1979; external assessor U. Pertanian Malaysia, 1994-97. Author: Pesky Plants, 1994, 7th edit., 2006; co-author: Scientific Style and Format, 1994, 7th edit., 2006; editor Minn. Fulbright newsletter, 1995—2002, Procs. IX Internat. Congress Plant Protection, 2 vols., 1981, Corn Disease newsletter, 1970—76, assoc. editor The Boghopper, 1996—, cons. editor McGraw Hill Ency. Sci. and Tech., 1972—78, editor-in-chief Phytopathology, 1964—67; sr. editor: Challenging Problems in Plant Health, 1982, Plant Disease Reporter, 1979; contbr. articles to profl. jours. Bd. mem. Park Bugle, 1998—2007. Recipient Elvin Charles Stakman award, 1990, award of merit, Gamma Sigma Delta, 1994, Ed Stevens Vol. award, Roseville, 2007; Guggenheim fellow, 1961, Fulbright scholar, 1968. Fellow AAAS, Am. Phytopathol. Soc. (councilor 1958-60, pres. 1971, publs. coord. 1978-84, Disting. Svc. award 1984, 93, sci. adv. 1984—, adv. bd. office internat. programs 1987-93, editor Focus 1981—); mem. Am. Inst. Biol. Scis., Bot. Soc. Am., Coun. Sci. Editors, Internat. Soc. Plant Pathology (councilor 1971-78, sec.-gen. and treas. 1983-88, treas. 1988-93, editor newsletter 1983-93), Mycol. Soc. Am., Minn. Acad. Sci., NY Acad. Scis., Weed Sci. Soc. Am. (award of excellence 1968), Fulbright Assn. (editor newsletter Minn. chpt. 1995-2002). Baptist. Home: 1666 Coffman St Apt 322 Saint Paul MN 55108-1340 Office: U Minn Dept Plant Pathology 495 Borlaug Hall 1991 Upper Buford Cir Saint Paul MN 55108-6030 Office Phone: 612-625-3164. Office Fax: 612-625-9728. Business E-Mail: thork@umn.edu.

KOMOROSKI, LEN, professional sports team executive; m. Denise Komoroski; children: Kristin, Kelly, Jamie, Zachary. Grad. cum laude, Duquesne U., 1982. With Maj. Indoor Soccer League Pitts. Spirit, 1982; mgmt. position NHL Pitts. Penguins; with Maj. Indoor Soccer League Minn. Strikers; regional mgr. sports mktg. Miller Brewing Co.; v.p. sales, sr. sales and mktg. ofcl. NBA Minn. Timberwolves, 1988—94; sr. v.p., COO Internat. Hockey League Cleve. Lumberjacks; sr. v.p., chief bus. ops. NFL Phila. Eagles; pres. NBA Cleve. Cavaliers/Quicken Loans Arena. Bd. dirs. Cleve. chpt. City Year, ARC, United Way; bd. mem. Greater Cleve. Conv. and Visitors Bur. Office: Cleve Cavaliers One Center Ct Cleveland OH 44115-4001

KONECK, JOHN MICHAEL, lawyer; b. Mpls., Aug. 16, 1953; s. Robert W. and Bernice V.; m. Debra K. Plotz, Aug. 16, 1980; 1 child, Robert John. BS, N.D. State U., 1975; JD, Yale Law Sch., Mpls., 1978. Bar: N.D. 1978, Minn. 1979. Jud. law clk. N.D. Supreme Ct., Bismarck, 1978-79; ptnr., pres. Fredrikson & Byron, Mpls., 1979—. Real property law specialist, mem. Minn. Bd. Legal

Cert., Supreme Ct. Minn., 1994-99, chmn., 1996-99; mem. Vol. Lawyers Network; assoc. prof. William Mitchell Coll. Law, 1997—. Mem. ABA (chair litig. and dispute resolution, com. of sect. real property, probate and trust law 1995-98, chief editor newsletter of litig. and dispute resolution com. 1991-93, vice chair 1991-95), Am. Coll. Real Estate Lawyers, Minn. State Bar Assn. (co-chair real property cert. coun. 1990—, mem. rules of profl. conduct com.), State Bar Assn. N.D., Hennepin County Bar Assn. (co-chair rules of profl. conduct com. 1994-96). Office: Fredrikson & Byron 200 S 6th St Ste 4000 Minneapolis MN 55402-1425 Home Phone: 651-483-3198; Office Phone: 612-492-7038. Business E-Mail: jkoneck@fredlaw.com.

KONENKAMP, JOHN K., state supreme court justice; b. Oct. 20, 1944; m. Geri Konenkamp; children: Kathryn, Matthew. JD, U. S.D., 1974. Dep. state's atty., Rapid City; pvt. practice, 1977-84; judge SD Cir Ct. (7th cir.), 1984—88, presiding judge, 1988-94; assoc. justice SD Supreme Ct., Pierre, 1994—. Bd. dirs. Alt. Dispute Resolution Com., Adv. Bd. for Casey Family Program. Served in USN. Mem. Am. Judicature Soc., State Bar S.D., Pennington County Bar Assn., Nat. CASA Assn., Am. Legion. Office: SD Supreme Ct 500 E Capitol Ave Pierre SD 57501-5070

KONERKO, PAUL, professional baseball player; b. Providence, Mar. 2, 1976; First baseman Chgo. White Sox, 1999—. Host Starlight Children's Found., Comiskey Park. Achievements include mem. Major League Baseball World Champions, 2005. Office: Chgo White Sox 333 W 35th St Chicago IL 60616

KONICEK, MICHAEL, city official; b. Cleve., Oct. 5, 1943; m. Paula Lauracella; children: David, John. B Chem. Engring., Ohio State U., 1966, MSChemE, 1966. Rsch. engr. Sohio, Cleve., 1966-69; sr. rsch. engr. Monsanto Rsch. Corp., Dayton, Ohio, 1969-72; R & D group leader, tech. supt., staff engr. Diamond Shamrock, Cleve., mgr. R & D and market devel., mgr. bus. devel., 1972-82; mgr. bus. devel. Eltech Sys. Corp., Chardon, Ohio, 1982-84; v.p., ptnr. Lectranator Corp., 1984-87; tech. mgr. Lectranator Corp. subs. Olin Corp., 1987-90; dir. pub. utilities City of Cleve., 1990—. Bd. dirs. N.E. Ohio Regional Sewer Dist., 1994—. Office: Cleve Dept Pub Utilities 1201 Lakeside Ave Cleveland OH 44114-1132

KÖNIG, PETER, pediatrician, educator; b. Cluj, Romania, Feb. 14, 1938; came to U.S., 1976; s. Rudolf and Irina (Grünwald) K.; m. Lea Schiffer, Sept. 30, 1965; 1 child, Orly. Graduate, Timisoara Med. Sch., Romania, 1959; MD, Hebrew U., Jerusalem, 1966; PhD, U. London, 1974. Resident Hadassah Hosp., Jerusalem, 1969—70, Bikur Cholim Hosp., Jerusalem, 1970-71, staff, 1974-76; fellow in pulmonary diseases Brompton Hosp., London, 1971-74; asst. prof. child health U. Mo., Columbia, 1976-80, assoc. prof. child health, 1980-84, prof. in child health, 1984—. Fellow Am. Acad. Allergy; mem. Am. Thoracic Soc., Acad. Allergy, Soc. Pediatric Research, Chilean Asthma Found., Sigma Xi. Home: 1310 Vintage Dr Columbia MO 65203-4878 Office: U Mo Child Health 1 Hospital Dr Columbia MO 65212-5276 Office Phone: 573-882-6978. Business E-Mail: KonigP@health.missouri.edu.

KONOPINSKI, VIRGIL JAMES, retired industrial hygienist, consultant; b. Toledo, July 11, 1935; BSChemE, U. Toledo, 1956; MSChemE, Pratt Inst., 1960; MBA, Bowling Green State U., 1971. Registered profl. engr., Ind., Calif., cert. safety profl. Assoc. engr. Owens Ill., Toledo, 1956, 60; real estate developer Grand Rapids, Ohio, 1961; chem. engr. USPHS, Cin., 1961-64; sr. environ. engr. Vistron Corp., Lima, Ohio, 1964-67; environ. specialist, asst. to dir. environ. control Owens Corning Fiberglas, Toledo, 1967-72; gen. mgr. Midwest Environ. Mgmt., Maumee, Ohio, 1972-73; staff specialist, indl. hygienist Williams Bros. Waste Control, Tulsa, 1973-75; dir. divsn. indsl. hygiene and radiol. health Ind. State Bd. Health, Indpls., 1975-87; exec. v.p. ACT Ind., Indpls., 1987-89; sr. cons. Occusafe, Chgo., 1990-91; regional safety engr., human resources analyst/safety U.S. Postal Svc., Bloomingdale, Ill., 1991—2003; cons. in field, 2003—. Bd. dirs. IOSHA Indsl. Hygiene, 1975—83; cons. indoor air, occupl. health abd safety, Zionsville, 1987—91; cons. indoor air, safety, Cary, 1991—2003, Maumee, Ohio, 2003—. Contbr. articles to profl. jours. With USNR, 1956—59. Mem.: Am. Soc. Safety Engrs., Mil. Officers Assn. Republican. Roman Catholic. Home and Office: 7206 Longwater Dr Maumee OH 43537 Office Phone: 419-878-3158.

KONTNY, VINCENT L., rancher, retired engineering executive; b. Chappell, Nebr., July 19, 1937; s. Edward James and Ruth Regina (Schumann) K.; m. Joan Dashwood FitzGibbon, Feb. 20, 1970; children: Natascha Marie, Michael Christian, Amber Brooke. BSCE, U. Colo., 1958, DSc honoris causa, 1991. Operator heavy equipment, grade foreman Peter Kiewit Son's Co., Denver, 1958-59; project mgr. Utah Constrn. and Mining Co., Western Australia, 1965-69, Fluor Australia, Queensland, Australia, 1969-72; sr. project mgr. Fluor Utah, San Mateo, Calif., 1972-73; sr. v.p. Holmes & Narver, Inc., Orange, Calif., 1973-79; mng. dir. Fluor Australia, Melbourne, 1979-82; group v.p. Fluor Engrs., Inc., Irvine, Calif., 1982-85, pres., chief exec. officer, 1985-87; group pres. Fluor Daniel, Irvine, Calif., 1987-88, pres., 1988-94, Fluor Corp., Irvine, 1990-94, COO, bd. dirs., vice chmn., 1994; ret., 1994; bd. dirs. Chgo. Bridge & Iron Co., Plainfield, Ill., 1997—; COO Washington Group Internat., Inc., Boise, Idaho, 2000—03. Purchased Last Dollar Ranch, Ridgway Co. 1989, Centennial Ranch, Colona Co., 1992, owner Double Shoe Cattle Co. Contbr. articles to profl. jours. Mem. engring. devel. coun., U. Colo.; mem. engring. adv. coun., Stanford U. Lt. USN, 1959-65. Mem.: Nat. Acad. Constrn. (pres. 2007, v.p. 2006), Center Club (Costa Mesa, Calif.). Republican. Roman Catholic. Avocations: skiing, hunting, fishing. Home and Office: 35000 S Highway 550 Montrose CO 81401-8477 Personal E-mail: vincekontny@starband.net.

KONTOS, MARK, treasurer; V.p. Citibank/Citicorp, NYC; CFO, v.p. fin. Armco Steel Co., 1993—94; CFO, v.p. fin., treas. AK Steel Corp., Middleton, Ohio, 1994; sr. v.p., CFO, treas. Battelle Meml. Inst., Columbus, Ohio, 1997—. Bd. dirs. Brookhaven Sci. Assocs., Omniviz, Inc.; trustee COSI Columbus, Middletown Regional Hosp. Office: Battelle Meml Inst 505 King Ave Columbus OH 43201

KONZ, GERALD KEITH, retired manufacturing executive; b. Racine, Wis., Apr. 3, 1932; m. Marianne Bubolz; children: Richard C., Brenda S. BS in Econs., U. Wis., 1957, LLB, 1960. V.p. in charge corp. tax dept. S.C. Johnson & Son, Inc., Racine, 1982-98, chmn. bd. trustees pension trust, employee profit sharing and savs. plan, 1982-98. Bd. dirs. Optique Funds, Inc. (formerly Johnson Family Funds, Inc.), Milw., Wis. Pub. Expenditure Survey, Madison, 1982-92; mem. adv. bd. Venture Investors, Inc., Madison, Wis., 1997—98. Treas. St. Catherines H.S. Found., Racine, 1994—97, pres., 1997—2001; bd. dirs. YMCA, Racine, 1988—98. Mem. ABA, Tax Execs. Inst. (pres. Wis. chpt. 1972), Wis. Bar Assn., Racine-Kenosha Estate Planning Coun. (pres. 1980). Office: 3515 Taylor Ave Racine WI 53405-4727 Home Phone: 262-554-7796; Office Phone: 262-554-7796. E-mail: gkonz@wi.rr.com.

KOOB, ROBERT DUANE, chemistry professor, academic administrator; b. Graetinger, Iowa, Oct. 14, 1941; s. Emil John and Rose Mary (Slinger) Koob; m. E. Yvonne Ervin, June 9, 1960; children: Monique, Gregory, Michael, Eric, David; children: Angela, Julie. BA in Edn., U. No. Iowa, 1962; PhD in Chemistry, U. Kans., 1967. From asst. prof. to prof. chemistry ND State U., Fargo, 1967—90, chmn. dept. chemistry, 1974—78, 1979—81, dir. Water Inst., 1975—85, dean Coll. Sci. and Math., 1981—84, v.p., 1985—90, interim pres., 1987—88; v.p. for acad. affairs, sr. v.p. Calif. Poly. State U., San Luis Obispo, 1990—95; pres. U. No. Iowa, Cedar Falls, 1995—, prof., 1995—. Cons. TransAlta, Edmondton, Alta., Canada, Alta. Rsch. Coun., Mitre Corp., Washington; bd. dirs. State Bank Fargo, Fargo Cass County Econ. Devel. Corp.; chair bd. dirs. Cal Poly Found.; chair Iowa Coordinating Coun. for Post-H.S. Edn., 1996—97. Contbr. articles to profl. jours. V.p. Crookston Diocesan Sch. Bd., Minn., 1982; pres. elem. sch. bd., St. Joseph's Ch., Moorhead, Minn., 1982, parish coun., Moorhead, Minn., 1983; pres. bd. Shanley H.S., Fargo, 1985; serves on Cedar Valley Promise, Cedar Valley Alliance, Cedar Valley United Way, Opportunity Works, Am. Coun. Edn., Am. Assn. of States Colls. and Univs. Named to Cedar Valley Bus. Hall of Fame; grantee in field. Mem.: Iowa Assn. Coll. Pres. (pres. 1996). Roman Catholic. Avocations: reading, flying, sailing, sports, bicycling. Office: Univ of Northern Iowa 1227 W 27th St Cedar Falls IA 50614-0002 Office Phone: 319-273-2566. E-mail: bob.koob@uni.edu.

KOONTZ, FRANK P., microbiology educator, research administrator; Prof. U. Iowa; dir. clin. microbiology lab. U. Iowa Hosps. and Clinics, Iowa City. Recipient Sonnenwirth Meml. award Am. Soc. Microbiology, 1995. Office: U Iowa Hosps and Clinics Dept Pathology Iowa City IA 52242 E-mail: franklin-koontz@viowa.edu.

KOOSER, TED (THEODORE J. KOOSER), poet; b. Ames, Iowa, Apr. 25, 1939; s. Theodore B. and Vera (Moser) Kooser; m. Kathleen Rutledge. BS, Iowa State U., 1962; MA, U. Nebr., 1968. Former v.p. Lincoln Benefit Life; 13th Poet Laureate Cons. in Poetry to the Libr. of Congress, 2004—05; founder Am. Life in Poetry project, 2005—. Vis. prof. English U. Nebr., Lincoln. Author: (poetry collections) Official Entry Blank, 1969, A Local Habitation and a Name, 1974, Not Coming to Be Barked At, 1976, Sure Signs, 1980 (Soc. of Midland Authors Poetry Prize, 1980), One World at a Time, 1985, The Blizzard Voices, 1986, Weather Central, 1994, Winter Morning Walks: One Hundred Postcards to Jim Harrison, 2000 (Nebr. Book Award for poetry, 2001), Delights & Shadows, 2004 (Pulitzer Prize for poetry, 2005); co-author (with Jim Harrison): Braided Creek: A Conversation in Poetry, 2003 (Soc. Midland Authors Poetry Prize, 2004); author: (chapbooks/spl. editions) Grass County, 1971, Twenty Poems, 1973, Shooting a Farmhouse/So This is Nebraska, 1975, Old Marriage and New, 1978, Etudes, Bits Press, 1992, A Book of Things, 1995, A Decade of Ted Kooser Valentines, 1996, Flying at Night: Poems, 1965-1985, 2005; co-author (with Harley Elliott): Voyages to the Inland Sea, 1976; co-author: (with William Kloefkorn) Cottonwood County, 1979; author: (essay collection) Local Wonders: Seasons in the Bohemian Alps, 2002 (Nebr. Book Award for nonfiction, 2003, Gold Award for Autobiography, ForeWord mag. Book of Yr. Awards), (non-fiction) The Poetry Home Repair Manual: Practical Advice for Beginning Poets, 2005. Recipient Prairie Schooner Prize in Poetry, 1976, 1978, Stanley Kunitz Poetry Prize, Columbia Mag., 1984, Pushcart Prize, 1984, Nebr. Governor's Art Award, 1988, Mayor's Art Award, Lincoln, Nebr., 1989, Richard Hugo Prize, Poetry N.W., 1994, James Boatwright Award, Shenandoah, 2000, Merit Award in Poetry, Nebr. Arts Coun., 2000, Mari Sandoz Award, Nebr. Libr. Assn., 2000; writing fellowship, Nat. Endowment Arts, 1976, 1984. Address: care Copper Canyon Press Bldg 313 Ft Worden State Pk PO Box 271 Port Townsend WA 98368

KOPELMAN, IAN STUART, lawyer; b. Chgo., Oct. 11, 1949; s. Ted and Norma (Hyman) K.; m. Nancy Henriette Stamp, Mar. 18, 1984; children: Meredith Samantha, Jason Lee. BA cum laude, Knox Coll., 1971; JD with distinction, U. Iowa, 1974. Bar: Ill. 1974, U.S. Dist. Ct. (no. dist.) Ill. 1974, U.S. Tax Ct. 1974. Ptnr. Arnstein & Lehr, Chgo., 1979-88; prin. Shefsky & Froelich Ltd., Chgo., 1988-96; ptnr., chair employee benefits/exec. compensation group Altheimer & Gray, Chgo., 1996-99, Rudnick & Wolfe, Chgo., 1999-2000; ptnr., chair employee benefits/exec. compensation dept. Piper, Marbury, Rudnick & Wolfe (now DLA Piper US LLP), Chgo., 2000—. Adj. prof. law John Marshall Law Sch., 2004—; lectr. in field. Contbr. articles to profl. publs. Pres. Chgo.-Knox Coll. Alumni Assn., Chgo., 1978-79. Recipient commendation Internat. Acad. Trial Lawyers, 1974, award Iowa Acad. Trial Lawyers. Mem. ABA, Ill. Bar Assn., Chgo. Bar Assn. (chmn. employee benefits com. 1981-82, commendation 1986), Profit Sharing/401k Coun. Am. (legal counsel 2005—, legal and legis. com. 1990—, bd. dirs. 1997-2005), Midwest Benefits Coun. (chmn. legal and legis. com. 1991-93), Chgo. Assn. Commerce and Industry, Phi Sigma Alpha, Omicron Delta Kappa, Phi Delta Phi. Jewish. Avocations: theater, history, reading, sports. Office: DLA Piper US LLP Suite 1900 203 N La Salle St Chicago IL 60601-1293 Office Phone: 312-368-2161. Office Fax: 312-236-7516. Business E-Mail: Ian.Kopelman@dlapiper.com.

KOPF, GEORGE MICHAEL, retired ophthalmologist; b. Chilton, Wis., Oct. 20, 1935; s. George and Mary (Schmid) K.; m. Sandra Mary Nolte, Dec. 29, 1962; children: Karen, Jennifer, Nancy. BS, U. Wis., 1958, MD, 1961. Diplomate Am. Bd. Ophthalmology. Intern Luther Hosp., Eau Claire, Wis., 1961-62; resident Milw. County Hosp., 1962-63, Detroit Gen. Hosp., 1965-68; ophthalmologist pvt. practice, Zanesville, Ohio, 1968—; ret., 1999. Mem. med. staff Bethesda Hosp., Zanesville; mem. med. Staff Good Samaritan Med. Ctr., Zanesville, pres., 1978, sec. bd. dirs., 1986-96. Capt. USAF, 1963-65. Fellow ACS, Am. Acad. Ophthalmology; mem. Ohio Ophthalmology Soc. (pres. 1976-77), Muskigum County Acad. Medicine (pres. 1983), Ohio State Med. Assn., Rotary. Republican. Roman Catholic. Avocations: tennis, swimming, hiking, reading, travel. Home: 22030 Longleaf Tr Bonita Springs FL 34135 Personal E-mail: kopfgs@comcast.net.

KOPF, RICHARD G., federal judge; b. 1946; BA, U. Nebr., Kearney, 1969; JD, U. Nebr., Lincoln, 1972. Law clk. to Hon. Donald R. Ross US Ct. Appeals (8th cir.), 1972-74; ptnr. Cook, Kopf & Doyle, Lexington, Nebr., 1974-87; U.S. magistrate judge, 1987-92; fed. judge US Dist. Ct. (Nebr. dist.), 1992—, chief judge, 1999—2004. Mem. ABA, ABA Found., Nebr. State Bar, Nebr. State Bar Found. Office: US Dist Ct 586 US Courthouse 100 Centennial Mall N Lincoln NE 68508-3859 Office Phone: 402-437-5252. Business E-Mail: richard_kopf@ned.uscourts.gov.

KOPP, BRUCE, newscaster; b. Chgo., Aug. 13, 1958; s. Joan K.; m. Paula Graves, Oct. 17, 1987; 1 child, Jonathan. BS in Radio, TV, So. Ill. U., 1980. Anchor, reporter Sta. WEHT-TV, Evansville, Ind., 1980-82, Sta. WOOD-TV, Grand Rapids, Mich., 1982-83, Sta. WTHR-TV, Indpls., 1983—. Recipient award Soc. Profl. Journalist (Best General News Reporting, 1986, 89, Best Feature, 1988, Best Spot News Coverage, 1988), AP (Best Live Report, 1988, Best Feature, 1988, Best Spot News Reporting, 1989). Avocations: home computing, golf, skiing, water-skiing. Office: Sta WTHR TV 1000 N Meridian St Indianapolis IN 46204-1015

KOPPELMAN, ANDREW MARTIN MAYER, law educator; b. Nyack, NY, Aug. 29, 1957; s. George Irving and Ruby Etta (Lee) K.; m. Valerie Jane Quinn, June 24, 1989; children: John Miles Isidore, Georgina Isabella, Emme Sophia. AB, U. Chgo., 1979; MA in Polit. Sci., Yale U., 1986, JD, 1989, PhD, 1991. Bar: Conn. 1990, NY 1991. Law clk. to Chief Justice Ellen A. Peters conn. Supreme Ct., 1991—92; asst. prof. politics Princeton U., NJ, 1992—97; asst. prof. law and polit. sci. Northwestern U., Chgo., 1997—2000, assoc. prof., 2000—03, George C. Dix prof. constitutional law, 2000—01, prof. law, 2003—07, John Paul Stevens prof. law and polit. sci., 2007—. Vis. prof. law U. Tex. at Austin, 1997. Author: Antidiscrimination Law and Social Equality, 1996 (Myers Center Award, 1997), The Gay Rights Question in Contemporary American Law, 2002, Same Sex, Different States: When Same-Sex Marriages Cross State Lines, 2006; contbr. articles to profl. jours. Summer rsch. fellow Ctr. for Studies in Law, Econs. and Pub. Policy Yale U., 1988, 90, 91, NEH summer rsch. stipend fellow, 1993, Harvard U. Program in Ethics and Professions fellow, 1994-95. Office: Northwestern U Sch Law 357 E Chicago Ave Chicago IL 60611 Business E-Mail: akoppelman@northwestern.edu.

KOPPES, CLAYTON R., academic administrator; s. Clinton and Effie Koppes. Grad., Bethel Coll., 1967; MA, Emory Coll., 1968; PhD, U. Kans., 1974. Sr. rsch. fellow Calif. Inst. Tech.; mem. faculty Oberlin Coll., 1978—, Irvin E. Houck prof. humanities, 1986—91, dean Coll. Arts and Scis., 1996—2004, v.p. acad. affairs, provost, 2004—05, prof. hist. dept., 2005—. Author: JPL and the American Space Program, 1982 (Dexter prize Soc. for the History of Tech.); co-author: Hollywood Goes to War: How Politics, Profits & Propaganda Shaped World War II Movies, 1987. Office: Oberlin Coll Rice Hall 305 Oberlin OH 44074 Office Phone: 440-775-8317.

KOPRIVA, ROBERT S., food products executive; BS in Acctg., U. Ill.; MS in Mgmt., Northwestern U. Audit mgr. Price Waterhouse, Chgo.; various positions Sara Lee Corp., Chgo., 1981—96; pres., CEO Jimmy Dean Foods, Chgo., 1996—2000; v.p. Sara Lee Corp., Chgo., 2000—03; pres. Sara Lee Foods U.S. -Supply Chain, Chgo., 2000—01; pres., CEO Sara Lee Foods, Chgo., 2001—; sr. v.p. Sara Lee Corp., Chgo., 2003—. Office: Sara Lee Corp 3 First Nat Plaza Chicago IL 60602-4260

KORANDO, DONNA KAY, journalist; b. Chester, Ill., Mar. 31, 1950; d. Samuel L. and Dorothy L. (Meyer) K.; m. James J. Heidenry, Nov. 28, 1981; children: Reid Samuel, Rachel. BA, So. Ill. U., 1972; MSL, Yale U., 1980. Tchr. journalism Lincoln H.S., Manitowoc, Wis., 1972-73; copy editor St. Louis Post-Dispatch, 1973-77, editorial writer, 1977-86, editor commentary page, 1986—. Mem. Lafayette Square Restoration Com., St. Louis, 1981—. Mem. Assn. Opinion Page Editors (bd. dirs.). Roman Catholic. Avocation: literature. Office: St Louis Post Dispatch 900 N Tucker Blvd Saint Louis MO 63101-1099

KORDONS, ULDIS, lawyer; b. Riga, Latvia, July 9, 1941; arrived in U.S., 1949; s. Evalds and Zenta Alide (Apenits) Kordons; m. Virginia Lee Knowles, July 16, 1966. AB, Princeton U., 1963; JD, Georgetown U., 1970. Bar: N.Y. 1970, Ohio 1978, Ind. 1989. Assoc. Whitman, Breed, Abbott, NYC, 1970-77, Anderson, Mori & Rabinowitz, Tokyo, 1973-75; counsel Armco Inc., Parsippany, NJ, 1977-84; v.p., gen. counsel, sec. Sybron Corp., Saddle Brook, NJ, 1984-88, Hillenbrand Industries Inc., Batesville, Ind., 1989-92; pres. Plover Enterprises, Cin., 1992—96, Kordons & Co., LPA, Cin., 1996—. Lt. USN, 1963—67. Mem.: ABA, Ind. Bar Assn., Ohio Bar Assn., N.Y. Bar Assn. Office: 8238 Wooster Pike Cincinnati OH 45227-4010 Home Phone: 513-272-2836; Office Phone: 513-272-1636. E-mail: ukordlaw@aol.com.

KOREN, YORAM, mechanical engineering educator; b. Tel Aviv, Aug. 1, 1938; came to U.S., 1985; s. Shlomo and Bathia (Rabinowitz) Shterwzis; m. Aliza Halina Palyard, Apr. 3, 1963; children: Shlomik, Esther. BS, Israel Inst. Tech., MS in Elec. Engring., PhD in Mech. Engring. Founding dir. NSF Engring. Rsch. Ctr. for Reconfigurable Mfg. Systems, 1996—; Paul G. Goebel prof. engring. U. Mich., Ann Arbor. Cons. Ford, Coldy Internat., Cybernet System, Metcut, SKF, Frat, 1980—. Author: Computer Control of Manufacturing Systems, 1983, Robotics for Engineers, 1985, Numerical Control of Machine Tools, 1978; contbr. articles to profl. jours.; patentee in field. Sgt. maj. USAF, 1957-61. Fellow SME, ASME; mem. IEEE (sr.), CIRP, NAE. Home: 4101 Thornoaks Dr Ann Arbor MI 48104-4255 Office: U Mich 2238 GG Brown Bldg Ann Arbor MI 48109-2125 Office Phone: 734-936-3596. E-mail: ykoren@umich.edu.

KORENIC, LYNETTE MARIE, librarian; b. Berwyn, Ill., Mar. 29, 1950; d. Emil Walter and Donna Marie (Harbutt) K. m. Jerome Dennis Reif, Dec. 31, 1988. BS in Art, U. Wis., 1977, MFA, 1979, MA in LS, 1981, MA in Art History, 1984; PhD in Art History, U. Calif., Santa Barbara, 2006. Asst. art libr. Ind. U., Bloomington, 1982-84; art libr. U. Calif., Santa Barbara, 1984-88, head Arts Libr., 1988-99; art libr. U. Wis., Madison, 1999—. Author articles. Mem. Art Librs. Soc. .Am. (sec. 1983-84, v.p. 1989, pres. 1990), Beta Phi Mu. Office Phone: 608-263-2256. E-mail: lkorenic@library.wisc.edu.

KORNBLET, DONALD ROSS, communications company executive; b. St. Louis, Nov. 7, 1943; s. Louis Yale and Mildred Fayette (Levey) K.; m. Ann Louise Vogel, Dec. 30, 1973; children: Ben Michael, David, Sarah. BA, Yale U., 1966. Dir. pub. info. Urban League St. Louis, 1968—71; midwestern dir. Coro Found., 1971—76; v.p., ptnr. Fleishman-Hillard, Inc., 1976—84; pres., co-owner USA-800, Inc., Kansas City, Mo., 1984—86; pres., owner BRI, St. Louis, 1986—2002; sr. v.p. Americall Group, Inc., 2002—05, Kornblet Consulting, 2006—. Instr. edn. St. Louis CC, 2006—. Prodr.: (radio show) Daily Essentials for Bus. Success. Mem. chancellor's coun. U. Mo., St. Louis, 1982-85; bd. dirs. Zelda Epstein Day Care Ctr., St. Louis, 1989; pres. Wellington Way Condominium, 1989; bd. dirs. Better Bus. Bur. Ea. Mo., 1990-2000, chmn., 1994-95, Coun. Better Bus. Burs., 1997-2005, The Nat. Conf., 1990, Coro Found., Midwestern Ctr., 1992, bd. trustees Coro Found., 1998; trustee Laumeier Sculpture Park, St. Louis County. Recipient merit award Opportunities Industralization Ctr., St. Louis, 1984; named One of Top 25 Small Bus. Owners, St. Louis U., 1988. Mem. Direct Mktg. Assn. (Direct Marketer of Yr. 1995), Bus. Mktg. Assn., Missouri Athletic Club, Yale Club. Jewish. Office: 6147 Lindell Saint Louis MO 63112 E-mail: drkornblet@yahoo.com.

KORNFELD, STUART A., hematology educator; b. St. Louis, Mo., Oct. 4, 1936; AB, Dartmouth Coll., 1958; MD, Washington U., 1962. Rsch. asst. biochemistry dept. sch. medicine Washington U., St. Louis, 1958-62, from instr. to asst. prof. medicine, 1966-70, from asst. to assoc. prof. biochemistry, 1968-72, prof. medicine dept. internal medicine, 1972—, prof. biochemistry, co-dir. divsn. hematology and oncology, 1976—, dir. divsn. oncology, 1973-76; intern med. ward Barnes Hosp., 1962-63, asst. resident, 1965-66; rsch. assoc. nat. inst. arthritis and metabolic disease NIH, 1963-65. Faculty rsch. assoc. Am. Cancer Soc., 1966-71; mem. cell biology study sect. NIH, 1974-77; mem. bd. sci. counselors Nat. Inst. Arthritis, Diabetes & Digestive & Kidney Disease, 1983-87; mem. sci. rev. bd. Howard Hughes Med. Inst., 1986—; mem. bd. sci. advisers Jane Coffin Childs Meml. Fund. Res., 1987—; Jubilee lectr. Biochemistry Soc., 1989. Assoc. editor Jour. Clin. Investigation, 1977-81, editor, 1981-82; assoc. editor Jour. Biol. Chemistry, 1982-87; author 145 publs. Recipient Borden award, 1962, Rsch. Career Devel. award NIH, 1971-76; named Harden Medallist, Biochemistry Soc., 1989, Passano Found. laureate, 1991. Mem. NAS (mem. inst. medicine), Am. Soc. Clin. Investigation (counselor 1972-75), Am. Soc. Hematology, Am. Soc. Biol. Chemists, Assn. Am. Physicians (sec. 1986—), Am. Acad. Arts and Sci., Am. Chem. Soc., Sigma Xi. Achievements include research in the structure, biosynthesis and function of glycoproteins, especially those which are found on the surface of normal and malignant cells, targeting of newly synthesized acid hydroloses to lysosomes. Office: 8826 Clin Scis Res Bldg PO Box 8125 Saint Louis MO 63156-8125

KORNGOLD, GERALD, law educator, former dean; b. Aug. 20, 1952; BA, U. Pa., 1974, JD, 1977. Bar: Pa. 1977, D.C. 1979, Ohio, 1995. Atty. Wolf, Block, Schorr & Solis-Cohen, Phila., 1977-79; asst. prof. N.Y. Law Sch., NYC, 1979—81, assoc. prof., 1981—84, assoc. dean for acad. affairs, 1984-86, prof., 1984—87, Case Western Res. U. Sch. Law, Cleve., 1987—, Everett D. and Eugenia S. McCurdy prof., 1994—, dean, 1997—2006, Case Western Res. U. Sch. Mgmt., Cleve., 2004. Author: Private Land Use Arrangements: Easements, Covenants, and Equitable Servitudes, 1990, (with Paul Goldstein) Real Estate Transactions, 1993. Named Prof. of the Yr., NY Law Sch., 1982—83, Case Western Reserve U. Sch. Law, 1989—90, 1995—96, 1996—97. Mem. Am. Law Inst., Phi Beta Kappa Office: Case Western Res U Sch Law 11075 East Blvd Cleveland OH 44106-5409 Office Phone: 216-368-3283. E-mail: slb11@case.edu.

KORNICK, MICHAEL, chef; Grad., Culinary Inst. Am., 1982. Chef Quilted Giraffe, NY, Windsor Ct. Hotel, New Orleans; mng. ptnr. KDK Restaurant Group; exec. chef Gordon, 1985, Lettuce Entertain You Enterprises, Four Seasons Hotel Aujord'hui, Boston, 1991, Marche, Red Light; owner, chef MK the Restaurant, Chgo., 1998—. Named Best New Chef de Cuisine, Boston mag., 1992; recipient award, James Beard Found., 2001. Office: 868 N Franklin Chicago IL 60610

KORNMANN, CHARLES BRUNO, judge; b. Watertown, SD, Sept. 14, 1937; BA, Coll. St. Thomas, 1959; LLB, Georgetown U., 1962. Bar: S.D. 1962. Ptnr. Richardson, Groseclose, Kornmann & Wyly, Aberdeen, S.D.; dist. judge U.S. Dist. Ct., Aberdeen, 1995—. Mem. S.D. Constnl. Revision Commn., 1974-77, S.D. Bd. Charities and Corrections, 1973-80, pres. 1978. Mem. Brown County Bar Assn., The State Bar of S.D. (bd. commrs. 1978-81, pres. 1988-89), Assn. Ins. Attys., S.D. Trial Lawyers Assn., Phi Delta Phi. Office: US District Judge Ste 408 102 4th Ave SE Aberdeen SD 57401-4309

KORPAN, RICHARD, retired energy executive; Exec. v.p., CFO Fla. Progress Corp., 1989-91, pres., COO, 1991-97, chmn., CEO, 1997—2000; ret., 2000. Bd. dirs. Progress Energy Corp., 2000—01, Black Hills Corp., Rapid City, SD, 2003—. Address: PO Box 33028 Saint Petersburg FL 33733-8028 Office: Black Hills Corp PO Box 1400 Rapid City SD 57709 Office Phone: 605-721-1700.

KORSCHOT, BENJAMIN CALVIN, retired investment company executive; b. LaFayette, Ind., Mar. 22, 1921; s. Benjamin G. and Myrtle P. (Goodman) K.; m. Marian Marie Schelle, Oct. 31, 1941; children: Barbara E. Korschot Haehlen, Lynne D. Korschot Gooding, John Calvin. BS, Purdue U., 1942; MBA, U. Chgo., 1947. V.p. No. Trust Co., Chgo., 1947-64; sr. v.p. St. Louis Union Trust Co., 1964-73; exec. v.p. Waddell and Reed Co., Kansas City, Mo., 1973-74, pres., 1974-79, vice-chmn. bd., 1979-85; pres. Waddell & Reed Investment Mgmt. Co., 1985-86; chmn. bd. Waddell & Reed Asset Mgmt. Co., 1973-86, retired, 1986. Pres. United Group of Mut. Funds, Inc., Kansas City, Mo., 1974-85, chmn., 1985-86; vice-chmn. Roosevelt Fin. Group, St. Louis, 1968-91, chmn. adv. bd., 1991-92; treas. Helping Hand of Goodwill Industries, 1993-95, chmn. investment com., 1995-2004; bd. dirs. Mo. United Meth. Found., 1995-2004, chmn. investment com., 2001-2004; chmn. bd. govs. Investment Co. Inst., 1980-82; chmn. bd. Fin. Analyst Fedn., 1978-79. Contbr. articles on investment fin. to profl. publs.; author autobiography, 1997. Mem. Civic Coun. Greater Kansas City, Mo., 1974-85; chmn. fin. com. ARC Retirement Sys.,

1986-87. With USN, 1942-45, 50-52. Mem. Inst. CFAs, Fin. Execs. Inst., Kansas City Soc. Fin. Analysts, Lakewood Oaks Golf Club. Republican. Home: 101 NW Hackberry St Lees Summit MO 64064-1477 Personal E-mail: bckorschot@yahoo.com.

KORT, BETTY, secondary school educator; English tchr. Hastings (Nebr.) Sr. High Sch., 1979—. Named Nebr. State English Tchr. of Yr., 1993. Office: Hastings Sen High Sch 1100 W 14th St Hastings NE 68901-3064

KOSKAN, JOHN M., state legislator; b. Winner, SD, Sept. 27, 1955; s. Milo Harlan and Juanita Mae (Mitchell) K.; m. Verna Gale Heying, 1973; children: Fawn Michelle, Tracy Michael, Joel Mathew, Joni Melissa. BS, S.D. Sch. Mines & Tech., 1977. Mem. Sch. Bd., Wood, S.D., 1984-90, S.D. Ho. of Reps., 1991-2000, mem. taxation and transp. coms.; design engr. Boeing Aircraft, Wichita, Kans., 1977-79, Cessna Aircraft Co., Wichita, 1979-80; design cons., mfr. Piper Advanced Technologies, Wichita, 1980-81; farmer, rancher Wood, S.D., 1980—; mem. S.D. Senate from 26th dist., Pierre, 2001—. Home: HC 1 Box 117A Wood SD 57585-9611 Office: State Capitol Senate 500 E Capitol Ave Pierre SD 57501-5070

KOSS, JOHN CHARLES, consumer electronics products manufacturing company executive; b. Milw., Feb. 22, 1930; s. Earl L. and Eda K.; m. Nancy Weeks, Apr. 19, 1952; children: Michael, Debra, John Charles, Linda, Pamela. Student, U. Wis., Milw., 1952; DEng (hon.), Milw. Sch. Engring., 1983. Founder Koss Corp., Milw., 1953, pres., 1958—72, 1984—86, chmn. bd., 1967—, chief exec. officer, 1973—90; creator home-stereophone, 1958. Created first high-fidelity stereophone, 1958. Bd. dirs. Milw. Hearing Soc.; bd. dirs., past pres. Jr. Achievement S.E. Wis. Assn.; dir. emeritus Milw. Sch. Engring.; With Air Force Band USAF, 1950-52. Named Entrepreneur of Yr. Research Dirs. Assn. Chgo., 1972, Mktg. Man of Yr. Am. Mktg. Assn. Milw. chpt., 1972; named to Audio Hall Fame, 1979, Consumer Electrics Hall of Fame, Consumer Electronics Assn., 2000, Wis. Bus. Hall of Fame Jr. Achievement, 2004; Mktg. Exec. of Yr. Sales and Mktg. Execs., 1976; recipient Debby award Soc. Audio Cons.'s, 1975, Pioneer award, Milw. Sch. Engring., 1980. Mem. Chief Execs. Orgn., Inst. High Fidelity (pres. 1968), Wis. Pres.'s Orgn., World Bus. Coun., World Pres.'s Org., Young Pres.'s Org. Clubs: Milw. Country, University; Les Ambassadeurs (London). Republican. Baptist. Office: Koss Corp 4129 N Port Washington Rd Milwaukee WI 53212-1029 Office Phone: 414-964-5000.

KOSTECKI, MARY ANN, financial tax consultant, small business consultant; b. St. Louis, Jan. 6, 1941; 4 children. Student, Forest Park Jr. Coll., 1969-72, Washington U., 1973-77. Dem. candidate for U.S House 2nd Dist., Mo., 1996. Home: 4256 State Road V De Soto MO 63020-3708

KOTEN, JOHN A., retired communications executive; b. Indpls., May 21, 1929; s. Roy Y. and Margaret (Neerman) K.; m. Catherine M. Hruska, Nov. 22, 1952; children: John, Mark, Sarah. BA, North Cen. Coll., Naperville, Ill., 1951, LLD (hon.), 1991; postgrad., Northwestern U., 1953; LLD (hon.), Quincy Coll., 1990. Supr. field advt. Montgomery Ward, Chgo., 1951-52; asst. dir. pub. rels. Am. Osteo. Assn., Chgo., 1952-53; editorial asst. Ill. Bell Tel. Co., Chgo., 1955-56, editor Telebriefs newsletter, 1956-57, supr. info., 1957-59, supr. comml. staff, 1959-60, supr. news svc. and advt. Springfield, 1960-62, dist. comml. mgr., 1962-63; supr. pub. info. AT&T, NYC, 1963, supr. customer rels., 1963-64; mgr. div. traffic Ill. Bell Tel. Co., Chgo., 1965-66, mgr. pub. rels., 1966-68, asst. v.p. civic affairs, 1968-69, asst. v.p. Chgo. ops., 1969-70, gen. mgr. upstate area Joliet, 1970-71; dir. state regulatory matters AT&T, Lisle, Ill., 1971-72; asst. v.p. pub. rels. Ill. Bell Tel. Co., Chgo., 1972-74; dir. pub. rels. AT&T, NYC, 1974-75; v.p. pub. rels. N.J. Bell Telephone Co., Newark, 1975-77, Ill. Bell Telephone Co., Chgo., 1977-80, v.p. corp. communications, 1980-87; sr. v.p. corp. communications Ameritech Corp., Chgo., 1987-92, ret., 1992; pres. The Wordsworth Group, Barrington Hills, Ill. Trustee Chgo. Symphony Orch., 1985-97, life trustee, 1997—; trustee Joint Coun. on Econ. Edn., N.Y.C.; trustee Am. Coun. Arts, 1987-98, treas., 1991-93; v.p. Ill. Arts Alliance, Chgo., 1986-91; trustee Arthur W. Page Soc., 1985—, pres., 1985-87; pres. Ameritech Found., Chgo., 1987-94; vice chmn. Am. Arts Alliance, Washington, 1983-92; bd. dirs. Am. Symphony Orch. League, Washington, 1982-94, Gt. Books Found., Chgo., 1991—, chmn. exec. com.; trustee SOS Children's Internat. Villages, Ill., 1996-00; trustee Assoc. Colls. Ill., Chgo., 1986-96, life trustee, 1997—; trustee Nat. Cultural Alliance, 1990-98; bd. visitors Medill Sch. Journalism, Northwestern U., 1988-94; assoc. trustee Wordsworth Trust, Eng., 1988; mem. corp. coun. Bus. Com. for Arts, 1988-96; mem. bd. overseers Curtis Inst. Music, Phila., 1997—; life trustee orth Ctrl. Coll., Ill., 1997—; bd. trustees Dist. 220 Edn. Found., vice chmn., 1999—. Mem. Pub. Rels. Soc. Am., Conf. Bd. Corp. Communications Coun., Chgo. Advt. Club (bd. dirs. 1978-82), Ind. Soc., Pub. Affairs Coun., Brookings Coun., Chgo. Club, Tavern Club, Econs. Club, Chgo. Yacht Club. Home and Office: The Wordsworth Group 271 Otis Rd Barrington IL 60010-5123

KOTHARI, RAJESH UJAMLAL, investment company executive; b. Pontiac, Mich., Dec. 4, 1967; s. Ujamlal and Kumud (Choksi) K. BA in Econ., U. Mich., 1989, MBA, 1992. CFA Assn. Investment Mgmt. and Rsch. Assoc. Zaske, Sarafa & Assoc., Bloomfield Hills, Mich., 1984-89; portfolio mgr. Masco Corp., Taylor, Mich., 1989—94; founder, treasurer, dir. internat. investing Cranbrook Capital Mgmt., Detroit, 1994—96; dir. GMA Capital, Farmington Hills, 1996; bd. dirs. Amicas, Inc., VerNova, Inc.; investment officer ProVen Pvt. Equity, London; co-founder, mng. dir. Seneca Partners Inc., Birmingham, 2002—. Dep. comdr. CAP, USAF Aux., Pontiac, 1981—. Recipient Comdrs. Commendations CAP, 1991, 92, 93, named on of 40 Under 40, Crain's Detroit Bus., 2006. Mem. Fin. Analyst soc. Detroit, at. Assn. Security Profls. (treas. Detroit chpt. 1995—), Mich. Venture Capital Assn. (bd. mem., exec. com.). Avocations: fencing, camping, jet skiing. Office: Seneca Partners Inc 300 Park St Ste 400 Birmingham MI 48009 Office Phone: 248-723-6650. Office Fax: 248-723-6651.

KOTLER, PHILIP, marketing educator, writer; b. Chgo., May 27, 1931; s. Maurice and Betty (Bubar) K.; m. Nancy Ruth Kellum, Jan. 30, 1955; children: Amy Elizabeth, Melissa Eve, Jessica Kellum. Student, DePaul U., 1948-50; MA, U. Chgo., 1953; PhD, MIT, 1956; postgrad., U. Chgo., 1957, Harvard, 1960; PhD (hon.), DePaul U., 1988, U. Zurich, Switzerland, 1989, Athens U. Econs. and Bus., 1995, Stockholm U., 1998, Crackow U. Econs., 1998; PhD (hon.), Budapest Sch. Econ. Sci. and Pub. Policy, B.I. Norwegian Sch. Mgmt. Sch. analyst Westinghouse Corp., Pitts., 1953; asst., then assoc. prof. Roosevelt U., Chgo., 1957-61; from asst. prof. to prof. marketing Northwestern U., Evanston, Ill., 1962-69, A. Montgomery Ward prof. marketing, 1969-73, Harold T. Martin prof. marketing, 1973-88, S.C. Johnson & Son disting. prof. internat. mktg., 1989—. Adv. mktg. editor Holt, Rinehart and Winston, 1965-78; chmn. Coll. on Mktg., Inst. Mgmt. Scis., 1968; mem. adv. bd. Yankelovich Ptnrs. Author: Simulation in Social and Administrative Science, 1971, Creating Social Change, 1971, The ew Competition, 1985, Marketing for Health Care Organizations, 1986, Marketing Models, 1992, Marketing for Congregations: Serving People More Effectively, 1992, Strategic Marketing for Education Institutions, 1995, High Visibility, 1997, Standing Room Only: Strategies for Marketing the Peforming Arts, 1997, The Marketing of Nations, 1997, Museum Strategy and Marketing, 1998, Kotler on Marketing, 1999, Marketing Places Europe, 1999, Marketing Asian Places, 2001, Marketing Moves, 2002, Repositioning Asia, 2002, Marketing Professional Services, 2002, Social Marketing: Improving the Quality of Life, 2002, A Framework for Marketing Management, 2003, Marketing Places: Attracting Investment, Industry and Tourism to Cities, States, and Nations, Marketing for Hospitality and Tourism, 2003, Marketing Global Biobrands, 2003, Rethinking Marketing, 2003, Marketing Insights A to Z, 2003, Lateral Marketing, 2003, Strategic Marketing for Nonprofit Organizations, 2003, Ten Deadly Marketing Sins, 2004, Attracting Investors, 2004, Corporate Social Responsibility: Doing the Most Good for Your Company and Your Cause, 2005, Principles of Marketing, 2005, Marketing Management: Analysis, Planning and Control, 2005, According to Kotler, 2005, The Elusive Fan: Reinventing Sports in a Crowded Marketplace, 2006. Bd. govs. Sch. of Art Inst. Chgo., 1985-2004. Mem. Am. Mktg. Assn. (bd. dirs. 1970-72, First Disting. Mktg. Educator 1985), Inst. Mgmt. Scis., Marketing Sci. Inst. (trustee 1974-84), Phi Beta Kappa. Office: Northwestern U Kellogg Sch Mgmt Evanston IL 60208-0001

KOTLOWITZ, ALEX, writer, journalist; Student, Wesleyan U. Former prodr. segments TV series MacNeil/ Lehrer NewsHour; former reporter The Wall Street Jour.; former contbr. NPR. Writer-i-residence Northwestern U.; Welch chmn. in Am. studies U. Notre Dame, South Bend, Ind. Author: There Are No Children Here: The Story of Two Boys Growing Up In the Other America, 1991 (Helen Bernstein award Excellence Journalism N.Y. Pub. Libr. 1992), The Other Side of the River: A Story of Two Towns, a Death and America's Dilemma, 1998 (Heartland prize for nonfiction Chgo. Tribune 1998), Never a City So Real, 2004; contbr. The N.Y. Times Mag., This Am. Life. Recipient George Polk award TV reporting Long Island U. Journalism dept. work on MacNeil/Lehrer NewsHour, 1984, Robert F. Kennedy award Coverage of Disadvantaged, George Foster Peabody award 2003. Office Phone: 708-445-8805. E-mail: akotlowitz@aol.com.

KOTOWICZ, WILLIAM EDWARD, dental educator; MS in Denture Prosthodontics, U. Mich., 1968, DDS, 1966. Asst. prof. U. Mich., 1969—71, interim dean, Sch. Dentistry, 1987—89, assoc. prof., 1971—74, sr. assoc. dean, 1989, prof. dentistry, prosthodontics, 1974—, acting dean, Sch. Dentistry Ann Arbor, 1995—97, dean, Sch. Dentistry, 1997—2002. Mem.: Am. Bd. Prothodontics, Am. Assn. Dental Sch., Internat. Assn. for Dental Rsch., Am. Assn. Dental Rsch., Phi Kappa Phi, Omicron Kappa Upsilon. Office Phone: 734-764-5060. Office Fax: 734-764-8046. E-mail: kotowicz@umich.edu.

KOTULAK, RONALD, newspaper science writer; b. Detroit, July 31, 1935; s. John and Mary (Roman) Kotulak; m. Jean Bond, May 6, 1961 (dec. July 1974); children: Jeffrey, Kerry, Christopher; m. Donna Clausonthue, July 19, 1980; stepchildren: Paul Clausonthue, Lisa Clausonthue. Student, Wayne State U., 1953—54; BJ, U. Mich., 1959. Mem. staff Chgo. Tribune, 1959—, sch. bd. reporter, 1961—63, writer, 1965—. Recipient 1st pl. sci. writing award, ADA, 1966, 1st pl. med. writing award, AMA, 1968, 1st pl. Howard Blakeslee Sci. Writing award, Am. Heart Assn., 1968, 1st prize Russell L. Cecil award, Arthritis Found., 1969, 1st pl. Claude Bernard Sci. Journalism award, Nat. Soc. Med. Rsch., 1971, James T. Brady award, Am. Chem. Soc., 1974, Lifeline award, Am. Health Found., 1976, Edward Scott Beck award, Chgo. Tribune, 1965, 1976, 1991, 1993, Outstanding Achievement award, U. Mich., 1978, Robert T. Morse Writers award, Am. Psychiat. Assn., 1982, 1989, Helen Carringer Nat. Mental Health Journalism award, Nat. Mental Health Assn., 1988, Excellence in Journalism award, Am. Aging Assn., 1992, Pulitzer Prize for explanatory journalism, 1994, others. Mem.: Nat. Assn. Sci. Writers (pres. 1972—73). Home: 737 N Oak Park Ave Oak Park IL 60302-1536 Office: The Chicago Tribune 435 N Michigan Ave Chicago IL 60611-4066

KOUCHOUKOS, NICHOLAS THOMAS, surgeon; b. Grand Rapids, Mich., Dec. 26, 1936; s. Thomas Paul and Antoinette (Karver) K.; m. Judith Buell, Aug. 24, 1966; children— Nicholas Thomas, Robert Buell, Thomas Paul. Student (James B. Angell scholar), U. Mich., 1954-57; MD cum laude, Washington U., 1961. Diplomate Am. Bd. Thoracic Surgery (bd. dirs. 1989-96). Intern Barnes Hosp., Washington U. Med. Ctr., St. Louis, 1961-62, asst. resident in surgery, 1962-65, chief adminstrv. resident, 1965-66; sr. clin. trainee in surgery USPHS, 1966-67; asst. in surgery Sch. Medicine Washington U., St. Louis, 1961-65, instr. surgery, 1965-67, John M. Shoenberg prof. cardiovascular surgery, 1984-96, vice chmn. dept. surgery, 1993-96; research fellow surgery Sch. Medicine, U. Ala., Birmingham, 1967-68, instr. surgery, 1967-69, advanced trainee thoracic and cardiovascular surgery, 1968-70, asst. prof. surgery, 1969-71, assoc. prof., 1971-74, prof., vice-dir. div. thoracic and cardiovascular surgery, 1974-81, John W. Kirklin prof. cardiovascular surgery, 1981, clin. prof., 1981-84; cardiovascular surgeon-in-chief Jewish Hosp. of St. Louis, 1984-96, surgeon in chief, 1988-96; mem. cardiovascular research study com. Am. Heart Assn., 1977-79; surgery study sect. USPHS, Bethesda, Md., 1977-80; vice chmn. dept. surgery Washington U. Sch. Medicine, St. Louis, 1991-96. Ad hoc cons. Specialized Centers in Research Arteriosclerosis, Nat. Heart and Lung Inst., Bethesda, 1971-72, mem. ad hoc rev. com. for collaborative studies on coronary artery surgery, 1973-75, surgery A study sect., 1976-77; mem. merit rev. bd. in cardiovascular studies VA, Washington, 1976-78 Editorial bd. Jour. Cardiac Rehab., 1979-84, Current Topics in Cardiology, 1977-92, Circulation, 1978-81, 86-88, Cardiology Update, 1979-92, Annals Thoracic Surgery, 1980-89, Cardiosat, 1984-92; assoc. editor Jour. Thoracic and Cardiovascular Surgery, 1994-98. Fellow: ACS, Am. Coll. Cardiology (asst. treas. 1997—99, sec. 1999—2000, finalist Young Investigators award 1962); mem.: AAUP, AMA, Internat. Cardiovascular Soc., Soc. Vascular Surgery, Soc. Univ. Surgeons, So. Surg. Assn., So. Thoracic Surg. Assn., St. Louis Thoracic Surg. Soc. (pres. 1993—95), Soc. Thoracic Surgeons (treas. 1992—97, v.p. 1998, pres. 1999—2000, historian 2007—), John Kirklin Soc., St. Louis Met. Med. Soc., Internat. Surg. Soc., Assn. Acad. Surgery, Assn. Clin. Cardiac Surgeons, Am. Surg. Assn., Am. Assn. Thoracic Surgery, Alpha Omega Alpha, Phi Beta Kappa. Home: 25 Picardy Ln Saint Louis MO 63124-1606 Office: Missouri Baptist Hosp 3009 N Ballas Rd Ste 360C Saint Louis MO 63131-2308 Office Phone: 314-996-5287. Personal E-mail: ntkouch@aol.com.

KOUCKY, JOHN RICHARD, metallurgical engineer, manufacturing executive; b. Chgo., Sept. 21, 1934; s. Frank Louis and Ella (Harshman) K.; m. Beverly Irene O'Dell, Aug. 16, 1958 (dec. May 1990); children: Deborah, Diane; m. Beverly Kay Cummins, Apr. 27, 1991 (dec. Jan. 1996); m. Mary Ann Hubbard, Jan. 4, 1997. BSMetE, U. Ill., 1957; MBA, Northwestern U., 1959. Metallurgist, asst. plant mgr. Fansteel Metall. Corp., North Chicago, Ill., 1957-64; supr. production engring. cen. foundry div. Gen. Motors Corp., Saginaw, Mich., 1964-67; asst. gen. mgr. Marion (Ind.) Malleable Iron, 1967-68; mgr. production engring. tech., plant mgr., v.p. engr. Wagner Castings Co., Decatur, Ill., 1968-79, 83-91; v.p., gen. mgr. Pa. mall iron div. Gulf & Western, Lancaster, 1979-82; v.p. tech. Wagner Laser Techs., 1989-94; v.p. Decatur Mfg. Co., 1993-95, 300 Below, Inc., Decatur, 1993—. Bd. dirs. Little Theater. 1st lt. US Army, 1957—58. Mem. Am. Soc. Metals (local chmn. 1976—), Am. Foundrymans Soc. (local vice chmn. 1968—), Ductile Iron Soc. (nat. bd. dirs. 1983—), Iron Castings Soc., Soc. Automotive Engrs., U. Ill. Dept. Materials Sci. Alumni Assn. (bd. dirs. 1983-98, Loyalty award 1986), Gray Iron Founders Assn., Soc. for Advancement Material and Process Engring., Country Club Decatur, Decatur Tennis Club (pres. 1976-78), Decatur Racquet Club. Republican. Avocations: tennis, golf, bridge, gardening. Home: 510 Greenway Ln Decatur IL 62521-2533 Office: 300 Below Inc 2999 Parkway Dr Decatur IL 62526 Office Phone: 217-423-3070. E-mail: jkoucky@300below.com.

KOUTSKY, DEAN ROGER, advertising executive; b. Omaha, Nov. 17, 1935; s. John Lewis and Ann Helen (Swan) K.; m. Kathryn Junette Strand; children: Linda, Lisa. BFA, Mpls. Coll. Art and Design, 1957. Art dir. Knox Reeves Advt., Inc., Mpls., 1958-65; v.p., exec. art dir. BBDO, Inc., Mpls., 1965-70; v.p., assoc. creative dir. Campbell-Mithun, Inc., Mpls., 1970-80, sr. v.p., creative dir., 1980-83, exec. v.p., exec. creative dir., 1983-85, vice chmn., 1985-89; exec. cons. Campbell-Mithun Esty, Inc., Mpls., 1989-90; ptnr., mgr. Harmon Ct., 1991-97. Bd. trustees Mpls. Coll. Art and Design, 1982-90, chmn., bd. trustees, 1985-89, adj. prof. advt./design divsn., 1995-2005. Office: 2005 James Ave S Minneapolis MN 55405-2404

KOUVEL, JAMES SPYROS, physicist, educator; b. Jersey City, May 23, 1926; s. Spyros and Ifegenia (Cassianos) K.; m. Audrey Lumsden, June 26, 1953; children: Diana, Alexander. B.Engring., Yale U., 1946, PhD, 1951. Research fellow U. Leeds, Eng., 1951-53, Harvard, 1953-55; physicist Gen. Electric Co. Research and Devel. Center, 1955-69; prof. physics U. Ill.-Chgo., 1969—2007. Vis. scientist Atomic Energy Rsch. Establishment, Harwell, Eng., 1967-68; vis. prof. U. Paris, Orsay, France, 1981; cons. Argonne (Ill.) Nat. Lab., 1969-89, mem. rev. com., 1970-72, vis. scientist, 1973-74; mem. materials rsch. adv. com. NSF, 1980-82, mem. materials rsch. groups spl. emphasis panel, 1993; mem. evaluation panel NRC, 1981-85. Author papers in field.; Editor: Magnetism Conf. proc, 1965-67; editorial bd.: Jour. Magnetism and Magnetic Materials, 1975—. Served with USNR, 1944-46. Guggenheim fellow, 1967-68; NSF rsch. grantee, 1973-96. Fellow Am. Phys. Soc., AAAS Home: 223 N Euclid Ave Oak Park IL 60302-2107 Office: U Ill Physics Dept Chicago IL 60607-7059 Office Phone: 312-996-5348. Business E-Mail: kouvel@uic.edu.

KOUYOUMJIAN, ROBERT G., electrical engineering educator; b. Apr. 26, 1923; BS in Physics, Ohio State U., 1948, PhD in Physics, 1953. Prof. emeritus dept. elec. engring. Ohio State U. Mem. URSI Commn. B. Fellow IEEE (Fellow award, Disting. Lectr., Centennial medal 1984); mem. Sigma Xi, Eta Kappa Nu, Sigma Pi Sigma. Office: Ohio State U Dept of Elec Engring Rm 256 2015 Neil Ave Dept Of Columbus OH 43210-1210

KOVAC, F. PETER, advertising executive; Pres., CEO NKH&W, Inc., Kansas City, Mo. Office: NKH&W Inc 5th Fl 600 Broadway Kansas City MO 64105

KOVACIK, THOMAS L., chief operating officer and safety director; b. Toledo, Ohio, Aug. 9, 1947; BS in Chemistry, Bowling Green State U., 1969, MA, 1971. Chemist water treatment City of Toledo, 1967-69, chief chemist water plant, chief chemist, dir. pollution control, dir. pub. utilities, 1982-89; pres. Envirosafe, Toledo, 1989-92, Great Lakes N-Viro, 1992-94; cons. Toledo, 1994-96; COO, safety dir. City of Toledo, 1996—. Office: City of Toledo Ste 2200 1 Govt Ctr Toledo OH 43604

KOVACS, ROSEMARY, newpaper editor; BS in Journalism, Bowling Green State U., 1968. Mng. editor prodn. The Plain Dealer, Cleve., 1990—. Named to Bowling Green State U. Journalism Hall of Fame, 1988. Mem. Press Club of Cleve. (pres.). Office: Plain Dealer Pub Co 1801 Superior Ave Cleveland OH 44114-2198

KOVEL, RALPH MALLORY, writer, antique expert; b. Milw. s. Lester and Dorothy K.; m. Terry Horvitz; children: Lee R., Karen. Attended, Ohio State U. Pres., chmn. U.S. Brands, Inc.; pres. Lucayan Aquaculture, Freeport, Bahamas. V.p., treas. Antiques, Inc.; trustee WVIZ-TV, Western Res. Hist. Soc., Cleve., Cleve. Pops Orch., Inc., Sara Lee Foods; Hiram fellow, former tchr. course in antiques Western Res. U., John Carroll U. Writer: (with Terry Kovel) syndicated column Kovels Antiques and Collecting, 1955—, Ask the Experts, House Beautiful, 1979-2000, Medio, CD-Rom Mag., 1995, The Kovels on Collecting, Forbes Mag., 2000-02; editor: monthly newsletters Kovels on Antiques and Collectibles, 1974—, Kovels Sports Collectibles, 1992-97; Know Your Antiques, Pub. TV, 1969-70; syndicated TV series Kovels on Collecting, 1981, 87, Collector's Journal TV, 1989-93, Flea Market Finds with the Kovels HGTV, 2000-04; numerous appearances on radio and TV talk shows; author: (with Terry Kovel) Kovels' Dictionary of Marks-Pottery and Porcelain, 1953, rev. edit., 1995, Directory of American Silver, Pewter and Silver Plate, 1958, American Country Furniture, 1780-1875, 1963, Kovels' Know Your Antiques, rev. edit., 1993, Kovels Antiques and Collectibles Price List, 39th edit., 2007, Kovels' American Art Pottery, 1993, Kovels' Bid, Buy & Sell Online, 2001, The Kovels' Bottle Price List, 13th edit., 2006, Kovels' Price Guide for Collector Plates, Figurines, Paperweight and Other Ltd. Editions, 1978, Kovels' Collector's Guide to American Art Pottery, 1974, Kovels' Collector's Guide to Limited Editions, 1974, Kovels' Know Your Collectibles, 1981, 1992, Kovels' Book Antique Labels, 1982, Kovels' Depression Glass and Dinnerware Price List, 8th edit. 2004, Kovels' Illustrated Price Guide to Royal Doulton, 2d edit., 1984, Kovels' Organizer for Collectors, rev. edit., 1983, Kovels' Collectors' Source Book, 1983, Kovels' New Dictionary of Marks Pottery and Porcelain, 1850 to the Present, 1986, Kovels' Advertising Collectibles Price List, 1986, 05, Kovels' Guide to Selling Your Antiques and Collectibles, rev. edit., 1990, Kovels' American Silver Marks 1650 to Present, 1989, Kovels' Antiques and Collectibles Fix-It Source Book, 1990, Kovels' Quick Tips: 799 Helpful Hints on How to Care For Your Collectibles, 1995, Kovels' Guide to Selling, Buying and Fixing Your Antiques and Collectibles, 1995, The Label Made Me Buy It, 1998, Kovel's Yellow Pages 2d edit., 2003, Kovel's American Antiques 1750-1900, 2004, Kovels American Collectibles 1900-2000, 2007; (video tape series) Collecting With the Kovels, Art Pottery I, Art Pottery II, 1995, Kovels' Page-A-Day Collectibles Calendar 1990, 1991, Kovels' Antiques and Collectibles 2003 Day-At-A-Time Calendar; contbr. numerous articles on antiques to publs, chapt. to books. Former mem. rev. and allocations com. United Torch Fund, Cleve.; past pres. E. End eighborhood Settlement House; past chmn. adv. com. Woodhill Homes; past bd. dirs. Soc. Collectors, Silver Mus. Religious Art. Recipient Lane Bryant award, 1966; Peirce Award for Outstanding Cmty. Svc. Sta. WVIZ-TV, 1980, Cleve. Emmy award best entertainment, 1971, Cleve. Emmy award cultural affairs programming, 1987, Cleve. Pops Orch. Star award, 2005, Telly award, Flea Market Finds. Mem.: Union League Club (Chgo.), Oakwood Club (Cleve.). Office: PO Box 22200 Cleveland OH 44122-0200

KOVEL, TERRY HORVITZ, writer, antiques authority; b. Cleve. d. Isadore and Rix Horvitz; m. Ralph Kovel; children: Lee R., Karen. BA, Wellesley Coll., 1950. Tchr. math. Hawken Sch. for Boys, Shaker Heights, Ohio, 1961-71; now pres. Antiques Inc.; past tchr. course in antiques Western Res. U., John Carroll U. Writer: (with Ralph Kovel) syndicated column Kovels Antiques and Collecting, 1955—, Ask the Experts, House Beautiful, 1979-00, Medio, CD-Rom mag., 1995, The Kovels on Collecting, Forbes Mag., 2000-02; editor: monthly newsletters Kovels on Antiques and Collectibles, 1974-, Kovels Sports Collectibles, 1992-97; TV series Know Your Antiques, Pub. TV, 1969-70; syndicated TV Series Kovels on Collecting, 1981, 87, Collector's Journal TV, 1989-93, Flea Market Finds with the Kovels HGTV, 2000-04; numerous appearances on radio and TV talk shows; author: (with Ralph Kovel) Kovels' Dictionary of Marks-Pottery and Porcelain, 1953, rev. edit., 1995, Directory of American Silver, Pewter and Silver Plate, 1958, American Country Furniture, 1780-1875, 1963, Kovels' Know Your Antiques, rev. edit, 1993, Kovels' American Art Pottery, 1993, Kovels' American Antiques 1750-1900, 2004, Kovels American Collectibles 1900-2000, 2007, Kovels' Antiques and Collectibles Price List, 39th edit., 2007, Kovels' Know Your Collectibles, 1981, 92, Kovels' Bottle Price List, 13th edit., 2006, Kovels' Organizer for Collectors, 1978, revised, 1983, Kovels' Price Guide for Collector Plates, Figurines, Paperweights and Other Limited Editions, 1978, Kovels' Collector's Guide to American Art Pottery, 1974, Kovels' Collector's Guide to Limited Editions, 1974, Kovels' Depression Glass and Dinnerware Price List, 8th edit., 2004, Kovels' Illustrated Price Guide to Royal Doulton, 2d edit., 1984, Kovels' Collectors' Source Book, 1983, Kovels' ew Dictionary of Marks Pottery and Porcelain, 1850 to the Present, 1986, Kovels' Advertising Collectibles Price List, 1986, 05, Kovels' Guide to Selling Your Antiques and Collectibles, 1987, 2d edit., 1990, Kovels' Book of Antique Labels, 1982, Kovels' American Silver Marks 1650 to the Present, 1989, Kovels' Antiques and Collectibles Fix-It Source Book, 1990, Kovels' Guide to Selling, Buying and Fixing Your Antiques and Collectibles, 1995, Kovels' Quick Tips: 799 Helpful Hints on How To Care for Your Collectibles, 1995, The Label Made Me Buy It, 1998, Kovels' Yellow Pages, 2d. edit., 2003, Kovels' Bid, Buy and Sell Online, 2001; (Video tape series) Collecting With the Kovels, 1995, Art Pottery I, Art Pottery II, Kovels' Page-A-Day Collectibles Calendar 1990, 1991, Kovels' Antiques and Collectibles 2003 Day-At-A Time-Calendar; contbr. numerous articles on antiques to publs, chapt. to books. Trustee Hiram Coll., 1989—99, hon. trustee, 2000; bd. mem. Shaker Hist. Soc. Hiram fellow; recipient Peirce award for outstanding cmty. svc. Sta. WVIZ-TV, 1980, Cleve. Emmy award for best entertainment, 1971, Cleve. Emmy award for cultural affairs programming, 1987; Laurel Sch. Alumanae of Yr., Telly award, Flea Market Finds, 2002. Office: PO Box 22200 Cleveland OH 44122-0200

KOWALSKI, KENNETH LAWRENCE, physicist, researcher; b. Chgo., July 24, 1932; s. Florian Lawrence and Emily Helen (Sinoga) K.; m. Audrey Bellin; children: Eric Clifford, Claudia Gail. BS, Ill. Inst. Tech., 1954; PhD, Brown U., 1963. Aero. rsch. scientist Lewis Rsch. Ctr., NACA, 1954-57; rsch. assoc. in physics Brown U., summer 1962, Case Inst. Tech., Cleve., 1962-63, asst. prof. physics, 1963-67, assoc. prof., 1967-73, Case Western Res. U., 1967-73, prof., 1973—, exec. officer dept. physics, 1970-71, chmn. dept. physics, 1971-76. Vis. prof. Inst. Theoretical Physics U. Louvain, Belgium, 1968-69; scientist-in-residence Argonne Nat. Lab., 1986-87, User Fermilab, 1993—. Author: (with S.K. Adhikari) Dynamical Collision Theory and It's Applications, 1991; editor: (with W.J. Fickinger) Modern Physics in America, 1988; contbr. articles to profl. jours. NSF grantee, 1972-96. Mem. Am. Phys. Soc. Achievements include research on theoretical physics. Home: 2172 Bellfield Ave Cleveland Heights OH 44106 Office: Case Western Res U Dept Physics 10900 Euclid Ave Dept Physics Cleveland OH 44106-1712 Office Phone: 216-368-4011. Business E-Mail: klk3@po.cwru.edu.

KOWALSKI, RICHARD SHELDON, hospital administrator; b. Detroit, Feb. 18, 1944; s. Richard Joseph and Margaret Lucile (Sheldon) K.; m. Doris Kay Smith, Nov. 20, 1982; children: Renée Marie, Jerrod Patrick, Sterling Prescott. BBA, Ea. Mich. U., 1966; MS in Health Adminstrn., Trinity U., San Antonio, 1971. Adminstrv. asst. Univ. Hosp.-U. Wash., Seattle, 1969-70; med. facilities cons. Ill. Dept. Health, Des Moines, 1970-72; asst. adminstr. Mercy Hosp., Cedar Rapids, Iowa, 1972-79; chief exec. officer St. Mary Med. Ctr., Galesburg, Ill., 1979—. Mem. coun. for govt. rev. Crescent Counties Found. for Med. Care, aperville, Ill., 1986—; bd. dirs. Assn. Venture Corp., Naperville; chmn. bd. dirs. United Health Properties, Galesburg, 1985—; mem. adv. bd. Physician Hosp. Inst.; mem. comty. bd. Wells Fargo. Mem. strategic planning steering com. City of Galesburg, 1986—; bd. dirs. Econ. Devel. Coun., Galesburg, 1986—, Knox County Devel. Corp., 1986, Civic Ctr. Authority, 2001—. Named hon. alumnus Grad. Program in Hosp. and Health Adminstrn., U. Iowa, 1990. Fellow Am. Coll. Healthcare Execs. (regent Ctrl. Ill.); mem. Ill. Hosp. Assn. (pres. region

1-B, bd. dirs. 1987—, Disting. Leadership award 1986), Galesburg Area C. of C. (chmn. 1990), Soangetaha Country Club (bd. dirs. 1990), Rotary. Avocations: golf, tennis. Office: St Mary Med Ctr 3333 N Seminary St Galesburg IL 61401-1251

KOWEL, STEPHEN THOMAS, electrical engineer, educator; b. Phila., Nov. 20, 1942; s. Abraham and Anna K.; m. Janis Zoltan, June 7, 1970; children: Ann, Eugene, Rose. BSEE, U. Pa., 1964; PhD in Elec. Engring., 1968; MSEE, Poly. Univ., 1966. Rsch. assoc. U. Pa., Phila., 1968-69; asst. prof. elec. and computer engring. Syracuse (N.Y.) U., 1969-74, assoc. prof., 1974-79, prof., 1979-84; prof. elec. engring. and computer sci. U. Calif., Davis, 1984-90, vice-chair dept., 1986-90, dir. organized rsch. program on polymeric ultrathin film systems, 1988-90; chmn. elec. and computer engring. U. Ala., Huntsville, 1990-97, dir. PhD program in optical sci. and engring., 1992-97, interim dean engring., 1997—98, dir., lab. for integrated computing and optoelectric systems, 1998-99, prof elec. and computer engring., 1998-99; dean engring. U. Cin., 1999—2004, prof. elec. engring., 2004—. Vis. prof. Cornell U., Ithaca, N.Y., 1982-83; cons. in field. Contbr. articles to profl. jours.; patentee in field. Grantee NASA, USAF, U.S. Army, NSF, Advanced Rsch. Projects Agy. Fellow OSA, IEEE (Centennial medal 1984); mem. AAUP, Am. Soc. Engring. Edn., Sigma Xi. Home: 3787 Brighton Manor Ln Cincinnati OH 45208-1965 Business E-Mail: stephen.kowel@uc.edu.

KOZAK, JOHN W., bank executive; b. Zanesville; With Mut. Fed. Savs. Bank (now named Century Nat. Bank), Park Nat. Corp. (formerly Mut. Fed. Savs. Bank), 1990, Park Nat. Bank, Newark, 1991-98, CFO, 1998, sr. v.p., 1998—. Office: Park Nat Bank 50 N 3d St Newark OH 43055 Fax: 740-349-3787.

KOZIURA, JOSEPH FRANK, state representative; b. Aug. 21, 1946; m. Kitti Wheatley; 1 child, Mary. Grad., Lorain County C.C.; BA in Bus., Dyke Coll., 1968. Chief dep. auditor, Lorain, Ohio, 1971-76; city auditor, 1976-83; state rep. Dist. 55 Ohio State Congress, 1985-92, state rep. Dist. 61, 1993-95; mayor City of Lorain, Ohio, 1996—99; state rep. Dist. 56, 2001—. Precinct committeeman Lorain Dems.; exec. com. mem. Lorain County Dems., fin. advisor securities. Mem. VFW, Lorain C. of C., Amvets, Vietnam Vets. Am.

KOZMA, ADAM, electrical engineer; b. Cleve., Feb. 2, 1928; s. Desire and Vera (Nagy) K.; m. Eileen Marie Somogyi, Oct. 24, 1956 (dec. Jan. 1978); children: Paul A. (dec.), Peter A.; m. Rebecca Chelius, Feb. 6, 1993. BSME, U. Mich., 1952, MS in Engring.-Instrumentation Engring., 1964; MS in Engring. Mechanics, Wayne State U., 1961; PhD in Elec. Engring., U. London, 1968; diploma of membership, Imperial Coll., 1969. Design engr. US Broach Co., Detroit, 1951-57; rsch. engr. Inst. Sci. & Tech., Willow Run Labs. U. Mich., Ann Arbor, 1958-69; gen. mgr. Electro Optics Ctr. Harris, Inc., Ann Arbor, 1969-73; sr. rsch. engr. radar div. Environ. Rsch. Inst. Mich., Ann Arbor, 1973-75, mgr. elec. and electromagnetics dept., 1975-76, mgr. tech. staff, 1976-77, v.p., dir. radar div., 1977-85, v.p., corp. devel., 1985-86; v.p., dir. def. electronics engring. div. Syracuse (N.Y.) Rsch. Corp., 1986-88; head intelligence systems dept. MITRE Corp., Bedford, Mass., 1988-89, head advanced systems dept., 1990-93; adj. prof. Coll. Engring. U. Mich., Ann Arbor, 1993—2002, vis. scholar, 2003—06. Cons. Conductron Corp., Ann Arbor, 1966, IBM, Endicott, N.Y., 1967-68, U.S. Army Missile Command, Huntsville, Ala., 1974-76, MITRE Corp., 1993-2001, Veridian-ERIM-Internat., Inc., 1998-2001; lectr. various univs.; engring. cons., 1993-2005. Co-author: Hologram Visual Displays (Motion Picture TV Engrs. honorable mention 1977); patentee in field. With US Army, 1946—47, with USAR, 1947—51, with reserve USAF, 1953—61. Fellow IEEE (life), Optical Soc. Am.; mem. Aero. and Electronics Systems Soc. of IEEE (radar sys. panel 1984-2006, emeritus, 2006-bd. govs. 91-93), Geosci. and Remote Sensing Soc. of IEEE, Am. Def. Preparedness Assn. (chmn. various coms. avionics sect. 1975-88, Ordnance medal 1984), Soc. Photo-Optical Instrumentation Engrs., Sigma Xi. Lutheran. Avocations: tennis, skiing, bicycling. Home and Office: 2996 Appleway Ann Arbor MI 48104-1808 Business E-Mail: akozma@umich.edu.

KRAEMER, HARRY M. JANSEN, JR., investment and former medical products executive; BA in Math. and Econs. summa cum laude, Lawrence U., Wis., 1977; M in fin. and acctg., orthwestern U. Kellogg Sch., 1979. CPA Ill. With N.W. Industries, Bank of Am.; dir. corp. devel. Baxter Internat. Inc., Deerfield, Ill., 1982, various positions in domestic and internat. ops., sr. v.p., CFO, 1993-97, mem. Office Chief Exec., 1995—, pres., 1997, CEO, 1999—2004, bd. dirs., 1995, chmn., 2000; exec. ptnr. Madison Dearborn Partners, Chgo., 2005—. Bd. dirs. Sci. Applications Internat. Corp., Evanston Northwestern Healthcare; mem. Bus. Roundtable, Healthcare Leadership Coun. Bd. trustees, deans' adv. bd. Northwestern U. J.L. Kellogg Grad. Sch. Mgmt.; bd. trustees Lawrence U. Recipient Schaffner award, Northwestern U. Kellogg Sch., 1996. Mem.: Chgo. Club, Comml. Club Chgo. Office: Madison Dearborn Partners 9 W 57th St # 42 New York NY 10019-2701

KRAFT, ARTHUR, dean; b. Eden, NY, May 7, 1944; s. Arthur Brauer and Mary Jane (Forti) K.; m. Joan Marie Brown, Sept. 3, 1966; children: Arthur G., Stephen Michael, Leigh Judith. BS, St. Bonaventure U., 1966; MA, SUNY, Buffalo, 1969, PhD, 1970. Asst. prof. Ohio U., Athens, 1969—72, assoc. prof., 1972—75; prof. U. Nebr., Lincoln, 1975—77, assoc. dean Coll. Bus., 1977—83; dean Coll. Bus. and Econs. W.Va. U., Morgantown, 1983—87; dean sch. bus. Rutgers U., ew Brunswick, NJ, 1987—93; dean Sch. Mgmt. Ga. Inst. Tech., Atlanta, 1993—97; dean Coll. Commerce, Charles H. Kellstadt Grad Sch. Bus. DePaul U., Chgo., 1997—2005; dean Robert J. and Carolyn A. Waltos, Jr. chair in bus. and econs. George L. Argyros Sch. Bus. and Econs. Chapman U., Orange, Calif., 2006—. Mem. pension adv. com. Monongalia County Hosp., Morgantown, 1985-87., 1985—87. Recipient NASA fellowship Stanford U., 1973, fellow Sears-Roebuck Fellowship Found., Washington, 1974-75; named Outstanding Young Individual Jaycees, Lincoln, 1978 Mem. Am. Econ. Assn., Am. Assembly of Collegiate Schs. of Bus. (chmn. bd. 2006-07, visitation com. 1977—, continuing accreditation com. 1987, bus. accreditation com. 1995—), North Ctrl. Assn. (evaluator 1986-87), Beta Gamma Sigma. Avocations: trivia, sports. Office: Chapman Univ George L Argyros Sch Business Economics Beckman Hall One University Dr Orange CA 92866 Office Phone: 714-628-2839. Personal E-mail: artkraft07@yahoo.com.

KRAFT, BURNELL D., agricultural products company executive; b. Chester, Ill., July 24, 1931; s. Herman F. and Ella Kraft; m. Shirley Ann Huch, Dec. 30, 1950; children: Jon B., Julie Ann Kraft Schwalbe. BS, So. Ill. U., 1956. Acct., mcht. Tabor and Co., Decatur, Ill., 1956-59, v.p., 1959-61, exec. v.p., 1961-70, pres., 1970-75; with Archer Daniels Midland Co. (merged with Tabor and Co.), Decatur, 1975-84, corp. v.p., 1984-94, group v.p., 1994-97, sr. v.p., 1997—, pres. ADM/GROWMARK River System div., 1985—, pres. Collingwood Grain div., 1989-94. Bd. dirs. Alfred C. Toepfer Internat., United Grain Growers. Trustee Millikin U., Decatur, 1983-95, chmn. trustees, 1990-94; bd. dirs. Decatur Meml. Hosp., 1970-80. With U.S. Army, 1952-53, Korea. Mem. N.Am. Export Grain Assn., Nat. Feed Grains Council, Nat. Grain and Feed Assn., St. Louis Mchts. Exchange, Chgo. Bd. Trade, Decatur C. of C. (past bd. dirs.), Phi Kappa Phi, Beta Gamma Sigma. Clubs: Decatur, Country Club Decatur (bd. dirs. 1974-78). Republican. Lutheran. Avocations: aviation, golf, boating, tennis. Office: Archer Daniels Midland Co 4666 Faries Pkwy PO Box 1470 Decatur IL 62525-1820

KRALEWSKI, JOHN EDWARD, health service research educator; b. Durand, Wis., May 20, 1932; s. Joseph and Esther (Hetrick) K.; m. Marjorie L. Gustafson; Apr. 22, 1957; children: Judy, Ann, Sara. BS in Pharmacy, U. Minn., 1956, MHA, 1962, PhD, 1969. Asst. prof. U. Minn., Mpls., 1965-69, prof. health svcs. rsch., 1979—; prof. U. Colo., Denver, 1969-78. 1st lt. USAF, 1957-60. Kellogg fellow Kellogg Found., 1962-65, Valencia (Spain) Acad. Medicine fellow, 1993. Mem. APHA, Assn. Health Svcs. Rsch. Avocation: oenology. Office: U Minn Health Svc Rsch 420 Delaware St SE Box 729 Minneapolis MN 55455-0374

KRAMER, ANDREA S., lawyer; b. Chgo., Mar. 15, 1955; BA summa cum laude with high distinction, U. Ill., 1975; JD cum laude, Northwestern U., 1978. Bar: Ill. 1978, U.S. Tax Ct. 1980, U.S. Ct. Fed. Claims 1982, Ill. Ct. Appeals (no. dist., 7th cir.). With Coffield, Ungaretti & Harris, Chgo.; ptnr. McDermott Will & Emery LLP, Chgo. Adj. law prof. Northwestern U. Sch. Law. Author: Financial Products: Taxation, Regulation and Design, 2000; mem. editorial bd. Jour. Criminal Law and Criminology, 1976-78; contbr. articles to profl. jours., chpts. to books. Founding bd. mem. The Women's Treatment Ctr., Chgo., chmn. bd. dirs.; bd. dirs. Dance Art. Named one of The 50 Most Influential Women Lawyers in Am., Nat. Law Jour., 2007; recipient Bronze Tablet, U. Ill., 1975, Unsung Heroine Award, Cook County Bd. Commrs., 2004. Mem. Anti-Defamation League, Internat. Bar Assn., Chgo. Bar Assn. (sect. taxation), Chgo. Fin. Exchange, Alpha Lambda Delta, Phi Alpha Theta, Phi Beta Kappa, Phi Kappa Phi. Office: McDermott Will & Emery LLP 227 W Monroe St Chicago IL 60606-5096 Office Phone: 312-372-2000, 312-984-6480. Office Fax: 312-984-7700. Business E-Mail: akramer@mwe.com.

KRAMER, DALE VERNON, retired language educator; b. Mitchell, SD, July 13, 1936; s. Dwight Lyman and Frances Elizabeth (Corbin) K.; m. Cheris Gamble Kramarae, Dec. 21, 1960; children: Brinlee, Jana. BS, SD State U., Brookings, 1958; MA, Case Western Res. U., Cleve., 1960, PhD, 1963. Instr. English Ohio U., Athens, 1962-63, asst. prof., 1963-65, U. Ill., Urbana, 1965-67, assoc. prof., 1967-71, prof. English, 1971-96; prof. emeritus, 1997—; acting head English dept. U. Ill., Urbana, 1982, 86-87, assoc. dean Coll. of Arts & Scis., 1992-95. Assoc. vice provost, prof. English, U. Oreg., 1990. Author: Charles Robert Maturin, 1973, Thomas Hardy: The Forms of Tragedy, 1975, Thomas Hardy: Tess of the d'Urbervilles, 1991; editor: Critical Approaches to the Fiction of Thomas Hardy, 1979, Thomas Hardy, The Woodlanders, 1981, 85, Thomas Hardy, The Mayor of Casterbridge, 1987, Critical Essays on Thomas Hardy: The Novels, 1990, The Cambridge Companion to Thomas Hardy, 1999; Chmn. bd. editors Jour. English and Germanic Philology, 1972-95; mem. bd. editors Cambridge Edit. of the Works of Joseph Conrad, 1995-2008. Served to capt. US Army, 1958-66. Mem. Ctr. Advanced Study, 1971; Am. Philos. Soc. grantee, 1969, 86, NEH grantee, 1986. Mem.: Thomas Hardy Assn. (v.p. 2007—). Congregationalist.

KRAMER, DARREN, newscaster; b. Wis. BA in Comm., U. Wis., Stevens Point. With KDNL-TV, St. Louis; co-anchor Good Morning Conn. WRNH-TV, New Haven, 1999—2003, co-anchor News at Noon; weekend anchor and reporter WMAQ-TV, Chgo., 2003—. Office: WMAQ-TV NBC Tower 454 N Columbus Dr Chicago IL 60611

KRAMER, DAVID J., state representative, lawyer; b. Omaha, Sept. 5, 1964; BA in Polit. Sci., Loyola Univ., 1987; JD, Georgetown Univ., 1990. Bar: Nebr. 1990, U.S. Dist. Ct. Nebr., U.S. Ct. Appeals (8th cir.). Atty. Baird Holm Law Firm, Omaha, 1990—96, 1999—; chmn. Nebr. Rep. Party, 2001—. Dir. resident program Internat. Rep. Inst., Luanda, Angola, 1997, Luanda, 98; chmn. Douglas County Rep. Party, 1995—96. Mem. Douglas County, 1991—, State Ctrl. Com., 1991—; vol. U.S. Senate Campaign, U.S. House Rep. Campaign, State Legislature Campaign, County Treas. Campaign, City Council Campaign, Sch. Bd. Campaign. Named One of Ten Outstanding Omahans, Jaycees, 1999. Mem.: ABA, State Ctrl. Com., Douglas County Com. (chmn. 1995—96). Republican. Office: Nebr Rep Party 421 S 9th St Ste 233 Lincoln NE 68508 Address: Baird Holm Mceachen Pedersen Hamann & St 1500 Woodmen Tower Omaha NE 68102 E-mail: dkramer@bairdholm.com.

KRAMER, EUGENE LEO, lawyer; b. Barberton, Ohio, Nov. 7, 1939; s. Frank L. and Portia I. (Acker) Kramer; m. JoAnn Stockhausen, Sept. 19, 1970; children: Martin, Caroline, Michael. AB, John Carroll U., 1961; JD, U. Notre Dame, 1964. Bar: Ohio 1964. Law clk. U.S. Ct. Appeals (7th cir.), Chgo., 1964-65; ptnr. Squire, Sanders & Dempsey, Cleve., 1965-91, Roetzel & Andress, A Legal Profl. Assn., Cleve. and Akron, Ohio, 1992-97; spl. counsel Ohio Atty. Gen., 2003—06. Cons. Ohio Constl. Revision Commn., Columbus, 1970—74. Trustee Regina Health Ctr., 1997—, pres., 2001—04; past pres. HELP Found., Inc., HELP, Inc., Cleve., 1981—92, Playhouse Sq. Assn., Cleve., 1980—84; pres. N.E. Ohio Transit Coalition, 1992—; mem. policy com. Build-Up Greater Cleve. Program, 1982—98; mem. Greater Cleve. Partnership; trustee Consultation Ctr. Diocese Cleve., 1990—96; mem. Future Ch. Leadership Coun., 2005—; trustee Citizens League Greater Cleve., 1984—90, 1993—, Citizens League Rsch. Inst., 1995—97, Lyric Opera Cleve., 1995—2006, Beck Ctr. for the Arts, 2007—, St. Ann Found., 1990—92. Recipient Disting. Leadership award, HELP, Inc., 1986, Pioneer Achievement award, HELP-Six Chimneys, Inc., 1986, Disting. Svc. award, Assn. Retarded Citizens, 1990, Vol. Svc. award, City of Lakewood, 2001. Mem.: ABA, Cleve. Bar Assn., Ohio State Bar Assn. (chmn. local govt. law com. 1986—90), Club Key Tower. Democrat. Roman Catholic. Avocations: music, theater, sports, travel. Home and Office: 1422 Euclid Ave Ste 1162 Cleveland OH 44115-2001 Home Phone: 216-228-7442; Office Phone: 216-621-7974. Personal E-mail: elkramer5@aol.com.

KRAMER, JOEL ROY, journalist, newspaper executive; b. Bklyn., May 21, 1948; s. Archie and Rae (Abramowitz) Kramer; m. Laurie Maloff, 1969; children: Matthew, Elias, Adam. BA, Harvard U., Cambridge, 1969. Editor-in-chief Harvard Crimson; reporter Sci. Mag., Washington, 1969—70; free lance writer Washington, 1970—72; from copy editor to news editor, exec. news editor, asst. mng. editor Newsday, LI, NY, 1972—80; exec. editor Buffalo Courier-Express, 1981—82, Star Tribune, Mpls., St. Paul, 1983—91, pub., pres., 1992—98; sr. fellow Sch. Journalism and Mass Comms., U. Minn., Mpls., 1998—. Bd. dirs. Harvard Crimson Inc., World Press Inst. Chmn. bd. Mpls. Children's Theatre Co., 1994—96. Co-recipient Pulitzer Prize for pub. svc. for the Heroin Trail, Newsday, 1973; recipient Best Legal Writing on Large Daily award, N.Y. Bar Assn., 1974. Address: Sch Journalism U Minn 111 Murphy Hall 206 Church St SE Minneapolis MN 55455-0488

KRAMER, KENT, state representative, finance company executive; b. Newton, Iowa, Oct. 21, 1961; s. Kay and Mary Kramer; m. Kim Thompson, May 1984; children: Kelsey, Kallen, Karsen, Kennedy. BBA in Fin. with high distinction, U. Iowa, 1984. CFP. Mem. staff Campus Crusade for Christ, 1985—94; fin. exec. Atlantic Capital Mgmt., 1994—99; v.p. and investment mgr. dept. trust Bankers Trust, 1999—2001; sr. planner Foster Group, 2001—; state rep. dist. 69 Iowa Ho. of Reps., 2003—; mem. econ. growth com.; mem. edn. com.; mem. govt. oversight com.; mem. judiciary com.; vice chair ways and means com.; mem. oversight subcom. Coach youth soccer and basketball; mem. Broadlawns Hosp. Devel. Coun., Greater Des Moines Leadership Bd. Govs.; chair Transformational Leadership Program; founding mem. and sec. Francophone Ptnrs. Found.; tchr. adult Sunday sch.; bd. elders Westchester Evang. Free Ch. Mem.: Fin. Planning Assn. Iowa, Downtown Des Moines AM Rotary. Republican.

KRAMER, MARY ELIZABETH, ambassador, former state legislator; b. Burlington, Iowa, June 14, 1935; d. Ross L. and Geneva M. (McElhinney) Barnett; m. Kay Frederick Kramer, June 13, 1958; children: Kent, Krista. BA, U. Iowa, 1957, MA, 1971. Cert. tchr., Iowa. Tchr. Newton (Iowa) Pub. Schs., 1957-61, Iowa City Pub. Schs., 1961-67, tchr., asst. supt., 1971-75; dir. pers. Younkers, Inc., Des Moines, 1975-81; v.p. Wellmark, Inc., Des Moines, 1981-99; mem. Iowa Senate from 37th dist., Des Moines, 1990—2004; pres. of the senate, 1997—2004; US amb. to Barbados and Ea. Caribbean, 2004—06. Mem. Olympic adv. com. Blue Cross and Blue Shield Assn., Chgo., 1988—92; presdl. appointee White House Commn. on Presdl. Scholars, 2001, now chmn.; Bd. dirs. Polk County Child Care Rsch. Ctr., Des Moines, 1986—96, YWCA, Des Moines, 1989—94. Named Mgr. of Yr. Iowa Mgmt. Assocs., 1985, Woman of Achievement YWCA, 1986, Woman of Vision Young Women's Resource Ctr., 1989. Mem. Soc. Human Resource Mgmt. (Profl. of Yr. 1996), Iowa Mgmt. Assn. (pres. 1988), Greater Des Moines C. of C. (bd. dirs. 1986-96), exus, Rotary Internat. Republican. Presbyterian. Avocations: music, public speaking.

KRAMER, RICHARD J., manufacturing executive; b. Cleve., Oct. 30, 1963; married; 4 children. BS in Bus. Adminstrn., John Carroll U., 1986. CPA. With PricewaterhouseCoopers, 1987—2000, ptnr.; v.p. corp. fin. Goodyear Tire & Rubber Co., 2000, v.p. fin. North American Tire, 2002—03, sr. v.p. strategic planning & restructuring, 2003—04, exec. v.p., CFO, 2004—. Office: Goodyear Tire & Rubber Co 1144 East Market St Akron OH 44316

KRAMER, WEEZIE CRAWFORD, former broadcast executive; Student, U. Ky., 1977, Wheaton Coll. Sales/local sales mgr. WKQQ, Lexington, Ky., 1977-80; local sales mgr. WHBQ, Memphis, 1980-81; gen. sales mgr. KBPI/KNUS, Denver, 1981-85, WFYR, Chgo., 1985-88, WMAQ All News 67, Chgo., 1988-94, sta. mgr., 1994, v.p., gen. mgr., 1994-99. Office: WMAQ-AM 455 N Cityfront Plaza Dr Chicago IL 60611-5503

KRANITZ, THEODORE MITCHELL, lawyer; b. St. Joseph, Mo., May 27, 1922; s. Louis and Miriam (Saferstein) K.; m. Elaine Shirley Kaufman, June 11, 1944; children: Hugh David, Karen Gail and Kathy Jane (twins). Student, St. Joseph Jr. Coll., 1940-41; BS in Fgn. Svc., Georgetown U., 1948, JD, 1950. Bar: Mo. 1950, U.S. Supreme Ct. 1955. Pres., sr. ptnr. Kranitz & Kranitz, PC, St. Joseph, 1979—. Author: articles in field. Pres. St. Joseph Comty. Theatre, Inc., 1958-60; bd. dirs. United Jewish Fund St. Joseph, 1957—, pres., 1958-63; sec. Boys' Baseball St. Joseph, 1964-68; trustee Temple Adath Joseph, 1970-74, 77-80; bd. dirs. Temple B'nai Sholem, 1976—, Lyric Opera Guild Kansas City, 1980-91; founder, pres. St. Joseph Light Opera Co., Inc., 1989-90; mem. St. Joseph Postal Customers Adv. Coun., 1993-2005, chmn., 1993-95; mem., sec. St. Joseph Downtown Assn., 1995-97 Mem. Mo. Bar, St. Joseph Bar Assn. (pres. 1977-78), Am. Legion, Air Force Assn., B'nai B'rith (dist. bd. govs. 1958-61). Home: 2609 Gene Field Rd Saint Joseph MO 64506-1615 Office: Kranitz & Kranitz PC Boder Bldg 107 S 4th St PO Box 968 Saint Joseph MO 64502-0968 Office Phone: 816-232-4409. Office Fax: 816-232-8558. Business E-Mail: tkranitz@kranitzlaw.com.

KRANTZ, STEVEN GEORGE, mathematics professor, writer; b. San Francisco, Feb. 3, 1951; s. Henry Alfred and Norma Oliva (Crisafulli) K.; m. Randi Diane Ruden, Sept. 7, 1974. BA, U. Calif., Santa Cruz, 1971; PhD, Princeton U, 1974. Asst. prof. UCLA, 1974-81; assoc. prof. Pa. State U., University Park, 1981-84, prof., 1984-86; prof. dept. math. Washington U., St. Louis, 1986—, chmn. dept. math., 1999—, divsn. head for sci. depts., 2002—. Adv. bd. Am. Inst. Math., dep. dir., 2006—08; adv. bd. Am. Math. Soc. book series; mng. editor Jour. Math. Analysis and Applications. Founder, mng. editor Jour. Geometric Analysis; editor-in-chief Jour. of Math. Analysis and Apps.; Author: Function Theory of Several Complex Variables (monograph), 1982, 2d edition, 1992, Complex Analysis: The Geometric Viewpoint, 1990, Real Analysis and Foundations, 1991, Partial Differential Equations and Complex Analysis, 1992, A Primer of Real Analytic Functions, 1992, Geometric Analysis and Function Spaces, 1993, How to Teach Mathematics, 1993, 2nd edit., 1999, A Tex Primer for Scientists, 1995, The Elements of Advanced Mathematics, 1995, 2d edit., 2002, Techniques of Problem Solving, 1996, Function Theory of One Complex Variable, 1997, A Primer of Mathematical Writing, 1996; (with H. R. Parks) The Geometry of Domains in Space, 1999, Contemporary Issues in Mathmatics Education, 1999, A Handbook of Complex Variables, 1999, A Panorama of Harmonic Analysis, 1999, Handbook of Typography for the Mathematical Sciences, 2000, The Implicit Function Theorem, 2002, Mathematical Apocrypha, 2002, Graduate School and Careers in Mathematics: A Survival Guide, 2003; cons. editor Birkhäuser Pub., 2002-, McGraw-Hill, 2002-; contbr. numerous rsch. articles to profl. publs. Recipient Disting. Tchg. award, UCLA Alumni Found., 1979:NSF rsch. grantee, 1975—, Kemper grantee, 1994; Richardson fellow Australian Nat. U., 1995. Mem. Am. Math. Soc. (prin. organizer summer rsch. inst. 1989), Math. Assn. Am. (Chauvenet prize, Beckenbach prize 1994), Am. Inst. Math. (dep. dir. 2006—), Textbook Authors Assn. Office Phone: 650-845-2072. Business E-Mail: sk@math.wustl.edu.

KRANZ, KENNETH LOUIS, human resources company executive; b. Evanston, Ill., July 7, 1946; s. Kenneth Louis Sr. and Florence A. (Knapton) K.; m. Susan Emilie Mueller, Apr. 3, 1976. BA, Tarkio Coll., 1969. Cert. compensation profl.; lic. IRS enrolled agt., adminstrv. svc. mgr., life and health agt. Cost acct. Fluid Power, Wheeling, Ill., 1969-71, Wells Lamont Corp., Chgo., 1971-74, sr. cost acct., 1974-76, asst. mgr. cost, audit, 1977-80, asst. mgr. taxes, employee benefits, 1980-81, mgr. taxes, employee benefits, 1981-84; benefits mgr. Keeler Brass Co., Grand Rapids, 1984-86, employee benefits, compenstion mgr., 1986-90; human resources mgr. GRM Industries, Grand Rapids, 1990-92; co-owner Profl. Benefits Svcs., Inc., Grand Rapids, 1992-95; pres. Magna Benefits Solutions, Inc., Grand Rapids, 1995—. Mem. Home Health Svcs. (treas. 1986-90), Internat. Soc. Pre-Retirement Planners, West Mich. Compensation Assn., Am. Compensation Assn., Human Resource Mgmt. Assn., Life Underwriters Assn. Republican. Avocations: coin collecting/numismatics, sports. Office: Magna Benefits Solutions Inc 6140 28th St SE Ste 200 Grand Rapids MI 49546-6934

KRASHESKY, ALAN, newscaster; married; 3 children. BS in Comm. Mgmt., Ithaca Coll., NYC, 1981. Weekend sports anchor, weathercaster and reporter WBNG-TV, Binghamton, NY, 1981; weathercaster and reporter KTBC-TV, Austin, Tex., 1982; reporter WLS-TV, Chgo., 1982—89, co-anchor morning news, 1989—94, co-anchor 5pm news, 1994—98, co-anchor 6pm news, 1998—, co-anchor 4pm news, 2005—, host NewsViews. TV Journalist Francis Cardinal George: Journey of Hope, 1999 (Silver Angels award, 1999), Pilgrimage of Peace: The Pope in the Holy Land, 2000 (Chgo. Emmy award, 2000). Named Alumnus of Yr., Milton Hershey Sch., 2005; recipient Outstanding Young Alumni award, Ithaca Coll., 1992, Father of Yr., Chgo. Father's Day Coun., 1996, Communicators award, Archdiocese of Chgo., 1997, Heritage Media award, Polish Am. Congress, 1997, Outstanding Achievement in Broadcast Journalism award, Milton Hershey Sch., 1997. Mem.: ATAS (Chgo. chpt.), Chgo. Headline Club. Office: WLS-TV 190 N State St Chicago IL 60601

KRASNEWICH, KATHRYN, water transportation executive; b. 1973; BS, U. Ill., 1995. Investment banker Arthur Andersen & cO., 1995—2000, Deutsche Bank, 2000—03; dir. mergers and acquisitions Brunswick Corp., Chgo., 2003—. Named one of 40 Under Forty, Crain's Bus. Chgo., 2005. Office: Brunswick Corp 1 Northfield Ct Lake Forest IL 60045-4811 Office Phone: 847-735-4700. Office Fax: 847-735-4765.

KRASNY, MICHAEL P., investment company executive; BS in Fin., U. Ill., 1975. Founder, chmn., CEO, sec. CDW Computer Ctrs., Vernon Hills, Ill., 1984—2001, pres., 1984—90, bd. mem. emeritus, 2001—; pres. Sawdust Investment Mgmt. Corp. Bd. mem. Kellogg Sch. of Mgmt., Northwestern U. Bd. dirs. Ctr. for Enriched Living, The Anti-Defamation League, B'nai Brith Beber Camp. Named one of Forbes' Richest Americans, 2006; recipient Entrepreneur of Yr., Ernest and Young, 1993, CEO of Yr., Fin. World, 1996, Torch award for marketplace ethics, Nat. BBB, 2000. Mem.: Young Pres. Orgn., Econ. Club of Chgo. Office: CDW 200 N Milwaukee Ave Vernon Hills IL 60061-1577

KRASNY, PAULA J., lawyer; b. Phila., Pa., Sept. 29, 1963; Student, Harvard U., 1984; AB, Vassar Coll., 1985; JD, Northwestern U., 1988. Bar: Ill. 1988. Atty. McDermott, Will & Emery, Chgo., ptnr., 1995—99, Baker & McKenzie, Chgo., 1999—. Mem. adv. bd. Northwestern Jour. Tech. and Intellectual Property; bd. dir. Frances Lehman Loeb Art Ctr. Vassar Coll. Mem.: ABA, Internat. Trademark Assn., Am.-Israel C. of C. Office: Baker & McKenzie One Prudential Plz 130 East Randolph Dr Chicago IL 60601

KRATT, PETER GEORGE, lawyer; b. Lorain, Ohio, Mar. 7, 1940; s. Arthur Leroy and Edith Ida (Dietz) K.; m. Sharon Amy Maruska, June 15, 1968; children: Kevin George, Jennifer Ivy. BA, Miami U., Oxford, Ohio, 1962; JD, Case Western Res. U., 1966. Bar: Ohio 1966. Atty. Cleve. Trust Co., 1966-74; assoc. counsel AmeriTrust Co., 1974-84, sec., assoc. counsel, 1985-87, sec., sr. assoc. counsel, 1987-92; ret. v.p., mgr. personal trust adminstrn. Huntington Trust Co., 1993-99. Mem. Ohio Bar Assn., Lions. Methodist. Avocations: hiking, gardening. E-mail: pkratt@centurytel.net.

KRAUSE, ARTHUR B., retired telecommunications industry executive; BBA in Acctg., Marquette U. Various positions in acctg. and contr. depts. Gen. Tel. and Electronics; asst. contr. United Tel. Co. Sprint, 1971-75, contr., 1975, v.p. fin., 1977, sr. v.p. adminstrn. tel. hdqrs., 1980, pres. United Tel.-Ea. Group, 1986; exec. v.p., CFO Sprint Corp., 1990—2002. Office: Sprint 6391 Sprint Pkwy Overland Park KS 66251-6100

KRAUSE, CAROLYN H., state legislator, lawyer; m. David Krause. BA, U. Wis.; JD, IIT. Assoc. Foss, Schuman & Drake, Chgo., 1966-73; lawyer, solo practice Mt. Prospect, Ill., 1973-76; pvt. practice Krause & Krause, Mt. Prospect, Ill., 1976—; mayor Mt. Prospect, 1973-76; Dist. 56 rep. Ill. Ho. Reps., Springfield, 1993—. Spokesman appropriations, gen. svcs., cities and villages, fin. instns., healthcare, and human svcs. coms., Ill. Ho. Reps. Apptd. by Gov. James Thompson (Ill.) to local govt. fin. study commn., 1980, criminal justice info. authority, 1985-87; past dir. Clearbrook Ctr.; chair Mcpl. Conf.; dir. Pub. Action to Deliver Shelter of Northwest Cook County. Mem. Ill. and Chgo. Bar Assns. Home: 204 S George St Mount Prospect IL 60056-3430 Office: Ill Ho of Reps State Capitol Springfield IL 62706-0001 Also: 111 E Busse Ave Ste 605 Mount Prospect IL 60056-3249

KRAUSE, CHARLES JOSEPH, otolaryngologist; b. Des Moines, Apr. 21, 1937; s. William H. and Ruby I. (Hitz) Krause; m. Barbara Ann Steelman, June 14, 1962; children: Sharon, John, Ann. BA, State U. Iowa, 1959, MD, 1962.

Diplomate Am. Bd. Otolaryngology. Intern Phila. Gen. Hosp., 1962—63; resident in surgery U. Iowa, 1965—66, resident in otolaryngology, 1966—69; fellow dept. plastic surgery Marien Hosp., Stuttgart, Germany, 1970; asst. prof. otolaryngology U. Iowa, 1969—72, asso. prof., 1972—75, vice chmn. dept. otolaryngology, 1973—77, prof., 1975—77; prof., chmn. dept. otolaryngology U. Mich. Med. Sch., Ann Arbor, 1977—92; pres. Am. Bd. Otolaryngology, Houston. Prof. dept. otolaryngology U. Mich., 1977—2000, emeritus prof., 2000—, asst. dean for clin. affairs, 1986—89, sr. assoc. dean med. sch., 1992—96, chief clin. affairs, 1992—95, sr. assoc. hosp. dir., 1995—96; chief clin. affairs U. Mich. Hosps., Ann Arbor, 1986—89; bd. dirs. Am. Bd. Otolaryngology, 1984—2002, pres., 1998—2000. Author: book in field; contbr. chapters to books, articles to profl. jours. Capt. USAF, 1963—65. Fellow: Am. Soc. Head and Neck Surgery (coun. 1980—83, chmn. rsch. com. 1980—83, pres. 1987—88); mem.: Am. Bd. Otolaryngology (bd. dirs. 1984—, exam. com. chair 1993—, pres.-elect 1996—98, pres. 1998—2000), Centurions of Deafness Rsch. Found., Am. Laryngol. Assn., Am. Laryngol., Rhinol. and Otol. Soc., Am. Cancer Soc. (med. adv. com. Washtenaw County unit), Walter P. Work Soc. (pres. 1987), Soc. United Otolaryngologists, Am. Acad. Depts. Otolaryngology, Mich. Otolaryngol. Soc., Mich. State Med. Soc., Washtenaw County Med. Soc. (exec. com. 1979—82), Assn. Rsch. in Otolaryngology, Am. Asssn. Cosmetic Surgeons, Assn. Head and Neck Oncologists, ACS (adv. coun. otolaryngology 1979—83), Am. Acad. Facial Plastic and Reconstructive Surgery (regional v.p. 1977—80, chmn. rsch. com. 1977—80, pres. 1981—82), Am. Acad. Otolaryngology Head and Neck Surgery (bd. dirs. 1987—93, sec.-treas. 1987—93, pres.-elect 1995, pres. 1996), AMA. Republican. Presbyterian. Home and Office: 880 Sea Dune Ln Marco Island FL 34145-1840 E-mail: cjkrause1@aol.com.

KRAUSE, CHESTER LEE, publishing executive; b. Iola, Wis., Dec. 16, 1923; s. Carl and Cora E. (Neil) K. Grad. high sch., Iola. Ind. contractor, 1946-52; chmn. bd. Krause Publs., Inc., Iola, 1952-95. Co-editor: Standard Catalog of World Coins Chmn. bldg. fund drive Iola Hosp., 1975-80; active Village Bd., 1963-72, Assay Commn., 1961, Marshfield Clinic Nat. Adv. Coun., 1992-96. With AUS, 1943-46 Named Wis. Small Businessman of Yr. Wis. Small Bus. Adminstrn. Adv. Coun., 1990; Melvin Jones fellow, 1990; recipient Meguiar award, 1995, Friend of Automotive History award Soc. Automotive Historians, 1995, Marshfield Clinic Heritage Found. award, 2001. Mem. Soc. of Automobile Historians (Friends of Automobile Historians 1995), Am. Numis. Assn. (medal of merit, Farren Zerbe award, Hall of Fame, Lifetime Achievement award, Exemplary Svc. award 2005, Profl. Numis. Guild Lifetime Achievement award, 2007, Amb. Numis. award, 2007, mem. bd. govs.), Can. Numis. Assn. Home: 290 E Iola St Iola WI 54945-9620 Office: 160 N Chet Krause Dr Iola WI 54945 E-mail: ckrause@ethenet.net.

KRAUSE, HARRY DIETER, law educator; b. Germany, 1932; naturalized, 1954; m. Eva Maria Disselnkötter, 1957; children: Philip Renatus, Thomas Walther, Peter Herbert. Student, Freie U., Berlin, 1950-51; BA, U. Mich., 1954, JD, 1958. Bar: Mich. 1959, D.C. 1959, Ill. 1963, U.S. Supreme Ct. 1963. With firm Covington & Burling, 1958-60; with Ford Motor Co., Dearborn, Mich., 1960-63; asst. prof. to prof. law U. Ill., Champaign, 1963-82, Alumni Disting. prof. law, 1982-89, Max L. Rowe prof. law, 1989-94, tchg. prof. emeritus, 1994—. Fulbright prof. U. Bonn, Germany 1976-77; vis. assoc. Ctr. Socio-Legal studies, 1977; vis. fellow Wolfson Coll. Oxford U., Eng., 1984; US Del. to Hague Conf. on Pvt. Internat. Law Treaty on Internat. Adoptions, 1990-93; commr. Uniform State Laws, Ill., 1991-97; reporter Uniform Parentage Act, 1969-73, Rev. Uniform Adoption Act, 1979-84, Uniform Putative Fathers Act, 1985, Nat. Conf. Commr. on Uniform State Laws; mem. Internat. Acad. Comparative Law Rapporteur US, Uppsala, 1966, Teheran, 1974, Budapest, 1978, Caracas, 1983, Sydney, 1986, Brisbane, 2002, Utrecht, 2006; gen. rep. Athens, 1994; cons. on family law and social legis. to fed. and state legis., jud. and exec. commns.; vis. prof. law U. Mich., 1981, U. Miami, 1987; Culverhouse prof. Stetson U., 1991. Author: Illegitimacy: Law and Social Policy, 1971, Family Law: Cases and Materials, 1976, 5th edit., (with Elrod, Garrison,Oldham), 2003, Kinship Relations, 1976, Family Law in a Nutshell, 1977, 4th edit. (with D. Meyer), 2003, Child Support in America: The Legal Perspective, 1981; law editor: (with R. Walker et. al.) Inclusion Probabilities in Parentage Testing, 1983, (with D. Meyer) Family Law (Thomson-West's Blackletter Series), 1988, 3d edit., 2004, International Library of Essays in Law and Legal Theory: Family Law I: Society and Family, 1992, Family Law II: Cohabitation, Marriage and Divorce, 1992, Child Law: Parent, Child and State, 1992; bd. editors Mich. Law Rev., 1957-58, Family Law Quar., 1971—, Jour. Legal Edn., 1988-91, Am. Jour. Comparative Law, 1991-2004, and others. With US Army, 1954-56. Recipient von Humboldt Found. rsch. prize, 1992, 2004; Guggenheim fellow, 1969-70; assoc. Ctr. Advanced Study U. Ill., 1970, 79; German Marshall Fund US fellow, 1977-78; Hewlett fellow, Australia, 1984; German Acad. Exch. Svc. fellow, 1985. Mem. ABA (past mem. coun. sect. family law, com. chmn.), Am. Law Inst. (life; adviser family law project 1990-2001), Ill. Bar Assn. (past mem. coun. sect. on family law, internat. law), Am. Assn. Comparative Study of Law (dir. 1980-2000), Internat. Soc. Family Law (v.p. 1973-77, exec. coun. 1977-97), Order of Coif. Office: U Ill Coll Law Champaign IL 61820 Business E-Mail: hkrause@law.uiuc.edu.

KRAUSE, JERRY (JEROME RICHARD KRAUSE), former professional basketball team executive; b. Chgo., Apr. 6, 1939; s. Paul and Gertrude (Sherman) Krause; m. Sharon Bergofsky, Oct. 16, 1969 (div. 1971); m. Thelma Frankel, July 1, 1979; children: Stacy, David. Student, Bradley U., 1957—61. Dir. scouting Balt. Bullets Basketball Club, 1962—65; gen. mgr. Portland Baseball Club, Pacific Coast League, 1966; scout Cleve. Indians Baseball Club, 1967—72; dir. scouting Chgo. Bulls Basketball Club, 1969—72, v.p. basketball ops., 1985—2003; dir. scouting Phoenix Suns Basketball Club, 1972; scout Oakland (Calif.) Athletics Baseball Club, 1973—75; dir. scouting L.A. Lakers Basketball Club, 1977—79; supr. Midwestern scouting Seattle Mariners Baseball Club, 1977—79; spl. assignment scout Chgo. White Sox Baseball Club, 1979—85. Mem. competition com. NBA. Contbr. articles to profl. jours. Named to Bradley U. Athletic Hall of Fame, 1992; recipient Exec. of Yr., NBA, 1988.

KRAUSS, LAWRENCE MAXWELL, physicist, astronomy educator, researcher, author; b. NYC, May 27, 1954; s. Alfred and Geraldine (Title) Krauss; m. Katherine Anne Kelley, Jan. 19, 1980; 1 child. BSc with first class honours in Math. and Physics, Carleton U., Ottawa, Ont., Can., 1977; PhD in Physics, MIT, Cambridge, 1982; DSc (hon.), Carleton U., Ottawa, Ont., Can., 2003. Jr. fellow Harvard Soc. Fellows, Cambridge, Mass., 1982-85; asst. prof. depts. physics and astronomy Yale U., New Haven, 1985-88, assoc. prof., 1988-93; Ambrose Swasey prof. physics, prof. astronomy Case Western Res. U., Cleve., 1993—. Assoc. European Orgn. uc. Rsch. (CERN), 1983, sci. assoc., 1996—97; vis. rschr. Smithsonian Astrophysy. Obs., 1984—88, Inst. Theoretical Physics, Santa Barbara, Calif., 1984, 85, 88, 89, 92, 2002, 03, U. Chgo., 1989, Inst. Nuc. Theory, Seattle, 1994, Lawrence Berkeley Lab. Inst. Nuc. and Particle Astrophysics, 1995, 96, 98, Institut des Hautes Études Scientifiques, Bures-sur-Yvette, France, 1997—98, Cambridge U. Isaac Newton Inst., 1999, Perimeter Inst., 2003; vis. scientist Boston U. and Smithsonian Astrophysy. Obs., 1985—86, Harvard-Smithsonian Ctr. Astrophysics, Cambridge, Mass., 1986—89; assoc. dept. physics Harvard U., 1987—95; mem. panel astronomy and astrophysics survey com. NRC, Washington, 1989—90; chmn. dept. physics Case Western Res. U., 1993—2005, dir. Ctr. Edn. and Rsch. in Cosmology and Astrophysics, 2002—, dir. office of sci., pub. policy and bio-entrepreneurship Sch. Medicine, 2005; Hooker disting. vis. prof. McMaster U. Origins Inst., 2005; mem. Inst. Advanced Study, 2005. Contbr. articles to profl. jours., to popular media; author: The Fifth Essence, 1989, Fear of Physics, 1993, Physics of Star Trek, 1995, Quintessence: The Mystery of the Missing Mass, 2000, Atom: A Single Oxygen Atom's Journey from the Big Bang to Life on Earth.and Beyond, 2002 (Am. Inst. Physics Sci. Writing award, 2002), Hiding in the Mirror: The Mysterious Allure of Extra Dimensions, from Plato to String Theory and Beyond, 2005; mem. adv. bd.: Odyssey Mag., 1997—; editor: Modern Physics Letter A, 1998—2000, Internat. Jour. Modern Physics, 1998—2000. Trustee Cleve. Mus. Natural History, 2002—; bd. advisors Def. of Constutution, 2005; bd. advisors, mem. guidance com. Sci. Fiction Experience, Seattle, 2003; trustee, mem. exec. com. Great Lakes Sci. Ctr., 1998—2004; mem. internat. adv. com. Internat. Conf. on Dark Matter Detection, 2000; mem. Aspen Ctr. Physics, 1998—; bd. dirs. Faststart Found., 2003—. Recipient First Prize award, Gravity Rsch. Found., 1984, Prize award, 1989, 1991, 1995, 1999, Presdl. Young Investigator award, 1986, Glover award, Distinction in Physics Achievement and Physics Edn., Dickenson Coll., Pa., 1997, Andrew R. Gemant award, Am. Inst. Physics, 2001, Humanism award, Free Inquirers of N.E. Ohio, 2003, Oersted medal, Am. Assn. Physics Tchrs., 2004, No. Ohio Live award of Achievement, Sci. and Tech., 2004; Vis. scholar, Phi Beta Kappa, 2007—. Fellow: AAAS (chmn.-elect physics divsn. 2006—, Award for Pub. Understanding of Sci. and Tech. 2000), Am. Phys. Soc. (mem. exec. com. divsn. astrophysics 1997—2000, chair forum physics and soc., Julius Edgar Lilienfeld prize 2001, Joseph A. Burton Forum award 2005); mem.: Bulletin Atomic Scientists (bd. sponsors), Am. Astron. Soc., Skeptics Soc. (bd. advisors 2001—). Office: Case Western Res U Physics Dept 10900 Euclid Ave Cleveland OH 44106-7079 E-mail: krauss@cwru.edu.

KRAUTER, AARON JOSEPH, state legislator, farmer; b. Dickinson, ND, July 21, 1956; s. Adam Robert and Ann Christine (Grundhauser) K.; m. Cynthia Marie Nordquist, June 28, 1986; children: Emily Christine, Mitchell Aaron, Hannah Marie. BSEd., U. Mary, Bismarck, 1978, BSBA, 1981. Music instr. Cooperstown (N.D.) High Sch., 1978-79; store mgr. Best Product, Inc., Bismarck, 1979-85, ops. mgr. Richmond, Va., 1985-87; farmer Regent, N.D., 1987—; mem. N.D. Senate, 1990—. Mem. .D. Gov.'s Coun. on Children and Youth, Bismarck, 1989-94, N.D. Gov.'s Coun. on Phys. Fitness and Health, 1992-94; mem. agronomy seed adv. bd. N.D. State U., 1991—, mem. ext. adv. coun., 1991—; chair N.D. Senate Dem. Caucus, 1993-97; asst. minority leader, 1997—. Recipient Know Your State award N.D. Bar Assn., 1974, Excellence in Govt. award Assn. Counties, 1993, Flemming Fellow Leadership award Ctr. for Policy Alternatives, Washington, 1995. Mem. KC, Elks. Democrat. Roman Catholic. Home and Office: HC 1 Box 27 Regent ND 58650-9721

KRAVITT, JASON HARRIS PAPERNO, lawyer; b. Chgo., Jan. 19, 1948; s. Jerome Julius and Shirley (Paperno) K.; m. Beverly Ray Niemeier, May 11, 1974; children: Nikola Wedding, Justin Taylor Paperno. AB, Johns Hopkins U., 1969; JD, Harvard U., 1972; diploma in comparative legal studies, Cambridge U., Eng., 1973. Bar: Ill. 1973, .Y. 2002, U.S. Dist. Ct. (no. dist.) Ill. 1973, U.S. Dist. Ct. (so. dist.) N.Y. 2002. Assoc. Mayer, Brown Rowe & Maw (formerly Mayer, Brown & Platt), Chgo., 1973-78, ptnr., 1979—, co-chmn., 1998-2001. Adj. prof. law Northwestern U., Evanston, Ill., 1994—, adj. prof. fin. Kellogg Sch. Mgmt., 1998—. Editor: Securitization of Financial Assets, 2d edit., 1996. Bd. dirs. Chgo. Met. YMCA, 1998—2001, Mus. Contemporary Art, Chgo., 1974—75; dir., chmn. The Cameron Kravitt Found., 1984—; sec., chair legal, regulatory tax and acctg. com. Am. Securitization Forum, 2001—. Fellow Am. Coll. Comml. Lawyers; mem. ABA, Chgo. Coun. Lawyers, Chgo. Bar Assn., NY State Bar Assn., NYC Bar Assn., Econ. Club of Chgo., Execs. Club Chgo. Home: 250 Sheridan Rd Glencoe IL 60022-1948 Office: Mayer Brown Rowe & Maw 190 S La Salle St Ste 3100 Chicago IL 60603-3441 Office Phone: 212-506-2622. Business E-Mail: jkravitt@mayerbrown.com.

KRAWCZYK, JUDY, state representative; b. Green Bay, Wis., Jan. 24, 1939; married; 3 children. Grad., Joseph Acad. H.S., 1957. Owner supper club; state assembly dist. 88 mem. Wis. State Assembly, Madison, 2000—, mem. colls. and univs., health, natural resources, small bus. and consumer affairs, state affairs, and vets. and mil. affairs coms. Mem.: Nat. Assn. Sportsmen Legislators, YWCA of Green Bay, Wis. Restaurant Assn., Zool. Soc. Inc. Brown County. Republican. Office: State Capitol Rm 9 N PO Box 8952 Madison WI 53708-8952

KRAWETZ, STEPHEN ANDREW, molecular medicine and genetics scientist, educator; b. Fort Frances, Ont., Can., Sept. 17, 1955; s. Stephen and Michaelene (Medynski) K.; m. Lorraine Ruth St. John, Aug. 19, 1977; children: Rhochelle Tairaesa, Alexandra Renée. BSc, U. Toronto, Ont., 1977, PhD, 1983. Tchr. Scarborough Bd. Edn., Ont., 1976-77; Alberta Heritage Found. Med. Rsch. postdoc. fellow U. Calgary, Alta., Canada, 1983-89; asst. prof. rsch. ctr. for molecular biology Wayne State U., Detroit, 1989, asst. prof. molecular biology and genetics, 1989-92, asst. prof. obstetrics and gynecology and molecular biology and genetics, 1992-94, assoc. prof. ob/gyn. and molecular medicine and genetics, 1994-2000, prof. ob-gyn. and molecular medicine and genetics Inst. Sci. Computing, 2000, Charlotte B. Failing prof. ob-gyn. and molecular medicine and genetics and Inst. Sci. Computing, 2001—07, dir. Bioinformatics Node Mich. Life Scis. Corridor, 2001—07, dir. Ctr. of Excellence for Combating the Paternal Impact of Toxicol. Waste on the Next Generation, dir. translational reproductive sys., 2007—. Biotech. cons., Calgary, 1985-89, Grosse Pointe Woods, Mich., 1989—; co-founder Genetic Imaging, Inc., 1988. Mem. editl. bd. BioTechniques, Ag Biotech News and Info., Cellular and Molecular Biology Letters, Gene Therapy and Molecular Biology, EIC SBiRM Systems Biology in Reproductive Medicine; contbr. numerous articles to scholarly jours. Recipient B.C. Childrens Hosp. Rsch. award, Vancouver, 1984, Computer Applications in Molecular Biology award IntelliGenetics Inc., Mountain View, Calif., 1988, others, Bd. of Govs. award Wayne State U., 2004; named Outstanding Basic Scientist, C.S. Mott Ctr., 1999; Alta. Heritage Found. Med. Rsch. fellow, 1985-88. Mem. AAAS, Am. Soc. Human Genetics, Soc. for the Study of Reprodn. Achievements include development of a computer-based imaging system for biological data, of the basis of biological sequence alignment algorithm; first definition of sequence interpretation errors in the GenBank database; first to define a genic domain in human sperm; research in gene therapy targeted to the amelioration of human disease; showed that selective potentiation of our genome mediates cell-phenotype.

KREBS, EUGENE KEHM, II, state legislator; b. Hamilton, Ohio, Aug. 4, 1953; s. Eugene Kehm and Martha Logan (Magaw) K.; m. Janet Lynn Krepp, Dec. 27, 1975; children: Kindra, Alaina. BS, Bowling Green State U., 1975. Farmer, Camden, Ohio, 1975—; mem. Ohio Ho. of Reps., Columbus, 1993—. Contbr. article to Wall St. Jour. Mem. Sch. Bd., Eaton (Ohio) City Schs., 1990-92. Republican. Methodist. Avocations: creative writing, tree plantations, fencing. Home: 12173 State Route 732 Camden OH 45311-9642 Office: Ohio Ho of Reps 77 S High St Columbus OH 43215-6108

KREBS, WILLIAM HOYT, industrial hygienist, health science association administrator; b. Detroit, Apr. 6, 1938; s. William Thomas and Mary Louise (Hoyt) K.; m. Susan Kathryn Bartholomew, Aug. 8, 1964 (div. July 1976); children: Elizabeth Louise, William Thomas II; m. Jane Germer Meikle, June 18, 1983 (dec. May 2004); stepchildren: David Andrew, Sarah Elizabeth. BS, U. Mich., 1960, MPH (IH), 1963, MS, 1965, PhD, 1970. Rsch. asst. U. Mich., Ann Arbor, 1962-63; indsl. hygienist Lumbermens Mut. Casualty Co., Chgo., 1963-64, GM Corp., Detroit, 1970-77, mgr. toxic materials control activity, 1977-81, dir. toxic materials control activity, 1981-90, dir. indsl. hygiene activity, 1990-93; v.p. Indsl. Health Scis., Inc., Grosse Pointe Park, Mich., 1993—94, pres., 2004—. Mem. asbestos adv. com. Mich. Occupational Health Standards Commn., Lansing, 1984—. Contbr. articles to profl. jours. Mem. Grosse Pointe Meml. Ch., Grosse Pointe Farms, 1954; mem. health and safety com. Detroit Area coun. Boy Scouts Am., 1980; mem. environment and energy com. Detroit Regional Chamber. Fellow Am. Indsl. Hygiene Assn. (hon. mem.; bd. dirs. 1976-79, v.p. 1986-87, pres. 1988-89); mem. AAAS, APHA, Mich. Indsl. Hygiene Soc. (pres. 1980-81), Brit. Occupational Hygiene Soc., Internat. Occupational Hygiene Assn. (v.p. 1990-91, pres. 1992-93), Internat. Commn. on Occpl. Health, Soc. Automotive Engrs. Presbyterian. Home: 1014 Bishop Rd Grosse Pointe Park MI 48230-1421 Office: Indsl Health Scis Inc 1014 Bishop Rd Grosse Pointe Park MI 48230-1421 Office Phone: 313-885-8225.

KREBSBACH, KAREN K., state legislator; m. Paul Krebsbach; 2 children. BS, Minot State U. Corp. sec. Krebsbach's, Inc.; mem. N.D. State Senate from 40th and 50th dists., 1989—. Mem. adv. bd. SBA. Bd. dirs. Trinity Med. Ctr. Mem. Minot (N.D.) C. of C., Kiwanis Club, Trinity Med. Ctr. Republican. Home: PO Box 1767 Minot ND 58702-1767

KREER, IRENE OVERMAN, association and meeting management executive; b. McGrawsville, Ind., Nov. 11, 1926; d. Ralph and Laura Edith (Sharp) Overman; m. Henry Blackstone Kreer, Dec. 22, 1946 (dec.); children: Laurene (dec.), Linda Kreer Witt. BS in Speech Pathology, Northwestern U., 1948. Speech pathologist Ill. pub. schs., 1947-49; staff asst., lectr. Art Inst. Chgo., 1962—; pres. Irene Overman Kreer & Assocs., Inc., 1962—. TV appearances representing Art Inst. edn. programs; lectr. in field. Past bd. dirs. Glenview (Ill.) Pub. Libr.; mem. The Art Inst. Chgo., Glenview Cmty. Ch., Field Mus., Chgo. Architecture Found., Smithsonian Assocs. Mem. Nat. Trust Hist. Preservation, Assn. Alumnae Northwestern U. (bd. dirs. 1975—), Delta Delta Delta. Republican. Avocations: travel, archaeology, tennis.

KREGEL, JAMES R., publishing executive; b. Grand Rapids, Mich., Apr. 18, 1950; BA, Mich. State U., 1972. Pres. Kregel Publs., Grand Rapids, Mich., 1989—. Office: Kregel Publs Box 2607 733 Wealthy St SE Grand Rapids MI 49503-5553

KREHBIEL, FREDERICK AUGUST, II, electronics executive; b. Chgo., June 2, 1941; s. John Hammond and Margaret Ann (Veeck) K.; m. Kay Kirby, Dec. 21, 1973; children: William Veeck, Jay Frederick. BA, Lake Forest Coll., 1963. Advt. and human resources mgr. Molex, Inc., Lisle, Ill., 1965—67, export mgr., 1967—69, v.p. internat., 1970—75, exec. v.p., dir., from 1976, vice chmn., CEO, 1988-93, chmn., CEO, 1993—98, co-chmn., co-CEO, 1998—2001, co-chmn., 2001—, CEO, 2004—05. Bd. dirs. Tellabs Inc., Molex, Inc., DeVry, Inc. Trustee Rush Med. Ctr., Chgo., Lyric Opera, Chgo., Chgo. Hist. Soc., Mus. Sci. and Industry, Chgo., Chgo. Orch. Assn., Trinity Found., Ireland; trustee, chmn. Chgo. Zool. Soc. Mem. Hinsdale (Ill.) Golf Club, Chgo. Club, Casino Club (Chgo.), Racquet Club Chgo., Everglades Club, Bath and Tennis Club Palm Beach. Home: 505 S County Line Rd Hinsdale IL 60521-4725 Office: Molex Inc 2222 Wellington Ave Lisle IL 60532-3820 Business E-Mail: fkrehbiel@molex.com.

KREHBIEL, ROBERT JOHN, lawyer; b. Waukegan, Ill., Dec. 8, 1948; BA magna cum laude, Knox Coll., 1971; JD, Washington U., 1980. Bar: Mo. 1980, U.S. Dist. Ct. (ea. dist.) Mo. 1980, U.S. Dist. Ct. (we. dist.) Mo. 1992, Ill. 1981, U.S. Ct. Appeals (8th cir.) 1981, U.S. Supreme Ct. 1987. Mem. Evans & Dixon, St. Louis. Mem. Mo. Bar, Bar Assn. Met. St. Louis, Order of Coif, Phi Beta Kappa.

KREIBICH, ROBIN G., state legislator; b. June 4, 1959; BA, U. Minn.; postgrad., Brown Inst. Broadcasting. Former TV anchorman; former media specialist U. Wis., Eau Claire; mem. from dist. 93 Wis. State Assembly, Madison, 1992—. Address: 3437 Nimitz St Dr Eau Claire WI 54701-7200

KREIDER, JIM, farmer, former state legislator; b. Nurnburg, Germany, June 24, 1955; (parents Am. citizens); m. Debbie Kreider; children: Lacey, Neeley. Student, S.W. Mo. State U. Farmer, Nixa, Mo.; mem. Mo. Ho. of Reps., Jefferson City, 1992—2002, spkr. pro tem, 1997—2001, spkr., 2001—02. Mem. agr.-bus. com., agr. com., edn. com., energy environ. com. Mem. com. Am. Soil Conservation Svc. Named Farm Family of Yr., 1992. Mem. Christian County Farm Bur. (v.p., legis. chmn.). Democrat. Home and Office: PO Box 1980 Nixa MO 65714-1980

KREIDER, LEONARD EMIL, retired economics professor; b. Newton, Kans., Feb. 25, 1938; s. Leonard C. and Rachel (Weaver) K.; m. Louise Ann Pankratz, June 10, 1963; children: Brent Emil, Todd Alan, Ryan Eric. Student, Bluffton Coll., 1956-58; BA, Bethel Coll., 1960; student, Princeton U., 1960-61; MA, Ohio State U., 1962, PhD, 1968. Economist So. Ill. U., Carbondale, 1965-70; asst. prof. Beloit (Wis.) Coll., 1970—, prof., 1978—2007, chmn. dept. econ. and mgmt., 1984-89, acting v.p. acad. affairs, 1987-88, Allen Bradley prof. econ., 1991—2003. Chief of Party Devel. Assocs., Asuncion, Paraguay, 1970; economist Deere and Co., 1973, Castle and Cooke, San Francisco, 1975-76, AmCore, Rockford, Ill., 1984, Rockford Meml. Hosp., 1990-91, Stone Container, San Jose, Costa Rica, 1996, Rock Island Co., Chgo., 2003; cons. corps. and attys. Author: Development and Utilization of Managerial Talent, 1968; contbr. numerous articles, reports to profl. jours. Mem. Nat. Assn. Bus. Economists, Am. Econ. Assn., Am. Assn. Higher Edn., Soc. Internat. Devel. (pres. So. Ill. chpt. 1969), Indsl. Rels. Rsch. Assn. (elections com. 1974). Presbyterian. Home: 1528 Hawthorne Cir Harrisonburg VA 22802 Home Phone: 540-564-3688. Business E-Mail: kreidere@beloit.edu.

KREIMAN, KEITH, state senator, lawyer; b. Fargo, ND, June 28, 1954; m. Rose Ann Kreiman. AA, Ellsworth C.C., 1974; BA, Seattle U., 1976; JD, U. Iowa, 1978. Laborer United Hydraulics Corp., 1971—76; pvt. practice atty., 1978—; mem. Iowa State Senate, DesMoines, 2003—, ranking mem. judiciary com., mem. edn. com., human resources com. and local govt. com. Active Davis County Child Abuse Prevention Coun., Iowa Rural Econ. Devel. Coun., Good Shepard Luth. Ch. Mem.: Centerville C. of C., Iowa Trial Lawyers Assn., Iowa State Bar Assn., Bloomfield Lions Club. Democrat. Home: 406 Parkview Dr Bloomfield IA 52537 Office: State Capitol Bldg East 12th and Grand Des Moines IA 50319

KREINDLER, MARLA J., lawyer; b. Cin., Feb. 20, 1963; Attended, London Sch. Econs., 1982; BA, U. Mich., 1984, JD, 1987. Bar: Ill. 1987. Ptnr., chair Employee Benefits and Exec. Compensation Dept., sr. mem. Corp. and Fin. Svcs. Dept. Katten Muchin Zavis Rosenman, Chgo. Mem.: WEB, Women in Financial Svcs. (founding mem. Chgo. chap.), Stable Value Investment Assn., Pension Real Estate Assn., Art Inst. Chgo.

KREININ, MORDECHA ELIAHU, economics professor; b. Tel Aviv, Jan. 20, 1930; came to U.S., 1951, naturalized, 1960; m. Marlene Miller, Aug. 29, 1956; children: Tamara, Elana, Miriam. BA, U. Tel Aviv, 1951; MA, U. Mich., 1952, PhD, 1954. Asst. prof. econs. Mich. State U., East Lansing, 1957-59, assoc. prof., 1959-61, prof., 1961-90, univ. disting. prof. econs., 1990—. Vis. prof. econs. UCLA, 1969, UN, Geneva, 1971-73, NYU, 1975, 93, 96, U. Toronto, 1978, others; vis. scholar Inst. Internat. Econs. Studies, U. Stockholm, 1978-80, U. B.C., summer, 1983, Monash U., Melbourne, Australia, 1987-94, 2002, NYU, 1993, 96, Copenhagen Bus. Sch., Denmark, 1994-95, Kobe (Japan) U., 1997, Ctr. Southeast Asian Studies, U. Singapore, 1998, Johns Hopkins U., 2002; adj. rsch. assoc. East-West Ctr., Honolulu, 1990—; world lectr. tours on behalf of U.S. Info. Svc., 1974-96; cons. to Dept. Commerce, 1964-66, Dept. State, 1972-74, UN Coun. Fgn. Rels, N.Y.C., 1965-67, Brockings Instn., 1972-75, Ctrl. Am. Common Market, 1972-75, Internat. Monetary Fund, 1976, East-West Ctr., Honolulu, 1987—; mem. internat. econs. rev. bd. NSF, 1981, 85; bd. dirs. Internat. Trade and Fin. Assn., pres. 1993; sr. Fulbright specialist, 2001—. Author: Israel and Africa: A Study in Technical Cooperation, 1964, Alternative Commercial Policies*Their Effects on the American Economy, 1967, International Economics-A Policy Approach, 10th edit., 2005, Trade Relations of the EEC*An Empirical Investigation, 1974, International Commercial Policy: Issues for the 1990's, 1993, Contemporary Issues in Trade Policy, 1995, (with L. Officer) The Monetary Approach to the Balance of Payments: A Survey, 1978, Economics, 1983, 3d edit., 1999, 4th edit., 2003; co-author: Economic Integration on Asia, 2000, Economic Integration and Development, 2002; editor: Can Australia Adjust?, 1988, International Commercial Policy: Issues for the 90's, 1993, Contemporary Issues in Trade Policy, 1995, The U.S.-Canada Free Trade Agreement, 1999, Empirical Modeling in International Trade, 2005; co-editor: Asia-Pacific Economic Linkages, 1997; contbr. articles to profl. jours. NSF fellow, 1964-73, Ford Found. fellow, 1960-61; recipient Disting. Faculty award Mich. State U., 1968, State of Mich. Collegiate award, 1984, Whitefield Winslow Faculty award, 1994; Festschrift in his honor, Washington, 2003; essays pub. in his honor Empirical Models in International Trade, 2005 Mem. AAUP, Am. Econ. Assn., Midwest Econ. Assn., Western Econ. Assn., Royal Econ. Assn., Internat. Trade and Fin. Assn. (bd. dirs. 1991-94, pres. 1992). Jewish. Home: 1431 Sherwood Ave East Lansing MI 48823-1851 Office: Mich State U Dept Econs East Lansing MI 48824 E-mail: kreinin@msu.edu.

KREIS, JASON, professional soccer coach, retired professional soccer player; b. Omaha, Dec. 29, 1972; Student, Duke U. Midfielder Dallas Burn, 1998—2005, Real Salt Lake, 2005—07, U.S. Nat. Team, 1999—2007; head coach Real Salt Lake, 2007—. U.S. Nat. Soccer Team debut 1996; finished 9th in MLS scoring, 1996, scored goal in all-star game; 3-time All-Am., Duke U. Office: US Soccer Fedn 1801-1811 S Prairie Ave Chicago IL 60616

KREITLOW, PAT, newscaster; m. Sharry Kreitlow; 2 children. Degree in journalism, U. Wis., Eau Claire. News dir. radio stas., Rice Lake and West Bend, Wis.; mem. staff WAXX-WAYY radio, Eau Claire, Wis.; prodr., reporter, co-anchor, weekend anchor NewsCenter 13 WEAU-TV, Eau Claire, Wis., 1996—. Bd. dirs. Chippewa Valley chpt. Literacy Vols. Am. Office: WEAU-TV PO Box 47 Eau Claire WI 54702

KREITZER, MELVYN, II, optical engineer; b. Cape Town, South Africa, Oct. 21, 1945; came to U.S., 1973; s. Charles and Lucy (Faktor) K.; m. Sharon Meyerowitz, Apr. 6, 1971; children: Jason, David. BS, U. Cape Town, South Africa, 1964, BS (hon.), 1966; MS, Rochester Inst. Tech., 1968; MS, PhD, U. Ariz., 1976. Co-author chpt. to book; patentee in field. Mem. Optical Soc. Am. (Engring. Excellence award 1995). Avocations: reading, movies, golf. Home: 3681 Carpenters Creek Dr Cincinnati OH 45241-3824 Office: Opcon Assocs Inc 3997 Mcmann Rd Cincinnati OH 45245-2307

KREMER, EUGENE R., architecture educator; b. NYC, Jan. 4, 1938; s. John and Ida (Applegreen) K.; m. Sara Lillian Kimmel, June 26, 1960; children: Michael, Ian. BArch, Rensselaer Poly. Inst., 1960; postgrad., U. Pa., 1960-61; MArch, U. Calif., 1967; grad. coll. mgmt. program, Carnegie Mellon U., 1991. Registered architect, N.Y., Kans. Architect Ulrich Franzen Assoc., NYC, 1963-66; asst. prof. Washington U., St. Louis, 1967-70; lectr. Portsmouth (Eng.) Poly. Inst., 1970-71, Poly. Ctrl. London, 1971-72; dir. Inst. Environ. Design, Washington, 1972-73; prof., head dept. architecture Kans. State U., Manhattan, 1973-85, 92-95, dir. program devel. Coll. Architecture and Design, 1985-92, asst. dean, 1988-90. Dir. Boston Architecture and Design, summer, 1983—90; vis. faculty mem. Czech Tech U., Prague, 1999; scholar in residence AIA, Washington, 2002; mem. State Bldg. Adv. Bd., Topeka, 1984—86, Topeka, 1992—95; mem. editl. bd. Jour. Arch. and Planning Rsch., College Station, Tex., 1983—. Author: Careers in Architecture, 1967, Leadership Meetings in Environmental Design, 1973; author/editor newsletter Architecture Update, 1984-86, 92—; editor Architecture and Design News, 1990-92; contbr. Architects Handbook of Professional Practice, 13th and 14th edits., also articles to profl publs. Chmn. Adv. Bd. Gifted, Talented, Creative, Manhattan, 1974-75; mem. Convocations Com., Manhattan, 1974-93, chn., 1984-88, 90-93; mem. Truman Scholarship Com., Manhattan, 1980-2003; pres. Friends Kans. State U. Librs., Manhattan, 1985-86. Fellow AIA (Spl. Svc. award Kans. 1984, 88, 91, 94, 98, 99, Presdl. citation Kansas City 1993); mem. Environ. Design Rsch. Assn., Assn. Collegiate Schs. Architecture (treas. 1976-80, pres. 1981-82, Svc. award 1983), AIA Kans. (sec. 1989, v.p./pres.-elect 1990, pres. 1991, past pres. 1992, univ. liaison 1993-2002, Henry Schirmer Disting. Svc. award 2002), AIA Flint Hills (pres. 1998), Golden Key (hon.), Tau Sigma Delta, Tau Beta Pi, SCARAB (hon.), Tau Epsilon Phi (pres. 1959-60). Avocations: reading, photography. Office: Kans State U Coll Architecture Planning and Design 211 Seaton Hall Manhattan KS 66506-2900 Home: Apt 310 3800 Fairfax Dr Arlington VA 22203-1786

KREMER, ROBERT M., state legislator; b. Aurora, Nebr., Dec. 8, 1936; m. Beverly Jackson, July 19, 1958; children: Mark Kremer, Sheila Miller, Sherri Holm, Shauna Moody. BS, Northwestern Coll., 1958. Farmer, cattle feeder; mem. Nebr. Legislature from 34th dist., Lincoln, 1998—. County pres., state bd. dirs., mem. state edn. adv. com., mem. state policy devel. com. Nebr. Farm Bur.; county pres., state bd. dirs., mem. nat. com. Nebr. Cattlemen; bd. dirs. Edgerton Explorit Ctr., Nebr. Energy Coop.; chmn., youth leader Pleasant View Bible Ch.; mem. Ag Builders Nebr.; former mem. Aurora Dist 4-R Bd. Edn. Mem. Nebr. Corn Growers Assn. (bd. dirs.), Aurora C. of C. (mem. agr. com.), Rotary, 4-H Club (leader). Office: State Capitol Dist 34 PO Box 94604 Rm 1529 Lincoln NE 68509-4604 Home: 186 Donegal Rd Aurora NE 68818-1430

KREMKAU, PAUL, principal; Prin. Highland Middle Sch. (formerly Highland Upper Grade Ctrl. Sch.), Libertyville, Ill., 1984—. Recipient Blue Ribbon Sch. award U.S. Dept. Edn., 1990-91. Office: Highland Mid Sch 310 W Rockland Rd Libertyville IL 60048-2739

KRENDL, KATHY, dean; BA in english, Lawrence U., 1972; MA in journalism, Ohio St. U., 1977; PhD in comm., U. Mich., 1982. Dean Ind. U., Sch. of Continuing Studies, 1994—96, Ohio U. Coll. Comms., Athens, 1996—. Office: Ohio U Coll Comm RTVC 483B Athens OH 45701-2905

KRENT, HAROLD J., dean, law educator; BA, Princeton U.; JD, NYU Sch. Law. Clerk for Hon. William H. Timbers Second Cir.; atty. Dept. Justice, Appellate Staff Civil Div.; prof. law Chgo.-Kent Coll. Law, Ill Inst. Tech., 1994—, assoc. dean, 1997—2002, interim dean, 2002—03, dean, 2003—. Cons. Adminstrn. Conf. of U.S. Author: Presidential Powers, 2005; contbr. articles to law jours. Office: Chgo-Kent Coll Law Ill Inst Tech 565 W Adams St Chicago IL 60661-3691 Office Phone: 312-906-5010. E-mail: hkrent@kentlaw.edu.

KRENTZ, JANE, former state legislator, elementary school educator; b. Mpls., Dec. 24, 1952; children: Leah, Sarah, Jeremy. BA, Hamline U., 1971; MEd, U. Minn., 1996. Elem. sch. tchr.; former mem. Minn. Senate from 51st dist., St. Paul, 1993—2003; now Midwest coord. Nat. Caucus Environ. Legislators. Mem. C. of C. Stillwater, Forest Lake, Anoka County (all Minn.). Office: Nat Caucus Environ Legislators 14177 Paris Ave N Stillwater MN 55082

KRESGE, CHARLES T., chemicals executive; B in Chemistry, Swarthmore Coll.; PhD in Phys. Chemistry, U. Calif., Santa Barbara. Rsch. chemist catalyst synthesis & devel. grp. Mobil Corp., Paulsboro, NJ, 1979, head exploratory synthesis & characterization grp., 1987—93, head catalyst synthesis, characterization and applications Paulsboro and Princeton, 1993—97, tech. leader, chief scientist exploratory materials chemistry rsch., 1997, sr. mem. tech. leadership strategic rsch. ctr. Mobil Tech. Co.; grp. head fluid catalytic cracking rsch. W.R. Grace & Co., 1985—87; global R & D dir. Dow Chem. Co., Midland, Mich., 1999—2000, global R & D dir. chem. scis., 2000—05, head rsch. and engring. scis., 2005, v.p. R & D. Mem. Nat. Acad. of Engrs.; bd. chem. scis. & tech. RC. Contbr. articles to profl. publs.; mem. editl. bd.: Advanced Functional Materials. Co-recipient Donald W. Breck award in Molecular Sieve Sci., Internat. Zeolite Conf., 1994; recipient R & D 100 award for Innovation. Mem.: Am. Chem. Soc. Achievements include patents in field. Office: 2020 Dow Ctr Midland MI 48674

KRESS, WILLIAM F., manufacturing executive; s. Jim Kress. Pres. Green Bay (Wis.) Packaging. Bd. dir., Shenandoah Energy Inc., 2000—. Office: Green Bay Packaging 1700 North Webster Ct Green Bay WI 54302-1166

KRETSCHMAR, WILLIAM EDWARD, state legislator, lawyer; b. St. Paul, Aug. 21, 1933; s. William Emanuel and Frances Jane (Peterson) K BS, Coll. St. Thomas, 1954; LLB, U. Minn., 1961. Bar: N.D. 1961, U.S. Dist. Ct. N.D. 1961. Pvt. practice Kretschmar Law Office, Ashley, ND, 1962—; mem. N.D. Ho. of Reps., Bismarck, 1972-98, speaker, 1988-90, 2000—. Mem. N.D. Commn. Uniform State Laws, 1987—; del. N.D. Constl. Conv., Bismarck, 1971-72 Mem. State Bar Assn. ND, Lions (pres. local club 1972-73, 93-94), Elks, Eagles. Republican. Roman Catholic. Avocations: hunting, swimming, hiking, bicycling, skiing. Home: 201 E 3d St Venturia D 58413-4015 Office: Kretschmar Law Office 117 1st Ave NW Ashley ND 58413-7037

KRETSCHMER, CHARLES J., electronics executive; b. 1956; V.p. ESCO, St. Louis, Mo., 1999, v.p., CFO, 1999-00, sr. v.p., CFO, 2000—. Office: ESCO Electronics Corp 8888 Ladue Rd Ste 200 Saint Louis MO 63124-2090

KREUSER, JAMES E., state legislator; b. Kenosha, Wis., May 20, 1961; s. Harold Floyd and LaVerne Kreuser; m. Jane, 1990; children: Justin, James Jr. BA, U. Wis.-Parkside, 1983, MPA, 1986. Adminstrv. asst. Kenosha County Exec. Bd., Wis.; assemblyman Wis. State Assembly Dist. 64, 1993—. Elections & constnl. law com. Wis. State Assembly, hwy. & transp. com., mandates com., spl. com. on electronic benefit transfer sys., legal council com. on Indian affairs. Past exec. bd. ARC. Mem. Kenosha Area Devel. Corp., Sr. Action Coun., Rotary, Masons, Danish Brotherhood, Kenosha Sport Fishing and Conservation Assn. Office: PO Box 8952 Madison WI 53708-8952

KREUTER, GRETCHEN V., academic administrator; b. Mpls., May 7, 1934; d. Sigmund and Marvyl (Larson) von Loewe; m. Robert L. Sutton, 1993; children: David Karl, Betsy Ruth Rymes. BA, Rockford Coll., 1955; MA, U. Wis., 1958, PhD, 1961; LLD (hon.), Rockford Coll., 1992, Coll. St. Mary, 1994. Lectr. in Am. Studies Colgate U., Hamilton, N.Y., 1962-67; lectr. in history Coll. St. Catherine, St. Paul, 1969-71, Hamline U., St. Paul, 1971-72; prof. of history Macalester Coll., St. Paul, 1972-73, St. Olaf Coll., Northfield, Minn., 1975-80; asst. to pres. Coll. St. Catherine, St. Paul, 1980-84; asst. to v.p. acad. affairs U. Minn., Mpls., 1984-87; pres. Rockford Coll., Ill., 1987-92, Olivet (Mich.) Coll., 1992-93; sr. fellow Am. Coun. Edn., Washington, 1993-94; hon. fellow Inst. for Rsch. in Humanities U. Wis., Madison, 1994—; interim pres. Coll. of St. Mary, Omaha, 1995-96. Mem., chmn. Minn. Humanities Coun., St. Paul, 1974-83; mem. Mich. Humanities Coun., 1993; bd. dirs. Nat. Assn. State Humanities Commn., Washington, 1984-86. Author: An American Dissenter, 1969 (McKnight prize 1978), Running the Twin Cities: editor: Women of Minnesota, 1977, 2d edit., 1998, Two Career Family, 1978, Forgotton Promise: Race and Gender Conflict on a Small College Campus: A Memoir, 1996. Bd. dirs. Kobe Coll. Corp., Rockford Mus. Ctr., ACE Commn. on Minorities in Higher Edn., 1991-92, Mich. Humanities Coun., 1993-94. Address: 1666 Coffman St Apt 123 Falcon Heights MN 55108-1326 E-mail: gkreuter@facstaff.wisc.edu.

KRIEGEL, DAVID L., retail executive; b. 1946; Grad., Bliss Bus. Coll., 1968. With Lake End Sales, Inc. subs. of Scot Lad Foods, Inc., Fort Wayne, Ind., 1968-73; pres. Am. Merchandising Assocs., Inc., Van Wert, Ohio, 1973-88; chmn., pres., CEO Diamond Distributing, Inc., Lima, Ohio, 1978—, Kriegel Holding Co., Inc., Van Wert, Ohio, 1978—; corp. v.p. Roundy's, Inc., 1988-90; v.p. Cardinal Health and Mktg. Group, divsn. of Cardinal Distribution, Inc., 1990-93; CEO Drug Emporium, Inc., Powell, Ohio, 1993—. Office: Drug Emporium Inc 14525 Highway 7 Minnetonka MN 55345-3734

KRIEGER, IRVIN MITCHELL, retired chemistry professor; b. Cleve., May 14, 1923; s. William I. and Rose (Brodsky) K.; m. Theresa Melamed, June 9, 1965; 1 dau., Laura. BS, Case Inst. Tech., 1944, MS, 1948; PhD, Cornell, 1951. Rsch. asst. Case Inst. Tech., Cleve., 1946-47; teaching fellow Cornell U., Ithaca, NY, 1947-49; instr. Case Western Res. U., 1949-51, asst. prof., 1951-55, assoc. prof., 1955-68, prof., 1968-88, prof. emeritus, 1988—; dir. Center for Adhesives, Sealants and Coatings, 1983-88. Vis. prof. U. Bristol, 1977-78; cons. for chem. firms; prof. invité Ecole Nat. Supérieure de Chimie de Mulhouse, 1987, Louis Pasteur U., Strasbourg, France, 1989. Contbr. articles to profl. jours. With USNR, 1943—46. NSF fellow Université Libre De Bruxelles, 1959-60; sr. fellow Weizmann Inst., 1970 Mem. Am. Chem. Soc., Am. Inst. Chem. Engrs., AAUP, Soc. Rheology (pres. 1977-79, Bingham medalist 1989). Home: 3460 Green Rd Apt 101 Beachwood OH 44122-4076 Office Phone: 216-921-6133. E-mail: imk@case.edu.

KRIER, HERMAN, mechanical and industrial engineering educator; b. Maribor, Yugoslavia, Feb. 15, 1942; came to U.S., 1950; s. Jacob and Katherine (Kless) K.; m. Marion Puleio, June 12, 1965; children: Melissa, Daniel Herman. BS, U. Pitts., 1964; MA, Princeton U., NJ, 1966, PhD, 1968. Asst. prof. mechanical and indsl. engring. U. Ill., Urbana, 1969-73, assoc. prof., 1973-78, prof., 1978—. Chief scientist Combustion Scis., Inc., Champaign, Ill., 1977-92. Editor: Proceedings of the 18th Combustion Symposium, 1980, Proceedings of the 19th Combustion Symposium, 1982; co-editor: Progress in Aeronautics and Astronautics, 1979; contbr. articles to profl. jours. Fellow AIAA, mem. ASME, The Combustion Inst. Achievements include being author or co-author of more than 100 publications in the field of combustion. Office: U Ill Dept Medh and Ind Engring 1206 W Green St Urbana IL 61801-2906

KRIER, JAMES EDWARD, law educator, writer; b. Milw., Oct. 19, 1939; s. Ambrose Edward and Genevieve Ida (Behling) Krier; m. Gayle Marian Grimsrud, Mar. 22, 1962 (div.); children: Jennifer, Amy; m. Wendy Louise Wilkes, Apr. 20, 1974; children: Andrew Wilkes-Krier, Patrick Wilkes-Krier. BS, U. Wis., 1961, JD, 1966. Bar: Wis. 1966, U.S. Ct. Claims 1968. Law clk. to chief justice Calif. Supreme Ct., San Francisco, 1966-67; assoc. Arnold & Porter, Washington, 1967-69; acting prof., then prof. law UCLA, 1969-78, 80-83; prof. law Stanford U., Calif., 1978-80, U. Mich. Law Sch., Ann Arbor, 1983—, Earl Warren DeLano prof., 1988—. Cons. Calif. Inst. Tech., EPA; mem. pesticide panel NAS, 1972—75, mem. com. energy and the environment, 1975—77. Author: (book) Environmental Law and Policy, 1971; author: (with Stewart) Environmental Law and Policy, 2d edit., 1978; author: (with Ursin) Pollution and Policy, 1977; author: (with Dukeminier) Property, 1981; author: (with Alexander and Schill) Property, 6th edit., 2006; contbr. articles to profl. jours. Served to lt. US Army, 1961—63. Mem.: Order of Coif, Artus, Phi Kappa Phi. Office: U Mich Law Sch 625 S State St Ann Arbor MI 48109-1215 Office Phone: 734-763-4701. Business E-Mail: jkrier@umich.edu.

KRIMM, SAMUEL, physicist, researcher, educator, administrator; b. Morristown, NJ, Oct. 19, 1925; s. Irving and Ethel (Stein) K.; m. Marilyn Marcy Neveloff, June 26, 1949; children: David Robert, Daniel Joseph. BS in Chemistry, summa cum laude, Poly. Inst. Bklyn., 1947; MA in Phys. Chemistry, Princeton U., 1949, PhD in Phys. Chemistry, 1950. Postdoctoral fellow U. Mich., Ann Arbor, 1950-52, mem. faculty, 1952—, prof. physics, 1963-2001, prof. emeritus, 2001—, mem. Macromolecular Rsch. Ctr., 1968—, mem. biophysics rsch. divsn., 1962—, chmn. biophysics rsch. div., 1976-86, dir. program in protein structure and design, 1985-94, assoc. dean research Coll. Lit., Sci. and Arts, 1972-75. Chmn. infrared spectroscopy Gordon Rsch. Conf., 1968; mem. NAS/NRC NBS Polymers divsn. Evaluation Panel, 1973-76, chmn., 1975-76; materials rsch. adv. com. NSF, 1981-86, chmn., 1984; mem. DOE Coun. on Material Scis., 1986-89; program adv. com. Internat. Conf. on Raman Spectroscopy, 1984-86, exec. com., 1988-90; Fraser Price Meml. lectr., 1988; disting. lectr. Inst. Materials Sci. U. Conn., 1995; com. on promoting rsch. collaboration NAS/IOM, 1987-89; cons. B.F. Goodrich, 1956-86, Allied 1963-93, Monsanto, 1987-92; vis. prof. Lab. Molecular Biology, Cambridge, 1962-63, Weizmann Inst., 1970, U. Mainz, 1983, U. Paris, 1991. Author papers on vibrational spectroscopy of polymers and proteins, x-ray diffraction studies of natural and synthetic polymers, potential energy function devel.; mem. editorial bd. Jour. Polymer Sci. Polymer Physics Edn., 1967-99; Biopolymers, 1973-2006; Macromolecules, 1968-71; Jour. Macromolecular Sci.-Rev. Macromolecular Chemistry, 1983-92. Served with USNR, 1944-46. Recipient Humboldt award, 1983; U. Mich. Disting. Faculty Achievement award, 1986; Textile Research Inst. fellow, 1947-50; NSF sr. postdoctoral fellow, 1962-63; sr. fellow U. Mich. Soc. Fellows, 1971-76 Fellow AAAS, Am. Phys. Soc. (High Polymer Physics prize 1977, chmn. div. biol. physics 1979, div. councilor 1981, exec. com. 1983, planning com. 1992); mem. Am. Chem. Soc., Biophys. Soc., Coblentz Soc. (hon., bd. mgr. 1967-70). Office: U Mich LSA Biophysics 930 N University Ave Ann Arbor MI 48109-1055 Home Phone: 734-663-1978. Business E-Mail: skrimm@umich.edu.

KRINGEL, JEROME HOWARD, lawyer; b. Milw., Apr. 2, 1940; s. Lester E. and Irene A. (Kreutzer) K.; m. Mary Kathleen McAuliffe, Sept. 8, 1962; children: Anne, Mary Karen, Jennifer, Elisabeth, Katherine. AB, Marquette U., 1962; postgrad., U. Heidelberg, Germany, 1963; LLB, Yale U., 1966. Bar: Wis. 1966, U.S. Dist. Ct. (ea. dist.) Wis. 1966, U.S. Ct. Appeals (7th cir.) 1966. Ptnr., coord. bus. practice Michael, Best & Friedrich, Milw., 1966—. Trustee Shorewood (Wis.) Village Bd., 1974-80. Mem. ABA, Wis. Bar Assn. (chmn. bus. law sect. 1990-91), Milw. Bar Assn. Office: Michael Best & Friedrich LLP 100 E Wisconsin Ave Ste 3300 Milwaukee WI 53202-4108 Business E-Mail: jhkringel@michaelbest.com.

KRINGEN, DALE ELDON, state legislator, transportation executive; b. Chester, SD, May 8, 1935; s. Palmer and Madeline (Amundson) K.; children from previous marriage: Brian, Brad, Kevin, Kane; m. Katherine T. Krinteh, Aug. 27, 1990; 1 child, Anne. BS, S.D. State U., 1967, MEd, 1960. Tchr., coach, Ruthton, Minn.; prin.; supt. schs. Alexandria, S.D.; rep. Scott, Foresman Pub. Co., Glenview, Ill.; dir. S.D. Job Svc., Pierre, S.D.; owner Allied Transp. Svcs., Inc., 1983—, Continental Transp. Svcs., Inc., 1983—, Truck Bonding, USA, 1983—, Truck Process Agents Am., Inc., 1983—, Assist Fin. Svcs., 1986—. Home: RR 1 Box 86H Wentworth SD 57075-9602

KRINGSTAD, EDROY, state legislator; m. Faye Kringstad; 3 children. BS, Valley City State U.; MS, U. N.D. Senator Dist. 49 N.D. Senate, mem. natural resources com., appropriations com., vice chmn. fin. and taxation com. Named to Hall of Fame, Valley City State U., Nat. Wrestling Hall of Fame; named Nat. Coach of Yr. Nat. Jr. Coll. Athletic Assn., Athletic Dir. and Dance Tchr. of Yr. N.D. Health, Phys. Edn. Recreation and Dance. Mem. Amvets, Am. Legion, Nat. Coaches Assn. (past pres.), Am. Fedn. Tchrs., Elks, Eagles. Republican.

KRINKIE, PHILIP B., state legislator; b. St. Paul, Feb. 3, 1950; s. Frederic W. and Helen (Trieglaff) K.; m. Mary Ramsey, 1984. BA, Coe Coll., Cedar Rapids, Iowa, 1975. Pres. Shelling Co., 1981—; Dist. 53A rep. Minn. Ho. of Reps., St. Paul, 1991—. Mem. govt. op. and gaming-state govt. fin. divsn., local govt. and met. affairs, and transp. and transit coms., Minn. Ho. of Reps. Chmn. 4th Congrl. Dist. Rep. Com., 1983-84. Recipient spl. achievement award, Army Corps of Engrs., 1976. Mem. Sigma Nu. Office: 100 Constitution Ave Saint Paul MN 55155-1232

KRISCH, ALAN DAVID, physics professor; b. Phila., Apr. 19, 1939; s. Kube and Jeanne (Freiberg) K.; m. Jean Peck, Aug. 27, 1961; 1 child, Kathleen Susan. AB, U. Pa., 1960; PhD, Cornell U., 1964. Instr. Cornell U., 1964; mem. faculty U. Mich., Ann Arbor, 1964—, assoc. prof. high energy physics, 1966-68, prof., 1968—, dir. Spin Physics Ctr., 1994—. Vis. prof. Niels Bohr Inst., Copenhagen, 1975-76; trustee Argonne Nat. Lab., 1972-73, 80-82, chmn. zero gradient syncrotron users group, 1973-75, 78-79, chmn. internat. com. high energy spin physics symposia, 1977-94, past chmn., 1995-2006, mem., 2007—, chmn. organizing com. conf. on particle and nuclear physics intersections, 1983-86, mem., 1987-91, hon. mem., 1994—; chmn.-elect, chmn. IUCF Users Group, 1997-2002; spokesperson NEPTUN-A Expt. at 400 GeV UNK accelerator in Russia, 1989-99, SPIN@FERMI collaboration Fermilab, 1991-95, SPIN@HERA collaboration DESY in Germany, 1996-99, SPIN@U-70 Exp. at 70 Gev IHEP accelerator in Protvino, Russia, 2000—, SPIN@COSY Expt. COSY accelerator, Jülich, Germany, 2002-, SPIN@J-PARC Collaboration, Tokai, Japan, 2003—. Trustee Ann Arbor Hands On Mus., 1999-2005. Fellow NSF, 1963, Guggenheim Found., 1971-72, Denmark Nat. Bank, 1975-76. Fellow Am. Phys. Soc.; mem. AAAS. Achievements include discovery of heavy elementary particles, of structure within the proton, of scaling in inclusive reactions, of spinning core within proton, of large spin forces in violent proton collisions, of precise confirmation of large spin forces; invention of inclusive reactions; development of first high energy spin-polarized proton beam, of first strong focusing spin-polarized proton beam; demonstration of "Siberian snake" technique for accelerating spin-polarized beams; first spin-flipping of polarized boson beam. Office: U Mich Randall Lab Ann Arbor MI 48109-1120

KRISHNAN, PADMANABAN, food scientist, educator; BS in Botany, U. Madras, India, 1977; MS in Food & Nutrition, ND State U., Fargo, 1983, PhD in Cereal Sci., 1989. Lab. tech. IV, Dept. Food and Nutrition ND State U., Fargo, ND, 1987—88; instr., dept. nutrition, food sci. & hospitality SD State U., Brookings, SD, 1988—89, asst. prof., dept. nutrition, food sci. & hospitality, 1989—94, assoc. prof., dept. nutrition, food sci. & hospitality, 1994—2001, prof., dept. nutrition, food sci. & hospitality, 2001—05, prof., acting dept. head, dept. nutrition, food sci. & hospitality, 2005—07, prof., dept. nutrition, food sci. & hospitality, 2007—. Chair U. Harding Disting. Lecture; mem.-at-large Great Plains Subsection IFT, 1999; exec. com., academic senate SD State U., 2006. Mem.: Midwest Assn. Official Analytical Chemists (technical chair, food, nutraceutical, and pharm. analysis sect. 2000), Am. Assn. Cereal Chemists (co-chair, vitamin methods com. 2000, chair, vitamins methods com. 2006), Am. Assn. for Clinical Chemistry (assoc. mem. oats products com. 1999, voting mem., vitamin methods technical com. 1999). Office: Dept Nutrition Food Sci & Hospitality South Dakota State U SNF 415 Box 2275A Brookings SD 57007 Office Phone: 605-688-4040. Office Fax: 605-688-5603. Business E-Mail: padmanaban.krishnan@sdstate.edu.*

KRISLOV, MARVIN, academic administrator, lawyer, educator; b. Balt., Aug. 24, 1960; s. Joseph and Evelyn (Moreida) K.; m. Amy Ruth Sheon, Aug. 25, 1993; children: Zachary Jacob, Jesse Harris, Eve Rose. BA in Econs. summa cum laude, Yale U., 1982; BA/MA in Modern History, Oxford U., Eng., 1985; JD, Yale U., 1988. Bar: Calif. 1988, DC 1989, Mich. 1999. Law clk to Judge Marilyn Hall Patel US Dist. Ct. (no. dist.) Calif., San Francisco, 1988-89; trial atty. civil rights divsn. US Dept. Justice, Washington, 1989-93; spl. asst. U.S. atty. US Atty.'s Office, Washington, 1989-90; spl. counsel Office of Counsel to the Pres., Washington, 1993-94, asst. counsel, 1994, assoc. counsel, 1995-96; dep. solicitor US Dept. Labor, Washington, 1996-98, acting solicitor, 1997-98; v.p., gen. counsel U. Mich., Ann Arbor, 1998—2007; pres. Oberlin Coll., Ohio, 2007—. Adj. prof. law, George Washington U. Law Sch., Washington, 1991-93; adj. prof. U. Mich. Law Sch., 2000—, U. Mich. polit. sci. dept., 2001—. Mem. New Haven Bd. Aldermen, 1982-83. Rhodes scholar, 1983. Mem. Phi Beta Kappa. Office: Oberlin Coll Office of Pres 70 N Professor St Oberlin OH 44074 E-mail: Marvin.Krislov@oberlin.edu.

KRISS, GARY W(AYNE), priest; b. Balt., Dec. 29, 1946; s. Warren B. and Margaret L. (Austin) K. AB cum laude, Dartmouth Coll., 1968; MDiv, Yale U. Div. Sch., 1972; postgrad. studies, The Gen. Theol. Sem., NYC, 1972, St. George Coll., Jerusalem, 1978; DD, Nashotah House, 2001. Ordained to ministry Episcopal Ch. as deacon, 1972, as priest 1972. Chaplain to the congregation Cathedral Ch. of St. Paul, Burlington, Vt., 1972-74; coord. Rock Point (Vt.) Summer Confs., 1973-77; vicar St. Mark's, St. Luke's Parishes, Castleton and Fair Haven, Vt., 1974-78; asst. to dean The Cathedral of All Saints, Albany, N.Y., 1978-79, canon precentor, 1979-84, dir. inst. Christian studies, 1979-84; dean Cathedral of All Saints, Albany, 1984-91; dean and pres. Nashotah (Wis.) House, 1992—2001; interim rector St. Paul's Epis. Ch., Troy, NY, 2001—02, assoc. priest, 2002—04; vicar St. Paul's Ch., Salem, NY, 2003—. Bd. dirs. Brookhaven Home for Boys, Chelsea, Vt., 1975-79, Albany Collegiate Interfaith Ctr., 1982-90, pres. 1984-90; Episcopal campus priest, SUNY, Albany, 1980-84; bd. dirs. Capital Area Coun. of Chs., Albany, N.Y., 1989-91, chmn. of Faith and Learning Commn.; The Living Ch. Found., 1994—. Bd. dirs. Samaritan Shelters, Glenmont, N.Y., 1979-91, The Child's Hosp., Albany, 1986-90, Child's Nursing Home, Albany, 1987-91, pres. 1990-91. Episcopalian. Home and Office: PO Box 26 Cambridge NY 12816

KRISS, ROBERT J., lawyer; b. Cleve., Dec. 15, 1953; BA summa cum laude, Cornell U., 1975; JD cum laude, Harvard U., 1978. Bar: Ill. 1978, U.S. Dist. Ct. (no. dist.) Ill. 1978, U.S. Ct. Appeals (7th cir.) 1983, U.S. Dist. Ct. (no. dist. trial bar) Ill. 1982. Ptnr. Mayer, Brown LLP, Chgo. Presenter in field; adj. prof. trial practice Northwestern U. Law Sch. Author: published short story. Chmn. consent degree task force Chgo. Park Dist., 1986-87; bd. dirs. Chgo. Legal Assistance Found., 1996-2000, Victory Gardens Theater, 2003-04, Chgo. Coun. Sci. Tech., 2007. Named a Leading Lawyer in Ill., Ill. Super Lawyer, 2005, 2008. Mem.: ABA (sect. on litigation, bus. law). Avocation: writing. Office: Mayer Brown Rowe & Maw 71 S Wacker Dr Chicago IL 60606-4637 Home Phone: 847-501-3813; Office Phone: 312-701-7165. Business E-Mail: rkriss@mayerbrown.com.

KRISTENSEN, DOUGLAS ALLAN, former state legislator; b. Kearney, Nebr., Jan. 4, 1955; s. Donald M. and Mary Lou (Martin) K.; m. Terri S. Harder; children: Morgan Claire, Paige Nicole. BA, U. Nebr., 1977; JD, Drake U., 1980. Bar: US Supreme Ct. Ptnr. Lieske & Kristensen, 1981—2002; atty. Kearney County, 1982-88; mem. Nebr. Legislature from 37th dist., Lincoln, 1988—; chmn. transp. com. Nebr. Legislature, Lincoln, 1991-98, mem. intergovtl. coop. and revenue coms., mem. exec. bd., chair transp. com., 1991-97, speaker of the legislature, 1998—2002; chancellor U. Nebr., 2002—. Bd. dirs. young lawyers ssect. Nebr. Bar, 1984-88, ebr. CLE Inc., 1986-90. Pres. Rocky Mountain Athletic Conf., 2005—06. Henry Toll fellow, 1991; recipient Pres.' award Nebr. Assn. County Ofcls., 1987. Mem. Nebr. Bar Assn. (award of spl. merit 2002), Iowa Bar Assn., Nebr. County Atty.'s Assn. (bd. dirs. 1985-88), Rotary Internat., Optimists Club. Office: University of Nebraska at Kearney 905 W 25th St Lincoln NE 68849 Home: 219 N Brown Ave Minden NE 68959-1524

KRITZER, PAUL ERIC, publishing executive, lawyer; b. Buffalo, May 5, 1942; s. James Cyril and Bessie May (Biddlecombe) K.; m. Frances Jean McCallum, June 20, 1970; children: Caroline Frances, Erica Han. BA, Williams Coll., 1964; MS in Journalism, Columbia U., 1965; JD, Georgetown U., 1972. Bar: U.S. Supreme Ct. 1978, Wis. 1980. Reporter, copy editor Buffalo Evening News, 1964, 69, 70; instr. English Augusta Coll., Ga., 1968-69; law clk. Office of FCC Commr., Washington, 1971, MCI, Washington, 1972; counsel US Ho. of Reps., Washington, 1972-77; assoc. counsel Des Moines Register & Tribune, 1977-80; editor, pub. Waukesha Freeman, Wis., 1980-83; legal v.p., sec. Jour. Comm. Inc., Milw., 1983—. Trustee Carroll Co., Waukesha, 1981-89; producer Waukesha Film Festival, 1982; bd. dirs. Des Moines Metro Opera, Inc., 1979-80, Milw. Youth Symphony Orch., 1992-2001, pres. 1994-97; bd. dirs. United Performing Arts Fund, 1994-97, Milw. Symphony Orch., 1997-2004, Waukesha Landmarks Commn., 2005-06; adj. instr. Marquette U., 2007—. With US Army, 1965—68. Presbyterian. Avocations: bridge, gardening. Home: 211 Oxford Rd Waukesha WI 53186-6263 Office: Jour Communications Inc 333 W State St PO Box 661 Milwaukee WI 53201-0661 Home Phone: 262-548-9666; Office Phone: 414-224-2374. Business E-Mail: pkritzer@journalcommunications.com.

KRIVIT, JEFFREY SCOT, surgeon; b. Aug. 15, 1955; m. Mary Hoyme, July 6, 1986; children: Bradley, Alex, Elyse, Hanna. BS, U. Ill., 1977, MD, 1981. Resident Ill. Eye & Ear Infirmary, Chgo., 1982-86; physician Carle Clinic Assoc., Urbana, Ill., 1986-89, Linn Head & Neck Surgery, Cedar Rapids, Iowa, 1989-92, Cedar Rapids ENT, 1992-96, Ea. Iowa ENT, Cedar Rapids, 1996—. Chief surgery St. Luke's Hosp., Cedar Rapids, 1995-96. Fellow Am. Rhinol. Soc., Am. Acad. Otolaryngology Head & Neck Surgery, Am. Soc. Head & Neck Surgery, Am. Acad. Facial Plastic & Reconstructive Surgery, Am. Coll. Surgeons; mem. AMA, Linn County Med. Soc., Iowa Med. Soc. Office: PCI ENT Dept 2d Fl 600 7th St SE Fl 2D Cedar Rapids IA 52401-2112

KRIVKOVICH, PETER GEORGE, advertising executive; b. Bad Ischl, Austria, Oct. 25, 1946; came to U.S., 1953; s. George M. Krivkovich and Ada (Kalenkiewicz) Bajor; children: Peter A., Alexis C. BS, U. Ill., 1969; postgrad.,

Loyola U., Chgo., 1972-73. Advt. asst. Kemper Ins. Co., Chgo., 1969-71; account exec. Nader-Lief, Chgo., 1971-72; account mgr. Leo Burnett, Chgo., 1972-73; ptnr. Hackenberg, Normann, Krivkovich, Chgo., 1973-80; pres. Cramer-Krasselt, Chgo., 1981-86, pres., COO, 1987-98, pres., CEO, chmn. bd., 1999—; pres., CEO CKPR, 2002—. Mem. Nat. Advt. Rev. Bd. Bd. dirs. Off The Street Club, 1997—, Prentice Hosp., 1998—, Chgo. Humanities Festival, 2002—03. Named One of 100 Best and Brightest Advt. Execs. of Yr. Advt. Age mag., 1986, Midwest Advt. Exec. of Yr. Adweek mag., 1987. Mem. Am. Assn. Advt. Agys. (chmn. Chgo. chpt. 1992, 93, regional bd. govs. 1996, 97, nat. bd. govs. 1998-2002, 06—, bd. dirs. Ad coun. 2007—), Direct Mktg. Assn., Chgo. Assn. Direct Mktg., Chgo. Advt. Club, Glenview (Ill.) C. of C., Tavern Club, Exec. Club. Office: Cramer-Krasselt 225 N Michigan Ave Ste 800 Chicago IL 60601-7690 E-mail: pkrivkov@c-k.com.

KRIZEK, RAYMOND JOHN, engineering educator, consultant; b. Balt., June 5, 1932; s. John James and Louise (Polak) K.; m. Claudia Stricker, Aug. 1964; children: Robert A., Kevin J. BE, Johns Hopkins U., 1954; MS, U. Md., 1961; PhD, Northwestern U., 1963; doctorate (hon.), U. Cantabria, Spain, 2003. Instr. U. Md., College Park, 1957-61; rsch. asst. civil engring. Northwestern U., Evanston, Ill., 1961-63, asst. prof. civil engring., 1963-66, assoc. prof. civil engring., 1966-70, prof. civil engring., 1970—, chmn. dept. civil engring., 1980-92, dir. Master of Project Mgmt. program, 1994—, Stanley F. Pepper chair prof., 1987—. Cons. to industry. Editor books; contbr. numerous articles to profl. jours. Served to lt. U.S. Army Corp Engrs., 1955-57. Decorated Palmes Academiques (France); recipient Hogentogler award ASTM, 1970; named disting. vis. scholar NSF, 1972; inducted Innovation Hall of Fame U. Md. Sch. Engring., 2007. Mem.: ASCE (pres. GEO Inst. 1997—98, Huber Rsch. prize 1971, Karl Terzaghi award 1997, Ill. sect. Civil Engr. of Yr. 1999, Hon. mem. 2002, Wallace Hayward Baker award Geo-Inst. 2003, G. Brooks Earnest award 2005, Karl Terzaghi lecture 2006), Internat. Soc. Soil Mechanics and Geotech. Engring., Nat. Acad. Engring., Spanish Royal Acad. Engring. (corr.). Roman Catholic. Home: 1366 Sanford Ln Glenview IL 60025-3165 Office: Dept Civil Engring Northwestern U 2145 Sheridan Rd Evanston IL 60208-3109 Office Phone: 847-491-4040. Business E-Mail: rjkrizek@northwestern.edu.

KROCK, CURTIS JOSSELYN, pulmonologist; b. Fort Smith, Ark., Oct. 11, 1935; s. Frederick Henry and Hazel Armiger (Josselyn) Krock; m. Ruth Leone Johnson, Apr. 27, 1968; children: Eric Gregory, Lynn Alyson; m. Susan de la Fuente, July 15, 2006. BA, Stanford U., 1957; MD, Johns Hopkins U. Sch. Medicine, 1961. Diplomate Am. Bd. Internal Medicine, Am. Bd. Pulmonary Medicine. Intern Barnes Hosp., St. Louis, 1961-62, resident in internal medicine, 1963-65; resident in pathology Johns Hopkins U. Sch. Medicine, Balt., 1962-63; pulmonary fellow Duke U., Durham, NC, 1965-66; pvt. practice Holt-Krock Clinic, Ft. Smith, Ark., 1968-72, Carle Clinic, Urbana, Ill., 1972-2001, also bd. dirs., 1978-80, chief medicine dept., 1996-99; clin. asst. prof. U. Ill., Urbana, 1976-99, clin. assoc. prof., 2000—; interim chief of medicine UICOM-UC; chief of medicine Carle Found. Hosp., 2003—. Capt. US Army, 1966—68. Fellow: ACP; mem.: Sierra Club, Sigma Xi. Avocations: violin, reading. Home: 2125 Lynwood Dr Champaign IL 61821-6606 Office: Carle Clin Edn Ctr Forum Bldg 611 W Park Urbana IL 61801-2530 Office Phone: 217-383-4617. Personal E-mail: ckrock1935@aol.com. Business E-Mail: curtis.krock@carle.com.

KROENERT, ROBERT MORGAN, retired lawyer; b. Kansas City, Mo., July 19, 1939; s. Robert Andrew and Marion Leona (Morgan) K.; m. Susan Aldrich, Aug. 18, 1962; children: Kathleen Susan, Ann Elizabeth, Robert Aldrich. BS, U. Kans., 1961; JD, U. Mich., 1964. Bar: Mo. 1964, U.S. Dist. Ct. (we. dist.) Mo. 1965, U.S. Ct. Appeals (8th cir.) 1984, U.S. Ct. Appeals (5th, 10th and D.C. cirs.) 1986, U.S. Supreme Ct. 1991. Assoc. Morrison & Hecker L.L.P., Kansas City, 1964-69; ptnr. Morrison & Hecker, Kansas City, 1969—2002. Bd. dirs. Guadalupe Ctr., Inc., Kansas City, 1978-87; mem. adv. bd. greater univ. fund, U. Kans., Lawrence, 1985-88; Mem. fin. com. Johnson County Rep. Com., 1987-90, Mo. Supreme Ct. Disciplinary Com. for Jackson County, 1992-2000, divsn. chair, 1995-97; mem. coun. Colonial Congregtional Ch., 1990-93, moderator, 1991-93. Mem.: Mo. Bar, Internat. Assn. Def. Counsel, Lawyers Assn. Kansas City (bd. dirs., pres. 1998—99, past. pres., past pres. found.), Mission Hills Country Club, Rotary. Avocation: golf.

KROEPLIN, KENNETH, state legislator; b. Grand Forks, ND, Jan. 15, 1952; m. Sharon; 3 children. Farmer; supr. Township, N.D., Edendale, N.D.; mem. House of Rep., .D., N.D. Senate from 23rd dist., Bismark, N.D., 1996—. Bd. dirs. Steele County Farmers Union, Steele County Mut. Ins.; mem. Hope Rural Fire Protection Dist. With N. D. Nat. Guard, 1970-76; Hope Am. Legion (vice cmdr.) Democrat. Lutheran. Office: Dist 23 Rt 1 Box 39 Hope ND 58046 E-mail: kkroepli@state.nd.us.

KROGSTAD, JACK LYNN, associate dean, accounting educator; b. Harlan, Iowa, Jan. 27, 1944; s. Chester Milo and Geraldine Elizabeth (Archibald) K.; m. Nancy Ellen Coffin, June 18, 1967; children: Kristine Ellen, Brian Lynn. BS, Union Coll., 1967; MBA, U. Nebr., 1971, PhD, 1975. Staff acct. Trachtenbarg & Grant CPAs, Lincoln, Nebr., 1967-68; asst. prof. U. Tex., Austin, 1975-78; assoc. prof. Kans. State U., Manhattan, 1978-80; John P. Begley prof. acctg. Crieghton U., Omaha, 1980-96, prof. acctg., 1997—, assoc. dean, 2000—. Vis. assoc. prof. U. Mich., Ann Arbor, 1980; vis. prof. U. Ill. 2000-; dir. rsch. Nat. Commn. Fraudulent Fin. Reporting, 1985-87. Editor: Auditing: A Journal of Practice and Theory; contbr. articles to profl. jours. With U.S. Army, 1968-70. Recipient Disting. Faculty Svc. award Crieghton U., 1988; Arthur Anderson & Co. doctoral fellow, 1974-75, Paton Acctg. Ctr. rsch. fellow, 1980, Barret Disting. Svc. award, 2002, Coll. Faculty of the Yr. award, 2001. Mem. AICPA, Nebr. Soc. CPAs (Acctg. Educator of Yr. award 1983), Am. Acctg. Assn. (regional v.p. 1984-85, auditing sect. chmn. 1984-85, Outstanding Auditing Educator award 1994), Beta Gamma Sigma, Beta Alpha Psi. Republican. Seventh-Day-Adventist. Home: 56717 Deacon Rd Pacific Junction IA 51561-4169 E-mail: jkrogstad@creighton.edu.

KROHNKE, DUANE W., retired lawyer; b. Keokuk, Iowa, June 29, 1939; s. Ward Glenn and Marian Frances (Brown) K.; m. Mary Alyce Luschen, June 25, 1963; children: Alan Duane, Brian Douglas. BA, Grinnell Coll., Iowa, 1961, Oxford U., 1963, MA, 1970; JD, U. Chgo., 1966; DHL, Grinnell Coll., 1999. Bar: N.Y. 1967, Minn. 1970, U.S. Supreme Ct. 1970, U.S. Ct. Appeals (2d cir.) 1967, U.S. Ct. Appeals (8th cir.) 1970, U.S. Ct. Appeals (D.C.) 1974, U.S. Dist. Ct. (so., ea. dists.) N.Y. 1967, U.S. Dist. Ct. Minn. 1970. Assoc. atty. Cravath, Swaine, Moore, NYC, 1966-70, Faegre & Benson, Mpls., 1970-73, ptnr., 1974-2000, of counsel, 2001; ret., 2001. Adj. prof. U. Minn. Law Sch., 2002—. Editl. bd.: U. Chgo. Lit. Rev., 1964—66. Co-chair Bicentennial com. U.S. Dist. Ct. Minn. dist., Mpls., 1986-88; elder Westminster Presbyn. Ch., Mpls., 1985-91; trustee United Theol. Seminary, New Brighton, Minn., 1988-98. Recipient Alumni award Grinnell Coll., 1982; Rhodes scholar Rhodes Trustees, Oxford, Eng., 1961-63; Mecham scholar U. Chgo., 1963-66. Mem. Minn. State Bar Assn. (co-chair antitrust sect. 1982-84, co-chair ethics/standards of practice com. of ADR sect. 1995-96, chair elect ADR sect. 1996-97, chair ADR sect. 1997-98), Minn. Human Rights Advocates (vol. award 1991, 99, 2002), Order of Coif, Phi Beta Kappa. Avocations: reading, exercise.

KROLL, BARRY LEWIS, retired lawyer; b. Chgo., June 8, 1934; s. Harry M. and Hannah (Lewis) K.; m. Jayna Vivian Leibovitz, June 20, 1956; children: Steven Lee, Joan Lois Kroll Dolgin, Nancy Maxine Kroll Richardson. AB in Psychology with distinction, U. Mich., 1955, JD with distinction, 1958. Bar: Ill. 1958. Assoc. firm Jacobs & McKenna, Chgo., 1958-66, Epstein, Manilow & Sachnoff, Chgo., 1966-68, Schiff, Hardin, Waite Dorschel & Britton, Chgo., 1968-69; ptnr. Wolfberg & Kroll, Chgo., 1970-74, Kirshbaum & Kroll, Chgo., 1972-74; of counsel Jacobs, Williams & Montgomery, Ltd., Chgo., 1973-74; ptnr. Jacobs, Williams & Montgomery Ltd., Chgo., 1974-85, Williams & Montgomery Ltd., Chgo., 1985—2001; of counsel Williams Montgomery & John, Ltd., 2002—. Faculty John Marshall Law Sch., Chgo., 1969-73; atty. for petitioner in U.S. Supreme Ct. decision Escobedo vs Ill., 1964; mem. legal and legis. com. Internat. Franchise Assn., 1976-80 Asst. editor: Mich. Law Rev, 1957-58. Chmn. Park Forest Bd. Zoning Appeals, Ill., 1971-78. Served to Capt., Judge Advocate Gen. Corps, US Army, 1959-63. Named Outstanding Young Man, Park Forest Jr. C. of C., 1966. Mem. Ill. Bar Assn., Chgo. Bar Assn. (chmn. legis. com. 1974-75), Ill. Appellate Lawyers Assn. (treas. 1978-79, sec. 1979-80, pres. 1981-82), Bar Assn. 7th Fed. Circuit, Order of Coif, Tau Epsilon Rho, Alpha Epsilon Pi. Jewish (trustee congregation 1966-70, 72-75, 90—, pres. men's club 1965-66). Home: 1440 N State Pkwy Apt 21B Chicago IL 60610-6509 Personal E-mail: jaynabarry@msn.com, blk@willmont.com.

KROLL, STEVEN L., lawyer; b. Ft. Belvoir, Va., 1959; m. Jane Patterson; children: Harry, Annie. BA, Dartmouth Coll., 1981; JD, U. Mich., 1984. Bar: Ill. 1984. Assoc. Chapman and Cutler, Chgo., 1984—86, McDermott, Will & Emery, 1986—91; pvt. practice Chgo., 1991—97; part-time fill-in Cancer Treatment Ctrs. Am., Arlington Heights, Ill., 1997—2000, gen. counsel, v.p., 2000—.

KROMKOWSKI, THOMAS S., state legislator; b. South Bend, Ind., Sept. 2, 1942; m. Janeen Kromkowski, 1963; 2 children. With A M Gen. Corp.; rep. Dist. 7 Ind. Ho. of Reps., 1980—, chmn. elec. and apportionment com., ranking minority mem., mem. labor and employment com., mem. pub. health, aged and aging com. Mem. Westside Dem. and Civic Club, South Bend; vice chmn. United Auto Workers; mem. St. Joseph County Coun. Mem. VFW, Polish Falcons Am. Club.

KRON, RANDY, farmer, agricultural association administrator; m. Joyce Kron; children: Victoria, Benjamin. B Agrl. Econs., Purdue U., 1983. Dir. Ind. Farm Bur, Indpls., 1995—, now v.p.; owner farm Evansville, Ill. Chmn. polit. action com. Ind. Farm Bur., mem. state young farmer com., 1986—87. Mem. Vanderburgh County Soil and Water Conservation Bd.; past pres. county extension bd.; rep. agrl. adv. com. Rep. John Hostettler; sr. youth sponsor Salem United Ch. of Christ, Darmstadt, Ill. Recipient Young Farmer Achievement Bd., Ind. Farm Bur., 1989. Office: Ind Farm Bur Inc PO Box 1290 Indianapolis IN 46206

KRONICK, SUSAN D., retail executive; b. NYC; Grad., Conn. Coll. Exec. trainee Bloomingdale's Macy's Inc. (formerly Federated Dept. Stores Inc.), 1973—85; operating v.p., divsn. merchandise mgr. Bloomingdale's Macy's Inc., 1985—88, sr. v.p., divsn. merchandise mgr. Bloomingdale's, 1988—90, exec. v.p., gen. mgr. Bloomingdale's, 1990—91, sr. v.p. dir. stores, Bloomingdale's, 1991—93, pres. RLG Divsn. Atlanta, 1992—97, chmn. Burdines Fla., 1997—2000, group pres. regional dept. stores Cin., 2001—03, vice chmn., 2003—. Bd. dirs. Pepsi Bottling Group. Recipient Nat. Human Rels. award, Am. Jewish Com., 1999. Office: Macy's Inc 7 W Seventh St Cincinnati OH 45202

KRONMILLER, JAN E., dean, academic administrator; BS in Chemistry, Ohio State U., DDS, 1978; PhD in biomedical sciences, U. Conn., 1991. Cert. pediatric dentistry and orthodontics. NIH rsch. fellow U. Conn. Health Ctr.; asst. prof. pediatric dentistry U. Pitts.; pvt. practice; head orthodontics section, Coll. Dentistry U. Ky.; prof. and chair. dept. orthodontics, Sch. Dentistry Oreg. Health Scis. U., prof., grad. program, Sch. Medicine; dean, Coll. Dentistry Ohio State U., 2001—. Recipient Nat. Rsch. Svc. award, NIH, Individual Physician Scientist award. Fellow: Internat. Coll. Dentists, Am. Coll. Dentists. Office: 305 W 12th Ave Columbus OH 43210 Office Phone: 614-292-9755. Office Fax: 614-292-7619. Business E-Mail: kronmiller.1@osu.edu.

KRSUL, JOHN ALOYSIUS, JR., lawyer; b. Highland Pk., Mich., Mar. 24, 1938; s. John A. and Ann M. (Sepich) K.; m. Justine Oliver, Sept. 12, 1958; children: Ann Lisa, Mary Justine. BA, Albion Coll., 1959; JD, U. Mich., 1963. Bar: Mich. 1963. Assoc. Dickinson Wright PLLP, 1963-71, ptnr. Detroit, 1971-99, consulting ptnr., 2000—. Asst. editor: U. Mich. Law Rev, 1962-63. Recipient Disting. Alumnus award Albion Coll., 1984; Sloan scholar, 1958-59; Fulbright scholar, 1959-60; Ford. Found. grantee, 1964 Fellow: Am. Bar Found. (life; chmn. Mich. chpt. 1988—89); mem.: ABA (ho. of dels. 1979—2002, chmn. standing com. on membership 1983—89, exec. coun. 1984—91, chmn. sect. gen. practice 1989—90, tort and ins. practice sect., exec. coun. 1991—94, bd. govs. 1991—99, chmn. fin. com. 1993—94, exec. com. 1993—94, 1996—99, treas. 1996—99, editl. bd. ABA Jour. 1996—99, chmn. audit com. 2003—07), Am. Bar Ins. Cons. Inc. (bd. dirs. sec. 1988—95), Am. Bar Endowment (bd. dirs. 1996—99), Nat. Conf. Bar Pres. (exec. coun. 1986—89), Am. Judicature Soc. (dir. 1971—79, exec. com. 1973—74), Fellows of Young Lawyers Am. Bar (bd. dirs. 1977—86, pres. 1983—84, chmn. bd. 1984—86), Mich. State Bar Found. (trustee 1982—83, 1985—99, chmn. fellows 1986—87), State Bar Mich. (commr. 1973—83, pres. 1982—83), Detroit Bar Assn. Found. (dir. 1971—84, pres. 1979—80), Detroit Bar Assn. (dir. 1971—80, pres. 1979—80), Am. Bar Retirement Funds (bd. dirs. 1999—2005, sec. 2003—05, v.p. 2005—06, pres. 2006—07, bd. dirs. 2007—), Sixth Cir. Jud. Conf. (life), Detroit Club, Orchard Lake Country Club, Delta Tau Delta, Phi Eta Sigma, Omicron Delta Kappa, Phi Beta Kappa. Office: Dickinson Wright PLLC 500 Woodward Ave Ste 4000 Detroit MI 48226-3416 Home: 10048 Weko Dr Bridgman MI 49106-4310

KRUEGER, BONNIE LEE, editor, writer; b. Chgo., Feb. 3, 1950; d. Harry Bernard and Lillian (Soyak) Krueger; m. James Lawrence Spurlock, Mar. 8, 1972. Student, Morraine Valley Coll., 1970. Adminstrv. asst. Carson Pirie Scott & Co., Chgo., 1969-72; traffic coord. Tatham Laird & Kudner, Chgo., 1973-74, J. Walter Thompson, Chgo., 1974-76, prodn. coord., 1976-78; editor-in-chief Assoc. Pubs., Chgo., 1978—, Sophisticate's Hairstyle Guide, 1978—, Sophisticate's Beauty Guide, 1978—, Complete Woman, 1981—; pub., editorial svcs. dir. Sophisticate's Black Hair Guide, 1983—, Sophisticate's Soap Star Styles, 1994-95. Active Statue of Liberty Restoration Com., NYC, 1983, Chgo. Architecture Found.; campaign worker Cook County State's Atty., Chgo., 1982; poll watcher Cook County Dem. Orgn., 1983. Recipient Exceptional Woman in Pub. award, Women in Periodical Pub., 2000. Mem. Soc. Profl. Journalists, Am. Health and Beauty Aids Inst. (assoc., Communicator of Yr. award), Lincoln Park Zool. Soc., Landmarks Preservation Coun. of Ill., Art Inst. Chgo., Chgo. Hist. Soc., Mus. Contemporary Art, Peta, Headline Club, PAWS (Pets Are Worth Saving), Historymakers, Sigma Delta Chi, City Club Chgo. Lutheran. Office: Associate Pubs 875 Michigan Ave Chicago IL 60611-1803 Business E-Mail: krueger@associatedpub.com.

KRUEGER, DARRELL WILLIAM, academic administrator; b. Salt Lake City, Feb. 9, 1943; s. William T. and E. Marie (Nelson) K.; m. Verlene Terry, July 1, 1965 (dec. Jan., 1969); 1 child, William; m. Nancy Leane Jones, Sept. 2, 1969; children: Antonia, Amy, Susan. BA summa cum laude, So. Utah State Coll., 1967; MA in Govt., U. Ariz., 1969, PhD in Govt., 1971. Asst. prof. polit. sci. N.E. Mo. State U., Kirksville, 1971-73, v.p. acad. affairs, dean of instrn., 1973-89; pres. Winona State U., Minn., 1989—2005, pres. emeritus, 2005—. Facilitator The 7 Habits of Highly Effective People, 1993, Crucial Conservations, 2003; mem. adv. bd. U.S. Bank, Rochester, Minn., 1989—. Mem. Gamehaven Coun. Boy Scouts Am., 1989—. Recipient Outstanding Alumnus award, So. Utah State, 1992. Mem.: Am. Assn. Higher Edn., Am. Assn. State Colls. and Univs., Rotary, Phi Beta Kappa. Mem. Lds Ch. Avocations: running, golf. Office: Winona State U Somsen 201 8th & Johnson Winona MN 55987 Home: 303 E 3810 N Cedar City UT 84720-7262 Office Phone: 507-457-5003.

KRUEGER, JAMES H., social service association executive; With Aid Assn. for Luths., Appleton, Wis., 1965—, from dist. reps. to gen. agt., 1965-83, gen. agt., dir. of agys. Agy. and Sales, 1987—, mem. mktg. and strategy couns. Instr. CLU. Recipient Jack Nussbaum Disting. Svc. award Wis. Assn. Life Underwriters, 1989. Mem. Chartered Life Underwriters, Chartered Fin. cons., Gen. Agts. and Mgrs. Assn. (chmn. internat. mktg. com.), Nat. Assn. Life Underwriters, Life Underwriting Tng. Coun. (bd. dirs.), Golden Key Soc. Office: Aid Assn for Lutherans 4321 N Ballard Rd Appleton WI 54919-0001

KRUEGER, RAYMOND ROBERT, lawyer; b. Portage, Wis., Aug. 29, 1947; s. Earl Andrew and Catherine Virginia (Klenert) K.; m. Barbara Bowen, June 21, 1969; children: Lindsey, Michael. BA in Econs., U. Wis., 1969, JD, 1972. Bar: Wis. 1972. Assoc. Charne, Glassner, Tehan, Clancy & Taitelman S.C., Milw., 1973-79, shareholder, 1979-91; ptnr. Charne Clancy Krueger Pollack & Corris S.C., Milw., 1991—92, Michael, Best & Friedrich LLP, Milw., 1992—. Chmn. Georgia O'Keeffe Found., Abiquiu, N.Mex., 1989—; trustee Village of Whitefish Bay, Wis., 1989—2003; mem. Milwaukee River Revitalization Coun., 1988—, vice chair, 1989—96, chair, 1996—; dir. River Revitalization Found., Inc., 1998—, chair, 2001—03; trustee Milw. Art Mus., 2003—, mem. bldg. com., 1996—2003; chair Whitefish Bay Cmty. Devel. Authority, 2002—. Capt. USAF, 1969—78. Mem. ABA (natural resources sect.), State Bar Wis. (environ. law sect.), Milw. Bar Assn. (environ. law sect.), Environ. Law Inst. Avocation: visual arts. Office: Michael Best & Friedrich LLP 100 E Wisconsin Ave Ste 3300 Milwaukee WI 53202-4108 Office Phone: 414-271-6560. Business E-Mail: rrkrueger@michaelbest.com.

KRUEGER, RICHARD ARNOLD, technology executive; b. St. Paul, Feb. 13, 1949; s. Richard Earnest and Shirley Mae (Popp) K.; m. Diane Susan Schiller, Apr. 14, 1973; children: Melissa, Ryan, Alisha. BA, Winona State Coll., 1971; MA in Teaching, Coll. of St. Thomas, 1973; MPA, Harvard U., 1992; PhD, U. Minn., 1997. Program dir. Midway YMCA, St. Paul, 1971-72; tchr. Lakeville (Minn.) Pub. Schs., 1973-79; dir. Staples (Minn.) Tchr. Ctr., 1979-82; owner Computer etworx, Inc., Staples, 1983-89; mem. Minn. Ho. of Reps., St. Paul, 1983-94, asst. majority leader, 1987-90, chair internat. trade and tech. com., 1989-90, speaker pro tempore, 1991-92, chair state govt. fin., 1993-94; info. mgmt. cons., Staples, 1990-94; pres. Minn. High Tech. Assn., Inc., Eagan, 1994-99; CEO, pres. KeyTech, Inc., 1999-2000; v.p. Key Investment, Inc., Mpls., 2000-01, JLT Group, Inc., 2001—03; pres. Million Zillion Software, 2003, Minn. Transp. Alliance, 2003—. Contbr. articles to profl. publs. Named Outstanding Alumnus, Winona State U., 1990; recipient Top Tech. Legis. Group award Am. Electronic Assn., 1992, Top Pub. Sector award Med. Alley, 1993, Chairs award Minn. High Tech. Assn., 1999. Mem. Democrat Farm Labor Party. Lutheran. Avocations: swimming, reading. Home: 11605 177th St W Lakeville MN 55044-7676 Office: 601 2nd Ave S Ste 5200 Minneapolis MN 55402-4317

KRUEGER-HORN, CHERYL, apparel executive; B in Home Econs. and Bus., Bowling Green State U., 1974. Buyer Burdine's Dept. Store, 1974-76; mdse. mgr. The Limited, 1976; v.p. sale Chaus Sportswear, CEO, until 1985; owner Cheryl's Cookies; pres., CEO Cheryl & Co. Bd. dirs. Bob Evans. Recipient Columbus Area Small Bus. Person of Yr. award Small Bus. Adminstrn., 1986, Woman of Achievement award YWCA, 1992, Outstanding Innovation Achievement award Innovation Alliance, 1992, Ctrl. Ohio Entrepreneur of Yr. award Inc. Mag. and Ernest & Young, 1994, Salesperson of Yr. award Columbus C. of C. Sales Exec. Club, Businessperson of Yr. award Ohio State U., Rosabeth Moss Kantor Excellence in Enterprise award Ohio Dept. Devel., 1996. Mem. Young Pres. Orgn. Office: 646 Mccorkle Blvd Westerville OH 43082-8778

KRUESI, FRANK EUGENE, lobbyist, former government executive; b. Marblehead, Mass., July 12, 1950; s. William Rogers and Lydia Abigail (Fuller) K.; m. Susan Francis Boyd, Sept. 1, 1971 (div. Jan. 1993); children: Elizabeth Ann, William Shepardson; m. Barbara Grochala, Oct. 16, 1993. BA in Econs. cum laude, Middlebury Coll., 1972; MA in Polit. Sci., U. Chgo., 1979. Lectr. polit. sci. Loyola U., Chgo., 1974, DePaul U., Chgo., 1979, Rosary Coll., Chgo., 1979; assoc. prof. pub. policy U. Chgo., 2000—; rsch. assoc. Ill. Gov.'s Commn. Individual Liberty & Personal Privacy, Chgo., 1975; cons. Ill. Gov.'s Commn. Mental Health Code, Chgo., 1975-77; exec. officer Cook County State's Atty. Office, Chgo., 1980-89; chief policy officer Office of Mayor of City of Chgo., 1989-93; asst. sec. for policy US Dept. Transp., Washington, 1993—97; pres. Chgo. Transit Authority, 1997—2007; chief lobbyist City of Chgo., Washington, 2007—. Vis. lectr. Harris Sch. Pub. Policy, U. Chgo., 2000—. Dir. internat. affairs Wash. DC Off., Chgo., 2007-; Issues dir. Daley for State's Atty. and Mayor campaigns, Chgo., 1980-89. Democrat. Office Phone: 202-783-0911.

KRUG, SHIRLEY, state legislator; b. Milw., Jan. 29, 1958; BS, U. Wis., Milw., 1981, MA, 1983. Mem. from dist. 13 Wis. State Assembly, Madison, 1984-96, mem. from dist. 12, 1984—. Former adj. prof. econs. U. Wis., Parkside. Commr. Mils. Met. Sewerage Dist.; former v.p. Jobs with Peace. Office: Wis State Assembly State Capitol PO Box 8952 Madison WI 53708-8952 Address: 9352 W Terra Ct Milwaukee WI 53224-2949

KRUKOWSKI, LUCIAN, philosopher, educator, artist; b. NYC, Nov. 22, 1929; s. Stefan and Anna (Belcarz) Krukowski; m. Marilyn Denmark, Jan. 14, 1955; 1 child, Samantha. BA, CUNY, 1952; BFA, Yale U., 1955; MS, Pratt Inst., 1958; PhD, Wash. U., St. Louis, 1977. Faculty mem. Pratt Inst., NYC, 1955-69; dean Sch. Fine Arts Washington U., St. Louis, 1969-77, prof. philosophy, 1977-96, chmn. dept. philosophy, 1986-89, prof. philosophy emeritus, 1996—. Author: Art and Concept, 1987, Aesthetic Legacies, 1992; contbr. articles to profl. jours.; one-man shows include Staempfli Gallery, NYC, 1960, 1963, Cee Je Gallery, 1967, Gallery Loretto Hilton Ctr., St. Louis, 1970, Terry Moore Gallery, 1975, 1978, Timothy Burns Gallery, 1981, LI U., NYC, 1985, Messing Gallery, St. Louis, 1992, Vernissage, 2000, exhibited in group shows at Tanager Gallery, NYC, 1958, Bklyn. Mus., 1958—60, U. Nebr., 1960, San Francisco Mus. Modern Art, 1961, Mus. Modern Art, NYC, 1962, St. Louis Art Mus., 1972, Fogg Mus., Cambridge, 1972, Timothy Burns Gallery, 1979—80, Represented in permanent collections Fogg Mus., Mass., San Francisco Mus., Washington U. Cpl. USMC, 1952—54. Mem.: Am. Philos. Assn., Am. Soc. Aesthetics. Avocations: climbing, hiking. Office: Washington U Dept Philosophy 1 Brookings Dr Saint Louis MO 63130-4899 Office Phone: 314-935-6670. Personal E-mail: lkruko@hotmail.com.

KRULITZ, LEO MORRION, retired business executive, director; b. Wallace, Idaho, June 15, 1938; s. John Morrion and Myrtle (Parker) K.; m. Donna Eileen Ristau, June 18, 1960; children— Cynthia, Pamela. BA, Stanford U., 1960; JD cum laude, Harvard U., 1963; MBA, Stanford U., 1969. Bar: Idaho 1963, Ind. 1969, DC 1978, U.S. Supreme Ct. 1978. Ptnr. firm Moffatt, Thomas, Barrett & Blanton, Boise, Idaho, 1963-67; v.p., treas. Irwin Mgmt. Co., Columbus, Ind., 1969-77; solicitor Dept. of the Interior, Washington, 1977-79; gen. counsel Cummins Engine Co., Columbus, Ind., 1979-80, v.p., 1980-92; pres. Cummins Fin., Inc., 1984-92, Cummins Cash and Info. Svcs., Inc., 1988-92; pres., CEO Saunders, Inc., Birmingham, Ala., 1992-93; pres., CEO, dir. Parkland Mgmt. Co., Cleve., 1994—2005; endowment trustee Euclid Ave. Christian Ch., 2005—06; dir. Horvitz Newspapers, Inc., Bellevue, Wash., 1994—2005. Trustee Lois U. Horvitz Found., 1998-2005; exec. dir. H.R.H. Family Found., 1994-98; treas. Irwin-Sweeney-Miller Found., Columbus, 1976-77; dir. L'Enfant Plaza Properties, Washington, 1974-77; mem. U.S. delegation Soviet Union Conf. on Environ. Law, 1978 Active Bartholomew Consol. Sch. Bd., 1982-88; trustee Wheelright Mus. of the Am. Indian, 2002—; pres., bd. trustee Wheelright Mus. Endowment Found., 2005—, Wheelwright Mus., 2007-. Democrat.

KRULL, DOUGLAS ARTHUR, lawyer; b. Grundy Center, Iowa, Oct. 11, 1958; s. Harm Henry and Esther S. (Schipper) K.; m. Jennifer Jo Shuldhiess, Aug. 23, 1986. BA, Upper Iowa U., 1981; JD, U. Iowa, 1984. Bar: Iowa 1985, U.S. Dist. Ct. (no. dist.) Iowa 1986. Assoc. Law Office John H. Greve, Northwood, Iowa, 1985-86; ptnr. Greve & Krull, Northwood, 1986—; county atty. Worth County, Northwood, 1986—. Chmn. Worth County Repub. Cen. Com., 1988—. Mem. Iowa Bar Assn., 2A Bar Assn., Worth County Bar Assn., Masons (Iowa Young Mason Yr. Award 1990), Northwood Area C. of C. Home: 401 11th St S Northwood IA 50459-1817 Office: Greve & Krull 736 Central Ave # 167 Northwood IA 50459-1518

KRULL, JEFFREY ROBERT, library director; b. North Tonawanda, NY, Aug. 29, 1948; s. Robert George and Ruth Otilie (Fels) K.; m. Alice Marie Hart, Apr. 12, 1969; children: Robert, Marla. BA, Williams Coll., Williamstown, Mass., 1970; MLS, SUNY, Buffalo, 1974. Cert. profl. libr., NY, Ohio, Ind. Traffic mgr. New Eng. Tel. Co., Burlington, Vt., 1970—71; tchr. English and German, varsity basketball coach Harrisburg Acad., Pa., 1971—72; reference libr. bus. and labor dept. Buffalo and Erie County Pub. Libr., 1973—76; head libr. Ohio U., Chillicothe, 1976—78; dir. Mansfield-Richland County Pub. Libr., Ohio, 1978—86, Allen County Pub. Libr., Ft. Wayne, Ind., 1986—. Mem. exec. com. Ft. Wayne Area Libr. Svc. Authority, 1986-90, v.p., 1989; mem. exec. com. Ind. Coop. Libr. Svcs. Authority, 1992-96, pres., 1994-95; mem. Online Computer Libr. Ctr. Pub. Libr. Adv. Coun., 1994-97; pres. Ft. Wayne Area INFONET, 1995-2001. Pres. Three Rivers Literacy Alliance, 1997—99; trustee Ohionet, Columbus, 1984—86; mem. Ind. Libr. and Hist. Bd., 2006—. Named Sagamore of the Wabash, Gov. Ind., 2001. Mem. ALA, Pub. Libr. Assn. (pres. met. librs. sect. 1990-91, statis. report adv. com.), Libr. Adminstrn. and Mgmt. Assn. (sec. libr. orgn. and mgmt. assn. 1996-97), Ohio Libr. Assn. (bd. dirs. 1985-86), Ind. Libr. Fedn. (vice chmn. legis. com. 1987-2006), Indiana Libr. ans Hist. Bd. (2006-), Urban Librs. Coun., Beta Phi Mu, Ft. Wayne Rotary Club. Home: 3017 Oak Borough Run Fort Wayne IN 46804-7808 Office: Allen County Pub Libr 900 Library Plz Fort Wayne IN 46802 Office Phone: 260-421-1200. E-mail: jkrull@acpl.lib.in.us.

KRULL, STEPHEN KEITH, lawyer; b. Peoria, Ill., Jan. 1965; m. Elizabeth A. Krull. BBA, Ea. Ill. U., 1986; JD with high honors, Chgo.-Kent Coll. Law, 1990. Assoc. atty. Sidley & Austin, Chgo.; corp. counsel A.B. Dick Co., Chgo.; divsn. counsel Roofing Systems Bus. Owens Corning, Toledo, 1996—99, v.p. corp. comm., gen. counsel, 1999—2003, sr. v.p., gen. counsel, sec., 2003—. Chmn. legal adv. bd. Nat. Ctr. Missing and Exploited Children, Washington; mem.

assoc. bd. dirs. Boys & Girls Clubs Toledo, 2004—; bd. mem. Habitat for Humanity Ohio, 2005—. Office: Owens Corning 1 Owens Corning Pky Toledo OH 43659 Office Phone: 419-248-8000. Office Fax: 419-248-5337. E-mail: stephen.k.krull@owenscorning.com.

KRUMLAUF, ROBERT EUGENE, neuroscientist, educator; B in Chem. Engring., Vanderbilt U., 1970; PhD in Devel. Biology, Ohio State U., 1979. Chief chem. engr. Capital City Products Inc., Columbus, Ohio, 1970—75; fellow dept. biochemistry Ohio State U., 1975—79; postdoctoral fellow Dr A. Balmain Beatson Inst. Cancer Rsch., Glasgow, Scotland, 1979—82, Dr S. Tilghman Inst. Cancer Rsch., Phila., 1982—85; from group leader to adj. group leader NIMR, England, 1985—2000, adj. group leader, 2000; sci. dir. Stowers Inst. Med. Rsch., Kansas City, Mo., 2000—. Prof. oral biology Sch. Dentistry U. Mo., Kansas City, 2000—; prof. oral biology Dept. Anatomy and Cell Biology U. Kans. Med. Sch., Kansas City, 2001—; prof. neuroscience Graduate Program U. Kans., Kansas City, 2002—. Editor: Devel. Biology, 1995—; mem. editl. bd.: New Biologist, 1989—92, Mechanisms of Devel., 1990—, Nucleic Acids Rsch., 1992—, Current Biology, 1993—2000, Portland Press, 1994—2000, Devel., 1994—, Molecular and Cellular Neurobiology, 1995—, Human Molecular Genetics, 1996—98, Genes and Function, 1997—98, InScight, 1998—. Fellow: Acad. Med. Scis.; mem.: Am. Acad. Arts and Scis., Soc. Pathology and Teratology, Acad. Med. Scis. UK, The Genetical Soc., Am. Soc. Microbiology, Am. Assn. Anatomists, Soc. Devel. Biology, Brit. Soc. Devel. Biology, European Molecular Biology Org., European Devel. Biology Org. (sec. 1997—2001). Office: Stowers Inst 1000 E 50th St Kansas City MO 64110 Home: 5407 Mission Dr Mission Hills KS 66208 Home Phone: 913-831-7680; Office Phone: 816-926-4051. Business E-Mail: rek@stowers-institute.org.

KRUMMEL, DONALD WILLIAM, librarian, educator; b. Sioux City, Iowa, July 12, 1929; s. William and Leta Margarete (Fischer) K.; m. Marilyn Darlene Frederick, June 19, 1956; children: Karen Elisabeth, Matthew Frederick. Mus.B., U. Mich., 1951, Mus.M., 1953, MA in Library Sci, 1954, PhD, 1958. Instr. in music lit. U. Mich., 1952-56; reference librarian Library of Congress, Washington, 1956-61; head reference dept., asso. librarian Newberry Library, Chgo., 1962-69; asso. prof. library sci. U. Ill., 1970-71, prof. library sci. and music, 1971—, assoc. Center Advanced Study, 1974; univ. scholar, 1991; Centennial scholar, 1994. Middle mgmt. intern U.S. Civil Svc., 1960; scholar in residence Aspen Inst., 1969; mem. faculty Rare Book Sch. Columbia U., 1990-91, U. Va., 1993—; archival cons. Kneisel Hall, 1990-94. Author: Bibliotheca Bolduaniana, 1972, Guide for Dating Early Published Music, 1974, English Music Printing, 1553-1700, 1975, Bibliographical Inventory to the Early Music in the Newberry Library, 1977, Organizing the Library's Support, 1980, Resources of American Music History, 1981, Bibliographies, Their Aims and Methods, 1984, Bibliographical Handbook of American Music, 1987, The Memory of Sound, 1988, Grove-Norton Handbook of Music Printing and Publishing, 1990, The Literature of Music Bibliography, 1993, Fiat Lux, Fiat Latebra, 1999; contbr. numerous articles and revs. to profl. jours. Recipient awards Huntington Libr., 1965, Am. Coun. Learned Socs., 1966-77, Am. Philos. Soc., 1969, Coun. Libr. Resources, 1967; Newberry libr. travelling fellow, 1969-70; Univ. Coll. (London) hon. rsch. fellow, 1974-75; Guggenheim fellow, 1976-77. Mem. ALA (G.K. Hall award 1987, Beta Phi Mu award 1999), Music Libr. Assn. (pres. 1981-83, spl. citation award), Bibliog. Soc. (London), Bibliog. Soc. Am., Sonneck Soc. (Lowens award 1989), Am. Antiquarian Soc., Am. Printing Hist. Assn. (laureate 2004), Caxton Club (Chgo.), Grolier Club. Home: 702 W Delaware Ave Urbana IL 61801-4807 Office: U Ill 501 E Daniel St Champaign IL 61820-6211 Home Phone: 217-344-6311; Office Phone: 217-344-6311. E-mail: donkay@uiuc.edu.

KRUPINSKI, JERRY W., state legislator; b. Feb. 27, 1941; m. Eileen Krupinski; children: Scott, Erin, Todd. Commr. Jefferson County, Ohio, 1981-86; state rep. Dist. 98 Ohio State Congress, 1987—. Recipient Caritas medal Diocese of Steubenville, Excellence in Govt. award Steubenville C. of C., Consumer of Yr. award Ohio Consumer Coun., 1991. Mem. Polish Nat. Alliance, Gen. George Custer Com., Farm Bur., Indian Club, KC, Moose.

KRUPNICK, ELIZABETH RACHEL, human resources consulting firm and former insurance company executive; b. NYC, Oct. 21, 1949; d. Julius Michael and Doris (White) K.; children: Tobias Perse, Jacob. BA in Art History, Colby Coll., 1973; MA, U. Mo., 1976. Instr. journalism Emerson Coll., Boston, 1976-78; asst. prof. journalism U. Maine, Orono, 1978-79, Portland Oreg. State U., 1979-83; asst. v.p. Aetna Life & Casualty, Hartford, Conn., 1985-89, v.p. corp. affairs, 1989—92, sr. v.p. corp. affairs; sr. v.p. corp. comm. NY Life; pres. Dewe Rogerson, 1997—98; sr. v.p., US corp. practice dir. Manning, Selvage & Lee, 2000—01; exec. v.p. global corp. comm. Bcom3, 2001—03; sr. v.p. global comm. Mastercard Internat., Purchase, NY, 2003—04; founder TKO Comm. Cons., 2004—07; sr. v.p., chief mktg. officer Heidrick & Struggles Internat., Inc., Chgo., 2007—. Co-author: From Despair to Decision, 1982. Mem. Women in Communications, Ins. Info. Inst. communications com., 1987, pub. relations com., 1986. Office: Heidrick & Struggles Internat Inc 233 S Wacker Dr Sears Tower Ste 4200 Chicago IL 60606

KRUSE, DENNIS K., state legislator; b. Auburn, Ind., Oct. 7, 1946; s. Russell Wayne and Luella Marie (Boger) K.; m. Kay Adele Yerden, 1968; children: Dennis K. II, John Mark, Timothy James, Daniel Webster. Student, Anderson U., 1967—68; BS, Ind. U., 1970; postgrad., Purdue U. Auctioneer Kruse Auctioneers, 1964—; realtor Kruse Realtors, 1968—; asst. to corp. officer Ambassador Steel Corp., 1981—95; rep. Dist. 51 Ind. Ho. of Reps., 1990—, ranking mem. county and twp. com., interstate coop. and pub. safety com., mem. ways and means com. Precinct committeeman Jackson Twp. S. DeKalb County, 1968—72; mem. U.S. Electoral Com., Ind., 1972—; trustee Jackson Twp., 1983—89; del. Ind. Rep. State Conv., 1990—; chmn. Ind. Conservative Assembly, Legis. Coalition to Reduce Underage Drinking; parade marshall Gradili County Fair, Ind., 1990—; mem. DeKalb County Right to Life; adv. bd. DeKalb County Am. Family Assn., 1988—; mem. Child Evangelism Fellowship N.E. Ind., DeKalb Coun. Pregnancy, Right-to-Life, Ind. Family Inst.; bd. dirs. Northeastern Ind. Child Evangelism, 1986—96.

KRUSE, JOHN ALPHONSE, lawyer; b. Detroit, Sept. 11, 1926; s. Frank R. and Ann (Nestor) K.; m. Mary Louise Dalton, July 14, 1951 (dec. Apr. 2006); children: Gerard, Mary Louise, Terence, Kathleen, Joanne, Francis, John, Patrick. BS, U. Detroit, 1950, JD cum laude, 1952. Bar: Mich. bar 1952. Ptnr. Alexander, Buchanan & Conklin, Detroit, 1952-69, Harvey, Kruse, PC, Detroit, 1969—. Guest lectr. U. Mich., U. Detroit, Inst. Continuing Legal Edn.; city atty. Allen Park, Mich., 1954-59; twp. atty., Van Buren Twp., Mich., 1959-61. Co-founder Detroit and Mich. Cath. Radio. Past pres. Palmer Woods Assn.; mem. pres.'s cabinet U. Detroit; bd. dirs. Providence Hosp. Found. Named one of 5 Outstanding Young Men in Mich., 1959, Outstanding Alumnus, U. Detroit Sch. Law, 1989; recipient Humanitarian award Neuromuscular Inst. 1988, Voice of Life award Mich. Right to Life, 2006. Mem. Detroit Bar Assn., State Bar Mich. (past chmn. negligence sect.), Assn. Def. Trial Counsel (bd. dirs. 1966-67), Am. Judicature Soc., Internat. Assn. Def. Counsel, Equestrian Order of the Holy Sepulchre. Clubs: Detroit Golf (past pres.). Roman Catholic. Home: 5569 Hunters Gate Dr Troy MI 48098-2342 Office: 1050 Wilshire Dr Ste 320 Troy MI 48084-1526 Home Phone: 248-641-7681; Office Phone: 248-649-7800. Business E-Mail: jkruse@harveykruse.com. E-mail: johnakruse@yahoo.com.

KRUSE, LOWEN V., state legislator; b. Boelus, Nebr., 1929; BA, Wesleyan U., 1951; M, Northwestern U., 1955. Pastor Buffalo, Custer and Douglas Counties, Nebr.; supt. chs. N.E. Nebr., 1972; dir. ministries Nebr. Meth. Chs., 1974; exec. min. Omaha 1st United Meth. Ch., 1979; supt. Omaha dist. United Meth. Ch., 1988; mem. Nebr. Legislature from 13th dist., Lincoln, 2001—. Author: 3 Nebr. history books. Mem. Kiwanis, Lions, North Omaha Comml. Club. Office: Rm 1117 State Capitol Lincoln NE 68509

KRUSE, RONIA, information technology executive; b. 1970; MS in Taxation, Wayne State U., 1994. Lectr. Wayne State U.; sr. tax cons. Deloitte & Touche L.L.P., 1995—99; pres., CEO OpTech L.L.C., Detroit, 1999—. Named one of 40 Under 40, Crain's Detroit Bus., 2006. Office: OpTech LLC Guardian Bldg 500 Griswold Ste 1690 Detroit MI 48226 Office Phone: 313-962-9000. Office Fax: 313-962-9001. Business E-Mail: rkruse@optechus.com.

KRUSICK, MARGARET ANN, state legislator; b. Milw., Oct. 26, 1956; d. Ronald J. and Maxine C. K. BA, U. Wis., 1978; postgrad., U. Wis., Madison, 1979-82. Legal asst. Milw. Law Office, 1973-78; teaching asst. U. Wis., Milw., 1978-79; staff mem. Govs. Ombudsman Program for the Aging & Disabled, Madison, Wis., 1980; administrv. asst. Wis. Higher Edn. Aids Bd., Madison, 1981; legis. aide Wis. Assembly, Madison, 1982-83, state rep., 1983—. Author: Wisconsin Youth Suicide Prevention Act, 1985, Wisconsin Nursing Home Reform Act, 1987, Wisconsin Truancy Reform Act, 1988, Elder Abuse Fund, 1989, Stolen Goods Recovery Act, 1990, Fair Prescription Drug Pricing Act, 1994, Anti-Graffiti Act, 1996, Caregiver Criminal Background Checks and Abuse Prevention Act, 1997, Child Abuse Prosecution Act, 1998, Nursing Home Resident Protection Act, 1998, Seniorcare Prescription Drug Program, 2002, Criminal Background Checks for School Van and Bus Drivers, 2003, Child Protection and Clergy Abuse Reporting Act, 2004, Child Support Collection Act, 2004. Mem. St. Gregory Great Cath. Ch., Milw., 1960—, Dem. Party, Milw., 1980—; bd. dirs. Alzheimer's Assn., 1986-88. Named Legislator of Yr. award Wis. Sch. Counselors, Madison, 1986, Wis. County Constnl. Officers Legislator of Yr., 1999; recipient Sr. Citizen Appreciation Allied Coun. for Sr. Milw., 1987, Crime Prevention award Milw. Police Dept., Milw., 1988, Cert. Appreciation, Milw. Pub. Sch., 1989, Friends of Homecare award, 1989, Environ. Decades' Clean 16 award, 1986-90, 95-96, Badger State Sheriff's Law and Order award, 1993, Appreciation award Coalition of Wis. Aging Groups, 1998, 2001. Mem. Jackson Park Neighborhood Assn.(Wis. Coun. Sr. Citizens award, 2003), U. Milw. Alumni Assn. (trustee 1986-90). Achievements include development of Alliance for attendance truancy abatement task force, which led to the Govenores state call to action to end child abuse and neglect. Office: Wis Assembly State Capitol Madison WI 53702-0001 Home: 128 State Capital PO Box 8952 Madison WI 53708 Business E-Mail: rep.kusick@legis.state.wi.us.

KRUTSCH, PHYLLIS, academic administrator; MS, U. Wis. Regent U. Wis., 1990—97, 2000—, chmn. edn. com., 1994—97, chmn. com. bd. effectiveness. Grantee, Bradley Found. Mailing: 727 Superior Ave Washburn WI 54891

KRUTTER, FORREST NATHAN, lawyer; b. Boston, Dec. 17, 1954; s. Irving and Shirley Krutter. BS in Econs., MS in Civil Engring., MIT, 1976; JD cum laude, Harvard U., 1978. Bar: Nebr. 1978, U.S. Supreme Ct. 1986, NY 1991. Antitrust counsel Union Pacific R.R., Omaha, 1978-86; sr. v.p. law, sec. Berkshire Hathaway Group, Omaha, 1986—; pres. Republic Ins., Dallas, 2000—. Co-author: Impact of Railroad Abandonments, 1976, Railroad Development in the Third World, 1978; author: Judicial Enforcement of Competition in Regulated Industries, 1979; contbr. articles Creighton Law Rev. Mem. ABA, Phi Beta Kappa, Sigma Xi. Office: Berkshire Hathaway Group 100 First Stamford Pl Stamford CT 06902 Office Phone: 402-536-3214. Business E-Mail: fkrutter@berkre.com.

KRUZAN, MARK R., state legislator; b. Hammond, Ind., Apr. 11, 1960; BA, Ind. U., 1982, JD, 1985. Pvt. practice law; state rep. Dist. 61 Ind. Ho. of Reps., 1986—, mem. pub. policy, ethics, vet. affairs and judiciary coms., vice chmn. environ. affairs com., ranking minority mem., mem. ways and means and caucus campaign com., legis coun., chmn. environ. policy com. Adj. prof. Ind. U. Mem. Cmty. Svc. Coun. Mem. Ind. U. Alumni Assn. (life), Ind. State Bar Assn., Greater Bloomington C. of C., Bloomington Press Club, Sigma Delta Chi. Home: 2976 N Lakewood Ct Bloomington IN 47408-1081

KRYGIER, ROMAN J., automotive executive; b. 1944; BME, Purdue Univ., 1964; MIT, 1974. Joined and held a variety of positions at the Chgo. Stamping Plant Ford Motor Co., 1964, named asst. plant ops. mgr. at the metal stamping division's gen. office, 1974, apptd. plant mgr. of the Buffalo stamping plant, 1977, held several mgmt. positions within the body and assembly ops., 1983—94; named exec. dir. of the advanced mfg. engring. and process leadership, Ford Automotive Ops., 1994; v.p. advanced mfg. engring. and process leadership Ford Motor Co., 1997—98; v.p. power train ops., Ford Automotive Ops., 1999—2001; group v.p. Mfg. and Quality Ford Motor Co., Dearborn, Mich., 2001—.

KRYSTKOWIAK, LARRY BRETT, former professional basketball coach; b. Missoula, Mont., Sept. 23, 1964; m. Jan Krystkowiak; children: Cameron, Luc, Ben. Student, U. Mont., 1982—86, BA in Bus. Adminstrn., 1996. Profl. basketball player San Antonio Spurs, 1986—87, Milw. Bucks, 1987—92, Utah Jazz, 1992—93, Orlando Magic, 1993—94, Chgo. Bulls, 1994—95, Levallois Basketball Club, Paris, 1996, LA Lakers, 1996—97, Continental Basketball Assn. Idaho Stampede, 1997—98; asst. coach U. Mont., 1998—2000, Old Dominion U., 2001—02, Norfolk Collegiate HS, Va., 2002—03; head coach Continental Basketball Assn. Idaho Stampede, 2003—04, U. Mont., 2004—06; asst. coach Milw. Bucks, 2006—07, head coach, 2007—08.*

KSIENSKI, AHARON ARTHUR, retired electrical engineer; b. Warsaw, June 23, 1924; came to U.S., 1951, naturalized, 1959; s. Isreal and Rebecca K.; married; children: David, Ruth. B.E. in Mech. Engring, Inst. Mech. Engring., London, 1947; M.Sc. in Elec. Engring, U. So. Calif., 1952, PhD, 1958. Sr. staff engr., head antenna dept. research staff Hughes Aircraft Co., Culver City, Calif., 1958-67; prof. elec. engring., tech. dir. communication systems electrosci. lab. Ohio State U., 1967-76, prof. elec. engring., chmn. communication and propagation com. electrosci. lab., 1976-87, prof. emeritus, 1987—; ret., 1987. Bd. dirs. Ohio State U. Research Found., 1975-79; cons. in field. Editor trans., revs. in field. Recipient Brabazon award Inst. Electronic and Radio Engrs., London, 1967, 76 Fellow IEEE; mem. Internat. Union Radio Sci. (chmn. commns. B and C 1972-75) Home: 665 Trafalgar Dr Hagerstown MD 21742 Personal E-mail: aharon@myactv.net.

KUBALE, BERNARD STEPHEN, lawyer; b. Reedsville, Wis., Sept. 5, 1928; s. Joseph and Josephine (Novak) Kubale; m. Mary Thomas, Apr. 21, 1956 (dec. Jan. 13, 2001); children: Caroline, Catherine, Anne stepchildren: Lauren Ziedonis, Nicholas Ziedonis; m. Karen Robinson, Jan. 23, 2004. BBA, U. Wis., 1950, LLB, 1955; LLD (hon.), St. Norbert Coll., 1985. CPA Wis.; bar: Wis. 1955. Acct. John D. Morrison and Co., Marquette, Mich., 1950-51; atty., ptnr. Foley and Lardner, Milw., 1955—, chmn. mgmt. com., 1985-94. Bd. dirs. Green Bay Packers, E. R. Wagner Mfg. Co., Wausau Homes. Chmn. bd. dirs. St. Norbert Coll., DePere, Wis., 1980—84, Children's Hosp. Wis., Milw., 1982—91. 1st lt. USAF, 1951—53. Mem.: ABA, Milw. Bar Assn., Wis. Bar Assn., Wis. Inst. CPAs, Milw. Club, Chenequa Country Club. Republican. Roman Catholic. Avocations: fishing, skiing. Office: Foley & Lardner 1st Wisconsin Ctr 777 E Wisconsin Ave Ste 3800 Milwaukee WI 53202-5367 Home: PO Box 544 Merton WI 53056 Personal E-mail: bskubale@aol.com.

KUBIDA, JUDITH ANN, museum administrator; b. Chgo., Aug. 29, 1948; d. William and Julia Ann (Kun) K.; m. Benjamin Kocolowski, Nov. 22, 1980. Attended, Southeast Coll. Adminstrn. asst. in vis. svcs. and sci. and edn. depts. Mus. Sci. and Industry, Chgo. Columnist monthly community newspaper Pullman Flyer. Vice-pres. pub. rels. Hist. Pullman Found., Hist. Pullman Dist., Chgo., editor quarterly newsletter Update, create publicity brochures, liaison with Ill., Chgo. Film Offices, publ. chmn., mem. annual house tour com., prodr. commemorative plate. Democrat. Home: 11334 S Langley Ave Chicago IL 60628-5126 Office: Hist Pullman Found Hotel Florence 11111 S Forrestville Ave Chicago IL 60628-4649

KUCERA, DANIEL WILLIAM, archbishop emeritus; b. Chgo., May 7, 1923; s. Joseph F. and Lillian C. (Petrzelka) K. BA, St. Procopius Coll., 1945; MA, Catholic U. Am., 1950, PhD, 1954. Professed Order of St. Benedict, 1944, ordained priest, 1949; registrar St. Procopius Coll. and Acad., Lisle, Ill., 1945—49, St. Procopius Coll., Lisle, Ill., 1954—56, acad. dean, head dept. edn., 1956—59, pres., 1959—65; abbot St. Procopius Abbey, Lisle, 1964—71; pres. Ill. Benedictine Coll. (formerly St. Procopius Coll.), Lisle, 1971—76, chmn. bd. trustees, 1976—78; ordained bishop, 1977; aux. bishop Diocese of Joliet, Ill., 1977—80; bishop Diocese of Salina, Kans., 1980—83; archbishop Archdiocese of Dubuque, Iowa, 1983—95. Mem.: KC (4 degree). Roman Catholic. Personal E-mail: dwkucera@aol.com.

KUCINICH, DENNIS JOHN, congressman; b. Cleve., Oct. 8, 1946; s. Frank and Virginia Kucinich; m. Elizabeth Harper, Aug. 21, 2005; 1 child. Student, Cleve. State U.; BA in Speech and Comm., Case Western Res. U., 1973, MA in Speech and Comm. V.p. sales & mktg. Town and Country Printing, Cleve.; mem. city coun. City of Cleve., 1970—75, Ohio, 1981—82, mayor, 1977-79; clk. of cts. Mcpl. Ct., Cleve., 1976—77; pres. K Comm., Cleve., 1985—95; mem. Ohio State Senate, 1994—96, US Congress from 10th Ohio dist., 1997—, mem. edn. and labor com., mem. oversight and govt. reform com., chmn. domestic policy subcommittee. US del. UN Conv. Climate Change, 1998, 2004. Author: A Prayer for America, 2003. Recipient Outstanding Senator of Yr. award NASW, 1996, Green Thumb award, League of Conservation Voters, 1997, Charles Van Riper award, Nat. Coun. Communicative Disorders, 1998, Oak Tree award Ohio PTA, 1999, Congl. Appreciation award, Operation Lifesaver, 2000, Champion for Peace award, Military Families Speak Out, 2007; named Outstanding Pub. Official, Internat. Eagles. Mem.: Internat. Alliance of Theatrical Stage Employees, Moving Picture Technicians, Artists and Allied Crafts of the US. Democrat. Roman Catholic. Office: 14400 Detroit Ave Lakewood OH 44107 Office Phone: 202-225-5871, 216-228-8850. Office Fax: 216-228-6465.

KUDISH, DAVID J., financial executive; b. NYC, Aug. 10, 1943; s. L. Ben and Nellie D. (Kaufman) K.; m. Sheri K. Ross-Kudish; children: Lisa, Seth, Debra, Stephanie, Samantha. BS, U. Rochester, 1965; MS, U. Minn., 1967; postgrad., Harvard. U., 1996. With Dean Witter & Co., Inc., NYC, 1968-73; with Oppenheimer & Co., NYC, 1973-74; ptnr., dir. investment cons. Hewitt Assocs., Lincolnshire, Ill., 1974-82; pres., mng. dir. Stratford Advisory Group, Inc., Chgo., 1982—2001; pres. Stratford Investment Group, Inc., 1983-2000, Advocate Investment Advisors, LLC (now called Advocate Asset Mgmt., LLC), Chgo., 2001—. Asset mgr. pension, endowment and charitable funds. Editor Benefits Quar. Mem. Mayor's Energy Task Force, City of Chgo.; gov. mem. Sustaining Fellows, Art Inst. Chgo., Contemporary Art Cir. of Mus. Contemporary Art; benefactor Lyric Opera of Chgo.; mem. gala com. Chgo. Abused Women's Coalition; bd. dirs. Com. for Accuracy in Mid. East Reporting in Am., Aspen Cmty. Campaign; mem. Jewish Cmty. Rels. Coun., Jewish Fedn. Met. Chgo.; mem. exec. bd. Chgo. chpt. Am. Jewish Com.; bd. govs. The Investigative Projecton Terrorism; mem. adv. bd. Middle East Forum; regent Ctr. Security Policy; lectr (Aspen, Chgo., Cleve.) Terrorism and the Media. With USAF, 1968, Air NG, 1968-73. Minn. Mining and Mgr. fellow U. Minn., 1967; NSF grantee, 1967 Mem. Tau Beta Pi, Sigma Alpha Mu. Clubs: Standard. Republican. Jewish. Office: Advocate Asset Mgmt LLC Ste 1510 10 S Riverside Plz Chicago IL 60606 Office Phone: 312-756-0074. Office Fax: 312-756-0084.

KUDO, IRMA SETSUKO, not-for-profit executive director; b. Ica, Peru, Feb. 25, 1939; arrived in U.S., 1944; d. Seiichi and Angelica (Yoshinaga) Higashide. Asst. dir. coun. annual session ADA, Chgo., 1971-80; exec. dir. Am. Assn. of Endodontists, Chgo., 1980—. Recipient Warren Wakai medal Japan Endodontic Assn., 1992. Mem. ADA Alumni Assn. Student Clinicians (hon.), Am. Assn. Endodontists (hon.), Am. Soc. of Assn. Execs., Profl. Conv. Mgmt. Assn., Assn. Forum Chicagoland. Office: Am Assn of Endodontists 211 E Chicago Ave Ste 1100 Chicago IL 60611-2687 E-mail: ikudo@aae.org.

KUDRLE, ROBERT THOMAS, economist, educator; b. Sioux City, Iowa, Aug. 23, 1942; s. Chester John and Helen Marguerite Kudrle; m. Venetia Hilary Mary Thomas, July 20, 1970; children: Paul John Reginald, Thomas David Chester. AB, Harvard U., 1964, AM, 1969, PhD, 1974; MPhil., U. Oxford, Eng., 1967. Grad. rsch. assoc. Ctr. Internat. Affairs Harvard U., Cambridge, Mass., 1969-71; instr. Tex. A & M Univ., College Station, 1971-72; asst., assoc. prof. Humphrey Inst. U. Minn., Mpls., 1972-83, asst., assoc. dir. Ctr. Internat. Studies, 1972-82, prof. Humphrey Inst., 1983—, dir. MA program pub. affairs, 1984-86, dir. Freeman Ctr. Internat. Econ. Policy, 1990-97, assoc. dean rsch. Humphrey Inst., 1992-96, Freeman prof. internat. trade and investment policy, 2006—. Cons. U.S. Dept. Justice, U.S. AID, Urban Inst., UN Ctr. Transnat. Corps., Consumer and Corp. Affairs Can., WHO, others. Author: Agricultural Tractors: A World Industry Study, 1975; co-author State Evaluation of Foreign Sales Efforts, 1988; co-editor Reducing the Cost of Dental Care, 1983, The Industrial Future of the Pacific Basin, 1984, Jour. Internat. Studies Quarterly, 1980-84, 85; mem. editorial bd. Internat. Political Economy Yearbook, 1983—, Jour. Health Politics, Policy & Law, 1981-92; contbr. articles to profl. jours., chpts. to texts. 1st v.p. UN Assn. Minn., Mpls., 1976—78, mem. adv. coun., 1978—88. Graduate prize fellow Harvard U., 1967-69, Pew Faculty fellow in Internat. Affairs Harvard U., 1990-91; Nuffield Coll. studentship, Oxford, Eng., 1966-67; Rhodes scholar, Oxford, Eng., 1964-67. Mem. Assn. Pub. Policy Analysis and Mgmt. (instl. rep. 1988-97), Internat. Studies Assn. (v.p. 1998-99), Am. Econ. Assn., Harvard Club Minn. Avocations: running, gardening. Home: 4650 Fremont Ave S Minneapolis MN 55419-2263 Office: Humphrey Inst Pub Affairs 301 19th Ave S Ste 300 Minneapolis MN 55455-0429 Business E-Mail: bkudrle@hhh.umn.edu.

KUEHN, GEORGE E., lawyer; b. NYC, June 19, 1946; m. Mary Kuehn; children: Kristin, Rob, Geoff. BBA, U. Mich., 1968, JD, 1973. Bar: Mich. 1974. Assoc. Hill, Lewis et al, Detroit, 1974-78; ptnr. Butzel, Long et al, Detroit, 1978-81; exec. v.p., gen. counsel, sec. The Stroh Brewery Co., Detroit, 1981-99—; shareholder Butzel Long, Detroit, 2000—. With U.S. Army, 1969-71. Office: Butzel Long 350 S Main St Ste 200 Ann Arbor MI 48104 Office Phone: 734-213-3257. Business E-Mail: Kuehn@butzel.com.

KUEHNE, CARL W., food products executive; CEO, pres. Am. Foods Group, Dakota Pork Industries. Office: Am Foods Group PO Box 8547 544 Acme St Green Bay WI 54308-8547

KUENNEN, THOMAS GERARD, journalist; b. St. Louis, June 30, 1953; s. George Glennon and Earline (Doherty) K.; m. Anne L. Gillette, Sept. 10, 1988; 1 child, Madeline Livingston. BJ, U. Mo., 1975. Copy editor Macon (Ga.) Telegraph & News, 1976-77; news editor Mascoutah (Ill.) Herald, and related newspapers, 1977-79; pub. rels. assoc. Booker Assocs., Inc., St. Louis, 1979-80, Fru Con Corp., St. Louis, 1980-81; assoc. editor Rock Products Mag., Chgo., 1981-84; editor Roads & Bridges Mag., Des Plaines, Ill., 1984-95; prin., editor Expresswaysonline.com, Buffalo Grove, Ill., 1995—. Mem. editl. com. Am. Bus. Press, .Y.C., 1984-85. Contbg. editor: Concrete Products, Better Roads. Recipient Jesse H. Neal award Am. Bus. Press, 1983, Svc. award La. Associated Gen. Contractors, 1990, Editl. Excellence award Am. Soc. Bus. Press Editors, 1998, finalist Jesse H. Neal award, 2005. Mem. Constrn. Writers Assn. (bd. dirs. 1985-86, 95-99, Robert F. Boger award 1985, 93, 95, 98, Hon. Mention 2003), The Rd. Info. Program (bd. dirs. 1999—), Road Gang, Nat. Asphalt Pavement Assn. (Hot Mix Hall of Fame), Women in Comm. (treas. 1983-84, Cub's Cup 1985). Roman Catholic. Office: Expresswaysonline.com 251 N Milwaukee Ave Ste 224B Buffalo Grove IL 60089

KUENSTER, JOHN JOSEPH, editor; b. Chgo., June 18, 1924; s. Roy Jacob and Katheryn (Holechek) Kuenster; m. Mary Virginia Maher, Feb. 15, 1947 (dec. Feb. 1983); m. Suely Brazâo, July 1, 1995. Editor The Columbian, Chgo., 1948-57; staff writer Chgo. Daily News, Chgo., 1957-65; dir. devel. and pub. rels. Mercy Hosp., Chgo., 1965-66; sr. writer The Claretians, Chgo., 1966—2007; editor Baseball Digest, Evanston, Ill., 1969—; exec. editor Century Pub. Co., Evanston. Author: Cobb to Catfish, 1975; co-author: To Sleep with the Angels, 1996; author: Heartbreakers, 2001, At Home and Away, 2003, How St. Jude Came to Chicago, 2004, The Best of Baseball Digest, 2006, (booklets) The Police, Money, Mission in Guatemala, Honesty, Is it the Best Policy?. Mem.: Baseball Writers' Assn. Am. Roman Catholic. Office: Baseball Digest Lakeside Publishing Co 990 Grove St Evanston IL 60201-6510 Office Phone: 847-491-6440. Business E-Mail: jkuenster@centurysports.net.

KUESTER, DENNIS J., diversified financial services company and bank executive; b. Milw., Mar. 7, 1942; m. Sandy Kuester. BBA in Acctg. & Fin., U. Wis.-Milw., 1966, DCS (hon.), 1996. Various sales and sales mgmt. positions IBM Corp., Milw., Mpls., Chgo., 1966—75; v.p. M & I Data Services, Inc. (now Metavante Corp.), Milw., 1976—85, pres, 1985—93, chmn., CEO, 1993—98; chmn. Metavante Corp., 1998—; pres. Marshall & Ilsley Corp., Milw., 1987—2005, CEO, 2002—07, chmn., 2005—; pres. M&I Marshall & Ilsley Bank, 1989—2001, CEO, 2001—07, chmn., 2001—. Mem. adv. coun. FRS, 2004—; bd. dirs. Modine Mfg. Co., Krueger Internat., Super Steel Products Corp., Wausau Paper Corp. Bd. dirs. Froedtert Meml. Lutheran Hosp., Lynde and Harry Bradley Found.; chmn. Christian Stewardship Found.; mem. U. Wis.-Milw., 1994—, pres., 1990—92. Recipient Disting. Alumnus award, U. Wis.-Milw. Alumni Assn., 1988. Office: Marshall & Ilsley Corporation 770 N Water St Milwaukee WI 53202-3509

KUFFEL, EDMUND, electrical engineering educator; b. Poland, Oct. 28, 1924; s. Franciszek and Marta (Glodowska) K.; m. Alicja, Oct. 4, 1952; children: Anna, John, Richard, Peter. BSc, U. Coll., Dublin, 1953, MSc, 1954, PhD, 1959; DSc, U. Manchester, 1967. Rsch. engr. Met. Vickers Electric Co., Manchester, England, 1954-60; mem. faculty elec. engring. U. Manchester Inst. Sci. and Tech., 1960-68; head of elect. engring. U. Windsor, Ont., Canada, 1970-78; prof.

elec. engring. U. Man., Winnipeg, Canada, 1968-70, head of elec. engring., 1978-79, dean of engring., 1979-89, prof. elec. engring., dean emeritus, 1989—. Cons. various mfrs. high voltage cables; bd. dirs. Man. Hydro Elec. Bd., 1978-96; cons. prof. Xi'an Jiaotong U., People's Rep. China, 1986—. Author or co-author 4 textbooks and more than 200 pub. tech. papers on high voltage engring. Fellow IEEE, Can. Acad. Engring. Home: 2661 Knowles Ave Winnipeg MB Canada R2G 2K7 Office: U Manitoba Fac Engring Winnipeg MB Canada R3T 2N2 E-mail: ekuffel@shaw.ca.

KUFFNER, GEORGE HENRY, dermatologist, educator; b. S.I., NY, Aug. 22, 1949; s. George Henry and Wilmouth Anne (Clendenin) K.; m. Lynne Diane Blakeslee, May 17, 1975; children: Kevin, Todd A. BA, Johns Hopkins U., 1971, MD, 1975. Intern U. Hosps. Cleve., 1975-78, resident, 1978-81; staff dermatologist Cleve. Clinic Wooster, Ohio, 1981—. Asst. clin. prof. dermatology U. Hosps. Cleve., 1981—. Contbr. articles to profl. jours. Fellow Am. Acad. Dermatology; mem. Ohio State Med. Assn., Ohio Dermatological Assn., Akron Dermatology Staff, Am. Med. Assn., Cleve. Dermatology Soc. Methodist. Avocations: swimming, piano, reading, travel. Office: Cleveland Clinic Wooster 1740 Cleveland Rd Wooster OH 44691-2204

KUHI, LEONARD VELLO, astronomer, academic administrator; b. Hamilton, Ont., Can., Oct. 22, 1936; came to U.S., 1958; s. John and Sinaida (Rose) K.; m. Patricia Suzanne Brown, Sept. 3, 1960 (div.); children: Alison Diane, Christopher Paul; m. Mary Ellen Murphy, July 15, 1989. BS, U. Toronto, 1958; PhD, U. Calif., Berkeley, 1964. Carnegie postdoctoral fellow Hale Obs., Pasadena, Calif., 1963-65; asst. prof. U. Calif., Berkeley, 1965-69, assoc. prof., 1969-74, prof., 1974-89, chmn. dept. astronomy, 1975-76, dean phys. scis. Coll. Letters and Sci., 1976-81, provost, 1983-89; sr. v.p. for acad. affairs, provost U. Minn., Mpls., 1989-91, prof. astronomy, 1989—, chmn. dept. astronomy, 1997—. Vis. prof. U. Colo., 1969, Coll. de France, Paris, 1972-73, U. Heidelberg, 1978, 80-81; bd. dirs. Am. Inst. Physics. Contbr. articles to profl. jours. Recipient Alexander von Humboldt Sr. Scientist award, 1980-81; NSF research grantee, 1966—. Fellow AAAS; mem. Am. Astron. Soc. (treas. 1987, 96—), Astron. Soc. Pacific (pres. 1978-80), Internat. Astron. Union, Assn. Univ. for Rsch. Astronomy (chair bd. dirs. 1998-2001). Office: U Minn Dept Astronomy 116 Church St SE Minneapolis MN 55455-0149 Home Phone: 952-470-0856; Office Phone: 612-624-7053. Business E-Mail: kuhi@astro.umn.edu.

KUHL, DAVID EDMUND, nuclear medicine physician, educator; b. St. Louis, Oct. 27, 1929; s. Robert Joseph and Caroline Bertha (Waldermeyer) Kuhl; m. Eleanor Dell Kasales, Aug. 7, 1954; 1 child, David Stephen. AB, Temple U., Phila., 1951; MD, U. Pa., 1955; LHD (hon.), Loyola U. Chgo., 1992. Diplomate Am. Bd. Radiology, Am. Bd. Nuc. Medicine (a founder; life trustee 1977-). Intern, then resident in radiology Sch. Medicine and Hosp. U. Pa., 1955—56, 1958—63, mem. faculty, 1963—76, chief div. nuc. medicine, 1963—76, prof. radiology, 1970—76, vice chmn. dept., 1975—76; prof. bioengring. Moore Sch. Electrical Engring. U. Pa., 1974—76; prof. radiol. scis. UCLA Sch. Medicine and Hosp., 1976—86, chief div. nuc. medicine, 1976—84, vice-chmn. dept., 1977—86; prof. internal medicine and radiology U. Mich. Sch. Medicine, Ann Arbor, 1986—2000, chief divsn. nuc. medicine, dir. PET Ctr., 1986—2002, prof. radiology, 2000—. Disting. faculty lectr. in biomed. rsch. U. Mich. Med. Sch., 1992, Henry Russel lectr., 98; mem. adv. com. Dept. Energy, NIH, Internat. Commn. on Radiation Units and Measures, Max Planck Soc. Mem. editl. bd.: various jours.; contbr. articles to med. jours. Served as officer M.C. USNR, 1956—58. Recipient Rsch. Career Devel. award, USPHS, 1961—71, Ernst Jung prize for medicine, Jung Found., Hamburg, 1981, Emil H. Grubbe gold medal, Chgo. Med. Soc., 1983, Berman Found. award peaceful uses atomic energy, 1985, Steven C. Beering award for advancement med. sci., Ind. U., 1987, Disting. Grad. award, U. Pa. Sch. Medicine, 1988, William C. Menninger Meml. award, ACP, 1989, Javits Neurosci. Investigator award, NIH, 1989, Charles F. Kettering prize, GM Cancer Rsch. Found., 2001, Hon. Lifetime Mem. award, Einstein Soc., Nat. Atomic Mus. Found., 2001. Fellow: Am. Inst. for Med. and Biol. Engring., Am. Coll. Nuc. Physicians, Am. Coll. Radiology; mem.: Inst. Medicine Nat. Acad. Scis., Am. Neurol. Assn. (Foster Elting Bennett Meml. lectr. 1981), Soc. Nuc. Medicine (ann. lectr. 1991, Nuc. Pioneer citation 1976, Disting. Scientist award 1981, Herman L. Blumgart, M.D. Pioneer award 1979, George Charles de Hevesy Nuc. Medicine Pioneer award 1995, Benedict Cassen prize for rsch. 1996), Radiol. Soc. N.Am. (ann. orator 1982, Outstanding Rschr. award 1996), Assn. Univ. Radiologists, Assn. Am. Physicians, Alpha Omega Alpha. Office: U Mich Hosp Divsn Nuc Medicine 1500 E Medical Center Dr Ann Arbor MI 48109-0028 Business E-Mail: dkuhl@umich.edu.

KUHLER, DEBORAH GAIL, grief therapist, retired state legislator; d. Robert Edgar and Beverly Maxine Ecker; m. George Kuhler, Dec. 28, 1973; children: Karen, Ellen. BA, Dakota Wesleyan U., 1974; MA, U. N.D., 1977. Cert. profl. counselor, in thanatology. Outpatient therapist Ctr. for Human Devel., Grand Forks, ND, 1975-77; mental health counselor Community Counseling Services, Huron, SD, 1978-88, 91-93; owner, dir. bereavement svcs. Kuhler Funeral Home, Huron, 1978—; adj. prof. Huron U., 1979—83, 1990—2002; mem. from dist. 23 S.D. Ho. Reps., Pierre, 1987-90; mem. House Judiciary com., chair House Health and Welfare Com., Pierre, 1990. Active First United Meth. Ch. Named Young Alumnus of Yr., Dakota Wesleyan U., 1989, Woman of Yr. Bus. and Profl. Women, 1989. Mem. ACA, PEO, Am. Mental Health Counselors Assn., Assn. for Death Edn. and Counseling. Methodist. Avocations: reading, sewing, piano, quilting.

KUHLMAN, JAMES WELDON, retired county extension education director; b. Amarillo, Tex., Feb. 13, 1937; s. Herman and Alma Marie (Gerdsen) K.; m. Ann Bullock Davis, Dec. 23, 1967; children: Lisa Ann, Jennifer Shawn. BS, West Tex. State U., 1959; MS, U. Nebr., 1961. Tchr. West Tex. State U., Canyon, 1958—59; grad. asst. U. ebr., Lincoln, 1959—61; Buffalo County ext. agt., chair, 1967—72; Worth County ext. dir. Iowa State U., Northwood, 1972—81, Cerro Gordo County ext. edn. dir. Mason City, 1981—97; ret., 1997; farmer Randall County, Tex., 1955—, Buffalo County, Nebr., 1955—97. Spkr. various civic clubs, 1980—, flower garden Buchart Gardens in Victoria, Can., 1990-2001. Author: The History of the Nance Hereford Ranch, 1996, The Block Pasture, 1998, From Kirchhatten to Canyon, 2001, Reflections through a Milk Bottle--The Nebraska Years, 2004. Past pres., past treas. No. Iowa Figure Skating Club, Mason City, 1984-89; active Mason City Iowa Conv. and Visitors Bur., chair grants com., 1998-2000; treas. River City Trees, 1998-2004; bd. dirs. Ctrl. Gardens, Clear Lake, Iowa, treas., 2005—; with Congo agr. project North Ctrl. Office Presby, 2006—. With U.S. Army Res., 1961-67. Recipient Disting. Pres. award Sertoma Club Internat., Kearney, Nebr., 1966, Top award Lions Club Internat., Northwood, Iowa, 1979; named to Iowa's 4-H Hall of Fame, 2005. Mem. Nat. Assn. County Agrl. Agts. (nat. com., voting dir. 1984, 90, Disting. Svc. award 1984), Nat. Assn. Ret. Fed. Employees (pres. local chpt. 1998-1999, co-chair state conv. 2001), Iowa Fedn. of Nat. Assn. of Ret. Fed. Employees (chair nat. legislation com., chair Iowa PAC 2005—), Am. Hereford Assn., Iowa Hereford Assn. (dir. 1991-99), Iowa Hereford Breeders Assn. (dir.), Holstein Assn. Am., North Ctrl. Iowa Geneology Club (past vice chair, pres. 1999-2000), Rotary Club Mason City (com. chair 1988, 97—, bd. dirs. 2000-03), Mason City C. of C. (agr. com. 1981-2004, chmn. regional issues com. 1990-91), Iowa State U. Ext. Assn. (dir. 1980s), Iowa State U. Coun. Ex Profls. (chair retiree sect. 1999-2000), Epsilon Sigma Phi (dir.). Presbyterian. Avocations: cattle breeding and cattle history of Hereford breed, genealogy, writing, gardening, photography. Home: 722 N Hampshire Ave Mason City IA 50401-2440

KUHLMANN, FRED MARK, lawyer; b. St. Louis, Apr. 9, 1948; s. Frederick Louis and Mildred (Southworth) K.; m. Barbara Jane Nierman, Dec. 30, 1970; children: F. Matthew, Sarah Ann Morgan. AB summa cum laude, Washington U., St. Louis, 1970; JD cum laude, Harvard U., 1973. Bar: Mo. 1973. Assoc. atty. Stolar, Heitzmann & Eder, St. Louis, 1973-75; from tax counsel to staff v.p. McDonnell Douglas Corp., St. Louis, 1975—87, sr. v.p., gen. counsel, 1991—97; exec. v.p. McDonnell Douglas Health Systems Co., 1987—89; pres. McDonnell Douglas Systems Integration Co., 1989—91; of counsel Bryan Cave, St. Louis, 1997-98; pres. Sys. Svc. Enterprises, St. Louis, 1998—2004, co-CEO, 2004—. Bd. dirs. Republic Health Corp., Dallas, 1988-90, Grace Place Retreats, 2005—; mem. governing bd. Luth. Med. Ctr., 1989-95, chmn., 1990-92. Bd. dirs. Luth. Charities Assn., 1982-91, sec. 1984-86, chmn. 1986-89; elder Luth. Ch. of Resurrection, 1977-80; mem. Regents Coun. Concordia Sem., 1981-84; chmn. cub scout pack 459 Boy Scouts Am., 1984-86; bd. dirs. Luth. H.S. Assn., 1978-84, 91-97, pres. 1992-97, long range planning com. 1990-92, chmn. alumni assn., 1981; chmn. North Star dist. Boy Scouts Am., 1990-93; bd. dirs. Mcpl. Theatre Assn., St. Louis, 1991—; chmn. long range planning com. St. Paul's Luth. Ch., 1988-91, 98-2001, pres., 1996-97, 2002-03; bd. dirs., mem. exec. com. United Way of Greater St. Louis, 1994-97, chmn. Vanguard divsn., 1994-97; mem. amb. coun. Luth. Family and Children's Svcs. of St. Louis, 1998—; bd. dirs. Luth. Found. St. Louis, 1998—, chmn., 2004-06; mem. adv. bd. Webster U. Bus. and Tech. Sch., 1999-2001; mem. bd mgrs. worker benefit plans Luth. Ch.-Mo. Synod, 2001—, vice-chmn., 2006—; bd. dirs. KFUO Radio Arts Bd., 2005—, Thrivent Fin. for Luths., 2006—. Recipient Disting. Leadership award Luth. Assn. for Higher Edn., 1981. Mem. ABA, Mo. Bar Assn., Bar Assn. Met. St. Louis, Bellerive Country Club, Phi Beta Kappa, Omicron Delta Kappa. Republican. Avocations: tennis, golf, racquetball. Home: 1711 Stone Ridge Trails Dr Saint Louis MO 63122-3546 Office: Sys Svc Enterprises 77 Westport Plz Ste 500 Saint Louis MO 63146-3126 Home Phone: 314-821-4833; Office Phone: 314-439-4702. Business E-Mail: fmkuhlmann@sseinc.com.

KUHN, EDWIN P., travel company executive; BS in bus. adminstrn., Ohio State U.; grad. work, Wright State U., Dayton, Ohio. Named pres., CEO TravelCenters of Am., Inc., 1992—, now chmn. Mem. Nat. Assn. Truck Stop Operators (chmn. long-range planning com.). Office: TravelCenters of Am Inc 24601 Center Ridge Rd Ste 200 Westlake OH 44145 Office Phone: 440-808-9100.

KUHN, MARK A., state representative, farmer; b. Charles City, Iowa, Sept. 10, 1950; Student, Iowa State U. Farmer, Floyd County, Iowa, 1979—; mem. Floyd County Bd. Suprs., 1992—98; state rep. dist. 14 Iowa Ho. of Reps., 1999—; ranking mem. agr. com.; mem. local govt. com.; mem. transp., infrastructure, and capitals appropriations com.; mem. ways and means com. Confirmation mentor Trinity United Meth. Ch. Democrat. Office: State Capitol East 12th and Grand Des Moines IA 50319 Address: 2667 240th St Charles City IA 50616

KUHN, ROBERT MITCHELL, retired rubber company executive; b. NYC, May 9, 1942; s. Robert M. and Marie (Mildenberger) K.; m. Edda Clorinda Barsotti, Sept. 7, 1968; children— Marisa A., Michele T. BA in Psychology, Alfred U., 1964; MBA, NYU, 1970. Various fin. and operational positions Singer Co., Stamford, Conn., 1970-75, United Techs., Hartford, Conn., 1975-82; exec. v.p., dir. Armstrong Rubber Co., New Haven, 1982; pres. Dayco Products, Inc., Dayton, Ohio, 1986-98; ret., 1998. Bd. dirs. Copolymer Rubber & Chem. Corp., Baton Rouge. Served to capt. USMC, 1964-68, Vietnam Republican. Roman Catholic. Office: Goss Graphics Systems 700 Oakmont Ln Westmont IL 60559-5551 Home: 128 Smedley Rd Fairfield CT 06824-5249

KUHN, ROSEANN, sports association administrator; Staff mem. Women's Internat. Bowling Congress, Greendale, Wis., 1974-96, exec. dir., 1996—. Office: Womens Internat Bowling Congress (WIBC) 5301 S 76th St Greendale WI 53129-1128

KUHN, RYAN ANTHONY, investment banker; b. Framingham, Mass., Sept. 15, 1947; s. Robert Anthony Kuhn and Julia (Scott) McMillan; m. Cynthia Lynn DeVore, June 4, 1988; 1 child, Ryan R. BA in Psychology, Trinity Coll., Hartford, Conn., 1970; MBA, Harvard U., 1979. Mgr. corp. acquisitions McGraw-Hill, NYC, 1979-85; sr. assoc. venture capital Golder Thoma Cressey, Chgo., 1985-86; pres. Reid Psychol. Systems, Chgo., 1986-90, Lilly Pulitzer, Chgo., 1990-93; prin. Kuhn Capital, Chgo., 1990—. Contbr. articles to profl. pubis. and mags.; guest spkr. TV and radio talk show. Bd. dirs. Infant Welfare Soc. Chgo., Harvard Bus. Sch. of Chgo. Republican. Episcopalian. Office: Kuhn Capital Ste 200 500 Western Ave Lake Forest IL 60045 Office Phone: 847-457-2400.

KUHN, WHITEY, advertising executive; Pres. Kuhn & Wittenborn Advt., Kansas City, Mo., 1978—. Office: Kuhn & Wittenborn Advt Ste 600 2405 Grand Blvd Kansas City MO 64108

KUHRMEYER, CARL ALBERT, manufacturing executive; b. St. Paul, May 12, 1928; s. Carl and Irma Luella (Lindeke) K.; m. Janet E. Pedersen, Oct. 31, 1953; children: Karen Graden, John, Paul. BSME, U. Minn., 1949. Registered profl. engr., Minn. Design engr. Magney, Tusler & Setter, St. Paul, 1950-51; with 3M Co., St. Paul, 1951-93, successively product devel. engr., machine devel. engr., project leader, copy machine prodn. supr., process engring. and contracting supr., process engring. mgr., project mgr., until 1964, tech. dir., 1964-66, div. v.p., 1967-70, corp. group v.p., 1970-80, corp. v.p., 1980-93. Bd. dirs., chmn. bd. Product Level Control, Eagan, Minn., 1995—. Patentee in field. Mem. nat. adv. coun. Nat. Multiple Sclerosis Soc., 1973—; trustee United Theol. Sem., St. Paul, 1986-2002; bd. dirs. Minn. Protestant Found., St. Paul, 1987—, pres., 1997—; bd. dirs. Minn. Pvt. Coll. Fund, St. Paul, 1986-95, St. Paul Winter Carnival Assn., 1987-93, chmn., dir., 1990-91; bd. dirs., v.p. Family Resources Devel. Inc., St. Paul. Mem. St. Paul C. of C. (bd. dirs. 1988-95, chmn. bd. 1993), Minn. Club (bd. dirs. 1994-2002), White Bear Yacht Club (bd. dirs. 1995-97), North Oaks Country Club (bd. dirs. 1981-83, pres. 1983), Osman Temple. Mem. United Church of Christ. Office: 3050 Minnesota World Trade Ctr 30 7th St E Saint Paul MN 55101-4914 E-mail: cakuhrmeyer@mmm.com.

KUJALA, WALFRID EUGENE, musician, educator; b. Warren, Ohio, Feb. 19, 1925; s. Arvo August and Elsie Fannie (Ojajarvi) K.; m. Sherry Henry, Dec. 29, 1989; children by previous marriage: Stephen, Gwen, Daniel. MusB, Eastman Sch. Music, 1948, MusM, 1950. Flutist Rochester Philharm. Orch., 1948—54; soloist, flutist, piccoloist Chgo. Symphony Orch., 1954—2001; prof. flute Northwestern U., Evanston, Ill., 1962—. Vis. prof. of flute Shepherd Sch. Music, Rice U., 1995-97. Author: The Flutist's Progress, 1970, The Flutist's Vade Mecum of Scales, Arpeggios, Trills and Fingering Technique, 1995, Orchestral Techniques for Flute and Piccolo, 2006; consulting editor Flute Talk Mag., 1991—; contbr. articles to profl. jours.; performed world premiere of Concerto for Flute by Gunther Schuller with Chgo. Symphony Orch., conducted by Sir Georg Solti, 1988. Served with AUS, 1943-45, ETO, PTO. Recipient Exemplar of Music Tchg. award, orthwestern U., 1992, Cultural Leadership award, Ill. Coun. Orch., 2007, Lifetime Achievement award, Chgo. Flute Club, 2007. Mem.: Nat. Flute Assn. (past pres., Lifetime Achievement award 1997). Office: Sch Music Northwestern U Evanston IL 60208-2400 E-mail: walfridkujala@aol.com.

KUJAWA, SISTER ROSE MARIE, academic administrator; b. Detroit; d. Francis and Anne Kujawa. BS in math., Madonna U., Livonia, Mich., 1966; MS in edn. and math., Wayne State U., Detroit, 1971, PhD in higher edn. adminstrn., 1979. Dept. chair math. Bishop Borgess H.S.; asst. prin. and curriculum coord. Ladywood H.S.; prof. Madonna U., Livonia, Mich., 1975, academic dean, academic v.p., acting dean Coll. of Arts and Sci., pres., 2001—. Office: Madonna U 36600 Schoolcraft Rd Livonia MI 48150-1173 Office Phone: 800-852-4951 5315. E-mail: srosemarie@madonna.edu.

KULCINSKI, GERALD LAVERNE, nuclear engineer, educator, dean; b. La Crosse, Wis., Oct. 27, 1939; s. Harold Franklin and June Kramer K.; m. Janet Noreen Berg, Nov. 25, 1961; children: Kathryn, Brian, Karen. BS in Chem. Engring., U. Wis., 1961, MS in Nuclear Engring., 1962, PhD in Nuclear Engring., 1965. Rschr. Los Alamos (N.Mex.) Nuclear Lab., 1963; lectr. Ctr. Grad. Study, Richland, Wash., 1965-71; sr. rsch. sci. Battelle Northwest Lab., Richland, 1965-71; prof. U. Wis., Madison, 1972—, dir. Fusion Tech. Inst., 1973-75, 79—, Grainger Prof. Nuclear Engring., 1984—, assoc. dean coll. engring., 2001—. Vis. scientist Karlsruhe (Germany) Nuclear Rsch. Ctr., 1977, Bechtel Corp., San Francisco, 1989, 95; active Gov. Energy Policy Task Force, Wis., 1980; U.S. del. to Internat. Tokamak Reactor Project, Vienna, Austria, 1979-81; mem. adv. panel INTOR, 1987; mem. numerous review panels, including Los Alamos Nat. lab., Sandia Nat. Lab., Argonne Nat. Lab.; mem. NASA Adv. Coun., 2005—. Assoc. editor: Fusion Engring. and Design. Recipient Curtis W. McGraw Rsch. award Engring. Rsch. Com. Am. Assn. Engring. Edn., 1978, John Randle Grumman Achievement award Grumman Aircraft Corp., 1987, Leadership Fusion award Fusion Power Assocs., 1992, NASA Pub. Svc. medal, 1993, Disting. Faculty award Wis. Alumni Assn., 1994, Big 10 Centennial award, 1995. Fellow Am. Nuclear Soc. (sec. Richland sect. 1970, student advisor Wis. chpt. 1972-73, chmn. 2nd topical meeting on fusion tech. 1976, bd. dirs. 1987-90, chmn 16th topical meeting on fusion tech. 2004, Outstanding Achievement award 1980); mem. NAE. Home: 6013 Greentree Rd Madison WI 53711-3125 Office: U Wis 1500 Johnson Dr Madison WI 53706-1609 Business E-Mail: kulcinski@engr.wisc.edu.

KULLBERG, DUANE REUBEN, accounting firm executive; b. Red Wing, Minn., Oct. 6, 1932; s. Carl Reuben and Hazel Norma (Swanson) K.; m. Sina Nell Turner, Oct. 19, 1958 (dec. Sept. 1989); children: Malissa Kullberg, Caroline Godellas; m. Susan Turley, Dec. 30, 1992; stepchildren: Betsy Lucas, Jane Magnuson. BBA, U. Minn., 1954. With Arthur Andersen & Co., S.C., 1954-89, ptnr., 1967-89, mng. ptnr., Mpls., 1970-74, dep. mng. ptnr., Chgo., 1975-78, vice chmn. acctg. and audit practice worldwide, 1978-80, mng. ptnr., CEO, 1980-89, ret., 1989. Bd. dirs. Chgo. Bd. Options Exch. Life trustee Northwestern U., Art Inst. Chgo., U. Minn. Found., chmn. bd. trustees, 1993-95; chair Swedish Coun. Am. Found., 1999-2001. With U.S. Army, 1956-58. Decorated comdr. Royal Order of Polar Star (Sweden), 1989; recipient Legend in Leadership award Emory U., 1992, Regents award U. Minn., 1995, Outstanding Achievement award U. Minn., 1990. Mem. Chgo. Club, Comml. Club, Mpls. Club. Home (Summer): 55 East Erie St Apt 1703 Chicago IL 60611-2247 Home (Winter): 6444 N 79th St Scottsdale AZ 85250-7919 Office Phone: 312-953-3083. Personal E-mail: drkchicago@mac.com, dkullberg@mac.com.

KUMAR, PANGANAMALA RAMANA, electrical and computer engineering educator; b. Nagpur, Maharashtra, India, Apr. 21, 1952; arrived in U.S., 1973; s. Panganamala Bhavanarayana and Panganamala Kamala (Avasarala) Murthy; m. Devarakonda Jayashree Sundaram, Jan. 22, 1982; children: P. Ashwin, Shilpa P. BTech in Elec. Engring., Indian Inst. Tech., Madras, 1973; MS, Washington U., St. Louis, 1975, DSc, 1977. Asst. prof. dept. math. and computer sci. U. Md., Baltimore County, 1977—82, assoc. prof., 1982—84; assoc. prof. dept. elec. and computer engring. and coordinated sci. lab. U. Ill., Urbana, 1985—87, prof. dept. elec. and computer engring., 1987—, rsch. prof. coordinated sci. lab., 1987—, Franklin W. Woeltge prof. elec. and computer engring., 2000—. Co-author: Stochastic Sys., 1986; assoc. editor: Sys. and Control Letters, 1984-93, Math. of Control Signals and Sys., 1986-2005, SIAM Jour. on Control and Optimization, 1989-93, Jour. Discrete Event Dynamic Systems: Theory and Application, 1993-2004; mem. editl. bd. Jour. on Adaptive Control and Signal Processing, 1986-99, Math. Problems in Engring., 1995—, ACM Trans. on Sensor Networks, 2004-06, Foundations and Trends in Networking, 2004, IEEE Trans. on Mobile Computing, 2005-06; editor Comm. Info. and Sys., 1999; assoc. editor IEEE Trans. on Automatic Control, 1982-83, assoc. editor at large, 1989-97; mem. editl. bd. Sadhana, 2005—, Academy Proceedings in Engineering Sciences, 2005—; contbr. articles to profl. jours., chpts. to books. Recipient Donald P. Eckman award, Am. Automatic Control Coun., 1985. Fellow: IEEE (Field award Control Sys. 2006); mem.: NAE. Avocation: ping pong/table tennis. Office: Univ Ill Ubrana Champaign Coord Sci Lab 1308 W Main St Urbana IL 61801-2307 Office Phone: 217-333-7476. E-mail: prkumar@uiuc.edu.

KUMAR, ROMESH, chemical engineer; b. Rajpura, India, Oct. 18, 1944; arrived in U.S., 1966; s. Kundan Lal and Pushpa (Wati) Agarwal; m. Kumkum Khanna, Feb. 22, 1976. BS, Panjab U., India, 1965; MS, U. Calif., Berkeley, 1968, PhD, 1972. From postdoctoral appointee to sr. chem. engr. Argonne Nat. Lab., Ill., 1972—2004, sr. chem. engr., 2004—; with Chem. Scis. and Engring. Dept. Tchr. fuel cell power sys. design and analysis for transp. applications. Contbr. to Weissberger's Techniques in Chemistry, 1975; patentee in field. Recipient Silver medal Panjab U., 1965, Medal for Disting. Performance U. Chgo., 2004. Hindu. Home: 1549 Ceals Ct Naperville IL 60565-6148 Office: 9700 Cass Ave Argonne IL 60439-4803 Office Phone: 630-252-4342. Business E-Mail: kumar@anl.gov.

KUMMER, FRED S., construction company executive; b. 1929; BS, U. Mo., 1952. Engr. William Ittner & Co., 1952-56; with Buckley Constrn. Co., Inc., 1957-59, Kummer Constrn. Co., Inc., from 1959; pres., treas. HBE Corp., St. Louis, now chmn., pres., CEO; CEO Adam's Mark Hotels. Address: HBE PO Box 419039 Saint Louis MO 63141-9039 Office: Adam's Mark Hotels 11330 Olive St Rd Box 27239 Saint Louis MO 63141

KUMMEROW, ARNOLD A., superintendent of schools; b. Framingham, Mass., Mar. 25, 1945; s. Arnold A. Sr. and Elizabeth Patricia (Westfield) K.; m. Constance Booth, July 10, 1971. BME, Eastern Mich. U., 1968, MA, 1975; PhD, U. Mich., 1989. Cert. adminstrn., Mich. Instrumental music dir. Vandercook Lake Pub. Schs., Jackson, Mich., 1968-74; instrumental music dir., asst. prin., prin. L'Anse Creuse Pub. Schs., Mt. Clemens, Mich., 1975-89; asst. supt. curriculum and pers. Lincoln Consol. Schs., Ypsilanti, Mich., 1989-91; asst. supt. Ypsilanti Pub. Schs., 1991-93; mem. curriculum devel. staff Mich. Dept. Edn., 1993-94; supt. Carsonville-Port Sanilac (Mich.) Schs., 1994-97, Armada (Mich.) Area Schs., 1997—. Named Exemplary Sch. Prin., Mich. Dept. Edn. and U.S. Dept. Edn. Mem. AASA, MASA, ASCD. Home: 17201 Knollwood Dr Clinton Township MI 48038-2833 Office: Armada Area Schs 74500 Burk St Armada MI 48005-3314

KUMMLER, RALPH H., chemical engineer, educator, dean; b. Jersey City, Nov. 1, 1940; m. Jean Evelyn Helge, Aug. 25, 1962; children: Randolph Henry, Bradley Rolf, Jeffrey Ralf. BSChemE, Rensselaer Poly. Inst., 1962; PhD, Johns Hopkins U., 1966. Chem. engr. GE Space Scientist Lab., Valley Forge, Pa., 1965—69; assoc. prof. chem. engring. Wayne State U., Detroit, 1970—75, prof., 1975—, chmn. dept., 1974—93, dir. hazardous waste mgmt. programs, 1986—, assoc. dean rsch., 1997—2001, interim dean, 2001—04, dean, 2004—. Contbr. articles to publs. Bd. dirs., past pres. Kirkwood Lake Assn. Fellow: Engr. Soc. Detroit (Young Engr. of Yr. award 1975, Gold award 1990, Disting. Svc. award 1994, Horace Rackham Humanitarian award 1999, Disting. Svc. award 2004), Am. Inst. Chemists; mem.: AIChE (past pres. Detroit chpt.), Svc. award 1981, Chem. Engr. of Yr. award 1981), Mich. Air and Waste Mgmt. Assn. ((past pres.), Waste Mgmt. award 2002), Am. Chem. Soc., Tau Beta Pi, Sigma Xi. Achievements include co-patentee in chem. innovations. Office: Wayne State U Coll Engring Detroit MI 48202 Office Phone: 313-577-3775. Business E-Mail: rkummler@wayne.edu.

KUNC, KAREN, artist, educator; b. Omaha, Dec. 15, 1952; BFA, U. Nebr., Lincoln, 1975; MFA, Ohio State U., 1977. Assoc. prof. printmaking U. Nebr., Lincoln, 1983-97, full prof. printmaking, 1997—, gallery dir., 1988-91. Prof., art, Univ. Neb., 1983-, vis. asst. prof. U. Calif., Berkeley, 1987; vis. artist, instr. Carleton Coll., Northfield, Minn., 1989; rsch. fellow Kyoto Seika U., Japan, 1993; vis. artist Icelandic Coll. Arts & Crafts, Rekyavik, 1995. One-woman show Columbus (Ohio) Mus. Art, 1983, Sheldon Meml. Art Gallery, Lincoln, 1984, Mus. Art, U. Iowa, City, 1994, Joslyn Art Mus., Omaha, 1995, Gallery APA, Nagoya, Japan, 1995, Kutna Hora, Czech Republic, 1996, Galleria Harmonia, Jyvasklya, Finland, 1996; exhibited in group shows San Francisco Mus. Modern Art, 1980, Honolulu Acad. Arts, 1985, Mednorodini Graficni Likovni Ctr., Ljubljana, Yugoslavia, 1987, Zimmerli Art Mus., Rutgers U., New Brusnwick, N.J., 1988, Greenville (S.C.) County Mus. Art, 1988, Calif. Palace Legion of Honor, San Francisco, 1989, Nat. Mus. Women in Arts, Washington, 1991, Elvehjem Mus. Art, U. Wis., Madison, 1993, 9th Seoul Internat. Print Biennale, 1994, Tama Art Mus., Japan, 1995, Graphicstudio Gallery, Tampa, Fla., 1996, Nat. Mus. Am. Art, Washington, 1997; represented in permanent collections Mus. of Modern Art, N.Y., Nat. Mus. Am. Art, Smithsonian Instn., Washington, Libr. Congress, Washington, Worcester (Mass.) Art Mus., Sheldon Meml. Art Gallery, U. Nebr., Nat. Art Libr., Victoria and Albert Mus., London, Mus. Modern Art, N.Y.C., Bklyn. Mus. Art, Fogg Art Mus. Harvard U.; commns. include woodcut print Madison Print Club, 1994, Benziger Winery Imagery Series, Glen Ellen, Calif., 1996, prints Zimmerli Art Mus., 1995, Rutgers Archives Printmaking Studios, 1995, artists book Nat. Mus. Women Arts, Washington, 1996; co-author, editor: Polish Prints: A Contemporary Graphic Tradition, 1989; author: Woodcut and the Contemporary Impressions, 1993; represented by Jane Haslem Gallery, Washington. Recipient 1st prize Graphica Atlaantica, Reykjavik, Iceland, 1987, purchase award U. Del., 1988, prize Machida City Mus. Graphic Art, Tokyo, 1993; fellow Nat. Endowment Arts, 1984, 96; Fulbright scholar, 1996. Mem. NAD (academician, 1994-), Mid-Am. Print Coun., Coll. Art Assn., Ctr. Book Arts, Calif. Soc. Printmakers, Boston Printmakers, Print Club. Office: Art & History 303B NCW Univ Nebraska Lincoln NE 68588-0114 also: Atrium Gallery 4729 Mcpherson Ave Saint Louis MO 63108-1918 Office Phone: 402-472-5541. E-mail: kkunc@unlserve.unl.edu.

KUNDTZ, JOHN ANDREW, lawyer; b. Cleve., June 23, 1933; s. Ewald E. and Elizabeth (O'Neill) K.; m. Helen Margaret Luckiesh, Aug. 31, 1957; children— John M., Helen E., Margaret L. BS in Social Studies, Georgetown U., 1955; JD, Case Western Reserve U., 1958. Bar: Ohio 1958, U.S. Dist. Ct. (no. dist.) Ohio 1961. Ptnr. Falsgraf, Kundtz, Reidy & Shoup, Cleve., 1961-69; ptnr. Thompson Hine and Flory, Cleve., 1970-90; pvt. practice Cleve., 1990—. Dir. Investment

Advisors Internat., Inc., Cleve. Trustee Hathaway Brown Sch., Shaker Heights, Ohio, Chagrin River Land Conservancy, Chagrin Falls, Ohio, Cleve. Soc. for the Blind. 1st lt. USAF, 1958-60. Mem. Ohio State Bar Assn., Assn. Transp. Practitioners. Republican. Roman Catholic. Home: 32540 Creekside Dr Pepper Pike OH 44124-5224 Office: 3000 Aurura Rd Ste 250 Cleveland OH 44139

KUNG, HAROLD HING-CHUEN, engineering educator; b. Hong Kong, Oct. 12, 1949; s. Shien C. and Kai Sau (Wong) K.; m. Mayfair Chu, June 12, 1971; children: Alexander, Benjamin. BS in chem. engring., U. Wis., 1971; PhD in chemistry, Northwestern U., 1974. Rsch. sci. ctrl. rsch. and devel. dept. E.I. duPont de Nemours & Co., Wilmington, Del., 1974-76; asst. prof. chem. engring. Northwestern U., 1976, asst. prof. chem. engring. and chemistry, 1977, assoc. prof., 1981, prof. chem. engring. and chemistry, 1985-97, chmn. chemical engring., 1986-92; dir. Ctr. for Catalysis and Surface Sci., 1993-97. Chmn. Gordon rsch. Conf. on Catalysis, 1995; tech. advisor UNIDO Mission, 1995; John McClanahan Henske Disting. lectr. Yale U., 1996; mem. com. to rev. PNGV program Nat. Rsch. Coun., 1996-2000; Olaf Hongen vis. prof. U. Wis., Madison, 1999. Author: Transition Metal Oxides, Surface Chemistry and Catalysis, 1989, Catalyst Modificaton-Selective Oxidation Processes, 1991; editor: Methanol Production and Use, 1994, Applied Catalysis A = General, 1996—; patents include Photolysis of Water Using Rhodate Semiconductive Electrodes, and Oxidative Dehydrogenation of Alkanes to Unsaturated Hydrocarbons. Japanese Soc. for Promotion of Sci. fellow, 1996. Mem. AIChE, Am. Chem. Soc., Chgo. Catalysis Club (program chair 1992, pres. 1993, Herman Pines award 1999), N.Am. Catalysis Soc. (Paul H. Emmett award 1991, Robert L. Barwell lectr. 1999), Phi Lambda Epsilon. Office: Dept of Chem Engring Northwestern University 2145 Sheridan Rd Evanston IL 60208-0834 E-mail: hkung@northwestern.edu.

KUNKEL, RICHARD W., state legislator; BS, Minot State; MEd, EdD, U. N.D.; PhD, Columbia U. Retired supt. of schs.; mem. N.D. Ho. of Reps., 1991-98, vice chmn. appropriations com., vice chmn. edn. com., vice chmn. environ. divsn. com. Past pres. United Way; exec. coun. Boy Scouts Am.; bd. dirs. N.D. Bd. Higher Edn., 1999—. Mem. Elks, Rotary (past pres.), Eagles, Cmty. Concert Assn. (past pres.). Home: 1312 6th St Devils Lake ND 58301-2812

KUNKEL, STEVEN, pathologist, educator; BS, N.Dak. State U., 1973, MS, 1974; PhD in Microbiology, U. Kans., 1978. Postdoctoral rschr. U. Conn. Health Ctr., Farmington, Conn., 1978—80; from instr. to prof. Dept. Pathology U. Mich. Med. Sch., Ann Arbor, 1980—91, prof. pathology, 1991—. Divisional dir. gen. pathology U. Mich., 1991—, assoc. dean Rackham Grad. Sch., 1995—. Editor: Jour. Clin. Investigation, Am. Jour. Pathology, Jour. Clin. Immunology. Named to Endowed Chair, U. Mich. Med. Sch., 1997; grantee, NIH. Achievements include patents in field. Office: Univ Mich General Path M5214 MSI 0602 1301 Catherine Street Ann Arbor MI 48109-0602

KUNKLE, WILLIAM JOSEPH, judge, lawyer; b. Lakewood, Ohio, Sept. 3, 1941; s. William Joseph and Georgia (Howe) K.; m. Sarah Florence Nesti, July 11, 1964; children: Kathleen Margaret, Susan Mary. BA, Northwestern U., Evanston, Ill., 1963, JD, 1969. Bar: Ohio 1969, U.S. Dist. Ct. (no. dist.) Ill. 1969, Ill. 1969, U.S. Ct. Appeals (7th cir.) 1991, U.S. Supreme Ct. 1991. Process control engr. Union Carbide Corp., Cleve., 1964-65, prodn. supr. Greenville, SC, 1965-66; assoc. Hauxhurst, Sharp, Mollison & Gallagher, Cleve., 1969-70; asst. pub. defender Cook County Pub. Defender, Chgo., 1970-73; asst. states atty. Cook County States Atty., Chgo., 1973-85; ptnr. Phelan, Cahill & Quinlan, Ltd., Chgo., 1985-96, Cahill, Christian & Kunkle, Ltd., Chgo., 1996—2002, Wildman, Harrold, Allen & Dixon, Chgo., 2002—04; judge Cir. Ct. Cook County, 2004—. Chmn. The Ill. Gaming Bd., 1990—93; dep. spl. outside counsel U.S. Ho. Reps., Washington, 1988—89; adj. prof. I.I.T. Chgo. Kent Sch. Law, 1980—84; instr. Nat. Inst. Trial Advocacy, 1978—82, 1986; lectr. Nat. Coll. Dist. Attys., 1978—85, Nat. Law Enforcement Inst., 1983—85; 1st asst. states atty. of Cook County, 1983—85; spl. state's atty. 18th Jud. Cir., DuPage County, 1995—99. Contbg. author: Punishment Prosecutor's Viewpoint, 1983, 1989, Trial Techniques Compendium, Nat. College of Dist. Attys. (2d, 3rd, 4th, 5th, 6th eds.). Recipient Disting. Faculty award Nat. Coll. Dist. Attys., 1980, Award for Prosecution Svc. Chgo. Assn. Commerce & Industry, 1981. Fellow Am. Coll. Trial Lawyers, ABA; mem. Internat. Soc. Barristers, Nat. Dist. Attys. Assn. (bd. dirs. 1984-85), Assn. Govt. Attys. in Capital Litigation (pres. 1983-84), Chgo. Bar Assn. (bd. mgrs. 1983-84), Ill. State Bar Assn. (LAWPAC trustee 1989-95), Internat. Assn. Gaming Attys., Chgo. Crime Commn. (bd. dirs.). Avocations: golf, softball, carpentry, motorcycling.

KUNTZ, WILLIAM HENRY, lawyer, mediator; b. Indpls., Feb. 27, 1954; s. Herman William and Ethel Cleora (Stangle) K. BA in Chemistry, Purdue U. at Indpls., 1984; MS in Chemistry, Purdue U., Indpls., 1986; JD, Ind. U., Indpls., 1989. Bar: Ind. 1989, U.S. Dist. Ct. (so. and no. dists.) Ind. 1989, U.S. Patent Office 1992, U.S. Supreme Ct. 1993. Assoc. Urdal, Tarvin and Alexander, P.C., Connersville, Ind., 1989-90; dep. prosecutor County of Fayette, Connersville, 1990, chief dep. prosecutor, 1991-92; pvt. practice Indpls., 1992-94; chief dep. prosecutor Fayette County, Connersville, 1995-98; with Baker and Bodwell, P.C., Connersville, Ind., 1999—. Mem. ABA, Nat. Bar Assn., Ind. State Bar Assn. (bd. dirs. ADR sect. 1997—), Indpls. Bar Assn. (chmn. legal awareness com. 1996, chmn. law student liaison com. 1996), Fayette County Bar Assn. (sec.-treas. 1989-90), Marion County Bar Assn., Ind. Trial Lawyers Assn., Ind. Assn. Mediators (sec. 1993-94, 97—, pres.-elect 1994-95, pres. 1995-96), Soc. Profls. in Dispute Resolution, Acad. Family Mediators, Purdue U. Indpls. Sch. Sci. Alumni Bd. (v.p. 1998—). Home: 2065 Lick Creek Dr Indianapolis IN 46203-4922 also: 105A E 16th St Connersville IN 47331-2735

KUNZE, RALPH CARL, retired savings and loan association executive; b. Buffalo, Oct. 31, 1925; s. Bruno E. and Esther (Graubman) K.; m. Helen Hites Sutton, Apr. 1978; children by previous marriage: Bradley, Diane Kunze Cowgill, James. BBA, U. Cin., 1950, postgrad., 1962-63; grad., Ind. U. Grad. Sch. Savs. and Loan, 1956, U. Calif., 1973. With Mt. Lookout Savs. & Loan Co., Cin., 1951-63, sec., mng. officer, 1958-63; with Buckeye Fed. Savs. & Loan Assn., Columbus, Ohio, 1963-77, exec. v.p., sec., 1967-70, pres., sec., vice chmn. bd. dirs., 1970-77; pres., chief operating officer, dir. Gate City Savs. and Loan Assn., Fargo, ND, 1977-81; chief exec. officer, dir. United Home Fed., Toledo, 1981-91, also chmn. bd. dirs., 1985-91; ret., 1991. Former trustee Ohio Savs. and Loan League, Toledo C. of C.; mem. investment adv. com. City of Toledo; mem. media contact group and legis. com. U.S. Savs. League. Mem. Toledo Com. 100, Toledo Zool. Soc., St. Vincent Hosp. Found.; past pres. Toledo Zoo; past pres. coun. Hope Luth. Ch.; pres. Toledo Neighborhood Housing Svcs., 1981-83; pres., chmn. pers. com. United Way Franklin County, Ohio; past pres. Ohio Soc. Prevention Blindness; bd. dirs. Revitalization Corp. Toledo, 1983-84, Bittersweet Farms, Autistic Cmty. of N.W. Ohio, Inc.; past mem., trustee Kidney Found. Northwestern Ohio and Luth. Social Svcs., Wesley Glen Retirement Meth. Ctr., Columbus, 1974-77. Served with USNR, 1944-45. Mem.: Lambda Chi Alpha. Home: 2606 Emmick Dr Toledo OH 43606-2701

KUNZEL, ERICH, JR., conductor, arranger, educator; b. NYC, Mar. 21, 1935; s. Erich and Elisabeth (Enz) Kunzel; m. Brunhilde Gertrud Strodl, Sept. 5, 1965. AB in Music, Dartmouth Coll., 1957; postgrad., Harvard U., 1957—58; AM, Brown U., 1960; LittD, No. Ky. State U., 1973; D of Arts, Coll. Mt. St. Joseph, 1996; D in Musical Arts, U. Cin., 2000. Condr. Sante Fe Opera, 1957, Santa Fe Opera, 1964, 1965; music faculty Brown U., 1958—65; asst. condr. R.I. Philharmonic, 1963—65; resident condr. Cin. Symphony Orch., 1965—77; condr. Cin. Summer Opera, 1966, 1973, Cin. Ballet Co., 1966—68; assoc. prof. U. Cin. Coll.-Conservatory Music, 1965—71, chmn. opera dept., 1968—70; music dir. Philharmonia Orch., 1967—71, New Haven (Conn.) Symphony Orch., 1974—77, San Francisco Art Commn. Pops, 1981—83; condr. Cin. Pops Orch., 1977—; prin. pops condr. Naples Philharm. Orch., 1993—. Guest condr. Boston Symphony, Cleve. Orch., Boston Pops, Phila. Orch., San Francisco Symphony, Buffalo Philharm., Rochester Philharm., Pitts. Symphony, Atlanta Symphony, Chgo. Symphony Orch., Interlochen Arts Festival, Dallas Symphony, Detroit Symphony, Toronto Symphony, Montreal Symphony, St. Louis Symphony, Nat. Symphony, London Symphony, China Nat. Symphony, Can. Opera Co., San Francisco Opera, others. Editor, arranger choral works, recs. for Decca Gold Label, Atlantic Records, Telarc Internat., Vox Records, Caedmon Records, Pro Arte Records, Fanfare, MMG, MCA Classics Gold. V.p. Pierre Monteux Meml. Found., Met. Opera Guild; chmn. Greater Cin. Arts and Edn. Ctr., 1998—. Named Billboard Crossover Artist of Yr., 1988, 1989, 1990, 1991; named to Hon. Order Ky. Cols.; recipient Grand Prix du Disque, 1989, Sony Tiffany award, 1989, Classical Record of Yr. award, Japan, 1989, Grammy nomination, 1989, 1991, 1993, 1995, Ohioana Pegasus award, 2000, Nat. Medal Arts, Nat. Endowment Arts, 2006. Mem.: Am. Symphony Orch. League, Delta Omicron, Phi Mu Alpha Sinfonia, Phi Delta Theta (Disting. Alumnus award 1996). Mailing: c/o Peter Throm Mgmt LLC 2040 Tibbitts Court Ann Arbor MI 48105

KUPCHELLA, CHARLES EDWARD, academic administrator, writer, educator; b. Nanty Glo, Pa., July 7, 1942; s. Charles Francis and Margaret (Bouite) Kupchella; m. R. Adele Kiel, July 20, 1963; children: Richard Charles, Michele Louise, Jason Charles. BS in Edn., Indiana U. of Pa., 1964; PhD in Physiology, St. Bonaventure U., 1968. Asst. prof. Bellarmine Coll., Louisville, 1968-72, assoc. prof., 1972-73; assoc. dir. cancer rsch. ctr. Sch. of Medicine, assoc. prof. U. Louisville, 1973-79; prof., chmn. dept. biology Murray State U., Ky., 1979-85; dean Ogden Coll. of Sci., Tech. and Health Western Ky. U., Bowling Green, 1985—93; provost S.E. Mo. State U., Cape Girardeau, 1993—99; pres., prof. biology U. ND, 1999—. Author: Sights/Sounds: Special Senses, 1976, Environmental Science, 1986, 3rd rev. edit., 1993, Dimensions of Cancer, 1987; contbr. chpts. to books, over 50 articles to profl. jours. Bd. dirs. Ky. Ctr. for Pub. Issues, Lexington, 1990-93; mem. cancer edn. rev. com. NIH/Nat. Cancer Inst., 1993-97; mem. inst. rsch. grant rev. com. Am. Cancer Soc., 1993-96; chmn. N.D. Cancer Coalition, 2006—; trustee ND Hist. Soc., 2002—; ptnr. Nat. Dialogue Cancer, 2000—. NDEA fellow, 1964-68. Mem. AAAS (nominating com. sect. on sci. and engring. 1995-97), Ky. Acad. Sci. (pres. 1977), Ky. Sci. and Tech. Coun. (sec., treas. Lexington 1988-93), Am. Assn. Cancer Edn. (chair fin. com. 1990-93, treas. 1993-96, pres. 1999-2000, exec. coun., mem. midwest higher edn. commn. 1999-2001, mem. accreditation rev. coun. higher learning commn. 2005-06). Office: U ND Office of Pres PO Box 8193 Grand Forks ND 58202-8193 Office Phone: 701-777-2122. Office Fax: 701-777-3866. E-mail: ckupchella@mail.und.edu.

KUPPER, BRUCE DAVID, advertising executive; b. Geneva, NY, Nov. 17, 1952; s. Alan D. and Leila (Winograd) K.; m. Karen Ryan Kupper, Sept. 12, 1976; children: David, Laura. BA, Bates Coll., 1975. Account exec. Lieberman Advt., St. Louis, 1976-77; account supr. Young & Rubicam, Detroit, 1977-78; sr. ptnr., chief exec. officer Kupper Advt., Inc., St. Louis, 1978—; pres. Kupnic, Inc., 1991—; sr. ptnr. Kupper Parker Communications Inc., 1992—. Author: (Book) French Canadians in Am., 1975. Fellow: Coro Found.; mem. St. Louis Advt. Club, Am. Assn. Advt. Agys. (regional bd. mem.), Westborough Country Club.

KUPST, MARY JO, psychologist, researcher; b. Chgo., Oct. 4, 1945; d. George Eugene and Winifred Mary (Hughes) K.; m. Alfred Procter Stresen-Reuter Jr., Aug. 21, 1977. BS, Loyola U., 1967, MA, 1969, PhD, 1972. Lic. psychologist, Ill., Wis. Postdoctoral fellow U. Ill. Med. Ctr., Chgo., 1971—72; rsch. psychologist Children's Meml. Hosp., Chgo., 1972—89; assoc. prof. psychiatry and pediatrics Northwestern U. Med. Sch., Chgo., 1981—89; prof. pediatrics Med. Coll. Wis., Milw., 1989—, dir. pediatric psychology, 1995—. Practice clin. psychology, Chgo., 1975-89, McHenry, Ill., 1987-89; co-chair pediat. oncology group psychology com., 1995-2001, vice chair psychology discipline Children's Oncology Group, 2002-06. Editor: (with others) The Child with Cancer, 1980; contbr. articles to profl. jours. V.p. McHenry County Mental Health Bd., 1997—2001; co-chair Alliance for Childhood Cancer, 2005—. Fellow: APA (pres. divsn. 54 2004—05, charter fellow); mem.: Wis. Psychol. Assn. Office: Med Coll Wis Dept Pediats 8701 W Watertown Plank Rd Milwaukee WI 53226-3548 E-mail: mkupst@mcw.edu.

KURIT, NEIL, lawyer; b. Cleve., Aug. 31, 1940; s. Jay and Rose (Rainin) K.; m. Doris Tannenbaum, Aug. 9, 1964 (div.); m. Donna Chernin, Aug. 24, 1986. BS, Miami U., Oxford, Ohio, 1961; JD, Case Western Res. U., 1964. Bar: Ohio 1964. Prin. Kahn, Kleinman Co., L.P.A., Cleve., 1964—. Co-author Handbook for Attys. and Accts., Jewish Cmty. Fedn. Endowment Fund. Trustee, v.p. Montefiore Home, 1983-87; trustee Jewish Cmty. Fedn. Cleve., 1983-86, 90-95. Mem. ABA, Ohio State Bar Assn. Home: 2870 Courtland Blvd Cleveland OH 44122-2802 Office: Kahn Kleinman Co LPA 2600 Tower at Erieview Cleveland OH 44114 Office Phone: 216-736-3352. E-mail: nkurit@kahnkleinman.com.

KURNICK, ROBERT H., JR., automotive executive, lawyer; b. 1961; BA, Mich. State U.; JD, U. Notre Dame. Ptnr. Honigman Miller Schwartz and Cohn, Detroit, 1986—95; asst. gen. counsel Penske Corp., 1995—99; sr. v.p., gen. counsel Penske Auto Ctrs., Inc., 1995—2001, Penske Motorsports, Inc., 1996—99; exec. v.p., gen. counsel United Auto Group, Inc., 2000—; pres. Penske Corp., 2002—08, Penske Automotive Group, 2008—.

KURTENBACH, JAMES, state representative, finance educator; b. Feb. 1957; Assoc. prof. acctg. Coll. Bus. Iowa State U., Ames; state rep. dist. 10 Iowa Ho. of Reps., 2003—, commerce, regulation and labor com., vice-chmn. ways and means com., human svc. appropriations subcom. Republican. Office: Coll Business Iowa State Univ Gerrin Bus Bldg Ames IA 50011 also: State Capitol East 12th and Grand Des Moines IA 50319 Business E-Mail: jim.kurtenbach@legis.state.ia.us.

KURTH, RONALD JAMES, retired academic administrator, military officer; b. Madison, Wis., July 1, 1931; s. Peter James and Celia (Kuehn) K.; m. Esther Charlene Schaefer, Dec. 21, 1954; children: Steven, Audrey, John, Douglas. BS, U.S. Naval Acad., 1954; MPA, Harvard U., 1961, PhD, 1970. Commd. ensign U.S. Navy, 1954, advanced through grades to rear adm., 1981; U.S. naval attache Moscow, 1975-77; comdg. officer NAS, Memphis at Millington, Tenn., 1977-79; mil. fellow Council Fgn. Relations, NYC, 1979-80; exec. asst. to dep. chief naval ops. Dept. Navy, Washington, 1980-81, dir. Pol-Mil Policy and Current Plans, 1981-83, dir. Long Range Planning Group, 1983-84; U.S. def. attache Moscow, 1985-87; pres. U.S. Naval War Coll., Newport, RI, 1987-90, Murray (Ky.) State U., 1990-94; dean acad. affairs Air War Coll., Maxwell AFB, Ala., 1994-98; pres. St. John's Northwestern Mil. Acad., Delafield, Wis., 1998—2004, pres. emeritus, 2004—. Teaching fellow Harvard U., Cambridge, Mass., 1969-70. Author: The Politics of Technological Innovation in the Navy, 1970. Former mem. nat. adv. bd. Boy Scouts Am. Decorated Def. D.S.M., Navy D.S.M., Legion of Merit with 2 gold stars, Meritorious Svc. medal with gold star. Mem. U.S. Naval Inst. (life), Naval War Coll. Found. (life), U.S. Naval Acad. Alumni, Harvard U. Alumni, Washington Inst. Foreign Affairs. Episcopalian. Home: 8106 Ainsworth Ave Springfield VA 22152 Personal E-mail: randckurth@verizon.net.

KURTZ, CHARLES JEWETT, III, lawyer; b. Columbus, Ohio, May 13, 1940; s. Charles Jewett, Jr. and Elizabeth Virginia (Gill) K.; m. Linda Rhoads, Mar. 18, 1983. BA, Williams Coll., 1962; JD, Ohio State U., 1965. Bar: Ohio 1965, D.C. 1967, U.S. Dist. Ct. (so. dist.) Ohio 1967, U.S. Dist. Ct. (no. dist.) Ohio 1976, U.S. Ct. Appeals (6th cir.) 1992. Law clk. to justice Ohio State Supreme Ct., Columbus, 1965-67; assoc. Porter, Wright, Morris & Arthur, Columbus, 1967-71, ptnr., 1972—2004, mng. ptnr. litigation dept., 1988-91, mem. directing ptnrs. com., 1988-89, of counsel, 2005—. Mem. faculty Ohio Legal Ctr. Inst. Trustee Ballet Met., Columbus, 1990-94; mem. vestry St. Albans Episcopal Ch., 1986-89. Mem. ABA, Am. Arbitration Assn. (mem. panel comml. arbitrators), Columbus Bar Assn. (common pleas ct. com.), Columbus Bar Found., Columbus Def. Assn. (pres. 1976), Athletic Club, Columbus Country Club, Capital Club. Office: Porter Wright Morris & Arthur 41 S High St Ste 2900 Columbus OH 43215-6194 Personal E-mail: cjkurtz3@yahoo.com. Business E-Mail: Ckurtz@porterwright.com.

KURTZ, DAVID S., lawyer; b. Cleve., July 12, 1954; BA, Case Western Res. U., 1976, JD, 1979. Bar: Ohio 1979, Ill. 1980. Mem. Jones, Day, Reavis & Pogue, Chgo.; sr. ptnr. reorganization grp. Skadden, Arps, Slate, Meagher & Flom, Chgo.; mng. dir., co-head restructuring grp. Lazard, Chgo., 2002—. Recipient Bankruptcy Dealmaker of Yr., The Am. Lawyer mag., 2000. Office: Lazard Ste 2200 200 W Madison St Chicago IL 60606 Mailing: 1913 N Fremont St Chicago IL 60614-5016 Home Phone: 773-929-9112; Office Phone: 312-407-6600. Office Fax: 312-407-6620.

KURTZ, HARVEY A., lawyer; BA, U. Wis., 1972; JD, U. Chgo., 1975. Bar: Wis. 1975, U.S. Dist. Ct. (ea. dist.) Wis. 1980. Ptnr. Foley & Lardner LLP, Milw., 1989—. Mem. ABA, State Bar of Wis. Assn., Milw. Bar Assn. (chmn. employee benefits sect. 1993-94), Greater Milw. Employee Benefit Coun., Wis. Retirement Plan Profls. (pres. 1987-88), Kiwanis, Phi Beta Kappa. Home: 3927 N Stowell Ave Milwaukee WI 53211-2461 Office: Foley & Lardner LLP Ste 3800 777 E Wisc Ave Milwaukee WI 53202-5306 Office Phone: 414-297-5819. Business E-Mail: hkurtz@foley.com.

KURTZ, SHELDON FRANCIS, lawyer, educator; b. Syracuse, NY, May 18, 1943; s. Abraham Kurtz and Rosalyn (Bronstein) Stern; m. Alice Kaufman, June 22, 1968; children: Andrea, Emily. AB, Syracuse U., 1964, JD, 1967. Bar: N.Y. 1967, Iowa 1973. Assoc. Nixon, Mudge, Guthrie, Alexander & Mitchell, NYC, 1967-69, Cleary, Gottlieb, Steen & Hamilton, NYC, 1970-73; prof. U. Iowa Coll. Law, Iowa City, 1973-89, U. Va. Sch. Law, Charlottesville, 1979-80; dean Coll. Law, Fla. State U., Tallahassee, 1989-91; prof. Coll. Law U. Iowa, Iowa City, 1991—, prof. Coll. Med. Author: Kurtz on Iowa Estates, 3 vols., 1981, 2d edit., 2 vols., 1989, Problems, Cases and Materials on Family Estate Planning, 1983; (with Hood and Shors) Estate Planning for Shareholders of a Closely Held Corporation, 2 vols. and supplement, 1986, (with Hovenkamp) American Property Law, 1987, 4th edit., 2003, The Law of Property, 2001; (with McGovern) Wills, Trusts and Estates, 3d edit., 2004, Introduction to the Law of Real Property, 4th edit., 2005; contbr. articles to profl. jours. Recipient Burlington No. tchg. award U. Iowa, 1987, Michael J. Brody Disting. Svc. award, 2001. Mem. Iowa Bar Assn. (commr. Uniform State Laws), Am. Law Inst. Avocations: cooking, hiking. Office: U Iowa Coll Law Rm 446 Iowa City IA 52242 Home Phone: 319-337-7185; Office Phone: 319-335-9069. Business E-Mail: sheldon-kurtz@uiowa.edu.

KURTZMAN, CLETUS PAUL, microbiologist, researcher; b. Mansfield, Ohio, July 19, 1938; s. Paul A. and Marjorie M. (Gartner) K.; m. Mary Ann Dombrink, Aug. 4, 1962; children: Mary, Mark, Michael. BS, Ohio U., 1960; MS, Purdue U., 1962; PhD, W.Va. U., 1967. Microbiologist Nat. Ctr. Agrl. Utilization Rsch./USDA, Peoria, Ill., 1967-85, rsch. leader, 1985—. U.S. rep. Internat. Commn. on Yeasts, 1980—, World Fedn. Culture Collections, 1988—2000. Editor: Yeasts in Biotechnology, 1988, The Yeasts, A Taxonomic Study, 4th edit., 1998; contbr. papers to sci. jours. 1st lt. U.S. Army, 1962-64. Named Midwest Area Outstanding Scientist USDA, 1986; recipient Medal of Merit award Ohio U., 1992. Fellow AAAS, Am. Acad. Microbiology; mem. Internat. Mycol. Assn. (sec.-gen. 1990-94, v.p. 1994-2002), Mycol. Soc. Am., Am. Soc. Microbiology (divsn. chair 1991-92, J. Roger Porter award 1990), U.S. Fedn. Culture Collections (pres. 1976-78), Soc. Gen. Microbiology. Achievements include patent for xylose fermentation in yeasts; research in the correlation of DNA relatedness and fertility in yeasts, correlation of ribosomal RNA divergence. Office: Nat Ctr Agrl Utilization Rsch 1815 N University St Peoria IL 61604-3902 Business E-Mail: kurtzman@ncaur.usda.gov.

KURY, BERNARD EDWARD, lawyer; b. Sunbury, Pa., Sept. 11, 1938; AB, Princeton U., 1960; LLB, U. Pa., 1963. Bar: NY 1964. Assoc. Dewey, Ballantine, Bushby, Palmer & Wood, NYC, 1963-71, ptnr., 1971—2004; v.p., gen. counsel Guidant Corp., Indpls., 2004—06. Contbg. editor Ency. of Venture Capital; bd. trustees Keck Grad. Inst. (KGI), 2006—. Editor: Pa. Law Sch. Review. Mem.: NY State Bar Assn., Assn. of the Bar of the City of NY, ABA. Mailing: Keck Grad Inst 535 Watson Dr Claremont CA 91711

KUSHNER, JEFFREY L., manufacturing executive; b. Wilmington, Del., Apr. 7, 1948; s. William and Selma (Kreger) K.; m. Carolyn Patricia Hypes, May 2, 1975; children: Tawnya Lynne. BBA summa cum laude, U. Hawaii, 1970; MBA, Columbia U., 1972. Sr. fin. analyst Black & Decker, Towson, Md., 1972-73, div. controller Solon, Ohio, 1973-74; asst. div. controller Rockwell Internat., Pitts., 1974-75; div. contr. Carborundum Corp., Niagara Falls, NY, 1975-77; mgr. fin. planning United Techs. Corp., Hartford, Conn., 1977-80, corp. v.p. fin. planning, 1986-88, corp. v.p. asset mgmt., 1989-92; asst. contr. Sikorsky Aircraft, Stratford, Conn., 1980-82, div. controller, 1982-83, v.p. fin., chief fin. officer, 1983-85; v.p. fin. and adminstrn. MasterBrand Industries Inc., Deerfield, Ill., 1993-98; sr. v.p. fin. and CFO Lorillard Tobacco Co., 1998; exec. v.p., CFO Cookson Electronics, 1999—2005; ret., 2005. Bd. dirs. ACR, Hartford, 1987-88. Recipient Bronfman Found. fellowship, 1970-71. Mem. Conf. Bd. (coun. 1987-88), Fin. Execs. Inst. Home: 195 Woodland Rd Westwood MA 02090-2631 Business E-Mail: jlk95@columbia.edu.

KUSHNER, MARK JAY, engineering and physics educator, dean; s. Leonard Harry and Muriel (Chelin) K. BA, BS, UCLA, 1976; MS, Calif. Inst. Tech., 1977, PhD, 1979. Postdoctoral Calif. Inst. Tech., Pasadena, 1979-80; physicist Sandia Nat. Labs, Albuquerque, 1980-81, Lawrence Livermore (Calif.) Nat. Labs, 1981-83; dir. electron, atomic and molecular physics Spectra Tech., Bellevue, Wash., 1983-86; prof., Founder prof. engring. U. Ill., Urbana, 1986—2004; dean, Coll. Engring. Iowa St. U., 2005—, Melsa Prof. Engring., 2005—. Chairperson Gaseous Electronics Conf., 1996-98, Gordon Rsch. Conf. Plasma Processing Sci., 2002-04; mem. plasma sci. com. NRC, 1998-2003. Assoc. editor Transactions Plasma Sci., 1989-; editl. bd. Plasma Sources Sci. and Tech., 1991-, Jour. Vacuum Sci. & Tech. A, 1998-2000, Jour. Phys. D, 2004—, Plasma Processes and Polymers, 2004—; Plasma Chemistry and Plasma Processing, 2006-; contbr. over 230 articles to tech. jours. Recipient Tech. Excellence award, Semiconductor Rsch. Corp., 1995. Fellow IEEE (Plasma Sci. and Applications award 2000), Am. Phys. Soc., Optical Soc. Am., Inst. Physics, Am. Vacuum Soc. (Plasma Sci. and Tech. award 1999), Japanese Soc. Advancement Sci.; mem. Materials Rsch. Soc., Am. Soc. Engring. Edn., Soc. Women Engrs. Office: Iowa St Univ Coll Engring 104 Marston Hall Ames IA 50011-2151 Office Phone: 515-294-9988. Business E-Mail: mjk@iastate.edu.

KUTA, JEFFREY THEODORE, lawyer; b. Oak Park, Ill., Aug. 30, 1947; s. Stanley Joseph and Helen Mary (Terpin) K.; m. Diane LaVerne Jancovic, June 22, 1969; children: Jonathan Paul, Joseph Anthony. BA with honors, U. Chgo., 1969, JD, 1972. Bar: Ill. 1972, U.S. Dist. Ct. (no. dist.) Ill. 1972. Assoc. Hopkins & Sutter, Chgo., 1972-76; assoc. to ptnr. Newman, Stahl & Shadur, Chgo., 1976-80; ptnr. Holleb & Coff, Chgo., 1981—2000, Schiff Hardin LLP, Chgo., 2000—. Instr. Chgo. Kent Coll. Law, 1978-79; adj. prof. John Marshall Law Sch., 1996—. Sec. Chgo. Equity Fund, Inc., 1985-2000; sec. Nat. Equity Fund, Inc., 1987-89, sec. Cmty. Reinvestment Fund, Inc., 1997—. Mng. editor U. Chgo. Law Rev., 1971-72. Mem. ABA (mem. spl. com. on housing and urban devel. law 1987-91, editor ABA Jour. Affordable Housing and Cmty. Devel. Law 1991-93, mem. governing com. of forum on affordable housing and cmty. devel. law 1992-95, chmn. 1993-94), Chgo. Bar Assn. (chmn. mag. 1982-83), Chgo. Coun. Lawyers, U. Chgo. Alumni Assn. (v.p. 1973-76, chmn. law jour. 1973-76), Lambda Alpha Internat. Home: 442 W Melrose St Chicago IL 60657-3834 Office Phone: 312-258-5777.

KUTLER, STANLEY IRA, historian, lawyer, educator; b. Cleve., Aug. 10, 1934; s. Robert P. and Zelda R. (Coffman) K.; m. Sandra J. Sachs, June 24, 1956; children: Jeffrey, David, Susan, Andrew. BA, Bowling Green State U., 1956; PhD, Ohio State U., 1960. Instr. history Pa. State U., State College, 1960-62; asst. prof. San Diego State U., 1962-64; from asst. prof. to prof. U. Wis., Madison, 1964-80, E. Gordon Fox prof. Am. instns., law and history, 1980—. Disting. exchange scholar to China Nat. Acad. Scis., 1982; Kenneth Keating lectr. Tel Aviv U., 1984; sr. Fulbright lectr. to Japan, 1977, to Israel, 1985, China, 1986; disting. vis. Fulbright scholar, Peru, 1987; Bicentennial prof. Tel Aviv U., 1985; cons. NEH, 1975—, The Constitution Project, 1985—; disting. chair Polit. Sci., U. Bologna, 1991; hist. cons. BBC/Discovery series Watergate, 1994. Author: Judicial Power and Reconstruction, 1968, Privilege and Creative Destruction, 1971, 2d edit., 1990, The American Inquisition, 1983, The Wars of Watergate: The Last Crisis of Richard Nixon, 1990, 92, Abuse of Power: The ew Nixon Tapes, 1997; editor: Supreme Court and the Constitution, 1969, 3d edit., 1984, Looking for America, 1975, 80, The Encyclopedia of the Vietnam War, 1995, Encyclopedia of 20th Century America, 1995, American Perspectives: Historians on Historians, 1996, Watergate: The Fall of Richards Nixon, 1996, Dictionary of American History, 10 vols., 1996—; founding editor Rev. in Am. History, 1972-97; mem. adv. editor Greenwood Pub., 1968-73, Johns Hopkins U. Press, 1982—. Recipient Silver Gavel award ABA; fellow Sage Found., 1967-68, Emmy award, 1994, Peabody award, 1994, Best Reference Work award, Am. Assn. Pubs., 1996; fellow Guggenheim Found., 1971-72, Rockefeller Found., 1979-80. Jewish. Office: U Wis Dept History Madison WI 53706 Business E-Mail: sikutler@wisc.edu.

KUTZ, KENNETH L., district attorney; b. Hibbing, Minn., Oct. 20, 1953; s. Leroy Dennis and Rosemary Helen (Marold) K.; m. Mary Patricia McConnell, July 18, 1981; children: Brian, Sean, Brendan. BA, U. Minn., Duluth, 1976; JD, Marquette U. Law Sch., Milw., 1979. Bar: Wis. 1979, U.S. Dist. Ct. (ea. dist., we. dist.) Wis. 1979. Assoc. atty. Sorenson Law Office, Ripon, Wis., 1979-83; asst. dist. atty. Burnett Cty. Dist. Atty., Siren, Wis., 1983-86, dist. atty., 1987—. Mem., past chmn. Burnett Cty. Dem. Party, Siren, 1983—; dir. Cmty. Referral Agy., Milltown, 1986-90;, mem. bd. Burnett Med. Ctr. 1993-1998, 2002—, bd. pres. Burnett Med. Ctr. 1996-1998, Grantsburg, Wis., 1993—. Recipient Integrity award U.S. Inspector Gen's. Office, Chgo., 1993. Mem. Wis. Bar Assn., Wis. Dist. Atty's. Assn. Democrat. Roman Catholic. Home: PO Box 231 Grantsburg WI 54840-0231 Office: Burnett Cty Dist Atty 7410 County Road K Ste 113 Siren WI 54872-9067

KUWAYAMA, S. PAUL, physician, immunologist, allergist; b. Sapporo, Hokkaido, Japan, Nov. 8, 1932; s. Satoru and Chiyoko (Nishikawa) K.; m. Barbara Ann Dresback, June 29, 1974; children: David, Steven, Jason. BS, Hokkaido U., Sapporo, 1955, MD, 1959. Diplomate Am. Bd. Pediatrics, 1965, Am. Bd. Allergy & Immunology, 1972, Am. Bd. Pediatric Allergy, 1970; lic. Nat. Bd. Med. Examiners of Japan, 1960, Wis. State Bd. Med. Examiners, 1968, Ariz. State Bd. Med. Examiners, 1987, N.Mex. State Bd. Med. Examiners, 1987, Tenn. State Bd. Med. Examiners, 1992. Intern U.S. Naval Hosp., Yokosuka, 1959-60, St. Mary's Hosp., Milw., 1960-61; jr. resident in pediatrics Temple U. Sch. of Medicine, Phila., 1961-62; chief pediat. resident W.Va. U. Sch. of Medicine, Morgantown, 1962-63; postdoctoral fellow in immunology, jr. fellow in pediatric allergy The Children's Mercy Hosp.-U. Kans. Sch. of Medicine, Kansas City, 1964-65; staff pediatrician Atomic Bomb Casualty Commn. in Hiroshima, U.S. Nat. Acad. of Scis.-U.S. Atomic Energy Commn., 1966-67; sr. pediatric allergist, dept. immunobiology U. Kans. Sch. of Medicine, 1967-68. Asst. clin. prof. pediatric allergy and immunology Med. Coll. Wis., Milw., 1970—. Contbg. author texts and forward to books. Fulbright scholar, 1960-63. Fellow Am. Acad. Pediat. (sect. on allergy and immunology), Am. Coll. Allergy, Asthma and Immunology, Am. Assn. Cert. Allergists, Am. Acad. Allergy, Asthma and Immunology, Am. Assn. Clin. Immunology and Allergy; mem. AMA, Fulbright Scholarship Grantee Alumni Assn., Milw. Pediatric Soc. Office: 11035 W Forest Home Ave Hales Corners WI 53130-2541

KUZMAN, ROBERT DANIEL, state representative; Grad., Ball State U., 1989, Thomas Cooley Law Sch., 1993. Atty.; state rep. dist. 19 Ind. Ho. of Reps., Indpls., 1996—, vice chmn. judiciary com., mem. environ. affairs, and pub. policy ethics and vets. affairs coms. Democrat. Office: Ind Ho of Reps 200 W Washington St Indianapolis IN 46204-2786

KUZNESOF, ELIZABETH ANNE, history educator; BA, U. Wash., 1961, MA, 1968; PhD, U. Calif., Berkeley, 1976. Vis. prof. history U. Kans., Lawrence, 1976-77, asst. prof. history, 1977-80, assoc. prof., 1980-85, prof., 1985—, asst. prof. history, 1977-80, assoc. prof., 1981-87, prof., 1987—, dir. L.Am. Studies, 1992—. Author: Household Economy and Urban Development in Sao Paulo 1765 to 1836, 1986; guest editor, author Jour. Family History, 1985; contbr. articles to profl. jours. Numerous fellowships and grants NEH, 1980, 91, Social Sci. Rsch. Coun., 1991-92, Fulbright/S.Am. Today Grant, 1986, Fulbright Tchg. Rsch. Grant to Brazil, 1988; Tinker fellow, 1981-82; John Carter Brown Libr., Hall Found. for Humanities, 1985-86, Utah Eccles Fellowship, 1991-92. Office: Univ of Kansas Ctr Latin Am Studies Lawrence KS 66045-0001

KVALSETH, TARALD ODDVAR, mechanical engineer, educator; b. Brunkeberg, Telemark, Norway, Nov. 7, 1938; married; 3 children. BS, U. Durham, King's Coll., Eng., 1963; MS, U. Calif., Berkeley, 1966, PhD, 1971. Rsch. asst. engring. expt. sta. U. Colo., Boulder, 1963-64, tchg. asst. dept. mech. engring.; mech. engr. Williams & Lane Inc., Berkeley, Calif., 1964-65; rsch. asst. dept. indsl. engring. and ops. rsch. U. Calif., Berkeley, 1965-71, rsch. fellow, 1973; asst. prof. Sch. Indsl. and Systems Engring. Ga. Inst. Tech., Atlanta, 1971-74; sr. lectr. indsl. mgmt. div. Norwegian Inst. Tech. U. Trondheim, 1974-79, head indsl. mgmt. divsn., 1975-79; assoc. prof. dept. mech. engring. U. Minn., Mpls., 1979-82, prof., 1982—2005, prof. emeritus, 2005—. Guest worker NASA Ames Research Ctr., Calif., 1973; mem. organizing com. 1st Berkeley-Monterey Conf. Timespan, Pay and Discretionary Capacity, 1973; steering com. Internat. Conf. Human Factors in Design and Op. Ships, Gothenburg, Sweden, 1977; gen. session chmn. Conf. Work Place Design and Work Environ. Problems, Trondheim, 1978; presenter in field. Contbr. articles to profl. jours., chapters to books. Fellow AAAS; mem. IEEE, Inst. Indsl. Engrs. (sr.), Human Factors and Ergonomics Soc. (pres. upper Midwest chpt.), Nordic Ergonomics Soc. (coun. 1977-80), Internat. Ergonomics Assn. (gen. coun. 1977-80, v.p. 1982-85), Ergonomics Soc., Psychonomic Soc., Am. Psychol. Soc., Am. Statis. Assn., Math. Assn. Am., Sigma Xi. Lutheran. Achievements include patents in field. Home: 4980 Shady Island Cir Mound MN 55364 Office: U Minn Dept Mech Engring Minneapolis MN 55455 Office Phone: 612-625-5051. Business E-Mail: kvals001@umn.edu.

KWAN, NESITA, newscaster; b. Canada; BA English, U. Va. Reporter Sta. WINA-AM, Charlottesville, Va., 1986; anchor, reporter Sta. WDBJ-TV, Roanoke, Va., 1987—90; co-anchor, reporter Sta. WVEC-TV, Norfolk, Va., 1990—92; co-anchor weekend news Sta. KHOU-TV, Houston, 1992—94; co-anchor weekend evening edition BC 5 Chgo. News, 1994, co-anchor weekday morning show, anchor late night news. Office: NBC 454 N Columbus Dr Chicago IL 60611

KWONG, EVA, artist, educator; b. Hong Kong, 1954; came to the U.S., 1967; d. Tony and Ivory Kwong; m. Kirk Mangus, 1976; children: Una, Jasper. BFA, RISD, 1975; MFA, Tyler Sch. Art/Temple U., Phila., 1977. Vis. artist, 1977—; vis. faculty Cleve. Inst. Art, 1982-83; part-time faculty U. Akron, Ohio, 1987, 89, 95, Kent (Ohio) State U., 1990—. Lectr. in field. Works in over 300 exhbns. Visual Arts Regional fellow Arts Midwest, Mpls., 1987, Visual Arts fellow Nat. Endowment for the Arts, Washington, 1988, Ohio Arts Coun., Columbus, 1988, 94, 99, 2004, Ohio Arts Coun. fellow in visual arts, 2004; recipient Internat. award China NCECA, 2003. Mem. Nat. Coun. on Edn. for the Ceramic Arts (dir.-at-large 1995-97).

KYFF, KIMBERLY, elementary school educator; BA in Edn., Univ. Mich., Dearborn, 1979; M in Art of Tchg., Marygrove Coll., 1999. Cert. middle childhood generalist at. Bd. Tchg. Standards, 2003. Tchr., 1987—, Jamieson Elem. Sch., Detroit, 1996—. Facilitator, master's edn. program Univ. Phoenix, Southfield, Mich. named Mich. Tchr. of Yr., 2007. Office: Jamieson Elem Sch 2900 W Philadelphia Detroit MI 48206 Personal E-mail: kimberyff@aol.com.

KYLE, KIMBERLY, lawyer; b. Lexington, Ky., June 27, 1975; BA in Hist., Ohio State U., 1997, BA in Polit. Sci., 1997; JD, U. Cin., 2000. Bar: Ohio 2000, Ky. 2001, US Dist. Ct. Southern Dist. Ohio 2001, US Dist. Ct. Eastern Dist. Ky. 2001, US Ct. of Appeals Sixth Cir. 2002. Assoc. Kohnen & Patton LLP, Cin. amed one of Ohio's Rising Stars, Super Lawyers, 2006, 2007. Mem.: Ky. Bar Assn., Ohio State Bar Assn., Cin. Bar Assn. Office: Kohnen & Patton LLP PNC Ctr Ste 800 201 E Fifth St Cincinnati OH 45202 Office Phone: 513-381-0656. Office Fax: 513-381-5823.

KYLE, RICHARD HOUSE, federal judge; b. St. Paul, Apr. 30, 1937; s. Richard E. and Geraldine (House) K.; m. Jane Foley, Dec. 22, 1959; children: Richard H. Jr., Michael F., D'Arcy, Patrick G., Kathleen. BA, U. Minn., 1959, LLB, 1962. Bar: Minn. 1962, U.S. Dist. Ct. Minn. 1992. Atty. Briggs and Morgan, St. Paul, 1963-68, 1970-92; solicitor gen. Minn. Atty. Gen. Office, St. Paul, 1968-70; judge U.S. Dist. Ct., St. Paul, 1992—. Pres. Minn. Law Rev., Mpls., 1962. Mem. Minn. State Bar Assn., Ramsey County Bar Assn. Office: Federal Courts Bldg 316 Robert St N Saint Paul MN 55101-1495 E-mail: rhkyle@mnd.uscourts.gov.

KYLE, ROBERT ARTHUR, medical educator, oncologist; b. Bottineau, ND, Mar. 17, 1928; s. Arthur Nichol and Mabel Caroline (Crandall) K.; m. Charlene Mae Showalter, Sept. 11, 1954; children: John, Mary, Barbara, Jean. AA, N.D Sch. Forestry, 1946; BS, U. N.D., 1948; MD, Northwestern U., 1952; MS, U. Minn., 1958. Diplomate Am. Bd. Internal Medicine; subsplty. Hematology. Fellow Mayo Grad. Sch., Rochester, Minn., 1953-59; clin. asst. Tufts U. Sch. Medicine, Boston, 1960-61; cons. internal medicine Mayo Clinic, Rochester, 1961—; prof. medicine and lab. medicine Mayo Med. Sch., Rochester, 1975—. Pres. med. subjects unit Am. Topical Assn., Johnstown, Pa., 1976-81; chmn. standards, ethics and peer rev. orgn. Cancer & Acute Leukemia Group B, Scarsdale, NY, 1978-82; Robert A. Hettig lectr. in hematology Baylor U. Coll. Medicine, Houston, 1984; Waldenström lectr., Stockholm, 1988; Redlich Meml. lectr Cedars-Sinai Med. Ctr., U. Calif., LA; vis. prof. St. Elizabeth's Med. Ctr., Tufts U. Sch. Medicine, Boston, 1998 Author: The Monoclonal Gammopathies, 1976, Medicine and Stamps, vols. 1 and 2, 1980, vol. 3, 2004; author, editor: Neoplastic Disease of the Blood, 4th edit., 2003, Myeloma: Biology and Management, 1995, 3rd edit. 2004 Chmn. bd. trustees First Presbyn. Ch., Rochester, Minn., 1967; chmn. Rochester Med. Ctr. Ministry, 1979-86; chmn. adv. bd. Internat. Waldenstrom's Macroglobulinemia Found. Capt. USAF, 1955-57. Named Disting. Topicl Philatelest, Am. Topical Soc., 1982; Recipient Waldenström award Internat. Workshop for Myeloma, Italy, 1991, Henry S. Plummer Distinguished Internist award Mayo Clin., 1995, Mayo Distinguished Clinician award 1996, Sioux award U. N.D., 1998, Robert A. Kyle Lifetime Achievement award IMF, 2003, Mayo Clinic Disting. Alumni award, 2005; Bruce Wiseman lectr. Ohio State U., 1991, Kauffman Meml. lectr. Meml. Sloan Kettering Med. Ctr., N.Y.C., 1997; Clement Finch prof. U. Wash., 1993, Joseph Michaeti award for Myeloma, 2006, David A. Karnofsky award and Lectr., ASCO, 2007. Master ACP; mem. Royal Coll. Pathologists (hon.), N.Y. Acad. Scis., Am. Soc. Hematology, Internat. Soc. Hematology (sec.-gen. Inter-Am. divsn. 1990-96), Am. Assn. Cancer Rsch., Internat. Myeloma Found. (chmn. sci. adv. bd. 1995), Internat. Soc. Amyloidosis (pres. 2001-), Phi Beta Kappa. Republican. Avocation: stamp collecting/philately. Home: 1207 6th St SW Rochester MN 55902-1918 Office: Mayo Clinic 200 1st St SW Rochester MN 55905-0002 also: 6-26 Stabile Rochester MN 55905-0001 Home Phone: 507-285-9138; Office Phone: 507-284-3039. Business E-Mail: kyle.robert@mayo.edu.

KYLE, ROBERT CAMPBELL, II, publishing executive; b. Cleve., Jan. 6, 1935; s. Charles Donald and Mary Alice (King) K.; children: Peter F., Kit C., Scott G. BS, U. Colo., 1956; MA, Case Western Res. U., 1958; MBA, Harvard U., 1963, DBA, 1966. Ptnr. McLagan & Co., Chgo., 1966-67; founder, pres. Devel. Sys. Corp. (subs. Longman Group USA), Chgo., 1967-82; pres. Longman Group USA, Chgo., 1982-89; chmn., CEO Dearborn Pub. Group, Inc. (formerly Longman Group USA), 1989-98. Chmn. CTS Fin. Pub., 1997-2000. Author: Property Management, 1979; co-author: Modern Real Estate Practice, 1967, How to Profit From Real Estate, 1988 (Chgo. Book Clinic Lifetime Achievement award 1998). Mem. dean's adv. coun. Coll. Bus. U. Colo., 1992-98, Ctr. for Entrepreneurship Adv. Bd., U. Colo., 1996-2002; trustee Mystic Seaport Mus., 1989—, exec. com., 1999—2004, vice chair, 2001—2004; dir. Chgo. Maritime Soc., pres. 1999-2000; trustee The Burnham Inst., 2002—, San Diego Maritime Mus., 2002—, exec. com., 2003—, chair audit com., 2003—. Mem. Real Estate Educators Assn. (pres. 1981), Internat. Assn. Fin. Planning, Chgo. Book Clinic (bd. dirs.), Harvard Club NY, Chgo. Econs. Club, San Diego Yacht Club (chair history com. 2004—, bd. dirs. 2006—), Y Yacht Club, Explorers Club, Rotary. Avocations: yacht racing, skiing. Home: 2910 Owens St San Diego CA 92106 E-mail: rckyle@aol.com.

LABAN, MYRON MILES, physician, hospital administrator; b. Detroit, Mar. 9, 1936; s. Larry Max and Mary Marsha (Harris) LaBan; m. Rita Joyce Hochman, Aug. 17, 1958; children: Terry, Amy, Craig. BA, U. Mich., Ann Arbor, 1957, MD, 1967; M.Med. Sci., Ohio State U., Columbus, 1965. Diplomate Am. Bd. Phys. Medicine and Rehab. Intern Sinai Hosp., Detroit, 1961-62; resident Ohio State U. Hosp., 1962-65; assoc. dir. phys. medicine and rehab. Letterman Gen. Hosp., San Francisco, 1965-67; dir. phys. medicine and rehab. William Beaumont Hosp., Royal Oak, Mich., 1967—; Licht lectr. Ohio State U., 1986, clin. prof., 1993. Bd. dirs. Oakland County Med. Bd., Birmingham, Mich., 1982—87; clin. prof. Oakland U., Rochester, Mich., 1983, Wayne State U., Detroit, 1990, Ohio State U., Columbus, 1992; rep. to Commn. Phys. Medicine and Rehab. Mich. State Med. Soc. Contbr. chapters to books, articles to profl. jours. Med. dir. Oakland County March of Dimes, Mich., 1969—83; pres. Bloomfield Art Ctr., 2003—. Served to capt. US Army, 1965—67. Fellow: Am. Acad. Phys. Medicine and Rehab. (bd. dirs. 1980, pres. 1985—86, Bernard Baruch Rsch. award 1961, R. Rosenthal Rsch. award 1982, Zeiter lectureship, Disting. Clinician award 1991, Top Doc PM& R Detroit Monthly 1993, 1996, Frank H. Krusen award 1997); mem.: AMA, Mich. Acad. Phys. Med. and Rehab. (pres. 1982—84, jud. commr. 1991—95, mem. editl. bd. Jour. Phys. Med. and Rehab.), Mich. State Med. Soc., Oakland County Med. Soc. (treas. 1983, pres.-elect 1987, pres. 1988—89), Am. Assn. Electromyography adn Electrodiagnosis (program dir. 1972), Am. Congress Rehab. Medicine. Republican. Jewish. Avocations: gardening, model building. Office: LMT Rehabilitation Assocs 3535 W 13 Mile Rd Rm 703 Royal Oak MI 48073-6710 Home Phone: 248-642-2547; Office Phone: 248-288-2210. Personal E-mail: myjoy@comcast.net.

LABUDDE, ROY CHRISTIAN, lawyer; b. Milw., July 21, 1921; s. Roy Lewis and Thea (Otteson) LaB.; m. Anne P. Held, June 7, 1952; children: Jack, Peter, Michael, Susan, Sarah. AB, Carleton Coll., 1943; JD, Harvard U., 1949. Bar: Wis. 1949, U.S. Dist. Ct. (ea. and we. dists.) Wis. 1950, U.S. Ct. Appeals (7th cir.) 1950, U.S. Supreme Ct. 1957. Assoc. Michael, Best & Friedrich, Milw., 1949-57, ptnr., 1958—. Dir. DEC-Inter, Inc., Milw. Western Bank, Western Bancshares, Inc., Superior Die Set Corp., Aunt Nellie's Farm Kitchens, Inc. Bd. dirs. Wis. Hist. Soc. Found.; chmn., bd. dirs. Milw. div. Am. Cancer Soc. Served to lt. j.g. USNR, 1943-46. Mem. Milw. Estate Planning Coun. (past pres.), Wis. Bar Assn., Wis. State Bar Attys. (chmn. tax sch., bd. dirs. taxation sect.), Univ. Club, Milw. Club, Milw. Country Club. Republican. Episcopalian. Home: 4201 W Stonefield Rd Mequon WI 53092-2771 Office: Michael Best & Friedrich 100 E Wisconsin Ave Ste 3300 Milwaukee WI 53202-4108

LACEY, GARY EUGENE, lawyer; b. Scottsbluff, Nebr., Oct. 2, 1942; s. Harold Kenneth and Chelsa (Hiatt) L.; m. Carol Leitschuck, June 6, 1965 (div. Nov. 1992); children: David, Anne; m. Janet England, July, 1993. BA, U. Nebr., 1965, JD, 1971. Bar: Nebr. 1972, U.S. Dist. Ct. Nebr. 1972, U.S. Ct. Appeals (8th cir.) 1980. Econ. reporter So. Ill., Carbondale, 1965-66; staff atty. Centel Corp., Lincoln, Nebr., 1971-75; dep. county atty. Lancaster County, Lincoln, Nebr., 1975-90, county atty., 1991—. Prosecutor Lancaster County, Lincoln, 1990—; bd. dirs. YMCA, Lincoln, 1989—. 1st lt. U.S. Army, 1967-69. Mem. Nebr. County Atty. Assn. (bd. dirs. 1985—), Nebr. Bar Assn. (Ho. of Dels. 1986-90), Univ. Club, Shriners, Masons. Republican. Methodist. Avocations: reading, writing, politics, cooking. Office: Lancaster County Atty 555 S 10th St Lincoln NE 68508-2810

LACH, JOSEPH THEODORE, physicist; b. Chgo., May 12, 1934; s. Joseph and Kate (Ziemba) L.; m. Barbara Ryan, June 26, 1965; children— Michael, Elizabeth AB, U. Chgo., 1953, MS, 1956; PhD, U. Calif.-Berkeley, 1963. Rsch. assoc. in physics Yale U., Hew Haven, 1963-65, asst. prof. physics, 1966-69; physicist Fermi Nat. Accelerator Lab., Batavia, Ill., 1969—, chmn. dept. physics, 1974-75; chmn. Gordon Rsch. Conf. in Elem. Particle Physics, 1975. Mem. joint rsch. program with USSR and People's Republic of China. Fellow Am. Phys. Soc., Physicians for Social Responsibility, Ill. Geol. Survey (rsch. affiliate). Home: 28w364 Indian Knoll Trl West Chicago IL 60185-3013 Office: Fermilab PO Box 500 Batavia IL 60510-0500 E-mail: lach@fnal.gov.

LACROSSE, JAMES, retail executive; b. 1932; BA, Wesleyan Univ., 1954; MBA, Harvard Univ., 1956. Miller Stevenson Chemical Co., 1956-59; Amerace-Ense Co., 1960-69; Bio-Dynamics Co. Inc., 1965-59; owner Nat. Wine & Spirits Corp., 1973—, pres., CEO, CFO, chmn. bd. dirs., 1991—. Office: Nat Wine & Spirits Corp 700 W Morris St PO Box 1602 Indianapolis IN 46206-1602

LACY, ALAN JASPER, retired retail executive; b. Cleveland, Tenn., Oct. 19, 1953; s. W. Jasper Lacy and Mary (Leigh) Lou; m. Caron Lacy. BSIM, Ga. Inst. Tech., 1975; MBA, Emory U., 1977. CFA. Fin. analyst Holiday Inns, Inc., Memphis, 1977-79; mgr. investor rels. Tiger Internat., LA, 1979-80, Dart Industries, LA, 1980-81; dir. corp. fin. Dart & Kraft, Northbrook, Ill., 1981-82, asst. treas., 1982-83, treas., v.p., 1984-86, v.p. fin. and adminstrn. internat., 1987-88; v.p., treas., CFO Minnetonka Corp., Bloomington, Minn., 1988-89; sr. v.p. strategy and devel. Kraft Gen. Foods, Glenview, Ill., 1989-90, sr. v.p. fin., 1990-92, sr. v.p. fin., strategy, sys., 1992-93; v.p. fin. svcs. and sys. Philip Morris Cos., Glenview, Ill., 1993-95; exec. v.p., CFO Sears, Roebuck & Co., Hoffman Estates, Ill., 1995-97, pres, Sears credit, 1997—99, pres., services, 1999—2000, pres., CEO, 2000—05, chmn., 2000—05; vice chmn. Sears Holdings Corp., Hoffman Estates, Ill., 2005—06. Bd. dir. Western Union. Trustee Nat. Pks. Conservation Assn., Field Mus. Natural History. Mem. Econ. Club (Chgo.).

LACY, ANDRE BALZ, industrial executive; b. Indpls., Sept. 12, 1939; s. Howard J. Lacy II and Edna B. (Balz) Lacy; m. Julia Lello, Feb. 23, 1963; children: Mark William, Peter Lello, John Andre. BA Econs., Denison U.; DEng (hon.), Rose-Hulman Inst. Various mgmt. positions U.S. Corrugated, Indpls., 1961-69, exec. v.p., 1969-72; exec. v.p., chief ops. officer Lacy Diversified Industries, Indpls., 1972-78, chmn. bd. subs., 1973-78, pres., chief ops. officer, 1978-83; pres., chief exec. officer Lacy Diversified Industries, now LDI, Ltd., Indpls., 1983—, chmn., 1992. Bd. dirs. Herff Jones, Inc., Indpls., Patterson Dental Co., Mpls., Nat. Bank Indpls. Chmn. United Way Greater Indpls., 1989—91; Mem. bd. mgrs. Rose-Hulman Inst., Terre Haute, Ind.; pres. Indpls. Bd. Sch. Commn., Indpls., 1985—86; hon. mem. 500 Festival Assocs., Inc., Indpls.; bd. dirs. Indpls. Conv. and Visitors Assn., 1996; dir. Ctrl. Ind. Corp. Partnership, Indpls. Downtown, Inc. Mem.: Nat. Assn. Wholesaler Distbrs. (dir.), Ind. Pres. Orgn., Kiwanis Club of Indpls., Young Pres. Orgn., Ind. C. of C. (bd. dirs. 1989), Columbia Club, Meridian Hills Golf and Country Club (Indpls.), Lost Tree Club. Republican. Episcopalian. Avocation: sailing. Home: 450 E Vermont St Indianapolis IN 46202-3680 Office: LDI Ltd 54 Monument Cir Ste 800 Indianapolis IN 46204-2928

LACY, STEPHEN M., publishing and broadcasting executive; m. Cathy Lacy; 2 children. B in acctg., Kans. State U., 1976, M in acctg., 1977. CPA. Sr. audit mgr. Deloitte & Touche, Des Moines, Kansas City, Mo.; v.p., CFO Commtron Corp., Des Moines, 1986—92; with Johnson & Higgins/Kirke-Van Orsdel Inc., Des Moines, 1992—98, v.p., CFO, exec. v.p., pres.; v.p., CFO Meredith Corp., Des Moines, 1998—2000, pres. mktg. group, 2000, COO, pres. publ. group, 2004—06, pres., CEO, 2006—. Bd. dirs. Advt. Coun. Chair bd. dirs. United Way Cent. Iowa; bd. dirs. Am. Red Cross, Jr. Achievement Cent. Iowa. Named Publ. Exec. Yr., Advt. Age, 2003. Mem.: Direct Mktg. Assn. (bd. dirs., exec. com., treas.). Office: Meredith Corp 1716 Locust St Des Moines IA 50309-3023

LADD, JEFFREY RAYMOND, lawyer; b. Mpls., Apr. 10, 1941; s. Jasper Raymond and Florence Marguerite (DeMarce) L.; m. Kathleen Anne Crosby, Aug. 24, 1963; children: Jeffrey Raymond, John Henry, Mark Jasper, Matthew Crosby. Student, U. Vienna, Austria; BA, Loras Coll.; postgrad., U. Denver; JD, Ill. Inst. Tech. Bar: Ill. 1973, U.S. Dist. Ct. 1973. V.p. mktg. Ladd Enterprises, Des Plaines, Ill., 1963-66, v.p. mktg. and fin. Crystal Lake, Ill., 1966-70; ptnr. Ross & Hardies, Chgo., 1973-81, Boodell, Sears, et al., 1981-86, Bell, Boyd & Lloyd, Chgo., 1986—. Spl. asst. atty. gen. for condemnation State of Ill., 1977-82; chmn. Metra, 1984-2006. Mem., chmn. Ill. Bd. Govs. of State Colls. and Univs., 1972—75; mem. bd. regents Loras Coll., 2003—; del. 6th Ill. Constnl. Conv., 1969—70. Recipient W. Graham Claytor, Jr. award for disting. svc. to passenger transp., 1995, Disting. Svc. award IIT/Chgo.-Kent Law Sch., 1997; named Citizen of Yr., Chgo. City Club, 1995. Mem. ABA, Chgo. Bar Assn., Nat. Assn. Bond Lawyers, Ill. Assn. Hosp. Attys., Am. Acad. Hosp. Attys., Am. Health Lawyers Assn., Crystal Lake Jaycees (Disting. Svc. award), Crystal Lake C. of C. (past pres.), Econ. Club, Legal Club, Union League Club, Bull Valley Golf Club, Woodstock Country Club, Lambda Alpha. Roman Catholic. Avocations: golf, hunting, fishing, tennis, skiing. Office: Bell Boyd & Lloyd 3 First National Pla 70 W Madison St Ste 3100 Chicago IL 60602-4284

LADEHOFF, LEO WILLIAM, metal products manufacturing executive; b. Gladbrook, Iowa, May 4, 1932; s. Wendell Leo and Lillian A. L.; m. Beverly Joan Dreessen, Aug. 1, 1951; children: Debra K., Lance A. BS, U. Iowa, 1957. Supt. ops. Square D Co., 1957-61; mfg. mgr. Fed. Pacific Electric Co., 1961; v.p. ops. Avis Indsl. Corp., 1961-67; pres. energy products Group Gulf & Western Industries, Inc., 1967-78; chmn. bd., pres., chief exec. officer, dir. Amcast Indsl. Corp., Ohio, 1978-95, chmn. bd. dirs. Ohio, 1995—97, Ohio, 2001—02. With USAF, 1951—54, Korea. Mem. Soc. Automotive Engrs., U. Iowa Alumni Assn., Forest Highlands Country Club, The Estancia Club, Pinnacle Peak Country Club. Republican. also: Elkhart Products Corp 1255 Oak St Elkhart IN 46514-2277 E-mail: lladehoff@aol.com.

LADSON-BILLINGS, GLORIA J., education educator; BA, Stanford U., 1984. Prof. urban edn. Dept. Curriculum and Instrn. U. Wis., Madison, project dir. Wis. Ctr. Edn. Rsch.; vis. scholar Ctr. Advanced Study in Behavioral Sci., Stanford, Calif., 2003—04. Editor: Am. Edn. Rsch. Jour., sect. on teaching, learning & human devel.; author: The Dreamkeepers: Successful Teachers of African American Children, 1994; contbr. Fellow: Annenberg Inst. Sch. Reform, Brown U. (sr.); mem.: Nat. Acad. Edn. (mem. 2005—), Am. Edn. Rsch. Assn. (mem. 1989—, pres. 2005, coun. mem. at large, mem. profl. devel. and tng. com., Palmer O. Johnson award, Early Career award). Office: U Wis Sch Edn 464c Teacher Edn 225 N Mills St Madison WI 53706 Office Phone: 202-223-9485, 608-263-1006. Office Fax: 202-775-1824. E-mail: gjladson@facstaff.wisc.edu.

LADWIG, BONNIE L., state legislator; b. Dec. 11, 1939; married. Student, U. Wis. Mem. from dist. 63 Wis. State Assembly, Madison, 1992—. Mem. Racine County and Coastal Mgmt. Coun.; mem. County Human Svc. Bd., past chmn. Office: 6437 Norfolk Ln Racine WI 53406-1859

LAESSIG, RONALD HAROLD, preventive medicine and pathology educator, state official; b. Marshfield, Wis., Apr. 4, 1940; s. Harold John and Ella Louise L.; m. Joan Margaret Spreda, Jan. 29, 1966; 1 child, Elizabeth Susan. BS, U. Wis., Stevens Point, 1962; PhD, U. Wis., 1965. Cert. chem. chemist Nat. Registry Cert. Chemists, 1968. Jr. faculty Princeton (N.J.) U., 1966; chief clin. chemistry Wis. State Lab. Hygiene, Madison, 1966-80, dir., 1980—2007, emeritus dir., 2007; asst. prof. preventive medicine U. Wis., Madison, 1966-72, assoc. prof., 1972-76, prof., 1976—2007, emeritus prof., 2007, prof. pathology, 1980—. Cons. Ctrs. Disease Control, Atlanta, bd. sci. counselors Nat. Ctr. Environ. Health Ga., 2004-; dir. Nat. Com. for Clin. Lab. Stds., Villanova, Pa., 1977-80; chmn. invitro diagnostic products adv. com. FDA, 1974-75; mem. rev. com. Nat. Bur. Stds., 1983-86; legis. coun., State of Wis., 2003-04; chair Pub. Health Adv. Com., Wis., 2003-05, mem. 1998-. Mem. editl. bd. Analytical Chemistry, 1970-76, Health Lab. Sci., 1970-76, Med. Electronics, 1970-80; contbr. articles to profl. jours. Mem. State of Wis. Tech. Com. Alcohol and Traffic Safety, 1970-88; mem. adv. com. Newbon Screening, Wis. Recipient Excellence in Advocacy award, March of Dimes, 2004, APHL, Gold Std. for Pub. Health Excellence award, 2004; Sloan Found. grantee, 1966; recipient numerous grants. Mem. APHA (Difco award 1974), Am. Assn. Clin. Chemistry (chmn. safety com. 1984-86, bd. dirs. 1986-89, Natelson award 1989, Contbns. Svc. to Profession award 1990, Reiner award 1998, Eiler award 1999), Am. Soc. for Med. Tech., Nat. Com. Clin. Lab. Stds. (pres. 1980-82, bd. dirs. 1984-87), Assn. Pub. Health Labs. (chmn. environ. health com. 2001-04, Gold Std. Pub. Health Excellence award 2004), Nat. Ctr. Environ. Health/CDC (bd. counselors 2004-07), Sigma Xi. Avocation: woodworking. Office: State Lab Hygiene 465 Henry Mall Madison WI 53706-1578 Office Phone: 608-262-3911. Business E-Mail: rhl@mail.slh.wisc.edu.

LAFAVE, JOHN, state legislator; Mem. Wis. St. Assembly, 1993—. Home: 1129 N Jackson St Apt 1401 Milwaukee WI 53202-3268

LAFLEY, A.G. (ALAN GEORGE LAFLEY), consumer products company executive; b. Keene, NH, June 13, 1947; AB, Hamilton Coll., 1969; MBA, Harvard Bus. Sch., 1977. Brand asst. Joy The Procter & Gamble Co., 1977-78, sales tng. Denver Sales Dist., 1978-80, asst. brand mgr. Tide, 1978-80, brand mgr. Dawn & Ivory Snow, 1980-81, brand mgr. spl. assignment and Ivory Snow, 1981-82, brand mgr. Cheer, 1982-83, assoc. advt. mgr. PS&D Divsn. to advt. mgr., 1983-86, 86-88, gen. mgr. laundry products PS&D Divsn., 1988-91, v.p. laundry & cleaning products, 1991-92, group v.p., pres. laundry and cleaning products, 1992-94, group v.p., pres. Far East Divsn., 1994-95, exec. v.p., pres. Asia Divsn., 1995-98, exec. v.p., pres. N.Am. Divsn., 1998-99, pres. Global Beauty Care & North Am., 1999-2000, pres., CEO, 2000—, chmn., 2002—. Bd. dirs. The Procter & Gamble Co., 2000—, Gen. Electric Co., 2002—, Dell, Inc., 2006—. Co-author (with Ram Charan): The Game-Changer: How You Can Drive Revenue and Profit Growth with Innovation, 2008. Bd. dirs., United Negro Coll. Fund; bd. trustees Hamilton Coll., 2007-, US Coun. Internat. Bus., Xavier U., Cin. Playhouse in the Park, Cin. Symphony Orchestra, Cin. Inst. of Fine Arts, The Seven Hills Sch.; past mem. Am. C. of C. in Japan, adv. coun. Schulich Sch. of Bus., York U., Toronto. With USN, 1970-75. Named one of 25 Most Powerful People in Bus., Fortune Mag., 2007; recipient Golden Plate award, Acad. Achievement, 2004. Mem. Hamilton Club of So. Ohio, Harvard Club of Cin., Met. Club, Commonwealth Club of Cin. Office: The Procter & Gamble Co 1 Procter & Gamble Plz Cincinnati OH 45202-3315 E-mail: lafley.ag@pg.com.*

LAFLEY, ALAN GEORGE See LAFLEY, A.G.

LA FOLLETTE, DOUGLAS J., state official; b. Des Moines, June 6, 1940; s. Joseph Henry and Frances (Van der Wilt) La Follette. BS, Marietta Coll., 1963; MS, Stanford U., 1964; PhD, Columbia U., 1967. Asst. prof. chemistry and ecology U. Wis.-Parkside, 1969-72; mem. Wis. State Senate, 1973-75; sec. state State of Wis., Madison, 1975-79, 83—. Author: Wisconsin's Survival Handbook, 1971, The Survival Handbook, 1991. Mem. Coun. Econ. Priorities; mem. Lake Michigan Fed., Wis. Environ. Decade, 1971, S.E. Wis. Coalition for Clean Air, Dem. candidate for US Congress, 1970, for Wis. lt. gov., 1978, for US Senate, 1988. Recipient Environ. Quality EPA, 1976, Fulbright Disting. Am. scholar, 2003. Mem. Am. Fedn. Tchrs., Fedn. Am. Scientists, Phi Beta Kappa, Sierra Club (nat. bd. mem.). Democrat. Office: Office Sec of State PO Box 7848 Madison WI 53707-7848 Office Phone: 608-266-8888. Office Fax: 608-266-3159. E-mail: statesec@sos.state.wi.us.

LAGALLY, MAX GUNTER, physics professor; b. Darmstadt, Germany, May 23, 1942; came to U.S., 1953, naturalized, 1960; s. Paul and Herta (Rudow) L.; m. Shelley Meserow, Feb. 15, 1969; children: Eric, Douglas, Karsten BS in Physics, Pa. State U., 1963; MS in Physics, U. Wis.-Madison, 1965, PhD in Physics, 1968. Registered profl. engr., Wis. Instr. physics U. Wis., Madison, 1970-71, asst. prof. materials sci., 1971-74, assoc. prof., 1974-77, prof. materials sci. and physics, 1977—, dir. thin-film deposition and applications ctr., 1982-93, John Bascom Prof. materials sci., 1986—, E.W. Mueller Prof. materials sci. and physics, 1993—. Gordon Godfrey vis. prof. physics, U. New South Wales, Sydney, Australia, 1987; cons. in thin films, 1977—; vis. scientist Sandia Nat. Lab., Albuquerque, 1975; founder, pres. Piezomax Techs., Inc. (now nPoint, Inc.), 1997—, now chmn., chief sci. officer; founder, chmn., chief sci. officer Sonoplot, Inc., 2003—. Editor: Kinetics of Ordering and Growth at Surfaces, 1990, (with others) Methods of Experimental Physics, 1985, Evolution of Surface and Thin-Film Microstructure, 1993, Morphological Organization in Epitaxial Growth and Removal, 1998; mem. editl. bd., also editor spl. issue Jour. Vacuum Sci. and Tech., 1978-81; prin. editor Jour. Materials Rsch., 1990-93; mem. editl. bd. Surface Sci., 1994-2001, Revs. Sci. Instruments, 1997-2000, Diffusion and Defect Data, 1997-2002, Jour. Phys. D, 2004—, Nanotechnology Rsch. Letters, 2005-; contbr. articles to profl. jours.; patentee in field. Max Planck Gesellschaft fellow, 1968, Alfred P. Sloan Found. fellow, 1972, H.I. Romnes fellow, 1976, Humboldt Sr. Rsch. fellow, 1992, 93; grantee fed. agys. and industry; recipient Outstanding Sci. Alumnus award Pa. State U., 1996, Tibbetts award U.S. SBA, 2002. Fellow AAAS, Am. Phys. Soc. (D. Adler award 1994, Davisson-Germer prize 1995), Australian Inst. Physics, Am. Vacuum Soc. (M.W. Welch prize 1991, trustee 1995-97); mem. Materials Rsch. Soc. (medal 1994), Leopoldina-German Acad. Scis., Nat. Acad. Engring. Home: 5110 Juneau Rd Madison WI 53705-4744 Office: U Wis Materials Sci & Engring 1509 University Ave Madison WI 53706-1538 Office Phone: 608-263-2078. Personal E-mail: max.lagally@npoint.com. Business E-Mail: lagally@engr.wisc.edu. E-mail: lagally@sonoplot.com.

LAGANI, DANIEL, publishing executive; married; 2 children. BA, SUNY, Oneonta, 1985. Pub. George mag.; assoc. pub. New Woman mag. Primedia, 1994—96; assoc. pub. Traveler mag. Condé Nast, 1997—99; ea. advt. mgr. & group advt. mgr. Better Homes and Gardens and Country Home mag. Meredith Corp., 1988—94, v.p., pub. Ladies Home Jour., 2001—02, v.p., pub. Better Homes & Gardens NYC, 2002—05; v.p., pub. Fairchild Bridal Group, NYC, 2002—05; pres. Fairchild Fashion Group, 2006—. Nominee Under 40 Hall of Fame, Am. Advt. Fedn., 2002—03. Office: Fairchild Fashion Group 750 Third Ave 8th Fl New York NY 10017

LAGARDE, CHRISTINE, French government official, lawyer; b. Paris, Jan. 1, 1956; d. Lallouette Robert and Carre Nicole; m. Wilfrid Lagarde, June 17, 1982 (div. Apr. 1992); children: Pierre-Henri, Thomas. BA, U. Avignon, France, 1979; M of Law, U. Paris, 1979; M Polit. Scientist, Polit. Scis. Inst., 1977. Assoc. Baker McKenzie, Paris, 1981-87, ptnr., 1987-91, mng. ptnr., 1991-95, chmn. exec. com. Chgo., 1999—2004, chmn. policy com., 2004—05; min. trade Govt. France, Paris, 2005, min. economy, fin. & employment, 2007—. Author: Breaking New Ground, 1991, Into France, 1993. Mem. French Prime Min. Adv. Bd. on Attractivity of France. Decorated chevalier de la Legion d'Honneur; named one of 100 Most Powerful Women in World, Forbes mag., 2005—07. Mem. Cercle Interallie Paris. Office: Ministry of Economy Fin and Employment 139 rue de Bercy 75572 Paris France Office Phone: 3315384200, 1-40 04 04 04.

LAGRAND, KENNETH, technology products company executive; b. 1941; married. BS in Mech. Engring., Mich. State U., 1964. Dir. mktg. Grayson Divsn. Robertshaw Controls Co., 1975-79; v.p., gen. mgr. Simicon Divsn. Robertshaw Controls Co., Holland, Mich., 1979-87; exec. v.p., dir. Gentex, 1987—. Mem. Soc. Automotive Engrs. Office: Gentex Corp 600 N Centennial St Zeeland MI 49464-1318

LAGUNOFF, DAVID, pathologist, educator; b. NYC, Mar. 14, 1932; s. Robert and Cicele (Lipman) L.; m. Susan P. Powers, Mar. 8, 1958; children: Rachel, Liza, Michael. MD, U. Chgo., 1957. Rsch. asst. microbiology U. Miami, Coral Gables, Fla., 1951-53; intern U. Calif. San Francisco Hosp., 1957-58; postdoctoral fellow dept. pathology U. Wash., Seattle, 1958-59, trainee in pathology, 1959-60, instr. pathology, 1960-62, asst. prof., 1962-65, assoc. prof., 1965-69, prof., 1969-79; prof. dept. pathology St. Louis U., 1979—2003, chmn. dept. pathology, 1979-89, 91-96, asst. v.p., 1989-93, prof. emeritus, 2003—; assoc. rsch. scientist dept. biochem. and molecular biology Columbia U., NYC, 2004—05; adj. prof. cell biology U. Med. & Dental NJ, 2005—. Assoc. dean rsch. St. Louis U. Sch. Medicine, 1989—96; vis. lectr. dept. pathology Sackler Sch. Medicine, Tel Aviv, 1988; vis. prof. dept. pathology U. Wash., Seattle, 2001—02; adj. prof. pathology SUNY Downstate, 2004—05. Nat. Heart Inst. fellow Carlsberg Laboratorium, Copenhagen, 1962-64, Nat. Cancer Inst. fellow Sir William Dunn Sch. Pathology, Oxford, Eng., 1970. Mem.: AAUP, AAAS, Am. Soc. Investigative Pathologists, Am. Soc. Cell Biology. Office Phone: 973-975-1511. Business E-Mail: lagunoda@umdnj.edu.

LAHAIE, PERRY, radio director; m. Teresa LaHaie, 1985; children: Kali, Taylor. Asst. mgr. Family Life Radio WUGN, Midland, Mich., 1989—. Performer: 4 CDs of original songs. Avocations: basketball, mountain biking. Office: 510 E Isabella Rd Midland MI 48640

LAHAINE, GILBERT EUGENE, retail lumber company executive; b. Owosso, Mich., Jan. 30, 1926; s. Eric Eugene and Martha Dorothy (Wetzel) LaH.; m. Dorothy Jean Williams, July 1, 1945; children: Gilbert Eugene Jr., Susan, Karen, David, Barbara, Ruth, Marianne, Steven, Eric. BA, Mich. State U., 1949. Acct. Hazen Lumber Co., Lansing, Mich., 1949-56; pres., mgr. Gilbert Lumber Co., Lansing, 1956-94, also bd. dirs., sec., 1994—. Sec. bd. dirs. Duane Bone Builder, Inc., East Lansing, Mich. Bd. dirs. Mo. Synod, Luth. Ch., St. Louis, 1987-95. With USN, 1944-46. Avocations: fishing, softball, reading, hunting. Home: 2401 Stirling Ave Lansing MI 48910-2755 Office: Gilbert Lumber Co 3501 S Pennsylvania Ave Lansing MI 48910-4734

LAHANN, JOERG, chemist; BSc in chemistry, U. Saarland, 1993; MS in chemistry, RWTH Aachen, 1995; PhD in macromolecular chemistry, RWTH Achen, 1998; postdoctoral rsch., MIT, 1999—2003, Harvard U., 1999—2003. Asst. prof. dept. chemical engring. U. Mich., 2003—. Contbr. articles to profl. jour. Named one of Top 100 Young Innovators, MIT Tech. Review, 2004. Mem.: Sigma Xi. Office: U Mich Dept Chemical Engring 2300 Hayward St Ann Arbor MI 48109-2136 Business E-Mail: lahann@umich.edu.

LAHEY, JOSEPH PATRICK, engineering executive; b. Pitts., Apr. 3, 1947; s. Michael Patrick and Henrietta (Szczesny) L.; m. Diane Ruth Lapp, July 24, 1971; children: Brendan, Meghan. BSME magna cum laude, U. Pitts., 1973, MBA, 1978. Registered profl. engr., Pa. Engring., mktg. Dravo Corp., Pitts., 1973-81; dir. mktg. M.W. Kellogg, Houston, 1981-83; v.p., gen. mgr. Combustion Engring., Stamford, Conn., 1985-88; pres., CEO Barnard & Burk Group, Inc., Baton Rouge, 1988—94; sr. exec. positions with various firms, 1994—96; pres., CEO Worldwide, Inc., Dallas, 1996—2002; co-founder Pluris Capital Advisors Co., 2002—04; pres., CEO Corrpro Cos., Inc., Medina, Ohio, 2004—. Mem. Am. Soc. Mech. Engrs., Soc. Petroleum Engrs., Constrn. Industry Inst. (bd. dirs.), Constrn. Industry Pres.'s Forum, Omicron Delta Kappa, Tau Beta Pi. Republican. Roman Catholic. Avocations: golf, fishing, jogging. Office: Corrpro Cos Inc 1090 Enterprise Dr Medina OH 44256

LAHOOD, RAY H., congressman; b. Peoria, Ill., Dec. 6, 1945; m. Kathleen (Kathy) Dunk LaHood; children: Darin, Amy, Sam, Sara. Student, Canton Jr. Coll., Ill.; BS in Edn. and Sociology, Bradley U., 1971. Tchr. Catholic and pub. jr. high schs., 1971-77; dist. administrv. asst. to congressman Tom Railsback, 1977; mem. Ill. Ho. of Reps., 1982—83; Chief of Staff to Congressman Bob Michels Ho. of Reps., 1993—94; mem. U.S. Congress from 18th Ill. dist., 1995—. Mem. appropriations com. US Congress, legis. br. subcom., intelligence task force. Mem. ITOO Soc., Downtown Rotary Club, Holy Family Ch. (Peoria), Peoria Area C. of C. Republican. Roman Catholic. Office: US Ho Reps 1424 Longworth Ho Office Bldg Washington DC 20515-1318 also: Peoria Dist Office Rm 100 100 NE Monroe St Peoria IL 61602-1003

LAIDIG, GARY W., state legislator; b. York, Pa., Aug. 15, 1948; s. Robert Vance and Daisy (Harvey) L.; m. Paula Jane Kinney, 1972; two children. Student, Morningside Coll., 1966-67, U. Wis., River Falls. Dist. 51A rep. Minn. Ho. of Reps., St. Paul, 1972-82; Dist. 56 senator Minn. State Senate, St. Paul, 1982—. Mem. ethics and campaign reform, crime prevention fin. divsn., environ. and natural resources and fin. divsn., and fin. and rules and adminstrn. coms., Minn. State Senate. Decorated Nat. Defense Medal, two Vietnamese Svc. ribbons. Named Outstanding Young Man of Stillwater, Minn., 1974; recipient Disting. Svc. awared Stillwater Jaycees, 1975. Mem. VFW, Am. Legion, Jaycees. also: State Senate 100 Constitution Ave Saint Paul MN 55155-1232 Mailing: 10202 Country Club Curv Saint Paul MN 55129-4209

LAIDLAW, ANDREW R., lawyer; b. Durham, NC, Aug. 28, 1946; BA, Northwestern U., 1969; JD, U. NC, 1972. Bar: Ill. 1972. Ptnr. Seyfarth Shaw LLP, Chgo., mem. exec. com., head Contracts Practice Area, head Litig. Practice Area. Contbr. articles to profl. jour. Mem.: Barristers, ABA (securities law com. 1982—, antitrust com.). Office: Seyfarth Shaw LLP Mid Continental Plz 55 E Monroe St Ste 4200 Chicago IL 60603-5863 Office Phone: 312-269-8823. Office Fax: 312-269-8869. Business E-Mail: alaidlaw@seyfarth.com.

LAIKIN, ROBERT J., electronics executive; V.p. Centruy Cellular Network, 1986-87, pres., 1988—93; v.p., treas. Brightpoint, Inc., Indpls., 1989-92, pres., 1992—96, chmn., CEO, 1994—. Office: Brightpoint Inc 501 Airtech Pkwy Plainfield IN 46168-7408

LAIMBEER, BILL, professional basketball coach, retired professional basketball player; b. Boston, May 19, 1957; s. William Laimbeer Sr.; m. Chris Laimbeer, 1979; children: Eric, Kerlann. Grad. in Econs., U. Notre Dame, 1979. Draft pick Cleve. Cavaliers, 1979, basketball player, 1980-82, Detroit Pistons, 1982-93; spl. cons. WNBA Detroit Shock, 2002, head coach, 2002—. Head coach WNBA Ea. Conf. All-Star Team, 2007. Named Coach of Yr., WNBA, 2003; named to BA All-Star Team, 1983, 1984, 1985, 1987. Achievements include winning back-to-back NBA Championships as a member of the Pistons, 1989, 90; led Detroit to the WNBA Championship twice as head coach, 2003, 06. Office: Detroit Shock Palace Sports & Entertainment 5 Championship Dr Auburn Hills MI 48326

LAING, KARELANN, publishing executive; b. Mpls., July 5, 1939; d. Edward Francis and Elizabeth Jane Karel (Templeton) Hannon; m. G. R. Cheesebrough, Dec. 19, 1959 (div. 1969); 1 child, Jennifer Read; m. Ronald Harris Laing, Jan. 6, 1973; 1 child, Christopher Harris. Grad., U. Minn., 1960. With Guthrie Symphony Opera Program, Mpls., 1969-71; account supr. Colle & McVoy Advt. Agy., Richfield, Minn., 1971-74; owner The Cottage, Edina, Minn., 1974-75; salespromotion rep. Robert Meyers & Assocs., St. Louis Park, Minn., 1975-76; cons. Webb Co., St. Paul, 1976-77, custom pub. dir., 1977-89; pres. K.L. Publs., Inc., Bloomington, Minn., 1989—. Contbr. articles to profl. jours. Cmty. vol. Am. Heart Assn., Am. Cancer Soc., Edina PTA; charter sponsor Walk Around Am., St. Paul, 1985. Mem.: Minn. Mag. Pub. Assn. (founder, bd. govs.), Direct Mail Mktg. Assn., Am. Bankers Assn., Advt. Fedn. Am., Fin. Instn. Mktg. Assn., Bank Mktg. Assn., St. Andrews Soc. Republican. Presbyterian. Avocations: painting, gardening, reading, travel. Office: KL Publs 2001 Killebrew Dr Minneapolis MN 55425-1865

LAKIN, JAMES DENNIS, allergist, immunologist, director; b. Harvey, Ill., Oct. 4, 1945; s. Ora Austin and Annie Pitranella (Johnson) L.; m. Sally A. Stuteville, July 22, 1972 (dec. July 27, 2002); children: Tracey A., Margaret K., Matthew A., Christian J., Anne E.; m. Debra J. Franz, May 29, 2004. PhD, Northwestern U., 1968, MD, 1969; MBA in Med. Group Mgmt., U. St. Thomas, 1996. Diplomate Am. Bd. Internal Medicine, Am. Bd. Allergy and Immunology; cert. comml. pilot FAA, cert. flight instr., sr. aviation med. examiner. Dir. allergy rsch. Naval Med. Rsch. Inst., Bethesda, Md., 1974-76; clin. prof. U. Okla., Oklahoma City, 1976-89; dir. lab., chmn. allergy and immunology dept. Oxboro Clinics, Bloomington, Minn., 1989—2001; dir. Fairview Allergy and Asthma Svcs., Bloomington, 1995-2001; mng. ptnr. Minn. Allergy and Asthma Consultants, LLP, 2001—. Bd. dirs. Okla. Med. Rsch. Found., Oklahoma City, 1980-89; regional cons. Diver Alert Network, Duke U., Chapel Hill, N.C., 1987—; cert. diving med. officer NOAA, 1988. Co-author: Allergic Diseases, 1971, 3d edit., 1986; contbr. articles, revs. to profl. publs. Councilperson Our Lord's Luth. Ch., Oklahoma City, 1978-88, Faith Luth. Ch., Lakeville, Minn., 1990-91. Lt. comdr. USN, 1970—76, Vietnam, ret. Fellow ACP, Am. Acad. Allergy and Immunology, Am. Coll. Allergy and Immunology,Am. Coll. Chest Physicians, Am. Coll. Med. Practice Execs. (E.B. Stevens Article of Yr. award 1998); mem. Am. Assn. Immunologists, Med. Group Mgmt. Assn. (bd. dirs. 2002-06, E.B. Stevens Article of Yr. award, 1998), Am. Coll. Physician Execs. Achievements include research in characterization of the immunoglobulin system of the rhesus monkey, alterations in allergic reactivity during immunosuppression. Office: 303 E Nicollet Ave # 362 Burnsville MN 55337-4559 Office Phone: 952-223-3040. Business E-Mail: jdlakin@minnesotaallergy.com.

LAKIN, SCOTT BRADLEY, insurance agent; b. Kansas City, Mo., Dec. 28, 1957; s. John Bradley and Marilyn (Marr) L.; m. Cynthia Kay Wohlgemuth, May 26, 1979; children: Kyle, Caroline, Christopher. BS, William Jewell Coll., 1980. Congl. aide Congressman Richard Bolling, Kansas City, Mo., 1979-83; mem. Mo. State Legislature, 1992-2000. Gov. apptd. dir. Mo. Dept. Ins., 2001—. Bd. dirs. Safe Haven Domestic Violence Shelter. Mem. Sertoma (bd. dirs. 1989-92), Kansas City C. of C., Gladstone C. of C., Northland Regional C. of C. Democrat. Baptist. Avocations: jogging, tennis, reading. Home: 6020 N Chelsea Ave Kansas City MO 64119-3059 E-mail: slakin@services.state.mo.us, xrep33@hotmail.com.

LALIME, PATRICK, professional hockey player; b. St. Bonaventure, PQ, Can., July 7, 1974; Goaltender Pitts. Penguins, 1996—97, Ottawa Senators, 1999—2004; goaltender St. Louis Blues, 2004—. Named to NHL All-Star game, 2003. Office: c/o St Louis Blues Savvis Center 1401 Clark Ave Saint Louis MO 63103

LALK, DAVID, state representative, farmer; b. Oelwein, Iowa, Nov. 13, 1948; Student, N. Fayette Cmty. Sch. Farmer; state rep. dist. 18 Iowa Ho. of Reps., 2003—; mem. agr. com.; mem. econ. growth com.; mem. ways and means com.; vice chair adminstrn. and regulation appropriations subcom. Deacon and Sunday sch. supt. local ch. With Air Nat. Guard. Republican. Office: State Capitol East 12th and Grand Des Moines IA 50319

LALONDE, BERNARD JOSEPH, finance educator; b. Detroit, June 3, 1933; s. John Bernard and Fannie (Napier) LaL.; m. Barbara Elaine Eggenberger, Sept. 6, 1958; children— Lisa Renee, Michell Ann, Christopher John. AB, U. Notre Dame, 1955; MBA, U. Detroit, 1957; PhD, Mich. State U., 1961. Asst. prof. mktg. U. Colo., Boulder, 1961-65; assoc. prof. Mich. State U., East Lansing, 1965-69; James R. Riley prof. mktg. and logistics Ohio State U., Columbus, 1969-85, Raymond E. Mason prof. transp. and logistics, 1985-95, prof. emeritus, 1995. Author: Physical Distribution Management, 2d edit, 1968, Customer Service: A Management Perspective, 1988; Editor: Jour. Bus. Logistics; Jour. book and monographs editor, Am. Mktg. Assn.; Contbr. articles to profl. jours. Pres. Transp. Research Found. Recipient John Drury Sheehan award, 1976; Formerly Ford scholar; Gen. Electric fellow. Mem. Am. Marketing Assn., Regional Sci. Assn., Council Logistic Mgmt., Soc. Logistics Engrs., Beta Gamma Sigma, Alpha Kappa Psi. Roman Catholic. Home: 8538 Pitlochry Ct Dublin OH 43017-9770 Office: Ohio State U Coll Bus Supply Chain Mgmt Rsch Grp 351 Fisher Hall 2100 Neil Ave Columbus OH 43210

LAMB, GORDON HOWARD, academic administrator; b. Eldora, Iowa, Nov. 6, 1934; s. Capp and Ethel (Hayden) L; m. Nancy Ann Painter; children: Kirk, Jon, Phillip. B in Music Edn., Simpson Coll., 1956; M of Music, U. Nebr., 1962; PhD, U. Iowa, 1973. Choral dir. Iowa Pub. Schs., Tama/Paullina, Sac City, 1957-68; asst. prof. music U. Wis., Stevens Point, 1969-70, U. Tex., Austin, 1970-74, prof., dir. divsn. music San Antonio, 1974-79, prof., v.p. acad. affairs, 1979-86; pres. Northeastern Ill. U., Chgo., 1986-95, pres. emeritus, 1996—; interim chancellor U. Wis., Parkside, 1997—98, U. Mo., Kansas City, 1999—2000; sr. v.p. EFL Assocs./TranSearch, Overland Park, Kans., 2000—07; interim pres. U. Mo. Sys., Columbia, 2007—. Vis. prof. music dept. Western Ill. U., 1996-97 Author: Choral Techniques, 1974, 3d edit. 1988; editor: Guide for the Beginning Choral Director; contbr. articles to scholarly and profl. jours.; composer numerous pieces choral music. Served with U.S. Army, 1957-58. Recipient Most Supportive Pres. or Chancellor award Am. Assn. Colls. for Tchr. Edn., 1992. Mem. Am. Assn. Higher Edn., Am. Assn. State Colls. and Univs., Am. Choral Dirs. Assn. (life, chmn. nat. com. 1970-72). Office: U Mo Office of Pres 321 University Hall Columbia MO 65211 Office Phone: 573-882-2011.

LAMB, STEVEN G., financial executive; BSEE, U.S. Mil. Acad.; MBA, Harvard U. Mgmt. and operational positions Internat. Paper, 1988-92; exec. asst. to pres. Tenneco Inc.; mng. dir. Europe Case Corp., Racine, Wis., 1993-95, exec. v.p., COO, 1995-97, pres., COO, 1997—. Office: 700 State St Racine WI 53404-3343

LAMBERT, DANIEL MICHAEL, retired academic administrator; b. Kansas City, Mo., Jan. 16, 1941; s. Paul McKinley and Della Mae Lambert; m. Carolyn Faye Bright, Dec. 27, 1969; children: Kristian Paige, Dennis McKinley. AB, William Jewell Coll., 1963; MA, Northwestern U., 1965; postgrad., Harvard U., 1965-66; PhD, U. Mo., Columbia, 1977. Dean student affairs William Jewell Coll., Liberty, Mo., 1970-77, exec. asst. to pres., 1977-80, v.p., 1980-85; pres. College Hill Investments Inc., Liberty, 1985-87; prof. edn. Baker U., Baldwin City, Kans., pres., 1987—2006. Bd. dirs. Ferrell Co., Liberty; dir. Kansas City Bd. of Trade, 1988-90; hon. trustee Dohto U., Japan. Bd. dirs. Nat. Assn. Intercollegiate Athletics, The Barstow Sch., Kans. Ind. Colls. Assn.; trustee Midwest Rsch. Inst., Bishop Seabury Acad., Kans., Douglas County Cmty. Found., Kans. Capt. U.S. Army, 1966-70, Vietnam. Recipient Civic Leadership award Mo. Mcpl. League, 1986. Mem. Nat. Assn. Ind. Colls. and Univs. (bd. dirs.), KC. E-mail: dmlambert@bakeru.edu.

LAMBERT, GEORGE ROBERT, lawyer, realtor; b. Muncie, Ind., Feb. 21, 1933; s. George Russell and Velma Lou (Jones) L.; m. Mary Virginia Alling, June 16, 1956; children: Robert Allen, Ann Holt, James William. BS, Ind. U., Bloomington, 1955; JD, Chgo.-Kent Coll. Law, 1962. Bar: Ill. 1962, U.S. Dist. Ct. (no. dist.) Ill. 1962, Iowa 1984, Pa. 1988, Ind. 1999. V.p., gen. counsel, sec. Washington Nat. Ins. Co., Evanston, Ill., 1970-82; v.p., gen. counsel Washington Nat. Corp., Evanston, 1979-82; sr. v.p., sec., gen. counsel Life Investors Inc., Cedar Rapids, Iowa, 1982-88; v.p., gen. counsel Provident Mut. Life Ins. Co., Phila., 1988-95; pres. Lambert Legal Consulting, Inc., Wilmington, Del., 1995—2002; realtor Coldwell Banker, North Palm Beach, Fla., 1996—2001, Cressy and Everett GMAC Real Estate, South Bend, Ind., 1999-2000; ind. real estate broker Granger, Ind., 2001—03; realtor Martinique II Realty Inc., Port St. Lucie, Fla., 2002—; ind. real estate broker Bloomington, Ind., 2004—. Alderman Evanston (Ill.) City Coun., 1980-82; mem. bd. edn. Lake Bluff (Ill.) Elementary Sch. Dist., 1970-71. Lt. USAF, 1955-57. Mem.: Assn. of Life Ins. Counsel (past pres.). Home: 7958 Poppy Hills Ln Port Saint Lucie FL 34986 Home (Summer): 9411 Harbour Pointe Dr Bloomington IN 47401 Personal E-mail: glamb10100@aol.com.

LAMBERT, JOHN BOYD, chemical engineer, consultant; b. Billings, Mont., July 5, 1929; s. Jean Arthur and Gail (Boyd) L.; m. Jean Wilson Bullard, June 20, 1953 (dec. 1958); children: William, Thomas, Patricia, Cathy, Karen; m. Ilse Crager, Sept. 20, 1980 (dec. 1995). BS in Engring., Princeton U., 1951; PhD, U. Wis., 1956. Rsch. engr. E.I. DuPont de Nemours Co., Wilmington, Del., 1956-69; sr. rsch. engr. Fansteel, Inc., Balt., 1969, mktg. mgr., plant mgr. North Chicago, Ill., 1970-73, mgr. mfg. engring. Waukegan, Ill., 1974-80, corp. tech. dir. North Chicago, 1980-86, gen. mgr. metals, 1987-90, v.p., corp. tech. dir., 1990-91. IESC vol., Brazil, 1995; ind. cons., Lake Forest, Ill., 1991—. Contbr. articles to profl. jours. Recipient Charles Hatchett medal Inst. Metals, London, 1986. Mem. AIChE, Am. Chem. Soc., Am. Soc. Metals, Sigma Xi. Episcopalian. Achievements include patents in field of dispersion-strengthened metals, refractory metals, chemical vapor deposition, both products and processes. Home and Office: 617 Greenbriar Ln Lake Forest IL 60045-3214 Home Phone: 847-234-7645; Office Phone: 847-234-7645. Office Fax: 847-234-7649. Personal E-mail: drjbl@aol.com.

LAMBERT, JOSEPH BUCKLEY, chemistry professor; b. Ft. Sheridan, Ill., July 4, 1940; s. Joseph Idus and Elizabeth Dorothy (Kirwan) L.; m. Mary Wakefield Pulliam, June 27, 1967; children: Laura Kirwan, Alice Pulliam, Joseph Cannon. BS, Yale U., 1962; PhD (Woodrow Wilson fellow 1962-63, NSF fellow 1962-65), Calif. Inst. Tech., 1965. Asst. prof. chemistry Northwestern U., Evanston, Ill., 1965-69, assoc. prof., 1969-74, prof. chemistry, 1974-91, Clare Hamilton Hall prof. chemistry, 1991—, Charles Deering McCormick prof., 1999—2002, chmn. dept., 1986-89, dir. integrated sci. program, 1982-85. Vis. assoc. Brit. Mus., 1973, Polish Acad. Scis., 1981, Chinese Acad. Scis., 1988. Author: Organic Structural Analysis, 1976, Physical Organic Chemistry through Solved Problems, 1978, The Multinuclear Approach to NMR Spectroscopy, 1983, Archaeological Chemistry III, 1984, Introduction to Organic Spectroscopy, 1987, Recent Advances in Organic NMR Spectroscopy, 1987, Acyclic Organonitrogen Stereodynamics, 1992, Cyclic Organonitrogen Stereodynamics, 1992, Prehistoric Human Bone, 1993, Traces of the Past, 1997, Organic Structural Spectroscopy, 1998, Nuclear Magnetic Resonance Spectroscopy, 2004; audio course Intermediate NMR Spectroscopy, 1973; editor in chief Journal of Physical Organic Chemistry; contbr. articles to sci. jours. Recipient Nat. Fresenius award, 1976, James Flack Norris award, 1987, Fryxell award, 1989, Nat. Catalyst award, 1993, Mosher award, 2003; Alfred P. Sloan fellow, 1968-70, Guggenheim fellow, 1973, Interacad. exch. fellow (U.S.-Poland), 1985, Air Force Office sci. rsch. fellow, 1990. Fellow AAAS, Japan Soc. for Promotion of Sci., Brit. Interplanetary Soc., Ill. Acad. Sci. (life); mem. Am. Chem. Soc. (chmn. history of chemistry divsn., 1996, F.S. Kipping award 1998, S.M. Edelstein award 2004), Royal Soc. Chemistry, Soc. Archaeol. Scis. (pres. 1986-87), Phi Beta Kappa, Sigma Xi (hon. lectr. 1997-98). Home: 1956 Linneman St Glenview IL 60025-4264 Office: Northwestern University Dept of Chemistry 2145 Sheridan Rd Evanston IL 60208-3113 Office Phone: 847-491-5437.

LAMBERT, ROBERT FRANK, electrical engineer, educator, consultant; b. Warroad, Minn., Mar. 14, 1924; s. Fred Joseph and Nutah (Gibson) L.; m. June Darlene Flatten, June 30, 1951; children: Cynthia Marie, Susan Ann, Katherine Cheryl. B.E.E., U. Minn., 1948, MS in Elec. Engring, 1949, PhD, 1953. Asst. prof. U. Minn. Inst. Tech., Mpls., 1953-54, assoc. prof., 1955-59, prof. elec. engring., 1959-94, prof. emeritus, 1994, assoc. dean, 1967-68; dir. propagation research lab. U. Minn., 1968-87; asst. prof. Mass. Inst. Tech., 1954-55. Cons. elec. engr., also in acoustics, 1953—; guest scientist Third Phys. Inst., Göttingen, Fed. Republic Germany, 1964; vis. scientist NASA, Hampton, Va., 1979; dir. Inst. Noise Control Engring., Washington, 1972-75 Contbr. numerous articles to tech. jours. Served with USNR, 1943-46. Fellow IEEE, Acoustical Soc. Am. (assoc. editor jour. 1985-93); mem. Am. Soc. Engring. Edn., Am. Soc. Engring. Sci., AAAS, Inst. Noise Control Engring. (dir., John C. Johnson Meml. award), Sigma Xi, Tau Beta Pi, Eta Kappa Nu, Gamma Alpha. Lutheran. Achievements include rsch. in acoustics, communication tech. random vibrations. Home: 2503 Snelling Curv N Saint Paul MN 55113 Office: U Minn Inst Tech Dept Elec Engring Minneapolis MN 55455 Business E-Mail: lambe024@tcumn.edu.

LAMBERTI, DONALD, convenience store executive; Chmn., CEO, co-founder Casey's Gen. Stores, Inc., Ankeny, Iowa, chmn., 1998—. Office: Casey's Gen Stores Inc 1 Convenience Blvd Ankeny IA 50021-8045

LAMBERTI, JEFF, state legislator, lawyer; b. Des Moines, Oct. 21, 1962; m. Shannon Lamberti; 2 children. BA, Drake U., 1985, MBA, JD, Drake U., 1989. Assoc. Ahlers, Cooney, Dorweiler, Haynie, Smith & Albee, P.C., 1989-94; prin. Jeffrey M. Lamberti Law Firm, 1995—; shareholder Handley, Gocke, Block, Lamberti, Barnes and Moore, P.C., 1998—; mem. Iowa Ho. of Reps., Des Moines, 1994-98, Iowa Senate from 33rd dist., Des Moines, 1998—; vice chair state govt. com., mem. ways and means com.; vice chair jud. com., mem.

commerce com. Iowa Senate, Des Moines, mem. appropriations com. Bd. dirs. Polk County Health Svcs.; chair, bd. dirs. On with Life; mem. Neveln Cmty. Resource Ctr.; bd. dirs. Family Futures Network, Homeless Child Day Care and Family Suppot Ctr.; mem. Ankeny Area Hist. Soc. Mem. ABA, Nat. Assn. Bond Lawyers, Iowa State Bar Assn., Polk County Bar Assn., Ankeny C. of C., Polk City C. of C., KC, Vittoria Lodge. Republican. Roman Catholic. Office: State Capitol 9th And Grand Ave Des Moines IA 50319-0001 E-mail: jeff_lamberti@legis.state.ia.us.

LAMBORN, LEROY LESLIE, law educator; b. Marion, Ohio, May 12, 1937; s. LeRoy Leslie and Lola Fern (Grant) Lamborn. AB, Oberlin Coll., 1959; LLB, Western Res. U., 1962; LLM, Yale U., 1963; JSD, Columbia U., 1973. Bar: N.Y. 1965, Mich. 1974. Asst. prof. law U. Fla., 1965-69; prof. Wayne State U., Detroit, 1970-97, prof. emeritus, 1997—. Vis. prof. State U., Utrecht, 1981. Author: (book) Legal Ethics and Professional Responsibility, 1963; contbr. articles on victimology to profl. jours. Mem.: World Soc. Victimology (exec. com. 1982—94), Nat. Orgn. Victim Assistance (bd. dirs. 1979—88, 1990—91), Am. Law Inst.

LAMBRIGHT, STEPHEN KIRK, brewing company executive, lawyer; b. Kansas City, Mo., Dec. 3, 1942; s. Ray B. and Janet Lambright; m. Gail T. Tabler; children: Stephen K. Jr., James H., Sarah E., Catherine L. BS in Acctg., U. Mo., 1965; JD cum laude, St. Louis U., 1968, MBA in Fin., 1977, civil mediation tng., 2004; Transitional Tng., USA&M, 2005. Bar: Mo. 1968, Va. 1979, DC 1979, CPA Mo. 1969, U.S. Dist. Ct. (ea. dist.) of Mo., U.S. Ct. of Appeals (8th Cir.), U.S. Supreme Ct., Cir. Ct. of St. Louis County (21st Jud. Cir.), Cir. Ct. City of St. Louis (22nd Jud. Cir.). Tax acct. Arthur Andersen & Co., 1965-69; atty. Lashly, Caruthers, Thies, Rava & Hamel, 1970-77; asst. gen. counsel Anheuser-Busch Cos., St. Louis, 1977-78, exec. asst. chmn. bd., 1978-79, v.p., nat. affairs Washington, 1979-81, v.p., industry and govt. affairs St. Louis, 1981-83, mem. corp. policy com., 1981—, v.p. group exec., 1983—, group v.p., gen. counsel; of counsel Williams, Venker & Sanders LLC, St. Louis. Served USCGR, intelligence Officer(commander) USNR ret. 1983. Mem. Shriner's Hosp. for Crippled Children, Keep Am. Beautiful. Mem. C. of C. of U.S., Mo. Bar Assn., DC Bar Assn., Va. State Bar Presbyterian. Home: 7 Bonhomme Grove Ct Chesterfield MO 63017-6053 Office: Williams Venker & Sanders LLC Ste 1600 Equitable Bldg 10 S Broadway Saint Louis MO 63102 Office Phone: 314-345-5000, 314-345-5060. Office Fax: 314-345-5055. Business E-Mail: slambright@wvslaw.com.

LAMKIN, FLETCHER M., JR., academic administrator; b. Lakehurst, NJ, Apr. 2, 1942; married; 3 daus. BS, U.S. Mil. Acad., 1964; MS in Engring., U. Calif., Berkeley; DPhil, U. Wash.; grad., Army Command Gen. Staff Coll., Naval War Coll. Commd. 2d lt. U.S. Army, 1964; early assignments include battery exec. officer 7th bn., 11th field arty., Republic South Vietnam, bn. fire support officer, battery comdr., 1966-67; comdr. 1st spl. tng. co. Ft. Gordon, Ga., 1967-68; bn. ops. officer 1st bn., 38th field arty., Korea, 1975-76; bn. exec. officer, tng. officer, dep. ops. officer 9th infantry divsn., Ft. Lewis, Wash., 1976-80; inspections team chief, Office of Inspector Gen. U.S. Army Europe, Heidelberg, Germany, 1980—81; bn. comdr. 4th bn., 77th field arty., Babenhausen, FRG, Germany, 1981—83; instr., asst. prof. dep. mechs. U.S. Mil. Acad., West Pt., NY, 1971-74, assoc. prof. dept. engring., 1987-89, prof., dep. head dept. civil and mech. engring., 1989-92, vice dean acad. bd., 1993-94, prof., head dept. civil and mech. engirng., 1994-95, dean acad. bd., 1995—2000; pres. Westminster Coll., Fulton, Mo., 2000—. Office: Office of the President Westminster College 501 Westminster Ave Fulton MO 65251-1299

LAMM, MICHAEL EMANUEL, pathologist, immunologist, educator; b. Bklyn., May 19, 1934; s. Stanley S. and Rose (Lieberman) L.; m. Ruth Audrey Kumin, Dec. 16, 1961; children: Jocelyn, Margaret. Student, Amherst Coll., 1951-54; MD, U. Rochester, 1959; MS in Chemistry, Western Res. U., 1962. Diplomate Am. Bd. Pathology. Intern, asst. resident in pathology Inst. Pathology Western Res. U. and Univ. Hosps. of Cleve., 1959-62; research assoc. NIMH, Bethesda, Md., 1962-64; asst. prof. pathology NYU Sch. Medicine, NYC, 1964-68, assoc. prof., 1968-73, prof., 1973-81; prof. dept. pathology Case We. Res. U. Sch. Medicine, 1981—; chmn. dept. Case Western Res. U. Sch. Medicine, 1981-2001. Vis. sci. dept. biochemistry U. Oxford, 1968; vis. prof. dept. pathology U. Geneva, 1976-77; mem. cancer spl. program adv. com. Nat. Cancer Inst., Bethesda, 1976-79, mem. bd. sci. counselors divsn. cancer biology, diagnosis and ctrs., 1993-95; mem. sci. adv. com. Damon Runyon-Walter Winchell Cancer Fund, N.Y.C., 1978-82; mem. immunol. sci. study sect. NIH, Bethesda, 1988-92; mem. immunotoxicology subcom. NRC, 1989-90; mem. toxin peer rev. panel Am. Inst. Biol. Sci., 1990—; bd. dirs. Univ. Associated for Rsch. and Edn. Pathology. Mem. editl. bd. Procs. Soc. Exptl. Biology and Medicine, 1973-82, Molecular Immunology, 1979-83, Jour. Immunol. Methods, 1980—, Jour. Immunology, 1981-85, Am. Jour. Pathology, 1982-92, Regional Immunology, 1988-95, Modern Pathology, 1989-96; contbr. articles to profl. jours. Recipient Excellence in Tchg. award NYU Sch. Medicine, 1974, Gold-Headed Cane award Am. Soc. for Investigative Pathology, 2004; named Career Scientist Health Rsch. Coun., City of NY, 1966-75; NIH grantee 1965—. Fellow AAAS, N.Y. Acad. Scis.; mem. Am. Assn. Pathologists (councilor 1986-88, sec. treas. 1988-90, v.p. 1990-91, pres. 1991-92), Am. Assn. Immunologists, Am. Soc. Biochemistry and Molecular Biology, Coll. Am. Pathologists, U.S. and Can. Acad. Pathology, Soc. for Exptl. Biol. Medicine, Clin. Immunology Soc., Soc. Mucosal Immunology, Am. Soc. Clin. Pathologists, Harvey Soc., Sigma Xi, Alpha Omega Alpha. Home: Apt 6B 13515 Shaker Blvd Cleveland OH 44120-5602 Home Phone: 216-561-6470. Business E-Mail: mel6@case.edu.

LAMP, BENSON J., tractor company executive; b. Cardington, Ohio, Oct. 7, 1925; m. Martha Jane Motz, Aug. 21, 1948; children: Elaine, Marlene, Linda, David. BS in Agr. and B in Agrl. Engring., Ohio State U., Columbus, 1949, MS in Agrl. Engring., 1952; PhD in Agrl. Engring., Mich. State U., East Lansing, 1960. Registered profl. engr., Ohio. Prof. agrl. engring. Ohio State U., Columbus, 1949-61, 87-91, prof. emeritus, 1991—; product mgr. Massey Ferguson Ltd., Toronto, Can., 1961-66; product planning mgr. Ford Tractor Ops. div. Ford Motor Co., Troy, Mich., 1966-71, mktg. mgr., 1971-76, bus. planning mgr., 1978-87; v.p. mktg. and devel. Ford Aerospace div. Ford Motor Co., Dearborn, Mich., 1976-78. Author: Corn Harvesting, 1962. Served to 2d lt. USAF, 1943-45. Fellow Am. Soc. Agrl. Engrs. (pres. 1985-86, Gold medal 1993); mem. Nat. Acad. Engring., Country Club at Muirfield Village (Dublin, Ohio). Avocations: golf, tennis, bridge. Office: BJM Company Inc 6128 Inverurie Dr E Dublin OH 43017-9472 Office Phone: 614-761-9745. Personal E-mail: blamp2@aol.com.

LAMPERT, LEONARD FRANKLIN, mechanical engineer; b. Mpls., Nov. 13, 1919; s. Arthur John Lampert and Irma (Potter) Smith. BME, U. Minn., 1943, B in Chem. Engring., 1959, MS in Biochemistry, 1964, PhD in Biochemistry, 1969. Registered profl. engr., Minn. With flight measurement rsch. dept. Douglas Aircraft Corp., El Segundo, Calif., 1943-47; researcher, tchr. U. Minn., Mpls., 1947-83; with rsch. engring. dept. Mpls. Honeywell Corp., 1950-55; info. scientist Control Data Corp., Mpls., 1982-88; mech. engr. Leonard Lampert Co., White Bear Lake, Minn., 1988—. Scientist Eurasion Watermilfoil Control, White Bear Lake, 1989—; stockholder rep. Lampert Lumber Co., St. Paul, 1988—. Contbr. articles to profl. jours. Mem. Am. Inst. Chem. Engrs. (award 1959), Am. Chem. Soc., U. Minn. Alumni Assn. (advisor) MIT Alumni Assn. (advisor), Phi Gamma Delta (advisor), Gamma Alpha, Phi Lambda Upsilon. Republican. Avocations: ballroom dancing, water-skiing, bicycling, geography, travel. Home and Office: 2467 S Shore Blvd Saint Paul MN 55110-3820 Home Phone: 651-429-1881.

LAMPERT, STEVEN A., lawyer; b. Chgo., Nov. 11, 1944; BS, U. Ill., 1966; JD cum laude, Northwestern U., 1969. Bar: Ill. 1969. Ptnr. Neal, Gerber & Eisenberg, Chgo. Mem. editorial bd. Northwestern U. Law Rev., 1968-69. Mem. ABA, Ill. State Bar Assn., Chgo. Bar Assn., Chgo. Estate Planning Coun. Office: Neal Gerber & Eisenberg 2 N La Salle St Ste 2200 Chicago IL 60602-3801

LAMPINEN, JOHN A., newspaper editor; b. Waukegan, Ill., Nov. 26, 1951; s. Walter Valentine and Patricia Mae Irene (Pruess) L.; m. Belinda Walter, Oct. 20, 1973; children: Amanda Michelle, Heidi Elizabeth. BS in Comm., U. Ill., 1973. Staff writer Paddock Cir. Newspapers, Libertyville, Ill., 1973-75; regional editor The Jour., New Ulm, Minn., 1975-76; various positions Daily Herald, Arlington Heights, Ill., 1976-90, asst. v.p., mng. editor, 1990—97, asst. v.p., exec. editor, 1997—99, v.p., exec. editor, 1999—2001, sr. v.p., editor, 2001—. Adj. prof. Medill Sch. Journalism, Northwestern U., Evanston, Ill., 1995-98. Mem. Assoc. Press Mng. Editors, Soc. Profl. Journalists, Am. Soc. Newspaper Editors. Avocations: baseball, long-distance running, coaching girls softball, sports memorabilia. Office: Daily Herald 155 E Algonquin Rd Arlington Heights IL 60005-4617

LAMPING, KATHRYN G., medical educator, medical researcher; BS in Biology, U. Ill., 1976; MS in Pharmacology, Med. Coll. Wis., 1982, PhD in Pharmacology, 1983. Postdoctoral rsch. fellow Dept. Internal Medicine, U. Iowa, Iowa City, 1983-86, asst. rsch. scientist, 1986-89, adj. asst. prof., 1989-95, asst. prof., 1995—. Contbr. articles to profl. jours. Mem. Am. Heart Assn. (Established Investigator award 1995), Am. Physiol. Soc., Microcirculatory Soc. Office: U Iowa Ctr on Agin 2159 Westlawn S Iowa City IA 52242-1100

LANANE, TIMOTHY S., state legislator, lawyer; m. Cynthia Lanane; children: Angelique Boyle, Katie, Meaghan. BS, Ball State U.; JD, Ind. U. Atty. City of Anderson, Ind.; mem. Ind. Senate from 25th dist., Indpls., 1997—; ranking minority mem. commerce and consumer affairs; mem. ins. and fin. instns. com.; mem. jud. com., mem. natural resources com. Mem. East Ctrl. Legal Svcs. Bd., Anderson City Sister Cities Com., Madison County Urban League. Mem. ABA, Madison County Bar Assn., Ind. Trial Lawyers Assn. Democrat. Avocations: reading, golf, running. Office: 200 W Washington St Indianapolis IN 46204-2728

LANCASTER, JOAN ERICKSEN, judge; b. 1954; BA magna cum laude, St. Olaf Coll., Northfield, Minn., 1977; spl. diploma in social studies, Oxford U., 1976; JD cum laude, U. Minn., 1981. Atty. LeFevere, Lefler, Kennedy, O'Brien & Drawz, Mpls., 1981-83; asst. U.S. atty. Dist. Minn., Mpls., 1983-93; shareholder Leonard, Street and Deinard, Mpls., 1993-95; dist. ct. judge 4th Jud. Dist., Mpls., 1995-98; assoc. justice Minn. Supreme Ct., 1998—2002; judge U.S. Dist. Ct., St. Paul, 2002—. Office: US District Court 316 N Robert St Saint Paul MN 55101

LANCASTER, PETER MCCREERY, lawyer; b. 1954; AB, Princeton U., 1976; JD, Yale U., 1980. Bar: Minn. 1984. Ptnr., co-chair intellectual property litig. group Dorsey & Whitney LLP, Mpls. Mem.: Minn. Intellectual Property Law Assn., Am. Intellectual Property Law Assn. Office: Dorsey & Whitney LLP Ste 1500 50 S Sixth St Minneapolis MN 55402-1498 Office Phone: 612-340-7811. Office Fax: 612-340-2868. Business E-Mail: lancaster.peter@dorsey.com.

LAND, SUZANNE PRIEUR, lawyer; b. Youngstown, Ohio, Oct. 26, 1964; AB in Acctg. and Econs. summa cum laude, Youngstown State U., Ohio, 1987; JD summa cum laude, Case Western Res. Sch. Law, Cleve., 1990. Bar: Ohio 1990, Ky. 2005. Atty. Greenebaum, Doll & McDonald, Covington, Ky. Adj. prof. law U. Cin. Law Sch., 1998—; bd. advs. No. Ky. C. of C. Bd. visitors Salmon P. Chase Coll. Law; bd. trustees St. Luke Cmty. Found., Redwood Rehab. Ctr., Boys & Girls Clubs Greater Cin.; corp. guild mem., steering com. mem. Dressed for Success Cin. Named one of Top 100 Attys., Worth mag., 2005—06. Mem.: ABA, Ky. State Bar Assn., Ohio State Bar Assn., Cin. Bar Assn. Office: Greenebaum Doll & McDonald 1800 RiverCenter I 50 E RiverCenter Blvd Covington KY 41011-1660 Office Phone: 513-455-7619. Office Fax: 513-762-7919. E-mail: spl@gdm.com.

LAND, TERRI LYNN, state official; b. Grand Rapids, Mich., June 30, 1958; m. Dan Hibma; children: Jessica Hibma, Nicholas Hibma. BA in Polit. Sci., Hope Coll., Holland, Mich. County clk. Kent County, Mich., 1992—2000; sec. state State of Mich., 2003—. Atty. Grievance Commn., 1999—2002; sec. Atty. Grievance Commn., 2001—02; mem. Secchia Millennium Commn., 2000, Cmty. Archives & Rsch. Ctr., 1997—, 54 Jefferson Study Com., 1997—. Mem. Grandville Rotary, 1990—99; bd. dirs. Am. Heart Assn., 1995—99, Jr. Achievement Alumni Bd., 1997—99, Project Rehab Found., 1997—98. Mem.: Mich. Supreme Ct. Hist. Soc., US Supreme Ct. Hist. Soc., Women's Resource Ctr. (v.p., bd. of dirs. 2001—02), Grand Rapids Pub. Mus. Found. Bd., Grand Rapids Rotary, Grand Rapids Early Morning Riser's Club, Friends of John Ball Zool. Pk., Byron Ctr. Fine Arts Found. (pres. 1999—), Friends of Van Andel Mus., Frederick Meijer Gardens, Grand Rapids C. of C., Byron Ctr. Hist. Soc. (pres. 1990—92), Byron Ctr. Cmty. Fine Arts Coun., Potters House Found. (mem., bd. dirs. 1997—). Republican. Office: Office Sec of State Treasury Bldg First Floor 430 West Allegan St Lansing MI 48918 Office Phone: 517-373-2510. Office Fax: 517-373-0727.

LANDAU, WILLIAM MILTON, neurologist, department chairman; b. St. Louis, Oct. 10, 1924; s. Milton S. and Amelia (Rich) L.; m. Roberta Anne Hornbein, Apr. 3, 1947; children: David, John, Julia, George. Student, U. Chgo., 1941-43; MD cum laude, Washington U., St. Louis, 1947. Diplomate: Am. Bd. Psychiatry and eurology (dir. 1967, pres. 1975). Intern U. Chgo. Clinics, 1947; resident St. Louis City Hosp., 1948; fellow Washington U., St. Louis, 1949-52, NIH, Bethesda, Md., 1952-54; instr. neurology Washington U., 1952-54, asst. prof., 1954-58, assoc. prof., 1958-63, prof., 1963—, dept. head, 1970-91, co-head dept. neurology and neur. surgery, 1975. Chmn. Nat. Com. for Research in Neurol. and Communicative Disorders, 1980 Editorial bd.: Neurology, 1963, A.M.A. Archives Neurology, 1965, Annals Neurology, 1977. Mem. ACLU (trustee East Mo. 1956—), Am. Neurol. Assn. (pres. 1977), Am. Acad. Neurology, Assn. U. Profs. eurology (pres. 1978), Soc. Neurosci., Am. Physiol. Soc., Am. Electro-encephalography Soc. Rsch. in neurophysiology. Office: Washington U Sch Med Dept eurology 660 S Euclid Ave Saint Louis MO 63110-1010 E-mail: landauw@neuro.wustl.edu.

LANDER, JOYCE ANN, retired nursing educator, retired medical/surgical nurse; b. Benton Harbor, Mich., July 27, 1942; d. James E. and Anna Mae Remus LPN, Kalamazoo Practical Nursing, Ctr., 1967; AAS, Kalamazoo Valley C.C., 1981, Grad. Massage Therapy Program, 1995. LPN-RN Bronson Meth. Hosp., Kalamazoo, 1972-82; RN med./surg. unit Borgess Med. Ctr., Kalamazoo, 1982-84; RN pediat. Upjohn Home Health Care, Kalamazoo, 1984-88; supr. nursing lab Kalamazoo Valley Comm. Coll., 1982—2005, ret., 2005. Therapeutic massage therapist in client homes with Business Kneading Peace Therapeutic Massage, Kalamazoo, 1995—; nursing asst., instr. State of Mich. Observer, 1990-96. Author: What Is A Nurse, 1980. Address: 3300 Woodstone Dr E Apt 108 Kalamazoo MI 49008-2548

LANDES, STEPHEN J., lawyer; b. Chgo., Sept. 27, 1945; BA with distinction, Northwestern Univ., 1967, JD cum laude, 1970. Bar: Ill. 1970, DC 1977. Asst. gen. counsel Bank of Israel, Jerusalem, 1974; ptnr. Wildman Harrold Allen & Dixon LLP, Chgo. Projects editor Northwestern Univ. Law Rev., 1969—70. Dir. Mt. Sinai Hosp. Med. Ctr. Named Russell Sage Scholar, 1967—70. Mem.: ABA, DC Bar, Chgo. Bar Assn. Office: Wildman Harrold Allen & Dixon LLP Ste 3000 225 W Wacker Dr Chicago IL 60606-1229 Office Phone: 312-201-2772. Office Fax: 312-201-2555. Business E-Mail: landes@wildmanharrold.com.

LANDES, WILLIAM M., law educator; b. 1939; AB, Columbia U., 1960, PhD in Econs., 1966. Asst. prof. economics Stanford U., 1965—66, U. Chgo., 1966—69; assoc. prof. Columbia U., 1969—72, CUNY Grad. Ctr., 1972—74; prof. economics U. Chgo. Law Sch., 1974—80, Clifton R. Musser prof. economics, 1980—92, Clifton R. Musser prof. law & economics, 1992—; founder, chmn. Lexecon, Inc., 1977—98, chmn. emeritus, 1998—; mem. bd. examiners GRE in Econs., ETS, 1967—74. Author (with Richard Posner): The Economic Structure of Tort Law, 1987; editor (with Gary Becker): Essays in the Economics of Crime and Punishment, 1974; editor: Jour. Law and Econs., 1975—91, Jour. Legal Studies, 1991—. Mem.: Am. Law and Econ. Assn. (v.p. 1991—92, pres. 1992—93), Am. Econ. Assn., Mont Pelerin Soc. Office: U Chgo Sch Law 1111 E 60th St Chicago IL 60637-2776 also: Lexecon Inc 332 S Michigan Ave Ste 1300 Chicago IL 60604-4406

LANDGREBE, DAVID ALLEN, electrical engineer; b. Huntingburg, Ind., Apr. 12, 1934; s. Albert E. and Sarah A. L.; m. Margaret Ann Swank, June 7, 1959; children: James David, Carole Ann, Mary Jane. BSEE, Purdue U., 1956, MSEE, 1958, PhD, 1962. Mem. tech. staff Bell Telephone Labs., Murray Hill, NJ, 1956; electronics engr. Interstate Electronics Corp., Anaheim, Calif., 1958, 59, 62; mem. faculty Purdue U., West Lafayette, Ind., 1962—, dir. lab. for applications of remote sensing, 1969-81, prof. elec. engring., 1970—2002, assoc. dean engring., 1981-84, acting head sch. elec. and computer engring. West Lafayette, 1995-96, prof. emeritus of elec. and computer engring., 2002—. Rsch. scientist Douglas Aircraft Co., Newport Beach, Calif., 1964; dir. Univ. Space Rsch. Assn., 1975-78. Author: Signal Theory Methods in Multispectral Remote Sensing, 2003, (with others) Remote Sensing: The Quantitative Approach, 1978. Recipient medal for exceptional sci. achievement NASA, 1973, William T. Pecora award NASA/U.S. Dept. Interior, 1990. Fellow IEEE (pres. Geosci. and Remote Sensing Soc. 1986-87, Exceptional Svc. award 1988, Sci. Achievement award 1992, Edn. award 2003), AAAS, Am. Soc. Photogrammetry and Remote Sensing; mem. AE, Am. Soc. for Engring. Edn., Sigma Xi, Tau Beta Pi, Eta Kappa Nu. Office: Purdue U Dept Elec Engring West Lafayette IN 47907-1285 Business E-Mail: landgreb@ecn.purdue.edu.

LANDGREBE, JOHN ALLAN, chemistry professor; b. San Francisco, May 6, 1937; s. Herbert Frederick and Janet Miller (Allan) L.; m. Carolyn Jean Thomson, Dec. 23, 1961; children— Carolyn Janet, John Frederick BS, U. Calif.-Berkeley, 1959; PhD, U. Ill., 1962. Asst. prof. U. Kans., Lawrence, 1962—67, assoc. prof., 1967—71, prof., 1971—2002, prof. emeritus, 2002—, dept. chmn., 1970—80. Vis. prof. U. Calif.-Berkeley, 1974 Author: Theory and Practice in the Organic Laboratory, 1973, 5th edit., 2005. NSF fellow, 1960-62; E. Watkins Faculty fellow U. Kans., 1963; recipient Career Tchg. award Chancellors Club, 1999. Mem. Am. Chem. Soc., Royal Soc. of Chemistry, Phi Lambda Upsilon. Republican. Lutheran. Avocations: gardening, camping, hiking. Home: 1125 Highland Dr Lawrence KS 66044-4523 Office: U Kansas Dept Chemistry Lawrence KS 66045-0001

LANDIS, DAVID MORRISON, state legislator; b. Lincoln, Nebr., June 10, 1948; m. Melodee Ann McPherson, June 6, 1969; children: Matthew, Melissa. BA, U. Nebr., 1970, JD, 1971, M. in Cmty. Regional Planning, 1995; MPA, U. Nebr., Omaha, 1984. Bar: Nebr. 1972. Practice law, Lincoln, 1972—74; mem. Nebr. Legislature from 46th dist., 1978—; chmn. govt. mil. and vets. affairs com. Nebr. Legislature, 1983—87, chmn. banking, commerce and ins., 1988—2002, chair revenue com., 2003—. Instr. Coll. Law, U. Nebr., 1990—; adj. faculty mem. dept. pub. adminstrn. U. Nebr., Omaha, 1984—; adj. faculty mem. Nebr. Wesleyan U., 1995—96, 1999—; adj. mem. faculty Doane Coll., 1985—95. Bd. dirs. Lower Platte S. Natural Resources Dist., 1971—78; adminstrv. law judge Dept. Labor, 1977—78; officer PTA, 1979—80; mem. Nebr. Humanities Coun., 1990—96. Named Tchr. of the Yr., Doane Coll., 1987, 1988, 1992; named to Hall of Fame, Nebr. Repertory Theatre, 2002; recipient Disting. Alumni award, Lincoln S.E. H.S., 1998. Mem. Innocents Soc. (hon.), Golden Key Soc. (hon., U. Nebr.), Purple Mask (hon., U. Nebr., Lincoln), Pi Alpha Alpha (hon. U. Nebr. at Omaha), Tau Sigma Delta (hon. U. Nebr., Lincoln). Office: Nebr State Legislature Rm 1116 State Capitol Lincoln E 68509 E-mail: dlandis@unicam.state.ne.us.

LANDO, JEROME BURTON, macromolecular science educator; b. Bklyn., May 23, 1932; s. Irving and Ruth (Schwartz) L.; m. Geula Ahroni, Dec. 2, 1962; children: Jeffrey, Daniel, Avital. AB, Cornell U., 1953; PhD, Poly. Inst. Bklyn., 1963. Chemist Camille Dreyfus Lab., Research Triangle Inst., Durham, NC, 1963-65; asst. prof. macromolecular sci. Case Western Res. U., Cleve., 1965—68, assoc. prof., 1968—74, prof., 1974—2005, prof. emeritus, 2005—; pres., CEO Edison Polymer Inovation Corp., 2000—. Dept. chmn. Case Western Res. U., Cleve., 1978—85; Erna and Jakob Michael vis. prof. Weizmann Inst. Sci., Rehovot, Israel, 1987; Lady Davis vis. prof. Technion, Haifa, Israel, 1992—93. Author: (with S. Maron) Fundamentals of Physical Chemistry, 1974; mem. editl. adv. bd. Polymers for Advanced Techs. Served to lt. U.S. Army, 1953-55. Named Alexander Von Humboldt Sr. Am. Scientist U. Mainz, Germany, 1974, disting. alumnus Poly. U., 1990. Fellow Am. Phys. Soc.; mem. Am. Chem. Soc., Am. Crystallographic Assn., Soc. Plastics Engrs. (rsch. award 1994, edn. award 1999), Sigma Xi. Jewish. Home: 21925 Byron Rd Cleveland OH 44122-2942 Office: Case Western Res U Dept Macromolecular Sci Kent Hale Smith Bldg 321 Cleveland OH 44106 Office Phone: 216-368-6366. Business E-Mail: jbl2@case.edu.

LANDON, ROBERT GRAY, retired manufacturing company executive; b. Portsmouth, Ohio, Dec. 22, 1928; s. Herman Robert and Hazel Ruth Landon; m. Carole A. Beaumont, Aug. 30, 2001; children: Geoffrey, Suzanne. Student, Cornell U., 1947-49; BA in Econs., U. Pa., 1955; grad. advanced mgmt. program, Harvard Sch. Bus., 1978. Loan officer Nat. City Bank, Cleve., 1955-60; SEC adminstr. Smith Kline Corp., 1960-64; controller, treas. Grumman Allied Industries, Inc., Garden City, .Y., 1964-76, v.p., 1977-82; v.p. investment mgmt. Grumman Corp., Bethpage, N.Y., 1978-79; pres. Grumman Ohio Corp., Worthington, Ohio, 1979-88. Served with AC, USN, 1949-53. Mem. The Oaks Club.

LANDOW-ESSER, JANINE MARISE, lawyer; b. Omaha, Sept. 23, 1951; d. Erwin Landow and Beatrice (Hart) Appel; m. Jeffrey L. Esser, June 2, 1974; children: Erica, Caroline. BA, U. Wis., 1973; JD with honors, George Washington U., 1976. Bar: Va. 1976, DC 1977, Ill. 1985. Atty. U.S. Dept. Energy, Washington, 1976-83, Bell, Boyd & Lloyd, Chgo., 1985-86, Seyfarth, Shaw, Fairweather & Geraldson, Chgo., 1986-88, Holleb & Coff, Chgo., 1988-2000, Quarles & Brady, Chgo., 2000—. Contbr. articles to profl. jours. Bd. dirs. Bernard Zell Anshe Emet Day Sch. Parent-Tchr. Orgn., 1991-95. Mem. ABA, Chgo. Bar Assn. (vice chmn. environ. law com. 1990-91, chmn. 1991-92), Nat. Brownfield Assn. (Ill. chpt. chmn. legis. and policy com. 2005—), Am. Jewish Congress (bd. dirs., pres. Midwest Region 2001-04). Office: Quarles & Brady 500 W Madison St Ste 3700 Chicago IL 60661-2592 Office Phone: 312-715-5055. Business E-Mail: je3@quarles.com.

LANDRY, PAUL LEONARD, lawyer; b. Mpls., Nov. 23, 1950; s. LeRoy Robert Landry and Alice Ruth (Swain) Stephens; m. Lisa Yvonne Yeo, Dec. 13, 1984; children: Marc, Lauren, Matthew. BA, Macalester Coll., 1974; postgrad., Georgetown U., 1976-77; JD, Boston U., 1977. Bar: Va. 1977, D.C. 1978, Minn. 1984, U.S. Dist. Ct. D.C., U.S. Dsit. Ct. Va., U.S. Dist. Ct. Minn., U.S. Ct. Appeals (D.C., 2d, 4th and 8th cirs.). Dancer Dance Theater Harlem, NYC, 1971-72; prin. dancer Dance Theatre Boston, 1972-75; atty. EPA, Washington, 1976-77; assoc. Reed, Smith, Shaw & McClay, Washington, 1977-83; officer, shareholder Fredrikson & Byron, P.A., Mpls., 1984—. Adj. prof. law William Mitchell Coll. Law, St. Paul, 1985-89. Bd. dirs. Ind. Sch. Dist. 284, Wayzata, Minn., 1989-96, 2002-, chmn., 1992-93; bd. dirs. Walker Art Ctr., Mpls., 1992—; bd. dirs., vice chair Greater Twin Cities Youth Symphonies, 1999-2001; advisor Kevin McCary Scholarship Fund. Mem. ABA (conf. of minority ptnrs. adv. com.), Nat. Bar Assn., Minn. State Bar Assn. (art and entertainment sect., labor and employment sect.), D.C. Bar, Hennepin Conty Bar Assn., Black Entertainment and Sports Lawyers Assn., Barristers. Avocations: golf, music, basketball. Office: 3624 78th Ave N Brooklyn Park MN 55443-2827 E-mail: plandry@fredlaw.com.

LANDSBERG, LEWIS, dean, endocrinologist, medical researcher; b. NYC, Nov. 23, 1938; AB, Williams Coll., 1960; MD, Yale U., 1964. Intern Yale-New Haven Hosp., 1964—65, resident in internal medicine, 1965—66, 1968—69; fellow in endocrinology NIH, 1966—68; from instr. to asst. prof. medicine Sch. Medicine Yale U., 1969-72; from asst. prof. to assoc. prof. Harvard Med. Sch., 1972-77, from assoc. prof. to prof., 1977-86; Irving S. Cutter prof., chmn. dept. medicine orthwestern U. Feinberg Sch. Medicine, Chgo., 1990—2000, dir. Ctr. Endocrinology, Metabolism & Nutrition, 1990-93, dean, v.p. for medical affairs, 2000—. Assoc. physician Yale-New Haven Hosp., 1969-71, attending physician, 1971-72, Beth Israel Hosp., 1974-79, physician, 1979-88, sr. physician, 1988-90; attending physician West Haven VA Hosp., 1970-72; assisting physician Boston City Hosp., 1972-73, assoc. vis. physician, 1973-74; physician-in-chief dept. medicine Northwestern Meml. Hosp., 1990—. Fellow ACP, AAAS; mem. Am. Fedn. Clin. Rsch., Endocrine Soc., N.Y. Acad. Scis., AHA, Am. Soc. Pharmacology and Exptl. Therapeutics, Am. Physiology Soc., Am. Soc. Clin. Investigators, Am. Clin. and Climatological Assn., Assn. Am. Physicians. Achievements include rsch. in catecholamines and the sympathoadrendal system, nutrition and the sympathetic nervous system, obesity and hypertension. Office: Northwestern Univ Med Sch Morton 4-656 310 East Superior St Chicago IL 60611-2958

LANDSKE, DOROTHY SUZANNE (SUE LANDSKE), state legislator; b. Evanston, Ill., Sept. 3, 1937; d. William Gerald and Dorothy Marie (Drewes) Martin; m. William Steve Landske, June 1, 1957; children: Catherine Suzanne Jones, Jacqueline Marie Basilotta, Pamela Florence Snyder, Cheryl Lynn Boisson, Eric Thomas. Student, St. Joseph Coll., Ind. U., U. Chgo. Owner, operator Sues Bridal House, 1967-75; dep. clk.-treas. Cedar Lake, 1975; chief dep. twp. assessor Center Twp., Crown Point, Ind., 1976-78, twp. assessor, 1979-84; mem. Ind. Senate, 1984—. Asst. pres., chair elections protem-senate. Vice chair Lake County Rep. Cen. Com., 1978-89, 97—. Lt. col. NG Res. Mem.

LWV, Coun. State Govts., Nat. Order Women Legislators, Nat. Coun. State Legislators, Bus. and Profl. Women, Grange Ind. Farm Bur. Roman Catholic. Office: Ind Senate Dist 6 200 W Washington St Indianapolis IN 46204-2728

LANDSMAN, STEPHEN A., lawyer; b. Chgo., Aug. 28, 1942; s. Sam W. and Jeanne N. (Engerman) L.; m. Beth Landsman; Children: Mark, Scott, Sari. BS in Econs., U. Pa., 1964; JD summa cum laude, U. Mich., 1967. Bar: Ill. 1967, U.S. Dist. Ct. (no. dist.) Ill. 1967, U.S. Ct. Appeals (7th cir.) 1967, U.S. Tax Ct. 1975. Assoc. Mayer, Brown & Platt, Chgo., 1967-69, Rudnick & Wolfe, Chgo., 1969-70, ptnr., 1970—99; ptnr., nat. chmn. mergers & acquisitions practice group Piper Rudnick LLP, Chgo., 1999—2004; ptnr., co-chair Mergers and Acquisitions practice group DLA Piper US LLP, Chgo., 2005—. Contbr. articles to profl. jours. Chmn. Chgo. Do the Write Thing Challenge, bd. dirs., treas. St. Joseph Hosp. Assocs., Chgo., 1978-82. Named one of Ill. Super Lawyer, Chgo. mag., 2005, 2006, Am. Leading Lawyers in Bus., Chambers USA, 2007; recipient Jane Addams medal, Juvenile Protective Assn., Judge Abraham Lincoln Marovitz Civil Rights award, Anti-Defamation League. Mem. Am. Arbitration Assn. (mem. Panel of Arbitrators), Ill. Bar Assn., Chgo. Bar Assn., Order of Coif. Office: DLA Piper US LLP Suite 1900 203 N La Salle St Chicago IL 60601-1293 Office Phone: 312-368-4050. Office Fax: 312-236-7516. Business E-Mail: stephen.landsman@dlapiper.com.

LANDSMAN, STEPHEN N., lawyer; BA, U. Ill., Urbana, 1981, JD, 1984. Sr. atty. Nalco Holding Co., Naperville, Ill., now v.p., gen. counsel, corp. sec. Office: Nalco Holding Co 1601 W Diehl Rd Naperville IL 60563 Office Phone: 630-305-1000. Fax: 630-305-2922.

LANDWEHR, BRENDA, state legislator, corporate financial executive; Mem. Kans. Ho. of Reps. Address: 2837 N Edwards Street Wichita KS 67204

LANDWEHR, STEVEN J., manufacturing executive; m. Barbara Landwehr. BS in Bus. Adminstrn., Minn. State U., 1970, MS in Bus. Adminstrn., 1974. Sales rep. 3M Co., mng. dir., 3M Norway, European bus. dir. Brussels, gen. mgr., automotive aftermarkets divsn., 1997—99, v.p., automotive aftermarkets divsn., 1999—2002, exec. v.p., transp. bus., 2002—. Recipient Disting. Alumni Award, Minn. State U., 2003. Office: 3M Co 3M Ctr Saint Paul MN 55144

LANE, AL, state legislator; m. Peggy Lane. Grad. Ohio State U. Kans. state rep. Dist. 25, 1989—; internat. airline capt., ret., 1964-88. Home: 6529 Sagamore Rd Shawnee Mission KS 66208-1946

LANE, JEFFREY H., lawyer; b. NYC, Apr. 14, 1949; AB, Columbia U., 1970; JD cum laude, Boston U., 1975. Bar: Wis. 1975. With Foley & Lardner, Milw., 1975—96, ptnr.; sr. v.p., gen. counsel, sec. MGIC Investment Corp., 1996—. Mem. ABA, State Bar Wis. Office: MGIC Investment Corp MGIC Plz 250 E Kilbourn Ave PO Box 488 Milwaukee WI 53201-0488 Office Phone: 414-347-6406. Office Fax: 414-347-6696.

LANE, KENNETH EDWIN, retired advertising agency executive; b. Orange, NJ, Sept. 30, 1928; s. Clarence Edwin and Erma Catherine (Kinser) L.; children by previous marriage— Kenneth, Laura, Linda, Katherine; m. Susan Spafford Zimmer, Sept. 13, 1980; stepchildren— Todd and Margaret Zimmer. BA, U. Chgo., 1947, MA, 1950. Mgr. media Toni div. Gillette Co., 1953-63; media dir. MacParland-Aveyard Co., 1963-64; assoc. media dir. Leo Burnett Co., Chgo., 1964-71, mgr. media dept., 1971-75, sr. v.p. media services, 1975-84. Bd. dirs. Traffic Audit Bur. Maj. USAR, ret. Mem. Am. Assn. Advt. Agys., Media Dirs. Council., Phi Beta Kappa Office: Leo Burnett Agy 35 W Wacker Dr Chicago IL 60601-1614

LANE, MEREDITH ANNE, botany educator, museum director; b. Mesa, Ariz., Aug. 4, 1951; d. Robert Ernest and Elva Jewell (Shilling) L.; m. Donald W. Longstreth, Apr. 6, 1974 (div. Feb. 1985). BS, Ariz. State U., 1974, MS, 1976; PhD, U. Tex., 1980. Asst. prof. U. Colo., Boulder, 1980-88, assoc. prof., 1988-89; assoc. prof., curator div. botany Natural History Mus., U. Kans., Lawrence, 1989-96, prof., 1997—. Vis. asst. prof. U. Wyo., Laramie, 1985-86; vis. scholar U. Conn., Storrs, 1989; cons. editor McGraw-Hill Ency. of Sci. and Tech., N.Y.C., 1985-92; program dir. Nat. Sci. Found., 1995-97; rsch. assoc. Smithsonian Inst., 1995—; agy. rep. Nat. Sci. and Tech. Coun., 1997. Editor Plant Sci. Bull., 1990-94; contbr. over 25 articles to profl. jours. Mem. Am. Soc. Plant Taxonomists (sec. 1986-88, program dir. 1986-90, councillor 1993-96, Cooley award 1982), Bot. Soc. Am. (sect. chmn. 1984-86, sect. sec. 1986-90), Internat. Orgn. for Plant Biosystematics (councillor 1989-92), Internat. Assn. Plant Taxonomists, Calif. Bot. Soc. Avocations: reading, conversation, country dance, hiking, furniture refinishing. Office: R L McGregor Herbarium 2045 Constant Ave Lawrence KS 66047-3729

LANE, MICHAEL HARRY, steel company executive; b. St. Louis, Jan. 8, 1943; s. Harry T. and Margaret (Cody) L.; m. Karen Numi, June 13, 1964; children: Michael P., Kelly, Richard. BS in Commerce, St. Louis U., 1964. C.P.A., Mo., Fla. Mgr. Price Waterhouse, Miami, Fla., 1964-72, St. Louis, 1964-72; v.p. fin. Laclede Steel Co., St. Louis, 1972—. Mem. Fin. Execs. Inst., Am. Inst. C.P.A.s, Mo. Soc. C.P.A.s Clubs: Mo. Athletic.

LANE, N. GARY, retired paleontologist; Emeritus prof. of paleontology Ind. U. Recipient Raymond C. Moor Paleontology medal Soc. for Sedimentary Geology, 1995. Office: Geology Dept Ind U Bloomington IN 47401

LANE, ROBERT W., farm equipment manufacturing executive; b. Washington, Nov. 14, 1949; m. Patricia Lane; 3 children. BA with high honors, Wheaton Coll., Ill., 1972; MBA, U. Chgo. Grad. Sch. Bus., 1974. First Nat. Bank Chgo., Europe; various positions Deere & Co., Moline, Ill., 1982—, CFO, sr. v.p. fin./tax/acctg., 1996—98, sr. v.p., mng. dir. mfg. mktg. Europe, Africa, Middle East, 1998—99, pres. worldwide agrl. equip. divn., 1999, pres., COO, 2000, chmn., CEO, 2000—. Bd. dirs. Deere & Co., 2000—, Verizon Communications Inc., 2004—, GE Co., 2005—; trustee Com. for Econ. Devel.; mem. Bus. Roundtable, Bus. Coun. Mem. Nat. Adv. Coun. Figge Art Mus., Iowa. Mem.: Lyric Opera bd. in Chgo. Office: Deere & Co 1 John Deere Rd Moline IL 61265-8098

LANE, RONALD ALAN, lawyer; b. Ames, Iowa, July 15, 1950; s. Raymond Oscar and Beverly (Burdge) L.; m. Eileen Smietana, June 17, 1972; children: Andrew, Audrey. AB, Miami U., Oxford, Ohio, 1972; JD, Northwestern U., 1975; MBA, U. Chgo., 1987. Bar: U.S. Dist. Ct. (no. dist.) Ill. 1975, U.S. Ct. Appeals (7th cir.) 1975, U.S. Supreme Ct. 1980. Atty. Atchison, Topeka & Santa Fe Ry. Co., Chgo., 1975-78; from asst. gen. atty. to gen. atty. Santa Fe So. Pacific Corp., Chgo., 1979-86, gen. corp. atty., 1986-87; asst. v.p. pers. and labor rels. Atchison, Topeka & Santa Fe Ry. Co., 1987-90; v.p., gen. counsel Ill. Ctrl. R.R. Co., Chgo., 1990-99; of counsel Franczek Sullivan, P.C., 1999—2000; ptnr. Fletcher & Sippel, LLC, 2001—. Dir. Chgo. Ctrl. Area Com., 1995-99, Transp. Tech. Ctr., Inc., 1997-99; mem. railroad shipper trans. adv. coun. Surface Transp. Bd., 1996-99. Office: Fletcher & Sippel LLC 29 N Wacker Blvd Ste 920 Chicago IL 60606

LANER, RICHARD WARREN, lawyer; b. Chgo., July 12, 1933; s. Jack E. and Esther G. (Cohon) L.; m. Barbara Lee Shless, Aug. 15, 1954 (dec. Oct. 1997); children: Lynn, Kenneth; m. Daryl Lynn Homer, Sept. 17, 1998. Student, U. Ill., 1951-54; BS, Northwestern U., 1955, LLB, 1956. Bar: Ill. 1956. Assoc. Laner, Muchin, Dombrow, Becker, Levin & Tominberg, Ltd., Chgo., 1956-62, ptnr., 1962-99, of counsel, 1999. Editor Northwestern Law Rev., 1954-56; contbr. articles to profl. jours. Mem. Chgo. Bar Assn. (chmn. com. labor law 1972-73), Chgo. Assn. Commerce and Industry, Order of Coif. Home: 161 E Chicago Ave Unit 41de Chicago IL 60611-2601 Office: Laner Muchin Dombrow Becker Levin & Tominberg Ltd 515 N State St Fl 28 Chicago IL 60610-4325 Office Phone: 312-467-9800. Business E-Mail: rlaner@lanermuchin.com.

LANEVE, MARK R., automotive executive; b. Beaver Falls, Pa., Mar. 8, 1959; m. Paula LaNeve; children: Jake, Drew. Bachelor in bus. comm., Univ. Va. Sales & mktg. positions GM, 1981—95, brand mgr., Pontiac Bonneville, 1995—97, gen. mgr. Cadillac, 2001—04, v.p. mktg. & advt., GM No. Am., 2004—05, v.p. vehicle sales, svc. & mktg., GM N Am., 2005—; v.p. mktg. Volvo Cars No. Am., 1997—2000, pres. & CEO, 2000—01. Trustee Judson Ctr. Named Grand Marketer of the Year, Brandweek mag., 2003. Office: General Motors Corp 300 Renaissance Ctr Detroit MI 48265-3000

LANEY, SANDRA EILEEN, information technology executive; b. Cin., Sept. 17, 1943; d. Raymond Oliver and Henrietta Rose (Huber) H.; m. Dennis Michael Laney, Sept. 30, 1968; children: Geoffrey Michael, Melissa Ann. AS in Bus. Adminstrn., Thomas More Coll., 1988, BA in Bus. Adminstrn., 1993. Adminstrv. asst. to chief exec. officer Chemed Corp., Cin., 1982, asst. v.p., 1982-84, v.p., 1984-91, v.p., chief adminstrv. officer, 1991-93, sr. v.p., chief adminstrv. officer, 1993-2001, bd. dirs., 1986—, exec. v.p. chief adminstrn. officer, 2001—02; CEO, chmn. Cadre Computer Resources Co., 2001—. Bd. dirs. Omnicare Inc., Covington, Ky., Ind. U. Found., Chem. Corp. 1986—; bd. visitors Ind. U. Sch. Public and Environ. Affairs. Mem. bd. advisors Sch. Nursing U. Cin., 1992—; bd. overseers Cin. Symphony Orch., 1998; trustee Lower Price Hill Cmty. Sch., Cmty. Land Coop. of Cin. Mem. AAUW, NOW, Internat. Platform Assn., Amnesty Internat., World Affairs Coun., Women's Action Coun. Roman Catholic. Office: Cadre Computer Resources Co 1200 Chemed Ctr 255 E 5th St Cincinnati OH 45202-4700

LANFORD, LUKE DEAN, retired electronics company executive; b. Greer, SC, Aug. 4, 1922; s. John D. and Ethel W. (Ballenger) L.; m. Donna Marie Cellar, Dec. 20, 1945 (dec. Apr. 29, 1984); 1 dau., Cynthia Lea Lanford Brown; m. Jacquelyn Sue Carr Bussell, Feb. 14, 1986 BSE.E., Va. Poly. Inst., 1943. With Western Electric Co., Inc., 1946-78, asst. mgr. tng. NYC, 1957-60, mgr. engring. Kansas City, 1960-63, asst. works mgr. Allentown, Pa., 1963-65; plant mgr. Reading, Pa., 1965-69; gen. mgr. Indpls., 1969-78. Dir. Met. Indpls. Television Assn., Inc., Sta. WFYI-TV, 1970—, pres., 1975-79 Served with U.S. Army, 1943-46. Mem. IEEE, Telephone Pioneers Am., Jacaranda West Country Club, Eta Kappa Nu, Tau Beta Pi, Phi Kappa Phi. Republican. Roman Catholic. Home: 1935 Pebble Beach Ct Venice FL 34293-3830

LANG, CRAIG, farmer, farm association officer; m. Mary Lang; 4 children. Grad., Iowa State U. Co-owner dairy operation, Iowa; pres. Iowa Farm Bur., West Des Moines, 2001—. Mem. polit. action com., dairy adv. com. Iowa Farm Bur., mem. state bd., 1992, v.p.; bd. dirs. Am. Farm Bur. Sunday sch. tchr. Madison Ch. of Christ. Office: Iowa Farm Bur 5400 University Ave West Des Moines IA 50266

LANG, DANIEL W., trust company executive; BSBA, U. Colo.; MBA, U. Mo., Kansas City. With trust dept. Commerce Bank, 1982, NationsBank; exec. v.p., personal trust mgr. The Midwest Trust Co., Overland Park, Kans. Mem. planned gift coun. Children's Mercy Hosp. Mem.: Estate Planning Soc. Kansas City. Office: Midwest Trust Company 5901 College Blvd Ste 100 Leawood KS 66211-1834

LANG, LOUIS I., state legislator, lawyer; b. Chgo., Nov. 26, 1949; s. Eugene and Shirley (Busel) L.; m. Teri Rosenbaum, 1987; children: David, Adam, Matthew Paul, Chad Paul, Rebecca. BA in Polit. Sci. with high honors, U. Ill., 1971; JD with honors, DePaul U., 1974. Litigation ptnr. Feingold, Lang & Levy, 1977-93; attorney Niles Twp. Govt., Ill., 1977-87; Dist. 16 rep. Ill. Ho. Reps., Springfield, 1987—; of counsel Baker & Miller, 1993-95; chief counsel Cook County Emergency Telephone Svc. Bd., 1994—; of counsel Goldberg Weisman & Cairo Ltd., Chgo., 1995—. Ill. Ho. Reps. Dem. fl. rep., vice chmn. state govt. adminstrn. com. and judiciary I com., mem. appropriations II, cities and villages, human svcs., higher edn., children, aging coms.; chmn. mental health select, health care, real estate law, and rules coms., and spl. com. on flicts of interest. Mem. Mayor's Task Force on Traffic, Skokie; campaign mgr. Samuel Berger for State Senate, Ill., 1980; bd. dirs. Holocaust Meml. Found., 1987—; bd. dirs. Jewish Cmty. Ctr., 1987—, North Ctrl. Skokie Homeowners Assn.; mgr. Little League Baseball. Named Citizen of the Month, Lerner Newspapers, 1986, Legislator of the Yr. Ill. Hosp. Assn., Ill. Pub. Action Coun., Ill. Social Workers Assn., Chgo. Tchrs. Union, Ill. Coun. on Sr. citizens, Suburban Area Agy. on Aging, Nat. Assn. Social Workers, Ill. Assn. Social Workers, Svc. Employees Union, Ind. Voters of Ill., Ethel Parker award Ind. Voters of Ill., 1993 Maccabean award Zionist Orgn. Chgo., Kit Pfau Voters Rights award Ind. Voters of Ill., Best Legis. Voting Record award, 1995 Activator Friend of Agr. award Ill. Farm Bur., Statesman of the Yr. award Internat. Union Operating Engrs., 1996. Mem. Niles Twp. Dem. Orgn., Decalogue Soc. of Lawyers, Ill. Bar Assn., Chgo. Bar Assn., Hillel Found., Pi Lambda Phi. Home: 5123 Jerome Ave Skokie IL 60077-3359

LANG, MARVEL, urban affairs educator; b. Bay Springs, Miss., Apr. 2, 1949; s. Otha and Hattie (Denham) L.; children: Martin E., Maya S. BA cum laude, Jackson State U., 1970; MA, U. Pitts., 1975; PhD in Urban/Social and Econ. Geography, Rural Settlement and Quantitative Methods/Computer Applications, Mich. State U., 1979; postgrad., St. John's Coll., Santa Fe, 1973, Miss. State U., 1979, Murray State U., 1980. Grad. teaching fellow dept. geography U. Pitts., 1970-72; instr. geography Jackson (Miss.) State U., 1972-74, asst. prof. geography, 1978-82, assoc. prof. geography, 1982-83; assoc. prof., dir. geography program Jackson (Miss.) State U. Ctr. Urban Affairs, 1983-84; grad. teaching & rsch. asst. dept. geography Mich. State U. Computer Inst. Social Sci. Rsch., East Lansing, 1974-76; grad. teaching fellow dept. geography Mich. State U., East Lansing, 1976-78; grad. asst. to dir. Mich. State U. Ctr. Urban Affairs, Coll. Urban Devel., East Lansing, 1977-78; dir. Ctr. Urban Affairs, assoc. prof. urban affairs programs Mich. State U., East Lansing, 1986-91, dir. Ctr. Urban Affairs, prof. urban affairs programs, 1991-93, prof. urban affairs programs, 1993—2003; profl. geographer Bureau of the Census, Washington, 1984-85, rsch. geographer, 1985-86. Instr. geography Lansing C.C., 1976-78, vis. prof., 1990-91; vis. prof. grad. sch. edn. & allied professions Fairfield (Conn.) U., 1990, 91, Egeler correctional facility prison edn. program Spring Arbor Coll., Jackson, 1990, McNair summer rsch. opportunity program, Mich. State U., 1989, 90, Wilberforce U., 1991, 92; rsch. cons. Mich. State U. Ctr. Urban Studies, 1978-79; prin. investigator NASA, 1979-81, Inst. Rsch., Devel. & Engring. in Nuclear Energy, 1980-81, U.S. Dept. Energy, 1980-82; co-prin. investigator & dir. U.S. Bureau of the Census, 1988—; mem. commn. geography & Afro-Am. fellowship U. Pitts, 1970-72; mem. numerous coms. Jackson State U., Mich. State U.; commentator on various radio and television programs; conductor seminars, workshops, and presentations; cons.; speaker in field. Author: (with others) The World at Your Fingertips: A Self Instructional Geography Handbook, 1991, Gone to Hell This Morning, 2005; editor: Contemporary Urban America: Problems, Issues and Alternatives, 1991, (with C. Ford) Black Student Retention in Higher Education, 1988, Strategies for Retaining Minorities in Higher Education, 1992; author (with others) Introduction to Remote Sensing of the Environment, 1982, Black Student Retention in Higher Education, 1988, Politics and Policy in the Age of Education, 1990, International Science, Technology, and Development: Philosophy, Theory and Policy, 1990, The Second Handbook of Minority Student Services, 1990, Contemporary Urban America: Problems, Issues, and Alternatives, 1991, The Guide to College Success: For Black Students Only, 1992, numerous tech. reports; mem. editorial bd. Jour. Urban Affairs, Urban Affairs Quarterly, 1992—; referee Urban Affairs Quarterly, Jour. Urban Affairs, Social Devel. Issues Jour., Econ. Devel. Quarterly, Urban Geography Jour.; contbr. articles and reviews to profl. jours. Mem. Gov.'s Coun. Selective Svc. in the State of Miss., 1969-80; bd. dirs. Boys and Girls Clubs of Lansing, 1986-89; chair bd. program com., bd. dirs. St. Vincent Children's Home/Catholic Social Svcs. of Lansing, 1986-89; mem. com. community rels. Tri-County Coun. Aging, 1987-89; mem. adv. com. Mich. Legis. Black Caucus Found., 1987—, hon. host Ann. Black History Month Celebration, 1989-91; mem. coordinating com. Friendship Baptist Ch. Acad. Enrichment Program, 1986-89; bd. dirs. Mich. Protection & Advocacy Svcs., 1991—; faculty advisor MSU Black Grad. Student's Assn., 1989-90; active CIC Acad. Leadership Devel. Program, 1989-90; co-founder, v.p. Black Men Inc. of Greater Lansing, 1992—. Acad. and Marching Band scholar Jackson State U., 1966-70; recipient Outstanding Leadership award Friendship Bapt. Ch. Laymen's League, 1988, Meritorious Svc. award Mich. Legis. Black Caucus Found., 1988; grantee Commn. on Geography and Afro-America and the Nat. Office of Edn., 1973, Jackson State U. Grad. Sch. Rsch. and Publ. Com., 1979, NASA, 1979-80, 80-81, U.S. Dept. Energy, 1980-81, 81-82, Inst. Rsch., Devel. & Engring. Nuclear Energy, 1980-81, NSF, 1980-82, Kellogg Found., 1981-84, Miss. Coun. Humanities, 1982-83, U.S. Bureau of the Census, 1988-90, C.S. Mott Found., 1990-93. Mem. Urban Affairs Assn. (nominating com. 1987-88, membership com. 1987—, site selection com. 1988-89, governing bd. 1989—, chair membership com. 1990-91, sec., treas. 1991-92, vice chair 1992—, chair 1993—), Assn. Am. Geographers (chair com. on the status of Afro-Am. geographers 1980-83, com. affirmative action 1983—, census adv. com. 1990—), Southeast Divsn. Assn. Am. Geographers (steering com. 1980-81, com. edn. 1981-86, program com. 1982), Nat. Coun. Geog. Edn. (remote sensing com. 1981-84), Assn. Advancement of Policy, Rsch. and Devel. in the Third World (conf. program planning com. 1988-89, chair health and population sect. 1988-89), Miss. Coun. Geog. Edn. (pres., chair program com. 1979-80), Population Assn. Am., Assn. Social and Behavioral Scientists, Mich. Acad. Scis., Sigma Rho Sigma Nat. Honor Soc., Gamma Theta Upsilon Nat. Honor Soc., Alpha Kappa Mu Nat. Honor Soc., Alpha Phi Alpha Frat., Inc. Home: 3700 Colchester Rd Lansing MI 48906-3418 Office: Mich State U Ctr for Integrative Social Sci S-G Berkey Hall East Lansing MI 48824 Office Phone: 517-355-6618. Business E-Mail: lang@msu.edu.

LANG, OTTO, retired gas industry executive, former Canadian cabinet minister; b. Handel, Sask., Can., May 14, 1932; s. Otto T. and Maria (Wurm) L.; m. Adrian Ann Merchant, 1963-88; children: Maria (dec.), Timothy, Gregory, Andrew, Elisabeth, Amanda, Adrian; m. Deborah McCawley, 1989; stepchildren: Andrew, Rebecca. BA, U. Sask., 1951, LLB, 1953; BCL (Rhodes scholar), Oxford U., Eng., 1955; LLD (hon.), U. Man., 1987. Bar: Sask. 1956, Ont., Yukon and .W.T 1972, Man. 1988; created Queen's counsel 1972. Mem. faculty Law Sch., U. Sask., 1956-68, assoc. prof. law, 1958-61, prof., dean law, 1961-68; M.P. for Sask.-Humboldt, 1968-79; Canadian min. without portfolio, 1968-69; min. for energy and water, 1969; min. of manpower and immigration, 1970-72; min. of justice, 1972-75, 78-79; min. transport, 1975-79; min.-in-charge Canadian Wheat Bd., 1969-79; exec. v.p. Pioneer Grain Co. Ltd., James Richardson & Sons Ltd., Winnipeg, Manitoba, Can., 1979-88; chmn. Transp. Inst., U. Man., Winnipeg, 1988-93; mng. dir. Winnipeg Airports Authority, Inc., 1992-93, vice chmn., 1993—2005; pres., CEO Centra Gas Manitoba, Inc., Winnipeg, 1993-99; cons. Winnipeg, 1999—; sr. counsel Fleishman-Hillard Can., 2000—. Mem. Queen's Privy Coun. for Can.; hon. consul gen. for Japan, 1993-97; bd. dirs. Investors Group Trust Co., London Life Trust Co., Winnipeg Airports Authority. Editor: Contemporary Problems in Public Law, 1967. V.P. Sask. Liberal Assn., 1956-62, fed. campaign chmn., Sask., 1963-64; campaign chmn. Winnipeg United Way, 1983; chmn. Royal Winnipeg Ballet Capital Campaign, 1996-99; co-chmn. Man. Fed. Liberal Campaign, 2005-06. Decorated officer Order of Can. Mem.: St. Charles Golf Club. Roman Catholic. Office: GPC 6 Liss Rd Saint Andrews MB Canada R1A 2X2

LANGBO, ARNOLD GORDON, retired food products company executive; b. Richmond, BC, Can., Apr. 13, 1937; s. Osbjourn and Laura Marie (Hagen) Langbo; m. Martha Marie Miller, May 30, 1959; children: Sharon Anne, Maureen Bernice, Susan Colleen, Roderick Arnold, Robert Wayne, Gary Thomas, Craig Peter, Keith Edward. Student, U. B.C. Retail salesman Kellogg Co., Vancouver, 1956-57, dist. mgr. Prince George, B.C., 1957-60, supermarket salesman Vancouver, 1960, dist mgr. Winnipeg, Man., 1964-65; acct. mgr. Kellog Co. of Can., Ltd., Toronto, 1965-67; sales staff asst. Kellogg Co., Battle Creek, Mich., 1967-69, adminstrv. asst. to pres., 1969; exec. v.p. Kellogg Co. of Can. Ltd., London, Ont., 1970; v.p. sales and mktg. Kellogg Salada Can. Ltd., Toronto, 1971-74, sr. v.p. sales and mktg., 1974-76, pres., CEO, 1976-78; pres. food products divsn. Kellogg U.S., Battle Creek, 1978-81; group exec. v.p. Kellogg Co., Battle Creek, 1983-86, exec. v.p., 1986—; pres. Mrs. Smith's Frozen Foods Co. subs. Kellogg Co., Battle Creek, 1983-85, chmn., CEO, 1985—86; pres. Kellogg Internat., 1986—90, pres., COO, internat. bd. dirs., 1990-99; chmn., CEO, pres. Kellogg Co., Battle Creek, 1992-99. Bd. dirs. Johnson & Johnson, 1991—, Whirlpool Corp., 1994—, Weyerhaeuser Co., 1999—, The Hershey Co., 2007—, Atlantic Richfield Co.; chmn. Grocery Mfrs. Am. Co-trustee W.K. Kellogg Found. Trust; chmn. trustees Albion Coll. Bd.; bd. dirs. Internat. Youth Found., America's Promise; mem. adv. bd. J.K. Kellogg Grad. Sch. of Mgmt., Northwestern U. Mem.: Bus. Roundtable.

LANGE, DAVID CHARLES, journalist; b. Natrona Heights, Pa., Oct. 14, 1949; s. Charles Manfred Lange and Helga (Hingst) Faverty; m. Linda Gaiduk, June 29, 1974; children: Erik David, Anthony Charles. BA in Journalism, Kent State U., 1975; postgrad., Akron U., 1980—83. Placement specialist Goodwill Industries Cleve., 1976-77; mng. editor, sports editor Chagrin Valley Times, Chagrin Falls, Ohio, 1977-82; editor Chagrin Valley Times/Solon Times, Chagrin Falls, 1988—; features editor, Sunday editor Lake County Telegraph, Painesville, Ohio, 1982-83; editor Geauga Times Leader, Chardon, Ohio, 1983-84; editor-in-chief Habitat, Cleve., 1984-88. Asst. swim coach Kenston H.S., 1999-2005, head swim coach, 2005-06. With USN, 1968-71, Vietnam. Recipient Democracy in Housing award Cleve. Assn. Real Estate Brokers, 1988. Mem. Soc. Profl. Journalists (Excellence in Journalism award human interest reporting 1981, Best Columnist in Ohio 2000), Ohio Newspaper Assn. (Hooper award for editl. writing 1991-92, 94, 96-2002, 04, 07, Hooper award for column writing 1993, 97, 2001-02, 04, 07, 08), Chagrin Valley C. of C., Solon C. of C., Cleve. Press Club, Nat. Newspaper Assn., VFW, Am. Legion, Vietnam Vets. Am. Avocations: swimming, skiing, tennis. Home: 8353 Chagrin Rd Chagrin Falls OH 44023-4757 Office: Chagrin Valley Times PO Box 150 Chagrin Falls OH 44022-0150

LANGE, GERALD F., state legislator; b. Devils Lake, ND, Sept. 19, 1928; m. Alice Lange; 4 children. BA Philosophy, U. N.D., 1951; student, Georgetown U., 1957, U. avarra, Pampaloma, Spain, 1964. High school teacher, 1954-62; prof. of history & govt. Dakota State U., 1964-90; mem. S.D. Senate, 1990—, mem. transp. retirement laws and taxation coms., chmn. local govt. com.; farmer. With US Army Signal Corps, 1946-47, with Army of Occupation, Japan, 1946-47.n Home: RR 3 Box 109 Madison SD 57042-9342

LANGE, MARILYN, social worker; b. Milw., Dec. 6, 1936; d. Edward F. and Erna E. (Karstaedt) L.; divorced; children: Lara Cash, Gregory Cash. B of Social Work, U. Wis., Milw., 1962, MSW, 1974. Cert. ind. clin. social worker. Recreation specialist Dept. Army, Europe, 1962-63; social worker Family Svc. Milw., 1967-75, dir. homecare divsn., 1975-85; nat. field rep. Alzheimers Assn., Chgo., 1986-90; exec. dir. Village Adult Svcs., Milw., 1991—. Mem. Nat. Coun. Aging, Wis. Adult Daysvcs. Assn. (past pres.), Dementia Care Network, Older Adult Svc. Providers Consortium, U. Wis.-Milw. Alumni Assn. Home: 8959 Woodbridge Dr Greendale WI 53129 Office: Village Adult Svcs 336 W Walnut St Milwaukee WI 53212-3811 E-mail: marilyn_lange@aurora.org.

LANGER, EDWARD L., trade association administrator; b. Cleve., May 8, 1936; s. Edward L. and Evelyn (Palmer) L.; m. Sheila Mary Fitzpatrick, Nov. 5, 1957 (div. Sept. 1976); children— Dennis, Edward, Michael, Thomas, Michele; m. Carol E. Stower, Aug. 4, 1979; children— Tamara, Troy BS, John Carroll U., 1958, MA, 1964; postgrad., Ohio U., 1962-63, Cleve. State U., 1967-68. Asst. dean admissions and records John Carroll U., University Heights, Ohio, 1964-65; head guidance Wickliffe City Schs., Ohio, 1965-67; successively dir. mem. relations, mktg., planning, asst. mng. dir. Am. Soc. for Metals, Materials Park, Ohio, 1967-84, mng. dir., 1984-96; bd. dirs., vice-chmn. Kolene Corp, 1997—. Bd. dirs. Kolene Corp. Author: Solid State Structures and Reactions, 1968 Bd. dirs., vice chmn. Cleve. Conv. Bur., 1984-98. Mem. Am. Soc. Assn. Execs. (bd. dirs., vice chmn. 1988-92), Coun. Engring. and Sci. Soc. Execs. (bd. dirs. 1987-93, pres. 1992), numerous other engring. and sci. socs. Avocations: fishing, golf.

LANGER, RICHARD J., lawyer; b. Rockford, Ill., June 10, 1944; s. John W. and Dorothy E. (Brunn) Langrehr; m. Audrey A. Russo, Jan. 28, 1967; children: Kathleen M., Michael R. BS, U. Ill., 1967; JD, U. Wis., 1974. Bar: Wis. 1974, U.S. Dist. Ct. (we. dist.) Wis. 1974. Assoc. Ela, Esch, Hart & Clark, Madison, Wis., 1974-76; ptnr. Stolper, Koritzinsky, Brewster & Neider, Madison, 1976-91, Michael, Best & Friedrich, Madison, 1991—. Pres. Hospice Care Found., Inc. Author: The Marital Property Classification Handbook, 1986, 2d edit., 1998, Workbook For Wisconsin Estate Planners, 1997, Family Estate Planning in Wisconsin, 1996, Conservation Easements: An Important Estate Planning Tool, 2002; contbr. articles to profl. jours. Named Outstanding Vol. Fund Raiser, Hospice Care Found., Inc., 2002. Fellow Am. Coll. Trust and Estate Coun.; mem. ABA, State Bar Wis., Madison Estate Coun. Avocations: scuba diving, travel, bicycling. Home: 1502 Windfield Way Madison WI 53562-3808 Office: Michael Best & Friedrich 1 S Pinckney St Madison WI 53703-2892 Office Phone: 608-283-2248. Business E-Mail: rjlanger@michaelbest.com.

LANGER, STEVEN, human resources specialist, consultant, psychologist; s. Israel and Anna (Glaisner) L.; m. Jacqueline White, Oct. 11, 1954 (dec. Dec. 1969); children: Bruce, Diana, Geoffrey; m. Elaine Catherine Brewer, Dec. 29, 1979 (dec. Feb. 1992). BA in Psychology, Calif. State U., Sacramento, 1950; MS in Pers. Svcs., U. Colo., 1958; PhD, Walden U., 1972. Lic. psychologist, Ill; cert.

sr. human resources specialist. Asst. to pers. dir. City and County of Denver, 1956-59; pers. dir. City of Pueblo, Colo., 1959-60; pers. cons. J.L. JAcobs & Co., Chgo., 1961-64, adminstrv. mgr., 1966-67; sales selection mgr. Reuben H. Donnelly Corp., Chgo., 1964-66; pres. Abbott, Langer & Assocs., Crete, Ill., 1967—2007, Langer Human Resources Group, LLP, Park Forest, Ill., 2007—. Vis. prof. mgmt. Loyola U., Chgo., 1969-71; community prof. behavioral scis. Purdue U., Calumet campus, Hammond, Ind., 1973-75. Contbr. articles to profl. jours. Mem. Ill. Psychol. Assn. (chmn. sect. indsl. psychologists 1971-72), Chgo. Psychol. Assn. (pres. 1974-75, 94-95), Chgo. Indsl./Orgnl. Psychologists, Soc. Human Resources Mgmt. (accredited, chmn. rsch. award com. 1966-69), World at Work, Chgo. Compensation Assn. (sec. 1976-77), Mensa (pres. Chgo. chpt. 1972-74). Unitarian Universalist. Office: Langer Human Resources Group LLP 247 Manhattan Dr Boulder CO 80303 Office Phone: 720-304-2171. Business E-Mail: SLanger@LangerHR.com.

LANGLEY, GRANT F., municipal lawyer; b. Worcester, Mass., July 20, 1945; BA, U. Wis., 1967; JD, Marquette U. Bar: State of Wis. Asst. city atty. City of Milw., 1971-84, city atty., 1984—. Mem. Supreme Ct. Selection Com., 2001—. Mem. Internat. Mcpl. Lawyers Assn. Office: Office of City Atty City Hall Rm 800 200 E Wells St Milwaukee WI 53202-3515

LANGSETH, KEITH, state legislator, farmer; b. Moorhead, Minn., Jan. 20, 1938; s. Norman Clifford and Ruth (Rosenquist) L.; m. Lorraine Mae Ersland, 1957; children: Danny, Gayle, Joy. Farmer; Dist. 9B rep. Minn. Ho. of Reps., St. Paul, 1975-78; mem. Minn. Senate from 9th dist., St. Paul, 1980—. Chmn. agr., transp. and semi-states divsn., Minn. State Senate; mem. Edn., Edn. Funding, Fin., Transp., and Met. Affairs coms.; bonding chair (capital investment), policy environ. & natural resources, fin.-edn. budget divn. transp. policy & budget divn., rules & adminstrn. Chmn. Dist. 9 Dem.-Farmer-Labor party, Minn., 1973-74, chmn. Clay County Dem.-Farmer-Labor party, 1974. Office: 14043 70th Ave SO Glyndon MN 56547-9531 also: State Senate State Capital Building Saint Paul MN 55155-0001

LANGSLEY, PAULINE ROYAL, psychiatrist; b. Lincoln, Nebr., July 2, 1927; d. Paul Ambrose and Dorothy (Sibley) Royal; m. Donald G. Langsley, Sept. 9, 1955; children: Karen Jean, Dorothy Ruth Langsley Runman, Susan Louise. BA, Mills Coll., 1949; MD, U. Nebr., 1953. Cert. psychiatrist, Am. Bd. Psychiatry and Neurology. Intern Mt. Zion Hosp., San Francisco, 1954; resident U. Calif., San Francisco, 1954-57, student health psychiatrist Berkeley, 1957-61, U. Colo., Boulder, 1961-68; assoc. clin. prof. psychiatry U. Calif. Med. Sch., Davis, 1968-76; student health psychiatrist U. Calif., Davis, 1968-76; assoc. clin. prof. psychiatry U. Cin., 1976-82; pvt. practice psychiatry Cin., 1976-82; cons. psychiatrist Federated States of Micronesia, Pohnpei, 1984-87; fellow in geriatric psychiatry Rush-Presbyn./St. Luke Hosp., Chgo., 1989-91. Mem. accreditation rev. com. Accreditation Coun. for Continuing Med. Edn., 1996-98. Trustee Mills Coll., Oakland, 1974-78, 2001—; bd. dirs. Evanston Women's Club. Fellow Am. Psychiat. Assn. (chair continuing med. edn. 1990-96); mem. AMA, Am. Med. Womens Assn., Ohio State Med. Assn., Ill. Psychiat. Soc. (sec. 1993-95, pres.-elect 1995-96, pres. 1996-97, accreditation coun. 1996-98). Home and Office: 1111 Race St 10A Denver CO 80206 Home Phone: 303-321-4193; Office Phone: 303-321-4193.

LANGSTON, EDWARD LEE, physician, pharmacist; b. Logansport, Ind., Sept. 28, 1944; m. Linda Langston; 2 children. BS in pharmacy, Purdue U. Sch. Pharmacy; MD, Ind. U. Sch. Medicine. Bd. cert. in family practice. Resident in family practice St. Mary's Grad. Med. Ctr., Evansville, Ill.; chair Commn. on Legis.; dir. family practice program, assoc. prof. Tex. Med. Ctr., 1993—96; v.p. med. affairs and med. edn. Trinity Regional Health Sys., Rock Island, Ill., 1996—2000; pvt. practice family physician Lafayette, Ind., 2000—. Affiliate asst. prof. Purdue U., Sch. Pharmacy, West Lafayette, Ind.; mem. adv. com. State Medicaid Prescription Drug; coord., sec. Lafayette Med. Edn. Found., 2001—; vol. faculty Cmty. Hosp. Family Practice Residency Program, dir., 1988—92; mem. bd. trustees US Pharmacopoeia, 1995—2000; bd. dir. Accreditation Coun. on Grad. Med. Edn., 1998—2003; bd. commr. Joint Commn. on Accreditation of Healthcare Orgn., 2005—. Mem.: Ind. State Med. Assn., Am. Acad. Family Physicians (bd. dir. 1991—93, v.p. 1994, chair delegation 1999—2002), AMA (house del. 1987—, mem., coun. on med. edn. 1997—2003, bd. trustees 2003—, chair-elect bd. trustees 2006—07, chmn. bd. trustees 2007—, mem., chair, specialty and svc. soc.), Ind. Acad. Family Physicians (pres. 1982—83), Alpha Omega Alpha. Avocations: jogging, reading, furniture refinishing. Office: 2323 Ferry St Ste 101 Lafayette IN 47904 Office Phone: 765-448-4511.

LANGSTON, MALINDA L., lawyer; b. Lexington, Ky., May 10, 1971; BS, Ga. Southern U., 1993; JD, U. Dayton, 1997. Bar: Ohio 1997, Ky. 1999. Asst. pros. atty. Montgomery County, Ohio; assoc. Kohnen & Patton LLP, Cin. Named one of Ohio's Rising Stars, Super Lawyers, 2006. Mem.: Northern Ky. Bar Assn., Ky. Bar Assn., Ohio State Bar Assn., Cin. Bar Assn. Office: Kohnen & Patton LLP PNC Ctr Ste 800 E Fifth St Cincinnati OH 45202 Office Phone: 513-381-0656. Office Fax: 513-381-5823.

LANGWORTHY, AUDREY HANSEN, state legislator; b. Grand Forks, ND, Apr. 1, 1938; d. Edward H. and Arla (Kuhlman) Hansen; m. Asher C. Langworthy Jr., Sept. 8, 1962; children: Kristin Langworthy McLaughlin, Julia Langworthy Steinberg. BS, U. Kans., 1960, MS, 1962; postgrad., Harvard U., 1989. Tchr. jr. high sch. Shawnee Mission Sch. Dist., Johnson County, Kans., 1963-65; councilperson City of Prairie Village, Kans., 1981-85; mem. Kans. Senate from 7th dist., Topeka, 1985-2001. Alt. del. Nat. Conf. State Legislatures, 1985-87, del., 1987—, nominating com., 1990-92, vice chair fed. budget and taxation com., 1994, chair fed. budget and taxation com., 1995-96, vice chair assembly on federal issues, 1996-97, mem. exec. com., 1997-2000; del. Midwestern Conf. State Legislatures, 1989-98; mem. strategic planning com. Coun. State Govts., 1997-98; bd. dirs. St. Luke's/Shawnee Mission Med. Ctr. Found., 1997—. City co-chmn. Kassebaum for U.S. Senate, Prairie Village, 1978; pres. Jr. League Kansas City, Mo., 1977, Kansas City Eye Bank, 1980-82, chmn., 1983-85, bd. mem., 1977-98; mem. bd. Greater Kansas City ARC, 1975—, pres., 1984, chmn. midwestern adv. coun., 1985-86, nat. bd. govs., 1987-93; mem. Johnson County C.C. Found., 1999—; mem. Leadership Kans., Germany Today Program, 1991; bd. dirs. Kans. Wildlife & Parks Fund; trustee Found. on Aging, 1992-96; hon. co-chair Shawnee Mission Edn. Found. Benefit Showtime 99, 1999; mem. Johnson County adv. com. Met. Orgn. to Counter Sexual Assault, 1999—; bd. dirs. Cmty. Found. of Johnson County, 1999—, Heart of Am. United Way, 2000—; chair Kans. 3rd dist. George W. Bush-Pres., 2000; elected precinct committeewoman, 2000—; del. Rep. Nat. Conv., 2000, mem. platform com. Recipient Outstanding Vol. award Cmty. Svcs. Award Found., 1983, Confidence in Edn. award Friends of Edn., 1984, Pub. Svc. award as Kans. Legislator of Yr., Hallmark Polit. Action Com., 1991, Clara Barton Honor award Greater Kans. City ARC, Intergovtl. Leadership award League Kans. Mcpls., 1994, Disting. Pub. Svc. award United Cmty. Svcs. of Johnson County, 1995, Outstanding Achievement in Hist. Preservation award Alexander Majors Hist. House, 1995, Kansas City Spirit award, 1996, disting. pub. svc. award Prairie Village, 1995, Audrey Langworthy award Univ. Mo-Kansas City Women's Coun. Grad. Asst. Fund, 1997, Audrey Langworthy award Outstanding Youth Vol. Work Greater Kansas City ARC, 1996, Regional Leadership award Mid-Am. Regional Coun., 1999, award of appreciation Kans. Rep. Party, 2000, Cmty. Svc. award Greater Kansas City Women's Polit. Caucus, 2000, Recognition for Leadership and Svc., Greater Kansas City C. of C., 2000; named 1st hon. chair The Genevieve Byrn Series, Greater Kansas City ARC, 2000. Mem. LWV, Women's Pub. Svc. Network, U. Kans. Alumni Assn. Episcopalian. Avocations: hunting, running. Home: 6324 Ash St Prairie Village KS 66208-1369 E-mail: alangwo622@aol.com.

LANGWORTHY, ROBERT BURTON, lawyer; b. Kansas City, Mo., Dec. 24, 1918; s. Herman Moore and Minnie (Leach) L.; m. Elizabeth Ann Miles, Jan. 2, 1942 (dec. Dec. 2006); children: David Robert, Joan Elizabeth Langworthy Tomek, Mark Burton. AB, Princeton U., 1940; JD magna cum laude, Harvard U., 1943. Bar: Mo. 1943, U.S. Supreme Ct. 1960, Kans. 2006. Pvt. practice, Kansas City, 1943—; assoc., then mem. and v.p. Linde, Thomson, Langworthy, Kohn & Van Dyke, P.C., 1943—91; pres., mng. shareholder Blackwood, Langworthy & Schmelzer, P.C., Kansas City, 1991—96; mng. mem. Blackwood, Langworthy & Tyson, L.C., and predecessor, Kansas City, 1996—. Lectr. on probate, law sch. CLE courses U. Mo., Kansas City. Mem. bd. editors Harvard Law Rev., 1941-43; contbr. chpts. to Guardian and Trust, Powers, Conservatorships and Nonprobate Desk Books of Mo. Bar. Mem. edn. appeal bd. U.S. Dept. Edn., 1982-86; commr. Housing Authority Kansas City, 1963-71, chmn., 1969-71; chmn. Bd. Election Commrs. Kansas City, 1973-77; chmn. bd. West Ctrl. area YMCA, 1969-95; bd. dirs. Mid-Am. region YMCA, 1970-83, vice chmn., 1970-73, chmn., 1973-78; pres. Met. Bd. Kansas City (Mo.) YMCA (now YMCA Greater Kansas City), 1965, bd. dirs., 1965-2004, nat. bd. 1971-78, 79-83; bd. dirs. YMCA of Rockies, 1974-2003, bd. sec., 1994-99, adv. dir., 2004—; bd. dirs. YMCA Found. Kansas City, 2005-; trustee Sioux Indian YMCAs, 1983-2002, chmn. bd. trustees, 1983-2002, chmn. hon. trustees, 2003—; bd. dirs. Armed Svcs. YMCA, 1984-85; pres. Met. Area Citizens Edn., 1969-72; chmn. Citizens Assn. Kansas City (Mo.), 1967, bd. dirs., 1995-96; bd. dirs. Presbyn. Ch. Kans.-Mo., 1967-80, pres., 1970-72, treas., 1972-73, sec., 1973-76; 1st v.p. Human Resources Corp. Kansas City, 1969-73, bd. dirs., 1965-73; hon. v.p. Am. Sunday Sch. Union (now Am. Missionary Fellowship), 1965—; vice chmn. bd. trustees Kemper Mil. Sch., 1966-73; U.S. del. YMCA World Coun., Buenos Aires, 1977, Estes Park, Colo., 1981, Nyborg, Denmark, 1985; bd. dirs. Mo. Rep. Club, 1960-2001; del., platform com. Rep. Nat. Conv., 1960; Rep. nominee U.S. Congress, 1964; mem. gen. assembly Com. on Representation Presbyn., 1991-97, moderator, 1993-94; commr. to gen. assembly Presbyn. Ch., 1984, gen. assembly com. on location of hdqrs. 1984-87; moderator Heartland Presbytery, 1984. Lt. (j.g.) USNR, 1943-46, capt. Res. ret. Mem.: ABA, Kans. Bar Assn., Harvard Law Sch. Assn. Mo. (v.p. 1973—74, pres. 1974—75, 1985—87), Lawyers Assn. Kansas City, Mo. State Bar (chmn. probate and trust com. 1983—85, chmn. sr. lawyers com. 1991—93), Kansas City Met. Bar Assn. (chmn. probate law com. 1988—90, 1999—2000, living will com. 1989—91), Kansas City Club. Presbyterian. Home: Claridge Ct Apt 305 8101 Mission Rd Prairie Village KS 66208-5238 Office: 1220 Washington St Ste 300 Kansas City MO 64105-1439 Home Phone: 913-381-2787; Office Phone: 816-474-6200. Business E-Mail: robert.langworthy@blackwoodlaw.com.

LANIGAN, JOHN, radio personality; b. Pgallala, Nebr., 1942; With WGAR, 1971—85; radio host WMJI, Cleve., 1985—. Co-host (radio shows) The Lanigan & Malone Show. Co-recipient (with Jimmy Malone) Large Market Personality of Yr., NAB Marconi Radio Awards, 2005; named Cleveland's Favorite Radio Performer (twice), WJW Cleve. Office: WMJI 105.7 6200 Oak Tree Blvd 4th Fl Independence OH 44131 also: WMJI 105.7 FM Fl 6 310 W Lakeside Ave Cleveland OH 44113 E-mail: lanigan@wmji.com.

LANNERT, ROBERT CORNELIUS, manufacturing executive; b. Chgo., Mar. 14, 1940; s. Robert Carl and Anna Martha (Cornelius) L.; children: Jacqueline, Krista, Kevin, Meredith. BS in Indsl. Mgmt., Purdue U., 1963; MBA, Northwestern U., 1967; grad. Advanced Mgmt. Program, Harvard U., 1978. With Navistar Internat. Corp. (formerly Internat. Harvester), Chgo., 1963—; staff asst. overseas fin. Navistar Internat. Transp. Corp. (formerly Internat. Harvester), Chgo., 1967-70; asst. mgr., treas. and contr. IH Finanz AG, Zurich, Switzerland, 1970-72; mgr. overseas fin. corp. hdqrs. Internat. Truck & Engine Co., Chgo., 1972—76, asst. treas., 1976—79, v.p., treas., 1979—90; exec. v.p., chief fin. officer Navistar Internat. Corp., Chgo., 1990—2002, vice chmn., CFO, 2002—, also bd. dirs. Bd. dirs. Internat. Truck and Engine Co., Harbour Assurance Co., Bermuda, Navistar Fin. Corp., Chgo. Home: 904 Kenmare Dr Burr Ridge IL 60527 Office: Navistar Internat Corp 4201 Winfield Rd PO Box 1488 Warrenville IL 60555

LANPHEAR, BRUCE PERRIN, health facility administrator, educator; BA in Biology, U. Mo., Kansas City, 1985, MD, 1986; MPH, Tulane Sch., 1988. Diplomate Am. Bd. Gen. Preventive Medicine and Pub. Health. Resident in gen. preventive medicine and pub. health Tulane Sch. of Pub. Health and Tropical Medicine, 1989; fellowship in gen. acad. pediatric rsch. U. Rochester Sch. Medicine and Dentistry, 1995; assoc. prof. pediatrics; dir. children's environtl. health ctr. Cin. Children's Hosp. Med. Ctr. Sci. and rsch. work group EPA's Office of Children's Environtl. Health Protection; scientific cons. Nat. Ctr. for Lead-Safe Housing, Columbia, Md.

LANSAW, JUDY W., public utility executive; b. Dayton, Ohio, July 12, 1951; d. Edwin Columbus and Stella Sabra (Roark) Wyatt; m. James L. Schaefer, Oct. 16, 1971 (div. 1975); m. Charles Edward Lansaw, Dec. 30, 1982; 1 child, Eric. BA in Organizational Communications, Wright State U., Dayton, 1988. Legal sec. Robert Abrahamson, atty., Dayton, 1970-78; exec. adminstrv. asst. Dayton Power & Light Co., 1978-81, mktg. rsch. energy specialist, 1981-84, exec. asst. to chief exec. officer, 1984-88, corp. sec., 1988—, v.p., 1989—; corp. sec. DPL Inc., Dayton, 1988—, v.p., 1989—. Trustee Jobs for Grads., Inc., Dayton, 1989-92, Victoria Theatre Assn., Dayton, 1990—. Mem. Am. Soc. Corp. Secs., Dayton Club, Racquet Club. Republican. Avocations: tennis, skiing, golf, sailing. Home: PO Box 750130 Dayton OH 45475-0130 Office: DPL Inc 1065 Woodman Dr Dayton OH 45432-1438

LANTZ, JOANNE BALDWIN, retired academic administrator; b. Defiance, Ohio, Jan. 26, 1932; d. Hiram J. and Ethel A. (Smith) Baldwin; m. Wayne E. Lantz. BS in Physics and Math., U. Indpls., 1953; MS in Counseling and Guidance, Ind. U., 1957; PhD in Counseling and Psychology, Mich. State U., 1969; LittD (hon.), U. Indpls., 1985; LHD (hon.), Purdue U., 1994; LLD (hon.), Manchester Coll., 1994. Tchr. physics and math. Arcola (Ind.) High Sch., 1953-57; guidance dir. New Haven (Ind.) Sr. High Sch., 1957-65; with Ind. U.-Purdue U., Fort Wayne, 1965—, interim chancellor, 1988-89, chancellor, 1989-94, chancellor emeritus, 1994—. Bd. dirs., hon. dir. Ft. Wayne Nat. Corp.; bd. dirs. Foellinger Found., 1992-2007. Contbr. articles to profl. jours. Mem. Ft. Wayne Econ. Devel. Adv. Bd. and Task Force, 1988-91, Corp. Coun., 1988-94; bd. advisors Leadership Ft. Wayne, 1988-94; mem. adv. bd. Ind. Sml. Bus. Devel. Ctr., 1988-90; trustee Ancilla System, Inc., 1984-89, chmn. human resources com., 1985-89, exec. com., 1985-89; trustee St. Joseph's Med. Ctr., 1983-84, pers. adv. com. to bd. dirs., 1978-84, chmn., 1980-84; bd. dirs. United Way Allen County, sec., 1979-80; bd. dirs. Anthony Wayne Vocat. Rehab. Ctr., 1969-75. Mem.: AAUW (Am. women fellowship com. 1978—83, program com. 1981—83, chmn. 1981—83, internat. fellowship com. 1986—88, trust rsch. grantee 1980), APA, Southeastern Psychol. Assn. (referee conv. papers 1987—88), Ft. Wayne Ind.-Purdue Alumni Soc. (hon.), Ind. Sch. Women's Club (v.p. program chair 1979—81), Delta Kappa Gamma (leadership devel. com. 1978—82, dir. N.E. region 1982—84, exec. bd. 1982—84, adminstrv. bd. 1982—84, gen. chair conv. 1985—86, editl. bd. 1986—88, bd. trustees ednl. found. 1996—2002, nominating com. 2002—06), Sigma Xi, Pi Lambda Theta. Avocations: swimming, reading, knitting, boating. Personal E-mail: joalantz@aol.com.

LANZINGER, JUDITH ANN, state supreme court justice; b. Toledo, Apr. 2, 1946; m. Robert C. Lanzinger, Jr., 1967; 2 children. BA in Edn., U. Toledo, 1968, JD, 1977; MS in Jud. Studies, Nat. Jud. Coll., U. Nev., Reno, 1992. Bar: Ohio, U.S. Supreme Ct., U.S. Dist. Ct. for Northern Dist. of Ohio, U.S. Dist. Ct. for Eastern Dist. of Mich., Sixth Circuit Ct. of Appeals. Atty. environmental law Toledo Edison Co., 1978—81; atty. employment law and litigation Shumaker, Loop and Kendrick, 1981—85; judge Toledo Municipal Ct., 1985—88, Lucas County Common Pleas Ct., 1989—2003, Ohio Sixth Dist. Ct. of Appeals, 2003—04; justice Ohio Supreme Ct., 2005—. Adjunct prof. U. Toledo Coll. of Law, 1988—2006; prof. Nat. Jud. Coll., 1990—; mem. Ohio Criminal Sentencing Commn., 1991—97; co-chair Public Ed. and Awareness Task Force Ohio Cts. Futures Commn., 1996—2000; chair Ohio Jud. Coll., 2000—01; former mem. Ohio Supreme Ct. Bd. of Grievances and Discipline; chair Commn. Rules of Superintendence, Ohio Cts., 2006—. Recipient Superior Jud. Service award, Ohio Supreme Ct., 1985, Arabella Babb Mansfield award, Toledo Women's Bar Assn., 1995, Service to Judicial Ed. award, Ohio Jud. Coll., 2002, Golden Gavel award, Ohio Common Pleas Judges' Assn., 2002. Fellow: Ohio Bar Found.; mem.: Thurgood Marshall Assn., Am. Judicature Soc., Nat. Assn. of Women Judges, Am. Judges Assn., Ohio Bar Assn., Morrison R. Waite Am. Inn of Ct. (pres. 2000—02). Office: Ohio Supreme Ct 65 S Front St Columbus OH 43215-3431 Office Phone: 614-387-9090.

LANZINGER, KLAUS, language educator; b. Woergl, Tyrol, Austria, Feb. 16, 1928; arrived in U.S., 1971, naturalized, 1979; m. Aida Schuessl, June, 1954; children: Franz, Christine. BA, Bowdoin Coll., 1951; PhD, U. Innsbruck, Austria, 1952. Rsch. asst. U. Innsbruck, 1957-67; assoc. prof. modern langs. U. Notre Dame, Ind., 1967-77, prof., 1977-97, prof. emeritus, 1997—. Resident dir. fgn. study program, Innsbruck, 1969-71, 76-78, 82-85; acting chmn. dept. Modern and Classical Langs., U. Notre Dame, fall 1987, chmn. dept. German and Russian, 1989-96. Author: Epik im amerikanischen Roman, 1965, Jason's Voyage: The Search for the Old World in Am. Lit., 1989, America-Europe: A Transatlantic Diary 1961-1989, 2007; editor: Americana-Austriaca, 5 vols., 1966-83; contbr. articles to profl. jours. Fgn. Student scholar Bowdoin Coll., 1950-51; Fulbright Rsch. grantee U. Pa., 1961; U. Notre Dame Summer Rsch. grant Houghton Libr., Harvard U., 1975, 81; named to Internat. Order of Merit, 2001; recipient Lifetime Achievement award Internat. Biographical Ctr., Cambridge, Eng., 2007. Mem. MLA, Deutsche Gesellschaft für Amerikastudien, Thomas Wolfe Soc. (Zelda Gitlin Lit. prize 1993). Home: 52703 Helvie Dr South Bend IN 46635-1215 Office: Dept German Russian Langs & Lits U Notre Dame Notre Dame IN 46556

LANZNAR, HOWARD S., lawyer; b. Champaign, Ill., Aug. 15, 1955; BA, Amherst Coll., 1977; JD, U. Chgo., 1983. Bar: Ill. 1983. Ptnr. Katten Muchin Zavis Rosenman, Chgo. Mem.: ABA, Chgo. Bar Assn., Lincoln Park Zoological Soc. Office: Katten Muchin Zavis Rosenman 525 W Monroe St Chicago IL 60661 Office Phone: 312-902-5696, 312-577-8798. E-mail: howard.lanznar@kmzr.com.

LAPACZ, STEVEN P., social services association executive; b. Green Bay, Wis. Former tchr. jr. h.s.; sr. programmer Aid Assn. for Luths., Appleton, Wis., 1974-79, sr. programmer analyst, 1979-87, dir. micro-devel. svcs., 1987-88, asst. v.p., 1988-95, 2d v.p. micro-devel. svcs., 1995, 2d v.p. application devel. svcs., 1995—. Mem. Ops. Coun., Soc. for Info. Mgmt. Office: Aid Assn for Luths 4321 N Ballard Rd Appleton WI 54919-0001

LAPHEN, JAMES A., investment company executive; Pres., COO Comml. Fed. Bank, Omaha, 1988-2000; CEO 1st Fed. Lincoln Bank, Nebr., 2000—01; pres., COO TierOne Corp., Lincoln, Nebr., 2001—. Office: TierOne Corp 1235 N St Lincoln NE 68508

LAPIN, HARVEY I., lawyer; b. St. Louis, Nov. 23, 1937; s. Lazarus L. and Lillie L. Lapin; m. Cheryl A. Lapin; children: Jeffrey, Gregg. BS, Northwestern U., 1960, JD, 1963; LLM in Tax Law, Georgetown Law Ctr., Washington, 1967. CPA Ill.; bar: Ill. 1963, Fla. 1980, Wis. 1985, cert.: Fla. (tax lawyer). Atty. Office Chief Counsel, IRS, Washington, 1963-65; trial atty. Office Regional Counsel, IRS, Washington, 1965-68; from assoc. to ptnr. Fiffer & D'Angelo, Chgo., 1968-75; pres. Harvey I. Lapin, P.C., Chgo., 1975-83; mng. ptnr. Lapin, Hoff, Spangler & Greenberg, Chgo., 1983-88, Lapin, Hoff, Slaw & Laffey, Chgo., 1989-91; ptnr. Gottlieb and Schwartz, Chgo., 1992-93; prin. Harvey I. Lapin & Assocs., P.C., Northbrook, Ill., 1993—2003, Harvey I. Lapin, P.C. (formerly Harvey I. Lapin & Assocs., P.C.), Northbrook, 2004—. Instr. John Marshall Law Sch., 1969—; facility adv. lawyers asst. program Roosevelt U., Chgo.; mem. cemetery adv. bd. Ill. Comptr., 1974—96, 1999—; mem. IRS Gt. Lakes TE/EO Coun., 2001—. Asst. editor: Fed. Bar Jour., 1965—67; contbg. editor: (book) Cemetery and Funeral Service Business and Legal Guide; contbr. articles to profl. jours. Bd. mem. Cotswold Homeowners Assn., 1994—, pres., 1994—97, treas., 1997—; bd. mem. Art Alliance Contemporary Glass, 2006—, Midwest Contemporary Glass Arts Group, 2003—, pres., 2007—. Mem.: ABA, Chgo. Bar Assn., Ill. Bar Assn., Wis. Bar Assn., Fla. Bar Assn. Jewish. Office: Harvey I Lapin PC PO Box 1327 Northbrook IL 60065-1327 Business E-Mail: harv4law@sbcglobal.net.

LAPIN, JEFFRY MARK, magazine publisher; b. Pawtucket, RI, Mar. 18, 1953; s. Nathan and Jeannette Mildred (Rose) L.; m. Lynne Miller, June 7, 1975. BA, Bethany Coll., 1975; MBA, Xavier U., 1984. Fashion illustrator, copywriter L.S. Good & Co., Wheeling, W.Va, 1975; mgr. mktg. Writer's Digest Books, Cin., 1976-80; dir. circulation Harvest Pub. Co., Cleve., 1980-82, bus. mgr., 1982-84; dir. circulation F&W Pubs., Inc., Cin., 1984-85, v.p., gen. mgr. mag. div., 1986—; pub. Artist's Mag., Cin., 1985—. Cons. copy/design, Cleve., 1980-84. Author Circulation Mgmt., 1987—. Mem. Mag. Pubs. Assn., Hobby Industries Am., Nat. Art Materials Trade Assn., Cin. Art Club, Cin. Direct. Mktg. Club. Avocations: music, art, home remodeling. Office: F&W Pubs 1507 Dana Ave Cincinnati OH 45207-1000

LAPINSKY, JOSEPH F., manufacturing executive; married; 2 daughters. MS in Indsl. Rels., W.Va. U., 1973; MBA in Mgmt., Youngstown State U., 1984. Early career positions include conditioning foreman Copperweld Steel Co., then ops., mgr. human resources, v.p. human resources, 1974-91, also exec. v.p.; ind. industry cons., 1991-95; gen. mgr. hot rolled bar ops. Republic Techs. Internat., Akron, Ohio, 1995-97, pres. Hot Rolled Bar divsn., 1997-98; pres., COO Republic Engineered Steels and Bar Techs., Akron, 1998—99; COO Republic Techs. Internat., Akron, 1999—2002; CEO, pres. Republic Engineered Products (formerly Republic Techs. Internat.), 2002—.

LAPLANTE, R. BROOKS, state representative; b. Rockville Center, NY, July 6, 1953; married; 3 children. BA in Gen. Sci., U. Rochester, NYC, NROTC. Materials mgr. Ontario Metal Supply, 1977—84; customer svc. mgr. Alcan Rolled Products (formerly ARCO), 1984—87; exec. v.p., ptnr. Splty. Blanks, Inc., 1987—99; COO, ptnr. Doughmakers, LLC, 1999—; rep. dist. 46 Ind. Ho. of Reps., Indpls., 2002—04, mem. commerce and econ. devel., fin. instns., and interstate and internat. cooperation coms. Mem. Wabash Valley Youth for Christ, Ind. Officer NROTC USN, 1973—77. Mem.: Ind. Mfrs. Assn., NRA, Jr. Achievement of Wabash Valley, Ind. Right to Life, Boy Scouts of Am., Sigma Chi. Republican. Office: Doughmakers PO Box 10034 Terre Haute IN 47801

LA PLATA, GEORGE, federal judge; b. 1924; m. Frances Hoyt; children: Anita J. La Plata Rard, Marshall. AB, Wayne State U., 1951; LLB, Detroit Coll. Law, 1956. Pvt. practice law, 1956-79; judge Oakland County (Mich.) Cir. Ct., Pontiac, 1979-85, U.S. Dist. Ct. (ea. dist.) Mich., Ann Arbor, 1985-96; spl. litigation counsel Allan Miller, P.C., Mich., 1996—. Prof. Detroit Coll. Law, 1985-86. Trustee William Beaumont Hosp., 1979—, United Found., 1983—. Served to col. USMC, 1943-46, 52-54. Mem. ABA, Oakland County Bar Assn., Hispanic Bar Assn. Lodges: Optimists. Office: Allan Miller PC 370 E Maple Rd Fl 4 Birmingham MI 48009-6303

LAPTEWICZ, JOSEPH E., JR., medical products executive; married; 3 children. MS in Biochem. Engring., Cornell U., 1972; BSChemE, Worcester Polytechnic Inst., 1971; MBA in Mktg. and Fin., U. New Haven, 1978. Prodn. supr. Pfizer Chem. Divsn., Southport and Groton, 1972-77; project leader fermentation recovery Pfizer Ctrl. Rsch. Divsn., Groton, 1977-80; contr. Howmedica R&D Pfizer Hosp. Products Group, Groton, 1981-83, dir. ventures, 1984-86, dir. corp. R&D, 1987-89; v.p., gen. mgr. Schneider U.S. Stent Divsn., Plymouth, Minn., 1990-91; pres., exec. v.p. Schneider (USA) Inc., Plymouth, Minn., 1991-94; pres., CEO, Empi, Inc., St. Paul, 1994—; dir. Angiodynamics, Inc. Patentee in field. Key account exec. Mpls. chpt. United Way; bd. advisors Coll. of St. Catherine. Mem. AIChE, Worcester Polytechnic Inst. Alumni Assn. Avocations: sailing, golf. Office: EMPI,Inc 599 Cardigan Rd Saint Paul MN 55126-4099

LARBALESTIER, DAVID CHISTOPHER, materials scientist, educator; b. Castle Carey, U.K., May 22, 1943; came to U.S., 1976; s. Basil Douglas and Anna (Felder) L.; m. Karen Anne Williams, May 6, 1967; children: Nikolai David, Laura Jane, Eleanor Lucy. BS, U. London, 1965, PhD, 1970. Staff scientist Battelle Lab., Geneva, 1970-72; sr. sci. officer Rutherford Lab., Chilton Didcot, U.K., 1973-76; asst. prof. U. Wis., Madison, 1976-78, assoc. prof., 1978-81, prof., 1981—, L.V. Shubnikov prof., 1990—, dir. Applied Superconductivity Ctr., 1991—, Grainger prof. superconducting materials, 1996—. Panel mem. NAS, Washington, 1987. Contbr. articles to profl. jours. Recipient Matthey prize U. London, 1970, IEEE particle Accelerator Conf. award, 1991, Byron award U. Wis., 1992, others. Fellow Am. Phys. Soc.; mem. NAE, Materials Rsch. Soc., Metall. Soc. Office: U Wis Appl Superconductivity Ctr 915 Engring Rsch Bldg 1500 Engineering Dr Madison WI 53706-1609 Office Phone: 608-263-2194. E-mail: larbales@engr.wisc.edu.

LARDAKIS, MOIRA GAMBRILL, insurance executive, lawyer; b. Cleve., Sept. 14, 1951; d. Merle LC. and Ellen K. (Moore) Gambrill; m. Tony E. Lardakis, Aug. 31, 1985; children: Christopher E., Michael A. BA, Cleve. State U., 1972; JD, Cleveland Marshall Coll. Law, 1981. Bar: Ohio 1981. Child care supr. Lake County Comprehensive Ctr., Cleve., 1973-75, work adjustment counselor, 1975-78; with Progressive Casualty Ins. Co., Mayfield Village, Ohio, 1978—, gen. mgr., 1985-87, div. pres., 1987—. Mem. Ohio Bar Assn.

LARDY, HENRY A(RNOLD), biochemistry professor; b. Roslyn, SD, Aug. 19, 1917; s. Nicholas and Elizabeth (Gebetsreiter) L.; m. Annrita Dresselhuys, Jan. 21, 1943; children: Nicholas, Diana, Jeffrey, Michael. BS, S.D. State U.,

1939, DSc (hon.), 1979; MS, U. Wis., 1941, PhD, 1943. Asst. prof. U. Wis., Madison, 1945-47, assoc. prof., 1947-50, prof., 1950-88, Vilas prof. biol. sci., 1966-88, prof. emeritus, 1988—. Henry Lardy annual lectr. S.D. State U., Brookings, 1985. Mem. editl. bd. Archives Biochemistry and Biophysics, 1957-60, Jour. Biol. Chemistry, 1958-64, 80-85, Biochem. Preparations, Methods of Biochem. Analysis, Biochemistry, 1962-73, 75-81; contbr. over 470 articles to profl. jours. Pres. Citizens vs McCarthy, Wis., 1950. Recipient Neuberg medal Am. Soc. European Chemists, 1956, Wolf prize in agr., Wolf Found., Israel, 1981, Nat. award Agrl. Excellence, 1982. Fellow Wis. Acad. Arts and Scis.; mem. Am. Chem. Soc. (chmn. biol. divsn. 1958, Paul-Lewis Labs. award 1949), Am. Soc. Biol. Chemists (pres. 1964, William Rose award 1988), Am. Acad. Arts and Scis. (Amory prize 1984), Am. Philos. Soc., Am. Diabetes Assn., Nat. Acad. Scis., Biochem. Soc. Great Britain, Harvey Soc., Soc. for Study of Reprodn. (Carl Hartman award 1984), The Endocrine Soc., Japanese Biochem. Soc. (hon.), Golden Retriever Club Am. (pres. 1964). Democrat. Achievements include patents for steroid compounds and lab. apparatus. Home: 1829 Thorstrand Rd Madison WI 53705-1052 Office: U Wis 1710 University Ave Madison WI 53726-4087 Home Phone: 608-233-1584; Office Phone: 608-262-3372. Business E-Mail: halardy@wisc.edu.

LARDY, SISTER SUSAN MARIE, academic administrator; b. Sentinel Butte, ND, Nov. 9, 1937; d. Peter Aloysius and Elizabeth Julia (Dietz) L. BS in Edn., U. Mary, Bismarck, ND, 1965; MEd, U. N.D., 1972. Entered Order of St. Benedict, Bismarck, 1957. Elem. tchr. Cathedral Grade Sch., Bismarck, 1958-67, Christ the King Sch., Mandan, N.D., 1967-68, 70-72, St. Joseph's Sch., Mandan, 1968-70; asst. prof. edn. U. Mary, Bismarck, 1972-80; adminstr., asst. prioress Annunciation Priory, Bismarck, 1980-84, prioress, major superior, 1984-96; dir. U. Mary-Fargo (N.D.) Ctr., 1997—. Dir. Fargo Ctr. U. Mary, 1997—. Mem. Delta Kappa Gamma. Home: 1101 32nd Ave S Fargo ND 58103-6036 Office: U Mary Fargo Ctr 3001 25th St S Fargo ND 58103-5055

LARIVIERE, RICHARD WILFRED, academic administrator, educator; b. Chgo., Jan. 27, 1950; s. Wilfred Francis and Esther Irene Lariviere; m. Janis Anne Worcester, June 5, 1971; 1 child, Anne Elizabeth. BA, U. Iowa, Iowa City, 1972; PhD, U. Pa., Phila., 1978. Lectr. U. Pa., Phila., 1978-79; asst. prof. U. Iowa, Iowa City, 1980-82; prof. U. Tex., Austin, 1982—, Ralph B. Thomas Regents prof. Asian studies, 1993—, assoc. v.p., 1995-99, dean Coll. Liberal Arts, 1999—2006; exec. vice chancellor, provost U. Kans., 2006—. Dir. Sinha & Lariviere Ltd., Austin; founder Doing Bus. in India seminar; cons. Perot Sys. Corp., Dallas, 1993—; bd. dirs. eMR Tech. Ventures, Coun. Am. Overseas Rsch. Ctrs., Washington; Mossiker chair in humanities, 2003-06; mem. Kans. Bio. Kans. Tech. Enterprise Corp. Author: Ordeals in Hindu Law, 1981, Narada Smrti, 2003; gen. editor Studies in South Asia. Fellow NEH, 1979-83. Fellow Royal Asiatic Soc.; mem. Am. Oriental Soc., Am. Inst. Indian Studies (sr.fellow 1989, 95, v.p. 1990), Assn. Asian Studies, Coun. on Fgn. Rels. Home: 1006 Avalon Rd Lawrence KS 66044 Office Phone: 785-864-4904.

LAROCCA, PATRICIA DARLENE MCALEER, middle school educator; b. Aurora, Ill., July 12, 1951; d. Theodore Austin and Lorraine Mae (Robbins) McAleer; m. Edward Daniel LaRocca, June 28, 1975; children: Elizabeth S., Mark E. BS in Edn./Math., No. Ill. U., 1973, postgrad., 1975. Tchr. elem. sch. Roselle (Ill) Sch. Dist., 1973-80; instr. math. Coll. DuPage, Glen Ellyn, Ill., 1988-90; tchr. math. O'Neill Mid. Sch., Downers Grove, Ill., 1995—. Pvt. cons., math. tutor, Downers Grove, Ill., 1980-88, 90-95. Bd. dirs. PTA, Hillcrest Elem. Sch., Downers Grove; active Boy Scouts Am.; mem. 1st United Meth. Ch. Ill. teaching scholar, 1969. Methodist. Avocations: antiques, softball, organ, dance. Home and Office: 5648 Dunham Rd Downers Grove IL 60516-1246 Home Phone: 630-960-5933. Personal E-mail: roc4meep@comcast.net.

LARRICK, MONTE, radio personality; b. Chgo., Oct. 26; Sr. news corr. Sta. WMBI Radio, Chgo. Avocations: swimming, softball, reading, music. Office: WMBI 820 N LaSalle Blvd Chicago IL 60610

LARSEN, EDWARD WILLIAM, mathematician, nuclear engineering educator; b. Flushing, NY, Nov. 12, 1944; BS, Rensselaer Polytech Inst., 1966, PhD in Math., 1971. Asst. prof. math. NYU, 1971-76; assoc. prof. U. Del., 1976-77; mem. staff math. Los Alamos (N.Mex.) Nat. Lab., 1977; prof. dept. nuc. engring. U. Mich., Ann Arbor. Editor Transport Theory and Stats. Physics, 1975—, Jour. Applied Math., 1976—; contbr. articles to profl. jours. Recipient Ernest Orlando Lawrence Meml. award U.S. Dept. Energy, 1994. Mem. Am. Nuc. Soc. (Arthur Holly Compton award 1996), Soc. Indsl. and Applied Math. Office: U Mich Dept Nuc Engring & Radiol Scis 1906 Cooley Bldg Ann Arbor MI 48109-0001

LARSEN, PAUL EMANUEL, religious organization administrator; b. Mpls., Oct. 5, 1933; s. David Paul and Myrtle (Grunnet) L.; m. Elizabeth Helen Taylor, Mar. 19, 1966; children: Kristin, Kathleen (dec.). BA, Stanford U., 1955; MDiv, Fuller Theol. Sem., 1958; STD, San Francisco Theol. Sem., 1978; DD, North Park U., 1998. Ordained to ministry Evang. Ch., 1963. Asst. pastor Evang. Ch., Eagle Rock, Calif., 1958-59; pastor Pasadena, Calif., 1963-70, Peninsula Covenant Ch., Redwood City, Calif., 1971-86; pres. Evang. Covenant Chs., Chgo., 1986—. Chmn. meeting U.S. ch. leaders, 1992—. Author: Wise Up and Live, Mission of a Covenant. Mem. Internat. Fedn. of Free Evang. Chs. (pres. 1996—). Home: 36125 Avenida De Las Montana Cathedral City CA 92234-1516 Office: Evang Covenant Ch 5101 N Francisco Ave Chicago IL 60625-3611

LARSEN, PEG, state legislator; b. Aug. 10, 1949; m. Thomas Larsen; 4 children. BA, U. Slippery Rock. Minn. state rep. Dist. 56B, 1994—. Former ednl. asst. spl. needs. Address: 409 Quixote Ave N Lakeland MN 55043-9645 Also: 100 Constitution Ave Saint Paul MN 55155-1232

LARSEN, ROBERT EMMETT, federal judge; b. Queens, NY, Sept. 9, 1946; s. Robert Ludwig and Elizabeth Catherine (Colgan) L.; m. Roberta Barclay, Sept. 22, 1973; children: Matthew Robert, Thomas Barclay, Paige Barclay. BA, Rockhurst Coll., 1969; JD, U. Mo., Kansas City, 1973. Bar: Mo. 1973, U.S. Dist. Ct. (we. dist.) Mo. 1973, U.S. Ct. Appeals (D.C. cir.) 1974, U.S. Ct. Appeals (8th cir.) 1977, U.S. Supreme Ct. 1977. Staff atty. criminal div. U.S. Dept. Justice, Washington, 1974-76; asst. U.S. atty. U.S. Atty.'s Office, Kansas City, 1976-81, chief criminal div., 1981-83, atty.-in-charge organized crime drug enforcement task force, 1983-88, 1st asst. U.S. atty., 1988-90, sr. litigation counsel, 1990-91; U.S. magistrate judge U.S. Cts., Kansas City, 1991—. Commr. Mental Health Commn., Mo., 1990—; chmn. Metro. Kansas City Task Force on Alcohol and Drug Abuse, 1986-90; chmn., adv. bd. Mo. Fedn. of Parents for Drug Free Youth, Springfield, Mo., 1987-88; bd. trustees Nat. Coun. Alcoholism for Drug Free Youth, Kansas City, 1988-90; bd. dirs. YouthNet, Good Samaritan Project, Kansas City Consensus, Della Lamb Community Svcs.; bd. regents Rockhurst Coll. Regents, 1994—; mem. adv. bd. drug awareness Park Hill Sch. Dist., 1988-90; mem. steering com. Coalition for Positive Family Relationships, 1992—; mem. divsn. alcohol and drug abuse States Adv. Coun., 1987-88. Author: Pretrial Preparation, 1985; contbr.: 8th Circuit Criminal Institute, 1992. Co-chmn. Harmony in World of Difference, Kansas City, 1989—; mem., bd. dirs. Life Edn. Ctr., Kansas City, 1990—, Genesis, Kansas City, 1992; active Northland Citizen's Crusade Coun., Inc., 1989—, Ad Hoc Group Against Crime, 1986—. Recipient Community Svc. award Nat. Coun. Alcohol and Drug Abuse, 1988, Cert. Appreciation, 1988, Pub. Adv. award Dept. Mental Health, State of Mo., 1988, Law Enforcement award Ad Hoc Group Against Crime, 1989, GEICO Pub. Svc. award, 1990. Mem. ABA, Mo. Bar Assn., D.C. Bar Assn., Kansas City, Mo. Bar Assn. Roman Catholic. Home: 420 NW Briarcliff Pky Kansas City MO 64116-1670 Office: US Dist Ct 231 US Courthouse 811 Grand Blvd Ste 201 Kansas City MO 64106-1904

LARSEN, ROBERT LEROY, artistic director; b. Walnut, Iowa, Nov. 28, 1934; s. George Dewey and Maine M. (Mickel) L. MusB, Simpson Coll., Indianola, Iowa, 1956; MusM, U. Mich., 1958; MusD, Ind. U., 1972. Music prof. Simpson Coll., 1957—, chmn. music dept., 1965-99. Founder, artistic dir. Des Moines Met. Opera, 1973—, mus. and stage dir. over 100 prodns., 1973—. Mus. coach Tanglewood, Lenox, Mass., 1963, Oglebay Pk. (W.Va.) Opera, 1965, Chgo., N.Y. studios; condr., stage dir. Simpson Coll., Des Moines Met. Opera, Miss. Opera, U. Ariz.; solo pianist, song recital coach and accompanist; adjudicator Met. auditions and competitions, Mpls., Chgo., Kansas City, Mo., Tulsa, San Antonio; stage dir., condr. operas, Simpson Coll., Des Moines Met. Opera, 1973—; editor Opera Anthologies by G. Schirmer; piano rec. artist for G. Schirmer Libr. Recipient Gov's. award State of Iowa, 1974, Iowa Arts award for long term commitment to excellence in the arts, 1998. Mem. Am. Choral Dir. Assn., Nat. Opera Assn., Music Tchrs. Nat. Assn., Pi Kappa Lambda, Phi Kappa Phi, Phi Mu Alpha Sinfonia (faculty advisor). Presbyterian. Avocations: reading, theater, coaching students. Office: Des Moines Metro Opera 106 W Boston Ave Indianola IA 50125-1836 Home Phone: 515-961-4036; Office Phone: 515-961-1571.

LARSEN, STEVEN, orchestra conductor; b. Oak Park, Ill., Feb. 10, 1951; s. Edwin Earnest and Sylvia Nila Larsen; divorced; children: Vanessa, Krista; m. Martha Jane Bein, Mar. 21, 1993. MusB, Am. Conservatory Music, Chgo., 1975; MusM, Northwestern U., 1976. Cert. Nederlandse Dirigenten Kursus. Instr. music theory, chair instrumental dept Am. Conservatory Music, Chgo., 1976-82, orch. dir., 1978; music dir. Opera Theatre of San Antonio, 1987-90; orch. dir. Rockford (Ill.) Symphony Orch., 1991—; instr. music lit. Rock Valley Coll., Rockford, 2002—. Music dir., acting artistic dir. Chgo. Opera Theater, 1981-92; interim artistic dir. Dayton (Ohio) Opera, 1996; music dir. Champaign-Urbana (Ill.) Symphony, 1996—; lectr. opera performance Chgo. Mus. Coll., 1989-96. Recipient Disting. Svc. award Rockford Park Dist., 1997, Condr. of Yr., Ill. Coun. of Orchs., 1998-99, Mayor's Arts award Rockford Area Arts Coun., 1999. Mem. Rockford Downtown Rotary (bd. dirs. 2000-2002). Office: Rockford Symphony Orch 711 N Main St Rockford IL 61103-7204 E-mail: steve@larsenbein.com.

LARSEN, WILLIAM LAWRENCE, engineering educator; b. Crookston, Minn., July 16, 1926; s. Clarence M. and Luverne (Carlisle) L.; m. Gracie Lee Richey, June 19, 1954; children— Eric W., Thomas R. BME, Marquette U., Milw., 1948; MS, Ohio State U., 1950, PhD, 1956; postgrad., U. Chgo., 1950—51. Registered profl. engr., Iowa. Research assoc. Ohio State U., Columbus, 1951-56; research metallurgist E. I. duPont de Nemours & Co., Wilmington, Del., 1956-58; metallurgist Ames Lab., AEC, Iowa, 1958-73; assoc. prof. Iowa State U., Ames, 1958-73, prof. materials sci. and engring., 1973-93; prof. emeritus, 1993—. Cons. metallurgical engring., 1960— Contbr. articles to profl. jours. Served with USNR, 1944-46 Mem.: NSPE, NACE Internat., ASTM, ASM Internat. (life). Home and Office: 2332 Hamilton Dr Ames IA 50014-8201

LARSON, ALLAN LOUIS, political scientist, educator, lay worker; b. Chetek, Wis., Mar. 31, 1932; s. Leonard Andrew and Mabel (Marek) L. BA magna cum laude, U. Wis., Eau Claire, 1954; PhD, Northwestern U., 1964. Instr. Evanston Twp. High Sch., Ill., 1958-61; asst. prof. polit. sci. U. Wis., 1963-64; asst. prof. Loyola U., Chgo., 1964-68, assoc. prof., 1968-74, prof., 1974—. Author: Comparative Political Analysis, 1980, Soviet Society in Historical Perspective: Polity, Ideology and Economy, 2000, (essay) The Human Triad: An Introductory Essay on Politics, Society, and Culture, 1988; (with others) Progress and the Crisis of Man, 1976; contbr. articles to profl. jours. Assoc. mem. Paul Galvin Chapel, Evanston, Ill. Norman Wait Harris fellow in polit. sci. Northwestern U., 1954-56 Mem. AAAS, ASPCA, AAUP, Humane Soc. U.S., Northwestern U. Alumni Assn., Am. Polit. Sci. Assn., Am. Acad. Polit. and Social Sci., Acad. Polit. Sci., Midwest Polit. Sci. Assn., Nat. Assn. Scholars, Spiritual Life Inst., Anti-Cruelty Soc., Nat. Wildlife Fedn., N.Am. Butterfly Assn., Acad. of Am. Poets (assoc.), Policy Studies Orgn., Noetic Scis. Inst., Nat. Assn. Scholars, Humane Soc. U.S., Kappa Delta Pi, Pi Sigma Epsilon, Pi Sigma Alpha. Roman Catholic. Home: 11152 43d Ave Chippewa Falls WI 54729-6626 Office: Loyola U 6525 N Sheridan Rd Damen Hall Rm 915 Chicago IL 60626

LARSON, BRIAN FOIX, architect; b. Eau Claire, Wis., July 6, 1935; s. Albert Foix and Dorothy Jean (Thompson) L.; m. Mildred Anne Nightswander, Feb. 13, 1961; children: Urban Alexander, Soren Federick. BArch, U. Ill., 1959. Registered architect, Wis., Minn., Colo., Mass., N.H., Fla. Architect-in-tng. Geometrics, Inc., Cambridge, Mass., 1959-60, Bastille Halsey Assoc., Boston, 1960-62; ptnr. Larson, Playter, Smith, Eau Claire, 1962-72; v.p. Larson, Hestekins, Smith, Ltd., Eau Claire, 1962-80, Ayres Assocs., Eau Claire, 1980—. Sec. Wis. Bd. Archtl. Examiners, 1985-88, chmn., 1988-89; master juror Nat. Coun. Archtl. Reg. Bd. Bldg. Design Exam, 1987-96. Prin. works include One Mill Plaza, Laconia, N.H. (Honor award New Eng. Regional Council AIA 1974), Eau Claire County Courthouse, Wis., (Honor award Wis. Soc. Architects 1978), St. Croix County Courthouse, Wis., Dunn County Jud. Ctr. Mem. Hist. Bldg. Code Adv. Com., Wis., 1985. Mem. AIA (bd. dirs. 1996-98), Wis. Soc. Architects (pres. 1983), Wis. Architects Found. (bd. dirs. 1992-98), Soc. Archtl. Historians. Home: 215 Roosevelt Ave Eau Claire WI 54701-4065 Office: Ayres Assocs PO Box 1590 Eau Claire WI 54702-1590 E-mail: larsonb@ayresassociates.com.

LARSON, CAL, state legislator; b. Aug. 10, 1930; m. Loretta Larson; two children. BA, Concordia Coll., Moorhead, Minn. Formerly real estate/ins. broker; mem. Minn. Ho. of Reps., St. Paul, 1967-74, Minn. Senate from 10th dist., St. Paul, 1986—. Mem. edn.-higher edn. divsn. and edn. funding, fin., commerce, elections, and rules and adminstrn. Minn. State Senate. Address: 153 State Office Bldg Saint Paul MN 55155-0001

LARSON, CHARLES W., SR., retired prosecutor; m. Ellen Larson; 2 children. Grad., Kans. State U., U. Iowa Sch. Law, US Army War Coll., US Army Command and Gen. Staff Coll. Magistrate Iowa 5th Judicial Ct., 1973; commr. Iowa Dept. Public Safety, 1973—79; mgr. law enforcement Sanders and Assocs., Kingdom of Saudi Arabia, 1979—82; ptnr. Walker, Larson and Billingsley, Newton, Iowa, 1982—86; US atty. (no. dist.) Iowa US Dept. Justice, Cedar Rapids, 1986—93, 2001—07; dir. Iowa Office Drug Control, 1993—98; chmn. Iowa Bd. Parole, 1998—2001.

LARSON, DAVID LEE, surgeon; b. Kansas City, Mo., Dec. 9, 1943; s. Leonard Nathaniel and Mary Elizabeth (Stuck) L.; m. Sherrill Ankli, Apr. 16, 1977; children: Jeffrey David, Dawn Elizabeth, Bradley Jesse. BS, Bowling Green State U., 1965; MD, La. State U., 1969. Diplomate Am. Bd. Plastic Surgery (bd. dirs. 1996—, sec.-treas. 1998—). Intern Charity Hosp. of La., New Orleans, 1969-70; resident otolaryngology Baylor Coll. Medicine, Houston, 1972-76; plastic surgery resident Ind. U., Indpls., 1976-78; surgeon M.D. Anderson Cancer Ctr., Houston, 1978-85; prof., chmn. dept. plastic and reconstructive surgery Med. Coll Wis., Milw., 1986—, George S. Korkos prof. plastic surgery, 2007. Alano J. Ballantyne prof. in head and neck surgery M.D. Anderson Cancer Ctr., Houston, 1985; sec.-treas. Am. Bd. Plastic Surgery, 1996-2002. Editor: Cancer in the Neck, 1987, Essentials of Head and Neck Oncology, 1998. Capt. USNR, 1991—. Mem. Am. Assn. Plastic Surgeons, Nat. Inst. Healthcare Rsch. (chmn. bd. dirs. 1995-2000), Plastic Surgery Edn. Found. (pres. 2001—02). Avocations: reading, exercise. Home: 13510 Braemar Dr Elm Grove WI 53122-2509 Office: Med Coll Wis 8700 Watertown Plank Rd Milwaukee WI 53226-3522 E-mail: dlarson@mcw.edu.

LARSON, EDWARD, retired state supreme court justice; m. Mary Loretta Thompson; children: Sarah, John, Mary Elizabeth. BS, Kans. State U., 1954; JD, Kans. U., 1960. Pvt. practice, Hays, Kans., 1960—87; judge Kans. Ct. Appeals, 1987—95; justice Kans. Supreme Ct., Topeka, 1995—2003; ret., 2003. Mcpl. judge City of Hays, 1965—72. 2nd lt. USAF. Home: 2761 SW Plass Ave Topeka KS 66611

LARSON, GARY, cartoonist; b. Tacoma, Wash., Aug. 14, 1950; s. Vern and Doris Larson; married. BA in Communications, Wash. State U., 1972. Jazz musician, 1973-76; with music store, Seattle, 1976-77, Humane Soc., Seattle, 1978-80; cartoonist Seattle Times, 1978-79; syndicated cartoonist The Far Side Chronicle Features Syndicate, San Francisco, 1979-84; syndicated cartoonist The Far Side cartoon panel Universal Press Syndicate, Kansas City, Mo., 1984-94; cartoonist, 1994—. Prodr. books, calendars, greeting cars, t-shirts, day runner organizers, computer calendars, screen savers, coffee mugs.; since The Far Side was retired in 1994, it still appears syndicated in over 200 newspapers in fgn. market by Creators Syndicate Internat. Exhbns. include The Far Side of Sci. (exhibited at Calif. Acad. Scis., 1987, Smithsonian Instn., 1987, Denver Mus. Natural History, L.A. County Mus., Shedd Aquarium, Chgo., other mus.), The Far Side of the Zoo, Washington Park Zoo, Portland, Oreg., 1987; author: (cartoon collections) The Far Side, 1982, Beyond The Far Side, 1983, In Search of The Far Side, 1984, Bride of The Far Side, 1985, Valley of the Far Side, 1985, It Came from The Far Side, 1986, The Far Side Observer, 1987, Hound of the Far Side, 1984, Night of the Crash-Test Dummies, 1988, Wildlife Preserves, 1989, The Prehistory of the Far Side: A 10th Anniversary Exhibit, 1989, Weiner Dog Art, 1990, Unnatural Selections, 1991, Cows of Our Planet, 1992, The Chickens are Restless, 1993, The Curse of Madame "C", 1994, Last Chapter and Worse, 1996, (cartoon anthologies) The Far Side Gallery, 1984, The Far Side Gallery II, 1986, The Far Side Gallery III, 1988, The Far Side Gallery IV, 1993, The Far Side Gallery V, 1995, There's A Hair in My Dirt! A Worm's Story, 1998; animated film and CBS TV Halloween spl. Gary Larson's Tales from The Far Side, 1994 (Grand prix Annecy Film Festival, 1995), 2d animated film Gary Lason's Tales from The Far Side II, 1997. Recipient award for Best Humor Panel, Nat. Cartoonists Soc., 1986, Reuben award for Outstanding Cartoonist of Yr. Nat. Cartoonists Soc., 1991, 94, Max and Moritz prize for best internat. comic strip panel Internat. Comics Salon, 1993, other awards. Avocation: jazz music. Address: Creators Syndicated Internat 5777 W Century Blvd Ste 700 Los Angeles CA 90045 also: care Andrews McMeel Pub 4520 Main St Ste 700 Kansas City MO 64111-7701

LARSON, GREGORY DANE, lawyer; b. Mpls., Mar. 11, 1947; s. Allen L. and Lohma (Rogers) L.; m. Susan K. Strand, Sept. 8, 1973; children: Jennifer, Dane, Kyle, Kathleen. BA, Bemidji State Coll., 1969; JD, William Mitchell Coll. of Law, 1976. County atty. Hubbard County, Park Rapids, Minn., 1986—. With U.S. Army, 1970-72. Mem. Minn. State Bar Assn. (15th dist. pres.), Am. Legion (judge advocate 1982—). Democrat. Roman Catholic.

LARSON, JERRY LEROY, state supreme court justice; b. Harlan, Iowa, May 17, 1936; s. Gerald L. and Mary Eleanor (Patterson) L.; m. Debra L. Christensen; children: Rebecca, Jeffrey, Susan, David. BA, State U. Iowa, 1958, JD, 1960. Bar: Iowa. Partner firm Larson & Larson, 1961-75; dist. judge 4th Jud. Dist. Ct. of Iowa, 1975-78; justice Iowa Supreme Ct., 1978—. Office: Supreme Ct Iowa PO Box 109 Des Moines IA 50319-0001

LARSON, JOHN DAVID, insurance company executive, lawyer; b. Madison, Wis., July 6, 1941; s. Lawrence John and Anna Mathilda (Furseth) Larson; m. Evelyn Vie Smith, Jan. 22, 1966 (div. Apr. 1980); children: Eric John, Karen Annette; m. Nancy With Jay, Nov. 29, 1980 (div. Dec. 1998); stepchildren: Andrew Zachary Jay, Anne Elizabeth Jay, Christopher Allen Jay; m. Sherri Ann Sturtz Kliczak, July 12, 2002; 1 stepchild, Cristopher Howard Kliczak. BBA, U. Wis., 1964, JD, 1965, MBA, 1966. CPA Wis.; CLU; bar: Wis. 1965, U.S. Ct. Mil. Appeals 1966; chartered fin. cons. With Nat. Guardian Life Ins. Co., Madison, 1969—, exec. v.p., treas., 1973, pres., dir., 1974—, pres., CEO, 1989—2004, chmn., pres., CEO, 2004—. Bd. advisors U.S. Bank, Madison; bd. dirs. TV Wis., Inc., KELAB, Inc. Chmn. Madison chpt. ARC, 1974—75; pres. United Way Dane County, Wis., 1975, Wis. N.G. Assn., 1992—96; trustee Village of Maple Bluff, Wis., 1997—2003, pres., 2003—07. With US Army, 1966—69, brig. gen. Wis. Army N.G., 1998. Named Disting. Bus. Alumnus, U. Wis.-Madison, 1996; recipient Know Your Madisonian award, Wis. State Jour., 1973. Mem.: ABA, Am. Soc. Fin. Svc. Profls., State Bar Wis., U. Wis. Bus. Alumni (bd. dirs. 1986—90), Madison C. of C. (dir. 1976—80), Maple Bluff Club (bd. dirs. 1974—80), Rotary. Lutheran. Home: 401 New Castle Way Madison WI 53704-6070 Office: PO Box 1191 Madison WI 53701-1191 Business E-Mail: jdlarson@nglic.com.

LARSON, JOHN M., retired educational consultant; BS in Bus. Adminstrn., U. Calif., Berkeley, Calif.; diploma in Exec. Mgmt. Program, Stanford U., 2000. With Mktg. Dept. DeVry Inc.; v.p. mktg. Nat. Edn. Ctrs., Inc., 1980—89; sr. v.p. ops. Geneva Cos., 1989; sr. v.p. Coll. Ops. Phillips Colls., Inc., 1989—93; ea. regional operating mgr. Ednl. Med., Inc., 1993; cons. Heller Equity Capital Corp., 1993—94; pres. Career Edn. Corp., Hoffman Estates, Ill., 1994—2006, CEO, 1994—2006, chmn. bd., 2000—06. Named Entrepreneur of Yr. Ill. and N.W. Ind. Region, Ernst & Young.

LARSON, LARRY GENE, financial planner; b. Sioux Falls, SD, July 9, 1948; s. L. Dale and Doris L. (Iverson) L.; m. Mary Kemppainen, Aug. 13, 1977; children: Kay, Lynn, Bret. BA, Augustana Coll., 1970. Republican. Lutheran. Avocations: fishing, golf. Home: 2172 Center St Marquette MI 49855-1302 Office: Am Express 2400 Us Highway 41 W Marquette MI 49855-2261

LARSON, PAUL WILLIAM, public relations executive; b. Wilmington, NC, May 28, 1956; s. Robert WIlliam and Helen Joyce (Hillen) L. BA, U. Calif., Berkeley, 1981; MS in Journalism Medill Sch. of Journalism, Northwestern U., Evanston, Ill., 1991. Reporter Turlock (Calif.) Daily Jour., 1982-84; writer, editor Paul Larson Commns., Modesto, Calif., 1984-90, Evanston, Ill., 2002—; dir. external affairs and pubs. Medill Sch. Journalism, Northwestern U., Evanston, 1991-96; mgr. strategic com. AMA, Chgo., 1996-98, dir. membership com., 1998-2000, v.p. mem. and bus. comms., 2000—02; prin. Paul Larson Comms., 2002—. Bd. dirs. Housing Options for Mentally Ill, Evanston, 1993-2000, chmn. comm. com. 1995-2000; docent Evanston Hist. Soc., 1992-95. Recipient Rotary Group Study Exchg. award Rotary Internat., 1986, Rotary Found. Dist. Svc. award, 1995, Leadership Evanston Evanston Cmty. Rels., 1995-96, Vol. of the Yr. award Evanston McGaw YMCA, 1995. Mem. Rotary (bd. dirs. Evanston 1991-95). Home: 1017 Greenleaf St Evanston IL 60202-1235

LARSON, PETER N., manufacturing executive; b. 1939; BS, Oreg. State U.; JD, Seton Hall U. With Johnson & Johnson, N.J., 1967-78, 91-95, Kimberly Clark; chmn. bd., CEO Brunswick Corp., Lake Forest, Ill., 1995—. Office: Brunswick Corp One Northfield Ct Lake Forest IL 60045

LARSON, ROBERT CRAIG, real estate company officer; b. Mpls., June 15, 1934; s. Eugene and Frances (Wescott) L.; m. Lucy Ann Ballinger, June 20, 1957 (div. 1981), m. Karen Chase, Sept. 5, 1981; children: Elizabeth, Eric, Kathryn. BA in Govt. and Internat. Rels., Carleton Coll., Northfield, Minn., 1956. Various staff positions Inland Steel Co., Chgo., 1956-67; gen. mgr. Inland Steel Container Co., Cleve., 1967-70; v.p. Inland Steel Devel. Co., Washington, 1970-74; gen. mgr. Georgetown Inland Corps., Washington, 1970-74; sr. v.p. Taubman Co., Washington, 1974-78, pres., COO, 1978—88, CEO, 1988—90, vice chmn., Taubman Ctrs. Inc., 1990—2000, chmn., Taubman Realty Group, 1990—98; prin., non-exec. chmn. Larson Realty Group; chmn. Lazard Real Estate Partners, LLC; mng. dir. Lazard Alternative Investments, LLC. Bd. dirs. Intercontinental Hotels Group PLC, Brandywine Realty Trust; chmn. United Dominion Realty Trust, Inc.; bd. dirs. Atria Senior Living Group, Inc., Destination Europe Limited, Commonwealth Atlantic Properties, Inc., ARV Assisted Living, Inc., Taubman Co. Chmn. at. Urban League, N.Y.C.; bd. govs. Cranbrook Acad. Art, Bloomfield Hills, Mich.; trustee, vice chmn. Children's Hosp. of Mich., Cranbrook Ednl. Community, Detroit, Citizens Rsch. Coun. of Mich., Detroit, Detroit Med. Ctr., Detroit Symphony Orch., Inc.; dir. Detroit Econ. Growth Corp.; trustee Kresge Found. Mem. Nat. Realty Com. (chmn. 1986—), Urban Land Inst., Internat. Coun. Shopping Ctrs., Bloomfield Open Hunt (Bloomfield Hills), City Tavern (Washington), World Trade (San Francisco). Office: Larson Realty Group 91 W Long Lake Rd Bloomfield Hills MI 48304-2747 Office Phone: 248-593-8010. Office Fax: 248-593-8011.*

LARSON, ROY, journalist, publishing executive; b. Moline, Ill., July 27, 1929; s. Roy W. and Jane (Beall) L.; m. Dorothy Jennisch, June 7, 1950; children: Mark, Bruce, Jodie, Bradley. AB, Augustana Coll., Rock Island, Ill., 1951; M.Div., Garrett Theol. Sem., 1955. Ordained to ministry Methodist Ch., 1956; min. Covenant United Meth. Ch., Evanston, Ill., 1963-68, First United Meth. Ch., Elmhurst, Ill., 1968-69; religion editor Chgo. Sun-Times, 1969-85; pub. The Chgo. Reporter, 1985-94; exec. dir. Garrett-Medill Ctr. for Religion and News Media, Evanston, Ill., 1995—2002; dir. comm. Chgo. Temple, 2003—. Home: 1508 Hinman Ave Evanston IL 60201-4664 Office: Chgo Temple 77 W Washington Chicago IL 60602 Office Phone: 312-236-4548. E-mail: drlarson29@comcast.net.

LARSON, SANDRA B., nursing educator; b. Chgo., Apr. 21, 1944; d. Richard Milward and Eldred Gertrude (Piehl) Blackburn; m. Eric Richard Larson, Nov. 25, 1967; children: Sarah, Keith. BS, No. Ill. U., 1966, MS, 1978. RN, Ill. Nursing educator Luth. Hosp., Moline, Ill., 1968-70; charge nurse ICU Peninsula Hosp., Burlingame, Calif., 1970-72; staff nurse Illini Hosp., Silvis, Ill., 1972-76; nursing educator Black Hawk Coll., Moline, 1976—. Co-author: Anatomy and Physiology Testbank, 1994, 97, 99. Mem. ANA, Ill. Nurses Assn. (5th dist. treas. 1982-84, pres. 1984-86, 1st v.p. 1986-87, pres. 1988-92, 2nd v.p. 1993-95), Sigma Theta Tau. Democrat. Roman Catholic. Avocations: reading, quilting. Home: 3009 29th St Moline IL 61265-6950 Office: Black Hawk Coll 6600 34th Ave Moline IL 61265-5870 Business E-Mail: larsons@bhc.edu.

LARSON, SIDNEY, art educator, artist, writer, painting conservator; b. Sterling, Colo., June 16, 1923; s. Harry and Ann Levin; m. George Ann Madden, Aug. 30, 1947; children: Sara Catherine, Nancy Louise. BA, U. Mo., 1949, MA in Art, 1950. Prof. art Columbia Coll., Mo., 1951—; art curator State Hist. Soc. Mo., 1962—; painting conservator, Columbia, 1960—. Exhibited paintings and drawings in group shows in Midwest, Washington, N.Y. and Japan; executed murals Daily News, Rolla, Mo., Shelter Ins., Columbia, Mo., Guitar Bldg., Columbia, Mcpl. Bldg., Jefferson City, Mo., Centerre Bank, Columbia, chs. in Okla. and Ark. Adv. Mo. State Council on Arts, 1960, Boone County Courthouse, Columbia. Served with USN, 1943-46, PTO. Fellow Huntington Hartford Found., 1962; rRecipient Commendation award Senate of State of Mo., 1977, 87, Nat. Prof. of Yr. award, Bronze medalist, Mo. State Prof. of Yr. award Coun. for Advancement and Support Edn., 1987, Disting. Svc. award State Hist. Soc. Mo., Mo. State Arts Coun. award, 1991. Mem. Am. Inst. Conservation of Hist. and Artistic Works (assoc. mem.), Nat. Assn. Mural Painters. Avocations: world travel, reading. Office: Columbia Coll Dept Art Columbia MO 65216-0001 Home: 605 Manor Dr Columbia MO 65203-1745

LARSON, VERNON LEROY, state official; b. Vivian, SD, Oct. 25, 1948; s. Melvin Anton and Ruth (Hudspeth) Larson; 2 children. BS in Polit. Sci. and English, No. State U., 1970. Tchr. Hill City H.S., 1970—72; aide to Rep. Jim Abdnor SD, 1974—78; adv. SD Fedn. Teen Age Rep, 1976—78, 1987—95; state auditor State of S.D., Pierre, 1979—2003, state treas., 2003—. Mem.: Nat. Assn. State Auditors, Comptrollers & Treasurers (bd. mem. 1997—2002, 2004—), Kiwanis, Elks, Masons (Elk of the Yr., SD 1982). Republican. Lutheran. Achievements include being the longest serving constitutional officer in South Dakota history. Office: Office of State Treasurer Capitol Bldg 2d Fl 500 E Capitol Pierre SD 57501-5070*

LARSON, VICKI LORD, academic administrator, communication disorders educator; b. Prentice, Wis., Sept. 21, 1944; d. Edward A. and Stella Mae Lord; m. James Roy Larson, Sept. 3, 1966. BSEd, U. Wis., Madison, 1966, MS, 1968, PhD, 1974. Speech-lang. pathologist Coop. Ednl. Svc. Agy. 2, Minoqua, Wis., 1967—69; instr. U. Wis., Whitewater, 1969—71, rsch. asst. Madison, 1971—73, asst. prof. Eau Claire, 1973-77, assoc. prof., 1977—81, prof. communication disorders, 1981—91, dept. chair, 1978—83, asst. dean grad. studies and univ. rsch., 1984—89, assoc. dean grad. studies and univ. rsch., 1989—91, interim chancellor, 2005—06, prof. comm. Oshkosh, 1991—2000, dean Grad. Sch. Rsch., 1991—94, provost, vice chancellor acad. affairs, 1994—2000. Acquistions editor Thinking Publs., Eau Claire, 2001—04, acquistions mgr., 2004—06. Author: Adolescents: Communication Development and Disorder, 1983, Communication Assessment and Intervention Strategies for Adolescents, 1987; contbr. Handbook of Speech-Language Pathology and Audiology, 1988, Language Disorders in Older Students, 1995, Working Out With Listening, 2002, Communication Solutions for Older Students, 2003, S-MAPs curriculum-based assessment, 2004, Aspergers Syndrome: Strategies for Solving the Social Puzzle, 2005; contbr.: Working Out With Writing, 2005. Fellow: Am. Speech, Lang., Hearing Assn. (councilor); mem.: Wis. Speech, Lang., Hearing Assn. (pres. 1976, honors 1991, pres. found. 2000—04, v.p. 2005—07, treas. 2005—07), Golden Key, Phi Kappa Phi, Omicron Delta Kappa. Avocations: traveling, quilting, reading. E-mail: larsonvl@uwec.edu.

LARUE, PAUL HUBERT, retired lawyer; b. Somerville, Mass., Nov. 16, 1922; s. Lucien H. and Germaine (Choquet) LaR.; m. Helen Finnegan, July 20, 1946; children: Paul Hubert, Patricia Fell, Mary Hogan. PhB, U. Wis., 1947, JD, 1949. Bar: Ill. 1955, Wis. 1949, U.S. Supreme Ct. 1972. Grad. asst. instr. polit. sci. dept. U. Wis., 1947-48; mem. staff Wis. Atty. Gen., 1949-50; trial atty., legal advisor to commr. FTC, 1950-55; pvt. practice Chgo.; mem. Chadwell & Kayser, Ltd., 1958-90; ptnr. Vedder, Price, Kaufman & Kammholz, 1990-93; of counsel, 1993-99; ret., 1999. Spkr. profl. meetings; mem. Com. Modern Cts. in Ill., 1964; mem. Com. for Constl. Conv. Ill., 1968, Better Govt. Assn., 1966-70 Contbr. articles to profl. jours. Mem. lawyers com. Met. Crusade of Mercy, 1967-68, United Settlement Appeal, 1966-68; apptd. pub. mem. Ill. Conflict of Interest Laws Commn., 1965-67. With AUS, 1943-45, ETO; capt. JAGC, USAFR, 1950-55. Fellow Ill. Bar Found. (charter mem.); mem. ABA (mem. coun. sect. antitrust law 1980-83, chmn. Robinson-Patman Act com. 1975-78), Ill. State Bar Assn., Chgo. Bar Assn. (chmn. antitrust com. 1970-71), Wis. State Bar (emeritus mem.), Rotary. Roman Catholic. Home: 250 Cuttriss St Park Ridge IL 60068 Personal E-mail: paullarue@sbcglobal.net.

LA RUSSA, TONY, JR., (ANTHONY LA RUSSA JR.), professional baseball manager; b. Tampa, Fla., Oct. 4, 1944; m. Elaine Coker, Dec. 31, 1973; children: Bianca, Devon. Student, U. Tampa; BA, U. So. Fla., 1969; LLB, Fla. State U., 1978. Bar: Fla., 1979. Player numerous major league and minor league baseball teams, 1962-77; coach St. Louis Cardinals orgn., 1977; mgr. minor league team Knoxville, 1978, Iowa, 1979; coach Chgo. White Sox, 1978, mgr., 1979-86, Oakland A's, 1986-95, St. Louis Cardinals, 1996—. Mgr. Am. League All-Star Team, 1988, Nat. League All-Star Team, 2005 Co-founder Tony LaRussa's Animal Rescue Found., 1991—. Mgr., Am. League Champions, 1988-90; Nat. League Champions, 2004, 2006; World Series Champions, 1989, 2006; Named Am. League Mgr. Yr. Major League Baseball Writers' Assn., 1983, 88, 92; Nat. League Mgr. Yr., 2002; named to Mo. Sports Hall of Fame, 2006; recipient C.I. Taylor award Negro League Hall of Fame, 2004 Achievements include becoming the second manager in major league baseball history to win the World Series in both leagues, 1989, 2006. Office: St Louis Cardinals Busch Stadium 250 Stadium Plz Saint Louis MO 63102-1722

LARUSSO, NICHOLAS F., gastroenterologist, educator, scientist; Dir. Ctr. Basic Rsch. Digestive Disorders Mayo Clinic Coll Medicine, Rochester, Minn., 1977—2002, prof., chmn. dept. internal medicine, 1977—, Charles H. Weinman endowed prof. medicine, 2006—. Office: Mayo Clinic Ctr Basic Rsch Digestive Disease Guggenheim 17 Rochester MN 55905-0001 Home Phone: 507-292-1877; Office Phone: 507-284-3725. Business E-Mail: larusso.nicholas@mayo.edu.

LASANSKY, LEONARDO, artist, educator; b. Iowa City, Mar. 29, 1946; s. Maurcio Lasansky and Emilia Barragan; 1 child, Amadeo Galgo. B of Gen. Studies, U. Iowa, 1971, MA, MFA, U. Iowa, 1972. Prof. art Hamline U., St. Paul, 1972—, chair fine arts divsn., 1981—85; artist-in-resident Dartmouth Coll., Hanover, NH, 1982—82; dir. exhbns. Hamline U., St. Paul, 1995—, chair dept. studio arts and art history, 1995—; artist-in-resident Hamline U. Coll. of Liberal Arts, St. Paul, 2004—. Mem. adv. panel Minn. State Arts Bd., St. Paul, 1988—90; academician Nat. Acad., NYC, 1994—. Curator (exhibitions) España: The Legacy of War: Works by Francisco Goya (Best Curated Exhbn. in the Twin Cities, Mpls. Star Tribune, 1998), Africa: A Legacy in Memory, Hamline U., loan from Mus. African Art, YC, 2004, Star Tribune, Mary Abbe, Icons of Perfection: Figurative Scuplture from Africa, 2005—06; exhibitions include Norfolk Mus. of Arts and Scis., Va., 1969, Figura 3, IBA, Leipzig, Germany, 1982, Bklyn. Mus., 1983, Internat. Triennial of Coloured Graphic Prints, Grenchen, Switzerland, 1985, Internat. Print Triennial, Krakow, Poland, 1986, 1988, 1994, Am. Printmaking, Belgrade, Yugoslavia, 1989, Premio Internazionale, Biella, Italy, 1987, Grabado Latinoamericano, San Juan, Puerto Rico, 1988, 1998, Jane Haslem Gallery, Washington, 1990, Prefectural Mus. of Art, Fukuoka, Japan, 1990, Mus. Modern Art, Wakayoma, Japan, 1991, Heard Mus., Phoenix, 1993, Nat. Acad. and Mus., NYC, 1995, 1998, Ball State Univ. Mus. of Art, 1996, AAAL, NYC (Spl. Purchase Award, 1979), Intergrafic '80, Berlin, Germany, Intergrafia '94, Prague, Czechoslovakia, Augsburg, Germany, Krakow and Torun, Poland, rep. in numerous permanent collections, included in publ., Icons of Perfection: Figurative Sculpture from Africa, 2006. Grantee, Regis Found., 2007—. Mem.: Nat. Acad. Office: Hamline Univ Dept Studio Arts and Art History 1536 Hewitt Ave Saint Paul MN 55104 Office Phone: 651-523-2386. Office Fax: 651-523-3057.

LASANSKY, MAURICIO, artist; b. Buenos Aires, 1914; arrived in U.S., 1943, naturalized, 1952; m. Emilia Lasansky; 6 children. Attended, Superior Sch. Fine Arts, Argentina; DFA (hon.), Iowa Wesleyan Coll., 1959, Pacific Lutheran Univ., 1969; HHD (hon.), Associated Colls. Twin Cities, 1977; DFA (hon.), Carleton Coll., 1979, Coe Coll., 1985. Dir. Free Fine Arts Sch., Cordoba, Argentina, 1936—39, Taller Manualidades, Cordoba, Argentina, 1939—45; prof. Univ. Iowa, 1945—67, Virgil M. Hancher disting. prof., 1967—84, Virgil M. Hancher prof. emeritus, 1984—. Exhibitions include over 250 one-man shows in the U.S. and other countries; represented in collections of over 140 museums. Recipient 2 Eyre Medals, Pa. Acad. Fine Art, 1957—59, Posada award, Primera Exposicion Bienal Interamericana, Mexico City, 1959, Accadamico Onorario, Classe de Incisione, Accademia della Arti del Designo, Florence Italy, 1965, Arts award, Dickinson Coll., 1974, Disting. Svc. citation, Nat. Assn. Sch. Art, 1978, Honored Artist award, Fourth Latin Am. Bienal Graphic Arts, 1979, Disting. Tchg. Art award, Coll. Art Assn. Am., 1980, Honorary award, Arts & Humanities Commn. for the Aging, Iowa, 1983, Iowa Arts Council, 1990, Cert. of Recognition for Disting. Svc., State of Iowa, 1991, Iowa award, 1999, 14th Recipient of State of Iowa Highest Honor award, Gov. Iowa, 2000, Hon. Artist Mem. LA Soc. Printmakers, 2001; grantee 5 Guggenheim Fellowships, 1943—63. Fellow: Inst. Advanced Study, Indiana Univ.; mem.: L.A. Soc. Printmakers (Honorary Artist 2001), NAD (academician 1990). Best known for series of Nazi Drawings, 1961-66. Office: Lasansky Corporation 216 E Washington St Iowa City IA 52240 Office Phone: 319-337-9336. Business E-Mail: info@lasanskyart.com.

LASEE, ALAN J., state legislator; b. Rockland, Wis., July 30, 1937; married; 7 children. Mem. Wis. Senate from 1st dist, Madison, 1977—, pres. pro tempore, 1995—2002, pres., 2003—. Mem. Great Lakes Water Quality Commn., 1988—89. Town chmn., 1973—82, 1985—. Office: 2259 Lasee Rd De Pere WI 54115-9663 also: RR 2 De Pere WI 54115-9802 also: State Senate State Capitol Rm 919 Madison WI 53702-0001

LASEE, FRANK G., state legislator; b. Dec. 11, 1961; BA, U. Wis., Green Bay. Chmn. Town of Ledgeview, 1993-97. Wis. state assemblyman, Dist. 2, 1994—. Office: PO Box 8952 Madison WI 53708-8952 Home: 2380 Bluestone Pl Green Bay WI 54311-6430

LASHBROOKE, ELVIN CARROLL, JR., law educator, consultant; b. Dec. 14, 1939; s. Elvin Carroll Sr. and Lois Lenora (Weger) L.; m. Margaret Ann Jones, Dec. 19, 1964; children: Michelle Ann, David C. BA, U. Tex., 1967, MA, 1968, JD, 1972, LLM, 1977; PhD, Mich. State U., 1993. Bar: Tex. 1972, Fla. 1973. Legis. counsel Tex. Legis. Coun., Austin, 1972-75; pvt. practice law, 1975-77; asst. prof. coll. of law DePaul U., Chgo., 1977-79, Stetson U., St. Petersburg, Fla., 1979-80; assoc. prof. sch. law Notre Dame, South Bend, Ind., 1981-85; prof., chmn. bus. law dept. Mich. State U., East Lansing, 1985-95; assoc. dean adminstrn. Eli Broad Coll. Bus., East Lansing, 1993-97; pvt. practice cons., 1986-97; dean Coll. Bus. U. Nev., Las Vegas, 1997-99; assoc. dean Broad Grad. Sch. of Mgmt. Mich. State U., East Lansing, 1999—2001, dir. study abroad and e-learning initiatives, 2001—03, dir. edn., 2003—04, assoc. dean emeritus, 2004—; exec. mem. Lashbrooke of Barrowfield, LLC, 2004—. Instr. St. Edward's U., Austin, 1975-76. Author: Tax Exempt Organizations, 1985, The Legal Handbook of Business Transactions, 1987; contbr. articles to profl. jours. Mem. Tex. Bar Assn., Fla. Bar Assn. Avocation: computers. Home: 6204 E Golfridge Dr East Lansing MI 48823 Office: Mich State Univ Broad Grad Sch of Mgmt East Lansing MI 48824-1122 Home Phone: 517-337-1847; Office Phone: 517-353-4336. Business E-Mail: lashbrooke@bus.msu.edu.

LASHUTKA, GREGORY S., mayor, lawyer; b. NYC, 1944; m. Catherine (Adams); children: Nicholas, Lara, Stephanie, Michael. BS, Ohio State U., 1967; JD, Capital U., 1974. Bar: Ohio, 1974, Fla. and D.C., 1975. Ptnr. Squire, Sanders, and Dempsey, Columbus, Ohio; elected mayor City of Columbus, Ohio, 1991—99; former Columbus City Atty., Ohio; sr. v.p. corp. rels. Nationwide, Columbus, Ohio, 2000—. Past chmn. Columbus Area Sports Devel. Corp.; pres. Nat. League of Cities; comentator of the Ohio State U. Football Color, 1983-90; active civic and charitable orgn.; bd. dir. Simon Kenton, coun. Boy Scouts Am.; bd. dir. Cath. Social Svc., lt., USN. Named Mcpl. Leader of the Yr., Am. City and County mag., 1993. Mem. Nat. Acad. Pub. Adminstr. Office: Nationwide One Nationwide Plz Columbus OH 43215-2220

LASKOWSKI, LEONARD FRANCIS, JR., microbiologist; b. Milw., Nov. 16, 1919; s. Leonard Francis and Frances (Cyborowski) L.; m. Frances Bielinski, June 1, 1946; children— Leonard Francis III, James, Thomas. BS, Marquette U., 1941, MS, 1948; PhD, St. Louis U., 1951. Diplomate: Am. Bd. Microbiology. Instr. bacteriology Marquette U., 1946-48; mem. faculty St. Louis U., 1951—, prof. pathology and internal medicine, Div. Infectious Diseases, 1969-90, prof. emeritus, 1990—, assoc. prof. internal medicine, 1977-90—. Dir. clin. microbiology sect. St. Louis U. Hosps. Labs., 1965—; cons. clin microbiology Firmin Desloge Hosp., St. Louis U. Group Hosps., St. Marys Group Hosps.; cons. bacteriology VA Hosp.; asst. dept. chief Pub. Health Lab., St. Louis Civil Def., 1958—; cons. St. Elizabeths Hosp., St. Louis County Hosp., St. Francis Hosp., Alexian Bros. Hosp., St. Clements Hosp., St. Mary's Hosp., East St. Louis. Contbr. articles to profl. jours. Health and tech. tng. coordinator for Latin Am. projects Peace Corps, 1962-66. Served with M.C. AUS, 1942-46. Fellow Am. Acad. Microbiology; mem. Soc. Am. Bacteriologists, N.Y. Acad. Scis., Am., Mo. pub. health assns., AAUP, Med. Mycol. Soc. Am., Alpha Omega Alpha. Home: 505 Cedar Summit Ln Villa Ridge MO 63089

LASKOWSKI, MICHAEL, JR., chemist, educator; b. Warsaw, Mar. 13, 1930; came to U.S., 1947, naturalized, 1955; s. Michael and Maria (Dabrowska) L.; m. Joan Claire Heyer, ov. 29, 1957; children: Michael Christopher, Marta Joan. BS magna cum laude, Lawrence Coll., 1950; PhD (NIH fellow), Cornell U., 1954, postgrad., 1954-55, Yale U., 1955-56. Research asst. Marquette U., 1949-50; instr. Cornell U., 1956-57; asst. prof. chemistry Purdue U., 1957-61, asso. prof., 1961-65, prof., 1965—. Chmn. Gordon Rsch. Conf. Physics and Phys. Chemistry Biopolymers, 1966, Proteolytic Enzymes and Their Inhibitors, 1982; mem. study sect. NIH, 1967-71, NSF, 1989, sci. adv. bd. Receptor, Inc., 1993-94, Khepri Pharms., Inc., 1993-95, BioNona Dynamics, 2002-. Mem. editorial bd. Archives Biochemistry and Biophysics, 1972-90, Biochemistry, 1973-78, Jour. Protein Chemistry, 1981-97, Jour. Biol. Chemistry, 1983-88; mem. expert sci. coun. Protein Identification Resource, 2000—; contbr. articles to profl. jours. Recipient McCoy award Purdue U., 1975; co-recipient award in biol. scis. Alfred Jurzykowski Found., 1977 Mem. Am. Chem. Soc. (chmn. sect. 1968-69, treas. div. biol. chemistry 1981-84, councillor 1985-88), Am. Soc. Biol. Chemists, Biophys. Soc., Protein Soc., AAAS, AAUP, Polish Inst. Arts, Sci. Am., ACLU, Sigma Xi. Home: 222 E Navajo St West Lafayette IN 47906-2155 Office: Purdue U Dept Chemistry West Lafayette IN 47907 Office Phone: 765-494-5291. E-mail: michael.laskowski.1@purdue.edu.

LASKOWSKI, RICHARD E., retail hardware company executive; b. 1941; With Ace Hardware Corp., Oak Brook, Ill., 1962-98, now chmn. bd. dirs., also pres. subs., ret. from bd. dirs., 1998; now mgr., owner Ace Hardware Stores, Round Lake, Ill., 1998—. Office: Ace Hardware Corp 659 Railroad Ave Round Lake IL 60073-3299

LASORDA, TOM (THOMAS W. LASORDA), automotive executive; b. Windsor, Ont., Can., July 24, 1954; s. Frank and Bea LaSorda; m. Doreen LaSorda; 2 children. BA, U. Windsor, 1977, B of Commerce, 1977, MBA, 1980. Mfg. & labor rels. assignments Gen. Motors Corp., 1977—83, with labor rels. & pub. rels., 1983—85, mgr. quality assurance GM Can., 1985—87, dir. svc. engring. Buick Motor divsn., 1987—90, dir. prodn., 1990—91, v.p. prodn. CAMI Automotive Inc. (GM/Suziki Jount Venture, 1991, pres. Opel Eisenach GmbH Germany, 1991—93, mfg. mgr. Cadillac Luxury Car Group, 1993—96, exec. in charge Lean Mfg., 1996—98, v.p. quality, reliability & competitive ops. implementation, 1998—2000; sr. v.p. powertrain mfg. Chrysler Group, 2000—02, exec. v.p. mfg., 2002—04, COO, 2004—05; dep. mem. bd. mgmt. Chrysler Group, 2004—05; pres., CEO Chrysler Group, 2005—07, mem. bd. mgmt., 2005—07; vice-chmn., pres., mfr. & purchasing ops. Chrysler LLC, Auburn Hills, Mich., 2007—; vice chmn. Cerberus Operating & Advisory Co. LLC, 1997. Bd. dirs. Chrysler LLC, 2007—, Econ. Alliance for Mich. Bd. dirs. Detroit Renaissance; bd. dirs Detroit Econ. Club; bd. dirs. Automotive Youth Ednl. Systems. Recipient Disting. Svc. Citation, Automotive Hall of Fame, 2005. Mem.: Mich. Bus. Roundtable. Achievements include being President of Opel-Eisenach GmbH from 1991-93, the first auto assembly plant in eastern Germany after the fall of the Berlin Wall. Office: Chrysler LLC 1000 Chrysler Dr Auburn Hills MI 48326*

LASSA, JULIE M., state representative; b. Oct. 21, 1970; married. BS, U. Wis., Stevens Point, 1993. Former exec. dir. Plover Area Bus. Assn., Wis.; former legis. aide Wis.; mem. state assembly dist. 71 Wis. State Assembly, Madison, 1998—, mem. child abuse and neglect bd., mem. agr., colls. and univs., econ. devel., and labor and workforce devel. coms., minority caucus sec., 1999. Former chair Portage County Dem. Party, Wis.; mem. town bd. Dewey, Wis., 1993—94. Mem.: Portage County Bus. Coun., Portage County Hist. Soc. Democrat. Office: State Capitol Rm 122N PO Box 8952 Madison WI 53708-8952 E-mail: rep.lassa@legis.state.wi.us.

LASSAR, SCOTT R., lawyer, former prosecutor; b. Evanston, Ill., Apr. 5, 1950; s. Richard Ernest and Jo (Ladenson) Lassar; m. Elizabeth Levine, May 22, 1977; children: Margaret, Kate. BA, Oberlin Coll., 1972; JD, Northwestern U., 1975. Bar: Ill. 1975. With Office US Atty. (No. dist) Ill. US Dept. Justice, Chgo., 1975—86, first asst., 1993—97; ptnr. Keck, Mahin & Cate, 1986—93, Sidley, Austin, Brown & Wood LLP, 2001—; interim US atty., 1997; US atty., 1997—2001. Fellow Am. Coll. Trial Lawyers. Recipient Bill of Rights in Action award, Constl. Rights Found., 2002. Office: Bank One Plaza 10 South Dearborn St Chicago IL 60603

LASSETER, ROBERT HAYGOOD, electrical engineering educator, consultant; b. Miami, Fla., Apr. 4, 1938; s. J. Haygood and Elsiemae (Davis) L.; m. Lucy Taylor, Sept. 2, 1979; children: Courtney M., Malahn P., Robert M., Lauren L. BS in Physics, N.C. State U., 1963, MS in Physics, 1967; PhD in Physics, U. Pa., 1971; postgrad., U. Pa., Phila., 1971—73. Cons. engr. GE Co., Phila., 1973—80; asst. prof U. Wis., Madison, 1980—82, assoc. prof., 1982—85, prof., 1985—. Dir. power sys. Engring. Rsch. Ctr.-Wis., 1994—; cons. engr. Siemens AG, Germany, 1985-86. Contbr. articles to profl. jours. Fellow IEEE. Achievements include pioneering work in application of digital methods to the design of high voltage direct current power systems; basic development of analytical methods for design and study of power electronic controllers in power systems; creating a concept of Microgrids as applied to distributed resources in power systems. Office: Univ Wisconsin Electrical & Computer Engineering 1415 Engineering Dr Madison WI 53706-1607

LASTER, DANNY BRUCE, animal scientist; b. Scotts Hill, Tenn., Nov. 29, 1942; married 1960; 2 children. BS, U. Tenn., 1963; MS, U. Ky., 1964; PhD in Animal Breeding, Okla. State U., 1970. Rsch. specialist U. Ky., Lexington, 1965-68; asst. prof. endocrinology Iowa State U., 1970-71; rsch. leader reproduction rsch. unit, Clay Ctr. Agr. Rsch. Svc. USDA, Nebr., 1971-78, nat. program leader, assoc. dep. adminstr. Agrl. Rsch. Svc., 1981-88; dir. Roman L. Hruska U.S. Meat Animal Rsch. Ctr. Clay Ctr., Nebr., 1998-2000. Mem. Am. Soc. Animal Sci.

LATELL, ANTHONY A., JR., state legislator; m. Dorothy Kreeger; children: Jacqueline, Kurt, Tod. BS, U. Dayton; postgrad., Wright State U., Youngstown State U. Councilman-at-large, coun. pres., Girard City, Ohio, 1976-80; state senator Dist. 32 Ohio Senate, 1992-2000; state rep. Ohio Ho. of Reps., 2001—. Ranking minority mem. Ohio Senate, mem. finance and fin. instns. com., hwys. and transp. com., ins., commerce and labor com., state and local govt. and vets. affairs com., joint com. agy. rule rev.; precinct com. person, mem. Trumbull County Dems., 1970—; commr. Trumbull County, 1980—. Active United Way, Big Brothers/Big Sisters, Leadership Geauga County, Geauga County Libr.; trustee Found. Extended. Mem. Internat. Narcotics Enforcement Offices Assn., Sons of Italy, Elks, KC Office: 862 Krehl Ave Girard OH 44420-1903 also: Rm # 050, Ground Fl Senate Bldg Columbus OH 43215

LATHAM, TOM, congressman; b. Hampton, Iowa, July 14, 1948; s. Willard and Evelyn L.; m. Kathy Swinson, 1975; children: Justin, Jennifer, Jill. Student, Watrburg Coll., Iowa State U. Bank teller, bookkeeper, Brush, Colo., 1970-72; ind. ins. agent Fort Lupton, Colo., 1972-74; mktg. rep. Hartford Ins. Co., Des Moines, 1974-76; with Latham Seed Co., Alexander, Iowa, 1976—, now v.p., co-owner; mem. US Congress from 4th Iowa dist. (formerly 5th), 1994—, Ho. Appropriations Com. Sec. Republican Party of Iowa; rep. 5th dist. Republican State Ctrl. com.; co-chair Francklin County Republican Ctrl. com.; whip Iowa del. Republican Nat. Conv., 1992. Past chair Franklin County Extension Coun.; mem. Nazareth Lutheran Ch., past pres.; citizens adv. coun. Iowa State U. Mem. Am. Soybean Assn., Am. Seed Trade Assn., Iowa Farm Bur. Fedn., Iowa Soybean Assn., Iowa Corn Growers Assn., Iowa Seed Assn., Agribusiness Assn. of Iowa. Republican. Lutheran. Office: US Ho Reps 440 Cannon Ho Office Bldg Washington DC 20515-1504 Office Phone: 202-225-5476. Office Fax: 202-225-3301. E-mail: tom.latham@mail.house.gov.

LATIMER, KENNETH ALAN, lawyer; b. Chgo., Oct. 26, 1943; s. Edward and Mary (Schiller) L.; m. Carole Ross, June 23, 1968; children: Cary, Darren, Wendy. BS, U. Wis., 1966; JD with honors, George Washington U., 1969. Bar: D.C. 1969, Ill. 1970. Atty. U.S. Office of Comptroller, Washington, 1969-70; assoc. Berger, Newmark & Fenchel, Chgo., 1970-74, ptnr., 1975-86, Holleb & Coff, Chgo., 1986-99, Duane, Morris LLP, Chgo., 1999—. Guest speaker Ill. Inst. for Continuing Legal Edn., Chgo., 1975-87; lectr. Banking Law Inst., 1996—. Pres. North Suburban Jewish Cmty. Ctr., Highland Park, Ill., 1985; bd. dirs. Jewish Cmty. Ctrs. Chgo., 1985-95. Mem. ABA Fellows, Ill. Bar Assn. (chmn. sect. coun. on comml. banking and bankruptcy 1990-91), ABA (com. on banking and comml. finance), Chgo. Bar Assn. (com. on fin. instns.), Comml. Fin. Assn. Ednl. Found. (founders coun.), Assn. Comml. Fin. Attys., Am Coll. Comml. Fin Attys.(bd. regents), Standard Club. Avocations: jogging, travel. Office: Duane Morris LLP 227 W Monroe St Ste 3400 Chicago IL 60606-5098 Home Phone: 847-433-8116; Office Phone: 312-499-6730. E-mail: kalatimer@duanemorris.com.

LATOURETTE, STEVEN C., congressman; b. Cleve., July 22, 1954; 5 children. BA in Hist., U. Mich., 1976; JD, Cleve. State U. Marshall Coll. Law, 1979. Asst. pub. defender Lake County, Ohio, 1980-83, prosecutor Ohio, 1987—94; assoc. Cannon, Stern, Aveni & Krivok, Painesville, 1983-86; with Baker, Hackenberg & Collins, Painesville, 1986-88; mem. US Congress from 14th Ohio dist., 1994—, mem. US Holocaust Meml. Coun., 1995—, mem. transp. and infrastructure com., ranking mem. subcommittee on Coast Guard and maritime transp., mem. fin. svcs. com. Bd. dirs. Regional Forensic Lab.; bd. trustees Cleve. Police Hist. Soc. Recipient Anchor award, Nat. Credit Union Found., 1998, Consumers Choice award, Credit Union Nat. Assn., 1998, Leading Light of Long-Term Care award, Am. Health Care Assn., 2005. Mem.: Ohio Prosecuting Attys. Assn., Nat. Dist. Attys. Assn. Republican. Methodist. Office: 1 Victoria Pl Rm 320 Painesville OH 44077 Office Phone: 202-225-5731, 440-352-3939.

LATSHAW, JOHN, entrepreneur, director; b. Kansas City, Dec. 10, 1921; s. Ross W. and Edna (Parker) L.; m. Barbara Haynes, Nov. 13, 1954 (div. Dec. 1975); children: Constance Haynes, Elizabeth Albright. Student, Kansas City Jr. Coll., 1938-40; BS, Mo. U., 1942. Mgr. trading dept. Harris, Upham & Co., 1943-49; ptnr. Uhlmann & Latshaw, 1949-53, E.F. Hutton & Co. (merger with Uhlmann & Latshaw), 1954-87, exec. v.p., mgn. dir., 1987—. Chmn. bd. dirs., chief exec. officer B.C. Christopher & Co., 1987-89, chmn. emeritus, 1989-90; chmn., chief exec. officer Conchemco Inc.; chmn., chief exec. officer, mng. dir. Latshaw Enterprises, 1990—; past chmn. bd. dirs. Bus. Communications, Inc., Install, Maintain and Repair. Inc., Interior Designs, Inc.; mem. Kansas City Bd. Trade; gov. Midwest Stock Exchange, 1966-68; moderator, opening speaker Plenary Panel on Needs and Opportunities in Key Bus. Sectors, Miami Conf. on the Caribbean, 1980; pres. World Cable Ltd. Past Chmn. Key Men's Council; past pres. Friends of Zoo, 1970; mem. exec. com. Religious Heritage Am., Starlight Theatre, Performing Arts Kansas City; v.p., mem. exec. bd. Am. Cancer Soc., 1970, 71; mem. Jackson County and Crusade Adv. Com., Gov.'s Com. on Higher Edn.; bd. dirs. Kansas City Theatre Guild Council, The Curry Found., Am. Urban Devel. Found., Kansas City Crime Commn.; trustee City Employees Pension Plan, St. Andrew's Episcopal Ch. Meml. and Res. Trust Fund, U. Mo., Kansas City; bd. govs. Am. Royal, Agrl. Hall of Fame, 1976-77; exec. bd. Kansas City Area council Boy Scouts Am., 1970-72, adv. bd., 1973, chmn. patriotism program, 1970; hon. bd. dirs. Rockhurst Coll.; past pres. Kansas City Soccer Club, Inc.; mem. exec. com. N.Am. Soccer League, 1968, 69; bd. govs. Invest-In-Am. Nat. Council; mem. Central Region exec. com.; regional chmn. Invest-in-Am. Week Liaison, 1958—; mem. fin. com. Mayor's Prof. Theater; mem. Univ. Assos. of U. Mo. of Kansas City; chmn. hon. trustees YWCA, 1968-69; trustee Midwest Research Inst.; mem. chancellor's adv. council Met. Community Colls., 1976-77; mem. pres.'s council bd. hon. trustees Kansas City Art Inst.; mem. Pres.' Scholarship Club Avila Coll.; bd. dirs., mem. fin. com. Mayor's Christmas Tree Assn.; chmn. bd. trustee Conservatory of Music; community adv. com. U. Mo. Kansas City Sch. Nursing; mem. Civic Council Greater Kansas City; chmn. Brotherhood Citation Dinner for NCCJ, 1980; trustee Westminster Coll., 1981; hon. bd. govs. Hyman Brand Hebrew Acad.; adv. com. Metro Energy Ctr., 1982; mem. NASA adv. bd. to Pres. U.S., 1983-86. Recipient citation of merit U. Mo., 1957, Golden Eagle award Nat. Invest in Am. Coun., 1970, Chaturathabhorn of Most Exalted Order of White Elephant award, Thailand, 1983; named hon. consul Thailand, Royal Consulate Gen., 1986, The Knight Comdr. of the Most Noble Order of the Crown of Thailand, 1993; decorated Knight Hospitaller of Malta Sovereign Order St. John Jerusalem. Mem. Internat. Trade Assn. (chmn. bd.), Kansas City C. of C. (dir., past pres.), Bus. and Profl. Assn. Western Mo. (mem. adv. bd.), Kansas City Security Traders Assn. (past pres.), Nat. Security Traders Assn. (past exec. v.p.), Wine Soc. of World, Order Jim Daisy, Sigma Nu. Episcopalian (trustee). Clubs: Carriage,

Mission Hills Country. Home: 5049 Wornall Apt 2C Kansas City MO 64112-2409 also: 4560 Gulf Shore Blvd N Unit 113 Naples FL 34103 Office: 800 W 47th St Ste 716 Kansas City MO 64112-1249

LATTA, BRENT, consumer products company executive; From v.p. mktg. to pres., CEO Landauer, Inc., Glenwood, Ill., 1987—98, pres., 1998—, CEO, 1998—. Office: Landauer Inc 2 Science Rd Glenwood IL 60425

LATTA, ROBERT EDWARD (BOB LATTA), congressman, former state legislator; b. Bluffton, Ohio, Apr. 18, 1956; s. Delbert Leroy Latta & Rose Mary (Kiene) L.; m. Marcia Sloan, 1986; children: Elizabeth, Maria BA, Bowling Green State U., 1978; JD, U. Toledo, 1981. Bar: Ohio 1981. Atty. Marshall & Melhorn, 1981—82, Cheetwood & Davies, 1982—83; assoc. counsel Truscorp, 1982—89; commr. Wood County, Ohio, 1990—96; mem. Ohio State Senate, Columbus, 1997-2001, Ohio Ho. of Reps. from 6th dist. (formerly 4th dist.), Columbus, 2001—07, chair criminal justice com., mem. civil & comml. law ways and means and pub. utility, criminal sentencing commn., correctional instn. inspection com.; mem. US Congress from 5th Ohio Dist., 2007—. Mem. Wood County Arthritis Found., Wood County Hist. Soc. Recipient: Legis. Appreciation award, Ohio Assn. Alcohol Drug Addiction & Mental Health Svcs., Watchdog of Treas. award, United Conservatives of Ohio, 1998, 2000, 2005, Maj. Gen. Charles Dick award for Legis. Excellence Ohio N.G. Assn., 1999, Svc. award, The Ohio State U. SeaGrant, 1999, Patriot award, US Sportsmen's Alliance, 2002, Cooperator award, Ohio Soil & Water Conservation Districts, 2004, Disting. Legis. award, Ohio Econ. Devel. Assn., 2007; named Outstanding Freshman Legis., 1998, Legis. of Yr., Ohio Farmers Union, 2000, League of Ohio Sportsmen, 2000; cert. Appreciation Ohio Supts. Ednl. Svc. Ctr. Assoc. Mem. Wood County Farm Bur., Wood County Bar Assn. (trustee 1991-95), Wood County HIstorical Soc., Friends of Camp Perry, Bowling Green C. of C., Kiwanis (v.p., 1990-91, pres. 1991-92), Omicron Delta Kappa, Ohio Rifle & Pistol Assn., NRA, NFIB Office: US Congress 1203 Longworth Ho Office Bldg Washington DC 20515 also: 96 S Washington St Ste 400 Tiffin OH 44883

LATTO, LEWIS M., broadcast executive; b. Duluth, Minn., Jan. 21, 1940; s. Lewis M. and Ethel S. L.; divorced; children: Aaron, Caroline. BA, U. Minn., 1963. Owner, mgr. Sta. KXTP, Duluth, 1965-94, Sta. WAKX-FM, 1974-94; owner Sta. KRBT-AM, WEVE-FM, Eveleth, Minn., 1978—, Sta. KGPZ-FM, Grand Rapids, Minn., 1995—. Mem. Duluth City Council, 1969-75, pres., 1974. Mem. Nat. Radio Broadcasters Assn. (dir.), Minn. Broadcasters Assn. (pres. 1992-93). Republican. Methodist. Office: Northland Radio Stas 5732 Eagle View Dr Duluth MN 55803-9498 E-mail: lewlatto@aol.com.

LAU, PAULINE YOUNG, chemist; b. Harbin, China, June 18, 1943; d. Ching-ju and Chuan-erh (Fu) Young; m. Roland Lau, Sept. 16, 1967 (div. 1990); 1 child, Joan Mann. BS in Med. Tech., Nat. Taiwan U., 1964; MS in Chemistry, Wayne State U., Detroit, 1967; PhD in Chemistry, 1984. Med. technologist Detroit Gen. Hosp., 1967-68; adminstrv. asst. in rsch. Purdue U., W. Lafayette, Ind., 1970-72; supr. chemistry dept. Raritan Valley Hosp., Greenbrook, N.J., 1973-75; head chemistry dept. Princeton (N.J.) Med. Ctr., 1975-80; mgr. S.E. region RIA Ctr., Columbia, S.C., 1980-82; rsch. chemist Med. Product dept. DuPont Co., Wilmington, Del., 1984-88; mgr. rsch./devel. Boehringer Mannheim Diagnostics, Indpls., 1988—. Com. mem. Nat. Com. on Clin. Lab. Stds., 1989—. Author: Clinical Chemistry Laboratory Procedures, 1977. Recipient Outstanding Product Devel. award, Boehringer Mannheim Co., 1990. Mem. Chinese Acad. and Profl. Assn. in Mid-Am. (bd. dirs. 1990—), Ind. Assn. Chinese Ams. (pres. 1993), Mt. Jade Assn. (chmn. biomed. div. 1990—), Ctrl. Ind. Clin. Biochemistry Forum (pres. 1993—), Am. Assn. Clin. Chemistry (chpt. treas. 1989-92, divsn. sec. 1992-93), Am. Chem. Soc. (chpt. bd. dirs. 1990-91), Ind. Chinese Profl. Assn. (v.p. 1990-91, pres. 1992-93), N.Am. Chinese Clin. Chemists Assn. (bd. dirs. 1988-91, pres. 1992—). Office: Roche Diagnostic Corp 9115 Hague Rd Indianapolis IN 46256-1025 Home: 4238 Suzanne Dr Palo Alto CA 94306-4335

LAUER, RICHARD T., lawyer; b. Cin., Feb. 26, 1969; BA, U. Mass. Amherst, 1991. Bar: Ohio 1994, US Dist. Ct. Southern Dist. Ohio 1995, US Ct. of Appeals Sixth Cir. 2000, Ky. 2001, US Dist. Ct. Eastern Dist. Ky. 2002. Ptnr. Robbins, Kelly, Patterson & Tucker, Cin. Named one of Ohio's Rising Stars, Super Lawyers, 2006. Office: Robbins Kelly Patterson & Tucker Federated Bldg Ste 1400 7 W 7th St Cincinnati OH 45202-2417 Office Phone: 513-721-3330. Office Fax: 513-721-5001.

LAUER, RONALD MARTIN, pediatric cardiologist, researcher; b. Winnipeg, Man., Can., Feb. 18, 1930; m. Eileen Pearson, Jan. 12, 1959; children: Geoffrey, Judith Lauer. BS, U. Man., 1953, MD, 1954. Diplomate Am. Bd. Pediatrics. Asst. prof. pediatrics U. Pitts., 1960-61; asst. prof. pediatrics U. Kans., 1961-67, assoc. prof. pediatrics, 1967-68; prof. pediatrics, dir. pediatrics cardiology U. Iowa, 1968-95, vice chmn. pediatrics, 1974-82, prof. pediatrics and preventive medicine 1980—. Recipient Sci. Couns. Disting. Achievement award Am. Heart Assn., 1991, award of meritorious achievement, 1998, Eugene Braunwald Mentorship award, 2002, named Disting. Scientist, 2004; Founder's award Am. Acad. Pediatrics, 1997. Office: U Iowa Coll Medicine Divsn Pediat Cardiology 200 Hawkins Dr Iowa City IA 52242-1009 Office Phone: 319-356-2839. Business E-Mail: ronald-lauer@uiowa.edu.

LAUFF, GEORGE HOWARD, biologist; b. Milan, Mich., Mar. 23, 1927; s. George John and Mary Anna (Klein) L. BS, Mich. State U., 1949, MS, 1951; postgrad., U. Mont., 1951, U. Wash., 1952; PhD, Cornell U., 1953. Fisheries research technician Mich. Dept. Conservation, 1950; teaching asst. Cornell U., 1952-53; instr. U. Mich., 1953-57, asst. prof., 1957-61, asso. prof., 1961-62; research asso. Gt. Lakes Research Inst., U. Mich., 1954-59; dir. U. Ga. Marine Inst., 1960-62; asso. prof. U. Ga., 1960-62; research coord. Sapelo Island Research Found., 1962-64; dir. Kellogg Biol. Sta., 1964-90; prof. dept. fisheries and wildlife and zoology Mich. State U., East Lansing, 1964-91, prof. emeritus, 1991—. Mem. cons. and rev. panels for Smithsonian Inst., Nat. Water Commn., NSF, Nat. Acad. Sci., Am. Inst. Biol. Sci., U.S. AEC, Inst. Ecology, others. Editor: Estuaries, 1967, Experimental Ecological Reserves, 1977. Served with inf. U.S. Army, 1944-46. Office of Naval Research grantee; U.S. Dept. Interior grantee; NSF grantee; others. Fellow AAAS; mem. Am. Inst. Biol. Sci., Am. Soc. Limnology and Oceanography (pres. 1972-73), Ecol. Soc. Am., Freshwater Biology Assn., INTECOL, Societas Internationalis Limnologiae, Orgn. Biol. Field Stas., Sigma Xi, Phi Kappa Phi. Home: PO Box 53185 Kalamazoo MI 49005-3185 Office: 3700 E Gull Lake Dr Hickory Corners MI 49060-9505 Business E-Mail: lauff@msu.edu.

LAUFMAN, LESLIE RODGERS, hematologist, oncologist; b. Pitts., Dec. 13, 1946; d. Marshall Charles and Ruth Rodgers; m. Harry B. Laufman, Apr. 25, 1970 (div. Apr. 1984); children: Hal, Holly; m. Rodger Mitchell, Oct. 9, 1987. BA in Chemistry, Ohio Wesleyan U., 1968; MD, U. Pitts., 1972. Diplomate Am. Bd. Internal Medicine and Hematology. Intern Montefiore Hosp., Pitts., 1972-73, resident in internal medicine, 1973-74; fellow in hemotology and oncology Ohio State Hosp., Columbus, 1974-76; dir. med. oncology Grant Med. Ctr., Columbus, 1977-92; practice medicine specializing in hematology and oncology Columbus, 1977—. Bd. dirs. Columbus Cancer Clinic; prin. investigator Columbus Cmty. Clin. Oncology Program, 1989-98. Contbr. articles to profl. jours. Mem. AMA, Am. Women Med. Assn. (sec./treas. 1985-86, pres. 1986-87), Am. Soc. Clin. Oncology, Southwest Oncology Group, Nat. Surg. Adjuvant Project for Breast and Bowel Cancers. Avocations: tennis, piano, sailing, hiking, travel. also: 8100 Ravines Edge Ct Columbus OH 43235-5426 Office: 8100 Ravines Edge Ct Columbus OH 43235-5426 Office Phone: 614-846-0044.

LAUGHLIN, NANCY, newspaper editor; Nation/world editor Detroit Free Press, 1992—. Office: Detroit Free Press Inc 600 W Fort St Detroit MI 48226-2706

LAUGHLIN, STEVEN L., advertising executive; b. 1948; Copy writer Fuller Biety Connell Agy., Milw., 1968-74, Cramer Krusselt Co., Milw., 1974-75; with Laughlin/Constable Inc., Milw., 1976—, pres., ptnr., creative dir., writer, ptnr. Office: Laughlin/Constable Inc 207 E Michigan St Milwaukee WI 53202-4996

LAUGHREY, NANETTE KAY, federal judge; b. Cheyenne, Wyo., Feb. 11, 1946; m. Christopher Sexton Kelly; children: Hugh, Jessica Katherine. BA, UCLA, 1967; JD, U. Mo. Columbia, 1975. Bar: Mo. 1975, U.S. Dist. Ct. (we. dist.) Mo. 1975, U.S. Ct. Appeals (8th cir.) 1976, U.S. Supreme Ct. 1978. Asst. atty. gen. Mo. Atty. Gen.'s Office, Kansas City, 1975-79; assoc. Craig Van Matre, P.C., Columbia, 1980-83; assoc. prof. law U. Mo. Columbia, 1983-87, prof. law, 1987-89, William H. Pittman prof. law, 1989-96; judge U.S. Dist. Ct. (we. dist.) Mo., Kansas City, 1996—. Mcpl. judge City of Columbia, 1979-83; vis. prof. law U. Iowa, 1990; dep. atty. gen. Mo. Atty. Gen.'s Office, 1992-93. Contbr. articles to profl. jours. Bd. dirs. Columbia Housing Authority. Mem.: ABA, Mo. Bar Assn., Am. Law Inst., U. Mo. Alumni Assn., Am. Whitewater Assn., Mo. Whitewater Assn. Office: US Dist Ct 400 E 9th St Ste 7452 Kansas City MO 64106-2670

LAUMANN, EDWARD OTTO, sociology educator; b. Youngstown, Ohio, Aug. 31, 1938; m. Anne Elizabeth Solomon, June 21, 1980; children: Christopher, Timothy; children by previous marriage: Eric, Lisa. AB summa cum laude, Oberlin Coll., 1960; MA, Harvard U., 1962, PhD, 1964. Asst. prof. sociology U. Mich., Ann Arbor, 1964-69, assoc. prof., 1969-72; prof. sociology U. Chgo., 1973—, George Herbert Mead Disting. Service prof., 1985—, dean divsn. of social scis., 1984—92, provost, 1992—93, chmn. dept., 1981—84, 1997—99, 2002—03. Bd. govs. Argonne Nat. Lab., 1992-93. Author: Prestige and Associations in an Urban Community, 1966, Bonds of Pluralism, 1973, (with Franz U. Pappi) Networks of Collective Action, 1976, (with John P. Heinz) Chicago Lawyers, 1982, (with David Knoke) The Organizational State, 1987, (with John P. Heinz, Robert Nelson and Robert Salisbury) The Hollow Core, 1993, (with John Gagnon, Robert Michael, Stuart Michaels) The Social Organization of Sexuality, 1994, (with Robert Michael, John Gagnon, Gina Kolata) Sex in America, 1994, (with Robert T. Michael) Sex, Love and Health, 2001, (with Stephen Ellison, Jenna Mahay, Anthony Pain, Yoosik Youm), The Sexual Organization of the City, 2004, (with John Heinz, Robert elson, Rebecca Sandefur) Urban Lawyers, 2005; editor Am. Jour. Sociology, 1978-84, 95-97. Mem. sociology panel NSF, Washington, 1972-74; commr. CBASSE, RC, 1986-91; chair bd. trustees NORC, 2001—; trustee U. Chgo. Hosps., 1992-93; mem. Panel on Elder Mistreatment, 2000-02; bd. dirs. Family Inst., 2004—. Fellow AAAS (chmn. sect. K 2001-04), Soc. Sci. Study Sexuality, Internat. Acad. Sex Rsch.; mem. Sociol. Rsch. Assn., Am. Sociol. Assn., Population Assn. Am.; Chgo. Coun. Fgn. Rels. (pres.'s cir.). Office: U Chgo 1126 E 59th St Chicago IL 60637 Home Phone: 312-587-0097; Office Phone: 773-702-8691. Business E-Mail: e-laumann@uchicago.edu.

LAURENCE, MICHAEL MARSHALL, editor; b. NYC, May 22, 1940; s. Frank Marshall and Edna Ann (Roeder) L.; m. Patricia Ann McDonald, Mar. 1, 1969; children: Elizabeth Sarah, John Marshall. AB cum laude, Harvard U., 1963. From sr. editor to asst. pub. Playboy mag., Chgo., 1967—77, asst. pub., 1977—82; mng. editor Oui mag., Chgo., 1973-77; editor, pub. Linn's Stamp News, Sidney, Ohio, 1982—2002, also columnist Editor's Choice; sr. v.p., editl. dir. Amos Hobby Pub., Sidney, 2002—05; exec. dir. Philatelic Found., NYC, 2006—07. Co-founder, dir. U.S. 1869 Pictorial Rsch. Assocs., 1975-82. Author: Playboy's Investment Guide, 1971; editor-in-chief The Chronicle of the U.S. Philatelic Classics Society, 2005—; editor: U.S. Mail and Post Office Assistant, 1975; author articles. Recipient G.M. Loeb award for disting. mag. writing U. Conn., 1968; named to Writers Hall of Fame, Am. Philatelic Soc., 1994. Mem. U.S. Philat. Classics Soc. (life, Elliott Perry award 1975, bd. dirs. 1975-81, Disting. Philatelist award 2003), Harvard Club (N.Y.C.), Collectors Club Chgo. (bd. dirs. 1978-82), Collectors Club N.Y.C. Avocations: stamp collecting/philately, gardening.

LAURIE, WILLIAM, sports team executive; b. Versailles, Mo. m. Nancy, 1974; 1 child. B in Secondary Edn., Memphis State Coll., 1974. Tchr., basketball coach Christian Bros. Coll. High Sch., Memphis, 1974-78, Rock Bridge High Sch., Columbia, Mo., 1978-83; exec. Crown Ctr. Farms, Columbia, Mo., 1983-99; chmn., owner St. Louis Blues Hockey Team, 1999—; chmn. Savvis Ctr., St. Louis. Booster U. Mo. Tiger Sport. Office: Savvis Ctr 1401 Clark Ave Saint Louis MO 63103-2709

LAURITZEN, BRUCE RONNOW, banker; b. Omaha, June 21, 1943; s. John Ronnow and Elizabeth Ann (Davis) L.; m. Kimball McKay Bowles, Nov. 26, 1965; children: Margaret, Blair, Clarkson. AB, Princeton U., 1965; MBA, U. Va., 1967. With First Nat. Bank Omaha, 1967—, 2d v.p., 1972, v.p., 1972-83, exec. v.p., 1983-87, pres., 1987—, chmn., 1999, also bd. dirs., mem. exec. com., 1968—. Pres. Farmers Savs. Bank, Shelby, Iowa, 1969-82, Harlan County Bank, Alma, Nebr., 1972-96, Landmands at. Bank, Audubon, Iowa, 1972—, Sibley (Iowa) Ins. Agy., 1972-98, Sibley State Bank, 1972-91, First Nat. Bank, Elm Creek, Nebr., 1974-77, Landmands Ins. Agy., Kimballton, Iowa, 1974-98, K.B.J. Enterprises, Iowa, 1975—, Viking Corp., Iowa, 1975—, Lauritzen Corp., Nebr. and Iowa, 1985—, Emerson (Iowa) State Bank, 1980-84; chmn. Crawford County Bank, Denison, Iowa, 1976-98, MCV Acceptance Corp., Omaha, 1986—, Sibley State Bank, 1991—; bd. dirs. York State Bank. Chmn. Charlson Regional Health Svcs.; bd. dirs. Creighton U., Omaha; trustee Joslyn Art Mus., Omaha, Nebr.; bd. govs. Ak-Sar-Ben; trustee, regional rep. St. Paul's Sch.; pres., dir. Omaha Riverfront Devel. Corp. Recipient Bus. Leadership award UNL Coll. Bus. Adminstrn., 1989. Mem. Young Pres. Orgn. (chpt. chmn. 1988-89), Omaha C. of C. (chmn. 1989, named Outstanding Young Omahan, 1978). Clubs: Omaha Country, Omaha, Omaha Press; Univ. Cottage (Princeton, N.J.); Minnesouri Angling (Alexandria, Minn.), Roaring Fork (Basalt, Colo.). Republican. Episcopalian. Avocations: skiing, golf, hunting. Home: 608 Fairacres Rd Omaha NE 68132-1806 Office: One First National Ctr 1 First National Ctr Omaha NE 68102

LAUSE, MICHAEL FRANCIS, lawyer; b. Washington, Mo., Aug. 3, 1948; s. Walter Francis and Junilla Rose (Marquart) L.; m. Ann G. Hellman, Aug. 29, 1981; children: Andrew Edward, Scott Michael. BA, St. Benedict's Coll., 1970; JD, U. Ill., 1973. Bar: Mo. 1973. Ptnr. Thompson Coburn LLP, St. Louis, 1973—, mem. exec. com., 2002—. Chmn. corp. dept. Thompson Coburn LLP, St. Louis, 2002-, exec. com. Gen. counsel Mo. Health and Ednl. Facilities Authority, 1986—, St. Louis Zoo, 1992—. Mem. ABA, Mo. Bar Assn., St. Louis Bar Assn., Nat. Assn. Bond Lawyers, Bellerive Country Club. Roman Catholic. Home: 9822 Old Warson Rd Saint Louis MO 63124-1066 Office: Thompson Coburn LLP One US Bank Plz Saint Louis MO 63101 Office Phone: 314-552-6000. Business E-Mail: mlause@thompsoncoburn.com.

LAUTENSCHLAGER, PEGGY A., former state attorney general; b. Fond du Lac, Wis., Nov. 22, 1955; d. Milton A. and Patsy R. (Oleson) L.; m. Rajiv M. Kaul, Dec. 29, 1979 (div. Dec. 1986); children: Joshua Lautenschlager Kaul, Ryan Lautenschlager Kaul; m. William P. Rippl, May 26, 1989; 1 child, Rebecca Lautenschlager Rippl. BA, Lake Forest Coll., 1977; JD, U. Wis., 1980. Bar: Wis., U.S. Dist. Ct. (we. dist.). Pvt. practice atty., Oshkosh, Wis., 1981-85; dist. atty. Winnebago County Wis., Oshkosh, 1985-88; mem. Wis. State Assembly, Fond du Lac, 1988-92; U.S. atty. (we. dist.) Wis. US Dept. Justice, Madison, Wis., 1992—2000, 2006; atty. gen. State of Wis., Madison, 2003—07; ptnr. Lawton & Cates, SC, Madison. Former mem. Govs. Coun. on Domestic Violence, Madison, State Elections Bd., Madison; bd. dirs. Blandine House, Inc., Mahala's Hope, Inc., ASTOP, Inc. Active Dem. Nat. Com., Washington, 1992-93; com. Wis., 1989-92. amed Legislator of Yr., Wis. Sch. Counselors, 1992, Legislator of Yr., Wis. Corrections Coalition, 1992. Mem. Wis. Bar Assn., Dane County Bar Assn., Fond du Lac County Bar Assn., Phi Beta Kappa. Democrat. Avocations: gardening, house renovation, sports, cooking. Office: Lawton & Cates SC 10 E Doty St Ste 400 Madison WI 53703 Office Phone: 608-282-6200. Business E-Mail: peglautenschlager@lawtoncates.com.

LAUZEN, CHRISTOPHER J., state legislator; b. Aurora, Ill., Dec. 30, 1952; MBA, Harvard U. Owner Comprehensive Acct. Svcs., Geneva, Ill.; mem. Ill. Senate from dist. 21, Springfield, 1992—. Office: 613B Capitol Bldg Springfield IL 62706

LAVELLE, ARTHUR, anatomy educator; b. Fargo, ND, Nov. 29, 1921; s. Frank and Lillie (Hanson) LaV.; m. Faith Evelyn Wilson, 1947; 1 dau., Audrey Anne. BS, U. Wash., 1946; MA, Johns Hopkins, 1948; PhD, U. Pa., 1951. USPHS postdoctoral fellow U. Pa., Phila., 1951-52; mem. faculty dept. anatomy U. Ill. Coll. Medicine, Chgo., 1952—, assoc. prof., 1958-65, prof., 1965-87, prof. emeritus, 1987—. Vis. prof. UCLA, 1968-69; cons. Galesburg (Ill.) State Rsch. Hosp., 1965-68; mem. Biol. Stain Commn., 1953-93, trustee, 1978-93, pres., 1981-86, v.p., 1991-92. Mem. editorial bd. Biotechnic and Histochemistry, 1989-93; contbr. articles to profl. jours. USPHS research grantee, 1953-70; Cerebral Palsy Found. grantee, 1964-68; Guggenheim fellow, 1968-69 Mem. Am. Assn. Anatomists, Am. Soc. Cell Biology, Cajal Club, AAAS, Soc. Neurosci., Sigma Xi. Personal E-mail: arthurlavelle@cs.com.

LAVELLE, AVIS, consulting firm executive; b. Chgo., Mar. 5, 1954; d. Adolph Eugene and Mai Evelyn (Hicks) Sampson. BS in Comms. cum laude, U. Ill., 1975. Announcer, pub. affairs dir. Sta. WTAX Radio, Springfield, Ill., 1977-78; news dir., anchor Sta. WLTH Radio, Gary, Ind., 1978-79; reporter, anchor Stas. WJJD/WJEZ, Chgo., 1979-84; chief polit. reporter Sta. WGN-Radio/TV, Chgo., 1984-88; campaign press sec. Richard M. Daley for Mayor, Chgo., 1988-89; mayoral press sec. Officer of the Mayor, Chgo., 1989-92; nat. press sec. Clinton/Gore for Pres., Little Rock, 1992; spl. asst. to chmn. Vernon Jordan Presdl. Transition, Washington, 1992-93; asst. sec. pub. affairs U.S. Dept. Health and Human Svcs., Washington, 1993—95; v.p. comm. Waste Mgmt. Inc., 1995—99; v.p. govt. and pub. affairs U. Chgo. Hosps., 1999—2001; sr. ptnr. bus. devel. The Foster Group, Chgo., 2001—04; pres. A LaVelle Consulting Svcs. LLC, Chgo., 2004—. Mem. Delta Sigma Theta Pub. Svc., Chgo., 1973—; mem. steering com. Black Adoption Taskforce of Ill., Chgo., 1987; v.p. Chgo. Bd. Edn., 1997-2003; bd. dirs. Project Image, Inc., Chgo., 1988-89, Human Resources Devel. Inst., Chgo., 1988; founding mem. bd. dirs. After Sch. Matters Found.; mem. resource com. Met. Planning Coun.; campaign mgr. Mayor Richard M. Daley's Re-election, 1999; commr. Chgo. Cable Commn., 2003—; state dir. Ill. Kerry for Pres. Campaign, 2004. Recipient African Am. Bus. and Profl. Women award Dollars and Sense Mag., 1989, Women at Work award Nat. Commn. Working Women, 1980, First Place Team award AP, 1984; named one of Chicago's 100 Most Influential Women, Crain's Chgo. Bus., 2004. Democrat. Office: A LaVelle Consulting Svcs LLC 25 E Washington St #908 Chicago IL 60602 Office Phone: 312-223-0581.

LAVERS, RICHARD MARSHALL, lawyer; b. Oak Ridge, Tenn., Apr. 15, 1947; s. Willard Douglas and Athena Vashti (Compton) L.; m. Christine Anne Jandl, June 2, 1973; children: Christian Douglas, Ansley McKay, Ti-Patrice, Rickey Elizabeth. BA, U. Mich., 1968; postgrad., Columbia U., 1968-69; JD cum laude, U. Mich., 1972; postdoctoral, U. Wis., 1977-81. Bar: Colo. 1972, U.S. Dist. Ct. (Colo.) 1972, U.S. Ct. Appeals (10th cir.) 1975, Wis. 1978, La. 1983, U.S. Dist. Ct. (mid. dist.) La. 1983, U.S. Ct. Appeals (5th cir.) 1983, N.Y. 1986. Dep. dist. atty. 9th Jud. Dist., Glenwood Springs, Colo., 1972-73; assoc. Martin Dumont, Glenwood Springs, 1972-74, Rovira, Demuth & Eiberger, Denver, 1974-76; assoc. resident counsel Nat. Presto Industries, Eau Claire, Wis., 1976-82; asst. counsel Ethyl Corp., Baton Rouge, 1982-87; ptnr. Mulcahy & Wherry, S.C., Milw., 1987-90, Michael, Best & Friedrich, Milw., 1990-94; gen. counsel RMT, Inc., Madison, Wis., 1994—97; of counsel Whyte Hirschboeck Dudek, S.C., 1994—97; gen. counsel MK Rampage, Inc., 1995—99; exec. v.p., sec., gen. counsel Coachmen Industries, Inc., Elkhart, Ind., 1997—. Gen. counsel Wis. World Trace Ctr., 1987-91; bd. dirs. Nexus Internat., Ltd.; adj. prof. bus. law Cardinal Stritch Coll. Mem. editorial bd. U.S. Trademark Assn., Guide to the Internat. Sale of Goods Conv., Bus. Laws Inc. Counsel U.S. Rep. Steve Gunderson campaign, Eau Claire, Wis., 1980; bd. dirs. Milw. Kickers Soccer Club, Inc., pres., 1992—95. Mem. ABA, N.Y. Bar Assn., Wis. Bar Assn. (bd. dirs. internat. practice sect. 1992—), La. Bar Assn., Eau Claire Jaycees (bd. dirs. 1976-80), Meridian Club (pres. 1981). Republican. Congregationalist. Office: RMT Inc PO Box 8923 Madison WI 53708-8923

LAVEY, MARTHA, performing company executive; b. Lawrence, Kans. BA in Comms., Northwestern U., 1979, PhD in Performance Studies, 1994. Mem. ensemble Steppenwolf Theatre Co., Chgo., 1993—, artistic assoc., 1994—95, artistic dir., 1995—. Recipient Sarah Siddons award. Office: Steppenwolf Theatre Company 758 W North Ave 4th Fl Chicago IL 60610*

LAVEY, WARREN G., lawyer; AB in Applied Math., MS in Applied Math., Harvard U., 1975, JD magna cum laude, 1979; diploma in Econ., Cambridge U., 1976. Spl. asst. to chief of Common Carrier Bur. FCC, 1983, 1984; practice leader for comm. Skadden, Arps, Slate, Meagher & Flom, LLP, Chgo. Lectr and panelist at telecommunications seminars; adj. prof. Kellogg Sch. of Mgmt., Northwestern U.; bd. legal advisors Intelsat; mem. Blue Ribbon Panel Ill. Commerce Comm.; mem. steering com. on fgn. telecommunications privatizations and competition US Dept. Commerce; chmn. of conf. on telecommunications mfg. joint ventures, Shanghai; lead spkr. at conf. on global telecom regulatory developments, Tel Aviv. Authorships (to profl. jours.); author: "Can I Do the Deal? Terminated Rules, Bad Rules and Phantom Rules at the FCC", The M&A Lawyer, 2004.

LAVIK, BRICKER L., lawyer; b. 1950; BA magna cum laude, U. Minn., 1974; JD cum laude, Hamline U., 1977. Bar: Minn. 1977. Atty. Legal Aid Soc., Mpls., 1977—86; atty., trial dept. Dorsey & Whitney LLP, Mpls., 1986—93, ptnr., sr. counsel, trial group, dir., pro bono program, 1994—, dir., pro bono dept., 1996—. Adj. prof. Hamline Univ. Sch. Law., 1986—92, 1995, William Mitchell Coll. Law., 1989—92. Lectr. in field. Named a Super Lawyer, Minn. Law & Politics, 2002; recipient Outstanding Svc. award, Minn. Justice Found., 1992, Pro Bono Publico award, Hennepin County Bar Assn., 1994, Disting. Alumni award, Hamline Univ. Law Sch., 2000, Pro Bono Atty. award, Minn. Legal Services Coalition, 2001. Mem.: Minn. State Bar Assn. (construction Law sect. 1998—, gov. coun.), Hennepin County Bar Assn. (co-chair, delivery legal svcs. com. 2001—). Office: Dorsey & Whitney LLP Ste 1500 50 S Sixth St Minneapolis MN 55402-1498 Office Phone: 612-340-5645. Office Fax: 612-340-2868. Business E-Mail: lavik.bricker@dorsey.com.

LAVORATO, LOUIS A., retired state supreme court justice; s. Charles Lavorato; m. Janis M. Lavorato; children: Cindy, Natalie, Anthony, Dominic. BS in Bus. Adminstrn., Drake U., 1959, JD, 1962. Sole practice, Des Moines, 1962-79; judge Iowa Dist. Ct., Des Moines, 1979-86; justice Iowa Supreme Ct., Des Moines, 1986—2000, chief justice, 2000—06, sr. judge, 2006—. Mem. Iowa Supreme Ct. Administrative Subcom.; former chair Iowa Supreme Ct. Equality in the Courts Task Force Subcom. Recipient Judicial Achievement award, Iowa Assn. of Trial Lawyers, 1985, Merit award, Iowa Judges Assn., 1996. Home: 1123 SW Rose Ave Des Moines IA 50315

LAW, VELDON LEE, college administrator; b. Ft. Eustis, Va., Dec. 12, 1952; s. Vernon and VaNita (McGuire) L.; m. D. Lorraine Schultz, Apr. 21, 1974; children: Allison, Garrett, Jesse, Lindsay, Blake. BS, Brigham Young U., 1976, MREA, 1977; EdD, U. Nev., Las Vegas, 1988. Asst. dir. community svcs. Snow Coll., Ephraim, Utah, 1976-78; extended svcs. coord. N.Mex. Jr. Coll., Hobbs, 1978-79, dir. community devel., 1979-82; asst. dean continuing edn. Santa Barbara (Calif.) City Coll., 1982-84; exec. dir. community edn. Clark County Community Coll., Las Vegas, 1984-88; dean instrn. John Wood Community Coll., Quincy, Ill., 1988-96; pres. Barton County C.C., Great Bend, Kans., 1996—. First counselor Ch. Jesus Christ of Latter-day Saints, Quincy, 1989—. Mem. Exchange Club, Ill. Community Coll. Coun. Adminstrs. (chair 1989, instrnl. svcs. commn. 1990). Avocations: camping, golf. Office: Barton County Community College 245 NE 30 Rd Great Bend KS 67530-9107

LAWFER, I. RONALD, state legislator; BA, U. Ill. Dir. Kent Bank; Dist. 74 rep. Ill. Ho. Reps. Mem. Jo Daviess County bd.; bd. dirs. Northwestern Ill. Cmty. Action Agy., Jo Daviess Farm Bur., Jo Daviess Agrl. Extension Coun. Address: 14123 Burr Oak Ln Stockton IL 61085-9514 Also: 19 S Chicago Ave Freeport IL 61032-4229

LAWLER, GREGORY FRANCIS, mathematics professor; b. Alexandria, Va., July 14, 1955; s. Thomas Comerford and Patricia Ann (Fullerton) L.; m. Marcia Fenker Curtis, May 5, 1990. BA, U. Va., 1976; PhD in Math., Princeton U., 1979. Asst. prof. math. Duke U., Durham, NC, 1979-85, assoc. prof. math., 1985-91, prof. math., 1991—2001, A. Hollis Edens prof. math., 2001—03; prof. math. Cornell U., Ithaca, NY, 2001—06; prof. math. & statistics U. Chgo., 2006—. Vis. assoc. prof. Cornell U., 1989; vis. rsch. scientist U. BC, 1994—95. Author: Intersections of Random Walks, 1991, Introduction to Stochastic Processes, 1995, Conformally Invariant Processes in the Plane, 2005. Sloan Found. rsch. fellow, 1986-90; recipient: George Polya prize, 2006 Fellow Inst. Math. Stats. Office: U Chgo Dept Math 5734 S University Ave Chicago IL 60637 E-mail: lawler@math.uchicago.edu.

LAWLER, JAMES EDWARD, physics professor; b. St. Louis, June 29, 1951; s. James Austin and Dolores Catherine Lawler; m. Katherine Ann Moffatt, July 21, 1973; children: Emily Christine, Katie Marie. BS in Physics summa cum laude, U. Mo., Rolla, 1973; MS in Physics, U. Wis., 1974, PhD in Physics, 1978. Rsch. assoc. Stanford (Calif.) U., 1978-80; asst. prof. U. Wis., Madison, 1980-85, assoc. prof., 1985-89, prof., 1989—, Arthur & Aurelia Schawlow prof., 1999—. Product devel. cons. Nat. Rsch. Group, Inc., Madison, 1977-78; cons. GE, Schenectady, N.Y., 1985-96, Teltech, Inc., 1990—; exec. com. Gaseous

Electronics Conf., 1987-89, treas., 1992-94, DAMOP program com., 1993-95. Editor: (with R.S. Stewart) Optogalvanic Spectroscopy, 1991; contbr. articles to profl. jours. Recipient Penning award Internat. Conf. on Phenomena in Ionized Gases, 1995; Schumberger scholar U. Mo., 1971-72; grad. fellow U. Wis. Alumni Rsch. Found., 1973-74, NSF, 1974-76, H.I. Romnes faculty fellow U. Wis., 1987. Fellow Am. Phys. Soc. (Will Allis prize 1992), Optical Soc. Am.; mem. Sigma Xi. Achievements laser and lighting patents; development of laser diagnostics for glow discharge plasmas, of methods for measuring accurate atomic transition probabilities and radiative lifetimes. Office: U Wis Dept Physics 1150 University Ave Madison WI 53706-1302 Home Phone: 608-231-1473. Business E-Mail: jelawler@wisc.edu.

LAWLER, JAMES F., state senator; b. Howard, SD, Dec. 14, 1935; m. Christine A. Lawler; children: Jeff, James, Lisa. BS in Math., Sci., Dakota State U., Madison, SD, 1958; MPH, U. Minn., 1962. Dist. environ. sanitarian S.D. Dept. of Health, Sioux Falls, 1959-62; mild and food cons. USPHS Bur. of State Svcs., Washington, 1962-64; radiation surveillance officer USPHS, DHHS, Kansas City, Mo., 1964-67, spl. asst. to area dir., chief tng. svcs. Aberdeen Area Indian Health Svc. Aberdeen, 1964-67, chief tng. ops. Desert Willow Tng. Ctr. Tucson, 1972-77, spl. asst. to area dir. Aberdeen Area Indian Health Svc. Aberdeen, 1977-79, area instnl. environ. control officer Aberdeen Area Indian Health Svc., 1979-85, spl. project dir. Aberdeen Area Indian Health Svc., 1985-92, retire, 1992; rep. for dist. 3 S.D. State Senate, 1992—. Guest speaker numerous colls. and univs.; prof. No. State U., Aberdeen. Contbr. articles to mags. and newsletters. Mem. PTA, Aberdeen Conv. and Visitors Bur.; bd. dirs. Boys and Girls Club Aberdeen, Salvation Army, Am. Lung Assn. S.D.; past pres. adv. coun. Foster Grandparent Program, Kiwanis Club Aberdeen; past mem., bd. dirs. Adjustment Tng. Ctr., Aberdeen. With S.D. N.G., 1954-62, capt. USPHS, 1962-92. Recipient Acad. scholarship 1954-58, Exemplary Performance award U. S.D. Sch. Medicine, 1989, Surgeon Gen.'s Exemplary Svc. medal, 1992; named Vol. Family Yr., S.D. Spl. Olympics, 1989. Mem. Nat. Environ. Health Assn., Internat. Assn. Milk, Food and Environ. Sanitarians, S.D. Pub. Health Assn. (pres. 1988-89, G.J. Van Heuvelen award 1990), S.D. Environ. Health Assn. (pres. 1983-84, Sanitarian Of Yr. 1988), Commd. Officers Assn. USPHS (Aberdeen area past pres.), Nat. Assn. Retarded Children, Nat. Coun. Exceptional Children, Elks, Moose, Kappa Sigma Iota. Address: SD Senate 602 W 5th St Pierre SD 57501-1413

LAWLER, JAMES RONALD, French language educator; b. Melbourne, Australia, Aug. 15, 1929; married, 1954; 2 children. BA, U. Melbourne, 1950, MA, 1952; DUniv., U. Paris, 1954. Lectr. French U. Queensland, Australia, 1955-56; sr. lectr. U. Melbourne, 1957-62; prof., head dept. U. Western Australia, 1963-71; prof., chmn. dept. UCLA, 1971-74; McCulloch prof. Dalhousie U., Halifax, N.S., Canada, 1974-79; prof. French U. Chgo., 1979—, Edward Carson Waller Disting. Svc. prof., 1983-97, prof. emeritus, 1998. Vis. prof. Coll. de France, 1985, Tokyo, 1996, 98-99; chmn. vis. com. Romance Langs. and Lits. Harvard U., 1991-94, Soc. Amis U. Paris coun. Author: Form and Meaning in Valery's Le Cimetiere Marin, 1959, Lecture de Valery: Une Etude de Charmes, 1963, The Language of French Symbolism, 1969, The Poet as Analyst, 1974, Rene Char: The Myth and the Poem, 1978, Edgar Poe et les Poetes Francais, 1989, Rimbaud's Theatre of the Self, 1992, Poetry and Moral Dialectic: Baudelaire's Secret Architecture, 1997; co-author: Paul Valery; Poems, 1971, Paul Valery: Leonardo, Poe, Mallarme, 1972, Paul Claudel: Knowing the East, 2004, Edgar Allan Poe: Histoires, Essais, Poèmes, 2007; editor: An Anthology of French Poetry, 1960, Paul Valery: An Anthology, 1977, Paul Valery, 1991, Rimbaud Vivant; founding editor Essays in French Literature, 1964, Dalhousie French Studies, 1980. Decorated officier Palmes Academiques; recipient Prix Internat. Amities Françaises, Prix du rayonnement de la langue francaise Acad. Francaise, 1999; Brit. Coun. interchange scholar, 1967; Australian Acad. Humanities fellow, 1970, Guggenheim Found. fellow, 1974, NEH fellow, 1985; Grad. Students Tchg. award U. Chgo., 1998. Mem. MLA (coun. 1978-82), Internat. Assn. French Studies (pres. 1998-2001), Australian Acad. the Humanities, Soc. Amis de Rimbaud (pres. 2006—). Achievements include rsch. in modern French poetry, poetics, 20th century novel. Office: U Chgo Dept Romance Langs & Lit 1050 E 59th St Chicago IL 60637-1559

LAWNICZAK, JAMES MICHAEL, lawyer; b. Toledo, Sept. 11, 1951; m. Christine Nielsen, Dec. 31, 1979; children: Mara Katharine, Rachel Anne, Amy Elizabeth. BA, U. Mich., 1974, JD, 1977. Bar: Mich. 1977, Ill. 1979, Ohio 1989. Law clk. to the Honorable Robert E. DeMascio U.S. Dist. Ct. (ea. dist.) Mich., Detroit, 1977-79; assoc. Levy and Erens, Chgo., 1979-83; assoc. then ptnr. Mayer, Brown & Platt, Chgo., 1983-88; ptnr. Calfee, Halter & Griswold, LLP, Cleve., 1988—. Contbg. author: Collier on Bankruptcy, 15th edit. rev., 1997—. Mem. Chgo. Bar Assn. (subcom. on bankruptcy 1983-88), Cleve. Bar Assn. (trustee 2005—). Home: 14039 Fox Hollow Dr Novelty OH 44072-9773 Office: Calfee Halter & Griswold LLP 800 Superior Ave E Ste 1400 Cleveland OH 44114-2601 E-mail: jlawniczak@calfee.com.

LAWRENCE, DAVID, radio personality; b. Denver, Sept. 08; m. Deanna Joy Utrecht, Mar. 16, 1985; children: Dan, Bailey. Radio host WDAF/61 Country, Westwood, Kans., 1973—. Avocations: collecting 45rmp records, gardening. Office: WDAF/61 Country 4935 Belinder Rd Westwood KS 66205

LAWRENCE, JAMES A., food products executive; m. Mary G. Lawrence; 3 children. BA, Yale U., 1974; MBA with distinction, Harvard U., 1976. With Fidelity Funds, Boston Cons. Group; ptnr. Bain & Co.; co-founder, ptnr. The LEK Partnership, 1983—92; pres., CEO Asia, Africa & Mid. E. bus. units The Pepsi-Cola Co., 1992—96; exec. v.p., CFO Northwest Airlines, St. Paul, 1996—98, General Mills, Inc., Mpls., 1998—2006, exec. v.p. internat. ops., 2000—06, vice-chmn., CFO, 2006—07; CFO Unilever, Englewood Cliffs, NJ, 2007—. Bd. dirs. Avnet Inc. Mem. bd. overseers Carlson Sch. Bus. Univ. Minn.; bd. mem. Univ. Minn. Found. Office: Unilever 800 Sylvan Ave Englewood Cliffs NJ 07632

LAWRENCE, JAMES KAUFMAN LEBENSBURGER, lawyer; b. New Rochelle, NY, Oct. 8, 1940; s. Michael Monet and Edna (Billings) L.; m. George-Ann Adams, Apr. 5, 1969; children: David Michael, Catherine Robin. AB, Ohio State U., 1962, JD, 1965. Bar: Ohio 1965, U.S. Dist. Ct. (so. dist.) Ohio 1971, U.S. Ct. Appeals (6th cir.) 1971, U.S. Ct. Appeals (4th cir.) 1978. Field atty. NLRB, Cin., 1965-70; ptnr. Frost Brown Todd LLC, Cin., 1970—. Adj. prof. econs. dept. and Coll. Law U. Cin., 1975—; treas. Potter Stewart Inn of Ct., Cin., 1988—90; tchg. fellow Harvard Negotiation Project, 1991; chmn. adv. panel on appointment of magistrate judges US Dist. Ct. for So. Dist. Ohio, 1993—97; adj. prof. McGregor Sch., Antioch U., 1993—98; adj. prof. Moritz Coll. Law Ohio State U., 1995—; adj. prof. Xavier U., 1995; adj. prof. MBA program Otterbein Coll., 2002—05; adj. prof. Pepperdine U., 2007—, Stravs Inst. for Dispute Resolution, 2007—. Contbr. articles to profl. jours.; editor: (newsletter) Pass the Gavel, 2002—03. Mem. nat. coun. Ohio State U. Coll. Law, 1974—; steering com. Leadership Cin., 1985-89; mem. Seven Hills Neighborhood Houses, Cin., 1973-95, pres., 1992-94; bd. dirs. Beechwood Home, Cin., 1973-85; adv. bd. Emerson Behavioral Health Svcs., 1990-95, chmn., 1995; chmn. Labor Dept., 1978-89, Franciscan Hosp. Devel. Coun., 1995-99, chmn., 1996-97; trustee Ctr. for Resolution of Disputes, Inc., 1988-91, treas., 1990-91; mem. Ohio Gov.'s Ops. Improvement Task Force, 1991. Recipient Outstanding Adj. Faculty award, U. Cin., 1998. Fellow Coll. Labor and Employment Lawyers; mem. ABA, Cin. Bar Assn. (chmn. labor law com. 1979-82, comm. adv. com. 1994-96, alternative dispute resolution com. 1996—), Ohio Bar Assn. (cert. specialist in labor and employment law, vice chmn. labor and employment law sect. 1987-90, chmn. 1990-92, Ohio's Friend of Legal Edn. award 2003), Indsl. Rels. Rsch. Assn. (bd. govs. 1977-80), Alumni Assn. Coll. Law Ohio State U. (pres. 1984-85), Assn. for Conflict Resolution, Cincinnatus Assn. (pres. 1985-86), Collaborative Law Ctr. (steering com. 1996—2004), Univ. Club; master Potter Stewart Inn of Ct. Avocations: collecting movie posters, Lionel trains. Home: 3300 Columbia Pkwy Cincinnati OH 45226-1044 Office: Frost Brown Todd LLC 2200 PNC Ctr 201 E 5th St Cincinnati OH 45202-4182 Home Phone: 513-871-2220; Office Phone: 513-651-6822. Business E-Mail: jlawrence@fbtlaw.com.

LAWRENCE, JENNIFER L., lawyer; b. Cin., May 30, 1971; BA, Ohio State U., 1993; JD, Salmon P. Chase Coll. Law, 1996. Bar: Ohio 1996, Ky. 1997, US Dist. Ct. Southern Dist. Ohio. Assoc. The Lawrence Firm L.P.A., Cin. Bd. mem. Birth Trauma Litig. Grp., Commn. CLE, Ohio. Co-author: Medical Malpractice: Understanding the Evolution, Rebuking the Revolution. Named one of Ohio's Rising Stars, Super Lawyers, 2006. Mem.: Salmon P. Chase Am. Inn of Ct., Assn. Trial Lawyers of Am., Ohio Acad. Trial Lawyers, Ky. Acad. Trial Lawyers, Northern Ky. Bar Assn., Cin. Bar Assn. Office: The Lawrence Firm LPA 8804 Montgomery Rd Ste 700 Cincinnati OH 45202 Office Phone: 513-651-4130. Office Fax: 513-651-0525.

LAWRENCE, JEREMY, radio director; m. Jennifer Lawrence, 1997; 1 child. Alexander. Cmty. rels. dir WUGN, Midland, Mich., 1998—. Avocation: golf. Office: WUGN 510 E Isabella Rd Midland MI 48640

LAWRENCE, JOAN WIPF, former state legislator; m. Wayman; children: Wayman, Anne, David. RN, L.I. Coll. Hosp. Sch. Nursing, 1952; student, Douglass Coll., 1952-53, Rutgers U., 1953, Ohio State U., 1968-70. Rep. Dist. 87 Ohio Ho. Dist., 1983-92, rep. Dist. 80, 1993-99; dir. Ohio Dept. Aging, 1999—. Mem. Big Walnut Bd. Edn., 1970-73. Mem. LWV (Ohio pres. 1975-77), YWCA, Women's Polit. Caucus, Ohio Reps. for Choice, Farm Bur. Office: Ohio Dept Aging 9th Fl 50 W Broad St Fl 9 Columbus OH 43215-3301

LAWRENCE, WALTER THOMAS, plastic surgeon; b. Balt., Md., Sept. 5, 1950; s. Walter Jr. and Susan (Shryock) L.; m. Marsha Blake, May 30, 1987. BS, Yale U., 1972; MPH, Harvard U., 1976; MD, U. Va., 1976. Diplomate Am. Bd. Surgery, Am. Bd. Plastic Surgery. Intern and resident in gen. surgery U. NC, Chapel Hill, 1976-78; resident gen. surgery Med. Coll. Va., Richmond, 1978-81; resident plastic surgery U. Chgo., 1981-83; expert NIH, Bethesda, Md., 1983-85; asst. prof. U. C, Chapel Hill, 1985-92, assoc. prof., div. chmn., 1992-95; prof., divsn. chmn. U. Mass. Med. Ctr., 1995-99, U. Kans. Med. Ctr., Kansas City, 1999—. Treas. Plastic Surgery Rsch. Coun., 1991—94, Plastic Surgery Ednl. Found., 2005—06; mem. Residency Rev. Com. for Plastic Surgery, 2000—06; pres. Assn. Academic Chmn. in Plastic Surgery, 2006—07. Contbr. articles to profl. jours. Fellow ACS; mem. Am. Assn. Plastic Surgeons, Am. Soc. Plastic and Reconstructive Surgeons, Assn. Academic Chmn. Plastic Surgery, Plastic Surgery Rsch. Coun., Humera Soc., Womack Soc., Wound Healing Soc. Avocations: skiing, sailing, tennis. Office: U Kans Med Ctr Sutherland Inst/Pl Surgery 3901 Rainbow Blvd Kansas City KS 66160-0001 Office Phone: 913-588-2000. Business E-Mail: tlawrence@kumc.edu.

LAWRENCE, WAYNE ALLEN, publisher; b. Cin., Dec. 11, 1938; s. Clarence E. and Edna M. (Newman) L.; m. Carol SueAnn Wisecup, July 28, 1959; children: Jeffrey Thomas, Jon Christopher, Jeremy Wayne. Student public schs., Seaman, Ohio. Advt. salesman Amos Press, Inc., Sidney, Ohio, 1957-61, v.p., 1973-83, sr. v.p., 1983-92, ret., 1992, also bd. dirs. Pub. Stamp World, Linns Stamp News, 1977-82; v.p. advt. Coin World, Sidney, 1973-78; advt. mgr. World Coins, Sidney, 1964-68, advt. dir., 1968-73, v.p., 1973-77; adv. mgr. Numis. Scrapbook, Sidney, 1967-68, advt. dir., 1968-73, v.p. advt., 1973-78; pub. Cars & Parts, Sidney, 1978-85; propr., dir. Sidney Camera, 1981-87; pres. Scott Pub. Co., 1984-92. Contbr. articles and editorials on coins, stamps and cars to Amos publs. Bd. dirs. Shelby County (Ohio) United Way, 1970-76, 1st United Meth. Ch., Sidney, 1982—; bd. dirs. Sidney-Shelby County C. of C., 1982-85, sec., 1985; mem. U.S. Assay Commn., 1975. Mem. Am. Mgmt. Assn., Am. Numis. Assn., Am. Philatelic Assn., Numis. Lit. Guild, Am. Stamp Dealers Assn., Mag. Pubs. Assn., Am. Motorcycle Assn., Soc. Automotive Historians. Home: 1444 Double D Dr Sevierville TN 37876-0287 Office: 911 S Vandemark Rd Sidney OH 45365-8974

LAWSON, A. PETER, lawyer; AB, Dartmouth Coll., 1968; JD, Columbia U., 1971. Bar: NY 1971, Ill. 1979. Assoc. Sullivan & Cromwell, 1971-78; sr. counsel Baxter Internat., 1978-79; assoc. gen. attorney Motorola Inc., 1980—84, v.p., gen. attorney, 1985—87, corp. v.p., asst. gen. counsel, 1987—94, sr. v.p., asst. gen. counsel, 1994—96, sr. v.p., sec., gen. counsel, 1996-98, exec. v.p., gen. counsel, sec., 1998—. Mem.: Am. Soc. Corporate Sec., North Shore Gen. Counsel Assn., CLO Roundtable, American Corporate Counsel Assoc., ABA, Association of Gen. Counsel. Office: Motorola Inc 1303 E Algonquin Rd Schaumburg IL 60196-1079 Office Phone: 602-732-3188.

LAWSON, CONNIE, state legislator; b. Indpls., Apr. 20, 1949; m. Jack Lawson; 2 children: Brandon, Kylie. Diploma, Assn. Ind. Counties, 1996. Owner Lawson Bros. Auctioneers, Jack Lawson Realtors; mem. Ind. Senate from 24th dist., Indpls., 1996—; mem. agr. and small bus. com., mem. elections com. Ind. Senate, Indpls. Mem. liaison com. Nat. Election Ctr. Recipient Outstanding Election Admistr. award Ind. State Election Bd., 1994, Cir. Ct. Clk. of Yr., 1993, Cert. Appreciation Hendricks County Bar Assn., 1996. Mem. Assn. Cir. Ct. Clks. Ind. (pres.), Ind. Supreme Ct. Records (mgmt. com.), Assn. Ind. Counties (legis. com., bd. dirs., Clk. of Yr. 1996). Republican. Office: 200 W Washington St Indianapolis IN 46204-2728

LAWSON, KENNETH L., lawyer; b. Cin., Apr. 19, 1963; m. Marva Lawson; 5 children. BA, Wittenberg U., 1986; JD, U. Cin., 1989. Bar: OH 1989, OH Supreme Ct. 1989. Assoc. Taft, Stettinius & Hollister, 1989—93; mng. ptnr. Kenneth L. Lawson & Assocs., Cin., 1993—. Adj. prof. U. Cin. Bd. dir. Evanston-Walnut Hills Cmty. Health Ctr., 1992, SUMA, 1991, v.p., 1991. Named Nat. Atty. of Yr., WCIN; named one of Am.'s Top Black Lawyers, Black Enterprise Mag., 2003; recipient Wright-Overstreet award, NAACP, 2002, Imagemaker's Pub. Svc. award, US Dist. Ct. (so. dist.), OH, Outstanding and Dedicated Svc. award, Nat. African Am. Leadership Summit, Coalition Concerned Citizens. Mem.: Am. Bar Assn., OH State Bar Assn., Cin. Bar Assn., Black Lawyers Assn. Cin. (v.p., bd. dir.).

LAWSON, LINDA, state senator; Grad., Gavit H.S., 1966. Ret. police Capt.; state rep. dist. 1 Ind. Ho. of Reps., Indpls., 1998—, chair judiciary com., vice chair cts. and criminal code com., mem. labor and employment com. Mem. Hammond Sch. Bd., 12 yrs. Democrat. Office: Ind Ho of Reps 200 W Washington St Indianapolis IN 46204-2786

LAWSON, ROBERT DAVIS, theoretical nuclear physicist; b. Sydney, July 14, 1926; came to U.S., 1949; s. Carl Herman and Angeline Elizabeth (Davis) L.; m. Mary Grace Lunn, Dec. 16, 1950 (div. 1976); children: Dorothy, Katherine, Victoria; m. Sarah Virginia Roney, Mar. 13, 1976 (dec. 1994). BS, U. B.C., Can., 1948; MS, U. B.C., 1949; PhD, Stanford U., 1953. Research assoc. U. Calif., Berkeley, 1953-57; research assoc. Fermi Inst. U. Chgo., 1957-59; assoc. physicist Argonne (Ill.) Nat. Lab., 1959-65; sr. physicist Argonne Nat. Lab., 1965—. Vis. scientist U.K. Atomic Energy Authority, Harwell, Eng., 1962-63, Oxford U., Eng., 1970, 85; vis. prof. SUNY, Stony Brook, 1972-73; vis. fellow Australian Nat. U., Canberra, 1982; vis. prof. U. Groningen, 1973, U. Utrecht, 1974, Technische Hochschule, Darmstadt, 1975, 78, Free U., Amsterdam, 1976, 81, others; TRIUMF, U. B.C., Vancouver, Can., 1984. Author: Theory of the Nuclear Shell Model, 1980; contbr. articles to profl. jours. Fellow Weizmann Inst. Sci., 1967-68, Niels Bohr Inst., 1976-77; Sir Thomas Lyle fellow U. Melbourne, Australia, 1987. Fellow Am. Phys. Soc. Office: Argonne Nat Lab Bldg 203 Argonne IL 60439 Home: 35 N Main #25 Glen Ellyn IL 60137 Office Phone: 630-972-4092.

LAWSON, WILLIAM HOGAN, III, electrical motor manufacturing executive; b. Lexington, Ky., Feb. 3, 1937; s. Otto Kirsky and Gladys (McWhorter) L.; div.; children: Elizabeth, Cynthia; m. Ruth Stanat, 1995. BSME, Purdue U., 1959; MBA, Harvard U., 1961. Gen. mgr. svc. divsn. Toledo Scale Corp., 1964-68; exec. v.p., COO Skyline Corp., Elkhart, Ind., 1968-85; chmn. bd. dirs., CEO Franklin Elec. Co., Inc., Bluffton, Ind., 1985—, also bd. dirs. Bd. dirs. JSJ Corp., Skyline Corp., Sentry Ins. (a Mut. Ins. Co.); instr. U. Toledo, 1966-67. With US Army, 1961—63. Mem.: Harvard U. Bus. Sch. Assn., Bird Key Yacht Club, Summit Club Ft. Wayne, Ft. Wayne Country Club. Republican. Presbyterian. also: 232 Bird Key Dr Sarasota FL 34236-1602 Office: Franklin Electric Co Inc 400 E Spring St Bluffton IN 46714-3798

LAWTON, BARBARA, lieutenant governor; b. Milw., Wis., July 5, 1951; m. Cal Lawton; children: Joseph, Amanda Krupp. BA summa cum laude, Lawrence U., 1987; MA, U. Wis., 1991. Lt. gov. State of Wis., Madison, 2003—. Founding mem. Ednl. Resource Found.; founding trustee Cmty. Found.; founding mem. Latinos Unidos; mem. adv. bd. Green Bay Multicultural Ctr., Women's Polit. Voice; mem. bus. planning and resource team Entrepreneurs of Color; bd. mem. Planned Parenthood Advs. Wis., Northeastern Wis. Tech. Coll. Edn. Found. Named Feminist of the Yr., Wis. Chpt. NOW, 1999; recipient Ft. Howard Founds. Humanitarian award. Mem.: AAUW, LWV, Nat. Women's Polit. Caucus. Democrat. Office: Office of Lt Governor 19 East State Capitol PO Box 2043 Madison WI 53702 Office Phone: 608-266-3516. Office Fax: 608-267-3571. E-mail: ltgov@ltgov.state.wi.us.

LAWTON, FLORIAN KENNETH, artist, educator; b. Cleve., June 20, 1921; m. Lois Mari Ondrey, June 19, 1948; children: Kenneth R., David F., Dawn M., Patricia A. Student, Cleve. Sch. Art, 1941-43, Cleve. Inst. Art, 1948-51, John Huntington Polytech. Inst., 1946-50. Instr. Cooper Sch. Art, Cleve., 1976-80, Cleve. Sch. Art, 1980-82. Cons., instr. Orange Art Ctr., Pepper Pike, Ohio, 1978—; cons. in field, juror, 1968—. Exhbns. include Am. Watercolor Soc., N.Y., Cleve. Mus. Art, Butler Mus., Youngstown, Ohio, Canton (Ohio) Mus., Massillon (Ohio) Mus., Nat. Arts Club, N.Y.C., Pitts. Watercolor Soc., Audubon Artists, N.Y.C., Salmagundi Club, N.Y.C., Parkersburg (W.Va.) Art Ctr., Boston Mills Arts Festival, Peninsula, Ohio, Marietta (Ohio) Coll., Nat. Pks. Assn. Exhbn., 1996, 97, 2000, many others; 25 yrs. retrospective exhbn. Amish paintings, Butler Inst. Am. Art, 1989; represented in collections including Am. Soc. Metals, Ctrl. Nat. Bank, Diamond-Shamrock, Diocese Cleve., Kaiser Found., Ohio Conservation Found., Nat. City Bank Ohio, TRW, Standard Oil Co., Huntington Bank, at. Mennonite Mus., Lancaster, Pa., Ohio Bell Telephone Co., Day-Glo Corp., Soc. Bank Corp., The White House Collection, Washington, numerous others U.S. and internat., also pvt. collections; featured mags., calendars; Mill Pond Press; cons., artist (documentary) Amish Romance, 1979; official Coast Guard artist; artist Amish Documentary-PBS, 1996. Cons. Aurora (Ohio) Community Libr., 1990—. Cpl. USAF, 1943-46, PTO. Recipient Disting. Alumni award Garfield Hgts. (Ohio) High Sch., 1990, 1st place award Grand Invitational Exhbn., Akron, Ohio, 1996, numerous others. Mem. Ohio Watercolor Soc. (signature, charter, Grand Buckeye award 1983), Am. Watercolor Soc. (signature, Strathmore award 1977), Nat. Watercolor Soc. (signature), Akron Soc. Artists, Assoc. Audubon Artists, Artists Fellowships Inc. (N.Y.), Ky. Watercolor Soc. (signature), Midwest Watercolor Soc., Pa. Watercolor Soc. (signature), Ga. Watercolor Soc., Whiskey Painters Am., Rotary Club Chagrin Valley (Paul Harris fellow 1989). Office: 410-29 Willow Cir Aurora OH 44202-9131 Fax: 330-562-4102.

LAWTON, MATT, professional baseball player; b. Gulfport, Miss., Nov. 3, 1971; Baseball player Minn. Twins, 1995—2001, Cleveland Indians, 2002—04, Pitts. Pirates, 2004—05, Chgo. Cubs, 2004—05, New York Yankees, 2005, Seattle Mariners, 2006—. Office: Seattle Mariners PO Box 4100 Seattle WA 98194

LAYMAN, DALE PIERRE, retired medical educator, researcher, writer; b. Niles, Mich., July 3, 1948; s. Pierre Andre and Delphine Lucille (Lenke) L.; m. Kathleen Ann Jackowiak, Aug. 8, 1970; children: Andrew Michael, Alexis Kathryn, Allison Victoria, Amanda Elizabeth. AS in Life Sci., Lake Mich. Coll., Benton Harbor, 1968; BS in Anthropology and Zoology with distinction, U. Mich., Ann Arbor, 1971, MS in Physiology, 1974; EdS in Physiology and Health Sci., Ball State U., Muncie, Ind., 1979; PhD in Health and Safety Studies, U. Ill., Champaign-Urbana, 1986; Grand PhD in Medicine, World Info. Distributed U., Belgium, 2003. Histological technician in neuropathology U. Mich. Med. Sch., Ann Arbor, 1971-72, tchg. fellow human physiology, 1972-74; instr. human anatomy, physiology, and histology Lake Superior State U., Sault Ste. Marie, Mich., 1974-75; prof. med. terminology, human anatomy and physiology Joliet Jr. Coll., Ill., 1975—2007; ret., 2007. Author: The Terminology of Anatomy and Physiology, 1983, The Medical Language: A Programmed Body-Systems Approach, 1995, Biology Demystified, 2003, Anatomy Demystified, 2004, Physiology Demystified, 2004, Medical Terminology Demystified, 2005; contbr. articles to profl. jours. Founder Robowatch. Mem. Ill. C.C. Faculty Assn. (campus coord.), London Diplomatic Acad. (mem. acad. coun.), European Acad. Informatization (cavalier-knight, prof.), Internat. Assn. Bus. Leaders (life), Phi Kappa Phi, Kappa Delta Pi. Avocations: running, swimming, reading. Home: 509 Westridge Ln Joliet IL 60431-4883 Business E-Mail: drdlayman@sbcglobal.net.

LAZAR, JILL SUE, home healthcare company executive; b. Oak Park, Ill., June 15, 1954; d. Norton David and Carol Ellen (Kaufmann) Freyer; m. Bruce Horwich, Aug. 21, 1976 (div. Sept. 1982); 1 child, Mathew Freyer Horwich; m. Neil Lazar, Nov. 23, 1986. BS in Mktg., No. Ill. U., 1975. Mktg. rsch. assoc. McDonald's Corp., Oak Brook, Ill., 1976-80; renewal coord. Time, Inc., Chgo., 1984-87; product mgr. Macmillan Directory Div., Wilmette, Ill., 1987-92; with DependiCare, Broadview, Ill., 1992—. Mem. provider adv. panels Chad Therapeutics, Aradigm Corp., others. Mem. Chgo. Health Execs. Forum. Avocations: swimming, reading. Office: DependiCare 1815 Gardner Rd Broadview IL 60155-4401

LAZAR, KATHY PITTAK, lawyer; b. Lorain, Ohio, Nov. 12, 1955; BA summa cum laude, Kent State U., 1978; JD, Case Western Res. U., 1982. Bar: Ohio 1982. Sr. counsel TRW Inc. Rsch. editor Case Western Res. U. Law Rev., 1981-82. Mem. ABA, Ohio State Bar Assn., Cleve. Bar Assn., Order of Coif, Phi Beta Kappa.

LAZAR, RAYMOND MICHAEL, lawyer, educator; b. Mpls., July 16, 1939; s. Simon and Hessie (Teplin) L.; children: Mark, Deborah; m. Judith Mares Lazar. BBA, U. Minn., 1961, JD, 1964. Bar: Minn. 1964, U.S. Dist. Ct. Minn. 1964. Spl. asst. atty. gen. State of Minn., St. Paul, 1964-66; pvt. practice Mpls., 1966-72; ptnr. Lapp, Lazar, Laurie & Smith, Mpls., 1972-86; ptnr., officer Fredrikson & Byron P.A., Mpls., 1986—. Lectr. various continuing edn. programs, 1972—; adj. prof. law U. Minn., Mpls., 1983-99. Fellow Am. Acad. Matrimonial Lawyers; mem. ABA (chair divorce laws and procedures com. family law sect. 1993-94), Minn. Bar Assn., Hennepin County Bar Assn. (chair family law sect. 1978-79). Home: 400 River St Minneapolis MN 55401 Office: Fredrikson & Byron PA 200 S 6th St Ste 4000 Minneapolis MN 55402-3314 Office Phone: 612-492-7121. E-mail: rlazar@fredlaw.com.

LAZARUS, LILA, announcer; m. Jeff Lazarus, June 7, 1997. BA in Polit. sci., German, Kalamazoo Coll., 1984; MA in Journalism, U. Mich.; MA in Polit. sci., U. Mass.; postgrad., U. Freiburg, German, U. Bonn, Hebrew U., Israel. Prin. primet time anchor New Eng. Cable News, Boston, 1994—96; anchor Fox 25 News at 10, Boston, 1994—96; gen. assignment reporter WBAL-TV, Balt.; anchor/reporter/prodr. WJRT-TV, Flint, Mich.; anchor/reporter WWTV, Cadillac, Mich.; fgn. corr./staff reporter Ann Arbor News, Mich. Recipient award, Am. Soc. Colon and Rectal Surgeons, 1998, 1999, Emmy, 2001, Best News Spl. award, Mich. Assn. Broadcasters, 2002; fellow Hanns-Seidel, West Germany; scholar Fulbright. Office: WDIV-TV 550 W Lafayette Blvd Detroit MI 48226

LAZARUS, STEVEN, technology company exective; b. NYC, May 31, 1931; s. Jesse and Dorothy (Gold) L.; m. Arlene Doris Travin, June 18, 1953; children: Paul M., Scott R., Jeffrey T. AB, Dartmouth Coll., 1952; MBA, Harvard U., 1965. Commd. ensign USN, 1953, advanced through grades to capt., 1973, ret., 1969; asst. maritime adminstr. U.S. Dept. Commerce, Washington, 1969-72, dept. asst. sect. commerce for east-west trade, 1972-74; various positions to group v.p. for health care systems Baxter Travenol Labs. Inc., Chgo., 1974-86; assoc. dean grad. sch. of bus. U. Chgo., 1986—94; founder, mng. dir. Arch Venture Partners, 1986—; chief exec. officer, pres. Arch Devel. Corp., Chgo., 1986—94. Bd. dirs. Amgen Corp., Thousand Oaks, Calif., Primark Corp., McLean, Va, First Consulting Group, R2 Tech., Inc. Trustee Highland Park (Ill.) Hosp., 1985—. Office: Arch Venture Partners 8725 W Higgins Rd Ste 290 Chicago IL 60631

LAZERSON, EARL EDWIN, retired academic administrator; b. Detroit, Dec. 10, 1930; s. Nathan and Ceil (Stashefsky) L.; m. Ann May Harper, June 11, 1966; children from previous marriage: Joshua, Paul. BS, Wayne State U., Detroit, 1953; postgrad., U. Leiden, Netherlands, 1957-58; MA, U. Mich., 1954, PhD, 1982. Mathematician Inst. Def. Analyses, Princeton, NJ, 1960-62; asst. prof. math. Washington U., St. Louis, 1962-65, 66-69; vis. asso. prof. Brandeis U., 1965-66; mem. faculty So. Ill. U., Edwardsville, 1969—, prof. math., 1973—, chmn. dept. math. studies, 1972-73, dean Sch. Sci. and Tech., 1973-76, univ. v.p., provost, 1977-79, pres., 1980-93; pres. emeritus, 1994—. Chmn. Southwestern Ill. Devel. Authority, City of East St. Louis Fin. Adv. Authority; active Leadership Coun. Southwestern Ill., Gateway Ctr. Met. St. Louis, Inc., St. Louis Symphony Soc.; trustee Jefferson Nat. Expansion Meml. Assn., Ill. Econ. Devel. Bd. Recipient Sr. Teaching Excellence award Standard Oil Found.,

1970-71 Mem. Am. Math. Soc., Math. Assn. Am., European Math. Soc., London Math. Soc., Soc. Mathematique France, Fulbright Alumni Assn., Sigma Xi. Home: 122 Forest Grove Dr Glen Carbon IL 62034 E-mail: elazerson@sbcglobal.net.

LAZO, JOHN, JR., physician; b. Passaic, NJ, Nov. 29, 1946; s. John and Mary (Beley) Lazo; m. Donnalynn Margaret Materna, July 22, 1972; children: Jonathan Christopher, Ashley Jude. BS, Fairleigh Dickinson U., 1974; MD, Univ. Autonoma de Guadalajara, Mex., 1978. Diplomate Am. Bd. Emergency Medicine, Am. Bd. Forensic Examiners, Am. Bd. Forensic Medicine. Intern Akron (Ohio) City Hosp., 1980-81, resident in emergency medicine, 1981-83, chief resident in emergency medicine, 1982-83; med. dir. emergency svcs. Parma (Ohio) Cmty. Gen. Hosp., 1986-93, chmn. emergency dept., 1994-95, vice-chmn. emergency dept., 1995-99, chmn. emergency dept., 2000—05. Dir. Paramedic Edn. Program, Parma, 1986—93; med. dir. Emergeny Medicine Physicians -Cuyahoga County, LLC, 2002—03. Sgt. USAF, 1966—70. Fellow: Am. Coll. Emergency Physicians; mem.: Cleve. Acad. Medicine, Ohio Am. Coll. Emergency. Republican. Russian Orthodox. Avocations: photography, cooking. Home: 545 Eastwood Dr Hinckley OH 44233-9496 Office: Parma Cmty Gen Hosp 7007 Powers Blvd Parma OH 44129-5437 Office Phone: 440-743-2375. Personal E-mail: doclexus@aol.com. E-mail: jlazo@emp.com.

LAZUKA, ROBERT, artist, art educator; BFA in painting, Art Inst. Chgo.; MFA, Ariz. State U. Prof. Sch. Art, Ohio. U., 1984—, interim dir. Represented in permanent collections, Whitney Mus. Art, N.Y., Smithsonian Nat. Mus. Am. Art, Washington, DC, Nelson-Atkins Mus. Art, Kans. City, MO, Clemson U., S.C., Chattahoochee Valley Art Mus., Ga., Baseball Hall Fame Mus. Mem.: Coll. Bd. Advanced Placement Program (mem. 1988—, chief faculty consultant, studio art 1996—2000, devel. com.). Office: Ohio University School of Art 417 Seigfred Hall Athens OH 45701 Office Phone: 740-593-1676. Office Fax: 740-593-0457. E-mail: lazuka@ohiou.edu.

LAZZARA, DENNIS JOSEPH, orthodontist; b. Chgo., Mar. 14, 1948; s. Joseph James and Jacqueline Joan (Antonini) L.; m. Nancy Ann Pirhofer, Dec. 18, 1971; children: Kristin Lynn, Bryan Matthew, Matthew Dennis, Kathryn Marie, David Brady. BS, U. Dayton, 1970; DDS, Loyola U., 1974, MS in Oral Biology, 1976, cert. orthodontics, 1976. Practice dentistry specializing in orthodontics, Geneva, Ill., 1976—. Mem. dental staff Delnor Cmty. Hosp., Geneva and St. Charles, Ill., 1976—; sec. dental staff, Geneva, 1978-80, v.p., 1980-82, pres., 1982-84, exec. com., 1982-84. Leader Boy Scouts Am., 1988-90. Recipient award of merit Am. Coll. Dentists, 1974. Mem. ADA, Am. Assn. Orthodontists (presenter ann. meeting 1997, Harry Sicher hon. mention award 1977), Midwestern Soc. Orthodontists, Ill. Soc. Orthodontists, Fox River Valley Dental Soc. (bd. dirs. 1983-86), Blue Key Nat. Honor Soc. Roman Catholic. Avocations: sailing, golf. Office: PO Box 431 Geneva IL 60134-0431 Office Phone: 630-232-2277.

LEA, LORENZO BATES, lawyer; b. St. Louis, Apr. 12, 1925; s. Lorenzo Bates and Ursula Agnes (Gibson) L.; m. Marcia Gwendolyn Wood, Mar. 21, 1953; children— Victoria, Jennifer, Christopher. BS, MIT, 1946; JD, U. Mich., 1949; grad. Advanced Mgmt. Program, Harvard U., 1964. Bar: Ill. 1950. With Amoco Corp. (formerly Standard Oil Co. Ind.), Chgo., 1949—89, asst. gen. counsel, 1963-71, assoc. gen. counsel, 1971-72, gen. counsel, 1972-78, v.p., gen. counsel, 1978-89. Trustee Village of Glenview, Ill., 1963-64, mem. Zoning Bd., 1961-63; bd. dirs. Chgo. Crime Commn., 1978—, Midwest Coun. for Internat. Econ. Policy, 1973—, Chgo. Bar Found., 1981—, Chgo. Area Found. for Legal Svcs., 1981—; bd. dirs. United Charities of Chgo., 1973—, chmn., 1985—; bd. dirs. Cmty. Found. Collier County, 1997—, Naples Bot. Garden, 2000—. Served with USNR, 1943-46. Mem. ABA, Am. Petroleum Inst., Am. Arbitration Assn. (dir. 1980—), Ill. Bar Assn., Chgo. Bar Assn., Assn. Gen. Counsel (bd. dirs. 1983-89), Order of Coif, Law Club, Econs. Club, Legal, Mid-Am. (Chgo.), Glen View, Wyndemere, Hole-In-The-Wall, Sigma Xi. Republican. Mem. United Ch. of Christ.

LEACH, JANET C., publishing executive; b. 1956; m. John Leach; 3 children. Degree in Journalism, Bowling Green State U. Mng. editor The Cin. Enquirer, until 1998; editor Akron Beacon Jour., 1998—2003; profl. in residence Sch. Journalism and Mass Comm. Kent State U., 2003—; police reporter The Rev. Times, Fostoria. Mem. staff Ariz. Republic, Phoenix (Ariz.) Gazette; instr. journalism No. Ky. U., U. Cin. Mem. Knight Found. Recipient 4 Pulitzer prizes, Golden medal Meritorious Svc., 1994. Mem.: Am. Soc. Newspaper Editors, Akron Press Club, Soc. Profl. Journalists.

LEACH, MICHAEL, financial executive; Degree in acctg., Miami U., Ohio. CPA, Ohio. With Ernst & Young; contr. Drug Emporium, Powell, Ohio, 1993-98, CFO, 1998—. Pres. DrugEmporium.com.; CFO Healthcite.com. Office: Drug Emporium Inc 14525 Highway 7 Minnetonka MN 55345-3734

LEACH, RALPH F., banker; b. Elgin, Ill., June 24, 1917; s. Harry A. and Edith (Sanders) L.; m. Harriet C. Scheuerman, Nov. 18, 1944; children: C. David, H. Randall, Barbara E. AB, U. Chgo., 1938. Investment analyst Harris Trust & Savs. Bank, Chgo., 1940-48, Valley Nat. Bank, Phoenix, 1948-50; chief govt. finance sect. Fed. Res. Bd., Washington, 1950-53; treas. Guaranty Trust Co., NYC, 1953-59, v.p., 1958-59; v.p., treas. Morgan Guaranty Trust Co., NYC, 1959-62, sr. v.p., treas., 1962-64, exec. v.p., treas., 1964-68, vice chmn. bd. dirs., 1968-71, chmn. exec. com., 1971-77; dir. Merrill Lynch and Co., YC, 1978—89. Chmn. emeritus Energy Conversion Devices Inc. Bd. trustees The Juilliard Sch., 1963—87, vice chmn., 1968—87. Capt. USMC, 1940—45. Mem.: Phi Kappa Psi. Home: Apt 446 2855 W Commercial Blvd Fort Lauderdale FL 33309-2973 Office Phone: 954-777-3188.

LEACH, RONALD GEORGE, education educator, librarian; b. Monroe, Mich., Feb. 22, 1938; s. Garnet William and Erma (Erbadine) L.; m. Joy Adeline Moore, Dec. 21, 1956; children— Ronald George, Debra Mabel, Catherine Louise, Shane John. BS in Secondary Edn, Central Mich. U., 1966; MA in L.S. (U.S. Office Edn. fellow 1968-69), U. Mich., 1969; PhD in Higher Edn. Adminstrn, Mich. State U., 1980. Head libr. Ohio State U., Mansfield, 1969-70; asst. dir., then acting dir. libr. Lake Superior State Coll., Sault Ste. Marie, Mich., 1970-76; assoc. dir. librs. Central Mich. U., 1976-80; dean libr. svcs. Ind. State U., Terre Haute, 1980-93, assoc. v.p. info. svcs., dean of librs., 1994-97, prof. higher ednl. adminstrn., 1997—. Prof. edn., mem. accreditation teams North Ctrl. Assn. Author articles in field. Served with N.G., 1955-61. Mem. ALA, INFORMA (steering com. 1990—), Assn. Coll. and Rsch. Librs., Libr. Info. and Tech. Assn., Ind. Libr. Assn., Am. Soc. Info. Sci., Libr. Adminstrn. and Mgmt. Assn. (pres. 1985-86), Online Computer Libr. Ctr. User Council (exec. com. 1986, 88). Office: Ind State U Dept Leadership Admin Found Terre Haute IN 47809-0001

LEADBETTER, TIFFANY, hotel executive; b. Tex., 1976; BA, Cornell U., 1998; MBA, U. Chgo. Grad. Sch. Bus. Sales mgmt. trainee Hyatt Regency McCormick Place, Chgo., 1998; from intern to dir. devel. Global Hyatt Corp., Chgo., 1999—2006, asst. v.p. N.Am. acquisitions & devel., 2006—. Named one of 40 Under 40, Crain's Chgo. Bus., 2006. Office: Global Hyatt Corp 71 S Wacker Dr Chicago IL 60606

LEAGUE, DAVID, hardware company executive; V.p., gen. counsel Ace Hardware Corp., Oak Brook, Ill. Office: Ace Hardware Corp 2200 Kensington Ct Hinsdale IL 60523-2100

LEAHY, CHRISTINE A., lawyer, information technology executive; b. Providence, June 1964; m. Adam Weinberg; children: Annika, Sammantha. BA, Brown U., 1986; JD, Boston Coll., 1991. Ptnr. Sidley, Austin, Brown & Wood, Chgo., 1991—2001; sr. v.p., gen. counsel, corp. sec. CDW Corp, Vernon Hills, Ill., 2002—. Mem. YWCA Cir. Friends, Chgo. Women in Tech. Grp. Mem.: DC Bar Assn., Chgo. Bar Assn., ABA. Office: CDW Corp 200 N Milwaukee Ave Vernon Hills IL 60061

LEARNER, HOWARD ALAN, lawyer; b. Chgo., June 1, 1955; s. Donald and Patricia Learner; m. Lauren S. Rosenthal, Oct. 22, 1988; children: Daniel J., Samuel D., David N. AB, U. Mich., 1976; JD, Harvard Law Sch., 1980. Bar: Ill 1980, U.S. Dist. Ct. (no. dist.) Ill. 1980, U.S. Ct. Appeals (7th cir.) 1981, U.S. Supreme Ct. 1993. Gen. counsel Bus. and Profl. People for Pub. Interest, Chgo., 1980-93; pres., exec. dir. Environ. Law and Policy Ctr. Midwest, Chgo., 1993, now exec. dir. Chmn., pres., dir. Citizens Utility bd., Chgo., 1984-93; bd. govs. Chgo. Coun. Lawyers, 1986-90; dir. Environ. Law Inst., Washington, 1998—. Treas., dir. Ill. Environ., Springfield, 1982-88; legal counsel Ill. chpt. Sierra Club, Chgo., 1984—; dir. Jewish Coun. Urban Affairs, Chgo., 1984-92, Jewish Fund Justice, N.Y.C., 1990—, Leadership Greater Chgo. Fellows' Assn., 1995—, Pub. Interest Law Initiative, 1983-99. Environ. fellowship German Marshall Fund U.S. Fellow Leadership Greater Chgo., Royal Soc. Arts, Mfg. and Commerce. Office: Environ Law & Policy Ctr Midwest 35 E Wacker Dr Ste 1300 Chicago IL 60601-2110

LEARY, MARGARET A., law library director; b. 1942; BA, Cornell U., 1964; MLS, U. Minn., 1966; JD, William Mitchell Coll. Law, St. Paul, 1973. Bar: Minn. 1973, Mich. 1974. Chpt. cataloger U. Minn. Law Libr., 1968—69; cataloger William Mitchell Coll. Law, 1970—72; atty. Legal Aid Soc., Mpls., 1972—73; lectr. U. Mich. Sch. Info. and Libr. Studies, 1974—88; asst. dir. U. Mich. Law Sch. Libr., 1973—81, assoc. dir. Ann Arbor, 1982—84, dir., 1984—. Exec. com. mem. Inst. for Continuing Legal Edn., 2004, Am. Assn. Law Libraries, 1983—86, pres., 1988—89. Contbr. articles to profl. jours. Trustee William Mitchell Coll. Law, 1993—2002; vice chmn. Planning Commn. City of Ann Arbor, 1994—2002, mem. Planning Commn., 1994—2002. Named Volunteer of Yr., Habitat for Humanity, Huron Valley, 2002. Achievements include being first woman to head a library at one of the top 5 US law schools. Office Phone: 734-764-4468. Fax: 734-615-0178. Business E-Mail: mleary@umich.edu.

LEASE, ROBERT K., lawyer; b. Cleve., 1948; AB magna cum laude, Dartmouth Coll., 1970; JD cum laude, U. Conn., 1976. Bar: Ohio. Ptnr. Baker & Hostetler LLP, Cleve. Mem. Phi Beta Kappa. Office: Baker & Hostetler LLP 3200 Nat City Ctr 1900 E 9th St Ste 3200 Cleveland OH 44114-3485 Office Phone: 216-621-0200. E-mail: rlease@bakerlaw.com.

LEAVITT, JEFFREY STUART, lawyer; b. Cleve., July 13, 1946; s. Sol and Esther (Dolinsky) L.; m. Ellen Fern Sugerman, Dec. 21, 1968; children: Matthew Adam, Joshua Aaron. AB, Cornell U., 1968; JD, Case Western Res. U., 1973. Bar: Ohio 1973. Assoc. Jones Day, Cleve., 1973—80, ptnr., 1981—. Contbr. articles to profl. jours. Trustee Bur. Jewish Edn., Cleve., 1981-93, v.p., 1985-87; trustee Fairmount Temple, Cleve., 1982-2002, v.p., 1985-90, pres., 1990-93; trustee Citizens League Greater Cleve., 1982-89, 92-94, pres., 1987-89; trustee Citizens League Rsch. Inst., Cleve., 1989-98, Great Lakes Region of Union Am. Hebrew Congregations, 1990-93; mem. bd. govs. Case Western Res. Law Sch. Alumni Assn., 1989-92; sec. Kulas Found., 1986-88, 93-99, asst. treas., 1989-92. Named Ohio Super Lawyer, Cin. Mag. and Law and Politics, 2004, 2005, Leading Lawyer, Chanmbers USA Guide, 2006. Mem.: ABA (employee benefits coms. 1976—). Jewish. Home: 7935 Sunrise Ln Novelty OH 44072-9404 Office: Jones Day N Point 901 Lakeside Ave E Cleveland OH 44114-1190 Home Phone: 440-338-4485; Office Phone: 216-586-7188. Business E-Mail: jleavitt@jonesday.com.

LEAVITT, JUDITH WALZER, history of medicine educator; b. NYC, July 22, 1940; d. Joseph Phillip and Sally (Hochman) Walzer; m. Lewis Arger Leavitt, July 2, 1966; children: Sarah Abigail, David Isaac. BA, Antioch Coll., 1963; MA, U. Chgo., 1966, PhD, 1975. Asst. prof. history of medicine U. Wis., Madison, 1975-81, assoc. prof., 1981-86, prof., 1986—, Evjue-Bascom prof., 1990-95, chmn. dept., 1981-93, assoc. dean for faculty, 1996-99, Ruth Bleier prof., 1997—. Author: The Healthiest City, 1982, Brought to Bed, 1986, Typhoid Mary, 1996; editor: Women and Health, 1984, 2d edit., 1999, Sickness and Health in America, 1985, 3d edit., 1998. Office: U Wis Dept History Medicine 1300 University Ave Madison WI 53706-1510

LEAVITT, LEWIS A., pediatrician, educator; b. NYC, Nov. 7, 1941; s. Isidore and Sarah (Fishkowitz) L.; m. Judith E. Walzer, July 2, 1966; children: Sarah Abigail, David Isaac. BS, U. Chgo., 1961, MD, 1965. Diplomate Am. Bd. Pediat. Intern, then resident Albert Einstein Coll. Medicine, Jacobi Hosp., Bronx, N.Y., 1965-68; prof. pediat. U. Wis., Madison, 1984—; head infant devel. lab. Weisman Ctr. Mental Retardation and Human Devel., U. Wis., 1973—. Editor books on Down's syndrome and children's exposure to violence; contbr. artcles to profl. jours. Lt. comdr. USN, 1968-70. Mem. Soc. Rsch. in Child Devel., Am. Acad. Pediat. Office: U Wis 1500 Highland Ave Madison WI 53705-2274

LEBANO, EDOARDO ANTONIO, foreign language educator; b. Palmanova, Italy, Jan. 17, 1934; came to U.S., 1957, naturalized, 1961; s. Nicola and Flora (Puccioni) L.; m. Mary Vangell, 1957; children: Tito Nicola, Mario Antonio. Student, U. Florence, Italy, 1955; MA, Cath. U. Am., 1961, PhD, 1966. Tchr. high sch., Florence, 1955-57; Italian lang. specialist Bur. Programs and Stds., CSC, Washington, 1958; lang. instr. Sch. Langs., Fgn. Svcs. Inst., Dept. State, Washington, 1959-61; lectr. Italian, U. Va., Charlottesville, 1961-66; asst. prof. Italian, U. Wis., Milw., 1966-69, assoc. prof., assoc. chmn. dept. French and Italian, 1969-71; assoc. prof. dept. French and Italian, Ind. U., Bloomington, 1971-83, prof., 1983—2000, prof. emeritus, 2000—. Dir. Sch. Italian, Middlebury Coll., Vt., 1987-95. Author: A Look at Italy, 1976, Buon giorno a tutti, 1983, L'Insegnamento dell'italiano nei colleges e nelle universita del nordamerica, 1983; author introduction and notes to Morgante by Luigi Pulci, 1998; contbr. articles to profl. jours. Decorated cavaliere Ordine al Merito della Repubblica Italiana; recipient Uhrig award U. Wis.-Milw. faculty, 1968. Mem. MLA, AAUP, Am. Assn. Tchrs. Italian (sec.-treas. 1980-84, pres. 1984-87, exec. dir. 2006-, Disting. Svc. award 1994), Dante Soc. Am., Renaissance Soc. Am., Boccaccio Soc. Am., Nat. Italian Am. Found., Am. Italian Hist. Assn., Am. Assn. Italian Studies, Midwest MLA. Home: 4323 Falcon Dr Bloomington IN 47403-9044 Office: Ind U Ctr for Italian Studies Bloomington IN 47405 Home Phone: 812-824-6145; Office Phone: 812-855-2508. Business E-Mail: lebano@indiana.edu.

LEBEDOFF, DAVID MILLER, lawyer, writer; b. Mpls., Apr. 29, 1938; s. Martin David and Mary Louise (Galanter) Lebedoff; m. Randy Louise Miller, Feb. 7, 1981; children: Caroline, Jonathan, Nicholas. BA magna cum laude, U. Minn., 1960; JD, Harvard U., 1963. Bar: Minn. 1963. Spl. asst. atty. gen. Atty. Gen. of Minn., St. Paul, 1963-65; pvt. practice law Mpls., 1967-81; ptnr. Lindquist & Vennum, Mpls., 1981-91, Briggs & Morgan, Mpls., 1991-95; of counsel Gray, Plant, Mooty, Mooty & Bennett, Mpls., 1995—. Spl. master U.S. Dist. Ct., Mpls., 1974—75. Past bd. dirs. Guthrie Theatre, 1980—85, Coun. Crime and Justice, 1999—2007, U. Minn. Found., Blake Sch., 1988—94, Ctr. Am. Experiment; bd. dirs. Mpls. Inst. Art, 1975—, chmn., 1989—91, life trustee, 1997—; bd. regents U. Minn., Mpls., St. Paul, 1977—89, chmn. bd. regents, 1987—89. Recipient Outstanding Achievement award, U. Minn., 1991, Minn. Book award, 1998. Mem.: Minikahda Club, Mpls. Club (former bd. dirs.), Phi Beta Kappa. Home: 1738 Oliver Ave S Minneapolis MN 55405-2222 Office Phone: 612-632-3214.

LEBEDOFF, JONATHAN GALANTER, retired judge, mediator; b. Mpls., Apr. 29, 1938; s. Martin David and Mary (Galanter) L.; m. Sarah Sargent Mitchell, June 10, 1979; children: David Shevlin, Ann McNair. BA, U. Minn., 1960, LLB, 1963. Bar: Minn. 1963, U.S. Dist. Ct. Minn. 1964, U.S. Ct. Appeals (8th cir.) 1968. Pvt. practice, Mpls., 1963-71; judge Hennepin County Mcpl. Ct., State Minn., Mpls., 1971-74; dist. ct. judge State of Minn., Mpls., 1974-91; U.S. magistrate judge U.S. Dist. Ct., Mpls., 1991—2002, chief U.S. magistrate judge, 2002—05; pvt. mediator and arbitrator Mpls., 2005—. Mem. Gov.'s Commn. on Crime Prevention, 1971-75; mem. State Bd. Continuing Legal Edn.; mem. Minn. Supreme Ct. Task Force for Gender Fairness in Cts., mem. implementation com. of gender fairness in cts. Jewish. Avocation: bridge. Office: 4900 IDS Ctr 80 S 8th St Minneapolis MN 55402 Home Phone: 952-473-1414; Office Phone: 612-338-0505. E-mail: jglebedoff@yahoo.com.

LEBEDOFF, RANDY MILLER, lawyer; b. Washington, Oct. 16, 1949; m. David Lebedoff; children: Caroline, Jonathan, Nicholas. BA, Smith Coll., 1971; JD magna cum laude, Ind. U., 1975. Assoc. Faegre & Benson, Mpls., 1975-82, ptnr., 1983-86; v.p., gen. counsel Star Tribune, Mpls., 1989—2001; asst. sec. Star Tribune Cowles Media Co., Mpls., 1990—98; pvt. practice Mpls., 2001—02; v.p., gen. counsel Twin Cities Public Television, 2002—. Bd. dirs. Milkweed Editions, 1989-96. Bd. dirs. Minn. Opera, 1986-90, YWCA, 1984-90, Planned Parenthood Minn., 1985-90, Fund for Legal Aid Soc., 1988-96, Abbott-Northwestern Hosp., 1990-94. Mem. ewspaper Assn. Am. (legal affairs com. 1991-2002), Minn. Newspapers Assn. (bd. dirs. 1995-2002, pres. 2002). Home: 1738 Oliver Ave S Minneapolis MN 55405-2222 Office: 172 E Fourth St Saint Paul MN 55101

LEBEDOW, AARON LOUIS, consulting company executive; b. Chgo., Aug. 19, 1935; s. Isidor and Fannie (Perchikoff) L.; m. Madeleine Hellman; children: Ellen, Francine, Sheri, Tracey, Schildee Sheral. BS in Indsl. Engring, Ill. Inst. Tech., 1957; MBA, U. Mich., 1958. Cert. mgmt. cons. Asst. marketing mgr. Imperial-Eastman, Chgo., 1960-61; mgr. Corplan Assos., Chgo., 1961-66; chmn. bd. Technomic, Inc., Chgo., 1966-87, Technomic Consultants Internat., Deerfield, Ill., 1981-93, Global Devel. Network, Inc., 1993—. Bd. dirs. Coun. for Jewish Elderly. Served to 1st lt. USAF, 1958-60. Mem. Am. Mgmt. Assn., Am. Mktg. Assn., Tau Epsilon Phi. Office: Global Devel Network Inc 6540 N Kilbourn Ste A100 Lincolnwood IL 60712-3437 Office Phone: 847-674-7300. Personal E-mail: lebedowa@aol.com.

LEBLOND, RICHARD FOARD, internist, educator; b. Seattle, July 17, 1947; s. Donald E. and Ruth Elizabeth (Foard) LeB.; m. Anita Caraig Garcia, Dec. 28, 1994; children: Sueno Emmeline, Edgardo Alan. AB, Princeton U., 1969; MD, U. Wash., 1972. Diplomate Am. Bd. Internal Medicine (bd. dirs. 1993-98, sec.-treas. 1996-98). Intern Harlem Hosp., NYC, 1972-73; resident in medicine, clin. fellow in oncology U. Wash., Seattle, 1975-78; pvt. practice, Livingston, Mont., 1978-96; dir. Livingston Meml. Hosp., 1979-91, 93-96, chmn. bd. dirs., 1984-91. Clin. asst. prof. medicine Mont. State U., Bozeman, 1979-96, U. Wash., 1991-96, U. Calif., San Francisco, 1991-92; acting instr. Makerere U., Kampala, 1991-92; prof. clin. medicine U. Iowa, Iowa City, 1996—, med. dir. U. Iowa Hosps. and Clinics Family Care Ctr., 1997-2002; bd. dirs. Am. Bd. Family Practice, RRC-1M, 1998-2003, vice chair 2002-03; bd. dirs. Inst. for Clin. Evaluation, treas., 1999-2001. Bd. dir. Park County Friends of the Arts, Livingston, Iowa, 1981—87, Livingston Cmty. Trust, 1986—91. Served in Indian Health Svc. USPHS, 1973—75, Poplar, Mont. Named Regional Trustee of Yr., Am. Hosp. Assn., 1989; recipient med. achievement award Deaconess Found., 1995, Mont. ACP Laureate award, 1996. Fellow ACP; mem. AMA, Am. Soc. for Internal Medicine, Iowa Med. Soc. Avocations: fishing, hunting, hiking, reading, gardening. Home: 2023 Laurence Ct NE Iowa City IA 52240-9150 Office: Univ Iowa Hosps and Clinics 200 Hawkins Dr Iowa City IA 52242-1009 E-mail: richard-leblond@uiowa.edu.

LEBOWITZ, ALBERT, lawyer, writer; b. St. Louis, June 18, 1922; s. Jacob and Lena (Zemmel) L.; m. Naomi Gordon, Nov. 26, 1953; children: Joel Aaron, Judith Leah. AB, Washington U., St. Louis, 1945; LL.B., Harvard U., 1948. Bar: Mo. bar 1948. Assoc. Frank E. Morris, St. Louis, 1948-55; partner firm Morris, Schneider & Lebowitz, St. Louis, 1955-58, Crowe, Schneider, Shanahan & Lebowitz, St. Louis, 1958-66; counsel firm Murphy & Roche, St. Louis, 1966-67, Murphy & Schlapprizzi, St. Louis, 1967-81; partner firm Murphy, Schlapprizzi & Lebowitz, 1981-86; editor lit. quar. Perspective, 1961-80; of counsel Donald L. Schlapprizzi, P.C., 1986—, John T. Murphy, Jr., 1986-88. Author: novel Laban's Will, 1966, The Man Who Wouldn't Say No, 1969, A Matter of Days, 1989; also short stories. Served as combat navigator USAAF, 1943-45, ETO. Decorated Air medal with 3 oak leaf clusters. Mem. Mo. Bar Assn., Phi Beta Kappa. Home: 743 Yale Ave Saint Louis MO 63130-3120

LECHLEITER, JOHN C., pharmaceutical executive; b. 1953; BS in Chemistry summa cum laude, Xavier U., Cin., 1975; MS in Organic Chemistry, Harvard U., 1980, PhD, 1980; D in Bus. Adminstrn. (hon.), Marian Coll., Indpls., 2006. Sr. organic chemist process R & D Eli Lilly & Co., 1979—82, head process R & D, 1982—84, dir. pharm. product devel. Lilly Rsch. Ctr. Ltd. Windlesham, England, 1983—86, mgr. rsch. devel. projects Europe Indpls., 1986—88, dir. devel. projects mgmt., pharm. regulatory affairs, 1988, dir. chemistry, mfg. and control, 1989, exec. dir. pharm. product devel., 1991—93, v.p. pharm. prodn. & devel., 1993—94, v.p. regulatory affairs, 1994—96, v.p. devel. & regulatory affairs, 1996—98, sr. v.p. pharm. products, 1998—2001, exec. v.p. pharm. products & corp. devel., 2001—04, exec. v.p. pharm. ops., 2004—05, pres., COO, 2005—08, pres., CEO, 2008—. Bd. dirs. Great Lakes Chemical Corp., 1999—2005, Eli Lilly & Co., 2005—. Vis. com. Harvard Bus. Sch., 2004—; health policy and mgmt. coun. Harvard Sch. Pub. Health, 2004—; bd. trustees Xavier U., Cin.; disting. advisor Children's Mus. Indpls.; Dean's adv. bd. Ind. U. Sch. Med.; bd. dirs. United Way Ctrl. Ind. Mem.: Am. Chem. Soc. Office: Eli Lilly and Co Lilly Corp Ctr Indianapolis IN 46285 Office Phone: 317-276-2000.*

LECHTENBERG, VICTOR L., agricultural studies educator; b. Butte, Nebr., Apr. 14, 1945; m. Grayce Lechtenberg; 4 children. BS, U. Nebr., 1967; PhD in Agronomy, Purdue U., 1971. Prof. agronomy Purdue U., West Lafayette, Ind., 1971—, assoc. dir. Agrl. Experiment Sta., 1982-89, exec. assoc. dean agr., 1989-93, dean agr., 1994—2004, vice provost engagement, 2004—07, interim provost, 2007—. Contbr. articles to profl. jours., chpts. to books. Scoutmaster Boy Scouts Am., 1983-85. Recipient Nebr. 4-H Dist. Alumni award, 1981. Fellow Am. Soc. Agronomy (Ciba-Geigy award), Crop Sci. Soc. Am. (past pres.); mem. Crop Sci. Soc. Agrnomy, Coun. Agrl. Sci. and Tech. (past pres., bd. dirs.), USDA (past chmn. nat. agrl. rsch., extension, edn. and econs. adv. bd.). Sigma Xi, Alpha Zeta, Gamma Sigma Delta. Roman Catholic. Avocation: woodworking. Office: Purdue Univ Hovde Hall 610 Purdue Mall West Lafayette IN 47907 Office Phone: 765-494-9095. Business E-Mail: vll@purdue.edu.

LECKEY, ANDREW A., financial columnist; b. Chgo., Sept. 22, 1949; s. Alexander and Ellen (Martin) Leckey. BA, Trinity Coll., Deerfield, Ill., 1971; MA in Journalism, U. Mo., 1975; postgrad., Columbia U., 1978—79, Rutgers U., 1981. Fin. editor Oreg. Statesman, Salem, 1975—76; statehouse reporter Phoenix Gazette, 1976—78; fin. columnist Chgo. Sun-Times, 1979—85, Chgo. Tribune and N.Y. Daily News, 1985—; fin. commentator Sta. WBEZ, Chgo., 1981—83; syndicated fin. columnist L.A. Times Syndicate, 1983—85, Tribune Media Svcs., 1985—; dir. Bus. Reporting Prog., Grad. Sch. Journalism U. Cal., Berkeley, 1999—2002; vis. prof., Bus. & Econ. Journalism B.U., 2002—03; dir., Donald C. Reynolds Nat. Ctr. Bus. Journalism Amer. Press Inst., Reston, Va., 2003—. Author: (book) Make Money with the New Tax Laws, 1987, The 20 Hottest Investments for the 21st Century, 1994, The Morningstar Approach to Investing: Wiring into the Mutual Fund Revolution, 1997, Global Investing, 1999, 2000, (annual anthology) The Best Business Stories of the Year, 2001—, (book) The Lack of Money is the Root of All Evil: Mark Twain's Timeless Wisdom on Money and Wealth for Today's Investor, 2001. Office: Tribune Media Svcs 435 N Michigan Ave Ste 1500 Chicago IL 60611-4012

LECLAIR, DON (DONAT R. LECLAIR JR.), automotive executive; b. 1952; B in Econs., U. Mich., MBA. Fin. analyst Lorain Assembly Plant Ford Motor Co., 1976, various leadership positions in product devel., mfg. and fin., contr. Ford Australia, contr. Global Product Devel. and Mfg., contr. N.Am., 2001—03, group v.p., CFO, 2003—05, exec. v.p., CFO, 2005—. Office: Ford Motor Co One American Rd Dearborn MI 48126-1899 Office Phone: 313-322-3000. Office Fax: 313-845-0570.

LEDERMAN, LEON MAX, physicist, researcher; b. NYC, July 15, 1922; s. Morris and Minna (Rosenberg) Lederman; m. Florence Gordon, Sept. 19, 1945; children: Rena S., Jesse A., Heidi R.; m. Ellen Carr, Sept. 17, 1981. BS, CCNY, 1943, DSc (hon.), 1980; AM, Columbia U., 1948, PhD, 1951; DSc (hon.), No. Ill. U., 1984, U. Chgo., 1985, Ill. Inst. Tech., 1987; 35 additional hon. degrees. Assoc. in physics Columbia U., NYC, 1951, asst. prof., 1952—54, assoc. prof., 1954—58, prof., 1958—89, Eugene Higgins prof. physics, 1972—79; Frank L. Sulzberger prof. physics U. Chgo., 1989—92; dir. Fermi Nat. Accelerator Lab., Batavia, Ill., 1979—89, dir. emeritus, 1989—; Pritzker prof. sci. Ill. Inst. Tech., Chgo., 1992—; resident scholar Ill. Math. and Sci. Acad., 1998—. Dir. Nevis Labs., Irvington, NY, 1962—79; guest scientist Brookhaven Nat. Labs., 1955; cons. Nat. Accelerator Lab., European Orgn. for Nuc. Rsch. (CERN), 1970—; mem. high energy physics adv. panel AEC, 1966—70; mem. adv. com. to divsn. math. and phys. scis. NSF, 1970—72; sci. advisor to gov. State of Ill., 1989—93; chmn. XXIV Internat. Physics Olympiad, 1991—93; co-chair com. on capacity bldg. in sci. Internat. Sci. Unions, 1994—2001; pres. bd. sponsors Bull. Atomic Scientists, 2000—; mem. adv. com. to dean U. Chgo., 2000—; pres.'s coun. The Cooper Union, 2002—. Author: Quarks to the Cosmos, 1989, The God Particle, 1993, Symmetry and the Beautiful Universe, 2005; editor, contbr.: Portraits of Great American Scientists, 2001; editor: Science Education (NATO Sci. series), 2002; contbr. articles over 200 to profl. jours. including. Commr. White House Fellows Program, 1997—2000; Univ. Rsch. Assocs., 1967—71, 1992—;

founder sci. edn. program ARISE, 1995; mem. sci. adv. bd. Sec. of Energy, 1991—2001; bd. dirs. Mus. Sci. and Industry, Chgo., 1989—, Weizmann Inst. Sci., Israel, 1988—. Named Hon. Prof., Beijing Normal U., The Lederman Sci. Edn. Ctr. in his name, Fermi Nat. Accelerator Lab., 1997; recipient Nat. medal of Sci., 1965, Townsend Harris medal, CUNY, 1973, Elliot Cresson medal, Franklin Inst., 1976, Wolf prize in physics, Wolf Found., Israel, 1982, Nobel prize in Physics, 1988, Enrico Fermi prize, Pres. William J. Clinton, 1993, Rosenblith lectr. in Sci. and Tech., NAS, Joseph Priestly award, Dickinson Coll., 1996, Pres.'s medal, CCNY, 1993, Heald prize, Ill. Inst. Tech., 2000, Pupin Med. award, Columbia U., 2000, Faraday award, NSTA, Discover, 2002, Dedication of Science Literacy in the 21st Century, to him and including one of his articles; fellow Guggenheim, 1958—59, Ford Found., European Ctr. for Nuc. Rsch., Geneva, 1958—59, NSF, 1967, Presdl., World Bank, 1996—59; scholar Great Minds program, Ill. Math. Sci. Acad. Fellow: AAAS (pres. 1990—91, chmn. 1991—92, Abelson award 2001), Am. Phys. Soc. (mem. coun., pres., Compton medal 2005); mem.: IEEE, NAS (U.S., Argentina, Finland, Mex., Russia), World Assn. Young Scientists (hon. pres. 2004—), Russian Acad. Scis. (fgn. mem.), Coun. Advancement of Sci. Writing, Italian Phys. Soc. (hon.), Tchrs. Acad. for Math. and Sci. in Chgo. (co-chmn. 1990—2001), Ill. Math. Sci. Acad. (founding vice chmn. 1985—98), Aspen Inst. Physics (pres. 1990—92).

LEDWIDGE, PATRICK JOSEPH, lawyer; b. Detroit, Mar. 17, 1928; s. Patrick Liam and Mary Josephine (Hooley) L.; m. Rosemary Lahey Mervenne, Aug. 3, 1974; stepchildren: Anne Marie, Mary Clare, John, David, Sara Edleman. AB, Coll. Holy Cross, 1949; JD, U. Mich., 1952. Bar: Mich. 1952. Assoc. firm Dickinson, Wright, Moon, Van Dusen & Freeman, Detroit, 1956-63; mem. Dickinson Wright PLLC, Bloomfield Hills, Mich., 1964—. Served to lt. j.g. U.S. Navy, 1952-55. Mem. Mich. Bar Assn., Detroit Bar Assn., Am. Law Inst. Clubs: Detroit Athletic, Detroit Golf. Roman Catholic. Office: Dickinson Wright PLLC 38525 Woodward Ave Ste 2000 Bloomfield Hills MI 48304-5092

LEE, ALAN, announcer; b. Chgo. m. Sean Lee; 1 child, Spencer. BA in Journalism, Purdue U. Sports dir. WBNB, St. Thomas, V.I., WEHT, Evansville, Ind.; morning news anchor, gen. assignment reporter WRC, Washington; gen. assignment reporter WTTG, Washington; co-anchor Fox 2 News Morning, WJBK-TV, Detroit, 1996—. Office: WJBK Fox 2 PO Box 2000 Southfield MI 48037-2000

LEE, ANDREA JANE, academic administrator, nun; 1 adopted child, Lahens. AA in Italian, Villa Walsh Coll.; BA in music and elem. edn., Northeastern Ill. U.; MEd, Pa. State U., PhD in edn. adminstrn. Instr. tchr. edn. Pa. State U.; dean continuing edn. and cmty. svcs. Marygrove Coll., 1981—84, exec. v.p. and COO, 1984—97, interim pres., 1998; pres. Coll. of St. Catherine, St. Paul, 1999—. Office: Coll of St Catherine 2004 Randolph Ave Saint Paul MN 55105

LEE, BERNARD SHING-SHU, research company executive; b. Nanking, People's Republic of China, Dec. 14, 1934; came to U.S., 1949; s. Wei-Kuo and Pei-fen (Tang) L.; m. Pauline Pan; children: Karen, Lesley, Tania. BSc, Poly. Inst. Bklyn., 1956, DSc in Chem. Engring., 1960. Registered profl. engr., N.Y., Ill. With Arthur D. Little, Inc., Cambridge, Mass., 1960-65, Inst. Gas Tech., Chgo., 1965-78, pres., 1978—. Chmn. M-C Power Corp., Burr Ridge, Ill., Shanghai Zhihai Gasification Tech. Devel.; chmn. steering com. LNG-13; bd. dirs. NUI corp., Bedminster, N.J., Nat. Fuel Gas Co., Buffalo, Peerless Mfg. Co., Dallas. Contbr. over 60 articles to profl. jours. Recipient Outstanding Personal Achievement in Chem. Engring. award Chem. Engring. mag., 1978. Fellow AAAS, Am. Inst. Chem. Engrs. (33d inst. lectr. 1981); mem. Am. Chem. Soc., Am. Gas Assn. (Gas Industry Rsch. award 1984, Disting. Svc. award 1998). Office: Inst Gas Tech 1700 S Mount Prospect Rd Des Plaines IL 60018-1800

LEE, BRANT THOMAS, lawyer, educator, federal official; b. San Francisco, Feb. 17, 1962; s. Ford and Patricia (Leong) L.; m. Marie Bernadette Curry, Sept. 20, 1991. BA in Philosophy, U. Calif., Berkeley, 1985; JD, Harvard U., 1990, M in Pub. Policy, 1994. Bar: Calif. 1992. Counsel subcom. on Constitution, U.S. Senate Judiciary Com., Washington, 1990-92; assoc. Breon, O'Donnell, Miller, Brown & Dannis, San Francisco, 1992-96; dep. staff sec., spl. asst. to Pres. (acting) The White House, Washington, 1993; vis. asst. prof. Syracuse (N.Y.) U. Coll. Law, 1996-97; asst. prof. U. Akron (Ohio) Sch. Law, 1997-2001, assoc. prof., 2001—. Commr. San Francisco Ethics Commn., 1995-96. Bd. dirs., Asian Svcs. in Action, Inc., Akron, 1998—; trustee Chinese for Affirmative Action, San Francisco, 1992-96; bd. dirs. Conf. Asian Pacific Am. Leadership, Washington, 1990-92; staff mem. Dukakis for Pres., Boston, 1988. Mem. ABA, at. Asian Pacfic Am. Bar Assn. Office: U Akron Sch Law Akron OH 44325-0001 Office Phone: 330-972-6616. Business E-Mail: btlee@uakron.edu.

LEE, CATHERINE M., business owner, educator; b. Grand Rapids, Mich., Aug. 21, 1941; m. Gordon Timothy Lee; 4 children. BA, Aquinas Coll., 1963; MA, U. Mich., 1964; postgrad., Wayne State U., 1965-67. Pres. CDL & Assocs., Barrington, Ill., 1988—. Mem. Unit Dist. 220 Bd. Edn., 1984-93; Dem. candidate Ill. Ho. of Reps., 1992; Dem. candidate 16th dist. Ill. U.S. Ho. of Reps., 1996. Roman Catholic. Office: CDL & Assocs 445 Shady Ln Barrington IL 60010-4141

LEE, DAVE, radio personality; m. Julie Lee; 3 children. Grad., U. N.D. With Sta. KFGO-Radio, Fargo, ND, program dir.; with morning show Sta. WCCO Radio, Mpls. PA announcer Minn. Gopher Football Games; vol. Children's Heartlink, Mt. Olivet Rolling Acres for the Develop. Disabled, Pennies for Patients for Leukemia Soc. Recipient 3 Minn. Play by Play Broadcaster of Yr. awards, AP. Office: WCCO 625 2nd Ave S Minneapolis MN 55402

LEE, EDWARD L., retired bishop; b. Fort Washington, Pa., 1934; m. Kathryn Fligg, 1961; 1 child, Kathryn E. Grad. cum laude, Brown U., 1956; MDiv, Gen. Theol. Seminary, 1959. Ordained diaconate, priesthood Episc. Ch., 1959. Curate Ch. Holy Trinity, Phila., 1959-64; Episc. advisor Univ. Christian Movement Temple Univ., Phila., 1964-73; rector St. James Ch., Florence, Italy, 1973-82, St. John's Ch., Washington, 1982-89; bishop Episcopal Diocese We. Mich., 1989—; ret. Sunday, pastoral asst. Ch. Annunciation, Phila.; parish cons. St. Peters Ch., Germantown; lectr. homiletics Phila. Divinity Sch.; nat. chair Episc. Peace Fellowship, 1970-73; with Convocation of Am. Chs. Europe, pres. coun. advice; dep. Gen. Conv., 1976, 79; chair Coun. Coll. Preachers; active Washington Diocesan Coun., chmn. exec. com.; com. inquiry on the nuclear issues Diocesan Peace Commn. Former chair bd. advisors Am. Internat. Sch. Florence. Episcopalian. Office: Episcopal Diocese Western Mich 2600 Vincent Ave Portage MI 49024-5600

LEE, E(UGENE) STANLEY, engineering educator; b. Hopeh, China, Sept. 7, 1930; arrived in US, 1955; s. Ing Yah and Lindy (Hsieng) L.; m. Mayanne Lee, Dec. 21, 1957 (dec. June 1980); children: Linda J., Margaret H.; m. Yuan Lee, Mar. 8, 1983; children— Lynn Hua Lee, Jin Hua Lee, Ming Hua Lee. BS, Chung Cheng Inst. Tech., Taiwan, Republic of China, 1953; MS, N.C. State U., 1957; PhDChemE, Princeton U., 1962. Rsch. engr. Phillips Petroleum Co., Bartlesville, Okla., 1960-66; asst. prof. chem. engring. Kans. State U., Manhattan, 1966-67, assoc. prof. indsl. engring., 1967-69, prof. indsl. engring., 1969—; prof. chem. and elec. engring. U. So. Calif., 1972-76. Hon. prof. Chinese Acad. Sci., 1987—; chaired prof. Yuan-ze Inst. Tech., Taiwan, Republic of China, 1993—; cons. govt. and industry. Author: Quasilinearization and Invariant Imbedding, 1968, Coal Conversion Technnology, 1979, Operations Research, 1981, Fuzzy and Evidence Reasoning, 1996, Fuzzy and Multi-level Decision Making, 2000; editor: Energy Sci. and Tech., 1975; assoc. editor: Jour. Math. Analysis and Applications, 1974—, Computers and Mathematics with Applications, 1974—; mem. editl. bd. Jour. Engring. Chemistry and Metallurgy, 1989—, Jour. of Nonlinear Differential Equations, 1992—, Jour. Chinese Fuzzy Sys. Assn., 1995—, Internat. Jour. Applied Fuzzy Sets Theory, 1995—, Fuzzy Optimization and Decision Making, 2000—, Internat. Jour. Modeling and Optimization, 2001—, Internat. Jour. Ops. Rsch., 2005, Jour. Uncertain Sys., 2006—; contbr. articles to profl. jours. Grantee Dept. Def., 1967-72, Office Water Resources, 1968-75, EPA, 1969-71, NSF, 1971—, USDA, 1978-90, Dept. Energy, 1979-84, USAF, 1984-88. Mem. Soc. Indsl. and Applied Math., Ops. Rsch. Soc. Am., N. Am. Fuzzy Info. Processing Soc., Internat. Neural Network Soc., Sigma Xi, Tau Beta Pi, Phi Kappa Phi. Office: Kans State U Dept Indsl Engring Manhattan KS 66506 Business E-Mail: eslee@ksu.edu.

LEE, GREGORY A., human resources specialist; BS in Mktg., Southern Ill. U. V.p. human resources PepsiCo, 1983—92; sr. v.p. human resources St. Paul Companies, 1992—98, Whirpool, 1998—2000, Sears, Roebuck and Co., 2001—. Bd. dirs. Boys and Girls Club of Chgo. Mem.: Human Resources Policy Assn. (bd. dirs.). Avocations: photography, woodworking, golf, history. Office: Sears Roebuck and Co 3333 Beverly Rd Hoffman Estates IL 60179 Office Phone: 847-286-2500. Office Fax: 847-286-7829.

LEE, HOWARD D., academic administrator; B Indsl. Edn., M Indsl. Edn., U. Wis., Stout; PhD Edn., U. Minn., 1981. Grad. program dir. master's program vocat. and tech. edn. U. Wis., exec. dir. Stout Solutions Menomonie, 2002—. Office: U Wis Stout Solutions 140 Vocat Rehab Bldg Menomonie WI 54751-0790

LEE, HWA-WEI, librarian, educator, consultant; b. Guangdong, China, Dec. 7, 1933; came to U.S., 1957, naturalized, 1962; s. Luther Kan-Chun and Mary Hsiao-Huei (Wang) L.; m. Mary F. Kratochvil, Mar. 14, 1959; children: Shirley, James, Pamela, Edward, Charles, Robert. BEd, Nat. Taiwan Normal U., 1954; MEd, U. Pitts., 1959, PhD, 1964; MLS, Carnegie Mellon U., 1961. Asst. libr. U. Pitts. Librs., 1959-62; head tech. svcs. Duquesne U. Libr., Pitts., 1962-65; head libr. U. Pa., Edinboro, 1965-68; dir. libr. and info. ctr. Asian Inst. Tech., Bangkok, 1968-75; assoc. dir. librs., prof. libr. adminstrn. Colo. State U., Fort Collins, 1975-78; dean librs., prof. Ohio U., Athens, 1978-99, dean emeritus, librs., 1999—; disting. vis. scholar OCLC, 2000—02; chief Asian divsn. Libr. of Congress, 2003—08. Fulbright sr. specialist, 2001; cons. FAO, UNESCO, U.S. AID, World Bank, Internat. Devel. Rsch. Ctr., Asia Found., OCLC; del.-at-large White House Conf. Libr. and Info. Svcs., 1991. Author: Librarianship in World Perspectives, 1991, Fundraising for the 1990s: The Challenge Ahead, 1992, Modern Library Management, 1996, Knowledge Management: Theory and Practice, 2002; exec. editor Jour. Ednl. Media and Libr. Sci., 1982—; mem. editl. bd. Internat. Comm. in Libr. Automation, 1975-76, Jour. Libr. and Info. Sci., 1975-78, Libr. Acquisition: Practice and Theory, 1976-83; adv. bd. Jour. Info., Comm. and Libr. Sci., 1994—; contbr. articles to profl. jours. Recipient Disting. Svc. award Libr. Assn. of China (Taiwan), 1989; new bldg. on Ohio U. campus named in his honor: Hwa-wei Lee Libr. Annex, and 1st flr. of the main libr.: Hwa-wei Lee Ctr. for Internat. Collections, 1999. Mem. ALA (councilor 1988-92, 93-97, John Ames Humphry/Forest Press award 1991), Acad. Libr. Assn. Ohio, Am. Soc. Info. Sci., Asian-Pacific Am. Librs. Assn. (Disting. Svc. award 1991), Internat. Fedn. Libr. Assns. and Instns. (standing com. univ. librs. and other gen. rsch. librs. 1989-93), Assn. Coll. and Rsch. Librs. Chinese-Am. Librs. Assn. (Disting. Svc. award 1983), Internat. Assn. Orientalist Librs., Ohio Libr. Coun. (bd. dirs. 1991-92, Libr. of the Yr. 1987, Hall of Fame Libr. 1999), Online Computer Libr. Ctr. (users coun. 1987-91), Ohio Chinese Acad. and Profl. Assn. (founding pres. 1988-90), China Soc. Libr. Sci (hon. life). Home: 13698 W M Davis Pky W Jacksonville FL 32224 Home Phone: 703-919-9005. E-mail: leeh@ohio.edu.

LEE, JACK (JIM SANDERS BEASLEY), broadcast executive; b. Buffalo Valley, Tenn., Apr. 14, 1936; s. Jesse McDonald and Nelle Viola (Sanders) Beasley; m. Barbara Sue Looper, Sept. 1, 1961; children: Laura Ann, Elizabeth Jane, Sarah Kathleen. Student, Wayne State U., Detroit, 1955-57; BA, Albion Coll., Mich., 1959. Announcer Sta. WHUB-AM, Cookeville, Tenn., 1956; news dir., program dir. Sta. WALM-AM, Albion, Mich., 1957-59; radio-TV personality WKZO-Radio-TV, Kalamazoo, 1960-62; prodn. dir. Sta. WKMH-WKNR, Detroit, 1962-63; gen. mgr. Sta. WAUK-AM-FM, Waukesha, Wis., 1963-65; asst. program mgr. Sta. WOKY, Milw., 1965-70; program mgr. Sta. WTMJ-WKTI, Milw., 1970-76; gen. mgr. Sta. WEMP-WMYX, Milw., 1976-88; pres. Jack Lee Enterprises Ltd., Milw., 1977—; pres., CEO, Milw. Area Radio Stas., 1989—2006; dir. integrated media Lake Front Comm. LLC, Milw., 2006—. Instr. dept. mass comm. U. Wis.-Milw., 1972-81. With US Army, 1959, 61-62; maj. CAP, 1964-01, ret. Decorated Army Commendation medal; cert. radio mktg. cons., Broadcasters Hall of Fame, 1999; Milw. Air awards Lifetime Achievement, 2003 Mem. AFTRA, Actors Equity, Omicron Delta Kappa, Alpha Epsilon Rho. Office: Milw Radio Group 5407 W McKinley Ave Milwaukee WI 53208 Office Phone: 414-978-9470. Office Fax: 414-978-4001.

LEE, JANIS K., state legislator; b. Kensington, Kans., July 11, 1945; m. Lyn Lee; children: David, Brian, Daniel. BA, Kans. State U., 1970. Mem. from dist. 36 Kans. State Senate, 1988—. Mem. Kappa Delta Pi, Phi Kappa Phi. Democrat. Home: RR 1 Box 145 Kensington KS 66951-9801 Office: Kansas Senate State Capitol Rm 402-S Topeka KS 66612

LEE, JUDITH, state legislator; b. Redding, Calif., Mar. 7, 1942; m. Duane Lee, 1964; 2 children. BS, U. N.D., 1964. Real estate broker; mem. govt. & vet. affairs com. N.D. Senate 13th dist., West Fargo, ND, 1994—, human svcs., chair human svcs. com. Mem. West Fargo (N.D.) Planning and Zoning Com., 1982—94; bd. dirs. United Way of Cass-Clay, 1987—93, 2005—06, Hospice of Red River Valley, 1997—2002, Fargo-Moorhead Symphony, 2000—. Named Realtor of Yr., Fargo-Moorhead Area Assn. Realtors, 1988, YWCA Woman of the Yr. in Vol. Category, 1994, Legislator of Yr., N.D. Assn. Township Officers, 1998, N.D. Mental Health Assn., 2003; recipient Guardian of Sm. Bus. award, Nat. Fedn. Ind. Businesses, 1998, Legislator of Yr., N.D. Assn. Nurses, 2003, Legislator Svc. award, ARC, N.C., 2004, NDAR Polit. Improvement award, 2005. Mem.: Park County Realtors, Fargo-Moorhead C. of C. (bd. dirs. 1993—99), West Fargo C. of C. (bd. dirs. 1985—88). Office: PO Box 89 Fargo ND 58107-0089 Office Phone: 701-237-5031.

LEE, KAREN, art appraiser; B Polit. Sci., Tung-hai U., Taiwan; JD, Washburn U., 1983. Ind. art dealer, Topeka. Bd. regents Washburn U., 1999—. Home and Office: 132 SW Fairlawn Rd Topeka KS 66606

LEE, KRISTI, broadcast executive, reporter; b. Indpls., July 17, 1960; d. Sammy Cecil Gibson and Mary Scott (Pounds) Crawley. Student, Ind. U., 1978—. T.v. engr. WRTV-Channel 6, Indpls., 1980-86; t.v. engr., dir. KOAT-TV, Albuquerque, 1986-88; radio news dir. Bob and Tom Show WFBQ-095, Indpls., 1988—; sports reporter ESPN, ESPN 2, 1993—. Dir. Musicians Against Child Abuse, Indpls., 1995—; fundraiser, vol. Hope Lodge. Mem. Am. Women in Radio and TV (95 Radio Personality of the Yr. award). Avocations: movies, golf, sports events, gardening, travel. Office: WFBQ-Q95 6161 Fall Creek Rd Indianapolis IN 46220-5032

LEE, MARCELLA, announcer; BBA, U. Mich. Photographer/reporter WLNS-TV, Lansing, Mich.; with WBNS-TV, Columbus, Ohio, KCNC-TV, Denver. Recipient, 3 Emmy award, 2003, Cmty. Svc. award, Filipino Am. Cmty. Coun. of Metro Detroit. Office: WDIV-TV 550 W Lafayette Blvd Detroit MI 48226

LEE, MARGARET BURKE, college president, language educator; b. San Diego, Dec. 28, 1943; d. Peter John and Margaret Mary (Brown) Burke; m. Donald Harry Lee, June 30, 1973 (dec. June 2002); children: Katherine Louise, Kristopher Donald. BA summa cum laude, Regis Coll., 1966; MA with honors, U. Chgo., 1970, PhD, 1978; IEM Cert., Harvard U., 1992, Seminar for New Pres., 1996. Asst. to humanities MIT, Cambridge, 1969; instr. Dover-Sherborn H.S., Dover, 1973-75, Alpena (Mich.) C.C., 1975-80, dean liberal arts, 1980-82; dean instrn. Kalamazoo Valley C.C., 1982-85; v.p. Oakton C.C., Des Plaines, Ill., 1985-95, pres., 1995—; bd. dirs. Am. Academic Leadership Inst., 2007—. Vice chair Am. Coun. on Internat. Intercultural Edn., 2000—, chair, 2002-05; cons., field faculty Vt. Coll., Montpelier, 1982-85; admissions com. Ill. Math and Sci. Acad., 1988—; bd. govs. North Cook Ednl. Svc. Ctr., 1988-2004, vice chair, 1990-91, chair, 1992-94, bd. dirs.; bd. dirs. Academic Search Cons. Svcs., Internat. Chair Acad., Am. Assn. CC, 2000-2003 Bd. edn. Dist. 39, Wilmette, Ill., 1990-92, Des Plaines Sister Cities, 1995—; mem. 50th ann. leadership cir. Sister Cities Internat.; bd. dirs. Ill. C.C. Atty.'s Assn., 1994—; mem. Career Edn. Planning Dist., Kalamazoo, 1982, Kalamazoo Forum/Kalamazoo Network, 1982, Needs Assessment Task Force, 1984. Ford Found. fellow, 1969—73, Woodrow Wilson Found. fellow, 1975, fed. grantee, 1978—84. Mem. Am. Assn. CC (bd. dirs. 2000-04, exec. com. 2002-04), Am. Assn. Cmty. and Jr. Colls., Mich. Assn. C.C. Instrnl. Adminstrs. (pres. 1983-85), Mich. Occupl. Deans Adminstrs. Coun. (exec. bd. 1983-85), Mich. Women's Studies Assn. (hons. selection com. 1984), North Ctrl. Assn. Acad. Deans (pres. 1988-90, cons. evaluator Chgo., 1982—, commr.-at-large, 1988-92, commn. on inst. of higher edn. bd. dirs. 1992—, vice chair, 1996-98, chair 1998-2001, v.p.), Kalamazoo Consortium Higher Edn. (pres.'s coun. coord. com. 1982-85), Kalamazoo C. of C. (vocat. edn. subcom. indsl. coun. 1982), North Ctrl. Assn. Acad. Deans (v.p., pres. 1985-87), Des Plaines C. of C. (bd. dirs. 1995—). Democrat. Lutheran. Avocations: quilt collecting, reading, listening to classical music, sports spectating, theatre-going. Home: 2247 Lake Ave Wilmette IL 60091-1410 Office: Oakton CC 1600 E Golf Rd Des Plaines IL 60016-1234 Business E-Mail: plee@oakton.edu.

LEE, MARIE CATHERINE, medical educator; MD, Northeastern Ohio U. Coll. Medicine, 2001. Resident, gen. surgery Lenox Hill Hosp., 2005, chief resident, gen. surgery, 2006; fellow, surgical breast oncology U. Mich. Cancer Ctr., 2007, rsch. fellow, breast oncology, 2007; asst. mem. H. Lee Moffitt Cancer Ctr & Rsch. Inst., Fla., 2007; clin. lectr., dept. surgery Mich. Comprehensive Care Ctr., 2007—. Contbr. articles to profl. jours. Office: 3302 Cancer & Geriatrics Center 1500 E Medical Center Dr Ann Arbor MI 48109-0932 Office Phone: 734-936-8771.*

LEE, MORDECAI, political scientist, educator; b. Milw., Aug. 27, 1948; s. Jack Harold and Bernice (Kamesar) L.; 1 child, Ethan. BA, U. Wis., Madison, 1970; MPA, Syracuse U., NYC, 1972, PhD, 1975. Guest scholar Brookings Instn., Washington, 1972-74; legis. asst. to Congressman Henry Reuss Washington, 1975; asst. prof. polit. sci. U. Wis.-Whitewater and Parkside, 1976; mem. Wis. Ho. Reps., 1977-82, Wis. Senate, 1982-89; exec. dir. Milw. Jewish Coun. Cmty. Rels., 1990-97; asst. prof. govt. U. Wis.-Milw., 1997—2002, assoc. prof., 2002—06, prof., 2006—. Author: The First Presidential Communications Agency: FDR's Office of Government Reports, 2005, Institutionalizing Congress and the Presidency: The U.S. Bureau of Efficency, 1916-1933, 2006; editor: Govt. Pub. Rels., A Reader, 2008. Grantee, Franklin and Eleanor Roosevelt Inst., 2002, Hoover Presdl. Libr. Assn., 2003, IBM Ctr. for Bus. of Govt., 2003. Mem.: ASPA (co-chair program com. 64th conf. 2003, exec. com. sect. pub. adminstrn. edn. 1998—2003), Assn. for Rsch. on Nonprofit Orgns. and Voluntary Action (vice-chair sect. tchg. 2001—03). Business E-Mail: mordecai@uwm.edu.

LEE, ROBERT LLOYD, pastor, religious association executive; b. Escanaba, Mich., Jan. 3, 1943; s. Lloyd Benjamin and Eleanor Mae (Leece) L.; m. Gloria Jeanne James, June 3, 1967; children: Adam Robert, Amy Vicary Lee Skogerboe. BA, Augsburg Coll., 1965; MDiv, Free Luth. Sem., 1968; ThM, Bethel Theol. Sem., 1988. Ordained min. Luth. Ch., 1968. Pastor Tioga (N.D.) Luth. Parish, 1966-72, Grace & Zion Luth. Chs., Valley City, N.D., 1972-79, Helmar Luth. Ch., Newark, Ill., 1990-92; prof. hist. theology Free Luth. Schs., Mpls., 1979-89, adj. prof., 1996—; pres. Assn. Free Luth. Congregations, Mpls., 1992—. Author: Fever Saga, 1987, A New Springtime, 1997; editor: Do the Work of An Evangelist, 1990; co-author: Free and Living Congregations, 2002; editor The Luth. Ambassador, 1990-93. Co-chmn. Luth. Estonian Am. Friends, 1992—. Mem. Valdres Samband, Norwegian-Am. Hist. Assn., N.Am. Manx Assn, George Sverdrup Soc. Office: Assn Free Luth Congregations 3110 E Medicine Lake Blvd Minneapolis MN 55441-3008

LEE, SHUISHIH SAGE, pathologist; b. Soo-chow, Kiang su, China, Jan. 5, 1948; came to U.S., 1972, naturalized, 1979; m. Chung Seng Lee; children: Yvonne Claire, Michael Chung. MD, Nat. Taiwan U., 1972; PhD, U. Rochester, 1976. Resident in pathology Strong Meml. Hosp., Rochester, NY, 1976-78, Northwestern Meml. Hosp., Chgo., 1978-79; dir. cytology and electron microscopy Parkview Meml. Hosp., Ft. Wayne, Ind., 1979—. Clin. prof. Ind. U. Med. Sch. Contbr. articles to profl. jours. Fellow: Am. Soc. Clin. Pathologists, Coll. Am. Pathologists; mem.: AMA, Internat. Assn. Chinese Pathologists (pres. 1999—2001), Ft. Wayne Acad. Physicians and Surgeons (pres. 1990), Ft. Wayne Med. Soc. (pres. 2001—02, chair bd. 2002—), Electron Microscopy Soc. Am., Internat. Acad. Cytology, Internat. Acad. Pathology, Am. Soc. Cytology, Am. Assn. Pathologists, N.Y. Acad. Scis., Ind. Assn. Pathologists, N.E. Ind. Pathologists Assn. (sec. 1984), Ind. Med. Assn. Home: 5728 The Prophets Pass Fort Wayne IN 46845-9659 Office: Parkview Meml Hosp 2200 Randallia Dr Fort Wayne IN 46805-4699

LEE, STEPHEN W., lawyer; b. New Castle, Ind., Oct. 25, 1949; s. Delmer W. Lee and Loma F. (Thurston) McCall; m. Pamela A. Summers, Aug. 2, 1969; children: Erin E., Stephanie M. BS, Ball State U., 1971; JD summa cum laude, Ind. U., 1977. Bar: Ind. 1977, U.S. Dist. Ct. (so. dist.) Ind. 1977, U.S. Ct. Appeals (7th cir.) 1977, U.S. Supreme Ct. 1982. Officer, lt.(j.g.) USNR, Phila., 1971-74; law clk. U.S. Dist. Ct. (no. dist.) Ind., Ft. Wayne, 1977-78; assoc. Barnes, Hickam, Pantzer & Boyd, Indpls., 1978-82, Barnes & Thornburg, Indpls., 1982-83, ptnr., 1984—. Dir. The Julian Ctr., Indpls., 1999-2005; mem. Ind. U. Sch. of Law Bd. of Visitors, 1999—. Editor-in-chief: Indiana Law Jour., 1976-77. Dir. Ind. Repertory Theatre, Indpls., 1986-91; exec. coun. Ind. U. Alumni Assn., Bloomington, 1989; dir. Ind. U. Sch. of Law Alumni Assn., Bloomington, 1984-90, pres., 1991-92; mem. Ball State U. Coll. Bus. Alumni Bd., 1991-2000, Ball State U. Entrepreneurship Adv. Bd., 1994-2002; mem. United Way Ctrl. Ind. Projects Commn., 1996—. Mem. Ind. State Bar Assn., Indpls. Bar Assn. (chmn. bus. sect. 1985), Highland Golf & Country Club. Republican. Avocation: golf. Office: Barnes & Thornburg 11 S Meridian St Indianapolis IN 46204-3535 Office Phone: 317-231-7200. Business E-Mail: slee@btlaw.com.

LEE, WILLIAM CHARLES, judge; b. Ft. Wayne, Ind., Feb. 2, 1938; s. Russell and Catherine (Zwick) L.; m. Judith Anne Bash, Sept. 19, 1959; children: Catherine L., Mark R., Richard R. AB, Yale U., 1959; JD, U. Chgo., 1962; LLD (hon.), Huntington Coll., 1999. Bar: Ind. 1962. Ptnr. Parry, Krueckeberg & Lee, Ft. Wayne, Ind., 1964—70, chief dep., 1966-69; U.S. atty. No. Dist. Ind., Ft. Wayne, 1970-73; ptnr. Hunt, Suedhoff, Borror, Eilbacher & Lee, Ft. Wayne, 1973-81; U.S. dist. judge U.S. Dist. Ct. (no. dist.) Ind., Ft. Wayne, 1981—; dep. pros. atty. Allen County Ind., 2006. Instr. Nat. Inst. Trial Advocacy; lectr. in field. Co-author: Business and Commercial Litigation in Federal Courts, 1998; author: Volume I Federal Jury Practice and Instructions, 1999; contbr. to numerous publs. in field. Co-chmn. Fort Wayne Fine Arts Operating Fund Drive, 1978; past bd. dirs., v.p., pres. Fort Wayne Philharm. Orch.; past bd. dirs., v.p. Hospice of Fort Wayne, inc.; past bd. dirs. Fort Wayne Fine Arts Found., Fort Wayne Civic Theatre, Neighbors, Inc., Embassy Theatre Found.; past bd. dirs., pres. Legal Aid of fort Wayne, Inc.; past mem. chm. coun., v.p. Trinity English Lutheran Ch. Coun.; past trustee, pres. Fort Wayne Cmty. Schs., 1978-81, pres., 1980-81; trustee Fort Wayne Mus. Art, 1984-90; past bd. dirs., pres. Fort Wayne-Allen County Hist. Soc. Griffin Scholar, 1955-59; chmn. Fort Wayne Cmty. Schs. Scholarship Com.; bd. dirs. Arts United of Greater Fort Wayne, Fort Wayne Ballet. Weymouth Kirkland scholar, 1959-62; named Ind. Trial Judge of Yr., 1988; recipient Nat. Conservative award Izack Walter League of Am., Jorgenson Leadership award Sagamore of the Wabash, Nieman citation excellence and professionalism. Fellow Am. Coll. Trial Lawyers, Ind. Bar Found.; mem. ABA, Allen County Bar Assn., Ind. State Bar Assn., Fed. Bar Assn., Seventh Cir. Bar Assn., Benjamin Harrison Am. Inn of Ct., North Side High Alumni Assn. (bd. dris., pres.), Fort Wayne Rotary Club (bd. dirs.), Phi Delta Phi (chmn. Indian Pro Bono Commn.). Republican. Lutheran. Office: US Dist Ct 2145 Fed Bldg 1300 S Harrison St Fort Wayne IN 46802-3495

LEE, WILLIAM JOHNSON, lawyer; b. Jan. 13, 1924; s. William J. and Ara (Anderson) L. Student, Akron U., 1941—43, Denison U., 1943—44, Harvard U., 1944—45; JD, Ohio State U., 1948. Bar: Ohio 1948, Fla. 1962, US Dist. Ct. (no. dist.) Ohio 1960, US Dist. Ct. (so. dist.) Fla. 1965, US Dist. Ct. (so. dist.) Ohio 1970. Rsch. asst. Ohio State U. Law Sch., Columbus, 1948—49; asst. dir. Ohio Dept. Liquor Control, chief purchases, 1956—57, atty. examiner, 1951—53, asst. state permit chief, 1953—55, state permit chief, 1955—56; asst. counsel, staff Hupp Corp., 1957—58; spl. counsel City Attys. Office, Ft. Lauderdale, Fla., 1963—65; pvt. practice Ft. Lauderdale, 1965—66; asst. atty. gen. Office Atty. Gen. State of Ohio, 1966—70; administr. State Med. Bd. Ohio, Columbus, 1970—85. Mem. Federated State Bd.'s Nat. Commn. for Evaluation of Fgn. Med. Schs., 1981-83; mem. Flex I/Flex 2 Transitional Task Force, 1983-84; acting mcpl. judge, Ravenna, Ohio, 1960; instr. Coll. Bus. Adminstrn., Kent State U., 1961-62. chmn. legal aid com. Portage County, Ohio, 1960. Mem. editl. bd. Ohio State Law Jour., 1947—48; contbr. articles to profl. jours. Mem. pastoral rels. com. Epworth United Meth. Ch., 1976; chmn. troop awards Boy Scouts Am., 1965; mem. ch. bd. Melrose Park Meth. Ch., Fla., 1966. Served with USAAF, 1943-46. Mem. Fla. Bar Assn., Ohio State Bar Assn., Broward County Bar Assn., Franklin County Trial Lawyers Assn., Columbus Bar Assn., Akron Bar Assn., Exptl. Aviation Assn. SW Fla., Am. Legion, Delta Theta Phi, Phi Kappa Tau, Pi Kappa Delta. Home: Apple Valley 704 Country Club Dr Howard OH 43028-9530

LEE, WILLIAM MARSHALL, lawyer; b. NYC, Feb. 23, 1922; s. Marshall McLean and Hazel (Letts) L.; m. Lois Kathryn Plain, Oct. 10, 1942; children: Marsha Derynck, William Marshall Jr., Victoria C. Nelson. Student, U. Wis., 1939-40; BS, Aero. U., Chgo., 1942; postgrad., UCLA, 1946-48, Loyola U. Law Sch., LA, 1948-49; JD, Loyola U., Chgo., 1952. Bar: Ill. 1952, U.S. Supreme Ct., 1972. Thermodynamicist Northrop Aircraft Co., Hawthorne, Calif., 1947-49; patent agt. Hill, Sherman, Meroni, Gross & Simpson, Chgo., 1949-51, Borg-Warner Corp., Chgo., 1951-53; ptnr. Hume, Clement, Hume & Lee, Chgo., 1953-72; pvt. practice Chgo., 1973-74; ptnr. Lee and Smith (and predecessors), Chgo., 1974-89, Lee, Mann, Smith, McWilliams, Sweeney & Ohlson, Chgo., 1989—2002; ind. expert intellectual property Barrington, Ill., 1999—. Cons. Power Packaging, Inc., 1982-2002, spkr. in field. Contbr. articles to profl. jours. Pres. Glenview (Ill.) Citizens Sch. Com., 1953-57; v.p. Glenbrook High Sch. Bd., 1957-63. Lt. USNR, 1942-46, CBI. Recipient Pub. Svc. award Glenbrook High Sch. Bd., 1963 Mem. ABA (chmn. sect. intellectual property law 1986-87, sect. fin. officer 1976-77, sect. sec. 1977-80, sect. governing coun. 1980-84, 87-88), Ill. Bar Assn., Chgo. Bar Assn., 7th Fed. Cir. Bar Assn., Am. Intellectual Property Law Assn., Intellectual Property Law Assn. Chgo., Licensing Execs. Soc. (pres. 1981-82, treas. 1977-80, trustee 1974-77, 80-81, 82-83, internat. del. 1980—), VFW, Phi Delta Theta, Phi Alpha Delta. Republican. Office: 84 Otis Rd Barrington IL 60010-5128

LEEKLEY, JOHN ROBERT, lawyer, consumer products company executive; b. Phila., Aug. 27, 1943; s. Thomas Briggs and Dorothy (O'Hora) L.; m. Karen Kristin Myers, Aug. 28, 1965 (dec. Mar. 1997); children: John Thomas, Michael Dennis; m. Gerry Lee Gildner, June 5, 1999. BA, Boston Coll., 1965; LLB, Columbia U., 1968. Bar: Y 1968, Mich. 1976. Assoc. Curtis, Mallet-Prevost, Colt & Mosle, NYC, 1968-69, Davis, Polk & Wardwell, NYC, 1969-76; asst. corp. counsel Masco Corp., Taylor, Mich., 1976-77, corp. counsel, 1977-79, v.p., corp. counsel, 1979-88, v.p., gen. counsel, 1988-96, sr. v.p., gen. counsel, 1996—. Bd. visitors Columbia U. Law Sch., NYC, 1994-96; mem. Freedom Twp. Bd. Tax Appeals, 1984-85. Mem. ABA (com. long range issues affecting bus. practice 1976-96), Mich. State Bar Assn. Democrat. Roman Catholic. Avocations: percheron horse breeding, hunting, fishing, outdoor activities. Office: Masco Corp 21001 Van Born Rd Taylor MI 48180-1300

LEEMPUTTE, PETER G., manufacturing executive; BS in chem. engring., Wash. U.; MBA, U. Chgo. Grad. Sch. of Bus. Product devel. engr. Proctor & Gamble Co.; fin. Armco Inc., FMC Corp., BP Amoco; v.p., ptnr. Mercer Mgmt. Cons., 0196—1998; Exec. v.p., CFO, admin. officer Chgo. Title Corp., 1998—2000; v.p., contr. Brunswick Corp., Lake Forest, Ill., 2000—03, sr. v.p., CFO, 2003—. Office: Brunswick 1 N Field Ct Lake Forest IL 60045-4811

LEER, STEVEN F., mining executive; b. Vermillion, SD; m. Beverly Uhl; 1 child. BSEE, Univ. Pacific, 1975; MBA, Washington Univ., 1977; D (hon.), Univ. Pacific, 1993. Exec. mgmt. positions Ashland Inc., Ashland Coal, Valvoline Co.; pres., CEO Arch Mineral Corp., Arch Coal Inc., St. Louis, 1997—2006, chmn., CEO, 2006—. Bd. dir. Norfolk Southern Corp., USG Inc., Mineral Info. Inst., We. Bus. Roundtable; bd. dir., past chmn. Nat. Coal Council, Ctr. for Energy & Econ. Develop., Nat. Mining Assn.; delegate Coal Ind. Adv. Bd. Internat. Energy Agency, Paris. Mem.: Bus. Roundtable, NAM. Office: Arch Coal 1 City Pl Saint Louis MO 63141

LEFF, ALAN RICHARD, medical educator, researcher; b. May 23, 1945; s. Maurice D. and Grace Ruth (Schwartz) Leff; m. Donna Rae Rosene, Feb. 14, 1975; children: Marni, Karen, Alison. AB cum laude, Oberlin Coll., 1967; MD, U. Rochester, 1971. Diplomate Am. Bd. Internal Medicine, Am. Bd. Pulmonary Disease. Intern U. Mich. Hosp., Ann Arbor, 1971—72, resident, 1974—76; fellow U. Calif., San Francisco, 1976—77, postdoctoral fellow, 1977—79; asst. prof. medicine U. Chgo., 1979—85, assoc. prof. medicine and clin. pharm., 1985—89, prof. medicine, anesthesia, critical care and clin. pharm., 1989—, prof. cell physiology, 1992—, prof. pediats., neurobiology, physiology, 1999—, dir. pulmonary medicine svc., 1984—87, dir. Pulmonary Function Lab., 1979—87, chief sect. pulmonary and critical care medicine, 1987—2000, sr. dir. R&D biol. scis., 2000—02. Dir. NIAID Asthma and Allergic Disease Coop. Rsch. Ctr., Chgo., 1993—97; co-chair asthma sect. NIAID Task Force on Immunology, 1996—98; advisor San Francisco Dept. Pub. Health, 1977—79, Chgo Dept. Health, 1979—89; dir. Ctr. of Excellence in Asthma Glaxo Smith Kline, 2000—. Cons. editor, mem. editl. bd. Jour. Clin. Investigation, mem. editl. bd. Am. Jour. Physiology, Jour. Applied Physiology; editor: Am. Jour. Respiratory Critical Care Medicine, 1994—99, Procs. Am. Thoracic Soc., 2004—; editor, assoc. editor: Am. Rev. Respiratory Diseases, 1989—94, Pulmonary Pharmacology, 1987—92, assoc. editor: European Respiratory Jour., 2006—; contbr. articles to profl. jours. Bd. dirs. Chgo. Lung Assn., 1984—93. With USPHS, 1972—74. Recipient Citation of Merit, Chgo. Lung Assn., 1974, Am. Lung Assn., 1998; fellow, Leopold Schepp Found., 1967—69. Fellow: Am. Coll. Chest Physicians; mem.: Am. Assn. Immunologists, Ctrl. Soc. for Clin. Investigation, Am. Thoracic Soc. (Spl. Citation 1999), Assn. Am. Physicians, Am. Physiol. Soc., Am. Soc. Clin. Investigation, Am. Fedn. Clin. Rsch. (councilor 1983—86), Sigma Xi. Avocation: music. Home: 5730 S Kimbark Ave Chicago IL 60637-1615 Office: U Chgo Pritzker Sch Medicine Div Biological Scis MC 6076 5841 S Maryland Ave Chicago IL 60637-1463 Home Phone: 773-955-9555. Business E-Mail: aleff@medicine.bsd.uchicago.edu.

LEFFERTS, WILLIAM GEOFFREY, internist, educator; b. Towanda, Pa., Mar. 24, 1943; s. William LeRoy and Beatrice (Smith) L.; m. Susan Lynn Hiles, Oct. 31, 1970. BA, Hamilton Coll., 1965; MD, Hahnemann Med. Coll., 1969. Intern Hahnemann Hosp., 1969-70; resident in internal medicine Cleve. Clinic Hosp., 1970-73, chief med. resident, 1972-73; asst. prof. internal medicine Hahnemann Med. Coll., 1973-77; assoc. prof. Med. Coll. Pa., 1978-82, dir. primary care unit, 1978-82, dir. div. gen. internal medicine, 1979-82; staff physician Cleve. Clinic Found., 1982—. Fellow ACP. Office: 9500 Euclid Ave Cleveland OH 44195-0001

LEFFLER, CAROLE ELIZABETH, retired women's and mental health nurse; b. Sidney, Ohio, Feb. 18, 1942; d. August B. and Delores K. Aselage; children: Veronica, Christopher. ADN, Sinclair C.C., Dayton, Ohio, 1975. Cert. psychiat. nurse supr. Nurse Grandview Hosp, Dayton, 1961—76; substitute sch. nurse Fairborn City Schs., Ohio, 1981—82; dir. nursing Fairborn Nursing Home, 1983; supr. psychiat. nurse Twin Valley Behavioral Health Ctr., 1984—; ret., 2006. Mem. exec. bd. 1199; chmn. disaster mental health com. ARC Ohio. Vol., instr., disaster health nurse ARC, chmn. State of Ohio disaster mental health com.; officer, leader, camp nurse for Girl Scouts, Boy Scouts; Ch. Parish Coun. Recipient Fleur de Lis award Girl and Boy Scouts, Svc. award ARC, Fairborn Mayor's Cert. of Merit for Civic Pride, State of Ohio Govs. award Innovation Ohio, Ohio State Gov.'s award for assistance in N.Y.C. disaster, 2001. Mem. ANA, Ohio Nurses Assn., BPOE and Women of the Moose. Home: 1711 Port Jefferson Rd Sidney OH 45365-1939

LEFKOW, JOAN HUMPHREY, federal judge; b. Kans., Jan. 9, 1944; d. Otis L. and Donna Grace (Glenn) Humphrey; m. Michael F. Lefkow (dec. 2005), June 21, 1975 AB, Wheaton Coll., 1965; JD, Northwestern U., 1971. Bar: Ill. 1971, U.S. Dist. Ct. (no. dist.) Ill. 1972, U.S. Ct. Appeals (7th cir.) 1972, U.S. Ct. Appeals (5th cir.) 1980. Law clerk to Hon. Thomas E. Fairchild U.S. Ct. Appeals (7th cir.), 1974—75; atty. Legal Assistance Found. Chgo., 1975—79; adminstrv. law judge Ill. Fair Employment Practices Commn., 1975—77; instr. sch. law U. Miami, Fla., 1980—81; exec. dir. Cook County Legal Assistance Found., 1981—82; magistrate judge U.S. Dist. Ct. (no. dist.) Ill., 1982—96; judge U.S. Bankruptcy Ct. (no. dist.) Ill., 1997—2000. Mem. editl. bd. Northwestern U. Law Rev. Mem. Chgo. Bar Assn. (Alliance for Women 1992—), Chgo. Coun. Lawyers (gov. bd. 1975-77), 7th Cir. Bar Assn. Episcopalian. Office: Everett McKinley Dirksen Bldg Ste 1956 219 S Dearborn St Chicago IL 60604

LEFKOWITZ, IRVING, engineering educator; b. NYC, July 8, 1921; s. Adolph and Celia (Berko) L.; m. Madelyn I. Moinester, July 3, 1955; children: Deborah, Daniel. BS in Chem. Engring., Cooper Union, 1943; MS in Instrumentation Engring., Case Inst. Tech., 1955, PhD, 1958. With J.E. Seagram & Sons, 1943-53, dir. instrumentation research, 1951-53; faculty Case Inst. Tech., 1953-87, prof. engring., 1965-87, prof. emeritus, 1987—, dir. research group in control of complex systems, 1960-85; acting chmn. systems engring. dept. Case Western Res. U., 1972-76, chmn., 1980-83; v.p. techs. devel. Control Soft, Inc., Cleve., 1994—. Mem. sci. staff Internat. Inst. Applied Systems Analysis, Austria, 1974-75; Cons. in field, 1959— Contbr. papers to profl. lit.; Editorial adv. bd.: Jour. Dynamic Systems, Measurement and Control, 1972-77. NATO postdoctoral fellow, 1962-63 Fellow IEEE, AAAS; mem. Systems Sci. and Cybernetics Soc. (adminstr. com. 1969-72), Am. Automatic Control Council (chmn. systems engring. com. 1968-69, Control Heritage award 1982), IFAC (vice-chmn. systems engring. com. 1975-78, chmn. com. 1978-81, vice chmn. tech. bd. 1981-84), IEEE Control Systems Soc. (chmn. control of indsl. systems tech. com. 1983-87, bd. govs. 1985-86). Office: Case Western Res U Sys Engring Dept 706 Olin Bldg Cleveland OH 44106 Home: Apt 301 3330 Warrensville Center Rd Shaker Heights OH 44122-3790 E-mail: ixl@po.cwru.edu.

LEGAN, KENNETH, state legislator, farmer; b. Halfway, Mo., Aug. 3, 1946; s. Adolphus J. and June (Jones) L.; m. Rebecca M. Bodenhamer, 1969; children: Brock Alan, Stephanie Kaye. BS, U. Mo., 1969. Owner, mgr. Legan Farms, Halfway, 1971—; mem. Mo. Ho. of Reps., Jefferson City, 1981—, sr. rep., 1992—. Mem. Polk County (Mo.) Rep. Ctrl. Com., 1971—, chmn., 1976-80, vice chmn., 1980-86. Recipient Farm Mgmt. award Kansas City C. of C., 1976, Disting. Legislator award MCCA, 1992; named hon. chpt. farmer Halfway Future Farmers Am., 1978. Mem. Farm Bur., Legis. Exch., Lions, Masons, Shriners. Home: 1901 E 487th Rd Half Way MO 65663-9281

LEGER, JAMES ROBERT, engineering educator; BS in Applied Physics, Calif. Inst. Tech., 1974; PhD in Elec. Engring., U. Calif., San Diego, 1980. With 3M; mem. rsch. staff Lincoln Lab. MIT, 1984-91; mem. faculty U. Minn., 1991, prof. electrical and computer engineering. Contbr. articles to profl. jours., chpt. to book. Achievements include application of new techniques in Fourier optics and holography to modern electrooptic devices, leading to new applications ranging from optical pattern recognition to novel laser systems; first application of multi-level diffractive micro-optics to diode laser arrays; development of the Talbot caivty and Dammann grating techniques; application of diffractive optics in laser reesonators. Home: 19000 31st Ave N Plymouth MN 55447-1085 Office: U Minn Dept Elec & Computer Engring 200 Union St SE Minneapolis MN 55455-0154 Fax: (612) 625-4583. E-mail: leger@ece.umn.edu.

LEGG, J. IVAN, academic administrator; BA in Chemistry, Oberlin Coll., 1960; PhD in Chemistry, U. Mich., 1965. Faculty Wash. State U., 1966—87, chair chemistry, 1978—86; dean sci. and math. Auburn U., 1987—92; provost U. Memphis, 1992—2001; exec. v.p., provost No. Ill. U., DeKalb, 2001—. NIH fellow, Harvard Med. Sch., 1972, 1973. Office: No Ill U Office Of Provost Dekalb IL 60115-2886 Office Phone: 815-753-0493. Business E-Mail: ilegg@ntu.edu.

LEGGE KEMP, DIANE, architect, landscape consultant; b. Englewood, NJ, Dec. 4, 1949; d. Richard Claude and Patricia (Roney) L.; m. Kevin A. Kemp; children: Alloy Hudson, McClelland Beebe, Logan Roney. BArch, Stanford U., 1972; MArch, Princeton U., 1975. Registered arch., Ill., landscape arch., Ill. Arch. Northrop, Kaelber & Kopf, Rochester, NY, 1971—73, Michael Graves, Architect, Princeton, NJ, 1973—75, The Ehrenkrantz Group, NYC, 1975-77; ptnr. Skidmore Owings & Merrill, Chgo., 1977-89; pres. Diane Legge Kemp Architecture and Landscape Consulting, Riverside, Ill., 1993—, DLK Architecture, 1993—, DLK Civic Design. Mem. bd. govs. Sch. of Art Inst., Chgo., 1991—; dir., past pres. Soc. for Contemporary Art, Chgo., 1991—. Office: DLK Civic Design 410 S Michigan Ave Chicago IL 60605-1308 Office Phone: 312-322-2550. Business E-Mail: dleggekemp@dlkinc.com.

LEGGETT, ANTHONY JAMES, physics professor, researcher; b. London, 1938; Student, Balliol Coll., Oxford, Eng.; degree in physics, Merton Coll., Oxford, PhD in Theoretical Physics. Mem. faculty U. Sussex (UK), 1967-71, reader, 1971-78, prof., 1978-83; John D. and Catherine T. Macarthur prof. U. Ill., Urbana-Champaign, 1983—. Rschr. Urbana, Ill., Kyoto, Japan; lectr. in field. Author: The Problems of Physics, 1987, Quantum Tunnelling in Condensed Media, 1992; contbr. articles to profl. jours. Recipient Maxwell Medal and Prize, Inst. Physics, UK, 1975, Simon Meml. prize, 1981, Fritz London Meml. award, 1981, Paul Dirac Medal and prize, Inst. Physics, UK, 1992, John Bardeen prize, 1994, Wolf prize in physics, Wolf Found., Israel, 2003, Nobel prize in physics, 2003. Fellow: American Physical Soc., Inst. Physics, UK (hon.), Royal Soc., UK; mem.: Russian Acad. of Sciences, Nat. Acad. of Sciences (assoc.), Am. Acad. Arts & Sciences, Am. Philol. Soc. Achievements include research in condensed matter physics, high-temperature superconductivity, foundations of quantum mechanics. Office: U Ill 1110 W Green St Urbana IL 61801-9013 E-mail: aleggett@uiuc.edu.

LEHE, DONALD J., state representative; BS, Purdue U., 1970. Co-owner Lehe Farms, Inc.; rep. dist. 15 Ind. Ho. of Reps., Indpls., 2002—. Pres., bd. mem. White County Agr. Assn.; state exec. com. Ind. Pork Prodrs.; mem. White County 4-H adv. com., bd. dirs.; state exec. com. Ind. Farm Bur.; pres., bd. mem. Frontier Sch. Corp.; bd. mem. White County Cmty. Found. Mem.: Nat. Fedn. Ind. Bus., Nat. Corn Growers Assn., Ind. Sch. Bds. Assn., Eagle Forum, Nat. Right to Life, Frontier PTO, NRA, KC, Am. Legion. Republican. Office: Ind Ho of Reps 200 W Washington St Indianapolis IN 46204-2786

LEHMAN, HARRY JAC, lawyer; b. Dayton, Ohio, Aug. 29, 1935; s. H. Jacques and Mildred (Benas) L.; m. Linda L. Rocker, June 7, 1964 (div. Mar. 1977); children: Sara Beth, Adam Henry, Matthew Daniel; m. Patricia L. Steele, Aug. 30, 1980; 1 child, Alexandra Steele. BA, Amherst Coll., 1957; JD, Harvard U., 1960. Bar: Ohio 1960. Assoc. Burke, Haber & Berick, Cleve., 1960-61, Falsgraf, Kundtz, Reidy & Shoup, Cleve., 1961-66, ptnr., 1967-70; of counsel Benesch, Friedlander, Coplan & Aronoff, Cleve., 1971-80; ptnr. Jones, Day, Reavis & Pogue, Columbus, 1980-99. Adj. prof. law Ohio State U., Columbus, 1980-84, 86-87; mem. Bd. Bar Examiners, State of Ohio, Columbus, 1983-85. Contbr. articles to profl. jours. Mem. Ohio Ho. of Reps., Columbus, 1971-80; chmn. House Judiciary Com., 1975-80; mem. Ohio Elections Com., Columbus, 1983-88, State Underground Parking Com., Columbus, 1983-87, chmn., 1984-86. Served with USAR, 1960-66. Named one of Ten Outstanding Young Men, Cleve. Jaycees, 1968-69; recipient Disting. Service award NAACP, 1968, Outstanding Freshman Legislator award Ohio Legis. Correspondents Assn., 1971-72, Disting. Service award Ohio Edn. Assn., 1972, Most Effective Legislator award Ohio Legis. Correspondents Assn., 1973-74, Pub. Service award Ohio Pub. Defender Assn., 1974, Outstanding Pub. Service award Ohio Pub. Transit Assn., 1978, Disting. Service award ACLU Ohio Found., 1978, Most Effective Legislator 112th Gen. Assembly Ohio award Columbus Monthly Mag., 1980, Most Effective Legislator 113th Gen. Assembly Ohio award Columbus Monthly Mag. Mem. Ohio Bar Assn., Columbus Bar Assn., Cleve. Bar Assn., Columbus Athletic Club, New Albany Country Club. Democrat. Jewish. Avocations: reading, golf. Home: 5 Pickett Pl New Albany OH 43054-8415 Office: Jones Day PO Box 165017 Columbus OH 43216-5017

LEHMAN, JOHN W., state representative; b. Rhinelander, Wis., Aug. 2, 1945; m. Catherine Lehman; children: Rachel, Martha, Catherine. Student, U. Wis., Parkside and Madison; BA, Luther Coll., 1967; MEd, Carthage Coll., 1979. H.s. tchr. Racine (Wis.) Unified Sch. Dist., 1971—96; mem. state assembly dist. 62 Wis. State Assembly, Madison, 1996—, ranking mem. edn. com., mem. edn. reform, environ., and natural resources coms. Mem. Racine Bd. Health; mem. Racine Pub. Libr. Bd.; former pres. Racine Sister City Planning Coun.; alderman City of Racine, Wis., 1988—2000. Mem.: Racine Edn. Assn. Democrat. Lutheran. Office: State Capitol Rm 303 W PO Box 8952 Madison WI 53708-8952

LEHMAN, MICHAEL A., state legislator; Mem. Wis. State Assembly Dist. 58, 1988—. Republican. Home: 1317 Honeysuckle Rd Hartford WI 53027-2614 Office: State Capitol Rm 103 West Madison WI 53708-0952

LEHODEY, JOHN FRANCOIS, hotel company executive; b. Paris, July 27, 1933; came to U.S., 1960; s. Jacques and Gabrielle (Godard) L.; 1 child, Jacques. BS in Hotel Adminstrn., Hotel Sch., Thonon, France, 1953. Purser S.S. Liberté, S.S. Ile de France, French Line, Le Havre, N.Y., 1955-60; mgr. rooms divsn. Waldorf Astoria Hotel, NYC, 1963-71; mgr. Novotel, Paris, 1972-78; gen. mgr., v.p. Sofitel divsn. Accor N.Am., Mpls., 1979-97, pres. Scarsdale, N.Y., 1997—. Served with French Navy, 1953-55. Mem. French-Am. C. of C., Chaine des Rotisseurs. Home: 5601 W 78th St Minneapolis MN 55439-3105

LEIBHAM, JOSEPH K., state senator; b. June 6, 1969; BA, U. Wis., 1991. Former food svc. industry acct. exec.; assembly mem. Wis. State Assembly, Madison, 1998—2002; state sen. Wis. State Senate, Madison, 2002—, chair, audit com., co-chair, joint com. on audit, mem. census and redistricting, energy and utilities, state and local fin., tax and spending limitations, and transp. coms. Membership devel. mgr. Sheboygan (Wis.) C. of C. Republican. Office: State Capitol Rm 409 PO Box 7882 Madison WI 53707-7882 also: Dist Office 3618 River Ridge Dr Sheboygan WI 53081

LEIBOWITZ, DAVID PERRY, lawyer; b. Bronx, NY, Jan. 21, 1950; s. Bernard B. and Annette (Friedman) L.; children: Rachel, Saryn. BA in Econs., Northwestern U., 1970; JD cum laude, Loyola U., 1974. Bar: Ill. 1974, U.S. Dist. Ct. (no. dist) Ill. 1974, U.S. Ct. Appeals (7th cir.) 1974, U.S. Supreme Ct. 1982, U.S. Ct. Appeals (11th cir.) 1985. Assoc. Goebel & Kal, Chgo., 1974-75; judicial clerk Ill. Appellate Ct., Chgo., 1975-76; ptnr. Schwartz, Cooper, Kolb & Gaynor, Chgo., 1976-91, Freeborn & Peters, Chgo., 1992-99; pvt. practice Waukegon, 1999—. Adj. prof. John Marshall Law Sch., 1997—. Mem. bd. edn. Highland Park (Ill.) Sch. Dist., 1987-92; pres. bd. edn. North Shore Sch. Dist. 112, Highland Park, 1992-98; pres. bd. trustees Highland Park Pub. Libr., 1991-92. Mem. Am. Bankruptcy Inst., Ill. Bar Assn., Chgo. Bar Assn., Lake County Bar Assn. Office: Law Offices Of David P Leibowitz 420 W Clayton St Waukegan IL 60085-4216 E-mail: dpl@lakelaw.com.

LEIBRECHT, JOHN JOSEPH, bishop emeritus; b. Overland, Mo., Aug. 8, 1930; PhD, Cath. U., Washington, 1961. Ordained priest Archdiocese of Saint Louis, Mo., 1956, supt. schs., 1962-81; ordained bishop, 1984; bishop Diocese of Springfield-Cape Girardeau, 1984—2008, bishop emeritus, 2008—. Roman Catholic. Office: The Catholic Ctr 601 S Jefferson Ave Springfield MO 65806-3107 Office Phone: 417-866-0841. Office Fax: 417-866-1140. E-mail: jleibrecht@dioscg.org.*

LEIDEN, JEFFREY MARC, venture capitalist, molecular biologist, cardiologist; b. Chgo., Oct. 12, 1955; s. Irving and Rosemary (Rebelsky) Leiden; m. Lisa Leyland, June 23, 1982; children: Benjamin Bradford, Alexander Dow. BA in Biol. Sci. with honors, U. Chgo., 1975, MD with honors, 1979, PhD, 1981. Diplomate Am. Bd. Internal Medicine, Am. Bd. Cardiovascular Diseases, lic. cardiologist Mass., Ill. Chief cardiology, Frederick H. Rawson prof. medicine and pathology U. Chgo.; Elkan R. Blout prof. biological sciences Harvard Sch. Public Health; prof. medicine Harvard Medical Sch.; founder Cardiogene, Inc.; bd. dirs. Abbott, 1999, sr. v.p., chief scientific officer, 2000, exec. v.p. pharmaceuticals, 2000, pres., COO pharmaceutical products group, 2001—06; ptnr. Clarus Ventures, 2006—. Cons. Pfizer, Bristol Meyers-Squibb, Boston Scientific Inc. Bd. dirs. Chgo.'s Mus. Sci. and Industry, Ravinia Festival, Keystone Symposia. Fellow: Am. Acad. Arts and Sciences; mem.: Am. Assn. Physicians, Am. Soc. Clinical Investigation, IOM. Office: Clarus Ventures One Memorial Drive Ste 1230 Cambridge MA 02142

LEIER, CARL VICTOR, internist, cardiologist; b. Bismarck, ND, Oct. 20, 1944; married; 3 children. Grad., Creighton U., MD cum laude, 1969. Diplomate Am. Bd. Internal Medicine, Cardiovascular Medicine, Critical Care Medicine, Geriatric Medicine, Electrocardiography, Nat. Bd. Med. Examiners; lic. med., surgical ebr., med. Ohio. Intern Ohio State U. Coll. Medicine, Columbus, 1969-70, med. resident (instr.) dept. medicine, 1971-73, chief resident (instr.), 1973-74, fellowship divsn. cardiology, 1974-76; pathology resident dept. pathology St. Vincent Hosp., Worcester, Mass., 1970-71; trainee NIH Tng. Grant, 1974-75; asst. prof. medicine cardiology dept., Ohio State U. Coll. Medicine, Columbus, 1976-80, asst. prof. pharmacology, 1976-80, assoc. prof., 1980-84, faculty mem. grad. sch., 1980—, dir. rsch. divsn. cardiology, 1980-83, James W. Overstreet prof. of medicine, 1983—, prof. of medicine divsn. cardiology, 1984—, prof. pharmacology, dept. pharmacology, 1984—, dir. divsn. cardiology, 1986-98. Mem. rsch. com. ctrl. Ohio chpt. Am. Heart Assn., 1977-84, bd. trustees, 1979-88, exec. rsch. com., 1979-84, vice chmn. rsch. com., 1980-82, chmn. rsch. peer rev. com., 1982-84, v.p., 1984-86, pres. elect, 1986-88; numerous other coms.; cons. AMA on Drugs and Tech., 1985—. FDA Cardiorenal adv. com. 1986-92; mem. chmn. Annual Sci. Sessions of the Am. Coll. of Cardiolog, 1996-97; vis. prof., lectr. and presenter at numerous sci. confs., insts. in U.S. and internationally. Editor: (book) Cardiotonic Drugs, 1986, 2d rev. edit., 1991; co-author: (with H. Boudoulas) CardioRenal Disorders and Diseases, 1986, 2d edit., 1992 (with J. Vincent) Critical Care Medicine: Recent Advances in Cardiovascular Medicine, 1990; contbr. more than 40 chpts. to other medical books and almost 200 articles to peer reviewed jours. including: Circulation, Brit. Heart Jour., Jour. Clin. Investigation, Jour. Am. Coll. Cardiology, Am. Jour. Cardiology, Chest, Am. Jour. Medicine, Am. Heart Jour., Annals of Internal Medicine and others; editor in chief Congestive Heart Failure: Index and Revs., 1988-94; mem. editorial bds. of ten medical jours. concerned with heart diseases, the review bds. of others including New Eng. Jour. Medicine, Internat. Jour. Cardiology, Jour. of Lab. and Clin. Medicine. Recipient Upjohn award, 1969, Lange Scholar award, 1969, Golden Apple Student Tchg. award, 1973, 75, Young Investigator award Ctrl. Ohio Heart Chpt., Am. Heart Assn., 1976-78, Rsch. Recognition award, 1978. Fellow Am. Heart Assn., Am. Coll. Cardiology, Am. Coll. Physicians, Coun. on Geriatric Cardiology; mem. AAAS, Am. Fedn. for Clin. Rsch., Ctrl. Soc. for Clin. Rsch., Am. Soc. Clin. Investigation, Assn. Univ. Cardiologists. Office: Ohio State U Med Ctr Divsn Cardiology 473 W 12th Ave Columbus OH 43210-1250 Office Phone: 614-293-8963.

LEIGH, SHERREN, communications and publishing executive, editor; b. Cleve., Dec. 22, 1942; d. Walter Carl Maurushat and Treva Eldora (Burke) Morris; m. Norman J. Hickey Jr., Aug. 23, 1969 (div. 1985). BS, Ohio U., 1965. Communications dir. Metal Lath Assn., Cleve., 1965-67; creative dir. O'Toole Inc., Chgo., 1967-69; sr. v.p. RLC Inc., Chgo., 1969-77; pres. Leigh Communications Inc., Chgo., 1978—; chmn. Today's Chgo. Woman mag., 1982—. Pres. Ill. Ambassadors, Chgo., 1985-86; bd. dirs. Chgo. Fin. Exchange, 1985-87. Author: How to Write a Winning Resume, How to Negotiate for Top Dollar, How to Find, Get and Keep the Job You Want. Bd. dirs. Midwest Women's Ctr., Chgo., 1984-86, Girl Scouts Chgo., 1985-87, Black Women's Hall of Fame Found., Chgo., 1986—, Apparel Industry Bd., Chgo., 1988, Auditorium Theater of Roosevelt U.; pres. Today's Chgo. Woman Found., 1998; mem. adv. bd. Salvation Army, 1998. Recipient Corp. Leadership award YWCA Met. Chgo., 1979, Entrepreneurship award, 1988, Media Advocate of Yr. award U.S. SBA, 1994, Achievement award Network of Women Entrepreneurs, 1998, Golden Heart award Ill Assn. Non-Profit Orgns., 1998, Women with A Vision award Women's Bar Assn. Ill., 1998; named one of 10 Women of Achievement Midwest Women's Ctr., Chgo., 1987, Advt. Woman of Yr. Women's Advt. Club, Chgo., 1988; inducted City of Chgo. Women's Hall of Fame, 1988. Mem. Chgo. Network, Econ. Club Chgo., Execs. Club Chgo., Com. of 200 (founding mem.). Office: Leigh Communications Inc 150 E Huron St Ste 1001 Chicago IL 60611-2947 E-mail: sleigh@todayschicagowomen.com.

LEIGHTON, GEORGE NEVES, retired judge; b. New Bedford, Mass., Oct. 22, 1912; s. Antonio N. and Anna Sylvia (Garcia) Leitao; m. Virginia Berry Quivers, June 21, 1942; children: Virginia Anne, Barbara Elaine. AB, Howard U., 1940; LLB, Harvard U., 1946; LLD, Elmhurst Coll., 1964; LLD., John Marshall Law Sch., 1973; LLD, U. Mass., 1975, New Eng. U. Sch. Law, 1978, R.I. Coll., 1992, So. New Eng. Sch. Law, 2000; LLD (hon.), Loyola U., Chgo., 1989. Bar: Mass. 1946, Ill. 1947, U.S. Supreme Ct. 1958. Ptnr. Moore, Ming & Leighton, Chgo., 1951-59, McCoy, Ming & Leighton, Chgo., 1959-64; judge Cook County Circuit Ct., Chgo., 1964-69, Ill. Appellate Ct. (1st dist.), 1969-76; U.S. dist. judge U.S. Dist. Ct. (no. dist.) Ill., 1976-86, sr. dist. judge, 1986-87; ret.; of counsel Earl L. Neal & Assocs., 1987—. Adj. prof. John Marshall Law Sch., Chgo., 1965—; commr., mem. character and fitness com. for 1st Appellate Dist., Supreme Ct. Ill., 1955-63, chmn. character and fitness com., 1961-62; joint com. for revision Ill. Criminal Code, 1959-63; chmn. Ill. adv. com. U.S. Commn. on Civil Rights, 1964; mem. pub. rev. bd. UAW, AFL-CIO, 1961-70; Asst. atty. gen. State of Ill., 1950-51; pres. 3d Ward Regular Democratic Orgn., Cook County, Ill., 1951-53; v.p. 21st Ward, 1964; spl. counsel to chmn. bd. Chgo. Transit Authority, 1988. Contbr. articles to legal jours. Bd. dirs. United Ch. Bd. for Homeland Ministries, United Ch. of Christ, Grant Hosp., Chgo.; trustee U. Notre Dame, 1979-83, trustee emeritus, 1983—; bd. overseers Harvard Coll., 1983-89. Capt., inf. AUS, 1942-45. Decorated Bronze Star; recipient Civil Liberties award Ill. div. ACLU, 1961, U.S. Supreme Ct. Justice John Paul Stevens award, 2000, Father Agustus Tolton award Cath. Archdioceses Chgo., 2000; named Chicagoan of Year in Law and Judiciary Jr. Assn. Commerce and Industry, 1964, Laureate, Acad. Ill. Lawyers, 2000; named Main US Post Office Bldg. in his honor, New Bedford, Mass., 2005 Fellow ABA (chmn. coun. 1976, mem. coun. sect. legal edn. and admissions to bar, medal 2005), Am. Coll. Trial Lawyers; mem. NAACP (chmn. legal redress com. Chgo. br.), John Howard Assn. (bd. dirs.), Chgo. Bar Assn., Ill. Bar Assn. (joint com. for revision jud.

article 1959-62, sr. counselor 1996), Nat. Harvard Law Sch. Assn. (mem. coun.), Howard U. Chgo. Alumni Club (chmn. bd. dirs.), Phi Beta Kappa. Office: Neal & LeRoy LLC 203 N LaSalle Ste 2300 Chicago IL 60601-1213 Office Phone: 312-641-7144. Business E-Mail: gleighton@nealandleroy.com.

LEIGHTON, ROBERT JOSEPH, lawyer; b. Austin, Minn., July 7, 1965; s. Robert Joseph Sr. and JoAnn (Mulvihill) L. BA, U. Minn., 1988; JD, U. Calif., Berkeley, 1991. Minn. state rep. Dist. 27B, 1995—2002; atty. Nolan, MacGregor, Thompson & Leighton, St. Paul, 2002—. Presdl. and Waller scholar U. Minn., 1988. Mem. Minn. Bar Assn., Minn. Trial Lawyers Assn., Phi Beta Kappa. Home: 4243 Wexford Way Eagan MN 55122 Office: Nolan MacGregor Thompson & Leighton Lawson Commons Ste 710 380 St Peter St Saint Paul MN 55102 Home Phone: 651-686-4467; Office Phone: 651-227-6661. Business E-Mail: rleighton@nmtlaw.com.

LEIKEN, EARL MURRAY, lawyer; b. Cleve., Jan. 19, 1942; s. Manny and Betty G. L.; m. Ellen Kay Miner, Mar. 26, 1970; children: Jonathan, Brian. BA magna cum laude, Harvard U., 1964, JD cum laude, 1967. Asst. dean, assoc. prof. law Case Western Res. U., Cleve., 1967-71; ptnr. Hahn, Loeser, Freedheim, Dean & Wellman, Cleve., 1971-86, Baker & Hostetler, Cleve., 1986—. Adj. faculty, lectr. law Case Western Res. U., 1971-86. Pres. Shaker Heights (Ohio) Bd. Edn., 1986-88, Jewish Community Ctr., Cleve., 1988-91, Shaker Heights Family Ctr., 1994-97; mem. Shaker Heights City Coun., 2000—. Named one of Greater Cleve.'s 10 Outstanding Young Leaders, Cleve. Jaycees, 1972; recipient Kane award Cleve. Jewish Community Fedn., 1982. Mem. ABA, Greater Cleve. Bar Assn. (chmn. labor law sect. 1978). Home: 20815 Colby Rd Cleveland OH 44122-1903 Office: Baker & Hostetler 3200 Nat City Ctr 1900 E 9th St Ste 3200 Cleveland OH 44114-3475

LEINENWEBER, HARRY D., federal judge; b. Joliet, Ill., June 3, 1937; s. Harry Dean and Emily (Lennon) L.; m. Lynn Morley Martin, Jan. 7, 1987; 5 children; 2 stepchildren. AB cum laude, U. Notre Dame, 1959; JD, U. Chgo., 1962. Bar: Ill. 1962, U.S. Dist. Ct. (no. dist.) Ill. 1967. Assoc. Dunn, Stefanich, McGarry & Kennedy, Joliet, Ill., 1962-65, ptnr., 1965-79; city atty. City of Joliet, 1963-67; spl. counsel Village of Park Forest, Ill., 1967-74; spl. prosecutor County of Will, Ill., 1968-70; spl. counsel Village of Bolingbrook, Ill., 1975-77, Will County Forest Preserve, 1977; mem. Ill. Ho. of Reps., Springfield, 1973-83, chmn. judiciary I com., 1981-83; ptnr. Dunn, Leinenweber & Dunn, Joliet, 1979-86; fed. judge U.S. Dist. Ct. (no. dist.) Ill., Chgo., 1986—. Bd. dirs. Will County Bar Assn., 1984-86, State Jud. Adv. Coun., 1973-85, sec. 1975-76; tchr. legis. process seminar U. Ill., Chgo., 1988-2001; coord. U. Ill. Disting. Lecture Series, 2002--; mem. U. Ill. Inst. Govt. and Pub. Affairs Nat. Adv. Com., 1998-2001. Bd. dirs. Will County Legal Assistance Found., 1982-86, Good Shepard Manor, 1981—, Am. Cancer Soc., 1981-85, Joliet (Ill.) Montessori Sch., 1966-74; del. Rep. Nat. Conv., 1980; precinct committeeman, 1966-86; mem. nat. adv. com. U. Ill. Inst. Govt. and Pub. Affairs, 1998-2001. Recipient Environ. Legislator Golden award. Mem. Will County Bar Assn. (mem. jud. adv. coun., 1973-85, sec. 1975-76, bd. dirs. 1984-86), Nat. Conf. Commrs. on Uniform State Laws (exec. com. 1991-93, elected life mem. 1996), The Law Club of Chgo. (bd. dirs. 1996-98). Roman Catholic. Office: US Dist Ct 219 S Dearborn St Ste 1946 Chicago IL 60604-1801 Home Phone: 773-935-4205; Office Phone: 312-435-7612. E-mail: harry_leinenweber@ilnd.uscourts.gov.

LEINIEKS, VALDIS, classicist, educator; b. Liepaja, Latvia, Apr. 15, 1932; came to U.S., 1949, naturalized, 1954; s. Arvid Ansis and Valia Leontine (Brunaus) L. BA, Cornell U., 1955, MA, 1956; PhD, Princeton U., 1962. Instr. classics Cornell Coll., Mount Vernon, Iowa, 1959-62, asst. prof. classics, 1962-64; assoc. prof. classics Ohio State U., 1964-66, U. Nebr., Lincoln, 1966-71, prof. classics, 1971—2005, chmn. dept. classics, 1967-95, chmn. program comparative lit., 1970-86, interim chmn. dept. modern langs., 1982-83, prof. emeritus, 2005—. Author: Morphosyntax of the Homeric Greek Verb, 1964, The Structure of Latin, 1975, Index Nepotianus, 1976, The Plays of Sophokles, 1982, The City of Dionysos, 1996; contbr. articles to profl. jours. Mem. AAUP, Am. Philol. Assn Home: 2505 A St Lincoln NE 68502-1841 Office: U Nebr Dept Classics Lincoln NE 68588-0337

LEININGER, MADELEINE MONICA, nursing educator, consultant, retired anthropologist, editor, writer, theorist; b. Sutton, Nebr., July 13, 1925; d. George M. S. and D. Irene (Sheedy) L. BS in Biology, Scholastic Coll., 1950, LHD, 1976; MS in Nursing, Cath. U. Am., 1953; PhD in Anthropology, U. Wash., 1965; DSc (hon.), U. Indpls., 1990; PhDN (hon.), 1990, U. Kuopio, Finland, 1991. RN; cert. transcultural nurse FAAN/Am. Acad. Nursing. Instr., mem. staff, head nurse med.-surg. unit, supr. psychiat. unit St. Joseph's Hosp., Omaha, 1950-54; assoc. prof. nursing, dir. grad. program in psychiat. nursing U. Cin. Coll. ursing, 1954-60; research fellow Nat. League Nursing, Papua New Guinea, 1960—62, 1978, 1992, 1994; research assoc. U. Wash. Dept. Anthropology, Seattle, 1964-65; prof. nursing and anthropology, dir. nurse-scientist PhD program U. Colo., Boulder and Denver, 1966-69; dean sch. nursing, prof. nursing, lectr. anthropology U. Wash., Seattle, 1969-74; dean coll. nursing, prof. nursing and anthropology U. Utah, Salt Lake City, 1974-80; Anise J. Sorell prof. nursing Troy (Ala.) State U., 1981; prof. nursing, adj. prof. anthropology, dir. Ctr. for Health Research, dir. transcultural nursing offerings Wayne State U., Detroit, 1981-95, prof. emeritus, 1995—; prof. Coll. Nursing U. Nebr. Med. Ctr., 1997—2001; ret., 2001—. Adj. prof. anthropology U. Utah, 1974-81; adj. prof. nursing U. Nebr., 1997—; disting. vis. prof. over 200 univs., U.S. and overseas, 1970—; docent Boys and Girls Town of Am., Omaha Father Flanaghan Ctr., 1996; cons. and lectr. in field. Author: 30 books including Nursing and Anthropology: Two Worlds to Blend, 1970, Contemporary Issues in Mental Health Nursing, 1973, Caring: An Essential Human Need, 1981, Reference Sources for Transcultural Health and Nursing, 1984, Basic Psychiatric Concepts in Nursing, 1960, Care: The Essence of Nursing and Health, 1984, Qualitative Research Methods in Nursing, 1985, Care: Discovery and Clinical-Community Uses, 1988, Ethical and Moral Dimensions of Caring, 1990, Culture Care, Diversity and Universality: A Theory of Nursing, 1991, 3d edit., 2005, Care: The Compassionate Healer, 1991, Caring Imperative for Nursing Education, 1991, (co-authored with Marilyn McFarland and James Bartlett) Transcultural Nursing, 3d edit., 2005, Transcultural Nursing Concepts, Theories, Research and Practice, 3d edit., 2004, Transcultural Nursing Culture Care Theory Diversity and University. a Worldwide Theory, 3d edit., 2005; editor, founder Jour. Transcultural Nursing, 1988-00, 05 (AJN award 2003); contbr. over 400 articles to profl. jours., chpts. to books; prodr. Leininger Nursing Autobiography, 2005. Recipient Outstanding Alumni award Cath. U. Am., 1969, Hon. award Am. Assn. Colls. Nursing, 1976, 96, Nurse of Yr. award Dist. 1 Utah Nurses Assn., 1976, Lit. award Utah Nurses Assn., 1978, Trotter Disting. Pub. Lectr. award U. Tex., 1985, Disting. Faculty Tchg. Recognition award Wayne State U., 1985, Outstanding Faculty Rsch. scholar award Wayne State U. and Gerontology Inst., 1985, Gershenson Rsch. award Wayne State U., 1985, Pace Inst. Rsch. award, 1992, Hewlett Packard Rsch. award, 1992, award for Acad. Excellence AAUW-Detroit, 1986, Disting. award Bd. Govs., 1987, Pres. Excellence in Tchg. award, 1988, Women of Sci. award U. Calif., Fullerton, 1990, Outstanding U. Grad. Mentor award Wayne State U., 1995, 97, Nightingale Rsch. award Oakland U., 1995, Outstanding Nursing Leader Russell Sage Coll, Sigma Theta Tau Intl. Disting. scholar award Russell Sage Coll., 1995, Nobel prize nominee, 1999, Can. Outstanding Rsch. award Can. Nurses Assn., 2003, Deans award Wayne State U. Coll. Nursing, 2005, Outstanding Public Nursing Svc. award Wayne State U., 2005, others; Womens Hall of Fame, 2004, Leininger Learning and Transcultural Nursing Collection libr. and reading sects. at Madonna U., Livonia, Mich. named in her honor, 1996; Leininger Archival Room at Trinity Coll., Moline, Ill. named in her honor, 2002; Mary Boynton Disting. lectr., 1998; Disting. vis. scholar Jimmy Crockett Lectr. Series, Disting. Vis. scholar U. Nebr., 1999, U. (Fresno) Calif. State U., 2005; named Disting. scholar U. Wis., 2001-02, Disting lectr. Arab Am. Internat. Conf., 2005, Deana Excellence Pub. Svc. award Wayne State U., 2005, Outstanding Achievement Health Care award Wayne State U., 2005, others; Worldwide Transcultural ursing Ctr. named in her honor, 2001; Dist. honoree Worldwide Transcultural Nursing Soc., 2003; nominee Women's Hall of Fame, 2003, Nobel Peace prize, 2000. Fellow ANA, Am. Anthropol. Soc. for Applied Anthropology (exec. com. 1980-84, nominee Nobel Perce award), Am. Acad. Nursing (Living Legend award 1998), Royal Coll. Nursing Australia (First Internat. Achievement award 2000, First Qualitative Achievement award 2003); mem. Am. Assn. Humanities, Am. Applied Anthropol. Soc., Royal Coll. Nursing Australia, Mich. Nurses Assn. (Bertha Culp Human Rights award 1994), Ctrl. States Anthropology, Amnesty Internat., Transcultural Nursing Soc. (founder, bd. dirs., pres. 1974-80), Cultural Cmty. Group Assn. (ethics, humanities heritage study group), Australian Nat. Rsch. Care Confs. (leader human care rsch.), Internat. Assn. Human Caring (founder, pres., bd. dirs.), Nordic Caring Soc. Sweden (hon.), Sigma Xi, Pi Gamma Mu, Sigma Theta Tau (Lectr. of Yr. 1987—, Disting. Spkr. at conf. 1995-2005), Delta Kappa Gamma, Alpha Tau Delta.

LEISTEN, ARTHUR GAYNOR, lawyer; b. Chgo., Oct. 17, 1941; s. Arthur Edward Leisten and Mary (Francis) Gaynor; m. Florence T. Kelly, May 11, 1968; children: Thomas, Hillary. AB magna cum laude, Loyola U., Chgo., 1963; JD, Harvard U., 1966; grad. exec. mgmt. program, Northwestern U., Chgo., 1983 and 1986, Pa. State U., 1985. Bar: Ill. 1966, U.S. Dist. Ct. (no. dist.) Ill. 1967, U.S. Ct. Appeals 1967. Assoc. prof. Sch. Law Loyola U., 1966-69; assoc. Chadwell & Kayser, Ltd., Chgo., 1969-74; staff atty. Texaco, Inc., Chgo., 1974-75; atty. USG Corp., Chgo., 1975-78, sr. atty., 1978-82, sr. gen. atty., 1982-85, assoc. gen. counsel, 1985, v.p., assoc. gen. counsel, 1985-86, v.p., gen. counsel, 1986-90, sr. v.p., gen. counsel, 1990-93, sr. v.p., gen. counsel, sec., 1993—. Mem. ABA (corp. counsel com.), Chgo. Bar Assn., Am. Corp. Counsel Assn., Univ. Club, Law Club (Chgo.), Mich. Shores Club (Wilmette, Ill.), Westmoreland Country Club. Office: USG Corp PO Box 6721 125 S Franklin St Fl 2 Chicago IL 60606-4678

LEITCH, DAVID G., automotive executive, lawyer; b. 1960; m. Ellen Leitch; 3 children. Grad., Duke U., 1982; JD, U. Va. Sch. Law, 1985. Law clk. to Hon. J. Harvie Wilkinson III US Ct. Appeals (4th Cir.); law clk. to Chief Justice William H. Rehnquist US Supreme Ct.; dep. asst. atty. gen., sr. counsel, Office Legal Counsel US Dept. Justice, Washington; assoc. Hogan and Hartson, LLP, Washington, 1987—94, ptnr., 1994—2001; chief counsel FAA, Washington, 2001—02; counsel, Transition Planning Office US Dept. Homeland Security, Washington; dep. asst. to the Pres, dep. counsel The White House, Washington, 2002—05; gen. counsel, sr. v.p. Ford Motor Co., Dearborn, Mich., 2005—. Office: Ford Motor Co 1 Am Rd Dearborn MI 48126

LEITCH, DAVID R., state legislator; b. Three Rivers, Mich., Aug. 22, 1948; m. Marlene Leitch; three children. BA, Kalamazoo Coll., 1970. Dist. 47 senator Ill. Senate, Springfield, 1986-87; Dist. 93 rep. Ill. Ho. Reps., Springfield, 1988—. Asst. majority leader, mem. appropriations II, utilities, environ. and energy, rules, Medicaid, labor and commerce, reapportionment, and legis. rsch. unit coms., Ill. Ho. Reps. Mem. Rep. ctrl. and fin. coms., Peoria County, Ill., 1975—; v.p. First of Am.-Ill. Named Outstanding Young Man in Peoria; recipient Disting. Svc. award, 1981. Mem. Inst. Physical Medicine, Heartland Health Clinic, United Way, Komen Found., Rotary. Address: 5921 N Cypress Dr Apt 1602 Peoria IL 61615-2627 Also: 3114 N University St Peoria IL 61604-1317

LEIWEKE, TOD, professional sports team executive; m. Tara Leiweke; children: Tyler, Tori. Prin. Leiweke & Co., Kansas City, 1982—87; v.p. mktg. and broadcasting Golden State Warriors, NBA, 1987—91, pres. arena devel. co., 1994; exec. v.p. Orca Bay Sports and Entertainment; exec. dir. First Tee, World Golf Found.; pres. Minn. Wild Minn. Hockey Ventures Group LP, St. Paul, 1999—2001, COO, 2001—04; CEO Seattle Seahawks, 2004—; interim gen. mgr. Portland Trailblazers, 2007—. Office: Seattle Seahawks 11220 NE 53rd St Kirkland WA 98033

LELAND, BURTON, state legislator; b. Detroit, Nov. 24, 1948; s. Morris Leland and Beatrice (Bernstein) L.; m. Rosanne Letvin; children: Zachary Levi, Gabriel Daniel. BS, Wayne State U., 1971; MSW, U. Mich., 1977. Social worker Wayne County Dept. Social Svc., 1972-80; state rep. Dist. 13 Mich. Ho. of Reps., 1981-98; mem. Mich. Senate from 5th dist., Lansing, 1999—. Mem. Joint Com. on Adminstrv. Rules, Elec. Consumers, Pub. Health & Transp. Coms. Mich. Ho. of Reps.; vice-chmn. Tourism, Fisheries & Wildlife Com. Mem. NASW, Nat. Conf. State Legislators, Alpha Epsilon Pi. Home: 17254 Bentler St Detroit MI 48219-4746 Office: 315 Farnum Bldg PO Box 30036 Lansing MI 48909-7536

LELAND, DAVID J., political association executive; m. Cindy Leland; children: Ben, Maria. BA, Ohio State U., 1975; JD, Capital U., 1978. Committeeman 19th ward Dem. Com., 1972—; vice-chmn. Franklin County Dem. Com., 1972-77; state assemblyman dist. 28 Ohio State Assembly, 1983-84; alt. del. Nat. Dem. Conv., 1988; fin. dir. polit. campaigns Mayor candidate Ben Epsy, Columbus, 1991-94, Coun. Pres. Cynthia Lazarus, 1991-94, Atty. Gen. Lee Fisher, 1991-94; rep. State of Ohio Nat. Dem. Conv. Platform com., 1992; chmn. Dem. Nat. Conv., 1996, mem. Rules & By-Laws com., 1996—; del. State of Ohio Dem. State Party, 1996—; chmn. Ohio Dem. State Party, 1996—; staff coun. Ohio Civil Svc. Employees Assn., 1980-82. Instr. bus. and govt. law Columbus Tech. Inst., 1983-84; atty. Gibson and Robbins-Penniman, 1985-86, Schwartz, Warren and Ramirez, 1991-96; dir. transp. dept. Pub. Utilities Commn., Ohio, 1986-90. Named one of Ten Outstanding Young Citizens, Columbus Jaycees, 1975, 79, Dem. of Yr. Franklin County Dem. Party, 1982, Outstanding Freshman State Rep. Columbus Monthly Mag., 1983-84. Home: 6805 Oak Creek Dr Columbus OH 43229-1573

LEMAHIEU, DANIEL R., state official; b. Nov. 5, 1946; Student, U. Wis., Milw. Pub.; state assemblyman Wis., 2002—. Mem. aging and long-term care com.; mem. rural devel. com.; vice chair urban and local affairs com.; mem. small bus. com. With US Army, Vietnam. Republican. Office: State Capitol Rm 17 N PO Box 8952 Madison WI 53708-8952

LEMAIRE, JACQUES, professional hockey coach; b. Lasalle, Que., Can., Sept. 7, 1945; Forward Montreal Canadiens, 1967-79, head coach, 1983-85, dir. of hockey pers., 1985-87, asst. to mng. dir., 1987-93, cons. to gen. mgr., 1998-00; head coach, player Sierre Hockey Club, Switzerland, 1979-81; asst. coach SUNY Coll., Plattsburgh, 1981-82; coach Longueuil Chevaliers, 1982-83; head coach NJ Devils, 1993-98, Minnesota Wild, Saint Paul, 2000—. Named NHL Coach of Yr., Sporting News, 1993, 94; recipient Jack Adams Award, NHL, 2003. Achievements include being a member of Stanely Cup Champion Montreal Canadiens, 1968, 1969, 1971, 1973, 1976, 1977, 1978, 1979; being the coach of Stanley Cup Champion NJ Devils, 1995; being inducted into the Hockey Hall of Fame, 1984. Home: Minn Wild 317 Washington St Saint Paul MN 55102*

LEMAN, EUGENE D., meat industry executive; b. Peoria, Ill., Dec. 1, 1942; s. Vernon L. and Viola L. (Beer) L.; m. Carolyn Leman, June 14, 1964; children— Jill C., Jennifer A. BS, U. Ill., 1964. Dir. various depts. Wilson Foods, Oklahoma City, 1964-78, v.p. fresh and processed pork, 1978-80, v.p. fresh meat group, 1980-81; group v.p. IBP, Inc., Dakota City, Nebr., 1981-86, exec. v.p., 1986—95, CEO, exec. v.p., 1986—95, pres. Allied Group, 1996—98; pres. IBP Fresh Meats, Dakota City, Nebr., 1998, CEO, 2000, sr. group v.p., 2001, Tyson Fresh Meats, Dakota City, Nebr., 2003. Bd. dirs. Wells Fargo Bank, Dakota Valley Bus. Coun.; bd. trustees BSA Mid-Am. Coun. Bd. mem. United Way of Siouxland, 2003—05, campaign chmn., 2004—05; bd. trustees Siouxland Cmty. Found. Mem. Am. Meat Inst. (chmn. pork com. 1980-81), Nat. Pork Producers Council (packer rep. Pork Value Task Force 1981-82, 88, pork export com. 1985) Clubs: Sioux City Country (Iowa), Dakota Dunes Country Club. Republican. Office: Tyson Fresh Meats Ste 820 800 Stevens Port Dr Dakota Dunes SD 57049-5005 E-mail: gene.leman@tyson.com.

LEMANSKE, ROBERT F., JR., allergist, immunologist; b. Milw., 1948; MD, U. Wis., 1975. Diplomate Am. Bd. Pediats., Am. Bd. Allergy and Immunology. Intern U. Wis. Hosp., Madison, 1975-76, resident in pediats., 1976-78, prof. pediats. medicine, divsn. head pediat. allergy, immunology & rheumatology. Fellow: Am. Acad. Allergy and Immunology, Am. Acad. Pediat. Office: Clin Sci Ctr Rm K4/916 600 Highland Ave Madison WI 53792-0001 Office Phone: 608-265-2206.

LE MASTER, DENNIS CLYDE, retired forester, economist, educator; b. Startup, Wash., Apr. 22, 1939; s. Franklin Clyde and Delores Ilene (Schwartz) Le M.; m. Kathleen Ruth Dennis, Apr. 4, 1961; children: Paul, Matthew. BA, Wash. State U., Pullman, 1961; MA, Wash. State U., 1970, PhD, 1974. Asst. prof. dept. forestry and range mgmt. Wash. State U., Pullman, 1972-74, assoc. prof., 1978-80, prof., chair dept., 1980-88; prof., head dept. forestry and natural resources Purdue U., West Lafayette, Ind., 1988—2004; dir. resource policy Soc. Am. Foresters, Bethesda, Md., 1974-76; staff counsel subcom. on forests Ho. of Reps., Washington, 1977-78, ret., 2005. Cons. USDA Forest Svc., Washington, 1978—, Com. on Agr., Ho. of Reps., 1979-80, Forest History Soc., Durham, N.C., 1979-83, The Conservation Found., 1989-90, Office Tech. Assessment, Washington, 1989-91, Consultative Group on Biol. Diversity, 1991, Colo. State Forest Svc., 2006-07. Author: Decade of Change, 1984; co-editor 8 books; contbr. articles to profl. jours. Bd. dirs. Pinchot Inst. for Conservation, treas., 1996-97, vice-chair, 1998-99, chair, 2000-01. Sr. fellow, Pinchot Inst. for Conservation. Mem. AAAS, Soc. Am. Foresters (chair ho. of dels. 1982, coun. 1999), Inst. Forest Biotech., Internat. Union Forest Rsch. Orgns., Beta Gamma Sigma, Epsilon Sigma Phi, Omicron Delta Epsilon, Xi Sigma Pi. Democrat. Episcopalian. Avocation: fishing. Home: 626 40th Pl Everett WA 98201 Office: Purdue U Dept Forestry and Natural Resources West Lafayette IN 47907 Home Phone: 425-252-1391; Office Phone: 425-252-1391. Personal E-mail: dclmstr@comcast.net.

LEMAY, RONALD T., telecommunications industry executive; Former pres., chief oper. officer long distance div. U.S. Sprint, Westwood, Kans. Office: Sprint 6391 Sprint Pkwy Overland Park KS 66251-6100

LEMBERGER, LOUIS, pharmacologist; b. Monticello, NY, May 8, 1937; s. Max and Ida Lemberger; m. Myrna Sue Diamond, 1959; children: Harriet Felice Schor, Margo Beth. BS magna cum laude, Bklyn. Coll. Pharmacy, LI U., 1960; PhD in Pharmacology, Albert Einstein Coll. Medicine, 1964, MD, 1968; Doctorate (hon.), LI U., 1994. Pharmacy intern VA Regional Office, Newark, summer 1960; postdoctoral fellow Albert Einstein Coll. Medicine, 1964-68; intern in medicine Met. Hosp. Ctr., NY Med. Coll., NYC, 1968-69; rsch. assoc. NIH, Bethesda, Md., 1969-71; clin. pharmacologist Lilly Lab. for Clin. Rsch., Eli Lilly & Co., Indpls., 1971-75, chief clin. pharmacology, 1975-78, dir. clin. pharmacology, 1978-89, clin. rsch. fellow, 1982-93; asst. prof. pharmacology Ind. U., 1972-73, asst. prof. medicine, 1972-73, assoc. prof. pharmacology, 1973-77, assoc. prof. medicine, 1973-77, prof. pharmacology, 1977—, prof. medicine, prof. psychiatry, 1977—, mem. grad. faculty, 1975—; adj. prof. clin. pharmacology Ohio State U., 1975-86; physician Wishard Meml. Hosp., 1976-98. Cons. US at. Commn. on Marijuana and Drug Abuse, 1971-73, Can. Commn. Inquiry into Non-Med. Use of Drugs, 1971-73; mem. Pharm. Mfrs. Assn. Commn. on Medicines for Drug Dependence and Abuse, 1990-93, Ind. Optometric Legend Drug Adv. Com., 1991-96; guest lectr. various univs., 1968—; lectr. U. Minn., 1993—; mem. adv. com. Faseb Life Scis. Rsch. Office, 1993-96. Author: (with A. Rubin) Physiologic Disposition of Drugs of Abuse, 1976; contbr. numerous articles on biochemistry and pharmacology to sci. jours.; editorial bd.; Excerpta Medica, 1972-96, Clin. Pharmacology and Therapeutics, 1976-96, Communications in Psychopharmacology, 1975-91, Pharmacology, Internat. Jour. Exptl. and Clin. Pharmacology, 1978-94, Drug and Alcohol Abuse Rsch., 1979-86, Drug Devel. Rsch., 1980-87, Trends in Pharmcol. Scis., 1980-85. Post adviser Crossroads of Am. coun. Boy Scouts Am., 1972-77; comdr. Jewish War Vet. Post 114, 2005—06. Lt. comdr. USPHS, 1969-71. Recipient Disting. Alumnus award, Albert Einstein Coll. Medicine, 1989, LI U., 1990, Pres. award, 1998, Cornerstone award for Outstanding Lifetime Achievement in Health Scis., Am. Drugstore Mus., 2000. Fellow ACP, AAAS, Am. Coll. Neuropsychopharmacology (chmn. credentials com. 1993), Am. Coll. Clin. Pharmacology; mem. Am. Soc. Pharmacology and Exptl. Therapeutics (com. div. clin. pharmacology 1972-78, chmn. com. 1978-83, coun. 1980-83, chmn. long-range planning com. 1984-86, pres. 1987-88, ASPET award in Therapeutics, 1985, Harry Gold award for rsch. and teaching excellence in clin. pharmacology 1993), Am. Soc. Clin. Pharmacology and Therapeutics (chmn. sect. neuropsychopharmacology 1973-80, chmn. fin. com. 1976-83, 89-92, v.p. 1981-82, pres. 1983-84, dir. 1975-81, 84-87, Rawls-Palmer award 1986, Henry Elliot Disting. Svc. award 1992, Oscar B. Hunter award for outstanding achievement in exptl. therapeutics 2003), Am. Soc. Clin. Investigation, Collegium Internat. Neuro-Psychopharmacologicum, Am. Fedn. Clin. Rsch. Ctrl. Soc. Clin. Rsch., Soc. Neurosci., Jewish War Vets (comdr. Post 114 2005-06), Sigma Xi, Alpha Omega Alpha, Rho Chi. Jewish. Achievements include being first person to administer and study the actions in humans of the antidepressant drug Prozac (fluoxetine), Permax (pergolide) the drug used to treat Parkinson's disease, and the cannabinoid drug Cesamet (nabilone) utilized for the treatment of nausea and vomiting secondary to cancer chemotherapy and Zyprexa (Olanzepine) the drug utilized in schizophrenia and Strattera (atomoxetine) the drug utilized in attention deficit hyperactivity disorder; responsible for directing and spearheading the clinical development of Prozac, Permax and Cesamet through clinical trials, regulatory approval and eventually into the marketplace. Home: 3315 Walnut Creek Dr N Carmel IN 46032-9038 Office: Ind Univ Sch Medicine Dept Pharmacology and Medicine Indianapolis IN 46202

LE MENAGER, LOIS M., incentive merchandise and travel company executive; b. Cleve., Apr. 25, 1934; d. Lawrence M. and Lillian C. (Simicek) Stanek; m. Charles J. Blabolil (dec. 1982); children: Sherry L., Richard A.; m. Spencer H. Le Menager, Mar. 23, 1984. Grad. high sch. Travel counselor Mktg. Innovators Internat. Inc., Rosemont, Ill., 1978-80, mktg. dir., 1980-82, chmn., CEO, owner, 1982—. Dir. Northwest Commerce Bank, Rosemont. Featured in (articles) Crain's Chgo. Bus. Recipient Entrepreneurial Success award U.S. Small Bus. Adminstrn., 1999; named Supplier of Yr., J.C. Penney Co., Inc. Mem. NAFE, Am. Inst. Entrepreneurs (Entrepreneur of Yr. 1988), Am. Mktg. Assn., Internat. Soc. Mktg. Planners, Soc. Incentive Travel Execs., Am. Soc. Travel Agts., Nat. Fedn. Ind. Bus., Nat. Assn. Women Bus. Owners, Des Plaines C. of C., Rosemont C. of C., Chicagoland C. of C. (dir.), The Chgo. Network, Exec. Club (Chgo.). Congregationalist. Office: Mktg Innovators Internat Inc 9701 W Higgins Rd Rosemont IL 60018-4717 Office Phone: 847-696-1111.

LEMIEUX, JOSEPH HENRY, manufacturing executive, researcher; b. Providence, Mar. 2, 1931; s. Mildred L. Lemieux; m. Frances Joanne Schmidt, Aug. 11, 1956; children: Gerald Joseph, Craig Joseph, Kimberly Mae Lemieux Wolff, Allison Jo. Lemieux Smith. Student, Stonehill Coll., 1949-50, U. R.I., 1950-51; BBA summa cum laude, Bryant Coll., 1957. From mem. staff to CEO Owens-Ill., Toledo, 1957—91; CEO Owens-Ill., Inc., 1991—2003, ret., 2003, chmn. bd., 1991. Bd. dirs. at. City Bank Northwest, Toledo, Nat. City Corp., Cleve. Trustee Bryant Coll. Staff sgt. USAF, 1951—55. Named one of Outstanding Young Men Am., Jaycees, 1965; recipient glass industry's Phoenix award, 1997. Mem.: Glass Packaging Inst. (chmn. 1984—86), Inverness Club (Toledo). Roman Catholic. Avocations: golf, tennis. Office: Owens-Illinois Inc 1 Seagate Toledo OH 43666-0001

LEMKE, ALAN JAMES, environmental specialist; b. Appleton, Wis., May 22, 1945; s. Edwin R. and Ethel Mae (Noe) L.; m. Joyce Eileen Kruse, May 24, 1975; 1 child, David Edwin. BS in chemistry, Coll. Idaho, 1968. Rsch. chemist Am. Med. Ctr., Denver, 1972-74; chemist U.S. Geol. Survey, Denver, 1975-77; chemist II Occupl. Health Lab., Portland, Oreg., 1977-80, State Hygienic Labs., Des Moines, 1980-82; indsl. hygienist Iowa Divsn. Labor, Des Moines, 1982-88; environ. specialist Iowa Dept. Natural Resources, Spencer, 1988—. Small bus. owner Al's Stamps and Collectables. Author: The Noe Family's Involvement in the Civil War: A History of Wisconsin's 19th Volunteer Infantry Regiment, 1994. Republican. Evangelical. Avocations: camping, hiking, fishing, history, reading. Home: 1110 15th Ave W Spencer IA 51301-2943 Office: Iowa Dept Natural Resources 1900 N Grand Ave Spencer IA 51301-2200

LEMON, DON, newscaster; b. Baton Rouge; Degree in TV/Radio and Broadcast Journalism, Bklyn. Coll.; at, La. State U. Reporter WBRC-TV, Birmingham, Ala.; investigative reporter KTVI-TV, St. Louis; weekend anchor and reporter WCAU-TV, Phila., 1999—2002; corr. NBC and MSNBC, NYC, 2002—03; substitute anchor Weekend Today show NBC, NYC, 2002—03; co-anchor 5pm news and reporter WMAQ-TV, Chgo., 2003—. Named one of Black Achievers in Bus. and Industry, YMCA, Phila., 2001; recipient Outstanding Achievement in Comm. award. Office: WMAQ-TV NBC Tower 454 N Columbus Dr Chicago IL 60611-5555

LEMPERT, RICHARD OWEN, lawyer, educator; s. Philip Leonard and Mary (Steinberg) L.; m. Cynthia Ruth Willey, Sept. 10, 1967 (div.); 1 child, Leah Rose; m. Lisa Ann Kahn, May 26, 2002. AB, Oberlin Coll., 1964; JD, U. Mich., 1968, PhD in Sociology, 1971. Bar: Mich. 1978. Asst. prof. law U. Mich., Ann Arbor, 1968-72, assoc. prof., 1972-74, prof. law, 1974—, prof. sociology, 1985—, Francis A. Allen collegiate prof. law, 1990—2001, acting chair dept. sociology, 1993-94, chair dept. sociology, 1995-98, dir. life scis., values and society program, 2000—04, Eric Stein Disting. Univ. prof. law and sociology, 2001—; dir. divsn. social and econ. scis. NSF, 2002—06. Mason Ladd disting. vis. prof. U. Iowa Law Sch., 1981; vis. fellow Centre for Socio-Legal Rsch., Wolfson Coll., Oxford (Eng.) U., 1982; mem. adv. panel for law and social sci. div. NSF, 1976-79, mem. exec. com. adv. com. for social sci., 1979; mem. com. law enforcement and adminstrn. of justice NRC, vice chmn., 1984-87, chmn., 1987-89; mem. adv. panel NSF program on Human Dimensions of Global

Change, 1989, 92-94; mem. com. on DNA technology in forensic sci. NRC, 1989-92, com. on drug testing in workplace, 1991-93; vis. scholar Russell Sage Found., 1998-99; vis. scholar Russell Sage Found., 1998-99. Author: (with Stepehn Saltzburg) A Modern Approach to Evidence, 1977, 2d edit., 1983, 3d edit. (with Sam Gross and James Liebman), 2000; (with Joseph Sanders) An Invitation to Law and Social Science, 1986, Under the Influence, 1993; editor: (with Jacques Normand and Charles O'Brien) Under the Influence? Drugs and the American Work Force, 1994, Evidence Stories, 2006; editorial bd. Law and Soc. Rev., 1972-77, 89-92, 98—, editor, 1982-85; mem. editl. bd. Evaluation Rev., 1979-82, Empirial Legend Studies 2003-; Jour. Law and Human Behavior, 1980-82; contbr. articles to profl. jours. Fellow Ctr. for Advanced Study in Behavioral Scis., 1994-95; vis. scholar Russell Sage Found., 1998-99. Fellow Am. Acad. Arts and Scis.; mem. Am. Sociol. Assn. (chair sect. sociology of law 1995-96, mem. coun. 2005-), Am. Assn. Advancement Sci. (sec. sect. K 2006-) Law and Society Assn. (trustee 1977-80, 90-93, 06-, exec. com. 1979-80, 82-87, 2006-, pres., 2007-; Harry Kalven Jr. Prize), Order of Coif, Phi Beta Kappa, Phi Kappa Phi. Jewish. Personal E-mail: rol25@hotmail.com.

LEMPKE, MICHAEL R., treasurer; Sr. v.p., treas. Fort James Corp., Deerfield, Ill., 1998—. Office: Fort James Corp 1919 S Broadway Green Bay WI 54304-4905

LENKOSKI, LEO DOUGLAS, retired psychiatrist, educator; b. Northampton, Mass., May 13, 1925; s. Leo L. and Mary Agnes (Lee) L.; m. Jeannette Teare, July 12, 1952; children— Jan Ellen, Mark Teare, Lisa Marie, Joanne Lee. AB, Harvard, 1948, spl. student, 1948-49; MD, Western Res. U., 1953; grad., Cleve. Psychoanalytic Inst., 1964. Intern Univ. Hosps., Cleve., 1953-54, resident in psychiatry, 1956-57, dir. psychiatry, 1970-86, chief of staff, 1982-90; dir. profl. services Horizon Ctr. Hosp., 1980; asst. resident in psychiatry Yale U., New Haven, 1954-56; teaching fellow Case Western Res. U., Cleve., 1957-60, from instr. to prof. psychiatry, 1960-93; prof. emeritus, 1993—; assoc. dean Sch. Medicine Case Western Res. U., Cleve., 1982-93, dir. Substance Abuse Ctr., 1990-93. Cons. Cleve. Ctr. on Alcoholism, DePaul Maternity and Infant Home, St. Ann's Hosp., Def. Dept., Cleve. VA Hosp., Psychiat. Edn. br. NIMH; mem. Cuyahoga County Mental Health and Retardation Bd., 1967-73, 94-2002, 2004—, Health Planning and Devel. Commn., 1967-73, Ohio Mental Health and Retardation Commn., 1976-78; mental health advisor Jewish Family Svcs. Assocs., 2003—. Contbr. articles to profl. jours. Bd. dirs. Hough-Norwood Health Ctr., Hitchcock Ctr., Hopewell Inn, Woodruff Found, 2001—. 1st lt. USAAF, 1943-46. Decorated D.F.C., Air medal with oak leaf cluster.; Career Tchr. grantee IMH, 1958-60 Fellow Am. Psychiat. Assn. (life), Am. Coll. Psychiatrists, Am. Coll. Psychoanalysts (pres. 1988-89); mem. AMA, AAAS, Ohio Psychiat. Assn. (pres. 1974—), Am. Psychoanalytic Assn., Assn. Am. Med. Colls., Cleve. Acad. Medicine (bd. dirs. 1987-90), Ohio Med. Assn., Pasteur Club, Am. Assn. Chairmen Depts. Psychiatry (pres. 1978-79), Alpha Omega Alpha. Home: 1 Bratenahl Pl Apt 1010 Cleveland OH 44108-1155 Office: 11000 Euclid Ave Cleveland OH 44106-1714

LENN, STEPHEN ANDREW, investment banker; b. Ft. Lauderdale, Fla., Jan. 6, 1946; s. Joseph A. and Ruth (Kreis) L.; 1 child, Daniel Lenn. BA, Tufts U., 1967; JD, Columbia U., 1970. Assoc. Kronish, Lieb, Shainswit, Weiner & Hellman, NYC, 1970-72, Shereff, Friedman, Hoffman & Goodman, NYC, 1972-75; exec. v.p., gen. counsel Union Commerce Bank, Union Commerce Corp., Cleve., 1975-83; ptnr., mng. ptnr. Porter, Wright, Morris & Arthur, Cleve., 1983-88; ptnr. Baker & Hostetler, Cleve., 1988-97; CEO Capital Strategies Inc., Cleve., 1997—. Trustee Gt. Lakes Sci. Ctr.; corp. bd. mem. Ohio Motorists Assn.; bd. dirs. Cuyahoga County Pub. Libr. Found. Mem.: ABA. Office: Capital Strategies Inc Two Bratenahl Pl #7BC Cleveland OH 44108 Office Phone: 216-523-1850.

LENNES, GREGORY, manufacturing and financing company executive; b. Chgo., Aug. 5, 1947; s. Lawrence Dominic and Genevieve (Karoll) L.; m. Kathie Lennes; children: Robert, Sandra, Ryan, Bonnie. BA, U. Ill., 1969, MA, 1971, postgrad., 1971-73. Corp. archivist Navistar Internat. Corp. (formerly Internat. Harvester Co.), Chgo., 1973-80, records mgr., 1980—, asst. sec., 1980—; dir. document mgmt., 1997—; sec. Navistar Fin. Corp., Schaumburg, Ill., 1980—, Internat. Truck and Engine Corp., 1987—. Editor: Historical Records in the Farm Equipment Industry, 1977. Mem. Am. Soc. Corp Secs., Assn. Records Mgrs. and Adminstrs., Soc. Am. Archivists, Midwest Archives Conf., Assn. Info. and Image Mgmt., Nat. Assn. Stock Plan Profls. Home: 530 LaMelodia Dr Las Cruces M 88011 Office: Internat Truck and Engine Corp 4201 Winfield Rd Warrenville IL 60555

LENNON, RICHARD GERARD, bishop; b. Arlington, Mass., Mar. 26, 1947; AB, St. John's Sem., Brighton, Mass., 1969, MTh, 1973, MA, 1984. Ordained priest Archdiocese of Boston, 1973; ordained bishop, 2001; aux. bishop Archdiocese of Boston, 2001—06, apostolic adminstr., 2002—03; bishop Diocese of Cleve., 2006—. Mem.: Equestrian Order of the Holy Sepulchre of Jerusalem, Knights of Malta. Roman Catholic. Office: Chancery Bldg 1027 Superior Ave Cleveland OH 44114 Office Phone: 216-696-6525 ext. 2030. Office Fax: 216-621-7332.*

LENNOX, HEATHER, lawyer; b. Cleve., Sept. 22, 1967; d. Rand Tru and Leilani Marie L.; m. Douglas Robert Krause, Sept. 17, 1994. BA summa cum laude, John Carroll U., 1989; JD cum laude, Georgetown U., 1992. Bar: Ohio 1992, US Dist. Ct. (no. dist.) Ohio 1993, US Ct. Appeals (6th cir.) 2006. Ptnr. Jones Day, Cleve., 1992—. Contbr. articles to profl. jours. Named an Outstanding Young Prof., Turnarounds & Workouts, 2006, Ohio Super Lawyer, Law Politics & Pubs. of Cin. mag., 2005, 2006, Law Politics & Pubs. of Cin. Mag., 2007; named one of The Best Lawyers in Am., 2006, 2007. Mem.: Am. Bankruptcy Inst., Cleve. Bar Assn. Office: Jones Day N Point 901 Lakeside Ave E Cleveland OH 44114-1190 Office Phone: 216-586-7111. Office Fax: 216-579-0212. Business E-Mail: hlennox@jonesday.com.

LENON, RICHARD ALLEN, chemical corporation executive; b. Lansing, Mich., Aug. 4, 1920; s. Theo and Elizabeth (Amon) L.; m. Helen Johnson, Sept. 13, 1941; children: Richard Allen, Pamela A., Lisa A. BA, Western Mich. Coll., 1941; postgrad., Northwestern U., 1941-42. Mgr. fin. div. Montgomery Ward & Co., Chgo., 1947-56; v.p. fin. Westinghouse Air Brake Co., 1963-67, treas., 1965-67; v.p., treas. Internat. Minerals & Chem. Corp., Skokie, Ill., 1956-63, group v.p. fin. and adminstrn., 1967-68, exec. v.p., 1968-70, pres., 1970-78, chmn., 1977-86, chmn. exec. com., 1986-88, IMC Global Inc., 1989-96. Lt. comdr. USNR, 1942-47. Mem.: University (Chgo.); Glen View (Ill.). Home: 803 Solar Ln Glenview IL 60025-4464 Office: 100 Saunders Rd Ste 300 Lake Forest IL 60045-2502

LENSING, VICKI, state representative, funeral home business owner; b. Iowa City, June 1957; m. Rich Templeton; children: Amanda, Alex, Nick. BA, U. Iowa, 1979. Co-owner Lensing Funeral and Cremation Svc.; state rep. dist. 78 Iowa Ho. of Reps., 2001—; mem. econ. growth com.; mem. judiciary com.; mem. local govt. com.; ranking mem. govt. oversight com. Facilitator adult bereavement support groups, 1985—, S.E. Jr. High bereavement support group, 1998—2001, ICARE AIDS bereavement support group, 1995—97. Mem. econ. well-being task force City of Iowa City, 1994, mem. citysteps task force, 1994; pres. Johnson County Women's Network, 1997—98; co-pres. Dist. Parent Orgn., 1998—99; parent rep. site-based decision-making team City H.S., 1995—99; site coun. facilitator Weber Elem. Sch., 1998—2000; mem. Old Brick Adv. Coun., 1999—2000; bd. dirs. Iowa City Cmty. Sch. Dist. Found., 1998—2000; co-chair women's leadership cir. United Way, 1999. Named Disting. Alumni, Iowa City W. High, 1992; recipient Gov.'s Vol. award in edn., 1998. Mem.: Preferred Funeral Dirs. Internat. (pres.), Iowa City Area C. of C. (bd. dirs. 1991, 1994—96, 1998—2000, chair 2000, 2000). Democrat. Office: State Capitol East 12th and Grand Des Moines IA 50319

LENSKI, RICHARD EIMER, evolutionary biologist, educator; b. Ann Arbor, Mich., Aug. 13, 1956; BA in Biology, Oberlin Coll., 1976; PhD in Zoology, U. NC, 1982. Postdoctoral rsch. assoc. dept. zoology U. Mass., Amherst, 1982-85; vis. asst. prof. Dartmouth Coll., Hanover, NH, 1984; asst. prof. dept. ecology and evolutionary biology U. Calif., Irvine, 1985—88, assoc. prof., 1988-91; Hannah prof. of Microbial Ecology Mich. State U., East Lansing, 1991—. Vis. asst. prof. dept. biol. scis. Dartmouth Coll., Hanover, N.H., 1984; mem. NRC Commn. on Life Scis., 1990-96, NRC Bd. Biology, 1990-96. Assoc. editor Evolution, 1990-93; editorial bd. Microbial Ecology, 1991-93; contbg. author: Coevolution, 1983; contbr. articles to Sci., Nature, Ecology, Am. Naturalist. NSF fellow, 1977-81; Presdl. Young Investigator NSF, 1988-93; rsch. fellow Guggenheim Found., 1992-93; vis. fellow All Souls Coll., Oxford U., 1992-93; McArthur fellow, 1996. Fellow Am. Acad. Arts Sci.; mem. Am. Soc. Microbiology, Am. Soc. Naturalists, Ecol. Soc. Am.(com. on environ. applications genetically engineered organisms 1988), Genetics Soc. Am., Soc. Study Evolution, Sigma Xi, NAS. Achievements include research on ecology, genetics and evolution of microbial populations including studies on coevolution of bacteria, viruses and plasmids, causes of mutation. Office: Ctr Microbial Ecology Mich State U 288 Plant And Soil Science East Lansing MI 48824-1325 Office Phone: 517-355-3278. E-mail: lenski@msu.edu.

LENTS, DON GLAUDE, lawyer; b. Kansas City, Mo., Nov. 4, 1949; s. Donald Victor and Helen Maxine (Draper) L.; m. Peggy Lynn Iglauer, Aug. 27, 1972; children: Stacie Lee, Kelsey Lynn. BA magna cum laude, Harvard Coll., 1971; JD magna cum laude, Harvard Law Sch., 1974. Bar: Mo. 1974, U.S. Dist. Ct. (ea. dist.) Mo. 1975, U.S. Ct. Appeals (8th cir.) 1975. Jr. ptnr. Bryan Cave LLP, St. Louis, 1974-81, ptnr., 1982, 84—, London, 1982-84, mem. exec. com., 1988—, mgr. internat. dept., 1984-88, mgr. corp. and bus. dept., 1988-95, chair corp. and bus. dept., 1995-96, head transactions group, 1996—2002, vice chmn., 2003—04, chmn., 2004—. Instr. law Washington U., 1979-80, adj. prof., 2002-03. Co-author: Missouri Corporate Law and Practice, 1989, 5th edit., 2007, and ann. supplements. Bd. dirs. Leadership St. Louis, Inc., 1978-81, 86-91, pres., 1989-91; bd. dirs. Coro Found., St. Louis, Inc., 1986-91, gen. counsel, sec., 1988-90; vol. St. Louis Lawyers and Accts. for Arts, 1988-93, v.p., 1990-92, pres., 1992-93; bd. dirs. Brit. Am. Project, 1989-94, pres., 1993-94; bd. dirs., exec. com. Confluence St. Louis, 1995-96; bd. dirs., exec. com. Focus St. Louis, 1996-2000; bd. dirs. Grand Ctr., Inc., 2002—, chmn. bd., 2004—07; bd. dirs. St. Louis Regional Chamber and Growth Assn., 2005-, exec. comm. 2008-; exec. bd. dirs. St. Louis coun., Boy Scouts Am., 2004—; bd. dirs. United Way Greater St. Louis, 2007—. Sheldon fellow Harvard U., 1974-75. Mem. ABA, Mo. Bar Assn. (coun. corp. and bus. law sect. 1987-93, vice chmn. 1988-92), Met. St. Louis Bar Assn. (sec. bus. law sect. 1980-81), Harvard Alumni Assn. (regional dir. 1993-96), Hasty Pudding Club, Harvard Club (exec. com. St. Louis Club 1978-82, v.p. 1987-92, pres. 1992-93). Office: Bryan Cave One Metropolitan Sq 211 N Broadway Saint Louis MO 63102-1705 Office Phone: 314-259-2119. Office Fax: 314-259-2020. Business E-Mail: dglents@bryancave.com.

LENZMEIER, ALLEN U., consumer products company executive; Joined Best Buy Co., Inc., Mpls., 1984, exec. v.p., CFO, 1991—2001, pres., COO, 2002—04, vice chmn., 2004—. Bd. dir. UTStarcom, Inc, Best Buy Inc., 2001—. Nat. trustee Boys and Girls Clubs Am. Office: Best Buy Co Inc PO Box 9312 Minneapolis MN 55440-9312

LEON, ARTHUR SOL, research cardiologist, exercise physiologist; b. Bklyn., Apr. 26, 1931; s. Alex and Anne (Schrek) L.; m. Gloria Rakita, Dec. 23, 1956; children: Denise, Harmon, Michelle. BS in Chemistry with high honors, U. Fla., 1952; MS in Biochemistry, U. Wis., 1954, MD, 1957. Intern Henry Ford Hosp., Detroit, 1957-58; fellow in internal medicine Lahey Clinic, Boston, 1958-60; fellow in cardiology Jackson Meml. Hosp.-U. Miami (Fla.) Med. Sch., 1960-61; dir. clin. pharmacology research unit Hoffmann-La Roche Inc.-Newark Beth Israel Med. Ctr., 1969-73; from instr. to assoc. prof. medicine Coll. Medicine and Dentistry N.J., Newark, 1967-73; from assoc. prof. to prof. div. epidemiology U. Minn., Mpls., 1973—, H.L. Taylor prof. exercise sci. and health enhancement, dir. lab. physiol. hygiene and exercise sci., div. kinesiology, Coll. Edn., 1991—, dir. applied physiology and nutrition, 1973-91. Mem. med. eval. team Gemini projects NASA, 1964-67. Editor Procs. of the NIH Consensus Conf. on Phys. Activity and Cardiovasc. Health, 1997; assoc. editor Surgeon Gen.'s Report on Health Benefits of Exercise, 1996; contbr. numerous articles to profl. pubs. Trustee Vinland Nat. Sports Health Ctr. for Disabled, 1978—; mem. gov.'s coun. physical fitness sports, 1979-90. Served as officer M.C. U.S. Army, 1961-67, 90-91, col. Res. 1978-92, ret. Recipient Meritorious Svc. medal U.S. Army, 1993, Anderson award AAHPER, 1981, Presdl. award for exercise sci. rsch. Internat. Olympic Com., 1999; Am. Heart Assn. fellow, 1960-61 Fellow Am. Coll. Cardiology, Am. Coll. Chest Physicians, Am. Coll. Clin. Pharmacology, N.Y. Acad. Scis., Am. Coll. Sports Medicine (trustee 1976-78, 82-83, v.p. 1977-79, pres. Northland chpt. 1975-76, Citation award 1995), Am. Assn. Cardiovasc. and Pulmonary Rehab. (trustee 1989-90), Am. Acad. Kinesiology and Phys. Edn.; mem. Am. Physiol. Soc., Am. Soc. Pharmacology and Exptl. Therapeutics, Am. Inst. Nutrition, Am. Heart Assn. (v.p. Hennepin County divsn. 1980-81, pres. 1982-83), Am. Coll. Nutrition, Am. Fedn. Clin. Rsch., Minn. Lung Assn. (trustee 1978-81), Phi Beta Kappa, Phi Kappa Phi. Jewish. Home: 5628 Glen Ave Minnetonka MN 55345-6610 Office: U Minn Sch Kinesiology 202 Cooke Hall Minneapolis MN 55455-0136 Home Phone: 952-937-5271; Office Phone: 612-624-8271. Business E-Mail: leonx002@umn.edu.

LEONARD, DANIEL J., state representative; BS, Purdue U. Owner South Side Furniture, Huntington, Ind.; state rep. dist. 50 Ind. Ho. of Reps., Indpls., 2002—. Leader Cub and Boy Scouts; bd. dirs. Salvation Army. Mem.: South Side Bus. Assn. in Huntington County (past pres.), Huntington C. of C. (past pres.). Republican. Office: Ind Ho of Reps 200 W Washington St Indianapolis IN 46204-2786

LEONARD, EUGENE ALBERT, banker; b. St. Louis, Aug. 27, 1935; s. Albert Hiram and Mary (Crowson) L.; m. Mary Ann Sampson, Aug. 31, 1956 (div. 1994); children: Charles, James, Susan; m. Constance Anne Deschamps, June 3, 1995. BS, U. Mo., 1957, MS, 1958, PhD, 1962; postgrad., Rutgers U., 1964-66. Instr. agrl. econs. U. Mo. at Columbia, 1959-60; with Fed. Res. Bank St. Louis, 1961-77; v.p., mgr. Fed. Res. Bank St. Louis (Memphis br.), 1967-70, sr. v.p., 1970-71, 1st v.p., 1971-77; on loan to bd. govs. FRS as asst. sec., Washington, 1970-71; sr. v.p. Merc. Bancorp. Inc., St. Louis, 1977-87; pres. Corp. for Fin. Risk Mgmt., St. Louis, 1987—. Instr. econs. Central States Sch. Banking, 1962-69, Ill. Bankers Sch., 1962-74, Sch. Banking South, 1970-83, Stonier Grad. Sch. Banking, 1975-80, bd. regents, 1978-81; adj. assoc. prof. econs. Memphis State U., 1969-70; bd. dirs. Ctrl. West End Bank, St. Louis, 1997—. Bd. dirs. Logos Sch., St. Louis, 1977-85, chmn., 1985; bd. dirs. Repertory Theater of St. Louis, 1981-87. Mem. Mo. Bankers Assn. (treas. 1984-85, pres. 1986-87), U. Mo. Columbia Alumni Assn. (nat. pres. 1980-81, bd. dirs. devel. fund 1981-89, Faculty Alumni award 1986), Gamma Sigma Delta, Kappa Sigma. Unitarian Universalist. Home: 30 Portland Pl Saint Louis MO 63108-1204 Office: Corp for Fin Risk Mgmt 1829 Belt Way Dr Saint Louis MO 63114-5815

LEONARD, KURT JOHN, retired plant pathologist, director; b. Holstein, Iowa, Dec. 6, 1939; s. Elvin Elsworth and Irene Marie (Helkenn) L.; m. Maren Jane Simonsen, May 28, 1961; children: Maria Catherine, Mary Alice, Benjamin Andrew. BS, Iowa State U., 1962; PhD, Cornell U., 1968. Plant pathologist Agrl. Rsch. Svc. USDA, Raleigh, NC, 1968-88, dir. Cereal Disease Lab. U. Minn. St. Paul, 1988—2001. Author: (with others) Annual Review of Phytopathology, 1980; co-editor: Plant Disease Epidemiology, vol. 1, 1986, vol. 2, 1989, Fusarium Head Blight of Wheat and Barley, 2003; editor-in-chief: Phytopathology, 1981-84, Am. Phytopathol. Soc. Press, 1994-97; contbr. over 130 articles to profl. jours., chpts. to books. Fellow Am. Phytopathol. Soc. (coun. 1981-84, 94-97); mem. Am. Mycol. Soc., Internat. Soc. Plant Pathology (councilor 1982-93), Brit. Soc. Plant Pathology, Phi Kappa Phi, Sigma Xi, Gamma Sigma Delta. Achievements include description of new species and genera of plant pathogenic fungi; research on spread of disease through crop mixtures, on relationships between virulence and fitness in plant pathogenic fungi. Office: U Minn Dept Plant Pathology Saint Paul MN 55108

LEONARD, LAURA L., lawyer; b. 1956; AB, U. Calif., Davis, 1978; JD, Loyola U., Chgo., 1983. Bar: Ill. 1983. With Sidley & Austin, Chgo., 1983—, ptnr., 1991—. Lectr. on environ. aspects of bus. trans., including Northwestern U. Kellogg Grad. Sch. Mgmt.; mem. adv. bd. BNA's Environ. Due Digigence Guide. Office: Sidley & Austin Bank One Plz 10 S Dearborn St Chicago IL 60603 Fax: 323-853-7620. E-mail: lleonard@sidley.com.

LEPPARD, RAYMOND JOHN, conductor, musician; b. London, Aug. 11, 1927; arrived in U.S., 1976; s. Albert Victor and Bertha May (Beck) Leppard. MA, U. Cambridge, Eng., 1955; DLitt (hon.), U. Bath, Eng., 1973; PhD (hon.), U. Indpls., 1991, Purdue U., 1992, Butler U., 1994, Wabash Coll., 1995; MusD (hon.), Ind. U., 2001. Fellow Trinity Coll., Cambridge; lectr. music U. Cambridge, 1958—68; music dir. English Chamber Orch., London, 1959—77; prin. condr. BBC Philharm., Manchester, England, 1972—80; condr. symphony orchs. in Am. and Europe, Met. Opera, NYC, Santa Fe Opera, N.Mex., San Francisco Opera, Calif., Covent Garden, Glyndebourne, Paris Opera, Paris; prin. guest condr. St. Louis Symphony Orch., St. Louis, 1984—90; music dir. Indpls. Symphony Orch., 1987—2001, condr. laureate, 2001—. Music dir. European tours, 1993, 97. Rec. artist, composer numerous film scores; author: Authenticity in Music, 1989, Raymond Leppard on Music/An Anthology of Critical and Personal Writings, 1993; composer: (film scores) Lord of the Flies, Laughter in the Dark, Hotel New Hampshire. Decorated Commendatore Della Republica Italiana, comdr. Order Brit. Empire; recipient Gov.'s Arts Award, 1997, Deutsche Schallplattenpreis, Grammy award, Grand Pro/Am Music Prix du Disque, Edison prize. Office: care Michal Schmidt 59 E 54th St Ste 83 New York NY 10022 also: Indianapolis Symphony Orchestra 32 E Washington St Ste 600 Indianapolis IN 46204-3585

LEPPIK, MARGARET WHITE, municipal official; b. Newark, June 5, 1943; d. John Underhill and Laura (Schaefer) White; m. Ilo Elmar Leppik, June 18, 1967; children: Peter, David, Karina. BA, Smith Coll., 1965. Rsch. asst. Wistar Inst., U. Pa., Phila., 1967-68, U. Wis., Madison, 1968-69; mem. Minn. Ho. Reps., St. Paul, 1991—2003, chair higher edn. fin. com.; mem. Met. Coun., 2003—. Active Golden Valley (Minn.) Planning Commn., 1982—90, Golden Valley Bd. Zoning Appeals, 1985—87; commr. Midwest Higher Edn. Commn., 1999—2003; bd. dirs. Minn. Partnership Action Against Tobacco, 1998—2003. Named Citizen of Distinction, Hennepin County Human Svcs. Planning Bd., 1992, Legislator of Yr., U. Minn. Alumni Assn., 1995, 1998—2001, Minn. State U. Student Assn., 1999; recipient Presdl. medallion, North Hennepin CC, 2003. Mem.: LWV (v.p., dir. 1984—90), Hubert H. Humphrey Inst. (adv. coun. 2003—), Nature Conservancy (bd. trustees 2003—), Minn. Opera Assn. (pres. 1986—88), Optimists, Rotary. Republican. Avocations: gardening, bicycling, canoeing. Home: 7500 Western Ave Golden Valley MN 55427-4849 Personal E-mail: peggy@leppik.net.

LERNER, HARRY JONAS, publishing executive; b. Mpls., Mar. 5, 1932; s. Morris and Lena (Liederschneider) Lerner; m. Sharon Ruth Goldman, June 25, 1961 (dec. 1982); m. Sandra Karon Davis, Aug. 24, 1996. Student, U. Mich., 1952, Hebrew U., Jerusalem, 1953-54; BA, U. Minn., 1957. Founder Lerner Publs. Co., Mpls., 1959, chief exec. officer, 1959—; founder Muscle Bound Bindery, Inc., 1967, chief exec. officer, 1967—; founder Carolrhoda Books, Inc., 1969; gen. mgr. Interface Graphics Inc., 1969—, CEO, 1993—. Bd. visitors U. Minn. Press; chmn. N. Loop Bus. Assn., Mpls., 1972—79, Minn. Books Pubs. Roundtable, 1974; del. White House Conf. Libr. and Info. Svcs., 1979; bd. overseers Hill Monastic Manuscript Libr. St. John's U., Collegeville, Minn., 1986—89; bd. dirs., libr. dir. Jewish Cmty. Ctr.; mem. adv. coun. small bus. and labor Fed. Res. Bank, Mpls., 2006—. Pres. Twin City chpt. Am. Jewish Com., 1980—85; bd. dirs. Fgn. Policy Assn. Minn., 1970—71, Children's Book Coun., NYC, 1991—94, Minn. Libr. Assn. Found., 1997; bd. advisors Books for Africa, 1996. Recipient Brotherhood award, NCCJ, 1961, Kay Sexton award, 2002, numerous graphic arts awards, Minn. Innovative Communicator award, Minn. State U., 2004. Mem.: Jewish Hist. Soc., St. Paul-Mpls. Com. Fgn. Affairs, Walker Art Ctr., Mpls. Inst. Art, Daybreakers Breakfast Club (Mpls.), Upper Midwest Ampersand Club. Home: 2215 Willow Ln N Minneapolis MN 55416-3862 Office: Lerner Pub Group 241 1st Ave N Minneapolis MN 55401-1676 Business E-Mail: hjl@lernerbooks.com.

LERNER, RANDOLPH D., finance company executive; s. Alfred and Norma Lerner. BA, Columbia U., 1984, JD, 1987. Bar: N.Y., D.C. With Bear Stearns; ptnr. Securities Advisors, L.P., 1991—2001; dir. MBNA Corp., 1993—2006, vice chmn., 2002, chmn., 2002—06; owner, chmn. Cleve. Browns, 2002—. Chmn. bd. trustees NY Acad. Art, 1998—2003; trustee Hosp. for Spl. Surgery, NYC. Named one of 400 Richest Americans, Forbes, 2006. Mem.: D.C. Bar Assn., N.Y. State Bar Assn. Office: Cleveland Browns Stadium 100 Alfred Lerner Way Cleveland OH 44114

LERNER, WAYNE M., healthcare executive; b. Chicago, Ill. BS, U. Ill.; MHA, U. Mich., DPH, 1988. Adminstrv. positions Rush Presbyterian St. Luke's Med. Ctr., Chicago; pres. Jewish Hosp., St. Louis, 1991—96; developer. exec. v.p. BLC Health System, 1993—96; v.p. Lash Group, Bannockburn, Ill., 1996; pres., CEO Rehab. Inst. Chgo., 1997—. Chmn. Am. Hosp. Assn. Com. of Commissioners; mem. exec. com., bd. of commissioners Joint Commn. on Accreditation of Healthcare Orgn. Fellow Am. Coll. of Healthcare Executives. Office: Rehab Inst Chgo 345 E Superior St Chicago IL 60611-2654 Office Phone: 312-908-2720.

LEROY, SPENCER, III, lawyer; b. Oak Park, Ill., Apr. 13, 1946; s. Spencer and Priscilla LeRoy; m. Barbara LeRoy. AB with high honors, U. Mich., 1968, JD, 1974. Bar: Ill. 1974, US Dist. Ct. No. Dist. Ill. 1974. Assoc. Lord, Bissell & Brook, 1974—82, ptnr., 1982—92; sr. v.p., sec., gen. counsel Old Republic Internat. Corp., Chgo., 1992—. Sgt. US Army, 1970—73. Mem.: Ill. State Bar Assn., ABA, Phi Beta Kappa. Office: Old Republic International Corp 19th Fl 307 N Michigan Ave Chicago IL 60601

LESEWSKI, ARLENE, state legislator, insurance agent; b. Apr. 12, 1936; m. Thomas Lesewski; three children. Student, Southwest State U., Minn. Ins. agent; mem. Minn. Senate from 21st dist., St. Paul, 1993—. Address: 807 Columbine Dr Marshall MN 56258-2406

LESNIK, STEVEN HARRIS, public relations and sports marketing executive; b. Newark, May 1, 1940; s. Seymour J. and Ida (Rosenblatt) L.; m. Madeline Sigfried, June 1, 1963; children: Blaine R., Joshua W. BA, Brown U., 1962; postgrad., Am. U., 1969. Reporter, columnist The Stamford (Conn.) Advocate, 1963-65; press rels. rep. Ins. Info. Inst., NYC, 1966, asst. mgr. Chgo., 1967; ea. corp. rels. mgr. Kemper Ins. Cos., Washington, 1968-72, asst. to pres. for corp. affairs Long Grove, Ill., 1972; dir. communications and pub. affairs Kemper Group, Long Grove, 1973, v.p., 1977; pres. Kemper Sports Mgmt., Northbrook, Ill., 1977; chmn., chief exec. officer Kemper Lesnik Orgn. (now KemperSports Inc.), Northbrook, 1977—. Chief exec. officer Sioux Falls Skyforce; mem. Conf. Bds. Pub. Affairs Rsch. Coun., 1975-79; pres. Insurers Pub. Rels. Coun., 1975-79; bd. dirs. Career Educn. Corp., Hoffman Estates, Ill., 2006-. Vice-chmn. Community Action Com., Montgomery County, Md., 1969-72; mem. Winnetka (Ill.) Caucus Com., 1979; pres. Met. Chgo. Housing Corp., 1974-79; mem. Ill. Econ. Bd., 1990—. Mem. Internat. Pub. Rels. Assn., Pub. Rels. Soc. Am., Nat. Press Club, Publicity Club Chgo., N.Y. Publicity Club, Ill. Profl. Golfers Assn. (adv. com.), Ill. Math. and Sci. Acad. Fund for Advancement of Edn., Internat. Assn. Bus. Communicators. Office: KemperSports Inc 500 Skokie Blvd Ste 444 orthbrook IL 60062-2867

LESSEN, LARRY LEE, federal judge; b. Lincoln, Ill., Dec. 25, 1939; s. William G. and Grace L. (Plunkett) L.; m. Susan Marian Vaughn, Dec. 5, 1964; children: Laura, Lynn, William. BA, U. Ill., 1960, JD, 1962. Bar: Ill. 1962, U.S. Dist. Ct. (ctrl. dist.) Ill. 1964, U.S. Bankruptcy Ct. 1964, U.S. Tax Ct. 1982, U.S. Ct. Appeals (7th cir.) 1981, U.S. Supreme Ct. 1981. Law clk. to presiding justice U.S. Dist. Ct., 1962-64; asst. state's atty. State of Ill., Danville, 1964-67; mng. ptnr. Sebat, Swanson, Banks and Lessen, Danville, 1967-85; judge U.S. Bankruptcy Ct., Danville, 1973-85, U.S. Magistrate, Danville, 1973-84; chief judge U.S. Bankruptcy Ct., Springfield, Ill., 1985-93; U.S. bankruptcy judge Springfield divsn., 1993—. Mem. ABA, FBA, Sangamon County Bar Assn., Vermilion County Bar Assn, Nat. Conf. Bankruptcy Judges (bd. govs. 1994-97), Am. Bankruptcy Inst., Lincoln-Douglas Inn of Cts. Office: US Bankruptcy Ct 235 U S Courthouse 600 E Monroe St Springfield IL 62701-1626

LESTON, PATRICK JOHN, judge; b. Maywood, Ill., May 2, 1948; s. John R. and Lorraine (McQueen) L.; m. Kristine Brzezinski; children: Alison, Adam. BS in Comm., U. Ill., 1970; JD cum laude, Northwestern U., Chgo., 1973. Bar: Ill. 1973, U.S. Dist. Ct. (no. dist.) Ill. 1973, U.S. Ct. Appeals (7th cir.) 1973. Ptnr. Jacobs & Leston, Villa Park, Ill., 1973-79; atty. Patrick J. Leston Ltd., Glen Ellyn, Ill., 1979-89; ptnr. Keck, Mahin & Cate, Oakbrook Terrace, Ill., 1989-95; judge 18th Cir. Ct., DuPage County, Ill., 1995—. Presiding judge juvenile divsn. DuPage County, 2006-, supervising judge juvenile ct.; presenter at profl. confs. Editor Ill. State Bar Assn./Young Lawyers Divsn. Jour., 1983-85. Class rep. Northwestern U. Law Sch. Fund, 1982-88; organizer DuPage County (Ill.) Law Explorers. Recipient Honor award, Am. Acad. Opthalmology, 1999, Sr. Achievement award, 2007, Secretariat award, 2007. Fellow ABA (Ill. del. to ABA/Young Lawyers divsn. assembly 1982-85), Ill. Bar Assn. (chmn. fellows 1991-92, bd. govs. 1990-97, chmn. young lawyers divsn. 1985, chmn. agenda com. 1986, del. to 18th jud. cir. assembly 1982-88), Ill. Judges Assn. (bd. dirs. 1997-2004, chmn. benefits and pension com. 1999—, chmn. govt. affairs 2004—), Ill. Bar Found.

(charter), Am. Bar Found.; mem. DuPage County Bar Assn. (bd. dirs. 1979-84, pres. 1987, chmn. judiciary com. 1988, gen. counsel 1989), Lions, Chi Psi. Avocations: volleyball, skiing, scuba diving, travel, golf. Office: 18th Jud Cir Ct 505 N County Farm Rd Wheaton IL 60187-3907 Office Phone: 630-407-8860. Business E-Mail: patrick.leston@dupageco.org.

LESZINSKE, WILLIAM O., investment company executive; Chief investment officer Texas Commerce Investment Mgmt. Co.; sr. ptnr. and and equity portfolio mgr. Harris Investment Mgmt. Inc., Harris Bankcorp., Inc., Chgo., 1995, pres., chief investment officer, 1966—. Office: Harris Bankcorp Inc 190 S Lasalle St Chicago IL 60603-3410

LETARTE, CLYDE, state legislator; BA, Muskegon C.C., Hope Coll.; MA, Mich. State U. Pres. Jackson C.C.; state rep. Mich., until 1998; mem. appropriations com.; cons. New Horizons Tour and Travel, Jackson, Mich., 1999—. Office: New Horizons Tour and Travel 2727 Springharbor Rd Jackson MI 49201

LETHAM, DENNIS J., wholesale company executive; CFO, exec. v.p. Anixter Inc., Glenview, Ill., 1993—; CFO, sr. v.p. fin. Anixter Internat. Inc., Glenview, Ill., 1995—. Office: Anixter Internat Inc 2301 Patriot Blvd Glenview IL 60025

LETSINGER, ROBERT LEWIS, chemistry professor; Student, Ind. U., 1939-41; BS in Chemistry, MIT, 1943, PhD in Organic Chemistry, 1945; DSc (hon.), Acadia U., Can., 1993. Research assoc. MIT, 1945-46; research chemist Tenn. Eastman Corp., 1946; faculty Northwestern U., 1946—, prof. chemistry, 1959—, chmn. dept., 1972-75, joint prof. biochemistry and molecular biology, 1974—92, Clare Hamilton Hall prof. chemistry, 1986—91, Clare Hamilton Hall prof. emeritus chemistry, 1991—; co-founder Nanosphere Inc., 2000—; adj. prof. Ind. U., 2002—. Med. and organic chemistry fellowship panel NIH, 1966-69, mem. physiol. chemistry review group, 1984, bio-organic and natural products chemistry study sect., 1985, chmn. spl. proposal rev. com., 1992; medicinal chem. A study sect., 1971-75; bd. on chem. scis. and tech. NRC, 1987-90, chmn. site visit NRC rsch. assocs., Frank J. Seiler rsch. lab, 1990; mem. steering com. Inst. Medicine Workshop; mem. AIDS project concept rev. panel, 1987; mem. program rev. divsn. biochem. and biophysics, FDA; mem. spl. rev. com. human genome program, 1992; mem. spl. emphasis panel for nat. coop. drug discovery groups for treatment of HIV infection. Bd. editors: Nucleic Acids Rsch., 1990—2002, Oligonucleotides, 2002—. Recipient Rosenstiel medallion, 1985, MIH merit award, 1988, Arthur C. Cope scholar award, 1993, B.F. Goodrich Collegiate Inventors award, 1997, Humboldt prize, Germany, 1989; Guggenheim Fellow, 1956, JSPS fellow, Japan, 1978. Fellow AAAS, Am. Acad. Arts and Scis., Nat. Acad. Scis., Am. Assn. Arts and Scis.; mem. Am. Chem. Soc. (bd. editors 1969-72, adv. bd. for bioconjugate chemistry 1992—, editl. bd. oligonucleotides, 2004—), Sigma Xi, Phi Lambda Upsilon (hon. mem.). Achievements include development of base for efficient automated synthesis of gene fragments that has facilitated rapid development of molecular biology; introduction of rapid chemical methods for synthesis of DNA segments, including solid phase synthesis and application of phosphite intermediates. Avocations: golf, hiking. Home: 1034 Sassafras Cir Bloomington IN 47408

LETT, PHILIP W., engineering executive; b. Newton, Ala, May 4, 1922; s. Philip Wood Sr. and Lily Octavia (Kennedy) L.; m. Katy Lee Howell, June 26, 1948; children: Kathy, Warren, Lisa. B MechE, Auburn U., 1943; MS in Engring., U. Ala., 1947; PhD MechE, U. Mich., 1950; MS in Indsl. Mgmt., MIT, 1960. Registered profl. engr., Mich. Lab. engr., engring. div. Chrysler Corp., 1950-52, project engr., def. engring. div., 1952-54, chief engr., def. engring. div., 1954-61, operating mgr., def. engring. div., 1961-73, head M1 Tank task force Sterling Heights, Mich., 1973-76; gen. mgr. Sterling Def. div. Chrysler Corp., 1976-79; v.p. engring. Chrysler Def. Inc., Ctr. Line, Mich., 1980-82; v.p. rsch. & engring. Gen. Dynamics Land Systems Div., Ctr. Line, 1982-86, v.p., asst. to gen. mgr., 1986-87; pres. PWL Inc., 1987—. Mem. US delegation to NATO Indsl. Adv. Group. Contbr. articles to tech. jour. and to Internat. Def. Rev. Trustee Judson Ctr., 1989—. Capt. US Army, 1943-46. Decorated Cheonsu medal Republic of Korea; awarded membership US Nat. Acad. Engring., 1984; recipient Outstanding Engr. award Auburn U., 1984, Ben S. Gilmer award Auburn U., 1991, Gold medal Am. Def. Preparedness Assn., 1997; named Disting. Engring. fellow U. Ala. Coll. Engring., 1992; elected to Ala. Engring. Hall of Fame, 1992; Sloan fellow MIT, 1960-61. Mem. Orchard Lake Country Club. Baptist. Home: 1330 Oxford Rd Bloomfield Hills MI 48304-3952 Office: PO Box 2074 Warren MI 48090-2074

LETTS, TRACY, actor, playwright; b. Tulsa, July 4, 1965; s. Dennis and Billie Letts. Ensemble mem. Steppenwolf Theatre Co., Chgo. Writer (plays) Bug, 1996, Killer Joe, 1996, Man From Nebraska, 2003 (Finalist Pulitzer prize for drama, 2004), August: Osage County, 2007 (Pulitzer prize for drama, 2008); actor: (plays) Who's Afraid of Virginia Woolf?, Picasso at the Lapin Agile, Three Days of Rain, The Dazzle, The Glass Menagerie, Glengarry Glen Ross, Homebody/Kabul, The Dresser, Orson's Shadow, 2004, The Pain & the Itch, 2005; (films) Paramedics, 1987, Straight Talk, 1992, US Marshals, 1998, Chicago Cab, 1998, Guinevere, 1999, (TV appearances) Home Improvement, 1995, Seinfeld, 1997, The Drew Carey Show, 1998, Profiler, 2000, The District, 2001; dir.: (plays) Great Men of Science, 21 & 22. Office: Steppenwolf Theatre Co 1650 N Halsted St Chicago IL 60614*

LEUCK, CLAIRE M., state legislator; m. Richard Leuck. Student, Ind. Vo-Tech. Coll., Ind. State U. Clk. Benton County Cir. Ct., Ind., 1974-82, bailiff, sec., 1984-86; state rep. Dist. 25 Ind. Ho. of Reps., 1986—, chmn. agr. com., mem. natural resources, rds. and transp. com., mem. county and twp. elec., agr. and rural devel. com., ranking minority mem. Farmer. Bd. dirs. Coun. for Acad. Excellence-Dollars for Scholars; mem. St. Anne Soc.; mem. dean's adv. coun. Purdue U. Agr. Mem. Am. Legion Aux., No. Dist. Cir. Ct. Clks., Kappa Kappa Kappa. Home: RR 1 Box 203 Fowler IN 47944-9772 Also: 2816 N 400 E Fowler IN 47944-8081

LEUTHOLD, RAYMOND MARTIN, agricultural economics professor; b. Billings, Mont., Oct. 13, 1940; s. John Henry and Grace Irene L.; m. Jane Hornaday, Aug. 20, 1966; children— Kevin, Gregory. Student, Colo. U., 1958-59; BS, Mont. State U., 1962; MS, U. Wis., 1966, PhD, 1968. Faculty U. Ill., Urbana-Champaign, 1967—, now prof. emeritus dept. agrl. econs., T.A. Hieronymus disting. prof. Vis. scholar Stanford U., 1974, Chgo. Mercantile Exch., 1990, 91. Co-author: The Theory and Practice of Futures Markets, 1989; editor: Commodity Markets and Futures Prices, 1979; co-editor: Livestock Futures Research Symposium, 1980. With US Army, 1962—64. Fulbright research scholar Institute de Gestion Internationale Agro-Alimentaire, Cergy, France, 1981 Mem. Am. Econ. Assn., Am. Agrl. Econs. Assn. (Disting. Policy award 1980, Outstanding Instr. award 1986, 88, 90, 92, College Funk award 1993). Office: 305 Mumford Hall 1301 W Gregory Dr Urbana IL 61801-9015

LEVCO, STANLEY M., lawyer; BA in English, U. Mass., 1968; JD, Ind. U., 1971. Bar: Ind. 1972. Chief dep. prosecutor, Posey County, Ind., 1972-75; judge Posey and Gibson County, Ind., 1976-80; dep. prosecutor, pvt. practice Vanderburgh County, Ind., 1981-90; prosecutor, 1991—. Tchr. English jr. h.s., Cleve., 1969-71; lectr. Ind. Prosecutor's Assn., Ind. Coroner's Assn. Author: The Best of Stan Levco, 1986, Problems with Documentary Evidence, 1989, Impeachment: A Practical and Tactical Approach, National College of District Attorneys, 1996; weekly columnist Evansville Press and Evansville Courier, 1981-90. Mem. at. Dist. Attys. Assn., Ind. State Bar Assn. (lectr.), Assn. Govt. Attys. in Capital Litigation. Office: Vanderburgh County Prosecuting Atty 1 NW Martin Luther King Jr Blv Evansville IN 47708-1831

LEVEN, CHARLES LOUIS, economics professor; b. Chgo., May 2, 1928; s. Elie H. and Ruth (Reinach) R.; m. Judith Danoff, 1950 (div. 1970); m. Dorothy Wish, 1970 (div. 1999); children: Ronald L., Robert M., Carol E., Philip W., Alice S. Student, Ill. Inst. Tech., 1945-46, U. Ill., 1947; BS, Northwestern U., 1950, MA, 1957, PhD, 1958. Economist Fed. Res. Bank of Chgo., 1950-56; asst. prof. Iowa State U., 1957-59, U. Pa., 1960—62; assoc. prof. U. Pitts., 1962-65; chmn. dept. econs. Washington U., St. Louis, 1975-80, prof. econs., 1965-91, 2005—, prof. emeritus, 1991—; dir. Inst. Urban and Regional Studies, 1965-85. Disting. prof. U. Mo., St. Louis, 1991—2001; disting. vis. prof. George Mason U., 2007; cons. EEC, Ill. Auditor Gen., Polish Ministry of Planning and Constrn., St. Louis Sch. Bd., Ukrainian Ctr. for Markets and Entrepreneurship, City of Chgo.; mem. internat. adv. bd., com. spatial econ. and regional planning Polish Acad. Sci. Author: Theory and Method of Income and Product Accounts for Metropolitan Areas, 1963, Development Benefits of Water Resource Investment, 1969, An Analytical Framework for Regional Development Policy, 1970, Neighborhood Change, 1976, The Mature Metropolis, 1978. Served with USNR, 1945-46. Ford Found. fellow, 1956, Weiner Sch. Real Estate Fin. and Urban Econ. hon. fellow, 2005; recipient Disting. Alumni award Sullivan HS, Chgo., 2002; grantee Social Sci. Rsch. Coun., 1960, Com. Urban Econ., 1965, NSF, 1968, 73, Merc. Bancorp., 1976, HUD, 1978, NIH, 1985, 2001 Mem.: Am. Econ. Assn., Regional Sci. Assn. (pres. 1964—65, Walter Isard award for disting. scholarship 1995), Western Regional Sci. Assn. (pres. 1974—75, Disting. Fellow 1999), So. Regional Sci. Assn. (Disting. Fellow 1991). Office: Washington U Box 1208 1 Brookings Dr Saint Louis MO 63130-4899 Home: 1111Ontario Apt 1007 Oak Park IL 60302 Personal E-mail: charlessleven@yahoo.com.

LEVENFELD, MILTON ARTHUR, lawyer; b. Chgo., Mar. 18, 1927; s. Mitchell A. and Florence B. (Berman) Levenfeld; m. Iona R. Wishner, Dec. 18, 1949; children: Barry, David, Judith. Ph.B., U. Chgo., 1947, JD, 1950. Bar: Ill. 1950. Ptnr. Altman, Levenfeld & Kanter, Chgo., 1961-64, Levenfeld and Kanter, Chgo., 1964-80, Levenfeld, Eisenberg, Janger & Glassberg, Chgo., 1980-99; of counsel Levenfeld Pearlstein, Chgo., 1999—. Lectr. in fed. taxation. Contbr. articles to profl. jours. Co-gen. chmn. Chgo. Jewish United Fund, 1977, vice chmn. campaign, 1979; gov. mem. Orchestral Assn. Chgo. Symphony Orch.; 1st nat. v.p. legacies and endowments com., 1982—84, chmn.; bd. dirs. Jewish Fedn. Chgo., 1975—84, Spertus Coll. Judaica; mem. vis. com. U. Chgo. Law Sch., 1989—91. With USNR, 1944—45. Recipient Keter Shem Tov award, Jewish Nat. Fund, 1978. Mem.: ABA, Chgo. Bar Assn., Ill. Bar Assn., Am.-Israel C. of C. (pres. Met. Chgo. 1993—95, 1996—98). Home: 866 Stonegate Dr Highland Park IL 60035-5145 Office: 400 Skokie Blvd Ste 700 Northbrook IL 60062 Office Phone: 312-476-7531. Business E-Mail: mlevenfeld@lplegal.com.

LEVENSON, CAROL A., corporate bond research company executive; BA, New Coll.; MA in English, Univ. Chgo., MBA. Sr. bond analyst, portfolio security selection Harris Investment Mgmt. Co., 1984—94; co-founder, dir. rsch. Gimme Credit, Chgo., 1994—; and editor Gimme Credit daily newsletter. Named one of 100 Most Influential Women, Crain's Chicago Bus., 2004. Office: Gimme Credit Ste 210 333 W Wacker Dr Chicago IL 60606 Office Phone: 847-920-9286, 312-781-1036. Business E-Mail: clevenson@gimmecredit.com.

LEVENTHAL, BENNETT LEE, psychiatry and pediatrics educator, academic administrator; b. Chgo., July 6, 1949; s. Howard Leonard and Florence Ruth (Albert) L.; children: Matthew G., Andrew G., Julia G. Student, Emory U., Atlanta, 1967—68; BS, La. State U., New Orleans, 1972, MD, 1974. Diplomate Am. Bd. Psychiatry and eurology in Psychiatry, Am. Bd. Psychiatry and Neurology, Child Psychiatry; lic. physician NC, La., Ill., Va. Undergrad. rsch. assoc. Lab. Prof. William A. Pryor dept. chemistry La. State U., 1968-70; house officer 1 Charity Hosp. at New Orleans, 1974; resident in psychiatry Duke U. Med. Ctr., Durham, NC, 1974-78, chief fellow divsn. dept. psychiatry, 1976-77, chief resident dept. psychiatry, 1977-78, clin. assoc. dept. psychiatry, 1978-80; staff psychiatrist, head psychiatry dept. Joel T. Boone Clinic, Virginia Beach, Va., 1978-80; staff psychiatrist, faculty mem. dept. psychiatry Naval Regional Med. Ctr., Portsmouth, Va., 1978-80; asst. prof. psychiatry and pediats. U. Chgo., 1978-85, dir. Child Psychiatry Clinic, 1978—2005, dir. Child and Adolescent Psychiatry Fellowship tng. program, 1979-88, Irving B. Harris prof. child and adolescent psychiatry, 1998—, emeritus, 2005—, dir. Sonia Shankman Orthogenic Sch., 2002—05; prof. psychiatry, dir. Ctr. Child Mental Health U. Ill., Chgo., 2005—. Psychiat. cons. Caledonia State Prision/Halifax Mental Health Ctr., Tillery, NC, 1976-77, Fed. Correctional Inst., Butner, NC, 1977-78; cons. Norfolk Cmty. Mental health Ctr., 1978-80; adj. prof. psychology, biopsychology, and devel. psychology U. Chgo., 1990, adj. assoc. prof. dept. psychology and com. on biopsychology, 1987-90; meed. dir. Child Life and Family Edn. program Wyler Children's Hosp. of U. Chgo., 1983-95; dir. child and adolescent programs Chgo. Lakeshore Hosp., 1986-2000; Pfizer vis. prof. dept. psychiatry U. PR, 1992; examiner Am. Bd. Psychiatry and Neurology in Gen. Psychiatry and Child Psychiatry, 1982—; mem. steering com. Harris Ctr. for Devel. Studies, U. Chgo., 1983—; mem. com. on evaluation of GAPS project AMA, 1993-97; treas. Chgo. Consortium for Psychiat. Rsch., 1994; pres. Ill. Coun. Child and Adolescent Psychiatry, 1992-94; vis. scholar Hunter Inst. Mental Health and U. New Castle, NSW, Australia, 1995; mem. Gov.'s Panel on Health Svcs., 1993-94; prof. psychiatry & pediats. U. Chgo., 1990-2005, chmn. dept. psychiatry, 1991-98, Irving B. Harris prof. child & adolescent psychiatry, 1998-2004; presenter in field. Mem. editl. bd. Univ. Chgo. Better Health Letter, 1994-96; cons. editor: Jour. Emo tional and Behavioral Disorders, 1992-96; reviewer: Archives of Gen. Psychiatry, 1983—, Biol. Psychiatry, 1983—, Am. Jour. Psychiatry, 1983—, Jour. AMA, 1983—, Jour. Am. Acad. Child and Adolescent Psychiatry, 1983—, Sci., 1983—; book rev. editor Jour. Neuropsychiatry and Clin. Neuroscis., 1989-92, mem. editl. bd., 1989-92; contbr. articles to profl. jours. Lt. comdr. MC USNR, 1978—80. Recipient Crystal Plate award Little Friends, 1994, Individual Achievement award Autism Soc. Am., 1991, Merit award Duke U. Psychiat. Resident's Assn., 1976, Bick award La. Psychiat. Assn., 1974; Andrew W. Mellon Found. faculty fellow U. Chgo., 1983-84; John Dewey lectr. U. Chgo., 1982. Fellow Am. Acad. Child and Adolescent Psychiatry (Outstanding Mentor 1988, dep. chmn. program com. 1979—, chmn. arrangements com. 1979—, new rsch. subcom. for ann. meeting 1986—, mem. work group on rsch. 1989—), Am. Psychiat. Assn. (Falk fellow, mem. Ittleson Award Bd. 1994-97, mem. Am. Psychiat. Assn./Wisniewski Young Psychiatrists Rsch. Award Panel 1994—), Am. Acad. Pediats., Am. Orthopsychiat. Assn.; mem. AAAS, Am. Coll. Psychiatrists, Brain Rsch. Inst., Ill. Coun. Child and Adolescent Psychiatry, Ill. Psychiat. Soc., Soc. for Rsch. in Child Devel., Soc. of Profs. of Child and Adolescent Psychiatry, Soc. Biol. Psychiatry, Nat. Bd. Med. Examiners, Mental Health Assn. Ill. (profl. adv. bd. 1991—), Sigma Xi. Office: Inst for Juvenile Rsch Dept Psychiatry (M/C 747) U Ill at Chgo 1747 W Roosevelt Rd Rm 155 Chicago IL 60608 Office Phone: 312-355-3026. Business E-Mail: bll@uic.edu.

LEVER, ALVIN, health science association administrator; b. St. Louis, Jan. 27, 1939; s. Jack I. and Sabina (Vogel) L.; m. Norine Sue Schwedt, Jan. 27, 1963; children: Daniel Jay, Michael Leonard. BS in Archtl. Scis., Washington U., St. Louis, 1961, BArch, 1963; MA in Applied Psychology, U. Santa Monica, 1992. Registered architect, Mo., Ill. Project designer Sir Basil Spence, Architects, Edinburgh, Scotland, 1963-65; sr. project designer Hellmuth, Obata & Kassabaum, St. Louis, 1965-68, v.p., project mgr., 1968-72; v.p. facility devel. Michael Reese Med. Ctr., Chgo., 1972-74; v.p., gen. mgr. Apelco Internat., Ltd., Northbrook, Ill., 1974-90; dir. membership and fin. Am. Coll. Chest Physicians, Northbrook, 1990-92, exec. dir., 1992-95, exec. v.p., CEO, 1995—. Pub. jour. Chest. Pub. Chest. Bd. dirs. Chest Found., 1997; v.p. Congregation B'nai Tikvah, 1987-91, pres., 1993-95. Mem. Profl. Conv. Mgmt. Assn., Am. Soc. Med. Soc. Execs., Am. Soc. Assn. Execs., Chgo. Soc. Assn. Execs., Chgo. Assn. Healthcare Execs., Alliance for Continuing Med. Edn., Mission Hills Country Club. Avocations: scuba diving, bicycling, travel, golf. Office: Am Coll Chest Physicians 3300 Dundee Rd Northbrook IL 60062-2303 Office Phone: 847-498-8300. E-mail: alever@chestnet.org.

LEVERETT, ALLEN L., energy executive; BS summa cum laude in elec. engring., Vanderbilt U.; MS in elec. engring., Stanford U.; MBA in fin., Auburn U. Various positions in transmission planning, integrated resource planning, startegic planning, wholesale mktg. and fin.; v.p., treas. Southern Co. Svcs.; exec. v.p., CFO Ga. Power Co.; CFO Wis. Energy Corp., Milw., 2003—. Mem.: Ga. Coun. Econ. Edn. (dir.), Energy Ins. Mutual (dir.), Piedmont Pk. Conservancy (resource devel. dir.), Agnes Scott Coll. (trustee), Decatur-DeKalb YMCA (dir.). Office: Wisconsin Energy Corporation PO Box 1331 Milwaukee WI 53201-1331

LEVI, JOHN G., lawyer; b. Chgo., Oct. 9, 1948; s. Edward H. and Kate (Sulzberger) L.; m. Jill Felsenthal, Oct. 7, 1979; children: Benjamin E., Daniel F., Sarah K.H BA honors, U. Rochester, 1969; JD, Harvard U., 1972, LLM, 1973. Bar: Ill. 1973, U.S. Dist. Ct. (no. dist.) Ill. 1973, U.S. Ct. Appeals (7th cir.) 1973, U.S. Supreme Ct. 1977. Ptnr. Sidley Austin LLP, Chgo., 1973—. Chmn. bd. Francis W. Parker Sch., Chgo.; bd. dirs. Chgo. Child Care Soc., U. Chgo. Brain Rsch. Found., Jane Addams Juvenile Ct. Found., Ctr. for Wrongful Convictions, Chgo. Inst. for Psychoanalysis, High Jump Mem. ABA, Ill. Bar Assn., Chgo. Bar Assn., Lawyers Club Chgo Office: Sidley Austin LLP One S Dearborn St Chicago IL 60603

LEVI, PETER STEVEN, municipal official, lawyer; b. Washington, June 3, 1944; s. Kurt and Ruth (Neumann) L.; m. Enid Goldberg, Jan. 26, 1969; children: Joshua, Jeff. BA, Northwestern U., 1966; JD, U. Mo., Kansas City, 1969, LLM in Urban Legal Affairs, 1971. Bar: Mo. 1969. Gen. counsel Mid Am. Regional Coun., Kansas City, 1971-77, exec. dir., 1977-90; pres. Greater Kansas City C. of C., 1990—. Participant internat. local govt. mgmt. exch. program with Israel, Internat. City Mgmt. Assn., 1985-86. Author: Model Subdivision Regulations, 1975; contbr. numerous articles to legal and pub. adminstrn. jours. Bd. dirs. Downtown Coun., Full Employment Coun., City of Fountains; past pres. Kehilath Israel Synagogue. Recipient Pub. Adminstr. of Yr. award Am. Soc. Pub. Adminstrn., 1985, L.P. Cookingham Pub. Adminstrn. award, 1989; Walter Scheiber Regional Leadership award Nat. Assn. Regional Couns., 1990; fellow U.S. Dept. Transp., 1975. Mem. Assn. C.C. Execs., Rotary. Office: Greater Kans City C of C 911 Main St Ste 2600 Kansas City MO 64105-5303 Home: 11512 High Dr Leawood KS 66211-3081 E-mail: levi@kcchamber.com.

LEVIN, ARNOLD MURRAY, social worker, psychotherapist, educator; b. Bklyn., Dec. 26, 1924; s. William and Pauline Levin; m. Elaine M. Zimmerman, Dec. 19, 1946 (dec. Aug. 1971); children: Michael, Nancy Jo Noteman, Amy Louise. BA, U. Mass., 1948; MA, U. Chgo., 1950, PhD, 1975; Cert., Chgo. Inst. Psychoanalysis, 1955. ACSW, LCSW, BCD. Case worker Jewish Family Svcs., Chgo., 1950-53; group therapist Portal House Clinic Alcoholism, Chgo., 1952-55; exec. dir. Family Svc., Mental Health Ctr. So. Cook County, Park Forest, Ill., 1953-60; pvt. practice in social work Chgo., 1960—. Founder, pres. Inst. Clin. Social Work, Chgo., 1979—; bd. dirs. Jewish Childrens Bur., Chgo., 1987—; founder, pres., Ill. Soc. Clin. Social Workers, Chgo., 1971-76; mem. 90 for the 90's, Ill. Author: Private Practice of Psychotherapy, 1983. Sgt. U.S. Army, 1943-46. NIMH grantee, 1971; recipient Gov.'s award, Chgo., 1975, Alumnus of Yr. award U. Chgo., 1976. Mem. Nat. Registry of Health Care Providers in Clin. Social Wk. (bd. dirs. 1985-88), Nat. Fedn. Socs. for Clin. Social Work (founder 1971-75), Am. Acad. of Practice (diplomate, disting. practitioner). Avocations: acting, theater, bicycling.

LEVIN, BURTON, diplomat; b. NYC, Sept. 28, 1930; s. Benjamin and Ida (Geller) L.; m. Lily Lee, Jan. 4, 1960; children: Clifton, Alicia. BA, CUNY, 1952; M Internat. Affairs, Columbia U., 1954; postgrad., Harvard U., 1964; LLD (hon.), Carleton Coll., 1993. Commd. fgn. service officer Dept. State, 1954; counselor/econ. officer Am. Embassy, Taipei, Taiwan, 1954-56, polit. officer, 1969-74; intelligence research specialist Dept. State, Washington, 1956-58, dir. Republic China affairs, 1974-77; polit. officer Am. Embassy, Jakarta, Indonesia, 1959-63, Am. Consulate Gen. Hong Kong, 1965-69, dep. chief mission, 1977-78, consul gen., 1981-86; dep. chief mission Am. Embassy, Bangkok, Thailand, 1978-81; amb. to Burma, 1987-90; dir. Asia Soc. Hong Kong Ctr., 1990-95. Vis. prof. Carleton Coll., 1995; vis. fellow Stanford U., 1974; vis. lectr. Harvard U., 1986, Carleton Coll., 1994; bd. dirs. Mansfield Found., Noble Resources Ltd.; mem. coun., chmn. emeritus Hopkins-Nanjing U. Ctr. for Chinese and Am. Studies Johns Hopkins U. Mem. Am. Fgn. Service Assn. Clubs: Am., Hong Kong Country. Home: 314 2nd St E Northfield MN 55057-2204 Office Phone: 507-645-0086. Personal E-mail: burtlevin@comcast.net.

LEVIN, CARL MILTON, senator; b. Detroit, June 28, 1934; m. Barbara Halpern, 1961; children: Kate, Laura, Erica. BA in Polit. Sci., Swarthmore Coll., 1956; LLB, Harvard U., 1959. Bar: Mich. 1959. Ptnr. Grossman, Hyman & Grossman, Detroit, 1959-64; asst. atty. gen., gen. counsel Mich. Civil Rights Commn., 1964-67; chief appellate defender City of Detroit, 1968-69, mem. coun., 1970-73, pres. coun., 1974-77; ptnr. Schlussel, Lifton, Simon, Rands & Kaufman, 1971—73, Jaffe, Snider, Raitt, Garratt & Hever, 1978—79; US Senator from Mich., 1979—. Past instr. Wayne State U., U. Detroit; chmn. Armed Svcs. Com., Homeland Security and Govtl. Affairs Com., Com. on Small Bus., Senate Dem. Steering & Coordination Com., Senate Select Com. on Intelligence, Congressional-Executive Commn. on China. Mem. ABA, Mich. Bar Assn., Detroit Bar Assn., Democrat. Jewish. Office: US Senate 269 Russell Senate Ofc Bldg Washington DC 20510-2202 also: Patrick V McNamara Fed Bldg Rm 1860 477 Michigan Ave Detroit MI 48226-2576 Office Phone: 202-224-6221, 313-226-6020. Office Fax: 202-224-1388, 313-226-6948. E-mail: senator@levin.senate.gov.

LEVIN, CHARLES EDWARD, lawyer; b. Chgo., Oct. 6, 1946; m. Barbara Serwer, Dec. 28, 1975. BA with high honor, DePaul U., 1968; JD cum laude, Northwestern U., Chgo., 1971. Bar: Ill. 1971. Asst. instr. legal writing and rsch. Northwestern U. Law Sch., 1970-71; assoc. D'Ancona & Pflaum, Chgo., 1971-76, ptnr., 1977-90, Jenner & Block, Chgo., 1990-2000, McDermott, Will & Emery, Chgo., 2000—. Governing bd. Comml. Fin. Assn. Edn. Found., 1990-2000; asst. instr. legal writing, rsch. Northwestern U., 1970-71. Mem. bd. editors Northwestern U. Law Rev., 1970-71. Aux. bd. Chgo. Architecture Found., 1989-99; founders leadership coun. C omml. Fin. Assn. Edn. Found., NY. Mem. ABA (bus. sect. 1992—), Chgo. Bar Assn. (vice chmn. architecture and law com. 1974-75, vice chmn. divsn. D, mem. exec. com. fed. tax com. 1983-84, comml. fin. and trans. com. 1990—, Article 9 drafting subcom.), East Bank Club Chgo. Avocations: acquisition fine arts, support arts organizations, jogging. Office: McDermott Will & Emery LLP 227 W Monroe St Ste 4400 Chicago IL 60606-5016

LEVIN, CHARLES LEONARD, state supreme court justice; b. Detroit, Apr. 28, 1926; s. Theodore and Rhoda (Katzin) L.; children: Arthur, Amy, Fredrick. BA, U. Mich., 1946, LLB, 1947; LLD (hon.), Detroit Coll. Law, 1980. Bar: Mich. 1947, N.Y. 1949, U.S. Supreme Ct. 1953, D.C. 1954. Pvt. practice law, NYC, 1948-50, Detroit, 1950-66; ptnr. Levin, Levin, Garvett & Dill, Detroit, 1951-66; judge Mich. Ct. Appeals, Detroit, 1966-73; assoc. justice Mich. Supreme Ct., 1973-96. Mem. Mich. Law Revision Commn., 1966 Trustee Marygrove Coll., 1971-77, chmn., 1971-74; mem. vis. coms. to Law Schs., U. Mich., U. Chgo., 1977-80, Wayne State U. Mem. Am. Law Inst. Office: Mich Supreme Ct 500 Woodward Ave Fl 20 Detroit MI 48226-5498

LEVIN, GEOFFREY ARTHUR, botanist; b. Los Alamos, N.Mex., Dec. 7, 1955; s. Jules Samuel and Jane Walden (Settle) L.; children: Tobias, Madeline; m. Lori E. Davis, 2001. BA, Pomona Coll., 1977; MS, U. Calif., Davis, 1980, PhD, 1984. Asst. prof. Ripon (Wis.) Coll., 1982-84; curator, chmn. botany dept. San Diego Natural History Mus., 1984-93; lectr. U. San Diego, 1984-90; asst. profl. scientist Ill. Natural History Survey, Champaign, 1994-96, assoc. profl. scientist to profl. scientist, dir. Ctr. for Biodiversity, 1996—2006; dir. Divsn. Biodiversity and Ecol. Entomology, 2006—. Adj. asst. prof. dept. plant biology U. Ill., 1995—; rsch. assoc. Mo. Bot. Garden, 1994—. Contbr. articles to jours. in field. Bd. dirs. Fond du Lac Audubon Soc., 1983-84, San Diego Audubon Soc., 1986-87; pres. Summit Unitarian Universalist Fellowship, El Cajon, Calif., 1989-91; treas. Unitarian Universalist Ch., Urbana, Ill., 1996-98, moderator, 1998-2000. Recipient Jesse M. Greenman award. Mo. Bot. Garden, 1987; NSF grad. fellow, 1977-81. Mem. Am. Inst. Biol. Scis., Am. Soc. Plant Taxonomists, Bot. Soc. Am., Soc. Systematic Biologists, Calif. Bot. Soc. (bd. editors 1992-95), Phi Beta Kappa, Sigma Xi. Democrat. Office: Illinois Natl History Survey Ctr Biodiversity 1816 S Oak St Ste A Champaign IL 61820-6954 Business E-Mail: glevin@inhs.uiuc.edu.

LEVIN, JACK S., lawyer; b. Chgo., May 1, 1936; s. Frank J. and Judy G. (Skerball) L.; m. Sandra Sternberg, Aug. 24, 1958; children: Lisa, Laura, Leslie, Linda. BS summa cum laude, Northwestern U., 1958; LL.B. summa cum laude, Harvard U., 1961. Bar: Ill. 1961; C.P.A. (gold medalist), Ill., 1958. Law clk. to chief judge U.S. Ct. of Appeals 2d Circuit, NYC, 1961-62; asst. for tax matters to Solicitor Gen. of U.S., Washington, 1965-67; assoc. law firm Kirkland & Ellis, Chgo., 1962-65, ptnr., 1967—. Frequent lectr. legal aspects of pvt. equity and venture capital transactions, mergers, acquistions, buyouts, workouts, fed. income tax matters; vis. com. Harvard Law Sch., 1987-93, lectr., 1997—; lectr. Law Sch. U. Chgo., 1988—. Author book on structuring venture capital, pvt. equity and entrepreneurial transactions; co-author 4-volume treatise on mergers, acquisitions and buyouts; case editor Harvard Law Rev., 1959-61; contbr. numerous articles to legal jours. and chpts. to law books. Parliamentarian Winnetka (Ill.) Town Meetings, 1974-83, 89, 93-96; chmn. nat. fundraising drives Harvard Law Sch., 1985-86, 90-91, 95-96, 2001, 03-06, chmn. lawyer's divsn. Jewish United Fund Chgo., 1993-95. Recipient Learned Hand award, Am. Jewish Com., 2000, Fellows award, Ill. Venture Capital Assn., 2002, Chambers Internat. Lifetime Achievement award, 2005, Humanitarian award, Ill. Holocaust Mus., 2005. Mem. ABA (chmn. subcom. 1968-79), Fed. Bar Assn., Chgo. Bar Assn. (tax sect. exec. com. 1985-00), Am. Jewish Com. (nat. bd. govs.

2005—, Midwest bd. dirs., exec. com. 2003-), Am. Coll. Tax Consel, Mid-Am. Club (bd. dirs. 1985-88), Birchwood Club (pres. 1980-82). Home: 985 Sheridan Rd Winnetka IL 60093-1558 Office: Kirkland & Ellis 200 E Randolph St 57th Fl Chicago IL 60601-6608 Office Phone: 312-861-2004. Business E-Mail: jlevin@kirkland.com.

LEVIN, LAWRENCE DANIEL, lawyer; b. Chgo., May 10, 1959; s. Sandra Morrison, June 22, 1986; children: Phillip David, Laura Michelle. BS in Accountancy, U. Ill., 1981, JD, 1985. Bar: Ill. 1985, U.S. Dist. Ct. (no. dist.) Ill. 1985. Ptnr. Katten Muchin Rosenman LLP, Chgo., 1985—. Mem. ABA, Chgo. Bar Assn. (chmn. securities law com. 1996-97). Office: Katten Muchin Rosenman LLP 525 W Monroe St Ste 1900 Chicago IL 60661-3693

LEVIN, MARVIN EDGAR, physician; b. Terre Haute, Ind., Aug. 11, 1924; s. Benjamin A. and Bertha Levin; m. Barbara Yvonne Symes; 3 children. BA, Washington U., St. Louis, 1947; MD, Washington U., 1951. Diplomate Am. Bd. Internal Medicine. Intern Barnes Hosp., St. Louis, 1951-52, asst. resident in internal medicine, 1952-53; Nat. Polio Found. fellow in metabolism and endocrinology Sch. Medicine, Washington U., St. Louis, 1953-55; adj. prof. medicine Washington U. Sch. Medicine, St. Louis, 1980—98. Vis. prof. endocrinology and diabetes People's Republic of China, 1982, Jakarta, Indonesia, Cairo, 92, Taipei, 94, Malvern, England, 96; med. dir. Harry and Flora D. Freund Meml. Found., adj. prof. medicine endocrine, diabetes and metabolism, 2000—. Co-author: Levin and O'Neal's The Diabetic Foot, 7th edit., 2007; co-editor: The Uncomplicated Guide to Diabetes Complication, 3d edit., 2008; contbr. articles to profl. jours., book chpts. Recipient Disting. Alumni award, Washington U., 1989, Arts and Scis. Disting. award, 1998. Fellow ACP, Soc. Vascular Medicine and Biology, Am. Coll. Endocrinology; mem. AMA, Am. Diabetes Assn. (nat. bd. dirs. 1984-86, chmn. publ. com. 1986-87, bd. dirs. Mo. chpt. 1987-93, editor in chief Clin. Diabetes 1988-93, co-editor Diabetes Spectrum 1988-93, Outstanding Clinician award 1979, Outstanding Physician Educator award 1991), Am. Dietetic Assn. (hon., Marvin E. Levin, MD Scholarship Program for rsch. in diabetic lower extremity disease named for him), St. Louis Clin. Diabetes Assn. (pres. 1965-66), Am. Thyroid Assn., Endocrine Soc., St. Louis Soc. Internal Medicine, St. Louis Internist Club (pres. 1972), Sigma Xi, Alpha Omega Alpha. Avocations: golf, art. Office: 732 Fairfield Lake Dr Town And Country MO 63017-5928 Office Phone: 314-469-6918. Personal E-mail: blevin0001@aol.com.

LEVIN, MICHAEL DAVID, lawyer; b. Chgo., Oct. 11, 1942; s. Joseph F. and Libbie (Landman) L.; children: Victoria, David, Elizabeth, Emma, Madeline; m. Carol A. McErlean, Oct. 10, 1993. AB, U. Mich., 1964, JD, 1967. Bar: Ill. 1967. Assoc. Arnstein, Gluck, Weitzenfeld & Minow, Chgo., 1967-73, ptnr., 1973-81, Latham & Watkins, Chgo., 1982-95; sr. v.p., sec. & gen. counsel Sears Roebuck & Co., Hoffman Estates, Ill., 1996-98; ptnr. Latham & Watkins, 1998—. Mem. ABA, Chgo. Bar Assn. (chmn. securities law 1982-83), Met. Club. Republican. Jewish. Office: Sears Roebuck & Co 5800 Sears Tower Chicago IL 60684-0001

LEVIN, SANDER MARTIN, congressman, lawyer; b. Detroit, Sept. 6, 1931; s. Saul R. and Bess (Levinson) L.; m. Victoria Schlafer, 1957; four children. BA, U. Chgo., 1952; MA in Internat. Relations, Columbia U., 1954; LLB, Harvard U., 1957. Atty. priv. practice, 1957—64; supr. Oakland County Bd. Suprs., Mich., 1961-64; mem. Mich. Senate, 1965-70; atty. priv. practice, 1971—77; fellow Kennedy Sch. Govt., Inst. Politics, Harvard U., Cambridge, Mass., 1975; asst. adminstr. Agency for Internat. Develop., Washington, 1977-81; mem. U.S. Congresses from 12th (formerly 17th) Mich dist., 1983—; mem. ways and means com. Adj. prof. law Wayne State U., Detroit, 1971—74. Chmn. Mich. Dem. Com., 1968-69; Dem. Candidate for Gov., 1970, 74. Recipient Public Policy award, Am. Soc. Tng. and Devel. award, 1997. Democrat. Jewish. Office: US House Reps 2300 Rayburn House Office Bldg Washington DC 20515-0001 also: District Office 27085 Gratiot Ave Roseville MI 48066-2947 Office Phone: 202-225-4961, 586-498-7122. Office Fax: 202-226-1033, 586-498-7123.

LEVINE, DONALD NATHAN, sociologist, educator; b. New Castle, Pa., June 16, 1931; s. Abe and Rose (Gusky) L.; m. Joanna Bull, Nov. 6, 1955 (div. 1967); children: Theodore, William; m. Ruth Weinstein, Aug. 26, 1967; 1 child, Rachel. AB, U. Chgo., 1950, MA, 1954, PhD, 1957; postgrad., U. Frankfurt, Germany, 1952-53; PhD (hon.), Addis Ababa U., Ethiopia, 2004. Asst. prof. sociology U. Chgo., 1962-65, assoc. prof., 1965-73, prof., 1973-86, dean of Coll., 1982-87, Peter B. Ritzma prof., 1986—; founder, pres. Aiki Extensions, 1998—. Author: Wax and Gold: Tradition and Innovation in Ethiopian Culture, 1965, Georg Simmel on Individuality and Social Forms, 1971, Greater Ethiopia: The Evolution of a Multiethnic Society, 1974, Simmel and Parsons: Two Approaches to the Study of Society, 1980, The Flight from Ambiguity: Essays in Social and Cultural Theory, 1985, Visions of the Sociological Tradition, 1995, Powers of the Mind: The Reinvention of Liberal Learning in America, 2006; editor: The Heritage of Sociology series, 1988—. Mem. adv. bd. Ethiopian Cmty. Assn. Chgo., 1993—. Recipient Quantrell award, U. Chgo., 1971, Cert. of award, Ethiopian Rsch. Coun., 1993, Disting. Contbn. to Undergrad. Tchg. award, Amoco Found., 1996, Outstanding Cmty. Support award, Ethiopian Cmty. Assn. Chgo., 2000; fellow, Guggenheim Found., 1980, Ctr. Advanced Study in Behavioral Scis., 1980—81. Mem. Internat. Soc. Comparative Study Civilization, Am. Sociol. Assn. (chair theory sect. 1996-97). Jewish. Office: U Chgo 1126 E 59th St Chicago IL 60637-1580 Business E-Mail: dlok@uchicago.edu.

LEVINE, JAY, newscaster; Degree in Engring., Cornell U. News and sports anchor, reporter WHCU-AM/FM, Ithaca, NY; news reporter WCAU-AM, Phila., 1972—74; reporter WLS-TV, Chgo., 1974—90; weekend anchor and reporter WBBM-TV, Chgo., 1990—91, chief corr., 1991—98, 2001—, anchor early morning news, 1998—2001. Recipient AP honors, UPI honors, 4 Chgo. Emmys, Nat. RTNDA award, Jacob Scher award Investigative Reporting. Avocation: golf. Office: WBBM-TV 630 N McClurg Ct Chicago IL 60601

LEVINE, LAURENCE HARVEY, lawyer; b. Cleve., Aug. 23, 1946; s. Theodore and Celia (Chaikin) Levine; m. Mary M. Conway, May 13, 1978; children: Abigail, Adam, Sarah. BA cum laude, Case Western Res. U., 1968; JD, Northwestern U., 1971. Bar: Ill. 1971, U.S. Dist. Ct. (no. dist.) Ill. 1972, U.S. Ct. Appeals (6th, 7th, 10th, 11th and D.C. cirs.), U.S. Ct. Claims 1997, U.S. Ct. Appeals (fed. cir.) 2000. Law clk. to presiding judge U.S. Ct. Appeals (6th cir.), Detroit, 1971-72; assoc. Kirkland & Ellis, Chgo., 1972-76; ptnr. Latham & Watkins, Chgo., 1976—. Bd. editors Northwestern Law Rev., 1968-71. Mem. ABA, Chgo. Bar Assn., Mid-Am. Club. Office: Latham & Watkins Sears Tower Ste 5800 Chicago IL 60606-6306 E-mail: laurence.levine@lw.com.

LEVINE, NORMAN M., academic administrator; b. Chgo., 1943; BS Engring., Ill. Inst. Tech., 1964; MBA, Marquette U., 1969. Sr. v.p., CFO DeVry Inc., Oakbrook Terrace, 2001—. Mem. Fin. Execs. Internat. Office: DeVry Inc Ste 1000 One Tower Ln Oakbrook Terrace IL 60181 Office Phone: 630-574-1906. Business E-Mail: nlevine@devry.com.

LEVINE, PETER S., corporate lawyer; b. Cleve., Jan. 15, 1959; BA with honors, Northwestern U., 1981; JD, U. Mich., 1984. Bar: Ohio 1984. Assoc. Benesch, Friedlander, Coplan & Aronoff, 1984-85; trial atty. Equal Employment Opportunity Commn., 1985-88; law instr. Case We. Res. U., 1988-90; trustee Cleve. Legal Aid Soc., 1988-90; counsel TRW Inc., Washington, Mich., 1990-93, sr. counsel, 1993-99, v.p., asst. gen. counsel, 1999—. Mem.: ABA, Ohio State Bar Assn., Cleve. Bar Assn. Office: TRW Inc 4505 26 Mile Rd Washington MI 48094-2600

LE VINE, VICTOR THEODORE, retired political science professor; b. Berlin, Dec. 6, 1928; came to U.S., 1938; s. Maurice and Hildegard (Hirschberg) LeV.; m. Nathalie Jeanne Christian, July 19, 1958; children: Theodore, Nicole. BA, UCLA, 1950, MA, 1958, PhD, 1961. Research assoc. UCLA, 1958-60; prof., head dept. polit. sci. U. Ghana, Legon, 1969-71; Fulbright prof. U. Yaounde, Cameroon, 1981-82; prof. polit. sci. Washington U., St. Louis, 1961—2003, prof. emeritus, 2003—. Cons. U.S. Dept. State, Dept. Def., 1971—; lectr. USIA, 1981—; mem. U.S. Nat. Commn. UNESCO, 1964; dir. Office Internat. Studies, Washington U., 1975-76; vis. lectr. Fudan U., U. Nanjing (China), 1987, Ibn Saud and King Abdulazziz Univs., Saudi Arabia, 1990; mem. Carter Ctr. Internat. monitoring team to Ghana nat. elections, 1992; vis. prof. Hebrew U., Jerusalem, 1978, U. Tex., Austin, 1980, Sabanci U., Turkey, 2003, Athens U., Greece, 2003. Author: Cameroons: Mandate to Independence, 1964, 70, Cameroon Federal Republic, 1971, Political Corruption: Ghana, 1975, (with Timothy Luke) Arab-African Connection, 1979; (with Heidenheimer and Johnston) Political Corruption: A Handbook, 1990; Conceptualizing Ethnicity and Ethnic Conflict: A Controversy Revisited, 1997 Paraspolitics: Mapping The Terrain of Informal Politics, 2002, Politics in Francophone Africa, 2004. Mem., dir. UN Assn., St. Louis, 1964-74; mem. Coun. on World Affairs, 1969-2000; pres. Ctr. for Internat. Understanding, 1988-2000. With U.S. Army, 1951-54. Ford. Found. fellow Cameroon, 1960-61; Hoover Instn. fellow, 1974; Lester Martin fellow Truman Instn., Jerusalem, 1978; Fulbright lectr. U.S. Fulbright Commn., Yaounde, Cameroon, 1981-82, Greece and Turkey, 2003. Mem. Am. Polit. Sci. Assn., African Studies Assn., Mideast Studies Assn., Midwest Polit. Sci. Assn., Mo. Polit. Sci. Assn. Office: Washington U Dept Polit Sci Saint Louis MO 63130 Office Phone: 314-935-5867. Business E-Mail: vlevine@wustl.edu.

LEVINGS, THERESA LAWRENCE, lawyer; b. Kansas City, Mo., Oct. 24, 1952; d. William Youngs and Dorothy (Neer) Frick; m. Darryl Wayne Levings, May 25, 1974; children: Leslie Page, Kerry Dillon. BJ, U. Mo., 1973; JD, U. Mo., Kansas City, 1979. Bar: Mo. 1979, U.S. Dist. Ct. (we. dist.) Mo. 1979, U.S. Ct. Appeals (8th cir.) 1982, U.S. Ct. Appeals (10th cir.) 1986, U.S. Dist. Ct. (ea. dist.) Mo. 1989, U.S. Dist. Ct. Kans. 1995. Copy editor Kansas City Star, 1975-78; law clk. to judge Mo. Supreme Ct., Jefferson City, 1979-80; from assoc. to ptnr. Morrison & Hecker, Kansas City, 1980-94; founding ptnr. Badger & Levings, L.C., Kansas City, 1994—. Mem. fed. practice com. U.S. Dist. Ct. (we. dist.), 1990-95; mem. fed. adv. com. U.S. Ct. Appeals (8th cir.), 1994-97, Kans. 2006, U.S. Supreme Ct. 2006. Mem. ABA (house dels., 2006—), Mo. Bar (bd. govs. 1990—03, pres. 2001-02), Assn. Women Lawyers Greater Kansas City (pres. 1986-87, Woman of Yr. 1993), Kansas City Met. Bar Assn. (chair civil practice and procedure com. 1988-89, chair fed. practice com. 1990-91, Inns of Court (master 1996-2000, 2002-06). Office: Badger & Levings LC Ste 1920 920 Main St Kansas City MO 64105 Office Phone: 816-421-2828. Business E-Mail: tlevings@badgerlevings.com.

LEVI-SETTI, RICCARDO, physicist, director; b. Milan, July 11, 1927; married; 2 children. PhD Degree in Physics, U. Pavia, Italy, 1949; Libera Docenza in Physics, U. Rome, 1955. Asst. prof. U. Pavia, Italy, 1949-51; rsch. mem. Nat. Inst. for Nuclear Rsch. U. Milan, 1951-56; rsch. assoc. Enrico Fermi Inst. U. Chgo., 1956-57, asst. prof., 1957-62, assoc. prof., 1962-65, prof. physics, 1965—, emeritus prof. physics, 1992—. Hon. rsch. assoc. Field Mus. Natural History, Chgo., 1976—. Author: Trilobites, 1975, 1993. Decorated Commendatore dell'Ordine al Merito (Italy); John Simon Guggenheim fellow, 1963, Angelo della Riccia fellow Italian Phys. Soc., 1954. Fellow Am. Phys. Soc.; mem. Phi Beta Kappa. Office: U Chgo Enrico Fermi Inst 5640 S Ellis Ave Chicago IL 60637-1433

LEVIT, WILLIAM HAROLD, JR., lawyer; b. San Francisco, Feb. 8, 1938; s. William Harold and Barbara Janis Kaiser L.; m. Mary Elizabeth Webster, Feb. 13, 1971; children: Alison Jones Baumler, Alexandra Bradley Kovacevich, Laura Elizabeth Fletcher, Amalia Elizabeth Webster Todryk, William Harold, III. BA magna cum laude, Yale U., 1960; MA Internat. Rels., U. Calif., Berkeley, 1962; LLB, Harvard U., 1967. Bar: N.Y. 1968, Calif. 1974, Wis. 1979. Fgn. service officer Dept. State, 1962-64; assoc. Davis Polk & Wardwell, NYC, 1967—73; assoc. ptnr. Hughes Hubbard & Reed, NYC., L.A., 1973-79; sec. and gen. counsel Rexnord Inc., Milw., 1979-83; ptnr., chair internat. practice group, loss prevention ptnr., former dir and chair litigation practice group Godfrey & Kahn, Milw., 1983—. Substitute arbitrator Iran-U.S. Claims Tribunal, The Hague, 1984-88; lectr. Practicing Law Inst., ABA, 7th Cir. Bar Assn., Nat. Assn. Corp. Dirs., Calif. Continuing Edn. of Bar, State Bar of Wis.; trustee State of Wis. Investment Bd., 2003—. Chmn. Bd. Ad Oversight Supreme Ct. Wis. Office Lawyer Regulation, 2000—06; bd. dirs. Wis. Humane Soc., 1980—90, pres., 1986—88; bd. dirs. Vis. Nurse Corp., Milw., 1980—90, chmn., 1985—87; bd. dirs. Vis. Nurse Found., 1986—95, chmn., 1986—91; bd. dirs. Aurora Health Care Inc., 1988—93, Aurora Health Care Ventures, 1993—2004, chair, 1998—2000, 2002—03; trustee Columbia Coll. Nursing, 1992—, chair, 2002—04; trustee Mt. Mary Coll., 2002—04; dir. adv. bd. Med. Coll. Wis. Cardiovasc. Ctr., 1994—, chmn., 1999—2002; rep. Assn. Yale Alumni, 1976—79, 1981—84, 1990—93; pres. Yale Club So. Calif., 1977—79; neutral advisor panel, gen. counsel, franchise and ins. panels Internat. Inst. for Conflict Prevention and Resolution. Ford Found. fellow, U. Pa., 1960—61, NDEA fellow, U. Calif., Berkeley, 1961—62. Fellow: Wis. Law Found., Am. Bar Found., Chartered Inst. Arbitrators (London) (chartered arbitrator); mem.: ABA, Internat. C. of C. (arbitration panel), Am. Arbitration Assn. (comml., internat., large complex case, and mediation panels), Inst. Jud. Adminstrn., Am. Soc. Internat. Law, N.Am. Coun. London Ct. of Internat. Arbitration, N.Y. Stock Exch. (panel arbitrators 1988—), Nat. Assn. Security Dealers (panel arbitrators 1988—), Am. Br. Internat. Law Assn., Bar Assn. 7th Cir. (pres. 2002—03), State Bar Wis. (dir. internat. bus. transactions sect. 1985—92, dist. 2 Wis. Supreme Ct. bd. attys. profl. responsibility com. 1985—94, chmn. 1993—94), L.A. County Bar Assn. (ethics com. 1976—79), State Bar Calif. (com. on continuing edn. of bar 1977—79), Assn. Bar City N.Y., Am. Soc. Corp. Secs. (dir. 1981—92, pres. Wis. chpt. 1982—83), Am. Law Inst., Mountain Lake Club, Milw. Athletic Club, Town Club, Phi Beta Kappa. Office: 780 N Water St Ste 1200 Milwaukee WI 53202-3512 Office Phone: 414-273-3500. Business E-Mail: wlevit@gklaw.com.

LEVITT, SEYMOUR HERBERT, radiologist, educator; b. Chgo., July 18, 1928; s. Nathan E. Levitt and Margaret (Chizever) D.; m. Phillis Jeanne Martin, Oct. 31, 1952 (div. Oct. 1981); children: Mary Jeanne, Jennifer Gaye, Scott Hayden; m. Solveig I. Ostberg, Feb. 6, 1983. BA, U. Colo., 1950, MD, 1954, DSc (hon.), 1997. Diplomate Am. Bd. Radiology. Intern Phila. Gen. Hosp., 1954-55; resident in radiology U. Calif. at San Francisco Med. Center, 1957-61; instr. radiation therapy U. Mich., Ann Arbor, 1961-62, U. Rochester, NY, 1962-63; asso. prof. radiology U. Okla., Oklahoma City, 1963-66; prof. radiology, chmn. div. radiotherapy Med. Coll. Va., Richmond, 1966-70; prof., head dept. therapeutic radiology U. Minn., Mpls., 1970—99. Cons. in field. Exec. bd. Am. Joint Com. for End Result Reporting and Cancer Staging; com. radiation oncology studies Nat. Cancer Inst.; trustee Am. Bd. Radiology, 1977-89; chmn. bd. dirs. Found. for Rsch. and Edn.; fgn. adj. prof. Karolinska Inst., Stockholm, 2002. Bd. dirs., mem. exec. com. Am. Cancer Soc., 1990-95. With M.C., AUS, 1955-57. Recipient Disting. Svc. award U. Colo., 1988, Gold Medal award Gilbert Fletcher Soc., 1987, Silver and Gold award Med. Sch., U. Colo., 1992. Fellow: Am. Soc. Therapeutic Radiologists (exec. bd. 1974—78, pres. 1978—79, chmn. bd. 1979—80, Gold medal 1991), Am. Coll. Radiology (bd. chancellors, Gold medal 1995), Royal Coll Radiology (hon.); mem.: Am. Soc. Clin. Oncology, Soc. Nuclear Medicine, Internat. Soc. Radiation Oncology (pres. 1981—85), Soc. Chmn. Acad. Radiation Oncology Programs (pres. 1974—76), German Soc. Radiation Oncology (hon.), European Cong. Radiology (hon.), German Soc. Radiology (hon.), Am. Roentgen Ray Soc., Am. Cancer Soc. (pres. Minn. divsn. 1979—80, nat. bd., exec. com.), Am. Assn. Cancer Rsch., Radiol. Soc. N.Am. (bd. dirs. 1991—2000, chmn. bd. dirs. 1997—98, pres.-elect 1998, pres. 1999—, Gold medal 2004), Am. Radium Soc. (sec. 1981—83, pres. 1983—84, Janeway medal 1989), Alpha Omega Alpha, Sigma Xi, Phi Beta Kappa.

LEVMORE, SAUL, dean, law educator; b. 1953; BA, Columbia Coll., 1973, PhD, 1978; JD, Yale U., 1980; LLD (hon.), Ill. Inst. Tech. Chgo.-Kent Law Sch., 1995. Bar: Va. 1983. Dean Jonathan Edwards Coll. Yale U., 1979-80; asst. prof. U. Va., Charlottesville, 1980-84; prof. U. Va., Charlottesville, 1984—98, Brokaw prof. of law; William B. Graham prof. law U. Chgo. Law Sch., 1998—, dean, 2001—. Lectr. econs. Yale U., 1976-80, vis. prof., 1986-87; vis. prof. Harvard U., 1990-91, U. Chgo., 1993. Author: (book) Superstrategies for Puzzles and Games, 1981. Recipient Alumni Assn. Teaching Award, U. Va., 1984, Traynor Award, 1997. Mem.: Am. Law Deans Assn. (pres.), Am. Acad. of Arts and Sciences. Office: U Chgo Law Sch 1111E 60th St Chicago IL 60637 Office Phone: 773-702-9590. Office Fax: 773-702-0730. Business E-Mail: s-levmore@uchicago.edu.

LEVY, DEBORAH, security company executive; b. Chgo. d. Sam and Ruth Gadlin; m. Barry W. Levy (dec.); children: Scott B., Todd B. Student, So. Ill. U. Exec. v.p., sec., officer, dir. Levy Security Corp., Chgo., until 1994, chair, CEO, 1994—. Mem. Women Bus. Enterprise Initiative (Mem. of Yr. award 1997), Nat. Assn. Women Bus. Owners, Am. Soc. Indsl. Security. Achievements include being listed in Working Woman 500 Magazine. Office: Levy Security Corp Ste 1200 8750 W Bryn Mawr Ave Chicago IL 60631-3560 Home Phone: 847-392-0343; Office Phone: 773-867-9204. Business E-Mail: dlevy@levysecurity.com.

LEVY, DONALD HARRIS, chemistry professor; b. Youngstown, Ohio, June 30, 1939; s. Gabriel and Minnie (Lerner) L.; m. Susan Louise Miller, June 14, 1964; children— Jonathan G., Michael A., Alexander B. BA, Harvard U., 1961; PhD, U. Calif.-Berkeley, 1965. Asst. prof. chemistry U. Chgo., 1967-74, assoc. prof., 1974-78, prof., 1978—, chmn. dept. chemistry, 1983-85, Ralph and Mary Otis Isham prof., 1994-97, Albert A. Michelson Dist. Svc. prof., 1997—, v.p. rsch. and nat. labs., 2007—. Mem. chemistry adv. com. NSF; Lady Davis vis. prof. The Technion, Haifa, Israel, 1998; Jeremy Musher Meml. lect. Hebrew U., Jerusalem, Israel, 2002; Powell lectr. U. Richmond, 2006. Assoc. editor Jour. Chem. Physics, 1983-98; editor Jour. Chem. Physics, 1998-07. Fellow AAAS, Am. Phys. Soc. (Plyler prize 1987, Bright Wilson award 2006), Optical Soc. Am. (Ellis A. Lippencott award 2000—); mem. Am. Chem. Soc.(E. Bright Wilson award in Spectroscopy, 2006), Am. Acad. Arts and Scis., Nat. Acad. Scis. Office: U Chgo Dept Chemistry 5801 S Ellis Ave Chicago IL 60637-1433 Business E-Mail: d_levy@uchicago.edu.

LEVY, EDWARD CHARLES, JR., manufacturing executive; b. Detroit, Nov. 14, 1931; s. Edward Charles and Pauline (Birndorf) Levy; 2 children. SB, MIT, 1952. From staff to exec. v.p. Edw. C. Levy Co., Detroit, 1952-70, pres., 1970—. Bd. dirs. Julie and Ed Levy Jr.Found., Karmanos Cancer Inst., Detroit, Round Table of Christians and Jews, Mackinac Ctr. for Pub. Policy; trustee Children's Hosp. of Mich., Citizens Rsch. Coun. Mich., Washington Inst. for Near East Policy; officer Am. Israel Pub. Affairs Com. Mem. ASTM, Am. Concrete Inst., Engring. Soc. Detroit, Detroit Athletic Club, Renaissance Club, Franklin Hills Country Club. Jewish. Office: Edw C Levy Co Inc 8800 Dix St Detroit MI 48209-1096

LEVY, NELSON LOUIS, immunologist, educator, surgeon; b. Somerville, NJ, June 19, 1941; s. Myron L. and Sylvia (Cohen) L.; m. Joanne Barnett, Dec. 21, 1963 (div. 1972); children: Scott, Erik, Jonathan; m. Louisa Douglas Stiles, Dec. 21, 1974; children: Michael, Andrew, David. BA/BS summa cum laude, Yale U., 1963; MD, Columbia U., 1967; PhD, Duke U., 1972. Diplomate Am. Bd. Allergy and Immunology. Intern U. Colo. Med. Ctr., Denver, 1967-68; resident Duke U. Med. Ctr., Durham, NC, 1970-73; rsch. assoc. NIH, Bethesda, Md., 1968-70; asst. prof. immunology Duke U. Med. Ctr., Durham, 1972-75, assoc. prof. immunology and neurology, 1975-80, prof., 1980-81; dir. biol. rsch. Abbott Labs., Abbott Park, Ill., 1981, v.p. rsch., 1981-84; pres. Fujisawa Pharm., Deerfield, Ill., 1992-93; CEO Ill. Tech. Devel. Corp., 1993-95, The Core Techs Corp., Lake Forest, Ill., 1984—92, chmn. bd. dirs., CEO, 1995—. Chmn. bd. dirs. Horizon Quest Inc., Laguna Hills, Calif., 1996—97, ColesCraft Corp., 1997—, IMM UVA Corp., New Orleans, 1997—, ChemBridge Pharms., Inc., 2006—; bd. dirs. ChemBridge Corp., San Diego, Targeted Genetics Corp., Seattle, Biona PTY Ltd., Laguna Beach, Cary Pharm. Co., Bethesda, Md., ChemBridge Rsch. Labs., LLC, San Diego, zuChem, Inc., Chgo.; chmn. sci. adv. bd. Neoprobe Corp., First Horizon Pharms., Inc.; mem. sci. adv. bd. Ligand Pharms. Inc.; cons. Alcide Corp., 1991—, Ameritech, 1993—, US Dept. Treasury, FTC, 1999—; others. Contbr. chapters to books, articles to profl. jours. Mem. Gov.'s Task Force on Econ. Devel., 1993-98; mem. corp. adv. bd. Family Svc. of South Lake County, 1991—; commr. Lake County, Ill., 1998—. Surgeon USPHS, 1968-70. Grantee Am. Cancer Soc., 1970-75, NIH, 1971-81, Nat. Multiple Sclerosis Soc., 1974-81, Ill. Dept. Commerce and Cmty. Affairs, 1993—. Mem. Am. Assn. Immunologists, Am. Assn. Cancer Rsch., Licensing Execs. Soc., Rotary, Phi Beta Kappa, Sigma Xi, Alpha Omega Alpha, Phi Gamma Delta. Avocations: triathlons, biking, rhythm 'n blues. Office: 1391 Concord Rd Lake Forest IL 60045-1506 Office Phone: 847-295-3720.

LEVY, PETER A., lawyer; b. Apr. 17, 1949; BA, U. Ill., Urbana-Champaign, 1971; JD, U. Chgo., 1974. Bar: Ill. 1974. Ptnr., co-chmn. Lodging & Timeshare practice group DLA Piper Rudnick Gray Cary, Chgo. Lectr. Practicing Law Inst., Georgetown Univ. Law Ctr. Co-author: Ill. Real Estate Forms. Mem.: ABA, Ill. State Bar Assn., Chgo. Bar Assn., Phi Beta Kappa. Office: DLA Piper Rudnick Gray Cary 203 N LaSalle St Chicago IL 60601-1293 Office Phone: 312-368-4068. Office Fax: 312-630-5342. Business E-Mail: peter.levy@dlapiper.com.

LEVY, SUSAN C., lawyer; b. Chgo., Oct. 10, 1957; BA magna cum laude, Cornell U., 1979; JD, Harvard Law Sch., 1982. Bar: Ill. 1982, No. Dist. Ill., US Ct. Appeals (7th cir., 8th cir., fed. cir.). Ptnr. Jenner & Block LLP, Chgo. Chair Jenner and Block campaign United Way, 2005—; exec. com., women of achievement com. Anti-Defamation League; devel. com. Broader Urban Devel. Leadership Devel., co-chair fundraising dinners, 2006—07. Contbr. articles to profl. jours. Bd. trustees Ravinia Festival, Chgo. Named Ill. Super Lawyer, 2005—08. Mem.: ABA, United Way Tocqueville Soc., Phi Beta Kappa. Office: Jenner & Block LLP 330 N Wabash Chicago IL 60611 Office Phone: 312-923-2772. Office Fax: 312-840-7772. Business E-Mail: slevy@jenner.com.

LEWALLEN, DAVE, announcer; m. Sandra LewAllen; 2 children. B of Journalism, Ctrl. Mich. U. Sports anchor WJIM-TV, Lansing, Mich.; sports reporter/anchor WJR-AM; sports dir. CKLW-AM, Detroit, 1983—84; play-by-play announcer U. Detroit basketball, WMTG Radio; with WJBK-TV, Southfield, Mich., 1985—88; sports reporter WXYZ-TV, Detroit, 1988—90, weekend sports anchor, host Sports Update, 1990—. Mem.: Am. Sportscasters Assn., Detroit Sports Broadcasters Assn. (past pres.). Office: WXYZ-TV 20777 W Ten Mile Rd Southfield MI 48037

LEWAND, F. THOMAS, lawyer; b. San Diego, July 24, 1946; s. Barbara (Boening) L.; m. Kathleen Sullivan, Aug. 3, 1968; children: Thomas, Kevin, Kristen, Carrie. BA, U. Detroit, 1968; JD, Wayne State U., 1970. Bar: Mich. 1970, U.S. Dist. Ct. (ea. dist.) 1970. Law clk. to judge U.S. Ct. Appeals (6th cir.), Detroit, 1970; commr. Oakland County, Pontiac, Mich., 1978-80; chief of staff to Gov. J. Blanchard Lansing, Mich., 1982-83; ptnr. Jaffe, Raitt & Heuer, Detroit, 1970-92, Bodman LLP, Detroit, 1992—. Trustee Gov. Blanchard Found., Lansing, 1982—; dir. Wayne County Econ. Devel. Corp., 1997—, Nat. Conf. on Cmty. and Justice, 1999—2001; trustee U. Detroit Mercy, 1996—, chmn., 2001—06; spl. master US Dist. Ct., 2003—. Campaign mgr. Gov. James J. Blanchard, Mich., 1978; chmn. Mich. Dems., 1989-91, Mackinac Island (Mich.) Dept. Pub. Works, 2006—; treas. Govs. Residence Found., 2003; mem. Mich. Civil Svc. Com., 2003—; mem. exec. com. Mich. Econ. Devel. Corp., 2006—. Mem. State Bar Mich., Nat. Assn. Bond Lawyers. Office: Bodman LLP 1901 Saint Antoine St Fl 6 Detroit MI 48226-2310 Office Phone: 313-393-7573. E-mail: tlewand@bodmanllp.com.

LEWELLEN, WILBUR GARRETT, management educator, consultant; b. Charleroi, Pa., Jan. 21, 1938; s. Anthony Garrett and Cozie Harriett (Watson) L.; m. Jean Carolyn Vanderlip, Dec. 8, 1962 (div. 1982); children— Stephen G., Jocelyn A., Jonathan W., Robyn E.; m. Eloise Evelyn Vincent, Mar. 5, 1983 BS, Pa. State U., University Park, 1959; MS, MIT, Cambridge, 1961, PhD, 1967; LhD (hon.), Budapest U. of Econ. Scis., 1996. Asst. prof. mgmt. Purdue U., West Lafayette, Ind., 1964-68, assoc. prof. mgmt., 1968-72, prof., 1972-83, Loeb prof. mgmt., 1983-88, Krannert disting. prof. mgmt., 1988—, dir. exec. edn. programs, 1985—2006. Cons. Bank Am., San Francisco, 1975—90, Ind. Bell Tel. Co., Indpls., 1976—90, Am. Water Works Co., Wilmington, Del., 1978—94, Indpls. Power and Light Co., 1993—99, NiSource, Inc., 2000—; bd. dirs. Indsl. Dielectrics, Inc. Author: Executive Compensation in Large Industrial Corporations, 1968, Ownership Income of Management, 1971, The Cost of Capital, 1981, Financial Management: An Introduction to Principles and Practice, 2000. Recipient Salgo-Noren award as Outstanding Tchr. in Grad. Prof. Programs, Salgo-Noren Found., 1973, 77, 79, 84. Mem. AAUP, Fin. Mgmt. Assn. (v.p. 1973-74), Am. Fin. Assn., Western Fin. Assn. Methodist. Office: Purdue Univ Grad Sch Mgmt West Lafayette IN 47907 Office Phone: 765-494-4493.

LEWINE, MARK SAUL, anthropology professor; b. Jan. 29, 1946; Prof. anthropology, sociology and urban studies, dir. Ctr. for Community Rsch. Cuyahoga CC, Cleve. Recipient President's Award, Soc. for Anthropology in CC, US Professors of Yr. Award for Outstanding CC Prof., Carnegie Found. for Advancement of Tchg. and Coun. for Advancement and Support of Edn., 2006. Office: Cuyahoga CC Metro Campus 2900 Community College Ave Cleveland OH 44115 E-mail: Mark.Lewine@tri-c.edu.

LEWIS, ANDRÉ LEON, performing company executive; b. Hull, Que., Can., Jan. 16, 1955; s. Raymond Lincoln and Theresa Lewis. Student, Classical Ballet Studio, Ottawa, Royal Winnipeg (Man.) Ballet Sch., 1975; studies with David Moroni, Arnold Spohr, Rudi van Dantzig, Jiri Kylian, Peter Wright, Hans van Manen, and Alicia Markova, among others. Mem. corps de ballet Royal Winnipeg (Man.) Ballet, 1979-82, soloist, artistic coord., 1984-89, interim artistic dir., 1989-90, assoc. artistic dir., 1990-96, artistic dir., 1996—. Staged Danzig's Romeo and Juliet, Teatro Comunale, Florence, Italy, Greek Nat. Opera, Athens. Dancer soloist (ballets) Song of a Wayfarer, Fall River Legend, Nuages, Lento A Tempo E Appassionatto, Nutcracker, Four Last Songs, Romeo and Juliet, The Ecstasy of Rita Joe, (TV films) Belong, Romeo and Juliet, The Big Top, Firebird, (ballets) performed at many events including the opening Gala in Jackson Miss., Le Don Des Etoiles, Montreal, spl. gala honoring Queen Beatrix of Holland and at a Gala performance in Tchaikovsky Hall, Moscow, appeared as a guest artist throughout, N.Am., the Orient and USSR. Avocation: listening to opera. Office: Can Royal Winnipeg Ballet 380 Graham Ave Winnipeg MB Canada R3C 4K2 Office Phone: 204-956-0183. E-mail: ballet@rwb.org.

LEWIS, AYLWIN B., former retail executive, former food service company executive; b. Houston, May 28, 1954; m. Noveline L. Lewis. BS in Bus. Mgmt. & English Lit, Houston U., 1976, MBA, 1990. Regional gen. mgr KFC, 1991—93, divsn. v.p. ops., 1993—95, sr. v.p. mktg. & ops. devel., 1995—96; sr. v.p. ops. Pizza Hut, Inc., 1996—97, COO, 1997—99; exec. v.p. ops. & new bus. devel. YUM! Brands, Inc. (formerly Tricon Global Restaurants), 2000, COO, 2000—03, pres., chief multi-branding & oper. officer, 2003—04; pres., CEO Kmart Holding Corp., Troy, Mich., 2004—05, Sears Holdings Corp., Hoffman Estates, Ill., 2005—08. Bd. dirs. Halliburton Co., 2001—05, The Walt Disney Co., 2004—, Kmart Holding Corp., 2004—05, Sears Holdings Corp., 2005—08.*

LEWIS, CALVIN FRED, architect, educator; b. Chgo., Mar. 27, 1946; s. Howard George and Fern Teresa (Voelsch) L.; m. L. Diane Johnson, Aug. 24, 1968; children: athan, Miller, Cooper, Wilson. BArch, Iowa State U., 1969. Architect Charles Herbert and Assocs., Des Moines, 1970-86; prin. Herbert Lewis Kruse Blunck Architecture, Des Moines, 1987—2004; prin., owner Lewis Studio, Des Moines, 2005—; prof. Iowa State U., 2000—, chmn. Dept. Arch., 2000—. Peer reviewer Design Excellence Program GSA, 2003—; lectr., awards juror. More tha 50 projects published in profl. jours. Recipient Best in Design award Time mag.; named one of Top Young Architects in Country, Met. Home mag.; firm named Nat. AIA Firm of Yr., 2001. Fellow AIA (more than 70 design awards 1972—, 3 Nat. Honor awards, Interior Design award Bus. Week/Archtl. Record 1998, 2 interior design mag. awards, Nat. Design award AIA-AISC 1999). Avocations: sports, photography. Office: Dept Arch Iowa State U 156 Coll of Design Ames IA 50011 Office Phone: 515-294-2665. E-mail: calewis@iastate.edu.

LEWIS, CHARLES A., foundation administrator; b. Orange, NJ, Oct. 23, 1942; s. F. Donald and Edna H. L.; m. Gretchen Smith, July 1967 (div.); m. Penny Bender Sebring, June 9, 1984. BA, Amherst Coll., 1964; MBA, U. Pa., 1966; LHD (hon.), Amherst Coll., 2003. Asst. to pres. Computer Tech., Inc., Skokie, Ill., 1969-70; 1st v.p. White, Weld, & Co., 1970-78; vice chmn. investment banking Merrill Lynch & Co., Chgo., 1978—2004. Mem. adv. com. Database of Black Performers of Instrumental Concert Music, 1999—. Life trustee Amherst Coll., Folger Shakespear Libr., 1989—; life trustee, vice chair Chgo. Symphony Orch., 1989—; life dir. Juvenile Diabetes Rsch. Found. Ill.; trustee U. Chgo., vis. com. divsn. social scis.; trustee Ravinia Festival, 1995—98; leadership coun. Chgo. Pub. Edn. Fund, 2000—; governing bd. North Kenwood/Oakland Charter Sch., 2000—03; co-chair The Amherst Coll. Campaign, 1993—2001; mem. policy bd. Ctr. Urban Sch. Improvement U. Chgo., 2003—; bd. dirs. Juvenile Diabetes Rsch. Found. Internat., 1994—95. Named to, Shaker H.S. Sports Hall of Fame, 2003; recipient Cmty. Ptnr. award, People's Music Sch., 2002. Mem. Chgo. Club, Glen View Club. Office: Coach House Capital and Lewis-Sebring Family Found 2735 Sheridan Rd Evanston IL 60201 Home Phone: 847-328-4310; Office Phone: 847-864-9615. E-mail: calewis@lewissebringff.org.

LEWIS, DAN ALBERT, education educator; b. Chgo., Feb. 14, 1946; s. Milton and Diane (Sabath) L.; m. Stephanie Riger, Jan. 3, 1982; children: Matthew, Jake. BA cum laude, Stanford U., 1968; PhD, U. Calif., Santa Cruz, 1980. Rsch. assoc. Arthur Bolton Assocs., Sacramento, 1969-70; survey contr. Sci. Analysis Corp., San Francisco, 1971; dir. Stanford Workshops on Polit. and Social Issues Stanford (Calif.) U., 1971-74; projects adminstr. Ctr. Urban Affairs and Policy Rsch., Northwestern U., Evanston, Ill., 1975-80, asst. prof. edn., 1980-86, assoc. prof. edn., 1986-90, assoc. dir., chair grad. program human devel./social policy, 1987-90, prof. edn., 1990—. Vis. scholar Sch. Edn., Stanford U., 1990-91; mem. task force on restructuring mental health svcs. Chgo. Dept. Health, 1982; mem. human rights authority Ill. Guardianship and Advocacy Commn., 1980-82; adv. mem. com. on planning and inter-agy. coordination Commn. Mental Health and Devel. Disabilities, 1979; interim adv. com. on mental health City of Chgo., 1978; adv. mem. Gov.'s Commn. to Revise Mental Health Code Ill., 1975-77;dir. Univ. Consortium on Welfare Reform, 1999-2003; presenter at profl. confs.; presenter workshops. Editor: Reactions to Crime, 1981; co-author: Fear of Crime: Incivility and the Production of a Social Problem, 1986, The Social Construction of Reform: Crime Prevention and Community Organizations, 1988, The Worlds of the Mentally Ill, 1991, The State Mental Patient in Urban Life, 1994, Race and Educational Reform, 1995; contbr. articles, book revs. to profl. publs. Bd. dirs. Designs for Change, Ill. Mental Health Assn.; rsch. adv. com. Chgo. Urban League, Chgo. Panel Pub. Sch. Finances, 1989-91; needs assessment tech. com. United Way Chgo., 1989-90; ednl. coun. Francis W. Parker Sch., Chgo., 1988-90; task force on restructuring mental health svcs. Chgo. Dept. Health, 1982; com. on mentally disabled Ill. State Bar Assn., 1983-89; dir. U. Consortium on Welfare Reform, 1999-2002; rsch. policy com. Ill. Dept. Mental Health, 1978; bd. dirs. Mental Health Assn. Greater Chgo., 1977-84, v.p. pub. policy, 1979-83 Recipient Excellence in Tchg. award Northwestern U. Alumni Assn., 1998; named to Faculty Honor Roll Associated Student Govt., 2001-04. Office: Northwestern Univ 2040 Sheridan Rd Evanston IL 60208-0855 Business E-Mail: dlewis@northwestern.edu.

LEWIS, DARRELL L., retail executive; b. Mason City, Iowa, Nov. 20, 1931; s. Milton Loren and Blanche Ione (Wilson) L.; m. Mary Jo Bahnsen, Oct. 22, 1950; children— John L., Lonnette Ann, Sherri Jo. MBA, Stanford U., 1970. With Osco Drug, Inc. subsidiary Jewel Cos., Inc., 1949-62; with Jewel Turn-Style, 1962; pres. Turn-Style Family Centers, Franklin Park, Ill., 1967-74, head Jewel Hypermarket, 1974; pres. Osco Drug, Inc., 1974-75, v.p. store and sales devel., 1976-77; pres. D.L. Lewis Drug Co. Inc., Bensenville, Ill., 1978—, chmn. bd., 1987—. Office: DL Lewis Drug Co 12338 Sunset Dr Three Rivers MI 49093-9580

LEWIS, DAVID BAKER, lawyer; b. Detroit, June 9, 1944; BA, Oakland U., 1965; MBA, U. Chgo. Grad. Sch. Bus., 1967; JD, U. Mich. Law Sch., 1970. Bar: Mich. 1970. Law clk. to Honorable Theodore Levin, US Dist. Ct., Ea. Dist. Mich., 1970—71; pres. Lewis, Clay & Munday, Detroit, 1972—82, chmn. corp. svcs. practice group, 1982—, founder, shareholder; assoc. prof. law, law and social change Detroit Coll. Law, 1973—78, former asst. prof.; chmn. Lewis & Munday, A Profl. Corp., CEO; bd. dirs. Kroger Co., 2008—, H&R Block, 2008—; former dir. Comerica, Inc.; chmn. L&M's Corp. Svcs. Practice Group. Mem., sec. State of Mich. Atty. Discipline Bd., 1978—83; mem. steering com. Bond Attys. Workshop, 1979, 89; mem. exec. com. Met. Ctr. High Tech., 1983—90, bd. dirs., 1983—90; mem. exec. com. HGH Health Sys., 1984—88, bd. trustees, 1984—88, Inst. Am. Bus., 1985—, mem. exec. com., 1985—; mem. Met. Affairs Corp., 1985—91, vice-chmn., 1989—91, bd. dirs., 1989—91, Booker T. Washington Bus. Assn., 1989—91; former dir. Consolidated Rail Corp. (Conrail), bd. dirs., 1989—, mem. audit com., 1989—, mem. fin. com., 1989—; former dir. LG&E Energy Corp., mem. audit com., 1992—, mem. devel. com., 1992—, bd. dirs., 1992—; former dir. TRW, Inc., bd. dirs., 1995—, mem. compensation com., 1995—, mem. retirement funding com., 1995—; mem. audit and legal com. Comerica Bank, Mich., 1995—, mem. trust and investment com., 1995—, bd. dirs., 1995—; life mem. Sixth Circuit Judicial Conf.; former dir. Mass. Hanna Co. Mem. Greater Detroit Area Hosp. Coun., Inc., 1977—79, 1983—87, Detroit Inst. Arts Dir. Search Com., 1983—85, Greater Detroit and Windsor Japan-Am. Soc., 1989; bd. trustees Harper-Grace Hosp., 1979—88, mem. exec. com., 1979—88; bd. trustees Oakland U., 1970—81, vice chmn. bd. trustees, 1976—78, chmn. bd. trustees, 1978—80, trustee emeritus bd. trustees; pres. Franklin-Wright Settlement, Inc., 1975—76; v.p. Mich. Assn. Governing Bds. Colls. and Univs., 1977—79; chmn. com. vis. U. Mich. Law Sch.; bd. trustees Ctr. Creative Studies, 1983—95, Grosse Pointe Acad., 1984—87, 1993—94; bd. dirs. Detroit Symphony, 1983—, Detroit. Zoological Soc., 1983—89, Musical Hall Ctr. Performing Arts, 1983—94, Founders Soc., Detroit Inst. Arts, 1984—89, Greater Detroit Interfaith Round Table, Nat. Conf. Christian and Jews, Inc., 1990—, Detroit Club, 1989—95, sec., 1989—95. Named one of Am. Top Black Lawyers, Black Enterprise Mag., 2003. Mem.: Nat. Assn. Securities Profl., Inc. (sec. 1985—87, chair-elect 1987, chair 1988, exec. com.), Nat. Assn. Bond Lawyers (bd. dirs. 1993—95, past dir.). Office: Lewis & Munday 2490 First Nat Bldg 660 Woodward Ave Detroit MI 48226-3531 Home Phone: 313-823-0471; Office Phone: 313-961-2550 4110. Business E-Mail: dlewis@lewismunday.com.

LEWIS, DIANE, announcer; m. Glenn Lewis; 2 children. Grad., Ctrl. State U., Wilburforce, Ohio. With WPVI, Phila., KABC, LA; co-anchor WXYZ, Southfield, Mich., 1977—85; career in TV and film industry Calif., 1985—88; co-anchor WXYZ, Southfield, Mich., 1988—. Actor: (plays) Rocky, Rocky 5 and others. Recipient Silver Cir. award, 1995, 2 Emmy awards, 2002, Gov.'s Lifetime Achievement award, 2002, Best News Anchor, 2002. Office: WXYZ-TV 20777 W Ten Mile Rd Southfield MI 48037

LEWIS, DONALD JOHN, mathematics professor; b. Adrian, Minn., Jan. 25, 1926; s. William J. and Ellanora (Masgai) L.; m. Carolyn Dana Hauf, Dec. 28, 1953. BS, Coll. St. Thomas, 1946; PhD, U. Mich., 1950. Instr. Ohio State U., Columbus, 1950-52; asst. prof. U. Notre Dame (Ind.), 1953-57, assoc. prof., 1957-61, U. Mich., Ann Arbor, 1961-63, prof. maths., 1963-2000, prof. emeritus, 2000—, dept. chair, 1983-94; dir. Divsn. Math. Scis. Nat. Sci. Found., 1995-99. Mem. Inst. for Adv. Study, 1952-53, 90-91; vis. scientist U. Manchester (Eng.), 1959-61, Cambridge (Eng.), 1960-61; vis. fellow Trinity Coll., Cambridge, 1965, 69, Japanese Soc. for Promotion of Sci., Tokyo, 1974, Braesnose Coll., Oxford, Eng., 1976; visitor U. Heidelberg, Germany, 1980-81, 83; adv. bd. math. sci. NSF, 1983-86, math panel sci., 1993. Author: Introduction to Algebra, 1965, Calculus and Linear Algebra, 1970; editor: Proceedings of Symposia in Pure Math., 1971; contbr. 55 articles on number theory to profl. jours. Recipient Humboldt Preis award, Alexander von Humboldt Soc., Germany, 1980; Fellow, NSF, 1952—53, 1959—61. Mem.: Soc. Indsl. and Applied Math., Am. Math. Soc. (Disting. Svc. award 1995). Roman Catholic. Avocation: gardening. Home: 2250 Glendaloch Rd Ann Arbor MI 48104-2832 Office: Math Dept U Mich East Hall Ann Arbor MI 48109-1009 E-mail: djlewis@umich.edu.

LEWIS, EDWARD ALAN, religious organization adminstrator; b. Brazil, Ind., July 22, 1946; s. Edward and Ruth Margaret (Eberwein) L. B in Music Edn., Grace Coll., 1969; M in Divinity, Grace Sem., 1973. Asst. to pastor, youth dir. Grace Brethren Ch., Winona Lake, Ind., 1969-73; nat. dir. youth ministries Grace Brethren Ch. Christian Edn., Winona Lake, 1973-85; dir. candidate pers. Grace Brethren Fgn. Missions, Winona Lake, 1982-88; exec. dir. Grace Brethren Ch. Christian Edn., Winona Lake, 1985—. Mem. Grace Brethren Ch., Winona Lake, 1969—, exec. mem. denominational youth com., 1984—; moderator Nat. Fellowship of Grace Brethren Chs., 1994-95. Mem. Grace Sem. Alumni Assn. (pres. 1984-85), Ind. Dist. Ministerium, Nat. Ministerium Assn. Avocations: music, piano, singing, jogging, travel. Home and Office: PO Box 365 Winona Lake IN 46590-0365 Office Phone: 574-267-6622.

LEWIS, FRANK RUSSELL, JR., surgeon; b. Willards, Md., Feb. 23, 1941; m. Janet Christensen, 1996. AB in Physics, Princeton U., 1961; MD, U. Md., 1965; postgrad. in med. physics, U. Calif., Berkeley, 1970. Surg. dir. M/SICU San Francisco Gen. Hosp., 1973-80, dir. emergency dept., 1980-83, chief of staff, 1983-85, asst. chief of surgery, 1981-86, chief of surgery, 1986-92; prof. surgery Case We. Res. U., Cleve., 1994—2002; chmn. dept. surgery Henry Ford Hosp., Detroit, 1992—2002; former exec. dir. Am. Bd. Surgery. Fellow: ACS (gov. 1988—93, 1st v.p. 1995—96); mem.: So. Surg. Assn., Shock Soc. (coun. 1978—, pres.), We. Surg. Soc., Ctrl. Surg. Soc., Am. Assn. for Surgery of Trauma (pres. 1999—2002), Am. Surg. Assn. Office: Am Bd Surgery 1617 JFK Blvd Ste 860 Philadelphia PA 19130 Home Phone: 267-514-1125; Office Phone: 215-568-4000. Business E-Mail: flewis@absurgery.org.

LEWIS, GENE DALE, historian, educator; b. Globe, Ariz., Feb. 20, 1931; s. Abner E. and May J. (Hyatt) L.; m. Dottie Ladd Bidlingmeyer, Aug. 3, 1963. BA, Ariz. State U., 1951, MA, 1952; PhD, U. Ill., 1957. Lectr. Ariz. State U., 1953, So. Ill. U., 1957-58; vis. assoc. prof. history U. Ill., Urbana, 1965, Case Western Res. U., Cleve., 1966; prof. history U. Cin., 1958—, acting head dept., 1981-82, dir. grad. studies, 1989, head dept., 1989-98. Sr. v.p., provost, 1973-76 Author: Charles Ellet Jr., Engineer as Individualist, 1968; editor: New Historical Perspectives: Essays on the Black Experience in Antebellum America, 1984; co-editor Greater Cincinnati Bicentennial History Series, 1988—. Recipient Barbour award for excellence U. Cin., 1969, Nat. award Omicron Delta Kappa, 1968 Mem. AAUP, So. Hist. Assn., Am. Hist. Assn., Orgn. Am. Historians. Home: 444 Rawson Woods Ln Cincinnati OH 45220-1142 Office: U Cin Dept History Cincinnati OH 45221-0001

LEWIS, JAMAL, professional football player; b. Atlanta, Aug. 29, 1979; Degree, U. Tenn. Running back Balt. Ravens, 2000—07, Cleve. Browns, 2007—. Named NFL Offensive Player of Yr., 2003; named to Am. Football Conf. Pro-Bowl Team, 2003. Achievements include being a member of Super Bowl XXXV Champion Baltimore Ravens, 2001; setting an NFL record for single game rushing (295 yards), 2003; led NFL in rushing yards (2,066), 2003. Mailing: Cleve Browns 76 Lou Groza Blvd Berea OH 44017

LEWIS, JAMES A., state legislator; b. Highland, Ky., Dec. 26, 1930; m. Anna Mae Spencer; children: David, Thomas, Charles. Student, Purdue U. Bldg. contr.; mem. Ind. Ho. of Rep., 1970-72, Ind. Senate from 45th dist., 1974—; minority caucus chmn.; mem. natural resources, fin., agr. and small bus. coms.; mem. labor and pensions com.; ranking minority mem.; mem. appointments and claims com.; mem. consumer affairs com. Mem. City Council, 1960-68; mem. Clark County, Ind. coun., 1981-82; precinct committeeman; scoutmaster Boy Scouts Am. Recipient Best Citizen award Jaycees, 1959. Mem. So. Home Bldrs. Assn., Clark County Conservation Club, Masons, Scottish Rite, Moose.

LEWIS, JEFFREY E., dean, law educator; BA, Duke U., 1966, JD, 1969. Asst. prof. law U. Akron Sch. Law, 1970—72, U. Fla. Coll. Law, 1972—75, assoc. prof., 1975—77, prof., 1977—99, prof. emeritus, 1999—, assoc. dean, 1982—88, dean, 1988—96, dean emeritus, 1996—; dean. prof. law Saint Louis U. Sch. Law, 1999—. Vis. prof. law Escuela Libre de Derecho, 1996, Johann Wolfgang Goethe U., 1997, U. Ala., 1999. Contbr. articles to law jours. Fellow: ABA; mem.: Omicron Delta Kappa, Phi Kappa Phi. Office: St Louis U Sch Law 3700 Linden Blvd Saint Louis MO 63108 E-mail: lewisje@slu.edu.

LEWIS, JOHN BRUCE, lawyer; b. Poplar Bluff, Mo., Aug. 12, 1947; s. Evan Bruce and Hilda Kathryn (Kassebaum) L.; m. Diane F. Grossman, July 23, 1977; children: Samantha Brooking, Ashley Denning. BA, U. Mo., 1969, JD, 1972; LLM in Labor and Employment Law, Columbia U., 1978; diploma, Nat. Inst. Trial Advocacy, 1982. Bar: Mo. 1972, U.S. Ct. Appeals (8th cir.) 1973, U.S. Dist. Ct. (ea. dist.) Mo. 1974, U.S. Dist. Ct. (no. dist.) Ohio 1979, Ohio 1980, U.S. Ct. Appeals (6th cir.) 1982, U.S. Dist. Ct. (ea. dist.) Mich. 1983, U.S. Ct. Appeals (3d cir.) 1987, U.S. Supreme Ct. 1987, U.S. Dist. Ct. (no. dist.) Calif. 1987, U.S. Ct. Appeals (7th cir.) 1990, U.S. Dist. Ct. (so. dist.) Ohio 2003. Assoc. Millar, Schaefer & Ebling, St. Louis, 1972-77, Squire, Sanders & Dempsey, Cleve., 1979-85; ptnr. Arter & Hadden, Cleve., 1985-2001, Baker & Hostetler, Cleve., 2001—, chair nat. employment and civil rights class action team, 2005—. Lectr. in field. Author: Employment Practices Self-Assessment Guide, 3d edit., 2006; contbr. articles to legal jours. Mem. Cleve. Council on World Affairs. Fellow: Coll. Labor and Employment Lawyers; mem. ABA (sec. labor and employment law, com. EEO law, comm. law forum), Ohio State Bar Assn. (sec. labor and employment law), Cleve. Bar Assn. (sec. labor law), St. Louis Met. Bar Assn., Am. Law Inst., Selden Soc., Ohio C. of C. (employment law com.), William K. Thomas Inn of Ct. (master bencher). Office: Baker & Hostetler LLP 3200 Nat City Ctr 1900 E 9th St Cleveland OH 44114-3485 Office Phone: 216-861-7496. Business E-Mail: jlewis@bakerlaw.com.

LEWIS, JOHN D., banking official; Various mgmt. positions with Comerica, Inc., Detroit, 1970-95, vice-chmn., 1995—, also bd. dirs. Office: Comerica Inc Comerica Twr/500 Woodward A Detroit MI 48226

LEWIS, JOHN FRANCIS, lawyer; b. Oberlin, Ohio, Oct. 25, 1932; s. Ben W. and Gertrude D. Lewis; m. Catharine Monroe, June 15, 1957; children: Ben M., Ian A., Catharine G., William H. BA, Amherst Coll., 1955; JD, U. Mich., 1958. Bar: Ohio 1958, U.S. Dist. Ct. (no dist.) Ohio 1959, U.S. Supreme Ct. 1972. Assoc. firm Squire, Sanders & Dempsey, Cleve., 1959—67; ptnr. Squire, Sanders & Dempsey LLP, 1967—2002, mng. ptnr. Cleve. office to sr. coun., 1985—2002, sr. coun., 2002—. Co-author: Baldwin's Ohio School Law, 1980-91, Ohio Collective Bargaining Law, 1983. Hon. life trustee Found. for Sch. Bus. Mgmt., Leadership Cleve., 1977—78; trustee Playhouse Sq. Found., chmn., 1980—85; chair Cleve. Initiative for Edn., 1988—95; chmn. Cleanland Cleve., 1992—95; trustee Ohio Found. Ind. Colls. Case Western Res. U., chmn., 1995—2006; trustee, chmn. Ohio Aerospace Coun., 2001—03; trustee Ohio Aerospace Inst., Inst. for Rsch. on Unlimited Love. Recipient Malcolm Daisley Labor-Mgmt. Rels. award, 1991, Tree of Life award Jewish Nat. Fund, 1993, NCCJ award, 1995, Franklin D. Roosevelt March of Dimes award, 1999, Case Western Reserve U. Presdl. medal, 2001, Goff award The Cleveland Found., 2005. Mem.: ABA, Ohio Coun. Sch. Bd. Attys. (founding chair), Ohio Assn. Sch. Bus. Ofcls. (Marion McGehey Edn. Law award 1996), Edn. Law Assn. (past pres.), Nat. Sch. Bd. Assn., Ohio Bar Assn., Cleve. Bar Assn., Edn. Law Inst., Fifty Club of Cleve. Episcopalian. Home: 2 Bratenahl Pl Ste 7ef Bratenahl OH 44108-1183 Office: Squire Sanders & Dempsey 4900 Key Tower 127 Public Sq Ste 4900 Cleveland OH 44114-1304 Office Phone: 216-479-8553. Personal E-mail: capeoceans@aol.com. Business E-Mail: Jlewis@ssd.com.

LEWIS, JORDAN D., federal judge; b. 1932; JD, Ind. U., 1959. Atty. Lewis & Lewis, 1959-96; part-time magistrate judge U.S. Dist. Ct. (so. dist.) Ind., Terre Haute, 1979—. Served with U.S. Army, 1952-55. Office: 207 Federal Bldg Terre Haute IN 47808

LEWIS, LISA, psychologist, administrator; B of Psychology and Biology, Pa. State U.; M of Clin. Psychology, Conn. Coll.; D of Clin. Psychology, Miami U., Oxford, Ohio. Intern Fla. Med. Sch.; dir. clin. psychology Menninger, Topeka. Presenter in field. Contbr. articles to profl. jours. Recipient David Rappaport Excellence in Teaching award; postdoctoral fellow Menninger. Address: Menningers PO Box 809045 Houston TX 77280

LEWIS, PETER BENJAMIN, insurance company executive; b. Cleve., Nov. 11, 1933; s. Joseph M. and Helen (Rosenfeld) Lewis; children: Ivy, Jonathan, Adam. AB, Princeton U., NJ, 1955. Underwriting trainee Progressive Ins. Cos., 1955; exec. trainee Progressive Casualty Ins. Co., pres., CEO, 1965-94, The Progressive Corp., Ohio, 1965-2000, chmn. bd., 2000—. Bd. trustees Solomon R. Guggenheim Mus. Named one of Top 200 Collectors, ARTnews Mag., 2004, Forbes' Richest Ams., 2006. Achievements include a contribution to Princeton University, which allowed the university to establish a science library and the Lewis-Sigler Institute for Integrative Genomics; one of the most significant benefactors in all of Princeton University's history in 2006, recent contribution will allow for the expansion of the creative & performing arts program. Avocation: Collector of Contemporary art including Am. conceptualism. Office: Progressive Corp 6300 Wilson Mills Rd Cleveland OH 44143-2109 Office Phone: 440-461-5000. E-mail: peter_lewis@progressive.com.

LEWIS, PHILLIP HAROLD, museum curator; b. Chgo., July 31, 1922; s. Bernard and Sonia (Pimstein) L.; m. Sally Leah Rappaport, Aug. 25, 1949; children— David Bernard, Betty Alice and Emily Ruth (twins). B.F.A., Art Inst. Chgo., 1947; MA, U. Chgo., 1953, PhD, 1966; postgrad. (Fulbright ednl. grant), Australian Nat. U., Canberra, 1953-54. Conducted field research projects on art and soc. of New Ireland, 1953-54, 70, 81; asst. curator primitive art Field Mus. Natural History, Chgo., 1957-59, asso. curator, 1960, curator, 1961-67, curator primitive art and Melanesian ethnology, 1968-92, ret., 1992, chmn. dept. anthropology, 1975-79, co-chmn. dept., 1980-81, acting chmn. dept., 1987; curator emeritus, 1994—. Served with USAAF, 1942-45. Fellow Royal Anthrop. Inst. Gt. Britain and Ireland, Am. Anthrop. Assn. Home: 1222 Chicago Ave Apt 303b Evanston IL 60202-1338

LEWIS, RICHARD PHELPS, cardiologist, educator; b. Portland, Oreg., Oct. 26, 1936; s. Howard Phelps and Wava Irene (Brown) L.; m. Penny A. Brown, Oct. 12, 1982; children: Richard Phelps, Heather Brown. BA, Yale U., 1957; MD, U. Oreg., 1961. Intern Peter Bent Brigham Hosp., Boston, 1961-62, resident, 1962-63; Howard Irwin fellow in cardiology U. Oreg., Portland, 1963-65; sr. resident Stanford U., 1965-66, instr. dept. medicine, 1968-69; asst. chief cardiology Madigan Gen. Hosp., Tacoma, 1966-68; asst. prof. medicine div. cardiology Ohio State U., 1969-71, assoc. prof., 1971-75, prof., 1975-2000, dir. Divsn. Cardiology, 1972-86, dir., 1972-86, assoc. chmn. for hosp. and clin. affairs, 1980-86, prof. emeritus, 2000—. Mem. cardiovascular sect. Am. Bd. Internal Medicine, 1981-87, critical care medicine, 1988-92. Contbr. articles to profl. jours. Served with M.C. U.S. Army, 1966-68, col. res. Decorated Army Commendation medal Master Am. Coll. Cardiology (Ohio gov. 1988-91, chmn. bd. govs. 1990-91, trustee 1991-2000, editor self assessment program ACCSAP, 1991-96, 2000—, v.p. 1994-95, pres.-elect 1995-96, pres. 1996-97); fellow ACP (gov. Ohio chpt. 1976-80, chmn. MKSAP cardiovascular sect. 1989-82, master tchr. 1998), Am. Heart Assn. (coun. on clin. cardiology), Am. Clin. and Climatological Assn.; mem. Am. Fedn. Clin. Rsch., Ctrl. Soc. Clin. Rsch., Laennec Soc., Am. Heart Assn., Assn. U. Cardiologists, Alpha Omega Alpha. Republican. Episcopalian. Home: 5088 Stratford Ave Powell OH 43065-8771 Office: 473 W 12th Ave Columbus OH 43210-1240 E-mail: richard.lewis@osumc.edu.

LEWIS, ROBERT ENZER, editor, educator; b. Windber, Pa., Aug. 12, 1934; s. Robert Enzer and Katharine Torrence (Blair) L.; m. Julie Fatt Cureton, May 14, 1977; children: Perrin Lewis Rubin, Torrence Evans Lewis; stepchildren: Sarah Cureton Kaufman, James S. Cureton. BA, Princeton U., 1959; MA, U. Pa., 1962, PhD, 1964. Tchr. English Mercersburg (Pa.) Acad., 1959-60; teaching fellow U. Pa., Phila., 1961-63; lectr. Ind. U., Bloomington, 1963-64, asst. prof., 1964-68, assoc. prof., 1968-75, prof. English, 1975-82, U. Mich., Ann Arbor, 1982—2003, prof. emeritus, 2004—. Author: (with A. McIntosh) Descriptive Guide to the Manuscripts of the Prick of Conscience, 1982, (with others) Index of Printed Middle English Prose, 1985; editor: De Miseria Condicionis Humane (Lotario dei Segni), 1978; co-editor: Middle English Dictionary, 1982-83, editor-in-chief: vols. 8, 9, 10, 11, 12, 13, 1984-2001; gen. editor: Chaucer Libr., 1970—, chmn. editl. com., 1978-89, 97—. Bd. regents Mercersburg Acad., 1975-87. U.S. Army, 1954-56. Recipient Sir Israel Gollancz Meml. prize for English studies Brit. Acad., 2003; vis. rsch. fellow Inst. Advanced Studies in the Humanities, U. Edinburgh, 1973-74; Am. Coun. Learned Socs. fellow, 1979-80. Fellow: Dictionary Soc. N.Am. (mem. nominating com. 2005—); mem.: Medieval Acad. Am. (mem. publs. com. 1987—92). Episcopalian. Office: U Mich Dept English 3187 Angell Hall Ann Arbor MI 48109-1003 Business E-Mail: relewis@umich.edu.

LEWIS, STEPHEN RICHMOND, JR., economist, educator; b. Englewood, NJ, Feb. 11, 1939; s. Stephen Richmond and Esther (Magan) Lewis; m. Judith Frost, 1996; children from previous marriage: Virginia, Deborah, Mark. BA, Williams Coll., 1960, LLD, 1987; MA, Stanford U., 1962, PhD, 1963; LHD, Doshisha U., 1993, Macalester Coll., 2002; LLD, Carleton Coll., 2002. Instr. Stanford U., 1962—63; research advisor Pakistan Inst. Devel. Econs., Karachi, 1963—65; asst. prof. econs. Harvard U., 1965—66, Williams Coll., 1966—68, assoc. prof., 1968—73, prof., 1973—76, Herbert H. Lehman prof., 1976—87, provost of coll., 1968—71, 1973—77, spl. asst. to pres., 1979—80, dir. Williams-Botswana Project, 1982—88, chmn. dept. econs., 1984—86; vis. sr. research fellow Inst. Devel. Studies, airobi, Kenya, 1971—73; econ. cons. to Ministry of Finance and Devel. Planning, Govt. of Botswana, 1975—; vis. fellow Inst. Devel. Studies, Sussex, England, 1986—87; pres., prof. econs. Carleton Coll., Northfield, Minn., 1987—2002, pres. emeritus, 2002—; chmn. RiverSource Funds, 2007—, also bd. dirs.; assoc. scientist Lingman U., 2007. Trustee Carnegie Endowment for Internat. Peace, 1988—, Minn. Humanities Commn., 2004—; bd. dirs. William Mitchell Coll. Law, XDX Innovative Refrigeration, Inc., Xenomosis, LLC, Valmont Industries, Inc.; cons. in field. Author (with others): Relative Price Changes and Industrialization in Pakistan, 1969; author: Economic Policy and Industrial Growth in Pakistan, 1969, Pakistan: Industrialization and Trade Policy, 1970, Williams in the Eighties, 1980, Taxation for Development, 1983, South Africa: Has Time Run Out?, 1986, Policy Choice and Development Performance in Botswana, 1989, The Economics of Apartheid, 1989; editor: Very Brave or Very Foolish? Memoirs of an African Democrat, 2006; mem. editl. bd.: Jour. Econ. Lit., 1985—87; contbr. chapters to books, articles to profl. jours. Mem. chmn.'s coun. No. Star coun. Boy Scouts Am., 1989—. Decorated Presdl. Order of Meritorious Svc. Botswana; recipient Disting. Eagle Scout award, 1993, Biscentenniel medal, Williams Coll, 2007; fellow, Danforth Found., 1960—63, Ford Found., 1962—63. Mem.: Nat. Tax Assn., Coun. on Fgn. Rels., Phi Beta Kappa. Office: 901 Marquette Ave S Ste 2810 Minneapolis MN 55402

LEWIS-WHITE, LINDA BETH, elementary school educator; b. Fresno, Calif., June 30, 1950; d. Lloyd Ernest and Anne Grace (Barkman) Lewis; m. Francis Everett White, Feb. 15, 1975; children: Anna Justine, Christopher Andrew Arthur. BA in Home Econs., Calif. State U., Sacramento, 1972, MA in Social Scis., 1973; postgrad., Tex. Women's U., 1976-79; PhD in Reading, East Tex. State U., 1994. Cert. bilingual and elem. edn. tchr., Tex. Tchr. bilingual Arlington Sch. Dist., 1977-96; prof. reading Eastern Mich. U., 1996—. Adj. prof. reading Tex. Women's U., Denton, 1989, adj. prof. ESL East Tex. State U., 1993; mem. tchr. trainer cadre, Dallas Ind. Sch. Dist., 1985-92; freelance cons., 1987—; presenter TESOL Internat. Conf., San Antonio, 1989. Cons., writer (book) Ciencias-Silver Burdett, 1988. Troop leader Girl Scouts U.LS., Dallas, 1980-82. Recipient Ronald W. Collins Provost Disting. Faculty award, Eastern Mich. U., 2007. Mem. at. Reading Conf., Nat. Writing Project, Internat. Reading Assn., Tchrs. of English to Spkrs. of Other Langs. (nominating com. 1990-91), TEXTESOL V (chair elem. edn. com. 1989-91), Tex. Assn. Bilingual Edn., Phi Delta Kappa, Phi Mu. Mem. Christian Ch. Avocations: sewing, knitting, quilting, reading, gourmet cooking. Office: Eastern Mich U 313A Porter Bldg Ypsilanti MI 48197-2210 Business E-Mail: llewiswh@emich.edu.

LEX, WILLIAM JOSEPH, college official; b. Temple, Tex., Sept. 3, 1944; s. Henry Joseph and Mary Dorothy (Jeske) L.; m. Diane Chostner, Nov. 25, 1967; 1 child, Carolyn Kimberly. AA, San Francisco City Coll., 1965; BA, U. Calif., Santa Barbara, 1967; MS, Oreg. State U., 1973; PhD, U. Tex., 1984. Head resident Oreg. State U., Corvallis, 1971-73; head resident edn. and programs U. Alaska, Fairbanks, 1973-76; dir. vocat. and tech. studies Tanana Valley C.C., Fairbanks, 1976-86; assoc. dean, dir. North Campus Pa. Coll. Tech., Wellsboro, 1986-91; dean Mendocino Coast Campus, Ft. Bragg, Calif., 1991-96; pres. Frontier C.C., Fairfield, Ill., 1996—. Chmn. community devel. com. Mendocino Pvt. Industry Coun.; mem. coastal com. Mendocino County Econ. Summit Steering Com.; mem. adv. com. Ft. Bragg Police Dept., Mendocino County Arts Coun. Mem. Nat. Coun. Instrnl. Adminstrs., Wellsboro Area C. of C. (bd. dirs. 1987-91), Mendocino Coast C. of C. (chmn. community devel. com.), Rotary (bd. dirs. GAleton, Pa. chpt. 1988-89, active Ft. Bragg chpt.), Phi Kappa Phi, Kappa Delta Pi. Democrat. Avocations: reading, gardening, music, outdoor sports.

LEYLAND, JIM (JAMES RICHARD LEYLAND), professional baseball manager; b. Toledo, Dec. 15, 1944; m. Katie Leyland. Player various minor league teams Detroit Tigers, 1964-69, coach minor league system, 1970-71, mgr. minor league system, 1971-81; coach Chgo. White Sox, 1981-85; mgr. Pitts. Pirates, 1985-96, Fla. Marlins, Miami, 1997-98, Colo. Rockies, Denver, 1998—99, Detroit Tigers, 2005—. Christmas chmn. Salvation Army, 1990-91. Named Nat. League Mgr. Yr. Baseball Writers' Assn., 1988, 1990, 2006; Sporting News, 1990, Man of Yr. Arthritis Found., 1989, Epilepsy Found., 1991; lead Detroit to playoffs two years after having worst record in Major League Baseball, 2006 Office: Detroit Tigers Comerica Pk 2100 Woodward Ave Detroit MI 48201

LHOTA, WILLIAM J., electric company executive; Exec. v.p. Am. Electric Power Svc. Corp., Columbus, Ohio. Office: Am Electric Power Svc Corp 1 Riverside Plz Columbus OH 43215-2355

LI, CHU-TSING, art historian, educator; b. Canton, China, 1920; came to U.S., 1947; m. Yao-wen; children: Ulysses, Amy. BA, U. Nanking, 1943; MA in English Lit., U. Iowa, 1949, PhD in Art History, 1955. Instr. U. Iowa, 1954-55, 56-58, asst. prof., 1958-62, assoc. prof., 1962-65, rsch. prof., 1963—64, prof., 1965-66; prof. art history U. Kans., Lawrence, 1966-78, dept. chmn., 1972-78, Judith Harris Murphy Disting. prof., 1978-90, prof. emeritus, 1990—, dir. EH summer seminar on Chinese art history, 1975, 78, coord. Mellon faculty seminar, 1979; acting asst. prof. Oberlin Coll., 1955-56; asst. prof. Ind. U., summer 1956; coord. N.Y. state faculty seminar on Chinese Art History, SUNY, 1965; rsch. curator Nelson Gallery of Art, Kansas City, 1966—. Vis. prof. fine arts Chinese U., Hong Kong, 1972-73, summer 1971, leader China visit group, 1973; vis. prof. Grad. Inst. Art History, Nat Taiwan U., 1990; vis. Andrew W. Mellon prof. U. Pitts., 1995; dir. NEH Summer Inst. Modern Chinese Art and Culture, 1991; participant Internat. Symposiums on Chinese Painting, at. Palace Mus., Taipei, 1970, Cleve. Mus. Art, 1981, Huangshan Sch. Painters, Hefei, Ahnui, Rep. China, 1984, on Words and Images in Chinese Painting, Met. Mus. Art, N.Y.C., 1985, on the Elegant Brush: Chinese Painting under the Qianlong Emperor, Phoenix Art Mus., 1985, to celebrate 60th anniversary Nat. Palace Mus., Taipei, Taiwan, 1985, on History of Yuan Dynasty, Nanjing U., China, 1986, on art of Badashanren (Chu Ta), Nanchang, China, 1986; on Dunhuang Grottoes, China, 1987; on the Four Monk Painters, Shanghai Mus., 1987; on art of Chang Dai-chien, Nat. Mus. History, Taipei, 1988; Symposium on Contemporary Artistic Development, Nanjing, 1988; Symposium on Chinese Painting of Ming Dynasty Chinese U. Hong Kong, 1988; Symposium on Chinese Painting of the Ming and Qing Dynasties from the Forbidden City, Cleve. Mus. Art, 1989, Symposium on Hist. Studies, since 1911, Nat. Taiwan U., 1989, Symposium on 40th Anniversary of Founding of Liaoning Provincial Mus., Shenyang, China, 1989, Symposium on Painting of Wu Sch., Palace Mus., Beijing, 1990; Internat. Colloquium on Chinese Art History, Nat. Palace Mus. Taipei, 1991, Internat. Symposium on Art of Four Wangs, Shanghai, 1992, VIIeme Colloque Internat. de Sinologie, Chantilly, France, 1992, Symposium Painting at Close Qing Empire, Phoenix, 1992, Symposium on Ming & Qing Painting, Beijing, 1994, Symposium on Art of Zhao Meng-fu, Shanghai, 1995, Symposium on 20th Century Chinese Painting, Hong Kong Mus. Art, 1995, Symposium on Contemporary Chinese Painting, Biennale of Shanghai Art Mus., 1998; spl. cons. Chinese U., Hong Kong, 1971, Symposium on Painting and Calligraphy by Ming Loyalists, Early Ch'ing Period, 1975, Symposium on the Art of Liu Kuo-sung, Mus. of History, Beijing, 2002, Palace Mus., Beijing, 2007, Symposium on Chinese Painting of 1850-1950, Kaohshing Mus. of Art, Taiwan, 2007. Author (books and exhbn. catalogues): The Autumn Colors on the Ch'iao and Hua Mountains, A Painting by Chao Meng-fu, 1254-1322, 1965; author: Liu Kuo-sung: The Development of a Modern Chinese Artist, 1970, A Thousand Peaks and Myriad Ravines: Chinese Paintings in the Charles A Drenowatz Collection, 2 vols., 1974, Trends in Modern Chinese Painting, 1979; co-author: History of Modern Chinese Painting, Part 1: Late Qing, 1998, Part 2: Republican China, 2001, Part 3: Contemporary, 2003, Tradition and Transformation: Studies in Chinese Art in Honor of Chu-Tsing Li, 2005; editor: Artists and Patrons: Some Social and Economic Aspects of Chinese Painting, 1990; co-editor: Chinese Scholar's Studio: Artistic Life in Late Ming, Asia Soc., 1987; contbr. articles to profl. jours. Ford Found. Fgn. Area Tng. fellow, 1959-60; grantee Am. Coun. Learned Socs. and Social Sci. Rsch. Coun., 1963-64, NEH, 1975, 78, 91, Com. for Scholarly Communication with People's Republic of China NAS, 1979, Am. Coun. Learned Socs., 1980, Asian Cultural Coun., N.Y., 1981, Kans. U., summers 1966-80; Fulbright-Hayes faculty fellow, 1968-69 Mem. Coll. Art Assn. Am., Assn. for Asian Studies, Midwest Art History Soc., Min-chiu Soc. Hong Kong, Phi Tau Phi, Phi Beta Kappa (hon.), Phi Beta Delta. Home: 1108 Avalon Rd Lawrence KS 66044-2506 Office: Univ Kans Kress Found Dept Art History Lawrence KS 66045-0001 Personal E-mail: ctsli@earthlink.net. Business E-Mail: ctsli@ku.edu.

LI, NORMAN N., chemicals executive; b. Shanghai, Jan. 14, 1933; naturalized, US, 1969; s. Lieh-wen and Amy H. Li; m. Jane C. Li, Aug. 17, 1963; children: Rebecca H., David H. BSChemE, Nat. Taiwan U., Taipei, 1955; MS, Wayne State U., 1957; PhD, Stevens Inst. Tech., 1963. Sr. scientist Exxon Rsch. and Engring. Co., Linden, NJ, 1963-81; dir. separation sci. and tech. UOP, Des Plaines, Ill., 1981-88; dir. engineered products and process tech. Allied-Signal Inc., Des Plaines, Ill., 1988-92, dir. rsch. and tech., 1993-95; pres., CEO NL Chem. Technology, Inc., 1995—. Mem. NRC, 1985-89; lectr. AIChE, 1975-86. Editor 20 books on separation sci. and tech.; contbr. articles to profl. jours.; patentee in field. Fellow: AIChE (dir. divsn. food, pharms. and bioengring. 1988—91, bd. dirs. 1992—94, founder award for Outstanding Contributions to Chem. Engring. field 2006, Alpha Chi Sigma rsch. award 1988, Ernest Thiele award 1995, Chem. Engring. Practice award 2000, Lifetime Achievement award 2001, Gerhold award in separation tech. 2002); mem.: Acad. Sinica, Chinese Acad. Scis., N.Am. Membrane Soc. (pres. 1991—93, Perkin medalist 2000), Am. Chem. Soc. (Separation Sci. and Tech. award 1988), NAE. Home: 620 N Rolling Ln Arlington Heights IL 60004-5820 Office Phone: 847-824-2888. Personal E-mail: NLChem@aol.com.

LI, TZE-CHUNG, lawyer, educator; b. Shanghai, China, Feb. 17, 1927; came to U.S., 1956; s. Ken-hsiang Li and Yun-hsien (Chang) Li; m. Dorothy In-lan Wang, Oct. 21, 1961; children— Lily, Rose LL.B., Soochow U., Shanghai, 1948; Diploma, Nat. Chengchi U., Nanking, 1949, China Research Inst. of Land Econs., Taipei, 1952; M.C.L., So. Meth. U., Dallas, 1956; LL.M., Harvard U., Cambridge, 1958; MS, Columbia U., NYC, 1965; PhD, New Sch. for Social Research, NYC, 1963. Judge Hwa-lien Dist. Ct., Hwa-lien, Taiwan, Republic of China, 1949-51; dist. atty. Ministry of Justice, Tapei, 1951-52; chief law sect. Ministry of Nat. Def., Tapei, 1952-56; asst. prof. library sci. Ill. State U., Normal, 1965-66; asst. prof. polit. sci., library sci. Rosary Coll., River Forest, Ill., 1966-69, assoc. prof. library sci., 1969-70, 72-74, prof. library sci., 1974-82, dean, prof. Grad. Sch. Library and Info. Sci., 1982-88; prof. Dominican U., River Forest, Ill., 1988-99, dean, prof. emeritus, 2000—; vis. assoc. prof. law Nat. Taiwan U., 1969; vis. assoc. prof. polit. sci. Soochow U., Taipei, 1969; dir. Nat. Central Library, Taipei, 1970-72; pres. One China Comm., 2005—. Chmn. Grad. Inst. Library Sci., Nat. Central Library, Taipei, 1970-72; commr. Ministry of Examination, Examination Yuan, Taipei, 1971; chmn. com. on library standards, Ministry of Edn., Taipei, 1972; library cons. Soochow U., Nat. Chengchi U., Dr. Sun Yat-sen Meml. Library; mem. library adv. com. Ency. Britannica, 1982-95; hon. prof. library and info. sci. Jiangxi U., People's Republic of China, 1985—; vis. prof. law Suzhou U., Peking U., 1991, Nat. Taiwan U., 1991; hon. cons. univ. library, 1985—; hon. cons. Jiangxi Med. Coll., 1985—; adv. prof. East China Normal U., 1987—; cons. Nova U., 1987-88; mem. ad hoc adv. com. Chgo. Pub. Library Bldg. Planning, 1987-88; CEO LLD Group, 1972—; bd. chmn. Li Ednl. Found., 1977—; legacy leader Nat. Conf. Asian Pacific Am. Librarians, 2001. Author books including: Social Science Reference Sources, 1980, 3d edit., 2000, Mah Jong, 1982, 2d edit., 1991, An Introduction to Online Searching, 1985; also numerous articles in profl., scholarly jours.; founding editor Jour. Library and Info. Sci., 1975-80, mem. editl. bd. 1986-90; founding chmn., mem. editl. bd. Internat. Jour. of Revs., 1984-89; editor: World Libraries, 1996-99. Pres. Chinese Am. Ednl. Found., Chgo., 1968—70. Recipient Govt. Citation Republic of China, 1956, 1972, Philip D. Sang Excellence in Teaching award Rosary Coll., 1971, Disting. Service award Phi Tau Phi, Chgo., 1982, Service award HUD, Chgo. region, 1985, Disting. Service award Chinese Am. Librarians Assn., 1988. Mem. Chinese Am. Librarians Assn. (founding pres. 1976-80), China Assn. Libr. and Info. Sci. Edn. (hon.), Library Assn. China (Taipei), Phi Tau Phi (pres. 1985-87) Roman Catholic. Home: 135 E 54th St 11H New York NY 10022 Business E-Mail: richard@chamonline.org, chiamonline@att.net.

LI, WEN-HSIUNG, geneticist; b. Pinq-Tung, Taiwan, Sept. 22, 1942; s. Linder and Piau Wang; m. Sue J. Li, Mar. 31, 1975; children: Vivian, Herman, Joyce. BE, Chungyuan Coll. Sci. & Engr., Chung-li, Taiwan, 1965; MS, Nat. Ctrl. U., Mio-li, Taiwan, 1968; PhD in Applied Math, Brown U., Providence, RI, 1972. Project assoc. U. Wis., Madison, 1972-73; asst. prof. U. Tex.-Houston, 1973-78, assoc. prof., 1978-84, prof., 1984-98, U. Chicago, 1998—. Assoc. editor Genetics, 1984-86; editor Molecular Phylogenetics & Evolution, San Diego, 1991—. Author: Fundamentals of Molecular Evolution, 1991, Molecular Evolution, 1997. Grantee: Nat. Inst. Health, Bethesda, Md., 1983, 96, 87, 98, 99, 00. Fellow AAAS, Soc. for Molecular Biology & Evolution (pres. 2000), George Beadle Prof. Democrat. Avocations: sports, music, movies. Office: Dept Ecology & Evolution 1101 E 57th St Dept Ecology& Chicago IL 60637-1503 Fax: 773-702-9740. E-mail: whli@uchicago.edu.

LIAO, SHUTSUNG, biochemist, molecular oncologist; b. Tainan, Taiwan, Jan. 1, 1931; s. Chi-Chun Liao and Chin-Shen Lin; m. Shuching Liao, Mar. 19, 1960; children: Jane, Tzufen, Tzuming, May. BS in Agrl. Chemistry, Nat. Taiwan U., 1953, MS in Biochemistry, 1956; PhD in Biochemistry, U. Chgo., 1961. Rsch. assoc., 1960-63; asst. prof. U. Chgo., 1964-69; assoc. prof. dept. biochemistry and molecular biology Ben May Lab. Cancer Rsch., U. Chgo., 1969-71; prof. depts. biochemistry, molecular and cancer biology Ben May Inst. for Cancer Rsch., 1972—; dir. Tang Ctr. Herbal Medicine Rsch., 2000—02. CEO, chmn. bd., Anagen Therapeutic Co., 2000—; cons. in field. Mem. editl. bd. Jour. Steroid Biochemistry and Molecular Biology, The Prostate, Receptors, Signal Transduction, J. Formosan Med. Assoc., Biomedical Sci.; assoc. editor Cancer Rsch., 1982-89; contbr. over 250 articles to profl jours. V.p. Chgo. Formosan Fed. Credit Union, 1977-79; trustee Taiwanese United Fund in U.S., 1981-85; mem. adv. com. Taiwan-U.S. Cultural Exch. Ctr., 1984-87. Recipient Sci-Tech. Achievement prize Taiwanese-Am. Found., 1983, Pfizer Lecture fellow award Clin. Rsch. Inst. Montreal, 1972, Gregory Pincus medal and award Worcester Found. for Exptl. Biology, 1992, Tzongming Tu award Formosan Med. Assn., 1993, C.H. Li Meml. Lecture award, 1994; NIH grantee, 1962—; Am. Cancer Soc. grantee, 1971-81. Fellow Am. Acad. Art and Scis.; mem. Am. Soc. Biochemistry and Molecular Biology, Am. Assn. Cancer Rsch., Endocrine Soc., .Am.-Taiwanese Profs. Assn. (pres. 1980-81, exec. dir. 1981—), Nat. Acad. Taiwan. Achievements include discovery of androgen activation mechanism and androgen receptors; cloning and structural determination of androgen receptors and other novel nuclear receptors, and their genes, and receptor gene mutation in hereditary abnormalities and cancers; rsch. on regulation of hormone-dependent gene expression and cell growth, molecular bases of cancer cell growth and progression, chemoprevention, and therapeutic treatment of hormone-sensitive and insensitive cancers and diseases, molecular bases of cholesterol modulation and control in cardiovascular and neurodegenerative diseases and cancer progression. Home: 5632 S Woodlawn Ave Chicago IL 60637-1623 Office: U Chgo Ben May Inst Cancer Rsch 929 E 57th St Chicago IL 60637

LIBBY, WENDY B., academic administrator; m. Richard Libby; children: Glenn, Gregg. BS in Biology, Cornell U., 1972; MBA, Johnson Grad. Sch. of Mgmt. at Cornell U., 1977; PhD in Ednl. Adminstrn., U. Conn., 1994. Dir. adminstrn. pub. mgmt. program Johnson Grad. Sch. of Mgmt. at Cornell U., Ithaca, NY, 1979—80; dir. adminstrv. ops. Coll. of Architecture, Art and Planning, Ithaca, NY, 1980—84; adminstrv. mgr. Coll. Edn. Ohio State U., Columbus, 1984—85, adminstrv. assoc. Office of Fin., 1984—85; asst. dir. U. Conn. Med. Ctr. John Dempsey Hosp., Farmington, Conn., 1985—87, asst. to assoc. exec. dir., 1985—87; spl. asst. to pres. and sr. human resources officer U. Hartford, Conn., 1987—89; chief fin. and bus. officer Westbrook Coll., Portland, Maine, 1989—95; v.p. bus. affairs and CFO Furman U., Greenville, SC, 1995—2003; pres. Stephens Coll., Columbia, Mo., 2003—. Founding bd. dirs. Tuition Plan Consortium, Caribbean Inst. Tech.; bd. dirs. Greenville Literacy Assn., Women's Coll. Coalition. Mem.: Boone County Nat. Bank Coun. Ind. Coll. (bd. mem.), Soc. Coll. and U. Planning, So. Assn. of Coll. and U. Bus. Officers, Ea. Assn. of Coll. and U. Bus. Officers (bd. dirs.), Nat. Assn. of Coll. and U. Bus. Officers. Office: Stephens Coll 1200 E Broadway Columbia MO 65215

LIBERT, DONALD JOSEPH, lawyer; b. Sioux Falls, SD, Mar. 23, 1928; s. Bernard Joseph and Eleanor Monica (Sutton) L.; m. Jo Anne Murray, May 16, 1953; children: Cathleen, Thomas, Kevin, Richard, Stephanie. BS magna cum laude in Social Scis., Georgetown U., 1950, LLB, 1956. Bar: Ohio. From assoc. to ptnr. Manchester, Bennett, Powers & Ullman, Youngstown, Ohio, 1956-65; various positions to v.p., gen. counsel and sec. Youngstown Sheet & Tube Co., 1965-78; assoc. group counsel LTV Corp., Youngstown and Pitts., 1979; v.p. and gen. counsel Anchor Hocking Corp., Lancaster, Ohio, 1979-87; pvt. practice Lancaster, 1987—. Served to lt. (j.g.) USN, 1951-54. Mem. Ohio Bar Assn., Fairfield County Bar Assn., Lancaster Country Club, Rotary. Republican. Roman Catholic. Home: 2198 William T Cir Lancaster OH 43130-1087

LICATA, ANTHONY R., lawyer, real estate developer; b. DuQuoin, Ill., July 19, 1954; s. Jack and Juanita (Keeler) L.; m. Susan A. Licata, May 8, 1982; 1 child, Haley M. BS, MacMurray Coll., 1976; JD, Harvard U., 1979. Bar: Ill. Assoc. Sidley & Austin, Chgo., 1979-84, of counsel, 1984—; pres. Broadacre Ptnrs., Inc., Chgo., 1989—. Bd. dirs. McClier Corp., Chgo.; lectr. J.L. Kellogg Grad. Sch. Mgmt., Northwestern U., Chgo., 1989—. Contbr. articles to profl. publs. Bd. dirs. Make A Wish Found., 1988, Chgo. Osteo. Health Systems, 1990—; chmn. adv. com. Senator Paul Simon.

LICHTER, ALLEN S., oncologist, educator, dean; BS, U. Mich., 1968, MD, 1972. Intern St. Joseph Hosp., Denver; resident U. Calif., San Francisco, 1976; former dir. radiation therapy sect. radiation oncology br. Nat. Cancer Inst.; dir. breast oncology program Comprehensive Cancer Ctr., U. Mich., Ann Arbor, 1984-91, chmn. dept. radiation oncology, 1984-97, interim dean Med. Sch., 1998-99, prof. radiation oncology, 1999—, dean Med. sch., 1999—. Bd. dirs. Accreditation Coun. for Grad. Med. Edn. Assoc. editor Jour. Clin. Oncology; editl. bd. Jour. Nat. Cancer Inst., Internat. Jour. Radiation Oncology; co-editor Clinical Oncology, 1995, 2d edit., 1999. Mem.: Am. Soc. Therapeutic Radiology and Oncology (bd. dirs.), Am. Soc. Clin. Oncology (past pres.). Achievements include research in effective breast cancer treatment. Office: U Mich M4101 Med Science Bldg I-C Wing MSI 0624, 1301 Catherine St Ann Arbor MI 48109

LICHTER, PAUL RICHARD, ophthalmology educator; b. Detroit, Mar. 7, 1939; BA, U. Mich., 1960, MD, 1964, MS, 1968. Diplomate Am. Bd. Ophthalmology. Asst. to assoc. prof. ophthalmology U. Mich., Ann Arbor, 1971-78, prof., chmn. dept. ophthalmology and visual scis., 1978—. Chmn. Am. Bd. Ophthalmology, 1987. Editor-in-chief Ophthalmology jour., 1986-94; assoc. editor Am. Jour. Ophthalmology, 2004—. Served to lt. comdr. USN, 1969-71. Fellow: Am. Acad. Ophthalmology (bd. dirs. 1981—97, pres. 1996, sr. hon. award 1986, Lifetime Achievement award 2001); mem.: Acad. Ophthalmologica Internat. (sec.-gen. 2002—), Assn. Univ. Profs. Ophthalmology (trustee 1986—93, pres. 1991—92), Mich. Ophthalmol. Soc. (pres. 1993—95), Washtenaw County Med. Soc., Mich. State Med. Soc., Pan Am. Assn.Ophthalmology (bd. dirs. 1988—, sec.-treas. English-speaking countries 1991—95, pres. 1999—2001), Am. Ophthalmol. Soc. (pres. 2000—01), AMA, Alpha Omega Alpha. Office: U Mich Med Sch Kellogg Eye Ctr 1000 Wall St Ann Arbor MI 48105-1912 Business E-Mail: Plichter@umich.edu.

LICHTWARDT, ROBERT WILLIAM, mycologist; b. Rio de Janeiro, Nov. 27, 1924; s. Henry Herman and Ruth Moyer Lichtwardt; m. Elizabeth Thomas, Jan. 27, 1951; children: Ruth Elizabeth, Robert Thomas. AB, Oberlin Coll., 1949; MS, U. Ill., 1951, PhD, 1954. Postdoctoral fellow NSF, Panama, Brazil, 1954-55; postdoctoral rsch. assoc. Iowa State U., Ames, 1955-57; asst. prof. U. Kans., Lawrence, 1957-60, assoc. prof., 1960-65; sr. postdoctoral fellow NSF, Hawaii, Japan, 1963-64; prof. U. Kans., Lawrence, 1965-94, prof. emeritus, 1994—. Author: The Trichomycetes, Fungal Associates of Arthropods, 1986; contbr. 130 articles to profl. jours. Mem. Mycological Soc. Am. (life, pres. 1971-72, editor-in-chief 1965-70, William H. Weston award for tchg. excellence in mycology 1982, Disting. Mycologist award 1991), Brit. Mycological Soc. (hon.), Japan Mycological Soc. (hon.). Office: U Kans Dept Ecology Evol Biology Lawrence KS 66045-7534 Office Phone: 785-864-3740. Business E-Mail: licht@ku.edu.

LICKHALTER, MERLIN, architect; b. St. Louis, May 4, 1934; s. Frank E. and Sophia (Geller) L.; m. Harriet Braen, June 9, 1957; children: Debra, Barbara. BArch, MIT, 1957. Registered arch., Mo., Calif., Fla., Man. Ptnr. Drake Partnership, Architects, St. Louis, 1961-77; pres. JRB Architects, Inc., St. Louis, 1977-81; sr. v.p., mng. dir. Stone, Marraccini & Patterson, St. Louis, 1981-93; sr. v.p., dir. Cannon, 1993—2002; pres. Lickhalter & Assocs. LLC, 2003—. Owner, pres. mgmt. program Harvard U. Bus. Sch., 1992; cons. Dept. Def., Washington, 1977-78; lectr. Washington U. Sch. Medicine, 1989—. Prin. projects include The Mayo Clinic, Jacksonville, Fla., Washington U. Med. Ctr., St. Louis, U.S. Army Hosp., Frankfurt, Germany, Nat. AIDS Rsch. Ctr., NIH, Washington, Evanston (Ill.) Hosp., Loma Linda (Calif.) U. Med. Ctr., U. Mo. Health Scis. Ctr., Columbia, St. Louis U. Health Scis. Ctr., Children's Hosp. Rsch. Inst., ew Orleans, U. Ala. Birmingham Sch. Medicine, U. Ala. Sch. Optometry. Trustee United Hebrew Congregation, St. Louis, 1980-88, 93-98, 2000—; exec. com. bd. dir. Arts & Edn. Coun. St. Louis, 1991-2002; pres. Acad. Architecture for Health Found., 2002-06; exec. com., bd. dir. United Arts Coun. Collier County, 2003—, pres., 2007-08; vice chair, bd. mem., Pelican Bay Found., 2005—; Capt. U.S. Army, 1957-59. Recipient Renovation Design award St. Louis Producers Coun., 1976, USAF Europe Design Award, 1990. Fellow: AIA (pres. nat. acad. arch. for health 1993, bd. dir. 2003—, exec. com.), Am. Coll. Healthcare Architects; mem.: Acad. Arch. Health Found. (pres., trustee 2000—06), MIT Club Southwest Fla. (dir. 2005—), Club Pelican Bay. Jewish. Home and Office: 6825 Grenadier Blvd Naples FL 34108 Personal E-mail: mlickhalter@comcast.net.

LICKLITER, TODD, men's college basketball coach; b. Apr. 17, 1955; s. Arlan Lickliter; m. Joez Lickliter; children: Ry, Garrett, John. A, Ctrl. Fla. CC, 1977; BS in Secondary Edn., Butler U., 1979. Head coach Pk. Tudor HS, Indpls., 1979—87, Danville HS, Ind., 1987—88, 1989—92, Ah Ahli Sports Club, Jeddah, Saudi Arabia; asst. coach Butler U., 1988—89, 1999—2001, adminstrv. asst., 1996—97, head coach, 2001—07, U. Iowa, 2007—; asst. coach Ea. Mich. U., Ypsilanti, 1997—99. Named Horizon League Coach of Yr., 2006, 2007, Divsn. I Coach of Yr., Nat. Assn. Basketball Coaches, 2007. Office: Iowa Basketball 240 Carver Hawkeye Arena Iowa City IA 52242-1020 Office Phone: 319-335-9444.

LIDDY, BRIAN, food products executive; CFO Schreiber Foods, Inc., Green Bay, Wis. Office: Schreiber Foods Inc PO Box 19010 Green Bay WI 54307 Office Fax: (920) 437-1617.

LIDDY, EDWARD M., insurance company executive; b. New Brunswick, NJ, Jan. 28, 1946; m. Marcia Liddy; 3 children. BA, Cath. U. Am., 1968; MBA, George Washington U., 1972. With Internat. Harvester Co., Ford Motor Co., Ryder Systems Inc., 1968-79; sr. v.p. G.D. Searle & Co., Skokie, Ill., 1979-85; exec. v.p., CFO ADT Inc., NYC, 1986-88; CFO Sears, Roebuck and Co., 1988-94; pres., COO The Allstate Corp. and Allstate Ins. Co., Northbrook, Ill., 1994-98, chmn., pres., CEO, 1999—2005, chmn., CEO, 2005—06, chmn., 2007—. Bd. dirs. The Kroger Co., 3M, Ins. Information Inst., Goldman Sachs Group, Inc. Chmn. elect, nat. gov. Boys & Girls Clubs Am.; bd. dirs. Northwestern Meml. Hosp., Jr. Achievement of Chgo. Mem.: Catalyst, Bus. Roundtable, Fin. Svcs. Forum. Office: The Allstate Corp 2775 Sanders Rd Northbrook IL 60062-6127

LIDSTROM, NICKLAS, professional hockey player; b. Vasteras, Sweden, Apr. 28, 1970; Defenceman Detroit Red Wings, 1991—, capt., 2006—; player NHL All-Rookie Team, 1992, NHL All-Star Game, 1996, 1998—2004. Named to All-Rookie Team, NHL, 1992, NHL All-Star Game, 1996, 1998—2004, 2007, 2008, First All-Star Team, NHL, 1998—2003, 2006, 2007; recipient James Norris Meml. Trophy, 2001, 2002, 2003, 2006, 2007, Conn Smythe Trophy, 2002. Achievements include being a member of Stanley Cup Champion Detroit Red Wings, 1997, 1998, 2002; being a member of gold medal winning Swedish Hockey Team, Torino Olympics, Italy, 2006; over 600 assists, 2006. Office: Detroit Red Wings Joe Louis Arena 600 Civic Ctr Detroit MI 48226*

LIE, ERIK, finance educator; b. 1968; s. Rolf Lie. BS summa cum laude, U. Ore., 1990, MBA, 1991; PhD, Purdue U., 1996. Asst. prof. bus. Coll. William & Mary, Williamsburg, Va., 1996—2002, Wilson P. and Martha Claiborne Stephens assoc. prof., 2002—04; assoc. prof., Henry B. Tippie rsch. fellow U. Iowa, Iowa City, 2004—. Contbr. articles to profl. jours. Served with Norwegian Navy, Norwegian Coast Guard, 1991—92. Named one of The World's 100 Most Influential People, TIME mag., 2007; recipient Alumni Fellowship award for Excellence in Teaching, Coll. William & Mary, 2002. Office: Henry B Tippie Coll Bus U Iowa Iowa City IA 52242-1000 Office Phone: 319-335-0846. Office Fax: 319-335-3690. E-mail: erik-lie@uiowa.edu.

LIEB, MICHAEL, English educator, humanities educator; AB in Eng. Lit., Rutgers U., 1962, AM in Eng. Lit., 1964, PhD in Eng. Lit., 1967; student, U. Iowa, 1962-63, U. Chgo. Divinity Sch., 1974-75, Spertus Coll. of Judaica, 1987-92. Asst. prof. Eng. Coll. of William and Mary, Williamsburg, Va., 1967-70; assoc. prof. Eng. U. Ill., Chgo., 1970-75, prof. Eng., 1975-88, rsch. prof. humanities, 1988—. Vis. professorial lectr. U. Chgo. Divinity Sch., 1979; bd. dirs. Friends of Milton's Cottage; mem. exec. com. U. Chgo. Renaissance Seminar, 1977—; mem. exec. com. Divsn. 17th Century Eng. Lit. MLA, 1982-86, Divsn. Religious Approaches to Lit., 1987-91; mem. exec. com. Ctr. Renaissance Studies Newberry Libr., 1979—, mem. com. Brit. Acad. Fellowships, 1982-83, mem. search com. for dir., 1984; mem. adv. com. 2d Internat. Milton Symposium, 1983, 4th, 1990; campus rep. Woodrow Wilson Found., 1982-83; mem. numerous coms. U. Ill. Author: The Dialectics of Creation: Patterns of Birth and Regeneration in Paradise Lost, 1970, Poetics of the Holy: A Reading of Paradise Lost, 1981 (James Holly Hanford award Milton Soc. Am.), The Sinews of Ulysses: Form and Convention in Milton's Works, 1989, The Visionary Mode: Biblical Prophecy, Hermeneutics and Cultural Change, 1991, Milton and the Culture of Violence, 1994; co-editor, contbg. author: Achievements of the Left hand: Essays on the Prose of John Milton, 1974, Eyes Fast Fixt: Current Perspectives in Milton Methodology, 1975, Literary Milton: Text, Pretext, Context, 1994, The Miltonic Samson, 1996; contbr. articles to profl. jours.; symposia speaker in field; panelist; invited speaker; cons. edit. bds., univ. presses, profl. jours., librs., depts. Eng., Comparative Lit., Divinity. Pres., co-founder Oak Park Housing Ctr., 1971-73, Advocate award 1992; mem. hon. com. Ill. Humanities Coun., 1986; mem. Am. Jewish Com. Academicians

Seminar, Israel, 1986. NEH U. Tchrs. fellow, 1991-92, John Simon Guggenheim Meml. Found. fellow 1987-88, U. Ill. Chgo. Inst. for Humanities sr. fellow 1983, Newberry Libr. Nat. Endowment for Humanities sr. fellow 1981-82, NEH Younger Humanist Study fellow 1974-75; recipient Am. Coun. Learned Societies Grant-in-Aid, 1985, Am. Philosophical Soc. Grant-in-Aid, 1983, Folger Shakespeare Libr. fellow, 1970, 74; Honors Coll. U. Ill. Chgo. fellow 1986—; others. Mem. Milton Soc. Am. (chair James Holly Hanford awards com. 1991-93, treas. 1973-77, v.p. 1980, pres. 1981, honored scholar 1992), Modern Lang. Assn., Milton Soc. of Japan, Southeastern Renaissance Conf., Renaissance Soc. of Am., Calif. Renaissance Conf., Northeastern Modern Lang. Assn., Newberry Libr. Milton Seminar (co-founder, co-chair 1986—), Newberry Libr. Dante Lectures. Home: 212 S Ridgeland Ave Oak Park IL 60302-3226 Office: U Ill Chgo Coll Liberal ARts & Scis Dept Eng M/C 162 601 S Morgan St Chicago IL 60607-7100

LIEB, PETER, lawyer; BA, Yale U.; JD, U. Mich. Law clk. to Chief Justice Warren Burger US Supreme Ct.; asst. atty. US Dist. Ct. (so. dist. NY); ptnr. Jones, Day, Reavis & Pogue; asst. gen. counsel GTE Svc. Corp.; v.p., dep. gen. counsel Internat. Paper Co., 1998—2003; sr. v.p., gen. counsel, sec. Symbol Technologies, Inc., Holtsville, NY, 2003—06; sr. v.p., gen. counsel NCR Corp., 2006—. Adj. prof. Fordham U. Office: NCR Corp 1700 S Patterson Blvd Dayton OH 45479 Office Phone: 631-738-4765. Office Fax: 631-738-5980.

LIEBERMAN, EDWARD JAY, lawyer; b. Evansville, Ind., Apr. 8, 1946; s. Heiman George and Anna Sharp (Blacker) L.; m. Ellen Ackerman Wegusen, June 1, 1969; 1 child: Laura Amy. BSBA, Washington U., St. Louis, 1968, JD, 1971. Bar: Mo. 1971. Jr. ptnr. Bryan Cave, St. Louis, 1972-76; assoc. counsel 1st Nat. Bank in St. Louis, 1976-80; ptnr. Lowenhaupt, Chasnoff, Armstrong & Mellitz, St. Louis, 1980-84, Husch & Eppenberger, LLC, St. Louis, 1984—. Mem. ABA, Mo. Bar, Bar Assn. Met. St. Louis, Am. Coll. Mortgage Attys., Nat. Health Care Lawyers Assn. Office: Husch & Eppenberger LLC 190 Carondelet Plz Ste 600 Saint Louis MO 63105 E-mail: ed.lieberman@husch.com.

LIEBERMAN, LAURENCE, poet, educator; b. Detroit, Feb. 16, 1935; s. Nathan and Anita (Cohen) L.; m. Bernice Clair Braun, June 17, 1956; children—Carla, Deborah, Isaac. BA, U. Mich., 1956, MA in English, 1958; postgrad., U. Calif.-Berkeley. Prof. English Coll. V.I., 1964-68; prof. English and creative writing U. Ill., Urbana, 1968—. U. Ill. Ctr. for Advanced Study Creative Writing fellow, Japan, 1971-72 Author: The Unblinding, 1968, The Achievement of James Dickey, 1969, The Osprey Suicides, 1973, Unassigned Frequencies: American Poetry in Review (1964-77), 1977, God's Measurements, 1980, Eros At the World Kite Pageant, 1983, The Mural of Wakeful Sleep, 1985, (poems) The Creole Mephistopheles, 1989, The Best American Poetry, 1991 (award), New and Selected Poems (1962-92), 1993, The St. Kitts. Monkey Feuds, 1995, Beyond the Muse of Memory: Essays on Contemporary Poets, 1995, Dark Songs: Slave House and Synagogue, 1996, Compass of the Dying, 1998, The Regatta in the Skies: Selected Long Poems, 1999, Flight From the Mother Stone, 2000, Hour of The Mango Black Moon, 2004, Carib's Leap: Selected and New Poems, 2005, numerous poems; poetry editor U. Ill. Press, 1970—. Recipient award for Best Poems of 1968, at. Endowment for Arts, 1969, Jerome P. Shestack award Am. Poetry Rev., 1986; creative writing fellow U. Ill. Ctr. for Advanced Study, 2000—, Nat. Endowment Arts, 1986-87. Office: U Ill English Dept 608 S Wright St Urbana IL 61801-3630

LIEBERMAN, MYRON, lawyer; b. Chgo., Feb. 14, 1931; s. Louis and Ethel (Shulman) L.; m. Eleanor Levy, July 22, 1954; children: Elizabeth Lieberman Keller, Peter Harold. BS, Stanford U., 1952; LLB, Northwestern U., Chgo., 1954. Bar: Ill. 1954. Assoc. Law Office of Bernard Mamet, Chgo., 1954-55, Law Office of Swiren & Heineman, Chgo., 1955-57; ptnr. Lieberman, Levy, Baron & Stone, Chgo., 1958-80; sr. ptnr. Altheimer & Gray, Chgo., 1980—. Dir. Columbia Nat. Bank of Chgo., Montgomery Ward & Co., Inc., Chgo., Mid-Town Bank & Trust Co., Chgo. Bd. dirs. Anti-Defamation League, Chgo., 1991—. Mem. Standard Club. Home: 360 Deere Park Dr E Highland Park IL 60035-5350

LIEBLER, ARTHUR C., automotive executive; b. Pitts., June 19, 1942; s. Arthur Cyril and Frances (Coyle) L.; m. Nancy Elizabeth Cullen, Sept. 19, 1964; children: Molly, Katie, Patrick. AB in Journalism, Marquette U., 1964; postgrad., Wayne State U. Reporter WRJN Radio Racine Journal Times, Wis., 1964; jr. acct. exec. The Selz Orgn., Chgo., 1965-66; staff reporter, employer Ford Motor Co., Dearborn, Mich., 1966-67, corporate pub. rels. staff, 1967-76; sr. v.p. acct. mgmt. and supv. Ross Roy Inc., Detroit, Mich., 1976-80; dir. corp. mdse. Chrysler Corp., Detroit, 1980-82, dir. communications programs, 1982, gen. mktg. mgr., 1983-87, dir. mktg. svcs., 1987-98, v.p. mktg., 1998—; sr. v.p. mktg. Daimler Chrysler, Auburn Hills, Mich., 1998-2000, sr. v.p. global brand mktg., 2000—. Bd. dirs. Common Ground (Drug Prevention) Birmingham Mich., 1966-70; committeeman Dem. Party Chectenham Township Pa., 1971-72; miscellaneous Sch. Bd. Activities, Birmingham Mich., 1974-77. Mem. Detroit Adcraft Club (accreditied, bd. dirs.), Pub. Rels. Soc. Am. (bd. dirs.), Am Advt. Fedn. (bd. dirs.), Detroit Golf Club.

LIEDER, BERNARD L., state legislator, civil engineer; m. Shirley B. Lieder; three children. Student, U. Ill., Purdue U. Engineer; Dist. 2A rep. Minn. Ho. of Reps., St. Paul, 1984—. Vice chmn. agr., transp. and semi-state divsn. appropriations com., chmn. transp. fin. divsn. appropriations Minn. Ho. of Reps.; mem. local govt. and met. affairs and transp. coms.; former chmn. ethics com.; mem. capital investments, econ. devel., infrastructure and regulation fin. coms. Home: 911 Thorndale Ave Crookston MN 56716-1150

LIEGEL, CRAIG A., meat packing company executive; CFO Packerland Packing Co., Green Bay, Wis. Office: Packerland Packing Co PO Box 23000 Green Bay WI 54305-3000

LIEN, BRUCE HAWKINS, minerals and oil company executive; b. Waubay, SD, Apr. 7, 1927; s. Peter Calmer and LaRece Catherine (Holm) L.; m. Deanna Jean Browning, May 4, 1978. BS in Bus., Wyo. U., 1953; doctorate in Bus. (hon.), SD Sch. Mines & Tech., 1996. Corp. exec. Pete Lien & Sons, Inc., Rapid City, S.D., 1944-60, bd. chmn., 1960—, Concorde Gaming Corp., 1990—, Browning Resources U.S., 1989—. Chmn. Cmty. Chest. Rapid City, S.D., 1956; pres. U. Wyo. Found., 1989-90; life bd. dirs. Salvation Army. 1st lt. U.S. Army, 1945-47, 50-52. Recipient Disting. Svc. award S.D. Sch. Mines, Rapid City, 1972, Disting. Svc. award Cosmopolitan Internat., Rapid City, 1983; named Disting. Alumnus, Wyo. U., Laramie, 1982, 1996. Mem. Internat. Lime Assn. (pres. 1973-75), Nat. Lime Assn. (pres. 1973-75, Merit award 1973, bd. dirs.), VFW, Am. Legion, Cosmopolitan Club, Masons, Elks. Republican. Lutheran. Home: PO Box 440 Rapid City SD 57709-0440 Office: Pete Lien & Sons Inc I 90 & Deadwood Ave PO Box 440 Rapid City SD 57709-0440

LIEN, JOHN DONOVAN, lawyer; b. LaCrosse, Wis., Dec. 30, 1943; s. Arthur Marvin and Alverda (Larson) L.; m. Kathleen McHenry, June 17, 1967 (div. Mar. 1983); m. Molly Warner, Apr. 2, 1983. BA, U. Wis., 1965; JD, Harvard U., 1968. Bar: Wis. 1968, Ill. 1972, U.S. Dist. Ct. (no. dist.) Ill. 1972, U.S. Ct. Appeals (7th cir.) 1977. Assoc. Wilson & McIlvaine, Chgo., 1972-77, ptnr., 1978-86, Antonow & Fink, Chgo., 1986-88, Foley & Lardner LLP, Chgo., 1988—, chmn. construction practice group. Trustee Village of Winnetka, Ill., 1997-2001, Winnetka Libr. Dist., 1985-93. Capt. USAF, 1968-72. Republican. Episcopalian. Office: Foley & Lardner LLP One IBM Plz Chicago IL 60611 Office Phone: 312-832-4370. Business E-Mail: jlien@foley.com.

LIENEMANN, DELMAR ARTHUR, SR., accountant, real estate developer; b. Papillion, Nebr., May 17, 1920; s. Arthur Herman and Dorothea M. (Marth) L.; m. Charlotte Peck, Jun 17, 1944 (dec. Mar. 1995); children: Delmar Arthur Jr., David (dec.), Diane, Douglas, Dorothy, Daniel, Denise. BS, U. Nebr., 1941. CPA, Nebr. Acct. Wickstrom Supply, Lincoln, Nebr., 1941, L.L. Coryell & Sons, Lincoln, 1942, Lester Buckley, CPA, Lincoln, 1943-45; pvt. practice Lincoln, 1945—. Pres., v.p., sec., treas., bldg. chmn., charter mem. Christ Luth. Ch., Lincoln, 1949-70; co-commr. Lancaster County, Lincoln, 1954-58; pres. Lincoln Symphony Orch. Found., 1984—, Ethel S. Abbott Charitable Found. Mem. AICPA, N.E. Soc. CPA, Colo. Soc. CPA, Tex. Soc. CPA, Sertoma (sec.-treas. Lincoln chpt. 1952-68, Internat. Sertoman of Yr. 1962), Nebr. Soc. CPA (Pub. Svc. award, 2003), Hillcrest Country Club, Nebr. Club, Nebr. Chancellors Club, Nebr. Touchdown Club, Nebr. Power Club, Nebr. Rebounders Club. Republican. Avocation: travel. Office: PO Box 81407 Lincoln NE 68501-1407

LIESE, CHRISTOPHER A., benefits and financial consulting company owner, state legislator; b. St. Louis, Mar. 24, 1963; s. Albert Joseph and Rose Clare (Kaufmann) L.; m. Sheila Marie Bercier, May 8, 1993. BA, St. Louis U., 1985. CFP. Owner Liese & Assocs., St. Louis; mem. Mo. Ho. of Reps. Dist. 85, Jefferson City, 1992—. Legal intern Legal Svcs. for Ea. Mo., Inc., 1984-85; vol. athletic instr. Mo. Athletic Club, 1983—; mem. St. John Bosco Ch., St. Blaise Alumni Com., Mo. River Twp. Dem. Club, N.W. River Twp. Dem. Club, Young Dems. Greater St. Louis. Mem. Mo. Assn. Life Underwriters, Maryland Heights/Westport C. of C. (econ. devel. com. 1990, 91), Jaycees, Delta Sigma Phi (pres. 1983-84). Home: 12230 Foxpoint Dr Maryland Heights MO 63043-2110 Office: House Post Office State Capitol 201 W Capitol Ave Jefferson City MO 65101-1556

LIFKA, MARY LAURANNE, history educator; b. Oak Park, Ill., Oct. 31, 1937; d. Aloysius William and Loretta Catherine (Juric) L. B.A., Mundelein Coll., 1960; M.A., Loyola U., Los Angeles, 1965; Ph.D., U. Mich., 1974; postdoctoral student London U., 1975. Life teaching cert. Prof. history Mundelein Coll., Chgo., 1976-84, coordinator acad. computer, 1983-84, prof. history Coll. St. Teresa, Winona, Minn., 1984-89, Lewis U., Romeoville, Ill., 1989—; chief reader in history Ednl. Testing Service, Princeton, N.J., 1980-84; cons. world history project Longman, Inc., 1983—; cons. in European history Coll. Bd., Evanston, Ill., 1983—; mem. Com. on History in the Classroom. Author: Instructor's Guide to European History, 1983; contbr. articles to publs. Recipient Br. Miguel Febres Cordero award for scholarship, 1998. Mem. Am. Hist. Assn., Ednl. Testing Service Devel. Com. of History. Democrat. Roman Catholic.

LIGGETT, HIRAM SHAW, JR., retired diversified financial services company executive; b. St. Louis, Jan. 12, 1932; s. Hiram Shaw and Lucille (Gardner) L.; m. Margaret McGinness, Jan. 21, 1961; children: Lucille Gardner, Frances Shelby. BA, Colo. Coll., 1953; LLD (hon.), Maryville U., 1991. Cashier Brown Group, Inc., St. Louis, 1957-64, asst. treas., 1964-68, treas., 1968—, v.p., 1983-86 (ret.). Bd. dirs. Roosevelt Fed. Savs. and Loan, St. Louis Past trustee, vice chmn. bd. dirs. McKendree Coll., Lebanon, Ill., 1980-88; trustee, past chmn. bd. trustees Maryville U., St. Louis, 1982-91; past chmn. Provident Counseling, 1983; past v.p., bd. dirs. Jr. Achievement Miss. Valley, 1983; past dir. bi-state chpt. ARC, 1983; bd. dirs., pres. Cardinal Ritter Inst.; bd. dirs., chmn. devel. bd. Paraquad. Capt. USNR, 1953-79. Mem. Fin. Execs. Inst. (pres., dir. 1983—), St. Louis Coun. Navy League (bd. councilors 1982), Univ. Club (St. Louis, chmn. house com. 1975-78), Strathalbyn Farms Club (chmn. house com., pres. bd. dirs.), Alpha Kappa Psi, Tau Kappa Alpha. Republican. Presbyterian. Office: Liggett-Black & Co 8000 Bonhomme Ave #320 Saint Louis MO 63105 Home: 14304 Quiet Meadow Ct E Chesterfield MO 63017 Personal E-mail: hligg498@aol.com.

LIGGETT, RONALD DAVID, state legislator; m. Frances Liggett. Student, Ball State U., Muncie, Ind., 1963-65. Owner/contr. Liggett Constrn. Co.; rep. Dist. 33 Ind. Ho. of Reps., 1992—, mem. cities and towns, elec. and apportionment coms., mem. labor and employment com.; vice chmn. agr. and rural devel. com. Mem. Pvt. Industry Coun. Mem. Lions, Moose, Masons. Address: RR 1 Box 482 Redkey IN 47373-9797 Also: 7483 S 1000 W Redkey IN 47373-9398

LIGGIO, CARL DONALD, lawyer; b. NYC, Sept. 5, 1943; AB, Georgetown U., 1963; JD, NYU, 1967. Bar: N.Y. 1967, D.C. 1967, Wis. 1983, Ill. 1998. Cons. Arent, Fox, Kintner, Plotkin & Kahn, Washington, 1968-69; assoc. White & Case, NYC, 1969-72; gen. counsel Arthur Young & Co., NYC, 1972-89, Ernst & Young, NYC, 1989-94; ptnr. Dickinson, Wright, Moon, Van Dusen & Freeman, Chgo., 1995-97, of counsel, 1998-99, McCullough, Campbell & Lane, 1999—. Mem. Brookings Civil Justice Reform Task Force, 1988, bd. regents, 2005-. Trustee Fordham Prep. Sch., 1988-96. Mem. ABA, Assn. Corp. Counsel Assn. (chmn. bd. dirs. 1984, mem. exec. com. 1982-95), Am. Judicature Soc. (bd. dirs. 1988-92), Coll. Law Mgmt., N.Y. State Bar Assn., Wis. Bar Assn., Ill. Bar Assn., D.C. Bar Assn. Home: 233 E Walton St Chicago IL 60611-1510 Office: 205 N Michigan Ave Ste 4100 Chicago IL 60601 Office Phone: 312-923-4103. Business E-Mail: cliggio@mcandl.com.

LIGHT, CHRISTOPHER UPJOHN, freelance/self-employed writer, photographer; b. Kalamazoo, Jan. 4, 1937; s. Richard and Rachel Mary (Upjohn) L.; m. Lilykate Victoria Wenner, June 22, 1963 (div. 1986); children: Victoria Mary, Christopher Upjohn Jr.; m. Margo Ruth Bosker, Jan. 2, 1994. AB, Carleton Coll., 1958; MS, Columbia U., 1962; MBA, We. Mich. U., 1967; PhD, Washington U., St. Louis, 1971. Editor, pub. Kalamazoo Mag., 1963-66; pres. Mich. Outdoor Pub. Co., Kalamazoo, 1965-68; product planner Upjohn Co., Kalamazoo, 1967-68; asst. prof. U. Utah, Salt Lake City, 1971-72; assoc. prof., chmn. fin. dept. Roosevelt U., Chgo., 1975-78; vis. prof. fin. No. Ill. U., 1978-79; freelance writer, computer musician, 1979—. Editor: Charles Dickens' Village Coquettes, 1992; mgr. spl. projects Sarasota Music Archive, 1992-96. Contbr. articles to profl. and microcomputer jours.; composer: Ten Polyrhytmic Etudes, 1991, Piano Sonata #1, 1992, (albums) Apple Compote, One-Man Band, 1985, Ultimate Music Box, Vol. I, 1988, Ultimate Music Box, Vol. II, 1993; Aspects of Flowers, Ann Arbor, Mich., 1996, East Lansing, Mich., 1997, Kalamazoo, 1997, Aspects of Flowers II, Ann Arbor, 1997, Aspects of Flowers III, Fontana Festival, 1998, Portraits of Engines, Kalamazoo, 1998, Aspects of Flowers: Selections, Ann Arbor, 1999, Pathways, Kalamazoo, 1999, Aspects of Flowers IV, 2001, Landscapes, 2001, Aspects of Flowers, Sarasota, Fla., 2005, Portraits of Engines, Kalamazoo, 2006. Trustee Harold and Grace Upjohn Found., 1965-85, 94-2002, pres., 1997-2002; trustee, bd. dirs. Kalamazoo Symphony Orch. Assn., 1990-99; trustee Sarasota Music Archive, 1990-95, Kalamazoo Coll., 1991-93; bd. dirs. Am. Symphony Orch. League, 1992-2000, sec., 1996-99; bd. dirs. Fontana Chamber Arts, 2002—. Recipient ann. press award Mich. Welfare League, 1967. Mem. ASCAP, ARAS (voting com.), Fin. Mgmt. Assn., Soc. Profl. Journalists, Univ. Club Chgo., Sarasota Concert Assn. (bd. dirs. 1998—, v.p., 2003—), Gull Lake Country Club, Columbia U. Club. N.Y. Home: 1808 Greenlawn Ave Kalamazoo MI 49006-4325

LIGHT, TERRY RICHARD, orthopedic hand surgeon; b. Chgo., June 22, 1947; BA, Yale U., 1969; MD, Chgo. Med. Sch., 1973. Diplomate in orthopedic surgery and in hand surgery Am. Bd. Orthopaedic Surgery. Asst. prof. Yale U., New Haven, 1977-80, Loyola U., Maywood, Ill., 1980-82, assoc. prof., 1982-88, prof., 1988-90, Dr. William M. Scholl prof., chmn. orthop. surgery and rehab, 1991—. Attending surgeon Hines (Ill.) VA Hosp., 1980—, Shriner's Hosp., Chgo., 1981—, Foster McGaw Hosp., Maywood, 1980—; hand cons. Chgo. White Sox, 1986-2003; bus. mgr. Jour. Hand Surgery, 1995-99. Editor Am. Acad. Orthop. Surgeons Hand Surgery Update, 1999, 2d edit. V.p. Frank Lloyd Wright Home and Studio Found., Oak Park, Ill., 1985-88, pres., 1988-90; chmn. bd. Fairfield Pub. Gallery, Sturgeon Bay, Wis., 1998-99; bd. dirs. Loyola U. Health Sys., 1999—. Fellow: ACS, Am. Acad. Orthop. Surgeons (editor Instrnl. Cruise Lects. vol. 55 2006); mem.: Am. Orthop. Assn. (2d v.p. 2004—05, 1st v.p. 2005—06, pres. 2006—), Ill. Orthop. Soc. (v.p. 1995, pres.-elect 1996, pres. 1997), Twenty-First Century Orthop. Assn. (pres. 1979—), Acad. Orthopaedic Soc. (pres. 2001—02), Chgo. Soc. for Surgery of Hand (sec. 1985—87, pres.-elect 1987—88, pres. 1988—89), Am. Assn. Hand Surgery (bd. dirs. 1989—91), Am. Soc. for Surgery of Hand (chair Jour. Hand Surgery com. 1995—99, treas. 1999—2002, v.p. 2002—03, pres. 2004—05), Alpha Omega Alpha. Avocation: collecting American arts and crafts and pottery. Office: Loyola U Med Ctr 2160 S 1st Ave Maywood IL 60153-3304 Office Phone: 708-216-4570. Personal E-mail: tlight1320@aol.com. Business E-Mail: tlight@lumc.edu.

LIGHTFOOT, EDWIN NIBLOCK, JR., retired chemical engineering educator; b. Milw., Sept. 25, 1925; married 1949, 5 children. BS, Cornell U., 1947, PhD in Chem. Engring., 1951; D in Tech. (hon.), Tech. U. Norway, 1985, Tech. U. Denmark, 2000. Asst prof., prof. biochem engr. U. Wis., Madison, 1953-80, prof. chem. engr., 1980-95, prof. emeritus, 1995—. Vis. prof. Tech. U. Norway, 1962, Stanford U., 1971, U. Canterbury, New Zealand, 1972. Author 14 books; contbr. articles to profl. jours. Recipient William H. Walker award Am. Inst. Chem. Engrs., 1975, Food, Pharm. and Bioengring. award, 1979, Warren K. Lewis award, 1991, Nat. medal sci. in engring., 2004, James E. Bailey award Soc. Biol. Engring., 2006. Mem. NAS, AAAS, Nat. Acad. Engr., Royal Norwegian Soc. Sci. and Letter, Am. Inst. Chem. Engr., Am. Chem. Soc. (E.V. Murphree award, 1994). Achievements include research on physical separation technology mass transfer and biomedical engineering. Office: U Wis 3639 Engineering Bldg 1415 Engineering Dr Madison WI 53706-1691 Business E-Mail: lightfoot@engr.wisc.edu.

LIGHTFORD, KIMBERLY A., state legislator; BA in Pub. Comm., Western Ill. U.; MPA, U. Ill., Springfield. Mem. Ill. Senate, Springfield, 1998—, chair edn. com., vice chair higher edn. com., mem. fin. instns. com., mem. pub. health com., mem. revenue com. Former trustee Village of Maywood. Democrat. Address: 10001 W Roosevelt Rd Ste 202 Westchester IL 60154 Office Phone: 217-782-8505, 708-343-7444. Business E-Mail: klightford@senatedem.ilga.gov.

LIGOCKI, KATHLEEN A., former auto parts company executive; b. 1956; BA, Ind. U., 1978; MBA, U. Penn., 1985; doctorate (hon.), Ind. U., 2002. Dir. bus. strategy Ford Motor Co., 1998—2000; pres., CEO Ford Mex., 2000—01; corp. v.p. Can., Mex. and N.Am. strategy Ford Motor Co., 2001—02; corp. officer, v.p. Ford Customer Svc. Divsn., 2002—03; pres., CEO Tower Automotive, Inc., 2003—07. Bd. dirs. Tower Automotive, Inc., 2003—07.

LILEY, PETER EDWARD, retired engineering educator; b. Barnstaple, North Devon, Eng., Apr. 22, 1927; came to U.S., 1957; s. Stanley E. and Rosa (Ellery) L.; m. Elaine Elizabeth Kull, Aug. 16, 1963; children: Elizabeth Ellen, Rebecca Ann. BSc, U. London, 1951, PhD in Physics, 1957, DIC, 1957. With Brit. Oxygen Engring., London, 1955-57; asst. prof. mech. engring. Purdue U., West Lafayette, Ind., 1957-61, assoc. prof., 1961-72; assoc. sr. researcher Thermophys. Properties Research Ctr., Purdue U., West Lafayette, Ind., 1961-72, prof. mech. engring., 1972-98; sr. rschr. Ctr. for Info. and Numerical Data Analysis and Synthesis, Purdue U., West Lafayette, Ind., 1972-92; ret., 1997. Cons. in field. Author: Sect. 2 Perry's Chemical Engineers Handbook, 7th edit., 1997; author: (with Hartnett et al.) Handbook of Heat Transfer Fundamentals, 2d edit., 1985; author: (with others) Marks Mechanical Engineers Handbook, 11 edit., 2006, Schaums 2000 Solved Problems in Mechanical Engineering Thermodynamics, 1995, Kutz Mechanical Engineers Handbook, 3d edit., 2006; co-author: Steam and Gas Tables with Computer Equations, 1985, Thermal Conductivity of Nonmetallic Liquids and Gases, 1970;: Properties of Nonmetallic Fluid Elements, 1981, Properties of Inorganic and Organic Fluids, 1988; editor, mem. editl. bd. Internat. Jour. Thermophysics, 1980—86; contbr. chpts. to handbooks in field, articles to profl. jours.; reviewer profl. jours. Served with Royal Corps Signals, Brit. Army, 1945-48. Lutheran. Home: 3608 Mulberry Dr Lafayette IN 47905-3937 E-mail: petereliley@insightbb.com.

LILJEGREN, FRANK SIGFRID, art association administrator, artist, educator; b. NYC, Feb. 23, 1930; s. Josef Sigfrid and Ester (Davidsson) L.; m. Donna Kathryn Hallam, Oct. 12, 1957. Student, Art Students League, NYC, 1950—55. Instr. painting, drawing, composition Westchester County Ctr., White Plains, NY, 1967-77, Art Students League, 1974-75, Wassenberg Art Ctr., Van Wert, Ohio, 1978-80, Wright State U. Br. Western Ohio Campus, Celina, 1981—. Corr. sec. Allied Artists Am., N.Y.C., 1967, exhbn. chmn., 1968-, pres., 1970-72, also bd. dirs. Exhibited at Suffolk Mus., Stonybrook, NY, Springfield (Mass.) Mus., Marion Kugler McNay Art Inst., San Antonio, Philbrook Mus., Tulsa, NAD, NYC, New Britain (Conn.) Mus. Art, Ft. Wayne (Ind.) Mus. Art; represented in permanent collections Art Students League, Univ. Mus., S.E. Mo. State U., Cape Girardeau, Manhattan Savs. Bank, NYC, Am. Ednl. Pubs. Inst., NYC, New Britain Mus. Am. Art, Conn., U. St. Francis, Ft. Wayne, Ft. Wayne Mus. Art. With AUS, 1951. Recipient numerous awards for still life oil paintings. Mem. Fine Arts fedn. N.Y, Art Students League (life), Acad. Artists Assn., Allied Artists Am. (life), Coun. Am. Artists Socs., Artists Fellowship, Salmagundi. Home Phone: 419-238-1159.

LILLEHAUG, DAVID LEE, lawyer; b. Waverly, Iowa, May 22, 1954; s. Leland Arthur and Ardis Elsie (Scheel) L.; m. Winifred Sarah (Smith), May 29, 1982; one child, Kara Marie. BA, Augustana Coll., Sioux Falls, SD, 1976; JD, Harvard U., 1979. Bar: Minn., 1979, US Dist. Ct. Minn., 1979, DC, 1981, US Ct. Appeals (8th cir.), 1981, US Dist. Ct. DC, 1982. Law clk. to presiding judge US Dist. Ct., Mpls., 1979-81; assoc. Hogan and Hartson, Washington, 1981-83, 84-85; issues aide, exec. asst. to Walter Mondale, Washington, 1983-84; assoc. Leonard, Street, and Deinard, Mpls., 1985-87, ptnr., 1988—93, 1998—99; US atty. Dist. of Minn., 1994-98; atty. Fredrikson & Byron, P.A., Mpls., 2002—. Candidate, US Senate, 1999-2000. Recipient Outstanding Alumnus award, Augustana Coll., 2006; Mondale Policy Forum fellow, U. Minn., 1990—91. Mem. Minn. Bar Assn. (past chair constrn. law sect., Author's Award 1990). Lutheran. Avocations: fishing, golf. Office: Fredrikson & Byron PA 200 S Sixth St Minneapolis MN 55402 Home: 6701 Parkwood Ln Edina MN 55436 Office Phone: 612-492-7000. Business E-Mail: dlillehaug@fredlaw.com.

LILLESAND, THOMAS MARTIN, engineer, educator; b. Laurium, Mich., Oct. 1, 1946; m. Theresa Hofmeister, 1968; children: Mark, Kari, Michael. BS, U. Wis., 1969, MS, 1970, PhD in Civil Engring., 1973. Prof. remote sensing SUNY, Syracuse, 1973-78, U. Minn., 1978-82, U. Wis., Madison, 1982—. Cons., 1973—. Recipient SAIC/Estes Meml. Tchg. award, 2005. Mem. Am. Soc. Photogrametry and Remote Sensing (pres. 1998-99, Alan Gordon award 1979, 93, Talbert Abrams award 1984, Fennell award 1988, SAIC/Estes Meml. Tchg. award 2005). Office: U Wis Environ Remote Sensing Ctr 1225 W Dayton St Rm 1239B Madison WI 53706-1612

LILLESTOL, JANE BRUSH, educational consultant; b. Jamestown, ND, July 20, 1936; d. Harper J. and Doris (Mikkelson) Brush; m. Harvey Lillestol, Sept. 29, 1956; children: Kim, Kevin, Erik. BS, U. Minn., 1969, MS, 1973, PhD, 1977; grad. Inst. Ednl. Mgmt., Harvard U., 1984. Dir. placement, asst. to dean U. Minn., St. Paul, 1975-77; assoc. dean, dir. student acad. affairs ND State U., Fargo, 1977-80; dean Coll. Human Devel. Syracuse U., NY, 1980-89, v.p. for alumni rels., 1989-95, project dir. IBM Computer Aided Design Lab., 1989—92; prin. Lillestol Assocs.; emeritus faculty Syracuse U., 1995—; faculty U. Phoenix, 2002—, curriculum devel. specialist, 2003. Charter mem. Mayor's Commn. on Women, 1986-90; NAFTA White House Conf. for Women Leaders, 1993. Rev. bd. rsch. jour.: U. Phoenix, 2007—. Bd. dirs. Univ. Hill Corp. Syracuse, 1983-93; mem. steering com. Consortium for Cultural Founds. of Medicine, 1980-89; trustee Manlius Pebble Hill Sch., 1990-94, Archbold Theatre, 1990-95, ND State U., 1992—. Recipient award US Consumer Product Safety Commn., 1983, Woman of Yr. award AAUW, 1984, svc. award Syracuse U., 1992; named among 100 Outstanding Alumni Over Past 100 Yrs., U. Minn. Coll. Human Ecology, 2001. Office: Lillestol Associates 3207 Casa Marina Rd NW Alexandria MN 56308 Personal E-mail: janelillestol@gmail.com.

LILLIE, JOHN CANFIELD, III, lawyer; b. Rochester, Minn., May 7, 1970; m. Shelley Lillie; 1 child. BA, Hope Coll., 1992; JD, Hamline U. Sch. Law, 1998. Bar: Minn. 1998. Atty. Dudley and Smith, P.A., St. Paul. Named a Rising Star, Minn. Super Lawyers mag., 2006. Mem.: Nat. Assn. Criminal Def. Lawyers, Minn. Assn. Criminal Def. Lawyers, Washington County Bar Assn., ABA, Minn. State Bar Assn., Ramsey County Bar Assn. Office: Dudley & Smith PA 2602 US Bank Ctr 101 E 5th St Saint Paul MN 55101 Office Phone: 651-291-1717. E-mail: jcl@dudleyandsmith.com.

LILLY, KRISTINE MARIE (KRISTINE LILLY HEAVEY), professional soccer player; b. NYC, July 27, 1971; m. David Heavey, Jan. 24, 2006. BA in Comm., U. NC, 1993. Midfielder US Women's Nat. Soccer Team, Chgo., 1987—, capt., 2005—, Boston Breakers, 2001—03; midfielder Tyreso Football Club, Sweden, 1994, Continental Indoor Soccer League Washington Warthogs, 1995, W League Delaware Genies, 1998, KIF Orebro in Swedish First Divsn., 2005. Bd. mem. Clifford's Gift. Named Most Valuable Offensive Player, CAA Championship, 1989, 1991, US Soccer Female Athlete of Yr., 1993, 2005, 2006, Tournament MVP, Nike US Women's Cup, 1999, Peace Queen Cup, 2006, CONCACAF Women's Gold Cup, 2006, First Team All-WUSA, 2001—03; named to All-Tournament Team, Nike US Women's Cup, 1995—97, WUSA All-Star Team, 2003; recipient Hemann Trophy, 1991. Achievements include winning a gold medal at the Olympics, 1996, 2004, and the Goodwill Games, 1998; member, winning FIFA Women's World Cup Team, 1991; member, World Cup Team, 1999; member, U. NC NCAA National Championship Teams, 1989-92; became first player, male or female, to play in 200 international matches, May 7, 2000, against Canada; second leading scorer in women's soccer history; second in career assists (98) in women's soccer. Avocations: music, reading, movies. Office: US Soccer Fedn 1801 S Prairie Ave Chicago IL 60616-1319

LIM, HENRY WAN-PENG, dermatologist; b. Bandung, Indonesia, July 19, 1949; s. Budiman Ruslim and Nietje Tedjasuryani; m. Mamie Wong, July 20, 1975; children: Christopher T., Kevin T. BS in Biochemistry with honors, McGill U., 1971; MD cum laude, SUNY, Bklyn., 1975. Diplomate Am. Bd.

Dermatology, Nat. Bd. Med. Examiners. Intern Albert Einstein Coll. Medicine, Bronx, NY, 1975-76; resident dept. dermatology NYU Sch. Medicine, NYC, 1976-79, NIH fellow in dermatology, 1979, Dermatology Found. fellow, 1979-80, from instr. to assoc. prof. dermatology, 1979-93, prof. dermatology, 1993-97, asst. dean vet. affairs, 1993-97; chmn., Clarence S. Livingood chair dermatology Henry Ford Hosp., Detroit, 1997—, dir. acad. programs, 2002—03, v.p. for acad. affairs, 2003—; assoc. dean Wayne State U./Henry Ford Health Sys., Wayne State U. Sch Medicine, Detroit, 2004—. Chief dermatology svc. N.Y. VA Med. Ctr., NYC, 1985—94, chief staff, 1993—97, staff physician dermatology svc., 1994—97; prof. pathology Sch. Medicine Wayne State U., Detroit, 2003—. Editor: Photodermatology, Photoimmunology & Photomedicine, 2000—03; assoc. editor: Jour. Investigative Dermatology, 2003—; mem. editl. bd. Jour. Am. Acad. Dermatology, 1993—. Recipient numerous awards; scholar, McGill U., 1968—70. Mem.: AMA, AAAS, Internat. Union Photobiology (v.p. 2004—), Photomedicine Soc. (pres. 1992—99), Am. Assn. Immunologists, Am. Soc. Photobiology (councilor 1998—2001, pres. 2002—03, chair sci. program com. 2003—04), Am. Fedn. for Clin. Rsch., Assn. Profs. Dermatology (bd. dirs. 2000—03), Am. Dermatol. Assn. (chair membership com. 2002—03, bd. dirs. 2006—, program com. 2007—08, chair), Dermatology Found. (trustee 2003—), Soc. Investigative Dermatology, Am. Acad. Dermatology (bd. dirs. 2002—06, exec. com. 2004—08, v.p. 2007—08), Alpha Omega Alpha. Avocation: travel. Office: Henry Ford Med Ctr New Ctr One Dept Dermatology 3031 W Grand Blvd Dept Ste 800 Detroit MI 48202-2689 Home Phone: 313-886-5002; Office Phone: 313-916-4060. Business E-Mail: hlim1@hfhs.org.

LIMBACK, E(DNA) REBECCA, vocational education educator; b. Higginsville, Mo., Mar. 23, 1945; d. Henry Shobe and Martha Pauline Rebecca (Willard) Ernstmeyer; m. Duane Paul Limback, Nov. 9, 1963; children: Lisa Christine, Derek Duane. BE, Cen. Mo. State U., 1968, MEd, 1969, EdS, 1976; EdD, U. Mo., 1981. Cert. bus., English and vocat. tchr. Supervising tchr. Lab. Sch. Ctrl. Mo. State U., Warrensburg, 1969-76, asst. to grad. dean, 1977-79, asst. prof., asst. to bus. dean, 1981-83, assoc. prof. computer and office info. systems, 1984-95, 1986-95, prof. computer and office info. sys., 1996—2003, prof. emeritus, 2003—. Mem. manual editing/revision staff State of Mo., Jefferson City, 1989-90; textbook reviewer Prentice-Hall, Englewood Cliffs, N.J., 1990-91. Author various curriculum guides; mem. editl. bd. Cen. Mo. State U. Rsch., 1982-92. Recipient Mo. Gov.'s Excellence in Tchg. award, 2001; grantee, RightSoft Corp., 1988. Mem. DAR, Nat. Bus. Edn. Assn. (conf. profl. opportunities com. 1989-99, info. processing editor Bus. Edn. Forum 1991), Assn. Career and Tech. Edn., North Cen. Bus. Edn. Assn. (Mo. rep., Collegiate Disting. Svc. award 1993), Mo. Bus. Edn. Assn. (all-chpt. pres. 1988-89, chair strategic planning com. 1999—, Postsecondary Tchr. of Yr. 1992), Assn. Bus. Comms., Mid-Mo. Artists, Phi Delta Kappa (all-chpt. pres. 1985), Delta Pi Epsilon (rsch. rep. 1989-92, nat. publs. com. 1993—). Lutheran. Avocations: archaeology, painting, photography, fishing. Office: Dockery 200-B/COIS Dept Ctrl Mo State U Warrensburg MO 64093 E-mail: rlimback@iland.net.

LIMBAUGH, STEPHEN NATHANIEL, federal judge; b. Cape Girardeau, Mo., Nov. 17, 1927; s. Rush Hudson and Bea (Seabaugh) L.; m. DeVaughn Anne Mesplay, Dec. 27, 1950; children— Stephen Nathaniel Jr., James Pennington, Andrew Thomas. BA, S.E. Mo. State U., Cape Girardeau, 1950; JD, U. Mo., Columbia, 1951. Bar: Mo. 1951. Prosecuting atty. Cape Girardeau County, Mo., 1954-58; judge U.S. Dist. Ct. (ea. and we. dists.) Mo., St. Louis, 1983—. With USN, 1945-46. Recipient Citation of Merit for Outstanding Achievement and Meritorious Service in Law, U. Mo., 1982 Fellow Am. Coll. Probate Counsel, Am. Bar Found.; mem. ABA (ho. of dels. 1987-90), Mo. Bar Assn. (pres. 1982-83). Republican. Methodist. Office: US Dist Ct Thomas F Eagleton Courthouse 111 S 10th St Ste 3 125 Saint Louis MO 63102 Office Phone: 314-244-7400. Business E-Mail: stephen_limbaugh@moed.uscourts.gov. E-mail: limbaugh@moed.uscourts.gov.

LIMBAUGH, STEPHEN NATHANIEL, JR., state supreme court judge; b. Cape Girardeau, Mo., Jan. 25, 1952; s. Stephen N. and Anne (Mesplay) L.; m. Marsha Dee Moore, July 21, 1973; children: Stephen III, Christopher K. BA, So. Meth. U., 1973, JD, 1976; LLM, U. Va., 1998. Bar: Tex. 1977, Mo. 1977. Assoc. Limbaugh, Limbaugh & Russell, Cape Girardeau, 1977-78; pros. atty. Cape Girardeau County, Cape Girardeau, 1979-82; shareholder, ptnr. Limbaugh, Limbaugh, Russell & Syler, Cape Girardeau, 1983-87; cir. judge 32d Jud. Cir., Cape Girardeau, 1987-92; judge Mo. Supreme Ct., Jefferson City, 1992—. Mem. ABA, State Bar Tex., Mo. Bar. Office: Supreme Ct Mo 207 W High St Jefferson City MO 65101-1516 Office Phone: 573-751-4375.

LIMMER, WARREN E., state legislator, real estate broker; m. Lori Limmer; two children. BA, Cloud State U. Real estate broker; Dist. 33B rep. Minn. Ho. of Reps., St. Paul, 1988-95; mem. Minn. Senate from 33rd dist., St. Paul, 1995—. Former mem. govt. op., labor-mgmt. rels., judiciary, edn.-higher edn. fin. divsn., and environ. and natural resources coms., Minn. Ho. of Reps. Home: 12888 73rd Ave N Maple Grove MN 55369-5247

LIN, CHUN CHIA, research physicist, educator; b. Canton, China, Mar. 7, 1930; s. Yue Hang Lam and Kin Ng. BS, U. Calif., Berkeley, 1951, MA, 1952; PhD, Harvard U., 1955. Asst. prof. physics U. Okla., Norman, 1955-59, assoc. prof. physics, 1959-63, prof. physics, 1963-68, U. Wis., Madison, 1968—. Cons., univ. retainee Tex. Instruments Inc., 1960-68; cons. Sandia Labs., 1976-81; sec. Gaseous Electronics Conf., 1972-73, chmn., 1990-92. Contbr. articles ot profl. jours. Sloan Found. fellow, 1962-66; rsch. grantee NSF and Air Force Office Sci. Rsch. Fellow Am. Phys. Soc. (sec. divsn. electron and atomic physics 1974-77, chair divsn. atomic molecular and optical physics 1994-95, Will Allis prize 1996). Home: 1652 Monroe St Apt C Madison WI 53711-2046 Office: U Wis Dept Physics Madison WI 53706 Office Phone: 608-262-0697.

LIN, JAMES CHIH-I, biomedical and electrical engineer, educator; b. Dec. 29, 1942; m. Mei Fei, Mar. 21, 1970; children: Janet, Theodore, Erik. BS, U. Wash., 1966, MS, 1968, PhD, 1971. Engr. Crown Zellerbach Corp., Seattle, 1966-67; asst. prof. U. Wash., Seattle, 1971-74; prof. Wayne State U., Detroit, 1974-80, U. Ill., Chgo., 1980—, head dept. bioengring., 1980-92, dir. robotics and automation lab., 1982-89, dir. spl. projects Coll. Engring., 1992-94, rsch. chair SC, 1993-97. Vis. prof., Beijing, Rome, Shan Dong, Taiwan Univs.; lectr. short courses, 1974—; cons. Battelle Meml. Inst., Columbus, Ohio, 1973-75, SRI Internat., palo Alto, Calif., 1978-79, Arthur D. Little Inc., Cambridge, Mass., 1980-83, Ga. Tech. Rsch. Inst., Atlanta, 1984-86, Walter Reed Army Inst. Rsch., 1973, 87, 88, Naval Aerospace Med. Rsch. Labs., Pensacola, 1982-83, U.R.S. Corp., San Francisco, 1985-87, CBS Inc., N.Y., 1988, U. Va., 1991-92, ACS Inc., Santa Clara Calif., 1989-90, Luxtron Corp., Mountainview, Calif., 1991-92, Commonwealth Edison, Chgo., 1991-95, Lucent Tech./Bell Labs., 1998-2000, Biopac, Santa Barbara, Calif., 2006-07; program chmn. Frontiers of Engring. and Computing Conf., Chgo., 1985; chmn., convener URSI Jt. Symposium Electromagnetic Waves in Biol. Sys., Tel Aviv, 1987, Internat. Conf. on Sci. and Tech., 1989-91; chmn. Chinese-Am. Acad. and Profl. Conv., 1993; mem. Congrl. Health Care Adv. Coun., 13th dist., Ill., 1987-99; panelist NSF Presdl. Young Investigator award com., Washington, 1984, 89; mem. NIH diagnostic radiology, 1981-85, chmn. spl. study sect., 1986—2004; mem. U.S. Nat. Commn. for URSI, NAS, 1980-82, 90-99, chair Commn. K., 1990-99, Extremely Low Frequency Field monitoring com., 1995-97; mem. Internat. Commn. on Non-ionizing Radiation Protection, 2004—; mem. Pres. Com. Nat. Medal of Sci., 1992-93; mem. Nat. Coun. Radiation Protection and Measurement, 1992—, chmn. radio frequency sci. com., 1995—, v.p. 2005-07; chmn. Internat. Union of Radio Scis. Commn., Electromagnetics in Biology and Medicine, 1996-99; chmn. Internat. Sci. Meeting on Electromagnetics in Medicine, 1997; mem. citizens adv. coun. Hinsdale Ctrl. H.S., 1988-93 Author: Microwave Auditory Effects and Applications, 1978, Biological Effects and Health Implications of Radiofrequency Radiation, 1987, Electromagnetic Interaction with Biological Systems, 1989, Mobile Comm. Safety, 1996; editor: Advances in Electromagnetic Fields in Living Systems, 1994—, EMB Mag., 1997—99, Wireless Networks, 1996—97; editor in chief: Bioelectromagnetics, 2006—; contbr. articles to profl. jours., columns to mags. Recipient Nat. Rsch. Svcs. award 1982, Disting. Svc. award, Outstanding Leadership award Chinese Am. Acad. and Profl. Assn. MidAm., 1989. Fellow AAAS, AIMBE, IEEE (tech. policy coun. 1990-91, chmn. com. on man and radiation, 1990-91, assoc. and guest editor transactions on biomed. engring., guest editor transaction on microwave theory and techniques, disting. lectr. engring. in medicine and biology 1991—, com. chair 2007-, Transaction Best Paper award 1975); mem. Biomed. Engring. Soc. (sr. mem.), Robotics Internat. (sr. mem.), Am. Soc. Engring. Edn., Bioelectromagnetics Soc. (charter, pres.-elect 1993-94, pres. 1994-95, chmn. ann. meeting 1994, d'Arsonval medal 2003), Marconi Found. (sci. com. 1996—), Golden Key, Sigma Xi, Phi Tau Phi (v.p.), Tau Beta Pi. Office: U Ill Coll Engring 1030 SEO MC/154 851 S Morgan St Chicago IL 60607-7042 Office Phone: 312-413-1052. Business E-Mail: lin@uic.edu.

LIN, PEN-MIN, electrical engineer, educator; b. Liaoning, China, Oct. 17, 1928; arrived in US, 1954; s. Tai-sui and Tse-san (Tang) Lin; m. Louise Shou Yuen Lee, Dec. 29, 1962; children: Marian, Margaret, Janice. BSEE, Taiwan U., 1950; MSEE, N.C. State U., 1956; PhD in Elec. Engring., Purdue U., 1960. Asst. prof. Purdue U., West Lafayette, Ind., 1961-66, assoc. prof., 1966-74, prof. elec. engring., 1974-94, prof. emeritus, 1994—. Author: (with L.O. Chua) Computer Aided Analysis of Electronic Circuits, 1975, Symbolic Network Analysis, 1991, (with R.A. DeCarlo) Linear Circuit Analysis, 1995, 2d edit., 2001. Fellow: IEEE (life). Home: 3029 Covington St West Lafayette IN 47906-1107 Office: Purdue Univ Sch Of Elec Engring West Lafayette IN 47907

LIND, JON ROBERT, lawyer; b. Evanston, Ill., July 4, 1935; s. Robert A. and Ruth (Anderson) L.; m. Jane Langfitt, Aug. 29, 1959; children: Jon Robert Jr., Elizabeth Neal, Susan Porter. AB, Harvard U., 1957, LLB, 1960; diploma in comparative law, Cambridge U., Eng., 1961. Bar: Ill. 1961. Assoc. Isham, Lincoln & Beale, Chgo., 1961-68, ptnr., 1968-88, McDermott, Will & Emory, Chgo., 1988-96, of counsel, 1997—. Atty. Winnetka (Ill.) Park Dist., 1973-78; bd. dirs. Swedish-Am. Mus. Ctr., 1988-96. Mem. ABA, Chgo. Bar Assn., Harvard U. Alumni Assn. (sec. 1970-73), Econ. Club Chgo., Law Club Chgo. Home: 644 Walden Rd Winnetka IL 60093-2035 Office: McDermott Will & Emery 227 W Monroe St Ste 3100 Chicago IL 60606-5096

LINDA, GERALD, advertising and marketing executive; b. Boston, Nov. 25, 1946; s. Edward Linda and Anne Beatrice (Lipofsky) Coburn; m. Claudia Wollack, Sept. 24, 1978; children— Jonathan Daniel Rezny, Jessica Simone. BS in Bus. Adminstrn., Northeastern U., 1969, MBA, 1971; postgrad., U. Mich., 1971-75. Faculty U. Ky., Lexington, 1975-77; ptnr. Tatham-Laird & Kudner, Chgo., 1977-80; v.p. Marsteller, Chgo., 1980-84; sr. v.p. HCM, Chgo., 1984-86; pres. Gerald Linda & Assocs., Chgo., 1986-89; prin. Kurtzman/Slavin/Linda, Inc., Chgo., 1990-93, Kapuler Mkgt. Rsch., Chgo., 1993-94; pres. Gerald Linda & Assocs., Glenview, Ill., 1994—. Mem. editorial review bd. Jour. Current Issues and Rsch. in Advt., 1984—. Named scientific lectr., Inst. Food Technologists. Mem.: Am. Mgmt. Assn. (mktg. faculty mem.). Office Phone: 847-729-3403. Personal E-mail: glinda@gla-mktg.com.

LINDAAS, ELROY NEIL, state legislator; b. Mayville, ND, Aug. 10, 1937; m. Janice Roberta Pederson; 7 children. 3d generation farmer; mem. N.D. Senate from 20th dist., Bismark, 1991—; mem. appropriations com. N.D. Senate. Past mem. agrl. stblzn. and conservation com. Trail Co.; mem. Farmers Home Adminstrn. Com.; past emergency coord. N.D. Radio; mem. Amateur Civil Emergency Svc.

LINDAHL, DENNIS, retail executive; With Arthur Andersen LLP, Holiday Cos., Mpls., 1986—2003, v.p., CFO, 1997—2003; asst. sec. Gander Mountain, St. Paul, 1997—2004, acting CEO, 1997, exec. v.p., CFO, 2003—, sec., treas., 2004—. Office: Gander Mountain Ste 1300 180 E Fifth St Saint Paul MN 55101

LINDAU, PHILIP, commodities trader; b. 1936; With Pillsbury Co., 1964-93; pres. Pillsbury Flour Milling & Spl. Commodities Ops., Mpls.; pres., CEO Commodity Specialists Co., Mpls. Office: Commodity Specialists Co 400 S 4th St Minneapolis MN 55415-1015 Business E-Mail: csc@world.com.

LINDBERG, DUANE R., bishop, historian; b. Thief River Falls, Minn., Apr. 16, 1933; s. Edgar and Alice (Amundson) L.; m. E. Mardell Kvitne, June 6, 1954; children: Erik Duane, Karen Kristin Kelle, Karl Stephen, Martha Alice Stone, Kristian John. BS in Chemistry, U. N.D., 1954; MDiv in Theology, Luther Sem., St. Paul, 1961; MA in Am. Studies, U. Minn., 1969, PhD in Am. Studies, 1975. Rsch. chemist DuPont Co., 1954; asst. ops. and tng. office Army Chem. Corps Sch., Ft. McClelland, Ala., 1955—56; tchg. asst. chemistry dept. U. Wis., Madison, 1956-57; chemist Minn. Farm Bur. Lab., St. Paul, 1957-59; pastor Epping and Wheelock (N.D.) Luth. Chs., 1961-68; rsch. historian Minn. State Hist. Soc., St. Paul, 1969-71; pastor Zion Luth. Ch., West Union, Iowa, 1971-78; sr. pastor Trinity Luth. Ch., Waterloo, Iowa, 1978-87, Acension Luth. Ch., Waterloo, 1987—98, sr. pastor emeritus, 1998—; nat. ch. body founder, presiding pastor Am. Assn. Luth. Chs., Mpls., 1987-99, presiding pastor emeritus, 1999—; interim pastor St. Luke Luth. Ch., Traer, Iowa, 2003—05. Vis. prof. Upper Iowa U., Fayette, 1976-77; adj. prof. Am. Luth. Theol. Sem., St. Paul, 1996—; chemistry instr. Valley Luth. HS, Cedar Falls, Iowa, 2005—. Author: Uniting Word, 1969, Men of the Cloth, 1980; contbr. articles to profl. jours. Bd. dirs. Palmer Meml. Hosp., West Union, Iowa, 1972-78, Allen Meml. Hosp., Waterloo, 1979-05, Northeast Iowa Med. Edn. Found., Waterloo, 1983-02; founder, bd. mem. Buffalo Trails Mus., Epping, N.D., 1964-68; founder, bd. mem. Fayette County Hist. Soc., West Union, 1975-78; dean Decorah Conf. Am. Luth. Ch., 1976-78, exec. com. Iowa Dist., 1976-78; bd. dirs. Great Plains Inst. Theology, 1965-68; pres. Eastern Iowa Luth. H.S. Assn., 1997-04, major gifts dir., 2006—. 1st lt. U.S. Army, 1954-56. Recipient award of commendation Concordia Hist. Inst., St. Louis, 1980, Nehemiah award Abiding World Ministries, Mpls., 1990, award of excellence Allen Meml. Hosp., Waterloo, 1995. Mem. numerous profl. ministerial groups and ch. bds., Rotary, Sons of Norway. Lutheran. Office: Valley Luth HS 4520 Rownd St Cedar Falls IA 50613

LINDBERG, GEORGE W., federal judge; b. Crystal Lake, Ill., June 21, 1932; s. Alger Victor and Rilla (Wakem) L. BS, Northwestern U., 1954, JD, 1957. V.p., legal counsel John E. Reid & Assocs., Chgo., 1955-68; ptnr. Franz, Franz, Wardell & Lindberg, Crystal Lake, 1968-73; comptr. State of Ill., Springfield, 1973-77, dep. atty. gen. Chgo., 1977-78; justice Ill. Appellate Ct., Elgin, 1978-89; dist. judge U.S. Dist. Ct. (no. dist.) Ill., Chgo., 1989—. Chmn. Ill. House Com. on Judiciary, Com. on Ethics, Springfield, 1970-73. Holder numerous govt. offices, 1966—. Office: US Dist Ct 219 S Dearborn St Ste 1472 Chicago IL 60604-1705

LINDBERGH, REEVE, writer, poet; d. Charles A. Lindbergh and Anne Morrow L.; m. Nathaniel Tripp. Graduate, Radcliffe Coll., 1968. Bd. dir. Charles A. and Anne Morrow Lindbergh Found., 1977—, v.p., 1986—95, pres, 1995—2004, hon. chairwoman, 2004—. Author: (memoirs) Under a Wing, 1998, No More Words: A Journal of My Mother, Anne Morrow Lindbergh, 2001, (novels) Moving to the Country, 1983, The Names of the Mountains, 1992, (book of essays) View from the Kingdom, 1987, (children's books) The Midnight Farm, 1987, Benjamin's Barn, 1990, There's a COW in the Road, 1993, What Is The Sun?, 1994, Grandfather's Lovesong, 1995, The Day the Goose Got Loose, 1995, If I'd Known Then What I Know Now, 1996, Awful Aardvarks Shop for School, 2000, The Circle of Days, 2002, On Morning Wings, 2002, My Hippie Grandmother, 2003, Our Nest, 2004, The Visit, 2005. Office: Charles A and Ann Morrow Lindbergh Foundation Ste 310 2150 Third Ave N Anoka MN 55303-2200

LINDBLOOM, CHAD M., transportation executive; BS, MBA, Univ. Minn. Staff acct. CH Robinson Worldwide Inc., Eden Prairie, Minn., 1990—98, corp. contr., 1998—99, v.p., CFO, 1999—. Office: CH Robinson Worldwide 8100 Mitchell Rd Eden Prairie MN 55344-2248

LINDE, MAXINE HELEN, lawyer, corporate financial executive, investor; b. Chgo., Sept. 2, 1939; d. Jack and Lottie (Kroll) Stern; m. Ronald K. Linde, June 12, 1960. BA summa cum laude, UCLA, 1961; JD, Stanford U., 1967. Bar: Calif. 1968. Applied mathematician, rsch. engr Jet Propulsion Lab., Pasadena, Calif., 1961—64; law clk. U.S. Dist. Ct. No. Calif., 1967—68; mem. firm Long & Levit, San Francisco, 1968—69, Swerdlow, Glikbarg & Shimer, Beverly Hills, Calif., 1969—72; sec., gen. counsel Envirodyne Industries, Inc., Chgo., 1972—89; pres. The Ronald and Maxine Linde Found., 1989—; vice chmn. bd., gen. counsel Titan Fin. Group, LLC, Chgo., 1994—98. Mem. bd. visitors Stanford Law Sch., 1989—92, law and bus. adv. coun., 1991—94, dean's adv. coun., 1992—94. Mem.: Alpha Lambda Delta, Pi Mu Epsilon, Phi Beta Kappa, Order of Coif.

LINDELL, ANDREA REGINA, dean, nurse; b. Warren, Pa., Aug., 21, 1943; d. Andrew D. and Irene M. (Fabry) Lefik; m. Warner E. Lindell, May 7, 1966; children: Jennifer I., Jason M. B.S., Villa Maria Coll., 1970; M.S.N. Catholic U., 1975, D.N.Sc., 1976; diploma R.N., St. Vincent's Hosp., Erie, Pa. Instr. St. Vincent Hosp. Sch. Nursing, 1964-66; dir. Rouse Hosp., Youngsville, Pa., 1966-69; supr. Vis. Nurses Assn., Warren, Pa., 1969-70; dir. grad. program Cath. U., Washington, 1975-77; chmn., assoc. dean U. N.H., Durham, 1977-81; dean, prof. Oakland U., Rochester, Mich., 1981-90, dean, Schmidlapp prof. nursing U. Cin., 1990—; bd. dirs. CHEMED Corp.; cons. Moorehead U., Ky., 1983. Editor; Jour. Profl. Nursing, 1985; contbr. articles to profl. jours. Mem. sch. bd. Strafford Sch. Dist., N.H., 1977-80; Gov.'s Blue Ribbon Commn. Direct Health Policies, Concord, N.H., 1979-81; vice chmn. New England Commn. Higher Edn. in Nursing, 1977-81; mem. Mich. Assn. Colls. Nursing, 1981—. Named Outstanding Young Woman Am., 1980. Mem. Nat. League Nursing, Am. Assn. Colls. Nursing (pres. 1996—), Sigma Theta Tau. Democrat. Roman Catholic. Avocations: water skiing, roller skating, reading, fishing, camping. Office: College of Nursing & Health 3110 Vine St Cincinnati OH 45221-0001

LINDELL, EDWARD ALBERT, academic and religious organization administrator; b. Denver, Nov. 30, 1928; s. Edward Gustaf and Estelle (Lundin) L.; m. Patricia Clare Eckert, Sept. 2, 1965; children: Edward Paul, Erik Adam. BA, U. Denver, 1950, MA, 1956, Ed.D., 1960, L.H.D. (hon.), 1975; Litt.D. (hon.), Tusculum Coll., 1979; D.H.L. (hon.), Roanoke Coll., 1981; Litt.D (hon.), Christ Coll., Irvine, 1992. Tchr. North Denver High Sch., 1952-61; asst. dean Coll. Arts and Scis., U. Denver, 1961-65, dean, 1965-75; pres. Gustavus Adolphus Coll., St. Peter, Minn., 1975-80, Luth. Brotherhood Mut. Funds, Mpls., 1980—. V.p. Luth. Brotherhood Found., 1980—, also exec. dir. Mem. exec. bd. Rocky Mountain Synod Luth. Ch. Am., 1968—, Luth. Coun. U.S.A., v.p., 1975—; also pres. bd. coll. edn. and ch. vocations; trustee Midland Luth. Coll., Fremont, Nebr., Kans. Wesleyan U., Colo. Assn. Ind. Colls. and Univs., Luth. Med. Center, Wheatridge, Colo., Luth. Sch. Theology, Chgo., 1975—, St. John's U., Minn., 1978—; bd. dirs. Swedish Coun. in Am., 1978—, pres., chmn.-elect, 2001, pres., 2002; adv. bd. Royal Swedish Acad. Scis., 1980; v.p. Am.-Swedish Inst., 1980; exec. v.p. external affairs Luth. Brotherhood, 1981—; pres. Nat. Fraternal Congress Am., 1988—; bd. dirs. Pacific Luth. Theol. Sem., 1978-80, Loretto Heights Coll., Colo., 1978-86, Gettysburg Theol. Sem., 1981-83, Wittenberg U., 1988, Bethany Coll., 1991—, Minn. Orch., 1983—, Am. Scandinavian Found., 1982—, Fairview Hosp., 1982—, Luth. Internat. Congress, 1996-2000; bd. dirs. U.S. Swedish Found. Internat. Sci. Rsch., 1981—, v.p. 1986—; bd. dirs. Habitat for Humanity Internat., 1992—, mem. global leadership com., 2003—; pres. U.S. Wittenberg Found., 1996—. Named Outstanding Faculty Mem. Coll. Arts and Scis., U. Denver, 1964; decorated knight King of Sweden, 1976; recipient Suomi Disting. Svc. award, 1989; named to Hall of Fame North Denver HS, 2006. Mem. Good Samaritan Soc. (bd. dirs. 1997—, vice-chmn. 98-99, chmn.-elect 1999, chmn. 2000—), Swedish Pioneer Hist. Soc. (dir. 1979—), U. Denver Alumni Assn. (Career Alumni Achievement award 1994), Phi Beta Kappa. Office: Swedish Coun Am 2600 Park Ave S Minneapolis MN 55407 E-mail: 2swedes@outtech.com.

LINDENBAUM, SHARON, publishing executive; b. Johannesburg; B., U. Kans.; M in acctg., Wichita State U. Sr. acct. Main Hurdman, Wichita, Kans.; mng. partner Lindenbaum & O'Sullivan, Wichita, Kans.; controller Pennypower Shopping News Inc., Wichita, Kans.; v.p. fin. Kansas City (Mo.) Star, 1995—. Office: Kansas City Star 1729 Grand Blvd Kansas City MO 64108-1458

LINDENLAUB, JOHN CHARLES, electrical engineer, educator; b. Milw., Sept. 10, 1933; m. Deborah Hart, 1957; children: Brian, Mark, Anne, David. BS, MIT, 1955, MS, 1957; PhD in Elec. Engring., Purdue U., 1961. From asst. prof. to prof. Purdue U., West Lafayette, Ind., 1961-72, prof. elec. engring., 1972—99, dir. Ctr. Instrnl. Devel. Engring., 1977-81, prof. emeritus, 1999—. Mem. tech. staff Bell Telephone Labs., 1968-69; cons. Western Elec., N.Y. State Bd. Regents, Control Data Corp., J. Warren Rsch. in Higher Edn., Nat. Technol. U. Contbr. articles to profl. jours. Recipient Helen Plants award Frontiers in Edn. Conf., 1980, 87, 93; Danforth Found. assoc., 1966. Fellow IEEE (Edn. Soc. Achievement award 1984, Schmitz award FIE Conf.), Fellow Am. Soc. Engring. Edn. (Chester F. Carlson award 1988, Disting. Svc. citation 1993, E.R.M. Disting. Svc. award 1999). Office: Purdue Univ Elec Engring Bldg 465 Northwestern Ave Lafayette IN 47907-2035 E-mail: john.c.lindenlaub.1@purdue.edu.

LINDGREN, A(LAN) BRUCE, church administrator; b. Grand Rapids, Mich., July 1, 1948; m. Carole Coonce; children: Stacey, Michael, David (dec.). BS in Sociology, Mich. State U., 1970; MDiv, St. Paul Sch. Theology, 1975. Ordained high priest. Campus minister Park Coll., 1975-77; dir. ministerial edn. Temple Sch., 1986-92; exec. min., World Ch. sec., exec. asst. to 1st presidency Cmty. of Christ, 1992—. Dir. devel. basic leadership curriculum Temple Sch., 1977-86. Editor: Leaders Handbook, 1985-92. Office: Cmty of Christ 1001 W Walnut Independence MO 64050

LINDNER, ARLON, state legislator; b. Aug. 3, 1935; m. Shirlee Lindner; 4 children. BA, Tex. State U.; MDiv, Cen. Bapt. Theol. Sem., Mpls. Minn. state rep. Dist. 33A, 1993—. Self-employed businessman. Address: 19508 Country Cir E Rogers MN 55374-9709

LINDNER, CARL H., III, insurance company executive; s. Carl H. Lindner, Jr. and Edith Lindner. With Great Am. Ins. Co. (subs. Am. Fin. Group Inc.), 1975—, various ins. ops. positions, 1987—, now vice chmn., pres.; co-pres. Am. Fin. Group, 1996—2005, co-CEO, co-pres., 2005—. Office: Am Fin Group Inc 1 E 4th St Cincinnati OH 45202

LINDNER, CARL HENRY, JR., insurance company executive, professional sports team owner; b. Dayton, Ohio, Apr. 22, 1919; s. Carl Henry and Clara (Serrer) Lindner; m. Edyth Bailey, Dec. 31, 1953; children: Carl Henry III, Stephen Craig, Keith Edward. HHD (hon.), Xavier U., 1991. Co-founder United Dairy Farmers, 1940; pres. Am. Fin. Group, Cin., 1959—84, chmn., 1959—, CEO, 1984—2005; owner, CEO Cin. Reds, 1999—. Chmn. Great Am. Fin. Resources, Inc., Great Am. Ins. Group. Bd. advisors Bus. Adminstrn. Coll., U. Cin. Named one of Forbes' Richest Americans, 2006; recipient Heritage award, Urban League of Greater Cin., 1997. Republican. Baptist. Office: Am Fin Group 1 E 4th St Cincinnati OH 45202-3717

LINDNER, CRAIG, financial services company executive; Co-pres. Am. Fin. Group, Inc., Cin., 1999—. Office: Am Fin Group Inc One E 4th St Cincinnati OH 45202

LINDNER, ROBERT DAVID, finance company executive; b. Dayton, Ohio, Aug. 5, 1920; s. Carl Henry and Clara (Serrer) L.; m. Betty Ruth Johnston, Mar. 29, 1947; children: Robert David, Jeffrey Scott, Alan Bradford, David Clark. Chmn. bd. United Dairy Farmers, Cin., 1940—; With Am. Financial Corp., Cin., 1950-95, former v.p., vice chmn. bd., now vice chmn. bd. dirs.; founder, former pres., chmn. bd. United Dairy Farmers. Trustee No. Bapt. Theol. Sem. Served with U.S. Army, 1942-45. Mem. Masons (33 degree). Home: 6950 Given Rd Cincinnati OH 45243-2840 Office: United Dairy Farmers 3955 Montgomery Rd Cincinnati OH 45212-3798

LINDNER, S(TEPHEN) CRAIG, insurance company executive; s. Carl H. Lindner Jr. and Edith Lindner. BBA, U. Cinn., 1977. With Am. Fin. Group Inc., Cin., 1977—, co-pres., 1996, co-CEO, 2005—. Pres., CEO Great Am. Fin. Resources; pres. Am. Money Mgmt. Corp. Office: Am Fin Group Inc 1 E 4th St Cincinnati OH 45202-3717

LINDQUIST, SUSAN LEE, biology and microbiology professor; b. June 5, 1949; BA in Microbiology with honors, U. Ill., 1971; PhD in Biology, Harvard U., 1976. Asst. prof. dept. molecular biology U. Chgo., 1978-84, assoc. prof., 1984—99, full prof., 1988, Albert D. Lasker prof. med. sciences, 1999—2001, investigator Howard Hughes Med. Inst., 1988—2001; dir. Whitehead Inst. Biomedical Rsch., Cambridge, Mass., 2001—04, mem., 2001—; prof. biology MIT, Cambridge, Mass., 2001—; investigator Howard Hughes Med. Inst., 2006—. Mem. com. genetics, com. devel. biology U. Chgo., 1999—; cons. Mus. Sci. & Industry, Chgo., 1983-87; vis. scholar Cambridge U., 1983; cons., prin. in film Lights Breaking, 1985; mem. sci. adv. com. Helen Hay Whitney Found., 1997—; bd. dirs. Johnson & Johnson, 2004-; lectr. in field. Co-editor: The Stress Induced Proteins, 1988, Heat Shock, 1990; assoc. editor The New Biologist, 1991-93; mem. editl. bd. Cell Regulation, 1989—, Molecular and Cell Biology, 1984—, Gene Expression, 1994-95, Cell Stress and Chaperones, 1995—, Current Biology, 1996—, Molecular Biology of the Cell, 1996—; monitoring editor Jour. Cell Biology, 1993—; contbr. articles to profl. jours. Teaching fellow Harvard U., 1973-74, Postdoctoral fellow Am. Cancer Soc., 1976-78, U. Chgo.; recipient Novartis Drew award in Biomedical Rsch., 2000, Dickson prize in Medicine, 2003, Sigma Xi William Procter prize for Scientific Achievement, 2006, Emil Christian Hansen Gold medal, 2006, U. Ill. Alumni Achievement award, 2006; named one of Top 50 Women Scientists, Discover Mag., 2002. Fellow Am. Acad. Microbiology, AAAS, NAS, Am. Acad. Arts and Sci.; mem. Am. Soc. Cell Biology, Am. Soc. Microbiology, Fedn. Am. Scientists for Exptl. Biology, Genetics Soc. Am. (former sec.), Molecular Medicine Soc., Inst. Medicine. Achievements include research in the impact of protein-conformational changes on diverse processes in cellular and organismal biology. Office: Whitehead Inst Nine Cambridge Ctr Cambridge MA 02142-1479 Office Phone: 617-258-5184. E-mail: lindquist_admin@wi.mit.edu.

LINDSAY, JOHN CONAL, state legislator; b. Omaha, June 27, 1959; m. Mary Beth Barbina, 1988; children: John, Patrick, Robert. BA, Creighton U., 1981, JD cum laude, 1984; postgrad., U. Nebr., 1981-82. Bar: Nebr., 1984. Ptnr. Lindsay & Lindsay, 1985-97; mem. from dist. 9 Nebr. State Senate, Lincoln, mem. govt., mil. and vet. affairs coms., 1989-97, mem. banking, commerce and ins. coms., com. on coms., chmn. judiciary com.; lobbyist O'Hara & Assocs., 1997—. Vis. asst. prof. bus. law Nebr. Wesleyan U., 1985-86; del. Dem. Nat. Conv., 1992, 96. Mem. Archdiocesan Social Min. Commn., 1997—. Named One of Ten Outstanding Young Omahans, 1990. Mem. Nebr. Bar Assn., Omaha Bar Assn., KC, Rotary Club, Omaha Barristers Club (v.p. 1986-87, pres. 1987-88). Home: 1537 Skylark Dr Omaha NE 68144-1758

LINDSAY, MICHAEL ANTHONY, lawyer; b. Omaha, Nebr., May 9, 1958; s. William J. and Mary F. Lindsay. BA summa cum laude, Marquette U., 1980; Gen. Studies with first class honors, London Sch. Econ., 1980; JD cum laude, U. Chgo., 1983. Bar: Minn. 1985, US Dist. Ct. Minn. 1985. Law clk. to judge Richard Posner US Ct. Appeals, Chgo., 1983—84; assoc. Dorsey & Whitney, Mpls., 1985-90, ptnr., trial practice group, 1991—, and co-chmn., anti-trust group. Adj. prof. Law Sch. Hamline U., St. Paul, 1988-99, U. St. Thomas, Mpls., Minn., 2002—. Pres. Prevention Alliance, Mpls., 1991-96. Mem.: Phi Beta Kappa, Order of Coif. Office: Dorsey & Whitney Ste 1500 50 S Sixth St Minneapolis MN 55402-1498 Office Phone: 612-340-7819. Office Fax: 612-340-2868. Business E-Mail: lindsay.michael@dorsey.com.

LINDSEY, DAVID HOSFORD, lawyer; b. Kingsville, Tex., July 25, 1950; s. Ernest Truman and Helen Elizabeth (Hosford) L.; m. Marilyn Kay Williams, June 8, 1974; children: Seth Williams, Brooks Daniel. BS in Bus. Adminstrn., U. Mo., 1972; JD, Washburn U., 1975. Bar: Mo. 1975. With trust dept. Commerce Bank, Kansas City, Mo., 1974—75, from asst. v.p. to sr. v.p., 1979—94, chief credit officer, 1989—, exec. v.p., 2000—; mgr., sales dept. Pioneer Pallet, Inc., North Kansas City, Mo., 1976; from asst. cashier to v.p. Nat. Bank, North Kansas City, 1977—79. Vice-chmn. planning and zoning com. City of Liberty, Mo., 1981-93, tax increment fin. commr., 2002—; bd. dirs. Kansas City Met. YMCA. Mem. Mo. Bar Assn., Lawyers Assn. Kansas City, Kansas City Met. Bar Assn., Robert Morris Assn. (bd. dirs. Kansas City chpt.), Kansas City C. of C., Kansas City Alumni Assn. (bd. dirs.), Clayview Country Club, Phi Gamma Delta, Omicron Delta Kappa. Baptist. Home: 602 Camelot Dr Liberty MO 64068-1176 Office: Commerce Bank 1000 Walnut St Ste 1800 Kansas City MO 64106-2123

LINDSEY, SUSAN LYNDAKER, zoologist; b. Valley Forge, Pa., Aug. 23, 1956; d. Howard Paul and Lillian Irene (Whitman) Lyndaker; m. Kevin Arthur Lindsey, July 17, 1982; children: Ryan Howard, Shannon Marie. BS in Biology, St. Lawrence U., 1978; MA in Zoology, So. Ill. U., Carbondale, 1980; PhD in Zoology, Colo. State U., 1987. Rschr. St. Lawrence U., Kenya, East Africa, 1978; tchr. Beth Jacob H.S., Denver, 1986-87; rschr. mammal dept. Dallas Zoo, 1988-93; exec. dir. Wild Canid Survival and Rsch. Ctr., Eureka, Mo., 1993—. Adj. prof. Cedar Valley Coll., 1992-93, So. Ill. U., Carbondale, 1996—; mgmt. group mem. Red Wolf Species Survival Plan, Tacoma, Wash., 1994—, Mexican Gray Wolf Species Survival Plan, Albuquerque, 1993—, Maned Wolf Species Survival Plan, Washington, 1999—, African Wild Dog Species Survival Plan, 2005—, Swift Fox Species Survival Plan, 2006—; advisor Mex. Gray Wolf Species Survival Plan Behavioral. Author: (with others) The Okapi: Mysterious Animal of Congo-Zaire, 1999; contbr. articles to profl. jours. Docent Denver Zool. Found., Denver Zoo, 1985-88. Recipient Disting. Alumni citation, St. Lawrence U., 2003. Mem. Acad. Sci. St. Louis, Assn. Zoos and Aquariums, Am. Behavior Soc., Am. Soc. of Mammalogists, Beta Beta Beta, Phi Beta Kappa, Psi Chi. Avocations: horseback riding, canoeing, gardening, photography, travel. Office: Wild Canid Survival Rsch Ctr Wash U PO Box 760 Eureka MO 63025-0760 Home Phone: 636-742-4956; Office Phone: 636-938-5900.

LINEHAN, LOU ANN, political organization worker; m. Kevin Linehan; 4 children. Student, U. Nebr. Campaign mgr. Congl. Campaign for Ally Milder, 1990; exec. dir. Douglas County Rep. Party, 1991-93; adminstrv. asst. to Dr. Ron Roskens Action Internat., 1993-95; campaign mgr. U.S. Senate Campaign for Chuck Hagel, 1995-96; chief of staff U.S. Senator Chuck Hagel, 1997—. CCD tchr. Christ the King Ch., 1993-94; chmn. Celebrity Waiter's GOP Fundraiser, 1993; treas. Loveland Parents' Assn., 1994; active Women's Guild-Meyer Children's Rehab. Inst., 1988-95, pres. 1993. Named Vol. of Yr. Douglas County, 1988. Home: 2353 S 87th St Omaha NE 68124-2143 Office: Office of Senator Chuck Hagel 346 Russell Senate Off Bldg Washington DC 20510-0001 also: 294 Federal Bldg 100 Centennial Mall N Lincoln NE 68508 E-mail: louann_linehan@hagel.senate.gov.

LINEHAN, SCOTT, professional football coach; b. Sunnyside, Wash., Sept. 17, 1963; m. Kristen Linehan; 3 children. Grad., U. ID, 1982—86. Quarterbacks coach U. ev., Las Vegas, 1991—92; wide receivers coach U. Idaho, 1989—91, offensive coord., quarterbacks coach, 1992—94; wide receivers coach U. Nebr., 1994—96, offensive coord., 1996—98; offensive coord., quarterbacks coach U. Louisville, 1999—2001, Minn. Vikings, 2002—05; offensive coord. Miami Dolphins, 2005—06; head coach St. Louis Rams, 2006—. Office: c/o St Louis Rams 1 Rams Way Saint Louis MO 63045

LING, TA-YUNG, physicist; b. Shanghai, Feb. 2, 1943; married, 1969; 3 children. BS, Tunghai U., Taiwan, 1964; MS, U. Waterloo, Ont., Can., 1966; PhD in Physics, U. Wis., 1971. Rsch. asst. U. Wis., 1967-71; rsch. assoc. physics U. Pa., Phila., 1972-75, asst. prof., 1975-77; from asst. prof. to assoc. prof. Ohio State U., Columbus, 1977-83, prof. physics, 1983—. Recipient Outstanding Jr. Investigator award Dept. of Energy, 1977. Mem. Am. Phys. Soc. Achievements include research in experimental high energy physics; deep inelastic neutrino-nucleon scattering, neutrino masses and mixing, neutrino oscillations, deep inelastic electron-proton scattering, high energy proton-proton collisions. Office: Dept Physics 191 W Woodruff Ave Columbus OH 43210-1117 E-mail: ling@mps.ohio-state.edu.

LINHARDT, ROBERT JOHN, chemistry professor; b. Passaic, NJ, Oct. 18, 1953; s. Robert J. and Barbara A. (Kelley) L.; m. Kathryn F. Burns, May 31, 1975; children: Kelley, Barbara. BS in Chemistry, Marquette U., 1975; MA in Chemistry, Johns Hopkins U., 1977, PhD in Organic Chemistry, 1979; postgrad., Mass. Inst. Tech., 1979-82. Rsch. assoc. Mass. Inst. Tech., Cambridge, 1979-82; asst. prof. U. Iowa, Iowa City, 1982-86, assoc. prof., 1986-90, prof. medicinal and natural products chemistry, 1990—2003, prof. chem. and biochem. engring., 1996—2003, F. Wendell Miller Disting. prof., 1996—2003, prof. chemistry, 1999—; constellation chair in biocatalysis and metabolic engring. Rensselaer Poly. Inst., Troy, NY. Cons. in field.; interacad. exchange scientist to USSR NAS, 1988. Mem. editl. bd. Applied Biochemistry and Biotech., 1985—, Carbohydrate Rsch., 1990—, Jour. Carbohydrate Chemistry, 1995—, Jour. Biol. Chem., 1995-2000, Analytical Biochemistry, 1991-97, 2001—; contbr. numerous articles to profl. jours. Johnson and Johnson fellow MIT, 1981; NIH grantee, 1982—. Mem. AAAS, AACP (Volwiler award 1999), Am. Chem. Soc. (Horace S. Isbell award Carbohydrate Chemistry 1994, Claude S. Hudson award in carbohydrate chemistry 2003), Soc. Glycobiology. Office: Rensselaerp Poly Inst 110 8th St Troy NY 12180 Home: 214 Lancaster St Albany NY 12210-1132 E-mail: linhar@rpi.edu.

LINK, DAVID THOMAS, dean, lawyer; b. 1936; BS magna cum laude, U. Notre Dame, 1958, JD, 1961; postgrad., Georgetown U., 1965—66. Bar: Ohio 1961, Ill. 1966, Ind. 1975, U.S. Supreme Ct. 1965. Trial atty. Office of Chief Counsel, IRS, 1961—66; ptnr. Winston, Strawn, Smith & Patterson, Chgo., 1966—70; prof. U. Notre Dame Law Sch., Notre Dame, Ind., 1970—99, dean, 1975—99, dean, prof. emeritus, 1999—; pres. vice chancellor U. Notre Dame, Australia, 1990—92, pres., vice chancellor emeritus, bd. trustees, bd. govs., 1992—; founding dep. vice chancellor, provost St. Augustine U. Coll., South Africa, 1999—; pres., CEO Internat. Ctr. Healing and Law, 2001—; assoc. coun. Office Ind. Counsel. Cons. to GAO. Author (with Soderquist): Law of Federal Estate and Gift Taxation, Vol. 1, 1978, Vol. 2, 1980, Vol. 3, 1982, Healing and the Law, 2 vols., 2004. Mem. Ind. Gov.'s Com. on Individual Privacy; mem. pres.' task force New Methods for Improving the Quality of Lawyers' Svcs. to Clients; chair Ind. State Ethics Commn., 1988—90, Pub. Officers' Compensation Adv. Commn., 2004—; acad. coun., provost's adv. com., athletic affairs, acad. affairs, faculty affairs coms. of bd. trustees U. Notre Dame Ctr. for Civil and Human Rights. Served to lt. comdr. USN. Mem.: ABA (coun. on sci. and tech., com. on advt., sect. on legal edn., com. on professionalism 1993—97), Future of Russia Found., Woodrow Wilson Internat. Ctr. for Scholars, Miracle of Nazareth Internat., World Law Inst., Soc. for Values in Higher Edn.

LINK, TERRY, state legislator; b. Waukegan, Ill., Mar. 20, 1947; m. Susan McCall; 4 children. Student, Stout State U. Ptnr. Lake County Indsl. Equipment; mem. Ill. Senate, Springfield, 1997—, mem. commerce & industry, exec. appts., state govt. ops. com. Democrat. Office: State Capitol 119-b Capitol Bldg Springfield IL 62706-0001 also: 425 Sheridan Rd Ste B Highwood IL 60040-1308

LINKLATER, WILLIAM J., lawyer; b. Chgo., June 3, 1942; s. William John and Jean (Connell) L.; m. Dorothea D. Ash, Apr. 4, 1986; children: Erin, Emily. BA, U. Notre Dame, 1964; JD, Loyola U., 1968. Bar: Ill. 1968, U.S. Dist. Ct. (no. dist.) Ill. 1968, U.S. Ct. Appeals (7th cir.) 1971, U.S. Supreme Ct. 1971, U.S. Ct. Appeals Wash. 1978, Calif. 1981, U.S. Dist. Ct. (cen. dist.) Calif. 1981, U.S. Tax Ct. 1982, U.S. Dist. Ct. (no. dist.) Calif. 1983, U.S. Dist. Ct. (ea. dist.) Mich. 1989, Colo., 1990, U.S. Ct. Appeals (6th cir.) 1990, U.S. Dist. Ct. Hawaii 1992, U.S. Ct. Appeals (11th cir.), 1999, U.S. Ct. Appeals (5th cir.), 1999, Wyo. 2005. Atty. Fed. Defender Project, Chgo.; assoc. Baker & McKenzie, Chgo., 1968-75, ptnr., 1975—, dir. profl. responsibility. Contbr. articles to profl. jours. Named one of World's Leading White Collar Crime Lawyers, Euromoney, World's Leading Competition and Antitrust Lawyers. Mem.: FBA, ABA (past co-chmn. com. on internat. criminal law criminal justice sect., mem. criminal practice and procedure com. antitrust sect., others), Wyo. Bar Assn., Nat. Assn. Criminal Def. Lawyers, Am. Bd. Criminal Lawyers, Am. Coll. Trial Lawyers, Colo. Bar Assn., Calif. Bar Assn., Chgo. Bar Assn. (pres. 2000—01, bd. mgrs. 1997—2002, past v.p. jud. candidates evaluation com., chmn. large law firm com.), 7th Cir. Bar Assn., Ill. Bar Assn., Wong Sun Soc. San Francisco (internat. proctor), Chgo. Inn of Ct., Alpha Sigma Nu. Office: Baker & McKenzie LLP 130 E Randolph Dr Ste 2500 Chicago IL 60601 Office Phone: 312-861-2794.

LINNELL, NORMAN C., lawyer; BA, U. Minn., 1981, JD, 1984. Bar: Minn. 1984. Ptnr. Dorsey & Whitney; gen. counsel, sec. Donaldson Co. Inc., Mpls., 1996—99, v.p., gen. cousel, sec., 2001—. Office: Donaldson Co Inc PO Box 1299 Minneapolis MN 55440 Office Phone: 952-887-3631. E-mail: nlinnell@mail.donaldson.com.

LINS, DEBRA R., bank executive; BA magna cum laude, Lakeland Coll., 1979; MBA, U. Wis., 1984. Loan officer Farm Credit Svcs., Baraboo, Wis., 1979—83; v.p., sr. lender M&I Bank So. Wis., Sauk City, Wis., 1983—90, First Bus. Bank Madison, Wis., 1990—93; pres., CEO, dir. Cmty. Bus. Bank, 1993—. Bd. dir. Sauk Prairie Meml. Hosp., 1992—98, Sauk Prairie United Way, Inc., 1996—2001, benedictine Life Found. Wis., Inc., 2000—02. Named Disting. Woman in Banking, N.W. Fin. Rev., 1994, Outstanding Entrepreneurial Woman in Dane County, Tempo Madgen, Outstanding Woman in Agr., Assn. Women in Agr., 1998, Wis. Woman of Century, Wis. Woman Mag., 2000, One of 25 Most Powerful Women in Banking, U.S. Banker Mag., 2003; recipient, 2004. Mem.: Am. Banker's Assn. (mem. cmty. bankers coun. 2001—). Office: Community Business Bank 1111 Sycamore St PO Box 636 Sauk City WI 53583-0636 Office Phone: 608-643-6300.

LINSON, ROBERT EDWARD, retired academic administrator; b. Indpls., Dec. 10, 1922; s. William Albert and Anne Charlotte (Karstedt) L.; m. Nancy Sue Hughes, June 6, 1948; children: Cynthia, Lawrence, LuAnn. BS, Ball State U., Muncie, Ind., 1947, MS, 1948; EdD, U. Denver, 1957. Prin., acting supt. Jonesboro Pub. Schs., Ind., 1948-49; prin J.C. Knight Sch., Jonesboro, 1949-50, 51-52, Spiceland Pub. Schs., Ind., 1952-55; dir. alumni rels. Ball State Tchrs. Coll., Muncie, 1955-75; exec. dir. alumni and devel. Ball State U., Muncie, 1975-80, v.p. univ. relations, 1980-87, v.p. univ. relations emeritus, 1987—. Cons. in field. Contbr. articles to profl. jours. Bd. dirs. Planned Parenthood of East Ctrl. Ind., 1988-91, United Way of Delaware County, Muncie, 1982-86, Muncie YMCA, 1980-84; mem. task force on govtl. rels. United Way of Ind., Indpls., 1985-91; founder Coun. Advancement and Support of Edn., 1974; bd. dirs. Ind. Basketball Hall of Fame. With USAF, 1943-46, 50-51. Named Outstanding U.S. Advancement Officer, Coun. for Advancement & Support of Edn., 1986; Alumni Disting. Svc. award, Ball State U., 1980, Ball State U. Athletic Hall of Fame, others. Mem. Am. Alumni Coun. (chmn. bd. dirs. 1972-73), Sagamore of the Wabash, Rotary. Democrat. Presbyterian. Avocations: travel, reading, intercollegiate athletics. Home: 909 N Meadow Ln Muncie IN 47304-3326

LINSTROTH, TOD BRIAN, lawyer; b. Racine, Wis., Feb. 19, 1947; s. Eugene and Gloria Linstroth; m. Jane Kathryn Zedler, June 23, 1972; children: Kathryn, Krista, Kassandre, Kyle. BBA in Acctg., U. Wis., 1970, JD, 1973. Bar: Wis. Assoc. Michael, Best & Friedrich, Madison, Wis., 1973-79, ptnr., 1980—, past chmn., mem. firm mgmt. com., 1997—2005. Chmn. Wis. Tech. Coun., Inc., 2001—. Mem. Wis. Gov.'s Sci. and Tech. Coun., Madison, 1993—95; pres. Madison Repertory Theatre; bd. visitors U. Wis. Sch. Bus., 1991—94. Mem.: Wis. Venture Fair (chair steering com. 1997—), Greater Madison Area C. of C. Avocations: skiing, sailing, reading. Office: Michael Best & Friedrich 1 S Pinckney St Ste 700 Madison WI 53703-4236 Office Phone: 608-283-2242. Business E-Mail: TBLinstroth@michaelbest.com.

LINTON, WILLIAM CARL, state legislator; b. Ft. Worth, Tex., Nov. 26, 1929; s. Carl Gustav and Mary Zola (Delashamit) L.; m. Lois Anne Reeder, Dec. 16, 1935; children: David, Rebecca, Angela, Steven. BS in Indsl. Engring., Washington U., 1951; MS in Engring. Mgmt., U. Mo., Rolla, 1974. Registered profl. engr., Mo. Indsl. engr. Laclede Steel, Alton, Mo., 1953-54; sales engr. Nooter Corp., St. Louis, 1954-84; sales rep. Hill Equip. Co., St. Louis, 1984-86; state rep. Mo. Ho. of Reps., Jefferson City, 1986—. Mem. Rockwood Bd. of Edn., St. Louis County, 1976-82, pres., 1981. With U.S. Army, 1951-53. Mem. Nat. Assn. Corrosion Engrs. (chmn. 1964), Eureka C. of C., West St. Louis C. of C. Republican. Presbyterian. Avocation: sports. Office: Ho of Reps State Capitol Building Jefferson City MO 65101-1556 Home: 322 Algonquin Dr Ballwin MO 63011-2534

LINTZ, ROBERT CARROLL, retired financial holding company executive; b. Cin., Oct. 2, 1933; s. Frank George and Carolyn Martha (Dickhaus) L.; m. Mary Agnes Mott, Feb. 1, 1964 (dec.); children— Lesa, Robert, Laura, Michael. B.B.A., U. Cin., 1956. Staff accountant Alexander Grant, Cin., 1958-60; dist. mgr. Uniroyal, Memphis, 1960-65; v.p. Am. Fin. Corp., Cin., 1965—2002; dir. Rapid-American Corp., McGregor Corp., Faberge Inc., all N.Y.C., H.R.T. Industries Inc., Los Angeles. Fisher Foods Inc., Cleve., Am. Agronomics, Tampa, Fla. Trustee, St. Francis-St. George Hosp., Cin., 1974-81. Served to capt. U.S. Army, 1956-58, 61-62. Republican. Roman Catholic. Home: 5524 Palisades Dr Cincinnati OH 45238-5620 Office: Am Fin Corp 1 E 4th St Cincinnati OH 45202-3717

LINVILLE, RANDAL L., agricultural company executive; married; 1 child. BS in Bus. Finance and Agrl. Economics, Kans. State U., 1976, MS in Agrl. Economics, 1977. Merchandise mgr. The Scoular Co., 1984, v.p., gen. mgr. grain divsn., 1992, CEO, 1999—.

LINVILLE, RONALD G., lawyer; b. Youngstown, Ohio, Oct. 28, 1954; BA cum laude, Wittenberg U., 1977; JD summa cum laude, Capital U., 1980. Bar: Ohio 1980, US Supreme Ct., 1994. Ptnr. Baker & Hostetler, Columbus, Ohio, chair, nat. employment and labor group, 2000—. Named an Ohio Super Lawyer, 2004. Mem. ABA (labor and employment law section), Ohio State Bar Assn., Columbus Bar Assn. Office: Baker & Hostetler 65 E State St Ste 2100 Columbus OH 43215-4260 Office Phone: 614-462-2647. Office Fax: 614-462-2616. Business E-Mail: rlinville@bakerlaw.com.

LIOI, SARA ELIZABETH, judge; b. Canton, Ohio, Dec. 17, 1960; BA summa cum laude, Bowling Green State U., 1983; JD, Ohio State U., 1987. Bar: Ohio 1987. Assoc. Day, Ketterer, Raley, Wright & Rybolt, Ltd., 1987—93, ptnr., 1993—97; judge Stark County Ct. Pub. Pleas, 1997—2007, US Dist. Ct. (no. dist.) Ohio, 2007—. Mem. Leadership Stark County, Cmty. Svcs. Stark County, Walsh U. Adv. Bd., Plain Local Schools Found., Stark County Humane Soc.

LIONE, GAIL ANN, lawyer; b. NYC, Oct. 22, 1949; d. James G. and Dorothy Ann (Marsino) L.; 1 child, Margo A. Peyton. BA magna cum laude in Polit. Sci., U. Rochester, 1971; JD, U. Pa., 1974. Bar: Pa. 1974, Ga. 1975, DC 1990, NC 1998. Atty. Morgan, Lewis & Bockius, Phila., 1974-75, Hansell & Post, Atlanta, 1975-80; v.p. 1st Nat. Bank Atlanta, 1980-86; sr. v.p., corp. sec., gen. counsel Sun Life Group of Am., Inc., Atlanta, 1986-89; v.p. Md. Nat. Bank, Balt., 1989-90; gen. counsel, sec. US News & World Report, LP, Applied Graphics Technologies, Atlantic Monthly Co., Washington, 1990—97; exec. v.p., gen. counsel, sec. Harley-Davidson, Inc., Milw., 1997—. Bd. dirs. Sugar Imperial Co., 2007—, Sargento Foods, Inc., 2006. Sec., dir., com. chair State Bar Ga. (Young Lawyers Sect.), 1976-84; Chmn. bd. Spl. Audiences, Inc., 1983-85, bd. dirs., 1975-89; trustee Client Security Fund State Bar Ga., 1985-89; vice chmn. Metro Atlanta United Way Campaign, 1986-87; chmn. bd. Atlanta Ballet, 1985-86, bd. dirs., 1975-89; mem. Atlanta Legal Aid Soc., 1981-89; bd. mgrs. U. Pa. Law Sch., 1982-85; mem. U. Rochester Trustee Coun., 1994—; bd. dirs. YMCA Balt., 1989-90; past bd. dirs. Metro YMCA, Atlanta, Sudden Infant Death Syndrome Inst., Atlanta Cmty. Food Bank; mem. Leadership Atlanta, 1988; mem. fin. com. Nat. Symphony Ball, 1995; adv. bd. Cardiovascular Ctr. Medical Coll. Wis., 1999-2002; mem., bd. dirs. Bradley Ctr. Sports & Entertainment Corp., 2003-; Milw. Art Mus., 2004-, Outstanding Atlanta award, TOYPA, 1982, outstanding Vol. Golden Rule award, 1984; named one of Top 40 Under 40 Atlanta Mag., 1984, Top 20 Women in Atlanta by Atlanta Bus. Chronicle, 1987; teaching fellow Salzburg Inst., 1989. Mem. ABA (mem. ho. dels., 1980-84, chmn. standing com. comm. on assn. comm., 1993-96, co-chair. litig. sect. com. fed. legis. 1994—96, regional co-chair forum on comm. law, 1996—98, standing com. on pub. oversight and strategic comm., 1996-2000), Copywright Soc. USA (trustee 1996-99), Mfg. Inst., 2002-, Nat. Assn. Mfrs., Phi Beta Kappa. Office: Harley-Davidson 3700 W Juneau Ave PO Box 653 Milwaukee WI 53201-0653 Office Phone: 414-343-4044. Office Fax: 414-343-4189.

LIPFORD, ROCQUE EDWARD, lawyer; b. Monroe, Mich., Aug. 16, 1938; s. Frank G. and Mary A. (Mastromarco) L.; m. Marcia A. Griffin, Aug. 5, 1966; children: Lisa, Rocque Edward, Jennifer, Katherine. BS, U. Mich., 1960, MS, 1961, JD with distinction, 1964. Bar: Mich. 1964, Ohio 1964. Instr. mech. engring. U. Mich., 1961—63; atty. Miller, Canfield, Paddock & Stone, Detroit, 1965—66; asst. gen. counsel Monroe Auto Equipment Co., 1966—70, gen. counsel, 1970—72, v.p., gen. counsel, 1973—77, Tenneco Automotive, 1977—78; ptnr. firm Miller, Canfield, Paddock & Stone, Detroit, 1978—, mng. ptnr., 1988—91. Bd. dirs. La-Z-Boy Inc., MBT Fin. Mem.: Knights of Malta, Legatus, Mich. Bar Assn., Mariner Sands Golf and Country Club, Monroe Golf and Country Club, North Cape Yacht Club, Otsego Ski Club, Pi Tau Sigma, Tau Beta Pi. Home: 1065 Hollywood Dr Monroe MI 48162-3045 Office: Miller Canfield Paddock & Stone 214 E Elm Ave Ste 100 Monroe MI 48162-2682 Office Phone: 734-243-2000. Business E-Mail: lipford@mcps.com.

LIPINSKI, ANN MARIE, publishing executive; b. Trenton, Mich. m. Steve Kagan; 1 child, Caroline. B in Am. Studies, U. Mich. Joined Chgo. Tribune, 1978, named head investigative team, 1990, assoc. mng. editor met. news., 1991—93, dep. mng. editor, 1994—95, mng. editor, 1995—2000, v.p. & exec. editor, 2000—01, sr. v.p. & exec. editor, 2001—. Juror Pulitzer Prize, 2001, 02; mem. Pulitzer Prize Bd., 2003—. Bd. visitors Poynter Inst., U. Mich. Journalism Fellows program, Stanford U. Journalism Fellows program. Recipient Pulitzer Prize for investigative reporting, 1988; Nieman Fellowship Harvard U., 1989-90. Office: Chgo Tribune 435 N Michigan Ave Chicago IL 60611-4066 E-mail: ctc-editor@tribune.com.*

LIPINSKI, DANIEL, congressman; b. Chgo., July 15, 1966; s. William and Marie Lipinski; m. Judy Lipinski. BS, Northwestern Univ., 1988; MA, Stanford Univ., 1989; PhD in polit. sci., Duke Univ., 1998. Assoc. prof. Notre Dame Univ., 2000—01, Univ. Tenn., 2001—04; mem. U.S. Congress from 3d Dist Ill., 2005—; mem. sci. com., small bus. com. U.S. Ho. of Reps. Democrat. Roman Catholic. Office: US House Reps 1217 Longworth House Office Bldg Washington DC 20515-1303 Office Phone: 202-225-5701. Office Fax: 202-225-1012.

LIPINSKI, WILLIAM OLIVER, former congressman; b. Chgo., Dec. 22, 1937; s. Oliver and Madeline (Collins) L.; m. Rose Marie Lapinski, Aug. 29, 1962; children: Laura, Daniel. Student, Loras Coll., Dubuque, Iowa, 1957-58. Various positions to area supr. Chgo. Parks, 1958-75; alderman Chgo. City Coun., 1975-83; mem. 98th-108th Congresses from 5th (now 3rd) Dist. Ill., 1983—2005, mem. transp. and infrastructure com. Dem. ward committeeman, Chgo., 1975—; del. Dem. Nat. Midterm Conv., 1974, Dem. Nat. Conv., 1976, 84, 88; pres. Greater Midway Econ. and Community Devel. Com.; mem. Chgo. Hist. Soc., Art Inst., Chgo., pres.'s coun. St. Xavier Coll.; mem. Congl. Competitive Caucus, Congl. Caucus for Women's Issues, Congl. Hispanic Caucus, Congl. Human Rights Caucus, Congl. Populist Caucus, Dem. Study Group, Export Task Force, Inst. for Ill., Maritime Caucus, N.E.-Midwest Congl. Coalition, Urban Caucus. Named Man of Yr. Chgo. Park Dist. 4, 1983; recipient Archer Heights Civic Assn. award 1979, 23d Ward Businessmen and Mchts. award Chgo., 1977, Garfield Ridge Hebrew Congregation award Chgo., 1975-77, Installing Officer award Vittum Park Civic Assn., 23d Ward Minuteman award, Friends of Vittum Park Polish award, Nathan Hale Grand award from S.W. Liberty Soc., S.W. Am. Edn. and Recreation program award, Sentry of Yr. award Stars & Stripes Soc., Ill. State Minuteman award 1991. Mem. Polish Nat. Alliance, Kiwanis (Disting. Svc. award, pres., Peace Through Strength Leadership award 1991). Democrat. Roman Catholic.

LIPMAN, DAVID, retired journalist, multi-media consultant; b. Springfield, Mo., Feb. 13, 1931; s. Benjamin and Rose (Mack) L.; m. Marilyn Lee Vittert, Dec. 10, 1961; children: Gay Ilene, Benjamin Alan. BJ, U. Mo., 1953, LHD (hon.), 1997. Sports editor Jefferson City (Mo.) Post-Tribune, 1953, Springfield Daily ews, 1953-54; gen. assignment reporter Springfield Leader and Press, 1956-57; reporter, copy editor Kansas City (Mo.) Star, 1957-60; sports reporter St. Louis Post-Dispatch, 1960-66, asst. sports editor, 1966-68, news editor, 1968-71, asst. mng. editor, 1971-78, mng. editor, 1979-92; chmn. Pulitzer 2000 Pulitzer Pub. Co., St. Louis, 1992-96, multimedia cons., 1997-2000. Guest lectr. Am. Press Inst., Columbia U. Journalism Sch., 1967-70; chmn. bd. advisors U. Mo. Sch. Journalism, 1989-2001, chmn. bd. dirs. multi-cultural mgmt. program, 1995-97; bd. dirs. Columbia Missourian; chmn. U. Mo. Jounalism Sch. task force, 2001-02; 1st v.p. Mo. Press Found., 2003—. Author: Maybe I'll Pitch Forever, The Autobiography of LeRoy (Satchel) Paige, 1962, reissued, 1993, Mr. Baseball, The Story of Branch Rickey, 1966, Ken Boyer, 1967, Joe Namath, 1968; co-author: The Speed King, The Story of Bob Hayes, 1971, Bob Gibson Pitching Ace, 1975, Jim Hart Underrated Quarterback, 1977. Bd. dirs. Mid-Am. Press Inst., 1973-97, chmn., 1975-77; mem.-at-large nat. coun., bd. dirs. Am. Jewish Com. St. Louis, 1997—, life time adv. bd. mem., 2005—; bd. dirs. Rabbi Samuel Thurman Ednl. Found., 1997—; trustee United Hebrew Congregation, 1975-77; bd. dirs. Parkview Housing Corp., 1999-2004; chmn. com. 21st Century, U. Mo., 1993-94; vice chair Mo. Gov.'s Commn. on Info. Tech., 1994-95; chmn. ethics commn. City of Creve Coeur, 2001-02, chair new tech. com., 1997-2001; mem. Creve Coeur Charter Commn., 2000-2001; cons. Mo. Press-Bar Commn., 1995-2002; mem. adv. bd. Jewish Light, 2001—. 1st lt. USAF, 1954-56. Named a St. Louis Media Hall Fame, 2007; named to Writers Hall of Fame of Am., Springfield, Mo., 2002, Mo. Newspapers Hall of Fame, 2002; recipient Univ. Mo. Faculty and Alumni award, 1988, Univ. Mo. Disting. Svc. in Journalism medal, 1989, St. Louis Jermiah award, 1991. Mem. Am. Soc. Newspaper Editors, Newspaper Assn. Am. (mem. industry devel. com. 1993-96), Mo. Editors and Pubs. Assn. (pres. 1990-91), Mo. Soc. Newspaper Editors (bd. dirs. 1990-97, vice chmn. 1992-93, chmn. 1993), Mo. Press Assn. (1st v.p. 1994-95, pres. 1997, bd. dirs. 1998-2002), Mo. AP Mng. Editors Assn. (pres. 1990), U. Mo. Sch. Journalism Nat. Alumni Assn. (chmn. 1980-83), Press Club of St. Louis (chmn. 1987-94), Soc. Profl. Journalists (pres. St. Louis chpt. 1976-77), Kappa Tau Alpha, Omicron Delta Kappa. Jewish.

LIPO, THOMAS A., electrical engineer, educator; b. Milw., Feb. 1, 1938; married; 4 children. BEE, Marquette U., 1962, MSEE, 1964; PhD, U. Wis., 1968. Grad. trainee Allis-Chalmers Mfg. Co., Milw., 1962-64, engring. analyst,

1964; instr. U. Wis., Milw., 1964-66; NRC rsch. fellow U. Manchester (Eng.) Inst. Sci. and Tech., 1968-69; elec. engr. Gen. Electric Co., Schenectady, 1969-79; prof. Purdue U., West Lafayette, Ind., 1979-80, U. Wis., Madison, 1981-90, W.W. Grainger prof. pwoer electronics and elec. machines, 1990—. Co-dir. Wis. Elec. Machines and Power Electronics Consortium, 1981—. Fellow IEEE, IEEE Power Engring. Soc., IEEE Indsl. Applications Soc., IEEE Power Electronics Soc. Office: U Wis Dept Elec & Comp Eng 1415 Engineering Dr Dept Elec& Madison WI 53706-1607

LIPOVSKY, ROBERT P., marketing executive; b. Chgo., Apr. 15, 1950; s. Rudoplh John and Anna Mary (Nemec) L.; m. Sharon Sue Zelienka, July 1, 1972; children: Katherine Michelle, Robert Paul. BS, Western Ill. U., 1972. Dist. mgr. W.R. Grace and Co., Peoria, Ill., 1972-78; mktg. mgr. Doane Agrl. Svc., St. Louis, 1978-82; v.p., div. mgr. Maritz Mktg. Rsch. Inc., St. Louis, 1982—, pres., Maritz Performance Improvement Co., Fenton, Mo. Mem. Nat. Agrl. Mktg. Assn. Republican. Lutheran. Avocations: golf, hunting, sports, skeet shooting. Office: Maritz Performance Improvement Co 14 S Hwy Dr Fenton MO 63099-0001

LIPP, ROBERT I., insurance company executive; b. 1938; m. Martha Berman; 5 children. Grad., Williams Coll.; grad. in bus., Harvard U.; JD, NYU, 1969. With Chem. Bank, NYC, 1963-86, sr. trainee, 1963-65, office asst. control div., 1965-66, asst. controller, 1966-67, asst. v.p. corp. planning, 1967-69, corp. sr. v.p., dep. head ops., 1972-74, exec. v.p., head ops. div., 1974-77, exec. v.p., head met. div., 1977-79, corp. sr. exec. v.p., head met. div., 1979, sr. exec. v.p., 1979-83, pres., 1983-86; v.p. corp. planning, treas. Chem. NY Corp., 1969-70, dep. mgr. ops. div., 1970-72; exec. v.p. for consumer fin. services group Comml. Credit Co., Balt., 1986-89, chmn. consumer fin. svcs., 1999; exec. v.p. consumer fin. svcs. Primerica Corp. (parent co.), NYC, 1988; exec. v.p., chmn., CEO Travelers Aetna Property, Hartford, Conn., 2001—04; exec. chmn. St. Paul Travelers Cos., Inc., Minn., 2004—05, also bd. dirs. Bd. dirs. J.P. Morgan Chase & Co., 2003—, sr. advisor, 2005—; bd. dirs. Accenture Ltd. Dir. NYC Ballet; trustee Jackie Robinson Found., Carnegie Hall Society; chmn. exec. com. Williams Coll. Office: St Paul Travelers 385 Washington St Saint Paul MN 55102 also: JP Morgan Chase 270 Park Ave 39th Fl New York NY 10017

LIPPINCOTT, JAMES ANDREW, retired biochemistry and biological sciences educator; b. Cumberland County, Ill., Sept. 13, 1930; s. Marion Andrew and Esther Oral (Meeker) L.; m. Barbara Sue Barnes, June 2, 1956; children—Jeanne Marie, Lisa Ellen, John James. AB, Earlham Coll., 1954; A.M., Washington U., St. Louis, 1956, PhD, 1958. Lectr. botany Washington U., 1958-59; Jane Coffin Childs Meml. fellow Centre Nat. de la Recherche Scientifique, France, 1959-60; asst. prof. biol. scis. Northwestern U., Evanston, Ill., 1960-66, assoc. prof., 1966-73, prof., 1973-81, prof. biochemistry, molecular biology and cell biology, 1981-94, prof. emeritus Evanston, Ill., 1994—, assoc. dean biol. scis., 1980-83; ret., 1994. Vis. assoc. prof. U. Calif., Berkeley, 1970-71; vis. prof. Inst. Botany U. Heidelberg (Germany), 1974. Contbr. articles to profl. jours. Grantee NIH, NSF, Am. Cancer Soc., USDA Mem. Am. Soc. Biol. Chemists, Am. Soc. Plant Physiologists, Bot. Soc. Am., Am. Soc. Microbiology

LIPSCHUTZ, MICHAEL ELAZAR, chemistry professor, consultant, researcher; b. Phila., May 24, 1937; s. Maurice and Anna (Kaplan) L.; m. Linda Jane Lowenthal, June 21, 1959; children: Joshua Henry, Mark David, Jonathan Mayer. BS, Pa. State U., 1958; S.M., U. Chgo., 1960, PhD, 1962. Gastdocent U. Bern, Switzerland, 1964-65; from asst. prof. chemistry to assoc. head dept. Purdue U., West Lafayette, Ind., 1965—93, prof. chemistry, 1973—2007, prof. emeritus, 2007—, assoc. head dept. of chemistry, 1993—2001; dir. chemistry ops. Purdue Rare Isotope Measurement Lab. (PRIME), 1990—2002. Vis. assoc. prof. Tel Aviv U., 1971-72; vis. prof. Max-Planck Inst. fuer Chemie, Mainz, Fed. Republic Germany, 1987; mem. panel space sci. experts Com. on Space Rsch., Space Agy. Forum of the Internat. Space Yr., Internat. Coun. Sci. Unions, 1990-92; cons. in field. Assoc. editor 11th Lunar and Planetary Sci. Conf., 3 vols., 1980; fin. editor Meteoritics and Planetary Sci., 1992-2000; contbr. numerous articles to profl. jours. Served to 1st lt. USAR, 1958-64. Recipient Cert. of Recognition, ASA, 1979, Cert. of Spl. Recognition, 1979, Group Achievement award, 1983, Cert. Appreciation, Nat. Commn. on Space, 1986; postdoctoral fellow NSF, 1964-65, NATO, 1964-65; Fulbright fellow, 1971-72 Fellow Meteoritical Soc. (treas. 1978-84, mem. joint com. on pubs. of Geochem. and Meteoritical Socs. 1985-93, fin. officer 1985-93, chmn. 1988-90); mem. AAAS, Am. Chem. Soc., Am. Geophys. Union, Planetary Soc., Internat. Astron. Union (US rep. 1988—), Sigma Xi. Achievements include having minor planet named in honor of Lipschutz by Internat. Astron. Union, 1987, Cert. of Recognition, Dept. Def., 1999. Office: Purdue U Dept Chemistry West Lafayette IN 47907 Home Phone: 765-463-2895; Office Phone: 765-494-5326. Business E-Mail: rnaapuml@purdue.edu.

LIPSHAW, JEFFREY MARC, lawyer, chemicals executive, educator; b. Detroit, June 16, 1954; s. Harold Melvin Lipshaw and Renata Adele Freed; m. Alene Susan Franklin, Apr. 10, 1959; children: Arielle, Matthew, James. AB, U. Mich., 1975; JD, Stanford U., 1979. Bar: Mich. 1979, U.S. Supreme Ct. 1984, Ind. 2001. Assoc. Dykema Gossett, Detroit, 1979—87, ptnr., 1987—92, of counsel, 1998—99; sr. counsel automotive Allied Signal, Inc., Southfield, Mich., 1992—93, v.p., gen. counsel automotive, 1993—97; sr. v.p., gen. counsel, sec. Gt. Lakes Chem. Corp., Indpls., 1999—. Adj. prof. Ind. U. Sch. Law, Indpls., 2004—; vis. prof. Wake Forest U. Sch. Law, 2005. Co-author: Litigating the Commercial Case, 1992; contbr. articles to profl. jours. Bd. dirs. Temple Beth El, Bloomfield Hills, Mich., 1994—97, New Enterprise Forum, Ann Arbor, 1999, Park Tudor Sch., Indpls., 2003—. Recipient Disting. Brief award, Thomas M. Cooley Law Sch., 1987. Jewish. Avocations: tennis, running. Office: Great Lakes Chemical Corp 199 Benson Rd Waterbury CT 06749-0001 Office Phone: 317-715-3072. Business E-Mail: jlipshaw@glcc.com.

LIPTON, LOIS JEAN, lawyer; b. Chgo., Jan. 14, 1946; d. Harold and Bernice (Reiter) Farber L.; m. Peter Carey, May 30, 1978; children: Rachel, Sara. BA, U. Mich., 1966; JD summa cum laude, DePaul Coll. Law, Chgo., 1974; postgrad., Sheffield U., Eng., 1966. Bar: Ky. 1974, U.S. Dist. Ct. (we. dist.) Ky. 1974, U.S. Ct. Appeals (6th cir.) 1974, Ill. 1975, U.S. Dist. Ct. (no. dist.) Ill. 1975, U.S. Ct. Appeals (7th cir.) 1976. Staff counsel Roger Baldwin Found. of ACLU, Inc., Chgo., 1975-79, dir. reproductive rights project, 1979-83; atty. McDermott, Will & Emergy, Chgo., 1984-86, G.D. Searle, Skokie, Ill., 1988-90; sr. atty. AT&T, Chgo., 1990—. Del. White House Conf. on Families, Mpls., 1980; chmn. elect Chgo. Found. for Women. Recipient Durfee award, 1984, Roger Baldwin Lifetime Achievement award 2004. Mem. ACLU (v.p.), ABA, Chgo. Coun. Lawyers. Office: AT&T # R15 222 W Adams St Chicago IL 60606-5017 Home Phone: 847-491-1850; Office Phone: 312-230-2667. Personal E-mail: llipton@att.com.

LIPTON, RICHARD M., lawyer; b. Youngstown, Ohio, Feb. 25, 1952; s. Sanford Y. Lipton and Sarah (Kentor) Goldman; m. Jane Brennan, May 24, 1981; children: Thomas, Anne, Martin, Patricia. BA, Amherst Coll., 1974; JD, U. Chgo., 1977. Bar: Ill. 1977, D.C. 1978, U.S. Dist. Ct. (no. dist.) Ill. 1979, U.S. Dist. Ct. Appeals (D.C. and 7th cirs.) 1979, U.S. Tax Ct. 1977, U.S. Ct. Claims 1979. Law clk. to judge Hall U.S. Tax Ct., Washington, 1977—79; assoc. Isham, Lincoln & Beale, Chgo., 1979—83; ptnr. Ross & Hardies, Chgo., 1983—86; v.p. Pegasus Broadcasting, Chgo., 1986—88; ptnr. Sonnenschein Nath & Rosenthal, Chgo., 1988—99, McDermott, Will & Emery, 2000—02, Baker & McKenzie, 2003—. Contbr. articles to profl. jours. Recipient Order of Coif award, U. Chgo. Law Sch., 1977. Fellow: Am. Coll. Tax Counsel (regent 1998—2004, sec., treas. 2004—06, vice chair 2006—); mem.: ABA (coun. dir. 1990—93, vice chair taxation sect. 1993—96, chair taxation sect. 2001—02), Chgo. Bar Assn. (subcom. chair, chair fed. taxation com. 1991—92), Conway Farms Club, Mich. Shores Club, Union League Club. Republican. Office: Baker & McKenzie 130 E Randolph Chicago IL 60601

LISAK, ROBERT PHILIP, neurologist, researcher, educator; b. Bklyn., Mar. 17, 1941; s. Irving Arthur and Sylvia Lillian (Kadish) L.; m. Deena Freda Penchansky, Aug. 2, 1964; children: Ilene Ann, Michael Loren. BA, NYU, 1961; MD, Columbia U., 1965; MA (hon.), U. Pa., 1976. Diplomate Am. Bd. Neurology. Intern in medicine Montefiore Hosp. and Med. Ctr., Bronx, 1965-66; rsch. assoc. NIMH, Bethesda, Md., 1966-68; resident in medicine Bronx Mcpl. Med. Ctr., 1968-69; resident in neurology Hosp. of the U. of Pa., Phila., 1969-72; with Sch. of Medicine U. Pa., Phila., 1972-87, prof. neurology Sch. of Medicine, 1980-87, vice chmn. dept. neurology Sch. of Medicine, 1985-87; prof., chmn. dept. neurology Sch. of Medicine Wayne State U., Detroit, 1987—. Mem. adv. bd. Guillain-Barre Syndrome Internat., Wynnewood, Pa., 1985—; mem. med. adv. bd. Myasthenia Gravis Found., Mpls., 1988—, Nat. Multiple Sclerosis Soc., N.Y.C., 1988—. Co-author: Myasthenia Gravis, 1982; mem. editl. bd. Jour. Neuroimmunology, 1984-98, Muscle and Nerve Jour., 1981-86, 92-95, 98-2002, Neurology, 1981-86, Annals of Neurology, 1990-95, Jour. Peripheral Nervous Sys., 1995-2006, Clin. Neuropharm., 1997—; editor-in-chief Jour. Neurol. Sci., 1998—; contbr. articles to profl. jours. With USPHS, 1966-68. Fulbright rsch. scholar, London, 1978-79; recipient Disting. Teaching award U. Pa., 1985, Drs. award Myasthenia Gravis Found., 1991. Fellow Am. Acad. Neurology (sci. issues com. 1987-93); mem. Am. Neurol. Assn. (membership com. 1989-91, chmn. 1990-91, sci. program com. 1994-96, councillor 2002—), Internat. Soc. Neuroimmunology (exec. com. 1987-91, 95-2001, sec.-treas. 1991-95), Am. Assn. Immunologists, Soc. for Neurosci., Norwegian Neurol. Assn., Royal Soc. Medicine. Office: Wayne State U Sch Medicine 8DE-UHC 4201 St Antoine Detroit MI 48201 Home Phone: 248-646-2974. Business E-Mail: rlisak@med.wayne.edu.

LISHER, JOHN LEONARD, lawyer; b. Indpls., Sept. 19, 1950; s. Leonard Boyd and Mary Jane (Rafferty) L.; m. Mary Katherine Sturmon, Aug. 17, 1974. BA in History with honors, Ind. U., 1975, JD, 1975. Bar: (Ind.) 1975. Dep. atty. gen. State of Ind., Indpls., 1975-78; asst. corp. counsel City of Indpls., 1978-81; assoc. Osborn & Hiner, Indpls., 1981-86; ptnr. Osborn, Hiner & Lisher, P.C., 1986—. Pres. Brendonwood Common Inc.; asst. vol. coord. Marion County Rep. Com., Indpls., 1979-80; vol. Don. Bogard for Atty. Gen., Indpls., 1980, Steve Goldsmith for Prosecutor, Indpls., 1979-83, Mayflower Classic, Indpls., 1981-86. Recipient Outstanding Young Man of Am. award Jaycees, 1979, 85, Indpls. Jaycees, 1980. Mem. ABA, Ind. Bar Assn., Indpls. Bar Assn. (membership com.), Assn. Trial Lawyers Am., Ind. U. Alumni Assn., Hoosier Alumni Assn. (charter, founder, pres.), Ind. Trial Lawyers Assn., Ind. Def. Lawyers Assn., Ind. U. Coll. Arts and Scis. (bd. dirs. 1983-92, pres. 1986-87), Wabash Valley Alumni Assn. (charter), Founders Club, Pres. Club, Phi Beta Kappa, Eta Sigma Phi, Phi Eta Sigma, Delta Xi Alumni Assn. (Outstanding Alumnus award 1975, 76, 79, 83), Delta Xi Housing Corp. (pres.), Pi Kappa Alpha (midwest regional pres. 1977-86, parliamentarian nat. conv. 1982, del. convs. 1978-80, 82, 84, 86, trustee Meml. Found. 1986-91, 2004—). Presbyterian. Avocations: reading, golf, jogging, roman coin collecting. Home: 5725 Hunterglen Rd Indianapolis IN 46226-1019 Office: Osborn Hiner & Lisher PC 8500 Keystone Xing Ste 480 Indianapolis IN 46240-2460 Office Phone: 317-257-2400. Business E-Mail: jlisher@ohllaw.com.

LISHKA, EDWARD JOSEPH, underwriter, consultant; b. Chgo., Oct. 8, 1949; s. Edward John and Virginia Nelly (Powers) L.; m. Marie Ann Slawniak, June 7, 1975 (dec. Dec. 1993); 1 child, Ann. BS, Bradley U., 1971, MA, 1972. CPCU. Design engr. Forest Electric Co., Melrose Park, Ill., 1972-73; tech. writer Advance Schs. Inc., Des Plaines, Ill., 1973-74; design engr. Universal Oil Products, Des Plaines, 1974-75; account engr. Oil Ins. Assn., Chgo., 1975-81; policy cons. CNA Ins. Co., Chgo., 1981-85; underwriter Service Ins. Agy., Mount Prospect, Ill., 1985-86; sr. acct. underwriter Arkwright Mut. Inst. Co., Schaumburg, Ill., 1986-92; acct. analyst Mack & Parker, Chgo., 1992—2002; exec. risk mgmt. rep. Arthur J. Gallagher & Co., Itasca, Ill., 2002—. Mem. Schaumburg Village Ins. Com., 1983—. Mem. Soc. CPCUs (speaker 1987—, chmn. candidate devel. 1987-88, Profl. Devel. award 1986, 88, 89, 90, 92), Accredited Advisers in Ins. (assoc. in risk mgmt., assoc. in marine ins. mgmt.), Four Winds Ski Club (Itasca, Ill.). Republican. Roman Catholic. Avocations: skiing, golf, bicycling, fishing. Home: 100 Idlestone Ln Schaumburg IL 60194-4044 Office: Arthur J Gallagher & Co Two Pierce Pl Itasca IL 60143-3141 Personal E-mail: edlishka@aol.com. Business E-Mail: edward_lishka@ajg.com.

LISIO, DONALD JOHN, historian, educator; b. Oak Park, Ill., May 27, 1934; s. Anthony and Dorothy (LoCelso) Lisio; m. Suzanne Marie Swanson, Apr. 22, 1958; children: Denise Anne, Stephen Anthony. BA, Knox Coll., 1956; MA, Ohio U., 1958; PhD, U. Wis., 1965. Mem. faculty overseas div. U. Md., 1958-60; from asst. prof. history to prof. emeritus Coe Coll., Cedar Rapids, Iowa, 1964—2002, prof. emeritus, 2002—. Author: (book) The President and Protest: Hoover, Conspiracy, and the Bonus Riot, 1974, Hoover, Blacks, and Lily-Whites: A Study of Southern Strategies, 1985; contbg. author: book The War Generation, 1975; contbr. articles to hist. jours. Mem. exec. com. Cedar Rapids Com. Hist. Preservation, 1975—77. With US Army, 1958—60. Fellow William F. Vilas Rsch., U. Wis., 1963—64, NEH, 1969—70, Rsch., 1984—85, Am. Coun. Learned Socs., 1977—78; grantee, 1971—72, Rsch., U.S. Inst. Peace, 1990. Mem.: AAUP, Am. Hist. Assn., Orgn. Am. Historians, Rancho Bernardo Rotary Club. Roman Catholic. Home Phone: 858-676-1226.

LISKA, PAUL J., communications executive, former insurance compny executive; b. Oct. 12, 1955; married; 3 children. Grad., U. Notre Dame, 1977; MBA, orthwestern U. CPA. With Price Waterhouse & Co., Am. Hosp. Supply Corp., Quaker Oats Co.; CFO Kraft Gen. Foods, 1988-94; pres., CEO Specialty Foods Corp., 1994-96; exec. v.p., CFO The St. Paul Cos., 1997-2001, Sears, Roebuck & Co., 2001—02, exec. v.p., pres. credit & fin. products, 2002—03; ptnr. Ripplewood Holdings L.L.C., 2004—08; exec. chmn. US Freightways Corp., 2004—06; exec. v.p., CFO Motorola, Inc., Schaumburg, Ill., 2008—. Office: Motorola Inc 1303 E Algonquin Rd Schaumburg IL 60196*

LISS, WILLIAM J., lawyer; b. LA, Jan. 29, 1971; BA in English, Ohio U., 1993; JD, U. Cin., 1997; LLM in Taxation, U. Fla., 1999. Bar: Ohio 1997, Nev. 1998, US Dist. Ct. Southern Dist. Ohio 1998, Fla. 1999, US Tax Ct. Assoc. Santen & Hughes, Cin. Named one of Ohio's Rising Stars, Super Lawyers, 2006. Mem.: Ohio State Bar Assn., Cin. Bar Assn., Phi Beta Kappa. Office: Santen & Hughes Ste 3100 312 Walnut St Cincinnati OH 45202 Office Phone: 513-721-4450. Office Fax: 513-721-0109.

LISSKA, ANTHONY JOSEPH, humanities educator, philosopher; b. Columbus, Ohio, July 23, 1940; s. Joseph Anthony and Florence (Wolfel) L.; m. Marianne Hedstrom, Mar. 16, 1968; children: Megan Catherine, Elin Elizabeth. BA in Philosophy cum laude, Providence Coll., 1963; AM in Philosophy, St. Stephen's Coll., Dover, Mass., 1967; PhD in Philosophy, Ohio State U., 1971; Cert., Harvard U., Cambridge, 1979. Asst. prof. Denison U., Granville, Ohio, 1969—76, assoc. prof., 1976—81, dean of coll., 1978—83, prof. philosophy, 1981—, dir. honors program, 1987—2002, Charles and Nancy Brickman disting. svc. chair, 1998—2001, Maria Theresa Barney chair in philosophy, 2004—. Project reviewer NEH, Washington, 1979-90, evaluator; adv. bd. Midwest Faculty Seminar, Chgo., 1981-90; vis. scholar U. Oxford, Eng., 1984; mem. scholarship com. Sherex Chem. Co., Dublin, Ohio, 1984-92; cons. Franklin Pierce Coll., Ringe, N.H., 1991, Hampden-Sydney Coll., Va., 1998, Luther Coll., 2005; referee various philosophy jours.; lectr. in field. Author: Philosophy Matters, 1977, Aquinas's Theory of Natural Law, 1996, paperback edit. 1997, 2002, Illustrated History of Buckeye Lake Yacht Club, 2007; co-editor: The Historical Times, 1988—, Bi-centennial History of Granville, 2004; contbr. numerous articles to profl. jours., chpts. to books. Bd. mgmt. Granville Hist. Soc., 1987-2002; precinct rep. Dem. Party, Granville, 1994—; convener Civil War Roundtable, Granville, 1989-95; v.p. The Granville Found., 2003-, pres. 2004, acting pres. 2007-08; mem. Granville Bicentennial Commn., 1996-2006. Named Carnegie Prof. of Yr., Carnegie Found., 1994; recipient Sears Found. Teaching award, 1990, Historian of Yr. award, 2005; NEH grantee, 1973, 77, 85; R.C. Good fellow, 1990, 96, 02. Mem. Am. Philos. Assn. (program com. 2003, Tchg. award 1994), Am. Cath. Philos. Assn. v.p., 2004-05, pres., 2005-06, exec. coun., 2004-07), Nat. Collegiate Honors Coun., Soc. for Ancient Greek Philosophy, Soc. for Medieval and Renaissance Philosophy, Internat. Thomas Aquinas Soc., NE Polit. Sci. Assn., Phi Beta Kappa. Democrat. Roman Catholic. Avocations: history, photography. Home: 285 Burtridge Rd Granville OH 43023-1214 Office: Denison U Dept Philos Knapp Hall Granville OH 43023 Office Phone: 740-587-5616. Business E-Mail: lisska@denison.edu.

LISTECKI, JEROME EDWARD, bishop; b. Chgo., Mar. 12, 1949; BA, Loyola U., 1971; MDiv, St. Mary of the Lake, Mundelein, Ill., 2975, STB, 1973, STL, 1978; JD, DePaul U., 1976; JCL, Pontifical U. St. Thomas, Rome, 1980, JCD, 1981. Ordained priest Archdiocese of Chgo., 1975; ordained bishop, 2000; aux. bishop Archdiocese of Chgo., 2000—04, episcopal bishop of Vicariate I, 2002—04; bishop Diocese of La Crosse, Wis., 2004—. Legal counsel Archdiocese of Chgo., 1985—87; host WIND Cath. Conversation, 1978—79. Lt. col. USAR. Roman Catholic. Office: Diocese of La Crosse 3710 E Ave S PO Box 4004 La Crosse WI 54602-4004 Office Phone: 608-788-7700. Office Fax: 608-788-8413.*

LITAN, ROBERT ELI, lawyer, economist; b. Wichita, Kans., May 16, 1950; s. David and Shirley Hermine (Krischer) Litan. BS in Econs., U. Pa., 1972; MPhil in Econs., Yale U., 1976, JD, 1977, PhD in Econs., 1987. Bar: (DC) 1980. Rsch. asst. Brookings Instn., 1972-73; instr. to lectr. econs. Yale U., 1975-76; energy cons. NAS, 1975-77; regulation and energy specialist Pres.'s Coun. Econ. Advs., 1977-79; assoc. Arnold & Porter, Washington, 1979-82; assoc., then ptnr. and counsel Powell, Goldstein, Frazer & Murphy, Washington, 1982-90; sr. fellow Brookings Instn., Washington, 1984-92, 2003—, dir. Ctr. for Econ. Progress, 1987-93, v.p., dir. econ. studies, Cabot family chair in econs., 1996—2003; dep. asst. atty. gen. Dept. Justice, Washington, 1993-95; assoc. dir. Office of Mgmt. and Budget, Washington, 1995-96. Cons. Inst. Liberty and Democracy, Lima, Peru, 1985—88; vis. lectr. Yale U. Law Sch., 1985—86; mem. Presdl. Congl. Commn. Causes of Savs. and Loan Crisis, 1991—92; cons. U.S. Dept. Treasury, 1996—97, 1999—2000; v.p. rsch. and policy The Kauffman Found., 2003—; sr. fellow The Brookings Inst., 2003—. Author: What Should Banks Do?, 1987, Blueprint for Restructuring America's Financial Institutions, 1989; co-author: Energy Modeling for an Uncertain Future, 1978, Reforming Federal Regulation, 1983, Saving Free Trade: A Pragmatic Approach, 1986; author: Banking Industry in Turmoil, 1990, The Revolution in U.S. Finance, 1991, The Liability Maze, 1991; co-author: Liability: Perspectives and Policy, 1988, American Living Standards: Threats and Challenges, 1988, Down in the Dumps: Administration of the Unfair Trade Laws, 1991, The Future of American Banking, 1992, Growth With Equity, 1993, Assessing Bank Reform, 1993, Verdict, 1993, Financial Regulation in a Global Economy, 1994, Footing the Bill for Superfund Cleanups, 1995, American Finance for the 21st Century, 1997, Globaphobia: Confronting Fears of Open Trade, 1998, None of Your Business: World Data Flows and the European Privacy Directive, 1998, The GAAP Gap, 2000, Beyond the Dot.Coms, 2001, Sticking Together: The Israeli Experiment in Pluralism, 2002, Protecting the American Homeland, 2002, Following the Money: Corporate Disclosure After Enron, 2003, Financial Statecraft, 2005, Worldwide Financial Reporting, 2006, Good Capitalism, Bad Capitalism and the Economics of Growth and Prosperity, 2007, Competitive Equity: An Alternative Model for Mutual Funds, 2007; contbr. articles to profl. jours. Recipient Class of 1964 award, U. Pa., W. Gordon award, 1972, Albert A. Berg award, 1971, 1972, Felix S. Cohen award, Yale U., 1976, Silver medal, Royal Soc. Arts, 1972; fellow Thouron, Eng., 1972. Mem.: ABA, Coun. on Fgn. Rels., Am. Econs. Assn. Democrat. Home: 5437 Mohawk St Fairway KS 66205-2732 Office: The Kauffman Found 4801 Rockhill Rd Kansas City MO 64110 Home Phone: 913-262-0731; Office Phone: 816-932-1179. Business E-Mail: rlitan@brookings.edu, rlitan@kauffman.org.

LITFIN, A. DUANE, academic administrator; b. Mich. m. Sherri Litfin; 3 children. B in Bibl. Studies, Phila. Coll. of the Bible, 1966; ThM, Dallas Theol. Seminary; PhD in Interpersonal Comm., Purdue U.; DPhil in N.T. Studies, Oxford U. Tchr. Purdue U., Ind. U.; pastor Metea Bapt. Ch., Lucern, Ind.; assoc. prof. pastoral ministries Dallas Theol. Sem., 1974—84; sr. pastor First Evang. Ch., Memphis, 1984—93; pres. Wheaton Coll., Ill., 1993—. Author: Public Speaking: A Handbook for Christians, 1992, St. Paul's Theology of Proclamation, 1994. Office: Wheaton Coll 501 College Ave Wheaton IL 60187-5593 Office Phone: 630-752-5002. E-mail: Duane.Litfin@wheaton.edu.

LITTLE, BRUCE WASHINGTON, professional society administrator; b. Feb. 22, 1936; m. Nancy J. Mains; children: Elizabeth, Thomas, David. BS, Kans. State U., 1963, DVM, 1965. Pvt. practice assoc., Normal, Ill., 1965-69; pvt. practice Americana Animal Hosp., Bloomington, Ill., 1969-85; asst. exec. v.p. AVMA, Schaumburg, Ill., 1986-96, exec. v.p., 1996—. Rabies control officer McLean County, Ill., 1968-72; instr. U. Ill. Extension Svc., 1974, adv. Mclean County Bd. of Health, 1980-85; pres., ops. mgr. Blooming Grove Farm, Inc., Bloomington, 1983—; bd. dirs. Assn. Forum Chicagoland, 2003—, Am. Vet. Med. Found., 1996-, at. Commn. of Vet. Econ. Issues, 1998-; spkr. in field. Contbr. articles to profl. jours. Coach, Ill. 4-H Equine Judging Teams, 1974-76; bd. dirs. Mclean County Assn. Commerce Industry, 1983-85, Assn. Forum Chicagoland, 2003—, Am. Vet. Med. Found., 1996—, Nat. Commn. on Vet. Econ. Issues, 1999—; v.p. Ill. State U. Athletic Booster Club, 1980-82, pres., 1982-84. With U.S. Army, 1955-57. Named an alumni fellow, Kans. State U., 1998. Mem. AVMA, Ill. State Vet. Med. Assn., Chgo. Vet. Med. Assn., (hon.) Brit. Vet. Assn., Rotary (Paul Harris Fellow), Alpha Zeta. Avocations: sports, golf, reading, horse breeding. Office: Am Vet Med Assn 1931 N Meacham Rd Schaumburg IL 60173-4364

LITTLE, CHRISTOPHER MARK, publishing company executive, lawyer; b. Tazewell, Va., Mar. 11, 1941; s. Haskin Vincent and Janet Koe (Kessinger) L.; m. Virginia Elizabeth Silver, Dec. 27, 1963 (div. Oct. 1988); children: Timothy Mark, Margaret Elizabeth; m. Elizabeth Foster Anderson, Oct. 15, 1988. BA, Yale U., 1963; LLB, U. Tex., 1966. Bar: D.C. 1966. Assoc. Covington & Burling, Washington, 1966-68, 70-75; adminstrv. asst. to Congressman Bob Eckhardt, U.S. Ho. of Reps., Washington, 1968-70; asst. gen. counsel EPA, Washington, 1975-76; v.p., counsel The Washington Post, 1976-80; pres., pub. The Herald, Everett, Wash., 1980-84; sr. v.p. adminstrn. Newsweek, Inc., NYC, 1984-86, pres., 1986-89, Cowles Mags., Inc., Harrisburg, Pa., 1989-92; v.p. pub. dir. Meredith Corp., Des Moines, Iowa, 1992-94, pres. mag. group, 1994—. Internat. bd. trustees Am. Field Svc., N.Y.C., 1989-95, chmn., 1992-95. Mem. Mag. Pubs. Am. (chmn. govt. affairs coun. 1990—), Wakonda Club, Des Moines Club. Episcopalian. Avocations: landscape architecture, 18th century american history, classical music. Office: Meredith Corp 1716 Locust St Des Moines IA 50309-3023

LITTLE, DANIEL EASTMAN, philosopher, educator, director; b. Rock Island, Ill., Apr. 7, 1949; s. William Charles and Emma Lou (Eastman) L.; m. Ronnie Alice Friedland, Sept. 12, 1976 (div. May 1995); children: Joshua Friedland-Little, Rebecca Friedland-Little. BS in Math. with highest honors, AB in Philosophy with high honors, U. Ill., 1971; PhD in Philosophy, Harvard U., 1977. Asst. prof. U. Wis.-Parkside, Kenosha, 1976-79; vis. assoc. prof. Wellesley (Mass.) Coll., 1985-87; vis. scholar Ctr. Internat. Affairs Harvard U., 1989-91, assoc. Ctr. Internat. Affairs, 1991-95; asst. prof. Colgate U., Hamilton, NY, 1979-85, assoc. prof., 1985-92, prof., 1992-96, chmn. dept. philosophy and religion, 1992-93, assoc. dean faculty, 1993-96; v.p. academic affairs Bucknell U., Lewisburg, Pa., 1996-2000, prof. philosophy, 1996-2000; chancellor U. Mich., Dearborn, 2000—, prof. philosophy, 2000—; faculty assoc. Inter-U. Consortium for Social and Political Rsch., 2000—. Teaching fellow Harvard U., 1973-76; participant internat. confs. Ctr. Asian and Pacific Studies, U. Oreg., 1992, Social Sci. Rsch. Coun./McArthur Found., U. Calif., San Diego, 1991, Budapest, Hungary, 1990, Morelos, Mex., 1989, Rockefeller Found., Bellagio, Italy, 1990, U. Manchester, Eng., 1986; mem. screening com. on internat. peace and security Social Sci. Rsch. Coun./MacArthur Found., 1991-94; manuscript reviewer Yale U. Press, Cambridge U. Press, Princeton U. Press, Oxford U. Press, Westview Press, Harvard U. Press, Can. Jour. Philosophy, Philosophy Social Scis., Synthese, Am. Polit. Sci. Rev.; grant proposal reviewer NSF, Social Sci. Rsch. Coun., Nat. Endowment for Humanities; tenure and promotion reviewer U. Tenn., Bowdoin Coll., Duke U., U. Wis.; faculty assoc. Inter-Univ. Consortium for Social and Polit. Rsch., 2000—. Author: The Scientific Marx, 1986, Understanding Peasant China: Case Studies in the Philosophy of Social Science, 1989, Varieties of Social Explanation: An Introduction to the Philosophy of Social Science, 1991 (Outstanding Book award Choice 1992), On the Reliability of Economic Models, 1995, Microfoundations Method and Causation: On the Philosophy of the Social Sciences, 1998, The Paradox of Wealth and Poverty: Mapping the Ethical Dilemmas of Global Development, 2003; contbr. articles to profl. jours., books. Social Sci. Rsch. Postdoctoral fellow MacArthur Found., 1989-91, Rsch. grantee NSF, 1987, Woodrow Wilson Grad. fellow, 1971-72. Mem. Am. Philos. Assn., Assn. Asian Studies, Internat. Devel. Ethics Assn., Social Sci. History Assn., Soc. for the History of Tech., Phi Beta Kappa. Office: Chancellor U Mich Dearborn 4901 Evergreen Rd Dearborn MI 48128 E-mail: delittle@umich.edu.

LITTLE, ROBERT EUGENE, engineering educator; b. Enfield, Ill., May 24, 1933; s. John Henry and Mary (Stephens) L.; m. Barbara Louina Farrell, Feb. 4, 1961; children: Susan Elizabeth, James Robert, Richard Roy, John William. BSME, U. Mich., 1959; MSME, Ohio State U., 1960; PhDME, U. Mich., 1963. Asst. prof. mech. engring. Okla. State U., Stillwater, 1963-65; assoc. prof. U.

Mich., Dearborn, 1965-68, prof., 1968—. Author: Statistical Design of Fatigue Experiments, 1975, Probability and Statistics for Engineers, 1978, Mechanical Reliability Improvement, 2003. Mem. ASTM, Am. Statis. Assn. Home: 3230 Pine Lake Rd West Bloomfield MI 48324-1951 Office: U Mich 4901 Evergreen Rd Dearborn MI 48128-1491 Office Phone: 313-593-5122.

LITTLE, WILLIAM G., manufacturing executive; m. Corinne Little. Grad., U. Mo. Sales exec. Lathe divsn. Amsted Industries, South Bend, Ind.; distbr. sales mgr. Quam-Nichols Co., 1970, pres., CEO Chgo. Co-chair U.S. del. U.S.-Japanese Electronic Industries Plenary Session, Tokyo, 1988; participant Dept. of Def. Joint Civilian Orientation Conf., 1990; bd. dirs. Ohmite Mfg. Co., Skokie, Ill., Aerovox, Inc., New Bedford, Mass. Inductee Hall of Fame, Electronic Distbrs. Rsch. Inst., 1981. Mem. Electronic Industries Assn. (chmn., chmn. distbr. products divsn.), Electronic Industry Show Corp. (officer), U.S. C. of C. (dir. 1994—, vice chmn. 1997-98). Office: Quam-Nichols Co 234 E Marquette Rd Chicago IL 60637-4090

LITTLEFIELD, ROBERT STEPHEN, communications educator, training consultant; b. Moorhead, Minn., June 21, 1952; s. Harry Jr. and LeVoyne Irene (Berg) L.; m. Kathy Mae Soleim, May 24, 1974; children: Lindsay Jane, Brady Robert. BS in Edn., Moorhead State U., 1974; MA, N.D. State U., 1979; PhD, U. Minn., 1983. Tchr. Barnesville (Minn.) Pub. Schs., 1974-78; teaching asst. N.D. State U., Fargo, 1978-79, lectr., 1979-81; teaching assoc. U. Minn., Mpls., 1981-82; instr. N.D. State U., Fargo, 1982-83, asst. prof., chmn., 1983-89, assoc. prof., chmn., 1989-90, interim dean, 1990-92, assoc. prof., chmn., 1992-94, prof., 1994—; dir. Inst. for Study of Cultural Diversity, 1992-97. Owner KIDSPEAK Co., Moorhead, 1987-97. Author/co-author: (series) KIDSPEAK, 1989-92; lyricist (centennial hymn) Built on a Triangle with Faith in the Triune, 1989; contbr. more than 50 articles to profl. jours. Vol. forensic coach Fargo Cath. Schs. Network, 1992—; mem. N.D. dist. com. Nat. Forensic League, 1995—; advisor to exec. coun. Nat. Jr. Forensic League, 1995—. Recipient Burlington No. award N.D. State U., 1988-89; named Outstanding Speech Educator, Nat. Fedn. High Sch. Activities Assn., 1990-91. Mem. Am. Forensic Assn. (sec. 1990-92), N.D. Speech and Theatre Assn. (historian 1989—, pres. 1985-87, Hall of Fame 1989, Scholar of Yr. 1989), N.D. Multicultural Assn., Speech Comm. Assn., Pi Kappa Delta (nat. coun. 1983—, nat. pres. 1991-93, nat. sec.-treas. 1993—), Fargo Lions Club (pres. 1990-91). Democrat. Lutheran. Office: ND State U 321G Minard Hall Fargo D 58105

LITTLEFIELD, VIVIAN MOORE, nursing educator, administrator; b. Princeton, Ky., Jan. 24, 1938; children: Darrell, Virginia. BS magna cum laude, Tex. Christian U., 1960; MS, U. Colo., 1964; PhD, U. Denver, 1979. Staff nurse USPHS Hosp., Ft. Worth, 1960-61; instr. nursing Tex. Christian U., Ft. Worth, 1961-62; nursing supr. Colo. Gen. Hosp., Denver, 1964-65; pvt. patient practitioner, 1974-78; asst. prof. nursing U. Colo., Denver, 1965-69, asst. prof., clin. instr., 1974-76, acting asst. dean, assoc. prof. continuing edn. regional perinatal project, 1976-78; assoc. prof., chair dept. women's health care nursing U. Rochester Sch. Nursing, N.Y., 1979-84; clin. chief ob-gyn., nursing U. Rochester Strong Meml. Hosp., N.Y., 1979-84; prof., dean U. Wis. Sch. Nursing, Madison, 1984-99, prof., 2000—. Cons. and lectr. in field. Author: Maternity Nursing Today, 1973, 76, Health Education for Women: A Guide for Nurses and Other Health Professionals, 1986; mem. editl. bd. Jour. Profl. Nursing; contbr. articles to profl. jours. Bur. Health Professions Fed. trainee, 1963-64. Recipient Nat. Sci. Service award, 1976-79. Mem. MAIN, AACN (bd. dirs.), NLN (bd. dirs.), Am. Acad. Nursing, Am. Nurses Assn., Consortium Prime Care Wis. (chair), Health Care for Women Internat., Midwest Nursing Research Soc., Sigma Theta Tau (pres. Beta Eta chpt., co-chair coun. nursing practice and edn. 1995). Avocations: golf, bicycling. Office: U Wis Sch Nursing 600 Highland Ave # H6150 Madison WI 53792-3284

LITWIN, BURTON HOWARD, lawyer; b. Chgo., July 26, 1944; s. Manuel and Rose (Boehm) L.; m. Nancy I. Stein, Aug. 25, 1968; children: Robin Litwin Levine, Keith Harris, Jill Stacy. BS with honors, BA with honors, Roosevelt U., Chgo., 1966; JD cum laude, Northwestern U., 1970. Bar: Ill. 1970, U.S. Dist. Ct. (no. dist.) Ill. 1970, U.S. Tax Ct. 1971, U.S. Ct. Fed. Claims 1983; CPA, Ill. Sr. counsel Neal, Gerber & Eisenberg, Chgo., 2002—. Author chpts. of books; contbr. articles to profl. jours. Recipient Gold Watch award Fin. Execs. Inst., Chgo., 1965. Mem. ABA (chmn. nonfiler task force for No. Ill. 1992-94), Chgo. Bar Assn. (chmn. adminstrv. practice subcom., fed. taxation subcom. 1982-83) Avocations: painting, photography. Office: Neal Gerber & Eisenberg LLP Two N LaSalle St Ste 2200 Chicago IL 60602-3801 Home Phone: 847-398-5377; Office Phone: 312-269-5986. Business E-Mail: blitwin@ngelaw.com. E-mail: gosox13@aol.com.

LITWIN, STUART M., lawyer; b. Skokie, Ill., June 17, 1959; BS summa cum laude, U. Ill., 1981; MBA, U. Chgo., 1985, JD cum laude, 1985. CPA Ill., 1981; bar: Ill. 1985. Assoc. Mayer Brown Rowe & Maw, Chgo., 1985—94, ptnr., co-head securitization practice, 1994—. Bd. dir. Chgo. Lawyers Com. for Civil Rights Under Law, treas., 1996—97, sec., 1997—98, v.p., 1998—99, pres., 1999—2000. Contbr. articles to profl. jours. Bd. dir. Pegasus Players Theatre, Cameron Kravitt Found., East Village Youth Prog., CityPAC, Am. Jewish Congress Midwest Region, United Jewish Appeal Nat. Cabinet. Mem.: ABA, Chgo. Bar Assn. (chmn. corp. control subcom. 1996—98, chmn. securities law com. 1998—99). Office: Mayer Brown Rowe & Maw LLP 71 S Wacker Dr Chicago IL 60606-4637 Office Phone: 312-701-7373. Office Fax: 312-706-8165. Business E-Mail: slitwin@mayerbrownrowe.com.

LITZSINGER, RICHARD MARK, retail executive; b. Houston, Sept. 7, 1955; s. Paul Richard and Dona Lucy (Follett) L. BFA, Tex. Christian U., 1978. Mgmt. trainee Saddleback C.C. Bookstore, Mission Viejo, Calif., 1978, Follett Coll. Stores, Elmhurst, Ill., 1978-79; bookstore mgr. U. Ill., Champaign, 1979-81, Northwestern U., Evanston, Ill., 1981-83; dir. of mktg. Follett Coll. Stores, Elmhurst, Ill., 1983-85, spl. asst. to pres., 1985-88; dir. of devel. Follett Corp., Chgo., 1989—91, also bd. dirs., pres. Custom Acad. Pub. Co., 1991—98, vice chmn., 1998—2001, chmn., 2001—. Trustee Follett Ednl. Found. Republican. Presbyterian. Avocations: tennis, skiing, running, paddle tennis, golf. Office: Follett Corp 2233 N West St River Grove IL 60171-1895

LIU, BEN-CHIEH, economist; b. Chungking, China, Nov. 17, 1938; came to U.S., 1965, naturalized, 1973; s. Pei-juang and Chung-su L.; m. Jill Jyh-huey, Oct. 2, 1965; children— Tina Won-ting, Roger Won-jung, Milton Won-ming. BA, Nat. Taiwan U., 1961; MA, Meml. U. Nfld., 1965, Washington U., St. Louis, 1968, PhD, 1971. Economist Chinese Air Force and Central Customs, Taiwan, 1961-63; resource economist Canadian Land Inventory and Forest Services, Nfld., 1963-65; research project dir. St. Louis Regional Indsl. Devel. Corp., 1966-72; prin. econs. Midwest Research Inst., Kansas City, Mo., 1972-80; mgr. Energy and Environ. Systems Div., Argonne (Ill.) Nat. Lab., 1980-81. Prof. econs., assoc. dir. rsch. Oklahoma City U., 1981-82; prof. mgmt., mktg. and info. systems Chgo. State U., 1982—; pres. Liu & Assocs., Inc., 1982—; vis. prof. econs. U. Mo., 1970-78, Nat. Taiwan U., 1991-92; Fulbright prof., dir. Internat. Enterprises Inst., Nat. Dong-Hwa U., Taiwan, 1997-98; dean Coll. Bus., Chung-Yuan Christian U., Taiwan, 2000-01; cons. UN, NSF; mem. Gov. Thompson's Adv. Com. on Agrl. Export, 1985-87, Congressman Fawell's Adv. Com. on Sci. and Tech., 1985-98; commr. Nat. Commn. on Librs. and Info. Svcs., 1991-94. Author: Interindustrial Structure Analysis: An Input-Output Study for St. Louis Region, 1968, The Quality of Life in the United States, 1970, Rating, Index and Statistics, 1973, Quality of Life Indicators in U.S. Metropolitan Areas, 1975, Physical and Economic Damage Functions for Air Pollutants by Receptors, 1976, Earthquake Risk and Damage Functions, An Integrated Model, 1981, Income, Energy and Quality of Life: An Information Systems Approach to Decisions, 1988; mem. editl. bd.: Internat. Jour. Math. Social Sci, Am. Jour. Econs. and Sociology, 1978—, Hong Kong Jour. Bus. Mgmt., Internat. Jour. of Bus.; Internat. Jour. Mgmt.; contbr. articles to profl. jours. Recipient rsch. study award, Am. Indsl. Devel. Coun., 1969—, Fulbright scholar awards, 1992, 1996, Faculty Meritorious awards, Chgo. State U., 1983, 1986, 1989, 1990, 2002, Disting. Prof. Advancement Increase awards, 1990, 1996, 2003, Outstanding Rsch. award, Nat. Sci. Coun., 1997—98; U.S. Econ. Devel. Adminstrn. fellow, 1967—68, Korean Govt. scholar, 1963—65, Fulbright scholar, Mgmt. Devel. Inst., Delhi U., 1992. Fellow Am. Statis. Assn. (com. mem.); mem. Am. Econ. Assn. (com. mem.), Econometric Soc., Royal Econ. Soc., Internat. Statis. Instn., Assn. for Social Econs. (com. mem.), Tax Inst. Am., Chinese Acad. and Profl. Assn. (pres. 1984-85), Chinese Econ. Assn. in N.Am. (pres. 1988-90), Chinese Am. Profs. Assn. (pres. 1996—). Home: 5360 Pennywood Dr Lisle IL 60532-2032 Office: Chgo State U Chicago IL 60628 Home Phone: 630-964-0236. Personal E-mail: liuasso1982@yahoo.com. E-mail: bencliu678@hotmail.com.

LIU, BENJAMIN YOUNG-HWAI, engineering educator; b. Shanghai, Aug. 15, 1934; s. Wilson Wan-su and Dorothy Pao-ning (Cheng) L.; m. Helen Hai-ling Cheng, June 14, 1958; 1 son, Lawrence A.S. Student, Nat. Taiwan U., 1951-54; BS in Mech. Engring., U. Nebr., 1956; PhD, U. Minn., 1960; doctorate (hon.), U. Kupio, Finland, 1991. Asso. engr. Honeywell Co., Mpls., 1956; research asst., instr. U. Minn., 1956-60, asst. prof., 1960-67, asso. prof., 1967-69, prof., 1969-93, regents prof., 1993—2002, regents prof. emeritus, 2002—, dir. Particle Tech. Lab., 1973-95; dir. Ctr. for Filtration Rsch., 1995—2002, prof. emeritus, 2002; pres. MSP Corp., Shoreview, Minn., 2002—. Vis. prof. U. Paris, 1968-69; patentee in field. Contbg. author: Aerosol Science, 1966; editor: Fine Particles, 1976, Application of Solar Energy for Heating and Cooling Buildings, 1977, Aerosols in the Mining and Industrial Work Environment, 1983, Aerosols: Science, Technology and Industrial Application of Airborne Particles, 1984; editor-in-chief: Aerosol Sci. and Tech., 1983-93; contbr. articles to Ency. Chem. Tech., Ency. Applied Physics. Guggenheim fellow, 1968-69; recipient Sr. U.S. Scientist award Alexander von Humboldt Found., 1982-83. Mem. ASME, ASHRAE, Inst. Environ. Scis. (v.p. 1993-95), Air and Waste Mgmt. Assn., Am. Assn. for Aerosol Rsch. (pres. 1986-88), Chinese Am. Assn. Minn. (pres. 1971-72), NAE (Fuchs' prize 1994), Am. Filtration and Separation Soc. Home: 1 N Deep Lake Rd North Oaks MN 55127-6504 Office: Mech Engring Rm 3101-B 111 Church St SE Minneapolis MN 55455 Office Phone: 612-625-6574. Business E-Mail: liuxx001@umn.edu.

LIU, CHUNG-CHIUN, chemical engineering educator; b. Canton, Kwangtun, China, Oct. 8, 1936; came to U.S., 1961, naturalized, 1972; s. Pay-Yen and Chi-Wei (Chen) L.; children: Peter S.H. BS, Nat. Cheng-Kung U., Taiwan, 1959; MS, Calif. Inst. Tech., 1962; PhD, Case Western Res. U., 1968. Grad. asst. Case Western Res. U., Cleve., 1963-68, postdoctoral fellow, 1968, prof. chem. engring., 1978—; asst. prof. chem. engring. U. Pitts., 1968-72, assoc. prof., 1972-76, prof., 1976-78; prof. chem. engring. Case Western Res. U., Cleve., 1978—; assoc. dir. Case Center for Electrochem. Scis., Cleve., 1982-86, dir. electronics design ctr., 1986-89, Wallace R. Persons prof. sensor tech. and control, 1989—. Contbr. articles in field to profl. jours.; patentee in field. Mem. Electrochem. Soc. (summer fellowship award 1963, 66), Am. Inst. Chem. Engrs. Home: 2917 E Overlook Rd Cleveland OH 44118-2433 Office: Case Western Res U Dept Chem Engr 10900 Euclid Ave Dept Chem Cleveland OH 44106-1712 E-mail: cxl9@cwru.edu.

LIU, LEE, utility company executive; b. Hunan, People's Republic of China, Mar. 30, 1933; came to U.S., 1953; s. Z. Liang and Swai Chin (Chan) L.; m. Andrea Pavageau, Dec. 19, 1959; children: Monica, Christine BS, Iowa State U. With Iowa Electric Light & Power Co., Cedar Rapids, 1957—, jr. engr.; chmn., pres., chief exec. officer Iowa Electric Light & Power Co., Iowa So. Utilities Co., Cedar Rapids, 1983—; also bd. dirs. Iowa Electric Light & Power Co., Cedar Rapids; chmn., CEO IES Industries, Cedar Rapids, 1991—, IES Utilities, Cedar Rapids. Bd. dirs. Firstar Bank Cedar Rapids, N.A., Edison Electric Inst., Electric Power Rsch. Inst., Hon Industries, Muscatine, Iowa, Prin. Fin. Group, Des Moines, McLeod, Inc., Eastman Chemical Comp.; bd. visitors Univ. Iowa Coll. Bus.; bd. trustees U. No. Iowa; mem. Iowa State U. Pres.'s Coun.; chmn. Iowa Bus. Coun. Trustee Mercy Med. Ctr., Iowa Natural Heritage Found., Hoover Presdl. Libr. Assn., Iowa Utility Assn.; chmn., bd. dirs. Cedar Rapids C. of C. (Cmty. Recognition award for work with Priority One campaign); adv. bd. United Way; exec. adv. coun., U. Northern Iowa, Sch. Bus.; adv. com., Engring. Coll. Iowa State U.; pres. Mercy Care Mgmt., Inc. Recipient Profl. Achievement citation Iowa State Univ., 1984, Achievement award for Bus. and Industry, Orgn. Chinese Americans, 1989, Achievement award in Engring. Mgmt., Chinese-Am. Engineers and Scientists Assn., 1991, Marston Medal award, Iowa State Univ., Coll. Engring., 1996, Excellence 2000 award for Bus., US Pan Asian Am. C. of C., 1997, Ellis Island Medal of Honor, 1998; named Iowa Bus. Leader of Yr., Des Moines Register, 1989. Mem. Iowa Utility Assn., Iowa Bus. Coun. (chmn.), Iowa Group for Econ. Devel., Cedar Rapids Country Club. Republican. Roman Catholic. Office: Alliant Energy PO Box 77007 Madison WI 53707-1007

LIU, MING-TSAN, computer engineering educator; b. Peikang, Taiwan, Aug. 30, 1934; BSEE, Nat. Cheng Kung U., Tainan, Taiwan, 1957; MSEE, U. Pa., 1961, PhD, 1964. Prof. dept. computer and info. sci. Ohio State U. Recipient Engring. Rsch. award Ohio State U., 1982, Best Paper award Computer Network Symposium 1984, Disting. Achievement award Nat. Cheng Kung U., 1987, Disting. Scholar award Ohio State U., 1991, Ameritech prize for excellence in telecom. Ameritech Found., 1991. Fellow IEEE (chmn. tech. com. on distbtd. processing Computer Soc. 1982-84, editor IEEE Transactions on Computers 1982-86, chmn. Eckert-Mauchly award com. 1984-85, 91-92, bd. govs. Computer Soc. 1984-90, chmn. tutorials com. 1982, program chmn. 1985, gen. chmn. 1986, chmn. steering com. 1989, gen. co-chmn. Internat. Conf. on Distbtd. Computing Sys. 1992, chmn. steering com. Symposium on Reliable Distbtd. Sys. 1986-89, v.p. membership and info. Computer Soc. 1984, mem. fellow com. 1986-88, editor-in-chief IEEE Transactions on Computers 1986-90, program chmn. IEEE Internat. Conf. on Data Engring. 1990, mem. TAB awards and recognition com. 1990-91, program chmn. Internat. Symposium on Comm. 1991, Internat. Phoenix Conf. on Computers and Comm. 1992, mem. TAB new tech. directions com. 1992-93, gen. co-chmn. Internat. Conf. on Parallel and Distbtd. Sys. 1992, Meritorious Svc. award Computer Soc. 1985, 87, 90, Outstanding Mem. Columbus sect. 1986-87). Office: Ohio State U 279 Dreese Labs 2015 Neil Ave Columbus OH 43210-1210

LIU, RUEY-WEN, electrical engineering educator; b. Kiang-en, China, Mar. 18, 1930; came to U.S., 1951, naturalized, 1956; s. Yen-sun and Wei-en (Chang) L.; m. ancy Shao-lan Lee, Aug. 18, 1957; children— Alexander, Theodore BS, U. Ill., 1954, MS, 1955, PhD, 1960. Asst. prof. elec. engring. U. Notre Dame, Ind., 1960-63, assoc. prof. Ind., 1963-66, prof. Ind., 1966—, Frank M. Freimann prof elec. and computer engring. Ind., 1989—. Vis. prof. U. Calif.-Berkeley, 1965-66, Nat. Taiwan U., Taipei, spring 1969, U. Chile, Santiago, summer 1970; hon. prof. Fu-dan U., Shanghai, 1986, Inst. Electronics, Academia Sinica, Beijing, China, 1989. Trustee Calif. Buddhism Assn., 1974-76 U. Ill. fellow, 1954; Gen. Electric fellow, 1958; NSF grantee, 1962 Fellow IEEE (editor transaction on circuits and systems jours. 1989—, pres. circuits and sys. soc., 1995); mem. N.Y. Acad. Scis., Am. Math. Soc., Soc. Indsl. and Applied Math., Chinese Acad. Sci., Beijing (hon.), Inst. Electronics, Info. and Communications Engrs. (overseas adv. com. transactions in fundamentals of electronics, communications and computer scis., 1991—), Sigma Xi, Tau Beta Pi, Pi Mu Epsilon Home: 1929 Dorwood Dr South Bend IN 46617-1818 Office: Notre Dame Univ Dept Elec Engring Notre Dame IN 46556

LIU, WING KAM, mechanical engineering educator, civil engineer, educator; b. Hong Kong, May 15, 1952; came to U.S., 1973, naturalized, 1990; s. Yin Lam and Siu Lin (Chan) L.; m. Betty Hsia, Dec. 12, 1986; children: Melissa Margaret, Michael Kevin. BSc with highest honors, U. Ill., Chgo., 1976; MSc, Calif. Inst. Tech., 1977, PhD, 1981. Registered profl. engr., Ill. Asst. prof. mech. and civil engring. Northwestern U., Evanston, Ill., 1980-83, assoc. prof., 1983-88, prof., 1988—, Walter F. Murphy Prof. Mech. Engring., 2003—; dir. NSF Summer Inst. on Nano Mechanics and Materials, 2003—. Prin. cons. reactor analysis and safety div. Argonne (Ill.) Nat. Lab., 1981—, Dir. of NSF Summer Inst. on Nano Mechanics and Materials. Co-author: Nonlinear Finite Elements for Continua and Structures, 2000; co-editor: Innovative Methods for Nonlinear Problems, 1984, Impact-Effects of Fasts Transient Loadings, 1988, Computational Mechanics of Probabilistic and Reliability Analysis, 1989; co-author (with Shaofan Li): Meslifree Particle Method, 2004; co-author: Nano Mechanics and Materials: Theory, Multiscale Analysis and Applications, 2005. Recipient Thomas J. Jaeger prize Internat. Assn. for Structural Mechanics in Reactor Tech., 1989, Ralph R. Teetor award Soc. Automotive Engrs., 1983, Computational Mechanics award Internat. Assn. for Computational Mechanics, 2002; named among 93 most highly cited rschrs. in engring. Inst. for Sci. Info., 2001; grantee USF, Army Rsch. Office, NASA, AFSOR, ONR, GE, Ford Motor, Chrysler, Japan Soc. of Mechanical Engineers Computational Mechanics award, 2004 Fellow ASCE, ASME (exec. mem. applied mechanics divsn. 2001, Melville medal 1979, Pi Tau Sigma gold medal 1985, Gustus L. Larson Meml. award 1995), U.S. Assn. Computational Mechanics (pres. 2000—, Computational Structural Mechs. award 2001), Am. Acad. Mechanics, Internat. Assn. Computational Mechanics (exec. 2002—, Computational Mechanics award 2002), Japan Soc. Mech. Engrs. (computational mechanics award 2004). Office: Northwestern U Dept Mech Engring 2145 Sheridan Rd Evanston IL 60208-0834 E-mail: w-liu@northwestern.edu.

LIU, YUAN HSIUNG, drafting and design educator; b. Tainan, Taiwan, Feb. 24, 1938; came to U.S., 1970; s. Chun Chang and Kong (Wong) L.; m. Ho Pe Tung, July 27, 1973; children: Joan Anshen, Joseph Pinyang. BEd, Nat. Taiwan Normal U., Taipei, 1961; MEd, Nat. Chengchi U., Taipei, 1967, U. Alta., Edmonton, 1970; PhD, Iowa State U., 1975. Cert. tchr. Tchr. indsl. arts and math. Nan Ning Jr. H.S., Tainan, Taiwan, 1961-64; tech. math. instr. Chung-Cheng Inst. Tech., Taipei, 1967-68; drafter Sundstrand Hydro-Transmission Corp., Ames, Iowa, 1973-75; assoc. prof. Fairmont (W.Va.) State Coll., 1975-80; per course instr. Sinclair C.C., Dayton, Ohio, 1985; assoc. prof. Miami U., Hamilton, Ohio, 1980-85, Southwest Mo. State U., Springfield, 1985—. Cons. Monarch Indsl. Precision Co., Springfield, 1986, Gen. Electric Co., Springfield, 1988, Fasco Industries, Inc., Ozark, Mo., 1989, 95, Springfield Remfg. Corp., 1990, 92, Ctrl. States Indsl., Intercont Products, Inc., L&W Industries, Inc., ZERCO Mfg. Co., 1994-95, Paul Mueller Co., 1996. 2d lt. R.O.C. Army, 1962-63. Recipient Excellent Teaching in Drafting award Charvoz-Carsen Corp., Fairfield, N.J., 1978. Mem. Am. Design Drafting Assn. Avocations: walking, tv. Office: SW Mo State U Dept Indsl Mgmt 901 S National Ave Springfield MO 65804-0094 E-mail: yhl045f@smsu.edu.

LIVERIS, ANDREW N., chemical company executive; b. Darwin, Australia; married; 3 children. BS in Chemical Engring., U. Queensland, 1976. Joined Dow Chem. Co., 1976, gen. mgr. all ops. Thailand, 1989—92, group bus. dir. Midland, Mich., 1992—93, gen. mgr., 1993—94, v.p., 1994—95, pres., Dow chem. pacific Hong Kong, 1995—98, v.p. splty. chems. Midland, 1998—2000, bus. group pres., 2000—04, pres., 2003—, COO, 2003—04, CEO, 2004—, chmn., 2006—. Bd. mem., exec. com. OPTIMAL Group, Malaysia; bd. dirs. Dow Corning Corp., Dow Chemical Co., 2004—, Citigroup, 2005—; bd. trustees Herbert H. and Grace A. Dow Found. Bd. mem. Lake Huron Area Coun., Boy Scouts Am. Mem.: Am. Chemistry Coun., Soap and Detergent Assn., Comerica Bank (Midland advisory bd. mem.), Inst. Chem. Engrs. (UK) (corp. mem.), Midland Ctr. for the Arts (bd. mem.). Office: The Dow Chem Co 47 Building Midland MI 48667

LLEWELLYN, JOHN T., state legislator; m. Becky; children: Evan, Elizabeth, Matthew. BA, Alma Coll. Commr. Newago County, Mich., 1989-92; mem. Pub. Health Bd., 1990-92; mem. Newago County Zoning & Planning Bd., 1990-92; state rep. Dist. 100 Mich. Ho. of Reps., 1993-98; owner, operator family orchard Fremont, Mich., 1996—; dep. dir. Rep. caucus svcs. Mich. Ho. Reps., 1998—. Chair Consumers Com. Mich. Ho. of Reps., vice-chair Ins. Com., 1993—, mem Conservation, Edn. Great Lakes & Higher Edn. Coms., 1993—, mem. task force to study advt. impact, house oversight ethics com., 1996—, chmn. Ins. Com., 1996—, vice chmn. Human Resources & Labor Com., 1996—, co-chair. Mem. Mich. Agrl. Coop. Mktg. Assn. Home: 5588 W 32nd St Fremont MI 49412-7723 Office: 720 House Office Bldg Lansing MI 48909

LLOYD, JOHN RAYMOND, mechanical engineering educator; b. Mpls., Aug. 1, 1942; s. Raymond Joseph and Wilma Mable (Epple) L.; m. Mary Jane Whiteside, Dec. 20, 1963; children: Jay William, Stephanie Christine. BS in Engring., U. Minn., 1964, MSME, 1966, PhDME, 1971; D in Tech. Sci. (hon.), Russian Acad. Scis., 2000. Devel. engr. Procter & Gamble Co., Cin., 1966-67; prof. mech. engring. U. Notre Dame, South Bend, Ind., 1970-83; disting. prof. Mich. State U., East Lansing, 1983—, chmn. dept. mech. engring., 1983-91, dir. Inst. Global Engring. Edn., 1997—2001. Cons. LeRoy Troyer & Assocs., Mishawaka, Ind., 1980—90, Azdel Inc., Shelby, NC, 1987—90; advisor NSF, Washington, 1987—90; Nat. Bur. Stds. assessment panel NRC, Washington, 1987—93; mem. exec. com. Internat. Ctr. Heat and Mass Transfer, 2003—; chmn. Midwest Energy Consortium, 1993—2000; adv. editor McGraw Hill, Inc., 1990—. Adv. editor Internat. Jour. Heat and Fluid Flow, 1985—, Jour. Engring. Physics and Thermodynamics, 1993—; contbr. over 100 articles to profl. jours., chpts. to books. Recipient Outstanding Faculty award U. Notre Dame, 1975, 82, Ralph R. Teetor Ednl. award Soc. Automotive Engrs., 1986. Fellow: ASME (nat. bd. comm. 1983—90, rsch. and tech. devel. bd. 1985—99, editor Jour. Heat Transfer 1989—95, coun. on edn., critical techs. com. 1991—93, v.p. rsch. 1995—98, sr. v.p. engring. 1999—2002, gov. 2002—05, Outstanding Paper award 1977, Melville medal 1978, Heat Transfer Meml. award 1995, Dedicated Svc. award 1999); mem.: European Acad. Scis. Office: Mich State U Dept Mech Engring 2242 Engring Bldg East Lansing MI 48824 E-mail: lloyd@egr.msu.edu.

LLOYD, PATRICK M., dean, dental educator; B in Mathematics, Marquette U., 1974; DDS, Marquette U. Sch. Dentistry, 1978; MS, Marquette U. Grad. Sch., 1989. Cert. in Prosthodontics Vet. Adminstrn. Med. Ctr., 1981, diplomate Am. Bd. Prosthodontics. Chief dental geriatrics VA Med. Ctr., Milwaukee, 1981—85; nat. coord. geriatric dental programs Dept. Vet. Affairs, 1985—92; head, Special Patient Care Clinic Marquette U. Sch. Dentistry-, 1992—96; head dept. family dentistry U. Iowa Coll. Dentistry, 1996—2003; dean U. Minn. Sch. Dentistry, 2004—. Editor-in-chief: Journal of Prosthodontics, 1993—. Fellow: Gerontological Soc. Am., Clin. Med. Sect. (mem. fellowship com. 1998—), Am. Coll. Prosthodontics (pres. elect); mem.: Publs. Com., Greater NY Acad. of Prosthodontics, Scientific Investigation Com., Greater NY Acad. of Prosthodontics, Internat. Coll. Prosthodontics (co-pres. 2001—03). Office: U Minn Sch Dentistry Room 15-209 MoosT 1291 515 Deleware St SE Minneapolis MN 55455 Office Phone: 612-624-2424. Business E-Mail: plloyd@umn.edu.

LOBB, WILLIAM K., dean, dental educator; Student, Notre Dame U., Nelson, BC, U. Calgary, 1970—72; DDS, U. Alberta, Edmonton, 1977; MS in orthodontics, U. Mich., Ann Arbor, 1981. Resident in dentistry U. Alberta Hosp., Edmonton, Canada; pvt. orthodontics practice Edmonton; mem. faculty U. Alberta, Edmonton, 1981—89; chair dept. orthodontics Dalhousie U., Halifax, 1989—94; assoc. dean acad. affairs Sch. Dentistry Marquette U., 1994—97, dean, 1997—. Recipient W.W. Wood award for excellence in dental edn., Assn. Can. Faculties Dentistry, Disting. Service Award, Marquette Sch. of Dentistry. Fellow: Internat. Coll. Dentists, Pierre Fachard Acad., Am. Coll. Dentists; mem.: ADA, Wis. Dental Assn., Omicron Kappa Upsilon. Office: Marquette Univ Sch Dentistry 1801 W Wisconsin Ave Milwaukee WI 53233 Office Phone: 414-288-7485. Office Fax: 414-288-3586. Business E-Mail: william.lobb@marquette.edu.

LOBBIA, JOHN E., retired utility company executive; b. 1941; married. BSEE, U. Detroit, 1964. Asst. primary svc. engr. sales dept. Detroit Edison Co., 1964-68, acting asst. dist. mgr., 1968-69, dir. svc. planning, 1969-72, project mgr. constrn., 1972-74, dir. generation constrn. dept., 1974-75, mgr. Ann Arbor div., 1975-76, asst. mgr. Detroit div., 1976-78, mgr. Oakland div., 1978-80, asst. vice chmn., 1980-81, asst. v.p., mgr. fuel support, 1981-82, v.p. fin. svcs., 1982-87, exec. v.p., 1987-88, pres., COO, 1988-94, chmn., CEO, 1990-98, also bd. dirs. Bd. dirs. Nat. Bank of Detroit; bd. dirs. NBD Bancorp, Inc., DTE Energy Co., Detroit Investment Fund.

LOCHNER, JAMES V., food products executive; Exec. v.p., then pres. mfg. fresh meats IBP, Inc., Dakota Dunes, SD, 1998—2001; group v.p. through sr. v.p. purchasing Tyson Foods, Springdale, Ark., 2001—. Office: Tyson Foods PO Box 2020 Springdale AR 72765-2020

LOCK, RICHARD WILLIAM, packaging company executive; b. NYC, Oct. 5, 1931; s. Albert and Catherine Dorothy (Magnus) L.; m. Elizabeth Louise Kenney, Nov. 2, 1957; children— Albert William, Dorothy Louise Lock Kuhl, John David. BS, Rutgers U., 1953; MBA, N.Y. U., 1958. Acct. Gen. Electric Co., 1953-54, Union Carbide Co., NYC, 1956-58; div. controller St. Regis Paper Co., Houston, 1959-62, Owens-Illinois, Inc., Toledo, 1962-64, supr. programmer office methods and data processing, 1964-65, asst. mgr. data processing procedures, 1965-67, mgr. systems analysis and devel., 1967-68, mgr. corp. systems analysis and devel., 1968-70, dir. corp. systems and data processing, 1970-72, gen. mgr. electro/optical display, 1972-75, treas., 1975-80, v.p., dir. corp. planning, 1980-84, v.p., asst. chief fin. officer, treas., 1984-88; mng. dir. Magnus Assocs., 1989—. Mem. adv. bd. Toledo Salvation Army, 1973—, chmn., 1974-77; pres. Toledo Area Govtl. Rsch. Assn., 1978-79; bd. dirs. Riverside Hosp. Found., Toledo, 1982—. Served with USAF, 1954-56. Mem. Fin. Execs. Inst., Am. Soc. Corp. Secs., Phi Beta Kappa. Clubs: Toledo. Republican. Lutheran.

LOCKE, CARL EDWIN, JR., academic administrator, engineer, educator; b. Palo Pinto County, Tex., Jan. 11, 1936; s. Carl Edwin Sr. and Caroline Jane (Brown) L.; m. Sammie Rhae Batchelor, Aug. 25, 1956; children: Stephen Curtis, Carlene Rhae. BSChemE, U. Tex., 1958, MSChemE, 1960, PhDChemE, 1972. Rsch. engr. Continental Oil Co., Ponca City, Okla., 1959-65; prodn. engr. R.L. Stone Co., Austin, Tex., 1965-66; prodn. rsch. engr. Tracor Inc., Austin, 1966-71; vis. assoc. prof. U. Tex., Austin, 1971-73; from asst. prof. to prof., dir. chem. engring. U. Okla., Norman, 1973-86; dean engring. U. Kans., Lawrence, 1986—2002, prof. chem. and petroleum engring., 1986—2005, prof. emeritus, 2005—. Co-author: Anodic Protection, 1981; contbr. articles to profl. jours. Recipient Disting. Engring. Svc. award U. Kans. Sch. Engring., 2002; named Disting. Engring. grad. U. Tex., 1993, Kansas Engr. of Yr. Kansas Engring. Soc., 1996. Fellow AIChE, NSPE; mem. ASTM, Nat. Assn. Corrosion Engrs. (regional chair 1988-89, Eben Junkin award South Cen. region 1990), Am. Soc. Engring. Edn. (vice-chair engring. deans coun. 1999-2001, chair 2001-02), Lawrence C. of C., Rotary (pres. 2001-02). Democrat. Presbyterian. Office: U Kans Sch Engring 4132D Learned Hall 1530 W 15th St Lawrence KS 66045-7526 Office Phone: 785-864-2929. Office Fax: 785-864-4967. E-mail: lok@ku.edu.

LOCKHART, GREGORY GORDON, prosecutor; b. Dayton, Ohio, Sept. 2, 1946; s. Lloyd Douglas and Evelyn (Gordon) L.; m. Paula Louise Jewett, May 20, 1978; children: David H., Sarah L. BS, Wright State U., 1973; JD, Ohio State U., 1976. Bar: Ohio 1976, US Dist. Ct. (so. dist.) Ohio 1977, US Ct. Appeals (6th cir.) 1988, US Supreme Ct. 1993. Legal advisor Xenia and Fairborn (Ohio) Police Dept., 1977-78; asst. pros. atty. Greene County Prosecutor, Xenia, 1978-87; ptnr. DeWine & Schenck, Xenia, 1978-82, Schenck, Schmidt & Lockhart, Xenia, 1982-85, Ried & Lockhart, Beavercreek, Ohio, 1985-87; asst. US atty. (so. dist.) OH US Dept. Justice, Columbus, 1987-2001, US atty. (so. dist.) Ohio, 2001—. Adj. prof. Coll. Law U. Dayton, 1990—, Wright State U., Dayton, 1979—. Co-author: Federal Grand Jury Practice, 1996. Pres. Greene County Young reps., Xenia, 1977-79. With USAF, 1966-70; Vietnam. Named Outstanding Alumni, Wright State U., 2005; named to Xenia H.S. Hall of Honor, 2006; recipient Outstanding Contributions in Field of Drug Law Enforcement, 1989. Mem. Fed. Bar Assn. (chpt. pres. 1994-95), Dayton Bar Assn., Kiwanis (pres. 1983-84, lt. gov. 1986-87), Jaycees (pres. 1976-79), Am. Inns of Ct. (master of bench emeritus), Dayton Lawyer's Club. Methodist. Avocations: golf, tennis, hiking. Office: US Attys Office Federal Bldg 200 W 2d St Rm 602 Dayton OH 45402 Office Phone: 937-225-2910. E-mail: gregory.lockhart@usdoj.gov.

LOCKHART, JOHN MALLERY, management consultant; b. Mellen, Wis., May 17, 1911; s. Carl Wright and Gladys (Gale) L.; m. Judith Anne Wood, Feb. 26, 1938 (dec. June 1991); children: Wood Alexander, Gale, Thomas. BS, Northwestern U., 1931; JD, IIT, 1938. CPA, Ill. Teaching fellow Northwestern U., 1931; asst. v.p. Welsh, Davis & Co. (investment bankers), Chgo., 1935-41; treas. Transcontinental & Western Air, Inc., Kansas City, Mo., 1941-47; exec. v.p., CEO TACA Airways, S.A., 1944-45; v.p., dir. The Kroger Co., 1947-71, exec. v.p., 1961-71; pres. Kroger Family Ctr. Stores, 1969-71, Lockhart Co. (mgmt. cons.), 1971—; v.p. corp. fin. Gradison & Co., 1973-86. Chmn. bd. dirs., CEO Ohio Real Estate Investment Co., Ohio Real Estate Equity Corp., 1974-76; bd. dirs. Employers Mut. Cos., Des Moines, Witt Co.; chmn. bd. dirs. Autotronics Systems, Inc., 1976-78; bd. dirs. Vectra Internat., Inc., Hamilton Mut. Ins. Co. Chmn. Hamilton County Hosp. Commn., 1965-84; mem. adv. bd. Greater Cin. Airport, 1961-86. Mem. Comml. Club, Cin. Country Club, Conquistadores del Cielo Club. Home and Office: 2770 Walsh Rd Cincinnati OH 45208-3425

LOCKINGTON, DAVID, conductor; b. Eng. arrived in U.S., 1978; m. Dylana Jenson; 3 children. BA, U. Cambridge, Eng.; MA in cello performance, Yale U. Prin. cellist at. Youth Orch. Great Britain; cellist New Haven Symphony Orch.; asst. prin. cellist Denver Symphony Orch., asst. conductor; music dir. Cheyenne Symphony Orch., Denver Young Artist's Orch., Boulder Bach. Festival; founder, conductor Acad. Wilderness Chamber Orch.; asst. conductor Opera Colo., Balt. Symphony Orch., 1992, assoc. conductor, 1993-95; music dir. N.Mex. Symphony Orch., 1995—2000, Ohio Chamber Orch., Long Island Philharmonic, 1996—97, 1999—2000, Grand Rapids Symphony, Grand Rapids, Mich., 1999. Guest conductor St. Louis Symphony, Colo. Symphony, Grand Rapids (Mich.) Symphony, Pacific Symphony, Wichita (Kans.) Symphony, Honolulu Symphony, Harrisburg (Pa.) Symphony, Fla. Orch., Dayton (Ohio) Philharmonic, La. Philharmonic, World Youth Symphony, Interlochen Arts Acad. Office: Grand Rapids Symphony 300 Ottawa Ave NW Ste 100 Grand Rapids MI 49503-2314

LOCKMAN, STUART M., lawyer; b. Jersey City, July 18, 1949; s. Albert Korey and Edna Sally (Easton) Lockman; m. Deena Laurel Young, Dec. 27, 1970; children: Jeffrey, Alison Susan, Stephen, Karen. BA, U. Mich., 1971, JD, 1974. Bar: Mich. 1974, Fla. 1991; bd. cert. health law specialist, Fla. Ptnr. Honigman Miller Schwartz and Cohn LLP, Detroit, 1974—. Named one of Best Lawyers in Am., Superlawyers, 2007. Office: Honigman Miller Schwartz & Cohn 2290 1st National Bldg Detroit MI 48226 Office Phone: 313-465-7500. Business E-Mail: sml@honigman.com.

LOCKNER, VERA JOANNE, farmer, rancher, state legislator; b. St. Lawrence, SD, May 19, 1937; d. Leonard and Zona R. (Ford) Verdugt; m. Frank O. Lockner, Aug. 7, 1955; children: Dean M., Clifford A. Grad., St. Lawrence (S.D.) High Sch., 1955. Bank teller/bookkeeper First Nat. Bank, Miller, SD, 1963-66, Bank of Wessington, SD, 1968-74; farmer/rancher Wessington, 1955-2000. Sunday sch. tchr. Trinity Luth. Ch., Miller, 1968-72; treas. Trinity Luth. Ch. Women, 2005—; treas. PTO, Wessington, 1969-70; treas., vice chmn., chmn., state com. woman Hand County Dems., Miller, 1978-2003, state com. woman, 2007-; SD state legislator, 1992-2000; mem. SD Dem. Exec. Bd., 1997-2000. Named one of Outstanding Young Women of Am., Women's Study Club, Wessington, 1970. Mem. Order of Ea. Star (warder, marshall, chaplain 1970-2002). Democrat. Avocations: painting, crafts, gardening, photography. Home and Office: 301 3rd St NW Saint Lawrence SD 57373-2324

LOCKWOOD, BERT BERKLEY, JR., law educator; b. Utica, NY, Feb. 12, 1944; s. Bert Berkley and Mildred (Dowling) L.; m. Lynn Grigoli, Dec. 23, 1979; children: Matthew, Dylan, Courtney, Meredith. BA, St. Lawrence U., 1966; JD, Syracuse U., 1969; LLM, U. Va., 1971. Bar: Ohio 1981. Exec. dir. Procedural Aspects of Internat. Law Inst., NYC, 1980-89; asst. dir., sr. fellow Ctr. for Internat. Studies NYU, NYC, 1971-74; program dir. World Peace Through Law Ctr., Washington, 1974-76; assoc. dean Am. U. Law Sch., Washington, 1976-79; assoc. prof. U. Cin. Law Sch., 1979-86, prof., 1986—, dir. Urban Morgan Inst. for Human Rights, 1979—; vis. scholar U. Essex, Colchester, U.K., 1994. Adv. bd. Internat. Human Rights Law Group, Washington, 1978—, Can. Found. on Human Rights, Montreal, Quebec, Can., 1984—. Editor in chief Human Rights Quar., 1982—, Amnesty Internat. USA Legal Support Network Newsletter, 1990-93; series editor Pennsylvania Studies in Human Rights, 1988—. Coord. Group 86 Amnesty Internat., Cin., 1984—; adv. bd. Diana Project, 1994—. Recipient Sol Feinstein Alumni award St. Lawrence U., 1990; honoree Cin. chpt. ACLU, 1991. Mem. ABA, Cin. Bar Assn., Am. Soc. Mag. Editors, Internat. Law Assn. (human rights com. 1982—). Office: U Cincinnati Coll of Law Urban Morgan Institute PO Box 210040 Cincinnati OH 45221-0040 Office Phone: 513-556-6805. Office Fax: 513-556-2391.

LOCKWOOD, GARY LEE, lawyer; b. Woodstock, Ill., Dec. 3, 1946; s. Howard and Luella Mae (Behrens) L.; m. Cheryl Lynn Wittrock, Jan. 5, 1967; children: Jennifer, Lee, Cynthia. BA magna cum laude, Iowa Wesleyan Coll., 1969; student, Albert Ludwig U., Freiburg in Breisgau, Fed. Republic Germany, 1968-69; JD, Northwestern U., 1976. Bar: Ill. 1976, U.S. Dist. Ct. (no. dist.) Ill. 1976, U.S. Ct. Appeals (7th cir.) 2000, U.S. Ct. Appeals (9th cir.) 2002. Assoc. Lord, Bissell & Brook, Chgo., 1976-85, ptnr., 1985—2005; ptnr., founder Walker, Wilcox, Matousek LLP, 2005—. Bd. dirs. McHenry Sch. Dist. 15, Ill., 1974-85, pres., 1979-80. Served to sgt. U.S. Army, 1970-72. Mem. ABA. Methodist. Avocation: sports. Home: 333 N Canal St Chicago IL 60606 Office: Walker Wilcox Matousek LLP 225 West Washington St Ste 2400 Chicago IL 60606 Office Phone: 312-244-6701. Business E-Mail: glockwood@wwmlawyers.com.

LOCKWOOD, JOHN LEBARON, plant pathologist, educator; b. Ann Arbor, Mich., May 28, 1924; s. George LeBaron and Mary Bonita (Leininger) L.; m. Jean Elizabeth Springborg, Mar. 21, 1959; children: James L., Laura A. Student, Western Mich. Coll., 1941-43; BA, Mich. State Coll., 1948, MS, 1950; PhD, U. Wis., 1953. Asst. prof. Ohio Agrl. Expt. Sta., Wooster, 1953-55, Mich. State U., East Lansing, 1955-61, assoc. prof., 1961-67, prof., 1967-90, prof. emeritus, 1990—. Served with U.S. Army, 1943-46 NSF research fellow, 1970-71. Fellow Am. Phytopathol. Soc. (pres. 1984-85). Home: 1929 Danbury W Okemos MI 48864-1873

LOEB, DEANN JEAN, nurse; b. West Union, Iowa, Aug. 1, 1960; d. Dale Alfred and Annagene Helen (Suhr) Ungerer; m. Thomas Allan Loeb, Sept. 1, 1985; children: Ryan, Jennifer, Andrea, Cody. Diploma in nursing, NE Iowa Tech. Inst., 1982. Lic. practical nurse, Iowa. Laundry aide Good Samaritan Ctr., West Union, 1977, kitchen aide, cook, 1977-79, nurses asst., 1979-81, practical nurse, 1982-84, Ind. (Ind.) Care Ctr., 1985-89, Dr. Jose C. Aguiar, Waterloo, Iowa, 1989-93, Dr. John Musgrave-Dr. Mary O'Connell, Waterloo, Iowa, 1993-94; nurse Waterloo Asthma and Allergy Clinic, 1994—, staff nurse, office mgr., 2002—; on call nurse Interim Health, 2001—. Leader Brownies, asst. leader Girl Scouts U.S.; tchr. Bible, Sunday sch., mem. parish bd. edn., mem. parish life com. Zion Jubilee Luth. Ch., Jesup, Iowa, altar com., worship com., chair altar guild; mem. Cub Scout Com. Republican. Home: 7144 Spring Creek Rd Jesup IA 50648-9568

LOEB, JANE RUPLEY, academic administrator, educator; b. Chgo., Feb. 22, 1938; d. John Edwards and Virginia Pentland (Marthens) Watkins; m. Peter Albert Loeb, June 14, 1958; children: Eric Peter, Gwendolyn Lisl, Aaron John. BA, Rider Coll., 1961; PhD, U. So. Calif., 1969. Clin. psychology intern Univ. Hosp., Seattle, 1966-67; asst. prof. ednl. psychology U. Ill., Urbana, 1968-69, asst. coord. rsch. and testing, 1968-69, coord. rsch. and testing, 1969-72, asst. to vice chancellor acad. affairs, 1971-72, dir. admissions and records, 1972-81, assoc. prof. ednl. psychology, 1973-82, assoc. vice chancellor acad. affairs, 1981-94, prof. edn. psychology, 1982—. Author: College Board Project: the Future of College Admissions, 1989; co-editor: Academic Couples: Problems and Promises, 1997. Chmn. Coll. Bd. Coun. on Entrance Svcs., 1977-82; bd. govs. Alliance for Undergrad. Edn., 1988-93; active charter com. Coll. Bd. Acad. Assembly, 1992-93. HEW grantee, 1975-76. Mem. APA, Am. Ednl. Rsch. Assn., Nat. Coun. Measurement in Edn., Harvard Inst. Ednl. Mgmt. Avocation: french horn. Home: 1405 N Coler Ave Urbana IL 61801-1625 Office: U Ill 1310 S 6th St Champaign IL 61820-6925

LOEBSACK, DAVE, congressman, former political science professor; b. Mount Vernon, Iowa, Dec. 23, 1952; m. Terry Loebsack; children: Jennifer, Sarah stepchildren: Marcos Melendez, Madeleine Melendez. BS in Polit. Sci., Iowa State U., 1974, MA in Polit. Sci., 1976; PhD in Polit. Sci., U. Calif. Davis, 1985. Prof. polit. sci. Cornell Coll., 1982—2006; mem. US Congress from 2nd Iowa dist., 2007—, mem. armed svcs. com., edn. & labor com. Former chair Cornell Coll. Politics Dept.; former pres. Iowa Conf. Polit. Scientists; bd. mem. UN Am. Linn County coord. Howard Dean for Pres., 2000; local leader Bill Bradley Presdl. Campaign, 2000; chair Linn Phoenix Club, 2002—05. Mem.: Humanities Iowa Speakers Bur. Democrat. Methodist. Office: 1513 Longworth House Office Bldg Washington DC 20515 also: 125 S Dubuque St Iowa City IA 52240

LOEFFELHOLZ, GABE, state representative; b. Dickeyville, Wis., Nov. 11, 1940; m. Joyce Loeffelholz; children: Jodi, Gary. Self-employed farmer, 1968—2000; mem. state assembly dist. 49 Wis. State Assembly, Madison, 2000—, mem. agr., criminal justice, edn., govt. ops., hwy., and rural affairs and forestry coms., caucus mem., Cuha City Cmty. Faiir, Dairy Land Antique Tractors, Grant County Fair, Platteville Dairy Days. Mem. Platteville (Wis.) Sch. Bd., 1990—2000, Farm Svc. Agy., 1990—2000. Served to SP4, combat sujpport US Army, 1959—62. Mem.: NRA, Farm Bur., KC, Am. Legion. Republican. Roman Catholic. Office: State Capitol Rm 317N PO Box 8952 Madison WI 53708-8952

LOEFFLER, FRANK JOSEPH, physicist, educator; b. Ballston Spa, NY, Sept. 5, 1928; s. Frank Joseph and Florence (Farrell) Loeffler; m. Eleanor Jane Chisholm, Sept. 8, 1951; children: Peter, James, Margaret, Anne Marie. BS in Engring. Physics, Cornell U., 1951, PhD in Physics, 1957. Rsch. assoc. Princeton U., 1957-58; mem. faculty Purdue U., Lafayette, Ind., 1958-97, prof. physics, 1962-97, prof. emeritus, 1997—. Vis. prof. Hamburg U., Germany, 1963—64, Heidelberg U., Germany, CERN, Switzerland, 1971, Stanford U. Linear Accelerator Ctr., 1980—83, U. Hawaii, 1985—86; trustee, mem. exec. com., chmn. high energy com. Argonne Univs. Assn., 1972—76, 1978—79, mem. com. fusion program, 1979—80. Contbr. articles to profl. jours. Recipient Antarctic Svc. medal, NSF/USN, 1990, Ruth and Joel Spira award for Outstanding Tchg., 1992. Fellow: Am. Phys. Soc., Sigma Xi, Tau Beta Pi. Achievements include development of undergraduate physics laboratory experiments and lecture demonstration apparatus; research in astophysics; high energy gamma ray astronomy; high energy particle interactions and on-line data acquisitions-processing systems; established gamma ray astronomy lab at South Pole, Antarctica. Home: 341 Hokulani St Makawao HI 96768-8612 Office: Purdue U Dept Physics Lafayette IN 47907 Home Phone: 808-572-8804; Office Phone: 808-572-8804. Personal E-mail: fjloef@aol.com.

LOEHR, MARLA, chaplain; b. Cleve., Oct. 7, 1937; d. Joseph Richard and Eleanore Edith (Rothschuh) L. BS, Notre Dame Coll., South Euclid, Ohio, 1960; MAT, Ind. U., 1969; PhD, Boston Coll., 1988; Degree (hon.), Notre Dame Coll. Ohio, 1995. Cert. high sch. tchr., counselor, Ohio; cert. spiritual dir., pastoral min. Dean students Notre Dame Coll., South Euclid, Ohio, 1972-85, acting acad. dean, 1988, pres., 1988-95; chaplain Hospice of Western Res., Cleve., 1995—, spiritual dir., 1997—. Author: Mentor Handbook, 1985; co-author: Notre Dame College Model for Student Development, 1980. Hon. mem. Leadership Cleve. Class of 1990; v.p., trustee SJ Wellness Ctr., 1999; mem. leadership coun. Future Ch., Diocese of Cleve. Recipient Career Woman of Achievement award YWCA, 1992; named One of 100 Cleve.'s Most Powerful Women. Mem. Spiritual Dirs. Internat., Nat. Hospice Assn., Alpha Sigma Nu, Kappa Gamma Pi. Avocations: photography, hiking, reading, sports. Office: Hospice Western Res 29101 Health Campus Dr Ste 400 Westlake OH 44145-5268 E-mail: marlajlo@cs.com.

LOESCH, KATHARINE TAYLOR, communications educator, theater educator; b. Berkeley, Calif., Apr. 13, 1922; d. Paul Schuster and Katharine (Whiteside) Taylor; m. John George Loesch, Aug. 28, 1948; 1 child, William Ross. Student, Swarthmore Coll., 1939-41, U. Wash., 1942; BS, Columbia U., 1944, MA, 1949; grad., Neighborhood Playhouse Sch., 1946; postgrad., Ind. U., 1953; PhD, Northwestern U., 1961. Instr. speech Wellesley (Mass.) Coll., 1949-52, Loyola U., Chgo., 1956; asst. prof. English and speech Roosevelt U., Chgo., 1957, 62-65; assoc. prof. comm. and theatre U. Ill., Chgo., 1968-87, assoc. prof. emeritus, 1987—. Contbr. articles to profl. jours.; author numerous poems; performer of poetry. Active ERA, Ill., 1975-76. Grantee, Am. Philos. Soc., 1970, U. Ill., Chgo., 1970; Fgn. Travel grantee, 1983, Dylan Thomas scholar. Mem. MLA, Am. Soc. for Aesthetics, Linguistic Soc. Am., Chgo. Linguistic Soc. (co-chmn. 1954-56), Nat. Comm. Assn. (chair interpretation divsn. 1979-80, Golden Ann. award 1969), Celtic Studies Assn. N.Am., Pi Beta Phi. Episcopalian. Office: Univ Ill Dept Performing Arts M/C 255 1040 W Harrison St Chicago IL 60607-7130 Home: 2400 Lakeview 1901 Chicago IL 60614 Personal E-mail: dpa@uic.edu. Business E-Mail: william.loesch@goldberg.kohn.com.

LOEWENBERG, GERHARD, political science professor; b. Berlin, Oct. 2, 1928; came to U.S., 1936, naturalized, 1943; s. Walter and Anne Marie (Cassirer) L.; m. Ina Perlstein, Aug. 22, 1950; children: Deborah, Michael. AB, Cornell U., 1949, A.M., 1950, PhD, 1955. Mem. faculty Mount Holyoke Coll., 1953-69, chmn. dept. polit. sci., 1963-69, acting academic dean, 1968-69; prof. polit. sci. U. Iowa, Iowa City, 1970—2003, U. Iowa Found. Disting. prof. emeritus, 2003—, chmn. dept., 1982-84, dean Coll. Liberal Arts, 1984-92, dir. Comparative Legis. Research Center, 1971-82, 92—; vice chair East-West Parliamentary Practice Project, 1990-2000. Vis. assoc. prof. Columbia, UCLA, 1966, U. Mass. summer session at Bologna, Italy, 1967, Cornell U., 1968; mem. council Inter-Univ. Consortium for Polit. Research, 1971-74, chmn., 1973-74 Author: Parliament in the German Political System, 1967, Parlamentarismus im politischen System der Bundesrepublik Deutschland, 1969, Modern Parliaments: Change or Decline, 1971; co-author: Comparing Legislatures, 1979; co-editor: Handbook of Legislative Research, 1985, Legislatures: Comparative Perspectives on Representative Assemblies, 2002; contbr. articles to profl. jours. Trustee Mt. Holyoke Coll., 1971-84, chmn., 1979-84. Fulbright fellow, 1957-58, Rockefeller fellow, 1961-62, Social Sci. Rsch. Coun. Faculty Rsch. fellow, 1964-65, Guggenheim fellow, 1969-70. Fellow Am. Acad. Arts and Scis.; mem. Am. Polit. Sci. Assn. (coun. 1971-73, v.p. 1990-91, Frank J. Goodnow award 2001), Midwest Polit. Sci. Assn., Phi Beta Kappa, Phi Kappa Phi, Pi Sigma Alpha. Office: U Iowa 336 Schaeffer Hall Iowa City IA 52242-1409 Business E-Mail: g-loewenberg@uiowa.edu.

LOFGREN, CHRISTOPHER B., trucking executive; BS in Indsl. and Mgmt. Engring., MS in Indsl. and Mgmt. Engring., Mont. State U.; PhD in Indsl. and Systems Engring., Georgia U. Tech. With Symantec Corp., Motorola Inc., CAPS Logistics; v.p. Schneider Nat., Inc., Green Bay, Wis., 1994—96, chief tech. officer, 1996—99, chief info. officer, 1999—2000, COO, 2000—02, pres., CEO, 2002—, also bd. dir. Bd. dir. Computer Assocs. Internat., Inc. (now called CA), Islandia, NY, 2005—. Bd. dir. Green Bay Chpt. of the Boys and Girls Club Am.; bd. advisors Sch. Indsl. and Sys. Engring., Ga. Inst. Tech. Office: Schneider Nat Inc PO Box 2545 3101 S Packerland Dr Green Bay WI 54306-2545

LOFGREN, KARL ADOLPH, retired surgeon, educator; b. Killeberg, Sweden, Apr. 1, 1915; s. Hokan Albin and Teckla Elizabeth (Carlsson) L.; m. Jean Frances Taylor, Sept. 12, 1942; children: Karl Edward, Anne Elizabeth. Student, Northwestern U., 1934-37; MD, Harvard U., 1941; MS in Surgery, U. Minn., 1947. Diplomate Am. Bd. Surgery. Intern U. Minn. Hosps., Mpls., 1941-42; Mayo Found. fellow in surgery, 1942-44, 46-48; asst. surgeon Royal Acad. Hosp., Uppsala, Sweden, 1949; asst. to surg. staff Mayo Clinic, Rochester, Minn., 1949-50, cons. sect. peripheral vein surgery, 1950-81; instr. in surgery Mayo Grad. Sch. Medicine, 1951-60, asst. prof. surgery, 1960-74; comdg. officer USNR Med. Co. Mayo Clinic, 1963-67, head sect. peripheral vein surgery, dept. surgery, 1966-79, sr. cons., 1980-81. Assoc. prof. surgery Mayo Med. Sch., 1974-79, prof., 1979-81, emeritus prof., 1982—; cons. surg. staff Rochester Meth. Hosp., St. Mary's Hosp. Contbr. chpts. to textbooks, articles to profl. jours. Mem. adv. bd. Salvation Army, Rochester, 1959-81, 82—, pres., 1962-63. Served to capt. M.C. USNR, 1944-46. Decorated Bronze Star Fellow ACS; mem. Soc. Vascular Surgery, Midwestern Vascular Surgery Soc., Internat. Cardiovascular Soc., Minn. Surg. Soc., Swedish Surg. Soc. (hon.), Swiss Soc. Phlebology (co-worker), So. Minn. Med. Assn. (pres. 1972-73), Scandinavian Soc. Phlebology (hon.), Am. Venous Forum, Rotary Club, Sigma Xi. Baptist. Office: Mayo Clin Rochester MN 55905-0001 Home: 211 2nd St NW Apt 1916 Rochester MN 55901

LOFTON, THOMAS MILTON, lawyer; b. Indpls., May 12, 1929; s. Milton Alexander and Jane (Routzong) L.; m. Betty Louise Blades, June 20, 1954; children: Stephanie Louise, Melissa Jane. BS, Ind. U., 1951, JD, 1954, LLD (hon.), 2000, Wabash Coll., 2001. Bar: Ind. 1954, U.S. Ct. Appeals (7th cir.) 1959, U.S. Supreme Ct. 1958. Law clk. to justice U.S. Supreme Ct., Washington, 1954-55; ptnr. Baker & Daniels, Indpls., 1958-91. Dir. Ind. U. Found., Bloomington, 1978-91, Clowes Fund, 1980-2001; chmn. bd. Lilly Endowment, Indpls., 1991—; mem. bd. visitors Ind. U. Law, Bloomington, 1976—. Editor-in-chief Ind. Law Jour., 1953. Trustee Earlham Coll., 1988—91; dir. Allen Whitehill Clowes Charitable Found., 1990—. 1st lt. US Army, 1955—58. Recipient Peck award Wabash Coll., 1982, Disting. Alumni Svc. award Ind. U., 1997. Mem.: Ind. Acad., Masons, Order of Coif, Sigma Nu, Beta Gamma Sigma. Republican. Presbyterian. Home: 9060 Pickwick Dr Indianapolis IN 46260-1714 Office: Lilly Endowment 2800 N Meridian St Indianapolis IN 46208-4713

LOGA, SANDA, physicist, researcher; b. Bucharest, Romania, June 13, 1932; came to U.S., 1968; d. Stelian and Georgeta (Popescu) L.; m. Karl Heinz Werther, Mar. 1968 (div. 1970); m. Radu Zaciu, 1996. MS in Physics, U. Bucharest, 1955; PhD in Biophysics, U. Pitts., 1978. Asst. prof. faculty medicine and pharmacy, Bucharest, 1963-67; rsch. asst. Presbyn./St. Luke's Hosp., Chgo., 1968-69; assoc. rsch. scientist Miles Labs., Elkhart, Ind., 1969-70; rsch. asst. U. Pitts., 1971-78; rsch. assoc. Carnegie-Mellon U., Pitts., 1978-80; health physicist VA Med. Ctr., Westside, Chgo., 1980; med. physicist, VA Med. Ctr. N. Chgo, 1980-97. Assoc. prof. Chgo. Med. Sch., N. Chgo., 1985-2004. Mem. Am. Assn. Physicists in Medicine, Health Physics Soc. Office: Chgo Med Sch U Health Scis 3333 Green Bay Rd North Chicago IL 60064-3037 Business E-Mail: sanda.loga@rosalindfranklin.edu.

LOGAN, JAMES KENNETH, lawyer, retired judge; b. Quenemo, Kans., Aug. 21, 1929; s. John Lysle and Esther Maurine (Price) Logan; m. Beverly Jo Jennings, June 8, 1952; children: Daniel Jennings, Amy Logan Sliva, Sarah Logan Sherard, Samuel Price. AB, U. Kans., 1952; LLB magna cum laude, Harvard U., 1955. Bar: Kans. 1955, Calif. 1956. Law clk. U.S. Cir. Judge Huxman, 1955—56; with firm Gibson, Dunn & Crutcher, LA, 1956—57; asst. prof. law U. Kans., 1957—61, prof., dean Law Sch., 1961—68; ptnr. Payne and Jones, Olathe, Kans., 1968—77; judge U.S. Ct. Appeals (10th cir.), 1977—98; pvt. practice Logan Law Firm LLC, Olathe, 1998—2001, Foulston Siefkin LLP, Overland Park, Kans., 2002—. Ezra Ripley Thayer tchg. fellow Harvard Law Sch., 1961—62; vis. prof. U. Tex., 1964, Stanford U., 1969, U. Mich., 1976; sr. lectr. Duke U., 1987, 91, 93; commr. U.S. Dist. Ct., 1964—67; mem. U.S. Jud. Conf. Adv. Com. Fed. Rules of Appellate Procedure, 1990—97, chair, 1993—97. Author (with W.B. Leach): Future Interests and Estate Planning, 1961; author: Kansas Estate Administration, 5th edit., 1986; author: (with A.R. Martin) Kansas Corporate Law and Practice, 2d edit., 1979; author: The Federal Courts of the Tenth Circuit: A History, 1992, also articles. Candidate for U.S. Senate, 1968. With US Army, 1947—48. Recipient Disting. Svc. citation, U. Kans., 1986, Francis Rawle award, ABA-ALI, 1990; scholar Rhodes Scholarship, 1952. Mem.: ABA, Kans. Bar Assn., Order of Coif, Phi Delta Phi, Alpha Kappa Psi, Pi Sigma Alpha, Omicron Delta Kappa, Beta Gamma Sigma, Phi Beta Kappa. Democrat. Presbyterian. Office Phone: 913-498-2100. Business E-Mail: jlogan@foulston.com.

LOGAN, SEAN D., state legislator; b. Salem, Ohio, Feb. 11, 1966; s. Robert C. and Dorothy (Hall) L.; m. Melissa Logan. BA, Muskingum Coll., 1988. Intern Legis. Svc. Commn., 1988; legis. aide Ho. Rep. Ohio State Congress, 1989-90, state rep. Dist. 3, 1990—. Recipient Friendship Pin Beaver Creek Lodge N FOP, Svc. award Columbiana County Fedn. Conservation Club, 1993, Ohio/W.Va. Pub. Svc. award Am. Heart Assn., 1996; named Regional Pub. Servant of Yr. Nat. Soc. Social Workers, 1993. Mem. Nat. Conf. State Legislators, Ohio Farm Bur. (hon.), Sons of Am. Legion (hon.), Ruritan Internat., Columbiana County Twp. Trustees and Clks. Assn. (hon.). Home: 32927 Lucille Dr Lisbon OH 44432-8440

LOGEMANN, JERILYN ANN, speech pathologist, educator; b. Berwyn, Ill., May 21, 1942; d. Warren F. and Natalie M. (Killmer) L. BS, Northwestern U., 1963; MA, 1964, PhD, 1968. Grad. asst. dept. communicative disorders Northwestern U., 1963-68; instr. speech and audiology DePaul U., 1964-65; instr. dept. communicative disorders Mundelein Coll., 1967-71; rsch. assoc. dept. neurology and otolaryngology and maxillo, 1970-74; asst. prof., 1974-78; dir. clin. and rsch. activities of speech and lang., 1975—; assoc. prof. depts. neurology, otolaryngology and comm. scis, 1978-83; prof., 1983; chmn. dept. comm. scis. and disorders, 1982-96; Ralph and Jean Sundin Prof. of Comm. Scis. and Disorders, 1995—; mem. assoc. staff Northwestern meml. Hosp., 1976—; Evanston (Ill.) Hosp., 1988—. Cons. in field; assoc. dir. cancer control Ill. Comprehensive Cancer Coun., Chgo., 1980-82; mem. rehab. com. Ill. divsn. Am. CAncer Soc., 1975-79, chmn., 1979—; mem. upper aerodigestive tract organ site com. Nat. Cancer Inst., 1986-89; postdoct. fellow Nat. Inst. Neurologic Disease, Communicative Disorders and Stroke,Northwestern U., 1968-70. Author: The Fisher-Logeman Test of Articulation Competence, 1971, Evaluation and Treatment of Swallowing Disorders, 1983, 2nd edit., 1998, Manual for the Videofluorographic Evaluation of Swallowing, 1985, 93; assoc. editor: Jour. Speech and Hearing Disorders, Dysphagia Jour., 1978—. Fellow Inst. Medicine Chgo., 1981—; grantee Nat Cancer Inst., 1975—, Am. Cancer Soc., 1981-82, Nat. Inst. Dental Rsch., 1996-2000, Nat. Inst. Deafness and Other Comm. Disorders, 1997—; recipient Honors award Conn. Speech Lang. Hearing Assn., 1995, Am. Acad. Otolaryngology-Head Neck Surgery, 1997, Appreciation award Coun. Grad. Prgrams in Comms. Scis. and Disorders, 1995, Cellular One award Vanderbilt U., Am. Special Lang. Hearing Assn., 2003. Fellow Speech, Lang. and Hearing Assn. (pres. 1994, 2000, Honors award 2003), Inst. Medicine, Ill. Speech-Lang. Hearing Assn.(Honors 2003); mem. Internat. Assn. Logopedics and Phoniatrics, AAUP, Acoustic Soc. Am. (program com. Chgo. regional chpt.), Linguistic Soc. Am., Speech Comm. Assn., Am. Cleft Palate Assn., Ill. Speech and Hearing Assn. (DiCarlo award 1988), Chgo. Heart Assn., Chgo. Speech Therapy and Auditory Soc. Office: Northwestern U Feinberg Sch Medicine 10-205 Galter Pavilion 201 E Huron Chicago IL 60611 also: Northwestern U Dept Comm Sci and Disorder 2240 Campus Dr Evanston IL 60208-0001 Home Phone: 847-492-9527; Office Phone: 847-491-2490.

LOGGIE, JENNIFER MARY HILDRETH, retired physician, educator; b. Lusaka, Zambia, Feb. 4, 1936; arrived in U.S., 1964, naturalized, 1972; d. John and Jenny (Beattie). M.B., B.Ch., U. Witwatersrand, Johannesburg, South Africa, 1959. Intern Harare Hosp., Salisbury, Rhodesia, 1960-61; gen. practice medicine Lusaka, 1961-62; sr. pediatric house officer Derby Children's Hosp., also St. John's Hosp., Chelmsford, England, 1962-64; resident in pediatrics Children's Hosp., Louisville, 1964, Cin. Children's Hosp., 1964-65; fellow clin. pharmacology Cin. Coll. Medicine, 1965-67; mem. faculty U. Cin. Med. Sch., 1967—, prof. pediatrics, 1975-98, assoc. prof. pharmacology, 1972-77, prof. emeritus pediatrics, 1998—; ret., 1998. Contbr. articles to med. publs.; editor Pediatric and Adolescent Hypertension, 1991. Grantee, Am. Heart Assn., 1970—72, 1989—90. Mem. Am. Pediatric Soc. (Founder's award 1996), Midwest Soc. Pediatric Rsch. Episcopalian. Home: 1133 Herschel Ave Cincinnati OH 45208-3112 Personal E-mail: jennlog@webtv.net.

LOGIE, JOHN HOULT, SR., former mayor, lawyer; b. Ann Arbor, Mich., Aug. 11, 1939; s. James Wallace and Elizabeth (Hoult) Logie; m. Susan G. Duerr, Aug. 15, 1964; children: John Hoult Jr., Susannah, Margaret Elizabeth. Student, Williams Coll., 1957-59; BA, U. Mich., 1961, JD, 1968; MS, George Washington U., 1966; D of Pub. Svc. (hon.), Ferris State U., 2004. Bar: Mich. 1969, U.S. Dist. Ct. (we. and ea. dists.) Mich. 1969, U.S. Ct. Appeals (6th cir.) 1987. Assoc. Warner, Norcross & Judd, Grand Rapids, Mich., 1969-74, ptnr., 1974—2001, of counsel, 2002—; mayor City of Grand Rapids, 1991—2003. Instr. U.S. Naval Acad., 1964—66; chmn. civil justice adv. group U.S. Dist. Ct. (we. dist.) Mich., 1995—99; bd. vis. Sch. Bus. and Pub. Mgmt. George Washington U., 1995—2004; program coord. condemnation law sect. Inst. CLE; guest lectr. Grand Rapids CC, Grand Valley State U., Western Mich. U., Mich. State U.; mem. Mich. Land Use Inst., 2004—07. V.p., bd. dirs. Am. Cancer Soc., Grand Rapids, 1970—81; pres. Grand Rapids PTA Coun., 1971—73; pres., trustee Heritage Hill Assn., 1971—84, pres., 1976; v.p., bd. dirs. Goodwill Industries, Grand Rapids, 1973—79; chmn. Grand Rapids Urban Homesteading Commn., 1975—80, Grand Rapids Hist. Commn., 1985—90, Grand Rapids/Kent County Sesquicentennial Com., 1986—88, Clarke Hist. Libr., Ctrl. Mich. U., 2000—; pres., trustee Hist. Soc. Mich., 1984—90; mem. Headlee Blue Ribbon Commn., 1993—94, Mich. Workforce Devel. Bd., 2002—04; trustee Grand Valley State U. Found., 1998—; bd., sec. Mich. Land Use Inst., 2004. Lt. USN, 1961—66. Recipient Media Access Leadership award, Cmty. Media Ctr., 2000, Lifetime Achievement award, Mich. Hist. Preservation Network, 2000, Econ. Club, 2004, Emeritus award, Aquinas Coll., 2002, Disting. Trustee award, Leadership Grand Rapids, 2005, Disting. Cmty. Trustee award, Grand Rapids C. of C., 2005, Cmty. Leadership award, Convention/Arena Authority, 2006, Baxter History award, Grand Rapids Hist. Soc., 2007. Mem.: ABA (mem. forum com. healthlaw 1980—), Mich. Soc. Hosp. Attys. (pres. 1976—77), Grand Rapids Bar Assn. (dir. young lawyers sect. 1970, Worsfold Lifetime Svc. award 2004), Mich. Bar Assn. (chmn. condemnation com. real property sect. 1985—88), Am. Health Lawyers Assn., Univ. Club (dir. 1979—82, pres. 1980—82). Avocations: motor cruising, hunting, fishing. Home: 601 Cherry St SE Grand Rapids MI 49503-4726 Office: Warner Norcross and Judd 111 Lyon St NW Ste 900 Grand Rapids MI 49503-2487 Home Phone: 616-458-0951; Office Phone: 616-752-2111. Business E-Mail: jlogie@wnj.com.

LOGRASSO, DON, state legislator, lawyer; b. Kansas City, Mo., May 31, 1951; m. Leelah Lograsso; children: Chad, Scott. BA, MA, JD, U. Mo., Kansas City. Bar: Mo. Mem. Mo. Ho. of Reps. Dist. 54, Jefferson City, 1991—. Mem. civil and criminal law, ethics, judiciary and state instn. and property coms. Address: 404 E Stonewall Dr Blue Springs MO 64014-1759 Office: Mo Ho Rep House Post Office 201 W Capitol Ave Jefferson City MO 65101-1556

LOGSTROM, BRIDGET A., lawyer; b. 1958; BS magna cum laude, U. Minn., 1980; JD magna cum laude, William Mitchell Coll. Law, 1983. Bar: Minn. 1983. Assoc. Dorsey & Whitney LLP, Mpls., 1983—90, ptnr, individual, estate & trust svcs. group, 1983. Fellow: Am. Coll. of Trust and Estate Counsel; mem.: Hennepin County Bar Assn., Minn. State Bar Assn.

LOH, HORACE H., pharmacology educator; b. Canton, Republic of China, May 28, 1936; BS, Nat. Taiwan U., Taipei, Republic China, 1958; PhD, U. Iowa, 1965. Lectr. dept. pharmacology U. Calif. Sch. Medicine, San Francisco, 1967; assoc. prof. biochem. Wayne State U., Detroit, 1968-70; lectr., rsch. assoc. depts. psychiatry, pharmacology Langley Porter Neuropsychiatric Inst. U. Calif. Sch. Medicine, San Francisco, 1970-72, assoc. prof. depts. psychiatry, pharmacology Langley Porter Neuropsychiatric Inst., 1972-75, prof. depts. psychiatry, pharmacology Langley Porter Neuropsychiatric Inst., 1975-88; prof., head dept. pharmacology U. Minn. Med. Sch., Mpls., 1989—, Frederick and Alice Stark prof., head dept. pharmacology, 1990—. Chmn. ann. meeting theme com. on receptors Fedn. Am. Socs. for Exptl. Biology, 1984; mem. exec. com. Internat. Narcotic Rsch. Conf., 1984—87, chair sci. program ann. meeting, 1986; mem. adv. com. Nat. Tsing Hua U. Inst. Life Scis., Taiwan, China, 1985—89; mem. exec. com. Com. on Problems of Drug Dependence, Inc., 1985—88; mem. sci. adv. coun. Nat. Found. for Addictive Diseases, 1987—; cons. U.S. Army R & D Dept. Def., 1980—84. Mem. editl. adv. bd. Life Scis., 1978—, Substance and Alcohol Abuse, 1980—, Neurochemistry Internat., 1980—88, Neuropharmacology, 1992—, Neurosci. Series, 1982—83, Ann. rev. Pharmacology and Toxicology, 1984—89, Jour. Pharmacology and Exptl. Therapeutics, 1987—, assoc. editor CRC Critical Rev. in Pharmacol. Scis., 1987—88, Ann. Rev. Pharmacology and Toxicology, 1990—95; contbr. 56 chpts. in books, 300 articles to profl. jours. Recipient Career Devel. award, USPHS, 1973—78, 1978—83, Rsch. Scientist award, 1983—88, 1989—94, Humboldt award for sr. U.S. scientists, 1977. Mem.: We. Pharmacology Soc. (councilor 1980—83, pres. 1984—85), Soc. Chinese Bioscientists in Am. (pres. 1985—86), Am. Soc. Pharmacology and Exptl. Therapeutics (program com. 1976—86, trustee bd. publs. 1987—93, com. on confs. 1990—93), Am. Coll. Neuropsychopharmacology (honorific awards com. 1988—). Office: U Minn Med Sch Dept Pharmacology 6-120 Jackson 321 Church St SE Minneapolis MN 55455-0217 Office Phone: 612-625-9997. Business E-Mail: lohxx001@umn.edu.

LOH, ROBERT N. K., engineering educator; b. Lumut, Malaysia; arrived in Can., 1962, came to U.S., 1968; m. Annie Loh; children: John, Peter, Jennifer. BSc in Engring., Nat. Taiwan U., Taipei, 1961; MSc in Engring., U. Waterloo, Ont., Can., 1964, PhD, 1968. Asst. prof. U. Iowa, Iowa City, 1968-72, assoc. prof., 1973-78; prof. Oakland U., Rochester, Mich., 1978—, John F. Dodge prof., 1984—, assoc. dean, 1985-98, dir. Ctr. for Robotics and Advanced Automation, 1984—. Mem. editorial bd. Info. Systems, 1975—, Jour. of Intelligent and Robotic Systems, 1987—, Asia-Pacific Engring. Jour., 1990—; contbr. over 190 jour. publs. and tech. reports. Recipient numerous research grants and contracts from Dept. Def., NSF and pvt. industry. Mem. IEEE, Soc. Machine Intelligence (bd. dirs. 1985—), Assn. Unmanned Vehicle Systems, 1987—, Sigma Xi, Tau Beta Pi. Office: Oakland U Ctr for Robotics and Advanced Automation Dodge Hall Engring Rochester MI 48309-4401

LOKEN, JAMES BURTON, federal judge; b. Madison, Wis., May 21, 1940; s. Burton Dwight and Anita (Nelson) Loken; m. Caroline Brevard Hester, July 30, 1966; children: Kathryn Brevard, Kristina Ayres. BS, U. Wis., 1962; LLB magna cum laude, Harvard U., 1965. Law clk. to Hon. J. Edward Lumbard US Ct. Appeals (2d Cir.), YC, 1965—66; law clk. to assoc. justice Byron White US Supreme Ct., Washington, 1966—67; assoc. atty. Faegre & Benson, Mpls., 1967—70, ptnr., 1973—90; gen. counsel Pres.'s Com. on Consumer Interests, Office of Pres. of U.S., Washington, 1970; staff asst. Office of Pres. of U.S., Washington, 1970—72; judge US Ct. Appeals (8th cir.), St. Paul, 1990—2003, chief judge, 2003—. Editor: Harvard Law Rev., 1964—65. Mem.: Am. Law Inst., Phi Beta Kappa, Phi Kappa Phi. Avocations: golf, running. Office: US Courthouse 300 S 4th St Ste 11W Minneapolis MN 55415-0848 also: US Ct Appeals 8th Cir 111S 10th St Rm 24-32 Saint Louis MO 63102

LOMAS, LYLE WAYNE, agricultural research administrator, educator; b. Monett, Mo., June 8, 1953; s. John Junior and Helen Irene Lomas; m. Connie Gail Frey, Sept. 4, 1976; children: Amy Lynn, Eric Wayne. BS, U. Mo., 1975, MS, 1976; PhD, Mich. State U., 1979. Asst. prof., animal scientist S.E. Agrl. Rsch. Ctr., Kans. State U., Parsons, 1979-85, assoc. prof., 1985-92, prof., 1992—, head, 1985—. Contbr. articles to refereed sci. jours. Mem. Am. Soc. Animal Sci., Am. Registry Profl. Animal Scientists, Am. Forage and Grassland Coun., Rsch. Ctr. Adminstrs. Soc. (bd. dirs. 1993—, sec. 1999-2000, 2d v.p. 2000-01, v.p. 2001-02, pres. 2002-03), Rotary (bd. dirs. Parsons 1992—96 v.p. 1994-95, pres. 1995-96), Phi Kappa Phi, Gamma Sigma Delta. Presbyterian. Achievements include research in ruminant nutrition, forage utilization by grazing stocker cattle. Home: 24052 Douglas Rd Dennis KS 67341-9014 Office: Kans State U SE Agrl Rsch Ctr PO Box 316 Parsons KS 67357-0316 Home Phone: 620-421-0033; Office Phone: 620-421-4826. Business E-Mail: llomas@oznet.ksu.edu.

LOMBARD, ARTHUR J., judge; b. NYC, Nov. 30, 1941; s. Maurice and Martha (Simons) L.; m. Frederica Koller, Aug. 18, 1968; children: David, Lisa. BS in Acctg. magna cum laude, Columbia U., 1961; JD, Harvard U., 1964. Bar: N.Y. 1964, U.S. Ct. Appeals (2d cir.) 1965, U.S. Supreme Ct. 1970, U.S. Ct. Appeals (6th cir.) 1972, Mich. 1976. Law clk. to J. Edward Lumbard chief judge U.S. Ct. Appeals (2d cir.), NYC, 1964-65; teaching fellow law sch. Harvard U., Cambridge, Mass., 1965-66; instr. Orientation Program in Am. Law, Assn. Am. Law Schs., Princeton, N.J., 1966; prof. law Wayne State U., Detroit, 1966-87, assoc. dean law, 1978-85; prof. Detroit Coll. Law, 1987-94, dean, chief adminstrv. officer, 1987-93; judge Wayne County (Mich.) Cir. Ct., 1994—. Chmn. revision of Mich. class action rule com. Mich. Supreme Ct., 1980-83; reporter rules com. U.S. Dist. Ct. (ea. dist.) Mich., 1978-94. Contbr. articles to profl. jours. Mem. Mich. Civil Rights Commn., 1991-94, co-chmn., 1992-93, chmn. 1993-94. Office: 1913 City County Bldg Detroit MI 48226

LOMBARDI, CORNELIUS ENNIS, JR., lawyer; b. Portland, Oreg., Feb. 12, 1926; s. Cornelius Ennis and Adele (Volk) L.; m. Ann Vivian Foster, Nov. 24, 1954; children— Cornelius Ennis, Gregg Foster, Matthew Volk. BA, Yale, 1949; JD, U. Mich., 1952. Bar: Mo. Since practiced in, Kansas City, Mo.; mem. firm Blackwell, Sanders, Peper, Martin, 1957-92, of counsel. Former pres. Kansas City Mus. Assn., Estate Planning Coun. of Kansas City; trustee Pembroke Country Day Sch.; chmn. soc. of fellows Nelson Gallery Found.; bd. dirs., Mo. Parks Assn. Mem.: Kansas City Country Club, Order of Coif, Phi Alpha Delta. Home: 5049 Wornall Rd Kansas City MO 64112-2423 Office Phone: 816-983-8000.

LOMBARDI, FREDERICK MCKEAN, lawyer; b. Akron, Ohio, Apr. 1, 1937; s. Leonard Anthony and Dorothy (McKean) L.; m. Margaret J. Gessler, Mar. 31, 1962; children: Marcus M., David G., John A., Joseph F. BA, U. Akron, 1960; LLB, Case Western Res., 1962. Bar: Ohio 1962, U.S. Dist. Ct. (no. and so. dists.) Ohio 1964, U.S. Ct. Appeals (6th cir.) 1966. Prin., shareholder Buckingham, Doolittle & Burroughs, Akron, 1962—, chmn. comml. law and litigation dept., 1989-99. Bd. editors Western Res. Law Rev., 1961-62. Trustee, mem. exec. com., v.p. Ohio Ballet, 1985-93; trustee Walsh Jesuit H.S., 1987-90; life trustee Akron Golf Charities, NEC World Series of Golf; bd. mem. Summa Health Sys. Found., Downtown Akron Partnership, St. Hilary Parish Found. Mem. Ohio Bar Assn. (coun. of dels. 1995-97), Akron Bar Assn. (trustee 1991-94, 97-2000, v.p., pres.-elect 1997-98, pres. 1998-99), Case Western Res. U. Law Alumni Assn. (bd. mem. 1995-98, 2003—06), Case Western Res. Soc. Benchers, Fairlawn Swim and Tennis Club (past pres.), Portage Country Club, Pi Sigma Alpha Democrat. Roman Catholic. Office: Buckingham Doolittle & Burroughs 3800 Embassy Pkwy Ste 300 Akron OH 44333 Office Phone: 330-376-5300. Business E-Mail: flombardi@bdblaw.com.

LONDON, TERRY, former state legislator; b. Apr. 15, 1940; married 1980. Rep. Mich. Ho. of Rep., 1985-86, state rep. Dist. 81, 1988-98; chmn. St. Clair County Rep. Com. Home: 1020 Illinois St Marysville MI 48040-1575

LONERGAN, ROBERT C., financial executive; b. Conn., 1943; BSBA in Fin., Georgetown U.; MBA, Case Western Res. U. Mgmt. positions GE Plastics; pres. Reb Plastics; pres. window group Owens Corning, 1993, pres. sci. and tech. ops., 1995, v.p., pres. bldg. materials Europe and Africa, 1998, sr. v.p. strategic resources. Office: Owens Corning One Owens Corning Pkwy Toledo OH 43659 Home: 261 Linkside Cir Ponte Vedra Beach FL 32082-2034

LONEY, MARY ROSE, former airport administrator, aviation industry consultant; b. Ohio, 1952; B in Sociology and Philosophy, U. Pitts., 1973; MPA, U. Nev., Las Vegas, 1983. Ticket sales staff Grand Canyon Airlines, 1973—75; mgr. Lucky's Grocery Stores, 1976—78; planning svcs. mgr. McCarran Internat. Airport, Las Vegas, Nev., 1979-84; asst. aviation dir. Albuquerque Internat. Airport, 1984-86; asst. dir. aviation San Jose (Calif.) Internat. Airport, 1986-89; first dep. commr. aviation Chgo. Airport Sys., 1989-92; dep. exec. dir. fin. and adminstrn. Dallas/Ft. Worth Internat. Airport, 1992-93; dir. aviation Phila. Internat. Airport, 1993-96; commr. aviation Chgo. Airport Sys., 1996—99; pres. Travelways, Inc., NJ, 1999—2000; pres., CEO The Loney Group, Satellite Beach, Fla., 2000—. Bd. dirs. Chgo. Tourism and Visitors Bur., 1993—2000, Phila. Conv. and Visitors Bur., 1993—2000, Chgo.-Gary Airport Authority, 1996—2000; bd. mem. Chgo. Econ. Devel. Commn., 1996—2000. Trustee St. Joseph's U., Phila., 1994—97; bd. dirs. Chgo. Pub. Art Commn., 1996—2000. Named Santa Clara County Woman of Achievement, 1988, Woman of Yr., Phila. Customs Brokers and Freight Forwarders Assn., 1994, one of State Pa. Honor Roll of Women, 1996; recipient YWCA's Tribute to Women in Industry award, 1989, Bus. Woman of Yr. award Great Valley Regional C. of C., 1994, Transp. award March of Dimes, 1995. Mem. FAA (appointed rsch. engring. and devel. adv. com.), Am. Assn. Airport Execs. (accredited airport exec., nat. bd. dirs. 1995-97, chmns. award 1994), St. Joseph's U. (bd. trustees). Home: 1290 Highway A1A Ste 102 Satellite Beach FL 32937-2477

LONG, CHRISTOPHER HOWARD, professional football player; b. Santa Monica, Calif., Mar. 28, 1985; s. Howie and Diane Long. Student in sociology, U. Va., 2004—08. Defensive lineman St. Louis Rams, 2008—. Finalist Rotary Lombardi award, Bronko Nagurski Trophy, Ronnie Lott Trophy, 2007—08; named Defensive Player of Yr., Atlantic Coast Conf., 2007—08, First-Team All-America, Am. Football Coaches Assn., rivals.com, 2007—08; recipient Ted Hendricks Defensive End of Yr. award, Dudley award, 2007—08. Office: St Louis Rams One Rams Way St. Louis MO 63045*

LONG, CLARENCE WILLIAM, accountant; b. Hartford City, Ind., Apr. 17, 1917; s. Adam and Alice (Weschke) L.; m. Mildred Bernhardt, Aug. 8, 1940; children: William Randall, David John, Bruce Allen. BS, Ind. U., 1939. With Ernst & Young, Indpls., 1939-78, ptnr., 1953-78, ret., 1978. Mem. econ. exec. com. Gov. Ind., 1968-73. Mem. nat. budget and consultation com. United Way of Am., 1968-70; bd. dirs. United Fund Greater Indpls., 1966—, treas., 1968—; bd. dirs. Jr. Achievement, Ind., 1966-67; mem. exec. com. Nat. Jr. Achievement, 1966-67; mem. fin. com. Indpls. Hosp. Devel. Assn., 1966-67; trustee Ind. U., 1975-84; trustee Art Assn. Indpls., pres., 1977-86; mem. adv. com. to dir. NIH, 1986-92. Mem. Am. Inst. C.P.A.'s (council 1959-62), Ind. Assn. C.P.A.'s, Nat. Assn. Accountants, Ind. C. of C. (dir.), Delta Chi, Beta Alpha Psi, Alpha Kappa Psi. Clubs: Woodstock (Indpls.) (dir. 1958-60), Columbia (Indpls.) (dir. 1971-77, pres. 1976), Royal Poinciana Golf Club (Naples, Fla.). Republican. Lutheran. Home: 607 Somerset Dr W Indianapolis IN 46260-2924 Office: 1 Indiana Sq Indianapolis IN 46204-2004

LONG, DAVID C., state legislator, lawyer; m. Melissa Long; children: Adam, Erik. BA, U. Calif.-Davis; JD, U. Santa Clara. Gen. counsel Pizza Hut of Ft. Wayne, Inc.; mem. Ind. Senate, Indpls., 1996—, ranking mem. commerce and consumer affairs com., mem. corrections, criminal and civil procedures com., former mem. jud. com., mem. pensions and labor com. Mem. Ft. Wayne Plan Commn., Urban Enterprise Zone Bd., Ft. Wayne; former mem. cable TV negotiation team City of Ft. Wayne; former mem. Ft. Wayne City Coun., 1988-95; mem. Utility Privatization Study Com.; bd. dirs. Arts United. Office: 200 W Washington St Indianapolis IN 46204-2728

LONG, EDWIN TUTT, surgeon; b. St. Louis, July 23, 1925; s. Forrest Edwin and Hazel (Tutt) L.; m. Mary M. Hull, Apr. 16, 1955; children: Jennifer Ann, Laura Ann, Peter Edwin. AB, Columbia U., 1944, MD, 1947. Diplomate Am. Bd. Surgery, Am. Bd. Thoracic Surgery. Rotating intern Meth. Hosp., Bklyn., 1947—48; surg. intern U. Chgo. Clinics, 1948-49, resident in gen. surgery, 1952-55, resident in thoracic surgery, 1955-57; asst. prof. surgery U. Chgo., 1957-59; thoracic and cardiovasc. surgeon Watson Clinic, Lakeland, Fla., 1960-69, chief surgery dept., 1969; dir. Watson Clinic Rsch. Found., 1965—69; assoc. prof. surgery U. Pa., Phila., 1970-73; attending thoracic and cardiovasc. surgeon Allegheny Cardiovasc. Surg. Assocs., Pitts., 1973-88; exec. v.p. Mailings Clearing House and Roxbury Press, Inc., 1988-90, pres., 1990-96, chmn. bd. dirs., 1991—; regent Rockhurst U., 2002—. Disting. lectr., curriculum advisor Healthcare Leadership Program, Helzberg Sch. Mgmt., Rockhurst U., 2001—, mem. dean's adv. com., 2004—; nat. adv. panel Ctr. for Practical Health Reform, 2003—, regional co-chair Kansas City chpt., 2003—. Author: (book) Life Stability And The Persuit of Health Care. Capt. USAF, 1950—52. Pressure Vectorography Rsch. grant Alfred P. Sloan Found., 1963; Nelson-Atkins Mus. fellow, 1997—. Fellow Heart Rhythm Soc.; mem. AMA, ACS, Am. Coll. Cardiology, Soc. for Vascular Surgery, Allegheny Vascular Soc. (pres. 1987), Ea. Vascular Soc., Soc. Thoracic Surgery, Ctr. for Practical Bioethics, Kansas City Concensus, Woodside Club, Rotary, Sigma Xi, Beta Theta Pi. Achievements include patents for gas sterilizer. Home: 4550 Warwick Blvd # 1204 Kansas City MO 64111-7725 Office: 4550 Warwick Blvd # 1209 Kansas City MO 64111 also: Roxbury Press Inc 601 E Marshall St Sweet Springs MO 65351-0295 Office Phone: 816-753-0089. E-mail: elongmd@kc.rr.com.

LONG, ELIZABETH L., state legislator, small business owner; m. Kent Long; children: Amie, Dana, Sarah. Student, Drury Coll. County clk. Laclede County, Mo., 1982-90; owner, mgr. retail gift shop, Lebanon; mem. Mo. Ho. of Reps. Dist. 146, Jefferson City, 1991. Mem. election fed.-state rels. and vet. affairs, fees and salaries, state parks, recreation and natural resources and tourism, recreation and cultural affairs coms. Mem. Lebanon Area Found. Mem. Lebanon C. of C. Republican. Office: Rm 201E State Capitol Jefferson City MO 65101

LONG, GARY, former insurance company executive; CFO Northwestern Mutual Life, Milw. Office: Northwestern Mutual Life 720 E Wisconsin Ave Milwaukee WI 53202-4703

LONG, GARY R., lawyer; b. Sikeston, Mo., June 30, 1951; BS, U. Mo., 1973, JD, 1976. Bar: Mo. 1976. Ptnr., mem. Exec. Com., chmn. Nat. Product Liability Litig. Group Shook, Hardy & Bacon LLP, Kansas City, Mo. Note and comment editor Mo. Law Rev., 1975-76. Mem. ABA, Def. Rsch. Inst. (mem. product, liability adv. coun.), Mo. Def. Lawyers Assn., Order of Coif. Office: Shook, Hardy & Bacon LLP 2555 Grand Blvd Kansas City MO 64108 Office Phone: 816-474-6550. Office Fax: 816-421-5547. E-mail: glong@shb.com.

LONG, JAN MICHAEL, judge; b. Pomeroy, Ohio, May 31, 1952; s. Lewis Franklin and Dorothy (Clatworthy) L.; m. Susan Louise Custer, May 12, 1978; children: John D., Justin M., Jason M. BA, Ohio State U., 1974; JD, Capital U., 1979. Adminstrv. asst. Congressman Doug Applegate, Washington, 1974-77; asst. prosecuting atty. Pickaway County, Circleville, Ohio, 1979-80; mem. Ohio State Senate, Columbus, 1987-97; asst. minority whip Ohio Senate, Columbus, 1995-97; juvenile/probate judge for Pickaway County Circleville, Ohio, 1997—. Named one of Outstanding Young Men Am. U.S. Jaycees, 1987. Mem. Pickaway County Bar Assn. (treas. 1985-86, sec. 1986-87). Democrat. Home: 522 Glenmont Dr Circleville OH 43113-1523 Office: Juvenile Ct 207 S Court St Circleville OH 43113-1648

LONG, LARRY, state attorney general; b. Brookings, SD, Sept. 30, 1947; m. Jan Anderson; children: Claire, Craig. BA, SD State U., 1969; JD, U. SD, 1972. Pvt. practice, Martin, 1972—73; state's atty. Bennett County, 1973—90; chief dep. atty. gen. SD, 1991—2002; atty. gen. State of SD, 2003—. With US Army. Republican. Office: Office of Atty Gen Ste 1 1302 East Highway 14 Pierre SD 57501-8501 Office Phone: 605-773-3215.

LONG, PHILLIP CLIFFORD, retired museum director; b. Tucson, Oct. 11, 1942; s. Hugh-Blair Grigsby and Phyllis Margaret (Clay) L.; m. Martha Whitney Rowe, Aug. 26, 1972; children— Elisha Whitney, Charlotte Clay, Elliot Sherlock BA, Tulane U., 1965. Sec. Fifth Third Bancorp, Cin., 1974-94; sr. v.p., sec. Fifth Third Bank, Cin., 1974—94; dir. Taft Mus. Art, Cin., 1994—2006; ret., 2007. Trustee Contemporary Arts Ctr., 1974-84, Art Acad. Cin., 1980-94, Cin. Symphony Orch., 1981-87, Cin. Nature Ctr., 1982-88, Taft Mus., 1987-94, Cin. Country Day Sch., 1991-97; trustee, treas. Cin. Music Hall, 1981-92, Convalescent Hosp. for Children, 1989—, Spring Grove Cemetery, 1989—, Cin. Assn. for Arts, 1992—. Mem. The Camargo Club, Queen City Club. Home: 4795 Burley Hills Dr Cincinnati OH 45243-4007

LONG, ROBERT EUGENE, retired banker; b. Yankton, SD, Dec. 5, 1931; s. George Joseph and Malinda Ann (Hanson) L.; m. Patricia Louise Glass, June 19, 1959; children: Malinda Ann, Robert Eugene, Jennifer Lynn, Michael Joseph. BS in Acctg., U. S.D., 1956; MBA, U. Mich., 1965; grad., Madison Grad. Sch. Banking, 1973, Nat. Comml. Lending Grad. Sch., U. Okla., 1977. Cert. comml. lender. Financial analyst Chrysler Corp., 1958-59; supr. finance Ford Motor Co., 1966-67; with First Wis. Bankshares Corp., Milw., 1967—, v.p. fin., 1973—; exec. v.p. 1st Wis. Fond du Lac, 1978—; dir. 1st Wis. Nat. Bank of, Southgate, Waukesha and Fond du Lac; exec. v.p., dir. West Allis State Bank, 1979-81, pres., dir., 1981—, chief exec. officer, 1983—; sr. v.p. adminstrn. Park Banks, 1987—; chmn., pres., CEO Robert E. Long & Assoc., L.L.C., 2002—. Speaker/chmn. banking seminars Am. Mgmt. Assn., 1970— Pres. local br. Aid Assn. Luth., 1970—, corp. bd. dirs., 1982—, vice chmn. bd., 1989—; pres. Mt. Carmel Luth. Ch., Milw., 1972; team capt. Re-elect Nixon campaign, 1972; bd. dirs. Luth. Social Svcs. of Wis. and Upper Mich., 1978—, chmn. bd., 1983—; bd. dirs. Luther Manor, 1981, Luther Manor Found., 1984, pres. bd. dirs. United Luth. Program for Aging, 1986—; bd. dirs. Wis. Inst. Family Medicine, 1985, pres., 1992—, elected corp. adv. coun., 1996; vice chmn. adv. coun. West Allis Meml. Hosp., 1993—; bd. dirs. Luth. Sem. Theology at Chgo., 1997. With USAF, 1951-52. Recipient Good Citizenship award Am. Legion, 1948 Mem. Wis. Assn. Family Practice (bd. dirs. 1992—), Wauwatosa C. of C. (bd. dirs. 1992—), Alpha Tau Omega. Clubs: Western Racquet (Elm Grove, Wis.) (dir. 1976—); Bluemound Golf and Country; Elmbrook Swim (pres. 1977-78). Lodges: Masons, Shriners, Jesters, Scottish Rite. Lutheran. Home and Office: N21w24052 Dorchester Dr Unit 6D Pewaukee WI 53072-4692 E-mail: PattyLou4@aol.com.

LONG, ROBERT M., newspaper publishing executive; m. June Long; children: Shannon, Bob. BBA, Dyke Coll. CPA, Ohio. From acct. to treas. and contr. Plain Dealer Pub. Co., Cleve., 1965-92, exec. v.p., 1992—. V.p. Plain Dealer Charities, Inc., Delcom, Inc. Trustee Dyke Coll., Cleve. Ballet, St. Vincent Quadrangle, Inc.; bd. dirs. Jr. Achievement; active Leadership Cleve., 1993. Mem. Internat. Newspaper Fin. Execs. (bd. dirs.), Ohio Soc. CPAs, Cleve. Treas. Club. Office: The Plain Dealer Pub Co 1801 Superior Ave E Cleveland OH 44114-2198

LONG, SARAH ANN, librarian; b. Atlanta, May 20, 1943; d. Jones Lloyd and Lelia Maria (Mitchell) Sanders; m. James Allen Long, 1961 (div. 1985); children: Andrew C., James Allen IV; m. Donald J. Sager, May 23, 1987. BA, Oglethorpe U., 1966; M in Librarianship, Emory U., 1969. Asst. libr. Coll. of St. Matthias, Bristol, England, 1970-74; cons. State Libr. Ohio, Columbus, 1975-77; coord. Pub. Libr. of Columbus and Franklin County, Columbus, 1977-79; dir. Fairfield County Dist. Libr., Lancaster, Ohio, 1979-82, Dauphin County Libr. Sys., Harrisburg, Pa., 1982-85, Multnomah County Libr., Portland, Oreg., 1985-89; sys. dir. North Suburban Libr. Sys., Wheeling, Ill., 1989—. Chmn. Portland State U. Libr. Adv. Coun., 1987-89, bd. dirs. Am. Libr., Paris, 2000-02. Contbr. to weekly column in Daily Herald; monthly cable show Whats New in Libraries; contbr. articles to profl. jours. Bd. dirs. Dauphin County Hist. Soc., Harrisburg, 1983-85, ARC, Harrisburg, 1984-85; pres. Lancaster-Fairfield County YWCA, Lancaster, 1981-82; vice chmn. govt. and ednl. divsn. Lancaster-Fairfield County United Way, Lancaster, 1981-82; sec. Fairfield County Arts Coun., 1981-82; adv. bd. Portland State U., 1987-89; mentor Ohio Libr. Leadership Inst., 1993, 95; mentor Synergy. Leadership Inst. Ill. State Libr., 2006; moderator Congl. Ch., Deerfield Ill., 2006—. Recipient Dir.'s award Ohio Program in Humanities, Columbus, 1982, Emory medal Emory U., 2006, Ken Haycock award ALA, 2005; Sarah Long Day established in her honor Fairfield County, Lancaster, Bd. Commrs., 1982. Mem. ALA (pres. 1999-2000, elected coun. 1993-97, chair Spectrum fund raising com. 2001-02), Pub. Libr. Assn. (pres. 1989-90, chair legis. com. 1991-95, chair 1998, nat. conf. com. 1995-98), Ill. Libr. Assn. (pub. policy com. 1991-97, Librarian of Yr. award 1999), Ill. Libr. Sys. Dirs. Orgn. (pres. 2000-05), Libr. Cmty. Found. (bd. dirs. 1995-2005) Office: N Suburban Libr Systems 200 W Dundee Rd Wheeling IL 60090-4750 Business E-Mail: slong@nsls.info.

LONG, SARAH ELIZABETH BRACKNEY, physician; b. Sidney, Ohio, Dec. 5, 1926; d. Robert LeRoy and Caroline Josephine (Shue) Brackney; m. John Frederick Long, June 15, 1948; children: George Lynas, Helen Lucille Corcoran, Harold Roy, Clara Alice Lawrence, Nancy Carol Sieber. BA, Ohio State U., 1948, MD, 1952. Intern Grant Hosp., Columbus, Ohio, 1952—53; resident internal medicine Mt. Carmel Med. Ctr., Columbus, 1966—69, chief resident internal medicine, 1968—69; med. cons. Ohio Bur. Disability Determination,

Columbus, 1970—. Physician student health Ohio State U., Columbus, 1970-73; sch. physician Bexley City Schs., Ohio, 1973-83; physician advisor to peer rev. Mt. Carmel East Hosp., Columbus, 1979-86, med. dir. employee health, 1981-96; physician cons. Fed. Black Lung program U.S. Dept. Labor, Columbus, 1979-98. Mem.: AMA, Gerontol. Soc. Am., Columbus Med. Assn., Ohio State Med. Assn., Ohio Hist. Soc., Phi Beta Kappa, Alpha Epsilon Delta. Home: 2765 Bexley Park Rd Columbus OH 43209-2231

LONG, THOMAS LESLIE, lawyer; b. Mansfield, Ohio, May 30, 1951; s. Ralph Waldo and Rose Ann (Cloud) L.; m. Peggy L. Bryant, Apr. 24, 1982. AB in Govt., U. Notre Dame, 1973; JD, Ohio State U., 1976. Bar: Ohio 1976, U.S. Dist. Ct. (so. dist.) Ohio 1976, U.S. Dist. Ct. (no. dist.) Ohio 1977, U.S. Ct. Appeals (6th cir.) 1978. Assoc. Alexander, Ebinger, Fisher, McAlister & Lawrence, Columbus, Ohio, 1976-82, ptnr., 1982-85, Baker & Hostetler, Columbus, 1985—. Mem. ABA, Ohio Bar Assn., Columbus Bar Assn., Fed. Bar Assn., Assn. Trial Lawyer Am. Clubs: Capitol (Columbus). Democrat. Roman Catholic. Home: 2565 Leeds Rd Columbus OH 43221-3613 Office: Baker & Hostetler 65 E State St Ste 2100 Columbus OH 43215-4260 Office Phone: 614-228-1541.

LONG, TOM, brewery executive; BA, U. NC, Chapel Hill; MBA, Harvard U. With Gulf & Western, McCann Erickson, Goldman Sachs; mktg. exec. Coco-Cola Co., 1988—2005, mgr. market planning Atlanta, v.p. 7-Eleven account, 1993, v.p. Wal-Mart global account, 1995, v.p. nat. sales, dir. rsch. and trends, dir. global strategic mktg., pres. Great Britain & Ireland, pres. N.W. Europe Div. London; chief mktg. officer Miller Brewing Co., Milw., 2005—06, pres., CEO, 2006—. Office: Miller Brewing Co 3939 W Highland Blvd Milwaukee WI 53208

LONG, WILLIS FRANKLIN, electrical engineering educator, researcher; b. Lima, Ohio, Jan. 30, 1934; s. Jesse Raymond and Cerelda Elizabeth (Stepleton) L.; m. Ginger Carol Miller; children: Andrew Mark, Kristin Kay, David Franklin. BS in Engring. Physics, U. Toledo, 1957, MSEE, 1962; PhD, U. Wis., 1970. Registered profl. engr., Wis. Project engr. Doehler Jarvis div. Nat. Lead Co., Toledo, 1957, 59-60; instr. U. Toledo, 1962-66; mem. tech. staff Hughes Rsch. Labs., Malibu, Calif., 1969-73; asst., then assoc. prof. depts. extension engring. and elec. engring. U. Wis., Madison, 1973-80, prof., chair dept. extension engring., 1980-83, prof. depts. engring., profl devel. and elec. and computer engring., 1985—, prof. emeritus, 2001—; dir. ASEA Power System Ctr., New Berlin, Wis., 1983-85. Prin. Long Assocs., Madison, 1973—; cons. Dept. Energy, Washington, 1978—, ABB Power Systems, Raleigh, N.C., 1985—. Editor EMTP Rev., 1987-91; contbr. articles to profl. jours.; patentee power switching. Mem. adv. com. energy conservation Wis. Dept. Labor, Industry and Human Rels., 1976-77; mem. rural energy mgmt. coun. Wis. Dept. Agrl., Trade and Comsumer Protection, 1999-2001; chmn. Wis. chpt. Sierra Club, 1977; pres. bd. dirs. Madison Urban Ministry, 1993-95. 2d lt. Signal Corps., U.S. Army, 1958. Recipient Disting. Engring. Alumnus award U. Toledo, 1983, award of excellence U. Wis.-Extension, 1987; Sci. Faculty fellow NSF, 1966. Fellow IEEE (life, Meritorious Achievement in Continuing Edn. award 1991); mem. Internat. Coun. on Large Electric Systems (expert advisor 1979—). Mem. United Ch. of Christ. Avocation: canoeing. Home: 125 N Hamilton St #906 Madison WI 53703 Office: U Wis 432 N Lake St Rm 737 Madison WI 53706-1415

LONGABERGER, TAMI, home decor accessories company executive; BSBA in Mktg., Ohio State U., 1984. Joined Longaberger Co., Newark, Ohio, 1984, pres., 1994, CEO, 1998. Mem. 60th commn. human rights United Nation; bd. dirs. Woodrow Wilson Internat. Ctr. Scholars; chair Nat. Women's Bus. Coun.

LONGENECKER, MARK HERSHEY, JR., lawyer; b. Akron, Ohio, Feb. 16, 1951; s. Mark Hershey and Katrina (Hetzner) L.; children: Emily Irene, Mark Hershey III; m. Marcie Garrison, June. 5, 2004. BA, Denison U., 1973; JD, Harvard U., 1976. Bar: Ill. 1976, Ohio 1979. Atty. Lord, Bissell & Brook, Chgo., 1976-79; ptnr. Frost Brown Todd LLC (and predecessor firms), Cin., 1979—2002, chmn. bus.-corp. dept., 1996—2002; mem. Greenebaum, Doll & McDonald, PLLC, 2002—06; ptnr. Porter Wright Morris & Arthur LLP, Cin., 2006—. Dir. ST Media Group Internat., HealthPro Brands, Inc. Bd. govs. Ohio Fair Plan Underwriting Assn., Columbus, 1989-92; bd. dirs. Salvation Army, Cin., 2000—, Cin. Union Bethel, 2006—. Mem. Cin. Country Club, Harvard Club (Cin. pres. 1993-94). Home: 7708 Chumani Ln Cincinnati OH 45243 Office: Porter Wright Morris & Arthur ILP Ste 2200 250 E Fifth St Cincinnati OH 45202 Business E-Mail: mlongenecker@porterwright.com.

LONGHOFER, RONALD STEPHEN, financial consultant; b. Junction City, Kans., Aug. 30, 1946; s. Oscar William and Anna Mathilda (Krause) L.; m. Elizabeth Norma McKenna; children: Adam, Nathan, Stefanie. BMus, U. Mich., 1968, JD magna cum laude, 1975, MBA with distinction, 2004. CPA Ill., accredited in bus. valuation; bar: Mich. 1975, U.S. Dist. Ct. (ea. dist.) Mich., U.S. Ct. Appeals (6th cir.), U.S. Supreme Ct.; cert. chartered fin. analyst, fraud examiner. Law clk. to judge U.S. Dist. Ct. (ea. dist.) Mich., Detroit, 1975-76; ptnr. Honigman, Miller, Schwartz & Cohn, Detroit, 1976—2003, chmn. litigation dept., 1993-96; dir. Stout, Risius, Ross, Inc., 2004—06; prin. RSL Financial Cons., LLC, Plymouth, Mich., 2003—. Co-author: Courtroom Handbook on Michigan Evidence, 2007, Michigan Court Rules Practice, 1998, Michigan Court Rules Practice-Evidence, 2002, Introducing Evidence at Trial, 2007; author: Courtroom Handbook on Michigan Civil Procedure, 2007, Michigan Court Rules Practice, 2004; editor Mich. Law Rev., 1974-75. Bd. dir. Plymouth Canton Symphony Soc. With US Army, 1968—72. Mem. Acad. Ct. Appointed Masters, FBA, Am. Inst. CPAs, Oakland County Bar Assn., CFA Soc. Detroit, CFA Inst., Assn. Cert. Fraud Examiners, Ill. CPA Soc., Mich. Assn. Cert. Pub. Accts., Inst. Bus. Appraisers, U. Mich. Pres.' Club, Order of Coif, Phi Beta Kappa, Phi Kappa Phi, Pi Kappa Lambda, Beta Gamma Sigma. Home: 974 Penniman Ave Plymouth MI 48170 Office: RSL Fin Cons LLC 249 S Main St Plymouth MI 48170 Home Phone: 248-252-5459; Office Phone: 734-207-1004. Business E-Mail: rlonghofer@rslfinancialconsulting.com.

LONGO, AMY L., lawyer; BSN, Creighton U., 1970, JD, 1979. Bar: Nebr. 1979. Ptnr. Ellick, Jones, Buelt, Blazek & Longo, Omaha. Mem. moot ct. bd., adj. asst. prof. law Coll. Medicine, U. Nebr., 1987—. Fellow Am. Bar Found.; mem. ABA (del. 1993), Nebr. State Bar Assn. (pres.-elect, ho. dels. 1984—, chair 1996), Omaha Bar Assn. Office: Ellick Jones Buelt Blazek & Longo 8805 Indian Hills Dr Ste 280 Omaha NE 68114-4077

LONGONE, DANIEL THOMAS, chemistry professor; b. Worcester, Mass., Sept. 16, 1932; s. Daniel Edward and Anne (Novick) L.; m. Janice B. Bluestein, June 13, 1954. BS, Worcester Poly. Inst., 1954; PhD, Cornell U., 1958. Research fellow chemistry U. Ill., Urbana, 1958-59; mem. faculty dept. chemistry U. Mich., Ann Arbor, 1959—, assoc. prof., 1966-71, prof., 1971-87, emertius prof., 1988—. Cons. Gen. Motors Research Co., 1965-77 Am. Chem. Soc.-Petroleum Research Fund internat. fellow, 1967-68; Fulbright scholar, 1970-71 Mem. Am. Chem. Soc., Sigma Xi, Tau Beta Pi, Phi Lambda Upsilon. Home: 1207 W Madison St Ann Arbor MI 48103-4729 Office: U Mich 3533 Chemistry Ann Arbor MI 48109 E-mail: dtlongwfl@netscape.net.

LONGSTAFF, RONALD EARL, federal judge; b. Pittsburg, Kans., Feb. 14, 1941; m. Norma Jeanne Miller, July 25, 1970. BA, Kans. State Coll., 1962; JD with distinction, U. Iowa, 1965. Assoc. McWilliams, Gross and Kirtley, Des Moines, 1967-68; law clk. to Hon. Roy L. Stephenson US Dist. Ct. (so. dist.) Iowa, 1965-67, ct. clk., 1968-76, magistrate judge, 1976-91, judge Des Moines, 1991—2001, chief judge, 2001—06, sr. judge, 2006—. Adj. prof. law Drake U., 1973-76. Mem. Iowa State Bar Assn. (chmn. spl. commn. to revise Iowa exemption law 1968-70, mem. adv. com. 8th cir. ct. appeals 1988—). Office: US Dist Ct 422 US Courthouse 123 E Walnut St PO Box 9344 Des Moines IA 50306-9344

LONGSWORTH, ROBERT MORROW, language educator; b. Canton, Ohio, Feb. 15, 1937; s. Robert H. and Margaret Elizabeth (Morrow) L.; m. Carol Herndon, Aug. 16, 1958; children: Eric D., Margaret W., Ann E. AB, Duke U., 1958; MA, Harvard U., 1960, PhD, 1965. Asst. prof. Oberlin Coll., 1964-70, assoc. prof., 1970-75, prof. English, 1975—, emeritus prof., 2001—, dean Coll. Arts and Scis., 1974-84. Author: The Cornish Ordinalia, 1967, The Design of Drama, 1972 A Decade of Campus Language at Oberlin College, 2003; contbr. articles to profl. jours. Danforth Found. fellow Fellow Am. Coun. Learned Socs., Nat. Humanities Ctr.; mem. MLA, Medieval Acad. Am., Cornwall Archaeol. Soc., Phi Beta Kappa.

LONGWORTH, RICHARD COLE, journalist, writer; b. Des Moines, Mar. 13, 1935; s. Wallace Harlan and Helen (Cole) L.; m. Barbara Bem, July 19, 1958; children: Peter, Susan. BJ, Northwestern U., 1957; postgrad., Harvard U., 1968-69. Reporter UPI, Chgo., 1958-60, parliamentary corr. London, 1960-65, corr. Moscow, 1965-68, Vienna, 1969-72, diplomatic corr. Brussels, 1972-76; econ. and internat. affairs reporter Chgo. Tribune, 1976-86, bus. editor, econ. columnist, 1987-88, chief European corr., 1988-91, sr. writer, 1991—2002, sr. corr., 2002—03; internat. affairs commentator Sta. WBEZ-FM, Chgo., 1984—; exec. dir. Global Chgo. Ctr. of Chgo., Coun. on Fgn. Rels., 2003—06; sr. fellow Chgo. Coun. Global Affairs, 2006—. Adj. prof. Northwestern U., 1998—, guest scholar, 2001; disting. vis. scholar DePaul U., 2008-. Author: Global Squeeze: The Coming Crisis for First-World Nations, 1998, Global Chicago, 2000, Caught in the Middle: America's Heartland in the Age of Globalism, 2008. With U.S. Army, 1957-58. Nieman fellow, 1968-69; recipient award for econ. reporting U. Mo., 1978, 80, John Hancock, 1978, 79, 82, Gerald Loeb award for econ. reporting, 1979, Media award for econ. understanding Dartmouth Coll., 1979, award Inter-Am. Press Assn., 1979, Peter Lisagor award Sigma Delta Chi, 1979, Sidney Hillman award, 1985, Lowell Thomas award for travel writing, 1985, Beck award for fgn. corr., 1986, Domestic Reporting award, 1987, Overseas Press Club award, 1994, 97, Alumni Merit award Northwestern U., 2000, finalist, Pulitzer prize, 1979, 2003 Mem. Coun. Fgn. Rels. N.Y., Assn. Am. Corrs. in London, Internat. Music Found. (dir.), Ednl. Found. for Nuclear Sci. (dir.). Office: Chgo Coun Global Affairs 332 South Michigan Ave 11th Fl Chicago IL 60604 Office Phone: 312-821-7508. Business E-Mail: rlongworth@thechicagocouncil.org.

LONNGREN, KARL ERIK, electrical and computer engineering educator; b. Milw., Aug. 8, 1938; s. Bruno Leonard and Edith Irene (Osterlund) L.; m. Vicki Anne Mason, Feb. 16, 1963; children: Sondra Lyn, Jon Erik. BS in Elec. Engring., U. Wis., 1960, MS, 1962, PhD, 1964. Postdoctoral appointment Royal Inst. Tech., Stockholm, 1964-65; asst. prof. elec. engring. U. Iowa, Iowa City, 1965-67, assoc. prof., 1967-72, prof., 1972—. Vis. scientist Inst. Plasma Physics, Nagoya, Japan, 1972, Math Rsch. Ctr., Madison, 1976, Los Alamos (N.Mex.) Sci. Labs., 1979, 80, Inst. Space and Astron. Sci., Tokyo, 1981, Danish Atomic Energy, Riso, 1982, others. Author: Introduction to Physical Electronics, 1988, Electromagnetics with MATLAB, 1997; co-author: Introduction to Wave Phenomena, 1985, Fundamentals of Electromagnetics with MATLAB, 2005, 2d edit., 2007; co-editor: Solitons in Action, 1978. Recipient Disting. Svc. citation U. Wis. Madison, 1992. Fellow Am. Phys. Soc., IEEE Presbyterian. Office: U Iowa Dept Elec & Computer Engring Iowa City IA 52242 Home: 1 Oaknoll Ct Apt G657 Iowa City IA 52246-5250 Home Phone: 319-887-5204; Office Phone: 319-335-5959. E-mail: lonngren@engineering.uiowa.edu.

LONSBERG, JOHN V., lawyer; BA summa cum laude, U. Notre Dame, 1976; JD cum laude, U. Mich., 1979. Bar: Mo. 1979. Ptnr. Fulbright & Jaworski LLP, St. Louis, leader Mid. East practice. Mem.: Pi Sigma Alpha, Phi Beta Kappa. Office: Fulbright & Jaworski LLP 8000 Maryland Ave Ste 1190 Saint Louis MO 63105 Office Phone: 314-505-8800. Business E-Mail: jlonsberg@fulbright.com.

LOO, NANCY, newscaster; b. Hong Kong; m. Brian Jenkins; 2 children. BA in Broadcast Journalism, U. Oreg. Former journalist English-language news stations, Hong Kong and Japan, NY 1 News, NYC, 1992—94; former news anchor, reporter WABC-TV, NYC, 1994—2001; anchor morning and noon newscasts WFLD-TV (Fox Chicago), 2001—. Named Reporter/Anchor of the Yr., Women in Cable, 1994; recipient Emmy awards, NY Gov.'s award of excellence, 1992. Office: Fox Chicago WFLD-TV 205 N Michigan Ave Chicago IL 60601

LOOK, DONA JEAN, artist; b. Port Washington, Wis., Mar. 30, 1948; m. Kenneth W. Loeber. BA, U. Wis., Oshkosh, 1970. Art tchr. Dept. Edn., NSW, Australia, 1976-78; ptnr. Look and Heaney Studio, Byron Bay, NSW, 1978-80; studio artist Algoma, Wis., 1980—. One person shows include Perimeter Gallery, Chgo., 1991; exhibited in group shows Perimeter Gallery, Chgo., 1983, 93, 94, Phila. Mus. Art, 1984, Civic Fine Arts Mus., Sioux Falls, S.D., 1985, Dacotah Prairie Mus., Aberdeen, S.D., 1985, Bergstrom-Mahler Mus., Neenah, Wis., 1985, Lawton Gallery, U. Wis.-Green Bay, 1985, J. B. Speed Art Mus., Louisville, 1986, Laguna (Calif.) Art Mus., Am. Craft Mus., N.Y.C., 1985, 86, 87, 89, Ark. Arts Ctr. Decorative Arts Mus., Little Rock, 1987, Cultural Ctr., Chgo., 1988, Erie (Pa.) Art Mus., 1988, Maine Crafts Assn., Colby Coll. Mus. Art, 1989, Ft. Wayne (Ind.) Mus. Art, 1989, The Forum, St. Louis, 1990, Palo Alto (Calif.) Cultural Ctr., 1990, Neville Pub. Mus., Green Bay, Wis., 1992, Waterloo (Iowa) Mus. Art, 1993, Sybaris Gallery, Royal Oak, Mich., 1993, 95, Sun Valley Ctr. for Arts and Humanities, Ketchum, Idaho, 1995, Nat. Mus. Am. Art, Smithsonian Instn., Washington, 1995; represented in permanent collections The White House Collection, Phila. Mus. Art, MCI Telecomms. Corp., Inc., Washington, Am. Craft Mus., N.Y.C., Ark. Arts Ctr., Little Rock, C. A. Wustum Mus. Fine Arts, Racine, Erie Art Mus.; works included in publs. The White House Collection of American Crafts, 1995, Craft Today: Poetry of the Physical, 1986, International Crafts, 1991, FIBERARTS Design Book Four, 1991, The Tactile Vessel, 1989, Creative Ideas for Living, 1988, The Basketmaker's Art: Contemporary Baskets and Their Makers, 1986. Recipient 1st prize award Phila. Craft Show, 1984, 2d prize award, 1985, Design award Am. Craft Mus., 1985, Craftsmen's award Phila. Craft Show, 1986; Nat. Endowment for Arts/Arts Midwest fellow, 1987, Nat. Endowment for Arts Fellowship grantee, 1988. Office: Perimeter Gallery 210 W Superior St Chicago IL 60610-3508

LOOMAN, JAMES R., lawyer; b. Vallejo, Calif., June 5, 1952; s. Alfred R. and Jane M. (Halter) L.; m. Donna G. Craven, Dec. 18, 1976; children: Alison Marie, Mark Andrew, Zachary Michael. BA, Valparaiso U., Ind., 1974; JD, U. Chgo., 1978. Bar: Ill, 1978, U.S. Dist. Ct. (no dist.) Ill. 1978, U.S. Claims Ct. 1979. Assoc. Isham, Lincoln & Beale, Chgo., 1978—83, Sidley & Austin, Chgo., 1983—86; ptnr. Sidley Austin LLP, 1986—. Assoc. gen. counsel Comml. Fin. Assn., 2002—. Bd. dirs. Valparaiso U., Ind., 2006—. Fellow Am. Coll. Comml. Fin. Lawyers; mem. ABA, Chgo. Bar Assn. (chmn. comml. and fin. transactions com. 1996-97, 2002-03), Chgo. Athletic Assn., Skokie Country Club, Mid-Day Club, Univ. Club Chgo. Lutheran. Office: Sidley Austin LLP One South Dearborn St Chicago IL 60603-2003 Home Phone: 847-835-2457; Office Phone: 312-853-7133. Business E-Mail: jlooman@sidley.com.

LOORY, STUART HUGH, journalist; b. Wilson, Pa., May 22, 1932; s. Harry and Eva (Holland) L.; m. Marjorie Helene Dretel, June 19, 1955 (div. July 1995); children: Joshua Alan, Adam Edward, Miriam Beth; m. Nina Nikolaevna Kudriavtseva, Aug. 17, 1995. BA, Cornell U., 1954; MS with honors, Columbia U., 1958; postgrad., U. Vienna, Austria, 1958. Reporter Newark News, 1955-58, N.Y. Herald Tribune, 1959-61, sci. writer, 1961-63, Washington corr., 1963-64, fgn. corr. Moscow, 1964-66; sci. editor Metromedia Radio Stas., 1962-64, Moscow corr., 1964-66; sci. writer N.Y. Times, 1966; White House corr. Los Angeles Times, 1967-71; fellow Woodrow Wilson Internat. Center for Scholars, Washington, 1971-72; exec. editor WNBC-TV News, 1973; Kiplinger prof. pub. affairs reporting Ohio State U., Columbus, 1973-75; assoc. editor Chgo. Sun-Times, 1975-76, mng. editor, 1976-80; v.p., mng. editor Washington bur. Cable News Network, 1980-82, Moscow bur. chief, 1983-86, sr. correspondent, 1986, exec. producer, 1987-90; exec. dir. internat. rels. Turner Broadcasting System, Inc., Atlanta, 1988—; editor-in-chief CNN World Report, 1990-91; v.p., CNN, 1990-95; exec. v.p. Turner Internat. Broadcasting, Russia, 1993-97; v.p., supervising prodr. Turner Original Prodns., 1995. Lee Hills chair in free press studies U. Mo., Columbia, 1997—; lectr. in field. Author: (with David Kraslow) The Secret Search for Peace in Vietnam, 1968, Defeated: Inside America's Military Machine, 1973, (with Ann Imse) Seven Days That Shook the World: The Collapse of Soviet Communism, 1991; Editor IPI Report (Internat. Press Inst.), 1998-1999, IPI Global Journalist, 1999-2005, Global Journalist, 2005; contbr. articles mags. and encys. Recipient citation Overseas Press Club, 1966; Raymond Clapper award Congl. Press Gallery, 1968; George Polk award L.I.U., 1968; Du Mont award U. Calif. at Los Angeles, 1968; Distinguished Alumni award Columbia, 1969; 50th Anniversary medal Columbia Sch. Journalism, 1963; Edwin Hood award for diplomatic corr. Nat. Press Club, 1987; Pulitzer traveling scholar, 1958. Jewish. Office: U Mo Sch Journalism 132A Neff Annex Columbia MO 65211-1200 Office Phone: 573-884-1599. Business E-Mail: loorys@missouri.edu.

LOOYENGA, ROGER L., insurance company executive; BS, Minot State Coll. CLU, CPCU. Exec. v.p. Auto-Owners Ins. Co., Lansing, Mich., 1999—2004, chmn., CEO, 2004—. Trustee Am. Inst. for CPCU, 2004—, Ins. Inst. Am., 2004—. Office: Auto Owners Insurance Co 6101 Anacapri Blvd Lansing MI 48917

LOPATIN, DENNIS EDWARD, immunologist, educator; b. Chgo., Oct. 26, 1948; s. Leonard Harold and Cynthia (Shifrin) L.; m. Marie S. Ludmer, June 6, 1971 (div. 1983); 1 child, Jeremy; m. Constance Maxine McLeod, July 24, 1983. BS, U. Ill., 1970, MS, 1972, PhD, 1974. Postdoctoral fellow Northwestern U. Med. Sch., Chgo., 1974-75; rsch. scientist U. Mich., Ann Arbor, 1976-90, prof., 1982—. Contbr. articles to sci. jours. Mem. Am. Assn. Immunologists, Am. Soc. Microbiology, Internat. Assn. Dental Rsch., Sigma Xi. Office: U Mich Sch Dentistry 1011 N University Ave # 1078 Ann Arbor MI 48109-1078

LOPER, CARL RICHARD, JR., metallurgical engineer, educator; b. Wauwatosa, Wis., July 3, 1932; s. Carl Richard S. and Valberg (Sundby) Loper; m. Jane Louise Loehning, June 30, 1956; children: Cynthia Louise Loper Koch, Anne Elizabeth. BS in Metall. Engring., U. Wis., 1955, MS in Metall. Engring., 1958, PhD in Metall. Engring., 1961; postgrad., U. Mich., 1960. Metall. engr. Pelton Steel Casting Co., Milw., 1955-56; instr., rsch. assoc. U. Wis., Madison, 1956-61, asst. prof., 1961-64, assoc. prof., 1964-68, prof. metall. engring., 1968-88, prof. materials sci. and engring., 1988-2001, ret. prof. materials sci. and engring., 2001, assoc. chmn. dept. metall. and mineral engring., 1979-82; pres. CRL Corp., 1979—. Rsch. metallurgist Allis Chalmers, Milw., 1961; adj. prof. materials U. Wis., Milw., 2002—; cons., lectr. in field. Author: (book) Principles of Metal Casting, 1965; contbr. articles to profl. jours. Chmn. 25 Anniversary Ductile Iron Symposium, Montreal, Canada, 1973; pres. Ygdrasil Lit. Soc., 1989—90. Recipient Adams Meml. award, Am. Welding Soc., 1963, Howard F. Taylor award, 1967, Svc. citation, 1969, 1972, others, Silver medal award, Sci. Merit Portuguese Foundry Assn., 1978, medal, Chinese Foundrymen's Assn., 1989, E.J. Walsh Award, 2002, Merton Flemings award, Materials Processing Inst., 2006; fellow Foundry Ednl. Found., 1953—55, Wheelbrator Corp., 1960, Ford Found., 1960. Fellow: Am. Soc. Metals (chmn. 1969—70), Am. Inst. Mgmt.; mem.: Yedrasil-Norwegian-Am. Lit. Soc., Tau Beta Pi, Korean Inst. Metals and Materials (hon.), Foundry Ednl. Found. (E.J. Walsh award 2002), Am. Welding Soc., Am. Foundry Soc. (Wis. bd. dirs. 1967-70, 76-79, Foundry Ednl. Found. dirs. award 1994, Cast Iron Hon. Lecture 2006, Best Paper award 1966, 67, 85, John A. Penton gold medal 1972, Hoyt Meml. lectr. 1992, Aluminum Divsn. award sci. merit 1995), Blackhawk Country Club, Torske Klubben (bd. dirs., co-founder 1978—, Foundry Hall of Honor 2001), Gamma Alpha, Alpha Sigma Mu, Sigma Xi. Lutheran. Achievements include research in understanding the solidifcation and metallurgy of ferrous and non-ferrous alloys; solidification and cast iron metallurgy, education in metallurgy and materials science. Office Phone: 608-836-1296. Business E-Mail: loper@engr.wisc.edu.

LOPEZ, CAROLYN CATHERINE, physician; b. Chgo., Oct. 13, 1951; d. Joseph Compean and Angela (Silva) L. BS, Loyola U., Chgo., 1973; MD, U. Ill., 1978. Diplomate Am. Bd. Family Practice. Intern, resident Rush/Christ Hosp., Chgo., 1978-81; med. dir. Wholistic Health Ctr., Oak Lawn, Ill., 1981-82; clin. dir. Anchor HMO, Oak Brook, Ill., 1982-84, assoc. med. dir., 1984-87; med. dir. Chgo. Pk. Dist., 1987-91; v.p. Rush Access HMO, Chgo., 1992-93; asst. dean Rush Med. Coll., 1990-93; med. dir. Rush Access HMO, Chgo., 1991-93, v.p., 1992-93; v.p. for profl. affairs Rush Anchor HMO, 1993; sr. v.p. and chief med. officer Rush-Prudential Health Plans, 1993-95; chair dept. family practice Cook County Hosp., 1996—. Pres. Inst. Medicine, Chgo., 2006—; interim co-chief Cook County Bur. Health, 2006. Mem. Chgo. Bd. Health, 2004—; bd. govs. Inst. Medicine, Chgo., 2003—. Primary Care Policy fellow USPHS, 1993. Fellow: Inst. Medicine Chgo. (bd. govs. 2003—, pres. 2006—, 2006—); mem.: AMA, Am. Med. Women's Assn., Ill. Acad. Family Physicians (bd. dirs. 1987—89, spkr. 1990—91, bd. chair 1990—91, pres.-elect 1991—92, pres. 1992—93), Am. Acad. Family Physicians (alt. del. 1992—95, del. 1996—99, vice-spkr. 1999—2002, spkr. 2002—04). Roman Catholic. Avocations: swimming, cooking. Office: Cook County Hosp Dept Family Practice 1900 W Polk St Chicago IL 60612-3736

LOPICCOLO, JOSEPH, psychologist, educator, author; b. LA, Sept. 13, 1943; s. Joseph E. and Adeline C. (Russo) Lo P.; m. Leslie Joan Matlen, June 20, 1964 (div. 1978); 1 child, Joseph Townsend; m. Cathryn Gail Pridal, Dec. 20, 1980; 1 child, Michael James. BA with highest honors, UCLA, 1965; MS, Yale U., 1968, PhD, 1969. Lic. psychologist, Mo. Asst. prof. U. Oreg., Eugene, 1969-73; assoc. prof. U. Houston, 1973-74; prof. SUNY, Stony Brook, 1974-84, Tex. A&M U., College Station, 1984-87; prof. psychology U. Mo., Columbia, 1987—, chmn. dept., 1987-90. Vis. scholar Cambridge (Eng.) U., 1991. Author: Becoming Orgasmic, 1976, 2d edit., 1988, also book chpts.; editor: Handbook of Sex Therapy, 1978; contbr. numerous articles to profl. jours. Woodrow Wilson Found. fellow; NIH rsch. grantee, 1973-84 Fellow Am. Psychol. Assn.; mem. Internat. Acad. Sex Rsch., Soc. for Sci. Study of Sex (pres. 1983-84, Alfred Kinsey Meml. Rsch. award), Soc. for Sex Therapy and Rsch. (Masters and Johnson Rsch. award 1997), Phi Beta Kappa, Sigma Xi. Office: U Mo Dept Psychology 210 McAlester Hall Columbia MO 65211-2500 Office Phone: 573-882-7752. Business E-Mail: LoPiccoloJ@missouri.edu.

LOPRETE, JAMES HUGH, lawyer; b. Detroit, Sept. 17, 1929; s. James Victor and Effie Hannah (Brown) LoP.; m. Marion Ann Garrison, Sept. 11, 1952; children: James Scott, Kimberly Anne, Kent Garrison, Robert Drew. AB, U. Mich., 1951, JD with distinction, 1953. Bar: Mich. 1954. Practiced law, Detroit, 1954—; atty. Chrysler Corp., Detroit, 1953; assoc. Monaghan, LoPrete, McDonald, Yakima, Grenke & McCarthy, P.C. and predecessor firms, Detroit, 1954, mem. firm, 1966—2001, pres., 1979—2001; assoc. LoPrete & Lyneis PC, 2008. Bd. dirs. Drake's Batter Mix Co.; instr. legal writing Wayne State U., Detroit, 1955-57. Trustee scholarship fund U. Mich. Club of Detroit, 1961, pres., 1982—; trustee Samuel Westerman Found., 1971—, pres., 1984; trustee John R. and M. Margrite Davis Found.; pres., dir. Louis and Nellie Sieg Found., 2000—, Frank G. and Gertrude Dunlap Found., 2001— Named Disting. Alumnus, U. Mich. Club, Detriot. Fellow Am. Coll. Trust and Estate Counsel (litig. com. 1997-, state chair 2006-), Internat. Acad. Estate and Trust Law; mem. ABA, Oakland County Bar Assn., State Bar Mich. (chmn. probate and estate planning sect. 1977), Detroit Athletic Club (dir. 1983-88, sec. 1986-88), Orchard Lake Country Club, U. Mich. of Greater Detroit (pres. 1966). Avocations: travel, sailing, swimming. Home: 2829 Warner Dr Orchard Lake MI 48324-2449 Office: LoPrete & Lyneis PC 40950 Woodward Ave Ste 306 Bloomfield Hills MI 48304 Office Phone: 248-594-5770. Business E-Mail: bqasawa@lopreteandlyneispc.com.

LORCH, KENNETH F., lawyer; b. Indpls., July 24, 1951; BSBA, Washington U., 1973; JD, John Marshall Sch. Law, 1976. Bar: Ill. 1976, U.S. Dist. Ct. (no. dist.) Ill. 1977; CPA, Ill. Ptnr. Hamilton Thies Lorch & Hagnell LLP, Chgo. Mem. planned giving adv. coun. Chgo. Symphony Orch.; mem. Chgo. bd. Am. Technion Soc.; mem. Chgo. Coun. on Planned Giving; mem., exec. com. Coun. for Jewish Elderly; mem. profl. adv. com. Chgo. Cmty. Trust; mem. planned giving adv. coun. Lincoln Park Zoo, Chgo.; mem., prof. Affiliates Comm. Care. Mem. Chgo. Bar Assn. (exec. com., Cook County Probate Ct. rules and forms com., mem. legis. com., mem. probate practice com. 1991, mem. trust law com., chmn. estate planning com., mem. young lawyers sect. 1983-85), Chgo. Estate Planning Coun., Jewish Fedn. Chgo. (past chair profl. adv. com.). Office: Hamilton Thies Lorch & Hagnell LLP 200 S Wacker Dr Ste 3800 Chicago IL 60606 Home Phone: 847-251-3027; Office Phone: 312-650-8640. Business E-Mail: lorch@htlhlaw.com.

LORCH, ROBERT K., corporate financial executive; V.p. global picture tube bus. Thomson Multimedia; sr. v.p., CFO Marmon Group, 2002—. Exec. positions GE, RCA Corp.; with mgmt., fin., global gen. mgmt., sales and mktg., and strat. planning. Office: Marmon Group 225 Washington St Ste 1900 Chicago IL 60606

LORELL, BEVERLY H., medical products executive, consultant; BA with distinction, Stanford U., 1971; MD, Stanford Sch. Medicine, 1975. Intern to resident physician Stanford U. Hosp.; clin. rsch. fellowship, cardiology Mass. Gen. Hosp., Harvard Med. Sch.; dir., program in heart failure, also mem. interventional cardiology team Besth Israel Deaconess Med. Ctr.; prof., medicine Harvard U. Med. Sch.; v.p., chief med. tech. officer Guidant Corp., Indpls., 2003—06; sr. med. and policy advisor King & Spalding LLP, Washington,

2006—. Served as an advisor to the fed. govt., including svc. on study sect. of the NIH and Cardiovascular and Renal Drugs Adv. Com. of the FDA; lectr. at various heart conf. and symposiums around the world. Contbr. articles to profl. jours. Mem.: Besth Israel Intervention Cardiology Team, Am. Coll. Cardiology, Heart Failure Soc. of Am., Am. Heart Assn., Guidant Compass Bd. Office: King & Spalding LLP Ste 200 1700 Pennsylvania Ave. NW Washington DC 20006-4706 Office Phone: 202-383-8937. Office Fax: 202-626-3737. E-mail: blorell@kslaw.com.

LORENTZ, JOSHUA A., lawyer; b. Orlando, Fla., Feb. 12, 1975; BA in Polit. Sci., Ohio U., 1998, BS in Bio., 1997; JD, U. Dayton Sch. Law, 2001. Bar: Ohio 2001, US Dist. Ct. Southern Dist. Ohio 2001, US Ct. of Appeals Sixth Cir. 2001, US Ct. of Appeals Fed. Cir. 2001, US Patent and Trademark Office. Assoc. Dinsmore & Shohl LLP, Cin. Named one of Ohio's Rising Stars, Super Lawyers, 2006. Mem.: Licensing Exec. Soc., Am. Intellectual Property Law Assn., Ohio State Bar Assn., Cin. Bar Assn. Office: Dinsmore & Shohl LLP 255 E Fifth St Ste 1900 Cincinnati OH 45202-4700 Office Phone: 513-977-8564. Office Fax: 513-977-8141.

LORENZ, JOHN DOUGLAS, college official; b. Talmage, Nebr., July 2, 1942; s. Orville George and Twila Lucille (Larson) L.; m. Alice Louise Hentzen, Aug. 26, 1967; 1 child, Christian Douglas. BS, U. Nebr., 1965, MS, 1967, PhD, 1973. Systems analyst U. Nebr., Lincoln, 1967-73; asst. prof. Kettering U., Flint, Mich., 1973-74, assoc. prof., 1974-78, prof., 1978—, dept. head, 1984-87, asst. dean, 1986-88, provost, dean faculty, 1988-92, Richard L. Terrell prof. acad. leadership, 1990—, v.p. for acad. affairs, provost, 1992—, Robert and Claire Reiss prof. indsl. engring., 2002—. Cons. GM, Detroit, 1973-82, various orgns. Contbr. articles to profl. jours. Judge Internat. Sci. and Engring. Fair, various locations, 1989—. Mem. NSPE, Soc. Mfg. Engrs. (sr.), So. Automotive Engrs., Accreditation Bd. for Engring. and Tech., Am. Soc. Engring. Edn., Antique Auto Racing Assn., Model Engine Collectors Assn., Antique Model Race Car Club. Home: 8165 Shady Brook Ln Flushing MI 48433-3007 Office: Kettering U 1700 W 3rd Ave Flint MI 48504-4898 E-mail: jlorenz@kettering.edu.

LORENZ, KATHERINE MARY, bank executive; b. Barrington, Ill., May 1, 1946; d. David George and Mary (Hogan) L. BA cum laude, Trinity Coll., 1968; MBA, Northwestern U., 1971; grad., Grad. Sch. for Bank Adminstrn., 1977. Ops. analyst Continental Bank, Chgo., 1968, supr. ops. analysis, 1969—71, asst. mgr. customer profitability analysis, 1971—73, acctg. officer, mgr. customer profitability analysis, 1973—77, 2d v.p., 1976, asst. gen. mgr. contr.'s dept., 1977—80, v.p., 1980, contr. ops. and mgmt. svcs. dept., 1981—84, v.p., sector contr. retail banking, corp. staff and ops. depts., 1984—88, v.p., sr. sector contr. pvt. banking, centralized ops. and corp. staff, 1988—90, v.p., sr. sector contr. bus. analysis group/mgmt. acctg., 1990—94, mgr. contrs. dept. adminstrn. and tng., 1990—94; v.p., chief of staff to chief adminstrv. officer Bank Am. Ill., Chgo., 1994—96, sr. v.p., mgr. adminstrv. svcs., 1996—97, mng. dir., mgr. adminstrv. svcs., 1998—99; sr. v.p., Chgo. adminstrn. exec. Bank Am., 1999—. Mem.: Execs. Club Chgo. Office: Bank of Am ILI-231-13-20 231 S La Salle St Chicago IL 60697 Office Phone: 312-828-4756.

LORENZ, MARK C., automotive executive; BBA, U. Mich., 1972; MBA, Ctrl. Mich. U., 1986. Analyst, accts. payable GM, Flint, Mich., 1973, various pos. in mfg. and materials mgmt., including gen. supr. material handling and gen. supr. prodn. control, 1973—85, supt. materials, C-P-C Stamping Hamilton, Ohio, 1985—87; asst. mgr. tech. liaison office NUMMI, Fremont, Calif., 1987—89; advisor C-P-C Prodn. Systems GM, Warren, Mich., 1989—90, mgr. synchronous orgn., 1990—92, dir. materials mgmt., exptl. mfg., 1992—93, dir. materials mgmt. for N.Am. ops. prototype shops, 1993—96; exec. dir. PC&L Delphi Corp., Troy, Mich., 1996—98, v.p. in charge of PC&L, 1998—2000, v.p. ops. and logistics, 2000—. Mem. mfg. and engring. external adv. bd. Broad Grad. Sch. Mgmt. and Coll. Engring., Mich. State U.; mem.-at-large, bd. dirs. Nat. Safety Coun. Office: World Hdqrs Delphi Corp 5725 Delphi Dr Troy MI 48098-2815

LORENZO, ALBERT L., academic administrator; BS, U. Detroit, 1965, MBA, 1966; LLD (hon.), Walsh Coll. Accountancy and Bus. Adminstrn., 1987. Asst. dir. housing U. Detroit, 1964-65; staff acct. McManus, McGraw and Co., Detroit, 1964-66; asst. prof. acctg. Macomb Community Coll., Warren, Mich., 1966-68, bus. mgr., 1968-74, contr., 1974-75, v.p. bus., 1975-79, pres., 1979—. Lectr., pub. speaker, presenter in field. Dir. rsch. SBA, 1966; mem. Mayor's Adv. Com. Small Bus., Detroit, 1967-70, base-community coun. Selfridge Air NG, 1978-86, steering com. March of Dimes, 1980-86, adv. coun. Met. Affairs Corp., 1982—, Mich. Competitive Enterprise Task Force, 1988-90, adv. bd. Nat. Inst. Leadership Devel., 1988—, Community Growth Alliance Macomb County, 1982—, selection panel Heart of Gold ann. awards Southeastern Mich. United Way, 1990; chair div. II United Found., 1981; apptd. commr. State Mich. High Edn. Facilities Authority, 1988-90; bd. dirs. N.E. Guidance Community Mental Health Ctr., 1976-79, Mich. Nat. Bank Macomb, 1981-87, Indsl. Tech. Inst., 1982—; trustee Nat. Commn. Coop. Edn., 1985—; trustee St. Joseph Hosp., 1984-87, sec. 1985-87, mem. adv. bd. 1981-83. Recipient Resolution of Tribute Mich. State Senate, 1979, Italian-Am. Citizen Recognition award, 1980, Volkswagen Am. Recognition award, 1982, Excellence in Speech Writing award Internat. Assn. Bus. Communicators, 1988, Nat. Leadership award U. Tex., 1989, Thomas J. Peters Nat. Leadership award, 1989; named Pres. of Yr. Am. Assn. Women in Community and Jr. Colls., 1985. Mem. Am. Assn. Community and Jr. Colls., World Future Soc., Met. Mus. Art, Mich. Community Coll. Assn., Econ. Club Detroit. Office: 14500 E 12 Mile Rd Warren MI 48088-3870

LOSEE, JOHN FREDERICK, JR., manufacturing executive; b. Milw., Apr. 27, 1951; s. John Frederick and Helen (Joslyn) L.; m. Jane Agnes Trawicki, Aug. 25, 1973; children: icole Marie, John Michael. BSME, Marquette U., 1973, MS in Indsl. Engring., 1982. Registered profl. engr., Wis.; cert. numerical control mgr., Wis. Mfg. engr. OMC-Evinrude div. Outboard Marine Corp., Milw., 1975-78, mfg. engr. supr., 1978-80, mgr. tool engring., 1980-85, mgr. process and tool engring., 1985-86, dir. mfg. engring., 1986-88; v.p. ops. Rytec Corp., Jackson, Wis., 1988-90; v.p. adminstrn. Custom Products Corp., 1990-91; part-owner Nat. Mfg. Co. Inc., Milw., 1991-96; owner JFL Mfg., Inc., Sussex, Wis., 1996—. Mem. Numerical Control Soc., Soc. Mfg. Engrs., Computer and Automated Systems Assn. Republican. Roman Catholic. Home: W264 N6565 Hillview Dr Sussex WI 53089-3452 Office Phone: 262-820-9090. Personal E-mail: jflmfg27@aol.com.

LOSH, J. MICHAEL, former automotive company executive; b. 1946; BSME, Gen. Motors Inst., 1970; MBA, Harvard U., 1970. With GM, Detroit, 1964—2000, v.p., gen. mgr., 1984—94; exec. dir. fin. GM do Brasil SA, 1980-82; dep. mng. dir. GM de Mexico, 1982-84; exec. v.p., CFO GM, 1994—2000; non-exec. chmn. Metaldyne Corp., 2000—02; interim CFO Cardinal Health Inc., 2004—05. Bd. dir. AON, 2003—, MASCO Corp., TRW Corp., 2003—. Mailing: Bd Dir AON Corp 200 E Randolph St Chicago IL 60601

LOTHIAN, THOMAS A., state official; b. Cleve., Dec. 14, 1928; m. Carol Ann Lothian; children: Thomas, John. BS, Ohio State U., 1953; MS in Chemistry, Ill. Inst. Tech., 1965. Tchr. Wickliff H.S.; lab dir. dept. chemistry U. Ill., dir. dept. space utilization, exec. sec. dept. chemistry; trustee Williams Bay Village Bd., 1979—82; supr. Walworth County Bd., 1992—2002; state assemblyman Wis., 2002—. Dir. Comty. Action Inc., 1992—2002. Mem.: Internat. Lions Clubs. Republican. Office: State Capitol Rm 306 N PO Box 8952 Madison WI 53708-8952

LOTOCKY, INNOCENT HILARION, bishop emeritus; b. Petlykivci Stari, Buchach, Ukraine, Nov. 3, 1915; arrived in U.S., 1946; s. Stefan and Maria (Tytyn) L. Student, various religious insts., Ukraine; PhD in Sacred Theology, U. Vienna, Austria, 1994. Ordained priest Order of St. Basil the Great, 1940, superior-novice master Dawson, Pa., 1946—51, provincial superior US province NY, 1951—53, novice master Glen Cove, NY, 1958—60; pastor-superior St. George Ch., NYC, 1953—58; pastor St. Nicholas Ch., Chgo., 1960—62; pastor-superior Immaculate Conception Ch., Hamtramck, Mich., 1962—81, also tchr., 1962—81; ordained bishop, 1981; bishop St. Nicholas Ukrainian Cath. Eparchy, Chgo., 1981—93, bishop emeritus, 1993—. Provincial counselor U.S. province Order St. Basil, 1962—80, del. to gen. chpt. Rome, 1963. Active numerous civic orgns. Mem.: Nat. Council Cath. Bishops. Roman Catholic. Office: Eparchy of St Nicolas 2245 W Rice St Chicago IL 60622-4858 Office Phone: 773-276-5080. Office Fax: 773-276-6799.*

LOUCKS, KATHLEEN MARGARET, lawyer; b. Milw., 1971; Student, Bethel Coll., 1989—92; BA, U. Minn., Mpls., 1995; JD, William Mitchell Coll. Law, 1999. Bar: Minn. 1999, US Dist. Ct. (dist. Minn.), Iowa 2005. Assoc. Gislason & Hunter, L.L.P., Minnetonka. Named a Rising Star, Minn. Super Lawyers mag., 2006. Mem.: Minn. Trial Lawyers Assn., Minn. State Bar Assn., ABA, Minn. Women Lawyers, Hennepin County Bar Assn., Minn. Def. Lawyers Assn. Office: Gislason & Hunter LLP 701 Xenia Ave S Ste 500 Minneapolis MN 55416 Office Phone: 763-225-6000. E-mail: kloucks@gislason.com.

LOUGHEAD, JEFFREY LEE, physician; b. Mystic, Conn., May 11, 1957; s. Lawrence L. and Alice M. Loughead; m. Melinda K., Apr. 29, 1995; children: Brittany, Molly, Connor, Graham. BA, Miami U., 1979; MD, U. Cin., 1983; postgrad. in bus. adminstrn., Wright State U., 1997-98. Intern Children's Hosp. Med. Ctr., Cin., 1983-84, resident, 1984-86, chief resident, 1986-87; fellow in neonatal-perinatal medicine U. Cin., 1987-90; med. dir. spl. care unit Good Samaritan Hosp., Dayton, 1991-95; dir. quality assurance Children's Med. Ctr., Dayton, 1991-97, physician advisor nursing rsch. com., 1993-97, clin. dir., 1995-97; dir. neonatal intensive care unit Ctrl. Dupage Hosp.; dir. strategic ops. Midwest Neoped Assocs. Ltd., 1998—2005; dir. pediatrics Children's Meml. at Ctrl. Dupage Hosp., 2005—. Contbr. chpts. to books; nutrition editor: Neonatal Network, 2000—. Fellow Am. Coll. Nutrition (Young Investigator award 1988), Am. Acad. Pediatrics (diplomate pediatrics, neonatal perinatal medicine); mem. Phi Beta Kappa, Alpha Omega Alpha, Beta Gamma Sigma. Avocation: auto racing. Office: Ctrl Dupage Hosp 25 N Winfield IL 60190 Office Phone: 630-933-6602.

LOUGHNANE, DAVID J., lawyer; b. Chgo., Sept. 3, 1947; BA, U. Wis., 1969; student, U. So. Calif.; JD, Loyola U., 1972. Bar: Ill. 1972, Wis. 1972, U.S. Dist. Ct. (no. dist.) Ill., 1972. With Johnson & Bell, Chgo., 1996—. Author: Institutional Negligence, 1989. Mem. Am. Acad. Hosp. Attys., Def. Rsch. Inst. Office: Johnson & Bell Ste 4100 55 E Monroe Chicago IL 60603-5896

LOUGHREY, F. JOSEPH, manufacturing executive; b. Holyoke, Mass., Oct. 27, 1949; s. F. Joseph and Helen T. (Barrett) Loughrey; m. Deborah Jane Welsh, July 23, 1988; 1 stepchild, Blair Edward Boehmer. BA in Econs., African Studies, U. Notre Dame, 1971. Pres. AIESEC-U.S. Inc., NYC, 1971-73; mgr. corp. employment Cummins Engine Co., Columbus, Ind., 1974-75, mgr. internat. personnel, 1975-79, dir. personnel (mktg.), 1979-81, dir. personnel (mktg. and subs.), 1981-83, dir. internal mgmt., 1983-84; mng. dir. Holset Engring. Co. Ltd., Huddersfield, Eng., 1984-86; v.p. employee rels. Cummins Engine Co., Columbus, Ind., 1986-87, from. v.p. So. Ind. ops. to v.p. heavy duty engines, 1988-90, group v.p. worldwide ops., 1990-95, exec. v.p., group pres. indsl. and chief tech. officer, 1996-99, pres.-engine bus., 1999—2005, pres., COO, 2005—. Sr. mem. nat. adv. bd. Tauber Mfg. Inst. U. Mich.; vice. chmn. adv. coun. coll. arts and letters U. Notre Dame; pres. bd. disr. Developmental Svcs., Inc.; bd. dirs. Sauer-Danfoss, Inc., Cummins Found., Columbus Edn. Coalitim, 2003—, Cummins Inc.; chmn. Mfg. Inst., 2005—. Mem.: NAM (bd. dirs. 2002—), AIESEC Interna. (sr.), Conexus Ind. (chmn.). Democrat. Roman Catholic. Office: Cummins Inc PO Box 3005 Columbus IN 47202-3005 Office Phone: 812-377-5123. Business E-Mail: joe.loughrey@cummins.com.

LOUIS, KENNETH R.R. GROSS, academic administrator; m. Diana Louis; children: Amy Katherine, Julie Jeannette. BA, Columbia U., 1959, MA, 1960; PhD, U. Wis., 1964. Asst. prof. Ind. U., 1964—67, assoc. prof. English and Comparative Lit., 1967—73, prof., 1973—, assoc. chmn. comparative lit. dept., 1967—69, assoc. dean arts and scis., 1970—73, chmn. English dept., 1973—78, dean arts and scis., 1978—80, v.p. acad. affairs, 1980—2001, chancellor Bloomington, 1980—2001, sr. v.p. for acad. affairs, chancellor, 2004—. Active Friends of the Lilly Libr.; chair Com. on Instnl. Cooperation, 1986—2000; active Commn. for Downtown Revitalization, Inc., NEH Commn. Humanities and the Am. People. Mem.: AAUP, MLA, Coun. for Acad. Affairs, Nat. Assn. Univs. and Land Grant Colls., Monroe County Libr. Assn., North Ctrl. Assn., Nat. Coun. Tchrs. English, Christianity and Lit., Woodburn Guild, Univ. Club, Phi Beta Kappa. Office: Ind Univ Bloomington Bryan Hall 100 107 S Indiana Ave Bloomington IN 47405-7000 Office Phone: 812-855-9011. E-mail: grosloui@indiana.edu.

LOUSBERG, PETER HERMAN, former lawyer; b. Des Moines, Aug. 19, 1931; s. Peter J. and Otillia M. (Vogel) L.; m. JoAnn Beimer, Jan. 20, 1962; children: Macara Lynn, Mark, Stephen. AB, Yale U., 1953; JD cum laude, U. Notre Dame, 1956. Bar: Ill. 1956, Fla. 1972, Iowa 1985; cert. mediator, Iowa. Law clk. to presiding justice Ill. Appellate Ct., 1956-57; asst. states atty. Rock Island County, Ill., 1959-60; ptnr. Lousberg, Kopp, Kutsunis and Weng, P.C., Rock Island, Ill.; opinion commentator Sta. WHBF, 1973-74. Lectr., chmn. Ill. Inst. Continuing Edn.; lectr. Ill. Trial Lawyers seminars; chmn. crime and juvenile delinquency Rock Island Model Cities Task Force, 1969; chmn. Rock Island Youth Guidance Coun., 1964-69; mem. adv. bd. Ill. Dept. Corrections Juvenile Divsn., 1976; Ill. commr. Nat. Conf. Commrs. Uniform State Laws, 1976-78; treas. Greater Quad City Close-up Program, 1976-80; mem. nominations commn. U.S. Senate Judicial Nominations Commn. Ctrl. Dist., Ill., 1995; bd. visitors No. Ill. U. Coll. Law. Contbr. articles to profl. jours. Bd. dirs. Rock Island Indsl.-Comml. Devel. Corp., 1977-80; bd. govs. Rock Island Cmty. Found., 1977-82. 1st lt. USMC, 1957-59. Fellow Am. Bar Found. (rsch. adv. com., chair 1993-96, Ill. chair of fellows 1995—), Am. Coll. Trial Lawyers, Ill. Bar Found. (bd. dirs. 1986-93, chmn. fellows 1987-88); mem. ABA (ho. of dels. 1990-93, com. on client protection 1997—), Am. Law Inst., Ill. State Bar Assn. (bd. govs. 1969-74, 88-94, chmn. spl. survey com. 1974-75, com. on mentally disabled 1979-80, spl. com. on professionalism 1986-87, task force on professionalism 1987-89, atty.'s fees 1988, bd. dirs. 1989—, pres. 1992-93, pres./chair bd. Mutual Ins. Co. 1993-94), Rock Island Bar Assn., Assn. Trial Lawyers Am., Ill. Trial Lawyers Assn. (bd. mgrs. 1974-78), Am. Judicature Soc., Nat. Legal Aid and Defenders Assn. (regional coord. 1989-90), Ill. Inst. Continuing Legal Edn. (bd. dirs. 1980-83, chmn. 1981-82), Lawyers Trust Fund Ill. (bd. dirs. 1984-88), Fla. Bar Assn. (chmn. out-of-state practitioners com. 1985-86), Rock Island C. of C. (treas. 1975, pres. 1978), Quad Cities Coun. of C. of C. (1st chmn. 1979-80), Notre Dame Club, Quad Cities Club, Rotary (bd. dirs. Quad Cities). Roman Catholic. Office: 322 16th St Rock Island IL 61201-8626 Home: 6575 99th Way N Apt 22103 Saint Petersburg FL 33708-5500

LOUX, P. OGDEN, distribution company executive; b. 1942; Grad., Drexel U. Mgmt. positions GE; fin. mgmt. positions W.W. Grainger, Inc., Lake Forest, Ill., 1987—94, v.p. fin., 1994—96, sr. v.p. fin., CFO, 1997—2008, vice chmn., 2008—. Past bd. dir. Condell Med. Ctr. Office: WW Grainger Inc 100 Grainger Pkwy Lake Forest IL 60045-5201*

LOVE, JOSEPH LEROY, history professor, former cultural studies center administrator; b. Austin, Tex., Feb. 28, 1938; s. Joseph L., Sr. and Virginia (Ellis) Love; m. Laurie Reynolds, Dec. 23, 1978; children: Catherine R., David A.;children from previous marriage: James A., Stephen N. AB in Econs. with honors, Harvard U., 1960; MA in History, Stanford U., 1963; PhD in History with distinction, Columbia U., 1967. From instr. to prof. U. Ill., Urbana-Champaign, 1966—, dir. ctr. Latin Am. and Caribbean studies, 1993-99. Rsch. assoc. St. Anthony's Coll. Oxford U.; vis. prof. Pontifical Cath. U., Rio de Janeiro; presenter in field. Author: Rio Grande do Sul and Brazilian Regionalism, 1882-1930, 1971, São Paulo in the Brazilian Federation, 1889-1937, 1980, Crafting the Third World: Theorizing Underdevelopment in Rumania and Brazil, 1996; editor (with Robert S. Byars): Quantitative Social Science Research on Latin America, 1973; editor: (with Nils Jacobsen) Guiding the Invisible Hand: Economic Liberalism and the State in Latin American History, 1988; editor: (with Werner Baer) Liberalization and Its Consequences: A Comparative Perspective on Latin America and Eastern Europe, 2000; bd. editors Latin AM. Rsch. Rev., 1974—78, Hispanic Am. Hist. Rev., 1984—89, The Americas, 1995—99; contbr. articles to profl. jours. Fellow, Social Sci. Rsch. Coun., IREX, Guggenheim; vis. scholar, U. São Paulo, Inst. Ortega y Gasset, Madrid, U. Nova, Lisbon; Fulbright-Hays Rsch. grantee, Sr. Rsch. fellow, NEH, others, Sr. Univ. scholar, U. Ill., 1993—96. Mem.: Latin Am. Studies Assn., Conf. Latin Am. History (chair Brazilian studies com. 1973, mem. gen. com. 1983, Conf. prize 1971), Am. Hist. Assn. Unitarian Universalist. Office: U Ill Dept History 309 Gregory Hall 810 S Wright St Urbana IL 61801-3644 Office Phone: 217-333-3182. Business E-Mail: j-love2@uiuc.edu.

LOVE, LISA A., lawyer; b. 1959; BS, U. Tenn., Knoxville; JD, Salmon P. Chase Coll. of Law. Assoc. counsel, mgr. insurance ops. Cincinnati Insurance Co., 2000—03, sr. counsel, 2003—. Office: Cincinnati Insurance Co PO Box 145496 6200 S Gilmore Rd Cincinnati OH 45250

LOVEDAY, WILLIAM JOHN, hospital administrator; b. Lynn, Mass., Nov. 4, 1943; married. B, Colby Coll., 1967; MHA, U. Chgo., 1970. Adminstrv. asst. Meml. Med. Ctr., Long Beach, Calif., 1970—71, asst. adminstr., 1971—74, v.p., 1974—82, exec. v.p., 1982—88; pres., chief exec. officer Meth. Hosp. Ind., Inc., Indpls., 1988—97; pres., CEO Clarian Health Ptnrs., Inc., Indpsl., 1997—. Office: Clarian Health PO Box 1367 Indianapolis IN 46206-1367

LOVEJOY, PAUL ROBERT, lawyer, air transportation executive; b. Rochester, NY, Jan. 30, 1955; s. V. Paul and Jean M. Lovejoy; m. Susan Seyfarth, Dec. 30, 1978; 1 child, Kate Hightower. BA summa cum laude, New Eng. Coll., 1977; JD, Case Western Res. U., 1981. Bar: Ohio 1981, NY 1988, Ill. 2005. Assoc. Squire, Sanders & Dempsey, Cleve., 1981—89, ptnr., 1989—90; asst. gen. counsel Texaco Inc., White Plains, NY, 1990—99; ptnr. Weil, Gotshal & Manges, NYC, 1999—2003; sr. v.p., gen. counsel, sec. UAL Corp., Chgo., 2003—. Trustee New Eng. Coll., Henniker, NH, 1993—2002. Office: UAL Corp 77 W Wacker Dr Chicago IL 60601

LOVELL, EDWARD GEORGE, mechanical engineering educator; b. Windsor, Ont., Can., May 25, 1939; s. George Andrew and Julia Anne (Kopacz) Lovell; m. Roxann Engelstad; children: Elise, Ethan. BS, Wayne State U., 1960, MS, 1961; PhD, U. Mich., 1967. Registered profl. engr., Wis. Project engr. Bur. Naval Weapons, Washington, 1959, Boeing Co., Seattle, 1962; test engr. Ford Motor Co., Troy, Mich., 1960; instr. U. Mich., Ann Arbor, 1963-67; design engr. United Tech., Hartford, Conn., 1970; prof. engring. U. Wis., Madison, 1968—, chmn. dept. engring. mechanics and astronautics, 1992-95, assoc. chmn. dept. of mech. engring., 1999—. Cons. structural engring. to govt. labs., indsl. orgns., maj. textbook pubs., 1968— Contbr. numerous articles to profl. jours. Postdoctoral research fellow Nat. Acad. Sci., 1967; NATO Sci. fellow, 1973; NSF fellow, 1961 Mem. Wis. Fusion Tech. Inst., Wis. Ctr. for Applied Microelectronics, Sigma Xi, Tau Beta Pi, Phi Kappa Phi Office: U Wis Dept Mech Engring 1513 University Ave Madison WI 53706-1572

LOVIN, KEITH HAROLD, retired academic administrator, philosopher, educator; b. Clayton, N.Mex., Apr. 1, 1943; s. Buddie and Wanda (Smith) L.; m. Marsha Kay Gunn, June 11, 1966; children: Camille Jenay, Lauren Kay BA, Baylor U., 1965; postgrad., Yale U., 1965-66; PhD, Rice U., 1971. Prof. philosophy Southwest Tex. State U., San Marcos, 1970-77, chmn. dept. philosophy, 1977-78, dean liberal arts, 1978-81; provost, v.p. acad. affairs Millersville U., Pa., 1981-86; provost, v.p. acad. and student affairs U. So. Colo., Pueblo, 1986-92; pres. Maryville U. St. Louis, 1992—2005, pres. emeritus, 2005—. Adv. bd. Southwest Studies in Philosophy, 1981—90. Contbr. articles to profl. jours. Bd. dirs. St. Louis Symphony Orch., 1995-2001, United Way Greater St. Louis, 1992-99, Boys Hope, Jr. Achievement Mississippi Valley, Inc., 1992-2001, Nat. Coun. Alcohol and Drug Abuse Adv. Bd., St. Louis Intercollegiate Athletic Conf., Higher Edn. Coun., St. Luke's Hosp., vice-chmn., 2001-03, chmn., 2003—; bd. dirs., pres. Ind. Colls. and Univs. Mo., 1999-2002, vice chair, 2002-03; mem. pres.'s adv. com. Mo. Coordinating for Bd. Higher Edn., 2002-05; trustee KETC Channel 9, 2003—05. Mem.: Chesterfield C. of C., Gov. Bus. Edn. Roundtable, St. Louis Club. Avocation: fly fishing. Home: 3006 Hawthorne Cove Georgetown TX 78628 Office Phone: 512-869-2053. Personal E-mail: klovin@yahoo.com.

LOVING, CHARLES ROY, museum director, curator; b. Waukesha, Wis., June 2, 1957; s. Wesley E. and Ruth A. (Zieskie) L.; m. Annick P. Gendre, Apr. 28, 1984. BFA, U. Wis., 1980; MFA, U. Utah, 1982, MA, 1985. Asst. coord. Utah Arts Coun., Salt Lake City, 1982-84; asst. dir. Utah Mus. of Fine Arts, Salt Lake City, 1984—, Snite Mus. Art, U. Notre Dame, dir., curator modern sculpture, 1999—. Juror Park City (Utah) Arts Festival, 1985-90; grants reviewer Inst. Mus. Svcs., Washington, 1988-89. Curator (exhibit) Power Dressing, 1989; co-curator (exhibit) Recent Fires, 1990. Bd. dirs. Utah Citizens for the Arts, Salt Lake City, 1984-88, Salt Lake City Art Design Bd., 1987—, Moab (Utah) Arts Ctr., 1990—. Mem. Am. Assn. Mus. (state rep.), Utah Fundraising Soc. Office: Snite Mus Art U Notre Dame PO Box 368 Notre Dame IN 46556-0368 E-mail: loving.1@nd.edu.

LOW, ROBERT E., transportation executive; Student, U. Mo. Founder, pres. Prime, Inc., Urbana, Mo., 1970-80, Springfield, Mo., 1980—. Avocations: golf, horse racing, basketball, gaming. Office: Prime Inc 2740 N Mayfair Ave Springfield MO 65803-5084

LOWE, ALLEN, state legislator; Rep. Dist. 105 Mich. Ho. of Rep., 1993-98; city mgr. Grayling, Mich., 2000—. Home: 1101 Ottawa St Grayling MI 49738-1323

LOWE, JOHN BURTON, medical association administrator, molecular biologist, educator, pathologist; b. Sheridan, Wyo., June 13, 1953; s. Burton G. and Eunice D. Lowe. BA, U. Wyo., 1976; MD, U. Utah, 1980. Diplomate Am. Bd. Pathology. Asst. med. dir. Barnes Hosp. Blood Bank, St. Louis, 1985-86; instr. Sch. of Medicine Washington U., St. Louis, 1985, asst. prof. Sch. of Medicine, 1985-86; asst. investigator Howard Hughes Med. Inst., Ann Arbor, Mich., 1986-92, assoc. investigator, 1992-96, investigator, 1997—2005; asst. prof. Med. Sch. U. Mich., Ann Arbor, 1986-91, assoc. prof. Med. Sch., 1991-95, prof. Med. Sch., 1995—2005; Henry Willson Payne prof. and chair dept. pathology Case Western Res. U. Sch. Medicine, Cleve., 2005—, prof., chmn. dept. pathology, 2005. Dep. editor Jour. Clin. Investigation, 1997—2002, mem. editl. bd. FEBS Jour., 2001—; contbr. articles to profl. jours. including Jour. Biol. Chemistry, Genes and Devel., Nature, Cell, Sci. Fellow: AAAS; mem.: Am. Assn. Physicians, Am. Soc. Clin. Investigation. Office: Dept Pathology Case We Reserve Univ Sch Medicine 10900 Euclid Ave Cleveland OH 44106-7288

LOWE, KENNETH W., multimedia executive; BA radio, television, motion pictures, UNC. With Southern Broadcasting, 1969, Harte-Hanks Broadcasting, 1970—80; gen. mgr., Radio Properties E.W. Scripps Co., 1980—88, v.p., programming, promotion, marketing, 1988—94; CEO Scripps Network, 1994—2000; pres., CEO E.W. Scripps Co., 2000—. Bd. dir. Greater Cincinnati Chamber of Commerce; chmn. Cincinnati USA Partnership; bd. dir. Cincinnati Center City Development Center; trustee Fine Arts Fund; bd. of advisors U.N.C. Dept. of Communication. Office: c/o EW Scripps 312 Walnut Street 2800 Scripps Center Cincinnati OH 45202

LOWE, MARVIN, artist, educator; b. Bklyn., May 19, 1922; m. Juel Watkins, Apr. 1, 1949; 1 dau., Melissa. Student, Julliard Sch. Music, 1952-54; BA, Bklyn. Coll., 1956; MFA, U. Iowa, 1961. Prof. fine arts Ind. U., Bloomington, 1968-92, prof. emeritus, 1992—. Vis. artist-lectr., 1970-91. Exhibited in 64 one-person shows; over 200 group and invitational exhbns.; participated in U.S. info. exhbns. in Latin Am., Japan, USSR, and most European countries; represented in 84 permanent collections including Phila. Mus. Art, Bklyn. Mus., Smithsonian Instn., Brit. Mus., Japan Print Assn., N.Y.C. Pub. Libr., Calif. Palace Legion of Honor, San Francisco, Boston Pub. Libr., Columbia U., Libr. of Congress, Indpls. Mus. Art, Ringling Mus., Honolulu Acad. Art, Ft. Wayne Mus. Art, Purdue U. Mus. Fine Art, Springfield, Mass, Retrospective exhbn. Ind. U. Art Mus., 1998 Served with USNR, 1942-45. Fellow Nat. Endowment for Arts, 1975; fellow Ford Found., 1979, Ind. Arts Commn., 1987; recipient numerous Purchase awards, 1960—; grantee: Ind. Arts. Commn., 1997, Florsheim, 1997. Office: Ind U Sch Fine Arts Bloomington IN 47405

LOWELL, SCOTT, restaurant manager, real estate developer; b. 1967; m. Carolyn Howard. Degree in Bus., Wayne State U., 1993. Pres. Traffic Jam & Snug, Detroit, 1998—, Pied A Terre Inc., Detroit; ptnr. Bronx Bar, Detroit, Cliff Bell's, Detroit, 2006—. Named one of 40 Under 40, Crain's Detroit Bus., 2006. Mem.: U. Cultural Ctr. Assn. (bd. mem.). Office: Traffic Jam & Snug 511 W Canfield Detroit MI 48201 Office Phone: 313-831-9470.

LOWENBERG, DAVID A., pharmaceutical executive; Pres. Healthcare Devel. Consulting; sr. v.p., dir. site ops. Express Scripts, Inc., Md. Heights, Mo., 1993—99, exec. v.p., COO, 1999—2006, CEO CuraScript, Inc., 2006—; dep. dir. Ariz. Health Care Cost Containment Sys. Bd. dirs. Logos Sch. Office: Express Scripts Inc 13900 Riverport Dr Maryland Heights MO 63043

LOWERY, CHRISTOPHER M., men's college basketball coach; b. Evansville, Ind., July 7, 1972; m. Erika Lowery. B in Phys. Edn., So. Ill. U., 1995. Asst. coach Rend Lake CC, Ina, Ill.; head coach Mo. So. State Coll.; asst. coach S.E. Mo. State, U. Ill., 2003, So. Ill. U., Carbondale, head coach, 2004—. Named a Divsn. I All-Dist. Coach (Dist. 11), Nat. Assn. Basketball Coaches, 2007; named Mo. Valley Conf. Coach of Yr., 2005, 2007. Office: Intercollegiate Athletics So Ill U Mailcode 6620 Carbondale IL 62901 Office Phone: 618-453-4667. E-mail: cmlowery@siu.edu.

LOWERY, DOUG, principal; BS in Edn., Ohi9o Dominican Coll.; MA in Edn. Adminstrn., U. Dayton. Prin. Hilliard Meml. Middle Sch., Ohio. Mem.: Nat. Assn. Secondary Sch. Principals (bd. dirs., Ohio Meddle Level Prin. of Yr. 2003, Nat. Middle Level Prin. of Yr. 2004). Avocations: farming, horseback riding, coaching, team roping. Office: Hilliard Meml Middle School 5600 Scioto Darby Rd Hilliard OH 43026 Office Phone: 614-334-3057. Office Fax: 614-334-3058. E-mail: Doug_Lowery@hboe.org.

LOWERY, ELIZABETH, automotive executive; b. New Britain, Conn., Oct. 24, 1955; BBA cum laude, Ea. Mich. U., 1978; JD magna cum laude, Wayne State U., 1981. Ptnr. Honigman Miller Schwartz and Cohn; law clerk Mich. Supreme Ct. Chief Justice G. Mennen Williams, 1981—83; atty. GM, 1989—94, practice area mgr. environ. and energy, 1994—97, v.p. N.Am., gen. counsel, 1997—2000, v.p. environ. and energy, 2000—. Bd. dirs. World Environ. Ctr., Keystone Ctr., Haven, Women's Leadership Forum. Named One of 100 Most Influential Women, Crain's Detroit Bus., 2002. Office: GM Corp 300 Renaissance Ctr Detroit MI 48265-3000

LOWINGER, FREDERICK CHARLES, lawyer; b. Chgo., July 18, 1955; s. Alexander I. and Muriel (Rosencranz) L.; m. Lynn T. Wollins, July 12, 1981; children: Lauren, Daniel, Stephen. BS in Acctg., MS in Acctg., U. Pa., 1977; JD, U. Chgo., 1980. CPA. Bar: Ill. 1982. Law clk. to Judge J. Skelly Wright US Ct. Appeals (DC cir.), Washington, 1980-81; clk. to Justice William J. Brennan Jr. US Supreme Ct., Washington, 1981-82; assoc. Sidley & Austin, Chgo., 1982—88; ptnr. Sidley Austin LLP, Chgo., 1988—, mem. exec. com., 1996—, head, Chgo. office corp. group, 1999—. Dir. Jewish Vocat. Svc., Chgo., 1993-98. Mem. ABA, Chgo. Bar Assn., Lawyers Club Chgo. Avocations: golf, skiing. Office: Sidley Austin LLP One S Dearborn St Chicago IL 60603 Office Phone: 312-853-7238. Office Fax: 312-853-7036. Business E-Mail: flowinger@sidley.com.

LOWRIE, WILLIAM G., former oil company executive; b. Painesville, Ohio, Nov. 17, 1943; s. Kenneth W. and Florence H. (Strickler) L.; m. Ernestine R. Rogers, Feb. 1, 1969; children: Kristen, Kimberly. BChemE, Ohio State U., 1966. Engr. Amoco Prodn. Co. subs. Standard Oil Co. (Ind.), New Orleans, 1966-74, area supt., Lake Charles, La., 1974-75, div. engr., Denver, 1975-78, div. prodn. mgr., Denver, 1978-79, v.p. prodn., Chgo., 1979-83; v.p. supply and marine transp. Standard Oil Co. (Ind.), Chgo., 1983-85; pres., Amoco Can., 1985-86; sr. v.p. prodn., Amoco Prodn. Co., 1986-87, exec. v.p. USA, 1987-88; exec. v.p. Amoco Oil Co., Chgo., 1989-90, pres., 1990-92; pres. Amoco Prodn. Co., 1992-94; exec. v.p. E&P sector Amoco Corp., 1994-95, pres. 1996-98, dep. CEO BP Amoco. Bd. dirs. Jr. Achievement, Northwestern Meml. Corp.; trustee, bd. dirs. Nat. 4-H Coun. Named Outstanding Engring. Alumnus, Ohio State U., 1979, Disting. Alumnis Ohio State U., 1985. Mem. Am. Petroleum Inst., Soc. Petroleum Engrs., Mid-Am. Club (Chgo.). Republican. Presbyterian.

LOWTHER, GERALD HALBERT, lawyer; b. Slagle, La., Feb. 18, 1924; s. Fred B. and Beatrice (Halbert) L.; children by previous marriage: Teresa, Craig, Natalie, Lisa. AB, Pepperdine Coll., 1951; JD, U. Mo., 1951. Bar: Mo. 1951. Since practiced in, Springfield; ptnr. firm Lowther, Johnson, Joyner, Lowther, Cully & Housley. Mem. Savs. and Loan Commn. Mo., 1965-68, Commerce and Indsl. Commn. Mo., 1967-73; lectr. U. Tex., 1955-57, Crested Butte, Colo., 1958-59 Contbr. articles law jours. Past pres. Ozarks Regional Heart Assn.; Del., mem. rules com. Democratic Nat. Conv., 1968; treas. Dem. Party Mo., 1968-72, mem. platform com., 1965, 67, mem. bi-partisan commn. to reapportion Mo. senate, 1966; Bd. dirs. Greene County Guidance Clinic, Ozark Christian Counseling Service, Greene County, Mo.; past pres. Cox Med. Center. Served with AUS, 1946-47; Col. staff of Gov. Hearnes 1964, 68, Mo. Mem. ABA, Mo. Bar Assn., Greene County Bar Assn., Def. Orientation Conf. Assn., Internat. Assn. Ins. Counsel, Def. Rsch. Inst., Springfield C. of C. Clubs: Kiwanian (pres. 1962), Quarterback (pres. 1958), Tip Off (pres. 1960). Office: 540 Foggy River Rd Hollister MO 65672

LOWTHIAN, PETRENA, academic administrator; b. Feb. 10, 1931; d. Leslie Irton and Petrena Lowthian; m. Clyde Hennies (div.); children: David L. Hennies, Geoffrey L. Hennies; m. Nisson Mandel. Grad., Royal Acad. Dramatic Art, London, 1952. Retail career with various orgns., London and Paris, 1949-57; founder, pres. Lowthian Coll. divsn. Lowthian Inc., Mpls., 1964-97. Mem. adv. coun. Minn. State Dept. Edn., St. Paul 1974-82; mem. adv. bd. Mpls. Comty. Devel. Agy., Mpls., 1983-85; mem. Downtown Coun. St. Paul, 1972, chmn. retail bd., 1984-92; mem. Bd. Bus. Indsl. Advisors U. Wis.-Stout, Menomonie, 1983-89. Mem. Fashion Group, Inc. (regional bd. dirs. 1980), Rotary (mem. career and econ. edn. 1988—). Address: 10 Creekside Dr Long Lake MN 55356-9431

LOYD, WARD EUGENE, lawyer; b. Henderson, Ky., Feb. 8, 1943; s. Ward Beecher Loyd and Maxine Watkins; m. Suzanne Keeler, Dec. 29, 1966; children: Katherine Marie, Keele Suzanne. BA, Southwestern Coll., 1965; JD with honors, Washburn U., Kans., 1968. Bar: Kans. 1968, US Dist. Ct. Kans. 1968, US Ct. Appeals (10th cir.) 1969. Pvt. practice, Garden City, Kans., 1968—; mem. Kans. Ho. of Reps., 1998—2006. Gen. counsel Garden City Urban Renewal Agy., 1969-75, Garden City Pub. Sch. Sys., 1972-91, Garden City C.C., 1971-, S.W. Kans. Area Coop., Ensign, 1995—; mem. Kans. Supreme Ct. Stds. Com., Topeka, 1980, Kans. Supreme Ct. Client Protection Fund Commn., 2000-06, Kans. Supreme Ct. child support guidelines adv. commn., 2002-06, bd. dirs. Western State Bank, Garden City; chmn. Kans. Criminal Justice Recodification, Rehab. and Restoration Commn., 2004-07, Kans. Reentry Policy Coun., 2006-07, Kans. Adv. Group Juvenile Justice and Delinquency Prevention, 2006—; co-chmn. Pub. Safety and Justice Task Force, 2005-06; mem. governing body/exec. bd. Coun. State Govts., 2004-06; mem. Interstate Migrant Edn. Coun., 2005-2007. Comments editor Washburn Law Jour., 1967-68. City commr. City of Garden City, 1985-89, 90-94, 97, mayor, 1986, 88; mem. First United Meth. Ch., Garden City; past bd. mem., past pres. Cmty. Day Care Ctr.; past mem. Kans. League Municipalities. Recipient Award of Merit, Garden City Area C. of C., 1992, Outstanding Pub. Ofcl. of Yr., Kans. Assn. Addition Profls., 2003, Intergovtl. Leadership award League of Kans. Municipalities, 2006. Fellow Kans. Bar Found.; mem. Nat. Assn. Sch. Bds. (coun. sch. attys.), Kans. Bar Assn. (mem. ethics com. 1978-82), S.W. Kans. Bar Assn. (pres. 1986-88, sec. 1992-93, dir.), Kans. Sch. Attys. Assn. (regional dir. 1980-84), Kans. Assn. Def. Counsel, Finney County Bar Assn., Garden City C. of C. (bd. dirs. 1990-92), Phi Alpha Delta (justice 1968). Republican. Home: 2203 Center Garden City KS 67846-3525 Office: Ward Loyd Law Office LLC PO Box 834 118 W Pine St Garden City KS 67846-5444 Office Phone: 620-275-1415. Business E-Mail: loyd@gcnet.com.

LOYND, RICHARD BIRKETT, consumer products company executive; b. Norristown, Pa., Dec. 1, 1927; s. James B. and Elizabeth (Geigus) L.; m. Jacqueline Ann Seubert, Feb. 3, 1951; children: Constance, John, Cynthia, William, James, Michael. BS in Elec. Engring., Cornell U., 1950. Sales engr. Lincoln Electric Co., Cleve., 1950-55; with Emerson Electric Co., St. Louis, 1955-68, pres. Builder Products div., 1965-68, v.p. Electronics and Space div., 1961-65; v.p. ops. Gould, Inc., Chgo., 1968-71; exec. v.p. Eltra Corp., NYC, 1971-74, pres., 1974-81; chmn. Converse, Inc., 1982-88; CEO Furniture Brands Internat., Inc (formerly Interco Inc.), St. Louis, 1989-96; chmn. Interco Inc., St. Louis, 1989-98; chmn. exec. com. Furniture Brands Internat. Inc., St. Louis, 1998—, mem. gov. and nominating com. Home: 19 Randall Dr Short Hills NJ 07078-1957 Office: Furniture Brands Internat Inc 101 S Hanley Rd Saint Louis MO 63105-3406

LOZANO, RUDOLPHO, federal judge; b. East Chgo., Ind., 1942; BS in Bus., Ind. U., 1963, LLB, 1966. Mem. firm Spangler, Jennings, Spangler & Dougherty, P.C., Merrillville, Ind., 1966-88; judge U.S. Dist. Ct. (no. dist.) Ind., Hammond, 1988—2007; sr. judge US Dist. Ct. (no. dist.) Ind., 2007—. With USAR, 1966-73. Mem. ABA, Ind. State Bar Assn., Def. Rsch. Inst. Office: US Dist Ct 205 Fed Bldg 507 State St Hammond IN 46320-1533

LOZOFF, BETSY, pediatrician, educator; b. Milw., Dec. 19, 1943; d. Milton and Marjorie (Morse) L.; 1 child, Claudia Brittenham. BA, Radcliffe Coll., 1965; MD, Case Western Res. U., 1971, MS, 1981. Diplomate Am. Bd. Pediat. From asst. prof. to prof. pediatrics Case Western Res. U., Cleve., 1974-93; prof. pediat. U. Mich., Ann Arbor, 1993—, dir. Ctr. Human Growth and Devel., 1993—2004, rsch. prof. Ctr. Human Growth and Devel., 2004—. Recipient Rsch. Career Devel. award Nat. Inst. Child Health and Human Devel., 1984-88. Fellow Am. Acad. Pediatrics; mem. Soc. for Pediatric Rsch., Soc. Rsch. in Child Devel. (program com. 1991-97), Soc. Behavioral Pediatrics (exec. com. 1985-88), Ambulatory Pediatric Soc. Office: Univ Mich Ctr Human Growth and Devel 300 N Ingalls St Ann Arbor MI 48109-2007 Office Phone: 734-764-2443. E-mail: blozoff@umich.edu.

LU, YI, chemistry professor; BS, Beijing Univ.; PhD, UCLA; postdoctoral rsch., Calif. Inst. Tech. Assoc. prof., dept. chem., dept. biochem. and computational biology Univ. Ill. Urbana-Champaign. Faculty Environ. Coun., Ctr. for Nanoscale Sci., Tech., Univ. Ill. Urbana-Champaign; rsch. prof. Howard Hughes Med. Inst., 2002—. Adv. bd. Jour. of Biological Inorganic Chemistry; contbr. articles to profl. journals. Recipient Nat. Sci. Found. Career award, Arnold and Mabel Beckman Young Investigator award, 1996, Rsch. Corp. Cottrell Scholars award, 1997, Alfred P. Sloan Rsch. Fellowship, 1998, Camille Dreyfus Teacher-Scholar award, 1999, Howard Hughes Med. Inst. grant, 2002. Office: Dept Chem A322 Chem & Life Sci Univ Ill 600 S Mathews Ave Urbana IL 61801 Office Phone: 217-333-2619. Office Fax: 217-333-2685. Business E-Mail: yi-lu@uiuc.edu.

LUBAWSKI, JAMES LAWRENCE, healthcare consultant; b. Chgo., June 4, 1946; s. Harry James and Stella Agnes (Pokorny) L.; m. Kathleen Felicity Donnellan, June 1, 1974; children: Kathleen N., James Lawrence, Kevin D., Edward H. BA, Northwestern U., 1968, MBA, 1969, MA, 1980. Asst. prof. U. Northern Iowa, Cedar Falls, 1969-72; instr. Loyola U., Chgo., 1974-76; dir., market planning Midwest Stock Exchange, Chgo., 1976-77; dir. mktg. Gambro Inc., Barrington, Ill., 1977-79; mktg. mgr. Travenol Labs., Deerfield, Ill., 1979-82; dir. mktg. Hollister Inc., Libertyville, Ill., 1982-84; pres., chief exec. officer Neomedica Inc., Chgo., 1984-86; v.p. bus. devel. Evangl. Health Svcs., Oak Brook, Ill., 1986-87; pres., chief exec. officer Cath. Health Alliance Met. Chgo., 1987-95; mng. dir. Ward Howell Internat., Chgo., 1995-98; v.p. A.T. Kearney, Chgo., 1998-2000; pres. Zwell Internat., Chgo., 2000—02; founder Lubawski & Assocs., Northfield, 2002—. Author: Food and Man, 1974, Food and People, 1979; co-editor: Consumer Behavior in Theory and in Action, 1970. Mem. Evanston Golf Club (pres. 2000-02). Avocations: golf, fishing. Office: 1765 Maple St Ste 15 Northfield IL 60093 Office Phone: 847-441-7300. Personal E-mail: Jim@Lubawski.com.

LUBBEN, DAVID J., retired lawyer; b. Cedar Rapids, Iowa, 1951; BA, Luther Coll., 1974; JD, U. Iowa, 1977. Bar: Minn. 1977. Ptnr. Dorsey & Whitney LLP, Mpls., 1977—96; gen. counsel, sec. UnitedHealth Group, Inc., Minnetonka, Minn., 1996—2006.

LUBBERS, AREND DONSELAAR, retired academic administrator; b. Milw., July 23, 1931; s. Irwin Jacob and Margaret (Van Donselaar) L.; m. Eunice L. Mayo, June 19, 1953 (div.); children— Arend Donselaar, John Irwin Darrow, Mary Elizabeth; m. Nancy Vanderpol, Dec. 21, 1968; children— Robert Andrew, Caroline Jayne. AB, Hope Coll., 1953; AM, Rutgers U., 1956; LittD, Central Coll., 1977; DSc, U. Sarajevo, Yugoslavia, 1987; LHD, Hope Coll., 1988; DSc, Akademia Ekonomiczna, Krakow, Poland, 1989, U. Kingston Univ., Eng., 1995. Rsch. asst. Rutgers U., 1954-55; rsch. fellow Reformed Ch. in Am., 1955-56; instr. history and polit. sci. Wittenberg U., 1956-58; v.p. devel. Central Coll., Iowa, 1959-60, pres., 1960-69, Grand Valley State U., Allendale, Mich., 1969-2001; ret., 2001. Mem. Am. Assn. State Colls. and Univs. seminar in India, 1971, Fed. Commn. Orgn. Govt. Conduct Fgn. Policy, 1972; USIA insp., Netherlands, 1976; mem. pres.'s commn. NCAA, 1984-87, 89—, chmn. pres.'s commn., 1998-2002; bd. dirs. Grand Bank, Grand Rapids, Mich., Macatawa Bank; cons. Grand Valley State U., Hackley Hosp., Olivet Coll., Pierce Cedar Creek Inst. Environ. Rsch. and Edn. Student Cmty. amb. from Holland (Mich.) to Yugoslavia, 1951; bd. dirs. Grand Rapids Symphony, 1976-82, 99, Butterworth Hosp., 1988; chmn. divsn. II NCAA Pres.'s Commn., 1992-95, 98-99, mem. pres.'s coun., 1997; mem. Michigan Cmty. Svc. Commn., 2001-; mem. exec. com. West Mich. Sports Commn., 2007. Recipient Golden Plate award San Diego Acad. Achievement, 1962, Golden-Emblem Order of Merit Polish Peoples Republic, 1988, trustee's award cmty. leadership Aquinas Coll., 1998, Lifetime Achievement award Econ. Club Grand Rapids, 2001; named 1 of top 100 young men in U.S. Life mag., 1962. Mem. Mich. Coun. State Univs. Pres. (chmn. 1988, 2000—), Grand Rapids World Affairs Council (pres. 1971-73), Phi Alpha Theta, Pi Kappa Delta, Pi Kappa Phi. Home: 4195 N Oak Pointe Ct Grand Rapids MI 49525 Office Phone: 616-331-6607. Business E-Mail: lubbers@gvsu.edu.

LUBBERS, TERESA S., state legislator, public relations executive; b. Indpls., July 5, 1951; d. Richard and Evelyn (Ent) Smith; m. R. Mark Lubbers, Oct. 7, 1978; children: Elizabeth Stone, Margaret Smith. AB, Ind. U., 1973; MPA, Harvard U., 1981. Tchr. English Warren Ctrl. High Sch., 1973-74; pub. info. officer Office of Mayor Richard Lugar, 1974-75; dep. press sec., legis. asst. Office of U.S. Senator Richard Lugar, 1976-78; legis. rep. Nat. Fedn. Ind. Bus., 1978-80; dir. info. INC. Mag., 1981-82; press sec. Dielmann for Congress, 1982-83; pres. pub. rels. firm Capitol Communications, 1983—; mem. Ind. Senate from 30th dist., Indpls., 1992—. Co-founder, v.p. Richard G. Lugar Excellence in Pub. Svc. Series, 1990—; bd. dirs. Young Audiences Ind., Nat. Policy Forum. Bd. deacons Tabernacle Presbyn. Ch.; mem. cultural enrichment com. Immaculate Heart Sch., Meridian Kessler Neighborhood Assn., Rep. Profl. Women's Roundtable; mem. steering com. Forum Series, Girls Inc.; bus. mem. Broad Ripple Village Assn.; vol. Dick Lugar's 1974 Senate Campaign; pub. info. officer Mayor's Office, 1974-75; office mgr., Friends of Dick Lugar, 1976; senate staff Office of Senator Richard Lugar, 1976-78; adv. com. Ind. Sch. for Blind; bd. dirs. Brebeuf Prep. Sch., St. Vincent New Hope; cmty. adv. bd. Jr. League of Indpls.; exec. bd., crossroads coun. Boy Scouts of Am.; mem. devel. commn. White River State Park. Republican. Office: Ind Senate Dist 30 200 W Washington St Indianapolis IN 46204-2728

LUBIN, BERNARD, psychologist, educator; b. Washington, Oct. 15, 1923; s. Israel Harry and Anne (Cohen) L.; m. Alice Weisbord, Aug. 5, 1957. BA, George Washington U., 1952, MA, 1953; PhD, Pa. State U., 1958. Diplomate: Am. Bd. Profl. Psychology, Am. Bd. Psychol. Hypnosis; lic. psychologist, Mo., Tex. Intern St. Elizabeths Hosp., 1952-53, Roanoke (Va.) VA Hosp., 1954-55, Wilkes-Barre (Pa.) VA Hosp., 1955; USPHS postdoctoral fellow, postdoctoral residency in psychotherapy U. Wis. Sch. Medicine, 1957-58; staff psychologist, instr. dept. psychiatry Ind. U. Sch. Medicine, Indpls., 1958-59, chief psychologist adult outpatient service, 1960-62, assoc. prof., 1964-67; dir. psychol. services Dept. Mental Health, Indpls., 1962-63, dir. div. research and tng., 1963-67; dir. div. psychology Greater Kansas City (Mo.) Mental Health Found., 1967-74; prof. dept. psychiatry U. Mo. Sch. Medicine, Kansas City, 1967-74, 76—; prof., dir. clin. tng. program dept. psychology U. Houston, 1974-76; prof., chmn. dept. psychology U. Mo. at Kansas City, 1976-83, Curators' prof., 1988; trustees' faculty fellow, 1994. Cons. Am. Nurses Assn., Panhandle Eastern Pipeline Co., Eli Lilly Pharm. Co., U.S. Sprint, Am. Mgmt. Assn., Inst. Psychiat. Research, Ind. U. Med. Center, Ind. U. Sch. Dentistry, Goodwill Industries, USPHS Bur. Health Services, mental retardation div., (univ.-affiliated facilities br.), U.S. VA, Baylor U. Med. Sch., U. Tex. Health Scis. Center, Houston, 1974-76; Mem. tng. staff Nat. Tng. Labs. Inst.; dean or faculty mem. numerous confs., 1960—; exec. sec. Ind. Assn. for Advancement Mental Health Research and Edn., 1962-67 Author: (with M. Zuckerman) Multiple Affect Adjective Check List: Manual, 1965, 2d edit., 1985, 3d edit., 1999, (with E.E. Levitt) The Clinical Psychologist: Background, Roles and Functions, 1967, Depression: Concepts, Controversies, and Some New Facts, 1975, 2d edit., 1983, Depression Adjective Check Lists: Manual, 1967, rev. edit., 1994, (with L.D. Goodstein and A.W. Lubin) Organizational Development Sourcebooks I and II, 1979; (with W.A. O'Connor) Ecological Approaches to Clinical and Community Psychology, 1984, (with Alice W. Lubin) Comprehensive Index to the Group Psychotherapy Literature: 1906-1980, 1987, (with A.W. Lubin) Family Therapy: A Bibliography, 1937-86, 1988, (with R. Gist) Psychosocial Aspects of Disaster, 1989 (with R.V. Whitlock) Homelessness in America: A Bibliography with Selective Annotations, 1894-1994, 1994, (with D. Wilson, S. Petren and A. Polk) Research on Group Methods of Treatment: 1970-1996, 1996, (with D. Wilson) Annotated Bibliography on Organizational Consultation, 1997, (with P. G. Hanson) Answers to the Most Frequently Asked Questions About Organization Development, 1995, (with R. Gist) Ecological and Community Approaches to Disaster Response, 1999, (with R.V. Whitlock) Mental Health Services in Criminal Justice Settings, 1999, also articles; editorial bd. Jour. Community Psychology; mem. editorial bd. Internat. Jour. Group Psychotherapy, Profl. Psychology: Research and Practice; cons. reader, bd. dirs. Jour. Cons. and Clin. Psychology. Pres. Midwest Group for Human Resources, Inc., 1965-69, trustee, 1965. Recipient N.T. Veatch award for disting. rsch. and creative activity, 1983; faculty fellow U. Kansas City, 1994. Mem. APA (chmn. sponsor approval com., exec. bd. dirs. cons. psychology, coun. rep., Disting. Sr. Contbr. to Counseling Psychology award 1995, Harry Levinson award for excellence in consultation 1996), AAAS, Mo. Psychol. Assn. (exec. bd., Richard Wilkinson Lifetime Achievement award 1997), Am. Group Psychotherapy Assn. (edit. com.); mem. Midwestern Psychol. Assn., Ind. Psychol. Assn. (pres. 1967), World Fedn. for Mental Health, Conf. Psychologist Dirs. and cons. in State, Fed. and Territorial Mental Health Programs (editor conf. procs. 1966-68, Perspective 1966-68, mem. exec. com. 1946-68), Inter-Am. Congress Psychology, Cert. Cons. Internat. (charter), NTL Inst. (bd. dirs. 1986-92), Sigma Xi, Phi Kappa Phi, Psi Chi (v.p. for midwest, mem. nat. coun. 1986-90, pres.-elect 1991-92, pres. 1992-93, past pres. 1993-94). Office: U Mo Kansas City Dept Psychology 5307 Holmes St Kansas City MO 64110-2437

LUBIN, DONALD G., lawyer; b. NYC, Jan. 10, 1934; s. Harry and Edith (Tannenbaum) L.; m. Amy Schwartz, Feb. 2, 1956; children: Peter, Richard, Thomas, Alice Lubin Spahr. BS in Econs., U. Pa., 1954; LLB, Harvard U., 1957. Bar: Ill. 1957. Ptnr. Sonnenschein Nath & Rosenthal LLP, Chgo., 1957—, chmn. exec. com., 1991-96. Past exec. com., fin. com., chmn. nominating and corp. governance com. McDonald's Corp.; bd. dirs. Molex, Inc., Daubert Industries Inc., Charles Levy Co.; founding bd. dirs. Lake County Cmty. Trust; former bd. dirs., First Nat. Bank Highland Park. Former mem. Navy Pier Redevel. Corp., Highland Park Cultural Arts Commn., Chgo. Bicentennial Commn.; life trustee, former chmn. bd. Highland Park Hosp., Ravinia Festival Assn.; chmn. Chgo. Metropolis 2020, Renaissance Schs. Fund; trustee, exec. com. Rush U. Med. Ctr.; life trustee Chgo. Symphony Orch.; bd. dirs., v.p. Ronald McDonald House Charities, Inc., Chgo. Found. for Edn.; mem. Evanston Northwestern Healthcare Found.; pres., bd. dir. Barr Fund; former bd. dirs., v.p., sec. Ragdale Found.; bd. govs. Art Inst. Chgo.; former bd. overseers Coll. Arts and Sci., U. Pa.; former dir. Smithsonian Inst., Washington, Nat. Mus. Am. History, Washington. Woodrow Wilson vis. fellow Fellow Am. Bar Found., Ill. Bar Found., Chgo. Bar Found.; mem. Chgo. Bar Assn., Civic Com. (mem. steering com.), Lawyers Club Chgo., Chgo. Hort. Soc. (past bd. dirs.), Comml. Club, Std. Club, Lakeshore Club, Beta Gamma Sigma. Home: 2269 Egandale Rd Highland Park IL 60035-2501 Office: Sonnenschein Nath & Rosenthal LLP 233 S Wacker Dr Ste 7800 Chicago IL 60606-6491 Office Phone: 312-876-8007. Personal E-mail: dlubin@sonnenschein.com.

LUBIN, PETER SCOTT, lawyer; b. Chgo., Dec. 3, 1957; s. Donald Gilbert and Amy (Schwartz) L.; m. Tara K. Lubin, Dec.3, 1968. AB, Dartmouth Coll., 1980; LLB, U. Chgo., 1983. Bar: Ill. 1983, US Dist. Ct. (no., ctrl. dists.) Ill. 1984, US Ct. Appeals (2nd, 3rd, 5th, 7th, 10th, 11th, DC circuits) 1993, US Supreme Ct. 1993. Pvt. practice, Oakbrook Terrace, Ill., 1983—. Assoc. bd. mem. Ravinia Music Festival, Highland Park, Ill., 1990—. Mem. ABA (bus. torts com.), Chgo. Coun. of Lawyers, Am. Inns of Ct., Ill. State Bar Assn., Chgo. Bar Assn. Democrat. Jewish. Avocations: skiing, hiking. Office: D tommass and Loubin PC Ste 200 17 W 220 22nd St Villa Park IL 60181 Home Phone: 630-710-4940; Office Phone: 630-333-0002. Office Fax: 630-333-0333. Business E-Mail: psh@ditommasolaw.com.

LUBY, ELLIOT DONALD, psychiatrist, educator; b. Detroit, Apr. 3, 1924; m. Ideane Maura Levenson, June 28, 1950; children: Arthur, Howard, Joan. Student, U. Chgo., 1943-44; BS, U. Mo., 1945-47; MD, Wash. U., St. Louis, 1947-49. Clin. dir. Lafayette Clinic, Detroit, 1957-74; chief psychiatry Harper Hosp., Detroit, 1978-91. Prof. psychiatry and law Wayne State U., 1965—, endowed chair in psychiatry, 2005; pres. Comprehensive Psychiatry Svcs., Southfield, Mich., 1972-98. Contbr. numerous articles to various publs., also several book chpts. Served to lt. USPHS, 1950-52. Recipient Gold Medal award Am. Acad. Psychosomatic Medicine, 1962, Career Achievement award Mich. Mental Health Assn., 1999 Endowed Chair award Wayne State U., 2005. Fellow Am. Psychiat. Assn. (disting., life), Am. Coll. Psychiatrists; mem. AMA, N.Y. Acad. Sci., Sigma Xi. Jewish. Office: 28800 Orchard Lake Rd Ste 250 Farmington Hills MI 48334-2922 Home: 27540 Lakehills Dr Franklin MI 48025-1742 Office Phone: 248-932-2500.

LUCAS, ALEXANDER RALPH, child psychiatrist, educator, writer; b. Vienna, July 30, 1931; came to U.S., 1940, naturalized, 1945; s. Eugene Hans and Margaret Ann (Weiss) L.; m. Margaret Alice Thompson, July 6, 1956; children: Thomas Alexander, Nancy Elizabeth Watson, Alexander Eugene, Peter Clayton. BS, Mich. State U., 1953; MD, U. Mich., 1957. Diplomate Am. Bd. Psychiatry and Neurology (psychiatry and child and adolescent psychiatry), Am. Bd. of Med. Specialties. Intern U. Mich. Hosp., 1957-58; resident in child psychiatry Hawthorn Ctr., Northville, Mich., 1958-59, 61-62, staff psychiatrist, 1963-65, sr. psychiatrist, 1965-67; resident in psychiatry Lafayette Clinic, Detroit, 1959-61, rsch. child psychiatrist, 1967-71, rsch. coord., 1969-71; asst. prof. psychiatry Wayne State U., 1967-69, assoc. prof., 1969-71; cons. child and adolescent psychiatry Mayo Clinic, 1971-97; assoc. prof. Mayo Med Sch., 1973-76, prof., 1976-97; emeritus prof., 1998—; head sect. child and adolescent psychiatry Mayo Clinic, Rochester, Minn., 1971-80, emeritus cons., 1998—. Dir. com. on certification in child and adolescent psychiatry Am. Bd. Psychiatry and Neurology, 1997-2001; residency rev. com. Accreditation Coun. for Grad. Med. Edn., 1999-2001. Author (with C. R. Shaw): The Psychiatric Disorders of Childhood, 1970; author: Demystifying Anorexia Nervosa, 2004. Recipient Eating Disorders Scientific Achievement award, 1998. Fellow Am. Acad. Child and Adolescent Psychiatry (life, editl. bd. jour. 1976-82), Am. Orthopsychiat. Assn. (life), Am. Psychiat. Assn. (life); mem. Minn. Soc. Child and Adolescent Psychiatry (pres. 1993-95), Soc. Profs. Child and Adolescent Psychiatry (pres. 2000-02), Sigma Xi Achievements include research in biol. aspects of child psychiatry, psychopathology, psychopharmacology, eating disorders, psychiat. treatment of children, adolescents, and young adults. Office: Mayo Clinic 200 1st St SW Rochester MN 55905-0002 Office Phone: 507-284-2691.

LUCAS, BERT ALBERT, pastor, social services administrator, consultant; b. Hammond, Ind., Mar. 26, 1933; s. John William and Norma (Gladys) Graham; m. Nanci Dai Hindman, Sept. 10, 1960; children: Bradley Scott, Traci Dai. BA, Wheaton Coll., 1956; BD, No. Bapt. Theol. Sem., 1960, ThM, 1965; MSW, U. Mich., 1971; D in Marriage and Family, Ea. Bapt. Theol. Sem., 1988. Lic. social worker, Ohio; ordained clergyman Am. Baptist Conv.; cert. family life educator. Chaplain Miami Children's Ctr., Maumee, Ohio, 1967-83; assoc. pastor First Bapt. Ch., La Porte, Ind., 1959-62; pastor Maumee Bapt. Ch., 1963-67; adminstrv. social work supr. Lucas County (Ohio) Children Svcs., 1967-97; pastor Holland (Ohio) United Meth. Ch., 1979-90, Broadway United Meth. Ch., 1994-97, Bono Bapt. Ch., Toledo, 1997-99. Adj. prof. Bowling Green (Ohio) State U., 1972-79; family life cons. New Horizon's Acad., Holland, 1984-86, co-dir. family svcs. 1985-86; cons. parenting, marriage enrichment, Toledo, 1986—. Rep. precinct capt., Toledo, 1984. Bert A. Lucas Day proclaimed City of Holland, 1984. Mem.: AACD, First Bapt. Ch. Greater Toledo (ch. officer 2003—), Council Family Rels., Hist. Preservations of Am. (Comty. Leader and Noteworthy Ams. award 1976—77), Assn. for Couples in Marriage Enrichment, Am. Assn. Marriage and Family Therapy (assoc.). Personal E-mail: bert.lucas@sbcglobal.net.

LUCAS, GEORGE J., bishop; b. St. Louis, June 12, 1949; s. George J. Lucas and Mary Catherine Kelly. BA, Cardinal Glennon Coll., 1971; MTh, Kenrick Sem., 1975; MA, St. Louis U., 1986. Ordained priest Archdiocese of St. Louis, 1975; assoc. pastor St. Justin Martyr, Sunset Hills, Mo., 1975—80, St. Dismas, Florissant, Mo., 1980—81, Our Lady of Mt. Carmel, St. Louis, 1981—84, Ascension, Normandy, 1984—86, St. Ann, Normandy, 1986—89, St. Peter, Kirkwood, 1989—90; chancellor Archdiocese of St. Louis, 1990—94, vicar gen., 1994—95; rector Kenrick-Glennon Seminary, 1995—99; ordained bishop, 1999; bishop Diocese of Springfield, Ill., 1999—. Vice-prin. St. Louis Prep. Sem. North, 1982—87; dean of students St. Louis Prep. Sem., 1987—90; bd. trustees Kenrick-Glennon Sem., 1990—99; mem. editl. bd. St. Louis Rev., 1988—99. Roman Catholic. Office: Diocese of Springfield 1615 W Washington St PO Box 3187 Springfield IL 62708-3187 Office Phone: 217-698-8500. Office Fax: 217-698-0802.*

LUCAS, LARRY JAMES, state legislator; b. Jan. 10, 1951; m. Debera Lucas; 4 children. Student, S.D. State U., 1969-74. Mem. S.D. Ho. of Reps., 1991—, mem. edn. and state affairs coms.; tchr. Todd County Sch. Dist., 1975—. Democrat. Home: PO Box 182 Mission SD 57555-0182

LUCAS, ROBERT ELMER, soil scientist, researcher; b. Malolos, The Philippines, June 27, 1916; (parents Am. citizens); s. Charles Edmund and Harriet Grace (Deardorff) L.; m. Norma Emma Schultz, Apr. 27, 1941; children: Raymond and Richard (twins), Milton, Keith, Charles. BSA, Purdue U., 1939, MS, 1941; PhD, Mich. State U., 1947. Research asst. Va. Agrl. Research Sta., Norfolk, 1941-43; farmer Culver, Ind., 1943-44; grad. asst. Mich. State U., East Lansing, 1945, assoc. prof. soil sci., 1951-57, prof., 1957-77, prof. emeritus, 1977—; agronomist William Gehring, Inc., Rensselaer, Ind., 1946-50, 77-78. Vis. prof. Everglades Research Sta. U. Fla., Belle Glade, 1979-80. Author chpts. in books, research reports. Leader Boy Scouts Am., Lansing, Mich., 1961-72, dist. chmn. Chief Okemos (Mich.) Coun. Boy Scouts Am., 1965-66; pres. Okemos Cmty. Sr. citizens, 1987-88, pres. Lansing Area Farmers Agrl. Club, 1992, sec.-treas., 1994-99. amed Outstanding Specialist Mich. Coop. Extension Specialist Assn., 1967. Fellow Soil Sci. Soc. Am., Am. Soc. Agronomy (contbr. articles to jour.); mem. Internat. Peat Soc. (del. 1963—), U.S. Peat Soc., Mich. Onion Growers Assn. (sec. 1953-72), Mich. Muck Farmers Assn. (sec. 1953-72, Assoc. Master-Farmers award 1966), Mich. Mint Growers Assn. (sec. 1953-60). Republican. Lutheran. Avocations: travel, gardening, sports, genealogy. Home: 3827 Dobie Rd Okemos MI 48864-3703 Office: Mich State Univ Dept Of Crop & Soil Sci East Lansing MI 48824

LUCAS, ROBERT EMERSON, JR., economist, educator; b. Yakima, Wash., Sept. 15, 1937; BA, U. Chgo., 1959, PhD, 1964; PhD (hon.), U. Paris-Dauphine, 1992, Athens U. Econ. and Bus., 1994; DSc (hon.), Technion-Israel Inst. Tech., 1996; PhD (hon.), U. Montréal, 1998. Lectr. U. Chgo., 1962-63; asst. prof., economics Carnegie-Mellon U., Pittsburgh, 1963-67; assoc. prof., 1967-70; prof., 1970-75; prof., economics U. Chgo., 1975—, vice chmn. Dept. Econs., 1975—83, named John Dewey Disting. Svc. prof., 1980, chmn. Dept. Econs., 1986—88. Ford Found. vis. rsch. prof. U. Chgo., 1974-75; vis. prof. econ. Northwestern U., Chgo., 1981-82. Author: Studies in Business-Cycle Theory, 1981, Models of Business Cycles, 1987, Lectures on Economic Growth, 2001; co-author: Recursive Methods in Economic Dynamics, 1989; co-editor: Rational Expectations and Econometric Practice, 1981; assoc. editor Jour. Econ. Theory, 1972-78, Jour. Monetary Econs., 1977—; editor Jour. Polit. Theory, 1978-81, 1988-; contbr. articles to profl. jours. Woodrow Wilson fellow, 1959-60, Brookings fellow, 1961-62, Woodrow Wilson Dissertation fellow, 1963, Ford Found. Faculty fellow, 1966-67, Guggenheim Found. fellow, 1981-82; Proctor and Gamble scholar, 1955-59; recipient Nobel Prize in Econs., 1995. Fellow AAAS, Econometric Soc. (2nd v.p. 1995, pres. 1997), Am. Acad. Arts and Scis.; mem. NAS, Econometric Soc. (2nd v.p., v.p. 1995, pres. 1997), Am. Econ. Assn. (v.p. 1987, pres. 2001), European Acad. Arts, Scis. and Humanities, Am. Philosophical Soc., Phi Beta Kappa. Achievements include developing and applying the hypothesis of rational expectations, and thereby having transformed macroeconomic analysis and deepened out understanding of economic policy. Office: U Chgo Dept Econs 1126 E 59th St Chicago IL 60637-1580

LUCAS, WAYNE LEE, sociologist, educator; b. Joliet, Ill., Jan. 6, 1947; s. Cecil Elmer and Mabel (Torkelson) L.; m. Nancy Jean Floyd, Aug. 23, 1969; children: Jeffrey, Keri. BS, Ill. State U., 1969, MS, 1972; PhD, Iowa State U., 1976. Prof. U. Mo. Kansas City, 1976—. Contbr. articles to profl. jours. Mem. Acad. Criminal Justice Scis., Am. Soc. Criminology, Soc. for Study of Social Problems, Midwestern Criminal Justice Assn. Democrat. Presbyterian. Avocations: fishing, guitar, woodworking. E-mail: lucasw@umkc.edu.

LUCE, MICHAEL LEIGH, lawyer; b. Mitchell, S.D., Mar. 2, 1952; s. John Russell and Irene (Merkel) L.; m. Mary Claire Goad, Sept. 7, 1979; children: Juliann Marie, Colin Thomas. B.S., Augustana Coll., Sioux Falls, S.D., 1974; J.D., U. S.D., 1977. Bar: S.D. 1977, U.S. Dist. Ct. S.D. 1977, U.S. Ct. Appeals (8th cir.) 1979. Law clk. to Judge Fred J. Nichol, U.S. Dist. Ct. S.D., Sioux Falls, 1977-78; assoc. Davenport Law Firm, Sioux Falls, 1978-80, ptnr., 1981—. Lead articles editor S.D. Law Rev., 1977. Mem. ABA, S.D. Bar Assn. (com. on rules of evidence), Am. Trial Lawyers Assn., Am. Bd. Trial Attys., S.D. Trial Lawyers Assn., Nat. Sch. Bd. Assn. Counsel Sch. Attys., Internat. Soc. Barristers. Democrat. Home: 336 Aspen Cir Sioux Falls SD 57105-6934 Office: Davenport Evans Hurwitz 206 W 14th St Sioux Falls SD 57104-6858 Office Phone: 605-336-2880.

LUCHINS, DANIEL JONATHAN, psychiatrist; b. NYC, July 1, 1948; s. Abraham Samuel and Edith (Hirsch) L.; children: Kerith, Matthew. BSc, McGill U., Montreal, Que., Can., 1971, MD, 1973. Diplomate in psychiatry and geriatric psychiatry Am. Bd. Psychiatry and Neurology. Vis. scientist NIMH, Washington, 1977-81; assoc. prof. U. Chgo., 1981—; med. coord. mental health Ill. Dept. Mental Health, Chgo., 1989-91; chief of adult psychiatry U. Chgo., 1991-93; chief clin. svcs. Office Mental Health, Ill. Dept. Human Svcs., Chgo., 1995—2005; chief pub. psychiatry U. Chgo., 1996; chief, Mental Health Rsch. Ctr. Jesse Brown VAMC, 2007—. Dir. SGA Youth and Family Svcs., 2001—. Contbr. articles to profl. publs. Recipient A.E. Bennett award Soc. Biol. Psychiatry, Geriatric Mental Health acad. award NIMH, 1984-87, Exemplary Psychiatrist award NAMI, 1998. Fellow Am. Psychiat. Assn. (disting.); mem. Ill. Psychiat. Assn. (councillor 1989-91, pres. 1995, Am. Psychiat. Assn. rep.). Jewish. Achievements include development of criteria for hospice care for demented patients. Office: U Chgo Dept Psychiatry 5841 S Maryland Ave Chicago IL 60637-1463 also: Jesse Brown VAMC 820 S Damen Ave Chicago IL 60612 Home Phone: 773-667-5947; Office Phone: 312-567-8072. Business E-Mail: daniel.luchins@va.gov.

LUCK, JAMES I., foundation executive; b. Akron, Ohio, Aug. 28, 1945; s. Milton William and Gertrude (Winer) L.; children: Andrew Brewer, Edward Aldrich. L. BA, Ohio State U., 1967; MA, U. Ga., 1970. Caseworker Franklin County Welfare Dept., Columbus, Ohio, 1967-69; dir. forensics Tex. Christian U., Ft. Worth, 1970-74; assoc. dir. Bicentennial Youth Debates, Washington, 1974-76; exec. dir. Nat. Congress on Volunteerism and Citizenship, Washington, 1976-77; fellow Acad. Contemporary Problems, Columbus, Ohio, 1977-79; exec. dir. Battelle Meml. Inst. Found., Columbus, 1980-82; pres. Columbus Found., 1981—2001, pres. emeritus, 2001—; exec. dir. Columbus Youth Found. and Ingram-White Castle Funds, 1981—2001; chmn. Am Resource Devel., LLC, Columbus, 2002—; pres., CEO Global 3E, 2003—. Co-chmn. Task Force on Citizen Edn., Washington, 1977; mediator Negotiated Investment Strategy, Columbus, 1979; chmn. Ohio Founds. Conf., 1985; cons. HEW, Peace Corps., U. Va. Author: Ohio-The Next 25 Years, 1978, Bicentennial Issue Analysis, 1975; editor: Proceedings of the Nat. Conf. on Argumentation, 1973; contbr. articles to profl. jours. Trustee Godman Guild Settlement House, Columbus, 1979-81, Am. Diabetes Assn., Ohio, 1984-88; chmn. spl. com. on displacement Columbus City Coun., 1978-80; bd. dirs. Commn. on the Future of the Professions in Soc., 1979. Mem. Donors Forum Ohio. Clubs: Capital, Columbus Club, Columbus Met., Kit-Kat. Lodges: Rotary. Avocations: travel, reading. Home: 799 Pinecliff Pl Worthington OH 43085-1906 Home Phone: 614-846-3303; Office Phone: 614-364-7111. E-mail: jluck@ard501.cm.

LUCK, RICHARD EARLE, astronomy educator; b. Mar. 9, 1950; BA, U. Va., 1972; MA, U. Tex., 1975, PhD in Astronomy, 1977. Chmn., Warner prof. astronomy Case Western Res. U., Cleve. Mem. Am. Astron. Soc., Royal Astron. Soc. Office: Dept Astronomy Case Western Res Univ University Circle Cleveland OH 44106

LUCKE, ROBERT VITO, investment company executive; b. Kingston, Pa., July 26, 1930; s. Vito Frank and Edith Ann (Adders) L.; m. Jane Ann Rushin, Aug. 16, 1952; children: Thomas, Mark, Carl. BS in Chemistry, Pa. State U., 1952; MS in Mgmt., Rensselaer Polytech Inst., 1960. Polymer chemist Uniroyal Naugatuck Chem. Div., Conn., 1954-60; comml. devel. engr. Exxon Enjay Div., Elizabeth, NJ, 1960-66; group gen. mgr. Celanese Advanced Composites, Summit, NJ, 1966-70; bus. mgr. polymer div. Hooker Chem., Burlington, NJ, 1970-74; gen. mgr. Oxy Metal Industries Environ. Equipment. Divs., Warren, Mich., 1974-79; corp. v.p., group gen. mgr. Hoover Universal Plastic Machinery Divs., Manchester, Mich., 1979-84; pres. Egan Machinery, Somerville, NJ, Bone Markem UK, Bone Cravens, England, 1984—87; pres., chief exec. officer Krauss Maffei Corp., Cin., 1987—90; pres. Adventa Global LLC, 1990—2007. Instr., Chem. Market Rsch. Assn., 1974. Author: (with others) Plastics Handbook, 1972. 1st lt. corp. engrs., 1952—54, Korea. Senatorial scholar, Pa. State U., 1948-52. Mem. Am. Chem. Soc., Soc. Plastics Engrs. (sect. engr. STDS com. 1969), Tech. Assn. Pulp Paper Industry, Comml. Devel. Assn., Assn. Corp. Growth (pres. So. Ohio Chpt, 1998). Achievements include 6 patents in field. Avocations: golf, skiing, travel, gardening. Office: Arvel LLC subs Adevnta Global LLC 2260 Heather Hill Blvd Cincinnati OH 45244-2664 Home Phone: 513-474-2999; Office Phone: 513-474-2999. Personal E-mail: wiseowl726@aol.com.

LUCKE, STEPHEN P., lawyer; b. 1957; AB in Econ. magna cum laude, Coll. Holy Cross, 1980; JD magna cum laude, Georgetown Univ., 1983. Bar: Minn. 1984, Wis. 1990. Law clerk, Hon. Myron H. Bright US Ct. Appeals (8th cir.), 1983—84; assoc. Dorsey & Whitney, Mpls., 1984—90, ptnr., trial group, co-head, ERISA litig., 1991. Mng. editor Georgetown Law Jour., 1982—83. Mem.: ABA, Hennepin County Bar Assn., Minn. State Bar Assn., Alpha Sigma Nu, Phi Beta Kappa. Office: Dorsey & Whitney LLP Ste 1500 50 S Sixth St Minneapolis MN 55402-1498 Office Phone: 612-340-2600. Office Fax: 612-340-8800. Business E-Mail: lucke.steve@dorsey.com.

LUCKERT, MARLA JO, state supreme court justice; b. Goodland, Kans., July 20, 1955; d. William Gottleib and Gladys Iona (Rohr) L.; m. Steven. K. Morse, May 25, 1980; children: Sarah, Alisa. BA, Washburn U., 1977, JD, 1980. Bar: Kans. 1980, U.S. Dist. Ct. Kans. 1980, U.S. Ct. Appeals (10th cir.) 1980. Assoc. Goodell, Stratoon, Edmond & Palmer, Topeka, 1980—92; judge Third Jud. Dist., Kans. Supreme Ct., Kans., 1992—2000, chief judge Kans., 2000—03; justice Kans. Supreme Ct., Kans., 2003—. Adj. prof. Washburn Univ. Sch. Law, Topeka, 1980-81, 1990—. Author: Kansas Consent Manual, 1988, Record Relations Guide, 1988, Kansas Law for Physicians, 1989. Pres. Mobile Meals of Topeka (Kans.), Inc., 1987-89, Mobile Meals of Topeka (Kans.) Found., 1989—; co-chair YWCA ominating Com., Topeka, 1988-89. Recipient Woman of Excellence Award, YWCA, Topeka, Kans. Mem. ABA (co-chair young lawyers health law com. 1988-90), Am. Acad. Hosp. Attys., Kans. Assn. Hosp. Attys., Kans. Assn. Def. Counsel (bd. dirs. 1988—, disting. svc. award 1990), Kans. Bar Assn. (pres. young lawyers 1989-90, outstanding svc. award 1990), Topeka Bar Assn. (chair law day pubs. com.), Women Attys. Assn. Kans., Topeka (pres. 1988-89), Sam A. Crow Inn of Ct., Am. Judges Assn., Nat. Assn. Women Judges, Nat. Ctr. State Courts, Supreme Ct. Historical Soc., Am. Judicature Soc.; fellow Am. Bar Found., Kans. Bar Found. Office: Kansas Judicial Ctr 301 SW 10th Ave Topeka KS 66612-1507

LUCKETT, BYRON EDWARD, JR., chaplain, retired military officer; b. Mineral Wells, Tex., Feb. 2, 1951; s. Byron Edward and Helen Alma (Hart) L.; m. Kathryn Louise Lambertson, Dec. 30, 1979; children: Florence Louise, Byron Edward III, Barbara Elizabeth, Stephanie Hart. BS, U.S. Mil. Acad., 1973; MDiv, Princeton Theol. Sem., 1982; MA, Claremont Grad. Sch., 1987. Commd. 2d lt. U.S. Army, 1973, advanced through grades to lt. col.; stationed at Camp Edwards E., Korea, 1974-75; bn. supply officer 563rd Engr. Bn., Kornwestheim, Germany, 1975-76; platoon leader, exec. officer 275th Engr. Co., Ludwigsburg, Germany, 1976-77; boy scout project officer Hdqrs., VII Corps, Stuttgart, Germany, 1977-78; student intern Moshannon Valley Larger Parish, Winburne, Pa., 1980-81; Protestant chaplain Philmont Scout Ranch, Cimarron, N.Mex., 1982; asst. pastor Immanuel Presbyn. Ch., Albuquerque, 1982-83, assoc. pastor, 1983-84; tchr. Claremont High Sch., 1985-86; Protestant chaplain 92nd Combat Support Group, Fairchild AFB, Wash., 1986-90; installation staff chaplain Pirinclik Air Station, Turkey, 1990-91; Protestant chaplain Davis-Monthan AFB, Ariz., 1991-95; dir. readiness ministries Offutt AFB, Nebr., 1995-96, sr. Protestant chaplain Nebr., 1996-98, Elmendorf AFB, Alaska, 1998-2000; wing chaplain Minot AFB, ND, 2000—01; sr. career advisor Bernard Haldane Assocs., Las Vegas, 2001—02; on-call chaplain St. Rose Dominican Hosp., Henderson, Nev., 2002—; sr. cons. IDC, Henderson, Nev., 2003—04, account exec., 2004—05; pres. Luckett Capital Group, Las Vegas, 2005—. Mem. intern program coun. Claremont (Calif.) Grad. Sch.; affiliate faculty Regis U., Las Vegas, 2003—,; campaign dir. combined fed. campaign, So. Nev., 2007—, lead faculty, Cmty. Outreach, Regis U., 2008-. Contbr. articles to profl. jours. Bd. dirs. Parentcraft, Inc., Albuquerque, 1984, United Campus Ministries, Albuquerque, 1984, Proclaim Liberty, Inc., Spokane, 1987-90, Amazing Grace Ministry, Las Vegas, 2005—; bd. dirs. western region Nat. Assn. Presbyn. Scouters, Irving, Tex., 1986-89, chaplain, 1991-93; mem. N.Mex. Employer Co, in Support of the Guard and Reserve, Albuquerque, 1984, Old Baldy coun. Boy Scouts Am., 1986; chmn. Fairchild Parent Coop., Fairchild AFB, 1986-87; pres. Co. Grade Officers Coun., Fairchild AFB, 1987-88; pres. Luckett Family Found. Capt. U.S. Army Reserve; chaplain USAF Res., 1983-86; lt. col. 1998. Recipient Dist. Award of Merit for Disting. Svc. Boy Scouts Am., 1977, Aubrey Douglas award, Claremont Grad. U., 1986, Excellence Tchg. award, Regis U., 2007. Mem. Soc. Cin. Md., Mil. Order Fgn. Wars U.S., Civil Affairs Assn., Huguenot Soc. Tex. Presbyterian. Home and Office: 6024 Mustang Breeze trail #103 Henderson NV 89011 Home Phone: 702-360-3342. Personal E-mail: ekluckett@cox.net. Business E-Mail: luckettcapital@mac.com.

LUCKING, PAUL, telecommunications executive; Various sr. mgmt. positions Fed. Express, SysteMed, CitiCorp.; founder, pres. Interface Solutions, Inc.; chief tech. officer, sr. v.p. ADT; COO, pres. subsidiaries Davel Comms., Inc., Tampa, Fla., 2000—. Office: Davel Communications 200 Public Sq Ste 700 Cleveland OH 44114-2323

LUCKY, ANNE WEISSMAN, dermatologist; b. NYC, May 11, 1944; d. Jacob and Gertrude (Tetelman) Weissman; m. Paul A. Lucky, May 19, 1972; children: Jennifer, Andrea. BA, Brown U., 1966; MD, Yale U., 1970. Diplomate Nat. Bd. Med. Examiners, Am. Bd. Pediatrics/subspecialty of pediatric endocrinology, Am. Bd. Dermatology (pres. 1998—). Intern and resident in pediatrics The Children's Hosp. Med. Ctr., Boston, 1970-73; fellow in human genetics and pediatrics Yale U. Sch. Medicine, New Haven, Conn., 1973-74, resident in dermatology, 1979-81, instr. pediatrics, 1980-81, assoc. prof. dermatology and pediatrics, 1981-83; clin. assoc. Reprodn. Rsch. Br./Nat. Inst. Child Health/NIH, Bethesda, Md., 1974-76; asst. prof. pediatrics Wyler Children's Hosp./Pritzker Sch. Med./U. Chgo. Hosps., 1976-79; assoc. prof. dermatology, pediatrics U. Cin. Coll. Medicine, 1983-88; pvt. practice Dermatology Assocs. of Cin, Inc., 1988—; pres. Dermatology Rsch. Assocs., Inc., Cin., 1988—; dir. Dermatology Clinic Children's Hosp. Med. Ctr., Cin., 1989—. Vol. prof. dermatology and pediatrics U. Cin. Coll. Medicine, 1988-94. Editorial bd. Pediatric Dermatology, 1982—, Archives of Dermatology, 1983-94; contbr. numerous articles to profl. jours., publs. Recipient the Janet M. Glasgow Meml. Scholarship, Am. Women's Med. Assn., 1970, the Ramsey Meml. Scholarship award Yale U. Sch. Medicine, 1968, others; grantee USPHS, 1964-66, 67, 68-70, NIH, 1977-79, 79-82, 82-87, 84-87, 87-93, others. Mem. Lawson Wilkins Pediatric Endocrine Soc., Soc. for Pediatric Endocrinology (bd. dirs. 1984-87, pres. 1990-91), Am. Acad. Dermatology, Soc. Investigative Dermatology, Soc. for Dermatologic Genetics of the Am. Acad. Dermatology, Endocrine Soc., Acad. Medicine/Cin. Women's Faculty Assn./The Children's Hosp. Med. Ctr., Women's Derm. Soc. (bd. dirs. 1993—), Ohio State Med. Assn., Soc. Pediatric Rsch., Cin. Derm. Soc. (pres. elect 1995-96), Phi Beta Kappa, Sigma Xi, Alpha Omega Alpha. Office: Derm Assocs of Cin 7691 5 Mile Rd Cincinnati OH 45230-4348

LUDEMA, KENNETH C., mechanical engineer, educator; b. Dorr, Mich., Apr. 30, 1928; BS, Calvin Coll., 1955, U. Mich., 1955, MS, 1956, PhD in Mechanical Engring., 1963; PhD in Physics, Cambridge U., 1965. Instr. mechanical engring. U. Mich., 1955-62, from asst. prof. to assoc. prof. Ann Arbor, 1964-72, prof. mechanical engring., 1972—. Mem. ASME (Mayo D. Hersey award 1995), Am. Soc. Testing & Mat. Achievements include research in sliding friction and wear behavior of solids, steels, plastics and rubbers; fundamental adhesion mechanisms between dissimilar materials; skid resistance properties of tires and roads. Office: U Mich Dept Mechanical Engring 2250GGBL 2350 Hayward St Ann Arbor MI 48109-2125

LUDES, JOHN T., financial executive; Pres., CEO Acushnet Co., 1982-94; group v.p. Fortune Brands, 1988-94; chmn. bd., CEO Fortune Brands Internat. Corp., 1990-94; pres., COO Fortune Brands, Inc., Lincolnshire, Ill., 1995-98, vice-chmn., 1999—. Bd dirs. Fortune Brands, Inc., mem. exec. com., conflicts of interest com., capital appropriations com. Dir. New Eng. Zenith Fund. Office: Fortune Brands Inc 300 Tower Pkwy Lincolnshire IL 60069-3640

LUDINGTON, THOMAS LAMSON, federal judge; b. Midland, Mich., Dec. 28, 1953; s. John S. and Dorothy (Lamson) L.; m. Katrina McGuire, Sept. 20, 1986. BA, Albion Coll., Mich., 1976; JD, U. San Diego, 1979. Bar: Calif. 1980, Mich. 1981. Assoc. Currie & Kendall, P.C., Midland, 1979-2000; cir. ct. judge Midland County Ct. House, Mich., 2000—06; dist. judge US Dist. Ct. (Ea. dist.) Mich., Bay City, 2006—. Mem. hearing panel Atty. Discipline Bd., Detroit, 1987—. Bd. dirs. Ir. Achievement of Midland County, Gerstacker Found.; mem. Midland Found.; bd. trustees Saginaw Valley State U. Found., Albion Coll. Mem. ABA, State Bar Mich., State Bar Calif., Midland County Bar Assn., Assn. Trial Lawyers Am., Nat. Order Barristers. Methodist. Office: US Dist Ct PO Box 913 Bay City MI 48707 Office Phone: 989-894-8810.

LUDMERER, KENNETH MARC, medical educator; b. Long Beach, Calif., Jan. 13, 1947; s. Sol and Norma (Helfer) L.; m. Loren Rae Starobin, Aug. 9, 1987. AB, Harvard U., 1968; MA, Johns Hopkins U., 1971, MD, 1973. Med. resident, fellow Washington U., St. Louis, 1973-78; chief resident internal medicine Barnes Hosp., St. Louis, 1978-79; asst. prof. medicine, asst. prof. history Faculty Arts and Scis. Washington U., St. Louis, 1979-86, assoc. prof. medicine, assoc. prof. history, 1986-92, prof. medicine, prof. history, 1992—. Clin. scholars adv. com. mem. Robert Wood Johnson Found., Princeton, N.J., 1988-92; new pathway program evaluation com. mem. Assn. Am. Med. Colls., 1986-88; mem. nat. adv. com. Robert Wood Johnson Found. Clin. Scholars Program, Princeton, N.J., 1988-92; mem. adv. bd. Culpeper Found. Program in Med. Humanities, Stanford, Conn., 1992-93; mem. task force on med. edn. Acadia Inst.-Med. Coll. Pa., Phila., 1992-96; mem. vis. com. Harvard Med. Sch., Boston, 2000-2002, North Shore-L.I. Jewish Health Sys., Manhasset, N.Y., 2003—; med. edn. cons. numerous schs., hosps., profl. orgns., state govts., 2000—. Author: Genetics and American Society: A Historical Appraisal, 1972, Learning to Heal: The Development of American Medical Education, 1985, Time to Heal: American Medical Education from the Turn of the Century to the Era of Managed Care, 1999 (William Welch medal 2004); mem. editl. bd. Am. Jour. Medicine, 1981-96, Jour. History Medicine, 1981-83, 88-90, The Pharos, 1986—, History Edn. Quar., 1993-96, Annals Internal Medicine, 1993—. Med. adv. com. St. Louis Sci. Ctr., 1985-87; trustee Mo. Hist. Soc., St. Louis, 1987-93, St. Louis History Mus., 1987-93, Jewish Fedn. St. Louis, 2002—, Sommers Children's Welfare Bur., St. Louis, 2000—; chair cmty. rsch. peer rev. com. St. Louis Heart Assn., 1988-89. Faculty scholar gen. internal medicine Henry J. Kaiser Family Found., 1981-86; recipient Rsch. award Joseph Macy Jr. Found., 1989-96. Master ACP (com. on publ. policy 1988-93, Tchg. and Rsch. scholar 1980-83); fellow AAAS, Am. Acad. Arts and Scis. (Midwest coun.); mem. Assn. Am. Physicians, Am. Clin. and Climatol. Assn., Am. Assn. History Medicine (coun. 1984-87, 2000—, v.p. 2000-02, pres. 2002-04), Am. Fedn. for Clin. Rsch., History Sci. Soc., Am. Osler Soc. (bd. govs. 1988-96, v.p. 1992-94, pres. 1994-95), Phi Beta Kappa, Alpha Omega Alpha, Sigma Xi. Avocations: music, running, travel. Home: 42 Rio Vista Dr Saint Louis MO 63124-1745 Office: Washington U Sch Medicine Dept Medicine Box 8066 660 S Euclid Ave Saint Louis MO 63110 Business E-Mail: kludmere@im.wustl.edu.

LUDWIG, RICHARD JOSEPH, small business owner; b. Lakewood, Ohio, July 28, 1937; s. Mathew Joseph and Catherine Elizabeth (Sepich) L.; m. Erleen Catherine Halambeck Ramus, July 22, 1977; children: Charleen, Tracey, Charles, Cassandra. Student, Ohio State U., 1955-59; BBA Fenn Coll., Cleve. State U, 1963. C.P.A., Ohio. Sr. acct. Ernst & Whinney, Cleve., 1964-66; supervising acct. Ernst & Young, 1966-70; asst. treas. Midland Ross Corp., Cleve., 1970-71, treas., 1971-76; v.p. fin., treas. U.S. Realty Investments, 1976-78, v.p.-fin., chief fin. officer, 1978-79; owner Boston Mills Ski Resort, Inc., Peninsula, Ohio, 1979—2002; ptnr. White Oak Winery, Healdsburg, Calif., 1988—; owner Brandywine Ski Resort, Inc., Sagamore Hills, Ohio, 1990—2002; ptnr. Honor Mansion, Healdsburg, 2003—. Mem. Firestone Country Club (Akron, Ohio), Black Diamond Ranch Club (Lecanto, Fla.), Mayacama Golf Club (Santa Rosa, Calif.), The Club at Mediterra (Naples), Stonewater Golf Club (Highland Heights, Ohio). Home: 15911 Roseto Way Naples FL 34110

LUDWIG, WILLIAM JOHN, advertising executive; b. Detroit, Apr. 7, 1955; s. Albert Donald and Vivian Delores (Bantle) L.; m. Karen Sue Ward, Sept. 25, 1981; children: Adam, Gunnar. BA, Western Mich. U., 1978. Writer, producer Patten Corp., Southfield, Mich., 1978-80; writer D'Arcy, MacManus & Masius, Bloomfield Hills, Mich., 1980-82; sr. writer Campbell-Ewald, Warren, Mich., 1982-83, v.p., group head, 1983-85, sr. v.p., group supr., 1985, sr. v.p., creative dir., 1985-87, group sr. v.p., creative dir., 1987-89; exec. v.p., creative dir. Lintas: Campbell-Ewald, Warren, Mich., 1989; vice chmn., chief creative officer Lintas: Campbell-Ewald (now Campbell Ewald), Warren, Mich., 1998—. Recipient numerous awards. Mem. Adcraft, Bloomfield Open Hunt Club. Office: Campbell Ewald 30400 Van Dyke Ave Warren MI 48093-2368

LUEBBERS, JEROME F., state legislator; m. Judy Luebbers; children: Joe, Jerry, Jim, Julie, Jill, Jesse. Student, Quincy Coll. State rep. Dist. 21 Ohio State Congress, 1979-92, state rep. Dist. 33, 1993-2000. Trustee Delhi Twp., 1970-78; pres. Cin. Newsmonth Inc. Recipient Certificate Support Ohio Farmers Union, 1990, Appreciation award Boy Scouts Am. Troop 483, 1991, Things Keep Looking Up award Downs Syndrome Assn. Greater Cin., 1991, Jack Wolf Meml. award Ohio Sec. State, 1991, Legis. Appreciation award Ohio Right to Life, 1991, Guardian of Small Bus. Nat. Fedn. Ind. Bus., 1992; named Legislator of Yr. Hamilton County Assn. Trustees and Clks., 1985, Hamilton County Twp. Assn., 1990. Mem. Delhi Twp. Civic Assn., Prince Hill Civic Assn., Easter Seals (Mary Schloss award selection com.), Oak Hills Local Sch. Dist. (Hall Honor selection com.), Cath. Soc. Svc. Bd. Cin. Archdiocese, Delhi/Riverview Kiwanis, Diamond Oaks Adv. Com. Office: 417 Anderson Ferry Rd Cincinnati OH 45238-5228 Home: 5540 Timber Top Ct Cincinnati OH 45238-5167

LUECHTEFELD, DAVID, state legislator; b. Lively Grove, Ill., Nov. 8, 1940; m. Flo; 4 children. B, St. Louis U., 1962; M, So. Ill. U., Edwardsville, 1970. Tchr., athletic dir., coach, basketball, baseball; mem. Ill. Senate, Springfield, 1995—, mem. agrl. & conservation, state govt. ops. coms. Republican. Office: State Capitol Capitol Bldg M122 Springfield IL 62706-0001 also: 700 E North St Frnt Okawville IL 62271-1178

LUECK, MARTIN R., lawyer; b. St. Paul, Sept. 25, 1956; BS, Winona State U., 1978; JD cum laude, William Mitchell Coll. Law, 1984. Bar: Minn. 1984, US Dist. Ct. (dist. Minn.) 1984, US Dist. Ct. (no. dist. Calif.) 1987, US Supreme Ct. 1997, US Dist. Ct. (dist. Ariz.) 1998, US Ct. Appeals (11th and fed. cirs.) 1998, Y Supreme Ct. Appellate (3rd jud. dist.) 2003, NY 2003, US Dist. Ct. (dist. Colo.). Law clk. Sahr Kunert & Tamornino, Mpls., 1981—83; ptnr. Robins, Kaplan, Miller & Ciresi LLP, Mpls., 1983—, mem. exec. bd., 1996—, chmn. bus. litigation group, 1999—. Spkr, lectr. in field, 1992—. Contbr. articles to profl. jour. Named one of Minn. Lawyer's 15 Attys. of Yr., 2003, Top 10 Trial Lawyers in Am., Nat. Law Jour., 2004, Best Lawyers in Am., 2006—07. Fellow: Am. Coll. Trial Lawyers; mem.: ABA (mem. tng. the trial lawyer task force), Am. Assn. Justice, Internat. Bar Assn., Fed. Cir. Bar Assn., Hennepin County Bar Assn., Minn. Intellectual Property Law Assn., Am. Intellectual Property Law Assn. Office: Robins Kaplan Miller & Ciresi LLP 2800 LaSalle Plz 800 LaSalle Ave Minneapolis MN 55402-2015 Office Phone: 612-349-8500. Office Fax: 612-339-4181. E-mail: mrlueck@rkmc.com.

LUEDERS, WAYNE RICHARD, lawyer; b. Milw., Sept. 23, 1947; s. Warren E. and Marjorie L. (Schramek) L.; m. Patricia L. Rasmus, Aug. 1, 1970 (div. Nov. 1990); children: Laurel, Daniel, Kristin; m. Kristine Harbrecht, May 22, 2004. BBA with honors, U. Wis., 1969; JD, Yale U., 1973, Yale Law Sch. Bar: Wis. 1973. Acct. Arthur Andersen & Co., Milw., 1969-70; atty. Foley & Lardner, Milw., 1973-80, ptnr., 1980—. Bd. dirs. numerous cos. Bd. dirs. Riveredge Nature Ctr., Milw., 1983-92, 96-99, Wis. Pro Soccer, 1986-2003, Milw. Art Mus., 1992-2001, Child Abuse Prevention Fund, Milw., 1989-2003, Michael Fields Agrl. Inst., 1991—, Florentine Opera Co., 1992—; class agt. Yale Law Sch., 1978—. With U.S. Army, 1969-75. Mem. ABA, AICPA (Wisc.), Wis. Bar Assn., Milw. Bar Assn., Estate Counselors Forum, Univ. Club (Milw.), Phi Kappa Phi. Avocations: theater, racquetball, violin. Office: Foley & Lardner LLP 777 E Wisconsin Ave Ste 3500 Milwaukee WI 53202-5306 Home Phone: 414-271-6452; Office Phone: 414-297-5786. Business E-Mail: wlueders@foley.com.

LUE-HING, CECIL, civil engineer; Dir. R&D Met. Water Reclamation Dist. Gtr. Chgo. V.p. Environ. and Water Resources Inst. Mem. NAE. Office: Metro Water Reclamation Dist Gtr Chgo 100 E Erie St Chicago IL 60611

LUEKEN, HAROLD W., retail executive; b. Bayshore, NY, Apr. 28, 1962; BA summa cum laude, Slippery Rock U., 1984; JD cum laude, Fordham U., 1988. Mng. dir., gen. counsel corp. investment Banc of Am. Securities, 2000—03;

prin. Morgan Stanley Dean Witter & Co., NYC, 1994—2000; corp. assoc. Cravath, Swaine & Moore, YC, 1989—94; fgn. assoc. Boden Oppenhoff & Schneider, Cologne, Germany, 1988—89; sr. v.p., gen. counsel, sec. Kmart Corp, Troy, Mich., 2003—.

LUENING, ROBERT ADAMI, retired agricultural studies educator; b. Milw., Apr. 20, 1924; s. Edwin Garfield and Irma Barbara (Adami) L.; m. Dorothy Ellen Hodgskiss, Aug. 27, 1966. BS, U. Wis., 1961, MS, 1968. Dairy farmer, Hartland, Wis., 1942-58; fieldman Waukesha County Dairy Herd Improvement Assn., Waukesha, Wis., 1958; adult agr. instr. Blair Sch. Dist., Wis., 1961-63; extension farm mgmt. agt. U. Wis.-Racine, 1963-69; extension farm record specialist dept. agrl. and applied econs. U. Wis.-Madison, 1969-88; free-lance work, 1988—. Author: (with others) The Farm Management Handbook, 1972, 7th edit., 1991, Teacher's Manual, 1991, Managing Your Financial Future Farm Record Book Series, 1980, 4th edit., 1987, USDA Yearbook of Agriculture, 1989, Beef, Sheep and Forage Production in Northern Wisconsin, 1992, Dairy Farm Business Management, 1996, Poultry Farm Business Management, 1999, 2d edit., 2000, revised, 2004; writer mag. column: Agri-Vision, 1970-88. Founder, exec. pres. Lüning Family Orgns. U.S.A., Inc.; bd. dirs. Friends of the Max Kade Inst. for German-Am. Studies. Recipient John S. Donald Excellence in Teaching award U. Wis.-Madison, 1980; recipient Wis. State Farmer award Vocat. Agr. Inst. Wis., 1980, Second Mile award Wis. County Agts. Assn., 1980, Outstanding Svc. to Wis. Agr. award Farm and Industry Short Course, 1989. Mem. Wis. Soc. Farm Mgrs. and Rural Appraisers (hon., coll. v.p. 1976, chmn. editl. com. 1978-80, sec.-treas. 1968-80, pres. 1982, Silver Plow award 1988), Wis. State Geneal. Soc. (pres. S.C. chpt. 1995-96, pres. PAF Users group 1995), Epsilon Sigma Phi (Disting. Service award 1988), Alpha Gamma Rho, Kiwanis. Lodges: Masons. Presbyterian. Personal E-mail: rluening@wisc.edu.

LUEPKER, RUSSELL VINCENT, epidemiology educator; b. Chgo., Oct. 1, 1942; s. Fred Joseph and Anita Louise (Thornton) L.; m. Ellen Louise Thompson, Dec. 22, 1966; children: Ian, Carl. BA, Grinnell Coll., 1964; MD with distinction, U. Rochester, 1969; MS, Harvard U., 1976; PhD (hon.), U. Lund, Sweden, 1996. Intern U. Calif., San Diego, 1969-70; resident Peter Bent Brigham Hosp., Boston, 1973-74; cardiology fellow Peter Bent Brigham Hosp./Med., Boston, 1974-76; asst. prof. divsn. epidemiology med. lab. physiol. hygiene U. Minn., Mpls., 1976-80, assoc. prof., 1980-87, prof. divsn. epidemiology and medicine, 1987—, dir. divsn. epidemiology, 1991—2004, Mayo prof. pub. health, 2000—. Cons. NIH, Bethesda, Md., 1980—, U. So. Calif., L.A., 1985—, Armed Forces Epidemiology Bd., 1993-97; vis. prof. U. Goteborg, Sweden, 1986, Ninewells Med. Sch., Dundee, Scotland, 1995. With USPHS, 1970—73. Harvard U. fellow, 1974-76, Bush Leadership fellow, 1990; recipient Prize for Med. Rsch. Am. Coll. Chest Physicians, 1970, Nat. Rsch. Svc. award Nat. Heart, Lung and Blood Inst., Bethesda, 1975-77, Disting. Alumni award Grinnell Coll., 1989. Fellow ACP, Am. Coll. Cardiology, Am. Heart Assn. (chmn. coun. on epidemiology 1992-94, chair program com. sci. sessions 1995-97, award of merit 1997), Am. Coll. Epidemiology; mem. Am. Epidemiol. Soc., Am. Soc. Preventive Cardiology (Joseph Stokes award 1999), Delta Omega Soc. (Nat. Merit award 1988). Office: Univ Minn Sch Pub Health Div Epidemiology 1300 S 2nd St Minneapolis MN 55454-1087 Home Phone: 612-729-2659; Office Phone: 612-624-6362. Business E-Mail: luepker@epi.umn.edu.

LUETKENHAUS, WILLIAM JOSEPH, state legislator; b. Josephville, Mo., Sept. 15, 1962; s. Elmer William and Marilyn (Jenkins) L.; m. Patricia Ann Schulte; children: Katie, Andrew. Attended, Ranken Tech Coll., 1982-84. Lic. real estate broker, Mo. Plumber Lic. Journeymen, 1984—; owner, pres. Luetkenhaus Properties, Inc.; village trustee Town Bd., Josephville, 1989-90; county commr. St. Charles County, 1991-92; mem. Mo. Ho. of Reps. 12th Dist., Jefferson City, 1992—. Active St. Joseph Ch., Josephville. Mem. Plumbers and Pipefitters Local 567, Ranken Alumni Club, Lions. Roman Catholic. Avocations: hunting, travel. Home: 742 Hancock Rd Wentzville MO 63385-3104 Office: Ho of Reps State Capital Jefferson City MO 65101

LUGAR, DICK (RICHARD GREEN LUGAR), senator; b. Indpls., Apr. 4, 1932; s. Marvin L. and Bertha (Green) L.; m. Charlene Smeltzer, Sept. 8, 1956; children: Mark, Robert, John, David. BA, Denison U., 1954; BA, MA (Rhodes scholar), Oxford U., Eng., 1956. Mayor, Indpls., 1968-75; vis. prof. polit. sci. U. Indpls., 1976; US Senator from Ind., 1977—; chmn. com. fgn. rels. US Senate, 1985-86, 2003—06, chmn. com. on agr., nutrition and forestry, 1995-2001; chmn. Nat. Rep. Senatorial Com., 1983-84. Pres. Lugar Stock Farm, Inc.; mem. Indpls. Sch. Bd., 1964-67, v.p., 1965-66; vice chmn. Adv. Commn. on Intergovtl. Relations, 1969-75; pres. Nat. League of Cities, 1970-71; mem. Nat. Commn. Standards and Goals of Criminal Justice System, 1971-73; Del., mem. resolutions com. Republican Nat. Conv., 1968, del., mem. resolutions com., 1992, Keynote speaker, 1972, del., speaker, 1980., 88, 92, 96. Author: Letters to the Next President, 1988. Trustee Denison U., 1966—, U. Indpls., 1970-2002; bd. dirs. Nat. Endowment for Democracy, 1992-2000, Nuclear Threat Initiative, 2000—. Served to lt. (j.g.) USNR, 1957-60. Pembroke Coll., Oxford U. hon. fellow Mem. Rotary, Blue Key, Phi Beta Kappa, Omicron Delta Kappa, Pi Delta Epsilon, Pi Sigma Alpha, Beta Theta Pi. Republican. Methodist. Office: US Senate 306 Hart Senate Bldg Washington DC 20510-0001 Office Phone: 202-224-4814. Office Fax: 202-228-0360. E-mail: senator_lugar@lugar.senate.gov.

LUGAR, THOMAS R., manufacturing executive; BS mech. engring., Purdue Univ. With Allison Div. Gen. Motors Co., Indpls., 1955-57; pres. Thomas L. Green & Co., Indpls., 1957—2001; chmn. Thomas L. Green LLC (Divsn. of Reading Bakery Systems). Served US Army. Mem.: Cookie and Snack Bakers Assn., Biscuit & Cracker Manufacturers Assn. Office: Thomas L Green LLC 7802 Moller Rd Indianapolis IN 46268-2117

LUHMAN, GARY LEE, lawyer; b. Milford, Ill., July 13, 1957; s. Edgar C. and Ruth A. (Schuldt) L.; m. Beth Luhman, Aug. 25, 1984; children: Christopher, Ethan. BA, U. Ill., 1979; JD, U. Wis., Madison, 1982. Asst. dist. atty. County of Green, Monroe, Wis., 1983-88, County of Lafayette, Darlington, Wis., 1988-89; assoc. Ewald Law Offices, Monroe, 1989—. Village atty. Village of Browntown, Wis., 1989—; asst. city atty. City of Monroe, 1989—. Rep. candidate for Green County Dist. Atty., Monroe, 1989-90; pres. Jordan Luth. Ch., 1985-90. Mem. Kiwanis, Phi Beta Kappa. Home: 9440W Coon Creek Rd Browntown WI 53522-9765 Office: Ewald Law Offices 1112 17th Ave Monroe WI 53566-2007

LUKAN, STEVEN, state representative; b. New Vienna, Iowa, Dec. 17, 1978; BS in Polit. Sci., Laras Coll. State rep. dist. 32 Iowa Ho. of Reps., 2003—; mem. human resources com.; mem. natural resources com.; mem. ways and means com.; mem. justice sys. appropriations subcom.; vice chair econ. growth com. With USN. Republican. Roman Catholic. Office: State Capitol East 12th and Grand Des Moines IA 50319

LUKE, RANDALL DAN, retired manufacturing executive, lawyer; b. New Castle, Pa., June 4, 1935; s. Randall Beamer and Blanche Wilhelmina (Fisher) L.; m. Patricia Arlene Moody, Aug. 4, 1962 (div. Jan. 1977); children: Lisa Elin, Randall Sargent; m. Saralee Frances Krow, Mar. 1, 1979; 1 stepchild, Stephanie Sogg. BA in Econs. with honors, U. Pa., 1957, JD, 1960. Bar: Ohio 1960, Calif. 1962, Ill. 1989. Assoc., ptnr. Daus, Schwenger & Kottler, Cleve., 1965-70; ptnr. Kottler & Danzig, Cleve., 1970-75, Hahn, Loeser, Freedheim, Dean & Wellman, Cleve., 1975-81; assoc. gen. counsel The Firestone Tire & Rubber Co., Akron, Ohio, 1981-82, v.p., assoc. gen. counsel and sec., 1982-88, Bridgestone/Firestone, Inc., Akron, 1988-91, ret., 1991; of counsel Hahn Loeser & Parks, Cleve., 1991-2000; ret., 2000. Trustee, Akron Art Mus., 1982-87, Akron Symphony Orch., 1986-87, Cleve. Opera League, 1992-98. Served to Capt. USNR, 1960-81; ret. 1981. Mem.: Ohio Bar Assn., Ill. Bar Assn., Calif. Bar Assn., Union Club, Mayfield Country Club, Cleve. Skating Club. Republican. Avocations: tennis, golf, skiing, swimming, exercise. Home: 13901 Shaker Blvd Cleveland OH 44120-1582

LUMENG, LAWRENCE, physician, educator; b. Manila, Aug. 10, 1939; came to US, 1958; s. Ming and Lucia (Lim) Lu; m. Pauline Lumeng, Nov. 26, 1966; children: Carey, Emily. AB, Ind. U., 1960, MD, 1964, MS, 1969. Intern U. Chgo., 1964-65; resident Ind. U. Hosps., Indpls., 1965-67, fellow, 1967-69, asst. prof. Sch. of Medicine, 1971-73, assoc. prof. Sch. of Medicine, 1974-79, prof. Sch. of Medicine, 1979—2003, dir. div. gastroenterology and hepatology Sch. of Medicine, 1984—; chief gastroenterology sect. VA Med. Ctr., Indpls., 1979—2003. Merit rev. bd. VA. Cen. Office, Washington, 1981-84; alcohol biomed. res. rev. com. IAAA, Washington, 1982-86; grant rev. panel USDA, Washington, 1985-2003. Contbr. over 290 articles to profl. jours. Maj. U.S. Army, 1969-71. Fellow ACP; mem. Am. Soc. Clin. Investigation, Am. Soc. Biol. Chemists, Rsch. Soc. on Alcoholism (treas. 1985-87, sec. 1987-89), Am. Gastroenterological Assn., Am. Assn. Study Liver Diseases, Am. Assn. Physicians, Cen. Soc. Clin. Rsch., Am. Liver Found. (vet. hepatitis C liver disease coun.), Am. Coll. Gastroenterology. Avocations: painting, music, gardening. Office: Ind U Med Ctr 975 W Walnut St Indianapolis IN 46202-5181 Home Phone: 317-873-6679; Office Phone: 317-274-3505. Business E-Mail: lluming@iupui.edu.

LUMPE, SHEILA, commissioner, retired state legislator; b. Apr. 17, 1935; m. Gustav H. Lumpe, 1958. AB, Ind. U.; postgrad., Johns Hopkins U.; MA, U. Mo. Formerly mem. Mo. Ho. of Reps.; now. Mo. Pub. Svc. Commn. Active Women's Polit. Caucus; bd. dirs. Mo. Humanities Coun., Partnership for Outstanding Schs. Democrat. Office: Pub Svc Commn PO Box 360 Jefferson City MO 65102-0360 Home: 6908 Amherst Ave Saint Louis MO 63130-3124

LUMPKINS, ROBERT L., food products executive; b. Lawrenceburg, Tenn., Jan. 25, 1944; s. Robert L. and Maude (Holthouse) L.; m. Sara Jane O'Connell, Dec. 29, 1966; 1 child, Christine Jane. BS in Math. magna cum laude, U. Notre Dame, 1966; MBA, Stanford U., 1968. Fin. analyst Cargill Inc., Mpls., 1968-70, mgr. fin. info. svcs. dept., 1970-73, gen. mgr. Cargil Leasing corp., 1973-75, group contr., 1975-82, sec., fin. com., 1975-82, pres. fin. svcs. divsn., 1983-88, chief fin. offficer Cargill Europe London, 1988-89, CFO, 1989—2005, vice chmn., 1995—. Chmn. Mosaic Co.; bd. dir. Ecolab Inc., Wherenet Corp. Mem. sci. adv. coun. U. Notre Dame, 1994--; bd. dirs. Minn. Orch. Assn., Mpls., 1993-2000; trustee Minn. Med. Found., Mpls., 1992-2000; bd. dirs. Greater Mpls. Met. Housing Corp., 1996-99, Technoserve Inc., 1997—; trustee Howard U., 1998—; mem. adv. coun. Stanford Bus. Sch., 2000—. Mem. Minikahda Club. Roman Catholic. Office: Cargill Inc PO Box 9300 Minneapolis MN 55440-9300

LUMSDAINE, EDWARD, mechanical engineering educator, dean; b. Hong Kong, China, Sept. 30, 1937; came to U.S., 1953; s. Clifford Vere and Ho Miao Ying Lumsdaine; m. Monika Amsler, Sept. 8, 1959; children: Andrew, Anne Josephine, Alfred, Arnold BS in Mech. Engring., N.Mex. State U., Las Cruces, 1963, MS in Mech. Engring., 1964, PhD, 1966. Research engr. Boeing Co., Seattle, 1966-67, 68; asst. prof. to assoc. prof. S.D. State U., Brookings, 1967-72; assoc. prof. to prof. U. Tenn., Knoxville, 1972-77; prof., sr. research engr. phys. sci. lab., dir. N.Mex. solar energy inst. N.Mex. State U., Las Cruces, 1977-81; prof., dir. energy, environ. and resources ctr. U. Tenn., Knoxville, 1981-83; dean engring., prof. U. Mich., Dearborn, 1982-88, U. Toledo, 1988-93; dean of engring. Mich. Technol. U., Houghton, 1993-95, prof. mech. engring., 1993—; mgmt. cons. Ford Motor Co., 1995—. Vis. prof. Cairo U., Egypt, 1974, Tatung Inst. Tech., Taipei, China, 1978, Qatar U., Doha, 1983, Inst. Enterprise and Innovation U. Nottingham, Eng., 1999-2000; spl. prof. bus. U. Nottingham, 2000—; UNESCO expert cons. to Egypt, 1979-80; cons. E&M Lumsdaine Solar Cons., Hancock, Mich., 1979—; cons. Oak Ridge (Tenn.) Nat. Lab., 1979-82, BDM Corp., Albuquerque, 1984, Ford Motor Co., Dearborn, Mich., 1984-95, Am. Supplier Inst., Dearborn, 1986-95. Author: Industrial Energy Conservation for Developing Countries, 1984, (with Monika Lumsdaine) Creative Problem Solving: An Introductory Course for Engineering Students, 1990, Creative Problem Solving: Thinking Skills for a Changing World, 1995, (with Monika Lumsdaine and J. William Shelnutt) Creative Problem Solving and Engineering Design, 1999, (with Martin Binks) Keep On Moving! Entrepreneurial Creativity and Effective Problem Solving, 2003, (with Martin Binks) Entrepreneurship, Creativity and Effective Problem Solving, 2005, (with Monika Lumsdaine, J. William Shelnutt and George E. Dieter) Creative Problem Solving and Engineering Design 2, 2005, (with Martin Binks) Entrepreneurship from Creativity to Innovation, 2007; contbr. software packages, articles to profl. jours. Served with USAF, 1954-58 Recipient Am. Soc. Engring. Edn./Xerox Chester F. Carlson award for innovation in engring. edn., 1994; NASA faculty fellow, 1969, 70; grantee NSF, ASA, U.S. Dept. Energy, Dept. Navy, ASHRAE, AID, Ford Motor Co. Fellow AIAA, ASME, Royal Soc. Arts; mem. Am. Soc. Engring. Edn., Am. Creativity Assn. Baptist. Office: Mich Tech U Dept Mech Engring Houghton MI 49931 Office Phone: 906-487-2977. Business E-Mail: lumsdain@mtu.edu.

LUND, DARYL BERT, retired food science educator; b. San Bernardino, Calif., Nov. 4, 1941; married June 15, 1963; children: Kristine, Eric. BS in Math., U. Wis., 1963, MS in food Sci., 1965, PhD in Food Sci., 1968. Rsch. asst. in food sci. U. Wis., Madison, 1963-67, instr., 1967-68, asst. prof., 1968-72, assoc. prof., 1972-77, prof. food sci., 1977-87, chmn. dept. food sci., 1984-87; chmn. dept. food sci., assoc. dir. agrl. experiment sta. Rutgers, the State U., ew Brunswick, 1988-89, interim exec. dean agr. and natural resources, 1989-91, exec. dean agr./natural resources, 1991-95, exec. dir. N.J. Agrl. Experiment Sta., dean Cook Coll., 1991-95; Ronald P. Lynch dean of agr. and life scis. Cornell U., Ithaca, NY, 1995-2000; exec. dir. North Ctrl. Regional Assn. U. Wis., Madison, 2001—06; emeritus prof food sci. U. Wis., Madison, 2007—. Vis. engr. Western Regional Rsch. Lab., Berkeley, Calif., 1970-71; advisor for evaluation of food tech. dept. Inst. Agr., Bogor, Indonesia, 1973; mem. four-man evaluation team to review grad. edn. programs Brazilian univs., 1976; vis. prof. food process engring. Agrl. U., Wageningen, The Netherlands, 1979; invited vis. prof. food process engring. Univ. Coll., Dublin, 1982; invited advisor Inter-Univ. Ctr. on Food Sci. and Nutrition, Bogor, 1991; advisor Agrl. U., Bogor, 1992; Woodroof lectr. U. Ga., 2003; lectr. in field Contbr. over 200 articles to profl. jours.; editor 5 books; co-author text book. Fellow Inst. Food Sci. and Tech., UK, 2000; recipient Food Engring. award Dairy and Food Industries Supply Assn. and Am. Soc. Agrl. Engring., 1987, Internat. award Inst. Food Technologists, 2001, Irving award Svc., Am. Distance Edn. Consortium 2001, Carl Fellers award IFT, 2003, Harris award Ohio State U., 2006. Fellow Inst. Food Technologists (Wis. sect. 1968-87, N.Y. sect. 1988-95, ctrl. N.Y. 1995-2000), Internat. Union Food Sci. and Tech.; mem. AIChE, Am. Inst. Nutrition, Internat. Acad. Food Sci. and Tech., 1999 (charter mem.), Sigma Xi, Gamma Sigma Delta, Phi Tau Sigma. Avocations: golf, travel, woodworking. Home: 151 E Reynolds St Cottage Grove WI 53527

LUND, DORIS HIBBS, retired dietitian; b. Des Moines, Nov. 10, 1923; d. Loyal Burchard and Catharine Mae (McClymond) Hibbs; m. Richard Bodholdt Lund, Nov. 9, 1946; children: Laurel Anne, Richard Douglas, Kristi Jane Lund Lozier. Scholar, Duchesne Coll., 1941-42; BS, Iowa State U., 1946; postgrad., Grand View Coll., 1965; MS in Mgmt., Iowa State U., 1968. Registered dietitian, lic. dietitian. Clk. Russell Stover Candies, Omaha, 1940-42; chemist Martin Bomber Plant, Omaha, 1942-43; Dietitian Grand Lake (Colo.) Lodge, 1946; tailoring instr. Ottumwa Pub. Schs., 1952-53; cookery instr. Des Moines Pub. Schs., 1958-62; dietitian Calvin Manor, Des Moines, 1965; home economist Am. Wool Coun./Am. Lamb Coun., Denver, 1963-65, The Merchandising Group of N.Y., 1965-68, Thomas Wolff, Pub. Rels., 1968-70; home economist weekly TV program Iowa Power Co., 1968-70; cons. in child nutrition programs Iowa Dept. Edn., Des Moines, 1970-95; ret. Nutritioneering, Ltd., 1995. Mem. Iowa Home Economists in Bus. (pres. 1962-63), PEO. Pres. Callanan Jr. H.S. PTA, 1964, Roosevelt H.S. PTA, 1966; amb. Friendship Force Internat., 1982—; alliance mem. Des Moines Symphony; guild mem. Civic Music Des Moines Met. Opera; mem. Civic Music Guild, Bot. Ctr. Des Moines, Des Moines Art Ctr., Des Moines Civic Ctr.; chmn. Met. Opera Previews; chair Wesley Grand Coun., 2005; pres. Ctrl. Presbyn. Mariners, Des Moines; ruling elder, clk. of session Ctrl. Presbyn. Session, Des Moines, 1972—78; bd. dirs. Ctrl. Found., Ctrl. Pastor Seeking Nomination Com., 1996; chair cmty. concerns Calvin Cmty. Found., 1998, chair support and edn., 1999—. Duchesne Coll. 4 yr. scholar. Mem. Am. Dietetic Assn., Iowa Home Economists in Bus. (pres. 1962-63), Drake Univ. Lifelong Learning, PEO, Pi Beta Phi (pres. 1945-46). Republican. Avocations: travel, writing, sailing, sewing, cooking.

LUNDBERG, JOE, meteorologist, radio personality; Meteorologist Sta. WMBI Radio, Chgo. Avocations: bowling, softball, golf, singing, playing games. Address: PO Box 263 Pine Grove Mills PA 16868

LUNDBERG, SUSAN ONA, musical organization administrator; b. Mandan, ND, Mar. 15, 1947; d. Robert Henry and Evelyn (Olson) L.; m. Paul R. Wick, July 2, 1972 (div. May 1976); 1 child, Melissa. BA, Stephens Coll., 1969; MLS, Western Mich. U., 1970; MPA, Calif. State U., Fullerton, 1980. Children's and reference libr. Bismarck (N.D.) Pub. Libr., 1970-71; reference libr. U. Tenn., Knoxville, 1971-72; coord. children's svcs. Orange County (Calif.) Pub. Libr., 1972-75; exec. dir. Bismarck-Manda Orch. Assn., 1992—. Exec. dir., founder Sleepy Hollow Summer Theatre, Bismarck, 1990—; trustee Gabriel J. Brown Trust, Bismarck, 1989—. Exhibitions include of paintings Scandinavian Threads of Inheritance, 2002. Chair Nat. Music Week N.D., 1990—, Friends of the Belle, 1997—; chair small budget orchs. Am. Symphony Orch. League, 2000-03; mem. civic chorus Bismarck-Mandary. Named Outstanding Leaders of Yr. Bismarck Tribune, 1995; recipient hon. portrait, Belle Mehus City Auditorium, Vol. award, DAR, 2004, Family Vol. award, Folk Fest, 2004. Mem. DAR (Vol. award 2004), Calif. Libr. Assn. (pres. children's svcs. 1971-72), Bismarck Art Assn. (pres. 1982-84), Bismarck Art and Galleries Assn. (bd. dirs. 1985-2000, pres. 1986-88, Honor Citation award 1992), Jr. Svc. League. Lutheran. Avocations: painting, singing. Home: 112 Ave E W Bismarck ND 58501 Office Phone: 701-258-8345.

LUNDBY, MARY A., state legislator; b. Carroll County, Feb. 2, 1948; d. Edward A. and Elizabeth Hoehl; m. Michael Lundby, 1971; 1 child, Daniel. BA in History, Upper Iowa U., 1971. Former staff asst. Senator Roger Jepsen; mem. Iowa Senate from 26th dist., Des Moines, 1995—2002, Iowa Senate from 18th dist., Des Moines, 2003—. Active Solid Waste Adv. Com. Republican. Office: Iowa State Senate State Capitol Des Moines IA 50319-0001 Home: PO Box 648 Marion IA 52302-0648

LUNDE, HAROLD IRVING, retired management educator; b. Austin, Minn., Apr. 18, 1929; s. Peter Oliver and Emma (Stoa) L.; m. Sarah Jeanette Lysne, June 25, 1955; children: Paul, James, John, Thomas. BA, St. Olaf Coll., 1952; MA, U. Minn., 1954, PhD, 1966. Assoc. prof. econs. Macalester Coll., St. Paul, 1957-64; fin. staff economist Gen. Motors Corp., NYC, 1965-67; corp. sec. Dayton Hudson Corp., Mpls., 1967-70; mgr. planning and gen. research May Dept. Stores Co., St. Louis, 1970-72, v.p. planning and rsch., 1972—78; exec. v.p. adminstrn. Kobacker Stores, Inc., Columbus, Ohio, 1979; prof. mgmt. Bowling Green (Ohio) State U., 1980-98, emeritus, 1998—. Bd. dir. and trustee AgCredit, Fostoria, Ohio, Goodwill Industries N.W. Ohio, U.S. Naval War Coll. Found., ewport, RI. Mem. Acad. Mgmt., Am. Econ. Assn., Nat. Assn. Bus. Economists, Decision Scis. Inst., Phi Beta Kappa, Phi Kappa Phi, Omicron Delta Kappa, Beta Gamma Sigma. Home: 880 Country Club Dr Bowling Green OH 43402-1602 Personal E-mail: hlunde@bgsu.edu.

LUNDERGAN, BARBARA KEOUGH, lawyer; b. Chgo., Nov. 6, 1938; d. Edward E. and Eleanor A. (Erickson) Keough; children: Matthew K., Mary Alice. BA, U. Ill., Urbana, 1960; JD, Loyola U., Chgo., 1964. Bar: Ill. 1964, Ga. 1997, Minn. 2004, U.S. Dist. Ct. (no. dist.) Ill. 1964, U.S. Tax Ct. 1974. Ptnr. Seyfarth Shaw LLP, Chgo., 1971—98, of counsel, 1998—2004, Hristendahl Moersch and Dorsey PA, Northfield, Minn., 2004—. Fellow Am. Coll. Trust and Estate Counsel; mem. ABA (com. on fed. taxation), Ill. Bar Assn. (coun. sect. on fed. taxation 1983-91, chair 1989, coun. sect. on trusts and estates sect. coun. 1992-97, sec. 1996-97, editl. bd. Ill. Bar Jour. 1993-96), Chgo. Bar Assn. (chmn. trust law com. 1982-83, com. on fed. taxation). Office: Hristendahl Moersch and Dorsey PA 311 Water St Northfield MN 55057 Home Phone: 507-645-6713; Office Phone: 507-645-9358. Business E-Mail: bkl@hvmd.com.

LUNDGREN, TERRY J., retail company executive; b. Long Beach, Calif., 1953; m. Nancy (div.); two children. BA, U. Ariz., 1974. From. v.p. Bullock's to pres. Bullock's Wilshire Federated Dept. Stores, Inc., NYC, 1975-88; chmn., CEO Neiman Marcus Stores Neiman Marcus Group Inc., 1990—94; chmn., CEO Federated Merchandising Group Federated Merchandising Group, 1994—98; pres., chief merchandising officer Macy's Inc. (formerly Federated Dept. Stores, Inc.), 1997—2002; COO Macy's Inc., 2002—03, pres., CEO, 2003—, chmn., 2004—. Bd. dirs. Dallas Symphony Orch., Dallas Citizens Coun. Office: Macy's Inc 7 W 7th St Cincinnati OH 45202

LUNDRIGAN, NICOLE M., lawyer; b. Piqua, Ohio, 1977; BA, U. Dayton, 1998; JD, Ohio Northern U., 2002. Bar: Ohio 2002, US Dist. Ct. Southern Dist. Ohio 2002, US Ct. of Appeals Sixth Cir. 2003. Assoc. Strauss & Troy, Cin. Named one of Ohio's Rising Stars, Super Lawyers, 2006. Mem.: Ohio State Bar Assn., Cin. Bar Assn., Dayton Bar Assn. Office: Strauss & Troy Federal Reserve Bldg 150 E Fourth St Cincinnati OH 45202-4018 Office Phone: 513-621-2120. Office Fax: 513-241-8259.

LUNDSTEDT, SVEN BERTIL, behavioral and social scientist, educator; b. NYC, May 6, 1926; s. Sven David and Edith Maria L.; m. Jean Elizabeth Sanford, June 16, 1951; children: Margaret, Peter, Janet. AB, U. Chgo., 1952, PhD, 1955; SM, Harvard U., 1960. Lic. in psychology, N.Y., Ohio; cert. Council for Nat. Register of Health Services. Asst. dir. Found. for Research on Human Behavior, 1960-62; asst. prof. Case-Western Res. U., Cleve., 1962-64, assoc. prof., 1964-68; assoc. prof. adminstrv. sci. Ohio State U., Columbus, 1968-69, prof. pub. policy and mgmt., 1969—, Ameritech Research prof., 1987-89, prof. internat. bus. and pub. policy, 1988—, prof. mgmt. and human resources, 1990—2005, prof. emeritus, 2005—, mem. John Glenn Inst. for Pub. Svc. and Pub. Policy, 1999—, emeritus prof. pub. policy and mgmt., 2004—. Affiliate scientist Battelle PNL, 1974—; chmn. Batelle Endowment Program for Tech. and Human Affairs, 1976—80; mem. Univ. Senate, 2002—; dir. project on edn. of CEO Aspen Inst., 1978—80; advisor Task Force on Innovation, US Ho. of Reps., 1983—84; advisor Citizens Network for Fgn. Affairs, 1988—; mem. Am. Com. on US Soviet Rels., 1985—, chair trade and negotiation project; cons. E.I. duPont de Nemours & Co., B.F. Goodrich Co., Bell Tel. Labs., Battelle Meml. Inst., Nat. Fulbright Award Com.; invited spkr. Royal Swedish Acad. Scis., 1989. Author: Higher Education in Social Psychology, 1968; co-author: Managing Innovation, 1982, Managing Innovation and Change, 1989; author, editor: Telecommunications, Values and the Public Interest, 1990; contbr. articles to profl. jours. Pres., Cleve. Mental Health Assn., 1966-68; mem. Ohio Citizen's Task Force on Corrections, 1971-72. Served with U.S. Army, 1944-46 Harvard U. fellow, 1960; grantee Bell Telephone Labs., 1964-65, NSF, 1965-67, Kettering Found., 1978-80, Atlantic Richfield Found., 1980-82, German Marshall Fund of U.S. to conduct internat. ednl. joint ventures on econ. negotiations, Budapest, Hungary, 1990; recipient Ohio Ho. of Reps. award, 1986. Mem.: APA, Internat. Soc. Panetics (mem., sec. bd. govs., founding mem.), Am. Soc. for Pub. Adminstrn. (pres. Central Ohio chpt. 1975—77, founder, chmn. com. on bus. govt. relations 1977—79, editl. bd. Pub. Adminstrn. Rev. 1978—82), Am. Acad. Arts and Scis. (chmn. PIN com. on east/west trade negotiation), Internat. Inst. for Applied Systems Analysis (innovation task force, nat. adv. com. project. internat. negotiation with AAAS, founder, chmn. U.S. Midwest Assn. for IIASA 1986—, sr. social sci. advisor 1994—). Unitarian Universalist. E-mail: lundstedt.1@osu.edu.

LUNDY, SHERMAN PERRY, secondary school educator; b. Kansas City, Mo., July 26, 1939; s. Loren F. and O. Metta (Brown) L.; m. Beverly J., Feb. 25, 1960; children: Paul, Carolyn. BA, U. Okla., 1963; MA, So. Meth. U., 1966; EdS, U. Iowa, 1975. Cert. tchr., Iowa. Tchr. Platte Canyon High Sch., Bailey, Colo., 1964-65, Lone Grove (Okla.) High Sch., 1966-68, Ardmore (Okla.) High Sch., 1968-69; tchr., sci. dept. chair Burlington (Iowa) High Sch., 1969—. Geologist Basic Materials Corp., Waterloo, Iowa, 1983—, Raid Quarries, Burlington, 1975-80. Contbr. articles to profl. jours.; author curriculum guide: Environmental Activities, 1975. Mem., commr. Regional Solid Waste Commn., Des Moines County, 1990—; mem., pres. Conservation Bd., Des Moines County, 1978-88; bd. dirs. Iowa Conservation Bd. Assn., 1984-85; mem. Civil Rights Commn., City of Burlington, 1970-76; pres. Burlington Trees Forever, 1998-99. With USMC, 1960-64. Recipient Silver Beaver Boy Scouts Am., 1975, Service Recognition, Des Moines County Conservation Bd., 1988, Project ESTEEM agt., Harvard/Smithsonian, 1992, Soil Conservation Water Shed Achievement award State of Iowa, 1998, DAR Award for Conservation, 1998, Environ. Educator of Yr. award U.S. EPA, Region 7, Iowa, 1998. Mem. Geol. Soc. Am. (North Cen. edn. com. 1989—), Iowa Acad. Sci. (edn. com. 1990-91, chair earth sci. tchrs. sect. 1993-94, exec. bd. 1992-94), Nat. Assn. Geology Tchrs. (Outstanding Earth Sci. Tchr. 1992, v.p. ctrl. sect. 1994-95, pres. ctrl. sect. 1996-98), Soc. Econ. and Sedimentary Geology, Geol. Soc. Iowa, Am. Chem. Soc. (Excellence in Sci. Tchg. award consortiums 1996, Chem. Cos. award), Unitarian Fellowship, Sons of Confederate Vets. (comdr. Camp 1759 1998—), SE Iowa Civil War Round Table (chair 1992-94). Unitarian Universalist. Avocations: history, stamp collecting/philately, fossil collecting. Home: 1103 Ellen St Cedar Falls IA 50613-2366

LUNGSTRUM, JOHN W., federal judge; b. Topeka, Nov. 2, 1945; s. Jack Edward and Helen Alice (Watson) L.; m. Linda Eileen Ewing, June 21, 1969; children: Justin Matthew, Jordan Elizabeth, Alison Paige. BA magna cum laude, Yale Coll., 1967; JD, U. Kans., 1970. Bar: Kans. 1970, Calif. 1970, admitted to practice: US Dist. Ct. (Ctrl. Dist.) Calif., US Ct. Appeals (10th Cir.). Assoc. Latham & Watkins, LA, 1970-71; ptnr. Stevens, Brand, Lungstrum, Golden & Winter, Lawrence, Kans., 1972-91; U.S. Dist. judge Dist. of Kans., Kansas City, 1991—2001, chief judge, 2001—07. Lectr. law U. Kans. Law Sch., 1973—; mem. faculty Kans. Bar Assn. Coll. Advocacy, Trial Tactics and Techniques Inst., 1983-86; chmn. Douglas County Rep. Ctrl. Com., 1975-81; mem. Rep. State Com.; del. State Rep. Conv., 1968, 76, 80; chair com. on ct. adminstrn. and case mgmt. Jud. Conf. US, 2000-05, mem. budget com., 2005-. Chmn. bd. dirs. Lawrence C. of C., 1990-91; pres. Lawrence United Fund, 1979; pres. Independence Days Lawrence, Inc., 1984, 85, Seem-to-be-Players, Inc., Lawrence Rotary Club, 1978-79; bd. dirs. Lawrence Soc. Chamber Music, Swarthout Soc. (corp. fund-raising chmn.); mem. Lawrence Art Commn., Williams Scholarship Fund, Lawrence League Women Voters, Douglas County Hist. Soc.; bd. trustees, stewardship chmn. Plymouth Congl. Ch.; pres. Lawrence Round Ball Club; coach Lawrence Summertime Basketball; vice chmn. U. Kans. Disciplinary Bd.; bd. govs. Kans Sch. Religion; bd. dirs. Kans. Day Club, 1980, 81. National Merit scholar, Yale Nat. scholar. Fellow Am. Bar Found.; mem. ABA (commn. Am. Jury 2004-05, past mem. litig. and ins. sect.), Douglas County Bar Assn., Johnson County Bar Assn., Wyandotte County Bar Assn., Kans. Bar Assn. (vice chair legis. com., subcom. litig., mem.CLE com.), U. Kans. Alumni Assn. (life), Judge Hugh Means Inn of Ct. (pres. 2005-), Phi Beta Kappa, Phi Gamma Delta, Phi Delta Phi. Avocations: basketball, hiking, skiing. Office: Robt J Dole US Courthouse Ste 517 500 State Ave Rm 517 Kansas City KS 66101-2400

LUNING, THOMAS P., lawyer; b. St. Louis, Oct. 11, 1942; AB magna cum laude, Xavier U., 1964; JD, Georgetown U., 1967. Bar: D.C. 1968, Ill. 1968. Law clk. to Hon. Spottswood W. Robinson III and to ct. U.S. Ct. Appeals (D.C. cir.), 1967-68; atty. Schiff Hardin & Waite, Chgo. Mng. editor Georgetown Law Jour., 1966-67. Mem. ABA, Ill. State Bar Assn., Chgo. Bar Assn., 7th Cir. Bar Assn., Chgo. Coun. Lawyers. Office: Schiff Hardin & Waite 6600 Sears Tower Chicago IL 60606 E-mail: tluning@schiffhardin.com.

LUPULESCU, AUREL PETER, medical educator, researcher, physician; b. Manastiur, Banat, Romania, Jan. 1, 1923; came to US, 1967, naturalized, 1973; s. Peter Vichentie and Maria Ann (Dragan) L. MD magna cum laude, Sch. Medicine, Bucharest, Romania, 1950; MS in Endocrinology, U. Bucharest, 1965; PhD in Biology, U. Windsor, Ont., Can., 1976. Diplomate Am. Bd. Internal Medicine. Chief lab. investigations Inst. Endocrinology, Bucharest, 1950-67; rsch. assoc. SUNY Downstate Med. Ctr., 1968-69; asst. prof. medicine Wayne State U., 1969-72, assoc. prof., 1973—. Vis. prof. Inst. Med. Pathology, U. Rome, 1967; cons. VA Hosp., Allen Park, Mich., 1971-73; sr. cancer rsch. scientist Wayne State U., 1991—. Author: Steroid Hormones, 1958, Advances in Endocrinology and Metabolism, 1962, Experimental Pathophysiology of Thyroid Gland, 1963, Ultrastructure of Thyroid Gland, 1968, Effect of Calcitonin on Epidermal Cells and Collagen Synthesis in Experimental Wounds As Revealed by Electron Microscopy Autoradiography and Scanning Electron Microscopy, 1976, Hormones and Carcinogenesis, 1983, Hormones and Vitamins in Cancer Treatment, 1990, Cancer Cell Metabolism and Cancer Treatment, 2001; reviewer various sci. jours.; contbr. chpts., numerous articles to profl. publs. Recipient Lifetime Sci. Achievement award, Internat. Biographical Ctr., 2003. Fellow Fedn. Am. Socs. for Exptl. Biology; mem. AMA, AAAS, Electron Microscopy Soc. Am., Soc. for Investigative Dermatology, NY Acad. Scis., Am. Soc. Cell Biology, Soc. Exptl. Biology and Medicine. Republican. Achievements include research on hormones and tumor biology; studies regarding role of hormones and vitamins in cancer treatment and prevention. Office: Wayne State U Sch Medicine 540 E Canfield St Detroit MI 48201-1928

LURAIN, JOHN ROBERT, III, gynecologist; b. Princeton, Ill., Oct. 27, 1946; s. John Robert Jr. and Elizabeth Helen (Grampp) L.; m. Nell Lee Snavely, June 14, 1969; children: Alice Elizabeth, Kathryn Anne. BA, Oberlin Coll., 1968; MD, U. N.C., 1972. Diplomate Am. Bd. Ob-Gyn., Am. Bd. Gynecologic Oncology. Resident in ob-gyn. U. Pitts./Magee-Womens Hosp., 1972-75; fellow in gynecologic oncology Roswell Park Cancer Inst., Buffalo, 1977-79; prof. gynecology and cancer rsch. Northwestern U., Feinberg Sch. Medicine, Chgo., 1979—; chief gyn. oncology svc. Northwestern Meml. Hosp., 1985—2004. Contbr. over 170 articles to profl. jours., chapters to books. Lt. comdr. USN, 1975-77. Fellow: Am. Coll. Ob-Gyn.; mem.: Internat. Soc. Study Trophoblastic Diseases, Internat. Gynecol. Cancer Soc., Am Soc. Colposcopy and Cervical Pathology, Ctrl. Assn. Ob-Gyn., Am. Soc. Clin. Oncology, Soc. Gynecologic Oncologists. Avocations: golf, tennis. Office: Northwestern U Med Sch 250 E Superior St Chicago IL 60611-3015 Home Phone: 708-383-4950; Office Phone: 312-472-4684. Business E-Mail: jlurain@nmff.org.

LURIE, ANN LASALLE, foundation administrator; b. Fla. m. Robert H. Lurie (dec. 1990); 6 children. BS in Nursing, Univ. Fla. Former pub. health, pediatric intensive care nurse; pres. Lurie Investments, Chgo., 1990—; pres., treas. Ann and Robert H. Lurie Foundation, Chgo., 1992—; founding pres. Africa Infectious Disease (AID) Village Clinic, Kenya, 2002—. Bd. trustees Northwestern Univ. Named one of Top 10 Women in Philanthropy, Chgo. Sun-Times, 100 Most Influential Women, Crain's Chicago Bus., 2004; recipient Jane Addams History Maker award for distinction in social services. Office: Ann and Robert H Lurie Found Ste 1500 2 N Riverside Plz Chicago IL 60606

LUSCOMBE, GEORGE A., II, lawyer; b. Jefferson, Iowa, Oct. 22, 1944; BS, U. Ill., 1966, JD, 1969; LLM, George Washington U., 1972. Bar: Ill. 1969, U.S. Supreme Ct. 1972, U.S. Claims Ct. 1972, D.C. 1972. Asst. br. chief legislation and regulations divsn. IRS Office Chief Counsel, 1972-73; ptnr. Mayer, Brown, LLP, Chgo. Adj. prof. law IIT, 1987-93; speaker in field. Mem. ABA (chmn. com. depreciation and investment tax credit, sect. taxation 1980-82), Ill. State Bar Assn. (chmn. fed. tax sect. coun. 1991-92), Chgo. Bar Assn. (chmn. gen. income tax divsn., fed. tax com. 1977-79), D.C. Bar. Office: Mayer Brown LLP 71 S Wacker Dr Chicago IL 60606-4637 Office Phone: 312-701-7099.

LUSHER, JEANNE MARIE, pediatric hematologist, educator; b. Toledo, June 9, 1935; d. Arnold Christian and Violet Cecilia (French) L. BS summa cum laude, U. Cin., 1956, MD, 1960. Resident in pediat. Tulane divsn. Charity Hosp. La., New Orleans, 1961-64; fellow in pediat. hematology-oncology Child Rsch. Ctr. Mich., Detroit, 1964-65, St. Louis Children's Hosp./Washington U., 1965-66; instr. pediat. Washington U., St. Louis, 1965-66; from instr. to prof. Sch. Medicine Wayne State U., Detroit, 1966—97, disting. prof., 1997—; dir. divsn. hematology-oncology Children's Hosp. Mich., Detroit, 1976—. Marion I. Barnhart prof. hemostasis rsch. Sch. Medicine Wayne State U., Detroit, 1989—; med. dir. Nat. Hemophilia Found., NYC, 1987—94, chmn. med. and sci. adv. coun., 1994—2001, bd. dirs., 1997—2001, co-chmn. gene therapy working group, 2000—; pres. Wayne State U. Acad. of Scholars, 2004—05. Author, editor: Treatment of Bleeding Disorders with Blood Components, 1980, Sickle Cell, 1974, 76, 81, Hemophilia and von Willebrand Disease in the 1990's, 1991, Acquired Bleeding Disorders in Children, 1981, F VIII/von Willebrand Factor and Platelets in Health and Disease, 1987, Inhibitors to Factor VIII, 1994, Blood Coagulation Innhibitors, 1996. Mem. Citizens Info. Com., Pontiac Township, Mich., 1980-82; apptd. mem. Hazardous Waste Incinerator Commn., Oakland County, Mich., 1981. Recipient Disting. Alumnus award U. Cin. Alumni Assn., 1990, Lawrence Weiner award Wayne State U. Sch. Medicine Alumni Assn., 1991, Disting. Career award Am. Soc. Pediat. Hematology-Oncology, 2000, Disting. Career award Nat. Hemophilia Found., 2003. Mem. Am. Bd. Pediat. (chmn. sub-bd. on hematology-oncology 1988-90), Am. Soc. Hematology (chmn. sci. com. pediat. 1991-92, sci. com. hemostasis 1998—), Am. Pediat. Soc., Soc. Pediat. Rsch., Internat. Soc. Thrombosis-Hemostasis (chmn. factor VIII/IX subcom. 1985-90, chmn. sci. and standardization com. 1996-98), Mich. Humane Soc., Humane Soc. U.S., Wayne State U. Acad. Scholars (pres. 2004-05). Avocations: nature, wildlife. Office: Children's Hosp Mich 3901 Beaubien Blvd Detroit MI 48201-2119 E-mail: jlusher@med.wayne.edu.

LUSSEN, JOHN FREDERICK, pharmaceutical laboratory executive; b. NYC, Jan. 5, 1942; s. Frederick Maurice and Kathleen (Herlihy) L.; m. Kathleen Elizabeth Sheppard; children: Tara, Eric, Gregory. BS in Fin., Fordham U., 1963, JD, 1967; LLM in Tax, NYU, 1971. Bar: N.Y. 1967. Tax atty. Pfizer Inc., NYC, 1971-74; mgr. taxes SCM Corp., NYC, 1974-79; v.p. taxes Abbott Labs., Abbott Park, Ill., 1979—. PhRMA tax com. Fin. Execs. Inst. Capt. U.S. Army, 1968-70. Mem. ABA, Tax Execs. Inst., Bus. Roundtable (mem. tax subcom.), P.R. USA Found. (pres.). Avocations: tennis, golf. Home: 1055 Westleigh Rd Lake Forest IL 60045 Office: Abbott Labs D367 AP6D 100 Abbott Park Rd Abbott Park IL 60064-6057 E-mail: john.lussen@Abbott.com.

LUSTER, JORY F., president of manufacturing company; Prin., owner Luster Products, Inc., Chgo., 1991—. Office: Luster Products Inc 1104 W 43rd St Chicago IL 60609-3342

LUSTREA, ANITA, radio personality; b. Blue Hill, Maine, May 28; m. Bob Lustrea; 1 child, John. Radio host Sta. WMBI, Chgo. Office: WMBI 820 LaSalle Blvd Chicago IL 60610

LUTHER, ROBERT K., college president; BA, MA, Eastern Ill. U.; PhD, U. Mich. V.p. Carl Sandburg Coll., Galesburg, Ill.; pres. Columbia-Greene Cmty. Coll., Hudson, .Y., Lake Land Coll., Mattoon, Ill., 1988—. Pres. East Ctrl. Ill. Dev. Corp., Coles Together; v.p. Ill. Council Cmty. Coll. Pres.; mem. Ill. Human Resource Investment Council (chmn. employment opportunities com.), Ill. Cmty. Coll. Bd., Ill. Bd. Higher Edn. Workforce Dev. Task Force. Office: Lake Land College 5001 Lake Land Bvld Mattoon IL 61938-9366

LUTHER, WILLIAM P., former congressman; b. Fergus Falls, Minn., June 27, 1945; s. Leonard and Eleanor L.; m. Darlene Luther, Dec. 16, 1967; children: Alexander, Alicia. BS in Elec. Engring. with high distinction, U. Minn., 1967; JD cum laude, U. Minn. Law Sch., 1970. Judicial clerkship 8th cir. U.S. Ct. Appeals, 1970-71; atty. Dorsey & Whitney Law Firm, Mpls., 1971-74, William P. Luther Law Office, Mpls., 1974-83; founder, sr. ptnr. Luther, Ballenthin & Carruthers Law Firm, Mpls., 1983-92; state sen. 47th dist. State of Minn., 1977-94, asst. maj. leader, 1983-94; mem. U.S. Congress from 6th Minn. dist., 1995—2003; mem. commerce com., telecomm., trade & consumer protection, fin., hazardous materials subcoms. Democrat. Home: 12310 Singletree Ln Apt 2444 Eden Prairie MN 55344-7976

LUTHRINGSHAUSEN, WAYNE, brokerage house executive; b. 1945; Commodities sys. analyst Howard, Weil, Labouesse, Friedricks, Inc., New Orleans, 1968-70; planning specialist Chgo. Bd. Trade, 1970-72; with Options Clearing Corp., Chgo., chmn., CEO.

LUTHRINGSHAUSER, DANIEL RENE, manufacturing executive; b. Fontainebleau, France, July 23, 1935; came to U.S., 1937; s. Ernest Henri and Jeanne (Guerville) L.; m. Carol King; children: Mark Ernest, Heidi Elizabeth. BS, NYU, 1956, MBA, 1970. With exec. tng. program, internat. pub. relations Merck & Co. Inc., Rahway, N.J. and YC, 1962-65; dep. mktg. dir. Merck Sharp & Dohme Internat., Brussels, 1965-66; mktg. service dir. Paris, 1966-69; gen. mgr. Merck Sharp & Dohme/Chibret, Paris, 1970-74; v.p. mktg. Merrell (France), Paris, 1974-78; v.p. gen. mgr. Revlon Devel. Corp., Paris, 1978-82, Medtronic Europe, Paris, Africa, Middle East, 1982-86; v.p. internat. Medtronic Inc., Mpls., 1986-98; prin. DRL Internat. Cons., 1998—. Bd. dirs. Medtronic Found., Mpls., 1986—91, French-Am. C. of C., 2003—06; chmn. Internat. Assn. of Prosthesis Mfrs., Paris, 1983—85; adj. prof. Grad, Sch. of Bus., Univ. St. Thomas. Bd. dirs. Am. Hosp. Paris, 1983-86, 94-95, Minn. Internat. Ctr., 1990—2003; mem. Am. Club Paris, 1970-80, Medtronic Found., Mpls., 1986-91. Served to capt. USAF, 1956-62. Recipient Gold medal Am. Mktg. Assn., 1956. Mem.: Mpls. Club, Ausable Club (Keene Valley, N.Y.). Avocations: gardening, golf, squash, skiing. Home: 480 Peavey Rd Wayzata MN 55391-1529 Office: PO Box 718 Wayzata MN 55391 Personal E-mail: dluthring@aol.com.

LUTTER, PAUL ALLEN, lawyer; b. Chgo., Feb. 28, 1946; s. Herbert W. and Lois (Muller) L. BA, Carleton Coll., 1968; JD, Yale U., 1971. Bar: Ill. 1971, U.S. Tax Ct. 1986. Assoc. Ross & Hardies, Chgo., 1971-77, ptnr., 1978—2003, McGuire Woods, Chgo., 2003—04, Bryan Cave, Chgo., 2004—. Co-author: Illinois Estate Administration, 1993. Office: Bryan Cave 161 N Clark St Ste 4300 Chicago IL 60601 Home: 437 N Canal St Chicago IL 60610 Office Phone: 312-602-5121.

LUTTIG, J(OHN) MICHAEL (JOHN MICHAEL LUTTIG), aerospace transportation executive, former federal judge; b. Tyler, Tex., June 13, 1954; s. John and Bobbie Luttig; m. Elizabeth Ann Luttig; children: Morgan, John. BA, Washington and Lee U., 1976; JD, U. Va., 1981. Asst. counsel to Pres. The White House, Washington, 1981—82; law clk. to Hon. Antonin Scalia US Ct. Appeals (DC Cir.), 1982—83; law clerk to Chief Justice Warren Burger US Supreme Ct., 1983—84, spl. asst. to Chief Justice Warren Burger, 1984—85; assoc. Davis Polk & Wardwell, 1985—89; prin. dep. asst. atty. gen., Office of Legal Counsel US Dept. Justice, 1989—90, asst. atty. gen., Office of Legal Counsel, counselor to atty. gen., 1990—91; judge US Ct. Appeals (4th Cir.), McLean, Va., 1991—2006; sr. v.p., gen. counsel The Boeing Co., Chgo., 2006—. Mem. Nat. Adv. Com. of Lawyers for Bush, 1988, Lawyers for Bush Com., 1988. Mem.: ABA, D.C. Bar Assn., Va. Bar Assn. Office: The Boeing Co 100 N Riverside Plz Chicago IL 60606

LUTZ, LARRY EDWARD, state legislator; b. Evansville, Ind., Oct. 28, 1938; s. Edward George and Bertha (Eberhardt) L.; m. Mary Lotus Toelle, 1961; 1 child, Chris Edward. Student, Lockyears Bus. Coll., Evansville, Ind., 1963, U. so. Ind., 1985. Lt. Evansville Fire Dept., 1963-65, inspector, 1966-68, dist. chief, 1979-83; master firefighter State of Ind., 1979; assessor Perry Twp., Vanderburgh County, Ind., 1979-82; mem. Ind. Ho. of Reps. from 76th dist., 1982-96; chmn. environ. affairs com.; mem. ins. corp. and sml. bus. com.; mem. pub. safety com., labor com., rds. and transp. com.; mem. Ind. Senate from 49th dist., 1999—. Named Hon. State Fire Marshal, 1980-83, Firfighter of Yr., Kiwanis, Ind., 1980. Mem. Ind. Firefighters Assn. (pres. 1976-77), Ind. Assessors Assn. (v.p. 1981), Kiwanis. Home: 5530 Whippoorwill Dr Evansville IN 47712-7120

LUTZ, ROBERT ANTHONY (BOB LUTZ), automotive executive; b. Zurich, Switzerland, Feb. 12, 1932; came to U.S., 1939; s. Robert H. and Marguerite (Schmid) L.; m. Betty D. Lutz, Dec. 12, 1956 (div. 1979); children: Jacqueline, Carolyn, Catherine, Alexandra; m. Heide Marie Schmid, Mar. 3, 1980 (div. Dec. 1992); m. Denise Ford, Apr. 17, 1994; 2 stepchildren. BS in Prodn. Mgmt., U. Calif., Berkeley, 1961, MBA in Mktg. with highest honors, 1962; LLD (hon.), Boston U., 1988; DM (hon.), Kettering U., 2003. Research assoc., sr. analyst IMEDE, Lausanne, Switzerland, 1962-63; sr. analyst forward planning GM, NYC, 1963-65, mgr. vehicle div. Paris, 1966-69; staff asst., mng. dir. Adam Opel, Russelsheim, Germany, 1965-66, asst. mgr. domestic sales, 1969, dir. sales Vorstand, 1969-70; v.p. Vorstand BMW, Munich, 1972-74; gen. mgr. Ford of Germany, Cologne, Germany, 1974-76; v.p. truck ops. Ford of Europe, Brentwood, Eng., 1976-77, pres., 1977-79, chmn., 1979-82; exec. v.p. Ford Internat., Dearborn, Mich., 1982-84, Chrysler Motors Corp., Highland Park, Mich., 1986-88; pres. ops., pres., COO Chrysler Corp., Highland Park, Mich., 1988-96, vice chmn., 1996—98; chmn. Exide Corp., 1998—2002, pres., 1998—2000, CEO, 1998—2001; chmn. General Motors . Am., 2001—05; vice chmn., prod. devel. General Motors Corp., 2001—; pres. GM Europe, 2004. Bd. dirs. Exide Technologies, 1998-, Kepner-Tregoe, Silicon Graphics, ASCOM, Switzerland; mem., former chmn. Hwy. Users Fedn. for Safety and Mobility. Author: Guts: The Seven Laws of Business That Made Chrysler the World's Hottest Car Company, 1998, Guts: 8 Laws of Business from One of the Most Innovative Business Leaders of our Time, 2003. Trustee: Mich. Cancer Found., USMC U. Found.; vice-chmn, bd. trustees, Marine Military Acad.; bd. dirs. United Way of Southeastern Mich.; mem. adv. bd. Walter A. Haas Sch. Bus., U. Calif., Berkeley, 1979—; chmn., The New Common School Found.; Capt. USMC, 1954-65. Named Alumnus of Yr., Sch. Bus., U. Calif., 1983; Kaiser Found. grantee, 1962; named one of 12 People to Watch, Newsweek mag., 2008 Mem. NAM (exec. com.), Phi Beta Kappa. Republican. Avocations: skiing, motorcycling, bicycling, helicopter flying, vintage cars, fixed-wing flying. Office: GM Corp PO Box 300 Detroit MI 48265-3000*

LYALL, KATHARINE CULBERT, former academic administrator, economist, educator; b. Lancaster, Pa., Apr. 26, 1941; d. John D. and Eleanor G. Lyall. BA in Econs., Cornell U., 1963, PhD in Econs., 1969; MBA, NYU, 1965. Economist Chase Manhattan Bank, NYC, 1963-65; asst. prof. econs. Syracuse U., 1969-72; assoc. prof. econs. Johns Hopkins U., Balt., 1972-77, dir. grad. program in pub. policy, 1979-81; dep. asst. sec. for econs. Office Econ. Affairs, HUD, Washington, 1977-79; v.p. acad. affairs U. Wis. Sys., 1981-85; prof. of econ. U. Wis., Madison, 1982—; acting pres. U. Wis. Sys., Madison, 1985-86, 91-92, exec. v.p., 1986-91, pres., 1992—2004, pres. emeritus, 2005—. Bd. dirs. Marshall & Ilsley Bank, Alliant, Carnegie Found. for Advancement of Tchg. Author: Reforming Public Welfare, 1976, Microeconomic Issues of the 70s, 1978, True Genius of America At Risk, 2006. Mem. Mcpl. Securities Rulemaking Bd., Washington, 1990-93. Mem. Am. Econ. Assn., Phi Beta Kappa. Business E-Mail: klyall@wisc.edu.

LYALL, LYNN, consumer products company executive; Sr. v.p. fin., info. svcs. & tech. Cadbury Schweppes, PLC; exec. v.p., CFO Blockbuster Entertainment, Inc.; exec. v.p. Alticor Inc., 1999—, CFO. Office: Alticor Inc 7575 Fulton St E Ada MI 49355

LYBARGER, JERRY, lawyer; b. 1947; BA, Northeast Mo. State U., 1969; JD, Calif. Western Sch. Law, 1972. Bar: 1973. Atty. Furniture Brands Internat., 1977—80, asst. gen. counsel, 1980—96, asst. gen. counsel, asst. sec., 1996—97, assoc. gen. counsel, dir. legal services, asst. sec., 1997—2000, gen. counsel, asst. sec., 2000—. Office: Furniture Brands Internat 101 S Hanley Rd Saint Louis MO 63105 E-mail: j.lybarger@furniturebrands.com.

LYBYER, MIKE JOSEPH, former state legislator, farmer; b. Waynesville, Mo., Feb. 23, 1947; m. Mary Jane Rockill, 1981. BS, U. Mo., 1969. Farmer, Huggins, Mo., 1969—; mem. Mo. Senate, Jefferson City, 1976-98. Mem. edn. and transp. bill coms., chmn. agr., conservation and parks com.; govt. cons. Mem. Masons, Shriners, Odd Fellows. Democrat. Address: 12743 Highway 38 Huggins MO 65484-9108

LYKAM, JIM, state representative; Mem. Iowa Ho. Reps., DesMoines, 2003—, mem. natural resources com., mem. state govt. com., mem. transp. com. Democrat. Office: State Capitol East 12th and Grand Des Moines IA 50319 also: 2906 W 35th St Davenport IA 52806

LYNCH, BILL, university football coach; b. Indpls., June 12, 1954; m. Linda Lux; children: Billy, Kelly, Joe, Kevin. BS, Butler U., 1972, MS, 1979. Offensive coord. football team Butler U., Indpls., 1977-83, No. Ill. U., DeKalb, 1984; head coach Butler, Indpls., 1985-89; quarterbacks coach Ind. U., Bloomington, 1993-94; asst. coach Orlando (Fla.) Renegades U.S. Football League, 1984; offensive coord. Ball State U., Muncie, Ind., 1990-92, head coach, 1995—.

LYNCH, DANIEL C., state legislator; b. Omaha, Aug. 9, 1929; m. Jane Lynch, 1950; children: Debby, Julia, Marrianne, Maureen, Dan Jr. Student, Loras Coll. Pres. Lynch Plumbing & Heating Co.; mem. from 13th dist. Nebr. State Senate, Lincoln, 1984—, chmn. rules com., past mem. com. on coms., appropriations com., past mem. Nebr. retirement sys. com.; v.p. consumer and govt. affairs Blue Cross/Blue Shield, Omaha, 1984—. V.p. consumer and govt. affairs Blue Cross/Blue Shield, Nebr. Commr. Douglas County, 1960-81; mem. Pres.' Coun. on Intergovtl. Affairs; mem. adv. com. Ea. Nebr. Office on Aging. Mem. Assn. Counties, Omaha Comml. Club. Office: Blue Cross/Blue Shield 7261 Mercy Rd Omaha NE 68124-2349

LYNCH, DAVID WILLIAM, physicist, retired educator; b. Rochester, NY, July 14, 1932; s. William J. and Eleanor (Fouratt) L.; m. Joan N. Hill, Aug. 29, 1954 (dec. Nov. 1989); children: Jean Louise, Richard William, David Allan; m. Glenys R. Bittick, Nov. 14, 1992. BS, Rensselaer Poly. Inst., 1954; MS, U. Ill., 1955, PhD, 1958. Asst. prof. physics Iowa State U., 1959-63, assoc. prof., 1963-66, prof., 1966—2003, chmn. dept., 1985-90, disting. prof. liberal arts and scis., 1985—; on leave at U. Hamburg, Germany; and U. Rome, Italy, 1968-69; sr. physicist Ames Lab. of Dept. of Energy; acting assoc. dir. Synchrotron Radiation Ctr., Stoughton, Wis., 1984. Vis. prof. U. Hamburg, summer 1974; dir. Microelectronics Rsch. Ctr., Iowa State U., 1995-99. Fulbright scholar U. Pavia, Italy, 1958-59. Fellow: AAAS, Am. Phys. Soc. Achievements include research on solid state physics. Home: 2020 Elm Cir West Des Moines IA 50265-4294 Home Phone: 525-440-1716; Office Phone: 515-294-3476. Business E-Mail: dwl@ameslab.gov.

LYNCH, EDWARD FRANCIS, professional sports team executive; b. Bklyn., Feb. 25, 1956; m. Kristin Kacer; children: Meghan, James. BA in Fin., U. S.C., 1977; JD, U. Miami, 1990. Pitcher Chgo. Cubs, 1977-80, 86-87, gen. mgr., v.p., 1994—; spl. asst. to exec. v.p. baseball ops. N.Y. Mets, 1980-86; dir. minor leagues San Diego Padres, 1990-93; pitcher Tex. Rangers, 1977-79, N.Y. Mets, 1980-86, dir. ops., 1993. Office: Chicago Cubs 1060 W Addison St Chicago IL 60613-4397

LYNCH, GEORGE MICHAEL, auto parts manufacturing executive; b. Ft. Lauderdale, Fla., Apr. 7, 1943; s. Jack Traverse and Ruth Margarite (Koehler) L.; m. Carol Rollins, June 18, 1966; children: Kristin Ruth, Michael Scott. BSEE, Cornell U., 1965, MEE, 1966; MS in Indsl. Adminstrn., Carnegie-Mellon U., 1968. Fin. analyst, various supervisory positions Ford Motor Co., Dearborn, Mich., 1968-73, mgr. car product analysis, 1973-76, mgr. N.Am. ops. N.Am. contrs. analysis dept. office, 1976-77, mgr. programming and capacity dept., 1977-81, mgr. facilities and fin. staff mgmt. svcs., 1981-83, dir. fin. Ford of Australia, 1983-86, contr. Ford Tractor div. Troy, Mich., 1986-87; exec. v.p., chief fin. officer Ford New Holland, Inc., New Holland, Pa., 1987-97; v.p., contr. Dow Chem. Co., 1997-2000; exec. v.p., CFO Fed.-Mogul Corp., Southfield, Mich., 2000—. Mem. Orchard Lake Country Club, Birmingham Athletic Club (tennis chmn. 1977—), Phi Kappa Phi, Tau Beta Pi. Avocations: tennis, bicycling. Office: Fed Mogul Corp 26555 Northwestern Hwy Southfield MI 48034 Home: 2566 Kent Ridge Ct Bloomfield Hills MI 48301-2276 Office Phone: 248-354-9935.

LYNCH, HENRY THOMSON, medical educator; b. Lawrence, Mass., Jan. 4, 1928; s. Henry F. and Eleanor (Thomson) L.; m. Jane Smith, Nov. 9, 1951; children— Patrick, Kathleen, Ann. BS, Okla., 1951; MA, Denver U., 1952; MD, U. Tex., Galveston, 1960. Intern St. Mary's Hosp., Evansville, Ind., 1960; resident U. Nebr. Sch. Medicine, 1961-64, sr. clin. cancer trainee, 1964-66; practice medicine specializing in internal medicine and medical oncology Omaha, 1967—; asst. prof. medicine U. Tex. M.D. Anderson Hosp., Houston, 1966-67; assoc. prof. Creighton U. Sch. Medicine, Omaha, 1967-70, prof., chmn. dept. preventive medicine and pub. health, 1970—, prof. medicine, 1982—. Editor: Hereditary Factors in Carcinoma, 1967, Dynamic Genetic Counseling for Clinicians, 1969, Cancer and You, 1971, Skin, Heredity and Malignant Neoplasms, 1972, Cancer Genetics, 1975, Genetics and Breast Cancer, 1981, Cancer Associated Genodermatoses, 1982, Colon Cancer Genetics, 1985, Biomarkers, Genetics and Cancer, 1985; contbr. over 600 sci. articles. Served with USNR, 1944-46. Recipient Bristol-Myers Squibb Co. unrestricted cancer rsch. grantee, 1996. Office: Creighton U Sch Med Dept Preventive Med Criss Ii Omaha NE 68178-0001 Business E-Mail: htlynch@creighton.edu.

LYNCH, JOHN PETER, lawyer; b. Chgo., June 5, 1942; s. Charles Joseph and Anne Mae (Loughlin) Lynch; m. Judy Godvin, Sept. 21, 1968; children: Julie, Jennifer. AB, Marquette U., 1964; JD, Northwestern U., 1967. Bar: Ill. 1967, U.S. Ct. Appeals (7th cir.) 1979, U.S. Ct. Appeals (5th cir.) 1976, U.S. Supreme Ct. 1979. Atty. Kirkland & Ellis, Chgo., 1970—73, ptnr., 1973—76, Hedlund, Hunter & Lynch, Chgo., 1976—82, Latham, Watkins, Hedlund, Hunter & Lynch, Chgo., 1982—85, Latham & Watkins, Chgo., 1985—, and vice chair, global litig. dept., also resident ptnr. Paris, 2001—. Former mem. exec. com. Latham & Watkins. Notes and Comments editor: Northwestern U. Law Rev., 1967. Mem. vis. com. Northwestern U. Law Sch. Lt. USN, 1968—71. Mem.: ATLA, ABA, Ill. Bar Assn., Order of Coif, Met. Club, Exec. Club, City Club. Home: 439 Sheridan Rd Kenilworth IL 60043-1220 Office: Latham & Watkins Ste 5800 Sears Tower 233 S Wacker Dr Chicago IL 60606 also: Latham & Watkins 53 quai d'Orsay 75007 Paris France

LYNCH, KIRSTEN, food products executive; b. Chgo., 1968; BA, Ill. State U., 1990; MA, Washington U., St. Louis, 1990. With Kraft Foods, Chgo., 1996—; mktg. dir., Macaroni & Cheese Kraft Foods, Inc., 2005—. Avocation: snowboarding. Office: Kraft Foods Inc 3 Lakes Dr Northfield IL 60093 Office Phone: 847-646-2000, 847-646-0372. Office Fax: 847-646-6005. E-mail: klynch@kraft.com.

LYNCH, LELAND T., advertising executive; Co-founder, chmn., CEO Carmichael Lynch, Mpls., 1962—. Co-founder Leading Ind. Agy. Network. Bd. dis. Planned Parenthood Minn., Minn. Pub. Radio; chair-elect Mpls. Downtown Coun., 1996—. Mem. Am. Assn. Advt. Agys. (regional pres., nat. sec./treas.). Office: Carmichael Lynch Inc 800 Hennepin Ave Minneapolis MN 55403-1817

LYNCH, MATTHEW J., information technology executive, retail executive; Grad., No. Ariz. U., Coll. Engring. Tech. Software engr. Sperry Aerospace; info. sys. mgmt. Air Wis. Airlines, Am. West Airlines, Honeywell, Aerospace Electronics Sys., 1985—93; v.p., info. tech. svcs. Runzheimer Internat.,

1993—98; v.p., oper. tech. svcs. ShopKo, Green Bay, Wis., 1998—2003, sr. v.p., chief info. officer, 2003—. Named one of Premier 100 IT Leaders, Computerworld, 2006. Office: ShopKo 700 Pilgrim Way Green Bay WI 54304

LYNCH, MICHAEL, lawyer, staffing company executive; BSBA, JD, Marquette U. Tax mgr. Arthur Andersen & Co.; dir. corp. tax Manpower, Inc., Milw., 1990—93, v.p. corp. tax, 1993, v.p. internat. support services., internat. gen. counsel, 1999—. Office: Manpower Inc 5301 N Ironwood Rd Milwaukee WI 53217

LYNCH, MIKE, meteorologist, radio personality; Instr. astronomy Wood Lake Nature Ctr., Richfield, Minn., 1973; instr. Minn., 1973—, Wis., 1973—; broadcast meteorologist Sta. WCCO Radio, Mpls., 1981—. Office: WCCO 602 2nd Ave S Minneapolis MN 55402

LYNCH, PRISCILLA A., nursing educator, psychotherapist; b. Joliet, Ill., Jan. 8, 1949; d. LaVerne L. and Ann M. (Zamkovitz) L. BS, U. Wyo., 1973; MS, St. Xavier Coll., Coll., 1981. RN, Ill. Staff nurse Rush-Presbyn.-St. Luke's Med. Ctr., Chgo., 1977-81, psychiat.-liaison cons., 1981-83, asst. prof. nursing, unit dir., 1985—. Mgr. and therapist Oakside Clinic, Kankakee, Ill., 1987—; mem. adv. bd. Depressive and Manic Depression Assn., Chgo., 1986—; mem. consultation and mental health unit Riverside Med. Ctr., Kankakee, 1987—; speaker numerous nat. orgns. Contbr. numerous abstracts to profl. jours., chpts. to books. Bd. dirs. Cornerstone Svcs., ARC of Ill. Recipient total quality mgmt. award Rush-Presbyn.-St. Luke's Med. Ctr., 1991, named mgr. of the quarter, 1997, Wayne Lerner Leadership award, 1998. Mem. APNA, ISPN, Ill. Nurses Assn. (coms.), Coun. Clin. Nurse Specialists, Profl. Nursing Staff (sec. 1985-87, mem. coms.). Presbyterian. Home: 606 Darcy Ave Joliet IL 60436-1673 Office Phone: 312-942-5100. Business E-Mail: priscilla_lynch@rush.edu.

LYNCH, RICHARD GREGORY, medical educator; b. Apr. 9, 1934; BA, U. Mo., 1961; MD, U. Rochester, 1966. Resident Washington U., St. Louis, 1966-69, from asst. prof. to assoc. prof. pathology, 1972-80; dir. NIH Tng. Program, 1980-81, 84-87; prof., head dept. pathology U. Iowa, Iowa City, 1981-99, prof. microbiology, 1982-99, Hanson prof. immunology, 1992—. Chmn. pathology B study sect. NIH, 1983-86. Postdoctoral immunology fellow Washington U., St. Louis, 1969-72; recipient Rous-Whipple award, 1997. Office: U Iowa Dept Pathology 200 Hawkins Dr Rm 1117 ML Iowa City IA 52242-1009 E-mail: Richard-Lynch@uiowa.edu.

LYNCH, THOMAS JOSEPH, museum director; b. Omaha, Feb. 15, 1960; s. James Humphery and Patricia Mae (Gaughan) L. BA in History, U. Nebr., 1984. Mus. asst. Father Flanagan's Boys' Home, Boys Town, Nebr., 1986-88, mus. assoc., 1988-93; CEO, dir. Boys Town Hall of History and Fr. Flanagan's House, 1993—. Mem. adv. bd. RSVP; bd. dirs. Union Pacific R.R. Mus. Mem. Am. Assn. for State and Local History, Am. Mus. Assn., Nebr. Mus. Assn. (bd. dirs., former pres.), Nat. Hist. Landmark Stewards Assn. Office: Boys Town Hall of History 14057 Flanagan Blvd Boys Town NE 68010-7509 Business E-Mail: lyncht@boystown.org.

LYNCH, WILLIAM THOMAS, JR., advertising executive; b. Evergreen Park, Ill., Dec. 3, 1942; s. William T. and Loretta J. L.; m. Kathleen; children: Kelly, Maureen, Kim, Meagan, Molly. BA, Loras Coll., 1964; MBA, U. Iowa, 1966. Media trainee Leo Burnett Co. Inc., Chgo., 1966-68, asst. account exec., 1968-76, v.p., 1976-79, sr. v.p., 1979-82, exec. v.p., 1981—86; vice chmn. Leo Burnett USA, Chgo., 1985-89, chmn., CEO, 1987—91; pres. Leo Burnett Worldwide, Chgo., 1993; CEO, pres. Leo Burnett Worldwide, Leo Burnett Co. Inc., Chgo., 1993-97; pres., CEO Liam Holdings, Prospect Heights, Ill., 1997—. Bd. dirs. Pella Corp., Smurfit-Stone Container Corp. Bd. dir. U. Chgo. Grad. Sch. Bus., Northwestern Meml. Found.; bd. dirs., mem. exec. com. Big Shoulders Archdiocese of Chgo., Loras Coll. Mem. Econ. Club Chgo., Comml. Club Chgo. Roman Catholic. Avocations: running, skiing, gardening, golf. Office: Liam Holdings 206 N Pine St Prospect Heights IL 60070-1524

LYNE, TIMOTHY JOSEPH, bishop emeritus; b. Chgo., Mar. 21, 1919; Grad., St. Mary of the Lake Sem., Mundelein, Ill. Ordained priest Archdiocese of Chgo., 1943; ordained bishop, 1983; aux. bishop Archdiocese of Chgo., 1983—85, aux. bishop emeritus, 1995—. Roman Catholic. Office: Archdiocese of Chgo 155 E Superior St PO Box 1979 Chicago IL 60690 Office Phone: 312-751-8200. Office Fax: 312-337-6379.*

LYNHAM, C(HARLES) RICHARD, manufacturing executive; b. Easton, Md., Feb. 24, 1942; s. John Cameron and Anna Louise (Lynch) L.; m. Elizabeth Joy Card, Sept. 19, 1964; children: Jennifer Beth, Thomas Richard. BME, Cornell U., 1965; MBA with distinction, Harvard U., 1969. Sales mgr. Nat. Carbide Die Co., McKeesport, Pa., 1969-71; v.p. sales Sinter-Met Corp., North Brunswick, NJ, 1971-72; sr. mgmt. analyst Am. Cyanamid Co., Wayne, NJ, 1972-74; gen. mgr. ceramics and additives div. Foseco Inc., Cleve., 1974-77, dir. mktg. steel mill products group, 1977-79; pres., chief exec. officer Exomet, Inc. subs. Foseco, Inc., Conneaut, Ohio, 1979-81, Fosbel Inc. subs. Foseco, Inc., Cleve., 1981-82; gen. mgr. splty. ceramics group Ferro Corp., Cleve., 1982-84, group v.p. splty. ceramics, 1984-92; owner, pres. Harbor Castings, Inc., North Canton, Ohio, 1992—, Island Castings, Inc., Muskegon, Mich., 2000—; owner, CEO Blue Ridge Castings, Inc., Piney Flats, Tenn., 2000—07. Bd. dirs. Western Res. Bancorp., Inc. Patentee foundry casting ladle, desulphurization of metals. Past pres. bd. trustees Hospice of Medina County; treas., past pres. bd. trustees Bridges Home Health Care. Capt. C.E. US Army, 1965—71. Decorated Bronze Star with one oak leaf cluster; recipient Frank H.T. Rhodes Exemplary Alumni Svc. award, Cornell U., 1999. Mem. Am. Foundrymen's Soc., Cornell U. Alumni Coun., Cornell U. Alumni Class 1963 (past v.p., past pres.), Cornell U. Alumni Fedn. (past pres., bd. dirs., past v.p.), Chippewa Yacht Club (commodore 1982), Cornell Club of N.E. Ohio (past pres., bd. dirs.), Harbor Bay Yacht Club. Republican. Congregationalist. Avocations: sailing, genealogy. Home: 970 Hickory Grove Ave Medina OH 44256-1616 Office: Harbor Castings Inc 4321 Strausser St NW North Canton OH 44720-7144

LYNN, NAOMI B., academic administrator; b. NYC, Apr. 16, 1933; d. Carmelo Burgos and Maria (Lebron) Berly; m. Robert A. Lynn, Aug. 28, 1954; children: Mary Louise, Nancy Lynn Francis, Judy Lynn Chance, Jo-An Lynn Cooper. BA, Maryville Coll., Tenn., 1954; MA, U. Ill., 1958; PhD, U. Kans., 1970. Instr. polit. sci. Cen. Mo. State Coll., Warrensburg, Mo., 1966-68; asst. prof. Kans. State U., Manhattan, 1970-75, assoc. prof., 1975-80, acting dept. head, prof., 1980-81, head polit. sci. dept., prof., 1982-84; dean Coll. Pub. and Urban Affairs, prof. Ga. State U., Atlanta, 1984-91; chancellor U. Ill., Springfield, 1991-2001, chancellor emerita, 2001—. Cons. fed., state and local govts., Manhattan, Topeka, Altanta, 1981-91; bd. trustees Maryville Coll., 1997—. Author: The Fulbright Premise, 1973; editor: Public Administration, The State of Discipline, 1990, Women, Politics and the Constitution, 1990; contbr. articles and textbook chpts. to profl. pubs. Bd. dirs. United Way of Sangamon County, 1991-98, Ill. Symphony Orch., 1992-95, Urban League, 1993-99, Ill. State Mus. Soc., 2002-05; v.p. World Affairs Coun. Ctrl. Ill., 2006—. Recipient Disting. Alumni award Maryville Coll., 1986; fellow Nat. Acad. Pub. Adminstrn. Mem. Nat. Assn. Schs. Pub. Affairs and Adminstrn. (nat. pres.), Am. Soc. Pub. Adminstrn. (nat. pres. 1985-86, chair endowment bd. 2005—), Am. Polit. Sci. Assn. (mem. exec. coun. 1981-83, trustee 1993-96, Am. Assn. State Colls. and Univs. (bd. dirs.), Midwest Polit. Sci. Assn. (mem. exec. coun. 1976-79), Women's Caucus Polit. Sci. (pres. 1975-76), Greater Springfield C. of C. (bd. dirs. 1991-99, mem. U.S. Senate jud. nominations commn. State Ill. 1999-01), Pi Sigma Alpha (nat. pres.). Presbyterian. Personal E-mail: nblynn416@aol.com.

LYNNES, R. MILTON, advertising executive; b. Chgo., Apr. 16, 1934; s. Roy Milton and Ethel (Wolfe) L.; m. Carol Rinehart, Aug. 30, 1958; children: Christopher, Katherine, Jeffrey, Jennifer. BS, Iowa State U., 1957. Advt. sales promotion supr. Interlake Steel, Chgo., 1961-62; copywriter Garfield-Linn, Chgo., 1963; account exec. Biddle Co., Appleton, Wis., 1964-66; exec. v.p. Marsteller HCM, Chgo., 1966-84, bd. dirs., 1978-84; prin. Grant, Jacoby Inc., Chgo., 1985-89, pres., 1989-94, chmn. CEO, 1994—. Bd. dirs. Worldwide Ptnrs., Denver, chmn. N.Am. region, 1996-97. Bd. dirs. MTW/WWP Media Venture, 1995, Better Bus. Bur., Chgo., 1984-87. Mem. Am. Assn. Advt. Agys. (vice chmn. ctrl. region, bd. dirs. 1981-82), Chicagoland C. of C. (bd. dirs. 1999), Chgo. Advt. Club (bd. dirs. 1985-86), Exmoor Country Club (pres. 1998-99), Bob O Link Golf Club, Pelican Bay Golf Club, Econs. Club, Tavern Club, Chicago Club. Republican. Congregationalist. Office: Grant Jacoby 20 W Kinzie St Ste 1610 Chicago IL 60610-6198

LYON, BOB, state legislator; m. Rita Lyon. Mem. Kans. State Senate, 2001—, mem. membership fed. and state affairs com., mem. state bldg. constrn. com., mem. transp. com., mem. utilities com. Republican. Address: 14431 Saline Rd Winchester KS 66097 Office: 1201 Walnut St Kansas City MO 64106-2149 E-mail: lyon@senate.state.ks.us, blyon55@hotmail.com.

LYON, JEFFREY, journalist, author; b. Chgo., Nov. 28, 1943; s. Herbert Theodore and Lyle (Hoffenberg) L.; m. Bonita S. Brodt, June, 20, 1981; children: Lindsay, Derek. BS in Journalism, Northwestern U., 1965. Reporter Miami (Fla.) Herald, 1964-66, Chgo. Today, 1966-74, Chgo. Tribune, 1974-76, columnist, 1976-80, 94—, feature writer specializing in sci., 1980—, editor Tempo sect., 1997. Creative writing adj. prof.; coord. joint sci. and journalism programs Columbia Coll., Chgo., 1987—, dir., 1988—. Author: Playing God in the Nursery, 1985, Altered Fates: Gene Therapy and the Retooling of Human Life, 1995; also newspaper series Altered Fates, 1986 (Pulitzer Prize 1987). Mem. State of Ill. Perinatal Adv. Com., Springfield, 1986-90; mem. pediat. ethics com. U. Chgo. Hosps., 1985-90; bd. dirs. Shore Cmty. Svcs. to Retarded Citizens, Evanston, Ill., 1985-90; mem. bd. Little City, Palatine, Ill., 1979—. Recipient at. Headliner award Atlantic City Press Club, 1984, Citizen Fellow award Inst. Medicine of Chgo., 1987, Peter Lisagor award, 1990. Office: The Chgo Tribune 435 N Michigan Ave Chicago IL 60611-4066 E-mail: jlyon@tribune.com.

LYON, THOMAS L., agricultural organization administrator; b. Toledo, Iowa, Sept. 12, 1940; m. Barbara Lyon; children: Jeff, Melissa, Scott. BS in Dairy Sci., Iowa State U., 1962. Exec. sec. Iowa State Dairy Assn.; with 21st Century Genetics, gen. mgr., 1976-93; pres. Coop. Resources Internat., Shawano, Wis., 1993—, now CEO. Bd. dirs. Am. Farmland Trust, Coop. Bus. Internat., Coop. Devel. Found.; chmn. Nat. Coop. Bus. Assn.; mem. Nat. Rural Devel. Task Force & Coop. 2000 com., Dairy Shrine Club, steering com. Wis. Dairy Inititative 2020, Kellogg Found. Food Systems; bd. advisors U. Wis., Eau Claire; bd. visitors U. Wis., Madison; trustee Grad. Inst. Coop. Leadership, Coop. Found.; cons. U. Wis. Bus. Schs. Review. Recipient Friend of Extension award U. Wis., 1981, Wis. Friend of County Agents award, 1984, Dairy Industry Person of Yr. award World Dairy Expo, 1985, Nat. Coop. Pub. Svc. award, 1991, Disting. Citizen Shawano award, 1993, Agribus. award Iowa State U. Coll. Agr. Alumni Soc., 1995. Office: Coop Resources Internat 100 NBC Dr PO Boox 469 Shawano WI 54166

LYONS, DUDLEY E., manufacturing executive; Sr. v.p. Brunswick Corp., Lake Forest, Ill., 1999—. Office: Brunswick Corp 1 N Field Ct Lake Forest IL 60045-4811

LYONS, GORDON, marketing executive; V.p. supermarket devel. Schnuck Market Inc., St. Louis, Mo. Office: Schnuck Market Inc 11420 Lackland Rd Saint Louis MO 63146-3559

LYSON, STANLEY W., state legislator; b. Porshall, ND, Mar. 5, 1956; m. Shirley; 3 children., MInot STate U. Sheriff; retired; mem. N.D. Senate from 1st dist., Bismark, 1999—. With U.S. Army. REcipient Lone Eagle award. Mem. N.D. Assn. Counties (pres.), N.D. Peace Officers Assn. (pres.), Am. Legion, VFW, Elks. Office: Dist 1 1608 4th Ave W Williston ND 58801-4127 E-mail: sysonstate@nd.us.

LYST, JOHN HENRY, former newspaper editor; b. Princeton, Ind., Mar. 28, 1933; s. John Henry and Marguerite (McQuinn) L.; m. Sharon Long, Dec. 29, 1956; children: Shannon M., Bettina A., Audrey K., Ellen K. AB, Ind. U., 1955. Reporter Indpls. Star, 1956-67, bus. columnist, from 1967, editor editl. page, 1979—2000. Corr. N.Y. Times, from 1964. Served with AUS, 1956-59. Mem. Indpls. Press Club (pres. 1968, bd. dirs. 1969), Sigma Delta Chi. Office: Indpls Newspapers Inc PO Box 145 Indianapolis IN 46206-0145

LYTHCOTT, MARCIA A., newspaper editor; d. William and Florence; m. Stephen Lythcott (dec.). BA in journalism, U. Wisc., Madison. Assoc. food guide editor Chicago Tribune, Ill., editor, style section Ill., editor, home section Ill., 1993—94, op-ed editor Ill., 1995—. Office: Chicago Tribune 435 N Michigan Ave Chicago IL 60611-4066

LYTLE, L(ARRY) BEN, insurance company executive, lawyer; b. Greenville, Tex., Sept. 30, 1946; children: Hugh, Larry. BS in Mgmt. Sci. and Indsl. Psychology, East Tex. State U., 1970; JD, Ind. U., 1980. Computer operator/programmer U.S. Govt., Ft. Smith, Ark., 1964-65; customer engr. Olivetti Corp., San Antonio, 1965-66; mgr. computer ops. and computer software LTV Electrosystems, Greenville, 1966-70; project mgr. electronic fin. system, dir. systems planning Assocs. Corp. N.Am., South Bend, Ind., 1970-75; asst. v.p. systems Am. Fletcher Nat. Bank, Indpls., 1975-76; with Anaheim Ins. Cos., Inc., Indpls., 1976-99; pres. Assoc. Ins. Cos., Inc., Indpls., 1987-99, COO, 1987-89, CEO, 1989-99. Chmn. bd. dirs. Anthem Cos., Inc., Acordia, Inc.; chmn. bd. dirs. AdminaStar, Inc., Health Networks Am., Inc., Novalis, Inc., Robinson-Conner Nev., Inc.; bd. dirs. The Shelby Ins. Group, Raffensperger, Hughes & Co., Inc., Indpls. Power and Light Co. Enterprises; mem. adv. bd. CID Venture Ptnrs., Ltd. Partnership; rschr., cons. state and fed. govt. orgns., including, Adv. Coun. on Social Security, Pepper Commn. of U.S. Congress, others. Chmn. health policy commn. State of Ind., Indpls., 1990-92; active various civic orgns., including United Negro Coll. Fund, Indpls. Mus. Art. Mem. ABA, Ind. Bar Assn., Indpls. Bar Assn., Ind. State C. of C. (bd. dirs.), Indpls. C. of C. (bd. dirs.). Home: PO Box 441830 Indianapolis IN 46244-1830

LYTLE, MARKT L., state legislator; Student, Oakland City Coll., Ball State U., Muncie, Ind.; grad., Ky. Sch. Mortuary Sci. Mng. dir. Lytle-Gans-Andrew Funeral Home; state rep. Dist. 69 Ind. Ho. of Reps., 1992—, mem. county and twp. ways and means com., vice chmn. natural resources com. Mem. agriculture, natural resources and rural devel. com. (chmn.), evniron. affairs com., local govt. com. Mayor, City of Madison Ind.; recorder Jefferson County, Ind.; precinct committeeman; mem. Southeastern Ind. Regional Planning Commn. Mem. Sons of Legion, Elks. Home: 423 W Main St Madison IN 47250-3736

MAAS, DUANE HARRIS, distilling company executive; b. Tilleda, Wis., Aug. 26, 1927; s. John William and Adela (Giessel) M.; m. Sonja Johnson, Mar. 11, 1950; children: Jon Kermit, Duane Arthur, Thomas Ervin. BS, U. Wis., 1951. With Shell Chem. Corp., 1951-59; plant mgr. Fleischmann Distilling Corp., Owensboro, Ky., 1959-63, Plainfield, Ill., 1963-65; asst. to v.p. Barton Distilling Co., Chgo., 1965-68, exec. asst. to pres., 1968, v.p. adminstrn., 1968; v.p., gen. mgr. Barton Brands, Inc., Chgo., 1968— 72; pres. Leaf Confectionery div. W.R. Grace, Chgo., 1972-74; v.p., gen. mgr. Romano Bros., Chgo., 1974-79; v.p., sec.-treas. Marketing Directions Inc., Chgo., 1974-77; pres. Associated Wine Producers, Inc., 1979-80; exec. v.p., chief exec. officer Mohawk Liqueur, Detroit, 1980-86; v.p. McKesson Wine & Spirits Group of N.Y., Detroit, 1982-86; pres. Mgmt. Cons. Services Co., Chgo., 1986—, U.S. Distilled Products Co., Princeton, Minn., 1996-99, Am. Distilled Products Corp., 2001—, Midwest Custom Bottling, 2007—. Chmn. Qingdao Johnson Distiller Co. Ltd., Qingdao, China, 1996-99; past pres. Bart on Distilling (Can.), Ltd.; past mng. dir. Barton Distilling (Scotland), Ltd.; past dir. Barton Distillers Europe, Barton Internat., Ltd. Sec.-treas. Plainfield Twp. Park Dist., 1967-70; chmn. Plainfield Planning and Zoning Commn., 1965-70. Served with USAAF, 1945-47. Mem.: Wis. Alumni Assn. Lutheran. Home and Office: N28W22312 Foxwood Ln Waukesha WI 53186 Home Phone: 762-522-1063; Office Phone: 262-522-6953. Personal E-mail: dhm@mcservices.com.

MAATMAN, GERALD LEONARD, insurance company executive; b. Chgo., Mar. 11, 1930; s. Leonard Raymond and Cora Mae (Van Der Laag) M.; children: Gerald L. Jr., Mary Ellen; m. Bernice Catherine Brummer, June 3, 1971. BS, Ill. Inst. Tech., 1951. Asst. chief engineer Ill. Inspection & Rating Bur., Chgo., 1951-58; prof., dept. chmn. Ill. Inst. Tech., Chgo., 1959-65; v.p. engring. Kemper Group, Chgo., 1966-68, pres. Nat. Loss Control Svc. Corp., 1969-74, v.p. corp. planning Long Grove, Ill., 1974-79, sr. v.p. info. svcs. group, 1979-85, exec. v.p. ins. ops., 1985-87; pres. Kemper Nat. Ins. Co., Long Grove, Ill., 1987-92, CEO, 1989-95, also bd. dirs., chmn. bd. dirs., 1991-95. Bd. dirs. Advs. for Auto and Hwy. Safety, 1992-98; chmn. bd. trustees Underwriters Labs., 1991-2002. Lt. (j.g.) USCGR, 1952-54. Mem. Knollwood Golf Club, Tau Beta Pi. Republican.

MABEE, KEITH V., communications and investor relations executive; BS in Journalism, Bowling Green State U., 1969; MEd in Sociology, Wayne State U., 1972; MBA, Pepperdine U., 1980. Comm. specialist Internat. Paper Co., NYC, 1969-70, 73; pub. affairs officer, U.S. Army NATO, Europe, 1970-72; sr. lectr. Coll. Mgmt., Queensland U. Tech., Australia, 1973-77; organizational/effectiveness officer U.S. Army, Pacific, 1978-80; sr. v.p., corp. comm. AMFAC, Inc., San Francisco, 1980-89; v.p. comm. Indsl. Indemnity, San Francisco, 1989-93; v.p. corp. rels. Figgie Internat. Inc., 1993-98; sr. exec. v.p. Dix & Eaton, 1997-98, pres., 1998—2001, pres., COO, 2001—. Former pres. San Francisco chpt. Nat. Investor Rels. Inst., former officer, former dir. nat. bd., chmn. sr. roundtable; founding trustee, lectr. San Francisco Acad.; vice chmn. bd. dirs. Ohio Tuition Trust Authority. Accredited mem. Pub. Rels. Soc. Am. Office: Dix & Eaton Inc Ste 1400 200 Public Square Cleveland OH 44114-1882 Office Phone: 216-241-3068. Fax: 216-241-3070.

MACAULEY, EDWARD C., retired company executive; b. St. Louis, Mar. 22, 1928; s. Charles J. and Josephine (Durkin) M.; m. Jacqueline Combs, July 12, 1952; children: Mary Ann, Robert, Teresa, Michael, Kathleen, Margaret. BS, St. Louis U., 1949. Basketball player Boston Celtics, 1950-56, St. Louis Hawks, 1957-58, coach, 1959-60; sports dir. Stas. KTVI-TV and KSDK-TV, St. Louis, 1960-70; stockbroker A.G. Edwards-Shearson Lehman, St. Louis, 1970-81; pres. Macauley Kremjet, St. Louis, 1981—, Eagle Communications, St. Louis, 1982-86. Bd. dirs. Color Art Printing Co., St. Louis. Trustee Basketball Hall of Fame, Springfield, Mass., 1980—, Mo. Basketball Hall of Fame, Columbia, 1988—, Marianist Apostolic Ctr., St. Louis, 1988—; mem. St. Liborius Food Pantry, St. Louis, 1988-89; organizer St. Nicholas Food Pantry, St. Louis, 1989; ordained deacon Archdiocese of St. Louis, Roman Cath. Ch., 1989—. Named to All Am. Basketball Team, AP, UP, Life, Colliers mag., 1948, 49, All Pro Team, NBA, 1951, 52, 53; inducted into Basketball Hall of Fame, 1961. Avocations: golf, travel, preaching. Home and Office: 13277 Barrett Chase Cir Ballwin MO 63021-3825

MACCARTHY, JOHN L., lawyer; b. St. Louis, Dec. 26, 1959; BA magna cum laude, Williams Coll., 1982; JD, Stanford U., 1985. Bar: Ill. 1985, U.S. Dist. Ct. Ill. (no. dist.) 1985. Assoc. to ptnr. Winston & Strawn LLP, Chgo., 1985—; sr. v.p., gen. counsel Nuvren Investments LLC, 2006—. Bd. dirs. Met. Family Svcs., Renaissance Soc. U. Chgo., Nature Conservancy Chgo. Mem.: Phi Beta Kappa, Order of Coif.

MACCARTHY, TERENCE FRANCIS, lawyer; b. Chgo., Feb. 5, 1934; s. Frank E. and Catherine (McIntyre) MacC.; m. Marian Fulton, Nov. 25, 1961; children— Daniel Fulton, Sean Patrick, Terence Fulton, Megan Catherine BA in Philosophy, St. Joseph's Coll., 1955; JD, DePaul U., 1960. Bar: Ill. 1960, U.S. Dist. Ct. (no. dist.) Ill. 1961, U.S. Ct. Appeals (7th cir.) 1961, U.S. Supreme Ct. 1966. Assoc. prof. law Chase Coll. Law, Cin., 1960-61; law clk. to chief judge U.S. Dist. Ct., 1961-66; spl. asst. atty. gen. Ill., 1965-67; exec. dir. Fed. Defender Program, U.S. Dist. Ct. (no. dist.) Ill., Chgo., 1966—. Mem. nat. adv. com. on criminal rules; 7th cir. criminal jury instrn. com.; chmn. Nat. Defender Com.; chmn. bd. regents Nat. Coll. Criminal Def.; faculty Fed. Jud. Ctr., Nat. Coll. Criminal Def., Nat. Inst. Trial Advocacy, U. Va. Trial Advocacy Inst., Harvard Law Sch. Trial Advocacy Program, Western Trial Advocacy Inst., orthwestern U., U. Ill. Defender Trial Advocacy course, Nat. Criminal Def. Coll., Loyola U. Trial Advocacy Program; lectr. in field Contbr. articles on criminal law to profl. jours. Bd. dirs. U.S.O. Served as 1st lt. USMC, 1955-57 Recipient Nat. Legal Aid and Defender Assn./ABA Reginald Heber Smith award, 1986, Alumni Merit award St. Joseph Coll., 1970, Cert. of Distinction USO, 1977, Harrison Tweed Spl. Merit award Am. Law Inst./ABA, 1987, Bill of Rights award Ga. chpt. ACLU, 1986, William J. Brennan award U. Va., 1989, Alumni Svc. award DePaul U. Coll. Law, 1994, Ann. Significant Contbns. award Calif. Attys. for Criminal Justice, Defender of the Century Fed. Defenders Assn., Inns of Ct. and Ct. of Appeals (7th cir.) Professionalism award; named to Outstanding Young Men of Am., 1970. Mem. ABA (past chmn. criminal justice sect., ho. of dels., bd. govs., Charles English award criminal justice sect.), Ill. Bar Assn., Chgo. Bar Assn., 7th Cir. Bar Assn., Nat. Assn. Criminal Def. Lawyers (Disting. Svc. award 1993), Nat. Legal Aid and Defender Assn., Nat. Coll. Criminal Def. (chair), Union League of Chgo. (pres.). Democrat. Roman Catholic. Office: US Dist Ct No Dist Ill 55 E Monroe St Ste 2800 Chicago IL 60603-5802

MACDONALD, JOHN, marketing executive; V.p. mktg. Chrysler Corp., Auburn Hills, Mich., 1996-98, v.p. sales and svc., 1997-99; sr. v.p. sales and svc. DaimlerChrysler Corp., Auburn Hills, 1999—.

MACDOUGAL, GARY EDWARD, corporate board member, foundation trustee; b. Chgo., July 3, 1936; s. Thomas William and Lorna Lee (McDougall) MacD.; children: Gary Edward, Michael Scott; m. Charlene Gehm, June 15, 1992. BS in Engring., UCLA, 1958; MBA with distinction, Harvard U., 1962. Cons. McKinsey & Co., LA, 1963-68, ptnr., 1968-69; chmn. bd., chief exec. officer Mark Controls Corp. (formerly Clayton Mark & Co.), Evanston, Ill., 1969-87; gen. dir. N.Y.C. Ballet, 1993-94; chmn. Gov. Task Force on Human Svcs. Reform State of Ill., 1993-97. Sr. advisor and asst. campaign mgr. George Bush for Pres., Washington, 1988; pub. del. alt. rep. U.S. Del. apptd. by Pres. Bush, UN 44th Gen. Assembly, 1989-90; chmn. Bulgarian-Am. Enterprise Fund, Chgo. and Sophia, Bulgaria, 1991-93, bd. dirs., 1991—; apptd. to U.S. Commn. on Effectiveness of UN, 1992-93; bd. dirs. United Parcel Svc. Am., Inc., Atlanta, 1973-07; adv. dir. Saratoga Ptnrs., N.Y.; instr. UCLA, 1969. Author: Make a Difference: How One Man Helped Solve America's Poverty Problem, 2000, 2nd edit. 2005; contbr. articles to Harvard Bus. Rev., Wall St. Jour., N.Y. Times, Chgo. Tribune, other publs., chpts. to books. Trustee Annie E. Casey Found., 1983-2006, UCLA Found., 1973-79, W.T. Grant Found., 1992-94, Russell Sage Found., 1981-91, chair, 1987-90; co-chmn. Americans for Bulgaria Found., 2008-; chmn. MacDougal Family Found.; commr. Sec. Labor's Commn. on Workforce Quality and Productivity, Washington, 1988-89; Lt. USN, 1958-61. Mem. Coun. Fgn. Rels., Author's Guild, Harvard Club, Kappa Sigma. Episcopalian. Home: 505 N Lake Shore Dr Apt 3611 Chicago IL 60611-3406 Personal E-mail: gemacd@aol.com.

MACE, JERILEE MARIE, performing arts association administrator; BA in Speech Comm. and Mgmt. magna cum l, Simpson Coll., 1991. Mem. adminstrv. staff Des Moines Metro Opera, 1976, dir. mktg., exec. dir., 1988—. Developer OPERA Iowa, Des Moines Metro Opera; cons. various opera cos. On-site evaluator NEA; grad., bd. dirs. Greater Des Moines Leadership Inst.; founding mem. Warren County Leadership Com. Named Iowa Arts Orgn. of Yr., 2000, Employee of Yr., Indianola C. of C., 2004; recipient Outstanding Achiever award, Ft. Dodge C. of C., 1994, Best Kept Secret award for bus. excellence, Greater Des Moines Partnership 2001, Women of Influence award, Des Moines Bus. Record, 2001; fellow exec., OPERA Am., 1993. Office: Des Moines Metro Opera 106 W Boston Ave Indianola IA 50125-1836 E-mail: jerimace@aol.com.

MACFARLANE, ALASTAIR IAIN ROBERT, manufacturing executive, consultant; b. Sydney, Mar. 7, 1940; arrived in U.S., 1978; s. Alexander Dunlop and Margaret Elizabeth (Swan) M.; m. Madge McCleary, Sept. 24, 1966; children: Douglas, Dennis, Robert, Jeffrey. B in Econs. with honors, U. Sydney, Australia, 1961; MBA, U. Hawaii, Honolulu, 1964; postgrad., Columbia U., NYC, 1964; AMP, Harvard Bus. Sch., Cambridge, Mass., 1977. Comml. cadet B.H.P. Ltd., Australia, 1958-62; product mgr. H.J. Heinz Co., Pitts., 1965-66, gen. mgr. new products divsn. Melbourne, Australia, 1967-72; ptnr., dir., gen. mgr. Singleton, Palmer & Strauss McAllan Pty. Ltd., Sydney, 1972-73; dir., gen. mgr. successor co. Doyle Dane Bernbach Internat. Inc., Sydney, 1973-77, group sr. v.p. NYC, 1978-84; pres., CEO PowerBase Systems, Inc., 1984-85, Productivity Software Internat. L.P., NYC, 1985-86; divsn. pres., pub. Whittle Comm. L.P., Knoxville, Tenn., 1987-88; chmn., CEO Phyton Techs. Inc., Knoxville, 1988-94; pres., CEO Knox Internat. Corp., Knoxville, 1988-94; chmn., CEO Mich. Bulb Co., Grand Rapids, 1988-94; dir. Univ. of Sydney USA Found., 1994—; chmn., CEO Creative Pub. Internat., Inc., Minnetonka, Minn., 1997-99; sr. v.p. Pleasant Co., Middleton, Wis., 2000-2001; CEO Centric Strategies Internat., Inc., Mpls., 2001—02; sr. v.p. The Middleton Doll Co., Waukesha, Wis., 2002—04; CEO Lee Middleton Original Dolls, Inc., Columbus, Ohio, 2002—04; pres. Biz Coaching & Assocs., LLC dba Action COACH Bus. Coaching, Madison, Wis., 2004—. Ind. mgmt. cons., Melbourne, 1970—72;

lectr. Faculty Econ., Politics Monash U., Melbourne, Australia, 1970—71; chmn., CEO Lansinoh, Labs., Inc., Oak Ridge, Tenn., 1994—96; dir. World Future Soc., Madison, Wis.; bd. dirs. Hilton Oceanfront Resort Hotel, Hilton Head Island, SC, U. Sydney Found.; dir. franchisee adv. bd. ActionCOACH Bus. Coaching; lectr. in field. Contbr. articles to profl. jours. V.p. Waverley Dist. Cricket Club, 1975-77. East-West Ctr. fellow, 1962-64; Australian Commonwealth scholar, Australian Steel Industry scholar, 1958-61. Fellow Australian Inst. Mgmt. (assoc.); mem. Australian Soc. Accts. (assoc.), Harvard Club N.Y.C., Blackhawk Country Club, Tenn. Nat. Golf Club. Home: 6219 S Highlands Ave Madison WI 53705 Office Phone: 608-238-7844. Business E-Mail: iainmacfarlane@actioncoach.com.

MACFARLANE, JOHN CHARLES, utilities executive; b. Hallock, Minn., Nov. 8, 1939; s. Ernest Edward and Mary Bell (Yates) MacF.; m. Eunice Darlene Axvig, Apr. 13, 1963; children: Charles, James, William. BSEE, U. N.D., 1961. Staff engr. Otter Tail Power Co., Fergus Falls, Mn., 1961-64, div. engr. Jamestown, N.D., 1964-71, div. mgr. Langdon, N.D., 1972-78, v.p. planning and control Fergus Falls, 1978-80, exec. v.p., 1981-82, pres. and chief exec. officer, 1982—, also bd. dirs., now chmn. Bd. dirs. Wells Fargo, Fergus Falls, Pioneer Mut. Ins. Co. Pres. Langdon City Commn., 1974-78; chmn. Fergus Falls Port Authority, 1985-86; bd. dirs. Minn. Assn. Commerce and Industry, Minn. Safety Coun., Edison Electric Inst., Village Family Svcs., Fargo; bd. dirs. U. N.D. Energy Rsch. Adv. Coun. Served with U.S. Army, 1962-64. Mem. Am. Mgmt. Assn., IEEE (chmn. Red River chpt.), U. N.D. Alumni Assn., Fergus Falls C. of C. Lodges: Rotary, Masons. Republican. Presbyterian.

MACFARLANE, MALCOLM HARRIS, physicist, educator; b. Brechin, Scotland, May 22, 1933; came to U.S., 1956; s. Malcolm P. and Mary (Harris) M.; m. Eleanor Carman, May 30, 1957; children: Douglas, Kenneth, Sheila, Christine. MA, U. Edinburgh, Scotland, 1955; PhD, U. Rochester, 1960. Research asso. Argonne (Ill.) Nat. Lab., 1959-60; asst. prof. physics U. Rochester, 1960-61; asso. physicist Argonne Nat. Lab., 1961-68, sr. physicist, 1968-80; prof. physics U. Chgo., 1968-80, Ind. U., Bloomington, 1980—2003, prof. emeritus, 2003—. Vis. fellow All Souls Coll., Oxford (Eng.) U., 1966-67; mem. nuclear scis. adv. com. Dept. Energy-NSF, 1983-87; cons. Ency. Brit. Contbr. articles of theoretical nuclear physics to profl. jours. Guggenheim fellow physics, 1966-67; Alexander von Humboldt Found. sr. scientist award, 1985. Fellow Am. Phys. Soc.; mem. Nuclear Physics sect. Am. Phys. Soc. (mem. exec. com. 1969-71) Home: 1008 S Meadowbrook Dr Bloomington IN 47401-4217 Office: Dept Physics Indiana U Bloomington IN 47405 Office Phone: 812-855-3709. E-mail: macfarla@indiana.edu.

MACH, ELYSE, music educator, author, pianist; b. Chgo., Jan. 12, 1942; d. Theodore August and Minna Louise (Holz) M.; children: Sean, Aaron, Andrew. B in Music Edn., Valparaiso U., 1962; MusM, Northwestern U., 1963, PhD in Music, 1965. Mem. faculty Northeastern Ill. U., Chgo., 1964—, prof. music, 1974—, assoc. chair dept. music, 1983-86; concert tours of Netherlands, Germany, Switzerland; recitalist, guest soloist; guest lectr. Northwestern U., Yale U., Juilliard Sch. Music, St. Catherine's Coll. of Oxford U.; cons., book reviewer Harcourt Brace Jovanovich and Macmillan, Oxford; writer monthly column Practice Notes for Clavier music mag.; disting. prof. of bd. govs. state colls. and univs. in Ill., 1990-91. Author: The Liszt Studies, 1973, Contemporary Class Piano, 1976, rev. 6th edit., 1993, 88, 6th edit., 2003, Great Pianists Speak for Themselves, 1980, (London) 81, (Tokyo) 86, The Rare and the Familiar: Twenty-eight Piano Pieces by Franz Liszt, 1982, Great Pianists Speak for Themselves, Vol. 2, 1988, Vols. 1 and 2, 1991, Great Contemporary Pianists Speak for Themselves, 1991, (with others) The Well-Tempered Keyboard Teacher, 1991, 2d edit., 2001, Contemporary Class Piano, Vol. 2, 1994, Learning Piano: Piece by Piece, 2005; contbg. music critic Chgo. Sun-Times. Mem. Edgebrook Cmty. Assn., Chgo., 1975—. Recipient Presdl. Merit award Northeastern Ill. U., 1978, 81, 89, 92, 95, 96, 98, 2000, 02, Bd. Govs. Disting. Prof. award, 1990-91; ortheastern Ill. U. Found. grantee, 1980. Mem. Am. Liszt Soc. (bd. dirs.), Music Educators Nat. Conf., Ill. Music Tchrs. Assn., Midland Soc. Authors. Avocations: traveling, film, reading, theater. Home: 6551 N Waukesha Ave Chicago IL 60646-2726 Office: Northeastern Ill U 5500 N Saint Louis Ave Chicago IL 60625-4679 Office Phone: 773-442-5913.

MACH, MICHAEL J., state agency administrator; BA, U. Wis. -Superior; MA, Grad. Sch. Banking, U. Wis. -Madison; MBA, U. Wis. -Oshkosh. Bank examiner Divsn. Fin. Insts., Oshkosh, Wis., 1971—78, field office supr. La Crosse, Wis., 1978—84, various positions Madison, Wis., adminstr., divsn. banking. Instr. Grad. Sch. Banking, U. Wis., Madison, Wis.; bd. dirs. Am. Coun. State Savings Suprs., Conf. State Bank Suprs. Regulatory Com.; co-chair fin. com. Gov.'s Blue Ribbon Commn. on Year 2000 Preparedness; fin. cons. and speaker. Contbr. articles to profl. jours. Vol. Boy Scouts Am. Office: Wis Div of Banking PO Box 7876 Madison WI 53707-7876

MACH, RUTH, principal; m. Stan Mach; 2 children. Grad., Truman State U., 1958; M, U. Mo.; PhD, St. Louis U. Cert. elem. sch. adminstr., reading specialist, tchr. of learning disabled, tchr. behaviorally disturbed. Tchr. Affton Sch. Dist., Lindbergh Sch. Dist.; elem. sch. prin. Mehlville Sch. Dist.; prin. Meramec Elem. Sch., Clayton, Mo. Bd. dirs. Truman State U. Found.; apptd. bd. govs. Truman State U., 1995—. Mem.: ASCD, St. Louis Suburban Prins. Assn. (past pres., Disting. Prin. award), Conf. on Edn., Mo. Assn. Elem. Sch. Prins. (Disting. Elem. Prin. award), Nat. Assn. Elem. Sch. Prins. Office: Meramec Elem Sch 400 S Meramec Clayton MO 63105

MACHASKEE, ALEX, retired newspaper publishing company executive; b. Warren, Ohio; m. Carol Machaskee. BA in Mktg., Cleve. State U., 1972, LHD (hon.), 1995, U. Akron, 1998. Sports reporter The Warren (Ohio) Tribune; asst. to pub., promo dir. to dir. labor rels. & pers. to v.p., gen. mgr. The Plain Dealer, Cleve., 1985—90, pres., pub., 1990—2006; ret., 2006. Chmn. Cleve. Coun. on World Affairs, 2006—. V.p. Mus. Arts Assn. (Cleve. Orch.); chmn. bd. United Way, 2000; mem. bd. governance, fin. and adminstrn. com. Cleve. Found.; bd. dirs. Univ. Cir. Inc., Greater Cleve. Partnership, St. Vladimir's Orthodox Theol. Sem., Crime Stoppers of Cuyahoga County, Urban League Greater Cleve.; chmn. bd. dirs. United Way Svcs., 2002—03; bd. trustees Cleve. Mus. Art; nat. bd. dirs. IOCC. Named to N.E. Ohio Bus. Hall of Fame, 2001. Mem.: Am. Soc. Newspaper Editors, Newspaper Assn. Am. Office: Plain Dealer Pub Co 1801 Superior Ave E Cleveland OH 44114-2198 Business E-Mail: publisher@plaind.com.

MACHER, FRANK E., automotive executive; b. Detroit, Mar. 1, 1941; BSME, GMI Engring & Mgmt. Inst., Flint, Mich., 1963; MBA, Mich. State U., 1975. Various positions Ford Motor Co., Saline, Mich., mfg. engr. mgr., 1971, prodn. mgr., 1972, mfg. mgr., 1973, mgr. plastics, paint and vinyl div. Saline Plastics and Instrumentation Plant, 1975—, v.p., gen. mgr., Automotive Components Divsn.; pres., CEO ITT Automotive, 1997—99; CEO, chmn. Federal-Mogul, 2001—04; pres., CEO Collins & Aikman, 2005—07. Bd. dir. Dacoma Intern., Tenneco Automotive. Bd. trustees Kettering U., Flint, Mich.

MACHIN, BARBARA E., lawyer; b. Kansas City, Mo., Mar. 26, 1947; d. Roger H. and Doris D. (Dunkel) Elliott; m. Peter A. Machin, June 1, 1969; 1 child, Andrew D. BS in Sec. Edn., U. Kans., 1969, MA in Curriculum Devel./Anthropology, 1973; JD, U. Toledo Coll., 1978. Bar: Ohio 1978, U.S. Dist. Ct. (no. dist.) Ohio 1978, U.S. Ct. Appeals (6th cir.) 1981, U.S. Supreme Ct. 1987. Instr. rsch. and writing U. Toledo Coll. of Law, 1978-79; law clerk Lucas County Ct. of Common Pleas, Toledo, 1979-80; assoc., ptnr. Doyle, Lewis & Warner, Toledo, 1980-87; assoc. Shumaker, Loop & Kendrick, Toledo, 1987-92; gen. counsel U. Toledo, 1993—. Pres., v.p., mem. bd. trustees Toledo Legal Aid Soc., 1983-93; pres. Toledo Civil Trial Attys., 1990-93; trustee Esworth Found., 1993-96. Contbr. articles to profl. jours. Mem. house corp. bd. Gamma Phi Beta Sorority, 1985—; mem. bd. trustees Epworth Found., 1993—, St. Luke's Hosp., 1994—. Mem. Ohio State Bar Assn., Toledo Bar Assn., Toledo Women's Bar Assn., Toledo Civil Trial Attys. (pres. 1983-92). Home: 414 Grenelefe Ct Holland OH 43528-9232

MACIAS, EDWARD S., chemistry professor, dean, academic administrator; b. Milw., Feb. 21, 1944; s. Arturo C. Macias and Minette (Schwenger) Wiederhold; m. Paula Wiederhold, June 17, 1967; children: Matthew Edward, Julia Katherine. AB, Colgate U., 1966; PhD, MIT, 1970. From asst. prof. to Barbara and David Thomas Disting. prof. Arts and Scis. Washington U., St. Louis, 1970—2005, Barbara and David Thomas Disting. prof. Arts and Scis., 2005—, exec. vice chancellor and dean Faculty Arts and Scis., 1995—. Cons. Meteorology Rsch., Inc., Altadina, Calif., 1978-81, Salt River Project, Phoenix, 1980-83, Santa Fe Rsch., Bloomington, Minn., 1985-88, AeroVironment, Inc., Monrovia, Calif., 1986-88. Author: Nuclear and Radiochemistry, 1981; editor: Atmospheric Aerosol, 1981; contbr. numerous articles to profl. jours. Bd. dirs. Mark Twain Summer Inst., St. Louis, 1984-87, 88-90, The Coll. Sch., St. Louis, 1984-88, Colgate U., 1997—. Grantee NSF, EPA, Electric Power Rsch. Inst., So. Calif. Edison Co., Dept. Energy, AEC. Mem. Am. Chem. Soc., Am. Assn. Aerosol Rsch. (editorial bd.), Am. Phys. Soc., AAAS. Home: 6907 Waterman Ave Saint Louis MO 63130-4333 Office: Washington U Campus Box 1094 One Brookings Dr Saint Louis MO 63130 Office Phone: 314-935-6800.

MACINNIS, AL, professional sports team executive, retired professional hockey player; b. Inverness, NS, Can., July 11, 1963; Defenceman Calgary Flames, 1981-94, St. Louis Blues, 1994—2005, v.p. hockey ops., 2006—. Mem. Team Can., Olympic Games, Nagano, Japan, 1998, Salt Lake City, 2002; player NHL All-Star Game, 1985, 1987—92, 1994, 1996—2001, 2003. Named to Sporting News All-Star First Team, 1990, 1991, First All-Star Team, NHL, 1990, 1991; recipient Max Kaminsky Trophy, 1983, Conn Smythe Trophy, 1989, James Norris Meml. Trophy, 1999. Achievements include being a member of Stanely Cup Champion Calgary Flames, 1989; being a member of gold medal Canadian Hockey team, Salt Lake City Olympic Games, 2002; having his number, 2, retired by St. Louis Blues, 2006; being inducted into the Hockey Hall of Fame, 2007. Office: St Louis Blues Hockey Club Scottrade Ctr 1401 Clark Ave Saint Louis MO 63103

MACIUSZKO, KATHLEEN LYNN, librarian, educator; b. Nogales, Ariz., Apr. 8, 1947; d. Thomas and Stephanie (Horowski) Mart; m. Jerzy Janusz Maciuszko, Dec. 11, 1976; 1 child, Christina Aleksandra. BA, Ea. Mich. U., 1969; MLS, Kent State U., 1974; PhD, Case Western Res. U., 1987. Reference libr. Baldwin-Wallace Coll. Libr., Berea, Ohio, 1974-77, dir. Conservatory of Music Libr., 1977-85; dir. bus. info. svcs. Harcourt Brace Jovanovich, Inc., Cleve., 1985-89; staff asst. to exec. dir. Cuyahoga County Pub. Libr., Cleve., 1989-90; dir. Cleve. Area Met. Library System, Beachwood, Ohio, 1990; media specialist Cleve. Pub. Schs., 1991-93, Berea (Ohio) City Sch. Dist., 1993—. Author: OCLC: A Decade of Development, 1967-77, 1984; contbr. articles to profl. jours. Named Plenum Pub. scholar, 1986. Mem. Spl. Librs. Assn. (pres. Cleve. chpt. 1989-90, v.p. 1988-89, editor newsletter 1988-89), Baldwin-Wallace Coll. Faculty Women's Club (pres. 1975), Avocation: music. Office: Midpark HS 7000 Paula Dr Middleburg Heights OH 44130

MACK, JIM, advertising executive; With Frankel & Co., Chgo., 1979-89, pres., 1989-98, pres., CEO, 1998—2002, Chmn., 2002—.

MACK, RICHARD L., lawyer, software company executive; BS in Acctg., Moorhead State U.; JD, Hamline U. Bar: 1993. Counsel administrative div. Norwest Corp.; sr. atty. Cargill, Inc., 1994—2004; sr. v.p., gen. counsel, corp. sec. Mosaic Co. (formerly IMC Global & Cargill, Inc.), 2004—. Mem.: Am. Corp. Counsel Assn., Hennepin County Bar Assn., Minnesota State Bar Assn. Office: Mosaic Co Atria Corp Ctr, Ste E490 3033 Campus Dr Plymouth MN 55441

MACK, ROBERT EMMET, retired hospital administrator; b. Morris, Ill., 1924; MD, St. Louis U., 1948. Diplomate: Am. Bd. Internal Medicine. Intern St. Marys Hosp. Group, 1948-49; asst. resident, then resident internal medicine St. Louis U., 1949-52; asst. chief radioisope clinic Walter Reed Army Med. Center, 1954-56; chief med. service, chief radioisotope service St. Louis VA Hosp., 1956-61; vis. physician St. Louis City Hosp., 1957-61; chmn. dept. medicine Womans Hosp., Detroit, 1961-66; dir. Hutzel Hosp., Detroit, 1966-71, pres., 1971-80; v.p. for academic affairs Detroit Med. Center Corp., 1980-96; ret. Asst. prof. medicine St. Louis U., 1957-61; assoc. prof. medicine, Wayne State U., Detroit, 1961-66, prof., 1966-96, emeritus prof. internal medicine, 1996—, dir. admissions, 1978-81, asst./assoc. dean Med. Ctr. Rels., 1981-96. Fellow ACP, Am. Coll. Hosp. Adminstrs., Soc. Med. Adminstrs. (pres. 1987-89); mem. AMA, Am. Fedn. Clin. Rsch., Cen. Soc. Clin. Rsch., Am. Endocrine Soc., Am. Physiol. Soc. Home: 3020 S Westview Ct Bloomfield Hills MI 48304-2472 E-mail: rmack@intmed.wsu.edu.

MACK, STEPHEN W., financial planner; b. Chgo., Mar. 4, 1954; s. Walter M. and Suzanne (Charbonneau) M.; m. Dayle A. Rothermel, Nov. 19, 1983; children: Michael, Veronica, Kevin. BBA in Fin., U. Mich., 1976; cert., Coll. Fin. Planning, Denver, 1987. NASD Lic. Series 63 Uniform Securities Agent State Law Exam., Series 7 Gen. Securities Rep., Series 5 Interest Rate Options, Series 8 Gen. Securities Sales Supr., Series 15 Fgn. Currency Options, Series 24 Gen. Securities Prin., Series 4 Registered Options Prin., Series 53 Municipal Securities Prin. Gen. sales mgr. Mack Cadillac Corp., Mt. Prospect, Ill., 1976-81; sales rep. Merrill Lynch Co., Chgo., 1981-84, resident mgr. Rockford, Ill., 1984-85, asst. v.p. Skokie, Ill., 1985-86; pres., chief exec. officer Mack Investment Securities, Inc., Glenview, Ill., 1986—. Editor, distributor Mack Tracks (trademark), monthly newsletter; creator, developer Money Mgrs. Plus Program and Website. Bdi. dirs. Glenview Youth Baseball, 1994-99, pres., 1999-2001. Mem. Inst. Cert. Fin. Planners, Internat. Assn. Registered Fin. Planners (cert. sr. adv. 2006—), Nat. Assn. Securities Dealers, Internat. Assn. Fin. Planners, Am. Assn. Cert. Fin. Planners, Am. Assn. Registered Fin. Planners, Am. Assn. Registered Investment Advisers, Soc. Asset Allocation and Fund Timers, Mensa, Nat. Football League Players Assn. (registered, player fin. advisor 2005—). Avocations: skiing, tennis, running. Office: Mack Investment Securities Inc 1939 Waukegan Rd Glenview IL 60025-1715

MACK, TOM, retired professional football player; b. Cleve., Nov. 1, 1943; Guard L.A. Rams, 1966—78. Named to Pro Football Hall of Fame, 1999. Achievements include Rams No. 1 draft pick, 1966; player 4 NFC championship games; player 3 NFL Pro Bowls; 8 AFC-NFC Pro Balls; All-Pro 1970, 71, 73, 84; All-NFL, 1969; All-NFC, 1970, 71, 72, 73, 74, 75, 77, 78; All-Am., Mich., 1965; playing in 184 consecutive games; never missed a game in 13-season career. Office: Pro Football Hall of Fame 212 George Halas Dr NW Canton OH 44708

MACKAY, ALFRED F., dean, philosophy educator; b. Ocala, Fla., Oct. 1, 1938; s. Kenneth Hood and Julia Horsey (Farnum) MacK.; m. Ann Nadine Wilson, Feb. 4, 1962; children: Douglas Kevin, Robert Wilson. AB, Davidson Coll., 1960; PhD, U. N.C., 1967. Prof. philosophy Oberlin Coll., Ohio, 1967-84, 96—, dean Coll. Arts and Scis. Ohio, 1984-95, acting pres. Ohio, 1991, provost Ohio, 2005—. Vis. asst. prof. philosophy dept. U. Ill., Urbana/Champaign, 1970-71; vis. prof. philosophy dept. Wayne State U., Detroit, 1983. Author: Arrow's Theorem: The Paradox of Social Choice, 1980; editor: Society: Revolution and Reform, 1971, Issues in the Philosophy of Language, 1976. Campaign cons. Buddy MacKay for U.S. Senate, Fla., 1988. 1st lt. U.S. Army, Airborne, 1961-63. Fellow Woodrow Wilson Found., 1963-66, Am. Coun. of Learned Socs., 1973, Humanities fellow Rockefeller Found., 1981. Democrat. Avocations: choral singing, automobiles. Office: Oberlin Coll Provost Cox Administration Building Oberlin OH 44074 Office Phone: 440-775-8410. Office Fax: 440-775-8944. E-mail: al.mackay@oberlin.edu.

MACKAY, DAVID (A.D. DAVID MACKAY), food products executive; b. Hamilton, New Zealand, Aug. 16, 1955; m. Michelle Mackay; 2 children. B of Bus., Charles Stuart U., Australia, 1977. Group product mgr. Kellogg Australia, 1985—87; category dir. ready-to-eat cereals corp. hdqrs. Kellogg Co., Battle Creek, Mich., 1987—91; mng. dir. Sara Lee Bakery, Australia, 1992—98, Kellogg Australia, Battle Creek, 1998; mng. dir. U.K. and Republic of Ireland Kellogg Co., Battle Creek, 1998—2000; sr. v.p. Kellogg USA, Battle Creek, 2000, pres., 2000—03; exec. v.p. Kellogg Co., Battle Creek, Mich., 2000—03, pres., COO, 2003—06, pres., CEO, 2007—. Bd. dir. Kellogg Co., 2005—, Fortune Brands Inc., 2006—. Office: Kellogg PO Box 3599 1 Kellogg Sq Battle Creek MI 49016-3599

MACKENZIE, GEORGE ALLAN, company director; s. George Adam and Annette Louise MacKenzie; m. Valerie Ann Marchand, June 30, 1971; children from previous marriage: Richard Michael, Barbara Wynne. Student, Jamaica Coll., Kingston, 1944-48. Commd. flying officer Canadian Air Force, 1951, advanced through grades to lt. gen., 1978; comdr. Canadian Forces Air Command, Winnipeg, Man., 1978-80, resigned, 1980; exec. v.p., COO Gendis Inc., 1980-89, pres., COO, 1989-99, pres., CEO, 1999—2002; bd. dirs. Sony of Can. Ltd., Willowdale, Ont., Canada; dir. O.V. Assocs. LTD.; pres., CEO CANUSA MedExpress Ltd., 2003—07. Mem. regional adv. bd. Carleton U. Decorated comdr. Order of Mil. Merit, Order St. Johns, Can. Decoration, Knight of St. Lazarus of Jerusalem. Mem. United Services Inst. Can. (hon. v.p.), Can. Corps Commissionaires (gov.), Police Chiefs Rsch. Found. (co-chmn.), Manitoba Club, Royal Mil. Inst. Manitoba. Home: 383 Christie Rd Winnipeg MB Canada R2N 4A5 Personal E-mail: gallanmac@hotmail.com.

MACKENZIE, NANCI, gas company executive; m. Len Mackenzie, 1988. Co-founder (with Sue Palmer) Lucky Lady Oil Co., 1976—82; founder, pres. USGT/Aquila (formerly U.S. Gas Transp. before sale to Aquila), Dallas, 1986—2001; pres. Aquila Dallas Marketing LP. Recipient Entrepreneur of the Yr, 1998. Mem.: Nat. Assn. Women's Bus. Owners, Am. Gas Assn. Office: Aquila Inc 20 W Ninth St Kansas City MO 64105

MACKENZIE, RONALD ALEXANDER, anesthesiologist; b. Detroit, Mar. 31, 1938; s. James and Elizabeth Mackenzie; m. Nancy Lee Vogan, Aug. 25, 1962; children: Margaret, James. BS, Alma Coll., 1961; DO, Kansas City Coll., 1967. Diplomate Am. Bd. Anesthesiology. Resident in anesthesiology Detroit Osteo. Hosp., 1970-72, Cleve. Clinic, 1972-73, Mayo Clinic, Rochester, Minn., 1973-74, cons. in anesthesia, 1974—87, vice-chmn. anesthesiology, 1988—99, chmn. GYN/ENT anesthesia, 1998—99; pres. ceo Am. Soc. Anesthesiologists. Vice-chmn. dept. anesthesiology Mayo Clinic, 1988-98. Pres. Minn. Orch., Rochester, 1987-89. Fellow Am. Coll. Anesthesiologists; mem. Am. Soc. Anesthesiologists (bd. dirs. 1983-87, sec. 1991-97, 1st v.p. 1998, pres.-elect 1999), Sigma Xi. Avocations: sailing, photography. Office: Mayo Clinic 200 1st St SW Rochester MN 55905-0002

MACKEY, MAURICE CECIL, university president, economist, lawyer; b. Montgomery, Ala., Jan. 23, 1929; s. M. Cecil and Annie Laurie (Kimrey) M.; m. Clare Siewert, Aug. 29, 1953; children: Carol, John, Ann. BA, U. Ala., 1949, MA, 1953, LL.B., 1958; PhD, U. Ill., 1955; postgrad., Harvard U., 1958-59. Bar: Ala. 1958. Asst. prof. econs. U. Ill., 1955-56; assoc. prof. econs. U.S. Air Force Acad., 1956-57; asst. prof. law U. Ala., 1959-62; with FAA, 1963-65, U.S. Dept. Commerce, 1965-67; asst. sec. U.S. Dept. Transp., 1967-69; exec. v.p., prof. law Fla. State U., Tallahassee, 1969-71; pres. U. South Fla., Tampa, 1971-76; pres., prof. law Tex. Tech U., Lubbock, 1976-79; pres., prof. econs. Mich. State U., East Lansing, 1979-85, prof. econs., 1985—. Asst. counsel Subcom. on Antitrust and Monopoly, U.S. Senate, 1962-63; bd. dirs. Community First Bank, Lansing, Mich.; mem. adv. com. U.S. Coast Guard Acad., 1969-71; chmn. Fla. Gov.'s Adv. Com. on Transp., 1975, Nat. Boating Safety Adv. Council, 1975—; mem. adv. council NSF, 1978-81; assoc. China Council, 1979—; Disting. vis. prof. United Arab Emirates U., 1990, 91, 92, 93; bd. dirs. Summit Holding Corp., Lansing. Bd. dirs. Gulf Ridge council Boy Scouts Am.; pres. Chief Okemos council, 1981-82; bd. dirs. Tampa United Fund, Lubbock United Way; chmn., bd. dirs. Debt for Devel. Coalition, 1989—. Served with USAF, 1956-57. Recipient Arthur S. Flemming award Washington Jaycees, 1967 Mem. Fla. Council 100, Tampa C. of C. (bd. govs.), Am. Assn. State Colls. and Univs. (pres., dir.), Artus, Chi Alpha Phi. Office: Mich State U Dept Econs 101 Marshall Hall East Lansing MI 48824-1038

MACKIE, RICHARD H., orchestra executive; married; 3 children. Grad., Tulane U.; M in Arts Adminstrn., U. Wis., Madison. Jazz musician New Hyperion Oriental Foxtrot Orch.; pres. Friends of WHA-TV; dir. devel. Edgewood Coll.; exec. dir. Madison (Wis.) Symphony Orch., 1999—. Office: Madison Symphony Orchestra 222 W Washington Ave Ste 460 Madison WI 53703-2744

MACKIEWICZ, LAURA, advertising agency executive; Formerly with D'Arcy Advt.; with BBDO, Chgo., 1973—, now sr. v.p., dir. broadcast and print svcs. Office: BBDO Chgo 410 N Michigan Ave Ste 8 Chicago IL 60611-4273

MACKINNEY, ARCHIE ALLEN, physician; b. St. Paul, Aug. 16, 1929; s. Archie Allen and Doris (Hoops) MacK.; m. Shirley Schaefer, Apr. 9, 1955; children— Julianne, Theodore, John. BA, Wheaton Coll., Ill., 1951; MD, U. Rochester, 1955. Intern, resident in medicine U. Wis. Hosp., 1955-59; clin. assoc. NIH, 1959-61; clin. investigator VA, 1961-64; asst. prof. medicine U. Wis., Madison, 1964-68, assoc. prof., 1968-74, prof., 1974-98, med. alumni prof., 1987. Mentor class of '03 U. Wis. Med. Sch.; chief hematology VA Hosp., Madison, 1964-98, chief nuclear medicine, 1964-73, 78-79 Author (editor): Pathophysiology of Blood, 1984, Hematology for Students, 2002; contbr. articles to profl. jours. Trustee Intervarsity Christian Fellowship, 1985-88. Served with USPHS, 1959-61. Danforth assoc., 1962 Mem. Am. Soc. Hematology, Am. Fedn. Clin. Research, Central Soc. Clin. Research. Republican. Baptist. Home: 190 N Prospect Ave Madison WI 53705-4071 Office: 2500 Overlook Ter Madison WI 53705-2254

MACKINNON, CATHARINE ALICE, lawyer, educator, writer; d. George E. and Elizabeth V. (Davis) MacKinnon. BA in Govt. magna cum laude with distinction, Smith Coll., 1969; JD, Yale U., 1977, PhD in Polit. Sci., 1987; doctorate (hon.), Hebrew U., Jerusalem, 2008. Prof. law U. Mich., Ann Arbor, 1990—, Elizabeth A. Long Prof. Law. Long term vis. prof. U. Chgo., 1997-2005; co-dir. LAW Project Equality Now, 2001-05; fellow Ctr. for Advanced Study, 2005-06; Roscoe Pound Vis. Prof. Law, Harvard Law Sch., 2007; vis. prof. various univs. Author: Sexual Harassment of Working Women, 1979, Feminism Unmodified, 1987, Toward a Feminist Theory of the State, 1989, Only Words, 1993, Sex Equality, 2001, 2nd. edit., 2007, Women's Lives, Men's Laws, 2005, Are Women Human? and other international dialogues, 2006; co-author: In Harm's Way, 1997, Directions in Sexual Harassment Law, 2003. Mem.: AAAS (assoc.), Am. Bar Found. (Disting. Rsch. award 2007). Office: U Mich Law Sch 625 S State St Ann Arbor MI 48109-1215 Office Phone: 734-647-3595. Office Fax: 734-764-8309. E-mail: camtwo@umich.edu.

MACKINNON, KEVIN SCOTT, lawyer; b. San Jose, Calif., June 29, 1958; s. Hector Neil and Margie Lou (Riggs) MacK.; m. Hanna T. Piech, Sept. 1, 1984. BA, U. Calif., Santa Barbara, 1980; JD, U. Santa Clara, 1983. Assoc. Fisher & Hurst, Chgo., 1983-84, Isham, Lincoln & Beale, Chgo., 1984-86, Schiff, Hardin & Waite, Chgo., 1986; sr. corp. counsel, staff dir. McDonald's Corp.; ptnr. Katten Muchin Zavis Rosenman, Chgo. Mem.: ABA, Lawyers for Creative Arts (v.p.), Internat. Franchise Assn., Chgo. Bar Assn., Internat. Trademark Assn.

MACKLIN, CROFFORD JOHNSON, JR., lawyer; b. Columbus, Ohio, Sept. 10, 1947; S. Crofford Johnson, Sr. and Dorothy Ann (Stevens) M.; m. Mary Carole Ward, July 5, 1969; children: Carrie E., David J. BA, Ohio State U., 1969; BA summa cum laude, U. West Fla., 1974; JD cum laude, Ohio State U., 1976. Bar: Ohio 1977, U.S. Tax Ct. 1978. Acct. Touche Ross, Columbus, 1976-77; assoc. Smith & Schnacke, Dayton, 1977-81, shareholder, 1988-89; sole practice Dayton, 1981-82; ptnr. Porter, Wright, Morris & Arthur, Dayton, 1983-88, Thompson, Hine LLP, 1989—, practice group leader pers. and succession planning, 2001—06. Adj. faculty Franklin U., 1977; adj. prof. U. Dayton Law Sch., 1981. Contbr. articles to profl. jours. Bd. dirs. Great Lakes Nat. Bank Ohio, 1997, Easter Seals, 1984-86. Served to capt. USMCR, 1969-74. Fellow Am. Coll. Trust and Estate Counsel; mem. ABA, Dayton Bar Assn. (chmn. probate com. 1981-83), Dayton Trust & Estate Planning (pres. 1983-84), Ohio Bar Assn. Presbyterian. Home: 7276 Wetherington Dr West Chester OH 45069 Office: Thompson Hine LLP 2000 Courthouse Pla NE PO Box 8801 Dayton OH 45401-8801 Home Phone: 513-759-0504; Office Phone: 937-443-6730.

MACKLIN, MARTIN RODBELL, psychiatrist; b. Raleigh, NC, Aug. 27, 1934; s. Albert A. and Mitzi (Robdell) M.; m. Ruth Chimacoff (div.); children: Meryl, Shelley; m. Anne Elizabeth Warren, May 25; children: Alicia, Aaron. BME, Cornell U., 1957, M in Indsl. Engring., 1958; PhD in Biomed. Engring., Case Western Res. U., 1967, MD, 1977. Diplomate Am. Bd. Psychiatry and Neurology; cert. in alcoholism and other drug dependencies Am. Soc. Addiction Medicine. Investigator Am. Heart Assn., Cleve., 1969-74; vis. fellow U. Sussex, Brighton, England, 1970; assoc. prof. biomed. engring. Case Western Res. U., 1972-81, asst. prof. psychiatry, 1981—; clin. dir. Horizon Ctr. Hosp., Warrensville Township, Ohio, 1981-83; adminstrv. dir. Riverview Psychiat. Assocs., 1983-94; med. dir. Woodside Hosp., 1989-94; v.p. med. affairs UHHS Geauga Regional Hosp., Chardon, Ohio, 1994—2007; physician surveyor The Joint Commn., 2007—. Psychiat. cons. Glenbeigh Hosp., Ohio and Fla.; chair quality intervention panel Ohio State Med. Bd.; cons. in field. Contbr. articles to profl. jours; patentee in field. NIH rsch. grantee Kellogg Found., Cleve., 1967-81;

Laughlin fellow Am. Coll. Psychiatry, 1980. Mem. Am. Psychiat. Assn., Am. Coll. Physician Execs., Cleve. Acad. Medicine, Cleve. Psychiat. Soc., AMA. Avocations: woodworking, gardening. Home: 843 Haywood Dr South Euclid OH 44121 Home Phone: 216-691-5950; Office Phone: 440-269-6595. E-mail: martin.macklin@case.edu.

MACKLIN, PHILIP ALAN, retired physics professor; b. Richmond Hill, NY, Apr. 13, 1925; s. Egbert Chalmer and Margaret Griswold (Collins) M.; m. Cora Baldwin Galindo, Sept. 5, 1953 (dec. Feb. 2005); children: Susan, Steven, Peter. BS cum laude, Yale U., 1944; MA, Columbia U., 1949, PhD, 1956. Physicist Carbide & Carbon Chems. Corp., Oak Ridge, 1946-47; research scientist AEC, Columbia U., 1949-51; instr. physics Middlebury Coll., Vt., 1951-54, acting chmn. dept., 1953-54; mem. faculty Miami U., Oxford, Ohio, 1954—, prof. physics, 1961-93, chmn. dept., 1972-85, prof. emeritus, 1993—; ret., 1993. Research scientist Armco Steel Co., summers 1955-56; vis. prof. U. N.Mex., summers 1957-68, Boston U., fall 1985-86; physicist Los Alamos Sci. Labs., summers 1960-62; participant NSF summer insts., 1970-71; vis. scientist MIT, 1985-86 Author publs. in field; patentee in field. Vestryman Holy Trinity Episcopal Ch., Oxford, 1959-61, 67, 71-73, 75-77, mem. fin. com., chmn. blood assurance program, 1980—, lector, 1989—. With USN, 1944-46. Mem. AAAS, LWV of Oxford (treas. 1986-88, dir. governance 1997—), Am. Phys. soc., Forum Physics and Soc., Kiwanis (bd. dirs. 1994-97), Torch Club of Butler County (pres. 1982-83, 96-97, mem. editl. adv. com. The Torch), 1809 Club (pres. 1964-65), Campus Ministry Ctr. (trustee 1994-2002), Union of Concerned Scientists, Ctr. for Voting and Democracy (charter), Membership Assn. Miami U. Art Mus. (exec. com. 1999-2002), Phi Beta Kappa (pres. Iota of Ohio chpt. 1987-88), Sigma Xi, Sigma Pi Sigma, Omicron Delta Kappa. Democrat. Home: 211 Oakhill Dr Oxford OH 45056-2710 Office: Culler Hall Miami Univ Oxford OH 45056 Office Phone: 513-529-5625. E-mail: macklipa@muohio.edu.

MACKUS, ELOISE L., food products company executive; Asst. gen. counsel J.M. Smucker Co., Orrville, Ohio, 1994-99, dir. internat., 1999, v.p., gen. mgr. internat. market, 2000—. Office: 1 Strawberry Ln Orrville OH 44667-1241

MACLAUGHLIN, HARRY HUNTER, retired judge; b. Breckenridge, Minn., Aug. 9, 1927; s. Harry Hunter and Grace (Swank) MacL.; m. Mary Jean Shaffer, June 25, 1958; children: David, Douglas. BBA with distinction, U. Minn., 1949, JD, 1956. Bar: Minn. 1956. Law clk. to justice Minn. Supreme Ct.; ptnr. MacLaughlin & Mondale, MacLaughlin & Harstad, Mpls., 1956-72; assoc. justice Minn. Supreme Ct., 1972-77; U.S. sr. dist. judge Dist. of Minn., Mpls., 1977—92. Part-time instr. William Mitchell Coll. Law, St. Paul, 1958-63; lectr. U. Minn. Law Sch., 1973-86; mem. 8th Cir. Jud. Council, 1981-83. Bd. editors: Minn. Law Rev, 1954-55. Mem. Mpls. Charter Commn., 1967-72, Minn. State Coll. Bd., 1971-72, Minn. Jud. Council, 1972; mem. nat. adv. council Small Bus. Adminstrn., 1967-69. Served with USNR, 1945-46. Recipient U. Minn. Outstanding Achievement award, 1995; named Best Fed. Dist. Ct. Judge in 8th Cir., Am. Lawyer mag., 1983. Mem. ABA, Minn. Bar Assn., Hennepin County Bar Assn., Beta Gamma Sigma, Phi Delta Phi. Congregationalist. Office: US Dist Ct 8E US Courthouse 300 S Fourth St Minneapolis MN 55415

MACLEAN, DOUG, former professional hockey coach, former sports team executive; b. Summerside, PEI, Can., Apr. 12, 1954; m. Jill MacLean; children: Clark, Mackenzie. Student, P.E.I.; M in Ednl. Psychology, We. Ont. Asst. coach London Knights of OHL, 1984-85, St. Louis Blues, 1986-87, 87-88, Washington Capitals, 1988-89, 89-90, Detroit Red Wings, 1990-91, asst. gen. mgr., 1992-93, 93-94; gen. mgr. Adirondack, Red Wing orgn., 1992-93, 93-94; dir. player devel., scout Fla. Panthers, 1994-95, head coach, 1995—98; gen. mgr Columbus Blue Jackets, 1998—2007, pres., 1998—2007, head coach, 2003—04.

MACLIN, ALAN HALL, lawyer; b. DuQuoin, Ill., Dec. 22, 1949; s. John E. and Nora (Hall) M.; m. Joan Davidson (div. Dec. 1981); children: Molly, Tess, Anne; m. Jeanne Sittlow, Nov. 17, 1984. BA magna cum laude, Vanderbilt U., 1971; JD, U. Chgo., 1974. Bar: Minn. 1974, U.S. Dist. Ct. Minn. 1974, U.S. Ct. Appeals (8th cir.) 1974, U.S. Ct. Appeals (5th cir.) 1975. U.S. Supreme Ct. 1978. Asst. atty. gen. Minn. Atty. Gen., St. Paul, 1974-80; chief anti-trust divsn. Briggs & Morgan, St. Paul, 1980—, mem. bd. dirs., 1993-96. Mem. Minn. State Bar Assn. (treas. anti-trust sect. 1978-80, 96-98, chair 1998—), Ramsey County Bar Assn. (sec. jud. com. 1980-82), Phi Beta Kappa. Unitarian Universalist. Office Phone: 612-977-8400. Personal E-mail: amaclin@briggs.com.

MACMILLAN, SHANNON ANN, professional soccer player; b. Syosset, NY, Oct. 7, 1974; Student in social work, U. Portland. Profl. soccer player San Diego Spirit, 2001—03. Mem. U.S. Nat. Women's Soccer Team, 1993—, including silver medal World Univ. Games team, 1993, gold medal U.S. Olympic Team, 96; mem. U.S. Women's Under-20 Nat. Team, 1993—94, including championship Internat. Women's Tournament, France, 1993; mem. LaJolla (Calif.) Nomads club soccer team, winning state club championship, 1991, 92, Japanese Women's Profl. League, 1996, 97. Named 1995 Soccer Am. Player of Yr., Female Athlete of Yr., 1993, 1995, U. Portland, World Cup Champion, 1999; named to San Diego Union Tribune All-Acad. team; recipient Mo. Athletic Club award, 1995, Hermann award, U. Portland, 1995, Bill Hayward award, 1995, Silver medal, Sydney Olympic Games, 2000. Office: US Soccer Fedn 1801-1811 S Prairie Ave Chicago IL 60616

MACMILLAN, STEPHEN P., health products executive; b. July 19, 1963; married; 2 children. BA in econ., Davidson Coll.; grad. advanced mgmt. program, Harvard Bus. Sch. Various mktg. positions Procter & Gamble; with over the counter div. McNeil Consumer and Specialty Pharm. Johnson & Johnson Corp., mktg. dir. J&J/Merck over-the-counter franchise worldwide England; mgr. dir. Johnson & Johnson MSD (Merck), England, 1995; v.p., mktg. and profl. sales McNeil Consumer and Splty. Pharm. Johnson & Johnson Corp., 1997; pres. Johnson & Johnson-Merck Consumer Pharmaceuticals; sector v.p. global splty. ops. Pharmacia & Upjohn, 1999—2003; COO Stryker Corp., 2004—05, pres., CEO, 2005—. Office: Stryker Corp 2725 Fairfield Rd Kalamazoo MI 49002

MACPHEE, CRAIG ROBERT, economist, educator; b. Annapolis Royal, NS, Can., July 10, 1944; came to U.S., 1950; s. Craig and Dorothy (Seney) MacP.; m. Kathleen Gray McCown, Feb. 6, 1966 (div. 1981); children: Paul, Heather, Rob; m. Andrea Joy Sime, June 26, 1983. BS, U. Idaho, 1966; MA, Mich. State U., 1968, PhD, 1970. Asst. prof., then assoc. prof. econs. U. Nebr., Lincoln, 1969-89, prof., 1989—, chmn. econs. dept., 1980—83, 1989—98. Econ. affairs officer UN, Geneva, 1975-77; internat. economist US Dept. Labor, Washington, 1983-84; econ. adv. Republic of Ga., 1998-2001, Republic of Montenegro, 2001, Mongolia, 2006; cons. in field. Author: Economics of Medical Equipment and Supply, 1973, Restrictions on International Trade in Steel, 1974, Roll Over Joe Stalin, 2005. Mem. Am. Econ. Assn., Nebr. Econ. and Bus. Assn., Phi Eta Sigma, Omicron Delta Epsilon. Avocations: running, skiing, sailing, reading. Home: 631 Hazelwood Dr Lincoln NE 68510-4325 Office: U Nebr Coll Bus Dept Econs Lincoln NE 68588-0489 Office Phone: 402-472-2449. Business E-Mail: cmacphee@unl.edu.

MAC WATTERS, VIRGINIA ELIZABETH, singer, music educator, actress; b. Phila. d. Frederick-Kennedy and Idoleein (Hallowell) Mac W.; m. Paul Abée, June 10, 1960. Grad., Phila. ormal Sch. for Tchrs., 1933; student, Curtis Inst. Music, Phila., 1936. With New Opera Co., NYC, 1941-42; artist-in-residence Ind. U. Sch. Music, 1957-58; assoc. prof. U. Ind. Sch. Music, 1958-68, prof. voice, 1968-82, prof. emeritus, 1982—. Singer: leading roles Broadway mus. Rosalinda, 1942-44, Mr. Strauss Goes to Boston, 1945, leading opera roles New Opera Co., N.Y.C., 1941-42, San Francisco, 1944, N.Y.C. Ctr., 1946-51; leading soprano for reopening of Royal Opera House, Covent Garden, London, 1947-48, Guatemala, El Salvador, Cen. Am., 1948-49; debut at Met. Opera, N.Y.C., 1952; TV spls. on BC include Menotti's Old Maid and the Thief, 1949, Would-be Gentleman (R. Strauss), 1955; leading singer with Met. Opera Co. on coast to coast tour of Die Fledermaus, 1951-52, Met. Opera debut, N.Y.C., 1952, leading soprano Cen. City Opera Festival, Colo., 1952-56; performed with symphony orchs. in U.S., Can., S.Am.; concert recitalist U.S., Can., 1950-62; opened N.Y. Empire State Music Festival in Ariadne auf Naxos (Strauss), 1959; soloist Mozart Festival, Ann Arbor, Mich. Recipient Mile award Album Familiar Music, 1949, Ind. U. Disting. Tchg. award, 1979; named One of 10 Outstanding Women of the Yr.; Zeckwer Hahn Phila. Mus. Acad. scholar, 1941-42; MacWatters chair donated by New Auer Grand Concert Hall, U. Ind. Sch. Music. Mem. Nat. Fedn. of Music Clubs, Nat. Soc. Arts and Letters, Nat. Soc. Lit. and Arts, Soc. Am. Musicians, Nat. Assn. Tchrs. of Singing, Internat. Platform Assn., Sigma Alpha Iota. Clubs: Matinee Musical (hon. mem. Phila., Indpls. chpts.). Achievements include having only original recorded version of Zerbinetta aria from Ariadne auf Naxos (Strauss). Home: 3800 Arlington Rd Bloomington IN 47404-1347 Office: Ind U Sch Music Bloomington IN 47405

MACY, JOHN PATRICK, lawyer; b. Menomonee Falls, Wis., June 26, 1955; s. Leland Francis and Joan Marie (LaValle) M. BA, Carroll Coll., 1977; JD, Marquette U., 1980. Bar: Wis. 1980, U.S. Dist. Ct. (we. and ea. dists.) Wis. 1980, U. S. Ct. Appeals (7th cir.) 1980. Assoc. Hippenmeyer Reilly Arenz Molter Bode & Gross, Waukesha, Wis., 1980-83; ptnr. Arenz Molter Macy & Riffle, S.C., Waukesha, 1983—. Lectr. in field. Mem. ABA, Waukesha County Bar Assn. (chair 1995-96). Republican. Roman Catholic. Home: 4839 Hewitts Point Rd Oconomowoc WI 53066-3320 Office: Arenz Molter Macy & Riffle SC PO Box 1348 720 N East Ave Waukesha WI 53186-4800 Office Phone: 262-548-1340. Business E-Mail: ammrlaw@ammr.net.

MADANSKY, ALBERT, statistics educator; b. Chgo., May 16, 1934; s. Harry and Anna (Meidenberg) M.; m. Paula Barkan, June 10, 1990; children from previous marriage: Susan, Cynthia, Noreen, Michele. AB, U. Chgo., 1952, MS, 1955, PhD, 1958. Mathematician Rand Corp., Santa Monica, Calif., 1957-65; sr. v.p. Interpub. Group of Companies, NYC, 1965-68; pres. Dataplan Inc, NYC, 1968-70; prof. computer scis. CCNY, 1970-74; prof. bus. adminstrn. grad. sch. U. Chgo., 1974—, assoc. dean, 1985-90, dep. dean, 1990-93, H.G.B. Alexander prof. bus. adminstrn., 1996-99, H.G.B. Alexander emeritus bus. adminstrn., 1999—. Bd. dirs. Analytic Services, Washington, 1975—. Author: Foundations of Econometrics, 1975, Prescriptions for Working Statisticians, 1988. Fellow: Ctr. for Advanced Study in Behavioral Scis., Am. Statis. Assn., Inst. Math. Stats., Econometric Soc. Home: 200 E Delaware Pl Apt 23F Chicago IL 60611-5799 Office: U of Chicago Grad Sch Business Chicago IL 60637 E-mail: albert.madansky@gsb.uchicago.edu.

MADARA, JAMES LEE, dean, pathologist, educator, epitheliologist; b. Altoona, Pa., Sept. 16, 1950; s. Daniel Rodman and Margaret Jane (Hauser) M.; m. Victoria Mollenkopf, May 14, 1975; children: J. Maxwell, Alexis Lindsy. BA, Juniata Coll., 1971; MD, Hahnemann Med., 1975. Cert. anatomic and clin. pathology. Intern Deaconess Hosp., Boston, 1975—76, resident in pathology, 1976—78; fellow in internal medicine Harvard Med. Ctr., Boston, 1978—80; instr. pathology Harvard Med. Sch., Boston, 1980-81, asst. prof. pathology, 1981-85, assoc. prof. pathology, 1985-91, prof. pathology, 1993-97; assoc. prof. of health scis. and tech. Harvard-M.I.T., Boston, 1986-91; Timmie prof., chmn. dept. pathology & lab. medicine Emory U. Sch. Medicine, Atlanta, 1997—2002; dean, v.p. for medical affairs Pritzker Sch. of Med. and Div. of Biological Sciences, U. of Chicago, Chicago, Ill., 2002—, Sara and Harold Lincoln Thompson disting. svc. prof. Assoc. editor Gastroenterology, 1986-91; mem. editl. bd. Jour. Clin. Investigation, 1987—; editor-in-chief Am. Jour. Pathology, 2000; contbr. over 160 articles to profl. jours. Grantee NIH, 1980—. Mem. Am. Soc. for Clin. Investigation (elected), Am. Soc. for Cell Biology, Am. Gastroenterological Assn. (rsch. coun. 1988-90, Ross Rsch. scholar award 1982), Am. Physiol. Soc., Am. Assn. Pathology (Parke/Davis award 1990), Assn. Am. Physicians. Achievements include description of functional sequellae of neutrophil-epithelial cell interactions; recognition that tight junctions between epithelial cells are regulated under physiological conditions. Office: Biological Sci U Chicago 5812 S Ellis St Chicago IL 60637 Office Fax: 773-702-1897. E-mail: jmadara@bsd.uchicago.edu.

MADDEN, CHERYL BETH, state legislator; b. Burke, SD, Nov. 15, 1948; d. Herman and Ida Denker; m. Michael K. Madden, 1977; children: Pamela, Jessica, Rachel. Grad. high sch. Mem. S.D. Ho. of Reps., Pierre, 1992-98, mem. edn., health and human svc. coms.; mem. S.D. Senate from 35th dist., Pierre, 1999—. Chaplain, chmn. Fedn. Rep. Women. Address: 63 Langdon Rd Buffalo WY 82834-9341

MADDEN, LAURENCE VINCENT, plant pathology educator; b. Ashland, Pa., Oct. 10, 1953; s. Lawrence Vincent and Janet Elizabeth (Wewer) M.; m. Susan Elizabeth Heady, July 7, 1984. BS, Pa. State U., 1975, MS, 1977, PhD, 1980. Research scientist Ohio State U., Wooster, 1980-82, asst. prof., 1983-86, assoc. prof., 1986-91, prof., 1991—. Invited univ. lectr. on plant disease epidemiology in more than 10 countries. Author: Introduction to Plant Disease Epidemiology; sr. editor Phytopathology, 1988-90, APS Press, 1988-90; editor-in-chief Phytopathology, 1991-93; contbr. 140articles to profl. jours. U.S. Dept. Rsch. grantee, 1984, 85, 86, 87, 89, 90, 91, 95, 99, 2000; Disting. scholar Ohio State U., 1991,; recipient Outstanding Alumni award Pa. State U. Coll. Agrl. Scis. Fellow AAAS, The Linnean Soc. of London, Am. Phytopathol. Soc. (chmn. com. 1983, 86, coun. 1991-93, Ciba Geigy Agrl. Achievement award 1990, v.p. 1994-95, pres.-elect 1995-96, pres. 1996-97); mem. Biometric Soc., Brit. Soc. Plant Pathology, Sigma Xi (chpt. pres. 1985). Achievements include development of statistical and mathematical models for understanding, predicting and comparing botanical epidemics and assessing crop losses. Home: 1295 Briarcrest Cir Wooster OH 44691 Office: Ohio State U OARDC Dept Plant Pathology Wooster OH 44691 E-mail: madden.1@osu.edu.

MADDOX, O. GENE, state legislator, lawyer; b. Peoria, Ill., Aug. 23, 1938; BS, Northwestern U., 1960, JD, 1963. Pvt. practice, Des Moines, 1963—; gen. counsel, employee rels. v.p. Mid-Continent Industries, Des Moines, 1987—; mem. Iowa Senate from 38th dist., Des Moines, 1992—; vice chair commerce com., mem. appropriations com.; mem. jud. com., mem. state govt. com.; mem. ways and means com. Mayor City of Clive, 1978-93; mem. Grace United Meth. Ch.; v.p. Iowa Affiliate, Am. Diabetes Assn.; mem. Iowa Natural Heritage Found.; vol. reader Visually Impaired Persons; mem. Iowa Hist. Soc., Polk-Des Moines Taxpayers. Mem. ABA, Iowa Bar Assn., Polk County Bar Assn., Iowa Jaycees (pres.), Iowa League of Cities (pres. 1987-88), Iowa Municipalities (bd. dirs. 1983-89, pres. 1987-88), Greater Des Moines C. of C., Rotary (N.W. Des Moines chpt.), Lions. Republican. Office: State Capitol 9th And Grand Ave Des Moines IA 50319-0001 E-mail: omaddox@legis.state.ia.us.

MADDOX, WILMA, health facility administrator; Grad., Truman State U., 1979. Bus. mgr. Vision Care Assocs., Macon, Maine. Bd. govs. Truman State U., 1994—; mem. Ko. K-16 Coalition; mem. bd. edn. Macon County R-I Sch. Dist.; vol. aftersch. program Macon United Meth. Ch. Mem.: Am. Found. for Vision Awareness (past pres. Mo. affiliate). Office: Vision Care Associates 1705 Prospect Drive Macon MO 63552

MADDUX, GREGORY ALAN, professional baseball player; b. San Angelo, Tex., Apr. 14, 1966; m. Kathy Maddux; children: Amanda Paige, Chase Alan. Grad., H.S., Las Vegas. Pitcher Chgo. Cubs, 1986—92, 2004—06, Atlanta Braves, 1993—2003, LA Dodgers, 2006, San Diego Padres, 2007—. Co-founder Maddux Found., 1993—. Named Nat. League Pitcher of Yr., The Sporting News, 1992—95; named to All-Star team, 1988, 1992, 1994—98, 2000, All-Time Rawlings Gold Glove Team, 2007; recipient Cy Young award, 1992—95, Gold Glove award, 1990—2002, Gold Glove Award, 2004—07. Achievements include being the first pitcher in Major League history to win the Cy Young award for four consecutive years, 1992-95; being a member of the World Series Champion Atlanta Braves, 1995; becoming 13th pitcher in MLB history to throw 3,000 strikeouts, 2005; setting a new all-time record for Golden Glove awards with 17 in 2007. Office: San Diego Padres 9449 Friars Rd San Diego CA 92108

MADGETT, NAOMI LONG, poet, editor, publisher, educator; b. Norfolk, Va., July 5, 1923; d. Clarence Marcellus and Maude Selena (Hilton) Long; m. Julian F. Witherspoon, Mar. 31, 1946 (div. Apr. 1949); 1 child, Jill Witherspoon Boyer; m. William H. Madgett, July 29, 1954 (div. Dec. 1960); m. Leonard P. Andrews, Mar. 31, 1972 (dec. May 1996). BA, Va. State Coll., 1945; MEd, Wayne State U., 1955; PhD, Internat. Inst. for Advanced Studies, 1980; LHD (hon.), Siena Heights Coll., 1991, Loyola U., 1993; DFA (hon.), Mich. State U., 1994. Reporter, copyreader Mich. Chronicle, Detroit, 1946; svc. rep. Mich. Bell Telephone Co., Detroit, 1948-54; tchr. English pub. high schs. Detroit, 1955-65, 66-68; rsch. assoc. Oakland U., Rochester, Mich., 1965-66; mem. staff Detroit Women Writers Conf. Ann. Writers Conf., 1968—; lectr. English U. Mich., 1970-71; assoc. prof. English Eastern Mich. U., Ypsilanti, 1968-73, prof., 1973-84, prof. emeritus, 1984—; editor-pub. Lotus Press, 1974—. Editor Lotus Poetry Series, Mich. State U. Press, 1993-98. Author: (poetry) Songs to a Phantom Nightingale (under name Naomi Cornelia Long), 1941, One and the Many, 1956, Star by Star, 1965, 2d edit., 70, (with Ethel Tincher and Henry B. Maloney) Success in Language and Literature B, 1967, (textbook) Pink Ladies in the Afternoon, 1972, 2d edit., 90, Exits and Entrances, 1978, A Student's Guide to Creative Writing, 1980, (textbook) Phantom Nightingale: Juvenilia, 1981, Octavia and other Poems (Creative Achievement award Coll. Lang. Assn.), 1988, Remembrances of Spring: Collected Early Poems, 1993, Octavia: Guthrie and Beyond, 2002, Connected Islands, 2004, (autobiography) Pilgrim Journey, 2006; editor: (anthology) A Milestone Sampler: 15th Anniversary Anthology, 1988, Adam of Ife: Black Women in Praise of Black Men, 1992; In Her Lifetime tribute Afrikan Poets Theatre, 1989 Participant Creative Writers in Schs. program. Recipient Esther R. Beer Poetry award Nat. Writers Club, 1957, Disting. English Tchr. of Yr. award, 1967; Josephine Nevins Keal award, 1979; Mott fellow in English, 1965, Robert Hayden Runagate award, 1985, Creative Artist award Mich. Coun. for the Arts, 1987, award Nat. Coalition 100 Black Women, 1984, award Nat. Coun. Tchrs. English Black Caucus, 1984, award Chesapeake/Virginia Beach chpt. Links, Inc., 1981, Arts Found. Mich. award, 1990, Creative Achievement award Coll. Lang. Assn., 1988; Arts Achievement award Wayne State U., 1985, The Black Scholar Award of Excellence, 1992; Am. Book award, 1993, Mich. Artist award, 1993; Creative Contbrs. award Gwendolyn Brooks Ctr. Black Lit. and Creative Writing Chgo. State U., 1993, Lifetime Achievement award Furious Flower, 1994, George Kent award, 1995, Lifetime Achievement award Gwendolyn Brooks Ctr., 2003; Naomi Long Madgett Poetry award named for her, 1993—, Alain Locke award Detroit Inst. Arts, Friends of African and African Am. Art, 2003, Creative Scholarship award, Coll. Lang. Assn.; inducted Sumner H.S. Hall of Fame, St. Louis, 1997, Nat. Lit. Hall Fame for Writers of African Descent, Chgo. State U., 1999, Mich. Women's Hall of Fame, 2002; named Poet Laureate, City of Detroit, 2001—, Mayor's award Literary Excellence, 2005; named one of 23 Enterprising Women, Detroit Hist. Soc., 2004; Bronze Bust created by Artis Lane unveiled at Charles H. Wright Mus. African Am. History, 2005. Mem. NAACP, Coll. Lang. Assn., So. Poetry Law Ctr., Langston Hughes Soc., Charles H. Wright Mus. of African Am. History, Detroit Working Writers, Detroit Inst. Arts, Fred Hart Williams Geneal. Soc., Alpha Kappa Alpha. Congregationalist. Home: 18080 Santa Barbara Dr Detroit MI 48221-2531 Office: PO Box 21607 Detroit MI 48221-0607 Office Phone: 313-861-1280. Personal E-mail: nlmadgett@aol.com.

MADIA, WILLIAM JUUL, chemist; b. Pitts., May 20, 1947; s. William Anthony and Joanna (VanKerchkoven) M.; m. Audrey Marie Madia, May 23, 1970; children: Joseph Anthony, Benjamin Paul, William Byron. BS in Chemistry, Ind. U. of Pa., 1969, MS in Nuclear Chemistry, 1970; PhD in Radiochemistry, Va. Polytech. Inst., 1975. With Battelle, 1975—; chemist, researcher Battelle Columbus (Ohio) div., 1975-77, assoc. sect. mgr., 1977-80, sect. mgr., 1980-83, mgr. office of nuclear waste isolation, 1983-85; pres. Battelle Project Mgmt. div., 1985-86; sr. v.p. Battelle Meml. Inst., 1988-89, 89—; pres. Battelle Tech. Internat., 1988-89, corp. sr. v.p., 1990-91, gen. mgr. environ. systems and tech. divsn., corp. sr. v.p., 1992-94; dir. Pacific Northwest Nat. Lab., 1994—99, Oak Ridge Nat. Lab., Tenn., 2000—03; pres., CEO UT-Battelle, Oak Ridge, Tenn., exec. v.p., 2003—. Mem. adv. bd. Ohio State U. Coll. Engring.; bd. dirs. Mason & Hanger. Mem. editl. bd. R&D Mag.; contbr. articles to profl. jours. Bd. dirs. Franklin U., 1987-94, Franklin County Children Svcs., 1988-94; editorial adv. bd. High Tech. Bus., 1988—; bd. dirs. Tri-City Indsl. Devel. Coun., Washington Roundtable; hon. bd. dirs. Mid-Columbia Edn. Alliance; adv. bd. Jr. Achievement Greater Tri-Cities; bd. dirs. Reading Found.; co-chair Tri-Cities Corp. Coun. Arts; mem. exec. com. Children's Ctr. Capital Campaign. With U.S. Army, 1970-72. Mem. AAAS, Indsl. Rsch. Inst. (fed. sci. and tech. com.), Midwest Rsch. Inst. (trustee), Nat. Renewable Energy Lab. (bd. govs.), Brookhaven Sci. Assocs. (bd. dirs.), U.S. Dept. Energy Lab. Ops. Bd., Washington Tech. Alliance. Roman Catholic. Office: Battelle 505 King Ave Columbus OH 43201

MADIGAN, JOHN WILLIAM, publishing executive; b. Chgo., June 7, 1937; s. Edward P. and Olive D. Madigan; m. Holly Williams, Nov. 24, 1962; children: Mark W., Griffith E., Melanie L. BBA, U. Mich., 1958, MBA, 1959. Fin. analyst Duff & Phelps, Chgo., 1960—62; audit mgr. Arthur Andersen & Co., Chgo., 1962—67; v.p. investment banking Paine, Webber, Jackson & Curtis, Chgo., 1967—69; v.p. corp. fin. Salomon Bros., Chgo., 1969—74; v.p., CFO, dir. Tribune Co., Chgo., 1975—81, exec. v.p., 1981—91; pub. Chgo. Tribune, 1990—94; pres., CEO Tribune Pub. Co., Chgo., 1991—94; pres., COO Tribune Co., Chgo., 1994—95, pres., 1994—2001, CEO, 1995—2002, chmn., 1996—2004; spl. ptnr. Madison Dearborn Ptnrs. LLC, 2005—. Bd. dir. AP, AT&T Wireless Svcs.; former dir. Morgan Stanley. Trustee Rush-Presbyn.-St. Luke's Med. Ctr., Mus. TV and Radio in N.Y., Northwestern U., Ill. Inst. Tech.; mem. bd. overseers Hoover Instn. Mem.: Chgo. Coun. on Fgn. Rels. (chmn.), Robert R. McCormick Tribune Found. Office: Madison Dearborn Ste 3800 Three First National Plz Chicago IL 60602

MADIGAN, LISA, state attorney general; m. Pat Byrnes; 1 child, Rebecca. BA, Georgetown U., 1988; student, Loyola U. Asst. dean adult, continuing edn., dir. Sr. Acad. Lifelong Learning Wrights Family Coll. Wilbur Wright Coll., with positive alts. project; litigator Sachnoff & Weaver, Ltd., Chgo.; mem. Ill. Senate, Springfield, 1998—2002, mem. senate appropriations com., edn. com., joint com. adminstrv. rules; atty. gen. State of Ill., 2002—. Former vol. tchr., South Africa. Bd. dirs. AIDS Living Rememberance Com. Named one of Top 40 Lawyers Under 40, Nat. Law Jour., 2005. Mem. Ill. Bar Assn., Women's Bar Assn. Ill., Chgo. Bar Assn. Republican. Office: Office of Atty General James R Thompson Ctr 100 W Randolph St Chicago IL 60601 Office Phone: 312-814-3000.

MADIGAN, MICHAEL JOSEPH, state legislator, political organization administrator; b. Chgo., Apr. 19, 1942; m. Shirley Roumagoux; children: Lisa, Tiffany, Nicole, Andrew. Ed., U. Notre Dame, Loyola U., Chgo. Mem. Ill. Ho. of Reps., 1971—, majority leader, 1977-80, minority leader, 1981-82, house spkr., 1983-94, Dem. leader, 1995-96, ho. spkr., 1997—; private atty. Sec. to Alderman David W. Healey; hearing officer Ill. Commerce Commn.; del. 6th Ill. Constnl. Conv.; trustee Holy Cross Hosp.; ex officio mem. adv. com. to pres. Richard J. Daley Coll.; adv. com. Fernley Harris Sch. for Handicapped; committeeman 13th Ward Democratic Orgn.; chmn. Dem. Party of Ill., 1998-. Mem. Council Fgn. Relations, City Club Chgo. Democrat. Office: House Reps 300 State Capital Bldg Springfield IL 62706-0001 also: Dem Party Ill PO Box 518 Springfield IL 62705*

MADISON, ROBERT PRINCE, architect; b. Cleve., July 28, 1923; s. Robert J. and Nettie (Brown) M.; m. Leatrice L. Branch, Apr. 16, 1949; children: Jeanne Marie, Juliette Branch. Student, Howard U., 1940—43, HHD, 1987; BArch, Western Res. U., 1948; MArch, Harvard U., 1952; DFA (hon.), Cleve. State U., 2000; HHD (hon.), Kent State U., 2001; DSc (hon.), Case We. Res. U., 2004. Mem. various archtl. firms, 1948; instr. Howard U., Washington, 1952—54; chmn., CEO Robert P. Madison Internat., architects, engrs. and planners, Cleve., 1954—. Trustee Am. Automobile Assn.; vis. prof. Howard U., 1961-62; lectr. Western Res. U., 1964-65; mem. U.S. architects del. Peoples Repub. China, 1974 Prin. works include U.S. Embassy Dakar, Senegal, West Africa, 1966, State of Ohio Computer Ctr., 1988, Cuyahoga County Jail, 1990, Continental Airlines Hub Concourse, Cleve. Internat. Airport, 1991. Mem. tech. adv. com. Cleve. Bd. Edn., 1960—; mem. adv. com. Cleve. Urban Renewal, 1963—; mem. fine arts adv. com. to mayor, Cleve.; mem. archtl. adv. coun. Cornell U.; trustee Case Western Res. U., Cleve. Opera, 1990, NCCJ, 1990, Commn. on Higher Edn., 1990, Cleve. (Ohio) Orch., 1998, Cleve. (Ohio) Arts Prize, 2001; bd. dirs. Jr. Achievement Greater Cleve.; trustee Cuyahoga County Hosp. Found., 1983—, Univ. Circle Inc., Midtown Corridor Inc.; mem. Ohio Bd. Bldg. Standards, 1986, Cleveland Heights City Planning Commn., 1987. 1st lt., inf. AUS, 1943-46. Decorated Purple Heart; Fulbright fellow, 1952-53; recipient Disting. Svc. award Case Western Res. U., 1989, Disting. Archtl. Firm award Howard U., 1989, Entrepreneur of Yt. award Ernst Young, Inc., Merrill Lynch, 1991, Arch. of Yr. Nat. Tech. Assn., 1996, Martin Luther King Jr. Crp. award African-Am. Archives Aux. Western Res. Hist. Soc., 1997, Disting. Alumni award Case We. Res. U., 1997; named to Corp. Hall of Fame, Ohio Assembly of Couns., 1991, Pres. award Kent State U., 1999; named to Cleve. Bus. Hall of Fame, 2002. Fellow AIA (chpt. pres., nat. task force for creative econs. 1976, mem. jury of fellows 1983-85, mem. nat. judicial coun. 1993, Gold Medal Firm award Ohio 1994, Gold Medal award Ohio 1997, Whitney M. Young Jr. award 2002); mem. Architects Soc. Ohio, Epsilon Delta Rho, Alpha Phi Alpha, Sigma Pi Phi. Office: Robert P Madison Internat Inc 2930 Euclid Ave Cleveland OH 44115-2416 Home: 18975 Van Aken Blvd Apt 410 Shaker Heights OH 44122-3539 Office Phone: 216-861-8195. Business E-Mail: rmadison@rpmadison.com.

MADORI, JAN, art gallery director; Founder, CEO Personal Preference Inc., Bolingbrook, Ill., 1979—. Named Illinois/Northwest Indiana Entrepreneur of the Year, Ernst & Young; named to U. Illinois Entrepreneurship Hall of Fame. Office: Personal Preference Inc 800 Remington Blvd Bolingbrook IL 60440-4800

MADSEN, H(ENRY) STEPHEN, retired lawyer; b. Momence, Ill., Feb. 5, 1924; s. Frederick and Christine (Landgren) Madsen; m. Carol Ruth Olmstead, Dec. 30, 1967; children: Stephen Stewart, Christie Morgan, Kelly Ann. MBA, U. Chgo., 1948; LLB, Yale U., 1951. Bar: Wash. 1951, Ohio 1953, U.S. Supreme Ct. 1975. Rsch. asst. Wash. Water Power Co., Spokane, 1951; assoc. Baker, Hostetler & Paterson, Cleve., 1952-59, ptnr., 1960-88, sr. ptnr., 1989-92; ret., 1992. Danish consul for Ohio, 1973—98. Active Bus. Advisers Cleve.; trustee Ohio Presbyn. Ret. Svcs. With AC US Army, 1943—46. Decorated Knight Queen of Denmark. Fellow: ABA (life); mem.: Cleve. Bar Assn., Am. Law Inst., Am. Coll. Trial Lawyers (life), Country Club Cleve.

MADSEN, MATTHEW J., lawyer; b. Feb. 26, 1969; BBA in Fin., U. Iowa, 1991; JD, Stanford U., Calif., 1998. Bar: Mo. 1998. Atty. Lewis, Rice & Fingersh, LC, St. Louis, 2004—. Contbr. articles to profl. jours. Outside gen. counsel St. Louis Cmty. Found.; mem. planned giving adv. coun. Cardinal Glennon Childrens Hosp.; mem. gift planning coun. Variety Club of St. Louis. Named one of Top 100 Attys., Worth mag., 2006, Best Lawyers, Am. Trust and Estate; recipient 40 under 40 award, St. Louis Bus. Jour., 2008. Mem.: Estate Planning Coun. St. Louis, Bar Assn. Met. St. Louis, ABA (real property, probate and trust law sect.). Office: Lewis Rice & Fingersh LC 500 N Broadway Ste 2000 Saint Louis MO 63102 Office Phone: 314-444-7878. Office Fax: 314-612-7878. E-mail: mmadsen@lewisrice.com.

MADURA, JAMES ANTHONY, surgeon, educator; b. Campbell, Ohio, June 10, 1938; s. Anthony Peter and Margaret Ethel (Sebest) M.; m. Loretta Jayne Sovak, Aug. 8, 1959; children: Debra Jean, James Anthony II, Vikki Sue. BA, Cogate U., 1959; MD, Western Res. U., 1963. Diplomate Am. Bd. Surgery. Intern in surgery Ohio State U., Columbus, 1963—64, resident in surgery, 1966—71; asst. prof. surgery Ind. U., Indpls., 1971—76, assoc. prof. Surgery, 1976—80, prof. Surgery, 1980—, J.S. Battersby prof. surgery, 2001—. Dir. gen. surgery Ind. U. Sch. Medicine, Indpls., 1985—, vice-chmn., 1985—. Contbr. articles to profl. jours. Bd. dir. Indpls. Opera. Capt. med. corps US Army, 1965—66, Vietnam, 85th Evacuation Hosp. Fellow Am. Coll. Surgeons; mem. Cen. Surg. Assn., Western Surg. Assn., Soc. Surgery Alimentary Tract, Midwest Surg. Assn., Internat. Biliary Assn., Assn. Acad. Surgeons, The Columbia Club. Republican. Roman Catholic. Home: 9525 Copley Dr Indianapolis IN 46260-1422 Personal E-mail: jmadura1@comcast.net. Business E-Mail: jmadura@iupui.edu.

MAEHR, MARTIN LOUIS, psychology professor; b. Guthrie, Okla., June 25, 1932; s. Martin J. and Regina (Meier) M.; m. Jane M. Pfeil, Aug. 9, 1959; children— Martin, Michael, Katherine BA, Concordia Coll., 1953, MA, 1959; PhD, U. Nebr., 1960. Counselor U. Nebr., Lincoln, 1959-60; asst. prof. to assoc. prof. Concordia Sr. Coll., Fort Wayne, Ind., 1960-67; assoc. prof. ednl. psychology U. Ill., Urbana, 1967-70, prof., 1970—, chmn. dept. ednl. psychology, 1970-75, assoc. dean grad. and internat. programs prof., 1975-77, research prof., dir. Inst. Research on Human Devel., prof. ednl. psychology, 1977-88, assoc. dir. Office Gerontology and Aging Studies, 1980-82; prof. edn. and psychology U. Mich., Ann Arbor, 1988—, chair combined program edn. and psychology, 1988-92. Vis. prof. U. Queensland, Australia, 1981; vis. prof., cons. to dean Faculty Edn. U. Tehran, Iran, 1973-74 Author: Sociocultural Origins of Achievement, 1974, (with Jane Maehr) Being a Parent in Today's World, 1980, (with L.A. Braskamp) The Motivation Factor, 1986, (with Carol Midgley) Transforming School Cultures, 1996; editor: Advancement in Motivation and Achievement series; contbr. articles to profl. jours. Lutheran. Office Phone: 734-647-0627. Business E-Mail: mlmaehr@umich.edu.

MAGEE, MARK E., lawyer, financial executive; b. 1948; BA, Miami U.; JD, U. Cin. Bar: Ohio 1975. V.p., gen. counsel, sec. Provident Bancorp, Inc., Cin. Office: 1 E 4th St Cincinnati OH 45202-3717

MAGEE, PAUL TERRY, geneticist and molecular biologist, educator; b. Los Angeles, Oct. 26, 1937; s. John Paul and Lois Lorene (Cowgill) M.; m. Beatrice Buten, Aug. 6, 1964; children: Alexander John, Amos Hart. BS, Yale U., 1959; PhD, U. Calif., Berkeley, 1964. Am. Cancer Soc. postdoctoral fellow Lab. Enzymologie, Gif-sur-Yvette, France, 1964-66; mem. faculty Yale U., 1966-77, asst. prof. microbiology, 1966-72, assoc. prof. microbiology and human genetics, 1972-75, assoc. prof. human genetics, 1975-77; dean Trumbull Coll., 1969-72; prof. microbiology, chmn. dept. microbiology and pub. health Mich. State U., East Lansing, 1977-87, dir. Biotech. Research Ctr., 1985-87; dean Coll. Biol. Scis. U. Minn., 1987-95, Morse Alumni Disting. prof. genetics and cell biology, 2000—. Mem. genetics adv. panel NSF, 1978-83, mem. adv. com. biology directorate, 1992-97, chair, 1995-96; chmn. BBS task force looking to 21st century, 1991; cons. Corning Glass Works, 1978-80, Pillsbury Rsch., 1990-96; mem. pers. com. Am. Cancer Soc., 1983-87; mem. microbial genetics and physiology study sect. NIH, 1984-88; co-chmn. com. grad. record exam. biochemistry cell and molecular biology Ednl. Testing Svc., 1988-98; co-chair Gordon Rsch. Conf. on Cellular and Molecular Mycology, 1996; mem. microbiology and infectious disease rsch. com. NIH, 1994-99, chair, 1996-99; chair Burroughs Wellcome Fund Award Com. in Molecular Pathogenic Mycology, 1995-2001; traveling fellow Japanese Soc. for Promotion of Sci., 1995; lectr. in field. Mem. editorial bd. Jour. Bacteriology, 1975-80, Molecular and Cell Biology, 1981-92, Fungal Genetics and Biology, 1996—. Named Mich. champion masters swimming, 1978-84, 86, Minn. champion masters swimming, 1988, 89, 91-99, nat. YMCA swimming champion, 1990, nat. Can. swimming champion, 1999. Mem. AAAS, Am. Soc. Microbiologists, Am. Acad. Microbiology, Genetics Soc. Am. Jewish. Office: U Minn Dept Genetics and Cell Bio 6-160 Jackson 321 Church St SE Minneapolis MN 55455

MAGERS, RON, newscaster; b. San Bernadino, Calif. married; 3 children. Contbg. reporter KEZI-TV, Eugene, Oreg., 1965—67; reporter and anchor KPIX-TV, San Francisco, 1968—74; prin. news anchor KGW-TV, Mpls., 1974—81; news anchor and reporter WMAQ-TV, Chgo., 1981—97, WLS-TV, Chgo., 1998—. Supports Heartland Alliance, Baseball Cancer Charities, Northwestern U. Settlement Ho., Bears Care. Recipient Chgo. Emmy awards, Peter Lisagor award, Nat. Press Club citation, AP award, Ill. Broadcasters award, Ohio State award, Ethics award, Soc. Profl. Journalists. Mem.: AFTRA. Office: WLS-TV 190 N State St Chicago IL 60601

MAGGS, PETER BLOUNT, lawyer, educator; b. Durham, NC, July 24, 1936; s. Douglas Blount and Dorothy (Mackay) M.; m. Barbara Ann Widenor, Feb. 27, 1960; children: Bruce MacDowell, Gregory Eaton, Stephanie Ann, Katherine Ellen. AB, Harvard U., 1957, JD, 1961; postgrad. (exchange student), Leningrad State U., USSR, 1961-62. Bar: D.C. 1962. Research assoc. Law Sch. Harvard U., 1963-64; asst. prof. law U. Ill., 1964-67, assoc. prof., 1967-69, prof., 1969-88, William and Marie Corman prof., 1988-98, Peer & Sarah Pedersen prof., 1998—2002, acting dean, 1990, Clifford M. and Bette A. Carney chair in law, 2002—; dir. Rule of Law Program Washington, 1994. Fulbright lectr. Moscow State U., 1977; reporter Uniform Simplification of Land Transfers Act.; vis. prof. George Washington U., 1998. Author: (with others) The Mandelstam File, 1996; co-translator Civil Code of the Russian Federation, translation, 2003, Civil Code of the Republic of Armenia, translation, 1999, Intellectual Property (in Russian), 2000, Internet and Computer Law, 2001, Trademark and Unfair Competition, 2002; designer talking computers for the blind. Fulbright rsch. scholar, Yugoslavia, 1967; Fulbright disting. chair, Trento, 2002; East-West Ctr. fellow, 1972, Guggenheim fellow, 1979. Mem. ABA, D.C. Bar, Am. Assn. Advancement Slavic Studies, Assn. Am. Law Schs., Am. Law Inst. (consultative group, UCC Article 2), Internat. Acad. Comparative Law. Office: U Ill Coll Law 504 E Pennsylvania Ave Champaign IL 61820-6909 Office Phone: 217-333-6711. E-mail: p-maggs@uiuc.edu.

MAGID, CREIGHTON (CHIP) REID, lawyer; b. Cedar Rapids, Iowa, Dec. 11, 1961; s. Frank N. and Marilyn (Young) M. AB, Princeton U., 1984; JD, U. Mich., 1987. Bar: Iowa 1987, Minn. 1987, Mont. 1988, U.S. Dist. Ct. Minn., U.S. Dist. Ct. (no. dist.) Iowa. Ptnr., trial, regulatory, tech. group Dorsey & Whitney PLLP, Mpls., 1987—, and co-chmn., products and tech. liability litig. group. Mem. Mpls. Rowing Club (pres. 1991-95). Avocation: rowing. Office: Dorsey & Whitney Ste 1500 50 S 6th St Minneapolis MN 55402-1498 Office Phone: 612-340-5661. Office Fax: 612-340-2868. Business E-Mail: magid.chip@dorsey.com.

MAGILL, FRANK JOHN, federal judge; b. Verona, ND, June 3, 1927; s. Thomas Charles and Viola Magill; m. Mary Louise Timlin, Nov. 22, 1955; children: Frank Jr., Marguerite Connolly, R. Daniel, Mary Elizabeth, Robert, John. BS in Fgn. Svc., Georgetown U., 1951, LLB, 1955; MA, Columbia U., 1952. Ptnr. Nilles, Hansen, Magill & Davies, Ltd., Fargo, ND, 1955—86; judge US Ct. Appeals (8th cir.), Fargo, 1986—2000, sr. judge, 2000—. Chmn. fin. disclosure com. US Jud. Conf., 1993—98. Fellow: Am. Coll. Trial Lawyers; mem.: Cass County Bar Assn. (Pres. 1970). Republican. Avocations: tennis, sailing, skiing.

MAGILL, KENT B., lawyer; b. Kansas City, Mo., Dec. 2, 1952; m. Teresa A. Magill. BS, Kent State U., 1975; JD, U. Iowa, 1977. Bar: Mo. 1977, Kans. 1987, US Dist. Ct. Dist. Kans. Assoc. Shughart, Thomson & Kilroy, Kansas City, Mo., 1977—80, atty., 1980—89; assoc. gen. counsel, v.p. The Marley Co., Mission Woods, Kans., 1989—92; v.p., gen. counsel, sec. Layne Christensen Co., Mission Woods, Kans., 1992—2000; assoc. gen. counsel Interstate Brands Corp., 2000—02, v.p., gen. counsel, sec., 2002—, Interstate Bakeries Corp., Kansas City, Mo., 2002—. Office: Interstate Bakeries Corp 12 E Armour Blvd Kansas City MO 64111

MAGNUS, KATHY JO, religious organization executive; b. Brainerd, Minn., Oct. 22, 1946; d. Fred L. and Doris K. (Anderson) Kunkel; m. Richard A. Magnus, Dec. 17, 1966; children: Erica Jo, Cory Allan. BS, U. Minn., 1968. Tchr. St. Paul Schs., 1968-69, Denver Pub. Schs., 1969-75; dir. comm. St. Paul Luth. Ch., Denver, 1979-81; adminstrv. asst. to bishop Rocky Mountain Synod Luth. Ch. Am., Denver, 1981-87; exec. staff Rocky Mountain Synod Evang. Luth. Ch. Am., Denver, 1988—; v.p. Evangel. Luth. Ch. in Am., 1991-97, assoc. dir. for missionary support svcs./candidate screening Chgo., 1997—, assoc. dir. internat. personnel, 1997—. Mem. ctrl. com. World Coun. Chs., Geneva, 1995—. Named exemplar of univ. Calif. Luth. U., 1992. Avocations: writing, reading. Office: Evang Luthern Ch in Am 8765 W Higgins Rd Chicago IL 60631-4101

MAGNUSON, JOHN JOSEPH, zoology educator; b. Evanston, Ill., Mar. 8, 1934; BS, U. Minn., 1956, MS, 1958; PhD in Zoology, U. B.C., 1961. Chief tuna behavior program Biol. Lab. Bur. Comml. Fisheries U.S. Fish and Wildlife Svc., Honolulu, 1961-67; program dir. ecology NSF, Washington, 1975-76; asst. prof. to assoc. prof. U. Wis., Madison, 1968-74, chmn. oceanography and limnology grad. program, 1978-83, 86, prof. zoology, limnology, ecology fishes, dir. Trout Lake Biol. Sta., 1974-82, prof. zoology, 1982-2000, prof. emeritus, 2000—, dir. Ctr. Limnology, 1982-2000. Lead investigator North Temperate Lakes Long Term Ecol. Rsch. site, NSF, U. Wis., 1981-99; chmn. Aquatic Ecol. sect. Ecol. Soc. Am., 1975-76; chair Com. Fisheries, Nat. Rsch. Coun., 1981-83, 93-94; chmn. Com. Sea Turtle Protection & Mgmt., 1989-90, chmn. Com. Pacific N.W. Anadromous Salmonids, 1992-94; chmn. com. Assessment Atlantic Bluefin, 1994; mem. Ocean Studies Bd., 1995-97, com. Sustainable Fisheries, 1995-99; working group on hydrology and aquatic ecology Intergovernmental Panel on Climate Change, 1993-95, and Ecosystems, 1998-2000, interim chmn. long term ecol. rsch. network coord. com., 2005-06; chmn. com. Dynamic Changes in Marine Ecosystems: Fishing, Food Webs and Future Options, 2005— Named Team Mem. Month, NOAA, 2002; recipient Wis. Idea award in Natural Policy, 1990, Hilldale award Biological Sci. Div., U. Wis., Madison, 1999—2000, Outstanding Achievement award, U. Minn., 2003, co-chair Waters of Wis. Project, Wis. Acad. Sci. Arts Letters, 2001—03; NSF midcareer fellow, U. Wash., 1992. Fellow AAAS; mem. Am. Fisheries Soc. (pres. 1981, Disting. Svc. award 1980, award of excellence 2000), Am. Soc. Limnology and Oceanography (at large 2000-03, Lifetime Acheivement award, 2002), Ecol. Soc. Am., Soc. Internat. Limnology, Nature Conservancy, (trustee Wis. chpt. 2003—). Office: Univ Wisconsin Madison Ctr Limnology 680 N Park St Madison WI 53706-1413 E-mail: jjmagnus@wisc.edu.

MAGNUSON, PAUL ARTHUR, federal judge; b. Carthage, SD, Feb. 9, 1937; s. Arthur and Emma Elleda (Paulson) Magnuson; m. Sharon Schultz Magnuson, Dec. 21, 1959; children: Marlene Peterson, Margaret(dec.), Kevin, Kara Berger. BA, Gustavus Adolphus Coll, 1959; JD honors causa, William Mitchell Coll., 1963; DLL (hon.), Wm. Mitchell Coll., 1991; DLL (hon.), Gustavus Adolphus Coll., 1982. Bar: Minn. 1963, U.S. Dist. Ct. Minn. 1968. Asst. registrar William Mitchell Coll. of Law, 1959-60; claim adjuster Agrl. Ins. Co., 1960-62; clk. Bertie & Bettenberg, 1962-63; ptnr. LeVander, Gillen, Miller & Magnuson, South St. Paul, Minn., 1963-81; judge U.S. Dist. Ct. Minn., St. Paul, 1981—, chief judge, 1994—2001. Jurist-in-residence Hamline U., 1985, Augsberg Coll., 1986, Bethel Coll., 1986, Concordia Coll., St. Paul, 1987, U. Minn., Morris, 1987; instr. William Mitchell Coll. Law, 1984-92, Corcordia Coll., Moorhead, 1988, St. John's U., 1988, Coll. of St. Benedict, 1988; mem. jud. conf. com. on adminstrn. of Bankruptcy Sys., 1987-96; mem. Eighth Cir. Edn. Com., 1992-97, chmn. 1994-97; mem. jud. conf. com. on Internat. Jud. Rels., 1996—, chair, 1999—; mem. com. on dist. judges edn. Fed. Jud. Ctr., 1998—; mem 8th cir. Edn. com., 1992-97, chmn. 1994-97. Mem. Met. Health Bd., St. Paul, 1970-72; legal counsel Ind. Rep. Party Minn., St. Paul, 1979-81. Recipient Disting. Alumnus award Gustavus Adolphus Coll., 1982; First Disting. Svc. award William Mitchell Coll. Law, 1999, Dr. of Laws Honors Causa, William Mitchell Coll. of Law, 1991. Mem. Minn. State Bar Assn., 1st Dist. Bar Assn. (pres. 1974-75), Dakota County Bar Assn., 10th Jud. Dist. Bar Assn., Am. Judicature Soc., Fed. Bar Assn., Fed. Cir. Bar Assn., Fed. Judges Assn. (bd. dirs., treas. 1997-2001, v.p. 2001-). E-mail: PAMagnuson@mnd.uscourts.gov.

MAGNUSON, ROGER JAMES, lawyer; b. St. Paul, Jan. 25, 1945; s. Roy Gustaf and Ruth Lily (Edlund) M.; m. Elizabeth Cunningham Shaw, Sept. 11, 1982; children: James Roger, Peter Cunningham, Mary Kerstin, Sarah Ruth, Elizabeth Camilla, Anna Clara, John Edlund, Britta Kristina. BA, Stanford U., 1967; JD, Harvard U., 1971; BCL, Oxford U., 1972. Bar: Minn. 1973, U.S. Dist. Ct. Minn. 1973, U.S Ct. Appeals (8th, 9th, 10th, 11th cirs.) 1974, U.S. Supreme Ct. 1978. Chief pub. defender Hennepin County Pub. Defender's Office, Mpls., 1973; ptnr., trial group Dorsey & Whitney, Mpls., 1972—, and head, strategic litig. group. Dean Oak Brook Coll. of Law and Govt. Policy, 1995—; chancellor Magdalen Coll., 1999—. Author: Shareholder Litigation, 1981, Are Gay Rights Right, The White-Collar Crime Explosion, 1992, Informed Answers to Gay Rights Questions, 1994, Internat. Judicial Asst. in Civil Matters, 1999, Barracuda Bait, 2007; contbr. articles to profl. jours. Elder, Straitgate Ch., Mpls., 1980—. Fellow, Ctr. of Internat. Legal Studies, Mem. Christian Legal Soc., The Am. Soc. Writers of Legal Subjects, Mpls. Club, White Bear Yacht Club. Republican. Office: Dorsey & Whitney LLP 50 S 6th St Ste 1500 Minneapolis MN 55402-1498 Home Phone: 651-429-0579; Office Phone: 612-340-2738. Office Fax: 612-340-2807. Business E-Mail: magnuson.roger@dorsey.com.

MAGOON, PATRICK MICHAEL, hospital administrator; b. Chgo., Mar. 9, 1953; s. Albert George and Elizabeth Jane (Nolan) M.; m. Robin L. Gaeski, June 4, 1977. BA, Western Ill. U., 1976; MS in Urban Policy and Planning, U. Ill., Chgo., 1978. Asst. planner Children's Meml. Hosp., Chgo., 1977-78, adminstrv. svcs. mgr., 1978-80, dir. adminstrv. svcs., 1980-81, asst. v.p., 1981-83, v.p. adminstrn., 1983-90, v.p. adminstrn. ambulatory and satellite svcs., 1990, exec. v.p. corp. svcs., pres., CEO, 1998—. Bd. dirs. Nr. North Health Svcs. Corp., Chgo.; mem. profl. adv. com. Pediatric Excellence Program, Westchester, Ill., 1990—; chmn., Nat. Assn. Children's Hospitals and Related Instns., 2005-. Mem. Am. Hosp. Assn., Nat. Assn. Children's Hosp. and Related Instns., Ill. Hosp. Assn., Soc. for Ambulatory Care Profls, Met. Chgo. Healthcare Coun. (bd. dirs.), Comml. Club, Econ. Club, Exec. Club, City Club Chgo. Office: Children's Meml Hosp 2300 N Childrens Plz Chicago IL 60614-3394

MAGORIAN, JAMES, poet, writer; b. Palisade, Nebr., Apr. 24, 1942; s. Jack and Dorothy (Gorthey) M. BS, U. Nebr., 1965; MS, Ill. State U., 1969; postgrad., Oxford U., 1972, Harvard U., 1973. Author children's books: School Daze, 1978, 17%, 1978, The Magic Pretzel, 1979, Ketchup Bottles, 1979, Imaginary Radishes, 1980, Plucked Chickens, 1980, Fimperings and Torples, 1981, The Witches' Olympics, 1983, At the City Limits, 1987, The Beautiful Music, 1988, Magic Spell #207, 1988; author numerous books of poetry, including: Ideas for a Bridal Shower, 1980, The Edge of the Forest, 1980, Spiritual Rodeo, 1980, Tap Dancing on a Tight Rope, 1981, Training at Home to Be A Locksmith, 1981, The Emily Dickinson Jogging Book, 1984, Keeper of Fire, 1984, Weighing the Sun's Light, 1985, Summer Snow, 1985, The Magician's Handbook, 1986, Squall Line, 1986, The Hideout of the Sigmund Freud Gang, 1987, Haymarket Square, 1998, Dragon Bones, 1999, Millennial Journal, 2000, Voices, 2006, (novels) America First, 1992, Hearts of Gold, 1996, (poetry) The Bookbinder's Daughter, 2007; contbr. poems and stories to numerous publs. Home and Office: 2626 North 49th St 402 Lincoln NE 68504

MAGRUDER, JACK, retired academic administrator; m. Sue Brimer; children: Julie Magruder Lochbaum, Kerry, Laura Magruder Mann. BS in Chemistry and Math., Truman State U., 1957; postgrad., La. State U., 1959; MA in Chemistry and Sci. Edn., U. No. Iowa, 1960; EdD in Chemistry and Sci. Edn., U. No. Colo., 1966; grad., Harvard U. Inst. Ednl. Mgmt., 1992. Asst. prof. chemistry Truman State U., Kirksville, Mo., 1964—86, prof., head divsn. sci., 1986—89, acting dean instrn., 1989—91, v.p. acad. affairs, 1991—94, pres., 1994—2003; ret., 2003. Cons.-evaluator Higher Learning Commn. North Ctrl. Assn. Colls. and Schs.; chmn. com. on transfer and articulation Mo. Coord. Bd. for Higher Edn.; past pres. Coun. of Pub. Liberal Arts Colls., Coun. Pub. Higher Edn. for Mo. Mem.: Sci. Tchrs. Mo., Am. Chem. Soc., Sigma Beta Delta, Phi Kappa Phi, Phi Delta Kappa, Beta Gamma Sigma, Phi Beta Kappa. E-mail: wjm@truman.edu.

MAGUIRE, JOHN PATRICK, investment company executive; b. New Britain, Conn., Apr. 1, 1917; s. John Patrick and Edna Frances (Cashen) M.; m. Mary-Emily Jones, Sept. 8, 1945; children: Peter Dunbar (dec.), Joan Guilford. Student, Holy Cross Coll., 1933-34; degree in bus. adminstrn. with distinction, Babson Inst., 1936; AB cum laude, Princeton U., 1941; BS (hon.), Babson Inst., 1995, Babson Coll., 1995; JD, Yale U., 1943; PhD (hon.), St. Bonaventure U., 1965. Bar: Conn. 1943, N.Y. 1944. Assoc. Cravath, Swaine & Moore (and predecessor), NYC, 1943-50, 52-54; v.p., dir. Forbes, Inc.; also mng. editor Investors Adv. Inst., 1951-52; asst. counsel Gen. Dynamics Corp., 1954-60, sec., 1962-87, v.p., 1981-87; sec., gen. counsel Tex. Butadiene and Chem. Corp., 1960-62; with J.P. Maguire Investment Advisors, 1987-95; exec. v.p. Fiduciary Asset Mgmt. Co., 1995—2002. Mem. bd. govs. N.Y. Young Rep. Club, 1951-52; chmn. fin. and investment coms. St. Louis Art Mus., 1984-94; trustee St. Bonaventure U., 1965-71, Webster U., 1983-85, John Burroughs Sch. (chmn. investment com.) 1976-85. Mem. ABA. Clubs: Piping Rock (Locust Valley, L.I.); Yale (St. Louis); St. Louis Country; Princeton (St. Louis); Tiger Inn (Princeton).

MAHALEY-JOHNSON, HOSANNA, school system administrator; b. 1968; 3 children. BA, Marquette U., Milw., 1991; MEd, U. Ill., Chgo.; MBA, Northwestern U. Chief of staff Chgo. Pub. Schools, 2001—07, dir. New Schools Devel., dir. Renaissance 2010 initiative, 2006—07; pres. Atlanta Local Edn. Fund, 2007—. Bd. dirs. City Yr. Chgo.; bd. advisors Chgo. Comty. Trust; bd. dirs. Nat. Assn. Charter Sch. Authorizers. Named one of 40 Under 40, Crain's Chgo. Bus., 2006; fellow Entrepreneurial Leaders for Public Edn. Program, Aspen Inst., 2007. Office: 250 Williams St Ste 2115 Atlanta GA 30303 Office Phone: 773-553-1530. Office Fax: 773-553-2199.

MAHAN, JAMES T., manufacturing executive; V.p., engineered adhesives divsn. 3M Co., gen. mgr., bonding sys. divsn., exec. v.p., engring., mfg., and logistics, 2003—. Mem. Engring. Coll. Indsl. Adv. Coun., Iowa State U. Office: 3M Co 3M Ctr Saint Paul MN 55144

MAHAR, WILLIAM F., JR., state legislator; b. Chgo. Heights, Ill., Feb. 13, 1947; m. Elizabeth Mahar; two children. BA, So. Ill. U.; MS, Purdue U. Trustee Village of Homewood, Ill., 1979-85; Dist. 19 senator Ill. Senate, Springfield, 1985—. Mem. election and reapportionment, local govt., appropriations I, energy and environment, econ. devel., fin. and credit regulations, pub. health, welfare and corrections, and state govt. orgn. and adminstrn. coms., Ill. Senate. Office: State Senate State Capital Springfield IL 62706-0001 Also: 14700 S Ravinia Ave Orland Park IL 60462-3134

MAHER, DAVID WILLARD, Internet company executive; b. Chgo., Aug. 14, 1934; s. Chauncey Carter and Martha (Peppers) M.; m. Jill Waid Armagnac, Dec. 20, 1954; children: Philip Armagnac, Julia Armagnac. BA, Harvard, 1955, LLB, 1959. Bar: NY 1960, Ill. 1961, Wis. 1996, US Patent Office 1961. Pvt. practice, Boston, NYC, 1958-60; assoc. Kirkland & Ellis, and predecessor firm, 1960-65, ptnr., 1966-78, Reuben & Proctor, 1978-86, Isham, Lincoln and Beale, 1986-88, Sonnenschein, Nath & Rosenthal, Chgo., 1988—2003; ret., 2003; chmn. bd. dirs. Publ. Interest Registry, 2003—04, sr. v.p law and policy, 2004—. Dir. BBB Chgo. and No. Ill., 2004—; lectr. DePaul U. Sch. Law, 1973—79, Loyola U. Law Sch., Chgo., 1980—84. Contbr. articles to profl. jours. Vis. com. U. Chgo. Div. Sch., 1986—. 2nd lt. USAF, 1955—56. Recipient Torch of Integrity award, Better Bus. Bureau, Chgo. and N. Ill., Inc. Fellow Am. Bar Found. (life); mem. ABA, Am. Law Inst., Wis. State Bar, Chgo. Bar Assn., Chgo. Lit. Club. Roman Catholic. Home: 501 N Clinton St Apt 1503 Chicago IL 60610-8886 Office: Pub Interest Registry 1775 Wiehle Ave Ste 102A Reston VA 20190 Office Phone: 312-876-8055. Business E-Mail: dmaher@pir.org.

MAHER, FRANCESCA MARCINIAK, lawyer, former air transportation executive; b. Chgo., Oct. 27, 1957; BA, Loyola U., 1978, JD, 1981. Ptnr. Mayer, Brown & Platt, Chgo., 1981—84, 1987—93; v.p. law, corp. sec. UAL Corp., Elk Grove Village, Ill., 1993-97, v.p., gen. counsel, sec., 1997-98, sr. v.p., gen. counsel, sec., 1998—2003; spl. counsel Mayer, Brown, Rowe & Maw, Chgo., 2003—. Bd. dirs. YMCA Met. Chgo., Lincoln Park Zool. Soc. Mem. Ill. Humane Soc. (pres. 1996-98).

MAHER, FRANK ALOYSIUS, research and development company executive; b. Jamaica, NY, Mar. 31, 1941; s. Frank A. and Gertrude F. (Peterson) M.; m. Barbara A. Eggers, Aug. 14, 1965 (div. 1978); children: B. Kelly, F. Scott, Erin K.; m. Karen S. Adcock, June 28, 1980. BA, U. Dayton, 1966, MS, 1971. Lic. psychologist, Ohio. Research psychologist Ritchie Inc., Dayton, Ohio, 1965-68, Bunker Ramo, Dayton, 1968-70; lectr., research assoc. Wright State U., Dayton, 1970-71; research psychologist USAF, Wright Patterson AFB, Ohio, 1971-84; dir. Perceptronics, Inc., Dayton, 1984-87; rsch. and devel. exec. Unisys, Dayton, 1987-92; bus. devel. Black Tech. Corp., Dayton, 1992—2001; dir. Gibson Fisher Ltd, Dayton, 1997—. Counseling psychologist Eastway Mental Health Ctr., Dayton, 1974-75, Good Samaritan Mental Health Ctr., Dayton, 1979. Conbtg. author: Perceptions in Information Sciences; editor: Developmental Learning Handbook. Bd. dirs. Miami Valley Mental Health Assn., Dayton, 1974-77, Greene Mental Health Assn., Xenia, Ohio, 1977; dir. Ft. McKinley UMC Pantry. Roman Catholic. Avocations: tennis, skiing, sailing, sports car racing. Office: Gibson Fisher 3070 Riverside Dr Columbus OH 43221 Personal E-mail: frankamaher@netserver.net. Business E-Mail: fmaher@gibsonfisher.com.

MAHER, L. JAMES, III, molecular biologist; b. Mpls., Nov. 28, 1960; s. Louis James and Elizabeth Jane (Crawford) M.; m. Laura Lee Moseng, July 2, 1983; children: Elizabeth Lillian, Christina Ailene. BS in Molecular Biology, U. Wis., 1983, PhD in Molecular Biology, 1988. Fellow U. Wis., Madison, 1983-84, rsch. asst., 1984-88; postdoctoral fellow Calif. Inst. Tech., Pasadena, 1988-91; asst. prof. molecular biology Eppley Inst., U. Nebr. Med. Ctr., Omaha, 1991-95; assoc. prof. biochem. molecular biology Mayo Clinic Coll. Medicine, Rochester, Minn., 1995-2000, prof., 2000—02, vice chmn., 2002—, assoc. dean for academic affairs, 2003—. Editorial bd. Antisense and Nuclear Acid Drug Design, 1991—, Nucleic Acids Rsch. Jour., 1988—; contbr. articles to profl. jours. Musician, Madison Symphony Orch., 1983-88, Calif. Inst. Tech. Symphony Orch., L.A., 1988-91. Gosney fellow, 1988; Am. Cancer Soc. postdoctoral fellow, 1988. Mem. AAAS, Phi Beta Kappa. Evangelical Christian Ch. Achievements include research in chemical and biochemical agents designed to artificially regulate the flow of genetic information in biological systems. Office: Mayo Clinic Coll Medicine Dept Biochem and Molec Biol 200 1st St SW Rochester MN 55905-0001 Home Phone: 507-287-0275; Office Phone: 507-284-9041. Business E-Mail: maher@mayo.edu.

MAHER, LOUIS JAMES, JR., geologist, educator; b. Iowa City, Iowa, Dec. 18, 1933; s. Louis James and Edith Marie (Ham) M.; m. Elizabeth Jane Crawford, June 7, 1956; children: Louis James, Robert Crawford, Barbara Ruth. BA, U. Iowa, 1955, MS, 1959; PhD, U. Minn., 1961. Mem. faculty dept. geology and geophysics U. Wis.-Madison, 1962—, prof., 1970—2003, chmn. dept., 1980-84, prof. emeritus, 2003—. Contbr. articles to profl. jours. With US Army, 1956—58, with counter intelligence corps US Army, 1957—58, Duty

Sta., La Rochelle, France. Danforth fellow, 1955-61; NSF fellow, 1959-61; NATO fellow, 1961-62 Fellow AAAS, Geol. Soc. Am.; mem. Am. Quaternary Assn., Ecol. Soc. Am., Wis. Acad. Sci., Arts and Letters, Sigma Xi. Episcopalian. Office: U Wis Dept Geology and Geoph 1215 W Dayton St Madison WI 53706-1600 Office Phone: 608-262-9595. E-mail: maher@geology.wisc.edu.

MAHERN, EDMUND M., state representative; b. Beech Grove, Ind., Jan. 1, 1946; Grad., Ball State U., 1967; M, Eastern Mich. U., 1969. Pres. Mahern Assocs.; state rep. dist. 97 Ind. Ho. of Reps., Indpls., 1996—, chmn., elections com., mem. fin. instns. and judiciary coms. Democrat. Roman Catholic. Office: Ind Ho of Reps 200 W Washington St Indianapolis IN 46209-2786

MAHNKE, KURT LUTHER, psychotherapist, clergyman; b. Milw., Feb. 18, 1945; s. Jonathan Henry and Lydia Ann (Pickron) M.; m. Dana Moore, Mar. 19, 1971; children: Rachel Lee, Timothy Kurt, Jonathan Roy. BA, Northwestern Coll., Watertown, Wis., 1967; MDiv, Wis. Luth. Sem., 1971; MA, No. Ariz. U., 1984. Lic. profl. counselor, marriage and family therapist, ind. clin. social worker, cert. trauma counselor. Pastor Redeemer/Grace Luth. Chs., Phoenix & Casa Grande, Ariz., 1971-75, St. Philips Luth. Ch., Milw., 1975-78, 1st Luth. Ch., Prescott, Ariz., 1978-82; counselor NAU Counseling/Testing Ctr., Flagstaff, Ariz., 1983-84, Wis. Luth. Child & Family Svc., Wausau, Wis., 1984-86, area adminstr. Appleton, Wis., 1986-89; founder, psychotherapist Family Therapy & Anxiety Ctr., Menasha, Wis., 1989—. Part-time min. St. Paul Luth. Ch., Appleton, 1993-94; presenter Nat. Police Week, Washington, 1995—, 13th Nat. Conf. on Anxiety Disorders, Charleston, S,C., 1993; cons. editor Northwestern Pub. House, Milw., 1990-97; adj. faculty Fox Valley Tech. Coll., Appleton, 1993—; on-call critical incident stress debriefer, U.S. Marshall's Svc., 1999—; critical incident stress cons., Appleton Police Dept., Brillion Police Dept., Menasha Police Dept., Neenah Police Dept., Two Rivers Police Dept., Outagamie County Sheriff's Dept., 1999—, New London Police Dept., Winnebago County Sheriff's Dept., 2000—. Cons. editor Counseling at the Cross, 1990; contbr. articles to profl. publs. Cons. Wis. Evang. Luth. Synod, Milw., 1986—; cons. crisis counselor Fox Valley Luth. H.S., Appleton, Appleton Police Dept., Menasha Police Dept., Brillion Police Dept. Outagamie County Sheriff's Dept., 1998—, New London Police Dept., Winnegago County Sheriff's Dept., U.S. Marshall's Office, 1999—; crisis counselor, clin. dir. Critical Incident Stress Debriefing Team, Fox Cities, 1991—, U.S. Atty.'s Office, 1995-99; victim crisis response coord. Appleton Police Dept., 1996-99, Neenah Police Dept., Menasha Police Dept., Town of Menasha Police Dept., 1997-99. Mem. Internat. Critical Stress Found., Nat. Anxiety Found., Obsessive Compulsive Found. Republican. Lutheran. Office: Family Therapy/Anxiety Ctr 1477 Kenwood Ctr Menasha WI 54952-1160 Office Phone: 920-729-6780. Personal E-mail: klmahnke@aol.com.

MAHONE, BARBARA JEAN, automotive executive; BS, Ohio State U., 1968; MBA, U. Mich., 1972; program for mgmt. devel., Harvard U., 1981. Sys. analyst GM, Detroit, 1968-71, sr. staff asst., 1972-74, mgr. career planning, 1975-78, dir. pers. adminstrn. Rochester, NY, 1979-81, mgr. indsl. rels. Warren, Ohio, 1982-83, dir. human resources mgmt. Chevrolet-Pontiac-Can. group, 1984-86, dir. gen. pers. and pub. affairs Inland divsn. Dayton, Ohio, 1986-88, gen. dir. pers. Indland Fisher Guide divsn. Detroit, 1989-91, gen. dir. employee benefits, 1991-93, dir. human resources truck group Pontiac, Mich., 1994—2000, exec. dir. human resources, 2001—. Chmn. Fed. Labor Rels. Authority, Washington, 1983-84, Spl. Panel on Appeals; dir. Metro Youth; mem. bd. govs. U. Mich. Alumni. Bd. dirs. ARC, Rochester, 1979-82, Urban League Rochester, 1979-82, Rochester Aea Multiple Sclerosis; mem. human resources com. YMCA, Rochester, 1980-82; mem. exec. bd. Nat. Coun. Negro Women; mem. allocations com. United Way Greater Rochester. Recipient Pub. Rels. award Nat. Assn. Bus. and Profl. Women, 1976, Mary McLeod Bethune award Nat. Coun. Negro Women, 1977, Senate resolution Mich. State Legislature, 1980; named Outstanding Woman, Mich. Chronicle, 1975, Woman of Yr., Nat. Assn. Bus. and Profl. Women, 1978, Disting. Bus. Person, U. Mich., 1978, one of 11 Mich. Women, Redbook mag., 1978. Mem. Nat. Black MBA Assn. (bd. dirs., nat. pres. Disting. Svc. award, bd. dirs., nat. pres. Outstanding MBA), Women Econ. Club (bd. dirs.), Indsl. Rels. Rsch. Assn., Internat. Assn. for Pers. Women, Engring. Soc. Detroit. Republican. Home: 2697 Melcombe Cir Unit 402 Troy MI 48084

MAHONEY, CAROLYN RAY, academic administrator; b. Memphis, Dec. 22, 1946; d. Stephen and Myrtle (Gray) Boone; m. Charles Augustus Mahoney, May 20, 1972; children: Cindy Rae, Megan Ruth, Carolyn Bernadette. BS, Sienna Coll., 1970; MS in Math., Ohio State U., 1972, PhD in Math., 1983. Asst. prof. math. Denison U., Granville, Ohio, 1984-87; founding faculty prof. math. Calif. State U., San Marcos, 1989—2000; dean sch. math. sci. and tech. Eiizabeth City State, Elizabeth City, NC, provost, vice chancellor academic affairs; pres. Lincoln U., Jefferson City, Mo., 2005—. Interim v.p. acad. affairs, Calif. State U. San Marcos, 1985-86; sabatical Math. Scis. Rsch. Inst., 1986-87; vis. asst. prof. math. Ohio State U., Columbus, 1987-89; program dir. NSF 1994-95; vis. scholar Carnegie Found. the Advancement Tchg., 2000-01, Am. Coun. Edn. Commn. on Internat. Initiatives, 2006-08. Contbr. articles to profl. jours. including Jour. Combinatorial Theory, Soc. Indsl. and Applied Math, Notices the Am. Math. Soc., others; contbr. articles to books. Active Edn. Commn. of States Task Force on Improving Achievement of Minorities in Higher Edn., 1990. Grantee NSF, 1987, 90, 92, Math. Assn. Am., 1992, Charles A. Dana Found, 1989, Ohio Bd. Regents, 1989, Math. Scis. Edn. Bd., 1989; named to Women's Hall of Fame, Ohio, 1989; recipient Ralph S. Brown award Am. Assn. Univ. Profs., 2007. Mem. Am. Math. Soc., Assn. for Women in Math., Math. Assn. Am., Nat. Assn. Mathematicians, Rotary, Phi Kappa Phi. Achievements include becoming the first female president of Lincoln University; being among the first 25 African American females to receive a PhD in mathematics. Avocations: reading, walking, gardening. Office: Lincoln Univ 820 Chestnut St Jefferson City MO 65102-0029 Business E-Mail: president@lincolnu.edu.

MAHONEY, JOAN, law educator; AB, AM, U. Chgo.; JD, Wayne State U.; PhD, Cambridge U. Assoc. Honigman Miller Schwartz and Cohn, Detroit; mem. law faculty U. Mo., Kansas City, 1980—94; mem. faculty, dean Western New Eng. Coll. Law, 1994—96; mem. faculty Wayne State U. Law Sch., Detroit, 1994—, dean, 1996—. Contbr. articles to profl. jours., chpts. to books. Office: Wayne U Law Sch 471 W Palmer Detroit MI 48202

MAHONEY, JOHN JEREMY, former state legislator; m. Ann Christianson; 4 children. BS, U. N.D., 1975, JD, 1978. Atty. Center City, N.D., 1979—; ptnr. Mahoney & Mahoney, Center City, 1979—; mem. N.D. Ho. of Reps., 1990—2002. Oliver County States Atty., 1979—. Mem. KC, Elks, Oliver County Gun Club. Home: PO Box 355 Center D 58530-0355

MAHONEY, MARY C., radiologist, educator; BA magna cum laude, Brown U., Providence; MD, U. Cin. Diplomate Nat. Bd. Med. Examiner, 1984, lic. NY, 1984, Ohio, 1986, Amer. Bd. Radiology, 1988, Fla., 1993. Chief resident dept. radiology U. Cin., 1987—88; clin. instr. radiology U. Cin. Coll. Medicine, 1988—89, asst. prof. radiology, 1989—92, 1996—2001, assoc. prof. radiology, 2001—07, prof. radiology, 2008—; fellow dept. radiology U. Cin. Med. Ctr., 1988—89. Dir. divsn. ultrasound, radiology dept. U. Med. Ctr., Cin., 1990—92; dir. breast intervention, dept. radiology U. Cin. Med. Ctr., 1999—2001, dir. breast imaging and intervention, dept. radiology, 2001—. Contbr. scientific papers in field. Oral bd. examiner for breast imaging Am. Bd. Radiology, 2001—08; written bd. item writer for breast imaging, 2002—08; written bd. exam. com. for breast imaging, 2003—08; sci. session presiding officer, 2003—08; mem. pub. info. advisors network, 2004—08; oral bd. examiner for chair relief, 2004—08; pub. info. com. and media rels. subcom., 2006—08; written bd. exam. com., chair breast sect., 2006—08. Finalist Health Care Hero, Cin. Bus. Courier, 2003, 2006; recipient Leading Woman of Cin. award, Cin., 2005. Mem.: Radiol. Soc. N.Am., Ohio State Radiol. Soc., Ohio State Med. Assn., Cin. Radiol. Soc., Cin. Acad. Medicine, Am. Roentgen Ray Soc., Am. Coll. Radiology, Am. Assoc. Women Radiologists, Soc. Breast Imaging, Alpha Omega Alpha.*

MAHONEY, PATRICK MICHAEL, federal judge; b. 1946; BA, St. Ambrose Coll., 1968; JD, U. Ill., 1971. Magistrate judge U.S. Dist. Ct. (no. dist.) Ill., We. Divsn., 1976—. Office: US Dist Ct 211 S Court St Ste 204 Rockford IL 61101-1226

MAHONEY, ROBERT WILLIAM, electronic and security systems manufacturing executive; b. NYC, Sept. 10, 1936; s. Francis Jospeh and Margaret (Colleton) Mahoney; m. Joan Marie Sheraton, Oct. 3, 1959; children: Linda Marie, Stephen Francis, Brian Michael. BS, Villanova U., 1958; MBA, Roosevelt U., Chgo., 1961. With sales dept. NCR, Inc., Phila., 1961—70, sales mgr. Allentown, Pa., 1971—76, v.p. Dayton, Ohio, 1977—80; pres. NCR Can. Ltd., Toronto, 1981—82; sr. v.p. Diebold, Inc., Canton, Ohio, 1983—84, pres., COO, 1984—85, pres., CEO, 1985—88, chmn. bd., 1988—2000, bd. dirs. Chmn. Fed. Res. Bank Cleve. Mem. adv. bd. C. of C. Leadership Canton, 1987, Firestone County, Arkon, Brookside County, Canton; bd. dirs. Timken Co., Sherwin-Williams Co., Cin. Bell., Akron U. Econ. Devel. Bd., Ohio, 1982, timken Mercy Med. Ctr., Canton, 1983—, Canton Symphony Orch., 1985, Northeast Ohio Coun., Cleve., 1986—, Stark County Devel. Bd., 1986—, Profl. Football Hall of Fame, Canton, 1987—, Jr. Achievement, 1984; trustee Canton City Sch.s, 1986, Mt. union Coll., 1988—, Ohio Found. Ind. Colls., 1988—. Served with USN, 1958—61. Republican. Roman Catholic.

MAHOWALD, ANTHONY PETER, geneticist, developmental biologist, educator; b. Albany, Minn., Nov. 24, 1932; s. Aloys and Cecilia (Maus) Mahowald; m. Mary Lou Briody, Apr. 11, 1971; children: Maureen, Lisa, Michael. BS, Spring Hill Coll., 1958; PhD, Johns Hopkins U., 1962. Asst. prof. Marquette U., Milw., 1966-70; asst. staff mem. Inst. Cancer Rsch., Phila., 1970-72; assoc. prof. Ind. U., Bloomington, 1972-76, prof., 1976-82; Henry Willson Payne prof. Case Western Res. U., Cleve., 1982-90, chmn. dept. anatomy, 1982-88, chmn. dept. genetics, 1988-90; Louis Block prof., chmn. dept molecular genetics and cell biology U. Chgo., 1990—2002, Louis Block prof. emeritus, 2002—. Chmn. Com. Devel. Biology U. Chgo., 1991-99. Woodrow Wilson Found. fellow, 1958, NSF fellow, 1958-62. Fellow AAAS, Am. Acad. Arts and Scis., Soc. Scholars Johns Hopkins U.; mem. Nat. Acad. Scis., Genetics Soc. Am. (sec. 1986-88), Soc. Devel. Biology (pres. 1989, editor-in-chief jour. 1980-85), Am. Soc. Cell Biology (coun. mem. 1996-98). Office: U Chgo Dept Molec Genet/Cell Biol 920 E 58th St Chicago IL 60637-5415 Business E-Mail: am29@uchicago.edu.

MAHSMAN, DAVID LAWRENCE, writer, church administrator; b. Quincy, Ill., Aug. 16, 1950; s. Alvin Henry and Dorothy Marie (Schnack) M.; m. Lois Jean Mohn, July 27, 1975. BS in Journalism, So. Ill. U., 1972; MDiv, Concordia Theol. Seminary, Fort Wayne, Ind., 1983; STM, Concordia Sem., St. Louis, 1995. Staff writer Paddock Publs., Arlington Heights, Ill., 1972-73, Decatur (Ill.) Herald & Rev., 1973-76; press asst. Hon. Tom Railsback U.S. Ho. Reps., Washington, 1976-79, campaign press sec. Hon. Dan Coats Ft. Wayne, Ind., 1979-80, 82; pastor Trinity Luth. Ch., Glen Cove, NY, 1983-85; dir. news and info. Luth. Ch.-Mo. Synod, St. Louis, 1985—2005; exec. editor, contbr. Luth. Witness, St. Louis, 1985—2005; exec. editor Reporter, St. Louis, 1985—2005; asst. to exec. dir. Bd. Mission Svcs. Mo. Synod, 2005—. Mem. Inter-Luth. task force on pornography Luth. Coun. U.S.A., 1986; mem. Washington adv. coun. Mo. Synod, Office of Govt. Info., Washington, 1987-2000. Editor: Augsburg Today: This We Believe, Teach and Confess, 1997. Recipient Jacob Scher Investigative Reporting award Women in Comm., 1974, Commendation award Concordia Hist. Inst., 1988, 98, 1st Place Reporting award Evang. Press Assn., 2003. Mem. Concordia Hist. Inst. (life). Republican. Lutheran. Avocations: travel, photography. Office: Luth Ch-Mo Synod 1333 S Kirkwood Rd Saint Louis MO 63122-7226 E-mail: david.mahsman@lcms.org.

MAIBACH, BEN C., JR., consumer products company executive; b. Bay City, Mich., 1920; With Barton-Malow Co., Detroit, 1938—, v.p., dir.-in-charge field ops., 1949-53, exec. v.p., 1953-60, pres., 1960-76, chmn. bd., 1976; chmn. and dir. Barton-Malow Ent.; chmn. bd. Cloverdale Equipment Co. Trustee Barton-Malow Found, Maibach Found., 1967—; chmn. Apostolic Christian Woodhaven, Detroit; bishop Apostolic Christian Ch., Mich., Ont., Fla.; bd. dirs. S.E. Mich. chpt. ARC, Rural Gospel and Med. Missions of India. Home: 29711 Wentworth St Apt 207 Livonia MI 48154-3887 also: 5525 Azure Way Sarasota FL 34242-1857

MAIBACH, BEN C., III, construction company executive; b. May 5, 1946; BS, Mich. State U., 1969. With Barton-Malow Corp., Oak Park, Mich., 1964—, v.p. field ops., 1964-68, systems analyst, programmer, 1968-70, project adminstr., 1970-72; officer mgr., purchasing agt. Barton-Malow Co., Oak Park, Mich., 1972-73, v.p., 1973-76, exec. v.p., 1976-81, pres., 1981—. Office: Barton Malow Co 26500 American Dr Southfield MI 48034

MAIDA, ADAM JOSEPH CARDINAL, cardinal, archbishop; b. East Vandergrift, Pa., Mar. 18, 1930; BA, St. Vincent Coll., Latrobe, Pa., 1952; STL, St. Mary's U., Balt., 1956; JCL, Lateran U., Rome, 1960; JD, Duquesne U., 1964. Bar: Pa., US Dist. Ct., We. Pa., US Supreme Ct. Ordained priest Diocese of Pitts., 1956, assoc. pastor through vice-chancellor & gen. counsel, 1956—84; ordained bishop, 1984; bishop Diocese of Green Bay, Wis., 1984—89; archbishop Archdiocese of Detroit, 1990—; elevated to cardinal, 1994; cardinal-priest Ss. Vitale, Valerian, Gervasio & Protasio, 1994—; superior Cayman Islands, Antilles, 2000—. Past asst. prof. theology, LaRoche Coll.; past adj. prof., Duquesne Univ. Sch. Law; Mem. Congregation for Catholic Edn., Congregation for the Clergy, Pontifical Council for Interpretation of Legis. Texts, Pontifical Council for Pastoral Care of Migrants & Itinerant Peoples, Cardinal Commn. for the Supervision of the Inst. for Works of Religion, Roman Curia. Author, Ownership Control & Sponsorship of Catholic Institutions, 1975, Church Property, Church Finances and Church-Related Corporations, A Canon Law Handbook, 1983; ed., The Tribunal Reporter, 1970, Issues in the Labor-Mgmt. Dialogue: Church Perspectives, 1983. Trustee, Basilica of the Nat. Shrine of the Immaculate Conception, Catholic Univ. Am., Mich. Catholic Conf., Papal Found. Phila.; chmn. bd. trustees, Sacred Heart Major Sem., S.S. Cyril & Methodius Sem.; mem. bd. gov. Ave Maria Sch. Law; bd. dir. Nat. Catholic Bioethics Ctr. Mem.: U.S. Conf. Bishops. Roman Catholic. Home and Office: Archdiocese of Detroit 1234 Washington Blvd Detroit MI 48226-1825

MAIER, DONNA JANE-ELLEN, history professor; b. St. Louis, Feb. 20, 1948; d. A. Russell and Mary Virginia Maier; m. Stephen J. Rapp, Jan. 3, 1981; children: Alexander John, Stephanie Jane-Ellen. BA, Coll. of Wooster, 1969; MA, Northwestern U., 1972, PhD, 1975. Asst. prof. U. Tex. at Dallas, Richardson, 1975-78; asst. prof. history U. No. Iowa, Cedar Falls, 1978-81, assoc. prof., 1981-86, prof., 1986—. Cons. Scott, Foresman Pub., Glenview, Ill., 1975-94; editl. cons. Children's Press, 1975-76, Macmillan Pubs., 1989-90, Harper-Collins Pubs., 1994. Co-author: History and Life, 1976, 4th edit., 1990; author: Priests and Power, 1983; co-editor African Economic History, 1992—; contbr. articles to profl. jours, Encyclopedia Britannica. Mem. Iowa Dem. Cen. Com., 1982-90, chmn. budget com., 1986-90; chmn. 3d Congl. Dist. Cen. Com., 1986-88. Fulbright-Hays fellow, Ghana, 1972, Arab Republic Egypt, 1987; fellow Am. Philos. Soc., London, 1978; recipient Iowa Bd. Regents Faculty Excellence award, 1996, U. No. Iowa Rsch. Assignment, Tanzania, 2002-04. Mem. African Studies Assn., AAUW (fellow Ghana 1973), pres. Quota Internat. of Waterloo, 1999-2000, Quota Club. Office: U No Iowa Dept History Cedar Falls IA 50614-0001 E-mail: Donna.Maier@uni.edu.

MAIESE, KENNETH, neurologist, neuroscientist; b. Audubon, NJ, Dec. 5, 1958; s. Charles and Margaret (Fioretti) M. BA summa cum laude, U. Pa., 1981; MD, Cornell U., 1985. Intern N.Y. Hosp., 1985—86, resident neurology, 1986—89, asst. attending physician, 1989—94; asst. prof. Cornell U. Med. Coll., NYC, 1989—94; assoc. prof. dept. neurology, anatomy and cell biology Ctr. Molecular Toxicology and Medicine Wayne State U., Detroit, 1994—99, dir. lab. molecular and cellular cerebral ischemia Ctr. Molecular Toxicology, 1994—, prof. dept. neurology, anatomy, cell biology Ctr. Molecular Toxicology, 1999—. Dir. neurol. diagnosis NY Hosp., 1991—94; chmn. nat. brain/stroke consortium Am. Heart Assn., 2000—01, exec. coun., 2001—, nat peer rev. steering com., 2002—, mem. rsch. com., 2003—; mem. study sect. cell death and injury NIH/CDIN, 2003—; mem. neurobiology study sect. Vet.'s Adminstrn., 2004—; spkr. in field. Author: eurology and General Medicine, 1989, Neurological and Neurosurgical ICU Medicine, 1988; editor-in-chief Current Neurovascular Rsch., 2002—, Oxidative Stress and Cellular Longevity, 2007—; editor: Neuronal and Vascular Plasticity, 2003; mem. editl. bd. Letters in Drug Design and Discovery, 2002—, Histology and Histopathology, 2002—, Jour. Histological Histopathology, 2002—, Drug Design Revs., 2003—, Medicinal Chemistry, 2004—, Current Drug Targets-Heme Agts., Jour. Heart Digest, 2005—, Internat. Jour. Molecular Medicine, 2005—, Ctrl. Nervous Sys. Agts., Medicinal Chemistry, 2006—, Open eurosci. Jour., 2007—, Open Biochem. Jour., 2007—; editl. bd. contbr. The Merck Manual Profl. Home Edit., 2007; contbr. articles to profl. jours. Joseph Collins scholar, 1981-85, Grupe Found. scholar, 1985; grantee NIH, 1990—, Nat. Stroke Assn., 1992-94, Alzheimer's Assn., 1994—, Am. Heart Assn., 1995—, United Cerebral Palsy Found., 1995—, Janssen Found., 1995—; recipient Young Scientist award Jours. Cerebral Blood Flow, 1991, Hoechst Investigator award, 1993, Robert G. Siekert award in stroke, 1994, Johnson and Johnson Disting. Investigator award, 1996-98, Maiese Lab. Neurosci. Tng. award J & J/Janssen, 1998, Boehringer Investigator award, 1999, NIH/NIEHS award, Learn Found. award, 2002-03, MI Challenge award, Bugher Found. award, 2005, Am. Diabetes Assn. award, 2006, NIH/NIA award, 2007; named one of Am.'s Top Physicians, 2005-06, Best of US Physicians, 2006. Mem. NIH (minority edn. tng. 2002—, spl. emphasis cellular pathophysiologyspl., emphasis panel cellular degeneration 2004—), Am. Acad. Neurology, NY Acad. Scis., Assn. for Rsch. in Nervous and Mental Diseases, Am. Neurol. Assn. (elected), Soc. Neurosci., Internat. Acad. Cardiology (sci. com. 2003-, Bugher Found. award 2005-), Am. Diabetes Assn. (Sr. Investigator award 2006), Alzheimer's Soc. UK, Diabetes Found. UK, Rsch. Coun. Hong Kong, Rsch. Coun. Spain, NIH Applied Metabolom Techs., Austrian Sci. Fund., Nat. Swiss Sci. Found. Roman Catholic. Achievements include rsch. in imidazole receptors, cerebral ischemia, nitric oxide toxicity, growth factor neuroprotection, signal cellular transduction mechanisms, metabotropic glutamate receptors, gene regulation, and gene therapy, patents in field. Office: Wayne State U Sch Medicine 8C-1 U Health Ctr Dept Neur 4201 Saint Antoine St Detroit MI 48201-2153 Business E-Mail: kmaiese@med.wayne.edu.

MAIMON, ELAINE PLASKOW, academic administrator; b. Phila., July 28, 1944; d. Louis J. and Gertrude (Canter) Plaskow; m. Morton A. Maimon, Sept. 30, 1967; children: Gillian Blanche, Alan Marcus. AB, U. Pa., 1966, MA, 1967, PhD, 1970. Asst. prof. Haverford Coll., 1971-73; lectr. Arcadia U., Glenside, Pa., 1973-75, asst. prof., dir. writing, 1975-77, assoc. prof., 1977-83, assoc. dean, 1980-84, assoc. v.p., prof. English, 1984-86; adj. assoc. prof. U. Pa., Phila., 1982-83; assoc. dean of coll. Brown U., Providence, 1986-88; dean, prof. English Queens Coll. CUNY, Flushing, NY, 1988-96; campus CEO, provost Ariz. State U. West, Phoenix, 1996—2004; v.p. Ariz. State U., 1996—2004; chancellor U. Alaska, Anchorage, 2004—07; pres. Govs. State U., University Park, Ill., 2007—. at. bd. cons. NEH, 1977-81; mem. adv. bd. Cox Comm., 1997-2001; bd. dirs. Arrowhed Cmty. Bank. Co-author: Writing in the Arts and Sciences, 1981, A Writer's Resource, 2003; co-editor: Readings in the Arts and Sciences, 1984, Thinking, Reasoning and Writing, 1989, A Writer's Resource, 2003, 2d edit., 2007, The New McGraw Hill Handbook, 2007, Writing Intensive, 2007, The Brief McGraw Hill Handbook, 2008. Trustee Heard Mus., Phoenix, 1999—2005. Recipient Golden Heart award, Today's Ariz. Woman, 2000, Women of Distinction award, YMCA, Maricopa County, 2001, YWCA award in Edn., 2002, World award, Girl Scouts Am., Ariz. Cactus-Pine Coun., 2002, Woman of Vision award, Phoenix Bus. Jour.; Elaine Maimon award for Excellence in Writing named in her honor, Arcadia U., 1994. Mem.: MLA (exec. com., tchg. of writing divsn.), Am. Assn. Colls. and Univs. (exec. bd. 2002—06), Conf. on Coll. Composition Comm. (exec. com. 1985—87), ACE Nat. Commn. Women, Nat. Coun. Tchrs. English (nominating com. 1986—87, teaching of writing divsn. 1991), Phi Beta Kappa. Office: Govs State U Office of Pres 1 University Parkway University Park IL 60466-0975 Home Phone: 708-367-0990; Office Phone: 708-534-4130. Business E-Mail: e-maimon@govst.edu.

MAINE, MICHAEL ROLAND, lawyer; b. Anderson, Ind., Feb. 22, 1940; s. Roland Dwight and Vivian Louise (Browning) M.; m. Suzanne Bauman, Aug. 25, 1962; children: Christopher Michael (dec.), Melinda Louise. AB with high distinction, DePauw U.; JD with distinction, U. Mich. Bar: Ind., D.C., U.S. Dist. Ct. (so. dist.) Ind., U.S. Ct. Appeals (7th cir.), U.S. Supreme Ct. Assoc. Baker & Daniels, Indpls., 1964-71, ptnr., 1972—2004. Contbr. articles to profl. jours. Bd. dirs. Ind. Repertory Theatre, Indpls., 1986—2003, Cmty. Hosp. N., 1988—91, Japan-Am. Soc. Ind. Inc., 1988—2003, Royal Palm Players, 2005—; pres. Mental Health Assn. Ind., Indpls., 1985; bd. visitors Sch. Law Ind. U., Indpls.; trustee De Pauw U., Greencastle, Ind., 1990—; bd. dirs. U.S.-China Bus. Coun. Legal Cooperation Fund, 2002—05. Capt. USAF, 1965—68. Named Sagamore of Wabash, Gov. Ind., 1986. Fellow: Indpls. Bar Found., Ind. Bar Found.; mem.: Indpls. Bar Assn. (sec. 1983, pres. 1985, extraordinary svc. award 1985), Ind. Bar Assn. (chmn. fed. judiciary com. 1986—88), Kiwanis (lt. gov. Ind. club 1972, pres. Indpls. club 1969), Masons, Kiwanis (lt. gov. Ind. club 1972, pres. Indpls. club 1969), Masons, Phi Beta Kappa, Order of Coif. Avocation: golf. Home: 13100 Joseffa Ct Placida FL 33946 Office: Baker & Daniels 300 N Meridian St Ste 2700 Indianapolis IN 46204-1782

MAIR, DOUGLAS DEAN, pediatrician, educator, consultant; b. Mpls., May 29, 1937; s. Lester Alexander and Irene Clare (Fisher) M.; m. Joanne Mary Elliott, Aug. 18, 1963; children: Scott, Michele, Todd. BA, U. Minn., 1959, MD, 1962. Bd. cert. pediats. and pediat. cardiology. Cons. Mayo Clinic, Rochester, Minn., 1971—; from asst. prof. pediats. to assoc. prof. pediats. Mayo Med. Sch., Rochester, 1972-80, prof. pediats., 1980—, assoc. prof. internal medicine, 1978—. Contbr. numerous articles and book chpts. to profl. publs. Capt. USAF, 1966-67.

MAITLAND, JOHN W., JR., state legislator; b. Normal, Ill., July 19, 1936; m. Joanne Sieg; three children. Student, Ill. State U. Grain farmer; Dist. 44 senator Ill. Senate, Springfield, 1979—. Asst. majority leader, Ill. Senate; mem. elem. and secondary edn. appropriations I, energy and environment, and appropriations II coms.; minority spokesman; mem. commn. intergovernmental cooperation, con. and fiscal commn., task force on sch. fin. Office: 525 N East St Bloomington IL 61701-4087

MAJERUS, PHILIP WARREN, physician; b. Chgo., July 10, 1936; s. Clarence Nicholas and Helen Louise (Mathis) Majerus; m. Janet Sue Brakensiek, Dec. 28, 1957; children: Suzanne, David, Juliet, Karen; m. Elaine Michelle Flansburg, 1996. BS, Notre Dame U., 1958; MD, Washington U., 1961. Resident in Medicine Mass. Gen. Hosp., Boston, 1961—63; research assoc. NIH, Bethesda, Md., 1963—66; asst. prof. biochemistry Washington U., St. Louis, 1966—75, asst. prof. medicine, 1966—69, assoc. prof. medicine, 1969—71, prof. medicine, 1971—, dir. div. hematology, 1973—, prof. biochemistry, 1976—. Mem. editl. bd. numerous jours. and profl. mags.; contbr. articles to profl. jours. Recipient Faculty Rsch. Assoc. award, Am. Cancer Soc., 1966—75, Disting. Career award for contbns. to hemostasis, Internat. Soc. for Thrombosis and Hemostasis, 1985, Alumni Faculty award, Washington U. Sch. Medicine, 1986, The Robert J. and Claire Pasarow Found. award, 1994, Bristol-Myers Squibb prize for cardiovascular rsch., 1998, numerous others. Fellow: ACP; mem.: Inst. of Medicine of NAS, Am. Soc. Clin. Investigation (pres. 1981—82), Am. Soc. Biol. Chemists, Am. Fedn. Clin. Rsch., Am. Soc. Hematology (pres. 1991), Assn. Am. Physicians, Am. Acad. Arts and Scis., Alpha Omega Alpha, Sigma Xi. Home: 7220 Pershing Ave Saint Louis MO 63130-4248 Office: Wash Univ Sch of Med Dept Int Med Saint Louis MO 63110

MAKELA, JONATHAN JAMES, engineering educator; BS in Elec. Engring with honors, Cornell U., Sch. Elec. Engring., Ithaca, NY, 1999, PhD in Elec. & Computer Engring., 2003. Student researcher The Cleve. Clinic Found., 1995, 1996; co-op engr. 3M Co., 1997; undergraduate researcher Cornell U., Sch. Elec. & Computer Engring., Ithaca, NY, 1998—99, grad. rsch. asst., 1999—2002; Nat. Rsch. Coun. Rsch. Assoc., Thermospheric and Ionospheric Rsch. and Applications group aval Rsch. Lab., Washington, 2002—04; with U. Ill, Urbana-Champaign, 2004—, asst. prof., dept. elec. & computer engring., 2004—, asst. rsch. prof., Coordinated Sci. Lab., 2004—. Mem. academic excellence workshop Cornell U., 1998, tchg. asst. fellow, 2000—01, head cooperative learning trainer, Learning Initiatives for Future Engineers, 2000—02; Discovery Station vol. Nat. Air and Space Mus., 2002—04; co-convener in the field, 2002—; sci. definition team member, Communication/Navigation Outage Forecasting System (C/NOFS) satellite, 2002—; team mem. calibration/validation effort for the Special Sensor Ultraviolet Spectrographic Imager (SSUSI), 2002—, Special Sensor Ultraviolet Limb Imager (SSULI) on the next generation Defense Meteorological Support Program (DMSP) satellites, 2002—; presenter in field; invited lectr. in field. Contbr. articles to profl. publications; referee for papers in several profl. publications, panel reviewer for proposals at NSF and NASA, reviewer for proposals Journal of Geophysical Research, Geophysical Research Letters, Radio Science, Annales Geophysicae, Planetary and Space Science, Journal of Atmospheric and Solar-Terrestrial Physics, and Advances in Space Research. Recipient Einwecther award for outstanding service to the Coll. Engring, 1999, Editors' Citation for Excellence in Refereeing for Geophysical Rsch. Letters, 2005; Cornell U. Grad. Rsch. Fellowship, 1999—2002, NSF Grad. Rsch. Fellowship, 1999—2002, NRC Post-Doctoral Rsch. Associateship, 2002—04. Mem.: Am. Geophysical Union, IEEE. Achievements include development of new instrumentation to forcast the weather in the ionosphere. Office:

Dept Elec & Computer Engring U Ill 316 Coordinated Science Laboratory 1308 W Main St Urbana IL 61801-2307 Office Phone: 217-265-9470. Office Fax: 217-333-4303. Business E-Mail: jmakela@uiuc.edu.

MAKI, DENNIS G., epidemiology educator; b. River Falls, Wis., May 8, 1940; m. Gail Dawson, 1962; children: Kimberly, Sarah, Daniel. BS in Physics with honors, U. Wis., 1962, MS in Physics, 1964, MD, 1967. Diplomate Am. Bd. Internal Medicine, Am. Bd. Infectious Diseases, Am. Bd. Critical Care Medicine. Physicist, computer programmer Lawrence Radiation Lab., AEC, Livermore, Calif., 1962; intern, asst. resident Harvard Med. unit Boston City Hosp., 1967-69, chief resident, 1972-73; with Hosp. Infections sect. Ctrs. for Disease Control, USPHS, Atlanta, 1969-71; acting chief nat. nosocomial infections study Ctr. for Disease Control, USPHS, Atlanta, 1970-71; sr. resident dept. medicine Mass. Gen. Hosp., 1971-72, clin. and research fellow infectious disease unit, 1973-74; asst. prof. medicine U. Wis., Madison, 1974-78, assoc. prof., 1978-82, prof., 1982—; hosp. epidemiologist, U. Wis. Hosp. and Clinic, Madison, 1974—; Ovid O. Meyer prof. medicine U. Wis., Madison, 1975—, head sec. infectious diseases, 1979—2007, attending physician Ctr. for Trauma and Life Support, 1976—. Clinician, rschr., educator in field; mem. program com. Intersci. Conf. on Antimicrobial Agts. and Chemotherapy, 1987-94; mem. Am. Bd. Critical Care Medicine, 1989-95. Sr. assoc. editor Infection Control and Hosp. Epidemiology, 1979-93; mem. editl. bd. Jour. Lab. and Clin. Investigation, 1980-86, Jour. Critical Care, 1985-96, Jour. Infectious Diseases, 1988-90, Critical Care Medicine, 1989-94, 97—, Mayo Clinic Procs., 2002-07; contbr. articles to med. jours. Recipient 1st award for disting. rsch. in Antibiotic Rev., 1980, Internat. CIPI award, 1994, SHEA lectr., 1999, numerous tchg. awards and hon. lectrs. Master ACP; fellow Infectious Diseases Soc. Am. (coun. 1993-96, citation 2000), Am. Acad. Microbiology, Soc. for Critical Care Medicine, Surg. Infection Soc., Wis. Acad. Scis., Arts and Letters; mem. Soc. Hosp. Epidemiologists Am. (pres. 1990), Ctrl. Soc. for Clin. Rsch., Am. Soc. Microbiology, Am. Fedn. Clin. Rsch., Alpha Omega Alpha (nat. bd. dirs. 1983-89). Office: U Wis Hosp and Clinics H4/574 Madison WI 53792 Office Phone: 608-263-1545. Fax: 608-833-0327. Personal E-mail: dgmaki@yahoo.com. Business E-Mail: dgmaki@medicine.wisc.edu.

MAKINEN, MARVIN WILLIAM, biophysicist, educator; b. Chassell, Mich., Aug. 19, 1939; s. William John and Milga Katarina (Myllyla) M.; m. Michele de Groot, July 30, 1966; children: Eric William, Stephen Matthew. AB, U. Pa., 1961; postgrad., Free U. Berlin, 1960-61; MD, U. Pa., 1968; DPhil, U. Oxford, Eng., 1976. Diplomate Am. Bd. Med. Examiners. Intern Columbia-Presbyn. Med. Ctr., NYC, 1968-69; rsch. assoc. NIH, Bethesda, Md., 1969-71; vis. fellow U. Oxford, Eng., 1971-74; asst. prof. biophysics U. Chgo., 1974-80, assoc. prof., 1980-86, prof. biochemistry and molecular biology, 1986—, chmn. dept., 1988-93. Established investigator Am. Heart Assn., 1975-80; lectr. in field. Contbr. numerous articles to profl. jours. Sr. surgeon USPHS, 1969-71. John Simon Guggenheim fellow 1997-98, John E. Fogarty Sr. Internat. fellow, 1984-85, European Molecular Biology Orgn. sr. fellow, 1984-85, NIH spl. fellow, 1971-74, Berquist fellow Am. Scandinavian Found., 1970. Fellow Am. Inst. Chemists; mem. Am. Chem. Soc., Biophys. Soc., Am. Soc. Biochemistry and Molecular Biology, The Protein Soc., AAAS. Office: U Chgo Center Integrative Science 929 E 57th St Chicago IL 60637-5415 Home Phone: 773-684-6507; Office Phone: 773-702-1080. Business E-Mail: makinen@uchicago.edu.

MAKRI, NANCY, chemistry professor; b. Athens, Greece, Sept. 5, 1962; came to the U.S., 1985; d. John and Vallie (Tsakona) M.; m. Martin Gruebele, July 9, 1992; children: Alexander Makris Gruebele, Valerie Gruebele Makri. BS, U. Athens, 1985; PhD, U. Calif., Berkeley, 1989. Jr. fellow Harvard U., Cambridge, Mass., 1989-91; from asst. prof. to assoc. prof. U. Ill., Urbana, 1992-99, prof., 1999—. Recipient Beckman Young Investigator award Arnold & Mabel Beckman Found., 1993, Ann. medal Internat. Acad. Quantum Molecular Sci., 1995, Camille Dreyfus Tchr.-Scholar award The Camille and Henry Dreyfus Found., 1997, Agnes Fay Morgan award Iota Sigma Pi, 1999, physics prize Bodossaki Found., 1999; named NSF Young Investigator, 1993; Packard fellow for sci. and engring. David and Lucile Packard Found., 1993, Sloan Rsch. fellow Alfred Sloan Found., 1994, Cottrell scholar Rsch. Corp., 1994; univ. scholar U. Ill., 1999. Fellow: AAAS, Am. Phys. Soc. Home: 2722 Valley Brook Dr Champaign IL 61822-7634 Office: U Ill Urbana Dept Chem 601 S Goodwin Ave Urbana IL 61801-3709 E-mail: nancy@makri.scs.uiuc.edu.

MAKUPSON, AMYRE PORTER, broadcast executive; b. River Rouge, Mich., Sept. 30, 1947; d. Rudolph Hannibal and Amyre Ann (Porche) Porter; m. Walter H. Makupson, Nov. 1, 1975; children: Rudolph Porter, Amyre Nisi. BA, Fisk U., 1970; MA, Am. U., Washington, 1972. Asst. dir. news Sta. WGPR-TV, Detroit, 1975-76; dir. pub. rels. Mich. Health Maintenance Orgn., Detroit, 1976-77; mgr. pub. affairs, news anchor Sta. WKBD-TV, Southfield, Mich., 1977—2004, Children's Miracle etwork Telethon, 1989—. Mem. Co-Ette Club, Inc., Met. Detroit Teen Conf. Coalition; mem. adv. com., bd. dirs. Alzheimers Assn.; bd. dirs. com. March of Dimes; bd. dirs. Providence Hosp. Found., Sickle Cell Assn., Covenant House Mich., AAA, Home Fed. Savs. Bank, Skillman Found. Recipient 6 Emmy awards 4 Best Commentary/Best Anchor, Best Interview/Discussion Show, 26 Emmy nominations NATAS, Editl. Best Feature award AP, Media award UPI, Oakland County Bar Assn., TV Documentary award, Detroit Press Club, Bishop Gallagher award Mental Illness Rsch. Assn., Svc. award Arthritis Found. Mich., Mich. Mchts. Assn., DAV, Jr. Achievement, City of Detroit, Salvation Army, Spirit award City of Detroit, Spirit award City of Pontiac, Golden Heritage award Little Rock Bapt. Ch., 1993, Neal Shine award outstanding contbn. Nat. Soc. Fundraising Execs., Virginia Merrick award outstanding contbn. Christ Child Soc., Outstanding Achievement award Tuskegee Airmen, Best Feature Story award Mich. Assn. Broadcasters; named Media Person of the Yr., So. Christian Leadership Conf., 1994, Humanitarian of the Yr., March of Dimes, 1995, Michiganian of the Yr., Detroit News, Outstanding Woman of the Yr., GM Women's Club. Mem. Pub. Rels. Soc. Am., Am. Women in Radio and TV (Outstanding Achievement award 1981, Outstanding Woman in TV Top Mgmt. 1993, Mentor award 1993), Women in Comm., Nat. Acad. TV Arts and Scis., Detroit Press Club, Ad-Craft, Howard U. Nat. Gold Key Honor Soc. (hon.). Roman Catholic. Office: 26955 W 11 Mile Rd Southfield MI 48034-2292

MALACARNE, C. JOHN, insurance company executive, lawyer; b. St. Louis, Dec. 26, 1941; s. Claude John and Virginia E. (Miller) M.; m. Kathleen M. Morris, Aug. 27, 1966; children: Tracy, Kristen, Lisa. AA, Harris-Stowe State Coll., 1962; BS in Pub. Adminstrn., U. Mo., 1964, JD, 1967. Bar: Mo. 1967. Asst. counsel Kansas City (Mo.) Life, 1967-71, assoc. counsel, 1971-74, asst. gen. counsel, 1974-76, assoc. gen. counsel, 1976-80, gen. counsel, 1980-81, v.p., gen. counsel, sec., 1981—. Bd. dirs. Kansas City Life Ins. Co., Sunset Life Ins. Co. Am., Alaska Life & Health Guarangy Assn., Calif. Life and Health Ins. Guaranty Assn., Mo. Life and Health Guaranty Assn.; sec., bd. dirs. Old Am. Ins. Co. Sec., bd. dirs. Mid-Continent coun. Girl Scouts U.S.A., Kansas City, 1986-88; v.p., bd. dirs. Kansas City Eye Bank, 1986-91; pres., bd. dirs. Shepherd's Ctr., Kansas City, 1982-84; bd. dirs. Shepherd's Ctr. Internat., 1986-92, Community Mental Health Svcs. Found., sec. rsch., 1992-94, v.p., 1995—; mem. Bd. Edn. Consolidated Sch. Dist. #4, Jackson County, Mo., 1989-91. Mem. ABA, Kansas City Met. Bar Assn. (vice chmn. corp. counsel com. 1986-87, vice chmn. corp. law 1993-94, chmn. corp. law com. 1994-95), Lawyers Assn. Kansas City (bd. dirs. 1976), Internat. Assn. Def. Counsel (chmn. accident health and life sect. 1982-84, ins. exec. com. 1986, v.p., mem. exec. com. 1988-90), Jr. C. of C. (bd. dirs. 1972), Kiwanis (pres. Kansas City 1975-76). Home: 604 Tam O Shanter Dr Kansas City MO 64145-1240 Office: Kansas City Life Ins Co PO Box 219139 Kansas City MO 64121-9139

MALANGONI, MARK ALAN, surgeon, educator; b. East Chicago, Ind., Nov. 3, 1949; s. Roland G. and Cornelia (Marza) M.; m. Nancy Knapp, Aug. 12, 1972; children: Joseph, Michael, Jonathan. AB in Zoology cum laude, Ind. U., 1971, MD, 1975. MD; diplomate Am. Bd. Surgery. Asst. prof. surgery Med. Coll. Wis., Milw., 1980-84, assoc. program dir., gen. surgery, 1981-84; assoc. prof. Surgery U. Louisville, 1984-90, chief surgery Humana Hosp., 1985-90; prof. surgery Case Western Res. U., Cleve., 1990—. Chmn. dept. surgery MetroHealth Med. Ctr., Cleve., 1990—. Merit Rev. grantee VA, Louisville, 1985-88. Fellow Am. Coll. Surgeons; mem. Cen. Surg. Assn., So. Surg. Assn., Am. Surg. Assn., Phi Beta Kappa, Alpha Omega Alpha. Office: MetroHealth Med Ctr 2500 Metrohealth Dr # 914 Cleveland OH 44109-1998 Office Phone: 216-778-4558.

MALCOLM, CHRISTINE ANNE, university hospital administrator; b. St. Paul, Jan. 25, 1950; d. Harold Thomas and Velma Lucille (Kuefler) Lehto; m. Mark Justin Malcolm, Sept. 18, 1971; children: Justine Emily, Benjamin Alexander. AB with hons., U. Chgo., 1972, MBA in Hosp. Adminstrn., 1978. Clinic mgr. Hennepin County Med. Ctr., Mpls., 1972-76; adminstrv. resident Ingalls Meml. Hosp., Harvey, Ill., 1977-78; cons. A.T. Kearney, Chgo., 1977, Coopers & Lybrand, Chgo., 1978-80; mgr. Amherst Assocs., Chgo., 1980-81; dir. Coopers & Lybrand, Chgo., 1981-86; v.p. planning and corp. devel. U. Chgo. Hosps., 1986—93; v.p. managed care and network devel. U. HealthSystem Consortium, Chgo.; v.p. provider solutions Global Health Solutions Group Computer Sci. Corp.; sr. v.p. strategic planning, mktg. and program devel. Rush U. Med. Ctr., Chgo., 2002—. V.p. Q.V., Inc., Chgo., 1987—. Author: (Digital Perspectives column) Healthcare Fin. Mgmt. mag. Sec., treas. and bd. dirs. Chgo. Child Care Soc., 1978—. Recipient Am. Mktg. Assn. Innovator award, 1988; named one of Chicago's 100 Most Influential Women, Crain's Chgo. Bus., 2004; NSF grantee, 1971. Mem. U. Hosp. Consortium, Am. Coll. Healthcare Execs., Am. Mktg. Assn. Lutheran. Avocations: gardening, canoeing, cooking. Office: Rush Univ Med Ctr 1653 W Congress Pkwy Chicago IL 60612

MALICKY, NEAL, academic administrator; b. Sour Lake, Tex., Sept. 14, 1934; s. George and Ethel L. (Reed) M.; m. Margaret A. Wilson, Sept. 2, 1956; children: Michael Neal, Eric Scott, David Matthew. AB, Baker U., 1956; B.D., So. Meth. U., 1959; PhD, Columbia U., 1968; postgrad., Harvard U., 1978. Ordained to ministry Meth. Ch., 1959, pastor Moran, Kans., 1959-62, Van Cortlandtville, N.Y., 1962-66; asst. prof., dir. semester on UN Drew U., 1966-69; prof. polit. sci., dean Coll., Baker U., Baldwin City, Kans., 1969-75, acting pres., 1973-75; v.p. acad. affairs, also dean Baldwin-Wallace Coll., Berea, Ohio, 1975-81, pres., 1981-99; ret., 2000. Author: To Keep the Peace, 1965, Non-Governmental Organizations at the United Nations, 1968; contbr. articles to profl. jours. Mem. Leadership Cleve., Nat. Conf. Christian and Jews, Cleve. Commn. Higher Edn., Cleve. Coun. World Affairs, Greater Cleve. Roundtable (chmn. edn. com.), Cleve. Initiative Edn. (vice chmn.), Summit on Edn. (co-convenor), Assn. Independent Colls. Ohio (chmn.). Mem. UN Assn. Clubs: Union of Cleve., Fifty of Cleve. Office: Baldwin-Wallace Coll Office of Pres 275 Eastland Rd Berea OH 44017-2005

MALKASIAN, GEORGE DURAND, JR., obstetrician, educator; b. Springfield, Mass., Oct. 26, 1927; s. George Dur and Gladys Mildred (Trombley) M.; m. Mary Ellen Koch, Oct. 16, 1954; children: Linda Jeanne, Karen Diane, Martha Ellen. AB, Yale U., 1950; MD, Boston U., 1954; MS, U. Minn., 1963. Diplomate Am. Bd. Ob-Gyn. Intern Worcester (Mass.) City Hosp., 1954-55; resident in ob-gyn Mayo Grad. Sch. Hosp., Rochester, Minn., 1955-58, 60-61; mem. faculty Mayo Med. Sch., 1962—, prof. ob-gyn, 1976—, chmn. dept. ob-gyn, 1976-86. Author articles in field. Served to lt. comdr. M.C., USNR, 1958-60. Named Tchr. of Yr., Mayo Grad. Sch. Medicine, 1973, 77, Alumnus of Yr., Boston U. Sch. Med., 1990. Fellow Royal Coll. Obstetricians and Gynecologists (ad eundum); mem. ACS, Am. Coll. Ob-Gyn (pres. 1989-90), Am. Ob-Gyn Soc., Am. Radium Soc., Soc. Ob-Gyn, Assn. Profs. Ob-Gyn., N.Am. Ob-Gyn. Soc., Ctrl. Assn. Ob-Gyn, Minn. Soc. Ob-Gyn, Internat. Fedn. Ob-Gyn (v.p. 1997-2000), Zumbro Valley Med. Soc. (exec. dir. 1996-2002). Home: 211 NW 2nd St #503 Rochester MN 55901 Office: Mayo Clinic 200 1st St SW Rochester MN 55905-0001

MALKIN, CARY JAY, lawyer; b. Chgo., Oct. 6, 1949; s. Arthur D. and Perle (Slavin) Malkin; m. Lisa Kimley, Oct. 27, 1976; children: Dorothy R., Victoria S., Lydia R. BA, George Washington U., 1971; JD, Northwestern U., 1974. Bar: Ill. 1974, U.S. Dist. Ct. (no. dist.) Ill. 1974, N.Y. 2001. Assoc. Mayer, Brown & Platt, Chgo., 1974—80, ptnr., 1981—2002, Mayer, Brown, Rowe & Maw LLP, Chgo., 2002—, Mayer Brown LLP, Chgo., 2007—. Chmn. spl. events com. Mental Health Assn., 1984—85; mem. steering com. Endowment Campaign Latin Sch. Chgo., 1990—91, trustee, 1991—2000, nat. trustee, 2000—02, sr. trustee, 2002—; chmn. Campaign Latin Sch. Chgo., 1995—98; mem. exec. com. Friends Prentice Women's Hosp., 1991—92; bd. dirs. SOS Children's Village Ill., 1992—96; mem. M. S. Weiss fund bd. Children's Meml. Hosp., 1993—96, mem. Graziano fund bd., 1993—96; trustee Field Mus., 1999—, mem. fin. com., 2002—05, mem. investment com., 2003—05, mem. budget com., 2005—, mem. founder's coun., 1995—, chmn. founder's coun., 1999—2003. Mem.: Saddle and Cycle Club (bd. govs. 1998—2001, 2006—), Chgo. Club, Phi Beta Kappa, Order of Coif. Home: 233 E Walton St Chicago IL 60611-1526 Office: Mayer Brown LLP 71 S Wacker Dr Chicago IL 60606

MALKINSON, FREDERICK DAVID, dermatologist, educator; b. Hartford, Conn., Feb. 26, 1924; s. John Walter and Rose Malkinson; m. Una Zwick, June 15, 1979; children by previous marriage: Philip, Carol, John. Student, Loomis Inst., 1937-41; 3 yr. cert. cum laude, Harvard U., 1943, DMD, 1947, MD, 1949. Intern Harvard-Beth Israel Hosp., Boston, 1949-50; resident in dermatology U. Chgo., 1950-54, from instr. to assoc. prof. dept. dermatology, 1954-68; prof. medicine and dermatology U. Ill., Chgo., 1968-71; chmn. dept. dermatology Rush Med. Coll. and Rush-Presbyn.-St. Luke's Med. Ctr. (now Rush U. Med. Ctr.), Chgo., 1968-92, Clark W. Finnerud, M.D. prof. dept. dermatology, 1981-95, 95—; trustee Sulzberger Inst. Dermatol. Comm. and Edn., 1976-96; pres. Sulzberger Inst. Dermatol. Communication and Edn., 1983-88, 93-96; prof. emeritus Rush U. Med. Ctr., Chgo., 2000—. Editor: Year Book of Dermatology, 1971-78; chief editor: AMA Archives of Dermatology, 1979-83; bd. editors, 1976-84, Jour. AMA, 1979-83; editorial cons. World Book Medical Encyclopedia, 1991-2000; contbr. articles to profl. jours., chpts. to books. Active Evanston (Ill.) Libr. Bd., 1988-94, pres., 1993-94. With M.C. USNR, 1950-52. Grantee, U.S. Army, 1955—61, USPHS, 1962—70. Fellow AAAS; mem. Am. Acad. Dermatology (v.p. 1987-89, dir. 1964-67), Am. Dermatol. Assn., Soc. Investigative Dermatology (v.p. 1978-79, dir. 1963-68), Am. Fedn. Med. Rsch., Cen. Soc. Clin. Rsch., Radiation Rsch. Soc., Assn. Profs. of Dermatology (dir. 1982-85), Dermatology Found. (exec. com., trustee 1980-93, pres. 1983-85, Lifetime Career Educator award 2006), Nat. Coun. on Radiation Protection and Measurements (mem. com. on cutaneous radiobiology 1986-92), Chgo. Dermatol. Soc. (pres. 1964-65, Gold Medal award 1992, established ann. lectureship, 2004), Chgo. Lit. Club (v.p. 1997-99, 2000-03, pres. 1999-2000). Office: Rush Univ Med Ctr Dept Dermatology 707 S Wood St 220 Annex Bldg Chicago IL 60612 Office Fax: 312-942-7778.

MALKUS, DAVID STARR, mathematician; b. Chgo., June 30, 1945; s. Willem V.R. Malkus and Joanne (Gerould) Simpson; m. Evelyn R. (div.); children: Christopher, Annelise, Byron, Renata. AB, Yale U., 1968; PhD, Boston U., 1976. Mathematician U.S. Nat. Bur. Standards, Gaithersburg, Md., 1975-77; asst. prof. math. Ill. Inst. Tech., Chgo., 1977-83, assoc. prof., 1983-84; assoc. prof. mechanics U. Wis., Madison, 1984-87, prof., 1987—2002, chmn. Rheology Rsch. Ctr., 1991-94, prof. emeritus, 2002—. Chair prof. Nanjing (People's Republic China) Aero. Inst., 1986. Co-author: Concepts and Applications of Finite Element Analysis, 1989; contbr. articles to Computer Methods Applied Mech. Engring., Jour. Computational Physics. Achievements include research on finite element methods--reduced and selective integration techniques, a unification of concepts. Home: 2710 Mason St Madison WI 53705-3716 Home Phone: 608-232-1455. Business E-Mail: malkus@engr.wisc.edu.

MALL, SANFORD J., lawyer; Cert.: Nat. Elder Law Found. (elder law atty.), Soc. Sr. Advs. (sr. adv.). Founder, sr. ptnr. Mall Malisow & Cooney PC, Farmington Hills, Mich. Instr. estate planning Cert. Fin. Planning prog. Coll. Fin. Planning, Denver. Named one of Top 100 Attys., Worth mag., 2006. Mem.: State Bar Mich. (chair elder law & disability rights sect.). Office: Mall Malisow & Cooney PC 30445 Northwestern Hwy Ste 250 Farmington Hills MI 48334 Office Phone: 248-538-1800. Office Fax: 248-538-1801. E-mail: sjmjd@teclf.com.

MALLAK, JAMES A., auto parts company executive; BS in Acctg., Mich. StateU.; MBA, Mich. State U. Numerous fin. mgmt. positions ITT Automotive, 1977—98; v.p. fin. Heavy Vehivle Systems divsn. Arvin/Meritor, 1998—99; exec. v.p., chief fin. officer Textron Automotive Corp., 1999—2001; chief fin. officer Tower Automotive Inc, Novi, Mich., 2004—. Mem. adv. bd. acctg. and fin. dept. Oakland U., Mich. Office: Tower Automotive Inc 27175 Haggarty Rd Novi MI 48377

MALLETT, CONRAD LEROY, JR., former state supreme court chief justice, hospital administrator; b. Detroit, Oct. 12, 1953; s. Conrad LeRoy and Claudia Gwendolyn (Jones) M.; m. Barbara Straughn, Dec. 22, 1984; children: Alex Conrad, Mio Thomas, Kristan Claudia. BA, UCLA, 1975; MPA, JD, U. So. Calif., 1979; MBA, Oakland U. Bar: Mich. 1979. Legal asst. to congressman, Detroit, 1979-80; dep. pol. div. Dem. Nat. Com., Washington, 1980-81; assoc. Miller, Canfield, Paddock & Stone, Detroit, 1981-82; legal counsel, dir. to gov. State of Mich., Lansing, 1983-84; sr. exec. asst. to Mayor City of Detroit, 1985-86; ptnr. Jaffe, Raitt, Heuer & Weiss, Detroit, 1987-90; justice Mich. Supreme Ct., Lansing, 1990—98, chief justice, 1997—98; pvt. practice Miller Canfield, Detroit, 1999; gen. counsel, chief adminstrv. officer Detroit Med. Ctr., 1999—2001, exec. v.p., chief adminstrv. officer, 2003—; COO City of Detroit, 2002; pres., gen. counsel Hawkins Food Group, 2002—03; interim pres. Sinai Grace Hosp., Detroit, 2003—. Bd. mem. Lear Corp., TechTeam Global, Inc. Mem. NAACP, Kappa Alpha Psi. Democrat. Roman Catholic. Avocations: writing, fiction. Office: Sinai-Grace Hosp 6071 W Outer Dr Detroit MI 48235-2624

MALLORY, MARK L., mayor, former state legislator; b. Cin., Apr. 2, 1962; s. William L. Mallory. Student, Xavier U.; BS in Adminstrv. Mgmt., U. Cin. Dept. mgr. Hamilton County Pub. Libr. Graphic Prodn., Cin., 1981—95; rep. dist. 31 Ohio Ho. Reps., Columbus, 1995—98; mem. Dist. 9 Ohio State Senate, Columbus, 1998—2005, asst. minority whip, 2000—03, asst. minority leader, 2003—05; mayor City of Cin., 2005—. Bd. trustees Friar's Club; advisory coun. 4C for Children; advisory bd. Ronald McDonald House of Cin. Recipient Devel. Leadership award, Bowhay Inst. for Legis. Leadership, 1996, Myrl Shoemaker Legis. of the Year award, 1998, Excellence in Correctional Edn. award, Correctional Edn. Assn., 1999, Pub. Svc. award, Gothic Lodge 122, 2000, Legis. of the Year award, Nat. Assn. Social Workers, 2001, Wolfe award of Excellence, OH Assn. Elected Officials, 2002, Pub. Svc. award, Nat. Assn. Grad. & Profl. Students, 2003, Passport to Excellence award, Phi Delta Kappa, 2003, Andrew Carnegie award, OH Library Coun., 2003, Legis. of the Year award, OH Community Corrections Assn., 2004. Mem. NAACP, Libr. Staff Assn., Black Male Coalition, Friends of Pub. Libr., Urban League of Cin., Pub. Libr. Staff Assn., Internat. TV Assn. Achievements include being the first African American directly elected by the people of Cincinnati, 2005. Office: Office of Mayor 801 Plum St Cincinnati OH 45202

MALLORY, ROBERT MARK, controller, finance company executive; b. Mattoon, Ill., Apr. 15, 1950; s. Robert Monroe and Betty Ann (Mudd) M.; m. Diana Marie Burde, Aug. 19, 1972; 1 child, Laura Elizabeth. BS in Accountancy, U. Ill., 1972; MBA, Northwestern U., 1985. CPA Ill. Staff acct. Price Waterhouse, Chgo., 1972-74, sr. acct., 1974-77, mgr., 1977-79; dir. internal audit Mark Controls Corp., Skokie, Ill., 1979-81, corp. contr., 1981-86, v.p., contr., 1986-88; contr., dir. planning Tribune Co., Chgo., 1988-91, v.p., contr., 1991—. Bd. dirs. Met. Family Svcs. Mem. AICPA (Elijah Watts Sells award 1972), Ill. CPA Soc., Fin. Execs. Internat. (bd. dirs.), Internat. Newspaper Fin. Execs. (bd. dirs.), Beta Gamma Sigma. Methodist. Home: 3312 Lakewood Ct Glenview IL 60026-2505 Office: Tribune Co 435 N Michigan Ave Chicago IL 60611-4066 Home Phone: 847-998-1467. Personal E-mail: mallory435@aol.com.

MALLOY, EDWARD ALOYSIUS, academic administrator; b. Washington, May 3, 1941; s. Edward Aloysius and Elizabeth (Clark) Malloy. BA, U. Notre Dame, 1963, MA, 1967, ThM, 1969; PhD, Vanderbilt U., 1975. Ordained to ministry Cath. Ch., 1970. Instr. U. Notre Dame, South Bend, Ind., 1974—75, asst. prof., 1975—81, assoc. prof., 1981—88, prof. theology, 1988—, assoc. provost, 1982—86, pres. elect, 1986, pres., 1987—2005, pres. emeritus, 2005—. Established chair Cath. Studes in name of Edward A. Malloy Vanderbilt U., 1997; editl. adv. bd. The Presidency mag.; bd. dir. Nat. Com. on Higher Edn. and Health of Youth; co-chmn. Nat. Inst. on Alcohol Abuse and Alcoholism; chmn. Nat. Commn. on Substance Abuse and Sports; regent U. Portland, 1985—; bd. govs., trustee Notre Dame, Australia, 1990—. Author: Culture & Commitment: The Challenge of Today's University, 1992, Notre Dame: The Unfolding Vision, 1994, Monk's Reflection: A View from the Dome, 1999, Monk's Travels People, Places & Events, 2004, Monk's Notre Dame, 2005; co-author: Colleges and Universities as Citizens, 1999. Chmn. Am. Coun. Edn.; mem. Pres. Adv. Coun. on Drugs, 1989—; adv. bd. AmeriCorps and Nat. Civilian Cmty. Corps, 1994—97; interim chmn. Ind. Commn. Cmty. Svc., 1994—97; active Boys and Girls Clubs Am., 1997—; trustee U. St. Thomas, 1997—, Vanderbilt U., 1999; bd. advisors Berrnadin Ctr., 1997—2005; founding dir., bd. dir. Points of Light Found.; past chmn. Campus Impact; bd. regents U. Portland, 1985; bd. govs. Notre Dame Australia, 1990; mem. Bishopps and pres. com. Assn. Cath. Colls. and Univs., 1988—2005; bd. dirs. Internat. Fedn. Cath. Univs., 1988—2005, NCAA Found., 1989—. Mem.: Nat. Assn. Ind. Colls. and Univs. (bd. dirs. 1997), The Conf. Bd., Assn. Governing Bds. of Univs. and Colls. (vice chair 1996—2004), Bus.-Higher Edn. Forum, Am. Soc. Christian Ethics, Cath. Theol. Soc. Roman Catholic. Office: Univ Notre Dame Pres Emeritus Notre Dame IN 46556 Office Phone: 574-631-6755.

MALMBERG, AL, radio personality; m. Kathy Malmberg, 1971; 2 children. Gen. mgr., corp. program dir., network anchorman, syndicated talk show host; radio host late night show Sta. WCCO, Mpls. Office: WCCO 625 2nd Ave S Minneapolis MN 55402

MALOF, KEVIN K., lawyer; b. Cin., Nov. 27, 1967; BS, Miami U., 1990; JD, Salmon P. Chase Coll. Law, 2000. Bar: Ohio 2000. Sr. assoc. Frost Brown Todd LLC, Cin. Mem. Nat. Moot Ct. Bd., 1998—2000. Mem. Miami Twp. Zoning Bd.; bd. mem. NWCCSAY Soccer; coach Miami Twp. Soccer, Miami Twp. Baseball. Named one of Ohio's Rising Stars, Super Lawyers, 2006. Mem.: Ohio State Bar Assn., Cin. Bar Assn., ABA. Office: Frost Brown Todd LLC 2200 PNC Ctr 201 E Fifth St Cincinnati OH 45202-4182 Office Phone: 513-651-6431. Office Fax: 513-651-6981.

MALONE, JIMMY, radio personality; m. April Malone; 1 child, Angela. Radio host WMJI, Cleve., 1961—. Stand-up comedian. Co-host (radio shows) Knuckleheads in the News, 1961—, The Lanigan & Malone Show, 1991—. Active Cleve. Scholar Program, Providence House, Greater Cleve. Hunger Task Force. Co-recipient (with John Lanigan) Large Market Personality of Yr., NAB Marconi Radio Awards, 2003; named Radio and TV Coun. Students' Bordcaster of Yr.; named to, Shaker Heights Alumni Hall of Fame. Office: WMJI 105.7 4th Fl 6200 Oak Tree Blvd Independence OH 44131 also: WMJI 105.7 FM 6th Fl 310 W Lakeside Ave Cleveland OH 44113 E-mail: malone@wmji.com.

MALONE, MICHAEL W., manufacturing executive; Grad., St. John's U. CPA. With Arthur Andersen & Co., Polaris Industries Inc., Medima, Minn., 1984—, asst. treas., CFO, treas., 1993—. Office: Polaris Industries Inc 2100 Highway 55 Medina MN 55340-9100

MALONE, ROBERT ROY, artist, educator; b. McColl, SC, Aug. 8, 1933; s. Robert Roy and Anne (Matthews) M.; m. Cynthia Enid Taylor, Feb. 26, 1956; 1 child, Brendan Trevor. BA, U. N.C., 1955; MFA, U. Chgo., 1958; postgrad., U. Iowa, 1959. Instr. art Union U., Jackson, Tenn., 1959-60, Lambuth Coll., 1959-61; asst. prof. art Wesleyan Coll., Macon, Ga., 1961-67, assoc. prof., 1967-68, W.Va. U., 1968-70, So. Ill. U., Edwardsville, 1970-75, prof., 1975—2000, prof. emeritus, 2000—. One-man shows at Gallery Illien, Atlanta, 1969, De Cinque Gallery, Miami, 1968, 71, Ill. State Mus., Springfield, 1974, U. Del., Newark, 1978, Elliot Smith Gallery, St. Louis, 1985, Merida Galleries, Louisville, 1985, Yvonne Rapp Gallery, Louisville, 1990, 92-93, 96, 98, 2000, 04, St. John's Coll., Santa Fe, 1991, Uzelac Gallery, Pontiac, Mich., 1997, others; group shows include Bklyn. Mus., 1966, Assoc. Am. Artists Gallery, NYC, 1968, Mus. d'Art Modern, Paris, 1970, DeCordova Mus., 1973-74, St. Louis Art Mus., 1985, Wake Forest U., 1985, New Orleans Mus. Art, 1990, Dakota Internat., Vermillion, 1994, Springfield Art Mus., Mo., 2004; represented in permanent collections including Smithsonian Instn., Washington, USIA, Washington, Libr. of Congress, Calif. Palace of Legion of Honor, San Francisco, NY Pub. Libr., NYC, Victoria and Albert Mus., London, Chgo. Art Inst., Indpls. Mus. Art, Humana Inc., Louisville, State of Ill. Ctr., Chgo., Speed Mus., Louisville, N. Ill. U., Capital Devel. Bd., Ill.; co-editor: Contemporary American Printmakers, 1999 (English and Chinese edits.). Recipient numerous regional, nat. awards in competitive exhbns.; Ford fellow, 1977, So. Ill. U. at Edwardsville sr. research scholar, 1976, 1984. Home: 600 Chapman St Edwardsville IL 62025-1260

MALONEY, EDWARD DENNIS, state senator, assistant principal; b. Chgo., May 22, 1946; s. John Frances and Lucille Veronica (Wiechern) M.; m. Norine Marie Smith, Oct. 26, 1968; children: Brian, Matthew, Daniel, Martin. BA in Polit. Sci., Lewis U., 1968; MEd, Chgo. State U., 1976. Tchr., counselor Oak

Lawn HS, Ill., 1968—91, dept. chair Ill., 1991—97; dep. dir. Chicago park dist., 1997—2001; asst. prin. Brother Rice HS, 2001—; senator, dist. 18 State of Ill., 2002—. Mem. S.W. Counselors Assn., Ill. Personel and Guidance Assn., Cen. Ofcls. Assn. Clubs: Bull Baseball (Chgo.) (commr.). Democrat. Roman Catholic. Avocations: triathlons, basketball officiating. Office: 311 Capitol Bldg Springfield IL 62706

MALONEY, MARY D., lawyer; BA, U. Akron, 1984; JD summa cum laude, Cleve. State U., 1987; LLM, Case Wester Res. U., 1995. Bar: Ohio 1987. With Jones Day, Cleve., 1987—, ptnr., 2001—. Mem.: Ohio State Bar Assn. Office: Jones Day North Point 901 Lakeside Ave Cleveland OH 44114-1190

MALONEY, RITA, radio personality; With Sta. WBVP, Pitts., news dir.; radio host Sta. WCCO radio, Mpls. Named one of Pitts. 50 Finest Young Profls.; recipient Best Regularly Scheduled Newscast award, 3 AIR awards for Best Traffic Reporter, Best Spot News Coverage award, Pa. AP. Office: WCCO 625 2nd Ave S Minneapolis MN 55402

MALOVANY, HOWARD, lawyer; b. Dayton, Ohio, July 6, 1950; m. Cynthia Jane Shilt, Sept. 18, 1976. BA, Ohio State U., 1972; JD, U. Toledo, 1977; MBA, U. Dayton, 1985. Bar: Ohio 1977, Ill. 1997. Staff atty., asst. sec. Nat. Cash Register Corp., Dayton, 1977-85; counsel Outboard Marine Corp., Waukegan, Ill., 1985-89, asst. sec., counsel, 1989—93, sec., sr. counsel, 1993—96; asst. sec., sr. counsel William Wrigley Jr. Co., Waukegan, 1996-98, sec., gen. counsel Chgo., 1998-2001, v.p., sec., gen. counsel, 2001—. Mem.: ABA, Am. Soc. Corp. Secretaries (mem. corp. practice & technology com. 1995—97), Toledo Internat. Law Soc. (founder), Ohio State Bar Assn., Ill. State Bar Assn. Office: William Wrigley Jr Co 410 N Michigan Ave Chicago IL 60611-4213 Office Phone: 312-645-4223. Business E-Mail: hmalovany@wrigley.com.

MALTER, JAMES SAMUEL, pathologist, educator; b. Tooele, Utah, May 18, 1956; s. Robert Henry Malter and Evvajean (Harris) Mintz; m. Elaine Gadzicki, May 26, 1988. AB, Dartmouth Coll., 1979; MD, Washington U., 1983. Diplomate Am. Bd. Clin. Pathology. Resident in pathology U. Pa., Phila., 1983-88, chief resident, 1987-88; asst. prof. pathology Tulane U., New Orleans, 1988-91; dir. exptl. pathology Tulane Med. Ctr., New Orleans, 1988-91, dir. Blood Ctr., 1989-91; asst. prof. pathology Sch. Medicine U. Wis., Madison, 1991-97; med. dir. Blood Bank U. Wis. Hosp. & Clinic, Madison, 1991—; prof. pathology Sch. Medicine U. Wis., Madison, 1997—. Mem. editl. bd. Hepatology jour., 1991—. Recipient Nat. Rsch. Svc. award NIH, 1986-88, Clin. Investigator award NCI-NIH, 1988-91, Ind. Investigator award NIH, 1991—. Mem. Am. Assn. Blood Banks, Am. Assn. Pathologists, Am. Coll. Pathologists (diplomate). Office: U Wis Hosp & Clinic Dept of Pathology 600 Highland Ave # B4 263 Madison WI 53792-0001

MAMAT, FRANK TRUSTICK, lawyer; b. Syracuse, NY, Sept. 4, 1949; s. Harvey Sanford and Annette (Trustick) M.; m. Kathy Lou Winters, June 23, 1975; children: Jonathan Adam, Steven Kenneth. BA, U. Rochester, 1971; JD, Syracuse U., 1974. Bar: D.C. 1976, U.S. Ct. Appeals (D.C. cir.) 1976, Fla. 1977, U.S. Supreme Ct. 1979, US. Dist. Ct. (ea. dist.) 1983, U.S. Ct. Appeals (6th cir.) 1983, Mich. 1984, U.S. Dist. Ct. (no. dist.) Ind. 1984. Atty. NLRB, Washington, 1975—79; assoc. Proskauer, Rose, Goetz & Mendelsohn, Washington, NYC and L.A., 1979—83, Fishman Group, Bloomfield Hills, Mich., 1983—85, ptnr., 1985—87; sr. ptnr. Honigman, Miller, Schwartz and Cohn, 1987—94; pres., CEO Morgan Daniels Co., Inc., West Bloomfield, Mich., 1994—; ptnr. Clark Klein & Beaumont, P.L.C., Detroit, 1995—96, Clark Hill, P.L.C., Detroit, 1996—2003, mem. exec. com., 1999—2001; ptnr. Dickinson Wright, PLLC, 2003—. Bd. dirs. Mich. Food and Beverage Assn., Air Conditioning Contractors of Am., Air Conditioning Contractors of Mich., Am. Subcontractors Assn., Mich. Mfrs. Assn. Labor Counsel, Jewish Vocat. Svcs., Constrn. Fin. Mgmt. Assn., Mich. Assn. Home Builders. Gen. counsel Rep. Com. of Oakland County, 1986—; chmn. Constrn. Code Commn. Mich., 1993—; bd. dirs. 300 Club, Mich., 1984-90; pres. 400 Club, 1990-93, chmn., 1993—; mem. Associated Gen. Contractors Labor Lawyers Coun.; mem. Rep. at. Com. Nat. Rep. Senatorial Com., Presdl. Task Force, Rep. Labor Coun., Washington; city dir. West Bloomfield, 1985-87; pres. West Bloomfield Rep. Club, 1985-87; chmn. bd. trustees Am. Soc. Edn. Found., 2005—; fin. com. Rep. Com. of Oakland County, 1984-93; pres. Oakland County Lincoln Rep. Club, 1989-90; bd. dirs. camping svcs. and human resources com. YMCA, 1989-93, Anti-Defamation League, 1989—; vice chmn. Lawyers for Reagan-Bush, 1984; v.p. Fruehauf Farms, West Bloomfield, Mich., 1985-88; mem. staff Exec. Office of Pres. of US Inquiries/Comments, Washington, 1981-83. Fellow Coll. Labor and Employment Attys.; mem. ABA, FBA, Mich. Bar Assn., Fla. Bar Assn. (labor com. 1977—), Rep. Nat. Lawyers Assn., Mich. Bus. and Profl. Assn., Am. Acad. Constrn. and Labor Attys. (exec. dir. 1998—), Am. Subcontractors Assn. (Southeastern Mich., bd. dirs.), Founders Soc. Detroit Bar Assn., Assn. Corp. Growth (Detroit chpt.), Oakland County Bar Assn., Mich. Infrastructure and Transp. Assn., Constrn. Mgmt. Fin. Assn., B'nai B'rith (v.p. 1982-83, trustee 1987-88, bd. dirs. Detroit Barristers unit 1983-91, pres. 1985-87), Am. Soc. Employers (chmn. 2003-05, chmn. ednl. found. 2005—), Oakpointe Country Club, Detroit Soc. Clubs, Skyline Club, Fairlane Club, Detroit Athletic Club, Renaissance Club, Econ. Club Detroit. Office: Dickinson Wright PLLC 500 Woodward Ave Ste 4000 Detroit MI 48226 also: Morgan Daniels Co Inc 5484 Crispin Way Rd West Bloomfield MI 48323-3402 Home Phone: 248-626-4107; Office Phone: 313-223-3169, 313-333-7174. Personal E-mail: fmamat@aol.com. Business E-Mail: fmamat@dickinsonwright.com.

MAMAYEK, TELLY, radio personality; married; children: Emily, Nathan. BA Journalism, U. Wis., 1985. With Stas. WBIZ/WJJK Radio, Eau Claire, Wis., Stas. KZIO/WDSM Radio, Duluth, Minn., Sta. WNIU Pub. Radio, DeKalb, Ill., Sta. WCKY Radio, Cin., Sta. WCCO Radio, Mpls., 1991—, morning news editor, anchor. Mem.: Minn. AP Broadcast Bd., Minn. Chpt. Profl. Journalists (pres.). Avocation: bicycling. Office: WCCO 625 2nd Ave S Minneapolis MN 55402

MAMER, STUART MIES, lawyer; b. East Hardin, Ill., Feb. 23, 1921; s. Louis H. and Anna (Mies) M.; m. Donna E. Jordan, Sept. 10, 1944; children: Richard A., John S., Bruce J. AB, U. Ill., 1942, JD, 1947. Bar: Ill. bar 1947. Assoc. Thomas & Mulliken, Champaign, 1947-55; partner firm Thomas, Mamer & Haughey, Champaign, 1955—. Lectr. U. Ill. Coll. Law, Urbana, 1965-85; Mem. Atty. Registration and Disciplinary Commn. Ill., 1976-82 Chmn. fund drive Champaign County Community Chest, 1955; 1st pres. Champaign County United Fund, 1957; Pres., dir. U. Ill. McKinley Found., Champaign, 1957-69; trustee Children's Home and Aid Soc. of Ill., v.p., 1977-96. Served as pilot USAAC, 1943-45. Mem. Am. Coll. Trust and Estate Counsel (bd. regents 1984-90), Pillar of Champaign County Bar Assn., Phi Beta Kappa, Phi Gamma Delta. Republican. Presbyterian. Home: 101 W Windsor Rd # 3105 Urbana IL 61802-6663 Office: Thomas Mamer & Haughey LLP 30 E Main St Fl 5 Champaign IL 61820-3629 Office Phone: 217-351-1500. Business E-Mail: smamer@tmh-law.com.

MAMET, DAVID ALAN, playwright, scriptwriter; b. Chgo., Nov. 30, 1947; s. Bernard Morris and Lenore June (Silver) Mamet; m. Lindsay Crouse, Dec. 1977 (div.); m. Rebecca Pidgeon, Sept. 22, 1991. BA, Goddard Coll., Plainfield, Vt., 1969; DLitt (hon.), Dartmouth Coll., 1996. Artist-in-residence Goddard Coll., 1971-73; artistic dir. St. Nicholas Theatre Co., Chgo., 1973-75; guest lectr. U. Chgo., 1975, 79, NYU, 1981; assoc. artistic dir. Goodman Theater, Chgo., 1978; assoc. prof. film Columbia U., 1988. Chmn. bd. Atlantic Theater Co. Author: (plays) The Duck Variations, 1971, Sexual Perversity in Chicago, 1973 (Village Voice Obie award, N.Y. Drama Critics Cir. award), Reunion, 1973, Squirrels, 1974, American Buffalo, 1976, A Life in the Theatre, 1976, The Water Engine, 1976, The Woods, 1977, Lone Canoe, 1978, Prairie du Chien, 1978, Lakeboat, 1980, Donny March, 1981, Edmond, 1982 (Village Voice Obie award, 1983), The Disappearance of the Jews, 1983, The Shawl, 1985, Glengarry Glen Ross, 1984 (Pulitzer prize for drama, N.Y. Drama Critics Cir. award), Speed-the-Plow, 1987, Bobby Gould in Hell, 1989, The Old Neighborhood, 1991, Oleanna, 1992, The Cryptogram, 1994, Ricky Jay and His 52 Assistants, 1994, Death Defying Acts, 1995, Boston Marriage, 1999, Romance, 2005, November, 2007; dir.: (plays) Dangerous Corner, 1995; author: (screenplays) The Postman Always Rings Twice, 1979, The Verdict, 1980, The Untouchables, 1986, House of Games, 1986, We're No Angels, 1987, Homicide, 1991, Hoffa, 1991, Oleanna, 1994, The Edge, 1996, The Spanish Prisoner, 1996, Wag the Dog, 1997, Ronin, 1998, The Winslow Boy, 1999, State & Main, 2000, Lakeboat, 2001, Hannibal, 2001; co-author (with Shel Silverstein) Things Change, 1987; author: (novels) The Village, 1994, The Old Religion, 1996, Wilson: A Consideration of the Sources, 2001, (non-fiction) True and False: Heresy and Common Sense for the Actor, 1996, 3 Uses of the Knife: On the Nature and Purpose of Drama, 1996, The Wicked Son: Anti-Semitism, Self-Hatred and the Jews, 2006, Bambi vs. Godzilla: On the Nature, Purpose and Practice of the Movie Business, 2007, (children's books) Warm and Cold with drawings by Donald Sultan, 1985, Passover, The Duck and the Goat, 1996, The Duck and the Goat, Jafsie & John Henry, 1999, Bar Mitzvah, 1999, Henrietta, 1999, (essays) Writing In Restaurants, 1986, SomeFreaks, 1989, On Directing Film, 1990, The Cabin, 1992, Make-Believe-Town, 1996, (poetry) The China Man, 1999, The Hero Pony, 1990; dir.: (films) House of Games, 1986, The Winslow Boy, 1988, Things Change, 1988, Homicide, 1991, Oleanna, 1994, The Spanish Prisoner, 1996, State and Main, 2000, Catastrophe, 2000; writer, dir. (films) Heist, 2001, assoc. prodr. Hoffa, 1992; exec. prodr.: (TV films) Lansky, 1999, A Life in the Theater, 1993; prodr.: Lip Service, 1988; creator, writer (TV series) The Unit, 2006. Recipient Outer Critics Circle award for contbn. to Am. theater, 1978, Acad. award nominee for best screenplay adaptation, 1983, 1998, Common Wealth Award Distinguished Svc., 2004, Screen Laurel Award, Writers Guild Am., 2005; Rockefeller grantee, 1977, CBS Creative Writing fellow, Yale U. Drama Sch, 1976—77. Office: David Mamet 2 Northfield Plz Northfield IL 60093-1294

MAMMEL, RUSSELL NORMAN, retired food distribution company executive; b. Hutchinson, Kans., Apr. 28, 1926; s. Vyvian E. and Mabel Edwina (Hursh) M.; m. Betty Crawford, Oct. 29, 1949 (dec. Oct. 1994); children: Mark, Christopher, Elizabeth, Nancy. BS, U. Kans., 1949. With Mammel's Inc., Hutchinson, 1949-57, pres., 1957-59; retail gen. mgr. Kans. divsn. Nash Finch Co., Hutchinson, 1959-61, retail gen. mgr. Iowa divsn. Cedar Rapids, 1961-66, dir. store devel. Mpls., 1966-75, v.p., 1975-83, exec. v.p., 1983-85, pres., COO, 1985-91, also bd. dirs., 1991-97; pvt. investments, 1991—. With AUS, 1944-46. Office: Nash Finch Co 7600 France Ave S Ste 200 Minneapolis MN 55435-5920 Home: c/o B Howard 155 Gleason Lake Rd Apt 205 Wayzata MN 55391-1350

MANCOFF, NEAL ALAN, lawyer; b. Chgo., May 7, 1939; s. Isadore and Sarah (Leviton) M.; m. Alys Belofsky, June 26, 1966; children: Wesley, Frederick, Daniel. BBA, U. Wis., 1961; JD, Northwestern U., 1965. Bar: Ill. 1965, U.S. Dist. Ct. (no. dist.) Ill. 1965. Assoc. Aaron Aaron Schimberg & Hess, Chgo., 1965-72, ptnr., 1972-80, Schiff Hardin & Waite, Chgo., 1980—. Author: Qualified Deferred Compensation Plans, 1983, Nonqualified Deferred Compensation Agreements, 1987. Lst lt. U.S. Army, 1961-62. Mem. Chgo. Bar Assn. (chmn. employee benefits com. 1984). Office: Schiff Hardin LLC 7500 Sears Tower Chicago IL 60606

MANDEL, JACK N., manufacturing executive; b. Austria, July 16, 1911; s. Sam and Rose M.; m. Lilyan, Aug. 14, 1938 (dec.) Student, Fenn Coll., 1930-33. Founder, former pres., chmn. Premier Indsl. Corp., Cleve.; chmn., pres. Manbro Corp.; exec. dir. Parkwood Corp.; gen. ptnr. Courtland Assocs. Former mem. exec. com. NCCJ; former life trustee Wood Hosp.; trustee Fla. Soc. for Blind; life trustee South Broward Jewish Fedn., Cleve. Jewish Welfare Fedn.; former pres., life trustee Montefiore Home for Aged; pres. adv. bd. Barry U.; hon. trustee Hebrew U.; trustee Tel Aviv U. Mus. of the Diaspora; life trustee The Temple, Woodruff Found.; trustee Cleve. Play House. Mem. Beachmont Country Club, Commede Club, Union Club. Office: Parkwood Corp 2829 Euclid Ave Cleveland OH 44115-2413 Office Phone: 216-875-6502.

MANDEL, SHELDON LLOYD, dermatologist, educator; b. Mpls., Dec. 6, 1922; s. Maurice and Stelle R. M.; m. Patricia E., Oct. 15, 1978; 1 child, Melissa A. MA in Spl. Edn., St. Thomas U., St. Paul; BA, U. Minn., Mpls., 1943, BS, 1944, BM, MD, U. Minn., Mpls., 1946. Diplomate Am. Bd. Dermatology, 1953. Intern U. Okla., 1946-47; resident Valley Forge (Pa.) Gen. Hosp., 1947—49, VA Hosp., Mpls., 1949—51, VA Hosp. and U. Minn., Mpls., 1949—51; pvt. practice dermatology Mpls., 1951—; prof. clin. dermatology U. Minn., Mpls., 1970—. Contbr. articles to profl. jours. Capt. MC, U.S. Army, 1947-49. Fellow Royal Soc. Medicine (Britain), Am. Acad. Dermatology (life); mem. AMA, Minn. Med. Soc., Noah Worcester Dermatol. Soc. (bd. dirs. 1988-91), Internat. Dermatol. Soc. Address: Downtown Dermatology PA 825 Nicollet Mall Ste 1629 Minneapolis MN 55402-2705

MANDELL, FLOYD A., lawyer; b. Chgo., June 17, 1948; s. Marvin M. and Estelle (Witt) M.; m. Pamela Sue Cohen, Aug. 31, 1975; children: Chad, Craig. BA magna cum laude, No. Ill. U., 1970; JD, U. Ill., Champaign, 1973. Bar: Ill. 1973, Fla. 1973. Assoc. Dettishell, McAuliffe & Hifestiter, Chgo., 1973-76; sr. ptnr. Katten Muchin Zavis Rosenman, Chgo., 1976—. Dir. Chgo. Bar Assn., 1978-80; planning chmn. Ill. Continuing Legal Edn., Intellectual Property Litigation, Chgo., 1985—. Cpl. USAR, 1969-73. Office: Katten Muchin Zavis Rosenman 525 W Monroe St Ste 1600 Chicago IL 60661-3693 Office Fax: 312-577-8982. E-mail: floyd.mandell@kmzr.com.

MANDELSTAMM, JEROME ROBERT, lawyer; b. St. Louis, Apr. 3, 1932; s. Henry and Estelle (London) M.; m. Carolyn A. White; stepchildren: John M. Gagliardi, Maria A. Amundson, Amy E. Gagliardi. AB, U. Pa., Phila., 1954; LLB, Harvard U., Cambridge, Mass., 1957. Bar: Mo. 1957. Since practiced in, St. Louis; ptnr. Greenfield, Davidson, Mandelstamm & Voorhees, 1969—81, Schmitz, Mandelstamm, Hawker & Fischer, 1981—82; pvt. practice St. Louis, 1982—. Bd. dirs. Legal Aid Soc. City and County St. Louis, 1967-75, pres. 1969-70; bd. dirs. Lawyers Reference Service Met. St. Louis, 1976-83, chmn., 1978-83; bd. dirs. Mo. Legal Aid Soc., 1977-82; mem. 22d Jud. Cir. Bar Com., 1983-85, gen. chmn., 1984-85. Mem. St. Louis County Bd. Election Commrs., 1973-77. Served with AUS, 1957. Mem. ABA, Mo. Bar Assn., Am. Arbitration Assn. (panel of arbitrators 1984-2003), Bar Assn. Met. St. Louis (v.p. 1974-75, treas. 1975-76, William L. Weiss award for Svcs. to the Bar and the Cmty. 2004), Legal Svcs. Ea. Mo. Inc. F. Wm. McCalpin Wall of Justice award, 2002. Home: 7217 Princeton Saint Louis MO 63130-3000 Office: 1010 Market St Ste 1600 Saint Louis MO 63101-2082

MANDERSCHEID, LESTER VINCENT, agricultural economics educator; b. Andrew, Iowa, Oct. 9, 1930; s. Vincent John and Alma (Sprank) M.; m. Dorothy Helen Varnum, Aug. 29, 1953; children: David, Paul, Laura, Jane. BS, Iowa State U., 1951, MS, 1952; PhD, Stanford U., 1961. Grad. asst. Iowa State U., Ames, 1951-52, Stanford (Calif.) U., 1952-56; asst. prof. Mich. State U., East Lansing, 1956-65, assoc. prof., 1965-70, prof., 1970-73, prof., assoc. chmn., 1973-87, prof., chmn., 1987-92, prof., 1992-95, prof. emeritus, 1996—, coord. Grad. Sch., 1993—. Reviewer Tex. A&M Agrl. Econ. Program, College Station, 1989; cons. Consortium Internat. Earth Sci. Info. Network, Ann Arbor, 1990. Co-author: Improving Undergraduate Education, 1967; contbr. articles to jours. in field. Pres. parish coun. St. Thomas, East Lansing, 1984-87; coll. coord. United Way, East Lansing, 1983-84; pres. bd. dirs. Cristo Rey Cmty. Ctr., 1998-2001. Recipient Disting. Faculty award Mich. State U., 1977. Mem. Am. Agrl. Econ. Assn. (pres. 1988-89, bd. dirs. 1982-85, excellence in teaching award 1974), Am. Statis. Assn., Am. Evaluation Assn., Am. Econ. Assn., University Club, Sigma Xi (pres. 1986-87), Phi Kappa Phi (pres. 1979-80). Roman Catholic. Home: 2372 Burcham Dr East Lansing MI 48823-3885 Office: Mich State U Dept of Agrl Econs Circle Dr East Lansing MI 48824-1039 Office Phone: 517-355-0301. Business E-Mail: mandersc@msu.edu.

MANETTA, RICHARD L., chemicals executive, lawyer; b. 1945; BA, U. Mich.; JD, Wayne State U. Legal advisor Detroit City Coun., 1973—74; chief supervising asst./corp. counsel City of Detroit Law Dept., 1974—78; asst. gen. counsel for automotive safety and product litigation Ford Motor Co., 1989—94, asst. gen. counsel for discovery, 1994—99, assoc. gen. counsel for litigation, 1999—2000, dep. gen. counsel, dir. regulatory compliance, 2000—01; corp. v.p., gen. counsel The Dow Chem. Co., Midland, Mich., 2001—04, corp. v.p., spl. counsel to pres., 2004—05. Spkr. in field. Recipient Pres. award, Nat. Bar Assn., 2001, award, Wolverine Bar Assn., 2001, Access to Justice award, State of Mich., 2003. Fellow: Mich. State Bar Found. (life); mem.: ABA, Mich. Gen. Counsel Assn., Mich. State Bar. Home: 59 Lake Shore Rd Grosse Pointe MI 48236

MANGANELLO, TIMOTHY M., auto parts company executive; B of Mech. Engring., U. Mich.; postgrad., Harvard U.; grad., Chrusler Inst. Program. Product engring. mgr. Chrysler Corp., 1973—81; sales mgr. PT Components, 1981—88; v.p. ops. BorgWarner TorqTransfer Systems, Inc., Muncie, Ind., 1995—99, pres., gen. mgr. Chgo., 1999—2001; v.p. BorgWarner, Inc., 1999—2001, exec. v.p., 2001—02, pres., COO, 2002—03, pres., CEO, 2003, chmn., CEO, 2003—. Mem. bd. dir. Bemis Co., Inc. Office: Borgwarner 3850 Hamlin Rd Auburn Hills MI 48326-2872

MANGIERI, PAUL L., lawyer; b. Galesburg, Ill., Jan. 17, 1959; s. Joseph L. and Dorothy Fern (McKinley) M.; m. Lori A. Armstrong, Nov. 17, 1979 (div. Oct. 1990); children: Regina A., Joseph P., Amy E., Michael T.; m. Felicia E. Hunt, Feb. 14, 1991; children: Jessica E. Fredrickson, Rudena J. Fredrickson, Dorothy D., Allison L. BA, Coe Coll., 1981; JD, St. Louis U., 1984. Bar: Ill. 1984, Mo. 1985, U.S. Dist. Ct. (ctrl. dist.) Ill. 1988. Judge adv. gen. USN-USS Saratoga, 1984-88; ptnr. Barash & Stoerzbach, Galesburg, Ill., 1988—. Lt. comdr. USN, 1984-88. Mem. KC. Democrat. Roman Catholic. Avocations: farming, hunting. Office: Barash & Stoerzbach 139 S Cherry St Galesburg IL 61401-4511 Home: 876 Willard St Galesburg IL 61401-2976

MANGLER, ROBERT JAMES, lawyer, judge; b. Chgo., Aug. 15, 1930; s. Robert H. and Agnes E. (Sugrue) M.; m. Geraldine M. Delich, May 2, 1959; children: Robert Jr., Paul, John, Barbara. BS, Loyola U., Chgo., 1952, MA, 1983; JD, Northwestern U., 1955. Bar: Ill. 1958, U.S. Dist. Ct. (no. dist.) Ill. 1959, U.S. Supreme Ct. 1976, U.S. Ct. Appeals (7th cir.) 1980. Author: (with others) Illinois Land Use Law, Illinois Municipal Law. Village atty., prosecutor Village of Wilmette, 1965-93; mcpl. prosecutor City of Evanston, 1963-65, adminstrv. law judge, 2000—; chmn. Ill. Traffic Ct. Conf., 1977—; pres. Ill. Inst. Local Govt. Law; mem. home rule attys. com. Ill. Mcpl. League. Mem. ABA (chmn. adv. com. traffic ct. program), Nat. Inst. Mcpl. Law Officers (past pres.), Ill. Bar Assn. (former chmn. traffic laws and ct. com.), Chgo. Bar Assn. (former chmn. traffic ct. seminar, former chmn. traffic laws com.), Caxton Club, Phi Alpha Delta.

MANGUN, CLARKE WILSON, JR., public health physician, consultant; b. Iowa Falls, Iowa, Feb. 12, 1919; s. Clarke Wilson and Vallie Hazel (Hoffman) M.; m. Edith Lauretta DuBois, May 13, 1945; children: Edith Ann, Nancy June, Laura Jane. BS, U. Iowa, 1940, MD, 1943; MPH, Columbia U., 1947. Diplomate Am. Bd. Preventive Medicine. Commd. officer USPHS, 1945-66; med. adminstr. Am. Hosp. Assn., Chgo., 1966-67, Chgo. Heart Assn., 1967-68, AMA, Chgo., 1969-80; long-term cons. Abbott Labs., North Chicago, Ill., 1980—2004. Recipient award Nat. Bd. Med. Examiners, 1944. Fellow APHA, Am. Coll. Preventive Medicine; mem. AMA (Physician's Recognition award, 1970—). Avocations: photography, travel, gardening. Home: 14001 W 92s St Apt 322 Lenexa KS 66215 Home Phone: 913-495-9995.

MANIN, YURI IVANOVICH, mathematician; b. Simferopol, Crimea, Russia, Feb. 16, 1937; s. Ivan Gavrilovich and Rebecca Zinovievna (Miller) M.; m. Marianna Z. Rosenfeld (div.); 1 child, Dimitri Yurievic; m. Xenia Glebovna Semenova, May 30, 1975. MS, Moscow U., 1958; PhD in Math., Math. Inst., Acad. Scis., Moscow, 1960. Leading rsch. scientist Steklov U., 1960—; prof. & chair mathematics Moscow U., 1965—91; dir. Max Planck Inst. for Mathematics, Bonn, 1995—2005; trustee prof. mathematics Northwestern U., 2002—. Vis. prof. Harvard U., MIT, Coll. de France, Montreal (Que., Can.) U., Utrecht (The Netherlands) U., others. Author: Cubic Forms, 1972, Mathematics and Physics, 1981, Gauge Fields and Complex Geometry, 1988, Frobenius Manifolds, Quantum Cohomology and Moduli Spaces, 1999. Recipient award Moscow Math. Soc., 1963, Lenin award for work in algebraic geometry USSR Govt., 1967, Brouwer medal Netherlands Math. Soc., 1987, Erwin Plein Nemmers prize in mathematics, Northwestern U., 1994, King Faisal Internat. prize in sci., 2002. Fellow Am. Acad. Arts and Scis.; mem. Acad. Scis. Russia (corr.), Royal Acad. Scis. of the Netherlands (fgn. mem.), Academia Europaea, Acad. de Scis. Inst. France (fgn.), Order Pour le Mérite Germany. Avocations: literary criticism, studies in psycholinguistics. Office: Northwestern U 2033 Sheridan Rd Evanston IL 60208 Business E-Mail: manin@mpim-bonn.mpg.de.

MANION, DANIEL ANTHONY, federal judge; b. South Bend, Ind., Feb. 1, 1942; s. Clarence E. and Virginia (O'Brien) Manion; m. Ann Murphy Manion, June 29, 1984. AB, U. otre Dame, 1964; JD, Ind. U., 1973. Bar: Ind., US Dist. Ct. (no. dist.) Ind., US Dist. Ct. (so. dist.) Ind. Dir., indsl. devel. Ind. Dept. Commerce, 1968—73; dep. atty. gen. State of Ind., 1973—74; from assoc. to ptnr. Doran, Manion, Boynton, Kamm & Esmont, South Bend, 1974—86; judge US Ct. Appeals (7th Cir.), South Bend, 1986—2007, sr. judge, 2007—. Mem. Ind. State Senate, Indpls., 1978—82; dir. St. Joseph Bank & Trust Co., 1979—86. With US Army, 1965—66. Office: US Ct Appeals US Courthouse & Federal Bldg 204 S Main St Rm 301 South Bend IN 46601-2122

MANION, THOMAS A., chancellor; b. Aug. 10, 1934; m. Maureen O'Mara; children: Gregory, Marcy, Andrew, Margaret, Vicki, Tina, Thomas. BBA, St. Bonaventure U., 1959; MBA, Boston Coll., 1962; PhD, Clark U., 1968; D.Pedagogy, Bryant Coll., 1973. Chmn. econs. dept., dean grad. sch., acad. provost v.p. Bryant Coll., Smithfield, R.I.; pres. Coll. Saint Rose, Albany, N.Y., 1973-83, St. Nobert Coll., De Pere, Wis., 1983-2000, chancellor, 2000—. Bd. dirs. Associated Kellogg Bank, Green Bay, Wis. Bd. dirs. Higher Edn. Aids Coun., State of Wis. Mem. NCAA, Nat. Assn. Ind. Colls. and Univs. (mem. commn. on campus concerns), Am. Assn. Higher Edn., Am. Coun. Edn., Nat. Cath. Edn. Assn., Assn. Cath. Colls. and Univs., Coun. Ind. Colls. (bd. dirs.), Wis. Assn. Ind. Colls. and Univs. (pres.), Wis. Found. Ind. Colls., Delta Epsilon, Delta Mu Delta. Office: St Norbert Coll 100 Grant St De Pere WI 54115-2002

MANKA, RONALD EUGENE, lawyer; b. Wichita, Kans., Dec. 12, 1944; s. James Ashford and Jane Bunn (Meeks) M.; m. Frances Ann Patterson, Aug. 7, 1965 (dec. Dec. 1985); children: Kimberly Ann, Lora Christine; m. Linda I. Bailey, Mar. 11, 1995. BBA cum laude, U. Kans., 1967; JD cum laude, U. Mich., 1970. Bar: Conn. 1970, Mo. 1974, Kans. 1985, Colo. 2001. Assoc. Day, Barry & Howard, Hartford, Conn., 1970-73, Lathrop & Gage L.C., Kansas City, Mo., 1973-78, mem., 1979-82, 85—; group counsel Butler Mfg. Co., Kansas City, 1982-83, div. gen. mgr., 1983—84. Legal com. Boulder County Cmty. Found., Colo., 2002—. Trustee, clk., elder Village Presbyn. Ch., Prairie Village, Kans.; dir., treas. Lyric Opera of Kansas City, 1995—; pres. Genesis Sch., Kansas City, 1987-89; devel. chmn. Kansas City Friends of Alvin Ailey, 1987-89; chmn. Kansas City Mus., 1988-92, gen. counsel, 1994—; gen. counsel Kansas City C. of C., 1989-2001; pres. Ctr. for Mgmt. Assistance, Kansas City, 1991-93; dir. Colo. Music Festival, 2002-. Mem. ABA, Mo. Bar Assn. (alt. dispute resolution com. 1986-2002), Lawyers Assn. Kansas City, Silicon Prairie Tech. Assn. (bd. dirs. 1990-92), Homestead Country Club (pres. 1984-85). Democrat. Avocations: bicycling, swimming. Home: 875 11th St Boulder CO 80302 Office: Colorado Venture Mgmt 2575 Park Ln #200 Lafayette CO 80026-3200 Fax: 720-931-3001. E-mail: RManka@LathropGage.com.

MANLEY, ROBERT EDWARD, lawyer, economist; b. Cin., Nov. 24, 1935; s. John M. and Helen Catherine (McCarthy) M.; m. Roberta L. Anzinger, Oct. 21, 1971 (div. 1980); 1 child, Robert Edward. ScB in Econs, Xavier U., 1956; AM in Econ. Theory, U. Cin., 1957; JD, Harvard U., 1960; postgrad., London Sch. Econs. and Polit. Sci., 1960, MIT, 1972. Bar: Ohio 1960, U.S. Supreme Ct. 1970. Pvt. practice law, Cin., 1960—; chmn. Manley Burke, 1977. Taft teaching fellow econs. U. Cin., 1956-57, vis. lectr. community planning law Coll. Design, Architecture and Art, 1967-73, adj. assoc. prof. urban planning Coll. Design, Architecture, Art and Planning, 1972-81, adj. prof., 1981—, adj. prof. law, 1980—. Author: Metropolitan School Desegregation, 1978, (with Robert N. Cook) Management of Land and Environment, 1981, others; chmn. editl. adv. bd. Urban Lawyer, 1986-95. Mem. Hamilton County Pub. Defender Commn., 1976-79; trustee HOPE, Cin., Albert J. Ryan Found.; counsel, co-founder Action Housing for Greater Cin.; mem. Spl. Commn. on Formation U. Cin. Health Maintenance Orgn., Mayor Cin. Spl. Com. on Housing; chmn. Cin. Environ. Adv. Coun., 1975-76; trustee The Americas Fund for Ind. Univs., 1987-2000; trustee Ohio Planning Conf., 1982-91, pres., 1987-89, trustee, 1987-90; sec. Cin. Mounted Patrol Com., 1993—; active Bd. Cin. Downtown Coun., 1991-98. Mem. ABA (coun. sect. local govt. law 1976-80, 81-85, 88-92), Ohio Bar Assn., Cin. Bar Assn., Am. Judicature Soc., Law and Soc. Assn., Nat. Coun. Crime and Delinquency, Harvard U. Law Sch. Assn. Cin. (pres. 1970-71), Am. Econ. Assn., Am. Acad. Polit. and Social Sci., Queen City Club, Explorers Club (N.Y.C.) (trustee, sec. Clark chpt. 1992—), Athenaeum Club (Phila.), S.Am. Explorers (Lima, Peru). Republican. Roman Catholic. Office: Manley Burke 225 W Court St Cincinnati OH 45202-1052 Office Phone: 513-721-5525. E-mail: rmanley@manleyburke.com.

MANN, DAVID SCOTT, lawyer, former congressman; b. Cin., Sept. 25, 1939; s. Henry M. and Helen Faye M.; m. Elizabeth Taliaferro, Oct. 5, 1963; children:

Michael, Deborah, Marshall. AB cum laude, Harvard Coll., 1961, LLB magna cum laude, 1968. Bar: Ohio 1968. Assoc. Dinsmore & Shohl, Cin., 1968-74, ptnr., 1974-83, Taliaferro and Mann, Cin., 1983-92; councilman City of Cin., 1974-92, mayor, 1980-82, 91; mem. 103d Congress 1st Ohio dist., Washington, 1993-94; mem. armed svcs. com., mem. jud. com. Washington; of counsel Thompson, Hine and Flory, Cin., 1995-96; pvt. practice Mann & Mann, LLC, Cin., 1997—. Adj. prof. Coll. Law U. Cin., 1995—2002. Editor Harvard Law Rev., 1966-68, notes editor, 1967-68; contbr. articles to profl. jours. Mem., chmn. Cin. Bd. Health, 1972-74. With USN, 1961-65. Mem. Cin. Bar Assn. Democrat. Methodist. Home: 568 Evanswood Pl Cincinnati OH 45220-1527 Office Phone: 513-621-2888. Business E-Mail: david@mannandmannlaw.com.

MANN, DAVID WILLIAM, minister; b. Elkhart, Ind., Apr. 17, 1947; s. Herbert Richard and Kathryn (Bontrager) M.; m. Brenda Marie Frantz, June 7, 1969; children: Troy, Todd, Erika. BA, Bethel Coll., 1969; MS, Nat. Louis U., 1986. Ordained to ministry Missionary Ch., 1978. Campus life dir. Youth for Christ, Elkhart, 1969-77; denominational youth dir. Missionary Ch., Ft. Wayne, Ind., 1977-81, Christian edn. dir., 1981-88, U.S. dir. missions, 1990—; assoc. dir. World Ptnrs., Ft. Wayne, 1988-90. Dir. Missionary Ch. Vol. Svc., Ft. Wayne, 1983—, World Ptnrs. USA, 1998—. Author: (with others) Youth Leaders Source Book, 1985; contbr. articles to prof. jour. Mgr. Little League, Ft. Wayne, 1981-89, bd. dirs. 1986. Recipient Alumnus of the Year award, Bethel Coll., 2003. Mem. Nat. Assn. Evangelicals, Evangelical Fellowship of Mission Agys. (nat. bd. dirs. 1999—), Denominational Execs. in Christian Edn. (chmn. 1988), Aldersgate Pub. Assn. (bd. dirs. 1985, 87), Nat. Christian Edn. Assn. (exec. com. 1987-89). Avocations: baseball, skiing, fishing, woodworking. Office: Missionary Ch PO Box 9127 Fort Wayne IN 46899-9127 Home Phone: 260-396-2509; Office Phone: 260-747-2027. E-mail: manndw@aol.com.

MANN, HENRY DEAN, accountant, bank executive; b. El Dorado, Ark., Feb. 8, 1943; s. Paul L. and Mary Louise (Capps) M.; m. Rebecca Balch, Aug. 14, 1965; children: Julie Elizabeth, Betsey Sawyer Mann. BSBA, U. Ark., 1965. CPA, Mo., Tex. Staff acct., mgr. Ernst & Whinney, Houston, 1967-76, ptnr., 1976-77; regional personnel ptnr. Ernst & Whinney (now Ernst & Young), St. Louis, 1977-78, mng. ptnr., 1978-88; pres. Mann Industries, Inc., St. Louis, 1988-89; pres., dir. 1st Capital Corp., Ft. Scott, Kans., 1989—, chmn., CEO, dir., 1989—, Citizens Bank, N.A., Fort Scott, Kans., 1989—. CEO, chmn. bd. dirs. Humble (Tex.) at. Bank, 1992-98; adv. bd. U. Mo. Sch. Accountancy, Columbia, 1979-82; bd. dirs. Cupples Co. Mfrs., St. Louis. Treas. Jr. Achievement, St. Louis, 1984-98, bd. dirs., 1986-98; treas., bd. dirs. United Way, St. Louis, 1986-92, Art and Edn. Coun., St. Louis, 1986-91; bd. dirs. St. Louis Symphony, 1988-89, Mercy Hosp. Found., Ft. Scott, Kans., 2000—, Bankers Bank of Kans., Wichita, 2000—; bd. dirs. Kammergild Chamber Orch., St. Louis, 1986, pres., 1983-85. Mem. AICPA, Mo. Soc. CPAs, Ft. Scott C. of C. (bd. dirs., pres.2001—), Bellerive Country Club (treas. 1986-87, v.p. 1988-89), Beta Gamma Sigma, Beta Alpha Psi. Presbyn. Office: Citizens Bank NA 200 S Main St Fort Scott KS 66701-2045

MANN, PHILLIP LYNN, data processing company executive; b. Charleston, W.Va., July 26, 1944; s. Clarence Edward and Virginia Charlotte (Rupe) M.; m. Edith Jane Dewell, Dec. 28, 1966 (div. 1977); 1 child, Cynthia Lynn; m. Phyllis Anita Berg, May 18, 1979; children: Stacia Lynn, Brandon Granville. BSEE, Purdue U., 1970; MBA, U. Chgo., 1975. Devel. engr. Western Electric Co., Inc., Lisle, Ill., 1970-77; v.p. Uniq Digital Techs., Inc., Batavia, Ill., 1977-88; pres. ProTech Computer Group, Inc., Batavia, 1988—. Served with USN, 1962-66. Avocations: radio control helicopters, fishing. Home: 428 Meadowrue Ln Batavia IL 60510-2815 Office: ProTech Computer Group Inc 428 Meadowrue Ln Batavia IL 60510-2815 Office Phone: 630-879-1566.

MANNA, JOHN S., fraternal organization administrator; Office: Woodmen of the World 1700 Farnam St Ste 2200 Omaha NE 68102-2007

MANNA, MARTIN, public relations executive, marketing executive; b. 1972; Pres. Chaldean Am. Chamber of Commerce, Farmington Hills, Mich., 2003—; co-founder Bank of Mich.; mng. ptnr. Interlink Media, Farmington Hills, Mich. Co-publisher The Chaldean News. Named one of 40 Under 40, Crain's Detroit Bus., 2006. Office: Chaldean American Chamber of Commerce 30095 Northwestern Hwy Ste 102 Farmington Hills MI 48334 Office Phone: 248-538-3700. Office Fax: 248-932-9161.

MANNING, BLANCHE M., federal judge; b. 1934; BEd, Chgo. Tchrs. Coll., 1961; JD, John Marshall Law Sch., 1967; MA, Roosevelt Univ., 1972; LLM, Univ. of Va. Law Sch., 1992; DHL (hon.), Chgo. State U., 1998. Asst. states atty. State's Atty.'s Office (Cook County), Ill., 1968-73; supervisory trial atty. U.S. EEOC, Chgo., 1973-77; gen. atty. United Airlines, Chgo., 1977-78; asst. U.S. atty. U.S. Dist. Ct. (no. dist.) Ill., 1978-79; assoc. judge Cir. Ct. of Cook County, 1979-86, circuit judge, 1986-87; appellate court judge Ct. of Review Ill. Appellate Ct., 1987-94; district judge U.S. Dist. Ct. (no. dist.) Ill., Chgo., 1994—. Tchr. A. O. Sexton Elem. Sch. James Wadsworth Elem. Sch., Wendell Phillips H.S. Adult Program, Morgan Park H.S. Summer Sch. Program, South Shore H.S. Summer Sch. Program, Carver H.S. Adult Edn. Program; lectr. Malcolm X C.C., 1970-71; adj. prof. NCBL C.C. of Law, 1978-79, DePaul Univ. Law Sch., 1992—; tchg. team mem. Trial Advocacy Workshop, Harvard Law Sch., U. Chgo. Law Sch., 1991—; chmn. Com. on Recent Devels. in Evidence, Ill. Judicial Conf., 1991; faculty mem. New Judges Seminar, Ill. Judicial Conf.; past faculty mem. Profl. Devel. Seminar for New Assoc. Judges, Cook County Cir. Ct.; past mem. bd. dirs., trained intervenor Lawyers' Assistance Program, Inc.; past mem. adv. coun. Lawyer's Asst. Program, Roosevelt U. Former trustee Sherwood Music Conservatory Bd.; clarinetist Cmty. Concert band Chgo. State U.; saxophonist Jazz ensemble, Chgo. State U. Jazz Band, jazz band Diversity. Mem. Cook County Bar Assn. (second v-p 1974), Nat. Bar Assn., Nat. Judicial Coun., Ill. Judicial Coun. (treas. 1982-85, chmn. 1988, chmn. judiciary com. 1992), Ill. State Bar Assn. (past mem. bd. dirs. Lawyers Assistance Program Inc.), Am. Bar Assn. (fellow 1991), Chgo. Bar Assn. (clarinetist Symphony Orch., saxophonist), John Marshall Law Sch. Alumni Assn. (bd. dirs.), Chgo. State Univ. Alumni Assn. (bd. dirs.). Office: US Dist Ct 2156 US Courthouse 219 S Dearborn St Ste 2050 Chicago IL 60604-1800

MANNING, DANIEL RICARDO, professional basketball player; b. Hattiesburg, Miss., May 17, 1966; s. Ed Manning. Student, U. Kans. Forward L.A. Clippers, 1988-93, Atlanta Hawks, 1993-94, Phoenix Suns, 1994-99, Milw. Bucks, 1999—. Recipient Bronze medal U.S. Olympic Basketball Team, 1988; named Most Outstanding Player NCAA Divsn. I Tournament, 1988, Naismith award, 1988, Wooden award, 1988; named to Sporting News NCAA All-Am. first team, 1987, 88, NBA All-Star Team, 1993-94. Achievements include first pick overall NCAA draft, 1988; mem. NCAA Divsn. I Championship team, 1988. Office: Milw Bucks 1001 N 4th St Milwaukee WI 53203-1314

MANNING, JOHN WARREN, III, retired surgeon, medical educator; b. Phila., Nov. 24, 1919; s. John Warren Jr. and Edith Margaret (Reagan) M.; m. Muriel Elizabeth Johnson, Oct. 11, 1944; children: John, Melissa, Susan. BS in Chemistry with honors, Ursinus Coll., 1940; MD, U. Pa., 1943; postgrad., 1978. Diplomate Am. Bd. Surgery. Naval intern Pa. Naval Hosp., 1946; resident Saginaw (Mich.) Gen. Hosp., 1947-50; preceptor Dr. H.M. Bishop, 1950-52; pvt. practice Saginaw, 1950—. Sr. staff mem. Saginaw Gen. Hosp., St. Luke's Hosp., Saginaw; past chief of surgery, chmn. tissue com. St. Mary's Hosp., Saginaw; cons. VA Hosp., Saginaw; assoc. clin. prof. surgery Mich. State U., assoc. prof. surgery, 1976-92, prof. emeritus, 1992—; mem. search com. Saginaw Coop. Hosp. Contbr. articles to profl. publs. Lt. USN, 1942-46, PTO. Fellow ACS; mem. AMA, Mich. State Med. Soc., Saginaw Surg. Soc., Soc. Abdominal Surgeons, Am. Coll. Angiology, Soc. Am. Gastrointestinal Endoscopic Surgeons. Office Phone: 989-793-0712.

MANNING, KENNETH PAUL, specialty chemical company executive; b. NYC, Jan. 18, 1942; s. John Joseph and Edith Helen (Hoffmann) M.; m. Maureen Lambert, Sept. 12, 1964; children: Kenneth J., John J., Elise, Paul, Carolyn, Jacqueline. BME, Rensselaer Poly. Inst., 1963; postgrad., George Washington U., 1965-66; MBA in Ops. Rsch., Am. U., 1968. With W.R. Grace & Co., NYC, 1973-87, v.p. European consumer divsn., 1975-76, pres. edol. products divsn., 1976-79, pres. real estate divsn., 1979-81, v.p. corp. tech. group, 1981-83, pres., CEO, Ambrosia Chocolate Co. divsn. Milw., 1983-87; group v.p. Sensient Technologies Corp., Milw., 1987-89, exec. v.p., dir., 1989-92, pres., COO, dir., 1992-96, pres., CEO, dir., 1996—, chmn., CEO, 1997—. Bd. dirs. Badger Meter, Inc., Milw., Sealed Air Corp., Saddle Brook, N.J. Served as lt. USN, 1963-67; rear adm. USNR, ret. Decorated Legion of Merit, Nat. Def. medal, others. Mem. ASME, Am. Chem. Soc., avy League, US Naval Inst., Naval Res. Assn., Milw. Metro Assn. Commerce, Knights of Malta. Republican. Roman Catholic. Office: Sensient Technologies Corp 777 E Wisconsin Ave Milwaukee WI 53202-5304

MANNING, PEYTON, professional football player; b. New Orleans, Mar. 24, 1976; s. Archie and Olivia Manning; m. Ashley Thompson, Mar. 17, 2001. BA in Speech Comm., U. Tenn., 1998. Quarterback Indpls. Colts, 1998—. Founder PeyBack Found., 1999. Co-recipient NFL MVP award, AP, 2003; named NFL Player of Yr., The Sporting News, 2003, NFL Offensive Player of Yr., 2004, NFL Pro Bowl MVP, 2005, Super Bowl XLI MVP, 2007; named one of The Most Influential People in the World of Sports, Bus. Week, 2007; named to Am. Football Conf. Pro-Bowl Team, 1999—2000, 2002—06, NFL All-Pro First-Team, 2003—06; recipient Am. Dream award, Hudson Inst., 2001, Henry P. Iba Citizen Athlete award, 2002, Bert Bell award, Maxwell Club, 2003—04, John Wooden trophy, Athletes for a Better World, 2004, Espy award for best NFL player, 2004, NFL MVP, AP, 2004, Byron "Whizzer" White Humanitarian award, 2005, Walter Payton Man of Yr. award, 2005, Espy award for Best Championship Performance, 2007. Achievements include leading the NFL in completions and passing yards in the 2000 and 2003 seasons; holding the NFL's single season record for most touchdown passes (49), 2004. Office: Indianapolis Colts PO Box 535000 Indianapolis IN 46253-5000 also: Indianapolis Colts 7001 West 56th Streeet Indianapolis IN 46254

MANNING, SYLVIA, language educator; b. Montreal, Que., Can., Dec. 2, 1943; came to U.S., 1967; d. Bruno and Lea Bank; m. Peter J. Manning, Aug. 20, 1967; children— Bruce David, Jason Maurice BA, McGill U., 1963; MA, Yale U., 1964, PhD in English, 1967. Asst. prof. English Calif. State U.-Hayward, 1967-71, assoc. prof., 1971-75, assoc. dean, 1972-75; assoc. prof. U. So. Calif., 1975-94, prof., assoc. dir. Ctr. for Humanities, 1975-77, assoc. dir. Ctr. for Humanities, 1975-77, chmn. freshman writing, 1977-80, chmn. dept. English, 1980-83, vice provost, exec. v.p., 1984-94; prof. English U. Ill., Champaign, 1994—, v.p. for acad. affairs, prof. English, 1994—, interim chancellor Chgo., 1999-2000, chancellor, 2000—. Author: Dickens as Satirist, 1971; Hard Times: An Annotated Bibliography, 1984. Contbr. essays to mags. Woodrow Wilson fellow, 1963-64, 66-67 Mem. MLA, Dickens Soc. Office: U of Ill Office of Chancellor 2833 University Hall 601 S Morgan St Chicago IL 60607-7100 Office Phone: 312-413-3350.

MANNING, WILLIAM DUDLEY, JR., retired specialty chemical company executive; b. Tampa, Fla., Mar. 7, 1934; s. William Dudley and Rebecca (Reid) M.; m. Carol Randolph Gillis, June 30, 1962; children: Carol Randolph, Rebecca Barrett, Anne Gillis. BA in Chemistry, Fla. State U., 1957. Sales rep. Amoco Chem. Co., St. Louis and Cleve., 1959-63; sales engr. The Lubrizol Corp., Tulsa, 1963-64, southwestern regional sales mgr., 1964-66, mgr. chem. product sales Wickliffe, Ohio, 1966-72, sales mgr., western U.S., 1972, gen. sales mgr., asst. div. head-sales, 1972-79, mktg. mgr., asst. div. head-sales, 1979-80, v.p. mktg., 1980-81, v.p., bus. devel. div., 1981-85, sr. v.p. sales and mktg., 1985-87; pres. Lubrizol Petroleum Chems. Co., Wickliffe, 1987-94; sr. v.p., asst. to pres. The Lubrizol Corp., 1994; cons., investor, 1994—. Bd. dirs. NYCO Am. LLC, Gates Missionio, Robbins and Myers, Dayton, Ohio, N.Y. Trustee Vocat. Guidance Svcs., Cleve., 1991-2000, Borromeo Sem., 2000—. With USAR, 1957-63. Mem. Soc. Automotive Engrs. (assoc.), Kirtland Country Club (v.p. 1986-88, pres. 1988-89), Tavern Club (trustee 1986-91), Chagrin Valley Hunt Club. Republican. Roman Catholic. Office Phone: 440-423-0561. E-mail: wdmann4@cs.com.

MANNING, WILLIAM HENRY, lawyer; b. Dallas, Feb. 5, 1951; BA, Creighton U., 1973; JD, Hamline U., 1978. Bar: Minn. 1978, U.S. Dist. Ct. Minn. 1978, U.S. Ct. Appeals (8th cir.) 1979; cert. civil trial specialist. Spl. asst. atty. gen. Minn. Atty. Gen.'s Office, St. Paul, 1980-83, dir. tort litigation div., 1984-86; ptnr. Robins, Kaplan, Miller & Ciresi, Mpls., 1986—. Office: Robins Kaplan Miller & Ciresi 800 Lasalle Ave Ste 2800 Minneapolis MN 55402-2015

MANNIX, PATRICK C., manufacturing executive; Various positions Ralston Purina, Co. (formerly part of Union Carbide), Sydney, Australia, 1963-85; chmn. Eveready Battery Co. Asia Pacific, Hong Kong, 1985-91; exec. v.p. to corp. v.p. Ralston Purina, 1991, 92-95, pres. Eveready Specialty Bus., 1995-98; v.p., pres. Eveready Battery Co., Inc. Ralston Purina, Co., St. Louis, 1998—. Office: Ralston Purina Co Checkerboard Sq Saint Louis MO 63164-0001

MANOOGIAN, RICHARD ALEXANDER, consumer products company executive; b. Long Branch, NJ, July 30, 1936; s. Alex and Marie (Tatian) Manoogian; m. Jane Manoogian; children: James, Richard, Bridget. BA in Econs, Yale U., 1958. Asst. to pres. Masco Corp., Taylor, Mich., 1958-62, exec. v.p., 1962-68, pres., 1968-85, chmn. bd., CEO, 1985—. Chmn., dir. Mascotech, Inc., Trimas Corp.; dir. First Chgo. NBD Corp., Bank One Corp., Ford Motor Co., Metaldyne Corp., Detroit Renaissance, Am. Bus. Conf. Chmn. Alex & Marie Manoogian Found.; pres. & treas. Richard & Jane Manoogian Found.; co-founder Mackinac Island Cmty. Found., 2003; trustee U. Liggett Sch., State Dept. Fine Arts Comsn., Founder's Soc., Detroit Inst. Arts, Center for Creative Studies; trustee coun. Nat. Gallery Art. Mem. Yale Alumni Assn. Clubs: Grosse Pointe Yacht, Grosse Pointe Hunt, Country Club Detroit, Detroit Athletic. Office: Masco Corp 21001 Van Born Rd Taylor MI 48180-1300

MANOS, JOHN, editor-in-chief; Editor-in-chief Consumer's Digest, Chgo., 1987—.

MANOUS, PETER J., lawyer; m. Susan Severtson Manous. BS in pub. adminstrn. & mgmt., Ind. Univ., 1984; law degree, Valparaiso U., 1987. Bar: Ind. State Bar Assn. Pvt. atty., 1994—; coord. Frank O'Bannon's Campaign, 1996—2000; adv. Governor Residence Commn. Bd. dirs. Lake Area United Way; past pres. Millennium Housing Found.; Lake County Welfare to Work Coun.; mem. N.W. Ind. Quality Life Coun.; bd. dirs. Tradewinds; mem. Ind. Dem. Party Deputy Chairmen; regional coord. Evan Bayh U.S. Senate; vol. Kennedy for Pres. Campaign, 1980; mem. St. George Greek Orthodox Ch. Mem.: Am. Bar Assn., Lake County Bar Assn. Democrat. Office: 9111 Broadway Ste GG Merrillville IN 46410

MANSELL, KEVIN B., retail executive; b. St. Louis; Student, U. Mo. With Venture Store divsn. May Dept. Stores, 1975, positions in merchandising and buying; divisional mdse. mgr. Kohl's Corp., Menomonee Falls, Wis., 1982—87, gen. mdse. mgr., 1987, sr. exec. v.p. merchandising and mktg., 1998—99, pres., 1999—, bd. dirs., 1999—. Office: Kohls Corp N56 W17000 Ridgewood Dr Menomonee Falls WI 53051-5660 Office Phone: 262-703-7000.

MANSKE, PAUL ROBERT, orthopedic hand surgeon, educator; b. Ft. Wayne, Ind., Apr. 29, 1938; s. Alfred R. and Elsa E. (Streufert) M.; m. Sandra H. Henricks, Nov. 29, 1975; children: Ethan Paul, Claire Bruch, Louisa Hendricks. BA, Valparaiso U., 1960, DSc (hon.), 1985; MD, Washington U., St. Louis, 1964. Diplomate Am. Bd. Surgery. Intern U. Wash., Seattle, 1964-65, resident in surgery, 1965-66; resident in orthopedic surg. Washington U., St. Louis, 1969-72; hand surgery fellow U. Louisville, 1971; instr. orthopedic surgery Washington U. Med. Sch., St. Louis, 1972-76, asst. prof. orthopedic surgery, 1976-83, prof., 1983—, chmn. dept., 1983-95. Editor-in-chief Jour. Hand Surgery, 1996—; contbr. over 215 articles to profl. jours. Lt. comdr. USN, 1966-69, Vietnam. Fellow AMA, Am. Acad. Orthopaedic Surgery (Elizabeth Winston Lanier award, 1985Am. Orthopaedic Assn.; mem. Am. Soc. Surgery of the Hand, Alpha Omega Alpha. Office: Washington Univ Sch Medicine Dept Orthop Surgery Box 8233 660 S Euclid Ave Saint Louis MO 63110-1036

MANSOORI, G. ALI, chemical engineer, educator; b. Naragh, Iran, Oct. 8, 1940; came to the U.S., 1964; s. Abbas and Khanam (Eslami) M.; m. Manijeh Mansoori, Jan. 10, 1992; 1 child,:Rana Mariam. BSChE, U. Tehran, 1963; MSChE, U. Minn., 1967; PhD, U. Okla., 1969; postdoctoral fellow, Rice U., 1969-70. Prof. U. Ill., Chgo., 1970—. Vis. scientist Argonne (Ill.) Nat. Lab., 1974-80, Nat. Inst. Standards and Tech., Boulder, Colo., 1983, 87, CRN-Pisa, Italy, 1985, 86; vis. prof. Bandug (Indonesia) Inst. Tech., 1992, 94; cons. numerous orgns. including Chevron, ARCO, Pertamina, NIOC, PEMEX, IMP, PETROBAS. Editor several jours.; series editor: Advances in Thermodynamics, 1987—; contbr. over 170 articles to profl. jours. Mem. AIChE, SPE, Internat. Non-Renewable Energy Source Conf. (tech. program chair 1993—), Internat. Fluid and Thermal Energy Conf. (tech. program co-chair 1994—). Avocations: mountain climbing, tennis, racquetball, swimming. Home: 1530 N Dearborn Pkwy Apt 23S Chicago IL 60610-1496

MANSOUR, GEORGE P., Spanish language and literature educator; b. Huntington, W.Va., Sept. 4, 1939; s. Elia and Marie (Yazbek) M.; m. Mary Ann Rogers, Dec. 27, 1961; children: Alicia, Philip. AB, Marshall U., 1961; MA, Mich. State U., 1963, PhD, 1965. Assoc. prof. Mich. State U., East Lansing, 1968-77, prof., 1977—, chmn. dept. Romance and Classical langs., 1982—. Cons. Mich. Dept. Edn., Lansing, 1984-85. Contbr. articles to profl. jours., including Hispania, Revista de estudias, hispanicos, also chpts. to books. Mem. Am. Assn. Tchrs. Spanish and Portuguese (v.p. 1969-71), Mich. Fgn. Lang. Assn. (pres. 1982-84). Democrat. Mem. Eastern Orthodox Ch. Avocations: pysanky, golf. Home: 1303 Lucerne Dr Dewitt MI 48820-9528 Office: Mich State U Dept Romance & Classical Langs East Lansing MI 48824 Office Phone: 517-285-1487. Personal E-mail: mansour1515@yahoo.com.

MANSUETO, JOSEPH DANIEL, publisher; b. East Chicago, Ind., Sept. 3, 1956; s. Mario Daniel and Sara Wilda (Smart) M. BBA, U. Chgo., 1978, MBA, 1980. Securities analyst Harris Assocs., Chgo., 1983-84; founder, chmn., prin. Morningstar, Chgo., 1984—, CEO, 1984—96, 2000—. Named one of Forbes' Richest Americans, 2006; recipient Rosenthal Award for Excellence in Investment Research, Univ. Chgo., 1992, KPMG Peat Marwick High Tech Entrepreneur of Yr. award, 1993, Disting. Entrepreneurial Alumnus award, Univ. Chgo., 2000. Office: 225 W Wacker Dr Chicago IL 60606 Office Phone: 312-696-6000.

MANTERNACH, GENE, state representative, farmer; b. Dec. 1953; Farmer, Cascade, Iowa; state rep. dist. 31 Iowa Ho. of Reps., 2001—; mem. agr. com.; mem. econ. devel. com.; mem. transp. com.; vice chair appropriations com. Republican.

MANTHEY, THOMAS RICHARD, lawyer; b. St. Cloud, Minn., May 5, 1942; s. Richard Jesse and Dolores Theresa (Terhaar) M.; m. Janet S. Barth, Dec. 18, 1965; children: Molly, Andrew, Luke. BA cum laude, St. John's U., Collegeville, Minn., 1964; JD cum laude, Harvard U., 1967. Bar: Minn. 1967. Assoc. Dorsey & Whitney, Mpls., 1967-73, ptnr. real estate dept., 1974—, also mem. Indian and gaming law practice group, chmn. real estate workout practice group. Contbr. articles to profl. jours. Capt. U.S. Army, 1968-70. Mem. Minn. State Bar Assn. (real estate sect.), Hennepin County Bar Assn. (real estate sect.). Roman Catholic. Avocations: volleyball, golf, fishing. Home: 9958 Wellington Ln Woodbury MN 55125-8459 Office: Dorsey & Whitney 50 S 6th St Ste 1500 Minneapolis MN 55402-1553

MANTIL, JOSEPH CHACKO, nuclear medicine physician, researcher; b. Kottayam, Kerala, India, Apr. 22, 1937; came to U.S., 1958; s. Chacko C. and Mary C. Manthuruthil; m. Joan J. Cunningham, June 18, 1966; children: Ann Marie, Lisa Susan. BS in Physics, Chemistry and Math. with distinction, Poona U., India, 1956; MS, U. Detroit, 1960; PhD, Ind. U., 1965; MS in Biological Scis., Wright State U., 1975; MD, U. Autonoma de Ciudad Juarez, Mex., 1977. Diplomate Am. Bd. Internal Medicine, Am. Bd. Nuclear Medicine; lic. physician, Ohio, Ind., Ky. Rsch. physicist Aerospace Rsch. Lab, Wright Patterson AFB, Ohio, 1964-75; chief resident, resident in internal medicine Good Samaritan Hosp., Dayton, Ohio, 1977-80; chief resident, resident in nuclear medicine Cin. Med. Ctr., 1980-82; assoc. dir., divsn. nuclear med. Kettering (Ohio) Med. Ctr., 1982-86, dir. dept. nuclear medicine/PET, 1986—; dir. Kettering-Scott Magnetic Resonance Lab., Kettering Med. Ctr. Wright State U. Sch. Medicine, Kettering, 1985—, clin. prof. medicine, chief divsn. nuclear medicine, dept. medicine, 1988—. Served as session chmn., speaker, amd co-organizer for five internat. confs. Author: Radioactivity in Nuclear Spectroscopy Vol. I and II, 1972; contbr. 38 articles to profl. jours. Mem. ACP, Am. Physical Soc., Soc. Nuclear Medicine, Soc. Magnetic Resonance in Medicine, Soc. Magnetic Resonance Imaging. Achievements include research in proton and phosphorous NMR spectroscopy and glucose metabolism (using PET) in various types of dementia; use of NMR spectroscopy (both proton and phosphorous) and positron emission tomography (measurement of glucose and protein metabolism) in the study of tumors and assessment of thier reponse to chemotherapy and radiation therapy; positron emission tomography in the study of myocardial viabilty; PET in the diagnosis of coronary artery disease; PET in seizire disorders; PET in solid tumors, devel. of positron probe as an aid in the surgical vesection of tumors, gene therapy of glioblastoma mustiforme. Home: 6040 Mad River Rd Dayton OH 45459-1508 Office: Kettering Med Ctr 3535 Southern Blvd Kettering OH 45429-1221

MANTONYA, JOHN BUTCHER, lawyer; b. Columbus, Ohio, May 26, 1922; s. Elroy Letts and Blanche (Butcher) M.; m. Mary E. Reynolds, June 14, 1947 (dec. 1987); children: Elizabeth Claire, Mary Kay, Lee Ann; m. Carole L. Lugar, Sept. 28, 1989. AB cum laude, Washington and Jefferson Coll., 1943; postgrad., U. Mich. Law Sch., 1946—47; JD, Ohio State U., 1949. Bar: Ohio 1949. Assoc. A.S. Mitchell, Atty., Newark, Ohio, 1949—50, C.D. Lindrooth, Newark, 1950—57; ptnr. firm Lindrooth & Mantonya, Newark, 1957—74; firm John B. Mantonya, 1974—81, John B. Mantonya, L.P.A., 1981—. Mem. North Fork Local Bd. Edn., 1962-69; adv. com. Salvation Army, Licking County, 1965—, Mayor of Utica, Ohio, 1953-59. Served with AUS, 1943-45. Mem. ABA, Ohio Bar Assn., Licking County Bar Assn. (pres. 1967), Phi Delta Phi, Beta Theta Pi. Home: 11055 Reynolds Rd Utica OH 43080-9549 Office: 3 N 3rd St Newark OH 43055-5506 Business E-Mail: jb.mantonya@alltel.com.

MANTULIN, WILLIAM W., biophysicist, lab administrator; b. Munich, Bavaria, Germany, Apr. 5, 1946; came to U.S., 1950; BS, U. Rochester, 1968; PhD, Northeastern U., 1972. Postdoctoral fellow Tex. Tech U., Lubbock, 1972-74, U. Ill., Urbana, 1975-77, adj. assoc. prof., 1986—, dir. Lab. Fluorescence Dynamics, 1986—; instr. Baylor Coll. Medicine, Houston, 1978-83, asst. prof., 1984-86. Cons. Exxon Corp., Houston, 1980-84. Author: (book chpt.) Fluorescent Biomolecules, 1989; contbr. articles to Bioimaging, Biochemistry. Recipient Paul Naney award Am. Heart Assn., 1987. Mem. Am. Chem. Soc., Am. Assn. Biochemistry and Molecular Biologists, Biophys. Soc. Achievements include patent for near infrared optical imaging. Office: U Ill Lab Fluorescence Dynamics 1110 W Green St Urbana IL 61801-3080 E-mail: lfd@uiuc.edu.

MANUEL, JERRY, former professional sports team manager; b. Hahira, Ga., Dec. 23, 1953; m. Renette Caldwell; children: Angela, Jerry, Anthony, Natalie. Switch-hitting infielder Detroit Tigers, 1972, Class A Lakeland, Class AAA Toledo, 1973, Class AAA Evansville, 1974-75, Detroit Tigers, 1975-76, Montreal, Can., 1980-81, San Diego, 1982, Class AAA Iowa, 1983, Class AAA Denver, 1984; scout White Sox, 1985; player, coach Indpls. orgn., 1986, infield instr., 1987; minor-league fielding coord. Expos orgn., 1988-89; mgr. Class AAA Indpls. Montreal Expos Sys., 1991; coach maj. league baseball Montreal Expos, 1991-96; mgr. Chgo. White Sox, 1997—2003. Bench coach Fla. Marlins, 1997. Named So. League Mgr. of Yr., 1992.

MANUEL, RALPH NIXON, retired private school executive; b. Frederick, Md., Apr. 21, 1936; s. Ralph Walter and Frances Rebecca (Nixon) M.; m. Sarah Jane Warner, July 22, 1960; children: Mark, David, Stephen, Bradley. AB, Dartmouth Coll., 1958; M.Ed., Boston U., 1967; PhD, U. Ill., 1971. Assoc. dean Dartmouth Coll., Hanover, NH, 1971-72, dean of freshmen, 1972-75, dean, 1975-82; pres. Culver (Ind.) Acad. and Culver Edn. Found., 1982-99. Bd. dirs. Ind. Sch. Cen. States, 1986-99, chair, 1993-95. Mem. Assn. Mil. Colls. and Schs. of U.S. (pres., bd. dirs.), Nat. Assn. Ind. Schs. (bd. dirs. 1995-99).

MANWARING, STEVE R., mechanical engineer; b. Conneaut, Ohio, Feb. 4, 1959; m. Rebecca Manwaring; children: Jonathan, Alyssa. BSME, Ohio U., 1982, MSME, 1984; PhD, Purdue U., 1989. Mech. engr. GE Aircraft Engines, Cin., 1989—. Recipient Gas Turbine award ASME, 1994. Mem. Internat. Gas Turbine Inst. Office: GE Aircraft Engines 1 Neumann Way Cincinnati OH 45215-1915

MANZ, JOHN R., bishop; BA in Philosophy, Niles Coll. Seminary, Loyola, Ill., 1967; MDiv, U. St. Mary of the Lake, Mundelein, Ill., 1971. Ordained priest Archdiocese of Chgo., 1971, aux. bishop, 1996—; assoc. pastor Providence of God, Chgo., 1971—78, St. Roman, Chgo., 1978—83; pastor St. Agnes of Bohemia, Chgo., 1983—96; dean Chgo.'s Lower West Side, 1987—96; ordained bishop, 1996; vicar for Vicariate III, 1996—. Mem.: US Conf. Catholic Bishops (chmn. Ch. Latin Am., mem. adminstrv. com., mem. Migration and Refugee Svcs. Ch. Latin Am.). Roman Catholic. Home: 1850 S Throop St Chicago IL 60608-3149*

MANZULLO, DONALD A., congressman, lawyer; b. Rockford, Ill., Mar. 27, 1944; s. Frank A. Sr. and Catherine M.; m. Freda Teslik; children: Neil, Noel, Katie. BA in Polit. Sci./Internat. Rels., American U., 1967; JD, Marquette U. Law Sch., 1971. Atty., 1970—; mem. U.S. Congress from 16th Ill. Dist., 1993—. Mem. House Com. on Internat. Rels., subcom. internat. econ. policy and trade, subcom. on Asia and the Pacific, House Com. on small bus., chmn. on subcom. on tax, fin. and exports, Banking Com. and its capital markets, securities and govt.-sponsored enterprises subcom. Mem. No. Ill. Alliance for Arts, Friends of Severson Dells, Citizens Against Govt. Waste, Rep. Nat. Com. Recipient George Washington honor medal for excellence in pub. comm. Freedoms Found., Valley Forge, Pa., 1991. Mem. ABA, Ill. Bar Assn., Ogle County Bar Assn. (pres. 1971, 73), Nat. Legal Found., Acad. Polit. Sci., Ill. Press Assn., Ill. C. of C., Oregon City C. of C., Nat. Land Inst., Nat. Fedn. Ind. Bus., Ogle County Hist. Soc., Aircraft Owners and Pilots Assn., Ogle County Pilots Assn., Ill. Farm Bur., Ogle County Farm Bur. Republican. Office: US House Reps 2228 Rayburn House Office Bldg Washington DC 20515-1316

MAPOTHER, DILLON EDWARD, physicist, academic administrator; b. Louisville, Aug. 22, 1921; s. Dillon Edward and Edith (Rubel) M.; m. Elizabeth Beck, June 29, 1946; children: Ellen, Susan, Anne. BS in Mech. Engring, U. Louisville, 1943; D.Sc. in Physics, Carnegie-Mellon U., 1949. Engr. Westinghouse Rsch. Labs., East Pittsburgh, Pa., 1943-46; instr. Carnegie Inst. Tech., Pitts., 1946; mem. faculty U. Ill., Urbana, 1949-94, prof. physics, 1959-94, dir. acad. computing services, 1971-76, assoc. vice chancellor for rsch., 1976-94, acting dean grad. coll., vice chancellor research, 1977-78, assoc. dean grad. coll., 1979-94, assoc. vice chancellor rsch. emeritus Urbana, 1995—, assoc. dean emertus grad. coll., prof. emeritus physics, 1995—. Cons. in field. DuPont fellow, 1947-49; Alfred P. Sloan fellow, 1958-61; Guggenheim fellow, 1960-61 Fellow Am. Phys. Soc.; mem. AAAS, Assn. Univ. Tech. Mgrs., Am. Assn. Physics Tchrs., Sigma Xi. Achievements include research on ionic mobility in alkali halides, thermodynamic properties of superconductors, calorimetric study of critical points, administration of university research, commercialization of academic research technology. Office: U Ill Physics Dept Loomis Lab 1110 W Green St Urbana IL 61801-9013 Home: 401 Burwash Ave Apt 142 Savoy IL 61874-9574 Business E-Mail: mapother@uiuc.edu.

MARANS, ROBERT WARREN, planning consultant, architect, educator; b. Detroit, Aug. 3, 1934; s. Albert and Anne Rose Marans; m. Judith Ann Bloomfield, Jan. 24, 1956; children: Gayl Elizabeth, Pamela Jo. BArch, U. Mich., 1957; M in Urban Planning, Wayne State U., 1961; PhD, U. Mich., 1971. Reg. architect, Mich. Archtl. engr., planner Detroit City Planning Comn., 1957-61; planning cons. Blair & Stein Assocs., Providence, 1961-64; architect-urban designer Artur Glikson, Architect, Tel Aviv, Israel, 1964-65; regional planner Detroit Area Transp. Land Use Study, 1965-67; asst. prof. Fla. State U., Talahassee, 1967; rsch. assoc., sr. study dir. Inst. Social Rsch., Ann Arbor, Mich., 1968-74, sr. rsch. scientist, 1974—; from lectr. to assoc. prof. Coll. Architecture Urban Planning, Ann Arbor, 1971-78; prof. architecture and urban planning U. Mich., Ann Arbor, 1978—. Cons. TVA, 1972, UN, 1974; chmn. urban and regional planning program, 1987-98. Co-author: Planned Residential Environments, 1970, Quality of NonMetropolitan Living, 1978, Evaluating Built Environments, 1981, Retirement Communities: An American Original, 1984; co-editor: Methods of Environmental and Behavioral Research, 1987, Environmental Stimulation: Research and Policy Perspectives, 1993, Advances in Environment, Behavior and Design, vol. IV, 1997; contbr. articles to profl. jours. and tech. reports. Vice chair Washtenaw County Parks Recreation Commn., Ann Arbor, 1972—; commr. Huron-Clinton Met. Parks Authority, Brighton, Mich., 1986—; chair Mich. Land Use Inst., 2002—; trustee Detroit Riverfront Conservancy, 2003—; v.p. Washtenaw Land Trust. Recipient fellow Social Sci. Rsch. Coun., 1969-70; Fulbright Rsch. award Coun. Internat. Exchange Scholars, Israel, 1977; Progressive Architecture Applied Rsch. award Progressive Architecture Mag., 1982; Design Rsch. Recognition award Nat. Endowment for Arts, 1983. Mem. Am. Planning Assn., Nat. Recreation Pk. Assn., Environ. Design Rsch. Assn. Avocations: swimming, stamp collecting/philately. Office: U Mich Inst for Social Rsch Ann Arbor MI 48106 E-mail: marans@umich.edu.

MARBLE, GARY, state legislator; Mem. dist. 130 Mo. Ho. of Reps., 1994—. Home: 1500 S Oaks Dr Jefferson City MO 65101-9775

MARCANTONIO, RICHARD L., uniform company executive; b. Chgo., Feb. 26, 1950; m. Carol Marcantonio; 3 children. BA in Bus. Admin., Elmhurst Coll., 1972. With Central Soya, 1973—76; pres., CEO Specialty Brands United Biscuits, 1976—95, sr. mgmt., sales and mktg. positions, Keebler Co.; sr. exec. including pres. indsl. svc. sectors Ecolab Inc., 1997—2002; pres., COO G&K Services Inc., Minneapolis, Minn., 2002—04, pres., CEO, 2004—, chmn., 2005—. Bd. dirs. H.B. Fuller Co., 2004—. Chmn. Minn. Public Radio; bd. dirs. Am. Public Media Group, YMCA Greater St. Paul.

MARCDANTE, KAREN JEAN, medical educator; b. Milw., Sept. 15, 1955; d. Willard Karl and Beth Elaine (Maule) Kohn; m. Mark Wendelberger, Aug. 5, 1978 (div. Sept. 1985); m. Anthony Marcdante, Oct. 17, 1998. Student, Marquette U., Milw., 1973-76; MD, Med. Coll. Wis., Milw., 1980. Diplomate Am. Bd. Pediat. & Pediat. Crit. Care. Resident in pediat. Med. Coll. Wis. affiliated hosps., Milw., 1980-83; instr. pediat. Med. Coll. Wis., Milw., 1983-85, asst. prof. pediat., 1987-94, assoc. prof. pediat., 1994-2000, prof. pediat., 2000—, assoc. dean curriculum, 1997—2003, vice-chair edn. dept. pediat., 1994—; fellow in pediatric critical care U. Calif., San Francisco, 1985-87; vice chief staff Children's Hosp. Wis., Milw., 1995-97. Dir. Respiratory Care Svcs., 1992-98, Transport Program, 1998—; chief dept. pediat. Children's Hosp. Wis., 1991-95, dept. critical care 1993-95, mem. numerous coms., including care mgmt. steering com., 1994-, critical care com., 1991—, pres.-elect, 2003-05; pres. med. dental staff, 2005-07. Contbr. numerous articles to profl. jours. Recipient New Investigator award Assn. Am. Med. Colls., 1992, Cert. Leadership award YWCA and Marquette Electronics Found., 1992, Laureate award Ctrl. Group Ednl. Affairs, 2004; grantee Dept. HHS, 1996—. Mem. Am. Acad. Pediat. (pub. rels. chair Wis. chpt. 1988-91, sec.-treas. 1990-95, v.p. 1995-96, chair careers and opportunities 1996-2001), Soc. Critical Care Medicine (chair task force on quality improvement pediat. 1994-96, quality indicator devel. work group 1997-98, Presdl. citation 1996, 97), Coun. on Med. Student Edn. in Pediat. (co-chair task force on tchg. methods 1991-96, nominating com. 1993-95, exec. com. 1996-99, sec.-treas. 1997-99). Business E-Mail: kwendel@mcw.edu.

MARCHESE, RONALD THOMAS, ancient history and archaeology educator; b. Fresno, Calif., Mar. 17, 1947; s. John Anthony and Julie Rita (Ferrarese) M.; m. Marcia Lynn Schneider, Apr. 6, 1974 (div. Apr. 1980); 1 child, Stephanie Jo; m. K. Werdin, 1988; children: Alexander Joseph, Kayla Marie. BA summa cum laude, Calif. State U., Fresno, 1970; MA, N.Y.U., 1972, PhD with distinction, 1976; postgrad., Columbia U., 1972-73. Asst. prof. Va. Poly. Inst., Blacksburg, 1976-77; asst. to assoc. prof. ancient history and archaeology U. Minn., Duluth, 1977-87, prof., 1987—. Rsch. assoc. dept. classics NYU, 1972—74; evaluator grant proposals NEH, NSF; excavator numerous sites in Israel, Turkey, and Greece; lectr. in field. Author, editor 7 books; author articles on nomadic material culture, religious textiles, and sacred relics from the American Orthodox Churches of Istanbul, Turkey. Recipient Fulbright-Hays Sr. Research fellowship, Turkey, 1984-85, 91-92, The Am. Council Learned Socs. fellowship, 1977-78, NDEA Title VI Fgn. Languages fellowship, 1972-75, Spl. Commendation for Excellence award Phi Alpha Theta, 1979; grantee NEH, 1978, 80, nat. Geographic Soc., 1974, Andrew Mellon Found., NSF, Ford Found., 1971-72, U. Minn., others; McKnight fellow, 2004—. Mem. NEH, Nat. Assn. Scholars, Coun. for Internat. Exchange, Am. Coun. Learned Socs., Fulbright Alumni Assn., Phi Alpha Theta, Sigma Xi, Alpha Phi Omega. Roman Catholic. Avocations: tennis, golf, horseback riding. Home: 5789 220th St N Forest Lake MN 55025-9677 Office Phone: 218-726-8507. Business E-Mail: rmarches@d.umn.edu.

MARCIL, WILLIAM CHRIST, SR., publisher, broadcast executive; b. Rolette, ND, Mar. 9, 1936; s. Max L. and Ida (Fuerst) M.; m. Jane Black, Oct. 15, 1960; children: Debora Jane, William Christ Jr. BSBA, U. N.D., 1958. Br. mgr. Community Credit Co., Mpls., 1959-61; with Forum Comms. Co., Fargo, N.D., 1961—, pres., pub., CEO, 1969—. Pres. Forum Comm. Found.; past bd. dirs. North Ctrl. region Boy Scouts Am. With U.S. Army, 1958-59. Mem. Inland Newspaper Press Assn., N.D. Press Assn., Am. Newspaper Pubs. Assn. (past dir., chmn.), Fargo Morehead C. of C., N.D. State C. of C. (past pres.), U.S. C. of C. (past chmn.), Sigma Delta Chi, Lambda Chi Alpha. Lodges: Masons, Shriners, Elks. Republican. Office: Forum Comm Co 101 5th St N Fargo ND 58102-4826 Home: 1618 S 8th St Fargo ND 58103

MARCIN, ROBERT H., automotive executive; BBA, SUNY, 1971; MBA, Calif. State U., 1973. With Ford Aerospace, San Jose, Calif., 1973—89; exec. v.p., dir., external & employee affairs First Nationwide Fin. Corp., 1989—93; dir., compensation planning office Ford Motor Co., 1993—95, dir., internat. labor affairs, 1995—98, exec. dir., labor affairs, 1998—2000; sr. v.p., human resources Visteon Corp., Dearborn, Mich., 2000—03, sr. v.p., corp. relations, 2003—. Bd. dirs. Med-i-bank, Inc., Am. Soc. Employers, Mich. Office: Visteon Corp 1700 Rotunda Dr Dearborn MI 48120

MARCOUX, WILLIAM JOSEPH, lawyer; b. Detroit, Jan. 20, 1927; s. Lona J. and Anna (Ransom) C.; m. Kae Marie Sanborn, Aug. 23, 1952; children: Ann K., William C. BA, U. Mich., 1949, JD, 1952. Bar: Mich. 1953. Pvt. practice, Pontiac, Mich., 1953; assoc. McKone, Badgley, Domke and Kline, Jackson, Mich., 1953-65, ptnr., 1965-75; dir. Marcoux, Allen, Schomer, Bower, Nichols, Kendall and Lindsey, PC, Jackson, Mich., 1975—. Mem. exec. bd. Great Sauk Trail council Boy Scouts Am., pres., 1965-66; bd. dirs. Jackson County United Way, pres., 1983-84. Served with USNR, 1945-46. Recipient Silver Beaver award Boy Scouts Am., 1969, Disting. Citizen award Land O'Lakes coun. Boy Scouts Am., 1991. Fellow Am. Coll. Trial Lawyers, Mich. State Bar Found.; mem. Mich. State Bar Assn., Jackson County Bar Assn. (pres. 1979-80), Jackson Rotary Club (pres. 1963-64), Country Club of Jackson, Clark Lake Yacht Club (commodore 1959). Methodist. Home: 1745 Malvern Dr Jackson MI 49203-5378 Office: Marcoux Allen et al PO Box 787 Jackson MI 49204-0787 Office Phone: 517-787-4100. Business E-Mail: wmarcoux@marcouxallen.com.

MARCOVICH, TOBY, lawyer; b. Superior, Wis., Jan. 6, 1930; BS, U. Wis., 1952, JD, 1954. Bar: Wis. 1954. Pres. bd. regents U. Wis. Instr. sociology U. Minn., Duluth, 1978—83; instr. trial practice U. Wis., Madison, Wis., 1987—88. Mem. bd. regents, pres. U. Wis., Wis., former mem. found. bd. Superior, Wis. Mem.: ATLA, Lawyer Pilots Bar Assn., Wis. Acad. Trial Lawyers (former bd. dirs.). Office: Marcovich Cochrane & Milliken Swansen & Kropp 1214 Belknap St Superior WI 54880 Home Phone: 715-394-4385; Office Phone: 715-394-6624.

MARCOVICI, MICHAEL, investment company executive; b. 1969; V.p., private banking and investment group Merrill Lynch & Co., Chgo. Named one of 40 Under Forty, Crain's Bus. Chgo., 2005. Office: Merril Lynch & Co Ste 2500 33 W Monroe St Chicago IL 60603-5409

MARCUM, JOSEPH LARUE, insurance company executive; b. Hamilton, Ohio, July 2, 1923; s. Glen F. and Helen A. (Stout) M.; m. Sarah Jane Sloneker, Mar. 7, 1944; children: Catharine Ann Marcum Lowe, Joseph Timothy (dec.), Mary Christina Marcum Manchester, Sarah Jennifer Marcum Shuffield, Stephen Sloneker. BA, Antioch Coll., 1947; MBA in Fin, Miami U., 1965. With Ohio Casualty Ins. Co. and affiliates, 1947—, now chmn. bd., also bd. dirs. Capt., inf. U.S. Army. Mem. Soc. CPCU, Queen City Club, Bankers Club, Princeton Club N.Y., Little Harbor club, Walloon Lake Country Club, Mill Reef Club. Presbyterian. Office: Ohio Casualty Corp 136 N 3rd St Hamilton OH 45011-2726 Home: 609 Lake Dr Vero Beach FL 32963-2166

MARCUS, JOHN, wholesale distribution executive; b. NYC, Oct. 18, 1941; s. Sam and Margaret (McCoy) M.; m. Helen S. Bondurant, Aug. 14, 1965; children: Lisa Marie, Lynn Michelle. AA, Wentworth Mil. Acad., Lexington, Mo., 1961. Buyer Foley Bros. Dept. Stores, Houston, 1963-65; owner JOMARC, Houston, 1965-66; sales mgr. Firestone Tire & Rubber Co., Houston, 1966-67; distbn. mgr. Matthews Book Co., St. Louis, 1967-69, office mgr., 1969, gen. mgr., 1970, v.p. ops., 1971, pres., 1972, chmn., CEO, 1974—. Pres., CEO McCoy Collegiate Svcs., St. Louis, 1969—, NACSCORP Inc., Oberlin, Ohio, 1983, Coll. Stores Rsch. and Edn. Found., 1984-85, chmn., CEO Founders Bookstore Svcs.; CEO Coll. Bookstores of Am., St. Louis, 1986—. Contbr. articles to pubs. Bd. dirs. YMCA, Wentworth Mil. Acad. Mem. Nat. Assn. Coll. Stores (pres. 1981-82), The Employee Stock Ownership Plans Assn. Office: Matthews Book Co 11559 Rock Island Ct Maryland Heights MO 63043-3596

MARCUS, JOSEPH, child psychiatrist; b. Cleve., Feb. 27, 1928; s. William and Sarah (Marcus) Schwartz; m. Cilla Furmanovitz, Oct. 3, 1951; children: Oren, Alon. B.Sc., Western Res. U., 1963; MD, Hebrew U., 1958. Intern Tel Hashomer Govt. Hosp., Israel, 1956-57; resident in psychiatry and child psychiatry Ministry of Health, Govt. of Israel, 1958-61; acting head dept. child psychiatry Ness Ziona Rehab. Ctr., 1961-62; sr. psychiatrist Lasker dept. child psychiatry Hadassah U. Hosp., 1962-64; research asso. Israel Inst. Applied Social Research, 1966-69; practice medicine specializing in psychiatry Jerusalem, 1966-72; assoc. dir. devel. neuropsychiatry Jerusalem Infant and Child Devel. Ctr., 1969-70; dept. head Eytanim Hosp., 1970-72; cons. child psychiatrist for Jerusalem Ministry of Health, 1970-72; dir. dept. child psychiatry and devel. Jerusalem Mental Health Ctr., 1972-75; prof. child psychiatry, dir. unit for research in child psychiatry and devel. U. Chgo., 1975-85, prof. emeritus, co-dir. unit for research in child psychiatry and devel., 1986—; vis. research psychiatrist UCLA Dept. Psychiatry, 1987—. Chief editor: Early Child Devel. and Care, 1972-76; mem. editorial bd.: Israel Annals of Psychiatry and Related Disciplines, 1965-70, Internat. Yearbook of Child Psychiatry and Allied Professions, 1968-74; contbr. articles to med. jours. Mem. Am. Acad. Child Psychiatry (com. on research, com. on psychiat. aspects of infancy), Soc. Research in Child Devel., Internat. Assn. Child Psychiatry and Allied Professions (asst. gen. sec. 1966-74), European Union Paedopsychiatry (hon.), World, Israel psychiat. assns., Internat. Coll. Psychosomatic Medicine, Israel Center Psychobiology. Home: 910 Chelham Way Santa Barbara CA 93108-1049

MARCUS, JOYCE (JOYCE MARCUS FLANNERY), anthropology educator; Student, U. Calif., Berkeley; MS, PhD, Harvard U. Prof. of anthropology, mus. anthropology U. Mich., Ann Arbor, curator, Latin American Archaeology. Serves on Smithsonian Coun. Contbr. articles to profl. jours. Mem.: Am. Acad. Arts and Sciences, NAS (councilor 2005—). Office: U Mich 101 West Hall 1092 Ann Arbor MI 48109 Office Phone: 734-763-5164. Business E-Mail: joymar@umich.edu.

MARCUS, LARRY DAVID, broadcast executive; b. NYC, Jan. 27, 1949; s. Oscar Moses and Sylvia (Ackerman) Marcus; children from previous marriage: Julia Ilene, Barbara Maureen. BBA, CUNY, 1970, postgrad. studies Bus. Admistrn., 1970-72. Computer systems analyst Johnson & Johnson, 1972—73; acctg. mgr. Sta. WPLG-TV, Miami, Fla., 1974-75; v.p., bus. mgr. Sta. KPLR-TV-Koplar Comm., Inc., St. Louis, 1976-82; chief fin. officer Koplar Comm., Inc., St. Louis, 1982-88, River City Broadcasting Co., St. Louis, 1988-96; gen. ptnr. Marcus Investments, L.P., 1996—; CEO Peak Media Holdings LLC, San Diego, 1997—. Computer design cons. PriceWaterhouse Coopers; ptnr. San Diego Social Venture. Scholarship com. Puo Kids, San Diego; bd. dirs. St. Louis Nat. Pub. Radio; pres. Del Mar TV Found. Mem.: Broadcast Cable Fin. Mgmt. Assn. (bd. dirs. 1976—89, treas. 1989—90, sec. 1990—91, v.p. 1991—92, pres. 1992—93). Avocations: skiing, golf. Office: Peak Media LLC 13748 Pine Needles Dr Del Mar CA 92014 E-mail: ldmarcus@aol.com.

MARCUS, RICHARD STEVEN, lawyer; b. Cin., May 26, 1950; s. Bernard Benjamin and Norma (Ginsberg) M.; m. Jane Iris Schreiber, Sept. 12, 1971; children: Rebecca, Sarah. BA in English, U. Wis., 1972; JD cum laude (hon.), Harvard U., 1975. Bar: Wis. 1975, U.S. Tax Ct. 1976, U.S. Ct. Appeals (7th cir.) 1977, U.S. Dist. Ct. (ea. dist.) Wis. 1979, U.S. Ct. Claims 1979. Assoc. Godfrey & Kahn, S.C., Milw., 1975—, Shareholder. Pres., Milw. Assn. for Jewish Edn., 1992; bd. dirs. Milw. Jewish Fedn., 1992, Milw. chpt. Jewish Nat. Fund, 1992. Mem.: Computer Law Assn., State Bar Wis., ABA. Office: Godfrey & Kahn SC 780 N Water St Ste 1500 Milwaukee WI 53202-3590 Business E-Mail: rmarcus@gklaw.com.

MARCUS, STEPHEN HOWARD, hospitality and entertainment company executive; b. Mpls., May 31, 1935; s. Ben D. and Celia Marcus; m. Joan Glasspiegel, Nov. 3, 1962; children: Greg, David, Andrew. BBA, U. Wis., Madison, 1957; LL.B., U. Mich., 1960. Bar: Wis. 1960. V.p. Pfister Hotel Corp., Milw., 1963-69, exec. v.p., 1969-75; pres. Marcus Hotel Corp., Milw., 1975-91; chmn., COO Marcus Corp., Milw., 1980—, COO, dir., 1988; exec. v.p. Marc Plaza Corp., Milw.; v.p. Wis. Big Boy Corp., Milw., Marcus Theatres Corp., Milw.; dir. Med. Coll. Wis., Milw., 1986—; chmn., CEO Marcus Corp., Milw. Dir. Preferred Hotels Assn., 1972—, chmn. bd., 1979; dir. Bank One N.A. Pres. Milw. Conv. and Visitors Bur., 1970-71, bd. dirs., mem. exec. com., 1968—; chmn. Wis. Gov.'s Adv. Council on Tourism, 1976-81; bd. dirs. Multiple Sclerosis Soc. Milw., 1965-67, Milw. Jewish Fedn., 1968-76, Milw. Jewish Chronicle, 1973-76, Children's Hosp. Found., Inc., Competitive Wis.; asso. chmn. bus. div. United Fund Campaign, Milw., 1971; co-chmn. spl. gifts com. United Performing Arts Fund, Milw., 1972-74, bd. dirs., 1973-81, chmn. maj. gifts, 1982, co-chmn., 1983—; bd. dirs. Friends of Art, Milw., 1973-74; pres. Summerfest, 1975; bd. dirs. MECCA, Milw., 1975-82, mem. exec. com., 1977; bd. dirs. Jr. Achievement, Milw., 1976—; trustee Mt. Sinai Med. Center, 1977—, Nat. Symphony Orchestra, 1985; bd. govs. Jewish Community Campus; co-chmn. Ann. Freedom Fund Dinner, NAACP, 1980-81; chmn. Icebreaker Festival, 1989. Served with U.S. Army, 1960-61. Recipient Ben ickoll award Milw. Jewish Fedn., 1969, Headliner award Milw. Press Club, 1986, Humanitarian award NCCJ, 1988, Lamplighter award Greater Milw. Conv. and Visitors Bur., 1991. Mem. Am. Hotel and Motel Assn. (dir. 1976-79, exec. com. 1978-79), Greater Milw. Hotel and Motel Assn. (pres. 1967-68), Wis. Innkeepers Assn. (pres. 1972-73), Variety Club, Milw. Assn. Commerce (bd. dirs. 1982-85), Downtown Assn., Young Pres.'s Orgn., Wis. Assn. Mfrs. and Commerce (dir. 1978-82), Greater Milw. Com. (dir. 1981) Office: The Marcus Corp 100 E Wisconsin Ave Ste 1900 Milwaukee WI 53202-1900

MARENDT, CANDACE L., state legislator; Student, Ind. U. Mem. Ind. State Ho. of Reps. Dist. 94, mem. commerce and econ. devel. com., mem. judiciary and pub. safety com., vice-chmn. families, children and human affairs com. Mem. MIBOR, Circle City Child Care Assn., N.W. Roundtable, Pike, Wayne, Washington and Eagle Creek GOP Clubs. also: Electronics Divsn 302 W Washington St Rm 204 Indianapolis IN 46204

MARES, HARRY, state legislator; b. Dec. 21, 1938; m. Geri Mares; 7 children. BA, Loras Coll., Dubuque, Iowa; MS, Winona State U. Minn. state rep. Dist. 55A, 1994—. Former tchr. Address: 24639 Madewood Ave Leesburg FL 34748-7881

MARGERUM, DALE WILLIAM, chemistry professor; b. St. Louis, Oct. 20, 1929; s. Donald C. and Ida Lee (Nunley) M.; m. Sonya Lora Pedersen, May 16, 1953; children: Lawrence Donald, Eric William, Richard Dale. BA, S.E. Mo. State U., 1950; PhD, Iowa State U., 1955. Research chemist Ames Lab., AEC, Iowa, 1952-53; instr. Purdue U., West Lafayette, Ind., 1954-57, asst. prof., 1957-61, assoc. prof., 1961-65, prof., 1965-97, disting. prof. chemistry, 1997—, head dept. chemistry, 1978-83. Inorganic-analytical chemist, vis. scientist Max Planck Inst., 1963, 70; vis. prof. U. Kent, Canterbury, Eng., 1970; mem. med. chem. study sect. IH, 1965-69; mem. adv. com. Research Corp., 1973-78; mem. chemistry evaluation panel Air Force Office Sci. Research, 1978-82 Cons. editor McGraw Hill, 1962-72; mem. editorial bd. Jour. Coordination Chemistry, 1971-81, Analytical Chemistry, 1967-69, Inorganic Chemistry, 1985-88. Recipient Grad. Rsch. award Phi Lambda Upsilon, 1954, Alumni Merit award S.E. Mo. State U., 1991, Sagamore of the Wabash, State of Ind., 1994; NSF sr. postdoctoral fellow, 1963-64. Fellow AAAS; mem. AAUP, Am. Chem. Soc. (chmn. Purdue sect. 1965-66, com. on profl. tng. 1993-2003, Disting. Svc. award in advancement of inorganic chemistry 1996), Sigma Xi (Monie A. Ferst award 2000), Phi Lambda Upsilon. Office: Dept Chemistry Purdue U West Lafayette IN 47907

MARGOLIASH, EMANUEL, biochemist, educator; b. Cairo, Feb. 10, 1920; s. Wolf and Bertha (Kotler) M.; m. Sima Beshkin, Aug. 22, 1944; children: Reuben, Daniel. BA, Am. U., Beirut, 1940, MA, 1942, MD, 1945. Rsch. fellow, lectr., acting head cancer rsch. labs. Hebrew U., Jerusalem, 1945-58; rsch. fellow Molteno Inst. Cambridge (Eng.) U., 1951-53; Dazian fellow Nobel Inst., 1958; rsch. assoc. U. Utah, Salt Lake City, 1958-60, McGill U., Montreal, Que., Canada, 1960-62; rsch. fellow Abbott Labs., North Chicago, Ill., 1962-69, sr. rsch. fellow, 1969-71, head protein sect., 1962-71; prof. biochemistry and molecular biology orthwestern U., Evanston, Ill., 1971-90, prof. chemistry, 1985-90, Owen L. Coon prof. molecular biology, 1988-90, Owen L. Coon prof. molecular biology emeritus, 1990—; prof. biol. scis. U. Ill., Chgo., 1989—, coord. lab. for molecular biology, 1990-93. Mem. com. on cytochrome nomenclature Internat. Union Biochemistry, 1962-75; mem. adv. com. Plant Research Lab., Mich. State U./AEC, 1967-72; co-chmn. Gordon Research Conf. on Proteins, 1967 Editl. bd. Jour. Biol. Chemistry, 1966-72, Biochem. Genetics, 1966-80, Jour. Molecular Evolution, 1971-82, Biochemistry and Molecular Biology Internat., 1981-99, Jour. Protein Chemistry, 1982-86, Chemtracts, Biochem. Molecular Biology, 1990-99; contbr. over 280 articles and revs. to sci. jours. Rudi Lemberg fellow Australian Acad. Sci., 1981; Guggenheim fellow, 1983 Fellow Am. Acad. Arts and Scis., Am. Acad. Microbiology, Am. Inst. Chemists; mem. Nat. Acad. Scis., Biochem. Soc. (Keilin Meml. lectr. 1970), Harvey Soc. (lectr. 1970-71), Am. Soc. Biochem. Molecular Biology (publs. com. 1973-76), Am. Chem. Soc., Am. Soc. Microbiology, Can. Biochem. Soc., Soc. Devel. Biology, Biophys. Soc. (exec. com. U.S. bioenergetics group 1980-83), N.Y. Acad. Sci., Ill. Acad. Sci., Am. Soc. Naturalists, Sigma Xi (nat. lectr. 1972-73, 74-77). Office: Biochemistry Molecular & Cell Biology Hogan Hall 2-100 Northwestern U Evanston IL 60208-3500 Home: 554 Oakdale Ave Glencoe IL 60022-2043 Office Phone: 847-491-5620.

MARGOLIS, JAY M., clothing executive; b. NYC, Feb. 11, 1949; s. Mac and Sarah Margolis; m. Donna Brenda Polsky, June 12, 1972; children: Jared Michael, Stacey Allyse. BA, Queens Coll., NYC, 1971. Asst. mdse. mgr. Manhattan Shirt Co., NYC, 1972-74; mdse. mgr. Arrow Shirt Co., NYC, 1974-78; pres. Yves St. Laurent-Biderman Inc., NYC, 1978-81, Ron Chereskin div. Cluett Peabody, NYC, 1981-83, Claiborne Mens-Liz Claiborne Inc., NYC, 1983-86; group pres., exec. v.p. corp. Liz Claiborne Inc., NYC, 1986-88, vice chmn., 1988—92; pres., vice chmn. Tommy Hilfiger, 1992—95; chmn., CEO Esprit de Corp., 1995—99, E7th.com, 1999—2001; pres. splty. bus. group Reebok Internat. Ltd., 2001, pres., COO, 2001—04; group pres. apparel Limited Brands, Inc., 2005—. Mem. bd. Fathers Day/Mothers Day Coun. Mem. City Athletic Club. Avocations: skiing, swimming, tennis, environmental studies. Office: Limited Brands Inc 3 Limited Pkwy Columbus OH 43216

MARGOLIS, PHILIP MARCUS, psychiatrist, educator; b. Lima, Ohio, July 7, 1925; s. Harry Sterling and Clara (Brunner) M.; m. Nancy Nupuf, July 26, 1959; children: Cynthia, Marc, David, Laurence. BA magna cum laude, U. Minn., 1945, MD, 1948. Diplomate Am. Bd. Psychiatry and Neurology, 1966 (examiner 1973—1999, 2003-), recert. com., 1998-2004. Intern Milw. County Hosp., 1948-49; resident VA Hosp. and U. Minn., 1949-52, Mass. Gen. Hosp. and Harvard U., Boston, 1952-54; instr. U. Minn., Milw., 1953-55; asst. prof. dept. psychiatry Med. Sch., U. Chgo., 1955-60, assoc. prof., 1960-66; prof. psychiatry Med. Sch. U. Mich., 1966—, prof. cmty. mental health, 1968—; prof. psychiatry emeritus L.S.A., 1997—, instr., 1977-97; chief psychiat. inpatient service U. Chgo. Hosps. and Clinics, 1956-66; dir. Civil Forensic Tng. Program, 1997—. Cons. Forensic Psychiat. Ctr., State of Mich., 1972—, coord. med. student edn. program, 1975-78, dir., 1978-82; cons. Turner Geriatric Clin., 1978-86, cons. Breast Cancer Clinic, 1988, Powertrain subs. Gen. Motors, 1984—. Dept. Mental Health, U.S. Dept. Justice; assoc. chief clin. affairs U. Mich. Hosps., 1981-85, chair legis. govt. com., 1996—, chmn. ethics com.; profl. rev. com. PSRO Area VII, 1982-86, PROM, 2003—; mem. Mich. State Bd. Medicine, 1986-94, chmn. 1992-94, senate adv. com. Univ. Affairs., 1986-89; spl. com. on profl. conduct and ethics Fedn. of State Med. Bds., 1998—, Mich. del., 1988-96, FLEX Com. Nat. Bd. Med. Examiners, 1988-98; civil liberties bd. U. Mich., 1995-2004, chmn., 1996-2002, gen counsel adv. com., 2002—; dir. Civil Forensic Tng. Program, 1997—. Author: Guide for Mental Health Workers, 1970, Patient Power: The Development of a Therapeutic Community in a General Hospital, 1974; also articles.; cons. editor: Community Mental Health jour, 1967—. Recipient Commonwealth Fund fellow award, 1964, Career Svc. award, 1992, Resident Appreciation award, 1991. Fellow: Am. Coll. Psychiatrists (chmn. bylaws com. 1997—, newsletter editor, Lifers 2003—), Am. Psychiat. Assn. (life; chmn. membership com. 1979—83, cons. ethics com. 1983—86, trustee 1985—88, sec. 1989—91, chmn. ethics appeals bd. 1989—, cons. steering com. on practical guidelines 1991—, budget com. 1991—, mem. assembly 1992, coun. med. edn. and career devel. 1993—, pres. Lifers 1994—, recertification com. 1998—, mem. pub. funding com. 2001—, assembly rep. 2003—, newsletter editor 2003—, cons. mem. com. 2004—, mem. audit com. 2004—, annual Lifers award 1999); mem.: Am. Acad. Psychiatry and Law (com. on psychoanalytic edn. 1995—, edn. com. 1998, treas. midwest chpt. 1998—2000, forensic tng. com. 2000—, pres. 2001—02), Am. Acad. Psychoanalysis, Mich. State Med. Soc. (bioethics com. 1989—, com. on med. licensure and discipline 1995—, legis. and regulations com. 1995—, mental health liaison com. 1995—, liaison com. Gen. Motors 1998—, chair 2000—, chair com. on med. licensure and discipline 2000—), Mich. Psychiat. Soc. (pres. 1980—81, chmn. ethics com. 1983—86, resolutions officer student rights responsibilities 1996—, chmn. legislation and govt. com. 1996—2005, v.p. 2000—, chmn. mem. com. 2004, 2004—, Career Achievement award 2000), Washtenaw County Med. Soc. (exec. coun. 1982—, chmn. ethics com. 1983—87, pres. 1987—88, editl. bd. 1995—, chair legis. commn. 1999—). Home: 228 Riverview Dr Ann Arbor MI 48104-1846 Office: 4250 Plymouth Rd Ann Arbor MI 48109 Office Phone: 734-647-8762. Business E-Mail: margolis@umich.edu.

MARGOLIS, ROB, publisher; m. Alycia Margolis; children: Zachary, Noah. Acct. mgr. TV Guide, 1982, assoc. publ., 1992-97, v.p., publ., 1997-98; sr. v.p. bus. devel. New Am. Mktg., Chgo., 1998—. Office: News Am Mktg 303 E Wacker Dr Fl 21 Chicago IL 60601-5212

MARGOLIS, SHERRY, newscaster; m. Jeffrey Zaslow, 1987; children: Jordan, Alexandra, Eden. BA in English, SUNY, Buffalo. Anchor and reporter WKBW-TV, Buffalo; reporter WJBK-TV, Detroit, 1984—, anchor "In the News", co-anchor 5am and noon news, anchor "Live at 11am", anchor "Fox-2 news at 5:30pm". Named Best ewscast in Mich., AP, 1990; recipient Best News Anchor Emmys, NATAS, 1993, 1999, Cmty. Involvement award, U. Mich., 2002, Emmy Reporting, NATAS, 2002, 2006, Pub. Affairs Emmy, 2004, Award of Excellence, Mich. Assn. Broadcasters, 2004, Edward R. Murrow award, 2006. Office: WJBK-TV Fox 2 PO Box 2000 Southfield MI 48037-2000

MARIANI, CARLOS, state legislator; b. July 13, 1957; m. Maritza Mariani; two children. Student, Macalester Coll.; postgrad., UJ. Miami. Social issues program dir.; Dist. 65B rep. Minn. Ho. of Reps., St. Paul, 1990—. Former vice chmn. econ. devel., infrastructure and regulations fin. com., Minn. Ho. of Reps.; asst majority leader; mem. edn.-higher edn., and housing and transp. and transit coms. Office: 187 Congress St W Saint Paul MN 55107-2114 Also: 100 Constitution Ave Saint Paul MN 55155-1232

MARIANO, ROBERT A., retail executive; BS, Univ. Ill., Chgo.; MBA, Univ. Chgo., 1987. V.p. dairy ops., mfg., retail ops. Dominick's Finer Foods, sr. v.p. mktg., perishable mdse., pres., COO, 1995—96, pres., CEO, 1996—98; commr. Ill. Gaming Bd., 2001—02; chmn., CEO, pres. Roundy's Supermarkets Inc., Milw., 2002—. Office: Roundy's Supermarkets Ste 100 875 E Wisconsin Ave Milwaukee WI 53202 Mailing: Roundy's Supermarkets PO Box 473 Milwaukee WI 53201-0473

MARINE, CLYDE LOCKWOOD, agricultural products supplier, consultant; b. Knoxville, Tenn., Dec. 25, 1936; s. Harry H. and Idelle (Larue) M.; m. Eleanor Harb, Aug. 9, 1958; children: Cathleen, Sharon. BS in Agr., U. Tenn., 1958; MS in Agrl. Econs., U. Ill., 1959; PhD in Agrl. Econs., Mich. State U., 1963. Sr. market analyst Pet Milk Co., St. Louis, 1963-64; mgr. market planning agr. chems. div. Mobile Chem. Co., Richmond, Va., 1964-67; mgr. ingredient purchasing Central Soya Co., Ft. Wayne, Ind., 1970-73, corp. economist, 1967-70, v.p. ingredient purchasing, 1973-75, sr. v.p., 1975-90; pres. Marine Assocs., Ft. Wayne, 1991—; bd. dirs. SCAN, 1992—. Mem. agrl. policy adv. com. U.S.D.A. Bd. dirs. Ft. Wayne Fine Arts Found., 1976-79, Ft. Wayne Pub. Transp. Corp., 1975-83; chair, Libr. Found., Metro Human Rels. Commn., Kids First Found. Bd., v.p. Ft. Wayne Philharm., 1974-76. Served with U.S. Army, 1959-60. Mem. at. Soybean Processors Assn. (chmn.), U.S. C. of C., Am. Agrl. Econs. Assn., Am. Feed Mfrs. Assn. (chmn. purchasing coun.). Clubs: Ft. Wayne Country. Episcopalian. Office: Marine Assocs 4646 W Jefferson Blvd Fort Wayne IN 46804-6842 Office Phone: 260-436-4180. Business E-Mail: lmarine@proparkwest.com.

MARINELLI, ROD, professional football coach; b. Rosemead, Calif., July 13, 1949; m. Barbara Marinelli; children: Chris, Gina. Attended, Univ. Utah, 1968, Calif. Lutheran, 1970—72. Asst. coach Rosemead Highschool, Calif., 1973—75; defensive line coach Utah St. U., 1976—81, offensive line/spl. teams coach, 1982; defensive line coach U. Calif., 1983—91; asst. coach, defensive line coach Ariz. State U., 1993—95; defensive line coach U.S.C., 1995—96, Tampa Bay Bucaneers, 1996—2006; head coach Detroit Lions, 2006—. Served in US Army, 1969, Vietnam. Recipient All-Am. honors, NAIA, 1972. Office: Detroit Lions 222 Republic Drive Allen Park MI 48101

MARING, MARY MUEHLEN, state supreme court justice; b. Devils Lake, ND, July 27, 1951; d. Joseph Edward and Charlotte Rose (Schorr) Muehlen: m. David Scott Maring, Aug. 30, 1975; children: Christopher David, Andrew Joseph. BA in Polit. Sci. summa cum laude, Moorhead State U., 1972; JD, U. N.D., 1975. Bar: Minn., N.D. Law clk. Hon. Bruce Stone, Mpls., 1975—76; assoc. Stefanson, Landberg & Alm, Ltd., Moorhead, Minn., 1976—82, Ohnstad, Twichell, Breitling, Rosenvold, Wanner, Nelson, Neugebauer & Maring, West Fargo, ND, 1982—88, Lee Hagan Law Office, Fargo, ND, 1988—91; pvt. practice Maring Law Office, Fargo, 1991—96; justice ND Supreme Ct., Bismarck, ND, 1996—. Women's bd. mem. 1st Nat. Bank, Fargo, 1977-82; career day speaker Moorhead Rotarians, 1980-83; mem. Court Svcs. Com., 1996-, Jud. Compensation, subcom. of Jud. Conf., 1998-, Five-State Jud. Conf. Planning Com., 1997-98, 99-2000; chmn. Gender Fairness Implementation Com., 1997-, Jud. Conf. Exec. Bd., 1998-, chair-elect, 2004-05, chair, 2005, Juvenile Drug Ct. Study, planning and Implementation Com., 1998-2000, Juvenile Drug Ct. Adv. Com., 2000-, Personnel Policy bd., 1999-2004, Govs. Drug and Alcohol Policy Adv. Bd., 1999-2001, N.Dak. Commn. on Drug and Alcohol Abuse, 2002-, No. Plains Ethics Inst., 2000-, Juvenile Policy Bd., 2001-, Jud. Edn. Com., 2005-, Jud. Planning Com., 2001-, Harold Schafer Leadership Ctr. Com. Contbr. note to legal rev.; note editor N.D. Law Rev., 1975. Mem. ABA (del. ann. conv. young lawyers sect. 1981-82, bd. govs. 1982-83), Minn. Women Lawyers, N.D. State Bar Assn. (bd. govs. 1991-93), Clay County Bar Assn. (v.p. 1983-84), N.D. Trial Lawyers Assn. (pres. 1992-93), Internat. Soc. of Barristers, Nat. Assn. of Women Judges (dist. 10 dir. 2001-03). Roman Catholic. Office: ND Supreme Ct 600 E Boulevard Ave Dept 180 Bismarck ND 58505-0530

MARITZ, W. STEPHEN, marketing professional, service executive; b. St. Louis; BS, Princeton U., 1980. With Maritz Inc., Fenton, Mo., 1983—, dir. sales, 1993—95, vice chmn. bd., 1994—, sr. v.p., 1995—97, pres., COO, 1997—98, CEO, pres., 1998—2001, chmn., CEO, 2001—. Bd. dir. Laclede Group Inc. Bd. dir. St. Louis Regional Chamber and Growth Assn. Office: Maritz 1375 N Highway Dr Fenton MO 63099

MARIUCCI, STEVE, professional football coach, former college football coach; b. Iron Mountain, Mich., Nov. 4, 1955; m. Gayle Mariucci; 4 children. Football coach o. Mich. U., 1978-79, Calif. State U., Fullerton, 1980-82; asst. head coach U. Louisville, 1983-84; receivers coach Orlando Renegades U.S. Football League, 1985; quality control coach L.A. Rams, 1985; receivers/spl. teams coach U. So. Calif. Trojans, LA, 1986, wide receivers/spl. teams coach, 1987-89, quarterbacks coach, offensive coord., 1990-91; quarterbacks coach Green Bay (Wis.) Packers, 1992-95; head coach U. Calif. Golden Bears, 1996-98, San Francisco 49ers, 1996—2003, Detroit Lions, 2003—05.

MARK, JAMES EDWARD, physical chemist, department chairman; b. Wilkes-Barre, Pa., Dec. 14, 1934; married, 1964; married, 1990; 2 children. BS, Wilkes Coll., 1957; PhD in Physical Chemistry, U. Pa., 1962. Rsch. chemist Rohm & Haas Co., 1955-56; rsch. asst. Stanford U., 1962-64; asst. prof. chemistry Polytechnic Inst. Brooklyn, N.Y., 1964-67; from asst. prof. to prof. chemistry U. Mich., Ann Arbor, 1967-77; disting. prof. polymer chemistry U. Cincinnati, 1977—. Cons. various industries, 1963—; vis. prof. Stanford U., 1973-74; spl. rsch. fellow NIH, 1975-76; lectr. short course program Am. Chem. Soc., 1973—. Recipient Am. Chem. Soc. award in Applied Polymer Sci., 1995. Mem. AAAS, Am. Chem. Soc. (Am. Chem. Soc. award in applied polymer sci. 1994), Am. Phys. Soc., N.Y. Acad. Sci. Research in statistical properties of chain molecules; elastic properties of polymer networks. Office: U Cincinnati Dept Chemistry Cincinnati OH 45221-0001

MARK, KELLY S., telecommunications industry executive, investment advisor; b. 1972; BS, U. Ill., 1994; MBA, Harvard Bus. Sch., 1999. With Davis Industries, Ford Motor Co., Motorola Future Bus. Group, 1999; investment mgr. Motorola Ventures, Schaumberg, Ill.; dir. bus. devel. Motorola, Inc., Schaumberg, Ill., 2004—. Named one of 40 Under 40, Crain's Chgo. Bus., 2006. Office: Motorola Inc 1303 E Algonquin Rd Schaumburg IL 60196

MARKEE, DAVID JAMES, academic administrator, education educator; b. Madison, Wis., Oct. 26, 1942; s. Richard L. and Cathrine Ann (Whalen) M.; m. Lou Ann Markee, Aug. 14, 1965; children: Jeffrey, Gregory. BS in English and Geography, U. Wis., Platteville, 1964, MEd in Counseling and Guidance, 1968; PhD in Counseling Psychology, U. Mo., 1974. Tchr. English, Platteville High Sch., 1964-67; asst. dir. residence halls U. Wis., 1967-69; asst. dir. student life U. Mo., Columbia, 1970-71, assoc. dir., 1971-72, dir., 1972-75; prof. edn. U. Wis., Whitewater, 1973-80, asst. chancellor student affairs, 1975-80; prof., v.p. for student svcs. No. Ariz. U., Flagstaff, 1980-94; v.p. instl. advancement, 1994-96; chancellor U. Wis., Platteville, 1996—. Contbr. articles to profl. jours. Pres., bd. dirs. Cath. Social Svcs., Flagstaff, 1983—; bd. dirs. Citizens Against Drug Abuse, Flagstaff, 1987-89, Flagstaff Arboretum, 1988—; chmn. Flagstaff Beautification Commn., 1988-93; co-chair Flagstaff United Way. Recipient Person of Yr. award U. Wis.-Whitewater Student Govt., 1975, Chief Manueleto award Navajo Nation, 1990. Mem. Nat. Assn. Student Pers. Adminstrs. (bd. dirs. 1989-90), Ariz. Assn. Student Pers. Adminstrs. (pres. 1986-87), Kiwanis (Outstanding Mem. award Flagstaff 1983-85), Kappaa Delta Pi. Democrat. Office: U Wis One Univ Plz Platteville WI 53818 E-mail: markee@uwplatt.edu.

MARKEL, HOWARD, physician, educator; b. Detroit, Apr. 23, 1960; s. Samuel and Bernice Markel; m. Marcia Deborah Gordin, Sept. 20, 1987 (dec. Oct. 1988); m. Kate Gelya Levin, Aug. 17, 1997; children: Bess Rachel, Samantha Louise. AB in English Lit. summa cum laude, U. Mich., 1982, MD cum laude, 1986; PhD in History of Sci., Medicine & Tech., Johns Hopkins U., 1994. Diplomate Am. Bd. Pediat., 1989. Intern, resident Johns Hopkins Hosp. & Sch. Medicine, Balt., 1986-89, fellow, gen. pediat. and adolescent medicine, 1989—91, fellow, history medicine, 1989—93; asst. prof. pediatrics, communicable diseases U. Mich., Ann Arbor, 1993-98, assoc. prof. pedicatrics, communicable diseases, 1998—2002, George E. Wantz disting. prof. history medicine, 2000—, prof. pediat. and communicable diseases, prof. history, 2002—, prof. pub. health, psychiatry, 2004—. Dir. Ctr. for History of Medicine, U. Mich., 1996—. Author: The H.L. Mencken Baby Book, 1990, The Portable Pediatrician, 1992, The Portable Pediatrician, 2nd edit., 2000, The Practical Pediatrician, 1996 (Child Mag. Book of Yr., 1997), Quarantine! East European Jewish Immigrants and the New York City, 1997 (Arthur Viseltear prize, APHA, 2003), When Germs Travel, 2004. Recipient Nat. Rsch. Svc. award, NIH, 1991, James A. Shannon Dirs. award, 1996, Burroughs Wellcome Fund 40th Ann. History Medicine award, 1996, History of Medicine award, Nat. Libr. Medicine, NIH, 2005—; scholar Robert Wood Johnson Found., 1996—2000. Fellow: Am. Acad. Pediat.; mem.: Am. Pediat. Soc., Soc. Pediat. Rsch., Am. Assn. History Medicine (exec. coun. 1994—97). Democrat. Jewish. Office: U Mich Ctr for History of Medicine 100 Simpson Meml Inst 102 Observatory Ann Arbor MI 48109-0725 Office Phone: 734-647-6914. Business E-Mail: howard@umich.edu.

MARKEY, JAMES KEVIN, lawyer; b. Springfield, Ill., July 15, 1956; s. James Owen and Marjorie Jean (Diesness) M.; m. Allison Markey; children: Lauren, Katherine. BBA with highest honors, U. Notre Dame, 1977; JD cum laude, U. Mich., 1980; MBA, U. Chgo., 1987; LLM in Taxation, DePaul U., 1993. CPA Ill., lic. Mich., 2002; bar: Ill. 1980. Assoc. Chapman & Cutler, Chgo., 1980-81; atty. Quaker Oats Co., Chgo., 1981-84; corp. counsel Baxter Healthcare Corp., Deerfield, Ill., 1984-90; v.p. law and other positions Motorola, Inc., Schaumburg, Ill., 1990-2000; v.p., chief counsel-securities and internat. Kellogg Co., Battle Creek, Mich., 2000—06; v.p., sec., gen. counsel MAG Industrial Automation Sys., LLC, Sterling Heights, Mich., 2006—. Mem. ABA, Beta Alpha Psi, Beta Gamma Sigma. Avocations: racquetball, running, bridge. Office: 13900 Lakeside Cir Sterling Heights MI 48313 Home: 1290 Grandview Rochester Hills MI 48306 Business E-Mail: james.markey@mag-ias.com.

MARKEY, JUDY, radio personality, writer; b. Calif., Feb. 18, 1944; BS in Journalism, Northwestern Univ., 1965. Reporter Chgo. Sun-Times; radio talk show host with Kathy O'Malley WGN-AM, Chgo., 1989—. Author: How to Survive Your High School Reunion and Other Mid-Life Crises, 1984, You Only Get Married for the First Time Once, 1988, The Daddy Clock, 1998, Just Trust Me, 2004. Named one of 100 Most Influential Women, Crain's Chicago Bus., 2004, 100 Most Important Talk Show Hosts in Am., Talkers Mag., 2005; named to Medill Sch. Hall of Achievement, Northwestern Univ., 2005. Office: WGN Radio 435 N Michigan Ave Chicago IL 60611 Office Phone: 312-222-4700. Office Fax: 312-222-5165. Business E-Mail: judymarkey@wgnradio.com.

MARKEY, MAURICE, food products executive; b. 1966; MBA, Ind. U., 1994. With Goodyear Tire & Rubber Co., Kraft Foods, Inc., 1994, mktg. dir., spoonables divsn. Chgo. Mktg. expert New Schools for Chgo., Ill., 2005. Named one of 40 Under 40, Crain's Chgo. Bus., 2005. Office: Kraft Foods Inc 3 Lakes Dr Winnetka IL 60093 Office Fax: 847-646-6005.

MARKIN, DAVID ROBERT, motor company executive; b. NYC, Feb. 16, 1931; s. Morris and Bessie (Markham) M.; children: Sara, John, Christopher, Meredith. BS, Bradley U., 1953. Foreman Checker Motors Corp., Kalamazoo, 1955-57, factory mgr., 1957-62, v.p. sales, 1962-70, pres., 1970—, dir. Bd. dirs. Jackpot Inc. Trustee Kalamazoo Coll. Served to 1st lt. USAF, 1953-55. Mem. Alpha Epsilon Pi Clubs: Standard (Chgo.); Park (Kalamazoo). Home: 2121 Winchell Ave Kalamazoo MI 49008-2205 Office: Checker Motors Corp 2016 N Pitcher St Kalamazoo MI 49007-1894

MARKLE, SANDRA, publishing company executive; 7th grade sci. tchr., Ohio; pres. CompuQuest, Inc., Bartlett, Ill. Office: CompuQuest Inc 366 S Main St Bartlett IL 60103-4423

MARKMAN, RONALD, artist, educator; b. Bronx, NY, May 29, 1931; s. Julius and Mildred (Berkowitz) M.; m. Barbara Miller, Sept. 12, 1959; 1 dau., Ericka Elizabeth. B.F.A., Yale U., 1957, M.F.A., 1959. Instr. Art Inst. Chgo., 1960-64; prof. fine arts Ind. U., 1964—. Color cons. Hallmark Card Co., 1959-60 One-man shows Kanegis Gallery, 1959, Reed Coll., 1966. Terry Dintenfass Gallery, 1965, 66, 68, 70, 76, 79, 82, 85, The Gallery, Bloomington, Ind., 1972, 79, Indpls. Mus., 1974, Tyler Sch. Art, Phila., 1976, Franklin Coll., 1980, Dart Gallery, Chgo., 1981, Patrick King Gallery, Indpls., 1983, 86, John Heron Gallery, Indpls., 1985, New Harmony Gallery, 1985, Mitchell Gallery, St. John's Coll., Annapolis, Md., 2005; two-man show Dintenfass Gallery, 1984; group shows include Kanegis Gallery, Boston, 1958, 60, 61, Boston Arts Festival, 1959, 60, Mus. Modern Art, 1959, 66, Whitney Mus., N.Y.C., 1960, Art Inst. Chgo., 1964, Gallery 99, Miami, Fla., 1966, Ball State Coll., 1966, Butler Inst., 1967, Indpls. Mus., 1968, 69, 72, 74, Phoenix Gallery, N.Y.C., 1970, Harvard U., 1974, Skidmore Coll., 1975, Am. Acad. Arts and Letters, 1977, 89, Tuthill-Gimprich Gallery, N.Y.C., 1980, Patrick King Gallery, 1988, numerous others; represented in permanent collections Met. Mus. Art, Mus. Modern Art, Art Inst. Chgo., Library of Congress, Cin. Art Mus., Bklyn. Mus., Ark. Art Center, others; commns. include 5 murals Riley Children's Hosp., Indpls., 1986; installation Evanston (Ill.) Art Ctr., 1989, 2-part installation Ortho Child Care Ctr., Raritan, N.J., 1991; illustrator Acid and Basics-A Guide to Acid-Base Physiology, 1992. Served with U.S. Army, 1952-54. Recipient Ind. Arts Commn. award, 1990, 93; Fulbright grantee, Italy, 1962, grantee Ctr. for New TV, Chgo., 1992; Lilly Endowment fellow, 1989, honorable mention, Ohio Film Festival, 1995. Home and Office: 1623 Saint Margarets Rd Annapolis MD 21401-5540

MARKMAN, STEPHEN J., state supreme court justice; b. Detroit, June 4, 1949; s. Julius and Pauline Markman; m. Mary Kathleen Sites, Aug. 25, 1974; children: James, Charles. BA, Duke U., 1971; JD, U. Cin., 1974. Legis. asst. to Rep. Edward Hutchinson, Mich., 1975, Rep. Tom Hagedorn, Minn., 1976—78; chief counsel, staff dir. subcom. on constn. Senate Com. on Judiciary, 1978—85, dep. chief counsel, 1983; asst. atty. gen. Office Legal Policy, Dept. Justice, Washington, 1985-89; U.S. atty. U.S. Dept. Justice, Detroit, 1989-93; mem. Miller, Canfield, Paddock & Stone, Detroit, 1993—95; judge Mich. Ct. Appeals, 1995—99; justice Mich. Supreme Ct., Lansing, Mich., 1999—. Prof. constitutional law Hillsdale Coll. Author numerous articles appearing in Stanford Law Review, U. Chicago Law Review, U. Mich. Jour. of Law Reform, Am. Criminal Justice Law Review, Barrister's Law Jour., Harvard Jour. of Law & Public Policy, Detroit Coll. of Law Review. Fellow: Mich. Bar Found.; mem.: ABA, One Hundred Club, Am. Inns of Ct. Office: Mich Supreme Ct Hall of Justice 925 W Ottawa St Fl 6 Lansing MI 48915 Office Phone: 517-373-9449.

MARKOS, CHRIS, retired real estate company executive; b. Cleve., Nov. 25, 1926; s. George and Bessie (Papathatou) Markos; m. Alice Zaharopoulos, Dec. 11, 1949 (dec.); children: Marilyn Martin, Irene Matthews, Betsy Feierabend; m. Marilyn Gardanier, Nov. 8, 2002; children: Kathleen Mitchell, Patricia Hickle. BA, Case Western Res. U., Cleve., 1960; LLB, LaSalle U., Chgo., 1964. Cert. gen. real estate appraiser Ohio. Pres. Brooklyn Realty Co., Cleve., 1953—63; vice-pres. Herbert Laronge Inc., Cleve., 1963-76; v.p. Calabrese, Racek and Markos Inc., Cleve., 1976-83, Herbert Laronge Inc., Cleve., 1983-87, pres., 1987-88; v.p. Cragin Lang, Inc., Cleve., 1989-91; sr. cons. Grubb & Ellis, Cleve., 1991-93; sr. v.p. Realty One Appraisal Divsn., Independence, Ohio, 1993-98. Pres. Alcrimar Inc., 1989—98. Co-author: Ohio Supplement to Modern Real Estate Practice, 5th-7th edits.; cons. editor, co-author: Modern Real Estate Practice in Ohio, 1st-3rd edits. Bd. dirs. Meyers U., Cleve., 1984-97; instr. real estate law Principals and Practices Real Estate, Real Estate Brokerage, 1961-79, Cleveland State U., Cuyahuga and Larain CC, Western Reserve U. divsn general studies; guest lectr. Kent State U. With US Army, 1945—46. Mem. Am. Soc. Appraisers (sr., pres. 1973, state dir. 1976), Cleve. Bd. Realtors (hon. life mem., pres. 1974, Realtor of Yr. award 1976). Republican. Greek Orthodox. Home: Corinthian Condominium 936 Intracoastal Dr Apt 6-H Fort Lauderdale FL 33304 Personal E-mail: alcrimar@bellsouth.net.

MARKOWSKY, JAMES J., retired utilities executive; BS, Pratt Inst.; MS, PhD, Cornell U. Lic. profl. engr. Ind., Ky., Mich., N.Y., Ohio, Tenn., Va., W.Va. Sr. engr. mech. engring. divsn. Am. Electric Power Co., Inc., Columbus, Ohio, 1971-77, program mgr., 1977-84, head mech. engring. divsn., asst. v.p., 1984-87, v.p. mech. engring., 1987-88, sr. v.p., chief engr., 1988-93, exec. v.p. engring. and constrn., 1993-96, exec. v.p. power generation, 1996-00; ret., 2000. Adj. assoc. prof. CUNY, 1975-77. Fellow ASME; mem. Nat. Acad. Engring., Nat. Rsch. Coun. (chmn. com. R & D opportunities for coal fired energy complexes), Assn. Edison Illuminating Cos.' (power generation com.), Coal Utilization Rsch. Coun. (chmn.), Office: Am Electric Power Co Inc 1 Riverside Plz Columbus OH 43215-2355

MARKS, ESTHER L., metals company executive; b. Canton, Ohio, Oct. 3, 1927; d. Jacob and Ella (Wisman) Rosky; m. Irwin Alfred Marks, June 29, 1947; children: Jules, Howard, Marilyn. Student, Ohio State U., 1945-46, Youngstown State U., 1946-47. V.p. Steel City Iron & Metal, Inc., Youngstown, Ohio. Pres. Jr. Hadassah, Youngstown, 1943-45, Pioneer Women, Youngstown, 1951, Anshe Emeth Sisterhood, Youngstown, Broadway Theatre League, Youngstown, 1958, B'nai B'rith Women, Youngstown, 1962, Dist. 2 B'nai B'rith Women, Cleve., 1969-70, Jewish Cmty. Ctr., Youngstown, Youngstown Area Jewish Fedn., 1988-90; v.p. United Way, Youngstown, 1991, chmn., 1996; grad. Leadership Youngstown, 1991; bd. Akiva Acad. Commn. for Jewish Edn., Temple El Emeth, Stambaugh Auditorium. Named Guardian of the Menorah B'nai B'rith, Youngstown, 1978; recipient B'nai B'rith Girls Alumda award, Washington, 1989, Woman of Valor award Jewish Fedn., 1996. Mem. LMV, YWCA, Ohio Hist. Soc. Democrat. Jewish. Avocations: knitting, organizational work. Home: 1295 Virginia Trl Youngstown OH 44505-1637 Office: 703 Wilson Ave Youngstown OH 44506-1445

MARKS, MARTHA ALFORD, writer; b. Oxford, Miss., July 27, 1946; d. Truman and Margaret Alford; m. Bernard L. Marks, Jan. 27, 1968. BA, Centenary Coll., 1968; MA, orthwestern U., 1972, PhD, 1978. Tchr. Notre Dame High Sch. for Boys, Niles, Ill., 1969-74; teaching asst. Northwestern U., Evanston, Ill., 1974-78, lectr., lang. coord., 1978-83; asst. prof. Kalamazoo (Mich.) Coll., 1983-85; writer Riverwoods, Ill., 1985—2002. Cons. WGBH Edn. Found., Boston, 1988-91, Am. Coun. on the Tchg. of Fgn. Langs., 1981-92, Ednl. Testing Svcs., 1988-90, Peace Corps., 1993. Co-author: Destinos: An Introduction to Spanish, 1991, 96, Al corriente, 1989, 93, 97, Que tal?, 1986, 90; author: (workbook) Al corriente, 1989, 93; contbr. articles to profl. jours. Mem. Lake County (Ill.) Bd., Forest Preserve Commn., 1992-2002; co-founder Lake County Conservation Alliance; co-founder Reps. for Environ. Protection, 1995, pres. Reps. for Environ. Protection. Office Phone: 505-889-4544.

MARKUS, KENT RICHARD, lawyer; b. Cleve., Feb. 1, 1959; s. Richard and Carol (Slater) M.; m. Susan Mary Gilles, Apr. 15, 1987; 1 child Robinson Reno. BS, Northwestern U., 1981; JD with honors, Harvard U., 1984. Bar: Ohio 1984, U.S. Dist. Ct. (no. dist.) Ohio 1984, U.S. Dist. Ct. (so. dist.) Ohio 1996, U.S. Ct. Appeals (6th cir.) 1986. Jud. clk. to Hon. Alvin I. Krenzler U.S. Dist. Ct. (no. dist.) Ohio, Cleve., 1984-86; litigation assoc. Gold, Rotatori, Schwartz & Gibbons, Cleve., 1986-89; transition dir. Ohio Atty. Gen. Office, Columbus, Ohio, 1990-91, first asst. atty. gen., chief of staff, 1991-93; counsel to dep. atty. gen. U.S. Dept. Justice, Washington, 1994, dep. assoc. atty. gen., 1994-95, acting asst. atty. gen. legis affairs, 1995, counselor to atty. gen, 1996-98, dep. chief of staff, 1997-98; prof., dir. Nat. Ctr. for Adoption Law & Policy, Capital U. Law Sch., 1998—. Adj. prof. law Cleveland-Marshall Coll. Law, 1987-88. Co-editor: Trial Handbook for Ohio Lawyers, 2nd edit., 1988; contbn. editor for law Webster's New World Dictionary, 4th edit., 1999. Past bd. dirs., past legis. chair Handgun Control Fedn. of Ohio, 1984-93; adv. coun. Northwestern U. Sch. Speech, 1985—; spl. projects dir. Celeste for Gov. Com., Cleve., 1986; campaign mgr. Lee Fisher for Atty. Gen., Cleve. and Columbus, 1989-90; bd. dirs., former trustee, life mem. Cleve. NAACP, 1986-87; chief of staff Dem. Nat. Com., Washington, 1993-94; at-large mem. bd. dirs. SEARCH, Inc., 2000-; bd. dirs. Ohio Legal Assistance Found. 2002-; chair Ctr. Ohio Neighborhood Safety Working Group, 2003-. Named Rising Star of Dem. Party, Campaigns and Elections mag., 1991. Mem. ABA, Ohio State Bar Assn. (former chair young lawyers divsn.), Columbus Bar Assn. Home: 5636 Indian Hill Rd Dublin OH 43017-8209 Office: Capital Univ Law Sch 303 E Broad St Columbus OH 43215-3201 E-mail: kmarkus@law.capital.edu.

MARKUS, LAWRENCE, retired mathematics professor; b. Hibbing, Minn., Oct. 13, 1922; s. Benjamin and Ruby (Friedman) M.; m. Lois Shoemaker, Dec. 9, 1950; children: Sylvia, Andrew. BS, U. Chgo., 1942, MS, 1946; PhD, Harvard U., Cambridge, Mass., 1951. Instr. meteorology U. Chgo., 1942-44; rsch. meteorologist Atomic Project, Hanford, 1944; instr. math. Harvard U., 1951-52; instr. Yale U., 1952-55; lectr. Princeton U., 1955-57; asst. prof. U. Minn., Mpls., 1957-58, assoc. prof., 1958-60, prof. math., 1960-93, assoc. chmn. dept. math., 1961-63, dir. control scis., 1964-73, Regents' prof. math., 1980-93, Regents' prof. emeritus, 1993—, dir. Control Sci. and Dynamical Sys. Ctr., 1980-89. Leverhulme prof. control theory, dir. control theory ctr. U. Warwick, Eng., 1970-73, uffield prof. math., 1970-85, hon. prof., 1985—; regional conf. lectr. NSF, 1969; vis. prof. Yale U., Columbia U., U. Calif., U. Warsaw, 1980, Tech. Inst. Zurich, 1983, Peking U. (China), 1983; dir. conf. Internat. Ctr. Math., Trieste, 1974; lectr. Internat. Math. Congress, 1974, Iranian Math. Soc., 1975, Brit. Math. Soc., 1976, Japan Soc. for Promotion Sci., 1976, Royal Instn., London, 1982, U. Beer Sheva, Israel, 1983; vis. prof. U. Tokyo, 1976, Tech. U., Denmark, 1979; mem. panel Internat. Congress Mathematicians, Helsinki, 1978; sr. vis. fellow Sci. Rsch. Coun., Imperial Coll., London, 1978; mem. UNESCO sci. adv. com. Control Symposium, U. Strasbourg, France, 1980; IEEE Plenary lectr., Orlando, Fla., 1982; Sci. and Engring. Rsch. Coun. vis. prof. U. Warwick, Eng., 1982-90; Neustadt Meml. lectr. U. So. Calif., 1985, prin. lectr. symposium U. Minn., 1988, dir. NSF workshop, 1989, prin. lectr. symposium in honor of his 75th birthday, 1997; Tate lectr. U. Cin., 1998; chmn. Conf. Markus-80, 2002; adv. bd. Office Naval Rsch., Air Force Office Sci. Rsch. Author: Flat Lorentz Manifolds, 1959, Flows on Homogeneous Spaces, 1963, Foundations of Optimal Control Theory, 1967, rev. edit., 1985, Lectures on Differentiable Dynamics, 1971, rev. edit., 1980, Generic Hamiltonian Dynamical Systems, 1974, Distributed Parameter Control Systems, 1991, Boundary Value Problems and Symplectic Algebra, 1998, Multi-Interval Linear Ordinary Boundary Value Problems and Complex Symplectic Algebra, 2001, Elliptic Partial Differential Operators and Symplectic Algebra, 2003, Infinite Dimensional Complex Symplectic Spaces, 2004; editor Internat. Jour. Nonlinear Mechanics, 1965-73, Jour. Control, 1963-67; mem. editl. bd. Proc. Georgian Acad. Sci. Math., 1993—; contbr. articles to profl. jours Lt. (j.g.) USNR, 1944-46. Recipient Rsch. prize Internat. Conf. Nonlinear Oscillations, Ukranian Acad. Sci., Kiev, 1969, Festschrift volume, 1993; Fulbright fellow Paris, 1950; Guggenheim fellow Lausanne, Switzerland, 1963. Fellow Royal Soc. Edinburgh (hon.); mem. Am. Math. Soc. (past mem. nat. coun.), Am. Geophys. Soc., Soc. Indsl. and Applied Math. (past nat. lectr.), Phi Beta Kappa, Sigma Xi. Office: 109 Vincent Hall 206 Church St S Minneapolis MN 55455 Business E-Mail: markus@math.umn.edu.

MARKUS, RICHARD M., judge, arbitrator; b. Evanston, Ill., Apr. 16, 1930; s. Benjamin and Ruby M.; m. Carol Joanne Slater, July 26, 1952; children: Linda, Scott, Kent. BS magna cum laude, Northwestern U., 1951; JD cum laude, Harvard U., 1954. Bar: D.C. 1954, Ohio 1956, Fla. 1994. Appellate atty., civil div. Dept. Justice, Washington, 1954-56; ptnr. civil litigation law firms Cleve., 1956-76, 89-98; judge Cuyahoga County (Ohio) Common Pleas Ct., 1976-80, Ohio Ct. Appeals, 1981-88. Instr. M.I.T., 1952-54; adj. prof. Case Western Res. U. Law Sch., 1972-78, 84-87, Cleve. State U. Law Sch., 1960-80, prof. 1999-2000; prof. Harvard Law Sch., 1980-81; mem. Nat. Commn. on Med. Malpractice, 1971-73; chmn. Nat. Inst. Trial Advocacy, 1978-81, trustee 1971—. Author: Trial Handbook for Ohio Lawyers, all edits., 1971—, Ohio Evidence Rules with Commentary, 1999; contbr. articles to profl. jours.; editor Harvard U. Law Rev, 1952-54. Republican nominee Justice of Ohio Supreme Ct., 1978; bd. dirs. Luth. Metro Ministry, 1988—, Fairview Luth. Hosp., 1985—. Mem. Ohio State Bar Assn. (pres. 1991-92), Cuyahoga County Bar Assn., Greater Cleve. Bar Assn. (trustee 1967-70, 85-90), Assn. Trial Lawyers Am. (nat. pres. 1970-71), Ohio Acad. Trial Lawyers (pres. 1965-66), Phi Beta Kappa, Pi Mu Epsilon, Delta Sigma Rho, Phi Alpha Delta. Home and Office: Pvt Judicial Svcs Inc 3903 N Valley Dr Cleveland OH 44126-1716 E-mail: judgemarkus1@cs.com.

MARKUSON, RICHARD K., former pharmaceutical association executive; Mem. adv. com. on pharmacy practice Nat. Assn. Bds. Pharmacy, pres.; exec. dir. Idaho State Bd. Pharmacy; adj. prof. pharmacy law Idaho State U.; chmn. Nat. Assn. Bds. Pharmacy, 2002—04. Mem.: Idaho State Pharm. Assn., Idaho Soc. Health Sys. Profls. (life). Office: 280 N 8th St Ste 204 Boise ID 83702

MARLETT, JUDITH ANN, nutritional sciences educator, researcher; b. Toledo; BS, Miami U., Oxford, Ohio, 1965; PhD, U. Minn., 1972; postgrad., Harvard U., 1973-74. Registered dietitian. Therapeutic and metabolic unit dietitian VA Hosp., Mpls., 1966-67; spl. instr. in nutrition Simmons Coll., Boston, 1973-74; asst. prof. U. Wis., Madison, 1975-80, assoc. prof. dept. nutritional scis., 1981-84, prof. dept. nutritional scis., 1984—. Cons. U.S. AID, Leyte, Philippines, 1983, Makerere U., Kampala, Uganda, 2005; acting dir. dietetic program dept. Nutritional Scis. U. Wis., 1977-78, dir., 1985-89; cons. grain, drug and food cos., 1985—, adv. bd. U. Ariz. Clin. Cancer Ctr., 1987-95; sci. bd. advisors Am. Health Found., 1988—; reviewer NIH, 1982-2004; vis. prof. Makerere U., Kampala, Uganada, 2005; spkr. in field. Mem. editl. bd. Jour. Sci. of Food and Agrl., 1989—, Jour. Food Composition and Analysis, 1994-2000, Jour. of utrition, 2002—; contbr. articles to profl. jours. Mem. NIH (Diabetes and Digestive and Kidney Disease spl. grant rev. com. 1992-96), Am. Soc. Nutrition, Am. Dietetic Assn. Achievements include research on human nutrition and disease, dietary fiber and gastrointestinal function. Office: U Wis Dept utritional Sci 1415 Linden Dr Madison WI 53706-1527 Home Phone: 623-972-5221; Office Phone: 623-972-5221. Business E-Mail: jmarlett@nutrisci.wisc.edu.

MARLING, KARAL ANN, art history educator, social sciences educator, curator; b. Rochester, NY, Nov. 5, 1943; d. Raymond J. and Marjorie (Karal) M. PhD, Bryn Mawr Coll., 1971. Prof. art history and Am. studies U. Minn., Mpls., 1977—. Author: Federal Art in Cleveland, 1933-1943: An Exhibition, 1974, Wall-to-Wall America: A Cultural History of Post-Office Murals in the Great Depression, 1982, 2d edit., 2001, The Colossus of the Roads: Myth and Symbol Along the American Highway, 1984, 2d edit., 2000, Tom Benton and His Drawings: A Biographical Essay and a Collection of His Sketches, Studies and Mural Cartoons, 1985, Frederick C. Knight (1898-1797), 1987, George Washington Slept Here: Colonial Revivals and American Culture, 1876-1986, 1988, Looking Back: A Perspective on the 1913 Inaugural Exhibition, 1988, Blue Ribbon: A Social and Pictorial History of the Minnesota State Fair, 1990; author: (with John Wetenhall) Iwo Jima: Monuments, Memories, and the American Hero, 1991; author: Edward Hopper, 1992, As Seen on T.V.: The Visual Culture of Everyday Life in the 1950's, 1994, Graceland: Going Home with Elvis, 1995; editor (with Jessica H. Foy): The Arts and the American Home, 1890-1930, 1994; editor: orman Rockwell, 1997, Designing the Disney Theme Parks: The Architecture of Reassurance, 1997, Merry Christmas! Celebrating America's Greatest Holiday, 2000, Looking North, 2003, Debutante, 2004, Old Glory Unfurled, 2004, Norman Rockwell: America's Favorite Painter, 2005, Behind The Magic: 50 Years of Disneyland, 2005, Designs on The Heart: The Homemade Art of Grandma Moses, 2006; contbr. essays to catalogs. Recipient award Minn. Humanities Commn., 1986, Book History award Minn., 1994, Robert C. Smith award Decorative Arts Soc., 1994, award Internat. Assn. Art Critics, 1998; Woodrow Wilson fellow, fellow Luce Found. Office: 1920 S 1st St Ste 1301 Minneapolis MN 55454-1190 Office Phone: 612-339-6172. Personal E-mail: kmarling@comcast.net. Business E-Mail: marli001@umn.edu.

MAROVICH, GEORGE M., federal judge; b. 1931; AA, Thornton Community Coll., 1950; BS, U. Ill., 1952, JD, 1954. Atty. Chgo. Title & Trust Co., 1954-59; mem. firm Jacobs & Marovich, South Holland, Ill., 1959-66; v.p., trust officer South Holland Trust & Savs. Bank, 1966-76; judge Cir. Ct. Cook County, Ill., 1976-88; dist. judge U.S. Dist. Ct. (no. dist.) Ill., Chgo., 1988—. Adj. instr. Thornton Community Coll., 1977-88. Mem. Ill. Judges Assn., Ill. Jud. Conf., Chgo. Bar Assn., South Suburban Bar Assn. Office: US Dist Ct Chambers 1956 219 S Dearborn St Ste 2050 Chicago IL 60604-1800

MAROVITZ, JAMES LEE, retired lawyer; b. Chgo., Feb. 21, 1939; s. Harold and Gertrude (Luster) M.; m. Gail Helene Florsheim, June 17, 1962; children: Andrew, Scott. BS, Northwestern U., 1960, JD, 1963. Bar: Ill. 1963, U.S. Dist. Ct. (no. dist.) Ill. 1963, U.S. Ct. Appeals (7th cir.) 1990. Assoc. Leibman, Williams, Bennett, Baird & Minow, Chgo., 1963-70, ptnr., 1970-72, Sidley & Austin, Chgo., 1972-99, sr. counsel, 2000—02, ret., 2002. Plan commr. Village of Deerfield, Ill., 1972-79, trustee, 1983-93, police commr. 1995—. Mem. Ill. Bar Assn., Univ. Club. E-mail: jmarovit@sidley.com.

MAROVITZ, SANFORD EARL, English language and literature educator; b. Chgo., May 10, 1933; s. Harold and Gertrude (Luster) M.; m. Eleonora Dimitsa, Sept. 1, 1964. BA with honors, Lake Forest Coll., 1960; MA, Duke U., 1961, PhD, 1968. Instr. English Temple U., 1963-65; Fulbright instr. U. Athens, Greece, 1965-67; from asst. prof. English to prof. Kent State U., Ohio, 1967-96, prof. emeritus, 1996—. Vis. prof. English, Shimane U., Matsue, Japan, 1976-77, chair, 1987-92; co-dir. Melville Among the Nations, Greece, 1997. Co-editor: Artful Thunder: Versions of Romanticism in American Literature in Honor of Howard P. Vincent, 1975, Melville Among the Nations: Proceedings, 2001; co-author: Bibliographical Guide to the Study of the Literature of the U.S.A., 5th edit., 1984; author: Abraham Cahan, 1996; contbr. articles to profl. jours. Nat. trustee Lake Forest Coll., 1990-98. With USAF, 1953-57. Woodrow Wilson fellow, 1960-61; recipient Disting. Svc. Citation Lake Forest Coll., 1985, Disting. Tchg. award Kent State U., 1985, Presdl. Citation Shimane U., 1998. Mem.: MLA, Jack London Soc., Coll. English Assn. (Robert Miller award for best article in CEA Critic 2000), R.W. Emerson Soc., Saul Bellow Soc., W.D. Howells Soc. (v.p. 2000—01, pres. 2002—03, editor The Howellsian 2004—07), Aldous Huxley Soc. (curator 1998—), Nathaniel Hawthorne Soc., Melville Soc. (sec. 1994—96, pres. 1998), Phi Beta Kappa, Phi Beta Delta, Omicron Delta Kappa. Democrat. Jewish. Home: 1155 Norwood St Kent OH 44240-3342 Office: Kent State U Dept English Kent OH 44242-0001 E-mail: smarovit@kent.edu.

MARQUARDT, CHRISTEL ELISABETH, judge; b. Chgo., Aug. 26, 1935; d. Herman Albert and Christine Marie (Geringer) Trolenberg; children: Eric, Philip, Andrew, Joel. BS in Edn., Mo. Western Coll., 1970; JD with honors, Washburn U., 1974. Bar: Kans. 1974, Mo. 1992, U.S. Dist. Ct. Kans. 1974, U.S. Dist. Ct. (we. dist.) Mo. 1992. Tchr. St. John's Ch., Tigerton, Wis., 1955-56; pers. asst. Columbia Records, LA, 1958-59; ptnr. Cosgrove, Webb & Oman, Topeka, 1974-86, Palmer & Marquardt, Topeka, 1986-91, Levy and Craig P.C., Overland Park, Kans., 1991-94; sr. ptnr. Marquardt and Assocs., L.L.C., Fairway, Kans., 1994-95; judge Kans. Ct. Appeals, 1995—. Mem. atty. bd. discipline Kans. Supreme Ct., 1984—86; mem. Kans. Sentencing Commn., 2004—, Kans. Criminal Justice Recodification, Rehab. and Restoration Com., 2004—; bd. regents Washburn U. Tokeka, 2007—. Mem. editorial adv. bd. Kans. Lawyers Weekly, 1992-96; contbr. articles to legal jours. Bd. dirs. Topeka Symphony, 1983-92, 96-, Arts and Humanities Assn. Johnson County, 1992-95, Brown Found., 1988-90; hearing examiner Human Rels. Com., Topeka, 1974-76; local advisor Boy Scouts Am., 1973-74; bd. dirs., mem. nominating com. YWCA, Topeka, 1979-81; bd. govs. Washburn U. Law Sch., 1987-2002, v.p., 1996-98, pres., 1998-2000, disting. alumni, 2004; mem. dist. bd. adjudication Mo. Synod Luth. Ch., Kans., 1982-88. amed Woman of Yr., Mayor, City of Topeka, 1982; Obee scholar Washburn U., 1972-74; recipient Jennie Mitchell Kellogg Atty. of Achievement award, 1999, Phil Lewis medal of Distinction, 2000, Atty. of Achievement award Kans. Women Attys. Assn., Disting. Svc. award Washburn U. Law Sch., 2002, 04; named Disting. Alumni, Washburn U. Fellow: Kans. Bar Found. (trustee 1987—89), Am. Bar Found.; mem.: ABA (mem. ho. dels. 1988—, chmn. specialization com. 1991—93, lawyer referral com. 1993—95, state del. 1995—99, bar svcs. and activities 1995—99, bd. govs., program and planning com. 1999—2002, bd. govs. 1999—2002, ctrl. and ea. European law initiative 2001—02, African law coun. 2002—04, del-at-large ho. of dels. 2002—, standing com. on jud. independence 2004—, SCOPE com. 2001—, SCOPE com. chair 2006—07), Scape and Correlation of Work (chair 2006—), Law and Organizational Econ. Ctr. (bd. dirs. 2000—02), Am. Bus. Women's Assn. (lectr., corr. sec. 1983—84, pres. career chpt. 1986—87, named one of Top 10 Bus. Women of Yr. 1985), Topeka Bar Assn., Kans. Trial Lawyers Assn. (bd. govs. 1982—86, lectr.), Kans. Bar Assn. (sec., treas. 1981—85, bd. dirs. 1983—, v.p. 1985—86, pres. 1987—88, mem., lawyer referral com. 1999—). Home: 3408 SW Alameda Dr Topeka KS 66614-5108 Office: 301 SW 10th Ave Topeka KS 66612-1502 Business E-Mail: marquardtc@kscourts.org.

MARQUARDT, MICHELE C., lawyer; b. Detroit, May 4, 1951; AB summa cum laude, Albion Coll., 1972; MA in Ednl. Psych., U. Mich., 1977; JD cum laude, Wayne State U., 1986. Bar: Mich. 1986, US Dist. Ct. (ea. dist. Mich.) 1986. Atty. DeMent & Marquardt, PLC, Kalamazoo. Named one of Top 100 Attys., Worth mag., 2006, 2007. Mem.: State Bar Mich. (mem. estate planning and real property sects., One of Mich. Superlawyers in Estate Planning 2007), ABA, Kalamazoo Bar Assn., Phi Beta Kappa. Office: DeMent and Marquardt PLC 211 E Water St Ste 401 Kalamazoo MI 49007-5806 Office Phone: 269-343-2106. Office Fax: 269-343-2107. E-mail: michele@dementandmarquardt.com.

MARQUARDT, STEVE ROBERT, advocate; b. St. Paul, Sept. 7, 1943; s. Robert Thomas and Dorothy Jean (Kane) M.; m. Judy G. Brown, Aug. 4, 1968; 1 child, Sarah. BA in History, Macalester Coll., 1966; MA in History, U. Minn., 1970, MLS, 1973, PhD in History, 1978. History instr. Macalester Coll., St. Paul, 1968—69; cataloger N.Mex. State U. Libr., Las Cruces, 1973—75; acting univ. archivist, acting dir. Rio Grande Hist. Collections N. Mex. State U. Libr., Las Cruces, 1973—74; acquisitions librarian Western Ill. U. Libr., Macomb, 1976—77, head cataloger, Online Computer Libr. Ctr. coord., 1977—79; asst. dir. resources & tech. svcs. Ohio U. Libr., Athens, 1979—81; dir. libns. U. Wis., Eau Claire, 1981—89; dir. univ. libns. No. Ill. U., DeKalb, 1989—90; dir. libns. U. Wis., Eau Claire, 1990—96; dean of libns. S.D. State U., Brookings, 1996—2006. Editor Jour. Rio Grande History, 1974; contbg. editor: Library Issues, 1994-2003; contbr. articles to profl. jours. Coord., adoption group 275 Amnesty Internat., Eau Claire, 1985—88, legis. coord. Minn., 2007—, freedom co-chair, 2006—; pres. Chippewa Valley Free-net, 1994—96. Mem.: ALA. Lutheran. Avocation: bicycling. Home and Office: Rancho Mosquito 9383 123rd Ave SE Lake Lillian MN 56253-4700 Home Phone: 605-690-6113; Office Phone: 605-688-5106, 320-664-4231. E-mail: marquardt.steve@gmail.com.

MARQUETTE, I. EDWARD, lawyer; b. Hannibal, Mo., Oct. 15, 1950; s. Clifford M. and Doris Elizabeth (McLane) M.; m. Ansie S. Goodrich, May 20, 1972; children: Brandeis, Brooks. BA in Econs., U. Mo., 1973; JD cum laude, Harvard U., 1976. Bar: Mo. 1976. Ptnr. Spencer, Fane, Britt & Browne LLP, 1976, Sonnenschein Nath & Rosenthal LLP. Contbr. articles to profl. jours., chpts. to books. Bd. dirs. Midwest Christian Counseling Combined Health Appeal, Kansas City, 1988-95. amed Best Lawyers Am. Mem. ABA (new info. tech. com.), Mo. Bar Assn. (tech. com.), Kansas City Bar Assn. (chmn. antitrust study grp. 1984, chmn. computer law com. 1989, 90, 95, 99), Silicon Prairie Tech. Assn., Phi Beta Kappa, Phi Kappa Phi & Delta Psi Omega. Democrat. Baptist. Avocation: computer programming. Office: Sonnenschein Nath & Rosenthal LLP 4520 Main St Ste 1100 Kansas City MO 64111 Office Phone: 816-460-2405. Office Fax: 816-531-7545. Business E-Mail: emarquette@sonnenschein.com.

MARRETT, CORA B., science educator; b. Richmond, Va., June 15, 1942; d. Horace Sterling and Clora Ann (Boswell) Bagley; m. Louis Everard Marrett, Dec. 24, 1968. BA, Va. Union U., 1963; MS, U. Wis., 1965, PhD, 1968. Asst. prof. U. N.C., Chapel Hill, 1968-69; from asst. to assoc. prof. Western Mich. U., Kalamazoo, 1969-73; from assoc. prof. to full prof. U. Wis., Madison, 1973-97; asst. dir. NSF, Arlington, Va., 1992-96; provost, vice chancellor for acad. affairs U. Mass., Amherst, 1997—2001; sr. v.p. for acad. affairs U. Wis. System, 2001—. Mem. sci. adv. panel U.S. Army, Washington, 1976-77; mem. Naval Rsch. Adv. Com., Washington, 1978-81, Pres. Commn. on the Accident at Three Mile Island, 1979; bd. govs. Argonne (Ill.) Nat. Lab., 1983-90, 96-99. Editor: Research in Race and Ethnic Relations, 1988, Gender and Classroom Interaction, 1990. Resident fellow NAS, 1973-74; fellow Ctr. for Advanced Study in Behavioral Scis., 1976-77. Mem. AAAS, ASA, Phi Kappa Phi. Avocations: reading, travel, film appreciation. Home: 7517 Farmington Way Madison WI 53717 Office: Office Acad Affairs U of Wisconsin System 1620 Van Hise Hall Madison WI 53706 Office Phone: 608-262-3826. E-mail: cmarrett@uwsa.edu.

MARRINAN, SUSAN FAYE, lawyer; b. Vermillion, SD, May 29, 1948; BA, U. Minn., 1969, JD, 1973. Bar: Minn. 1973, Wis. 1973. Atty. Carlson Cos., Plymouth, Minn., 1973-74, Prudential Ins. Co., Mpls., 1974-75; v.p., gen. counsel, corp. sec. H.B. Fuller Co., St. Paul, 1977—90; gen. counsel, sec. Snap-On, Inc., Kenosha, Wis., 1990—92, v.p., gen. counsel, sec., 1992—2004, v.p., sec., chief legal officer, 2004—. Fundraiser Am. Cancer Soc.; bd. dirs. Family Svcs. St. Paul, Childrens Theatre Co. Mem. Am. Assn. Corp. Counsel (bd. dirs. Minn. chpt. 1986—), Am. Corp. Counsel Assn. (bd. dirs. 1997-02). Republican. Avocation: running. Office: Snap-On Inc 2801 80th St Kenosha WI 53141

MARRISON, BENJAMIN J., editor-in-chief; b. Ashtabula, Ohio; BA, Bowling Green State U. With Toledo Blade, Cleve. Plain Dealer, 1990—99, Columbus bur. chief, 1996—99; mng. editor news Columbus Dispatch, Ohio, 1999, editor, 1999—. Named to Bowling Green State U. Hall of Fame. Mem.: AP Soc. Ohio, Columbus Met. Club. Office: Columbus Dispatch 34 S 3rd St Columbus OH 43215 Office Phone: 614-461-5200. E-mail: bmarrison@dispatch.com.*

MARSDEN, GEORGE M., history professor, writer; b. Feb. 25, 1939; BA in History, Haverford Coll., 1959; BD, Westminster Theol. Sem., 1963; MA, Yale U., 1961, PhD in Am. Studies, 1965. Asst. in instrn. Yale U., 1964—65, instr., asst. and assoc. prof., 1965—74; prof. dept. history Calvin Coll., 1974—86, dir. MA in Christian Studies Program, 1980—83; prof. history of Christianity in Am. Duke U., The Divinity Sch., 1986—92; Francis A. McAnaney prof. history U. Notre Dame, Ind., 1992—. Vis. prof. ch. history Trinity Evang. Div. Sch., Deerfield, Ill., 1976—77; vis. prof. history U. Calif., Berkeley, Calif., 1986, Berkeley, 90. Author: The Evangelical Mind and the New School Presbyterian Experience, 1970, Fundamentalism and American Culture: The Shaping of Twentieth-Century Evangelicalism, 1980, Reforming Fundamentalism: Fuller Seminary and the New Evangelicalism, 1987, Religion and American Culture, 1990, Understanding Fundamentalism and Evangelicalism, 1991, The Soul of the American University, 1994, The Outrageous Idea of Christian Scholarship, 1997, Jonathan Edwards: A Life, 2003 (The Grawemeyer award in Religion, U. Louisville, 2005); associate. editor: social scis. Christian Scholar's Rev., 1970—77; editor: (mem. sr. editl. bd.) The Reformed Jour., 1980—90. Fellow, Calvin Ctr. for Christian Scholarship, 1979—80, John Simon Guggenheim Meml. Found.; grantee, J. Howard Pew Freedom Trust, 1988—92; Younger Humanists fellow, NEH, 1971—72, Calvin Rsch. fellow, 1982—83. Mem.: Am. Soc. Ch. History (coun. mem. 1983—86, pres. 1992), Inst. for the Study of Am. Evangelicals (mem. adv. coun. 1989—). Office: Univ Notre Dame 321 Decio Faculty Hall Notre Dame IN 46556 E-mail: marsden.1@nd.edu.

MARSH, BENJAMIN FRANKLIN, lawyer; b. Toledo, Apr. 30, 1927; s. Lester Randall and Alice (Smith) M.; m. Martha Kirkpatrick, July 12, 1952; children: Samuel, Elizabeth. BA, Ohio Wesleyan U., 1950; JD, George Washington U., 1954. Bar: Ohio 1955. Pvt. practice law, Toledo, 1955—88; assoc., ptnr. Doyle, Lewis & Warner, Toledo, 1955—71; ptnr. Ritter, Boesel, Robinson & Marsh, Toledo, 1971—88; mem. Marsh & McAdams, Maumee, 1988—98; pers. officer AEC, 1950—54; asst. atty. gen. State of Ohio, 1969—71; asst. solicitor City of Maumee, 1959—63, solicitor, 1963—92; mem. Marsh McAdams, Ltd., Maumee, 1999—. Mem. U.S. Fgn. Claims Settlement Commn., Washington, 1990-94; counsel N.W. Ohio Mayors and Mgrs. Assn., 1990-2000; regional bd. rev. Indsl. Commn. Ohio, Toledo, 1993-94; mem. Ohio Dental Bd., 1995-2000; trustee Corp. for Effective Govt., 1998-2003; mem. Ohio Elections Commn., 2001-07, chmn. 2003-04 U.S. rep. with rank spl. amb. to 10th Anniversary Independence of Botswana, 1976; past pres. Toledo and Lucas County Tb Soc.; co-chmn. citizens for metro pks.; past mem. Judges Com. otaries Pub.; former mem. Lucas County Bd. Elections; former chmn. bldg. commn. Riverside Hosp., Toledo; past trustee Com. on Rels. with Toledo, Spain; past chmn. bd. trustee Med. Coll., Ohio; past treas. Coglin Meml. Inst.; chmn. Lucas County Rep. Exec. Com., 1973-74; precinct commiteeman, Maumee, 1959-73; legal counsel, bd. dirs. Nat. Coun. Rep. Workshops, 1960-65; pres. Rep. Workshops, Ohio, 1960-64; alt. del. Rep. Nat. Conv., 1964; candidate 9th dist. U.S. Ho. of Reps., 1968; adminstrv. asst. to Rep. state chmn. Ray C. Bliss, 1954; chmn. Lucas County Bush for Pres., 1980; co-chmn. Reagan-Bush Com. for Northwestern Ohio, 1980, vice chmn. fin. com. Bush-Quayle, 1992; co-chmn. Ohio steering com. Bush for Pres., mem. nat. steering com., 1988; del. Rep. at. Conv., 1988; past bd. dirs. Ohio Tb and Respiratory Disease Assn.; apptd. Ohio chmn. UN Day, 1980, 81, 82; adminstrv. asst. Legis. Svc. Commn., Columbus, 1954-55; mem. Lucas County Charter Commn., Toledo, 1959-60; vice-chmn. U.S. Nat. Commn. for UNESCO, mem. legal com., del. 17th gen. conf., Paris, 1972, U.S. observer meeting of nat. commns., Africa, 1974, Addis Ababa, Ethiopia; past mem. industry functional adv. com. on stds. trade policy matters; mem. nat. def. exec. res. Dept. Commerce; active Am. Bicentennial Presdl. Inauguration, Diplomatic Adv. Com. With USNR, 1945-46. Named Outstanding Young Man of Toledo, 1962. Mem. ABA, Maumee C. of C. (past pres.), UN Assn., Ohio State Bar Assn., Toledo Bar Assn., Ohio Mpcl. League (past pres.), Am. Legion (comdr. Toledo Post), Lucas County Maumee Valley Hist. Soc. (past pres.), Internat. Inst. Toledo, Ohio Mcpl. Attys. Assn. (past pres.), Orgn. Security and Cooperation in Europe (registration supr., adjudicator, elections supr. in Bosnia), Western Lake Erie Hist. Soc., Ohio Hist. Soc., Canal Soc. Ohio, Toledo Mus. Art, Ohio Wesleyan U. Alumni Assn. (past pres.), Ohio State Bar Found., Toledo Bar Found., Rotary, Toledo Country Club, Torch Club Toledo, Navy League, Omicron Delta Kappa, Delta Sigma Rho, Theta Alpha Phi, Phi Delta Phi. Presbyterian. Home: 1624 Swan Creek Ln Toledo OH 43614 Office: 204 W Wayne St Maumee OH 43537-2125 Office Phone: 419-893-4880. Personal E-mail: bmarsh124@aol.com.

MARSH, CHARLES ALAN, retail executive; b. Muncie, Ind., July 5, 1941; s. Ermal Woodrow and Garnet Rosetta (Gibson) Marsh; m. Janet Kaye Bradford, July 2, 1965; children: Charles Alan, Amanda Holt. BA, DePauw U., 1963; MBA, Ind. U., 1965; postgrad., Law Sch., 1966—68. Mgmt. trainee Marsh Supermarkets, Inc., Yorktown, Ind., 1965—66; local rsch. analyst Marsh Village Pantries, Yorktown, 1966—67, pres., 1982—. With Marsh Supermarkets, Inc., Yorktown, 1967—, dir. real estate, 1969—72, exec. v.p., 1972—85, pres., COO, bd. dirs., 1985—; dir. Miller Enterprises, Inc., Crescent City, Fla. Bd. dirs. Ind. Mental Health Meml. Found., 1986—90, chmn. bd., 1988—90. Mem.: Ind. Assn. Convenience Stores (bd. dirs.), Nat. Assn. Convenience Stores (bd. dirs., vice chmn. edn. 1983—85, vice chmn. ann. meeting 1985—86, vice chmn. fin., membership 1986—87, chmn. 1987—88), Crooked Stick Golf Club. Republican. Presbyterian. Home: 8650 Jaffa Court West Dr Apt 16 Indianapolis IN 46260-5335 Office: Marsh Village Pantries Inc 9800 Crosspoint Blvd Indianapolis IN 46256-3300 also: Marsh Supermarkets Inc 501 Depot St Yorktown IN 47396

MARSH, DON ERMAL, supermarket executive; b. Muncie, Ind., Feb. 2, 1938; s. Ermal W. and Garnet (Gibson) M.; m. Marilyn Faust, Mar. 28, 1959; children: Don Ermal, Jr., Arthur Andrew, David Alan, Anne Elizabeth, Alexander Elliott. BA, Mich. State U., 1961. With Marsh Supermarkets, Inc., Indpls., 1961—2006, pres., 1968—2006, chmn. CEO; ret. Chmn. FoodPAC, Washington, 1991; bd. dirs. Nat. City Bank, Indpls., Ind. Energy, Inc., Indpls.; gov. World Econ. Forum—Food & Agro, Geneva. Bd. dirs. Corp. Community Coun., Culver Fathers Assn., Food Industry Crusade Against Hunger, Charlene S. Lugar Birth Defects Grant Fund, Am. Arbitration Assn, Ctrl. Ind. Corp., Econ. Club Indpls., Hanover Coll., other; bd. mem. Ind. Assn. Cities and Towns; mem. adv. com. on food distbn. Western Mich. U.; mem. Conner Prairie Pioneer Settlement Adv. Coun.; mem. Indpls. Mus. Art.; mgmt. coun. Am. Mgmt. Assn. Mem. Am. Mgmt. Assn., Mgmt. Execs. Soc., Gen. Mgmt. Coun., Internat. Food Congress, Assn. of Publicly Traded Cos. (bd. dirs., past chmn.), Food Mktg. Inst. (bd. dirs.), Indpls. C. of C., Ind. State C. of C. (bd. dirs.), Ind. Retail Coun. (bd. dirs.), Ind. Soc. Chgo., Chief Execs. Orgn., World Bus. Coun., Newcomen Soc. N.Am., Internat. Ctr. for Cos. of Food Trade and Industry (past chmn., bd. dirs.), Food Merchandisers Edn. Coun., Nat. Assn. Convenience Stores, Nat. Assn. Food Rsch., World Pres. Orgn., Young Pres. Orgn. Alumni, Nat. Soc. Fund Raising Execs., Well House Soc., Am. Bus. Club, Ind. Fiscal Policy Inst., Ind. Soc. Chgo., Ind. U. Varsity Club, Crooked Stick Golf Club, Columbia Club, Delaware Country Club, The Hundred Club Indpls., Indpls. Athletic Club, Marco Polo Club, Meridian Hills Country Club, Skyline Club, Masons, Elks, Pi Sigma Epsilon, Lambda Chi Alpha Found., Sigma Phi Omega. Republican. Presbyterian.

MARSH, JAMES C., JR., secondary school principal; Headmaster Westminster Christian Acad., St. Louis, 1985—. Recipient Blue Ribbon Sch. award U.S. Dept. of Edn., 1990-91. Office: Westminster Christian Acad 10900 Ladue Rd Saint Louis MO 63141-8496

MARSH, MILES L., paper company executive; b. 1947; With various divsns. Dart & Kraft Inc., Gen. Foods USA; chmn., CEO Pet Inc., St. Louis, until 1995; pres., CEO Ft. James Corp., Richmond, 1995—, chmn. bd., 1996—, chmn., CEO Deerfield, Ill. Office: Fort James Corp 1919 S Broadway Green Bay WI 54304-4905

MARSH, RICHARD H., energy executive; BA, Kent State U.; MA in Clinical Psychology, U. Akron, MBA. CFA. Joined Ohio Edison, 1980, various financial positions, 1980—91; treasurer Ohio Edison (merged with Centerior Energy to form FirstEnergy), 1991—97; v.p. finance FirstEnergy Corp., Akron, Ohio, 1997, v.p., CFO, 1998—2001, sr. v.p., CFO, 2001—. Chmn. Utility Pension Fund Study Group; mem. fin. adv. com. Edison Elec. Inst. Mem. advancement coun. Coll. Bus. Admin. U. Akron, v.p. alumni coun.; chair We. Reserve Girl Scout Coun.; trustee FirstEnergy Found., H.M. Life Opportunity Services; mem. advisory com. for Master of Sci. in Fin. Engring. prog. Kent State U. Mem.: Cleve. Soc. Security Analysts. Office: First Energy Corp 76 S Main St Akron OH 44308-1890

MARSH, WILLIAM LYNN, retail executive; b. Muncie, Ind., May 12, 1944; s. Ermal W. and Garnet R. (Gibson) Marsh; m. Gail I. Turner (div. 1980); children: William L. II, Nicole D. BBA, U. Miami, 1966; postgrad. food mktg. mgmt., Mich. State U., 1967. With Marsh Supermarkets, Yorktown, Ind., 1961—. Market analyst Marsh Supermarkets, Yorktown, 1969—74, asst. dir. real estate, 1974—76, dir. real estate, 1976—81, v.p. real estate, 1981—85; v.p., gen. mgr. Marsh Properties, 1985—. Mem.: Nat. Assn. Real Estate Execs., Internat. Coun. Shopping Ctrs. Office: Marsh Supermarkets Inc 9800 Crosspoint Blvd Indianapolis IN 46256-3300

MARSHAK, MARVIN LLOYD, physicist, researcher; b. Mar. 11, 1946; s. Kalman and Goldie (Hait) M.; m. Anita Sue Kolman, Sept. 24, 1972; children: Rachel Kolman, Adam Kolman. AB in Physics, Cornell U., 1967; MS in Physics, U. Mich., PhD in Physics, 1970. Rsch. assoc. U. Minn., Mpls., 1970-74, from asst. prof. to assoc. prof., 1974-83, prof. physics, 1983-96, dir. grad. studies in physics, 1983-86, prin. investigator high energy physics, 1982-86, head Sch. Physics and Astronomy, 1986-96, sr. v.p. for acad. affairs, 1996-97, Morse-Alumni disting. tchg. prof. physics, 1996—, Inst. of Tech. prof., 2004—, dir. residential coll., 1997—2005, faculty legis. liason, 1997—2001, chair univ. senate consultative exec. com., 2004—05, dir. undergrad. rsch., 2007—. Contbr. articles to profl. jours. Trustee Children's Theater Co., 1989-94. Fellow: Am. Phys. Soc. Home: 2855 Ottawa Ave S Minneapolis MN 55416-1946 Office Phone: 612-624-1312. Business E-Mail: marshak@umn.edu.

MARSHALEK, EUGENE RICHARD, retired physics educator, researcher; b. NYC, Jan. 17, 1936; s. Frank M. and Sophie (Weg) M.; m. Sonja E. M. Lennhart, Dec. 8, 1962; children: Thomas, Frank. BS, Queens Coll., 1957; PhD, U. Calif., Berkeley, 1962. NSF postdoctoral fellow Niels Bohr Inst., Copenhagen, 1962-63; rsch. assoc. Brookhaven Nat. Lab., Upton, N.Y., 1963-65; asst. prof. physics U. Notre Dame, Ind., 1965-69, assoc. prof. Ind., 1969-78, prof. Ind., 1978—, prof. emeritus Ind., ret. Ind., 2002—. Contbr. articles to profl. jours. Recipient Alexander von Humboldt sr. scientist award, 1985. Fellow Am. Phys. Soc.; mem. AAAS, Sigma Xi. Office: U Notre Dame Dept Physics Notre Dame IN 46556

MARSHALL, CAROLYN ANN M., church official; b. Springfield, Ill., July 18, 1935; d. Hayward Thomas and Isabelle Bernice (Hayer) McMurray; m. John Alan Marshall, July 14, 1956 (dec. Sept. 1990); children: Margaret Marshall Bushman, Cynthia Marshall Kyrouac, Clinton, Carol Bentler. Student, De Pauw U., 1952-54; BSBA, Drake U., 1956; D of Pub. Svc. (hon.), De Pauw U., 1983; LHD (hon.), U. Indpls., 1990. Corp. sec. Marshall Studios, Inc., Veedersburg, Ind., 1956-89, exec. cons., 1989-93; sec. Gen. Conf., lay leader South Ind. conf. United Meth. Ch., Veedersburg, Ind., 1988-96; exec. dir. Lucille Raines Residence, Inc., Indianapolis, 1996—. Carolyn M. Marshall chair in women studies Bennett Coll., Greensboro, N.C., 1988; fin. cons. Lucille Raines Residence, Inpls., 1977-95. Pres. Fountain Ctrl. Band Boosters, Veedersburg, 1975-77; del. Gen. Conf., United Meth. Ch., 1980, 84, 88, 92, 96, 2000, pres. women's divsn. gen. bd. global ministries, 1984-88; bd. dirs. Franklin (Ind.) United Meth. Ch. Mem. United Meth. Ch. Home: 204 N Newlin St Veedersburg IN 47987-1358 Office: Lucille Raines Residence Inc 947 N Pennsylvania St Indianapolis IN 46204-1070 E-mail: cmarshall@sprintmail.com.

MARSHALL, CODY, bishop; Bishop Ch. of God in Christ, No. Ill. Mem. Ch. Of God In Christ. Office: Freedom Temple Church of God in Christ 1459 W 74th St Chicago IL 60636-4027 Office Phone: 773-483-1140.

MARSHALL, COLLEEN, newscaster; m. Gary Marshall; children: Garret, Shannon. BA, Point Park Coll.; postgrad., Capital U.; D (hon.), Roi Grande U., 2000, Park Point Coll, 2001. Writer, prodr., editor Sta. KQV, Pitts.; news dir., anchor, reporter Sta. WEIR, Weirton, W.Va.; anchor, reporter Sta. WWVA, Wheeling; reporter Sta.WTRF-TV, Sta. WCMH-TV, Columbus, Ohio, 1984—87, anchor, 1987—. Bd. dirs. Columbus AIDS Task Force, Cirrenton Family Svcs. Recipient Capital Area Humane Soc. Consumer Reporter award, 1988, Best Newscast and Best Spot News Coverage, The Associated Press, 1998, Emmy award, 1999, Stonewall Media award, 1999. Office: WCMH-TV 3165 Olentangy River Rd PO Box 4 Columbus OH 43202

MARSHALL, FRANCIS JOSEPH, aerospace engineer; b. NYC, Sept. 5, 1923; s. Francis Joseph and Mary Gertrude (Leary) M.; m. Joan Eager, June 14, 1952; children— Peter, Colin, Stephen, Dana. BS in Mech. Engring, CCNY, 1948; MS, Rensselaer Poly. Inst., 1950; Dr. Eng. Sci., N.Y. U., 1955. Engr. Western Union Co., NYC, 1948, Gen. Electric Co., Schenectady, 1948-50; engr. Wright-Aero Corp., Woodridge, NJ, 1950-52; group leader Lab. for Applied Scis., U. Chgo., 1955-60; instr. Ill. Inst. Tech., 1957-59; prof. Sch. Aeros. and Astronautics, Purdue U., West Lafayette, Ind., 1960—. Engr. U.S. Naval Underseas Warfare Center, Pasadena, Calif., 1966-68; faculty fellow NASA-Langley, 1969-70; vis. prof. Inst. Tech. Mara-Midwest Univs. Consortium for Internat. Activities, Malayasia, 1989. Contbr. articles to profl. jours. Served with U.S. Army, 1943-46. Decorated Combat Inf. badge.; Rsch. grantee NASA, 1970-76; Fulbright scholar, Turkey, 1988-89. Asso. fellow AIAA; mem. Am. Soc. Engring. Edn., AAUP. Home: 120 Leslie Ave West Lafayette IN 47906-2410 Office: Sch Aeros and Astronautics Purdue U West Lafayette IN 47907

MARSHALL, GARLAND ROSS, biochemist, biophysicist, medical educator; b. San Angelo, Tex., Apr. 16, 1940; s. Garland Ross and Jewel Wayne (Gray) M.; m. Suzanne Russell, Dec. 26, 1959; children: Chris, Keith, Melissa, Lee. BS, Calif. Inst. Tech., 1962; PhD, Rockefeller U., 1966; DSc (hon.), Politechnika, Lodz, Poland, 1993. Instr. Washington U., St. Louis, 1966-67, asst. prof., 1967-72, assoc. prof., 1972-76, prof. biochemistry, 1976—, prof. pharmacology, 1985-2000, dir. Ctr. for Molecular Design, 1988-2000; pres. MetaPhore Pharm. Inc., 1995—2003. Vis. prof. Massey U., Palmerston North, New Zealand, 1975; vis. prof. chemistry U. Florence, Italy, 1991; pres. Tripos Assocs., Inc., St. Louis, 1979-87; chmn. 10th Am. Peptide Symposium, St. Louis, 1986-88; councilor Am. Peptide Soc., 1990-93; established investigator Am. Heart Assn., Washington, 1970-75. Editor: Peptides: Chemistry and Biology, 1988, Peptides: Chemistry, Structure and Biology, 1990; editor-in-chief Jour. Computer-Aided Molecular Design, 1986-98. Recipient medal L-Lecia Tech. U., Lodz, Poland, 1987, Vincent de Vigneaud award Am. Peptide Soc., 1994, Sci. and Tech. award St. Louis Regl. Commerce and Growth Assn., 1996, Serial Entrepreneur award Mo. Biotech. Assn., 2003. Mem. Am. Chem. Soc. (Medicinal Chemistry award 1988, Midwest award 1996), Am. Soc. for Biochemistry and Molecular Biology, Am. Soc. for Pharmacology and Exptl. Therapeutics, Biophys. Soc., Am. Peptide Soc. (Vincent du Vigneaud award 1994, Merrifield award 2001), Chinese Peptide Soc. (Cathay award 2000). Office: Washington U Ctr for Computational Biol 700 S Euclid Ave Saint Louis MO 63110-1012 E-mail: garland@pcg.wustl.edu.

MARSHALL, GERALD FRANCIS, optical engineer, consultant, physicist; b. Seven Kings, Eng., Feb. 26, 1929; BSc in Physics, London U., 1952. Physicist Morganite Internat., London, 1954—59; sr. rsch. devel. engr. Ferranti Ltd., Edinburgh, Scotland, 1959—67; project mgr. Diffraction Limited Inc., Bedford, Mass., 1967—69; dir. engring. Medical Lasers, Inc., Burlington, Mass., 1969—71; staff cons. Speedring Systems, Troy, Mich., 1971—76; dir. optical engring. Energy Conversion Devices, Inc., Troy, Mich., 1976—87; sr. tech. staff specialist Kaiser Electronics, San Jose, Calif., 1987—89; cons. in optics design and engring., 1989—. Editor, contbg. author: Laser Beam Scanning, 1985, Optical Scanning, 1991, Handbook of Optical and Laser Scanning, 2004. Fellow: Inst. Physics, SPIE -Internat. Soc. Optical Engring. (bd. dirs. 1991—93), Optical Soc. Am. Achievements include patents in field. Home and Office: 410 Dusenbury St Niles MI 49120-1468 Office Phone: 269-687-1692.

MARSHALL, GREGG, men's college basketball coach; b. Greenwood, SC; m. Lynn Munday; children: Kellen, Maggie. BA in Econs./Bus., Randolph-Macon Coll., 1985; M in Sport Mgmt., U. Richmond, 1987. Asst. coach Randolph-Macon Coll., Ashland, Va., 1985—87, Belmont Abbey Coll., 1987—88, Coll. Charleston, 1988—96, Marshall U., 1996—98; head coach Winthrop U., Rock Hill, SC, 1998—2007, Wichita St. U., Kans., 2007—. Named Big South Conf. Coach of Yr., 1999, 2003, 2005. Office: Wichita State U Mens Basketball 1845 Fairmount St Wichita KS 67260

MARSHALL, IRL HOUSTON, JR., franchise consultant; b. Evanston, Ill., Feb. 28, 1929; s. Irl H. and Marjorie (Greenleaf) M.; m. Barbara Favill, Nov. 5, 1949; children: Alice Marshall Vogler, Irl Houston III, Carol Marshall Allen. AB, Dartmouth Coll., 1949; MBA, U. Chgo., 1968; cert. franchise exec., La. State U., 1991. Gen. mgr. Duraclean Internat., Deerfield, Ill., 1949-61; mgr. Montgomery Ward, Chgo., 1961-77; pres., chief exec. officer Duraclean Internat., 1977-98; pres. Franchise Cons. Svcs., 1998—. Cons. Exec. Svc. Corps., 1999—. Inventor/patentee in field. Pres. Cliff Dwellers, Chgo., 1977; exec. com., treas., dir. Highland Park Hosp., 1971-80; bd. dirs. Better Bus. Bur. Chgo. & No. Ill., Chgo., 1988—. Named to Hall of Fame, Internat. Franchise Assn., 2002. Mem. Internat. Franchise Assn. (bd. dirs. 1981-90, pres. 1985, chmn. 1985-86, bd. dirs. Ednl. Found. 1984—, Hall of Fame 2002), Inst. Cert. Franchise Execs. (bd. govs. 1995—), Econ. Club Chgo., Exmoor Country Club, Univ. Club Chgo. Presbyterian. Home: 1248 Ridgewood Dr Northbrook IL 60062-3725

MARSHALL, JOHN DAVID, lawyer; b. Chgo., May 19, 1940; s. John Howard and Sophie (Brezenk) M.; m. Marcia A. Podlasinski, Aug. 26, 1961; children: Jacquelyn, David, Jason, Patricia, Brian, Denise, Michael, Catherine. BS in Acctg., U. Ill., 1961; JD, Ill. Inst. Tech., 1965. CPA Ill.; bar: Ill. 1965, U.S. Tax Ct. 1968, U.S. Dist. Ct. (no. dist.) Ill. 1971. Ptnr. Mayer, Brown & Platt, Chgo., 1961—2006. Bd. dirs. Levinson Ctr. for Handicapped Children, Chgo., 1970—75. Mem. Ill. Bar Assn., Chgo. Bar Assn. (agribus. com. 1978—, trust law com. 1969-95, probate practice com. 1969—, com. on coms. 1983-00, vice chmn. 1988-89, chmn. 1989-90, legis. com. of probate practice com. 1983—, chmn. and vice chmn. legis. com. of probate practice com. 1983-84, rules and forms com., 1996—, chmn. exec. com. probate practice com. 1982-83, vice chmn. exec. com. 1981-82, sec. exec. com. 1980-81, div. chmn. 78-79, div. vice chmn. 1977-78, div. sec. 1976-77, Appreciation award 1982-83), Union League Club (Chgo.). Roman Catholic. Home: 429 N Willow Wood Dr Palatine IL 60074-3831 Office: Attorney at Law 1300 E Woodfield Rd Schaumburg IL 60173 Business E-Mail: jmarshall@ncc-cpa.com. E-mail: john.marshall@cliftons.com.

MARSHALL, JULI WILSON, lawyer; BA magna cum laude, Mich. State U., 1981; JD, U. Mich., 1984. Bar: Calif. 1984, Ill. 1995. Assoc. Latham & Watkins LLP, LA, 1984—91, named ptnr., 1991, now ptnr. Chgo., co-chair firm product liability and mass torts practice group. Office: Latham & Watkins LLP Sears Tower Ste 5800 233 S Wacker Dr Chicago IL 60606 Office Phone: 312-876-7700. Office Fax: 312-993-9767. E-mail: juli.marshall@lw.com.

MARSHALL, KATHRYN SUE, lawyer; b. Decatur, Ill., Sept. 12, 1942; d. Edward Elda and Frances M. (Minor) Lahniers; m. Robert S. Marshall, Sept. 5, 1964 (div. Apr. 1984); children: Stephen Edward, Christine Elizabeth; m. Robert J. Arndt, June 25, 1988 (dec. 1999). BA, Lake Forest Coll., 1964; JD, John Marshall Law Sch., Chgo., 1976. Intern U.S. Atty.'s Office, Chgo., 1974—76; mng. ptnr. Marshall and Marshall Ltd., Waukegan, Ill., 1976—84; pvt. practice Waukegan, 1984—93, Preemptive Solutions, Wash. Contbr. articles to profl. jours. Bd. dirs., v.p. Lake Forest (Ill.) Fine Arts Ensemble; bd. dirs. Island Hosp. Health Found.; mem. steering com. Equal Justice Coalition; cert. jud. Dem. candidate Lake County, Ill.; bd. dirs. Camerata Soc., Lake Forest. Fellow: ABA (gov. 1993—96), Coll. Law Practice Mgmt., Ill. Bar Assn.; mem.: Navy League (life). Avocations: boating, reading, travel. Office: 7610 Mid Town Rd # 30Z Madison WI 53719

MARSHALL, MARK F., lawyer; b. 1954; BS, U. SD, 1977, JD, 1981. Bar: SD 1981, US Dist. Ct. SD 1981, US Ct. Appeals (8th cir.) 1981, US Supreme Ct. 1984. Law clk. hon. Fred J. Nichol, 1981-83; ptnr. Bangs, McCullen, Butler, Foye & Simmons, Rapid City, SD, 1983-96; of counsel Johnson, Heidepriem, Miner, Marlow & Janklow, Sioux Falls, SD, 1996—2000; magistrate judge U.S. Dist. Ct. S.D., Sioux Falls, 1996-2000; ptnr. Davenport Law Firm, Sioux Falls, 2000—. Office: 206 W 14th St Sioux Falls SD 57105 Office Phone: 605-336-2880. Business E-Mail: mmarshall@dehs.com.

MARSHALL, RON, retail executive; BS with honors, Wright State U. V.p., CFO Barnes & Noble Bookstores; sr. v.p., CFO Dart Group Corp., Md., 1991-94; exec. v.p., CFO, Pathmark Stores, NJ, 1994-98; pres. Nash Finch Co., Mpls., 1998—2002, CEO, 1998—2006. Mem. Food Mktg. Inst. (bd. dirs.).

MARSHALL, SHERRIE, newspaper editor; Metro editor Star Tribune, Mpls., to 1998, editor news content, 1995—, dep. managing editor, 1999—. Office: Star Tribune 425 Portland Ave Minneapolis MN 55488-0002

MARSHALL, SIRI SWENSON, lawyer, retired consumer products company executive; b. 1948; BA, Harvard U., 1970; JD, Yale U., 1974. Bar: NY 1975. Assoc. Debevoise & Plimpton, 1974-79; atty., sr. atty., asst. gen. counsel Avon Products, Inc., NYC, 1979-85, v.p. legal affairs, 1985-89, sr. v.p., gen. counsel, 1990-94, Gen. Mills, Inc., Mpls., 1994—2007. Bd. dirs. CPR Internat. Inst. Dispute Resolution, Internat. Inst. for Conflict Prevention and Resolution, Ameriprise Fin., Equifax. Trustee Mpls. Inst. Arts.

MARSHALL, VINCENT DE PAUL, industrial microbiologist, researcher; b. Washington, Apr. 5, 1943; s. Vincent de Paul Sr. and Mary Frances (Bach) M.; m. Sylvia Ann Kieffer, ov. 15, 1986; children from previous marriage: Vincent de Paul III, Amy. BS, Northeastern State Coll., Tahlequah, Okla., 1965; MS, U. Okla. Health Sci. Ctr., Oklahoma City, 1967, PhD, 1970. Rsch. assoc. U. Ill., Urbana, 1970, postdoctoral fellow, 1971-73; rsch. scientist The Upjohn Co., Kalamazoo, Mich., 1973-74, rsch. head, 1975, sr. rsch. scientist, 1976-91, sr. scientist, 1991-2000; cons., 2000—. Mem. editl. bd. Jour. of Antibiotics, 1990-2001, Jour. Indsl. Microbiology, 1989-2001, Devels. in Indsl. Microbiology, 1990; contbr. numerous articles to profl. jours., chpts. to books; patentee in field. Served with U.S. Army Nat. Guard, 1960-65. NIH predoctoral fellow, 1967-70; NIH postdoctoral fellow, 1971-73. Fellow Am. Acad. Microbiology; mem. Soc. for Indsl. Microbiology (membership com. 1988-90, co-chair edn. com. 1989-93, local sects. com. 1991-96, chair nominating com. 1993-94, mem. nominating com. 1999-2000, co-chair program com. 1993-94, dir. 1994-96, pres. So. Great Lakes sect. 1992-95), Am. Soc. Microbiology, Am. Soc. Biochemistry and Molecular Biology, Internat. Soc. for Antimicrobial Activity of Non-Antibiotics (sci. adv. bd.), Sigma Xi. Republican. Lutheran. Home and Office: 203 Paisley Ct Kalamazoo MI 49006-4359 Home Phone: 269-349-3795; Office Phone: 269-349-3795. E-mail: vince3795@aol.com.

MARTEL, WILLIAM, radiologist, educator; b. NYC, Oct. 1, 1927; s. Hyman and Fanny M.; m. Rhoda Kaplan, Oct. 9, 1956; children: Lisa, Pamela, Caryn, Jonathan, David. MD, NYU, 1953. Intern, Kings County Hosp., N.Y., 1953-54; resident in radiology Mt. Sinai Hosp., NYC, 1954-57; instr. radiology U. Mich., Ann Arbor, 1957-60, asst. prof., 1960-63, asso. prof., 1963-67, prof., 1967—, Fred Jenner Hodges prof., 1984—, chmn. dept. radiology, 1981-92, dir. skeletal radiology, 1970-81, Fred Jenner Hodges prof. emeritus radiology, 1997—. Contbr. articles to Radiol. Diagnoses of Arthritic Diseases. Served with USAAF, 1945-46. Recipient Amoco U. Mich. Outstanding Teaching award, 1980; established William Martel professorship in radiology U. Mich., 1997. Mem. Radiol. Soc. N.Am., Am. Roentgen Ray Soc., Assn. Univ. Radiologists. Office: Univ Mich Hosps Dept Radiology 1500 E Med Ctr Dr Ann Arbor MI 48109 Home: 4020 Glacier Hills Dr Ann Arbor MI 48105-3651 E-mail: wmartel@umich.edu.

MARTEN, J. THOMAS, judge; BA, Washburn U., 1973, JD, 1976. Judge U.S. Dist. Ct. Kans., 1996—. Office: US Courthouse 401 N Market St Wichita KS 67202-2089

MARTEN, RANDOLPH L., transportation executive; Pres., chmn. Marten Transport, Ltd., Mondovi, Wis., 1974—. Office: Marten Transport Ltd 129 Marten St Mondovi WI 54755-1700

MARTIN, ALSON ROBERT, lawyer; b. Kansas City, Mo., Jan. 19, 1946; s. Keith U. and Hulda (Tully) M.; children: Scott Alson, Bradley A., Reid A. BA, U. Kans., 1968; JD cum laude, NYU, 1971, LLM in Taxation, 1976. Bar: N.Y. 1972, Kans. 1976, U.S. Supreme Ct. 1976, U.S. Ct. Appeals (10th cir.) 1979, U.S. Tax Ct. 1979. Dir. Shook, Hardy & Bacon LLP, Overland Park, Kans., 1986, ptnr., 1986—, co-chmn. Bus. and Fin. Divsn., 1986—2004, pres., 2004—, dir., 2004—. Mem. exec. com. Shook, Hardy & Bacon LLP, Overland Pk., Kans.; spkr. in field. Co-author: Kansas Corporation Law and Practice, 1977, rev. edit., 1992; author: Limited Liability & Partnership Answer Book, rev. edit., 2005 Trustee Johnson County C.C., 1979-83. Served to lt. USN. Fellow Am. Coll. Tax Counsel, Am. Coll. Employyee Benefits Coun.; mem. ABA (officer, tax sect. com. 1993—), Kans. Bar Assn. (exec. com. tax sect.), Johnson County Bar Assn., Estate Planning Coun. Kansas City, Internat. Assn. Fin. Planning (adv. bd., regulatory com.). Office: Shook Hardy & Bacon LLP # 84 Corp Woods 10801 Mastin Ste 1000 Overland Park KS 66210-2005 Office Phone: 913-451-6060. Office Fax: 913-451-8879. Business E-Mail: amartin@shb.com.

MARTIN, ARTHUR MEAD, lawyer; b. Cleve. Heights, Mar. 29, 1942; s. Bernard P. and Winifred (Mead) M. AB, Princeton U., 1963; LLB, Harvard U., 1966. Bar: Ill. 1966, U.S. Dist. Ct. (no. dist. Ill.) 1969, U.S. Ct. Appeals (7th cir.) 1970, U.S. Supreme Ct. 1980, U.S. Ct. Appeals (fed. cir.) 2000. Instr. law U. Wis., Madison, 1966-68; assoc. Jenner & Block, Chgo., 1968-74, ptnr., 1975—2003. Co-trustee Dille Family Trust, 1982—. Author: Historical and Practice Notes to the Illinois Civil Practice Act and Illinois Supreme Court Rules, 1968-88. Trustee 4th Presbyn. Ch., Chgo., 1996-99, sec. 1997-99, exec. com. 1997-99, mem. nominating com., 2006-07; bd. dirs. Stop Colon/Rectal Cancer Found., 1998—; founding bd. mem. Alliance for the Great Lakes, 2005—, chair nominating com., 2005—. Mem. ABA, Am. Law Inst. (mem. consultative group principles of law nonprofit orgns. 2004-), Ill. Bar Assn., Chgo. Bar Assn. (bd. editors 1972-86), Ill. State Hist. Soc. (adv. bd. 1998-99, bd. dirs. 1999—, exec. com. 1999—, fin. com. 1999—, treas. 2002—), Ill. Centennial Bus. Com., Lake Mich. Fedn. (bd. dirs. 1993-02, 03-, exec. com. 1994-02, treas. 1994-99, 01-02, sec. 1999-01), Law Club Chgo., Legal Club Chgo. Office: Jenner & Block 330 Wabash Ave FL 4400 Chicago IL 60611 Business E-Mail: amartin@jenner.com.

MARTIN, BRUCE JAMES, newspaper editor; b. Pontiac, Mich., Sept. 2, 1956; s. James Patrick and Patricia Ann (Taylor) M.; m. Elizabeth Hartley Nutting, July 30, 1988. BJ, U. Mo., 1982. Reporter Spinal Col. Newsweekly, Union Lake, Mich., 1982; sports editor Northville (Mich.) Record/Novi News, 1982-85; news editor Novi ews, Northville, 1984-85; copy editor Kalamazoo Gazette, 1985-89, Ann Arbor (Mich.) News, 1989-91, homes editor, 1991, arts and entertainment editor, 1991—. Recipient 1st Place in Sports Writing in Circulation Category, Mich. Press Assn., 1993. Avocations: songwriting, piano, guitar. Office: Ann Arbor ews 340 E Huron St Ann Arbor MI 48104-1900

MARTIN, EARL J., state representative; Owner Martin's Corner Deli; property developer, rental mgr.; state rep. dist. 57 Ohio Ho. of Reps., Columbus, 2002—. Mem. Avon Lake City Coun., Ohio. Republican. Office: 77 S High St 77th fl Columbus OH 63215-6111

MARTIN, FRANK (FRANCISCO J. MARTIN), men's college basketball coach; m. Anya Martin; children: Brandon, Amalia. B in Phys. Edn., Fla. Internat. U., Miami, 1993. Asst. varsity coach, head jr. varsity coach Miami Sr. HS, Fla., 1985—93, head coach, 1995—99, North Miami Sr. HS, 1993—95, Booker T. Washington HS, 1999—2000; asst. coach ortheastern U., Boston, 2000—04, recruiting coord., 2002—04; asst. coach U. Cin., 2004—06, Kans. State U., Manhattan, 2006—07, head coach, 2007—. Office: Kans State U Mens Basketball Bramlage Coliseum 1800 College Ave Manhattan KS 66502 Office Phone: 785-532-6531. E-mail: fjm@ksu.edu.

MARTIN, GARY JOSEPH, medical educator; b. Chgo., Mar. 12, 1952; m. Helen Gartner; children: Daniel T., David G. BA in Psychology, U. Ill., 1974, MD, 1978. Diplomate Am. Bd. Internal Medicine, Am. Bd. Cardiovascular Disease, Nat. Bd. Med. Examiners; lic. physician, Ill. Intern, resident internal medicine Northwestern U. Med. Sch., Chgo., 1978-81, instr. medicine, 1981-82, asst. prof. medicine, 1984-90, assoc. prof., 1990-96, prof., 1996—, divsn. chief, divsn. gen. internal medicine, 1988-2001, assoc. chmn. dept. medicine, 1998-2000, vice chmn. dept. medicine, 2001—; cardiology fellow Loyola U. Med. Ctr., 1982-84; attending physician Northwestern Meml. Hosp./Northwestern Med. Faculty Found., Chgo., 1984—; chief med. resident, attending physician Northwestern Meml. Hosp., Chgo., 1981-82; dir. primary care clerkship Nat. Ctr. for Advanced Med. Edn., 1984—. Chmn. outpatient utilization rev. and quality assurance com., 1985-93; chmn. Northwestern Meml. Hosp./Lakeside VA Rsch. Com., 1988-91; dir. tng. gen. internal medicine residency program, 1985-95; bd. dirs. com. orthwestern Med. Faculty Found., 1993—; cons. health care divsn. Ernst & Young, 1991—; peer reviewer Faculty Devel. Rev. Com. Panel 1, 1994. Contbr. articles to profl. jours. Fellow Buehler Ctr. on Aging. Fellow Am. Coll. Cardiology; mem. ACP, Soc. Gen. Internal Medicine, Am. Heart Assn. Office: orthwestern U Med Sch Divsn Gen Internal Medicine 675 N Saint Clair St Ste 18-200 Chicago IL 60611-5929

MARTIN, JACK, educational services company executive, former federal agency administrator; b. Frendale, Mich. m. Bettye Martin; children: Randy, Ingrid. BS, MBA, Wayne State U.; postgrad., U. Minn. CPA. With GM Corp., Detroit; various mgmt. positions Control Data; cons. acct. Touche Ross & Co. (now Deloitte and Touche); mng. dir., CEO, founder Jack Martin and Co. P.C., CPAs, 1975—2002; chmn., acting CEO Home Fed. Savings Bank, Detroit, 1995—2002; chmn. Provider Reimbursement Rev. Bd. US Dept. Health & Human Services, 1991—94; CFO US Dept. Edn., Washington, 2002—05; acting dir. Selective Svc. System, Arlington, Va., 2004; exec. v.p. White Hat Mgmt., Akron, Ohio, 2005—. Chmn. of bd. Health Alliance Plan; mem. investment com. Mercy Health Sys. (now Trinity Health); chair Mich. adv. com. U.S. Civil Rights Commn.; v.p. Merrill Palmer Inst. Wayne State U. Treas. Alzheimer's Assn. Recipient Pres. Quality award for Improved Fin. Performance, US Dept. Edn., Certificate of Excellence in Accountability Reporting, Assn. Govt. Accountants, Alexander Hamilton award for Tech., Treasury & Risk Mgmt. mag. Mem.: AICPA (mem. practice stds. subcom.), Det. Athletic Club (bd. dirs.). Office: White Hat Mgmt 159 S Main St Ste 600 Akron OH 44308

MARTIN, J(OSEPH) PATRICK, lawyer, judge; b. Detroit, Apr. 19, 1938; s. Joseph A. and Kathleen G. (Rich) Martin; m. Denise Taylor, June 27, 1964; children: Timothy J., Julie D. AB magna cum laude, U. Notre Dame, 1960; JD with distinction, U. Mich., 1963; postgrad., London Sch. Econs., 1964. Bar: Mich. 1963, U.S. Dist. Ct. (ea. dist.) Mich. 1963, U.S. Ct. Appeals (6th cir.) 1967, U.S. Supreme Ct. 1979, U.S. Dist. Ct. (we. dist.) Mich. 1981, U.S. Ct. Fed. Claims 1999. Spl. asst. to gen. counsel Ford Motor Co., Dearborn, Mich., 1962; assoc. Dykema, Wheat, Spencer et al, Detroit, 1963-66; from assoc. to ptnr. Poole Littell Sutherland, Detroit, 1966-76; sr. atty., ptnr., shareholder Butzel Long, Detroit and Birmingham, Mich., 1976-94; sr. atty., shareholder Vlcko, Lane, Payne & Broder PC, Bingham Farms, Mich., 1994-96; sr. atty. Gourwitz and Barr PC, Southfield, Mich., 1996-99; pvt. practice, 2000—; adminstrv. law judge State of Mich., 2002—. Arbitrator Am. Arbitration Assn., Southfield, Mich., 1968—, Nat. Assn. Security Dealers, 1988—, NY Stock Exch., 1991—, Constrn. Arbitration Svcs., Mt. Clemens, 2005—; adj. prof. remedies and alternative dispute resolution U. Detroit Law Sch., 1989—, Wayne State U. Law Sch., 1996—, Cooley Law Sch., 2001—; state ct. administrv. office approved mediator all Mich. cts. under new ADR rules; case evaluator, mediator, discovery master Oak County Cir. Ct., Pontiac, Mich., 1985—; mediator Lex Mundi, Coll. Mediators, 1992—; case evaluator, mediator Mediation Tribunal Assn. Wayne County Cir. Ct., 1992—, Oakland County Dist. Cts., 1998—, Wayne County Dist. Cts., 1998—, Wayne County Probate Ct., 2002—; moderator Mich. State Ct. Appeals, 1995—. Author, editor: Laches-Oak County Bar Assn. Legal Jour., 1984, 1992, 1996, Real Property Rev., 1989—90, Mich. Law Weekly, 1990, ADR ewsletter, 2000. Scholar, Cook Found., Ford Found., London, 1963—64. Mem.: ABA, Oakland County Bar Found., Mich. State Bar Found., Oakland County Bar Assn. (chair fed. ct. com., chair Mich. dist. ct. com., mem. ADR com., bd. dirs.), State Bar Mich. (chair alternative dispute sect.). Independent. Roman Catholic. Avocations: gardening, golf, walking. Home and Office: 1663 Hoit Tower Dr Bloomfield Hills MI 48302-2630 Home Phone: 248-932-8694. Home Fax: 248-932-0368. Personal E-mail: jpatrickmartin@comcast.net.

MARTIN, KATHRYN A., academic administrator; Dean Sch. Fine and Performing Arts Wayne State U., Detroit; chancellor U Minn, Duluth, 1995—. Office: Univ Minnesota-Duluth Office of Chancellor Admin Bldng 1049 University Dr Duluth MN 55812-3011

MARTIN, KEVIN JOHN, nephrologist, educator; b. Dublin, Jan. 18, 1948; came to U.S., 1973; s. John Martin and Maura Martin; m. Grania E. O'Connor, Nov. 16, 1972; children: Alan, John, Ciara, Audrey. MB BCh, Univ. Coll. Dublin, 1971. Diplomate Am. Bd. Internal Medicine, Am. Bd. Nephrology. Intern St. Vincent's Hosp., Dublin, 1971-72, resident, 1972-73. Barnes Hosp., St. Louis, 1973-74, fellow, 1974-77; asst. prof. Washington U., St. Louis, 1977-84, assoc. prof., 1984-89; prof., dir. div. nephrology St. Louis U., 1989—. Contbr. numerous articles to med. jours. Office: Saint Louis Univ Med Ctr 3635 Vista Ave Saint Louis MO 63110-2539

MARTIN, LAURA KEIDAN, lawyer; b. Detroit, Oct. 8, 1964; BA, U. Mich., 1986; JD, Harvard U., 1989. Bar: Ill. 1989. Ptnr. Katten Muchin Rosenman LLP, Chgo. Mem.: ABA, at. Health Lawyers Assn., Ill. Assn. Healthcare Attys. (bd. dirs. 2001—07, pres. 2006), Chgo. Bar Assn. (chair antitrust law com. 2004—05). Office: Katten Muchin Rosenman LLP 525 W Monroe St Chicago IL 60661 Office Fax: 312-902-5487, 312-577-8951. E-mail: laura.martin@kattenlaw.com.

MARTIN, LISA DEMET, lawyer; b. Pa., 1959; BA with honors, Wellesley Coll., 1980; JD, U. Pa., 1984. Bar: Mo. 1984. Ptnr., mem. exec. com. Bryan Cave LLP, St. Louis. Durant scholar Wellesley Coll. Mem. Phi Beta Kappa. Office: Bryan Cave LLP One Metropolitan Sq, Ste 3600 211 N Broadway Saint Louis MO 63102 Office Phone: 314-259-2125. E-mail: lmartin@bryancave.com.

MARTIN, NOEL, graphics designer, educator; b. Syracuse, Ohio, Apr. 19, 1922; s. Harry Ross and Lula (Van Meter) M.; m. Coletta Ruchty, Aug. 29, 1942; children— Dana, Reid Cert. in Fine Arts, Art Acad. Cin., Doctorate (hon.), 1994. Designer Cin. Art Mus., 1947-93, asst. to dir., 1947-55; freelance designer for various ednl., cultural and indsl. orgns., 1947—; instr. Art Acad. Cin., 1951-57, artist-in-residence, 1993—. Design cons. Champion Internat., 1959-82, Xomox Corp., 1961—, Federated Dept. Stores, 1962-83, Hebrew Union Coll., 1969—; designer-in-residence U. Cin., 1968-71, adj. prof., 1968-73; mem. adv. bd. Carnegie-Mellon U., R.I. Sch. Design, Cin. Symphony Orch., Am. Inst. Graphic Arts; lectr. Smithsonian Instn., Libr. of Congress, Am. Inst. Graphic Arts, Aspen Design Conf., various additional schs. and orgns. nationally. One man shows include Contemporary Arts Ctr., Cin., 1954, 71, Addison Gallery Am. Art, 1955,

R.I. Sch. Design, 1955, Soc. Typographic Arts, Chgo., 1956, White Mus. of Cornell U., 1956, Cooper & Beatty, Toronto, Ont., Can., 1958, Am. Inst. Graphic Arts, 1958, Ind. U., 1958, Ohio State U., 1971; exhibited in group shows at Mus. Modern Art, N.Y.C., Library of Congress, Musee d'Art Moderne, Paris, Grafiska Inst., Stockholm, Carpenter Ctr., Cambridge, Gutenberg Mus., Mainz, U.S. info. exhbns. In Europe, South America and USSR; represented in permanent collections Mus. Modern Art, Stedelijk Mus., Amsterdam, Cin. Art Mus., Boston Mus. Fine Arts, Cin. Hist. Soc., Library of Congress; contbr. to various publs. Served to sgt. U.S. Air Force, 1942-45 Recipient Art Directors medal, Phila., 1957, Sachs award, Cin., 1973, Lifetime Achievement award Cin. Art Dirs., 1989. Home Phone: 513-731-5519; Office Phone: 513-731-1287.

MARTIN, PATRICIA, dean, nursing educator; BSN, U. Cin.; MS, Wright State U.; PhD, Case Western Res. U. Dir. nursing rsch., interim dean, assoc. prof. Wright State U. Contbr. articles to profl. jours. Office: Wright State U 168 University Hall Dayton OH 45435-0001

MARTIN, PHILLIP HAMMOND, lawyer; b. Tucson, Jan. 4, 1940; s. William P. and Harriet (Hammond) M.; m. Sandra S. Chandler, June 17, 1961 (div. Mar. 1989); children: Lisa, Craig, Wade, Ryan; m. Erika Zetty, May 9, 1990. BA, U. Minn., 1961, JD, 1964. Bar: Minn. 1964, U.S. Tax Ct. 1967, U.S. Dist. Ct. Minn. 1968, U.S. Ct. Appeals (8th cir.) 1973, U.S. Supreme Ct. 1981, U.S. Claims Ct. 1983, U.S. Ct. Appeals (fed. cir.) 1988, U.S. Ct. Appeals (7th cir.) 1989. Assoc. Dorsey & Whitney, Mpls., 1964-69, ptnr., 1970—. Home: 487 Portland Ave Saint Paul MN 55102-2216 Office: Dorsey & Whitney LLP Ste 1500 50 S 6th St Minneapolis MN 55402-1498 Home Phone: 651-291-1933; Office Phone: 612-340-2845. Business E-Mail: martin.phil@dorsey.com.

MARTIN, QUINN WILLIAM, lawyer; b. Fond du Lac, Wis., 1948; s. Quinn W. and Marcia E. Martin; m. Jane E.; children: Quinn W., William J. BSME, Purdue U., 1969; postgrad., U. Santa Clara, 1969-70; JD, U. Mich., 1973. Bar: Wis. 1973, U.S. Dist. Ct. (ea. dist.) Wis. 1973, U.S. Ct. Appeals (7th cir.) 1973. Sales support mgr. Hewlett-Packard, Palo Alto, Calif., 1969-70; assoc. Quarles & Brady, Milw., 1973-80, ptnr., 1980—. Bd. dirs. Associated Bank Milw., U-Line Corp., Gen. Timber and Land, Inc., Fond du Lac. Chmn. Gov. McCallum Trans Com., Wis., U. Mich. Law Sch. Fund; bd. dirs. Milw. Zool. Soc., Found. for Wildlife Conservation. Mem. ABA, Wis. Bar Assn., Milw. Club, Ozaukee Country Club, Chaine des Rottiseurs, Delta Upsilon (sec.), Milw. Club, Rotary. Office: Quarles & Brady 411 E Wisconsin Ave Ste 2550 Milwaukee WI 53202-4497

MARTIN, REX, manufacturing executive; Chmn, pres., CEO Nibco, Elkhart, Ind. Office: NIBCO Inc 1516 Middleburry St PO Box 1167 Elkhart IN 46515-1167

MARTIN, ROBERT DAVID, judge, educator; b. Iowa City, Oct. 7, 1944; s. Murray and G'Ann (Holmgren) Martin; m. Ruth A. Haberman, Aug. 21, 1966; children: Jacob, Matthew, David. AB, Cornell Coll., Mt. Vernon, Iowa, 1966; JD, U. Chgo., 1969. Bar: Wis. 1969, US Dist. Ct. (we. dist.) Wis. 1969, US Supreme Ct. 1973, US Dist. Ct. (ea. dist.) Wis. 1974. Assoc. Ross & Stevens, S.C., Madison, Wis., 1969-72, ptnr., 1973-78; chief judge U.S. Bankruptcy Ct. We. Dist. Wis., 1978—. Instr. gen. practice course U. Wis. Law Sch., 1974, 76, 77, 80, lectr. debtor/creditor course, 1981-82, 83, 85, 87, 2001, 07, farm credit seminar, 1985, advanced bankruptcy problems, 1989, 91, 96; co-chmn. faculty Am. Law Inst.-ABA Fin. and Bus. Planning for Agr., Stanford U., 1979; faculty mem. Fed. Jud. Ctr. Schs. for New Bankruptcy Judges, 1985-96; chmn. Ann. Continuing Legal Edn. Wis. Debtor Creditor Conf., 1981—. Author: (book) Bankruptcy: Annotated Forms, 1989; co-author: Secured Transactions Handbook for Wisconsin Lawyers and Lenders, Bankruptcy-Text Statutes Rules and Forms, 1992, Ginsberg and Martin on Bankruptcy, 4th edit, 1996. Chmn., bd. dirs., mem. exec. com. Luth. Social Svc. Wis. and Upper Mich.; bd. dirs., mem. exec. com. Turnaround Mgmt. Assn., 1997—2007. Mem.: Wis. State Bar, Nat. Bankruptcy Conf., Nat. Conf. Bankruptcy Judges (bd. govs. 1989—91, sec. 1993—94, v.p. 1994—95, pres. 1995—96), Am. Coll. Bankruptcy. Office: 120 N Henry Rm 340 PO Box 548 Madison WI 53701-0548 Office Phone: 608-264-5188.

MARTIN, ROGER BOND, landscape architect; b. Virginia, Minn., Nov. 23, 1936; s. Thomas George and Audrey (Bond) M.; m. Janis Ann Kloss, Aug. 11, 1962; children: Thomas, Stephen, Jonathan. BS with high distinction, U. Minn., 1958; M. Landscape Arch., Harvard U., 1961. Asst. prof. U. Calif.-Berkeley, 1964-66; from assoc. prof. to prof. emeritus U. Minn., Mpls., 1966—99, prof. emeritus, 1999—; owner Roger Martin & Assoc., Mpls., 1966—68, 1999—; prin. InterDesign, Inc., Mpls., 1968-84, Martin & Pitz Assocs., Inc., Mpls., 1984-98. Vis. prof. U. Melbourne, Australia, 1979—80; vis. prof. coll. architecture U. Minn., Mpls., 2000—; sr. rsch. fellow Ctr. for Changing Landscapes, Mpls., 2003—. Prin. works include Minn. Zool. Gardens, 1978 (merit award Am. Soc. Landscape Archs., 1978), Mpls. Pkwy. Restorations, 1972—87 (merit award, 1978, Minn. Classic award Am. Soc. Landscape Archs., 1994), South St. Paul Ctrl. Sq., 1978 (merit award, 1978), Festival Park, Chisholm, Minn., 1986 (merit award, 1986), Miss. Wildlife Refuge Visual Image assessment (merit award, 1989), Nicollet Island Park, Hennepin Avenue Master Plan, 1995 (merit award, 1995), North Shore Scenic Byway Plan, 2005 (Honor award, 2005), Gitchi Gammi Trail Master Plan, 2005 (Honor award, 2006), Red Lake River Access Master Plan, 2007 (Honor award, 2007). Recipient Fredrick Mann award for svc. to edn. U. Minn., 1990, Disting. Educator award Sigma Lambda Alpha, 1990, Bradford Williams medals for outstanding articles in landscape Architecture mag., 1968, 69, Minn. chpt. Lob Pine award for outstanding svc. to Landscape architecture, 1988, Mpls. Com. on Urban Environ. award for design of Whittier Park, 1997; fellow Am. Acad. in Rome, 1962-64. Mem. Am. Soc. Landscape Archs. (pres. Minn. chpt. 1970-72, trustee 1980-84, nat. pres. 1987, chmn.-elect coun. fellows 1991, chmn. 1992-94, past chmn. 1994-96, Pub. Svc. award 1985, Minn. chpt. Classic award 1994, 1st Valued Places award 2005), Nat. Coun. Instrs. Landscape Architecture (pres. 1973-74), Can. Soc. Landscape Archs. (hon.). Home and Office: 2912 45th Ave S Minneapolis MN 55406-1829 Business E-Mail: marti009@umn.edu.

MARTIN, TERENCE D., food products executive; B in Polit. Sci., Holy Cross Coll.; M in Acctg., Northeastern U. Pub. acct. Arthur Andersen & Co., NYC, 1966—74; joined Price Waterhouse, 1974—86, ptnr., 1977—86; exec. v.p., fin. and adminstrn., also bd. dir. J. Walter Thompson, 1986—88; treas. Am. Cyanamid Co., 1988—91, CFO, mem. exec. com., 1991—95; exec. v.p., CFO Gen. Signal Corp., 1995—98; sr. v.p. fin., CFO Quaker Oats Co., Chgo., 1998—2001; dir. Del Monte Foods Co., San Francisco, 2002—. Office: Del Monte Food Co One Market @ The Landmark San Francisco CA 94105 Office Phone: 415-247-3000. Fax: 415-247-3565.

MARTIN, VINCENT LIONEL, retired manufacturing executive; b. Los Angeles, June 29, 1939; s. Arthur Seymon and Alice Maria (Miller) M.; m. Janet Ann Dowler, Mar. 25, 1961; children: Jennifer Lynn, Karen Arlene, Timothy Paul. BS, Stanford U., 1960; MBA, Harvard U., 1963. Various staff positions FMC Corp, Chgo, 1966-74, gen. mgr. Crane and Excavator div. Cedar Rapids, Iowa, 1974-79; pres. Equipment Systems div. AMCA Internat. Corp., Houston, 1979-81, group v.p. Brookfield, Wis., 1981-85; CEO, pres. Jason Inc., Milw., 1986-96, chmn. CEO, 1996-99, chmn., 1999—2004; ret. Bd. dirs. Jason Inc., Modine Mfg. Co., Proliance Internat. Inc. Mem. Phi Beta Kappa, Tau Beta Pi Republican. Presbyterian. Home: 2601 W Cedar Ln Milwaukee WI 53217-1138 Office: Jason Inc 411 E Wisconsin Ave Milwaukee WI 53202-4461 E-mail: Vmartin@jasoninc.com.

MARTIN, WILLIAM BRYAN, chancellor, lawyer, minister; b. Lexington, Ky., Apr. 11, 1938; s. William Stone and Alice Bryan (Spiers) Martin; m. Mary Ellen Matson, Aug. 11, 1973; children: Chanley Morgan, Matson Bryan, Evan Andrew. AB, Transylvania U., 1960; JD, U. Ky., 1964; LLM, Georgetown U., Washington, 1965; MDiv summa cum laude, Emory U., 1979. Bar: Ky. 1964, D.C. 1964; ordained to ministry Christian Ch. (Disciples of Christ), 1981. Legal intern Pub. Defender, Washingotn, 1964-65; asst. U.S. atty. Western Dist. Ky., 1965-67; assoc. McElwain, Denning, Clarke and Winstead, Louisville, 1967-69; asst. atty. gen. Commonwealth of Ky., 1969-70; prof. U. Louisville Sch. Law, 1970-81; dean Oklahoma City U. Sch. Law, 1982-83; pres. Franklin Coll. Ind., 1983-97. Bd. dirs. Coun. Ind. Colls., Washington, 1990-94; mem. Commn. on Pub. Rels. Nat. Assn. Ind. Colls. and Univs., 1992-99 (chmn. 1998-99); bd. dirs. Ind. Colls. Ind. Found., 1983-97, 1st vice chmn., 1992—, chmn., 1993-94, mem. spl. study com. and strategic planning com., mem. transition task force, 1991-92; mem. Ind. Colls. Ind., Ind. Conf. Higher Edn., 1983—; sec. Am. Bapt. Assn. Colls. and Univs., 1989-97; cons.-evaluator North Ctrl. Assn., Commn. on Instns. Higher Edn., 1985. Columnist Scripps Howard News Svc., 1991-97; contbr. articles to profl. jours. Mem. adv. bd. Heartland Film Festival, 1995—; bd. regents Ind. Acad., 1988-97, v.p. bd. 1986-98; bd. trustees Christian Theol. Sem., 1986-98, past mem. investment com., chair ednl. policies com.; bd. dirs., exec. com. Historic Landmarks Found. Ind., 1987-91, adv. coun., 1991—; first chmn. coun. pres. Ind. Collegiate Athletic Conf., 1987-90; elder Tabernacle Christian Ch., Franklin, 1983-91, North Christian Ch., Columbus, 1994-98; mem. Progress Forum Johnson County, 1987-92; mem. adv. bd. Greater Johnson County Cmty. Found., Inc., 1992-94; mem. Historic Preservation Task Force, Divsn. Historic Preservation and Archaeology, Ind. Dept. Natural Resources; mem. Nat. Environ. Task Force.ship com., tchr. family life class Douglass Blvd. Christian Ch.; deacon Crown Heights Christian Ch., Okla. Recipient Svc. award Franklin Heritage, 1986, Man of Yr. award Franklin C. of C., 1986, Disting. Svc. cert. Transylvania U., 1987, Assoc. Alumnus award Franklin Coll., 1998. Mem. Ben Franklin Soc., Ind. Soc. Chgo., Econ. Club Indpls., Junto Club Indpls., Columbia Club Indpls., Rotary of Franklin, Hillview Country Club, Alpha Soc. Home: Pres Residence & Reception Chancellors House 550 Davis Dr Franklin IN 46131 Office: Franklin Coll Ind 501 E Monroe St Franklin IN 46131-2512

MARTIN, WILLIAM F., retired transportation executive; V.p., legal and asst. sec. Yellow Freight System, Inc., Overland Park, Kans.; ret., 2002.

MARTIN, WILLIAM GIESE, lawyer; b. Canton, Ohio, Nov. 4, 1934; s. George Denman and Emily (Giese) M.; m. Martha Justice, June 14, 1958; children: William E.J., Peter J.D., George F.D. BA, Yale U., 1956; LLB, Harvard U., 1959. Bar: Ohio 1959, U.S. Dist. Ct. (so. dist.) Ohio 1963. Assoc. Porter, Stanley, Treffinger & Platt, Columbus, Ohio, 1963-68; ptnr. Porter, Wright, Morris & Arthur, Columbus, 1968-97, of counsel, 1997—. Trustee Coun. for Ethics in Econs., 1997—. Lt. USNR, 1959-63. Mem. ABA, Ohio State Bar Assn., Capital Club, Rocky Fork Hunt and Country Club, Yale Club of N.Y. Home: 6169 Havens Corners Rd Blacklick OH 43004-9676 Office: Porter Wright Morris & Arthur 41 S High St Ste 3100 Columbus OH 43215-6101

MARTIN, WILLIAM JOSEPH, II, dean, educator; m. Joyce Martin; 2 children. MD, U. Minn. Resident in internal medicine Mayo Grad. Sch. Medicine, Rochester, Minn., fellow in pulmonary medicine; faculty and med. staff Mayo Clinic, Rochester, Minn., 1981—88; Floyd and Reba Smith prof. respiratory disease Ind. U. Sch. Medicine, 1988—2002, exec. assoc. dean clin. affairs, dir. divsn. pulmonary, allergy, critical care and occupl. medicine, 1988—2000; acting sr. v.p. U. Cin., 2002—03, Christian R. Holmes prof., dean Coll. Medicine, 2002—04, rsch. prof., 2004—. Pres. and CEO Ind. U. Med. Group; health policy fellow U.S. Sen. for Sen. Labor and Human Resources Com., 1995—96; funded prin. investigator Nat. Heart, Lung and Blood Inst. Mem.: Am. Thoracic Soc. (pres. 2000—01), Assn. Pulmonary and Critical Care Medicine Program Dirs. (past pres.), Am. Lung Assn. Ind. (past pres.). Office: Coll Medicine 231 Albert Sabin Way Cincinnati OH 45267

MARTIN, WILLIAM RUSSELL, nuclear engineering educator; b. Flint, Mich., June 2, 1945; s. Carl Marcus and Audrey Winifred (Rosene) M.; m. Patricia Ann Williams, Aug. 13, 1967; children: Amy Leigh, Jonathan William. BSE in Engring. Physics, U. Mich., 1967; MS in Physics, U. Wis., 1968; MSE in Nuclear Engring., U. Mich., 1975, PhD in Nuclear Engring., 1976. Prin. physicist Combustion Engring., Inc., Windsor, Conn., 1976-77; asst. prof. nuclear engring. U. Mich., Ann Arbor, 1977-81, assoc. prof. nuclear engring., 1981-88, prof. nuclear engring., 1988—, dir. lab. for sci. computation, 1986—2001, chmn. nuclear engring., 1990-94, assoc. dean for acad. affairs Coll. Engring., 1994-99, dir. Ctr. for Advanced Computing, 2002—04; acting dir. Mich. Grid Ctr., 2002—04, chmn. nuclear engring., 2004—. Cons. Lawrence Livermore Nat. Lab., Livermore, Calif., 1982—, Los Alamos (N.Mex.) Nat. Lab., 1980-89, 2001—, IBM, Inc., Kingston, .Y., 1984, Rockwell Internat., Pitts., 1985. Author: Transport Theory, 1979; author tech. and conf. papers. Recipient Glenn Murphy award Am. Soc. for Engring. Edn., 1993; Disting. scholar U. Mich. Coll. Engring., 1967; vis. fellow Royal Soc., London, 1989. Fellow Am. Nuclear Soc.; mem. Am. Phys. Soc., Soc. for Indsl. and Applied Math., IEEE. Avocations: running, reading, skiing, sailing. Home: 420 Huntington Dr Ann Arbor MI 48104 Office: U Mich Dept uclear Engring Ann Arbor MI 48109 Home Phone: 734-665-3776; Office Phone: 734-764-5534. Business E-Mail: wrm@umich.edu.

MARTINEAU, ROBERT JOHN, retired law educator; b. Oconto, Wis., May 18, 1934; s. Francis Joseph and Gertrude (Schauer) Martineau; m. Constance Ann Zimmerman, Dec. 21, 1957; children: Robert John, Renee, Anne, Jeanne. BS, Coll. Holy Cross, 1956; JD, U. Chgo., 1959. Bar: Md. 1960, U.S. Supreme Ct. 1964, Iowa 1969, Wis. 1974. Law clk. to chief judge Md. Ct. Appeals, 1959-60; pvt. practice Md., 1960-68; asst. atty. gen. Md., 1964-65; assoc. prof. U. Iowa, 1968-71; prof., 1971-72; cir. exec. U.S. Ct. Appeals (8th cir.), Mo., 1972-74; exec. officer Wis. Supreme Ct., 1974-78; prof. U. Dayton, Ohio, 1978-80; prof. law U. Cin., 1980-88, disting. rsch. prof., 1988-93, emeritus, 1994—, assoc. dean, 1980—83, acting dean, 1985—86. Cons. Inst. Jud. Adminstrn., 1970—72, Fed. Jud. Ctr., 1978, Nat. Ctr. State Cts., 1978—79, 1987, Inst. Jud. Adminstrn., 1987—88, UN Devel. Program, Bhutan, 1999; spl. prof. U. Birmingham, England, 1987. Author: Wisconsin Appellate Practice, 1978, Judicial Reform in Wisconsin, in Court Reform in Seven States, 1980, Modern Appellate Practice-Federal and State Civil Appeals, 1983, Fundamentals of Modern Appellate Advocacy, 1985, Cases and Materials on Appellate Practice and Procedure, 1987; author: (with others) 2d edit., 2005; author: Appellate Justice in England and the United States: A Comparative Analysis, 1990, Drafting Legislation and Rules in Plain English, 1991; author: (with M. Salerno) Legal, Legislative, and Rule Drafting in Plain English. 2005. Reporter Wis. Supreme Ct. Com. Discipline Attys., 1975—77, Wis. Jud. Coun. Com. Appellate Practice and Procedure, 1976—78, Com. Contempt and Extraordinary Remedies, 1979—80; sec. Md. Constl. Conv. Commn., 1965—67, Md. Constl. Conv., 1967—68, Wis. Supreme Ct. Com. Study State Bar, 1975—77; mem. Iowa Mcpl. Laws Study Com., 1970—71, Wis. Legis. Coun. Com. Ct. Reorganization, 1977, Ohio Supreme Ct. Adv. Com. Rules, 1988—91; mem., reporter ABA Appellate Judges Conf. Com. Appellate Skills Tng., 1984—85, Com. Appellate Skills Tng., 1984—85; co-chair Com. Appellate Practice, 1986—88. Mem.: Am. Jud. Soc. (bd. dirs. 1966—68), Md. Bar Assn. (reporter com. jud. selection 1962—64, v.p. 1967), Assn. Am. Law Schs. (ho. reps. 1982—87). Democrat. Roman Catholic. Home Phone: 941-488-0455; Office Phone: 941-488-0455. Personal E-mail: r.j.martineau@gmail.com.

MARTINEZ, JIM, communications executive; Degree in Econ., Northwestern U., 1977. Editor Los Vecinos sect. Sun-Times, with Washington bur.; met. editor Chgo. Sun-Times, asst. editor; with Ogilvy Adams & Rinehart; leader Chgo. Advanced Tech. Team Hill & Knowlton Martinez; pres. pub. rels. KemperLesnik Comm., Chgo. Mem. adv. bd. multicultural journalism edn. Roosevelt U.; instr. grad. media mgmt. students Medill Sch. Journalism, Northwestern U. Office: Ste 1500 455 N Cityfront Plaza Dr Chicago IL 60611-5313 Fax: 312-755-0274.

MARTINEZ, NATALIE, newscaster; b. Buffalo; Degree, SUNY, Buffalo. Anchor, reporter, prodr. at upstate N.Y. radio and TV stations; reporter and weekend anchor WXAA-TV, Albany, NY, primary anchor; co-anchor weekend morning news and reporter WMAQ-TV, Chgo., 2001—. Mem.: Nat. League Female Execs., Nat. Assn. of Hispanic Journalists, One Voice. Office: WMAQ-TV NBC Tower 454 N Columbus Dr Chicago IL 60611-5555 Office Phone: 312-836-5830.

MARTINEZ, TODD J., chemistry professor; b. Mar. 22, 1968; BS, Calvin Coll., 1989; PhD, U. Calif., 1994. Fulbright fellow Fritz Haber Inst. Molecular Dynamics, Jerusalem; presdl. postdoctoral fellow U. Calif., LA, 1994—96; asst. prof. U. Ill., Urbana-Champaign, 1996—2002, assoc. prof., 2002—04, prof., 2004—, Gutsgell Chair of Chemistry, 2006—. Faculty affiliate theoretical and computational biophysics group Beckman Inst. Advanced Sci. and Tech.; ad hoc reviewer for numerous sci. journals; vice-chair ACS Theoretical Chemistry Subdivision, 2005—. Named a MacArthur fellow, John D. and Catherine T. MacArthur Found., 2005; recipient CAREER Award, NSF, 1998, Rsch. Innovation award, Rsch. Corp., 1998, Beckman Young Investigator award, Beckman Found., 1999, Camille Dreyfus Teacher-Scholar award, Camille & Henry Dreyfus Found., 2000—05. Mem.: Biophysical Soc., Am. Assn. for the Advancement of Sci., Am. Physical Soc., Am. Chem. Soc. Office: U Ill Dept Chemistry MC 712 600 S Mathews Urbana IL 61801 E-mail: tmartine@uiuc.edu.

MARTING, MICHAEL G., lawyer; b. Cleve., Nov. 5, 1948; BA summa cum laude, Yale U., 1971, JD, 1974. Bar: Ohio 1974. Assoc. Jones Day, Cleve., 1974-83, ptnr., 1984—. Mem.: Chagrin Valley Hunt Club, Tavern Club (trustee local chpt. 1985—88, 2004—06, treas., sec.), Cleve. Racquet Club. Avocations: fly fishing, hunting, squash. Office: Jones Day N Point 901 Lakeside Ave E Cleveland OH 44114-1190 Home Phone: 216-371-5185; Office Phone: 216-586-7194. Business E-Mail: mgmarting@jonesday.com.

MARTINO, FRANK DOMINIC, union executive; b. Albany, NY, Apr. 9, 1919; s. Benedetto and Rosina (Esposita) M.; m. Phyllis E. Higgins, June 15, 1963; children— Michael M., Lisa R. Student, Rutgers U., Cornell U., Oxford U. Timekeeper N.Y.C. R.R., 1937-41; chem. operator Sterling Drug Co., 1946-56; internat. rep. Internat. Chem. Workers Union, Akron, Ohio, 1956-70, internat. v.p., 1970-72, sec.-treas., 1972-75; internat. pres. Internat. Chem. Workers Union Coun./United Food Comml. Workers/UFCW, 1975—; Washington rep., dir. Internat. Chem. Workers Union Coun./USCW, 1962-70. Served with USAF, 1941-45. Democrat. Roman Catholic. Office: International Chemical Workers Union 1799 Akron Peninsula Rd # 300 Akron OH 44313-4847

MARTINO, ROBERT SALVATORE, orthopedic surgeon; b. Clarksburg, W.Va., May 31, 1931; s. Leonard L. and Sarafina (Foglia) M.; m. Lenora Cappellanti, May 22, 1954; children: Robert S. Jr., Leslie L. Reckziegel. AB, W.Va. U., 1953, postgrad., 1955-56, BS in Medicine, 1958; MD, Northwestern U., 1960. Diplomate Am. Bd. Orthop. Surgery; lic. Ill., Calif., Ind. Intern Chgo. Wesley, 1960-61; resident dept. orthopaedic surgery Northwestern U., 1961-65, Chgo. Wesley Meml., 1961-62, Am. Legion Hosp. for Crippled Children, 1962-63, Cook County Hosp., Chgo., 1964, 64-65; orthopeadic surgeon Gary, Ind., 1965-67; orthopaedic surgeon Merrillville, Ind., 1967—. Fellow Nat. Found. Infantile Paralysis, 1956, Office of Vocat. Rehab., Hand Surgery, 1965; chief of staff St. Mary Med. Ctr., 1976, chief of surgery, 1974-85; chief of staff Gary Treatment Ctr./Ind. Crippled Children's Svcs., 1974-84; adj. asst. prof. anatomy Ind. U., 1978, clin. asst. prof. orthop. surgery, 1980, emeritus asst. prof. anatomy and cell biology Ind. U., 2003, emeritus clin. asst. prof. orthop. surgery, 2003; mem. Zoning Bd., 1989-90. Chmn. Planning Bd. Town of Dune Acres, 1992-96; bd. dirs. United Steel Workers Union Health Plan, 1994—, St. Mary's Med. Ctr., Hobart, Ind.; com. on Health Care Reform. Capt. infantry US Army, 1953—55, active duty USAR, 1955—58. Fellow ACS (emeritus), Am. Acad. Orthop. Surgery (emeritus); mem. AMA, NRA, Ind. Med. Soc., Ill. Med. Soc., Chgo. Med. Soc., Ill. Orthop. Soc., Ind. Orthop. Soc., Mid-Am. Orthop. Assn., Tri-State Orthop. Soc., Clin. Orthop. Soc. Republican. Roman Catholic. Home: 22 Oak Dr Chesterton IN 46304-1016 Personal E-mail: indorth@aol.com, brutabobm@aol.com.

MARTINS, HEITOR MIRANDA, foreign language educator; b. Belo Horizonte, Brazil, July 22, 1933; came to U.S., 1960; s. Joaquim Pedro and Emilia (Miranda) M.; m. Teresomja Alves Pereira, Nov. 1, 1958 (div. 1977); children—Luzia Pereira, Emilia Pereira; m. Marlene Andrade, Jan. 11, 1984 AB, U. Federal de Minas Gerais, 1959; PhD, U. Federal de Minas Gerais, 1962. Instr. U. N.M., Albuquerque, 1960-62; asst. prof. Tulane U., New Orleans, 1962-66, assoc. prof., 1966-68; prof. dept. Spanish and Portuguese Ind. U., Bloomington, 1968—, chmn. dept., 1972-76. Vis. prof. U. Tex., Austin, 1963, Stanford U., 1968. Author: poetry Sirgo nos Cabelos, 1961; essay Manuel de Galhegos, 1964; essays Oswald de Andrade e Outros, 1973; critical anthology Neoclassicismo, 1982; Essays Do Barroco a Guimarães Rosa, 1983; editor: essays Luso-Brazilian Literary Studies. Social Sci. Research Council grantee, 1965; Fulbright-Hays Commn. grantee, 1966; Ford Found. grantee, 1970, 71 Mem. MLA, Renaissance Soc. Am., Am. Comparative Lit. Assn., Am. Assn. for 18th Century Studies. Home: 1316 S Nancy St Bloomington IN 47401-6050 Office: Indiana U Dept Spanish and Portuguese Bloomington IN 47405 E-mail: martins@indiana.edu.

MARTUCCI, WILLIAM CHRISTOPHER, lawyer; b. Asbury Park, NJ, Mar. 10, 1952; s. Frank and Evelyn (Gerrity) M.; children: Daniel Robert, William Sessions, John Andrew, James Christopher, Andrew Michael, Matthew Peter, Caroline Kenney. AB magna cum laude, Rutgers U., 1974; JD with honors, U. Ark., 1977; LLM with honors, Georgetown U., 1981; LLM in Exec. Edn., Harvard Bus. Sch., 1997. Bar: Mo. 1977. Law clk. to presiding justice Mo. Ct. Appeals, Kansas City, 1977-78; assoc. Spencer, Fane, Britt & Browne, Kansas City, 1981-86, ptnr., 1987-99, Shook, Hardy & Bacon LLP, Kansas City, 2000—, leader Nat. Employment Litig. & Policy Group. Mem. practice and procedure com. Nat. Labor Relations Act; charter mem. Am. Employment Coun., 1993—; adj. prof. employment law U. Mo. Law Sch., Kansas City, 1988-95, chair minority affairs com. 1992-2002. Editor-in-chief Ark. Law Rev., 1976-77; contbr. articles to profl. jours. Chmn. adv. coun. Urban League Greater Kansas City Tng. Ctr., chmn. mentor program, 1988-2005; mem. Kansas City Civic Coun.; mem. Kansas City Tomorrow Leadership Program, 1992-93; adv. bd. Boys and Girls Club Kansas City, Reviving Baseball in the Inner City. Served to lt. JAGC, USN, 1978-81. Decorated Navy Commendation medal. Mem. ABA (employment and labor rels. com., EEO litigation com.), Mo. Bar Assn. (exec. com. continuing legal edn. 1987—, chair 1993-2000), Kansas City Bar Assn. (chmn. continuing legal edn. 1984-86, mem. exec. com. 1985-98, leadership award 1985, chmn. labor and employment law com. 1988-90, Pres. award 1992, 97), Lawyers Assn. Kansas City (mem. exec. com. young lawyers sect. 1981-82), Kansas City Club, Homestead Country Club, Rotary. Clubs: Kansas City. Republican. Roman Catholic. Office: Shook Hardy and Bacon 2555 Grand Blvd Kansas City MO 64105-2613 Home: 6429 Overbrook Rd Mission Hills KS 66208-1939 Office Phone: 816-474-6550. Business E-Mail: wmartucci@shb.com.

MARTY, JOHN, state legislator, writer; b. Evanston, Ill., Nov. 1, 1956; s. Martin E. and Elsa Louise (Schumacher) M.; m. Connie Jaarsma, Nov. 29, 1980; children: Elsa, Micah. BA in Ethics, St. Olaf Coll., 1978. Rschr. Minn. Ho. of Reps., St. Paul, 1980-82, com. adminstr. com. criminal justice, 1982-84; corp. found. grant adminstr., 1984-86; mem. Minn. Senate from 54th dist., St. Paul, 1987—. Author Minn. Govt. Ethics Law, campaign fin. reform, DWI (driving while intoxicated) laws. Dem. Farm Labor gubernatorial candidate, 1994. Office: 325 Capitol 75 Constitution Ave Saint Paul MN 55155-1601

MARTY, MARTIN EMIL, theology studies educator; b. West Point, Nebr., Feb. 5, 1928; s. Emil A. and Anne Louise (Wuerdemann) Marty; m. Elsa Schumacher Marty, 1952 (dec. 1981); children: Frances, Joel, John, Peter, James, Micah, Ursula; m. Harriet Lindemann Marty, 1982. MDiv, Concordia Sem., 1952; STM, Luth. Sch. Theology, Chgo., 1954; PhD in Am. Religious and Intellectual History, U. Chgo., 1956; LittD (hon.), Thiel Coll., 1964; LHD (hon.), W.Va. Wesleyan Coll., 1967, Marian Coll., 1967, Providence Coll., 1967; DD (hon.), Muhlenberg Coll., 1967; LittD (hon.), Thomas More Coll., 1968; DD (hon.), Bethany Sem., 1969; LLD (hon.), Keuka Coll., 1972; LHD (hon.), Willamette U., 1974; DD (hon.), Wabash Coll., 1977; LLD (hon.), U. So. Calif., 1977, Valparaiso U., 1978; LHD (hon.), St. Olaf Coll., 1978, De Paul U., 1979; DD (hon.), Christ Sem.-Seminex, 1979, Capital U., 1980; LHD (hon.), Colo. Coll., 1980; DD (hon.), Maryville Coll., 1980, North Park Coll. Sem., 1982; LittD (hon.), Wittenberg U., 1983; LHD, Rosary Coll., 1984; LHD (hon.), Rockford Coll., 1984; DD (hon.), Va. Theol. Sem., 1984; LHD (hon.), Hamilton Coll., 1985, Loyola U., 1986; LLD (hon.), U. Notre Dame, 1987; LHD (hon.), Roanoke Coll., 1987, Mercer U., 1987, Ill. Wesleyan Coll., 1987, Roosevelt U., 1988, Aquinas Coll., 1988; LittD (hon.), Franklin Coll., 1988, U. Nebr., 1993; LHD (hon.), No. Mich. U., 1989, Muskingum Coll., Coe Coll., Lehigh U., 1989, Hebrew Union Coll. and Governors State U., 1990, Whittier Coll., 1991, Calif. Luth. U., 1993; DD (hon.), St. Xavier Coll. and Colgate U., 1990, Mt. Union Coll., 1991, Tex. Luth. Coll., 1991, Aurora U., 1991, Baker U., 1992; LHD (hon.), Luth. U., 1993; LHD, Calif. Luth. U., 1993, Midland Luth. Coll., 1995; DD, Hope Coll., 1993, Northwestern Coll., 1993; LHD (hon.), George Fox Coll., 1994, Drake U., 1994, Centre Coll., 1994, Fontbonne Coll., 1996; DD, Yale U., 1995; LHD (hon.), Otterbein Coll., 1996; ThD (hon.), Lycoming Coll., 1997; LHD, Dana Coll., 1998; LittD (hon.), Alma Coll., 1998, Concordia U. Portland, 1998, Niagara U., 1998; LHD (hon.), Kalamazoo Coll., 1999, William Jewell Coll., 1999; LittD, LittD, Lynchburg Coll., 2003; DD (hon.), Trinity Coll., 2001, Wake Forest U., 2003; DHum (hon.), Westminster Choir Coll., 2001; LHD (hon.), U. Scranton, 2001; DD (hon.), Wake Forest U., 2003; LHD (hon.), Ea. Mennonite U., 2003, Iona Coll.; LLD (hon.), Fordham U., 2005; LHD (hon.), Ill.

Coll., 2007, Augsburg Coll., 2007. Ordained to ministry Luth. Ch., 1952. Pastor, Washington, 1950—51; asst. pastor River Forest, Ill., 1952—56; pastor Elk Grove Village, Ill., 1956—63; prof. history of modern Christianity Div. Sch. U. Chgo., 1963—, Fairfax M. Cone Disting. Svc. prof., 1978—98, prof. emeritus, 1998—; assoc. editor Christian Century mag., Chgo., 1956—85, sr. editor, 1985—98; co-editor Ch. History mag., 1963—97. Pres. Park Ridge Ctr. for Study of Health Faith and Ethics, Ill., 1985—89, sr. scholar-in-residence, 1989—98; pres. Am. Inst. for Study of Health, Faith and Ethics, 1985—89; dir. The Pub. Religion Project, 1996—99; interim pres. St. Olaf Coll., 2000—01. Author: A Short History of Christianity, 1959, The New Shape of American Religion, 1959, The Improper Opinion, 1961, The Infidel, 1961, Baptism, 1962, The Hidden Discipline, 1963, Second Chance for American Protestants, 1963, Church Unity and Church Mission, 1964, Varieties of Unbelief, 1964, The Search for a Usable Future, 1969, The Modern Schism, 1969, Righteous Empire, 1970, Protestantism, 1972, You Are Promise, 1973, The Fire We Can Light, 1973, The Pro and Con Book of Religious America, 1975, A Nation of Behavers, 1976, Religion, Awakening and Revolution, 1978, Friendship, 1980, By Way of Response, 1981, The Public Church, 1981, A Cry of Absence, 1983, Health and Medicine in the Lutheran Tradition, 1983, Pilgrims in Their Own Land, 1984, Protestantism in the United States, 1985, Modern American Religion, The Irony of it All, Vol. 1, 1986, An Invitation to American Catholic History, 1986, Religion and Republic, 1987, Modern American Religion: The Noise of Conflict, Vol. 2, 1991, Lutheran Questions, Lutheran Answers, 2007, The Mystery of the Child, 2004; author: (with R. Scott Appleby) The Glory and the Power, 1992; editor (with Jerald C. Brauer): The Unrelieved Paradox: Studies in the Theology of Franz Bibfeldt, 1994; editor: (with Micah Marty) Places Along the Way, 1994; editor: Our Hope for Years to Come, 1995, Modern American Religion, Under God, Indivisible, Vol. 3, 1996, The One and the Many, 1997, The Promise of Winter, 1997, When True Simplicity is Gained, 1998, Politics, Religion, and the Common Good, 2000, Education, Religion, and the Common Good, 2001, Speaking of Trust, 2003, Vision of Utopia, 2003;: When Faiths Collide, 2004, Protestant Voice in American Pluralism, 2004, Martin Luther, 2004; editor: (jours.) Context, 1969—; editor: Second Opinion, The Mystery of Child, 2007, The Christian World: A Global History, 2008; sr. editor: The Christian Century, 1956—98; contbr. articles to religious publs. Chmn. bd. regents St. Olaf Coll., 1996—2001, sr. regent, 2002—; dir. The Pub. Religion Project, 1996—2000. Recipient Nat. Medal Humanities, 1997, Alumni medal, U. Chgo., 1998. Fellow: Am. Acad. Political and Social Scis. (Mohandas K. Gandhi Fellow, Mohandas K. Gandhi fellow), Soc. Am. Historians, Am. Acad. Arts and Scis. (dir. fundamentalism project 1988—94); mem.: Am. Antiquarian Soc., Am. Acad. Religion (pres. 1987—88), Am. Cath. Hist. Assn. (pres. 1981), Am. Soc. Ch. History (pres. 1971), Am. Philos. Soc. Lutheran. Personal E-mail: memarty@aol.com.

MARTZ, GARY R., lawyer; BA, U. Toledo, 1979; JD, Ohio State U., 1982. Bar: Ohio 1982. Ptnr. Baker & Hostetler, LLP, 1982—2001; sr. v.p., gen. counsel, sec. Greif, Inc., 2002—; pres. Soterra LLC, 2005—. Office: Greif Inc 425 Winter Rd Delaware OH 43015 Office Phone: 740-549-6188. E-mail: garymartz@greif.com.

MARUSKA, EDWARD JOSEPH, zoological park administrator; b. Chgo., Feb. 19, 1934; s. Edward M.; m. Nancy; children— Donna, Linda. Student, Wright Coll., Chgo., 1959-61; D.Sc. (hon.), Xavier U., 1986, U. Cin., 1989. Keeper hoofed animals Lincoln Park Zoo, Chgo., 1956-62; head keeper Children's Zoo, 1959-62; gen. curator Cin. Zoo, 1962-68, dir., 1968—. Lectr. biol. sci. U. Can.; numerous TV appearances. Recipient Cin. Conservation Man of Year award, 1973, Ambassador award Cin. Conv. and Visitors Bur., 1974 Fellow Am. Assn. Zool. Parks and Aquariums (pres. 1978-79); mem. Am. Soc. Ichthyologists and Herpetologists, Whooping Crane Conservation Assn., Internat. Union Zoo Dirs., Langdon Club, Cin. Naturalists Soc. Office: Zool Society of Cin 3400 Vine St Cincinnati OH 45220-1333

MARVIN, JAMES CONWAY, librarian, consultant; b. Warroad, Minn., Aug. 3, 1927; s. William C. and Isabel (Carlquist) M.; m. Patricia Katharine Moe, Sept. 8, 1947; children: James Conway, Jill C., Jack C. BA, U. Minn., 1950, MA, 1966. City librarian, Kaukauna, Wis., 1952-54; chief librarian Eau Claire, Wis., 1954-56; dir. Cedar Rapids (Iowa) Pub. Library, 1956-67, Topeka Pub. Library, 1967-92. ALA-Rockefeller Found. vis. prof. Inst. Libr. Sci., U. Philippines, 1964-65; vis. lectr. dept. librarianship Emporia (Kans.) State U., 1970-80; chmn. Kans. del. to White House Conf. on Librs. and Info. Svcs., Gov.'s Com. on Libr. Resources, 1980-81; mem. Kans. Libr. Adv. Commn., 1992—, chmn., 1998—. Served with USNR, 1945-46. Mem. ALA, Iowa Libr. Assn. (past pres.), Kans. Libr. Assn., Philippine Libr. Assn. (life), Mountain Plains Libr. Assn. Home: 40 SW Pepper Tree Ln Topeka KS 66611-2055

MARWEDEL, WARREN JOHN, lawyer; b. Chgo., July 3, 1944; s. August Frank and Eleanor (Wolgamot) M.; m. Marilyn Baran, Apr. 12, 1975. BS in Marine Engring., U.S. Merchant Marine Acad., 1966; JD, Loyola U., Chgo., 1972. Bar: Ill. 1972, U.S. Dist. Ct. (no. dist.) Ill. 1972, U.S. Supreme Ct. 1974. Pres. Marwedel Minichello & Reeb, P.C., Chgo. With U.S. Merchant Marines, 1966-70. Mem. ABA (Ho. of Dels. 1989-96), Ill. Bar Assn., Chgo. Bar Assn., Maritime Law Assn.(1st v.p.), Propeller Club (Chgo. pres. 1982). Avocations: boating, reading, history. Office: Marwedel Minichello & Reeb PC President 10 S Riverside Plz Ste 720 Chicago IL 60606-3708 Office Phone: 312-902-1600. Personal E-mail: wjmmmandr@aol.com. Business E-Mail: wmarwedel@mmr-law.com.

MARX, DAVID, JR., lawyer; b. Chgo., Nov. 15, 1950; BA cum laude, Amherst Coll., 1972; JD, Syracuse U., 1975. Bar: N.Y. 1976, Ill. 1986. Ptnr. McDermott, Will & Emery, Chgo. Mem. ABA, Chgo. Bar Assn. Office: McDermott Will & Emery 227 W Monroe St Fl 31 Chicago IL 60606-5016

MARX, THOMAS GEORGE, economist; b. Trenton, NJ, Oct. 25, 1943; s. George Thomas and Ann (Szymanski) Marx; m. Arlene May Varga, Aug. 23, 1969; children: Melissa Ann, Thomas Jeffrey, Jeffrey Alan. BS summa cum laude, Rider Coll., 1969; PhD, U. Pa., Phila., 1973. Fin. analyst Am. Cyanamid Co., Trenton, 1968; economist FTC, Washington, 1973; econ. cons. Foster Assocs. Inc., Washington, 1974-77; sr. economist GM, Detroit, 1977-79, mgr. indsl. econs., 1980-81, dir. econs. policy studies, 1981-83, dir. corp. strategic planning group, 1984-86, gen. dir. market analysis and forecasting, 1986-88, gen. dir. econ. analysis, 1988-90, gen. dir. issues mgmt. on industry govt. rels. staff, 1990-96, dir. econ. issues and analysis corp. affairs staff, 1996-97, dir. global climate issue, 1997—2005; coll. prof., dir. bus. adminstrn. doctorate program Coll. Mgmt. Lawrence Technol. U., 2005—. Mem. faculty Temple U., Phila., 1972—73, U. Pa., Phila., 1972—73; adj. prof. Wayne State U., 1981—89, U. Detroit, 1988—2005; prof., dir. bus. adminstrn. doctorate program Lawrence Technol. U., 2005—. Assoc. editor: Bus. Econs., 1980—98, mem. editl. bd.: Akron Jour. Bus. and Econs., 1981—90; contbr. articles to profl. jours. With USAF, 1961—65. Mem.: Assn. Pub. Policy Analysts, Planning Forum, Western Econ. Assn., So. Econ. Assn., Econ. Soc. Mich., Detroit Area Bus. Economists (v.p.), Nat. Assn. Bus. Economists, Am. Econ. Assn., Nat. Econs. Club, Beta Gamma Sigma, Pi Gamma Mu. Roman Catholic. Home: 3312 Bloomfield Park Dr West Bloomfield MI 48323-3514 Office Phone: 248-204-3081. Business E-Mail: tmarx@ltu.edu.

MARZLUF, GEORGE AUSTIN, biochemistry educator; b. Columbus, Ohio, Sept. 29, 1935; s. Paul Bayhan and Opal Faun (Simmons) M.; m. Zarife Sahenk; children: Bruce, Julie, Philip, Glenn. BS, Ohio State U., 1957, MS, 1960; PhD, Johns Hopkins U., 1964. Postdoctoral fellow U. Wis., Madison, 1964-66; asst. prof. biochemistry Marquette U., Milw., 1966-70; assoc. prof. Ohio State U., Columbus, 1970-75, prof., 1975—, chmn. dept. biochemistry, 1985-2000. Contbr. articles to profl. jours. Mem. Genetics Soc. Am., Am. Soc. Microbiology, AAAS, Am. Soc. Biochemists and Molecular Biologists. E-mail: Marzluf.1@osu.edu. Office: Ohio State U Dept of Biochemistry 484 W 12th Ave Columbus OH 43210-1214

MARZULLO, LARRY A., transportation executive; Chmn., CEO The Bekins Co., Inc., Hillside, Ill., 1995—. Office: The Bekins Co Inc 330 S Mannheim Rd Hillside IL 60162-1833

MASBACK, CRAIG, executive director United States track and field; BA, Princeton U.; JD, Yale U. Track and field broadcaster various television stations, 1982; asst. to dir. Olympic Mus., Lausanne, Switzerland, 1982-84; attorney Wash.; exec. dir. U.S.A. Track & Field, Indpls., 1997—. Creator Foot Locker Slam Fest. Keasbey scholar Trinity Coll., NCAA scholar Oxford U; runner, 1980 U.S. indoor mile champion, U.S. record holder 2000 meters, 1985 U.S. team World Cup Champion. Mem. TAC/USA (bd. dirs., athletes adv. com., internat. competition com., mktg. media com.). Office: USA Track & Field 1 Rca Dome Ste 140 Indianapolis IN 46225-1023

MASEK, MARK JOSEPH, writer; b. Joliet, Ill., June 13, 1957; s. Glenn James and Helen Margaret (Gleason) Masek; m. Theresa Marie Norton, Oct. 24, 1987. B, U. Ill., Urbana, 1979. Reporter The Daily Illini, Champaign, 1976—79, Joliet Herald-News, 1978—79; columnist, editor Elgin Daily Courier-News, Ill., 1979—88; editor The Daily Herald, Arlington Heights, Ill., 1988—90; publs. mgr. Argonne Nat. Lab., Ill., 1990—98; editor Riverside Press-Enterprise, Calif., 2003—05; news editor San Gabriel Valley Newspaper Group, Calif., 2005—. Author: Hollywood Remains to Be Seen, 2001. V.p. Recycle Now-Joliet, 1991—; active Environ. Commn. City of Joliet, 1993—96; bd. dirs. Will County Habitat for Humanity, 1994—99, pres., 1997—99. Recipient 1st pl. Pub. Svc. award, Ill. AP Editors' Assn., 3d pl. Pub. Svc. award, 1980, 2d pl. Columns award, No. Ill. Newspaper Assn., 1982, 1st pl. Columns award, Nat. Newspaper Assn., 1982. Mem.: Ind. Writers So. Calif., Soc. Profl. Journalists, Mensa. Democrat. Roman Catholic.

MASERU, NOBLE A.W., city health department administrator; b. Detroit; BS, Wayne State U.; MPH, Emory U. Sch. Medicine; PhD in Health Policy, Atlanta U. Founding dir., master of pub. health program Morehouse Sch. Medicine, Atlanta; health policy scientist Morehouse Coll., Pub. Health Scis. Inst.; v.p., cmty. health Greater Detroit Area Health Coun. Inc., 1998—2000; dir. and health officer Detroit Dept. Health and Wellness Promotion, 2003—. Office: Detroit Dept Health & Wellness Promotion Herman Kiefer Health Complex 1151 Taylor Detroit MI 48202 Office Phone: 313-876-4300.

MASH, DONALD J., college president; b. Oct. 12, 1942; children: Maria, Christina, Donnie (dec.). BS in Edn., Ind. U. Pa., 1960; MA in Geography, U. Pitts., 1966; PhD, Ohio State U., 1974. Teaching fellow U. Pitts., 1964-65; instr. geography U. Pitts.-Bradford, 1965-68; dean for student svcs. Ohio Dominican Coll., 1968-75; v.p. for student affairs George Mason U., Fairfax, Va., 1975-85, exec. v.p. adminstrn., 1985-88; pres. Wayne (Nebr.) State Coll., 1988-98; chancellor U. Wis.-Eau Claire, 1998—2005; exec. sr. v.p. U. Wis. Sys. Office: U Wis 1730 Van Hise Hall 1220 Linden Dr Madison WI 53706-4004 Office Phone: 608-262-4049. Business E-Mail: dmash@uwsa.edu.

MASON, EARL LEONARD, retired food products executive; b. Jersey City, July 12, 1947; s. Herman E. and Marguerite (Rondeau) Mason; m. Patricia Fladung; children: Holly Ann, Wendy Lynn; m. Bonita L. Blair, Dec. 11, 1976. BS, Fairleigh Dickinson U., 1969, MBA, 1984. With AT&T, N.J., 1969-79, dir. mktg. N.J., 1979-81; corp. contr. ATT Info. Sys., 1981-85; dir. fin. mgmt. and planning AT&T, N.J., 1985-87; contr. mfg. Digital Equipment Corp., Maynard, Mass., 1987-91, European CFO Geneva, 1990-91; v.p. fin., CFO Inland Steel Industries, Chgo., 1991-96, sr. v.p., 1995-96; sr. v.p., CFO Compaq Computer Corp., Houston, 1996-99; pres., CEO Alliant Foodservice, Chgo, 1999-2001. Dir. Family Inn, Boston, State of Ill.; chmn. bd. dirs. Computer Horizon's Corp. Mem.: Fin. Execs. Inst., Am. Iron and Steel Inst., City of Chgo. C. of C. (bd. dirs.), East Bank Club, Univ. Club. Avocations: squash, racquetball, tennis, golf, boating. Home: 195 N Harbor Dr Apt 2202 Chicago IL 60601-7530 Office: Alliant Food Service 9933 Woods Dr Skokie IL 60077-1057

MASON, EDWARD EATON, surgeon; b. Boise, Idaho, Oct. 16, 1920; s. Edward Files and Dora Bell (Eaton) M.; m. Dordana Fairman, June 18, 1944; children— Daniel Edward, Rose Mary, Richard Eaton, Charles Henry. BA, U. Iowa, 1943, MD, 1945; PhD in Surgery, U. Minn., 1953. Intern, resident in surgery Univ. Hosps., Mpls., 1945-52; asst. prof. surgery U. Iowa, 1953-55, asso. prof., 1956-60, prof., 1961-91, prof. emeritus, 1991—, chmn. gen. surgery, 1978-91. Cons. VA Hosp.; trainee Nat. Cancer Inst., 1949-52 Author: Computer Applications in Medicine, 1964, Fluid, Electrolyte and Nutrient Therapy in Surgery, 1974, Surgical Treatment of Obesity, 1981; developer gastric bypass and gastroplasty for treatment of obesity; contbr. articles profl. jours. Served to lt. (j.g.) USNR, 1945-47. Fellow ACS; mem. AMA, Am. Surg. Assn., Western Surg. Assn., Soc. Univ. Surgeons, Internat. Soc. Surgery, Ctrl. Surg. Assn., Soc. Surgery Alimentary Tract, Am. Thyroid Assn., Am. Soc. Bariatric Surgery, Sigma Xi, Alpha Omega Alpha. Republican. Presbyterian. Home: 5 Melrose Cir Iowa City IA 52246-2013 Office: Univ Hosp Dept Surgery Iowa City IA 52242 Business E-Mail: edward-mason@uiowa.edu.

MASON, JEREMY R., lawyer; b. Cin., Aug. 1, 1974; BS, Cornell U., 1997; JD, Ohio State U., 2000. Bar: Ohio 2000, US Dist. Ct. Southern Dist. Ohio 2001, Ky. 2006, US Dist. Ct. Northern Dist. Ohio 2006, US Dist. Ct. Eastern Dist. Ky. 2006, US Dist. Ct. Western Dist. Ky. 2006. Named one of Ohio's Rising Stars, Super Lawyers, 2006. Mem.: Am. Bankruptcy Inst. (Medal of Excellence 2000), Comml. Law League, Ky. Bar Assn., Ohio State Assn., Cin. Bar Assn., Bus. Assn. (CALI award 1998), Delta Kappa Epsilon (Scholar award). Office: Mason Schilling & Mason Co LPA 11340 Montgomery Rd Ste 210 Cincinnati OH 45249-2313 Office Phone: 513-489-0829. Office Fax: 513-489-0834.

MASON, LANCE T., state representative; BA with honors, Coll. of Wooster; JD, U. Mich. Trial atty. U.S. Dept. Agr., Washington; atty. Rucker, Sims & Assocs.; asst. pros. atty. Cuyahoga County Prosecutor's Office, Ohio; state rep. dist. 8 Ohio Ho. of Reps., Columbus, 2001—, ranking minority mem. criminal justice com., mem. civil and comml. law, juvenile and family law, and pub. utilities coms. Democrat. Office: 77 S High St 10th fl Columbus OH 43215-6111

MASON, PERRY CARTER, philosophy educator; b. Houston, Sept. 24, 1939; s. Lloyd Vernon and Lorraine (Carter) M.; m. Judith Jane Fredrick, June 11, 1960; children— Gregory Charles, Nicole Elizabeth BA, Baylor U., Waco, Tex., 1961; B.D., Harvard U., 1964; MA, Yale U., 1966, PhD, 1968. Asst. prof. philosophy Carleton Coll., Northfield, Minn., 1968-73, assoc. prof. philosophy, 1973-80, prof. philosophy, 1980—, v.p. for planning and devel., 1988-89, v.p. for external rels., 1989-91, John E. Sawyer prof. philosophy and liberal learning emeritus, 2000—. Contbr. articles to profl. publs. Mem. Minn. Philos. Soc., Am. Philos. Assn. Democrat. Home: 8629 Hall Ave Northfield MN 55057-4884 Office: Carleton College 1 N College St Northfield MN 55057-4044 E-mail: pmason@carleton.edu.

MASON, RACHEL J., lawyer; b. Cin., Dec. 8, 1977; BA, Lehigh U., 2000; JD, Dickinson Sch. of Law, Pa. State U., 2003. Bar: Ohio 2003. Named one of Ohio's Rising Stars, Super Lawyers, 2006. Mem.: Assn. Credit and Collection Professionals, Nat. Assn. Retail Collection Attorneys, Comml. Law League Am. (award of Excellence), ABA, Ohio State Bar Assn., Cin. Bar Assn. Office: Mason Schilling & Mason Co LPA 11340 Cincinnati OH 45249-2313 Office Phone: 513-489-0829. Office Fax: 513-489-0834.

MASON, RICHARD J., lawyer; b. Syracuse, NY, June 16, 1951; BA with high honors, U. Ill., 1973; MBA, U. Chgo., 1980; JD, U. Notre Dame, 1977. Bar: Ill. 1977. Ptnr., mem. exec. com. Ross & Hardies, Chgo., 1990—2003; ptnr. McGuireWoods, Chgo., 2003—. Adj. prof. law Kent Coll. Law, Ill. Inst. Tech., Chgo., 1984—. Bd. dirs. Ill. Farm Legal Assistance Found., 1985-88. Fellow Am. Coll. Bankruptcy; mem. ABA (chmn. bus. bankruptcy subcom. on use and disposition of property under the bankruptcy code 1989—), Am. Bankruptcy Inst., Ill. State Bar Assn. (mem. banking and bankruptcy law sect. coun. 1986-88), Chgo. Bar Assn. (mem. bankruptcy and reorgn. com. 1978—). Office: McGuireWoods LLP 77 W Wacker Dr Ste 4100 Chicago IL 60601

MASON, SALLY KAY FROST, academic administrator, biology professor; b. NYC, May 29, 1950; d. Michael and Alberta Viparina; m. John S. Frost, Aug. 1975 (div. Feb. 1982); m. Kenneth Andrew Mason, Mar. 17, 1990. BA in Zoology, U. Ky., 1972; MS in Cell/Devel. Biology, Purdue U., 1974; PhD in Cell/Devel. Biology, U. Ariz., 1978. Rsch. assoc. Ind. U., Bloomington, 1978-80; asst. prof. biology U. Kans., Lawrence, 1980—86, assoc. prof. biology, 1986-91, prof. biology, 1991-2001, chair dept. physiology and cell biology, 1986-89, assoc. dean scis., 1990-95, dean arts and scis., 1995-2001; provost, prof. biology Purdue U., West Lafayette, Ind., 2001—07; pres. U. Iowa, 2007—. Chmn. bd. Inproteo, 2003—07; chmn. EHR adv. bd. NSF, 2005—06; mem. exec. com. Nat. Assn. State U. and Land Grant Colls., 2002—; mem. Pres.'s Nat. Medal of Sci. Selection Com., 2006—. Mem. editl. bd. Pigment Cell Rsch., 1988-99; contbr. chpts. to books and articles to profl. jours. Dissertation fellow AAUW, 1977-78, Kemper Tchg. fellow U. Kans., Lawrence, 1997; grantee NSF, NIH, Washington, 1981—; Wesley Found. grantee Welsey Health Found., Wichita, Kans., 1991-93. Mem. Internat. Fedn. Pigment Cell Scis. (coun. mem. 1997-2000), Pan Am. Soc. for Pigment Cell Rsch. (coun. mem. 1988-98, pres. 1996-98), Coun. Colls. Arts and Scis. (bd. mem. 1997-99, pres. elect 1999-2000, pres. 2000-2001). Avocations: travel, reading, writing. Office: U Iowa Office of Pres 101 Jessup Hall Iowa City IA 52242-1316

MASON, THOMAS ALBERT, retired lawyer; b. Cleve., May 4, 1936; s. Victor Lewis and Frances (Speidel) M.; m. Elisabeth Gun Sward, Sept. 25, 1965; children: Thomas Lewis, Robert Albert. AB, Kenyon Coll., 1958; LLB, Case-Western Res. U., 1961. Bar: Ohio 1962. Assoc. Thompson, Hine and Flory, Cleve., 1965-73, ptnr., 1973—2001, ret., 2002—. Trustee Cleve. YMCA, 1975-94. Capt. USMCR, 1962-65. Mem. Am. Coll. Real Estate Lawyers, Ohio Bar Assn., Cleve. Bar Assn., The Country Club. Republican. Episcopalian. Avocations: tennis, golf. Office: Thompson Hine LLP 3900 Key Ctr 127 Public Sq Cleveland OH 44114-1291 Office Phone: 216-566-5519. E-mail: tom.mason@thompsonhine.com.

MASON, WILLIAM, opera company director; b. Chgo. m. Diana Davis; 2 children. MusB, Roosevelt U. Asst. to co-artistic dir. Pino Donati, 1962—66; asst. stage mgr. Lyric Opera Chgo., 1968—70; asst. to Felix Popper N.Y.C Opera, 1971; prod. stage mgr. Cin. Opera, 1972; stage mgr., asst. in musical preparation Light Opera of Manhattan, 1972; prod. mgr., asst. dir. Ohio-based Corbett Found., 1973; prod. dir. Lyric Opera Chgo., 1974—78, gen. dir., 1997—; artistic adminstr. San Francisco Opera, 1979—80. Mem. Lyric Children's Chorus, 1954—56. Office: Lyric Opera Chgo 20 N Wacker Dr Chicago IL 60606-2806

MASSENGALE, MARTIN ANDREW, agronomist, educator, university president; b. Monticello, Ky., Oct. 25, 1933; s. Elbert G. and Orpha (Conn) M.; m. Ruth Audrey Klingelhofer, July 11, 1959; children: Alan Ross, Jennifer Lynn. BS, Western Ky. U., 1952; MS, U. Wis., 1954, PhD, 1956; LHD (hon.), Nebr. Wesleyan U., 1987; DS (hon.), Senshu U., Tokyo, 1995. Cert. profl. agronomist, profl. crop scientist. Research asst. agronomy U. Wis., 1952-56; asst. prof., asst. agronomist U. Ariz., 1958-62, assoc. prof., assoc. agronomist, 1962-65, prof., agronomist, 1965-76, head dept., 1966-74, assoc. dean Coll. Agr. assoc. dir. Ariz. Agr. Expt. Sta., 1974-76; vice chancellor for agr. and natural resources U. Nebr., 1976-81; chancellor U. Nebr.-Lincoln, 1981-91, interim pres., 1989-91; pres. U. ebr., 1991-94, pres. emeritus, 1994, found. disting. prof. and dir., 1994—. Chmn. pure seed adv. com. Ariz. Agrl. Expt. Sta.; past chmn. bd., pres. Mid-Am. Internat. Agrl. Consortium; coord. com. environ. quality EPA-Dept. Agrl. Land Grand U.; past chmn. bd. dir. Am. Registry Cert. Profls. in Agronomy, Crops and Soils; bd. dir. Ctr. for Human Nutrition, Lincoln Ins. Group., Woodmen Accident & Life Co., LIG, Inc., Am. First, LLC, All Am. Enterprises, LLC; chair bd. dir. Agronomic Sci. Found., chmn. selection com; dir. devel. Secretariat, Filippo Maseri Florio World Prize Disting. Rsch. in Agr.; exec. com. U. Nebr. Tech. Park, LLC; mem. adv. bd. Nat. Agrl. Rsch., Ext., Edn. and Econs., 1998—, chair secs. nat. adv. bd., exec. com.; nat. adv. bd. Trees Am., 1998—. Chmn. NCAA Pres.'s Commn., 1988-91; distbn. revenue com., standing com. on appointments North Ctrl. Assn. Commn. on Insts. Higher Edn., 1991; trustee Nebr. Hist. Soc. Found.; bd. dir. Nebr. Hist. Soc.; bd. govs. Nebr. Sci. and Math. Initiative; mem. Knight Found. Commn. on Intercollegiate Athletics; bd. dir. Great Plains Funds, IBP, AGR Ednl. Found., 2004—; hon. life trustee Nebr. Coun. on Econ. Edn.; hon. lifetime trustee ebr. Coun. on Econ. Edn.; bd. dir., trustee U. Nebr. Found. With U.S. Army, 1956-58. Named Midlands Man of Yr., 1982, to We. Ky. U. Hall of Disting. Alumni, 1992, DeKalb Crop Sci. Disting. Career award, 1996, Outstanding Educator Am., 1970, Wayne County H.S., Monticello, Ky., Charter Hall of Fame, 2002; recipient faculty recognition award Tucson Trade Bur., 1971, Ak-Sar-Ben Agrl. Achievement award, 1986, Agrl. Builders Nebr. award, 1986, Walter K. Beggs award, 1986, Vol. of Yr. award for disting. svc. Nebr. Coun. on Econ. Edn., IANR Team Initiation award, Agri award Triumph of Agr. Expn., 1999, Exemplary Svc. to Agr. award Nebr. AgRels. Coun., 2000, Friend of LEAD award Nat. LEAD Alumni Assn., 2001, Outstanding Pres. award All-Am. Football Found., 2001, Wagonmaster award Nebraskaland Found., 2006; named to Charter Hall of Fame, USDA, 2004; hon. state farmer degrees Ky., Ariz., Nebr. Future Farmers Am. Assn. Fellow AAAS (sect. chmn.), Crop Sci. Soc. Am. (past dir., pres. 1972-73, past assoc. editor, pres. western soc., Disting. Career award 1996), Am. Soc. Agronomy (past dir., vis. scientist program, past assoc. editor Agronomy Jour., Disting. Svc. award 1984); mem. Am. Grassland Coun., Ariz. Crop Improvement Assn. (bd. dir.), Am. Soc. Plant Physiology, Nat. Assn. Colls. and Tchrs. Agr., Soil and Water Conservation Soc. Am., Ariz. Acad. Sci., ebr. Acad. Sci., Agrl. Coun. Am. (bd. dirs., issues com.), Coun. Agrl. Sci. and Tech. (bd. dir. budget and fin. 1979-82, 94-2005, treas., exec. com. 1997-2005), Nat. Assn. State Colls. and Land Grant Univs. (chmn. com. on info. tech. 1987-94, exec. com. 1990-92, bd. dir. 1992-94), Edn. Engring. Professions (mem. commn.), Coll. Football Assn. (chmn., bd. dir. 1986-88), Am. Assn. State Coll. and Univs. (task force instl. resource allocation), AAFL Enterprises LLC (bd. dir., 2004—), Assn. Am. Univs. Rsch. Librs. (steering com. 1992-94), Nebr. Crop Improvement Assn. (Disting. Svc. award), Grazing Lands Forum (pres.), Nebr. C. of C. and Industry, Nebr. Diplomats Inc. (hon. diplomate), Nebr. Vet. Med. Assn. (hon.), Sigma Xi, Phi Kappa Phi, Gamma Sigma Delta (Merit award), Alpha Zeta, Phi Sigma, Gamma Alpha, Alpha Gamma Rho (bd. dir. ednl. found. 2004—, Bros. of the Century award), Phi Beta Delta, Golden Key, Innocents Soc., AGR Ednl. Found. (bd. dir., 2004—). Office: U Nebr 220 Keim Hall Lincoln NE 68583-0953 Office Phone: 402-472-4101. Business E-Mail: mmassengale1@unl.edu.

MASSEY, DONALD E., automotive executive; CEO Don Massey Cadillac. Office: Don Massey Cadillac Inc 40475 Ann Arbor Rd E Plymouth MI 48170-4576

MASSEY, MICHAEL J., lawyer, retail executive; b. St. Louis, Mo., May 5, 1964; BA with honors, Indiana U., 1985; JD, Wash. U., 1989. Bar: Mo. 1989, Kans. 1997. Atty. The May Dept. Stores Co., 1990—96; sr. counsel Payless ShoeSource Inc., Topeka, 1996—98, v.p. group counsel intellectual property, 1998—2000, v.p. contract manufacturing, 2000, v.p. internat. develop., 2001, sr. v.p., gen. counsel, corp. sec., 2003—. Recipient John W. Foster prize. Mem.: ABA, Am. Soc. of Corp. Counsel, Assn. of Corp. Counsel, Mo. Bar Assn., Kansas Bar Assn. Office: Payless ShoeSource Inc PO Box 1189 3231 SE Sixth St Topeka KS 66601

MASSEY, RAYMOND LEE, lawyer; b. Macon, Ga., Sept. 25, 1948; s. Ford B. and Juanita (Sapp) M.; m. Lynn Ann Thielmeier, Aug. 23, 1967; children: Daniel, Caroline. BA, U. Mo., St. Louis, 1971; JD, U. Louisville, 1974. Bar: Mo. 1974, Ill. 1976, U.S. Dist. Ct. (ea. and we. dists.) Mo. 1974, U.S. Dist. Ct. (so. dist.) Ill. 1976, Tex. 1997. Assoc. Thompson & Mitchell, St. Louis, 1974-79; ptnr. Thompson & Mitchell (now Thompson & Coburn), St. Louis, 1979—. Mem. Maritime Law Assn. of U.S. (bd. dirs., chmn. ocean and river towing). Home: 3 Wild Rose Dr Saint Louis MO 63124-1465 Office: Thompson Coburn US Bank Ste 3400 Saint Louis MO 63101-1643 Home Phone: 314-991-1687; Office Phone: 314-552-6075. E-mail: rmassey@thompsoncoburn.com.

MASSEY, ROBERT JOHN, telecommunications executive; b. Montclair, NJ, July 12, 1945; s. William A. and Elizabeth (Grissing) M.; m. Sue A. Lavallee, July 26, 1968; children: Mary Beth, Michelle, Megan. BA, Holy Cross Coll., Worcester, Mass., 1967; MBA, Syracuse U., 1969. Mktg. rep. IBM, Washington, 1969-70, Boston, 1971-73; mktg. rep. Control Data Corp., Greenwich, Conn., 1974-75, mktg. mgr., N.Y.C., 1975-76; area mgr. CompuServe Inc., Eastern area, 1976-78, v.p. sales, Stamford, Conn., 1979-83, exec. v.p. bus. svcs., Columbus, Ohio, 1984-86, exec. v.p. software products, 1987-90, exec. v.p. network svcs., 1990, pres., until 1997; exec. v.p. bus. devel. Calltech Comm., Columbus, 1997-98; pres. Massey & Assocs., 1997-99; chmn. Calltech Comm. LLC, Columbus, 1999—. Bd. dirs. CompuServe. Coach Dublin (Ohio) Youth Athletics, 1978-85; parents coun. St. Mary's Coll., Notre Dame, Ind., 1988—. Mem. Dublin C. of C., Ohio State Fastbreakers, Holy Cross Alumni Assn., Syracuse U. Bus. Alumni Assn., Country Club of Muirfield Village (golf. com.). Avocations: golf, tennis. Office: Calltech Comm LLC 4335 Equity Dr Columbus OH 43228-3842

MASSIE, MICHAEL EARL, lawyer; b. Stambaugh, Mich., Aug. 12, 1947; s. Glen E. and Bernice L. (Lambert) M.; m. Vicki L. Colmark, June 11, 1977; children: Christopher, Adam. BA, U. Ill., 1969, JD, 1972. Bar: Ill. 1972, U.S. Dist. Ct. (cen. dist.) Ill. 1989, U.S. Ct. Appeals (7th cir.) 1989. Pvt. practice,

Galva, Ill., 1972—. Chair Ill. Com. Agrl. Edn. Fellow Am. Bar Found., Ill. Bar Found.; mem. ABA (chair, coun. mem. gen. practice sect. 1989—), Ill. State Bar Assn. (chmn. gen. practice sect. 1980, chmn. agrl. law com. 1980), Ill. Farm Legal Assistance Found. (chmn. bd. 1985-98), Henry County Bar Assn. (pres. 1977). Republican. Avocations: tennis, handball. Office: 115 NW 3rd Ave Galva IL 61434-1325

MASSIE, ROBERT JOSEPH, publishing company executive; b. NYC, Mar. 19, 1949; BA, Yale U., 1970; MBA, JD, Columbia U., 1974; diploma, U. d'Aix en Provence, France, 1969. Bar: D.C. 1974. Assoc. Covington & Burling, Washington, 1975-79; mgmt. cons. McKinsey & Co., NYC, 1979-82; v.p. Harlequin Enterprises, Toronto, Ont., Can., 1982-90; pres., CEO Gale Rsch., Inc., Detroit, 1990-92; dir. Chem. Abstracts Svc., Columbus, Ohio, 1992—. Chmn. bd. dirs. Harlequin Mondadori, Milan, Italy, 1985-88; bd. dirs. Harlequin Hachette, Paris, Cora Verlag, Hamburg, Fed. Republic Germany, Mills & Boon, Sydney, Australia. Contbr. articles to law jours. Bd. dirs. Mindleaders.com. Harlan Fiske Stone scholar, 1974. Office: Am Chem Soc Chem Abstracts Svcs PO Box 3012 Columbus OH 43210-0012

MAST, BERNADETTE MIHALIC, lawyer; BS, Ohio State U., 1982; JD magna cum laude, Case Western Res. U., 1988. CPA; bar: Ohio 1988; cert. prodn. and inventory mgr., systems profl. 1985. With Jones Day, Cleve., 1988—, ptnr., 2000—. Mem.: Cleve. Bar Assn. (real estate sect.), Ohio State Bar Assn. Office: Jones Day North Point 901 Lakeside Ave Cleveland OH 44114-1190

MASTERS, DAVID ALLEN, lawyer; b. Cape Girardeau, Mo., May 23, 1952; s. Elmo and Mary Louise (Davis) M.; m. Ginger N. Lloyd, May 28, 1977; children: Cecily, Phillip, Spencer, Rachel, Samuel. BA with honors, U. Ill., 1974; JD, U. Mo., 1984. Bar: Mo. 1984, U.S. Dist. Ct. (ea. dist.) Mo. 1985, U.S. Dist. Ct. (we. dist.) Mo. 1986, U.S. Ct. Appeals (8th cir.) 1987. Assoc. Oswald & Cottey, P.C., Kirksville, Mo., 1984-90; pvt. practice Macon, Mo.; prosecuting atty. County of Macon, 1990—. Instr. Peoples Law Sch. Program, Mo. Assn. Trial Attys., Kirksville, 1987-88. Mem. Assn. Trial Lawyers Am., Macon County Bar Assn. (pres.), Mo. Assn. Trial Attys. Avocations: hiking, camping.

MATASAR, ANN B., retired dean, finance educator; b. NYC, June 27, 1940; d. Harry and Tillie (Simon) Bergman; m. Robert Matasar, June 9, 1962; children—Seth Gideon, Toby Rachel AB, Vassar Coll., 1962; MA, Columbia U., 1964, PhD, 1968; M of Mgmt. in Fin., Northwestern U., 1977. Assoc. prof. Mundelein Coll., Chgo., 1965-78; prof., dir. Ctr. for Bus. and Econ. Elmhurst Coll., Elmhurst, Ill., 1978-84; dean Roosevelt U., Chgo., 1984-92; prof. Internat. Bus. and Fin. Walter E. Heller Coll. Bus. Adminstrn. Roosevelt U., 1992—2005, prof. bus. emerita, 2005—. Dir. Corp. Responsibility Group, Chgo., 1978-84; chmn. long range planning Ill. Bar Assn., 1982-83; mem. edn. com. Ill. Commn. on the Status of Women, 1978-81 Author: Corporate PACS and Federal Campaign Financing Laws: Use or Abuse of Power?, 1986; (with others) Research Guide to Women's Studies, 1974, (with others) The Impact of Geographic Deregulation on the American Banking Industry, 2002, Women of Wine: The Rise of Women in the Global Wine Industry, 2006; contbr. articles to profl. jours. Dem. candidate 1st legis. dist. Ill. State Senate, no. suburbs Chgo., 1972; mem. Dem. exec. com. New Trier Twp., Ill., 1972-76; rsch. dir., acad. advisor Congressman Abner Mikva, Ill., 1974-76; bd. dirs. Ctr. Ethics and Corp. Policy, 1985-90. Named Chgo. Woman of Achievement, Mayor of Chgo., 1978. Fellow AAUW (trustee ednl. found. 1992-97, v.p. fin. 1993-97); mem. Am. Polit. Sci. Assn., Midwest Bus. Adminstrn. Assn., Acad. Mgmt., Women's Caucus for Polit. Sci. (pres. 1980-81), John Howard Assn. (bd. dirs. 1986-90), Am. Assembly of Coll. Schs. of Bus. (bd. dirs. 1989-92, chair com. on diversity in mgmt. edn. 1991-92), North Ctrl. Assn. (commr. 1994-97), Beta Gamma Sigma. Democrat. Jewish. Avocations: walking, biking, opera, crosswords. Home Phone: 847-498-5959. E-mail: amatasar@roosevelt.edu.

MATCHETT, ANDREW JAMES, mathematics professor; b. Chgo., Jan. 30, 1950; s. Gerald James and Margaret Ellen (Stump) M.; m. Nancy Valentine Stasack, Aug. 7, 1976; children: Gerald Albert, Philip Joseph, Melanie Jeanne. BS, U. Chgo., 1971; PhD, U. Ill., 1976. Grad. teaching asst. U. Ill., Urbana, 1971-76; asst. prof. Tex. A&M U., College Station, 1976-82, U. Wis., La Crosse, 1982-86, assoc. prof., 1986—; grad. teaching asst. U. Ill., Urbana, 1971-76. Dir. Consortium for Core Math. Curriculum, Wis., 1987-88. Contbr. articles to profl. jours. Chmn. troop 18 com. Boy Scouts Am., La Crosse, 1990, charter rep. troop 18, 1992-94, scoutmaster, 1994-97, mem. com., 1997—. Mem.: AAAS, Math. Assn. Am. (sec.-treas. Wis. sect. 1989—, adminstr. 1999—), Am. Math. Soc. Unitarian Universalist. Achievements include development of a theory of class group homomorphisms. Home: 327 24th St N La Crosse WI 54601-3850 Office: U Wis Dept Math 1725 State St La Crosse WI 54601 Office Phone: 608-785-8382. Business E-Mail: matchett.andr@uwlax.edu.

MATELES, RICHARD ISAAC, biotechnologist; b. NYC, Sept. 11, 1935; s. Simon and Jean (Phillips) M.; m. Roslyn C. Fish, Sept. 2, 1956; children: Naomi, Susan, Sarah. BS, MIT, 1956, MS, 1957, DSc, 1959. USPHS fellow Laboratorium voor Microbiologie, Technische Hogeschool, Delft, The Netherlands, 1959-60; mem. faculty MIT, 1960-70, assoc. prof. biochem. engring., 1965-68; dir. fermentation unit Jerusalem, 1968-77; prof. applied microbiology Hebrew U., Hadassah Med. Sch., Jerusalem, 1968-80; vis. prof. dept. chem. engring. U. Pa., Phila., 1978-79; asst. dir. rsch. Stauffer Chem. Co., Westport, Conn., 1980, dir. rsch., 1980-81, v.p. rsch., 1981-88; sr. v.p. applied scis. IIT Rsch. Inst., Chgo., 1988-90; proprietor Candida Corp., Chgo., 1990—. Editor: Jour. Chem. Tech. and Biotech., 1972—; editor: (N.Am. edit.) Biotech., 2001—; editor: Penicillin: A Paradigm for Biotechnology, 1998, Directory of Toll Fermentation and Cell Culture Facilities, 2005; contbr. articles to profl. jours. Mem. Conn. Acad. Sci. Engring., 1981—; mem. vis. com., dept. applied biol. sci. MIT, 1980-88; mem. exec. com. Coun. on Chem. Rsch., 1981-85. Fellow Am. Inst. Med. and Biol. Engring.; mem. AICE, AAAS, SAR, Am. Chem. Soc., Am. Soc. Microbiology, Inst. Food Technologists, Soc. Chem. Ind. (U.K.) Union League, Sigma Xi. Home: 222 E Chestnut St Apt 10B Chicago IL 60611 Office: Candida Corp Ste 1310 220 S State St Chicago IL 60604 Office Phone: 312-431-1601. Business E-Mail: rmateles@candida.com.

MATHENY, EDWARD TAYLOR, JR., lawyer; b. Chgo., July 15, 1923; s. Edward Taylor and Lina (Pinnell) Matheny; m. Marion Elizabeth Shields, Sept. 10, 1947; children: Nancy Elizabeth, Edward Taylor III; m. Ann Spears, Jan. 14, 1984. BA, U. Mo., 1944; JD, Harvard, 1949. Bar: Mo. 1949. Pvt. practice, Kansas City, 1949-91; ptnr. firm Blackwell, Sanders, Matheny, Weary & Lombardi, 1954-91. Pres. St. Luke's Hosp., Kansas City, 1980-95; bd. dirs. Dunn Industries, Inc. Author: The Presence of Care (History of St. Luke's Hospital, Kansas City), 1997, A Long and Constant Courtship (The History of a Law Firm), 1998, The Rise and Fall of Excellence, 2000, The Pursuit of a Ruptured Duck (When Kansas Citians Went to War), 2001. Pres. Cmty. Svc. Broadcasting of Mid-Am., Inc., 1971—72; chmn. Citizens Assn. Kansas City, 1958; chmn. bd. dir. St. Luke's Found., 1989—95; trustee U. Kansas City, 1980—96, Kansas City Cmty. Found., 1983—94, Eye Found., 1990—2000, H&R Block Found., 1996—, Jacob L. and Ella C. Loose Found., 1996—2005. Mem. Kansas City Bar Assn., Mo. Bar, River Club, Mo. Acad. Squires, Mission Hills Country Club, Phi Beta Kappa, Sigma Chi (Balfour Nat. award 1944) Episcopalian (chancellor emeritus Diocese West Mo.). Home: 4900 Central St Kansas City MO 64112 Office: 4801 Main St Kansas City MO 64121-6777

MATHENY, RUTH ANN, editor; b. Fargo, ND, Jan. 17, 1918; d. Jasper Gordon and Mary Elizabeth (Carey) Wheelock; m. Charles Edward Matheny, Oct. 24, 1960. BE, Mankato State Coll., 1938; MA, U. Minn., 1955; postgrad., Universidad Autonoma de Guadalajara, Mex., 1956, Georgetown U., 1960. Tchr., U.S. and S.Am., 1938-61; assoc. editor Charles E. Merrill Pub. Co., Columbus, Ohio, 1963-66; tchr. Confraternity Christian Doctrine, Washington Court House, Ohio, 1969-70; assoc. editor Jr. Cath. Messenger, Dayton, Ohio, 1966-68; editor Witness Intermediate, Dayton, 1968-70; editor in chief, assoc. pub. Today's Cath. Tchr., Dayton, 1970—2002, editor-in-chief emeritus, 2002—; editor in chief Catechist, Dayton, 1976-89, Ednl. Dealer, Dayton, 1976-80; v.p. Peter Li, Inc., Dayton, 1980—. Editl. collaborator: Dimensions of Personality series, 1969—; co-author: At Ease in the Classroom; author: Why a Catholic School?, Scripture Stories for Today: Why Religious Education?; freelance writer, 1943— Bd. dirs. Friends Ormond Beach Libr. Mem.: 3d Order St. Francis (eucharistic min. 1990—2006), at. Coun. Cath. Women. Home: 26 Reynolds Ave Ormond Beach FL 32174-7043 Office: Peter Li Ednl Group 2621 Dryden Rd Ste 300 Dayton OH 45439 Personal E-mail: chilermat@aol.com.

MATHERN, DEB, state legislator; 2 children., N.D. State Coll. of Sc.; grad. Credit Union mgmt., U. Wis. Mem. N.D. Senate from 45th dist., Bismark, 1999—. Bd. dirs. N. D. Credit Union League, 1999—. Recipient Profl. of the Year, 1997. Mem. Fargo C. of C., NDCUL and affiliates. Office: Dist 45 3228 2nd St N Fargo D 58102-1109 E-mail: dmathern@state.nd.us.

MATHERN, TIM, state senator; b. Edgeley, ND, Apr. 19, 1950; m. Lorene Mathern, Feb. 12, 1971. BA, N.D. State U., 1971; MSW, U. Nebr., Omaha, 1980; MPA, Harvard U., 2000. Staff Cath. Family Svc., Fargo, ND, 1973-99; mem. N.D. Senate, Bismarck, 1986—, asst. majority leader, 1993, senate minority leader, 1995-99, mem. budget com. health care, emergency svcs. com., 2005—, mem. appropriations com., legal audit and fiscal rev. com., electricric competition com., 2005—; parish adminstr. Fargo, 2000—. Mem. Kennedy Sch. Student Govt., Cambridge, Mass., 1999—2000; mem. health care task force Coun. State Govts., 2003—; adv. bd. Med. Sch. U. N.D., Bismark, 2003—. Mem. Fargo-Cass County Econ. Devel. Corp., 1993—99; bd. dirs. Prairieland Home Care, 1993—99, Charism Cmty. Ctr., 1997—; pres., bd. dirs. Kaleidoscope, 2001—02; sch. coun. Martin Luther King Jr., Cambridge, 1999—2000; bd. dirs. Villa Nazareth, 2003—; treas. Clara Barton Neighborhood Assn., 2004—; mem. exec. com. N.D. Dem. Nonpartisan League Party, 1995—99; bd. dirs. Am. Diabetes Assn., 2004—. Named Legislator of the Yr., Red River Valley Mental Health Assn., 1989, 1991, N.D. Children's Caucus, 1993, 1998; recipient N.D. Prairie Peacemaker award, 2000, Pub. Svc. award, U. Nebr. Alumni Assn., 2002; Bush fellow, 1999, Littauer fellow, 2000. Mem.: NASW (Social Worker of the Yr. award 1987, Lifetime Achievement award 1998), Mental Health Assn. Democrat. Roman Catholic. Home: 429 16th Ave S Fargo ND 58103 E-mail: tmathern@state.nd.us.

MATHEWS, DAVID (FORREST DAVID MATHEWS), foundation executive, former secretary of health education and welfare; b. Grove Hill, Ala., Dec. 6, 1935; s. Forrest Lee and Doris (Pearson) M.; m. Mary Chapman, Jan. 24, 1960; children: Lee Ann Mathews Hester, Lucy Mathews Heegaard. AB, U. Ala., 1958; PhD, Columbia U., 1965; LL.D., U. Ala., 1969, Mercer U., 1976; L.H.D., William and Mary Coll., 1976, Med. U. S.C., 1976, Samford U., 1978, Transylvania U., 1978, Stillman Coll., 1980, Miami U., 1982; H.H.D., Birmingham-So. Coll., 1976, Wash. U., St. Louis, 1984; L.H.D., Ctr. Coll., 1985; L.L.D., Ohio Wesleyan U., 1987, Lynchburg Coll., 1987; L.H.D., U. New Eng., 1988, Hofstra U., 1999; L.L.D., Aquinas Coll. Exec. v.p. U. Ala., 1968-69, pres., 1969-80, prof. history, 1977-81; sec. US Dept. Health, Edn. and Welfare, 1975—77; pres., chief exec. officer Charles F. Kettering Found., Dayton, Ohio, 1981—. Dir. Birmingham br. Fed. Res. Bank of Atlanta, 1970-72, chmn., 1973-75; mem. council SRI Internat., 1978-85; chmn. Council Public Policy Edn., 1980— Contbr. articles to profl. jours. Trustee Judson Coll., 1968-75, Am. Univs. Field Staff, 1969-80; bd. dirs. Birmingham Festival of Arts Assn., Inc., 1969-75; mem. Nat. Programming Council for Public TV, 1970-73, So. Regional Edn. Bd., 1969-75, Ala. Council on Humanities, 1973-75; vice chmn. Commn. on Future of South, 1974; mem. So. Growth Policies Bd., 1974-75; mem. nat. adv. council Am. Revolution Bicentennial Adminstrn., 1975; mem. Ala. State Oil and Gas Bd., 1975, 77-79; bd. dirs. Acad. Ednl. Devel., 1975—, Ind. Sector, 1982-88,; chmn. Pres.'s Com. on Mental Retardation, 1975-77; chmn. income security com. aging com. Health Ins. Com. of Domestic Council, 1975-77; bd. govs. nat. ARC, 1975-77; bd. govs., bd. visitors Washington Coll., 1982-86; trustee John F. Kennedy Center for Performing Arts, 1975-77, Woodrow Wilson Internat. Center for Scholars, 1975-77; fed. trustee Fed. City Council, 1975-77; bd. dirs. A Presdl. Classroom for Young Americans, Inc., 1975-76; trustee Tchrs. Coll., Columbia U., 1977—85, Nat. Found. March of Dimes, 1977-83, Coun. om Learning, 1977-84, Miles Coll., 1978—; mem. nat. adv. bd. Nat. Inst. on Mgmt. Lifelong Edn., 1979-84; mem. Ala. 2000, 1980—; spl. adviser Aspen Inst., 1980-84; mem. bd. trustees Gerald R. Ford Found., 1988—, bd. visitors Mershon Ctr. Ohio State U., 1988-91; bd. dirs. Nat. Civic League, 1996—. Served with U.S. Army, 1959-60. Recipient Nicholas Murray Butler medal Columbia U., 1976, Ala. Adminstr. of Year award Am. Assn. Univ. Adminstrs., 1976, Educator of Year award Ala. Conf. Black Mayors, 1977, Brotherhood award NCCJ, 1979 Mem. Newcomen Soc. Am., Phi Beta Kappa, Phi Alpha Theta, Omicron Delta Kappa, Delta Theta Phi. Home: 6050 Mad River Rd Dayton OH 45459-1508 Office: Charles F Kettering Found 200 Commons Rd Dayton OH 45459-2788 Office Phone: 937-434-7300. E-mail: jenkyn@kettering.org.

MATHEWSON, JAMES L., state legislator; b. Warsaw, Mo., Mar. 16, 1938; m. Doris Angel Mathewson, 1964; 3 children. Student, Redding Jr. Coll., Calif. State U. Real estate appraiser, Sedalia, Mo.; mem. Mo. Ho. of Reps., Jefferson City, 1974-80, Mo. Senate, Jefferson City, 1980—, majority floor leader, 1984-88, pres. pro tem, 1989-96. Mem. Sedalia C. of C., Am. Legion, Masons, Elks, Moose. Democrat. Office: Rm 319 State Capitol Jefferson City MO 65101 Address: 2650 S Limit Court Sedalia MO 65301

MATHEWSON, JOHN JACOB, emergency and family practice physician; b. Greenville, Ill., Sept. 20, 1924; s. Henry Adolph and Grace Elizabeth (Kimbro) M.; m. Patricia Lou Hendrix, Aug. 31, 1946; children: John Jeffry, Craig Thomas, Susan Patricia. AB, Greenville Coll., 1948; BS, U. Ill., Chgo., 1950, MD, 1952. Bd. cert. Am. Bd. Emergency Medicine, Am. Bd. Family Practice, added qualifications in geriatrics; cert. wound care mgmt., 2002. Physician Pana (Ill.) Med. Group, 1954-71; emergency physician St. Johns Hosp., Springfield, Ill., 1971-74; assoc. prof. emergency medicine Tex. Tech. U. Sch. Medicine, Lubbock, 1974-78; dir., chair emergency dept. Lakeland (Fla.) Regional Med. Ctr., 1978-82; physician Flatonia (Tex.) Med. Clinic, 1982-84; emergency physician Watson Clinic, Lakeland, 1984-95; emergency and family physician Mult Hosp. and Fayette-Lavaca Family Med. Ctr., Lakeland and Shiner, Tex., 1995—. Bd. med. advisors Spectrum Emergency Med. Care, St. Louis, 1979-82; med. advisor Polk County Emergency Med. Svc., Lakeland, 1979—; tchr., organizer 1st course in emergency medicine Tex. Tech. U. Sch. Medicine, 1976; clin. asst. prof. U. So. Fla., Tampa, 1985—. Contbr. articles to med. jours. Mem. sch. bd., Pana, 1965. Col. U.S. Army, 1943-84. Mem. Polk County Med. Soc. (pres. 1993, del. 1992-95, trustee 1993-95), Fla. Coll. Emergency Physicians (bd. dirs. 1985-91), Christian County Med. Soc. (past pres. 1961-62).

MATHEWSON, MARK STUART, lawyer, editor; b. Pana, Ill., Mar. 6, 1955; s. Raymond Glenn and Frances (King) M.; m. Barbara Jean Siegert, Oct. 30, 1980; children: Margie, Molly. BA, U. Wis., Madison, 1978; JD, U. Ill., 1984; MA, U. Iowa, 1985. Bar: Ill. 1985. Reporter Ill. Times, Springfield, 1985; asst. prof. Culver Stockton Coll., Canton, Mo., 1985—86; pvt. practice Pana, Ill., 1987—88; mng. editor Ill. Bar Jour., Ill. State Bar Assn., Springfield, 1998—2000, dir. pub., 2000—. Office: Ill State Bar Assn Ill Bar Journal Ill Bar Ctr Springfield IL 62701 Home: 401 E Hargrave St Athens IL 62613-9787

MATHILE, CLAYTON LEE, pet food company executive; b. Portage, Ohio, Jan. 11, 1941; s. Wilbert and Helen (Good) Mathile; m. Mary Ann Maas, July 7, 1962; children: Cathy, Tim, Mike, Tina, Jennie. BA, Ohio No. U., 1962; postgraduate studies, Bowling Green State U., 1964; DBA (hon.), Ohio No. U., 1991. Acct. GM, apoleon, Ohio, 1962-63, Campbell Soup Co., Napoleon, 1963-65, buyer, 1965-67, purchasing agt., 1967-70; gen. mgr. The Iams Co., Dayton, Ohio, 1970-75, v.p., 1975-80, chief exec. officer, 1980-90, chmn., 1990-99, also dir.; ret., 1999. Mem. Pet Food Inst.; bd. dirs. Midwest Grp., Cin., Bush Bros. Co., Knoxville, Tenn., The Iams Co., 1999—. Author: A Bus. Owner's Perspective on Outside Bds. Trustee Chaminade-Julienne HS, Dayton, 1987—, U. Dayton; mem. adv. bd. coll. bus. Ohio No. U., Ada, 1987—, also trustee. Named Best of Best Ctr. for Values Rsch., Houston, 1987; named one of 400 Richest Ams. Forbes mag., 2006. Mem. Am. Mgmt. Assn., Am. Agt. Assn. Roman Catholic. Avocations: travel, swimming, golf. Office: The Iams Co PO Box 13615 Dayton OH 45413-0615

MATHIS, DAVID B., insurance company executive; b. Atlanta; BA, Lake Forest Coll., 1960. Leadership roles Kemper Corp., Long Grove, Ill., 1960—92, chmn., 1992—96, also bd. dirs.; chmn., pres., CEO, Kemper Ins. Cos., Long Grove, 1996—97. Office: Kemper Ins Cos 1 Kemper Dr Long Grove IL 60049-0001 E-mail: DMathis@Kemperinsurance.com.

MATHIS, GREG, judge, radio personality; Mem. staff Councilman Clyde Cleveland, 1983; civil rights activitist Operation P.U.S.H.; mgr. Detroit Neighborhood City Halls Mayor Coleman A. Young, 1986—93, campaign coord., 1988; judge 36th dist. Mich. Superior Ct., Detroit; host Judgement Call WCIU-TV, Chgo., 1995—. Performer: (musical stage play) Been There Done That, 2000. Mem.: So. Christian Leadership Conf. (nat. bd. dirs.), NAACP (life). Office: 36th Dist Ct 421 Madison Ave Detroit MI 48226

MATHISEN-REID, RHODA SHARON, international communications consultant; b. Portland, Oreg., June 25, 1942; d. Daniel and Mildred Elizabeth Annette (Peterson) Hager; m. James Albert Mathisen, July 17, 1964 (div. 1977); m. James Albert Mathisen, July 17, 164 (div. 1977); m. James A. Reid Sr., Jan. 1, 1991. BA in Edn., Music, Bible Coll., Mich., 1964. Cmty. rels. officer Gary-Wheaton Bank, Wheaton, Ill., 1971-75; br. mgr. Stiver Temporary Personnel, Chgo., 1975-79; v.p. sales Exec. Technique, Chgo., 1980-83; prin. Mathisen Assocs., Clarendon Hill., Ill., 1983—. Presenter seminars; featured speaker Women in Mgmt. Oak Brook Chpt., 1988.; cons. Haggai Inst., Atlanta; adv. mem. Nat. Bd. Success Group, 1986. Newsletter editor/publisher: 90th Divsn. Assn. (WWII Vets) 2001—. Mem. Downers Grove Twp. Precinct # 87 Rep. Com., 1998—; pres. chancel choir Christ Ch. Oak Brook, 1985—87; bd. dirs. Career Devel. Inst., Oak Brook, 1992—99, chair operational fin. com., 1997—98; bd. dirs. Crossroads Ministry Internat., 2000—; chmn. 1st Profl. Women's Seminar, 1995; judge Mrs. Ill., USI Pageant, 1994; exec. sec., treas. 90th Divsn. Assn., 2001—. Recipient Denby Steel award, 90th Divsn. Assn., 2001. Mem. Bus. and Profl. Women (charter mem., Woodfield chpt.), Execs. Club Oak Brook, Assn. Commerce and Industry (named Ambassdor of Month N.W. suuburban chpt. 1979), Oak Brook Assn. Commerce and Industry (membership com.), Women Entrepreneurs of DuPage County (membership chmn., featured speaker Ja 1988), Art. Inst., Willowbrook/Burr Ridge C. of C., 90th Divsn. Assn. (asst. sec., treas., 2001 Denby Steel award, editor newsletter), US Army WWII Vets. Orgn. (newsletter editor 2001-). Office: Mathisen Assocs 17 Lake Shore Dr Willowbrook IL 60527-2221

MATHISON, IAN WILLIAM, chemistry professor, dean, consultant; b. Liverpool, Eng., Apr. 17, 1938; came to U.S., 1963; s. William and Grace (Almond) M.; m. Mary Ann Gordon, July 20, 1968; children: Mark W., Lisa A. B. Pharm., U. London, 1960, PhD, 1963, D. Sci., 1976. Lic. pharmacist, Gt. Britain. Research assoc. U. Tenn. Ctr. for Health Scis., Memphis, 1963-65, asst. prof., 1965-68, assoc. prof., 1968-72, prof., 1972-76; medicinal chemistry prof. Ferris State U., Big Rapids, Mich., 1977—, dean, prof., 1977—. External examiner U. Sci., Malaysia, 1978-79; mem. Mich. dept. Mental Health Pharmacy Facilities Rev. Panel, Lansing, 1978-90, Quality Assurance Commn., 1979-90; cons. WHO, 1999; mem. adv. com. McKesson Medication Mgmt., 2002—; deans adv. com. Rite Aid, 2000—; cons. in field. Mem. editorial bd.: Jour. Pharm. Sci., 1981-86; contbr. articles to profl. jours.; sr. inventor, patentee in field. Marion Labs. awardee, 1965-74; NSF grantee, 1968-72; Beecham Co. grantee, 1974-79 Fellow Royal Inst. Chemistry, Royal Soc. Chemistry; mem. Am. Pharm. Soc., Am. Chem. Soc., Am. Assn. Coll. Pharmacy (bd. dirs. 1988-90), Nat. Assn. Retail Druggists (edn. adv. com. 1989-94), Royal Pharm. Soc. Gt. Britain, Nat. Assn. Chain Drug Stores (ednl. adv. com. 1993-2002). Home: 820 Osborn Cir Big Rapids MI 49307-2536 Office: Ferris State U 220 Ferris Dr Big Rapids MI 49307-2295

MATHOG, ROBERT HENRY, otolaryngologist, educator; b. New Haven, Apr. 13, 1939; s. William and Tiby (Gans) M.; m. Deena Jane Rabinowitz, June 14, 1964; children: Tiby, Heather, Lauren, Jason. AB, Dartmouth Coll., 1960; MD, NYU, 1964. Diplomate Am. Bd. Facial Plastic and Reconstructive Surgery. Intern Duke Hosp., Durham, C, 1964-65, resident surgery, 1965-66, resident otolaryngology, 1966-69; practice medicine, specializing in otolaryngology Mpls., 1971-77, Detroit, 1977—; chief of otolaryngology Hennepin County Med. Center, Mpls., 1972-77; asst. prof. U. Minn., 1971-74, asso. prof., 1974-77; prof., chmn. dept. otolaryngology Wayne State U. Sch. Medicine, 1977—. Chief otolaryngology Hennepin County Hosp., Mpls., 1972-77, Harper-Grace Hosps., Detroit, 1977—, Detroit Receiving Hosp., 1977-92; cons. staff VA Hosp., Allen Park, Minn., 1977—, Children's Hosp., Detroit, 1977—, Hutzel Hosp., Detroit, 1966, St. Joseph Mercy Hosp., Oakland, Mich., 2001; mem. adv. coun. Nat. Inst. Deaf and Other Communicable Disorders NIH, 1992-96; chief otolaryngology, head and neck surgery June Hosp., 1994-95. Author: Otolaryngology Clinics of North America, 1976, Textbook of Maxillofacial Trauma, 1983; editor in chief Videomed. Edn. Systems, 1972-75; editor: Atlas of Craniofacial Trauma, 1992; contbr. articles to med. jours. Bd. dirs. Bexer County Hearing Soc., 1969-71; adv. coun. WIDCB, 1993; chmn. Lions Hearing Ctr. S.E. Mich. Maj. USAF, 1969-71. Recipient Valentine Mott medal for proficiency in anatomy, 1961, Recognition award Wayne State Bd. Govs. Faculty, 1993; Deafness Rsch. Found. grantee, 1979-81, NIH grantee, 1986, 92, 96, Lawrence M. Weiner Alumni award Wayne State U. Sch. Med., 1999. Fellow ACS, Am. Acad. Otolaryngology, Head and Neck Surgery (Cert. award 1976, Cert. of Appreciation 1978), Am. Soc. Head and Neck Surgery, Triological Soc. (v.p. 1995-96, mtg. guest of honor 2002, Vice Presdl. Citation award 2004), Am. Otol. Soc., Am. Acad. Facial Plastic and Reconstructive Surgery (v.p. 1980), Am. Neurotology Soc.; mem. AMA, Am. Laryngol. Soc. (coun. 1994—), Am. Laryngol. Assn., Mich. Med. Soc., Am. Head and eck Soc., Soc. Univ. Otolaryngologists (pres. 1995), Assn. Acad. Depts. Otolaryngology, Assn. Rsch. Otolaryngology (pres. 1981). Home: 27115 Wellington Rd Franklin MI 48025-1329 Office: 43494 Woodward Ste 210 Bloomfield Hills MI 48312 Also: Wayne State U Sch Med 540 E Canfield St Detroit MI 48201-1928

MATIA, PAUL RAMON, lawyer; s. Leo Clemens and Irene Elizabeth (Linkert) M.; m. Nancy Arch Van Meter, Jan. 2, 1993. BA, Case Western Res. U., 1959; JD, Harvard U., 1962. Bar: Ohio 1962, US Dist. Ct. (no. dist.) Ohio 1969. Law clk. Common Pleas Ct. of Cuyahoga County, Cleve., 1963-66, judge, 1985-91; asst. atty. gen. State of Ohio, Cleve., 1966-69, adminstrv. ast. to atty. gen. Columbus, 1969-70; senator Ohio State Senate, Columbus, 1971-75, 79-83; ptnr. Hadley, Matia, Mills & MacLean Co., L.P.A., Cleve., 1975-84, Porter Wright Morris & Arthur LLP, Cleve., 2005—; judge U.S. Dist. Ct. (no. dist.) Ohio, 1991-99, chief dist. judge, 1999—2004, sr. judge, 2005; mem. 6th Cir. Jud. Coun., 1999—2004. Candidate Lt. Gov. Rep. Primary, 1982, Ohio Supreme Ct., 1988. Named Outstanding Legislator, Ohio Assn. for Retarded Citizens, 1974, Watchdog of Ohio Treasury, United Conservatives of Ohio, 1979; recipient Heritage award Polonia Found., 1988. Mem. Fed. Bar Assn., Ohio State Bar Assn., Cleve. Bar Assn., Cuyahoga County Bar Assn., Sixth Cir. (life), Judge John M. Manos Inn of Ct., Club at Key Ctr., Vineyards Country Club, Naples, Fla. Republican. Avocations: skiing, gardening, travel. Office: Porter Wright Morris & Arthur LLP 925 Euclid Ave Ste 1700 Cleveland OH 44115-1483 Office Phone: 216-443-2548. Business E-Mail: pmatia@porterwright.com.

MATIS, JIMMY, radio personality; b. Ind. married; 5 children. Radio host WFBQ-FM 94.7, Indpls. Owner Longacre Bar & Grill, Indpls. Writer (albums) Bob & Tom: Fun House, 1997, Bob & Tom: Gimme an F, 1998, Planet Bob & Tom, 2000, 2000, Bob & Tom: Radiogram, 2001, Bob & Tom Gone Wild, 2002, Bob & Tom: Odd Balls, 2004, Bob & Tom: Sideshow, 2004, Bob & Tom: Camel Toe, 2004, writer & performer Bob & Tom: You Guys Rock!, 2001; performer: (albums) Bob & Tom: Indiana Rocks, 2000. Recipient Marconi Radio award for Medium Market Personality of Yr., Nat. Assn. Broadcasters, 2000. Office: WFBQ 6161 Fall Creek Rd Indianapolis IN 46220

MATIS, NINA B., lawyer; b. NYC, June 23, 1947; AB cum laude, Smith Coll., 1969; JD, NYU, 1972. Bar: Ill. 1973. Ptnr. Katten Muchin Zavis Rosenman, Chgo. Adj. prof. law Northwestern U., 1984-87. Named one of 500 Leading Lawyer in Am., Lawdragon, 100 Most Influential Lawyers, Nat. Law Jour., 2006, The 50 Most Influential Women Lawyers in Am., 2007. Mem. Am. Bar Assn., Am. Coll. Real Estate Lawyers, Chicago Fin. Exchange, Chicago Real Estate Exec. Women, Chicago Real Estate Women, Econ. Club of Chicago, Lambda Alpha Internat. (Ely Chpt.), Internat. Coun. of Shopping Centers, Lakefront SRO, Pension Real Estate Assn., Real Estate Fin. Forum, The Chicago Network, Urban Land Inst. Office: Katten Muchin Zavis Rosenman 525 W Monroe St Ste 1600 Chicago IL 60661-3693 Office Fax: 312-577-8686. E-mail: nina.matis@kmzr.com.

MATKOWSKY, BERNARD JUDAH, mathematician, educator; b. NYC, Aug. 19, 1939; s. Morris N. and Ethel H. M.; m. Florence Knobel, Apr. 11, 1965; children: David, Daniel, Devorah. BS, CCNY, 1960; M.E.E., NYU, 1961, MS, 1963, PhD, 1966. Fellow Courant Inst. Math. Scis., NYU, 1961-66; mem. faculty dept. math. Rensselaer Poly. Inst., 1966-77; John Evans prof. applied math., mech. engring. & math. Northwestern U., Evanston, Ill., 1977—, chmn. engring. sci. and applied math. dept., 1993-99. Vis. prof. Tel Aviv U., 1972-73; vis. scientist Weizmann Inst. Sci., Israel, summer 1976, summer 1980, Tel Aviv U., summer 1980; cons. Argonne Nat. Lab., Sandia Labs., Lawrence Livermore Nat. Lab., Exxon Research and Engring. Co. Editor Wave Motion—An Internat. Jour., 1979-99, Applied Math. Letters, 1987—, SIAM Jour. Applied Math., 1976-95, European Jour. Applied Math., 1990-96, Random and Computational Dynamics, 1991-97, Internat. Jour. SHS, 1992—, Jour. Materials Synthesis and

Processing, 1992-2002, SIAM Mongraphs Math. Modeling and Computation, 2005—, Mathematical Modeling of atural Phenomena, 2007—; mem. editl. adv. bd. Springer Verlag Applied Math. Scis. Series; contbr. chpts. to books, articles to profl. jours. Fulbright grantee, 1972-73; Guggenheim fellow, 1982-83 Fellow: AAAS, Am. Phys. Soc., Am. Acad. Mechs.; mem.: Soc. Natural Philosophy, Com. Concerned Scientists, Conf. Bd. Math. Scis. (coun., com. human rights math. scientists), Am. Assn. Combustion Synthesis, Combustion Inst., Am. Math. Soc., Soc. Indsl. and Applied Math., Eta Kappa Nu, Sigma Xi. Home: 3704 Davis St Skokie IL 60076-1745 Office: Northwestern U Technological Institute Evanston IL 60208-0001 Office Phone: 847-491-5396. Business E-Mail: b-matkowsky@northwestern.edu.

MATLAK, JOHN, radio personality; Degree magna cum laude, U. Dayton, 1975. Radio host, sports dir. Grand Rapids First News Wood 1300, Grand Rapids, Mich. Recipient numerous awards, Mich. Assn. Broadcasters, AP. Office: Newsradio Wood 1300 77 Monroe Center Ste 100 Grand Rapids MI 49503

MATSAKIS, ELIAS N., lawyer; b. 1951; BA with honors, U. Chgo., 1971; JD cum laude, Harvard Law Sch., 1974. Bar: Ill. 1974. Ptnr. Holland & Knight LLP, Chgo., mem. dir. com. Staff mem. Harvard Civil Rights and Civil Liberties Law Review, 1972, lead author Navigating the Changing Tides of Managed Care and Health Reform, AMA. Mem. sch. bd. Dist. 225, Northfield Twp. Mem.: Comml. Law League Am., ABA, Hellenic Bar Assn. (Ill.), Ill. State Bar Assn., Chgo. Bar Assn. (chmn. pro se ct. com., young lawyers sect. 1977, David C. Hilliard award). Office: Holland & Knight LLP 131 S Dearborn St 30th Fl Chicago IL 60603 Office Phone: 312-715-5731. Business E-Mail: elias.matsakis@hklaw.com.

MATSLER, FRANKLIN GILES, retired education educator; b. Glendive, Mont., Dec. 27, 1922; s. Edmund Russell and Florence Edna (Giles) M.; m. Lois Josephine Hoyt, June 12, 1949; children— Linda, Jeanne, David, Winfield. BS, Mont. State U., Bozeman, 1948; MA, U. Mont., Missoula, 1952; PhD, U. Calif., Berkeley, 1959. Tchr. Missoula County (Mont.) High Sch., 1949-51, Tracy (Calif.) Sr. Elem. Schs., 1952-53, San Benito County (Calif.) High Sch. and Jr. Coll., 1953-55; grad. asst. U. Calif. at Berkeley, 1955-58; asst. prof. Humboldt State Coll., Arcata, Calif., 1958-62, assoc. prof., 1962-63, asst. exec. dean, 1958-63; chief specialist higher edn. Calif. Coordinating Council for Higher Edn., Sacramento, 1963-68; exec. dir. Ill. Bd. Regents, Springfield, 1968-84; prof. higher edn. Ill. State U., Normal, 1968-96, Regency prof. higher edn., 1984-96; ret., 1996. Chancellor Ill. Bd. Regents, 1995-96. Bd. dirs. Ill. Edn. Consortium, 1972-76; bd. dirs. Central Ill. Health Planning Agy., 1970-76, Springfield Symphony Orch. Assn.; pres. Bloomington/Normal Symphony Soc., 1988-90. Served to 1st lt. AUS, 1943-46. Mem. Nat. Assn. Sys. Heads (exec. v.p. 1985-92), Am. Assn. State Colls. and Univs. Assn. for Instl. Rsch., Phi Delta Kappa, Lambda Chi Alpha.

MATSON, TIMOTHY C., lawyer; b. Mpls., May 10, 1966; BA cum laude, St. Olaf Coll., 1988; JD, U. Minn., 1991. Bar: Minn. 1992, US Dist. Ct. Minn. 1993. Law clk. to Hon. Thomas H. Carey Minn. Dist. Ct. (4th Jud. Dist.), 1992—93; assoc. Lommen, Abdo, Cole, King & Stageberg, P.A., Mpls. Instr. music bus. prog. McNally Smith Coll. Music, 1996—98. Named a Rising Star, Minn. Super Lawyers mag., 2006. Mem.: Minn. State Bar Assn. (chair arts & entertainment law sect. 2003—04), Hennepin County Bar Assn. Office: Lomen Abdo Cole King & Stageberg PA 2000 IDS Ctr 80 S 8th St Minneapolis MN 55402 Office Phone: 612-336-9331. E-mail: tim@lommen.com.

MATTA, THAD MICHAEL, men's college basketball coach; b. Hoopeston, Ill., July 11, 1967; s. Jim Matta; m. Barbara Matta; children: Ali, Emily. Student, So. Ill. U.; BS, Butler U., 1990. Grad. asst. coach Ind. State U., 1990—91; academic coord., adminstrv. asst. Butler U., Indpls., 1991—94, asst. coach, 1997—2000, head coach, 2000—01; asst. coach Miami U., Ohio, 1994—95, 1996—97, Western Carolina U., 1995—96; head coach Xavier U., Cin., 2001—04, Ohio State U., Columbus, 2004—. Named Nat. Rookie Coach of Yr., CBS SportsLine.com and Coll. Insider.com, 2001, Coach of Yr., Midwestern Collegiate Conf., 2001, Atlantic 10 Conf., 2002, Columbus Dispatch, 2004, Big Ten Conf. and US Basketball Writers Assn. Dist. V, 2006. Office: Men's Basketball Ohio State U Jerome Schottenstein Ctr 555 Borror Dr Columbus OH 43210 Office Phone: 614-292-0505. E-mail: matta@osu.edu.

MATTHEI, EDWARD HODGE, architect; b. Chgo., Dec. 21, 1927; s. Henry Reinhard and Myra Beth (Hodge) M.; m. Mary Nina Hoffmann, June 30, 1951; children: Edward Hodge, Suzanne Marie, Christie Ann, Laura Jean, John William. BS in Archtl. Engring, U. Ill., 1951. Registered arch. 17 states, including Ariz., Fla., Ill., Mich., N.Y., Wis., Calif.; cert. NCARB. Dir. health facilities planning and constrn. Child & Smith (architects and engrs.), Chgo., 1951-60; sr. v.p. health facilities planning Perkins & Will, Chgo., 1960-74; ptnr. firm Matthei & Colin Assoc., Chgo., 1974-96; planning and archtl. design cons. Chgo., 1996—. Com. chmn. Am. Nat. Standards Inst., 1983-89; lectr. 1st Internat. Conf. on Rehab. of Handicapped, Beijing, 1986, Design USA, Novosibirsk and Moscow, USSR, 1990. Editor: Inland Architect, 1956-58; prin. works health facilities projects, med. ctr. master plans including Akron (Ohio) Gen. Hosp., Heritage Hosp., Taylor, Mich., Rose Meml., Denver, Silver Cross Hosp., Joliet, Ill., Shands Tchg. Hosp. & Med. Sch., U. Fla., Gainesville, Mercy Hosp., Davenport, Iowa, Westlake Cmty. Hosp., Chgo., Highland Park (Ill.) Hosp., Ctrl. DuPage Hosp., Winfield, Ill., Nebr. Meth. Hosp., Omaha, Rockford (Ill.) Meml. Hosp., U. Ala. Med. Ctr., Birmingham, U. Calif. Sch. Medicine, Irvine, Kent Hall, U. Chgo., Holy Cross Hosp., Md., West Mich. Cancer Ctr. Mem. profl. adv. com. Nat. Easter Seal Soc., 1965-1970, chair, 1988-89, second v.p., 1978; mem. bd. dirs. St. Scholastica H.S., Chgo., 1973-83, 86-96; mem. Welfare Coun. Greater Met. Chgo., 1965-72. With AUS, 1946-47. Recipient Leon Chatelain award for barrier-free environ. Nat. Easter Seals Soc., 1979, Disting. Svc. award, 1990, 99, Meritorious Svc. award Am. Nat. Standards Inst., 1987, Speedy award Paralyzed Vets. Am., 1993. Fellow: AIA (chmn. com. on arch. for health 1963—74, chmn. AMA joint com. on environ. health 1967—70, chmn. bldg. affairs com. Chgo. chpt. 1959—66, Disting. Svc. award Chgo. chpt. 1988); mem.: Builders Assn. Chgo., Nat. Center Barrier Free Environment (dir.), Internat. Hosp. Fedn., Am. Assn. Hosp. Planning, Am. Hosp. Assn., Chgo. Assn. Commerce and Industry. Home: 1437 W Glenlake Ave Chicago IL 60660-1801 Office: Matthei & Colin Assocs 332 S Michigan Ave Chicago IL 60604-4434

MATTHEWS, CHARLES DAVID, real estate appraiser, consultant; b. Anniston, Ala., June 15, 1946; s. James Boyd and Emma Grace (McCullough) M.; m. Stephanie Ann Woods, Dec. 28, 1968; children: Alison Paige, Dylan McCullough. BS, U. Tenn., 1968. County appraiser Assessor's Office, Freeport, Ill., 1969-71; staff appraiser Ill. Dept. Highways, Springfield, 1971-72; appraiser, dir. counseling Norman Benedict Assocs., Hamden, Conn., 1972-76; mgr. appraisal dept. Citizens Realty & Ins., Evansville, Ind., 1976-80; owner, mgr. David Matthews Assocs., Evansville, 1980—. Adj. real estate faculty U. Conn., 1974-76, U. Evansville, 1978-87, Appraisal Inst., 1989—; citizen amb. to Russia on Urban Valuation Team, 1993; AI edn. trust lead del. to Shanghi, China, 2004. Tympanist Chattanooga Symphony; drummer Temple Airs Big Band; author: (with others) Downtown Master Plan of Evansville, Indiana, 1984, 2002, The Appraisal of Real Estate, 10th edit. Mem. Leadership Evansville, 1982; bd. dirs. Raintree Girl Scouts. U.S.A., 2002—; bd. mem. WNIN (PBS-TV), 2003—; trustee Meth. Temple, 1994—2004; arbitrator Am. Arbitration Assn., 1986—91. Mem.: Counselors of Real Estate, Evansville Bd. Realtors (pres. 1986, chmn. computer com. 1987—, dir. 2007, Realtor of Yr. award 1987), Soc. Real Estate Appraisers (local pres. 1981), Appraisal Inst. (chmn. gen. appraiser bd. 1991—92, exec. com. 1991—92, chmn. pub. rels. 1993, exec. com. 1995—96, chmn. comm. 1995—96, chair edn. trust 2003—, Percy Wagner award 1992, Y.T. Lum award 1997), Am. Inst. Real Estate Appraisers (state pres. 1987, governing councillor 1989—90, vice chmn. nat. admissions 1990), Mensa, Evansville C. of C. (chair govt. affairs 1998—99, chair transp. 2002—04), Rotary. Avocations: videography, drums, travel, golf. Home: 430 S Boeke Rd Evansville IN 47714-1616 Office: 420 Main St Ste 1300 Evansville IN 47708-1719 Office Phone: 812-428-6000. E-mail: dma@evansville.net.

MATTHEWS, JACK (JOHN HAROLD MATTHEWS), language educator, writer; b. Columbus, Ohio, July 22, 1925; s. John Harold and Lulu Emma (Grover) M.; m. Barbara Jane Reese, Sept. 16, 1947; children: Cynthia Ann Matthews Warnock, Barbara Ellen Matthews Saunders, John Harold. BA, Ohio State U., 1949, MA, 1954. Clk. U.S. Post Office, Columbus, 1950-59; prof. English Urbana Coll., Ohio, 1959-64, Ohio U., Athens, 1964-77, disting. prof., 1977—2003, disting. prof. emeritus, 2003—. Author: Bitter Knowledge, 1964 (Ohioana fiction award 1964), Hanger Stout, Awake!, 1967, The Charisma Campaigns, 1972, Collecting Rare Bodies For Pleasure and Profit, 1977, Sassafras, 1983, Crazy Women, 1985, Booking in the Heartland, 1986 (Ohioana Non-fiction award 1986), Ghostly Populations, 1986, Memoirs of a Bookman, 1989, Dirty Tricks, 1990, On The Shore of That Beautiful Shore (play), 1991, An Interview with the Sphinx (play), 1992, Storyhood As We Know It and Other Tales (stories), 1993, Booking Pleasures, 1996, (essays) Reading Matter, 2000, Schopenhauerova Vule, 2002, others. Served with USCG, 1943-45. Recipient numerous ind. artist awards Ohio Art Council, Major Artist award, 1989-90, Ohioana Career award, 2005; Guggenheim fellow, 1974-75 Mem. Phi Beta Kappa Home: 4314 Fisher Rd Athens OH 45701-9333 Office: Ohio U Dept English Athens OH 45701 Business E-Mail: matthej1@ohio.edu.

MATTHEWS, JAMES SHADLEY, lawyer; b. Omaha, Nov. 24, 1951; s. Donald E. and Lois Jean (Shadley) M.; m. Mary Kvaal, May 3, 1991; 1 child, Katherine. BA cum laude, St. Olaf Coll., 1973; JD, U. Ill., 1976; MBA, U. Denver, 1977. Bar: Minn. 1976, U.S. Dist. Ct. Minn. 1978. With Northwestern Nat. Life Ins. Co., Mpls., 1978-89, v.p., asst. gen. counsel, 1985-89; ptnr. Lindquist & Venum, Mpls., 1990—. Sr. v.p., gen. counsel Washington Square Capital, Inc., 1989; sec. NWNL Health etwork, Inc., St. Paul, 1987-89; pub. dir. Minn. Health Reins. Assn., 1992-94; bd. dirs. Northstar Life Ins. Co., 2001-03; spkr. in field. Mem. ABA, Am. Health Lawyers Assn., Minn. Bar Assn. (chmn. health law sect. 1986-87). Office: Lindquist & Vennum IDS Ctr 80 S 8th St Ste 4200 Minneapolis MN 55402-2274 Office Phone: 612-371-3211. Business E-Mail: jmatthews@lindquist.com.

MATTHEWS, L. WHITE, III, railroad executive; b. Ashland, Ky., Oct. 5, 1945; s. L. White and Virginia Carolyn (Chandler) M.; m. Mary Jane Hanser, Dec. 30, 1972; children: Courtney Chandler, Brian Whittlesey. BS in Econs, Hampden-Sydney Coll., 1967; MBA in Fin. and Gen. Mgmt, U. Va., 1970. Corp. fin. Chem. Bank, NYC, 1970-72, asst. sec., 1972-74, asst. v.p., 1974-75, v.p., 1976-77; treas. Mo. Pacific Corp., St. Louis, 1977-82; v.p. fin. Mo. Pacific R.R. Co. subs. Mo. Pacific Corp., St. Louis, 1979-82; v.p., treas. Union Pacific Corp. and Union Pacific R.R. Co., NYC, 1982-87; sr. v.p. fin. Union Pacific Corp., Bethlehem, Pa., 1987-92, exec. v.p. fin., 1992-98; exec. v.p., CFO Ecolab Inc., 1999—. Bd. dirs. Union Pacific Corp., 1995, 98, Ecolab Inc., Lexent Inc., ortrax Inc., 2000—.

MATTHEWS, ROWENA GREEN, biological chemistry educator; b. Cambridge, Eng., Aug. 20, 1938; (father Am. citizen); d. David E. and Doris (Cribb) Green; m. Larry Stanford Matthews, June 18, 1960; children: Brian Stanford, Keith David. BA, Radcliffe Coll., 1960; PhD, U. Mich., 1969. Instr. U. S.C., Columbia, 1964-65; postdoctoral fellow U. Mich., Ann Arbor, 1970-75, asst. prof., 1975-81, assoc. prof. biol. chemistry, 1981-86, prof., 1986—, assoc. chmn., 1988-92, G. Robert Greenberg disting. univ. prof., 1995—, chair biophysics rsch. divsn., 1996—2001. Mem. phys. biochemistry study sect. NIH, 1982-86; mem. adv. coun. at. Inst. Gen. Med. Scis., NIH, 1991-94; adv. bd. NATO, 1994-96; mem. Commn. on Advancement of Women and Minorities in Sci., Engring. and Tech. Devel., 1999; mem. faculty Life Scis. Inst., 2002—. Mem. editl. adv. bd. Biochem. Jour., 1984-92, Arch. Biochemistry, Biophysics, 1992-97, Biochemistry, 1993—, Jour. Bacteriology, 1995-2003; contbr. articles to profl. jours. Recipient Merit award Nat. Inst. Gen. Med. Scis., 1991-2001; NIH grantee, 1978—, NSF grantee, 1992-2003. Fellow AAAS, NAS, Am. Acad. Arts & Scis, Inst. Medicine; mem. Am. Soc. Biochem. and Molecular Biology (program chair 1995, chair human resources 1996-98, William C. Rose award 2000), Am. Chem. Soc. (program chair biochemistry divsn. 1985, sec. biochemistry divsn. 1990-92, chair 1994-96, Repligen award 2001), Inst. Medicine (2004), Phi Beta Kappa, Sigma Xi. Office: Life Sci Inst U Mich 210 Washtenaw Ave Ann Arbor MI 48109-2216 Home: 1609 S University Ann Arbor MI 48104 Business E-Mail: rmatthew@umich.edu.

MATTHEWS, ROY S., management consultant; b. 1945; BS, Lewis U., 1967; MBA, No. Ill. U., 1971. With Regis Paper Co., Chgo., 1967-68, Continental Ill. Nat. Bank, Chgo., 1968-69; instr. acctg. Marquette U., Milw., 1971-72; asst. dean Lewis U. Coll. Bus., Romeoville, Ill., 1972-78; mgr. Peat, Marwick, Mitchell & Co., Chgo., 1978-84; with George S. May Internat. Co., Park Ridge, Ill., 1984—, now v.p. fin., sec.-treas. With USAR, 1968-74. Office: George S May Internat Co 303 S Northwest Hwy Park Ridge IL 60068-4232

MATTHIAS, JOHN EDWARD, English literature educator; b. Columbus, Ohio, Sept. 5, 1941; s. John Marshall and Lois (Kirkpatrick) M.; m. Diana Clare Jocelyn, Dec. 27, 1967; children— Cynouai, Laura. BA, Ohio State U., 1963; MA, Stanford U., 1966; postgrad., U. London, 1967. Asst. prof. dept. English U. Notre Dame, Ind., 1966-73, assoc. prof. Ind., 1973-80, prof. Ind., 1980—. Vis. fellow Clare Hall, Cambridge U., 1966-77, assoc., 1977—; vis. prof. dept. English, Skidmore Coll., Saratoga Springs, N.Y., 1975, U. Chgo., 1980. Author: Bucyrus, 1971, Turns, 1975, Crossing, 1979, Five American Poets, 1980, Introducing David Jones, 1980, Contemporary Swedish Poetry, 1980, Bathory and Lermontov, 1980, Northern Summer, New and Selected Poems, 1984, The Battle of Kosovo, 1987, David Jones: Man and Poet: A Gathering of Ways, 1991, Reading Old Friends, 1991, Swimming at Midnight, 1995, Beltane at Aphelion, 1995, Pages: New Poems and Cuttings, 2000, Working Progress, 2002, Three-Toed Gull: Selected Poems of Jesper Svenbro, 2003, New Selected Poems, 2004. Recipient Columbia U. Transl. award, 1978, Swedish Inst. award, 1981, Poetry award Soc. Midland Authors, 1984, Ingram Merrill Found. award, 1984, 90; Woodrow Wilson fellow, 1963, Lily Endowment fellow, 1993; Fulbright grantee, 1966. Mem. AAUP, PEN, Poets and Writers, Poetry Soc. Am. (George Bogin Meml. award 1990). Office: U otre Dame Dept English Notre Dame IN 46556

MATTHIES, FREDERICK JOHN, civil and environmental engineer; b. Omaha, Oct. 4, 1925; s. Fred. J. and Charlotte Leota (Metz) M.; m. Carol Mae Dean, Sept. 14, 1947; children: John Frederick, Jane Carolyn Matthies Goding BSCE, Cornell U., 1947; postgrad., U. Nebr., 1952-53. Bd. cert. Am. Acad. Environ. Engrs.; registered profl. engr., Nebr. Civil engr. Henningson, Durham & Richardson, Omaha, 1947-50, 52-54; sr. v.p. devel. Leo A. Daly Co., Omaha, 1954-90; cons. engr., 1990—. Lectr. in field; mem. dist. export coun. U.S. Dept. Commerce, 1981-83. Contbr. articles to profl. jours. Mem. Douglas County Rep. Cen. Com., ebr., 1968-72; bd. regents Augustana Coll., Sioux Falls., S.D., 1976-89; bd. dirs. Orange County Luth. Hosp. Assn., Anaheim, Calif., 1961-62, Nebr. Humanities Coun., 1988-94, Omaha-Shizuoka City (Japan) Sister City Orgn.; trustee Luth. Med. Ctr., Omaha, 1978-82; mem. adv. bd. Marine Mil. Acad., Harlingen, Tex. 1st lt. USMCR, 1943-46, 50-52, Korea. Fellow ASCE, Instn. Civil Engrs. (London), Euro Engr. European Econ. Commn.; mem. NSPE, Am. Water Works Assn. (life), Air Force Assn., Am. Legion, VFW. Home: 950 Southridge Greens Blvd # 15 Fort Collins CO 80525-6726

MATTSON, STEPHEN JOSEPH, retired lawyer; b. Abilene, Tex., Oct. 11, 1943; s. Joseph Martin and Dorothy Irene (Doyle) M.; m. Lynn Louise Mitchell, Mar. 13, 1965; children: Eric, Laura. BA (hon.), U. Ill., 1965, JD (hon.), 1970. Bar: Ill., 1970, U.S. Dist. Ct. (no. dist.) Ill. 1970. Assoc. Mayer, Brown, Rowe & Maw, Chgo., 1970—77, ptnr., 1978—2003, ret., 2003. Mem. ABA, Order of Coif.

MATZICK, KENNETH JOHN, hospital administrator; b. Chgo., May 31, 1943; married. B. U. Iowa, 1965, MHA, 1967. Adminstrv. resident VA Med. Ctr., Iowa City, 1966, Morristown (N.J.) Meml. Hosp., 1967-68, asst. to exec. v.p., 1968-69; asst. dir. William Beaumont Hosp., Royal Oak, Mich., 1969-76, dir. Troy, Mich., 1976-83, v.p., COO Royal Oak, 1983-97, exec. v.p., COO, 1997, now pres., CEO. Home: 22500 Lavon St Saint Clair Shores MI 48081-2076 Office: William Beaumont Hosp 3601 W 13 Mile Rd Royal Oak MI 48073

MATZKE, JAY, internist; b. Sidney, Nebr., Oct. 2, 1956; m. Ann Matzke, Feb. 13, 1982; children: Alex, Jered, Sloan. B Medicine, U. Nebr. Med. Ctr., 1979, MD, 1983. Diplomate Am. Acad. Family Physicians. Resident in family practice U. Nebr. Med. Ctr., Nebr., 1984—86; ptnr. Martin Med. Clinic/Sidney Meml. Hosp., 1987—90; med. dir. Sidney Meml. Hosp. Addiction Ctr., 1987—89; staff physician Omaha Family Practice, 1990—96; ptnr. Immanuel Clinic/Immanuel Med. Ctr., 1990—96; med. dir. Immanuel/Alegent Health Sports Medicine, 1995—96; staff physician Meml. Health Care Sys., Seward, Nebr., 1997—, chief med. staff, 1999; med. dir. S.W. Rural Fire Dept., Nebr., 1998—; med. advisor Lancaster County Red Cross, Nebr., 1999—. Chmn. emergency cardiac care com. for Nebr. Am. Heart Assn., 1995—, instr. ACLS, 1984—; instr. ATLS ACS, 1986—. Dist. chmn. Boy Scouts Am., 2000—, pack com. chmn., 1997—98; trustee Nebr. Children's Home Soc., Nebr., 1999—; bd. dirs. Emergency Med. Svcs., 1998—; mem. pres.' adv. com. U. Nebr., 1997—2000; den leader Boy Scouts Am., 1985—87; chmn. ACLS Task Force, Nebr., 1992—95; pres., v.p., treas. Millard Sch. Bd., 1993—97; mem. Sidney City Coun., 1988—90; pres., charter mem. Cheyenne County Cmty. Ctr. Found., Inc., 1988—90; mem. bd. mission outreach, trustee Faith Luth. Ch., 1997—. Named Outstanding Young Nebraskan, Nebr. Jaycees, 1989, Outstanding Chamber Mem., Cheyenne County C. of C., 1988; recipient award of achievement, Nebr. Assn. Sch. Bds., 1995, 1996. Mem.: Am. Med. Soc. Sports Medicine.

MAULE, THERESA MOORE, lawyer; b. Winner, SD, Jan. 20, 1966; d. Robert James and Serrilyn Rae (Belmer) M.; m. Brian Lee Kramer, Nov. 25, 1996. BA summa cum laude, Dakota Wesleyan U., 1988; MA, U. S.D., 1990, JD, 1994. Bar: S.D., U.S. Dist. Ct. S.D., Lower Brule Sioux Tribal Ct., Rosebud Sioux Tribal Ct. Prosecutor Rosebud (S.D.) Sioux Tribal Ct., 1994-96; ptnr. Maule & Maule Law Offices, Winner, S.D., 1995—; prosecutor Lower Brule (S.D.) Sioux Tribal Ct., 1996—; states atty Tripp County, Winner, 1997—. Mem. Tripp County Child Protection Team, Winner, S.D., 1997—. Mem. ABA, S.D. Bar Assn., Nat. Dist. Attys. Assn., S.D. Trial Lawyers Assn., Bus. and Profl. Women (Young Careerist 1996), Phi Kappa Phi, Phi Alpha Theta. Republican. Episcopalian. Avocations: camping, ceramics.

MAURER, DAVID LEO, lawyer; b. Evansville, Ind., Oct. 31, 1945; s. John G. Jr. and Mildred M. (Lintzenich) M.; m. Diane M. Kaput, Aug. 11, 1973; children: Eric W., Kathryn A. BA magna cum laude, U. Detroit, 1967, Cert. in Teaching, 1971; JD, Wayne State U., 1975. Bar: Mich., U.S. Dist. Ct. (ea. and we. dist.) Mich., U.S. Ct. Appeals (6th cir.) Cin. Law clk. Mich. Ct. Appeals, Detroit, 1976, Supreme Ct. Mich., Lansing, 1977-78; asst. U.S. atty. civil div. U.S. Dept. Justice, Detroit, 1978-81; assoc. to ptnr. Butzel, Long, Gust, Klein & Van Zile, Detroit, 1981-85; ptnr. Pepper Hamilton LLP), Detroit, 1985—2007. Guest lectr. Practicing Law Inst., 1988-2007, Nat. Bus. Inst., 1989—, U. Mich. Law Sch., U. Detroit Law Sch., 1990, Hazardous Waste Super Conf., 1986-87. Co-author: Michigan Environmental Law Deskbook, 1992; contbr. articles to profl. jours. and chpts. in books. Mem. Energy & Environ. Policy Com., 1988—, chairperson, 1989-90; mem. Great Lakes Water Resources Commn., 1986. Mem. State Bar Mich. (environ. couns. 1986-91, sec., treas., chairperson-elect, chairperson 1991-93). Office: 941 Sunningdale Dr Grosse Pointe MI 48236 Office Phone: 313-393-7448. Business E-Mail: maurerd@pepperlaw.com.

MAURER, HAROLD MAURICE, pediatrician; b. NYC, Sept. 10, 1936; s. Isador and Sarah (Rothkowitz) M.; m. Beverly Bennett, June 12, 1960; children: Ann Maurer Rosenbach, Wendy Maurer Linsky. AB, NYU, 1957; MD, SUNY, Bklyn., 1961. Diplomate Am. Bd. Pediatrics, Am. Bd. Pediatric Hematology-Oncology. Intern pediatrics Kings County Hosp., NYC, 1961-62; resident in pediatrics Babies Hosp., Columbia-Presbyn. Med. Center, NYC, 1962-64; fellow in pediatric hematology/oncology Columbia-Presbyn. Med. Center, 1966-68; asst. prof. pediatrics Med. Coll. Va., Richmond, 1968-71, asso. prof., 1971-75, prof., 1975—, chmn. dept. pediatrics, 1976-93; dean U. Nebr. Coll. Medicine, Omaha, 1993-98; chancellor U. Nebr. Med. Ctr., Omaha, 1998—. Chmn. Intergroup Rhabdomyosarcoma Study, 1972-98; exec. com. Pediatric Oncology Group. Editor: pediatrics, 1983, Rhabdomyosarcoma and Related Tumors in Children and Adolescence, 1991; mem. editorial bd. Am. Jour. Hematology, Journal Pediatric Hematology and Oncology, Medical and Pediatric Oncology, 1984-99; contbr. articles to profl. jours. Mem. Youth Health Task Force, City of Richmond., Gov.'s Adv. Com. on Handicapped., Gov.'s Homeland Security Policy Group, Nebr., 2002-; mem. coun. biodefense Assn. Academic Health Ctr., 2003—, coun. global health, 2003—, gov.'s homeland security policy group 2002—; mem. nat. com. on childhood cancer Am. Cancer Soc., bd. dirs. Va. divsn.; bd. dirs. Nebr. Med. Ctr., 1997—, Friends of Nat. Inst. Nursing Rsch., 2004-05; adv. com. Lisstratcom, 2004—. Served to lt. comdr. USPHS, 1964-66. Named Ak-Sar-Ben King C IX, 2005; recipient Midlander of Yr., Omaha World Herald Newspaper, 2004, Face on the Barroom Floor award, Omaha Press Club, 2007; grantee, NIH, 1974—98. Mem. Am. Acad. Pediatrics (com. oncology-hematology), Am. Soc. Hematology, Soc. Pediatric Rsch., Am. Pediatric Soc., Va. Pediatric Sic. (exec. com.), Assn. Med. Sch. Pediatric Dept. Chmn., Internat. Soc. Pediatric Oncology, Am. Soc. Clin. Oncology, Va. Hematology Soc., Am. Assn. Cancer Rsch., Am. Cancer Soc., Am. Soc. Pediatric Hematology-Oncology (v.p. 1990-91, pres. 1991-93, Lifetime Achievement award children's oncology group 2003), Sigma Xi, Coun. Deans AAMC, Gov.'s Blue Ribbon Commn., Alpha Omega Alpha. Republican. Jewish. Home: 9822 Ascot Dr Omaha NE 68114-3848 Office: U Nebr Med Ctr 986605 Nebraska Med Ctr Omaha NE 68198-6605 Business E-Mail: hmmaurer@unmc.edu.

MAURO, MICHAEL ANTHONY, state official; b. Sept. 29, 1948; m. Dorothy Fischer; children: Steven, Nick, Michael. Grad., Drake U., Des Moines, 1970. Lic. real estate broker, cert. elections/registration adminstr. 2003. HS govt. tchr., coach, referee; election dir. Polk County, Iowa, 1984—96, auditor Iowa, 1997—2007; sec. state State of Iowa, Des Moines, 2007—. Mem. I-VOTERS Standards com. Polk County, mem. HAVA State Plan Adv. Com., mem. Voting Equipment Users Grp., mem. Deferred Compensation Bd. Democrat. Office: Office Sec State State Capitol Rm 105 1007 E Grand Ave Des Moines IA 50319

MAURSTAD, DAVID INGOLF, federal agency administrator, insurance company executive; b. North Platte, Nebr., Aug. 25, 1953; s. Ingolf Byron and Marilyn Sophia (Gimble) M.; m. Karen Sue Micek, Sept. 7, 1974; children: Ingolf, Derek, Laura. A. in Fine Arts, Platte Community Coll., Columbus, Nebr., 1973; BSBA, U. Nebr., 1989, MBA, 2000. Asst. golf profl. Country Club of Lincoln (Nebr.), 1973-76; head golf profl. Westward Ho Country Club, Sioux Falls, S.D., 1977; ins. agt. Maurstad/Zimmerman Ins., Beatrice, Nebr., 1978-84; ins. agy. mgr. Maurstad Ins. Svcs., Inc., Beatrice, 1984-90, pres., 1990—; mayor City of Beatrice, 1991-94; mem. Nebr. Senate from dist. 30, 1995—99; lt. gov. State of Nebr., 1998—2001; regional dir. Fed. Emergency Mgmt. Agy. (FEMA), US Dept. Homeland Security, 2001—04, acting dir. mitigation divsn., acting fed. ins. adminstr., 2004—. Pres. Beatrice YMCA, 1982-83, Gage County United Way, Beatrice, 1985, founding trustee, 1st pres. Beatrice Ednl. Found., 1988-96; del., Rep. Nat. Conv., 2000; state vice chmn., Bush Cheney, 2000; mem. Nebr. Rep. State Cen. Com., Lincoln, 1985-90, 95-97, elected Bd. Edn. Sch. Dist. #15, Beatrice, 1988-90; candidate Nebr. Legislature, Lincoln, 1986; chmn. Highway 77 Improvement Assn., 1991-94; chair Nebr. Info. Tech. Commn., 1999-2001; trustee Beatrice Libr. Found., 1996-2001; bd. dirs. Madonna Found., 1997-2001. amed Outstanding Young Man of Am., Beatrice Jaycees, 1985, Citizen of Yr. Beatrice C. of C., 1993, Outstanding Amateur Golfer Nebr. Golf Assn., 1981, Harold Sieck Pub. Ofcl. of Yr., Arc of Nebr., 1998; recipient Young Alumnus award U. Nebr. Alumni Assn., 1993, Disting. Svc. award Nat. Fedn. Interscholastic Ofcls. Assn., 1989, Disting. Svc. award League of Nebr. Municipalities, 1998, Outstanding Alumnus award Ctrl. C.C. Platte Campus, Coll. Alumni Assn., 1998, Disting. Alumni award Nebr. C.C. System, 2000. Mem. Ind. Ins. Agts. Nebr. (Young Agt. of Yr. 1985), Blue Valley Life Underwriters (bd. dirs. 1988-94), Beatrice C. of C. (bd. dirs. 1985-87), U. Nebr.-Lincoln Coll. Bus. Adminstrn. Alumni Bd. (bd. dirs. 1989-96, pres. 1994-95, Leadership award 1994). Republican. Lutheran. Avocations: golf, reading, spectator sports. Office: Fed Emergency Mgmt Agy (FEMA) PO Box 25267 Bldg 710 A Denver Fed Ctr Denver CO 80225-0267

MAUST, JOSEPH J., agricultural products supplier; Pres. Active Feed Co., Pigeon, Mich., 1984—. Office: Active Feed Co 7564 Pigeon Rd Pigeon MI 48755-9701

MAUTINO, FRANK J., state legislator; b. Spring Valley, Ill., Aug. 7, 1962; BS, Ill. State U. Dist. 76 rep. Ill. Ho. Reps., Springfield, 1991—. Mem. housing ins., pub. safety,and infrastructure appropriations coms., Ill. Ho. Reps.

MAVES, MICHAEL DONALD, medical association executive; b. East St. Louis, Ill., Oct. 14, 1948; BS, U. Toledo, 1970; MD, Ohio State U., 1973; MBA, U. Iowa, 1988. Lic. physician, Iowa, Mo., Ill., D.C.; diplomate Am. Bd. Otolaryngology. Rsch. fellow Ohio State U. Coll. Medicine, Columbus, 1977; fellow head and neck surgery Columbia-Presbyn. Med. Ctr., NYC, 1978, U. Iowa Hosps. and Clinics, Iowa City, 1980-81; asst. prof. otolaryngology, head and neck surgery Ind. U. Sch. Medicine, Indpls., 1981-84, U. Iowa Hosps. and Clinics, Iowa City, 1984-87, assoc. prof., 1987-88; chmn. dept. otolaryngology St. Louis U. Sch. Medicine, St. Louis, 1988-94; exec. v.p. Am. Acad. Otolaryngology, Head and Neck Surgery, Alexandria, Va., 1994—2001; pres. Consumer Healthcare Products Assn., Wash., DC, 1999—2001; exec. v.p., CEO AMA, Chicago, 2002—. Lectr. in field. Contbr. articles to profl. jours. Capt. U.S.

Army, 1974-76. Recipient numerous awards including Honor award and Pres.'s award Am. Acad. Otolaryngology-Head and Neck Surgery; named one of Best 1000 Physicians in U.S., 1992, 94, One of Best 400 Cancer Doctors in Am., Good Housekeeping, 1992. Fellow ACS; mem. AMA (RBRVS update com.), Am. Cancer Soc., Am. Acad. Facial & Plastic Reconstructive Surgery.*

MAWARDI, OSMAN KAMEL, retired plasma physicist; b. Cairo, Dec. 12, 1917; arrived in U.S., 1946, naturalized, 1952; s. Kamel Ibrahim and Marie (Wiennig) M.; m. Betty Louise Hosmer, Nov. 23, 1950. BS, Cairo U., 1940, MS, 1945; A.M., Harvard U., 1947, PhD, 1948. Lectr. physics Cairo U., 1940-45; asst. prof. Mass Inst. Tech., 1951-56, assoc. prof., 1956-60; prof. engring., dir. plasma research program Case Inst. Tech., Cleve., 1960-88; dir. Energy Research Office, Case Western Res. U., 1977-82; ret., 1988. Pres. Collaborative Planners, Inc.; mem. Inst. Advanced Study, 1969-70; also cons. Contbr. articles to profl. jours. Past trustee Print Club Cleve., Cleve. Inst. Art. Recipient Biennial award Acoustical Soc. Am., 1952; CECON medal of achievement, 1979 Fellow AAAS, Acoustical Soc. Am., IEEE (Edison lectr. 1968-69, Centennial award 1984, Cleve. sect. Engr. of Yr. 1994); mem. N.Y. Acad. Scis., Sigma Xi, Eta Kappa Nu. Office: 2490 Lee Rd Cleveland OH 44118-4125 Home: 8505 Woodfield Crossing Blvd Ste 104 Indianapolis IN 46240 Office Phone: 216-932-9550. Business E-Mail: okm@case.edu.

MAWBY, RUSSELL GEORGE, retired foundation executive; b. Grand Rapids, Mich., Feb. 23, 1928; s. Wesley G. and Ruby (Finch) M.; m. Ruth E. Edison, Dec. 16, 1950 (dec. 2000); children: Douglas, David, Karen. BS in Horticulture, Mich. State U., 1949, PhD in Agrl. Econs., 1959, LL.D. (hon.), 1972; MS in Agrl. Econs, Purdue U., 1951, D.Agr. (hon.), 1973; L.H.D. (hon.), Luther Coll., Decorah, Iowa, 1972, Alma Coll., Mich., 1975, Nazareth Coll., 1976, Madonna Coll., 1983, N.C. Central U., 1986; LL.D. (hon.), N.C. A&T State U., Greensboro, 1974, Tuskegee Inst., 1978, Kalamazoo Coll., 1980; D.P.A. (hon.), Albion Coll., 1976; D.C.L. (hon.), U. Newcastle, Eng., 1977; D.Sc. (hon.), Nat. U. Ireland, 1980; D.Pub. Service (hon.), No. Mich. U., 1981; D.H.L. (hon.), So. Utah State Coll., 1983; HHD (hon.), Grand Valley State U., 1988; ScD (hon.), Calif. State U., 1989; LLD (hon.), Adrian Coll., 1990; LittD (hon.), Olivet Coll., 1991. Ext. specialist Mich. State U., East Lansing, 1952-56, asst. dir. coop. ext. svc., 1956-65; dir. div. agr. W.K. Kellogg Found., Battle Creek, Mich., 1965-66, mem., trustee, 1967—, v.p. programs, 1966-70, pres., 1970-82, chmn., CEO, 1982-95, chmn. emeritus, 1995—. Bd. dirs. Detroit br. Fed. Res. Bank Chgo., 1980-85, J.M. Smucker Co., 1983—; fellow Inst. for Children, Youth and Families Mich. State U., 1993; hon. fellow Kellog Coll., U. Oxford, Eng., 1990; mem. chancellor's ct. of benefactors U. Oxford, Eng., 1991; Disting. Vis. Prof. Inst. for Children, Youth and Families and Coll. of Edn., Mich. State U., 1996—. Trustee Youth for Understanding, 1973-79, Mich. State U. Coll. of Agr. and Natural Resources Alumni Assn., 1977-80, pres. 1978-79; trustee Arabian Horse Trust, 1978-90 (emeritus 1990—), Starr Commonwealth, 1987-97, 98—, (chmn. bd. trustees 1993-95), Found. Ctr., 1988-94 (chmn. bd. trustees 1989-94), Mich. Non-profit Assn., 1990-94 (chmn. bd. trustees 1990-94, emeritus 1994—), Mich. State U., 1992-96 (chmn. bd. trustees 1995); founding chmn. Coun. of Mich. Founds., 1972-74, chmn. emeritus 1994—; bd. dirs. Coun. on Founds., 1978-84, Mich.'s Children, 1995-98, emeritus 1998—; mem. Joint Coun. on Food and Agrl. Scis., USDA, 1984-88; mem. Com. on Agrl. Edn. in Secondary Schs., NRC, 1985-88, Gov.'s Task Force on Revitalization of Agr. Through Rsch. and Edn., 1986; mem. rural bus. partnership adv. bd. Mich. Dept. Commerce, 1989-90, Mich. Coop. Ext. Svc. Study Com., 1989; mem. pres.'s adv. coun. Clemson U., 1987-95; vis. com. Med. U. of S.C., 1990-95; steering com. Econ. Devel. Forum of Calhoun County, Mich., 1991—; mem. policy bd. Calhoun County Cmtys. in Schs., 1995-98; mem. Lt. Gov.'s Children's Commn., State of Mich., 1995-96; mem. leadership adv. coun. Olivet Coll., 1995—; trustee Battle Creek Community Found., 1996—, Mich. 4-H Found., 1996—, hon. trustee, 1996—; scholar-in-residence Ind. U. Ctr. on Philanthropy, 1996—; mem. State Officers compensation Commn., State of Mich., 1996-98; mem. bd. govs. Ind. U. Ctr. on Philanthropy, 2000—; bd. visitors Coll. of Nursing Mich. State U., 1997—; bd. dirs. Mich. State U. Found., 1998—. With AUS, 1953-55. Decorated knight 1st class Royal Order St. Olaf Norway, 1974; knight's cross Order of Dannebrog 1st class Denmark, 1976; comdr.'s medal Order of Finnish Lion Finland, 1981; recipient Disting. Service award U.S. Dept. Agr., 1963, Disting. Alumni award Mich. State U., 1971, Nat. Alumni award 4-H Clubs, 1972, Disting. Eagle Scout award Boy Scouts Am., 1973, Meritorious Achievement award Fla. A&M U., 1973, Nat. Ptnr. in 4-H award Dept. Agr. Ext. Svc., 1976; named hon. fellow Spring Arbor (Mich.) Coll., 1972; recipient Walter F. Patenge medal for pub. service Coll. Osteo. Medicine, Mich. State U., 1977, Disting. Service award Coll. Agr. and Natural Resources, 1980, Seaman A. Knapp Meml. lectr. U.S. Dept. Agr., 1983; recipient George award for cmty. svc. City of Battle Creek, 1986, Disting. Service award Rural Sociol. Soc., 1986, Centennial Alumnus award for Mich. State U. Nat. Assn. State Univs. and Land Grant Colls., 1988, Pres.'s award Clemson U., 1989, Disting. Citizen award Southwest Mich. Coun. Boy Scouts Am., 1989, Disting. Svc. award 1890 Land-Grant Colls. and Univs., 1990, Vol. of Yr. award Clemson U., 1990, Disting. Grantmaker award Coun. on Founds., 1992, Disting. Svc. award Nat. Assn. Homes and Svcs. for Children, 1992, Merit award Nat. Soc. Fund Raising Execs. West Mich. chpt., 1992, Red Rose award Rotary Club of Battle Creek, 1993, George W. Romney award Nat. Soc. Fund Raising Execs. Greater Detroit chpt., 1993, Director's award Arabian Horse Assn. of Mich., 1994, Disting. Svc. award Mich. Hort. Soc., 1994, Michiganian of Yr. The Detroit News, 1995, Gerald G. Hicks Child Welfare Leadership award Mich. Fedn. Private Child and Family Agys., 1995, Leon Bradley Humanitarian for Youth award No. Area Assn., Detroit, 1995, award of Honor Am. Hosp. Assn., 1995, Spirit of the Drum award, Nat. Youth Leadership Coun., 1996, Crystal Apple award Featherstone Soc. Coll. Edn. Mich. State U., 1996, Nat. Govs. Assn. award for disting. svc. to state govt., 1997, Nat. Interfraternity Conf. Gold Medal award, 1998, Govs. award for stewardship State of Mich., 1999; named Friend of the Coll., Mich. State U. Coll. Human Ecology, 1996, Internat. Adult and Continuing Edn. Hall of Fame, 1996, Owner of Yr. Mich. Harness Horsemen's Assn., 1999; Louis Harris fellow Rotary Club Battle Creek, 1998. Mem. Mich. Soc. Architects (hon.), Am. Agrl. Econ. Assn., Mich. State U. Alumni Assn. (bd. dirs. 1984-88), Alpha Gamma Rho (dir. 1976-82, grand pres. 1980-82, Man of Year Chgo. Alumni chpt. 1976, Hall of Fame 1986), Alpha Zeta, Phi Kappa Phi (Disting. Mem. award Mich. State U. 1978), Epsilon Sigma Phi (certificate of recognition 1974, Nat. Friend of Ext. 1982), Gamma Sigma Delta, Delta Sigma Pi (hon. mem., 1995). Home: 8400 N 39th St Augusta MI 49012-9713 Office: Heritage Tower 25 Michigan Ave W Ste 1701 Battle Creek MI 49017-7023

MAXSON, LINDA ELLEN, biologist, educator; b. NYC, Apr. 24, 1943; d. Albert and Ruth (Rosenfeld) Resnick; m. Richard Dey Maxson, June 13, 1964; 1 child, Kevin. BS in Zoology, San Diego State U., 1964, MA in Biology, 1966; PhD in Genetics, San Diego State U./U. Calif., Berkeley, 1973. Instr. biology San Diego State U., 1966-68; tchr. gen. sci. San Diego Unified Sch. Dist., 1968-69; instr. biochemistry U. Calif., Berkeley, 1974; asst. prof. zoology, dept. genetics and devel. U. Ill., Urbana-Champaign, 1974-76, asst. prof. dept. genetics, devel. and ecology, ethology & evolution, 1976-79, assoc. prof., 1979-84, prof., 1984-87, prof. ecology, ethology and evolution, 1987-88; prof., head dept. biology Pa. State U., State College, 1988-94; assoc. vice-chancellor acad. affairs/dean undergrad. acad. affairs, prof. ecology and evolutionary biology U. Tenn., Knoxville, 1995-97; dean Coll. Liberal Arts & Scis., prof. biol. scis. U. Iowa, Iowa City, 1997—. Exec. officer biology programs Sch. Life Scis., U. Ill., 1981-86, assoc. dir. acad. affairs, 1984-86, dir. campus honors program, 1985-88; vis. prof. ecology and evolutionary biology U. Calif., Irvine, 1988; mem. adv. panel rsch. tng. groups behavioral biol. scis. NSF, 1990-94; rsch. assoc. Smithsonian Instn. Author: Genetics: A Human Perspective, 3d edit., 1992; mem. editl. bd. Molecular Biology Evolution; exec. editor Biochem. Sys. & Ecology, 1993-2001; contbr. numerous articles to scientific jours. Recipient Disting. Alumni award, San Diego State U., 1989, Disting. Herpetologist award, Herpetologists' League, 1993. Fellow: AAAS; mem.: Soc. Molecular Biology and Evolution (treas. 1992—94, sec. 1992—95), Soc. Study Evolution, Soc. for Study of Amphibians and Reptiles (pres. 1991), Am. Men and Women in Sci., Phi Beta Kappa. Office: U Iowa 240 Schaeffer Hall Iowa City IA 52242-1409 Business E-Mail: linda-maxson@uiowa.edu.

MAXWELL, CHIP, state legislator; b. Omaha, Aug. 10, 1962; m. Pam Maxwell; children: Tomas, Oto. B in Polit. Sci., Boston Coll., 1984; M in Am. History, Oxford U., 1987; JD, U. Nebr., 1992. Law clk. Nebr. Ct. Appeals; editl. writer Omaha World-Herald; spl. asst. to U.S. Senater Chuck Hagel; devel. dir. Jesuit Mid. Sch., Our Lady Guadalupe & St. Agnes Mission Sch.; mem. Nebr. Legislature from 9th dist., 2001—. Mem. Nebr. BAr Assn. Home: 3835 California St Omaha E 68131 Office: Rm 1115 State Capitol Lincoln NE 68509

MAXWELL, DAVID E., academic executive, educator; b. NYC, Dec. 2, 1944; s. James Kendrick and Gertrude Sarah (Bernstein) M.; children: Justin Kendrick, Stephen Edward. BA, Grinnell Coll., 1966; MA, Brown U., 1968, PhD, 1974. Instr. Tufts U., Medford, Mass., 1971-74, asst. prof., 1974-78, assoc. prof. Russian lang. and lit., 1978-89, dean undergrad. studies, 1981-89; pres. Whitman Coll., Walla Walla, Wash., 1989-93; dir. Nat. Fgn. Lang. Ctr., Washington, 1993-99; pres. Drake U., Des Moines, 1999—. Chmn. steering com. Coop. Russian Lang. Program, Leningrad, USSR, 1981-86, chmn. 1986-90; cons. Coun. Internat. Ednl. Exch., 1974-94, bd. dirs., 1988-92, 93-94, vice chair, 1991-92, cons. Internat. Rsch. Exchs., 1976-83; mem. adv. bd. Israeli Lang. Policy Inst. Contbr. articles to scholarly jours. Cmty. bd. dirs. Wells Fargo; bd. dirs. Iowa Wellness Coun.; bd. dirs. Greater Des Moines Partnership; pres. Des Moines Higher Edn. Collaborative, 2000—; bd. dirs. Downtown Cmty Alliance, Des Moines. Fulbright fellow, 1970-71, Brown U., 1966-67, NDEA Title IV, 1967-70; recipient Lillian Leibner award Tufts U., 1970; citation Grad. Sch. Arts and Scis., Brown U., 1991. Mem. MLA, Am. Coun. Edn. (commn. on internat. edn., pres.'s coun. on internat. edn.), Assn. Am. Colls., Am. Assn. Higher Edn., Brown U. Alumni Assn. (exec. com.), Bus. Higher Edn. Forum (bd. trustees, coun. econ. devel.), Phi Beta Kappa. Democrat. Avocations: tennis, running, music. Office: Drake Univ Office of the Pres 2507 University Ave Des Moines IA 50311-4505 Home Phone: 515-277-2822; Office Phone: 515-271-2191. Business E-Mail: david.maxwell@drake.edu.

MAXWELL, DONALD ROBERT, pharmacologist; b. Paris, Mar. 30, 1929; s. Titus Bonner and Helen Marie-Camille M.; m. Catherine Marie Billon, Aug. 16, 1956; children— Monica, icholas, Christopher, Caroline, Denis, Dominic, Marie-Claire, Philip. BA in natural scis. (physics) (rsch. scholar), U. Cambridge, Eng., 1952, MA, 1956, PhD in med., 1955; MA in romance langs. and lit., U. Mich., 1994, PhD in romance langs. and lit., 1998. Attachée de recherches du C.N.R.S. Institut Pasteur, Paris, 1955-56; various appts. England, 1957—74; dir. preclin. research Warner-Lambert Co., Morris Plains, N.J., 1974-77; v.p. preclin. research Warner-Lambert/Parke-Davis, Ann Arbor, Mich., 1977-90, sr. v.p. rsch. and devel., exec. v.p. sci. affairs, 1990—. Vis. asst. prof. lectr. French, U. Mich. Author: The Abacus and the Rainbow: Bergson, Proust and the digital analogic Opposition, 1999, Science or Literature? The Divergent Cultures of Discovery and Creation, 2000; A Journey From Wartime Europe to Self-Discovery, 2003; contbr. articles to profl. jours. V.p., pres. Bd. Edn., Gabriel Richard H.S., Ann Arbor, 1981-85; adv. com. Cambridge U., U.S. Office, 1991—. Fellow Inst. Biology (Eng.), Royal Soc. Medicine (London); mem. Brit. Pharmacol. Soc., Physiol. Soc. (U.K.), Am. Soc. Pharmacology and Exptl. Therapeutics, Biochem. Soc., Internat. Coll. Neuro-Psychopharmacology, British Soc. Immunology, British Soc. Allergy and Clin. Immunology, European Soc. Study of Drug Toxicity. Office: U Mich Ann Arbor MI 48109 E-mail: maxwelld@umich.edu.

MAXWELL, ROBERT WALLACE, II, lawyer; b. Sept. 6, 1943; s. Robert Wallace and Margaret Maxwell; m. Mamie Lee Payne, June 18, 1966; children: Virginia, Robert, William. BS magna cum laude, Hampden-Sydney Coll., 1965; JD with honors, Duke U., 1968. Bar: Ohio 1968. Assoc. Taft, Stettinius & Hollister, Cin., 1968—75, ptnr., 1975—88, Keating, Muething & Klekamp, Cin., 1988—. Instr. U. Cin. Sch. Law, 1975-76. Elder Knox Presbyn. Ch.; bd. dir. Contemporary Arts Ctr. of Cin., Cin. Ballet Co. Mem.: ABA, Am. Assn. Mus. Trustees. Republican. Home: The Ascent, Unit 503 One Roebling Way Covington KY 41011 Office: Keating Muething & Klekamp 1 E 4th St Ste 1400 Cincinnati OH 45202-3752 Office Phone: 513-579-6594. E-mail: rmaxwell@kmklaw.com.

MAXWELL, WILLIAM HALL CHRISTIE, civil and environmental engineer, educator; b. Coleraine, No. Ireland, Jan. 25, 1936; came to U.S., 1958, naturalized, 1967; s. William Robert and Catherine Dempsey (Christie) M.; m. Mary Carolyn McLaughlin, Sept. 28, 1960; children: Katrina, Kevin, Wendy, Liam. BSc, Queen's U., Belfast, No. Ireland, 1956; MSc, Queen's U., Kingston, Ont., Can., 1958; PhD, U. Minn., 1964. Registered profl. engr., Ill. Site engr. Motor Columbus AG, Baden, Switzerland, 1956; tchg. asst. Queen's U., Kingston, 1956-58; from rsch. asst. to instr. U. Minn., Mpls., 1959-64; asst. prof. civil engring. U. Ill., Urbana, 1964-70, assoc. prof., 1970-82, prof., 1982-96, prof. emeritus civil and environ. engring., 1997—. Chmn. program com. 1st Internat. Conf. on ew/Emerging Concepts for Rivers, Chgo., 1996. Editor: Water Resources Management in Industrial Areas, 1982, Water for Human Consumption, Man and His Environment, 1983, Frontiers in Hydrology, 1984, New/Emerging Concepts for Rivers, 1996. Vestryman Emmanuel Meml. Episcopal Ch., Champaign, Ill., 1977-80; state exhibitor Ministry Edn., Stormont, No. Ireland, 1953-56. Queen's U. Found. scholar, Belfast, 1954-56, R.S. McLaughlin travel fellow Queen's U., Kingston, 1958-59. Fellow ASCE (com. chmn. 1982-83), Internat. Water Resources Assn. (editor-in-chief Water Internat. 1986-93, sr. editor 1994-98, mem. publs. com. 1980-98, v.p. U.S. geog. com. 1986-91, chmn. awards com. 1995-97, bd. dirs. 1995-97, Editl. award 1994); mem. Am. Geophys. Union, Internat. Assn. for Hydraulic Rsch., Nat. Assn. Scholars. Avocations: home construction, painting. Home: 1210 Devonshire Dr Champaign IL 61821-6527 Office: U Ill Dept Civil and Environ Engring 205 N Mathews Ave Urbana IL 61801-2350 Business E-Mail: wmaxwell@uiuc.edu.

MAY, ALAN ALFRED, lawyer; b. Detroit, Apr. 7, 1942; s. Alfred Albert and Sylvia (Sheer) M.; m. Elizabeth Miller; children: Stacy Ann, Julie Beth. BA, U. Mich., 1963, JD cum laude, 1966. Bar: Mich. 1967, D.C. 1976; former reg. nursing home adminstr., Mich. Ptnr. May and May PC, Detroit, 1979—2001; ptnr., shareholder, v.p. Kemp Klein, Umphrey and May, P.C., Troy, Mich., 2001—05; CEO NCCJ, 2005. Spl. asst. atty. gen. State of Mich., 1970—; pres., instr. Med-Leg Seminars, Inc., 1978; lectr. Wayne State U., 1974; instr. Oakland U., 1969. Chmn. Rep. 18th Congrl. Dist. Com., 1983-87, now chmn. emeritus; chmn. 19th Congrl. Dist. Com., 1981-83; mem. Mich. Rep. Com., 1976-84; del. Rep. Nat. Conv., 1984, rules com., 1984; del. Rep. Nat. Conv., 1988, platform com., 1988; former chmn. Mich. Civil Rights Commn.; mem., vice chair Mich. Civil Svc. Commn., 1984-88; former trustee, mem. exec. bd., vice chmn. nat conf. for cmty. and justice NCCJ; trustee Temple Beth El Birmingham, Mich., past pres. exec. bd.; mem. Electoral Coll.; former bd. dirs. ADL, Mich.; bd. dirs. exec. bd., past pres. Detroit Region/Nat. Conf. Cmty. and Justice, Charfoos Charitable Found. Named to Mich. Super Lawyers, 2007. Mem. Nat. Conf. Cmty. and Justice (former exec. bd., vice chmn., pres., CEO 2005—, interim pres. 2005), Detroit Bar Assn., Oakland County Bar Assn., Victors Club, Franklin Hills Country Club (past pres., bd. dirs.), President's Club. Home: 4140 Echo Rd Bloomfield Hills MI 48302-1941 Office: Kemp Klein Umphrey Endelman & May PC 201 W Big Beaver Rd Ste 600 Troy MI 48084 Office Phone: 248-528-1111. Business E-Mail: alan.may@kkue.com.

MAY, BRIAN HENRY, state legislator; b. St. Louis, Nov. 22, 1962; BS in Edn. summa cum laude, Harris-Stowe State Coll., 1986; JD, St. Louis U., 1989. Mem. dist. 108 Mo. Ho. of Reps.; with firm Casserly, Jones & Brittingham, P.C., St. Louis, 1990-95, Larsen, Feist & Bedell, P.C., St. Louis, 1995—. Office: 692 Meramec View Dr Eureka MO 63025-3716

MAY, GEORGIANA, biologist, educator; PhD, U. Calif., Berkeley, 1987. Assoc. prof. dept. plant biology U. Minn., St. Paul. Contbr. articles to profl. jours. Recipient Alexopoulos prize Mycological Soc. Am., 1997. Achievements include research on the interactions of fungi with plants, evolution of fungal populations and their interactions with other organisms, evolution of gene structure and function in mating compatibility loci, determining the genetic basis of smut resistance in maize, the impact of agricultural practice on host/pathogen interactions. Office: U Minn Dept Plant Biology 220 Biological Sci Ctr 1445 Gortner Ave Saint Paul MN 55108 Fax: 612-625-1738. E-mail: gmay@maroon.tc.umn.edu.

MAY, J. PETER, mathematics professor; b. NYC, Sept. 16, 1939; s. Siegmund Henry and Jane (Polachek) M.; m. Maija Bajars, June 8, 1963; children: Anthony D., Andrew D. BA, Swarthmore Coll., 1960; PhD, Princeton U., 1964. Instr. Yale U., New Haven, 1964-65, asst. prof., 1965-67; vis. prof. U. Chgo. (spring), 1967; assoc. prof. U. Chgo., 1967-70, prof., 1970—, chmn. dept. math., 1985-91, dir., Math. Disciplines Ctr., 1988—96, chmn. coun. on teaching, 1991-96, mem., policy com., Divsn. Physical Sciences, 1991—95, dir., VIGRE program, 2000—, co-chmn., grad. studies com., 2001—, co-chmn., grad. admissions com., 2002—. Mem. Inst. Advanced Study, Princeton, 1966; vis. prof. Cambridge U., England, 1971—72, 1977. Author: Simplicial Objects in Algebraic Topology, 1967, The Geometry of Iterated Loop Spaces, 1972, E-infinity Ring Spaces and E-infinity Ring Spectra, 1977, Equivariant Homotopy and Cohomology Theory, 1996, A Concise Course in Algebraic Topology, 1999; co-author: The Homology of Iterated Loop Spaces, 1976, H-infinity Ring Spectra and Their Applications, 1986, Equivariant Stable Homotopy Theory, 1987, Rings Modules and Algebras in Stable Homotopy Theory, 1997, Parametrized Honotopy Theory, 2006; also numerous articles and monographs. NSF grantee, 1967; Fulbright fellow, 1971-72; fellow Nat. Rsch. Coun., Eng., 1977. Mem.: Am. Math. Soc., AAUP. Office: U Chgo Dept Math 5734 S University Ave Chicago IL 60637-1514 Office Phone: 312-702-7381.

MAY, NICHOLAS G.B., lawyer; BA, U. Iowa, 1994; JD magna cum laude, William Mitchell Coll. Law, 1998. Bar: US Ct. Appeals (8th cir.), US Dist. Ct. (dist. Minn.), Minn. Supreme Ct. Ptnr. May & O'Brien, L.L.P., Hastings, Minn. Named a Rising Star, Minn. Super Lawyers mag., 2006. Mem.: Minn. Trial Lawyers Assn., Dakota County Bar Assn., Minn. Bar Assn. (mem. labor and employment sect.), ABA, Nat. Employment Lawyers Assn. (Minn. chpt.) (bd. mem., past pres.). Office: May & O'Brien LLP 204 Sibley St Ste 202 Hastings MN 55033 Office Phone: 651-437-6300. E-mail: nmay@mayobrien.com.

MAY, WALTER GRANT, chemical engineer, educator; b. Saskatoon, Sask., Can., Nov. 28, 1918; came to U.S., 1946, naturalized, 1954; s. George Alfred and Abigail Almira (Robson) M.; m. Mary Louise Stockan, Sept. 26, 1945 (dec. 1977); children: John R., Douglas W., Caroline O; m. Helen Dickerson, 1988. BSc, U. Sask., Saskatoon, 1939, MSc, 1942; ScD, MIT, 1948. Chemist Brit. Am. Oil Co., Moose Jaw, Sask., 1939-40; asst. prof. U. Sask., 1943-46; with Exxon Rsch. & Engring. Co., Linden, NJ, 1948-83, sr. sci. adv., 1976-83; prof. U. Ill., 1983-90, prof. emeritus, 1990—. With Advanced Research Projects Agy., Dept. Def., 1959-60; industry based prof. Stevens Inst. Tech., 1968-74, Rensselaer Poly. Inst., 1975-77 Recipient Process Indsl. Div. award ASME, 1972 Fellow AIChE (Chem. Engring. Practice award 1989); mem. Nat. Acad. Engring. Office: U Ill Dept Chem and Biochem Engring 1209 W California Ave Urbana IL 61801-3705 Home: 401 Burwash Ave 127 Savoy IL 61874

MAYANS, CARLOS, former mayor; b. Havana, Cuba, July 8, 1948; arrived in US, 1962; m. Linda Schreiner, 1975; children: Joseph, Matthew, Yvette. BA, Ga. State U., 1973; MA, Webster U., 1991. Owner, founder Mayans Insurance Services, 1978—2002; Kans. state rep. Dist. 100, 1993—2003; mayor Wichita, Kans., 2003—07. Republican. Roman Catholic. Home: 1842 N Valleyview St Wichita KS 67212-6738

MAYBERRY, ALAN REED, judge; b. Akron, Ohio, Mar. 15, 1954; s. Franklin Reed Mayberry and Mark K. (Kissane) Mayberry Alexander Botten; m. Lisa Renee Rush, Dec. 19, 1981; children: Reed Alan, Mason Rush, Clark Carroll. BS in Edn., Bowling Green State U., 1975; JD, U. Toledo, 1978; postgrad., Nat. Coll. Dist. Attys., at. Law Inst. Judge Ct. of Common Pleas. Faculty Nat. Advocacy Ctr. Office: Wood County Ct of Common Pleas 1 Court House Sq Bowling Green OH 43402-2427 E-mail: amayberry@co.wood.oh.us.

MAYER, FRANK D., JR., retired lawyer; b. Dec. 23, 1933; BA, Amherst Coll., 1955; student, Cambridge U.; JD, U. Chgo., 1959. Bar: Ill. 1959. Ptnr. Mayer, Brown, Rowe & Maw, Chgo., 1959—2006, ret., 2006. Mem. ABA, Chgo. Bar Assn., Order of Coif, Phi Beta Kappa. Office: Mayer Brown Rowe and Maw 190 S La Salle St Ste 3100 Chicago IL 60603-3441 E-mail: fmayer@mayerbrown.com.

MAYER, RAYMOND RICHARD, business administration educator; b. Chgo., Aug. 31, 1924; s. Adam and Mary (Bogdala) M.; m. Helen Lakowski, Jan. 30, 1954; children: Mark, John, Mary, Jane. BS, Ill. Inst. Tech., 1948, MS, 1954, PhD, 1957. Indsl. engr. Standard Oil Co., Whiting, Ind., 1948-51; orgn. analyst Ford Motor Co., Chgo., 1951-53; instr. Ill. Inst. Tech., Chgo., 1953-56, asso. prof., 1958-60; asst. prof. U. Chgo., 1956-58; Walter F. Mullady prof. bus. adminstrn. Loyola U., Chgo., 1960—. Author: Financial Analysis of Investment Alternatives, 1966, Production Management, 1962, rev. edit., 1968, Production and Operations Management, 1975, rev. edit., 1982, Capital Expenditure Analysis, 1978. Served with USNR, 1944-46. Ingersoll Found. fellow, 1955-56; Machinery and Allied Products Inst. fellow, 1954-55; Ford Found. fellow, 1962 Mem. Acad. Mgmt., Am. Econ. Assn., Am. Statis. Assn., Am. Inst. for Decision Scis., at. Assn. Purchasing Mgmt., Polish Inst. Arts and Scis. in Am., Alpha Iota Delta, Alpha Kappa Psi, Beta Gamma Sigma. Home: 730 Green Bay Rd Winnetka IL 60093-1912 Office: 820 N Michigan Ave Chicago IL 60611-2147 Office Phone: 312-915-6595.

MAYER, ROBERT ANTHONY, retired college president; b. NYC, Oct. 30, 1933; s. Ernest John and Theresa Margaret (Mazura) M.; m. Laura Wiley Christ, Apr. 30, 1960. BA magna cum laude, Fairleigh Dickinson U., 1955; MA, NYU, 1967. With N.J. Bank and Trust Co., Paterson, 1955-61, mgr. advt. dept., 1959-61; program supr. advt. dept. Mobil Oil Co., NYC, 1961-62; asst. to dir. Latin Am. program Ford Found., NYC, 1963-65, asst. rep. Brazil, 1965-67; asst. to v.p. adminstrn., 1967-73; officer in charge logistical services Ford Found., 1968-73; asst. dir. programs N.Y. Community Trust, NYC, 1973-76; exec. dir. N.Y. State Council on the Arts, NYC, 1976-79; mgmt. cons. NYC, 1979-80; dir. Internat. Mus. Photography, George Eastman House, Rochester, NY, 1980-89, mgmt. cons., 1989-90; pres. Cleve. Inst. of Art, 1990-97; ret., 1997. Author: (plays) La Borgia, 1971, Alijandru, 1971, They'll Grow No Roses, 1975; mem. editl. adv. bd. Grants mag., 1978—80, exhibited profl. photography, 1993—. Mem. state program adv. panel NEA, 1977—80; mem. Mayor's Com. Cultural Policy, NYC, 1974—75; mem. pres.'s adv. com. Bklyn. campus L.I. U., 1978—79; bd. dirs. Fedn. Protestant Welfare Agys., NYC, 1977—79, Arts Greater Rochester, 1981—83, Garth Fagan's Dance Theatre, 1982—86; trustee Internat. Mus. Photography, 1981—89, Lacoste Sch. Arts, France, 1991—96, sec., 1994—96; mem. dean's adv. com. Grad. Sch. Social Welfare, Fordham U., 1976; mem. N.Y. State Motion Picture, TV Devel. Adv. Bd., 1984—87, N.Y. State Martin Luther King Jr. Commn., 1985—90, Cleve. Coun. Cultural Affairs, 1992—94; chmn. Greater Cleve. Regional Transit Authority Arts in Transit Com., 1992—95; bd. dirs. Friends Ariz. State U. Ctr. Latin Am. Studies, 1997—99, Villa Solana Townhouse Assn., 2001—06, pres., 2000; bd. dirs. Mesa Art Ctr. Found., 2004—06; mem. nat. armed svcs. com. YMCA, 1976. Recipient Nat. award on advocacy for girls Girls Clubs Am., 1976 Mem. Nat. Assembly State Art Agys. (bd. dirs. 1977-79, 1st vice chmn. 1978-79), Alliance Ind. Colls. Art (bd. dirs. 1983-91, vice chmn. 1986-87, sec. 1987-89), N.Y. State Assn. Museums (bd. councilors 1983-86, pres. 1986-89), Assn. Ind. Colls. Art and Design (bd. dirs. 1991-97, exec. com. 1991-93, 96-97).

MAYER, VICTOR JAMES, geologist, educator; b. Mayville, Wis., Mar. 25, 1933; s. Victor Charles and Phyllis (Bachhuber) M.; m. Mary Jo Anne White, Nov. 25, 1965; children: Gregory, Maribeth. BS Geology, U. Wis., 1956; MS Geology, U. Colo., 1960, PhD Sci. Edn., 1966. Tchr. Colo. Pub. Schs., 1961—85; asst. prof. SUNY, Oneonta, 1965—67, Ohio State U., Columbus, 1967—70, assoc. prof., 1970—75, prof. ednl. studies, geol. scis. and natural resources, 1975—95, prof. emeritus, 1995—; affiliate prof. U. Northern Colo., 2005—. Co-organizer symposa 29th and 31st Internat. Geol. Congresses; internat. sci. edn. assistance to individuals and orgns. in Japan, Korea, Taiwan, Russia, and Venezuela; dir. NSF Insts., program leadership Earth Sys. Edn., 1990-95; dir. Korean Sci. Tchrs. Insts., 1986-88, 95, 2005-07; co-convenor Second Internat. conf. Geosci. Edn., Hilo, Hawaii, 1997; disting. vis. prof. SUNY, Plattsburg, 1994; vis. rsch. scholar Hyogo U., Japan, 1996; sr. Fulbright rschr. Shizuoka U., Japan, 1998; vis. prof. Korea Nat. U. Edn., 2000; Fulbright prof. Pusan Nat. U. Korea, 2003-04, spkr. in field. Author, editor: books Global Science Literacy, 2002, Implementing Global Science Literacy, 2003, with Jeonghee Nam and Hyonyong Lee The Earth System Approach to Integrated Science (in Korean), 2006; contbr. articles to profl. jours. With USAR. Recipient Lifetime Disting. Svc. award Internat. Earth Sci. Edn. Cmty., 1997; named Disting. Investigator Ohio Sea Grant Program, 1983 Fellow AAAS (chmn. edn. 1988-89), Ohio Acad. Sci. (v.p. 1978-79, exec. com. 1993-94, Outstanding univ. educator 1995); mem. NSTA (bd. dirs. 1984-86), Sci. Edn. Coun. Ohio (pres. 1987-88), Sigma Xi, Phi Delta Kappa Roman Catholic. Avocation: photography. Home and Office: 8483 Sand Dollar Dr Windsor CO 80528 Personal E-mail: mayer.4@osu.edu.

MAYERLE, THOMAS MICHAEL, lawyer; b. Grand Rapids, Minn., Jan. 5, 1948; s. James Raphael and Frances (Kosher) M.; m. Susan Terry Potter, Oct. 9, 1976; children— Jennifer Leigh, Scott Michael, Robert Michael. A.B., Dartmouth Coll., 1970; J.D. magna cum laude, U. Minn., 1973. Bar: Minn. 1973, U.S. Ct. Appeals (D.C. cir.) 1973. Law clk. to justice U.S. Ct. Appeals (D.C. cir.), Washington, 1973-74; ptnr. Faegre & Benson, Mpls., 1974—. Note and articles editor Minn. Law Rev., 1972-73. Mem. Minn. State Bar Assn., Hennepin

County Bar Assn., Am. Coll. Real Estate Lawyers, Order of Coif. Home: 5905 Chapel Dr Minneapolis MN 55439-1716 Office: Faegre & Benson 2200 Wells Fargo Ctr 90 S 7th St Minneapolis MN 55402-3901 E-mail: tmayerle@faegre.com.

MAYES, PAUL EUGENE, engineering educator, consultant; b. Frederick, Okla., Dec. 21, 1928; s. Robert Franklin and Bertha Ellen (Walter) M.; m. Lola Mae Davis, June 4, 1950; children: Gwynne Ellen, Linda Kay, Stuart Franklin, Patricia Gail, Steven Lee, David Thomas. BS in Elec. Engring., U. Okla., 1950; MS in Elec. Engring., Northwestern U., 1952, PhD, 1955. Rsch. asst. Northwestern U., Evanston, Ill., 1950-54; asst. prof. U. Ill., Urbana, 1954-58, assoc. prof., 1958-63, prof., 1963-93, prof. emeritus, 1994—. Tech. cons. Author: Electromagnetics for Engineers, 1965; contbr. articles to profl. jours.; inventor in field. Fellow IEEE. Avocations: woodworking, hiking, model railroading. Home: 1508 Waverly Dr Champaign IL 61821-5002 Office: U Ill 1406 W Green St Urbana IL 61801-2918 E-mail: p.mayes@insightbb.com.

MAYLAND, KENNETH THEODORE, economist; b. Miami, Fla., Nov. 17, 1951; s. Herbert and Vera (Bob) M; m. Gail Fern Bassok, Apr. 14, 1984. BS, MIT, Cambridge, Mass., 1973; MS, U. Pa., Phila., 1976, PhD, 1979. Cons. economist Data Resources, Inc., Lexington, Mass., 1973; economist, then chief economist First Pa. Bank, Phila., 1973-89; sr. v.p., chief economist Soc. Nat. Bank, Cleve., 1989-94; sr. v.p., chief fin. economist Key Corp., Cleve., 1994-96, sr. v.p., chief economist, 1996-2000; pres. ClearView Econs., LLC, 2000—. Econs. instr., Chartered Fin. Aanalysts Assn., Phila, 1984—; econ. adv. com. Phila. Econ. Devel. Coalition, 1984-86; chmn. econ. adv. com. Pa. Bankers Assn., Harrisburg, 1982-84; mem. Gov.'s Econ. Adv. Com., Ohio, 1989—. Contbr. semi-monthly periodical Money Markets, 1981-85, quar. periodical Regional Report, 1980-89, EconViewpoint/KeyViewpoint biweekly periodical, 1989-2000, Regional Rev. quar. periodical, 1989-94, ClearView on the Economy, 2000—. Mem. curriculum adv. com. Widener U., 1986-89. Named 2d Best Forecaster for 2003, USA Today survey panel, Top Forecaster mid-2003 to mid-2004, Bloomberg Mag., 2004, #1 Most Accurate Forecaster, BusinessWeek, 2006; recipient Lawrence R. Klein award, 2007. Mem. Am. Bankers Assn. (econ. adv. com. 1990-93), Internat. Econ. Roundtable (vice chmn. 1987-88, chmn. 1988-90), Nat. Assn. Bus. Economists (New Face for the Eighties award 1979), Phila. Coun. Bus. Economists (pres. 1982-84), Cleve. Bus. Economist Club (sec.-treas. 1990-91, v.p. 1991-92, pres. 1992-93). Avocations: fishing, badminton, gardening, camping. Office: 3237 Fox Hollow Dr Cleveland OH 44124-5426 Office Phone: 216-595-9931.

MAYNARD, JOHN RALPH, lawyer; b. Mar. 5, 1942; s. John R. Maynard and Frances Jane (Mitchell) Maynard Kendryk; m. Meridee J. Sagadin, Sept. 11, 1995; children: Bryce James, Pamela Ann. BA, U. Wash., 1964; JD, Calif. Western U., San Diego, 1972; LLM, Harvard U., 1973. Bar: Calif. 1972, Wis. 1973. Assoc. Whyte & Hirschboeck, Milw., 1973-78, Minahan & Peterson, Milw., 1979-91, Quarles & Brady, Milw., 1991-2000, Davis & Kuelthau, Milw., 2000—05, Maynard, McIlnay, Schmitt & Button, Grafton, Wis., 2005—. Bd. dirs. Transitional Living Svcs., Inc., 1999—2003; pres. Milw. Chamber Orch., 2000—02; mem. Wis. Adv. Coun. to U.S. SBA, 1987—89; bd. dirs. Am. Heart Assn., 1979—82, Found. Internal Medicine Exchange, 2004—, Bel Canto Chorus, 2004—. Mem.: ABA, Harvard Club (Wis.). Home: 809 E Lake Forest Ave Milwaukee WI 53217-5377 Office: Maynard McIlnay Schmitt & Button 1150 Washington St Grafton WI 53024 Office Phone: 262-387-4980. Business E-Mail: jmaynard@runbox.com.

MAYNARD, OLIVIA P., foundation administrator; m. S. Olof Karlstrom. BA, Geroge Washington U., 1959; MSW, U. Mich., 1971. Dir. Mich. Office Svcs. to Aging, 1983—90; tchr. Sch. Social Work U. Mich., Mich. State U.; tchr. Ctr. for Aging Edn. Lansing (Mich.) C.C.; pres. Mich. Prospect for Renewed Citizenship, Flint, Mich., 1992—. Del. White House Conf. on Aging, 1995. Regent U. Mich., Ann Arbor; chmn. Mich. Dem. Party, 1973—82; candidate Lt. Gov. of Mich., 1990; trustee Charles Stewart Mott Found.; bd. dirs. Nature Conservancy of Mich., McLaren Regional Medical Ctr., Council of Mich. Found. Democrat. Office: orthbank Ctr Ste 406 432 N Saginaw St Flint MI 48502 also: Mich Prospect 2248 Mt Hope Rd Ste 101 Okemos MI 48864

MAYNARD, ROBERT HOWELL, retired lawyer; b. San Antonio, Feb. 15, 1938; s. William Simpson Sr. and Lillian Isabel (Tappan) M.; m. Joan Marie Pearson, Jan. 6, 1962; children: Gregory Scott, Patricia Kathryn, Alicia Joan, Elizabeth Simms. BA, Baylor U., 1959, LLB, 1961; LLM, Georgetown U., 1965. Bar: Tex. 1961, D.C. 1969, Ohio 1973. Trial atty. gen. litigation sect. lands div. U.S. Dept. Justice, Washington, 1964-65; spl. asst. to solicitor U.S. Dept. Interior, Washington, 1965-69; legis. asst. U.S. Senate, Washington, 1969-73; ptnr., dept. head Smith & Schnacke, Dayton, Ohio, 1973-83; dir. Ohio EPA, Columbus, Ohio, 1983-85; ptnr., environ. policy and strategy devel., tech. law Vorys, Sater, Seymour and Pease, Columbus, 1985-2000; ret., 2000; pres. Tappan Woods LLC, 2001—. Trustee Ohio Found. for Entrepreneurial Edn., Bus. Tech. Ctr., 1994-2000, Episcopal Cmty. Svcs. Found., 1990-96, Columbus Technology Coun., 1992-2001, Johnson's Island Preservation Soc. USNR, 1962-65. Episcopalian.

MAYNE, LUCILLE STRINGER, finance educator; b. Washington, June 6, 1924; d. Henry Edmond and Hattie Benham (Benson) Stringer; children: Pat A., Christine Gail, Barbara Marie. BS, U. Md., College Park, 1946; MBA, Ohio State U., Columbus, 1949; PhD, Northwestern U., Evanston, Ill., 1966. Instr. fin. Utica Coll., 1949-50; lectr. fin. Roosevelt U., 1961-64, Pa. State U., 1965-66, asst. prof., 1966-69, assoc. prof., 1969-70; assoc. prof. banking and fin. Case-Western Res. U., 1971-76, prof., 1976-94, prof. emerita, 1994—, grad. dean Sch. Grad. Studies, 1980-84. Sr. economist, cons. FDIC, 1977-78; cons. Nat. Commn. Electronic Fund Transfer Sys., 1976; rsch. cons. Am. Bankers Assn., 1975, Fed. Res. Bank of Cleve., 1968-70, 73; cons. Pres.'s Commn. Fin. Structure and Regulation, 1971, staff economist, 1970-71; analytical statistician Air Materiel Command, Dayton, Ohio, 1950-52; asst. to promotion mgr. NBC, Washington, 1946-48; expert witness cases involving fin. instns. Assoc. editor: Jour. Money, Credit and Banking, 1980-83, Bus. Econs., 1980-85; contbr. articles to profl. jours. Vol. Cleve. Soc. for Blind, 1979-2004, Benjamin Rose Inst., 1995-2005; mem. policyholders nominating com. Tchrs. Ins. and Annuity Assn./Coll. Retirement Equities Fund, 1982-84, chair com., 1984; bd. dirs. Women's Cmty. Found., 1994-96. Grad. scholar, Ohio State U., 1949, doctoral fellow, orthwestern U., 1963—65. Mem. LWV (bd. dirs. Shaker Heights chpt. 1999--), Midwest Fin. Assn. (pres. 1991-92, bd. dirs. 1975-79, officer 1988-93), Phi Kappa Phi, Beta Gamma Sigma. Episcopalian. Home: 3723 Normandy Rd Cleveland OH 44120-5246 Office: Case Western Res U Weatherhead Sch Mgmt U Circle Cleveland OH 44106-7235 Business E-Mail: lucille.mayne@case.edu.

MAYR, JAMES JEROME, fertilizer company executive; b. Beaver Dam, Wis., Aug. 19, 1942; s. Alfred A. and Maxine E. (Kuehl) M.; m. Carol Ann Kaufman, Sept. 4, 1965; children: Christin and Carin (twins), Cathy, Conni. BS in Agrl. Econs., U. Wis., 1964. Mgr. trainee Oscar Mayer, Madison, Wis., 1964-65; v.p. Mayr's Seed and Feed, Beaver Dam, 1966-78; product mgr. Chem. Enterprises, Houston, 1978-80; gen. mgr. Coash, Inc., Bassett, Nebr., 1981-88, v.p., 1989; mgr. Blicks Agri-Farm Ctr., Inc., Scott City, Kans., 1990-91; area mgr. Rosen's Inc., Fairmont, Minn., 1992-95, Helena Chem. Co., Rochester, Minn., 1995—. Cons. Beaver Dam, 1971-75; spkr. fertilizer orgns., Wis. Advisor U. Wis. Coll. Agriculture; mem. com. Upper Elk Horn Natural Resources Dist., Oneill, Nebr., 1985-86. Mem. Wis. Fertilizer Assn. (bd. dirs. 1970-74), Nat. Fertilizer and Solutions Assn., Nebr. Fertilizer and Chem. Assn. Lodges: KC (dep. grand knight 1978-80, 81-85, Man of Yr. 1982). Republican. Roman Catholic. Avocations: target shooting, hunting, fishing, teaching target shooting. Home: 2550 Oak Hills Dr SW Rochester MN 55902-1263 Office Phone: 507-285-5886. Personal E-mail: jmayrusa@charter.net.

MAYS, CAROL JEAN, state legislator; b. Independence, Mo., July 16, 1933; m. Ronald H. Mays; children: Terri, Melanie, Hugh. Student, Baker U. State rep., chmn. consumer protection edn. appropriations com., mem. transp., ways & means & comm. coms. Mo. Ho. of Reps., Jefferson City. Restaurant owner. Mem. Mo. Restaurant Assn., Independence C. of C., Fairmount Comml. Club, Alpha Chi Omega. Democrat. Methodist. Home: 3603 S Hedges Ave Independence MO 64052-1167

MAYS, CAROLENE, state representative; 1 child, Jada. BA in Bus. Mgmt. and Mktg., Ind. State U. Various pos. in sales, corp. acct. mgmt., customer svc., and product distbn. Occidental Chem. Co., San Francisco, Dallas, and Mpls.; mgr. customer svc. and nat. accts. Mays Chem. Co.; pres., gen. mgr. The Indianapolis Recorder, 1998—; state rep. dist. 94 Ind. Ho. of Reps., Indpls., 2002—, mem. human affairs, judiciary, pub. health, and ways and means coms. Host, weekly TV news segment Community Link WISH-TV Ch. 8, Ctrl. Ind. Bd. dirs. Ind. Sports Corp. Bd., U. Indpls.; mem. Ind. Supreme Ct. Commn. for Racial and Gender Fairness; bd. dirs. Indpls. Downtown Mktg., Inc.; apptd. by mayor Indpls. Neighborhood Housing Partnership Bd.; adv. bd. Julian Ctr., NCAA Citizenship Through Sports Alliance/Common Ground; bd. dirs. Shrewsberry & Assocs., Peyton Manning's PeyBack Found.; apptd. by mayor Greater Indpls. Progress Com.; past bds. and coms. 2001 World Police and Fire Games Exec. Com., Indy Jazz Fest, Ind. Repertory Theatre, Ind. Sch. Champions, Ind. Pvt. Industry Coun., Girls, Inc., United Way's Ardeth Burkhart Series exec. com., Freetown Village Bd., chair Circle City Classic Coaches Luncheon 2000 NCAA Final Four Com., chair comm. World's Largest Christmas Tree, coord. Ind. Sch. Champions Camp, numerous other planning coms., workshops and speaking engagements. Named one of Women to Watch, Indpls. Bus. Jour.; recipient Disting. Alumni award, Ind. State U., Martin Luther King Ctr. Living the Legacy award, 2002, Media award, Ind. Black Expo, 2002, Trailblazer award, Women's Expo, 2001, Presdl. citation, Nat. Newspaper Pubs. Assn., 2000. Mem.: Nat. Coun. Negro Women (named Woman in the Bethune Tradition 2001), United Way Minority Key Club, Alpha Kappa Alpha (Regional Comm. award 2002). Democrat. Avocations: skiing, cooking. Office: Ind Ho of Reps 200 W Washington St Indianapolis IN 46204-2786

MAYS, DOUG, state representative, lawyer; b. 1947; m. Lena Mays. BA, U. Ky.; JD, U. Ark., Little Rock. Mem. Kans. State House, 1992—, House Spkr., 2002—. Mem. Calendar and Printing com.; vice chair Interstate Cooperation Legis. Branch Budget Select Com. on Revenue Amortization. Office: State Capitol, Rm 380-W Topeka KS 66612

MAYS, J. C., automotive executive; b. 1955; Grad., Art Ctr. Coll. of Design, 1980. Designer Audi AG, Ingolstad, Germany, 1980—83, BMW, Munich, 1983—84; sr. designer Audi AG, Ingolstad, Germany, 1984—89; chief designer Volkswagon of Am., Simi Valley, Calif., 1989—93; design dir. Audi AG, Ingolstad, Germany, 1993—95; v.p. design devel. SHR Perceptual Mgmt., Scottsdale, 1995—97; v.p. design Ford Motor Co., Dearborn, Mich., 1997—2003, group v.p. design, 2003—, chief creative officer, 2005—. Design (exhibitions) "Retrofuturism: The Car Design of J. Mays", Geffen Mus. Contemporary Art LA, 2002. Named a Master of Design, Fast Company mag., 2004; recipient Excellence in Design award, Harvard Design Sch., 2002, Don Kubly Profl. Attainment award, 2002. Office: Ford Motor Co One American Rd Dearborn MI 48126-1899

MAYS, M. DOUGLAS, state legislator, financial consultant; b. Pittsburg, Kans., Aug. 18, 1950; s. Marion Edmund and Lilliemae Ruth (Norris) M.; m. Lena M. Krog, June 10, 1971; children: Jessica, Aaron. BFA, Pittsburg State U., 1972; postgrad., Washburn U., 1973—. Registered rep. Waddell & Reed, Inc., Topeka, 1981-83, Paine Webber Jackson & Curtis, Topeka, 1983-85, Columbian Securities, Topeka, 1985-87; commr. securities State of Kans., Topeka, 1987-91; pres. Mays & Assocs., Topeka, 1991—; mem. Kans. Ho. Reps., Topeka, 1993—, asst. majority leader, 1997-99, spkr. pro tem, 1999—2001, spkr., 2003—. Adminstrv. law judge various securities proceedings, 1987—; with securities and commodities fraud working group U.S. Dept. Justice, 1988-90; with penny stock task force SEC, 1988-90; del. Commonwealth Secretariat Symposium Comml. Crime, Cambridge, Eng., 1989; securities arbitrator, 1991—. Rep. precinct committeeman Shawnee County, Kans., 1976—, county chmn., 1978-82; mem. 2d Dist. Rep. State Com., Kans., 1976-86, 92—; mem. Kans. Rep. State Com., 1976-87; Senate steering com. Kassebaum for Senate campaign, 1978; chmn., mgr. Hoferer for Senate campaign, 1984; campaign coord., dir. fin. Hayden for Gov., 1986; mem. pub. bldg. commn. City of Topeka, 1985-86, bldg. and fire appeals bd., 1986-89, dep. mayor, 1987-88; mem. Topeka City Coun., 1985-89; exec. bd. Topeka/Shawnee County Interngovtl. Coun., 1986-89; adv. bd. Topeka Performing Arts Ctr., 1989-90; active Topeka/Shawnee County Met. Planning Commn., 1992—, chmn., 1994-97. Mem. North Am. Securities Adminstrs. Assn. (chmn. enforcement sect. 1988-89, pres.-elect, bd. dirs. 1989-90, pres. 1990-91), Nat. Assn. Securities Dealers, Nat. Futures Assn. (bd. arbitrators), Internat. Orgn. Securites Commns. (inter-Am. activities consultative com. 1990, pres.'s com. 1990, del. 1990). Methodist. Home: 1920 SW Damon Ct Topeka KS 66611-1926 Office: Kans Ho Reps State Capitol Topeka KS 66612

MAYS, WILLIAM G., chemical company executive; MBA, Ind. U. Test chemist Linkbelt Facility, Indpls.; acct. mgr. Procter & Gamble; market planning Eli Lilly and Co.; asst. to pres. Cummins Engine Co.; founder, pres. Mays Chem. Co., Indpls., 1980—. Bd. dirs. NBD-Inc. Mem. exec. com., bd. dirs. United Way Ctrl. Ind., Ind. Conv. and Visitors Assn.; bd. dirs. Associated Group, Corp. Cmty. Coun., Ind. Univ. Found., Cmty. Leaders Allied for Superior Schs.; mem. dean's adv. coun. Ind. U. Sch. Bus.; mem. pres.'s coun. Ind. U.; co-chmn. Coca-Cola Circle City Classic; elder Witherspoon Presbyn. Ch. Recipient Man of Yr. award B'Nai B'Rith Isidora Feibleman award, 1990, Elder Watson Diggs Achievement award Kappa Alpha Psi, 1991, Ind. Minority Small Bus. Advocate of Yr. award, 1991, Sagamore of Wabash award Gov. Ind., 1991, Ind. Enterprise award, 1992, Ind. Christian Leadership Conf. Businessman of Yr. award, 1992, Disting. Hooser, 1992, 13th in Black Enterprise Mag. Top 100 Indsl./Svc Cos., 'Above and Beyond' award Ind. Black Expo, 1992, Pres.'s award Black Pres.'s Roundtable Assn., 1992, Vol. Fund Raiser award, 1992, Anti-Defamation League Americanizm award, 1993, Charles Whistler award, 1993, Indpls. Edn. Assn.'s Human Rights award, 1994, Ind. State Conf. NAACP Labor and Industry award, 1994, Robert W. Briggs Humanitarian award, 1995, and numerous others; carried Olympic flame during trip through Indpls., 1995. Mem. Ind. C. of C. (bd. dirs.), Indpls. C. of C. (exec. com., bd. dirs.). Office: Mays Chemical Co Inc PO Box 50915 Indianapolis IN 46250-0915

MAYSENT, HAROLD WAYNE, hospital administrator; b. Tacoma, Wash., June 26, 1923; s. Wayne L. Shivley and Esther Pierce M.; m. Marjorie Ellen Hodges, June 13, 1953; children: Jeffrey, Nancy, Brian, Gregory. BA, U. Wash., 1950; MS in Hosp. Adminstrn. with distinction, Northwestern U., 1954. Adminstrv. resident Passavant Meml. Hosp., 1953-54, adminstrv. asst., 1954-55; research asso. hosp. adminstrn. Northwestern U., Evanston, Ill., 1954-55; with Lankenau Hosp., Phila., 1955-72, dir., 1963-67, exec. dir., 1967-72; exec. v.p. Rockford (Ill.) Meml. Hosp., 1972-75, pres., 1975-91, Rockford Meml. Corp., 1983-91, pres. emeritus, 1991—; pres. The Rockford Group, 1983-91. Tchg. assoc. Rockford Sch. Medicine, U. Ill., 1974-89, adj. assoc. prof., 1989-92; mem. Ill. Health Facility Planning Bd., 1980-92; chmn. bd. Ill. Hosp. Joint Ventures, Inc., 1977-78, Vol. Hosps. Am. Midwest Partnership, 1985-89. Contbr. articles to profl. jours. Chmn.-elect Coll. Healthcare Execs., 1988-89, chmn., 1989; coach, adminstr. Broomal (Pa.) Little League, 1962-72; bd. dirs. Community Health Assn., 1964-70, Rockford Med. Edn. Found., 1972-87, Tri State Hosp. Assembly, 1978-80, Rockford Coun. 100, 1987-91, exec. com. 1987-91. With AUS, 1942-46. Recipient Malcolm T. MacEachern award Northwestern U., 1954, Laura G. Jackson Alumni Assn. award, 198, Disting. Svc. award Ill. Hosp. Assn., 1989. Fellow Am. Coll. Hosp. Adminstrs. (life, Ill. regent 1979-84, dist. bd. govs. 1984-88, gov. 1984-88, chmn. elect 1988-89, chmn. 1989-90, past chmn. 1990-91); mem. Am. Hosp. Assn. (com. on vols. 1976-80, coun. patient svcs. 1980-82, ho. of dels. 1977-84, rep. Am. Acad. Pediatrics com. on hosp. care 1983-85), Pa. Hosp. Assn. (bd. dirs. 1965-68), Ill. Hosp. Assn. (trustee 1973-79, sec. 1974-76, chmn. elect 1977, chmn. bd. trustees 1978, named Outstanding Leader in Hosp. Industry 1978, Disting. Svc. award 1989). Office: Rockford Meml 2400 N Rockton Ave Rockford IL 61103-3681

MAZANY, TERRY, foundation administrator; BA in Anthropology, MA in Anthropology, MBA, U. Ariz. Positions in public sch. adminstrn. Mich. Sch. Dist.; former assoc. superintendent for curriculum and instruction Oakland Unified Sch. Dist., Calif.; former dir. orgnl. learning and devel. Calif. Sch. Leadership Acad.; dir., sr. prog. officer for ed. initiative Chgo. Cmty. Trust, 2001—03, COO, 2003—04, pres., CEO, 2004—. Office: Chgo Cmty Trust 111 E Wacker Dr Ste 1400 Chicago IL 60601

MAZE, THOMAS H., engineering educator; b. St. Paul, June 1, 1952; s. Robert O. and Viola A.E. (Schultz) M.; m. Leslie Foster Smith, Aug. 2, 1979; children: Lauren L. Simonds, Julie W. Simonds. BS in Civil Engring., Iowa State U., 1975; M of Engring., Urban and Pub. Systems, U. Calif., Berkeley, 1977; PhD in Civil Engring., Mich. State U., 1982. Asst. prof. dept. civil engring. Wayne State U., 1979-82; assoc. prof. sch. civil engring. and environ. sci. U. Okla., Norman, 1982-87; prof. dept. civil and construction engring. Iowa State U., Ames, 1988—, prof. in-charge transp. planning program, 1987—, dir. ctr. for transp. rsch. and edn., ext. and applied rsch., 1988-99; v.p. H.R. Green Corp., St. Paul, 1999—. Assoc. dir. inst. urban transp., transp. rsch. ctr. Ind. U., Bloomington, 1987—; dir. Midwest Transp. Ctr., U.S. Dept. Transp.'s Univ. Transp. Ctr. Fed. Region VII, 1990-96. Mem. ASCE, Am. Pub. Transit Assn., Its Am. (founding, instl. issues com., CVO com.), Am. Pub. Works Assn. (adj. workshop faculty mem. 1986-91, exec. coun. inst. equipment svcs. 1991—), Coun. Univ. Transp., Transp. Rsch. Bd. (mem. various coms., chair 8th equipment mgmt. conf. 1990), Inst. Transp. Engrs. (assoc. mem. dept. 6 standing com., chmn. various coms., pres. U. Fla. student chpt. 1976-79), Chi Epsilon (faculty advisor U. Okla. 1985-87), Sigma Xi. Office: 2550 University Ave W #400N Saint Paul MN 55114-1052

MAZIAR, CHRISTINE M., academic administrator; BSEE, MSEE, Purdue U., PhD in Elec. Engring. Mem. faculty U. Tex., 1987—98, vice provost, 1995—98; faculty mem. U. Minn., Mpls., 1998—, v.p. for rsch., dean Grad. Sch., 1998—2002, exec. v.p., provost, 2002—04; mem. faculty U. Notre Dame, Ind., 2004—. Contbr. articles to profl. jours. Recipient Presdl. Young Investigator award, NSF, 1990, Tech. Excellence award, Semiconductor Rsch. Corp., 1992. Home: Office of Provost 800 Main Blvd Notre Dame IN 46556

MAZZE, ROGER STEVEN, medical educator, researcher; b. NYC, May 14, 1943; s. Harry Alan and Mollie (Schneider) M.; m. Rochelle Linda March, Dec. 28, 1969; children— Aaron, Rebekkah BA, Queens Coll., 1965, MA, 1967; PhD, U. Ill., 1971. Fellow in social psychiatry Brandeis U., Waltham, Mass., 1971; chmn. urban studies Fordham U., NYC, 1970-75; from assoc. to full prof. epidemiololgy and social medicine Einstein Coll. Medicine, NYC, 1975-87, exec. dir. Diabetes Research and Tng. Ctr., 1980-88; sr. v.p. research and devel. Internat. Diabetes Ctr., Mpls., 1988—; clin. prof. U. Minn. Med. Sch., 1988—; v.p. Inst. for Rsch. and Edn., Health Sys. Minn., Mpls., 1993—. Adv. bd. Nat. Diabetes Info. Clearinghouse, Washington, 1980-84, Pa. Diabetes Acad., Harrisburg, 1982—; co-dir. WHO Coll. Ctr. in Diabetes Care, Edn. and Computer Sci., Mpls., 1988—. Author: Narcotics, Knowledge and Nonsense, 1977, Professional Education in Diabetes, 1983, Frontiers of Diabetes Research, 1990, Staged Diabetes Management, 1995, Stage Diabetes Management: A Systemic Approach, 2000; editor: Practical Diabetes, 1987-89; contbr. articles to profl. jours. Active Internat. Diabetes Fedn., European Assn. for Study of Diabetes; chmn. Am. Diabetes Assn. Named Disting. vis. Scientist CDC, 1983-84; Hoechst lectr. Australian Diabetes Soc., 1985, 87, Japanese Diabetes Assn., 1983, 88, 93, 94, 99, Polish Diabetes Assn., 1993, 94, 95, 96, 99; named Best Spkr. of Yr., Soc. for Clin. Chemistry, 1991, Minn. Med. Alley award for excellence in rsch. and devel., 1995; grantee NIH, 1977—, ADA, 1991—, Juvenile Diabetes Found., 1992—; recipient Rschr. of Yr. award Inst. for Rsch. and Edn., 2000. Mem. Am. Diabetes Assn (chmn.), Internat. Diabetes Fedn., European Assn. for Study Diabetes. Home: 5870 Boulder Bridge Ln Excelsior MN 55331-7969 Office: Internat Diabetes Ctr 3800 Park Nicollet Blvd Minneapolis MN 55416-2527 E-mail: mazzer@hsmnet.com.

MCALISTER, ROBERT BEATON, lawyer; b. NYC, Oct. 5, 1932; s. Richard Charles and Martha Olive (Weisenbarger) McA.; widowed; children: Michael, Peter, Betsy. AB, Kenyon Coll., 1954; JD, U. Mich., 1957. Ptnr. Alexander, Ebinger, Fisher, McAlister & Lawrence, Columbus, Ohio, 1957-85; supt. Ohio Div. Savs. & Loan Assns., Columbus, 1985; ptnr. Baker & Hostetler, Columbus, 1985—, chmn. litigation dept., 1988-93. Exec. com. mem. Ohio Dem. Party, Columbus, 1967-74; active Dem. at. Com., Washington, 1972-76; counsel Gov. Richard F. Celeste, Columbus, 1982-90, Senator John Glenn, Washington, 1986-98. With USAF, 1968-64. Fellow Ohio Bar Found., Columbus Bar Found. Democrat. Episcopalian. Home: 77 E Nationwide Blvd Columbus OH 43215-2539 Office: Baker & Hostetler 65 E State St Ste 2100 Columbus OH 43215-4260

MCALLISTER, STEPHEN ROBERT, dean, law educator; b. Lawrence, Kans., Nov. 27, 1962; s. Stephen Ray and Rhoda Alice (Bening) McA.; m. Suzanne Carey McAllister, Feb. 26, 2004. BA in Econs., U. Kans., 1985, JD, 1988. Bar: Ill. 1989, U.S. Ct. Appeals (7th cir.) 1989. Law clk. to Hon. Richard Posner U.S. Ct. Appeals (7th cir.), Chgo., 1988-89; law clk. to Hon. Byron R. White U.S. Supreme Ct., Washington, 1989—91; assoc. Gibson, Dunn & Crutcher, Washington, 1992—93; vis. assoc. prof. U. Kans. Sch. Law, 1993—95, assoc. prof., 1995—98, prof., 1999—, assoc. dean Academic Affairs, 1999—2000, dean, 2000—05. Interim dir. Dole Inst. Politics, 2003—04. Recipient Dean Frederick J. Moreau Award, 1997; grantee W.T. Kemper Fellowship, 1999. Fellow: Am. Bar Found.; mem.: Supreme Ct. Hist. Soc. (trustee), Order of Coif. Office: U Kans Sch Law 1535 W 15th St Lawrence KS 66045 E-mail: stever@ku.edu.

MCARDLE, RICHARD JOSEPH, retired academic administrator; b. Omaha, Mar. 10, 1934; s. William James and Abby Marie (Menzies) McA.; m. Katherine Ann McAndrew, Dec. 27, 1958; children: Bernard, Constance, Nancy, Susan, Richard. BA, Creighton U., 1955, MA, 1961; PhD, U. Nebr., 1969. Tchr. pub. high schs., Nebr., 1955-65; grad. asst. romance langs. U. Nebr., 1965-66, instr. fgn. lang. methods, 1966-69; chmn. dept. edn. Cleve. State U., 1969-70; chmn. dept. elem. and secondary edn. U. North Fla., 1971-75; dean Coll. Edn. Cleve. State U., 1975-87, prof. edn., 1987-89, spl. asst. to pres. for campus planning, 1989-91, vice provost for strategic planning, 1991-92, acting provost, v.p. for acad. affairs, 1992-94, vice provost for strategic planning, 1994-96, prof. edn., 1996-2001, ret., 2001. Cons. in field. Author articles related to issues in tchr. edn. Mem. Am. Assn. Higher Edn. Office: CASAL Dept Cleve State U Cleveland OH 44115 Business E-Mail: r.mcardle@csuohio.edu.

MCAULIFFE, RICHARD L., church official; m. Janet Bettinghaus; children: Brian, Andrea Stephenson. Student, Carleton Coll.; MBA, Harvard U. Exec. v.p., treas., CFO Harris Bankcorp, Harris Trust and Savs. Bank, 1960-90; mng. agt. Resolution Trust Corp., 1990-92; treas. Evang. Luth. Ch. in Am., Chgo., 1992—. Pres. Grace Luth. Ch., Glen Ellyn, Ill., Evang. Luth. Ch. Am. Ch. Coun.; treas. English Synod and Christ Sem.-Seminex, AELC; bd. dirs./com. mem. Christian Century Found., Luth. Gen. Healthcare Sys.; active Luth. Social Svcs. Ill. Office: Evang Luth Ch Am 8765 W Higgins Rd Chicago IL 60631-4101

MCBREEN, MAURA ANN, lawyer; b. NYC, Aug. 18, 1953; d. Peter J. and Frances S. (McVeigh) McB. AB, Smith Coll., 1975; JD, Harvard U., 1978. Bar: Ill. 1978. Ptnr. Kirkland & Ellis, Chgo., 1978-86, Isham, Lincoln & Beale (merged with Reuben & Proctor), Chgo., 1986-88, Baker & McKenzie, Chgo., 1988—. Mem. bd. dir. Juvenile Protective Assn.; mem. Econ. Club Chgo., 2004—. Auth. several articles profl. jours. Mem. bd. dir. Lyric Opera Chgo. Mem. ABA, Chgo. Bar Assn., Ill. St. Bar Assn., Midwest Pension Conf. Office: Baker & McKenzie 1 Prudential Pla 130 E Randolph Dr Ste 3700 Chicago IL 60601-6342

MCBRIDE, ANGELA BARRON, nursing educator; b. Balt., Jan. 16, 1941; d. John Stanley and Mary C. (Szczepanska) Barron; m. William Leon McBride, June 12, 1965; children: Catherine, Kara. BS in Nursing, Georgetown U., Washington, 1962; MS in Nursing, Yale U., New Haven, Conn., 1964; PhD, Purdue U., West Lafayette, Ind., 1978; doctorate of Pub. Svc. (hon.), U. Cin., 1983; LittD (hon.), Purdue U., 1998; LLD (hon.), Ea. Ky. U., 1991; LHD (hon.), Georgetown U., 1993; DSc (hon.), Med. Coll. Ohio, 1995; LHD (hon.), U. Akron, 1997. Asst. prof., rsch. asst. inst. Yale U., New Haven, 1964-73; assoc. prof., chairperson Ind. U. Sch. Nursing, Indpls., 1978-81, 80-84, prof., 1981-92, assoc. dean rsch., 1985—91, interim dean, 1991—92, univ. dean, 1992—2003, disting. prof., 1992—2005, disting. prof., univ. dean emerita, 2006—; sr. v.p. acad. affairs, nursing Clarian Health Ptnrs., 1997—2003; Am. Acad. Nursing, Am. Nurses Found. scholar-in-residence Inst. Medicine, 2003—04; Helene Denne Schulte vis. prof. U. Wis., Madison, 2006. Mem. Nat. Adv. Mental Health Coun., 1987—91; adv. com. NIH Office of Women's Health Rsch., 1997—2001, NIH Office of Women's Health Rsch. Specialized Ctrs. Rsch. on Sex and Gender Factors, 2003—06; coun. mem. Yale U. Coun., 1999—2005; ext. acad. advisor Sch. Nursing, Hong Kong Poly. U., 2000—06; adv. bd. Meth. Health Found., 2000—; advisor U. Hong Kong, 2004—, Hong Kong Acad. Nursing, 2004—; appointed to Old Master Program Purdue U., 2007. Author: The Growth and Development of Mothers, 1973 (Best Book award 1973), Living with Contradictions, A Married Feminist, 1976, How to Enjoy A Good Life With Your Teenager, 1987; editor: Psychiatric-Mental Health Nursing: Integrating the Behavioral and Biological Sciences, 1996 (Best Book award 1996); compiler: Nursing and Philanthropy, 2000. Adv. bd. Women's Fund Indpls., 2000—05;

chair Nat. Adv. Com. Nurse Faculty Scholars Program Robert Wood Johnson Found., 2007—; bd. dirs. United Way of Ctrl. Ind., 2002—06, Clarian Health Ptnrs., 2004—, chair quality and patient safety com.; mem. Yale U. Sch. Nursing Adv. Bd., 2006—, chair, 2007—. Recipient Disting. Alumna award Yale U., Disting. Alumna award Purdue U., Univ. Medallion, U. San Francisco, 1993, Hoosier Heritage award, 2000, Disting. Nurse Educator award Coll. Mt. St. Joseph, Cin., 2000, Ross Pioneering Spirit award Am. Assn. Critical-Care Nurses, 2004, Lifetime Achievement award Assn. Fundraising Profls., Ind., 2005, Woman of Achievement award, Ball State U., 2005 Torchbearer award Ind. Commn. for Women, 2005, Melva Jo Hendrix Leadership award Internat. Soc. Psychiat. Nursing, 2006; named Influential Woman in Indpls., Indpls. Bus. Jour./Ind. Lawyer, 1999, HealthCare Hero Indpls. Bus. Jour., 2003, Adele Herwitz Disting. scholar Commn. Fgn. Nursing Schs., 2005, Harold Burdette award Behaovioral Coop. Oncology Group, 2007; Kellogg nat. fellow; Am. Nurses Found. scholar, Salute to Women award Indpls. YMCA, 1999, Sagamore of Wabash, 1999. Fellow: Nat. Acads. Practice, Am. Acad. Nursing (dir. leadership devel. bldg. acad. geriatric nursing capacity program 2000—, past pres., Living Legend 2006), APA (Nursing and Health Psychology award divsn. 38 1995); mem.: Soc. for Women's Health Rsch. (bd. mem. 2007—), Nat. Acad. Scis., Inst. of Medicine (mem. bd. health policy ednl. programs and fellowships 2006—), Soc. for Rsch. in Child Devel., Midwest Nursing Rsch. Soc. (Disting. Rsch. award 1985), Sigma Theta Tau (past pres., Mentor award 1993, disting. lectr 1995—99, Melanie Dreher award for contbns. as a dean 2001), Chi Eta Phi (hon.). Home: 744 Cherokee Ave Lafayette IN 47905-1872 Home Phone: 765-474-9187; Office Phone: 317-278-9076. Business E-Mail: amcbride@iupui.edu.

MCBRIDE, BEVERLY JEAN, lawyer; b. Greenville, Ohio, Apr. 5, 1941; d. Kenneth Birt and Glenna Louise (Ashman) Whited; m. Benjamin Gary McBride, Nov. 28, 1964; children: John David, Elizabeth Ann. BA magna cum laude, Wittenberg U., 1963; JD cum laude, U. Toledo, 1966. Bar: Ohio 1966. Intern Ohio Gov.'s Office, Columbus, 1962; asst. dean women U. Toledo, 1963-65; assoc. Title Guarantee and Trust Co., Toledo, 1966-69; spl. counsel Ohio Atty. Gen.'s Office, Toledo, 1975; assoc. Cobourn, Smith, Rohrbacher and Gibson, Toledo, 1969-76; v.p., gen. counsel, sec. The Andersons Inc., Maumee, Ohio, 1976—2005, of counsel, 2005—. Exec. trustee, bd. dirs. Wittenberg U., Springfield, Ohio, 1980-83; trustee Anderson Found., Maumee, 1981-93, Toledo Cmty. Found., 2006-; mem. Ohio Supreme Ct. Task Force on Gender Fairness, 1991-94, Regional Growth Partnership, 1994—; chmn. Sylvania Twp. Zoning Commn., Ohio, 1970-80; candidate for judge Sylvania Mcpl. Ct., 1975; trustee Goodwill Industries, Toledo, 1976-82, Sylvania Cmty. Svcs. Ctr., 1976-78, Toledo-Lucas County Port Authority, 1992-99; chair St. Vincent Med. Ctr., 1992-99; founder Sylvania YWCA Program, 1973; active membership drives Toledo Mus. Art, 1977-87. Recipient Toledo Women in Industry award YWCA, 1979, Outstanding Alumnus award Wittenberg U., 1981. Fellow Am. Bar Found.; mem. ABA, AAUW, Ohio Bar Assn., Toledo Bar Assn. (pres., treas., chmn., sec. various coms.), Toledo Women Attys. Forum (exec. com. 1978-82), Pres. Club (U. Toledo exec. com.). Home: 5274 Cambrian Rd Toledo OH 43623-2626

MCBRIDE, JERRY E., state legislator; b. Licking, Mo., May 20, 1939; m. Deloris Pearl Harris, 1971; children: Heather, Jarrett, Ginger Dee. Grad. high sch., Rolla, Mo. Mem. Mo. Ho. of Reps., Jefferson City, 1974-76, 78-80, 1982—. Chmn. state parks, recreation and natural resources com., mem. agribus., rules and joint rules and appropriations, natural and econ. resources com. Mem. SAR, Mo. Sch. Mines-U. Mo. Rolla Alumni Assn. (life), Order of Stars and Bars. Democrat. Home: PO Box 292 Edgar Springs MO 65462-0292

MCBRIDE, TED, prosecutor; Clk. Chief Judge Fred J. Nichol U.S. Dist. Ct. S.D.; fed. prosecutor Rapid City (S.D.) Office, 1980—; asst. U.S. atty. S.D.; asst. dir. Atty. Gen.'s Advocacy Inst., Washington, 1992-93; U.S. atty. S.D. dist. U.S. Dept. Justice. Office: 230 S Phillips Ave Ste 600 Sioux Falls SD 57104-6325

MC BRIDE, WILLIAM LEON, philosopher, educator; b. NYC, Jan. 19, 1938; s. William Joseph and Irene May (Choffin) McB.; m. Angela Barron, July 12, 1965; children: Catherine, Kara. AB, Georgetown U., Washington, DC, 1959; postgrad. (Fulbright fellow), U. Lille, 1959-60; MA (Woodrow Wilson fellow), Yale U., New Haven, Conn., 1962, PhD (Social Sci. Rsch. Coun. fellow), 1964. Instr. philosophy Yale U., New Haven, 1964-66, asst. prof., 1966-70, assoc. prof., 1970-73; lectr. Northwestern U., Evanston, Ill., summer 1972; assoc. prof. Purdue U., West Lafayette, Ind., 1973-76, prof., 1976-2001, Arthur G. Hansen disting. prof., 2001—. Senate chmn. Purdue U., 2004-05; lectr. Korcula Summer Sch., Yugoslavia, 1971, 73; Fulbright lectr. Sofia U., Bulgaria, 1997. Author: Fundamental Change in Law and Society, 1970, The Philosophy of Marx, 1977, Social Theory at a Crossroads, 1980, (with R.A. Dahl) Demokrati og Autoritet, 1980, Sartre's Political Theory, 1991, Social and Political Philosophy, 1994, Philosophical Reflections on the Changes in Eastern Europe, 1999, From Yugoslav Praxis to Global Pathos, 2001; editor: (with C.O. Schrag) Phenomenology in a Pluralistic Context, 1983, Sartre and Existentialism, 8 vols., 1997, (with M.B. Matustik) Calvin O. Schrag and the Task of Philosophy after Postmodernity, 2002, The Idea of Values, 2003, Social and Political Philosophy, 2006. Decorated chevalier Ordre des Palmes Académiques. Mem. AAUP (pres. Purdue chpt. 1983-86, pres. Ind. conf. 1988-89), Am. Philos. Assn. (chmn. com. on internat. coop. 1992-95, bd. dirs. 1992-95), N.Am. Soc. for Social Philosophy (v.p. 1997-2000, pres. 2000-05), Am. Soc. Polit. and Legal Philosophy, Soc. Phenomenology and Existential Philosophy (exec. co-sec. 1977-80), Sartre Soc. N.Am. (chmn. bd. dirs. 1985-88, 91-93), Am. Soc. Philosophy in the French Lang. (pres. 1994-96), Fed. Internat. Soc. Philosophie (steering com. 1998—, sec. gen. 2003—). Home: 744 Cherokee Ave Lafayette IN 47905-1872 Office: Purdue U Dept Philosophy 100 N Univ St West Lafayette IN 47907-2098 Office Phone: 765-494-4285. Business E-Mail: wmcbride@purdue.edu.

MCBRIEN, RICHARD PETER, theology educator; b. Hartford, Conn., Aug. 19, 1936; s. Thomas Henry and Catherine Ann (Botticelli) McB. AA, St. Thomas Sem., 1956; BA, St. John Sem., 1958, MA, 1962; STD, Gregorian U., 1967. Assoc. pastor Our Lady of Victory Ch., West Haven, Conn., 1962-63; prof., dean of studies Pope John XXIII Nat. Sem., Weston, Mass., 1965-70; prof. theology Boston Coll., Newton, Mass., 1970-80, dir. inst. of religious edn. and pastoral ministry, 1975-80; prof. theology U. Notre Dame, Ind., 1980—, chmn. dept. Ind., 1980-91. Cons. various dioceses and religious communities in the U.S. and Can., 1965—; vis. fellow John F. Kennedy Sch. Govt. Harvard U., Cambridge, 1976-77; mem. Council on Theol. Scholarship and Research Assn. of Theol. Schs., 1987-91. Author: Do We Need Church?, 1969, Catholicism, 2 vols., 1980, rev. edit., 1994 (Christopher award 1981), Caesar's Coin: Religion and Politics in America, 1987, Report on the Church: Catholicism after Vatican II, 1992, Responses to 101 Questions on the Church, 1996, Inside Catholicism, 1996; editor: Encyclopedia of Religion, 1987, HarperCollins Encyclopedia of Catholicism, 1995, Lives of the Popes: The Pontiffs from St. Peter to John Paul II, 1997, Lives of the Saints: from Mary and St. Francis of Assisi to John XXIII and Mother Teresa. Recipient Best Syndicated Weekly Column award Cath. Press Assn. of U.S. and Can., 1975, 77, 78, 84. Mem. Cath. Theol. Soc. of Am. (pres. 1973-74, John Courtney Murray award 1976), Coll. Theology Soc., Am. Acad. Religion. Office: U of Notre Dame Dept Theology 327 O'Shaughnessy Hall Notre Dame IN 46556

MCCAFFERTY, OWEN EDWARD, accountant, dental-veterinary consultant; b. Cleve., Sept. 5, 1952; s. Owen James and Ann Theresa (Barrett) McC.; m. Colleen Maura Mullen, Aug. 3, 1974; children: Owen Michael, Hugh Anthony, Maura Kathleen, Bridget Colleen. AB, Xavier U., 1974. CPA, Ohio, Ga., S.C., Tex., Nev.; cert. vet. practice mgr. Mem. staff to sr. accountant Deloitte, Haskins, & Sells, Cleve., 1974-78; ptnr., pres. Douglas, McCafferty & Co., Inc., Rocky River, Ohio, 1978-86; pres. Owen E. McCafferty, CPA, Inc., North Olmsted, Ohio, 1986—, McCafferty/Beach Devel., Inc., North Olmsted, 1989—, Anicare N.Am., Inc., 1994—, McCafferty/Beach Devel., Inc., North Olmsted, 1989—, Anicare N.Am., Inc., 1994—2005, Profl. Study Groups, Inc., Henderson, Nev., 2005—. Lectr. various vet. and dental assns.; cons. in field; pres. Virtual Profl. Publ. Inc., 1997—, Profl Study Groups, Inc., Henderson, N.V.; mng. unit holder Prescott/McCafferty Initiative, LLC; asst. treas. Vet. Study Groups, Inc; asst. sec. treas. Equine Med. Ctr. N.Am. Co-author: The Business of Veterinary Practice, 1993; mem. editl. adv. bd. Vet. Econs. Mag., 1977-97, Vet. Bus., 1999—; contbr. articles to acctg. and vet. jours.; co-author audiotape vet. practice mgmt. series, 1997; mem. editl. bd. Vet. Bus. Jour., 1999—. Mem. fin. com. St. Richard Parish, 1987-95, chmn. budgeting com., 1991-95. Recipient Meritorius Service award Ohio Vet. Med. Assn., 1986, Am. Animal Hosp. Assn. award, 1988; Pioneer award of Assn. Vet. Practice Mgmt. Consultants and Counselors. Fellow Am. Coll. Forensic Examiners Inst.; mem. AICPA (pvt. cos. practice sect., mgmt. cons. divsn., tax divsn.), Ohio Soc. CPAs (chmn. mgmt. adv. svcs. com. Cleve. chpt. 1987-89), mem. liaison com.), Vet. Hosp. Mgrs. Assn. (pres. 1993), Vet. Practice Mgrs. Assn. Gt. Britain and Republic of Ireland (hon. life), Am. Soc. Appraisers (candidate). Democrat. Roman Catholic. Office: PO Box 819 North Olmsted OH 44070-0819 Office Phone: 440-779-1099. Business E-Mail: oemccafferty@oemcpa.com.

MCCALEB, MALCOLM, JR., lawyer; b. Evanston, Ill., June 4, 1945; BA, Colgate U., 1967; JD, Northwestern U., 1971. Bar: Ill. 1971. Atty. McCaleb, Lucas & Brugman, Chgo., 1970—85; ptnr. Keck, Mahin & Cate, Chgo., 1985—95, Foley & Lardner, Chgo., 1995—2000, Barack Ferrazzano Kirschbaum Perlman & Nagelberg, LLP, Chgo., 2000—. Chmn. Northfield (Ill.) Village Caucus, 1981-82, active, 1977-82, Northfield Zoning Commn., 1985-88; pres. bd. dirs. Vols. Am., 1977-79; active Northfield Sch. and Park Bd. Caucus, 1980-87. Mem. Chgo. Bar Assn., Bar Assn. 7th Fed. Cir., Patent Law Assn. Chgo., Internat. Trademark Assn. Office: Barack Ferrazzano Kirschbaum Perlman & Nagelberg LLC 333 W Wacker Dr Chicago IL 60606 Office Phone: 312-984-3100. Business E-Mail: mac.mccaleb@bfkpn.com.

MCCALL, CHARLES BARNARD, retired health facility administrator; b. Memphis, Nov. 2, 1928; s. John W. and Lizette (Kimbrough) McCall; m. Carolyn Jean Rosselot, June 9, 1951 (dec. Feb. 2002); children: Linda, Kim, Betsy, Cathy; m. Ernestine Mann, Jan. 5, 2004. BA, Vanderbilt U., 1950, MD, 1953. Diplomate Am. Bd. Internal Medicine, Am. Bd. Pulmonary Diseases. Intern Vanderbilt U. Hosp., Nashville, 1953-54; clin. assoc., sr. asst. surgeon USPHS, Nat. Cancer Inst., NIH, 1954-56; sr. asst. resident in medicine U. Ala. Hosp., 1956-57, chief resident, 1958-59; fellow chest diseases Nat. Acad. Scis.-NRC, 1957-58; instr. U. Ala. Med. Sch., 1958-59; from asst. prof. to assoc. prof. medicine U. Tenn. Med. Sch., 1959-69, chief pulmonary diseases, 1964-69; mem. faculty U. Tex. Sys., Galveston, 1969-75, prof. med. br., 1971-73; assoc. prof. medicine Health Sci. Ctr., Southwestern Med. Sch., Dallas, 1973-75, also assoc. dean clin. programs, 1973-75; dir. Office Grants Mgmt. and Devel., 1973-75; dean, prof. medicine U. Tenn. Coll. Medicine, 1975-77, Oral Roberts U. Sch. Medicine, Tulsa, 1977-78; interim assoc. dean U. Okla. Tulsa Med. Coll., 1978-79; clin. prof. medicine U. Colo. Med. Sch., Denver, 1979-80; prof. medicine, assoc. dean U. Okla. Med. Sch., 1980-82; exec. dean and dean U. Okla. Coll. Medicine, 1982-85; v.p. patient affairs, prof. medicine U. Tex. M. D. Anderson Cancer Ctr., 1985-94; chief of staff VA Med. Ctr., Oklahoma City, 1980-82; ret., 2004. Exec. dir. Worldwide Healthcare Svcs., Inc., Waco, Tex., 1998—2002; clinic dir. Claremore Family Medicine, 2002—04, cons., 2002; bd. dirs. Amigos Internacionales, Inc. Contbr. articles to med. jours. Fellow: ACP, Am. Coll. Chest Physicians; mem.: AMA, Am. Fedn. Clin. Rsch., So. Thoracic Soc. (pres. 1968—69), Am. Thoracic Soc., Sigma Xi, Alpha Omega Alpha. Baptist. Home: Forest Lake Dr Branson West MO 65737 Personal E-mail: mccallcharles@centurytel.net.

MC CALL, JULIEN LACHICOTTE, banker; b. Florence, SC, Apr. 1, 1921; s. Arthur M. and Julia (Lachicotte) McC.; m. Janet Jones, Sept. 30, 1950; children: Melissa, Alison Gregg, Julien Lachicotte Jr. BS, Davidson Coll., 1942, LLD (hon.), 1983; MBA, Harvard U., 1947. With First Nat. City Bank, NYC, 1948-71, asst. mgr. bond dept., 1952-53, asst. cashier, 1953-55, asst. v.p., 1955-57, v.p., 1957-71; 1st v.p. Nat. City Bank, Cleve., 1971-72, pres., 1972-79, chmn., 1979-85, chief exec. officer, from 1979, also bd. dirs.; pres. Nat. City Corp., 1973-80, chmn., chief exec. officer, 1980-86, also bd. dirs., cons. Mem. fed. adv. coun. Fed. Res. Bd., 1984-87. Trustee St. Luke's Found., United Way Services, Boy Scouts Am., Playhouse Sq. Found., Cleve. Mus. Natural History. To 1st lt. Ordinance Corps US Army, 1942—46, Aftrica, ETO. Mem. Pepper Pike Club, Chagrin Valley Hunt Club, Mountain Lake Club (Lake Wales, Fla.), Rolling Rock Club (Ligonier, Pa.). Episcopalian. Office: 30195 Chagrin Blvd Ste 104W Pepper Pike OH 44124-5703 Home: Mountain Lake PO Box 832 Lake Wales FL 33859

MCCALL-RODRIGUEZ, LEONOR, healthcare services company executive, entrepreneur; b. Chgo., Feb. 21, 1958; d. Sixto Rodriguez Hernandez and Dolores Leonor Jimenez de Rodriguez; m. Dean W. McCall, July 14, 2002; stepchildren: Samantha Lynn McCall, Christopher Dean McCall. Licenciatura in Econs., Universidad Nacional Autónoma de México, Mexico City, 1982; MBA, Universidad de Las Americas, Mexico City, 1998. Lic. economist Secretaria de Educación Publica, Mexico. Mktg. mgr. Casa Pedro Domecq, Mexico City, 1984—90, Braun divsn. Gillette, Mexico City, 1990—91, PepsiCo-Frito Lay, Mexico City, 1991—97, La Opinion, LA, 1999—2000; pres. Bus. and Mktg. Solutions, Mexico City, 1997—99; v.p. Face to Face Mktg., Inc., Pasadena, Calif., 2000—03; gen. mgr. Walker Advt., Inc., San Pedro, Calif., 2000; pres., founder Mira Promo, Inc., Redondo Beach, Calif., 2003—04, Latino Speakers Bur., Redondo Beach, 2003—; v.p., emerging mkts. WellPoint Inc., Indianapolis, Ind., 2004—. Adj. prof. econs. Universidad Nacional Autónoma de México, Mexico City, 1982—84. Author: (short stories) Cuentos de Juanita La Ranita, 2004; editor, translator: novel La Quileña, 2004. Vol. art tchr. 1736 Family Crisis Ctr., LA, 2000—03; nat. bus. adv. coun. Rainbow Push Coalition. Named Corp. Leader of the Yr., Nat. Latina Bus. Women Assn., 2006. Mem.: Mexican Am. Nat. Assn. (assoc.), Women's Bus. Entrepreneurs Nat. Coun. (assoc.), Nat. Assn. Women Bus. Owners (assoc.), Latin Bus. Assn. (assoc.). Democrat. Roman Catholic. Avocations: writing, reef aquaria, travel.

MCCALLUM, J. D., manufacturing executive; b. 1920; With Darling & Co. (subs.), 1939—; v.p. Darling-Delaware Co., Chgo., 1965—75, pres., 1975—. Dir. Darling-Delaware Co. Office: Darling-Delaware Co Inc 4650 S Racine Ave Chicago IL 60609-3321

MCCALLUM, LAURIE RIACH, state government lawyer; b. Virginia, Minn., Aug. 19, 1950; d. Keith Kelvin and Maybelle Louella (Hanson) Riach; m. J. Scott McCallum, June 19, 1979; children: Zachary, Rory, Cara. BA, U. Ariz., Tucson, 1972; JD, So. Meth. U., Dallas, 1977. Bar: Wis. 1977. Consumer atty. Office of Commr. of Ins., Madison, Wis., 1977-79; asst. legal counsel Gov. of Wis., Madison, Wis., 1979-82; mng. ptnr. Petri and McCallum Law Firm, Fond du Lac, Wis., 1979-80; exec. dir. Wis. Coun. on Criminal Justice, Madison, 1981-82; commr. Wis. Pers. Commn., Madison, 1982—2002, chairperson, 1988—2002; commr. Wis. Labor and Industry Rev. Commn., 2002—03, sr. rev. atty., 2003—. Mem. gov.'s jud. selection com. Supreme Ct., 1993; dir. State Bar Labor Law Sect., Madison, 1988-91; faculty U. Wis. Law Sch., Madison, 1992-. Dir. Prevent Blindness Wis., Madison Symphony Orch., Wis. Women in Govt., Wis. Exec. Residence Found., Combat Blindness Found. Named Wis. Person of Vision, 2002, 1st Lady of Wis., 2001—03; recipient Disting. Svc. award, Wis. Coun. of the Blind, 2002. Mem.: State Bar Wis. Republican. Avocations: fabric art, piano. Office: LIRC PO Box 8126 Madison WI 53708-8126 Office Phone: 608-266-9850. Business E-Mail: mccalla@dwd.state.wi.us.

MCCALLUM, RICHARD WARWICK, medical researcher, clinician, educator; b. Brisbane, Australia, Jan. 21, 1945; came to U.S., 1969; MD, BS, Queensland U., Australia, 1968. Rotating intern Charity Hosp. La., New Orleans, 1969-70; resident in internal medicine Barnes Hosp., Washington, 1970-72; fellow in gastroenterology Wadsworth VA Hosp., LA, 1972-74, chief endoscopic unit, dept gastroenterology, 1974-76; dir. gastrointestinal diagnostic svcs. Yale-New Haven Med. Ctr., ew Haven, 1979-85; asst. prof. medicine UCLA, 1974-76, Yale U., New Haven, 1977-82, assoc. prof., 1982-85; prof., chief div. gastroenterology, hepatology and nutrition U. Va., Charlottesville, 1985-95; dir. GI Motility Ctr. U. Va. Health Sci. Ctr., Charlottesville, 1990-96; Paul Janssen prof. medicine U. Va., Charlottesville, 1987-96; prof. medicine and physiology U. Kans. Med. Ctr., Kansas City, 1996—, chief div. gastroenterology and hepatology, 1996—, dir. Ctr. for Gastrointestinal, Nerve and Muscle Function and Motility Disorders, 1996—. Patentee catheter for esophageal perfusion, gastrointestinal pacemaker usingphased multipoint stimulation, esophageal protection by mastication. Fellow ACP, Am. Coll. Gastroenterology (gov. Kans. 1998—), Royal Australasian Coll. Physicians, Royal Australian Coll. Surgeons; mem. Australian Gastroenterology Soc., Am. Fedn. Clin. Rsch., Am. Assn. Study Liver Diseases, Am. Soc. Gastrointestinal Endoscopy, Am. Soc. for Clin. Investigation, Am. Gastroenterology Assn., Am. Motility Soc. (host-organizer 11th biennial meeting Kansas City 2000), So. Soc. for Clin. Investigation (pres. 1997-98), Internat. Electrogastrography Soc. (pres. 1998-2000), So. Med. Assn. (chmn. gastrointestinal 1996-97). Office: U Kans Med Ctr Dept Internal Medicine 3901 Rainbow Blvd Kansas City KS 66160-0001 Office Phone: 913-588-3842. Business E-Mail: rmccallu@kumc.edu.

MCCANDLESS, JEFFRY SCOTT, lawyer; b. Kansas City, Mo., Apr. 14, 1954; s. Donald Eugene and June Marie (Winer) McC.; m. Elizabeth Ann Waugh, Nov. 3, 1984. JD, Washington & Lee U., 1979. Bar: Mo. 1979, U.S. Dist. Ct. (we. dist.) Mo. 1979. Assoc., then ptnr. Shook, Hardy & Bacon LLP, Kansas City, Mo., 1979—. Contbr. articles to mag. Mem.: ABA, Kan. City Met. Bar Assn. Avocations: reading, writing, baseball. Home: 4000 W 56th St Fairway KS 66205-2746 Office: Shook, Hardy & Bacon LLP 2555 Grand Blvd Kansas City MO 64108 Office Fax: 816-421-5547. Business E-Mail: smccandless@shb.Com.

MCCANLES, MICHAEL FREDERICK, retired English language educator; b. Kansas City, Mo., Mar. 8, 1936; s. Martin and Dorothy (Kaysing) McC.; m. Penelope A. Mitchell, May 27, 1967; children— Christopher, Stephanie, Jocelyn. BS, Rockhurst Coll., 1957; MA, U. Kans., 1959, PhD, 1964. Instr. dept. English U. Cin., 1962-64; asst. prof. Marquette U., 1964-68, assoc. prof., 1968-76, prof., 1976—2001, prof. emeritus, 2001. Author: Dialectical Criticism and Renaissance Literature, 1975, The Discourse of Il Principe, 1983, The Text of Sidney's Arcadian World, 1989, Jonsonian Discriminations: The Humanist Poet and the Praise of True obility, 1992; contbr. articles to profl. jours. Guggenheim fellow, 1978-79 Office: Dept English Marquette U Milwaukee WI 53233 E-mail: mmccanles@wt.rr.com.

MCCANN, DENNIS JOHN, columnist; b. Janesville, Wis., July 25, 1950; s. Thomas G. and Jean E. (Skelly) McC.; m. Barbara Jo Bunker, Sept. 11, 1971. BA, U. Wis., 1974. Reporter WMIR Radio, Lake Geneva, Wis., 1974, Janesville (Wis.) Gazette, 1975-83; reporter, columnist Milw. Jour. Sentinel, 1983—. Reporter Daily Herald, Arlington Heights, Ill., 1978. Author: The Wisconsin Story: 150 Stories, 150 Years, 1998, Dennis McCann Takes You for a Ride, 1999; contbg. author: Best of the Rest, 1993. Recipient Writing awards Milw. Press Club, Wis. Newspaper Assn., Newspaper Farm Editors. Avocations: golf, running. Office: The Milw Jour Sentinel 333 W State St Milwaukee WI 53203-1305

MCCANN, DIANA RAE, secondary school educator; b. Huron, SD, Nov. 16, 1948; d. Ralph Henry and Rosina Agnes (Rowen) Yager; m. Gregory Charles McCann, 1974; children: Grant Christopher, Holly Ann. BS, S.D. State U., 1972. Tchr. Bon Homme 4-2, Tyndall, SD, 1972—74, 1976—, Avon (S.D.) Sch., 1975—76. Math. curriculum adv. bd., SD, 1992—; coord. Presdl. awards in math., SD, 1998—. Leader 4-H Club, 1986—; sec.-treas. 4-H Leaders Assn., 1992—2000; tournament coord. Bon Homme Youth Wrestling Club, 1986—93. Recipient Elem. Math. Presdl. award for Excellence in Math. Tchgs., NSF, 1993, Disting. Svc. award for Math. in S.D., 2003, Bon Homme Outstanding Tchr. award, 2005. Mem.: S.D. Coun. Tchrs. Math. (pres.-elect 1990—92, pres. 1992—94, treas. 1999—), Nat. Coun. Tchrs. Math. Avocation: gardening. Personal E-mail: dm57062@valyou.net.

MCCANN, E. MICHAEL, lawyer; b. Chgo., 1936; BA, U. Detroit, 1959; LLB, Georgetown U., 1962; LLM, Harvard U., 1963; LLD honoris causa, Marquette U., 1997. Dist. atty. Milwaukee County, Wis. Lectr. Nat. Coll. Dist. Attys., Wis. Law Sch., Marquette Law Sch., Wis. Bar Continuing Legal Edn. Programs, State Prosecutor Edn. and Tng. Program, various state dist. atty. assns. Contbr. articles to law revs. Fellow Am. Bar Found., Am. Coll. Trial Lawyers; mem. ABA (resource team for high profile trials, past chair com. on victims, past chair criminal justice sect.), Nat. Dist. Attys. Assn. (lectr., bd. dirs.), Wis. Dist. Attys. Assn. (pres.), Pretrial Svcs. Resource Ctr. (bd. dirs.). Office: Milwaukee County Dist Atty's Office 821 W State St Rm 412 Milwaukee WI 53233-1427

MCCANN, RENETTA, advertising executive; b. Chgo., Dec. 8, 1956; d. Aditha Lorraine Collymore Walker; married; 2 children. BS in Speech, Northwestern U., 1978. Client svc. trainee Starcom, 1978, v.p., 1988, media dir., 1989, sr. v.p., 1995; CEO Starcom N.Am., Chgo., 1999—2004; CEO Americas Starcom MediaVest Group, 2004—. Bd. mem. Audit Bur. Circulations Northwestern U., mem. adv. bd. Media Mgmt. Ctr.; bd. mem. Chgo. United. Spkr. in field. Named a Woman to Watch, Crain's Chgo. Bus., 2007; named Media Maven, Advt. Age, 2001, Corp. Exec. of Yr., Black Enterprise, 2002, Advt. Woman of Yr., Women's Advt. Club Chgo., 2002; named one of 50 Women Who Are Changing the World, Essence, 2003, 50 Women to Watch, Wall Street Journal, 2005, Most Influential Black Americans, Ebony mag., 2006, Next 20 Female CEOs, Pink Mag. & Forté Found., 2006, 100 Most Powerful Women, Forbes mag., 2007; recipient Outstanding Women in Comm. award, Ebony, Vanguard award, Chgo. Mags. Assn., Media Strategies award, Bus. Week, Matrix award for Advt., NY Women in Comm. Inc., 2006. Mem.: Am. Advt. Fedn. (mem. multicultural bus. practices leadership coun.), Am. Assn. Advt. Agys. (chair media policy com.). Office: Starcom NAm 35 W Wacker Dr Chicago IL 60601

MCCANN, VONYA B., federal agency administrator, telecommunications industry executive; BA, U. Calif., LA, 1976; MA in Pub. Policy, U. Calif., Berkeley, 1979, JD, 1980. Bar: D.C., 1980. Law clk. Commr. Tyrone Brown, Fed. Comm. Commn.; policy analyst Nat. Telecommunications and Info. Adminstrn. Dept. Commerce; ptnr. Arent, Fox, Kintner, Plotkin and Kahn; amb., dep. asst. sec. internat. comm. & info. policy Dept. State, 1994—99, prin. dep. asst. sec. of state for econ. and bus. affairs, 1997—99; sr. v.p., fed. external affairs Sprint Corp., Overland, Kans., 1999—2005; v.p. govt. affairs Sprint Nextel Corp., Overland, 2005—. Office: Sprint World Hdqrs 6200 Sprint Pkwy Overland Park KS 66251

MCCARNEY, DAN, former college football coach; b. Iowa City, Iowa, July 28, 1953; m. Margy McCarney; children: Shane, Jillian, Melanie. BS, U. Iowa, 1975. Asst. coach Iowa U. Hawkeyes, 1977-89; defensive coord., defensive line coach U. Wis. Badgers, 1990-94; head coach Iowa State U. Cyclones, 1995—2006. Named Big-12 Coach of the Yr., Collegefootballnews.com, 2001. Mem. Am. Football Coaches Assn.

MCCARRON, JOHN FRANCIS, editor; b. Providence, Jan. 20, 1949; s. Hugh Francis and Katherine Anne (Brooks) McC.; m. Janet Ann Velsor, Sept. 3, 1971; children: Veronica, Catherine. BS in Journalism, Northwestern U., 1970, MS in Journalism, 1973. Gen. assignment reporter Chgo. Tribune, 1973-80, urban affairs writer, 1980-91, fin. editor, 1991-92, editorial bd. columnist, 1992-2000; v.p. strategy and comms. Met. Planning Coun. Chgo., 2000—02; adj. prof. Medill Sch. Journalism Northwestern U., 2002—; cons. local initiatives support ctr., 2003—. Contbr. to Planning Mag., World Book Ency., Preservation Mag., Land & People Mag. Lt. USNR, 1970-72. Recipient Editors award AP, 1983, 84, Ann. Journalism award Am. Planning Assn., 1983, Heywood Broun award Am. Newspaper Guild, Washington, 1989, Peter Lisagor award Soc. Profl. Journalists, 1994, Nat. Journalism award Lambda Alpha Internat., 2007. Home: 1425 Noyes St Evanston IL 60201-2639 E-mail: j.mccarron@att.net.

MC CARTAN, PATRICK FRANCIS, lawyer; b. Cleve., Aug. 3, 1934; s. Patrick Francis and Stella Mercedes (Ashton) Mc Cartan; m. Lois Ann Buchman, Aug. 30, 1958; children: M. Karen, Patrick Francis III. AB magna cum laude, U. Notre Dame, 1956, JD, 1959. Bar: Ohio 1960, U.S. Ct. Appeals (6th cir.) 1961, U.S. Ct. Appeals (3rd cir.) 1965, U.S. Ct. Appeals (DC cir.) 1980, U.S. Ct. Appeals (5th cir.) 1981, U.S. Ct. Appeals (4th cir.) 1989, U.S. Ct. Appeals (7th cir.) 1992, U.S. Supreme Ct. 1970. Law clk. to Hon. Charles Evans Whittaker, U.S. Supreme Ct., 1959; assoc. Jones Day, Cleve., 1961—65, ptnr., 1966—93, mng. ptnr., 1993—2002, sr. ptnr., 2003—. Trustee U. Notre Dame, 1989—, chair, 2000—07; trustee Cleve. Clinic Found.; standing com. on rules of practice and procedure Jud. Conf. of US. Fellow: Internat. Acad. Trial Lawyers, Am. Coll. Trial Lawyers; mem.: ABA, Bar Assn. Greater Cleve. (pres. 1977—78), Ohio Bar Assn., 6th Cir. Jud. Conf. (life), U.S.-Japan Bus. Coun., Coun. on Fgn. Rels., Greater Cleve. Growth Assn. (chmn. 1997—2000). Roman Catholic. Office: Jones Day North Point 901 Lakeside Ave E Cleveland OH 44114-1190 Office Phone: 216-586-3939, 216-586-7272. Business E-Mail: pmccartan@jonesday.com.

MCCARTER, CHARLES CHASE, lawyer; b. Pleasanton, Kans., Mar. 17, 1926; s. Charles Nelson and Donna (Chase) McC.; m. Clarice Blanchard, June 25, 1950; children: Charles Kevin, Cheryl Ann. BA, Principia Coll., 1950; JD, Washburn U., 1953; LLM, Yale U., 1954. Bar: Kans. 1953, U.S. Supreme Ct. 1962, Mo. 1968. Asst. atty. gen. State of Kans., 1954-57; lectr. law sch. Washburn U., 1956-57; appellate counsel FCC, Washington, 1957-58; assoc. Weigand, Curfman, Brainerd, Harris & Kaufman, Wichita, 1958-61; gen.

counsel Kans. Corp. Commn., 1961-63; ptnr. McCarter, Frizzel & Wettig, Wichita, 1963-68, McCarter & Badger, Wichita, 1968-73; pvt. practice law St. Louis, 1968-76; ptnr. McCarter & Greenley, St. Louis, 1976-85; mng. ptnr. Gage & Tucker, St. Louis, 1985-87, Husch and Eppenberger, St. Louis, 1987-89, McCarter & Greenley, LLC, St. Louis, 1990—. Prof. law, assoc. dir. law sch. Nat. Energy Law and Policy Inst. Tulsa U., 1977-79; prof. law, coach nat. moot ct. coll. of law Stetson U. Coll., St. Petersburg, Fla., 1980-84; mem. govtl. adv. coun. Gulf Oil Corp., 1977-81; legal com. Interstate Oil Compact Commn.; mem. adv. bd. Allegiant Bank, 1997—. Co-author: Missouri Lawyers Guide; assoc. editor Washburn U. Law Rev., 1952-53; contbr. articles to profl. jours. Chmn. Wichita Human Rels. Devel. Adv. Bd., 1967-68; bd. dirs. Peace Haven Assn.; active St. Louis Estate Planning Coun., 1987—; mem. bequests and endowment com. Salvation Army, 1995—; mem. YMCA endowment com., 1996—; mem. gifts and endowment bd. TV Channel 9, KETC, St. Louis, 2004—. With USNR, 1944-46. Recipient Excellent Prof. award U. Tulsa, 1979; vis. scholar Yale U., 1980 Mem. ABA (sect. real property, probate and trust law, bus. law sect.), Kans. Bar Assn., Mo. Bar Assn. (probate and trust com., tax com.), Am. Legion, VFW, Native Sons and Daus. Kans (pres. 1957-58), Kappa Sigma, Delta Theta Phi, Principia Dads Club (bd. dirs.) Republican. Office: One Metropolitan Sq Ste 2100 Saint Louis MO 63102-2751 Office Phone: 314-436-2100 ext. 107. Business E-Mail: cmccarter@mccartergreenley.com.

MC CARTER, JOHN WILBUR, JR., museum executive; b. Oak Park, Ill., Mar. 2, 1938; s. John Wilbur and Ruth Rebecca McC.; m. Judith Field West, May 1, 1965; children: James Philip, Jeffrey John, Katherine Field. AB, Princeton U., 1960; postgrad., London Sch. Econs., 1961; MBA, Harvard U., 1963. Cons., assoc., v.p. Booz Allen and Hamilton, Inc., Chgo., 1963-69; White House fellow Washington, 1966-67; dir. Bur. Budget and Dept. Fin., State of Ill., Springfield, 1969-73; v.p. DeKalb AgResearch, Ill., 1973-78, dir. Ill., 1975-86, exec. v.p. Ill., 1978-80, pres. Ill., 1981-82; pres., chief exec. officer DeKalb-Pfizer Genetics, 1982-86; pres. DeKalb Corp., 1985-86; sr. v.p. Booz Allen & Hamilton Inc., 1987-97; pres., CEO Field Mus., Chgo., 1996—. Bd. dirs. Divergence Inc., W.W. Grainger, Inc., Janus. Trustee Chgo. Pub. Television, 1973—, chmn., 1989-96, trustee Princeton U., 1983-87, U. Chgo., 1993—. Office: Field Museum 1400 S Lake Shore Dr Chicago IL 60605-2496

MCCARTER, W. DUDLEY, lawyer; b. St. Louis, Dec. 20, 1950; s. Willard Dudley and Vera Katherine (Schneider) McC.; m. Elizabeth Dunlop, June 14, 1986; children: Katherine, Elizabeth, Emily. BA, Knox Coll., 1972; JD, U. Mo., 1975. Bar: Mo. 1975, U.S. Dist. Ct. (ea. dist.) Mo. 1976, U.S. Ct. Appeals (8th cir.) Mo. 1977. Assoc. Mann & Poger, St. Louis, 1975-76, Suelthaus & Krueger, St. Louis, 1976-80; ptnr. Suelthaus & Kaplan, P.C., St. Louis, 1980-92, Behr, McCarter & Potter P.C., St. Louis, 1992—. Atty. City of Creve Coeur, Mo., 1992-2004. Author editor: Missouri Civil Litigation Handbook, 1992; author Jour. of the Mo. Bar, St. Louis Bar Jour. and Mo. Law Rev. Recipient W. Oliver Rasch award, 1985, 1989, Outstanding Young Lawyer award St. Louis County Bar Assn. 1983. Fellow ABA; mem. The Missouri Bar (pres. 1993-94). Office: Behr Mccarter And Potter 7777 Bonhomme Ave Ste 1400 Saint Louis MO 63105-1942

MCCARTHY, HAROLD CHARLES, retired insurance company executive; b. Madelia, Minn., Dec. 5, 1926; s. Charles and Merle (Humphry) McC.; m. Barbara Kaercher, June 24, 1949; children: David, Susan. BA, Carleton Coll., Northfield, Minn., 1950; postgrad. With Federated Mut. Ins. Co., Owatonna, Minn., 1950-67; with Meridian Mut. Ins. Co., Indpls., 1967-91, exec. v.p., then exec. v.p., gen. mgr., 1972-75, pres., 1975-90, bd. dirs., past chmn. bd., 1990-91; past pres. North Meridian Bus. Group; past pres., chmn. bd. Meridian Ins. Group, Inc. Chmn. bd., dir. Meridian Life Ins. Co.; past chmn., exec. com., bd. dirs. Ind. Ins. Inst.; mem. adv. bd. Harbor Fed. Savs. Bank. Former mem. Met. Devel. Commn., Corp. Cmty. Coun.; bd. dirs. Meth. Health Found., Family Services Assn., Boy Scouts Am., Indian River Symphony Assn.; trustee Butler U. With USNR, 1944-46. Named Sagamore of the Wabash. Mem. Skyline Club (Indpls.), Indian River Golf Club. Republican.

MCCARTHY, KAREN P., former congresswoman, former state legislator; b. Mass., Mar. 18, 1947; BS in English, Biology, U. Kans., 1969, MBA, 1985; MEd in English, U. Mo., Kansas City, 1976. Tchr. Shawnee Mission (Kans.) South High Sch., 1969-75, The Sunset Hill (Kans.) Sch., 1975-76; mem. Mo. House of Reps., Jefferson City, 1977-94; cons. govt. affairs Marion Labs., Kansas City, Mo., 1986-93; mem. U.S. Congress from 5th Mo. dist., Washington, 1995—2005; mem. commerce com.; mem. Ho. Select Com. on Homeland Security. Rsch. analyst pub. fin. dept. Stearn Bros. & Co., 1984-85, Kansas City, Mo.; rsch. analyst Midwest Rsch. Inst., econs. and mgmt. scis. dept., Kansas City, 1985-86. Del. Dem. Nat. Conv., 1992, Dem. Nat. Party Conf., 1982, Dem. Nat. Policy Com. Policy Commn., 1985-86; mem. Ho. Commerce Com. Energy and Power, Telecom., Trade and Consumer Protection; co-chair Dem. Caucus Task Health Care Reform. Recipient Outstanding Young Woman Am. award, 1977, Outstanding Woman Mo. award Phi Chi Theta, Woman of Achievement award Mid-Continent Coun. Girl Scouts U.S., 1983, 87, Annie Baxter Leadership award, 1993; named Conservation Legislator of Yr., Conservation Fed. Mo., 1987. Fellow Inst. of Politics; mem. Nat. Inst. of Politics; mem. Nat. Conf. on State Legis. (del. on trade and econ. devel. to Fed. Republic of Germany, Bulgaria, Japan, France and Italy, mem. energy com. 1978-84, fed. taxation, trade and econ. devel. com. 1986, chmn. fed. budget and taxation com. 1987, vice chmn. state fed. assembly 1988, pres.-elect 1993, pres. 1994), Nat. Dem. Inst. for Internat. Affairs (instr. No. Ireland 1988, Baltic Republics 1992, Hungary 1993). Democrat.

MCCARTHY, KEVIN, state representative, lawyer; b. June 1971; married. JD, Drake U. Former asst. atty. gen., Iowa; state rep. dist. 67 Iowa Ho. of Reps., 2003—; mem. ethics com.; mem. natural resources com.; mem. transp. com.; mem. justice sys. appropriations subcom.; ranking mem. pub. safety com. Democrat. Roman Catholic. Office: State Capitol East 12th and Grand Des Moines IA 50319

MCCARTHY, MARK FRANCIS, lawyer; b. Boston, July 8, 1951; s. William Alfred and Martha Louise (Blodgett) McC.; m. Karen Marie Umerley; children: Kevin Francis, Daniel Henry. AB in Theology, Georgetown U., 1973, JD, 1976. Bar: Ohio 1976. Assoc. Sweeney, Mahon, & Vlad, Cleve., 1976-80; ptnr. Arter & Hadden, 1980—2003, Tucker Ellis & West LLP, Cleve., 2003—. Atty. asst. to bd. pres. Bd. Cuyahoga County Commrs., Cleve., 1976-80; adj. prof. Case Western Reserve Law Ctr., Cleve., 1986-2004. Active Greater Cleve. Growth Assn. Leadership Cleve., 1979-80; trustee Parmadale, Parma, Ohio, Western Res. Hist. Soc., 1978-80, Cath. Charities Found.; chmn. Cath. Charities Svcs. Corp.; trustee, sec. Caritas Connection; founder, sec., gen. counsel St. Martin De Porres H.S., Cleve. Mem. Ohio Assn. Civil Trial Attys. (chmn. product liability sect. 1989—), Fedn. Ins. & Corp. Counsel, Ct. of Nisi Prius, Rowfant Club. Democrat. Roman Catholic. Avocations: book collecting, fly fishing, upland shooting. Home: 363 Britannia Pky Avon Lake OH 44012-2180 Office: Tucker Ellis & West LLP 1150 Huntington Bldg 925 Euclid Ave Cleveland OH 44115-1475 Office Phone: 216-696-3290. Business E-Mail: mfm@tuckerellis.com.

MCCARTHY, MICHAEL M., construction executive; CEO McCarthy, St. Louis, 1976—84, chmn., 1984—2002, chmn. emeritus, 2002—. Office: McCarthy Bldg Cos 1341 N Rock Hill Rd Saint Louis MO 63124-1441

MCCARTHY, MICHAEL SHAWN, health care company executive, lawyer; b. Evergreen Park, Ill., May 16, 1953; s. Martin J. and Margaret Anne (McNeill) McC.; m. Jane F. Alberding, Oct. 28, 1988; children: Caroline Margaret, Nicholas Michael, Claire Patricia. BA, Georgetown U., 1975; MS, U. Ill., 1976; JD, Loyola U., 1980. Bar: Ill. 1980, U.S. Dist. Ct. (no. dist.) Ill. 1980. V.p., sec., gen. counsel Luth. Gen. Health Care System, Park Ridge, Ill., 1980-85, sr. v.p., sec., gen. counsel, 1985-91, sr. v.p. corp. svcs., sec., gen. counsel, 1990-93; chmn., CEO Parkside Sr. Svcs., LLC, Skokie, Ill., 1993—. Life trustee Lake Forest Acad.; mem. coun. of regents Loyola U., Chgo., Ill. Mem. ABA, ASHA (exec. bd.), Ill. Hosp. Assn., Ill. Pub. Health Assn., Chgo. Bar Assn., ALFA Leadership Coun. Roman Catholic. Avocations: golf, travel. Home: 1026 Pine St Winnetka IL 60093-2024 Office: Parkside Sr Svcs LLC 5215 Old Orchard Rd Skokie IL 60077-1035 E-mail: McCarthy@parkside-sr.com.

MCCARTHY, MIKE, professional football coach; b. Pitts., Oct. 10, 1963; Grad., Baker U., 1986. Grad. asst. Fort Hays State, 1987—88; quarterbacks, wide receivers coach U. Pitts., 1989—92; offensive asst. Kans. City Chiefs, 1993—94, quarterbacks coach, 1995—98, Green Bay Packers, 1999, head coach, 2006—; offensive coord. New Orleans Saints, 2000—04, San Francisco 49ers, 2005. Named Nat. Football Conf. Asst. Coach of Yr., 2000, NFL Coach of Yr., NFL Alumni, 2007; recipient Motorola NFL Coach of Yr., 2007. Office: Green Bay Packers Lambeau Field 1265 Lombardi Ave Green Bay WI 54307*

MCCARTHY, PAUL FENTON, aerospace transportation executive, retired military officer; b. Boston, Mar. 3, 1934; s. Paul Fenton and Jane Gertrude (O'Connor) McC.; m. Sandra Williams, June 20, 1959; children: Paul Fenton III, Susan Stacy. BS in Marine and Elec. Engring., Mass. Maritime Acad., 1954; MS in Mgmt., U.S. aval Postgrad. Sch., 1964; D of Pub. Adminstrn. (hon.), Mass. Maritime Acad., 1987. Commd. ensign U.S. Navy, 1954, advanced through grades to vice adm., 1985; 7 command tours have included Aircraft Carrier USS Constellation, Carrier Group One, Task Force Seventy-seven; commdr. U.S. 7th Fleet, 1980-82; dir. R & D USN, Washington, 1980-83; negotiator Naval Air, Incidents at Sea Agreement, Moscow, 1980; ret., 1990; cons. in field Alexandria, Va., 1990-92; pres. McCarthy and McCarthy, Ltd.; v.p., chief engr., dep. gen.mgr. McDonnell Douglas Aerospace/Boeing, St. Louis, 1992-95; v.p. processes and sys. integration McDonnell Douglas Aerospace, St. Louis, 1995-97, dir. naval systems integration, 1997-2000; vis. disting. prof. Peter Conrad chair Naval Post Grad. Sch., 2000-02; sr. ptnr. McCarthy and McCarthy, LLC, 2002—; sr. lectr. grad studies U. San Diego, 2005—. Bd. visitors Mass. Maritime Acad., 1993. Decorated D.S.M., Legion of Merit, D.F.C., also by govts. of South Vietnam, Korea, Japan. Mem.: Mass. Maritime Acad. Alumni Assn. Episcopalian. Avocations: development and acquisition, aircraft and missile systems, financial management. Office Phone: 619-922-9494. E-mail: mcandmc@aol.com.

MC CARTHY, WALTER JOHN, JR., retired utilities executive; b. NYC, Apr. 20, 1925; s. Walter John and Irene McC.; m. Linda Lyon, May 6, 1988; children by previous marriage: Walter, David, Sharon, James, William. B.M.E., Cornell U., 1949; grad., Oak Ridge Sch. Reactor Tech., 1952; D.Eng. (hon.), Lawrence Inst. Tech., 1981; D.Sc. (hon.), Eastern Mich. U., 1983; LHD, Wayne State U., 1984; LLD, Alma Coll., Mich., 1985. Engr. Public Service Electric & Gas Co., Newark, 1949-56; sect. head Atomic Power Devel. Assos., Detroit, 1956-61; gen. mgr. Power Reactor Devel. Co., Detroit, 1961-68; with Detroit Edison Co., 1968-90, exec. v.p. ops., 1975-77, exec. v.p. divs., 1977-79, pres., chief operating officer, 1979-81, chmn., chief exec. officer, 1981-90. Author papers in field. Past chmn., bd. dirs. Inst. Nuclear Power Ops., Fed. Mogul Corp., Comerica Bank; past pres. Monterey County Symphony Orch., Detroit Symphony Orch.; past chmn. Detroit Econ. Growth Corp., Detroit Area Coun. Boy Scouts of Am. Fellow Am. Nuc. Soc., Engring. Soc. Detroit; mem. ASME, NAE. Methodist.

MCCARTNEY, N. L., investment banker; b. Jameson, Mo., Oct. 12, 1923; m. Helen M. Walsh, Feb. 11, 1950; children: Patricia, Deborah, Patrick. BS, U. Md., 1956; MBA, Syracuse U., 1959; MPA, George Washington U., 1963. Enlisted U.S. Army, 1944, advanced through grades to col., ret., 1972; dir. S.W. Mo. Health Care Foun., Springfield, 1974-88; pres. Resource Mgmt. Co., Springfield, 1988-96; exec. v.p. Spencer and Assocs., Springfield, 1990-94, Mo. Adv. Capital, 1995-99; pres. DMS, Inc., 1999—, CEO, 2001—. Instr. S.W. Mo. State U., Springfield, 1972-82. Pres. S.W. Mo. Adv. Coun. Govts., Ozarks Crime Prevention Coun., 1983-93, Vis. Nurse Assn.; mayor of Springfield, 1993-95. Mem. Rotary. Methodist. Home: 1233 E Loren St Springfield MO 65804-0041 Office: 330 N Jefferson Springfield MO 65806 Office Phone: 417-863-9992.

MCCASKEY, MICHAEL B., professional football team executive; b. Lancaster, Pa., Dec. 11, 1943; s. Edward B. and Virginia (Halas) McCaskey; m. Nancy McCaskey; children: John, Kathryn. Grad., Yale U., 1965; PhD, Case Western Res. U. Tchr. UCLA, 1972-75, Harvard U. Sch. Bus., Cambridge, Mass., 1975-82; pres., chief exec. officer Chgo. Bears (NFL), 1983-99, chmn. bd., 1999—. Author: The Executive Challenge: Managing Change and Ambiguity. Named Exec. of Yr. Sporting News, 1985. Office: 1000 Football Dr Lake Forest IL 60045-4829

MCCASKEY, RAYMOND F., insurance company executive; b. 1944; m. Judy McCaskey. With Continental Assurance Co., Chgo., 1963-73; assist v.p. Health Care Service Corp., 1973—79, chief actuary, 1979—82, CFO, 1982—91, pres., COO, 1991—98, pres., CEO, 1998—. Former bd. chmn. Lincoln Found. for Bus. Excellence. Office: Health Care Service Corp 300 E Randolph St Chicago IL 60601-5014 Office Phone: 312-938-6000.

MCCASKILL, CLAIRE C., senator, former auditor; b. Houston, July 25, 1953; d. William Y. and Betty Anne McCaskill; m. David Exposito (div. 1995); children: Austin, Maddie, Lily; m. Joseph Shepard, 2002; stepchildren: Benjamin, Carl, Marilyn, Michael. BS in Polit. Sci., U. Mo., Columbia, 1975, JD, 1978. Law clk. Mo. Ct. Appeals (we. dist.), Kansas City, 1978—79; asst. prosecutor County of Jackson, Mo., county prosecutor Mo., 1993—99; mem. Mo. Ho. of Reps., 1982—88; auditor State of Mo., Jefferson City, 1999—2007; US Senator from Mo., 2007—. Democrat. Office: US Senate 825A Hart Senate Office Bldg Washington DC 20510 Office Phone: 202-224-3121. Fax: 573-751-6539.

MCCASLIN, W. C., products and packaging executive; Owner, CEO Douglas Products and Packaging. Office: Douglas Products & Packaging 1550 E Old 210 Hwy Liberty MO 64068

MCCAULEY, MATTHEW D., lawyer; b. 1942; AB, Harvard U.; JD, U. Mich. V.p., assoc. gen. counsel Gen. Am. Corp., St. Louis, 1994—. Office: Gen Amer Life Ins 13045 Tesson Ferry Rd Saint Louis MO 63128-3407

MCCAUSLAND, THOMAS JAMES, JR., retired brokerage house executive; b. Cleve., Nov. 27, 1934; s. Thomas James and Jean Anna (Hanna) McC.; m. Kathryn Margaret Schacht, Feb. 9, 1957; children: Thomas James III, Andrew John, Theodore Scott. BA in Econs., Beloit Coll., Wis., 1956. V.p. A.G. Becker & Co., Inc., Chgo., 1959-74; v.p. The Chgo. Corp., 1974-76, sr. v.p., dir., 1976-83, exec. v.p., 1983-90, vice chmn., 1991-96; pres. The Chgo. Corp. Internat., 1990-96; ret., 2000. Treas. The LaSalle St. Coun., Chgo., 1990-95. V.p. Hospice the North Shore, Evanston, Ill., 1986-90; bd. dirs. McCormick Theol. Sem., Chgo., 1971-79, Presbyn. Home, Evanston, 1968-74; trustee Beloit Coll., 1987-90. Lt. USN, 1956-59. Mem. United Presbyn. Found. (trustee, vice-chmn. 1980-86), Skokie Country Club (bd. dirs. 1983-85, pres. 1993), Pelican Bay Club (Naples, Fla.)(chmn. 2001-03), Forum Club of Naples (bd. dirs.), Royal Poinciana Golf Club (Naples), Old Elm Club (Ill.). Republican. Avocations: travel, golf, history.

MCCLAIN, RICHARD WARNER, state legislator; m. Barrie L. McClain. BS, Purdue U., 1970. Sales mgr. east coast CTS Microelectronics; owner, mgr. The Spogge Shoppe, The Capt. Logan Hotel and Office Bldg.; sales and mktg. mgr. Controls, Inc.; trustee Jefferson Twp., 1978-80; city engr. Logansport, 1980-84; mem. Ind. Ho. Reps. Dist. 24. Mem. roads and transp. com., ways and means com. Active Boy Scouts Am., ARC, United Way, Farm Bur. Mem. Am. Legion, C. of C.

MCCLAIN, WILLIAM ANDREW, lawyer; b. Sanford, NC, Jan. 11, 1913; s. Frank and Blanche (Leslie) McClain; m. Roberta White, Nov. 11, 1944. AB, Wittenberg U., 1934; JD, U. Mich., 1937; LLD (hon.), Wilberforce U., 1963, U. Cin., 1971; LHD, Wittenberg U., 1972. Bar: Ohio 1938, U.S. Dist. Ct. (so. dist.) Ohio 1940, U.S. Ct. Appeals (6th cir.) 1946, U.S. Supreme Ct. 1946. Mem. Berry, McClain & White, 1937—58; dep. solicitor City of Cin., 1957—63, solicitor, 1963—72; mem. Keating, Muething & Klekamp, Cin., 1972—73; gen. counsel Cin. br. SBA, 1973—75; judge Hamilton County Common Pleas Ct., 1975—76, Mcpl. Ct., 1976—80; of counsel Manley, burke, Lipton & Cook, Cin., 1980—. Adj. prof. U. Cin., 1963—72, Salmon P. Chase Law Sch., 1965—72. Mem. exec. com. ARC, Cin., 1978—; bd. dirs. NCCJ, 1975—. 1st lt. JAG US Army, 1943—46. Decorated Army Commendation medal; recipient Nat. Layman award, A.M.E. Ch., 1963, Alumni award, Wittenberg U., 1966, Nat. Inst. Mcpl. Law Officers award, 1971, Ellis Island Medal of Honor, 1997. Fellow: Am. Bar Found.; mem.: ABA, Nat. Bar Assn., Ohio Bar Assn., Cin. Bar Assn., Am. Judicature Soc., Fed. Bar Assn., Bankers Club, Friendly Sons St. Patrick, Masons (32d degree), Sigma Pi Phi, Alpha Phi Alpha. Republican. Methodist. Home: 2101 Grandin Rd Apt 904 Cincinnati OH 45208-3346 Office Phone: 513-721-5525.

MCCLAMROCH, N. HARRIS, aerospace engineering educator, consultant, researcher; b. Houston, Oct. 7, 1942; s. Nathaniel Harris and Dorthy Jean (Orand) McC.; m. Margaret Susan Hobart, Aug. 10, 1963; 1 child, Kristin Jean BS, U. Tex., 1963, MS, 1965, PhD, 1967. Asst. prof. aerospace engring. U. Mich., Ann Arbor, 1967—71, assoc. prof., 1971—77, prof., 1977—, chair dept. aerospace engring., 1992—96. Research engr. Cambridge U., Eng., 1975, Delft U., Netherlands, 1976, Sandia Labs., Albuquerque, 1977, C.S. Draper Lab., Cambridge, Mass., 1982 Author: State Models of Dynamic Systems, 1980; contbr. numerous articles to profl. jours. Chmn. U. Mich. Faculty Senate, 1987-88. Fellow IEEE (v.p. Control Sys. Soc. 1998, editor Transactions on Automatic Control 1989-92, Millennium medal 2000); mem. AAAS. Home: 4056 Thornoaks Dr Ann Arbor MI 48104-4254 Office: U Mich Dept Aerospace Engring Ann Arbor MI 48109 Office Phone: 734-763-2355. Office Fax: 734-763-0578. E-mail: nhm@engin.umich.edu.

MC CLARREN, ROBERT ROYCE, librarian; b. Delta, Ohio, Mar. 15, 1921; s. Dresden William Howard and Norma Leona (Whiteman) Mc Clarren; m. Margaret Aileen Weed (dec. Oct. 2001); children: Mark Robert(dec.), Todd Adams. Student, Antioch Coll., 1938-40; AB, Muskingum Coll., 1942; MA in English, Ohio State U., 1951; MS in L.S., Columbia, 1954; DLitt (hon.), Rosary Coll. (now Dominican U.), 1989. Registration officer VA, Cin., 1946-47; instr. English Gen. Motors Inst., 1949-50; head circulation dept. Oak Park (Ill.) Pub. Libr., 1954-55, acting head librarian, 1955; head librarian Crawfordsville (Ind.) Pub. Libr., 1955-58, Huntington Pub. Libr., Western Counties Regional Pub. Libr., W.Va., 1958-62; dir. Ind. State Libr., 1962-67; system dir. North Suburban Libr. System, 1967-89, system dir. emeritus, 1990—; cons. libr. Chgo. Pub. Libr. Found., 1990. Del. White House Conf. on Librs., 1979; instr. U. Wis., summer 1964, Rosary Coll., 1968-80, U. Tex., summer 1979, 82, No. Ill. U., 1980; pres. W.Va. Libr. Assn., 1960, Ill. Libr. Assn., 1975; mem. Gov. Ind. Commn. Arts, 1964-65, Ill. State Libr. Adv. Com., 1972-79, 87-89, chmn., 1975-79, vice chmn., 1988-89; bd. dirs. Ill. Regional Libr. Coun., 1972-82, pres., 1977; chmn. adv. commn. Nat. Periodical System, Nat. Commn. on Librs. and Info. Sci., 1978-81; treas. Ill. Coalition Libr. Advs., 1982-89. Contbr. articles to profl. jours. Served to 1st lt. AUS, 1942-46, 51-52; maj. Res. Named Ill. Librarian of Yr., 1978; recipient Sagamore of Wabash (Ind.), 1966. Mem. ALA (councilor 1966-68, 74-78, treas. 1968-72, endowment trustee 1972-78, mem. publ. bd. 1972-75, pres. reference and adult svc. div. 1975-76, Joseph Towne Wheeler award 1954, Melville Dewey award 1989, Nat. Libr. Advocacy Honor Roll 2000), Assn. State and Coop. Libr. Agys. (prs. 1972), 14th Armored Divsn. Assn. (pres.-elect), Beta Phi Mu. Office: 200 W Dundee Rd Wheeling IL 60090-4750

MCCLELLAN, LARRY ALLEN, minister, educator; b. Buffalo, Nov. 3, 1944; s. Edward Lurelle McClellan and Helen (Denison) Greenlee; m. Diane Eunice Bonfoey, Aug. 19, 1973; children: Kara E., Seth C. Student, U. Ghana, 1964-65; BA in Psychology, Occidental Coll., 1966; MTh, U. Chgo., 1969, D Ministry, 1970. Ordained to ministry Presbyn. Ch. (U.S.A.), 1970. Prof. of sociology and community studies Govs. State U., University Park, Ill., 1970-86; interim pastor Presbyn. Ch. (U.S.A.), Chgo. area, 1980-86; sr. pastor St. Paul Community Ch., Homewood, Ill., 1986-96; adj. prof. Govs. State U., University Park, Ill., 1987-96; dir. South Met. Regional Leadership Ctr., Govs. State U., University Park, Ill., 1996—2001; cmty. rels. dir. Northeastern Ill. Planning Commn., 2001—05; pastor First Christian Ch. (Disciples), Chicago Heights, Ill., 2003—. Newspaper columnist Star Publs. Chgo., 1993-2004; trustee Internat. Coun. Community Chs., 1989-91, pres., 1991-93. Author: Local History South of Chicago, 1988; developer social simulation games; contbr. articles to profl. publs. Mayor Village of Park Forest South (name now University Park), Ill., 1975-79; co-organizer S. Region Habitat for Humanity, Chgo. area, 1989; pres. S. Suburban Heritage Assn., Chgo. area, 1988-91. Fellow Layne Found., 1966-70, NEH, 1979. Mem. Am. Assn. State and Local History, Ill. State Hist. Soc. (Spl. Achievement award 1989). Office Phone: 708-754-3792. E-mail: larryamcclel@msn.com.

MCCLELLAND, EMMA L., state legislator; b. Springfield, Mo., Feb. 26, 1940; m. Alan McClelland; children: Mike, Karen. BA, U. Mo., 1962. mem. appropriations, natural and econ. resources com., budget com., elem. and secondary edn. com., mcpl. corps. com., rules, joint rules and bills perfected and printed com., social services com., medicaid and elderly com. Dir. field office, corp. divsn. Mo. Sec. of State, St. Louis; committeewoman Gravois Twp.; mem. St. Louis County Rep. Cent. Com., Mo. Rep. State Com., Mo. Ho. of Reps., Jefferson City, 1991—; mem. appropriations, budget, edn., mcpl. corps., rules, joint rules and bills perfected and printed, social svcs., medicaid and the elderly coms. Bd. dirs. Ct. Apptd. Spl. Advocates, Family Support Network; elder Webster Groves Presbyn. Ch.; mem. Leadership St. Louis. Recipient Leadership award for govt. YWCA of St. Louis, Spirit of Enterprise award Mo. C. of C., Mental Health Assn. award for legis. svc., 1998, Mo. Child Adv. of Yr. award Mo. Child Care Assn., 1998. Mem. Webster Groves C. of C., Pi Lambda Theta. Republican. Presbyterian. Home: 455 Pasadena Ave Webster Groves MO 63119-3126

MCCLINTOCK, MARTHA K., biologist, educator; AB, Wellesley College, 1969; MA in Psychology, U. Penn., 1972, PhD in Psychology, 1974. With U. Chgo., 1976—, asst. prof., psychology and human devel., 1976, David Lee Shillinglaw Distinguished Svc. Prof. Psychology, dir., Inst. Mind & Biology; co-dir. Ctr. Interdisciplinary Health Disparities Rsch. Chmn. biopsychology com., 1986—99; mem. neurobiology com., evolutionary biology com., human develop. com. Contbr. articles to profl. jours. Recipient Disting. Sci. Award for Early Career Contbn. to Psychology, APA, 1982, MERIT Award, NIMH, 1992, Edith Krieger Wolf Disting. Vis. Prof., Northwestern Univ., 2000, Henry G. Walter Sense of Smell Award, Sense of Smell Inst., 2001. elected mem., Inst. of Medicine, 1999, Acad. of Arts and Sciences, 1999. Office: U Chgo 5730 S Woodlawn Ave Chicago IL 60637

MCCLINTON, JAMES ALEXANDER, mayor, former state agency administrator; b. Milw., Nov. 18, 1961; s. James Henry O'Neal and Essie Marie (McClinton) Jones; m. Hazel Marie Walker, July 19, 1986 (div. 1998); children: Tawana Nicolette, Jameika Alexandra. AA, Washburn U., 1985, BA, 1987; MPA, U. Kans., 1997. Unit team supr. Kans. Neurol. Inst., Topeka, 1983-85; corrections officer Kans. Dept. Corrections, Topeka, 1985-87, corrections counselor, 1987-91, asst. tng. mgr., 1991-95, adminstr. Prison Health Svcs. Lansing, 1995-96; personnel specialist City of Topeka, 1996-97; policy examiner Kans. Ins. Dept., Topeka, 1997-98; programs policy adminstr. Kans. Juvenile Justice Authority, Topeka, 1998—2003; mayor City of Topeka, 2004—. Mem. Topeka City Coun., 1989—93, 1997—2001. Bd. dirs. Habitat for Humanity, Topeka, Kans. State Bd. Nursing, 1993-97, pres. 1995-96; ward capt., precinct com. mem. Shawnee County Dem. Party, Topeka, 1994—; commr. Topeka/Shawnee County Planning Commn., 1994-97, Jaycees, 1998—, Sertoma, 1999—; trustee Antioch Missionary Bapt. Ch. Fellow Washburn U. Alumni, 1998. Mem. Jaycees, Sertoma Club, Pi Alpha Alpha. Bapt. Avocations: fishing, boating, travel, biking, baseball. Office: 215 SE 7th St Rm 352 Topeka KS 66603-3914 E-mail: jmcclinton@topeka.org.

MCCLOY, ELIZABETH K., lawyer; b. 1959; BA, Dartmouth Coll., 1981; JD, Northwestern U., 1984. Bar: Ill. 1984. With Sidley Austin Brown & Wood, Chgo., 1984—, ptnr., 1993—. Office: Sidley Austin Brown and Wood Bank One Plz 10 S Dearborn St Chicago IL 60603

MCCLURE, ALVIN BRUCE, watchmaker; b. Cin., Mar. 2, 1953; s. Alphonso Bruce McClure and Jewel Lee (Smith) Yates; m. Katherine Shenkar, Nov. 7, 1979; children: Jaina, Randi; m. Penny Bliss, July 7, 2000. Student, U. Mich., 1971-73, 76-77, Fanshawe Coll., London, Ont., Can., 1974-75, Coll. of St. Thomas, 1989-91, St. Paul Coll., 2005—06. Programmer Mfg. Data Systems, Ann Arbor, Mich., 1978-79; systems software specialist Mpls. Star and Tribune, 1979-81; systems analyst CR COMTEN, Inc., Roseville, Minn., 1981-84; software systems support programmer INTRAN Corp., Bloomington, Minn., 1984-85; programmer/analyst Minn. Dept. atural Resources, St. Paul, 1985-97; local area network adminstr. Minn. Pollution Control Agy., St. Paul, 1997-98; network mgr. Minn. Dept. Health, Mpls., 1998; info. sys. mgr. Van Wagenen Co., Eden Prairie, Minn., 1998-99; sr. tech. cons. Database/Network/WEB Lawson Software, St. Paul, 1999-2000; tech. cons. Productive Solutions Group, Mpls., 2000—01; pres. Reality Bytes, Inc., Elk River, 2001—; data mgmt. engr. Kroll Ontrack, Inc., Eden Prairie, 2002—03; watchmaker Ben Bridge Jewelers, Edina, Minn., 2007—. Mem. mgmt. info. svcs. tech. com. St. Paul, Miss., 1987—97. Mem. cmty. adv. bd. Sta. WCAL-FM, 1988-90; mem. Otsego Police Commn., 2003-. Mem. IEEE, AWI, Am. Inst. Physics, Audio Engring. Soc., Internat.

Platform Assn., Mgmt. Info. Svcs., Am. Watchmakers-Clockmakers Inst., Nat. Assn. Watch and Clock Collectors, Aikido Yoshinkai Mpls.-St. Paul (5th degree black belt, head instr.). Avocations: chess, photography, audiophile, sailing, aquaria. Home: 14348 96th St NE Elk River MN 55330-7376 Office: Reality Bytes Inc 14348 96th St NE Elk River MN 55330-7376 Office Phone: 952-922-1250. Personal E-mail: alvin@heisei.com. E-mail: alvin.mcclure@otsegomn.net.

MCCLURE, CHARLES G., automotive executive; BS in Mech. Engring., Cornell U.; MBA, U. Mich. Heavy truck sales engr., product engr. Ford Motor Co.; v.p., gen. mgr. automotive sys. groups for the Ams. Johnson Controls, Inc., pres., Detroit Diesel Corp., 1997—2003, CEO, 1999—2003; CEO, pres. Federal-Mogul Corp., 2003—04; chmn., pres., CEO ArvinMeritor Inc., Troy, Mich., 2004—. Mem. Bus. Roundtable; bd. dir. NAM, R.L. Polk and Co., Intermet Corp., Motor & Equip. Mfr. Assn. Bd. dir. Detroit Renaissance, Detroit Regional C. of C., Horizons Upward Bound; mem. exec. com. A World in Motion. Lt. (j.g.) USN, 1975—79. Office: ArvinMeritor Inc 2135 W Maple Rd Troy MI 48084

MCCLURE, JAMES A., lawyer, former senator; b. Payette, Idaho, Dec. 27, 1924; s. W. R. and Marie McC.; m. Louise Miller; children: Marilyn, Kenneth, David. JD, U. Idaho, 1950; DL (hon.), Coll. Idaho, 1986. Mem. Idaho State Senate, 1961-66; asst. majority leader, 1965-66; city atty. City of Payette, Idaho; pros. atty. Payette County, Idaho; mem. US Congress from 1st Idaho Dist., 1967-73; US Senator from Idaho, 1973-90; chmn. Energy and Natural Resources Com., 1981-86, Interior Appropriations Subcom.; co-founder, chmn. Steering Com.; mem. Com. on Rules and Adminstrn., Budget Com., Environment and Pub. Works Com., Spl. Com. Investigating the Iran/Contra Affair; pres. McClure, Gerard & Neuenschwander, Inc., Washington, 1990-99, of counsel; ptnr. Givens, Pursley, & Huntley, Boise, Idaho, 1990-99; of counsel Givens Pursley. Chmn. Senate Rep. Conf.; mem. Helsinki Commn. on Human Rights; mem. bd. dirs. Boise Cascade Corp., Coeur D'Alene Mines, Inc., Idaho Power Co., Mountain States Legal Found., Nat. Mus. Natural History, Williams Companies. Mem. bd. dirs. John F. Kennedy Ctr. for Performing Arts; trustee Meth. Ch. Aviation cadet USN, 1942—45. Named Outstanding Legislator of Yr., Nat. Assn. Towns and Twp., 1983; recipient Watchdog of Treasury award, Nat. Assn. Businessmen, Disting. Svc. award, Nat. Energy Resources Org., 1982, Leadership award, Coalition for Peace through Strength, 1982—83, Americans for Energy Ind., 1983. Mem. Elks, Masons, Kiwanis, Phi Alpha Delta, Am. Judicature Soc., Nat. & Idaho Reclamation Assns., Am. Legion. Republican. Methodist. Office: McClure Gerard & Neuenschwander Inc 201 Maryland Ave NE Washington DC 20002-5703 also: Givens Pursley PO Box 2720 Boise ID 83701 Business E-Mail: jam@givenspursley.com.*

MCCLURE, JAMES JULIUS, JR., lawyer, former city official; b. Oak Park, Ill., Sept. 23, 1920; s. James J. and Ada Leslie (Baker) McC.; m. Margaret Carolyn Phelps, Apr. 9, 1949; children: John Phelps, Julia Jean, Donald Stewart. BA, U. Chgo., 1942, JD, 1949. Bar: Ill. 1950. Ptnr. Gardner, Carton & Douglas, Chgo., 1962-91, of counsel, 1991—2007, 2007—08; mem. Oak Park Plan Commn., 1966-73, Northeastern Ill. Planning Commn., 1973-77, pres., 1975-77, Village of Oak Park, 1973-81, Oak Park Exch. Congress Inc., 1978—2002; ptnr. Drinker Biddle & Reath, 2007—. Mem. Bus. Leaders for Transp., 1998—. Pres. United Christian Cmty. Svcs., 1967-69, 71-73, Erie Neighborhood House, 1953-55, Oak Park-River Forest Cmty. Chest, 1967; moderator Presbytery Chgo., 1969; mem. Gov.'s Spl. Com. on MPO, 1978-79; bd. dirs. Leadership Coun. of Met. Open Cmtys., 1981-2002, sec., 1990-98; bd. dirs. Met. Planning Coun., 1982-93, hon. dir., 1993—; bd. dirs. Cmty. Renewal Soc., 1982-91, v.p., 1984-88, treas. 1988-91; bd. dirs. Christian Century Found., 1972—, chmn., 1981-2008; trustee McCormick Theol. Sem., 1981—, chmn. bd. 1987-90. hon. trustee, 1990—; mem. vocation agy., 1973-82; mem. ch. vocations unit, 1987-92, vice chair 1990; mem. gen. assembly coun. Presbyn. Ch. U.S.A., 1987-90, mem. gen. assembly Permanent Jud. Commn., 1997-2003; bd. dirs. Oak Park Edn. Found., 1991-96, Oak Park River Forest Cmty. Found., 1991-2002; mem. Vision 2000 (Oak Park) Coordinating Com., 1995. With USNR, 1942-46. Recipient Disting. Citizen award Oak Park, 1976; Silver Beaver award; Disting. Eagle Scout award Boy Scouts Am., Carl Winters Cmty. Svc. award Oak Park Rotary Club, 1996, William Staczak award Oak Park Edn. Found., 1997, Rita Johnson award Oak Park Family Svc. and Mental Health Ctr., 1997, Public Svc. award U. Chgo. Alumni Assn., 1997, Tradition of Excellence award Oak Pk. River Forest H.S., 1998, Alumni Svc. medal, Chgo. Alumni Assn., 2003, Gutenberg Award Chgo. Bible Soc., 2003; named one of 100 disting. Oak Parkers for Millenium, Wed Jour., 2002. Mem. ABA, Am. Coll. Trust and Estate Counsel, Ill. State Bar Assn., Chgo. Bar Assn., Am. Law Inst., Order of the Coif, Lambda Alpha. Clubs: Univ. (Chgo.). Office: Drinker Biddle & Reath 191 N Wacker Dr Chicago IL 60606-4719

MCCLURE, LAURA, state legislator; b. Hays, Kan., May 11, 1950; m. John D. McClure. Kans. state rep. Dist. 119, 1993—. Democrat. Friends Church. Office: Kans Ho of Reps State Capitol Topeka KS 66612

MCCLURE, WALTER F., risk management marketing company executive; b. 1934; Head retail brokerage network Arthur J. Gallagher & Co., Itasca, Ill., sr. v.p., dir., chmn., 1993—. Office: Arthur J Gallagher & Co 2 Pierce Pl Itasca IL 60143-3141 Fax: (630) 285-4000.

MCCLURG, JAMES EDWARD, research laboratory executive; b. Bassett, Nebr., Mar. 23, 1945; s. Warren James and Delia Emma (Allyn) McC. B.S., N.E. Wesleyan U., 1967; Ph.D., U. Nebr., 1973. Instr., U. Nebr. Coll. Medicine, Omaha, 1973-76, research instr., 1973-76, clin. asst. prof. Med. Ctr., 1984—; v.p., tech. dir. Harris Labs., Inc., Lincoln, Nebr., 1976-82, exec. v.p., 1982-84, pres., chief exec. officer, 1984—; bd. dirs. Lincoln Mut. Life Ins. Co., Lincoln Gen. Hosp. (chmn.), Unemed Corp., Lincoln, Harris Labs. Ltd, Belfast No. Ireland. Mem. editorial bd. Clin. Rsch. Practices and Drug Regulatory Affairs, 1984. Contbr. articles to profl. jours. Trustee Univ. Nebr. Found.; mem. Commn. on Human Rights, Lincoln, 1982-85; com. mem. Nebr. Citizens for Study Higher Edn., Lincoln, 1984; chmn. U. Nebr. Found. Recipient ann. research award Central Assn. Obstetricians and Gynecologists, 1982. Mem. Am. Assn. Lab. Accreditation (bd. dirs.). Republican. Clubs: Century (pres. Nebr. Wesleyan U. 1983-84), ebraska (Lincoln). Lodge: Rotary. Avocation: boating. Office: Harris Labs Inc PO Box 80837 Lincoln NE 68501-0837

MCCLUSKEY, LAURIE A., lawyer; b. Cin., Oct. 16, 1973; BSN, U. Cin., 1996; JD, Salmon P. Chase Coll. Law, 2002. Bar: Ohio 2002. Assoc. Undhorst & Dreidame Co., L.P.A., Cin. Named one of Ohio's Rising Stars, Super Lawyers, 2006. Mem.: Ohio State Bar Assn., ABA, Cin. Bar Assn. Office: Lindhorst & Dreidame Co LPA 312 Walnut St Ste 2300 Cincinnati OH 45202-4091 Office Phone: 513-421-6630. Office Fax: 513-421-0212.

MCCOLLEY, ROBERT MCNAIR, historian, educator; b. Salina, Kans., Feb. 2, 1933; s. Grant and Alice Elizabeth (McNair) McC.; m. Diane Laurene Kelsey, Aug. 30, 1958; children: Rebecca, Susanna, Teresa, Margaret, Carolyn, Robert Lauren. BA, Harvard U., 1954, MA, 1955; PhD, U Calif.-Berkeley, 1960. Instr. to prof. history U. Ill., Urbana, 1960—97. Mem. Com. for Advanced Placement Test in Am. History, 1987-90, chmn. 1988-90. Author: Slavery and Jeffersonian Virginia, 1964 (Dickerson award 1964); editor: Federalists, Republicans and Foreign Entanglements, 1969, Henry Adams, John Randolph, 1995, Jour. Early Ill. State Hist. Soc., 1998-2002, mem. editl. bd. 2002-07; co-editor: Refracting America, 1993; mem. editl. bd. Jour. Early Republic, 1981-85, Va. Mag. of History and Biography, 1994-98; classical recs. reviewer Fanfare mag., 1989-2006. Mem. Soc. Historians of Early Republic (pres. 1982), Orgn. Am. Historians, Va. Hist. Soc., Ill. Hist. Soc. (bd. dirs. 1978-81, 92-95, pres. 1997-99), Chgo. Hist. Soc., Cliff Dwellers. Home: 503 W Illinois St Urbana IL 61801-3927 Office Phone: 217-344-5138. E-mail: rmccolle@uiuc.edu.

MCCOLLUM, BETTY, congresswoman; b. Mpls., July 12, 1954; m. Douglas McCollum; 2 children. BS in Edn., Coll. St. Catherine, 1987. Retail store mgr., Minn.; mem. Minn. Ho. Reps., 1992-2000, mem. edn. com., environ. and natural resources com., mem. gen. legis. com., vet. affairs and elections com., mem. transportation and transit com., asst. majority leader, chair legis. commn. on econ. status of women, mem. rules and adminstrv. legis. com.; mem. U.S. Congress from Minn. 4th Dist., Washington, 2001—; mem. edn. and workforce com., resources com.; mem. Com. on Internat. Relations. Mem. St. Croix Valley Coun. Girl Scouts. Mem.: Am. Legion Aux., VFW Aux. Democrat. Office: US Ho Reps 1029 Longworth Ho Office Bldg Washington DC 20515-2304

MCCOLLUM, SUSAN, elementary school educator; Grad., Butler County C.C.; BA in Edn., Emporia State U., 1974, MA in Edn., 1979. Nat. bd. cert. tchr. 1998. Tchr. Santa Fe Trail Sch. Dist., Carbondale (Kans.) Sch. Named Disting. Alumni, Emporia State U., 2002. Mem.: NEA, Nat. Bd. for Cert. Tchrs. in Kans. (state chair 2003—), Nat. Bd. for Profl. Tchg. Stds. (bd. mem. 2002—). Office: Carbondale Attendance Ctr 315 N 4th Carbondale KS 66414

MCCOLLUM, W. LEE, chemical company executive; CFO SC Johnson & Son, Inc., Racine, Wis. Bd. dir. Sigma Aldrich Corp., Johnson Outdoors Inc., Johnson Bank, Cofresco. Office: SC Johnson & Son Inc 1525 Howe St Racine WI 53403

MCCOMBS, BILLY JOE (RED MCCOMBS), professional football team executive; m. Charlene McCombs; 3 daughters. Founder, dir. Clear Channel Communications, Inc, 1972—; former owner, chmn. bd. Denver Nuggets, 1982—86, San Antonio Spurs; chair. bd of trustees Southwestern Univ.; owner, chair., pres. Minnesota Vikings, Eden Prairie, 1998—2005. Film appearances: The Longest Yard, 2005. Chmn. bd. trustees Southwestern U.; former chmn. United Way of San Antonio, HemisFair World's Fair '68. Named to Bus. Hall of Fame; named one of Forbes Richest Americans, 2006. Mem. San Antonio C. of C. (former chmn.), Nat. Ford Dealers, U. Tex. Longhorn Club. Office: Winter Pk Admin Office 9520 Viking Dr Eden Prairie MN 55344-3898

MCCOMBS, CHARLINE, professional sports team executive; m. Red McCombs, 1950; children: Lynda, Marsha, Connie. DH (hon.), Southwestern U. Owner Minn. Vikings, Inc. Co-host Tex. Tuxedo fundraiser U. Minn., 1999; vol. Salvation Army, Cris Carter Viking Super Challenge; mentor San Antonio elem. schs.; mem. adv. bd. Friends of Ronald McDonald; bd. dirs. Las Casas Found., San Antonio, Susan G. Komen Breast Cancer Found., nat. adv. bd.; bd. dirs. Cancer Ctr. Coun.; former bd. dirs. Friends of Ronald McDonald, San Antonio; bd. dirs. McNay Art Mus., mem. art and edn. coms. Named Mother of Yr., Advance orgn.; recipient Trfoil award, Girl Scouts U.S., 1999, Spirit of Youth award, Boys Town, Sch. Arch. and Design award, U. Tex., Outstanding Philanthropist award, NAFE, Civic Virtue award, Freedom of Info. Found., Spirit of Philanthropy award, Non-Profit Resource Ctr. Office: 9520 Vikings Dr Eden Prairie MN 55344

MCCONKIE, GEORGE WILSON, education educator; b. Holden, Utah, July 15, 1937; s. G. Wilson and Mabel (Stephenson) McC.; m. Orlene Carol Johnson, Sept. 6, 1962; children: Lynnette Mooth, Heather Usevitch, April Rhiner, Faline Coffelt, George Wilson, Bryce Johnson, Camille Howard, Elissa, Esther Ostler, Bryna Fisher, Ruth Olson, Anna May Cox, Cynthia, Thomas Oscar. AA, Dixie Jr. Coll., 1957; BS, Brigham Young U., 1960, MS, 1961; PhD, Stanford U., 1966. Missionary LDS Ch., 1957-59; asst. prof. edn. Cornell U., 1964-70, asso. prof., 1970-75, prof., 1975-78, chmn. dept. edn., 1977-78; prof. U. Ill., Champaign, 1978—2003, chmn. dept. ednl. psychology, 1993-94, 95-97, prof. emeritus, 2003—. Sr. scientist Ctr. for Study of Reading, 1978-95, Beckman Inst., 1989-2004; rsch. fellow Cath. U. Louvain, Belgium, 1991-92; vis. prof. Nat. Yang Ming U., Taiwan, 1998, Beijing Normal U., 1999. Contbr. articles to profl. jours. Recipient Outstanding Sci. Contbn. award Soc. for Sci. Study of Reading, 1995; NIMH spl. fellow, 1971-72, NIH Fogarty Internat. fellow, 1991-92; grantee U.S. Office Edn., 1970-73, Nat. Inst. Edn., 1974-77, NIMH, 1974-84, NICHHD, 1983-89, 91-95, AT&T, 1986-89, NSF, 1989-91, 2000-03, CIA, 1991-97, Army Rsch. Lab., 1996-2001, Yamaha Motor Corp., 1997-99, GM, 2002-04; Fulbright scholar, Taiwan, 1998, Sr. scholar Chiang Chung Kuo Found., 1998-99. Mem. Lds Ch. Home: 2605 Berniece Dr Champaign IL 61822-7225 Office: Coll Education Dept Educational Psych 1310 S Sixth St Champaign IL 61820 Business E-Mail: gmcconk@uiuc.edu.

MCCONNAUGHEY, GEORGE CARLTON, JR., retired lawyer; b. Hillsboro, Ohio, Aug. 9, 1925; s. George Carlton and Nelle (Morse) McC.; m. Carolyn Schlieper, June 16, 1951; children: Elizabeth, Susan, Nancy. BA, Denison U., 1949; LLB, Ohio State U., 1951, JD, 1967. Bar: Ohio 1951. Sole practice, Columbus; ptnr. McConnaughey & McConnaughey, 1954-57, McConnaughey, McConnaughey & Stradley, 1957-62, Laylin, McConnaughey & Stradley, 1962-67, George, Greek, King, McMahon & McConnaughey, 1967-79, McConnaughey, Stradley, Mone & Moul, 1979-81, Thompson, Hine & Flory (merger McConnaughey, Stradley, Mone & Moul with Thompson, Hine & Flory), 1981—92, ret. ptnr., 1992—. Bd. dirs. N.Am. Broadcasting Co. (Sta. WMNI, WBZX and WTDA Radio); asst. atty. gen. State of Ohio, 1951-54. Pres. Upper Arlington (Ohio) Bd. Edn., 1967-69, Columbus Town Meeting Assn., 1974-76; chmn. Ohio Young Reps., 1956; U.S. presdl. elector, 1956; trustee Buckeye Boys Ranch, Columbus, 1967-73, 75-81, Upper Arlington Edn. Found., 1987-93; elder Covenant Presbyn. Ch., Columbus. With U.S. Army, 1943-45, ETO. Fellow Am. Bar Found., Ohio Bar Found., Columbus Bar Found.; mem. ABA, Ohio State Bar Assn., Columbus Bar Assn., Am. Judicature Soc., Scioto Country Club, Athletic Club, Rotary, Masons. Home: 1993 Collingswood Rd Columbus OH 43221-3741 Office: Thompson Hine LLP One Columbus 10 W Broad St Ste 700 Columbus OH 43215-3435 Office Phone: 614-469-3224.

MCCONNELL, E. HOY, II, advertising and public policy executive; b. Syracuse, NY, May 14, 1941; s. E. Hoy and Dorothy R. (Schmitt) McC.; m. Patricia Irwin, June 26, 1965; children: E. Hoy, III, Courtney. BA in Am. Studies magna cum laude with high honors, Yale U., 1963; MBA in Mktg, Harvard Bus. Sch., 1965. With Foote, Cone & Belding, Chgo., 1965-76, v.p. account supr., 1971—76; with D'Arcy-MacManus & Masius, Chgo., 1976-85, sr. v.p., dir. client services, then vice chmn., 1978-80, pres., 1980-84, chmn., 1984-85; mng. dir. D'Arcy Masius Benton & Bowles, Chgo., 1986-96, also bd. dirs.; sr. v.p., account dir. Leo Burnett Co., Chgo., 1996-98; exec. dir. Bus. and Profl. People for the Pub. Interest, 1999—. Bd. dirs. Evanston (Ill.) United Way, 1980-83, Evanston Youth Hockey Assn., 1980-89, pres. 1981-83; bd. dirs. Off-the-Street Club, 1980-90, Bus. Profl. People for Pub. Interest, 1981-, v.p. 1984-89, pres. 1990-95; co-chair Housing Ill., 2002-; bd. dirs. Harvard Bus. Sch. Club, 1990-92; bd. dirs. The Cradle Soc., 2000-07, mem. exec com., 2004-07, sec, 2004-05, treas., 2005-07; mem. Chgo. Coun. on Fgn. Rels., 1989-95, Wayfarers Club, 2001-. Mem. Am. Assn. Advt. Agys. (gov.-at-large Chgo. coun. 1984, sec. 1986, vice chmn. 1987, chmn. 1988-89), Glen View Country Club (bd. dirs. 1992-96), Dairymen's Country Club, Yale Club Chgo. (bd. dirs. 1996-99). Democrat. Unitarian Universalist. Home: 2703 Colfax St Evanston IL 60201-2035 Office: BPI 25 E Washington St Ste 1515 Chicago IL 60602-1804 Office Phone: 312-759-8259. Business E-Mail: hmcconnell@bpichicago.org.

MCCONNELL, JOHN P., metal products executive; With Worthington Industries, Columbus, Ohio, 1975—, v.p., gen. mgr., 1985, dir., 1990—, vice chmn., 1992—96, CEO, 1993—, chmn., 1996—. Bd. dir. Alltel Corp., The Wilds. Office: Worthington Industries 200 Old Wilson Bridge Rd Columbus OH 43085

MCCONNELL, JOHN THOMAS, publishing executive; b. Peoria, Ill., May 1, 1945; s. Golden A. and Margaret (Lyon) McC.; 1 child, Justin. BA, U. Ariz., 1967. Mgr. Fast Printing Co., Peoria, 1970-71; mgmt. trainee Quad-Cities Times, Davenport, Iowa, 1972-73; asst. gen. mgr., then v.p., gen. mgr. Peoria Jour. Star, 1973-81, pub., 1981—, pres., 1987—; v.p. The Copley Press, Inc., Peoria, 1997—. Bd. dirs. Peoria Downtown Devel. Council, Peoria Devel. Corp.; past trustee Methodist Hosp., Peoria. Served with USAR, 1967-69. Named Young Man of Year Peoria Jaycees, 1979 Mem. Peoria Advt. and Selling Club, Peoria C. of C. Clubs: Peoria Country, Mt. Hawley C.C. Congregationalist. Office: Peoria Jour Star Inc 1 News Plz Peoria IL 61643-0001 Business E-Mail: mac@pjstar.com.

MCCONNELL, MARY PATRICIA, lawyer; b. Mpls., Sept. 30, 1952; BS, U. Minn., 1978; JD, William Mitchell Coll. Law, St. Paul, 1984. Bar: Minn. 1988. Sr. biologist C.E., U.S. Army, St. Paul, 1979-84; asst. county atty. Dakota County, Hastings, Minn., 1985—92; ptnr. Lindquist & Vennum, Mpls., 1992—95; from v.p. environ. and regulatory affairs to sr. v.p., gen. counsel, sec. Genmar Holdings, Inc., 1995—2002; gen. counsel control products divsn. Honeywell, 2002—03; v.p., gen. counsel Polaris Industries, Inc., Medinia, Minn., 2003—. Master gardener U. Minn. Ext., St. Paul, 1992—. Contbr. articles to profl. jours. Dir. Wetlands Forum, Mpls., 1990—. Mem. Minn. Bar Assn. (governing coun. environ. and natural resources 1990—, law sect.), Mpls. C. of C. (Leadership Mpls. 1992). Office: Polaris Industries Inc 2100 Highway 55 Medina MN 55340 Office Phone: 763-542-0500. Office Fax: 763-542-0599. E-mail: mary.mcconnell@polarisind.com.

MCCONNELL, WILLIAM F., JR., medical products executive; b. LaGrange, Ill. BS in sys. analysis, Miami U., Oxford, Ohio, 1971. CPA. Staff mem. Arthur Andersen LLP, Indpls., 1971—75, mgr., 1975—81, ptnr., 1981—83, mng. ptnr., bus. cons., 1983—89, rejoined, 1997; CFO Resort Condo. Internat., 1989—90, COO, 1990—96, info. officer, worldwide, 1996—97; v.p., COO Guidant Corp., Indpls., Ill., 1998—2006; sr. v.p. adminstrn. Boston Scientific Corp., Natick, Mass., 2006—. Bd. dir. Global Healthcare Exchange, Vesalius Ventures. Former chmn. Children's Mus. of Indpls., Am. Red Cross of Greater Indpls., Red Cross of Conner Prairie; former bd. mem. Acordia Personal Ins. Svcs.; hon. trustee Children's Mus. of Indpls.; bd. gov. Nat. Am. Red Cross; chmn. bd. trustee Trustee Leadership Development; bd. mem., info. tech. com. Cmty. Hosp. of Indpls., Inc., Ind. U. Info. Tech. Advancement Coun. Office: Boston Scientific Corp One Boston Scientific Pl Natick MA 01760

MCCONNELL, WILLIAM THOMPSON, bank executive; b. Zanesville, Ohio, Aug. 8, 1933; s. William Gerald and Mary Gladys McC.; m. Jane Charlotte Cook, Aug. 25, 1956; children: Jennifer Wynne, William Gerald. BA, Denison U., 1955; MBA, Northwestern U., 1959. Pres. Park Nat. Bank, Newark, Ohio, 1979-83, pres., chief exec. officer, 1983-93, chmn., chief exec. officer, 1993-98, also bd. dirs., chmn., 1999—2004; pres., chief exec. officer Park Nat. Corp., Newark, 1987-94, chmn., CEO, 1994-98, chmn., 1999—2004, chmn. exec. com., 2005—. Mem. Newark Area C. of C. (past pres., dir. 1977-83), Ohio Bankers Assn. (pres., chmn. 1981-83), Am. Bankers Assn. (pres. 1997-98). Office: Park Nat Bank PO Box 3500 Newark OH 43058-3500

MCCONVILLE, RITA JEAN, finance executive; b. Chgo., July 7, 1958; d. Daniel Joseph and Rosemary (Smolinski) McC. BA, Northwestern U., 1979; MBA, U. Chgo., 1982. CPA, Ill. Fin. analyst Miami Valley Hosp., Dayton, Ohio, 1982-85; sr. cons. Health Facilities Corp., Northfield, Ill., 1985-87; sr. fin. analyst Lyphomed, Inc., Rosemont, Ill., 1987-88, mgr. fin. planning, 1988-90; controller Videocart, Inc., Chgo., 1990-93, OptionCare, Inc., Bannockburn, Ill., 1993-97; v.p., CFO, sec. Akorn, Inc., Buffalo Grove, Ill., 1997—. Mem. Ill. CPA Soc. Office: Akorn Inc 2500 Millbrook Dr Buffalo Grove IL 60089-4694 Home: 177 Willow Blvd Willow Springs IL 60480-1644

MCCOOLE, ROBERT F., construction company executive; b. St. Louis, Mar. 26, 1950; BS, St. Louis U., 1972. Project mgr. J.S. Alberici Constrn. Co. Inc., St. Louis, 1981-84, v.p. bus. devel., 1987-93, sr. v.p. bus. devel., 1993-96, pres., 1996—. Mem. Assoc. Gen. Contractors (chair 1997—). Office: JS Alberici Constrn Co Inc 2150 Kienlen Ave Saint Louis MO 63121-5505

MCCORKLE, LEON MARSHALL, JR., lawyer, educator; b. Alliance, Ohio, Mar. 2, 1941; s. Leon Marshall and Mary Carrington McC.; m. Patricia McCorkle Dec. 28, 1964 (div. Oct. 1982); children: Catherine Shapiro, Molly Carrington McCorkle; m. Virginia Marie Brotherton Trethewey, Nov. 28, 1986; children: Kyle, John Marshall. AB, Harvard Coll., Cambridge, Mass., 1964; JD, The Ohio State U. Coll. Law, Columbus, 1972. Bar: Supreme Ct. Ohio, 1972, U.S. Ct. (so. dist.), 1990. Sr. ptnr. Vorys, Sater, Seymour & Pease, LLP, Columbus, Ohio, 1972-98; adj. prof. Ohio State U. Coll. Law, Columbus, 1991-92, 95—; sr. v.p., gen. counsel Wendy's Internat., Inc., Dublin, Ohio, 1998, exec. v.p., gen. counsel, sec. Commr. Nat. Conf. Commissioners on Uniform State Laws, Chgo., 1988—. Editor in chief The Ohio State U. Law Jour., 1971-72. Lt. USN, 1963-69. Trustee Columbus Symphony Orchestra, Columbus, 1997-98, Columbus Bar Svcs., Inc., 1999; mem. bd. dirs. ACCA, Columbus, 1999. Fellow Columbus Bar Found.; mem. ABA, Ohio State Bar Found., Columbus Bar Found., Put-in-Bay Yacht Club, Am. Law Inst., Order of the Coif. Avocations: boating, weather instructor U.S. Power Squadrons, my children. Office: Wendys Internat Inc PO Box 256 Dublin OH 43017-0256 also: Wendy's International Inc One Dave Thomas Blvd Dublin OH 43017

MCCORMACK, MICHAEL, state supreme court justice; b. Omaha, July 20, 1939; JD, Creighton U., 1963. Asst. pub. defender, Douglas County, Nebr., 1963-66; pvt. practice Omaha, 1966-97; justice Nebr. Supreme Ct., 1997—. Fellow: Internat. Soc. Barristers; mem.: Sarpy County Bar Assn., Omaha Bar Assn., Colo. Bar Assn., Nebr. State Bar Assn. Office: State Capitol Bldg Rm 2218 Lincoln NE 68509 also: PO Box 98910 Lincoln NE 68509

MCCORMACK, MICHAEL JOSEPH, foundation administrator; b. St. Ignatius, Mont., July 19, 1952; s. Richard Joseph and Leona Julianna (Wasinger) McC.; m. Eileen Marie Turro, June 21, 1997. BA, Harvard U., 1974. Co-founder World Hello Day, 1973—. Author: Senti and Pigasso, 1997, Farewell Fillmore High, 1999; actor (play) My Antonia, 1994, Glory Years, 1995, Tony 'n Tina's Wedding, 1998-99, Farewell Fillmore High, 1999; (film) The Chess Murders, 1996, What Happened to Tully?, 1999; represented in permanent collections Internat. Mus. Peace and Solidarity, Samarkand, Uzbekistan, 1993. Recipient Freedoms Found. award Freedoms Found. Valley Forge, 1970. Mem. Signet Soc., Theatre Arts Guild, Alleged Perpetrators Improv, Nebr. Film, Video and TV Assn. Roman Catholic. Avocations: song writing, reading, violin, art, history.

MCCORMACK, ROBERT CORNELIUS, investment banker; b. NYC, Nov. 7, 1939; m. Mary Lester, Dec. 14, 1963; children: Robert Cornelius Jr., Walter, Scott. BA, U. N.C., 1962; MBA, U. Chgo., 1968. V.p. Dillon Read & Co. Inc., 1968-81; mng. dir. Morgan Stanley & Co., Inc., Chgo., 1981-87; dep. asst sec. def. prodn. support U.S. Dept. Def., Washington, 1987-88, dep. under sec. def. indsl. and internat. programs, 1988-89, acting dep. under sec. of def. acquisition, 1989-90, asst. sec. avy fin. mgmt. Washington, 1990-93; founding ptnr. Trident Capital L.P., Chgo., 1993—. Served to lt. USNR, 1963-66. Office: 277 83RD St #B2 Burr Ridge IL 60527-5846

MCCORMICK, JAMES HAROLD, academic administrator; b. Ind., Pa., Nov. 11, 1938; s. Harold Clark and Mary Blanche (Truby) McCormick; m. Maryan Kough Garner, June 7, 1963; children: David Harold, Douglas Paul. BS, Indiana U. of Pa., 1959; MEd, U. Pitts., 1961, EdD, 1963, postdoctoral, 1966, Columbia U., U. Mich., 1966-67, Harvard U., 1982. Tchr. Punxsutawney (Pa.) Area Joint Sch. Dist., 1959-61; adminstr. Baldwin-Whitehall Schs., Pitts., 1961-64; grad. asst. U. Pitts., 1962-63; asst. supt. instrn. Washington (Pa.) City Schs., 1964-65; prof. dept. edn. and psychology, asst. dean acad. affairs, acting dean acad. affairs, acting dean tchr. edn., asst. to pres., v.p. adminstrn. and fin. Shippensburg (Pa.) U., 1965-73; pres. Bloomsburg (Pa.) U., 1973-83, pres. emeritus, 1983—; founding chancellor Pa. State System Higher Edn., Harrisburg, 1983—2001; chancellor Minn. State Colls. and Univs., 2001—. Falk intern in politics, 1959; mem. adv. bd. Pa. Ednl. Policy Seminar; mem. Gov.'s Econ. Devel. Partnership Bd.; mem. higher edn. adv. coun. Pa. State Bd. Edn.; past commr. Edn. Commn. of the States; past chmn. Midwestern Higher Edn. Compact; bd. mem. Great North Alliance, Minn. Job Skills Partnership; founder, mem. Minn. P-16 Edn. Partnership; active Govs. Edn. Coun.; mem. postsecondary edn. and workforce devel. adv. com. Edn. Comm. States. Contbr. articles profl. jours. Named One of 10 Outstanding Young Men of Yr., Pa. Jr. C. of C.; recipient Young Leader in Edn. award Phi Delta Kappa, 1981, Disting. Alumnus award Indiana U. Pa., 1981, Outstanding Alumni award Bloomsburg U., 1984, Outstanding Alumnus award U. Pitts., 1985, Adler award Pa. Edn. Assn., 1992; selected CIVITAS Prague mission, 1995, Presdl. Lectures, Kuwait U., 1993, Svc. award Coll. and Univ. Pub. Rels., Assn. Pa., 1999, Disting. Svc. award Pa. Assn. Couns. of Trustees, 1998, Alumni Assn. Leadership award Bloomsburg U., 1999; McCormick Human Svcs. Ctr. named in his honor Bloomsburg U., 1983; McCormick House named in his honor Dixon U., 1994, Accreditation Team Negotiator US Dept. Edn., 2007. Mem. Am. Assn. State Colls. and Univs. (Pa. state rep. 1988-93, former chmn. acad. and student pers. com., mem. com. on state rels. and task force on ednl. equity, chmn. policies and purposes com., mem. Internat. Edn.), Am. Coun. on Edn. (commn. on women in higher edn.), Nat. Assn. Sys. Heads, (exec. com., past pres.), Commn. State Colls. and Univs. (mem. and past chmn. govt. rels. and student rels. coms.), Assn. Governing Bds. (adv. coun.), Am. Assn. for Affirmative Action, Am. Assn. Higher Edn., Am. Assn. Sch. Adminstrs., Am. Assn. Univ. Adminstrs. (Tosney Leadership award 1993), Pa. Assn. Colls. and Univs. (bd. dirs., chair 1982), Natl. Ctr. for the Study of Sport in Soc., Pa. Black Conf. on Higher Edn., State Higher Edn. Exec. Ofcrs. (exec. com., chair Fed. Relations Com.), Pers. Assn., Bloomsburg Area C. of C. (pres. 1983), Harrisburg Rotary (bd. dirs. to 1992), St. Paul Rotary (bd. dir. to 2007), Phi Delta Kappa. Office: Wells Fargo Pl 30 7th St East Ste 350 Saint Paul MN 55101 Home: 10560 Pinnacle Way Woodbury MN 55129 Office Phone: 651-296-7971.*

MCCORMICK, MICHAEL D., lawyer; b. Vincennes, Ind., Mar. 18, 1948; m. Margaret A. McCormick; children: Claire E., Brooks R. AB, Duke U., 1970; JD,

Ind. U., 1980. V.p. I & S McDaniel Inc., Vincennes, 1970-77; ptnr. Scopelitis & Garvin, Indpls., 1980-83; pres. Wales Transp. Co., Dallas, 1983-85; v.p., gen. counsel Overland Express Inc., Indpls., 1985-87, Bindley Western Industries Inc., Indpls., 1987—. Mem. ABA, Ind. Bar Assn., Indpls. Bar Assn.

MCCORMICK, STEVEN D., lawyer; b. Waterloo, Iowa, Apr. 24, 1946; AB, U. Notre Dame, 1968; JD, Northwestern U., 1971. Bar: Ill. 1972, NY 1992. Ptnr. Kirkland & Ellis LLP, Chgo., 1977—, head in-house trial advocacy prog., 1993—. Lectr., demonstrator, instr. Nat. Inst. Trial Advocacy, Chgo. and Boulder, Colo., 1989—98; adj. prof. integrated trial advocacy course Northwestern U. Sch. Law, 1997—. Articles editor: Northwestern U. Law Rev., 1970—71. Named one of Top 10 Trial Lawyers in Am., Nat. Law Jour., 2006, Am.'s Leading Lawyers for Bus., Chambers USA, 2006. Office: Kirkland & Ellis LLP 200 E Randolph Dr Fl 54 Chicago IL 60601-6636 Office Phone: 312-861-2246. Office Fax: 312-861-2200. E-mail: smccormick@kirkland.com.

MCCORMICK, TERRI, state legislator; b. Waupun, Wis., Oct. 24, 1956; married; 3 children. BS, U. Wis., 1980; postgrad., U. Windsor, Ont., Can., 1982, Lawrence U., 1993; MA, Marian Coll., 2000. Former edn. cons.; mem. Wis. State Assembly, Dist. 56, Madison, 2000—, mem. edn. reform, ins., judiciary, labor and workforce devel., pub. health and state/local fin. coms. Coach Xavier Mock Trial Team; mem. Winnebago County r. Mem.: Am. Legion Aux. Republican. Office: State Capitol Rm 127W PO Box 8953 Madison WI 53708-8953 Home: W6140 Long Ct Appleton WI 54914-8594

MCCOTTER, THADDEUS GEORGE, congressman; b. Livonia, Mich., Aug. 22, 1965; s. Dennis and Joan McCotter; m. Rita Michel; children: George, Timothy, Emilia. BA in Polit. Sci., summa cum laude, U. Detroit, 1987, JD, 1990. Bar: Mich. 1991. Trustee Schoolcraft C.C., 1989; commr. Wayne County, Mich., 1992-98; mem. 9th dist. Mich. Senate, Lansing, 1998—2002; mem. US Congress from 3rd Mich. dist., 2003—. Mem. com. budget US Congress, com. internat. relations, com. small bus. Rep. precinct del., 1986; chair Wayne County Rep. com. Recipient Outstanding Michigander award, Mich. Jaycees, 2001, Legis. of Yr., Police Officers Assn. of Mich., 2002. Republican. Roman Catholic. Office: District Office 17197 N Laurel Pk Dr Ste 533 Livonia MI 48152-7908 also: US Congress 1632 LHOB Washington DC 20515-2211 Office Phone: 202-225-8171, 734-632-0314. Office Fax: 202-225-2667, 734-632-0373.

MCCOY, FREDERICK JOHN, retired plastic surgeon; b. McPherson, Kans., Jan. 17, 1916; s. Merle D. and Mae (Tennis) McC.; m. Mary Bock, May 17, 1972; children: Judith, Frederick John, Patricia, Melissa, Steven. BS, U. Kans., 1938, MD, 1942. Diplomate Am. Bd. Plastic Surgery (dir. 1973-79, chmn. 1979). Intern Lucas County Hosp., Toledo, 1942-43; resident in plastic surgery U. Tex. Med. Sch., Galveston, 1946; preceptorship in surgery Grand Rapids, Mich., 1947-50; practice medicine specializing in plastic and reconstructive surgery Kansas City, Mo., 1950-93; staff St. Mary's Hosp., 1950-83, St. Joseph's Hosp., 1950—, N. Kansas City Meml. Hosp., 1955—; mem. staff, chief plastic surgery Kansas City Gen. Hosp. and Med. Center, 1952-72, Children's Mercy Hosp., 1954-93, Research Hosp., 1950—, St. Luke's Hosp., 1951—, Baptist Hosp., 1958—, Menorah Hosp., 1950—; chief div. plastic surgery Truman Med. Ctr., 1972-91; chmn. maxillo-facial surgery U. Kansas City Sch. Dentistry, 1950-57; assoc. prof. surgery U. Mo. Med. Sch., Kansas City, 1964-69, clin. prof. surgery, 1969—; pres. McCoy Enterprises, Kansas City, Mo. Contbr. articles to profl. jours.; editor: Year Book of Plastic and Reconstructive Surgery, 1971-88. Bd. govs. Kansas City Mus., 1959-93, pres., 1973-74. Served to maj. M.C. U.S. Army, 1943-46. Mem. ACS (pres. Mo. chpt. 1973), AMA, Am. Acad. Pediatrics, Am. Soc. Plastic and Reconstructive Surgeons (sec. 1969-73, dir. 1973-76, pres. 1976, chmn. bd. 1977, Spl. Achievement award 1988), Am. Soc. Pediat. Plastic Surgeons, Pan Pacific Surg. Soc., Singleton Surg. Soc. (v.p. 1965), Am. Assn. Plastic Surgeons (founder plastic surgery rsch. coun.), Internat. Soc. Aesthetic Plastic Surgery, Am. Soc. Aesthetic Plastic Surgery, Jackson County Med. Soc. (pres. 1964-65), Kansas City Southwest Clin. Soc. (pres. 1971), Mo. Med. Assn. (v.p. 1975), Internat. Coll. Surgeons (v.p. 1969), Royal Soc. Medicine (London), U. Tex. Sys. Chancellors Coun., Kansas City C. of C., Conservation Fedn. Mo., Natural Sci. Soc. (founder, chmn. 1973), Citizens Assn. Kansas City, Explorer's Club, Mission Hills Country Club, Boone and Crocket Club, Phi Delta Theta, Nu Sigma Nu. Republican. Mem. Christian Ch.

MCCOY, JOHN BONNET, retired bank executive; b. Columbus, Ohio, June 11, 1943; s. John Gardner and Jeanne Newlove (Bonnet) McC.; m. Jane Deborah Taylor, Apr. 21, 1968; children: Tracy Bonnet, Paige Taylor, John Taylor. BA, Williams Coll., Williamstown, Mass., 1965; MBA, Stanford U., Calif., 1967; LLD (hon.), Williams Coll., 1991; D of Bus. Adminstrn. (hon.), Ohio State U., Columbus, 1993; LLD (hon.), Kenyon Coll., Gambier, Ohio, 1994. With Banc One Corp., Columbus NA, Columbus, Ohio, 1970—, banking officer, 1970-73, v.p., 1973-77, pres., 1977-83; pres., COO Banc One Corp., Columbus, Ohio, 1983-84, pres., CEO, 1984-87, chmn., CEO, 1987-99, also bd. dirs., past chmn., CEO Chgo., 1999. Pres., COO Banc One Corp., Columbus, Ohio, 1983-84, pres., CEO, 1984-87, chmn. CEO, 1987—, also bd. dirs.; pres. Bank One Trust Co., 1979-81; bd. dirs. Cardinal Health, Inc., Fed. Home Loan Mortgage Corp., 1990-2005, AT&T, Choice Point, Inc.,; fed. adv. coun. Fed. Res. Sys., 1991-93. Trustee, chmn. bd. dirs. Kenyon Coll., 1992-95; trustee Stanford U., 1986-96, Williams Coll., 1996-2001, Battelle Meml. Inst.; bd. dirs., chmn. bd. PGA Tour; past pres. Columbus Area Growth Found.; chmn. Capitol South Urban Redevel. Corp., 1975-2007. Capt. USAF, 1967-70. Recipient Ernest C. Arbuckle award Stanford U., 1994. Mem. Columbus C. of C. (past chmn., trustee), Am. Bankers Assn., Bankers Roundtable (bd. dirs. 1989-94), Assn. Bank Holding Cos., Young Pres. Orgn. (chmn. Columbus chpt. 1982-83), Cypress Point Club, Seminole Golf Club, Links Club N.Y.C. Episcopalian. Office: Banc One Corp 191 W Nationwide Blvd Ste 625 Columbus OH 43215

MCCOY, JOHN JOSEPH, lawyer; b. Cin., Mar. 15, 1952; s. Raymond F. and Margaret T. (Hohmann) McC. BS in Math. summa cum laude, Xavier U., 1974; JD, U. Chgo., 1977. Bar: Ohio 1977, D.C. 1980. Ptnr. Taft, Stettinius & Hollister, Cin., 1977—, exec. com., 2002—. Lectr. Greater Cin. C. of C., 1984. Pro bono rep. Jr. Achievement Greater Cin., 1978; fund raiser Dan Beard coun. Boy Scouts Am., 1983; fund raising team leader Cin. Regatta, Cin. Ctr. Devel. Disorders, 1983; account mgr. United Appeal, Cin., 1984; mem. green areas trust adv. com. Village of Indian Hill, 1994-98. Named to Ohio Super Lawyers, 2006, Best Lawyers in Am. Mem. ABA, Ohio State Bar Assn. (banking, comml. and bankruptcy law com., corp. law com., fed. ct. practice com.), Cin. Bar Assn. (fed. cts., common pleas cts. and negligence law coms., trustee Vol. Lawyers for the Poor Found. 1994-2007, chmn. 1996-97), Cin. Inn. of Ct. (barrister 1984-86), Cin. Athletic Club (pres. bd. trustees 1986-89, nominating com. 1989—), Rhodesian Ridgeback Club of the U.S. (bd. dirs. 2000—). Office Phone: 513-357-9348.

MCCOY, JOHN V., lawyer; b. Waukesha, Wis., June 7, 1958; BS, U. Wis., Oshkosh, 1980; JD, Drake U., 1984. Bar: Wis. 1988, Iowa 1984, US Dist. Ct. (Ea. & We. Dist.), Wis. Ptnr. McCoy & Hofbauer, Waukesha, Wis. Pres. Propane Gas Defense Assn., 1994—95; chair & founding mem. Self-Insurance Inst. of Am., Wis. div., 1998; mem. Civil Trial Counsel of Wis., Defense Rsch. Inst., Federation of Defense and Corp. Counsel. Pres. & founding mem. Wis. Clean Cities-Southeast Area, Inc., 1994—; bd. dirs. Ctr. for Deaf and Hard of Hearing, 1990—96, 1999—. Mem.: Waukesha County Bar Assn., Milwaukee County Bar Assn., Wis. Bar Assn. Office: McCoy & Hofbauer Riverwood Corp Ctr N19 W24200 Riverwood Dr Ste 125 Waukesha WI 53188 Office Phone: 252-522-7000. Office Fax: 252-522-7020. Business E-Mail: jmccoy@mh-law.us.

MCCOY, MARILYN, director; b. Providence, Mar. 18, 1948; d. James Francis and Eleanor (Regan) McC.; m. Charles R. Thomas, Jan. 28, 1983. BA in Econs. cum laude, Smith Coll., 1970; M in Pub. Policy, U. Mich., 1972. Dir. Nat. Ctr. for Higher Edn. Mgmt. Systems, Boulder, Colo., 1972-80; dir. planning and policy devel. U. Colo., Boulder, 1981-85; v.p. adminstrn. and planning Northwestern U., Evanston, Ill., 1985—. Trustee JPMorgan Funds. Co-author: Financing Higher Education in the Fifty States, 1976, 3d edit., 1982. Bd. dir. Evanston Northwestern HealthCare Rsch. Inst., 1988—, Mather Found., 1995—; trustee Carleton Coll., 2003—. Mem. Soc. for Coll. and Univ. Planning (pres., v.p., sec., bd. dir. 1980—), Assn. for Instnl. Rsch. (pres., v.p., exec. com., publ. bd. 1978-87), Chgo. Network (chmn. 1992-93), Chgo. Econ. Club. Home: 1100 N Lake Shore Dr Chicago IL 60611-1070 Office: Northwestern U 633 Clark St Evanston IL 60208-0001

MCCOY, MATTHEW WILLIAM, state legislator; b. Des Moines, Mar. 29, 1966; s. William Paul and Mary Ann (Kenneally) McC.; 1 son, Jack William. BA in History and Polit. Sci., Briar Cliff Coll., 1988. V.p. industry rels. Ruan Transp. Mgmt. Systems, Des Moines, 1989-92; mem. Iowa Ho. of Reps., Des Moines, 1992-96, Iowa Senate Dist. 31, Des Moines, 1996—. Bd. dirs. Polk County (Iowa) Conservation Bd.; vice chair YMCA Bd. Mgrs.; mem. Youth Emergency Svcs. & Shelter Bd.; fundraising chair, Boy Scouts of Am. Mem.: Downtown Des Moines (Iowa) Cmty. Alliance (v.p.). Democrat. E-mail: mmccoy@ruan.com. Also: mmcoy@mccoyfor congress.com.

MCCOY, MICHAEL J., food products company executive; BS in Acctg., Loras Coll., 1969. With Hormel Foods Corp., Austin, Minn., 1992—, mem. staff treas.' office, co. treas., 1996-97, v.p., 1997-2000, sr. v.p. adminstrn., CFO, 2000—. Office: Hormel Foods One Hormel Pl Austin MN 55912-3680

MCCRACKEN, ELLIS W., JR., retired lawyer, corporation executive; BA, Lebanon Valley Coll., 1963; LLB, St. John's U., 1967. Bar: NY 1967, NJ 1969, Ohio 1972, Mo. 1993. Primary contract atty. foods divsn. Borden, Inc., 1970—74; assoc. Milbank, Tweed, Hadley & McCloy, 1967—70; v.p., gen. counsel Campbell Taggart, Inc., Dallas, 1980—92, Anheuser-Busch Co., St. Louis, 1992—.

MCCRACKEN, STEVEN R., former consumer products company executive; b. Tacoma, Wash., Apr. 11, 1953; m. Judy McCracken; children: Morgan, Kelsey. BS in Mech. Engring., Rose-Hulman Inst. Tech. Field engr. DuPont, Nonwovens-Tyvek, 1978—79, fin. mgr., 1981—84, mktg. dir. apparel, 1984—89; mng. dir. Lycra, Geneva, 1989—93, DuPont Corian, 1993—97, v.p., gen. mgr., 1997—2001; group v.p., gen. mgr. DuPont Apparel & Textile Scis., 2001—02; group v.p. DuPont Textiles & Interiors, Wilmington, Del., 2002—03; pres. Invista Inc. (formerly Dupont Textiles & Interiors), Wilmington, Del., 2003—04; CEO Invista Inc., 2003, COO, 2003—04; pres., CEO, chmn. Owens-Illinois, Inc., Toledo, 2004—06.

MCCRACKEN, THOMAS JAMES, JR., lawyer; b. Chgo., Oct. 27, 1952; s. Thomas J. Sr. and Eileen (Brophy) McC.; children: Catherine, Michael, Amanda, Quinn. BA, Marquette U., 1974; JD, Loyola U., 1977. Bar: Ill. 1977, U.S. Dist. Ct. (no. dist.) Ill., U.S. Ct. Appeals (7th cir.) 1984. Asst. state's atty. DuPage County State's Atty.'s Office, Wheaton, Ill., 1977—81; assoc. atty. McCracken & Walsh, Chgo., 1981—84; prin. Thomas J. McCracken Jr and Assoc., Chgo., 1984—. Commr. Nat. Conf. of Commns. on Uniform State Laws, 1989-. Contbr. articles to profl. jours. State rep. Ill. Gen. Assembly, Springfield, Ill., 1983-93, state senator, 1993; chmn. Regional Trans. Authority, Chgo., 1993-2004; dir. United Republican Fund, 2005-, Civic. Fedn. Chgo., 2006-. Named Top Ten Legislators Chgo. Mag., 1990. Mem.: Chgo. Bar Assn., Ill. State Bar Assn. Avocations: skiing, hunting, golf. Office: Thomas J McCracken Jr and Assoc 161 N Clark St Chicago IL 60601

MCCRAE, KEITH R., medical educator, researcher; b. Springfield, Mass., Dec. 4, 1956; m. Jo Ann McCrae; children: Brett, Kristen Ann. BA in Biochemistry summa cum laude, Dartmouth Coll., 1978; MD, Duke U., 1982. Diplomate Am. Bd. Internal Medicine, Am. Bd. Med. Oncology, Am. Bd. Hematology. Resident in internal medicine Duke U. Med. Ctr., Durham, 1982—85; fellow in hematology and oncology U. Pa., Phila., 1985—89, postdoctoral fellow, 1986—88, co-dir. clin. coagulation lab., 1991-93, dir. clin. coagulation course, 1992—93; rsch. assoc. U. Pa. Sch. Medicine, 1989, lectr. bridge curriculum, 1989—93, asst. prof. medicine, 1990—93, asst. prof. pathology and lab. medicine, 1991—93; lectr. basic curriculum U. Pa. Dental Sch., 1989—92; attending physician Hosp. of U. Pa., 1989—93, Phila. VA Hosp., 1990—93, Temple U. Hosp., 1993—; asst. prof. medicine Temple U. Sch. Medicine, 1993—96, lectr. bridge curriculum, 1993—, assoc. prof. medicine, 1996—. Tchg. attending hematology consult svc. U. Pa., 1989—93, tchg. attending hematology oncology inpatient unit, 1992—93; with hematology/oncology outpatient clinic, 1989—93; attending staff mem. hematology consult svc. Temple U. Sch. Medicine, 1993—, attending staff mem. hematology sickle cell outpatient clinic, 1993—, attending staff mem. gen. internal medicine svc., 1993; lectr. in field. Co-author (with M.D. Feldman): Blood: Hemostasis, Transfusion and Alternatives in the Perioperative Period, 1995; jour. reviewer: Blood, 1990—, Thrombosis and Haemostasis, 1991—, Annals of Internal Medicine, 1991—, Jour. Biol. Chem., 1992—, Placenta, 1992—, Jour. Exptl. Medicine, 1992—, Platelets, 1992—, Jour. Allergy and Clin. Immunology, 1992—, Cancer Rsch., 1993—, Am. Jour. Hematology, 1993—, Jour. Clin. Oncology, 1994—, Jour. Histochemistry and Cytochemistry, 1994—, Am. Jour. Physiol., 1995—, Thrombosis Rsch., 1995—; contbr. articles to profl. jours., chpts. to books. Mem.: AAAS, Am. Fedn. Clin. Rsch., Am. Soc. Hematology, Am. Heart Assn. (mem. thrombosis coun. 1994—, mem. arteriosclerosclerosis coun. 1994—, mem. southeastern Pa. peer rev. com. B 1995—), Phi Beta Kappa. Office: Case Western Res U Sch Med 2109 Adelbert Rd Cleveland OH 44106-2624

MCCRAY, CURTIS LEE, academic administrator; b. Wheatland, Ind., Jan. 29, 1938; s. Bert and Susan McCray; m. Mary Joyce Macdonald, Sept. 10, 1960; children: Leslie, Jennifer, Meredith. BA in psychology, Knox Coll., Galesburg, Ill., 1960; postgrad., U. Pa., 1960-61; PhD in English, U. Nebr., 1968. Mem. faculty Saginaw Valley Coll., Univ. Ctr., Mich., 1968—77, chmn. dept. English, 1972-73, dean arts and scis., 1973-75, v.p. acad. affairs, 1975-77; provost, v.p. acad. affairs Govs. State U., Chgo., 1977-82; pres. U. North Fla., Jacksonville, 1982-88, Calif. State U., Long Beach, 1988-93, Millikin U., Decatur, Ill., 1993-98, Nat.-Louis U., Chgo., 1998—. Chmn. high tech and industry coun., SUS, 1986-88; mem. state rels. and undergrad. edn. com., Am. Assn. State Colleges and Universities, 1985-88. Bd. dirs. Jacksonville United Way, 1982-88, campaign chmn., 1987; bd. dirs. Sta. WJCT Channel 7 and Stereo 90, Jacksonville, 1982-88, Jacksonville Art Mus., 1983-88, Meml. Med. Ctr., Jacksonville, 1983-88, Jacksonville Cmty. Coun. Inc., 1982-88, Arts Assembly Jacksonville, 1984-88, Jacksonville Urban League, 1985-88; hon. dir. Jacksonville Symphony Assn., 1983; mem. Dame Point Bridge Commn., Jacksonville, 1982; mem. Jacksonville High Tech. Task Force, 1982. George F. Baker scholar, 1956; Woodrow Wilson fellow, 1960-61; Johnson fellow, 1966; Ford Found. grantee, 1969; recipient Landee award for excellence in tchg. Saginaw State Coll., 1972. Mem. AAUP, Torch Club. Office: Nat-Louis U 122 S Michigan Ave Chicago IL 60603-6191

MCCUE, HOWARD MCDOWELL, III, lawyer, educator; b. Sumter, SC, Jan. 4, 1946; s. Howard McDowell and Carolyn Hartwell (Moore) McC.; m. Judith Weiss, Apr. 3, 1971; children— Howard McDowell IV, Leigh AB, Princeton U., 1968; JD, Harvard U., 1971. Bar: Mass. 1971, Ill. 1975, U.S. Tax Ct. 1977. Assoc. Hale and Dorr, Boston, 1971-72, Mayer Brown Rowe & Maw LLP, Chgo., 1975-77, ptnr., 1977—. Adj. prof. law master in tax program Chgo. Kent Coll. Law, 1981— Author: (with others) Drafting Wills and Trust Agreements, 1979, 82, 85, 87, 90; mem. editorial adv. bd. Trusts and Estates mag., 1981-2000; contbr. articles to profl. jours. Bd. dirs. Art Inst. Chgo., Arts Club Chgo.; former chmn. bd. govs. Northwestern U. Libr. Coun.; past vice-chmn. Ravinia Festival Assn.; chmn. Lloyd A. Fry Found. Lt. USN, 1972-75. Princeton U. scholar, 1965 Mem. ABA, Chgo. Bar Assn. (fed. tax com., past chmn., exec. coun.), Chgo. Bar Found. (past pres.), Am. Coll. Tax Counsel, Am. Coll. Trust and Estate Counsel (regent, past chair charitable planning and exempt orgns. com.), Harvard Law Soc. Ill., Internat. Acad. Estate and Trust Law, Phi Beta Kappa.

MCCUE, JUDITH W., lawyer; b. Phila., Apr. 7, 1948; d. Emanuel Leo and Rebecca (Raffel) Weiss; m. Howard M. McCue III, Apr. 3, 1971; children: Howard, Leigh. BA cum laude, U. Pa., Phila., 1969; JD, Harvard U., Cambridge, Mass., 1972. Bar: Ill. 1972, U.S. Tax Ct. 1984. Ptnr. McDermott Will & Emery LLP, Chgo., 1995—. Dir. Schawk, Inc., Des Plaines, Ill.; past pres. Chgo. Estate Planning Coun. Trustee Chgo. Symphony Orch., 1995—, vice chmn., 1998—2001, 2005—. Mem.: Chgo. Bar Assn. (chmn. probate practice com. 1984—85, chmn. estate and gift tax divsn. of fed. tax com. 1988—89), Am. Coll. Trust and Estate Counsel (com. chmn. 1991—94, regent 1993—2000, com. chmn. 1998—2001, pres. 2005—06). Office: McDermott Will & Emery LLP 227 W Monroe St Ste 3100 Chicago IL 60606-5096 Business E-Mail: jmccue@mwe.com.

MCCUEN, JOHN FRANCIS, JR., lawyer; b. NYC, Mar. 11, 1944; s. John Francis and Elizabeth Agnes McCuen; m. Christine McCuen; children: Sarah, Mary, John. AB, U. Notre Dame, 1966; JD, U. Detroit, 1969. Bar: Mich. 1970, Fla. 1970, Ohio 1978. Legal counsel Kelsey-Hayes Co., Romulus, Mich., 1970-77; corp. counsel Sheller-Globe Corp., Toledo, 1977-79, v.p., gen. counsel, 1979-86, sec., 1982-87, sr. v.p. gen. counsel, 1986-89; ptnr. Marshall & Melhorn, Toledo, 1989-92; pvt. practice Law Offices John F. McCuen, Toledo, 1992-93; counsel Butzel Long, Ann Arbor, Mich., 1993—94; v.p. legal Kelsey Hayes Co., Livonia, Mich., 1994-98, v.p., gen. counsel, 1998-99; of counsel Butzel Long, 1999—2001. Trustee Kidney Found. N.W. Ohio, 1979-88, pres., 1984-86. Mem. Mich. Bar, Forest Lake Country Club. Home: 1668 Trading Post Ln Bloomfield Hills MI 48302-1868

MCCULLAGH, GRANT GIBSON, retired architect; b. Cleve., Apr. 18, 1951; s. Robert Ernest and Barbara Louise (Grant) McC.; m. Suzanne Dewar Folds, Sept. 13, 1975; children: Charles Weston Folds, Grant Gibson Jr. BArch, U. Ill., 1973; MArch, U. Pa., 1975; MBA, U. Chgo., 1979. Registered architect, Ill. Dir. mktg. The Austin Co., Chgo., 1977-83, asst. dist. mgr., 1983-84, dist. mgr., 1984-88, v.p., 1987-88; chmn., CEO McClier Corp., Chgo., 1988—98; chmn. Holmes & Narver, Orange, Calif., 1997-2001; exec. v.p. AECOM, LA, 2000—03, vice chmn., 2003—04; chmn., CEO Global Integrated Bus. Solutions, Inc., 2004—; CEO The Facility Group, 2005—07. Contbr. articles to various indsl. publs. Trustee Newberry Libr., Brookfield Zoo/Chgo. Zool. Soc., 2004—, Chgo. Pub. Libr. Found.; council trustee Nat. Trust for Historic Preservation. Fellow: AIA; mem.: Design/Build Inst. Am., Calif. Club, Comml. Club, Indian Hill Country Club, Univ. Club, Casino Club, Chgo. Club, Econ. Club. Republican. Episcopalian. Home: 43 Locust Rd Winnetka IL 60093-3725 Office: 181 W Madison St Ste 3900 Chicago IL 60602 E-mail: grant.mccullagh@gibscorp.com.

MCCULLOH, JUDITH MARIE, editor; b. Spring Valley, Ill., Aug. 16, 1935; d. Henry A. and Edna Mae (Traub) Binkele; m. Leon Royce McCulloh, Aug. 26, 1961. BA, Ohio Wesleyan U., 1956; MA, Ohio State U., 1957; PhD, Ind. U., 1970. Asst. to dir. Archives of Traditional Music, Bloomington, Ind., 1964-65; asst. editor U. Ill. Press, Champaign, 1972-77, assoc. editor, 1977-82, sr. editor, 1982-85, exec. editor, 1985—2007, dir. devel., 1992—2003; asst. dir., 1997—2007. Advisor John Edwards Meml. Forum, LA, 1973—. Mem. Editorial Bd. Am. Music, 1980-89, 2007—, Jour. Am. Folklore, Washington, 1986-90; co-editor Stars of Country Music, 1975; editor (LP) Green Fields of Ill., 1963, (LP) Hell-Bound Train, 1964, Ethnic Recordings in America, 1982; gen. editor Music in American Life series, 1972-2007. Trustee Am. Folklife Ctr., Libr. of Congress, Washington, 1986—2004, chair, 1990—92, 1996—98, trustee emerita, 2004—. Fulbright grantee, 1958-59; NDEA grantee, 1961, 62-63; grantee Nat. Endowment for the Humanities, 1978; recipient Disting. Achievement citation Ohio Wesleyan U. Alumni Assn., Disting. Svc. award Soc. for Am. Music, Lifetime Achievement award Belmont U. Curb Music Industry, Disting. Achievement award Internat. Bluegrass Music Assn. Fellow: Am. Folklore Soc. (exec. bd. 1974—79, pres. 1986—87, exec. bd. 2001—03); mem.: Am. Musicological Soc. (mem. coun. 2005—07), Am. Anthropol. Assn., Soc. Ethnomusicology (hon.; treas. 1982—86, coun. 1976—79, 1983—86, 1990—93), Soc. Am. Music (1st v.p. 1989—93). Democrat. Office: U Ill Press 1325 S Oak St Champaign IL 61820-6903 Business E-Mail: jmmccull@uillinois.edu.

MCCULLOUGH, RICHARD LAWRENCE, advertising executive; b. Chgo., Dec. 1, 1937; s. Francis John and Sadie Beatrice McCullough; m. Julia Louise Kreimer, May 6, 1961; children: Stephen, Jeffery, Julie. BS, Marquette U., 1959. Commd. U.S. Army, 1959, advance through grades to sgt., 1966; account exec. Edward H. Weiss Advt., Chgo., 1960-66; account supr. Doyle Dane Bernbach, NYC, 1966-68; sr. v.p. J. Walter Thompson Co., Chgo., 1969-86; pres. E.H. Brown Advt., Chgo., 1986-97; exec. v.p. Space-Time Media Mgmt., Chgo., 1997—; ptnr. Callahan Group, Chgo., 2000—05. Developer Mktg. with Country Music nat. seminar, 1996; chmn. J. L. McCullough Advertising and Pub. Rels., Evanston, Ill., 2004—. Author: Building Country Radio, 1986, A New Look at Country Music Audiences, 1988, (video) Country Music Marketing, 1989. Bd. dirs. Gateway Found., Chgo., 1976—, chmn., 1988-91; bd. dirs., chmn. mktg. com. Cath. Charities, Chgo. Recipient Nat. Cmty. Svc. award, Gateway Found., 2002, Dennis Kelly Honor award, Cath. Charities, 2002. Mem. Country Music Assn. (Nashville bd. dirs. 1979-2004, pres. 1983-85, Pres.'s award 1987, elector Country Music Hall of Fame), NARAS (Nashville and Chgo. chpt.), North Shore Country Club (Glenview, Ill.), Dairymen's Country Club (Boulder Junction, Wis.). Roman Catholic. Home: 2720 Lincoln St Evanston IL 60201-2043 Office: Space-Time Media Mgmt Inc 35 E Wacker Dr Chicago IL 60601-2103 Home: 2720 Lincoln St Evanston IL 60201-2043 E-mail: dick@spacetimemedia.com, relchar@aol.com.

MCCURRY, STEPHANIE, historian, educator; BA, U. Western Ont., 1981; MA, U. Rochester, 1983; PhD, SUNY, Binghamton, 1988. Asst. prof. U. Calif., San Diego, 1988—94, assoc. prof., 1994—98, Northwestern U., Evanston, Ill., 1998—. Mem. grad. student award com. CCHWP-CGWH/Berkshire Conf. Women Historians, 1993, 94; mem. award selection com. NEH, 1995; dir. Calif. History Project U. Calif., San Diego, 1996—98; dir. Alice Berline Kaplan Ctr. for the Humanities Northwestern U., Evanston, 2002—03; reviewer Oxford U. Press, U. N.C. Press, Harvard U. Press, U. Ill. Press, Johns Hopkins U. Press, U. Ga. Press; referee Am. Hist. Rev., Jour. Am. History, Gender and History, Jour. So. History, Ark. Hist. Quarterly; lectr. in field. Author: Masters of Small Worlds: Yeoman Households, Gender Relations and the Political Culture of the Antebellum South Carolina Low Country, 1995 (nominated for Pulitzer prize in history, 1995); contbr. articles to profl. jours. Recipient Frances Weir prize for history and lit., U. Western Ont., 1981, John Hope Franklin prize, Am. Studies Assn., 1996; fellow, John Simon Guggenheim Meml. Found., 2003; grantee, Am. Coun. Learned Socs., 1990; Rush Rhees and History Dept. fellow, U. Rochester, 1981—83, Doctoral fellow, Social Scis. and Rsch. Coun. Can., 1983—85, Smithsonian Instn., 1985—86, AAUW, 1986—87, Vis. scholar, Inst. for Rsch. on Women and Gender, Stanford U., 1994—95. Mem.: Am. Hist. Assn. (mem. Joan Kelly prize com. 1997—99), So. Assn. Women Historians (chair Willie Lee Rose prize 1999, mem. A. Elizabeth Taylor prize com. 1996, Willie Lee Rose prize 1997), So. Hist. Assn. (chair Francis B. Simkins award com. 1999—2001, mem. program com. ann. meeting 1997, Charles Sydnor prize 1996, Francis Butler Simkins prize 1997), Orgn. Am. Historians (co-chair program com. 2003). Office: Northwestern Univ Dept History Harris Hall #202 1881 Sheridan Rd Evanston IL 60208

MCCUSKER, THOMAS J., lawyer, insurance company executive; b. South Bend, Ind., 1943; BA, U. Notre Dame, 1965, JD cum laude, 1969. Bar: NY 1970, Nebr. 1973, US Tax Ct. 1971. Exec. v.p., gen. counsel Mutual of Omaha Ins. Co. Mem.: Nebr. Bar Assn. Office: Mutual of Omaha Ins Co Mutual Of Omaha Plz Omaha NE 68175-1008

MCCUSKEY, MICHAEL PATRICK, federal judge; b. Peoria, Ill., June 30, 1948; s. Frank Morgan and Margaret Gertrude (Watkins) McC.; m. Linda A. Weers, July 1, 1978 (div. July 1985); 1 child, Melinda; m. Brenda Huber, Dec. 3, 1990; 1 child, Ryan Michael. BSEd, Ill. State U., 1970; JD, St. Louis U., 1975. Tchr. Ottawa (Ill.) Twp. High Sch., 1970-72; ptnr. Pace, McCuskey and Galley, Lacon, Ill., 1975-88; pub. defender Marshall County State of Ill., Lacon, 1976-88; judge 10th Jud. Circuit of Ill., Peoria, 1988-90; justice 3d Dist. Appellate Ct., Ottawa, 1990—98; judge US Dist. (ctrl. dist.) Ill., Urbana, Ill., 1998—, chief judge, 2005—. Bd. dirs. Ctrl. Ill. chpt. ARC, Peoria, 1989-95, Ill. State U. Alumni Assn., Normal, 1995—. Recipient Award of Excellence and Meritorious Svc, Ill. Public Defender Assn., 1991. Mem. Ill. Judges Assn., Ill. State Bar Assn. (gen. practice sect. coun. 1991—, assembly 1992—, criminal justice sect. coun. 1994—, family law sect. coun. 1997—), Peoria County Bar Assn., Rotary (Paul Harris fellow 1985—). Democrat. Methodist. Avocation: sports. Office: US Dist Ct 318 US Courthouse 201 S Vine St Urbana IL 61802 Office Phone: 217-373-5837. Office Fax: 217-373-5855.

MCCUTCHAN, GORDON EUGENE, retired lawyer, insurance company executive; b. Buffalo, Sept. 30, 1935; s. George Lawrence and Mary Esther (De Puy) McC.; m. Linda Brown; children: Lindsey, Elizabeth. BA, Cornell U., 1956, MBA, 1958, LLB, 1959. Bar: N.Y. 1959, Ohio 1964. Pvt. practice, Rome, NY, 1959-61; atty., advisor SEC, Washington, 1961-64; ptnr. McCutchan, Druen, Maynard, Rath & Dietrich, 1964-94; mem. office of gen. counsel Nationwide Mut. Ins. Co., Columbus, Ohio, 1964-94, sr. v.p., gen. counsel, 1982-89, exec. v.p., gen. counsel, 1989-94; exec. v.p. Law and Corp. Svcs., Nationwide Ins. Enterprise, 1994-98; ret., 1998. Trustee, bd. govs. Franklin U., 1992-97; trustee Ohio Tuition Trust Authority, 1992-97. Mem. Columbus Bar

Assn., Ohio Bar Assn., Am. Corp. Counsel Assn., Assn. Life Inst. Counsel (bd. govs. 1990-94), Fedn. Ins. and Corp. Counsel, Am. Coun. Life Ins. (chair legal sect. 1992-93). Home: 2376 Oxford Rd Columbus OH 43221-4011 E-mail: tunkpa@columbus.rr.com.

MCDADE, JOE BILLY, federal judge; b. 1937; BS, Bradley U., 1959, MA, 1960; JD, U. Mich., 1963. Staff atty. antitrust divsn. U.S. Dept. Justice, 1963-65; exec. trainee First Fed. Savs. and Loan Assn., 1965; exec. dir. Greater Peoria (Ill.) Legal Aid Soc., 1965-69; ptnr. Hafele & McDade, Peoria, Ill., 1968-77; pvt. practice Peoria, 1977-82; assoc. cir. judge State of Ill., 1982-88; cir. judge Cir. Ct. Ill., 1988-91; fed. judge U.S. Dist. Ct. (ctrl. dist.) Ill., 1991—. Bd. dirs. Peoria (Ill.) Pub. Libr., 1965-77, Peoria YMCA, ARC, Peoria Tri-Centennial; fin. chmn. St. Peters Cath. Ch.; active Peoria Civic Ctr. Authority, 1976-82; pres. Ill. Health Systems Agy., 1978-80, bd. dirs., 1975-82. Mem. Ill. State Bar Assn., Peoria County Bar Assn. (bd. dirs. 1980-82). Office: US Dist Ct 100 NE Monroe St Peoria IL 61602-1003

MCDANIEL, CHARLES-GENE, journalism educator, writer; b. Luxora, Ark., Jan. 11, 1931; s. Charles Waite and Edith Estelle (Kelly) McD. BS, Northwestern U., 1954, MS in Journalism, 1955. Reporter Gazette and Daily, York, Pa., 1955-58; sci. writer Chgo. bur. A.P., 1958-79; assoc. prof. journalism dept. Roosevelt U., Chgo., 1979-83, prof., 1984-96, chmn. dept., 1979-93, head faculty of journalism and communication studies, 1993-95, prof. emeritus, 1996—. Contbg. editor Libido; contbr. to anthologies, poems, Ency. Britannica, World Book Ency.; contbr. articles to profl. jours.; Chgo. corr. The Med. Post, Toronto, 1979-2000; columnist www.libidomag.com. Trustee Roosevelt U., 1985-94; bd. dirs. Internat. Press Ctr. Chgo., 1993-96. Recipient writing awards Erikson Inst. for Early Edn., 1972, writing award AMA, 1974, writing awards Chgo. Inst. for Psychoanalysis, 1971, 73, writing awards Ill. Med Soc., 1972, 73, writing awards ADA, 1975, Am. Psychol. Assn., 1982. Mem. ACLU, Fellowship of Reconciliation, War Registers League, Art Inst. Chgo. (life), Mus. Contemporary Art (charter), Ill. Arts Alliance, Handgun Control Inc., Hemlock Soc., Ptnrship in Caring. Home and Office: 5109 S Cornell Ave Chicago IL 60615-4215

MCDANIEL, JAMES EDWIN, lawyer; b. Dexter, Mo., Nov. 22, 1931; s. William H. and Gertie M. (Woods) McD.; m. Mary Jane Crawford, Jan. 22, 1955; children: John William, Barbara Anne. AB, Washington U., St. Louis, 1957, JD, 1959. Bar: Mo. 1959. Assoc. firm Walther, Barnard, Cloyd & Timm, 1959—60, McDonald, Barnard, Wright & Timm, 1960—63, ptnr., 1963—65, Barnard, Timm & McDaniel, St. Louis, 1965—73, Barnard & Baer, St. Louis, 1973—82, Lashly & Baer, St. Louis, 1982—2002, of counsel, 2002—; pros. atty. Glendale, Mo., 1968—. City atty. City of Glendale, Mo., 1996—; bd. dirs. Eden. Theol. Sem.; lectr. Latvian U., Riga, Inst. Fgn. Rels., Banking in Am., 1992-93. Leader legal del. Chinese-Am. Comparative Law Study, China, 1988, Russian-Am. Comparative Law Study, Russia, 1990; trustee, past chmn., past treas. 1st Congl. Ch. St. Louis. With USAF, 1951-55. Fellow Am. Bar Found. (life), St. Louis Bar Found. (life; bd. dirs. 2005-, pres. 2007—); mem. ABA (bd. govs. 1997-2000, ho. of dels. 1976-80, 84-92, 97-2000, state del. 1986-92, chmn. lawyers conf., jud. adminstrn. divsn. 1992-95, 8th cir. rep. standing com. on fed. jud. 1995-98, mem. standing com. on jud. qualification, tenure and compensation 1996-97, adv. com. law and nat. security 1999-), The Mo. Bar (pres. 1981-82, bd. govs. 1974-83), Mo. Assn. Def. Counsel, Bar Assn. Met. St. Louis (pres. 1972), Internat. Assn. Ins. Counsel, Assn. Def. Counsel St. Louis (past pres.), Phi Delta Phi. Home: 767 Elmwood Ave Saint Louis MO 63122-3216 Office: Lashly & Baer 714 Locust St Saint Louis MO 63101-1699 Office Phone: 314-621-2939. Personal E-mail: jemglendale@earthlink.net. Business E-Mail: jemcdaniel@lashlybaer.com.

MCDANIEL, JAN, broadcast executive; b. St. Louis, June 27, 1951; BA in Journalism, U. Mo., 1973. Pres., gen. mgr. Sta. KAKE-TV, 1991-96; gen. mgr. Sta. WCCO-TV, Mpls., 1996—. Mem. Women in Comm. Office: Sta WCCO-TV 90 S 11th St Minneapolis MN 55403-2414

MCDANIEL, MIKE, former political association executive; b. Muncie, Ind., Feb. 11, 1951; m. Gail McDaniel, 1978. BS, Ball State U., 1973, MPA, 1979. Legis. intern Rep. Caucus Ind. State Senate, 98th Session, Ind. Gen. Assembly; rsch. dir. City County Coun., Indpls., 1974-75; adminstrv. asst. to Pres. ProTem Ind. State Senate, 1975-76, minority caucus adminstr., 1977-78, spl. asst. to majority caucus, 1978-79; campaign dir. Rep. State Senate Campaign com., 1978; campaign mgr. John Mutz for Lt. Gov. campaign, 1980, 87-88; asst. to gov.-elect Hon. Judge Robert D. Orr, Ind.; chief of staff Lt. Gov. Ind., Hon. John M. Mutz, 1981-87; chmn. Ind. State Rep. Party; pub. rels. account exec. Caldwell Van Riper, Indpls. Instr. polit. sci. Ball State U., 1984—; exec. asst. to v.p. for bus. affairs, 1988-94, dir. govt. rels., 1994-95; exec. dir. Ind. State Election Bd., 1988; writer, producer, dir., editor video module series Ind. Gen. Assembly, 1990; bd. dirs. Bowen Inst. for Practical Politics. Recipient Sagamore of Wabash prize Gov. Otis R. Bowen, 1979, Gov. Robert D. Orr, 1981.

MCDAVIS, RODERICK J., academic administrator; b. Dayton, Ohio, Oct. 17, 1948; m. Deborah Moses; children: Ryan, Tony. BS in Social Scis. in Secondary Edn., Ohio U., 1970; MS in Student Pers. Adminstrn., U. Dayton, 1971; PhD in Counselor Edn., U. Toledo, 1974. Asst. prof. edn. grad. divsn. Siena Heights Coll., Adrian, Mich., 1973—74; asst. prof. edn. dept. counselor edn. Coll. Edn. U. Fla., Gainesville, 1974—79, assoc. prof. edn. dept. counselor edn. Coll. Edn., 1979—82, prof. edn. dept. counselor edn. Coll. Edn., 1982—89, acting asst. dean for grad. studies Grad. Sch., 1984—85, assoc. dean Grad. Sch. and Minority Programs Grad. Sch., 1986—89, prof. edn. dept. counselor edn. Coll. Edn., 1994—99, dean Coll. Edn., 1994—99; prof. counselor edn. dept. edn. leadership, counseling and founds. Coll. Edn. U. Ark., Fayetteville, 1989—94, dean Coll. Edn., 1989—94; prof. edn. divsn. ednl. studies Sch. Edn. Va. Commonwealth U., Richmond, 1999—2004, provost, v.p. acad. affairs, 1999—2004; pres. Ohio U., Athens, 2004—. Vis. prof. edn. dept. counselor edn. and human svcs. Grad. Sch. Edn. U. Dayton, 1979—83, 1992. Named Person of Yr. in Edn., The Gainesville Sun, 1995; recipient Disting. Svc. award for cmty. outreach through TV media, Fla. Assn. for Counselor Edn. and Supervision, 1978, Key to the City, City Commn., Gainesville, 1995, Outstanding Alumnus award, Ohio U. Coll. Edn., 1996, Black Achiever's award in edn., Fla. Conf. Black State Legislators, Tallahassee, 1997. Mem.: Nat. Alliance Black Sch. Educators, Am. Coll. Pers. Assn., Phi Kappa Phi, Phi Delta Kappa (Post-secondary Outstanding Educator award North Ctrl. Fla. chpt. 1996). Office: Office of the Pres 108 Cutler Hall Athens OH 45701 Home: 29 Park Pl Athens OH 45701 Office Phone: 740-593-1804. E-mail: mcdavis@ohio.edu.

MCDERMOTT, ALAN, newspaper editor; b. Kansas City, Mo., Sept. 5, 1951; Sr. editor Universal Press Syndicate, Kansas City, Mo., 1996—. Office: Universal Press Syndicate 4520 Main St Ste 700 Kansas City MO 64111-7701

MCDERMOTT, JOHN H., lawyer; b. Evanston, Ill., June 23, 1931; s. Edward Henry and Goldie Lucile (Boso) McD.; m. Ann Elizabeth Pickard, Feb. 19, 1966; children: Elizabeth A., Mary L., Edward H. BA, Williams Coll., 1953; JD, U. Mich., 1956. Bar: Mich. 1955, Ill. 1956. Assoc. McDermott, Will & Emery, Chgo., 1958-64, ptnr., 1964-99, of counsel, 2000—. Bd. dirs. Patrick Industries Inc. 1st lt. USAF, 1956-58. Mem. ABA, Chgo. Bar Assn. Clubs: Commerical of Chgo., Econ. of Chgo., Legal Chgo. (pres. 1981-82), Law Chgo. (pres. 1986-87). Home: 330 Willow Rd Winnetka IL 60093-4130 Office: McDermott Will & Emery 227 W Monroe St Ste 4400 Chicago IL 60606-5096 Home Phone: 847-446-2022; Office Phone: 312-984-7562. Personal E-mail: johnhmcdermott@comcast.net.

MCDERMOTT, KATHLEEN E., lawyer, corporate executive; b. July 1949; BS in fgn. svc., Georgetown U., JD. Bar: 1975. Assoc. Collier, Shannon, Rill & Scott, Washington, 1975—80, ptnr., 1981—93, 2000—01; exec. v.p., chief legal officer Am. Stores Inc. (now Albertson's Inc.), Salt Lake City, 1993—99; sr. v.p., gen. counsel ash Finch Inc., Mpls., 2002—06. Mem.: FTC Com. (chair), ABA (former vice chair corp. counseling com. antitrust sect.). Home: 29 E Churchhill Dr Salt Lake City UT 84103-2267 Office Phone: 801-703-1143. Personal E-mail: mcdermott.kathleen@gmail.com.

MCDERMOTT, KEVIN R., lawyer; b. Youngstown, Ohio, Jan. 26, 1952; s. Robert J. and Marion D. (McKeown) McD.; m. Cindy J. Darling, Dec. 11, 1976; children: Ciara, Kelly. AB, Miami U., Oxford, Ohio, 1974; JD, Ohio State U., 1977. Bar: Ohio 1977, U.S. Dist. Ct. (so. dist.) Ohio 1978, U.S. Dist. Ct. (no. dist.) Ohio 1988, U.S. Dist. Ct. (we. dist.) Mich. 1993, U.S. Supreme Ct. 1990, U.S. Ct. Appeals (3rd cir.) 1996, U.S. Ct. Appeals (6th cir.) 1988. Assoc. ptnr. Murphey Young & Smith, Columbus, Ohio, 1977-88; ptnr. Squire Sanders & Dempsey, Columbus, Ohio, 1988-90, Schottenstein Zox & Dunn, Columbus, Ohio, 1990—. Adv. bd. mem. Capital U. Legal Asst. Program, Columbus, Ohio, 1988—. Bd. pres. Easter Seal Soc. Ctrl. Ohio, Columbus, 1992-94, bd. mem. 1988-92; pres. Upper Arlington Civic Svc. Commn., Columbus, Ohio, 1988-93. Office: Schottenstein Zox & Dunn 250 West St Columbus OH 43215 Office Phone: 614-462-5001. Business E-Mail: kmcdermott@szd.com.

MCDERMOTT, MARY ANN, nursing educator; b. La Junta, Colo., June 23, 1938; d. George O. and Alice Agnes (Nohelty) Kelley; m. Dennis J. McDermott; children: Dennis, Michael, Sarah, William. BSN, Loyola U., 1960, MSN, 1969; EdD, No. Ill. U., 1980. RN, Ill. Staff nurse Evanston (Ill.) Vis. Nurse Assn., 1960-63, St. Francis Hosp., Sch. Nursing, Evanston, 1963-67; nurse, tchr. Head Start, Chgo. Bd. Edn., 1967-68; faculty mem. Niehoff Sch. Nursing Loyola U., Chgo., 1969—2004, prof. emeritus, 2004—, dir., Ctr. Faith and Mission, 1998—2002, faculty liaison Evoke project, 2004—; pres., nursing and humanities Hecktoen Inst. Medicine, Chgo. Bd. dirs. Park Ridge Ctr. Study Health, Faith and Ethics; adv. coun. Chgo. Dept. Aging, 1995—99; prin. Quality Life Tng., 2002—. Co-editor: Parish Nursing: The Developing Practice, 1990, Parish Nursing: Promoting Whole Person Health Within Faith Communities, 1998, Parish Nursing: Development, Education, Preparation and Administration, 2005. Adv. bd. St. Scholastica Acad., Chgo., 1996-2005; adv. coun. Chgo. Schweizer Urban Fellows, 1996-99; chair Civic Affairs com. U. Club. Chgo., 2001-03. Recipient Ill. Nurse Leader/Power of Nursing award, 2002. Fellow: Am. Acad. Nursing; mem.: ANA, Health Ministries Assn. (adv. bd. 1989—99), Ill. Nurses Assn., Am. Hosp. Assn. (nominating com. 1995—97). Democrat. Roman Catholic. Office: Loyola U Sch ursing Damen Hall 6525 N Sheridan Rd Chicago IL 60626-5344 Office Phone: 773-508-2904. Personal E-mail: maryannmcdermott@msn.com. Business E-Mail: mmcderm@luc.edu.

MCDILL, THOMAS ALLISON, minister; b. Cicero, Ill., June 4, 1926; s. Samuel and Agnes (Lindsay) McDill; m. Ruth Catherine Starr, June 4, 1949 (dec. Aug. 2001); children: Karen Joyce, Jane Allison, Steven Thomas; m. Doris E. McDill, July 27, 2002. Th.B., No. Baptist Sem., Oakbrook, Ill., 1951; BA, Trinity Coll., 1954; M.Div., Trinity Evang. Div. Sch., 1955, DD, 1989; D.Ministries, Bethel Theol. Sem., 1975. Ordained to ministry Evang. Free Ch. Am., 1949. Pastor Community Bible Ch., Berwyn, Ill., 1947-51, Grace Evang. Free Ch., Chgo., 1951-58, Liberty Bible Ch., Valparaiso, Ind., 1959-67, Crystal Evang. Free Ch., Mpls., 1967-76; v.p., moderator Evang. Free Ch. of Am., 1973-74, chmn. home missions bd., 1968-72, chmn. exec. bd., 1973-90, pres., 1976-90, ret., 1990; min. at large Evang. Free Ch. Am., 1991—. Contbr. articles to publs. Chmn. bd. Trinity Coll., Deerfield, Ill., 1974-76; bd. govs. Trinity Western U.; bd. dirs. Trinity Evang. Divinity Sch. Mem. Evang. Free Ch. Ministerial Assn., Evang. Ministers Assn., Nat. Assn. Evangelicals (bd. adminstrn. 1976—, mem. exec. com. 1981-88), Greater Mpls. Assn. Evangelicals (bd. dirs., sec. bd. 1969-73) Office: 901 E 78th St Bloomington MN 55420-1334

MCDONALD, CHRISTY, newscaster; m. Jamie Samuelsen, 2001. B in Polit. Philosophy, Mich. State U. Prodn. asst. WJBK, Southfield, Mich., 1994—95; prodr. WXYZ, 1996—98; with WJRT-TV, Flint, Mich., 1998—2000; co-anchor Action News at 7pm WXYZ TV, 2000—. Recipient Best Breaking News Reporting award, AP, award, Mich. Assn. Broadcasters, Detroit Press Club. Office: WXYZ-TV 20777 W Ten Mile Rd Southfield MI 48037

MCDONALD, JESS, state official; BA, Ill. State U.; MA in Social Svc. Adminstrn., U. Chgo.; postgrad., Harvard U. With Ill. Dept. Children and Family Svcs., Bloomington, acting dir., 1990-94; exec. dir. Ill. Assn. Cmty. Mental Health Agys., 1991; dir. Dept. Mental Health and Devel. Disabilities, 1992, Ill. Dept. Children and Family Svcs., Springfield, 1994—. Recipient award of excellence in pub. child welfare adminstrn. Nat. Assn. Pub. Child Welfare Adminstrs., 1996, Motorola award for excellence in pub. svc., 1997. Mem. Nat. Assn. Pub. Child Welfare Adminstrs. (exec. com.), Am. Pub. Welfare Assn. (chair children and family svcs. com.). Office: Children and Family Svcs Dept 406 E Monroe St Springfield IL 62701-1411

MCDONALD, JOHN J., JR., lawyer; b. St. Paul, Dec. 12, 1954; BA, Univ. St. Thomas, 1977; JD, Creighton Univ., 1981. Bar: Minn. 1982, Wis., US Dist. Ct. (Minn., Wis., ND dist.), US Ct. Appeals (1st, 7th, 8th cir.), US Supreme Ct. Ptnr., comml. litigation, mem. mgmt. com. Meagher & Geer PLLP, Mpls. Named a Minn. Super Lawyer, Minn. Law & Politics, 2000—04. Mem.: ABA, Am. Bd. Trial Advocates, Internat. Assn. Def. Counsel, Def. Rsch. Inst., Minn. State Bar Assn., Wis. State Bar Assn. Office: 33 S 6th St Ste 4400 Minneapolis MN 55402-3720 Office Phone: 612-347-9120. Office Fax: 612-338-8384. Business E-Mail: jmcdonald@meagher.com.

MCDONALD, PATRICK ALLEN, lawyer, educator, arbitrator; b. Detroit, May 11, 1936; s. Lawrence John and Estelle (Maks) Mc D.; m. Margaret Mercier, Aug. 10, 1963; children: Michael Lawrence, Colleen Marie, Patrick Joseph, Timothy, Margaret, Thomas, Maureen. PhB cum laude, U. Detroit, 1958, JD magna cum laude, 1961; LLM (E. Barrett Prettyman Trial scholar, Hugh J. Fegan fellow), Georgetown U., 1962. Bar: D.C. 1961, Mich. 1961, Colo. 1993. Case worker Dept. Pub. Welfare, Detroit, 1958; field examiner NLRB, Detroit, 1961; practiced in Washington, 1961-62; trial cons. NIH, Bethesda, Md., 1962; staff judge adv. USAF, France, 1962-65; ptnr. Monagham, LoPrete, Mc Donald, Yakima & Grenke, Detroit, 1965—. Bd. dirs., past chmn. Delta Dental Plan Mich.; past chmn. Delta Dental Plan Ohio; bd. dirs., chmn. Guest House, Lake Orion, Mich., Rochester, Minn., Detroit Athletic Club, Brighton Hosp.; instr. polit. sci. and law U. Md., 1963-65, U. Detroit Law Sch., adj. prof., 1965-2004; adj. prof. Ave Maria Law Sch., 2003—. Co-author: Law and Tactics in Federal Criminal Cases, 1963; author magnet plans for schs., Detroit, Boston. Mem. Detroit Bd. Edn., 1966-76, pres.; sec., trustee Mt. Elliott Cemetary Assn.; mem. U. Detroit Sports Hall of Fame; mem. adv. bd. Providence Hosp., Southfield, Mich.; exec. bd. U. Detroit Pres.'s Cabinet. Named one of Five Outstanding Young Men of Mich., Outstanding Young Man of Detroit. Mem. ABA, Detroit Bar Assn., State Bar Mich. (commr.), U. Detroit Alumni Assn. (bd. dirs.), Mensa, Blue Key, Alpha Phi Omega (pres. Eta Pi chpt. 1955), Alpha Sigma Nu (v.p. 1960). Home: 13066 Lashbrook Ln E Brighton MI 48114-6002 Office: 40700 Woodward Ave Bloomfield Hills MI 48304-2211 Office Phone: 810-220-3444. Office Fax: 248-642-9460. Personal E-mail: pmcd101@sbcglobal.net.

MCDONALD, PETER D., air transportation executive; m. Diane McDonald; children: Megan, Katie. B, Judson Coll., 1976. Various positions United Airlines Corp., 1969—, v.p., op. svcs., 1999—2001, sr. v.p. airport ops., 2001—02, exec. v.p. ops., 2002—04, exec. v.p., COO, 2004—.

MCDONALD, ROBERT ALAN (BOB MCDONALD), consumer products company executive; b. Gary, Ind., June 20, 1953; s. Ray Wellington and Froso (Manolios) McD.; m. Diane Janine Murphy, Dec. 31, 1977; children: Jennifer Elizabeth, Robert Wade. BS in Engring., U.S. Mil. Acad., 1975; MBA, U. Utah, 1978. Asst. Solo brand Procter & Gamble, Cin., 1980-81, asst. mgr. Dawn brand, 1981-82, asst. mgr. Cascade brand, 1982-83, mgr. Cascade brand, 1983-84, mgr. Tide brand, 1984—86, assoc. advt. mgr., 1986—89, mgr. laundry prod. P&G Canada, 1989—91, gen. mgr. P&G Far East, 1991—94, v.p., gen. mgr. P&G Far East, 1994—96, regional v.p. Japan, P&G Asia, 1996—99, v.p. NE Asia, 1999, pres. NE Asia, 1999—2001, pres. global fabric care & home care, 2001—04, vice chmn. global ops., 2004—07, vice chmn., COO, 2007—. Instr. econs. Meth. Coll., Golden Gate U., Campbell U., Fayetteville, N.C., 1979-80; bd. dir. Xerox Corp., GSI. Deacon Knox Presbyn. Ch., Cin., 1982-85, Mt. Washington Presbyn. Ch., Cin., 1986; mem. bd. vis. Fuqua Sch. Bus., Duke Univ.; mem. bd. adv. Northwestern Integrated Mktg. Communications. Advanced through grades to capt. US Army, 1975—80. Fellow Royal Soc. of Arts of London (Silver medal 1975); mem. Phi Kappa Phi, Beta Gamma Sigma, Commonwealth Club. Republican. Avocations: reading, running, painting. Office: Procter & Gamble 1 Procter And Gamble Plz Cincinnati OH 45202-3393 Mailing: Procter & Gamble PO Box 599 Cincinnati OH 45201-0599

MCDONALD, SALLY J., lawyer; b. Ind., 1964; d. Homer C. and Esteleen M. McD.; m. Richard M. Levin, Oct. 16, 1993. BS, Ind. U., 1986; JD, Duke U., 1990. Bar: Ill. 1990, Ill. Supreme Ct., US Dist. Ct. (no. dist. Ill.), US Ct. Appeals (7th cir.), Fed. Trial Bar. Assoc. Bell, Boyd & Lloyd, Chgo., 1990-92, Piper Rudnick, Chgo., 1992-98, hiring ptnr., 1998—99; ptnr., labor, employment group, co-nat. hiring ptnr. Piper Rudnick (now DLA Piper), 1999—. Gen. counsel Gtr. Chgo. Food Depository, 1995-99. Contbr. chpt. to book. Bd. mem. Pub. Interest Law Initiative; pres. bd. dir. CARPLS; outside counsel Greater Chgo. Food Depository. Mem. ABA, Chgo. Bar Assn. (bd. mgrs. 1998-2000, chair Young Lawyers sect. 1996-97, Maurice Weigle award 1994), Chgo. Bar Found. (bd. dir., treas.), Women's Bar Assn. Office: DLA Piper Suite 1900 203 N LaSalle St Chicago IL 60601-1293 Office Phone: 312-368-8927. Office Fax: 312-236-7516. Business E-Mail: sally.mcdonald@dlapiper.com.

MCDONALD, THOMAS ALEXANDER, lawyer; b. Chgo., Aug. 20, 1942; s. Owen Gerard and Lois (Gray) McD.; m. Sharon Diane Hirk, Nov. 25, 1967; children: Cristin, Katie, Courtney, Thomas Jr. AB, Georgetown U., Washington, DC, 1965; JD, Loyola U., Chgo., 1968. Bar: Ill. 1969, US Dist. Ct. (no. dist.) Ill. 1969. Ptnr. Clausen Miller, PC, Chgo., 1969—2001, McDonald & McCabe, LLC, Chgo., 2001—. Mem.: ABA, Chgo. Bar Assn., Ill. Bar Assn. Office: McDonald & McCabe LLC 225 S Wacker Dr Ste 2100 Chicago IL 60606-1299 Office Phone: 312-845-5190. Business E-Mail: tmcdonald@mcdonaldmccabe.com.

MCDONALD, WESLEY S., retail executive; b. 1962; B cum laude, Bucknell U., Lewisburg, Pa.; MBA, Wharton Sch., Phila., 1988. Various fin. positions Target Corp., 1988—2000; v.p., CFO Abercrombie & Fitch, New Albany, Ohio, 2000—03; exec. v.p., CFO Kohl's Corp., Menomonee Falls, Wis., 2003—. Office: Kohls Corp N56 W17000 Ridgewood Dr Menomonee Falls WI 53051-5660 Office Phone: 262-703-7000.

MCDONNELL, SANFORD NOYES, air transportation executive; b. Little Rock, Oct. 12, 1922; s. William Archie and Carolyn (Cherry) McD.; m. Priscilla Robb, Sept. 3, 1946; children: Robbin McDonnell MacVittie, William Randall. BA in Econs., Princeton U., 1945; BS in Mech. Engring., U. Colo., 1948; MS in Applied Mechanics, Washington U., St. Louis, 1954. With McDonnell Douglas Corp. (formerly McDonnell Aircraft Corp.), St. Louis, 1948—, v.p., 1959-66, pres. McDonnell Aircraft div., 1966-71, corp. exec. v.p., 1971, corp. pres., from 1971, chief exec. officer, from 1972, chmn., 1980-88, chmn. emeritus, 1988—. Mem. exec. bd. St. Louis and nat. councils Boy Scouts Am.; trustee, elder Presbyn. Ch.; chmn. emeritus Character Edn. Partnership, Washington, 1993-2005, chmn. emeritus, 2005—. Fellow AIAA; mem. Navy League U.S. (life), Tau Beta Pi Office: McDonnell Douglas Corp PO Box 516 Saint Louis MO 63166-0516

MCDONNELL, THOMAS A., information technology executive; b. Kansas City, Mo. BSBA in Acctg., Rockhurst Univ., 1966; MBA, Univ. Pa., 1968. With DST Systems, Inc., 1969—, pres., 1973—84, 1987—, treas., 1973—95, vice chmn., 1984—95, CEO, 1984—. Bd. dir. DST Systems Inc., 1971—, BHA Group Holdings Inc., Blue Valley Ban Corp., Commerce Bancshares Inc., Computer Sci. Corp., Euronet Worldwide Inc., Garmin Ltd., Janus Capital Corp., Ascential Software Inc., Asurion. Trustee Ewing Marion Kauffman Found., 2003—; chmn. Greater Kansas City C. of C., 1994, Civic Coun. Greater Kansas City, 1999—2001; bd. dir. Greater Kansas City Cmty. Found., Midwest Rsch. Inst., Harry S Truman Libr. Inst.; trustee Rockhurst Univ. Office: DST Systems 333 W 11th St Kansas City MO 64105 Office Phone: 816-435-1000.

MCDONOUGH, BRIDGET ANN, music theatre company director; b. Milw., June 19, 1956; d. James and Lois (Hunzinger) McD.; m. Gregory Paul Opelka, Sept. 20, 1986 (div. Aug. 1993); m. Robert Markey, Feb. 29, 2000. BS, Northwestern U., 1978. Bus. mgr. Organic Theater Co., Chgo., 1979-80; mng. dir., founder Light Opera Works, Evanston, Ill., 1980—. U.S. rep. European Congress Musical Theatre, 1995. Founder, mem. Chgo. Music Alliance, 1984—, pres., 1995-98; mem. Ill. Arts Alliance; bd. dirs., Nat. Alliance for Musical Theatre, 2001-2005, sec., 2001—04; bd. dirs. Evanston Convention Visitors Bur., 1999-2002; mem. alumni adv. bd. Northwestern U. Sch. Speech, 1999-2002; bd. dirs. Around the Coyote Arts Festival, 2002—. Recipient Women on the Move award Evanston YWCA, 1991. Mem. Evanston C. of C. (bd. dirs., 1993-99), North Shore Internat. Network, Rotary (pres. Evanston chpt. 1999-00), Union League Club. Avocation: birdwatching. Office: Light Opera Works 927 Noyes St Evanston IL 60201-6206

MCDONOUGH, JOHN J., household products company executive; V.p. fin. Litton med. products Litton Industries; v.p., treas. Am. TV and Comm., Denver; CFO, v.p. Blount, Inc., Montgomery, Ala.; sr. v.p. fin. Newell, 1981-83; founder, pres. GENDEX Corp. (merger with Dentsply Internat. 1993), 1983-93; vice chmn., CEO Dentsply Internat., 1993-95; CEO, vice chmn. bd. Newell Rubbermaid Inc., Freeport, Ill., 1997-2000, also bd. dirs. Chmn. bd. dirs. Juvenile Diabetes Found., 1998—, former mem. exec. and fin. coms., chmn. planned giving and vice chmn. $200 million internat. initiative. Named Man of Yr. Chgo. chpt. Juvenile Diabetes Found., 2000, Office: Newell Rubbermaid Inc 29 E Stephenson St Freeport IL 61032-4235

MCDONOUGH, JOHN MICHAEL, lawyer; b. Evanston, Ill., Dec. 30, 1944; s. John Justin and Anne Elizabeth (O'Brien) McD.; m. Susan J. Moran, Sept. 19, 1981; children: John E., Catherine Anne. AB, Princeton U., 1966; LLB, Yale U., 1969. Bar: Ill. 1969, Fla. 1991. Assoc. Sidley & Austin, Chgo., 1969-75, ptnr., 1975—. Bd. dirs. Met. Planning Coun., 1978—, pres., 1982-84; bd. dirs. Ctr. Am. Archeology, 1980-85, chmn., 1982-84; bd. dirs. Leadership Greater Chgo., 1984-90, sec.-treas., 1987-90; bd. dis. Brian Rsch. Found., 1985—, pres., 1989-94, chmn. 1999-. With JAGC, USAR, 1969-75. Mem. ABA, Racquet Club, Saddle & Cycle Club, Commonwealth Club, Phi Beta Kappa. Democrat. Episcopalian. Home: 1407 N Dearborn St Chicago IL 60610-1505

MCDOUGAL, ALFRED LEROY, publishing executive; b. Evanston, Ill., Feb. 12, 1931; s. Alfred L. and Mary (Gillett) McD.; m. Gudrun Fenger, May 7, 1960 (div. 1982); children: Thomas, Stephen; m. Nancy A. Lauter, Mar. 1, 1986. BA, Yale U., 1953; MBA, Harvard U., 1957. Asst. to pres. Rand McNally & Co., Skokie, Ill., 1962-65, mgr. sch. dept., 1965-69; pres. McDougal, Littell & Co., Evanston, Ill., 1969-91, chmn., CEO, 1991-94; dir. Houghton Mifflin Co., Boston, 1994-2001; CEO Alm Corp., 1994—. Chmn. McDougal Family Found.; gov. Yale U. Press, 1995—. Trustee Hadley Sch. for Blind, Winnetka, Ill., 1980-83; chmn. budget com. Evanston United Fund, 1974-76, bd. dirs.; bd. dirs. Evanston YMCA, 1988-94, Youth Job Ctr., 1987-93, chmn., 1989-91, Opportunity Internat., 1994-2000, Literacy Chgo., 1992-98, treas., 1994-96, Chgo. Symphony Orch., 2003-, Hubbard St. Dance, Chgo., 1995—, pres., 2003-. With U.S. Army, 1953-55. Mem. Assn. Am. Pubs. (exec. com. sch. divsn. 1981-94, chmn. 1988-89, 92-94, dir. 1987-89), No. Ill. Assn. (1st v.p. 1984, chmn. 1985). Office: ALM Corp 400 N Michigan Ave Ste 300 Chicago IL 60611-4130 E-mail: alfredmcdougal@yahoo.com.

MCDOWELL, RICHARD WILLIAM, academic administrator; b. McDonald, Pa., Aug. 20, 1936; s. William Murdock and Cora Josephine (Brackman) McD.; m. Ann Brammer, May 27, 1961; children: Susan, Kathleen, Karen. BS, Indiana U. of Pa., 1960, MEd, 1962; MS, Purdue U., 1967, PhD, 1969. Cert. tchr., Pa. Tchr. Penn Hills Sch. Dist., Pa., 1960-67; divsn. chmn. Cmty. Coll. Allegheny County, West Mifflin, Pa., 1969-71; dean, acting pres. C.C. Beaver County, Monaca, Pa., 1971-72; exec. dean C.C. Allegheny County, Monroeville, Pa., 1972-80, v.p. strategic planning Pitts., 1980-81; pres. Schoolcraft Coll., Livonia, Mich., 1981—. Mgmt. cons., Pa. and Ill., 1975-80; chmn., mem. evaluation team Middle States Assn., Phila., 1972-80; trainer workshop leaders Higher Edn. Mgmt. Inst., Washington, 1976-77. With USMC, 1954-56. Recipient Outstanding Tchr. award Spectroscopy Soc., Pitts., 1966, Edn. award Plymouth C. of C., Mich., 1982. Mem. Am. Assn. Cmty. and Jr. Colls., Mich. C.C. Assn. (bd. dirs. exec. com.), W.E. Mich. League C.C. (chmn.), North Central Assn., Assn. C.C. Trustees. Office: Schoolcraft Coll 18600 Haggerty Rd Livonia MI 48152-3932

MCDYESS, ANTONIO, professional basketball player; b. Quitman, Miss. Forward Denver Nuggets, 1995—97, 1998—2002, Phoenix Suns, 1997—98, N.Y. Knicks, 2003—04, Phoenix Suns, 2004, Detroit Pistons, 2004—. Named to NBA All-Rookie First Team, 1995—96, All-NBA Third Team, 1998—99. Avocations: bowling, rhythm and blues. Office: c/o Detroit Pistons Palace of Auburn Hills 2 Championship Dr Auburn Hills MI 48326

MCEACHEN, RICHARD EDWARD, banker, lawyer; b. Omaha, Sept. 24, 1933; s. Howard D. and Ada Carolyn Helen (Baumann) McE.; m. Judith Ann Gray, June 28, 1969; children: Mark E., Neil H. BS, U. Kans., Lawrence, 1955; JD, U. Mich., 1961. Bar: Mo. 1961, Kans. 1982; cert. trust and fin. advisor Inst.

for Cert. Bankers, 1991. Assoc. Hillix, Hall, Hasburgh, Brown & Hoffhaus, Kansas City, Mo., 1961-62; sr. v.p. First Nat. Bank, Kansas City, Mo., 1962-75; exec. v.p. Commerce Bank Kansas City, Mo., 1975-85, Centerre Bank of Kansas City N.A., 1985-87, Security Bank Kansas City, Kans., 1987-88; exec. v.p., trust officer UMB Overland Park Bank, 1988-93; atty. Ferree, Bunn, O'Grady & Rundberg, Chartered, Overland Park, 1994—2005. Gov. Am. Royal Assn., Kansas City, Mo., 1970-2002, amb., 1980-2004, com. mem., 1995-2005; bd. dirs. Harry S. Truman Med. Ctr., Kansas City, 1974-86, mem. fin. com., 1975-86, treas., 1979-84, bd. govs., 1986-2002, mem. bldg. and grounds com., 1993-2002, mem. pension com., 1976-93, 96-2000; trustee Clearinghouse for Midcontinent Founds., 1980-87; bd. dirs. Greater Kansas City Mental Health Found., 1963-69, treas., 1964-69, v.p., 1967-69; adv. bd. urban svcs. YMCA, Kansas City, 1976-83; cubmaster Kanza dist. Boy Scouts Am., 1982-83, dist. vice chmn., 1982-83, troop com., 1983-90, treas., 1986-88; bd. dirs. Scout Booster Club, Inc., 1989-94; mem. planned gift com. William Rockhill Nelson Gallery Art, Children's Mercy Hosp. Planned Gift Coun., 1991—2005; mem. adv. com. Legal Assistance Program Avila Coll., 1978-80, adv. coun. Future Farmers Am., 1972-82; mgr. Oppenstein Bros. Found., 1979-85; trustee Village Presbyn. Ch., 1987-90, chmn., 1989-90, elder, 1994-97, Golf Classic Com., 2005-; found. com. Am. Royal Charitable Found., 1995-2005; bd. dirs. Village Presbyn. Ch. Found., 1987-89, 94-97, chmn., 1996-97, mem. adv. bd., 1997-2001; bd. dirs. Estate Planning Coun., 1984-86; mem. Kansas City Fed. Estate Planning Symposium Com., 1992-98; bd. dirs. Shawnee Mission Med. Ctr. Found., 1988—, fin. com., 1989-92, 2002—, mem. planned giving com., 1996-, mem. investment com., 2000—; mem. adv. coun. Shawnee Mission Edn. Found., 2003. Recipient Eagle Scout, Boy Scouts Am., 1948. Mem. Nat. Assn. Securities Dealers Inc. (bd. arbitrators 1994—2004), Am. Arbitration Assn. (panel arbitrators 1994-96), Estate Planning Soc. Kansas City, Mo. Bar Assn., Kans. Bar Assn., Johnson County Bar Assn., Estate Planning Assn. (pres. 1974-75), Kansas City Jr. C. of C. (v.p. 1964-66), Ea. Kans. Estate Planning Coun., 40-Yrs. Ago Column Club (program com. 1999-2000, pres. 2001, trustee 2001-04), Indian Hills Club, Delta Tau Delta Alumni (v.p. Kansas City chpt. 1978-80, Hibbs Scholarship Com., 2007-). Republican. Home: 9100 El Monte St Shawnee Mission KS 66207-2627

MCELHATTON, JERRY, credit card company executive; m. Jane McElhatton. B degree in Indsl. Mgmt., Franklin U.; attended graduate degree program, Western Michigan U. Held exec. mgmt. positions in ops. and tech. Ameritrust, Cleve., Banl One, Columbus, Ohio; pres., CEO First Republic Bank Svcs. Corp., Payment Systems Tech. & Consulting, Inc., Dallas; sr. exec. v.p., global tech. and ops. Mastercard Internat., O'Fallen, Mo., 1994—. Bd. advisors BMC; bd. dir. Mascon. Mem. bd. trustee Nat. Coun. of the Washington U. Olin Sch. Bus., St. Louis U.; bd. dir. St. Louis Sci. Ctr., United Way, St. Louis Variety Club, Rainbow Village. Avocation: model trains. Office: Mastercard Internat 2200 Mastercard Blvd O Fallon MO 63366

MCELROY, DAN, state legislator; b. July 15, 1948; m. Mary McElroy. BA, U. Notre Dame. Minn. state rep. Dist. 36B, 1994—. Former mgmt. cons. Address: 12805 Welcome Ln Burnsville MN 55337-3623

MCELWREATH, SALLY CHIN, corporate communications executive; b. NYC, Oct. 15, 1940; d. Toon Guey and Jean B. (Wong) Chin; m. Joseph F. Callo, Mar. 17, 1979; 1 child, R.J. McElwreath III. BA, Pace Coll., 1963; MBA, Pace U., 1969. Copywriter O.E. McIntyre, NYC, 1963-65; editl. asst. Sinclair Oil Corp., NYC, 1966-70; account exec. Muller, Jordan & Herrick, NYC, 1970-71; regional mgr. pub. rels. United Airlines, NYC, 1971-79; dir. corp. comm. Trans World Airlines, NYC, 1979-86; v.p. pub. rels. TWA Mktg. Svcs., Inc. The Travel Ch. Divsn., NYC, 1986-88; ptnr. The Comm. Group, NYC, 1988-90; gen. mgr. corp. comm. Ofcl. Airline Guides, 1990-91; v.p. corp. comm. Macmillan, Inc., 1991-93; cons. NYC, 1993-94; sr. v.p. corp. comm. Aquila Inc., 1994—2005; dir. USS New York Commn. Com., 2006—. Pub. affairs officer USNR, 1973-2000. Ret. Capt. Named Woman of Yr., YWCA, 1980, Alumnus of Yr., Pace U., 1976. Mem. N.Am. Pub. Rels. Assn. (vice chair 2003—), Wings Club (N.Y.C.). Avocations: sailing, skiing, harpsichord. Personal E-mail: sallymc79@verizon.net.

MCENROE, PAUL, reporter; Gen. assignment reporter, National writer Mpls. Star Tribune, Mpls, to 1996, investigative reporter in projects unit, 1996—. Office: Star Tribune 425 Portland Ave Minneapolis MN 55488-0002

MCEVOY, THOMAS J., communications executive; BBA, Rollins Coll. Various pos. in fin., ops., bus. markets, consumer markets, and carrier markets bus. unit telecomm. industry, 22 yrs.; acct., so. ops. fin. area Sprint Corp., 1980, various other pos. in fin., including payroll mgr., oper. budgets mgr., and local exchange pricing and costing mgr., dir. consumer markets and carrier markets bus. units, v.p. sales and consumer care, local telecomm. divsn. consumer markets, pres., consumer markets, local telecomm. divsn., 2000—. Office: Sprint Corp 6200 Sprint Pkwy Overland Park KS 66251

MCFADDEN, JOHN VOLNEY, retired manufacturing company executive; b. NYC, Oct. 3, 1931; s. Volney and Mary Lucile (McConkie) McF.; m. Marie Linstead, June 27, 1953; children— Deborah, John Scott, David. BS in Commerce and Fin, Bucknell U., 1953; JD, Detroit Coll. Law, 1960. Pres., vice chmn. MTD Products, Inc., Cleve., 1960-92; pres. MTD Products Inc., Cleve., 1968-91, vice chmn., 1990-92; gen. ptnr. Camelot Ptnrs., Cleve.; pres. Parkside Acquisition Ptnrs. Ltd., Cleve., 1997—. Bd. dirs. C.E. White Co., Fusion Inc., Flambeau Corp., Hinkley Lighting, Inc., SGS Tool Co.; past chmn. financing adv. bd. State of Ohio Devel.; past pres. Cleve. World Trade Assn. Trustee Cleve. Eye Bank, former trustee Fairview Health Svcs, Cleve. Clinic. Lt. Supply Corps, USN. Mem. Cleve. Yachting Club. Office: Parkside Acq Ptnrs Ltd 20160 Parkside Dr Cleveland OH 44116-1347

MCFARLAND, KAY ELEANOR, state supreme court chief justice; b. Coffeyville, Kans., July 20, 1935; d. Kenneth W. and Margaret E. (Thrall) McF BA in English & History, Washburn U., Topeka, 1957, JD, 1964. Bar: Kans. 1964. Sole practice, Topeka, 1964-71; probate and juvenile judge Shawnee County, Topeka, 1971-73; dist. judge Topeka, 1973-77; assoc. justice Kans. Supreme Ct., 1977-95, chief justice, 1995—. Mem. Kans. Bar Assn., Women Attys. Assn. Topeka., Topeka Bar Assn Achievements include being the first woman appointed justice and chief justice of Kansas' Supreme Court. Office: Kans Supreme Ct Kans Jud Ctr 301 SW 10th Ave Topeka KS 66612-1507 Fax: (785) 291-3274.

MC FARLAND, ROBERT HAROLD, retired physicist; b. Severy, Kans., Jan. 10, 1918; s. Robert Eugene and Georgia (Simpson) McF.; m. Twilah Mae Seefeld, Aug. 28, 1940; children: Robert Alan, Rodney Jon. BS and BA, Kans. State Tchrs. Coll., Emporia, 1940; Ph.M. (Mendenhall fellow), U. Wis., 1943, PhD, 1947. Sci. instr., coach high sch., Chase, Kans., 1940-41; instr. navy radio sch. U. Wis., Madison, 1943-44; sr. engr. Sylvania Elec. Corp., 1944-46; faculty Kans. State U., 1947-60, prof. physics, 1954-60, dir. nuclear lab., 1958-60; physicist Lawrence Livermore Radiation Lab. U. Calif., 1960—69; dean Grad. Sch., U. Mo., Rolla, 1969-79, dir. instnl. analysis and planning, 1979-82; prof. physics U. Mo., Rolla, 1969-84, prof. emeritus physics dept., 1985—; v.p. acad. affairs U. Mo. System, 1974-75; Intergovtl. Personnel Act appointee Dept. Energy, Washington, 1982-84; vis. prof. U. Calif., Berkeley, 1980-81. Mem. Grad. Record Exams. Bd., 1971-75, chmn. steering com., 1972-73; cons. Well Surveys, Inc., Tulsa, 1953-54, Argonne Nat. Lab., Chgo., 1955-59, Kans. Dept. Pub. Health, 1956-57, cons. in residence Lawrence Livermore Radiation Lab., U. Calif., 1957, 58, 59, med. physics U. Okla. Med. Sch., 1971, grad. schs., PhD physics program, Utah State U., 1972; physicist, regional counselor Office Ordnance Research, Durham, N.C., 1955. Author: (with T. McFarland) McFarland Collections, 1985, Simpson Connections, 1987; co-author two family geneaol. books; contbr. over 113 articles to profl. jours.; patentee in field of light prodn., vacuum prodn., controlled thermonuclear reactions. Active Boy Scouts Am., 1952—, mem. exec. bd. San Francisco Bay Area council, 1964-68, Ozark Council, 1986—; chmn. Livermore (Calif.) Library Bond drive, 1964. Mem. Kans. N.G., 1936-40. Recipient Silver Beaver award Boy Scouts Am., 1968, Community Service award C. of C., 1965, Disting. Alumnus award Kans. State Tchrs. Coll., 1969. Fellow AAAS, Am. Phys. Soc., Kiwanis Internat.; mem. AAUP (chpt. pres. 1956-57), Am. Assn. Physics Tchrs., Mo. Acad. Sci., Mo. Assn. Phys. Sci. Tchrs., Am. Soc. Engring. Edn., Kiwanis (lt. gov. Mo.-Ark. dist. 1984-85, internat. accredited rep. 1985-92, Disting. Lt. Gov. 1985, Tablet of honor award 1997, 50 Yr. Perfect Attendance pin 2003), Sigma Xi, Lambda Delta Lambda, Xi Phi, Kappa Mu Epsilon, Kappa Delta Pi, Pi Mu Epsilon, Gamma Sigma Delta, Phi Kappa Phi. Home: 416 W Spring St Apt 3 Neosho MO 64850-1777 Office: U Mo Dept Physics Rolla MO 65401 Business E-Mail: robmcf@umr.edu.

MCFATE, KENNETH LEVERNE, trade association administrator; b. LeClaire, Iowa, Feb. 5, 1924; s. Samuel Albert and Margaret (Spear) McF.; m. Imogene Grace Kness, Jan. 27, 1951; children: Daniel Elliott (dec.), Kathryn Margaret, Sharon Ann. BS in Agrl. Engring., Iowa State U., 1950; MS in Agrl. Engring., U. Mo., 1959. Registered profl. engr., Mo. Agrl. sales engr. Ill. No. Utility Co., Aledo, 1950-51; extension agrl. engr. Iowa State U., Ames, 1951-53, rsch. agrl. engr., 1953-56; prof. agrl. engr. U. Mo., Columbia, 1956-86, prof. emeritus, 1986; dir. Mo. Farm Electric Coun., Columbia, 1956-75; exec. mgr. Nat. Farm Electric Coun., Columbia, 1975-86; pres. Nat. Food and Energy Coun., Columbia, 1986-91, pres. emeritus, 1991; mgr. Electrotechnology Rsch., 1991-93. Bd. dirs. Internat. Congress Agrl. Engrs., Brussels, 1989—94. Editor, author: (with others) Handbook for Elsevier Science, Electrical Energy in World Agriculture, 1989; mem. editl. bd. Energy in Agriculture for Elsevier Sci., Amsterdam, The Netherlands, 1981-88. With USAAF, 1943—45, 2d lt. USAAF, 1945. Recipient Outstanding Svc. awards Nat. Safety Coun., 1975, MOFEC, 1976, Nat. 4-H Coun., 1982, Nat. Hon. Extension Frat., 1984, Hon. Am. Future Farmers Assn. degree, 1991. Fellow Am. Soc. Agrl. Engrs. (George Kable elec. award 1974, Spl. Svc. award, 2000); mem. Alpha Epsilon, Gamma Sigma Delta. Republican. Presbyterian. Avocations: technical writing, gardening, woodworking.

MCFEE, WILLIAM WARREN, soil scientist; b. Concord, Tenn., Jan. 8, 1935; s. Fred Thomas and Ellen Belle (Russell) McF.; m. Barbara Anella Steelman, June 23, 1957; children— Sabra Anne, Patricia Lynn, Thomas Hallie. BS, U. Tenn., 1957; MS, Cornell U., 1963, PhD, 1966. Mem. faculty Purdue U., 1965—, prof. soil sci., 1973—, dir. natural resources and environ. sci. program, 1975-91, head dept. agronomy, 1991-2001. Vis. prof. U. Fla., 1986-87; cons. U.S. Forest Svc., Desert Rsch. Inst. Author articles in field, chpts. in books. Served with USAR, 1958-61. Alpha Zeta scholar, 1957; named Outstanding Agr. Tchr. Purdue U., 1972; recipient Am. Educator award Soil Sci. Soc., 1987. Fellow: Soil Sci. Soc. Am. (pres. 1991—92), Am. Soc. Agronomy (pres. 1996—97, resident edn. award 1989); mem.: Purdue Agrl. Alumni Assn. (cert. of distinction 2002), Ind. Seed Trade Assn. (hon.), Sigma Xi. Presbyterian. Home: 708 Mccormick Rd West Lafayette IN 47906-4915 Office: Purdue U Dept Agronomy West Lafayette IN 47907 E-mail: wmcfee@purdue.edu.

MCGAAN, ANDREW RAYMOND, lawyer; b. Highland Park, Ill., Oct. 15, 1961; s. Dean Bailey and Nancy Eva (Acheson) M. AB with honors, Cornell U., 1983, JD magna cum laude, 1986. Bar: Conn. 1986, Ill. 1991, US Dist. Ct. (dist. Conn.) 1987, US Dist. Ct. (so. & ea. dists. NY) 1988, US Dist. Ct. (no. & ctrl. dists. Ill.), US Ct. Appeals (2nd, 7th, 9th & 11th cirs.). Press sec. Com. to Elect Congressman Stewart B. McKinney, Fairfield, Conn., 1986; law clk. to Judge Warren W. Eginton US Dist. Ct. (dist. Conn.), Bridgeport, 1987-88; assoc. Cummings & Lockwood, Stamford, Conn., 1988—90; ptnr. Kirkland & Ellis, Chgo., 1990—. Elder, chmn. bd. trustees Fourth Presbyn. Ch. Chgo. Mem. ABA, Order of the Coif. Presbyterian. Office: Kirkland & Ellis 200 E Randolph Dr Chicago IL 60601 Office Phone: 312-861-2000. Office Fax: 312-861-2200. Business E-Mail: amcgaan@kirkland.com.

MCGAFFEY, JERE D., retired lawyer; b. Lincoln, Nebr., Oct. 6, 1935; s. Don Larsen and Doris McG.; m. Ruth S. Michelsen, Aug. 19, 1956; children: Beth, Karen. BA, BSc with high distinction, U. Nebr., 1957; LLB magna cum laude, Harvard U., 1961. Bar: Wis. 1961. Mem. firm Foley & Lardner LLP, Milw., 1961—2004, ptnr., 1968—2004. Dir. Wis. Gas Co., 1978-00, Smith Investment Co., Northwestern Mut. Trust Co., 2000-06, Lord Balt. Corp.; mem. take-over adv. com., Gov. Wis., 1988-89, commn on state/local partnerships 21st century 2000-01. Author works in field. Chmn. bd. dirs. Helen Bader Found.; former vice chmn. legis. Milw. Met. Assn. Commerce, 1984—2003; former chmn. Wis. Taxpayers Alliance, sec.-treas., 1994—; bd. dirs. Aurora Health Care, 1986—, chmn., 1986—90; chmn. bd. advisors U. Wis. Nursing Sch., Milw. Mem. ABA (chmn. tax sect. 1990-91, ho. dels. 1995-2000, Sect. Taxation Disting. Svc. award 2005), AICPA, Wis. Bar Assn., Wis. Inst. CPAs, Am. Coll. Tax Counsel (chmn. 1996-98), Am. Coll. Trust and Estate Counsel (chmn. bus. planning com. 1994-97, regent 2000-06), Am. Law Inst., Univ. Club, Milw. Country Club, Harvard Club, Phi Beta Kappa, Beta Gamma Sigma, Delta Sigma Rho. Home: 12852 NW Shoreland Dr Mequon WI 53097-2304 Office: Foley & Lardner 777 E Wisconsin Ave Ste 3600 Milwaukee WI 53202-5302 Home Phone: 262-242-1766. Business E-Mail: jmcgaffey@foleylaw.com.

MCGARITY, MARGARET DEE, federal judge; b. 1948; BA, Emory U., 1969; JD, U. Wis., 1974. Bar: Wis. 1974. Pvt. practice, 1974-87; bankruptcy judge U.S. Dist. Ct. (ea. dist.) Wis., 1987—. Lectr. on marital property, bankruptcy and family law Fed. Judicial Ctr., Nat. Conf. Bankruptcy Judges, State Bar Wis., Nat. Child Support Enforcement Assn., others. Co-author: Marital Property Law in Wisconsin, 2d edit. 1986, Collier Family Law and the Bankruptcy Code, 1991. Mem. at. Conf. Bankruptcy Judges, State Bar Wis., Nat. Assn. Women Judges, Milw. Bar Assn., Assn. Women Lawyers, Thomas E. Fairild Inn, Am. Coll. Bankruptcy, Am. Bankruptcy Inst. Office: 162 US Courthouse 517 E Wisconsin Ave Milwaukee WI 53202-4500

MCGARR, FRANK JAMES, retired federal judge, consultant; b. Feb. 25, 1921; married; 6 children. BA cum laude, Loyola U., Chgo., 1942, JD, 1950, degree (hon.), 2002. Bar: Ill. 1950. Assoc. Dallstream Schiff Stern & Hardin, Chgo., 1952—54; asst. U.S. atty., chief criminal divsn. No. dist. of Ill., 1954—55, first asst. U.S. atty., 1955—58; ptnr. McKay Solum & McGarr, Chgo., 1958—68; first asst. atty. gen. State of Ill., 1969—70; judge U.S. Dist. Ct. for No. Ill., 1970—88, chief judge, 1981—86, sr. judge, 1986—88; of counsel Phelan Cahill & Quinlan, Chgo., 1988—96, Foley & Lardner, Chgo., 1996—2001; arbitration and medication pvt. practice, 2001—. Instr. Eng. and pub. speaking Loyola U., 1946—48, administrv. asst. to pres., 1948—52; instr. law Loyola U. Law Sch., 1950—52, instr. criminal law, 1953—57, prof. admiralty and maritime law, 1953—57; instr. legal ethics John Marshal Law Sch., 1985—86. Chmn. law observance com. Chgo. Crime Comm., v.p., bd. dirs.; chmn. Law Enforcement Week Com.; pres. Constl. Rights Found., 1994; chmn. Ill Gov.'s Comm. on Death Penalty, 2000. With USN, 1942—45, Pacific Fleet. Named Man of Yr., Cath. Lawyers Guild Chgo., 1985; recipient Alumni Medal of Excellence, Loyola Law Alumni, 1964, Mother Cabrini award, Columbus-Cuneo-Cabrini Med. Ctr., 1978, Dei Gloriam award, St. Ignatius Coll. Prep, 1984, Disting. Jurist award, Loyola U. Law Sch., Chgo. Fellow: Am. Coll. Trial Lawyers; mem.: Soc. Trial Lawyers, Chgo. Bar Assn., Fed. Bar Assn. (pres. chgo. chpt. 1962—63, mem. exec. com.), 7th Cir. Bar Assn. Office: 4146 Venard Rd Downers Grove IL 60515-1908 Home Phone: 630-960-0985; Office Phone: 630-960-4655.

MCGARR, JOSEPH W., paper company executive; Dir. strategy, consumer products bus. James River Corp., 1982-96; v.p. cost and sys. effectiveness, 1996-97; sr. v.p. planning and strategy Ft. James Corp. (merger Ft. Howard Corp. and James River), Deerfield, 1997-2000; exec. v.p., CFO Ill., 2000—. Office: Fort James Corp 1919 S Broadway Green Bay WI 54304-4905

MCGAVRAN, FREDERICK JAEGER, lawyer; b. Columbus, Ohio, Apr. 24, 1943; s. James Holt and Marion (Jaeger) McG.; m. Elizabeth Dowlig, Jan. 5, 1980; children: Sarah Ann, Marian Katherine. BA, Kenyon Coll., 1965; JD, Harvard U., 1972. Bar: Ohio 1972, U.S. Supreme Ct. 1984, Ky. 1992. With Kyte, Conlan, Wulsin & Vogeler, Cin., 1972-78, Frost & Jacobs, Cin., 1978-2000, Frost, Brown & Todd, LLC, Cin., 2000—. Editor-in-chief Sixth Circuit Federal Practice Manual, 1999. Lt. USN, 1965—69. Mem. Fed. Bar Assn. (pres. Cin. chpt. 1984-85, mem. exec. com. Cin. chpt. 1985—), Ohio State Bar Assn. (chmn. com. on fed. cts. 1982-85), Univ. Club of Cin., The Literary Club (trustee). Home: 3528 Traskwood Cir Cincinnati OH 45208 Office: Frost Brown & Todd LLC 2200 PNC Ctr 201 E Fifth St Cincinnati OH 45202 Home Phone: 513-871-4840; Office Phone: 513-651-6940. Business E-Mail: fmcgavran@fbtlaw.com.

MCGEE, CHICK, radio personality; Radio host morning show Sta. WFBQ-FM, Indpls. Office: WFBQ 6161 Fall Creek Rd Indianapolis IN 46220

MCGEE, EDWIN C., JR., surgeon; b. SC, 1967; MD, Vanderbilt U. Sch. Medicine, 1993. Cert. surgery, thoracic surgery. Surg. resident Mass. Gen. Hosp.; fellow Cleveland Clinic Found., 2001—04; rsch. fellow NIH Nat. Cancer Inst.; surg. dir. heart transplant program Northwestern Meml. Hosp., Chgo., 2004—. Mem. Northwestern Med. Faculty Found.; asst. prof. Feinberg Sch. Medicine. Named one of 40 Under 40, Crain's Chgo. Bus., 2006. Mem.: Alpha Omega Alpha, Phi Beta Kappa. Avocations: fly fishing, dog training, hunting. Office: Galter 19-1000 675 N St Clair Chicago IL 60611 Office Phone: 312-695-4965. Office Fax: 312-695-1903.

MCGEE, HOWARD, radio personality; Weekend radio host Sta. WGCI-FM, Chgo., midday radio host, afternoon radio host, 1996—98, morning show radio host, 1998—. Office: Wgci Radio 233 N Michigan Ave Ste 2800 Chicago IL 60601-5704

MCGEE, PATRICK EDGAR, postal service clerk; b. Chgo., Jan. 13, 1944; s. Ralph and Minnie Odelia (Crutcher) McG. Machine clk. U.S. Postal Svc., Chgo., 1977—. Author of poems. Mem. The Art Inst. Chgo., Mus. Sci. & Industry, Chgo. Mem. Internat. Soc. Poets. Democrat. Roman Catholic. Avocations: painting, jazz, walking, jogging.

MCGEE, SHERRY, retail executive; b. Honolulu, Hawaii, Nov. 16, 1957; d. Winnie R. Johnson; 1 child, Michael L. BS, Wayne State U., 1987, MBA, 1991. Divsn. sales mgr. CDI Corp., 1978-89; sales tng. cons. McGee & Co., 1990-92; dir. mktg. Bartech, Inc., 1992-97; founder, pres. Apple Book Ctr., 1996—. Vol. Jr. Achievement.: Apple Book Center 18843 Gainsborough Rd Detroit MI 48223-1341 E-mail: apple001@aol.com.

MCGEGAN, NICHOLAS, music director; b. Eng. Student, Cambridge U., Oxford U. Music dir. San Francisco's Phila. Baroque Orch., 1985—, Irish Chamber Orch; artistic dir. Göttingen Handel Festival, Germany, 1990, Killaloe Festival; prin. guest condr. Scottish Opera, 1992-98; prin. condr. Drottningholm Ct. Theatre, 1993-95; founder, dir., harpsichordist The Arcadian Acad. Guest condr. San Francisco, St. Louis, Houston, Detroit, Indpls., Minn., Nat. Symphony orchs., City of Birmingham Symphony Orch., Halle Orch., Acad. of St. Martin-in-the-Fields in Breat Britain, Montreal Symphony, Nat. Arts Ctr. Orch., Ottawa, Orchestra de la Suisse Romande, Jerusalem Symphony, NY Philharm., Phila. Orch.; condr. Hanover Band, Freiburg Baroque Orch., Orch. of the Age of Enlightment; artist-in-residence, Milw. Symphony Orch.; condr. over 40 operas in Europe and US; artistic ptnr. St. Paul Chamber Orch. Condr. (Operas) Mostly Mozart Festival, NYC, 2003. Office: The St Paul Chamber Orchestra Third Fl of the Hamm Bldg 408 St Peter St Saint Paul MN 55102-1497

MC GEHEE, H. COLEMAN, JR., (HARRY COLEMAN MCGHHE), retired bishop; b. Richmond, Va., July 7, 1923; s. Harry Coleman and Ann Lee (Cheatwood) McG.; m. June Stewart, Feb. 1, 1946; children: Lesley, Alexander, Harry III, Donald, Cary. BS, Va. Poly. Inst., 1947; JD, U. Richmond, 1949; MDiv, Va. Theol. Sem., 1957, DD, 1973. Bar: Va. 1949, U.S. Supreme Ct. 1954; ordained to ministry Episcopal Ch., 1957. Spl. counsel dept. hwys. State of Va., 1949-51, gen. counsel employment svc., 1951, asst. atty. gen., 1951-54; rector Immanuel Ch.-on-the-Hill, Va. Sem., 1960-71; bishop Diocese of Mich., Detroit, 1971-90. Adv. bd. Nicaraguan Network, Ctr. for Peace and Conflict Studies, Wayne State U.; bd. dirs. Mich. Religious Coalition for Abortion Rights, 1976-84; trustee Va. Theol. Sem., 1978-93; pres. Episc. Ch. Pub. Co., 1978-85. Columnist Detroit News, 1979—85, weekly commentator pub. radio sta. WDET-AM, Detroit, 1984—90. Mem. Gov.'s Commn. on Status of Women, 1965-66, Mayor's Civic Com., Alexandria, 1967-68; sponsor Nat. Assn. for ERA, 1977-85; pres. Alexandria Legal Aid Soc., 1969-71; bd. dirs. No. Va. Fairhousing Corp., 1963-67; pres. Mich. Coalition for Human Rights, 1980-89 (Humanitarian award 2001); chmn. Citizens' Com. for Justice in Mich., 1983-84; sponsor Farm Labor Orgn. for Children, 1983-85; bd. dirs. Pub. Benefit Corp., Detroit, 1988-90, Mich. Citizens for Personal Freedom, 1989-92, Poverty and Social Reform Inst., Detroit, 1989—, Bread for the World, 1990-94, Ams. United for Separation of Ch. and State, 1990, ACLU Oakland County, Mich., 1991-94; co-chair Lesbian-Gay Found. Mich., 1991—. 1st lt. C.E., U.S. Army, 1943-46. Named Feminist of Yr., Detroit NOW, 1978, Person of Yr., Econ. Justice Commn. Mich., 1997; recipient Humanitarian award Detroit ACLU, 1984, Phillip Hart medal Mich. Women's Studies Assn., 1984, Sayre award for justice and peace Episc. Peace Fellowship, 1988, Spirit of Detroit award, 1989, Archbishop Romero award Mich. Labor Com., 1990, Brotherhood award AME Ch., Detroit, 1993, Ira Jayne award Detroit br. NAACP, 1993, Martin Luther King, Jr. award United Ch. of Christ, 1995, William Scarlett award Episc. Ch. Pub. Co., 1997, Humanitarian award Mich. Coalition for Human Rights, 2001. Mem.: Detroit Econ. Club (bd. dirs.). Episcopalian. Home: 1496 Ashover Dr Bloomfield Hills MI 48304-1215

MCGILL, JAMES C., manufacturing executive, director; b. Chgo., 1928; married. BA, Vaparaiso U., 1951. With McGill Mfg. Co., Inc., Valparaiso, Ind., 1950—, dir. sales electric divsn., 1953—56, mgr. distbn. sales Electric divsn., 1956—68, gen. mgr. Electric divsn., 1958—61, corp. sec., 1961—66, v.p. and sec., 1965—74, vice chmn. bd. and sec., 1974—76, CEO, chmn. bd. and mem. exec. com., 1976—, chmn., pres. and CEO. Dir. 1st Nat. Bank of Valparaiso, Gen. Telephone & Electric Corp. With US Army, 1951—53. Office: McGill Mfg Co Inc 909 Lafayette St Valparaiso IN 46383-4299

MCGILLIVRAY, DONALD DEAN, seed company executive, agronomist; b. Muscatine, Iowa, Aug. 28, 1928; s. Walter C. and Pearl E. McG.; m. Betty J. Anderson, June 24, 1951; children: Ann E., Jean M. BS in Agronomy, Iowa State U., 1950. Asst. mgr. Iowa, Minn., Wis. sect. Funk Seeds Internat., Belle Plaine, Iowa, 1965-69, mgr., 1969-70, mgr. hybrid corn ops. Bloomington, Ill., 1970-75, v.p. ops., 1976-82, pres., 1982-88; assoc. Smart Seeds, Inc., Bloomington, 1989—. Dir. U.S. Grains Coun., Washington, 1984-87. Bd. dirs. Ill. Agrl. Leadership Found., Macomb, 1985—, chmn. bd., 1990-2000; bd. dirs. Ill. Wesleyan Assocs., 1986-89, Ill. 4-H Found., 1996—; mem. adv. bd. Bro-Menn Hosp., 1985—, pres., 1989-90. Sgt. U.S. Army, 1951-53. Mem. Am. Seed Trade Assn. (bd. dirs. 1986-, divsn. chmn. 1978-79, 2d v.p. 1986-87, 1st v.p. 1987-88, pres. 1988-89), Am. Seed Rsch. Found. (bd. dirs. 1982-95, pres. 1984-87), Exch. Club, Masons.

MCGINN, BERNARD JOHN, theologian, educator; b. Yonkers, NY, Aug. 19, 1937; s. Bernard John and Catherine Ann (Faulds) McG.; m. Patricia Ann Ferris, July 10, 1971; children: Daniel, John. BA, St. Joseph's Sem., Yonkers, NY, 1959; Licentiate in Sacred Theology, Gregorian U., Rome, 1963; PhD, Brandeis U., 1970. Diocesan priest Archdiocese N.Y., NYC, 1963-71; prof. U. Chgo., 1969—, Naomi Shenstone Donnelly prof., 1992—2003, emeritus, 2003—. Program coord. Inst. for Advanced Study of Religion, Divinity Sch., U. Chgo., 1980-92. Author: The Calabrian Abbot, 1985, Meister Eckhart, 1986, Foundations of Mysticism, 1991, Growth of Mysticism, 1994, Antichrist, 1994, Flowering of Mysticism, 1998; editor: (series) Classics of Western Spirituality, 1978, (book) God and Creation, 1990. Fellow Medieval Acad. Am., Am. Acad. Arts and Scis. Home: 5701 S Kenwood Ave Chicago IL 60637-1718 Office: U Chgo Divinity Sch 1025 E 58th St Chicago IL 60637-1509 Business E-Mail: bmcginn@uchicago.edu.

MCGINN, MARY J., lawyer, insurance company executive; b. St. Louis, Apr. 9, 1947; d. Martin J. and Janet McGinn; m. Bernard H. Shapiro, Sept. 6, 1971; children: Sara, Colleen, Molly, Daniel. BA, Dominican U., River Forest, Ill., 1967; JD, St. Louis U., 1970. Bar: Mo. 1970, Ill. 1971. Atty. tax div. U.S. Dept. Justice, Washington, 1970-73; atty. Allstate Ins. Co., Northbrook, Ill., 1973—, v.p., dep. gen. counsel, 1980—. Mem. ABA, Am. Coll. Investment Counsel, Assn. Life Ins. Counsel. Roman Catholic. Home: 155 N Buckley Rd Barrington IL 60010-2607 Office: Allstate Ins Co 3075 Sanders Rd Ste G5A Northbrook IL 60062-7127 E-mail: mmcginn@allstate.com.

MCGINNIS, GARY DAVID, chemist, science educator; b. Everett, Wash., Oct. 1, 1940; BS, Pacific Lutheran U., 1962; MS, U. Wash., 1968; PhD in Organic Chem., U. Mont., 1970. Prodn. chemist Am. Cyanamid Co., 1964-67; fellow U. Mont., 1970-71; from asst. prof. wood chemistry to assoc. prof. wood sci. Forest Products Utilization Lab. Mich. State U., 1971—. Mem. Am. Chem. Soc., Forest Products Rsch. Soc., Sigma Xi. Office: Michigan Technology University Forestry Bldg Rm 150 Houghton MI 49931

MCGINNIS, KENNETH L., former state official; Dir. Corrections Dept., Lansing, Mich., til 1999. Office: Corrections Dept Grandview Plz PO Box 30003 Lansing MI 48909-7503

MCGINNIS, W. PATRICK, diversified company executive; BA in Political Science, Univ. Denver, 1970; MBA, Washington Univ, St. Louis, 1972. With Ralston Purina (now estle Purina), St. Louis, 1972—; dir. mktg, cons. prod. Ralston Purina Internat., 1978—80; exec. v.p., dir., grocery products Canadian div. Ralston Purina Co., Ontario, Canada, 1980—83, div. v.p., dir. mktg., grocery products St. Louis, Mo., 1983—84; pres., COO, grocery products group Ralston Purina, St. Louis, 1989—92; pres., CEO, grocery products group Ralston Purina Co., St. Louis, 1992—99, pres., CEO, 1999—2001, Nestle Purina, St. Louis, 2001—; corp. v.p., exec. v.p. Ralston Purina, St. Louis, 1984—89. Bd. dir Brown Shoe Co. Recipient Disting. Alumni Award, Olin Sch Bus., Washington Univ., 1993. Office: Nestle Purina Co Checkerboard Sq Saint Louis MO 63164-0001

MCGINNITY, MAUREEN ANNELL, lawyer; b. Monroe, Wis., Apr. 6, 1956; d. James Arthur and Marie Beatrice (Novak) McG.; m. Richard W. Ziervogel, July 17, 1982; 1 child, Brigitte Kathleen. BS, U. Wis., Milw., 1977; JD, U. Wis., 1982. Bar: Wis. 1982, U.S. Dist. Ct. (ea. and we. dists.) Wis. 1982, U.S. Ct. Appeals (7th cir.) 1989, U.S. Ct. Appeals (1st cir.) 1991, U.S. Tax Ct. 1995, U.S. Supreme Ct. 1991. Assoc. Foley & Lardner LLP, Milw., 1982-91, ptnr., 1991—, chairperson tax valuation & fiduciary litig. practice group. Mem. Wis. Supreme Ct. Planning and Policy Adv. Com., Madison, 1991-94; adv. bd. Domestic Violence Legal Clinic, Milw., 1991—. Treas. Waukesha (Wis.) Food Pantry, 1988-94; trustee Boys & Girls Club Greater Milw., 1991—; bd. dirs. Task Force on Battered Women & Children, Inc., 1994-2006. Recipient Outstanding Svc. award Legal Action Wis., Milw., 1984, 93 Outstanding Fundraising awards Boys & Girls Club Greater Milw., 1987-92, Cert. Recognition, Common Coun. Task Force on Sexual Assault & Domestic Violence, Milw., 1991, Cert. Appreciation, Wis. Equal Justice Task Force, Madison, 1991, Cmty. Svc. award Wis. Law Found., 1995. Mem. ABA, State Bar Wis. (bd. govs. 1992-96, Pro Bono award 1990, chair 1993-94), Assn. for Women Lawyers (various offices, pres. 1992-93), Milw. Young Lawyers Assn. (bd. dirs. 1987-92, pres. 1990-91, Pres.' award 1991), Profl. Dimensions. Office: Foley & Lardner LLP 777 E Wisconsin Ave Ste 3800 Milwaukee WI 53202-5367 Office Phone: 414-297-5510. Office Fax: 414-297-4900. Business E-Mail: mmcginnity@foley.com.

MCGIVERIN, ARTHUR A., former state supreme court chief justice; b. Iowa City, Nov. 10, 1928; s. Joseph J. and Mary B. McG.; m. Mary Joan McGiverin, Apr. 20, 1951; children: Teresa, Thomas, Bruce, Nancy. BSc with high honors, U. Iowa, 1951, JD, 1956. Bar: Iowa 1956. Pvt. practice law, Ottumwa, Iowa, 1956; alt. mcpl. judge, 1960-65; judge Iowa Dist. Ct. 8th Jud. Dist., 1965-78; assoc. justice Iowa Supreme Ct., Des Moines, 1978-87, chief justice, 1987-2000, sr. judge, 2000—. Mem. Iowa Supreme Ct. Commn. on Continuing Legal Edn., 1975. Served to 1st lt. U.S. Army, 1946-48, 51-53. Mem. Iowa State Bar Assn., Am. Law Inst. Roman Catholic. Avocation: golf. Office: Iowa Supreme Court State Capitol Building Des Moines IA 50319-0001

MC GLAMERY, MARSHAL DEAN, agronomist, educator, weed scientist; b. Mooreland, Okla., July 29, 1932; s. Walter Gaiford and Bernice (Gardner) McG.; m. Marilyn Hudson, June 2, 1957; children: Paul, Steve. BS, Okla. State U., 1956, MS, 1958; PhD, U. Ill., 1965. Instr. Panhandle A. and M. Coll., 1958-60; agronomist Agribus. Co., Lawrence, Kans., 1960-61; teaching asst. U. Ill., 1961-63, research fellow, 1963-65, asst. prof. weed sci., 1965-70, assoc. prof., 1970-76, prof., 1976-2000, prof. emeritus, 2002—, ext. crop scientist, 1965-2000, ret., 2000. Served with U.S. Army, 1953-55. NSF fellow, 1963 Mem. Weed Sci. Soc. Am., Coun. Agr. and Tech. Baptist. Home: 35 Lange Ave Savoy IL 61874-9705 Office: 1102 S Goodwin Ave Urbana IL 61801-4730 Business E-Mail: mmcglame@uiuc.edu.

MCGLAUCHLIN, TOM, artist; b. Turtle, Wis., Sept. 14, 1934; s. Charles Orion and Frances Lenore McGlauchlin; m. Patricia Ann Smith, Aug. 5, 1961; children: Christopher, Jennifer (dec.), Patrick (dec.). BS in Art, U. Wis., 1959, MS in Art, 1960; studied pottery with James McKinnell, 1962. Instr. dept. art and art edn. U. Wis., Madison, 1960-61; instr. art dept. Cornell Coll., Mt. Vernon, Iowa, 1961-64, asst. prof. art dept., 1964-68, assoc. prof., chmn. art dept., 1968-71; instr. Toledo Mus. Art, 1971-82, prof., dir. glass program, 1982-84. One-man exhbns. include Habatat Gallery, Dearborn, Mich., 1979, Glass Art Gallery, Toronto, 1981, 85, Glass Gallery, Bethesda, Md., 1981, 85, 87, 91, Heller Gallery, N.Y.C., 1983, B.Z. Wagman Gallery, St. Louis, 1983, Running Ridge Gallery, Santa Fe, 1990; selected group exhbns. include Toledo Mus. Art, 1972, 88, Glasmuseum Frauenau, Franenau, Germany, 1977, Habatat Gallery, 1980, 84, The Hand and the Spirit Gallery, Scottsdale, Ariz., 1980, Gallery of Contemporary Crafts, Detroit, 1980, The Naples (Fla.) Art Gallery, 1981, The Craftsman's Gallery, Scarsdale, N.Y., 1981, 84, The Nat. Mus. Modern Art, Kyoto and Tokyo, 1981, Perception Gallery, Houston, 1985, The AirLoft Gallery, Honolulu, 1986, The Corning (N.Y.) Mus. Glass, 1987; selected competitive exhbns. include Everson Mus. Art, Syracuse, N.Y., 1961, 62, Mus. Contemporary Crafts, N.Y.C., 1962, Corning Glass Mus., Met. Mus. Art, N.Y.C., Victoria and Albert Mus., London, Musee Ars Decoratif, Paris; public collections include Toledo Mus. Art, The Smithsonian Collection, Washington, Portland (Oreg.) Art Mus., New Orleans Mus. Art, Mus. Contemporary Crafts, Musee des arts decoratifs de la Ville de Lausanne, Switzerland, Minn. Mus. Art, St. Paul, Kunstmuseum, Dusseldorf, Germany, Corning Glass Mus. Grantee Associated Colls. Midwest, 1966-67; recipient First Jury award Toledo Glass Nat. II, 1968. Mem. Am. Crafts Coun., Internat. Sculpture Soc., Ohio Designer-Craftsmen, Glass Art Soc. Office: The Glass Studio 1940 W Central Ave Toledo OH 43606-3944 Office Phone: 419-461-4097. Business E-Mail: tom@mcglauchlin.com.

MCGOVERN, PETER JOHN, law educator; b. NYC, Dec. 6, 1938; s. John Phillip and Helen Marie (Gaisser) McG.; m. Catherine Bigley, Aug. 31, 1963; children: Brian Peter, Sean Daniel. AB, Notre Dame U., 1961; JD, Fordham U., 1964; EdD, U. S.D., 1980. Bar: N.Y. 1964, S.D. 1972, Ind. 1983, Ill. 1990, U.S. Supreme Ct. 1968. Atty. criminal divsn. Dept. Justice, 1971-72; prof. law U. S.D., Vermillion, 1972-83; from asst. dean to assoc. dean U. S.D. Sch. Law, Vermillion, 1972-77, dir. programs and planning, 1979-83; dean Valparaiso (Ind.) U. Sch. Law, 1983-85, St. Thomas U. Sch. Law, Fla., 1985-87, John Marshall Law Sch., Chgo., 1987-90, prof. law, 1990—. Dir. Ctr. for Internat. Bus. and Trade Law, 2000; dir. continuing legal edn. State Bar S.D., 1972-83; past chmn. S.D. Family Law Com.; bd. dirs. Legal Svcs. of Greater Gary Inc. Past pres. Vermillion Area Arts Coun., Nat. Anti-Vivisection Soc.; bd. dirs. Lawyer for Creative Arts, 1990-92. Lt. comdr. JAGC, USN, 1965-71. Recipient Legal Writing award Fed. Bar Assn., 1969. Fellow Ind. Bar Found.; mem. ABA, bd. dirs., mediator, arbitrator, Internat. Acad. Dispute Resolution Democrat. Roman Catholic. Home: 204 Benedictine Ln Yankton SD 57078-6878 Home Phone: 213-440-9705; Office Phone: 606-664-0101. E-mail: mcgowen@iw.net.

MCGRATH, BARBARA GATES, city manager; m. Pat McGrath; 1 child, Caitlin. BS summa cum laude, Ohio State U., 1976; JD magna cum laude, Capital U., 1979. Bar: Ohio 1979. Asst. city atty. Columbus (Ohio) City Atty.'s Office, 1979-85; dep. dir. Civil Svc. Commn. City of Columbus, 1985-90, exec. dir. Civil Svc. Commn., 1990—. Past chair bd. dirs. Lifescapes, Inc., A Place to Grow; grad. Columbus Area Leadership Program, 1989. Mem. Columbus Bar Assn. Office: City of Columbus Civil Svc Commn 50 W Gay St Fl 5 Columbus OH 43215-2821

MCGRATH, BRIAN W., lawyer; b. Milw., Dec. 18, 1955; BS, U. Wis., 1979; JD with honors, Harvard U., 1982. Bar: Wis. 1982. Ptnr. Foley & Lardner LLP, Milw., chmn. distribution & franchise practice group. Mem.: State Bar Wis. Office: Foley & Lardner LLP 777 E Wisconsin Ave Milwaukee WI 53202-5306 Office Phone: 414-297-5508. Office Fax: 414-297-4900. Business E-Mail: bmcgrath@foley.com.

MCGRATH, WILLIAM JOSEPH, lawyer; b. Cleve., July 6, 1943; s. William Peter and Marie Agnes (Wolf) McG.; m. Mary Ann Ostrenga; children: William Peter, Geoffrey Walton, Megan Joy. ABcl, John Carroll U., 1965; MA, Loyola U., 1967; JD, Harvard U., 1970. Bar: Ill. 1970. Assoc. McDermott, Will & Emery, Chgo., 1970-75, ptnr., 1976—, mem. mgmt. com., 1993-98, mem. exec. com., 1994-97. Vice chmn. investment com. Glencoe Capital LLC, 1997-2000, vice chmn., mng. dir., 2000—; bd. dirs. Tomy Am., Inc., Torrance, Calif. Trustee Boys and Girls Club Found., 1983; bd. dirs. Ctr. for Econ. Policy and Analysis, 1989—. Mem. ABA, Evanston Golf Club, Union League (Chgo.), Chgo. Club, Met. Club. Chgo. Democrat. Roman Catholic. Home: 943 Edgemere Ct Evanston IL 60202-1428 Office: Glencoe Capital LLC 222 W Adams St Chicago IL 60606

MCGREGOR, DOUGLAS HUGH, pathologist, educator; b. Temple, Tex., Aug. 28, 1939; s. Harleigh Heath and Joyce Ellen (Lambert) McG.; m. Mizuki Kitani, July 6, 1969; children: Michelle Sakuya, David Kenji. BA, Duke U., 1961, MD, 1966; postgrad., U. Edinburgh, Scotland, 1961-62. Diplomate Am. Bd. Pathology. Intern, chief resident in pathology UCLA Med. Ctr., 1966-68; surgeon, lt. comdr. Atomic Bomb Casualty Commn., Hiroshima, Japan, 1968-71; chief resident in pathology Queens Med. Ctr., Honolulu, 1971-73; asst., assoc. prof. pathology U. Kans. Med. Ctr., Kansas City, 1973-82, prof., 1982—. Dir. anat. pathology VA Med. Ctr., Kansas City, Mo., 1975-94, chief pathology and lab. medicine, 1994-2003, dir. surg. pathology, 2003—. Contbr. numerous articles to profl. jours., chpts. to books. Leader YMCA Indian Princess Program, Overland Park, Kans., 1977-79, Indian Guide Program, 1978-80, Cub Scout Am., Overland Park, 1980-82, Boy Scouts Am., Leawood, Kans., 1982—. Lt. comdr. USPHS, 1968-71, Japan. Grantee Merck, Sharp and Dohme, 1980. Fellow Coll. Am. Pathologists, Am. Soc. Clin. Pathologists; mem. Am. Assn. Pathologists, Internat. Acad. Pathologists, Soc. Exptl. Biology and Medicine, N.Y. Acad. Scis., AAAS, Kansas City Soc. Pathologists (sec.-treas. 1982-83, pres. 1983-84). Achievements include research in ultrastructure and pathobiology of neoplasms, radiation carcinogenesis, and morphogenesis of atherosclerosis. Home: 9400 Lee Blvd Shawnee Mission KS 66206-1826 Office: VA Med Ctr 4801 E Linwood Blvd Kansas City MO 64128-2226 Business E-Mail: douglas.mcgregor@va.gov.

MCGREGOR, JIM, state representative; b. 1948; married; 3 children. BA, U. Cin.; 40 grad. hrs. in pub. adminstrn., Ohio State U.; grad., Ohio Peace Officers Acad. Supt. parks City of Lebanon, Ohio; park naturalist Ohio Dept. Natural Resources, adminstr. field ops., divsn. natural areas, dep. chief to chief, divsn. civilian conservation; mayor Gahanna, Ohio; state rep. dist. 20 Ohio Ho. of Reps., Columbus, 2000—, vice chair, commerce and labor com., chair, vets. affairs subcom., chair, regulatory reform subcom., mem. conty and twp. govt., energy and environment, transp. and pub. safety, and ways and means coms. Past pres. Ctrl. Ohio Mayors Coun. Served 6 yrs. Ohio Army Res. NG. Recipient Disting. Cmty. Svc. and Leadership award, Columbus Jewish Fedn., 2001. Republican. Office: 77 S High St 11th fl Columbus OH 43215-6111

MCGUFF, JOSEPH THOMAS, professional sports team executive; m. Mary Heard; children: Nanch Thomas, Mike, Marianne, John, Elaine, Bill. Sportwriter Kansas City (Mo.) Star, 1948-66, sports editor, 1966-86, v.p., editor, 1986-92, ret., 1992; bd. dirs. Kansas City Royals, 1994—. Author: Winning It All, Why Me? Why Not Joe McGuff. Recipient 6 Outstanding Sports Writer in Mo. awards Sportswriters and Sportscasters Assn.; named Mr. Baseball, Kansas City Baseball Awards Dinner, 1983; named to writers wing Baseball Hall of Fame, 1986. Mem. Baseball Writers and AP Sports Editors (past nat. pres.), Mo. Sports Hall of Fame. Office: Kansas City Royals PO Box 419969 Kansas City MO 64141-6969

MCGUIRE, JOHN C., state legislator; b. Joliet, Ill. m. Marilyn McGuire; four children. Student, Joliet Jr. Coll., Ill.; BA, Colo. State Coll. Trustee, supr. Joliet Twp.; tchr., coach; Dist. 86 rep. Ill. Ho. Reps., Springfield, 1991—. Mem. labor and commerce, transp. and motor vehicles, econ. and urban devel., elem. and secondary edn., gen. svc. appropriations, and aging coms., Ill. Ho. Reps. Mem. VFW, Irish Am. Soc. Address: 1510 Glenwood Ave Joliet IL 60435-5832 Also: 121 Springfield Ave Joliet IL 60435-6561

MCGUIRE, MARY JO, state legislator; b. Mpls., 1956; BA in Bus. Adminstrn., Coll. of St. Catherine, 1978; JD, Hamline U., 1988; postgrad., Harvard U., 1995-97. Mem. Minn. Ho. of Reps., 1988—, mem. judiciary com., judiciary fin. divsn., vice chair family and early childhood edn. fin. divsn., mem. govt. ops., chair data practices subcom., lead minor mem. Democrat. Home: 1529 Iowa Ave W Saint Paul MN 55108-2128

MCGUIRE, TIM, editor; Mng. editor Star Tribune, Mpls., 1979—92, editor, sr. v.p., 1992—2002; syndicated columnist United Media, 2002—. Juror Pulitzer Prize, 2002; prof. Washington & Lee U., Lexington, Va., Davidson Coll. Sch. Journalism & Pub. Policy, NC. Author: (weekly column) More Than Work, 2002—. Mem.: Am. Soc. Newspaper Editors (pres. 2001—02). Roman Catholic. Office: Star Tribune 425 Portland Ave Minneapolis MN 55488-0002

MCGUIRE, WILLIAM W., retired insurance company executive; b. Troy, NY, 1948; m. Nadine M. McGuire; 2 children. BA, U. Tex., 1970, MD, 1974. Internal med. resident, chief resident & pulmonary fellow U. Tex. Health Sci. Ctr., San Antonio, 1974—78; rschr. Scripps Clinic & Rsch. Found., La Jolla, Calif., 1978—80; practicing physician Colo. Springs, 1980—85; v.p. health systems Peak Health Plan, 1985—86, med. dir., Coastguard, 1985—86, pres., COO, 1985—88; exec. v.p. United Healthcare Corp., Minnetonka, Minn., 1988—89, pres., 1989—91, CEO, chmn., 1991—98; CEO UnitedHealth Group., Inc., Minnetonka, Minn., 1998—2006; chmn. UnitedHealth Group Inc., Minnetonka, Minn., 1998—2006; founder William W. McGuire & Nadine M. McGuire Family Found. Chmn. Colo. Found. for Med. Care, Region 111, 1984—85; bd. dirs. UnitedHealth Grp. Inc. (formerly United HealthCare Corp.), 1989—, Minn. Bus. Partnership. Trustee Mpls. Inst. Arts; dir. Minn. Orch. Assn. Named one of Forbes' Richest Americans, 2006. Mem.: NIH Nat. Cancer Policy Bd. Home: 315 Woodhill Rd Wayzata MN 55391

MCGUIRE-RIGGS, SHEILA, Democratic party chairman; Chmn. Iowa Democrat Party, Iowa. Democrat. Mailing: 5661 Fleur Dr Des Moines IA 50321 E-mail: smriggs@iowademocrats.org.

MCGUNNIGLE, GEORGE FRANCIS, lawyer, judge; b. Rochester, NY, Feb. 22, 1942; s. George Francis and Mary Elizabeth (Curran) McG.; m. Priscilla Ann Lappin, July 13, 1968; children: Cynthia A., Brian P. AB, Boston Coll., 1963; LLB, Georgetown U., 1966; LLM, George Wash. U., 1967. Bar: Conn. 1971, Minn. 1972, U.S. Dist. Ct. D.C. 1967, U.S. Dist. Ct. Conn. 1971, U.S. Dist. Ct. Minn. 1972, U.S. Ct. Appeals (2d cir.) 1971, U.S. Ct. Appeals (8th cir.) 1977, U.S. Supreme Ct. 1986. Asst. U.S. atty. Office of U.S. Atty., Bridgeport, Conn., 1971—72; assoc. Leonard, Street and Deinard, Mpls., 1972—73, ptnr., 1974—2000; judge Fourth Jud. Dist., Mpls., 2000—. Editor: Business Torts Litigation, 1992. Bd. dirs. Cath. Charities, 1997—2003, North Ctrl. chpt. Arthritis Found., Mpls., 1986-92, 94—2003, mem. exec. com., 1988-92, 2001—03. Lt. JAGC, USN, 1967-71. Recipient Nat. Vol. Svc. citation Arthritis Found., 1992. Mem. ABA (litigation sect., chmn. bus. torts litigation com. 1988-91, divsn. dir. 1991-92, 97-98, coun. 1992-95, sect. of dispute resolution coun. 2000-01). Avocation: reading. Office: Fourth Judicial Dist C-1251 Hennepin County Govt Ctr Minneapolis MN 55487-0422 Office Phone: 612-596-8822.

MCGWIRE, MARK DAVID, retired professional baseball player; b. Pomona, Calif., Oct. 1, 1963; s. John and Kathy McGwire; 1 child, Matthew. Student, U. So. Calif. With Oakland Athletics, Calif., 1984—97, St. Louis Cardinals, 1997—2001. Named Am. League Rookie of Yr., 1987, Male Athlete of Yr., AP, 1998; named to All-Star Team, 1987—92, 1995—2000, MLB All-Century Team, 1999; recipient Gold Glove award, 1990. Achievements include being a member of U.S. Olympic Baseball Team, 1984; mem.of World Series Championship Team, 1989; led Am. League in Home Runs, 1987 (49), 1996 (52); led Nat. League in Home Runs, 1998 (70), 1999 (65); led Nat. League in RBI's (147), 1999.

MCHALE, JOHN JOSEPH, JR., major league baseball executive, former professional sports team executive; b. Detroit, 1949; s. John J. and Patricia (Cameron) McH.; m. Sally McHale; children: Duncan, William, Frances. Grad., U. Notre Dame, 1971; JD, Boston Coll., 1975; LLM, Georgetown U., 1982. Lawyer, Denver, 1981-91; chmn. bd. Denver MLB Stadium Dist., 1989-91; exec. v.p. baseball ops. Colo. Rockies, 1991-93, exec. v.p. ops., 1993; pres., CEO Detroit Tigers, 1995—2001; COO Tampa Bay Devil Rays, 2001—02; exec. v.p. adminstrn. MLB, 2002—. Dir. Maj. League Baseball Enterprises; mem. baseball ops. com. Maj. League Baseball. Chmn. Southeast Mich. WalkAm., March of Dimes, 1996, 97; mem. pres. adv. coun. Henry Ford Mus., Greenfield Village; bd. dirs. caring athletes team Children's Hosp., Henry Ford Hosp. Office: Major League Baseball 245 Park Ave 31st Fl New York NY 10165 Fax: 313-965-2138.

MCHALE, KEVIN EDWARD, professional sports team executive, retired professional basketball player; b. Hibbing, Minn., Dec. 19, 1957; m. Lynn McHale; children: Kristyn, Michael, Joseph, Alexandra, Thomas. Student, U. Minn., 1976—80. Player Boston Celtics, 1980—93; spl. asst. Minn. Timberwolves, 1993—94, asst. gen. mgr., 1994—95, v.p. basketball ops., 1995—, interim head coach, 2005. Named to NBA All Rookie Team, 1981, NBA All-Defensive Second Team, 1983, 89, 90, NBA All-Defensive First Team, 1986-88, All-NBA First Team, 1987, NBA All-Star Team, 1984, 86-91, Basketball Hall of Fame, 1999, Nat. HS Sports Hall of Fame, 2000; named one of Top 50 Players in first 50 years of NBA, 1995; named Top Player in U. Minn. hist.; recipient NBA Sixth Man award, 1984, 85. Achievements include winning NBA Championships as a member of the Celtics, 1981, 84, 86. Office: Minn Timberwolves 600 1st Ave N Minneapolis MN 55403-1416 Office Phone: 612-673-1600.

MCHALE, VINCENT EDWARD, political science professor; b. Jenkins Twp., Pa., Apr. 17, 1939; m. Ann Barbara Cotner, Nov. 8, 1963; 1 child, Patrick James. A.B., Wilkes Coll., 1964; M.A., Pa. State U., 1966, Ph.D. in Polit. Sci., 1969. Asst. prof. polit. sci. U. Pa., Phila., 1969-75, dir. grad. studies, 1971-73; assoc. prof. Case Western Res. U., Cleve., 1975-84, prof., 1984-03, chmn. dept. polit. sci., 1978-03; vis. lectr. John Carroll U., summer 1980, Beaver Coll., 1975; Marcus A. Hanna prof., 2006—. Author: (with A.P. Frognier and D. Paranzino) Vote, Clivages Socio-politiques et Developpement Regional en Belgique, 1974. Co-editor; contbr.: Evaluating Transnational Programs in Government and Business, 1980; Political Parties of Europe, 1983; edtl. adv. bd. Worldmark Ency. of Nations, 1994—. Contbr. chpts. to books, articles to profl. jours. Project cons. Council Econ Opportunity in Greater Cleve., 1978-81; mem. Morris Abrams Award Com., 1977—. Recipient Outstanding Prof. award Lux chpt. Mortar Bd., 1989, 90; named one of Most Interesting People of 1988, Cleve. Mag.; NSF grantee, 1971-72; HEW grantee, 1976-78; Woodrow Wilson fellow, 1968, Ruth Young Boucke fellow, 1967-68; All-Univ. fellow, 1967-68. Mem. Phi Kappa Phi. Home: 3070 Coleridge Rd Cleveland OH 44118-3556 Office: Case Western Res U Cleveland OH 44106 Office Phone: 216-368-2425. Business E-Mail: vem@case.edu.

MCHENRY, MARTIN CHRISTOPHER, physician, educator; b. Feb. 9, 1932; s. Merl and Marcella (Bricca) McH.; m. Patricia Grace Hughes, Apr. 27, 1957; children: Michael, Christopher, Timothy, Mary Ann, Jeffrey, Paul, Kevin, William, Monica, Martin Christopher. Student, U. Santa Clara, 1950-53; MD, U. Cin., 1957; MS in Medicine, U. Minn., 1966. Diplomate Am. Bd. Internal Medicine. Intern Highland Alameda County (Calif.) Hosp., Oakland, 1957-58; resident, internal medicine fellow Mayo Clinic, Rochester, Minn., 1958-61, spl. appointee in infectious diseases, 1963-64; staff physician Henry Ford Hosp., Detroit, 1964-67, Cleve. Clinic, 1967-72, chmn. dept. infectious diseases, 1972-92, sr. physician infectious diseases, 1992-98. Cons. infectious diseases, 1998—2006; asst. clin. prof. Case Western Res. U., 1970-77, assoc. clin. prof. medicine, 1977-91, clin. prof. medicine, 1991—2006; assoc. vis. physician Cleve. Met. Gen. Hosp., 1970-00; cons. VA Hosp., Cleve., 1973-74. Contbr. more than 100 articles to profl. jours., also chpts. to books. Chmn. manpower com. Swine Influenza Program, Cleve., 1976. With USNR, 1961-63. Named Disting. Tchr. in Medicine, Cleve. Clinic, 1972, 90; recipient 1st ann. Bruce Hubbard Stewart award Cleve. Clinic Found. for Humanities in Medicine, 1985, Nightingale Physician Collaboration award Cleve. Clinic Found. Divsn. ursing, 1995, Clinician of Yr. award Acad. Medicine of Cleve./No. Ohio Med. Assn., 2002. Fellow ACP, Infectious Diseases Soc. Am. (Clinician award 2000), Am. Coll. Chest Physicians (chmn. com. cardiopulmonary infections 1975-77, 81-83), Royal Soc. Medicine of Gt. Britain; mem. Am. Soc. Clin. Pharmacology and Therapeutics (chmn. sect. infectious diseases and antimicrobial agts. 1970-77, 80-85, dir.). Home: 2779 Belgrave Rd Pepper Pike OH 44124-4601 Office: 9500 Euclid Ave Cleveland OH 44195-0001

MCHENRY, POWELL, lawyer; b. Cin., May 14, 1926; s. L. Lee McHenry and Marguerite L. (Powell) Heinz; m. Venna Mae Guerrea, Aug. 27, 1948; children: Scott, Marshall, Jody Lee, Gale Lynn. AB, U. Cinn., 1949; LLB, Harvard U., 1951, JD, 1969. Bar: Ohio 1951, U.S. Ct. Appeals (6th cir.) 1964, U.S. Supreme Ct. 1966. Assoc. Dinsmore, Shohl, Sawyer & Dinsmore, Cinn., 1951-57; ptnr. Dinsmore, Shohl, Coates & Deupree (and predecessors), Cinn., 1958-75; gen. counsel Federated Dept. Stores, Inc., 1971-75; assoc. gen. counsel Procter & Gamble Co., 1975-76, v.p., gen. counsel, 1976-83, sr. v.p., gen. counsel, 1983-91; counsel Dinsmore & Shohl, Cin., 1991—; bd. dirs. Eagle Picher Industries, Inc., 1991-97. Mem. com. Hamilton County Pub. Defender, Cin., chmn., 1996-2000. With USNR, 1944-46. Recipient award of merit Ohio Legal Center Inst., 1969, Lifetime Achievement in Law award, Cin. Bar Found., 2004. Mem. ABA, Ohio Bar Assn., Cin. Bar Assn. (pres. 1979-80, exec. com. 1975-81), Harvard U. Law Sch. Assn. Cin. (pres. 1960-61), Am. Law Inst., Assn. Gen. Counsel (pres. 1986-88), Harvard Club, Western Hills Country Club (bd. dirs. 1964-70, sec. 1966-69, 87-89, treas. 1969-70, 89-90), Queen City Club, Commonwealth Club (pres. 1996-97). Republican. Methodist. Office: Dinsmore & Shohl 1900 Chemed Ctr 255 E 5th St Cincinnati OH 45202-4700 Office Phone: 513-977-8295.

MCHENRY, ROBERT (DALE), editor; b. St. Louis, Apr. 30, 1945; s. Robert Dale and Pearl Lenna (Nalley) McH.; m. Carolyn F. Amundson, Oct. 2, 1971; children: Curran, Zachary. BA in English Lit., Northwestern U., 1966; MA in English Lit., U. Mich., 1967; MBA in Mgmt., Northwestern U., 1987. Proofreader, prodn. editor Ency. Britannica, Inc., Chgo., 1967-69, editor, 1974-75, dir. yearbooks, 1985-86, mng. editor, 1986-90, gen. editor, v.p., 1990-92, editor-in-chief, 1992-97, editor-at-large, 1997—. Editor: Documentary History of Conservation in America, 1972, Webster's American Military Biographies, 1978, Liberty's Women, 1980, Webster's New Biographical Dictionary, 1983. Mem. United Ch. of Christ.

MCHUGH, RICHARD WALKER, lawyer; b. Sullivan, Ind., Dec. 9, 1952; s. Richard Harrison and Virginia Ann (Robinson) McH.; m. Marsha J. Marshall, May 24, 1975; children: Walker, Cora. BA, Wabash Coll., 1975; JD, U. Mich., 1978. Bar: Mich. 1984, Ky. 1979, U.S. Supreme Ct. 1987. Assoc. Youngdahl Law Firm, Little Rock, 1978-79; staff atty. Legal Aid Soc., Louisville, 1979-84; assoc. gen. counsel Internat. Union UAW, Detroit, 1984-95; pvt. practice, Ann Arbor, Mich., 1995-98; staff atty. Mich. Poverty Law Prgm., 1998-2000, Nat. Employment Law Project, Dexter, Mich., 2000—. Dir. Mich. Legal Svcs., Detroit, 1986-91. Mem. at. Acad. Social Ins. Democrat. Avocations: fishing, backpacking. Office: Nat Employment Law Project PO Box 369 Dexter MI 48130-0369

MCILROY, ALAN F., manufacturing executive; b. 1950; Internat. contr. Wheelabrator Corp., 1983-87; bus. unit contr. Gen. Chem., 1987-90; sr. v.p. Harris Chem.; head Greenock Group; CFO Dayton Superior Corp., Miamisburg, Ohio, 1997—2007.

MCINERNY, RALPH MATTHEW, philosopher, educator, writer; b. Mpls., Feb. 24, 1929; s. Austin Clifford and Vivian Gertrude (Rush) McI.; m. Constance Terrill Kunert, Jan. 3, 1953 (dec. May 2001); children: Cathleen, Mary, Anne, David, Elizabeth, Daniel. BA, St. Paul Sem., 1951; MA, U. Minn., 1952; PhD summa cum laude, Laval U., 1954; LittD (hon.), St. Benedict Coll., 1978, U. Steubenville, 1984; DHL (hon.), St. Francis Coll., Joliet, Ill., 1986, St. John Fisher Coll., 1994, St. Anselm's Coll., NH, 1995, Holy Cross Coll., New Orleans, 2001, Assumption Coll., Worcester, Mass., 2007. Instr. Creighton U., 1954-55; prof. U. Notre Dame, Ind., 1955—, Michael P. Grace prof. medieval studies Ind., 1988—, dir. dept. Ind., 1978-85, dir. Jacques Martin Ctr., 1978—2005. Vis. prof. Cornell U., 1988, Cath. U., 1971, Louvain, 1983, 95; founder Internat. Cath. U.; disting. vis. prof. Truman State U., Mo., 1999; Gifford lectr. Glasgow U., Scotland, 1999-2000, Joseph lectr. Pontifical Gregorian Inst., Rome, 2003; vis. lectr. Pontifical U. of Holy Cross, Rome, 2006, Ctr. of Applied Law, Cath. U. Chile, 2006. Author: The Logic of Analogy, 1961, History of Western Philosophy, vol. 1, 1963, vol. 2, 1968, Thomism in an Age of Renewal, 1966, Studies in Analogy, 1967, New Themes in Christian Philosophy, 1967, St. Thomas Aquinas, 1976, Ethica Thomistica, 1982, History of the Ambrosiana, 1983, Being and Predication, 1986, Miracles, 1986, Art and Prudence, 1988, A First Glance at St. Thomas: Handbook for Peeping Thomists,

1989, Boethius and Aquinas, 1989, Aquinas on Human Action, 1991, The Question of Christian Ethics, 1993, Aquinas Against the Averroists, 1993, The God of Philosophers, 1994, Aquinas and Analogy, 1996, Ethica Thomistica, 1997, Student Guide to Philosophy, 1999, Vernunftgemässes Leben, 2000, Characters in Search of Their Authors, 2001, Conversion of Edith Stein, 2001, John of St. Thomas, Summa Theologiae, 2001, Defamation of Pius XII, 2001, Very Rich Hours of Jacques Maritain, 2003, Aquinas, 2003; (novels) Jolly Rogerson, 1967, A Narrow Time, 1969, The Priest, 1973, Gate of Heaven, 1975, Rogerson at Bay, 1976, Her Death of Cold, 1977, The Seventh Station, 1977, Romanesque, 1977, Spinnaker, 1977, Quick as a Dodo, 1978, Bishop as Pawn, 1978, La Cavalcade Romaine, 1979, Lying Three, 1979, Abecedary, 1979, Second Vespers, 1980, Rhyme and Reason, 1981, Thicker than Water, 1981, A Loss of Patients, 1982, The Grass Widow, 1983, Connolly's Life, 1983, Getting Away with Murder, 1984, And Then There Were Nun, 1984, The Noonday Devil, 1985, Sine Qua Nun, 1986, Leave of Absence, 1986, Rest in Pieces, 1985, Cause and Effect, 1987, The Basket Case, 1987, Veil of Ignorance, 1988, Abracadaver, 1989, Body and Soil, 1989, Four on the Floor, 1989, Frigor Mortis, 1989, Savings and Loan, 1990, The Search Committee, 1991, The Nominative Case, 1991, Sister Hood, 1991, Judas Priest, 1991, Easeful Death, 1991, Infra Dig, 1992, Desert Sinner, 1992, Seed of Doubt, 1993, The Basket Case, 1993, Nun Plussed, 1993, Mom and Dead, 1994, The Cardinal Offense, Law and Ardor, 1995, Let's Read Latin, 1995, Aguinas and Analogy, 1996, The Tears of Things, 1995, Half Past Nun, 1997, On This Rockne, 1997, Penguin Classic Aquinas, 1997, The Red Hat, 1998, What Went Wrong With Vatican II, 1998, Lack of the Irish, 1998, Irish Tenure, 1999, Grave Undertakings, 1999, Heirs and Parents, 2000, Shakespearean Variations, 2000, Book of Kills, 2001, Triple Pursuit, 2001, Still Life, 2001, Sub Rosa, 2001, Emerald Aisle, 2001, John of St. Thomas, Summa Theologiae, 2001, Law and Ardor, 2001, As Good as Dead, 2002, Celt and Pepper, 2002, Prodigal Father, 2002, Last Things, 2002, Ablative Case, 2003, Irish Coffee, 2003, Requiem For A Realtor, 2004, Green Thumb, 2004, Blood Ties, 2005, Irish Gilt, 2005, Soul of Wit, 2005, (memoirs) Only I Have Escaped to Tell You, 2006, Prudence of the Flesh, 2006, Perambula Fidei, 2006, The Letter Killeth, 2006, The Widow's Mate, 2007; editor New Scholasticism, 1967-89; editor, pub. Crisis, 1982-96; pub. Catholic Dossier, 1995-2002, Fellowship of Cath. Scholars Quar., 2003—. Exec. dir. Wethersfield Inst., 1989-92; bd. govs. Thomas Aquinas Coll., Santa Paula, Calif., 1993-2001; bd. dirs. Southern Cross Found., 1999—; mem. Pres. Bush's Com. on the Arts and Humanities, 2002—. With USMC, 1946-47. Named to Cath. Edn. Found. Hall of Fame, 2007; recipient Thomas Aquinas medal U. Dallas, 1990, Thomas Aquinas Coll., 1991, St. Thomas Aquinas medal for eminence in philosophy, 1993, Maritain medal Am. Maritain Assn., 1994, P.G. Wodehouse award CRISIS Mag., 1995, Cardinal Journet medal Ave Maria U., Fla., 2007; Fulbright rsch. fellow, Belgium, 1959-60, NEH fellow, 1977-78, NEA fellow, 1983, Catholic Scholars fellow, 1992-95; Fulbright scholar, Argentina, 1986, 87, Outstanding Philosophical scholar Delta Epsilon Sigma, 1990; honoree Ralph McInerny Ctr. Thonistic Studies Thomas Internat. U., 2006. Fellow Pontifical Roman Acad. St. Thomas Aquinas; mem. Am. Philos. Assn., Am. Cath. Philos. Assn. (past pres., St. Thomas Aquinas medal 1993), Cath. Acad. Scis., Am. Metaphys. Soc. (pres. 1992), Am. Maritain Assn. (pres. 2004-06), Internat. Soc. for Study Medieval Philosophy, Medieval Acad., Mystery Writers Am. (Lifetime Achievement award 1993), Authors Guild, Fellowship Cath. Scholars (pres. 1992-95, Cardinal Wright award 1996, Premio Roncevalles de Navarre 2002). Office: U of Notre Dame Jacques Maritain Ctr 714 Hesburgh Notre Dame IN 46556-5677

MCINTOSH, DAVID M., former congressman; b. June 8, 1958; m. Ruthie McIntosh. Grad., Yale Coll., 1980, U. Chgo., 1983. Bar: Ind., U.S. Supreme Ct. Spl. asst. domestic affairs to Pres. Reagan; spl. asst. to Atty. Gen. Meese; liaison Pres.'s Commn. on Privatization; spl. asst. to V.P. Quayle, dep. legal counsel to; exec. dir. Pres.'s Coun. on Competitiveness; sr. fellow Citizens for a Sound Economy; founder Federalist Soc. for Law & Pub. Policy, now co-chmn.; mem. U.S. Congress from Ind., Washington, 1995-2001; ptnr. Mayer, Brown, Rowe and Maw, 2002—; prof., dept of econ. Ball St. Univ. Sch. of Bus., 2002—. Mem. State Bar of Ind. Republican. Office: Mayer Brown Rowe and Maw 1909 K St NW Washington DC 20006 Home: 3432 N George Mason Dr Arlington VA 22207-1840 E-mail: dmcintosh@mayerbrown.com.

MCINTOSH, ELAINE VIRGINIA, nutrition educator; b. Webster, SD, Jan. 30, 1924; d. Louis James and Cora Boletta (Bakke) Nelson; m. Thomas Henry McIntosh, Aug. 28, 1955; children: James George, Ronald Thomas, Charles Nelson. BA magna cum laude, Augustana Coll., Sioux Falls, SD, 1945; MA, U. S.D., 1949; PhD, Iowa State U., 1954. Instr., asst. prof. Sioux Falls Coll., 1945-48; instr. Iowa State U., Ames, 1949-53, rsch. assoc., 1955-62; postdoctoral rsch. assoc. U. Ill., Urbana, 1954-55; asst. prof. human biology U. Wis., Green Bay, 1968-72, assoc. prof., 1972-85, prof., 1985-90, emeritus prof., 1990—, writer, cons., 1990—, chmn. human biology dept., 1975-80, asst. to vice chancellor, asst. to chancellor, 1974-76. Author 3 books including American Food Habits in Historical Perspective, 1995, Lewis and Clark: Food, Nutrition, and Health, 2003; contbr. numerous articles on bacterial metabolism, meat biochemistry and nutrition edn. to profl. jours. Fellow USPHS, 1948-49. Avocation: travel. Office: LS 455 Human Biology U Wis Green Bay 2420 Nicolet Dr Green Bay WI 54311-7001

MCINTYRE, JOHN LAWRENCE, lawyer; b. St. Paul, Apr. 25, 1942; s. John F. and Mary E. (Clancy) McI.; m. Mary E. Seifert, May 6, 1967; children: Matthew, Aimee, Brendan. BA in Philosophy, Coll. St. Thomas, 1963; LLB, U. Minn., 1966. Bar: Minn. 1966, U.S. Ct. Appeals (8th cir.) 1966, U.S. Supreme Ct. 1984. Law clk. to judge U.S. Ct. Appeals (8th cir.), 1966-67; mem. Doherty, Rumble and Butler, St. Paul and Mpls., 1967-93; gen. counsel, v.p., sec. The Toro Co., Mpls., 1993—. Mem. ABA (law and acctg. com. bus. law sect.), Minn. Club, Minn. Bar Assn., Hennepin City Bar Assn., Minn. Corp. Counsel Assn. (dir.), Order of Coif. Roman Catholic. Office: The Toro Co 8111 Lyndale Ave S Minneapolis MN 55420-1196 Office Phone: 952-887-8059. Office Fax: 952-887-8920. Business E-Mail: larry.mcintyre@toro.com.

MCINTYRE, MICHAEL JOHN, lawyer, educator; b. Attleboro, Mass., Mar. 12, 1942; sd. John W. and Margaret E. (McBrien) McI.; m. May Ping Soo Hoo; children: Devin J., Colin J. AB, Providence Coll., 1964; JD, Harvard U., 1969. Bar: Mass. 1969, D.C. 1970. Vol. Peace Corps, Bhopal, India, 1964-66; assoc. Ivins, Phillips and Barker, Washington, 1969-71; dir. tng. Internat. Tax Program, Harvard U., Cambridge, Mass., 1971-75; prof. law Wayne State U., Detroit, 1975—. Cons. govt. of Egypt, State of N.Y., Navajo Tribe, govts. of Spain, Australia, 1975—; cons. UN Group Experts Internat. Coop. Tax Masters. Author: Readings in Federal Taxation, 1983, International Income Tax Rules of United States, 2d edit., 2001, (with Arnold) International Tax Primer, 1995, 2d edit., 2002; editor-in-chief Tax Notes Internat., 1989-91; contbr. articles to numerous publs. Office: Wayne State Univ Law Sch Detroit MI 48202 Office Phone: 313-577-3944. E-mail: mcintyre@wayne.edu.

MCKAY, BERNARD L., lawyer; b. Maysville, Ky., July 3, 1969; BBA, Morehead State U., 1991; JD, Salmon P. Chase Coll. Law, 1994. Bar: Ohio 1994, Ky. 1995. Ptnr. Frost Brown Todd LLC, Cin. Chmn., Local Rules Com. Hamilton County Probate Ct.; mem. Cin. Estate Planning Coun. Treasurer Salmon P. Chase Coll. Law Bd. Governors, 2003—04, pres. elect, 2004—05, pres., 2005—06; pres., Class of 2004 Leadership Northern Ky., mem., Class of 2005 Steering Com.; mem., Red Mass Com. St. Thomas More Soc.; mem. Friendly Sons of St. Patrick; mem., Bd. Dirs. Women's Crisis Ctr., chmn., Devel. Com.; mem., Bd. Dirs. Caracole, Inc. amed one of Ohio's Rising Stars, Super Lawyers, 2005, 2006, 40 Under 40, Cin. Bus. Courier, 2006; named to Best Lawyers in Am., 2006. Mem.: ABA (mem., Real Property, Probate and Trust Com.), Northern Ky. Bar Assn. (mem., Bus. and Tax Com., mem., Probate Com.), Ky. Bar Assn. (mem., Taxation Com., mem., Probate and Trust Law Com.), Ohio State Bar Assn. (mem., Estate Planning, mem., Trust and Probate Law Com.), Cin. Bar Assn. (mem., Taxation Com., mem., Adv. Estate Planning and Probate Inst. Com.). Office: Frost Brown Todd LLC 2200 PNC Ctr 201 E Fifth St Cincinnati OH 45202-4182 Office Phone: 513-651-6800. Office Fax: 513-651-6981.

MCKAY, MARK, radio personality; m. Marcia McKay; 3 children. Program dir. WRKO/FM, Boston, Y106, Orlando, Fla., KCMO-FM, Kansas City; radio host KFRC, San Francisco, KMEL, Oldies 95, Kansas City, Kans. Named one of Am.'s Most Influential Air Personalities of the Top 40 Era, Radio & Recs. Pub., 1998. Avocations: golf, baseball, travel. Office: Oldies 95 5800 Foxridge Dr 6th Fl Mission KS 66202

MCKAY, MELINDA, hotel executive; b. Sydney, Australia, 1974; Corp. mktg. devel., rsch. svcs. Jones Lang LaSalle Hotels Asia Pacific; mktg. rsch. Jones Lang LaSalle Hotels, rsch. mgr. Chgo., 1997—99, sr. v.p., 2001—. Named one of 40 Under Forty, Crain's Chgo. Bus., 2005.

MCKEACHIE, WILBERT JAMES, psychologist, educator; b. Clarkston, Mich., Aug. 24, 1921; s. Bert A. and Edith E. (Welberry) McK.; m. Virginia Mae Mack, Oct. 30, 1942; children: Linda, Karen. BA, Mich. State Normal Coll., 1942; MA, U. Mich., 1946, PhD, 1949; LLD, Ea. Mich. U., 1957, U. Cin.; ScD, Northwestern U., 1973, Denison U., 1975, Nat. Acad. Edn., 1977, Alma Coll., 1995; DLitt (hon.), Hope Coll., 1985; LHD (hon.), Shawnee State U., 1994. Faculty U. Mich., 1946—, chmn. dept., 1961-71, dir. Center for Research in Learning and Teaching, 1975-83. Mem. nat. adv. mental health council NIMH, 1976-80; mem. spl. med. adv. group VA, 1967-72 Author: (with J.E. Milholland) Undergraduate Curricula in Psychology, 1961, (with Charlotte Doyle and Mary Margaret Moffett) Psychology, 1966, 3d edit., 1977 (also Spanish edit. and instr.'s manual), Teaching Tips, 11th edit., 2002. Trustee Kalamazoo Coll., 1964-77; trustee-at-large Am. Psychol. Found., 1974-84, 92-96, pres., 1979-82. Officer USNR, 1943-45. Recipient Outstanding Tchr. award U. Mich. Alumni Assn., Am. Coll. Testing-Am. Edn1. Rsch. Assn. award for outstanding rsch. on coll. students, 1973, career contbns. award, 1990, award for disting. teaching in psychology Am. Psychol. Found., 1985, Gold medal award Am. Psychol. Found., others. Mem. APA (sec., dir., pres. 1976-77, Disting. Career Contbn. to Edn. and Tng. in Psychology award 1987, E.L. Thorndike award for outstanding rsch., 1988), Internat. Assn. Applied Psychology (pres. div. ednl. instrn. and sch. psychology 1982-86), Am. Assn. Higher Edn. (dir. 1974-80, pres. 1978), AAUP (pres. U. Mich. chpt. 1970-71), AAAS (chmn. sect. on psychology 1976-77), Sigma Xi. American Baptist. Home: 4660 Joy Rd Dexter MI 48130-9706 Office: U Mich Dept Psychology 525 E University Ave Ann Arbor MI 48109-1109 E-mail: billmck@umich.edu.

MCKEAGUE, DAVID WILLIAM, federal judge; b. Pitts., Nov. 5, 1946; s. Herbert William and Phyllis (Forsyth) McKeague; m. Nancy L. Palmer, May 20, 1989; children: Mike, Melissa, Sarah, Laura, Elizabeth, Adam. BBA, U. Mich., 1968, JD, 1971. Bar: Mich. 1971, US Dist. Ct. (we. dist.) Mich. 1972, US Dist. Ct. (ea. dist.) Mich. 1978, US Ct. Appeals (6th cir.) 1988. Assoc. Foster, Swift, Collins & Smith, Lansing, Mich., 1971-76, ptnr., 1976-92, sec.-treas., 1990-92; judge US Dist. Ct., (we. dist.) Mich., Lansing, Mich., 1992—2005, US Ct. Appeals (6th Cir.), Lansing, Mich., 2005—. Adm. prof. Mich. State U. Coll. Law, 1998—. Mem. nat. com. U. Mich. Law Sch. Fund, 1980—92, bd. trustees, 2007—; gen. counsel Mich. Rep. Com., 1989—92; mem. adv. coun. Wharton Ctr. Mich. State U., 1996—2002; adv. bd. Corp. Supportive Housing, 2002—. With USAR, 1969—75. Mem.: FBA (bd. dirs. Western Mich. chpt. 1991—), Federalist Soc. Law and Pub. Studies (lawyers divsn. Mich. chpt. 1996—), Am. Inns Ct. (pres. Mich. State U. Coll. Law chpt. 1999—2001), Mich. Bar Assn., Country Club Lansing (bd. govs. 1988—92, 1995—2001). Roman Catholic. Office: US Ct Appeals 315 W Allegan Rm 119 Lansing MI 48933 Office Phone: 517-377-1563. Business E-Mail: ca06-mckeague_chambers@ca6.uscourts.gov.

MCKEAN, ANDY, state legislator; b. June 23, 1949; m. Constance Hoefer. BS, SUNY, 1974; JD, U. Iowa, 1977. Lawyer; owner, operator Shaw Haw Bed and Breakfast; mem. Iowa Senate from 28th dist., Des Moines, 1992—; mem. ethics com., mem. local govt. com., mem. transp. com.; chair jud. com. Grad. sch. instr. U. Iowa. Square Dance caller Scotch Grove Pioneers; mem. Martella Christian Ch.; m. Jones County Hist. Soc. Mem. Jones County Bar Assn. Republican. E-mail: andy_mckean@legis.state.ia.us.

MCKECHNIE, ED, state legislator; b. July 31, 1963; m. Kristy McKechnie. Kans. state rep. Dist. 3. Mem. Lions. Home: 1124 N 250th St Arcadia KS 66711-4112

MCKEE, CHRISTOPHER FULTON, historian, educator; b. Bklyn., June 14, 1935; s. William Ralph and Frances McKee; m. Ann Adamczyk, 1993; children: Sharon, David. AB, U. St. Thomas, Houston, 1957; AMLS, U. Mich., 1960. Catalogue libr. Washington and Lee U., Lexington, Va., 1958-62; social sci. libr. So. Ill. U., Edwardsville, 1962-66, book selection officer, 1967-69, asst. dir., 1969-72; libr. of coll. Grinnell Coll., Iowa, 1972—2006, Samuel R. and Marie-Louise Rosenthal prof. Sec. of Navy rsch. chair naval history Naval Hist. Ctr., Washington, 1990—91; trustee Bibliog. Ctr. Rsch., Denver, 1984—88; scholar in res., Obermann Ctr. for Advanced Studies U. Iowa, 2006—. Author: (book) Edward Preble, 1972, A Gentlemanly and Honorable Profession: The Creation of the U.S. Naval Officer Corps 1794-1815, 1991, Sober Men and True: Sailor Lives in the Royal Navy 1900-1945, 2002. Mem. vestry Trinity Episcopal Ch., Iowa City. Recipient U.S. avl History prize, 1985, John Lyman Book award, N.Am. Soc. Oceanic History, 1991, Samuel Eliot Morison Disting. Svc. award, USS Constn. Mus., 1992; fellow NEH-Newberry Libr., 1978—79, Newberry Libr.-Brit. Acad., 1995—96. Mem.: U.S. Naval Inst., Soc. Historians Early Am. Republic, Orgn. Am. Historians, Soc. Mil. History, Navy Records Soc., Can. Nautical Rsch. Soc., Soc. Nautical Rsch. Democrat. Episcopalian. Home: 2382 Willowbrooke Ln Iowa City IA 52246-1834 Office: Obermann Ctr for Advanced Studies Univ Iowa N103 Oakdale Hall Iowa City IA 52242-5000 Home Phone: 319-351-7594; Office Phone: 319-335-4034.

MCKEE, KEITH EARL, manufacturing technology executive; b. Chgo., Sept. 9, 1928; s. Charles Richard and Maude Alice (Hamlin) McK.; children: Pamela Ann Houser, Paul Earl. BS, Ill. Inst. Tech., 1950, MS, 1956, PhD, 1962. Engr. Swift & Co., Chgo., 1953-54; rsch. engr. Armour Rsch. Found., Chgo., 1954-62; dir. design and product assurance Andrew Corp., Orland Park, Ill., 1962-67; dir. engring. Rsch. Ctr. Ill. Inst. Tech., Chgo., 1967-80, dir. mfg. prodn. ctr., 1977—. Prof. Ill. Inst. Tech., Chgo., 1979—, dir. indsl. programs, 1994—; coord. Nat. Conf. on Fluid Power, Chgo., 1983-88; mem. com. on materials and processing Dept. Def., Washington, 1986-92. Author: Productivity and Technology, 1988; co-author: Managing Technology Dependence Operation, 2004; editor: Automated Inspection and Process Control, 1987; co-editor: Manufacturing High Technology Handbook, 1987; mng. editor: Manufacturing Competitiveness Frontier, 1977-97. Capt. USMC, 1950-54. Recipient oustanding presentation award Am. Soc. of Quality Control, Milw., 1983. Fellow World Acad. Productivity Scis.; mem. ASCE, Am. Def. Preparedness Assn. (pres. Chgo. chpt. 1972-95), Am. Assn. Engring. Soc. (Washington) (coor. com. on productivity 1978-88), Inst. of Indsl. Engrs., Soc. Mfg. Engrs. (Gold medal 1991), Am. Assn. for Artificial Intelligence, Robotic Industry Assn. (bd. dir. 1978-81), Assn. for Mfg. Excellence, Soc. for Computer Simulation. Democrat. Roman Catholic. Home: Ste 504 3115 S Michigan Ave Chicago IL 60616 Office: Illinois Inst Tech Mfg Productivity Ctr 3424 S State St Ste 4001 S Chicago IL 60616 Office Phone: 312-567-3650. Business E-Mail: mckee@iit.edu.

MCKEE, RICHARD MILES, retired agricultural studies educator; b. Cottonwood Falls, Kans., Oct. 8, 1929; m. Marjorie Fisk, June 22, 1952; children: Dave, Richard, Annell, John. BS in Agriculture, Kans. State Coll. Agriculture and Applied Sci., 1951; MS in Animal Husbandry, Kans. State U., 1963; PhD in Animal Science, U. Ky., 1968. Herdsman Moxley Hall Hereford Ranch, Coun. Grove, Kans., 1951-52, 54-55, Luckhardt Farms, Tarkio, Mo., 1955-58; asst. mgr. L&J Crusoe Ranch, Cheboygan, Mich., 1958-59; asst. instr., cattle herdsman Kans. State U., Manhattan, 1959-65, from asst. prof. to assoc. prof., 1959-65, prof., departmental teaching coord., 1976-99; ret., 2005. Program participant and/or official judge numerous shows, field days including Kans. Jr. Hereford Field Day, Kans. Jr. Shorthorn Field Day, Better Livestock Day, Kans. Jr. Livestock Assn., Am. Jr. Hereford Assn. Field Day, Cheyenne, Wyo., 1973, Kans. Jr. Polled Hereford Field Day, Am. Jr. Shorthorn Assn., Kans. City, Mo., 1965, Am. Internat. Jr. Charolais Assn. Show, Lincoln, Nebr., 1976, Am. Royal 4-H Livestock Judging Contest, Kans. City, 1975, Jr. Livestock Activities various cattle breed assns. nationwide, 1977-81; served on many breed assn. coms.; judge County Fairs; official judge 14 different Nat. Beef Breed Shows U.S. and Can.; conducted 60 livestock judging and showmanship schs. at county level. Contbr. articles to profl. jours. Deacon 1st Presbyn. Ch., Manhattan, 1969-75, Sunday Sch. tchr., Chancel choir, elder; project leader com. mem. 4-H; foster parent Kans. State U. Football Program. Lt. USMC, 1952-54, Korea. Named Hon. State Farmer of Kans.; Hall of Merit Honoree for Edn. by Am. Polled Hereford Assn., 1985; NDEA scholar U. Ky., 1966-67; Miles McKee Student Enrichment Fund established at Kans. State U. Mem. Am. Soc. Animal Sci., Kans. Livestock Assn. (beef cattle improvement com. 1970-78, cow-calf clinic com. 1973, 74, 75, 76, 77, 78), Nat. Assn. Colls. and Tchrs. Agriculture, Block and Bridle Club, Am. Jr. Hereford Assn. (hon.), FarmHouse, Sigma Xi, Phi Kappa Phi, Alpha Zeta, Gamma Sigma Delta, Alpha Tau Alpha (hon.). Home: 901 Juniper Dr Manhattan KS 66502-3148 Office: Dept of Animal Scis & Industry Kansas State U Manhattan KS 66506 Office Phone: 785-532-1237. Personal E-mail: mmckee15@cox.net.

MCKEE, THOMAS FREDERICK, lawyer; b. Cleve., Oct. 27, 1948; s. Harry Wilbert and Virginia (Light) McK. BA with high distinction, U. Mich., 1970; JD with high distinction, Case Western Res. U., 1975. Bar: Ohio 1975, U.S. Dist. Ct. (no. dist.) Ohio 1975, U.S. Supreme Ct. 1979. Assoc. firm Calfee, Halter & Griswold, Cleve., 1975-81, ptnr., 1982—, also co-chmn. exec. com.; bd. dirs. Home Décor, Harden Furniture, Stanton Carpet, Data Trail Internat., Case We. Res.U., Musical Arts Assn. Contbg. editor Going Public, 1985. Mem. ABA (com. fed. regulation securities law sect.), Bar Assn. Greater Cleve., Order of Coif., Union Club, Tavern Club, Country Club, 50 Club, Pepper Pike Club. Office: Calfee Halter & Griswold 800 Superior Ave E Ste 1400 Cleveland OH 44114-2601 Home: 17429 Beech Grove Tr Chagrin Falls OH 44023

MCKEEN, ALEXANDER C., retired engineering executive, foundation administrator; b. Albion, Mich., Oct. 10, 1927; s. John Nisbet and Janet (Callander) McK.; m. Evelyn Mae Feldkamp, Aug. 18, 1951; Jeffrey, Brian, Andrew. BSME, U. Mich., 1950; MBA, Mich. State U., 1968. Registered profl. engr., Mich. From asst. supt. maintenance to supt. final assembly Cadillac Motor Car divsn. GM, Detroit, 1961-69; asst. dir. reliability cadillac motor car divsn. GM, Detroit, 1969-72, exec. engr. product assurance Warren, Mich., 1972-75, from asst. dir. to dir engring. analysis, 1975-87; pres., owner Engring. Analysis Assocs., Inc., Bingham Farms, Mich., 1987-99; cons. Detroit Exec. Svc. Corps, 1999—; pres. McKeen Found., 2002—. Pres. Dells of Bloomfield Home Owners Assn., Bloomfield Hills, Mich., 1987-88; trustee Kirk in Hills, Bloomfield Hills, 1990-93, 2003-06, elder, 1995-97. Mem. Soc. Auto. Engrs., Am. Soc. Quality Control, Econ. Club Detroit, Detroit Athletic Club, Bloomfield (Mich.) Lions Club (pres. 2004-05), Stonycroft Hills Golf Club (treas.), Pelican Nest Golf Club, Beta Gamma Sigma. Avocations: tennis, golf, photography, travel, gardening. Office: Detroit Executive Service Corps 16250 Northland Dr Ste 390 Southfield MI 48075

MCKELVEY, JOHN CLIFFORD, mental health services professional; b. Decatur, Ill., Jan. 25, 1934; s. Clifford Venice and Pauline Lytton (Runkel) McK.; m. Carolyn Tenney, May 23, 1980; children: Sean, Kerry, Tara, Evelyn, Aaron. BA, Stanford U., 1956, MBA, 1958. Rsch. analyst Stanford Rsch. Inst., Palo Alto, Calif., 1959—60, indsl. economist, 1960—64; with Midwest Rsch. Inst., Kansas City, Mo., 1964—2000, v.p. econs. and mgmt. sci., 1970—73, exec. v.p., 1973—75, pres., CEO, 1975—2000, The Menninger Clinic, Topeka, 2001—. Chmn. Trustee Vis. Coms. The Menninger Clinic, Topeka, 1978—86, chmn. bd. dirs., 1988—94; chmn. bd. The Menninger Found., 1994—97. Trustee Rockhurst Coll., 1993, Hoover Presdl. Libr. Assn., West Branch, Iowa, 1997; mem. Civic Coun. of Greater Kansas City; bd. dirs. Yellow Corp., Mid-Am. Mfg. Tech. Ctr., 1991; trustee The Menninger Found., 1975. Mem.: Carriage, Mission Hills. Home: 1156 W 103d St # 232 Kansas City MO 64114-4511 Address: Menningers PO Box 809045 Houston TX 77280

MCKENDRY, JOHN H., JR., lawyer; b. Grand Rapids, Mich., Mar. 24, 1950; s. John H. and Lois R. (Brandel) McK.; m. Linda A. Schmalzer, Aug. 11, 1973; children: Heather Lynn, Shannon Dawn, Sean William. BA cum laude, Albion Coll., Mich., 1972; JD cum laude, U. Mich., Ann Arbor, 1975. Bar: Mich. 1975. Assoc., then ptnr. Landman, Latimer, Clink & Robb, Muskegon, Mich., 1976-85; ptnr. Warner, Norcross & Judd, Muskegon, 1985—. Dir. debate Mona Shores High Sch., Muskegon, 1979-90; adj. prof. of taxation (employee benefits), Grand Valley State U., 1988—; debate instr. Muskegon C.C., 1999-2001. Pres. local chpt. Am. Cancer Soc., 1979; bd. dirs. West Shore Symphony, 1993-00, v.p. 1995-97, pres., 1997-99; bd. dirs. Cath. Social Svcs., 1998-04; chair profl. divsn. United Way, 1994, 98; chair bd. dirs. Deaf Hard of Hearing Connection, 2003—; bd. dirs. Mona Lake Watershed Coun., 2003-05, Hackley Life Counseling, 2007-; chair Charter Commn. City of Norton Shores, 2003-06. Recipient Disting. Service award Muskegon Jaycees, 1981; named 1 of 5 Outstanding Young Men in Mich., Mich. Jaycees. 1982; named to Hall of Fame, Mich. Speech Coaches, 1986, Diamond Key Coach Nat. Forensic League, 1987. Mem. ABA, Mich. Bar Assn., Muskegon County Bar Assn. (dir. 1992-98, pres. 1996-97), Muskegon C. of C. (bd. dirs. 1982-88), Mich. Interscholastic Forensic Assn. (treas. 1979-86), Optimists (pres. 1992). Republican. Roman Catholic. Home: 1575 Brookwood Dr Muskegon MI 49441-5276 Office Phone: 231-727-2637. Business E-Mail: mckendjh@wnj.com.

MCKENNA, ALVIN JAMES, lawyer; b. New Orleans, Aug. 17, 1943; s. Dixon N. Sr. and Mabel (Duplantier) McK.; m. Carol Jean Windheim, 1963; children: Sara, Alvin James Jr., Martha, Andrea, Erin, Rebecca. AB, Canisius Coll., 1963; JD, Notre Dame U., 1966. Bar: N.Y. 1966, Ohio 1967, U.S. Dist. Ct. (so. dist.) Ohio 1968, U.S. Dist. Ct. (no. dist.) Ohio 1978, U.S. Ct. Appeals (6th cir.) 1969, U.S. Supreme Ct. 1977. Law clk. to judge of U.S. Dist. Ct. (so. dist.), Columbus, Ohio, 1966-68; asst. U.S. atty., 1968-70; ptnr. Porter, Wright, Morris & Arthur, 1970—. Mem. Gahanna (Ohio) City Coun., 1972-80, 82-84; chmn. Gahanna Charter Rev. Commn., 1981, 06; pres. Cmty. Urban Redevel. Corp., Gahanna, 1984-. Named one of Ten Outstanding Young Persons in Columbus, Jaycees, 1974. Mem. ABA, Ohio Bar Assn., Fed. Bar Assn. (pres. Columbus chpt. 1973-74), Columbus Bar Assn. (chair fed. cts. com. 1972-74). Roman Catholic. Home: 202 Academy Ct Columbus OH 43230-2104 Office: Porter Wright Morris & Arthur 41 S High St Ste 2800 Columbus OH 43215-6194 Home Phone: 614-475-1511; Office Phone: 614-227-1945. Business E-Mail: amckenna@porterwright.com.

MCKENNA, ANDREW, JR., political organization administrator, printing company executive; BBA, U. Notre Dame, 1979; MBA, Northwestern U. With strategic planning dept. Kraft Foods; pres. Schwarz Paper Co., Morton Grove, Ill., 1981—; mem. Nat. Security Edn. Bd., 2004—; chmn. Ill. Rep. Party, 2005—. Treas. Kirk for Congress, mem. fin. com., 2000; mem. Vol. Polit. Action Com., 2002; chmn. Ill. Bus. Edn. Coalition, Ill. Bus. Roundtable. Chmn. Chicagoland C. of C., Christmas in April. Office: Schwarz Paper Source 8338 Austin Ave Morton Grove IL 60053*

MCKENNA, ANDREW JAMES, wholesale distribution, printing company executive, sports association executive; b. Chgo., Sept. 17, 1929; s. Andrew James and Anita (Fruin) McK.; m. Mary Joan Pickett, June 20, 1953; children: Suzanne, Karen, Andrew, William, Joan, Kathleen, Margaret. BS, U. Notre Dame, 1951; JD, DePaul U., 1954. Bar: Ill. Chmn. Schwarz Paper Co. (name now Schwarz Supply Source), Morton Grove, Ill., 1964—; non-exec. chmn. McDonald's Corp., 2004—. Bd. dir. Skyline Corp., AON Corp., McDonald's Corp., 1991—, Chgo. Bears Football CLub; chmn. Chgo. White Sox, 1975—81, Chgo. Cubs, 1981—84. Trustee, Univ. Notre Dame, chmn. 1992-2000; trustee, past chmn. Mus. Sci. and Industry, Chgo.; bd. dir. Cath. Charities of Chgo., Children's Meml. Med. Ctr. Chgo., Lyric Opera, United Way Metro. Chgo.; founding chmn. Chgo. Metropolis 2020. Mem. Comml. Club Chgo., Econ. Club Chgo., Lyric Opera (bd. dirs.), Execs. Club Chgo., Glenview Golf Club, Old Elm Club, Merit Club, Casino Club, The Island Club. Home: 60 Locust Rd Winnetka IL 60093-3751 Office: Schwarz 8338 Austin Ave Morton Grove IL 60053-3288 Business E-Mail: ajm@schwarz.com.

MCKENNA, GEORGE LAVERNE, art museum curator; b. Detroit, Dec. 7, 1924; s. John LaVerne and Carolyn Georgia (Schwab) McK.; m. Janice Ballinger, July 22, 1966. Student, U. Oreg., 1943-44, U. Calif., Berkeley, 1948-49, U. Chgo., 1950; AB, Wayne State U., 1948, MA, 1951. Curator prints, drawings and photographs Nelson-Atkins Mus. Art, Kansas City, Mo., 1952-96, cons, 1997—. Cons. Hallmark Cards, Inc., Kansas City, 1974-76. Curator, author exhbn. and coll. catalogues. With U.S. Army, 1943-46. Mem. Am. Assn. Mus., Print Coun. Am. Office: Nelson-Atkins Mus Art 4525 Oak St Kansas City MO 64111-1873

MCKENNA, WILLIAM JOHN, retired textile products executive; b. NYC, Oct. 11, 1926; s. William T. and Florence (Valis) McK.; m. Jean T. McNulty, Aug 27, 1949 (dec. Nov. 1984); children: Kevin, Marybeth, Peter, Dawn; m. Karen Lynne Hilgert, Aug. 6, 1988; children: Katherine Lynne, William John IV. BBA, Iona Coll., 1949; MS (Univ. Store Service scholar), NYU, 1950. V.p. Hat Corp. Am., NYC, 1961-63, v.p. mktg., 1961-63, exec. v.p., 1963-67; pres. Manhattan Shirt Co., NYC, 1967-74; pres., dir. Lee Co., Inc., Shawnee Mission, Kans., 1974-82, Kellwood Co., St. Louis, 1982—, chief exec. officer, 1984—, also bd. dirs., chmn., CEO, 1991-97, chmn., 1991-99, chmn. emeritus, 1999—.

Dir. United Mo. Bank of St. Louis. Trustee emeritus St. Louis U., Boys Hope; permanent deacon Archdiocese St. Louis. With USN, 1944-46, PTO. Mem. Sovereign Mil. Order Malta, St. Louis Club, Bellerive Country Club. Roman Catholic. E-mail: william_mckenna@kellwood.com.

MCKENZIE, LLOYD W., real estate development executive; V.p. Indpls. divsn. Crossman Cmtys., Inc., 1992—. Office: Crossman Cmtys Inc 9202 N Meridian St Ste 300 Indianapolis IN 46260-1833

MCKENZIE, ROBERT ERNEST, lawyer; b. Cheboygan, Mich., Dec. 7, 1947; s. Alexander Orlando and Edna Jean (Burt) McK.; m. Theresia Wolf, Apr. 26, 1975; 1 child, Robert A. BA in Pers. Adminstrn., Mich. State U., 1970; JD with high honors, Ill. Inst. Tech., 1979. Bar: Ill. 1979, US Dist. Ct. (no. dist.) Ill. 1979, US Tax Ct. 1979, US Ct. Appeals (7th cir.) 1979, US Supreme Ct. 1984; lic. pvt. pilot; enrolled agnet with IRS. Revenue officer IRS, Chgo., 1972-78; ptnr. McKenzie & McKenzie, Chgo., 1979-2000, Arnstein & Lehr LLP, 2000—. Author: Representation Before the Collection Divison of the IRS, 1989, 2007; co-author: Representing the Audited Taxpayer Before the IRS, 1990, 2007, Representation Before the US Tax Court, 2006; contbr. articles to profl. jours. Mem. tax adv. com. Nat. Bankruptcy Rev. Commn., 1997; bd. mem. Ctr. for Econ. Progress, 1999-2005; del. Rep. Nat. Conv., Detroit, 1980. 2nd lt. US Army, 1970, capt. US Army, 1978. Recipient scholarship Mich. State U., 1966-70, State of Mich., 1966-70, Silas Strawn scholarship ITT, 1977, Excellence in Edn. award, AEA Edn. Found., 2001; fellow Am. Bar. Fellow Am. Bar Found., mem. ABA (chmn. employment tax com. tax sect. 1992-94, co-chmn. bankruptcy task force 1997-98, coun. tax sect. 1998-2001, vice chmn. tax sect. 2003-05, chmn Pro Bono Com., 2007-), Chgo. Bar Assn. (chmn. com. devel. and tax coms. 1996-97), Am. Coll. Tax Counsel (bd. regents 2007-), Union League Chgo. Avocations: travel, flying. Office: Ste 1200 120 S Riverside Plz Chicago IL 60606 Home Phone: 847-981-1441; Office Phone: 312-876-6927. Business E-Mail: remckenzie@arnstein.com.

MCKEON, THOMAS JOSEPH, lawyer; b. Feb. 3, 1955; s. Thomas Michael and Mary Rose McKeon. BA, Ind. U., 1974; JD cum laude, Ind. U., Indpls., 1977. Bar: Ind. 1977, U.S. Dist. Ct. (so. dist.) Ind. 1977, U.S. Supreme Ct. 1979. Assoc. Nisenbaum & Brown, Indpls., 1977, Osborn & Hiner, Indpls., 1977; counsel Am. Family Ins., Indpls., 1982—; asst. counsel Radio Earth Internat., Inc., Radio Earth Curacao, Netherlands Antilles, 1985—. Author: (book) Post Traumatic Stress Disorder: Real or Imagined, 1986, Repetition Strain as a Compensable Injury, 1987; contbr. articles to profl. jours. Mem.: ABA, ATLA (assoc.), Ind. Arson and Crime Assn., Ind. Assn. Pvt. Detectives, Am. Corp. Counsel Assn., Def. Rsch. and Trial Lawyers Assn., Indpls. Bar Assn., Ind. Trial Lawyers Assn., Ind. Def. Lawyers Assn., Ind. Bar Assn., San Diego Turtle and Tortoise Soc. Office: 7330 Shadeland Sta Indianapolis IN 46256-3919

MCKEOWN, JAMES T., lawyer; b. Columbus, Ohio, Aug. 16, 1958; s. James J. and M. Eileen (O'Neill) McK.; m. Kathleen E. McKeown, Dec. 28, 1981; children: Bridget, Caitlin, Neil, Aislinn. BA in Econs., St. John's U., Collegeville, Minn., 1980; JD, U. Minn., 1984, MA in Pub. Affairs, 1985. Bar: Wis. 1984, U.S. Ct. Appeals (7th cir.) 1985, U.S. Dist. Ct. (ea. dist.) Wis. 1985, U.S. Supreme Ct. Law clk. Hon. Harlington Wood, Jr. U.S. Ct. Appeals for 7th Cir., Springfield, Ill., 1984-85; assoc. Foley & Lardner LLP, Milw., 1985-93, ptnr., 1993—, chmn. antitrust practice group. Adj. asst. prof. Marquette U., 1993-95. Contbr. articles to profl. jours. Civil svc. commr. Village of Shorewood, Wis.; fin. com. chmn. St. Robert Parish, Shorewood, 1993-94. Mem. Milw. Young Lawyers Assn. (Svc. award 1991). Office: Foley & Lardner LLP 777 E Wisconsin Ave Ste 3800 Milwaukee WI 53202-5367 Office Phone: 414-297-5530. Business E-Mail: jmckeown@foley.com.

MCKIBBEN, LARRY, state legislator, lawyer; b. Marshalltown, Iowa, Jan. 5, 1947; m. Marki McKibben; 2 children. BA, U. No. Iowa, 1970; JD, U. Iowa, 1972. Bar: Iowa 1972. Atty.; mem. Iowa Senate from 32nd dist., Des Moines, 1996—; mem. bus. and labor rels. com.; mem. jud. com., mem. appropriations com., mem. ethics com.; mem. transp. appropriations com., chair ways and means com. Republican. Office: State Capitol 9th And Grand Ave Des Moines IA 50319-0001 E-mail: larry.mckibben@legis.state.ia.us.

MCKINLEY, ANNE C., lawyer; b. 1974; m. John R. Wickstrom, May 6, 2000. BA, Northwestern U., 1996; grad., U. Ill. Coll. Law. With US SEC, Chgo., 1998—, br. chief enforcement divsn., 2003—. Named one of 40 Under 40, Crain's Chgo. Bus., 2006. Office: US SEC Midwest Regional Office Ste 900 175 W Jackson Blvd Chicago IL 60604 Office Phone: 312-353-7390. E-mail: chicago@sec.gov.

MCKINNELL, ROBERT GILMORE, retired zoologist, biology professor, geneticist; b. Springfield, Mo., Aug. 9, 1926; s. William Parks and Mary Catherine (Gilmore) McK.; m. Beverly Walton Kerr (dec.); children: Nancy Elizabeth, Robert Gilmore, Susan Kerr. B in Naval Sci., U. Notre Dame, 1946; AB, U. Mo., 1948; BS, Drury Coll., 1949, DSc (hon.), 1993; PhD, U. Minn., 1959. Rsch. assoc. Fox Chase Cancer Ctr., Phila., 1958-61; asst. prof. biology Tulane U., New Orleans, 1961-65, assoc. prof., 1965-69, prof., 1969-70; prof. zoology U. Minn., Mpls., 1970—76, prof. genetics and cell biology St. Paul, 1976—99, prof. emeritus, 1999—. Vis. scientist Dow Chem. Co., Freeport, Tex., 1976; guest dept. zoology U. Calif., Berkeley, 1979; Royal Soc. guest rsch. fellow Nuffield dept. pathology John Radcliffe Hosp., Oxford U., 1981-82; NATO vis. scientist Akademisch Ziekenhuis, Ghent, Belgium, 1984; faculty rsch. assoc. Naval Med. Rsch. Inst., Bethesda, Md., 1988; secretariat Third Internat. Conf. Differentiation, 1978; organizer, secretariat 6th Internat. Conf. on Pathology of Reptiles and Amphibians, 2001; mem. amphibian com. Inst. Lab. Animal Resources, NRC, 1970-73, mem. adv. coun., 1974; mem. panel genetic and cellular resources program NIH, 1981-82, spl. study sect., Bethesda, 1990. Author: Cloning: Amphibian Nuclear Transplantation, 1978, Cloning, A Biologist Reports, 1979; sr. editor: Differentiation and Neoplasia, 1980, Cloning: Leben aus der Retorte, 1981, Cloning of Frogs, Mice and Other Animals, 1985, (with others) The Biological Basis of Cancer, 1998, 2d edit., 2006, (with D.L. Carlson) Pathology of Reptiles and Amphibians, 2002, Prevention Cancer, 2008, also symposium procs. in field; mem. bd. advisors Marquis Who's Who; contbr. articles to profl. jours. Served to lt. USNR, 1944-47, 51-53. Recipient Outstanding Teaching award Newcomb Coll., Tulane U., 1970; Disting. Alumni award Drury Coll., 1979, Morse Alumni Tchg. award U. Minn., 1992; Rsch. fellow Nat. Cancer Inst., 1956-58, Prince Hitachi award Japanese Found. Cancer Rsch., 1998; Sr. Sci. fellow NATO, 1974. Fellow AAAS, Linnean Soc. (London); mem. Am. Assn. Cancer Rsch. (emeritus), Am. Assn. Cancer Edn. (sr.), Am. Assn. History of Medicine, Indian Soc. Devel. Biology (lifetime emeritus), Internat. Soc. Differentiation (pres. 1994-96), Minn. Acad. Medicine, Gown-in-Town Club, Sigma Xi. Office: 140 Gortner Lab Biochemistry 1479 Gortner Ave Saint Paul MN 55108 Home Phone: 651-646-3690. Business E-Mail: mckin002@umn.edu.

MCKINNEY, DENNIS, state legislator; m. Jean McKinney. Farmer, stockman, Greensburg, Kans.; mem. from dist. 108 Kans. State Ho. of Reps., Topeka, 1993—. Home: 1220 S Main St Greensburg KS 67054-9100

MCKINNEY, DENNIS KEITH, lawyer; b. Ottawa, Ill., May 12, 1952; s. Robert Keith and Delroy Louise (Clayton) McK.; m. Patricia Jean Boyle, Oct. 4, 1986; 1 child, Geoffrey Edward. BS, Ball State U., 1973; JD, Ill. Inst. Tech., 1976. Bar: Ind. 1977, U.S. Dist. Ct. (so. dist.) Ind. 1977, U.S. Supreme Ct. 1993. Appellate dep. Ind. Atty. Gen, Indpls., 1977-78, trial dep., 1978-79, sr. trial dep., 1979-81, chief real estate litigation sect., 1981-94; clk. to Hon. James S. Kirsch Ind. Ct. Appeals, Indpls., 1994-95; staff atty. Ind. Supreme Ct. Disciplinary Commn., Indpls., 1995—. Author: Eminent Domain, Practice and Procedure in Indiana, 1991, A Guide to Indiana Easement Law, 1995, A Railroad Ran Through It, 1996, Indiana Eminent Domain Practice and Procedure, 2003; contbg. author: Indiana Real Estate Transactions, 1996; contbr. articles to profl. jours. Active Indpls.-Scarborough Peace Games, 1983-84. Avocations: reading, volleyball, wargaming. Office: Ind Supreme Ct Disciplinary Ste 1060 115 W Wash St Indianapolis IN 46204-3420

MCKINNEY, E. KIRK, JR., retired insurance company executive; b. Indpls., Mar. 27, 1923; s. E. Kirk and Irene M. (Hurley) McK.; m. Alice Hollenbeck Greene, June 18, 1949; children: Kirk Ashley, Alan Brooks, Nora Claire McKinney Hiatt, Margot Knight. AB, U. Mich., 1948. Asst. treas. Jefferson Nat. Life Ins. Co., Indpls., 1949-52, asst. to pres., asst. treas., 1952-53, treas., asst. to pres., 1953-55, v.p., treas., 1955-59, pres., 1959-90, chmn. bd., 1970-90; vice chmn. bd. Somerset Group Inc., 1986-89; ret., 1990. Corp. rels. com. U. Mich.; former pres., former CEO, bd. govs., treas., bd. dirs., exec. com. Indpls. Mus. Art; past bd. dirs. (hon.) Greater Indpls. Progress Com.; former vice chmn. Indpls.-Marion County Bd. Ethics; former dir. Park Tudor Sch., Cmty. Svc. Coun. Indpls., Hosp. Devel. Corp., Ind. Repertory Theater; past adv. com. Indpls. Retirement Home; former bd. dirs., and pres. Episcopal Cmty. Svcs., Inc.; former vice chmn., life trustee Nature Conservancy; mem. adv. bd. Ind. U., Purdue U.; active Indpls. Symphony Orch.; former bd. dirs. Ind. Pub. Broadcasting Soc.; bd. dirs. Indpls. Civic Theater, 2001—, former bd. mem., 2008, Athenaeum Found., 2000—. Mem. Life Office Mgmt. Assn. (bd. dirs. 1981-83), Am. Coun. Life Ins. (state v.p. 1973-75, dir., exec. com. 1976-79), Assn. Ind. Life Ins. Cos. (pres. 1969-71), Indpls. C. of C., Sigma Chi. Clubs: Economic of Indpls. (bd. dirs.). Democrat. Home: 250 W 77th St Indianapolis IN 46260-3608 Office: 1330 W 38th St #100 Indianapolis IN 46208-4103 Office Phone: 317-925-2223. Personal E-mail: ekirkjr@sbcglobal.net.

MCKINNEY, JEFF, radio personality; b. Charlottesville, Va. married; 2 children. Student, Vanderbilt U.; BA English Lit., Washington U., St. Louis. With CBS Broadcasting, 1983; broadcast journalist Sta. WCCO radio, Mpls., 1994—. Recipient award, L.A. Press Club, Northwest Broadcasters Assn. Office: WCCO 625 2nd St S Minneapolis MN 55402

MCKINNEY, LARRY J., federal judge; b. South Bend, Ind., July 4, 1944; s. Lawrence E. and Helen (Byers) McK.; m. Carole Jean Marie Lyon, Aug. 19, 1966; children: Joshua E., Andrew G. BA, MacMurray Coll., Jacksonville, Ill., 1966; JD, Ind. U., 1969. Bar: Ind. 1970, U.S. Dist. Ct. (so. dist.) Ind. 1970. Law clk. to atty. gen. State of Ind., Indpls., 1969-70, dep. atty. gen., 1970-71; ptnr. Rodgers and McKinney, Edinburgh, Ind., 1971-75, James F.T. Sargent, Greenwood, Ind., 1975-79; judge Johnson County Cir. Ct., Franklin, Ind., 1979-87, U.S. Dist. Ct. (so. dist.) Ind., Indpls., 1987—, chief judge, 2001—. Presbyterian. Avocations: reading, jogging. Office: US Dist Ct 204 US Courthouse 46 E Ohio St Indianapolis IN 46204-1903

MCKINNEY, MYRON W., electronic company executive; b. Bolivar, Mo., 1945; m. Janet M.; children: Shannon Bowman, Rebecca McKinney. B in Bus. Adminstrn., SW Mo. State U., 1967. Sales cons. Empire Dist. Elec. Co., Joplin, Mo., 1967-82, v.p. commercial ops., 1982-94, v.p., 1994-95, exec. v.p. commercial ops., 1995-97, pres., CEO, 1997—. Mem. Mo. Valley Elec. Assn. Bd. dirs., Joplin Bus. and Indsl. Devel. Corp.; mem. Ozarks Pub. Telecomms., Joplin So. Corp., Rotary, Joplin C. of C., United Way. Office: Emprie Dist Electric Co PO Box 127 Joplin MO 64802-0127

MC KINNEY, ROBERT HURLEY, lawyer, corporate financial executive; b. Indpls., Nov. 7, 1925; s. E. Kirk and Irene (Hurley) McK.; m. Arlene Frances Allsopp, Nov. 28, 1951; children: Robert, Marni, Kevin, Kent, Lisa. BS, U.S. Naval Acad., 1946; JD, Ind. U., 1951. Bar: Ind. 1951. Since practiced in, Indpls.; sr. ptnr. Bose McKinney & Evans, 1963—; chmn., chief exec. officer The Somerset Group, Inc. and subs., Indpls., 1961-77, 79—, First & Loan Bank, Indpls., 1961—; chmn. Fed. Home Loan Bank Bd., 1977-79. Bd. dirs. Fed. Nat. Mortgage Assn., Wholesale Club, Inc., Lily Industries Coatings, Inc.; mem. adv. com. on internat. investment Dept. State. Chmn. Urban Reinvestment Task Force, Indpls.; bd. dirs. Children's Mus. Indpls., Ind. State Symphony Soc.; bd. dirs., mem. exec. com. Brebeuf Prep. Sch., 1970—; trustee Ind. U., U.S. Naval Coll.; del. Dem. Nat. Conv., 1968, 76, 80, 84. Lt. comdr. USNR, 1946-49, 51-53. Mem. Am., Ind., Indpls. bar assns., Com. for Econ. Devel., Young Pres. Orgn. (nat. chmn. for econ. edn. 1968-69, pres. Ind. chpt. 1973-74), Chief Exec. Orgn., Inc., Ind. C. of C. (bd. dirs.), Indpls. C. of C. (bd. dirs.), Knights of Malta. Office: First Ind Bank 2800 First Indiana Pla 135 N Pennsylvania St Fl 28 Indianapolis IN 46204-2400

MCKINNEY, WILLIAM T., psychiatrist, educator; b. Rome, Ga., Sept. 20, 1937; BA cum laude, Baylor U., 1959; MD, Vanderbilt U., 1963. Diplomate Nat. Bd. Med. Examiners (mem. psychiatry test com. 1982-87, chmn. 1984-87); cert. Am. Bd. Psychiatry and Neurology (sr. examiner 1979-90, bd. dirs. 1991—, mem. rsch. com., co-chair part I test com., chair added qualifications in geriatric psychiatry test com., mem. part II audio visual com., mem. disability accomodations com., rep. to residency rev. com.). Intern in medicine Bowman Gray Sch. Medicine, Wake Forest U., Winston-Salem, NC, 1963-64; resident dept. psychiatry Sch. Medicine, U. N.C., Chapel Hill., 1964-66, Sch. Medicine, Stanford (Calif.) U., 1966-67; clin. assoc. psychosomatic sect. adult psychiatry br., tng. specialist, asst. br. chief NIMH, Bethesda, Md., 1967-69; asst. prof. psychiatry dept. psychiatry Sch. Medicine, U. Wis., Madison, 1969-72, assoc. prof. psychiatry, 1972-74, prof. psychiatry, 1974-93; Asher prof. of psychiatry dept. psychiatry and behavioral scis., dir. Asher Ctr. for Study and Treatment of Depressive Disorders Med. Sch., Northwestern U., Chgo., 1993—. Part-time clin. pvt. practice, Bethesda, 1967-69; NIMH rsch. career investigator Sch. Medicine, U. Wis., Madison, 1970-75, rsch. psychiatrist Primate Lab., 1974-93, affiliate sci. Wis. Regional Primate Rsch. Ctr., 1974-93, affiliate prof. psychology dept. psychology, 1974-93, chmn. dept. psychiatry, 1975-80, dir. Wis. Psychiat. Rsch. Inst. Ctr. Health Scis., 1975-80; sr. staff psychiatrist William S. Middleton Meml. VA Hosp., Madison, Wis., 1974-93; rschr. sub dept. animal behaviour U. Cambridge, Eng., 1974; mem. rsch. rev. com. VA Behavioral Scis., 1976-79; Abbott Sigma XI Club lectr., 1976; Milw. Psychiat. Hosp. lectr., 1977; mem. program adv. com. and workshop chmn. Dahlem Found. Internat. Conf. on Depression, Berlin, 1982; U. Minn. lectr. at Festshrift, 1982; cons. grad. sch. U. Minn., 1982; fellow Ctr. Advanced Study in Behavioral Scis., Stanford, Calif., 1983-84; mem. external adv. bd. Clin. Rsch. Ctr. Dept. Psychiatry U. N.C., Chapel Hill, 1984—, cons., bd. advisors clin. rsch. fellow tng. program dept. psychology, 1988—; William F. Orr lectr. Vanderbilt U., 1985; vis. prof. dept. psychiatry U. Tex. Health Scis. Ctr., Dallas, 1986, U. Utah Sch. Medicine, Salt Lake City, 1987, U. Minn. Sch. Medicine, Mpls., 1988; cons. biol. scis. tng. br. divsn. manpower and tng. programs NIMH, 1975-76, mem. psychiatry spl. tng. com. 1983, plenary lectr., Clearwater, Fla., 1987, co-chairperson Workshop on Non-Human Primate Models of Psychopathology, 1987, mem. biol. psychopathology spl. rev. com., 1992—; mem. sci. core group MacArthur Found. Mental Health Rsch. Network I: The Psychobiology of Depression and Other Affective Disorders, 1988-93; vis. spkr. So. Calif. Psychiat. Soc., L.A., 1988; plenary lectr. Soc. Biol. Psychiatry ann. meeting, Montreal, 1988; vis. prof. Dalhousie U. Sch. Medicine, N.S., 1989, HCA Riveredge Hosp., Chgo., 1989, U. Pa., Phila., 1991, U. N.Mex., Albuquerque, 1992, Northwestern U., Chgo., 1992; invited spkr. Animal Models in Psychopharmacology Symposium, Duphar, Amsterdam, 1990; vis. spkr., cons. CIBA-GEIGY, Basel, Switzerland, 1990; mem. minority instns. rsch. devel. rev. com. Alcohol, Drug Abuse and Mental Health Adminstrn., 1990; guest spkr. Inst. Pa. Hosp., Phila., 1991; reviewer Human Frontier Sci. Program, 1992—; external cons. dept. psychiatry Mental Health Clin. Rsch. Ctr. U. Tex. Southwestern Med. Ctr., Dallas, 1992—; presenter in field. Author: Animal Models of Mental Disorders: A New Comparative Psychiatry, 1988; co-author: Mood Disorders: Towards a New Psychobiology, 1984; mem. editl. bd. Archives of Psychiatry and Neurol. Scis., Contemporary Psychiatry, 1981-82, Ethology and Sociobiology, Experientia, 1982-89, Trends in Neurosciences, 1982-86, Neuropsychopharmacology, 1987-90; manuscript and book reviewer numerous sci. jours.; contbr. articles to profl. jours. USHPS fellow in biostats. Vanderbilt U., 1962; recipient Beauchamp award Vanderbilt U. Med. Sch., 1963, Rsch. Career Devel. award NIMH, 1975, Rsch. Leave award U. Wis., 1983-84, Am. Acad. Pediats. award, 1991. Fellow Am. Psychiat. Assn. (cons. psychiat. edn. consultation svc. 1983—), Am. Coll. Psychiatrists, Am. Coll. Neuropsychopharmacology (mem. constn. and rules com. 1985-87, mem. ethics com. 1987-89, mem. fin. com. 1990-92, panel chair San Juan, P.R. 1992, panel presenter 1992); mem. Am. Soc. Primatologists, Am. Psychosomatic Soc. (mem. program com. 1975-76), Internat. Primatology Soc., Internat. Coll. Neurobiology, Biol. Psychiatry and Psychopharmacology (lectr. Zurich 1985), Internat. Soc. Devel. Psychobiology, Internat. Soc. Ethological and Behavioral Pharmacology (bd. advisors 1983—), Collegium Internat. Neuro-Psychopharmacologicum, Psychiat. Rsch. Soc., Soc. Neuroscience, Wis. Psychiat. Assn. (chmn. program com. 1972, co-chairperson task force on sexual misconduct and membership edn. 1986-88, pres.-elect 1989-91, pres. 1991-93).

MCKINNIS, MICHAEL BAYARD, lawyer; b. St. Louis, May 31, 1945; s. Bayard O. and Doris (Lammert) McK.; m. Patricia Butow, Aug. 24, 1968; children: Scott, Christopher, Elizabeth. BS, Drake U., 1967; JD, U. Mo., 1970. Bar: Mo. 1970, U.S. Dist. Ct. (ea. dist.) Mo. Ptnr. Bryan Cave LLP, St. Louis, gen. counsel. Editor U. Mo. Law Rev., 1969-70. Mem. ABA, Mo. Bar Assn., Order of Coif, Phi Delta Phi. Office: Bryan Cave LLP One Metropolitan Square 211 N Broadway, Ste 3600 Saint Louis MO 63102-2733 Office Phone: 314-259-2000. E-mail: mbmckinnis@bryancavellp.com.

MCKINSEY, ELIZABETH, humanities educator, consultant; b. Columbia, Mo., Aug. 10, 1947; d. J. Wendell and A. Ruhamah (Peret) McK.; m. Thomas N. Clough, June 18, 1977; children: Emily, Peter. BA, Radcliffe Coll., 1970; PhD, Harvard U., 1976. From instr. to asst. prof. English Bryn Mawr (Pa.) Coll., 1975-77; from asst. to assoc. prof. English Harvard U., Cambridge, Mass., 1977-85; dir. Bunting Inst. Radcliffe Coll., Cambridge, 1985-89; dean Carleton Coll., Northfield, Minn., 1989—2002, prof., 2002—. Author: Niagara Falls: Icon of the American Sublime, 1985; contbr. articles and revs. to profl. jours. and lit. mags. NEH fellow, 1980; Carnegie Found. for the Advancement of Tchg. vis. scholar, 2003. Mem. MLA, Am. Conf. Acad. Deans, Nat. Coun. for Rsch. on Women (assoc.), Am. Studies Assn., Nat. Assn. Women in Edn., Phi Beta Kappa (pres. Iota of Mass. chpt. 1986-89). Home: 801 Mayflower Ct Northfield MN 55057-2308 Office: Carleton Coll 1 N College St Northfield MN 55057-4001 Home Phone: 507-645-5754; Office Phone: 507-646-5900. E-mail: emckinse@carleton.edu.

MCKITRICK, JAMES THOMAS, retired retail executive; b. Cin., Sept. 14, 1945; s. Harry J. and L. May (Buck) McK.; m. Margaret J. Haynes, Sept. 6, 1975; children: Angela, Greg, Randal, Paul, Sheri, Richard, Mike. Student, Salem Coll., 1963-64. Dir. mdse. K Mart Corp., Troy, Mich., 1965-84; exec. v.p., gen. mgr. T.G. & Y. Stores, Oklahoma City, 1984-86, exec. v.p. merchandising and mktg., 1986; pres., chief exec. officer Warehouse Club, Skokie, Ill., 1986-87; pres., chief operating officer G.C. Murphy Co. subs. Ames, Rocky Hill, Conn., 1987-89; chmn. Zayre Discount, Rocky Hill, 1988-89; pres. & CEO Builders Emporium, Irvine, Calif., 1989-92, Quality Stores Inc. (formerly Central Tractor Farm & Country), Muskegon, Mich., 1992—2000. Republican. Methodist. Office: Quality Stores Inc PO Box 1002 Muskegon MI 49443-1002

MCLAREN, DERRYL, state legislator; b. Shenandoah, Iowa, Mar. 22, 1949; m. Carma Herrig. BS in Agr. Bus., Iowa State U., 1971, postgrad. Farmer; mem. Iowa Senate from 43rd dist., Des Moines, 1990—; chair appropriations com.; mem. state govt. com., mem. ways and means com. Mem. Iowa Corn Promotion Bd., 1985-87, Asia market com.; past chair Fremont County Reps. Mem. Nat. Corn Growers, Iowa Soybeans Assn., Iowa Farm Bur., Iowa Corn Growers, Nat. Corn Devel. Found., U.S. Feed Grains Coun., Farm Credit Task Force, Gamma Gamma Rho, Phi Kappa Phi, Alpha Zeta, Phi Eta Sigma. E-mail: derryl_mclaren@legis.state.ia.us.

MCLAREN, KAREN LYNN, advertising executive; b. Flint, Mich., Feb. 14, 1955; m. Michael L. McLaren, June 18, 1974. AA, Mott Community Coll., Flint, 1976; BA, Mich. State U., 1978. Writer Sta. WGMZ-FM, Flint, 1979-84; writer, producer Tracy-Stephens Advt., Flint, 1984-87; pres. McLaren Advt., Troy, Mich., 1987—. Contbr. articles to profl. jours. Mem. centennial com. Wolverine region ARC, 1981, pub. rels. com., 1981-84; vol. coord., pub. rels. tour guide Whaley Hist. Ho., Flint, 1980-91; home designer, tour guide Romeo (Mich.) Hist. Home Tour, 1992; mem. Nat. Trust for Hist. Preservation, 1991-95; com. chair Crim Festival of Races, Flint, 1992, 93, 94, 95; active Sta. WFUM-Pub. TV, Flint, 1980-91; panelist career fair Modona U., Livonia, Mich., 1994, 95, 96, 97; ad book chair Juvenile Diabetes Found./Detroit Evening of Brilliance, 1997; mem. Oakland Regional Bd. Barbara Ann Karmanos Cancer Instn., 1999. Recipient 3 awards, 2 Nat. Health Care Mktg. Competition awards, Women's Adv. Club Detroit Pres.'s award, 1994. Mem. NAFE, Women's Advt. Club Detroit (scholar chmn. 1988-88, bd. dirs. 1989, 92-93, chmn. scholarship fundraiser 1991, co-chmn. career fair 1989, 90, 92, career fair panelist 1993, v.p. 1990, pres. 1991, amb. 1992, chmn. woman of yr. award 1994-96, by-laws chmn. 1994), Women's Econ. Club Detroit (progam com. 1996, workplace of tomorrow com. 1996, vice chair 1997, chair 1999). Office: 3001 W Big Beaver Rd Ste 306 Troy MI 48084-3104

MCLAREN, RICHARD WELLINGTON, JR., lawyer; s. Richard Wellington and Edith (Gillett) McL.; m. Ann Lynn Zachrich, 1971; children: Christine, Richard, Charles. BA, Yale U., 1967; JD, Northwestern U., 1973. Bar: Ohio 1973, Ill. 1997, U.S. Dist. Ct. (no. dist.) Ohio 1973, U.S. Dist. Ct. (no. dist.) Ill. 1997, U.S. Ct. Appeals (6th cir.) 1978, U.S. Ct. Appeals (7th cir.) 1997, U.S. Ct. Appeals (fed. cir.) 1997, U.S. Supreme Ct. 1981. Assoc. Squire, Sanders & Dempsey, Cleve., 1973-82, ptnr., 1983-87; prin., counsel Ernst & Whinney, Cleve., 1988-89; assoc. gen. counsel Ernst & Young, Cleve., 1989-93; prin. counsel Centerior Energy Corp., Cleve., 1994-96; prin. Welsh & Katz, Ltd., Chgo., 1997—2007; ptnr. Duane Morris, 2007—. 1st lt. U.S. Army, 1967-70. Mem. ABA (litigation, intellectual property and corp. law), FBA, Am. Judicature Soc., Ohio Bar Assn., Ill. Bar Assn. Home: 638 S Monroe St Hinsdale IL 60521-3926 Office: 120 S Riverside Plz Fl 22 Chicago IL 60606-3913 Office Phone: 312-655-1500, 312-499-6754. Business E-Mail: rwmclaren@welshkatz.com, rwmclaren@doanemorris.com.

MCLAREN, RUTH, bank executive; BA in English, Dominican U., River Forest, Ill., MBA; grad., Am. Bankers Assn. Compliance Sch. and Robert Morris Assn. Commercial Lending Sch. With Madison Bank and Trust Co. (now Corus Bank), Chgo., 1985; pres., CEO Madison Nat. Bank of Niles, Ill.; with Resolution Trust Corp., Kansas City, 1991—96; charter employee to v.p., casher Cmty. Bank of Oak Park River Forest, Ill., 1996—2004, sr. v.p. retail banking Ill. Mem.: GALA Fireworks Orgn., Oak Park C. of C., Rotary Club of OPRF. Office: Cmty Bank Oak Park River Forest 1001 Lake St Oak Park IL 60301 E-mail: ruthm@cboprf.com.

MCLARNEY, CHARLES PATRICK, lawyer; b. Hemple, Mo., Mar. 28, 1942; s. Charles Joseph and Owatonna Mary (Sayles) McL.; m. Martina Borkowski, Aug. 28, 1965; children: Ellen, Megan, Michael. BS, St. Benedict's Coll., 1964; JD, U. Mo., 1968. Bar: Mo. 1968, U.S. Dist. Ct. (we. dist.) Mo. 1968, U.S. Ct. Appeals (8th cir.), U.S. Supreme Ct. 1968. Assoc. Shook, Hardy & Bacon LLP, Kansas City, Mo., 1968-72, ptnr., 1972-93, mng. ptnr., 1985-88, 91—, shareholder, pres., 1993-96, mng. ptnr., 1996. Active Friends of Art, Kans. City, 1980—; v.p. Civic Coun. Greater Kansas City. Named Outstanding Lawyer Kans. City Met. Bar Assn., 2004, Legal Leader of Yr. The Daily Record, 2005. Fellow Internat. Soc. Barristers (bd. dirs. 1989-94), Am. Coll. Trial Lawyers; mem. Kansas City Met. Bar, Lawyers Assn. Kansas City (pres. 1987-88), Mo. Bar (bd. govs., bd. dirs. 1991-94), Kansas City Soc. Fellows, Eight Twenty-Two Club, Kansas City Club, Plaza Bus. Breakfast Club (pres. 1983-84), Kansas City Met. Bar Assn. Democrat. Roman Catholic. Avocations: tennis, golf, skiing. Office: Shook, Hardy & Bacon LLP 2555 Grand Blvd Kansas City MO 64108 Office Phone: 816-474-6550. Home Fax: 816-421-5547. Business E-Mail: pmclarney@shb.com.

MCLAUGHLIN, CATHERINE G., healthcare educator; AB, Randolph-Macon Woman's Coll., 1971; MS in Econs., U. Wis., 1978, PhD in Econs., 1980. Prof. health mgmt. and policy U. Mich., 1983—, dir. Econ. Rsch. Initiative on the Uninsured, prof. dept. health mgmt. and policy, dir. Robert Wood Johnson Found. Scholars in Health Policy Rsch. Program. Dir. U. Mich. component Agy. for Healthcare Rsch. and Quality's Ctr. of Excellence on Managed Care Markets and Quality. Contbr. articles to profl. jours.; sr. assoc. editor Health Svcs. Rsch. Office: U Mich Dept Health Mgmt and Policy 109 S Observatory M3166 SPH II Ann Arbor MI 48109-2029 Business E-Mail: cmcl@umich.edu.

MCLAUGHLIN, HARRY ROLL, architect; b. Indpls., Nov. 29, 1922; s. William T. and Ruth E. (Roll) McL.; m. Linda Hamilton, Oct. 23, 1954. Registered Ind., Ohio, Ill., cert. Nat. Coun. Archtl. Registration Bds. Past pres. James Assocs. Inc., Indpls. Restorations include Old State Bank State Meml, Vincennes, Ind., Andrew Wylie House, Bloomington, Ind., Old Opera House State Meml, New Harmony, Ind., Old Morris-Butler House, Indpls. (Merit award 1972), Market St. Restoration and Maria Creek Baptist Ch., Vincennes, Benjamin Harrison House, Old James Ball Residence, Lafayette, Ind. (1st Design award 1972), Lockerbie Sq. Master Plan Park Sch., Indpls., Knox County Ct. House, Vincennes, 1972, J.K. Lilly House, Indpls., 1972, Waiting Station and Chapel, Crown Hill Cemetery, Indpls., 1972, Blackford-Condit House Ind. State U., Terre Haute, Indian houses Angel Mounds Archaeol. Site and Interpretative Ctr., Ind.; architect: Glenn A. Black Mus. Archaeology, Ind. U., Bloomington; Restoration Morgan County Ct. House, Indpls. City Market, Hist. Schofield House, Madison, Ind., Ernie Pyle Birthplace, Dana, Ind., Phi Kappa Psi Nat. Hdqrs, Indpls., 1980 (Design award), East Coll. Bldg, DePauw U., Greencastle, Ind., Pres.'s House Restoration, DePauw U., 1992; contbr.

articles to profl. jours.; Illustrator: Harmonist Construction. Past chmn. bd., past pres., now chmn. emeritus Historic Landmarks Found., Ind.; bd. dirs., past archtl. adviser, bd. advisers Historic Madison, Inc.; mem. adv. coun. Historic Am. Bldgs. Survey, Nat. Park Svc., 1967-73; past mem. Ind. profl. rev. com. for Nat. Register nominations, 1967-81; past adv. bd. Conner Prarie Mus., Patrick Henry Sullivan Found.; past adviser Indpls. Historic Preservation Commn.; past mem. preservation com. Ind. U.; past mem. Meridian St. Preservation Commn., Indpls., 1971-2001; hon. mem. Ind. Bicentennial Commn.; bd. dirs. Park-Tudor Sch., 1972-85; past nat. bd. dirs. Preservation Action; life bd. dirs. Historic New Harmony; trustee Masonic Heritage Found.; past bd. dirs. Ind. Masonic Home, 1984-91, Inpls. Pub. Libr. Found., treas. 1988, 95—, v.p., 1989, pres. 1990; past trustee Eiteljorg Mus. Western Art, mem. adv. and planning com., 1999; past mem. Hamilton County Tourism Commn., 1989-91. Recipient Gov.'s citation State of Ind., 1967, Sagamore of Wabash award, 1967, 80, 82, Mayor's citation City of Indpls., 1972, Sec. Interior citation U.S. Dept. Interior, 1970, Design and Environ. citation, 1975, Citation of Spl. Merit, Park Tudor Sch., 1993, Disting. Achievement award Ball State U., 2004, Disting. Alumni award Orchard Sch., 2007, Eli Lilly Lifetime Achievement award Ind. Hist. Soc., 2007, Citation Appreciation for Vol. Svc. Indpls. Pub. Libr. Found., 2007. Fellow AIA (nat. com. historic bldgs., chmn. 1970); mem. Ind. Soc. Architects (state preservation coord. 1960-85, Biennial award 1978, Design award 1978), at. Trust Historic Preservation (past trustee, bd. advisers), Soc. Archtl. Historians (Wilbur D. Peat award Ctrl. Ind. chpt. outstanding contbns. to understanding and appreciation of archtl. heritage 1993, past bd. dirs., Disting. Achievement in Hist. Preservation award 2005), Indpls. Mus. Art. (trustee, chmn. bldgs. com., bd. govs. 1986-95), Zionsville C. of C. (hon. bd. dirs.), U.S. Capitol (hon. trustee), Ind. Hist. Soc. (pres. 1999, trustee 1989-99, bldg. com.), Marion County Hist. Soc. (past v.p., bd. dirs.), Zionsville Hist. Soc. (hon. life), Navy League U.S. (life), Ind. State Mus. Soc. (life), English Speaking Union (past bd. dirs. Indpls.), Hamilton County Hist. Soc. (life), Woodstock Club (bd. dirs. 1982-86, pres. 1985, ex-officio 1986), Literary Club Found. (trustee 1990-2007), Skyline Club (life), Packard Club, Masons (33 deg.). Home and Office: 950 W 116th St Carmel IN 46032-8864

MCLAUGHLIN, PATRICK J., lawyer; b. 1947; BA summa cum laude, U. Minn., 1971, JD magna cum laude, 1975. Bar: Minn. 1975. Ptnr., banking, trial practice groups, chair, corp. trust svcs. group Dorsey & Whitney LLP, Mpls. Gen. counsel Minn. Police Relief Assn. Lectr. in field. Office: Dorsey & Whitney LLP Ste 1500 50 S Sixth St Minneapolis MN 55402-1498 Office Phone: 612-340-2975. Office Fax: 612-340-2643. Business E-Mail: mclaughlin.patrick@dorsey.com.

MCLAUGHLIN, PATRICK MICHAEL, lawyer; b. Monahans, Tex., July 23, 1946; s. Patrick John and Ann (Donnelly) M.; m. Christine Manos, Aug. 21, 1970; children— Brian Patrick, Christopher Michael, Conor Andrew B Gen. Studies, Ohio U., 1972; JD, Case We. Res. U., 1976. Bar: Ohio 1976, U.S. Dist. Ct. (no. dist.) Ohio 1978, U.S. Ct. Appeals (6th cir.) 1979, U.S. Supreme Ct. 1980; U.S. Dist. Ct. (so. dist.) Ohio 1989, U.S. Ct. Appeals (5th cir.). Dir. vets. edn. project. Am. Assn. Cmty. and Jr. Colls., Washington, 1972—73; law clk. Common Pleas Ct., Cleve., 1976—77; law clk. to judge 8th Jud. Dist. Ct. of Appeals, Cleve., 1977—78; asst. U.S. atty. No. Dist. Ohio, Cleve., 1978—82, chief civil divsn., 1982—84, U.S. atty. Cleve., 1984—88; ptnr. Janik & McLaughlin, Cleve., 1988—89, Mansour, Gavin, Gerlack & Manos Co., LPA, Cleve., 1989—97; apptd ind. spl. prosecutor Ohio Attys. Gen., 1993—96; mng. ptnr. McLaughlin & McCaffrey, LLP, Cleve., 1997—. Cons. Nat. League of Cities, U.S. Conf. Mayors, 1971-72; co-creator Opportunity Fair for Veterans Concept, 1971 Editor-in-chief Case Western Res. Jour. Internat. Law, 1975-76 Chmn. North Ohio Drug Abuse Task Force, 1986-88; chmn. Law Enforcement Coordinating Commn., North Ohio, 1985-88; chmn. civil issues subcom. Atty. Gen.'s Adv. Com., 1986-88; exec. v.p. Greater Cleve. Vets. Meml., Inc., 1993, pres., 1994—. Decorated Silver Star, Bronze Star, Purple Heart, Army Commendation medal, Vietnamese Cross of Gallantry with Silver and Bronze Stars; named to Ohio Vets. Hall of Fame, 2003, Ohio Mil.Hall of Fame for Valor, 2004. Fellow Am. Coll. Trial Lawyers; mem. ABA, FBA, Ohio Bar Assn., Cleve. Bar Assn., Nat. Assn. Former U.S. Attys., Soc. 1st Divsn., 18th Inf. Regiment Assn., Order of Ahepa, Vietnam Vets. Am., Nat. Vietnam Vets. Network (Disting. Vietnam Vet. award 1985), Nat. Assn. Concerned Vets. (nat. v.p. external affairs 1971-72, exec. dir. 1972-73), Cuyahoga County Vets. (award 1985), Nat. Soc. SAR (law enforcement commendation medal 1989), Judge John Manos Inn of Ct. (master bencher, 2005—). Republican. Roman Catholic. Office: McLaughlin & McCaffrey LLP Eaton Ctr 1111 Superior Ave Ste 1350 Cleveland OH 44114-2500 Home Phone: 216-371-0296; Office Phone: 216-623-0900. Business E-Mail: pmm@paladin-law.com.

MCLAUGHLIN, SHERRY, association administrator; m. Art McLaughlin; 3 children. With Emil H. Dutler unit 177 Am. Legion Aux., 1956, unit pres., 3d dist. pres., Dept. of Iowa pres., 1985—86, nat. v.p., nat. pres. Indpls., 2001—; counselor Iowa Girls State. Chmn. Aux. Emergency Fund; mem. numerous coms. Am. Legion Aux. Vol. Iowa Vets. Home, Iowa Braille, Vinton-Shellsburg Schs., Union Sch.; Ct. apptd. spl. advocate; confirmation tchr. Trinity Luth. Ch. Recipient Gov.'s Vol. of the Yr. award, 1999, 2000. Office: American Legion Auxiliary 777 N Meridian St 3rd Flr Indianapolis IN 46204

MCLAUGHLIN, T. MARK, lawyer; b. Salem, Mass., Apr. 20, 1953; s. Terrence E. and Mary E. (Donlon) McL.; m. Sandra L. Roman, Oct. 16, 1982; children: Daniel, Kathleen, Eileen. BA in Econs., U. Notre Dame, 1975, JD, 1978. Bar: Ill. 1978, U.S. Dist. Ct. (no. dist.) Ill. 1978, U.S. Dist. Ct. (cen. dist.) Ill. 1992, U.S. Dist. Ct. (ea. dist.) Wis. 1992, U.S. Ct. Appeals (7th cir.) 1982, U.S. Ct. Appeals (11th cir.) 1982, U.S. Ct. Appeals (8th cir.) 1998. Assoc. Mayer Brown LLP, Chgo., 1978-84, ptnr., 1985—. Adj. faculty law Loyola U., Chgo., 1983, 86-90. Bd. dirs. no. Ill. affiliate Am. Diabetes Assn., Chgo., 1985-94. Mem. ABA (franchising forum com. antitrust law sect.), Phi Beta Kappa. Office: Mayer Brown LLP 71 S Wacker Dr Chicago IL 60606-4637 Home Phone: 708-246-4234. Business E-Mail: mmclaughlin@mayerbrown.com.

MCLENDON, LLOYD, professional baseball coach, retired baseball player; Former infielder Cin. Reds, 1987—88, Chgo. Cubs, 1989—90, Toronto Blue Jays, 1990, Pitts. Pirates, 1990—94, former mgr.; bullpen coach Detroit Tigers, 2006, hitting coach, 2006—. Office: Detorit Tigers Comerica Park 2100 Woodward Ave Detroit MI 48201

MCLEOD, PHILIP ROBERT, publishing executive; b. Winnipeg, Man., Can., May 4, 1943; s. Donald G. and Phyllis (Brown) McL.; m. Cheryl Amy Stewart, Sept. 25, 1965 (div. 1992); children: Shawn Robert, Erin Dawn; m. Virginia Mary Corner, Nov. 6, 1992 (div. 2004); m. Shannon Diane Thompson, Dec. 8, 2004. Journalist Bowes Pub., Grande Prairie, Alta and Truro, N.S., Canada, 1962—76; journalist, dep. mng. editor Toronto (Ont., Can.) Star, 1976-87; editor-in-chief London (Ont.) Free Press, 1987-98; pub. Brockville (Ont.) Recorder & Times, 1998—2002; co-founding owner, editor The Londoner, ON, Canada, 2002—. Southam fellow Southam Newspapers, 1970. Mem. The Brockville Country Club. Avocations: canoeing, skiing. Office: The Londoner 332 Wellington Rd S Unit 1B London ON Canada N6C 4P6 Office Phone: 519-673-5005. Business E-Mail: pmcleod@thelondoner.ca.

MCLEVISH, TIMOTHY R., food products executive; BS in Acctg., U. Minn., 1982; MBA, Harvard U., 1985. CPA. Various mgmt. positions through div. pres. & gen. mgr. Mead Corp., Dayton, Ohio, 1987-99, v.p., CFO, 1999—2002; sr. v.p., CFO Ingersoll-Rand Co. Ltd., 2002—07; exec. v.p., CFO Kraft Foods Inc., Northfield, Ill., 2007—. Office: Kraft Foods Inc 3 Lakes Dr Northfield IL 60093

MCLIN, RHINE LANA, mayor, former state legislator; b. Dayton, Ohio, Oct. 3, 1948; d. C. Josef, Jr. and Bernice (Cottman) McL. BA in Sociology, Parsons Coll., 1969; MEd, Xavier U., 1972; postgrad. in law, U. Dayton, 1974-76; AA in Mortuary Sci., Cin. Coll., 1988. Lic. funeral dir. Tchr. Dayton Bd. Edn., 1970-72; divorce counselor Domestic Rels. Ct., Dayton, 1972-73; law clk. Montgomery Common Pleas Ct., Dayton, 1973-74; v.p., dir., embalmer McLin Funeral Homes, Dayton, 1972—; mem. Ohio Ho. of Reps. from 36th & 38th dists., Columbus, 1988-94, Ohio Senate from 5th dist., Columbus, 1994—2002; mem. Ways & Means Com.; controlling bd., ins. commerce comn. ranking mem.; state and local govt. com. Columbus; minority whip Ohio Senate, Columbus, 1994—2001; mayor City of Dayton, 2002—. Instr. Central State U., Wilberforce, Ohio, 1982-97; mem. Ohio Tuition Trust Authority. Mem. Dem. Nat. Com., Children's Def. Fund. Toll fellow; Paul Harris fellow; Flemming fellow; BLLD fellow; named Ohio Legislator of Yr., Ohio Social Workers Assn., 1999. Mem. Nat. Funeral Dirs. Assn., Ohio Funeral Dirs. Assn., Montgomery County Hist. Soc., NAACP (life), Nat. Coun. Negro Women (life), Delta Sigma Theta. Achievements include being first female mayor of Dayton. Office: City Hall 2nd Fl 101 W Third St Dayton OH 45402 Office Phone: 937-333-3653. Business E-Mail: Rhine.McLin@cityofDayton.org.

MCMAHON, DANIEL JOHN, lawyer; b. Rockville Centre, NY, Nov. 5, 1963; s. David Joseph and Colleen Anne (Phelan) McM.; m. Colleen Catherine Cary, Oct. 5, 1991; children: Maeve Colleen, Daniel John, Jr. BA, U. Notre Dame, 1986, JD, 1989. Bar: Ill. 1989, US Dist. Ct. (no. dist.) Ill. 1989, US Ct. Appeals (7th cir.) 1991, US Dist. Ct. (no. dist.) Ill. Trial Bar 1993, US Dist. Ct. (ctrl. and so. dists.) Ill. 1995, US Dist. Ct. (we. and ea. dists.) Wis. 1997, US Dist. Ct. (we. dist.) Mich. 2004, US Dist. Ct. (no. and so. dists.) Ind. 2004, US Ct. Appeals (6th cir.) 2001, US Ct. Appeals (8th cir.) 2005, US Supreme Ct. 1999. Law clk. William Mauzy & Assocs., Mpls., 1987; rsch. asst. Prof. Charles Rice, Notre Dame (Ind.) Law Sch., 1987-89; summer assoc. Peterson & Ross, Chgo., 1988, assoc., 1989-95, Wilson, Elser, Moskowitz, Edelman & Dicker LLP, Chgo., 1995-97, ptnr., 1997—, regional mng. ptnr. firm exec. com., 2004—. Contbr. article to profl. jour. Coach Near North Little League-Cabrini Green, Chgo., 1992-95; tutor St. Joseph's Grade Sch.-Cabrini Green, Chgo., 1992-95. Citizen's scholar Gen. Mills Corp., Mpls., 1982-86. Mem. ABA (torts and ins. practice sect.), Def. Rsch. and Trial Lawyers Assn. (life, health and disability com.), Chgo. Bar Assn., Ill. State Bar Assn., Profl. Liability Underwriting Soc. Roman Catholic. Avocations: reading, history, politics, sports. Office: Wilson Elser Moskowitz Edelman & Dicker 120 N La Salle St Fl 2600 Chicago IL 60602-2415 Office Phone: 312-704-0550. Business E-Mail: mcmahond@wemed.com.

MCMAHON, JAMES E., lawyer, former prosecutor; b. 1951; m. Kathy McMahon; 3 children. BS, Morningside U.; JD, U. S.D., 1977. Asst. atty. gen. State of SD, 1978—81; ptnr. Boyce, Murphy, McDowell & Greenfield, 1981—2002; pvt. practice Sioux Falls, SD, 2002—; US atty. Dist. SD US Dept. Justice, Sioux Falls, SD, 2002—05. Recipient Trial Lawyer of Yr. award, S.D. Trial Lawyers Assn., 2000.

MCMAINS, MELVIN L(EE), administrative executive; b. Oskaloosa, Iowa, Aug. 1, 1941; m. Kathryn Elaine Murphy; children: Kimberly, Lindsay. BA, U. Northern Iowa, 1966, MA, 1968. CPA, Iowa; CMA. V.p. adminstrv. svcs. HON Industries, Inc., Muscatine, Iowa, 1979—. Mem. AICPA, Fin. Execs. Inst., Iowa Soc. CPA's, Inst. Mgmt. Accts., Geneva Golf and Country Club.

MCMANAMAN, WILLIAM ROBERT, diversified financial services company executive; b. Chgo., May 1, 1947; s. William Joseph and Ursula Catherine (Geary) McM.; m. Elizabeth Ann Campbell, Sept. 10, 1948; children: Martin, Kara, Maureen. BA, Lewis U., Romeoville, Ill., 1969; MBA, U. Detroit, 1971; AMP, Harvard U., 1988. CPA, Ill. Mgr. in mfg. div. Arthur Andersen & Co., Chgo., 1971-79; mgr. reporting Brunswick Corp., Skokie, Ill., 1979-82, dir. acctg., 1982-86, corp. contr., 1986-88, v.p., fin., 1988—95; v.p., fin., CFO Dean Foods Co., 1995—2000; exec. v.p., CFO Aurora Foods, Inc., 2002—04; sr. v.p., CFO First Health Group Corp., 2004—05; exec. v.p., CFO Ubiquity Brands, 2005—08; CEO AMCORE Fin. Inc., Rockford, Ill., 2008—. Bd. dirs. AMCORE Fin. Inc., 1997—, Coolbrands Internat., Inc., 2006—. Mem. fin. com. St. Ignatius Coll. Pres. Sch., Chgo., 1986—; bd. dirs. Community Family Svcs. and Mental Health Ctr., LaGrange, Ill., 1989. Fellow Assn. Ill. CPAs, Ill. CPAs Soc. LaGrange Country Club, Mid-America Club, Univ. Club Chgo. Avocation: sports. Office: AMCORE Fin Inc 501 Seventh St Rockford IL 61104*

MC MANUS, EDWARD JOSEPH, federal judge; b. Keokuk, Iowa, Feb. 9, 1920; s. Edward W. and Kathleen (O'Connor) McM.; m. Sally A. Hassett, June 30, 1948 (dec.); children: David P., Edward W., John N., Thomas J., Dennis Q.; m. Esther Y. Kanealy, Sept. 15, 1987. Student, St. Ambrose Coll., 1936-38; BA, U. Iowa, 1940, JD, 1942. Bar: Iowa 1941. Gen. practice of law, Keokuk, 1946-62; city atty., 1946-55; mem. Iowa Senate, 1955-59; lt. gov. Iowa, 1959-61; chief U.S. judge No. Dist. Iowa, 1962-85, sr. U.S. judge, 1985—. Del Democratic Nat. Conv., 1956, 60. Served as lt. AC USNR, 1942-46. Office: US Dist Ct 329 US Courthouse 101 1st St SE Cedar Rapids IA 52401-1202 Office Phone: 319-286-2350. Business E-Mail: edward_mcmanus@iand.uscourts.gov.

MCMANUS, GEORGE ALVIN, JR., state legislator, cherry farmer; b. Traverse City, Mich., Dec. 12, 1930; s. George Alvin and Frieda Anna (Fromholz) McM.; m. Clara Belle Kratochvil, Aug. 16, 1949; children: Eliza J. Saints, Molly S. Agostinelli, Margaret L. Egelus, Kathleen E. Nurohammed, Kerry E. Canellos, George A., John K., Bridgett E. Popp,Matthew R. BS, Mich. State U., 1952, MS, 1953. Fruit grower pvt. practice, Traverse City, Mich., 1953—; coop. extension agt. Mich. State U., 1956-82; mem. Mich. Senate from 36th dist., Lansing, 1991—. Trustee Northwestern Mich. Coll., Traverse City, 1970-90; pres. Traverse City C.of C., 1982, Traverse City Rotary, 1993. Named Citizen of Yr. Traverse City C. of C., 1984. Mem. KC, Elks Club, Rotary Club. Republican. Roman Catholic. Avocation: golf. Office: Mich State Senate 52 Capital Bldg Lansing MI 48913-0001

MCMANUS, JAMES WILLIAM, lawyer; b. Kansas City, Mo., Aug. 1, 1945; s. Gerald B. and Mary M. McManus. BA, Rockhurst Coll., 1967; JD, St. Louis U., 1971. Bar: Mo. 1971, U.S. Dist. Ct. (we. dist.) Mo. 1972, U.S. Ct. Appeals (8th cir.) 1974, U.S. Supreme Ct. 1979, U.S. Ct. Appeals (10th cir.) 1984, U.S. Dist. Ct. Kans., 1995. Law clk. to presiding justice U.S. Dist. Ct. (we. dist.) Mo., 1971-73; assoc. Shughart, Thomson & Kilroy, P.C., Kansas City, 1973-76, dir., 1977-94; counsel Dysart, Taylor, Lay, Cotter & McMonigle, P.C., Kansas City, 1994—2002, DeWitt & Zeldin, L.L.C., Kansas City, 2002—04, McManus Law Offices, Kansas City, 2005—. Course lectr. med. jurisprudence U. Health Scis., Coll. Osteo. Medicine, Kansas City, 1994; lectr. in field. Adv. coun. St. Joseph Health Ctr., 1989-2002. Named to Best of the Bar, Appeals and Trials, Kansas City Bus. Jour., 2003, 2005, 2006; recipient Congenial Counselor award, Kansas City Metro Bar Assn., 2003, Exceptional Trial and Appellate atty. award, Mo. Ho. Reps., 2003. Fellow Am. Bar Found.; mem. ABA, AAJ (membership com. 2003-), Mo. Bar Assn., Kansas City Lawyers Assn., Kansas City Met. Bar Assn. (chmn. alternate dispute resolution com. 1996-97, vice chmn. 1994-95, chmn. med. malpractice com. 1989, Congenial Counselor award 2003), Mo. Assn. Trial Attys., Nat. Lawyers Assn., St. Louis Alumni Assn. (pres. 1984-92), St. Louis U. Law Sch. Alumni Assn. Home: 6824 Valley Rd Kansas City MO 64113-1929 Office: McManus Law Offices 1111 Main St Ste 700 Kansas City MO 64105 Office Phone: 816-474-3018. Business E-Mail: jamesmcmanus@justice.com.

MCMANUS, JOHN FRANCIS, association executive, writer; b. Bklyn., Jan. 24, 1935; s. V. Paul and Dorothy F. (Devenport) McM.; m. Mary Helen O'Reilly, Oct. 19, 1957; children: John G., Margaret A. Strauss, Paul J., Mary Anne Power. BS in Physics, Holy Cross Coll., 1957. Elec. engr. Transitron Corp., Wakefield, Mass., 1960-66; field coord. The John Birch Soc., Belmont, Mass., 1966-68, projects mgr., 1968-73, dir. pub. rels., 1973-91, pres. Appleton, Wis., 1991—. Author: An Overview of Our World, 1971, The Insiders: Architects of the New World Order, 1992, 5th edit., 2004, Financial Terrorism: Hijacking America Under the Threat of Bankruptcy, 1993, Changing Commands: The Betrayal of America's Military, 1995, William F. Buckley, Jr.: Pied Piper For the Establishment, 2002. Lt. USMC, 1957-60, capt., USMCR, 1960-68. Avocations: reading, sports. Home: PO Box 3076 Wakefield MA 01880-0772 Office: John Birch Society PO Box 8040 Appleton WI 54912-8040 Office Phone: 920-749-3780. Business E-Mail: jmcmanus@jbs.org.

MCMASTERS, JAMES, law librarian, educator; BS, Northwestern U., JD, 1990; MLIS, Dominican U. Litig. assoc. Bell, Boyd & Lloyd, Chgo., 1990—94; lectr. comm. and legal reasoning Northwestern U. Sch. Law, Chgo., staff mem. Pritzker Legal Rsch. Ctr., 2002—, acting dir.; reference libr. Loyola U., Chgo., 2000—02. Office: Pritzker Legal Rsch Ctr Northwestern U Sch Law 357 E Chicago Ave Chicago IL 60611 Office Phone: 312-503-8449. E-mail: j-mcmasters@law.northwestern.edu.

MCMEEKIN, DOROTHY, botanist, plant pathologist, educator; b. Boston, Feb. 24, 1932; d. Thomas LeRoy and Vera (Crockatt) McM. BA, Wilson Coll., 1953; MA, Wellesley Coll., 1955; PhD, Cornell U., 1959. Asst. prof. Upsala Coll., East Orange, NJ, 1959-64, Bowling Green State U., Ohio, 1964-66; prof. natural sci. Mich. State U., East Lansing, 1966-89, prof. botany, plant pathology, 1989—. Author: Diego Rivera: Science and Creativity, 1985; contbr. articles to profl. jours. Mem. Am. Phytopath. Soc., Mycol. Soc. Am., Soc. Econ. Bot., Mich. Bot. Soc. (former bd. dirs.), Mich. Women's Studies Assn., Sigma Xi, Phi Kappa Phi. Avocations: gardening, sewing, travel, drawing. Home: 1055 Marigold Ave East Lansing MI 48823-5128 Office: Mich State U Dept Botany-Plant Pathology 100 N Kedzie Hall East Lansing MI 48824-1031 E-mail: mcmeekin@msu.edu.

MC MEEL, JOHN PAUL, newspaper syndicate and publishing executive; b. South Bend, Ind., Jan. 26, 1936; s. James E. and Naomi R. (Reilly) McM.; m. Susan S. Sykes, Apr. 16, 1966; children: Maureen, Suzanne, Bridget. BS, U. Notre Dame, 1957. Sales dir. Hall Syndicate, 1960-67; asst. gen. mgr., sales dir. Publishers-Hall Syndicate, 1968-70; co-founder Universal Press Syndicate, Kansas City, Mo., 1970; pres. Andrews McMeel Universal, 1970—. Chmn. bd. Andrews McMeel Pub., 1973—; mem. arts and letters U. Notre Dame. Co-founder Christmas in October, Kansas City, 1984—, James F. Andrews fellowship program, U. otre Dame, 1981, adv. com. program in journalism; mem. The Civic Coun. Greater Kansas City. Mem. Fed. Assn. USA, Sovereign Mil. Order Malta. Home: Three Sunset Pl 5300 Sunset Dr Kansas City MO 64112-2358 Office: Andrews McMeel Universal 4520 Main St Kansas City MO 64111-1816 Office Phone: 816-932-6602. Business E-Mail: jmcmeel@amuniversal.com.

MCMENAMIN, JOHN ROBERT, lawyer; b. Evanston, Ill., Sept. 30, 1946; BA, U. Notre Dame, 1968, JD, 1971. Bar: Ill. 1971. Law clk. to presiding judge U.S. Ct. Appeals (7th cir.), 1971-72; ptnr. Mayer, Brown & Platt, Chgo., 1978-89, McDermott, Will & Emery, Chgo., 1989—. Chmn. adv. bd. Holy Trinity High Sch., Chgo., 1986-88; pres. Lawyer's Club Chgo., 2003-04. Mem. ABA, Lawyers Club, U. Club, Econ. Club. Roman Catholic. Office: McDermott Will & Emery 227 W Monroe St Ste 3100 Chicago IL 60606-5096

MCMILLAN, CARY D., food products executive; Grad. Coll. Commerce and Bus. Adminstrn., U. Ill., 1980. Mgr. Arthur Andersen, Chgo., 1985—92, mng. ptnr., 1992—2000; exec. v.p., CFO Sara Lee Corp., Chgo., 2000—, CEO, branded apparel div., 2001—. Office: Sara Lee Corp 3 1st Nat Plz Chicago IL 60602-4260

MC MILLAN, R(OBERT) BRUCE, retired museum director, anthropologist; b. Springfield, Mo., Dec. 3, 1937; s. George Glassey and Winnie Mae (Booth) McM.; m. Virginia Kay Moore, Sept. 30, 1961; children: Robert Gregory, Michael David, Lynn Kathryn. BS in Edn, S.W. Mo. State U., 1950; MA in Anthropology, U. Mo., 1963; PhD in Anthropology, U. Colo., 1971. Rsch. assoc. in archaeology U. Mo., 1963-65, 68-69; assoc. curator anthropology Ill. State Mus., Springfield, 1969-72, curator anthropology, 1972-73, asst. mus. dir., 1973-76, mus. dir., 1977—2005; exec. sec. Ill. State Mus. Soc., 1977—2005; ret., 2005. Lectr. anthropology orthwestern U., 1973. Editor: (with W. Raymond Wood) Prehistoric Man and His Environments, 1976. Mem. Ill. Spl. Events Commn., 1977-79, program chmn., 1977-78; commr. Ill. and Mich. Canal Nat. Heritage Corridor Commn., 1988-96; bd. dirs. Found. Ill. Archaeology, 1978-83. Grantee NSF, 1971-72, 80, NEH, 1978. Fellow AAAS, Am. Anthrop. Assn.; mem. Am. Assn. Mus. (coun. 1982-86), Midwest Mus. Conf. (pres.), Soc. Am. Archaeology, Current Anthropology (assoc.), Am. Quaternary Assn., Sigma Xi. Office: Ill State Mus 502 S Spring St Springfield IL 62706-5000 also: Dickson Mounds Museum Lewistown IL 61542 Home Phone: 217-529-2583; Office Phone: 217-524-0498. Business E-Mail: mcmillan@museum.state.il.us.

MCMILLIN, DAVID ROBERT, chemistry professor; b. East St. Louis, Ill., Jan. 1, 1948; s. Robert Cecil and Clara Rose McMillin; m. Nicole Wilson, Nov. 3, 1974; children: Robert Stephen, Andrew Wilson. BA, Knox Coll., 1969; PhD, U. Ill., 1973. Postdoctoral fellow Calif. Inst. Tech., Pasadena, 1974; asst. prof. chemistry Purdue U., West Lafayette, Ind., 1975-80, assoc. prof., 1980-85, prof., 1985—. Contbr. articles to profl. jours. Recipient F.D. Martin Teaching award Purdue U., 1975. Mem. Am. Chem. Soc., Inter-Am. Photochem. Soc. (sec. 1986-90, v.p. 1994-96, pres. 1996-98), Phi Beta Kappa, Sigma Xi. Presbyterian. Avocations: sports, reading. Office: Purdue U Dept Chemistry 560 Oval Dr West Lafayette IN 47907-2084 Home Phone: 764-463-4815. E-mail: mcmillin@purdue.edu.

MCMORROW, MARY ANN GROHWIN, retired state supreme court justice; b. Chgo., Jan. 16, 1930; m. Emmett J. McMorrow, May 5, 1962; 1 dau., Mary Ann. Attended, Rosary Coll., 1948—50; JD, Loyola U., 1953. Bar: Ill. 1953, U.S. Dist. Ct. (7th dist.) Ill. 1960, U.S. Supreme Ct. 1976. Atty. Riordan & Linklater Law Offices, Chgo., 1954—56; asst. state's atty. Cook County, Chgo., 1956-63; sole practice Chgo., 1963-76; judge Cir. Ct. Cook County, 1976-85, Ill. Appellate Ct., 1985-92; justice Ill. Supreme Ct., 1992—2006, chief justice, 2002—05. Faculty adv. Nat. Jud. Coll., U. Nev., 1984. Contbr. articles to profl. jours. Mem. Chgo. Bar Assn., Ill. State Bar Assn., Women's Bar Assn. of Ill. (pres. 1975-76, bd. dirs. 1970-78), Am. Judicature Soc., Northwestern U. Assocs., Ill. Judges Assn., Nat. Assn. Women Judges, Advocates Soc., Northwest Suburban Bar Assn., West Suburban Bar Assn., Loyola Law Alumni Assn. (bd. govs. 1985—), Ill. Judges Assn. (bd. dirs.), Cath. Lawyers Guild (v.p.), The Law Club of the City of Chgo., Inns of Ct.

MCMULLIN, RUTH RONEY, retired publishing executive; b. NYC, Feb. 9, 1942; d. Richard Thomas and Virginia (Goodwin) Roney; m. Thomas Ryan McMullin, Apr. 27, 1968; 1 child, David Patrick. BA, Conn. Coll., 1963; M Pub. and Pvt. Mgmt., Yale U., 1979. Market rschr. Aviation Week Mag., McGraw-Hill Co., NYC, 1962-64; assoc. editor, bus. mgr. Doubleday & Co., NYC, 1964-66; mgr. Natural History Press, 1967-70; v.p., treas. Weston (Conn.) Woods, Inc., 1970-71; staff assoc. GE, Fairfield, Conn., 1979-82; mng. fin. analyst GECC Transp., Stamford, Conn., 1982—84; credit analyst corp. fin. dept. GECC, Stamford, Conn., 1984-85; sr. v.p. GECC Capital Markets Group, Inc., NYC, 1985-87; exec. v.p., COO, CEO, John Wiley & Sons, NYC, 1987—90, pres., CEO; CEO Harvard Bus. Sch. Pub. Corp., Boston, 1991-94; mem. chmn.'s com., acting CEO UNR Industries Inc., Chgo., 1991-92, also bd. dirs.; mgmt. fellow, vis. prof. Sch. Mgmt. Yale U., New Haven, 1994-95; chairperson trustees Eagle-Picher Personal Injury Settlement Trust, 1996—; chairperson Claims Procesing Facility, Inc., 1998—. Bd. dirs. Bausch & Lomb, Rochester, NY, 1987-2007; vis. prof. Sch. Mgmt., Yale U., New Haven, 1994-95. Mem. dean's adv. bd. Sch. Mgmt. Yale U., 1985—92; bd. dirs. Yale U. Alumni fund, 1986—92, Yale U. Press, 1988—99, Math. Scis. Edn. Bd., 1990—93; bd. dirs., treas. Mighty Eighth Air Force Heritage Mus., 2000—; chmn. Mighty Eighth Found., 2003—; bd. dirs. Savannah Symphony, 1999—2003, The Landings Club, 2002—04. Mem. N.Y. Yacht Club, Yale Club, Landings Club. Avocations: sailing, skiing, golf, tennis. Home: 8 Breckenridge Ln Savannah GA 31411-1701 Office: Eagle Picher Trust 30 Garfield Pl Ste 730 Cincinnati OH 45202 Personal E-mail: rrmcmullin@aya.yale.edu. Business E-Mail: ruthmcmullin@mac.com.

MCNALLY, ALAN G., bank executive; b. Quebec, Can., Nov. 3, 1945; m. Ruth; 2 children. BSc., M Eng., Cornell U., 1967; Internat. MBA, York U., Can. With Aluminum Co. of Can.; vice chmn. personal and commercial fin. svcs. Bank of Montreal Group, 1975-93; CEO, vice chmn. Harris Bank and Haris Bankcorp Inc., 1993-1995, chmn. bd., CEO, 1995—. Trustee DePaul U., adv. bd. mem. Northwestern U. J.L. Kellogg Grad. Sch. Mgmt., bd. mem. Evenston Northwestern Healthcare, mem. bd. govs. York U., dir. Canadian Coun. for Aboriginal Bus. Gen. chair United Way/Crusade of Mercy fundraising campaign, 1996, dir. Chgo. Youth Ctrs., treas. Queen Elizabeth Hosp. Found., dir. Kid's Help Phone. Recipient Americanism award Anti-Defamation League, Community Builder award Christian Insudtrial League, Outstanding Exec. Leadership award York U. Schulich Sch. Bus., Toronto, Prime Movers award. Bd. dirs. Econ. Club Chgo., Chgo. Club, civic com. Commercial Club Chgo., Executive's Club Chgo., Glen View Club. Office: Harris Bank 111 W Monroe St Chicago IL 60603-4096

MCNALLY, ANDREW, IV, publishing executive, director; b. Chgo., Nov. 11, 1939; s. Andrew and Margaret C. (MacMillin) McN.; m. Jeanine Sanchez, July 3, 1966; children: Andrew, Carrie, Ward BA, U. NC, 1963; MBA, U. Chgo., 1969. Bus. mgr. edn. divsn. Rand McNally & Co., Chgo., 1967—70, exec. v.p., sec., 1970—74, pres., 1974—97, CEO, 1978—97, also chmn. bd. dirs., 1993—97; ptnr. McNally Investments, Chgo., 1998—. Bd. dirs. Hubbell Inc., Boyt Harness, Qualis. Trustee ewberry Libr.; bd. dirs. Children's Meml. Hosp. With Air Force N.G., 1963-69. Mem. Chgo. Club, Saddle and Cycle Club, Commonwealth Club, Racquet Club, Links (NYC) Office: 333 N Michigan Ave Ste 2200 Chicago IL 60601-4104

MCNAMARA, DAVID JOSEPH, financial and tax planning executive; b. Osceola, Iowa, Feb. 6, 1951; s. Loras Emmett and Nadine Evelyn (DeLancey) McN.; m. Ruth Ellen Hanken, Oct. 4,1974; children: Benjamin, Shawna, Heather. BGS, U. Iowa, 1974. Cert. fin. planner Coll. Fin. Planning, 1985; registered prin. Nat. Assn. Securities Dealers. Pres. The Planners Adv. Svcs., Inc., 1985; ptnr. VF Realty Ptnrs., West Desmoines, Iowa, 1987—. Mem.: Fin. Planning Assn. (bd. dirs. Iowa chpt. 1984—85). Republican. Office: The Planners Adv Svcs Inc 1012 Grand Ave West Des Moines IA 50265-3255

MCNEALEY, J. JEFFREY, lawyer, corporate executive; b. Cin., Feb. 8, 1944; s. J. Lawrence and Louise McNealey; m. Sara Wilson, Sept. 24, 1988; children: Anne Elizabeth, John Alexander. BA, Cornell U., 1966; JD, Ohio State U., 1969. Ptnr. Porter, Wright, Morris & Arthur, Columbus, Ohio, 1969—. Bd. dirs. TRC Cos., Windsor, Conn., 1985—; sec., bd. dirs. The Smoot Corp., Columbus, 1972—. Trustee Columbus Cancer Clinic, 1972—, past pres.; trustee German Village Soc., Columbus, 1986—, past pres.; bd. dirs. Columbus chpt. ARC, 1983-86, Columbus Urban League, 1984-90; active Union League Chgo., 1981—, Columbus/Dresden Sister City, Inc., 1996—; mem. vestry Trinity Episcopal Ch., 2000—. Mem. ABA, Ohio State Bar Assn. (past chmn. environ. com. 1978-84), Columbus Bar Assn., Columbus Country Club, Capital Club of Columbus, Cornell Club of Ctrl. Ohio (trustee 1978—, past pres.). Episcopalian. Avocations: flying, racquetball, woodworking, fly fishing. Office: Porter Wright Morris & Arthur 41 S High St Ste 30 Columbus OH 43215-6101

MCNEELY, JAMES LEE, lawyer; b. Shelbyville, Ind., May 4, 1940; s. Carl R. and Elizabeth J. (Orebaugh) McN.; m. Rose M. Wisker, Sept. 5, 1977; children: Angela, Susan, Meg, Matt. AB, Wabash Coll., 1962; JD, Ind. U., 1965. Bar: Ind. 1965, U.S. Dist. Ct. (so. dist.) Ind. 1965, U.S. Ct. Appeals (7th cir.) 1970. Assoc. Pell & Matchett, Shelbyville, 1965-70; ptnr. Matchett & McNeely, Shelbyville, 1970-74; sole practice Shelbyville, 1974-76; sr. ptnr. McNeely & Sanders, Shelbyville, 1976-86, McNeely, Sanders & Stephenson, Shelbyville, 1986-89, McNeely, Sanders, Stephenson & Thopy, Shelbyville, 1989-96, McNeely, Stephenson, Thopy & Harrold, Shelbyville, 1997—. Guest lectr. Franklin Coll., Ind., 1965-72; judge Shelbyville City Ct., 1967-71. Chmn. Shelbyville County Rep. Cen. Com., 1968-88; bd. dirs. Ind. Lung Assn., 1972-75, Crossroads Council Boy Scouts Am., 1982; trustee Wabash Coll., 2004—; bd. dirs., pres. Shelbyville Girls Club. Named Sagamore of the Wabash, Gov. Ed Whitcomb, 1971, Gov. Otis Bowen, 1977, Gov. Robert Orr, 1986, 88, Gov. Evan Bayh, 1996, Gov. Frank O'Bannon, 1999; recipient Lifetime Citizenship award for growth Shelby County C. of C., 2003. Fellow Ind. Bar Found. (patron, sec. 1999-2000, chair elect 2000-01, chmn. 2002-03); mem. ABA, Ind. Bar Assn. (sec. 1985-87, bd. dirs. 1976-78, chair-elect Ho. Dels. 1994-95, chair 1995-96, v.p. 1996-97, pres.-elect 1997-98, pres. 1998-99), Shelby County Bar Assn. (pres. 1975), Ind. Lawyers Commn. (pres., dir.), Fed. Merit Selection Commn. (adv. mem. 1988-92, chmn. 2001—), Shelbyville Jaycees (Distinguished Service award 1969, Good Govt. award 1970), Wabash Coll. Nat. Assn. Wabash Men (dir. 1983-89, sec. 1989-91, v.p. 1991-93, pres. 1993-95, Man of Yr. 1995), Kappa Sigma Alpha Pi chpt. (Hall of Fame 1995). Lodges: Lions, Elks, Eagles. Methodist. Avocations: golf, travel. Home: 1902 E Old Rushville Rd Shelbyville IN 46176-9569

MCNEELY, JOHN J., lawyer; b. Mpls., Oct. 8, 1931; s. John J. Sr. and Mae (Carlin) McN.; children: Mary Ann, John J. Jr., Michael F., Patricia C., David C. BS, Georgetown U., 1955, JD, 1958. Bar: Minn. 1958. Law clk. Minn. Supreme Ct., St. Paul, 1958-59; ptnr. Briggs & Morgan, St. Paul, 1959—. Sgt. USMC, 1950-52. Fellow Am. Coll. Trust and Estate Counsel; mem. ABA, Minn. State Bar Assn., Ramsey County Bar Assn., Mendakota Country Club. Home: 1183 Ivy Hill Dr Saint Paul MN 55118-1827 Office Phone: 651-808-6576.

MCNEIL, JOHN W., lawyer; b. Detroit, July 18, 1942; BA, Mich. State U., 1964; JD, U. Mich., 1967. Bar: Mich. 1968. Ptnr. Miller, Johnson, Snell & Cummiskey, PLC, Grand Rapids, Mich. Chmn. Goodwill Inds. Internat., Inc., 1992-94; bd. dirs. Goodwill Industries of Greater Grand Rapids, 1973-97, Goodwill Inds. Internat., Inc., 1988-97. Mem. State Bar Mich. (coun. of taxation sect. 1975-82, chmn. taxation sect. 1980-81), Grand Rapids Bar Assn. Office: Miller Johnson Snell & Cummiskey 250 Monroe Ave NW Ste 800 Grand Rapids MI 49503-2250

MCNEILL, G. DAVID, psychologist, educator; b. Santa Rosa, Calif., Dec. 21, 1931; s. Glenn H. and Ethel G. (Little) McN.; m. Nobuko Baba, Dec. 17, 1957; children: Cheryl, Randall L.B. AB, U. Calif., Berkeley, 1953, PhD, 1962. Research fellow Harvard U., 1962-65; asst. prof. psychology U. Mich., 1965-66, assoc. prof., 1966-68; prof. psychology and linguistics U. Chgo., 1969—2001, chmn. dept. psychology, 1991-97, prof. emeritus, 2001—. Vis. fellow Ctr. for Humanities, Wesleyan U., Middletown, Conn., 1970; mem. Inst. Advanced Study, Princeton, 1973-75; fellow Netherlands Inst. for Advanced Studies, 1983-84; visitor Max Planck Inst. for Psycholinguistics, Nijmegen, Netherlands, 1998-99 Author: The Acquisition of Language, 1970, The Conceptual Basis of Language, 1979, Psycholinguistics: A New Approach, 1987, Gengo Shinrigaku, 1991, Hand and Mind: What Gestures Reveal about Thought, 1992, Gesture and Thought, 2005; editor: Language and Gesture, 2000. Recipient Faculty Achievement award, 1991, Ann. Excellence in Pub. award Assn. Am. Pubs., Gordon G. Laing prize U. Chgo. Press, 1995; Guggenheim fellow, 1973-74; grantee NSF, 1983-89, 97—, Spencer Found., 1979-82, 89-92, 95-99, NIDCD, 1992-96, Advanced Rsch. and Devel. Agy., 2003—. Fellow AAAS, Am. Psychol. Soc.; mem. Internat. Soc. Gesture Studies (v.p. 2002-05, hon. pres. 2007—), Cognitive Sci. Soc., Linguistic Soc. Am., Violoncello Soc., Phi Beta Kappa, Sigma Xi Office: U Chgo Dept Psychology 5848 S University Ave Chicago IL 60637-1515 Office Phone: 773-702-8833. Business E-Mail: dmcneill@uchicago.edu.

MCNEILL, ROBERT PATRICK, investment advisor; b. Chgo., Mar. 17, 1941; s. Donald Thomas and Katherine (Bennett) McN.; m. Martha Stephan, Sept. 12, 1964; children— Jennifer, Donald, Victoria, Stephan, Elizabeth BA summa cum laude (valedictorian), U. Notre Dame, 1963; M.Letters, Oxford U., 1967. Chartered investment counselor. Assoc. Stein Roe & Farnham, Chgo., 1967-72, gen. ptnr., 1972-77, sr. ptnr., 1977-86, exec. v.p., 1986-89; pres., mng. dir. Stein Roe Internat., Chgo., 1989—. Underwriting mem. Lloyds of London, 1980—; dir. Comml. Chgo. Corp.; vice chmn. bd. Hill Internat. Prodn. Co., Houston, 1982—; dir., adv. bd. Touche Remnant Investment Counselors, London, 1983—; dir. TR Worldwide Strategy Fund, Luxembourg, Konrad Adenauer Fund for European Policy Studies, Fed. Republic Germany. Voting mem., sec Ill. Rhodes Scholarship Selection Com.; voting mem. Ill. rep. Great Lakes Dist. Rhodes Scholarship Selection Com.; bd. dirs. Kennedy Sch. for Retarded Children, Palos Park, Ill., 1972—, Winnetka United Way, Ill., 1984—, Division St. YMCA, Chgo., 1972—; assoc. Rush-Presbyterian-St. Lukes Med. Ctr., Chgo., 1975—; mem. leadership com. Rush Alzheimer's Disease Ctr. Rhodes scholar, 1963 Fellow Fin. Analysts Fedn.; mem. Chgo. Council on Fgn. Relations (bd. dirs., treas. 1975—), Inst. European Studies (bd. govs., vice-chmn. 1981—), Investment Analysts Soc. Chgo. (chgo. com., com. on fgn. affairs, com. on internat. and domestic issues), Assn. for Investment Mgmt. and Rsch., Chgo. Soc. Clubs, Econ. Club of Chgo, Sunset Ridge Country (bd. dirs. Northfield, Ill., 1983—). Avocations: coin collecting/numismatics, bridge, golf, skiing, art. Office Phone: 312-368-7684. Business E-Mail: rmcneill@sric.net.

MCNEILL, THOMAS B., director, retired lawyer; b. Chgo., Oct. 28, 1934; s. Donald T. and Katherine M. (Bennett) McN.; m. Ingrid Sieder, May 11, 1963; children: Christine, Thomas, Stephanie. BA, U. Notre Dame, 1956, JD, 1958. Ptnr. Mayer, Brown, Rowe & Maw, Chgo., 1962—99. Dir. Deltona Corp., Ocala, Fla. Served to capt. JAGC USAF, 1959-62. Fellow Am. Coll. Trial Lawyers; mem. Chgo. Bar Assn., Chgo. Council Lawyers, The Lawyers Club (Chgo. chpt.). Clubs: Indian Hill (Winnetka, Ill.). Home: 2418 Iroquois Rd Wilmette IL 60091-1335 E-mail: tomingrid@aol.com.

MCNERNEY, JAMES, JR., (W. JAMES MCNERNEY), aerospace transportation executive, former manufacturing executive; b. Providence, Aug. 22, 1949; m. Haity McNerney, 1987; 3 children. BA in American Studies, Yale U., 1971; MBA, Harvard U., 1975. Brand mgr. Proctor & Gamble, 1975—78; sr. mgr. McKinsey & Co., 1978—82; gen. mgr., GE Mobile Communications GE Co., 1982—86; pres. GE Info. Svcs., Rockville, Md., 1988—89; exec. v.p. GE Fin. Services and Capital, Stamford, Conn., 1989—91; pres., CEO GE Elec. Distribution and Control, Plainville, Conn., 1991—92, GE Lighting, Cleveland, Ohio, 1995—97; pres. GE Asia-Pacific, Hong Kong, 1993—95; pres., CEO GE Aircraft Engines, Cin., 1997—2000; chmn., CEO 3M Co, St. Paul, 2001—05; chmn., pres., CEO The Boeing Co., Chgo., 2005—. Bd. dir. The Boeing Co., 2001—, Proter & Gamble Co.; bd. trustee World Bus. Coun. for Sustainable Develop., Bus. Roundtable, Bus. Coun.; mem. spl. programs com. The Boeing Co. Dir. Greater Twin Cities United Way; bd. trustee Northwestern U. Named one of 25 Most Powerful People in Bus., Fortune Mag., 2007. Fellow: Am. Acad. Arts & Scis. Office: The Boeing Co 100 N Riverside Plz Chicago IL 60606-1596

MCPEEK, BRADLEY, lawyer; b. Cin., Feb. 5, 1973; BA, U. Notre Dame, 1995; JD, U. Cin., 1999. Bar: Ohio 1999, US Dist. Ct. Southern Dist. Ohio 2000. Ptnr. Lindhorst & Dreidame Co., L.P.A., Cin. Named one of Ohio's Rising Stars, Super Lawyers, 2006. Mem.: Ohio State Bar Assn., Cin. Bar Assn. Office: Lindhorst & Dreidame Co LPA 312 Walnut St Ste 2300 Cincinnati OH 45202-4091 Office Phone: 513-421-6630. Office Fax: 513-421-0212.

MCPHEE, MARK STEVEN, gastroenterologist, educator; b. Kansas City, Mo., Nov. 8, 1951; s. William Robert and Mary Kay (Paige) McP.; m. Christina Marie Luebke, July 14, 1974; children: Molly Amanda, Ian Andrew. BA magna cum laude, Pomona Coll., Claremont, Calif., 1973; MD summa cum laude, U. Kans., Kansas City, 1976. Diplomate Nat. Bd. Med. Examiners; diplomate in internal medicine and gastroenterology Am. Bd. Internal Medicine. Intern, resident, fellow Harvard U. Med. Sch., Boston, 1976-80; dir. gastrointestinal endoscopy unit Kans. U. Med. Ctr., Kansas City, 1980-85; chief sect. gastroenterology St. Luke's Hosp., Kansas City, Mo., 1988-93, chair dept. medicine, 1992-97, assoc. dir. med. edn., 1995-97, dir. med. edn., 1997—; assoc. dean U. Mo.-Kansas City Med. Sch., 1997—. Asst. prof. medicine U. Kans., KansasCity, 1980-85, assoc. prof., 1985; clin. prof. medicine U. Mo., Kansas City, 1970-97, prof. medicine, 1997—. Author: Annotated Key References in Gastroenterology, 1982; contbr. chpts. to textbook, articles to profl. jours. Bd. dirs. St. Luke's Hosp., Kansas City,Mo., 1993—, Am. Digestive Health Found., Bethesda, Md., 1996—. Fellow ACP, Am. Coll. Gastroenterology; mem. Am. Gastroent. Assn. (mem. governing bd., treas.), St. Lukes Hosp. Physicians Assn. (bd. dirs.), HealthNet Physician Ptnrs. (bd. dirs.), Alpha Omega Alpha. Episcopalian. Avocations: poetry, hiking/camping, golf, tennis, sporting clay target shooting. Office: St Lukes Hosp Dept Med Edn 44th and Wornall Rd Kansas City MO 64111

MCPHEETERS, F. LYNN, retired manufacturing executive; BS in Acctg., So. Ill. U.; grad., Duke U. Adv. Mgmt. Program, Stanford U. Adv. Fin. Mgmt. Trainee in acctg. Caterpillar, 1964, exec. v.p. fin. svcs. corp., 1990-96, corp. treas., 1996-98, v.p. corp. services div., CFO, 1998—2005. Dir. RLI Corp., Peoria, Ill., 2000—. Office: RELI Corp 9025 N Lindbergh Dr Peoria IL 61615

MCPHERSON, MICHAEL STEVEN, academic administrator, economist; b. June 6, 1947; married; 2 children. BA Math., U. Chgo., 1967, MA Econs., 1970, PhD Econs., 1974. Instr. econs. dept. U. Ill., Chgo., 1971—74; asst. prof. econs. Williams Coll., 1974—81, assoc. prof. econs., 1981—84, prof. econs., 1984—96, chmn. econs. dept., then dean of faculty, 1986—91; pres. Macalester Coll., St. Paul, 1996—2003, Spencer Found., Chgo., 2003—. Cons. Data Resources, Inc., 1979, Nat. Rsch. Coun. Commn. Human Resources, 1979, Modern Lang. Assn., 1980, Nat. Acad. Edn., 1980, Smith Coll., 1982, The Coll. Bd., 1983, Rand Corp., 1985—86, U.S. Dept. Edn. Ctr. Statis., 1986. Co-author (with M.O. Shapiro): Keeping College Affordable: Government and Educational Opportunity, 1991, The Student Aid Game: Meeting Need and Rewarding Talent in American Higher Education, 1998; co-author: (with D. Hausman) Economic Analysis and Moral Philosophy, 1996; editor: The Demand for the New Faculty in Science and Engineering, 1980, Democratic Development and the Art of Trespassing: Essays in Honor of Albert O. Hirschman, 1986; contbr. articles to profl. jours. Trustee Coll. Bd., 1997—. Fellow Study fellow, Am. Coun. Learned Socs., 1977—78, vis. fellow, Princeton U., 1977—78, sr. fellow, Brookings Inst., 1984—86; grantee, Ford Found., 1981—83, Mellon Found., 1984—86. Office: The Spencer Foundation 625 N Michigan Ave Ste 1600 Chicago IL 60611-3109

MCPHERSON, PETER (M. PETER MCPHERSON), publishing executive, educational association administrator; b. Grand Rapids, Mich., Oct. 27, 1940; s. Donald and Ellura E. (Frost) McP.; m. Joanne McPherson; 4 children. BA in Polit. Sci., Mich. State U., 1963; MBA, Western Mich. U., 1967; JD, Am. U., 1969; LLD (hon.), Mich. State U., 1984; LHD (hon.), Va. State U., Mt. St. Mary's Coll., 1996. Tax law specialist IRS, 1969—75; spl. asst. to Pres. Ford, dep. dir. presdl. pers. The White House, Washington, 1975—77; ptnr. Vorys, Sater, Seymour & Pease, Washington, 1977—80; adminstr. AID, 1981—87; dep. sec. US Dept. Treasury, Washington, 1987—89; group exec. v.p. Bank Am., 1989—93; pres. Mich. State U., East Lansing, 1993—2004, pres. emeritus, 2004—; co-chair, founder Partnership to Cut Hunger and Poverty in Africa, 2005—; pres. Nat. Assn. State Univs. and Land-Grant Colls., 2006—; chmn. Dow Jones & Co., NYC, 2007. Chmn. bd. Overseas Pvt. Investment Corp., 1981—87; dir. econ. policy Coalition Provisional Authority, Baghdad, Iraq, 2003. Vol. Peace Corps, Peru, 1964—65; gen. counsel Reagan-Bush Transition, 1980—81. Recipient Humanitarian of Yr. award, Am. Lebanese League, 1983, Jewish Nat. Fund Tree of Life award, 1998, UNICEF award for outstanding contributions to child survival, Disting. Svc. award, US Dept. Treasury, 2004, US Presdl. Certificate of Outstanding Achievement, Sec. State's Disting. Leadership award. Mem. DC Bar Assn., Mich. Bar Assn. Republican. Methodist. Office: 499 South Capitol St SW Ste 500B Washington DC 20003 also: ASULGC 1307 New York Ave NW Ste 400 Washington DC 20005-4722 Home Phone: 703-387-0222. E-mail: pmcpherson@nasulgc.org.

MCQUEEN, PATRICK M., bank executive; BBA, U. Mich., Dearborn; MBA, Mich. State U. Commr. Mich. Fin. Instns. Bur., 1993—; acting commr. Mich. Ins. Bur., 1995; pres., CEO Bank of Bloomfield Hills, Mich., 1999—. Mem.: Conf. State Bank Suprs. (bd. dir., legis. svcs. coun., internat. task force, strategic planning coun.). Avocations: hunting, fishing. Office: Bank of Bloomfield Hills 38505 Woodward Ave Bloomfield Hills MI 48304

MCROBBIE, MICHAEL ALEXANDER, academic administrator, computer scientist, educator; b. Melbourne, Australia, Oct. 11, 1950; s. Alexander Hewitt and Joyce Victoria (Gair) McRobbie; m. Andrea Shirley Gibson, Dec. 22, 1973; children: Josephine Elizabeth Joyce, Lucien Richard Vernon, Arabella Diana Grace. BA with honors I, U. Queensland, 1974; PhD, Australian Nat. U., 1979. Rsch. fellow La Trobe U., Melbourne, 1979-81, U. Melbourne, 1981-83, Australian Nat. U., Canberra, ACT, 1983-87; head Automated Reasoning Project, 1985-91; reader, exec. dir. Ctr. for Info. Sci. Rsch., 1987-90; prof., exec. dir. Ctr. for Info. sci. Rsch., 1990-96; CEO CRC for Advanced Computational Systems, 1992-96; v.p. info. tech., chief info. officer Ind. U., Bloomington, 1997—2006, prof. computer sci., prof. philosophy, prof. computer tech., 1997—, v.p. rsch., 2003—06, interim provost, v.p. academic affairs, 2006—07, pres., 2007—. Vis. prof. U. Kaiserlautern, Germany, 1987; Fulbright sr. fellow Argonne Nat. Lab., 1988. Co-author: (book) Automated Theorem Proving in Non-Classical Logics, 1986; author, co-author, editor: over 100 papers, articles, reports and books. Mem.: IEEE, Assn. Computer Machinery, Assn. Automated Reasoning, Columiba Club (Indpls.), Commonwealth Club (Canberra), Univ. Ho. (Australian Nat. U.). Avocations: art, book collecting, weightlifting, cricket. Office: Office of Pres Ind U 107 S Indiana Ave Bloomington IN 47405 E-mail: vpit@indiana.edu.

MCSWEENEY, MAURICE J. (MARC MCSWEENEY), lawyer; b. Chgo., July 3, 1938; s. Thomas J. and Margaret F. (Ahern) McS.; m. Sandra A. Panosh, Sept. 30, 1967; children: Erin, Sean. BS, DePaul U., 1960; JD, U. Chgo., 1963. Bar: Wis. 1963. With Foley and Lardner, Milw., 1963—, mem. mgmt. com., 1984—93, chmn. litig. dept., 1993—2002, chief diversity ptnr., 2003—. Bd. dirs. Harambee Elem. Sch., 1989-00, Internat. Clown Hall of Fame, 1995-02. Bd. dirs. Milw. Pub. Schs., 1973-79, Milw. chpt. ARC, 1979-85, Alverno Coll., Milw., 1984—, chmn., 2005-, Health Edn. Ctr. of Wis., 1987-96. Fellow Am. Coll. Trial Lawyers; mem. ABA, Wis. Bar Assn., Milw. Bar Assn., Am. Judicature Soc. (bd. dirs. 1988-93), Milw. Area Tech. Coll. Found., Rotary (bd. dirs. Milw. 1986-88). Avocations: skiing, tennis, Karate. Office: Foley & Lardner LLP 777 E Wisconsin Ave Ste 3800 Milwaukee WI 53202-5367 Office Phone: 414-297-5520. Business E-Mail: mmcsweeney@foley.com.

MCSWINEY, CHARLES RONALD, lawyer; b. Nashville, Apr. 23, 1943; s. James W. and Jewell (Bellar) Mc.; m. Jane Detrick McSwiney, Jan. 2, 1970. BA, Kenyon Coll., Gambier, Ohio, 1965; JD, U. Cin., 1968. Assoc. Smith & Schnacke, Dayton, Ohio, 1968-72, ptnr., 1972-89, pres. and mng. ptnr., 1984-89; sr. v.p., gen. counsel The Danis Cos., Dayton, 1989-92, 99-2000; vice chmn. Carillon Capital, Inc., Dayton, 1992-99; dir. devel. Youth Haven, Inc., 2002—. Chmn., CEO Crysteco, Inc., Wilmington, Ohio, 1995-99; pres. interchange exec. Presdl. Commn. on Pers. Interchange, Washington, 1972-73. Chmn., pres. bd. trustees Dayton Ballet Assn., 1985-88; trustee Columbus (Ohio) Symphony Orch., 1981-84; chmn. Dayton Performing Arts Fund, 1989-92, Dayton Devel. Coun., 1987-90, Wright State U. Found., Dayton, 1988-94, Miami Valley Sch., Dayton, 1988-94, Arts Ctr. Found., 1986-2000; mem. bd. advisors Wright State U. Coll. Bus. Adminstrn., 1988-98; bd. vis. U. Cin. Coll. Law, 1987-89; mem. pres.'s coun. Internat. Coll. Recipient Bronze Medal for Performance U.S. EPA, 1973. Mem. Dayton Area C. of C. (trustee 1987-90). Republican. United Ch. Of Christ. Home: 1872 Timarron Way Naples FL 34109 E-mail: ronmcswiney@comcast.net.

MC SWINEY, JAMES WILMER, retired pulp and paper manufacturing company executive; b. McEwen, Tenn., Nov. 13, 1915; s. James S. and Delia (Conroy) McS.; m. Jewel Bellar, 1940; children: Charles Ronald, Margaret Ann. Grad., Harvard Advanced Mgmt. Program, 1954. Lab. technician, shipping clk. Nashville div. The Mead Corp., 1934-39; asst. office mgr. Harriman div., 1939; plant mgr. Rockport, Ind., 1940; asst. office mgr. Kingsport (Tenn.) div.), 1941-44; exec. asst. to pres. Dayton, Ohio, 1954-57; v.p. devel., 1957-59; adminstrv v.p. Harriman div. (Kingsport (Tenn.) div.), 1959; group v.p., gen. mgr. Mead Bd. div., 1961-63, exec. v.p. corp., 1963-67, pres., chief exec. officer, 1968-71, chmn. bd., chief exec. officer, 1971-78, chmn. bd., 1978-82; ret., 1982. Acct., office mgr., asst. sec.-treas. Brunswick Pulp & Paper Co., Ga., 1944-45; bd. dirs. Ultra-Met, Gosiger, Inc., Sea Island Co. Trustee Com. for Econ. Devel. Aviation cadet USAAF, 1942-44. Home: PO Box 30604 401 Ocean Rd Sea Island GA 31561 Home Phone: 912-638-5262; Office Phone: 912-638-5262. E-mail: mcswineyj@bellsouth.net.

MCVISK, WILLIAM KILBURN, lawyer; b. Chgo., Oct. 8, 1953; s. Felix Kilburn and June (DePaur) Visk; m. Marlaine Joyce McDonough, June 20, 1975. BA, U. Ill, 1974; JD, orthwestern U., 1977. Bar: Ill. 1977, Ind. 1999, U.S. Dist. Ct. (no. dist.) Ill. 1977, U.S. Ct. Appeals (7th cir.) 1978, U.S. Dist. Ct. (no. and so. dists.) Ind. 1999, U.S. Ct. Appeals (10th cir.) 2001. Assoc. Jerome H. Torshen, Ltd., Chgo., 1977-80, Silets & Martin, Chgo., 1980-81, Peterson & Ross, Chgo., 1981-85, ptnr., 1985-95, Johnson & Bell Ltd., Chgo., 1995—. Contbr. articles to profl. jours. Mem.: Ill. Assn. Def. Trial Lawyers (chmn. ins. coverage com. 1999—2003), Ill. Assn. Hosp. Attys. (bd. dirs. 1997—2003, pres. 2002), Am. Health Lawyers Assn., Def. Rsch. Inst. Office: Johnson & Bell 33 W Monroe St Ste 2700 Chicago IL 60603-5713 Home Phone: 708-771-5421; Office Phone: 312-984-0229. Business E-Mail: mcviskw@jbltd.com.

MCWEENY, PHILIP, corporate lawyer; BS, Holy Cross Coll., 1961; JD, U. Mich., 1964. Bar: Ohio 1965. Asst. gen. counsel-antitrust Owens-Illinois, Inc., 1980-88, v.p., gen. counsel-corp., asst. sec., 1988—. Office: Owens-Illinois Inc 1 Seagate Toledo OH 43604-1558

MCWHIRTER, BRUCE J., retired lawyer; b. Chgo., Sept. 11, 1931; s. Sydney and Martha McWhirter; m. Judith Hallett, Apr. 14, 1960; children: Cameron, Andrew. BS, orthwestern U., 1952; LLB, Harvard U., 1955. Bar: DC 1955, Ill 1955, US Ct Appeals (7th cir) 1963, US Supreme Ct. Assoc. Lord, Bissell & Brook, Chgo., 1958-62; from assoc. to sr. ptnr. Ross & Hardies, Chgo., 1962-95, of counsel, 1996—2003. Editor: Donnelley SEC Handbook, 1972—87; contbr. articles to profl jours. With US Army, 1955—57. Mem.: ABA, Harvard Law Soc Ill., Chgo. Bar Assn., Harvard Club (N.Y.C.), Lawyers Club Chgo., Phi Beta Kappa. Democrat. Home: 111 Sheridan Rd Winnetka IL 60093-4223 Personal E-mail: jbmcw@aol.com.

MEAD, BEVERLEY TUPPER, physician, educator; b. New Orleans, Jan. 22, 1923; s. Harold Tupper and Helen Edith (Hunt) M.; m. Thelma Ruth Cottingham, June 8, 1947. BS, U. S.C., 1943; MD, Med. Coll. S.C., 1947; MS, U. Utah, 1958. Intern Detroit Receiving Hosp., 1947-48, resident, 1948-51; asst. prof. U. Utah, 1954-61; assoc. prof. U. Ky., 1961-65; prof. psychiatry and behavioral sci. Creighton U. Sch. Medicine, Omaha, 1965—2002, emeritus prof., 2002—, chmn. dept., 1965-77, assoc. dean for acad. and faculty affairs, 1980-88.

MEAD, JOHN STANLEY, university administrator; b. Indpls., Dec. 9, 1953; s. Judson and Jane Mead; m. Virginia Potter, Aug. 11, 1979; children: Christopher, Carolyn. BA, Ind. U., 1976; JD, U. Ill., 1979. Bar: Ill. Staff atty. Ill. Energy Resources Commn., Springfield, 1979-82, staff dir., 1982-85; mgr. coal rsch. Ill. Dept. Energy Natural Resources, Springfield, 1985-87, dir. office of coal devel. and mktg., 1987-89; dir. coal rsch. ctr. So. Ill. U., Carbondale, 1989—, assoc. dean Grad. Sch., 1996—. Bd. dirs. Mid-West Univ. Energy Consortium Inc., Chgo.; mem., past chair Ill. Clean Coal Inst., 1986—. Mem. Ill. Bd. atural Resources and Conservation, 1997—, sec., 2000—; mem. dist. com., scoutmaster Boy Scouts Am. Recipient gold medal Tech. Univ. Ostrava, Czech Republic, 1992, Georgius Agricola medal, 1994. Mem. Am. Radio Relay League, Ill. State Bar Assn., Carbondale Rotary Breakfast (pres. 2000-2001). Lutheran. Home: 78 Magnolia Ln Carbondale IL 62901-7665 Office: So Ill U Coal Rsch Ctr Mail Code 4623 Carbondale IL 62901 E-mail: jmead@siu.edu.

MEAD, PRISCILLA, state legislator; b. Columbus, Ohio, Feb. 7, 1944; m. John L. Mead; children: John, Willian, Neel, Sarah. Student, Ohio State U. Councilwoman, Upper Arlington, Ohio, 1982-90; mayor, 1986-90; mem. Ohio Ho. of Reps. from 28th dist., Columbus, 1992-2000, Ohio Senate from 16th dist., Columbus, 2001—. Mem. Franklin County Child Abuse and Neglect Found., Coun. for Ethics and Econs. Recipient Svc. award Northwest Kiwanis, Woman of Yr. award Upper Arlington Rotary, Citizen of Yr. award U.S. C. of C. Mem. LWV, Upper Arlington Edn. Found., Jr. League Columbus, Upper Arlington C. of C., Delta Gamma. Republican. Home: 2281 Brixton Rd Columbus OH 43221-3117

MEADOR, RON, newspaper editor, writer; b. Buffalo, Nov. 24, 1952; s. Meril E. and Evelyn (Lyons) M.; divorced; 1 child, Benjamin Brian. BA, Ind. U., 1975. Copy editor The Courier-Journal, Louisville, 1975-78, The New York Times, 1978-80; reporter, state editor, city editor, asst. mng. editor Star Tribune, Mpls., Minn., 1980-96, mem. editl. bd., editl. writer, 1996—. Mem. Investigative Reporters and Editors, Inc., Nat. Conf. Editl. Writers, Soc. Environ. Journalists, Insts. for Journalism and Natural Resources (mem. adv. bd.). Office: Star Tribune 425 Portland Ave Minneapolis MN 55488-0002

MEALMAN, GLENN, corporate marketing executive; b. Prescott, Kans., June 10, 1934; s. Edgar R. and Mary E. (Holstein) M.; m. Gloria Gail Proch, June 12, 1955; children: Michael Edward, Cathy Gail. BS in Bus., Kans. State Coll., Emporia, 1957; postgrad., Harvard U., 1970. With Fleming Cos., Topeka, 1957—, sr. v.p. mktg., 1981-82, exec. v.p. mktg., 1982-86, exec. v.p. Mid-Am. region, 1986-93, exec. v.p. nat. accts., 1994-96; mng. ptnr. Bus. Solutions Assocs. Dir. PBI-Gordon Co., Furrs Supermarkets. Pres. bd. Topeka YMCA, 1981; trustee Ottawa U., Kans., 1980. Served with USNR, 1954-56. Mem. Kans. State C. of C. and Industry (bd. dirs. 1991—), Blue Hills Country Club, Gainey Ranch Country Club, Rotary, Sigma Phi Epsilon (Kans. chpt.). Presbyterian. Office: PO Box 7448 Shawnee Mission KS 66207-0448

MEARS, PATRICK EDWARD, lawyer; b. Oct. 3, 1951; s. Edward Patrick and Estelle Veronica (Mislik) M.; m. Geraldine O'Connor, July 18, 1981. BA, U. Mich., 1973, JD, 1976. Bar: N.Y. 1977, Ill. 1996, U.S. Dist Ct. (so. and ea. dists) N.Y. 1977, Mich. 1980, U.S. Dist. Ct. (we. and ea. dists.) Mich. 1980, U.S. Ct. Appeals (6th cir.) 1983, Ill. 1996, U.S. Dist. Ct. (no. dist.) Ill. 1998. Assoc. Milbank, Tweed, Hadley & McCloy, NYC, 1976-79; ptnr. Warner, Norcross & Judd, Grand Rapids, Mich., 1980-91; sr. mem. Dykema Gossett PLLC, Grand Rapids, 1991—2002; equity mem. Dickinson Wright, PLLC, Grand Rapids, 2002—04; equity ptnr. Barnes & Thornburg LLP, 2004—. Adj. prof. Grand Valley State U., Allendale, Mich., 1981-84; dir. Children's Law Ctr., 1994, Grand Rapids Ballet, 1994-99, East Grand Rapids Pub. Sch. Found., 1994-98. Author: Michigan Collection Law, 1981, 2d edit., 1983, Basic Bankruptcy Law, 1986, Bankruptcy Law and Practice in Michigan, 1987, 1995, Revised Article 9 of the UCC in Michigan, 2001; co-author: Strategies for Secured Creditors in workouts and Foreclosures, 2004; contbg. author Collier Bankruptcy Practice Guide; contbr. articles to profl. jours.; editor: Jour. of the Hist. Soc. of the U.S. Dist. Ct. for the Western Dist. of Mich., 2003—. Chmn. legis. com. East Grand Rapids PTA, Mich., 1992—94; bd. dir. Grand Rapids Sister Cities Internat., 2004—06, sec., 2004—06. Fellow: Mich. State Bar Found. (sec. coun. real property sect. 1993—97, chair Uniform Comml. Code com. bus. law sect. 2000—), Am. Coll. Bankruptcy; mem.: ABA (chmn. workouts, bankruptcy and foreclosures 2002—04, vice chair real estate financing group 2004—06, chair real estate financing group 2006—), Fed. Bar Assn. (chmn. bankruptcy sect. We. Mich. chpt. 1992—94, newsletter editor 1998—2002, pres. 2001—02), Am. Law Inst., Am. Bankruptcy Inst., Mich. State Bar Assn., East Hills Athletic Club. Office: Barnes & Thornburg LLP 300 Ottawa Ave NW Ste 500 Grand Rapids MI 49503 Office Phone: 616-742-3936. Business E-Mail: pmears@btlaw.com.

MEASELLE, RICHARD LELAND, accountant; b. Detroit, Sept. 29, 1938; s. Leland Stanford and Jean Therese (Saydak) M; m. Alison Price, Dec. 2, 1995; seven children. BS in Bus., Miami U., Oxford, Ohio, 1961. Office mng. ptnr. Arthur Andersen, Barcelona, 1970-72, Detroit, 1975-87, mng. ptnr. acctg. and audit worldwide, 1987-89, worldwide mng. ptnr., 1989—; mng. ptnr. Andersen Worldwide, Mich., Ohio, Ky. and Wis., 1985-87, ret. 1997; CEO Exante Bank, Minn. Mem., bd. ptnrs., mem. exec. com. Arthur Andersen Worldwide Orgn. Co-author: Helping Public Schools Succeed, 1989. Chmn. bd. trustees U. Detroit, 1985; trustee Detroit Econ. Growth Corp., 1975-87; chmn. United Negro Coll. Fund, Detroit, 1982; hon. Spanish consul to Mich.; mem. vis. com. U. Mich. Sch. Bus. Adminstrn., Tax Found.'s Policy Coun, 1990; mem. com. Chgo. Coun. Fgn. Rels., 1991; mem. Brit. N.Am. Com.; bd. dirs. Field Mus. Natural History. With USMC, 1958-64, Res. Named Hon. Alumnus of Yr. U. Detroit, 1984, Acct. of Yr. Beta Alpha Psi-Miami U., 1989; recipient Pres.'s Cabinet award U. Detroit, 1989. Mem. AICPA, The Econ. Club of N.Y. Avocations: skiing, tennis. Office: Exant Bank 9900 Bren Rd E Hopkins MN 55343

MECHEM, CHARLES STANLEY, JR., retired broadcast executive; b. Nelsonville, Ohio, Sept. 12, 1930; s. Charles Stanley and Helen (Hall) Mechem; m. Marilyn Brown, Aug. 31, 1952; children: Melissa, Daniel, Allison. AB, Miami U., Oxford, Ohio, 1952; LLB, Yale U., New Haven, Conn., 1955. Bar: Ohio 1955. Practice in Cin., 1955—67; ptnr. Taft, Stettinius & Hollister, 1965—67; chmn. bd. Taft Broadcasting Co., Cin., 1967—90; commr. LPGA, Daytona Beach, Fla., 1990—95, commr. emeritus, 1995—; chmn. U.S. Shoe, 1993—95; chmn. Cin. Bell, Inc., 1996—98, Convergys Corp., 1998—2000; cons. Arnold Palmer Enterprises, Cin., 1996—. Bd. dirs. Messer Constrn., Inc. Capt. JAGC US Army, 1956—59. Mem.: Cin. C. of C. (pres. 1977), Comml. Club. Office: Taft Stettinius & Hollister LLP 425 Walnut St Ste 1800 Cincinnati OH 45202-4122

MECKLENBURG, GARY ALAN, retired hospital administrator; b. June 17, 1946; m. Lynn Kraemer; children: John, Sarah. BA, Northwestern U., 1968; MBA, U. Chgo., 1970. Adminstrv. resident Presbyn.-St. Luke's Hosp., Chgo., 1969-70, adminstrv. asst., 1970-71, asst. supt., 1971-76, assoc. supt., 1976-77, U. Wis. Hosps., Madison, 1977-80; adminstr. Stanford U. Hosp. Clinics, Calif.; pres., CEO St. Joseph's Hosp., Milw., 1980-85; pres. Franciscan Health Care Inc., Milw., 1985; pres., CEO Northwestern Meml. Hosp., Chgo., 1985—2001, Northwestern Meml. HealthCare, Chgo., 2001—06. Preceptor, guest lectr., mem. adv. bd. Kellogg Sch. Mgmt., Chgo., 1986—; pres., CEO, Northwestern Healthcare Network, 1990-92. Recipient Todd Scout award Boy Scouts Am., 1998, Chgo. Bus. Hall of Fame award Jr. Achievement, 2000, GSB Disting. Pub. Svc./Pub. Sector Alumnus award U. Chgo., 2000. Mem. Am. Hosp. Assn. (sect. met. hosps., governing coun. 1984-92, chmn. 1991, 2001, trustee 1996-2002, exec. com. 1997-2002, chmn., 2001, mem. regional policy bd., #5 1984, 87-89, 91-93, 95-99, chmn. 1996-99, 2001, mem. ho. dels. 1984, 87-89, 91—, mem. com. on med. edn. 1976-80), Ill. Hosp. Assn. (bd. dirs. 1988-95, chmn. 1994, mem. adv. panel coun. tchg. hosps. 1997—), U. Chgo. Hosp. Adminstrn. Alumni Assn. (pres. 1985-86), Econ. Club Chgo., Comml. Club Chgo.

MEDH, JHEEM D., medical educator, biochemist, researcher; BS in Chemistry and Biochemistry, U. Bombay, India, 1982; MS in Biochemistry, U. Bombay, 1984; PhD in Biochemistry, U. Tex. Med. Br., Galveston, 1990. Jr. rsch. fellow, dept. physiology L.T.M. Med. Coll., Bombay, 1984-86; rsch. asst., dept. human biol. chemistry and genetics U. Tex. Med. Br., 1986-90; postgrad. rsch. biochemist, dept. medicine U. Calif., San Diego, 1991-93; asst. rsch. scientist, adj. asst. prof., dept. medicine U. Iowa Coll. Medicine, Iowa City, 1993—. Presenter in field of role of LDL receptor-related protein, receptor-associated protein and lipoprotein lipase on the regulation of lipoprotein metabolism. Juvenile Diabetes Internat. Found. fellow 1992-93; recipient nat. grand-in-aid award Am. Heart Assn., 1995-98; recipient Gip Hudson award Nat. Student Rsch. Forum, 1989, Stephen C. Silverthorne award Grad. Sch. Biomed. Scis., U. Tex. Med. Br. Mem. Am. Heart Assn. (coun. for basic science), Am. Soc. Cell Biology, Juvenile Diabetes Found. Internat. Office: U Iowa Coll Med 200 CMAB Iowa City IA 52242

MEDLER, MARY ANN L., federal judge; JD, St. Louis U., 1983. Atty. Thompson Coburn, St. Louis, 1983-85; asst. cir. atty. Office of Cir. Atty. of City of St. Louis, 1985-92; atty. Union Pacific R.R., St. Louis, 1992-93; magistrate judge U.S. Dist. Ct. (ea. dist.) Mo., St. Louis. Office: 111 S 10th St Rm 13S Saint Louis MO 63102 Office Phone: 314-244-7490. Business E-Mail: Mary_Ann_Medler@moed.uscourts.gov.

MEDNICK, ROBERT, accountant; b. Chgo., Apr. 1, 1940; s. Harry and Nettie (Brenner) Mednick; m. Susan Lee Levinson, Oct. 28, 1962; children: Michael Jon, Julie Eden, Adam Charles. BSBA, Roosevelt U., Chgo., 1962. CPA Ill. Staff asst. Arthur Andersen, Chgo., 1962-63, sr. acct., 1963-66, mgr., 1966-71, ptnr., 1971-98, mng. dir. SEC policies, 1973-76, mng. dir. auditing procedures, 1976-79. Vice chmn. com. on profl. stds. Andersen Worldwide, 1979-82, chmn. com., 1982-98, mng. ptnr. profl. and regulatory matters, 1993-98; mem. faculty Northwestern U. Kellogg Grad. Sch. Mgmt., 1999; mem. panel disting. neutrals in banking, acctg. and fin. svcs. Internat. Inst. for Conflict Prevention and Resolution, 2003—. Contbr. articles to profl. jours. Bd. dirs. Roosevelt U., Chgo., 1977—, vice chmn., 1986-94, sr. vice chmn., 1994—, life trustee, 1999—; bd. dirs. Auditorium Theatre Coun., 1990-96, Lake Shore Drive Synagogue, 1992—; co-chmn. adv. coun. Chgo. Action for Soviet Jewry, Highland Park, Ill., 1983-87; bd. dirs., mem. exec. com. Am. Judicature Soc., 1990-95, vice chmn., 1993-95; bd. overseers Rand Corp. Inst. Civil Justice, 1994-98; bd. dirs. Nat. Bur. of Econ. Rsch., 1998—, treas., 1999—; acccountability adv. coun. to the Comptr. Gen. of the U.S., 2000—. Sgt. USAFR, 1965-69. Recipient Silver medal Ill. CPA Soc., 1962; named One of Ten Outstanding Young Men in Chgo., Chgo. Jr. C. of C., 1973-74; recipient Rolf A. Weil Disting. Service award, Roosevelt U., Chgo., 1983; Max Block award N.Y. State C.P.A. Soc., 1984; Ann. Literary award Jour. Accountancy, 1986, 88; Andrew D. Bradin award for distinctive contbns. to discipline of accountancy Case Western Res. U., Cleve., 1996; Disting. Alumni award Roosevelt U. Walter E. Heller Coll. Bus. Adminstrn., 1997; Disting. Vis. scholar Hebrew U., Jerusalem, 1999, 2000, Coll. Mgmt., Rishon Litzion, 2003, 05, 06, 07, hon. fellow, 2005. Mem. AICPA (bd. dirs. 1986-87, 92-94, 95-98, vice chmn. 1995-96, chmn. 1996-97, numerous coms., Elijah Watt Sells award 1962, Gold Medal for Disting. Svc. 1998), Ill. CPA Soc. (acctg. prins. com. 1973, legal liability com. 1986-89, mgmt. of acctg. practice com. 1991-94, regulation and legis. com. 1998—), Internat. Fedn. Accts. (chmn. compliance adv. panel 2003—). Jewish. Avocations: collecting art, travel. Home Phone: 312-642-4326; Office Phone: 312-642-0571. E-mail: bobmednick@aol.com.

MEDVED, PAUL STANLEY, lawyer; b. Milw., May 6, 1956; s. Frank F. and Evelyn F. (Poplawski) M.; m. Danita C. Cole, Aug. 27, 1988. BA with honors, Marquette U., 1978; JD, Columbia U., 1981. Bar: Wis. 1981, U.S. Dist. Ct. (ea. dist.) Wis. 1981, U.S. Dist. Ct. (we. dist.) Wis. 1984, U.S. Ct. Appeals (7th cir.) 1984. Assoc. Michael, Best & Friedrich, Milw., 1981-88, ptnr., 1988-97; shareholder Mallery & Zimmerman, S.C., Milw., 1997—. Office: Mallery & Zimmerman SC 731 Jackson St Ste 900 Milwaukee WI 53202-4697 E-mail: pmedved@mzmilw.com.

MEDVIN, HARVEY NORMAN, retired diversified financial services company executive; b. Chgo., Sept. 6, 1936; s. Benjamin and Clara (Edelstein) Medvin; m. Sheila S. Spitzner, July 5, 1965; children: Arla Risa, Steven Merrill. BS in Acctg., U. Ill., 1958. CPA Ill. Mem. audit staff Coopers & Lybrand, 1958-63; treas., v.p. The Martin Brower Co., Des Plaines, Ill., 1963-73; outside dir. Ryan Ins. Group, Inc. (now Aon Corp.), Chgo., 1972—73, exec. officer, 1973—82; exec. v.p., CFO, treas. Aon Corp., Chgo., 1987—2003, also bd. dirs. all subs.; ret., 2003. Bd. dir. Schwarz Paper Co., Morton Grove, Ill., La Salle Bank Corp., La Salle Nat. Bank, Chgo., Oshkosh Truck Corp., 2004—. Bd. dir. Highland Park Hosp., Ill.; bd. gov. Chgo. Lighthouse for Blind; trustee Ravina Festival Highland Park, Ill. With US Army, 1958—59. Mem.: AICPA. Office: Aon Corp 200 E Randolph St Chicago IL 60601

MEEK, VIOLET IMHOF, retired dean; b. Geneva, Ill., June 12, 1939; d. John and Violet (Krepel) Imhof; m. Devon W. Meek, Aug. 21, 1965 (dec. 1988); children: Brian, Karen; m. Don M. Dell, Jan. 4, 1992. BA summa cum laude, St. Olaf Coll., 1960; MS, U. Ill., 1962, PhD in Chemistry, 1964. Instr. chemistry Mount Holyoke Coll., South Hadley, Mass., 1964-65; asst. prof. to prof. Ohio Wesleyan U., Delaware, Ohio, 1965-84, dean for ednl. svcs., 1980-84; dir. annual programs Coun. Ind. Colls., Washington, 1984-86; assoc. dir. sponsored programs devel. Rsch. Found. Ohio State U., Columbus, 1986-91, dean, dir. Lima, 1992—2003; ret., 2003. Vis. dean U. Calif., Berkeley, 1982, Stanford U., Palo Alto, Calif., 1982, reviewer GTE Sci. and Tech. Program, Princeton, N.J., 1986-92, Goldwater Nat. Fellowships, Princeton, 1990-98. Co-author: Experimental General Chemistry, 1984; contbr. articles to profl. jours. Bd. dirs. Luth. Campus Ministries, Columbus, 1988-91, Luth. Social Svcs., 1988-91, Americom Bank, Lima, 1992-98, Art Space, Lima, 1993—, Allen Lima Leadership, 1993—, Am. House, 1992—, Lima Vets. Meml. Civic Ctr. Found., 1992—; chmn. synodical coms. Evang. Luth. Ch. Am., Columbus, 1982; bd. trustees Trinity Luth. Sem., Columbus, 1996—; chmn. Allen County C. of C., 1995—, chair bd. dirs., 1999; bd. dirs. Lima Syphony Orch., 1993—, pres. bd. dirs., 1997— Recipient Woodrow Wilson Fellowship, 1960. Mem.: Am. Assn. Higher Edn., Nat. Coun. Rsch. Adminstrs. (named Outstanding New Profl. midwest region 1990), Phi Beta Kappa. Avocations: music, skiing, woodworking, civil war history, travel. Home: 209 W Beechwold Blvd Columbus OH 43214-2012 Office: Ohio State Lima 8521 Libra Rd Dublin OH 43016-9022

MEEKS, ROBERT L., state legislator; b. Ft. Wayne, Ind., Feb. 3, 1934; m. Carol Meeks; children: Denise Schrock, Kevin, Layne, Kent. Mem. Ind. Senate from 13th dist., 1988—; sen. finance, nat. resources, local govt. issues coms.; chair budget sub-com. Past trustee Lakeland Sch. Bd. Recipient Maddox award FOP Life Savers Club, Allen County. Mem. Am. Legion, C. of C., Masons (Shriner). Home: 5840 E 025 N Lagrange IN 46761-9519

MEERS, BILL M., news executive; News bur. chief Met. Network News, 1999—. Office: Metro Networks 2120 County Road C W Saint Paul MN 55113-2501

MEERSCHAERT, JOSEPH RICHARD, retired physician; b. Detroit, Mar. 4, 1941; s. Hector Achiel and Marie Terese (Campbell) M.; m. Jeanette Marie Ancerewicz, Sept. 14, 1963; children: Eric, Amy, Adam. BA, Wayne State U., 1965, MD, 1967. Diplomate Am. Bd. Phys. Medicine and Rehab., Am. Bd. Pain Medicine. Intern Harper Hosp., Detroit, 1967-68; resident in phys. medicine and rehab. Wayne State U. Rehab. Inst., Detroit, 1968-71; chief divsn. phys. medicine Naval Hosp., Chelsea, Mass., 1971-73; attending physician William Beaumont Hosp., Royal Oak, Mich., 1973—2006, med. dir. rehab. unit, 1979-87; pvt. practice medicine specializing in phys. medicine and rehab. Royal Oak, 1973—2006; pvt. practice specializing in pain medicine, 1990—2006; ret., 2006. Mem. med. adv. bd. at. Wheelchair Athletic Assn., 1973—, U.S. team physician VII World Wheelchair Games, Stoke Mandeville, Eng.; clin. instr. Wayne State U., 1973-83, clin. asst. prof. phys. medicine and rehab., 1983—; mem. Mich. Dept. Licensing and Regulation State Bd. Phys. Therapy, 1978-81. Contbr. articles to profl. jours. With M.C. USN, 1971-73. Recipient John Hussey award Mich. Wheelchair Athletic Assn., 1981. Fellow Am. Coll. Pain Medicine; mem. Am. Acad. Phys. Medicine and Rehab. (reviewer, presenter) Am. Congress Rehab. Medicine, Mich. Phys. Medicine and Rehab. Soc., Am. Geriatrics Soc., Am. Assn. Electromyography and Electrodiagnosis, Mich. Rheumatism Soc., Mich. Acad. Phys. Medicine and REhab. (pres. 1986-87, chmn. program com. 1977-78, trustee 1980—, pres. bd. dirs. 1994-97), Oakland County Med. Soc. (bd. dirs. 1991, 97), Alpha Omega Alpha. Roman Catholic.

MEHLER, BARRY ALAN, humanities educator, journalist, consultant; b. Bklyn., Mar. 18, 1947; s. Harry and Esther Mehler; m. Jennifer Sue Leghorn, June 2, 1982; 1 child, Isaac Alan. BA, Yeshiva U., 1970; MA, CCNY, 1972; PhD, U. Ill., 1988. Rsch. assoc. Washington U., St. Louis, 1976-80, instr. history, 1977; NIMH trainee racism program U. Ill., Champaign, 1981-85, rsch. asst. IBM EXCEL project, 1986-88; asst. prof. humanities Ferris State U., Big Rapids, Mich., 1988-93, assoc. prof., 1993-99, prof., 1999—. Media cons. Scientist's Inst. for Pub. Info., NYC, 1980-98; cons. Calif. Humanities Coun., 1995, ZDF/arte (Zweite Deutsches Fernshen--German pub. TV), 1995, House Subcom. on Consumer Protection, 1994, McIntosh Commn. for Fair Play in Student-Athlete Admissions, 1994, Can. Broadcast Svc., Toronto, Ont., 1995-96, Am. Civil Liberties Union, Nat. Human Genome Rsch. Inst.; judge Women's Caucus Awards for Excellence, St. Louis, 1989-91, 93; dir. Inst. for Study of Acad. Racism, 1993—; mem. Pres.'s. Initiative on Race, 1998, One Am. initiative, named Promising Practices; presenter Performance Art in the Classroom, Minority Equity Conf. XI, 2001. Contbg. editor: Encyclopedia of Genocide, 1997; contbr. over 100 articles to profl. jours. Co-founder, sec.-treas. People Organized to Stop Rape of Imprisoned Persons, 1980; adv. bd. Stop Prison Rape, 2001, Immediate Family, Inc., 2003; advisor to project dir. Homeless Outreach Project and Evaluation, 2003; founder, bd. dirs. Internat. Com. to Free Russell Smith, 1977—80; co-founder Gay Peoples Alliance, St. Louis, 1978; exec. bd. Ferris Faculty Assn. Recipient cert. of recognition Ferris State Bd. of Control, 1994, Hesburgh award TIAA-CREFF and Am. Coun. on Edn., 2000; NSF rsch. fellow, 1976-80, Babcock fellow U. Ill., 1985-86; grantee Rockefeller Found., 1977, Office of Minority Affairs, Lansing, Mich., 1994-97. Mem. NAACP, B'nai B'rith (Anti-Defamation League. Jewish. Avocations: hiking, camping. Home: 216 Rust Ave Big Rapids MI 49307-1726 Office: Ferris State U 901 S State St Big Rapids MI 49307-2295 Business E-Mail: mehlerb@ferris.edu.

MEHLMAN, DAVID JOEL, cardiologist, educator; b. Chgo., 1948; AB, Princeton U., 1969; MD, Johns Hopkins U., 1973. Diplomate Am. Bd. Internal Medicine, Am. Bd. Cariology, Nat. Bd. Echocardiography with subspecialty in adult comprehensive echocardiography. Intern Johns Hopkins Hosp., Balt., 1973-74, resident in medicine, 1974-76; fellow cardiology U. Chgo. Hosps., 1976-78; asst. prof. medicine U. Chgo. Med. Sch., 1978-80, Northwestern U. Med. Sch., Chgo., 1980-86, assoc. prof. medicine, 1986—; dir. adult cardiovasc. disease tng. program McGaw Med. Ctr. Northwestern U., Chgo., 1988-95, assoc. dir., 1995—98. Assoc. dir. echocardiography lab. Northwestern Meml. Hosp., Chgo., 1980-95, co-dir. echocardiography lab., 1995— Fellow Am. Coll. Cardiology, ACP, AHA, Am. Soc. Echocardiography. Office: Northwestern U Med Sch Galter 8-203A 251 E Huron Chicago IL 60611-2914

MEHLMAN, MARK FRANKLIN, lawyer; b. LA, Dec. 18, 1947; s. Jack and Elaine Pearl (Lopater) M.; m. Barbara Ann Novak, Aug. 20, 1972; children: David, Jennifer, Ilyse. BA, U. Ill., 1969; LLB, U. Mich., 1973. Bar: Ill. 1973; U.S. Dist. Ct. (no. dist.) Ill. 1973. Assoc. Sonnenschein, Nath & Rosenthal LLP, Chgo., 1973—80, mem. policy and planning com., 1989—2006. Trustee Groveland Health Svcs., Highland Park (Ill.) Hosp., 1991-97; trustee, treas., exec. com. Spertus Inst. Jewish Studies, Chgo., 1992-97, vice chmn. bd. trustees, 1996—; vice-chmn. regional bd. Anti-Defamation League, 1987-89, hon. life mem. nat. commn., 1993—. Fellow Am. Bar Found.; mem. ABA (chmn. mortgages and other debt financing subcom. 1991-95, supervisory coun. 1997-2000, sec. RPPT sect. 2004-05), Am. Coll. Real Estate Lawyers (exec. com. bd. govs. 2000—, sec. 2003-04, treas. 2004-05, v.p. 2005-06, pres.-elect 2006—, chmn. MDP com. 2000—, chmn. mem. selection com. 2000-01), Anglo-Am. Real Property Inst., Legal Club of Chgo., Lake Shore Country Club, Standard Club, Exec. Club of Chgo. Office: Sonnenschein Nath & Rosenthal LLP Ste 7800 233 S Wacker Dr Chicago IL 60606-6491 Office Phone: 312-876-8023. Business E-Mail: mmehlman@sonnenschein.com.

MEHLMAN, MAXWELL JONATHAN, law educator; b. Washington, Nov. 4, 1948; s. Jacob and Betty (Hoffman) M.; m. Cheryl A. Stone, Sept. 15, 1979; children: Aurora, Gabriel. BA, Reed Coll., 1970, Oxford U., England, 1972; JD, Yale U., 1975. Bar: D.C. 1976, Ohio 1988. Assoc. Arnold & Porter, Washington, 1975-84; asst. prof. Case Western Res. U., Cleve., 1984-87, dir. Law-Medicine Ctr., 1986—, assoc. prof., 1987-90, prof. law, 1990-96, Arthur E. Petersilge prof., 1996—, prof. biomed. ethics, 1998—. Spl. counsel N.Y. State Bar, N.Y.C., 1988-94, Nat. Kidney Found., 1991; cons. Am. Assn. Ret. Persons, Washington, 1992. Editor: High Tech Home Care, 1991, (with T. Murray) Encyclopedia of Ethical, Legal and Policy Issues in Biotechnology; author: (with J. Botkin) Access to the Genome: The Challenge to Equality, 1998, (with Andrews and Rothstein) Genetics: Ethics, Law and Policy, 2002, 06, Wondergenes: Genetic Enhancement and the Future of Society, 2003; contbr. articles to profl. jours. Active steering com. AIDS Commn. Greater Cleve., 1986-90. Rhodes scholar, 1970; Rsch. grantee IH, 1992-94, 97—. Mem. Am. Assn. Law Schs. (chmn. sect. on law, medicine and health care 1990), Phi Beta Kappa. Avocations: skiing, music, kayaking. Office: Case Western Reserve U Sch Law-Law Medicine Ctr Gund Hall 11075 E Blvd Cleveland OH 44106 Office Phone: 216-368-3983. Business E-Mail: mjm10@case.edu.

MEHRBERG, RANDALL ERIC, lawyer, utilities executive; b. Bklyn., Dec. 29, 1955; s. Julius and June (Shapiro) M.; m. Michele Schara, Oct. 20, 1984; children: Dillon, Sam, Eric. BS magna cum laude in Econs., U. Pa., 1977; JD, U. Mich., 1980. Bar: Ill. 1980, US Dist. Ct. (no. dist. Ill.) 1980, US Ct. Appeals (7th cir.) 1981, US Supreme Ct. 1987. With Jenner & Block, Chgo., 1980—93, equity ptnr., 1997—2000; gen. counsel, lakefront dir. Chgo. Pk. Dist., 1993—97; sr. v.p., gen. counsel Exelon Corp., Chgo., 2000—02, exec. v.p., gen. counsel, 2002—, chief adminstrv. officer, chief legal officer. Asst. sec. Chgo. Pacific Corp., 1984—85; bd. mem. Nuc. Electric Ins. Ltd. V.p. bd. dirs. Gus Giordano Jazzdance Chgo. Recipient Hope for the People award, HOPE Fair Housing, Ill., 1982, commendation for work for the poor, Cath. Charities, 1986, award for def. of civil liberties, ACLU, 1987, Mex. Am. Legal Def. and Edn. Fund Legal Svcs. award, 2001. Mem. ABA, Chgo. Bar Assn. (exec. com. young lawyers sect. 1988-89, David C. Hilliard award), Chgo. Counsel Lawyers, Law Club Chgo. Avocations: tennis, skiing, hockey. Office: Exelon Corp 10 S Dearborn St 37th Fl PO Box 805398 Chicago IL 60680-5398 Office Phone: 800-483-3220.

MEIER, ARLENE, retail executive; BS, U. No. Iowa, 1974. Various acctg. and fin. planning positions Target Stores; v.p. controller Kohl's Corp., Menomonee Falls, Wis., 1989—94, CFO, 1994—2000, COO, 2000—, bd. dir., 2000—. Office: Kohls Corp N56 W 17000 Ridgewood Dr Menomonee Falls WI 53051 Office Phone: 262-703-1646.

MEIER, JOHN F., consumer products company executive; With Libbey Inc., Toledo, 1970-90, gen. mgr., 1990-93, CEO, 1993—, also chmn. bd. dirs.; pres. Owens-Ill., Inc., 1990. Bd. dirs. Tire & Rubber Co. Office: Libbey Inc 300 Madison Ave Fl 4 Toledo OH 43604-2634

MEIER, LISA M., lawyer; b. Springfield, Vt., Aug. 22, 1977; BA in Hist. and Russian Lang. and Lit., Smith Coll., 1999; JD, William Mitchell Coll. Law, 2002. Bar: Minn. 2002. Children's prog. intern Minn. Advocates for Human Rights, Mpls., 2000; devel. asst. Office of Instl. Advancement William Mitchell Coll. Law, St. Paul, 2000; law clk. Honsa & Michales, P.A., Mpls., 2001—02, atty., 2002—. Named a Rising Star, Minn. Super Lawyers mag., 2006. Mem.: Dakota County Bar Assn., ABA, Minn. State Bar Assn. (mem. family law sect.), Ramsey County Bar Assn. (mem. family law sect.), Hennepin County Bar Assn. (mem. family law sect., sec. family law exec. com.). Avocations: reading, hiking, walking. Office: Anne M Honsa 5500 Wayzata Blvd Ste 1075 Minneapolis MN 55416 Office Phone: 763-797-9855.

MEIERHENRY, JUDITH KNITTEL, state supreme court justice; b. Burke, SD, Jan. 20, 1944; m. Mark Vernon Meierhenry, May 14, 1961; children: Todd, Mary. BA in English, U. S.D., 1966, MA, 1968, JD, 1977. Bar: S.D. 1977. H.S. tchr. English Plattsmouth (Nebr.) Pub. Schs., 1966-67; instr. U. SD, 1968-70, Hiram Scott Coll., Scottbluff, Nebr., 1970; tchr. Todd County Pub. Schs., Mission, SD, 1971-74; ptnr. Meierhenry, DeVaney, Krueger & Meierhenry, Vermillion, SD, 1977-79; cabinet sec. SD Dept. Labor, Pierre, 1980-84; sr. mgr., asst. gen. counsel Citibank SD, 1985-88; cabinet sec. edn. and cultural affairs State SD, 1983-84, cir. ct. judge, 1988—2002; justice SD Supreme Ct., 2002—. Mem.: Nat. Assn. Women Judges, SD Bar Assn. Office: SD Supreme Ct 500 E Capital Ave Pierre SD 57501

MEIJER, DOUGLAS, retail company executive; b. 1954; With Meijer Inc., 1967—, co-chmn., 1990—. Office: Meijer Inc 2929 Walker Ave NW Grand Rapids MI 49544-9428

MEIJER, HANK, retail company executive; b. 1952; BA, U. Michigan, 1973. Asst. advt. dir. Meijer, Grand Rapids, Mich., mktg. dir., vice chmn. bd. dirs., co-chmn. bd. dirs., 1990—, CEO, 2002—05, co-CEO, 2005—. Office: 2929 Walker Ave NW Grand Rapids MI 49544

MEIJER, MARK, retail executive; With Bud's Ambulance Svc., Grand Rapids, Mich., 1977-79; pres. Life EMS Inc., Grand Rapids, Mich., 1979—; bd. dirs. Meijer Cos. Ltd., Grand Rapids, Mich. Office: Meijer Companies LTD 2929 Walker Ave NW Grand Rapids MI 49544-9428

MEINERT, JOHN RAYMOND, apparel executive, investment banker; b. White Cloud, Mich., Aug. 11, 1927; m. Joyce Macdonell, Nov. 5, 1955; children: Elizabeth Tinsman, Pamela Martin. Student, U. Mich., 1944-45; BS, Northwestern U., 1949. CPA Ill., 1952. With Hart Schaffner & Marx/Hartmarx Corp., Chgo., 1950-90, exec. v.p., 1975-80, vice chmn., 1981-85, sr. vice chmn., 1985-86, chmn., 1987-90, chmn. emeritus, 1990—, also bd. dirs.; prin. investment banking J.H. Chapman Group, LLC, Rosemont, Ill., 1990—, chmn., 1995—. Bd. dirs. County Seat Stores, Inc., N.Y.C., 1998-99, The John Evans Club, BBB, Chgo. C.of C.; trustee Amalgamated Ins. Fund, 1980-90, Rotary Internat. Retirement Fund, 2000-02; dir. Evanston Hosp., 1988-94, Clothing Mfrs. Assn., pres., 1982-87, chmn. 1987-90; instr. acctg. Northwestern U., 1949; faculty Lake Forest Grad. Sch. Mgmt., 1994-95; arbitrator Am. Arbitration Assn., 1993—. Chmn. bus. adv. coun. U. Ill., 1989-90; mem. Fin. Acctg. Stds. Adv. Coun., 1989-92, Chgo. Coun. Fgn. Rels., Sisters City Com.; mem. adv. coun. Northwestern U. Kellogg Grad. Sch. Recipient Alumni Merit award Northwestern U. Kellogg Grad. Sch., 1989; named Humanitarian of Yr., Five Hosp. Found., 1995. Mem. AICPA (v.p. 1985-86, bd. dirs. 1975-78, coun. 1971-93, trustee benevolent fund 1992-95, gold medal 1987), Ill. CPA Soc. (pub. svc. award 1996, pres. 1982-83, bd. dirs. 1966-68, 81-84, hon. award), Chicagoland C. of C. (bd. dirs.), Rotary (pres. Chgo. 1989-90, trustee found. 1991-95, asst. dist. gov. 1997-2000), Univ. Club, Execs. Club, Rolling Green Country Club. Presbyterian (elder). Home: 634 N Ironwood Dr Arlington Heights IL 60004-5818 Office: J H Chapman Group LLC 9700 W Higgins Rd Rosemont IL 60018-4796 Office Phone: 773-693-4800. Business E-Mail: jmeinert@jhchapman.com.

MEISEL, DAN, chemist; b. Tel Aviv, July 4, 1943; s. Arie and Mariasha Miriam (Ribak) M.; m. Osnat Meisel, Dec. 30, 1965; children: Einat, Omer. BSc, Hebrew U., 1967, MSc, 1969, PhD, 1974. Prof. chemistry U. Notre Dame, Ind., 1998—, dir. Radiation Lab. Ind., 1998—2004. Adv. bd.: Jour. Phys. Chem., 1993—2002; editor: Photochem. Energy Conversion, 1989, Semiconductors Nanoclusters, 1997. Mem. AAAS, Am. Chem. Soc., Am. Phys. Soc. Office: U Notre Dame Radiation Lab Notre Dame IN 46556 Office Phone: 574-631-5457. Business E-Mail: dani@nd.edu.

MEISEL, GEORGE VINCENT, lawyer; b. St. Louis, Sept. 24, 1933; s. Leo Otto and Margaret (Duggan) M.; m. Joy C. Cassin, May 18, 1963 BS summa cum laude, St. Louis U., 1956, JD cum laude, 1958. Bar: Mo. 1958. Assoc. Grand Peper & Martin, St. Louis, 1961-64, ptnr., 1965; jr. ptnr. Bryan Cave McPheeters & McRoberts, St. Louis, 1966-69; ptnr. Bryan Cave, LLP, St. Louis, 1970-2000, of counsel, 2000—. Served to 1st lt. USAF, 1958-61 Mem. ABA, Bar Assn. Met. St. Louis, Mo. Bar Assn. Clubs: Saint Louis, Mo. Athletic (St. Louis). Roman Catholic. Home: 2029 S Warson Rd Saint Louis MO 63124-1151 Office Phone: 314-259-2268. Business E-Mail: gvmeisel@bryancavellp.com.

MEISNER, GARY WAYNE, landscape architect; b. Terre Haute, Ind., Oct. 19, 1949; s. Ervin Gustav and Mary Lou (Marett) M.; children: Christopher Wayne, Kira Valora. BS in Landscape Architecture, Mich. State U., 1972. Lic. landscape architect, Ohio, Mich., Ind., Ill., Ky., W.Va. Designer Huron Clinton Metro Parks, Detroit, 1969, City of East Lansing, Mich., 1970, Fairfax County Park Authority, Annandale, Va., 1971; city design adminstr. Akron (Ohio) Dept. Planning and Urban Devel., 1972-79; prin. Bentley Meisner Assocs., Inc, Cin., 1979-94, Myers, Schmalenberger, Meisner Inc., Cin. and Columbus, Ohio, 1994-99, Meisner & Assocs., Cincinnati, 1999—. Designer Akron Downtown Plan, 1978, King Sch. Plan, 1980 (honor award 1982), master plan Toyota Regional Office, 1983 (honor award 1987), Falls at Cumberland Hill, 1987 (honor award 1989), Cin. Mus. Ctr., 1990 (honor award 1990), Walk Across Am. Garden, 1990 (honor award 1991), Dayton Nat. Cemetery, 1993 (honor award 1994), Piatt Park on Garfield Place, 1990 (honor award OPWA grand award 1992), Dayton Plaza of Flight (honor award 1995), Taylor Park Historic Riverwalk, 1995 (Ky. Gov.'s award 1996), Walnut Hills H.S. Master Plan (honor award 1999), Evermont County Land Use Vision Plan (AIA award 2000), Union

Ky. Town Plan (Honor award 2002), Hillside Trust-Cin. Viewshed Analysis Model (AIA award 2002), Flint Union Cemetery Master Plan (award 2003), Amreley Village Ohio CHCC Evaluation (award 2004), Ea. Corridor Cin. Land Use Vision Plan (award 2004), Ohio Gov.'s Residence Master Plan (AIA award 2004). Trustee Cin. Hillside Trust, 1987—, Capitol Square Renovation Found., Columbus, Ohio, 1987—93, Cin. Sculpture Coun., 1989—94, Hubbard Ednl. Trust, 1988—, Ohio Gov.'s Residence Commn., 2000—; bd. dirs. Arch. Found. Cin., 2005—. Recipient gov.'s commendation State of Ohio, 1985, Ohio Arts Coun. fellow, 1992-93, Apple award Architecture Found. of Cin., 1995. Fellow Am. Soc. Landscape Architects (nat. trustee 1982-89, chmn. nat. cmty. assistance team program 1983-86, chmn. editorial bd. Garden Design mag. 1986-90, mem. nat. publs. bd. 1988-92, 96-98, Nat. Com. Assistance Team commendation 1986, Trustee commendation 1989, Ohio Gov.'s commendation 2005); mem. Am. Soc. Botanic Garden and Arboretum, Urban Land Inst., Am. Underground Space Assn, Scenic Ohio (treas. 1985—). Mem. Unity Ch. Home: 4137 Jora Ln Cincinnati OH 45209-1406 Office: Meisner & Assocs 2043 Madison Rd Cincinnati OH 45208-3218

MEISSNER, ALAN PAUL, research engineer; b. Marshfield, Wis., Dec. 22, 1968; s. Arnold John and Viva Irene (Erickson) M.; m. Staci G. Olson, Oct. 8, 1994. Student, U. Wis., Eau Claire, 1987-89; BSME, U. Wis., Platteville, 1993. Registered profl. engr., Wis. Lab. technician Omnni Engrs., Appleton, Wis., summers 1989-91; project engr. Pella (Iowa) Corp., 1992; rsch. engr. Modine Mfg. Co., Racine, Wis., 1993—. Mem. Tau Beta Pi, Phi Eta Sigma, Pi Tau Sigma. Avocations: reading, computers, football, basketball, exercise. Office: Modine Mfg Co 1500 De Koven Ave Racine WI 53403-2552 Home: 8279 S 44th St Franklin WI 53132-8898

MEISSNER, EDWIN BENJAMIN, JR., retired real estate broker; b. St. Louis, Dec. 27, 1918; s. Edwin B. and Edna (Rice) Meissner; m. Nina Renard, Dec. 17, 1946; children: Edwin Benjamin III, Wallace, Robert; 1 child, Donald. BS, U. Pa., Phila., 1940. Joined St. Louis Car Co., 1934, asst. to pres., v.p., exec. v.p., 1950-56, pres., gen. mgr., 1956-61; pres. St. Louis Car div. Gen. Steel Industries, Inc., 1961-67; sr. v.p., dir. Gen. Steel Industries, Inc., 1968-74; v.p. Bakewell Corp., 1974-85; real estate broker, v.p. Hilliker Corp., St. Louis, 1985-96. Mem. pres.' coun. St. Louis U.; bd. dirs. Washington U. Med. Ctr. Redevel. Corp., Barnard Free Skin and Cancer Hosp.; past bd. dirs. James S. McDonnell USO; overseer St. Louis Symphony Soc.; hon. dir. Humane Soc. Mo.; v.p. Gateway Ctr. Met. St. Louis; past chmn. Ladue Police and Fire Commn., Mo.; mem. Jefferson Nat. Expansion Meml. Commn.; mil. affairs com. Regional Commerce; dir. Ctrl. Inst. for Deaf. Mem. Am. Ordnance Assn. (life), Internat. Assn. Chiefs of Police (assoc.), Mo. Assn. Chiefs of Police, Mo. Athletics Club, Westwood Country Club, Bridlespur Hunt Club, St. Louis Club, Beta Gamma Sigma. Office: Barton Bldg Ste 302 200 S Bemiston Saint Louis MO 63105-1915 Office Phone: 314-863-2440.

MEISTER, BERNARD JOHN, retired chemical engineer; b. Maynard, Mass., Feb. 27, 1941; s. Benjamin C. and Gertrude M. Meister; m. Janet M. White, Dec. 31, 1971; children: Mark, Martin, Kay Ellen. BSChemE, Worcester Poly. Inst., 1962; PhD in Chem. Engring., Cornell U., 1966. From engring. rschr. to rsch. scientist Dow Chem. Co., Midland, Mich., 1966—92, rsch. scientist, 1992—2005, ret., 2005. Contbr. articles to profl. jours. Mem.: AIChE, Soc. Rheology, Soc. Plastic Engrs., Am. Chem. Soc., Sigma Xi. Methodist. Home: 2925 Chippewa Ln Midland MI 48640-4181 Personal E-mail: bjjm1@att.net.

MEISTER, JULIA B., lawyer; b. Ft. Thomas, Ky., Nov. 16, 1969; BA, Xavier U., 1991; JD, Notre Dame Law Sch., 1995. Bar: Ohio 1995, Ct. of Appeals Sixth Cir., US Dist. Ct. Southern Dist. Ohio, US Dist. Ct. Southern Dist. Ind. Ptnr. Taft, Stettinius & Hollister LLP, Cin. Mem. Bd. for Cin. Area Sr. Services, Ky. Symphony Orch., Cin. Named a Rising Star, YWCA Acad. Career Women of Achievement; named one of Ohio's Rising Stars, Super Lawyers, 2006; named to Best Lawyers in Am. Mem.: Cin. Bar Assn. (chair, admissions com.). Office: Taft Stettinius & Hollister LLP 425 Walnut St Ste 1800 Cincinnati OH 45202-3957 Office Phone: 513-357-9330.

MEISTER, MARK JAY, museum director, professional society administrator; b. Balt., June 26, 1953; s. Michael Aaron and Yetta (Haransky) M.; m. Carla Steiger, Aug. 7, 1977; children: Rachel, Kaitlin. AB, Washington U., St. Louis, 1974; MA, U. Minn., 1976; cert. mus. mgmt., U. Calif., Berkeley, 1983. Asst. lectr. St. Louis Art Mus., 1974; asst. coord. young people's program Mpls. Inst. Arts, 1975—76, coord. mobile program, 1976, coord. tchrs. resource svcs., 1976—77; dir. Mus. Art and History, Port Huron, Mich., 1978—79, Midwest Mus. Am. Art, Elkhart, Ind., 1979—81; exec. dir. Children's Mus., St. Paul, 1981—86; dir. Mus. Art, Sci. and Industry, Bridgeport, Conn., 1986—89; exec. dir. Archaeol. Inst. of Am., Boston, 1989—99; exec. dir. Archl. Inst. Am. Inst. Archeologique d'Amerique, Boston and Toronto, 1994—99; exec. dir. Dayton Soc. Natural History, 2000—06, pres., CEO, 2006—. Adj. lectr. museology Kenyon Coll., Gambier, Ohio, 1977; adj. lectr. art history Ind. U., South Bend, 1980—81; regional reviewer Inst. Mus. Svcs., Washington, 1985—86, Washington, 1989; treas., vice chmn. Minn. Assn. Mus., St. Paul, 1983—86; ex-officio trustee U.S. com. Internat. Coun. on Monuments and Sites, 1995—99. Bd. dirs. Seaway Arts Coun., St. Clair County, Mich., 1978-79; bd. dirs. Dayton Sister Cities Com., 2000-05, chair, 2003-05; bd. dirs. Dayton Peace Accords Project, 2000-05, vice chair, 2003; bd. dirs. Glen Helen Ecology Inst., 2004—2007, Dayton Coun. on World Affairs, 2005-, pres.-elect 2006-; Greater Dayton Pub. TV, 2006-07, cmty. advisor bd, 2007-; mem. Mayor's Arts Adv. Com., Elkhart, 1981; mem. exec. com., Conf. Adminstrv. Officers, Am. Coun. Learned Socs., 1994-97; pres. Asian Arts Ctr., Dayton, 2002-05; bd. trustees, Dayton: A Peace Process, 2004-, co-chair, 2007-; Prevent Blindness Ohio, Dayton chpt. leadership coun., 2004—, chmn., 2006-. NEH museology fellow, Mpls. Inst. Arts, 1976-77, Kress fellow U. Minn. 1977-78, Bush leadership summer fellow, Bush Found., St. Paul, 1983; named One of Outstanding Young Men Am., 1981. Mem.: Assn. Midwest Mus., Archaeological Conservancy, Assn. Children's Mus., Ohio Mus. Assn., Assn. Sci. and Tech. Ctrs., Assn. Zoos and Aquariums, Assn. Sci. Mus. Dirs., Archaeological Inst. Am., Am. Assn. Mus. Office: Dayton Soc atural History 2600 Deweese Pkwy Dayton OH 45414-5499 Business E-Mail: mmeister@boonshoftmuseum.org.

MELAMED, LEO, global consulting firm executive; b. Bialystok, Poland, Mar. 20, 1932; arrived in U.S., 1941, naturalized, 1950; s. Isaac M. and Fayga (Barakin) M.; m. Betty Sattler, Dec. 26, 1953; children: Idelle Sharon, Jordan Norman, David Jeffrey. Student, U. Ill., 1950-52, LittD (hon.), 1999; JD, John Marshall Law Sch., Chgo., 1955. Bar: Ill. 1955. Sr. ptnr. Melamed, Kravitz & Verson, Chgo., 1956-66; chmn., CEO Dellsher Investment Co., 1965—93, Sakura Dellsher, Inc., Chgo., 1993—2000, Melamed & Assoc., Inc., Chgo., 1993—2002; co-chmn. Stevenson, Melamed and Assocs., Chgo., 2002—, Hua Mei Capital Co., 2005—, Stevenson, Melamed and Assocs., 2002—. Mem. Chgo. Merc. Exch., 1953—, mem. bd. govs., 1967—91, chmn. emeritus, 1991—, chmn. bd., 1969—71, 1975—77, chmn. exec. com., 1985—91, also spl. counsel, apptd. sr. policy advisor, 1997—; chmn. bd. Internat. Monetary Market, 1972—75, spl. counsel, 1976—91; mem. Chgo. Bd. Trade, 1969—; mem. corp. adv. bd. U. Ill., Chgo., 1991—; mayor Chgo. Coun. Manpower and Econ. Advisors, 1972; adv. coun. mem. Grad. Sch. Bus. U. Chgo., 1980—, Leo Melamed endowed chair future markets, 1991; hon. prof. Renmin U., Beijing, 2003; hon. dean Derivatives Sch. Peking U., China, 2007. Author: (sci. fiction novel) The Tenth Planet, 1987, Leo Melamed on the Markets, 1993, Escape to the Futures, 1996; editor: The Merits of Flexible Exchange Rates, 1988. Mem. bd. trustees John Marshall Law Sch., 1991—; coun. mem. US Holocaust Meml. Mus., 1992—, dir. Named Man Yr., Israel Bonds, 1975; recipient Human Rights medallion, Am. Jewish Com., 1991, Lifetime Achievement award, Anti-Defamation League, 2001; Betty and Leo Melamed Rsch. scholar biomed. rsch., Weizmann Inst. Sci., 1998, Leo Melamed fellow in internat. bus. and trade law, John Marshall Law Sch., 2000. Fellow: Internat. Assn. Fin. Engrs. (sr.); mem.: ABA, Chgo. Bar Assn., Ill. Bar Assn., Am. Judicature Soc., Nat. Futures Assn. (chmn. 1982—89, spl. advisor 1989—), Am. Contract Bridge League (life master), Standard Club, Union League Club, Econs. Club Chgo. Avocations: writing, jogging, bridge. Office: Melamed & Assocs Inc 10 S Wacker Dr Ste 3275 Chicago IL 60606-7442 Office Phone: 312-930-3310. Business E-Mail: lmelamed@melamedassoc.com. E-mail: lm@sdinet.com.

MELBINGER, MICHAEL S., lawyer; b. Chgo., Sept. 5, 1958; s. Donald G. and Joyce A. (Haynes) M.; m. Karen Mary Melbinger, June 16, 1984; children: Peter Donald, Charlotte Anna, Lucy Grace. BA, U. Notre Dame, 1980; JD, U. Ill., 1983. Bar: Ill., 1983. Assoc. McDermott, Will & Emery, Chgo., 1983-88, ptnr., 1989-93; ptnr., head employee benefits dept. Schiff, Hardin & Waite, Chgo., 1993—97; ptnr., chmn. employee benefits and exec. compensation Winston & Strawn LLP, Chgo., 1997—. Adj. prof. law Northwestern U., U. Ill. Mem. editorial bd. Practical Tax Strategies, Taxation for Lawyers, N.Y.C., 1989—, Employee Benefits Counselor, 1993—, Pension Management, 1995—; author Executive Compensation, 2004, author: Employee Benefit Trust Compliance Manual; contbr. articles to profl. jours. Pro bono Adoptive Families Am., Adoption Advocates. Mem. ABA, Nat. Assn. Stock Plan Profls. Home: 2699 Independence Ave Glenview IL 60025-7730 Office: Winston & Strawn LLP 35 W Wacker Dr Chicago IL 60601-9703 Office Phone: 312-558-7588. Office Fax: 312-558-5700. E-mail: mmelbinger@winston.com.

MELDMAN, ROBERT EDWARD, lawyer; b. Milw., Aug. 5, 1937; s. Louis Leo and Lillian (Gollusch) M.; m. Sandra Jane Setlick, July 24, 1960; children: Saree Beth, Richard Samuel. BS, U. Wis., 1959; LL.B., Marquette U., Milw., 1962; LL.M. in Taxation, NYU, 1963. Bar: Wis. 1962, Fla. 1987, Colo. 1990, U.S. Ct. Fed. Claims, U.S. Tax Ct. 1963, U.S. Supreme Ct. 1970. Practice tax law, Milw., 1963—; pres. Meldman, Case & Weine, Ltd., Milw., 1975-85; dir. tax div. Mulcahy & Wherry, SC, Milw., 1985-90; shareholder Reinhart, Boerner, Van Deuren, S.C., 1991—2006, of counsel, 2006—. Adj. prof. taxation U. Wis., Milw., 1970—2000, mem. tax adv. coun., 1978—2000, dir. Low Income Taxpayer Clinic, 2005—; adj. prof. Marquette U. Sch. Law, Milw., 2001—02, The U. of Queensland T.C. Beirne Sch. Law, 2002; vice chmn. Internat. Revenue Svc. Taxpayer Adv. Panel, 2003—04; sec. Profl. Inst. Tax Study, Inc., 1978—; bd. dirs. Wis. Bar Found., 1988—94; exec. in residence Deloitte & Touche Ctr. for Multistate Taxation, U. Wis., Milw., 1996—2000. Co-author: Federal Taxation Practice and Procedure, 1983, 1986, 1988, 1992, 1998, 2004, 2007, Practical Tactics for Dealing with the IRS, 1994, A Practical Guide to U.S. Taxation of International Transactions, 1996, 1997, 2004, Federal Taxation Practice and Procedure Study Guide/Quizzes, 1998; editor: Jour. Property Taxation, 1996—2002; mem. editl. bd.: Tax Litigation Alert, 1995—2000; contbr. articles to legal jours. Recipient Adj. Taxation Faculty award UWM Tax Assn., 1987; named Outstanding Tax Profl. 1992 Corp. Reports Wis. Mag. and UWM Tax Assn. Fellow Am. Coll. Tax Coun.; mem. ABA, Fed. Bar Assn. (pres. Milw. chpt. 1966-67), Milw. Bar Assn. (chmn. tax sect. 1970-71), Wis. Bar Assn. (bd. dirs. tax sect. 1964-78, chmn. 1973-74), Internat. Bar Assn., The Law Assn. for Asia and the Pacific (chair tax sect. 2000—, dep. chair bus. law sect.), Friends of Gold Meir Libr. (bd. dirs.), Marquette U. Law Alumni Assn. (bd. dirs. 1972-77), Milw. Athletic Club, Wis. Club (bd. dirs. 2003—), B'nai B'rith (trustee, Ralph Harris Meml. award Century Lodge 1969-70), Phi Delta Phi, Tau Epsilon Rho (chancellor Milw. chpt. 1969-71, supreme nat. chancellor 1975-76, v.p. Wis. chpt., tech. 1992-2000). Jewish (trustee congregation 1972-77). Office Phone: 414-298-8181. Business E-Mail: rmeldman@reinhartlaw.com.

MELENDEZ, BRIAN, lawyer, political organization administrator; b. Silver Creek, NY, Sept. 26, 1964; s. Gilbert Raymond and Dolores Maried (Valone) M. AB in Govt., Harvard U., 1986, MA in Theological Studies, 1991, JD cum laude, 1991. Bar: Minn., US Ct. Appeals (Fed. Cir.), US Dist. Ct. (Dist. Minn.). Adminstrv. sec. Harvard-Radcliffe Undergrad. Coun., Cambridge, Mass., 1983-84, 85-88; mgr. Copyrite Copy Ctrs., Winter Park, Fla., 1984; rsch. asst. Harvard U., Office of the Sec., Cambridge, 1985, Prog. on Info. Resources Policy, Cambridge, 1986-87; summer assoc. Avrell, Fons, Radey & Hinkle, Tallahassee, 1988, Greenberg, Travrig, Hoffman, Lipoff et al, Miami, Fla., 1989; ptnr. Faegre & Benson LLP, Minneapolis. Counselor Fla. Am. Legion Boys State, Tallahassee, 1982-89; v.p. Ctrl. Minn. Legal Services, 2003-05; bd. trustees Lawyers' Com. Civil Rights Under Law; bd. dirs. Vol. Lawyers Network, Ltd., Fair Vote Minn., 2002-05; mem. adv. com. on gen. rules of practice Supreme Ct. Minn., 2000-04, Minn. Citizens Commn. for Preservation of an Impartial Judiciary; chmn. Mpls. Dem.-Farmer-Labor Party, 1999-2005, Dem.-Farmer-Labor Congl. Dist. 5, 2004-05, Minn. Dem.-Farmer-Labor Party, 2005-; pres. Harvard Divinity Sch. Alumni Assn., 2001-03. Fellow, Am. Bar Found.; mem. ABA (law student div., chmn. young lawyers divsn. 2000-01, mem. House of Delegates 1997-2004, presdl. appointments com. 2003-04, coun. mem. bus. law sect. 2001-03), Nat. Sr. Classical League (nat. pres. 1985-86), Am. Inst. of Parliamentarians, Hennepin County Bar Assn. (pres. 2001-02), Minn. Bar Assn. (chmn. ct. rules and adminstrn. com., 1998-2001; pres.-elect 2006, pres. 2007), Nat. Assn. Parliamentarian; mem. Minn. Distance Running Assn. Office: Faegre & Benson LLP 2200 Wells Fargo Ctr 90 S 7th St Minneapolis MN 55402-3901 Office Phone: 612-766-7309. Office Fax: 612-766-1600. E-mail: bmelendez@faegre.com.*

MELGREN, ERIC FRANKLIN, prosecutor, lawyer; b. Minneola, Kans., Dec. 16, 1956; s. Carl James and Louise C. (Loechner) M.; m. Denise Melgren, June 16, 1979; children: David W., Susan C., Peter J., Abigail J. B, Wichita State U., 1979; JD, Washburn U., Topeka, 1985. Bar: Kans. 1985, US Dist. Ct. Kans. 1985, US Ct. Appeals (10th cir.) 1987, US Tax Ct. 1988, US Supreme Ct. 1995. Law clk. US Dist. Ct. Kans., Wichita, 1985-87; assoc. Foulston, Siefkin, Powers & Eberhardt, Wichita, 1987-92; ptnr. Foulston & Siefkin, Wichita, 1992—2002; US atty. dist. Kans. US Dept. Justice, 2002—. Trustee Leadership Wichita, 1994—. Mem. Christian Legal Soc. (state dir. 1989-94), Wichita State Alumni Assn. (exec. com. 1993—), West Wichita Rotary Club. Republican. Office: US Attys Office 1200 Epic Ctr 301 N Main Wichita KS 67202 Office Phone: 316-269-6481.

MELIN, ROBERT ARTHUR, lawyer; b. Milw., Sept. 13, 1940; s. Arthur John and Frances Magdalena (Lanser) M.; m. Mary Magdalen Melin, July 8, 1967; children: Arthur Walden, Robert Dismas, Nicholas O'Brien, Madalyn Mary. BA summa cum laude, Marquette U., Milw., 1962, JD, 1967. Bar: Wis. 1966, US Dist. Ct. (ea. dist.) Wis. 1966, US Ct. Appeals (7th cir.) 1966, US Ct. Mil. Appeals 1967, US Supreme Ct. 1975. Law clk. U.S. Dist. Ct. (ea. dist.), Wis., 1966; instr. bus. law U. Ga., Hinesville, 1968; lectr. bus. law U. Md., Asmara, 1970; lectr. law Haile Salassie I. U. Law Faculty, Addis Ababa, Ethiopia, 1971-72; with Walther & Halling, Milw., 1973-74, Schroeder, Gedlen, Riester & Moerke, Milw., 1974-82; ptnr. Schroeder, Gedlen, Riester & Melin, Milw., 1982-84, Schroeder, Riester, Melin & Smith, Milw., 1984—. Author: Evidence in Ethiopia, 1972; contbg. author Ann. Survey African Law, 1974; contbr. numerous articles to legal jours. Rep. Class of 2000, West Point Parent Assn. Wis., 1996—, exec. bd., 1997—; lectr. charitable solicitations and contracts Philanthropy Monthly 9th Ann. Policy Conf., NYC, 1985; chmn. Milw. Young Dems., 1963-64. Capt. JAGC, AUS, 1967-70. Mem.: ABA, Wis. Acad. Trial Lawyers, Wis. Bar Assn., Milw. Bar Assn., Friends Ethiopia, Am. Legion, Delta Theta Phi, Phi Alpha Theta, Pi Gamma Mu. Roman Catholic. Home: 8108 N Whitney Rd Milwaukee WI 53217-2752 Office: 135 W Wells St Milwaukee WI 53203-1807 Office Phone: 414-351-0539.

MELL, PATRICIA, dean; b. Cleve., Dec. 15, 1953; d. Julian Cooper and Thelma (Webb) M.; m. Michael Steven Ragland. AB with honors, Wellesley Coll., 1975; JD, Case Western Res. U., 1978. Bar: Ohio 1979, Pa. 1988, U.S. Dist. Ct. (so. and no. dists.) Ohio 1979. Asst. atty. gen. State of Ohio, Columbus, 1978-82, sec. of state corps. counsel, 1982-84; vis. asst. prof. Capital U. Law Sch., Columbus, 1984-85, U. Toledo Law Sch., 1985-86; asst. prof. law Widener U. (formerly Delaware Law Sch.), Wilmington, 1986—88; assoc. prof. law Mich. State U. Detroit Coll. of Law, East Lansing, Mich., 1992—2003, prof. law, 1996—2003, assoc. dean for academic affairs, 2000—02; dean John Marshall Law Sch., Chicago, Ill., 2003—. Mediator night prosecutor's program, Columbus, 1984-85. Mem. scholarship screening com. Black Am. Law Student Assn. U. Toledo Law Sch., 1985-86, governing bd. Case Western Res. U. Law Sch., Cleve., 1985-88, Alliance of Black Women, Columbus, 1983-85, Capers for Judge com., Cleve., 1980-86, century club Ohio Dems., 1985-86; chmn. law student com. Young Black Dems., Columbus, 1982-84; coordinator minority affiliations subcom. Citizens for Brown for Gov., Columbus, 1981-82; mem. Nat. Beach MBA, 1986—. Named Chgo. Midwest Honoree, Nat. Coun. Negro Women, 2003, one of Chgo.s 100 Most Influentianl Women, Crain's Chgo. Bus., 2004; recipient award, 2d Bapt. Ch., Evanston, 2003, Internat. Assn. Corps. Adminstrs., 1983, C.F. Stradford award, 2005. Mem. ABA, Nat. Bar Assn., Nat. Conf. Black Lawyers, Am. Arbitration Assn. (comml. arbitrator 1986—), Nat. Black MBA's, 1986-91. Lutheran. Avocations: modern languages, stained glass work, fencing, tennis, piano. Office: John Marshall Law Sch 315 S Plymouth Court Chicago IL 60604

MELLI, MARYGOLD SHIRE, law educator; b. Rhinelander, Wis., Feb. 8, 1926; d. Osborne and May (Bonnie) Shire; m. Joseph Alexander Melli, Apr. 8, 1950; children: Joseph, Sarah Bonnie, Sylvia Anne, James Alexander. BA, U. Wis., 1947, LLB, 1950. Bar: Wis. 1950. Dir. children's code revision Wis. Legis. Coun., Madison, 1950-53; exec. dir. Wis. Jud. Coun., Madison, 1955-59; asst. prof. law U. Wis., Madison, 1959-66, assoc. prof., 1966-67, prof., 1967-84, Voss-Bascom prof., 1985-93, emerita, 1993—. Assoc. dean U. Wis., 1970-72, rsch. affiliate Inst. for Rsch. on Poverty, 1980—; mem. spl. rev. bd. Dept. Health and Social Svcs., State of Wis., Madison, 1973—2002. Author: (pamphlet) The Legal Status of Women in Wisconsin, 1977, (book) Wisconsin Juvenile Court Practice, 1978, rev. edit., 1983, (with others) Child Support & Alimony, 1988, The Case for Transracial Adoption, 1994; co-editor: Child Support: The Next Frontier, 1999; contbr. articles to profl. jours. Bd. dirs. Am. Humane Assn., 1985-95, Frank Lloyd Wright -Wis., 2004-; chair A Fund for Women, Madison, Wis., 2002, 2003; mem. Dane County Ct. Ho. Art Acquisitions com. Named one of five Outstanding Young Women in Wis., Jaycees, 1961, Woman of Distinction, YWCA, Madison, Wis., 2007; grantee NSF, 1983; recipient Belle Case LaFollette award for outstanding svc. to the profession, 1994, Outstanding Contbn. to Advancement of Women in Higher Edn. award, 1991, Lifelong Contbn. to Advancement of Women in the Legal Prof. award, 1994, Sr. Svc. award Rotary, Madison, Wis., 2002, Woman of Distinction, Madison YMCA, 2007. Fellow Am. Acad. Matrimonial Lawyers (exec. editor jour. 1985-90); mem. Am. Law Inst. (cons. project on law of family dissolution), Internat. Soc. Family Law (v.p. 1994-2000, 2002-05), Wis. State Bar Assn. (reporter family law sect., 1976-2005), Nat. Conf. Bar Examiners (chmn. bd. mgrs. 1989, editl. adv. com.). Democrat. Roman Catholic. Avocations: walking, swimming, collecting art. Home: 2904 Waunona Way Madison WI 53713-2238 Office: U Wis Law Sch Madison WI 53706 Home Phone: 608-222-2003; Office Phone: 608-262-1610. Business E-Mail: msmelli@wisc.edu.

MELLOY, MICHAEL J., federal judge; b. Dubuque, IA, 1948; m. Jane Anne Melloy; children: Jennifer, Katherine, Bridget. BA, Loras Coll., 1970; JD, U. Iowa, 1974. With O'Conner & Thomas P.C. (formerly O'Conner, Thomas, Wright, Hammer, Bertsch & Norby, Dubuque, Iowa, 1974-86; judge US Bankruptcy Ct. (no. dist.) Iowa, 1986-92, US Dist. Ct. (no. dist.) Iowa, Cedar Rapids, 1992—2002; chief judge, 1992—99; judge US Ct. Appeals (8th cir.), 2002—. With US Army, 1970-72, USAR, 1972-76. Mem. ABA, Comml. Law League Am., Nat. Conf. Bankruptcy Judges, Eighth Cir. Judicial Coun. (bankruptcy judge rep., bankruptcy com.), Iowa State Bar Assn. (coun. mem. bankruptcy and comml. law sect.), Ill. State Bar Assn., Dubuque County Bar Assn., Linn County Bar Assn., Mason L. Ladd Inn of Ct., Rotary. Address: 625 1st St SE #200 Cedar Rapids IA 52401-2032

MELLUM, GALE ROBERT, lawyer; b. Duluth, Minn., July 5, 1942; s. Lester Andrew and Doris Esther (Smith) M.; m. Julie Murdoch Swanstrom, July 23, 1966; children: Eric Scott, Wendy Jane. BA summa cum laude, U. Minn., 1964, JD magna cum laude, 1968. Bar: Minn. 1968. Assoc. Faegre & Benson, Mpls., 1968-75, ptnr., 1976—, mem. mgmt. com., 1986-98. Mem. planning com. Garret Corp. and Securities Law Inst., Northwestern U. Law Sch., 1984—; bd. dirs., mem. adv. bd. Quali Tech Inc., Chaska, Minn., 1985-98; corp. sec. Excelsior-Henderson Motorcycle Mfg. Co., Belle Plaine, Minn., 1997-2000. Hockey chmn. LARC Bd., Mpls., 1980—85. Mem. ABA (fed. securities regulation com.), Minn. Bar Assn., Hennepin County Bar Assn. Republican. United Ch. Of Christ. Avocations: tennis, golf, snow and water skiing, handball, boating. Home: 3833 Thomas Ave S Minneapolis MN 55410 Office: Faegre & Benson 2200 Wells Fargo Ctr 90 S 7th St Ste 2200 Minneapolis MN 55402-3901 Home Phone: 612-926-1093; Office Phone: 612-766-7317. E-mail: gmellum@faegre.com.

MELMER, RICK, school system administrator; m. Valerie Melmer; children: Tara, Megan, Sean. BA in Elementary Edn. and Psychology, Dakota Wesleyan U.; MA in Elementary Edn., SD State U.; EdD in Ednl. Adminstrn., U. Wyo. Supt. schools Sioux Ctr. Cmty. Sch. Dist., Iowa, 1991—95, Watertown Sch. Dist., 1995—2003; sec. edn. SD Dept. Edn., Pierre, 2003—. Instructed grad. courses U. Sioux Falls, Morningside Coll., Iowa Area Edn. Agy., SD State Univ. Avocations: watching baseball, running, reading. Office: SD Dept Edn 700 Governors Dr Pierre SD 57501 Office Phone: 605-773-5669. Office Fax: 605-773-6139. Business E-Mail: rick.melmer@state.sd.us.

MELROSE, KENDRICK BASCOM, manufacturing executive; b. Orlando, Fla., July 31, 1940; s. Henry Bascom and Dorothy (Lumley) M.; children: Robert, Velia, Kendra. BS cum laude, Princeton U., 1962; M.Sc., MIT, 1965; MBA, U. Chgo., 1967. Mktg. mgr. Pillsbury Co., Mpls., 1967-69; dir. corp. planning Bayfield Techs., Inc., Mpls., 1969-70; dir. mktg., consumer products Toro Co. (mfrs. outdoor power equipment), Mpls., 1970—73, pres., Game Time Litchfield, Mich., 1973—76, v.p., outdoor power equipment Mpls., 1976—80, exec. v.p. outdoor power equipment div., 1980-81, pres., 1981-88, chief exec. officer, 1983—2005, chmn., 1987—2005, exec. chmn., 2005. Congregationalist. Office: Toro Co 8111 Lyndale Ave S Minneapolis MN 55420-1196

MELSHER, GARY WILLIAM, lawyer; b. Cleve., Mar. 8, 1939; BS, Ohio State U., 1961; JD, Case Western Reserve U., 1964. Bar: Ohio 1964. Ptnr. Jones, Day, Reavis & Pogue, Cleve. Mem. Order of Coif. Office: Jones Day Reavis & Pogue North Point 901 Lakeside Ave E Cleveland OH 44114-1190

MELSOP, JAMES WILLIAM, architect; b. Columbus, Ohio, June 2, 1939; s. James Brendan and Juanita Kathryn (Van Scoy) M.; m. Sandra Lee Minnich, Sept. 21, 1957; children: Deborah Lee, Susan Elizabeth, Kathryn Anne. BArch, Ohio State U., 1964; MArch, Harvard U., 1965; MBA, U. Chgo., 1975. Reg. architect, profl. engr. Architect The Austin Co., Chgo., 1967-69, mgr. bus. devel., 1969-74, asst. dist. mgr., 1974-75; pres., mng. dir. Austin Brasil, Sao Paulo, 1975-78; asst. dist. mgr. The Austin Co., Roselle, N.J., 1978-80, dist. mgr. Detroit, 1980-81, v.p., dist. mgr. Cleve., 1986, group v.p., dir., 1986—, exec. v.p. chief oper. officer, 1992, pres., CEO, 1992—, also chmn., bd. dirs.; founder, prin. owner Austin Holdings, Inc., 1997—. Named E&Y Entrepreneur of Yr., 1999. Mem. Am. Inst. Architects., Harvard Club N.Y.C., Presidents' Club, Ohio State U. (Disting. Alumnus award 1989). Home: 3165 Trillium Trail Cleveland OH 44124-5205

MELTON, DAVID REUBEN, lawyer; b. Milw., Apr. 4, 1952; s. Howard and Evelyn M.; m. Nancy Hillary Segal, May 22, 1981; children: Michelle, Hannah. BA, U. Wis., 1974; JD, U. Chgo., 1977. Bar: Ill. 1977, U.S. Dist. Ct. (no. dist.) Ill. 1977, U.S. Ct. Appeals (7th cir.) 1981, U.S. Supreme Ct. 1982, U.S. Fed. Cir. Ct. Appeals, 1991. Assoc. Karon, Morrison & Savikas, Ltd., Chgo., 1977-83; ptnr. Karon, Morrison & Saviskas, Ltd., Chgo., 1983-87, Karon, Savikas & Horn, Ltd., Chgo., 1987-88, Keck, Mahin & Cate, Chgo., 1988-96; counsel Mayer, Brown & Platt, Chgo., 1996-99, ptnr., 2000—07; sr. counsel Foley & Lardner, LLP, Chgo., 2007—. Office: Foley & Lardner LLP 321 N Clark St Ste 2800 Chicago IL 60610 Office Phone: 312-832-4599. Business E-Mail: dmetton@foley.com.

MELTON, EMORY LEON, lawyer, state legislator, publisher; b. McDowell, Mo., June 20, 1923; s. Columbus Right and Pearly Susan (Wise) M; m. Jean Sanders, June 19, 1949; children: Stanley Emory, John Russell. Student, Monett Jr. Coll., 1940-41, S.W. Mo. State U., 1941-42; LLB, U. Mo., 1945. Bar: Mo. 1944. Pvt. practice, Cassville, Mo., 1947—; pres. Melton Publs., Inc., 1959—; pros. atty. Barry County (Mo.), 1947-51; mem. Mo. Senate, 1973-97. Chmn. Barry County republican Com., 1964-68. Served with AUS, 1945-46. Recipient Meritorious Pub. Svc. award St. Lousi Globe-Democrat, 1976. Mem. Mo. Bar Assn., Lions, Masons. Office: PO Box 488 Cassville MO 65625-0488

MELTON, OWEN B., JR., banking company executive; b. 1946; BS, Indiana U., 1973. Chief adminstrv. officer Fed. Home Loan Bank Bd., Washington, 1977-79; exec. v.p. Skokie (Ill.) Fed. Savs. and Loan, 1979-81; chmn. bd. dirs., pres., chief exec. officer Diamond Savs. and Loan Co., 1981-83; with First Ind. Bank, Indpls., 1972—; now pres., CEO, also bd. dirs. First Ind. Fed. Savs. Bank, Indpls. Served with USAF, 1967-70. Office: 1st Ind Bank 135 N Pennsylvania St Indianapolis IN 46204-2400

MELTZER, BRIAN, lawyer; b. Chgo., Apr. 15, 1944; s. Maurice and Ethel (Goldstein) M.; m. Rosemary Labriola, Sept. 11, 1982; children: Stuart Joseph, Alan Phillip, Martin Angelo. BA in Math., Cornell U., 1966; JD, Harvard U., 1969. Bar: Ill. 1969. Assoc. atty. D'ancona & Pflaum, Chgo., 1969-72; assoc. then ptnr. Schwartz & Freeman, Chgo., 1972-88; ptnr. Keck, Mahin & Cate, Chgo., 1988-95, Meltzer, Purtill & Stelle, Schaumburg, Ill., 1996—. Office: 1515 E Woodfield Rd Schaumburg IL 60173-6046

MELTZER, DAVID OWEN, internist, educator, economist; b. NYC, Apr. 17, 1964; s. Herbert Yale and Sharon Bittenson Meltzer. BS, Yale U., 1986; PhD in Econs., U. of Chgo., 1992, MD in Econs., 1993. Diplomate Nat. Bd. Med. Examiners, 1994, Am. Bd. Internal Medicine, 1996. Lab. asst. Ill. State Psychiatric Inst., 1982; scientific rsch. asst. U. Chgo., 1983, econs. rsch. asst., dept. econs., 1984, econs. teaching asst., grad. sch. bus., 1988, econs. teaching asst., dept. econs., 1988, econs. rsch. asst., dept. econs., 1988—91, lectr., grad. sch. of pub. policy studies, 1991—93, asst. prof., dept. medicine, dept. econs., and grad. sch. pub. policy studies, 1996—2001, attending physician, Gen. Medicine Svcs., 1997—, physician care physician, Primary Care Group, 1997—, assoc. prof., dept. medicine, dept. econs., grad. sch. pub. policy studies, 2001—; genetics rsch. asst., dept. molecular biophysics and biochemistry Yale U., 1985, econs. rsch. asst., Econs. Growth Ctr., 1985—86; econs. tutor Yale Coll., 1985—86; resident in internal medicine Brigham & Women's Hosp. Harvard Med. Sch., Boston, 1993—96; associated faculty mem. Harris Sch., U. Chgo., 2001—, Dept. Econs., U. Chgo., 2001—. Faculty rsch. fellow Nat. Bur. Econ. Rsch., Cambridge, 1994—; dir. Ctrs. for Disease Control Chgo. Ctr. of Excellence in Health Promotion Econs.; co-dir., MD/PhD Program in the Soc. Sciences U. Chgo., 1997—, bd. dir., Graham Sch. Continuing Edn., 1998—, serves on faculty of graduate program in health adminstrn and policy, Population Rsch. Ctr., and Ctr. on Aging, mem., Com. to Assess Med. Informatics Initiative, 2000—, dir., Academic Hospitalist Iniatiative, dept. medicine, 2000—; co-dir. Robert Wood Johnson Clin. Scholars Program, 2001—; served on panel. "Future for Medicare" Nat. Acad. Social Insurance; served on tech. adv. panel Medicare for the Dept. Health and Human Svcs.; mem. steering com. Health and Retirement Survey, 2000—; invited lectr. and presenter; lectr. in field. Contbr. articles in profl. jours., chapters to books; reviewer Am. Econ. Review, Am. Jour. Medicine, Health Svcs. Rsch., Health Econs., JAMA, Jour. Gen. Internal Medicine, Jour. Health Econs., Jour. Human Resources, Jour. Labor Econs., Jour. Law & Econs., Jour. Polit. Economy, New England Jour. Medicine, Quality and Safety in Health Care, & Rand Jour. Econs., mem. editl. bd. Medical Decision Making, 1992—2002, Quality and Safety in Health Care, 2002—. Recipient Lee Lusted prize, NIH, 1996, Outstanding Paper award, 1998, Garfield award, Rsch. Am., 2002, Health Care Rsch. award, NIH Care Mgmt., Eugene Garfield Economic Impact award, Rsch. Am., Leaders in Gen. Medicine award, Midwest Soc. for Gen. Internal Medicine; John M. Olin Faculty Fellowship, 1999—2000. Mem.: Nat. Acad. Soc. Insurance, Phi Beta Kappa, Alpha Omega Alpha. Office: Univ Chgo 5841 S Maryland MC 2007 Chicago IL 60637 also: Univ Chgo 1155 E 60th St Ste 152 Chicago IL 60637 Office Phone: 773-702-0836. Office Fax: 773-834-2238. Business E-Mail: dmeltzer@medicine.bsd.uchicago.edu, dom2@midway.uchicago.edu.

MELVIN, STEWART WAYNE, engineering educator; BS in Agrl. Engring., Iowa State U., 1964, MS in Agrl. Engring., 1967, PhD, 1970. Registered agrl. engr., Iowa. With Soil Conservation Svc., USDA, 1963—67; asst. prof. Colo. State U., 1969-70, Iowa State U., Ames, 1970-74, assoc. prof. agrl. engring., 1974-79, prof. agrl. engring., 1979—2004, head agrl. engring., 1994—2001, prof. emeritus, 2004—; project mgr. Curry-Wille and Assocs., 2002—. Vis. prof. Silsoe Coll., Eng., 1985-86. Contbr. numerous articles to profl. jours. Fellow Am. Soc. Agrl. Engrs.; mem. Internat. Soil and Tillage Rsch. Orgn., Soil and Water Conservation Soc. Am., Am. Soc. Engring. Edn., Phi Kappa Phi, Tau Beta Pi, Gamma Sigma Delta, Sigma Xi, Epsilon Sigma Phi, Alpha Epsilon. Office: Curry Wille and Assocs PC 425 S 2d St Box 1732 Ames IA 50010 Office Phone: 515-232-9078. Office Fax: 515-232-9083. E-mail: smelvin@currywille.com.

MENARD, JOHN R., JR., home improvement retail executive; b. Eau Claire, Wisc., 1940; s. John Menard Sr. and Rosemary; 6 children. BA/BS, U. of Wis. Madison, 1963. Founder, pres., CEO Menard Inc., Eau Claire, Wis., 1972—; owner, pres. Menard Racing, 1979—. Bd. dirs. Polaris Industries. Named one of Forbes' Richest Americans, 1999—, World's Richest People, Forbes Mag., 2001. Avocation: auto racing. Office: Menard Inc 4777 Menard Dr Eau Claire WI 54703-9625

MENCER, JETTA, lawyer; b. Coshocton, Ohio, Apr. 7, 1959; d. William J. and Virginia M. (Fry) M. BS, Ohio State U., 1980, JD, 1983. Bar: Ohio, U.S. Dist. Ct. (so. dist.) Ohio. Assoc. Berry, Owens & Manning, Coshocton, 1983-86; asst. pros. atty. Coshocton County, 1983-86, Licking County, Newark, Ohio, 1986-88, asst. atty. gen., 1988-95; pvt. practice Coshocton, 1995-96; prosecuting atty. Coshocton County (Ohio) Prosecutor's Office, 1997-2001; atty. Lee Smith & Assocs., Columbus, Ohio, 2001—03; pvt. practice Columbus, 2003—. Treas. Coshocton County Dem. Cen. & Exec. Coms., 1984-86; chmn., 1986-88; sec., bd. dirs. Heart Ohio Girl Scout Council, Inc., Zanesville, Ohio, 1985-87; fin. chmn., bd. dirs. YMCA, Coshocton, 1985-87. Mem. Ohio State Bar Assn., Coshocton County Bar Assn., Lions Club. Democrat. Methodist. Office: One S Park Pl Newark OH 43055 Office Phone: 740-345-5171. Personal E-mail: jmencer@columbus.rr.com.

MENCHIK, PAUL LEONARD, economist, educator; b. NYC, Sept. 16, 1947; s. Irving and Elinor (Swedlow) M.; m. Bettie Ann Landauer, May 28, 1972; children: Daniel Aron, Jeremy Matthew. BA, SUNY, Binghamton, 1969; AM, U. Pa., 1971, PhD, 1976. Lectr. Rutgers Coll., New Brunswick, NJ, 1974-76; rsch. assoc. Inst. for Rsch. on Poverty, U. Wis., Madison, 1976-79; prof. dept. econs. Mich. State U., East Lansing, Mich., 1979—, chairperson dept. econs., 1992-96, dir. grad. studies, 2005—; sr. economist, econ. policy Office Mgmt. & Budget, Washington, 1990-91. Acad. visitor Stanford (Calif.) U., 1980, London Sch. Econ., 1987-88; vis. assoc. prof. U. Pa., Phila., 1982-83; vis. scholar Congrl. Budget Office, 1997-98; cons., advisor in field. Mem. editl. bd. Jour. Income Distbn., Amsterdam, 1992—; contbr. articles to profl. jour.; Hon. Rsch. Fellow, Univ. Coll., London, 2003. Grantee NSF, Social Security Adminstrn., U.S. Dept. Health and Human Svcs.; recipient Best Article of Yr. award Econ. Inquiry, 1987. Mem. Am. Econ. Assn., Nat. Tax Assn., Nat. Bur. Econ. Rsch. Conf. on Income & Wealth. Avocations: bowling, racquetball, golf, travel, camping. Office: Mich State U 101 Marshall Hall E Circle Dr East Lansing MI 48824 Home Phone: 517-349-5261; Office Phone: 517-355-4553. Business E-Mail: menchik@msu.edu.

MENDELSON, ELLEN B., radiologist, educator; MD, Northwestern U. Feinberg Sch. Medicine, 1980. Cert. diagnostic radiology 1984. Intern to resident, diagnostic radiology NW U. Meml. Hosp., Chgo., 1981—84, fellowship, 1984—85; radiologist Western Penn Hosp., Pitts.; bd. mem. Monongahela Valley Hosp., Pa.; assoc. prof., radiology U. Pitts. Sch. Medicine; prof. radiology NW U., Feinberg Sch. Medicine, Chgo.; dir. breast imaging NW Meml. Hosp. Office: NW U Feinberg Sch Medicine 675 N St Clair Galter 13th Fl Chicago IL 60611 Address: NW Meml Hosp 251 E Huron St Chicago IL 60611

MENDENHALL, CANDICE, former finance company executive; Sr. v.p. human resources Fed. Home Loan Mortgage Corp., McLean, Va. Home: 616 W Fulton St Apt 619 Chicago IL 60661-1141 Fax: 703-903-2447.

MENEFEE, FREDERICK LEWIS, advertising executive; b. Arkansas City, Kans., Oct. 22, 1932; s. Arthur LeRoy and Vera Mae (Rather) M.; m. Margot Leuze, Sept. 16, 1955; children: Gregory S., Christina Menefee-Anderson. AA, Arkansas City Jr. Coll., 1952; BA, U. Wichita, 1958. Sports editor, bus. mgr. Ark. Light and Tiger Tales, 1949-52; sports reporter Arkansas City Daily Traveler, 1949—52; advt. mgr. Derby Star, Haysville Herald and Sedgwick County News, 1956-57; v.p., account exec. Associated Advt. Agy., 1958-64; with McCormick-Armstrong Adv. Agy. (now Menefee and Ptnrs., Inc.), Wichita, 1964—, agy. mgr., 1964—, account. supr., 1965—, gen. mgr., 1972—, pres., CEO, 1979—, chmn. bd., 1986—2003. Vol. Wichita River Festival, 1974-98; pub. rels. chmn. Wichita Centennial Nat. Art Show and Exhibit, 1969-70. With AUS, 1953-55. Named Henry J. Lawrence Photo award, 1956, Wichita Beacon Advt. award, 1957, KANS Radio award, 1958, Advt. Man of Yr., Advt. Club of Wichita, 1964, Advt. Man of Yr., 9th Dist. Am. Advt. Fedn. Colo., Nebr., Iowa, Mo., Kans., 1965, Adm. Windwagon Smith III Wichita Festivals Inc., 1976. Mem. Am. Advt. Fedn. (nat. bd. dirs. 1969-70, dist. gov. 1968-69, chmn. nat. coun. govs. 1969-70, 1st lt. gov. awards chmn. 1967, 68), Wichita Wagonmasters (founding mem. 1973, capt. 1974-75, dir., charter, founder, commodore 1999), Wichita Advt. Club (bd. dirs. 1958-68), v.p. awards 1961-62, v.p. membership 1962, v.p. programs 1963, pres. 1964-65), PAWS Inc. (founder, 1st pres. 1978-86), Alpha Delta Sigma (pres. 1957-58, Outstanding Svc. award 1958), Quill & Scroll, 1949-50. Home: 2235 Red Bud Ln Wichita KS 67204-5346

MENG, JOHN C., food service executive; b. 1944; m. Engrid Meng; children: Molly, Katie, Preston, Spencer. BA, Wabash Coll., 1966; MBA, Washington U., 1967. From supr. to plant mgr. Schreiber Foods, Green Bay, Wis., 1968-74, v.p., sec. treas., 1974-77, sr. v.p. fin., 1977-81, exec. v.p., 1981-85, pres., COO, 1985-89, CEO, 1989-99, chmn., 1999—. Bd. dir. WPS Resources Corp., Green Bay, Associated Banc-Corp., Green Bay. Office: Schreiber Foods Inc 425 Pine St Green Bay WI 54301 Office Phone: 920-437-7601.

MENGEDOTH, DONALD ROY, commercial banker; b. Naperville, Ill., Aug. 10, 1944; s. Orville Gustav and Bernice Lydia (Fries) M.; m. Stacy K. Halverson; children: Paul Bernard, Daniel Lawrence, Mary Bernice. BS, Marquette U., 1968, MBA, 1973. Ops. officer 1st Bank, N.A.-Milw., 1968-69, asst. v.p., 1969-71, v.p., 1971-73, sr. v.p., 1973-79; v.p. 1st Bank System, Inc., Mpls., 1979-82, sr. v.p., 1983-87, pres., CEO, 1987—2000; chmn. Cmty. First Bankshares Inc., Fargo, ND, 1987—. Bd. dirs. Treasure Enterprises, Inc., Vail Banks Inc. Adv. bd. United Way Cass-Clay Campaign, Fargo, 1988-89; chmn. Cmty. 1st Polit. Action Com., Fargo, 1988-89; bd. dirs. Fargo Cath. Schs. Network Found., 1989-92; bd. dirs., vice chmn. Red River Zool. Soc., 1993-96; chmn. Diocesan God's Gift Appeals, Fargo, 1989. Mem. Am. Bankers Assn. (govt. rels. coun., pres. 2000-2001), Am. Mgmt. Assn., N.D. Bankers Assn., S.D. Bankers Assn., Greater N.D. Assn., Fargo Country Club. Avocations: tennis, golf, hunting, reading. Office: Cmty 1st Bankshares 520 Main Ave Fargo ND 58124-0001 E-mail: don_mengedoth@cfbx.com.

MENGEL, DAVID BRUCE, agronomy and soil science educator; b. East Chicago, Ind., May 1, 1948; s. Bill M. and Thelma Lee (Miller) M.; m. Susan Kay Haverstock, Aug. 30, 1968; children: David, Erin. BS in Agricultural Edn., Purdue U., 1970, MS in Agronomy, 1972; PhD in Soil Sci., N.C. State U., 1975. Cert. profl. agronomist, soil scientist. Asst. prof. agronomy La. State U., Crowley, 1975-79, Purdue U., West Lafayette, Ind., 1979-82, assoc. prof., 1982-86, prof. agronomy, 1986-98; prof., head agronomy Kans. State U., Manhattan, Kans., 1998—. Mem. Am Soc. Agronomy, Soil Sci. Soc. Am., Internat. Soil Sci. Soc., Sigma Xi, Gamma Sigma Delta, Epsilon Sigma Phi, Delta Tau Delta. Avocations: fishing, woodworking. Office: Plant Sci Ctr Dept Agronomy Kans State U 2004 Throckmorton Manhattan KS 66506-5501 E-mail: dmengel@ksu.edu.

MENGELING, CARL FREDERICK, bishop emeritus; b. Hammond, Ind., Oct. 22, 1930; s. Carl H. and Augusta Huke Mengeling. Attended, St. Meinrad Coll. and Sem., Ind.; Lic. in Sacred Theology, Angelicum U.; STD, Alfonsianum Acad. Ordained priest Diocese of Gary, Ind., 1957; assoc. pastor St. Mark Parish, Gary, 1957—61; tchr. Bishop Noll High Sch., Hammond, St. Joseph Calumet Coll., East Chgo., St. Procopius Sem., Lisle, Ill.; pastor All Saints Parish, Hammond, Ill., 1968—70, Holy Name Parish, Cedar Lake, Ill., 1970—71, Nativity of Our Savior, Portage, Ill., 1971—85, St. Thomas More Parish, Munster, Ill., 1985—95; named monsignor, 1984; founder, chair Inst. Religion, Diocesan of Gary; ordained bishop, 1995; bishop Archdiocese of Lansing, Mich., 1996—2008, bishop emeritus Mich., 2008—. Chair worship com. Diocese of Gary, chair vocations com., mem. Presbyteral coun., mem. ecumenical commn., mem. permanent diaconate formation team. Contbr. Faith Mag. Roman Catholic. Office: 300 W Ottawa St Lansing MI 48933-1530*

MENGLER, THOMAS M., dean; b. May 18, 1953; BA in Philosophy magna cum laude, Carleton Coll., 1975; MA in Philosophy, U. Tex., 1977, JD, 1981. Bar: Ill., Tex., D.C., U.S. Ct. Appeals (5th, 7th and 10th cirs.), U.S. Dist. Ct. (we. dist.) Tex. Law clk. to Hon. James K. Logan U.S. Ct. Appeals for 10thCir., Olathe, Kans., 1980-81; assoc. atty. Arnold & Porter, Washington, 1982-83; asst. atty. gen. Office of Atty. Gen. of Tex., Austin, 1983-85; asst. prof. law U. Ill. Coll. Law, Champaign, 1985-89, assoc. prof., 1989-91, prof. law, 1991—2002, assoc. dean for acad. affairs, 1992-93, dean, 1993—2002; dean, prof. law U. St. Thomas Sch. Law, Mpls., 2002—. Contbr. numerous articles to profl. jours. Mem. ABA, Ill. State Bar Assn., Order of Coif, Phi Beta Kappa. Office: U St Thomas Sch Law Mail TMH 440 1000 LaSalle Ave Minneapolis MN 55403-2005

MENNINGER, ROY WRIGHT, medical foundation executive, psychiatrist; b. Topeka, Oct. 27, 1926; s. William Claire and Catharine (Wright) M.; m. Beverly Joan Miller, Mar. 4, 1973; children: Heather, Ariel, Bonar, Eric, Brent, Frederick, Elizabeth. AB, Swarthmore Coll., Pa., 1947; MD, Cornell U., 1951; DHL, Ottawa U., Kans., 1977; LittD, William Jewell Coll., Liberty Mo., 1985. Diplomate Am. Bd. Psychiatry and Neurology, 1959. Intern N.Y. Hosp., 1951-52; resident in psychiatry Boston State Hosp., 1952-53, Boston Psychopathic Hosp., 1953-56; from resident psychiatrist to assoc. med. psychiatrist Peter Bent Brigham Hosp., Boston, 1956-61; teaching and rsch. fellow Harvard U. Med. Sch., Boston, 1956-61; staff psychiatrist Menninger Found., Topeka, 1961-63, dir. dept. preventive psychiatry, 1963-67, pres., CEO, 1967-93, chmn. trustees, 1991—. Bd. dirs. Bank IV Topeka N.A., CML Corp., The New Eng., U.S. Behavioral Health; mem. Karl Menninger Sch. Psychiatry, Topeka, 1972—, Ind. Sector, 1990—; clin. prof. psychiatry U. Kans. Med. Ctr., Wichita, 1977—; cons. Colmery-O'Neil VA Med. Ctr., Topeka, 1979—. Author: Trends in American Psychiatry: Implication for Psychiatry in Japan; co-author: The Medical Marriage, 1988, The Psychology of Postponement in the Medical Marriage; cons. editor Jour. Medical Aspects Human Sexuality, 1967-90; editor adv. bd. Parents mag., 1966-80, Clin. Psychiatry ews, 1973—; reviewer Am. Jour. Psychiatry, 1980—. Mem. sponsoring com. Inst. Am. Democracy, 1967-70; mem. adv. group Horizons '76 Am. Revolution Bicentennial Commn.; adv. bd., steering com. Topeka Inst. Urban Affairs, 1967-70; adv. bd. Highland Park-Pierce Neighborhood House, Topeka, 1967-70; bd. dirs. Shawnee council Campfire Girls, Topeka, 1962-69, A.K. Rice Inst., Washington, Sex Info. and Edn. Council U.S., 1972-73, mem. edn. com., long range planning com., 1972-73; bd. dirs. Goals for Topeka, Topeka Inst. Urban Affairs, 1969-74, v.p., 1973; med. adv. com. VA Hosp., 1972-78; mem. Gov.'s Com. on Criminal Adminstrn., 1971-74; trustee People-to-People, Kansas City, Mo., 1967-69, Baker U., 1968-72, Midwest Research Inst., 1967-1986, 86—, mem. exec. com., 1970-86; vis. lectr. Fgn. Service Inst., State Dept., 1963-66; chmn. social issues com. Group Advancement Psychiatry, 1972-82; community adv. bd. Kans. Health Workers Union, 1968-70; adv. com. to bd. dirs. New Eng. Mut. Life Ins. Co., 1968-70. With U.S. Army, 1953-55. Recipient Disting. Svs. citation U. Kans., 1985; Pacific Rim Coll. Psychiatry fellow. Fellow Am. Psychiat. Assn. (life), Joint Info. Svc. (exec. com.), Am. Coll. Psychiatry, Am. Orthopsychiat. Assn., Am. Coll. Mental Health Adminstrs.; mem. AAAS, Northeastern Group Psychotherapy (hon.), Physicians Social Responsibility, Kans. Psychiat. Soc., Greater Topeka C. of C. (dir.). Episcopalian. Avocations: stamp collecting/philately, chamber music, microcomputers. Office: Menningers PO Box 809045 Houston TX 77280

MENNINGER, WILLIAM WALTER, psychiatrist; b. Topeka, Oct. 23, 1931; s. William Claire and Catharine Louisa (Wright) Menninger; m. Constance Arnold Libbey, June 15, 1953; children: Frederick Prince, John Alexander, Eliza Wright, Marian Stuart, William Libbey, David Henry. AB, Stanford U., 1953; MD, Cornell U., 1957; LittD (hon.), Middlebury Coll., 1982; DSc (hon.), Washburn U., 1982; LHD (hon.), Ottawa U., 1986; LLD (hon.), Heidelberg Coll., 1993, Dominican U., 2007. Diplomate Am. Bd. Psychiatry and Neurology, Am. Bd. Forensic Psychiatry. Intern Harvard Med. Svc., Boston City Hosp., 1957-58; resident in psychiatry Menninger Sch. Psychiatry, 1958-61; chief med. officer, psychiatrist Fed. Reformatory, El Reno, Okla., 1961-63; assoc. psychiatrist Peace Corps, 1963-64; staff psychiatrist Menninger Found., Topeka, 1965—2001, coordinator for devel., 1967-69, dir. law and psychiatry, 1981-85, dir. dept. edn., dean Karl Menninger Sch. Psychiatry and Mental Health Scis., 1984-90, exec. v.p., chief staff, 1984-93, CEO, 1993—2001, pres., 1993—96, 1999—2001, chmn. bd. trustees, 2001—; clin. supr. Topeka State Hosp., 1969-70, sect. dir., 1970-72, asst. supt., clin., dir. residency tng., 1972-81; pres. Menninger Clinic, Topeka, 1991-96; staff Stormont-Vail Hosp., Topeka, 1984-94, assoc., 1994—2002. Adj. prof. Washburn U.; mem. Fed. Prision Facilities Planning Coun., 1970—73; mem. adv. bd. Nat. Inst. Corrections, 1975—88, chmn., 1980—84; cons. U.S. Bur. Prisons; mem. adv. bd. US Bank, Topeka, 1999—. Syndicated columnist: In-Sights, 1975—83; author: (book) Happiness Without Sex and Other Things Too Good to Miss, 1976, Caution: Living May Be Hazardous, 1978, Behavioral Science and the Secret Service, 1981, Chronic Mental Patient II, 1987; editor: Psychiatry Digest, 1971—74, Bull. of Menninger Clinic, 2001—; contbr. articles to profl. jours., chpts. to books. Mem. health and safety com. Boy Scouts Am., 1970—, chmn., 1980—85, mem. nat. exec. bd., 1980—90, mem. nat. adv. coun., 1990—; bd. dirs. Nat. Com. Prevention Child Abuse, 1975—83; mem. nat. adv. health coun. HEW, 1967—71; mem. Nat. Commn. Causes and Prevention Violence, 1968—69; rsch. adv. com. U.S. Secret Svc., 1990—2005; pres. Jayhawk coun. Boy Scouts Am., 1998—2001; mem. Kans. Gov.'s Adv. Commn. Mental Health, Mental Retardation and Cmty. Mental Health Svcs., 1983—90, Kans. Gov.'s Penal Planning Coun., 1970; chmn. Kans. Gov.'s Criminal Justice Coun., 1970; mem. Kans. Gov.'s Commn. on Crime Reduction and Prevention/Koch Commn., 1994—98; ruling elder 1st Presbyn. Ch., Topeka, 1992—95; trustee Kenworthy-Swift Found., 1980—; bd. dirs. Police Found., Washington, 1996—, Koch Crime Inst., 1998—2000; trustee Midwest Rsch. Inst., Kansas City, Mo., 1996—. With USPHS, 1959—64. Fellow: ACP, Am. Coll. Psychiatrists, Am. Psychiat. Assn. (chmn. com. chronically mentally ill 1984—86, chmn. Guttmacher award bd. 1990—96); mem.: AMA, Am. Acad. Psychiatry and Law, Am. Psychoanalytic Assn. (chmn. com. psychoanalysis, cmty. and soc. 1984—93), Inst. Medicine NAS, Group Advancement Psychiatry (chmn. com. mental health svcs. 1974—77, 1991—2002), Stanford Assocs. Office: PO Box 4406 Topeka KS 66604-0406 Office Phone: 785-235-3400. Business E-Mail: wmenninger@menninger.edu.

MENON, MANI, urological surgeon, educator; b Trichur, Kerala, India, July 9, 1948; came to U.S., 1972, naturalized, 1977; s. Balakrishna and Sumathie Menon; m. Shameem Ara Begum, Oct. 17, 1972; children: Nisha, Roshen. MBBS, Madras U., India, 1971. Diplomate Am. Bd. Urology. Intern Bryn Mawr (Pa.) Hosp., 1973-74; resident Brady Urol. Inst., The Johns Hopkins Hosp., Balt., 1974-80; asst. prof. urology Washington U. Med. Ctr., St. Louis, 1980-83, assoc. prof., 1983; prof. urology, chmn. div. urology and transplant surgery U. Mass. Med. Ctr., Worcester, 1983—; prof. physiology, U. Mass. Med. Ctr., Worcester, 1986—. Mem. AAAS, Am. Assn. Genito Urinary Surgeons, Am. Urol. Assn. (Gold Cytoscope award 1990), Am. Fedn. Clin. Rsch., Am. Soc. Transplantation and Vascular Surgery, Rschrs. on Calculus Kinetics, Johns Hopkins Med. and Surg. Assn., Mass. Med. Soc., Mass. Soc. Med. Rsch. Avocations: tennis, puzzles, mystery fiction. Office: U Mass Med Ctr Div Urology Worcester MA 01655 also: Henry Ford Hosp Vattikuti Urology Inst 2799 W Grand Blvd Detroit MI 48202 Office Phone: 313-916-2066. E-mail: mmenon1@hfhs.org.

MENSIK, MICHAEL, lawyer; BA with distinction, Stanford U., 1976; MA in Econs., U. Calif., Berkeley, 1980, JD, 1980. Bar: Ill. 1980. Ptnr. Baker & McKenzie LLP, Chgo. Contbr. articles to profl. jours. Office: Baker & McKenzie LLP One Prudential Plaza, Ste 2500 130 E Randolph Dr Chicago IL 60601 Office Phone: 312-861-8941. E-mail: michael.s.mensik@bakernet.com.

MENZEL, FEROL SCHRICKER, academic administrator; b. Cin., Mar. 12, 1946; d. Raymond and Esther (Meikle) Schricker; m. Bruce Willard Menzel, Aug. 9, 1969; children: Erich Leith, Evan Douglas. BS in Occupational Therapy, Ohio State U., 1968; MS in Child Devel., Iowa State U., 1975, PhD in Child Devel., 1979. Occupational therapist Spl. Children's Ctr., Ithaca, NY, 1969—70; work evaluator then dir. occupational therapy Woodward State Hosp.-Sch., Iowa, 1970—72, dir. Devel. Ctr., 1972—73; tchg. and rsch. asst. dept. child devel. Iowa State U., Ames, 1973—75; occupational therapist Iowa Area XI Edn. Agy., 1977—79; asst. prof. to prof. psych. Grand View Coll., Des Moines, 1980, prof., 1988, chair dept. psych., 1982—83, head social svcs. divsn., 1983, assoc. dean freshmen, 1986—88, dir. lifelong edn., 1989—90, dir. planning and instl. rsch., 1990; v.p. academic affairs, dean of faculty Wartburg Coll., Waverly, Iowa, 1999—. Lectr. dept. psych. Drake U., 1979; instr. in service tng. for tchrs. of severely and profoundly handicapped Drake U., 1978-79, U. Ga., 1978; instr. occupational therapy U. Iowa, 1981; cons. occupational therapy Iowa State Dept. Pub. Instrn., 1979-80, Mainstream Living, Inc., Ames, Iowa, 1975-76, Ames Pub. Schs., 1975-76; cons.-evaluator North Ctrl. Assn. Colls. and Schs., 1986, mem. accreditation rev. com., 1990, chair, Higher Learning Commn. Contbr. articles to profl. jours. Mem. Sawyer Sch. PTA, Ames, Crawford Sch. PTA, Ames, Supts. Adv. Com., Ames; bd. dirs. Coop. Presch., Ames, Ames Soccer Club; bd. deacons, chair Christian edn. com., tchr. Collegiate Presbyn. Ch., Ames. Mem. APA, Am. Assn. Higher Edn., Soc. Rsch. in Child Devel., Phi Kappa Phi, Phi Eta Sigma (chpt. advisor 1990). Office: Deans Office Wartburg Coll 100 Wartburg Blvd Waverly IA 50677-2215 E-mail: ferol.menzel@wartburg.edu.

MENZNER, DONALD, food products executive; CEO Marathon (Wis.) Cheese. Office: Marathon Cheese 304 East St Marathon WI 54448

MEOLA, TONY, professional soccer player, actor; b. Belleville, NJ, Feb. 21, 1969; s. Vincent and Maria Meola; m. Colleen Meola; 1 child, Jonathan. Student, U. Va., 1986—89. Goalkeeper U.S. Nat. Team, 1988—94, 1999—2002, U.S. World Cup Team, 1990, 1994, 2002, Brighton Football Club, England, 1990, Fort Lauderdale Strikers, 1991, Long Island Roughriders, 1994—95, NY-NJ MetroStars, 1996—98, 2005—, Kansas City (Mo.) Wizards, 1998—2004. Actor: (plays) Tony ' Tina's Wedding, 1995. Named Hermann Trophy winner, MVP, U.S. Cup, 1993; named to MLS All Star Team, 1996—98, 2000, 2002; recipient Mo. Athletic Club Player of Yr., 1989. Achievements include drafted ctr. fielder N.Y. Yankees; tried out as placekicker for N.Y. Jets, 1994; mem. N.J. State H.S. Soccer Champions, 1986; NCAA Division I Co-Champions, 1989. Office: NY NJ MetroStars 3d Fl 1 Harmon Plz Secaucus NJ 07094

MERANUS, LEONARD STANLEY, lawyer; b. Newark, Jan. 7, 1928; s. Norman and Ada (Binstock) M.; m. Jane B. Holzman, Sept. 20, 1989; children: Norman, James M., David. LittB, Rutgers U., 1948; LLB, Harvard U., 1954. Bar: Ohio 1954. Assoc. Paxton & Seasongood, cin., 1954-59, ptnr., 1959-85, pres., 1985-89; ptnr. Thompson, Hine and Flory, 1989-96, ptnr.-in-charge Cin. office, 1989-91, mem. firm mgmt. com., 1991-93, of counsel, 1998—; adj. prof. law U. Cin. Coll. Law, 1998-2000. Bd. dirs. Jewish Hosp., 1976-86, chmn. of the bd., 1983-86; trustee Andrew Jergens Found., 1962-97. Mem. ABA, Ohio Bar Assn., Cin. Bar Assn., Am. Arbitration Assn. (chmn. comml. arbitration adv. com., Ohio panel large, complex arbitration cases). Office: Thompson Hine LLP 312 Walnut St Ste 14 Cincinnati OH 45202-4089

MERCER, DAVID ROBINSON, cultural organization administrator; b. Van Nuys, Calif., Aug. 14, 1938; s. Samuel Robinson and Dorothy (Lenox) M.; m. Joyce Elaine Dahl, Aug. 23, 1958; children: Steven, Michael, Kimberly. BA, Calif. State U., LA, 1961. Exec. dir. YMCA of L.A., 1963-69, sr. v.p., 1969-80; reg. mgr. Am. City Bur., Hoffman Estates, Ill., 1980-82; pres. YMCA of San Francisco, 1982-90; nat. exec. dir. YMCA of USA, Chgo., 1990—. Cons. fin. devel. YMCAs throughout U.S., 1975—. Mem. The Family, Rotary (bd. dirs. 1987-89). Republican. Methodist. Avocations: golf, bridge, flying, backpacking. Office: YMCA of USA 101 N Wacker Dr Chicago IL 60606-7386

MERCER, RON, professional basketball player; b. May 18, 1976; Student, U. Ky. Guard Boston Celtics, 1997-99, Denver Nuggets, 1999-00, Orlando Magic, 2000, Chgo. Bulls, 2000—. Named SEC Player of the Yr., 1997. Office: c/o Chgo Bulls United Ctr 1901 W Madison St Chicago IL 60612-2459

MERCHANT, JAMES A., medical educator; MD, U. Iowa; PhD in Epidimiology, U. N.C. Resident Cleve. Metro. Gen. Hosp.; fellow Duke U.; Trudeau fellow Brompton Hosp., London; mem. faculty U. N.C., 1973-75; adj. prof. W.Va. U., 1985-81; mem. faculty Coll. Medicine U. Iowa, 1981—. Contbr. articles to profl. jours. Mem. APHA, Am. Coll. Radiology, Am. Lung Assn., Am. Occupl. Medicine Assn., Am. Thoracic Soc., Internat. Assn. Occupl. Health, Nat. Inst. Occupl. Safety and Health (mem. bd. sci. counselors), Alpha Omega Alpha. Office: U Iowa Coll Medicine 2707 Steindler Building Iowa City IA 52242-1008

MERCHANT, MYLON EUGENE, physicist, engineer; b. Springfield, Mass., May 6, 1913; s. Mylon Dickinson and Rebecca Chase (Currier) M.; m. Helen Silver Bennett, Aug. 4, 1937; children: Mylon David (dec.), Leslie Ann Merchant Alexander(dec.), Frances Sue Merchant Jacobson. BS magna cum laude, U. Vt., 1936, DSc (hon.), 1973; DSc, U. Cinn., 1941; DSc (hon.), U. Salford, Eng., 1980; D of Engring (hon.), Kettering U., 1994. Rsch. physicist Milacron, Inc., 1940-48, sr. rsch. physicist, 1948-51, asst. dir. rsch., 1951-57, dir. phys. rsch., 1957-63, dir. sci. rsch., 1963-69, dir. rsch. planning, 1969-81, prin. scientist, mfg. rsch., 1981-83; dir. advanced mfg. rsch. Metcut Rsch. Assocs., Inc., 1983-90; sr. cons. TechSolve, Cin., 1990—. Adj. prof. mech. engring. U. Cin., 1964-69, mfg. engring., 2001-; vis. prof. mech. engring. U. Salford, Eng., 1973—; hon. prof. U. Hong Kong, 1995—. Bd. dirs. Dan Beard coun. Boy Scouts Am., 1967-80, pres.'s coun., 1980—. Recipient Georg Schlesinger prize City of Berlin, 1980; Otto Benedikt prize Hungarian Acad. Scis., 1981, 1st Japan Soc. Precision Engring. prize, 1997; named to Automation Hall of Fame, 1995.

Fellow Soc. Tribologists and Lubrication Engrs. (pres. 1952-53), Am. Soc. Metals Internat., Ohio Acad. Sci., Soc. Mfg. Engrs. (hon. mem., pres. 1976-77); mem. NAE, ASME (hon., mfg. medal 1988), Internat. Instn. Prodn. Engring. Rsch. (hon., pres. 1968-69), Engrs. and Scientists of Cin. (pres. 1961-62), Fedn. Materials Socs. (pres. 1974), Phi Beta Kappa, Sigma Xi, Tau Beta Pi. Achievements include research on machining process and systems approach to manufacturing. Office: TechSolve 6705 Steger Dr Cincinnati OH 45237-3097 Home: 1943 N Summit Ave Apt 20 Milwaukee WI 53202-1385 Home Phone: 513-271-2258; Office Phone: 513-948-2067. Business E-Mail: merchant@techsolve.org. E-mail: gmerchant@fuse.net.

MERCURI, JOAN B., museum administrator; b. NYC; BA, Va. Commonwealth U., 1984. Mgmt. positions various corps., Ill., 1986-96; exec. dir. Frank Lloyd Wright Home and Studio Found., Oak Park, Ill., 1996—; pres., CEO Frank Lloyd Wright Preservation Trust, Oak Park, 2000—. Dir. Oak Park Area Conv. and Vis. Bur. Mem. Am. Assn. Museums, Nat. Trust for Hist. Preservation, Employment Mgmt. Assn., Soc. Human Resource Mgmt., Frank Lloyd Wright Bldg. Conservancy, Assn. Fundraising Profls., Board Source. Office Phone: 708-848-1976. Business E-Mail: mercuri@wrightplus.org.

MERIDEN, TERRY, physician; b. Damascus, Syria, Oct. 12, 1946; arrived in U.S., 1975; s. Izzat and Omayma (Aidi) Meriden; m. Lena Kahal, Nov. 17, 1975; children: Zina, Lana. BS, Sch. Sci., Damascus, 1968; MD, Sch. Medicine, Damascus, 1972, doctorate cum laude, 1973. Diplomate Am. Bd. Internal Medicine. Resident in infectious diseases Rush Green Hosp., Romford, Eng., 1973; house officer in internal medicine and cardiology Ashford Group Univ. Hosps., England, 1973-74; sr. house officer in internal medicine and neurology Grimsby Group Univ. Hosps., England, 1974; registrar in internal medicine and rheumatology St. Annes Hosp., London, 1974-75; jr. resident in internal medicine Shadyside Hosp., Pitts., 1975-76, sr. resident in internal medicine, 1976-77; fellow in endocrinology and metabolism Shadyside Hosp. and Grad. Inst., Pitts., 1976-77; clin. asst. prof. U. Ill., Peoria, 1979; pres. Am. Diabetes Assn., Peoria, 1982-84; dir. Proctor Diabetes Unit, Peoria, 1984—, 1984—. Adviser Gov. of Ill. on diabetes. Mem. editl. bd. Diabetes Forecast mag., Clin. Diabetes, 1990; contbr. articles to profl. jours. Fellow: ACP, Am. Coll. Endocrinology; mem.: ADA (chmn. profl. edn. and rsch. 1980—, mem. editl. bd., mem. Spanish lit. bd., nat. bd. dirs. 1986—, vice chmn. nat. com. on diabetes edn. and affiliate svcs. 1986—, Outstanding Svc. award 1984, Outstanding Diabetes Educator award 1986), AMA (Recognition award 1985), Am. Coll. Endocrinology, Am. Assn. Clin. Endocrinology (founding), Am. Cancer Soc. (Life Line award 1983), Obesity Found. (Century award 1984, Recognition award 1985). Home: 115 E Coventry Ln Peoria IL 61614-2103 Office: 900 Main St Ste 300 Peoria IL 61602-1049 Home Phone: 309-673-1616; Office Phone: 309-673-1717. Personal E-mail: tmeriden@aol.com.

MERIWETHER, HEATH J., newspaper consultant, retired publisher, educator; b. Columbia, Mo., Jan. 20, 1944; s. Nelson Heath and Mary Agnes (Immele) Meriwether; m. Patricia Hughes, May 4, 1979; children: Graham, Elizabeth. BA in History, BJ, U. Mo., 1966; MAT, Harvard U., 1967; Advanced Exec. Program, Northwestern U. Journalism fellow Stanford U.; reporter Miami (Fla.) Herald, 1970—72, editor Broward and Palm Beach burs., 1972—77, exec. city editor, 1977—79, asst. mgr. editor news, 1979—80, mng. editor, 1981—83, exec. editor, 1983—87, Detroit Free Press, 1987—95, pub., 1996—2004; newspaper cons., 2004—. Adj. prof. grad. sch. journalism City U. NY, 2006—. Chair Rails to Trails Conservancy, 2005—07. Lt. USNR, 1967—70. Office Phone: 646-758-7824. Personal E-mail: hjm4491@yahoo.com.

MERRICK, RAYMOND F., state representative; b. Smith, Alberta, Can., Oct. 18, 1939; m. Phyllis Merrick; children: Michael, Matthew. BBA, Washburn U., 1965. Mgr. sales Folger's Coffee; gen. mgr. Treat Am., sr. v.p., Myron Green Cafeterias Co., gen. mgr.; owner MSM Mgmt.; mem. Kans. Ho. Reps., Topeka, 2000—. Spkr. pro tem Kans. Ho. Reps., Topeka, 2005—. Pres. booster club Blue Valley H.S., 1995—98; pres. Blue Valley Riding Home Assn. Republican. Lutheran. Office: State Capitol 300 SW 10th Ave Topeka KS 66612 Address: 6874 W 164th Terr Stilwell KS 66085

MERRIGAN, WILLIAM A., food services company executive; Dir. distbn. Grand Union Co.; corp. dir. warehouse & transportation A&P Corp.; v.p. transportation & logistics Wakefern Food Corp.; sr. v.p. distbn. & logistics Nash Finch Co., Mpls. Office: Nash Finch Co 7600 France Ave S Minneapolis MN 55435-5924

MERRILL, CHARLES EUGENE, lawyer; b. San Antonio, Aug. 26, 1952; s. Charles Perry and Florence Elizabeth Merrill; m. Carol Ann Rutter, Apr. 28, 1984; children: Elizabeth C., Charles C. AB, Stanford U., 1974; JD, U. Calif., Berkeley, 1977. Bar: Mo. 1977, Calif. 1983, Ill. 1993. Mem. Husch & Eppenberger, LLC, St. Louis, 1977—. Mem. ABA, Bar Assn. of Met. St. Louis. Office: Husch & Eppenberger LLC 190 Carondelet Plz Ste 600 Saint Louis MO 63105-3441 Business E-Mail: charlie.merrill@husch.com.

MERRILL, CHRISTOPHER LYALL, writer; b. Northampton, Mass., Feb. 24, 1957; s. Charles Francis Merrill and Suzanne Sigmund France; m. Lisa Ellen Gowdy, June 4, 1983; children: Hannah Frances, Abigail Rose. BA, Middlebury Coll., 1979; MA, U. Wash., 1982. Dir. Santa Fe Writers Conf., 1987-90, Santa Fe Literary Ctr., 1988-92; William H. Jenks chair Contemporary Letters Coll. of the Holy Cross, Worcester, Mass., 1995-2000; dir. internat. writing program U. Iowa, Iowa City, 2000—. Author: The Old Bridge: The Third Balkan War and The Age of the Refugee, 1995, Watch Fire, 1994, The Grass of Another Country: A Journey Through The World of Soccer, 1993, From the Faraway Nearby: Georgia O'Keefe As Icon, 1992, Only the Nails Remain: Scenes from the Balkan Wars, 1999, Brilliant Water, 2001, Things of the Hidden God, 2005; poetry editor Orion Mag., 1993-2003; contbg. editor Paris Rev., 1991-95; gen. editor-poetry series Gibbs Smith Pub., Layton, Utah, 1987-2001. Recipient Ingram Merrill Found. award, 1991, Pushcart Prize in Poetry, 1990, Arts and Letters chevalier French Govt., 2006. Mem. Acad. Am. Poets (Peter Lavan Younger Poets award 1993, Bosnian Stecak award 2001, Kostas Kyriazis Internat. Lit. award 2005). Episcopalian. Avocations: gardening, hiking, reading. Office: U Iowa Internat Writing Program Shambaugh House Iowa City IA 52242-2020 Office Phone: 319-335-2609. Business E-Mail: christopher-merrill@uiowa.edu.

MERRILL, THOMAS WENDELL, lawyer, educator; b. Bartlesville, Okla., May 3, 1949; s. William McGill and Dorothy (Glasener) Merrill; m. Kimberly Ann Evans, Sept. 18, 1973; children: Jessica, Margaret, Elizabeth. BA, Grinnell Coll., 1971, Oxford U., 1973; JD, U. Chgo., 1977. Bar: Ill. 1980, U.S. Dist. Ct. (no. dist.) Ill. 1980, U.S. Ct. Appeals (5th cir.) 1982, U.S. Ct. Appeals (7th cir.) 1983, U.S. Ct. Appeals (9th and DC cirs.) 1984, U.S. Supreme Ct. 1985. Clk. U.S. Ct. Appeals (DC cir.), Washington, 1977-78, U.S. Supreme Ct., Washington, 1978-79; assoc. Sidley & Austin, Chgo., 1979-81, counsel, 1981-87, 90—; dep. solicitor gen. U.S. Dept. Justice, 1987-90; prof. law Northwestern U., Chgo., 1981—2003, John Paul Stevens prof., 1993—2003; Charles Keller Beckman prof. Columbia U., 2003—. Co-author: (book) Property: Takings, 2002; contbr. articles to profl. jours. Rhodes scholar, Oxford U., 1971, Danforth fellow, 1971. Fellow: Am. Acad. Arts & Sci. Office: 435 W 116th St, Rm 727 New York NY 10027 Office Fax: 212-854-7946. E-mail: tmerri@law.columbia.edu.

MERRITT, GILBERT STROUD, federal judge; b. Nashville, Tenn., Jan. 17, 1936; s. Gilbert Stroud and Angie Fields (Cantrell) M.; m. Louise Clark Fort, July 10, 1964 (dec.); children: Stroud, Louise Clark, Eli. BA, Yale U., 1957; LLB, Vanderbilt U., 1960; LLM, Harvard U., 1962. Bar: Tenn. 1960. Asst. dean Vanderbilt U. Law Sch., 1960-61, lectr., 1963-69, 71-75, assoc. prof. law, 1969-70; assoc. Boult Hunt Cummings & Conners, Nashville, 1962-63; asst. metro. atty. City of ashville, 1963-66; US Dist. atty. for (mid. dist.) Tenn., 1966-69; ptnr. Gullett, Steele, Sanford, Robinson & Merritt, Nashville, 1970-77; judge US Ct. Appeals (6th cir.), Nashville, 1977-2001, chief judge, 1989—96, sr. judge., 2001—. Exec. sec. Tenn. Code Commn., 1977. Mng. editor: Vanderbilt Law Rev, 1959-60; contbr. articles to law jours. Del. Tenn. Constl. Conv., 1965; chmn. bd. trustees Vanderbilt Inst. Pub. Policy Studies. Mem. ABA, Fed. Bar Assn., Tenn. Bar Assn., Nashville Bar Assn., Vanderbilt Law Alumni Assn. (pres. 1979-80), Am. Law Inst., Order of Coif. Episcopalian. Office: US Ct Appeals Customs House 701 Broadway Ste 303 Nashville TN 37203-3967

MERRITT, JAMES W., JR., state legislator, real estate developer; b. Indpls., July 28, 1959; s. James Warner and Marion Jane (Brown) M.; m. Kelley A. McCloskey, May 10, 1985. BS in Arts & Sci., Ind. State U., 1981. Candidate asst. Merchert for Congress, Indpls., 1981-82; campaign mgr. Hillis for Congress, Kokomo, 1982-83; dist. asst. U.S. Rep. Bud Hillis, Kokomo, 1983; property mgr. Circle Fin. Corp., Indpls.; mem. Ind. Senate from 31st dist., Indianapolis, 1990—. Mem. ward chmn. Marion County Rep. Party Lawrence Twp. 1987—. Mem. Jr. Achievement, Toastmasters. Republican. Office: Circle Fin Corp 9102 N Meridian St Indianapolis IN 46260-1860 Address: Ind Senate Dist 31 200 W Washington St Indianapolis IN 46204-2728

MERRYMAN, GEORGE, automotive executive; CFO Jordan Motors Inc., Mishawaka, Ind. Office: Jordan Motors Inc 609 E Jefferson Blvd Mishawaka IN 46545-6524

MERSEREAU, JOHN, JR., literature and language professor; b. San Jose, Calif., Apr. 16, 1925; s. John Joshua and Winona Beth (Roberts) M.; m. Nanine Landell, July 11, 1953; children: Daryl Landell, John Coates. AB, U. Calif., 1945, MA, 1950, PhD, 1957. Teaching fellow, Slavic dept. U. Calif., Berkeley, 1950-52, research asst., 1953-54; instr. Slavic dept. U. Mich., Ann Arbor, 1956-59, asst. prof., 1959-61, assoc. prof., 1961-63, prof., 1963—, chmn. dept., 1961-71, 85-89, prof. emeritus, 1990—, dir. Residential Coll., 1977-85. Mem. Joint Com. Eastern Europe of Am. Council Learned Socs./Social Sci. Research Council, 1971-74, chmn., 1973-74. Author: Mikhail Lermontov, 1962, Baron Delvig's Literary Almanac: Northern Flowers, 1967, Translating Russian, 1968, Russian Romantic Fiction, 1983, Orest Somov, 1989, How to Grill a Gourmet, 2000, Overdue at Immokalee, A Tale of Preemptive Assassination, 2003, The Russian Novel of Psychological Realism, 2005; assoc. editor Mich. Slavic Publs., 1962—; contbr. articles to profl. jours. Served to lt. (j.g.) USNR, 1943-46, PTO. Calmerton Slavic scholar U. Calif., Berkeley, 1954-55; Ford Found. fellow, London and Paris, 1955-56, Guggenheim fellow, 1972-73; recipient Disting. Service award U. Mich., Ann Arbor, 1961. Mem. Am. Assn. Advancement Slavic Studies, U. Mich. Research Club. Clubs: Waterloo Hunt (Grass Lake, Mich., sec. 1970-80); Commanderie de Bordeaux (Detroit). Avocations: flying, gourmet cuisine, raising horses. Office: U of Mich Slavic Dept Ann Arbor MI 48109 Business E-Mail: mersérea@umich.edu.

MERSHAD, FREDERICK J., retail executive; b. 1943; Exec. merchandising Rich's, McRae's, Millers; exec. v.p. Proffitt's, Inc., 1994-95, pres., CEO, 1995, Elder-Beerman, 1995—. Office: Elder-Beerman Stores Corp PO Box 1448 Dayton OH 45401-1448

MERSZEI, GEOFFREY E., corporate financial executive; BA, Albion Coll. With Dow Chem. Co., Midland, Mich., 1977—2001, treas. Germany Frankfurt, 1983—85, treas. Ea. Europe, 1985—86, fgn. exch. mgr. Midland, Mich., 1986—88, dir. fin. Asia Pacific Hong Kong, 1988—91, dir. fin. Europe Horgen, Switzerland, 1991—96, v.p., treas. Midland, Mich., 1996—2001; exec. v.p., CFO Alcan, Inc., 2001—05, Dow Chem. Co., Midland, Mich., 2005—, bd. dirs., mem. Office of the Chief Exec., 2005—. Bd. dir. Dow Corning Corpn.; mem. Conf. Bd. Com. Coun. Fin. Execs.; mem. corp. exec. bd. working coun. for CFOs. Office: Dow Chem Co 2030 Dow Ctr Midland MI 48674

MERTE, HERMAN, JR., mechanical engineering educator; b. Detroit, Apr. 3, 1929; s. Herman and Anna Marie (Mitterer) M.; m. Bernice Marie Brant, Sept. 17, 1952; children: Kenneth Edward, James Dennis, Lawrence Carleton, Richard Brant, Robert Paul. BS in Marine Engring, U. Mich., Ann Arbor, 1950, BS in Mech. Engring, 1951, MS, 1956, PhD, 1960. Faculty U. Mich., 1959—67, prof. mech. engring. Ann Arbor, 1967—2000, prof. emeritus, 2000—. Vis. prof. Tech. U. Munich, Germany, 1974-75 Served to lt. (j.g.) USNR, 1952-55. NSF sr. postdoctoral fellow, 1967-68 Mem. ASME, AIAA, Am. Soc. Engring. Edn., Am. Assn. U. Profs., Sigma Xi. Home: 3480 Cottontail Ln Ann Arbor MI 48103-1706 Office: U Mich Heat Transfer Lab 2026 G G Brown Lab Ann Arbor MI 48109-2125 Home Phone: 734-662-6253; Office Phone: 734-764-5240. Business E-Mail: merte@umich.edu.

MERTENS, THOMAS ROBERT, biology professor; b. Fort Wayne, Ind., May 22, 1930; s. Herbert F. and Hulda (Burg) M.; m. Beatrice Janet Abair, Apr. 1, 1953; children: Julia Ann, David Gerhard BS, Ball State U., 1952; MS, Purdue U., 1954, PhD, 1956. Research assoc. dept. genetics U. Wis.-Madison, 1956-57; asst. prof. biology Ball State U., Muncie, Ind., 1957-62, assoc. prof., 1962-66, prof., 1966-93, dir. doctoral programs in biology, 1974-93, George and Frances Ball disting. prof. biology edn., 1988-93, prof. emeritus, 1993—. Author: (with A. M. Winchester) Human Genetics, 1983 (with R.L. Hammersmith) Genetics Laboratory Investigations, 13th edit., 2006 (co-recipient William Holmes McGuffey Longevity award Text and Acad. Authors Assn. 1998); contbr. numerous articles to profl. jours. Co-recipient Gustav Ohaus award for innovative coll. sci. tchg. NSTA, 1986, recipient Disting. Svc. to Sci. Edn. citation, 1987; fellow NSF, 1963-64, Ind. Acad. Scis., 1969. Fellow AAAS; mem. Nat. Assn. Biology Tchrs. (pres. 1985, hon. mem. 1988), Am. Genetic Assn., Genetics Soc. Am. Episcopalian. Home: 4501 N Wheeling 9B-4 Muncie IN 47304-1277 Office: Ball State U Dept Biology Muncie IN 47306-0001 Personal E-mail: t.mertens@att.net.

MERTINS, JAMES WALTER, entomologist; b. Milw., Feb. 18, 1943; s. Walter Edwin and Harriet Ellen (Sockett) M.; m. Marilee Eloise Joeckel, Dec. 8, 1979. BS in Zoology, U. Wis., Milw., 1965; MS in Entomology, U. Wis., 1967, PhD in Entomology, 1971. Project assoc. dept. entomology U. Wis., Madison, 1971-75, rsch. assoc. dept. entomology, 1975-77; asst. prof. dept. entomology Iowa State U., Ames, 1977-84; entomol. cons. Ames, 1984-89; entomologist Nat. Vet. Svcs. Labs. USDA Animal and Plant Health Inspection Svc., Ames, 1989—. Co-author: (textbook) Biological Insect Pest Suppression, 1977, Russian edit., 1980, Chinese edit., 1988; contbr. articles to profl. jours. NSF Grad. fellow, 1970. Mem. Entomol. Soc. Am. (Insect Photography award 1984, 86, 2003), Entomol. Soc. Can., Mich. Entomol. Soc., Wis. Entomol. Soc. (pres., sec., treas., bd. dirs.), Cyclone Corvettes, Inc. (co-founder, pres. 1978, 79, sec., treas., bd. dirs., Mem. of Yr. 1982), Am. Mensa. Avocations: insect photography, Corvette automobile activities, gardening, movies, insect collecting. Office: USDA Animal and Plant Health Inspection Svc PO Box 844 Ames IA 50010-0844 Business E-Mail: James.W.Mertins@aphis.usda.gov.

MERTZ, DOLORES MARY, farmer, state legislator; b. Bancroft, Iowa, May 30, 1928; d. John Francis and Gertrude (Erickson) Shay; m. H. Peter Mertz (dec. 1983), Dec. 27, 1951; children: Peter, Mary Simpson, David, Ann Cornicelli, Helen Powell, Janice, Carol. AA, Briar Cliff Coll., 1948. Pres. Coun. Cath. Women, Sioux City, Iowa, 1986-88; state regent Cath. Daus. Am., Iowa, 1988-94; county supr. Kossuth County, Iowa, 1983-89; mem. Iowa Ho. of Reps., Des Moines, 1989—. Dem. precinct com. person, Kossuth County, Iowa, sec. 1975—. Recipient Womens Leadership award Iowa Lakes Community Coll., 1978; named Woman of Yr. Beta Sigma Phi Internat., West Bend, Iowa, 1989; recipient Iowa Lakes Community Coll. Disting. Svc. award, 1992, Guardian of Small Businsess award. Mem. Soroptomist Internat. (Woman of Distinction award 1987), Drama Club (pres. 1970's). Liberal. Roman Catholic. Office: Iowa Ho of Reps State Capitol Des Moines IA 50319-0001 Home: 607 110th St Ottosen IA 50570-8504

MERVIS, LOUIS, school system administrator; Chmn. Ill. Bd. Edn., Springfield, 1991-93, 97-99; owner Mervis Industries, Danville, Ill. Office: Mervis Industries 3295 E Main St Danville IL 61834-9382

MERWIN, DAVIS UNDERWOOD, newspaper executive; b. Chgo., June 22, 1928; s. Davis and Josephine (Underwood) M.; m. Nancy Snowden Smith Tailer, Nov. 14, 1958 (dec. Feb. 1995); children: Davis Fell, Laura Howell; m. Sharon Adkins Todd, May 12, 1998. AB, Harvard U., 1950; LLD (hon.), Ill. Wesleyan U., 1991. Pres. Evergreen Comm., Inc., Bloomington, Ill., 1969-80; pub. Daily Pantagraph, 1968-80; pres. Wood Canyon Corp., Tucson, 1989-93; vice-chmn. Bloomington Broadcasting Corp., 1993-99. Dir. State Farm Growth, Balanced Mcpl. Bond and Interim Funds, State Farm Variable Products Funds. Trustee emeritus Ill. Wesleyan U.; trustee Ill. Nature Conservancy. Recipient Disting. Svc. award U.S. Jaycees, 1959 Mem. Am. Newspaper Pubs. Assn., Inland Daily Press Assn. (pres. 1977, chmn. bd. dirs. 1978), Harvard Club (Chgo.), Phoenix-SK Club, Hasty Pudding Club, Bloomington Country Club, Ristigouche Salmon Club. Republican. Unitarian Universalist. Office: 2422 E Washington St Bloomington IL 61704-4478 Mailing: PO Box 1665 Bloomington IL 61702-1665 E-mail: DUMerwin@aol.com.

MERZ, JAMES LOGAN, electrical and materials engineering educator, researcher; b. Jersey City, Apr. 14, 1936; s. Albert Joseph and Anne Elizabeth (Farrell) M.; m. Rose-Marie Weibel, June 30, 1962; children: Kathleen, James, Michael, Kimarie. BS in Physics, U. Notre Dame, 1959; postgrad., U. Göttingen, Fed. Republic Germany, 1959-60; MA, Harvard U., 1961, PhD in Applied Physics, 1967; PhD (hon.), Linköping U., Sweden, 1993. Mem. tech. staff Bell Labs., Murray Hill, J, 1966-78; prof. elec. engring. U. Calif., Santa Barbara, 1978-94, prof. materials, 1986-94, chmn. dept. elec. and computer engring., 1982-84, assoc. dean for rsch. devel. Coll. Engring., 1984-86, acting assoc. vice chancellor, 1988, dir. semiconductor rsch. corp. core program on GaAs digital ICs, 1984-89, dir. Compound Semiconductor Rsch. Labs., 1986-92, dir. NSF Ctr. for Quantized Electronic Structures, 1989-94; Freimann prof. elec. engring. U. otre Dame (Ind.), 1994—, v.p. for grad. studies and rsch., dean Grad. Sch., 1996-2001, interim dean engring., 2006—. Mem. exec. com. Calif. Microelectronics Innovation and Computer Rsch. Opportunities Program, 1986-92; mem. NRC com. on Japan, NAS/NAE, 1988-90; mem. internat. adv. com. Internat. Symposium on Physics of Semiconductors and Applications, Seoul, Republic of Korea, 1990, Conf. on Superlattices and Microstructures, Xi'an, China, 1992; participant, mem. coms. other profl. confs. and meetings. Contbr. over 400 articles to profl. jours.; patentee in field. Fulbright fellow, Danforth Found. fellow, Woodrow Wilson Found. fellow; Alexander von Humboldt rsch. awardee, 2002. Fellow IEEE, Am. Phys. Soc.; mem. IEEE Lasers and Electro-Optics Soc. (program com. annual mtg. 1980), IEEE Electron Device Soc. (sec. 1994, 95), Am. Vacuum Soc. (exec. com. electronic materials and processing divsn. 1988-89), Materials Rsch. Soc. (editl. bd. jour. 1984-87), Soc. for Values in Higher Edn., Inst. Electronics, Info. and Comm. Engrs. (overseas adv. com.), Sigma Xi, Eta Kappa Nu. Achievements include research in field of optoelectronic materials and devices: semiconductors and ionic materials; optical and electrical properties of implanted ions, rapid annealing; semiconductor lasers, detectors, solar cells, other optoelectronic devices; low-dimensional quantum structures, nanostructures. Home: 1530 Marigold Way South Bend IN 46617-1016 Office: U Notre Dame Dept Elec Engring 203B Cushing Hall Notre Dame IN 46556-5637 Business E-Mail: jmerz@nd.edu.

MERZ, MICHAEL, federal judge; b. Dayton, Ohio, Mar. 29, 1945; s. Robert Louis and Hazel (Appleton) M.; m. Marguerite Logan LeBreton, Sept. 7, 1968; children: Peter Henry, Nicholas George. AB cum laude, Harvard U., 1967, JD, 1970. Bar: Ohio 1970, U.S. Dist. Ct. (so. dist.) Ohio 1971, U.S Supreme Ct. 1974, U.S. Ct. Appeals (6th cir.) 1975. Assoc. Smith & Schnacke, Dayton, Ohio, 1970-75, ptnr., 1976-77; judge Dayton Mcpl. Ct., 1977-84; magistrate judge U.S. Dist. Ct. (so. dist.) Ohio, 1984—. Adj. prof. U. Dayton Law Sch., 1979—; mem. rules adv. com. Ohio Supreme Ct., 1989-96. Bd. dirs. United Way, Dayton, 1981-95; trustee Dayton Metro Libr., 1991—, Montgomery County Hist. Soc., 1995—, Ohio Libr. Coun., 1997-2000; pastoral coun., Cincinnati Archdiocese; mem. nat. rev. bd. U.S. Conf. Cath. Bishops, 2004—. Fellow Am. Bar Found.; mem. ABA, Fed. Bar Assn., Am. Judicature Soc., Fed. Magistrate Judges Assn. (trustee 1997-2000), Ohio State Bar Assn. (chair Fed. Cts. Com., 2003-), Dayton Bar Assn. Republican. Roman Catholic. Office: US Dist Ct 902 Federal Bldg 200 W 2nd St Dayton OH 45402-1430 Office Phone: 937-512-1550. Business E-Mail: michael.merz@ohsd.uscourts.gov.

MESCHKE, HERBERT LEONARD, retired state supreme court justice; b. Belfield, ND, Mar. 18, 1928; s. G.E. and Dorothy E. Meschke; m. Shirley Ruth McNeil; children: Marie, Jean, Michael, Jill. BA, Jamestown Coll., 1950; JD, U. Mich., 1953. Bar: N.D. Law clk. U.S. Dist. Ct. N.D., 1953-54; practice law Minot, N.D., 1954-85; mem. N.D. Ho. of Reps., 1965-66, N.D. Senate, 1967-70; justice N.D. State Supreme Ct., 1985-98; of counsel Pringle & Herigstad Law Firm, Minot, 1999—. Mem. ABA, Am. Law Inst., Am. Judicature Soc., N.D. Bar Assn.

MESHBESHER, RONALD I., lawyer; b. Mpls., May 18, 1933; s. Nathan J. and Esther J. (Balman) M.; m. Sandra F. Siegel, June 17, 1956 (div. 1978); children: Betsy F., Wendy S., Stacy J.; m. Kimberly L. Garnaas, May 23, 1988; 1 child, Jolie M. BS in Law, U. Minn., 1955, JD, 1957. Bar: Minn. 1957, U.S. Supreme Ct. 1966. Prosecuting atty. Hennepin County, Mpls., 1958-61; pres. Meshbesher and Spence Ltd., Mpls., 1961—. Lectr. numerous legal and profl. orgns.; mem. adv. com. on rules of criminal procedure Minn. Supreme Ct., 1971-91; cons. on recodification of criminal procedure code Czech Republic Ministry of Justice, 1994. Author: Trial Handbook for Minnesota Lawyers, 1992; mem. bd. editors Criminal Law Advocacy Reporter; mem. adv. bd. Bur. Nat. Affairs Criminal Practice Manual; contbr. numerous articles to profl. jours. Mem.: ABA, ATLA (bd. govs. 1968—71),Calif. Attys. for Criminal Justice, Trial Lawyers for Pub. Justice, Minn. Assn. Criminal Def. Lawyers (pres. 1991—92, Disting. Svc. award 2001), Minn. Trial Lawyers Assn.(pres 1973—74, (Lifetime Achievement award 2001), at. Assn. Criminal Def. Lawyers (pres. 1984—85), Am. Acad. Forensic Scis., Am. Bd. Criminal Lawyers (v.p. 1983, bd.gov.) Am. Bd. Trial Advs., Am. Coll. Trial Lawyers (Lifetime Achievement sward, Minn. chpt., 2006), Internat. Acad. Trial Lawyers, Minn. Bar Assn. Avocations: bicycling, photography, travel, flying, theater. Office: Meshbesher & Spence 1616 Park Ave Minneapolis MN 55404-1695 Home Phone: 952-449-8700; Office Phone: 612-339-9121. E-mail: rmeshbesher@meshbesher.com.

MESHEL, HARRY, former state senator, political party official; b. Youngstown, Ohio, June 13, 1924; s. Angelo and Rubena (Markakis) Michelakis; children: Barry, Melanie. BSBA, Youngstown Coll., 1949; MS, Columbia U., 1950; LLD (hon.), Ohio U., Youngstown State U., Ohio Coll. Podiatric Medicine; LHD (hon.), Youngstown State U. Exec. asst. to mayor City of Youngstown, Ohio, 1964-68, urban renewal dir. Ohio, 1969; mem. 33d district Ohio Senate, Columbus, 1971-93, Dem. minority leader, 1981-82, 85-90, pres. and majority leader, 1983-84, com. mem. econ. develop., sci. & tech., state & local govt., ways & means, commerce & labor, controlling bd., state employment compensation bd., fin. chmn., 1974-81, rules chmn., 1983-84, com. mem. rules, reference & oversight, 1985-90; state chair Ohio Dem. Party, 1993-95. Real estate broker; adj. prof. polit. sci. Ohio U.; faculty mem. (limited svc.), bd. trustees Youngstown State U.; div. mgr. investment firm; Ohio Senate special com. mem. Task Force on Drug Strategies, Ohio Acad. Sci. Centennial Celebration Commn., Motor Vehicle Inspection & Maintenance Program, Legis. Oversight Com., Ohio Boxing Commn., Correctional Inst. Inspection Com., Ohio Small Bus. & Entrepreneurship Coun., Gov.'s Adv. Coun. Travel & Tourism, Legis. Svc. Commn., Capital Sq. Rev. & Adv. Bd., others. Past pres., past lt. gov. Am. Hellenic Ednl. Prog. Assn. (AHEPA); precinct committeeman Mahoning County Dem. Party, ward captain, mem. exec. com.; campaign mgr. local candidates, county campaign mgr. presdl. candidates; del. Dem. Mid-Term Conv., 1981; founder Great Lakes/N.E. Legis. Coalition; chmn., founder Nat. Dem. State Legis. Leaders Assn.; dir. State Legis. Leaders Found.; state/fed. assembly, mem. communications com. Nat. Conf. State Legis., legis. mgmt. com., govt. opers. com.; chair fiscal affairs com. Midwest Conf. Coun. State Govts., task force on econs. & fiscal affairs; del., exec. com. Dem. Nat. Com.; mem. Dem. Leadership Coun., State Dem. Exec. Com.; exec. com. Assn. State Dem. Chairs; bd. trustees Nat. Hall of Fame for Persons with Disabilities; mem. St. icholas Greek Orthodox Ch.; mem. Mill Creek Metro Park Bd. Commrs. With USN, 1943-46. Decorated two Bronze Battle Stars; recipient Dist. Svc. award Office of Pres., Top Legislator award Ohio Union Patrolmen Assn., Dist. Citizen award Med. Coll. Ohio, City of Hope Leadership award, 1993, Legis. Leadership award Ohio Coalition for Edn. of Handicapped Children, Phillips Medal of Pub. Svc., Ohio U., John E. Fogarty award Gov.'s Com. of Employment of Handicapped, Gov.'s award, 1992, U. Cin. Award for Excellence, Lamp of Learning award Ohio Edn. Assn., Black Cultural Soc. award East Liverpool, Mahoning Valley Man of Yr. award, Mahoning Valley Econ. Devel. Corp., Office Holder of Yr. award Truman-Johnson Dem. Women, Best Interest of Children award Fathers of Equal Rights, Founders Day award Circle of Friends Found., Helping Hand award Easter Seal Soc., Honorary Riverboat Captain award Mahoning County Dem. Party, Community Svc. and Special Svcs. awards Eastern Orthodox Men's Soc., Periclean award AHEPA, Academy of Achievement award Nat. AHEPA Ednl. Found., at. Svc. Dem. award AHEPA, 1994, Disting. Citizen award Youngstown State U. Alumni Assn., numerous appreciation and recognition awards; recipient Outstanding Legislator awards Ohio Acad. Trial Lawyers, Ohio Assn. Pub. Sch. Employees, Ohio Rehab. Assn., League Ohio Sportsmen; recipient Dist. Svc. awards Youngstown State U., Ohio Edn. Assn., Ohio Union Patrolmen Assn., Ohio Disabled Vets., AFL-CIO Ohio Barbers Union, AFL-CIO Nat. Assn. of Theatre Owners of Ohio; named

Guardian of the Menorah, Youngstown B'nai B'rith, Outstanding Dem., Fairfield Dem. Club, 1993; named to Ohio Vets. Hall of Fame. Mem. (life) NAACP, ACLU, AMVETS (Legislator of Yr. 1993), VFW, Am. Legion, Cath. War Vets (Dist. Legislator award), Vet. Boxers Assn. Mercer County, Pa., Trumbull County Boxers' Legends of Leather (Man of Yr. award Hall of Fame), William Holmes McGuffey Hist. Soc., Buckeye Elks Lodge (hon.); mem. Kiwanis Internat., Urban League, Alliance C. of C., Southern Community Jaycees (hon.), Soc. for Preservation of Greek Heritage, Greek Am. Progressive Assn., Pan Cretan Assn., Arms Hist. Mus. Soc., Eagles, Moose, The Stambaugh Pillars.

MESHII, MASAHIRO, materials science educator; b. Amagasaki, Japan, Oct. 6, 1931; arrived in US, 1956; s. Masataro and Kazuyo M.; m. Eiko Kumagai, May 21, 1959; children: Alisa, Erica. BS, Osaka U., Japan, 1954, MS, 1956; PhD, Northwestern U., 1959. Lectr., rsch. assoc. dept. materials sci. and engring. orthwestern U., Evanston, Ill., 1959-60, asst. prof., assoc. prof., then prof., 1960-88, chmn. dept. materials sci. and engring., 1978-82, John Evans prof., 1988—2003, John Evans prof. emeritus, 2003—. Vis. scientist Nat. Rsch. Inst. Metals, Tokyo, 1970-71; NSF faculty rsch. participant Argonne (Ill.) at. Lab., 1975; guest prof. Osaka U., 1985; Acta/Scripta Metallurgica lectr., 1993-95. Co-editor: Lattice Defects in Quenched Metals, 1965, Martensitic Transformation, 1978, Science of Advanced Materials, 1990; editor: Fatigue and Microstructures, 1979, Mechanical Properties of BCC Metals, 1982; contbr. over 245 articles to tech. publs. and internat. jours. Recipient Founders award Midwest Soc. Electron Microscopists, 1987; named Best Tchr. of Yr., Engring. Students of Northwestern U., 1978; Fulbright grantee, 1956; Japan fellow, 1957. Fellow ASM (Henry Marion Howe medal 1968, Best Acad. Paper award 1994), Japan Soc. Promotion of Sci.; mem. AIME (Meritorious award for Best Paper Iron and Steel Soc. 1993), Metall. Soc., Japan Inst. Metals (hon., Achievement award 1972), Toastmasters Internat. (Disting. Toast Master, 1987, 2007). Office: 22879 NE 127th Way Redmond WA 98053-5657 Office Phone: 425-836-2334. Personal E-mail: mmeshii@hotmail.com.

MESSER, RANDY KEITH, graphics designer, illustrator; b. Des Moines, Sept. 10, 1960; s. Delmar Keith and Thelma Darlene (Myers) M.; m. Jennifer Rae Harmeling, June 12, 1982; children: Joanna, Andrew. BA, Ctrl. Coll., Pella, Iowa, 1982; Assoc. in Applied Arts, Des Moines Area C.C., Ankeny, Iowa, 1984. Designer Eagle Sign and Advt., Des Moines, 1983-84, Perfection Form Co., Des Moines, 1984-90; asst. design dir. Perfection Learing Co., Des Moines, 1990-93, design dir., 1993—. Mem. adv. bd. Des Moines Area C.C., Ankeny, 1987—. Illustrator: Great Eagle and Small One, 1997. Elder Calvary Reformed Ch., Des Moines, 1989—. Recipient Silver awards Iowa Art Dirs. Exhbn., Des Moines, 1989, 91, Highest award Dale Carnegie Leadership, Des Moines, 1996; Art Dirs. Assn. Iowa scholar Iowa Art Dirs. Assn., Des Moines, 1984. Mem. Art Dirs. Assn. Iowa (treas. 1988-89, v.p. programs 1989-90, v.p. exhbn. 1990-91, pres. 1991-92, Gold award 1992). Avocations: hunting, fishing, photography, gardening, travel. Home: 9319 Lakewood Pointe Dr Norwalk IA 50211-1769 Office: Perfection Learning Corp 10520 New York Ave Des Moines IA 50322-3775

MESSIN, MARLENE ANN, plastics company executive; b. St. Paul, Oct. 6, 1935; d. Edgar Leander and Luella Johanna (Rahn) Johnson; m. Eugene Carlson (div. 1972); children: Rick, Debora, Ronald, Lori; m. Willard Smith (dec. 1975); m. Frank Messin, Sept. 24, 1982; 5 stepchildren. Bookkeeper Jeans Implement Co., Forest Lake, Minn., 1952-53, 1953—57, Great Plains Supply, St. Paul, 1960-62, Plastic Products Co., Inc., Lindstrom, Minn., 1962-75, pres., 1975—; co-owner, treas. Gustaf's Fine Gifts, Lindstrom, 1985—. Bookkeeper Trinity Luth. Ch., Lindstrom, 1976—81. Recipient award, Diversity 2000/Woman-Owned Bus. in Minn. Mem. Soc. Plastic Engrs., Swedish Inst., Soc. Plastic Industry, Minn. State Hist. Soc., Chgo. County Hist. Soc. Home: 28968 Olinda Trl Lindstrom MN 55045-9429 Office: 30355 Akerson St Lindstrom MN 55045-9456

MESSINGER, DONALD HATHAWAY, lawyer; b. Lyons, NY, July 1, 1943; s. Donald H. and Thelma (Hubbard) M.; m. Sara L. Stock, June 3, 1967; children: Michael David, Robert Stephen, Daniel Mark. BA, Colgate U., 1965; JD, Duke U., 1968. Bar: Ohio 1968. Assoc. Thompson Hine LLP, Cleve., 1968-76, ptnr., 1976—, vice chair corp. practice group, 1989-92, ptnr.-in-charge Cleve. office, 1991-96, mem. exec. com., 1996-2000. Sec., bd. dirs. Am. Steel and Wire Corp., 1986-93; sec., bd.dirs. Lee Wilson Engineering C., Inc., 1989-94; bd. dirs. Cedar Fair Mgmt. Co., 1993-2002. Trustee Cmty. Info.-Vol. Action Ctr., 1981-88, pres. 1981-84; trustee Free Med. Clinic Greater Cleve., 1970—, sec., 1970-82, v.p. 1982-86, 96-2002, pres. 2002-04; trustee Cleve. Hearing and Speech Ctr., 1980—, v.p. 1984-86, 92-93, pres., 1986-88, 98-2000; dir. Colgate U. Alumni Corp., 1979-83; trustee U. for Young Ams., 1982-95, sec.,1982-1982-86, pres., 1986-88, chmn. 1991-95; mem. exec. bd. Boy Scouts Am., 1983-88; Leadership Cleve., 1984—; trustee, sec. Bus. Vols. Unltd., 1992—; sec. Buckeye Area Devel. Corp., 1970-90; mem. adv. bd. Greater Cleve. New Stadium; dir., Cleve. Pops Orch., 2006-. Recipient Cmty. Svc. award Fedn. for Community Planning, 1981-82, Daniel D. Dauby award Cleve. Hearing & Speech Ctr. 2007.; named one of Outstanding Young Citizens of Greater Cleve., 1971-75, BTI Client Svc. All Star 2006. Mem. ABA, Ohio Bar Assn., Cleve. Bar Assn. (trustee 1975-79, chmn. securities law inst. 1983), Nat. Assn. Bond Lawyers Home: 21550 Shelburne Rd Shaker Heights OH 44122 Office: 3900 Key Ctr 127 Public Sq Cleveland OH 44114 Business E-Mail: don.messinger@thompsonhine.com.

MESSNER, JAMES W., advertising executive; b. 1939; Attended, 1959-61. With Sta. WCSM, Celina, Ohio, 1961-63, Sta. WTOD, Toledo, 1961-63, Detroit Advt. Agy., 1965-68, Norman, Navan, Moore & Bard, 1968-77; chmn., CEO J.W. Messner Inc., Grand Rapids, Mich., 1977—. Office: JW Messner Inc 161 Ottawa Ave NW Ste 403 Grand Rapids MI 49503-2760

METCALF, CHARLES DAVID, museum director, retired military officer; b. Anamosa, Iowa, June 18, 1933; m. Patricia (Sedlacek) M.; children: Christin, Karen. BA, Coe Coll., 1955; MBA, Mich. State U., 1964. Commd. 2d lt. USAF, 1955; advanced through grades to maj. gen., 1986; various fin. mgmt. duties USAF; asst. dir. Defense Security Assistance Agy.; commdr. Air Force Acctg. and Fin. Ctr.; ret., 1991; dir. USAF Mus., Wright-Patterson AFB, Ohio, 1996—. Decorated D.S.M. with one oak leaf cluster, Def. Superior Svc. medal, Legion of Merit. Office: USAF Mus 1100 Spaatz St Wright Patterson AFB OH 45433-7102

METCALF, DEAN, radio personality; Radio host morning show Sta. WFBQ-FM, Indpls. Office: WFBQ 6161 Fall Creek Rd Indianapolis IN 46220

METCALF, ROBERT CLARENCE, architect, educator; b. Nashville, Ohio, Nov. 7, 1923; s. George and Helen May (Drake) M.; m. Bettie Jane Sponseller, Sept. 15, 1943. Student, Johns Hopkins U., 1943; B.Arch., U. Mich., 1950. Draftsman G.B. Brigham, Jr., Architect, Ann Arbor, Mich., 1948-52; pvt. practice architecture Ann Arbor, 1953—; lectr. architecture U. Mich., Ann Arbor, 1955-58, asst. prof., 1958-63, asso. prof., 1963-68, prof., 1968-91, chmn. dept., 1968-74; dean U. Mich. (Coll. Architecture and Urban Planning), 1974-86; Emil Lorch prof. emeritus U. Mich., 1991—, dean emeritus, 1991—; pvt. practice, 1991—. Sec. Mich. Bd. Registration for Architects, 1975-79, chmn., 1980-82 Designer more than 140 bldgs., Ann Arbor, 1953—. Served with U.S. Army, 1943-46, ETO. Decorated Silver Star; recipient Sol King award for excellent teaching in architecture U. Mich., 1974; named Emil Lorch Professor of Architecture, 1989. Fellow AIA (Pres.'s award 1999); mem. AIA Mich., Assn. Collegiate Schs. Architecture, Phi Kappa Phi, Tau Sigma Delta. Home: 1052 Arlington Blvd Ann Arbor MI 48104-2816 Office: U Mich 2150 Art Architecture Bldg Ann Arbor MI 48109 also: Metcalf Architect 2211 Medford Rd Ann Arbor MI 48104-5004

METCALFE, WALTER LEE, JR., lawyer; b. St. Louis, Dec. 19, 1938; s. Walter Lee and Carol Metcalfe; m. Cynthia Williamson, Aug. 26, 1965; children: Carol, Edward. AB, Washington U., St. Louis, 1960; JD, U. Va., 1964. Bar: Mo. 1964. Ptnr. Armstrong, Teasdale, Kramer & Vaughan, St. Louis, 1964—81; sr. ptnr. Bryan Cave LLP, St. Louis, 1982—, former chmn.; chmn. Fed. Res. Bd., St. Louis. Bd. dirs. BJC Health Care, St. Louis. Bd. dirs. Washington U., St. Louis, Danforth Found., Pulitzer Found. Arts, St. Louis Children's Hosp. Named one of 100 Most Influential Lawyers, Nat. Law Jour., 2006. Mem.: ABA, St. Louis Bar Assn., Mo. Bar Assn., Noonday Club, Bogey Club. Episcopalian. Home: 26 Upper Ladue Rd Saint Louis MO 63124-1675 Office: Bryan Cave 211 N Broadway 1 Metropolitan Sq Ste 3600 Saint Louis MO 63102-2750 Office Phone: 314-259-2000.

METTE, VIRGIL LOUIS, publishing executive, biology educator; b. Moscow Mills, Mo., Jan. 8, 1942; s. Louis Charles Mette and Virginia Frances (Hustedde) Williams; m. Sharon Ann Werr, Aug. 15, 1964; children— Keith Douglas, Jeffrey Alan BS, U. Mo., 1964. Gen. mgr. Sci. Research Assocs., Chgo., 1976-78; mktg. mgr. C. V. Mosby Co., St. Louis, 1978-79, editor-in-chief, 1979-80, v.p., 1980-83, sr. v.p., 1983-85. Teaching asst. U. Mo., Columbia, 1961-64 Sec. sch. bd. Zion Luth. Sch., Harvester, Mo., 1982-84 Avocations: boating; golf; reading. Office: C V Mosby Co 11830 Westline Industrial Dr Saint Louis MO 63146-3318

METTERS, THOMAS WADDELL, sportswriter; b. Columbus, Ohio, Apr. 17, 1939; s. Thomas Hammond and Charlotte Ann (Waddell) M. BS in Journalism, Ohio U., Athens, 1965. Sports editor The Traveller, Ft. Lee, Va., 1960—62; sports writer The Athens Messenger, Ohio, 1965—. Asst. to officials Legion Baseball, Athens, 1962—. Contbr.: Ohio Interscholastic Athletic Media Guide, 1985. Bd. dirs. Athens H.S. Booster Club, 1975—07, Athens H.S. Athletic Hall of Fame, 2000; ofcl. scorekeeper Am. Legion World Series, Millington, Tenn., 1989. With US Army, 1959-62. Named to Ohio H.S. Basketball Coaches Assn. Hall of Fame, 1993; recipient Contributor award Ohio H.S. Track & Field Coaches Assn., 1995, Ohio H.S. Athletic Assn. Media Svc. award, 1998. Mem. Soc. Profl. Journalists (Recognition plaque 1973), Ohio Associated Press Sports Writers Assn. (pres. 1984), Green & White Club (sec. 1983-2004, historian 2004—, Jonesy Sams award 1987), Ohio Prep Sports Writers Assn. (Hall of Fame 1990), Ky. Colonels, Am. Legion. Republican. Avocation: bowling. Home: 71 Sunnyside Dr Athens OH 45701-1921 Office: The Athens Messenger 9300 Johnson Rd Athens OH 45701 Office Phone: 740-592-6612 x 221.

METTY, THERESA M., communications executive; Degree in Bus., Harvard U. Leader Associated Spring Divsn. Barnes Group, Inc., 1975—95; with IBM, 1995—98; v.p. global procurement IBM, 1998—2000; from sr. v.p. and gen. mgr. supply chain Personal Comms. Sector Motorola Inc., Schaumberg, Ill., 2000—03, sr. v.p. and chief procurement officer, 2003—. Active purchasing coun. Mfrs. Alliance Productivity and Innovation; bd. dirs. The Inst. Supply Mgmt., Nat. Minority Supplier Devel. Coun., Women's Bus. Enterprise Nat. Coun.; spkr. in field.

METZ, ADAM S., real estate company executive; BA, Cornell U.; MMgmt, Northwestern U. Corp. lending officer 1st Nat. Bank Chgo., 1983-87; v.p. Capital Markets Group, JMB Realty, 1987-93; treas., CFO, exec. v.p, dir. acquisitions Urban Shopping Ctrs., Inc., 1993-2000, pres., 2000—01; co-founding ptnr. Polaris Capital LLC, Northbrook, Ill., 2003—. Trustee Amli Residential Properties, 2003—, Ctr. for Urban Land Econs. Rsch., U. Wis., 1997—. Mem. Internat. Coun. Shopping Ctrs. Office: Polaris Capital LLC 1033 Skokie Blvd Ste 660 Northbrook IL 60062 Home Phone: 847-835-4171; Office Phone: 847-480-9180. E-mail: metza@comcast.net.

METZ, ANTHONY J., III, federal judge; Bankruptcy judge U.S. Dist. Ct. (so. dist.) Ind., Indpls., 1997—. Office: 317 US Courthouse 46 E Ohio St Indianapolis IN 46204-1903 E-mail: anthony_metz@insb.uscourts.gov.

METZ, CHARLES EDGAR, radiology educator; b. Bayshore, NY, Sept. 11, 1942; s. Clinton Edgar and Grace Muriel (Schienke) M.; m. Maryanne Theresa Bahr, July, 1967 (div. 1988); children: Rebecca, Molly. BA, Bowdoin Coll., 1964; MS, U. Pa., 1966, PhD, 1969. Instr. radiology U. Chgo., 1969-71, asst. prof., 1971-75, assoc. prof., 1976-80, dir. grad. programs in med. physics, 1979-85, prof., 1980—, prof. structural biology, 1984-86, prof. med. physics, 2003—. Mem. diagnostic rsch. adv. group Nat. Cancer Inst., 1980-81; mem. sci. com. Nat. Coun. on Radiation Protection and Measurements, 1982-85, 2001-, Internat. Commn. on Radiation Units and Measurements, 1988-96, chmn. sci. com., 1992-99; cons. and lectr. in field. Assoc. editor: Radiology Jour., 1986—91, Med. Physics Jour., 1992—95, mem. editl. bd.: Med. Decision Making Jour., 1980—84; contbr. over 250 articles to sci. jours. and chpts. to books. Recipient L.H. Gray medal, Internat. Commn. on Radiation Units and Measurements, 2005. Fellow Am. Assn. Physicists in Medicine; mem. Radiol. Soc. N.Am., Am. Assn. Physicists in Medicine, Soc. Med. Decision Making, Assn. Univ. Radiologists, Phi Beta Kappa, Sigma Xi. Achievements include development of software for ROC analysis used in more than 10,000 labs worldwide. Office: U Chgo Dept Radiology MC2026 5841 S Maryland Ave Chicago IL 60637-1463 E-mail: c-metz@uchicago.edu.

METZEN, JAMES P., state legislator, bank executive; b. Oct. 1943; m. Sandie Metzen; two children. Student, U. Minn. Banker; mem. Minn. Ho. of Reps., St. Paul, 1975-86, Minn. Senate from 39th dist., St. Paul, 1986—, pres., 2002—. Chmn. govt. op. and vets. com.; mem. jobs, energy and cmty. devel., state govt. fin. divsn. commerce and consumer protection, rules and adminstrn. Minn. State Senate. Office: 312 Deerwood Ct South Saint Paul MN 55075-2102 also: State Senate Rm 322 75 Rev Dr Martin Luther King Jr Blvd Saint Paul MN 55155-1606

METZGER, KERRY R., state legislator; m. Karen Metzger; children: Robert, Ryan. BS, Juniata Coll.; DDS, Temple U. Dentist pvt. practice, New Phila., Ohio; councilman City of New Phila., 1988-94; pres. City Coun. of New Phila., 1992-94; rep. dist. 97 Ohio Ho. of Reps., Columbus, 1994—. Mem. Tuscarawas County Rep. Exec. Com. Named Internat. Senator Jaycees; recipient Presidential award of honor, Ohio Jaycees. Mem. Am. Dental Assn., Ohio Dental Assn., Tuscarawas County Dental Soc., Soc. Forensic Odontology, Tuscarawas C. of C., Tuscarawas Valley Civil War Roundtable. Address: 1203 3rd St NW New Philadelphia OH 44663-1303 Home: 120 Prysi Pkwy SE New Philadelphia OH 44663-9389

MEULEMAN, ROBERT JOSEPH, banker; b. South Bend, Ind., May 1, 1939; s. Joseph and Louise (Dutrieux) M.; m. Judith Ann Mc Comb, July 1, 1961; children Joseph, Jennifer, Rachel. BA, U. Notre Dame, 1961; MBA, Mich. State U., 1962. Investment analyst Nat. Bank of Detroit, 1965-68, Heritage Investment Advisors, Milw., 1968-72; sr. investment officer St. Joseph Bank and Trust Co., South Bend, 1972-81; pres., CEO Amcore Financial, Inc., Rockford, Ill., 1981—. Bd. dirs. Amcore Fin. Bd. dirs. Swedish Am. Hosp. Found., Rockford, 1986—, Rockford Pro-Am., 1986—, Rockford YMCA, 1993. Served to 1st lt. U.S. Army, 1963-65. Mem. Chartered Fin. Analysts, Milw. Fin. Analysts, Rockford C. of C. (bd. dirs. 1985). Clubs: Rockford Country. Republican. Roman Catholic. Avocations: skiing, golf, tennis. Office: Amcore Financial Inc 501 7th St Rockford IL 61104-1200 Home: 5340 Winding Creek Dr Rockford IL 61114-5482

MEUSER, FREDRICK WILLIAM, retired church administrator, historian; b. Payne, Ohio, Sept. 14, 1923; s. Henry William and Alvina Maria (Bouyack) Meuser; m. Jeanne Bond Griffiths, July 29, 1951; children: Jill Martha, Douglas Griffiths. AB, Capital U., 1945, BD, 1948, DD (hon.), 1989; STM, Yale U., 1949, MA, 1953, PhD, 1956; DD (hon.), Tex. Luth. Coll., 1980, Capital U., 1989; LHD (hon.), Augustana Coll., 1985. Ordained to ministry Am. Lutheran Ch., 1948; asst. pastor 1st Luth. Ch., Galveston, Tex., 1948, Christ Luth. Ch., North Miami, Fla., 1949—51; campus minister Yale U., 1951—53; prof. ch. history Luth. Theol. Sem., Columbus, Ohio, 1953—78, dean grad. studies, 1963—69, pres., 1971—78; exec. sec. div. theol. studies Luth. Council in U.S.A., 1969—71; pres. Trinity Luth. Sem., Columbus, 1978—88; del. World Council Chs., 1968, Luth. World Fedn., 1970; v.p. Am. Luth. Ch., 1974—80; mem. Commn. for a New Luth. Ch., 1982—86; asst. pastor St. Paul Luth. Ch., Westerville, Ohio, 1995—97. Author: The Formation of the American Lutheran Church, 1958, Luther the Preacher, 1983; author: (with others) Church in Fellowship, 1963, Lutherans in North America, 1975; translator: (with others) What Did Luther Understand by Religion, 1977, The Reconstruction of Morality, 1979; editor and author: (with others) Interpreting Luther's Legacy, 1967. Recipient Disting. Churchman's award Tex. Luth. Coll., 1972, Joseph Sittler award Trinity Luth. Sem., 1990; named Outstanding Alumnus Capital U., 1977; Am. Assn. Theol. Schs. fellow, 1961-62 Home: 2055 S Floral Ave Lot 240 Bartow FL 33830-7157 Personal E-mail: fredmeuser@aol.com.

MEYER, AUGUST CHRISTOPHER, JR., broadcast executive, lawyer; b. Champaign, Ill., Aug. 14, 1937; s. August C. and Clara (Rocke) M.; m. Karen Haugh Hassett, Dec. 28, 1960; children: August Christopher F., Elisabeth Hassett. BA cum laude, Harvard U., Cambridge, Mass., 1959, LLB, 1962. Bar: Ill. 1962. Founding ptr. Meyer-Capel, Champaign, Ill., 1962-77, of counsel, 1977—2003; owner, dir., officer Midwest TV, Inc., Sta. KFMB-TV-AM-FM, San Diego, Sta. WCIA-TV, Champaign, Ill., Sta. WMBD-TV-AM, WMXP, Peoria, Ill., 1968—, pres., 1976—. Bd. dirs. BankIll., Main St. Trust Inc.; spl. asst. atty. gen. State of Ill., 1968-76. Chmn. bd. trustees Carle Found. Hosp., Urbana, Ill. Mem. Ill. Bar Assn., Champaign County Bar Assn. Clubs: Champaign Country. Office: Midwest TV Inc PO Box 197 100 W University Ave # 401 Champaign IL 61824-0197 also: Sta KFMB PO Box 85888 7677 Engineer Rd San Diego CA 92111-1515

MEYER, BRUD RICHARD, retired pharmaceutical executive; b. Waukegan, Ill., Feb. 22, 1926; s. Charles Lewis and Mamie Olive (Broom) M.; m. Betty Louise Stine (dec. 1970); children: Linda (Mrs. Gary Stillabower), Louise (Mrs. Donald Knochel), Janet (Mrs. Gerald Cockrell), Jeff, Karen, Blake, Amy; m. Barbara Ann Hamilton, Nov. 26, 1970. BS, Purdue U., 1949. With Eli Lilly & Co., Indpls., 1949-87, indsl. engr., 1949-56, supr. indsl. engr., 1956-59, sr. personnel rep., 1960-64, personnel mgr. Lafayette, Ind., 1964-67, asst. dir., 1967-69, dir. adminstrn., 1969-79, dir. personnel and public relations, 1980-87, ret., 1987. Bd. dirs. Lafayette Home Hosp., 1977—, Hanna Cmty. Ctr., 1983—, Tippecanoe Hist. Corp., 1985—; bd. dirs. United Way Tippecanoe County, 1970-76, pres., 1974; bd. dirs. Legal Aid Soc. Tippecanoe County, 1973—, Jr. Achievement, pres., 1979; bd. dirs. Lilly Credit Union, 1969-75, pres., 1973-74; mem. Citizen's Com. on Alcoholism, 1966-72; bd. dirs. Greater Lafayette Cmty. Ctrs., 1975-79, pres., 1977-78; bd. dirs. Tippecanoe County Child Care, 1990—, pres., 1998-99; mng. dir. Battle Tippecanoe Outdoor Drama Bd. With USAAF, 1943-45. Mem. Pi Tau Sigma, Lambda Chi Alpha, C. of C. Greater Lafayette (bd. dirs., v.p. 1969-73), Battleground Hist. Soc. Methodist. Home: 4217 Trees Hill Dr Lafayette IN 47909-3451 Office: Eli Lilly & Co PO Box 7685 Lafayette IN 47903-7685

MEYER, DAN, state legislator; b. Neenah, Wis., Jan. 1, 1949; married; 2 children. BBA, U. Wis., Oshkosh, 1978. Exec. dir. Eagle River C. of C. and Visitors Ctr.; mem. Wis. State Assembly, Madison, 2000—, mem. aging and long-term care com., mem. housing, natural resources coms., mem. sml. bus. and consumer affairs coms., mem. tourism and recreation coms., mem. urban and local affairs com. Mayor City of Eagle River, 1997—2001. With US Army. Republican. Office: State Capitol Rm 306 N PO Box 8953 Madison WI 53708-8953 Address: 1013 Walnut St Eagle River WI 54521

MEYER, DANIEL JOSEPH, machinery company executive; b. Flint, Mich., May 31, 1936; s. John Michael and Margaret (Meehan) M.; m. Bonnie Harrison, June 22, 1963; children: Daniel P., Jennifer. BS, Purdue U., 1958; MBA, Ind. U., 1963. CPA, N.Y. Mgr. Touche, Ross & Co., Detroit, 1964-69; contr. Cin. Milacron, Inc., 1969-77, v.p. fin., treas., 1977-83, exec. v.p. fin. and adminstrn., 1983-86, pres., COO, 1987-90, pres., CEO, 1990-91, chmn., CEO, 1991-92, also bd. dirs. Bd. dirs. E.W. Scripps Inc., Hubbell Inc., Cin. Bell Inc., AK Steel. With U.S. Army, 1959. Mem. Am. Inst. CPAs, Kenwood Country Club (Cin.). Clubs: Kenwood Country (Cin.). Home: 7655 Annesdale Dr Cincinnati OH 45243-4054

MEYER, G. CHRISTOPHER, lawyer; b. Fremont, Nebr., Mar. 27, 1948; s. Gerald William and Mildred Ruth (Clauson) M.; children: Kate, Stacy, Jon, Robert. Student, Grinnell Coll., Iowa, 1966—69; BA, U. Kans., 1970; JD, U. Pa. Law Sch., 1973. Bar: Ohio 1973, US Dist. Ct. (no. dist.) Ohio 1975, US Ct. Appeals (6th cir.) 1982. Assoc. Squire, Sanders & Dempsey, L.L.P., Cleve., 1973-82, ptnr., 1982—. Bd. mem. Cleve. Rape Crisis Ctr., past chmn. Named one of Best Lawyers in Am., Ohio Super Lawyers. Mem. ABA, Greater Cleve. Bar Assn., Am. Coll. Bankruptcy. Office: Squire Sanders & Dempsey LLP 4900 Key Tower 127 Public Sq Cleveland OH 44114-1304 Home: 5455 N Marginal Rd Cleveland OH 44114-3951 Office Phone: 216-479-8692. Business E-Mail: cmeyer@ssd.com.

MEYER, HELEN M., state supreme court justice; BSW, U. Minn.; JD, William Mitchell Coll. Law. Ptnr. Pritzker & Meyer, 1987—96, Meyer and Assocs., 1996—2002; assoc. justice Minn. Supreme Ct., St. Paul, 2002—. Office: Minn Jud Ctr 25 Rev Dr Martin Luther King Jr Blvd Saint Paul MN 55155

MEYER, JAMES B., retail executive; Dir. retail acctg. Spartan Stores, Grand Rapids, Mich., 1973-89, sr. v.p., CFO, 1989-96, COO, 1996-97, pres., CEO, 1997—, chmn., 2000—, also bd. dirs. Bd. dirs. Mich. Nat. Bank, Hope Network, Davenport Coll. Bd. dirs. Heart of West Mich. United Way, Employers Coalition Healing Racism, Mich. Econ. Devel. Coun.; corp. chair Year 2000 Juvenile Diabetes Found. Walk. Mem. Nat. Grocers Assn. (bd. mem.), Food Distbrs. Internat. (bd. mem.), Econ. Club Grand Rapids (bd. mem.). Office: Spartan Stores 850 76th St SW Grand Rapids MI 49518-8700

MEYER, JOHN FREDERICK, engineering educator; b. Grand Rapids, Mich., July 26, 1934; s. Frederick Albert and Harriet (Stibbs) M.; m. Nancy Shaw Briggs, July 4, 1959; children: John, Patricia, James. BS, U. Mich., 1957; MS, Stanford U., 1958; PhD, U. Mich., 1967. Data systems engr. Douglas Aircraft Corp., Santa Monica, Calif., 1957; research engr. Caltech, Jet Propulsion Lab., Pasadena, Calif., 1958-67; asst. prof. U. Mich., Ann Arbor, 1968-71, assoc. prof., 1971-76, prof. elec. engring. and computer sci., 1976—2002, dir. Computing Research Lab., 1984-89, prof. emeritus elec. engring. and computer sci., 2002—. Cons. Calif. Inst. Tech. Jet Propulsion Lab., 1979—91, Indsl. Tech. Inst., Ann Arbor, 1985-92, CIMSA, Paris, 1992, Bendix Advanced Tech. Ctr., Columbia, Md., 1977-85, Thomson CSF, Paris, 1975, Italtel, Milan, 1990—99, Applied Scis. Corp., Reading, Mass., 1993, U. Ill., 2002-05. Precinct chmn. 3d ward Democratic Party, Ann Arbor, 1971-74. Recipient Disting. Service Award U. Mich., 1964, Silver Core award IFIP, 1995, Golden Core award 1996; IBM fellow, 1957 Fellow IEEE; mem. AAAS, IEEE Computer Soc. (Cert. of Appreciation 1981, 95, Meritorious Svc. award 1985). Achievements include patents for time division multiplexer; admission control of mixed variable bitrate sources in broadband networks. Home: 1946 Ridge Ave Ann Arbor MI 48104-6306 Office: U Mich 3636 CSE Bldg Ann Arbor MI 48109-2121 Business E-Mail: jfm@umich.edu.

MEYER, JOHN P., communications executive; BA in Acctg., U. No. Iowa; grad. Program for Mgmt. Devel., Harvard Bus. Sch. CPA. Auditor Deloitte & Touche, 1973—82; various pos. Centel, Chgo., 1982—86, corp. controller, 1986—93, v.p., 1986—93; sr. v.p., controller Sprint Corp., Overland Park, Kans., 1993—. Dir. Kansas City Minority Supplier Coun. Mem.: Conf. Bd. Controllers Coun., Am. Inst. CPA's. Office: Sprint Corp 6200 Sprint Pkwy Overland Park KS 66251

MEYER, MAURICE WESLEY, retired physiologist, dentist, neurologist; b. Long Prairie, Minn., Feb. 13, 1925; s. Ernest William and Augusta (Warnke) M.; m. Martha Helen Davis, Sept. 3, 1946; children— James Irvin, Thomas Orville. BS, U. Minn., 1953, D.D.S., 1957, MS, 1959, PhD, 1961. Teaching asst. U. Minn. Sch. Dentistry, 1954-55, USPHS fellow, 1955-56, rsch. fellow, 1956-57, mem. faculty, 1960—; prof. physiology, dentistry and neurology U. Minn., 1976-88, prof. emeritus, 1988—; investigator Ctr. Rsch. and Cerebral Vascular Disease, 1969—; dir. lab. Center Research and Cerebral Vascular Disease, 1975—; postdoctoral research fellow Nat. Inst. Dental Research, 1957-60, research fellow, 1958-61, mem. faculty, 1961—, asso. prof. neurology, 1974-80, mem. grad. faculty, 1973—; trainee Inst. Advanced Edn. in Dental Research, 1964—. Vis. asso. prof., also vis. research fellow dept. physiology and Sch. Dentistry Cardiovascular Research Inst., U. Calif., San Francisco, 1971 Contbr. articles to profl. jours. Served to col. Dental Corps AUS, 1943-85. Decorated D.F.C., Air medal with 3 oak leaf clusters. Fellow AAAS; mem. ADA, Minn. Dental Soc., Internat. Assn. Dental Research (pres. Minn. sect. 1967-68), Soc. Exptl. Biology and Medicine, Am. Physiol. Soc., Microcirculatory Soc., Am. Assn. Dental Schs. (chmn. 1972-73), Can. Physiol. Soc., Sigma Xi, Omicron Kappa Upsilon. Clubs: Masons. Office: U Minn 6-255 Millard Minneapolis MN 55455 Home: 578 Longhurst Pl Brighton CO 80601-3402 E-mail: meyer109@tc.umn.edu.

MEYER, MICHAEL LOUIS, lawyer; b. Buffalo, Dec. 17, 1940; s. Bernard H. and Florence (Nusbaum) M.; m. Jo Ann Ackerman, Sept. 21, 1990. AB, Princeton U., 1962; LLB, Harvard U., 1965. Bar: Ill. 1965, D.C., 1978. Assoc. Schiff Hardin & Waite, Chgo., 1965-72, ptnr., 1972—. Lt. USN, 1965-68. Mem. ABA (mem. fed. regulation of security com.), Chgo. Bar Assn., Chgo. Coun. Lawyers, Chgo. Yacht Club, Metropolitan Club Office: Schiff Hardin & Waite 7200 Sears Tower Ste 1200 Chicago IL 60606

MEYER, PAUL REIMS, JR., orthopedic surgeon; b. Port Arthur, Tex. s. Paul Reims and Evelyn (Miller) M.; m. Lesa W. Meyer; children: Kristin Lynn, Holly Dee, Paul Reims III, Stewart Blair. BA, Va. Mil. Inst., 1954; MD, Tulane U., 1958; MA of Mgmt., J.L. Kellogg Grad. Sch. of Mgmt. (Northwestern U.), 1992. Dir. Spine Injury Ctr. (now Midwest Regional Spinal Injury Care System) Northwestern U., Chgo., 1972—, prof. orthopaedic surgery, 1981—. Cons. Nat. Inst. Disability and Rehab. Rsch. VA, Washington, 1978-2000; clin. prof. surgery Dept. Surgery, USUHS; mem. adv. com. World Rehab. Fund, 1990; mem. bd. councilors Am. Acad. Orthopaedic Surgeons, 1993-96. Author: Surgery of Spine Trauma, 1988; patentee cervical orthosis. Col. M.C., USAR. Fellow ACS, Am. Acad. Orthop. Surgeons; mem. Société Internationale de Chirurgie Orthopédique et de Traumatologie, Internat. Med. Soc. Paraplegia, Am. Trauma Soc. (bd. dirs. 1988), Am. Orthop. Assn., Am. Spinal Injury Assn. (past pres.), Soc. Med. Cons. to Armed Forces, Mid-Am. Orthop. Assn. Roman Catholic. Avocations: photography, fishing, amateur radio, aviation, boating.

MEYER, RICHARD CHARLES, microbiologist, educator; b. Cleve., May 2, 1930; s. Frederick Albert and Tekla Charlotte (Schrade) M.; m. Carolyn Yvonne Patton, Apr. 6, 1963; children: Frederick Gustav, Carl Anselm. B.Sc., Baldwin-Wallace Coll., 1952; M.Sc., Ohio State U., 1957, PhD, 1961. Teaching and research asst. Ohio State U., 1956-61, research assoc., 1961-62; microbiologist Nat. Cancer Inst., NIH, Bethesda, Md., 1962-64; asst. prof. vet. pathology and hygiene and microbiology U. Ill., Urbana-Champaign, 1965-68, assoc. prof., 1968-73, prof., 1973-89, prof. emeritus, 1989—. Served with C.E. U.S. Army, 1952-54. Mem. Am. Acad. Microbiology, AAAS, Am. Inst. Biol. Sci., Am. Soc. Microbiology, Sigma Xi, Gamma Sigma Delta, Phi Zeta. Republican. Lutheran. Home: 1504 S Buckthorn Ln Mahomet IL 61853-3632 Office: Dept Vet Pathobiology U Ill at Urbana-Champaign Urbana IL 61801

MEYER, RUSSELL WILLIAM, JR., air transportation executive; b. Davenport, Iowa, July 19, 1932; s. Russell William and Ellen Marie (Matthews) M.; m. Helen Scott Vaughn, Aug. 20, 1960; children: Russell William, III, Elizabeth Ellen, Jeffrey Vaughn, Christopher Matthews, Carolyn Louise. BA, Yale U., 1954; LLB, Harvard U., 1961. Bar: Ohio 1961. Mem. firm Arter & Hadden, Cleve., 1961-66; pres., chief exec. officer Grumman Am. Aviation Corp., Cleve., 1966-74; exec. v.p. Cessna Aircraft Co., Wichita, Kans., 1974-75, chmn. bd., CEO, 1975-2000, 2002—03, chmn., 2004, chmn. emeritus, 2005. Bd. dirs. Fourth Fin., 1975-1995, Westar Energy, 1978-2000, Gen. Dynamics, 1986-1992, Nations Bank, 1995-2001, Pub. Broadcasting Svc., Welfare to Work Partnership; presdl. appointee Aviation Safety Commn., 1987—; mem. Pres. Airline Commn., 1993, FAA Mgmt. Adv. Counsel, 2004—; dir. Pub. Broadcasting Sys. Chmn. bd. trustees 1st Bapt. Ch., Cleve., 1972-74; bd. dirs. United Way, Wichita and Sedgwick County; trustee Wesley Hosp. Endowment Assn., Wake Forest Univ.; bd. govs. United Way Am., 1993—. With USAF, 1955-58. Recipient Collier trophy Nat. Aeronautic Assn., 1986, George S. Dively award Harvard U., 1992, Wright Bros. Meml. trophy, 1995, Disting. Svc. Citation U. Kans., 2000; named Kansan of Yr., 1998. Mem. ABA, Ohio Bar Assn., Kans. Bar Assn., Cleve. Bar Assn., Gen. Aviation Mfrs. Assn. (chmn. bd. dirs. 1973-74, 81-82, 93-94), Wichita C. of C. (chmn. 1988—, bd. dirs.), Wichita Club, Wichita Country Club, Pine Valley Club, Cypress Point Club, Double Eagle Country Club, Flint Hills Nat. Club, Latrobe Country Club, Eldorado Country Club, The Tradition Golf Club. Home: 600 N Tara Ct Wichita KS 67206-1830 Office: Cessna Aircraft PO Box 7704 1 Cessna Blvd Wichita KS 67215-1424 Office Phone: 316-517-8000.

MEYER, SUSAN M., lawyer; b. 1943; BA in Philosophy and Psychology, Marquette U.; JD, Fordham U. Officer, investigator Washington Met. Police Dept.; gen. counsel Beatrice Consumer Durables, Northbrook, Ill., G.D. Searle & Co., Skokie, Ill.; sr. counsel Beatrice Cos., Inc., Chgo., 1986-91; v.p., sec., dep. counsel Gen. Instrument Corp., Chgo., 1991-98; v.p., sec., gen. counsel United Stationers Inc., Des Plaines, Ill., 1998—. Office: 2200 E Golf Rd Des Plaines IL 60016-1246

MEYERS, CHRISTINE LAINE, marketing and media executive, consultant; b. Detroit, Mar. 7, 1946; d. Ernest Robert and Eva Elizabeth (Laine) M.; 1 child, Kathryn Laine; m. Oliver S. Moore III, May 12, 1990. BA, U. Mich., 1968. Editor indsl. rels. diesel divsn. Gen. Motors Corp., Detroit, 1968; nat. advt. mgr. J.L. Hudson Co., Detroit, 1969-76, mgr. internal sales promotion, 1972-73, dir. pub., 1973-76; nat. advt. mgr. Pontiac Motor divsn., Mich., 1976-78; pres., owner Laine Meyers Mktg. Cos., Inc., Troy, Mich., 1978—; founder, owner CORP! Mag., 1998—. Dir. Internat. Inst. Met. Detroit, Inc. Contbr. articles to profl. publs. Bus. adv. coun. Ctrl. Mich. U., 1977-79; pub. adv. com. on jud. candidates Oakland County Bar Assn.; adv. bd. Birmingham Cmty. Hosp., Bank of Am., 1999-2001; bd. dirs. YMCA, Mich., 1992-98, Haven, 1997—, Automation Alley, Oakland County, 1999—. Named Mich. Ad Woman of Yr., 1976, one of Top 10 Working Women, Glamour mag., 1978, one of 100 Best and Brightest Advt. Age, 1987, one of Mich.'s top 25 female bus. owners Nat. Assn. Women Bus. Owners, One of Top 10 Women Owned Bus., Mich., 1994; recipient Vanguard award Women in Comm., 1986, Lifetime Achievement award Northwood U., 2002. Mem. Internat. Assn. Bus. Communicators, Adcraft Club, Women's Advt. Club (1st v.p. 1975), Women's Econ. Club (pres. 1976-77), Internat. Women's Forum Mich. (founding pres. 1986-97), Internat. Inst. Detroit (bd. dirs. 1986-89), Detroit C. of C., Troy C. of C., Mortar Bd., Quill and Scroll, Pub. Rels. Com. Women for United Found., Founders Soc. Detroit Inst. Arts, Fashion Group, Pub. Rels. Soc. Am., First Soc. Detroit (exec. com. 1970-71), Kappa Tau Alpha. Home: 604 Courtside Dr Naples FL 34105-7133 Office Phone: 248-458-2677 ext.301. Business E-Mail: cmyers@corpmagazine.com.

MEYERS, GERALD CARL, finance educator, writer, expert witness, consultant; b. Buffalo, Dec. 5, 1928; s. Meyer and Berenice (Meyers) M.; m. Barbara Jacob, Nov. 2, 1958. BS, Carnegie Inst. Tech., 1950, MS with distinction, 1954. With Ford Motor Co., Detroit, 1950-51, Chrysler Corp., Detroit and Geneva, 1954-62; with Am. Motors Corp., Detroit, 1962-84, v.p., 1967-72, group v.p. product, 1972-75, exec. v.p., 1975-77, pres., 1977-84, COO, 1977, chmn., CEO, 1977-82, ret., 1984; Ford disting. prof. Grad. Sch. Indsl. Adminstrn. Carnegie Mellon U., Pitts., 1985-96; prof. U. Mich. Bus. Sch., Ann Arbor, 1995—. Pres. Gerald C. Meyers Assocs., Inc., West Bloomfield, Mich.; adj. prof. Sch. Bus. U. Mich., Ann Arbor. Author: When It Hits the Fan, Managing the Nine Crises of Business; co-author: Dealers, Healers, Brutes and Saviors; bus. commentator Nat. Pub. Radio, Fox News Cable TV, CNBC TN Network; contbr. articles to N.Y. Times, Wall St. Jour., L.A. Times. 1st lt. USAF, 1951-53. Decorated Legion of Honor (France). Mem. Econ. Club Detroit, Tau Beta Pi, Phi Kappa Phi, Omicron Delta Kappa. Address: U Mich Bus Sch D 3246 701 Tappan Ave Ann Arbor MI 48109-1217 Office: 5600 W Maple Rd Ste B216 West Bloomfield MI 48322-3787

MEYERS, JOHN EDWARD, prosecutor; b. Ann Arbor, Mich., July 24, 1944; s. Roy E. and Emaline (Pryor) M.; m. Suzanne Meyers, June 7, 1966; children: Ben, Elizabeth, Tom, Peter. BA, David Lipscomb Coll., Nashville, 1966; JD, U. Toledo, 1969. Bar: Ohio 1969, U.S. Dist. Ct. (so. dist.) Ohio 1973, U.S. Dist. Ct. (no. dist.) Ohio 1976. Spl. agt. FBI, Washington/Savannah, 1969-73; pros. Mcpl. Ct. Bellevue (Ohio), 1974-84; atty. pvt. practice, 1974—; ptnr. Meyers & Wallingford, Bellevue, 1981—96; pros. Sandusky County Ct., Fremont, Ohio, 1985—2000. Pres. bd. trustees Bellevue Libr. Bd., 1977, Bellevue Soc. Arts, 2003—; v.p. trustees Bellevue Hosp. Bd., 1984. Mem. Ohio Pros. Attys. Assn. (exec. com. 1988—), Huron County Bar Assn. (sec. 1975), Bellevue C. of C. (pres. 1978-79), Rotary (pres. 1982). Republican. Ch. of Christ. Home: 412 W Main St Bellevue OH 44811-1334 Office: 117 W Main St Bellevue OH 44811-1329

MEYERS, PAMELA SUE, lawyer; b. Lakewood, NJ, June 13, 1951; d. Morris Leon and Isabel (Leibowitz) M.; m. Gerald Stephen Greenberg, Aug. 24, 1975; children: David Stuart Greenberg, Allison Brooke Greenberg. AB with distinction, Cornell U., 1973; JD cum laude, Harvard U., 1976. Bar: NY 1977, Ohio 1990. Assoc. Stroock & Stroock & Lavan, NYC, 1976-80; staff v.p., asst. gen. counsel Am. Premier Underwriters, Inc., Cin., 1980-96; legal counsel Citizens Fed. Bank, Dayton, Ohio, 1997-98; gen. counsel, sec. Mosler Inc., Hamilton, Ohio, 1998—2001. Bd. dirs. Hamilton County Alcohol and Drug Addiction Svc. Bd., 1996-2000, Adath Israel Congregation, 1999-2005; dir. Gorman Heritage Farm Found., 2006-2007; trustee Carpenters Creek Civic Assn., 2004-06; mem. Village Evendale Recreation Commn., 2006—. Mem. Cin. Bar Assn., Harvard Club of Cin. (pres. 1998-99, bd. dirs. 1993-2000), Phi Beta Kappa. Jewish. Avocations: piano, reading, tennis. Home: 3633 Carpenters Creek Dr Cincinnati OH 45241-3824 Personal E-mail: psmeyers@fuse.net.

MEYSMAN, FRANK L., food and consumer products executive; b. Belgium; Grad., U. Brussels, Ghent U., Belgium. Various mktg. positions Procter & Gamble, Brussels and Hamburg, Germany, 1977-86; v.p. mktg. Douwe Egberts Belgium, 1986-89, pres., 1989-90, sr. v.p. corp. strategy, bus. devel., 1990-91; mem. coffee and grocery bd. Sara Lee/DE, Utrecht, The Netherlands, 1991-92, corp. v.p., 1992-94, sr. v.p., 1992-94, also chmn. bd. mgmt., 1994—; exec. v.p. Sara Lee Corp., Chgo., 1997—. Office: Sara Lee Corp Three 1st National Plz Chicago IL 60602-4260

MICALLEF, JOSEPH STEPHEN, retired lawyer; b. Malta, Oct. 19, 1933; came to U.S., 1949; s. John E. and Josephine (Brownrigg) M.; m. Jane M. Yungers, Sept. 5, 1959; children: Lisa R., Maura J. Fisk, Sara M. Hulse, Amy A., Joseph S. Jr. BA cum laude, U. St. Thomas, 1958, LLB, JD, 1962. Pres., CEO Fiduciary Counselling, Inc., St. Paul, 1961-71, dir., cons., 1971-95. Trustee Gt. No. Iron Ore Properties Trust, St. Paul, The Charles A. Lindbergh Fund, Mpls.; mem. bd. visitors U. Minn. Law Sch., Mpls. Past pres., mem. exec. com. Minn. Hist. Soc., St. Paul; bd. dirs. Minn. Air NG Hist. Found., Inc., Plymouth Music Series, Ramsey County Hist. Soc.; bd. overseers Hill Monastic Manuscript Libr.; past regent St. John's U., Collegeville, Minn.; mem. investment adv. com. Archdiocese St. Paul/Mpls.; mem. fin. coun. Cathedral of St. Paul; dir. emeritus Sci. Mus. Minn., St. Paul; trustee James Jerome Hill Ref. Libr., St. Paul. Decorated Knight of the Sovereign Mil., Order of Malta, 1981, Knight of the Equestrian Order of Holy Sepulchre of Jerusalem, Hon. Consul Gen. of Malta, St. Paul/Mpls. Mem. ABA (com. on real property, probate and trust law), Minn. Bar Assn. (subcom. on the Minn. nonprofit corp. act trust law com.), Minn. Coun. on Founds. (govt. rels. com.), Minn. Club (bd. govs.), Town & Country Club, Casino Maltese Club, The Union Club (Malta). Office: Great orthern Iron Ore Properties W 1290 First National Bank 332 Minnesota St Saint Paul MN 55101-1361

MICHAEL, ALFRED FREDERICK, JR., physician, medical educator; b. Phila. s. Alfred Frederick and Emma Maude (Peters) M.; m. Jeanne Jones; children: Mary, Susan, Carol. MD, Temple U., 1953. Diplomate Am. Bd. Pediatrics (founding mem. sub-bd. pediatric nephrology, pres. 1977-79). Pediat. diagnostic lab. immunology and pediatric nephrology intern Phila. Gen. Hosp., 1953-54; resident St. Christopher's Hosp., Phila., 1954, Children's Hosp. and U. Cin. Coll. Medicine, 1957-60; postdoctoral fellow dept. pediatrics and biochemistry Med. Sch., U. Minn., Mpls., 1960-63, assoc. prof., 1965-68, prof. pediatrics, lab. medicine and pathology, 1968-88, co-dir. pediatric nephrology, 1968—86, Regents' prof., 1986—, head dept. pediatrics, 1986-97, dean, 1996—2002. Established investigator Am. Heart Assn., 1963-68. Past mem. editl. bd. Internat. Yr. Book of Nephrology, Am. Jour. Nephrology, Kidney Internat., Clin. Nephrology, Am. Jour. Pathology; contbr. articles to profl. jours. Physician founder Vikings Children's Fund, Univ. Pediat. Found.; bd. dirs. St. Mary's Health Clinics. Served with USAF, 1955—57. Recipient Alumni Achievement award Temple U. Sch. Medicine, 1988, John Peters award, 1992, Diehl award, 2003; NIH fellow, 1960-63, Guggenheim fellow, 1966-67, NIH Merit awardee, 1992-2002, Bolles Rogers award, Shotwell award. Fellow AAAS; mem. AMA, Am. Soc. Clin. Investigation, Assn. Am. Physicians, Am. Pediat. Soc., Soc. for Pediat. Rsch., Am. Assn. Investigative Pathology, Am. Soc. Cell Biology, Am. Soc. ephrology (coun., pres.-elect 1992—, pres. 1993, John Peters award), Internat. Soc. Nephrology, Soc. for Exptl. Biology and Medicine, Minn. Med. Assn. Home: 1986 Lower Saint Dennis Rd Saint Paul MN 55116-2820 Office Phone: 612-625-2715. Business E-Mail: micha003@umn.edu.

MICHAEL, JONATHAN EDWARD, insurance company executive; b. Columbus, Ohio, Mar. 19, 1954; BA, Ohio Dominican Coll., 1977. CPA, Ohio. Acct. Coopers & Lybrand, Columbus, Ohio, 1977-82; chief acct. RLI Ins. Co., Peoria, Ill., 1982-84, controller, 1984-85, v.p. fin., CFO, 1985—, exec. v.p., 1991-94, pres., COO, 1994-2000, pres., CEO, 2001—, chmn. bd., 2002—. Mem.: Mt. Hawley Country (Peoria). Roman Catholic. Avocation: golf. Office: RLI 9025 N Lindbergh Dr Peoria IL 61615-1499

MICHAEL, R. KEITH, theatre and dance educator; BS in Fine Art, State U. Pa.; MFA in Directing, U. Iowa; PhD in Theatre, U. Bristol, Eng. Mem. faculty Western Wash. U.; mem. theatre St. Cloud (Minn.) State U., chmn. dept. theatre, 1965-71; chmn. dept. theatre and drama Ind. U., Bloomington, 1971—. Program or archtl. cons. to 14 maj. theatres and State of Miss.; mem. adv. com. Nat. Soc. Arts and Letters. Host IU Jour. weekly PBS TV program. Recipient Ind. Gov.'s award, 1997. Mem. Nat. Assn. Schs. and Theatre (past pres.), Univ. and Coll. Theatre Assn. (past pres.), Univ./Resident Theatre Assn. (officer), Nat. Theatre Conf., North Ctrl. Assn. Colls. and Schs. Office: Ind U Bloomington Bryan Hall 100 Bloomington IN 47405-2618

MICHAELIDES, CONSTANTINE EVANGELOS, architect, educator; b. Athens, Greece, Jan. 26, 1930; came to U.S., 1955, naturalized, 1964; s. Evangelos George and Kalliopi Constantine (Kefallonitis) M.; m. Maria S. Canellakis, Sept. 3, 1955; children: Evangelos Constantine, Dimitri Canellakis. Diploma in Architecture, Nat. Tech. U., Athens, 1952; M.Arch., Harvard U., 1957. Practice architecture, Athens, 1954-55, St. Louis, 1963—; asso. architect Carl Koch, Jose Luis Sert, Hideo Sasaki, Cambridge, Mass., 1957-59, Doxiadis Assos., Athens and Washington, 1959-60, Hellmuth, Obata & Kassabaum, St. Louis, 1962; instr. Grad. Sch. Design Harvard U., 1957-59, Athens Inst. Tech., 1959-60; asst. prof. architecture Washington U., St. Louis, 1960-64, assoc. prof., 1964-69, prof., 1969-94, assoc. dean Sch. Architecture, 1969-73; dean Washington U., Sch. Architecture, 1973-93, dean emeritus, 1993—; Ruth and Norman Moore vis. prof. Washington U., St. Louis, 1995. Vis. prof. (Sch. Architecture), Ahmedabad, India, 1970; counselor Landmarks Assn. St. Louis., 1975-79 Author: Hydra: A Greek Island Town: Its Growth and Form, 1967, The Aegean Crucible: Tracing Vernacular Architecture in Post-Byzantine Centuries, 2003; contbr. articles to profl. jours. Mem. Mcpl. Commn. on Arts, Letters, University City, Mo., 1975-81. With Greek Army Res., 1952-54. Fellow AIA (Rsch. award 1963-64, Presdl. Citation 1992); mem. Tech. Chamber of Greece, Soc. Archtl. Historians, Modern Greek Studies Assn., Hellenic Soc. St. Louis (pres. 1991, 95, 96). Home and Office: 735 Radcliffe Ave Saint Louis MO 63130-3139 Business E-Mail: info@delospress.com.

MICHAELIS, ELIAS K., neurochemist; b. Wad-Medani, Sudan, Oct. 3, 1944; came to U.S., 1962; married, 1967; 1 child. BS, Fairleigh Dickinson U., 1966; MD, St. Louis U. Med. Sch., 1969; PhD in Physiology and Biophysics, U. Ky., 1973. Spl. fellow rsch. dept. physiology and biophysics U. Ky., 1972-73, from asst. prof. to prof. depts. human devel. and biochemistry, 1982-87; chair pharmacology and toxicology U. Kans., Lawrence, 1988—. Dir. ctr. biomed. rsch. and Higuchi bioscis. rsch. ctr. U. Kans., 1988—. Mem. AAAS, Am. Soc. Neurochemistry, Am. Soc. Biochemistry and Molecular Biology, Internat. Soc. Biomedical Rsch. on Alcoholism, Soc. Neuroscience, N.Y. Acad. Sci. Achievements include research in characterization of L-glutamate receptors in neuronal membranes, in membrane protein isolation and chemical analysis, in characterization of membrane transport systems for amino acids, sodium, potassium, and calcium, in neuronal membrane biophysics, in molecular neurobiology.

MICHAELS, DINAH, radio personality; m. Randy Michaels, Oct. 25, 1997. BA Mass Comm., Baker U. With KBNU Campus Sta.; radio host KUDL, Westwood, Kans. Author: The Bride's Guide to Reality (How to Have the Wedding You Want on the Budget You Have), 1999. Avocations: horseback riding, tennis, movies. Office: KULD 4935 Belinder Westwood KS 66205

MICHAELS, JACK D., manufacturing executive; BSME, U. Cin. Various postions Internat. Harvester Co., sr. v.p., gen. mgr. Paris, mng. dir. Germany, worldwide pres. agrl. and constrn. equipment ops., J. I. Case Co.; pres.-internat. Hussmann Corp., pres., CEO; pres. Hon Industries, Inc., Muscatine, Iowa, 1991—96, CEO, 1991—96, chmn., 1996—2004; chmn., pres., CEO Snap-on Inc., Kenosha, Wis., 2004—07, chmn., CEO, 2007, chmn., 2007—.

MICHAELS, JENNIFER TONKS, foreign language educator; b. Sedgley, England, May 19, 1945; d. Frank Gordon and Dorothy (Compston) Tonks; m. Eric Michaels, 1973; children: Joseph, David, Ellen. MA, U. Edinburgh, 1967, McGill U., 1971, PhD, 1974. Teaching asst. German dept. Wesleyan U., 1967-68; instr. German dept. Bucknell (Pa.) U., 1968-69; teaching asst. German dept. McGill U., Canada, 1969-72; prodn. asst. Pub. TV News and Polit. program, Schenectady, NY, 1974-75; from asst. prof. to assoc. prof. Grinnell (Iowa) Coll., 1975-87, prof., 1987—. Vis. cons. German dept. Hamilton Coll., 1981; cons. Modern Lang. dept. Colby Coll.; panelist NEH, 1985; spkr. in field. Author: D.H. Lawrence, The Polarity of North and South, 1976, Anarchy and Eros: Otto Gross' Impact on German Expressionist Writers, 1983, Franz Jung: Expressionist, Dadaist, Revolutionary and Outsider, 1989, Franz Werfel and the Critics, 1994; contbr. numerous articles, revs. to profl. jours. Mem. MLA, Rocky Mt. MLA (v.p. 2005), Am. Assn. Tchrs. of German, Soc. Exile Studies, German Studies Assn. (sec. treas. 1991-92, v.p. 1992-94, pres. 1995-96, numerous coms.). Democrat. Avocations: music, travel, reading. Office: Grinnell Coll German Dept PO Box 805 Grinnell IA 50112-0805 Business E-Mail: michaels@grinnell.edu.

MICHAELS, ROBERT A., real estate development company executive; BSBA, JD, U. S.D. With Gen. Growth, 1972—, gen. counsel, exec. v.p., dir. corp. leasing; pres., CEO Gen. Growth Mgmt., Inc.; pres., COO Gen. Growth Properties, Inc. Bd. dirs. Gen. Growth Properties, Inc., Gen. Growth Mgmt., Inc.; bd. dirs. Ctr. for Urban Land Econs. Rsch., Sch. of Bus. U. Wis.-Madison.; spkr. in field. Editor Law Rev., U. S.D.; contbr. articles to profl. jours. Mem. ABA, S.D. Bar Assn., Iowa Bar Assn., Minn. Bar Assn., Internat. Coun. of Shopping Ctrs. (exec. com., bd. trustees, govt. affairs chmn. states Iowa, Nebr., S.D., state dir. Minn., S.D., N.D.). Office: 110 N Wacker Dr Chicago IL 60606-1511

MICHALAK, EDWARD FRANCIS, lawyer; b. Evanston, Ill., Sept. 6, 1937; s. Leo Francis Michalak and Helen Sophie (Wolinski) Krakowski. BSBA, Northwestern U., 1959; LLB, Harvard U., 1962. Bar: Ill. 1962. Assoc. McDermott, Will & Emery, Chgo., 1963-69, ptnr., 1969—. Served to sgt. USAR, 1962-68. Mem. Ill. Bar Assn., Chgo. Bar Assn., Beta Gamma Sigma, Beta Alpha Psi. Roman Catholic. Avocations: golf, opera. Home: 3455 Harrison St Evanston IL 60201-4953 Office: McDermott Will & Emery 227 W Monroe St 47th Fl Chicago IL 60606-5096 Office Phone: 312-984-7506. Business E-Mail: emichalak@mwe.com.

MICHALIK, JOHN JAMES, legal association administrator; b. Bemidji, Minn., Aug. 1, 1945; m. Diane Marie Olson, Dec. 21, 1968; children: Matthew John, Nicole, Shane. BA, U. Minn., 1967, JD, 1970. Legal editor Lawyers Coop. Pub. Co., Rochester, NY, 1970—75; dir. continuing legal edn. Wash. State Bar Assn., Seattle, 1975—81, exec. dir., 1981—91; asst. dean devel. and cmty. rels. Sch. Law U. Wash., 1991—95; dir., CEO Assn. Legal Adminstrs., Lincolnshire, Ill., 1995—. Fellow: Coll. Law Practice Mgmt.; mem.: Nat. Trust Hist. Preservation, Am. Mgmt. Assn., Am. Soc. Assn. Execs. Lutheran. Office: Assn Legal Adminstrs 75 Tri-State Internat Ctr # 222 Lincolnshire IL 60069-4435 Home Phone: 847-821-9533; Office Phone: 847-267-1360. Business E-Mail: jmichalik@alanet.org.

MICHELI, FRANK JAMES, lawyer; b. Zanesville, Ohio, Mar. 23, 1930; s. John and Theresa (Carlini) Micheli; m. Doris Joan Clum, Jan. 9, 1954; children: Michael John, James Carl, Lisa Ann, Matthew Charles. Student, John Carroll U., Cleve., 1947-48, Xavier U., Cin., 1949-50; LL.D., Ohio No. U., Ada., 1953. Bar: Ohio 1953. Pvt. practice, Zanesville; ptnr. Leasure & Micheli, 1953-65, Kincaid, Micheli, Geyer & Ormond, 1965-75, Kincaid, Cultice, Micheli & Geyer (and predecessor), 1982-92, Micheli, Baldwin, Bopeley & Northrup, 1992—. Instr. bus. law Meredith Bus. Coll., Zanesville, 1956; lectr. med. malpractice, hosp. and nurse liability. Dir. pub. svc. City of Zanesville, 1954. Mem.: ABA, Am. Bd. Trial Advs. (bd. dirs. Ohio chpt. 1991—95, pres. 1997), Am. Arbitration Assn. (mem. nat. panel), Am. Judicature Soc., Ohio Bar Assn., Ohio Def. Assn., Def. Rsch. Inst., Internat. Assn. Ins. Counsel, Elk. Home: 160 E Willow Dr Zanesville OH 43701-1249 Office: PO Box 788 3808 James Ct Ste 2 Zanesville OH 43702-0788 Office Phone: 740-454-2545. E-mail: micheli@cyberzane.net.

MICHELS, MATTHEW, state representative, lawyer; b. 1960; BS, JD, U. S.D. Atty.; Rep. S.D. State House, 1998—, House Spkr., 2002—. Chair Legis. Procedure & Retirement Laws coms.; vice chair State Affairs Judiciary com.; candidate S.D. State House, Dist. 18, 1996. Office: 1213 Walnut St Yankton SD 57078

MICHELSEN, JOHN ERNEST, software and internet services company executive; b. New Brunswick, N.J., May 11, 1946; s. Ernest Arnold and Ursula (Hunter) M.; B.S., Northwestern U., 1969; M.S., Stevens Inst. Tech., 1972; M.B.A. in Fin. with honors, U. Chgo., 1978; m. Ruth Ann Flanders, June 15, 1969; children— Nancy Ellen, Rebecca Ruthann. Real-time programmer Lockheed Electronics Co., Plainfield, N.J., 1969-72; control system designer Fermi Nat. Accelerator Lab., Batavia, Ill., 1972-75; chief system designer Distributed Info. Systems Corp., Chgo., 1975-78, v.p., 1978-79; mgr. M.I.S. adminstrn. FMC Corp., Chgo., 1979-82; pres. Infopro, Inc., 1982—. Mem. Assn. Computing Machinery, Phi Eta Sigma, Tau Beta Pi, Beta Gamma Sigma. Office: 2920 Norwalk Ct Aurora IL 60504

MICHENER, CHARLES DUNCAN, entomologist, researcher, educator; b. Pasadena, Calif., Sept. 22, 1918; s. Harold and Josephine (Rigden) Michener; m. Mary Hastings, Jan. 1, 1941; children: David, Daniel, Barbara, Walter. BS, U. Calif., Berkeley, 1939, PhD, 1941. Tech. asst. U. Calif., Berkeley, 1939-42; asst. curator Am. Mus. atural History, NYC, 1942-46, assoc. curator, 1946-48, rsch. assoc., 1949—; assoc. prof. U. Kans., 1948-49, prof., 1949-89, prof. emeritus, 1989—, chmn. dept. entomology, 1949-61, 72-75, Watkins Disting. prof. entomology, 1959-89, acting chmn. dept. systematics, ecology, 1968-69, Watkins Disting. prof. systematics and ecology, 1969-89; dir. Snow Entomol. Museum, 1974-83, state entomologist, 1949-61. Vis. rsch. prof. U. Paraná, Curitiba, Brazil, 1955—56. Author: The Social Behavior of the Bees, 1974, The Bees of the World, 2000, 2d edit., 2007; author: (with Mary H. Michener) American Social Insects, 1951; author: (with S. F. Sakagami) (book) Nest Architecture of the Sweat Bees, 1962; author: (with M. D. Breed and H. E. Evans) The Biology of Social Insects, 1982; author: (with D. Fletcher) Kin Recognition in Animals, 1987; author: (with R. McGinley and B. Danforth) The Bee Genera of North and Central America, 1994; contbr. articles to profl. jours.; Am. editor: Insectes Sociaux, 1954—55, 1962—90; editor: (jour.) Evolution, 1962—64; assoc. editor: Ann. Rev. Ecology and Systematics, 1970—90. Served to capt. San Corps AUS, 1943—46. Recipient Disting. Rsch. medal, Internat. Soc. Hymenopterists, 2002; fellow Guggenheim, U. Paraná, 1955—56, Africa, 1966—67, Fulbright, U. Queensland, 1958—59; scholar Rsch., U. Costa Rica, 1963. Fellow: AAAS, Royal Entomol. Soc. London, Am. Acad. Arts and Sci., Am. Entomol. Soc., Entomol. Soc. Am. (C. V. Riley award 1999); mem.: NAS, Kans. Entomol. Soc. (pres. 1950), Linnean Soc. London (corr.), Russian Entomol. Soc. (hon.), Soc. Systematic Zoologists (hon.; pres. 1969), Netherlands Entomological Soc. (hon.), Brazilian Acad. Sci. (corr.), Internat. Union Study Social Insects (pres. 1977—82), Am. Soc. Naturalists (pres. 1978), Soc. Study Evolution (pres. 1967). Home: 1706 W 2nd St Lawrence KS 66044-1016 Office Phone: 785-864-4610. Business E-Mail: michener@ku.edu.

MICK, HOWARD HAROLD, lawyer; b. Newton, Kans., Oct. 21, 1934; s. Marvin Woodrow and Edith (Bergen) M.; m. Susan Siple, Sept. 5, 1957 (dec. July 1997); children: Martha, Julie, Elizabeth; m. Patricia Willson, Apr. 4, 1998. Student, U. Okla., 1952-54; BS, LLB, U. Colo., 1958. Bar: Colo. 1958, Mo. 1959. Assoc. Stinson, Mag & Fizzell, Kansas City, Mo., 1959—62, shareholder, 1962—2002; of counsel Stinson Morrison Hecker LLP, 2002—. Bd. dirs. Ctr. Mgmt. Assistance, Kansas City, Mo., 1984-88; mem. adv. coun. Kansas City Salvation Army, 1987—, Milbank Mfg. Co., Kansas City, Mo., 1996—; mem. adv. coun. Gordon Parks Elem. Sch., Kansas City, Mo., 2000—. Mem. ABA, Lawyers Assn. Kansas City, Kansas City Bar Assn., Rotary, Kansas City Club, Indian Hills Country. Democrat. Presbyterian. Avocations: golf, tennis, bridge. Office: Stinson Morrison Hecker LLP PO Box 419251 Kansas City MO 64141-6251 Office Phone: 816-691-3175. E-mail: howardmick@kc.rr.com.

MICKEL, EMANUEL JOHN, foreign language educator; b. Lemont, Ill., Oct. 11, 1937; s. Emanuel John and Mildred (Newton) M.; m. Kathleen Russell, May 31, 1959; children: Jennifer, Chiara, Heather. BA, La. State U., 1959; MA, U. N.C., 1961, PhD, 1965. Asst. prof. U. Nebr., Lincoln, 1965-67, assoc. prof., 1967-68, Ind. U., Bloomington, 1968-73, prof., 1973—, dir. Medieval Studies Inst., 1976-91, chmn. French and Italian, 1984-95. Cons. NEH; French advisor Soc. Rencesvals, 1995-98; adv. bd. mem. Nineteenth Century French Studies, 1995-, vis. scholar Pembroke Coll., U. Cambridge, 2006. Author: Marie de France, 1974, Eugene Fromentin, 1982, Ganelon Treason and the Chanson de Roland, 1989, Jules Vernes Complete Twenty Thousand Leagues Under the Sea, 1992, Enfances Godefroi and Retour de Cornumarant, 1999. Capt. U.S. Army, 1963-65. Grantee NEH, Washington, 1978-84; Lilly Open fellow Lilly Found., Indpls., 1981-82; Chevalier dans l'Ordre des Palmes Academiques, 1997.

Avocations: music, theater, sports, travel, ancient literature. Office: French & Italian Dept Indiana Univ 642 Ballantine Hall Bloomington IN 47401-5020 Office Phone: 812-855-8253. Business E-Mail: mickel@indiana.edu.

MICKELSON, JAN, radio personality; Radio host morning show Sta. WHO-AM, Des Moines. Office: WHO Radio 1801 Grand Ave Des Moines IA 50309

MICKELSON, STACEY, state legislator; BA, Minot State U., 1994. Govt. rels. dir. Artspace Projects, Inc.; rep. Dist. 38 N.D. Ho. of Reps., 1994-2000, mem. fin. and taxation com., vice-chmn. transp. com. Mem. interim taxation, adminstrv. rules coms. Bowhay Inst. for Legis. Leadership and Devel. fellow. Mem. Am. Coun. Young Polit. Leaders, Darden Program Emerging Polit. Leaders, Flemming Fellows. Home: 3120 Roosevelt St Ne Minneapolis MN 55418-2360

MIDDAUGH, JAMES (MIKE), former state legislator; b. Paw Paw, Mich., Sept. 4, 1946; s. Orson William and Phyllis Jean M.; m. Mary Ann. Student, Ferris State Coll., 1965-68; BS in Edn., Western Mich. U., 1969. Rep. Mich. Dist. 45, 1983-92, Mich. Dist. 80, 1993-98. Del. Van Buren County Mich. State Rep. Conv., 1965-73; adminstrv. asst. Mich. State Sen. Harry Gast, 1970—; chmn. issues com. Mich. Ho. Reps., 1974—, asst. minority whip, vice chmn. conservation, recreation & environ. com., mem. corps. and fin. com., pub. utilities & liquor control com. Mem. NRA, Farm Bur., N.Am. Hunting Club, Ferris State Coll. Alumni Assn. (pres. 1975), Southwestern Mich. Assn. Law Enforcement Officers. Home: 35361 51st Ave Paw Paw MI 49079-8852 Address: State Capitol PO Box 30014 Lansing MI 48909-7514

MIDDELKAMP, JOHN NEAL, pediatrician, educator; b. Kansas City, Mo., Sept. 29, 1925; s. George H. and Clara M. (Ordelheide) M.; m. Roberta Gill, Oct. 3, 1949 (div. 1970); children— Sharon Ann, Steven Neal, Susan Jean, Scott Alan; m. Lois Harper, Mar. 1, 1974 BS, U. Mo., 1946; MD, Washington U., St. Louis, 1948. Diplomate Am. Bd. Pediatrics. Intern D.C. Gen. Hosp., Washington, 1948-49; resident St. Louis Children's Hosp., 1949-50, 52-53; instr. pediatrics Washington U., 1953-57, asst. prof. pediatrics, 1957-64, assoc. prof., 1964-70, prof., 1970-98, prof. emeritus, 1998—; dir. ambulatory pediatrics St. Louis Children's Hosp., 1974-91. Author: Camp Health Manual, 1984; contbr. articles, chpts. to profl. publs. Served to comdr. M.C., USNR, 1943-66. NIH postdoctoral fellow, 1961-62 Mem. Am. Acad. Pediatrics, Am. Soc. Microbiology, Infectious Diseases Soc. Am., Am. Pediatric Soc., Ambulatory Pediatric Assn., Sigma Xi, Alpha Omega Alpha Home: 8845 Paragon Cir Saint Louis MO 63123-1114 Office: Office Assoc Dean for Grad Med Edn Washington Univ Sch Medicine 660 S Euclid Box 8033 Saint Louis MO 63110 Office Phone: 314-747-4479.

MIDDLEBROOK, JOHN G., automotive executive; b. Lansing, Mich., 1941; BS in Engring., GM Inst.; M in Mktg., Mich. State U. With GM Oldsmobile Divsn., 1959—67, GM Pontiac Divsn., 1967, asst. sales mgr., 1969—70, sales analysis mgr., 1970, dir. mktg. svcs., 1977; zone mgr. GM Corp., Washington, 1977—78, dir. mktg. ops., 1978—79, mgr. product planning, devel., 1979—81; dir. passenger car planning GM Worldwide, 1981—83; dir. car distbn., sales analysis, strategic planning GM Pontiac Divsn., 1983—84, asst. gen. sales mgr., merchandising, ops., 1984—85; v.p. sales, svc, mktg. Saturn Corp., 1985—87; v.p. mktg product planning staff GM Corp., 1987—89; gen. mgr. GM Pontiac Motor Divsn., 1989, GM Chevrolet Disnv., 1996—99, GM Corp., 1999—2000, v.p. mktg, advt., 2000—04, v.p. global sales svc. & mktg. ops., 2004—. Pres. Boy Scouts, Detroit. Recipient Outstanding Alumni award, Mich. State U., 2000. Office: GM Corp 300 Renaissance Ctr PO Box 300 Detroit MI 48265-3000*

MIDGLEY, A(LVIN) REES, JR., reproductive endocrinology educator, researcher; b. Burlington, Vt., Nov. 9, 1933; s. Alvin Rees and Maxine (Schmidt) M.; m. Carol Crossman, Sept. 4, 1955; children: Thomas, Debra, Christopher. BS cum laude, U. Vt., 1955, MD cum laude, 1958. Intern U. Pitts., 1958-59, resident dept. pathology, 1959-61, U. Mich., Ann Arbor, 1961-63, instr. pathology, 1963-64, asst. prof., 1964-67, assoc. prof., 1967-70, prof., 1970—, dir. Reproductive Scis. Program, 1968—. Chmn. BioQuant of Ann Arbor, Inc., 1985-89. Contbr. articles to med. jours. Recipient Parke-Davis award, 1970; Ayerst award Endocrine Soc., 1977; Smith Kline Bio-Sci. Labs. award, 1985; NIH grantee, 1960—; Mellon Found. grantee, 1979-91. Mem. Soc. Study Reprodn. (pres. 1983-84), Endocrine Soc., Am. Assn. Pathology, Am. Physiol. Soc. Home: 101 W Liberty St Apt 340 Ann Arbor MI 48104-1359 Office: U Mich Rm 1101 Reproductive Scis Program 300 N Ingalls Bldg Fl 11 Ann Arbor MI 48109-2007

MIGLIN, MARILYN, cosmetics executive; Student, Northwestern U. Profl. ballerina; model Marshall Fields; founder, owner Marilyn Miglin Cosmetic Co., 1963—. Active Mayor Richard M. Daley's spl. com. tourism; officer Chgo. Conv. and Tourism Bur.; apptd. Gov. James Edgar Econ. Devel. Bd.; past pres. Oak St. Coun.; founder Women of Destiny (mentoring program); bd. mem. Ctr. for Craniofacial Anomalies, U. Ill., Chgo. Named in her honor Marilyn Miglin Day, Chgo., 1998; named one of Chgos. 100 Most Influential Women, Crain's Chgo. Bus., 2004. Office: 120 E Oak St Chicago IL 60611-1204

MIHELIC, TRACEY L., lawyer; b. Lake Forest, Ill., Sept. 12, 1965; BA, Ill., 1990. With Gardner, Carton & Douglas, Chgo., 1990—2000, ptnr., 1998—2000, Baker & McKenzie, Chgo., 2000—. Mem.: ABA, Internat. Emissions Trading Assn., Emissions Mktg. Assn., Ill. State Bar Assn. Office: Baker and McKenzie One Prudential Plz 130 E Randolph Dr Chicago IL 60601

MIHM, MICHAEL MARTIN, federal judge; b. Amboy, Ill., May 18, 1943; s. Martin Clarence and Frances Johannah (Morrissey) M.; m. Judith Ann Zosky, May 6, 1967; children— Molly Elizabeth, Sarah Ann, Jacob Michael, Jennifer Leah BA, Loras Coll., 1964; JD, St. Louis U., 1967. Asst. prosecuting atty. St. Louis County, Clayton, Mo., 1967-68; asst. state's atty. Peoria County, Peoria, Ill., 1968-69; asst. city atty. City of Peoria, Ill., 1969-72; state's atty. Peoria County, Peoria, Ill., 1972-80; sole practice Peoria, Ill., 1980-82; U.S. dist. judge U.S. Govt., Peoria, Ill., 1982—; chief U.S. dist. judge U.S. Dist. Ct. (ctrl. dist.) Ill., 1991—98. Chmn. com. internat. jud. rels. U.S. Jud. Conf., 1994—96, mem. exec. com., 1995—97, mem. com. jud. br., 1987—93, mem. com. internat. jud. rels., 1998—2002; mem. Supreme Ct. Fellows Commn., 2000—; adj. prof. law John Marshall Law Sch., 1990—. Past mem. adv. bd. Big Brothers-Big Sisters, Crisis Nursery, Peoria; past bd. dirs. Salvation Army, Peoria, W.D. Boyce council Boy Scouts Am., State of Ill. Treatment Alternatives to Street Crime, Gov.'s Criminal Justice Info. Council; past vice-chmn. Ill. Dangerous Drugs Adv. Council; trustee Proctor Health Care Found., 1991-2002. Recipient Good Govt. award Peoria Jaycees, 1978, Vincent C. Immel Alumni Merit award St. Louis U. Sch. Law, 1997, Disting. Alumnus in Pub. Svc. award Loras Coll., 2000, U.S. AID award for Outstanding Vol. Svc. in Russia, 2004. Mem. Peoria County Bar Assn. Roman Catholic. Office: US Dist Ct 204 Federal Bldg 100 NE Monroe St Peoria IL 61602-1003 Office Phone: 309-671-7113. Business E-Mail: michael_mihm@ilcd.uscourts.gov.

MIKA, JOSEPH JOHN, library and information scientist, educator; b. McKees Rocks, Pa., Mar. 1, 1948; s. George Joseph and Sophia Ann (Stec) Mika; m. Marianne Hartzell; 4 children. BA in English, U. Pitts., 1969, MLS, 1971, PhD in Libr. Sci., 1980. Asst. libr., instr. Ohio State U., Mansfield, 1971-73; asst. libr., asst. prof. Johnson State Coll., Vt., 1973-75; grad. asst., tchg. fellow Sch. Libr. and Info. Sci., U. Pitts., 1975-77; asst. dean, assoc. prof. libr. svc. U. So. Miss., Hattiesburg, 1977-86; dir. libr. and info. sci. program Wayne State U., 1986—95, 2002—07, prof., 1986—. Co-owner Hartzell-Mika Consulting; cons. to librs. Editor: Jour. Edn. Libr. and Info. Sci., 1995—2005. Retired col. USAR. Decorated DSM. Mem.: ALA (councilor 1983—86, chmn. constn. and bylaws com. 1985—86, councilor 1998—2001), Mich. Ctr. for Book (chair 1994—2001), Soc. Miss. Archivists (treas., exec. bd. 1981—83), Assn. Coll. and Rsch. Librs. (chmn., chmn. budget com. 1982—83), Leadership Acad., Mich. Libr. Assn., Miss. Libr. Assn. (pres.-elect 1985, chair libr. edn. com. 1989), Assn. Libr. and Info. Sci. and Edn. (chmn. nominating com. 1982, chmn. membership com. 1982—83, exec. bd. 1986), Kiwanis (Hattiesburg), Phi Delta Kappa, Beta Phi Mu (pres-elect. 1987—89, pres. 1989—91). Home: 222 Abbott Woods Dr East Lansing MI 48823-1995 Office: Wayne State U Libr and Info Sci Program 106 Kresge Library Detroit MI 48202 Office Phone: 313-577-6196. Business E-Mail: aa2500@wayne.edu.

MIKAN, G. MIKE, healthcare services company executive; Mgmt. positions, corp. devel. group UnitedHealth Group, Minnetonka, Minn., CFO specialized care svcs., 2001—04, sr. v.p. fin., 2006, exec. v.p., CFO, 2006—; pres. UnitedHealth Networks, Minnetonka, Minn., 2004—06. Bd. dirs. Best Buy Co., Inc., 2008—. Bd. dirs. Make-a-Wish Found. Minn., 2004—. Office: UnitedHealth Group PO Box 1459 Minneapolis MN 55440-1459*

MIKESELL, MARVIN WRAY, geography educator; b. Kansas City, Mo., June 16, 1929; s. Loy George and Clara (Wade) M.; m. Reine-Marie de France, Apr. 1, 1957. BA, UCLA, 1952, MA, 1953; PhD, U. Calif.-Berkeley, 1959. Instr. to prof. geography U. Chgo., 1958—, chmn. dept. geography, 1969-74, 83-86. Del. U.S. Nat. Commn. for UNESCO Author: Northern Morocco, 1961; editor: Readings in Cultural Geography, 1962, Geographers Abroad, 1973, Perspectives on Environment, 1974. Fellow Am. Geog. Soc. (hon.); mem. Assn. Am. Geographers (pres. 1975-76, Disting. Career award 1995). Clubs: Quadrangle. Home: 1155 E 56th St Chicago IL 60637-1530 Office: Com Geog Studies 5828 S University Ave Chicago IL 60637-1583 Office Phone: 773-702-8313. Business E-Mail: mmikesel@uchicago.edu.

MILBERG, JOACHIM, retired automotive executive; b. 1943; Doctorate in prodn. engring., Tech. U. Berlin, 1971. Head automatic lathe divsn. Werkzeugmaschinenfabrik Gildemeister AG, 1978; prof. machine tools and ops. rsch. Munich Tech. U., 1981; mem. bd. mgmt. in charge of prodn. BMW, 1993, ret. chmn. bd. mgmt., 1999—2002, dir.; ret. CEO BMW A.G., 1999—2002. Mem. audit review com. Deere and Co., mem. corp. governance com.; dir. Allianza A.G., Festo A.G., MAN A.G. Achievements include raced in the 24hrs of LeMans and won with the BMW LMR.

MILBRETT, TIFFENY CARLEEN, professional soccer player; b. Portland, Oreg., Oct. 23, 1972; Degree in comms. mgmt., U. Portland. Mem. U.S. Women's Nat. Soccer Team; profl. soccer player N.Y. Power, 2001—03. Mem. championship team, Montricoux, France, 1993. Named World Cup Champion, 1999; recipient Gold medal, Centennial Olympic Games, 1996, 3d place medal, 1995, Silver medal, World Univ. Games, 1993, Sydney Olympic Games, 2000. Office: c/o US Soccer Fedn 1801 S Prairie Ave # 1811 Chicago IL 60616-1319

MILENTHAL, DAVID, advertising executive; B in Journalism, Ohio State U. Mgr. comms. Ohio Blue Shield; dir., organizer Pub. Interest Ctr., Ohio Environtl. Protection Agy.; pres., CEO Milenthal Advt. Agy.; exec. v.p. Hameroff/Milenthal, Inc.; pres., CEO HMS Ptnrs., chmn. Recipient Silver medal award Advt. Fedn. of Columbus; named Man of Yr. Temple Israel, Ten Outstanding Young Citizens Jaycees, People to Watch Columbus Monthly. Office: HMS Ptnrs Ste 5 250 Civic Center Dr S Columbus OH 43215-5086

MILES, WENDELL A., federal judge; b. Holland, Mich., Apr. 17, 1916; s. Fred T. and Dena Del (Alverson) M.; m. Mariette Bruckert, June 8, 1946; children: Lorraine Miles, Michelle Miles Kopinski, Thomas Paul. AB, Hope Coll., 1938, LLD (hon.), 1980; MA, U. Wyo., 1939; JD, U. Mich., 1942; LLD (hon.), Detroit Coll. Law, 1979. Bar: Mich. Ptnr. Miles & Miles, Holland, 1948-53, Miles, Mika, Meyers, Beckett & Jones, Grand Rapids, Mich., 1961-70; pros. atty. County of Ottawa, Mich., 1949-53; U.S. dist. atty. Western Dist. Mich., Grand Rapids, 1953-60, U.S. dist. judge, 1974—, chief judge, 1979-86, sr. judge, 1986—. Cir. judge 20th Jud. Cir. Ct. Mich., 1970-74; instr. Hope Coll., 1948-53, Am. Inst. Banking, 1953-60; adj. prof. Am. constl. history Hope Coll., Holland, Mich., 1979—; mem. Mich. Higher Edn. Commn.; apptd. Fgn. Intelligence Surveillance Ct., Washington, 1989—. Pres. Holland Bd. Edn., 1952-63. Served to capt. U.S. Army, 1942-47. Recipient Liberty Bell award, 1986. Fellow Am. Bar Found.; mem. ABA, Mich. Bar Assn., Fed. Bar Assn., Ottawa County Bar Assn., Grand Rapids Bar (Inns of Ct. 1995—), Am. Judicature Soc., Torch Club, Rotary Club, Masons. Office: US Dist Ct 236 Fed Bldg 110 Michigan St NW Ste 452 Grand Rapids MI 49503-2363 Home (Winter): 16380 Kelly Cove Dr #305 Fort Myers FL 33908 Home Phone: 616-942-8538; Office Phone: 616-456-2314. Business E-Mail: miles@miwd.uscourts.gov.

MILEWSKI, BARBARA ANNE, pediatrics nurse, neonatal/perinatal nurse practitioner, critical care nurse; b. Chgo., Sept. 11, 1934; d. Anthony and LaVerne (Sepp) Witt; m. Leonard A. Milewski, Feb. 23, 1952; children: Pamela, Robert, Diane, Timothy. ADN, Harper Coll., Palatine, Ill., 1982; BS, Northern Ill. U., 1992; postgrad., North Park Coll. RN Ill., cert. CPR instr. Staff nurse N.W. Cmty. Hosp., Arlington Heights, Ill., Resurrection Hosp., Chgo.; nurse neonatal ICU Children's Meml. Hosp., Chgo.; day care cons. Cook County Dept. Pub. Health; owner, CEO Child Care Health Cons. CPR instr. Stewart Oxygen Svcs., Chgo., Harper Coll., Children's Meml. Hosp.; instr., organizer parenting and well baby classes and clinics; health coord. CEDA Head Start; mem. adv. bd. Cook County Child Care Resource and Referral; dir. Albany Park Head Start. Vol. Children's Meml. Hosp., Boy Scouts Am. Mem.: Am. Mortar Bd., Sigma Theta Tau. Personal E-mail: barbmilewski@aol.com.

MILEY, GEORGE H., nuclear and electrical engineering educator, plasma engineer, energy conversion scientist; b. Shreveport, La., Aug. 6, 1933; s. George Hunter and Norma Angeline (Dowling) M.; m. Elizabeth Burroughs, Nov. 22, 1958; children: Susan Miley Hibbs, Hunter Robert. BS in Chem. Engring., Carnegie-Mellon U., 1955; MS, U. Mich., 1956, PhD in Chem.-Nuclear Engring., 1959. Nuclear engr. Knolls Atomic Power Lab., Gen. Electric Co., Schenectady, 1959-61; mem. faculty U. Ill., Urbana, 1961—, prof., 1967—, chmn. nuclear engring. program, 1975-86, dir. Fusion Studies Lab., 1976—, fellow Ctr. for Advanced Study, 1985-86; dir. rsch. Rockford Tech. Assocs. Inc., 1990-94; pres., dir. rsch. NPL Assocs. Inc., 1994—; chief scientist Lattice Energy, LLC, 2001—03. Vis. prof. U. Colo., 1967, Cornell U., 1969-70, U. New South Wales, 1986, Imperial Coll. of London, 1987; mem. Ill. Radiation Protection Bd., 1988—; mem. Air Force Studies Bd., 1990-94; chmn. tech. adv. com. Ill. Low Level Radioactive Waste Site, 1990-96; chmn. com. on indsl. uses of radiation Ill. Dept. uclear Safety, 1989-2000. Author: Direct Conversion of Nuclear Radiation Energy, 1971, Fusion Energy Conversion, 1976; editor Jour. Fusion Tech., 1980-2001; U.S. assoc. editor Laser and Particle Beams, 1982-86, mng. editor, 1987-91, editor-in-chief, 1991-2002; U.S. editor Jour. Plasma Physics, 1995-2003. Served with C.E. AUS, 1960. Recipient Western Electric Tchg.-Rsch. award, 1977, Halliburton Engring. Edn. Leadership award, 1990, Edward Teller medal, 1995, Scientist of Yr. award Inst. New Energy, 1996, Cert. Recognition award NASA, 2003; NATO sr. sci. fellow, 1975-76, Guggenheim fellow, 1985-86, Japanese Soc. Promotion of Sci. fellow, 1994, CMNS Preparata medal, 2006, Integrity in Rsch. award, 2006. Fellow IEEE (Fusion Engring. and Sci. award, 2004), Am. Nuclear Soc. (dir. 1980-83, Disting. Svc. award 1980, Outstanding Achievement award Fusion Energy divsn. 1992, Radiation Sci. and Tech. award 2004), Am. Phys. Soc., AIAA (assoc.); mem. Am. Soc. Engring. Edn. (chmn. energy conversion com. 1967-70, pres. U. Ill. chpt. 1973-74, chmn. nuclear divsn. 1975-76, Outstanding Tchr. award 1973), Sigma Xi, Tau Beta Pi. Presbyterian. Achievements include research in fusion, energy conversion, reactor kinetics, and fuel cells. Avocations: tennis, hiking. Office: U Ill 214 Nuc Engring Lab 103 S Goodwin Ave Urbana IL 61801-2901 Home Phone: 217-356-5402; Office Phone: 217-333-3772. E-mail: georgehm@aol.com.

MILKMAN, ROGER DAWSON, genetics educator, molecular biologist, researcher; b. NYC, Oct. 15, 1930; s. Louis Arthur and Margaret (Weinstein) M.; m. Marianne Friedenthal, Oct. 18, 1958; children: Ruth Margaret Milkman Atkinson, Louise Friedenthal, Janet Dawson Milkman Lussenhop, Paul David. AB, Harvard U., 1951, A.M., 1954, PhD, 1956. Student, asst., instr., investigator Marine Biol. Lab., Woods Hole, Mass., 1952-72, 88-96; instr., asst. prof. U. Mich., Ann Arbor, 1957-60; assoc. prof., prof. Syracuse U., NY, 1960-68; prof. biol. scis. U. Iowa, Iowa City, 1968-2001, prof. emeritus, 2001—, chmn. univ. genetics PhD program, 1992-93. Vis. prof. biology Grinnell (Iowa) Coll., 1990; mem. genetics study sect. NIH, 1986-87; NSF panelist, 1996-99; adj. scientist Marine Biol. Lab., Woods Hole, 2002—, Josephine Bay Paul Ctr. Translator: (from German) Developmental Physiology, 2d edit., 1971; editor: Perspectives on Evolution, 1982, Experimental Population Genetics, 1983, Evolution jour., 1984-86; mem. editl. bd. Jour. Bacteriology, 1998-2000; contbr. articles to profl. jours. Sec. Soc. Gen. Physiologists, 1963-65, Am. Soc. Naturalists, 1980-82; alumni rep. Phillips Acad., Andover, Mass., 1980-94. NSF grantee, 1959—; USPHS grantee, 1984-87. Fellow AAAS; mem. Am. Soc. for Microbiology, Genetics Soc. Am., Corp. Marine Biol. Lab., Soc. for Gen. Microbiology (U.K.), Soc. study Evolution. Jewish. Avocation: mountain hiking. Home and Office: 5901 Macarthur Blvd Nw Apt 498 Washington DC 20016-2549 Home Phone: 508-548-6248; Office Phone: 508-289-7390. Business E-Mail: rmilkman@mbl.edu, roger-milkman@uiowa.edu, rogmilkman@adelphia.net.

MILL, JETH, performing company executive; Exec. dir. Des Moines Symphony. Office: Des Moines Symph 221 Walnut St Des Moines IA 50309

MILL, SETH, orchestra executive; BA in Edn., Ohio U. With Nat. Pub. Radio, Washington, 1975-83; asst. mgr. Pitts. Symphony, 1983-89; mgr. Northeastern Pa. Philharmonic, Scranton, 1990-95; exec. dir. Lincoln (Nebr.) Symphony Orch., 1995-99, Des Moines Symphony, 1999—. Office: Des Moines Symphony 221 Walnut St Des Moines IA 50309-2101

MILLAR, JAMES F., pharmaceutical executive; Exec. v.p. No. Group Cardinal Health Inc., Dublin, Ohio, with distbn., pres. drug wholesaling opers., exec. v.p., Pharm. Distbn. and Med. Products. Office: Cardinal Health Inc 7000 Cardinal Pl Dublin OH 43017-1092

MILLARD, CHARLES PHILLIP, manufacturing executive; b. Janesville, Wis., Apr. 21, 1948; s. Duane Francis and Mary Lou (Ganley) M.; m. Mary Franzen, Oct. 7, 1967 (div. June 13, 1990); children: Katherine, Laura. Student, U. Wis., Janesville, 1966—67. Spot welder GM, Janesville, 1966—67; mgr. plant Insta-Foam Products, Addison, Ill., 1967—72; mgr. warehouse Ram Golf Corp., Elk Grove, Ill., 1972—77; master scheduler Gandalf Data Inc., Wheeling, Ill., 1977—84, coord. corp. mfg., 1984—85; coord. corp. mktg. Gandalf Technologies Inc., Wheeling, 1985—87, corp. strategist, 1988—89; analyst internat. rsch. Gandalf Data Inc., Wheeling, 1989—90; asst. mgr. safety/security Fellowes Mfg. Co., Itasca, Ill., 1990—93; process specialist, cons. Janesville, 1993—94; asst. mgr. Janesville Travel Ctr., 1994—95; coord. prodn. material Alliant Tech Sys., Janesville, 1995—96; mgr. prodn. inventory control fabrication divsn. Freedom Plastics, Janesville, 1997—99; staff armed security U.S. Attys. Office, Fed. Cthse. & FEMA Facilities, Madison, Wis., 2000. Patrol Officer Des Plaines (Ill.) Police Res., 1987-89; vol. with Alzheimer patients, 1999-2000. Mem. Am. Mgmt. Assn., Am. Mktg. Assn., Furniture Workers Union, Am. Fedn. Police, at. Rifle Assn. Avocations: physical fitness, motorcycling, home improvements, auto mechanics. Office Phone: 608-359-4821. E-mail: cpmillard@sbcglobal.net.

MILLEN, MATT, professional sports team executive; b. Hokendauqua, Pa., Mar. 12, 1958; m. Patricia Millen; children: Marianne, Michalyn, Marcus; 1 child, Matthew Jr. Student Pa. State U. Linebacker Oakland/L.A. Raiders, 1980—88, San Francisco 49ers, 1989—90, Washington Redskins, 1991; game analyst CBS, Fox TV; pres., CEO Detroit Lioins, 2001—. Named to NFL Pro Bowl Team, 1988. Office: Detroit Lions Inc 222 Republic Dr Allen Park MI 48101-3650

MILLER, ARTHUR HAWKS, JR., librarian, archivist; b. Kalamazoo, Mich., Mar. 15, 1943; s. Arthur Hawks and Eleanor (Johnson) M.; m. Janet Carol Schroeder, June 11, 1967; children: Janelle Miller Moravek, Andrew Hawks. Student, U. Caen, Calvados, France, 1963-64; AB, Kalamazoo Coll., 1965; AM in English, U. Chgo., 1966, AM in Librarianship, 1968; PhD, Northwestern U., 1973. Reference libr. Newberry Libr., Chgo., 1966-69, asst. libr. pub. svcs., 1969-72; coll. libr. Lake Forest (Ill.) Coll., 1972-94, archivist and libr. for spl. collections, 1994—. Co-author: 30 Miles North: A History of Lake Forest College, Its Town, and Its City of Chicago, 2000, Lake Forest Estates, People, and Culture, 2000, Classic Country Estates Lake Forest, 2003, One Hundred Rare and Notable Books, 2004, co-editor, Lake Forest College: A Guide to the Campus, 2007. Pres. Lake Forest/Lake Bluff Hist. Soc., 1982-85, bd. dirs., 2003—06; pres. Ill. Ctr. for Book Bd., 1992-93; pres. Ragdale Found., 1992-96; dir. Lake Forest Found. for Hist. Preservation, 1997—, v.p., 2000-02, 2006-07, pres., 2007—; dir Ctr. For Railroad Photography and Art, 1999—, sec., 2005—. Mem. Caxton Club. Presbyterian. Home: 169 Wildwood Rd Lake Forest IL 60045-2462 Office: Lake Forest Coll Donnelley and Lee Libr/LIT 555 N Sheridan Rd Lake Forest IL 60045-2399 Office Phone: 847-735-5064. E-mail: amiller@lakeforest.edu.

MILLER, ARTHUR J., JR., state legislator; b. Detroit, July 11, 1946; m. Marsha Ann; children: Holly A., Nicole M., Arthur J. III, Derek E. Student, Eastern Mich. U. Mem. Mich. Senate from 10th dist., Lansing, 1977—; Dem. Leader of the Senate, 1985—. City coun. Warren, Mich., v.p., pres. Address: PO Box 30036 Lansing MI 48909-7536 Also: State Senate 11139 Olive St Warren MI 48093-6557

MILLER, BENJAMIN K., retired state supreme court justice; b. Springfield, Ill., Nov. 5, 1936; s. Clifford and Mary (Luthyens) M. BA, So. Ill. U., 1958; JD, Vanderbilt U., 1961. Bar: Ill. 1961. Ptnr. Olsen, Cantrill & Miller, Springfield, 1964-70; prin. Ben Miller-Law Office, Springfield, 1970-76; judge 7th jud. cir. Ill. Cir. Ct., Springfield, 1976-82, presiding judge Criminal div., 1977-81, chief judge, 1981-82; justice Ill. Appellate Ct., 4th Jud. Dist., 1982-84, Ill. Supreme Ct., Springfield, 1984-2001, chief justice, 1991-93, ret., 2001. Adj. prof. So. Ill. U., Springfield, 1974—; chmn. Ill. Cts. Commn., 1988-90; mem. Ill. Gov.'s Adv. Coun. on Criminal Justice Legis., 1977-84, Ad Hoc Com. on Tech. in Cts., 1985—. Mem. editorial rev. bd. Illinois Civil Practice Before Trial, Illinois Civil Trial Practice Pres. Cen. Ill. Mental Health Assn., 1969-71; bd. govs. Aid to Retarded Citizens, 1977-80; mem. Lincoln Legals Adv. Bd., 1988—. Lt. USNR, 1964-67. Mem. ABA (bar admissions com. sect. of legal edn. and admissions to bar 1992—), Ill. State Bar Assn. (bd. govs. 1970-76, treas. 1975-76), Sangamon County Bar Assn., Ctrl. Ill. Women's Bar Assn., Am. Judicature Soc. (bd. dirs. 1990-95), Abraham Lincoln Assn. (bd. dirs. 1988-98). Address: 100 E Bellevue PL Apt 29F Chicago IL 60611-5194 Office Phone: 312-840-7216.

MILLER, BERNARD JOSEPH, JR., advertising executive; b. Louisville, July 31, 1925; s. Bernard J. Sr. and Myrtle (Herrington) M.; m. Jayne Hughes, Aug. 7, 1948 (div. Oct. 1970); children: Bernard J. III, Jeffrey, Janet Marie.; m. Brita Naujok, Nov. 24, 1970; 1 child, Brian. BS, Ind. U., 1949. Merchandising mgr. Brown-Forman Distillers, Inc., Louisville, 1949-54; v.p. Phelps Mfg. Co., Terre Haute, Ind., 1954-60; pres. Columbian Advt. Inc., Chgo., 1960-87, chmn., 1987—. 2d lt. USAF, 1943-46, PTO. Mem. Point of Purchase Advt. Inst. (dir. 1970-73). Saddle and Cycle Club (bd. dirs. 1987-90, 99—). Avocations: tennis, downhill skiing, collecting first edition autographed books.

MILLER, BEVERLY WHITE, former college president, educational consultant; b. Willoughby, Ohio, 1923; d. Joseph Martin and Marguerite Sarah (Storer) White; m. Lynn Martin Miller, Oct. 11, 1945 (dec. 1986); children: Michaela Ann, Craig Martin, Todd Daniel, Cass Timothy, Simone Agnes. AB, Western Res. U., 1945; MA, Mich. State U., 1957; PhD, U. Toledo, 1967; LHD (hon.), Coll. St. Benedict, St. Joseph, Minn., 1979; LLD (hon.), U. Toledo, 1988. Chem. and biol. researcher, 1945-57; tchr. schs. in Mich., also Mercy Sch. Nursing, St. Lawrence Hosp., Lansing, Mich., 1957-58; mem. chemistry and biology faculty Mary Manse Coll., Toledo, 1958-71, dean grad. div., 1968-71, exec. v.p., 1968-71; acad. dean Salve Regina Coll., Newport, RI, 1971-74; pres. Coll. St. Benedict, St. Joseph, Minn., 1974-79, Western New Eng. Coll., Springfield, Mass., 1980-96, pres. emerita, 1996—. Higher edn. cons., 1996—; cons. U.S. Office Edn., 1980; mem. Springfield Pvt. Industry Coun./Regional Employment Bd., exec. com., 1982-94; mem. Minn. Pvt. Coll. Coun., 1974-79, sec., 1974-75, vice chmn., 1975-76, chmn., 1976-77; cons. in field. Author papers and books in field. Corporator Mercy Hosp., Springfield, Mass. Recipient President's citation St. John's U., Minn., 1979; also various service awards; named disting. alumna of yr. U. Toledo, 1998. Mem. AAAS, Am. Assn. Higher Edn., Assn. Cath. Colls. and Univs. (exec. bd.), Internat. Assn. Sci. Edn., Nat. Assn. Ind. Colls. and Univs. (govt. rels. adv. com., bd. dirs. 1990-93, exec. com. 1991-93, treas. 1992-93), Nat. Assn. Biology Tchrs., Assn. Ind. Colls. and Univs. of Mass. (exec. com. 1981-96, vice chmn. 1985-86, chmn. 1986-87), Nat. Assn. Rsch. Sci. Tchg., Springfield C. of C. (bd. dirs.), Am. Assn. Univ. Adminstrs. (bd. dirs. 1989-92), Delta Kappa Gamma, Sigma Delta Epsilon. Office: 6713 County Road M Delta OH 43515-9778

MILLER, BRANT, meteorologist; m. Lisa Miller; 2 children. With Sta. WLS AM/FM, Sta. WTMX-FM; weather forecaster Fox 32, 1989; weekend weather forecaster NBC 5, Chgo., 1991—; weekday morning weather forecaster Sta. WUSN-FM, Sta. WJMK-FM. Recipient Chgo. Emmy awards, 1997, 1999, 2000, First pl. Silver Dome awards, Ill. Broadcasters Assn., 1999, 2000. Avocations: gardening, tinkerer, home repair aficionado. Office: NBC 5 454 N Columbus Dr Chicago IL 60611

MILLER, BRIDGET A., lawyer; BA, Ursuline Coll.; JD, Cleveland State U. Bar: Ohio 1983. Assoc. Mansour, Gavin, Gerlack & Manos, LPA, Cleveland; corp. insurance risk mgr. Invacare Inc., Elyria, Ohio, 1993, asst. gen. counsel, dir. risk mgmt., v.p., gen. counsel, 2002—. Mem.: ABA, Soc. Chartered Property Casualty Underwriters, Cleveland Bar Assn., Ohio State Bar Assn., Lorain County Bar Assn. Office: Invacare Corp One Invacare Way Elyria OH 44036

MILLER, CANDICE S., congresswoman; b. Clair Shores, Mich., May 7, 1954; m. Donald G. Miller; 1 child, Wendy Nicole. Student, Macomb County C.C., 1973—74, Northwood U., 1974. Sec., treas. D.B. Snider, Inc., 1972-79; trustee Harrison Twp., 1979-80, supr., 1980-92; treas. Macomb County, 1992-95; sec. of state State of Mich., Lansing, 1995—2003; mem. US Congress from 10th Mich. dist., 2003—. Mem. Lake St. Clair Blue Ribbon Commn. Chair John Engler for Gov. campaign, Macomb County; del. Rep. Nat. Conv., 1996; co-chair Rep. Platform Com., 1996, Dole/Kemp Presdl. Campaign, Mich., 1996, Bush/Cheney Presdl. Campaign, Mich., 2000; mem. Carehouse-Macomb County Child Adv. Ctr., Selfridge Air Nat. Guard Base Cmty. Coun., Detroit Econ. Club; mem. adminstrv. bd. Mich. State, mem. safety commn. Recipient Macomb Citizen of Yr. award, March of Dimes, 1997, Woman of Distinction award, Macomb County Girl Scouts, Adjutant General's Patriot award, Mich. Nat. Guard, 2002, GH award women in govt., Good Housekeeping mag., 2003, Econ. Excellence award, Macomb C. of C.; Paul Harris Internat. fellow. Mem.: Nat. Assn. Secretaries of State, Boat Town Assn. Republican. Presbyterian. Avocations: boating, yacht racing. Office: US Congress 228 Cannon HOB Washington DC 20515 also: District Office 48653 Van Dyke Ave Shelby Township MI 48317-2560 Office Phone: 202-225-2106, 586-997-5010. Office Fax: 202-226-1169, 586-997-5013.

MILLER, CHARLES S., clergy member, church administrator; Exec. dir. Division for Church in Society of the Evangelical Lutheran Church in America, Chicago, Ill. Office: Evangelical Lutheran Church Am 8765 W Higgins Rd Chicago IL 60631-4101

MILLER, CURTIS HERMAN, bishop; b. LeMars, Iowa, May 3, 1947; s. Herman Andrew and Verna Marion (Lund) M.; m. Sharyl Susan VanderTuig, June 2, 1969; children: Eric, athan, Paul. BA, Wartburg Coll., 1969; MDiv., Wartburg Sem., 1973; DD (hon.), Wartburg Coll., 1987. Assoc. pastor Holy Trinity Luth. Ch., Dubuque, Iowa, 1973-75; pastor St. Paul Luth. Ch., Tama, Iowa, 1975-82; coord. for congl. life Am. Luth. Ch. Iowa dist., Storm Lake, 1982-87; bishop Western Iowa Synod Evang. Luth. Ch. in Am., Storm Lake, 1987—. Bd. regents Waldorf Coll., Forest City, Iowa, 1987—; bd. dirs. Luth. Social Svcs. of Iowa, Des Moines, 1987. Office: Evang Luth Ch Am Western Iowa Synod PO Box 577 Storm Lake IA 50588-0577

MILLER, DALE ANDREW, city councilman; b. Cleve., Sept. 16, 1949; s. Leonard Allan and Margaret Eleanor (Kostur) M.; m. Carol Jean Pierse, Aug. 10, 1985. BS in Psychology, Case Western Reserve U., 1971; MS in Clin. Psychology, U. Utah, 1974, PhD in Clin. Psychology, 1976. Program evaluator Great Plains Mental Health Ctr., North Platte, Nebr., 1977, Community Guidance, Inc., Cleve., 1977-79; councilman City of Cleve., 1980—. Contbr. articles to profl. jours. Co-chmn. Charter Rev. Commn., Cleve., 1988; mem. spkrs. bur. Build Up Greater Cleve., 1985-86; trustee Cleve. Ptnr. Cities, 1987—; del. Nat. Dem. Midterm Conv., Salt Lake City, 1974; candidate for state senator, Ohio, 1990, 1994, apptd. state senator, 2004—; apptd. state rep. 1997, re-elected 1998, 2000, 2002; bd. dirs. Great Lakes Science Ctr; mem. Archwood United Ch. Christ. Named Outstanding Del., Utah Delegation, Salt Lake City, 1974. Mem. Wd 20 Democrat Club. Avocations: travel, camping, golf.

MILLER, DAVID GROFF, insurance agent; b. Kansas City, Kans., Aug. 17, 1949; s. Vincent G. and Ruth (Whitton) M.; m. Marjorie Zwiers, 1979. BA, U. Kans., 1972. CLU. Press aide to U.S. Senator James B. Pearson, 1974-75; fed. grant adminstr. Kans. Gov. Robert Bennett, 1975-78; brokerage rep. Paul Revere Co., Overland Park, Kans., 1979-85; prin. Miller Agy., Inc., Eudora, 1985—. Rep. dist. 43 Kans. State Reps., 1981-91; chmn. Kans. State Rep. Party, 1995-98. Mem.: Ind. Ins. Agts., Omicron Delta Kappa. Methodist. Office: Miller Agy Inc PO Box 460 Eudora KS 66025-0460

MILLER, DAVID PAUL, state legislator, lawyer; b. Batavia, Iowa, Nov. 24, 1946; m. Pam Miller; 4 children. BA, Denver U., 1969; JD, U. Iowa, 1974. Bar: Iowa 1974, U.S. Dist. Ct. Iowa 1984. Pvt. practice, Batavia, Iowa, 1974—; mem. Iowa Senate from 45th dist., Des Moines, 1998—; chair justice appropriations com. Iowa Senate, Des Moines, mem. ways and means com., mem. jud. com., vice chair local govt. com., mem. natural resources com. Specialist 6 US Army, 1970—72. Mem.: Farm Bur., Iowa State Bar Assn. Republican. Office: State Capitol 9th And Grand Des Moines IA 50319-0001 E-mail: david_miller@legis.state.ia.us.

MILLER, DAVID W., lawyer; b. Indpls., July 1, 1950; s. Charles Warren Miller and Katherine Louise (Beckner) Dearing; m. Mindy Miller, May 20, 1972; children: Adam David, Ashley Kay, Amanda Katherine Kupfer. BA, Ind. U., Bloomington, 1971; JD summa cum laude, Ind. U., Indpls., 1976. Bar: Ind. 1977. Investigator NLRB, Indpls., 1971-76; assoc. Roberts & Ryder, Indpls., 1977-80, ptnr., 1981-86, Baker & Daniels, Indpls., 1986—. Bd. dirs. Everybody's Oil Corp., Anderson, Ind. Bd. dirs. S. Madison Cmty. Found., Pendleton, Ind. Mem. Ind. Bar Assn. (chmn. labor law sect. 1981-82). Republican. Office: 300 N Meridian St Ste 2700 Indianapolis IN 46204-1750 Office Phone: 317-237-1316. E-mail: dwmiller@bakerd.com.

MILLER, DEMETRA FAY PELAT, elementary school educator, city official; b. Painesville, Ohio, June 15, 1933; d. William Anthony and Helen (Mimo) Pelat. Grad., Monticello Jr. Coll., Alton, Ill., 1953; BS in Edn., Kent State U., 1955, postgrad., 1957-63, John Carroll U., 1957-63. Tchr. Grant Elem. Sch., Cuyahoga Falls, Ohio, 1955-57, Benjamin Franklin Elem. Sch., Euclid, Ohio, 1957-58, Meml. Park Elem. Sch., Euclid, 1958-87, Lincoln Elem. Sch., Euclid, 1987—. Mem. Euclid City Coun., 1983—; sec. Citizens' Pet Responsibility Com., 1978—; trustee Shore Civic Cultural Ctr., 1988—; treas. Euclid Women's Caucus, 1978-79, v.p., 1981-83, pres., 1983; bd. dirs. YwCA-YMCA, Euclid, 1985—; mem. women's jr. bd., vol. Euclid Gen. Hosp., 1967—; mem. Euclid Devel. Corp., Euclid Recreation Commn., 1985—; former mem. citizens adv. bd. Regional Transit Authority; past mem. Euclid Charter Rev. Commn.; chmn. Euclid City Growth, Devel. and Zoning Commn., 1989—. Named Woman of Yr., Euclid Women's Caucus, 1985, Euclid Citizen of Yr., Am. Legion Post 343, 1986, cert. of appreciation YWCA-YMCA, 1989, One of Most Interesting People award Cleve. Mag., 1990. Mem. NEA (nat. del. 1978-89), Ohio Edn. Assn. (del. 1977—), Euclid Tchrs. Assn. (pres. 1978-79, 83-84, Outstanding Educator award 1979), Ednl. Coun. Cuyahoga County (pres. 1981-82), Coalition Major Ednl. Orgns., Delta Kappa Gamma. Greek Orthodox. Home: 25601 Zeman Ave Cleveland OH 44132-1816 Office: Euclid Bd Edn 651 E 222nd St Euclid OH 44123-2000

MILLER, DON WILSON, nuclear engineering educator; b. Westerville, Ohio, Mar. 16, 1942; s. Don Paul and Rachel (Jones) M.; m. Mary Catherine Thompson, June 25, 1966; children: Amy Beth, Stacy Catherine, Paul Wilson Thompson. BS in Physics, Miami U., Oxford, Ohio, 1964, MS in Physics, 1966; MS in Nuc. Engring., Ohio State U., 1970, PhD in Nuc. Engring., 1971. Rsch. assoc. Ohio State U., Columbus, 1966-68, univ. fellow, 1968-69, tchg. assoc., 1969-71, asst. prof. nuc. engring., 1971—74, assoc. prof., 1974-80, chmn. nuc. engring. program, 1977-97, prof., 1980—2004, dir. nuc. reactor lab., 1977—2002, prof. emeritus, 2004—, dir. Advanced Sys. and Safety, 2005—. Sec., treas. Cellar Lumber Co., Westerville, Ohio, 1972-84, 85—; cons. Monsanto Rsch. Corp., Miamisburg, Ohio, 1979, NRC, Washington, 1982-84, 99—, Scantech. Corp., Santa Fe, 1984-95, Neoprobe Corp., Columbus, 1990, Electric Power Rsch. Inst., Palo Alto, Calif., 1992-94; mem. adv. com. on reactor safeguards Nuc. Regulatory Commn., 1995-99. Patentee in field; contbr. articles to profl. jours. Mem. Westerville Bd. Edn., 1976-91, pres., 1977-78, 86-88; mem. Ohio Sch. Bd.'s Assn., Columbus, 1976-91; mem. fed. rels. com. Nat. Sch. Bd.'s Assn., Washington, 1984-86. With USAR, 1960-68. Named Tech. Person of Yr. Columbus Tech. Coun., 1979; named to All Region Bd. Ohio Sch. Bd.'s Assn., 1981, 86, Westerville South H.S. Hall of Fame, 1996; recipient Achievement award Mid Ohio Chpt. Multiple Sclerosis Soc., 1988. Fellow Am. Nuc. Soc. (chmn. edn. divsn. 1986-87, bd. dirs. 1989-91, chair human factors divsn. 1993-94, v.p./pres. elect 1995-96, pres. 1996-97, Cert. Appreciation 1991); mem. IEEE (sr. mem.), Am. Soc. Engring. Edn. (chmn. nuc. engring. divsn. 1978-79, Glenn Murphy award 1989), Nuc. Dept. Heads Orgn. (chmn. 1985-86), Westerville Edn. Assn. (Friend of Edn. award 1992), Rotary (Courtright Cmty. Svc. award 1989), Kiwanis, Hoover Sailing Club, Alpha Nu Sigma (chmn. 1991-93). Avocations: American history, travel, amateur radio. Home: Friendship Village 5675 Ponderosa Dr Columbus OH 43231 Office: Ohio State U Dept Mech Engring Nuc Engring Program E430 Scott Lab 201 W 19th Ave Columbus OH 43210-1142 Home Phone: 614-891-1858; Office Phone: 614-292-7979. Business E-Mail: miller.68@osu.edu.

MILLER, DONALD, food products executive; CFO Schwans Sales Enterprises, Marshall, Minn., v.p. fin., CEO. Office: Schwans Sales Enterprises 115 W College Dr Marshall MN 56258-1747

MILLER, DREW, financial management company executive; b. West Chester, Pa., Aug. 1, 1958; s. Raymond and Carol (Canfield) M.; m. Annabeth D.; 1 child, Anna Clarice. BS, USAF Acad., Colo., 1980; M in Pub. Policy, Harvard U., 1982, PhD, 1985. Cert. mgmt. acct., fin. planner, mergers and acquisitions advisor. Intelligence officer USAF, 1980-87; mgr. Con Agra, Inc., 1987-94; pres. Heartland Mgmt. Cons. Group, Papillion, Nebr., 1994—, Fin. Continuum, LLC, 1998-2000; mergers and acquisitions advisor, 2001—03. V.p. Fin. Dynamics, Inc., Papillion, 1997-98; bd. dirs. Signature Eyewear Inc. County commr. Sarpy County, Nebr., 1990-94; mem. Bd. Regents U. Nebr., 1994—. Home: 1904 Barrington Pkwy Papillion NE 68046-4152 E-mail: drmiller@drewmiller.com.

MILLER, ELLEN, advertising executive; Pres. health care mktg. svcs. Draft Worldwide (formerly DraftDirect Worldwide), Chgo. Office: Draft Worldwide 633 N Saint Clair St Chicago IL 60611-3234

MILLER, EUGENE ALBERT, retired bank executive; married. BBA, Detroit Inst. Tech., 1964; grad., Sch. Bank Adminstrn., Wis., 1968. With Comerica Bank-Detroit (formerly The Detroit Bank, then Detroit Bank & Trust Co.), 1955—, v.p., 1970-74, contr., 1971-74, sr. v.p., 1974-78, exec. v.p., 1978-81, pres., 1981-89, CEO, 1989—, chmn., 1990—2002; with parent co. Comerica Inc. (formerly DETROITBANK Corp.), 1973—, treas., 1973-80, pres., 1981—, CEO, 1989-92, chmn. bd., 1990-92; pres., COO Comerica Inc. (merged with Manufacturers Nat. Corp.), Detroit, 1992-2000; chmn., CEO Comerica Bank (merged with Manufacturers Nat. Corp.), Detroit, 1993—2002; ret., 2002. Bd. dir. DTE Energy, 1989—. Office: Comerica Inc Mail Code 7887 39400 Woodward Ave Ste 255 Bloomfield Hills MI 48304

MILLER, FRANCES SUZANNE, historic site curator; b. Defiance, Ohio, Apr. 17, 1950; d. Francis Bernard Johnson and Nellie Frances (Holder) Culp; m. James A. Batdorf, Aug. 7, 1970 (div. Aug. 1979); 1 child, Jennifer Christine Batdorf; m. Rodney Lyle Miller, Aug. 8, 1982 (div. Apr. 1987). BS in History/Museology, The Defiance Coll., 1990; AS in Bus. Mgmt., N.W. Tech. Coll., 1986. With accts. receivable dept. Ohio Art Co., Bryan, Ohio, 1984-87; leasing agent Williams Met. Housing Authority, Bryan, 1987-91; acting site mgr. James A. Garfield Nat. Historic Site, Mentor, Ohio, 1991—. Mem. AAUW (pres. 1993-95, treas. 1995-98), at. Trust Hist. Preservation, Ohio Mus. Assn., Ohio Assn. Host. Socs. and Mus., Cleve. Restoration Soc., Phi Alpha Theta. Avocations: needlecrafts, reading. Home: 8 Meadowlawn Dr Unit 19 Mentor OH 44060-6230

MILLER, GARY J., political economist; b. Urbana, Ill., Jan. 2, 1949; s. Gerald J. and Doris Elaine (Miner) M.; m. Anne Colberg, Jan. 29, 1971; children: Neil, Ethan. BA, U. Ill., 1971; PhD, U. Tex., 1976. Asst. prof. Calif. Inst. Tech., Pasadena, 1976-79; assoc. prof. Mich. State U., East Lansing, 1979-86; Taylor prof. polit. economy Washington U., St. Louis, 1986-97; assoc. dean for acad. affairs Olin Sch. Bus., St. Louis, 1995-96, prof. polit. sci. Author: Cities by Contract, 1981, Reforming Bureaucracy, 1987, Managerial Dilemmas, 1992. NSF grantee, 1981, 1983, 1992, 2003; recepient Herbert Simon award, 2004. Mem. Phi Beta Kappa, Phi Kappa Phi (Disting. Faculty award 1994). Democrat. Office: Washington U Dept Polit Sci 1 Brookings Dr Dept Polit Saint Louis MO 63130-4899 Home Phone: 314-822-9753; Office Phone: 314-935-5874. Business E-Mail: gjmiller@artsci.wustl.edu.

MILLER, HAROLD EDWARD, retired manufacturing conglomerate executive, consultant; b. St. Louis, Nov. 23, 1926; s. George Edward and Georgenia Elizabeth (Franklin) M.; m. Lilian Ruth Gantner, Dec. 23, 1949; children—Ellen Susan, Jeffrey Arthur. BSBA, Washington U., St. Louis, 1949. Vice pres. Fulton Iron Works Co., St. Louis, 1968-71, pres., 1971-79, chmn. bd., 1979-90; v.p. Katy Industries Inc., Elgin, Ill., 1976-77, exec. v.p., 1978-90, also dir., to 1990; pres. HM Consulting, Palatine, Ill., 1990—. Internat. cons. Vigel Spa, Italy; v.p. Vigel U.S.A. Inc., 1996—. Served with U.S. Army, 1945-46. Mem. Barrington Tennis Club, Inverness Golf Club. Presbyterian. Office Phone: 847-991-7852. Personal E-mail: hmillercons84@sbcglobal.net.

MILLER, HEIDI G., diversified financial company executive; b. 1951; married; 2 children. BA in History, Princeton U., 1974; PhD in History, Yale U., 1979. Various positions to mng. dir. emerging markets structured finance group Chemical Bank, 1979—92; joined as v.p. and asst. to the pres. Travelers Group, 1992, CFO, 1995—98, Citigroup (merger of Citibank and Travelers Group), NYC, 1998—2000; CFO, sr. exec. v.p. strategic planning and adminstrn. Priceline.com, Norwalk, Conn., 2000; vice chmn. Marsh & McLennan Co., Inc., NYC, 2001—02; exec. v.p. strategy and devel., CFO Bank One Corp., 2002—04; exec. v.p., CEO, treasury & securities div. J.P. Morgan Chase & Co. (merger of Bank One Corp. and J.P. Morgan Chase & Co.), NYC, 2004—. Bd. dirs. General Mills Inc., 1999—, Merck & Co., Inc., 2000—04, Bank One Corp., 2000—02, Local Initiatives Support Corp., 2004—. Trustee Princeton U., NYU Med. Sch. Named one of 50 Most Powerful Women in Bus., Fortune mag., 2006, 25 Most Powerful Women in Banking, US Banker, 2006. Avocation: yoga. Office: JP Morgan Chase & Co 270 Park Ave New York T 10017

MILLER, HELEN, state representative, lawyer; b. Newark, Nov. 1945; BA, Howard U.; MS, Our Lady of the Lake U.; JD, Georgetown U. Bar: (D.C.), (Iowa). Atty.; state rep. dist. 49 Iowa Ho. of Reps., 2003—, mem. internat. rels.com., mem. econ. growth com., mem. agr. com., mem. appropriations com., mem. adminstrn. and rules com., asst. minority leader. Vol. Cmty. Sch. Improvement Adv. Bd., Webster County Crime Stoppers; bd. govs. Leadership Iowa; cmty. task force adv. bd. Ft. Dodge Correctional Facility; exec. dir., bd. dirs. Young At Art. Democrat. Office: State Capitol East 12th and Grand Des Moines IA 50319 Address: PO Box 675 Fort Dodge IA 50501 Office Phone: 515-281-3221.

MILLER, IRVING FRANKLIN, chemical, biomedical engineer, academic administrator, educator; b. NYC, Sept. 27, 1934; s. Sol and Gertrude (Rochkind) M.; m. Baila Hannah Milner, Jan. 28, 1962; children: Eugenia Lynne, Jonathan Mark. BS in Chem. Engring., NYU, 1955; MS, Purdue U., 1956; PhD, U. Mich., 1960. Rsch. scientist United Aircraft Corp., Hartford, 1959-61; from asst. prof. to prof., head chem. engring. Poly. Inst. Bklyn., 1961-72; prof. bioengring., head bioengring. program U. Ill., Chgo., 1973-79, acting head sys. engring. dept., 1978-79, assoc. vice chancellor rsch., dean Grad. Coll., 1979-85, prof. chem. engring., head chem. engring., 1986-95, dir. Ctr. Advanced Edn. and Rsch., 1989-90, dir. Office Spl. Projects, 1990-92, dir. bioengring. program, 1992-95; dean Coll. Engring. U. Akron, Ohio, 1995-98, prof. biomed. engring., 1998-2000; dir. corp. ops. BioTechPlex Corp., 2002—06. Cons. to industry; cons. NAS, NIH, Exec. Sentence Corps, Chgo., 2007—; dir. distance learning programs Ohio Aerospace Inst., 1998—2000. Editor: Electrochemical Bioscience and Bioengineering, 1973; contbr. articles profl. jours. Mem. AIChE, AAAS, Am. Chem. Soc., Biomed. Engring. Soc., N.Y. Acad Scis. Home: 1746 N Larrabee St Chicago IL 60614-5634 Office Phone: 312-266-1728. Personal E-mail: ifmiller@sbcglobal.net. Business E-Mail: ifmiller@uic.edu.

MILLER, JAMES GEGAN, research scientist; b. St. Louis, Nov. 11, 1942; s. Francis John and Elizabeth Ann (Caul) M.; m. Judith Anne Kelvin, Apr. 23, 1966; 1 child, Douglas Ryan. AB, St. Louis U., 1964; MA, Washington U., 1966, PhD, 1969. Asst. prof. physics Washington U., St. Louis, 1970-72, assoc. prof., 1972-77, prof. physics, 1977—, dir. lab. for ultrasonics, 1987—, rsch. asst. prof. medicine, 1976-81, rsch. assoc. prof. medicine, 1981-88, rsch. prof. medicine, 1988-2000, prof. biomed. engring., 1998—, Albert Gordon Hill prof. physics, 1999—, prof. medicine, 2000—. Contbr. articles to profl. jours.; patentee in field. Recipient I-R 100 award, Indsl. Research Devel. Mag., 1974, 1978, Merit award, NIH, 1998, Tchg. award, Emerson U., 2004; grantee, NIH, NASA. Fellow IEEE (sr., gov. com. Ultrasonics, Ferroelectrics and Frequency Control Soc. 1978-80,86-88, 92-94, Achievement award 2006), Am. Inst. Ultrasound in Medicine, Acoustical Soc. Am. (Silver medal 2004), Am. Inst. Med. and Biol. Engring.; mem. Am. Phys. Soc., Sigma Xi (nat. lectr. 1981-82). Office: Washington Univ St Louis Physics Dept CB 1105 One Brookings Dr Saint Louis MO 63130 Office Phone: 314-935-6229. Business E-Mail: james.g.miller@wustl.edu.

MILLER, JAN PAUL, lawyer, former prosecutor; b. Md. married; 2 children. BA in polit. sci., U. N.C., 1982; JD cum laude, Harvard U., 1985. Assoc. Christy & Viener LLP, 1985—86, Casner, Edwards & Roseman LLP, 1986—88, Gordon, Feinblatt, Rothman, Hoffberger & Hollander LLP, 1988—89; asst. U.S. atty. dist. Md US Dept. Justice, 1989—2002, U.S. atty. Ctrl. dist. Ill. Springfield, 2002—05; ptnr. Thompson Coburn LLP, Belleville, Ill., 2005—. Adj. prof. George Washington U. Recipient numerous commendations from law enforcement agencies, including FBI, U.S. Customs Svc., Drug Enforcement Adminstrn., U.S. Secret Svc., U.S. Postal Ins. Office: Thompson Coburn LLP One US Bank Plaza Saint Louis MO 63101

MILLER, JOHN, foundation administrator; BA in Psychology, U. Del., 1970. Exec. v.p. Am. Cancer Soc., Jefferson City, Mo., 1979-83, Am. Coll. Sports Medicine, Indpls., 1983-88, Am. Camping Assn., Martinsville, Ind., 1988-97, Nat. Muzzle Loading Rifle Assn., Friendship, Ind., 1997—. Cons. CUBE, Inc., 1988-90. Vol. leadership devel. Am. Cancer Soc.; active numerous civic orgns., including Kingsway Christian Ch., Indpls., Indpls. Conv. and Vis. Assn., 1985-86, XXIII FIMS World Congress on Sports Medicine, Brisbane, Australia/speaker, 1986, others. Mem. Am. Soc. Assn. Execs. Office: Nat Muzzle Loading Rifle Assn PO Box 67 Friendship IN 47021-0067

MILLER, JOHN ALBERT, university educator, consultant; b. St. Louis County, Mo., Mar. 22, 1939; s. John Adam and Emma D. (Doering) M.; m. Eunice Ann Timm, Aug. 25, 1968; children: Michael, Kristin. AA, St. Paul's Coll., 1958; BA with high honors, Concordia Sr. Coll., 1960; postgrad., Wash. U., St. Louis, 1960-64; MBA, Ind. U., 1971, DBA in Mktg., 1972. Proofreader, editor Concordia Pub. House, St. Louis, 1960-62, periodical sales mgr., 1964-68; asst. prof. Drake U., Des Moines, 1971-74; cons. FTC, Washington, 1974-75; vis. assoc. prof. Ind. U., Bloomington, 1975-77; assoc. prof. U. Colo., Colorado Springs, 1977-79, prof., 1977-86, prof. mktg., resident dean, 1980-84; v.p. market devel. Peak Health Care Inc., Colorado Springs, 1984-85; dean Valparaiso (Ind.) U., 1986-96, prof. mktg., 1986—. Cons. and rschr. govt. and industry; dir. health maintenance orgn.; bd. dirs. Ind. Acad. Social Scis., 1988-90; adv. bd. .W. Ind. Small Bus. Devel. Ctr., 1989-91; consulting dean USIA project to form Polish Assn. of Bus. Schs., 1995. Author: Labeling Research The State of the Art, 1978; contbr. articles to profl. jours. Mem. Colorado Springs Symphony Orch. Coun., 1980-86; cons. Citizens Goals of Colorado Springs, 1985-86, Jr. League Colorado Springs, 1981-82; bd. dirs. Christmas in April-Valparaiso, 1991-96, Assn. Luth. Older Adults, 1998—. With U.S. Army, 1962-64. U.S. Steel fellow, 1970-71. Mem. Assn. Consumer Rsch. (chmn. membership 1978-79), Am. Mktg. Assn. (fed. govt. liaison com. 1975-76), Am. Acad. Advt., Ind. Acad. Social Scis. (bd. dirs. 1988-90), Greater Valparaiso C. of C. (accreditation com. 1991, planning com. 1989-92, chair 1992), Am. Assembly Collegiate Schs. Bus. (internat. affairs com. 1991-93, mem. peer rev. team 1994, 96, com. mem., seminar leader, faculty mem., program chair for New Deans seminar and other workshops 1992—), Beta Gamma Sigma, Alpha Iota Delta. Lutheran. Avocations: racquetball, jogging, walking. Office: Valparaiso U Dept Mktg Valparaiso IN 46383 Home: 6864 SW Alden St Portland OR 97223-1334

MILLER, JOHN ROBERT, oil industry executive; b. Lima, Ohio, Dec. 28, 1937; s. John O. and Mary L. (Zickafoose) M.; m. Karen A. Eier, Dec. 30, 1961; children: Robert A., Lisa A., James E. BSChE with honors, U. Cin., 1960, D.Comml. Sc. hon., 1983. With Standard Oil Co., Cleve., 1960-86, dir. fin., 1974-75, v.p. fin., 1975-78, v.p. transp., 1978-79, sr. v.p. tech. and chems., 1979-80, pres., COO, bd. dirs., 1980—86; chmn., CEO TBN Holdings, Cleve., 1986—2000, Petroleum Ptnrs., Cleve., 2000—03; chmn. SIRVA, Inc., 2006—. Bd. dirs. Cambrex Corp., Eaton Corp.; chmn. Graphic Packaging Corp., 2006—; former chmn. Fed. Res. Bank, Cleve. Mem. Pepper Pike Club, The Country Club, Chagrin Valley Hunt Club, Tau Beta Pi. Office: 7511 Creek View Tr Chagrin Falls OH 44023 Office Phone: 440-543-2128. Business E-Mail: office@johnrmiller.com.

MILLER, JOHN WILLIAM, JR., bassoonist; b. Balt., Mar. 11, 1942; s. John William and Alverta Evelyn M.; m. Sibylle Weigel, July 12, 1966 (div. 2000); children: Christian Desmond, Andrea Jocelyn, Claire Evelyn. BS, M.I.T., 1964; MusM with highest honors, New Eng. Conservatory, 1967, Artist's Diploma, 1969. Instr. bassoon Boston U., 1967-71, U. Minn., 1971—; prin. bassoonist, founding mem. Boston Philharmonia Chamber Orch., 1968-71; prin. bassoonist Minn. Orch., Mpls., 1971—. Dir. Boston Baroque Ensemble, 1963-71, John Miller Bassoon Symposium, 1984—; mem. Am. Reed Trio, 1977—; faculty Sarasota Music Festival, 1986—, Affinis Seminar, Japan, 1992; vis. faculty Banff Ctr. for Arts, 1987; faculty Nordic Bassoon Symposium, 1993—. Soloist on recs. for Cambridge, Mus. Heritage Soc., Pro Arte; featured guest artist 1st Internat. Bassoon Festival, Caracas, Venezuela, 1994. Recipient U.S. Govt. Fulbright award, 1964-65, Irwin Bodky award Cambridge Soc. Early Music, 1968 Mem. Internat. Double Reed Soc., Minn. Bassoon Assn. (founder) Home: 706 Lincoln Ave Saint Paul MN 55105-3533 Office: 1111 Nicollet Mall Minneapolis MN 55403-2406

MILLER, JOHN WINSTON, academic administrator; m. Barbara Miller; children: Lauren, Elizabeth, Raymond. BS in Journalism, Ohio U., 1969; MS in Edn., No. Ill. U., 1972; PhD in Edn., Purdue U., 1975. Pub. sch. tchr., Chgo. and Ind.; from asst. prof. to prof., assoc dean edn. Wichita State U., 1974—86; prof., dean Coll. Edn. Ga. So. U., 1986—93, Fla. State U., 1993—99; chancellor U. Wis., Whitewater, Wis., 1999—2005; pres. Ctrl. Conn. State U., New Britain, 2005—. Office: Ctrl Conn State U 1615 Stanley St New Britain CT 06050

MILLER, JOSEF M., otolaryngologist, educator; b. Phila., Nov. 29, 1937; married, 1960; 3 children. BA in Psychology, U. Calif., Berkeley, 1961; PhD in Physiology and Psychology, U. Wash., 1965; MD (hon.), U. Göteborg, Sweden, 1987; MD (h.c.), U. Turku, Finland, 1995. USPHS fellow U. Mich., 1965-67, rsch. assoc., asst. prof. dept. Psychology Ann Arbor, 1967-68, prof., dir. rsch. dept. Otolaryngology, dir. Kresge Hearing Rsch. Inst., 1984—; asst. prof. depts. Otolaryngology, Physiology and Biophysics U. Wash., Seattle, 1968-72, rsch. affiliate Regional Primate Rsch. Ctr., 1968-84, assoc. prof., 1972-76, acting chmn. dept. Otolaryngology, 1975-76, prof., 1976-84; Lunn and Ruth Townsend prof. comm., 1996—. Mem. study sect. Nat. Inst. Neurol. and Communicative Disorders and Stroke, NIH, 1978-84, ad hoc bd. dirs. sci. counselors, 1988; sci. rev. com. Deafness Rsch. Found., 1978-83, chair, 1983—; mem. faculty Nat. Conf. Rsch. Goals and Methods in Otolaryngology, 1982; adv. com. hearing, bio-acoustics and biomechanics Commn. Behavioral and Social Scis. and Edn., Nat. Rsch. Coun., 1983—; hon. com. Orgn. Nobel Symposium 63, Cellular Mechanisms in Hearing, Karlskoga, Sweden, 1985; cons. Otitis Media Rsch. Ctr., 1985-89, Pfizer Corp., 1988; faculty opponent U. Göteborg, Sweden, 1987; rsch. adv. com. Galludet Coll., 1987; chair external sci. adv. com. House Ear Inst., 1988-91; author authorizing legis. Nat. Inst. Deafness and Other Comm. Disorders, NIH, 1988, co-chair adv. bd. rsch. priorities com., bd. dirs. Friends adv. coun., 1989—, chair rsch. subcom., 1990-93, treas., bd. dirs., 1996—; grant reviewer Mich. State Rsch. Fund, NSF, VA; reviewer numerous jours. including Acta Otolaryngologica, Jour. Otology, Physiology and Behavior, Science. Mem. editorial bd. Am. Jour. Otolaryngology, 1981—, AMA, Am. Physiology Soc., Annals of Otology, Rhinology and Laryngology, 1980—, Archives of Oto-Rhino-Laryngology, 1985-93, Hearing Rsch., Jour. Am. Acad. Otolaryngology-Head and Neck Surgery, 1990—. Bd. dirs. Internat. Hearing Found., 1985—. Fellow U. Wash., 1962-65, Kresge Hearing Rsch. Inst., U. Mich., 1965-67; recipient award Am. Acad. Otolaryngology; grantee Deafness Rsch. Found., U. Wash., 1969-71; rsch. grantee NIH, 1969-73. Mem. AAAS, Am. Acad. Otolaryngology and Head and Neck Surgery (com. rsch. in otolaryngology 1971-82, continuing edn. com. 1975-79, NIH liaison com. 1988—, program steering com. jour. 1990, Pres. Citation 1997), Am. Auditory Soc., Am. Otological Soc., Am. Neurotological Soc., Am. Otologic Honor Soc., Acoustical Soc. Am. (com. rsch. psychol., physiol. acoustics 1969-78), Fedn. Am. Physiol. Soc., Fedn. Am. Socs. Exptl. Biology, Soc. Neurosci., Assn. Rsch. Otolaryngology (sec.-treas. 1979-80, pres. elect 1981, pres. 1982. program dir. mtg. 1983, award of merit com. 1985,

95-96, chair 1988, program dir., pres. symposium homeostatic mech. of inner ear 1993), Finnish Acad. Otolaryngology (hon.), Sigma Xi. Office: U Mich Kresge Hearing Rsch Inst 1301 E Ann St Rm R5032 Ann Arbor MI 48109-0506

MILLER, KAREN L., dean, nursing educator; BSN, Case Western Res. U.; MSN, U. Colo., PhD in Nursing. V.p. The Children's Hosp., Denver; assoc. prof. Coll. Nursing U. Colo. Health Scis. Ctr.; dean, prof. Sch. Nursing U. Kans., 1996—, dean Sch. Allied Health, 1998—. Mem. editl. bd. IMAGE: Jour. Nursing Scholarship. Grantee NIH, 1992. Fellow Am. Acad. Nursing; mem. ANA, ANA Coun. Nurse Rschrs., Am. Orgn. Nurse Execs., Coun. on Grad. Edn. for Nursing Adminstrn., Midwest Alliance in Nursing, Midwest Nursing Rsch. Soc., Sigma Theta Tau (collateral reviewer rsch. com.). Office: U Kans Sch Nursing 390 Rainbow Blvd Kansas City KS 66160-0001

MILLER, KENNETH W., lawyer; b. Chgo., Oct. 25, 1960; BS, U. Ill., 1982; JD magna cum laude, Northwestern U., 1985. Bar: Ill. 1985. Ptnr., co-chmn. pvt. equity practice Katten Muchin Rosenman LLP, Chgo. Mem.: ABA, Am. Inst. of CPAs. Office: Katten Muchin Rosenman LLP 525 W Monroe St Chicago IL 60661 Office Phone: 312-902-5261. Office Fax: 312-577-8747. Business E-Mail: ken.miller@kattenlaw.com.

MILLER, LEE I., lawyer; b. Nov. 16, 1947; BSBA, Georgetown U., 1969, JD, 1973. Bar: Md. 1973, Ill. 1976. Ptnr., Real Estate practice Rudnick & Wolfe, Chgo., mng. ptnr., 1992—99; ptnr, co-chmn. Piper Marbury Rudnick & Wolfe, Chgo., 1999—2004; ptnr., joint CEO DLA Piper Rudnick Gray Cary, Chgo., 2005—. Bd. dir. Griffindor Capital Ptnrs. LLC. Editorial asst. Tax Lawyer, 1972-73. Bd. visitors Georgetown Univ. Law Ctr.; mem. adv. bd. Georgetown Univ. Corp. Counsel Inst. Recipient Judge Learned Hand Human Rels. award, Am. Jewish Com., 2001. Mem.: Ill. State Bar Assn., Chgo. Bar Assn., Am. Coll. Real Estate Lawyers, Real Estate Roundtable (pres. club mem.), Phi Alpha Delta. Office: DLA Piper Rudnick Gray Cary Suite 1900 203 N La Salle St Chicago IL 60601-1293 Office Phone: 312-368-4029. Office Fax: 312-236-7516. Business E-Mail: lee.miller@dlapiper.com.

MILLER, MARK C., waste management administrator; BS in Computer Sci., Purdue U. From mgr. to v.p. Internat. Divsn. Abbott Labs., 1976—89, v.p. Internat. Divsn., 1989—92; pres. Stericycle Inc., Lake Forest, Ill., 1992—, CEO, 1992—. Bd. dir. Ventana Med. Sys., Inc., Lake Forest Hosp. Mem.: Phi Beta Kappa. Office: Stericycle Inc 28161 North Keith Drive Lake Forest IL 60045

MILLER, MARK F., state legislator; b. Boston, Feb. 1, 1943; m. Jo Miller; children: Chandra, Keiko, Sterling. BS, U. Wis., 1973. Pilot Wis. Air N.G., 1966—95; officer/mgr. Flagship, Inc., 1973—85; mem. Wis. State Assembly, Madison, 1998—, mem. com. on children and families, mem. environment com., mem. health com., mem. natural resources com. Bd. suprs. Dist. 24, Dane County, 1996—2000; mem. Dane County Bd. Health, 1996—2003, Wis. Environ. Edn. Bd., 2001—03; coord. coun. mem. Dane County, mem. environ. coun. Democrat. Office: State Capitol Rm 112 N PO Box 8953 Madison WI 53708-8953 Address: 4903 Roigan Terr Monona WI 53716

MILLER, ORLANDO JACK, obstetrician, gynecologist, educator, geneticist; b. Okla. City, May 11, 1927; s. Arthur Leroy and Iduma Dorris (Berry) M.; m. Dorothy Anne Smith, July 10, 1954; children: Richard Lawrence, Cynthia Kathleen, Karen Ann. BS, Yale U., 1946, MD, 1950. Intern St. Anthony Hosp., Okla. City, 1950-51; asst. resident in obstetrics and gynecology Yale-New Haven Med. Center, 1954-57, resident, instr., 1957-58; vis. fellow dept. obstetrics and gynecology Tulane U. Service, Charity Hosp., New Orleans, 1958; hon. research asst. Galton Lab., Univ. Coll., London, 1958-60; instr. Coll. Physicians and Surgeons Columbia U., NYC, 1960, asso. dept. obstetrics and gynecology, 1960-61, asst. prof., 1961-65, asso. prof., 1965-69, prof. dept. human genetics and devel., dept. obstetrics and gynecology, 1969-85; asst. attending obstetrician, gynecologist Presbyn. Hosp., NYC, 1964-65, assoc., 1965-70, attending obstetrician and gynecologist, 1970-85; prof. molecular biology, genetics and ob-gyn. Wayne State U. Sch. Medicine, Detroit, 1985-94, prof. Ctr. for Molecular Medicine and Genetics, 1994-96, prof. emeritus, 1996—, chmn. dept. molecular biology and genetics, 1985-93, dir. Ctr. for Molecular Biology, 1987-90. Bd. dirs. Am. Bd. Med. Genetics, 1983-85, v.p., 1983, pres., 1984, 85. Author: (with E. Therman) Human Chromosomes, 2000; editor Cytogenetics, 1970-72; assoc. editor: Birth Defects Compendium, 1971-74, Cytogenetics and Cell Genetics, 1972-97; mem. editl. bd. Cytogenetics, 1961-69, Am. Jour. Human Genetics, 1969-74, 79-83, Gynecologic Investigation, 1970-77, Teratology, 1972-74, Cancer Genetics and Cytogenetics, 1979-84, Jour. Exptl. Zoology, 1989-92, Chromosome Rsch., 1994-99; mem. editl. bd. com. Genomics, 1987-93, assoc. editor, 1993-96; mem. adv. bd. Human Genetics, 1978-98; cons. Jour. Med. Primatology, 1977-94; consulting editor McGraw-Hill Yearbook of Sci. and Tech., 1995-2007, Encyclopedia of Science and Technology, 1997-2007; contbr. chpts. to textbooks and articles to med. and sci. jours. Mem. sci. adv. com. on rsch. Nat. Found. March of Dimes, 1967-96, mem. sci. com., 1996—; mem. sci. rec. com. Basil O'Connor starter grants, 1973-77, 86-94; mem. human embryology and devel. study sect. NIH, 1970-74, chmn., 1972-74; mem. com. for study of inborn errors of metabolism NRC, 1972-74; mem. sci. adv. com. virology and cell biology Am. Cancer Soc., 1974-78, mem. sci. adv. com. cell and devel. biology, 1986-90; mem. human genome study sect. NIH, 1991-94; U.S. rep. permanent com. Internat. Congress of Human Genetics, 1986-91. With AUS, 1951-53. James Hudson Brown Jr. fellow Yale U., 1947-48; NRC fellow, 1953-54; Population Council fellow, 1958-59; Josiah Macy Jr. fellow, 1960-61; NSF sr. postdoctoral fellow U. Oxford, 1968-69; vis. scientist U. Edinburgh, 1983-84; Disting. vis. fellow, Fogarty Internat. fellow LaTrobe U., Melbourne, Australia, 1992; recipient Pres. Disting. Scientist award Soc. for Gynecol. Investigation, 1999. Fellow AAAS; mem. AAAS, Am. Soc. Human Genetics (bd. dirs. 1970-73, 86-90), Genetics Soc. Am., Acad. Scholars, Wayne State U. (life, pres. 1996-97), Sigma Xi. Home: 19365 Cypress Ridge Terr # 817 Lansdowne VA 20176 Office: 540 E Canfield St Detroit MI 48201-1928 E-mail: ojmiller@smartneighborhood.net.

MILLER, PATRICIA LOUISE, state legislator, nurse; b. Bellefontaine, Ohio, July 4, 1936; d. Richard William and Rachel Orpha (Williams) M.; m. Kenneth Orlan Miller, July 3, 1960; children: Tamara Sue, Matthew Ivan. RN, Meth. Hosp. Sch. Nursing, Indpls., 1957; BS, Ind. U., 1960. Staff nurse Cmty. Hosp., Indpls., 1958, Meth. Hosp., Indpls., 1959; office nurse A.D. Dennison, MD, 1960-61; rep. State of Ind. Dist. 50, Indpls., 1982-83; senator State of Ind. Dist. 32, Indpls., 1983—, chair senate health and provider svcs. com., 1999—; mem. labor and pension com., 1985—94; mem. edn. com., 1989—92; legis. appt. and elections com., chmn. interim study com. pub. health and mental health Ind. Gen. Assembly, 1986; chair Senate Environl. Affairs, 1990—91; health and environ affairs, 1992—; mem. election com., 1992—; mem. budget subcom. Senate Fin. Com., 1995—. Mem. Bd. Edn. Met. Sch. Dist., Warren Twop., 1974-82, pres., 1979-80, 80-81; mem. Warren Twp. Citizens Screening Com. for Sch. Bd. Candidates, 1972-84, Met. Zoning Bd. Appeals, Divsn. I, apptd. mem. City-County Coun. on Aging, Indpls. 1977-80; mem. State Bd. Vocat. and Tech. Edn., 1978-82, sec., 1980-82; mem. gov.'s Select Adv. Commn. for Primary and Secondary Edn., 1983; precinct committeeman Rep. Party, 1967-74, ward vice-chmn., 1974-78, ward chmn., 1978-85, twp. chmn., 1985-87; vice chmn. Marion County Rep., 1986-2000; sgt. at arms, 1982, mem. platform com., 1984, 88, 90, 92, co-chmn. Ind. Rep. Platform Com., 1992; rep. Presdl. Elector Alternate, 1992; active various polit. campaigns; bd. dirs. PTA, 1967-81; pres. Grassy Creek PTA, 1971-72; state del. Ind. PTA, 1978; mem. child car adv. com. Walker Career Ctr., 1976-80, others; bd. dirs. Ch. Fedn. Greater Indpls., 1979-82, Christian Justice Ctr., Inc., 1983-85, Gideon Internat. Aux., 1977, Ctrl. Ind. Coun. Aging; mem. United Meth. Bd. Missions Aux. Indpls., 1974-80, v.p., 1974-76, mem. nominating com., 1977; bd. dirs. Lucille Raines Residence, Inc., 1977-80; exec. com. S. Ind. Conf. United Meth. Women, 1977-80, lay del. s. Ind. Conf. United Meth. Ch., 1977—, fin. and adminstrn. com., 1979-88, planning and rsch. com., 1980-88, co-chmn. law adv. com., chmn. health and welfare, conf. coun. ministries, also mem. task force, bd. ordained ministry, also panel, chmn. com. on dist. superintendency, dist. coun. on ministries; sec. Indpls. S.E. Dist. Council on Minstries, 1977-78, pres. 1982; chmn. council on ministries Cumberland United Meth. Ch., 1969-76; chmn. stewardship com. Old Bethal United Meth. Ch., 1982-85, fin. com., 1982-85, adminstrv. bd., mem. council on ministries, 1981-85; co-chair Evangelism Com., 1994—; jurisdictional del. United Meth. Ch., 1988, 92, 96-2000; alternate del. United Methodist Ch. Gen. Conf., 1988, del. 1992; mem. adv. com. Warren Fine Arts Found., 1991—; mem. adv. bd. St. Francis Hosp., 1992-2005; mem. health and human svcs. com. Midwest Legis. Conf., 1995; del rep. various confs. and convs. Recipient Lambda Theta Honor for Outstanding contbr. in fiedl of end., 1976; named Woman of Yr. Cumberland Bus. and Profl. Women, 1979; Ind. Vocat. Assn. citation award, 1984, others. Mem. Indpls. dist. Dental Soc. Women's Aux., Ind. Dental Assn. Women's Aux., Am. Dental Assn. Women's Aux., Coun. State Govt. (intergovtl. affairs com.), Nat. Conf. State Legis. (vice chmn. health com. 1994—), Warren Twp. Rep., Franklin Rep., Lawrence Rep., Center Twp. Rep., Fall Creek Valley Rep, Marion County Coun. Rep. Women (3rd v.p. 1986-89), Ind. Women's Rep. (legis. chair 1988-89), Nat. Fedn. rep. Women, Beech Grove Rep., Perry Twp. Rep., Indpls. Women's Rep. Club (3rd v.p. 1989—), Indpls. Press Club. Office Phone: 317-232-9400. Business E-Mail: s32@in.gov.

MILLER, PATRICK WILLIAM, research scientist, educator; b. Toledo, Sept. 1, 1947; s. Richard William and Mary Olivia (Rinna) M.; m. Jean Ellen Thomas, Apr. 5, 1974; children: Joy, Tatum, Alex. BS in Indstrl. Edn., Bowling Green State U., 1971, MEd in Career Edn. and Tech., 1973; PhD in Indstrl. Tech. Edn., Ohio State U., 1977; Master's cert. Govt. Contract Adminstrn., George Washington U., 1995. Tchr. Montgomery Hills Jr. High Sch., Silver Spring, Md., 1971-72, Rockville (Md.) High Sch., 1973-74; asst. prof. Wayne State U., Detroit, 1977-79; assoc. prof., grad. coord. indstrl. edn. and tech. Western Carolina U., Cullowhee, NC, 1979-81; assoc prof. U. No. Iowa, Cedar Falls, 1981-86; dir. grad. studies practical arts and vocat.-tech. edn. U. Mo., Columbia, 1986-89; devel. editor Am. Tech. Pubs., Homewood, Ill., 1989-90; proposal mgr. Nat. Opinion Rsch. Ctr. U. Chgo., 1990-96; dir. grants & contracts City Colls. Chgo., 1996-99; assoc. v.p. acad. affairs Prairie State Coll., 1999—2001, also dean workforce devel. and career edn., 1999—2001; prof. Govs. State U., University Park, Ill., 2001—. Pres. Patrick W. Miller and Assocs., Munster, Ind., 1981—; presenter, cons. in field Author: Nonverbal Communication: Its Impact on Teaching and Learning, 1983, Teacher Written Tests: A Guide for Planning, Creating, Administering and Assessing, 1985, Nonverbal Communication: What Resarch Says to the Teacher, 1988, How To Write Tests for Students, 1990, Nonverbal Communication in the Classroom, 2000, Nonverbal Communication in the Workplace, 2000, Grant Writing: Strategies for Developing Winning Proposals, 2d edit., 2002, Test Development: Guidelines, Practical Suggestions and Examples, 2001, Body Language: An Illustrated Introduction for Teachers, 2005, Body Language on the Job, 2006, measurement and tchg., 2008; mem. editl. bd. Jour. Indsl. Tchr. Edn., 1981-88, Am. Vocat. Edn. Rsch. Jour., 1981-85, 94—, Tech. Tchr., 1982-84, Jour. Indsl. Tech., 1984—, Jour. Vocat. and Tech. Edn., 1987-90, Human Resource Devel. Quar., 1989-93; contbr. articles to profl. jours. Sec. U. No. Iowa United Faculty, Cedar Falls, 1983-84, pres., 1984-86. Lance cpl. USMC, 1966-68, Vietnam. Named one of Accomplished Grads. of Coll. Tech., Bowling Green State U., 1995; recipient editl. recognition award, Jour. Indsl. Tchr. Edn., 1984, 1986, 1988. Mem. ASTD, Am. Ednl. Rsch. Assn., Assn. for Career and Tech. Edn., Am. Vocat. Edn. Rsch. Assn., Nat. Assn. Indsl. Tech. (chmn. rsch. grants 1982-87, pres. industry divsn. 1991-92, chmn. exec. bd. 1992-93, past pres. 1993-94, Leadership award 1992, 93), at. Assn. Indsl. and Tech. Tchr. Educators (pres. 1988-89, past pres. 1989-90, trustee 1990-93, Outstanding Svc. award 1988, 90), Internat. Tech. Edn. Assn., Coun. Tech. Tchr. Edn., Epsilon Pi Tau, Phi Delta Kappa. Personal E-mail: patrickwmiller@sbcglobal.net.

MILLER, PAUL DAVID, aerospace transportation executive, retired admiral; BA, Fla. State U.; MBA, U. Ga. Commd. USN, advanced through grades to four star adm.; comdr.-in-chief U.S. Atlantic Command; supreme allied comdr.-Atlantic NATO; with Litton Marine Sys., 1995-99; pres. Sperry Marine Inc.; CEO Alliant Techsystems, Inc., Hopkins, Minn., 1999—2004, chmn., 1999—2005.

MILLER, PAUL DEAN, breeding consultant, geneticist, educator; b. Cedar Falls, Iowa, Apr. 4, 1941; s. Donald Hugh and Mary (Hansen) M.; m. Nancy Pearl Huser, Aug. 23, 1965; children: Michael, Steven. BS, Iowa State U., 1963; MS, Cornell U., 1965, PhD, 1967. Asst. prof. animal breeding cornell U., Ithaca, N.Y., 1967-72; v.p. Am. Breeders Svc., De Forest, Wis., 1972-95; exec. dir. Nat. Dairy Herd Improvement Assn., 1996—2003; pres. Windsor (Wis.) Park Inc., 1985—. Adj. prof. U. Wis., Madison, 1980—, sr. scientist, 2003—; dir. Internat. Com. on Animal Recording, 1998-2003. Contbr. articles to profl. jours. Mem. Beef Improvement Fedn. (disting. svc. award 1980), Am. Soc. Animal Sci., Am. Dairy Sci. Assn., Nat. Assn. Animal Breeders (dir. 1983-92, v.p. 1986). Republican. Office: Univ Wis 446 Animal Sci Bldg 1675 Observatory Dr Madison WI 53706-1284 Home: 6301 Fox Run Sun Prairie WI 53590-9357 E-mail: pdmil@aol.com, pdmiller2@wisc.edu.

MILLER, PAUL J., lawyer; b. Boston, Mar. 27, 1929; s. Edward and Esther M.; children— Robin, Jonathan; m. Michal Davis, Sept. 1, 1965; children— Anthony, Douglas BA, Yale U., 1950; LL.B., Harvard U., 1953. Bar: Mass. 1953, Ill. 1957. Assoc. Miller & Miller, Boston, 1953-54; assoc. Sonnenschein Nath & Rosenthal, Chgo., 1957-63, ptnr., 1963—; bd. dirs. Oil-DriCorp. Am., 1975—2004. Trustee Latin Sch. of Chgo., 1985-91. 1st lt. JAGC, U.S. Army, 1954-57. Fellow Am. Bar Found.; mem. Tavern Club, Saddle and Cycle Club, Law Club, Phi Beta Kappa. Avocation: gardening. Office: Sonnenschein Nath & Rosenthal 233 S Wacker Dr Ste 8000 Chicago IL 60606-6491 E-mail: pjm@sonnenschein.com.

MILLER, PEGGY GORDON ELLIOTT, retired academic administrator; b. Matewan, W.Va., May 27, 1937; d. Herbert Hunt and Mary Ann (Renfro) Gordon; m. Robert Lawrence Miller, Nov. 23, 2001; stepchildren: Rohn J., Robert K.;children from previous marriage: Scott Vandling Elliott III, Anne Gordon Elliott. BA, Transylvania Coll., 1959; MA, Northwestern U., 1964; EdD, Ind. U., 1975; degree (hon.), Transylvania U., 1993, Chungnam Nat. U., Korea, 2000; D in Pub. Svc., SD State U., 2006. Tchr. Horace Mann H.S., Gary, Ind., 1959-64; instr. English Am. Inst. Banking, Gary, 1969-70, Ind. U. N.W., Gary, 1965-69, lectr. Edn., 1973-74, asst. prof. edn., 1975-78, assoc. prof., 1978-80, supr. secondary student tchg., 1973-74, dir. student tchg., 1975-77, dir. Office Field Experiences, 1977-78, dir. profl. devel., 1978-80, spl. asst. to chancellor, 1981-83, asst. to chancellor, 1983-84, acting chancellor, 1983-84, chancellor, 1984-92; pres. U. Akron, Ohio, 1992-96, SD State U., 1998—2006, pres. emeritus, 2006—. Sr. fellow Nat. Ctr. for Higher Edn., 1996-97; vis. prof. U. Ark., 1979-80, U. Alaska, 1982; bd. dirs. Lubrizol Corp., A. Schulman Corp., Commn. on Women in Higher Edn., SD Mus. Art, Akron Tomorrow, Ohio Aerospace Consortium, Ohio Super Computer Com., Brookings C. of C.; holder VA Harrington disting. chair in edn., 1994-96, Charles G. Herbrich chair in leadership mgmt., 1996—; chmn. Growth partnership Rsch. Pk. Author: (with C. Smith) Reading Activities for Middle and Secondary Schools: A Handbook for Teachers, 1979, Reading Instruction for Secondary Schools, 1986, How to Improve Your Scores on Reading Competency Tests, 1981, (with C. Smith and G. Ingersoll) Trends in Educational Materials: Traditionals and the New Technologies, 1983, The Urban Campus: Educating a New Majority for a New Century, 1994, also numerous articles. Bd. dirs. Am. Humanics Meth. Hosp., N.W. Ind. Forum, N.W. Ind. Symphony, S.D. Art Mus., Boys Club N.W. Ind., Akron Symphony, NBD Bank, John S. Knight Conv. Ctr., Inventure Pl., Akron Roundtable, Cleve. Com. Higher Edn., 4-H Found., S.D. Art Mus., S.D. Value. Recipient Disting. Alumni award orthwestern U., UA Disting. Alumni award, 1994, Dist. Alumni award, Ind. U., 2004, Disting. Hon. Alumni, S.D. State U.; numerous grants; Am. Council on Edn. fellow in acad. adminstrn. Ind. U., Bloomington, 1980-81. Mem. Assn. Tchr. Educators (nat. pres. 1984-85, Disting. Mem. 1990), Ind. Assn. Tchr. Educators (past pres.), North Ctrl. Assn. (mem. commn. at large), Am. Assn. State Colls. and Univs. (acting v.p. divsn. acad. and internat. programs 1997, bd. dirs., treas., chmn. global priorities commn.), Am. Coun. Edn. (bd. dirs., exec. com.), Leadership Devel. Coun. ACE, Office Women Higher Edn. (mem. emerita of exec. bd), Am. Humanics (bd. dirs.), Ohio Inter Univ. Coun. (chairperson), Internat. Reading Assn., Akron Urban League (bd. dirs.), P.E.O., Cosmos Club, Phi Delta Kappa (Outstanding Young Educator award), Delta Kappa Gamma (Leadership/Mgmt. fellow 1980), Pi Lambda Theta, Pi Kappa Phi, Chi Omega. Episcopalian. Avocation: music. Home: 4834 Sweet Meadow Cir Sarasota FL 34238 Office Phone: 605-691-7391. Business E-Mail: peggy.miller@sdstate.edu.

MILLER, PETER C., lawyer; b. 1965; BA, Marquette U., 1987; JD, DePaul U., 1990. Bar: Ill. 1990. Ptnr. Seyfarth Shaw LLP, Chgo., chmn. Employee Benefits Practice Group. Mem.: Employee Stock Ownership Plans (ESOP) Assn., Ill. State Bar Assn., ABA. Office: Seyfarth Shaw LLP 55 East Monroe St Ste 4200 Chicago IL 60603 Office Phone: 312-269-8513. Office Fax: 312-269-8869. Business E-Mail: pmiller@seyfarth.com.

MILLER, RAY, state senator; BA in Polit. Sci., MA in Polit. Sci., Ohio State U. Pres., CEO Prof. Employment Svcs. Am.; state rep. Ohio Ho. of Reps., Columbus, 1981—93, 1998—2002; state sen., dist. 15 Ohio State Senate, Columbus, 2003—, ranking minority mem., fin. instns. and human svcs. and aging subcoms., and commerce and labor com., mem. fin. and fin. instns., health, and ins. coms. Founder, chmn. Ohio Commn. on Minority Health, Ohio Commn. on African-Am. Males; mem. exec. com. Ohio Dem. Party; chmn. Nat. Progressive Leadership Caucus. Recipient Dist. Legis. award, Am. Assn. Counseling and Devel., Trailblazer award, Ohio Legis. Black Caucus, C.J. Mclin, Jr. award, Urban Minority Alcoholism Drug Abuse Outreach Programs Ohio, Internat. Pathfinder award, World Congress on the Family, Dr. Martin Luther King Jr. Humanitarian award, Columbus Edn. Assn., 300 other cmty. and civic awards. Mem.: Coalition of 100 Black Men, Children's Hunger Alliance, NAACP, Alpha Phi Alpha. Democrat. Office: Senate Bldg Rm # 52 Ground fl Columbus OH 43215 E-mail: rmiller@maild.sen.state.oh.us.

MILLER, RICHARD J., pharmacologist, educator; b. London, Eng., July 8, 1950; BSc with 1st class honors, U. Bristol, 1972; MA, PhD, U. Cambridge, 1976. Tutor in biochemistry and pharmacology U. Cambridge, St. John's and Trinity Colls., England, 1972—75; postdoctoral rschr. Burroughs Wellcome Labs., Research Triangle Park, NC, 1976—77; from asst. prof. to assoc. prof. U. Chgo., 1977—81, prof. dept. pharmacol. and physiol. scis., 1981—95, William Mabie prof. neurosci., 1995—2001; prof. dept. molecular pharmacology and biol. chemistry Northwestern U., Chgo., 2001—. Mem. neurosci. study sect. NIH; mem. biomed. study sect. NIH, Nat. Inst. Drug Abuse; chmn. Gordon Conf. on Opiate Action, 1985; mem. sci. adv. bd. Nova Pharms., 1985—90, Synaptic Pharms., 1990—2000, Salk Inst. Biotech./Indsl. Assocs., 1991—2000; Rainbow Meml. lectr. U. Pa., 1988; Grass lectr. Emory U., 1990; Stirling Meml. lectr. U. Minn., 1990; Grass lectr. U. Ind., 1992, U. Man., 1992; Parke-Davis Disting. Neurosci. lectr., 94; Grass lectr. U. Utah, 1994, Tex. Tech. U., 1997. Mem. editl. adv. bd.: Molecular Biology, Brit. Jour. Pharmacology, Med. Biology, others, mem. molecular sect. editl. adv. bd.: European Jour. Pharmacology. Mem.: Brit. Pharmacol. Soc., Am. Soc. for Pharmacology and Exptl. Therapeutics (John Jacob Abel award 1983), Soc. for Neurosci., Internat. Soc. for Toxicology, Sigma Xi. Achievements include research in neuronal signal transduction. Office: Northwestern U Med Sch Molecular Pharmacology & Biol Chemistry 303 E Chicago Ave Chicago IL 60611

MILLER, RICK FREY, emergency physician; b. Peoria, Ill., July 27, 1946; s. Richard Ross and Mildred (Frey) M.; m. Cheryl Kay Hasty, June 1, 1968; children: Richard Andrew, Jennifer Caroline, Heidi Sue. BS in Math., BS in Chemistry, Bradley U., 1969; MD, U. Ill., 1974. Bd. cert. emergency medicine and pediats. Program dir. emergency medicine St. Francis Med. Ctr., Peoria, Ill., 1980-88, med. dir. Life Flight, 1985-91, chmn. dept. emergency medicine, dir. emergency med. svcs., 1988—. Contbr. book chpt.: Emergency Medicine Clinics of North America, 1992. Bd. dirs. Prevent Child Abuse-Ill., Springfield, 1991-98, Mental Health Assn. of Illinois Valley, Peoria, 1996-98; co-lay dir. Teens Encounter Christ, Peoria, 1997. Recipient Ptnrs. in Peace award Ctr. for Prevention of Abuse, 1996. Fellow Am. Coll. Emergency Physicians, Am. Acad. Pediats.; mem. Soc. Acad. Emergency Medicine. Avocations: skiing, bicycling. Office: OSF St Francis Med Ctr 530 NE Glen Oak Ave Peoria IL 61637-0001

MILLER, ROBERT ARTHUR, former state supreme court chief justice; b. Aberdeen, SD, Aug. 28, 1939; s. Edward Louis and Bertha Leone (Hitchcox) Miller; m. Shirlee Ann Schlim, Sept. 5, 1964; children: Catherine Sue, Scott Edward, David Alan, Gerri Elizabeth, Robert Charles. BSBA, U. S.D., 1961, JD, 1963. Asst. atty. gen. State of S.D., Pierre, 1963—65; pvt. practice law Philip, SD, 1965—71; state atty. Haakon County, Philip, 1965—71; city atty. City of Philip, 1965—71; judge State of S.D. (6th cir.), Pierre, 1971—86, presiding judge, 1975—86; justice S.D. Supreme Ct., Pierre, 1986—2001, chief justice, 1990—2001, ret., 2001—. Bd. dirs. Nat. Conf. of Chief Justices, 1996—97, State Justice Inst., 1998—, chair, 1998—; trustee S.D. Retirement Sys., Pierre, 1974—85, chmn., 1982—85; mem. faculty S.D. Law Enforcement Tng. Acad., 1975—85; bd. dirs. U. S.D. Law Sch. Found., 1990—. Mem. S.D. State Crime Commn., 1979—86; mem. adv. commn. S.D. Sch. for the Deaf, 1983—85, Comm. Svcs. to Deaf, 1990—92; cts. counselor S.D. Boy's State, 1986—, Nat. Awards Jury Freedoms Found., 1991. Mem.: S.D. Judge's Assn. (pres. 1974—75), State Bar of S.D., Elks. Roman Catholic. Avocations: golf, hunting. Office: SD Supreme Ct State Capitol Bldg 500 E Capitol Ave Pierre SD 57501-5070

MILLER, ROBERT EARL, engineering educator; b. Rockford, Ill., Oct. 4, 1932; s. Leslie D. and Marcia V. (Jones) M. BS, U. Ill., 1954, MS, 1955, PhD, 1959. Asst. prof. theoretical and applied mechanics U. Ill., Urbana, 1959-61, assoc. prof., 1961-68, prof., 1968-94, prof. emeritus, 1994—. Cons. in field to industry U.S. Army; in various positions in industry, summers, 1963-68 Contbr. articles to profl. jours. Mem. AIAA, Am. Soc. Engring. Edn. (Disting. Engring. award 1991), ASCE. Office: U Ill 216 Talbot Lab 104 S Wright St Urbana IL 61801-2935 Business E-Mail: rem@uiuc.edu.

MILLER, ROBERT G., retail executive; b. Cin., Sept. 7, 1936; s. Peter G. and Mildred (Behner) M.; m. Sharon T. Miller, Oct. 2, 1976 (div. July 1989); children: Lori A. Miller, Lynda S. Miller, Michael A. Miller., U. Cin., Cin., 1964. Store mgr. Mc Alpins, Cin., 1975—. Bd. dirs. YMCA, Blue Ash, Ohio, 1990—. Mem. Lions Club. Republican. Avocations: sports fisherman, tennis, golf. Home: 1815 Williams Ave Cincinnati OH 45212-3557 Office: Mc Alpins Kenwood 7913 Montgomery Rd Cincinnati OH 45236-4303

MILLER, ROBERT JAMES, educational association administrator; b. Mansfield, Ohio, Jan. 27, 1926; s. Dennis Cornelius and Mabel (Snyder) M.; m. Jerri Ann Burran, June 5, 1952; children: Robert James Jr., Dennis Burran. Student, Heidelberg Coll., 1946-47; BS, U. N.Mex., 1950, MA, 1952; postgrad., Miami U., Oxford, Ohio, 1951-55; MBA, Fla. Atlantic U., 1978. Asst. exec. sec. Phi Delta Theta Hdqrs., Oxford, Ohio, 1951—54, adminstrv. sec., 1954—55, exec. v.p., 1955—91, historian, 2006—; pres. Phi Delta Theta Found., Oxford, 1984—96, historian, 2006—; bus. mgr. The Scroll, Oxford, 1955—91; cons., 1997—. Editor: Phikeia—The Manual of Phi Delta Theta, 1951, 19 edits., 1989, Phis Sing, 1958, Constitution and General Statutes of Phi Delta Theta, Fraternity Education Foundations, 1962, Directory of Phi Delta Theta, 1973. Chmn. United Appeal, Oxford, 1960; bd. dirs. Interfrat. Found., 1995—, Oxford Cmty. Arts Ctr., 2005-06; bd. dirs. Knolls Oxford, 2007—; pres. Miami U. Art Mus., 1993-94, McCullough-Hyde Hosp., Oxford, 1966, chmn. endowment adv. com., 1988-89; vol. leader Boy Scouts Am., Oxford, 1966-79; historian Phi Delta Theta Found., 2006—. Named Citizen of Yr., City of Oxford, 1968; recipient citation Theta Chi, 1967, Order of Interfrat. Svc. Lambda Chi Alpha, 1994, Interfrat. Leadership award Sigma Nu, 1994, accolate for intrafraternity svc. Kappa Alpha, Meritorious Svc. award Boy. Scouts Am., 1977, others; Interfrat. Inst. fellow Ind. U., 1988. Mem. Nat. Intrafraternity Conf. (com. mem. 1954-96, Gold medal 1992), Am. Soc. Assn. Execs. (cert.), Cin. Soc. Assn. Execs., Fraternity Execs. Assn. (pres. 1962-63, Disting. Svc. award 1991), Edgewater Conf. (pres. 1978-79), Summit Soc., Country Club Oxford (bd. dirs.), Work Devel. Assn. (pres. 1999—), Order of Symposiarchs, Order of Omega, Rotary (founder Oxford club 1965, pres. 1966, Merit award 1974, dist. gov. S.W. Ohio 1978-79, study group exch. leader South Africa 1992), Blue Key, Phi Delta Kappa, Omicron Delta Kappa Home: 15 Woodcrest Way Oxford OH 45056-9485 Office: Phi Delta Theta Edni Found 2 S Campus Ave Oxford OH 45056-1801 Office Phone: 513-523-6966.

MILLER, ROBERT JUDD, lawyer; b. Ashland, Ohio, Nov. 18, 1950; s. Robert L. and Miriam A. (Willits) M.; m. Amy Louise McMullin, Aug. 29, 1980; children: Allison, Ashley, Abigail. BSIM, U. Cin., 1974; JD, U. Va., 1977. Bar: Ohio 1977, D.C. 1978, U.S. Dist. Ct. (so. dist.) Ohio 1977. Atty. Procter & Gamble Co., Cin., 1977-80, counsel, 1980-83, sr. counsel, 1983-87, v.p., gen. counsel, global legal, 2001—. Active in Big Bros., Cin. 1978. Mem. ABA, Ohio Bar Assn., Cin. Bar Assn., Cin. Athletic Club. Republican. Episcopalian. Office: Procter & Gamble Co 1 Procter And Gamble Plz Cincinnati OH 45202-3393 E-mail: miller.rj.1@pg.com.

MILLER, ROBERT L., JR., (BOB MILLER), federal judge; b. 1950; m. Jane Woodward. BA, Northwestern U., 1972; JD, Ind. U., 1975. Law clk. to Hon. Robert A. Grant U.S. Dist. Ct. (no. dist.) Ind., 1975; judge St. Joseph Superior Ct., South Bend, Ind., 1975-86, chief judge, 1981-83; judge US Dist. Ct. (no.

dist.) Ind., South Bend, Ind., 1985—, chief judge, 2003—. Mem. US Jud. Panel on Multidistrict Litig., 2003—. Office: US Dist Ct 325 Robert A Grant Fed Bldg 204 S Main St South Bend IN 46601-2122

MILLER, ROBERT STEVENS, JR., (STEVE MILLER), automotive parts company executive; b. Portland, Oreg., Nov. 4, 1941; s. Robert Stevens and Barbara (Weston) Miller; m. Margaret Rose Kyger, ov. 9, 1966 (dec. Aug. 11, 2006); children: Christopher John, Robert Stevens, Alexander Lamont. AB with distinction, Stanford U., 1963; LLB, Harvard U., 1966; MBA, Stanford U., 1968. Bar: Calif. 1966. Fin. analyst Ford Motor Co., Dearborn, Mich., 1968-71, spl. studies mgr. Mexico City, 1971-73; dir. fin. Ford Asia-Pacific, Inc., Melbourne, Australia, 1974-77, Ford Motor Co., Caracas, Venezuela, 1977-79; v.p., treas. Chrysler Corp., Detroit, 1980-81, exec. v.p. fin., 1981-90, vice chmn., 1990-92; sr. ptnr. James D. Wolfensohn, Inc., NYC, 1992-93; chmn. Morrison Knudsen, 1995—96; chmn., CEO Waste Management, 1997—99, Fed. Mogul Corp., Smithfield, Mich., 1999—2000, 2004—05, non-exec. chmn., 2001; chmn., CEO Bethlehem Steel Corp., Pa., 2001—03, Delphi Corp., Troy, Mich., 2005—06, exec. chmn., 2007—. Author: The Turnaround Kid: What I Learned Rescuing America's Most Troubled Companies, 2008. Office: Delphi Corp 5725 Delphi Dr Troy MI 48098*

MILLER, ROGER JAMES, lawyer; b. Yankton, SD, Oct. 6, 1947; s. Kenneth LeRoy and Bernice Mildred (Peterson) M.; m. Kristine Olga Christensen, June 12, 1971; children: David, Adam, Luke. BS, U. Nebr., 1970, JD, 1973. Bar: Nebr. 1973, U.S. Dist. Ct. Nebr. 1973, U.S. Ct. Appeals (5th, 8th and 10th cirs.) 1973, U.S. Ct. Appeals (D.C. cir.) 1974, U.S. Dist. Ct. (no. dist.) Calif. 1984. Assoc. Nelson & Harding, Lincoln, Nebr., 1973-74, ptnr. Omaha, 1974-84, McGrath, North, Mullin and Kratz, P.C., Omaha, 1984—. Mem. ABA (labor law sect., litigation sect.), Nebr. Bar Assn. Methodist. Avocations: golf, skiing, reading. Home: 567 S 152d St Elkhorn NE 68022 Office: McGrath North Mullin & Kratz PC First Nat Tower Ste 3700 1601 Dodge St Omaha NE 68102-1627 Office Phone: 402-341-3070. Business E-Mail: rmiller@mcgrathnorth.com.

MILLER, SAMUEL H., real estate company executive; Co-chmn. Forest City Mgmt. Inc., Cleve., 1989—. Office: Forest City Enterprises Inc 1100 Terminal Tower 50 Public Sq Ste 1170 Cleveland OH 44113-2203

MILLER, STEPHEN RALPH, lawyer; b. Chgo., Nov. 28, 1950; s. Ralph and Karin Ann (Olson) Miller; m. Sheila L. Krysiak, Feb. 2, 1998; children from previous marriage: David Williams, Lindsay Christine. BA cum laude, Yale U., 1972; JD, Cornell U., 1975. Bar: Ill. Assoc. McDermott, Will & Emery, Chgo., 1975-80, income ptnr., 1981-85, equity ptnr., 1986—2006, mgmt. com. mem., 1992-95, counsel, 2006—. Mem. spl. task force on post-employment benefits Fin. Acctg. Stds. Bd., orwalk, Conn., 1987—91. Contbr. articles to profl. jours. Trustee Police Pension Bd., Wilmette, Ill., 1992—98; mem. Chgo. Coun. Fgn. Rels., 1978—, mem. devel. com., 1997—2002, chair devel. subcom., 1999—2002, mem. external rels. com., 2002—03, mem. pres.'s cir. steering com., 2005—; trustee Seabury Western Theol. Sem., Evanston, Ill., 1994—2002, chancellor, 1996—97, 2004—05, chair trusteeship com., 2000—02; mem. Seabury Coun., 2004—. Mem.: ABA, Chgo. Bar Assn. (assoc.), Hundred Club Cook County, Cornell Club Chgo., Lawyers' Club Chgo., Yale Club Chgo. Avocations: sailing, water-skiing, cross country skiing. Office: McDermott Will & Emery 227 W Monroe St Ste 4700 Chicago IL 60606-5096 Office Phone: 312-984-7634. Business E-Mail: smiller@mwe.com.

MILLER, STEVEN, medical administrator; Grad., U. Mo., Kansas City. Hosp. staff, faculty Wash. U., 1990—, nephrology fellow, 1988, asst. prof., 1991—97, assoc. prof., 1997—, dir. hypertension clinic divsn. nephrology; med. dir. systemwide renal network Barnes-Jewish Hosp.; chief med. officer Wash. U. Sch. Medicine-Barnes Jewish Hosp., 1999—2005; now v.p. of rsch. Express Scripts Inc., St. Louis. Mem.: Internat. Soc. Nephrology, ACP. Office: Express Scripts Inc 13900 Riverport Dr Maryland Heights MO 63043

MILLER, SUSAN ANN, retired school system administrator; b. Cleve., Nov. 24, 1947; d. Earl Wilbur and Marie Coletta (Hendershot) M. BS in Edn., Kent State U., 1969; MEd, Cleve. State U., 1975; PhD, Kent State U., 1993. Cert. supt.; cert. elem. prin., cert. elem. supervisor; cert. Learning Disabled/Behavior Disabled tchr.; cert. tchr. grades 1-8; cert. sch. counselor; lic. counselor. Tchr., guidance counselor, interim prin. North Royalton City Schs., Ohio, 1969-84; dir. elem. and spl. edn., acting supt., asst. supt. Ednl. Svc. Ctr. of Cuyahoga County, Valley View, Ohio, 1984—2004. Contbr. articles to profl. jours. Grantee Latchkey Program, State Dept. Edn., North Coast Leadership Forum, Peer Assistance and Rev., Entry Yr. Program, Alt. H.S. Mem. ASCD, Coun. Exceptional Children, Phi Delta Kappa. Home: 7236 Morning Star Trail Sagamore Hills OH 44067 Personal E-mail: sumrtoi47@yahoo.com.

MILLER, SUZANNE MARIE, library director, educator; b. Feb. 25, 1954; d. John Gordon and Dorothy Margaret (Sabatka) M.; 1 child, Altinay Marie. BA in English, U. S.D., 1975; MA in Library Sci., U. Denver, 1976, postgrad. in law, 1984. Librarian II Law Sch. U. SD, Vermillion, 1977-78; law libr. U. LaVerne, Calif., 1978-85, law instr., 1980-85; asst. libr. tech. svcs. McGeorge Sch. Law, Calif., 1985-99, prof. advanced legal rsch., 1994-99; libr. SD State Library, Pierre, 1999—2004, Minn. State Libr. Svcs. and Sch. Tech., Roseville, 2004—. Co-author (with Elizabeth J. Pokorny) U.S. Government Documents: A Practical Guide for Library Assistants in Academic and Public Libraries, 1988; contbr. chapters to book, articles to profl. jours. Pres. Short Grass Arts Coun., 2001—03; bd. dirs. Black Hills Playhouse Bd., 1999—2004, S.D. Ctr. for the Book Bd., 2002—04. Recipient A. Jurisprudence award Bancroft Whitney Pub. Co., 1983. Mem.: ALA, Minn. Ednl. Media Orgn., Minn. Libr. Assn., Western Coun. State Librs. (sec. 2001—02), Chief Officers of State Libr. Agys. (sec. 2002—04, chair Rsch. & Stats. com. 2004—06), Western Pacific Assn. Law Librs. (sec. 1990—94, pres. elect 1994—95, pres. 1995—96, local arrangements chair 1997), o. Calif. Assn. Law Librs. (mem. program com., inst. 1988), Mt. Plains Libr. Assn. (S.D. rep. to exec. bd. 2001—04), So. Calif. Assn. Law Librs. (arrangements com. 1981—82), Am. Assn. Law Librs., S.D. Libr. Assn. Roman Catholic. Office: Minn Dept Edn 1500 Hwy 36 West Roseville MN 55113-4266 Office Phone: 651-582-8251. Business E-Mail: suzanne.miller@state.mn.us.

MILLER, TERRY ALAN, chemistry professor; b. Girard, Kans., Dec. 18, 1943; s. Dwight D. Miller and Rachel E. (Detjen) Beltram; m. Barbara Hoffmann, July 16, 1966; children: Brian, Stuart. BA, U. Kans., 1965; PhD, Cambridge U., Eng., 1968. Disting. tech. staff Bell Telephone Labs, 1968-84; vis. asst. prof. Princeton U., 1968-71; vis. lectr. Stanford U., 1972; vis. fgn. scholar Inst. Molecular Sci., Okazaki, Japan, summer 1983; Ohio eminent scholar, prof. chemistry Ohio State U., Columbus, 1984—. Chair Molecular Spectroscopy Symposium, Columbus, 1992—. Mem. editl. bd. Jour. Chem. Physics, 1978-81, Laser Chemistry, 1986—, Rev. of Sci. Instruments, 1986-89, Jour. Phys. Chemistry, 1989-95, Jour. Optical Soc. Am., 1989-95, Chemtracts, 1989-90, Ann. Revs. Phys. Chemistry, 1989-94, Jour. Molecular Structure, 1996-; mem. editl. bd. Jour. Molecular Spectroscopy, 1982-87, editor 2005-; contbr. articles to profl. jours. Recipient Bourke medal Royal Soc. Chemistry, 1998; Marshall fellow Brit. Govt., 1965-67, NSF fellow, 1967-68. Fellow Optical Soc. Am. (Meggars award 1993), Am. Phys. Soc. (H.P. Broida award 1999), AAAS; mem. Am. Chem. Soc. (councilor), Coblentz Soc. (Bomen-Michaelson award 1995). Office: Ohio State U 120 W 18th Ave Columbus OH 43210-1106

MILLER, TERRY MORROW, lawyer; b. Columbus, Ohio, Mar. 11, 1947; s. Robert E. and Elizabeth Jane (Morrow) M.; m. Martha Estella Johnson, Mar. 20, 1976; 1 child, Timothy. BS, Ohio State U., 1969, JD, 1975. Bar: Ohio 1975, U.S. Ct. Appeals (6th cir.) 1979, U.S. Supreme Ct. 1980. Asst. atty. gen. State of Ohio, Columbus, 1975—77; ptnr. Miller & Noga, Columbus, 1977—81; assoc. Vorys, Sater, Seymour and Pease, Columbus, 1981—85, ptnr., 1986—. Trustee Columbus Lit. Coun., 1997—2004. Sgt. U.S. Army, 1969-71, Okinawa. Mem. Am. Bankruptcy Law Forum, Columbus Bar Assn., Lakes Golf and Country Club, Rattlesnake Ridge Golf Club. Avocations: golf, Ohio history. Home: 288 E North Broadway Columbus OH 43214-4114 Office: Vorys Sater Seymour et al PO Box 1008 52 E Gay St Columbus OH 43216-1008 Home Phone: 614-263-7670; Office Phone: 614-464-5645. Business E-Mail: tmmiller@vorys.com.

MILLER, THOMAS J., state attorney general; b. Dubuque, Iowa, Aug. 11, 1944; s. Elmer John and Betty Maude (Kross) Miller; m. Linda Cottington, Jan. 10, 1981; 1 child, Matthew. BA, Loras Coll., Dubuque, 1966; JD, Harvard U., 1969. Bar: Iowa 1969. With VISTA, Balt., 1969—70; legis. asst. to US Rep. John C. Culver, 1970—71; legal edn. dir. Balt. Legal Aid Bur., part-time faculty U. Md. Sch. Law, 1971—73; pvt. practice McGregor, Iowa, 1973—78; city atty., 1973—79, Marquette, Iowa; atty. gen. State of Iowa, 1978—90, 1994—; ptnr. Faegre & Benson, Des Moines, 1991—95. Chmn. Microsoft case exec. com.; co-chmn. Airline Competition Working Grp.; pres. 2nd Dist. New Dem. Club, Balt., 1972. Mem.: ABA, Nat. Assn. Attys. Gen. (pres. 1989—90, chmn. consumer protection, ins., budget, and antitrust coms., Wyman award 1990), Iowa Bar Assn., Common Cause. Democrat. Roman Catholic. Office: Office of Atty Gen Hoover State Office Bldg 1305 E Walnut St Des Moines IA 50319-0112 Office Phone: 515-281-5164.

MILLER, THOMAS WILLIAMS, former university dean; b. Pottstown, Pa., July 2, 1930; s. Franklin Sullivan and Margaret (Williams) M.; m. Edythe Edwards, Dec. 20, 1952; children: Theresa, Thomas, Christine, Stefanie. BS in Music Edn, West Chester State Coll., Pa., 1952; MA, East Carolina U., Greenville, NC, 1957; Mus.A.D. (Univ. fellow), Boston U., 1964. Dir. instrumental music Susquenita (Pa.) High Sch., 1955-56; instr. trumpet East Carolina U., 1957-61; asst. dean East Carolina U. (Sch. Music), 1962-68, dean, 1969-71; vis. prof. U. Hawaii, Honolulu, 1968; dean Sch. Music Northwestern U., Evanston, Ill., 1971-89; dean emeritus Northwestern U., Evanston, Ill., 1989—. Contbr. articles to profl. jours. Assoc. Nat. Arts, 1989. Served with AUS, 1952-55. Named Distinguished Alumnus West Chester State Coll., 1975 Mem. Nat. Arts Assn., Music Educators Nat. Conf. (life), Nat. Assn. Schs. Music (hon. life, grad. commr. 1974-79, v.p. 1979-82, pres. 1982-85, chmn. grad. com. 1985-86, bd. dirs. 1986-89), Coll. Music Soc., Pi Kappa Lambda (hon. life regent, nat. pres. 1976-79), Phi Mu Alpha Sinfonia (hon. mem., Orpheus award 1989), Sigma Alpha Iota. Office: Sch of Music Northwestern U Evanston IL 60208-0001 Home: 108 South Dr Fairhope AL 36532-6310

MILLER, TICE LEWIS, theater educator; b. Lexington, Nebr., Aug. 11, 1938; s. Tice M. and Thyra V. (Lewis) M.; m. Carren J. Miller, Sept. 6, 1963; children: Dane, Graeme. BA, Kearney State Coll., 1960; MA, U. Nebr., 1961; PhD, U. Ill., 1968. Instr. Kansas City (Mo.) Jr. Coll., 1961-62; asst. prof. U. West Fla., Pensacola, 1968-72; from assoc prof. to prof. U. Nebr., Lincoln, 1972—, chair, 1989-96, pres. acad. senate, 2002—. Chair commn. on accreditation Nat. Assn. Schs. of Theatre, 1997-99. Author: Bohemians and Critics, 1981; co-editor: Shakespeare Around the Globe, 1986, Cambridge Guide World Theatre, 1988 (Hewitt award 1989), Cambridge Guide American Theatre, 1993, The American Stage, 1993; mem. editl. bd. Theatre History Studies, 1980--. Bd. dirs., ATHE, 1987-89, Lincoln Midwest Ballet Co., 1989-91, Theatre Arts for Youth, Lincoln, 1975-76, Pensacola Theatre, 1970-71. Lt. comdr. USNR 1962-65. Am. Theatre fellow, Mid-Am. Theatre Conf. fellow; inducted in Nebr. Repertory Theatre Hall of Fame. Mem. Am. Soc. for Theatre Rsch. Democrat. Unitarian Universalist. Office: U Nebr Dept Theatre Arts Lincoln NE 68588 Home Phone: 402-423-0494; Office Phone: 402-472-1617. E-mail: tmiller1@unl.edu.

MILLER, VERNON DALLACE, minister; b. McClure, Ill., Sept. 27, 1932; s. Homer Lee and Marie Kathleen (White) M.; m. Alice Elizabeth Wright, July 25, 1954; children: Ronald, Philip, Elizabeth, Annette, Douglas. Student, Moody Bible Inst., 1950-53, S.E. Mo. State, 1954, So. Ill. U., 1956-57; BA, Cedarville Coll., 1963, LittD, 1988. Ordained to min. Bapt. Ch., McClure, 1953. Pastor Camp Creek Bapt. Ch., Murphysboro, Ill., 1953-54, Bible Fellowship Bapt. Ch., Carterville, Ill., 1954-57, Faith Bapt. Ch., Mattoon, Ill., 1957-60, Immanuel Bapt. Ch., Arcanum, Ohio, 1961-63; editor, bus. mgr. Regular Bapt. Press, Chgo., 1963-70; pres. Ch. Bldg. Cons., Chgo., 1971-87; exec. editor, treas. Gen. Assn. of Regular Bapt. Chs., Schaumburg, Ill., 1987-97; min. christian edn. Berean Bapt. Ch., Portage, Mich., 1998—2005. Exec. bd. Awana Youth Assn., Streamwood, Ill., 1965-83, Grand Rapids (Mich.) Bapt. Coll. and Sem., 1981-91, Shepherds Bapt. Ministries, Union Grove, Wis., 1965-96. Editor: (mag.) The Baptist Bulletin, 1987-97. Del. Ill. Small Bus. Com., Springfield, Ill., 1984. Mem.: Christian Ministries Mgmt. Assn. Republican. Baptist.

MILLER, W. TIMOTHY, lawyer; b. Indpls., May 13, 1967; B in Music, DePauw U., 1989; JD, Cornell U., 1992. Bar: Ohio 1992. Named one of Ohio's Rising Stars, Super Lawyers, 2005, 2006; named to Best Lawyers in Am., Woodward/White Inc., 2006. Mem.: Tri-State Assn. for Corp. Renewal, Am. Bankruptcy Inst., ABA, Ohio State Bar Assn., Cin. Bar Assn. Office: Taft Stettinius & Hollister LLP 425 Walnut St Ste 1800 Cincinnati OH 45202-3957 Office Phone: 513-381-2838. Office Fax: 513-381-0205.

MILLER, WILLARD, JR., mathematician, educator; b. Ft. Wayne, Ind., Sept. 17, 1937; s. Willard and Ruth (Kemerly) Miller; m. Jane Campbell Scott, June 5, 1965; children: Stephen, Andrea. S.B. in Math., U. Chgo., 1958; PhD in Applied Math, U. Calif.-Berkeley, 1963. Vis. mem. Courant Inst. Math. Scis., NYU, 1963-65; mem. faculty U. Minn., 1965—, prof. math., 1972—, I.T. disting. prof. math., 2005—, head Sch. Math., 1978-86; co-prin. investigator Inst. Math. and its Applications, 1980-94, assoc. dir., 1987-94, dir., 1997—2001; assoc. dean Inst. of Tech., 1994-97; acting dean Inst. of Tech., 1995. Author: Lie Theory and Special Functions, 1968, Symmetry Groups and Their Applications, 1972, Symmetry and Separation of Variables, 1977; assoc. editor Jour. Math. Physics, 1973-75, Applicable Analysis, 1978-90. Mem. AAAS, Soc. Indsl. and Applied Math. (mng. editor Jour. Math. Analysis 1975-81), Am. Math. Soc., Sigma Xi. Home: 4508 Edmund Blvd Minneapolis MN 55406-3629 Office: Univ Minn Sch Math Minneapolis MN 55455

MILLER, WILLIAM CHARLES, theological educator, minister; b. Mpls., Oct. 26, 1947; s. Robert Charles and Cleithra Mae (Johnson) M.; m. Brenda Kathleen Barnes, July 24, 1969; children: Amy Renee, Jared Charles. BA, Ind. Wesleyan U., 1968; MLS, Kent State U., 1974, PhD, 1983; postgrad., U. Kans., 1984; MA in Religious Studies, Ctrl. Bapt. Theol. Sem., 1988; MBA, MidAm. Nazarene U., 1997; STM, Nashotah House, 2001. Ordained to ministry Ch. of Nazarene, 1986, received into communion and ordained Episcopal Ch., 2006, cert. ordained deacon Episcopal Ch., 2006, ordained priest Episcopal Ch., 2007. Libr. technician Kent State U., 1972—74; catalog libr. Mt. Vernon Nazarene Coll., Ohio, 1974—76, libr. catalog and acquisitions, 1976—78; dir. libr. svcs., prof. theol. bibliography Nazarene Theol. Sem., Kansas City, Mo., 1978—2005, dean adminstrn., 1996—98, 1999—2005; dir. accreditation Assn. Theol. Schs., Pitts., 2005—. Adj. rsch. assoc. U. Kans., 1984-85; adj. prof. MidAm. Nazarene U., Olathe, Kans., 1994-2000, Ind. Wesleyan U., 2005, Nazarene Theol. Sem., 2005-07; bd. dirs. Small Libr. Computing Inc.; pres. Mo. Libr. Network Corp., St. Louis, Mo., 1998-2001. Author: Holiness Works: A Bibliography, 1986; editor TUG ewsletter, 1984-87, bd. dirs., 1985-88; editor Jour. Religious and Theol. Info., 1990-98. With U.S. Army, 1968-72. Mem. Assn. Study Higher Edn., Am. Theol. Libr. Assn. (bd. dirs. 1985-88), Wesleyan Theol. Soc., Ch. Eng. Record Soc., Beta Phi Mu. Home: 18290 W 155th Ter Olathe KS 66062-6718 Office: Assn Theol Schs 10 Summit Park Dr Pittsburgh PA 15275-1103 Office Phone: 412-788-6505. Business E-Mail: miller@ats.edu.

MILLER, WILLIAM IAN, law educator; b. 1946; BA, U. Wis., 1969, M of Philosophy, 1973, PhD, 1975; JD, Yale U., 1980. Bar: Wis. 1980. Assoc. prof. U. Houston, 1981-85; prof. U. Mich. Law Sch., Ann Arbor, 1984—, Thomas G. Long Prof. Law. Vis. assoc. prof. U. Mich., An Arbor, 1984-85; vis. prof. Yale U., fall 1988. Author: Bloodtaking and Peacemaking: Feud, Law, and Society in Saga Iceland, 1990, Humiliation, 1993, The Anatomy of Disgust, 1997, The Mystery of Courage, 2000, Faking It, 2003, An Eye for an Eye, 2006. Mem. Law and Soc. Assn., Am. Soc. Legal History, Am. Hist. Assn. Office: U Mich Law Sch 411 Hutchins Hall 625 S State St Ann Arbor MI 48109-1215 Office Phone: 734-763-9014. Office Fax: 734-763-9375. E-mail: wimiller@umich.edu.

MILLER-LERMAN, LINDSEY, state supreme court justice; b. LA, July 30, 1947; BA, Wellesley Coll., Mass., 1968; JD, Columbia U., NYC, 1973; LHD (hon.), Coll. St. Mary, Omaha, 1993. Bar: NY 1974, US Dist. Ct. (so. dist.) NY 1974, US Ct. Appeals (2d cir.) 1974, Nebr. 1976, US Dist. Ct. (ea. dist.) NY 1975, US Dist. Ct. ebr. 1976, US Ct. Appeals (8th cir.) 1979, US Supreme Ct. 1982, US Ct. Appeals (6th cir.) 1984, US Ct. Appeals (10th cir.) 1987. Law clk. U.S. Dist. Ct., YC, 1973-75; from assoc. to ptnr. Kutak Rock, Omaha, 1975-92; judge Nebr. Ct. Appeals, Lincoln, 1992-98, chief judge, 1996-98; justice Nebr. Supreme Ct., 1998—. Contbr. articles to profl. jours. Office: Nebr Supreme Ct State Capitol Rm 2222 Lincoln NE 68509 Office Phone: 402-471-3734. Business E-Mail: lmiller-lerman@nsc.state.ne.us.

MILLICHAP, JOSEPH GORDON, neurologist, educator; b. Wellington, Eng., Dec. 18, 1918; came to U.S., 1956, naturalized, 1965; s. Joseph P. and Alice (Flello) M.; m. Mary Irene Fortey, Feb. 25, 1946 (dec. Oct. 1969); children: Martin Gordon, Paul Anthony; m. Nancy Melanie Kluczynski, Nov. 7, 1970 (dec. Apr. 1995); children: Gordon Thomas, John Joseph. MB Surgery honors, St. Bartholomew's Med. Coll., U. London, 1946, MD Internal Medicine, 1951, diploma child health, 1948. Diplomate Am. Bd. Pediat., Am. Bd. Neurology and Child Neurology, Am. Bd. Electroencephalography. Intern, resident St. Bartholomew's Hosp., 1946—49, Hosp. Sick Children, London, 1951—53, Mass. Gen. Hosp., Boston, 1958—60; pediat. neurologist NIH, 1955—56; USPHS fellow neurology Mass. Gen. Hosp., Boston, 1958—60; cons. pediat. neurology Mayo Clinic, 1960—63; pediat. neurologist Children's Meml. Hosp., Northwestern Med. Ctr., Chgo., 1963—; prof. neurology and pediat. Northwestern U. Med. Sch., 1963—. Cons. surgeon gen. USPHS; mem. med. adv. bds. Ill. Epilepsy League, Muscular Dystrophy Found., Cerebral Palsy Found., 1963—; vis. prof. Gt. Ormond St. Hosp., U. London, 1986-87 Author: Febrile Convulsions, 1967, Pediatric Neurology, 1967, Learning Disabilities, 1974, The Hyperactive Child with MBD, 1975, Nutrition, Diet and Behavior, 1985, Dyslexia, 1986, Progress in Pediatric Neurology, 1991, Vol. II, 1994, Vol. III, 1997, Environmental Poisons in Our Food, 1993, A Guide to Drinking Water, Hazards and Health Risks, 1995, Attention Deficit Hyperactivity and Learning Disorders, 1998, (with G.T. Millichap) The School in a Garden, 2000; editor Jour. Pediatric Neurology Briefs; contbr. articles to profl. jours., chpts. to books Chmn. rsch. com. med. adv. bd. Epilepsy Found., 1965—. Served with RAF, 1949-51 Named New Citizen of Year in Met. Chgo., 1965; recipient Americanism Medal DAR, 1972, Brennemann award Chgo. Pediat. Soc., 1998; USPHS rsch. grantee, 1957 Fellow Royal Coll. Physicians; mem. AMA, Am. Neurol. Assn., Am. Pediat. Soc., Am. Soc. Pediat. Rsch., Am. Acad. Neurology, Am. Soc. Pharmacology and Exptl. Therapeutics, Soc. Exptl. Biology and Medicine, Am. Bd. Psychiatry and Neurology (asst. examiner 1961—) Episcopalian. Office: Children's Meml Hosp Box 51 2300 N Childrens Plz Chicago IL 60614-3394 Home Phone: 312-943-1719.

MILLMAN, IRVING, microbiologist, educator, retired inventor; b. NYC, May 23, 1923; BS, City Coll. N.Y., 1948; MS, U. Ky., 1951; PhD, Northwestern U., 1954. Asst. prof. Northwestern U., 1954; formerly with Armour & Co., Pub. Health RSch. Inst. of N.Y.C., Merck Inst. Therapeutic Rsch.; adj. prof. Hahnemann U., Phila. Inducted Nat. Inventors Hall of Fame, 1993. Fellow Am. Acad. Microbiology; mem. N.Y. Acad. Scis., AAAS, Am. Soc. Microbiology. Achievements include development of test to identify Hepatitis B in blood samples. Office: Nat Inventors Hall Fame 221 S Broadway St Akron OH 44308-1505 also: Sch Med MCP Hahnemann U 2900 W Queen Ln Philadelphia PA 19129-1033

MILLNER, ROBERT B., lawyer; b. NYC, Apr. 20, 1950; s. Nathan and Babette E. (Leventhal) M.; m. Susan Brent, June 5, 1983; children: Jacob, Daniel, Rebecca. BA, Wesleyan U., 1971; JD, U. Chgo., 1975. Bar: Ill. 1975. Law clk. to Hon. George C. Edwards U.S. Ct. Appeals for 6th Cir., Cin., 1975-76; with Sonnenschein ath & Rosenthal, Chgo., 1976—, ptnr., 1982—. Contbr. articles to profl. jours. Trustee Anshe Emet Synagogue, Chgo., 1990-93; v.p. Am. Jewish Cong. midwest region, 1995—2006. Fellow: Am. Coll. Bankruptcy, Am. Bar Found. (life); mem.: ABA (co-chair bankruptcy and insolvency com. litigation sect. 1992—95, 2001—04, co-chair ins. subcom. bus. bankruptcy com.), Comml. Bar Assn. (hon. overseas mem.), Chgo. Bar Assn., Am. Bankruptcy Inst., Wesleyan Alumni Club Chgo. (pres. 1988—90), Std. Club, Legal Club, Phi Beta Kappa. Office: Sonnenschein Nath & Rosenthal 8000 Sears Tower Chicago IL 60606 Office Phone: 312-876-7994. E-mail: rmillner@sonnenschein.com.

MILLS, CHARLES N., healthcare supplies and products company executive; b. Sept. 30, 1961; BS, MBA, Cornell U. With IBM; then joined Medline Industries, Mundelein, Ill., 1986, pres. textile divsn., 1991—97, CEO, 1997—.

MILLS, EDWIN SMITH, economics professor; b. Collingswood, NJ, June 25, 1928; s. Edwin Smith and Roberta (Haywood) M.; m. Barbara Jean Dressner, Sept. 2, 1950; children: Alan Stuart, Susan Dorinda; m. Margaret M. Hutchinson, Jan. 22, 1977. BA, Brown U., 1951; PhD, U. Birmingham, Eng., 1956. Asst. lectr. Univ. Coll. North Staffordshire, Eng., 1953-55; instr. MIT, 1955-57; mem. faculty Johns Hopkins, Balt., 1957-70, prof. econs., 1963-70, chmn. dept. econs., 1966-69; prof. econs. and pub. affairs, Gerald L. Phillippe prof. urban studies Princeton U., 1970-75, prof. econs., 1975-87, chmn. dept., 1975-77; Gary Rosenberg prof. real estate and fin. Kellog Sch. Mgmt. Northwestern U., Evanston, Ill., 1987—96, emeritus prof., 1996—. Vis. rsch. fellow Cowles Found., Yale, 1961; sr. profl. staff Coun. Econ. Advisers, 1964—65. Author: Urban Economics, 1972, The Burden of Government, 1986; editor Jour. Urban Econs., 1973—90; contbr. articles to profl. jours. 2d lt. US Army, 1946—48. Recipient numerous rsch. grants and contracts, 1960—95. Mem.: Am. Econ. Assn., Phi Beta Kappa. Home: 1 Calvin Cir Apt A413 Evanston IL 60201-1953 Office: Northwestern U Ctr Real Estate Rsch Kellogg Graduate School 2001 Sheridan Rd Evanston IL 60208-2001 Office Phone: 847-491-8340. Business E-Mail: e_mills@kellogg.northwestern.edu.

MILLS, JAMES STEPHEN, medical supply company executive; b. Chgo., Sept. 29, 1936; s. Irving I. and Beatrice (Shane) M.; m. Victoria L. Krisch, Mar. 23, 1973; children: Charles, Donald, Margaret. BS in Bus., Northwestern U. Vice pres. sales Mills Hosp. Supply Co., Chgo., 1961-66; pres. Medline Industries Inc., orthbrook, Ill., 1966-75, co-chair, 1975—. Served with AUS, 1958-64. Jewish. Home: 500 N Green Bay Rd Lake Forest IL 60045-2146 Office: Medline Industries Inc 1 Medline Pl Mundelein IL 60060

MILLS, MORRIS HADLEY, state senator, farmer; b. Indpls., Sept. 25, 1927; s. Howard S. and Bernice H. (Sellars) M.; m. Mary Ann Sellars, 1954; children: Douglas, Fred, Gordon. BA in Econs., Earlham Coll., 1950; MBA, Harvard U., 1952. Treas. Maplehurst Farms, Inc., Indpls., 1952-62; ptnr. Mills Bros. Farms, Indpls., 1962—, treas., 1972—; also bd. dir.; mem. Ind. Ho. of Reps., 1970-72, Ind. Senate, 1972—, asst. pres. pro tem, chmn. budget subcom. fin., chmn. commerce and consumer affairs com. Chmn. bd. AMSCOR, Indpls., 1982—; dir. Maplehurst Group; mem. Pres. Reagan's adv. council on continuing edn., Washington, 1982—. Mem. Greater Indpls. Progress Com., Conner Prairie Settlement Adv. Coun.; bd. dirs. Corp. Sci. and Tech. Marion County Farm Bur.; asst. treas. Valley Mills Friends Ch.; mem. Decatur Township Rep. Club. Served with U.S. Army, 1946-47. Recipient Spl. award Ind. Vocat. Assn., 1976, Spl. award Ind. State Tchrs. award Assn., 1978. Mem. Lions. Republican. Mem. Soc. Of Friends. Office: Ind Senate Dist 35 200 W Washington St Indianapolis IN 46204-2728

MILLS, RICHARD HENRY, federal judge; b. Beardstown, Ill., July 19, 1929; s. Myron Epler and Helen Christine (Greve) M.; m. Rachel Ann Keagle, June 16, 1962; children: Jonathan K., Daniel Cass. BA, Ill. Coll., 1951; JD, Mercer U., 1957; LLM, U. Va., 1982. Bar: Ill. 1957, U.S. Dist. Ct. Ill. 1958, U.S. Ct. Appeals 1959, U.S. Ct. Mil. Appeals 1963, U.S. Supreme Ct. 1963. Legal advisor Ill. Youth Commn., 1958-60; state's atty. Cass County, Virginia, Ill., 1960-64; judge Ill. 8th Jud. Cir., Virginia, 1966-76, Ill. 4th Dist. Appellate Ct., Springfield, Ill., 1976-85, U.S. Dist. Ct. (cen. dist.) Ill., Springfield, 1985—. Adj. prof. So. Ill. U. Sch. Medicine, 1985-06; mem. adv. bd. Nat. Inst. Corrections, Washington, 1984-88, Ill. Supreme Ct. Rules Com., Chgo., 1963-85. Contbr. articles to profl. jours. Pres. Abraham Lincoln coun. Boy Scouts Am., 1978-80. With U.S. Army, 1952-54, Korea, col. res.; maj. gen. Ill. Militia. Recipient George Washington Honor medal Freedoms Found., 1969, 73, 75, 82, Disting. Eagle Scout Boy Scouts Am., 1985. Fellow Am. Bar Found.; mem. ABA, at. Conf. Fed. Trial Judges (chmn. 1999-00), Ill. Bar Assn., Chgo. Bar Assn., Cass County Bar Assn. (pres. 1962-64, 75-76), Sangamon County Bar Assn., 7th Cir. Bar Assn., Am. Law Inst., Fed. Judges Assn., Army and Navy Club (Washington), Sangamo Club, Masons (33 degree), Lincoln-Douglas Am. Inn of Ct. 150 (founding, pres. 1991-93). Republican. Office: US Dist Ct 600 E Monroe St Ste 117 Springfield IL 62701-1659 Office Phone: 217-492-4340.

MILLS, STEVEN R., agricultural company executive, accountant; b. July 12, 1955; BS in Mathematics, Ill. Coll, 1977. CPA 1981. Acct. State Farm Ins., Bloomington, Ind., 1977—79; joined Archer Daniels Midland Co., 1979—, contr., 1994—2000, v.p., contr., 2000—02, group v.p., contr., 2002—06, sr. v.p. strategic planning, 2006—08, exec. v.p., CFO, 2008—. Bd. dirs. Kirby Coll.; bd. trustees Ill. Coll. Office: Archer Daniels Midland Co 4666 Farus Pkwy Decatur IL 62526*

MILLSTONE, DAVID JEFFREY, lawyer; b. Morgantown, W.Va., 1946; AB, Johns Hopkins U., 1968; JD, W.Va. U., 1971. Bar: Ohio 1971. Ptnr. Squire, Sanders & Dempsey LLP, Cleve. Co-author: Wage Hour Law--How to Comply, 2001; editor: Ohio and Fed. Employment Law Manual, 2001; contbr. chapters to books. Past chair regional bd., nat commr., nat. exec. com. mem., chair edn. com. Anti-Defamation League, 2002—05. Mem.: ABA, Ohio Mgmt. Lawyers Assn., Cleve. Bar Assn. Office: Squire Sanders & Dempsey 4900 Key Tower 127 Public Sq Ste 4900 Cleveland OH 44114-1304 Office Phone: 216-479-8574. E-mail: dmillstone@ssd.com.

MILONE, ANTHONY MICHAEL, bishop emeritus; b. Omaha, Nebr., Sept. 24, 1932; BA, Conception Sem., 1954; STB, Gregorian U., Rome, 1956, STL, 1958. Ordained priest Roman Catholic Ch., 1957. Ordained priest Archdiocese of Omaha, Nebr., 1957; ordained bishop, 1982; aux. bishop Archdiocese of Omaha, Nebr., 1981—87; bishop Diocese of Great Falls-Billings, Mont., 1987—2006, bishop emeritus Mont., 2006—. Roman Catholic. Office: St Bernadette Ch So 42nd St Bellevue NE 68147-1702 also: Chancery Office 121 23rd St S PO Box 1399 Great Falls MT 59403-1399 Office Phone: 406-727-6683. Office Fax: 406-454-3480. E-mail: bishop@dioceseofgfb.org.*

MILSTED, AMY, biomedical educator; BSEd, Ohio State U., 1967; PhD, CUNY, 1977. Lectr. Hunter Coll./CUNY, 1970-76; instr. Carnegie-Mellon U., Pitts., 1976-77; postdoctoral fellow Muscular Dystrophy Assn./Carnegie-Mellon U., Pitts., 1978-79; rsch. assoc. Case Western Res. U., Cleve., 1979-82; rsch. chemist VA Med. Ctr., Cleve., 1982-87; project staff The Cleve. Clin. Found., 1987-89; asst. staff dept. brain and vascular rsch. Cleve. Clinic Found., 1989-93; grad. faculty Sch. Biomed. Scis. Kent (Ohio) State U., 1995—; assoc. prof. dept. biology U. Akron, Ohio, 1993-2000, prof. biology, 2000—. Contbr. articles to profl. jours. Fellow Am. Heart Assn.; mem. AAAS, Inter-Am. Soc. Hypertension, Am. Chem. Soc., Endocrine Soc., Assn. Women in Sci. Office: Univ Akron Dept Biology Asec 279 Akron OH 44325-3908 E-mail: milsted@uakron.edu.

MILTON, CHAD EARL, lawyer; b. Brevard County, Fla., Jan. 29, 1947; s. Rex Dale and Mary Margaret (Peacock) M.; m. Ann Mitchell Bunting, Mar. 30, 1972; children: Samuel, Kathleen, Kelsey. BA, Colo. Coll., 1969; JD, U. Colo., 1974; postgrad., U. Mo., 1976-77. Bar: Colo. 1974, Mo. 1977, U.S. Dist. Ct. Colo. 1974, U.S. Dist. Ct. (we. dist.) Mo. 1977. Counsel Office of Colo. State Pub. Defender, Colo. Springs, 1974-76; pub. info. officer, counsel Mid-Am. Arts Alliance, Kansas City, Mo., 1977-78; claims counsel Employers Reinsurance Corp., Kansas City, Mo., 1978-80; sr. v.p. Media/Profl. Ins., Kansas City, Mo., 1981-2000; sr. v.p. nat. practice leader, intellectual property & media Marsh, Kansas City, Mo., 2000—. Reporter, photographer, editor Golden (Colo.) Daily Transcript, 1970; investigator, law clk. Office of Colo. State Pub. Defender, Denver, Golden, 1970-74; participant Annenberg Project on the Reform of Libel Laws, Washington, 1987-88; adj. prof., comm. and advt. law Webster U., 1989-93; lectr. in field. Pres. bd. dirs. Folly Theater, 1992-94, Kans. City Chamber Orch., 1995—. Mem. ABA (chair intellectual property law com. of the torts and ins. practice sect., forum com. on comm. law, ctrl. and Ea. European law initiative), Mo. Bar Assn., Kansas City Met. Bar Assn., Libel Def. Resource Ctr. (editorial bd., exec. com.). Avocations: tennis, golf, skiing, sailing, antique maps. Home: 8821 Alhambra St Shawnee Mission KS 66207-2357 Office: Marsh 2405 Grand Blvd Kansas City MO 64108-2510 Office Phone: 816-556-4365. E-mail: chad.e.milton@marsh.com.

MINER, THOMAS HAWLEY, entrepreneur; b. Shelbyville, Ill., June 19, 1927; s. Lester Ward and Thirza (Hawley) M.; m. Lucyna T. Minciel, July 22, 1983; children: Robert Thomas, William John. Student, U.S. Mil. Acad., 1946—47; BA, Knox Coll., 1950; JD, U. Ill., 1953. Bar: Ill. 1954. Counsel Continental Ill. Nat. Bank & Trust Co., Chgo., 1953—55; pres. Harper-Wyman Internat. S.A., Venezuela and Mex., 1955—58, Hudson Internat. S.A., Can. and Switzerland, 1958—60, Thomas H. Miner & Assoc., Inc., Chgo., 1960—; chmn. Miner, Fraser & Gabriel Pub. Affairs, Inc., Washington, 1982—88, Miner Sys., Inc., 1981—; internat. dir. Urban Retail Properties Inc., 2005—; chmn., CEO Ill. Global Partnership, Inc., 2005—; dir. US-China C. of C., 2007—. Bd. dirs. Lakeside Bank, Worldschool, Bright Oceans Internat. Corp.; chmn. Ill. dist. export coun. U.S. Dept. Commerce, 1971—; sec. Consular Corps. Chgo., 1986—88; chmn. Mid-Am. China Mgmt. Tng. Ctr., Global Software Source, Geo Vision, Inc., U.S.-Iraq Bus. Alliance; dir. Global Heavy Lift Holdings LLc. Chmn. bd. dirs. Sch. Art Inst. Chgo., 1977-81; bd. govs., life mem., sustaining fellow Art Inst. Chgo.; former chmn. UN Assn., Chgo.; founder, chmn. Mid-Am. Com., 1968—; former mem. bd. dirs. UNICEF, NAM, Internat. Trade Policy Com. and Working Group on Commonwealth of Ind. States and Ea. Europe; trustee 4th Presbyn. Ch., Chgo., Roosevelt U., Chgo., 1996; bd. advisors Mercy Hosp.; vice chmn. Chgo. Sister Cities; mem. adv. bd. Internat. Inst. Edn.; bd. dirs. Internat. Sister Cities. With USNR, 1945-46; mem. Pres. Coun. U. Ill. Found.; dir. Internat. Urgan Retail Properties Co.; chmn. Ill. Global Partnership, Inc. Capt. U.S. Army, 1946-47. Decorated comdr. Crown of the Kingdom of Belgium, 2003, commendatore Ordine al Merito della Repubblica Italiana; recipient Alumni Achievement award Knox Coll., 1974, Gold Medallion award Internat. Visitors Ctr. Chgo., 1989; named One of Chgo.'s 10 Outstanding Young Men, 1962, Chicagoan of Year Chgo. Assn. Commerce and Industry, 1968, Alumni of Month Coll. Law U. Ill., Nov. 1970, Aug. 1984; hon. consul Republic of Senegal, 1970-88. Mem. Am. Mgmt. Assn., Chicagoland C. of C., Mid-Am. Arab C. of C. (founder, former pres.), Chgo. Bar Assn., Chgo. Com., Chgo. Coun. Fgn. Rels. (past dir.), Coun. of the Ams., Internat. Trade Club (past dir., pres.), Japan-Am. Soc., Nat. Coun. U.S.-China Trade, Nat. Acad. Scis. (pres. coun.), English Speaking Union (dir., past chmn.) Trade and Econs. Coun. USA-CIS (dir.), U.S.-Russia Bus. Coun., Mus. Contemporary Art, Newcomen Soc. N.Am., U.S.-China Bus. Coun., U.S.-Arab C. of C. (bd. dirs.), U.S.-Mex. C. of C. (bd. dirs.), Thomas Minor Soc., Chgo. Club, Econ. Club, Grant Park Concerts Soc., Chgo. Farmers Club, Mid-Am. Club, Univ. Club (Washington), Univ. Club (Milw.), Hillsboro Club (Fla.), Tryall Golf and Beach Club (Jamaica), Rotary, Phi Delta Phi, Phi Gamma Delta. Office: 900 N Michigan Ave Ste 900 Chicago IL 60611 Home Phone: 312-944-2453; Office Phone: 312-915-3336. Personal E-mail: ltminer@aol.com. Business E-Mail: minert@urbanretail.com.

MINGE, DAVID, former congressman, lawyer, law educator; b. Clarkfield, Minn., 1942; m. Karen Aaker; children: Erik, Olaf. BA in History, St. Olaf Coll., 1964; JD, U. Chgo., 1967. Atty. Faegre & Benson, Mpls., 1967-70; prof. law U. Wyo., 1970-77; atty. Nelson, Oyen, Torvik, Minge & Gilbertson, 1977-93; mem. 103d-106th Congresses from 2nd Minn. Dist., 1993-2001; judge Minn. Ct. Appeals, Minn., 2002—. Cons. Ho. Jud. Com., Subcom. Adminstrv. Law U.S. Congress, 1975; chair Agrl. Law Sect., Minn. State Bar Assn. 1990-92, adv. bd. Western Minn. Legal Svcs., 1978-84; bd. dirs. Legal Advice Clinics, Ltd., Hennepin County, Western Minn. Vol. Atty. Program; lectr. U. Minn., Morris, 2001-02 Coord. Montevideo area CROP Walk for the Hungry; clk. Montevideo Sch. Bd., 1989—92; dir. Montevideo Cmty. Devel. Corp.; steering com. Clean Up the River Environ., 1992. Fellow Kellogg Found. Food and Soc. fellow, 2002; scholar, Woodrow Wilson Ctr. for Internat. Studies, 2002. Mem.: Minn. Bar Assn. Office: 25 Dr Martin Luther King Jr Blvd Saint Paul MN 55155 Office Phone: 651-297-1003.

MINICHELLO, DENNIS, lawyer; b. Cleve., June 9, 1952; s. Ernest Anthony and Mary Theresa (Rocci) M.; m. Janine Stevens, Feb. 14, 1987. BA in Econs., MA in Econs., Ohio U., 1974; JD, Northwestern U., 1978. Bar: U.S. Dist. Ct. (no. dist.) Ill., U.S. Ct. Appeals (7th cir.), Supreme Ct. Ill., U.S. Supreme Ct. Assoc. Haskell & Perrin, Chgo., 1978-84; ptnr. Tribler & Marwedel, Chgo., 1984-89, Keck, Mahin & Cate, Chgo., 1989—97; shareholder Marwedel, Minichellot & Reeb, P.C., 1997—. Contbr. articles to profl. jours. Bd. dirs. Great Lakes Naval and Maritime Mus. Fulbright scholar, 1974-75. Mem. ABA, Ill. State Bar Assn., Chgo. Bar Assn. (mem. transp. com.), Maritime Law Assn. (proctor), Ohio U. Alumni Assn. (bd. dirs.), The Propeller Club US (pres. 1983-84), Port Chgo., Transp. Lawyers Assn., Conf. Freight Counsel, Midwest High Speed Rail Coalition (pres. 2000—), Def. Rsch. Inst., Leading Lawyers Network. Roman Catholic. Avocations: reading, exercise. Office: Marwedel Minichello & Reeb PC 10 S Riverside Plz Ste 720 Chicago IL 60606-3709 Office Phone: 312-902-1600 ext. 5065. Business E-Mail: dminichello@mmr-law.com.

MINISH, ROBERT ARTHUR, lawyer; b. Mpls., Dec. 25, 1938; s. William Arthur and Agnes Emilia (Olson) M.; m. Marveen Eleanor Allen, Sept. 16, 1961; 1 child, Roberta Ruth. BA, U. Minn., 1960, JD, 1963. Bar: Minn. 1963. Assoc. Popham, Haik, Schnobrich & Kaufman, Ltd., Mpls., 1963-67, ptnr., 1967-97, Hinshaw & Culbertson, Mpls., 1997—. Bd. dirs. Braas Co., Mpls. Mem. ABA, Minn. Bar Assn. Avocations: fishing, travel. Home: 331 Pearson Way NE Minneapolis MN 55432-2418 Office: Hinshaw & Culbertson 3100 Piper Jaffray Tower 222 S 9th St Minneapolis MN 55402-3389 Business E-Mail: rminish@hinshawlaw.com.

MINKOWYCZ, W. J., mechanical engineering educator; b. Libokhora, Ukraine, Oct. 21, 1937; came to U.S., 1949; s. Alexander and Anna (Tokan) M.; m. Diana Eva Szandra, May 12, 1973; 1 child, Liliana Christine Anne BS in Mech. Engring., U. Minn., 1958, MS in Mech. Engring., 1961, PhD in Mech. Engring, 1965. From asst. prof. to James P. Hartnett prof. U. Ill., Chgo., 1966—2006, James P. Hartnett prof., 2006—. Cons. Argonne Nat. Lab, Ill., 1970-82, U. Hawaii, Honolulu, 1974-94. Founding editor-in-chief (jour.) Jour. Numerical Heat Transfer, 1978—; editor-in-chief: Internat. Jour. Heat and Mass Transfer, 1968-, Rheologically Complex Fluids, 1972, Internat. Comms. in Heat and Mass Transfer Jour., 1974-, 1988, Handbook of Numerical Heat Transfer, 2006; editor: (book series) Computational and Physical Processes in Mechanics and Thermal Sciences, 1979—, Advances in Numerical Heat Transfer, 1996—, Vol. 1, 1997, Vol. 2, 2000; contbr. articles to profl. jours. Recipient Silver Circle for Excellence in Teaching, U. Ill.-Chgo., 1975, 76, 81, 86, 90, 94, Harold A. Simon award Excellence in Teaching, 1986, Ralph Coats Roe Outstanding Tchr. award Am. Soc. Engring. Edn., 1988, U. Ill. Disting. Tchr. award, 1989. Fellow: ASME (Heat Transfer Meml. award 1993, Classic Paper award 2006); mem.: Pi Tau Sigma, Sigma Xi. Republican. Ukrainian Catholic. Office: U Ill Dept Mech Engring Mail Code 251 842 W Taylor St Chicago IL 60607-7021 Office Phone: 312-996-3467. Business E-Mail: wjm@uic.edu.

MINNESTE, VIKTOR, JR., retired engineering executive; b. Haapsalu, Estonia, Jan. 15, 1932; s. Viktor and Alice (Lembra) M. BSEE, U. Ill., 1960. Elec. engr. Bell & Howell Co., 1960-69; microstatics divsn. A-M Co., 1969-71, multigraphics divsn., 1972-73; elec. engr. bus. products group Victor Comptometer Co. (merged with Walter Kidde Corp.), Chgo., 1973-74, svc. mgr. internat. group, 1974-75, supr. elecs. desing group, 1975-82; project engr. Warner Electric, 1982-84; systems engr. Barrett Elecs., 1984-85; phone engr. Williams Elecs., 1986-88; cons. engr., 1988-92; ind. contractor, 1993-95; ret., 1995. Pub. Motteid/Thoughts, 1962-68. Chmn. Estonian-Ams. Polit Action Com., 1968-72. With AUS, 1952-54. Home and Office: 3134 N Kimball Ave Chicago IL 60618-6856

MINOGUE, JOHN P., academic administrator, educator, priest; b. Chgo., Jan. 1946; B in Philosophy, St. Mary of the Barrens; MDiv, Deandreis Inst. Theology, 1972; M in Theology, DePaul U., 1975; PhD in Ministry, St. Mary of the Lake Sem., 1987. Ordained Vincentian priest, 1972. Vincentian priest Congregation of the Mission; instr. theology, dir. clin. pastoral placement programs St. Thomas Sem., Denver, 1972-76; instr. grad. theology, asst. then acad. dean DeAndreis Inst., 1976-83; pres. DePaul U., Chgo., 1993—. Trustee DePaul U., 1991—; bd. dirs. DePaul U. Corp., 1981-91; adj. prof. Sch. New Learning DePaul U., 1984—, instr. law and med. ethics Coll. Law DePaul U., 1989—; asst. prof. clin. ob.-gyn. Northwestern U.; instr. health care ethics St. Joseph Coll. ursing, Joliet, Ill., Northwestern Sch. Nursing, Chgo.; cons. nat. health care ethics, patient decision-making, mem. Congregation of the Missions Bd. mem. Children's Meml. Hosp. Mem.: NASA (bd. mem.). Office: De Paul U Office of the Pres 55 E Jackson Blvd 22nd Fl Chicago IL 60604-2287

MINOR, CHARLES DANIEL, lawyer, director; b. Columbus, Ohio, May 28, 1927; s. Walter Henry and Helen Margaret (Bergman) M.; m. Mary Jo Klinker, Dec. 27, 1950; children: Elizabeth, Daniel, Amy. BS in Bus. Adminstrn, Ohio State U., 1950, JD summa cum laude, 1952. Bar: Ohio 1952. Mem. firm Vorys, Sater, Seymour and Pease, Columbus, 1952—, ptnr., 1957-93, of counsel, 1993—. Bd. dirs. Inland Products, Inc., Worthington Industries, Inc. Served with USNR, 1945-46. Mem. Columbus, Ohio State bar assns., The Columbus Club, Double Eagle Club, Scioto Country Club. Republican. Office: Vorys Sater Seymour & Pease 52 E Gay St Columbus OH 43215-3161 E-mail: ldminor@vssp.com.

MINOR, MELVIN G., state legislator; b. Aug. 24, 1937; m. Carolyn Minor. Student, Emporia State U. Kans. state rep. Dist. 114; farmer. Mem. Masons, Shriners (Wichita Consistory).

MINOR, ROBERT ALLEN, lawyer; b. Washington, Oct. 20, 1948; s. Robert Walter and Joan (Allen) M.; m. Sue Ellyn Blose, June 13, 1981; children: Robert Barratt, Sarah Allen. AB in English, Duke U., 1970; JD, Ohio State U., 1975. Bar: Ohio 1975, US Dist. Ct. (so. dist.) Ohio 1976, DC 1979. Assoc. Vorys, Sater, Seymour & Pease, LLP, Columbus, Ohio, 1975-82, ptnr., 1982—. Author seminar articles. With U.S. Army, 1970-72. Mem. Ohio Bar Assn., Columbus Bar Assn., Scioto Country Club. Republican. Presbyterian. Office: Vorys Sater Seymour & Pease LLP PO Box 1008 52 E Gay St Columbus OH 43215-3161 Office Phone: 614-464-6410. Business E-Mail: raminor@vssp.com.

MINOR, RONALD RAY, minister; b. Aliceville, Ala., Nov. 3, 1944; s. Hershel Ray and Minnie Ozell (Goodson) M.; m. Gwendolyn Otella Newsome, July 25, 1970; 1 child, Rhonda Davis. BA in Ministerial, Southeastern U., 1971, BA in Secondary Edn., 1973; DDiv, So. Bible Coll., 1984. Ordained to ministry Pentecostal Ch. of God, 1968. Gen. sec. Pentecostal Ch. of God, Joplin, Mo., 1979—2005, dist. supt. Miss., 1975-79, pastor LaBelle, Fla., Bartow, Fla., Orient Park Tabernacle, Tampa, Fla., Lafayette (Ind.) Pentecostal Ch. of God. Pres. Pentecostal Young People's Assn., Fla. and Miss.; sec. Gen. Bd. Pentecostal Ch. of God, Joplin, 1979-2005; bd. dirs. Nat. Assn. Evangs., Wheaton, Ill., 1981-96; adv. coun. Am. Bible Soc., N.Y.C., 1979-2003; sec. Commn. Chaplains, Washington, 1991-95. Office: Pentecostal Ch of God 3511 S 9th St Lafayette IN 47909 Home Phone: 765-477-9803. E-mail: ronaldminor@insightbb.com.

MINOW, JOSEPHINE BASKIN, civic volunteer; b. Chgo., Nov. 3, 1926; d. Salem N. and Bessie (Sampson) Baskin; m. Newton N. Minow, May 29, 1949; children: Nell, Martha, Mary. BS, Northwestern U., Evanston, Ill., 1948. Asst. to advt. dir. Mandel Brothers Dept. Store, Chgo., 1948-49; tchr. Francis W. Parker Sch., Chgo., 1949-50; vol. in civil and charitable activities, 1950—; bd. dirs. Juvenile Protective Assn., Chgo., 1958—, pres., 1973-75. Bd. dirs. Parnham Trust, Beaminster, Dorset, England. Author: Marty the Broken Hearted Artichoke, 1997. Founder, coord. Children's divsn. Hospitality and Info. Svc., Washington, 1961-63; mem. Caucus Com., Glencoe, Ill., 1965-69; co-chmn. spl. study on juvenile justice Chgo. Cmty. Trust, 1978-80; chmn. Know Your Chgo., 1980-83; bd. dirs. Chgo. Coun. Fgn. Rels., 1977-2003, hon. life mem., 2003; trustee Chgo. Hist. Soc., Ravinia Festival Assn.; mem. women's bd. Field Mus., U. Chgo.; founding mem., v.p. women's bd. Northwestern U., 1978; bd. govs. Chgo. Symphony, 1966-73, 76-; mem. Citizens Com. Juvenile Ct. of Cook County, 1985-96; exec. com. Northwestern U. Libr. Coun., 1974-96; co-chair grandparents' adv. com. Chgo. Children's Mus., 1999; bd. dirs. Jane Addams Juvenile Ct. Found.; dir. Abraham Lincoln Presdl. Libr. and Mus., 2005—. Recipient spl. award Chgo. Sch. and Workshop for Retarded, 1975, Children's Guardian award Juvenile Protective Assn., 1993. Mem. Hebrew Immigrant Aid Soc. (bd. dirs. 1977-98, award 1988), Friday Club, The Arts Club. Democrat. Jewish. Office: Chgo Hist Museum Clark St at North Ave Chicago IL 60614

MINOW, NEWTON NORMAN, lawyer, educator; b. Milw., Jan. 17, 1926; s. Jay A. and Doris (Stein) Minow; m. Josephine Baskin, May 29, 1949; children: Nell, Martha, Mary. BS, Northwestern U., 1949, JD, 1950, LLD (hon.), 1965, U. Wis., Brandeis U., 1963, Columbia Coll., 1972, Govs. State U., 1984, De Paul U., 1989, RAND Grad. Sch., 1993, U. Notre Dame, 1994, Roosevelt U., 1996, Barat Coll., 1996, Santa Clara U. Sch. Law, 1998, Cath. Theol. Union, 2001. With firm Mayer, Brown & Platt, Chgo., 1950-51, 53-55; law clk. to chief justice U.S. Supreme Ct., 1951-52; asst. counsel to Ill. Gov. Stevenson, 1952-53; spl. asst. to Adlai E. Stevenson in presdl. campaign, 1952, 56; ptnr. firm Stevenson, Rifkind & Wirtz, Chgo., NYC and Washington, 1955-61; chmn. FCC, Washington, 1961-63; exec. v.p., gen. counsel, dir. Ency. Brit., Chgo., 1963-65; ptnr. Sidley Austin LLP, Chgo., 1965—91, sr. counsel, 1991—. Former trustee, past chmn. bd. dirs., adv. trustee Rand Corp.; past chmn. Chgo. Ednl. TV; chmn. pub. rev. bd. Arthur Andersen & Co., 1974—83; trustee Carnegie Corp. N.Y., 1987—97, chmn. bd. trustees, 1993—97; Annenberg prof. comm. law and policy Northwestern U., 1987—2003, prof. emeritus, 2003—, hon. trustee, 2007—; dir. Annenberg Washington Program, 1987—96; chmn. tech. and privacy adv. com. Sec. Def., 2003—04. Author: (book) Equal Time: The Private Broadcasters and the Public Interest, 1964; co-author: Presidential Television, 1973, Electronics and the Future, 1977, For Great Debates, 1987, Abandoned in the Wasteland: Children, Television, and the First Amendment, 1995, As We Knew Adlai. Bd. govs. Pub. Broadcasting Svc., 1973—80, chmn. bd. dirs., 1978—80; vice chmn. presdl. debates LWV, 1976, 1980, 1993—; chmn. bd. overseers Jewish Theol. Sem., 1974—77; trustee Notre Dame U., 1964—77, 1983—96, life trustee, 1996; trustee Mayo Found., 1973—81, Northwestern U., 1975—87, life trustee, 1987—. With US Army, 1944—46. Named one of Am.'s 10 Outstanding Young Men, 1961; recipient George Foster Peabody Broadcasting award, 1961, Ralph Lowell award, 1982, Lifetime Achievement award, The Am. Lawyer mag., 2004, Woodrow Wilson award for Pub. Svc., 2006, Legal Legend award, Am. Constitution Soc., 2006, Lifetime Achievement award, Common Sense Media, 2006, Paul Simon award for Pub. Svc., 2006. Fellow: Am. Acad. Arts and Scis., Am. Bar Found.; mem.: Northwestern U. Alumni Assn. (medal 1978), Century Club (N.Y.C.), Chgo. Club, Comml. Club (pres. 1987—88). Democrat. Office: Sidley Austin LLP One S Dearborn St Chicago IL 60603 Office Phone: 312-853-7555. Business E-Mail: nminow@sidley.com.

MIRACLE, GORDON ELDON, advertising educator; b. Olympia, Wash., May 28, 1930; s. Gordon Tipler and Corine Adriana (Orlebeke) M.; m. Christa Stoeter, June 29, 1957; children: Gary, Gregory, Glenn. BBA, U. Wis., 1952, MBA, 1958, PhD, 1962. Case officer, civilian intelligence analyst U.S. Army, Fed. Republic Germany, 1955-57; instr. commerce U. Wis. Grad. Sch. Bus., Madison, 1958-60; instr., then asst. prof. mktg. U. Mich., Ann Arbor, 1960-66; assoc. prof. advt. Mich. State U., East Lansing, 1966-70, chmn. PhD program in mass media, 1973-74, chmn. dept., 1974-80, prof. advt., 1970-99, prof. emeritus, 1999—. Vis. prof. mktg. mgmt. N. European Mgmt. Inst., Oslo, 1972-73; dir. InterSIP, 2007—; cons., lectr. in field. Author: Management of International Advertising, 1966; co-author: International Marketing Management, 1970, Advertising and Government Regulation, 1979, Instructor's Manual for International Marketing Management, 1971, European Regulation of Advertising: Supranational Regulation of Advertising in the European Economic Community, 1986, Voluntary Regulation of Advertising: A Comparative Analysis of the United Kingdom and the United States, 1987, (in Korean) Cultures in Advertising: Advertising in Cultures, 1990; contbr. articles to scholarly and profl. jours.; editor: Marketing Decision Making: Strategy and Payoff, 1965, Sharing for Understanding, Proc. Ann. Conf. Am. Acad. Advt., 1977. Served with AUS, 1952-55. Recipient first Biennial Excellence in Advt. award, U. Ill., 1995; Ford Found. fellow, 1961-62, 64, Am. Assn. Advt. Agys. fellow Marsteller, Inc., 1967, Advt. Ednl. Found. fellow McCann-Erickson Hakuhodo, 1985, Fulbright rsch. fellow Waseda U., Tokyo, 1985; recipient numerous grants; recipient Viktor-Mataja medal Austrian Advt. Rsch. Assn., Vienna, 1999. Fellow: Am. Acad. Advt. (treas., exec. com. 1978—79); mem.: Internat. Advt. Assn., Internat. Advt. Assn. ((ednl. accreditation com. 1993—95, internat. advt. edn. group 1996—2001), Am. Mktg. Assn., Acad. Internat. Bus. (sec., exec. com. 1973—75), Adcraft Club Detroit. Home: 10025 Oak Island Dr Laingsburg MI 48848-8718 Office: Mich State U Dept Advt East Lansing MI 48824 Business E-Mail: miracle@msu.edu.

MIRKIN, CHAD A., chemistry professor; BS in Chemistry, Dickinson Coll., 1986; PhD, Pa. State U., 1989; doctorate (hon.), Dickinson Coll. Asst. prof. chemistry orthwestern U., Evanston, Ill., 1991-95, assoc. prof. chemistry, 1995-97, prof. chemistry, 1997-2000, George B. Rathmann prof. chemistry, dir. Inst. anotechnology, 2000—. Contbr. articles to profl. jours. NSF postdoctoral fellow MIT, 1989-91; recipient Beckman Young Investigators award, 1992-94, Disting. New Faculty award Camille and Henry Dreyfus Found., 1991-96, Young Investigator Rsch. award NSF, Young Prof. award DuPont, Young Investigator award ONR, Inventors award B.F. Goodrich, Wilson prize, award in pure chemistry Am. Chem. Soc., Nobel Signature award, Am. Chem. Soc., Collegiate Inventors award, Nat. Inventors Hall of Fame, 2003, 04, Pioneer award, NIH, 2004; grantee USN. Mem. Am. Chem. Soc. Achievements include research nanotechnology biosensors and new ligand design in synthetic organometallic chemistry; over 50 patents in field. Office: Northwestern U Dept Chemistry 2145 Sheridan Rd K111 Evanston IL 60208-3113 E-mail: camirkin@chem.nwv.edu.

MIROWSKI, PHILIP EDWARD, economics professor; b. Jackson, Mich., Aug. 21, 1951; s. Edward and Elizabeth Mirowski. BA, Mich. State U., 1973; MA in Econs., U. Mich., 1976, PhD in Econs., 1979. Asst. prof. U. Santa Clara, Calif., 1978-81, Tufts U., Medford, Mass., 1981-84, assoc. prof. econs., 1984-90; Carl Koch prof. econs. and history and philosophy of sci. U. Notre Dame, Ind., 1990—. Vis. assoc. prof. Yale U., New Haven, 1987-88; vis. prof. Tinbergen Inst., Erasmus U., Rotterdam, Holland, 1991, U. Paris, 1997, U. Modena, Italy, 1998, Santa Fe Inst., 2001; Fulbright sr. fellow, 2003, Internat. Ctr. for Advanced Studies, YU, 2004. Author: Reconstruction of Economic Theory, 1986, Against Mechanism, 1988, More Heat Than Light, 1989, Machine Dreams, 2002, Science Bought and Sold, 2002, Effortless Economy of Science, 2004; editor: Natural Images in Economics, 1994, Edgeworth on Chance, 1994, Collected Works of William Thomas Thornton, 1999, Agreement on Demand, 2006; mem. editl. bd. History Polit. Econ., Duke U., 1986—, Social Concept, 1988-94, Jour. Instnl. Econs., 2004—, Jour. History of Econ., 2001—; contbr. articles to profl. jours. Mem. AAAS, Am. Econs. Assn., History Sci. Soc., History Econs. Soc., Soc. for Social Studies of Sci. (Ludwig Fleck prize 2006), Philosophy of Sci. Assn. Office: U Notre Dame 400 Decio Hall Notre Dame IN 46556 E-mail: mirowski.1@nd.edu.

MIRSKY, ARTHUR, retired geologist, educator; b. Phila., Feb. 8, 1927; s. Victor and Dorothy M.; m. Patricia Shorey, Dec. 22, 1961; 1 dau., Alexis Catherine. Student, Bklyn. Coll., 1944, student, 1946—48; BA, U. Calif., 1950; MS, U. Ariz., 1955; PhD, Ohio State U., 1960. Cert. geologist, Ind. Field uranium geologist AEC, S.W. U.S., 1951-53; cons. uranium geologist Albuquerque, 1955-56; asst. dir. Inst. Polar Studies, Ohio State U., 1960-67; adj. asst. prof. geology Ohio State U., 1964-67; from asst. prof. geology to prof. Ind. U.-Purdue U., Indpls., 1967-94, prof. emeritus, 1994—, coord. geology, 1967-69, chmn. dept. geology, 1969-93. Contbr. articles to profl. jours. Served with USN, 1944-46. Mem. AAAS, AAUP, Am. Inst. Profl. Geologists, Geol. Soc. Am., at. Assn. Geosci. Tchrs., Am. Geol. Inst., Soc. Sedimentary Geology, Ind. Acad. Sci., Sigma Xi. Office: Indiana U-Purdue U Dept Earth Scis 723 W Michigan St Indianapolis IN 46202-5132 Office Phone: 317-278-0229. E-mail: amirsky@iupui.edu.

MISCHKA, THOMAS, marketing professional; Degree in computer sci., U. Wis.-Oshkosh. Computer programmer Aid Assn for Lutherans, Appleton, Wis., 1982-98, v.p. nat. mktg., 1998—. Mem. Christus Luth. Ch., Greenville, Wis. Mem. Am. Mgmt. Assn. Office: Aid Assn for Lutherans 4321 N Ballard Rd Appleton WI 54919-0001

MISCHKE, CARL HERBERT, retired religious association executive; b. Hazel, SD, Oct. 27, 1922; s. Emil Gustav and Pauline Alvina (Polzin) M.; m. Gladys Lindloff, July 6, 1947; children: Joel, Susan Mischke Blahnik, Philip, Steven. BA, Northwestern Coll., Watertown, Wis., 1944; M.Div., Wis. Luth. Sem., Mequon, 1947. Ordained to ministry Evang. Lutheran Ch. Parish pastor Wis. Synod, 1947-79; pres. Western Wis. Dist. Evang. Luth. Ch., Juneau, 1964-79; v.p. Wis. Luth. Synod, Milw., 1966-79, pres., 1979-93; retired, 1993. Lutheran.

MISCHKE, CHARLES RUSSELL, mechanical engineering educator; b. Glendale, NY, Mar. 2, 1927; s. Reinhart Charles and Dena Amelia (Scholl) M.; m. Margaret R. Bubeck, Aug. 4, 1951; children: Thomas, James. BSME, Cornell U., 1947, MME, 1950; PhD, U. Wis., 1953. Lic. mechanical engr. Iowa, Kans. Asst. prof. mech. engring. U. Kans., Lawrence, 1953-56, assoc. prof. mech. engring., 1956-57; prof., chmn. mech. engring. Pratt Inst., NYC, 1957-64; prof. mech. engring. Iowa State U., Ames, 1964—, Alcoa Found. prof., 1974. Author: Elements of Mechanical Analysis, 1963, Introduction to Computer-Aided Design, 1968, Mathematical Model Building, 1972; editor: Standard Handbook of Machine Design, 1996, Mechanical Engineering Design, 7th edit., 2004, 8 Mechancal Designers Workbooks, 1990, Fundamentos de Diseno Mechanico, 4 vols., 1994. Scoutmaster Boy Scouts Am., Ames. With USNR, 1944-75, mem. Res. ret. Recipient Ralph Teetor award Soc. Automotive Engrs., 1977, best book award Am. Assn. Pubs., 1986, Legis. Teaching Excellence award Iowa Assembly, 1990, Ralph Coates Roe award Am. Soc. for Engring. Edn., 1991. Fellow ASME (life, Machine Design award 1990); mem. Am. Soc. Engring. Edn. (Centennial cert. 1993), Am. Gear Mfrs. Assn., Scabbard and Blade, Cardinal Key, Sigma Xi, Phi Kappa Phi, Pi Tau Sigma. Avocations: model building, railway history. Office: Iowa State U Dept Mech Engring Ames IA 50011-0001

MISHLER, CLIFFORD LESLIE, publisher; b. Vandalia, Mich., Aug. 11, 1939; s. Nelson Howard and Lily Mae (Young) M.; m. Sandra Rae Knutson, Dec. 21, 1963 (dec. July 8, 1972); m. Sylvia M. Leer, Feb. 27, 1976; children: Sheila, Sharon, Susan. Student, Northwestern U., 1957-58. Author, pub. ann. edits. Ann. Studies U.S. and Can. Commemorative Medals and Tokens, 1958-63; assoc. editor Numismatic News, Krause Publs., Iola, Wis., 1963-64, editor, 1964-66, numismatic editor all publs., 1966-75, exec. v.p., pub. all numismatic publs., 1975-78, exec. v.p., pub. all products, 1978-88, sr. v.p., pub. all Numismatic products, 1988-89, sr. v.p. ops., 1989-90; pres. Krause Publs., Iola, Wis., 1991-99, chmn. bd. dir., 2000—02, numismatic cons., 2002—05; dir. numismatic devel. Whitman Pub., 2005—. Bd. dirs. First State Bank Iola, 1972-83, Scandinavia Telephone Co., 1981-97, TDS Telecom cmty. bd., 1997-2000; mem. coins and medals adv. panel Am. Revolution Bicentennial Commn., 1970-75; mem. ann. assay commn. U.S. Mint, 1973. Co-author: Standard Catalog of World Coins, ann. 1972-2005; contbr. articles New Book Knowledge, ann. 1969-81. Co-founder Iola Old Car Show, Inc., 1972, ex-officio dir., 1985—2003; mem. Wis. Commemorative Quarter Coun., 2001—03; bd. dirs. William R. Higgins, Jr. Found., 1991—; chmn. fund drive Iola-Scandinavia Cmty. Fitness and Aquatic Ctr., 1999—2001. Recipient The Internat. Vreneli Preistrager: The "Friendly Prize" for lifetime numismatic achievements, Munzen-Revue, Basel, Switzerland, 2001, umis. Amb. award, Numis. News/Balt., Md., 2003. Fellow Am. Numismatic Soc. (life, coun. mem. 1997-2003, trustee 2003—); mem. Am. Numismatic Assn. (life, bd. govs. 2007—, Merit medal 1983, Farran Zerbe Meml. Disting Svc. award 1984, Glen Smedley meml. dedicated svcs. award 1991, Lifetime Achievement award 1997, named Numismatist of Yr. 2002, named to Hall Fame 2004, Burnett Anderson Meml. award for Excellence in Numismatic writing, 2005), Token and Medal Soc. (life, pres. 1976-78, editor jour. 1964-68, Disting. Svc. award 1966, 80), Numismatists of Wis. (life, pres. 1974-76, Meritorious Svc. award 1972), Soc. Internat. Numismatics (award of excellence 1981), Blue Ridge Numismatic Assn. (life, hall of fame 1994), Tex. Numismatic Assn. (life, hall of fame 1993), Ind. State Numismatic Assn. (life, founders award 1993), Ctrl. States Numismatic Soc. (life, medal of merit 1984), Iola Lions (Melvin Jones fellow 1996). Home: N 2253 Butternut Rd Waupaca WI 54981 Office: 105 N Main St Iola WI 54945-0001 Office Phone: 715-445-5050. Personal E-mail: mish@athenet.net.

MISKOWSKI, LEE R., retired automotive executive; b. Stevens Point, Wis., Mar. 27, 1932; s. Paul P. and Marie Grace (Glazer) M.; m. Billie Poulson, 1963; children: Christine, Katherine. BBA, U. Wis., 1954, MBA, 1957. V.p. Ford of Europe Ford Motor Co., Cologne, Germany, 1977-80, gen. mktg. mgr. Ford div. Dearborn, Mich., 1980-83, v.p., gen. mgr. parts and svc. div., 1989-91, v.p., gen. mgr. Lincoln-Mercury div., 1991-94, ret., 1994. Bd. dirs. Wolverine Brass, Inc., U. Wis. MC Found., Bradford Equities. Chmn. Hospice of Mich., 1996-98; vice chmn. Hospice of Mich. Found.; chmn. bd. dirs. Mich. Parkinson Found., Detroit, 1992-94, bd. dirs. Autocraft, 1994-2000. With U.S. Army, 1954-56. Mem. Oakland Hills Country Club. Roman Catholic. Avocations: tennis, golf, reading, travel.

MISSAD, MATTHEW J., lawyer; Gen. counsel, sec. Universal Forest Products, Grand Rapids, Mich., 1985—, v.p. corp. compliance, 1989—, exec. v.p., 1996—. Office: Universal Forest Products 2801 East Beltline, NE Grand Rapids MI 49525 Office Phone: 616-364-6161.

MITAU, LEE R., lawyer, bank executive; b. Oct. 17, 1948; AB cum laude, Dartmouth Coll., 1969; JD magna cum laude, U. Minn., 1972. Bar: Minn. 1972, NY 1973. Law clk. to Hon. George E. MacKinnon US Ct. Appeals (DC cir.), 1972-73; assoc. Cleary, Gottlieb, Steen & Hamilton, 1973—79; ptnr. Oppenheimer, Wolff & Donnelly, 1979—83, Dorsey & Whitney, Mpls., 1983—95, mem. policy com., 1988—99, chmn. corp. dept., 1989—95; exec. v.p., gen. counsel US Bancorp, Mpls., 1995—. Adj. prof. law William Mitchell Coll. Law, 1982—83; bd. dirs. H.B. Fuller Co., St. Paul, 1996—, Graco Inc., Mpls., 1990—, chmn., 2002—. Trustee Mpls. Inst. Arts, Minn. Pvt. Coll. Coun.; bd. govs. Mpls. Club. Office: US Bancorp US Bancorp Ctr 800 Nicollet Mall Minneapolis MN 55402

MITCHELL, BERT BREON, literary translator; b. Salina, Kans., Aug. 9, 1942; s. John Charles and Bernita Maxine (Breon) M.; m. Lynda Diane Fink, July 21, 1965; children: Kieron Breon, Kerry Archer. BA, U. Kans., 1964; PhD, Oxford U., 1968. Asst. prof. German and comparative lit. Ind. U., Bloomington, 1968-71, assoc. prof., 1971-78, prof., 1978—, assoc. dean Coll. Arts and Scis., 1975-77, chmn. comparative lit., 1977-85, dir. Wells Scholars program, 1988-98. Dir. The Lilly Libr., 2001—; chair adv. coun. Banff Internat. Lit. Translation Centre, 2002—. Author: James Joyce and the German Novel, 1922-1933, 1976, Beyond Illustration; The Livre d'Artiste in the Twentieth Century, 1976, The Complete Lithographs of Delacroix's Faust and Manet's The Raven, 1981; editor: Literature and the Other Arts, 1978, Metamorphosis and the Arts, 1979, Paul Morand, Fancy Goods/Open All Night, 1984; translator: Heartstop (Martin Grzimek), 1984, Selected Stories (Siegfried Lenz), 1989, The Musk Deer and Other Stories (Vilas Sarang), 1990, Looking Back (Lou Andreas-Salomé), 1991, Shadowlife (Martin Grzimek), 1991, Laura's Skin (J.F. Federspiel), 1991, The Color of the Snow (Rüdiger Kremer), 1992, Knife Edge (Ralf Rothmann) 1992, In the Kingdom of Enki (Vilas Sarang), 1993, The Silent Angel (Heinrich Böll), 1994, On the Glacier (Jürgen Kross), 1996, The God of Impertinence (Sten Nadolny), 1997, The Mad Dog (Heinrich Böll), 1997, The Trial (Franz Kafka), 1998, Morenga (Uwe Timm), 2003, Spies (Marcel Beyer), 2005. Rhodes scholar, 1964-68; Danforth fellow, 1964-68, Woodrow Wilson fellow, 1964, Alexander-von-Humboldt fellow, 1971, Translation fellow Nat. Endowment for Arts, 1989, Mellon fellow U. Tex., 1999; recipient Frederic Bachman Lieber Meml. award for disting. teaching, 1974, hon. citation Columbia Translation Ctr., 1990, Theodore Christian Hoepfner award So. Humanities Rev., 1995, Katharine and Daniel Leab award, 2001, Kurt and Helen Wolf prize for Disting. Translation, 2004. Mem. MLA (chair William Riley Parker prize selection com. 1994), P.E.N., Am. Comparative Lit. Assn., Am. Lit. Translators Assn. (pres. 1985-87, Alta prize for disting. translation 1992), Am. Translators Assn. (com. lit. transl. 1983-84, German Lit. prize for disting. translation 1987, chmn. honors and awards com. 1995. hon. citation for disting. transl. 1999), Nat. Coun. Tchrs. of English (chair com. on comparative and world lit. 1995-98), James Joyce Found., Franz Kafka Soc., Samuel Beckett Soc., So. Comparative Lit. Assn., Brit. Comparative Lit. Assn., Internat. Comparative Lit. Assn., Am. Antiquarian Soc., The Grolier Club. Office: BH657 Indiana U Bloomington IN 47405 E-mail: mitchell@indiana.edu.

MITCHELL, CAMERON M., restaurant executive; b. Columbus, Ohio, June 14, 1963; s. Earnest Edward and Joan (Kellough) M. Assoc. with honors, Culinary Inst. Am., Hyde Park, NY, 1986. Kitchen mgr. Max & Ermas Restaurants, Columbus, Ohio, 1981-84; chef Fifty Five at Crossroads Restaurant, Columbus, 1986-87, gen. mgr., 1989-90; exec. chef Fifty Five on the Blvd., Columbus, 1987, gen. mgr., 1987-89; ops. mgr. Fifty Five Restaurant Grove, Columbus, 1990-2000; prin., owner Cameron Mitchell Restaurants, Columbus, Ohio, 2000—. Dir. 55 Catering, Columbus; trustee Touchstone Cafe Inc., Columbus, 1988-90; alumni rep. Culinary Inst. Am.; chmn. Taste of Nation event, Columbus, 1990. Chmn., founder Core program, 1988—; mem. Downtown Columbus Planning Com., 1988; mem. Make Room Columbus Project. Named Citizen of Yr., Open Shelter, Columbus, 1990. Mem. Am. Culinary Fedn., Nat. Restaurant Assn., Ohio Restaurant Assn., Columbus Chefs Assn. Republican. Avocations: golf, reading, philanthropy, travel, food and wine. Office: Cameron Mitchell Restaurants 515 Park St Columbus OH 43215-2039

MITCHELL, CONNIE, director; m. George Mitchell, Sr.; children: Carlata, George Jr. Tchr. adv. Office Adminstrv./Instrnl. Pers. Detroit Pub. Schs. Dir. Ednl. Enrichment Acad.; mem. bd. dir. Nat. Bd. Profl. Tchg. Standards, 1995—2003. Active Meth. Children's Home Soc. Named Middle Sch. Tchr. of Yr., Newsweek Mag./WDIV-TV, 1994, Tchr. of Yr., Detroit Pub. Schs., 1994; recipient Golden Apple Tchr. award, Wayne County Regional Edn. Svc. Agy. Mem.: Nat. Bd. for Profl. Tchg. Stds. (bd. mem.), Alpha Kappa Alpha. Office: Detroit Pub Schs Schs Ctr Bldg 3031 W Grand Blvd Detroit MI 48202

MITCHELL, EARL WESLEY, clergyman; b. Excelsior Springs, Mo., Mar. 16, 1931; s. Earl Van and Ora Leah (Butterfield) M.; m. Mary Lou Bell, June 8, 1956; children: Susan Yvonne, Randall Bruce. Ordained to ministry Christian Union Ch., 1971. Min. Vibbard (Mo.) Christian Union Ch., 1962-69, Liberty (Mo.) Christian Ch., 1969—77, Barwick Christian Union Ch., Cameron, Mo., 1977-80, Independence (Mo.) Christian Union Ch., 1980—95; assoc. pastor Flack Meml. Christian Union Ch., Excelsior Springs, Mo., 1995—. Former mem. state exec. bd. Christian Union Mo., 1995-98; area rep. Mo. Christian Union USA; former mem. gen. exec. bd., former editor C.U. Witness. Sgt. USAF, 1951-55. Avocations: music, woodworking, painting, photography. Home and Office: 618 Henrie St Excelsior Springs MO 64024-2022

MITCHELL, EDWARD JOHN, economist, retired educator; b. Newark, Aug. 15, 1937; s. Edward Charles and Gladys (Werner) M.; m. Mary Josephine Osborne, June 14, 1958; children: Susan, Edward. BA summa cum laude, Bowling Green State U., 1960; postgrad., Oxford U., Eng., 1963-64; PhD in Econs., U. Pa., Eng., 1966. Lectr. in econs. Wharton Sch., U. Pa., 1964-65; economist Rand Corp., 1965-68; mem. Inst. Advanced Study, Princeton, NJ, 1968-69; sr. economist Pres.'s Council Econ. Advs., Washington, 1969-72; vis. assoc. prof. econs. Cornell U., 1972-73; assoc. prof. bus. econs. U. Mich., 1973-75, prof., 1975-88, prof. emeritus bus. econs. and pub. policy, 1988—; pres. Edward J. Mitchell Inc., Ann Arbor, 1977—94. Dir. nat. energy project Am. Enterprise Inst., 1974-76; pres. Fountainhead Investment Co., 1984—94. Author: U.S. Energy Policy: A Primer, 1974, Dialogue on World Oil, 1974, Financing the Energy Industry, 1975, Vertical Integration of the Oil Industry, 1976, The Deregulation of Natural Gas, 1983; contbr. articles to profl. jours. Home: 310 Penny Ln Santa Barbara CA 93108-2601 Office: Grad Sch Bus U Mich Ann Arbor MI 48109 Personal E-mail: ejmitchell@xtra.co.nz.

MITCHELL, GARY R., former state official; b. Dickinson County, Kans. BS in Econs. and History, Kans. State U., 1978, postgrad. Chief of staff U.S. Ho. of Reps. Com. on Agr.; mem. staff Senator Pat Roberts U.S. Ho. of Reps.; sec. Kans. Dept. Health and Environment, Topeka, 1997-99. Office: Kans Dept Health and Environment 900 SW Jackson St Rm 620 Topeka KS 66612-1220

MITCHELL, GERALD LEE, state legislator; b. Jacksonville, Ill., June 18, 1942; m. Janet L. Conway; 3 children. BS, Eureka Coll., 1968; MS, Ill. State U., 1974; EdS, Western Ill. U., 1992. Tchr., coach Eureka Mid. Sch., 1968-70; prin. elem. K-8 schs. Mt. Sterling, Ill., 1975-81; prin. Rock Falls Jr. H.S., 1983; asst. prin. Dixon H.S., 1986; prin. elem., mid., and h.s., 1974-86; dir. evaluation and edn. svc. Dixon Dist., 1986-92; asst. supt., 1992-93; from ctrl. adminstrn. through supt. schs. Dixon Cmty. Unit Schs. Dist. # 170, 1994; supt., 1993-94; mem. Ill. Ho. of Reps., 1995—. Mem. ASCD, Nat. Staff Devel., Coun., Am. Assn. Sch. Adminstrs., Ill. Assn. Sch. Bd. Address: 100 E 5th St Rock Falls IL 61071-1780 Office: 209-N Stratton Office Bldg Springfield IL 62706

MITCHELL, JAMES EDWARD, physician, educator; b. Chgo., June 19, 1947; s. James Edward and Elizabeth Latimer M.; m. Karen Antrim, June 14, 1969; children: James, Katherine. BA, Ind. U., 1968; MD, Northwestern U., 1972. Diplomate Am. Bd. Psychiatry Neurology. Intern Indpls. U., Mpls., 1972—73; resident U. Minn., Mpls., 1973—76, from asst. prof. to prof., 1979-90, prof., 1990-96; prof., chmn. dept. neuroscience sch. medicine & health sci. U. N.D., Fargo, 1996—. Pres., scientific dir. Neuropsychiat. Rsch. Inst., Fargo, 1996—. Named Tchr. of Yr., N.D. Psychiat. Residents Assn., 1997-98, 98-99. Fellow Am. Psychiat. Assn., Am. Assn. Social Psychiatry; mem. Acad. Eating Disorders (pres. 1999-2000), Eating Disorders Rsch. Soc. (sec.-treas. 1995—). Avocations: canoeing, art, travel. Office: Neuropsychiat Rsch Inst PO Box 1415 700 1st Ave S Fargo ND 58107 Office Phone: 701-293-1335. Fax: 701-293-3226. E-mail: mitchell@medicine.nodak.edu.

MITCHELL, JAMES W., state official, former state legislator; b. Springfield, Mo., June 30, 1950; s. James Robert and Shirley (Sharp) M.; m. Terri Lea Starmer; 1 child, Mona. BA, Drury Coll., 1973, MA, 1081. Pres. Mitchell Bros. Farms, Richland, Mo., 1980-86; owner, mgr. Jim Mitchell Ins. Agy., Richland, 1984—; mem. Mo. Ho. of Reps., Jefferson City, 1983—; bd. dirs. State Bd. of Probation and Parole, Mo., 1997—. Alderman City of Richland, 1978-83; bd. dirs. Mo. Ozarks Econ. Opportunity Corp., 1983—; pres. Cmty. Assn., 1976-79. Recipient award of merit Mo. Tchrs. Assn., 1979, Meritorious Svc. award St. Louis Globe Dem., 1984-86; named Outstanding Rural Freshman Legislator, 1982-84. Mem. NRA, Pulaski County Landowners Assn., Phi Delta Kappa, Sigma Nu. Republican.

MITCHELL, JOHN LAURIN AMOS, biological science educator; b. Lincoln, Nebr., July 18, 1944; s. William A. and Ruth Chilla (Cobbey) M.; m. Gail Ann Kurtz, July 13, 1968; children: Jill, Todd. BA, Oberlin Coll., 1966; PhD, Princeton U., 1970. Postdoctoral fellow McArdle Inst. Cancer Rsch., Madison, Wis., 1970-73; asst. prof. No. Ill. U., DeKalb, 1973-78, assoc. prof., prof., 1983—; dir. Ctr. Biochem. Biophys. Rsch., 1997—. Inventor in field; contbr. articles to profl. jours.

MITCHELL, LEE MARK, private equity investor, executive; b. Albany, NY, Apr. 16, 1943; s. Maurice B. and Mildred (Roth) M.; m. Barbara Lee Anderson, Aug. 27, 1966; children: Mark, Matthew. AB, Wesleyan U., 1965; JD, U. Chgo., 1968. Bar: Ill. 1968, D.C. 1969, U.S. Supreme Ct. 1972. Assoc. Leibman, Williams, Bennett, Baird & Minow, Chgo. and Washington, 1968-72, Sidley & Austin, Washington, 1972-74, ptnr., 1974-84, 92-94; exec. v.p. and gen. counsel Field Enterprises, Inc., Chgo., 1981-83, pres., CEO, 1983-84, Field Corp., 1984-92; prin. Golder, Thoma, Cressey, Rauner, Inc., Chgo., 1994-98; mng. ptnr. Thoma Cressey Bravo, Inc., Chgo., 1998—. Chmn. Chgo. Stock Exch., Inc., 2000—04. Author: Openly Arrived At, 1974, With the Nation Watching, 1979; co-author: Presidential Television, 1973. Bd. visitors U. Chgo. Law Sch., 1984—86, Medill Sch. Journalism, Northwestern U., 1984—91; pres. bd. govs. Chgo. Met. Planning Coun., 1988—91; mem. midwest regional adv. bd. Inst. Internat. Edn., 1987—99; trustee Ravinia Festival Assn., 1989—97, Northwestern U., orthwestern Meml. Hosp.; U.S. del. Brit. Legis. Conf. on Govt. and Media, Ditchley Park, England, 1974; adv. com. LWV Presdl. Debates, Washington, 1979—80, 1982; vice chair Chgo. Met. Planning Coun., 1999—2005, chair, 2005—. Mem.: Econ. Mid-Am. Club, ABA, Comml. Club Chgo. Home: 135 Maple Hill Rd Glencoe IL 60022-1252 Office: Thoma Cressey Bravo Inc Sears Tower Ste 9200 233 S Wacker Dr Chicago IL 60606-6331 Business E-Mail: lmitchell@tcb.com.

MITCHELL, NED, state legislator; Mayor City of Sesser (Ill.); auditor Ill. Comptroller, 1977—; mem. Ill. Senate, Springfield, 1999—. Democrat. Address: 112 E Market St Christopher IL 62822-1742

MITCHELL, ORLAN E., clergyman, academic administrator; b. Eldora, Iowa, Mar. 13, 1933; s. Frank E. and Alice G. (Brown) M.; m. Verlene J. Huehn, June 10, 1952; children: Jolene R., Stephen M., Nadene A., Timothy M., Mark E. BA, Grinnell Coll., 1955; B.D., Yale U., 1959, M.Div., 1965; D.Min., San Francisco Theol. Sem., 1976. Ordained to ministry United Ch. of Christ, 1959; pastor chs. Sheridan Twp., Iowa, 1954-55, New Preston, Conn., 1956-59, Clarion, Iowa, 1959-69, Yankton, SD, 1969-77; pres. Yankton (S.D.) Coll., 1977-96; conf. minister Iowa Conf. United Ch. Christ; ret., 1996. Cons. in field. Mem. Sch. Bd., Clarion, Iowa, 1965-69, mem., Yankton, S.D., 1973-77, pres., 1976; bd. dirs. Lewis and Clark Mental Health Center. Mem. S.D. Found. Pvt. Colls., S.D. Assn. Pvt. Colls., Colls. of Mid-Am. Lodges: Kiwanis; Masons. Democrat. Mem. United Ch. Of Christ. Office: 725 Park St Grinnell IA 50112-2235 Personal E-mail: orlanm@pcpartner.net.

MITSCHER, LESTER ALLEN, chemist, educator; b. Detroit, Aug. 20, 1931; s. Lester and Mary Athelda (Pounder) M.; m. Betty Jane McRoberts, May 29, 1953; children: Katrina, Kurt, Mark. BS, Wayne U., 1953, PhD, 1958. Rsch. scientist, group leader Lederle Labs., Pearl River, NY, 1958-67; prof. Ohio State U., Columbus, 1967-75, U. Kans., Lawrence, 1975—, chmn. dept. medicinal chemistry, 1975-92; intersearch prof. Victorian Coll. of Pharmacy, Monash U., Melbourne, Australia, 1975—. Author: (with D. Lednicer) The Organic Chemistry of Drug Synthesis, Vol. 1, 1976, Vol. 2, 1980, Vol. 3, 1984, Vol. 4, 1990, The Chemistry of the Tetracycline Antibiotics, 1978; co-author: The Green Tea Book, 1997; editor-in-chief Medicinal Research Reviews, 1995-99; contbr. over 250 articles to profl. jours. Recipient Disting. Alumnus award Sch. Pharmacy, Wayne State U., 1980, 97, Rsch. Achievement award Acad. Pharm. Scis., 1980, 97, Volweiler Rsch. award Am. Assn. Colls. Pharmacy, 1985, Higuchi-Simmons award U. Kans., 1986. Fellow AAAS; mem. Am. Soc. Pharmacognosy (pres. 1992-93, Rsch. Achievement award 2007), Am. Chem. Soc. (former chmn. councilor medicinal chemistry divsn., Bristol-Myers Smissman rsch. award 1989, Med. Chemistry award 2000, Medicinal Chemistry Hall of Fame medicinal chemistry divsn. 2007), Japanese Antibiotics Assn., Soc. Heterocyclic Chemistry, Internat. Orgn. for Chemistry in Developing Countries (steering com.). Presbyterian. Office: Dept Medicinal Chemistry U Kans Lawrence KS 66045 Office Phone: 785-864-4562. Business E-Mail: lmitscher@ku.edu.

MITSEFF, CARL, lawyer; b. Detroit, Nov. 16, 1928; s. Frank H. and Katherine (Schaffer) M.; m. Phyllis Schlitters, June 28, 1952; children: C. Randall, Bradley Scott, Julie, Emily, Faye. BS, Wayne State U., 1952, LL.B., 1955. Bar: Mich. 1956. Practiced in Detroit, 1956—; staff atty. Burroughs Corp., 1955-60; mem. firm LeVasseur, Mitseff, Egan & Capp, 1960-80, Mitseff & Baril, 1980-85, Fitzgerald, Hodgman, Cox, Cawthoren & McMahon, 1986-90, Cox & Hodgman, 1990—. Spl. asst. atty. gen. State of Mich.; lectr. in field. Named to Mich. Workers Compensation Hall of Fame, 2000. Mem. ABA, State Bar Mich., Internat. Assn. Ins. Counsel, Internat. Assn. Indsl. Accident Bds. and Commns., Detroit Athletic Club (bd. dirs.), Beavers (pres.), Exec. Club (pres.), Bus. Round Table (chmn.), Lochmoor Club, Grosse Pointe Yacht Club, Pi Kappa Alpha, Delta Theta Phi. Home: 612 N Brys Dr Grosse Pointe Woods MI 48236-1247 Office: 1001 Woodward Ave Ste 1000 Detroit MI 48226-1904 Office Phone: 313-963-3210. Personal E-mail: c.mitseff@aol.com.

MITSTIFER, DOROTHY IRWIN, honor society administrator; b. Gaines, Pa., Aug. 17, 1932; d. Leonard Robert and Laura Dorothy (Crane) Irwin; m. Robert Mitchell Mitsifer, June 17, 1956 (dec. Aug. 1984); children: Kurt Michael, Brett Robert. BS, Mansfield U., 1954; MEd, Pa. State U., 1972, PhD, 1976. Cert. home economist. Tchr. Tri-County High Sch., Canton, Pa., 1954-56, Loyalsock Twp. Sch. Dist., Williamsport, Pa., 1956-63; exec. dir. Kappa Omicron Phi, Williamsport, Pa., 1964-86, Kappa Omicron Phi, Omicron Nu, Haslett, Mich., 1986-90, Kappa Omicron Nu, East Lansing, Mich., 1990—. Prof. continuing edn. Pa. State U., University Park, 1976-80; prof. Mansfield (Pa.) U., 1980-86, pres.'s intern, 1984-86. Editor Kappa Omicron Nu Forum, 1986—; contbr. articles to profl. jours. Pres., bd. dirs. Profl. Devel. Ctr. Adv. Bd., Vocat. Edn., Pa. State U., 1980-86. Mem. ASCD, Am. Home Econs. Assn., Mich. Home Econs. Assn. (exec. dir. 1986-96), Am. Vocat. Assn., Am. Soc. Assn. Execs., Assn. Coll. Honor Socs. (sec.-treas. 1976—), Coll. Edn. Alumni Soc. Pa. State U. (pres. 1986-88, bd. dirs. 1980-90), Kappa Delta Pi. Avocations: sewing, camping, fishing. Home: 1425 Somerset Close St East Lansing MI 48823-2435 Office: Kappa Omicron Nu 4990 Northwind Dr Ste 140 East Lansing MI 48823-5031 Office Phone: 517-351-8335. E-mail: dmitstifer@kon.org, dmitstifer@achsnatl.org.

MITTEN, MATTHEW JOHN, law educator, lawyer; b. Tiffin, Ohio, Apr. 26, 1959; BA in Econs., Ohio State Univ., 1981; JD magna cum laude, Univ. Toledo, 1984. Bar: Ga. 1984. Atty. antitrust and intellectual property law Kilpatrick Stockton LLP, Atlanta, 1984—89; prof. law So. Tex. Coll. Law, Houston, 1990—99; prof. law, dir. Nat. Sports Law Inst. Marquette U. Law Sch., Milw., 1999—, assoc. dean academic affairs, 2002—04. Sr. fellow U. Melbourne Law Sch., 2005—06; faculty, comparative sports law TC Beirne Sch. Law, Univ. Queensland, Brisbane, Australia; vis. prof. Univ. Toledo Coll. Law; vis. lectr., sports medicine Univ. Tenn. Grad. Sch. Medicine; spkr. in field; cons. in field. Note and comment editor U. Toledo Law Review; contbr. articles i profl. jours. and chapters in books; co-author: Sports Law and Regulation-Cases, Materials and Problems, 2005. Chair NCAA Com. Competitive Safeguards and Med. Aspects Sports, 2002—05. Mem.: ABA (entertainment and sports law), Ct. Arbitration Sport, Am. Assn. Law Sch. (past chmn., sect. Law & Sports), Sports Lawyers Assn. (bd. dir.), Order of the Coif. Office: Marquette University Law School Sensenbrenner Hall PO Box 1881 Milwaukee WI 53201-1881 Office Phone: 414-288-7494. Business E-Mail: matt.mitten@marquette.edu.

MITYAS, SHERIF, management consultant; V.p., Midwest region AT Kearney, Inc., Chgo., also mng. ptnr., Midwest region. Mem.: Am. Lung Assn. (Jr. Achievement), Comml. Club (mem. civic com.). Office: AT Kearney Inc 222 W Adams St Chicago IL 60606

MIXON, AARON MALACHI, III, medical products executive; b. May 22, 1940; m. Barbara Weber; 2 children. BA, Harvard U., 1962, MBA, 1968. CEO, chmn. Invacare Corp., Elyria, Ohio, 1979—. Chmn. bd. trustees Cleve. Clinic Found. Recipient Alumni Achievement award, Harvard Bus. Sch., 2007. Office: Invacare Corp 1 Invacare Way PO Box 4028 Elyria OH 44036-2125 Office Phone: 440-329-6000. Office Fax: 440-366-9008.

MIYAMOTO, RICHARD TAKASHI, otolaryngologist; b. Feb. 2, 1944; s. Dave Norio and Haruko (Okano) Miyamoto; m. Cynthia VanderBurgh, June 17, 1967; children: Richard Christopher, Geoffrey Takashi. BS cum laude, Wheaton Coll., 1966; MD, U. Mich., 1970; MS in Otology, U. So. Calif., 1978; D Engring. (hon.), Rose Hulman Inst. Tech., 2001. Diplomate Am. Bd. Otolaryngology. Intern Butterworth Hosp., Grand Rapids, Mich., 1970—71, resident in surgery, 1971—72; resident in otolaryngology Ind. U. Sch. Medicine, Indpls., 1972—75; fellow in otology and neurotology St. Vincent Hosp. and Otologic Med. Group, LA, 1977—78; asst. prof. Ind. U. Sch. Medicine, Indpls., 1978—83, assoc. prof., 1983—88, prof., 1988—, chmn., 1987—, chief otology and neurotology dept. otology, head and neck surgery, 1982—, chmn. dept. otolaryngology, 1987—, Arilla DeVault prof. otolaryngology, 1991; chief otolaryngology, head and neck surgery Wishard Meml. Hosp., 1979—2002. Mem. editl. bd.: Laryngoscope, Am. Jour. Otology, Otolaryngology -Head and Neck Surgery, European Archives of Oto-Rhino-Laryngology, Anales de Otorrinolaringologia Mexicana; contbr. articles tto profl. jours. Mem. adv. coun. Nat. Inst. Deafness and other Commication Disorders, 1989—94, 2002—; mem. adv. bd. Alexander Graham Bell Assn. for the Deaf, The Ear Found., St. Joseph Inst. Deaf, chmn., 2004—. Maj. USAF, 1975—77. Fellow: ACS, Am. Auditory Soc. (mem. exec. com. 1985—2003), Am. Otological, Rhinological and Laryngological Soc. (v.p. mid. sect. 2002—03), Am. Acad. Otolaryngology (gov. 1982—); mem.: Assn. Acad. Depts. in Otolaryngology-Head and Neck Surgery (sec.-treas. 2002—04, pres.-elect 2004—06), Deafness Rsch. Inst. (bd. dirs., pres. Centurion group, comm. com.), Inst. of Medicine of NAS, Am. Neurotology Soc. (pres.-elect 1999—2000, pres. 2000—01), Collegium Oto-Laryntologicum Amecitiae Sacrum, Royal Soc. Medicine London, Assn. Rsch. Otol. (pres.-elect 2000—01, pres. 2001—), Am. Otol. Soc. (coun. 1992—), Otosclerosis Study Group (coun. 1993—), NY Acad. Scis., Am. Acad. Pediats., Marines Meml. Assn., Cosmos Club of Washington, Alpha Omega Alpha (pres. Ind. chpt. 2003—), Wheaton Coll. Scholastic Honor Soc., Psi Iota Xi. Office: Ind U Sch Med 702 Barnhill Dr Indianapolis IN 46202-5128

MIZRUCHI, MARK SHELDON, sociology professor, business administration professor; b. New Haven, Dec. 10, 1953; s. Ephraim Harold and Ruth M.; m. Katherine Teves, June 1981 (div. June 1995); 1 child, Joshua; m. Gail Schulman, Nov. 2006. BA, Washington U., 1975; MA, SUNY, Stony Brook, 1977, PhD, 1980. Statis. analyst Albert Einstein Coll. of Medicine, Bronx, NY, 1980-83, asst. prof. psychiatry, 1981-87, supr. statis. svcs., 1983-87; asst. prof. sociology Columbia U., YC, 1987-89, assoc. prof. sociology, 1989-91; prof. sociology and bus. adminstrn. U. Mich., Ann Arbor, 1991—. Author: The American Corporate Network, 1904-1974, 1982, The Structure of Corporate Political Action, 1992; editor (with M. Schwartz) Intercorporate Relations, 1987. Recipient Presdl. Young Investigator award NSF, 1988-93, Excellence in Edn. award U. Mich., 2004; grantee NSF, 1987-88, 93-95, 99-2000, 2002-03; invited fellow Ctr. for Advanced Study in the Behavioral Scis., 1989. Mem. Am. Sociol. Assn., Acad. Mgmt., Internat. Network for Social Network Analysis, Sociol. Rsch. Assn. Office: Dept Sociology Univ Mich Ann Arbor MI 48109-1382 Office Phone: 734-764-7444. Office Fax: 734-763-6887. Business E-Mail: mizruchi@umich.edu.

MLOCEK, SISTER FRANCES ANGELINE, financial executive; b. River Rouge, Mich., Aug. 4, 1934; d. Michael and Suzanna (Bloch) M. BBA, U. Detroit, 1958; MBA, U. Mich., 1971. CPA, Mich. Bookkeeper Allen Park (Mich.) Furniture, 1949-52, Gerson's Jewlery, Detroit, 1952-53; jr. acct. Meyer Dickman, CPA, Algaze, Staub & Bowman, CPAs, Detroit, 1953-58; acct., internal auditor Sisters, Servants of Immaculate Heart of Mary Congregation, Monroe, Mich., 1959-66, asst. gen. treas., 1966-73, gen. treas., 1973-76; internal auditor for parishes Archdiocese of Detroit, 1976-78; asst. to exec. dir. Leadership Conf. of Women, Silver Spring, Md., 1978-83; dir. of fin. Nat. Conf. of Cath. Bishops/U.S. Cath. Conf., Washington, 1989-94; CFO Sisters Servants of the Immaculate Heart of Mary, Monroe, Mich., 1994—. Trustee SSIHM Charitable Trust, Monroe, 1988—. Author: (manual) Leadership Conference of Women Religious/Conference of Major Superiors of Men, 1981. Treas. Zonta Club of Washington Found., Washington, 1983-88, pres., 1992-93; bd. dirs. Our

Lady of Good Counsel High Sch., Wheaton, Md., 1983-89. Mem. AICPA, D.C. Inst. CPAs (mem. not-for-profit com. 1992-94, CFOs com. 1990-94. Democrat. Roman Catholic. Office: Sisters Servants Immaculate Heart Mary 610 W Elm Ave Monroe MI 48162-7909

MOAWAD, ATEF, obstetrician, gynecologist, educator; b. Beni Suef, Egypt, Dec. 2, 1935; came to U.S., 1959; s. Hanna and Baheya (Hunein) M.; m. Ferial Fouad Abdel Malek, Aug. 22, 1966; children: John, Joseph, James. Student, Cairo U. Sch. Sci., 1951-52; MB, BCh, Cairo U. Sch. Medicine, 1957; MS in in Pharmacology, Jefferson Med. Coll., 1963. Diplomate Am. Bd. Ob-Gyn; licentiate Med. Coun Can. Rotating intern Cairo U. Hosp., 1958-59, Elizabeth (N.J.) Gen. Hosp., 1959-60; resident in ob-gyn. Jefferson Med. Coll. Hosp., Phila., 1961-64; lect. dept. pharmacology U. Alta., Can., 1966; asst. prof. dept. ob-gyn. and pharmacology U. Alta., Can., 1967-70, assoc. prof., 1970-72; assoc. prof. dept. ob-gyn. and pharmacology U. Chgo., 1972-75, prof. dept. ob-gyn. and pediatrics, 1975—, co-dir. perinatal ctr., 1974-80; obstetrician-gynecologist, chief obstetrics, co-dir. perinatal ctr. The Chgo. Lying-in Hosp. U. Chgo., 1980—, Blum Riese prof. ob-gyn., chief maternal fetal medicine, 2001—, interim chair dept. ob-gyn., 2002—. Vis. investigator dept. ob-gyn. U. Lund, Sweden, 1969. Co-author book chpts., jour. articles. Mem. perinatal adv. com. Chgo. March of Dimes, 1977—, health profl. adv. com., 1983—; mem. perinatal adv. bd. com. State of Ill., 1978—; mem. Chgo. Maternal Child Health Adv. Com., chmn., 1991—; mem. Mayor's Adv. Com. on Infant Mortality, 1991—. Fellow Jefferson Med. Coll., 1960-61, Case Western Res. U., 1964-65; grantee Brush Found., 1966-67, Maternal Fetal Medicine Units Network NIH, 1994; recipient award Phila. Obstet. Soc., 1964, Disting. Tchg. award Am. Profs. Gynecology and Obstetrics, 1993, DeLee Humanitarian award, 2003. Fellow Am. Coll. Ob-Gyn. (Purdue-Frederick award 1978), Royal Coll. Surgeons (Can.); mem. Soc. for Gynecol Investigation, Pharmacol. Soc. Can., Am. Gynecol. and Obstet. Soc., Soc. Perinatal Obstetricians, N.Y. Acad. Scis., Chgo. Gynecol. Soc., Can. Med. Assn., Christian Med. Soc., Edmonton Obstetrics Soc. Office: U Chgo Dept Ob-Gyn 5841 S Maryland Ave MC 2050 Chicago IL 60637-1463 E-mail: amoawad@babies.bsd.uchicago.edu.

MOBERG, DAVID OSCAR, sociology educator; b. Montevideo, Minn., Feb. 13, 1922; s. Fred Ludwig and Anna E. (Sundberg) M.; m. Helen H. Heitzman, Mar. 16, 1946 (dec. Oct. 16, 1992); children: David Paul, Lynette, Jonathan, Philip; m. Marlys Taege, July 23, 1994. AA, Bethel Jr. Coll., 1942; AB, Seattle Pacific Coll., 1947; MA, U. Wash., 1949; PhD, U. Minn., 1952. Assoc. instr. U. Wash., Seattle, 1948-49; faculty Bethel Coll., St. Paul, 1949-68, prof. sociology, 1959-68, chmn. dept. social scis., 1952-68; prof. sociology Marquette U., Milw., 1968-91, prof. emeritus, 1991—, chmn. dept. sociology and anthropology, 1968-77. Cons. Nat. Liberty Found., 1970-71, Fetzer Inst., 1995-96; rsch. cons. Internat. Luth. Women's Missionary League, 1997-99, Bonnie Walker & Assocs., 1997-99; cons. Nat. Interfaith Coalition on Aging, 1973-75, mem. nat. adv. bd., 1980-89; guest rschr. Sociology of Religion Inst., Stockholm, Sweden, summer 1978; adj. prof. San Francisco Theol. Sem., 1964-73, McCormick Theol. Sem., 1975-78, 81-82; vis. prof. U. So. Calif., 1979, Princeton Theol. Sem., 1979, So. Bapt. Theol. Sem., 1982, Soc. for Care of the Handicapped in the Gaza Strip of Palestine, 1995; mem. adv. bd. Ecumenical Ministry with Mature Adults, 1983-92; resource scholar Christianity Today Inst., 1985—; mem. bd. adv. editors Haworth Pastoral Press, 1998—. Author: The Church as A Social Institution, 1962, 2d edit. 1984, (with Robert M. Gray) The Church and the Older Person, 1962, 2d edit., 1977, Inasmuch: Christian Social Responsibility in the 20th Century, 1965, White House Conference on Aging: Spiritual Well-Being Background and Issues, 1971, The Great Reversal: Evangelism and Social Concern, 1972, 2d edit, 1977, 3d edit., 2007, Wholistic Christianity, 1985, Woman of God: An Assessment of the Spirituality of Women in the LCMS, 1999; also articles, chpts. in symposia.; editor: International Directory of Religious Information Systems, 1971, Spiritual Well-Being: Sociological Perspectives, 1979, Rev. Religious Research, 1968-72, Jour. Am. Sci. Affiliation, 1962-64, Adris Newsletter, 1971-76, Aging and Spirituality: Spiritual Dimensions of Aging Theory, Research, Practice, and Policy, 2001; co-editor Research in the Social Scientific Study of Religion, 1986-04; assoc. editor: Social Compass, 1968-2003; mem. editl. bd. Christian Univ. Press, 1979-84, Perspectives on Sci. and Christian Faith, 1988—, Jour. on Religion, Spirituality and Aging, 2006—; cons. editor Calif. Sociologist, 1982-96. Fulbright lectr. U. Groningen, Netherlands, 1957-58, Fulbright lectr. Muenster U., West Germany, 1964-65. Fellow Am. Sci. Affiliation (editor jour. 1962-64, publs. com. 1984-91, social ethics com. 1985-88, program chair 1995-96), Gerontol. Soc. Am.; mem. Am. Sociol. Assn., Internat. Sociol. Assn. (sociology of religion rsch. com. 1972—), Wis. Sociol. Assn. (pres. 1969-71), Midwest Sociol. Assn. (Wis. bd. dirs. 1971-73), Assn. Devel. Religious Info. Sys. (coord. ADRIS 1971—98, editor ADRIS newsletter 1971-76), Religious Rsch. Assn. (editor Rev. Religious Rsch. 1968-72, contbg. editor 1973-77, assoc. editor 1983-2000, bd. dirs. 1959-61, 68-72, pres. 1981-82, H. Paul Douglass lectr. 1986), Assn. for Sociology of Religion (exec. coun. 1971-73, pres. 1976-77), Soc. for Sci. Study Religion (exec. coun. 1971-74, sr. editl. cons. SSSR-RRA History Project 1995-99), Evangelicals for Social Action (planning com. 1973-75), Christian Sociol. Soc. (steering com. 1973-81, newsletter lit. reviewer 1981-93), Family Rsch. Coun. (assoc. 1985-88, rsch. network 1989-98), Internat Rsch. Found. Devel. (adv. bd. 1994-), Psychologists Interested in Religious Issues (profl. affiliate 1984-99), Univ. Faculty for Life, Midwest Coun. Social Rsch. on Aging (fellow 1961-64, 87—), Am. Soc. Aging, Village at Manor Pk. Ethics Com., Forum on Religion, Spirituality and Aging, Fairview Elder Enterprises (bd. dirs. 1989—, mem. profl. cons. com. for clin. pastoral edn. 2005—). Home and Office: 7120 W Dove Ct Milwaukee WI 53223-2766

MOBLEY, EMILY RUTH, library director, educator, dean; b. Valdosta, Ga., Oct. 1, 1942; d. Emmett and Ruth (Johnson) M. AB in Edn., U. Mich., 1964, AM in Libr. Sci., 1967, postgrad., 1973-76. Tchr. Ecorse (Mich.) Pub. Schs., 1964-65; adminstrv. trainee Chrysler Corp., Highland Park, Mich., 1965-66, engring. libr., 1966-69; libr. II Wayne State U., Detroit, 1969-72, libr. III, 1972-75; staff asst. GM Rsch. Labs. Libr., Warren, Mich., 1976-78, supr. reader svcs., 1978-81; libr. dir. GMI Engring. & Mgmt. Inst., Flint, Mich., 1982-86; assoc. dir. for pub. svcs. & collection devel., assoc. prof. libr. sci. Purdue U. Librs., West Lafayette, Ind., 1986-89, acting dir. librs., assoc. prof. libr. sci., 1989, dean librs., prof. libr. sci., 1989—2004; Esther Ellis Norton Disting. Prof. Libr. Sci. Purdue U., West Lafayette, Ind., 1997—. Adj. lectr. U. Mich. Sch. Libr. Sci., Ann Arbor, 1974-75, 83-86; grants reader Libr. of Mich., 1980-81; project dir. Mideastern Mich. Region Libr. Cooperation, 1984-86; cons. Libr. Coop. of Macomb, 1985-86, Clark-Atlanta U., 1990-91; search com. for new dir. of libr. Smithsonian Instn., 1988; mem. GM Pub. Affairs Subcom. on Introducing Minorities to Engring.; presenter in field. Author: Special Libraries at Work, 1984; mem. editl. bd. Reference Svcs. Rev., 1989-2004, Infomanage, 1993-97. Corp. vis. com. for librs. MIT, 1990-2004, Carnegie-Mellon U., 1998—; mem. Ind. Statewide Libr. Automation Task Force, 1989-90; state tech. strategy subcom. on info. tech. and telecomms. Ind. Corp. for Sci. & Tech., 1989; nat. adv. com. Libr. of Congress, 1988; trustee Libr. of Mich., 1983-86, v.p., 1986, long range plan com., 1979-82, task force on document access and delivery, 1977-79; info. project mem. Rep. Nat. Conv., 1980; bd. dirs. Small Farms Assn., Southfield, Mich., Lafayette Symphony Orch., YWCA. Recipient Bausch & Lomb award, 1960, Cert. for Outstanding Performance in Acad. Achievement State of Mich. Ho. of Reps., 1976, Spl. Tribute for Outstanding Contbns. Libr. of Mich. Bd. Trustees, 1986, Disting. Alumnus award U. Mich. Sch. Info. & Libr. Studies, 1989; U. Mich. Regents Alumni scholar, 1960-64; CIC doctoral fellow in libr. sci., 1973-76. Mem. ALA (com. on accreditation, subcom. to rev. 1972, standards for accreditation 1988-89, OLOS minority internship com. 1988-89, nominating com. 1992-93, mem. coun. resolutions com. 1993-97), Assn. Coll. & Rsch. Librs. (task force on libr. sch. curriculum 1988-89, com. on profl. edn. 1990-92), Libr. Adminstrn. & Mgmt. Assn., Assn. Rsch. Librs. (bd. dirs. 1990-93), Spl. Librs. Assn. (pres. 1987-88, fellow 1991, com. mem.), Alpha Kappa Alpha, Phi Kappa Phi, Sigma Xi, Iron Key. Office: Purdue U Librs Stewart Ctr Lafayette IN 47907 Business E-Mail: emobley@purdue.edu.

MOBLEY, TONY ALLEN, foundation administrator, former dean, recreation educator; b. Harrodsburg, Ky., May 19, 1938; s. Cecil and Beatrice (Bailey) M.; m. Betty Weaver, June 10, 1961; 1 child, Derek Lloyd. BS, Georgetown Coll., 1960; MS, Ind. U., 1962, D Recreation, 1965; MRE, So. Sem., Louisville, 1963. Chmn. dept. recreation and pks. Western Ill. U., Macomb, 1965-72, Pa. State U., University Park, 1972-76; prof., chmn. recreation and pks., dean Sch. Health, Phys. Edn. and Recreation Ind. U., Bloomington, 1976—; exec. dir. Ind. U. Found., Bloomington, 2002—. Chair health adv. coun. White River Park Commn., State of Ind., 1979—; v.p Ind. Sports Corp., Indpls., 1983-89; bd. dirs. Nat. Inst. for Fitness and Sport, Indpls., 1984-93; J.B. Nash scholar, lectr. Am. Assn. Leisure and Recreation, Reston, Va., 1985. Contbr. over 50 articles to profl. jours. Bd. dirs. Monroe County YMCA, Bloomington, 1984-88, United Way, Bloomington, 1994—; mem. Gov.'s Coun. for Phys. Fitness and Sport, 1991—. Am. Coun. Edn. adminstrv. internship fellow, N.C. State U., 1970-71. Fellow Am. Acad. Pk. and Recreation Adminstrn. (pres. 1985-86); mem. Nat. Recreation and Pk. Assn. (pres. 1978-79, Nat. Disting. Profl. award 1981), Assn. Rsch., Adminstrn., Profl. Couns. and Socs. (pres. 1986-87, award 1987), Am. Alliance Health, Phys. Edn., Recreation and Dance (Coll. and Univ. Adminstrs. Coun. Honor award 1986, R. Tait McKenzie award 1996), Soc. Pk. and Recreation Edn. (pres. 1974-75, award 1978), Ind. Pk. and Recreation Assn. (Outstanding Profl. award 1985). Avocations: golf, travel. Office: Ind U Found PO Box 500 Bloomington IN 47402

MODIC, STANLEY JOHN, business editor, publisher, retired columnist; b. Fairport Harbor, Ohio, Dec. 29, 1936; s. Frank and Mary (Zakrajsek) M.; m. Albina DiMichele, May 27, 1961; children— Mark Francis, Laurel Marie. BS in Commerce, Ohio U., 1958. Musician, band leader, 1953-58; Reporter The Telegraph, Painesville, Ohio, 1960-63, city editor, 1964-65; asst. editor Steel Mag., Cleve., 1965-67, news editor, 1968-70; mng. editor Industry Week (formerly Steel Mag.), Cleve., 1970-72, exec. editor, 1972, editor, 1972-86, sr. editor, 1986-89; editor-in-chief Purchasing World Mag., 1989-90, Tooling and Prodn. Mag., 1990—93, editor, pub., 1993—99; v.p. Adams Bus. Media, 1999—2002; ret. columist Tooling and Production, 2002—. Mcpl. clk. Fairport Harbor, 1960-61; mem. Fairport Harbor Village Council, 1962-63, pres., 1962-63. Recipient G.D. Crane award Am. Bus. Press, 1991; named Slovenian Man of Yr., Fedn. Slovenian Homes, Cleve., 1998. Mem.: Press Club (pres. Cleve. chpt. 1978—79), Hungarian Culture Club, Am. Slovenian Club (Fairport Harbor) (pres. 2002—05), KC, Elks, Sigma Delta Chi. Home: 5842 Woodhill St Painesville OH 44077-5167 E-mail: smodic@nelsonpub.com.

MODIN, FREDRIK, professional hockey player; b. Sundsvall, Sweden, Oct. 8, 1974; Left wing Brynas IF, Toronto Maple Leafs, 1996—99, Tampa Bay Lightning, 1999—2006, Columbus Blue Jackets, 2006—. Player NHL All-Star Game, 2001. Achievements include being a member of Stanley Cup Champion Tampa Bay Lightning, 2004; being a member of gold medal winning Swedish Hockey Team, Torino Olympics, Italy, 2006. Office: Columbus Blue Jackets Nationwide Arena 200 W ationwide Blvd Columbus OH 43215

MODISETT, JEFFREY A., lawyer, former state attorney general; b. Windfall, Ind., Aug. 10, 1954; s. James Richard and Diana T. Modisett; m. Jennifer Ashworth, June 9, 1990; children: Matthew Hunter Ashworth, Haden Nicholas. BA, UCLA, 1976; MA, Oxford U., Eng., 1978; JD, Yale U., 1981. Bar: Ind., Calif., D.C. Clk. to Hon. R. Peckham U.S. Dist. Ct. (no. dist.) Calif., San Francisco, 1981—82; asst. U.S. atty. Office U.S. Atty. (ctrl. dist.) Calif., LA, 1982—88; issues dir. Evan Bayh for Gov., Indpls., 1988; exec. asst. to gov. State of Ind., Indpls., 1988—90; prosecutor Marion County, Indpls., 1991—94; sr. counsel Ice Miller Donadio & Ryan, Indpls., 1995—96; atty. gen. State of Ind., 1997—2000; dep. CEO, gen. counsel Dem. Nat. Conv., 2000; co-CEO TechNet, Palo Alto, Calif., 2000—01; ptnr. Manatt Phelps & Phillips LLP, 2001—02; mng. ptnr. Bryan Cave LLP, LA, 2002—. Chmn. Gov. Commn. for Drug Free Ind., Indpls., 1989—, Gov. Coun. on Impaired and Dangerous Driving, Indpls., 1989—; pres. Family Advocacy Ctr., Indpls., 1991—94, Hoosier Alliance Against Drugs, Indpls., 1993—96; dir. Cmty. Couns. of Indpls., 1991—93; chmn. Ind. Criminal Justice Inst., Indpls., 1989—90, dir., 1989—; vice chmn. Juvenile Justice and Youth Gang Study Com., Indpls., 1992—94; legal analyst Sta. WTHR-TV, Indpls., 1995—96. Author: Prosecutor's Perspective, 1991—94; editor-in-chief: Yale Jour. Internat. Law, 1980—81. Co-chair Ind. State Dem. Coordinated Campaign, Indpls., 1996. Named Top Lawyer, Indpls. Monthly mag., 1993; named to Sagamore of Wabash, State of Ind., 1995; recipient Spl. Enforcement award, U.S. Customs, 1988, Child Safety Adv. award, Automotive Safety for Children, 1997, STAR Alliance Impact award, 1998, Spirit of Ind. award, Am. Lung Assn., 1999. Mem.: Indpls. Bar Assn., Ind. Bar Assn. Democrat. Avocation: bicycling. Office: Bryan Cave LLP 120 Broadway, Ste 300 Santa Monica CA 90401 Office Phone: 310-576-2370. Office Fax: 310-576-2200. E-mail: jamodisett@bryancave.com.

MOE, ROGER DEANE, former state legislator, secondary education educator; b. Crookston, Minn., June 2, 1944; s. Melvin Truman and Matheldia (Njus) M.; m. Paulette Moe; four children. BS, Mayville State Coll., 1966; student, Moorhead State Coll., 1969, N.D. State U., 1970. Tchr. Ada (Minn.) H.S., 1966—; v.p. Coleman, Christison Advt. Agy.; mem. Minn. Senate from 2nd dist., St. Paul, 1970—2002; majority leader Minn. State Senate, 1981. Chmn. rules and adminstrn. com., mem. ethics and campaign reform, edn., and higher edn. coms., Minn. State Senate. Ward del. Ada, Minn., 1970; state del. Minn. Dem.-Farmer-Labor Conv., 1970. Mem. NEA, Ada Edn. Assn., Jaycees. Dfl. Office: Rt 3 Box 86A Erskine MN 56535-9532

MOE, THOMAS O., lawyer; b. Des Moines, 1938; BA, U. Minn., 1960, LLB, 1963. Bar: Minn. 1963. Ptnr. Dorsey & Whitney LLP, Mpls., 1964-89, chmn., mng. ptnr., 1989-99, chmn., 1999—. Mem. Order of Coif. Office: Dorsey & Whitney 50 S 6th St Ste 1500 Minneapolis MN 55402-1553

MOEDDEL, CARL KEVIN, bishop emeritus; b. Cin., Dec. 28, 1937; s. Carl H. and Florence E. (Pohiking) Moeddel. AB, Athenaeum of Ohio; MA, MDiv., Mt. St. Mary's Sem. Ordained priest Archdiocese of Cin., 1962; asst. pastor St. Louis Ch., Cin., 1963; asst. chancellor Archdiocese of Cin., 1963, asst. treas., 1963—71, vice chancellor, 1975—76, dir. fin., 1978—85, auxiliary bishop, 1993—2007, aux. bishop emeritus, 2007—; pastor St. Peter in Chains Cathedral, 1976—85, St. James of the Valley Parish, 1985; dean Cathedral Deanery, 1976—83; ordained bishop, 1993. Exec. sec. Commn. Ecumenical and Interfaith Rels. Archdiocese of Cin., 1970—76, dir. Continuing Edn. of Priests, 1971—76, vicar Ecumenical and Interfaith Rels, 1973—78, chmn. Commn. Ecumenical and Interfaith Rels., 1973—76, vicar Fin., 1983—86, chmn. Fin. Coun., 1983—86; pres. Ohio Coun. Churches, 1973, chmn. fin. com., 1974—75, chmn. pub. policy com., 1976; pres. Met. Area Religious Coalition of Cin., 1976—77; Episcopal moderator Conf. Cath. Facility Mgmt. Chmn. governing bd. St. Rita Sch. for the Deaf. Roman Catholic. Office: 100 E 8th St Cincinnati OH 45202-2129*

MOEDDEL, MICHAEL J., lawyer; b. Cin., Apr. 6, 1978; BA, Ohio State U., 1999; JD, U. Cin. Coll. Law, 2002. Bar: Ohio 2002, US Dist. Ct. Southern Dist. Ohio 2002. Instr., Pre-Law Elder High Sch.; assoc. Keating Muething & Klekamp PLL, Cin. Commr. Cin. Recreation Commn.; mem., Caddie Classic Com. Evans Scholars; mem., Bd. Dirs. Greater Cin. Sports Corp. Named one of Ohio's Rising Stars, Super Lawyers, 2006. Mem.: Ohio State Bar Assn., Cin. Bar Assn., ABA, Order of Coif. Office: Keating Muething & Klekamp PLL One E Fourth St Ste 1400 Cincinnati OH 45202 Office Phone: 513-579-6400. Office Fax: 513-579-6457.

MOEDRITZER, MARK, lawyer; b. St. Louis, 1960; BA, U. Minn., 1983; JD, U. Mo., 1987. Bar: Mo. 1987. Ptnr. Shook, Hardy & Bacon LLP, Kansas City, Mo. Mem.: ABA, Kansas City Met. Bar Assn. Office: Shook, Hardy & Bacon LLP 2555 Grand Blvd Kansas City MO 64108 Office Phone: 816-559-2317. Office Fax: 816-421-5547. E-mail: mmoedritzer@shb.com.

MOELLER, ROBERT JOHN, management consultant; b. Mpls., July 20, 1938; s. Ben G. and Catheryn D. M.; m. Sharon Lee Holmberg, Sept. 1, 1962; children: Mark Thomas (dec.), Maria Therese. BBA, U. Minn., 1962, MBA, 1965; grad. exec. mgmt. program, Columbia U., 1972; grad. exec. internat. mgmt., Mankato U., 1990. Asst. brand mgr. toiletries Procter & Gamble, Cin., 1965-68; group product mgr. No. div. Am. Can Co., Greenwich, Conn., 1968-71, dir. mktg. Dixie div., 1971-73; v.p. mktg. and sales Tonka Toy Co., Mpls., 1973-77, Toro Co., Mpls., 1977-79, v.p. gen. mgr. outdoor appliance div., 1979-80, v.p. gen. mgr. irrigation div., 1980-84, exec. v.p. internat. and irrigation div., 1984-88; pres., COO Mackay Envelope Corp., Mpls., 1988-90; sr. v.p. mktg. meat sector Cargill, Inc., 1991-94; pres. Moeller Mgmt. Cons., 1994—. Bd. dirs. Vista Info. Solutions, 1992-98. Founding dir. Outward Bound USA, 2005—; founder, dir., trustee Voyageur Outward Bound Sch., 1993-2004, chmn. 2002-04; bd. dirs. State of Minn. Prison Industries, St. Paul, 1984—; commr. Chaska (Minn.) Planning Commn., 1988-98; pres. Dist. 112 Ednl. Found., Chaska, 1987-92; pres. Chaska Civic Theatre, 1978-80; commr. S.W. Metro Transit Commn., 1998—, Jonathan Archtl. Rev. Commn., 1976-78, Mpls. United Way, 1997-98, bd. dirs., 1999-2002. With USN, 1955-61. Recipient One award, 1976, Gold award Houston Film Festival, 1986, Crystal Achievement award for human svcs., Chaska, 1996. Avocations: skiing, sailing, tennis, music, golf.

MOELLER, WILLIAM E., cement, oil and gas company executive; b. 1942; married. BA, Yale Univ., 1964; MBA, Dartmouth Coll., 1966. V.p., area mgr. No. Ill., Ind., Ea. Wis., Western. Mich. Citicorp, 1966-81, also Citibank internat. supr.; exec. v.p., corp. ptnr. N.Am. banking group First Nat. Bank Chgo., 1981-88; exec. v.p. instl. banking S.E. Banking Corp., 1988; CEO United Healthcare of Ill. Inc., Chgo., 2004—. Office: United Healthcare of Illinois Inc 233 N Michigan Ave Chicago IL 60601

MOEN, RODNEY CHARLES, state legislator, retired naval officer; b. Whitehall, Wis., July 26, 1937; s. Edwin O. and Tena A. (Gunderson) M.; m. Catherine Jean Wolfe, 1959; children: Scott A., Jon C. (dec.), Rodd M., Catherine J., Daniel M. Student, Syracuse U., 1964-65; BA, U. So. Calif., 1972; postgrad., Ball State U., 1975-76. Gen. mgr. We. Wis. Comm. Coop., Independence, 1976-83; mem. Wis. Senate from 31st dist., Madison, 1983—; chair health, utilities, vets. and mil. affairs com. Wis. Senate, 1983—, asst. majority leader. Contbg. editor Govt. Photography, 1970-74. Lt. USN, 1955-76, Vietnam. Home: 18775 Dewey St Whitehall WI 54773-0215 Office: State Capitol PO Box 7882 Madison WI 53707-7882

MOESER, ELLIOTT, principal; Prin. Nicolet HS, Glendale, Ill., 1990—97, dist. adminstr., 1990—. Recipient Blue Ribbon Sch. award, 1990-91. Office: Nicolet HS 6701 Jean Nicolet Rd Glendale WI 53217-3799

MOFFATT, JOYCE ANNE, performing company executive; b. Grand Rapids, Mich., Jan. 3, 1936; d. John Barnard and Ruth Lillian (Pellow) M. BA in Lit., U. Mich., 1957, MA in Theatre, 1960; HHD (hon.), Profl. Sch. Psychology, San Francisco, 1991. Stage mgr., lighting designer Off-Broadway plays; costume, lighting and set designer, stage mgr. stock cos., 1954-62; nat. subscription mgr. Theatre Guild/Am. Theatre Soc., NYC, 1965-67; subscription mgr. Theatre, Inc.-Phoenix Theatre, NYC, 1963-67; cons. NYC Ballet and NYC Opera, 1967-70; asst. house mgr. NY State Theater, 1970-72; dir. ticket sales City Ctr. of Music and Drama, Inc., NYC, 1970-72; prodn. mgr. San Antonio's Symphony/Opera, 1973-75; gen. mgr. San Antonio Symphony/Opera, 1975-76, 55th St. Dance Theater Found., Inc., NYC, 1976-77, Ballet Theatre Found., Inc./Am. Ballet Theatre, NYC, 1977-81; v.p. prodn. Radio City Music Hall Prodns., Inc., NYC, 1981-83; artist-in-residence CCNY, 1981—; propr. mgmt. cons. firm for performing arts NYC, 1983—; exec. dir. San Francisco Ballet Assn., 1987-93; mng. dir. Houston Ballet Assoc., 1993-95; gen. mgr. Chgo. Music and Dance Theater, Inc., 1995—2004. Cons. Ford Found., NY State Coun. on Arts, Kennedy Ctr. Performing Arts, Lensic Performing Arts Ctr., Santa Fe, Bloomington Cultural Dist., Ill., Sheboygan Theater Found., Wis., The Arts Partnership Spartanburg, SC; mem. dance panels NY State Coun. on Arts, 1979-81; mem. panels for Support to Prominent Orgns. and Dance, Calif. Arts Coun., 1988-92. Appointee San Francisco Cultural Affairs Task Force, 1991; chmn. bd. dir. Tex. Inst. Arts in Edn., 1994—; trustee Internat. Alliance of Theatrical Stage Employees Local 16 Pension and Welfare Fund, 1991-94; bd. dir. Rudolf Nureyev Dance Found., Chgo., 1998—. Mem. Assn. Theatrical Press Agts. and Mgrs., Actors Equity Assn., United Scenic Artists Local 829, San Francisco Visitors and Conv. Bur. (bd. dirs.), Argyle Club (San Antonio). Office Phone: 864-457-4575.

MOFFETT, DAVID MCKENZIE, bank executive; b. Daytona Beach, Fla., Feb. 22, 1952; s. James Denny Jr. and Dorothy McCall (McKenzie) M.; m. Cynthia Ann Daugherty, Aug. 25, 1973 (div. Oct. 1977); m. Katherine Ann Martin, May 26, 1979; children: Jeffrey Martin, Layne McCall, Hilary Marie. BA, Okla. U., 1974; MBA, So. Meth. U., 1975; grad. Stonier Sch. Banking, Rutgers U., 1981. Planning analyst First Nat. Bank & Trust Co., Tulsa, 1975-76, fin. analyst, 1978, v.p., 1978-80, sr. v.p., 1981-86, exec. v.p., 1987—93; CFO Star Banc Corp. (merged with Firstar Corp.), 1993—98; CFO, vice chmn. Firstar Corp. (merged with US Bancorp), Milw., 1998—2001; CFO, vice chmn., dir. US Bancorp, Mpls., 2001—07. Faculty grad. sch. banking U. Wis., 1986; adj. prof. U. Tulsa. Bd. dirs. Leadership Tulsa, Inc., 1985-87, Arts & Humanities Council, Tulsa, 1986, Salvation Army, 1986, St. John's Episc. Ch., Tulsa, 1987. Recipient Chmn.'s award bd. dirs. First Nat. Bank, 1980. Mem. Nat. Asset/Liability Mgmt. Assn. (charter), Bank Adminstrn. Inst. (treasury mgmt. com. 1984, investment banking com. 1987). Republican. Episcopalian. Clubs: Tulsa, Cedar Ridge Country (Tulsa). Avocations: running, golf, skiing, scuba diving, bicycling.

MOFFITT, DONALD L., state legislator; b. Knox County, Feb. 18, 1947; s. Russell Wellington and Gertrude (Johnson) M.; m. Carolyn J. Lock; children: Linda J., Justin L., Amanda H. BS, U. Ill., 1969. Tchr.; Dist. 94 rep. Ill. Ho. Reps., Springfield, 1993—; treas. West Ill. Police Tng. Orgn. Mem. Knox County bd., 1978-84, chmn. 1982-84, treas. 1984-93; mem. Agr. Housing and Edn. Com. Ill. Ho. Reps., 1993—; sec. Agr. and Edn. Twp. and County Com., 1995—. Mem. Carver Cmty. Action Agy. Recipient Friend of Agr. award Ill. Farm Bur., 1994—. Mem. Ill. Farm Bur., Lions Club, Masons, Alpha Zeta, Omicron Delta Kappa. Address: RR 1 Box 160 Gilson IL 61436-9707 Also: 5 Weinberg Arcade Galesburg IL 61401

MOFORD, CRAIG S., prosecutor; b. Schenectady, NY; BA, Hope Coll.; JD, Valparaiso U. Atty. IRS, Cleveland, 1984—87; first asst. US atty. No. Dist., Ohio, 1987—2004; interim US atty. Eastern Dist., Mich., 2004—. Achievements include chief prosecutor, corruption trial of former Congressman James Traficant.

MOGERMAN, SUSAN, state agency administrator; Dir. State of Ill. Historic Preservation Agy., Springfield. Office: State Ill Hist Preservation Agy 500 E Madison Springfield IL 62701-1028

MOGK, JOHN EDWARD, law educator, association executive, consultant; b. Detroit, Feb. 10, 1939; s. Clifford Anthony and Evelyn Lenore (Paselk) M.; m. Lylas Heidi Good, Aug. 23, 1964; children: Marja, Tenley, Matthew. BBA, U. Mich., 1961, JD with distinction, 1964; diploma in comparative law, U. Stockholm, 1965. Bar: N.Y. 1966, Mich. 1970. Assoc. atty. Shearman & Sterling, NYC, 1964-68; mem. faculty Wayne State U. Sch. Law, 1968—, dir. grad. studies, 1990-95. Pres. MERRA Rsch. Corp., 1974-94; cons. econ. and urban devel., arbitrator; vis. prof. U. Utrecht, The Netherlands, 2000. Editor Michigan International Lawyer and Utilities Law Rev.; contbr. articles to profl. jours. Chmn. Mich. TOP Task Force, 1972; vice chmn. Mich. Constrn. Code Commn., 1973; mem. exec. com. Southeastern Mich. Coun. Govts., 1970; chmn. Detroit Sch. Boundary Commn., 1970, Downtown Detroit Vacant Bldg. Com., 1991-93; mem. Detroit Bd. Edn., 1970; mgr. Detroit Empowerment Zone Proposal, 1994; project exec. New Detroit Stadium, 1995; pres. Habitat for Humanity Detroit, 1999-2006. Named Outstanding Wayne State U. Assoc. Prof., 1971, Outstanding Wayne Law Sch. Prof., 1977, 83, 93, 97, 2003, Outstanding Young Man in Detroit, 1972, One of Ten Outstanding Young Men in U.S., 1973, One of Four Outstanding Vols. in U.S., 1974; recipient Presdl. citation Wayne State U., 1977, State of Mich., 1988, 94; Am.-Scandinavian fellow, 1965; vis. fellow U. Warwick, Eng., 1985-86. Mem. ABA, Mich. Bar Assn. (Outstanding Achievement award Internat. Law Sect. 2001). Home: 1000 Yorkshire Rd Grosse Pointe Park MI 48230-1432

MOGLIA, JOSEPH H., brokerage house executive; b. Apr. 1, 1949; m. Amy Jardine; 4 children from previous marriage. BA, Fordham U., 1971; MA, U. Del., 1974. Def. coord. Dartmouth Coll. football team, 1981—83; with Merrill Lynch, 1983—97, head global fixed income inst. sales, head mcpl. div., sr. v.p., head investment performance & product group, 1997—2001; CEO Ameritrade Holding Corp., 2001—. Author: Perimeter Attack Offense, 1981. Bd. dir. Creighton Univ., at. Italian Am. Found., 2005—, AXA Fin., 2002—. Office: Ameritrade Holding Corp 4211 S 102nd St Omaha NE 68127-1031 Mailing: Ameritrade Holding Corp PO Box 2760 Omaha NE 68103-2760 Office Phone: 402-331-2744. Business E-Mail: jmoglia@ameritrade.com.*

MOHAN, JOHN J., lawyer; b. St. Louis, May 22, 1945; s. John Joseph and Virginia Loretta (Durkin) M.; m. Elaine Bronwyn Lipe, May 29, 1982; children: Bryn Elizabeth, John Burke. BS Indsl. Engring., St. Louis U., Sch. Engring. and Earth Scis., 1967; JD, St. Louis U., 1971. Bar: Mo. 1971, Ill. 1971, U.S. Dist. Ct. (we. dist.) Mo. 1971, U.S. Dist. Ct. (ea. dist.) Mo. 1980, U.S. Dist. Ct. (so. dist.)

Ill. 1981, U.S. Ct. Appeals (8th cir.) 1987. Asst. prosecuting atty. St. Louis County, 1971-72; asst. cir. atty. St. Louis Cir. Atty's. Office, 1972-74; spl. asst. state's atty. St. Clair County Atty's. Office, Belleville, Ill., 1974—; assoc. Lashley, Caruthers, Theis, Rava & Hamel, St. Louis, 1979-80; ptnr. Schreiber, Tueth & Mohan, Clayton, Mo., 1981-83, Danis, Reid, Murphy, Tobben, Schreiber & Mohan, Ladue, Mo., 1983-87, Hinshaw & Culbertson, St. Louis, 1987-97, Blackwell, Sanders, Peper, Martin, St. Louis, 1998-2000, Tueth, Keeney, Cooper, Mohan & Jackstadt, P.C., 2000—; mcpl. judge City Wildwood, Mo., 2004—. Mem. U. Mo. Law Sch. Found. Scholarship. Mem. ABA, Am. Arbitration Assn. (cert. mediator, arbitrator 1988—), Ill. State Bar Assn., Mo. Bar, Bar Assn. Met. St. Louis, St. Clair County Bar, St. Louis County Bar, Def. Rsch. Inst., Mo. Orgn. Def. Lawyers, Pinnacle Arbitration and Mediation Svcs. (cert. mediator, arbitrator 1997—), Phi Delta Phi. Home: 529 Big Horn Basin Ct Wildwood MO 63011-4818 Office: Tueth Keeney Cooper Mohan Jackstadt PC Ste 600 34 N Meramec Clayton MO 63105

MOHIUDDIN, SYED MAQDOOM, cardiologist, educator; b. Hyderabad, India, Nov. 14, 1934; came to US, 1961, naturalized, 1976; s. syed Nizamuddin and Amat-Ul-Butool Mahmoodi Mohiuddin; m. Ayesha Sultana Mahmoodi, July 16, 0961; children: Sameena J., Syed R., Kulsoom S. MB, BS, Osmania U., 1960; MS, Creighton U., Omaha, 1967; DSc, Laval U., Que., Can., 1970. Diplomate in internal medicine and cardiovasc. disease Am. Bd. Internal Medicine. Intern Altoona Gen. Hosp., Pa., 1961-62; resident in cardiology Creighton Meml. Hosp., also St. Joseph Hosp., Omaha, 1963-65, mem. staff, 1965—; prof. adjoint Laval U. Med. Sch., 1970; practice medicine specializing in cardiology Omaha, 1970—; prof. Creighton U. Med. Sch., 1977—, assoc. dir. div. cardiology, 1983-96; prof. pharmacy practice Creighton U. Sch. Pharmacy, 1986—, dir. divsn. cardiology, 1996—2007, assoc. chair for acad. affairs dept. medicine, 1998—2007, Richard W. Booth MD prof. cardiology, 2005—, chair dept. medicine, 2007—. Cons. Omaha VA Hosp. Rsch. fellow Med. Rsch. Coun. Can., 1968; grantee Med. Rsch. Coun. Can., 1970, NIH, 1973, 2000-03. Fellow ACP, Am. Coll. Cardiology (gov. for Nebr. 1987-90), Am. Coll. Clin. Pharmacology, Am. Coll. Chest Physicians; mem. AAAS, Am. Heart Assn. (fellow coun. clin. cardiology, bd. dirs. 1973-75), Am. Fedn. Clin. Rsch., Nebr. Heart Assn. (chmn. rsch. com. 1974-76, dir. 1973—), Gt. Plains Heart Com. (Nebr. rep. 1976-84, pres. 1977-78), N.Y. Acad. Scis., Nebr. Cardiovasc. Soc. (pres. 1980-81), Creighton Med. Assn. (v.p. 2005—). Democrat. Muslim. Home: 12531 Shamrock Rd Omaha NE 68154-3529 Office: Cardiac Ctr Creighton U 3006 Webster St Omaha NE 68131-2027 Office Phone: 402-280-4566. Business E-Mail: smm@cardiac.creighton.edu.

MOHLER, STANLEY ROSS, preventive medicine physician, educator; b. Amarillo, Tex., Sept. 30, 1927; s. Norton Harrison and Minnie Alice (Ross) M.; m. Ursula Luise Burkhardt, Jan. 24, 1953; children: Susan Luise, Stanley Ross, Mark Hallock. BA, MA, U. Tex., 1953, MD, 1956. Diplomate Am. Bd. Preventive Medicine. Intern USPHS Hosp., San Francisco, 1956-57; med. officer Center Aging Research, NIH, Bethesda, Md., 1957-61; dir. Civil Aeromed. Rsch. Inst., FAA, Oklahoma City, 1961-66, chief aeromed. applications divsn. Washington, 1966-78; prof., vice chmn. dept. community medicine, dir. aerospace medicine Wright State U. Sch. Medicine, Dayton, Ohio, 1978—. Rsch. assoc. prof. preventive medicine and pub. health U. Okla. Med. Sch., 1961—; vice-chmn. Am. Bd. Preventive Medicine, 1978—, sec.-treas., 1980—. Co-editor: Space Biology and Medicine (5 vols.), 1995 (Life Scis. Book award Internat. Acad. Astronautics); contbr. articles to profl. jours. Bd. dirs. St. Citizens Assn. Oklahoma City, 1962—, Flying Physicians Assn., 1961—. Served with AUS, 1946-48. Recipient Gail Borden Rsch. award, Boothby award Aerospace Med. Assn., 1966, FAA Meritorious Svc. award, 1974, Cecil A. Brownlow Publ. award Flight Safety Found., 1998, Marie Marvingt award French Soc. Aerospace Medicine and Aerospace Med. Assn., 2006; co-recipient Life Scis. Book award in space, biology and medicine Internat. Acad. Astronautics, 1995. Fellow Geriatrics Soc., Aerospace Med. Assn. (pres. 1983, Harry G. Moseley award 1974, Lyster award 1984, Louis H. Bauer Founders award 1998), Am. Coll. Preventive Medicine, Gerontol. Soc.; mem. AMA, Aircraft Owners and Pilots Assn. (Sharples award 1984, Hubertus Strughold award 1991), Alpha Omega Alpha. Home: 6539 Reigate Rd Dayton OH 45459-3214 Office: Wright State U Sch Medicine PO Box 927 Dayton OH 45401-0927 Office Phone: 937-775-1400.

MOHLING, CHARLOTTE, middle school educator; BA in Home Econ. Edn., ND State Univ. Tchr. Wessington Springs (SD) Sch. Dist., 1975—. Bd. visitors ND State Univ. Named ESA Region 3 Tchr. of Yr., 2007, SD Tchr. of Yr., 2007; named to USA 2004 All-USA Tchr. Team; recipient Wessington Springs Disting. Svc. award (three times). Mem.: Nat. Coalition of Family and Consumer Sci., Assn. Edn. Comm. and Tech. Project, Assn. Career and Technical Edn. (pres., Family & Consumer Sci. Divsn.). Office: Wessington Springs Sch Dist 301 Dakota North PO Box 449 Wessington Springs SD 57382 Business E-Mail: charlotte.mohling@k12.sd.us.

MOHN, MELVIN PAUL, anatomist, educator; b. Cleve., June 19, 1926; s. Paul Melvin and Julia (Jacobik) M.; m. Audrey Faye Lonergan, June 28, 1952; children— Shorey Faye, Andrew Paul AB, Marietta Coll., 1950; Sc.M., Brown U., 1952, PhD in Biology, 1955. Instr. SUNY Downstate Med. Ctr., Bklyn., 1955-59, asst. prof., 1959-63; asst. prof. anatomy U. Kans. Sch. Medicine, Kansas City, 1963-65, assoc. prof., 1965-72, prof., 1972-89, prof. emeritus, 1989—. Cons. Nat. Med. Audiovisual Ctr., Atlanta, 1972; vis. lectr. U. Miami Sch. Medicine, Fla., 1966. Bd. dirs. U. Kans. Med. Ctr. Credit Union, 1968-77, Kansas City Youth Symphony, 1972-77; mem. U.S. Pony Club, 1964-71, Med. Arts Symphony, 1965-71, 90—, Spring Hill Chorale, 1990-96, Spring Hill Hist. Soc., 1997—. Served with USN, 1944-46, PTO. McCoy fellow, 1950, Arnold biology fellow, 1954 Fellow AAAS; mem. Am. Soc. Zoologists, Am. Assn. Anatomists, Am. Inst. Biol. Sci., Masons, Lions, Rotary, Ruritan, Olathe Trail Riders, Phi Beta Kappa, Sigma Xi, Beta Beta Beta. Republican. Methodist. Home: Yankee Bit Farm 23595 W 223rd St Spring Hill KS 66083-4029 Office: U Kans Med Ctr Dept Anatomy 39th and Rainbow St Kansas City KS 66103

MOHR, L. THOMAS, newspaper executive; b. Endicott, NY, Dec. 25, 1955; s. Lionel Charles and Anne (Tredwell) M.; m. Pageen Rogers, July 13, 1985; children: Mary Catherine, Jack. BA with honors, Queens U., Kingston, Ont., Can., 1979; MBA, U. Calif., Berkeley, 1987. Gen. mgr. Foster City (Calif.) Progress, 1981-82; classified advt. mgr. Peninsula Times Tribune, Palo Alto, Calif., 1982-85, mktg. mgr., 1985-86, advt. sales dir., 1986-87; dir. mktg. and advt. sales Bakersfield Californian, 1987-90; classified advt. dir. Star Tribune, Mpls., 1990-93, v.p., 1993-96, sr. v.p., gen. mgr., 1996-98, sr. v.p. mktg., 1998—. Chmn. bd. Cookie Cart; bd. dirs. Children's Theatre. Mem. Newspaper Assn. Am. (bd. dirs. mktg. com. 1997—, bd. dir. display fedn. 1997—). Republican. Roman Catholic. Avocations: running, tennis, golf, cross country skiing. Office: Star Tribune 425 Portland Ave Minneapolis MN 55488-0002 Home: 1810 University Way San Jose CA 95126-1560

MOHR, TERRENCE B., food company executive; With Quaker Oats Co., Chgo., 1987—, sr. v.p. customer orgn., 1997—. Office: The Quaker Oats Co 555 W Monroe St Chicago IL 60661-3716

MOHS, FREDERIC EDWARD, lawyer; b. Madison, Wis., Mar. 16, 1937; s. Frederic E. and Mary Ellen Reynolds M.; m. Mary M. Mohs, June 14, 1959; children: Paula A., Nicole L. BS, U. Wis., 1959, JD, 1964. Bar: Wis. 1964. Assoc. Axley, Brynelson, Madison, Wis., 1964-67; ptnr. Mohs, MacDonald, Widder & Maradise, Madison, 1967—. Bd. dirs. Madison Gas and Electric Co., Madison. Regent U. Wis., Madison, 1997-2004. Mem. Downtown Madison Rotary. Republican. Office: Mohs MacDonald Widder & Paradise 20 N Carroll St Madison WI 53703 Office Phone: 608-256-1978. E-mail: fred@mmwp-law.com.

MOLARO, ROBERT S., state legislator, lawyer; b. Chgo., June 29, 1950; BS, Loyola U.; JD, John Marshall Law Sch. Dist. 12 senator Ill. Senate, Springfield, 1993—. Del. Dem. Nat. Conv. 1988. Home: 2650 W 51st St Chicago IL 60632-1560

MOLDENHAUER, JUDITH A., graphic design educator; b. Oak Park, Ill., Feb. 28, 1951; d. Raymond L. and Jean Marie (Carqueville) M. BFA, U. Ill., 1973, MA, Stanford U., 1974; MFA, U. Wis., 1977. Design supr. N.E. Mo. State U., Kirksville, Mo., 1977-79; asst. prof. design Kansas City Art Inst., Mo., 1979-83; asst. prof. art, graphic design Sch. Art U. Mich., Ann Arbor, 1983-92; vis. lectr. Wayne State U., 1990-92, asst. prof. graphic design, 1992-98, assoc. prof. graphic design, 1998—, area coord. graphic design, 1992—. Free-lance designer The Detroit Inst. Arts, Toledo (Ohio) Mus. Art, Burroughs Corp. (Unisys) Detroit, Detroit Focus Gallery; vis. designer N.S. Coll. Art and Design, 1986; juror Ohio Mus. Assn., 1986, Collaborator Presdl. Initiative "Healthy Start": prenatal and pre-conceptional booklets and ednl. modules designs, 1992-1995; mem. organizing group health info. design Design Forum; presenter Congress Women's Health Issues, 1997, 98, Internat. Inst. Info. Design, Schwarzenberg, Austria, 1998, Vienna, 2005, Read Me exhbn., Bern, Switzerland, 1999, Expert Forum Manual Design, Malardalen U., Eskilstuna, Sweden, 2000, Vision Plus II, Internat. Inst. for Info. Design, 2005, others; co-chair info. design edn. Internat. Inst. Info. Design, 2004, faculty/vis. expert Summer Acad., Bolzano, Italy, 2005, co-dir. Summer Acad., Chgo., 2006, Health Comm. Forum, Boston, 2006 Contbr. articles to profl. jours. Recipient award of distinction, merit award Am. Assn. Museums, 1985, 86, Excellence Design award Beckett Paper Co., 1991, gold award for softcover books Printing & Pub. Competition, 1994, Am. Graphic Design award, 1996, 98; Rackham grantee U. Mich., 1987, grantee Nat. Endowment for Arts, 1988; US-EU FIPSE grantee U.S. Dept. Edn. student and faculty exch. info. design, 2003. 19th Internat. Bi-Ann. Graphic Design, Czech Republic, 2001; Fulbright fellow, Sweden, 2006—. Mem. Wood Engraving Network, Univ. and Coll. Designers Assn. (merit award 1979, gold award 1979), Coll. Art Assn. (chmn. panel 1991), Women's Caucus for Art (panel chmn. 1987), Amnesty Internat., Women in Design (excellence award Chgo. 1985, Sierra Club, Audubon Soc., Nat. Inst. Design. Lutheran. Office: Wayne State U Dept Art and Art History 150 Art Bldg Detroit MI 48202 Office Phone: 313-993-8165, 313-577-2980. Personal E-mail: FrogBoggd@aol.com.

MOLDENHAUER, WILLIAM CALVIN, soil scientist; b. New Underwood, SD, Oct. 27, 1923; s. Calvin Fred and Ida (Killam) M.; m. Catherine Ann Maher, Nov. 26, 1947; children— Jean Ann, Patricia, Barbara, James, Thomas BS, S.D. State U., 1949; MS, U. Wis., 1951, PhD, 1956. Soil surveyor S.D. State U., Brookings, 1948-54; soil scientist U.S. Dept. Agr., Big Spring, Tex., 1954-57, Ames, Iowa, 1957-72, Morris, Minn., 1972-75; rsch. leader Nat. Soil Erosion Rsch. Lab., Agrl. Rsch. Svc. U.S. Dept. Agr., West Lafayette, Ind., 1975-85; prof. dept. agronomy Purdue U., West Lafayette, 1975-85, prof. emeritus, 1985—. Contbr. articles to profl. jours. Served with U.S. Army, 1943-46 Fellow Am. Soc. Agronomy, Soil Sci. Soc., Soil Conservation Soc. Am. (pres. 1979), World Assn. Soil and Water Conservation (pres. 1983-85, exec. sec. 1985-2003, asst. treas. 2003-). Home and Office: 2400 Sunrise Ridge Cir #107 Brookings SD 57006 E-mail: moldwc@itctel.com.

MOLFENTER, DAVID P., former electronics executive; b. 1945; MEE, Purdue U.; M in bus. adminstrn., Ind. U. Pres., CEO Magnavox Electronic Sys. Co.; former CEO, pres. Hughes Def. Comm., Ft. Wayne, Ind.; v.p. Raytheon Sys., Ft. Wayne, 1995—2001; bd. dirs. Paravant Inc.

MOLL, CURTIS E., manufacturing executive; b. 1933; Diploma, Wesleyan Coll., 1961, So. Meth. U., 1963. Chmn., CEO MTD Products Inc. Office: MTD Products Inc PO Box 368022 Cleveland OH 44136-9722

MOLL, RUSSELL ADDISON, aquatic ecologist, science administrator; b. Bound Brook, NJ, Aug. 12, 1946; s. Addison and Celeste (Carrier) M. PhD, SUNY, Stony Brook, 1974; MS, U. Mich., 1983. Rsch. assoc. Brookhaven Nat. Lab., Upton, N.Y., 1972-74; rsch. investigator U. Mich., Ann Arbor, 1974-76, asst. rsch. scientist, 1976-81, assoc. rsch. scientist, 1981—; asst. dir. Mich. Sea Grant, Ann Arbor, 1988—; dir. Coop. Inst. Limnology and Ecosystems Rsch., U. Mich., 1989—. Univ. rep. Mich. Aquatic Scis. Consortium, 1989—; cons. Applied Scis. Assocs., Narragansett, R.I., 1988. Contbr. articles to profl. jours. Recipient numerous rsch. grants including NOAA, EPA, NSF, NASA, Agy. Internat. Devel. Mem. AAAS, Am. Soc. Limnology and Oceanography, Ecol. Soc. Am., Oceanographic Soc. Achievements include research in study of phytoplankton and bacteria dynamics in Great Lakes, effects of toxic materials on phytoplankton and bacteria, and ecological analysis of a large river and estuary in West Africa.

MOLL, WILLIAM GENE, broadcasting company executive; b. Sikeston, Mo., Dec. 25, 1937; s. John Alexander and Letha Ann (McDowell) M.; m. Marilyn Lewis, Aug. 2, 1957; children: David William, Craig Lewis. Student, So. Ill. U., 1955-57, Anderson Coll., 1957-58; BS in Edn., S.E. Mo. State Coll., 1960; MA, U. Tex., 1963. Announcer, program dir. Sta. KSIM, Sikeston, Mo., 1954-57, 58-59; announcer Sta. WCBC, Anderson, Ind., 1957; announcer, writer, dir., news anchor KFVS-TV, Cape Girardeau, Mo., 1959-62; producer, dir., writer KLRN-TV, Austin, Tex., 1962-64, mgr. sta. ops. San Antonio, 1964-69; v.p., gen. mgr. WSMW-TV, Worcester, Mass., 1969-72; with KENS-TV, San Antonio, 1972-87, pres., gen. mgr., 1977-81, chmn., 1981-87; pres., chief exec. officer Harte-Hanks TV Group, 1979-81, Harte-Hanks Broadcasting & Entertainment, 1981-87, chmn. TV group, 1981—; sr. v.p. Harte-Hanks Communications, Inc., 1981-87. Pres. WNBC-TV, .Y.C., 1989-92, WKRC-TV, Cin., 1992—. Bd. dirs. San Antonio Art Inst., 1974—, chmn., 1978-81; bd. dirs. Goodwill Industries, 1973-87, pres., 1987-88; bd. dirs. San Antonio Symphony Soc., 1979-85, United Way San Antonio, 1979-82, Friends of the McNay, 1979-81, Media-Advt. Partnership for Drug-Free Am., 1987—; pres., chmn. Dan Beard Coun. Boy Scouts of Am., Cin., 1996—. Mem. Tex. Assn. Broadcasters (dir. 1976—, sec.-treas. 1981—, pres. 1983), TV Bur. of Advt. (bd. dirs. 1980—, sec. 1981-83, chmn. 1983-85, pres./chief exec. officer 1987-89), CBS TV Affiliates Assn. (bd. dirs. 1980-83), Internat. Radio TV Found. (bd. dirs. 1985-88), Advt. Council (bd. dirs. 1987-89), Electronic Media Rating Council (bd. dirs. 1987-89). Clubs: Torch (San Antonio), Giraud (San Antonio); Oak Hills Country. Office: WKRC-TV 1906 Highland Ave Cincinnati OH 45219-3104

MOLLER, ANDREW K., finance company executive; CPA. Acctg. positions with Ladbroke Racing Canterbury, Inc., B Dalton Bookstores, Arthur Andersen LLP; asst. contr. Christopher & Banks, 1992—94, contr., 1995—98, v.p. finance, CFO, 1998—99, sr. v.p., CFO, 1999—. Office: Christopher & Banks Corp 2400 Xenium Ln N Minneapolis MN 55441

MOLLER, JAMES HERMAN, pediatrician, educator; b. Fresno, Calif., Aug. 12, 1933; s. Leonard Hansen and Eloise Jean (Hunter) M.; m. Carol Suzanne Eymann, Sept. 8, 1957; children: James, Elizabeth. AB, Stanford U., 1954, MD, 1958. Instr. pediat. U. Minn., Mpls., 1965-66, asst. prof., 1966-70, assoc. prof., 1970-73, prof., 1973—, Dwan prof., 1975—2005, interim head pediat., 1976-78, 97-99, chief pediat., 1976-78, head pediat., 1999—2003; chief of staff U. Minn. Hosp., Mpls., 1984-89. Vis. prof. Nat. Heart & Lung Inst., London, 1989-90, Inst. Child Health, London, 1989-90. Contbr. over 200 sci. articles to profl. jours. Bd. dirs. U. Minn. Hosp., 1984-89, Mpls. Children's Health Ctr., 1975-78, Children's Hosp., St. Paul, 1975-78, Minn. Assn. Pub. tchg. Hosps., Mpls., 1984-89, Variety Club Heart Assn., Mpls., 1980-83. Capt. U.S. Army, 1961-63. Fellow Am. Acad. Pediat. (exec. bd. 1991-92, dist. chmn. 1991-92, alternate dist. chmn. 1985-91, Ross Edn. award 1989), Am. Coll. Cardiology; mem. Am. Heart Assn. (pres. 1993-94, v.p. 1986-91, bd. dirs. 1986-95, award of Merit 1989), Am. Fedn. Clin. Rsch., Am. Pediatric Soc., Am. Bd. Pediat. Nat. Bd. Med. Examiners, Midwest Soc. Pediatric Cardiology Soc., Minn. Med. Assn. (inter-splty. coun. 1979-82, resource group child health 1980-82), Minn. Acad. Medicine, Mpls. Met. Pediatric Soc, No. Pediatric Cardiology Soc. (pres. 1978-79), Midwest Soc. Pediatric Rsch. Soc. Pediatric Rsch., Hennepin County Med. Soc. (bd. dirs. 1986-89), Irish Am. Paediatric Soc., British Paediatric Cardiac Assn., Coun. Med. Splty. Socs. (bd. dirs., 1991—), Sub-bd. Pediatric Cardiology (chmn. 1992-94), Internam. Heart Found. (pres. 1997-98), World Heart Fedn. (bd. dirs. 1999). Independent. Congregationalist. Avocations: gardening, travel, oriental carpets, reading. Home: 4816 Sheridan Ave S Minneapolis MN 55410-1917 Office: U Minn 420 Delaware St SE Minneapolis MN 55455-0374 Office Phone: 612-626-2790. Business E-Mail: molle002@umn.edu.

MOLNAR, DONALD JOSEPH, landscape architecture educator; b. Springfield, Ill., Dec. 24, 1938; s. Joseph and Mabel Irene (Woods) M.; m. Carol Jeanette Smith, Aug. 22, 1958; children: Elaina Deanne, Amy Lynn, Holly Suzanne. BFA in Landscape Architecture, U. Ill., 1960, MFA in Landscape Architecture, 1964. Landscape architect Simonds and Simonds, Pitts., 1961-63; landscape architect campus planning U. Ill., Urbana, 1963-72, asst. dir., planner capital programs Urbana and Chgo., 1971-81; assoc. prof. landscape architecture Purdue U., West Lafayette, Ind., 1981-85, dir. landscape architecture coop. program, 1983—, prof. landscape architecture, 1985—, chair landscape architecture program, 1987—, dir. internat. exch. landscape architecture, 1988—. Cons. to architect, engrs., park agys., 1964—, Mobile Homes Mfrs. Assn., Chgo., 966-76; prin. Profl. Searches for Landscape Archs., employment cons., 2000—; prin. Drumlin Group. Author: Anatomy of a Park, 2d edit., 1986, 3rd edit., 2003; illustrator: Anatomy of a Park, 1971, Visual Approach to Park Design, 1980; developer software CompuPave, 1992, PaveCAD, 1996. Mem., program coord. Champaign (Ill.) Devel. Coun., 1966-78. Named Hon. Parks Commr., Champaign Park Dist., 1981. Fellow Am. Soc. Landscape Architects (licensing com. Ill. chpt. 1968-70, registration com. Ind. chpt. 1982-85, pres. 1991-92, award 1982). Avocations: travel, computers.

MOLNAU, CAROL L., lieutenant governor, former state legislator; b. Waconia, Minn., Sept. 17, 1949; m. Steven F. Molnau, 1971; children: Heather, Kristen, Megan Attended, U. Minn. Mem. Chaska City Coun., 1989—92, Minn. Ho. of Reps., 1992—2003; commr. Minn. Dept. Transportation, 2003—08; lt. gov. State of Minn., St. Paul, 2003—. Active Corn Growers, Farm Bur., Soybean Growers, Norseland Ch. Mem. Agrl. Com., Econ. Devel., Infrastructure & Regulation Fin.-Transportation Fin. Divsn., Fin. Inst. & Ins.: Internat. Trade & Economic Devel. Republican. Lutheran. Office: Office Lt Governor 130 State Capitol 75 Rev Dr Martin Luther King Jr Blvd Saint Paul MN 55155 Office Phone: 651-296-3391. Office Fax: 651-296-2089.*

MOLONEY, THOMAS E., lawyer; b. Rockville Ctr., NY, Jan. 9, 1949; BS, U. Dayton, 1971; JD, U. Notre Dame, 1974. Bar: Ohio 1974. Prin. Am. Energy Svcs., Inc., Columbus, Ohio. Office: Am Energy Svcs Inc 1105 Schrock Rd Ste 602 Columbus OH 43229-1174 Office Phone: 614-885-1901. E-mail: amtem@sbcglobal.net.

MOLTENI, AGOSTINO, pathology educator; b. Como, Lombardy, Italy, Nov. 12, 1933; came to U.S., 1963; s. Enrico and Antonia (Signorini) M.; m. Loredana Brizio, Sept. 5, 1963; children: Claudio Enrico, Ronald Stephen. MD, U. Milan, Italy, 1957; PhD in Pathology, SUNY, Buffalo, 1970. Lic. Italian Bd. Internal Medicine, 1963. Intern and resident in internal medicine U. Milan (Italy), 1957-62; asst. prof. U. Milan, 1957-63; chief rsch. sect. Farmitalia Drug Co., Milan, 1963-65; rsch. assoc. SUNY, Buffalo, 1965-69, asst. prof., 1969-71; assoc. prof. U. Kans., Kansas City, 1971-76; prof. pathology Northwestern U., Chgo., 1976-96, prof. emeritus, 1996—; prof. pathology and pharmacology U. Mo., Kansas City, 1996—, adj. prof. basic med. scis. Vis. prof. Harvard U., 1983-84; dir. med. students rsch. program U. Mo. Kansas City, 2004-; adj. prof. anesthesia, U. Mo., Kansas City, 2007-. Editor, author: Endocrinology and Thermal Trauma, 1990, Menopause Update, 1992; exec. editor Current Pharmaceutical Design, 2000—, Nutrition Rsch., 2003, PPAR Rsch., 2005; contbr. articles to profl. jours., chpts. to books. Recipient Sharer in Lasker award Lasker Found., N.Y.C., 1983, Rsch. Career Devel. award NIH, Washington, 1970, award Am. Heart Assn., Chgo., 1982. Fellow Am. Acad. Clin. Biochemistry; mem. Am. Acad. Pathology, Am. Soc. Investigative Pathology, Clin. Chemistry Soc., Endocrine Soc. (emeritus), Am. Assn. Clin. Chemistry (emeritus). Achievements include patent for captopril as a cancer chemo-preventive agent; research on hypertension and hormonal regulation of cancer. Office: U Mo Truman Med Ctr 2301 Holmes St Kansas City MO 64108-2640 Office Phone: 816-235-5604. Business E-Mail: moltenia@umkc.edu.

MOLYNEAUX, DAVID GLENN, newspaper travel editor; b. Marion, Ind., Oct. 16, 1945; s. Glenn Ingersol and Barbara Wingate (Draudt) M.; children: Miles David, Rebecca Susan; m. Judi Dash, May 15, 1994. BS in Econs., Miami U., Oxford, Ohio, 1967. Reporter The Plain Dealer, Cleve., 1967-75, city editor, 1976-78, assoc. editor, 1979-80, editorial page editor, 1980-82, travel editor, 1982—. V.p. bd. trustees Soc. Am. Travel Writers Found., 2002—04, pres. bd. trustees, 2004—. Editor: 75 Years-An Informal History of Shaker Heights, 1987. Trustee Shaker Heights Pub. Libr., 1987—95. With U.S. Army, 1968-70. Mem. Cleve. Press Club. Office: Plain Dealer 1801 Superior Ave E Cleveland OH 44114-2198 Office Phone: 216-999-4560. E-mail: travel@plaind.com.

MONA, DAVID L., public relations executive; b. Mpls., May 4, 1943; BA in Journalism and Mass Communication, U. Minn, 1965. Reporter, editor Sta. WCCO-TV, 1962-65; reporter Mpls. Tribune, 1965-69; mgr. media rels. Luth. Brotherhood, 1969-70; dir. corp. communications Internat. Multifoods, 1970-78; v.p. communications The Toro Co., 1978-81; pres. David L. Mona Assocs., from 1981; chief exec. officer Mona, Meyer, McGrath & Gavin (now Weber Shandwick); chmn. Office: Weber Sgabdwick Ste 400 8000 Norman Center Dr Bloomington MN 55437-1180

MONA, STEPHEN FRANCIS, golf association executive; b. NYC, June 9, 1957; s. Francis Joseph and Lucille (Croce) M.; m. Mary Jo Abate, May 21, 1983 (div. 1990); 1 child, Meredith Iris; m. Cynthia Kaye Davidson, Aug. 29, 1992; stepchildren: Kinyon Murphy Vinson, Stephen Brett Vinson. BA in Journalism, San Jose State U., 1980. Sports writer Tri-Valley News, Danville, Calif., 1977-78, Tri-Valley Herald, Livermore, Calif., 1978-80; tournament dir. Northern Calif. Golf Assn., Pebble Beach, Calif., 1980-81; asst. mgr., press relations U.S. Golf Assn., Far Hills, N.J., 1981-83; exec. dir. Ga. State Golf Assn., Atlanta, 1983-93; CEO Golf Course Supt.'s Assn. of Am., 1993—. Bd. dirs. Ga. Turf Grass Found., Norcross, Ga., 1988-93; treas. Ga. Jr. Golf Found., Atlanta, 1986-93. Named Golf Writer of the Yr., Northern Calif. PGA, Calif. 1980; Sports Story of the Yr., Contra Costa Press Club, Walnut Creek, Calif., 1977, 1978. Mem. Ga. Soc. Assn. Execs. (pres. 1993), Internat. Assn. Golf Adminstrs. (pres. 1990), Am. Soc. Assn. Execs., K.C. Soc. Assn. Execs. (pres. 2000), Aluamar Country Club. Republican. Roman Catholic. Avocations: golf, reading. Office: GCSAA 1421 Research Park Dr Lawrence KS 66049-3858 E-mail: smona@gcsaa.org.

MONAGHAN, DAVID A., corporate lawyer; b. St. Louis, Mar. 9, 1956; BS, William Jewell Coll., 1978; JD, U. Mo., Columbia, 1985. Bar: Mo. 1985. Asst. gen. coun. Am. Family Ins. Group, Madison, Wis. Office: American Family Ins Group 6000 American Pkwy Madison WI 53783-0002

MONAGHAN, THOMAS JUSTIN, former prosecutor; JD, U. Nebr. Adj. faculty Coll. St. Mary, Nebr., 1985—91; ptnr. Monaghan, Tiedman & Lynch, Omaha, 1978—93; U.S. atty. Dept. Justice, Omaha, 1993—2001. Home: 327 S 71st St Omaha NE 68132-3343 E-mail: Tom@TheMonaghanGroup.com.

MONDALE, JOAN ADAMS, wife of former Vice President of United States; b. Eugene, Oreg., Aug. 8, 1930; d. John Maxwell and Eleanor Jane (Hall) Adams; m. Walter F. Mondale, Dec. 27, 1955; children— Theodore, Eleanor Jane, William Hall. BA, Macalester Coll., 1952. Asst. slide librarian Boston Mus. Fine Arts, 1952-53; asst. in edn. Mpls. Inst. of Arts, 1953-57; weekly tour guide Nat. Gallery of Art, Washington, 1965-74; hostess Washington Whirl-A-Round, 1975-76; ambassador to Japan, 1993-96. Author: Politics in Art, 1972, Letters from Japan, 1998. Bd. govs. Women's Nat. Dem. Club; hon. chmn. Fed. Coun. on Arts and Humanities, 1978-80; bd. dirs. Associated Coun. of Arts, 1973-75, Reading Is Fundamental, Am. Craft Coun., NYC, 1981-88, J.F.K. Ctr. Performing Arts, 1981-90, Walker Art Ctr., Mpls., 1987-93, 97-03, Minn. Orch., Mpls., 1988-93, 97-2003, St. Paul Chamber Orch., 1988-90, Northern Clay Ctr., 1988-93, St. Paul, 1988-93, Nancy Hauser Dance Co., Mpls., 1989-93, Minn. Landmarks, 1991-93; trustee Macalester Coll., 1986—00; mem. commn. Nat. Portrait Gallery, 1997—; chair Hiawatha Light Rail Transit Pub. Art and Design com., 2000-04; active Walker Art Ctr., 2003—07, Minn. Orch., 1997—; citizen's stamp adv. com. US Postal Svc., 2005— Mem.: Phi Beta Kappa Epsilon. Democrat. Presbyterian. Home: 2116 Irving Ave S Minneapolis MN 55405-2541 E-mail: joan.mondale@mac.com.

MONDALE, THEODORE ADAMS, former state senator; b. Mpls., Oct. 12, 1957; s. Walter Frederick and Joan (Adams) M.; m. Pamela Burris, June 12, 1988; children: Louis F., Amanda J., Berit C. BA in History, U. Minn., 1985; JD, William Mitchell Coll. Law, 1988. Assoc., law firm Larkin, Hoffman Daly & Lindgren, 1988-91; state senator Minn. State Senate, St. Paul, 1990—; v.p. pub. programs United HealthCare; atty. in pvt. practice Mpls. Legal counsel United HealtchCare Corp., Mpls. Press aide Carter for Pres. Com., 1976; surrogate speaker Carter Reelection Com., 1979-80, Mondale for Pres. Com., 1983-84; midwest dir. Dukakis for Pres. Com., 1988. Home: 3800 France Ave S Saint Louis Park MN 55416-4912 Address: 220 6th St NW Saint Paul MN 55112-6817

MONDALE, WALTER FREDERICK, lawyer, former Vice President of United States; b. Ceylon, Minn., Jan. 5, 1928; s. Theodore Sigvaard and Claribel Hope (Cowan) M.; m. Joan Adams, Dec. 27, 1955; children: Theodore, Eleanor,

William. BA cum laude, U. Minn., 1951, LLB cum laude, 1956. Bar: Minn. 1956. Law clk. Minn. Supreme Ct.; pvt. practice law, 1956-60; atty. gen. State of Minn., 1960-64; US Senator from Minn., 1964-77; v.p. U.S., 1977-81; mem. NSC, 1977-81; mem. firm Winston & Strawn LLP, 1981-87; US amb. to Japan US Dept. State, Tokyo, 1993-96, presdl. envoy to Indonesia, 1998; ptnr. Dorsey & Whitney LLP, Mpls., 1987—93, ptnr., internat. corp. practice group, sr. counsel, 1997—. Chmn. Nat. Democratic Inst. for Internat. Affairs, 1986—93. Author: The Accountability of Power*Toward a Responsible Presidency, 1975; mem. Minn. Law Rev. Dem. nominee for Pres. U.S., 1984. With U.S. Army, 1951-53. Named Disting. Univ. Fellow in law and pub. affairs, Hubert H. Humphrey Inst. of Pub. Affairs, Univ. Minn. Presbyterian. Democrat. Office: Dorsey & Whitney 50 S 6th St Ste 1500 Minneapolis MN 55402-1498 Office Phone: 612-340-2600. Office Fax: 612-340-2868.

MONDER, STEVEN I., orchestra executive; b. Newark, Mar. 12, 1945; B in Mus. Edn., Coll. Conservatory of Music, 1968, M in Mus. Edn., 1970. Tchr. orch., chorus, humanities McAuley H.S., Cin., 1970-71; prodn. mgr. Cin. Symphony Orch., 1971, asst. mgr., 1971-74, mgr., 1974-76, gen. mgr., 1976-89, exec. dir., 1989-98, pres., 1998—. Prodn. stage mgr. Cin. Opera Co., 1970, 71, adminstr., 1973. Office: Cin Symphony Orch Music Hall 1241 Elm St Cincinnati OH 45210-2231

MONDRY, DIANE, secondary school educator; b. Reginas, Sask., Can. 3 children. Career and tech. edn. tchr. Cmty. H.S., Grand Forks, ND. Part-time instr. dept. info. sys. and bus. edn. U. N.D. Recipient Outstanding Tchr. award, Nat. Assn. Vocat. Edn. Spl. Needs Pers. Mem.: NEA, Assn. for Career and Tech. Edn. (immediate past pres. 2001—02), Nat. Bd. for Profl. Tchg. Stds. (bd. mem.). Office: Cmty High Sch 500 Stanford Rd Grand Forks ND 58203-2748

MONE, ROBERT PAUL, lawyer; b. Columbus, Ohio, July 23, 1934; s. Henry P. and Ann E. (Freedlund) M.; m. Lucille L. Willman, May 3, 1960; children: Robert, Maria, Andrew, Richard. BA, U. Dayton, 1956; JD, U. Notre Dame, 1959. Bar: Ohio 1959. Law clk.to presiding judge U.S. Dist. Ct. (no. dist.) Ohio, Cleve., 1960-62; assoc. George, Greek, King, et al, Columbus, 1962-66, ptnr., 1966-79, McConnaughey, Stradley, et al, Columbus, 1979-81, Thompson Hine LLP, Columbus, 1981—. Cpl. U.S. Army, 1959-60. Mem. ABA, Ohio State Bar Assn., Energy Bar Assn., Columbus Bar Assn., Nat. Generation and Transmission Coop. Lawyers Assn. (1st pres.), Rotary. Home: 2300 Tremont Rd Columbus OH 43221-3706 Office: Thompson Hine LLP 10 W Broad St Ste 700 Columbus OH 43215-3435

MONGELLUZZO, JOHN ANDREW, lawyer; b. Lima, Ohio, Dec. 29, 1958; s. John Jr. and Virginia (Guagenti) M.; m. Kerry Jean Power, June 18, 1983. BA, U. Cin., 1981; JD, Capital U., 1984. Bar: Ohio 1984. Staff atty. savings and loan assns., securities Ohio Dept. Commerce, Columbus, 1985-86; counsel, sec. Structural Dynamics Rsch. Corp., Cin., 1986—. Vol. United Way, Clermont County, Ohio, 1987. Mem. ABA, Ohio State Bar Assn., Cin. Bar Assn., Am. Corp. Counsel Assn., Am. Soc. Corp. Secs. Republican. Roman Catholic. Office: Structural Dynamics Rsch 2000 Eastman Dr Milford OH 45150-2712 Home: 7875 Shawnee Run Rd Cincinnati OH 45243-3134

MONICAL, ROBERT DUANE, engineering company executive; b. Morgan County, Ind., Apr. 30, 1925; s. William Blaine and Mary Elizabeth (Lang) M.; m. Carol Arnetha Dean, Aug. 10, 1947 (dec. 1979); children: Mary Christine, Stuart Dean, Dwight Lee; m. Sharon Kelly Eastwood, July 13, 1980; 1 stepson, Jeffrey David Eastwood. BSC.E., Purdue U., 1948, MSC.E., 1949. Engr. N.Y.C. R.R., Cin., 1949-51, So. Rwy., Cin., 1951; design engr. Pierce & Gruber (Cons. Engrs.), Indpls., 1952-54; founder, partner Monical & Wolverton (Cons. Engrs.), Indpls., 1954-63, Monical Assocs., Indpls., 1963—, pres., 1975—; v.p. Zurwelle-Whittaker, Inc. (Engrs. and Land Surveyors), Miami Beach, Fla., 1975-90; pres. Monical Engring., Inc., 2004—. Mem. Ind. Adminstrv. Bldg. Council, 1969-75; chmn., 1973-75; mem. Meridian St. Preservation Commn., 1971-75, Ind. State Bd. of Registration for Profl. Engrs. and Land Surveyors, 1976-84, chmn., 1979, 83 Served with USNR, 1943-46, USAR, 1948-53. Mem. ASCE (Outstanding Civil Engr. award Ind. sect. 1987), Cons. Engrs. Ind. (pres. 1969, Cons. Recognition award 1986), Am. Cons. Engrs. Council (pres. 1978-79), Ind. Soc. Profl. Engrs. (Engr. of Yr. 1980), Nat. Soc. Profl. Engrs., Am. Concrete Inst., Am. Inst. Steel Constrn., Indpls. Sci. and Engring. Found. (pres. 1992-93), Am. Legion, Lions, Masons, Shriners. Mem. Christian Ch. Home and Office: 18831 Whitcomb Pl Noblesville IN 46062-8130 Office Phone: 317-770-1266. Personal E-mail: rduane1@sbcglobal.net.

MONK, SUSAN MARIE, pediatrician, educator; b. York, Pa., May 7, 1945; d. John Spotz and Mary Elizabeth (Shelly) M.; m. Jaime Pacheco, June 5, 1971; children: Benjamin Joaquin, Maria Cristina. AB, Colby Coll., 1967; MD, Jefferson Med. Coll., 1971. Diplomate Am. Bd. Pediatrics. Pediatrician Children's Med. Ctr., Dayton, Ohio, 1975—; asst. clin. prof. pediat. Wright State U., Dayton, 1976—83, assoc. clin. prof. pediat., 1983—2000, asst. prof. pediatrics, 2000—. Mem. bd. dirs. Children's Med. Ctr., Dayton, 1991-96, chief-of-staff, 1992-94. Mem. Am. Acad. Pediatrics, We. Ohio Pediatric Soc., Pediatric Ambulatory Care Soc. Avocations: reading, gardening, travel, movies, theater. Office: Childrens Health Clinic 730 C Valley St Dayton OH 45404-1845 Office Phone: 937-641-5355.

MONROE, CRAIG (KEYSTONE), professional baseball player; b. Texarkana, Tex., Feb. 27, 1977; s. Marilyn Monroe; m. Kasey Monroe; 1 child, Morgan. Outfielder Tex. Rangers, 2001, Detroit Tigers, 2002—07, Chgo. Cubs, 2007, Minn. Twins, 2008—. Outfielder Puerto Rican Winter League, 2003—04. Achievements include tying for second among all American League outfielders with 12 assists, 2006. Mailing: c/o Minnesota Twins Metrodome 34 Kirby Puckett Pl Minneapolis MN 55415*

MONROE, JEFF, state legislator; Rep. S.D. State Dist. 24. Health and human svcs. com. S.D. Ho. Reps., local govt. com.; pvt. practice chiropractic neurology. Address: 362 S Pierre St Pierre SD 57501-3137

MONROE, THOMAS EDWARD, business and financial executive; b. Ironton, Mo., Nov. 19, 1947; s. Donald Mansfield and Edwina Frances (Carr) M.; children: Thomas Edward II, Katherine Jenna. BA, Drury U., 1969; postgrad., Washington U. Sch. Bus. Adminstrn., St. Louis, 1970. Acctg. mgr., asst. contr. Am. Transit Corp., St. Louis, 1970-74; mgr. corp. devel., asst. treas. Chromalloy Am. Corp., St. Louis, 1974-77, v.p. fin., 1977-78, exec. v.p., 1978-82; dir. Chromalloy Fin. Corp., 1976-82, Am. Universal Ins. Co., 1978-82; chmn. Capital Assocs. Corp., 1982—, Fed. Air Ambulance, The Safe Deposit Co., CompuVault, Inc., James Flying Svc., Inc., Lindbergh Leasing, Inc., Vault II, LLC. Trustee Kingsbury Pl. Assn.; former trustee 2d Presbyn. Ch. With USMC, 1969—75, with USMC, 1969—75. Mem. Algonquin Club. Presbyterian. Office: Capital Assocs Corp 515 S Lindbergh Blvd Saint Louis MO 63131-2731 Office Phone: 314-991-3130.

MONSER, EDWARD L., electric power industry executive; BA, Ea. Mich. U., 1972; BS in Elec. Engring., Ill. Inst. Tech., 1980. Sr. engr. Rosemount divsn. Emerson, 1981, dir. tech., 1987—89, dir. new products and tech., 1989, v.p. pressure ops., v.p. pressure and temperature, 1994—95, v.p. and gen. mgr. pressure and temperature, 1995—96, pres., 1996—2001; COO Emerson Electric Co., St. Louis, 2001—. Office: Emerson Electric Co 8000 W Florissant Ave Saint Louis MO 63136

MONSON, DAVID CARL, school system administrator, state legislator, farmer; b. Langdon, ND, July 30, 1950; s. Carl Arthur and Shirley Jean (Klai) M.; m. Mary Kathryn Greutman, July 8, 1972; children: Cordell Carl, Cale David, Jared Arthur. Cert. tchr., adminstr., N.D. Sci. tchr. Hankinson (N.D.) Pub. Sch., 1972-75; tchr. Nekoma (N.D.) Pub. Sch., 1975-76; tchr., prin. NeKoma (N.D.) Pub. Sch., 1976-79; tchr., supt. Nekoma (N.D.) Pub. Sch., 1979-80; tchr., prin. Milton (N.D.)-Osnabrock H.S., 1981-84; supt. Adams (N.D.) Pub. Schs., 1984-88; ins. agt. N.Y. Life, Fargo, ND, 1988-95; self-employed ins. agt., Osnabrock, 1988—2003; farmer, 1975—; mem. N.D. Ho. of Reps., Bismarck, 1993—, asst. majority leader, 1998—; supt. Edinburg (N.D.) Pub. Schs., 1995—. Dir. Cavalier County Mut. Ins. Co., Osnabrock, N.D., 1990-98, Northeast Mut. Ins. Co., Cando, N.D., 1998-, N.Am. Indsl. Hemp Coun., 1999—. Leader Bobcats 4-H Club, 1988—2001; pres. Dovre Luth. Ch., Osnabrock, 2002—; mem. sch. bd. dirs. Osnabrock Sch. Bd., 1989—2001. Mem. N.D. Farm Bur., N.D. Coun. Sch. Adminstrs., Eagles, KP (grand sec. N.D. and Sask. 1985-93, award 1990). Republican. Lutheran. Avocations: skiing, gardening, hunting, coin collecting/numismatics. Business E-Mail: dmonson@nd.gov.

MONTAG, JOHN JOSEPH, II, librarian; b. Omaha, Jan. 8, 1948; s. John Joseph and Ruth Helen (Johnston) M.; m. Linda Kay Lubanski, Apr. 8, 1971; children: Nicole Elizabeth, Megan Kristine. BA, Midland Luth. Coll., 1970; postgrad., Wash. State U., 1970-74; MA, U. Iowa, 1976; postgrad., U. Nebr., 1982-84. English tchr. pub. schs., Nebr., Iowa, 1972-75; reference libr. Concordia Coll., Moorhead, Minn., 1976-81; asst. prof. libr. sci. U. Nebr., Lincoln, 1981-84; dir. Office of Info. State Libr. Iowa, Des Moines, 1984-86, state libr., 1986-87; dir. Thomas Libr. Wittenberg U., 1987-95, Cochrane-Woods Libr. Nebr. Wesleyan U., Lincoln, 1995-97, dir. libr. and computer svcs., 1997-99, univ. libr., 1999—. Trustee Bibliog. Ctr. for Rsch., Denver, 1986-87; adv. bd. No. Lights Libr. etwork, Detroit Lakes, Minn., 1980-81; chair Southwest Ohio Consortium Higher Edn. Libr. Coun., 1991-94; mem. exec. com. Nebr. Inst., 1998—; cons. U.S. Dept. of Edn. Contbr. articles to profl. jours. Co-founder Nebr. Found. for Oral History, 2001—. Univ. Found. libr. improvement grantee, U. Nebr., 1983; Challenge grantee NEH, 1992; Tchg. Am. History grantee Lincoln Pub. Schs., 2002, 04. Mem. ALA, Assn. Coll. and Rsch. Librs., Nebr. Ind. Coll. Libr. Consortium (chmn. libr. dirs. 2000—). Office: Cochrane Woods Libr Nebr Wesleyan U 5000 Saint Paul Ave Lincoln NE 68504-2760 Home Phone: 402-489-2418; Office Phone: 402-465-2401. E-mail: jmontag@nebrwesleyan.edu.

MONTAGUE, DROGO K., urologist; b. Alpena, Mich., Dec. 11, 1942; s. Frank Wright and Susan Alice (Kidder) M.; children: Mark Andrew, Lisa Joy. Student, U. Mich., 1960—63, MD cum laude, 1968. Diplomate Am. Bd. Urology. Intern Cleve. Clinic Hosp., 1968-69, resident in gen. surgery, 1969-70, resident in urology, 1970-73; assoc. staff urologist Cleve. Clinic Found., 1973-75, staff urologist, 1975—, head sect. prosthetic surgery, 1981—, urology residence program dir., 1985—2006, dir. Ctr. for Sexual Function, 1987—; prof. surgery Cleve. Clinic Lerner Coll. Medicine Case Western Res. U., 2004—. Trainee cardiovascular rsch. tng. program NIH, 1962-68; trustee Am. Bd. Urology, 1989-95, mem. examination com., 1975-80, examiner cert. exam., 1980-88, rep. to Am. Bd. Med. Specialties, 1989-95. Reviewer various publs. in field; contbr. numerous articles to profl. publs., chpts. to books; editor: Disorders of Male Sexual Function, 1988, Surgical Treatment of Erectile Dysfunction, 1993; author audiovisual tapes in field; mem. editl. bd. Jour. Urology. James B. Angell scholar, 1961, 62, Nat. Found. scholar, 1963-68; recipient Russell and Mary Hugh Scott Edn. award, 1989, Iowa Rsch. award, 1967. Fellow ACS; mem. Am. Urolog. Assn. (chmn. sci. exhibits com. North Cen. sect. 1977, mem. residency edn. com. 1979-83, vice chmn. audio visual com. 1989-95, mem. various coms., editor Am. Urolog. Assn. Video Libr. 1995-2000, chmn. audio visual com. 1996-2002, chmn. erectile dysfunction guidelines panel 1999—), Am. Assn. Genitourinary Surgeons, Cleve. Urolog. Soc. (sec.-treas. 1978-80, v.p. 1980-81, pres. 1981-82, 94-95), Soc. for Study of Impotence (pres. 1995). Office: Cleve Clinic Found Glickman Urol Inst A/100 9500 Euclid Ave Cleveland OH 44195-0001 Home Phone: 216-831-9937; Office Phone: 216-444-5590. Business E-Mail: montagd@ccf.org.

MONTELEONE, PATRICIA L., dean; MD, St. Louis U., 1961; MBA, MHA. V.p. med. affairs Cardinal Glennon Children's Hosp., 1986—93; prof. pediatrics St. Louis U. Sch. Medicine, 1967—, dean, 1994—. Office: St Louis U Sch Medicine 1402 S Grand Blvd Saint Louis MO 63104-1004

MONTGOMERY, ANN D., federal judge, educator; b. Litchfield, Minn., May 9, 1949; m. Theodore Smetak; 2 children; 1 stepchild. BS, U. Kans., 1971; JD, U. Minn., 1974. Bar: Minn. 1974, US Dist. Ct. Minn., US Ct. Appeals (8th cir.), US Supreme Ct. Law clk. DC Ct. Appeals, Washington, 1974-75; asst. US atty. Dist. Minn., Mpls., 1976-83; mcpl. judge Hennepin County, 1983-85; judge Hennepin County Dist. Ct., 1985-94, US Magistrate Ct., 1994-96; federal judge US Dist. Ct., Mpls., 1996—. Adj. prof. U. Minn. Law Sch., Mpls., 1988—; steering com. mem., dir. criminal divsn. Minn. Jud. Coll., 1990-94. Recipient Trial Judge of Yr. award Am. Bd. Trial Advocates, 1996. Mem. FBA, Minn. Dist. Judges Assn., Minn. Bar Assn., Minn. Women Lawyers (Myra Bradwell award 2000), Hennepin County Bar Assn. (Professionalism award 1993), Eighth Cir. Dist. Judges Assn. (pres. 2003-04). Office: US Dist Ct 300 S 4th St Minneapolis MN 55415-1320 Fax: 612-664-5097. E-mail: admontgomery@mnd.uscourts.gov.

MONTGOMERY, BETTY DEE, former state attorney general, retired state legislator; b. Apr. 3, 1948; BA, Bowling Green State U.; JD, Coll. Law U. Toledo, 1976. Criminal clk. Lucas County Common Pleas Ct.; asst. pros. atty. Wood County, Ohio, 1977—78, pros. atty. Ohio, 1980—88, City of Perrysburg, Ohio, 1978—81; mem. Ohio State Senate, Columbus, 1988—95; atty. gen. State of Ohio, Columbus, 1994—2002, auditor, 2002—06. Bd. dirs. Dominion Homes, Inc., 2007—. Mem. bd. dirs. Ohio Sch. Bd. Atty. Assn. Recipient Women of Achievement award, Toledo Women in Comms., 1984, Govt. Leaders Against Drunk Drivers, MADD, 1990, Senator of the Year, Ohio Hospice Assn., 1991, Disting. Svc. award, Ohio State Bar Assn., 1992, Ohio Women Hall of Fame award, 1996, Public Svc. award, Ohio Assn. of Big Brothers/Big Sisters, 1999, Advocacy award, Ohio Soc. Healthcare Consumer Advocacy, 1999, Child Adv. of the Year, Ohio Ct. Appointed Spl. Advs./Guardian Ad Litem Assn., 1999, Toledo YWCA Milestones award, Women in Govt., 2001, Presdl. award for Pro Bono Svc., The Ohio Legal Assistance Found., 2002, ABA Pro Bono award, to the Office of the Atty. Gen., 2002, Disting. Alumnus award, Bowling Green State Univ., 2003. Mem.: Ohio Prosecuting Atty. Assn. (mem. 1984), Legis. Com., Internat. Prosecutors Assn., Wood County Bar Assn., Alternative Edn. Adv. Com. (former chmn.), Wood County Child Abuse & Neglect Adv. Bd. (former vice-chmn., chmn.), Sexual Abuse Prevention Project, Wood County Sch. (mem. 1981—), Bowling Green C. of C. Republican.

MONTGOMERY, CHARLES BARRY, lawyer; b. Latrobe, Pa., Apr. 17, 1937; BA cum laude, Muskingum Coll., 1959; JD, U. Mich., 1962. Bar: Ill. 1962, U.S. Dist. Ct. (no. dist.) Ill. 1982, U.S. Supreme Ct. 1971. Atty. Jacobs & McKenna, 1962-67; founder, ptnr. Jacobs, Williams and Montgomery, Ltd., 1967-85; sr. ptnr., comml. and class action litig. and profl. liability litig. Williams Montgomery & John Ltd., Chgo., 1985—. Instr. advocacy inst. U. Mich., Ann Arbor, 1985, advanced program at. Inst. Trial Advocacy, 1986, trial acad. Internat. Assn. Def. Counsel, 1987, law inst. program Def. Rsch. Inst; pub. spkr. litigation. Contbr. articles to profl. jours. Fellow Internat. Acad. Trial Lawyers, Internat. Soc. Barristers; mem. ABA (vice-chair medicine and law com. 1989-90), Am. Bd. Trial Advs., Am. Arbitration Assn., Chgo. Bar Assn., Def. Rsch. Inst., Ill. Assn. Def. Trial Counsel, Ill. Assn. Hosp. Attys., Ill. State Bar Assn., Internat. Assn. Def. Counsel, Soc. Trial Lawyers, Legal Club of Chgo., Trial Lawyers Club of Chgo. Office: Williams Montgomery & John Ltd Ste 2100 20 N Wacker Dr Chicago IL 60606-3094 Office Phone: 312-443-3200. Office Fax: 312-630-8542. Business E-Mail: cbm@willmont.com.

MONTGOMERY, GARY B., manufacturing executive; CFO Amsted Industries Inc., Chgo. Office: Amsted Industries Inc 205 N Michigan Ave Chicago IL 60601

MONTGOMERY, LARRY (R. LAWRENCE MONTGOMERY), retail executive; b. 1949; BS in Math., Ferris State U., Mich. Pres., CEO Black's divsn. Allied Store Corp., 1985-87; sr. v.p., dir. stores, gen. mdse. mgr. Softlines, L.S. Ayres divsn. May Dept. Stores, 1987-88; sr. v.p., dir. stores Kohl's Corp., Menomonee Falls, Wis., 1988-93, exec. v.p., 1993-96, vice chmn., 1996—2000, CEO, 1999—, chmn., 2002—. Bd. dirs. Kohl's Corp., 1994—. Office: Kohls Corp N56 W17000 Ridgewood Dr Menomonee Falls WI 53051-5660 Office Phone: 262-703-7000.

MONTGOMERY, PHIL, state legislator; b. Hammond, Ind., July 7, 1957; married; 2 children. BS, U. Houston, 1988. Former systems engr.; mem. Wis. State Assembly, Madison, 1998—, mem. electronic democracy and govt. reform coms., mem. energy and utilities com., chair fin. instns. com., mem. health com., co-chair pub. and pvt. broadband com. Mem. Ashwaubenon Optimist Club, Green Bay Area Drug Alliance, Leadership Green Bay Alumni Assn.; active Spl. Olympics; mem. Ashwaubenon Cmty. Edn. Steering Com., Pioneer Fire Sta. Study Com., Waterfront Study Com. Republican. Office: State Capitol Rm 129 W PO Box 8953 Madison WI 53708-8953 Address: 1305 Oak Crest Dr Green Bay WI 54313

MONTGOMERY, REX, biochemist, educator; b. Halesowen, Eng., Sept. 4, 1923; came to U.S., 1948, naturalized, 1963; s. Fred and Jane (Holloway) M.; m. Barbara Winifred Price, Aug. 9, 1948 (dec.); children: Ian, David, Jennifer, Christopher. BSc, U. Birmingham, Eng., 1943, PhD, 1946, DSc, 1963. Rsch. assoc. U. Minn., 1951-55; mem. faculty U. Iowa, Iowa City, 1955—2005, prof. biochemistry, 1963—2005, assoc. dean U. Iowa Coll. Medicine, 1974-95, v.p. rsch., 1989-90, prof. emeritus, 2005—. Vis. prof. Nat. Australian U., 1969-70; mem. physiol. chemistry study sect. NIH, 1968-72; mem. drug devel. contract rev. com., 1975-87; chmn. com. biol. chemistry NAS, 1961-64; pesticide and fertilizer adv. bd. Iowa Dept. Agr., 1990-91; bd. dirs. Wallace Tech. Transfer Found., 1989-93; chmn. bd. dirs. Neurotron Inc., 1990-95; mem. rsch. com. Iowa Corn Promotion Bd., 1995-2001; rsch. dir. Biotech. Byproducts Consortium, 1989—; cons. in field. Author: Chemical Production of Lactic Acid, 1949, Chemistry of Plant Gums and Mucilages, 1959, Quantitative Problems in Biochemical Sciences, 2d edit., 1976, Biochemistry: A Case-Orientated Approach, 6th edit., 1996; mem. editl. adv. bd. Carbohydrate Rsch., 1968-80; mem. editl. bd. Molecular Biotherapy, 1988-92; contbr. articles to profl. jours. Postdoctoral fellow Ohio State U., 1948-49; fellow Sugar Research Found., Dept. Agr., 1949-51 Fellow: Royal Soc. Chemistry. Home: 1 Oaknoll Ct Iowa City IA 52246-5168 Office: U Iowa Coll Medicine Dept Biochemistry Iowa City IA 52242 Business E-Mail: rex-montgomery@uiowa.edu.

MONTGOMERY, ROBERT RENWICK, medical association administrator, educator; b. New Castle, Pa., June 3, 1943; BS in Chemistry, Grove City Coll., 1965; MD, U. Pitts., 1969. Diplomate Am. Bd. Pediatrics. Intern Childrens Hosp. Phila. U. Pa., 1969-70; resident Harriet Lane Svc. Johns Hopkins Hosp., 1972-73, fellow, 1972-73, U. Colo., 1973-76, Scripps Clinic and Rsch. Found., 1976-77; gen. med. officer USPHS, Chinle, Ariz., 1970-71, dep. chief pediatrics Tuba City, Ariz., 1971-72; rsch. clin fellow in pediatric hematology U. Colo., 1973-76; rsch. fellow in molecular immunology Scripps Clinic and Rsch. Found., 1976-77; acting dir. Mountain States Regional Hemphilia Program U. Colo., 1977-78, asst. prof. dept. pediatrics, 1977-80, co-dir. coagulation rsch. labs., asst. dir. mountain sates regional hemophilia program, 1978-80; asst. prof. dept. pediatrics Med. Coll. Wis., 1980-81; dir. hemostasis program Milwaukee Children's Hosp., 1980-84; med. dir. Great Lakes Hemophilia Found., 1980-84; dir. regional homeostasis reference lab. The Blood Ctr. Southeastern Wis., 1981—; cons. hemostasis lab., dept. pathology The Children's Hosp. Wis., 1981—; assoc. prof. dept. pediatrics Med. Coll. Wis., 1981-84; sr. investigator The Blood Ctr. Southeastern Wis., 1982—, section head hemostasis rsch.; scientific dir. Great Lakes Hemophilia Found., 1984-96; assoc. dir. rsch. The Blood Ctr. Southeastern Wis., 1984-86; assoc. clin. prof. dept. pediatrics Med. Coll. Wis., clin. prof. dept. pediatrics, 1986-96, prof. pediatrics, 1996—, vice chmn. rsch. dept. pediatrics, 1998—; dir. rsch. The Blood Ctr. Southeastern Wis., 1986-98; acting sect. head coagulation lab., dept. pathology Med. Coll. Wis., 1986-87; faculty med. tech. Marquette U., Milw., 1986-92; clin. prof. dept. pathology Med. Coll. Wis., 1987—; v.p., dir. rsch. to exec. v.p. and dir. rsch. The Blood Ctr. Southeastern Wis., 1988-96, 96-98. Mem. med. adv. com. Great Lakes Hemophilia Found., 1980-96, exec. com. 1995—; mem. libr. com., human rsch. rev. com. The Blood Ctr. Southeastern Wis., 1981—, mem. rsch. mgmt. group, rsch. strategic planning com., 1983—; mem. subcom. FVIII and von Willebrand factor Internat. Congress Thrombosis and Haemostasis, 1984—; mem. radiation safety com. The Blood Ctr. Southeastern Wis., 1984—; ad hoc reviewer Heart Lung and Blood Inst., NIH, 1984—; mem. Inst. Biosafety com. The Blood Ctr. Southeastern Wis., 1985—; chmn. rsch. review com. Nat. Hemophilia Found., 1987-96, mem. rsch. rev. com., 1996—; ad hoc reviewer com. B Nat. Heart, Lung and Blood Inst., 1991—; chmn. von Willebrand subcom. Hemophilia Rsch. Soc., 1990-97; pres. Hemophilia Rsch. Soc., 1990-93; exec. sec. Hemphilia Rsch. Soc. of N.A., 1993—; mem. med. scientific adv. com. Nat. Hemophilia Found., 1992-95; mem. bd. dirs. Wis. Sickle Cell Disease Comprehensive Ctr., 1992-93; chair med. adv. coun. Great Lakes Hemophilia Found., Milw., 1992-96; mem. blood diseases and resources adv. com. Nat. Heart, Lung, and Blood Inst., 1992-95; prof. pediat. Med. Coll. Wis., 1996—. Sr. asst. surgeon USPHS, Indian Health Svc., 1971-72. Recipient Nat. Rsch. Svc. award Heart Lung and Blood Inst., NIH, 1975-77, Young Investigator award, 1978-81, Established Investigator award Am. Heart Assn., 1982-87, Jack Kennedy Alumni Achievement award Groce City Coll., 1985, Dr. Murray Thelin award Nat. Hemophilia Found., 1991. Mem. AAAS, Am. Soc. Clin. Investigators, Am. Soc. Pediatric Hematology/Oncology, Am. Soc. Hematology, Am. Fedn. Clin. Rsch., Am. Heart Assn., Internat. Soc. Thrombosis and Hemostasis, Soc. Pediatric Rsch., Hemophilia Rsch. Soc. Office: Blood Center of SouthEastern Wis Blood Research Institute 1701 W Wisconsin Ave Milwaukee WI 53233-2113

MONTGOMERY, WILLIAM A., lawyer; b. Chgo., Aug. 15, 1960; s. William A. and Jane (Fauver) M. BA, Furman U., 1982; JD, Washington U., St. Louis, 1986. Bar: Mo. 1986, Ill. 1987. Of counsel Walgreen Co., Deerfield, Ill., 1987—. Contbr. articles to profl. jours. Mem. ABA, Ill. State Bar Assn., Mo. Bar Assn. Office: Walgreen Co 200 Wilmot Rd Deerfield IL 60015-4616

MONTGOMERY, WILLIAM ADAM, lawyer; b. Chgo., May 22, 1933; s. John Rogerson and Helen (Fyke) Montgomery; m. Jane Fauver, July 28, 1956 (div. Dec. 1967); children: Elizabeth, William, Virginia; m. Deborah Stephens, July 29, 1972; children: Alex, Katherine. AB, Williams Coll., 1955; LLB, Harvard U., 1958. Bar: D.C. 1958, Ill. 1959, U.S. Ct. Appeals (7th cir.) 1959, U.S. Supreme Ct. 1977. Atty. civil divsn., appellate sect. Dept. Justice, Washington, 1958—60; assoc. Schiff Hardin LLP, Chgo., 1960—68, ptnr., 1968—93, 1999—; v.p., gen. counsel State Farm Ins. Cos., Bloomington, Ill., 1994—97, sr. v.p., gen. counsel, 1997—99. Author: (39 corp. practice series) Tying Arrangements, 1984; co-author: Insurance Antitrust and Unfair Trade Practices Law, 2002; contbr. articles to profl. jours. Fellow: Am. Coll. Trial Lawyers; mem.: ABA (coun. antitrust sect. 1989—92), Seventh Cir. Bar Assn. (pres. 1988—89), Chgo. Bar Assn., Lawyers Club Chgo. Avocations: skiing, woodturning. Office: Schiff Hardin LLP 6600 Sears Tower Chicago IL 60606 Business E-Mail: wmontgomery@schiffhardin.com.

MONTO, ARNOLD SIMON, epidemiology educator; b. Bklyn., Mar. 22, 1933; s. Jacob and Mildred (Kaplan) M.; m. Ellyne Gay Polsky, June 15, 1958; children: Sarah D. Monto Maniaci, Jane E., Richard L., Stephen A. BA in Zoology, Cornell U., Ithaca, NY, 1954; MD, Cornell U., NYC, 1958. Diplomate Am. Coll. Epidemiology. Intern, asst. resident in medicine Vanderbilt U. Hosp., Nashville, 1958—60; USPHS postdoctoral fellow in infectious disease Stanford U. Med. Ctr., Palo Alto, Calif., 1960—62; mem. staff virus diseases sect. mid. Am. rsch. unit Nat. Inst. Allergy and Infectious Disease, Panama, 1962—65; assoc. prof. U. Mich. Sch. Pub. Health, Ann Arbor, 1965—76, prof., 1976—, chmn. dept. population planning and internat. health, 1993—97, dir. Ctr. for Population Planning, 1993—97, dir. U. Mich. Bioterrorism Preparedness Initiative, 2002—04. Vis. scientist Clin. Rsch. Ctr., Northwick Park Hosp., Harrow, Eng., 1976; scholar-in-residence bd. on sci. and tech. for internat. devel. NAS and Inst. Medicine, Washington, 1983-84; vis. scientist div. communicable diseases WHO, Geneva, 1986-87; mem. pulmonary diseases adv. com. Nat. Heart, Lung and Blood Inst., Bethesda, Md., 1979-83; mem. nat. adv. coun. Nat. Inst. Allergy and Infectious Diseases, Bethesda, 1989-93; mem. WHO Influenza Pandemic Task Force, 2006—. Contbr. articles to med. jours. Recipient career devel. award IH. Fellow Am. Coll. Epidemiology, Infectious Diseases Soc. Am.; mem. APHA (governing coun. 1978-80), Am. Epidemiol. Soc. (pres. 2004-05). Achievements include research on respiratory viral infections in the community; demonstration of effectiveness of influenza vaccine in severe disease in the elderly; prevention of spread of influenza virus and treatment of illness, occurrence, causes and treatment of common cold. Office: U Mich Sch Pub Health I 109 Observatory St Ann Arbor MI 48109-2029 Office Phone: 734-764-5453. Business E-Mail: asmonto@umich.edu.

MONTOYA, CARLOS, bank executive; b. 1960; BS, Loyola Univ., Chgo., 1981. Former loan officer Steel City Nat. Bank, Chgo., 1984; from loan officer to CEO Republic Bank Chgo., 1994—2002; founder, pres., CEO AztecAmerica Bancorp, Chgo., 2002—. Office: AztecAmerica Bank 4322 Ashland Ave Chicago IL 60609 Fax: 773-346-0388.

MONTPETIT, JEFFREY M., lawyer; b. St. Paul, 1972; BA, St. John's U., Collegeville, Minn., 1995; JD, William Mitchell Coll. Law, St. Paul, 1998. Bar: Minn. 1999, US Dist. Ct. (dist. Minn.) 1999, US Ct. Appeals (8th cir.) 1999. Atty. Sieben, Grose, Von Holtum & Carey, Ltd., Mpls., 1998—. Named a Rising Star, Minn. Super Lawyers mag., 2006. Mem.: Wis. Bar Assn., Hennepin County Bar Assn., ABA, Fed. Bar Assn., Minn. Trial Lawyers Assn., Assn. Trial

Lawyers of Am., Minn. State Bar Assn. Office: Sieben Grose Von Holtum & Carey Ltd 900 Midwest Plz East Bldg 800 Marquette Ave Minneapolis MN 55402 Office Phone: 612-333-9762. E-mail: jeffrey.montpetit@knowyourrights.com.

MONTROSS, ERIC SCOTT, professional basketball player; b. Sept. 23, 1971; s. Scott and Janice M.; m. Laura, Aug. 27, 1994. Student in Speech Comm., U. N.C. Ctr. Boston Celtics, 1994-96, N.J. Nets, 1996-97, Phila. 76ers, 1997-98, Detroit Pistons, 1998—. Named All-Am. Second team AP, All-ACC First team, All-Tournament teams ACC, NCAA East Region, NCAA Final Four, All-Rookie Second team, Schick, 1994-95. Avocations: reading, fishing, skeet shooting, travel, music. Office: Detroit Pistons The Palace of Auburn Hills Two Championship Dr Auburn Hills MI 48326

MONTY, MITCHELL, landscape company executive; Pres. Suburban Landscape Assocs., Inc., 1981—. Office: Suburban Landscape Associates Inc 20875 N Brady St Davenport IA 52804-9305

MONZON, CARLOS MANUEL, physician; s. Carlos Manuel and Amparo (Letona) Monzon; children: Carlos Rodolfo, Juan Pablo. MD, U. San Carlos, Guatemala, 1976; MSc, U. Minn., 1982. Diplomate Am. Bd. Pediat., Am. Bd. Pediat. Hematology and Oncology. Resident in pediat. U. San Carlos, 1976-77, U. Mo., Columbia, 1977-80; fellow in pediat. hematology and oncology Mayo Grad. Sch. Medicine, Rochester, Minn., 1980-82; instr. pediat. U. Mo., Columbia, 1982-83, asst. prof. child health, 1983-89; clin. asst. prof. in pediatrics Kansas U. Sch. Medicine, Kansas City, 1992—. Contbr. articles to med. jours. Recipient Fritz Kenny Meml. award in pediat. rsch. Midwest Soc. Pediat. Rsch., 1981. Fellow Am. Acad. Pediat. Home: 14201 Melrose St Overland Park KS 66221 Office: 20375 W 151st St Olathe KS 66061-7218

MOODY, JAMES T(YNE), federal judge; b. LaCenter, Ky., June 16, 1938; BA, Ind. U., 1960, JD, 1963. Bar: Ind. 1963, U.S. Dist. Ct. (no. and so. dists.) Ind. 1963, U.S. Supreme Ct. 1972. Atty. Cities of Hobart and Lake Station, Ind., 1963-73; sole practice Hobart, 1963-73; judge Lake County (Ind.) Superior Ct., 1973-79; magistrate U.S. Dist. Ct. (no. dist.) Ind., Hammond, 1979-82, judge, 1982—; mem. faculty bus. law Ind. U., 1977-80. Republican. Office: US Dist Ct 128 Fed Bldg 507 State St Hammond IN 46320-1533

MOOG, MATTHEW, Internet company executive; b. 1970; s. Robert A. and Shirleigh Moog; m. Lucy Morton Herman, Sept. 11, 1994. Grad. cum laude, George Washington U. Bus. devel. exec. Microsoft Corp., 1992—96; v.p. sales CoolSavings, Inc., Chgo., 1996—98, exec. v.p. sales, mktg., 1998—2001, pres., 2001—, COO, 2001, now CEO, 2001—. Named one of 40 Under Forty, Crain's Bus. Chgo., 2005.

MOON, HARLEY WILLIAM, veterinarian; b. Tracy, Minn., Mar. 1, 1936; s. Harley Andrew Moon and Catherine Mary (Engesser) Lien; m. Irene Jeannette Casper, June 9, 1996; children: Michael J., Joseph E., Anne E., Teresa J. BS, U. Minn., 1958, DVM, 1960, PhD, 1965. Diplomate Am. Bd. Veterinary Pathologists. Instr. Coll. Vet. Medicine U. Minn., St. Paul, 1960—62, NIH postdoctoral fellow, 1963—65; vis. scientist Brookhaven Nat. Lab., Upton, NY, 1965—66; assoc. prof. Coll. Vet. Medicine U. Sask., Saskatoon, Canada, 1966—68; rsch. vet. Nat. Animal Disease Ctr. Agrl. Rsch. Svc., USDA, Ames, Iowa, 1968—88, ctr. dir., 1988—95; Franklyn Ramnsey chair in veterinary medicine & prof. Ames, Iowa, 1996—; dir. Plum Island Animal Disease Ctr. USDA, 1995—96; prof. in charge Vet. Med. Rsch. Inst., 1996; now prof. emeritus, vet. med. Iowa State Univ. Assoc. prof. Iowa State U., Ames, 1970—73, prof., 1972—74; cons. U. N.C., Chapel Hill, 1985—92, Pioneer Hy-Bred Internat., Johnson, Iowa, 1986—92. Contbr. articles reporting rsch. on animal diseases. Recipient Superior Svc. award, USDA. Mem.: NAS, AAAS, NAS, AVMA, Am. Soc. Microbiologists, Am. Coll. Vet. Pathologists, Phi Zeta, Sigma Xi. Avocation: farming. Office: Iowa State University Veterinary Medicine Research Institute 1802 Elmwood Dr Ames IA 50011-0001

MOON, JAMES RUSSELL, retired technology education educator; b. St. Cloud, Minn., Apr. 12, 1950; s. Glenn Howard and Audrey Katherine (Berg) M.; m. Corrine Mae St. Aubin, July 14, 1978; children: Sheri Ann, Brian Michael. BS, St. Cloud State U., 1972; MS, Bemidji State U., 1975. Tech. edn. tchr. Minnetonka Pub. Schs., Minn., 1972—2005, dist. dept. chmn. tech. edn., 1993-95; ret., 2006. Voc. standards com. Minn. Dept. Edn., 1995; mem. State Planning Com., 1989-2005. Designer/engr.: Row Crop Tractor, 1975; contbr. articles to profl. jours. Recipient Anchor award Minn. Pub. Schs., 1991, Tchr. Excellence award Internat. Tech. Edn. Assn., 1994, Disting. Tech. Educator Citation, 2002, Minnetonka Co-curricular Advisor of Yr., 2001, Tchr. of Yr. Optimist Club of Glen Lake, 2005; named Disting. Tech. Educator, Internat. Tech. Edn. Assn., 2002. Mem. Minn. Valley Tech. Edn. Assn. (sec. 1974), Minn. Tech. Edn. Assn. (mem. supermileage state competition com. 1989-2005, Tech. Edn. Tchr. of Yr. 1993, Disting. Svc. award 1991, 92, 94, Joyce Gustafson Meml. award, 2003). Presbyterian. Avocations: auto restoration, outdoor activities. Home: 2037 20th St SE Buffalo MN 55313-4813 Home Phone: 763-682-3679.

MOON, JOHN C., healthcare company executive; B in Computer sci., No. Ill. U., M in Mgmt. Info. Sys. With Baxter Internat., Deerfield, Ill., 1983—, v.p. info. tech. renal bus., 1996—2000, chief info. officer, 2000—, v.p., 2002—. Bd. dirs. Global Healthcare Exch. Mem.: Assn. of Info. Tech. Profls., Soc. Info. Mgmt., Pharm. Info. Sys. Assn.

MOONE, ROBERT H., retired insurance company executive; BA in Psychology, Ohio State U., 1966. With State Auto Fin. Corp., Columbus, Ohio, 1970, br. underwriting mgr., 1980, mgr. sales devel., dir. mktg., dir. sales and mktg., pres., 1996—2006, CEO, 1999—2006, chmn., 2000—06.

MOONEY, BETH, bank executive; BA, U. Tex.; MBA, So. Meth. U. Sec. First Republic Bank, Dallas, bank mgr., 1980, Citicorp; head banking group AmSouth Bank, Tenn., No. La., 2000—04, sr. exec. v.p., CFO Birmingham, 2004—06; vice chairwoman KeyCorp, 2006—. Bd. dir. United Way Met. Nashville, 2001—, Vanderbilt Univ. Med. Ctr. Named one of 25 Most Powerful Women in Banking, US Banker, 2005, Top 10 CFOs in Banking, 2006, 25 Women to Watch, 2006. Office: KeyCorp 127 Public Sq Cleveland OH 44114 Office Phone: 615-748-2214. Office Fax: 205-326-4072.

MOONEY, KEVIN W., telecommunications executive; BS in Fin., Seton Hall U.; MBA in Fin., Ga. State U. Various mgmt. positions New Jersey Bell, AT&T, BellSouth Cellular, BellSouth, Inc.; CFO Cin. Bell, Inc.; exec. v.p. Broadwing, Inc., Cin. Office: 401 E 4th St PO Box 2301 Cincinnati OH 45201-2301

MOONEYHAM, BOBBY R., educational association administrator; D, U. Okla., 1975. Tchr., Yukon, Okla.; dir. Beaver County Cooperative Guidance Prog., Okla.; supt. Corn Pub. Schs., Okla., Okemah Pub. Schs., Okla.; exec. dir. Okla. State Sch. Bds. Assn., 1975—2000, Nat. Rural Edn. Assn., 2002—; adj. instr. dept. edn1. leadership and policy studies U. Okla., Norman. Creator Okla. Edn. Coalition, 1998. Named a Friend of Edn., Okla. Edn. Assn., 2004; named to Okla. Educators Hall of Fame, 2000. Office: U Okla 112 Fourth St Box 2 Norman OK 73019 Office Phone: 405-325-7959. E-mail: bmooneyham@ou.edu.

MOOR, ROB, professional sports team executive; b. Geneva; came to US, 1966; Grad., U. Calif., Irvine. Distbn. mgr. MGM Studios; mem. staff royalties, licensing and profits 20th Century Fox Studios; exec. v.p. NHL LA Kings; pres. Minn. Timberwolves, 1994—2005, CEO, 2005—; pres. Midwest Entertainment Grp. Bd. mem. Greater Mpls. Conv. and Visitors Assn., Downtown Coun. Mem. Greater Mpls. C. of C. (bd. dirs.). Office: Minn Timberwolves 600 First Ave N Minneapolis MN 55403-1416

MOOR, ROY EDWARD, finance educator; b. Riverside, Calif., Oct. 11, 1924; s. Hugh Erin and Clara Viola Moor; m. Beverly A. Colbroth, Aug. 29, 1959; children— Cynthia Ann, Sheryl Lynn BA, UCLA, 1949; PhD, Harvard U., 1958. Vice pres., chief economist Fidelity Bank, Phila., 1965-68; vice pres., chief economist Drexel Firestone, Phila., 1968-71, Warburg Paribas Becker, NYC, 1971-81; sr. v.p., chief economist First Chgo. Corp., 1981-86; prof. fin. Ill. Inst. Tech., Chgo., 1986—. Dir. Nat. Bur. Econ. Research, Cambridge, Mass. Author: Federal Budget as an Economic Document, 1962 Fellow Nat. Assn. Bus. Economists (pres. 1973) Home: 1013 Woodrush Ct Westmont IL 60561-8823 E-mail: rbmoor@kwom.com.

MOORADIAN, ARSHAG DERTAD, internist, educator; b. Aleppo, Syria, Aug. 20, 1953; arrived in U.S., 1981; s. Dertad and Araxi (Halajian) Mooradian; m. Deborah Lynn Miles, June 25, 1985; children: Arshag Dertad, Jr., Ariana Araxie. BS, Am. U., Beirut, 1976, MD, 1980. Diplomate Am. Bd. Internal Medicine. Asst. prof. medicine UCLA, 1985-88; assoc. prof. U. Ariz., Tucson, 1988-91; prof. St. Louis U., 1991—2006; prof. medicine, chmn. dept. medicine U. Fla., 2006—. Contbr. articles to profl. jours. Grantee VA, 1985—97. Mem.: Am. Diabetes Assn. (chmn. task force micronutrients 1990—91, chmn. coun. nutrition and metabolism 2000—02), Endocrine Soc., Gerontol. Soc. Am., Am. Fedn. Clin. Rsch., Phi Kappa Phi, Alpha Omega Alpha. Mem. Armenian Orthodox Ch. Achievements include identification of a potential biomarker of aging; research in on age-related changes in the blood-brain barrier; on age-related changes in thyroid hormone action; on diabetes related changes in the central nervous system. Office: U Fla Coll Medicine Dept Medicine 653-1 West Eighth St Jacksonville FL 32209 Business E-Mail: arshag.mooradian@jax.ufl.edu.

MOORE, ANDREA S., state legislator; b. Libertyville, Ill., Sept. 2, 1944; Attended, Drake U. m. William Moore; 3 children. Mem. Ill. Ho. of Reps., 1993—; mem. com. on elections and state govt.; mem. com. on aging; mem. cities and villages com.; mem. environ. and energy com.; mem. labor and commerce com.; mem. com. on healthcare; mem. revenue and commerce com. Republican. Home: 361 S Saint Marys Rd Libertyville IL 60048-9407 Office: Ill Ho of Reps State Capitol Springfield IL 62706-0001 also: 131 E Park Ave Libertyville IL 60048-2800

MOORE, C. BRADLEY, chemistry professor; b. Boston, Dec. 7, 1939; s. Charles Walden and Dorothy (Lutz) Moore; m. Penelope Williamson Percival, Aug. 27, 1960; children: Megan Bradley, Scott Woodward. BA magna cum laude, Harvard U., 1960; PhD, U. Calif., Berkeley, 1963. Predoctoral fellow NSF, 1960-63; asst. prof. chemistry U. Calif., Berkeley, 1963-68, assoc. prof., 1968-72, prof., 1972-2000, prof. emeritus, 2000—, vice chmn. dept., 1971-75, chmn. dept. chemistry, 1982-86, dean Coll. Chemistry, 1988-94; v.p. rsch. Ohio State U., Columbus, Disting. prof. math. and phys. sci., prof. chemistry, 2000—03, prof. emeritus, 2003—; prof. chemistry Northwestern U., 2003—08, v.p. rsch., 2003—07, prof. emeritus, 2008—. Assoc. prof. Faculty Scis., Paris, 1970, 75; Miller Rsch. Prof. U. Calif., Berkeley, 1972-73, 87-88; vis. prof. Inst. for Molecular Sci., Okazaki, Japan, 1979, Fudan U., Shanghai, 1979, adv. prof., 1988—; vis. fellow Joint Inst. for Lab. Astrophysics, U. Colo., Boulder, 1981-82; vis. prof., U. Gottingen, 1994, University Heidelberg, 1994, Max Planck Inst., Fiir Quantum Optic, 1997; faculty sr. scientist (Chemical Sci. Div.) Lawrence Berkeley Nat. Lab., 1974-2000, divsn. dir., 1998-2000: mem. editl. bd. Jour. Chem. Physics, 1973-75, Chem. Physics Letters, 1980-85, Jour. Phys. Chemistry, 1981-87, Laser Chemistry, 1982—; mem. Basic Energy Scis. adv. com. Office Sci. U.S. Dept. Energy, 2000-03. Editor: Chemical and Biochemical Applications of Lasers; assoc. editor Annual Review of Physical Chemistry, 1985-90; contbr. articles to profl. jours. Trustee Sci. Svc., 1995-2007, Sci. and Tech. Campus, 2000-03; mem. bd. govs. Ohio Supercomputer Ctr., 2000-03; rsch. officer Coun. of Ohio Bd. of Regents, 2000-03; pres., chmn. bd. Ohio State U. Rsch. Found., 2000-03; mem. governing bd. Argonne Nat. Lab., 2005-07, mem. sci. policy coun., 2005-07. Recipient Coblentz award, 1973, E.O. Lawrence Meml. award U.S. Dept. Energy, 1986, Lippincott award, 1987, 1st award Inter-Am. Photochem. Soc., 1988; nat. scholar Harvard U., 1958-60; fellow Alfred P. Sloan Found., 1968, Guggenheim Found., 1969, Humboldt Rsch. award for Sr. U.S. Scientists, 1994. Fellow AAAS (coun. 2007-, cheon coun. affairs, 2008-), Am. Acad. Arts and Scis., Am. Phys. Soc. (Plyler award 1994); mem. NSF adv. com. for education and human resources directorate, chair subcom. policy and planning 1997-99, NAS (chmn. com. undergrad. sci. edn. 1993-97, class I membership com., 1998-2000, 2002, 2000 nominating com.), Am. Chem. Soc. (past chmn. divsn. phys. chemistry, Calif. sect. award 1977). Avocation: bicycling. Office: Univ Calif Dept Chemistry 633 Clark St Berkeley CA 94720-1460 Home Phone: 510-528-4372; Office Phone: 847-491-3485, 510-206-1409. E-mail: moorecb@berkley.edu.

MOORE, DAVID SHELDON, statistics educator, researcher; b. Plattsburg, NY, Jan. 28, 1940; s. Donald Sheldon and Mildred (Roberts) M.; m. Nancy Kie Bok Hahn, June 20, 1964; children: Matthew, Deborah. AB in Mathematics, Princeton U., 1962; PhD in Mathematics, Cornell U., 1967. Asst., assoc. then prof. profl. stats. Purdue U., West Lafayette, Ind., 1967—96, Shanti S. Gupta disting. prof. stats., 1996, Shanti S. Gupta disting. prof. stats. emeritus, asst. dean Grad. Sch., 1977—80, dir. Stats. and Nat. Sci., 1980—81. Program dir. NSF, Washington, 1980-82, cons. 1981—; cons. NRC, Washington, 1982-85, content expert Annenberg/CPB project TV series, 1987, 89, 92; mem. U.S. Nat. Commn. Math. Instrn., 1999-2001. Author: Statistics Concepts and Controversies, 1978, 5th edit. 2001, Introduction to the Practice of Statistics, 1989, 3d edit., 1999, 5th edit., 2005, Basic Practice of Statistics, 1995, 2nd edit., 2000, 3rd edit., 2004; assoc. editor Internat. Stat. Rev., 1992-95, Jour. Stat. Edn., 1993-96; contbr. articles to profl. jours. Danforth Found. Grad. fellow, 1962-67. Fellow Am. Statis. Assn. (pres. 1998, Founders award 2001), Inst. Math. Statis. (governing coun. 1984-88); mem. Internat. Stat. Inc. (mem. coun. 1993-95), Math. Assn. Am. (Haimo award for Disting. Coll. and Univ. tchg. of Math, Ind. sect., 1994). Home: 4840 Jackson Hwy West Lafayette IN 47906-9209 Office: Purdue U Dept Stats Math Sciences Bldg 150 North University St West Lafayette IN 47907-1399 Office Phone: 765-494-6050. Office Fax: 765-494-0558. E-mail: dsmoore@stat.purdue.edu.

MOORE, DENNIS, congressman; b. Anthony, Kans., Nov. 8, 1945; m. Stephene; 7 children. BS, U. Kans., 1967; JD, Washburn U., 1970. Bar: Kans. 1970. Asst. atty. gen. State of Kans., 1971-73; pvt. practice, 1973-76; dist. atty. Johnson County, 1977-89; ptnr. Erker & Moore, LLC, 1991-98, Smith, Gill, Fisher & Butts, 1989-91; mem. U.S. Congress from 3d Kans. dist., 1999—, mem. com. on fin. svcs. and the budget. Elected to Johnson County C.C. bd. trustees, 1993; re-elected, 1997; bd. dirs. Johnson County Safehome, Coalition for Prevention of Child Abuse, Kans. Child Abuse Prevention Coun., CASA (Ct. Appointed Spl. Advocate), United Cmty. Svcs., Cmty. Corrections Adv. Bd.; unsuccessful Dem. candidate for state atty. gen., 1986. With U.S. Army, U.S. Army Res. Democrat. Achievements include personally prosecuting more than 25 felony jury trials; led Consumer Protection Divsn. in the investigation and successful prosecution of a nat. oil co. charged with rigging gas pumps to cheat consumers; established a victim assistance unit; was cited by an ind. cons. hired by the Johnson County Bd. Commrs. as running the most efficient office in Johnson County govt.; served as pres. Kans. County and Dist. Atty.'s Assn. Office: US Ho Reps 1727 Longworth Ho Office Bldg Washington DC 20515-1603

MOORE, DENNIS J., electronics executive; b. 1938; Grad., U.S. Naval Acad., 1961. bd. dirs. Instron Corp., adv. bd. Allendale Mutual Ins. Co., trustee Naval Acad. Found. Exec. mgmt. mktg., research and devel. Rosemount, Inc.; pres. Beckman Indsl., 1984-87, Electronics & Space Corp., 1987-89; group v.p. Emerson, 1989-90; pres., COO ESCO Techs., Inc., 1990-92, chmn., CEO, 1992—. Office: Esco Technologies 9900 Clayton Rd Ste A Saint Louis MO 63124-1186

MOORE, DORSEY JEROME, dentistry educator, maxillofacial prosthetist; b. Boonville, Mo., Feb. 8, 1935; s. Lloyd Elliott Moore and Mary Elizabeth (Day) Katemann; m. Mary Louise Foote, May 2, 1959; children: Elizabeth L., David J. DDS, U. Mo., Kansas City, 1959. Diplomate Am. Bd. Prosthodontics. Commd. ensign USN, 1955, advanced through grades to capt., 1973; gen. practice dentistry various naval stas., 1959-63; practice in prosthodontics USS Proteus AS-19, 1963-66; resident in prosthodontics and maxillofacial prosthetics Naval Dental Sch., Bethesda, Md., 1966-69, chief maxillofacial prosthetics divsn., 1969-70; sr. dental advisor Naval Adv. Group, Comdr. Naval Forces, Saigon, Vietnam, 1970-71; chief maxillofacial prosthetics div. Nat. Naval Dental Ctr., 1971-76; chief maxillofacial prosthetics br. Naval Regional Med. Ctr., Great Lakes, Ill., 1976-79, ret., 1979; vis. lectr. U. Mo. Sch. Dentistry, Kansas City, 1976-79, H.G.B. Robinson prof., chmn. dept. removable prosthodontics, 1979-2000, Hamilton G.B. Robinson emeritus prof. dentistry, 2000, ret., 2000; chief maxillofacial prosthetics Truman Med. Ctr., Kansas City, Mo., 2000—. Assoc. prof. U. Saigon Sch. Dentistry, 1970-71; advisor to Min. of Health, Saigon, 1970-71; profl. lectr. George Washington U., Washington, 1971-76; clin. assoc. prof. surgery U. Kans. City Sch. Medicine, 1987—; cons. maxillofacial prosthetics NIH Treatment Ctr., 1973—, Nat. Cancer Inst., 1973—, VA Hosp., North Chicago, Ill., 1976—, ADA Couns. Dental Edn., Hosp. Dental Svc. and Commn. on Accredition, 1978—; vice chancellor Devel. Adv. Com., 1983—; examiner Mo. Specialty Bd. Prosthodontics, 1982—; internat. cir. course lectr. Am. Prosthetics Soc., Indonesia, 1974, Guatelmala, 1975, N.Z., 1976, S.Africa, 1981, Japan, Taiwan, 1989, Mexico City, 1994, Beijing and Chengdu, China, 1998; nat. cons. U.S. Naval Dental Sch., Bethesda, 1991—; chief maxillofacial prosthetics Truman Med. Ctr., 2000-. Author: Practical Oral Rehabilitation of the Edentulous Patient, 8th edit., 1995; mem. editl. bd. Cancer of the Head and Neck: A Comprehensive Review of the Literature, 1982—; contbr. articles to profl. jours. Mem. adminstrv. ch. bd. Cen. Methodist Ch., 1981-88, pres. offcl. ch. bd., 1983-85; bd. dir. Ednl. Rsch. Found. Prosthodontics, 1982—, chmn. 1988—; bd. dir. Penn Valley Fitness Trail Assn. Decorated Legion of Merit with combat V, other awards; Navy Cross of Gallantry with palm (Republic of Vietnam); recipient Ackerman Meml. award outstanding contbns. to maxillofacial prosthetics, 1999. Fellow Am. Acad. Maxillofacial Prosthetics (bd. dir. 1972-75, mem. exec. com. 1973-76, pres. 1978-79, mem. exec. coun. 1979-82), Am. Coll. Prosthodontics (charter), Am. Coll. Dentists, Acad. Prosthodontics, Internat. Coll. Dentist, Midwest Acad. Prosthodontics; mem. ADA, Greater Kansas City Dental Soc. Avocations: jazz musician, string bassist. Office: Truman Med Ctrs Hospital Hill 2301 Holmes Kansas City MO 64108 Office Phone: 816-404-0500. E-mail: mooredj@umkc.edu.

MOORE, EMILY ALLYN, pharmacologist; b. Evansville, Ind., Apr. 3, 1950; m. Robert Alan Yount, Nov. 25, 1972 (div. Feb. 1986); 1 child, Joseph Taylor; m. Robert E. Moore Jr., Aug. 11, 1990; 1 child, Alexander Allyn. AB in Chem. Biology, Ind. U., Bloomington, 1971; MS in Applied Computer Sci., Purdue U., Indpls., 1985; PhD in Pharmacology, Ind. U., Indpls., 1976. Vis. asst. prof. biology Ind. U., Bloomington, 1979, rsch. assoc. in biochemistry Indpls., 1979-81, rsch. assoc., 1982-83, computer programmer for med. genetics, 1983-85, asst. scientist. med. genetics, 1985-87; tech. assessment specialist Boehringer Mannheim Corp., Indpls., 1987, mgr. sci. info., 1987-89; mgr. Tech. Assess, Indpls., 1989-93, quality process analyst, 1993-94. Contbr. articles to profl. jours. Officer or bd. dirs. LWV, Hendricks County, Ind., 1977-84; elder St. Luke's United Ch. of Christ, Speedway, Ind., 1983-85; mem. adv. bd. Operation SMART, Indpls., 1989-90. Achievements include participation in creation of first DNA bank for storage of DNA samples for future use in diagnosis of genetic diseases.

MOORE, GARRY ALLEN, state legislator; b. Yankton, SD, May 14, 1949; m. Connie Moore; 4 children. Student, S.D. State U., 1967-69. Mem. S.D. Ho. of Reps., 1991-98, mem. judiciary com., taxation com., local govt. com., health and human svcs. com.; mem. S.D. Senate from 18th dist., Pierre, 1999—; mem. judiciary com., govt. audit and ops. com. S.D. Senate, taxation com., transp. com., corrections commn. Sales mgr. Bob's Candy Svc., Yankton. Past mem. exec. bd. State Dem. Party; chmn. Yankton Sch. Bd., 1982-88. Mem. S.D. Wholesalers Assn. (past pres., mem. state affairs com.). Home: 2310 Western Ave Yankton SD 57078-1419

MOORE, GEORGE C., manufacturing executive; BA in Acctg., Loyola Coll. CPA. Acct. Arthur Andersen, 1977—87; pres., CFO Yield House, 1987—97; group fin. officer Tanaher Tools, Tool Products, Safety and Aviation and Automotive Danaher Corp., 1997—2003, group v.p. fin., 2000—03; exec. v.p. Maytag, Newton, Iowa, 2003—, CFO, 2003—. Office: Maytag 403 West 4th St N Newton IA 50208

MOORE, GWENDOLYNNE S. (GWEN MOORE), congresswoman; b. Racine, Wis., Apr. 18, 1951; 3 children. BA in Polit. Sci., Marquette U., Milw., 1978. Mem. Wis. State Assembly, 1989—92, Wis. State Senate from 4th dist., Madison, 1992—2004, US Congress from 4th Wis. dist., 2005—, mem. small bus. com., mem. fin. svcs. com. Named one of Most Influential Black Americans, Ebony mag., 2006. Democrat. Office: US House Reps 1408 Longworth House Office Bldg Washington DC 20515-4904 Office Phone: 202-225-4572.

MOORE, JOHN EDDY, former lieutenant governor; b. Charleston, W.Va., July 13, 1943; s. George Roy and Alvaretta (Hoskins) M.; m. Martha Clay Spangenberg, Aug. 7, 1966; children— Brian Clay, Stacia Hoskins BS in Comemrce, Washington and Lee U., 1965; JD, U. Ky., 1968. Group dir. Rockwell Internat., Cedar Rapids, Iowa, 1974-80, v.p. Dallas, 1980-81; v.p., ptnr. Korn/Ferry Internat., Dallas, 1981-82; sr. v.p. Cessna Aircraft, Wichita, Kans., 1982—2002; lt. gov. State of Kansas, 2003—07. Dir. Health Care Plus, Wichita, Kans., Riverside Hosp., Wichita; former mem. Spl. Commn. on Pub. Agenda for Kans.; sec. Kans. Foodbank Warehouse, Wichita; bd. dirs. Booth Meml. Residence, Wichita Mem. Midwest Aerospace Indsl. Relations Council, Machinery and Allied Products Inst. (human resources council), Wichita C. of C. (chmn. state legis. com.), Kans. C. of C. and Industry (bd. dirs.) Republican. Methodist. Avocation: golf.

MOORE, JOHN EDWIN, JR., academic administrator; b. Aurora, Mo., Nov. 7, 1942; s. John Edwin and Emma Lou (Harback) M.; children: John E. III, Catherine Porter. BA cum laude, Yale U., 1964, MA in Teaching, 1965; EdD, Harvard U., 1971. Tchr. N.C. Advancement Sch., Winston-Salem, 1965-66; rsch. asst. Tech. Edn. Rsch. Ctr., Cambridge, Mass., 1969-70; adminstrv. asst., treas. Kirkwood Sch. Dist. R-VII, St. Louis, 1970-73, asst. supt., treas., 1973-74; adj. prof. U. Mo., St. Louis, 1973-74; v.p. Athens (Greece) Coll., 1974-75; asst. commr. edn. Dept. Elem. and Secondary Edn., Jefferson City, Mo., 1975-83; pres. Drury U., Springfield, Mo., 1983—. Part-time instr. Far-East div. U. Md., 1967-68. Bd. dirs. United Way Ozarks, campaign chmn., 1988; bd. dirs. Mo. Colls. Fund, chmn., 1988-89; bd. dirs. Make-A-Wish Found.; chmn. bd. dirs. Am. Nat. Fish & Wildlife Mus., 1998—. With U.S. Army, 1966-68. Recipient Vincent Conroy Meml. award Harvard Grad. Sch. Edn., 1971; named one of Outstanding Young Men Am., 1973. Mem. Springfield Area C. of C. (v.p. 1988, bd. dirs. Springfieldian of Yr. 1989), Nat. Assn. Intercollegiate Athletics (coun. pres.'s), Rotary (pres. Springfield chpt. 1988-89). Presbyterian (elder). Avocations: hunting, fishing, gardening, conservation. Office: Drury U 900 N Benton Ave Springfield MO 65802-3712 Home: 1413 E River Oaks Ln Springfield MO 65804-7503

MOORE, JOHN RONALD, manufacturing executive; b. Pueblo, Colo., July 12, 1935; s. John E. and Anna (Yesberger) M.; m. Judith Russelyn Bauman, Sept. 5, 1959; children: Leland, Roni, Timothy, Elaine. BS, U. Colo., 1959; grad. advanced mgmt. program, Harvard Grad. Sch. Bus., 1981. Mgmt. trainee Montgomery Ward & Co., Denver, 1960-65; distbn. mgr. Midas Internat. Corp., Chgo., 1965-71; v.p., gen. mgr. Midas, Can., Toronto, Ont., 1972-75; pres. Auto Group Midas Internat. Corp., Chgo., 1976-82, pres., chief exec. officer, 1982-98. Bd. dirs. Lake Forest Grad. Sch. Mgmt., U. Colo. Found.; dir. Chgo. Crime Commn.; trustee U. Colo. Found. Mem. Harvard Bus. Sch. Alumni Assn., U. Colo. Alumni Assn., Chgo. Coun. Global Affairs, Econ. Club Chgo., Comml. Club Chgo. Republican.

MOORE, JOHN WILLIAM, former university president; b. Bayonne, NJ, Aug. 1, 1939; s. Frederick A. and Marian R. (Faser) M.; m. Nancy Baumann, Aug. 10, 1968; children: Matthew, Sarah, David. BS in Social Sci. and Edn., Rutgers U., 1961; MS in Counseling and Student Pers. Svcs., Ind. U., 1963; EdD, Pa. State U., 1970. Asst. to dean Coll. Edn. Pa. State U., University Park, 1968-70; asst. to dean students U. Vt., Burlington, 1970-71, asst. prof. edn. adminstrn., 1973-76, asst. v.p. acad. affairs, 1973-76, assoc. v.p. acad. affairs, 1976-77; v.p. policy and planning Old Dominion U., Norfolk, Va., 1977-78, exec. v.p., 1982-85; pres. Calif. State U., Stanislaus, Turlock, 1985-92, Ind. State U., 1992-2000. Author: (with others) The Changing Composition of the Work Force: Implications for Future Research and Its Application, 1982, also articles, papers presented at profl. meetings Pres. United Way, Modesto Calif., 1989; campaign chair United Way Wabash Valley, Terre Haute, Ind.; bd. dirs. Pvt. Industry Coun., Modesto, 1989, Union Hosp., Swope Mus., Am. Assn. Colls. and Univs.; bd. dirs., exec. com. Alliance for Growth and Progress, Terre Haute, Ind., 1992—, Terre Haute C. of C., Wabash Valley United Way, Bus. and Modernization Tech. Corp., Ind. Econ. Devel. Commn., PSI Energy. Recipient Disting. Svc. award Old Dominion U. Alumni Assn., 1985, Hispanic C. of C., 1982; recipient Community Svc. award Norfolk Commn. Edn., 1985, Leadership award United Way,1 986, Svc. award Pvt. Industry Coun., 1989; Alumni fellow Pa. State U., 1990. Mem. Am. Assn. State Colls. and Univs. (rep. Calif.

chpt. 1988-92, bd. dirs. 1994—), Gould Med. Found. (bd. dirs. 1988-92, trustee 1988-92), Modesto Symphony Orch. Assn. (bd. dirs. 1990-92), Am. Coun. Edn., Commn. on Women in Higher Edn., Turlock C. of C. (bd. dirs. 1988-92), Rotary. Methodist. Avocations: fitness training, skiing, coaching youth sports, golf. Office: Ind State U Condit House Terre Haute IN 47809-0001

MOORE, KAREN NELSON, judge; AB magna cum laude, Radcliffe Coll., 1970; JD magna cum laude, Harvard U., 1973. Bar: DC 1973, Ohio 1976, US Ct. Appeals (DC cir.) 1974, US Supreme Ct. 1980, US Ct. Appeals (6th cir.) 1984. Law clk. to Hon. Malcolm R. Wilkey US Ct. Appeals (DC Cir.), Washington, 1973—74; law clk. to Hon. Harry A. Blackmun US Supreme Ct., Washington, 1974—75; assoc. Jones, Day, Reavis & Pogue, Cleve., 1975—77; asst. prof. Case Western Res. Law Sch., Cleve., 1977—80, assoc. prof., 1980—82, prof., 1982—95; judge US Ct. Appeals (6th cir.), Cleve., 1995—. Vis. prof. Harvard Law Sch., 1990—91. Mem. Harvard Law Rev., 1971—73; contbr. articles to profl. jours. Trustee Lakewood Hosp., Ohio, 1978—85, Radcliffe Coll., Cambridge, 1980—84. Fellow: Am. Bar Found.; mem.: Harvard U. Alumni Assn. (bd. dirs. 1984—87), Am. Law Inst., Phi Beta Kappa. Office: US Ct Appeals 6th Cir Carl B Stokes US Courthouse 801 W Superior Ave Cleveland OH 44113-1831

MOORE, KENNETH CAMERON, lawyer; b. Chgo., Oct. 25, 1947; s. Kenneth Edwards and Margaret Elizabeth (Cameron) M.; m. Karen M. Nelson, June 22, 1974; children: Roger Cameron, Kenneth Nelson, Kristin Karen. BA summa cum laude, Hiram Coll., 1969; JD cum laude, Harvard U., 1973. Bar: Ohio 1973, U.S. Dist. Ct. Md. 1974, U.S. Ct. Appeals (4th cir.) 1974, D.C. 1975, U.S. Dist. Ct. (no. dist.) Ohio 1976, U.S. Ct. Appeals (6th cir.) 1977, U.S. Ct. Appeals (D.C. cir.) 1979, U.S. Supreme Ct. 1980. Law clk. to judge Harrison L. Winter U.S. Ct. Appeals (4th cir.), Balt., 1973-74; assoc. Squire, Sanders & Dempsey LLP, Washington, 1974—75, Cleve., 1975-82, ptnr., 1982—, profl. ethics ptnr., 1996—, mem. fin. com., 1990—, chair profl. ethics com., 2003—. Chmn. Ohio Fin. Com. for Jimmy Carter presdl. campaign, 1976; del. Dem. Nat. Conv., 1976; chief legal counsel Ohio Carter-Mondale Campaign, 1976; trustee Hiram Coll., 1997—, mem. exec. com., 1999, vice chair bd. trustees, 2000—, mem. bd. Laurel Sch., mem., 2005-, exec. com., 2006-, sec., 2006-, vice chair, 2007—. With AUS, 1970—76. Mem. ABA, Fed. Bar Assn., Ohio Bar Assn., Cleve. Bar Assn., Cleve. City Club. Home: 15602 Edgewater Dr Cleveland OH 44107-1212 Office: Squire Sanders & Dempsey LLP 4900 Key Ctr 127 Public Sq Ste 4900 Cleveland OH 44114-1304 Office Phone: 216-479-8500.

MOORE, KENNETH EDWIN, pharmacology educator; b. Edmonton, Alta., Can., Aug. 8, 1933; came to U.S., 1957, naturalized, 1966; s. Jack and Emily Elizabeth (Tarbox) M.; m. Barbara Anne Stafford, Sept. 19, 1953; children—Grant Kenneth, Sandra Anne, Lynn Susan. BS, U. Alta., 1955, MS, 1957; PhD, U. Mich., 1960. Instr. pharmacology Dartmouth Med. Sch., Hanover, N.H., 1960-61, asst. prof., 1962-66; assoc. prof. pharmacology Mich. State U., East Lansing, 1966-70, prof., 1970—, chmn. dept. pharmacology and toxicology, 1987—2001. Vis. scholar Cambridge (Eng.) U., 1974; instr. Lansing Community Coll., 1975-81; cons. NIH, also pharm. industry. Author 1 book; contbr. articles to profl. jours. Fellow Am. Coll. Neuropsychopharmacology; mem. Am. Soc. Pharmacology and Exptl. Therapeutics (chmn. bd. publs. trustees 1992-96, pres. 1998-2000), Soc. Exptl. Biology and Medicine, Soc. Neurosci. Home: 4790 Arapaho Trl Okemos MI 48864-1402 Office: Dept Pharmacology Mich State U East Lansing MI 48824 E-mail: moorek@msu.edu.

MOORE, KENNETH JAMES, agronomist, educator; b. Phoenix, June 6, 1957; s. George Taylor and Barbara Joyce (Amy) M.; m. Gina Marie McCarthy Aug. 11, 1979; children: Ellyn Elizabeth, David Taylor, Mark Daniel. BS in Agr., Ariz. State U., 1979; MS in Agronomy, Purdue U., 1981, PhD in Agronomy, 1983. Asst. prof. agronomy U. Ill., Urbana, 1983-87; assoc. prof. N.Mex. State U., Las Cruces, 1988-89; rsch. agronomist Agrl. Rsch. Svc., USDA, Lincoln, Nebr., 1989-93; prof. Iowa State U., Ames, 1993—. Adj. assoc. prof. U. Nebr. Lincoln, 1989-93, prof., 1993-96; sr. rsch. fellow Ag Rsch. Grasslands, New Zealand, 1998; dir. MS in Agronomy Distance Edn. program Iowa State U., 1995—, dir. Crop Advisor Inst., 2000—. Founding editor Crop Mgmt., 2001-02; assoc. editor Agronomy Jour., 1989-93, tech. editor, 1994-97; assoc. editor Crop Sci., 1994; editor: Forages: An Introduction to Grassland Ag, 2003, Forages: The Science of Grassland Agriculture, 2007, Native-Warm Season Grasses: Research Trends and Issues, 2000, Post-Harvest Physiology and Preservation of Forages, 1995; contbr. chpts. to books. Bd. dirs. Lincoln Children's Mus., 1991-93, Children's Svcs. of Ctrl. Iowa, 1996-97; bd. dirs. Children's Mus. Ctrl. Iowa, 1997-2002, pres., 2000-01; mem. mgmt. com. N.E. YMCA, Lincoln, 1991-93; mem. youth policy forum Lincoln YMCA, 1991-92. Recipient Point of Light award USDA, 1991. Fellow Am. Soc. Agronomy (bd. dirs. 2002-05 06—, pres.-elect 2007), Crop Sci. Soc. Am. (divsn. chmn. 1990-92, pres. 2003-04, exec. com. and bd. dirs. 2002-05, Young Crop Scientist award 1993); mem. Am. Forage and Grassland Coun. (Outstanding Young Scientist award 1982, merit award 1991). Independent. Methodist. Avocations: swimming, fishing, music. Office: Iowa State U Agronomy Dept 1571 Agronomy Hall Ames IA 50011-0001 Office Phone: 515-294-5482. Business E-Mail: kjmoore@iastate.edu.

MOORE, LORRIE, writer, English professor; b. Glens Falls, NY, Jan. 13, 1957; BA summa cum laude, St. Lawrence U., 1978; MFA, Cornell U., 1982. Now prof. English, U. Wis., Madison. Author: Self-Help, 1985, Anagrams, 1986, The Forgotten Helper, 1987, Like Life, 1990, Who Will Run the Frog Hospital?, 1994, Birds of America, 1998 (Nat. Book Critics Cir. award finalist, Irish Times Internat. Prize for Lit.); editor: I Know Some Things: Stories About Childhood by Contemporary Writers, 1992, The Best American Short Stories 2004; contbr. fiction reviews and essays to NY Times, NY Review of Books, Harper's, Paris Rev., New Yorker, others. Recipient Nat. Endowment Arts award, 1989, award, Irish Times, 1999, Rea award achievement in short story, 2004, PEN/Malamud award short fiction, 2005; Guggenheim fellow, 1991, Lannan Found. fellow, 2001. Mem.: Am. Acad. Arts and Letters. Office: 7187 Helen C White Hall Univ Wis Dept English 600 N Park St Madison WI 53706

MOORE, MCPHERSON DORSETT, lawyer; b. Pine Bluff, Ark., Mar. 1, 1947; s. Arl Van and Jesse (Dorsett) M. BS, U. Miss., 1970; JD, U. Ark., 1974. Bar: Ark. 1974, Mo. 1975, U.S. Patent and Trademark Office 1977, U.S. Dist. Ct. (ea. dist.) Mo. 1977, U.S. Ct. Appeals (8th, 10th and fed. cirs.). Design engr. Tenneco, Newport ews, Va., 1970-71; assoc. Rogers, Eilers & Howell, St. Louis, 1974-80; ptnr. Rogers, Howell, Moore & Haferkamp, St. Louis, 1981-89, Armstrong, Teasdale, Schlafly & Davis, St. Louis, 1989-95, Polster, Lieder, Woodruff & Lucchesi, St. Louis, 1995—. Engr. City of Ladue, Mo., 1998-2000; mem. intellectual property adv. bd. Washington U. Bd. dirs. Legal Svcs. Ea. Mo.; mem. Ladue Zoning and Planning Commn., 1998—; chmn. St. Michael's Houses, Ch. St. Michael and St. George. With USAR, 1970-76. Mem. ABA, Bar Assn. Met. St. Louis (chmn. young lawyers sect. 1981-82, sec. 1984-85, v.p. 1985-86, chmn. trial sect. 1986-87, pres. 1988-89), Ark. Bar Assn., St. Louis Bar Found. (sec. 1984-85, v.p. 1988-89, pres. 1989-90), The Mo. Bar (chmn. patent, trademark and copyright law com. 1992-94, co-chmn. 1994-95), St. Louis County Bar Assn., Women Lawyers Assn., Am. Intellectual Property Law Assn., Mound City Bar Assn., Phi Delta Theta Alumni (treas. St. Louis chpt. 1987-88, sec. 1988-89, v.p. 1989-90), Racquet Club (St. Louis). Home: 3 Mayfair Rd Saint Louis MO 63124-1663 Office: Polster Lieder Woodruff & Lucchesi Ste 200 12412 Powers Ct Dr Saint Louis MO 63131-3615 Office Phone: 314-238-2400.

MOORE, MITCHELL JAY, lawyer, educator; b. Lincoln, Nebr., Aug. 29, 1954; s. Earl J. and Betty Marie (Zimmerlin) M.; m. Sharon Lea Campbell, Sept. 5, 1987. BS in Edn., U. Mo., Columbia, 1977, JD, 1981. Bar: Mo. 1981, U.S. Dist. Ct. (we. dist.) Mo. 1981, Tex. 1982, U.S. Ct. Appeals (8th cir.) 1998. Tchr. Clinton Mid. Sch., 1978; sole practice Columbia, Mo., 1981—. Coordinating atty. student legal svcs. ctr. U. Mo., Columbia, 1983-89. Mem. Columbia Substance Abuse Adv. Commn., 1989—; bd. dirs. Planned Parenthood of Ctrl. Mo., Columbia, 1984-86, Opportunities Unltd., Columbia, 1984-86, ACLU of Mid-Mo., 1991-98; Libertarian candidate for Atty. Gen. of Mo., 1992, 2000, for 9th congl. dist. U.S. Ho. of Reps., 1994, 96, for Mo. State Rep. 23d dist., 1998, mem. Probation and Parole Citizens Adv. Bd., 1997-99. Recipient Pro Bono Publico award, Mid-Mo. Legal Svcs. Corp. Mem.: Tex. Bar Assn., Mo. Bar Assn., Boone County Bar Assn., Phi Delta Phi. Libertarian. Unitarian Universalist. Avocations: softball, camping, Tae Kwon Do, gardening. Office: 1210 W Broadway Columbia MO 65203-2126 Home Phone: 573-443-2642; Office Phone: 573-449-3318. Personal E-mail: mmoore259@mchsi.com.

MOORE, OLIVER SEMON, III, publishing executive, consultant; b. Jersey City, July 26, 1942; s. Oliver S. and Ann Loy (Spies) M.; m. Dina Downing DuBois, Feb. 23, 1961 (div. 1974); 1 child, Deborah; m. Christine Laine Meyers, May 12, 1990; 1 child, Kathryn Laine. BA, U. Va., 1964. Chief bur. Richmond (Va.) Times-Dispatch, 1964-66; corr. Time mag., NYC, 1966-67, contbg. editor, 1967-68; assoc. editor Newsweek, NYC, 1969-71; freelance writer, 1972-75; mng. editor Motor Boating and Sailing, NYC, 1976-78, editor, 1980-82; exec. editor US Mag., N.Y. Times Co., 1978-80; dep. editor Town & Country Mag., NYC, 1982-84; editor Sci. Digest Mag., NYC, 1984-86; pub. dir. Yachting Mag., NYC, 1986-95; editorial dir. Outdoor Life, NYC, 1993-95; v.p. The Outdoor Co., YC, 1994-95; editor-at-large Motor Boating & Sailing, 1995—2001; pres. Alamo Pub. Svcs., Inc., Detroit, 1995—. Co-founder, chmn. bd. Corp! (Mag.), 1998. Author: (poems) Voices International, 1969; contbg. editor Sports Afield, 1996—; photographer (mags.) Motor Boating and Sailing, Yachting, Working Woman Corp! (books) Lines to a Little Girl, Rancho Paradiso. Recipient Merit award Art Dirs. Club, 1981, award of merit Soc. Publ. Designers, 1981, Excellence in Media award Nat. Arbor Day Found., 1985. Mem. Am. Soc. Mag. Editors, Mag. Pubs. Assn. (nat. mag. award 1995), N.Y. Yacht Club, Grosse Pointe (Mich.) Club, Bayview (Mich.) Yacht Club, Wyndemere Country Club (Fla.). Republican. Episcopalian. Avocations: sailing, antique cars. Home and Office: 604 Courtside Dr Naples FL 34105-7133 Personal E-mail: omoore@comcast.net.

MOORE, PATRICK J., paper company executive; b. Sept. 7, 1954; m. Beth Moore; 3 children. BSBA, DePaul U., Chgo. Asst. treas. Jefferson Smurfit Corp., St. Louis, 1987-90, treas., 1990-93, v.p., treas., 1993-94; v.p., gen. mgr. Indsl. Packaging divsn. Indsl. Packaging divsn., St. Louis, 1994-96; v.p., CFO Jefferson Smurfit Corp., St. Louis, 1996—98, Smurfit-Stone Container Corp., Chgo., 1998—2002, pres., CEO, 2002—03, chmn., pres., CEO, 2003—06, chmn., CEO, 2006—. Serves on NASDAQ CEO Coun.; bd. dir. Am. Forest & Paper Assn., JP Morgan Nat. Adv. Bd., Intern. Corrugated Case Assn., Archer Daniels Midland. Mem. Civic Progress, St. Louis, Comml. Club, Chgo., Wash. U. John M. Olin Sch. Bus. Nat. Coun.; bd. dir. Met. YMCA, St. Louis, Boys Hope/Girls Hope, Big Shoulders Fund, Chgo. Office: Smurfit-Stone Container Corp 150 N Michigan Ave Chicago IL 60601-7568

MOORE, RANDALL CHARLES, biology professor; b. Columbus, Tex., June 21, 1954; s. Doyle Liles and Tillie Mae (Spross) M.; m. Kris Collum, May 20, 1989. BS in Biology, Tex. A&M U., 1977; MS in Botany, U. Ga., 1977; PhD in Biology, UCLA, 1980. Asst. prof. Baylor U., Waco, Tex., 1980—83, assoc. prof., 1983—88; prof., chmn. biology dept. Wright State U., Dayton, Ohio, 1988—93, asst. dean to assoc. dean Coll. Sci. and Math., 1990—93; prof. biology, dean Buchtel Coll. Arts and Sci. U. Akron, Ohio, 1993; with U. Louisville; faculty mem. to prof. biology Post Secondary Tchg. and Learning U. Minn., Twin Cities, 2000—. Sci. and tech. writer SciWrite, Waco and Dayton, 1983; corres. prof. Pontificia Universidad Catolica de Chile, Santiago, 1986. Editor: Compatibility Responses in Plants, 1982; author: Biology Laboratory Manual, 1985, 2nd edit. 1989, 3rd edit. 1992, The Living Desert, 1991, Writing to Learn Biology, 1992; mem. editl. bd.: Jour. Coll. Sci. Tchg., Issues in Writing, Jour. Biol. Edn. Sci. educator Trotwood Madison Sch. Dist., 1990. Fulbright scholar, 1988; named Most Outstanding Prof. Baylor U., 1986, Wright State U., 1993; grantee NSF, 1990, NASA, 1991; recipient Tchr. Exemplar award Soc. Coll. Sci. Tchrs., 1993, US Prof. of Yr. award, Carnegie Found. for Advancement of Tchg. and Coun. for Advancement and Support of Edn., 2006. Mem. AAAS, Am. Soc. Plant Physiologists, Bot. Soc. Am. (editor The Am. Biology Tchr., 1983-2002), Nat. Assn. Biology Tchrs. (hon.). Avocations: music, writing, running, movies, reading. Office: U Minn Post Secondary Tchg and Learning 374 Appleby Hall 128 Pleasant St SE Minneapolis MN 55455 Office Phone: 612-626-4458. Office Fax: 612-625-0709. E-mail: rmoore@umn.edu.

MOORE, RICHARD KERR, electrical engineering educator; b. St. Louis, Nov. 13, 1923; s. Louis D. and Nina (Megown) M.; m. Wilma Lois Schallau, Dec. 10, 1944 (dec. 1999); children: John Richard, Daniel Charles. BS, Washington U. at St. Louis, 1943; PhD, Cornell U., 1951. Test equipment engr. RCA, Camden, NJ, 1943-44; instr. and rsch. engr. Washington U., St. Louis, 1947-49; rsch. assoc. Cornell U., 1949-51; rsch. engr., sect. supr. Sandia Corp., Albuquerque, 1951-55; prof., chmn. elec. engring. U. N.Mex., 1955-62; Black and Veatch prof. U. Kans., Lawrence, 1962-94; prof. emeritus, 1994—; dir. remote sensing lab. U. Kans., 1964-74, 84-93. Pres. Cadre Corp., Lawrence, 1968-87; cons. cos., govt. agys. Author: Traveling Wave Engineering, 1960; co-author: (with Ulaby and Fung) Microwave Remote Sensing, Vol. I, 1981, Vol. II, 1982, Vol. III, 1986; contbr. to profl. jours. and handbooks. Lt. (j.g.) USNR, 1944-46. Recipient Achievement award Washington U. Engring. Alumni Assn., 1978, Outstanding Tech. Achievement award IEEE Geosci. and Remote Sensing Soc., 1982, Louise E. Byrd Grad. Educator award U. Kans., 1984, Irving Youngberg Rsch. award U. Kans., 1989, Australia prize, 1995. Fellow AAAS, IEEE (sect. chmn. 1960-61, Outstanding Tech. Achievement award coun. oceanic engring. 1978); mem., NAE, AAUP, Am. Soc. Engring. Edn., Am. Geophys. Union, Internat. Sci. Radio Union (chmn. U.S. commn. F 1984-87, internat. vice chmn. commn. F 1990-93, chmn. 1993-96), Kiwanis, Sigma Xi, Tau Beta Pi. Presbyterian (past elder). Achievements include research in submarine communications, radar altimetry, radar as a remote sensor, radar oceanography; patent for polypanchromatic radar. Home: 1712 Carmel Dr Lawrence KS 66047-1840 Office: U Kans R S & Remote Sensing Lab 2335 Irving Hill Rd Lawrence KS 66045-7612 Personal E-mail: rmoore@sunflower.com.

MOORE, ROBERT, protective services official; b. Pontotoc, Miss., Sept. 11, 1943; married; 2 children. Degree, Rock Valley C.C., Rockford, Ill., 1976; BA, U. Ill., Springfield, 1980, MA, 1985. Worker Chrysler Corp., Belvidere, Ill., 1966-70; dep. sheriff Winnebago County Sheriff's Dept., Rockford, 1970-72; dir. equal employment opportunity Ill. State Police, Springfield, 1976-84, dir. internal affairs, 1985; dep. chief of police Savannah (Ga.) Police Dept., 1985-87; dep. dir. children and family svcs. Springfield Police Dept., 1987, chief internal affairs, 1988-92, ret., 1993; U.S. marshal U.S. Ct., Ctrl. dist. Ill., 7th cir., Springfield, 1994—. Contbr. articles to profl. publs. Recipient NAACP Affirmative Action award, 1982, Human Rels. award Human Rels. Commn., 1993. Mem. Nat. Orgn. Black Law Enforcement Execs. (pres. local chpt. 1990-94), Internat. Police Chiefs Assn., Frontiers Internat. Baptist. Avocations: golf, writing, reading. Office: Office of US Marshal Fed Bldg US Ct 7th Cir 600 E Monroe St Springfield IL 62701-1626

MOORE, SCOTT, former state official; b. York, Nebr., 1960; m. Danene Tushar, 1989. BA in Polit Sci., U. Nebr. Legis. aide Nebr. Legislature, 1981-86, mem., 1986-94, chair appropriations com., 1991-94; sec. of state State of Nebr., 1995—2000; dir. gov. affairs Union Pacific R.R., 2000—. With Moore & Sons. Office: Union Pacific RR 1416 Dodge St Room 801 Omaha NE 68179 Home: 664 N 56th St Omaha NE 68132-2118

MOORE, SHERRY MILLS, lawyer; b. 1951; m. Tim Moore; 2 children. BA, Beloit Coll.; JD, Univ. ND, 1979. Bar: ND 1979. Pvt. practice, Bismarck, ND. Bd. mem. Mental Health Assn. of ND, Prevent Child Abuse ND; pres. Bismarck Library Bd.; chair Mayor's Task Force on Methamphetamine. Named Vol. Lawyer of Yr., Big Muddy Bar Assn., 2000. Mem.: State Bar Assn. ND (pres. 2004). Avocations: photography, reading, jetskiing. Office: Atty-at-Law 300 N 4th St PO Box 4144 Bismarck D 58502-4144 Office Phone: 701-222-4777. Office Fax: 701-222-8502.

MOORE, TERRY L., financial executive; CPA, Ohio. CFO, CEO Nationwise Automotive, Inc.; CFO, treas. Shoe Corp. Am.; contr. Drug Emporium, Inc., Powell, Ohio, CFO, 1999—. Office: Drug Emporium Inc 811 14525 Highway 7 Minnetonka MN 55345-3734

MOORE, THOMAS EDWIN, biologist, educator, museum director; b. Champaign, Ill. s. Gerald E. and Velma (Lewis) M.; m. E. Eleanor Sifferd, Feb. 4, 1951; children: Deborah S., Melinda S. BS, U. Ill., 1951, MS, 1952, PhD, 1956. Tech. asst. Ill. Natural History Survey, Urbana, 1950-56; instr. zoology U. Mich., Ann Arbor, 1956-59, asst. prof. zoology, 1959-63, assoc. prof. zoology, 1963-66, prof. biology, 1966—2000, curator insects, 1956—2000, dir. exhibit mus., 1988-93. Vis. prof. Orgn. Tropical Studies, San Jose, Costa Rica, 1970, 72; bd. dir. Orgn. Tropical Studies, San Jose, 1968-79; mem. steering com. tropical biome US Internat. Biol. Program, 1969-72; mem. conf. planning com. Nat. Inst. Environment, 1991-92; mem. steering com. Univ. Colloquium on Environ. Rsch. and Edn., 1991-93, grievance com. U. Mich., 1997-98, faculty handbook com., 1997-98. Co-editor: Lectures on Science Education, 1991, 92, 93; Cricket Behavior and Neurobiology, 1989; author movie 17-Year Cicadas, 1975, TV, 1998; co-author: Singing Insects of N.Am. Website, 2003—. County rep. Huron River Watershed Coun., Ann Arbor, 1987-95; mem. Mich. H.S. Accreditation Adv. Com., Ann Arbor, 1988-92; mem. U. Mich. Senate Adv. Com. on Univ. Affairs, 1993-96, vice chair, 1995-96; bd. mem. U. Mich. Acad. Freedom Lecture Fund, 1995—, treas., 1995-98; vol. Kempf House Ctr. for Local History, Ann Arbor, Mich.; cons. NSF Visual Tech. in Environ. Curricula, 1994-97; cons. Misery Bay exhibits ParksCanada, 2003-, bd. mem. Friends Misery Bay, 2007-Rsch. grantee NSF, 1963-66, 66-69, 96-97, rsch. equipment grantee, 1984-86, rsch. grantee Def. Advanced Rsch. Project Agy./Office of Naval Rsch. 1998—. Fellow AAAS, AAUP (pres. U. Mich. chpt. 1996-99, exec. bd. Mich. conf. 1996-98), Royal Entomol. Soc. London, Linnaen Soc. London; mem. Assn. Tropical Biology (pres. 1973-75), Sigma Xi (pres. U. Mich. chpt. 1994-96, coun. 1993-98) Home: 4243 N Delhi Rd Ann Arbor MI 48103-9485 Office: Mus of Zoology U Mich Ann Arbor MI 48109-1079 Office Phone: 734-764-0471. Business E-Mail: temoore@umich.edu.

MOORE, TIM J., lawyer; b. Wichita, Kans., June 1, 1964; s. Dennis F. and Mary Jane (O'Malley) M.; m. Kelly S. Belford, June 4, 1993; children: Henry, Charlotte. AB magna cum laude, Brown U., 1986; JD cum laude, Harvard U., 1989. Bar: Kans. 1989, US Dist. Ct. Kans. 1989, US Dist. Ct. (no. dist.) Tex. 1994, US Ct. Appeals (10th cir.) 1992, US Ct. Appeals (5th cir.) 1999. Ptnr. Morris, Laing, Evans, Brock & Kennedy, Chartered, Wichita, 1989—. Mem. bd. editors Wichita Barometer, 1989—; contbr. articles to profl. jours. Pres.& bd. dir. Wichita Pub. Libraries, v.p. Wichita Pub. Library Found., bd. dirs. Law and Pub. Policy Magnet Sch., Wichita, 1992-93; dist. rep. Boy Scouts Am., Wichita, 1993-95; state chair Nat. Alumni Schs. Program, Wichita, 1994—, mem. Kans. Library Trustee Assn., Brown Alumni Sch. Com., Kans., Boy Scouts of Am., Blackbear (advancement com.). Recipient Ratcliffe Hicks award Brown U, 1985, 86. Mem. Wichita Bar Assn. (bd. govs. 1998—, bd. of govs.), Wichita Young Lawyers Assn. (pres. 1992-93), ABA, Kans. Bar Assn., Am. Intellectual Property Law Assn., Kansas, Am. Trial Lawyers. Democrat. Roman Catholic. Sr. editor Harvard Jour. of Law and Pub. Policy. Office: Morris Laing Evans Brock & Kennedy Chartered Old Town 300 N Mead St Ste 200 Wichita KS 67202-2745 Office Phone: 316-262-2671. Office Fax: 316-262-6226.

MOORE, WARD WILFRED, medical educator; b. Cowden, Ill., Feb. 12, 1924; s. Cecil Leverett and Velma Leona (Frye) M.; m. Frances Laura Campbell, Jan. 29, 1949; children— Scott Thomas, Ann Gail, Brian Dean, Kevin Lee. AB, U. Ill., 1948, MS, 1951, PhD, 1952; DSc (hon.), Mahidol U., Bangkok, 2001. Instr., rsch. assoc. U. Ill., 1952-54; asst. prof. Okla. State U., Stillwater, 1954-55, Ind. U., Bloomington, 1955-59, assoc. prof., 1959-66, prof. physiology, 1966-89, prof. physiology and biophysics emeritus, 1989—, acting chmn. dept. anatomy, 1971-73, assoc. dean basic med. scis., 1971-89, assoc. dean, dir. med. scis. program, 1976-89. Vis. prof. Postgrad. Med. Center, Karachi, Pakistan, 1963-64; staff mem. Rockefeller Found., 1968-71; vis. prof., chmn. dept. physiology, faculty sci. Mahidol U., Bangkok, Thailand, 1968-71 Served with U.S. Army, 1943-46. Mem. Am. Physiol. Soc., Endocrine Soc., Am. Soc. ephrology, Soc. Study Reproduction, Am. Assn. Anatomists, Soc. Exptl. Biology and Medicine, Am. Assn. Med. Colls., AAAS, Am. Inst. Biol. Scis., AAUP, Ind. Acad. Sci., Ind. Hist. Soc., Shelby County (Ill.) Hist. Soc., Monroe County (Ind.) Hist. Soc., Soc. Sons of Am. Revolution, Sigma Xi, Phi Sigma. Home: 3500 E Bradley St Bloomington IN 47401-4201 Office: Indiana U Jordan Hall # 105 Bloomington IN 47405 Business E-Mail: moorew@indiana.edu.

MOORHOUSE, LINDA VIRGINIA, symphony orchestra administrator; b. June 26, 1945; d. William James and Mary Virginia (Wild) M. BA, Pa. State U., 1967. Sec. San Antonio Symphony, Tex., 1970-71, adminstrv. asst. Tex., 1971-75, asst. mgr. Tex., 1975-76; exec. dir. Canton (Ohio) Symphony, 1977—. Mem. Ohio Arts Coun. Music Panel, 1980-82, 87-89, Mich. Arts Coun. Music Panel, 1986. Bd. dirs. Stark County unit Arthritis Fedn., 1986-92, treas., 1989-91; bd. dirs. Canton Palace Theatre Assn., treas., 1994-96, pres., 1998-99; active Cen. Stark County United Way Allocations Panel, 1991-96. Mem. Met. Orch. Mgrs. Assn. (pres. 1983-85), Orgn. Ohio Orchs. (pres. 1985-86), Am. Symphony Orch. League (bd. dirs. 1983-85, nat. 1st ladies' site com. 1997—), Stark County Women's Hall of Fame (charter inductee), Soroptomist (Canton, Ohio, Women of Distinction 1992), Nat. First Ladies Libr. Office: Canton Symphony Orch 1001 Market Ave N Canton OH 44702-1024

MOOTY, BRUCE WILSON, lawyer; b. Mpls., May 27, 1955; s. John William and Virginia Mae (Nelson) M.; m. Ann Tracy Grogan, May 1, 1982; children: Katharine Grogan, Allison Taylor, Megan Ann. Student, Amherst Coll., 1973-74; BA summa cum laude, U. Minn., 1977, JD cum laude, 1980. Bar: Minn. 1980, U.S. Dist. Ct. Minn. 1980, U.S. Ct. Appeals 1983. Assoc., shareholder, officer, dir. Briggs & Morgan, P.A., Mpls., 1980-93; mng. ptnr. Gray, Plant, Mooty, Mooty & Bennett, P.A., Mpls., 1993—; also bd. dirs. Pres., chmn. bd. dirs. A Better Chance Found., Edina, Minn., 1988, Minn. Amateur Baseball Found., Mpls., 1992; mem. coun. Colonial Ch. Edina, 1992. Mem. ABA, Minn. Bar Assn. (community rels. com. 1992—), Hennepin County Bar Assn., Ramsey County Bar Assn., Minikahda Club (sec.), Phi Beta Kappa, Phi Kappa Phi. Home: 7021 Antrim Rd Minneapolis MN 55439-1709 Office: Gray Plant Mooty Mooty Bennett 80 S 8th St Ste 500 Minneapolis MN 55402-5383

MOOTY, JOHN WILLIAM, lawyer; b. Adrian, Minn., Nov. 27, 1922; s. John Wilson and Genevieve (Brown) M.; m. Virginia Nelson, June 6, 1952 (dec. 1964); children: David ., Bruce W., Charles W.; m. Jane Nelson, Jan. 15, 1972. BSL, U. Minn., 1943, LLB, 1944. Bar: Minn. 1944. Ptnr. Gray, Plant, Mooty & Bennett, Mpls., 1945—. Bd. dirs. Internat. Dairy Queen, Inc., Bur. of Engraving, Inc., Riverway Co. and subs.; chmn. Rio Verde Svcs., Inc., Ariz. Author (with others): Minnesota Practice Methods, 1956. Chmn. Gov.'s Task Force on Edn., 1981; pres. Citizens League Mpls., 1970; acting chmn. Republican Party of Minn., 1958. amed to Minn. Bus. Hall of Fame, 2003. Mem. ABA, Minn. Bar Assn., Hennepin County Bar Assn., U. Minn. Alumni Assn. (pres. 1982), Tonto Verde Country Club, Minikahda (Mpls.) Club, Mpls. Club. Home: 8106 Highwood Dr Apt Y232 Bloomington MN 55438-1054 Office Phone: 612-632-3200. Business E-Mail: john.mooty@gpmlaw.com.

MORA, ANTONIO GONZALEZ, III, broadcast journalist; b. Havana, Cuba, Dec. 14, 1957; came to U.S., 1960; s. Antonio Gonzalez Jr. and Natalia (Sandoval) M.; m. Julie Good, Aug. 27, 1994; children: Clara, Antonio Daniel. JD, U. Catolica Andres Bello, Caracas, Venezuela, 1980; LLM, Harvard U., Cambridge, Mass., 1981; DHL, Our Lady of Holy Cross, New Orleans, 2000; PhD (hon.), Ursinus Coll., 2001. Assoc. Debevoise & Plimpton, NYC, 1981-88; anchor Sta. WXTV, Secaucus, NJ, 1990-91, Sta. WNJU, Teterboro, NJ, 1991; anchor Nightside NBC, Charlotte, NC, 1992; reporter, anchor Sta. WTVJ-TV, Miami, 1992-93; host Good Day LA Tv Sta. KTTV, LA, 1993—94; host Good Morning America Sunday ABC, NYC, 1994-95; correspondent ABC News, NYC, 1995-99; news anchor Good Morning America ABC, NYC, 1999—2002; evening news anchor TV Sta. WBBM, Chgo., 2002—. Recipient Nat. Emmy award, 2000, Peabody award, 2000-01, Edward R. Murrow award, 2000, 5 Local Emmy awards, 2004-05. Mem.: Coun. Fgn. Rels.

MORACZEWSKI, ROBERT LEO, publisher; b. Saint Paul, Nebr., May 13, 1942; s. Leo and Florence (Wadas) M.; m. Virginia Kay Rohman, July 26, 1960; children— Mark, Matthew, Monika, Michael BS in Agrl. Journalism, U. Nebr., 1964. Assoc. editor Farmer Mag. Webb Co., St. Paul, 1964-72; mng. editor Farm Industry News Webb Co., St. Paul, 1972-74; editor Big Farmer Mag., Chgo., 1974-75; editorial dir. Webb Agrl. Services, St. Paul, 1976; editor The Farmer, The Dakota Farmer Webb Co., St. Paul, 1983-89; group pub. Webb Co., St. Paul, 1989-90; sr. v.p. Prism Bus. Media, St. Paul, 1990—. Chmn. Minn. Agri-Growth Coun. Contbr. articles to profl. jours. Mem. sponsors bd. Nat. FFA. Recipient numerous media awards. Mem. Am. Agrl. Editors Assn., Nat. Agrl. Mktg. Assn. Roman Catholic. Home: 32993 Kale Ave Chisago City MN 55013-2644 Office: Primedia Bus Media 7900 Internat Dr Minneapolis MN 55425 E-mail: bmoraczewski@prismb2b.com.

MORAN, DANIEL AUSTIN, mathematician, educator; b. Chgo., Feb. 17, 1936; s. Austin Thomas and Violet Lillian (Johnson) M.; m. Karen Krull, Sept. 14, 1963; children: Alexander, Claudia. BS summa cum laude, St. Mary's of Tex., 1957; MS, U. Ill., 1958, PhD, 1962. Research instr. U. Chgo., 1962-64; asst. prof. Mich. State U., 1964-68, assoc. prof., 1968-76, prof. math., 1976—. Vis. scholar U. Cambridge, 1970-71, U. North Wales, 1978 Contbr. articles to profl. jours. Mem. Math. Assn. Am., Sigma Xi, Pi Mu Epsilon, Delta Epsilon Sigma, Kappa Mu Alpha. Roman Catholic. Home: 2633 Roseland Ave East Lansing MI 48823-3870 Office: Dept Math Michigan State Univ East Lansing MI 48824

MORAN, GLENN J., corporate lawyer; BA, Pa. State U., 1969; JD, Temple U., 1972. Bar: Pa. 1972. Lawyer-major appliance group Gen. Electric, 1973-77; sr. lawyer Frito Lay, Inc., Pepsico, 1977-79; v.p., gen. counsel, sec. LTV Corp., Cleve. Office: LTV Steel Co 5800 Lombardo Ctr Ste 155 Seven Hills OH 44131-6913

MORAN, JAMES BYRON, federal judge; b. Evanston, Ill., June 20, 1930; s. James Edward and Kathryn (Horton) M.; m. Janet Remen; children: John, Jennifer, Sarah, Polly; stepchildren: Katie, Cynthia, Laura, Michael, Susan, Carol, Peggy, Tom, Lee. AB, U. Mich., 1952; LLB magna cum laude, Harvard U., 1957. Bar: Ill. 1958. Law clk. to judge U.S. Ct. of Appeals (2d cir.), 1957-58; assoc. Bell, Boyd, Lloyd, Haddad & Burns, Chgo, 1958-66, ptnr., 1966-79; judge U.S. Dist. Ct. (no. dist.) Ill., Chgo., 1979—. Dir. Com. on Ill. Govt., 1960-78, chmn., 1968-70; vice chmn., sec. Ill. Narcotic Drug Adv. Coun., 1967-74; dir. Gateway Found., 1969—; mem. Ill. Ho. of Reps., 1965-67; mem. Evanston City Council, 1971-75. Served with AUS, 1952-54. Mem. Chgo. Bar Assn., Chgo. Council Lawyers, Lawyers Club, Phi Beta Kappa. Home: 117 Kedzie St Evanston IL 60202-2509 Office: US Dist Ct 219 S Dearborn St Chambers 1846 Chicago IL 60604-1800 Home Phone: 847-475-3422; Office Phone: 312-435-5572. Personal E-mail: jbm117@aol.com.

MORAN, JERRY, congressman; b. Great Bend, Kans., May 29, 1954; m. Robba A. Moran; 2 children. BS, Kansas U., 1976, JD, 1981. Senator dist. 37 State of Kans., 1989—96, sen. majority leader, 1994—96; mem., asst. majority whip US Congress from 1st Kans. dist., 1997—, mem. agr., transp., infrastructure, vets. affairs coms., chmn. subcom. on gen. commodities; chmn. Rural Health Care Coalition. Republican. Office: US House Reps 1519 Longworth House Office Bldg Washington DC 20515-1601 Office Phone: 202-225-2715. Office Fax: 202-225-5124.

MORAN, JOHN, religious organization administrator; b. Oct. 4, 1935; m. Retha Jean Patrick; children: John II, James, Helen. Missionary, Nigeria, 1963—68; pastor, 1969-87, 2001—; vice dist. supt. North Ctrl. Dist., Missionary Church, Ind., 1977-81; pres. Missionary Ch., Ft. Wayne, Ind., 1987-2001. Mem. exec. bd. World Relief Corp., 1998-2001. Author: Joy in a Roman Jail, 1984, Taking the High Ground, 1997. Mem. Nat. Assn. Evang. (mem. exec. bd. 1987-97, pastor 2001-). Home Phone: 574-831-4354; Office Phone: 574-831-2414. E-mail: moranjr@bnin.net.

MORAN, JOHN FRANCIS, cardiologist; b. Chgo., Sept. 5, 1938; MD, Loyola U., Stritch Sch. Medicine, 1964. Cert. cardio. disease 1973. Office: Loyola U Med Ctr 2160 S 1st Ave Maywood IL 60153

MORAN, MICHAEL ROBERT, corporate lawyer; BS, U. Ill., 1967; JD, DePaul U., 1972. Bar: Ill. 1972. V.p.-adminstrn. Spiegel, Inc., 1982-87, v.p., sec. gen. counsel Downers Grove, Ill., 1988-96, sr. corp. v.p., sec., gen. counsel, 1996-97, pres., chief legal officer, 1997—, chmn. office of the pres., chief legal officer, 1998—. Mem. Ill. Retail Mchts. Assn. (chmn. bd. dirs., mem. credit com.), Nat. Retail Fedn. Office: Spiegel Inc 3500 Lacey Rd Downers Grove IL 60515-5421

MORAN, ROBERT FRANCIS, JR., library director; b. Cleve., May 3, 1938; s. Robert Francis Sr. and Jeanette (Mulholland) M.; m. Judith Mary Pacer, Dec. 28, 1968; children: Mary Jeanette, Catherine, Margaret. BA, Cath. U. Am., Washington, 1961, MLS, 1965; MBA, U. Chgo., 1976. Head librarian St. Patrick's Sem., Menlo Park, Calif., 1965-69; coordinator and reference librarian U. Chgo., 1969-72; serials librarian U. Ill., Chgo., 1972-78, acquisitions librarian, 1977-80; dir. library services Ind. U. Northwest, Gary, 1980—, asst. vice chancellor tech., 1991-99. V.p., sec., treas. Northwest Ind. Area Library Services Authority, Merrillville, 1982-91. Asst. editor Libr. Adminstrn. and Mgmt.; contbr. articles to profl jours. Mem. ALA, Libr. Adminstrn. and Mgmt. Assn. (com. chmn. 1981-86, sect. chmn. 1986-88, chmn. program com. 1988-91, chair nominating com. 1991-92, networked info. discussion group 1994-98, govtl. affairs com. 1998-2000). Democrat. Roman Catholic. Office: Ind Univ NW Library 3400 Broadway Gary IN 46408-1101

MORAVEC, CHRISTINE D. SCHOMIS, medical educator; b. LA, Apr. 26, 1957; BA, John Carroll U., 1978, MS, 1984; PhD, Cleve. State U., 1988. Tchr. Trinity H.S., Garfield Heights, Ohio, 1978-80; grad. teaching asst. dept. biology John Carroll U., Cleve., 1982-84; rsch. assoc. dept. cardiovascular biology Cleve. Clinic Found., 1990-93, project scientist dept. cardiovascular biology, 1990-93, asst. staff dept. cardiovascular biology, 1993-94; asst. prof. dept. physiology & biophys. Case Western Res. U. Sch. Medicine, Cleve., 1993—. Adj. asst. prof. Cleve. State U., 1994—; asst. staff Ctr. Anesthesiology Rsch. Cleve. Clinic Found., 1994—. Contbr. articles to profl. jours. Grad. fellow Cleve. Clinic Found., 1984-88, Postdoctoral fellow, 1988-89, recipient Tarazi fellow, 1989. Mem. Am. Physiol. Soc., Am. Heart Assn. (basic sci. coun. 1990—; Established Investigatorship award 1995), Ohio Physiol. Soc., Electron Microscopy Soc. ortheastern Ohio, Cardiac Muscle Soc. Office: Cleve Clin Found Ctr Anesthesiology Found 9500 Euclid Ave # FF40 Cleveland OH 44195-0001

MORDINO, JOSEPH T., lawyer; b. Buffalo, Feb. 27, 1971; BA, St. Lawrence University, 1992; JD, U. Cin., 1995. Bar: Ohio 1995, US Dist. Ct. Southern Dist. Ohio 1995, Ky. 2002, US Dist. Ct. Northern Dist. Ohio 2006, US Ct. of Appeals Sixth Cir. Ptnr. Faulkner & Tepe LLP, Cin. Named one of Ohio's Rising Stars, Super Lawyers, 2006. Mem.: Ky. Acad. Trial Attorneys, Def. Rsch. Inst., Ohio Assn. Civil Trial Attorneys, Ky. Bar Assn., Ohio State Bar Assn., Cin. Bar Assn., Phi Beta Kappa. Office: Faulkner & Tepe LLP 2200 Fourth and Vine Tower 1 W Fourth St Cincinnati OH 45202-3606 Office Phone: 513-421-7500. Office Fax: 513-421-7502.

MORDY, JAMES CALVIN, retired lawyer; b. Ashland, Kans., Jan. 3, 1927; s. Thomas Robson and Ruth (Floyd) M.; m. Marjory Ellen Nelson, Nov. 17, 1951; children: Jean Claire Mordy Jongeling, Rebecca Jane Mordy King, James Nelson. BA in Chemistry, U. Kans., 1947; JD, U. Mich., 1950; postgrad., George Washington U., 1952—53. Bar: Kans. 1950, Mo. 1950, cert.: Am. Bankruptcy Bd. (in bus. bankruptcy law). Assoc., Morrison, Hecker, Buck, Cozad & Rogers, Kansas City, Mo., 1950—59; ptnr. Morrison & Hecker LLP, Kansas City, 1959—96, sr. counsel, 1996—97, of counsel, 1997—2000; ret., 2000. Mem. Mich. Law Rev., 1948-49; contbg. author: Missouri Bar Insurance Handbook, 1968, Missouri Bar Bankruptcy Handbook, 1991, also supplements; contbr. articles to profl. jours. Chmn. bd. Broadway United Meth. Ch., Kansas City, 1964-70, chmn. bd. trustees, chmn. fin. com., 1988-90, 94, 2000-2002; bd. dirs. Broadway Child Enrichment Ctr., 1980-2006; bd. dirs., exec. com. Della Lamb Neighborhood House, Kansas City, 1973-80; bd. dirs., treas. Friends of Sacred Structures, Kansas City, 2000—; coun. mem. St. Paul Sch. Theology, Kansas City, 1986-; bd. dirs. Kingswood Sr. Living Cmty., Kansas City, 2004—, vice chmn., 2005-; del. 17th World Meth. Conf., Rio de Janeiro, 1996; ranger Rocky Mountain Nat. Park, 1948-1949. With USN, 1945-46, 51-53, comdr. USNR, ret. Recipient Shepherd of the Lamb award, Della Lamb Neighborhood House, 1980; Summerfield scholar, 1943—47. Fellow Am. Coll. Bankruptcy, Am. Bar Found. (life); mem. ABA, Am. Judicature Soc., Am. Bankruptcy Inst., Mo. Bar Assn., Kansas City Met. Bar Assn., Lawyers Assn. Kansas City, Workout Profs. Assn. Kansas City, Univ. Club (v.p., bd. dirs. 1983, 86), Barristers Soc., Phi Beta Kappa, Delta Tau Delta (pres. Kansas City alumni chpt. 1965-72, pres. U. Kans. House Corp. 1966-72), Alpha Chi Sigma, Phi Alpha Delta. Avocations: travel, geography (maps), history, music, theology. Home: 8741 Ensley Ln Leawood KS 66206-1615 Office: Stinson Morrison Hecker LLP 1201 Walnut St Kansas City MO 64106-2150

MOREHEAD, ANDREA, newscaster; BA in Comm./Journalism, Howard U., 1991; JD, Ind. U., 1996. Prodn. intern Koppel Comm., Washington; reporter, anchor Sta. WGMC-TV, Worchester, Mass., 1992—93; mgmt. coun. law clk. Nat. Football League, NY, 1995; reporter, asst. prodr. assignment editor WXIN-TV, Indpls.; anchor Sta. WOOD-TV, Grand Rapids, Mich., Sta. WTHR-TV, Indpls., 1999—. Recipient Up and Coming award, Ann. Minority Bus. and Profl. Achievers, Recognition award, Ctr. Leadership Devel., Indpls., 2002. Office: WTHR-TV 1000 N Meridian St Indianapolis IN 46204

MOREHOUSE, LAWRENCE GLEN, veterinarian, educator, academic administrator; b. Manchester, Kans., July 21, 1925; s. Edwy Owen and Ethel Merle (Glenn) M.; m. Georgia Ann Lewis, Oct. 6, 1956; children: Timothy Lawrence, Glenn Ellen. BS in Biol. Sci., Kans. State U., 1952, DVM, 1952; MS in Animal Pathology, Purdue U., 1956, PhD, 1960. Lic. vet. medicine. Veterinarian County Animal Hosp., Des Peres, Mo., 1952-53; supr. Brucellosis labs. Purdue U., West Lafayette, Ind., 1953-60; staff veterinarian lab. svcs. USDA, Washington, 1960-61; discipline leader in pathology and toxicology, animal health divsn. USDA Nat. Animal Disease Lab., Ames, Iowa, 1961-64; prof., chmn. dept. vet. pathology U. Mo. Coll. Vet. Medicine, Columbia, Mo., 1964—69, 1969—86, dir. Vet. Med. Diagnostic Lab., 1968-88, prof. emeritus, 1986—. Cons. USDA, to comdg. gen. U.S. Army R&D Command, Am. Inst. Biol. Scis., NAS, to Surg. Gen., Miss. State U., St. Louis Zoo Residency Tng. Program, Miss. Vet. Med. Assn., Okla. State U., Pa. Dept. Agr., Ohio Dept. Agr. Co-editor: Mycotoxic Fungi, Mycotoxins, Mycotoxicoses: An International Encyclopedic Handbook, 3 vols., 1977; contbr. articles on diseases of animals to profl. jours. Active Trinity Presbyn. Ch., Columbia, 1964-2002; bd. dirs. Mo. Symphony Soc., Columbia, 1989-92. Pharmacists mate second class USNR, 1943-46, PTO; 2d. lt. U.S. Army, 1952-56. Recipient Outstanding Svc. award USDA, 1959, merit cert., 1963, 64, Disting. Svc. award U. Mo. Coll. Vet. Medicine, 1987, Dean's Impact award, 1996, Kans. State U. Alumni award, 2004. Fellow Royal Soc. Health London; mem. AAAS, Am. Assn. Vet. Lab. Diagnosticians (E.P. Pope award 1976, chmn. lab. accreditation bd. 1972-79, 87-90, pres. 1979-80, sec.-treas. 1983-87), World Assn. Vet. Lab. Diagnosticians (bd. dirs. 1984-94, dir. emeritus 1994—), N.Y. Acad. Sci., U. S. Animal Health Assn., Am. Assn. Lab. Animal Sci., Mo. Soc. Microbiology, Am. Assn. Avian Pathologists, N.Am. Conf. Rsch. Workers in Animal Diseases, Mo. Univ. Retirees Assn. (pres. 1996-99). Presbyterian. Avocations: classic cars, boating, genealogy. Home: 916 Danforth Dr Columbia MO 65201-6164 Office: U Mo Vet Med Diagnostic Lab PO Box 6023 Columbia MO 65205-6023 Office Phone: 573-442-7069. Personal E-mail: gmoreho@att.global.net. Business E-Mail: lmorehou@coin.org.

MORELACK, MIKE, radio personality; b. Pensacola, Fla., Dec. 12; 1 child. Student, Marion Mil. Inst., U. Ala. Radio host WDAF, Westwood, Kans., 1980—. Avocations: horseback riding, collecting antique guns, classic cars. Office: WDAF 4935 Belinder Rd Westwood KS 66205

MORELLO, STEVEN JOHN, lawyer; b. Saginaw, Mich., Sept. 17, 1952; m. Francia S. Morello, Apr. 8, 1978; children: Steven Jr., Rebecca. BS in Fgn. studies, Georgetown U., 1974; JD, U. Detroit Mercy Sch. Law, 1977; MBA, Boston Coll. Law Sch., Heidelberg, Fed. Republic Germany, 1980; MA in Pastoral studies, Sacred Heart Major Seminary. Bar: Mich. 1977, Ill. 1984; cert. profl. contracts mgr., Nat. Contract Mgmt. Assn. (Fellow). Staff asst. U.S. Senator Philip A. Hart, Washington; mng. atty. regional offfice Digital Equipment Corp., Arlington Heights, Ill., 1984; atty. contract Northrop Corp. Def. Sys. Divsn., Rollings Meadows, Ill., 1982-84; v.p., gen. counsel Prechter Holdings Inc., Southgate, Mich.; gen. counsel, Dept. Army U.S. Dept. Def., Washington, 2001—05; gen. counsel Sault Ste. Marie Tribe of Chippewa Indians. Mem. Sault Ste. Marie Tribe of Chippewa Indians. Capt. JAGC US Army, 1978—85, trial counsel 21st Support Command, first mem. Trial Def. Svc., Karlsruhe, Germany, legal asst., adminstrv. law officer, Berlin Recruting Command, Ft. Sheridan, Ill., contract atty., 86th Army Reserve Command USAR, Ft. Sheridan, Ill. Fellow Nat. Contract Mgmt. Assn. (pres. Chgo. chpt. 1985-86). Office: Sault Tribe Legal Dept 523 Ashmun St Sault Sainte Marie MI 49783

MORENCY, PAULA J., lawyer; b. Oak Park, Ill., Mar. 13, 1955; AB magna cum laude, Princeton U., 1977; JD, U. Va., 1980. Bar: Ill. 1980, U.S. Dist. Ct. (no. dist.) Ill. 1980, U.S. Ct. Appeals (7th cir.) 1981, U.S. Ct. Appeals (5th cir.) 1990, U.S. Dist. Ct. (ctrl. dist.) Ill. 1999, U.S. Dist. Ct. (ea. dist.) Wis. 2000. Assoc. Mayer, Brown & Platt, Chgo., 1980-86, ptnr., 1987-94, Schiff Hardin LLP, Chgo., 1994—; practice group leader Intellectual Property, 2005—. Adj. prof. trial advocacy Northwestern U. Sch. Law, Chgo., 1997--; faculty Midwest Regional, Nat. Inst. for Trial Advocacy, 1988—; mem. pres.'s coun. Dominican U., 1998-2002. Author: Cross-Examination of a Franchise Executive, 1995, Insurance Coverage Issues in Franchise and Intellectual Property Litigation, 1996, Re-Emergence of Franchise Class Actions, 1997, Judicial and Legislative Update: ABA Forum on Franchising, 1999, How to Find, Use and Defend Against the Expert Witness, 2000, Dealing With System Change in a High-Tech World, 2001, A Decade After Daubert, 2004. Mem. ABA (forum franchising, governing com. 2001-04, litig. sect., antitrust sect., intellectual property sect.), Chgo. Coun. of Lawyers (bd. govs. 1989-93), Constnl. Rights Found. Chgo. (chair 2001, bd. dirs. 1994-). Office: Schiff Hardin LLP 6600 Sears Tower Chicago IL 60606 Office Phone: 312-258-5549.

MORFORD, JOANN (JOANN MORFORD-BURG), state senator, investment company executive; b. Miller, SD, Nov. 26, 1956; d. Darrell Keith Morford and Eleanor May Morford-Steptoe. BS in Agrl.-Bus., Comml. Econs., S.D. State U., 1979; cert. in personal fin. planning, Am. Coll., 1992. CLU; chartered fin. cons. Agrl. loan officer 1st Bank System, Presho, SD, 1980-82, Wessington Springs, SD, 1982-86, Am. State Bank, Wessington Springs, 1986; investment rep. ARM Fin. Svcs. Inc., Wessington Springs, 1986-96, Capital Financial Svcs., Inc., Miller, 1997—; mem. S.D. State Senate, Wessington Springs, 1990-96, majority whip, 1993-94, minority whip, 1995-96, mem., 1990-97, Miller, 1997-98; ins. agt. Western Fraternal Life Assn., 2001—03. Mem. transp. com., commerce com., taxation com. S.D. State Senate, Pierre, 1990—92, mem. appropriations com., 1993—98, chair ops. and audit com., 1993—94, mem. ops. and audit com., 1995—98; mem. fed. issues environ. com. Nat. Conf. State Legislators' Assembly, 1994—98, vice chair, 1996—97. Mem. midwestern-Can. task force Midwest Conf., 1990—94; treas. twp. bd. Wessington Springs, 1990—92; active Wessington Springs Sch. Improvement Coun., 1992—95; bd. dirs. Nyoda Coun. Girls Scouts U.S.; mem. fin. com. United Meth. Ch., Miller, 2001—04. Fleming fellow, Ctr. Policy Alternatives, 1996. Mem.: S.D. Farmers Union, Bus. and Profl. Women (2nd v.p. 2002), Alumni Coun. Young Polit. Leaders (China delegation 1996, host El Salvador delegation 1999), Future Farmers Am. (adv. bd. Wessington Springs chpt. 1984—96), S.D. State U. 4-H Alumni Assn., Order Ea. Star (various offices 1980—). Democrat. Home and Office: 1510 N Parkview Pl Miller SD 57362-0021

MORFORD, JOHN A., investment company executive; CFO V.T. Inc., Shawnee Mission, Kans. Office: VT Inc PO Box 795 Shawnee Mission KS 66201-0795

MORGAN, BETSY STELLE, lawyer; b. Terre Haute, Ind., Mar. 15, 1963; BA, DePauw U., 1985; JD, John Marshall Law Sch., 1988. Bar: Ill. 1989. With Baker & McKenzie, Chgo., 1988—, counsel, 1997—2002, ptnr., 2002—07, prin., 2007—. Co-chair N.Am. Pro Bono Initiative Baker & McKenzie, Chgo. Author: United States Business Immigration Manual, 2003. Office: Baker & McKenzie One Prudential Plz 130 E Randolph Dr Chicago IL 60601

MORGAN, DONNA EVENSEN, lawyer; b. Bklyn., Feb. 28, 1957; d. Edward Ivar and Judith (Larsen) Evensen; m. Charles S. Morgan, Sept. 3, 1988. BA, Colgate U., 1979; JD, U. Mich., 1984. Bar: Ill. 1985. Assoc. Chapman and Cutler, Chgo., 1985-86, Kirkland and Ellis, Chgo., 1987-89, Mayer Brown Rowe & Maw LLP, Chgo., 1989—. Office: Mayer Brown Rowe & Maw LLP 71 S Wacker Dr Chicago IL 60606-4637 Home Phone: 630-887-0192; Office Phone: 312-701-7138. Business E-Mail: dmorgan@mayerbrownrowe.com.

MORGAN, E. A., church administrator; Chaplain Ch. of the Living God Exec. Bd., Cin., 1984—. Office: Ch of the Living God 400 S Franklin St Decatur IL 62523-1316

MORGAN, JANE HALE, retired library director; b. Dines, Wyo., May 11, 1926; d. Arthur Hale and Billie (Wood) Hale; m. Joseph Charles Morgan, Aug. 12, 1955; children: Joseph Hale, Jane Frances, Ann Michele. BA, Howard U., 1947; MA, U. Denver, 1954. Staff Detroit Pub. Libr., 1954-87, exec. asst. dir., 1973-75, dep. dir., 1975-78, dir., 1978-87; ret., 1987. Mem. Mich. Libr. Consortium Bd.; exec. bd. Southeastern Mich. Regional Film Libr.; vis. prof. Wayne State U., 1989—. Trustee New Detroit, Inc., Delta Dental Plan of Mich., v.p. Delta Dental Fund, Delta Dental Plan of Ohio; v.p. United Southwestern Mich.; pres. Univ.-Cultural Ctr. Assn.; bd. dirs. Rehab. Inst., YWCA, Met. Affairs Corp., Literacy Vols. Am., Detroit, Mich. Ctr. for the Book, Interfaith Coun.; bd. dirs., v.p. United Comty. Svcs. Met. Detroit; chmn. Detroiters for Adult Reading Excellence; chmn. adv. coun. libr. sci. U. Mich.; mem. adv. coun. libr. sci. U. Mich., mem. adv. coun. libr. sci. Wayne State U.; dir. Met. Detroit Youth Found.; chmn. Mich. LSCA adv. coun.; mem. UWA Literacy Com., Attys. Grievance Com., Women's Commn., Mich. Civil Svc. Rev. Com.; vice-chair Mich. Coun. for Humanities; v.p. Commn. for the Greening of Detroit; adv. com. Headstart; mem. Detroit Women's Com., Detroit Women's Forum, Detroit Exec. Svc. Corps.; sec., treas. Delta Dental Fund, pres., 1999. Recipient Anthony Wayne award Wayne State U., 1981, Summit award Greater Detroit C. of C.; named Detroit Howardite of Year, 1983 Mem. ALA, AAUW, Mich. Libr. Assn., Women's at. Book Assn., Assn. Mcpl. Profl. Women, NAACP, LWV, Women's Econ. Club (bd. dirs.), Sorosis Club (v.p.), Alpha Kappa Alpha (pres.). Democrat. Episcopalian. Home: 7473 N Brynmawr Ct West Bloomfield MI 48322-3542

MORGAN, VICTORIA, performing company executive, choreographer; BFA, U. Utah, 1973, MFA magna cum laude, 1976. Prin. dancer Ballet West, 1969-78, San Francisco Ballet, 1978-87; resident choreographer San Francisco Opera, 1987—97; artistic dir. Cin. Ballet, 1997—. Dancer with lead roles in numerous classical, neoclassical and modern ballets including works by George Balanchine, Forsythe, and Kudelka, lead roles for TV and films, choreographer creating over 40 works for 20 ballet and opera cos. across U.S. including Utah Ballet, Pacific Northwest Ballet, Glimmerglass Opera, N.Y.C. Opera and Cin. Opera; creator, prodr. Ballet CD-ROM, choreography featured in documentary The Creation of O.M.O. Office: Cincinnati Ballet 1555 Central Pkwy Cincinnati OH 45214-2863

MORGAN, VIRGINIA MATTISON, judge; b. 1946; BS, Univ. of Mich., 1968; JD, Univ. of Toledo, 1975. Bar: Mich. 1975, Federal 1975, U.S. Ct. Appeals (6th cir.) 1979. Tchr. Dept. of Interior, Bur. of Indian Affairs, 1968-70, San Diego Unified Schs., 1970-72, Oregon, Ohio, 1972-74; asst. prosecutor Washtenaw County Prosecutor's Office, 1976-79; asst. U.S. atty. Detroit, 1979-85; magistrate judge U.S. Dist. Ct. (Mich. ea. dist.), 6th circuit, Detroit, 1985—. Mem. bd. Fed. Jud. Ctr., 1997-2001; mem. jud. conf. U.S. Com. on Long Range Planning, 1993-96. Recipient Spl. Achievement award Dept. of Justice, Disting. Alumni award U. Toledo, 1993. Fellow Mich. State Bar Found.; mem. FBA (chpt. pres. 1996-97), Fed. Magistrate Judges Assn. (pres. 1995-96). Office: US Courthouse 231 W Lafayette Blvd Detroit MI 48226-2700

MORGENSTERN, LEWIS B., medical educator; BA in Psychology, Pomona Coll., Claremont, Calif., 1984; MD, U. Mich. Med. Sch., Ann Arbor, 1990; postgrad., U. Tex. Sch. Pub. Health, Houston, 1996. Resident in neurology Johns Hopkins Hosp., Balt.; assoc. prof. neurology U. Tex. Med. Sch., Houston, 1994—2002; dir. stroke program U. Mich. Sch. Pub. Health, 2002—, prof. epidemiology, neurology emergency medicine, neurosurgery, 2005—. Recipient Clinician Scientist award, Am. Heart Assn., 1996. Mem.: Alpha Omega Alpha. Office: U Mich Sch Pub Health 1920 Taubman Ctr Ann Arbor MI 48109*

MORGENSTERN-CLARREN, PAT, federal judge; b. 1952; AB in Polit. Sci., U. Mich., 1974; JD, Case Western Res. U., 1977; LLM, London Sch. Econs./Polit. Sci., 1979. Law clk. to Hon. Jack Grant Day Ohio Ct. Appeals (8th dist.), 1977-78; assoc. to ptnr. Hahn Loeser & Parks, Cleve., 1979-87, 87-95; bankruptcy judge U.S. Bankruptcy Ct., Cleve., 1995—. Mem. bankruptcy appellate panel U.S. Ct. Appeals (6th cir.), 1999—2002. Assoc. editor Case Western Res. U. Law Rev. Mem. Order of Coif, Soc. of Benches. Office: Us Bankruptcy Court 201 Superior Ave E Ste 111 Cleveland OH 44114-1234

MORGENTHALER, DAVID TURNER, venture capitalist; b. Chester, SC, Aug. 5, 1919; s. Henry W. and Elizabeth (Taylor) Morgenthaler; m. Lindsay Anne Jordan, May 17, 1945; children: David T., Gary J., Todd W., Gaye Elizabeth. BS in Mech. Engring., MIT, MS, 1941. Sales mgr. Ervite Corp., 1945—47; mech. engr. Copes Vulcan/Blaw-Knox Co., 1947—50; v.p., dir. sales Delavan Mfg. Co., Des Moines, 1950—57; pres. Foseco Inc., Cleve., 1957—68; chmn. bd. Foseco Technik Ltd., Birmingham, England, 1964—68, API Instruments Co., 1968—70, dir., 1968—70; chmn. bd. Mfg. Data Sys., Inc., Ann Arbor, Mich., 1969—81; chmn. exec. com., dir. LFE Corp., Waltham, Mass., 1970—85; founding ptnr. Morgenthaler Assocs.; mng. ptnr. Morgenthaler Ventures, 1981—. Dir. Hausermand, Inc., Cleve., Tartan Labs., Inc., Pitts., Three Phoenix Co.; bd. dirs. Ribozyme Pharmas., 1992—2002, chmn., 1995—2002; cons. Brentwood Assocs. Trustee Cleve. Clinic Found.; bd. overseers Case Western Res. U. Served to capt. AUS, 1941—45. Mem.: Young Pres. Orgn. (sr. v.p., bd. dirs.), Chief Execs. Orgn., Inc. (past pres.), Nat. Venture Capital Assn. (past pres.), Lyford Cay Club, Westwood Country Club, Union Club, Sigma Nu. Home: 13904 Edgewater Dr Cleveland OH 44107-1416 Office: 50 Public Sq Ste 2700 Cleveland OH 44113

MORIARTY, DONALD WILLIAM, JR., bank executive; b. Amarillo, Tex., Sept. 15, 1939; s. Donald William and Lorraine Julia (Walck) Moriarty; m. Rita Ann Giller, Nov. 28, 1964; children: Mary Kathleen, Jennifer Ann, Anne Marie, Kerry Lee, Erin Teresa. Student, St. Benedict's Coll., 1957-59, 60-61; BSc, Washington U., 1962; MSc, St. Louis U., 1965, PhD, 1970. Cost acct. Emerson Electric, St. Louis, 1959-63; grad. fellow in econs. St. Louis U., 1963-65, instr., 1965-68; asst. prof. U. Mo., St. Louis, 1968-70; with Fed. Res. Bank of St. Louis, 1968-83, v.p., 1971-74, sr. v.p., controller, 1974-77, 1st v.p., 1977-83; sr. v.p. Gen. Bancshares Corp., 1983-86; exec. v.p. Commerce Bancshares, Inc., 1986-87; bank cons., 1987-89; pres., CEO, bd. dirs. Duchesne Bank, St. Peters, Mo., 1989-95; sr. cons. Universal Fin. Group, Inc., 1996—2003; assoc. prof. bus. Fontbonne U., St. Louis, 1998—2005; bus. cons., 2005—. Vis. instr. Webster Coll., 1975—82; adviser City of Des Peres, Mo., chmn. fin. com., 1976—78, chmn. mgmt. com., 1978—81, mem. pers. commn., 1978—81, mem. planning and zoning com., 1981—83; bd. dirs. Mid-Am. Payments Exch., Duchesne Bank; arbitrator N.Y. Stock Exch., 2006—. Mem. parent's coun. Creighton U., Omaha, 1995—97; mem. adv. bd. St. Joseph Acad., 1982—86; mem. pres.'s coun. St. Louis U., 1983—; dist. chmn. Boy Scouts Am., 1991—93, vice chmn., 1994—2001; Arbitrator NASD, 2006, FINRA, 2007; trustee, chmn. St. Joseph Hosp., 1982—93; bd. dirs. ea. Mo. region NCCJ, 1987—93. Recipient Alumni Merit award, St. Louis U., 1979. Mem.: Nat. Assn. Securities Dealers (arbitrator 2006—), Alpha Kappa Psi, Beta Gamma Sigma.

MORISATO, SUSAN CAY, actuary; b. Chgo., Feb. 11, 1955; d. George and Jessie (Fujita) M.; m. Thomas Michael Remec, Mar. 6, 1981. BS, U. Ill., 1975, MS, 1977. Actuarial student Aetna Life & Casualty, Hartford, Conn., 1977-79; actuarial asst. Bankers Life & Casualty Co., Chgo., 1979-80, asst. actuary, 1980-83, assoc. actuary, 1983-85, health product actuary, 1985-86, v.p., 1986-95, sr. v.p., 1996—2004, also bd. dirs., 2000—04; COO, sr. and retiree svcs. Ovations (a UnitedHealth Group co.), 2005—07; pres., fed. programs United Health Group Alliances, 2007—. Participant individual forum Am.'s Health Ins. Plans, 1983; spkr. in field. Adv. panel on long term care financing Brookings' Inst.; trustee Minn. Zoo Found., 2005—. Fellow Soc. Actuaries (workshop leader 1990, 93, news editor health sect. news 1988-90, conf. spkr. 2001, 02); mem. Am. Acad. Actuaries, Am.'s Health Ins. Plans (long term care task force 1988-04, chair 1993-95, tech. adv. com. 1991-93, legis. policy com. 1996-99, nominating com. 1996-98, other coms., policy coord. coun. 1999-03, sr. mktg. task force chair 2000-01, chmn. task force on Medicare modernization 2002-04, exec. com. 2004, bd. dirs. 2004, policy com. 2004, medicare com. 2005—, LTC leadership coun. 2006-, Founders award 1996), Health Ins. Assn. Am. (conf. spkr. 2000), LIMRA Internat. (strategic mktg. ins. com. 2001-06, bd. dirs. 2003-07, chmn. compensation and benefits com. 2004-05, vice-chair bd. dirs. 2005-06, chair bd. 2006), Nat. Assn. Ins. Commrs. (ad hoc actuarial working group for long term care nonforfeiture benefits 1992), Am. Coun. Life Ins. (accelerated benefits/long term care com. 1997-01), Chgo. Actuarial Assn. (sec. 1983-85, program com. 1987-89), Phi Beta Kappa, Kappa Delta Pi, Phi Kappa Phi. Office: Ovations UnitedHealth Group MN008-T440 9900 Bren Rd E Minnetonka MN 55343 Home Phone: 847-299-0560; Office Phone: 952-945-7555. Business E-Mail: susan_c_morisato@uhc.com.

MORITZ, DONALD BROOKS, mechanical engineer, consultant; b. Mpls., June 17, 1927; s. Donald B. and Frances W. (Whalen) M.; m. Joan Claire Betzenderfer, June 17, 1950 (dec. Dec. 21, 2004); children: Craig, Pamela, Brian. BS in Mech. Engring., U. Minn., 1950; postgrad., Western Res. U., 1956-58. Registered profl. engr., Ill. Minn., Ohio. V.p., gen. mgr. Waco Scaffold Shoring Co., Addison, Ill., 1950-72; group v.p. Bliss and Laughlin Industries, Oak Brook, Ill., 1972-83; sr. v.p. AXIA Inc. (formerly Bliss and Laughlin Industries, Oak Brook, 1983-84, exec. v.p., chief operating officer, 1984-88; cons. Exec. Svc. Corps Chgo., 1988—; pres. Image-A-Nation, Unltd., 1988—.

Bd. dirs. Am. Photographic Acad. Patentee in field. Served with USN, 1945-46. Mem. ASME, Scaffold and Shoring Inst. (founder, past pres.), Mensa, Five Seasons Country Club. Office: Moritz and Assocs PO Box 305 Clarendon Hills IL 60514-0305

MORK, GORDON ROBERT, historian, educator; b. St. Cloud, Minn., May 6, 1938; s. Gordon Matthew and Agnes (Gibb) Mork; m. Dianne Jeannette Muetzel, Aug. 11, 1963; children: Robert, Kristiana, Elizabeth. BA, Yale U., 1960; MA, U. Minn., 1963, PhD, 1966. Instr. history U. Minn., Mpls., 1966; lectr., asst. prof. U. Calif., Davis, 1966-70; mem. faculty Purdue U., West Lafayette, Ind., 1970—, assoc. prof., 1973-94, prof. history, 1994—, dir. honors program humanities, 1985-87, dir grad. studies history, Am. studies, 1987-93, mem. Jewish studies com., 1980—, head dept. history, 1998—2003; resident dir. Purdue U.-Ind. U. Program, Hamburg, Germany, 1975-76. Rsch. fellow in humanities U. Wis., Madison, 1969—70; mem. test devel. com. advanced placement European history Ednl. Testing Svc., 1993—99, chair, 1995—99; cons. Coll. Bd. and Ednl. Testing Svc., 1999—. Author: Modern Western Civilization: A Concise History, 3d edit., 1994, AP Instructor's Manual, 2007; editor: The Homes of Ober-Ammergau, 2000; mem. adv. bd. Teaching History, 1983—, History Teacher, 1986—2002. Mem. citizens task force Lafayette Sch. Corp., 1978—79; bd. dirs. Ind. Humanities Coun., 1986—89; bd. govs. Tippecanoe County Hist. Assn.; elder Ctrl. Presbyn. Ch., Lafayette, 1973—75, deacon, 1996—99, trustee, 2001—04; bd. dirs., sec. Murdock-Sunnyside Bldg. Corp., 1980—2000. Mem.: Soc. History Edn., German Studies Assn., Am. Hist. Assn., Internat. Soc. History Didactics (v.p. 1991—95, 1996—2000), Mortar Bd., Phi Beta Kappa. Home: 1521 Cason St Lafayette IN 47904-2642 Office: Purdue U Dept History 672 Oval Dr West Lafayette IN 47907-2087 Office Phone: 765-494-4138. Business E-Mail: gmork@purdue.edu.

MORLEY, HARRY THOMAS, JR., real estate executive; b. St. Louis, Aug. 13, 1930; s. Harry Thomas and Celeste Elizabeth (Davies) M.; m. Nelda Lee Mulholland, Sept. 3, 1960; children: Lisa, Mark, Marci. BA, U. Mo., 1955; MA, U. Denver, 1959. Dir. men's student activities Iowa State Tchrs. Coll., 1955-57; dir. student housing U. Denver, 1957-60; pvt. practice psychol. consulting St. Louis, 1960-63; dir. adminstrn. County of St. Louis, Mo., 1963-70; regional dir. HUD, Kansas City, Mo., 1970-71, asst. sec. adminstrn., 1971-73; pres. St. Louis Regional Commerce and Growth Assn., 1973-78, Taylor, Morley, Inc., St. Louis, 1978—2005, Morley Investments, Inc., 2005—. Teaching cons., lectr. Washington U., St. Louis, 1962-70; bd. dirs. Mid-Am. Alliance Corp., Life Ins. Co. Bd. dirs., exec. com. St. Louis Coll. Pharmacy; past chmn. Better Bus. Bur.; chmn. Mo. Indsl. Devel. Bd., Mo. State Hwy. Commn.; bd. dirs. St. Luke's Hosps., St. Johns Hosp., Downtown St. Louis, Inc., Laclede's Landing Redevel. Corp. With USN, 1951-53. Mem. Am. Nat. Assn. Homebuilders, St. Louis Homebuilders Assn. (pres.), St. Louis Advt. Club, Mo. Athletic Club, St. Louis Club, Noonday Club, Castle Oak Country Club, Round Table Club, Sunset Country Club. Republican. Methodist. Home: 14238 Forest Crest Dr Chesterfield MO 63017-2818 E-mail: morleyh@charter.net.

MORLEY, JOHN EDWARD, physician; b. Eshowe, Zululand, South Africa, June 13, 1946; came to U.S., 1977; s. Peter and Vera Rose (Phipson) M.; m. Patricia Morley, Apr. 4, 1970; children: Robert, Susan, Jacqueline. MB, BCh, U. Witwatersrand, Johannesburg, South Africa, 1972. Diplomate Am. Bd. Internal Medicine, subspecialty cert. endocrinology and geriatrics. Asst. prof. Mpls. VA Med. Ctr. and U. Minn., 1979-81; assoc. prof. U. Minn., Mpls., 1981-84; prof. UCLA San Fernando Valley, 1985-89; dir. GRECC Sepulveda (Calif.) VA Med. Ctr., 1985-89; Dammert prof. gerontology, dir. div. geriatric medicine St. Louis U. Med. Ctr., 1989—; dir. geriatric rsch., edn. and clin. ctr. St. Louis VA Med. Ctr., 1989—. Author: (with others) Nutritional Modulation of Neuronal Function, 1988, Neuropeptides and Stress, 1988, Geriatric Nutrition, 1990, 2d edit., 1995, Medical Care in the Nursing Home, 1991, 2d edit., 1997, Endocrinology and Metabolism in the Elderly, 1992, Memory Function and Aging Related Disorders, 1992, Aging and Musculoskeletal Disorders, 1993, Aging, Immunity and Infection, 1994, Sleep Disorders and Insomnia in the Elderly, 1993, Quality Improvement in Geriatric Care, 1995, Focus on Nutrition, 1995, Applying Health Services Research to Long-Term Care, 1996, Cardiovascular Disease in Older People, 1997, Hydration and Aging, 1997, Advances in Care of Older People with Diabetes, 1999, Endocrinology of Aging, 1999, Science of Geriatrics, 2000, Subacute Care, 2000, Anti-Aging, 2004, Principles and Practices of Geriatric Medicine, 4th edit., 2006; The Sci. Staying Young, 2007; mem. editl. bd. Peptides, 1983—, Internat. Jour. Obesity, 1986-89, Jour. utritional Medicine, 1990—, Clinics in Applied Nutrition, 1990-92; editor geriatrics sect. Yearbook of Endocrinology, 1987-2001, Nursing Home Medicine, 1992-97, Clin. Geriatrics, 1992-97, Sandwich Generation, 1997, others; editor Jour. Gerontology: Med. Scis., 2000-06, Jour. Am. Med. Dirs. Assn., 2006—. Mem. adv. bd. Alzheimer's Assn., St. Louis, 1990-92; mem. adv. com. for physicians Mo. Divsn. Aging, Jefferson City, 1990-2001; bd. dirs. Mo. Assn. Long Term Care Physicians, 1991—, Long Term Care Ombudsman Program, St. Louis, 1992, Fund for Psychoneuroimmunology, 1990-2001, Hamilton Hts. Health Resource Ctr., 1992—. Recipient Mead Johnson award, Am. Inst. Nutrition, 1985, Cmty. Svc. award, BREM, 1997, Robert H. Bollinger Disting. Acad. award, U. Kans., 1997, Longevity prize, Ispen Found., 1999, Circle award, Am. Dietetics Assn., 2001, Marsha Goodwin-Beck Interdisciplinary award for excellence in geriatric leadership, Dept. Vets. Affairs, 2005. Mem. ACP (geriatrics subcom. 1991-92), Am. Geriatric Soc. (Nasher/Manning award 2002), Internat. Soc. Study-Aging Male, Am. Soc. Clin. Investigation, Endocrine Soc., Am. Fedn. Clin. Rsch., Am. Acad. Behavioral Sci., Gerontology Soc. Am. (Freeman award, 2004), Am. Diabetes Assn., Am. Soc. Pharmacy and Therapeutics, Soc. for Neurosci., La Asociacion de Gerontologica y Geriatrica, A.C. (hon.), Assn. Dirs. Geriatric Acad. Programs, Internat. Soc. Study Male Aging, Phi Beta Kappa. Office: Saint Louis U Sch Medicine 1402 S Grand Blvd Rm M238 Saint Louis MO 63104-1004 Office Phone: 314-977-8462. E-mail: morley@slu.edu.

MORLEY, MICHAEL B., public relations executive; b. Madras, India, Nov. 18, 1935; s. Gordon and Violet M.; m. Ingrid Hellman, Aug. 20, 1957; children: Andrew, Helen, Ann. Attended, Eastbourne Coll. Dir. Harris & Hunter Pub. Rels., 1960-67; mng. dir. Daniel J. Edelman, 1967; pres. Edelman Internat., 1970, Edelman N.Y., 1994—; dep. chmn., pres. Edelman Worldwide, 2000—. Comms. Advt. and Mktg. Edn. Found. fellow, 1981; decorated Knight of First Class, Order of Lion, Rep. Finland, 1978. Mem. Internat. Pub. Rels. Assn., Internat. Pub. Rels., Brit. C. of C., Japan Soc., Bus. Coun. Internat. Understanding, Inc., Korea Soc. Home: 1 Devon Pl Cresskill NJ 07626-1608 Office: Edelman Pub Rels Worldwide 200 E Randolph St Fl 62 Chicago IL 60601-6436

MORNEAU, JUSTIN ERNEST GEORGE, professional baseball player; b. New Westminster, BC, Can., May 15, 1981; s. George and Audra Morneau. First baseman Minn. Twins, 2003—. Mem. Can. World Jr. Team, 1999, Can. Nat. Team,World Baseball Championship, 2001. Named Am. League MVP, 2006; named to Am. League All-Star Team, 2007; recipient Silver Slugger award, 2006. Mailing: c/o Minn Twins Metrodome 34 Kirby Puckett Plc Minneapolis MN 55415*

MORNEAU, ROBERT FEALEY, bishop; b. New London, Wis., Sept. 10, 1938; s. Leroy Frederick and Catherine (Fealey) M. MA, Catholic U., 1962; DD (hon.), 1979. Ordained priest Diocese of Green Bay, Wis., 1966; Instr. philosophy Silver Lake Coll., Manitowoc, Wis., 1966-78; dir. ministry to priests program Green Bay, Wis., 1979-85; aux. bishop Diocese of Green Bay, 1978—; ordained bishop, 1979. Chmn. Commn. on Prison Reform, Wis. Cath. Conf.; lectr. in field. Author: Our Father Revisited, 1978, Trinity Sunday Revisited, 1980, Discovering God's Presence, 1980, Mantras for the Morning, 1981, Mantras for the Evening, 1982, Principles of Preaching, 1982, Seasonal Themes, 1984, Mantras for Midnight, 1985 and others; author tape series from Alba House;; contbr. articles to profl. jours. Bd. trustees St. Norbert Coll. Mem. Nat. Conf. Cath. Bishops, Bishops Com. on Priestly Formation, Com. on Edn. US Cath. Conf. Roman Catholic. Office: PO Box 23825 Green Bay WI 54305-3825*

MOROF, JEFFREY W., lawyer; AB, U. Mich, 1976; JD, Washington U., St. Louis, 1979. Bar: Calif., Mo., US Dist. Ct. (Ctrl. & No. dists.) Calif., US Dist. Ct. Colo., US Dist. Ct. (So. dist.) Fla., US Dist. Ct. NJ. With Bryan Cave LLP, Chgo., 1979—, ptnr., 1988—, mng. ptnr., mem. exec. com.; settlement conference atty. US Dist. Ct. (Ctrl. dist.) Calif., 1998—2000, 2001—03. Office Phone: 312-602-5045. Office Fax: 312-602-5045. E-mail: jwmorof@bryancave.com.

MORRILL, R. LAYNE, real estate broker, executive, professional association administrator; m. Brenda Morrill; 1 child, Rochelle Dawn. Cert. real estate broker. Pres. Shepherhd of the Hills, Realtors, Kimberling City, Branson, Mo., 1960—; mem. exec. com. Nat. Assn. Realtors, 1988—, pres., 1998—99, also bd. dirs. and mem. exec. com., 1988—. Chair realtors polit. action com., 1988; regional v.p. Nat. Assn. Realtors, Ark., 1988, Kans., 88, Mo., 88, Okla., 88; dir. Bank Kimberling city, Mo., Rural Mo. Cable TV, Inc. White River Valley Electric Coop., Branson, Mo., KAMO Electric Coop., Vinita, Okla., Nat. Rural utilities Coop. Fin. Corp., Herndon, Va. Mem.: Tri-Lakes Bd. Realtors (pres.), Mo. Assn. Realtors (pres., bd. dirs. 1962—, Realtor of the Yr. award 1979). Office: Nat Assn Realtors 430 N Michigan Ave Chicago IL 60611-4011

MORRIS, G. RONALD, automotive executive; b. East St. Louis, Ill., Aug. 30, 1936; s. George H. and Mildred C. M.; m. Margaret Heino, June 20, 1959; children: David, Michele, James. BS in Metall. Engring, U. Ill., 1959. Metall. engr. Delco-Remy divsn. Gen. Motors Corp., 1959-60; factory metallurgist Dubuque Tractor Works, John Deere Co., Iowa, 1960-66; with Fed.-Mogul Corp., 1966-79, v.p., group mgr. ball and roller bearing group, 1979; pres. Tenneco Automotive divsn. Tenneco, Inc., Deerfield, Ill., 1979-82; pres., CEO PT Components, Inc., Indpls., 1982-88; vice-chmn. Rexnord Corp., Indpls., 1988-89; chmn., pres., CEO CTP Holdings Inc., 1986-88; chmn. Integrated Technologies, Inc., Indpls., 1990-92, also bd. dirs.; pres., CEO Western Industries, Inc., Milw., 1991-99. Bd. dirs. NN, Inc., Erwin, Tenn., Prism Capital Inc. Mem. Pres.'s Coun., U. Ill., mem. sr. adv. bd. Sch. Materials Sci. and Engring, U. Ill.; mem. U. Ill. Found. Mem. ASM, SAE, U. Ill. Alumni Assn. (bd. dirs.), The Landings Club (Savannah, Ga.), Masons, Scottish Rite, Kiwanis Internat. Republican. Presbyterian. E-mail: savannahronm@yahoo.com.

MORRIS, JOHN H., manufacturing executive; BS, U. W.Va.; MBA, Case Western Res. U. Mgmt. positions Gen. Tire & Rubber Co., Armstrong Cork Co.; dir. corp. mktg., corp. v.p. RPM, Inc., 1977-81, exec. v.p. Indsl. Group, 1981—. Dir. Fifth Third Bank, Northeastern Ohio. Office: 2628 Pearl Rd Medina OH 44256-7623

MORRIS, MATTHEW CHRISTIAN, professional baseball player; b. Middletown, NY, Aug. 9, 1974; Attended, Seton Hall Univ. Played Team USA, 1994; pitcher St. Louis Cardinals, 1997—. Named All-Am. Office: St Louis Cardinals 250 Stadium Plz Saint Louis MO 63102

MORRIS, MICHAEL DAVID, chemistry professor; b. NYC, Mar. 27, 1939; s. Melvin M. and Rose (Pollock) M.; m. Leslie Tuttle, June 5, 1961; children: Susannah, David, Rebecca, Ari. BA in Chemistry, Reed Coll., 1960; PhD in Chemistry, Harvard U., 1964. Asst. prof. Pa. State U., University Park, Pa., 1969; assoc. prof. U. Mich., Ann Arbor, 1969-82, prof., 1982—. Assoc. chmn. U. Mich., Ann Arbor, 1992-97. Editor: Spectroscopic and Microscopic Imaging of the Chemical State, 1993; mem. editorial bd. Applied Spectroscopy, 1994— (Gold medal N.Y. sect. 1993), Spectrochim Acta Rev., 1987-92, editor, 1993. Recipient Anachem award Assn. Analytical Chemists, 1997. Mem. Am. Chem. Soc. (award in Spectrochemical Analysis Divsn. Analytical Chemistry 1995), Soc. Applied Spectroscopy (Strock award 1995), Microbeam Analysis Soc. Office: Univ Mich Dept Chemistry Ann Arbor MI 48109 E-mail: mdmorris@umich.edu.

MORRIS, MICHAEL G., electric power industry executive; b. Fremont, Ohio, Nov. 11, 1946; married, Linda Lindstrom, 1970; two children. BS, Ea. Mich. U., MS, 1973; JD cum laude, Detroit Coll. Law, 1981. With environ. dept. Commonwealth Assocs., Jackson, Mich., 1973—76; pres. ANR Gathering Co.; exec. v.p. mktg., transp. and gas supply ANR Pipeline Co., 1982—87; pres. Colo. Interstate Gas Co., 1987—88; exec. v.p., natural gas & mktg. Consumers Energy subsidiary of CMS Energy Corp., 1988—92, COO, 1992—94, pres., CEO, 1994—97; chmn., pres., CEO Northeast Utilities, Berlin, Conn., 1997—2003; pres., CEO Am. Electric Power Co., Springfield, Mass., 2004—, chmn., 2004—. Past chmn. Conn. Bus. & Industry Assn.; chmn. Edison Electric Inst.; bd. dir. Nuclear Electric Ins. Ltd., Flint Ink Corp., Cincinnati Bell, Hartford Fin. Svc. Group Inc., Alcoa Inc., 2008—. Exec. com., trustee Inst. Gas Tech.; trustee Ea. Mich. U. Found.; trustee Detroit Coll. Law, Delta Sigma Phi Found.; mem. Olivet Coll. Leadership Adv. Coun.; US Dept. Energy, Electricity Adv. Bd.; Task Force Electricity Infrastructure, Nat. Gov. Assn.; Inst. Nuclear Power Ops.; Bus. Roundtable; Columbus Downtown Devel. Corp.; bd. dirs. Libr. Mich. Found.; bd. regents Ea. Mich. U., 1997—. Recipient Disting. Alumnus award Ea. Mich. U., 1995. Mem. Mich. Bar Assn., Delta Sigma Phi (pres.). Office: Am Electric Power Co 1 Riverside Plz Columbus OH 43215-2372

MORRIS, RALPH WILLIAM, chronopharmacologist; b. Cleveland Heights, Ohio, July 30, 1928; s. Earl Douglas and Viola Minnie (Mau) M.; m. Carmen R. Mueller; children: Christopher Lynn, Kirk Stephen, Timothy Allen and Todd Andrew (twins), Melissa Mary. BA, Ohio U., Athens, 1950, MS, 1953; PhD, U. Iowa, 1955; postgrad., Seabury-Western Theol. Sem., 1979-81, McHenry County Coll., 1986-88. Research fellow in pharmacology, then teaching fellow U. Iowa, 1952-55; instr. dept. pharmacology Coll. Medicine, 1955-56; asst. prof. dept. pharmacognosy and pharmacology Coll. Pharmacy, 1956-62, assoc. prof., 1962-69; prof. Med. Center, U. Ill., Chgo., 1969-98, prof. emeritus, 1998, adj. prof. dept. pharmacodynamics, 1998-2000. Mem. adv. com. 1st aid and safety Midwest chpt. ARC, 1972-83; cons. in drug edn. to Dangerous Drug Commn., Ill. Dept. Pub. Aid, Chgo., Ill. Dept. Profl. Regulataions, Ill. Dept. Corrections and suburban sch. dists.; adj. prof. edn. Coll. Edn., U. Ill., Chgo., 1976-85; vis. scientist San Jose State U., Calif., 1982-83, St. George Med. Sch., Grenada, 1994. Referee and contbr. articles to profl. and sci. jours., lay mags., radio and TV appearances. Trustee Palatine (Ill.) Pub. Libr., 1967-72, pres., 1969-70; trustee orth Suburban Libr. System, 1968-72, pres. 1970-72, mem. long-range planning com., 1975-81; chmn. Ill. Libr. Trustees, 1970-72, intellectual freedom com.; mem. Title XX Ill. Citizens Adv. Coun., 1981-83; trusteee McHenry (Ill.) Pub. Libr. Dist., 1987-89, pres., 1987-89; trustee St. Gregory's Abbey, Three Rivers, Mich., 1989-96; bd. dirs. North Suburban Libr. Found., Wheeling, Ill., 1998-99; bd. dirs. United Campus Ministry U. Ill. at Chgo., 1983-87; pres. R.W. Morris & Assocs., 1988—; v.p. Lake Barrington Shores Condo X Assn., bd. dirs., 1999—; mem. archtl. commn. Lake Barrington Shores Master Bd., 1999—. Recipient Golden Apple Teaching award U. Ill. Coll. Pharmacy, 1966; cert. of merit Town of Palatine, 1972 Mem. AAAS, Am. Assn. Coll. Pharmacists, Internat. Soc. Chronobiology, European Soc. Chronbiology, Am. Soc. Pharmacology and Exptl. Therapeutics, Am. Library Trustee Assn., Ill. Library Trustee Assn. (v.p. 1970-72, dir. 1969-72), Sigma Xi, Rho Chi, Gamma Alpha. Episcopalian. Home and Office: 584 Shoreline Dr Lake Barrington IL 60010-3883 Home Phone: 847-304-0605; Office Phone: 847-304-0605. Personal E-mail: raphaelmor@aol.com.

MORRIS, STEPHEN R., state legislator; b. Garden City, Kans., Jan. 4, 1946; m. Barbara Morris, 1968; children: Stephanie, Susan, Sara Beth. BS, Kans. State U., 1969. Farmer, Hugoton, Kans.; mem. from dist. 39 Kans. Senate, Topeka, 1992—; vice chmn. agr. com. Kans. State Senate, mem. energy and natural resources com., mem. emergency med. svc. bd., coord. coun. on early childhood devel. svc. With USAFR, 1974—. Mem. Kans. State U. Alumni Assn. Address: 600 S Trindle St Hugoton KS 67951-2734 Office: 120-S State Capitol 300 SW 10th Ave Topeka KS 66612

MORRIS, THOMAS WILLIAM, symphony orchestra administrator; b. Rochester, NY, Feb. 7, 1944; s. William H. and Eleanor E. M.; m. Jane Allison, Aug. 7, 1965; children: Elisa L., Charles A., William H. AB, Princeton U., 1965; MBA, Wharton Sch. U. Pa., 1969. Adminstrv. asst., Ford Found. fellow for adminstrv. interns in arts Cin. Symphony, 1965-67; payroll clk. bus. office Boston Symphony Orch., 1969-71, asst. mgr. bus. affairs, 1971-73, mgr., 1973-78, gen. mgr., 1978-86, v.p. spl. projects and planning, 1986; pres. Thomas W. Morris and Co., Inc., Boston, 1986-87; exec. dir. Cleve. Orch., 1987—2004; artistic dir. Ojai Music Festival, 2004—. Chmn. policy com. Maj. Orch. Mgrs., 1977-79; chmn. orch. panel Nat. Endowment for Arts, 1979-80. Chmn. Cleve. Cultural Coalition, 1992-95; mem. Cleve. Bicentennial Commn., 1993-97; mem. bd. overseers Curtis Inst. Music, 1998—. Mem. Am. Symphony Orch. League (dir. 1977-79) Office: 2533 Fairmount Blvd Cleveland OH 44106

MORRISON, ANDREW J., marketing professional; b. Pitts., Mar. 7, 1949; s. James E. and Doris A. (Addicks) M.; m. Kathleen Ann Steiner, Dec. 27, 1969; children: Alanna Christine, James Jason. BA, U. Mich., 1971, PhD, 1980. Sr. v.p. Market Opinion Rsch., Detroit, 1980-89; prin., founder Market Strategies, Inc., Livonia, Mich., 1989-93, pres., CEO, 1994—. Contbr. chpts. to books, also articles to profl. publs., including Mktg. Rsch. Mag., Comm. Rsch., Am. Behavioral Scientist. Mem. Am. Mktg. Assn. (editor mag. 1996-98), Am. Assn. Pub. Opinion Rsch. Office: Market Strategies Inc 20255 Victor Pkwy Ste 400 Livonia MI 48152-7003

MORRISON, CLINTON, banker; b. Mpls., Mar. 26, 1915; s. Angus Washburn and Helen (Truesdale) M.; m. Mary K. Morrison. BA, Yale U., 1937; MBA, Harvard U., 1939. With Shell Oil Co., NYC, St. Louis, 1939-41; with Vassar Co., Chgo., 1946-48, Holding Co., Mpls., 1948, First Nat. Bank, Mpls., 1955-80, former vice chmn. bd., chmn. trust com. Former dir. Gt. No. Ins. Co., Minn. Title Fin. Corp., Munsingwear, Inc.; Dep. Regional dir. Far East Fgn. Ops. Adminstrn. for U.S. Govt., 1953-55; mem. Internat. Pvt. Investment Adv. Council to AID, Dept. State, 1967-68, Nat. Adv. Council on Minority Bus. Enterprise, 1968-72 Former trustee Lakewood Cemetery Assn. Served to maj. Q.M.C. AUS, 1942-46. Mem. U.S. C. of C. (chmn. 1975-76), Bankers Assn. (exec. com. trust div. 1969-72), Twin Cities Soc. Security Analysts, Mpls. Econ. Roundtable. Office: 730 Second Ave South Ste 1350 Minneapolis MN 55402

MORRISON, CRAIG O., chemicals executive; Grad., Ea. Ky. Univ.; MBA, Harvard Univ., 1987. Cons. Bain & Co., 1987—90; sr. operational and bus. mgmt. pos. GE Co., 1990—93; pres., gen. mgr. Van Leer, Inc., 1993—98, Alcan Pharm. and Cosmetic Packaging, divsn. Alcan, Inc., Millville, NJ, 1998—2002; pres., CEO Hexion Specialty Chemicals Inc., Columbus, Ohio, 2002—, chmn., 2005—. Office: Hexion 180 E Broad St Columbus OH 43215

MORRISON, DEBORAH JEAN, lawyer; b. Johnstown, Pa., Feb. 18, 1955; d. Ralph Wesley and Norma Jean (Kinsey) Morrison; m. Ricardo Daniel Kamenetzky, Sept. 6, 1978 (div. ov. 1991); children: Elena Raquel, Julia Rebecca. BA in Polit. Sci., Chatham Coll., 1977; postgrad., U. Miami, Fla., 1977-78; JD, U. Pitts., 1981. Bar: Pa. 1981, Ill. 1985. Legal asst. Klein Y Mairal, Buenos Aires, 1978-79; legal intern Neighborhood Legal Svcs., Aliquippa, Pa., 1980-81; law clk. Pa. Superior Ct., Pitts., 1981-84; atty. John Deere Credit Co., Moline, Ill., 1985-89; sr. atty. Deere & Co., Moline, Ill., 1989-96, sr. counsel, 1996—2003, asst. gen. counsel, 2003—. Mem. ABA, Pa. Bar Assn., Phi Beta Kappa, Order of the Coif. Democrat. Mem. United Church of Christ. Office: Deere & Co 1 John Deere Pl Moline IL 61265-8098

MORRISON, DONALD WILLIAM, lawyer; b. Portland, Oreg., Mar. 31, 1926; s. Robert Angus and Laura Calista (Hodgson) M.; m. Elizabeth Margaret Perry, July 25, 1953; children: Elizabeth Laura, Carol Margaret. BSE.E., U. Wash., 1946; LL.B., Stanford U., 1950. Bar: Oreg. 1950, Calif. 1950, N.Y. 1967, Ill. 1968, Ohio 1974. Assoc. Pendergrass, Spackman, Bullivant & Wright, Portland, 1950-57, ptnr., 1957-60; gen. atty. Pacific N.W. Bell, Portland, 1960-66; atty. AT&T, NYC, 1966-68; counsel Ill. Bell Telephone Co., Chgo., 1968-74; v.p., gen. counsel Ohio Bell Telephone Co., Cleve., 1974-91; of counsel Arter & Hadden, Cleve., 1992—2003. Trustee Archael. Inst. Am., Cleve. Archaeol. Soc., Cleve. Chamber Music Soc., Cleve. Coun. on World Affairs; mem. adv. com. Cleve. Play House, Cleve. Bot. Garden; mem. Ohio adv. bd. Trust for Pub. Land. With USN, 1943—50. Recipient various bar and civic appreciation awards. Mem. ABA, Ohio State Bar Assn., Oreg. State Bar Assn., Calif. Bar Assn., Rowfant Club.

MORRISON, FRED LAMONT, law educator, dean; b. Salina, Kans., Dec. 12, 1939; s. Earl F. and Madge Louise (Glass) M.; m. Charlotte Foot, Dec. 27, 1971; children: Charles, Theodore, George, David. AB, U. Kans., 1961; BA, Oxford U., Eng., 1963, MA, 1968; PhD, Princeton U., 1966; JD, U. Chgo., 1967. Bar: Minn. 1973. Asst. prof. law U. Iowa, Iowa City, 1967-69; counselor on internat. law U.S. State Dept., Washington, 1982-83; assoc. prof. law U. Minn., Mpls., 1969-73, prof. law, 1973-90, Oppenheimer Wolff and Donnelly prof., 1990-97, acting dean, 1994-95, Popham Haik/Lindquist & Vennum prof., 1998—, interim co-dean, 2006—. Of counsel Popham, Haik, Schnobrich & Kaufman, Mpls., 1983-97. Dir. Am. Soc. for Comparative Study of Law; mem. adv. com. on internat. law U.S. Dept. State, Washington, 1987-89; mem. internat. adv. bd. Inst. on Internat. Law, Kiel, Germany, 1989—; mem. Am. Law Inst., bd. editors for Am. Jour. Comparative Law. Recipient President's Award for Outstanding Svc., U. Minn., 1997. Home: 1412 W 47th St Minneapolis MN 55419-5204 Office: U Minn Law Sch 229 19th Ave S Minneapolis MN 55455-0400 Office Phone: 612-625-0321. Business E-Mail: morrison@umn.edu.

MORRISON, HARRY, chemistry professor; b. Bklyn., Apr. 25, 1937; s. Edward and Pauline (Sommers) M.; m. Harriet Thurman, Aug. 23, 1958; children: Howard, David, Daniel. BA, Brandeis U., 1957; PhD, Harvard U., 1961. NATO-NSF postdoctoral fellow Swiss Fed. Inst., Zurich, 1961-62; rsch. assoc. U. Wis., Madison, 1962-63; asst. prof. chemistry Purdue U., West Lafayette, Ind., 1963-69, assoc. prof., 1969-76, prof., 1976—, dept. head, 1987-92, dean Sch. Sci., 1992—2002. Mem. acad. adv. com. Indsl. Rsch. Inst., 1993-96. Contbr. numerous articles to profl. jours. Bd. fellows Brandeis U. Mem. Am. Chem. Soc., Am. Soc. Photobiology, Inter-Am. Photochem. Soc., Coun. for Chem. Rsch. (chmn. 1995), Phi Beta Kappa Office: Purdue Univ Dept Chemistry Brown Bldg West Lafayette IN 47907-2084 Office Phone: 765-494-5246. Business E-Mail: hmorrison@purdue.edu.

MORRISON, JAMES FRANK, optometrist, state legislator; b. Colby, Kans., Apr. 11, 1942; s. Lloyd Wayne and Catherine Louise (Beckner) M.; m. Karen Jean Carr, Aug. 25, 1963; children: Mike, Jeff, Scott. Student, U. Kans., 1960-64; BS, OD, So. Coll. Optometry, 1967. Pvt. practice, 1969-75; founder, chief staff N.W. Kans. Ednl. Diagnostic and Referral Ctr. Children, Inc., Colby; asst. chief engr. Sta. KXXX-FM, 1977-80, chief engr., 1980-82; prof. vision dept. Colby Community Coll., 1979-84; mem. Kans. Ho. Reps., Topeka, 1992—. Cubmaster pack 140 Cub Scouts Am., 1970-80, dist. chmn., 1977-79. Fellow Am. Acad. Optometry, Coll. Optometrists in Vision Devel.; mem. Am. Optometric Assn., Am. Soc. Broadcast Engrs., Kans. Soc. Broadcast Engrs. (founder, pres. 1970-71), Kans. Optometric Assn., Kans. Assn. Children with Learning Disabilities, Mo. Optometric Assn., Thomas County Assn. Retarded Children, Rotary, Lions, Kiwanies (pres. 1971-72), Masons, Shriners. Rotary. Mem. Assemblies of God. Ch. Avocations: amateur radio, photography, astronomy. Home: 3 Cottonwood Dr Colby KS 67701-3902 Office: Morrison Optometric Assocs 180 W 6th St Colby KS 67701-2315

MORRISON, JOHN M., bank executive; Owner, CEO Ctrl. Bank Group, Golden Valley, Minn.; interim chmn., CEO Allina Health Sys., 2001—02, bd. chmn., 2004—. Mem. Fairview U. Med. Ctr. Bd., Fairview Health Sys. Corp. Bd.; chmn. exec. com. bd. trustees U. St. Thomas; former mem. bd. govs., chmn. bd.'s fin. com. U. Minn. Acad. Health Ctr.; former mem. Johns Hopkins Medicine bd. visitors Johns Hopkins U. Mem.: U. St. Thomas Sch. Law (mem. bd. govs., founder John. M. Morrison Ctr. Entrepreneurship).

MORRISON, JOSEPH YOUNG, transportation executive, consultant; b. Flushing, NY, Jan. 4, 1951; s. William Barrier and Barbara Helen (Lowe) Morrison; m. Shirley Morrison; children: Susan Parker, Travis Barrier. AS, Montreat Anderson Coll., NC, 1971; BA, Oglethorpe U., 1989. Dept. head J.C. Penny & Co., Atlanta, 1971-74; uniform patrol officer City of Atlanta, 1974-80; spl. agt. U.S. Dept. Transp., Atlanta, 1980-82; group dir. safety and ins. Western Express, Atlanta, 1982-85; dir. safety Taylor Maid Transp., Albany, Ga., 1985-86; v.p. risk mgmt. Burlington Motor Carriers, Inc., Daleville, Ind., 1986-96; pres. Motor Carrier Safety Cons. Inc., Noblesville, Ind., 1996-97, Nat. Transp. Cons., Inc., Noblesville, Ind., 1997—. Co-author: Guide to Handling Hazardous Material, 1986. Mem.: Am. Soc. Safety Engrs., Am. Trucking Assn. (mem. hazardous materials com. 1982—86, mem. safety mgmt. coun. 1982—, chmn. injury control com. 1984—88, mem. interstate carrier conf. 1985—, mem. nat. freight claims and security coun. 1985—, Safety Improvement award, Accident Reduction award, Injury Reduction award), Sertoma Club, Kenilworth Civic Club (treas. Stone Mountain Ga. chpt. 1981—83, pres. 1983—84), Sigma Alpha Epsilon. Methodist. Avocations: home remodeling, restoring old cars. Office: Nat Transp Cons 400 Lafayette Rd Noblesville IN 46060 Office Phone: 317-770-0953. E-mail: jmorrison@ntconsult.com.

MORRISON, KENNETH P., lawyer; BA, Yale Univ., 1977; MSM, MIT, 1983; JD magna cum laude, Boston Univ., 1983. Bar: Ill. 1983. Ptnr. in charge, asset fin. & securitization practice Kirkland & Ellis LLP, Chgo., 1990—. Adj. prof.

Northwestern Univ. Sch. Law, 1995—2001. Contbr. articles to profl. jours. Office: Kirkland & Ellis LLP 200 E Randolph Dr Chicago IL 60601-6636 Office Phone: 312-861-2347. Office Fax: 312-660-0967. Business E-Mail: kmorrison@kirkland.com.

MORRISON, PATRICIA B., electronics executive; BA in Math. & Stats. summa cum laude, Miami Univ., BS in Secondary Edn. Sys. mgmt., IT positions Procter & Gamble; CIO GE Indsl. Sys. Gen. Electric, 1997—2000; CIO Quaker Oats Co., Chgo., 2000—02; exec. v.p., CIO Office Depot, Inc., Delray Beach, Fla., 2002—05; sr. v.p., chief info. officer Motorola Inc., Schaumburg, Ill., 2005—07, exec. v.p., CIO, 2007—. Bd. dir. Jo-Ann Stores, Inc., SPSS Inc., 2007—. Bd. mem. Chgo. Symphony Orch., Lyric Opera Chgo. Office: Motorola Inc 1303 E Algonquin Rd Schaumburg IL 60196

MORRISON, PAUL J., former state attorney general, former prosecutor; b. Dodge City, Kans., June 1, 1954; m. Joyce Morrison; 3 children. Student, Kans. State U.; BA in Criminal Justice, Washburn U., Topeka; JD, Washburn U. Sch. Law, Topeka, 1980. Asst. dist. atty. Johnson County, Kans., 1980—89, dist. atty. Kans., 1989—2005; atty. gen. State of Kans., Topeka, 2007—08. Vice chair Kans. Sentencing Commn. Chmn. fundraising effort Johnson County United Way, 2004; mem. Good Shepherd Cath. Ch.; pres., bd. mem. Sunflower House, SafeHome, Inc. Named Prosecutor of the Yr., Kans. County & Dist. Attorney's Assn., 2001; recipient Clarence M. Kelley award for Excellence in Criminal Justice Adminstrn., Lifetime Achievement award, Kans. County & Dist. Attorney's Assn., 2007. Mem.: Johnson County Bar Found. (former pres.), Kans. County and Dist. Attys. Assn. (former pres.). Democrat. Roman Catholic. Office Phone: 785-296-2215.*

MORRISON, PORTIA OWEN, lawyer; b. Charlotte, NC, Apr. 1, 1944; d. Robert Hall Jr. and Josephine Currier (Hutchison) M.; m. Alan Peter Richmond, June 19, 1976; 1 child, Anne Morrison. BA in English, Agnes Scott Coll., 1966; MA, U. Wis., 1967; JD, U. Chgo., 1978. Bar: Ill. 1978. Sr. counsel DLA Piper U.S. LLP, Chgo., 1978—. Lectr. in field. Past pres. Girl Scouts of Chgo. Mem.: ABA, CREW Chgo., Chgo. Fin. Exch., Pension Real Estate Assn., Chgo. Bar Assn. (real property com., subcom. real property fin., alliance for women), Am. Coll. Real Estate Lawyers (past pres. bd. govs., bd. govs.). Office: DLA Piper US LLP 203 N La Salle St Chicago IL 60601-1210 Office Phone: 312-368-4013. Business E-Mail: portia.morrison@dlapiper.com.

MORRISS, FRANK HOWARD, JR., pediatrics educator; b. Birmingham, Ala., Apr. 20, 1940; s. Frank Howard Sr. and Rochelle (Snow) M.; m. Mary J. Hagan, June 29, 1968; children: John Hagan, Matthew Snow. BA, U. Va., 1962; MD, Duke U., 1966. Diplomate Am. Bd. Pediatrics, Am. Bd. Perinatal and Neonatal Medicine. Intern Duke U. Med. Ctr., Durham, NC, 1966-67, resident in pediatrics, 1967-68, fellow in neonatology, 1970-71, U. Colo., Denver, 1971-73; asst. prof. to prof. U. Tex. Med. Sch., Houston, 1973-86; prof. U. Iowa Coll. Medicine, Iowa City, 1987—, chmn. dept., 1987—2004. Editor: Role of Human Milk in Infant Nutrition and Health, 1986; contbr. numerous articles to profl. jours, chpts. to books. Lt. comdr. USN, 1968-70. Grantee, NIH, 1977—87, 1990—2004. Mem. Am. Pediatric Soc., Soc. Pediatric Rsch., Am. Acad. Pediatrics, Soc. Gynecol. Investigation, Midwest Soc. Pediatric Rsch. Office: U Iowa Hosps & Clinics Dept Pediatrics Iowa City IA 52242 Office Phone: 319-384-6530.

MORRISSEY, BILL, state agency administrator; Dir. Minn. Dept. Natural Resources, Office Ops. Pks. & Recreation, St. Paul, 1993—. Office: Minn Dept Natural Resources Office Ops Pks & Recreation 500 Lafayette Rd N Saint Paul MN 55155-4002 Fax: 651-296-4799.

MORRISSEY, MARY F. (FRAN), human resource consulting company executive; Cert. profl. employer specialist. Acctg., tax profl., small bus. cons., 10 yrs.; formre owner, mgr. profl. employer orgn.; co-founder, pres., CEO, Staff Mgmt., Inc., Rockford, Ill., 1983—. Part-owner John Morrissey, Accts., Rockford; presenter to state and fed. legislators, regulatory agys. and profl. orgns.; sec., mem. bd. Merc. Bank; bd. dirs. Inst. for Accreditation Profl. Employer Orgns. Bd. dirs. Swedish Am. Health Sys., Rockford; active numerous civic orgsn. Named One of Top 25 Women Bus. Owners, Crain's Chgo. Bus., 1993, 95, Connie Tremulis award for bus. owners YWCA, Rockford, 1998. Mem. Soc. for Human Resource Mgmt. (accredited sr. profl. in human resources), Nat. Assn. Profl. Employer Orgns. (past bd. dirs. and past pres.), former mem. profl. stds. com., also former chmn., past mem. comm. network, mgmt. performance, membership, govt. affairs, and edn. coms.), Midwest Assn. Profl. Employer Orgns. (past pres.), Nat. Assn. Women Bus. Owners (One of Top 25 Women Bus. Owners 1993, 95), Rockford Area C. of C. (coun. of 100, Woman Bus. Owner of Yr. 1998)), Rockford Women's Club, also others. Office: Staff Mgmt Inc 5919 Spring Creek Rd Rockford IL 61114-6447 Fax: 815-282-0515.

MORRIS-TATUM, JOHNNIE, state legislator; Mem. Wis. State Assembly. Address: 3711 W Douglas Ave Milwaukee WI 53209-3620

MORRONE, FRANK, electronics executive; b. Marano Marchesato, Cosenza, Italy, May 13, 1949; s. Luigi and Emma (Molinaro) M.; m. Katherine Ann Kuehn, Feb. 1, 1975; children: Louis H., Cecilia E., Joseph V. BSEE, U. Wis., 1972; MBA, Northwestern U., 1993. Project engr. 3M Co., St. Paul, 1972—73; product engr., mgr. Eaton Corp., Kenosha, Wis., 1973—79; chief elec. engr. Tree Machine Tool, Racine, Wis., 1979—80; v.p. engring. MacPower divsn. Manu-Tronics, Inc., Kenosha, 1980—84, exec. v.p., 1984—99, bd. dirs., sec., 1988—99; v.p. ops. Sanmina Corp., 1999—2001, sr. v.p., 2001—. Exec. bd. Southeast coun. Boy Scouts Am., Racine, 1987—2005, adv. bd. 2005-; bd. dirs. Kenosha Libr., 1987-98, U. Wis.-Parkside Benevolent Found., 2000—2007; mgmt. coun. Lakeview Tech. Acad., 1997-99. Mem. IEEE, Kenosha County Club (bd. dirs.). Office: Sanmina-SCI Corp 8701 100th St Pleasant Prairie WI 53158-2202 Office Phone: 262-947-7700.

MORROW, ANDREW NESBIT, interior designer, business owner; b. Fremont, Nebr., Feb. 22, 1929; s. Hamilton N. and May (Oberg) M.; m. Margaret M. Stoltinberg; children: Megan Beth, Molly Jean, Andrew C. BFA, U. Nebr., 1950. Interior designer Hardy Furniture, Lincoln, Nebr., 1950-61, Morrow Interiors, Lincoln, 1961—. Bd. visitors Found. for Interior Design Edn. and Rsch., 1976-84; mem. standards com. Found. for Interior Design Edn. and Research, N.Y.C. Exhibitor Fremont Art Gallery, 1986, Haymarket Art Gallery, 1984. Pres. First Luth. Ch., Lincoln, 1987-90; bd. dirs. Lincoln Symphony, 1988-91, Nebr. Republicans for Choice, 1992, Luth. Family Svcs. of Nebr., 1994, Luth. Family Svc. Nebr. Found., 1995—; treas. NCID, 1992—. Fellow Am. Soc. Interior Designers (bd. dirs. ebr.-Iowa chpt. 1974-78, pres. 1986-88); mem. Interior Design Educators Council (hon.). Republican. Avocations: gardening, horseback riding, cross country skiing. Home: 301 Park Vista Lincoln NE 68510 Office: Morrow Interiors Inc 1010 K St Lincoln NE 68508-2880

MORROW, GRANT, III, medical research director, pediatrician; b. Pitts., Mar. 18, 1933; married, 1960; 2 children. BA, Haverford Coll., 1955; MD, U. Pa., 1959. Intern U. Colo., 1959-60; resident in pediat. U. Pa., 1960-62, fellow neonatology, asst. instr., 1962-63, instr., 1963-66, assoc., 1966-68, asst. prof., 1968-70, assoc. prof., 1970-72, U. Ariz., 1972—78, prof., 1974-78, assoc. chmn. dept., 1976-78; med. dir. Columbus (Ohio) Children's Hosp., 1978-94; prof. neonatology and metabolism, chmn. dept. Ohio State U., 1978-94; med. dir. divsn. molecular and human genetics Children's Hosp. Rsch. Found., Columbus, 1994-98. Med. dir. Children's Rsch. Inst., Columbus, Ohio, 1978—. Mem. Am. Pediat. Soc., Am. Soc. Clin. Nutrition, Soc. Pediat. Rsch. Achievements include research on children suffering inborn errors of metabolism, mainly amino and organic acids. Office: Children's Rsch Inst 700 Childrens Dr Columbus OH 43205-2696 Home Phone: 614-253-5693; Office Phone: 614-722-2708. Office Fax: 614-722-2716. Business E-Mail: morrowg@ccri.net.

MORROW, RICHARD MARTIN, retired oil company executive; b. Wheeling, W.Va., Feb. 27, 1926; B.M.E., Ohio State U., 1948. With Amoco Corp., 1948-91; v.p. Amoco Prodn. Co., 1964-66; exec. v.p. Amoco Internat. Oil Co., 1966-70, Amoco Chem. Corp., 1970-74, pres., 1974-78, Amoco Corp., 1978-83, chmn. chief exec. officer, 1983-91; ret., 1991. Trustee U. Chgo. and Rush U. Med. Ctr. Office: 200 E Randolph Dr Ste 6952 Chicago IL 60601-7704

MORSCH, THOMAS HARVEY, lawyer, educator; b. Oak Park, Ill., Sept. 5, 1931; s. Harvey William and Gwenodyne (Maun) M.; m. Jacquelyn Casey, Dec. 27, 1954; children: Thomas H. Jr., Margaret, Mary Susan, James, Kathryn, Julia. BA, Notre Dame U., 1953; BSL., Northwestern U., 1953, JD, 1955. Bar: Ill. 1955, D.C. 1955. Assoc. Crowell & Leibman, Chgo., 1955-62; ptnr. Leibman, Williams, Bennett, Baird & Minow, Chgo., 1962-72, Sidley & Austin, Chgo., 1972-97, counsel, 1998-2000. Bd. dirs. Chgo. Lawyers Com. for Civil Rights Under Law, chmn., 1982-83; bd. dirs. Pub. Interest Law Initiative, pres., 1993-95; No. Dist. Ill. Civil Justice Reform Com., 1991-95, Ill. Equal Justice Commn., 1999—2003; mem. vis. com. Law Sch. Northwestern U., 1989-90, dir. Small Bus. Opportunity Ctr., 1998—, assoc. clin. prof., 1998-2003, clin. prof., 2003—; mem. adv. bd. Kellogg Ctr. for Nonprofit Mgmt., 2001-06. Pres. Republican Workshops of Ill., 1970; gen. counsel Ill. Com. to Re-elect the Pres., 1972; mem. LaGrange Plan Commn., Ill., 1972-80, LaGrange Fire and Police Commn., 1968-72; trustee LaGrange Meml. Hosp., 1983-89; mem. adv. bd. Cath. Charities of Chgo., 1985-2006; mem. bd. dir. Cath. Charities of Chgo., 2007-. Fellow Am. Coll. Trial Lawyers; mem. ABA, Ill. State Bar Assn., Chgo. Bar Assn. (bd. mgrs. 1979-81), DC Bar, 7th Cir. Bar Assn., Northwestern Law Sch. Alumni Assn. (pres. 1988-89), Chgo. Bar Found. (bd. dirs., pres. 1995-97), Univ. Club (Chgo.), LaGrange Country Club, Palisades Park Country Club (Mich.), Point O'Woods Country Club (Mich.). Roman Catholic. Home: 301 S Edgewood Ave La Grange IL 60525-2153 Office: Northwestern U Sch Law 357 E Chicago Ave Chicago IL 60611 Business E-Mail: tmorsch@law.northwestern.edu.

MORSE, PETER HODGES, ophthalmologist, educator; b. Chgo., Mar. 1, 1935; s. Emerson Glover and Carol Elizabeth (Rolph) M. AB, Harvard U., 1957; MD, U. Chgo., 1963. Diplomate: Am. Bd. Ophthalmology. Intern U. Chgo. Hosp., 1963-64; resident Wilmer Inst. Johns Hopkins Hosp., Balt., 1966-69; fellow, retina service Mass. Eye and Ear Infirmary, Boston, 1969-70; asst. prof. ophthalmology, chief retina service U. Pa., 1971-75, assoc. prof., 1975, U. Chgo., 1975-77; prof. ophthalmology, 1979-93; sec. dept. ophthalmology, 1976-77; chief retina service, prof., 1979-93; clin. prof. ophthalmology U. S.D. Sch. Medicine, Sioux Falls, 1993—. Prof. La. State U., 1978; chmn. dept. ophthalmology, chief retina service Ochsner Clinic and Found. Hosp., New Orleans, 1977-78; clin. prof. Tulane U., 1978 Author: Vitreoretinal Disease: A Manual for Diagnosis and Treatment, 1979, 2d edit., 1989, Practical Management of Diabetic Retinopathy, 1985; co-editor: Disorders of the Vitreous, Retina, and Choroid; bd. editors Perspectives in Ophthalmology, 1976—, Retina, 1980—; contbr. articles to profl. jours. Served with USNR, 1964-66. Fellow ACS, Coll. Ophthalmologists Eng., Am. Acad. Ophthalmology, Royal Soc. Health (Eng.), Royal Coll. Ophthalmologists (Eng.); mem. AMA, La. Med. Soc., Orleans Parish Med. Soc., New Orleans Acad. Ophthalmology, La. Ophthalmol. and Otolaryngol. Soc., Miss. Ophthalmol. and Otolaryngol. Soc., Assn. Rsch. Vision and Ophthalmology, Retina Soc., Soc. Heed Fellows, Ophthalmol. Soc. U.K., Pan Am. Assn. Ophthalmology, Oxford Ophthalmol. Congress, All-India Ophthalmol. Soc., Soc. Eye Surgeons, Vitreoretinal Soc. (India), Sigma Xi. Republican. Episcopalian. Home: 1307 S Holly Dr Sioux Falls SD 57105-0221

MORSS, LESTER ROBERT, chemist; b. Boston, Apr. 6, 1940; s. Sumner M. and Sylvia F. (Woolf) M.; m. Helaine Sue Gubin, June 19, 1966; children: Sydney, Benjamin, Rebecca, Alisa. BA, Harvard U., 1961; PhD, U. Calif., Berkeley, 1969. Postdoctoral rsch. assoc. Purdue U., West Lafayette, Ind., 1969-71; from asst. prof. to assoc. prof. Rutgers U., New Brunswick, N.J., 1971-80; chemist, sr. chemist Argonne (Ill.) Nat. Lab., 1980—. Vis. prof. U. Liège, Belgium, 1978-79, U. Paris, Orsay, 1993. Author, co-editor: The Chemistry of the Actinide Elements, 1986, Syntheses of Lanthanide and Actinide Compounds, 1991; editor procs. Rare Earth Rsch. Conf., 1986—. Lt. USN, 1961-65. Recipient Sr. Scientist award Alexander von Humboldt Found., 1992. Fellow AAAS; mem. Am. Chem. Soc. (sec. div. nuclear chemistry and tech. 1990-92, chair divsn. nuclear chemistry and tech. 1999), Am. Nuclear Soc., Sigma Xi (pres. Argonne chpt. 1988-89). Jewish. Home: 1s680 Verdun Dr Winfield IL 60190-1716

MORTENSON, KRISTIN OPPENHEIM, musician; b. San Antonio, July 14, 1964; d. Russell E. and Martha Kunkel Oppenheim; m. Gary Curtiss Mortenson; children: Leah Marie, Sarah Grace. Attended, U. Tex., 1984; MusB, La. State U., 1987, MusM, 1988. Violinist Austin Symphony Orch., Austin, Tex., 1981—84, Baton Rouge Symphony, Baton Rouge, 1985—89, Wichita Symphony Orch., Wichita, Kans., 1991—93, Des Moines Symphony, Des Moines, 1993—2001; assoc. concertmaster Topeka Symphony Orch., Topeka, 2001—; instr. music Kans. State U., 2004—. Assistant editor The International Trumpet Guild Jour., 2001—, violinist (live performances with) Ray Charles, Dionne Warwick, Bob Hope, Shirley Jones, Marvin Hamlisch, Rich Little. Mem. Lee Sch. Site Coun., Manhattan, Kans., 2000—02; pres. Lee Sch. PTO, Manhattan, Kans., 2000—01, 2005—06, treas., 2004—05. Mem.: Am. String Tchrs. Assn. (state pres. La. 1988—89), Sigma Alpha Iota (life; pres. U. Tex. 1983—84, Coll. Honor award, Sword of Honor 1984). Home: 522 Westview Dr Manhattan KS 66502

MORTENSON, M. A., JR., construction executive; Chmn., pres., ceo M. A. Mortenson Co., Mpls., 1960-98, chmn., CEO, 1998—. Office: M A Mortenson Co 700 Meadow Ln N Ste 710 Minneapolis MN 55422-4817

MORWAY, DAVID S., professional sports team executive; b. Bklyn., Nov. 9, 1959; s. Richard S. and Carol Morway; m. Karen E. Chellis, Oct. 10, 1996; children: Robbie, Michael. BS in Bus., U. Ariz., 1982; JD, U. San Diego, 1985. Bar: Calif. 1987. Asst. to pres. San Diego Padres, 1985—88; pres. Profl. Excellence in Sports, Inc., San Diego, 1989—95, DSM Inc., Salt Lake City, 1996—98; sr. v.p. basketball ops. Ind. Pacers, Indpls., 1999—. Mem.: Calif. Bar Assn. Avocations: tennis, golf. Office: Ind Pacers 125 S Pennsylvania St Indianapolis IN 46204-3610

MOSBERG, HENRY I., pharmacist, educator, medicinal chemist; b. Jan. 29, 1949; BS in Biophysical Chem., U. Ill., 1971, PhD in Chem., 1976. Postdoctoral rsch. assoc. U. Ill., Urbana, 1976—78, U. Ariz., Tucson, 1978—81, rsch. asst. prof. dept. chemistry, 1981—83; from asst. prof. to assoc. prof. U. Mich. Coll. Pharmacy, Ann Arbor, 1983—95, prof., 1995—. Ad hoc reviewer Human Frontier Sci. Program, Rsch. Corp., Med. Rsch. Coun. Can., NSF, NIH; mem. biochemistry rev. subcom. NIH, Nat. Inst. on Drug Abuse, 1989—93; mem. program com. Internat. Narcotic Rsch. Conf., 1996. Mem. editl. bd.: Jour. Medicinal Chemistry, Jour. Peptide Rsch., Letters in Peptide Sci.,:. Recipient Nat. Merit scholarship, 1967—71, James scholar, U. Ill., 1967—71, grad. fellowship, 1971—72, predoctoral fellowship, NIH, 1973—76, postdoctoral fellowship, Nat. Rsch. Svc. award, 1977—78, Rsch. Scientist Devel. award, NIH, Nat. Inst. Drug Abuse, 1989—99. Mem.: AAAS, Am. Chem. Soc., Protein Soc., Am. Chem. Soc. (ad hoc reviewer petroleum rsch. fund), Am. Peptide Soc. (awards com., publs. com., nominating com.), Phi Lambda Upsilon, Phi Kappa Phi. Achievements include research in modeling of opioid receptors and other GPCRs and of other membrane-bound proteins; synthesis and studies of nitric oxide synthase-derived calmodulin-binding peptides; design and synthesis of opioid peptide ligands and of peptidomimetics; developments of the theory of protein structure. Office: U Mich Coll Pharmacy 428 Church St Ann Arbor MI 48109-1065

MOSELEY-BRAUN, CAROL, former senator, former ambassador; b. Chgo., Aug. 16, 1947; d. Joseph J. and Edna A. (Davie) Moseley; m. Michael Braun, 1973 (div. 1986); 1 child, Matthew. BA, U. Ill., Chgo., 1969; JD, U. Chgo., 1972. Asst. U.S. atty. U.S. Dist. Ct. (no. dist.) Ill., 1973-77; mem. Ill. Ho. of Reps., 1979-88; recorder of deeds Cook County, Ill., 1988-92; U.S. senator from Ill. Washington, 1993-99; Am. ambassador to New Zealand and Samoa U.S. Dept. State, 1999—2001; adj. prof., mgmt. DePaul U., 2002.

MOSENA, DAVID R., museum administrator; BA in Bus. Adminstrn., U. Tenn., 1969, MA in City Planning, 1971. Dir. rsch. Am. Planning Assn., Chgo.; mem. staff City of Chgo., 1984-89, planning commr., 1989-91, chief of staff, 1991-92, aviation commr., 1991—96; pres. Chgo. Transit Authority, 1996—97; pres., CEO Mus. Sci. and Industry, Chgo., 1997—. Mem. vis. com., phys. scis. divsn. U. Chgo., 1998—. Chmn. bd. dirs. U. Chgo. Lab. Schs.; chmn. Commn. on Chicagoland Landmarks; bd. dirs. Exec. Coun. of Metropolis 2020, After Sch. Matters, Leadership Greater Chgo., South East Chgo. Commn. Mem.: Greater Chicagoland C. of C., Econ. Club Chgo., Comml. Club Chgo. Office: Mus Sci and Industry 5700 S Lake Shore Dr Chicago IL 60637 Office Phone: 773-684-1414.

MOSER, DEBRA KAY, medical educator; BSN magna cum laude, Humboldt State U., Arcata, Calif., 1977; M in Nursing, UCLA, 1988, D in Nursing Sci., 1992. RN, Calif., Ohio; cert. pub. health nurse, Calif. Staff nurse, relief supr. med.-surg. fl. Mad River Cmty. Hosp., Arcata, 1977-78, staff/charge nurse intensive care/cardiac care unit, 1978-86; clin. nursing instr. Humboldt State U., Arcata, 1985-86; staff/charge nurse surg. ICU Santa Monica (Calif.) Hosp., 1987-88; spl. reader UCLA Sch. Nursing, 1990-91, rsch. assoc., 1986-91, clin. rsch. nurse, 1988-92, project dir., 1991-92, asst. prof., 1992-94; asst. prof. dept. adult health and illness Ohio State U. Coll. Nursing, Columbus, 1994-98, assoc. prof. dept. adult health and illness, 1998—. Mem. working group on ednl. strategies to Prevent Prehosp. Delay in Patients at High Risk for Acute Myocardial Infraction, Nat. Heart Attack Alert Program, NIH, Nat. Heart, Lung and Blood Inst., 1993-95; abstract grader sci. sessions program Am. Heart Assn., 66th Sci. Sessions, 1993, 96; grad. advisor Sigma Theta Tau-Gamma Tau chpt., 1993-94; mem. med. adv. com. Westside YMCA Cardiac Rehab. Program, 1993-94; mem. Task Force on Women, Behavior and Cardiovasc. Disease NIH, Nat. Heart, Lung and Blood Inst., 1991; coord. cont. care CHF cmty. case mgmt. Mt. Carmel Health Sys., Columbus, Ohio, 1997—; presenter in field. Reviewer Am. Jour. Critical Care, 1992—, Heart and Lung, 1991—, Progress in Cardiovasc. Nursing, 1993—, Heart Failure: Evaluation and Care of Patients With Left-Ventricular Systolic Function, 1993, Intensive Coronary Care, 5th edit., 1994, Rsch. in Nursing & Health, 1995—, Jour. Am. Coll. Cardiology, 1995; co-editor Jour. Cardiovasc. Nursing, 1997—; mem. editl. bd. Am. Jour. Critical Care, 1994—, Jour. Cardiovasc. Nursing, 1995—; contbr. articles to profl. jours., chpts. to books. Recipient scholarship UCLA, 1988-90, scholarship Kaiser Permanente Affiliate Schs., 1990, Ednl. Achievement award LA-AACN, 1990, Alumni rsch. award UCLA, 1990, rsch. abstract award AACN-IVAC, 1993, Heart Failure Rsch. prize AHA Coun. Cardiovascular ursing/Otsuka Am. Pharm., Inc., 1995; grantee Sigma Theta Tau-Gamma Tau chpt., 1989-90, AACN, 1989-90, 92-93, NIH, Nat. Ctr. Nursing Rsch., 1990-92, UCLA Program in Psychneuroimmunology, 1992-93, UCLA Sch. Nursing, 1993, UCLA Acad. Senate, 1993-94, AACN/Sigma Theta Tau Internat., 1994-95, NIH, Nat. Inst. ursing Rsch., 1991-96, Sigma Theta Tau Epsilon chpt., 1995, Ohio State U., 1995, Nat. Am. Heart Assn., 1995—. Mem. AACN (Critical Care Rsch. Abstract award 1995, 98), Am. Heart Assn. Coun. Cardiovasc. Nursing (New Investigator award 1995, Heart Failure Rsch. prize 1995), Am. Psychol. Soc., Heart Failure Soc. Am., AHA (fellow Coun. Cardiovascular Nursing), Sigma Theta Tau (mem. rsch. com. 1990-94, Excellence in Rsch. award Gamma Tau chpt. 1993). Home: 4713 Scenicview Rd Lexington KY 40514-1443

MOSES, ABE JOSEPH, financial planner, consultant; b. Springfield, Mass., July 15, 1931; s. Mohammed Mustapha and Fatima (Merriam) M.; m. Donna C. Moses (dec. 1987); children: James Douglas, John C., Peter J.; m. Mary Jo Morris, Aug. 25, 2001. BA, Amherst Coll., 1955; MA in Internat. Affairs, Johns Hopkins U., 1957. Legis. aide Sen. J.F. Kennedy, 1955-57; Goodwill Amb. to Middle East and South Asia, 1957; fgn. service officer Dept. State, 1960-65; v.p., gen. mgr. Libyan Desert Oil Co., Texfel Petroleum Corp., Tripoli, Libya, 1965-67; v.p. adminstrn., fin. Occidental Petroleum Corp., Libya, 1967-70; v.p. fin., dir. Northrop Corp., 1970-74; chmn. Transworld Trade Ltd., Washington, 1971—; v.p., mng. dir. world adv. group Chase Manhattan Bank, 1974-80; pres. Berkshire Properties, 1976-95; pres., COO, Grolier Internat., Inc., Danbury, Conn., 1980-82; CEO, dir. Galadari Bros., Dubai, United Arab Emirates, 1982-86; internat. bus. and fin. cons. Traxol, Dubai, 1986—; fin. cons. Govt. Costa Rica, 1986-89. Chmn. Aviation Sys. Corp., Northampton, Mass., 1974, Dillon Internat., Akron, Ohio, 1986—; mem. bd. dirs. Near East Found. NYC, 1977—; mng. dir. Sheraton Suites Akron, Cuyahoga Falls, Ohio, 1990—; owner's rep. Monarch Sheraton Hotel, Springfield, Mass., 1993-95; bd. dirs., v.p. Morgan Freeport Co., Hudson, Ohio; bd. dirs. Seeds of Peace, Washington; gen. ptnr. BPM Ltd. Partnership, 1995—; bd. dirs. owners adv. bd. Starwood Hotels and Resorts, 2005-; bd. dir. ETRA Corp., Cuyahoga Falls, Ohio, 2005-. Pres., bd. dirs. Riverside Cmty. Urban Redevel. Corp.; mem. exec. com., bd. dirs. Near East Found., NYC, 1975-; pres. Riverfront Ctr. Assn., Cuyahoga Falls, 1992-95; bd. dirs. Gulfcoast Radio Ptnrs., 1997-99, Capitol City Radio Ptnrs., 1998-2000, Ind. Radio Ptnrs., Monroe (La.) Radio mems., LLC, Commonwealth Opera Co., Northampton, Mass., 2002—; bd. dir. N. Am. Owners Adv. Bd., 2005-07. From 1st lt. to capt. USAF, 1956—60. Ford Found. fellow Johns Hopkins U., 1955, Barr Found. fellow, 1955-57, Amherst Coll. fellow in Internat. Relations, 1955-57, Barr Found. fellow, Springfield, Mass., 1955-57; Obed Finch Slingerland award, Amherst Coll., Mass. Mem.: Assn. Starwood Franchise Owners N.Am. (bd. dirs. 2006—), Assn. Sheraton Franchise Owners N.Am. (bd. dirs. 2004—06). Democrat. Avocations: art, oriental carpet, flying. Home: 16 Highmeadow Rd Northampton MA 01062-2625 Office: Riverside CURC 1989 Front St Cuyahoga Falls OH 44221-3811 Office Phone: 330-920-7502. Personal E-mail: abejmoses@comcast.net.

MOSES, GREGORY H., JR., health services administrator; m. Johnella Moses. Lead engagement ptnr. Sister Mercy Health Corp.; ptnr.-in-charge Healthcare Consulting Group, .Y., N.J.; ptnr. Coopers & Lybrand; pres., COO United Am. Healthcare Corp., Detroit, 1998—. Office: United American Health Care 300 River Place Dr Ste 4950 Detroit MI 48207-5069 Fax: 313-393-7944.

MOSES, WINFIELD CARROLL, JR., state legislator, construction company executive; b. Ft. Wayne, Ind., Feb. 20, 1943; s. Winfield C. and Helen A. (O'Neil) M.; children: Elizabeth, Christopher. AB in Econs, Ind. U., 1964, MBA in Fin, 1966. Apt. builder, Ft. Wayne, 1966—; mem. Ft. Wayne City Coun., 1972-79; mayor City of Ft. Wayne, 1980-87; mem. Ind. Ho. of Reps., Indpls., 1992—. Founding pres. Washington House, 1973-76, Citizen Energy Coalition, 1974-75; active Art Mus.; mem. Ind. Urban Enterprise Zone Bd., Ind. Bus. Modernization Bd. Mem. C. of C., Rotary. Democrat. Unitarian Universalist. Office: 6000 N Oak Blvd Fort Wayne IN 46818-2438

MOSKAL, ROBERT M., bishop; b. Carnegie, Pa., Oct. 24, 1937; s. William and Jean (Popivchak) M. BA, St. Basil Coll. Sem., Stamford, Conn., 1959; lic. sacred theology, Cath. U. Am., 1963; student, Phila. Mus. Acad. and Conservatory of Mus., 1963—66. Ordained priest Archeparchy of Phila. (Ukrainian), 1963; founder, pastor St. Anne's Ukrainian Cath. Ch., Warrington, Pa., 1963—72; sec. Archbishop's Chancery, Phila., 1963—67; apptd. vice-chancellor Archeparchy of Phila. (Ukrainian), 1967—74; pastor Annunciation Ukrainian Cath. Ch., Melrose Park, Pa., 1972—74; named monsignor, 1974; chancellor archdiocese, pastor Ukrainian Cath. Cathedral of the Immaculate Conception, Phila., 1974—84; ordained bishop, 1981; aux. bishop Archeparcy of Phila. (Ukrainian), 1981—83; first bishop Diocese of St. Josaphat, Parma, Ohio, 1983—. Founder Ukrainian Cath. Hour, God is with Us, Sta. WIBF-FM, Phila., 1972—77, Christ Among Us, Sat. WTEL, 1975—; mem. Ukrainian Cath. Ch. Liturgical Subcommn., 1980—; host to His Holiness Pope John Paul II; Bd. dirs. Ascension Manor, Inc., Phila., 1964—84, sec.-treas., 1964—78, exec. v.p., 1977—84; pro-synodal judge Archdiocean Tribunal, Phila., 1965—67. Roman Catholic. Office: PO Box 347180 5720 State Rd Parma OH 44134-2500*

MOSKOS, CHARLES C., social studies educator; b. Chgo., May 20, 1934; s. Charles and Rita (Shukas) M.; m. Ilca Hohn, July 3, 1966; children— Andrew, Peter. BA cum laude, Princeton U., NJ, 1956; MA, UCLA, 1961, PhD, 1963; LHD (hon.), Norwich U., Northfield, Vt., 1992, Towson U., Md., 2002. Asst. prof. U. Mich., Ann Arbor, 1964-66; assoc. prof. sociology Northwestern U., Evanston, Ill., 1966-70, prof., 1970—. Fellow Progressive Policy Inst., 1992—; mem. Presdl. Commn. on Women in the Mil., 1992. Author: The Sociology of Political Independence, 1967, The American Enlisted Man, 1970, Public Opinion and the Military Establishment, 1971, Peace Soldiers, 1976, Fuerzas Armadas y Societdad, 1984, The Military--More Than Just A Job?, 1988, A Call to Civic Service, 1988, Greek Americans, 1989, Soldiers and Sociology, 1989, New Directions in Greek American Studies, 1991, The New Conscientious Objection, 1993, All That We Can Be, 1996, Reporting War When There Is No War, 1996, The Media and the Military, 2000, The Postmodern Military, 2000. Chmn. Theodore Saloutos Meml. Fund; mem. Archdiocesean Commn. Third Millenium, 1982-88; mem adv. bd. Vets. for Am., 1997—; mem. Congl. Commn. on Mil. Tng. and Gender-Related Issues, 1998-99, Nat. Security Study Group, 1998-2001. Served with AUS, 1956-58. Decorated D.S.M., Fondation pour les Etudes de Def. Nat. (France), S.M.K. (The etherlands); named to Marshall rsch. chair ARI, 1987-88, 95-96, 03; Ford. Found. faculty fellow, 1969-70; fellow Wilson Ctr., 1980-81, guest scholar, 1991; fellow Rockefeller Found. Humanities, 1983-84, Guggenheim fellow, 1992-93, fellow Annenberg Washington Program, 1995; grantee 20th Century Fund, 1983-87, 92-94, Ford Found., 1989-90; recipient Nat. Educator Leadership award Todd Found., 1997, Book award Washington Monthly, 1997, Honored Patriot award Selective Svc. Sys., 1998; Pub. Policy fellow Wilson Ctr., 2002; Eisenhower chair Royal Mil. Acad.

Netherlands, 2002. Mem. Am. Sociol. Assn., Internat. Sociol. Assn. (pres. rsch. com. on armed forces and conflict resolution 1982-86), Inter-Univ. Seminar on Armed Forces and Soc. (chmn. 1987-99), Am. Acad. Arts and Scis. Greek Orthodox. Address: 1040 4th St #309 Santa Monica CA 90403 Office Phone: 847-491-2705. Business E-Mail: c-moskos@northwestern.edu.

MOSKOW, MICHAEL H., retired bank executive; b. Paterson, NJ, Jan. 7, 1938; s. Jacob and Sylvia (Edelstein) M.; m. Constance Bain, Dec. 18, 1966; children: Robert Bain, Eliot Marc, Lisa Danielle. AB, Lafayette Coll., Easton, Pa., 1959; MA in Econs., U. Pa., 1962, PhD, 1965. Instr. econs. Lafayette Coll., 1964—65; asst. prof. mgmt. Drexel Inst. Tech., Phila., 1963-64, 65-67; assoc. prof. econs., dir. Bus. Econ. and Bus. Research, Temple U., Phila., 1967-69; sr. staff economist Coun. Econ. Advisers The White House, Washington, 1969-70; exec. dir. Constrn. Industry Collective Bargaining Commn., 1970-71; dep. under sec. US Dept. Labor, 1971-72, asst. sec. for policy, evaluation & research, 1972-73, under sec., 1976-77; asst. sec. for policy devel. and research US Dept. Housing & Urban Devel., 1973-75; dir. Council on Wage and Price Stability, 1975-76; cons. Com. for Econ. Devel., 1977; dir. corp. devel. and planning Esmark, Inc., 1977-78, v.p. corp. devel. and planning, 1978-80; exec. v.p. Estronics, Inc. div. Esmark, Inc., 1980-82; pres. Velsicol Chem. Corp. div. N.W. Industries, Inc., Chgo., 1982-84; v.p. corp. devel. Dart & Kraft, Inc., Northbrook, Ill., 1985-86; v.p. strategy and bus. devel. Premark Internat. Inc. (spinoff from Dart & Kraft), Deerfield, 1986-90; dep. US Trade Rep. Exec. Office of the Pres., Washington, 1991-93; prof. strategy & internat mgmt. Northwestern U. Kellogg Grad. Sch. Mgmt., Evanston, Ill., 1993-94; pres. Fed. Res. Bank Chgo., 1994—2007; sr. fellow Chgo. Coun. on Global Affairs, 2007—. Bd. dirs. Commonwealth Edison Co., 2008-Author: Teachers and Unions, 1966, Labor Relations in the Performing Arts: An Introductory Survey, 1970; co-author: Collective Negotiations for Teachers, 1966, Collective Bargaining in Public Employment, 1970, Strategic Planning in Business and Government, 1978; co-editor: Readings on Collective Negotiations in Public Education, 1967, Employment Relations in Higher Education, 1969, Women and Work, 1987; contbr. articles to profl. jours. Bd. trustees Lafayette Coll; mem. Coun. Foreign Location; bd. dirs. Chgo. Coun. Fgn. Rels., Coun. Fgn. Rels. YC, Northwestern Meml. Found., World Bus. Chgo., Chicagoland C. of C.; mem. governing bd. Ill. Coun. Econ. Edn.; 1st lt. AUS, 1959-60. Fellow Nat. Acad. Pub. Adnminstrn.; mem. Indsl. Rels. Rsch. Assn. (pres. 1987), Nat. Bur. Econ. Rsch. (chmn. 2002-05), Comml. Club Chgo. (civic com.), Econs. Club Chgo. (chmn. 2001-03).*

MOSKOWITZ, HERBERT, management educator; b. Paterson, NJ, May 26, 1935; s. David and Ruth (Abrams) Moskowitz; m. Heather Mary Lesgnier, Feb. 25, 1968; children: Tobias, Rebecca, Jonas. BS in Mech. Engring., Newark Coll. Engring., 1956; MBA, U.S. Internat. U., 1964; PhD, UCLA, 1970. Rsch. engr. GE, 1956-60; systems design engr. Gen. Dynamics Convair, San Diego, 1960-65; asst. prof. Purdue U., West Lafayette, Ind., 1970-75, assoc. prof., 1975-79, prof., 1979-85, Disting. prof. mfg. mgmt., 1985-87, James B. Henderson Disting. prof., 1987-91, dir. Dauch Ctr. Mgmt. Mfg. Enterprises, 1991—2005, Lewis B. Cullman Disting. prof. mfg. mgmt., 1991—. Cons. AT&T, Inland Steel Co.; adv. panelist NSF, 1990—. Author: Management Science and Statistics Texts, 1975—90; assoc. editor Decision Scis. Jour., 1984—90, Jour. Behavioral Decision Making, 1986—90; contbr. articles to jours. in field. Bd. dirs. Sons of Abraham Synagogue, Lafayette; mem. Lafayette Klezmorem, 1973—. Capt. USAF, 1956—60. Recipient Disting. Doctoral Student award, UCLA Alumni Assn., 1969—70; Fulbright Rsch. scholar, 1985—86. Fellow: Decision Scis. Inst. (sec. 1985—87, v.p. 1978—80); mem.: Ops. Rsch. Soc. Am./Inst. Mgmt. Sci. (liaison officer 1977—, panelist, advisor NSF and Fulbright Scholar program 1993—), Pi Tau Sigma, Tau Beta Pi. Jewish. Avocations: jewish music, tennis. Home: 1430 N Salisbury St West Lafayette IN 47906-2420 Office: Purdue Univ Krannert Sch Mgmt 100 S Grant St West Lafayette IN 47907-2076

MOSKOWITZ, ROLAND WALLACE, internist; b. Shamokin, Pa., Nov. 3, 1929; MD, Temple U., 1953. Intern Temple U. Hosp., Phila., 1953-54; fellow in internal medicine Mayo Clinic, Rochester, Minn., 1954-55, 57-60; mem. staff U. Hosps. Cleve.; prof. medicine Case Western Res. U. Sch. Medicine, Cleve. Mem.: ACR, Alpha Omega Alpha. Office: Parkway Med Ctr 3609 Park East Dr STe 307N Beachwood OH 44122

MOSNER, LAWRENCE J., retired financial administration company executive; BA, Midland Coll., Fremont, Nebr.; MBA, Roosevelt Univ. With Sears Roebuck & Co.; exec. v.p., COO Hanover Direct; pres. Deluxe Direct, Shoreview, Minn., 1995—97, Deluxe Fin. Svcs., Shoreview, Minn., 1997; exec. v.p. Deluxe Corp., Shoreview, Minn., 1997—2001, vice chmn., 1999—2001, chmn., CEO, 2001—05. Office Phone: 651-483-7111.

MOSS, GERALD S., medical educator; b. Cleve., Mar. 4, 1935; s. Harry and Lillian (Alter) M.; m. Wilma Jabak, Sept. 1, 1957; children: William Alan, Robert Daniel, Sharon Lynn. BA, Ohio State U., 1956, MD cum laude, 1960. Diplomate Am. Bd. Surgery (apptd. assoc. examiner com. 1989); lic. Ill. Intern Mass. Gen. Hosp., Boston, 1960-61, resident, 1961-65; from asst. prof. to assoc. prof. dept. surgery Coll. Medicine U. Ill., Chgo., 1968-72, prof., 1973-77, 89—; prof. dept. surgery Pritzker Sch. Medicine U. Chgo., 1977-89; head dept. surgery U. Ill., Chgo., 1989; dean U. Ill. Coll. of Medicine, Chgo., 1989—2004. Tutor in surgery Manchester (Eng.) Royal Infirmary, 1964; asst. chief surgical svcs. VA West Side Hosp., Chgo., 1968-70; attending surgeon dept. surgery Cook County Hosp., Chgo. 1970-72, chmn. 1972-77; dir. surgical rsch. Hektoen Inst. for Med. Rsch., Cook County Hosp., 1972-77, Michael Reese Hosp. and Med. Ctr., Chgo., 1977-89, chmn. dept. surgery, 1977-89, chief svc. 1989, trustee, 1981, and numerou coms.; appointed to Nat. Rsch. Coun., NAS, 1966-68, Ad Hoc Subcom., NAE, 1970, Ad Hoc Study Sect., 1970, del. to Third Joint U.S-USSR Symposium, 1983, Blood Diseases and Resources Adv. Com., 1984-88, Planning Com. for discussing key blood problems, Nat. Heart and Lung Inst., 1987, chmn. Plasma and Plasma Products Com., 1979, bd. dirs., 1983, v.p., 1985, Ad Hoc Transition Com., Am. Blood Commn., 1989, Panel on Rsch. Opportunities, Office Naval Rsch. Program, 1987, exec. com., coord. com., Nat. Blood Edn. Program, 1988, Tech. Adv. Task Force Am. Hosp. Assn., 1988, chmn. review panel contract proposals, NIH, 1975, program project site visit, 1976, chmn. site-visit review group, 1977, adv. com. Blood Resources Work group, 1978, Planning Com. for Consensus, 1987, Small Bus. Innovation Rsch., 1988, Med. Rsch. Scv. Merit Review Bd. VA, 1978-81, Liaison Com. Graduate Med. Edn. AMA, 1979, and numerous other coms. for various med. organizations; cons. at. Heart and Lung Inst., Transfusion Medicine Acad. Awardees Program; vis. prof. Montefiore Med. Ctr. Bronx, N.Y., 1986, Ohio State U., 1988, U. N.Mex., Albuquerque, 1989, Seton Med. Ctr., Austin, Tex., 1990, U. Ill. Coll. Medicine, Peoria, 1991; guest lectr., participant numerous meetings, symposiums; cons. in field. Contbr. numerous articles to profl. jours., chpts. to books. With USN, 1965—68, Vietnam. Teaching fellow Harvard Med. Sch., 1962; recipient Stitt Lectr. award Assn. Mil. Surgeons U.S.A., 1981; grantee U.S. Navy, 1969-84, U.S. Army, 1971-74, 75-78, NIH, 1969, 83-84, Dept. Pub. Health, 1973, HEW, 1974-77, UpJohn, 1974, Northfield Labs. 1985-89. Fellow ACS (pre and postoperative care com. 1975-83, rep. Am. blood commn. 1977—, mem. various coms., speaker various symposiums), Am. Soc. Surgery Trauma; mem. Am. Surgical Assn. (rep. Nat. Soc. Med. Rsch. 1984-88), Am. Trauma Soc., Am. Physicians Fellowship (rep. Israel Med. Assn.), Assn. Acad. Surgery (chmn. membership selection com. 1973-75, pres. elect 1974-75, pres. 1975-76, exec. coun. 1977-79), Soc. Univ. Surgeons (rep. Nat. Soc. Med. Rsch. 1973-77, com. Surgical Edn. 1979-81), Ctrl. Surgical Soc. (rep. Nat. Soc. Med. Rsch. 1973-77), Shock Soc. (chmn. planning com. 1986, chmn. program com. 1986, pres. elect 1986-87, pres. 1987-88), Soc. for Surgery Alimentary Tract (mem. com. west north ctrl. region 1978-82), Internat. Soc. Blood Transfusion, Surgical Biology Club II, Nat. Soc. for Med. Rsch., Collegium Internationale Chirugiae Digestivae, Societe Internationale de Chirugie, Sigma XI, Alpha Omega Alpha (faculty advisor 1972-73). Office: U Ill Coll Medicine Chgo 1853 W Polk St # M/C 784 Chicago IL 60612-4316 Home Phone: 847-433-6106; Office Phone: 312-996-3500. E-mail: gmoss@uic.edu.

MOSS, JOEL CHARLES, radio production director; b. NYC, Oct. 10, 1949; s. S. Herbert and Sylvia (Rosenberg) M.; m. Cynthia Louise Lamb, Nov. 27, 1983; children: Joshua David, Alyson Rachel. Student, N.Y. Tech., Old Westbury, 1968-70. Program dir. STa. WLIR-FM, Garden City, N.Y., 1975-77; air talent Sta. WNEW-FM, YC, 1979-81; program dir. Sta. WPFB, Middletown, Ohio, 1982-84; prodn. dir., soundtrack producer Sta WEBN, Cin., 1984—. Copywriter radio show VD Walk-In Clinic, 1974 (Clio awrd 1974); writer, producer radio commls. WEBN Tee-Shirts, 1987 (Addy award 1987), Omni-Netherland Plaza, 1987 (Addy award 1987); radio parody Without Radio, 1990 (Firsty award 1990), Fireworks Promos (Radio and Prodn. award 1991), 1991.

MOSS, RICHARD L., physiology educator; b. Fond du Lac, Wis., Nov. 2, 1947; s. Robert C. and Lenore H. Moss; m. Susan L. Rusch, Aug. 17, 1968; 1 child, James P. BS in Biology, U. Wis., Oshkosh, 1969; PhD in Physiology and Biophysics, U. Vt., 1975. Rsch. assoc. Boston Biomed. Rsch. Inst., 1975-79; asst. prof. physiology U. Wis., Madison, 1979-83, assoc. prof., 1983-87, prof., 1987—, chair dept. physiology, 1988—. Dir. U. Wis. Cardiovascular Rsch. Ctr., 1995—; mem. cellular pharmacology and physiology rsch. study com. Am. Heart Assn., Dallas, 1990-93, Established Investigator, 1981-86; mem. physiology study sect. NIH, 1994—. Mem. editl. bd. Biophys. Jour., 1985-92, Jour. Gen. Physiology, 1987-91, Am. Jour. Physiology: Cellular, 1990-96, Physiol. Revs., 1985-91, Jour. Physiology (London), 1995—; contbr. articles to Biophys. Jour., Circulation Rsch., Nature, Jour. Physiology. NRSA fellow NIH, 1976-78. Achievements include research on regulation of heart and skeletal muscle contraction by selective extraction and/or exchange of regulatory protein from permeabilized muscle preparations, implicating role of thick filament proteins (i.e. light chain-2 and C-protein) in regulation of tension and kinetics of contraction. Office: U Wis Med Sch 1300 University Ave Madison WI 53706-1510

MOSTER, MARY CLARE, public relations executive; b. Morristown, NJ, Apr. 7, 1950; d. Clarence R. and Ruth M. Moster; m. Louis C. Williams, Jr., Oct. 4, 1987. BA in English with honors, Douglass Coll., 1972; MA in English Lit., Univ. Chgo., 1973. Accredited pub. rels. counselor. Editor No. Trust Bank, Chgo., 1973-75, advt. supr., 1975-77, communications officer, 1977-78; account exec. Hill & Knowlton, Inc., Chgo., 1978-80, v.p., 1980-83, sr. v.p., 1983-87, sr. v.p., mng. dir., 1987-88; staff v.p. comms. Navistar Internat. Corp., Chgo., 1988-93; v.p. corp. comms. Comdisco, Inc., Rosemont, Ill., 1993—2002; sr. v.p. L.C. Williams and Assocs., Chgo., 2002—. Adj. prof. Integrated Mktg. Comm. Medill Sch., Northwestern U., 2000-05 Author poetry, poetry translation. Bd. govs. Met. Planning Coun., Chgo., 1988-94; fellow Leadership Greater Chgo., 1989-90; bd. dirs. New City YMCA, Chgo., 1986-92; corp. devel. bd. Steppenwolf Theatre Co., Chgo., 1988-90; active Chgo. Network, 1994—, bd. dirs., 1996-99. Mem. Nat. Investor Rels. Inst. (bd. dirs. 1988-89, 90-99, pres. Chgo. chpt. 1998-99), Arthur W. Page Soc., Pub. Rels. Soc. Am. Avocations: sailing, cross country skiing, book groups, biking. Office: L C Williams & Assocs 150 N Michigan Ave Ste 3800 Chicago IL 60601

MOTAWI, KARIM, textiles executive; b. 1970; s. Kamal and Karen. Grad., U. Mich. V.p., co-owner Motawi Tileworks Inc., Ann Arbor, Mich., 1992—. Sec. Ann Arbor Art Ctr. Named one of 40 Under 40, Crain's Detroit Bus., 2006. Office: Motawi Tileworks Inc 170 Enterprise Dr Ann Arbor MI 48103 Office Phone: 734-213-0017. Office Fax: 734-213-2569.

MOTTLEY, JAMES DONALD, state legislator, lawyer; b. Alamogordo, N.Mex., Aug. 29, 1954; s. Harry Edward Mottley Jr. and Linnie Sue (Tate) Johnson; m. Patricia Chris Cooper, June 30, 1980 (div. May 1984). BA in Polit. Sci. magna cum laude, Wright State U., 1975, MS in Econs., 1976; JD, Salmon P. Chase Coll. of Law, 1991. Bar: Ohio, 1991, U.S. Dist. Ct. (so. dist.) Ohio 1992. Fin. mgr. NCR Corp., Dayton, Ohio, 1977-81, mgr. cash mgmt. and investment banking, 1982-84; asst. to county commr. Montgomery County, Dayton, 1981-82; treas. NCR Credit Corp., Dayton, 1984-87; chief dep. county auditor Montgomery County Auditors Office, Dayton, 1987-91; assoc. Taft, Stettinius & Hollister, Cin., 1991-92; ptnr. Flanagan, Lieberman, Hoffman & Swaine, Dayton, 1993—; mem. Ohio Ho. of Reps., Columbus, 1993—. Mem. ctrl. and exec. coms. Orgn. Montgomery County Rep. Party, Dayton, 1985—. Mem. Optimists, Masons (master). Presbyterian. Avocation: flying. Home: 1641 Longbow Ln West Carrollton OH 45449-2344 Office: Ohio Ho of Reps 77 S High St Fl 13 Columbus OH 43215-6199

MOUL, MAXINE BURNETT, state official; b. Oakland, Nebr., Jan. 26, 1947; d. Einer and Eva (Jacobson) Burnett; m. Francis Moul, Apr. 20, 1972; 1 child, Jeff. BS in Journalism, U. Nebr., 1969; DHL (hon.), Peru State Coll., 1993. Sunday feature writer, photographer Sioux City Iowa Jour., 1969-71; reporter, photographer, editor Maverick Media, Inc., Syracuse, Nebr., 1971-73, editor, pub., 1974-83, pres., 1983-90; grant writer, asst. coord. Nebr. Regional Med. Program, Lincoln, 1973-74; lt. gov. State of Nebr., Lincoln, 1991-93; dir. Dept. Econ. Devel., Lincoln, 1993-99; pres. Nebr. Cmty. Found., 1999—. Mem. Dem. Nat. Com., Washington, 1988-92, Nebr. Dem. State Ctrl. Com., Lincoln, 1974-88; del. Dem. Nat. Conf., 1972, 88, 92; mem. exec. com. Nebr. Dem. Party, Lincoln, 1988-93. Recipient Margaret Sanger award Planned Parenthood, Lincoln, 1991, Champion of Small Bus. award Nebr. Bus. Devel. Ctr., Omaha, 1991, Toll fellowship Coun. State Govts., Lexington, Ky., 1992. Mem. Bus. and Profl. Womem, Nebr. Mgmt. Assn. (Silver Knight award 1992), Nat. Conf. Lt. Govs. (bd. dirs. 1991-93), Nebr. Press Women, Women Execs. in State Govt., Cmty. Devel. Soc., U. Nebr.-Lincoln Journalism Alumni. Democrat. Avocations: reading, gardening. Office: Nebr Cmty Found 317 S 12th St Lincoln NE 68508-2108

MOUL, WILLIAM CHARLES, lawyer; b. Columbus, Ohio, Jan. 12, 1940; s. Charles Emerson and Lillian Ann (Mackenbach) M.; m. Margine Ann Tessendorf, June 10, 1962; children: Gregory, Geoffrey. BA, Miami U., Oxford, Ohio, 1961; JD, Ohio State U., 1964. Bar: Ohio 1964, U.S. Dist. Ct. (so. dist.) Ohio 1965, U.S. Ct. Appeals (2d cir.) 1982, U.S. Ct. Appeals (6th cir.) 1984, U.S. Ct. Appeals (3d cir.) 1985. Assoc., ptnr. George, Greek, King, McMahon & McConnaughey, Columbus, 1964-79; ptnr. McConnaughey, Stradley, Mone & Moul, Columbus, 1979-81; ptnr.-in-charge Thompson, Hine & Flory, Columbus, 1981-89, exec. com., 1989-98. Chmn. Upper Arlington Civil Svc. Commn., Ohio, 1981-86. Mem. ABA, Ohio State Bar Assn. (labor sect. bd. dirs. 1983—), Columbus Bar Assn. (chmn. ethics com. 1980-82), Lawyers Club Columbus (pres. 1976-77), Athletic Club, Scioto Country Club, Wedgewood Country Club, Masons. Lutheran. Home: 2512 Danvers Ct Columbus OH 43220-2822 Office: Thompson Hine LLP 10 W Broad St Ste 700 Columbus OH 43215-3435 Office Phone: 614-469-3220. Business E-Mail: william.moul@thompsonhine.com.

MOULDER, WILLIAM H., police chief; b. Kansas City, Mo., Feb. 19, 1938; s. Roscoe B. and Charleen M. (Flye) M.; m. Louise M. Pollaro, Aug. 2, 1957; children: Deborah, Ralph, Robert. BA, U. Mo., Kansas City, 1971, MA, 1976. Cert. police officer, Mo., Iowa. From police officer to maj. Kansas City (Mo.) Police Dept., 1959-84; chief of police City of Des Moines, 1984—. Mem. Internat. Assn. Chiefs of Police, Police Exec. Rsch. Forum, Iowa Police Exec. Forum. Avocations: racquetball, travel. Office: Office of Police Chief 25 E 1st St Des Moines IA 50309-4800

MOURDOCK, RICHARD E., state official; BS, Defiance Coll.; MS in Geology, Ball State Univ. Lic. Profl. Geologist. Exec. Koester Companies, Inc.; cons., environ., energy bus.; state treas. State of Ind., 2006—; and chmn. Ind. Bond Bank. County commr. Vanderburgh County, 1995—2002. Office: State Treas 242 State House Indianapolis IN 46204 Office Phone: 317-232-6386. Office Fax: 317-233-1780.

MOUROU, GERARD A., research administrator; BS in Physics, U. Grenoble, France, 1967; MS in Physics, U. Orsay, France, 1970; PhD in Physics, U. Paris, 1973. Sci. cooperant Université Laval, Quebec, Canada, 1970-73; postdoctoral fellow San Diego State U., 1973-74; scientist Lab. for Laser Energetics U. Rochester, .Y., 1979-88, group leader Picosecond Rsch. Group, Lab. for Laser Energetics N.Y., 1979-88, sr. scientist Lab. for Laser Energetics N.Y., 1981-88, assoc. prof. Inst. Optics N.Y., 1983-87, divsn. dir. Ultrafast Science Divsn., Lab. for Laser Energetics N.Y., 1986-88, prof. Inst. Optics N.Y., 1987-89; prof. Dept. Elec. Engring. and Computer Scis., Coll. Engring. U. Mich., 1988—, dir. Ctr. for Ultrafast Optical Science NSF and Tech. Ctr., 1991—. Vis. prof. U. Tokyo, Japan, 1994; prof. physics, mcpl. chair Université Joseph Fourier, Grenoble, France, 1994; mem. editl. bd. Laser Focus. Contbr. numerous articles to scientific jours. Recipient R.W. Wood prize Optical Soc. of Am., 1995. Fellow Optical Soc. Am. Achievements include numerous patents in field including apparatus for switching high voltage pulses, light activated solid state switch, avalanche effect light activated solid state switching, microwave pulse generation with light activated semiconductor switch and control of transmission of microwaves using light activated semiconductors, laser system using organic dye laser and laser amplifier for generation of picosecond laser pulses, sweep drive circuit for streak camera image converter, photoelectron switching in semiconductors in the picosecond domain, measurement of electrical signal with Ps resolution, electro-optical wide band signal measurement system, CW pumped variable repetition rate regenerative laser amplifier, amplification of ultrashort pulses with Nd: glass amplifiers pumped by alexandrite free running laser. Office: Univeristy of Michigan Ctr for Ultrafast Optical Science 2200 Bonisteel Blvd Rm 6117 Ist Ann Arbor MI 48109-2099

MOUSER, LES (LYMAN MOUSER), advertising executive; Pres., COO Campbell Mithun Esty, Mpls., 1999—; CEO Campbell Mithun, Mpls., 2001—04, chmn. Office: Campbell Mithun Esty 222 S 9th St Minneapolis MN 55402-3389 Office Phone: 612-347-1000. Office Fax: 612-347-1515.

MOUSSEAU, DORIS NAOMI BARTON, retired elementary school principal; b. Alpena, Mich., May 6, 1934; d. Merritt Benjamin and Naomi Dora Josephine (Pieper) Barton; m. Bernard Joseph Mousseau, July 31, 1954. AA, Alpena Community Coll., 1954; BS, Wayne State U., 1959; MA, U. Mich., 1961, postgrad., 1972-75. Profl. cert. ednl. adminstr., tchr. Elem. tchr. Clarkston (Mich.) Community Schs., 1954-66; elem. sch. prin. Andersonville Sch., Clarkston, 1966-79, Bailey Lake Sch., Clarkston, 1979-94; ret., 1994. Oakland County rep. Mich. Elem. and Mid. Schs. Prins. Assn. Retirees Task Force, 1996. Cons., rsch. com. Youth Assistance Oakland County Ct. Svcs., 1968-88; leader Clarkston PTA, 1967-94; chair Clarkston Sch. Dist. campaign, United Way, 1985, 86; allocations com. Oakland County United Way, 1987-88. Recipient Outstanding Svc. award Davisburg Jaycees, Springfield Twp., 1977, Vol. Recognition award Oakland County (Mich.) Cts., 1984, Heritage Chair for 40 yrs. svc. with Clarkston (Mich.) Cmty. Schs., 1994. Fellow ASCD, MACUL (State Assn. Ednl. Computer Users); mem. NEA (del. 1964), Mich. Elem. and Middle Sch. Prins. Assn. (treas., regional del. 1982—, pres.-elect Region 7 1988-89, program planner, pres. 1989-90, sr. advisor 1990-91, Honor award Region # 7 1991), Mich. Edn. Assn. (pres. 1960-66, del. 1966), Clarkston Edn. Assn. (author, editor 1st directory 1963), Women's Bowling Assn., Elks, Spring Meadows Country Club (hole-in-one 1989, Sr. Ladies Net Champion 1999), The Dream Golf Club (hole-in-one 2003), Phi Delta Kappa, Delta Kappa Gamma (pres. 1972-74, past state and nat. chmn., Woman of Distinction 1982). Republican. Avocations: golf, gardening, reading, clarinet, genealogy. Home: 6825 Rattalee Lake Rd Clarkston MI 48348-1955 E-mail: dnbarmou@aol.com.

MOUSTAKIS, ALBERT D., prosecutor; b. Cairo, Feb. 5, 1956; came to U.S., 1959; s. David and Jeanette (Sayegh) M.; m. Anna Marie Marfredonia, 1982; m. Laura J. Moustakis, July 1, 1991; children: Matalyn Jean, Sydney Rae. BA, Loyola U., Chgo., 1978; JD, Nova Ctr. for Study Law, 1982. Pvt. practice, Downers Grove, Ill., Chgo.; atty. Nielsen & Nielsen, Eagle River, Wis.; pvt. practice Eagle River, Wis.; dist. atty. State of Wis., Eagle River. Pres. Walter E. Meml. Libr. Fund, Eagle River, 1993-94. Mem. Rotary (pres. 1995). Avocations: golf, hockey.

MOWBRAY, KEVIN D., publishing executive; b. 1962; m. Linda Mowbray; 4 children. BA, Western Ill. U. Advt. sales rep. Lee Enterprises, Inc., Kewanee, Ill., 1986, nat. sales mgr. corp. sales & mktg. Chgo.; advt. mgr. Lincoln Jour. Star, Nebr., 1995—98; gen. mgr. Missoulian, Missoula, Mont., 1998—2000; pub. Bismarck Tribune, ND, 2000—02, v.p. sales & mktg., 2002—04; v.p. pub., pub. Times of Northwest Ind., Munster, Ind., 2004—05; pres. & pub. St. Louis Post-Dispatch, 2006—. Office: St Louis Post-Dispatch 900 N Tucker Blvd Saint Louis MO 63101 Office Phone: 314-340-8970. E-mail: kmowbray@post-dispatch.com.*

MOWRIS, GERALD WILLIAM, lawyer; b. Grand Forks, ND, Oct. 2, 1948; s. Robert Earl and Lillian Vivian Mowris; m. Susan Leah Sachtjen; children: Danae E., Jeffrey W. Student, Mich. State U., East Lansing, 1966-67; JD, U. Wis., 1973. Bar: Wis. 1973, US Dist. Ct. (we. dist.) Wis. 1973, US Ct. Appeals (7th cir.) 1984, US Ct. Mil. Appeals 1984. Asst. dist. atty. Dane County Dist. Atty.'s Office, Madison, 1973-79; ptnr. Pellino, Rosen, Mowris & Kirkhuff, Madison, 1979—. Co-founder, mem. steering com. Wis. Criminal Justice Study Commn. Bd. dirs. YMCA of Met. Madison, 1991-94; mem. ARC Cmty. Svcs., Madison, 1980—, past pres., apptd. by gov. Wis. Sentencing Commn., 2003-. Major JAG Corp. USAR, 1970—92. Mem. State Bar Wis. (co-chmn. com. for local bar leaders 1995-97, bd. govs. 1999-2003, pres. 2001-02), Dane County Bar Assn. (pres. 1994-95), Wis. Assn. Criminal Def. Lawyers (pres. 1995-96), Nat. Assn. Criminal Def. Lawyers, Wis. Acad. Trial Lawyers, Nat. Ski Patrol (patroller 1967—). Avocations: skiing, fishing, hiking, canoeing, golf. Office: Pellino Rosen Mowris & Kirkhuff SC 131 W Wilson St Ste 1201 Madison WI 53703-3243 Office Phone: 608-255-4501. Office Fax: 608-255-4345. Business E-Mail: gmowris@prmk.com.

MOYER, J. KEITH, former publishing executive; b. Louisville, Ky. s. Billye Pearl (Watkins) Moyer; m. Marilyn Moyer; children: Austin, Alexis, Samantha. B in journalism, U. Fla., 1977. City hall reporter Tampa Times, Fla.; with Lakeland Ledger, Fla.; exec. editor News-Press, Fort Myers, Fla., 1986—90; named v.p., editor Ark. Gazette, Little Rock, 1990; v.p., editor Times-Union, Rochester, NY, Democrat & Chronicle, Rochester, NY; exec. editor The Fresno Bee, Calif., 1994—97, pub. Calif., 1997—2001; pub., pres. Star Tribune, Mpls., 2001—07. Mem. Itasca Project; bd. mem. Capital Cities Partnership, Minn. Bus. Partnership. Bd. mem. Walker Art Mus., Mpls.; mem. nat. adv. com. Sch. Journalism and Mass Communication, U. Minn. Named Editor of Yr., Gannett Co., 1989, Alumnus of Distinction, Coll. Journalism and Comm., U. Fla., 2003.

MOYER, THOMAS J., state supreme court chief justice; b. Sandusky, Ohio, Apr. 18, 1939; s. Clarence and Idamae (Hessler) M.; m. Mary Francis Moyer, Dec. 15, 1984; 1 child, Drew; stepchildren: Anne, Jack, Alaine, Elizabeth. BA, Ohio State U., 1961, JD, 1964. Asst. atty. gen. State of Ohio, Columbus, 1964-66; pvt. practice law Columbus, 1966-69; dep. asst. Office Gov. State of Ohio, Columbus, 1969-71, exec. asst., 1975-79; assoc. Crabbe, Brown, Jones, Potts & Schmidt, Columbus, 1972-75; judge U.S. Ct. Appeals (10th cir.), Columbus, 1979-86; chief justice Ohio Supreme Ct., Columbus, 1987—. Chair Conference of Chief Justices, 1995—96, Nat. Conf. on Ct. Security, 2005. Sec. bd. trustees Franklin U., Columbus, 1986-87; trustee Univ. Club, Columbus, 1986; mem. nat. council adv. com. Ohio State U. Coll. Law, Columbus. Recipient Award of Merit, Ohio Legal Ctr. Inst., Am. Judicature Soc. award, Disting. Service award at. Ctr. for State Cts., 1997, Innovative Program award Assn. Family & Conciliation Cts., 1998, Better World award Ohio Mediation Assn., 1999, Whitney orth Seymour medal Am. Arbitration Assn., 2000, James F. Henry award, 2003; named Outstanding Young Man of Columbus, Columbus Jaycees, 1969. Mem. Ohio State Bar Assn. (exec. com., council dels., Ohio Bar medal 1991), Columbus Bar Assn. (pres. 1980-81, Liberty Bell award), Critchon Club, Columbus Maennerchor Club; fellow Ohio State Bar Found. (Ritter award 1996). Republican. Avocations: sailing, tennis. Office: Ohio Supreme Ct 65 S Front St Columbus OH 43215

MOYNIHAN, WILLIAM J., museum executive; b. Little Falls, NY, Apr. 8, 1942; s. Bernard J. and Mary A. (Flynn) M.; m. Irene A. Sheilds, July 2, 1966; children: Patricia, Erin, Sean. BA, SUNY, Binghamton, 1964; MA, Colgate U., 1966; PhD, Syracuse U., 1973. From asst. to assoc. prof. Colgate U., Hamilton, NY, 1973—77, from asst. to assoc. dean faculty, 1977—80, dean students, 1980—83, dean coll., 1983—88; v.p.m. dir. Am. Mus. Natural History, NYC, 1988—95; pres., CEO Milw. Pub. Mus., 1995—2002; ret., 2002. Bd. dirs. N.Y. State Mus.; adv. com. arts and culture Congressman J. Nadler, N.Y.C., 1993-95. Adv. editor Curator jour., 1991-95. Mem. Am. Mus. Assn., Am. Assn. Museums (mem. ethics com., bd. dirs.), Wis. Acad. of Scis., Arts and Letters (councillor-at-large 1995-02), Univ. Club. Home: 84 Eaton St Hamilton NY 13346

MRAZEK, DAVID ALLEN, child and adolescent psychiatrist; b. Ft. Riley, Kans., Oct. 1, 1947; s. Rudolph George and Hazel Ruth (Schayes) M.; m. Patricia Jean, Sept. 2, 1978; children: Nicola, Matthew, Michael, Alissa. AB in Genetics, Cornell U., 1969; MD, Wake Forest U., 1973. Lic. psychiatrist, child psychiatrist, N.C., Ohio, Colo., D.C., Va., Md., Minn., Ariz., Fla. Lectr. child psychiatry Inst. of Psychiatry, London, 1977-79; dir. pediatric psychiatry Nat. Jewish Ctr. for Immunology and Respiratory Medicine, Denver, 1979-91; chmn. psychiatry Children's Nat. Med. Ctr., Washington, 1991-98; chair psychiatry and behavioral scis. George Washington U. Sch. Medicine, 1996-2000; dir. Children's Rsch. Inst. Neurosci., 1995-98; chair psychiatry and psychology Mayo Clinic, Rochester, Minn., 2000—; prof. psychiatry and pediatrics Mayo Sch. Medicine, Rochester, 2000—; dir. Mayo Clinic S.C. Johnson Genomics of Addictions Program, 2004—. Asst. prof. psychiatry U. Colo. Sch. Medicine, 1979-83, assoc. prof. psychiatry and pediatrics, 1984-89, prof., 1990-91; prof.

psychiatry and pediatrics George Washington U. Sch. Medicine, 1991-2000, Leon Yochelson prof. psychiatry and behavioral scis.; dir. Am. Bd. Psychiatry and Neurology, 2003-. Contbr. chapters to books, articles to profl. jours. Recipient Rsch. Scientist Devel. awards NIMH, 1983-88, 88-91, Irving Phillips Meml. award for outstanding rsch. in prevention Acad. Child and Adolescent Psychiatry, 2000, Simon Wile award Am. Acad. Child and Adolescent Psychiatry, 2005, Agnes Purcell McGavin award for Lifetime Achievement in Child and Adolescent Psychiatry, Am. Psychiatric Assn., 2008. Fellow Am. Acad. Child and Adolescent Psychiatry (Simon Wile award 2005), Royal Soc. Medicine, Am. Psychiat. Assn. (chmn. coun. children, adolescents and families 2006—, Blanche F. Ittleson award 1996, Agnes Purcell McGavin award 1999, 2008), Royal Coll. Psychiatrists, Am. Coll. Psychiatrists; mem. Group for the Advancement of Psychiatry, Colo. Child and Adolescent Psychiatry Soc. (pres. 1984), Benjamin Rush Soc., Am. Bd. Psychiatry Neurology (bd. dirs. 2003—). Office: Mayo Clinic Dept Psychiatry/Pschology 200 1st St SW Rochester MN 55905 Home Phone: 507-285-5656; Office Phone: 507-284-8891. Office Fax: 507-266-3319. Business E-Mail: mrazek.david@mayo.edu.

MROZEK, ERNEST J., customer service administrator; married; 2 children. Grad. in Acctg., U. Ill., 1976. CPA Ill. V.p. acctg. The ServiceMaster Co., Downers Grove, Ill., 1987, pres., COO, Consumer Svcs., 1997—98, group pres. consumer and comml. svcs., 1998—2002, pres., COO, 2002—04, pres., CFO, 2004—06, vice-chmn., 2006—. Bd. dir. G&K Services Inc., U.S. C. of C. Mem.: AICPAs, Ill. CPA Soc. Office: ServiceMaster 3250 Lacey Rd Downers Grove IL 60515

MRVAN, FRANK, JR., state legislator; b. East Chgo., Ind., Apr. 11, 1933; m. Jean Mrvan; three children, Judith, Frances, Frank., Ind. U., Am. Inst. Banking. Asst. v.p. First Nat. Bank East Chgo.; mem. Ind. Senate from 1st. dist., 1978-94, 98—; asst. chmn. minority caucus, 1981-82. Mem. health and environ. affaris com., ins. and fin. instns. com., edn. comm., appt. and claims com., govt. and regulatory coms. Mem. Hammond Planning Commn.; mem. Ind. State Commn. for Handicapped; mem. Hammond City Coun. Mem. KC, PTA (past pres.), Hammond Young Dems., Lake County Fish and Game Protective Assn., Am. Legion. Office: Ind Senate Dist 1 200 W Washington St Indianapolis IN 46204-2728

MUCHIN, ALLAN B., lawyer; b. Manitowoc, Wis., Jan. 10, 1936; s. Jacob and Dorothy (Biberfeld) M.; m. Elaine Cort, Jan. 28, 1960; children: Andrea Muchin Leon, Karen, Margery Muchin Goldblatt. BBA, U. Wis., Manitowoc, 1958, JD, 1961. Gen. counsel IRS, Chgo., 1961-65; assoc. Altman, Kurlander & Weiss, Chgo., 1965-68, ptnr., 1968-74; co-mng. ptnr. Katten Muchin Zavis Rosenman, Chgo., 1974-95, chmn. emeritus, 1995—. Bd. dirs. Chgo. Bulls, Chgo. White Sox, Alberto-Culver Co., Acorn Investment Trust; bd. visitors U. Wis. Law Sch.; trustee Noble St. Charter Sch. Pres. Lyric Opera Chgo., 1993—; mem. adv. com. Am. Com. for Weizmann Inst. of Sci., Chgo., 1991—. Mem. Econ. Club Chgo., Comml. Club Chgo. Avocations: travel, tennis, reading. Office: Katten Muchin Zavis Rosenman 525 W Monroe St Ste 1600 Chicago IL 60661-3693

MUCKERMAN, NORMAN JAMES, priest, writer; b. Webster Groves, Mo., Feb. 1, 1917; s. Oliver Christopher and Edna Gertrude (Hartman) M. BA, Immaculate Conception Coll., 1940, M. in Religious Edn., 1942. Ordained priest Roman Catholic Ch., 1942. Missionary Redemptorist Missions, Amazonas, Para, Brazil, 1943-53, procurator missions St. Louis, 1953-58; pastor, adminstr. St. Alphonsus Ch., Chgo., 1958-67, St. Gerard, Kirkwood, Mo., 1967-71; mktg. mgr. circulation Liguori Pubs., Liguori, Mo., 1971-76; editor Liguorian Mag., Liguori, Mo., 1977-89. Author: How to Face Death Without Fear, 1976, Redemptorists on the Amazon, 1992, Preparation for Death, 1998, Into Your Hands, 2001, From the Heart of St. Alphonsus, 2002; contbg. editor: Liguorian, 1989—95. Recipient Nota Dez award Caixa Fed. Do Para, Brazil, 1958 Mem. Cath. Press Assn. (cons. 1971-95, bd. dirs. 1976-85, pres. 1981-84, St. Francis De Sales award 1985). Avocations: reading, writing. Home Phone: 636-464-3666. Personal E-mail: nmuckerman@liguori.org.

MUDD, ANNE CHESTNEY, mediator, law educator, real estate broker; b. Macon, Ga., June 30, 1944; d. Bard Sherman Chestney and Betty (Bartow) Houston; children: Charles Lee Jr., Richard Chestney, Robert Jason. BA, U. Louisville, 1966, MA, 1976; JD cum laude, John Marshall Law Sch., 1998. Math statistican U.S. Bur. Census, Jeffersonville, Ind., 1966-70; instr. math. U. Louisville, 1975-77, Coll. DuPage, Glen Ellyn, Ill., 1978-85, 92; tchr. math and substitute tchr. Lyons Twp. High Sch., La Grange, Ill., 1986-91; realtor First United Realtors, Western Springs, Ill., 1989-92; owner, mgr. retail bus., 1992—2000; lawyer Mudd Law Offices, 1998—. Adj. prof. law. Editor: Mathematics Textbook, 1991-92. Steering com. Village Western Springs, 1986-87; bd. dirs. Children's Theater, 1987-91; sec. Collaborative Law Inst. of Ill., Leave a Legacy N.E. Ill. Outreach Com.; major gift task force Am. Cancer Soc. DuPage County. Mem.: LWV (pres. 1983—85, bd. dirs.), DuPage Assn. Women Lawyers, DuPage County Bar Assn., West Suburban Bar Assn., Ill. State Bar Assn., ABA, Collaborative Law Inst. Ill. (sec. bd. dir.), Suburban Chgo. Planned Giving Assn., Nat. Assn. Women Bus. Owners, Nat. Assn. Women Entrepreneurs (pres.), Assn. for Conflict Resolution, Mediation Coun. Ill. Avocations: gardening, politics, local govt. Office: Mudd Law Offices 3344 North Albany Ave Chicago IL 60618 Office Phone: 773-588-5410. Office Fax: 773-588-5440. E-mail: amudd@muddlawoffices.com.

MUEHLBAUER, JAMES HERMAN, manufacturing and distribution executive; b. Evansville, Ind., Nov. 13, 1940; s. Herman Joseph and Anna Louise (Overfield) M.; m. Mary Kay Koch, June 26, 1965; children: Stacey, Brad, Glen, Beth, Katy. BSME, Purdue U., West Lafayette, Ind., 1963, MS in Indsl. Adminstrn., 1964. Registered profl. engr., Ind., 1970. Engr. George Koch Sons, Inc., Evansville, 1966-67, chief estimator, 1968-72, chief engr., 1973-74, v.p., 1975-81, dir., 1978—98, exec. v.p., 1982-98; pres. George Koch Sons LLC, Evansville, 1999—2003, chmn., 2003—04; exec. v.p., bd. dirs. Koch Enterprises, Inc., 1999—; pres. Koch Air LLC, 2003—. V.p., bd. dirs. Brake Supply Co., Evansville, Gibbs Die Casting Corp., Henderson, Ky., Uniseal, Inc., Evansville, George Koch Sons LLC, Evansville, Southwestern Comm., Inc., Evansville, 2006-, Comfort Fin. Svcs. LLC, Evansville; bd. dirs. Fifth Third Bank Indiana, George Koch Sons Ltd., Lichfield, Eng., Red Spot Paint & Varnish Co., Inc., Evansville, George Koch Sons de Mex., Monterrey, Koch Air LLC, Evansville. Co-author: Tool & Manufacturing Engineering Handbook, 1976; patentee in paint finishing equipment. Bd. dirs., past pres. Evansville Indsl. Found., 1980—; bd. dirs., past pres., past campaign chmn. United Way S.W. Ind., Evansville, 1983—; bd. dirs., past vice-chmn. Univ. So. Ind. Found., Evansville, 1988-2001; bd. dirs. Deaconess Hosp., Evansville, 1986-2007, treas., 1991-96, vice-chmn., 1999-2003, chmn., 2003-07; bd. dirs. Cath. Found. Southwestern Ind., 1998-2004; dir. bd. advisors U. So. Ind. Sch. Bus., 1997—, chmn., 2001-02; bd. dirs. Ind. Assn. United Ways, 2000-06, Alliance Indpls., 1993-2004, pres. 1999; mem. Brute Soc., Cath. Diocese Evansville, 1997, Equestrian Order of the Holy Sepulchre of Jerusalem, 1996—. Named Engr. of Yr. S.W. chpt. Ind. Soc. Profl. Engrs., 1983; recipient Tech. Achievement award Tri-State Coun. for Sci. and Engring., Evansville, 1984, Purdue U. Alumni Citizenship award, 1991. Mem. Soc. Mfg. Engrs. (past nat. chmn. finishing and coating tech. divsn.), ASME, NSPE, Evansville Country Club, Evansville Kennel Club (bd. dirs. 1997-2001). Republican. Roman Catholic. Home: 2300 E Gum St Evansville IN 47714-2338 Office: Koch Enterprises 14 S 11th Ave Evansville IN 47744-0001 Home Phone: 812-477-8495; Office Phone: 812-962-5260. Business E-Mail: jmuehlbauer@kochair.com.

MUEHLBAUER, JAMES L., retail executive; b. 1961; BS in Acctg., St. Cloud State U. CPA. Sr. mgr. audit and consulting practice Coopers & Lybrand LLP; v.p., worldwide controller The Pillsbury Co.; CFO Musicland Best Buy Co., Inc., Richfield, Minn., 2002, sr. v.p., CFO US bus., 2006—07, interim CFO, 2007—08, exec. v.p. fin., CFO, 2008—. Office: Best Buy Co, Inc 7601 Penn Ave S Richfield MN 55423*

MUELLER, CHARLES FREDERICK, radiologist, educator; b. Dayton, Ohio, May 26, 1936; s. Susan Elizabeth (Wine) W.; m. Kathe Louise Lutterbei, May 28, 1966; children: Charles Jeffrey, Theodore Martin, Kathryn Suzanne. BA in English, U. Cin., 1958, MD, 1962. Diplomate Am. Bd. Radiology, Am. Bd. Nuclear Medicine. Asst. prof. radiology U. N.Mex., Albuquerque, 1968-72, assoc. prof. radiology, 1972-74, Ohio State U., Columbus, 1974-79, acting chmn. dept. radiology, 1975, prof. radiology, 1979—2002, prof. radiology, dir. post grad. program radiology, 1980-2000, acting chmn. dept. radiology, 1990—93, prof. emeritus, 2002—. Bd. dirs. Univ. Radiologists, Inc., Columbus, v.p., 1980—86; pres., founder Ambulatory Imaging, Inc., Columbus, 1985—2002. Author: Emergency Radiology, 1982; contbr. numerous articles to profl. jours.; editl. bd. Emergency radiology, 1995-2002; editor Internat. Trauma, Am. Jour. Roentgenology, 1997-2004. Com. chmn. Boy Scouts Am., Columbus, 1980—84; vol. Columbus Free Clinic, 2003—, Franklin Park Conservatory, 2003—. Capt. USAF, 1966—68. Research grantee Ohio State U. 1975, Gen. Electric Co., 1986-88; Gold medalist ASER, 2001. Fellow Am. Coll. Radiologists; mem. AMA, Assn. Univ. Radiologists, Am. Roentgen Ray Soc., Am. Soc. Emergency Radiology (founder 1988, pres. 1993-94, Gold medal 2001), Radiol. Soc. N.Am., N.Mex. Soc. Radiologists (pres. 1973-74), Ohio State Radiol. Soc. (pres. 1986-87). Republican. Presbyterian. Avocations: fly fishing, hiking, model railroading. Office: Ohio State Univ Hosps Dept Radiology 410 W 10th Ave Columbus OH 43210-1240 E-mail: cmueller@columbus.rr.com.

MUELLER, CHARLES WILLIAM, electric utility executive; b. Belleville, Ill., Nov. 29, 1938; s. Charles A. and Clara R. (Jorn) M.; m. Janet Therese Vernier, July 9, 1960; children: Charles R., Michael G., Craig J. BSEE, St. Louis U., 1961, MBA, 1966. Registered profl. engr., Mo., Ill. Engr. Union Electric Co., St. Louis, 1961-75, supervisory engr., 1975-77, asst. dir. corp. planning, 1977-78, treas., 1978-83, v.p. fin., 1983-88, sr. v.p. adminstrv. svcs., 1988-93; pres., CEO Ameren Corp., St. Louis, 1994-98, pres., CEO, chmn., 1998—2001, CEO, chmn., 2001—03, bd. dir.; ret., 2003. Dep. chmn. The Fed. Res. Bank of St. Louis; chmn. bd. Webster U.; bd. dirs. Electric Energy Inc., Regional Commerce and Growth Assn., Edison Electric Inst., Angelica Corp., United Way of Greater St. Louis, BJC Health Sys., Kiel Ctr. Corp.; dir. Assn. of Edison Illuminating Cos., St. Louis Children's Hosp., St. Louis Sci. Ctr., Civic Progress, The Mcpl. Theatre Assn. Mem.: IEEE, St. Louis Club, The Bogey Club, St. Clair Country Club, Mo. Athletic Club. Avocations: tennis, boating, travel.

MUELLER, JOHN ERNEST, political science professor, dance critic; b. St. Paul, June 21, 1937; s. Ernst A. and Elsie E. (Schleh) M.; m. Judy A. Reader, Sept. 6, 1960; children: Karl, Karen, Susan AB, U. Chgo., 1960; MA, UCLA, 1963, PhD, 1965. Asst. prof. polit. sci. U. Rochester, NY, 1965-69, assoc. prof., 1969-72, prof., 1972-2000, prof. film studies, 1983-2000, founder, dir. Dance Film Archive, 1973—; prof. polit. sci., Woody Hayes chair nat. security studies Ohio State U., 2000—. Lectr. on dance in U.S., Europe, Australia, 1973—; OP-ED columnist Wall St. Jour., 1984—, L.A. Times, 1988—, N.Y. Times, 1990—; mem. dance panel NEA, 1983-85; columnist Dance Mag., 1974-82; dance critic Rochester Dem. and Chronicle, 1974-82; mem. adv. bd. Dance in Am., PBS, 1975; mem. editl. bd. Ohio State U. Press, 2000—04. Author: War, Presidents and Public Opinion, 1973 (one of Fifty Books That Significantly Shaped Public Opinion Rsch. 1946-95 Am. Assn. Pub. Opinion Rsch. 1995, Mitofsky Award Roper Ctr., 2007), Dance Film Directory, 1979, Astaire Dancing: The Musical Films, 1985 (de la Torre Bueno prize 1983), Retreat From Doomsday: The Obsolescence of Major War, 1989, Policy and Opinion in the Gulf War, 1994, Quiet Cataclysm: Reflections on the Recent Transformation of World Politics, 1995, Capitalism, Democracy, and Ralph's Pretty Good Grocery, 1999, The Remnants of War, 2004 (Lepgold prize 2004), Overblown, 2006; co-author: Trends in Public Opinion: A Compendium of Survey Data, 1989; editor: Approaches to Measurement, 1969, Peace, Prosperity, and Politics, 2000; co-editor Jour. Policy Analysis and Mgmt., 1985-89; mem. editl. bd. Pub. Opinion Quar., 1988-91, Jour. Cold War Studies, 1999—, Internat. Polit. Sociology, 2005—; prodr. 12 dance films, 2 dance DVDs; commentator on 2nd soundtrack of laser disc edit. Swing Time, 1986, DVD edit., 2005; co-adapter (musical) A Foggy Day, 1998; prodr. Shaw Festival Niagara-on-the-Lake, Ont., 1998, 99. Grantee NSF, 1967-70, 74-75, NEH, 1972-73, 74-75, 77-78, 79-81; Guggenheim fellow, 1988. Mem. Am. Acad. Arts and Scis., Am. Polit. Sci. Assn., Dance Critics Assn. (bd. dirs. 1983-85). Home: 420 W 5th Ave Columbus OH 43201-3159 Office: Ohio State U Polit Sci Dept Columbus OH 43210-1373 Home Phone: 614-421-2448; Office Phone: 614-247-6007. Business E-Mail: bbbb@osu.edu.

MUELLER, KURT M., hotel executive; Pres. Motels Am., Des Plaines, Ill.; CFO MOA Hospitality Inc., Des Plaines, Ill., 1997—, pres., CFO. Office: Hospitality Inc 701 Lee St Ste 1000 Des Plaines IL 60016-4555

MUELLER, MARYLIN, graphic supply company executive; Pres., CEO Mueller Graphic Supply Co. Office: 11475 W Theodore Trecker Way Milwaukee WI 53214-1138

MUELLER, WALT, state legislator; b. Springfield, Mo., Dec. 12, 1925; BS, U. Kans. Mem. Mo. State Ho. of Reps. Dist. 93, 1973-93, Mo. State Senate Dist. 15, 1993—. Address: 12325 Manchester Rd Saint Louis MO 63131-4316

MUELLER, WILLARD FRITZ, economics professor; b. Ortonville, Minn., Jan. 23, 1925; s. Fritz and Adele C. (Thrmaehlen) Mueller; m. Shirley I. Liesch, June 26, 1948; children: Keith, Scott, Kay. BS, U. Wis., 1950, MS, 1951; PhD, Vanderbilt U., 1955. Asst. prof. U. Calif., Davis, 1954-57; prof. U. Wis., 1957-61, prof. agrl. and applied econs. dept. econ. Sch. Law Madison, 1969—; chief economist small bus. com. U.S. Ho. of Reps., 1961; chief economist, dir. bur. econs. FTC, 1961-68; exec. dir. Pres.'s Cabinet Com. Price Stability, 1968-69. Expert House and Senate Com., 1960—96; cons. in indsl. orgn. and pub. policy. Past bd. editors Rev. Ind. Orgn., Antitrust Law and Econ. Rev., Antitrust Bull., Jour. Reprints for Antitrust Law and Econs. Mem. Econ. Policy Inst., 1987—90. With USN, 1943—46. Named one of 20th Century Pioneers of Indsl. Org., 2006; recipient Disting. Svc. award, FTC, 1978. Fellow: Am. Agrl. Econs. Assn. (profl. excellence awards in policy contbn. 1980, in comm. 1985, in rsch. discovery 1988); mem.: Argus Econ. Svcs. (pres. 1985—), Indsl. Orgn. Soc. (pres. 1989—90), Assn. Evolutionary Econs. (pres. 1974—75). Unitarian Universalist. Office: U Wis 427 Lorch St Madison WI 53706-1513 Home: 8625 Wood Violet Way Madison WI 53717 Personal E-mail: wfritzmueller@aol.com.

MUFSON, ELLIOTT J., psychologist, director, neurologist, educator; b. Manhattan, NY, June 22, 1947; BA in Psychology, Hunter Coll., 1969; MA in Physiol. Psychology, Kans. State U., 1971; PhD in Biol. Psychology, SUNY, 1977. Rschr. and tchg. asst. Hunter Coll., NYC, 1968—69, Kans. State U., Manhattan, Kans., 1969—71; rsch. asst. Downstate Med. Ctr., Bklyn., 1971—72, tchg. asst., 1973—77, lab. instr. in nueroanatomy, 1975—77; rsch. fellow in neurology Beth Israel Hosp. and Harvard Neurology Unit, Boston, 1978—81; lab. instr. Harvard Med. Sch., Boston, 1980—87; assoc. dir. Bullard & Denny Brown Labs. Harvard Med. Sch., Beth Israel Hosp., 1986—87; dep. dir., head Divsn. Structural Studies Inst. Biogerontology Rsch., Sun City, Ariz., 1987—91; assoc. prof. Med. Sch. U. Ariz., Tucson, 1988—91; co-dir. Rush Brain Bank Rush Presbyn. St. Luke's Med. Ctr., Chgo., 1992—, prof. neurol. scis., 1992—; lab. instr. neuroanatomy Rush Med. Coll., Chgo., 1993—. Vis. fellow Heinz Werner Inst. Clark U., Worcester, Mass., 1977—78; instr. neurology Beth Israel Hosp. Harvard Neurology Unit, Boston, 1982—83; asst. prof. psychology Clark U., Worcester, 1983—84; asst. prof. neurology Harvard Med. Sch., 1983—87; lectr. and lab. instr. Clark U., 1984; lab. instr. neuroanatomy U. Ill. Med. Sch., 1992—97; cons. in field. Mem. editl. bd.: Neurobilogy of Aging, Neuropeptides, Jour. Alzheimer's Disease, Jour. Comparative Neurology, editl. cons.: Am. Jour. Pathology, Biol. Psychiatry, Brain Rsch., Exptl. Neurology, Jour. Chem. Neuroanatomy, Jour. Histochemistry and Cytochemistry, Jour. Neuroscience, Pharmacology, Biochemistry, and Behavior. Grantee Rsch. grant, NIH, 1978—81, 1988—92, Ariz. Disease Control Commn., 1988—92, award, Am. Health Assistance Found., 1989—92, Ill. State Pub. Health Svc., 1991—93, various grants, Nat. Inst. Aging, 1991—, Wash. Square Health Found., 1992—94, Ill. State Pub. Health Svc., 1994—95. Office: St Luke Medical Ctr RUSH PRS 1735 W Harrison St #406 Chicago IL 60612-3990

MUFSON, STUART LEE, astronomer, educator; b. Phila., May 16, 1946; BA, MS, U. Pa., 1968; MS, U. Chgo., 1970, PhD in Astronomy and Astrophysics, 1974. Rsch. assoc. at. Radio Astron. Obs., 1973-75; NRC assoc. Marshall Space Flight Ctr., NASA, 1975-77; chmn. dept. astronomy Ind. U., Bloomington. Prin. investigator ASA, 1977—. Mem. Internat. Astron. Union, Am. Astron. Soc. Achievements include research on high energy astrophysics, neutrino astronomy, cosmic ray research, evolution of supernova remnants. Office: Dept Astronomy Ind Univ Bloomington IN 47405-4200

MUGNAINI, ENRICO, neuroscience educator; b. Colle Val d'Elsa, Italy, Dec. 10, 1937; came to U.S., 1969. children: Karin E., Emiliano N.G. MD cum laude, U. Pisa, Italy, 1962; degree (hon.), U. Torino, 2005, U. Pisa, 2005, U. Salamanca, 2006. Microscopy lab. rsch. fellow dept. anatomy U. Oslo Med. Sch., 1963, asst. prof., head of electron microscopy lab., 1964-66, assoc. prof., 1967-69; prof. biobehavioral scis. and psychology, head lab. of neuromorphology U. Conn., Storrs, 1969-95; E.C. Stuntz prof. cell biology, dir. Inst. for Neurosci., Northwestern U., Chgo., 1995—2006. Vis. prof. dept. anatomy Harvard U., Boston, 1969-70; traveling lectr. Grass Found., 1986, 1990. Mng. editor USA Anatomy and Embryology Jour., 1989—; contbr. more than 200 articles to books and jours. Recipient Decennial Camillo Golgi award Acad. Nat. dei Lincei, 1981, Campano d'Oro award, 2005; Sen. Javits Neurosci. Rsch. Investigator grantee IH, 1985-92, Fernandez-Lindsay Lectureship grantee U. Chgo., 2003. Mem. AAAS, Am. Assn. Anatomists, Am. Soc. Cell Biology, Internat. Brain Rsch. Orgn., Internat. Soc. Developmental Neurosci., Norwegian Nat. Acad. Scis. and Letters, Soc. Neurosci., Inst. Lombardo, Acad. Sci. Lettere (corr. 2005-), Cajal Club (pres. 1987-88). Office: U Northwestern Feinberg Sch Medicine 5-474 Searle Bldg 320 E Superior St Chicago IL 60611-3010 Home Phone: 312-915-0922; Office Phone: 312-503-4333. Business E-Mail: e-mugnaini@northwestern.edu.

MUHAMMAD, AVA, minister and national spokesperson for the Nation of Islam; b. Columbus, Ohio, 1951; m. Darius Muhammad, 1988. JD, Georgetown U., 1975. Bar: NY 1976. Asst. DA Borough of Queens, NY; defense atty. NYC; joined Nation of Islam, 1981, min., 1985—, so. regional min., 1998, head Muhammad Mosque No. 15 Atlanta, 1998, nat. spokesperson, 2000—. Author: Queen of the Planet Earth, The Rebirth, Rise of the Original Woman. Achievements include first woman in Islam to be given authority over a Mosque; successfully sued the NY Post for defamation of Louis Farrakhan's character, 1994. Office: Nation of Islam 734 W 79th St Chicago IL 60620

MUIRHEAD, VINCENT URIEL, retired aerospace engineer; b. Dresden, Kans., Feb. 6, 1919; s. John Hadsell and Lily Irene (McKinney) M.; m. Bobby Jo Thompson, Nov. 5, 1943; children: Rosalind, Jean, Juleigh. BS, U.S. Naval Acad., 1941; BS in Aero. Engring, U.S. Naval Postgrad. Sch., 1948; Aero. Engr., Calif. Inst. Tech., 1949; postgrad., U. Ariz., 1962-64, Okla. State U., 1963. Midshipman U.S. Navy, 1937, commd. ensign, 1941, advanced through grades to comdr., 1951; nav. officer U.S.S. White Plains, 1945-46; comdr. Fleet Aircraft Service Squad, 1951-52; with Bur. Aeros., Ft. Worth, 1953-54; comdr. Helicopter Utility Squadron I, Pacific Fleet, 1955-56; chief staff officer Comdr. Fleet Air, Philippines, 1956-58; exec. officer Naval Air Tng. Center, Memphis, 1958-61; ret., 1961; asst. prof. U. Kans., Lawrence, 1961-63, assoc. prof. aerospace engring., 1964-76, prof., 1976-89, prof. emeritus, 1989—, chmn. dept., 1976-88. Cons. Black & Veatch (cons. engrs.), Kansas City, Mo., 1964— Author: Introduction to Aerospace, 1972, 6th edit., 2004, Thunderstorms, Tornadoes and Building Damage, 1975. Decorated Air medal. Fellow AIAA (assoc.); mem. Am. Acad. Mechanics, Am. Soc. Engring. Edn., Tau Beta Pi, Sigma Gamma Tau. Mem. Ch. of Christ (elder 1972-96). Achievements include research on aircraft, tornado vortices, shock tubes and waves. Home: 503 Park Hill Ter Lawrence KS 66046-4841 Office: Dept Aerospace Engring Univ Kans Lawrence KS 66045-0001 Personal E-mail: vmuirhead@sunflower.com.

MUKERJEE, PASUPATI, chemistry professor; b. Calcutta, India, Feb. 13, 1932; s. Nani Gopal and Probhabati (Ghosal) M.; m. Lalita Sarkar, Feb. 29, 1964 (dec.); m. Mina Maitra, Nov. 14, 1998. B.Sc., Calcutta U., 1949, M.Sc., 1951; PhD, U. So. Calif., 1957. Lectr., vis. asst. prof. U. So. Calif., 1956-57; rsch. assoc. Brookhaven Nat. Lab., LI, 1957-59; reader in phys. chemistry Indian Assn. Cultivation of Sci., Calcutta, 1959-64; guest scientist U. Utrecht, Holland, 1964; sr. scientist chemistry dept. U. So. Calif., 1964-66; vis. assoc. prof. U. Wis., Madison, 1966-67, prof. Sch. Pharmacy, 1967-94, emeritus prof., 1994—. Vis. prof. Indian Inst. Tech., Kharagpur, 1971-72; mem. commn. on colloid and surface chemistry Internat. Union Pure and Applied Chemistry Contbr. articles to profl. jours.; mem. editl. bd. Jour. Colloid and Interface Sci., 1978-80, Asian Jour. Pharm. Scis., 1978-85, Colloids and Surfaces, 1980-86. Grantee USPHS, NSF, Nat. Bur. Stds., Petroleum Rsch. Fund. Fellow AAAS, Acad. Pharm. Scis., Am. Inst. Chemistry; mem. Am. Chem. Soc. (editorial bd. Langmuir 1985-86), Am. Pharm. Assn., Acad. Pharm. Scis., Rho Chi. Home: 5526 Varsity Hl Madison WI 53705-4652 Office: 777 Highland Ave Madison WI 53705-2222 Office Phone: 608-262-7289.

MULANEY, CHARLES W., lawyer; AB summa cum laude, Georgetown U., 1971; JD, Yale Law Sch., 1974. Law clk. to the Honorable Judge Edward Weinfeld, So. Dist. NY, 1974—75; ptnr. Skadden, Arps, Slate, Meagher & Flom, LLP. Lectr. on mergers and acquisitions and corp. governance; faculty mem. pub. co. dir. programs U. Chgo. Grad. Sch. Bus., Kellogg Sch. Mgmt. Past pres. Midtown Edn. Found.; mem. exec. com. Corp. and Securities Law Inst., Northwestern Law Sch.

MULCAHY, MICHAEL J., light contruction and agricultural manfucturing; b. Detroit, Dec. 6, 1947; BS, U. Detroit, 1966, JD, 1969. Bar: Mich. 1969. Assoc. Raymond & Prokop, P.C., Southfield, Mich.; v.p., gen. counsel, sec. Gebl Co., West Bend, Wis. Office: Gebl Co PO Box 179 143 Water St West Bend WI 53095-3400 Fax: 262-334-6603.

MULCAHY, ROBERT WILLIAM, lawyer; b. Milw., Jan. 11, 1951; s. T. Larry and Mary Margaret (Chambers) M.; m. Mary M. Andrews, Aug. 3, 1974; children: Molly, Kathleen, Margaret, Michael. BS, Marquette U., 1973, JD, 1976. Staff atty. NLRB, Milw., 1976-79; ptnr. Mulcahy & Wherry, S.C., Milw., 1979-90, Michael, Best & Friedrich, Milw., 1990—. Co-author: Strike Prevention and Control Handbook, 1983, 2d edit., 2006, Comparable Worth: A Negotiator's Guide, 1985, Public Sector Labor Relations in Wisconsin, 1994. Bd. dirs. Milw. Repertory Theater, 1993-97, Gateway Tech. Coll. Found., 2004—; chmn. St. Monica Parish Coun., 1988-96, Charles Allis/Villa Terrace, 1991-, Whitefish Bay Police Commn.; divsn. chmn. United Performing Arts Fund, 1993-94; co-chmn. Villa Terrace Garden Renaissance Project, 2000-04, co-chair, Am. Diabetes Assn., Gala. Mem. ABA, State Bar Wis. (chair labor sect. 1986-87), Milw. Bar Assn. (co-chair labor sect. 1988-95), Nat. Assn. Counties, Nat. Pub. Employers Labor Rels. Assn., Nat. Assn. Coll. & Univ. Attys., Wis. Counties Assn., Indsl. Rels. Rsch. Assn., Mgmt. Resources Assn., Wis. Sch. Attys. Assn., Milw. Area Mcpl. Employers Assn., cmty leadership coun.(bd. mem. 2007) Office: Michael Best & Friedrich 100 E Wisconsin Ave Ste 3300 Milwaukee WI 53202-4108 E-mail: rwmulcahy@mbf-law.com, rwmulcahy@michaelbest.com.

MULCH, ROBERT F., JR., physician; b. Quincy, Ill., June 21, 1951; s. Robert Franklin and Martha Jo (Nisi) M.; m. Barbara Ann Best, Apr. 5, 1975; children: Matthew, Luke. BS, U. Ill., 1973; MD, Rush Med. Coll., Chgo., 1977. Diplomate Am. Bd. Family Practice; cert. in geriatrics. Intern Riverside Meth. Hosp., Columbus, Ohio, 1977-78, resident in family practice, 1978-80; family physician Hillsboro (Ill.) Med. Ctr., 1980—; ptnr., assoc. med. dir. Springfield Clin., 1998—; pres. med. staff Hillsboro Area Hosp. Asst. clin. prof. family medicine So. Ill. U., Springfield, 1981—90; reviewer Ctrl. Ill. Peer Rev. Orgn.; pres. med. staff Hillsboro Area Hosp. Fellow Am. Acad. Family Practice; mem. Am. Coll. Physician Execs. Lutheran. Avocations: computers, swimming. Office: Hillsboro Med Ctr SC 1250 E Tremont St Hillsboro IL 62049-1912 Office Phone: 217-532-6911. E-mail: rmulch@consolidated.net, rmulch@springfieldclinic.com.

MULDER, DONALD WILLIAM, physician, educator; b. Rehobath, N.Mex., June 30, 1917; s. Jacob D. and Gertrude (Hofstra) M.; m. Gertrude Ellens, Feb. 22, 1943. BA, Calvin Coll., 1940; MD, Marquette U., 1943; MS, U. Mich., 1946. Intern Butterworth Hosp., Grand Rapids, Mich., 1943-44; resident U. Hosp., Ann Arbor, Mich., 1944-46, Denver, 1947-49; asst. prof. medicine in neurology U. Colo., 1949-50; prof. neurology Mayo Found. Faculty, 1964—, Mayo Med. Sch., 1973—; cons. neurology Mayo Clinic, Rochester, Minn., 1950—, gov., 1962-69, chmn. dept. neurology, 1966-71, pres. staff, 1971—, Andersen prof. neurology, 1977-83, prof. emeritus, 1983—; sci. advisor ALS. Contbr. articles on neuromuscular disease to sci. jours. Ret. capt. USNR. Recipient Disting. Alumni award Calvin Coll., 1992. Fellow A.C.P., Am. Acad. Neurology; mem. Am. Neurol. Assn. (hon.). Office: 200 1st St SW Rochester MN 55905-0001 Home: Apt 1307 211 2nd St NW Rochester MN 55901-2897

MULDER, RICHARD DEAN, state legislator; b. Rock Valley, Iowa, May 8, 1938; m. Ruth Maxine Van Buren; 4 children. BS, S.D. State U., 1960; MD, U. Iowa, 1968. Intern McKennan Hosp., Sioux Falls, S.D., 1969; family practice, 1982—; Minn. state rep., 1994—. Presenter in field. Bush Clin. fellowship; recipient Disting. Alumnus award U. S.D. Sch. Medicine Alumni Found., 1991. Mem. AMA, Minn. Med. Assn., Am. Acad. of Family Physicians, Minn. Acad. of Family Physicians (S.W. chpt., Merit award 1984, 1989), Lyon/Lincoln Med.

Assn., Am. Assn. of Med. Examiners, Minn. Coroner's and Med. Examiners Assn., Phi Beta Phi. Office: Ivanhoe Clinic PO Box 76 Ivanhoe MN 56142-0076

MULLAN, JOHN FRANCIS (SEAN MULLAN), neurosurgeon, educator; b. County Derry, Northern Ireland, May 17, 1925; came to U.S., 1955; naturalized, 1962; s. John and Catharine Ann (Gilmartin) M.; m. Vivian C. Dunn, June 3, 1959; children: Joan Claire, John Charles, Brian Francis. MB, BCh, BAO, Queen's U., Belfast, Northern Ireland, 1947, DSc (hon.), 1976; postgrad., McGill U., 1953-55. Diplomate Am. Bd. Neurol. Surgery. Trainee gen. surgery Royal Victoria Hosp., Belfast, 1947-50, trainee in neurosurgery, 1951-53; trainee gen. surgery Guy's Hosp. and Middlesex Hosp., London, 1950-51, Montreal Neurosurg. Inst., Que., Canada, 1953—55; asst. prof. neurol. surgery U. Chgo., 1955-61, assoc. prof., 1961-63, prof., 1963—, John Harper Seeley prof., 1967—95, chmn. dept., 1967—93, emeritus, 1995—, dir. Brain Rsch. Inst., 1970-84. Author: Neurosurgery for Students, 1961; contbr. over 150 articles to profl. jours.; mem. editorial bd. Jour. eurosurgery, 1974-84, Archives of Neurology, 1976-87. Recipient Olivecrona medal Karolinska Inst., 1976, Wilder Penfield medal Can. Neurosurg. Soc., 1979, Jamieson medal Australian and New Zealand Neurosurg. Soc., 1980. Fellow ACS, Royal Coll. Surgeons; mem. Soc. Neurol. Surgeons (past pres.), Acad. eurol. Surgery, Am. Assn. Neurol. Surgeons, Am. Neurol. Assn., Cen. Neurosurg. Soc., Chgo. Neurol. Soc., World Fedn. of Neurosurg. Socs. (sec. 1989-93, hon. pres. 1993—). Roman Catholic. Achievements include conducting research on vascular diseases of the brain, pain, head injury.

MULLEN, EDWARD JOHN, JR., Spanish language educator; b. Hackensack, NJ, July 12, 1942; s. Edward J. and Elsie (Powell) Mullen; m. Helen Cloe Braley, Apr. 2, 1971; children: Kathleen, Julie Ann. BA, W.Va. Wesleyan Coll., 1964; MA, Northwestern U., 1965, PhD, 1968. Asst. prof. modern langs. Purdue U., West Lafayette, Ind., 1967-71; assoc. prof. Spanish U. Mo., Columbia, 1971-78, prof. Spanish, 1978—. Author: La Revista Contemporaneos, 1972, Carlos Pellicer, 1977, Langston Hughes in the Hispanic World and Haiti, 1977, The Life and Poems of Cuban Slave: Juan Francisco Manzano 1797-1854, 1981, Critical Essays on Langston Hughes, 1986, Sendas Literarias: Hispanoamerica, 1988, El Cuento Hispanico, 1980, 2007, Afro-Cuban Literature: Critical Junctures, 1998; editor: The Harlem Group of Negro Writers (Melvin B. Tolson), 2001; co-editor: Afro-Hispanic Rev., 1987—2005. Recipient diploma de honor, Inst. de Cultura Hispanica, 1964; fellow, Northwestern U., 1965—67; grantee, Am. Coun. Learned Socs., 1979; Woodrow Wilson fellow, 1964—65, Rsch. grantee, U. Mo., 1972, 1976. Mem.: MLA, Assn. Depts. Fgn. Langs. (pres. 1989—91), Am. Tchrs. Spanish and Protuguese. Home: 207 Edgewood Ave Columbia MO 65203-3413 Office: U Mo Dept Romance Langs 143 Arts And Sci Bldg Columbia MO 65211-0001 Office Phone: 573-882-5041. Business E-Mail: mullene@missouri.edu.

MULLEN, J. THOMAS, lawyer; b. Evanston, Ill., Aug. 27, 1940; BSE, Princeton U., 1963; JD cum laude, U. Mich., 1967. Bar: Ill. 1967. Atty. Mayer, Brown, Rowe & Maw LLP, Chgo., 1967—74, ptnr., 1974—, ptnr.-in-charge London office London, 1974-78, ptnr. Chgo., 1978—. Chmn., recruiting com. Mayer, Brown, Rowe & Maw LLP. Bd. dirs. Legal Assistance Found. Chgo., 1979-85. Mem. ABA, Chgo. Bar Assn., Chgo. Coun. Lawyers, Ill. State Bar Assn., Law Club of Chgo. Office: Mayer Brown Rowe & Maw 71 S Wacker Dr Chicago IL 60606-4637 E-mail: tmullen@mayerbrownrowe.com.

MULLEN, RUSSELL EDWARD, agricultural studies educator; b. Atlantic, Iowa, Sept. 4, 1949; AA, Southwestern C.C., Creton, Iowa, 1969; BS in Agriculture, N.W. Mo. State U., 1971, MS in Edn., 1972; PhD in Crop Physiology and Mgmt., Purdue U., 1975. Grad. asst. N.W. Mo. State U., Maryville, 1971-72; grad. teaching asst. Purdue U., West Lafayette, Ind., 1972-74, grad. instr., 1974-75, temporary asst. prof., 1975-76; asst. prof. U. Fla., Gainesville, 1976-78; from asst. prof. to prof. Iowa State U., Ames, 1978—86, prof., 1986—. Recipient Ensminger Interstate Disting. Tchr. award Nat. Assn. Colls. Tchrs. Agriculture, 1992, Am. Soc. Agronomy Resident Edn. award, 1999; Am. Soc. Agronomy fellow, 1998. Office: Iowa State U Dept Agronomy 1126 Agronomy Hl Ames IA 50011-0001

MULLENS, DELBERT W., automotive executive; b. Buffalo; children: Dorian, Mandy. BA in History and English, minor in Bus., Tenn. State U.; EdM, U. Buffalo, 1974; studied Metallurgy, Lehigh U. With Bethlehem Steel; CEO Wesley Ind., Inc., Bloomfield Hills, Mich. Trustee U. Buffalo; founder Thinking Outside the Box Scholarship award, U. Buffalo, 1992—; chmn., Campaign for U. Buffalo: Generation to Generation Com., Grad. Sch. Edn. U. Buffalo. Named Entrepreneur of Yr., Mich. Commerce Dept.; recipient Lifetime Achievement award, Nat. Black MBA Assn.

MULLER, JOHN BARTLETT, university president; b. Port Jefferson, NY, Nov. 8, 1940; s. Frederick Henry and Estelle May (Reeve) M.; m. Barbara Ann Schmidt, May 30, 1964 (dec. 1972); m. Lynn Anne Spongberg, Oct. 10, 1987. AB in Polit. Sci., U. Rochester, 1962; postgrad. in apologetics, Westminster Sem., Phila., 1962-63; MS in Psychology, Purdue U., 1968, PhD in Psychology, 1975. Asst. prof. psychology Roberts Wesleyan Coll., Rochester, NY, 1964-66, acting chmn. div. behavioral sci., dir. instl. research, 1967-70; vis. asst. prof. psychology Wabash Coll., Crawfordsville, Ind., 1970-71; research assoc. Ind. U.-Purdue U., Indpls., 1971-72; prof. psychology, v.p. for acad. affairs Hillsdale (Mich.) Coll., 1972-85; pres. BMW Assocs., Osseo, Mich., 1984-85, Bellevue (Nebr.) U., 1985—. Bd. dir. Nebr. Ind. Coll. Found., Omaha, Assn. Ind. Colls. Nebr., Lincoln; bd. advisors Applied Info. Mgmt. Inst., Gt. Western Bank. Contbr. articles to profl. jours. and textbooks. Bd. dir. Mid-American Coun. Boy Scouts Mental Health fellowship Purdue U., 1963, Nat. Tchg. fellowship Fed. Govt., 1967, Townsend fellowship U. Rochester, 1962. Mem. APA, Bellevue C. of C. (bd. dir. 1989-95), Phi Beta Kappa, Phi Kappa Phi. Republican. Home: 13303 Lochmoor Cir Bellevue NE 68123-3770 Office: Bellevue U Office of the Pres 1000 Galvin Rd S Bellevue NE 68005-3098 Business E-Mail: jmuller@bellevue.edu.

MULLER, MARCEL W(ETTSTEIN), electrical engineering educator; b. Vienna, Nov. 1, 1922; came to U.S., 1940; s. Georg and Josephine (David) M.; m. Esther Ruth Hagler, Feb. 2, 1947; children: Susan, George, Janet. BSEE, Columbia U., 1949, AM in Physics, 1952; PhD, Stanford U., 1957. Sr. scientist Varian Assocs., Palo Alto, Calif., 1952-66; prof. elec. engring. Washington U., St. Louis, 1966-91, prof. emeritus, rsch. prof., 1991—. Vis. lectr. U. Zurich, Switzerland, 1962-63; vis. prof. U. Colo., Boulder, summer 1969; vis. scientist Max Planck Inst., Stuttgart, Fed. Republic of Germany, 1976-77; cons. Hewlett-Packard Labs., Palo Alto, 1985-89, SRI Internat., Menlo Park, Calif., 1986—. Sgt. U.S. Army, 1943-46. Recipient Humboldt prize Alexander von Humboldt Soc., 1976; Fulbright grantee, 1977, grantee NSF, 1967—. Fellow IEEE, Am. Physical Soc. Achievements include development of Maser quantum noise theory; developments in micromagnetism; contributions to magnetic information storage; invention Magneprint security system.

MULLER, MERVIN EDGAR, computer scientist, consultant, statistician, educator; b. Hollywood, Calif., June 1, 1928; s. Emanuel and Bertha (Zimmerman) Muller; m. Barabara McAdam, July 13, 1963; children: Jeffrey McAdam, Stephen McAdam, Todd McAdam. AB, UCLA, 1949, MA, 1951, PhD, 1954. Instr. in math. Cornell U., 1954-56; rsch. assoc. in math. Princeton (NJ) U., 1956-59, sr. scientist statis. and elec. engring., 1968-69; sr. statistician, dept. mgr. IBM, NYC, White Plains, 1956-64; prof. computer sci. and stats. U. Wis., 1964-71; prof. computer sci. George Mason U., 1985; dept. dir. World Bank, Washington, 1971-81, sr. advisor, 1981-85; Robert M. Critchfield prof. computer info. sci. Ohio State U., 1985-98, prof. emeritus, 1994-98, dept. chair, 1985-94. Chair sci. and tech. info. bd. NAS; bd. dirs. Advanced Info. Tech. Ctr., Columbus, Ohio. Mem. editl. bd. Computation and Stats., 1990, Jour. Computational and Graphical Stats., 1990; contbr. articles to profl. jours. Trustee First Unitarian Ch., Bethesda, Md., 1975—79; bd. mem. Chamber Music Columbus, 2006. Rsch. grantee, AT&T, Columbus, 1987. Fellow: World Acad. Productivity Sci., Am. Statis. Assn.; mem.: Internat. Assn. Statis. Computing (sci. sec. 1979—83, pres. 1977—79), Internat. Statis. Inst. (mem. steering com. Internat. Rsch. Ctr. 1987—89). Avocations: reading, exercise, walking, bridge. Home: 4171 Clairmont Rd Upper Arlington OH 43220-4501 Office: Ohio State U Dept Computer Info Sci Rm 395 2015 Neil Ave Columbus OH 43210-1210 Office Phone: 614-292-4281. E-mail: mmuller@columbus.rr.com, muller.m@cse-ohio-state.edu.

MULLIGAN, MICHAEL DENNIS, lawyer; b. St. Louis, Mar. 9, 1947; s. Leo Virgil and Elizabeth (Leyse) M.; m. Theresa Baker, Aug. 7, 1971; children: Brennan, Colin. BA in Biology, Amherst Coll., 1968; JD, Columbia U., 1971. Bar: Mo. 1971, U.S. Dist. Ct. (ea. dist.) Mo. 1972, U.S. Ct. Appeals (8th cir.) 1982, U.S. Tax Ct. 1985. Law clk. to judge U.S. Dist. Ct. (ea. dist.) Mo., 1971-72; assoc. Lewis, Rice & Fingersh, L.C., St. Louis, 1972-80, ptnr., 1980—. Mem. editl. bd. Estate Planning Mag., 1985—, Jour. of Taxation, BNA Estates, Gifts and Trusts Jour. Served as cpl. USMC, 1968-70. Fellow Am. Coll. Trust and Estate Counsel; mem. ABA (mem. real property, probate and trust, and taxation sects.), Mo. Bar Assn. (mem. probate and trust, taxation sects.). Office: Lewis Rice & Fingersh LC 500 N Broadway Ste 2000 Saint Louis MO 63102-2147 Home Phone: 317-726-0139; Office Phone: 314-444-7757. Business E-Mail: mmulligan@lewisrice.com.

MULLIGAN, ROSEMARY ELIZABETH, legislator; b. Chgo., July 8, 1941; d. Stephen Edward and Rose Anne (Sannasardo) Granzyk; children: Daniel R. Bonaguidi, Matthew S. Bonaguidi. AAS, Harper Coll., Palatine, Ill., 1982; student, Ill. State U., 1959-60. Paralegal Miller, Forest & Downing Ltd., Glenview, Ill., 1982-91; ind. contractor mcpl. law, 1991—. Paralegal seminar educator Harper Coll. Program chair White House Women's Econ. Leadership Summit, 1997. Pro-choice activist and mem. Ill. Ho. of Reps., 1993—, chmn. human svcs. appropriations com.; gov.'s workgroup on early childhood; gov.'s wokforce investment bd., 1999—. Recipient Disting. Alumnus award Ill. C.C. Trustee Assn., 1993, Legislator of Yr. award Ill. Assn. Cmty. Mental Health Agys., 1996, Heart Start award Nat. Ctr. Clin. Infant Programs, Legis. Leadership award Ill. Alcoholism and Drug dependence Assn., 1996, Cert. Appreciation Ill. Libr. Assn., Legis. cert. appreciation Delta Kappa Gamma Soc., 1997, Ida B. Wells-Barnett award, 1996; named Top 100 Women Making a Difference Today's Chgo. Woman, 1997; Flemming fellow Ctr. for Policy Alts., 1994. Mem. LWV, Nat. Women's Polit. Caucus, Ill. Fedn. Bus. and Profl. Women (Outstanding Working Woman of the Yr. 1997), Ill. Women in Govt., Chgo. Women in Govt. Rels., Ill. Fedn. Bus. and Profl. Women (nat. legis. platform rep. 1991-92, chair Outstanding Working Women of Ill. 1991-92, state membership chair 1989-90, state legis. co-chair, nat. platform rep. 1988-89, state legis. chair, nat. platform rep. 1987-88). Roman Catholic. Avocations: politics, tennis, reading. Home: 856 E Grant Dr Des Plaines IL 60016-6260 Office: Ill Ho of Reps State Capitol Springfield IL 62706-0001 also: 932 Lee St Ste 201 Des Plaines IL 60016-6594

MULLIKIN, THOMAS WILSON, mathematics professor; b. Flintville, Tenn., Jan. 9, 1928; s. Houston Yost and Daisy (Copeland) M.; m. Mildred Virginia Sugg, June 14, 1952; children: Sarah Virginia, Thomas Wilson, James Copeland. Student, U. South, 1946-47; AB, U. Tenn., 1950; postgrad., Iowa State U., 1952-53; A.M., Harvard, 1954, PhD, 1958. Mathematician Rand Corp., Santa Monica, Calif., 1957-64; prof. math. Purdue U., 1964-93, interim v.p., dean grad. sch., 1991-93, dean grad. sch., prof. math emeritus, 1993—. Served with USNR, 1950-52. Mem.: AAAS, Am. Math. Soc. Home: 104 Club Ct Cape Carteret NC 28584-9736

MULQUEEN, MICHAEL PATRICK, food service executive, retired military officer; b. Newburgh, NY, Mar. 9, 1938; s. Michael Peter and Mary (O'Donavan) M.; m. Charna T. Endleman, Jan. 30, 1967; children: Alissa Mulqueen Reynolds, Brian D. BA, Fordham U., 1960; MS, Troy State U., 1973. Commd. 2d lt. USMC, 1961, advanced through grades to brig. gen., 1987, ret., 1991, commanding officer Marine Air Res. Tng. Unit Denver, 1973-75, commanding officer Marine Air Control Squadron Camp Pendleton, Calif., 1975-77, ops. and exec. officer Marine Air Control Group Okinawa, Japan, 1977-78, comdr. 3d Force Svc. Support Group, 1987-89, staff sec. Fleet Marine Force Pacific hdqrs. Hawaii, 1979-81, dep. for Marine Corps matters Office Program Appraisal Washington, 1982-84, spl. asst., aide Office Sec. of the Navy, 1984-87, comdr. U.S. Mil. Entrance Processing Command North Chicago, Ill., 1989—91; exec. dir. Greater Chgo. Food Depository, 1991—. Decorated Legion of Merit, Bronze Star, Meritorious Svc. medal with gold star, Navy Achievement medal. Mem. Army-Navy Club. Roman Catholic. Avocations: golf, skiing, hunting. Office: Greater Chgo Food Depository 4100 W Ann Lurie Pl Chicago IL 60632 E-mail: mpmulqueen@gcfd.org.

MULROW, PATRICK JOSEPH, medical educator; s. Patrick J. and Delia M.; m. Jacquelyn Pinover, Aug. 8, 1953; children: Deborah, Nancy, Robert, Catherine. AB, Colgate U., 1947; MD, Cornell U., 1951; MSc (hon.), Yale U., 1969; DSc (hon.), Med. Coll. Ohio, 2005. Intern N.Y. Hosp., 1951-52, resident, 1952-54; instr. physiology Med. Coll. Cornell U., 1954-55; research fellow Stanford U., 1955-57; instr. medicine Yale U., 1957-60, asst. prof., 1960-66, assoc. prof., 1966-69, prof. medicine, 1969-75; chmn. dept. medicine Med. Coll. Ohio, Toledo, 1975—95, prof. medicine, 1975—97, prof. emeritus, 1997—. Chmn. ednl. com. Council for high blood pressure rsch. Am. Heart Assn., 1968-70, mem. exec. com., 1986-96, vice-chmn. of coun., 1990-92, chmn. 1992-94, past chmn., 1995-96; mem. study sect. NIH, 1970-74. Editorial bd. Jour. Clin. Endocrinology and Metabolism, 1966-70, 75-79, Endocrine Rsch., 1974—, Jour. Exptl. Biology and Medicine, Hypertension, 1994-98; contbr. articles to profl. jours. With USNR, 1944-46. Mem. ACP, Am. Soc. Clin. Investigation, Assn. Am. Physicians, Am. Physiol. Soc., Endocrine Soc., Am. Fedn. Clin. Rsch., Am. Clin. and Climatol. Assn., Am. Heart Assn. (nat. rsch. com., chmn. cardiovasc. regulation rsch. study com. 1986-91), Assn. Profs. Medicine, Assn. Program Dirs. in Internal Medicine, Cen. Soc. Clin. Rsch. (pres. 1988-89), Internat. Soc. Hypertension, World Hypertension League (sec.-gen. 1995-2005), Inter-Am. Soc. Hypertension, Sigma Xi (pres. Yale chpt. 1965-66), Alpha Omega Alpha. Home: 9526 Carnoustie Rd Perrysburg OH 43551-3501 Office: Med Coll Ohio Dept Medicine 3120 Glendale Ave Toledo OH 43614-5809 Business E-Mail: pmulrow@meduohio.edu.

MULROY, THOMAS ROBERT, JR., lawyer; b. Evanston, Ill., June 26, 1946; s. Thomas Robert and Dorothy (Reiner) M.; m. Elaine Mazzone, Aug. 16, 1969. Student, Loyola U., Rome, 1966; BA, U. Santa Clara, Calif., 1968; JD, Loyola U., Chgo., 1972. Bar: Ill. 1973, U.S. Dist. Ct. (no. dist.) Ill. 1973, U.S. Ct. Appeals (7th cir.) 1973. Asst. U.S. atty. No. Dist. Ill., Chgo., 1972-76; ptnr. Jenner & Block, Chgo. 1976—, chmn. products liability group; adj. prof. Northwestern U. Sch. Law, Chgo., 1978-85, Loyola U. Sch. Law, 1983—, DePaul U. Sch. Law, Chgo., Nova U. Ctr. for Study of Law. Editor: Annotated Guide to Illinois Rules of Professional Conduct; contbr. articles to profl. jours.; bd. dirs. Loyola U. Trial Advocacy Workshop, 1982—, Legal Assistance Found., Ill. Inst. for Continued Legal Edn.; chmn. inquiry panel Ill. Atty. Registration and Disciplinary Commn., spl. counsel, 1989—. Mem. Chgo. Crime Commn., 1978—. Mem. ABA, (torts and ins. pratcie, chmn. rules and evidence com.), Am. Judicature Soc., Fed. Trial Bar, Legal Club Chgo., Law Club, 7th Fed. Cir. Bar Assn., Chgo. Bar Assn., Ill. Assn. Def. Trial Counsel, Ill. Bar Assn. Clubs: Univ., Execs. of Chgo., Union League.

MUMA, LESLIE M., former data processing company executive; b. 1944; BA, U. So. Fla., 1966. Pres. Fiserv, Inc., Brookfield, Wis., 1984—99, COO, 1995—99, CEO, 1999—2005. Bd. dirs. Fiserv, Inc., 1984—, Nat. Con-Serv, Inc., The Freedom Group, Inc., MGIC Investment Corp.; bd. trustees USF Found., 2003—; mem. Dean's cir. Coll. Bus. Adminstrn.

MUNDAY, DAVE, radio personality; children: Patrick, Chris. With KY 102, KEBQ; prodn. dir. KLSO, Fox & chiefs Radio Network; radio host Oldies 95 FM, Mission, Kans. Ack announcer State Fair Motor Speedway, Mo. State Fair Grounds, I-70 Speedway. Office: Oldies 95 5800 Ridgewood Dr 6th Fl Mission KS 66202

MUNGER, CHARLES T., diversified company executive; b. Omaha, Nebr., 1924; m. Nancy Munger; 8 children. Student, U. of Mich., 1941—42, Calif. Inst. Technol., 1943; JD, Harvard Law Sch., 1948. Joined Musick Peeler & Garrett, Los Angeles, Calif.; co-founder Munger, Tolles & Olson, 1962—, ptnr., 1962—65, Wheeler Munger & Co., LA, 1962—75; chmn., CEO, Blue Chip Stamps, 1976—; vice chmn. Berkshire Hathaway, Inc., Omaha, 1978—, also chmn., CEO Wesco Fin. subs., 1983—. Chmn. Daily Jour. Corp.; bd. dirs. Costco, 1997—. Meteorological officer USAF, World War II. Named one of Forbes' Richest Americans, 2006. Office: Berkshire Hathaway Inc 1440 Kiewit Plz Omaha NE 68131-3302 also: Munger Tolles and Olson 355 S Grand Ave Los Angeles CA 90071-1560

MUNGER, PAUL R., engineering educator; b. Hannibal, Mo., Jan. 14, 1932; s. Paul O and Anne M.; m. Frieda Anna Mette, Nov. 26, 1954; children: Amelia Ann Munger Fortmeyer, Paul David, Mark James, Martha Jane Munger Cox. BSCE, Mo. Sch. Mines and Metallurgy, 1958, MSCE, 1961; PhD in Engring. Sci., U. Ark., 1972. Registered profl. engr., Mo., Ill., Ark. Instr. civil engring Mo. Sch. Mines and Metallurgy, Rolla, 1958-61, asst. prof., 1961-65; assoc. prof. U. Mo., Rolla, 1965-73, prof., 1973-99; dir. Inst. River Studies, U. Mo., Rolla, 1976-93; exec. dir. Internat. Inst. River and Lake Systems, U. Mo., Rolla, 1984-93, interim chmn. CE dept., 1998-99, prof. emeritics of CE, 2000—. Mem. NSPE, Mo. Soc. Profl. Engr., Am. Soc. Engring. Edn., ASCE, Nat. Coun. Engring. Examiners (pres. 1983-84), Mo. Bd. Architects, Profl. Engr. and Land Surveyors (chmn. 1978-84, 95-2002).

MUNKVOLD, GARY P., plant pathologist, educator; BS in Forestry, U. Ill., 1986, MS in Plant Pathology, 1988; PhD in Plant Pathology, U. Calif., Davis, 1992. Grad. rsch. asst. Ill. Natural History Survey, Champaign, 1986-88; grad. rsch. asst. dept. plant pathology U. Calif., Davis, 1988-92; asst. prof., ext. plant pathologists dept. plant pathology Iowa State U., Ames, 1993-98, assoc. prof., ext. plant pathologist dept. plant pathology, 1998—. Recipient Novartis award Am. Phytopathol. Soc., 2000. Office: Iowa State U Dept Plant Pathology 317 Bessey Hall Ames IA 50010 Fax: 515-294-9420. E-mail: munkvold@iastate.edu.

MUNOZ, ANTONIO, state legislator; b. Chgo., Feb. 18, 1964; m. Patricia; 3 children. Officer Chgo. Police Dept.; mem. Ill. Senate, Springfield, 1999—, mem. edn., lic. activities, pub. health & welfare coms. Mem. mayor's lic. commn., Local Liquor Control Sect., Chgo., 1990, Dept. Aviation, Mayor's Office Budget & Mgmt. With U.S. Army. Mem. FOP. Democrat. Office: State Capitol Capitol Bldg M103 E Springfield IL 62706-0001 also: 3720 W 26th St Chicago IL 60623-3824

MUNRO, DONALD JACQUES, philosopher, educator; b. New Brunswick, NJ, Mar. 5, 1931; s. Thomas B. and Lucile (Nadler) M.; m. Ann Maples Patterson, Mar. 3, 1956; 1 child, Sarah de la Roche. AB, Harvard U., 1953; PhD (Ford Found. fellow), Columbia U., 1964. Asst. prof. philosophy U. Mich., 1964-68, assoc. prof., 1968-73, prof. philosophy, 1973—90, prof. philosophy and Asian langs., 1990-96; prof. emeritus philosophy and Chinese, 1996—; chmn. dept. Asian langs. and cultures U. Mich., 1993-95, with Ctr. Chinese Studies, 1964—; vis. rsch. philosopher Ctr. Chinese Studies U. Calif., Berkeley, 1969-70; mem. Assn. for Asian studies China and Inner Asia Coun., 1970—72; chmn. com. on studies of Chinese civilization Am. Council Learned Socs., 1979-81. Mem. Com. on Scholarly Comm. with People's Republic China, NAS, 1978-82, China Coun. of Asia Soc., 1977-80, Com. on Advanced Study in China, 1978-82; Evans-Wentz lectr. Stanford U., 1970; Fritz lectr. U. Wash., 1980; Gilbert Ryle lectr. Trent U., Ont., 1983; John Dewey lectr. U. Vt., 1989; Ch'ien Mu lectr. Chinese U. Hong Kong, 2002-03; Tang Chun I vis. prof. Chinese U. Hong Kong, 2006. Author: The Concept of Man in Early China, 1969, the Concept of Man in Contemporary China, 1977; editor: Individualism and Holism, 1985, Images of Human Nature: A Sung Portrait, 1988, The Imperial Style of Inquiry in Twentieth Century China, 1996, A Chinese Ethics for the New Century, 2005. Exec. com. Coll. Literature, Sci. and The Arts U. Mich., 1986-89. Lt. (j.g.) USNR, 1953-57. Recipient letter of commendation Chief Naval Ops.; Disting. Svc. award U. Mich., 1968, Excellence in Edn. award, 1992; Rice Humanities award, 1993-94; Nat. Humanities faculty fellow, 1971-72; John Simon Guggenheim Found. fellow, 1978-79; grantee Social Sci. Rsch. Coun., 1965-66, Am. Coun. Learned Socs., 1982-83, China com. grantee NAS, 1990; vis. rsch. scholar Chinese Acad. Social Scis. Inst. Philosophy, Beijing, 1983, dept. philosophy Beijing U., 1990. Home: 14 Ridgeway St Ann Arbor MI 48104-1739 Office: Dept Philosophy U Mich Ann Arbor MI 48104

MUNSON, BRUCE N., state legislator; BS, Ball State U.; JD, Ind. U., Indpls. Bar: Ind. Atty. in pvt. practice; mem. from 35th dist. Ind. State Ho. of Reps., 1992—, mem. commerce and econ. devel. com., mem. family, children and human affairs coms. Bd. dirs. Century Legal Svc. Program; mem. lega. adv. com. Habitat for Humanity. Mem. Century City Bus. Assn., Dalaware County Rep. Men's Club, Kiwanis, Century Ind. Old Car Club. Address: 7009 W Santa Fe Dr Muncie IN 47304-9342

MUNSON, DAVID ROY, state legislator; b. Sioux Falls, SD, Apr. 16, 1942; s. Roy Elmer Munson and Theil Severson; m. Linda Marie Carlson, 1972; children: Steven David, Paul James, John Jeffrey. BA, Sioux Falls Coll.; postgrad., Augustana Coll. Mem. S.D. Ho. of Reps., 1979-96, asst. majority whip, 1983-84, 89-90, mem. commerce and health and human svc. coms.; vice chmn. state affairs com.; banker; mem. S.D. Senate from 10th dist., Pierre, 1996—. Mem. commerce, labor and regulation coms., state-fed. assembly Nat. Conf. State Legislators. Past mem. Sioux Vocat. Bd.; mem. Multiple Sclerosis Bd., Luth. Social Svc. Consumers Credit Adv. Bd. and Cmty. Disabilities Svc. Bd.; mem. S.D. Devel. Corp.; mem. Sioux Empire Fire Bd. Fellow Augustana Coll. Mem. NEA. Home: 1009 Sycamore Ave Sioux Falls SD 57110-5748

MUNSON, DONALD E., state legislator; Mem. S.D. Ho. of Reps.; mem. govt., oper. and audit, taxation and transp. coms.; corp. mgr., acct. Address: PO Box 731 Yankton SD 57078-0731

MUNSON, RICHARD HOWARD, horticulturist; b. Toledo, Dec. 20, 1948; s. Stanley Warren and Margaret Rose (Winter) M. BS, Ohio State U., 1971; MS, Cornell U., 1973, PhD, 1981. Plant propagator The Holden Arboretum, Kirtland, Ohio, 1973-76; asst. prof. Agrl. Tech. Inst., Wooster, Ohio, 1976-78, Tex. Tech U., Lubbock, 1981-84; dir. botanic garden Smith Coll., Northampton, Mass., 1984-95; exec. dir. The Holden Arboretum, Kirtland, Ohio, 1995-2000; dir. botanic garden U. Mo., Columbia, Mo., 2001—04; mgr. The Conservatory, Miami U., Hamilton, Ohio, 2004—. Ret. lt. col. USAR, 1971-99. Recipient Disting. Alumnus award Ohio State U. Coll. Agr., 1998. Fellow Internat. Plant Propagator's Soc.; mem. Am. Pub. Garden Assn. (com. chmn. 1987-92, 01-03), Sigma Xi, Pi Alpha Xi, Gamma Sigma Delta. Avocations: fishing, fly-tying, golf, woodworking, gardening. Office: Miami U-Hamilton 1601 University Blvd Hamilton OH 45011 Home Phone: 513-523-5168; Office Phone: 513-785-3086. Business E-Mail: munsonrh@muohio.edu.

MUNYER, EDWARD ARNOLD, zoologist; b. Chgo., May 8, 1936; s. G. and M. Munyer; m. Marianna J. Munyer, Dec. 12, 1981; children: Robert, William, Richard, Laura, Cheryl. BS, Ill. State U., 1958, MS, 1962. Biology tchr. MDR High Sch., Minonk, Ill., 1961-63; instr. Ill. State U., Normal, 1963-64; curator zoology Ill. State Mus., Springfield, 1964-67, asst. dir., 1981-98, asst. dir. emeritus, 1998—; assoc. prof. Vincennes (Ind.) U., 1967-70; dir. Vincennes U. Mus., 1968-70; assoc. curator Fla. Mus. Natural History, Gainesville, 1970-81. Contbr. articles to profl. jours. Mem. Am. Assn. Mus. (bd. dirs. 1990-95), Assn. Midwest Mus. (pres. 1990-92, lifetime achievement award for disting. svc. 1998), Ill. Assn. Mus. (bd. dirs. 1981-86, lifetime profl. achievement award 1998), Wilson Ornithol. Soc. (life). Office: Ill State Mus Spring & Edward Sts Springfield IL 62706-0001 Personal E-mail: eammjm@insightbb.com.

MURAT, WILLIAM M., legislative staff member; b. Stevens Point, Wis., Dec. 4, 1957; s. James L. and Rose Murat. BS, U. Wis., Stevens Point, 1980; JD, U. Wis., Madison, 1983; MBA, Columbia U., 1992. Asst. dist. atty. to dist. atty. Portage County, Wis., 1983-88, dist. atty. Wis., 1988-91; assemblyman Wis. State Dist. 71, 1995-99; chief of staff Congressman Tammy Baldwin. Vice chmn. Portage County Dem. Com., 1976-80, chmn., 1985-86; exec. dir. Wis. Young Dems., 1978-79, pres., 1982-83; mem. exec. com. Seventh Dist. Dems., Wis., 1978-80, 82-90; adminstrv. com. Wis. Dem. Com., 1982-99; mem. Dem. Nat. Com., 1997-99; 1st vice chair Dem. Wis., 1997-99. Mem. Phi Delta Phi, Pi Kappa Delta.

MURATA, TADAO, engineering and computer science educator; b. Takayama, Gifu, Japan, June 26, 1938; arrived in U.S., 1962; s. Yonosuke and Ryu (Aomame) M.; m. ellie Kit-Ha Shin, 1964; children: Patricia Emi, Theresa Terumi. BSE.E., Tokai U., 1962; MSE.E., U. Ill., 1964, PhD in Elec. Engring., 1966. Rsch. asst. U. Ill., Urbana, 1962-66; asst. prof. U. Ill. at Chgo., 1966-68, assoc. prof., 1970-76, prof., 1977—, UIC disting. prof., 2002—; assoc. prof. Tokai U., Tokyo, 1968-70. Vis. prof. U. Calif., Berkeley, 1976-77; cons. Nat. Bur. Stds., Gaithersburg, Md., 1984-85; panel mem. NAS, Washington, 1981-82, 83-85; vis. scientist Nat. Ctr. For Sci. Rsch., France, 1981; guest rschr. Gesellschaft für Mathematik und Datenverarbeitung, Germany, 1979; Hitachi-Endowed prof. Osaka (Japan) U., 1993-94. Editor IEEE Trans. on Software Engring., 1986-92; assoc. editor Jour. of Cirs., Sysems and Computers, 1990—;

contbr. articles to sci. and engring. jours. Recipient C.A. Petri Disting. Tech. Achievement award Soc. Design and Process Scis., 2000; Sr. univ. scholar award U. Ill., 1990; NSF grantee, 1978—, U.S.-Spain coop. rsch. grantee, 1985-87. Fellow IEEE (life; golden core charter mem. IEEE Computer Soc., Donald G. Fink Prize award 1991), Inst. Electronics, Info. and Comm. Engrs.; mem. Assn. Computing Machinery, Info. Processing Soc. Japan, European Assn. for Theoretical Computer Sci., Upsilon Pi Epsilon. Avocations: golf, travel. Office: U Ill Dept Computer Sci m/c 152 851 S Morgan St Chicago IL 60607-7042 Personal E-mail: t.murata@ieee.org.

MURDOCK, CHARLES WILLIAM, lawyer, educator; b. Chgo., Feb. 10, 1935; s. Charles C. and Lucille Marie (Tracy) Murdock; m. Mary Margaret Hennessy, May 25, 1963; children: Kathleen, Michael, Kevin, Sean. BSChemE, Ill. Inst. Tech., 1956; JD cum laude, Loyola U., Chgo., 1963. Bar: Ill. 1963, Ind. 1971. Asst. prof. law DePaul U., 1968-69; assoc. prof. law U. Notre Dame, 1969-75; prof., dean Law Sch. Loyola U., Chgo., 1975-83, 86—; dep. atty. gen. State of Ill., Chgo., 1983-86; of counsel Chadwell & Kayser, Ltd., 1986-89. Vis. prof. U. Calif., 1974; cons. Pay Bd., summer 1972, SEC, summer 1973; co-founder Loyola U. Family Bus. Program; arbitrator Chgo. Bd. Options Exch., Nat. Assn. Securities Dealers, N.Y. Stock Exch., Am. Arbitration Assn.; co-founder, mem. exec. com. Loyola Family Bus. Ctr., 1990—; bd. dirs. Plymouth Tube Co., 1993—. Author: Business Organizations, 2 vols., 1996; editor: Illinois Business Corporation Act Annotated, 2 vols., 1975; tech. editor The Business Lawyer, 1989-90. Chmn. St. Joseph County (Ind.) Air Pollution Control Bd., 1971; bd. dirs. Nat. Center for Law and the Handicapped, 1973-75, Minority Venture Capital Inc., 1973-75. Capt. USMCR. Mem. ABA, Ill. Bar Assn. (cert. of award for continuing legal edn.), Chgo. Bar Assn. (cert. of award for continuing legal edn., bd. mgrs. 1976-78), Ill. Inst. Continuing Legal Edn. (adv. com) Roman Catholic. Home: 2126 Thornwood Ave Wilmette IL 60091-1452 Office: Loyola U Sch Law 1 E Pearson St Chicago IL 60611-2055 Office Phone: 312-915-7142. Business E-Mail: cmurdoc@luc.edu.

MURNANE, MARGARET MARY, engineering and physics educator; b. Limerick, Ireland, Jan. 23, 1959; d. Matthew and Helen (Bourke) M.; m. Henry Cornelius Kapteyn, Mar. 26, 1987. MSc, U. Coll. Cork, Ireland, 1983; PhD, U. Calif., Berkeley, 1989. Postdoctoral researcher U. Calif., Berkeley, 1990; asst. prof. Wash. State U., Pullman, 1990-95; assoc. prof. U. Mich., Ann Arbor, 1996—99; prof. physics U. Colo., 1999—, fellow, Joint Inst. Lab. Astrophysics. Presdl. Young Investigator awardee NSF, 1991, Sloan Found. fellow, 1992, Presdl. faculty fellow NSF, 1993, John D. and Catherine T. MacArthur fellow, 2000. Mem. NAS, Am. Phys. Soc. (Simon Ramo award 1990, Maria Goeppert-Mayer award 1997), Optical Soc. Am., Soc. Photo-Optical Instrumentation Engrs., Assn. Women in Sci.; Fellow Am. Acad. Arts & Sciences Office: Univ Colo Joint Inst Lab Astrophysics 440 UCB Boulder CO 80309-7789

MURPHY, ANDREW J., managing news editor; Mng. editor news The Columbus (Ohio) Dispatch, mng. editor, 1990—. Office: The Columbus Dispatch 34 S 3rd St Columbus OH 43215-4241

MURPHY, DANIEL J., JR., aerospace and defense manufacturing company executive, military officer; b. Newport, RI, May 30, 1948; m. Pam Murphy; children: Dan, Kate. BS, U.S. Naval Acad., 1970; M in Law and Diplomacy, Tufts U., 1981. Exec. asst. to chief of naval ops. USN; exec. asst. to Supreme Allied Comdr. Atlantic; adminstrv. aide to Sec. of Navy; plans officer Plans and Ops. Directorate; mil. analyst Bur. Intelligence and Rsch. Dept. of State; rear adm., dir. surface warfare USN, 1996-98, vice adm., comdr. Sixth Fleet, and NATO striking & support forces So. Europe, 1998—2000; group v.p., precision systems and pres. tactical systems Alliant Techsystems (ATK), Edina, Minn., 2000—03, chmn., CEO, 2003—. Comdr. Eisenhower Battle Group and Cruiser-Destroyer Group 8, comdr. Destroyer Squadron 14, commdg. officer USS Kidd, sea tours with USS Goldsborough, USS Richard L. Page, USS Edson, USN. Office: Alliant Techsystems 5050 Lincoln Dr Minneapolis MN 55436

MURPHY, DIANA E., federal judge; b. Faribault, Minn., Jan. 4, 1934; d. Albert W. and Adleyne (Heiker) Kuske; m. Joseph Murphy, July 24, 1958; children: Michael, John E. BA magna cum laude, U. Minn., 1954, JD magna cum laude, 1974; postgrad., Johannes Gutenberg U., 1954—55, U. Minn., 1955—58; LLD, St. Johns U., 2000, U. St. Thomas, 2003. Bar: Minn. 1974, US Supreme Ct. 1980. Assoc. Lindquist & Vennum, 1974—76; mcpl. judge Hennepin County, 1976—78, Minn. State dist. judge, 1978—80; judge US Dist. Ct. for Minn., Mpls., 1980—94, chief judge, 1992—94; judge US Ct. Appeals (8th cir.), Mpls., 1994—. Chair US Sentencing Commn., 1999—2004. Bd. editors: Minn. Law Rev., Georgetown U. Jour. on Cts., Health Scis. and the Law, 1989—92. Bd. dirs. Nat. Assn. Pub. Interest Law Fellowships for Equal Justice, 1992—95, Mpls. United Way, 1985—2001, treas., 1990—94, vice-chmn., 1996—97, chmn. bd. dirs., 1997—98; bd. dirs. Bush Found., 1982—2006, chmn. bd. dirs., 1986—91; organizer, 1st chmn. adv. coun. Amicus, bd. dirs., 1976—80; chair Mpls. Charter Commn., 1973—76; bd. dirs. Ops. De Novo, 1971—76, chmn. bd. dirs., 1974—75; mem., chmn. bill of rights com. Minn. Constl. Study Commn., 1971—73; regent St. Johns U., 1978—87, 1988—98, chmn. bd., 1995—98, bd. overseers sch. theology, 1998—2001; mem. Minn. Bicentennial Commn., 1987—88; trustee Twin Cities Pub. TV, 1985—94, chmn. bd., 1990—92; trustee U. Minn. Found., 1990—, chmn. of bd., 2003—05; bd. dirs. Sci. Mus. Minn., 1988—94, vice-chmn., 1991—94; trustee U. St. Thomas, 1991—, chair exec. com., 2006—; vice chair bd. govs. U. St. Thomas Law Sch., 2001—04, chair, 2004—06; bd. dirs. Spring Hill Conf. Ctr., 1978—84; bd. govs. Hill Mus. and Manuscript Libr., 2005—; bd. dirs. Minn. Opera, 1998—2004, 2005—. Recipient Amicus Founders' award, 1980, Outstanding Achievement award, U. Minn., 1983, YWCA, 1981, Disting. Citizen award, Alpha Gamma Delta, 1985, Devitt Disting. Svc. to Justice award, 2001, Disting. Alumnus award, U. Minn. Law Sch., 2002, Woman Who Makes a Difference award, Internat. Women's Forum, 2003, Iustitia et Lex award, 2006; scholar Fulbright. Fellow: Am. Bar Found.; mem.: ABA (ethics and profl. responsibility judges adv. com. 1981—88, standing com. on jud. selection, tenure and compensation 1991—94, standing com. on fed. jud. improvements 1994—97, Appellate Judges conf. exec. com. 1996—99, chmn. ethics and profl. responsibility judges adv. com. 1997—2000), Fed. Jud. Ctr. (bd. dirs. 1990—94, 8th cir. jud. coun. 1992—94, 1992—94, convener gender fairness task force 1993, U.S. jud. conf. com. on ct. adminstrn. and case mgmt. 1994—99, chair gender fairness implementation com. 1997—98), Hist. Soc. for 8th Cir. (bd. dirs. 1988—91), Fed. Judges Assn. (bd. dirs. 1982—2003, v.p. 1984—89, pres. 1989—91), U. Minn. Alumni Assn. (bd. dirs. 1975—83, nat. pres. 1981—82), Minn. Women Lawyers (Myra Bradwell award 1996), Nat. Assn. Women Judges (Leadership Judges Jud. Adminstrn. award 1998, Honoree of Yr. 2002), Nat. Assn. Governing Bds. Univs. Colls. (dir. 1998—, vice chair 2006—), Am. Judicature Soc. (bd. dirs. 1982—93, v.p. 1985—88, treas. 1988—89, chmn. bd. 1989—91), Am. Law Inst., Hennepin County Bar Assn. (gov. coun. 1976—81), Minn. Bar Assn. (bd. govs. 1977—81), Order of Coif, Phi Beta Kappa. Office: 11 E US Courthouse 300 S 4th St Minneapolis MN 55415-1320

MURPHY, GORDON JOHN, electrical engineer, educator; b. Milw., Feb. 16, 1927; s. Gordon M. and Cecelia A. (Knerr) M.; m. Dorothy F. Brautigam, June 26, 1948; children: Lynne, Craig. BS, Milw. Sch. Engring., 1949; MS, U. Wis., 1952; PhD, U. Minn., 1956. Asst. prof. elec. engring. Milw. Sch. Engring., 1949-51; systems engr. A C Spark Plug divsn. GM, 1951-52, cons., 1959-62; instr. U. Minn., 1952-56, asst. prof. elec. engring., 1956-57; assoc. prof. elec. engring. Northwestern U., Evanston, Ill., 1957-60, prof., 1960-97, head dept. elec. engring., 1960-69; pres. IPC Systems, Inc., 1975—2004; dir. Lab. for Design of Electronic Systems Northwestern U., Evanston, Ill., 1987-97, prof. emeritus, 1997—. Cons. numerous corps., 1959—; founder, 1st chmn. Mpls. chpt. Inst. Radio Engrs. Profl. Group on Automatic Control, 1956-57, Chgo. chpt., 1959-61; expert witness in numerous patent suits, 1997-2004. Author: Basic Automatic Control Theory, 1957, 2d edit., 1966, Control Engineering, 1959; contbr. numerous articles, papers to profl. jours.; patentee TV, electronic timers, periodontal instruments and motion control systems. Mem. indsl. adv. com. Milw. Sch. Engring., 1971-2001. Served with USN, 1945-46. Recipient ECE Centennial medal U. Wis., 1991, Outstanding Alumnus award Milw. Sch. Engring. Alumni Assn., 1974; named One of Chgo.'s Ten Outstanding Young Men Chgo. Jaycees, 1961. Fellow IEEE (for edn. and rsch. in automatic control 1967); mem. feedback control systems com. 1960-68, discrete systems com. 1962-68, adminstrv. com. profl. group on automatic control 1966-69, chmn. membership and nominating coms. 1966-67); mem. Am. Automatic Control Coun. (edn. com. 1967-69), Engr.'s Coun. for Profl. Devel. (guidance com. 1967-69), Nat. Electronic Conf. (bd. dirs. 1983-85), Am. Electronics Assn. (exec. com. M.W. coun. 1990-93), Sigma Xi, Eta Kappa Nu, Tau Beta Pi. Home: 638 Garden Ct Glenview IL 60025-4105 Office: Northwestern U Elec Engring Dept Evanston IL 60208 Office Phone: 847-491-7258.

MURPHY, HAROLD, state legislator; Student, Northeastern Ill. U. Owner, operator King's Lake Resort, Ind.; mem. Ill. Ho. of Reps. from 30th dist. Supervising mgr. Charles Chew Facility, Sec. of State of Ill.; alderman Markham, Ill. Democrat.

MURPHY, JANET GORMAN, college president; b. Holyoke, Mass., Jan. 10, 1937; d. Edwin Daniel and Catherine Gertrude (Hennessey) Gorman. BA, U. Mass., 1958, postgrad., 1960-61, EdD, 1974, LLD (hon.), 1984; MEd, Boston U., 1961. Tchr. English and history John J. Lynch Jr. H.S., Holyoke, 1958-60; tchr. English Chestnut Jr. H.S., Springfield, Mass., 1961-63; instr. English and journalism Our Lady of Elms Coll., Chicopee, Mass., 1963-64; mem. staff Mass. State Coll., Lyndonville, Vt., 1977-83; pres. Mo. Western State Coll., St. Joseph, 1983—. Mem. campaign staff Robert F. Kennedy Presdl. Campaign, 1967. Recipient John Gunther Tchr. award NEA, 1961, award Women's Opportunity Com., Boston Fed. Exec. Bd., 1963, Phi Delta Kappa Educator of Yr. award NAACP, 1992; named one of 10 Outstanding Young Leaders of Greater Boston Area, Boston Jr. C. of C., 1973. Office: Mo Western State Coll Office of the President 4525 Downs Dr Saint Joseph MO 64507-2246

MURPHY, JIM, state legislator; b. St. Louis, Feb. 4, 1925; s. William Francis and Jane Marie (Lavin) M.; m. Carol Pell Popovsky, 1961; children: Karen Ann, James William. BA, St. Louis U., 1948. Alderman, Crestwood, Mo., 1981-83; mem. Mo. State Ho. of Reps. Dist. 95, 1983—. Del. Mo. State Rep. Conv., 1984, 92. Recipient Globe-Dem. Meritorious Svc. award. Home: 9314 Cordoba Ln Saint Louis MO 63126-2708

MURPHY, JOHN F., lawyer; b. Jersey City, May 24, 1954; s. John Francis and Helen Joan (Makowski) M.; m. Bridget Fagan, Aug. 4, 1984; children: Helen Mary, John William. BA, U. Conn., 1976; JD, Washington & Lee U., 1979. Bar: Mo. 1979, US Dist. Ct. (we. dist.) Mo. 1979, US Ct. Appeals (8th cir.) 1982, US Supreme Ct. 1991. Assoc. Shook, Hardy & Bacon LLP, Kansas City, Mo., 1979-85, ptnr., 1985—, chmn., 2003—. Bd. dirs. Lakemary Ctr. Endowment Assn., Paola, Kans., Friends of Spl. People, Starlight Theatre, Cath. Edn. Found.; pres. Waterford Homes Assn., 1994. Mem. Fedn. Defense and Corp. Counsel, Mo. Bar Assn., Kansas City Met. Bar Assn., Greater Kansas City C. of C. (bd. dirs.), Kansas City Econ. Devel. Corp.(bd. dirs.), Civic Coun. Greater Kans. City, Phi Beta Kappa, Phi Kappa Phi, Omicron Delta Kappa. Republican. Roman Catholic. Avocations: running, spectator sports. Office: Shook Hardy & Bacon LLP 2555 Grand Blvd Kansas City MO 64108 Office Phone: 816-474-6550. Office Fax: 816-421-5547. Business E-Mail: jmurphy@shb.com.

MURPHY, JUDITH CHISHOLM, trust company executive; b. Chippewa Falls, Wis., Jan. 26, 1942; d. John David and Bernice A. (Hartman) Chisholm. BA, Manhattanville Coll., 1964; postgrad., New Sch. for Social Research, 1965-68, Nat. Grad. Trust Sch., 1975. Asst. portfolio mgr. Chase Manhattan Bank, N.A., NYC, 1964-68; trust investment officer Marshall & Ilsley Bank, Milw., 1968-72, asst. v.p., 1972-74, v.p., 1974-75; v.p., treas. Marshall & Ilsley Invesmtent Mgmt. Corp., Milw., 1975-94; v.p. Marshall & Ilsley Trust Co., Phoenix, 1982—, Marshall & Ilsley Trust Co. Fla., Naples, 1985—; v.p., dir. instnl. sales Marshall & Ilsley Trust Co., Milw., 1994-97, sr. v.p., 1997-98, M&I Investment Mgmt. Corp., 1998—. Coun. mem. Am. Bankers Assn., Washington, 1984-86; govt. relations com. Wis. Bankers Assn., Madison, 1982-88. Contbr. articles to profl. jours. Chmn. Milw. City Plan Commn., 1986—97; commr. Milw. County Commn. on Handicapped, 1988—90; bd. dirs. Cardinal Stritch Coll., Milw., 1980—89, Children's Hosp. Wis., Milw., 1989—98, Milw. Ballet Co., 1996—2001, Milw. Ctr. for Independence, 1999—2004, Girl Scouts Milw. Area, 2002—06, Milw. Symphony Orch., 2002—, Alzheimers Assn., 2007—. Recipient Outstanding Achievement award YWCA Greater Milw., 1985, Sacajawea award Profl. Dimensions, Milw., 1988, Pro Urbe award Mt. Mary Coll., 1988, Vol. award Milw. Found., 1992; named Disting. Woman in Banking, Comml. West Mag., 1988. Mem. Milw. Analysts Soc. (sec. 1974-77, bd. dirs. 1977-80), Fin. Women Internat. (bd. dirs., v.p. 1976-80), Am. Inst. Banking (instr. 1975-78), TEMPO (charter), Profl. Dimensions (hon.), University Club, Woman's Club Wis., Rotary. Democrat. Roman Catholic. Home: 3622 N Lake Dr Milwaukee WI 53211-2644 Office: M&I Investment Mgmt Corp 111 E Kilbourn Ave Milwaukee WI 53202-3197 Business E-Mail: judith.murphy@micorp.com.

MURPHY, KAREN, sports association executive; b. 1971; With Ernst & Young, Chgo., Walt Disney Co.; contr. Chgo. Bears Football Club Inc., Lake Forest, Ill., 1999—2002, CFO & treas., 2002—. Named one of 40 Under 40, Crain's Chgo. Bus., 2006. Office: Chgo Bears Football Club Inc 1000 Football Dr Lake Forest IL 60045

MURPHY, KATHLEEN M., lawyer; b. Evergreen Park, Ill. BA, St. Xavier Coll., 1980; MA, Loyola U., Chgo., 1982, JD, 1985. Bar: Ill. 1985, US Ct. Appeals, 7th Cir., US Ct. Appeals, Fed. Cir., US Ct. Internat. Trade, US Dist. Ct., No. Dist Ill. Ptnr., nat. chair Customs and Internat. Trade Dept. and Global Trade Adv. Group Katten Muchin Zavis Rosenman, Chgo. Mem.: ABA, Women in Internat. Trade, Midwest Importers Trade Assn., Joint Industry Group, Customs and Internat. Trade Bar Assn., Am. Assn. of Exporters and Importers.

MURPHY, KEVIN M., economics professor; AB, U. Calif., 1981; PhD, U. Chgo., 1986. Asst. prof. bus. economics and indsl. rels. U. Chgo., 1986—88, assoc. prof., 1988—89, prof., 1989—93, George Pratt Schultz prof., 1993—2002, George J. Stigler prof. economics, 2002—, George J. Stigler disting. svc. prof. economics, dept. economics and grad. sch. bus., 2005—. Faculty rsch. assoc. Nat. Bur. Econ. Rsch. Co-author: Social Economics: Market Behavior in a Social Environment, 2000; co-editor: Measuring the Gains from Medical Research: An Economic Approach, 2003; contbr. articles to profl. jours. Named MacArthur fellow, John D. and Catherin T. MacArthur Found., 2005; recipient John Bates Clark Medal, Am. Econ. Assn., 1998; fellow, Earhart Found., 1980—81, 1983—84, Friedman Fund, 1981—83, Sloan Found., 1989—91. Fellow: Econometric Soc.; mem.: Am. Acad. Arts and Scis., Phi Beta Kappa. Office: Univ Chgo Grad Sch Bus 5807 S Woodlawn Ave Chicago IL 60637 Office Phone: 773-702-7280. Office Fax: 773-702-2699. E-mail: murphy@chicagogsb.edu.

MURPHY, MARY C., state legislator; BA, Coll. St. Scholastica; postgrad., U. Wis., Superior, Am. U., Ind. U. H.s. tchr.; mem. Minn. Ho. of Reps., 1976—. Mem. judiciary fin. com., chair ethics com., mem. capital investments com., labor-mgmt. rels. com.; active del. Duluth Central Labor Body AFL-CIO; mem., lector St. Raphael's Parish; dir. State Democratic Farmer-Labor Party, 1972-74, chmn. 8th Dist. credentials com., 1974—, chmn. St. Louis County Legis. Delegation, 1985-86. Mem. Duluth Fedn. Tchrs. (1st v.p. 1976-77, various coms.), Minn. Fedn. Tchrs. (legis. com. 1972-75), Am. Fedn. Tchrs. (del. nat. convs.), Minn. Hist. Soc., Alpha Delta Kappa. Office: 100 Constitution Ave Saint Paul MN 55155-1232

MURPHY, MAX RAY, lawyer; b. July 18, 1934; s. Loren A. and Lois (Mink) M.; children: Michael Lee, Chad Woodrow. BA, DePauw U., 1956; JD, Yale U., 1959; postgrad., Mich. State U., 1960. Bar: Mich. 1960. Assoc. Glassen, Parr, Rhead & McLean, Lansing, Mich., 1960—67, Lokker, Boter & Dalman, Holland, Mich., 1967—69; ptnr. Dalman, Murphy, Bidol, & Bouwens, P.C., Holland, 1969—91, Cunningham Dalman, P.C., Holland, 1991—. Instr. Lansing Bus. U., 1963-67; asst. pros. atty. Ottawa County, Mich., 1967-69. Dem. candidate for Ingham County (Mich.) Pros. Atty., 1962, 1964. Mem. ABA, Ottawa County Bar Assn. (sec. 1970-71), Mich. Bar Assn. (mem. family law sect.). Home: 3169 E Crystal Waters 3 Holland MI 49424-8091 Office: 321 Settlers Rd Holland MI 49423-3778 Office Phone: 616-392-1821. Business E-Mail: mmurphy@sirus.com.

MURPHY, MICHAEL B., state legislator; m. Suzanne Thompson. BA, U. Notre Dame, 1979. TV, polit. reporter, 1979-87; dir. comm. Lt. Gov. John Mutz, 1987-89; pub. rels. mgr. Melvin Simons Assocs., 1989-92; dir. spl. projects Anthem, Inc., 1992—; mem. Ind. State Ho. of Reps. Dist. 90, asst. Rep. floor leader, mem. labor and employment coms. Chmn. bd. Monarch Inc. Sec. Rep. 6th Dist. Com., 1993-2001, mem. edn. com., 2001—.

MURPHY, MICHAEL EMMETT, retired food company executive; b. Winchester, Mass., Oct. 16, 1936; s. Michael Cornelius and Bridie (Curran) M.; m. Adele Anne Kasupski, Sept. 12, 1959; children: Leslie Maura, Glenn Stephen, Christopher McNeil. BS in Bus. Adminstrn, Boston Coll., 1958; MBA, Harvard, 1962. Financial analyst Maxwell House div. Gen. Foods Corp., White Plains, NY, 1962-64, cost mgr. San Leandro, Calif., 1964-65, controller Jacksonville, Fla., 1965-67, Hoboken, J, 1967-68, mgr. fin. planning and analysis, 1968-69; mgr. planning Hanes Corp., Winston-Salem, NC, 1969-70, corp. controller, 1970-72; v.p. adminstrn. Hanes Corp. (Hanes Knitwear), Winston-Salem, NC, 1972-74; v.p. fin. Ryder System Inc., Miami, Fla., 1974-75, exec. v.p., 1975-79; exec. v.p., dir. Sara Lee Corp., Chgo., 1979-93, vice chmn., 1993-97. Bd. dirs. GATX Corp., Payless Shoe Source, Inc., CNH Global N.V., Coach Inc., Bassett Furniture Industries, Inc., No. Funds. Mgmt. adviser Jr. Achievement, 1965-66; mem. exec. com. Hudson County Tax Rsch. Coun., 1967-68; trustee Boston Coll., 1980-88; chmn. Civic Fedn. Chgo., 1984-86; bd. dirs. Jobs for Youth, Chgo., 1983-86, Lyric Opera, 1986-2002; bd. dirs. Northwestern Meml. Hosp., Chgo., 1989-2000, Big Shoulders Fund, Chgo. Ctrl. Area Com., 1995—, Chgo. Cultural Ctr. Found., 1995—, Met. Pier and Exposition Authority, 2004—, Joffrey Ballet, 2006—; prin. Chgo. United, 1995-98. Mem. Nat. Assn. Mfrs. (bd. dirs. 1989-96, dir. Big Shoulders Fund 1995—), Fin. Execs. Inst., Hoboken C. of C., Winson-Salem C. of C., Miami C. of C., Internat. Platform Assn., UN Assn., Ouimet Scholar Alumni Group, Beta Gamma Sigma. Roman Catholic. Home: 1242 N Lake Shore Dr Chicago IL 60610-2361 Office: Sara Lee Corp 3 First National Plz Chicago IL 60602 Personal E-mail: mebmurphy@aol.com.

MURPHY, PATRICK JOSEPH, state representative; b. Dubuque, Iowa, Aug. 24, 1959; s. Lawrence John and Eileen (Heitz) M.; m. Therese Ann Gulick, Dec. 27, 1980; children: Jacob, John, Joey, Natalie. BA, Loras Coll., 1980. Transporter, security and safety officer, mental health technician Mercy Health Ctr., Dubuque, Iowa, 1975-88; documentation specialist software systems Cycare Systems Inc., Dubuque, 1988-90; state representative State of Iowa, Des Moines, 1989—99; instr. .E. Iowa C.C., 1999—. Adv. com. Iowa Birth Defects, 1995. Recipient Robert Tyson award Cmty. Action Assn., 1993, Pub. Svc. award Coalition for Family and Children's Svcs., 1994; Henry Toll fellow, 1996. Mem. NAACP, YMCA, Dubuque Mental Health Assn. (bd. dirs., Legis. of Yr.), Loras Club. Democrat. Roman Catholic. Avocations: weightlifting, jogging. Home: 155 N Grandview Ave Dubuque IA 52001-6325 Office: Ho Of Reps Des Moines IA 50319-0001

MURPHY, RAYMOND, state legislator; b. St. Louis, Dec. 15, 1937; m. Lynette; eight children. Student, Detroit Inst. Tech. Mem. Mich. Ho. of Reps from dist. 17, Lansing, 1983-94, Mich. Ho. of Reps from dist. 7, Lansing, 1995-98, Mich. Senate from 3rd dist., Lansing, 1998—. Spkr. pro tem Mich. Ho. Reps., chair labor com., mem bus. & fin. com., house oversight com., tourism & recreation coms. Real estate broker. Mem. NAACP, Nat. Black Caucus State Legis., Elks, Masons, Lions, Optimist. Office: State Capitol PO Box 30036 Lansing MI 48909-7514

MURPHY, SANDRA ROBISON, lawyer; b. Detroit, July 28, 1949; m. Richard Robin. BA, Northwestern U., 1971; JD, Loyola U., Chgo., 1976. Bar: U.S. Dist. Ct. (no. dist.) Ill. 1976. Assoc. Notz, Craven, Mead, Maloney & Price, Chgo., 1976-78; ptnr. McDermott, Will & Emery, Chgo., 1978—. Mem. ABA (family law sect.), Ill. Bar Assn. (chair sect. family law coun. 1987-88), Chgo. Bar Assn. (chair matrimonial law com. 1985-86), Am. Acad. Matrimonial Lawyers (sec. 1990-91, v.p. 1991-92, pres. Ill. chpt. 1992-93, pres.-elect 1994-95, pres. 1995-96), Legal Club Chgo. Business E-Mail: smurphy@mwe.com.

MURPHY, SHARON MARGARET, retired communications educator; b. Milw., Aug. 2, 1940; d. Adolph Leonard and Margaret Ann (Hirtz) Feyen; m. James Emmett Murphy, June 28, 1969 (dec. May 1983); children: Shannon Lynn, Erin Ann; m. Bradley B. Niemcek, Aug. 7, 1999. BA, Marquette U., 1965; MA, U. Iowa, 1970, PhD, 1973. Cert. K-14 tchr., Iowa. Tchr. elem. and secondary schs., Wis., 1959-69; dir. publs. Kirkwood C.C., Cedar Rapids, Iowa, 1969-71; instr. journalism U. Iowa, Iowa City, 1971-73; asst. prof. U. Wis., Milw., 1973-79; assoc. prof. So. Ill. U., Carbondale, 1979-84; dean, prof. Marquette U., Milw., 1984-94; prof. Bradley U., Peoria, Ill., 1994—2006, provost, v.p. acad. affairs, 1994-97, pres. Cmty. Career and Tech. Ctr., 1997-98, prof. emeritus, 2006—. Pub. rels. dir., editor Worldwide mag., Milw., 1965—68; reporter Milw. Sentinel, 1967; Fulbright sr. lectr. U. Nigeria, Nsukka, 1977—78; Fulbright sr. scholar U. Ljubljana, Slovenia, 2002. Author: Other Voices: Black, Chicano & American Indian Press, 1971; (with Wigal) Screen Experience: An Approach to Film, 1968; (with Murphy) Let My People Know: American Indian Journalism, 1981; (with Schilpp) Great Women of the Press, 1983; editor: (with others) International Perspectives on News, 1982. Mem. Peoria Riverfront Commn., 1995—2000; co-chair Peoria Race Rels. Com., 1999—2000; mem. NCA Higher Learning Commn.; bd. dirs. Dirksen Congl. Leadership Ctr., 1994—2000, Dow Jones Newspaper Fund, NY, 1986—95, Peoria Symphony, 1996—2002. Recipient Merit medal Journalism Edn. Assn., 1976, Tchg. Excellence award Amoco, 1977, Outstanding Achievement award Greater Milw. YWCA, 1989, Paul Snider Tchg. Excellence award Bradley U., 2005; named Knight of Golden Quill, Milw. Press Club, 1977; Nat. headliner Women in Comm., Inc., 1985. Mem. Assn. Edn. in Journalism and Mass Comm. (pres. 1986-87), Soc. Profl. Journalists, Nat. Press Club, Accrediting Coun.on Edn. in Journalism and Mass Comm. (v.p. 1983-86). Democrat. Roman Catholic. Office: Bradley U Global Comm Ctr Peoria IL 61625-0001 Home: 17193 Old 61 Rd Gays Mills WI 54631 Business E-Mail: smm@bradley.edu.

MURPHY, STEPHEN JOSEPH, III, prosecutor; b. St. Louis, Sept. 23, 1962; s. Stephen Joseph and Mary Elizabeth Murphy; m. Amy Elizabeth Uhl, June 8, 1996. BS, Marquette U., 1984; JD, St. Louis U., 1987. Bar: Mo. 1987, Mich. 1998. Trial atty. US Dept. Justice, Washington, 1987-92, asst. US atty. (ea. dist.) Mich. Detroit, 1992-2000, US atty. (ea. dist.) Mich., 2005—; asst. gen. counsel Gen. Motors Corp., Detroit, 2000—05. Adj. prof. trial practice, bus. crime U. Detroit Mercy, 1993-2000; adj. prof. evidence Ave. Maria, 2002; master of the bench Am. Inn of Ct., Detroit, 1996-99. Contbr. articles to profl. jours. Big brother Big Bros./Big Sisters of S.E. Mich., Southfield, 1993-96; co-chmn. Combined Fed. Campaign, Detroit, 1993. Recipient Commendation, Bur. ATF, 1993, Letter of Thanks from Dir. of FBI, 1996, Commendation, U.S. Secret Svc., 1998, Commendation, Detroit FBI, 1999, Commendation, Motion Picture Assn. Am., 1999. Mem. State Bar Mich. (bd. commrs. 2002-05, com. rules criminal procedure 2001-05), Fed. Bar Assn., Nat. Lawyers Assn., Pros. Attys. Assn. Mich. Roman Catholic. Office: US Attys Office 211 W Fort St #2001 Detroit MI 48226-3211 Business E-Mail: stephen.j.murphy@usdoj.gov.

MURPHY, STEVE, radio personality; Grad. History, Rutgers U. With Sta. WCCO Radio, Mpls., news anchor, mng. editor. Office: WCCO 625 2nd Ave S Minneapolis MN 55402

MURPHY, STEVEN LESLIE, state legislator, utilities company official; b. San Francisco, Sept. 9, 1957; s. Russell Jr. and Helen Glendora (Black) M.; m. Robin Estelle Stelling, Feb. 9, 1979; children: Nikolaas Russell, Matthew Steven. AS in Bus. Mgmt., Red Wing Tech. Coll., Minn., 1992. Operator No. St. Red Wing, 1981—; mem. Minn. Senate from 29th dist., St. Paul, 1992—. Steward Unit 47 Local 949 Internat. Brotherhood Elec. Workers, Red Wing, 1987—. Bd.dirs. CSAP Open/Charity Golf Tournament, Frontenac, Minn.; co-chair Fireman Caucus, Minn. Legislature, 1992—; vice-chair Vets. Com., Minn. Senate, 1992—. Served with USMC, 1976-80. Mem. Am. Legion, Marine Corps League. Mem. Democratic-Farmer Labor Party. Methodist. Avocations: hunting, fishing. Home: PO Box 40 Red Wing MN 55066-0040 Office: Minn State Senate State Capital Bldg 301 Saint Paul MN 55155-0001

MURPHY, THEODORE R., II, utilities executive; BA in Econs., Trinity Coll., 1980; MBA in Fin., Columbia U., 1986. Chartered fin. analyst. Asst. v.p., comml. loan officer Conn. Bank and Trust; dir. credit risk mgmt. Philbro Energy; v.p. power mktg. and trading AIG Trading; v.p., market risks Enron Corp., 1997—2000; sr. v.p., chief risk officer Enron Europe Ltd., 2001—02; sr. v.p. Cinergy Corp., Cin., 2002—, chief risk officer, 2002—. Mem. com. chief risk officers Cinergy Corp. Office: Cinergy Corp 139 E 4th St Cincinnati OH 45202

MURPHY, TOM, radio personality; b. Lorain, Ohio; m. Tracey Murphy; 1 child, Sean. Radio host WNWV, Elyria, Ohio. Avocation: auto racing. Office: WNWV 538 W Broad St PO Box 4006 Elyria OH 44036

MURRAY, ANDY, professional hockey coach; b. Gladstone, MB, Can., 1951; m. Ruth Murray; children: Braden, Jordan, Sarah. BA in Polit. Sci./Sociology, Brandon U., 1972, BA in Edn., 1974; MS in Sports Mgmt., St. Thomas U., 1986. Asst. coach Brandon U., 1974—76, head coach, 1978—81; asst. coach Hershey Bears, 1987—88; head coach Brandon Travelers, Manitoba Jr. A Hockey League, 1976—78; asst. coach Phila. Flyers, 1988-90, Minn. North Stars, 1990-92, Winnipeg Jets, 1993-95; head coach Can. Nat. Team, 1996-98, LA Kings, 1999—2006, St. Louis Blues, 2006—. Office: St Louis Blues Hockey Club Savvis Ctr 1401 Clark Ave Saint Louis MO 63103

MURRAY, CONNIE WIBLE, state official, former state legislator; b. Tulsa, Oct. 13, 1943; d. Carl Prince Lattimore and Jimmie Bell Henry; m. Jarrett Holland Murray, May 4, 1995. Cert. of oral hygiene, Temple U., 1965; BA, Loyola Coll., 1975; JD, U. Md., 1980. Registered dental hygienist, Bethlehem, Pa., 1965-66, Joppa, Md., 1966-77; law clk. Hon. Albert P. Close, Belair, Md., 1980-81; atty., 1981-85; realtor, 1985-90; mem. Mo. Ho. of Reps., Jefferson City, 1990-96; pub. svc. commr. State of Mo., Jefferson City, 1997—. House mgr. Articles ot Impeachment of Judith Moriarty, Mo. Sec. of State, 1994; mem. budget com. Mo. Ho. of Reps., also mem. appropriations social svcs. and corrections com., judiciary and ethics com., civil and criminal law and accounts, opers. and fin. com., interim com. for fed. funds and block grants, commn. on intergovtl. affairs, commn. on mgmt. and productivity, legis. oversight com. for ct. automation, ho. automation com. Bd. dirs. North Springfield Betterment Assn., 1989; vocat. adv. bd., dir. house intern programs Nat. Conf. State Legislators. Named Outstanding Freshman Legis. on Health Care Issues, Mo. Rep. Caucus, 1992; recipient Jud. Conf. Legis. award Mo. Jud. Conf., 1994, Outstanding Woman Legis. award Assn. Probate and Assoc. Cir. Judges, 1995. Mem. LWV (bd. dirs. Springfield 1989, treas.), Nat. Order Women Legis., Nat. Conf. State Legis., Nat. Women's Polit. Caucus, Women Legis. Mo., Mo. Bar Assn. (Adminstr. for Justice award), Am. Legis. Exch. Counsel, Ctr. for Am. Women in Politics, Greene County Bar Assn., Forum-A Women's Natwork, Women in Govt. Avocations: golf, bicycling, jogging, travel.

MURRAY, DANIEL RICHARD, lawyer; b. Mar. 23, 1946; s. Alfred W. and Gloria D. Murray. AB, U. Notre Dame, 1967; JD, Harvard U., 1970. Bar: Ill. 1970, U.S. Dist. Ct. (no. dist.) Ill. 1970, U.S. Ct. Appeals (7th cir.) 1971, U.S. Supreme Ct. 1974. Ptnr. Jenner & Block, Chgo., 1970—. Trustee Chgo. Mo. and Western Rlwy. Co., 1988-97; adj. prof. U. Notre Dame, 1997—. Co-author: Secured Transactions, 1978, Illinois Practice: Uniform Commercial Code Forms, 2006, Uniform Laws Annotated-Uniform Commercial Code Forms, 2007, Illinois Practice: Uniform Commercial Code with Illinois Code Comments, 2007. Bd. regents Big Shoulders Fund, Archdiocese of Chgo., Bernardin Ctr., Cath. Theol. Union. Mem.: Assn. Transp. Practitioners, Transp. Lawyers Assn., Am. Coll. Comml. Fin. Lawyers, Am. Bankruptcy Coll., Am. Law Inst., Am. Bankruptcy Inst., Cath. Lawyers Guild (bd. dirs.), Lawyers' Club Chgo. Roman Catholic. Home: 1307 N Sutton Pl Chicago IL 60610-2007 Office: Jenner & Block LLP 330 N Wabash Ave Ste 3800 Chicago IL 60611-3605 Office Phone: 312-923-2953. Business E-Mail: dmurray@jenner.com.

MURRAY, DIANE ELIZABETH, librarian; b. Detroit, Oct. 15, 1942; d. Gordon Lisle and Dorothy Anne (Steketee) LaBoueff; m. Donald Edgar Murray, Apr. 22, 1968. AB, Hope Coll., 1964; postgrad., Mich. State U., East Lansing, 1964-66; MLS, Western Mich. U., 1968; MM, Aquinas Coll., 1982. Catalog libr., asst. head acquisitions sect. Mich. State U. Librs., East Lansing, 1968-77; libr. tech. and automated svcs. Hope Coll., Holland, Mich., 1977-88; dir. librs. DePauw U., Greencastle, Ind., 1988-91; acquisitions libr. Grand Valley State U., Allendale, Mich., 1991—. Sec., vice chair, chairperson bd. trustees Mich. Libr. Consortium, Lansing, 1981—85. V.p. Humane Soc. Putnam County, Greencastle, 1990—91; bd. dirs. Loutit Dist. Libr., 1999—. Mem.: ALA. Methodist. Avocations: dog breeding and showing, handbell ringing. Office: Grand Valley State U Zumberge Libr Allendale MI 49401 Business E-Mail: murrayd@gvsu.edu.

MURRAY, GEORGE E., lawyer; b. Mo., 1954; BA magna cum laude, Dartmouth Coll., 1976; JD cum laude, U. Mo., 1979. Bar: Mo. 1979. Ptnr. Bryan Cave LLP, St. Louis, group co-leader Real Estate Devel. Construction and Project Fin. Note and comment editor: Mo. Law Rev., 1978-79. Mem. ABA, Order of Barristers, Order of Coif. Office: Bryan Cave LLP One Metropolitan Square 211 N Broadway, Ste 3600 Saint Louis MO 63102 Office Phone: 314-259-2344. E-mail: gemurray@bryancave.com.

MURRAY, JAMES A., bishop; b. Jackson, Mich., July 5, 1932; s. James Albert and Marcella Clare (Harris) Murray. BA, Sacred Heart Sem., Detroit; STB, St. John Sem., Plymouth, Mich.; JCL, Cath. U. Am., Washington. DC. Ordained priest Diocese of Lansing, Mich., 1958—, chancellor, moderator of curia, judge of tribunal; pastor St. Joseph Parish, St. Joseph, Mich., 1958—61, St. Mary Cathedral, 1962—73, rector, 1973—97; pastor St. Therese Parish, St. Gerard Parish, Lansing; monsignor, 1993; ordained bishop, 1998; bishop Diocese of Kalamazoo, Mich., 1997—. Roman Catholic. Office: Kalamazoo Diocese 215 N Westnedge Ave Kalamazoo MI 49007-3718*

MURRAY, JOHN PATRICK, psychologist, educator, researcher; b. Cleve., Sept. 14, 1943; s. John Augustine and Helen Marie (Lynch) M.; m. Ann Coke Dennison, Apr. 17, 1971; children: Jonathan Coke, Ian Patrick. PhD, Cath. U. Am., 1970. Rsch. dir. Office U.S. Surgeon Gen. NIMH, Bethesda, Md., 1969-72; asst. to assoc. prof. psychology Macquarie U., Sydney, 1973-79; vis. assoc. prof. U. Mich., Ann Arbor, 1979-80; dir. youth and family policy Boys Town Ctr., Boys Town, ebr., 1980-85; prof., dir. Sch. Family Studies and Human Svcs. Kans. State U., Manhattan, 1985-98, interim assoc. vice provost rsch., 1998—2000, emeritus prof. devel. psychology, 2008—; vis. scholar Ctr. on Media and Child Health Harvard U. Med. Sch., 2004—. Scholar-in-residence Mind Sci. Found., San Antonio, 1996-97; mem. children's TV com. CBS, 1996-99. Author: Television and Youth: 25 Years of Research and Controversy, 1980, The Future of Children's TV, 1984, (with H.T. Rubin) Status Offenders: A Sourcebook, 1983, (with E.A. Rubenstein, G.A. Comstock) Television and Social Behavior, 3 vols., 1972, (with A. Huston and others) Big World, Small Screen: The Role of Television in American Society, 1992, (with C. Fisher and others) Applied Developmental Science, 1996, Children and Television: 50 Years of Research (with N. Pecora and E. Wartella), 2006; contbr. numerous articles to profl. jours. Mem. Nebr. Foster Care Rev. Bd., 1982-84; mem. Advocacy Office for Children and Youth, 1980-85; mem. Nat. Coun. Children and TV, 1982-87; trustee The Villages Children's Homes, 1986—, Menninger Found., 1996—; mem. children's TV adv. bd. CBS-TV, 1996-99. Fellow Am. Psychol. Assn. (pres. div. child youth and family svcs. 1990); mem. Internat. Comm. Assn., Soc. Rsch. in Child Devel., Royal Commonwealth Soc. (London), Manhattan Country Club. Office: Kans State U 303 Justin Hall Manhattan KS 66506-1304 Home: 312 Landing Ln Chestertown MD 21620 Office Phone: 785-532-1456. E-mail: jpm@ksu.edu.

MURRAY, PETER See HAUTMAN, PETE

MURRAY, RAYMOND HAROLD, physician; b. Cambridge, Mass., Aug. 17, 1925; s. Raymond Harold and Grace May (Dorr) M.; children— Maureen, Robert, Michael, Margaret, David, Elizabeth, Catherine, Anne. BS, U. Notre Dame, 1946; MD, Harvard U., 1948. Diplomate Am. Bd. Internal Medicine, also Sub-bd. Cardiovascular Disease. Practice medicine, Grand Rapids, Mich., 1955-62; asst. prof. to prof. medicine Ind. U. Sch. Medicine, 1962-77; prof. dept. medicine Coll. Human Medicine Mich. State U., Lansing, 1977-95, chmn. dept. medicine Coll. Human Medicine, 1977-89, emeritus, 1995—. Chmn. aeromed.-bioscis. panel Sci. Adv. Bd., USAF, 1977-81; mem. adv. coun. Office Alternative Medicine/NIH, 1997-99. Contbr. numerous articles to profl. publs. Served with USNR, 1942-45; Served with USPHS, 1950-53. Master: ACP (gov. Mich. chpt. 1994—98); mem.: Am. Fedn. Clin. Rsch., Am. Heart Assn. (fellow coun. clin. cardiology). E-mail: Raymondmur@aol.com.

MURRAY, ROBERT WALLACE, chemistry professor; b. Brockton, Mass., June 20, 1928; s. Wallace James and Rose Elizabeth (Harper) M.; m. Claire K. Murphy, June 10, 1951; children: Kathleen A., Lynn E., Robert Wallace, Elizabeth A., Daniel J., William M., Padraic O'D. AB, Brown U., 1951; MA, Wesleyan U., Middletown, Conn., 1956; PhD, Yale U., 1960. Mem. tech. staff Bell Labs., Murray Hill, NJ, 1959-68; prof. chemistry U. Mo., St. Louis, 1968-81, chmn. dept., 1975-80, Curators' prof., 1981-2000, Curators' prof. emeritus, 2001—. Vis. prof. Engler-Bunte Inst. U. Karlsruhe, Fed. Republic Germany, 1982, dept. chemistry Univ. Coll., Cork, Ireland, 1989; cons. to govt. and industry. Co-editor: Singlet Oxygen, 1979; contbr. articles to profl. jours. Mem. Warren (N.J.) Twp. Com., 1962-63, mayor, 1963; mem. Planning Com. and Bd. Health, 1962-64, Bd. Edn., 1966-68. Served with USN, 1951-54; Lt. comdr. USNR. Grantee EPA, NSF, IH, Office of Naval Research. Fellow AAAS, Am. Inst. Chemists, N.Y. Acad. Scis.; mem. Am. Soc. Photobiology, Am. Chem. Soc., The Oxygen Soc., Sigma Xi. Home: 1810 Walnutway Dr Saint Louis MO 63146-3659 Office: Univ Mo Dept Chemistry Saint Louis MO 63121 Personal E-mail: kinsale63@aol.com.

MURRY, CHARLES EMERSON, lawyer, federal official; b. Hope, ND, June 23, 1924; s. Raymond Henry and Estelle Margarete (Skeim) M.; m. Donna Deane Kleve, June 20, 1948; children: Barbara, Karla, Susan, Bruce, Charles. BS, U. ND, Grand Forks, 1948, JD, 1950. Bar: ND 1950. Mem. firm Nelson and Heringer, Rugby, ND, 1950-51; dir. ND Legis. Council, 1951-75; adj. gen. with rank of maj. gen. State of ND, Bismarck, 1975-84; mgr. Garrison Diversion Conservancy Dist., 1985-93. Cons. Council State Govts.; mem. res. forces policy bd. Sec. of Def. Vice-pres. Mo. Slope Luth. Home of Bismarck, 1965-66. Served with AUS, 1942-45. Decorated D.S.M., Legion of Merit, Meritorious Service medal, Bronze Star, Army Commendation medal; Fourragere Belgium; Orange Lanyard Netherlands; recipient Sioux award U. ND, 1970; Gov.'s award of excellence, 1971; Nat. Leadership award Bismarck C. of C., 1971 Mem. Adjs. Gen. Assn. (exec. com., sec. 1983-84), Nat. Legis. Conf. (past chmn.), N.G. Assn., Am. Bar Assn., ND Bar Assn., Commrs. Uniform State Laws. Lodges: Elks, Masons. Lutheran. Office: 5505 Ponderosa Ave Bismarck ND 58503-9159

MURTAUGH, CHRISTOPHER DAVID, lawyer; b. Darby, Pa., Oct. 25, 1945; s. John Michael and Rita (Sullivan) M.; m. Nancy R. Hanauer, Nov. 30, 1968; children: Jason C., Colin M., Alison M. AB, U. Ill., 1967, JD, 1970. Bar: Ill. 1970, Fla. 1973, U.S. Dist. Ct. (no. dist.) Ill. 1975. Assoc. to ptnr. Winston & Strawn LLP, Chgo., 1974—, capital ptnr., 1987—, real estate dept. chmn., 1994—2005. Mem. Glen Ellyn (Ill.) Capital Improvements Com., 1985-89, Glen Ellyn Plan Com., 1989-96, Met. Planning Coun., 1995—; bd. visitors U. Ill. Coll. of Law, 1998-2001. bd. dirs. LifeSource Blood Svcs., 2005—; Lt. USNR, 1971-74. Mem. ABA, Am. Coll. Real Estate Lawyers, Fla. Bar Assn., Ill. State Bar Assn., Chgo. Bar Assn., Order of Coif. Office: Winston & Strawn LLP 35 W Wacker Dr Ste 4200 Chicago IL 60601-1695 Office Phone: 312-558-5600. E-mail: cmurtaugh@winston.com.

MUSACCHIO, ROBERT A., medical association administrator; B of Econs., SUNY; D of Econs., U. Wis. Sr. v.p. membership & info., chief info. officer AMA, Chgo. Bus. dir., mng. editor AMA's Health Insight, AMA's Website; mem. bd. advisors Intel. Contbr. articles to profl. jours. Office: Jour Am Med Assn 515 N State St Chicago IL 60610-4325

MUSCHLER, AUDREY LORRAINE, insurance broker; b. New Britain, Conn., May 24, 1928; d. Leonard Marl and Carolyn Dorothy (Low) Jackson; m. Arthur F. Muschler, Aug. 28, 1954; children: George F., James A., John L. Grad., Edgewood Coll., 1948. Agt. Fidelity Mut. Life Ins. Co., Chgo., 1953-63; ins. broker Oak Brook, Ill., 1975—. Co-author: Oak Brook, a concise history of the Village, 1990. Co-founder, 1st pres. Oak Brook Hist. Soc., 1975—, Fullersburg Hist. Found., Oak Brook, 1986—; co-founder, v.p., treas. Salt Creek Greenway Assn., Oak Brook, 1988-97; co-founder, co-dir, Mayslake Landmark Conservancy, Oak Brook, 1993-2000; active Grace Episcopal Churchwomen, 1970—, pres., 1987-89. Mem. Nat. Assn. Life Underwriters, DuPage Life Underwriters, PEO Sisterhood (pres. 1985-87). Republican. Avocation: historic preservation. Home: 55 Yorkshire Woods Oak Brook IL 60523-1472 E-mail: artimusm@aol.com.

MUSCOPLAT, CHARLES, dean; b. St. Paul; B in Chemistry, U. Minn., D in Vet. Microbiology. Faculty mem. vet. medicine U. Minn., 1976-83, prof. dept. animal sci., dean Coll. Agrl., Food and Environ. Scis., v.p. for agrl. policy, dir. Minn. Agrl. Experiment Sta., 1999—. Bd. dirs. Minn. Acad. Sci.; mem. bd. on agr. AS/NRC/ mem. bd. on sci. and tech. Internat. Devel.; mem. planning group Nat. Strategy for Biotech., U.S.-Indonesia Agrl. Biotechnology Workshop; sci. advisor State Dept. and the U.S. Agy. for Internat. Devel. Contbr. articles to profl. jours. Achievements include developed the nations first biotechnology animal health product (Genecol 99); played a key role in the development for the first U.S. biotechnology plant product herbicide-tolerant corn. Office: Coll Agrl Food & Environ Scis Rm 277 CofH 1420 Eckles Ave Saint Paul MN 55108

MUSHALA, MICHAEL C., career officer; BS in Materials Engring., Rensselaer Polytech. Inst., 1969, MS in Materials Engring., 1971, D in Materials Engring., 1973. Commd. 2d lt. USAF, 1969, advanced through grades to brig. gen., 1996; T-38 instr. pilot Vance AFB, Okla., 1975-76; chief T-38 pilot for operational test/evaluation Hdqrs. Air Tng. Command, Randolph AFB, Tex., 1976-78, ops. staff officer, dir. for ops. staff, 1978-79; instr. dept. of engring. mechanics USAF Acad., Colorado Springs, Colo., 1979-82; aide-de-camp to the chief of staff Hdqrs. Supreme Allied Powers Europe, Mons, Belgium, 1983-85; investment strategy mgr. Andrews AFB, Md., 1985-86; chief, plans divsn., sci. and tech. deputate, 1986-87; exec. officer to dep. chief of staff, tech. and plans, 1987-88; dep. program dir., space systems divsn. Nat. Aeronautics and Space Adminstrn. Advanced Launch Sys., LA, 1988-90; sr. mil. asst. to undersec. of def. for acquisition Office of the Sec. of Def., The Pentagon, Washington, 1991-92; F22 sys. program dir. Air Force Material Command, Hanscom AFB, Mass., 1996—. Sr. rsch. fellow Indsl. Coll. of the Armed Forces, 1991. Office: ASC/YF 2130 5th St Bldg 50 Wright Patterson AFB OH 45433-7003

MUSIAL, STAN(LEY) (FRANK MUSIAL), hotel and restaurant executive, former baseball team executive, former baseball player; b. Donora, Pa., Nov. 21, 1920; s. Lukasz M.; m. Lillian Labash, 1939; children: Richard, Geraldine, Janet, Jean. Baseball player St. Louis Cardinals Farm Team, 1938-41; 1st baseman, outfielder St. Louis Cardinals, Nat. League, 1941-63; sr. v.p. St. Louis Cardinals, 1963-91; pres. Stan Musial & Biggies, Inc., St. Louis. Author: Stan Musial: The Man's Own Story, 1964. Served with USNR, World War II. Voted Nat. League Rookie of Yr., 1943; named most valuable player Nat. League, 1943, 46, 48; mem. Nat. League All-Star Team, 1943-44, 46-63; voted most valuable player Baseball Writers Com., 1946; Maj. League Player of Year Sporting News, 1946, 51; Sid Mercer award N.Y. Baseball Writers, 1947; Kenesaw Mountain Landis Meml. plaque, 1948; Sports Illus. Sportsman of Yr., 1957; recipient Freedom Leadership medal, 1968; named to Baseball Hall of Fame, 1969; holder .331 lifetime batting average. Office: Stan the Man Inc 1650 Des Peres Rd Ste 125 Saint Louis MO 63131-1899

MUSSALLEM, MICHAEL A., healthcare company executive; BChemE, Rose-Hulman Inst. Tech., 1974. With Union Carbide, Baxter Healthcare, Deerfield, Ill., 1979—, various positions in mfg., engring. and product devel., gen. mgr. Access products, v.p. product devel. Parenterals, gen. mgr. Pharms. divsn., pres. Bentley divsn., group v.p. Baxter Surg. Group, chmn. Baxter Asia-Pacific Bd., group v.p. Baxter cardiovascular and biopharms.; chmn., CEO Edwards Life Sci. Corp., Irvine, Calif., 2000—. Bd. dirs. Calif. Health Care Inst., Advanced Med. Optics, Adva Med, UCI CEO Roundtable, Octane, Keck Grad. Inst. Office: Edwards Lifesciences 1 Edwards Way Irvine CA 92614

MUSSER, CHERRI M., information technology executive; m. Jack Musser. BA in Math., Miss. State Univ., 1973; MBA, Southern Methodist Univ. Various positions from programmer to dir. bus. sys. Texas Instruments, 1973—94, v.p. R&D, TI software, 1994—96; process information officer, bus. svcs. GM, 1996; acting chief information officer GM Europe; group v.p., CIO GMAC, Detroit, 2003—08; v.p., CIO Electronic Data Systems, Plano, Tex., 2008—. Recipient Coll. of Arts & Scis. Alumnus of Yr., Miss. State Univ., 1999. Mem.: Mich. Coun. Women in Tech. (pres. 2005—). Office: EDS 5400 Legacy Dr Plano TX 75024 Office Phone: 313-665-5906. Office Fax: 313-665-5908. Business E-Mail: cherri.musser@gm.com.*

MUSSER, TERRY M., state legislator; Mem. Wis. State Assembly. Home: W13550 Murray Rd Black River Falls WI 54615-5102

MUSTOE, THOMAS ANTHONY, physician, plastic surgeon; b. Columbia, Mo., June 29, 1951; s. Robert Moore and Carolyn (Swett) M.; m. Kathryn Claire Stallcup, Aug. 13, 1977; children: Anthony, Lisa. BA cum laude in biology, Harvard Coll., 1973, MD cum laude, 1978. Diplomate Am. Bd. Otolaryngology, Am. Bd. Plastic Surgery; licensed Miss. 1985, Ill. 1991. Rsch. assoc. dept. microbiology Harvard Med. Sch., Cambridge, Mass., 1976-77; intern in medicine Mass. Gen. Hosp., Boston, 1978-79; resident in surgery Peter Bent Brigham Hosp., Boston, 1979-80; resident in otolaryngology Mass. Eye and Ear Infirmary, Boston, 1980-82, chief resident, 1982-83; resident in plastic surgery Brigham and Women;s Hosp., Children's Hosp., Boston, 1983-84, chief resident, 1984-85; asst. prof. in surgery Wash. U. Sch. Medicine, St. Louis, 1985-89, assoc. prof., 1989-91; prof., chief divsn. plastic surgery Northwestern U. Med. Sch., Chgo., 1991—; plastic surgeon Northwestern Meml. Hosp., 1991—, Evanston Hosp., 1991—, Children's Meml. Hosp., 1992—, Shriner's Hosp. Chgo., 1994—. Co-chmn. Gorden Rsch. Conf., 1995; spl. cons. FDA, 1994—98; mem. sci. adv. panel Biologies, 1997, NCI, 1998; lectr. seminars, 2001. Editl. bd. Archives of Surgery, 1992-2004, Plastic and Reconstructive Surgery, 1993-2001, Wound Repair and Regeneration, 1992—, Jour. Surg. Rsch., 1997-2006; contbr. articles to profl. jours., more than 200 publs., book chpts.; book reviewer. Harvard Nat. scholar, 1969-73; Rhodes scholar candidate, Harvard Coll., 1973. Fellow: ACS (adv. coun. plastic surgery 1999—2002, surg. forum com. 1999—2002, editl. bd. jour. 2003—, surg. biology club III); mem.: AMA, Am. Soc. Plastic Surgery (sci. program chair 2005—), Am. Bd. Plastic Surgery, Coun. Plastic Surger Org., Double Boarded Soc. (pres. 1995—98), Chgo. Surg. Soc., Chgo. Plastic Surg. Soc. (sec. 1996—97), Wound Healing Soc. (program com. 1990, audit com. 1992, program com. 1992, bd. dir. 1993—96, program com. 1994, fin. com. 1994—96, program com. 1997, pres. 1997—99), Assn. Acad. Chmn. Plastic Surgery (matching program and ctrl. application svc. com. 1994), Soc. U. Surgeons, Soc. Head and Neck Surgeons (membership com. 1993—95), Plastic Surgery Rsch. Coun. (rep. coun. acad. surgeons 1991—94, com. indsl. rels. 1992, program com. 1992—94, 1995, Judge Snyder & Crikelair awards 1991), Midwest Assn. Plastic Surgeons, Lipoplasty Soc. N.Am. (lipoplasty edni. rsch. found. 1998—2000), Am. Assn. Plastic Surgery (rsch. and edn. com. 1994—96, chmn. 1996, mem. com. 1998—, co-chmn.ASPRS-ASAPS task force on emerging trends 1999—2000, chmn. instl. coun. com. 1999—), Am. Soc. Plastic and Reconstructive Surgery (rsch. fund proposal com. 1987—92, plastic surgery device com. 1989—93, resource book for plastic surgery residents com. 1991—93, socioecon. 1992—94, sci. program com. 1993—95, chmn. device and tecyhnique assessment com. 1994—96, co-chmn. gen. reconstruction subcom. 1995, ultrasonic lipectomy task force 1995—96, task force for outcomes and guidelines 1995—98, devices and tech. com. 1995—98, chmn. instrnl. com. 1999—2002, chmn. edn. com. 1999—, chmn. resource book com.), Aesculapian Club, Sigma Xi. Avocations: reading, golf, gardening, sports. Home: 144 Greenwood St Evanston IL 60201-4712

MUTCH, DUANE, state legislator; b. Grand Forks, ND, May 13, 1925; m. Dolores, 1949; children: Martha, John, Paul. Mem. N.D. Senate, 1959—, chmn. indsl., bus. and labor com., mem. transp. com. Distbr. bulk oil and propane. Mem. Am. Legion, Farm Bur. Address: PO Box 416 Larimore ND 58251-0416

MUTTI, ALBERT FREDERICK, retired minister; b. Hopkins, Mo., Feb. 13, 1938; s. Albert Frederick and Phyllis Margaret (Turner) M.; m. Etta Mae McClurg, June 7, 1959; children: Timothy Allen, John Frederick, Martin Kent. AB, Cen. Meth. Coll., 1960; MDiv., Garrett-Evang. Theol. Sem., 1963; DMin., St. Paul Sch. Theology, 1975; DD, Baker U., 1993, Ctrl. Meth. Coll., 2000. Pastor Union Star Charge, Mo., 1963-65; sr. pastor Crossroads Parish, Savannah, Mo., 1965-74; assoc. coun. dir. Mo. West Conf. UMC, Kansas City, 1974-80, coun. dir., 1980-82; sr. pastor First United Meth. Ch., Blue Springs, Mo., 1982-87; dist. supt. Cen. Dist. UMC, Mo., 1987-89; dist. supr. Kansas City N. Dist., 1989-92; bishop Kans. Area United Meth. Ch., Topeka, 1992—2004; bishop in residence Saint Paul Sch. Theology, 2004. Author: Breath of New Life, Dancing In a Wheelchair. Chair Savannah Cmty. Betterment, 1971; bd. mem. St. Mary's Hosp., Blue Springs, 1986; dir. ARC, Savannah, 1968; bd. Discipleship, Nashville, bd. Global Ministries, NY; pres. Mo. Coun. Chs., Jefferson City, Gen. Commn. on Christian Unity, Dean Mo. Area Ministers Sch., Curator, Ctrl. Meth. Coll.; trustee St. Paul Sch. Theology; organizer Rural, Religion and labor Coun. Kans; coordinating coun. Chs. Uniting in Christ, 2004—; fund coord. Global AIDS, 2004-. Named Disting. Alumni Ctrl. Meth. Coll.; recipient Grad. award St. Paul Sch. Theology. Methodist.

MUTZENBERGER, MARV, state legislator; m. Barbara; 3 children. Student, Wartburg Coll., Wartburg Sem. Mem. N.D. Ho. of Reps., 1991—, mem. human svcs. com., mem. vet. affairs com., mem. fed. govt. com., mem. judiciary com., mem. nat. resources com.; mem. N.D. Senate, Dist. 32. Prof.; minister. Mem. Social Svc. Bd. Bush fellow. Mem. AARP, Elks, Eagles. Home: 414 E Brandon Dr Bismarck ND 58503-0409

MYERS, ANNE M., developer; Sec., pub. rels. adminstr. Ch. of the Brethren, 1987-97; dir. devel. Timbercrest Retirement Cmty., North Manchester, Ind., 1990—. Office: Timbercrest Retirement Cmty 2201 East St North Manchester IN 46962-9654

MYERS, DANIEL N., lawyer, association executive; b. Independence, Kans., Sept. 17, 1942; s. James Kenneth and Evalyn Clair Petty (Feather) M.; m. Eileen Carruthers, Dec. 14, 1966; children: Yvette Christine, John Joseph. AA, Coffeyville Coll., 1961; BA, U. Okla., 1963; JD, Georgetown U., 1975. Bar: Va. 1976, U.S. Ct. Customs and Patent Appeals 1977, Ill. 1991. Asst. to pres. J.V. Hurson Assoc., Inc., Washington, 1968-74; mgr. fed. legis. affairs AICPA, Washington, 1974-77; dir. legis. svcs., assoc. counsel Nat. LP-Gas Assn., Arlington, Va., 1977-79; gen. counsel, v.p. govt. relations Nat. Propane Gas Assn., Arlington, Va., 1979-88, exec. v.p. Lisle, Ill., 1989—2003; exec. dir. Churchill Ctr., Washington, 2003—. Contbr. articles on good samaritan laws and genealogy to various publs. Bd. dirs. Washington Area State Rels. Group, 1980-82, mem. energy task force White House Conf. on Small Bus., 1980; chmn. good samaritan coaliton hazardous materials Adv. Coun., Washington, 1982-88; mem. motor carrier adv. com. Fed. Hwy. Adminstrn., Washington, 1982-88. Sgt. U.S. Army, 1964-68. Mem. Am. Soc. Assn. Execs. (legal sect. coun. 1980—, chmn. legal sect. 1991-92, bd. dirs. 1991-92), Spl. Indsl. Radio Svc. Assn. (bd. dirs. 1979-88), Indsl. Telecomm. Assn. (bd. dirs. 1995-97), Chgo. Soc. Assn. Execs., Nat. Vol. Firefighters Coun. Found. (bd. dirs. 1995-97). Avocations: golf, genealogy, racquetball, woodworking. Office: 4901 Forest Ave Downers Grove IL 60515 E-mail: dmyers@winstonchurchill.org.

MYERS, DON V., state legislator; m. Mary Myers. Rep. dist. 82 State of Kans., 1993—. Republican. Home: 613 N Briarwood Rd Derby KS 67037-2112

MYERS, FRANCES J., artist; b. Racine, Wis., Apr. 16, 1938; d. Stephen George and Bernadette Marie (Gales) M.; m. Warrington Colescott, Mar. 15, 1971. BA, U. Wis., 1959, MA, 1960, MFA, 1965. Lectr. St. Martin's Sch. Art, London, 1967; disting. prof. printmaking Mills Coll., Oakland, Calif., 1979; vis. lectr. U. Calif., Berkeley, 1982; asst. prof. art U. Wis., Madison, 1988-90, assoc. prof. art, 1990-. One-woman shows include Horwich Gallery, Chgo., 1977, 81, Haslem Gallery, Washington, 1981, 88, Madison Art Center, 1981, Carnegie Inst., Pitts., 1982, Wis. Acad. Arts, 1985, Perimeter Gallery, Chgo., 1986, 88, 91, 93, 97, Natasha Nicholson Works of Art, 1989, Dittmar Gallery, Northwestern U., Evanston, Ill., 1989, Peltz Gallery, Milw., 1990, 91, 94, 99, Wis. Acad. Gallery, 1997; group shows include U.S. Pavilion, World's Fair, Osaka, Japan, 1970, Biennale of Prints Musée d'Art Moderne, Paris, 1970, Bklyn. Mus. 20th Biennale Exhbns. of Prints, 1976, 23d Biennale, 1982, 14th and 16th Internat. Biennial Graphic Arts, Ljubljana, Yugoslavia, 1981, 85, Am. Biennial Graphic Arts, Cali, Colombia, 1981, Brit. Internat. Print Biennale, Bradford, Eng., 1984, Bklyn. Mus. 25th Print Biennale, 1986, prints displayed in Am. Consulate, Leningrad, USSR, 1987, USIA, Yugoslavia, 1989-90, Pace Gallery, N.Y.C., 1990, Figurative Graphics, Amerikahaus, Cologne, Fed. Rep. Germany, 1991, Portland (Oreg.) Art Mus., 1992, Milw. Mus. Art, 1990, Nat. Mus. Am. Art, Washington, 1991, Duke U. Mus. Art, Durham, N.C., 1993, Internat. Biennial of Prints, Bhopal, India, 1995, Madison Art Cen., Wis. Triennial, 1990, 92, 94, 99; represented in permanent collections Met. Mus. of Art, Victoria and Albert Mus., London, Chgo. Art Inst., Library of Congress, Phila. Mus. Art, Mus. Fine Arts, Boston. Nat. Endowment for the Arts fellow, 1974-75, 85-86, Stuart M. Egnal award, 1988, Purchase award, 22nd Bradley Nat. Print & Drawing Exhbn., 1989, H.I. Romnes fellow U. Wis., 1991. Mem. NAD (academician), Am. Print Alliance. Office: 6641d Humanities Building Univ Wisconsin 455 North Park St Madison WI 53706 Office Phone: 608-262-0719. Business E-Mail: fjmyers@facstaff.wisc.edu.

MYERS, GARY, public relations executive; BS, U. Mo., 1971. Pres., CEO Morgan & Myers, Jefferson, Wis., 1997—. Recipient Founder award Agrl. Rels. Coun., 1984. Mem. Pub. Rels. Soc. Am., Coun. Pub. Rels. Firms, Nat. Agrl. Mktg. Assn. Office: Morgan Myers Inc N16w23233 Stone Ridge Dr Ste 200 Waukesha WI 53188-1195

MYERS, JOHN JOSEPH, archbishop; b. Ottawa, Ill., July 26, 1941; s. M.W. and Margaret Louise (Donahue) M. BA maxima cum laude, Loras Coll., 1963; Licentiate in Sacred Theology, Gregorian U., Rome, 1967; Doctor of Canon Law, Cath. U. Am., 1977; DD (hon.), Apostolic See, Vatican City, 1987. Ordained priest Diocese of Peoria, Ill., 1966; asst. pastor Holy Family Parish, Peoria, Ill., 1967-70; asst. dept. internat. affairs US Cath. Conf., Washington, 1970-71; assoc. pastor St. Matthew Parish, Champaign, Ill., 1971-74; adminstr. St. Mary's Cathedral, Peoria, Ill., 1977—78, 1984; vice chancellor Diocese of Peoria, 1977-78, vocation dir., 1977-87, chancellor, 1978-87, vicar gen., 1982-90, mem. Presbyteral Coun., 1968—70, 1984—90, bd. Consultors, 1978—90; ordained bishop, 1987; coadjutor bishop Diocese of Peoria, 1987-90, bishop, 1990—2001; Superior Mission of Turks & Caicos, Turks and Caicos Islands, 2001—; archbishop Archdiocese of Newark, NJ, 2001—. Bd. govs. Canon Law Soc. Am., Washington, 1985-87; bd. dirs. Nat. Cath. Bio Ethics Ctr., Boston, 1999—, bd. gov.; mem. sem. com. Mt. St. Mary's Sem., Md., 1989-94; bd. trustees Cath. U. Am., Washington, 1999-; seminary com., fin. com., Ad Hoc Com. for By-Laws., Cat. U. Am., Washington; seminary bd. Kenrick-Glennon of the Archdiocese of St. Louis. Author: (commentary) Book V of the Code of Canon Law, 1983; contbr. numerous articles to religious publs. Mem. Canon Law Soc. Am., Nat. Conf. Cath. Bishops. (Canonical Affairs Com., 1988-2002, Com. on Shrines and Pilgrimages, 1990-, Com. on Vocations, 1995-1998, Ad Hoc Com. on Sexual Abuse, 2002, Com. on Hispanic Affiars, 2002-, and Com. on Aid to Eastern Europe, 1999-) Roman Catholic. Office: Archdiocese of Newark 171 Clifton Ave Newark NJ 07104-0500

MYERS, JON D., state legislator; m. Cheryl Myers; children: Shon, Jerrod, Ashley. BS, Urbana U. City councilman, Lancaster, Ohio; state rep. Dist. 78 Ohio State Congress, state rep. Dist. 6, 1993—. Employee Am. Electric Power, Lancaster. Named Freshman Legislator of Yr., 1992. Mem. Lancaster Law Commn. (chmn.), Friends of Lancaster Parks, Cameo and Cmty. Concerts, C. of C.

MYERS, LONN WILLIAM, lawyer; b. Rockford, Ill., Nov. 14, 1946; s. William H. and Leona V. (Janvrin) M.; m. Janet L. Forbes, May 14, 1968; children: Andrew, Hillary, Corwin. BA, Mich. State U., 1968; MBA, Ind. U., 1973; JD, Harvard U., 1976. Bar: Ill. 1976, U.S. Ct. of Fed. Claims 1977, U.S. Tax Ct. 1977, U.S. Ct. Appeals (7th cir.) 1977. Ptnr. McDermott Will & Emery LLP, Chgo., 1976—2005, counsel, 2006—. Served to maj. USAR, 1968—80. Mem. ABA (capital recovery and leasing com. tax sect., tax exempt fin. com. tax sect.). Episcopalian. Office: McDermott Will & Emery LLP 227 W Monroe St Chicago IL 60606-5096 Home: 1623 Glenview Rd Unit 316 Glenview IL 60025-2982 Office Phone: 312-984-7537. Business E-Mail: lmyers@mwe.com.

MYERS, MARY KATHLEEN, publishing executive; b. Cedar Rapids, Iowa, Aug. 19, 1945; d. Joseph Bernard and Marjorie Helen (Huntsman) Weaver; m. David F. Myers, Dec. 30, 1967; children: Mindy, James. BA in English and Psychology, U. Iowa, 1967. Tchr. Lincoln HS, Des Moines, 1967-80; editor Perfection Learning Corp., Des Moines, 1980-87, v.p., editor-in-chief, 1987-93; pres., founding ptnr. orgn. to promote Edward de Bono Advanced Practical Thinking Tng., Des Moines, 1992—; founder Myers House LLC, 2002. Pres. Innova Tng. & Cons., Inc., 2000-05. Editor: Six Thinking Hats, 1991, Lateral Thinking, 1993, Direct Attention Thinking Tools, 1997, Total Creativity, 1997 Focus on Facilitation, 2004, Simplicity, 2005 (Six Value Medals, 2007); pub. A Disgrace to the Profession, 2002; Pirateson the Prairie, 2008. Adv. bd. Sch. Bus., Econs. and Acctg., Simpson Coll., 1998—. Mem. ASTD, Am. Creativity Assn. (bd. dirs. 1997-2000, pres. 1999), Instrnl. Systems Assn. (mem. bd. dirs. 2002-04). Home: 813 56th St West Des Moines IA 50266-6314 Office: de Bono Thinking Systems 2570 106th St # A Des Moines IA 50322-3771 Home Phone: 515-225-7866; Office Phone: 515-334-2687. Business E-Mail: kmyers@debonosystems.com.

MYERS, PHILLIP WARD, otolaryngologist; b. Evanston, Ill., Nov. 11, 1939; s. R. Maurice and Vivian (Ward) M.; m. Lynetta Sargent, Dec. 22, 1963; children: Andrea, Ward, Alycia, Amanda, Andrew. BS, Western Ill. U., 1961; MD, U. Ill., 1965. Diplomate: Am. Bd. Otolaryngology. Intern St. Paul-Ramsey Hosp., 1965-66; resident in otolaryngology U. Louisville, 1966-68; resident Northwestern U., 1968-70, fellow, 1970-71; practice medicine specializing in otolaryngology Springfield, Ill., 1973—; clin. prof. otolaryngology So. Ill. U., Springfield, 1973—. Served to maj. M.C. AUS, 1971-73. Fellow Am. Soc. for Head and Neck Surgery, Am. Acad. Facial Plastic and Reconstructive Surgery; ACS, Am. Acad. Otolaryngology-Head and Neck Surgery. Achievements include research in perilymphatic fistulas. Home: 3423 N Oak Hill Rd Rochester IL 62563-9273 Office: So Ill Sch Medicine PO Box 19662 Springfield IL 62794-9662

MYERS, RICHARD E., state representative, trucking executive; b. Iowa City, Oct. 29, 1934; m. Doris Myers. Student, Kirkwood C.C., 1993, Iowa State U., U. Iowa. Pres. and CEO Hawk I Truck Stop Inc., 1962—, Hawk I Harley Davidson, 1994—; state rep. dist. 30 Iowa Ho. of Reps., 1994—; minority leader; mem. adminstrn. and rules com. Mem. Johnson County Bd. Suprs., 1982—93; mayor City of Coralville, 1969—78; mem. Coralville City Coun.; Iowa state dir. Farmers Home Adminstrn., 1980—81; past chair Iowa City Area Devel. Group, 1984—92; bd. dirs. MECCA, 1976—. With US Army, 1953—61, with USAR, 1961—62. Mem.: Nat. Assn. Truck Stop Operators, Iowa City Area C. of C. (bd. dirs. 1990—92). Democrat.

MYERS, RICHARD P., state legislator; Ill. state rep. Dist. 95, 1995—. Office: PO Box 170 331 N Lafayette St Macomb IL 61455-1505

MYERS, WILLIAM, food container manufacturing executive; CFO, treas. Dart Container, Mason, Mich., now treas. Office: Dart Container 500 Hogsback Rd Mason MI 48854-9547

MYERSON, ROBERT J., radiologist, educator; b. Boston, May 12, 1947; s. Richard Louis and Rosemarie M.; m. Carla Wheatley, Aug. 8, 1970; 1 child, Jacob Wheatley. BA, Princeton U., 1969; PhD, U. Calif., Berkeley, 1974; MD, U. Miami, 1980. Diplomate Am. Bd. Radiology. Asst. prof. dept. physics Pa. State U., State Coll., 1974-76; fellow Inst. Advanced Studies, Princeton, NJ, 1976-78; resident U. Pa. Hosp., Phila., 1981-84; assoc. prof. radiology Washington U. Sch. Medicine, St. Louis, 1984-97; prof. radiation oncology Wash. U. Sch. Medicine, St. Louis, 1997—. Contbr. articles to profl. jours. Recipient Career Devel. award Am. Cancer Soc., 1985. Fellow Am. Coll. Radiology; mem. Am. Coll. Radiation, Am. Soc. Therapeutic Radiologists, Am. Phys. Soc. Democrat. Jewish. Avocation: bicycling. Office: Washington U Radiation Oncology Ctr Box 8224 4921 Parkview Pl Saint Louis MO 63110-1001

MYERSON, ROGER BRUCE, economist, educator; b. Boston, Mar. 29, 1951; s. Richard L. and Rosemarie (Farkas) M.; m. Regina M. Weber, Aug. 29, 1982; children: Daniel, Rebecca. AB summa cum laude, Harvard U., 1973, SM in Applied Math., 1973, PhD in Applied Math., 1976; D (hon.), U. Basel, Switzerland, 2002. Asst. prof. managerial econs. and decision scis. Northwestern U., Evanston, Ill., 1976-78, assoc. prof., 1979-82, prof., 1982-2001, Harold Stuart prof. decision scis., 1986-2001, prof. econs., 1987-2001; W.C. Norby prof. economics U. Chgo., 2001—, Glen A. Lloyd Disting. Svc. Prof., 2007—. Guest researcher U. Bielefeld, Federal Republic of Germany, 1978-79; vis. prof. econs. U. Chgo., 1985-86, 2000-01. Author: Game Theory: Analysis of Conflict, 1991, Probability Models for Economic Decisions, 2005; creater: (software) Formlist.xla, Simtools.xla; mem. editorial bd. Internat. Jour. Game Theory, 1982-92, Games and Econ. Behavior, 1989-97; assoc. editor Jour. Econ. Theory, 1983-93; also articles. Guggenheim fellow, 1983-84; Sloan rsch. fellow, 1984-86; co-recipient Nobel Memorial Prize in Econ. Scis., 2007. Fellow Econometric Soc. (coun. mem. 1996-2002, 2005-, 2nd v.p. 2007), Am. Acad. Arts and Scis. (Midwest Coun. mem. 1995-2002, dir. Midwest Ctr. and v.p. 1999-2002). Office: U Chgo Dept Econs 1126 E 59th St Chicago IL 60637 Business E-Mail: myerson@uchicago.edu.

MYKLEBY, KATHY, newscaster, reporter; Degree, U. Iowa, 1976. With KRNA-FM Radio, Iowa City, 1976, WKY-Radio, Oklahoma City, 1976—80, WVTV-TV Channel 18, Milw., 1980; reporter, anchor WISN, Milw., 1980—. Active telethon Children's Miracle Network; co-chmn. Briggs and Stratton Run/Walk for Children's Hosp. of Wis. Recipient Regional award for best TV feature, UP Internat., 1984, Best Single Report Contbg. to Cmty. Welfare award, Milw. Press Club, 1987, Press Club award, 1992, Best Spot News award, Wis. Broadcasters Assn., 1997. Office: WISN PO Box 402 Milwaukee WI 53201-0402 Office Phone: 414-937-3331.

MYRA, HAROLD LAWRENCE, publisher; b. Camden, NJ, July 19, 1939; s. John Samuel and Esther (Christensen) M.; m. Jeanette Austin, May 7, 1966; children: Michelle, Todd, Gregory, Rick, Joshua, Lindsey. BS, East Stroudsburg State Coll., 1961; Litt.D., John Wesley Coll., 1976; D.Lit., Biola U., 1984; DLitt, Gordon Coll., 1992. Tchr. Pocono Mountain Jointure, Cresco, Pa., 1961; editorial asst. Youth for Christ Internat., Wheaton, Ill., 1961-62, asso. editor, 1962-64, mng. editor, 1964-65, dir. of lit., 1965-66; v.p. lit. div., pub. Campus Life, Wheaton, 1966-75; pres., chief exec. officer Christianity Today, Inc., Carol Stream, Ill., 1975—. Author: No Man in Eden, 1969, Michelle, You Scallawag, I Love You, 1972, The New You, 1972, The Carpenter, 1972, Elsbeth, 1975, Is There a Place I Can Scream?, 1976, Santa, Are You For Real?, 1979, Love Notes to Jeanette, 1979, The Choice, 1980, Halloween, 1982, Your Super-Terrific Birthday, 1985, Living By God's Surprises, 1988, Children in the Night, 1991, The Shining Face, 1993, Morning Child, 1994, Surprised by Children, 2001, The Leadership Secrets of Billy Graham, 2005. Presbyterian. Home: 1737 Marion Ct Wheaton IL 60187-3319 Office: Christianity Today 465 Gundersen Dr Carol Stream IL 60188-2498

MYRDAL, ROSEMARIE CARYLE, state official, former state legislator; b. Minot, North Dakota, May 20, 1929; d. Harry Dirk and Olga Jean (Dragge) Lohse; m. B. John Myrdal, (dec.) June 21, 1952; children: Jan, Mark, Harold, Paul, Amy. BS, N.D. State U., 1951. first grade tchr., N.D. Tchr., ND, 1951-71; bus. mgr. Edinburg Sch. Dist., ND, 1974-81; mem. N.D. Ho. of Reps., Bismarck, ND, 1984-92, mem. appropriations com., 1991-92; lt. gov. State of N.D., Bismarck, 1993—2001. Sch. evaluator Walsh County Sch. Bd. Assn., Grafton, N.D., 1983-84; evaluator, work presenter N.D. Sch. Bd. Assn., Bismarck, 1983-84; mem. sch. bd. Edinburg Sch. Dist., 1981-90; adv. com. Red River Trade Corridor, Inc., 1989-2001. Co-editor: Heritage '76, 1976, Heritage '89, 1989. Precinct committeewoman Gardar Twp. Rep. Com., 1980-86; leader Hummingbirds 4-H Club, Edinburg, 1980-83; bd. dir. Camp Sioux Diabetic Children, Grand Forks, N.D., 1980-90; N.D. affiliate Am. Diabetes Assn., Families First-Child Welfare Reform Initiative, Region IV, 1989-92; dir. N.D. Diabetes Assn., 1989-91; chmn. N.D. Ednl. Telecom. Coun., 1989-90; vice chmn. N.D. Legis. Interim Jobs Devel. Commn., 1989-90. Mem. AAUW (pres. 1982-84 Pembina County area), Pembina County Hist. Soc. (historian 1976-84); Northeastern N.D. Heritage Assn. (pres. 1986-92), Red River Valley Heritage Soc. (bd. dir. 1985-92); N.D. Sch. to Work Mgmt. Team chair-person Clubs: Agassiz Garden (Park River) (pres. 1968-69). Republican. Lutheran. Avocations: gardening, architecture, ethnic foods, history, cultural preservation. Home: 12987 80th St NE Edinburg ND 58227-9635

NAADEN, PETE, former state legislator; m. Mary Ellen; 12 children. farmer, rancher. City councilman; mem. N.D. Senate, 1973—, vice chm. appropriations com. Mem. Lions Club, Farm Bur., N.D. Pork Producers, N.D. Stockman's Assn. Home: PO Box 53 Braddock ND 58524-0053

NABEL, GARY JAN, virologist; b. July 2, 1953; BA in Biochemistry magna cum laude, Harvard Coll., 1975; PhD in Cell and Devel. Biology, Harvard U., 1980, MD, 1982. Instr. biology Harvard U., Boston, 1980-81, resident tutor in biology, 1980-83, clin. fellow medicine, 1983-85; intern and resident in internal medicine Brigham and Women's Hosp., Boston, 1983-85; instr. Harvard Med. Sch., Boston, 1984-87; assoc. Howard Hughes Med. Inst., Whitehead Inst., MIT, Lab. David Baltimore, 1985-87; assoc. physician Brigham and Women's Hosp., 1985-87; asst. prof. internal medicine and biol. chemistry U. Mich., Ann Arbor, 1987-90, asst. investigator Howard Hughes Med. Inst., 1987-91, assoc. prof. internal medicine and biol. chemistry, 1990-93, assoc. investigator Howard Hughes Med. Inst., 1991-94, prof. internal medicine and biol. chemistry, 1993—, investigator Howard Hughes Med. Inst., 1994—, Henry Sewall prof., 1995—99; dir. Vaccine Rsch. Ctr. NIH, 1999—. Mem. AIDS rsch. adv. com. Nat. Inst. Allergy and Infectious Diseases, NIH. Contbr. articles to profl. jours. Fellow Dana-Farber Cancer Inst., Harvard U., 1980-84; Harvard Nat. scholar, 1971-75, Harvard Grad. Nat. scholar, 1976-82; recipient Mallinkrodt Book prize, 1975, James Tolbert Shipley prize for rsch. Harvard Med. Sch., 1982, Ofcl. citation Conn. State Gen. Assembly for Contbns. to Human Gene Therapy, 1992, Young Investigator award Midwest Am. Fedn. for Clin. Rsch., 1992, Amgen award Am. Soc. Biochemistry and Molecular Biology, 1996. Mem. Am. Soc. Clin. Investigation, Assn. Am. Physicians. Office: Vaccine Rsch Ctr 40 Convent Dr Bldg 40 Rm 4502 Bethesda MD 20892 E-mail: gnabel@nih.gov.

NABOZNY, HEATHER, professional sports team groundskeeper; b. Milford, Mich., 1970; Grad. Turf Mgmt. Prog., Mich. State U., 1993. Groundskeeper Toronto Blue Jays spring tng. camp, Dunedin, Fla.; head groundskeeper Class A West Mich. Whitecaps, 1994, Detroit Tigers, 1999—. Named one of 40 Under 40, Crain's Detroit Bus., 2006. Achievements include becoming first female goundskeeper in Major League Baseball and World Series game. Office: c/o Detroit Tigers Comerica Park 2100 Woodward Ave Detroit MI 48201

NACLERIO, ROBERT MICHAEL, otolaryngologist, educator; b. NYC, Mar. 30, 1950; s. Albert Paul and Lee Ann (Rabinowitz) N.; m. Sharon Ann Silhan, Mar. 30, 1983; children: Jessica, Daniel. BA, Cornell U., 1972; MD with honors, Baylor U., 1976. Diplomate Am. Bd. Otolaryngology. Intern in surgery Johns Hopkins Hosp., Balt., 1976-77, resident in surgery, 1977-78; resident in otolaryngology Baylor Coll. Medicine, Houston, 1978-80, chief resident in otolaryngology, 1982-83; fellow in clin. immunology divsn. Johns Hopkins U. Sch. Medicine, Balt., 1980-82, asst. prof. medicine and otolaryngology, 1983-87, asst. prof. pediat., 1986-87, dir. divsn. pediat. otolaryngology, 1986-94, assoc. prof. otolargyngology, medicine and pediat., 1987-92, prof. otolaryngology, medicine and pediat., 1992-94; chief of otolaryngology, head and neck surgery U. Chgo., Chgo., 1994—. Cons. Richardson-Vicks Inc., 1986-89, 90, NIH, 1987, Proctor & Gamble, 1987, 94, Sandoz Rsch. Inst., 1988, Schering Rsch., 1988, Wallace Labs., 1989, Joint Rhinologic Conf., 1989, Internat. Congress Rhinology, 1991, orwich-Eaton Pharm. Inc., 1991-92, Ciba-Geigy Corp., 1991-92, Mktg. Corp. Am., 1993—, Astra, others; mem. med. bd. Children's Ctr., 1991-94, other local comms.; reviewer Am. Jour. Rhinology, others; lectr. in field. Editor: Rhinoconjunctivitis: New Perspectives in Topical Treatment, 1988; asst. editor: Am. Jour. Rhinology, 1986—, Rhinology, 1988—; mem. editl. bd. Otolaryngology-Head and Neck Surgery, 1990-97, Laryngoscope, 1990—, Jour. Allergy and Clin. Immunology, 1992-97; contbr. numerous chpts. to books, papers and abstracts to profl. jours. and procs. Fellow ACS, Am. Acad. Otolaryngology-Head and Neck Surgery (mem. com. 1985-90, 90-92, subcom. 1987-92), Am. Laryngol., Rhinol. and Otol. Soc., Inc.; mem. Am. Acad. Allergy and Immunology (mem. com. 1983-88, 88-89, 88-95, chmn. com. 1990-91, 91—, Jerome Glazer Meml. lectureship), Am. Fedn. Clin. Rsch., Am. Soc. Pediat. Otolaryngology (mem. rsch. com. 1990-94, chmn. subcom. 1990), Soc. Univ. Otolaryngologists-Head and Neck Surgeons, Pan-Am. Assn. Otorhinolaryngology, Internat. Symposium on Infection and Allergy of the Nose (v.p.). Office: U Chgo Sect O-HNS 5841 S Maryland Ave # 1035 Chicago IL 60637-1463 E-mail: rnacleri@surgery.bsd.uchicago.edu.

NADEAU, STEVEN C., lawyer; b. Schenectady, NY, July 6, 1954; AB magna cum laude, Boston Coll., 1974, JD cum laude, 1977. Bar: Mich. 1977. Mediator Wayne County Cir. Ct., 1983-88; mem., chair environ. law dept. Honigman Miller Schwartz and Cohn LLP, Detroit. Coord. dir. Sediment Mgmt. Work Group, 1998—. Mem. ABA (sect. natural resources), State Bar Mich. (sect. environ. law). Office: Honigman Miller Schwartz and Cohn LLP 660 Woodward Ave Ste 2290 Detroit MI 48226-3506 E-mail: snadeau@honigman.com.

NADER, ROBERT ALEXANDER, judge, lawyer; b. Warren, Ohio, Mar. 31, 1928; s. Nassef J. and Emily (Nader) N.; m. Nancy M. Veauthier. BA, Western Res. U., 1950, LL.B., 1953. Bar: Ohio 1953. Ptnr. Paul G. Nader, Warren, 1953-83. Pres. Warren City Police and Fire Pension Bds., 1960-66; trustee Office Econ. Opportunity, 1970-72; mem. Warren City Coun., 1960-66, pres. pro tem, 1964-66; mem. Ohio Ho. of Reps., 1971-83, chmn. reference com., 1977-81, chmn. judiciary com., 1981-83; presiding judge Trumbull County Ct. Common Pleas, 1983-91; judge Ohio 11th Dist. Ct. of Appeals, 1991-03; trustee Family Svc. Assn., 1959-65. With AUS, 1946-48. Recipient Outstanding Young Man of Yr. award, 1964, award Am. Arbitration Assn., 1965, Community Action award Warren Area Bd. Realtors, 1967, Outstanding Svc. award Kent State U., Trumbull campus. 1978, Outstanding Svc. award Children's Rehab. Ctr., 1980; named to Warren H.S. Disting. Alumni Hall of Fame, 1993, Sports Hall of Fame, 2003. Mem. Ohio State Bar Assn., Trumbull County Bar Assn. (past pres., Pres.'s award for disting. svc. 2003), Ct. Appeals Judges Assn. (chmn. legis. com. 1995-98), Trumbull County Law Libr. Assn. (trustee 1958-72), Trumbull New Theatre (past pres.), KC, Elks, Lambda Chi Alpha. Roman Catholic. Home: 798 Wildwood Dr NE Warren OH 44483-4458 Office: 11th Dist Ct of Appeals 111 High St NE Warren OH 44481

NADLER, JUDITH, library director; b. Romania; BA in English and Romance Studies, U. Jerusalem; MLS, Israel Grad. Sch. With U. Chgo. Libr., 1966—, cataloger fgn. language materials, dir., 2004—. Office: Joseph Regenstein Libr U Chgo 1100 E 57 St 180 Chicago IL 60637 Office Phone: 773-702-8743. Office Fax: 773-702-6623. E-mail: judi@uchicago.edu.

NAEGELE, ROBERT O., JR., professional sports team executive; m. Ellis Naegele; 4 children. BA in Sociology, Dartmouth Coll., 1961. Chmn. Naegele Comms., Inc.; ptnr. Rollerblade, Inc., 1985—95, chmn., 1995; chmn. Minn. Wild Minn. Hockey Ventures Group, St. Paul, 1997—. Mem.: Inline Skating Assn. (exec. com.), St. Paul Area C. of C. (chmn. bd. dirs.). Office: 317 Washington St Saint Paul MN 55102

NAEGER, PATRICK A., state legislator; Mem. dist. 155 Mo. Ho. of Reps. Office: 1083 Pcr 906 Perryville MO 63775-6141

NAFZIGER, ESTEL WAYNE, economics professor; b. Bloomington, Ill., Aug. 14, 1938; s. Orrin and Beatrice Mae (Slabaugh) N.; m. Elfrieda Nettie Toews, Aug. 20, 1966; children: Brian Wayne, Kevin Jon. BA, Goshen Coll., 1960; MA, U. Mich., 1962; PhD, U. Ill., 1967. Rsch. assoc. Econ. Devel. Inst., Enugu, Nigeria, 1964-65; asst. prof. Kans. State U., Manhattan, 1966-73, assoc. prof., 1973-78, prof., 1978-99, univ. disting. prof., 1999—; Fulbright prof. Andhra U., Waltair, India, 1970-71; fellow East West Ctr., Honolulu, 1972-73. Vis. scholar Cambridge U., 1976; vis. prof. Internat. U. Japan, Yamato-machi, 1983; external rsch. fellow World Acad. Devel. and Coop., College Park, Md., 1984-85; Indo-Am. Found. scholar Andura U., Waltair, India, 1993; World Inst. for Devel. Econ. Rsch., UN Univ., Helsinki, Finland, 1996-98. Author: African Capitalism, 1977, Class, Caste and Entrepreneurship, 1978; author: (with others) Development Theory, 1979; author: Economics of Political Instability, 1983, Economics of Developing Countries, 1984, 2nd edit., 1990, 3rd edit., 1997, Entrepreneurship Equity and Economic Development, 1986, Inequality in Africa, 1988 (one of Outstanding Acad. Books, Choice, 1989-90), The Debt Crisis in Africa, 1993, Poverty and Wealth, 1994, Learning From the Japanese, 1995, Fathers, Sons, and Daughters: Industrial Entrepreneurs under India's Liberalization, 1998; co-editor: War, Hunger, and Displacement, 2 vols., 2000, Prevention of Humanitarian Emergencies, 2002, Economic Development, Inequality, and War, 2003, Economic Development, 2006. Sec. bd. overseers Hesston Coll., Kans., 1980-85; chmn. Lou Douglas Lecture Series, 1984-91, 92-93; pres. faculty senate Kans. State U., 1990-92. Recipient Honor Lectr. award Mid Am. State U.'s Assn., 1984-85; grantee Social Sci. Found., 1969 Mem. Am. Econ. Assn., AAUP (pres. chpt. 1981-82), African Studies Assn., Assn. Comparative Econ. Studies, Omicron Delta Epsilon (hon.), Phi Kappa Phi (hon.) Democrat. Avocations: reading, running. Home: 1919 Bluestem Ter # 785 Manhattan KS 66502-4508 Office: Kans State U Dept Econs Waters Hall Manhattan KS 66506-4001 Office Phone: 785-532-4579.

NAGEL, SIDNEY ROBERT, physics professor; s. Ernest and Edith (Haggstrom) Nagel. BA, Columbia U., 1969; MA, Princeton U., 1972, PhD, 1974. Rsch. assoc. Brown U., Providence, 1974-76; asst. prof. physics U. Chgo., 1976-81, assoc. prof., 1981-84, prof., 1984—, assoc. dean divsn. phy. scis., 1997-2000, Louis Block prof., 1998-2000, assoc. dean divsn. phy. scis., 1997-2000, Stein-Freiler disting. svc. prof., 2001—. Contbr. articles to profl. jours. Recipient Quantrell award for Excellence in Undergrad. Tchg., U. Chgo., 1996; Klopsteg Meml. Lecture award Am. Assn. Physics Tchrs., 1998, Oliver E. Buckley prize Am. Phys. Soc., 1999; Alfred Sloan Found. fellow, 1978-82. Fellow AAAS, Am. Acad. Arts and Scis.; mem. NAS.

NAGLER, LORNA E., apparel executive; b. Oct. 5, 1956; Divisional merchandise mgr. Lane Bryant, Inc., Columbus, Ohio; v.p., divisional merchandise mgr. Kids 'R Us; sr. v.p., gen. merchandise mgr., apparel Kmart Corp., Hoffman Estates, Ill.; pres. Catherine Stores Corp., 2002—04, Lane Bryant, Inc., 2004—07; pres., CEO Christopher & Banks Corp., Plymouth, Minn., 2007—. Office: Christopher and Banks Corp 2400 Xenium Ln N Plymouth MN 55441-3626 Office Phone: 763-551-5000. Office Fax: 763-551-5198.*

NAGORSKE, LYNN A., bank executive; b. Minn., 1956; BA in Acctg., Minn. State U. CPA. Sr. mgr. Audit Dept. KPMG Peat Marwick; sr. v.p. and controller TCF Bank, 1985, treas., CFO, 1986, exec. v.p., 1988, pres., 1993, pres., COO, CEO, 2006—; pres., CFO TFC Bank Minn., 1997—98. Bd. dirs. TCF Bank, 1995—. Office: TCF Financial Corp 200 Lake St E Wayzata MN 55391

NAGY, DONNA M., dean, law educator; BA, Vassar Coll., 1986; JD cum laude, NYU Sch. Law, 1989. Assoc. Debevoise & Plimpton, Washington, DC, 1989—94; asst. prof. U. Cin. Sch. Law, 1994—98, assoc. prof., 1998—99, prof., 1999—2001, Charles Hartsock Prof. Law, 2001—, assoc. dean faculty devel., 2002—04, interim dean, 2004—. Vis. prof. law U. Ill. Coll. Law, Urbana-Champaign, 2001; vis. scholar U. Canterbury Sch. Law, New Zealand, 2002. Co-author: Ferrara on Insider Trading and the Wall, 1995, 2002, Securities Litigation and Enforcement: Cases and Materials, 2003; contbr. articles to law jours. Recipient Howard C. Schott Publ. Prize, 2002, 2003; Order of Coif. Mem.: ABA (mem. sec. Bus. Law), Am. Assn. Law Schs. (sec. Bus. Assns., Securties Regulation, and Women in Legal Edn.), Soc. Am. Law Tchrs., ACLU, Vassar Club of Cin. (Alumni Appointments Chair 1995—99).

NAGY, LOUIS LEONARD, engineering executive, researcher; b. Detroit, Jan. 15, 1942; s. Alex and Helen Nagy; m. Dianna M. Skarjune, Aug. 5, 1961; children: Tammy, Kimberly, Kristine, Amanda. BSEE, U. Mich., Dearborn, 1965; MSEE, U. Mich., Ann Arbor, 1969, PhDEE, 1974. Registered profl. engr. Rsch. engr. U. Mich., Ann Arbor, 1962-69; staff rsch. engr. GM R & D Ctr., Warren, Mich., 1969-98; sr. staff rsch. engr. Delphi Rsch. Labs., Warren, 1999—. Contbr. articles to profl. jours.; patentee in field. Bd. dirs. Convergence Ednl. Found., Birmingham, Mich., 1990-97, Convergence Transp. Electronics Assn., Birmingham, 1990-97. Recipient R&D 100 award R&D Mag., 1998. Fellow IEEE; mem. Convergence Fellowship (bd. dirs. 1988-96), Vehicular Tech. Soc. (Spl. Recognition award 1979, Avant Garde award 1986, Paper of Yr. 1975), Soc. Automotive Engrs., Tau Beta Pi, Eta Kappa Nu. Avocations: electronics, antennas, radar, automotive radar, microwaves. Office: Delphi Rsch Labs MC 483-478-105 51786 Shelby Pkwy Shelby Township MI 48315 Business E-Mail: Louis.L.Nagy@delphi.com.

NAHAT, DENNIS F., performing company executive, choreographer; b. Detroit, Feb. 20, 1946; s. Fred H. and Linda M. (Haddad) N. Hon. degree, Juilliard Sch. Music, 1965. Prin. dancer Joffrey Ballet, NYC, 1965-66; prin. dancer Am. Ballet Theatre, NYC, 1968-79; co-founder Cleve. Ballet, 1976, Sch. of Cleve. Ballet, 1972; founder, artistic dir. Sch. Cleve. San Jose Ballet, 1996; founder New Sch. of Cleve. San Jose Ballet, 1996—; founder, artistic dir. San Jose Cleve. Ballet (now Ballet San Jose), San Jose, 1985—. Co-chair Artists Round Table Dance USA, 1991; trustee Cecchetti Coun. Am., 1991; mem. adv. bd. Ohio Dance Regional Dance Am.; dir. dance USDAN Ctr. for the Creative Performing Arts, NY, 1999—. Prin. performer Broadway show Sweet Charity, 1966-67; choreographer Two Gentlemen of Verona (Tony award 1972), 1969-70; (ballet) Celebrations and Ode (resolution award 1985), 1985, Green Table, Three Virgins and a Devil (Isadora Duncan award 1985); conceived, directed, choreographed Blue Suede Shoes, PBS, 1997-98. Grantee Nat. Endowment Arts, 1978, Andrew Mellow Found., 1985; recipient Outstanding Achievement award Am. Dance Guild, 1995, 96, 2000—. Avocation: cooking. also: Ballet San Jose PO Box 1666 40 N 1st St San Jose CA 95109-1666 Office Phone: 408-288-2820 Ext.225. Business E-Mail: dnahat@balletsanjose.org.

NAHRWOLD, DAVID LANGE, surgeon, educator; b. St. Louis, Dec. 21, 1935; s. Elmer William and Magdalen Louise (Lange) Nahrwold; m. Carolyn Louise Hoffman, June 14, 1958; children: Stephen Michael, Susan Alane, Thomas James, Anne Elizabeth. AB, Ind. U., Bloomington, 1957; MD, Ind. U., Indpls., 1960. Diplomate Am. Bd. Surgery, Am. Bd. Thoracic Surgery. Intern, then resident in surgery Ind. U. Med. Ctr., Indpls., 1960-65; postdoctoral scholar in gastrointestinal physiology VA Ctr., UCLA, 1965; asst. prof. surgery Ind. U. Med. Sch., 1968-70; assoc. prof. Coll. Medicine Pa. State U., 1970-73; vice-chmn. dept. surgery Pa. State U., 1971-82, assoc. provost, dean health affairs, 1981-82, prof., chief divsn. gen. surgery, 1974-82; Loyal and Edith Davis prof., chmn. dept. surgery Northwestern U. Med. Sch., Chgo., 1982-97; surgeon-in-chief Northwestern Meml. Hosp., Chgo., 1982-97; pres., CEO Northwestern Med. Faculty Found., Inc., 1996-99; prof. surgery, exec. assoc. dean clin. affairs Northwestern U. Med. Sch., 1997-99, prof. emeritus, 1999—. Mem. Nat. Digestive Disease Adv. Bd., 1985—89; bd. dirs. Am. Bd. Surgery, vice chmn., 1994—95, chmn., 1995—96; bd. dirs. Northwestern Healthcare Network, Am. Bd. Med. Specialties, 1997—2005, pres., 2002—04; mem. exec. com. Accreditation Coun. for Grad. Med. Edn., 1999—2000; bd. commrs. Joint Commn. Accreditation Healthcare Orgns., 2002—, vice chmn. bd. commrs., 2004—, vice chmn. bd. dirs., 2005—06. Editor emeritus Jour. Laparoendoscopic Surgery, 1997-2004; mem. editl. bd. Surgery, 1981-94, Archives of Surgery, 1983-93, Digestive Surgery, 1986-99, Am. Jour. Surgery, 1994-2000, Jour. Gastrointestinal Surgery, 1996-2000, Current Opinion in Gen. Surgery, Jour. Lithotripsy and Stone Disease, 1988-92; contbr. articles to profl. jours. With MC US Army, 1966—68. Recipient John P. Hubbard award, Nat. Bd. Med. Examiners, 2003, Derrick Vail award, Am. Bd. Med. Specialties, 2007. Fellow: ACS (bd. govs. 1992—98, vice chmn. 1994—96, chmn. bd. govs. exec. com. 1996—98, interim dir. 1999—2000, 1st v.p. elect 2005—06, 1st v.p. 2006—07, bd. regents, Disting. Svc. award 2001), Philippine Coll. Surgeons (hon.); mem.: AMA, Chgo. Surg. Soc. (pres. 1993—94), Chgo. Med. Soc., We. Surg. Assn., Soc. Univ. Surgeons, Soc. Surgery Alimentary Tract (pres. 1989—90, trustee), Soc. Clin. Surgery (sec. 1984—88), Internat. Biliary Assn., Ill. Surg. Soc., Ill. State Med. Soc., Internat. Fedn. Surg. Colls. (hon.; treas. 1999—2002), Gastroenterology Rsch. Group, Collegium Internat. Chirurgiae Digestive (pres. U.S. chpt. 1988—90), Ctrl. Surg. Assn. (sec. 1994—97, pres.-elect 1997—98, pres. 1998—99, pres. Found. 2002—03), Assn. Surg. Edn., Assn. Acad. Surgery, Am. Surg. Assn. (2d v.p. 1993—94), Am. Phys. Soc., Alpha Omega Alpha, Sigma Xi. Office: Dept Surgery Galter 10-105 251 E Huron St Chicago IL 60611-2908 Home Phone: 847-714-1143; Office Phone: 312-695-4908. Business E-Mail: dnahrwol@nmh.org.

NAIR, RAGHAVAN D., accountant, educator; b. Dehradun, United Provinces, India, Oct. 23, 1951; came to U.S., 1973; s. Keshavan R. and Parvati Nair; m. Ruth Marie air, 1976; 1 child, Andrea. BA, U. Madras, India, 1970, MA, 1972; MBA, U. Mich., 1974, PhD, 1977. CPA, Wis. Prof. U. Wis., Madison, 1978—, sr. assoc. dean acad. affairs Sch. Bus., 1994—, dir. internat. programs, 1996—; faculty fellow Fin. Acctg. Standards Bd., Norwalk, Conn., 1984-86; faculty resident Arthur Andersen & Co., Chgo., 1991—, dir. PhD Program, 1987-90, chmn. dept. acctg., 1991-94; dir. Arthur Andersen Ctr. Fin. Reporting, 1992-93; prof. acctg. and info. systems Price Waterhouse, 1993—; dir. Ctr. Internat. Bus. Edn. and Rsch., Madison, 1998—. Invited speaker various corps., pub. acctg. firms, mgmt. and exec. edn. groups, 1982—. Contbr. articles to profl. jours. Pres. John Muir PTO, Madison, Wis., 1988-89. Recipient Excellence in Teaching award Lawrence J. Larson Sch. Bus., 1992. Mem. AICPA, Parkwood Hills Community Assn. (treas. 1987-89), Am. Acctg. Assn., Wis. Inst. CPAs (Outstanding Educator award 1989), Bascom Hill Soc., Blackhawk Country Club (bd. dirs. 1994-96). Avocations: golf, marathon running.

NAIR, VASU, chemist, educator; BSc in Chemistry with high honors, U. Otago, Dunedin, New Zealand, 1963; PhD, U. Adelaide, Australia, 1966, DSc (hon.), 1991. Rsch. assoc. U. Ill., Urbana, 1967-68; rsch. fellow Harvard U., Cambridge, Mass., 1968-69; from asst. prof. chemistry to assoc. prof. U. Iowa, Iowa City, 1969-79, prof., 1980—, U. Iowa Found. Disting. prof. chemistry, 1993—. Cons. Miles Lab., West Haven, Conn., 1987, Burroughs Wellcome Co., Rsch. Triangle Park, N.C., 1984-96, Nucleotide Chemistry, Integrated DNA Techs., Inc., Iowa City, 1988-93, Nucleoside Chemistry, San Diego, 1988-94, NIH, 1989—, Lipitek Internat., San Antonio, Tex., Gensia Pharms.; dir. U. Iowa HIgh-Field NMR Facility, 1982-86; assoc. chair dept. chemistry U. Iowa, 1991-93, mem. U. Iowa Biosci. Com., 1995—, Faculty Senate, 1996—. Contbr. over 200 articles and abstracts to profl. jours.; speaker in field; patentee: 3 U.S. patents, 2 on antiviral chemicals, 1 on a potential anti-AIDS agent. Recipient Disting. Vis. Scholar award U. Adelaide, Australia, 1987, Sci. medal, Iowa Acad. Scis., numerous rsch. grants and awards. Fellow AAAS; mem. Internat. Soc. Antiviral Rsch., Internat. Soc. Nucleic Acid Chemistry, Am. Soc. Microbiology, Am. Chem. Soc.

NAIR, VELAYUDHAN, pharmacologist, educator, academic administrator; arrived in U.S., 1956, naturalized, 1963; m. Jo Ann Burke, Nov. 30, 1957; children: David, Larry, Sharon. PhD in Medicine, U. London, 1956, DSc, 1976, LHD (hon.) h.c., 2003. Rsch. assoc. U. Ill. Coll. Medicine, 1956-58; asst. prof. U. Chgo. Sch. Medicine, 1958-63; dir. lab. neuropharmacology and biochemistry Michael Reese Hosp. and Med. Ctr., Chgo., 1963-68, dir. therapeutic rsch., 1968-71; prof. pharmacology FUHS/Chgo. Med. Sch., 1971—, disting. prof., 2001, vice chmn. dept. pharmacology and therapeutics, 1971—76, dean Sch. Grad. and Postdoctoral Studies, 1976—2003, v.p. rsch., 1999—2003, v.p., dean emeritus, 2003—, disting. prof., 2001. Vis. assoc. prof. pharmacology FUHS/Chgo. Med. Sch., 1963—68, vis. prof., 1968—71, Harvard U., 1994, Johns Hopkins Sch. Medicine, 1995. Contbr. articles to profl. jours. Recipient Morris Parker award, U. Health Scis./Chgo. Med. Sch., 1972. Fellow: AAAS, Am. Coll. Clin. Pharmacology, NY Acad. Scis.; mem.: AAUP, Internat. Soc. Devel. Neurosci., Am. Coll. Toxicology, Internat. Soc. Chronobiology, Soc. Neurosci., Soc. Exptl. Biology & Medicine, Pan Am. Med. Assn. (coun. on toxicology), Royal Inst. Chemistry (London), Brit. Chem. Soc., Am. Chem. Soc., Soc. Toxicology, Radiation Rsch. Soc., Am. Soc. Clin. Pharmacology & Therapeutics, Am. Soc. Pharmacology & Exptl. Therapeutics, Internat. Soc. Biochem. Pharmacology, Internat. Brain Rsch. Orgn., Cosmos Club (Washington), Alpha Omega Alpha, Sigma Xi. Office: Rosalind Franklin Univ Medicine and Sci 3333 Green Bay Rd North Chicago IL 60064-3037 Personal E-mail: velnair@comcast.net.

NAIRN, RODERICK, immunologist, educator, biochemist; b. Dumbarton, Scotland, Mar. 25, 1951; came to U.S., 1976; s. James Bell and Muriel Elizabeth (Hyde) N.; m. Morag Gilhooly, Dec. 29, 1971; 1 child, Carolyn Mhairi. BS, U. Strathclyde, Glasgow, Scotland, 1973; PhD, U. London, 1976. Postdoctoral fellow Albert Einstein Sch. Medicine, NYC, 1976-81; asst. prof. U. Mich. Med. Sch., Ann Arbor, 1981-87, assoc. prof., 1987-95, dir. student biomed. rsch. programs, 1989-92, dir. med. scientist tng. program, 1992-95; prof., chair dept. med. microbiology and immunology Sch. Medicine, Creighton U., Omaha, 1995—, interim dean, 1997-98, sr. assoc. dean academic affairs, 1998—. Contbr. chpts. to books, articles to profl. jours. Grantee NIH, Am. Cancer Soc. Mem. AAAS, Am. Che. Soc., Soc. for Microbiology, Am. Assn. Immunologists. Presbyterian. Office: Creighton U Sch Medicine Dept Med Microbiology & Immu Omaha NE 68178-0001 E-mail: rnairn@creighton.edu.

NAJARIAN, JOHN SARKIS, surgeon, educator; b. Oakland, Calif., Dec. 22, 1927; s. Garabed L. and Siranoush T. (Demirjian) N.; m. Arlys Viola Mignette Anderson, Apr. 27, 1952; children: Jon, David, Paul, Peter. AB with honors, U. Calif., Berkeley, 1948; MD, U. Calif., San Francisco, 1952; LHD (hon.), U. Athens, 1980; DSc (hon.), Gustavus Adolphus Coll., 1981; LHD (hon.), Calif. Luth. Coll., 1983. Diplomate Am. Bd. Surgery. Surg. intern U. Calif., San Francisco, 1952-53, surg. resident, 1955-60, asst. prof. surgery, dir. surg. research labs., chief transplant service dept. surgery, 1963-66, prof., vice chmn., 1966-67; spl. research fellow in immunopathology U. Pitts. Med. Sch., 1960-61; NIH sr. fellow and assoc. in tissue transplantation immunology Scripps Clinic and Research Found., La Jolla, Calif., 1961-63; Markle scholar Acad. Medicine, 1964-69; prof., chmn. dept. surgery U. Minn. Hosp., Mpls., 1967-93; med. dir. Transplant Ctr., clin. chief surgery Univ. Hosp., 1967-94; chief hosp. staff U. Minn. Hosp., Mpls., 1970-71, Regents' prof., 1985-95, Jay Phillips Disting. Chair in Surgery, 1986-95, prof. emeritus, prof. surgery, 1995—. Spl. cons. USPHS, NIH Clin. Rsch. Tng. Com., Inst. Gen. Med. Scis., 1965-69; cons. U.S. Bur. Budget, 1966-68; mem. sci. adv. bd. Nat. Kidney Found., 1968; mem. surg. study sect. A div. rsch. grants NIH, 1970; chmn. renal transplant adv. group VA Hosps., 1971; mem. bd. sci. cons. Sloan-Kettering Inst. Cancer Rsch., 1971-78; mem. screening com. Dernham Postdoctoral Fellowships in Oncology, Calif. div. Am. Cancer Soc. Editor: (with Richard L. Simmons) Transplantation, 1972; co-editor: Manual of Vascular Access, Organ Donation, and Transplantation, 1984; mem. editorial bd. Jour. Surg. Rsch., 1968—, Minn. Medicine, 1968—, Jour. Surg. Oncology, 1968—, Am. Jour. Surgery, 1967—, assoc. editor, 1982—; mem. editorial bd. Year Book of Surgery, 1970-85, Transplantation, 1970—, Transplantation Procs, 1970—, Bd. Clin. Editors, 1981-84, Annals of Surgery, 1972—, World Jour. Surgery, 1976—, Hippocrates, 1986—, Jour. Transplant Coordination, 1990—; assoc. editor: Surgery, 1971; editor-in-chief: Clin. Transplantation, 1986—. Bd. dirs., v.p. Variety Club Heart Hosp., U. Minn.; trustee, v.p. Minn. Med. Found. Served with USAF, 1953-55. Hon. fellow Royal Coll. Surgeons of Eng., 1987; hon. prof. U. Madrid, 1990; named Alumnus of Yr., U. Calif. Med. Sch., San Francisco, 1977; recipient award Calif. Trudeau Soc., 1962, Ann. Brotherhood award NCCJ, 1978, Disting. Achievement award Modern Medicine, 1978, Internat. Gt. Am. award B'nai B'rith Found., 1982, Uncommon Citizen award, 1985, Sir James Carreras award Variety Clubs Internat., 1987, Silver medal IXth Centenary, U. Bologna, 1988, Humanitarian of Yr. award, U. Minn., 1992, Najarian Festschrift award Am. Jour. Surgery, 1993, Jubilee medal Swedish Soc. Medicine, 1994. Fellow ACS; mem. AAAS, AMA, Internat. Pediat. Transplantation Assn. (pres. 1998-2000), Soc. Univ. Surgeons, Soc. Exptl. Biology and Medicine, Am. Soc. Exptl. Pathology, Am. Surg. Assn. (pres. 1988-89), Am. Assn. Immunologists, Transplantation Soc. (v.p. western hemisphere 1984-86, pres. 1994-96, Medawar prize 2004, Ellis Island medal of Hon, 2005), Am. Soc. Nephrology, Internat. Soc. Nephrology, Am. Assn. Lab. Animal Sci., Assn. Acad. Surgery (pres. 1969), Internat Soc. Surgery, Soc. Surg. Chairmen, Soc. Clin. Surgery, Ctrl. Surg. Assn., Minn. Med. Soc., Hennepin County Med. Socs., Minn. Surg. Soc., Mpls. Surg Soc, St. Paul Surg. Soc. Howard C. Nafziger Surg. Soc., Portland Surg Soc., Halsted Surg. Soc., Am. Heart Assn., Am. Soc. Transplant Surgeons (pres. 1977-78), Coun on Kidney in Cardiovasc. Disease, Hagfish Soc., Italian Rsch. Soc., Minn. Acad. Medicine, Minn. Med. Assn., Minn. Med. Found., Surg. Biology Club, Sigma Xi, Alpha Omega Alpha, others. Office: U Minn Surgery Dept Mayo Mail Code 195 420 Delaware St SE Minneapolis MN 55455-0374 Home Phone: 612-823-0051; Office Phone: 612-625-8444. Business E-Mail: najar001@umn.edu.

NAJITA, TETSUO, history professor; b. Honokaa, Hawaii, Mar. 30, 1936; s. Niichi and Kikuno (Manpuku) N.; m. Elinor Moon, Aug. 2, 1958; children: Mie Kim, Kiyoshi Young. BA, Grinnell Coll., 1958; MA, Harvard U., 1960, PhD, 1965; LLD, Grinnell Coll., 1989. Asst. prof. Carleton Coll., Northfield, Minn., 1964-66, Washington U., St. Louis, 1966-68; assoc. prof. U. Wis., Madison, 1968-69; Robert S. Ingersoll disting. prof. history/Japanese studies U. Chgo., 1969—2002, prof. emeritus, 2002—, dir. Ctr. for East Asian Studies, 1974-80, assoc. dean, 1983-87, master collegiate div. social scis., 1983-87. John A. Burns disting. visiting chair U. Hawaii, Manoa, 1994; chair dept. history U. Chgo., 1994-97; Ena H. Thompson lectr. Pomona Coll., 1996; Catherine Gould Chism vis. prof. U. Puget Sound, Tacoma; Maruyame Masao lectr. U. Calif., Berkeley, 2000; bd. dirs. Pacific Basin Inst., 2004. Author: Hara Kei in the Politics of Compromise, 1969 (J.K. Fairbank prize Am. Hist. Assn.), Intellectual Foundations of Modern Japanese Politics, 1974, Visions of Virtue in Tokugawa Japan, 1987, Tokugawa Political Writings, 1998. Grantee NEH 1973-74, 1980-81; Fulbright fellow 1961-63, 68, Guggenheim fellow 1980-81, Mellon Emeritus fellow, 2004-; recipient Yamagata Banto prize Prefecture of Osaka, 1989 Fellow Am. Acad. Arts and Scis.; mem. Am. Hist. Assn., Assn. for Asian Studies (v.p., pres. 1991-93), Phi Beta Kappa. Office: U Chgo Dept History 1126 E 59th St Chicago IL 60637-1580

NAKAJIMA, YASUKO, medical educator; b. Osaka, Japan, Jan. 8, 1932; came to U.S., 1962, 69; m. Shigehiro Nakajima; children: Hikeko H., Gene A. MD, U. Tokyo, 1955, PhD, 1962. Intern U. Tokyo Sch. Medicine, 1955-56, resident, 1956-57, instr., 1962-67; assoc. prof. Purdue U., West Lafayette, Ind., 1969-76, prof., 1976-88; prof. anatomy and cell biology U. Ill. Coll. Medicine, Chgo., 1988—. Vis. rsch. fellow Coll. Physicians and Surgeons, Columbia U., N.Y.C., 1962-64; asst. rsch. anatomist UCLA Sch. Medicine, 1964-65; vis. rsch. fellow Cambridge U., 1967-69; mem. study sect. NIH, 1996-98. Contbr. articles to sci. jours. Fulbright travel grantee, 1962-65; Univ. scholar U. Ill., 1997—. Mem. AAAS, Am. Physiol. Soc., Soc. Neurosci., Am. Soc. Cell Biology, Am. Assn. Anatomists, Biophys. Soc., Marine Biol. Lab. Corp. Office: U Ill Coll Medicine Dept Anatomy m/c 512 808 S Wood St Chicago IL 60612-7300 E-mail: YasukoN@uic.edu.

NAKER, MARY LESLIE, legal firm executive; b. Elgin, Ill., July 6, 1954; d. Robert George and Marilyn Jane (Swain). BS in Edn., No. Ill. U., 1976, MS in Edn., 1978, postgrad., 1980, Coll. Fin. Planning, 1990. Cert. tchr., Ill., fin. paraplanner. Retail sales clk. Fin'n Feather Farm, Dundee, Ill., 1972-75; pvt. practice tchr. South Elgin, Ill., 1974-78; tchg. asst. Sch. Dist #13, Bloomingdale, Ill., 1976-78, substitute tchr.; office mgr. Tempo 21, Carol Stream, Ill., 1978-82, LaGrange, Ill., 1982-85; sales coord. K&R Delivery, Hinsdale, Ill., 1986-89; fin. planner coord. Elite Adv. Svcs., Inc., Schaumburg, Ill., 1989-90; adminstrv. coord. Export Transports, Inc., Elk Grove Village, Ill., 1990-98; adminstrn. mgr. SBS Worldwide Chgo. Inc., Bensenville, Ill., 1998-99; office adminstr. DiMonte & Lizak, Attys. at Law, Park Ridge, Ill., 2000—. Leader Girl Scouts U.S.A., 1972—77, camp counselor, 1972—79; Sunday sch. tchr., 1999—. Music Scholar PTA, U. Wis., 1967, PTA, U. Iowa, 1968-69. Mem. Nat. Geographic Soc., Smithsonian Assn. Lutheran. Avocations: ceramics, bowling, knitting, camping, sewing. Home: 2020 Clearwater Way Elgin IL 60123-2588 Office: DiMonte & Lizak 216 Higgins Rd Park Ridge IL 60068-5706

NALBANDIAN, JOHN B., lawyer; b. Fort Ord, Calif., Feb. 15, 1969; BS in Econ., U. Pa., 1991; JD, U. Va., 1994. Bar: DC 1997, Ohio 2001. Clerk Hon. Jerry E. Smith. US Ct. of Appeals Fifth Cir.; worked in Issues and Appeals Sect., Litig. Grp. Jones, Day, Reavis & Pogue, Washington; ptnr. Taft, Stettinius & Hollister LLP, Cin. Named one of Ohio's Rising Stars, Super Lawyers, 2005, 2006. Mem.: Leadership Northern Ky. (Class of 2002), Telecom. Bd. Northern Ky., Cin. Bar Assn., DC Bar Assn., Va. Bar Assn., Order of Coif. Office: Taft Stettinius & Hollister LLP 425 Walnut St Ste 1800 Cincinnati OH 45202-3957 Office Phone: 513-381-2838. Office Fax: 513-381-0205.

NAMBU, YOICHIRO, physics professor; b. Toyko, Jan. 18, 1921; arrived in U.S., 1952; m. Chieko Hida Nambu, Nov. 3, 1945; 1 child, Jun-ichi. BS, U. Tokyo, 1942, DSc, 1952; DSc (hon.), Northwestern U., Evanston, Ill., 1987; degree (hon.), Osaka U., 1996. Research asst. U. Tokyo, 1945—49; prof. physics Osaka City U., Japan, 1950—56; mem. Inst. Advanced Study, Princeton, 1952—54; research assoc. U. Chgo., 1954—56, mem. faculty, 1956—, prof. physics, 1958, Henry Pratt Judson disting. svc. prof., 1978—91; Henry Pratt Judson Disting. Svc. prof. emeritus, dept. physics U. Chgo., Enrico Fermi Inst., 1991—. Contbr. articles to profl. jours. Recipient J. Robert Oppenheimer prize, 1976, Order of Culture, Japan Govt., 1978, US Nat. Medal Sci., 1982, Max Planck medal, German Physical Soc., 1985, Dirac medal, Internat. Centre for Theoretical Physics, 1986, Wolf prize in physics, Wolf Found., Israel, 1994, Gian Carlo Wick Commemorative medal, World Fedn. Scientists, 1995, Bogoliubov prize, Joint Inst. for Nuclear Rsch., 2003, Benjamin Franklin medal in Physics, Franklin Inst., 2005. Mem.: NAS, Georgian Acad. Sciences (fgn. fellow 1996), Am. Phys. Soc. (Sakurai prize 1994, Dannie Heineman prize for Math. Physics 1970), Am. Acad. Arts and Scis., Japan Acad. (hon.). Office: Univ of Chicago Enrico Fermi Inst 5640 S Ellis Ave EFI Box 29 RI 267 Chicago IL 60637 Office Phone: 773-702-7286. Business E-Mail: nambu@theory.uchicago.edu.

NANAGAS, MARIA TERESITA CRUZ, pediatrician, educator; b. Manila, Jan. 21, 1946; arrived in U.S., 1970; d. Ambrosio and Maria (Pasamonte) Cruz; m. Victor N. Nanagas, Jr.; children: Victor III, Valerie, Vivian. BS, U. of the Philippines, 1965, MD, 1970. Diplomate Am. Bd. Pediat. Intern, resident St. Elizabeth's Hosp., Boston, 1971-74; fellow in ambulatory pediat. North Shore Children's Hosp., Salem, Mass., 1974-75; active staff medicine Children's Med. Ctr., Dayton, Ohio, 1976—, head divsn. gen. pediat., 1988-90, 95-97, co-interim head ambulatory pediat., 1989-90, med. dir. ambulatory pediat., 1990—. Clin. asst. prof. pediat. Wright State U., Dayton, 1977-83, clin. assoc. prof. pediat., 1983—, selective dir., 1989—, assoc. prof. pediat., 2000—; clin. asst. prof. family practice Wright State U., Dayton, 1999—; dir., preceptor Wright State U. residents continuing clinic Children's Med. Ctr., 1989—, attending physician family practice programs, 1978—. Active Miami Valley Lead Poisoning Prevention Coalition, 19926. Fellow Am. Acad. Pediat.; mem. Western Ohio Pediat. Soc., Ambulatory Pediat. Assn. Office: Children's Med Ctr Health Clinic 1 Childrens Plz Dayton OH 45404-1898 Office Phone: 937-641-3500.

NANCE, FREDERICK, lawyer; b. Cleve., Oh., 1953; BA, Harvard U., 1975; JD, U. Mich., 1978. Bar: Ohio 1978, Fla. 1987, US Dist Ct., No. Dist Ohio, US Ct. Appeals Sixth Circuit. Mng. ptnr. Squire, Sanders & Dempsey, LLP, Cleve., 2002—. Mem. exec. com. Bus. Roundtable Cleve. Chmn. Cleveland Defense Indus. Alliance, 2004—05. Named one of Am. Best Corp. Lawyers, Corp. Board Mem. Mag., 2004, Best Lawyers in Am., Inside Bus. Mag, 2001—07. Mem.: ABA, US Ct Appeals Sixth Circuit Judicial Conf., Norman Minor Bar Assn., Ohio State Bar Assn. Office: Squire Sanders & Dempsey LLP 4900 Key Tower 127 Public Sq Cleveland OH 44114-1304

NAND, SUCHA, medical educator; b. Thiriewal, Punjab, India, Feb. 3, 1948; d. Narsingh Dass and Swaran Devi; m. Surinder S. Nand, June 15, 1973; children: Ranveer, Rahul. Pre-med. student, Dayanand Ayur Vedic Coll., Amritsar, India, 1966; MB, BS, Med. Coll., Amritsar, India, 1971. Diplomate Am. Bd. Internal Medicine, Am. Bd. Hemotology, Am. Bd. Med. Oncology. Asst. prof. Stritch Sch. Medicine Loyola U., Maywood, Ill., 1981-88, assoc. prof. Stritch Sch. Medicine, 1989-95; prof. medicine, 1996—. Editor Jour. of Med. Coll., 1969-71; contbr. articles to profl. jours. Clin. fellow Am. Cancer Soc., 1981; Brilliant Student scholarships, 1962-71. Mem. Am. Soc. Hematology, Am. Soc. Clin. Oncology, S.W. Oncology Group (mem. leukemia com. 1988—). Avocations: chess, reading, running. Office: Loyola Univ Med Ctr 2160 S 1st Ave Maywood IL 60153-3304 Office Phone: 708-327-3182.

NANNE, LOUIS VINCENT, professional hockey team executive; b. Sault Ste. Marie, Ont., Can., June 2, 1941; s. Michael and Evelyn N.; m. Francine Yvette Potvin, Aug. 27, 1962; children: Michelle, Michael, Marc, Marty. BS in Mktg., U. Minn., 1963. Mem. Minn. North Stars hockey club, 1967-78, v.p., gen. mgr., 1978-88, pres., 1988-91; sr. v.p. Piper Capital Mgmt., Mpls., 1991-95; exec. v.p. Voyageur Asset Mgmt., Mpls., 1995—. Bd. govs. Nat. Hockey League, 1981-91; mem. internat. com. USA Hockey. Bd. dirs. Mpls. C.C. Found., 1986-90, Children's Home Soc., 1998—. Recipient Lester Patrick award NHL, 1989; named among Top 50 Coll. Players in 50 Yrs.; inducted into U. Minn. Hall of Fame, U.S. Hockey Heritage Hall of Fame award, Sault St. Marie Hall of Fame, U.S. Hockey Hall of Fame, Internat. Ice Hockey Hall of Fame. Mem. Interlachen Country Club (bd. dirs. 1992-95), Spring Hill Golf Club (bd. dirs. 1996-2004). Roman Catholic. Office: Voyageur Asset Management 100 S 5th St Ste 2300 Minneapolis MN 55402-1230

NANNEY, DAVID LEDBETTER, geneticist, educator; b. Abingdon, Va., Oct. 10, 1925; s. Thomas Grady and Pearl (Ledbetter) Nanney; m. Jean Kelley, June 15, 1951; children: Douglas Paul, Ruth Elizabeth Beshears. AB, Okla. Bapt. U., 1946; PhD, Ind. U., 1951; Laurea honoris causa, U. Pisa, Italy, 1994. Asst. prof. zoology U. Mich., Ann Arbor, 1951-56, assoc. prof., 1956-58; prof. U. Ill., Urbana-Champaign, 1959-76, prof. genetics and devel., 1976-86, prof. ecology, ethology and evolution, 1987-91, prof. emeritus, 1991—. NIH sr. postdoctoral fellow Ind. U., 1949—51. Author (with Herbert Stern): The Biology of Cells, 1965, Experimental Ciliatology, 1980. Named Disting. Lectr., Sch. Life Scis., U. Ill., 1981; recipient Disting. Alumnus award, Okla. Bapt. U., 1972, Preisträger, Alexander von Humboldt Stiftung, Germany, 1984. Fellow: AAAS, Am. Acad. Arts and Scis.; mem.: Soc. Protozoologists, Am. Genetic Assn. (pres. 1982), Genetics Soc. Am. Home: 703 W Indiana Ave Urbana IL 61801-4835 Office: U Ill Dept Animal Biology 505 S Gregory St Urbana IL 61801 Business E-Mail: d-nanney@life.uiuc.edu.

NAPADENSKY, HYLA SARANE, engineering consultant; b. Chgo., Nov. 12, 1929; d. Morris and Minnie (Litz) Siegel; m. Arnaldo I. Napadensky; children: Lita, Yafa. BS in Math., MS in Math., U. Chgo. Design analysis engineer Internat. Harvester Co., Chgo., 1952-57; dir. rsch. Ill. Inst. Tech. Rsch. Inst., Chgo., 1957-88; v.p. Napadensky Energetics Inc., Evanston, Ill., 1988-94; engrng. cons., Lutsen, Minn., 1994-98. Contbr. numerous articles to profl. jours. Bd. overseers Armour Coll. Engring. Ill. Inst. Tech., 1988-93. Mem. NAE, Sigma Xi. Home and Office: 3284 W Highway 61 Grand Marais MN 55604-7537

NAPOLI, WILLIAM BILL, state legislator; Rep. S.D. State Dist. 35. Taxation com. S.D. Ho. Reps., transp. com.; owner Car Mus. Address: 6180 S Highway 79 Rapid City SD 57702-8467

NAPOLITANO, STEVEN V., lawyer; b. NYC, June 30, 1959; BA, U. Notre Dame; attended, London Sch. Econs.; JD, Boston U., 1985. Bar: Ill. 1985. Ptnr., co-chair Private Equity practice group, mem. bd. dirs. Katten Muchin Zavis Rosenman, Chgo., NYC. Mem.: ABA, Ill. State Bar Assn., Assn. for Corp. Growth. Office: 575 Madison Ave New York NY 10022 Office Phone: 312-902-5615. Office Fax: 312-577-8749. E-mail: steven.napolitano@kmzr.com.

NARAHASHI, TOSHIO, pharmacology educator; b. Fukuoka, Japan, Jan. 30, 1927; arrived in U.S., 1961; s. Asahachi and Itoko (Yamasaki) Ishii; m. Kyoko Narahashi, Apr. 21, 1956; children: Keiko, Taro. BS, U. Tokyo, 1948, PhD, 1960. Instr. U. Tokyo, 1951-65; research assoc. U. Chgo., 1961, asst. prof., 1962, Duke U., Durham, NC, 1962-63, 65-67, assoc. prof., 1967-69, prof., 1969-77, head pharmacology div., 1970-73, vice chmn. dept. physiology and pharmacology, 1973-75; prof., chmn. dept. pharmacology Northwestern U. Med. Sch., Chgo., 1977-94, Alfred Newton Richards prof., 1982—2005; John Evans prof. Northwestern U., Evanston, Ill., 1986—. Mem. pharmacology study sect. NIH, 1976-80; rsch. rev. com. Chgo. Heart Assn., 1977-82, vice chmn. rsch. coun., 1986-87, chmn., 1988-90; mem. Nat. Environ. Health Scis. Coun., 1982-86; rev. com. Nat. Inst. Environ. Health Scis., 1991-95. Editor: Cellular Pharmacology of Insecticides and Pheromones, 1979, Cellular and Molecular Neurotoxicology, 1984, Insecticide Action: From Molecule to Organism, 1989, Ion Channels, 1988—; specific field editor Jour. Pharmacology and Exptl. Therapeutics, 1972-97; assoc. editor Neurotoxicology, 1994—; contbr. articles to profl. jours. Recipient Javits Neurosci. Investigator award, NIH, 1986. Fellow AAAS, Acad. Toxicol. Scis.; mem. Am. Soc. for Pharmacology and Exptl. Therapeutics (Otto Krayer award 2000), Am. Physiol. Soc., Soc. for Neurosci., Biophys. Soc. (Cole award 1981), Soc. Toxicology (DuBois award 1988, Merit award 1991, Disting. Investigator Lifetime Achievement award 2001, Disting. Lifetime Toxicology Scholar award 2008), Agrochem. Divsn. Am. Chem. Soc. (Burdick L. Jackson Internat. award 1989). Home: 175 E Delaware Pl Apt 7911 Chicago IL 60611-7745 Office: Northwestern U Med Sch Dept Mol Pharmaco Biol Chem 303 E Chicago Ave Chicago IL 60611-3008 Home Phone: 312-337-0987; Office Phone: 312-503-8284. Business E-Mail: narahashi@northwestern.edu.

NARBER, GREGG ROSS, lawyer; b. Iowa City, Sept. 4, 1946; s. James R. and Marguerite Maxine (Lasher) N.; m. Kathleen Joyce Andriano; children: Joshua Ross, Zachary Edward. BA, Grinnell Coll., 1968; MA, JD, Washington U., St. Louis, 1971. Bar: Iowa 1971, U.S. Ct. Mil. Appeals 1974, U.S. Supreme Ct. 1974. Atty. The Principal Fin. Group, Des Moines, 1975-76, asst. counsel, 1976-80, assoc. counsel, 1980-85, counsel, 1985-89, v.p., gen. counsel, 1989-92, sr. v.p., gen. counsel, 1993—. Bd. dirs. Sargasso Mut. Ins. Co., Bermuda, Ban Renta Co. Seguros de Vida, Chile; prin. Life Compania de Seguros, S.A., Argentina, Internat. Argentina S.A., Compania de Seguros de Retiro S.A., Argentina; lectr. Iowa Humanities Bd., 1981-82, Arts Midwest, 1987. Co-author: New Deal Mural Projects in Iowa, 1982; also articles; artist various works. Pres. intercultural program Am. Field Svc. Internat., West Des Moines, 1990-94; mem. acquisitions com., bd. trustees Edmundson Art Found./Des Moines Art Ctr., 1989—, pres. 1998-99; bd. dirs. Des Moines Symphony, 1989-94, Metro Arts Coun. Greater Des Moines, 1990-94, Edmundson Art Found., 1992—, pres. 1998—. Mem. ABA (ho. of dels. 1995-98), Iowa Bar Assn., Polk County Bar Assn., Prairie Club (sec. 1982-84, 86-87, pres. 1991-92), West Des Moines Soccer Club (coach 1982-89, referee 1984-89). Democrat. Mem. Congregational Ch. Avocations: art history and collecting, soccer. Home: 711 High St Des Moines IA 50392-0001 Office: The Prin Fin Group 711 High St Des Moines IA 50392-0002

NARDELLI, ROBERT LOUIS, automotive executive, former consumer home products company executive; b. Old Forge, Pa., May 17, 1948; m. Sue Nardelli, 1971; 4 children. BS in Bus., Western Ill. U., 1971; MBA, U. Louisville, 1975; D in Bus. Adminstrn. (hon.), U. Louisville, 2001; LLD (hon.), Siena Coll., 2001; LHD (hon.), Western Ill. U., 2002. With GE, 1971-88; exec. v.p., gen. mgr. worldwide parts and components Case Corp., Racine, Wis., 1988-91; pres., CEO Can. Appliance Mfg. Co. subs. GE, Toronto, Ont., Canada, 1991-92, GE Transp. Sys., Erie, Pa., 1992-95, GE Power Sys., 1995-2000, The Home Depot, Atlanta, 2000—07, chmn., 2002—07; chmn., CEO Chrysler LLC, Auburn Hills, Mich., 2007—. Bd. dirs. The Home Depot, 2000—07, The Coca-Cola Co, 2002—05,

Chrysler LLC, 2007—. Named Exec. of Yr., Schenectady County C of C, 2000, Alumnus of Yr., U. Louisville, 2001; recipient Disting. Pennsylvanian Award, Gannon U., 1995, Disting. Alumni Award, Western Ill. U. Coll. Bus. & Tech., 1998. Mem.: President's Coun. on Service and Civic Participation, 2003. Office: Chrysler LLC 1000 Chrysler Dr Auburn Hills MI 48326*

NARKIEWICZ-LAINE, CHRISTIAN K., museum director, painter, poet; Student, U. de Strasbourg, France, 1970—72, Athens, Greece, 1972—73; grad., Lake Forest Coll., Ill., 1975. Arch. critic Chgo. Sun-Times, 1978—81; editor Inland Arch., 1979—81; pub. Met. Press Ltd., 1983; dir., pres. Chgo. Athenaeum, 1988—. Arch. cons.; tchr. arch. history and aesthetics Ill. Inst. Tech. Author: Helmut John, 1984, Landmark Springfield, 1985; author: (anthology of poetry) Distant Fires, 1997; author: Inspiration: Nature and the Poet (The Collected Poems of the Chicago architect, Louis H. Sullivan), 1999, Baltic Hours, 1999, Greenland, 2002, American Poets Against the War, 2006.

NARSAVAGE, GEORGIA ROBERTS, nursing educator, researcher; b. Pittston, Pa., Jan. 1, 1948; d. George H. Roberts and Betty (Smith) Brown; m. Peter P. Narsavage, Oct. 26, 1968; children: Peter A., Paul J., Marea L. BSN, U. Md., Washington DC, 1969; MSN, Coll. Misericordia, 1984; PhD in Nursing, U. Pa., Phila., 1990. RN, Ga.; cert. adult nurse practitioner, Ohio, Ga. Staff nurse Mercy Hosp., Scranton, Pa., 1970-72; pvt. duty nursing Pa., 1972-79; pvt. duty nurse Community Med. Ctr., Scranton, Pa., 1979; clinical instr. Lackawanna County Vo-Tech Practical Nursing Program, Dunmore, Pa., 1979-82; clinical and theoretical instr. Mercy Hosp. Sch. of Nursing, Scranton, Pa., 1982-84; asst. prof. nursing dept. nursing U. Scranton, Pa., 1984-93, assoc. prof., 1993—99, chmn. dept., 1991-94, dir. RN program dept. nursing, 1990-92, assoc. dean Panuska Coll. Profl. Studies, 1998—99; assoc. prof. Case Western Res. U., Cleve., 1999—2005, dir. MSN program Sch. Nursing, 1999—2004, assoc. dean Academic Programs, 2003—05; prof. and assoc. dean academic affairs Med. Coll. Ga., 2005—. Postdoctoral fellow U. Pa., Phila., 1995-97; cons. in field. Contbr. articles to profl. jours. Gifted program mentor Scranton Sch. Dist.; active in ch. and civic choirs. Grantee U. Scranton, 1989, 91, 94-98, NIH NRSA, 1995-97, Health Resources and Svcs. Adminstrn. Divsn. Nursing, 2004—; recipient Rsch. award European Respiratory Soc., 2002, Ednl. Rsch. award Midwest Nursing Rsch. Soc., 2004; Alumni award Nursing Edn. Coll. Misericordia, 2005. Fellow Am. Acad. Nursing; mem. ANA, APHA, Am. Thoracic Soc./Am. Lung Assn. (chmn. nursing assembly 2004—, bd. dirs., Abstract award 2002), Pa. Nurses Assn. (bd. dirs., chmn. com., conv. del., Excellence award 1996), Lackawanna Nurses Assn. (bd. dirs., com. chmn., dist. pres.), Nat. League for Nursing, Coun. ursing Informatics (chair nominating com. 1993-95), Pa. League for Nursing (chair nominating com.), Ohio Nurses Assn. (chmn. practice com.), Midwest ursing Rsch. Soc. (chmn. membership com., vice chmn. conf. com.), U. Md. Nurses Alumnae Assn., Ea. Nursing Rsch. Soc. (mem.-at-large bd. dirs., interim treas., rsch. grantee 1994), Theta Phi, Sigma Theta Tau (Rsch. award 1994), Iota Omega (Mentor award 2002). Lutheran. Office: Med Coll of Ga Son 997 St Sebastian Way Augusta GA 30912 Office Phone: 706-721-2787. Personal E-mail: narsavage1@hotmail.com. Business E-Mail: gnarsavage@mcg.edu.

NASH, DONALD GENE, federal investigator, economist; b. Paris, Ill., July 20, 1945; s. Lelan and Mildred (Washburn) N.; m. Jo Ann Bellew, Aug. 29, 1964; children: Stacey Alan, Ryan Christopher, Shaun Christian BS, So. Ill. U., 1967, MS, 1969; postgrad., DePaul U., Chgo., 1970-71. Farm mgr., test farms So. Ill. U., Carbondale, 1968-69; economist Commodity Futures Trading Commn., Chgo., 1969-77; v.p.-ops. Mid. Am. Commodity Exch., Chgo., 1977-86; sr. futures trading investigator Commodity Futures Trading Commn., Chgo., 1986—. Pres. Friends of Danada, Wheaton, Ill., 2001—. With N.G. US Army, 1968—74. Recipient Outstanding Mktg. award Wall St. Jour., 1966, award of merit Am. Farm Econ. Assn., 1967, cert. of merit Commodity Exch. Authority, merit award Naperville Art League, 1994, Honorable Mention award Danada Nature Show, 1995, 2002. Methodist. Avocations: photography, woodworking, sketching. Home: 923 Bainbridge Dr Naperville IL 60563-2002 Office: Commodity Futures Trading Comm 525 W Monroe St Ste 1100 Chicago IL 60661 Business E-Mail: dnash@cftc.gov.

NASH, GORDON BERNARD, JR., lawyer; b. Evergreen, Ill., Feb. 24, 1944; s. Gordon Bernard and Lilyan (Grafft) N.; m. Roseanne Joan Burke, Aug. 24, 1968; children: Caroline, Brian, Terry, Maureen. BA, Notre Dame U., 1966; JD, Loyola U., Chgo., 1969. Bar: Ill., U.S. Dist. Ct. (no. dist.) Ill. Atty. Office U.S. Atty. No. Dist. Ill., Chgo., 1971-78; prin. Gardner Carton & Douglas, LLC, Chgo., 1978—. Chmn. Ill. Bd. Ethics, Springfield, 1980-85. Served to capt. U.S. Army, 1969-71. Recipient John Marshall award U.S. Dept. Justice, 1978, Spl. Commendation award, 1975, Disting. Achievement award Internat. Acad. Trial Lawyers, 1969. Mem. ABA, Ill. Bar Assn., Chgo. Bar Found. Local Chpt. (bd. dirs. 1983-85, 87-89), Fed. Bar Assn. (bd. govs. 1986-91), Chgo. Bar Assn. (bd. mgrs. 1983-85, pres. 1990-91), Constl. Rights Found. Com. (bd. dirs. 1993—, chmn., 1998-2001), Am. Coll. Trial Lawyers, Ctr. for Conflict Resolution (bd. 1992-2000, v.p. 1995-2000), Chgo. Inn of Ct. (pres. 1996-97), Olympia Fields Country Club. Democrat. Roman Catholic. Home: 5101 Harvey Ave Western Springs IL 60558-2042 Office: Gardner Carton & Douglas LLC 191 N Wacker Dr Ste 3700 Chicago IL 60606-1698 E-mail: gnash@gcd.com.

NASH, JESSIE MADELEINE, journalist, science writer; b. Elizabeth City, NC, Sept. 11, 1943; d. John V. and Jessie B.; m. E. Thomas Nash, June 9, 1970. AB in History magna cum laude, Bryn Mawr Coll., 1965. Clip girl to sec. Time Mag., NYC, 1965-66, reporter rschr., 1966-70, stringer Bonn, Germany and Chgo., 1970-74, staff corr. Chgo., 1974-87, sr. sci. corr., 1987—. Mem. adv. com. on pub. infor. Am. Inst. of Physics, 1993-95. Author: El Niño: Unlocking the Secrets of the Master Weather-Maker, 2002. Recipient Page One award Newspaper Guild of N.Y., 1981, award Leukemia Soc. Am., 1994, Popular Sci. Writing award, Am. Astronomical Soc., 1997. David Perlman award, 2004. Mem. AAAS (Westinghouse award 1987, 90, Sci. Journalism award 1987, 91, 96,), Nat. Assn. Sci. Writers, Author's Guild, Sigma Xi (hon. mem). Avocation: travel. Office: Time Mag 303 E Ohio St Chicago IL 60611-3373

NASH, JOHN ARTHUR, bank executive; b. Indpls., Mar. 12, 1938; s. Basil and Harriet Nash; m. Susan Moss; children: John, Bill, Stacia. BS, Ind. U., 1960, MBA, 1961. Account officer Nat. City Bank, Cleve., 1961-66; v.p. Irwin Union Bank, Columbus, Ind., 1966-71, exec. v.p., 1971-75, pres., 1975-79; pres., bd. dirs. Irwin Fin. Corp., Columbus, 1975—2003. Bd. dirs. Irwin Union Bank, Irwin Mortgage Corp., Irwin Ventures, Irwin Home Equity Corp., Irwin Cap. Holdings. Chmn. bd. trustees Columbus Regional Hosp., Columbus Econ. Devel. Bd.; past chmn. Heritage Fund Bartholomew County, Columbus; mem. adv. bd. Ind. U.-Purdue U., Indpls. 2d lt. U.S. Army, 1961-63. Recipient Sagamore of Wabash award Gov. of Ind., 1991. Mem. Am. Bankers Assn. (mem. bank leadership coun.), Ind. Bankers Assn. (bd. dirs., past chmn., chmn. govt. rels. com.), Ind. U. Alumni Assn. (pres. 1991-92).

NASH, NICHOLAS DAVID, retail executive; b. Mpls., June 11, 1939; s. Edgar Vanderhoef and Nancy (Van Slyke) N. AB, Harvard U., 1962; MEd, Bowling Green State U., 1970; PhD, U. Minn., 1975. Head lower sch. Maumee Valley (Ohio) Country Day Sch., 1965-71; assoc. dir. Univ. Council for Ednl. Adminstrn.; adj. asst. prof. Ohio State U., 1975-78; v.p. programming Minn. Public Radio, St. Paul, 1978-82, Am. Pub. Radio, St. Paul, 1982-85; pres. The Nash Co., 1985—. Bd. dirs. Artspace Projects, Inc. Contbr. articles to profl. jours. Bd. dirs. Nash Found., 1975-04, Humane Soc. Companion Animals, 2002—06. Mem. Univ. Club St. Paul. Episcopalian. Home: 1340 N Birch Lake Blvd Saint Paul MN 55110-6716 Office: 2179 4th St Ste 2H Saint Paul MN 55110-3041 Business E-Mail: nicholasnash@post.harvard.edu.

NASH, RICK, professional hockey player; b. Brampton, Ont., Can., July 16, 1984; Left wing Columbus Blue Jackets, 2002—, capt., 2008—; left wing HC Davos, Switzerland, 2004—05. Mem. Team Can., IIHF World Championship, Vienna, 2005, Moscow, 07. Co-recipient Maurice Richard Trophy, 2004; named to NHL YoungStars Game, 2003, NHL All-Star Game, 2004, 2007, 2008; recipient All-Rookie Team, 2003. Achievements include being the first overall draft pick in HL entry draft, 2002. Avocation: golf. Office: Columbus Blue Jackets Nationwide Arena 200 W Nationwide Blvd, Ste Level Columbus OH 43215*

NASRALLAH, HENRY ATA, psychiatry researcher, educator; b. Apr. 30, 1947; came to U.S., 1972; s. Ata George and Rose G. (Yameen) N.; m. Amelia C. Tebsherani, June 9, 1972; children: Ramzy George, Rima Alice. BS in Biology, Am. U. of Beirut, 1967; MD, Am. U. Coll Medicine, Beirut-Lebanon, 1971. Intern Am. U. Med. Ctr., Beirut, 1972; resident in psychiatry U. Rochester, N.Y., 1972-75; rsch. assoc. NIMH, Washington, 1975-77; asst. prof. psychiatry U. Calif., San Diego, 1977-79; from assoc. prof. to prof. psychiatry U. Iowa, Iowa City, 1979-85; prof., chair psychiatry Ohio State U., Columbus, 1985-98; prof. psychiatry U. Miss. Med. Ctr., Jackson, 1998—2002; assoc. dean U. Cin. Coll. Medicine, 2003—. Staff psychiatrist VA Med. Ctr., La Jolla, Calif., 1977—79, chief psychiatry svc., Iowa City, 1979—85. Editor: (5 vol. book series) Handbook of Schizophrenia, 1986-90; co-editor: NMR Spectroscopy in Psychiatric Brain Disorders, 1995; editor-in-chief Schizophrenia Rsch., 1987—, Jour. Psychiatry Disorders, 1996—; author and co-author over 200 published articles, 1976—. Pres. Psychiat. Rsch. Found. of Columbus, 1985—; mem. Alliance for the Mentally Ill, Columbus, 1987—. Recipient VA grants, 1979-84, NIMH, 1983—. Fellow Am. Psychiat. Assn. (coun. on rsch.), Am. Coll. Neuropsychopharmacology (chmn. pubs. com. 1992-95), Am. Coll. Psychiatrists (Deans Award com. 1996—), Am. Acad. Clin. Psychiatrists (pres. 1989-90), Soc. Biol. Psychiatry (awards com. 1988-90). Avocations: photography, tennis, poetry. Office: U Cin Med Ctr Dept Psychiatry 231 Albert Sabin Way Cincinnati OH 45267-0559

NASS, CONNIE KAY, state auditor; m. Alan Nass; 3 children. V.p. Nass & Son, Inc., 1974—; auditor State of Ind., 1999—. Bd. Senator Richard Lugar's Excellence in Pub. Svc. Program. Bd. mem. Huntingburg Utility Bd., 1975—; city coun. mem., Huntingburg, 1979-88, mayor, 1988-96; mgr. municipally owned utility cos., Huntingburg, 1988-96; candidate for lt. gov. State of Ind., 1995-96; mem. GOP Platform Com., 1992; del. Rep. Nat. Conv., 1996; bd. dirs. Welborn Found. Evansville, S.W. Ind. Regional Health Care Ctr., Inc.; adv. bd. AAA, Evansville, 1990—; mem. fin. com. and emergency svcs. com. ARC Greater Indpls., 1999—; nat. gen. synod del. Ind.-Ky. Conf. United Ch. of Christ, 1981, com. on planning and evaluation, 1990—, bd. dirs., 1996—; Sunday sch. tchr., music dir. Salem United Ch. of Christ. Recipient Protect Our Woods Environtl. award, 1995; named Outstanding Rep. Woman Ind. Reps Mayor's Assn., 1995. Mem. Nat. Automated Clearing House Assn. (internet coun., electronic benefits coun., strategic expansion bd.), Nat. Assn. State Auditors, Comptrs. and Treas., etwork Women in Bus., Women Execs. in State Govt., Ind. State Auditor Adv. Coun., Ind. Farm Bur., Ind. Assn. of Cities and Towns (bd. dirs.), Dubois County GOP Women's Club (pres. 1996-98), Marion County GOP Women's Club, Huntingburg C. of C. Republican. Office: State House Rm 240 200 W Washington St Indianapolis IN 46204-2728

NATHAN, PETER E., psychologist, educator; b. St. Louis, Apr. 18, 1935; s. Emil and Kathryn (Kline) N.; m. Florence I. Baker, Nov. 26, 1959; children: David Edward, Anne Miller, Laura Carol, Mark Andrew. AB, Harvard U., 1957; PhD, Washington U., 1962. Research fellow psychology Harvard U., 1962-64, research asso., 1964-68, asst. prof. psychology, 1968-69; research psychologist Boston City Hosp., 1964-68, dir. alcohol study unit, 1967-70; prof. Rutgers U., New Brunswick, NJ, 1969-89, dir. clin. psychology tng., 1969-87, dir. Alcohol Behavior Research Lab., 1970-87, chmn. dept. clin. psychology, 1976-87, dir. Ctr. Alcohol Studies, 1983-89, Henry and Anna Starr prof. psychology, 1983-89; sr. program officer, health program MacArthur Found., 1987-89; v.p. acad. affairs, found. disting. prof. psychology U. Iowa, 1990—, dean faculties, 1990-93, provost, 1993-95, acting pres., 1995. Mem. advisory council VA, 1972-76; chmn. alcoholism com. Nat. Inst. on Alcohol Abuse and Alcoholism, 1973-76, co-chmn. spl. rev. com., 1985, mem. nat. adv. coun., 1990-94; mem. psychol. scis. fellowship rev. com. NIMH, 1977-79; chmn. N.J. State Community Mental Health Bd., 1981-84; mem. working group substance use disorders, DSM-IV. Author: Cues, Decisions, and Diagnoses, 1967, Psychopathology and Society, 1975, 2d edit., 1980, Experimental and Behavioral Approaches to Alcoholism, 1978, Alcoholism: New Directions in Behavioral Treatment and Research, 1978, Clinical Case Studies in the Behavioral Treatment of Alcoholism, 1982, Professionals in Distress, 1987, Neuropsychological Deficits in Alcoholism, 1987, Introduction to Psychology, 1987, 2d edit., 1990, Abnormal Psychology, 1992, 2d edit., 1996, A Guide to Treatments that Work, 1998, 2d edit., 2002; exec. editor: Jour. Studies Alcohol, 1983—90; assoc. editor Am. Psychologist, 1977—85, Contemporary Psychology, 1991—97, Prevention and Treatment, 1998—2001, Psychol. Bull., 2002—, mem. editl. bd. Jour. Clin. Psychology, 1969—95, Jour. Cons. Clin. Psychology, 1973—95, Profl. Psychology, 1976—89. Fellow Am. Psychol. Assn. (chmn. sect. 3 div. 12 1976-77, rep. to council 1976-79, 82-85, pres. div. 12 1984-85; Disting. Contbns. to Knowledge award 1999). Democrat. Jewish. Home: 248 Black Springs Cir Iowa City IA 52246-3800 Office: Univ Iowa E119 Seashore Hall Iowa City IA 52242-1316 Business E-Mail: peter-nathan@uiowa.edu.

NATHANSON, SAUL DAVID, oncologist, surgeon, educator; b. Johannesburg, Dec. 12, 1943; came to U.S., 1975; s. Hymie Barnett and Freda Charlotte (Weinberg) N.; m. Maxine Elaine Zacks, Nov. 29, 1966 (div. Sept. 1978); children: Laurence Cecil, Joshua Russel; m. Jerrilyn Marie Burke, Feb. 18, 1979; children: Abigail Mary, Alison Megan. MD, U. Witwatersrand, Johannesburg, 1966. Diplomate Am. Bd. Surgery. Resident in surgery U. Witwatersrand, 1967-74; fellow in immunology UCLA, 1975-77, fellow in surg. oncology, 1977-80; chief resident in surgery U. Calif.-Davis, Sacramento, 1980-82; surg. oncologist Henry Ford Health Sys., Detroit, 1982—, dir. breast cancer ctr., 1995—; prof. surgery Case Western Res. U., Cleve., 1993—2005. Assoc. clin. prof. surgery U. Mich., Ann Arbor, 1985—2000; adj. assoc. prof. med. physics Oakland U., Rochester, Mich., 1993—; cancer liaison physician, Commn. on Cancer; prin. investigator for HFHS, ACS Oncology Group; endowed chair Breast Cancer Rsch., 2001. Author: Ordinary Miracles, 2006; contbr. over 200 articles and abstracts to sci. jours., chpts. to books. Recipient Outstanding Tchr. awards U. Mich., 1982-2000, Humanitarian Cancer award, 2006; named Resident Tchr. of Yr., Henry Ford Health Sys. Dept. Surgery, 2006; NIH grantee Nat. Cancer Inst., 1989. Fellow ACS, Soc. Surg. Oncology, Royal Coll. Surgeons; mem. Am. Soc. Clin. Oncology, Western Surg. Assn., Am. Assn. Cancer Rsch., Wayne County Med. Soc. (alt. del. 1994—96). Office: Henry Ford Health Sys 2799 W Grand Blvd Detroit MI 48202-2608 Home Phone: 248-594-0045; Office Phone: 313-916-2917. Business E-Mail: dnathan1@hfhs.org.

NATOLI, JOSEPH, language educator; b. Bklyn., Aug. 24, 1943; m. Elaine Tuminelli, June 6, 1970; children: Amelia, Brenda. BA, Bklyn. Coll., 1965, MA, 1968; PhD, SUNY, Albany, 1973. Asst. prof. English New Eng. Coll., Henniker, NH, 1971-73, 1973-75; acting dir. libr., adj. lectr. English Bluefield State Coll., W.Va., 1975-77; head reference and bibliography libr. Wake Forest U., Winston Salem, NC, 1977-81; bibliographer, adj. lectr. humanities U. Calif., Irvine, 1981-83, Mich. State U., East Lansing, 1983—, dir. study abroad program Europe, 1996—. Series editor SUNY Press Postmodern Culture, Albany, 1990—. Author: Mots D'Ordre, 1992, Hauntings, 1994, Primer to Postmodernity, 1997, Speeding to the Millenium, 1998, Postmodern Journeys, 2000, Memory's Orbit, 2003, This is a Picture and Not the World, 2007; editor: Twentieth Century Blake Criticism, 1982, Psychological Perspectives on Literature, 1984, Psychocriticism, 1984, Tracing Literary Theory, 1987, Literary Theory's Future(s), 1989, A Postmodern Reader, 1993, Postmodernism: The Key Figures, 2002. Office: Mich State Univ Writing Rhetoric Am Culture Dept 241 Bessey Hall East Lansing MI 48824 Business E-Mail: natoli@msu.edu.

NATZ, JACQUES, news director; b. Paris, Dec. 3, 1955; BA in Journalism, U. Mo., 1977. News dir. WTHR-TV, Indpls., 1996—. Recipient Emmy award, 1985. Mem. Radio TV News Dir.'s Assn. Office: WTHR-TV 1000 N Meridian St Indianapolis IN 46204-1076

NAUGLE, ROBERT PAUL, dentist; b. Cleve., May 3, 1951; s. Paul Franklin Albert and Olga (Bigadza) N.; m. Nancy Elaine Baker, June 14, 1975; 1 child, Jennifer Elaine. BS, Heidelberg Coll., Tiffin, Ohio, 1973; DDS, Case Western Res. U., 1977. Pvt. practice, Uniontown, Ohio, 1980—. Capt. USAF, 1977-80. Mem. ADA, Ohio Dental Assn., Acad. Gen. Dentistry, Acad. Sports Dentistry, Stark County Dental Soc., Akron Dental Soc., Air Force Assn., Rotary (past program chmn. Uniontown, Student of Month chmn., past pres., past v.p., past treas., Paul Harris fellow, past sgt.-at-arms, past cmty. svc. chmn.). Republican. Mem. United Church of Christ. Office: 13027 Cleveland Ave NW Uniontown OH 44685-8430 Office Phone: 330-699-5995.

NAULT, WILLIAM HENRY, publishing executive; b. Ishpeming, Mich., June 9, 1926; s. Henry J. and Eva (Perrault) N.; m. Helen E. Matthews, Nov. 28, 1946; children: William Henry, Rebecca Nault Marks, Ronald, George, Peter, Julia Nault Doyle, Robert, David. AB, No. Mich. U., 1948, LittD (hon.), 1988; MA, U. Mich., 1949; EdD, Columbia U., 1953, LHD (hon.), 1980, LLD (hon.), 1986, LittD (hon.), 1988. Dir. adult edn., Battle Creek, Mich., 1948—49; guidance counselor, 1949-50; prin. W.K. Kellogg High Sch., Battle Creek, 1950-53; research assoc. Columbia U., 1953-54; asst. supt. Ridgewood, NJ, 1954-55; adj. prof. William Patterson U. N.J., 1954—55; dir. research World Book, Inc. (formerly Field Enterprises Edn. Corp.), Chgo., 1955-63, v.p., 1963-66, sr. v.p., editorial dir., 1966-68, exec. v.p. and editorial dir., 1968-83; pres., pub., chief operating officer World Book, Inc., 1983-84, gen. chmn. editorial adv. bds., 1968-99, pub., 1983-95, pub. emeritus, 1995—. Past vice chmn. Govt. Adv. Com. on Internat. Library and Book Programs, U.S. Dept. State; past mem. nat. adv. bd. Ctr. on Ednl. Media and Materials for Handicapped; past mem. exec. bd. Commn. Instns. Higher Edn., North Central Assn. Colls. and Secondary Schs.; mem. dean's adv. council Coll. Bus. and Pub. Adminstrn., U. Mo., Columbia; mem. nat. council Inst. Internat. Edn. Author material on courses of study. Mem. alumni com. Columbia Tchrs. Coll. Capital Campaign; mem. White House Conf. on Youth, White House Conf. on Librs., White House Conf. on Edn.; pres. Oak Park (Ill.) Bd. Edn., 1960-63; v.p. LaGrange (Ill.) Libr. Bd.; bd. regents Lincoln Acad., Ill.; past trustee Adler Planetarium, De Paul U., Chgo. Geol. Soc.; bd. dirs. H.V. Phalin Found. Grad. Study, World Book, Inc., A.J. Nystrom Co., Field Edn. Co., Libr. Movens, Inc.; mem. adv. bd. Rosary Coll.; mem. liberal arts and scis. adv. council De Paul U. Served with F.A., AUS, 1944-45. Recipient Columbia U. Tchrs. Coll. medal for disting. svc. in edn.; named Disting. Alumnus No. Mich. U., U. Mich., Columbia U. Fellow AAAS; mem. ALA, Chgo. Planetarium Soc. (trustee), Chgo. Geog. Soc. (dir.), Am. Acad. Polit. and Social Sci., Am. Edn. Rsch. Assn., Am. Assn. Sch. Adminstrs., ASCD, Chgo. Pubs. Assn. (past pres.), Ill. Assn. Sch. Adminstrs., Ill. Acad. Sci., NSTA, Nat. Council Tchrs. English, Assn. Am. Geographers, Assn. Childhood Edn. Internat., NAESP, Nat. Assn. Secondary Sch. Prins., Council for Advancement Sci. Writing, Internat. Platform Assn., Nat. Council Social Studies, Nat. Soc. Study Edn. Clubs: Mid-Am, Mchts. and Mfrs. Roman Catholic. Office: World Book Inc 525 W Monroe St Chicago IL 60661-3629 Personal E-mail: naultwh@aol.com, naultwh@comcast.net.

NAUMANN, JOSEPH FRED, archbishop; b. St. Louis, June 4, 1949; s. Fred and Louise (Lukens) Naumann. BA, Cardinal Glennon Coll., St. Louis, 1971; degree in theology, Kenrick Sem., St. Louis, 1975. Deacon St. Christopher's Parish, Florissant, Mo., 1974-75; ordained priest Archdiocese of St. Louis, 1975; assoc. pastor St. Dominic Savio Parish, Affton, Mo., 1975-79, Our Lady of Sorrows Parish, St. Louis, 1979-84; part-time assoc. pastor Most Blessed Sacrament Parish, St. Louis, 1984-89; pastor Ascension Parish, Normandy, Mo., 1989-94; vicar gen. Archdiocese of St. Louis, 1994—97, aux. bishop, 1997—2004, apostolic adminstr., 2003—04; coadjutor archbishop Archdiocese of Kansas City in Kans., 2004, archbishop, 2005—. Chmn. Kans. Cath. Conf.; trustee Kenrick-Glennon Sem. Roman Catholic. Office: Archdiocese of Kansas City 12615 Parallel Pkwy Kansas City KS 66109*

NAVARRE, RICHARD A., mining executive; Dir. fin. planning Peabody Group, St. Louis, 1993, v.p., CFO, exec. v.p., CFO, 2001—. Pres., v.p. fin., controller Peabody COALSALES; bd. advisors Coll. Bus. and Adminstrn. and Sch. Acct. So. Ill. U., Carbondale; chmn. Bituminous Coal Operators' Assn.; mem. Fin. Execs. Internat.; exec. comm. Civic Entrepeneurs Organization; advisor New York Mercantile Exchange. Bd. advsr. So. Ill. Univ. -Carbondale Coll. Bus. Admin. Office: Peabody Group 701 Market St Saint Louis MO 63101 E-mail: publicrelations@peabodygroup.com.

NAVARRE, ROBERT WARD, manufacturing executive, director; b. Monroe, Mich., May 21, 1933; s. Joseph Alexander N.; m. Barbara Anne Navarre, June 26, 1953; children— Veo Anne, Robert Ward, Jan Louise. BS in Commerce, U. Notre Dame, 1955; grad., exec. program Stanford U., 1979. Sales mgr. Marben Corp., Jackson, Mich., 1958-64; mktg. adminstr. Simpson Industries, Litchfield, Mich., 1964-67, pres., CEO, 1967-89, chmn., 1989-97, also bd. dirs. Bd. dirs. Webster Industries. Chmn. Jackson/Hillsdale Mental Health Service Bd., 1972-78; mem. Hillsdale Schs. Bd. Edn., 1972-76. Mem. NAM (regional vice chmn. 1978-79, chmn. membership com. 1979-80, bd. dirs.), Mich. Mfg. Assn. (bd. dirs., chmn. 1991—). Roman Catholic. Office: Simpson Industries Inc 47603 Halyard Dr Plymouth MI 48170-2429

NAVARRO, MONICA, lawyer; b. 1967; arrived in US, 1984; m. Mark Crane. BA in Polit. Sci. and Internat. Rels., Fla. Internat. U., 1990; JD, U. Mich. Law Sch., 1993. Bar: Ill., Mich., US Supreme Ct., US Ct. of Appeals Sixth Cir., US Dist. Ct. Eastern Dist. Mich., US Dist. Ct. Western Dist. Mich. Judicial clerk Hon. Julian Abele Cook, Jr., US Dist. Ct., Eastern Dist. Mich.; atty. Frank, Haron; prin. mem., ptnr. Frank, Haron, Weiner and Navarro, 2004—. Mem., HIPAA Compliance Com. Troy Chamber of Commerce; trustee Mich. Psychoanalytic Found., Southwest Solutions; chair tech. subcom. Health Law Sect. Mich. Bar. Guest Hospitals and Physicians: Friends and Foes, Bloomfield Cmty. TV, 2006. Named a Mich. Super Lawyer, 2007; named one of Top 10 Qui Tam Lawyers in Country, Corp. Crime Reporter, 40 Under 40, Crain's Detroit Bus., 2006; recipient Am. Jurisprudence award in Adminstrv. Law, Best Oralist award. Fellow: Oakland County Bar Found.; mem.: State of Mich. Bd. Psych. (mem. disciplinary subcom.), Mich. Trial Lawyers Assn., Assn. Trial Lawyers Am., Oakland County Women's Bar Assn. (Work Life balance award 2006), Oakland County Bar Assn. (Med./Legal Com.), Mich. Assn. Health Lawyers (mem. Tech. Subcommittee), Hispanic Bar Assn. Mich., Am. Health Lawyers Assn. Office: Frank, Haron, Weiner and Navarro 5435 Corporate Dr Ste 225 Troy MI 48098 Office Phone: 248-952-0400. Office Fax: 248-952-0890. Business E-Mail: mnavarro@fhwnlaw.com.

NAVRATIL, ROBERT J., financial executive; Prin. in charge of property The RREEF Funds, Chgo., 1989—. Office: 41st Fl 875 N Michigan Ave Fl 41 Chicago IL 60611-1803

NAYLOR, JAMES CHARLES, psychologist, educator; b. Chgo., Feb. 8, 1932; s. Joseph Sewell and Berniece (Berg) N.; m. Georgia Lou Mason, Feb. 14, 1953; children— Mary Denise, Diana Darice, Shari Dalice. BS, Purdue U., 1957, MS, 1958, PhD, 1960. Asst. prof. Ohio State U., 1960-63, asso. prof., 1963-67, prof. vice chmn. dept. psychology, 1967-68; prof. Purdue U., Lafayette, Ind., 1968-86, head dept. psychol. scis., 1968-79; prof., chmn. dept. psychology Ohio State U., Columbus, 1986-98, prof. emeritus, 1999—. Fulbright rsch. scholar, Umea, Sweden, 1976; Disting. scholar, vis. scientist Flinders U., South Australia, 1982-83, UNESCO ednl. cons. to Hangzhou U., Peoples Republic of China, 1984; chmn. Coun. Grad. Depts. Psychology, 1993-94; lead reviewer Psychology Program Rev., State U. Sys. Fla., 1996. Author: Industrial Psychology, 1968, A Theory of Behavior in Organizations, 1980; founder, editor: Organizational Behavior and Human Decision Processes; mem. editorial bd.: Prof. Psychology; Contbr. articles to profl. jours. Served with USN, 1950-54. Fellow AAAS, Am. Psychol. Soc., Am. Psychol. Assn.; mem. Psychonomic Soc., Psychmetric Soc., Internat. Assn. Applied Psychology, Soc. Organizational Behavior (founder), Midwestern Psychol. Assn. (coun. 1994-97), Phi Beta Kappa, Sigma Xi. Home: 176 Tucker Dr Columbus OH 43085-3064 Office: Ohio State U Dept Psychology Columbus OH 43210 E-mail: naylor.2@osu.edu.

NEAGLE, DENNIS EDWARD (DENNY NEAGLE), professional baseball player; b. Gambrills, Md., Oct. 13, 1968; Grad. high sch., Gambrills, Md.; student, U. Minn. With Minn. Twins, 1991; pitcher Pitts. Pirates, 1992-96, Atlanta Braves, 1996-98, Cin. Reds, 1999—. Selected to N.L. All-Star Team, 1995. Achievements include being a mem. Pitts. Pirates N.L. East Champions, 1992. Office: Cin Reds Cinergy Field 100 Cinergy Fld Cincinnati OH 45202-3543

NEAL, DIANE L., retail executive; BS in Retailing, Mich. State U., 1979. Various positions to pres. of Target subs. Mervyn's Target Corp., 1985—2001, pres. Mervyn's, 2001—04; sr. v.p. merchandising Gap, Inc., 2004—05, pres. Gap Inc. Outlet, 2005—06; pres., COO Bath & Body Works, Inc., Reynoldsburg, Ohio, 2006—07, CEO, 2007—. Bd. dirs. Nautilus Inc., 2004—. Mem. corp. fundraising com. San Francisco Museum Modern Art. Office: Bath and Body Works Inc Seven Limited Pkwy E Reynoldsburg OH 43068

NEAL, HOMER ALFRED, physics professor, researcher, academic administrator; b. Franklin, Ky., June 13, 1942; s. Homer and Margaret Elizabeth (Holland) Neal; m. Donna Jean Daniels, June 16, 1962; children: Sharon Denise, Homer Alfred Jr. BS in Physics with honors, Ind. U., 1961; MS in Physics (John Hay Whitney fellow), U. Mich., 1963, PhD in Physics, 1966. Asst. prof. physics Ind. U., 1967—70, assoc. prof., 1970—72, prof., 1972—81, dean research and grad. devel., 1976—81; prof. physics SUNY, Stony Brook, 1981—87, provost, 1981—86; prof. physics, chmn. U. Mich., Ann Arbor, 1987—93, v.p. rsch., 1993—97, interim pres., 1996—97, prof. of physics, 1987—2000, Samuel A. Goudsmit disting. prof. physics, 2000—, dir. of atlas project, 1997—. Bd. dirs. Ford Motor Co.; mem. Nat. Sci. Bd., 1980—86; mem. adv. coun. Oak Ridge Nat. Lab., 1993—99; mem. external adv. coun. Nat. Computational Sci. Alliance, 1997—; mem. applications strategy coun. Univ. Corp. for Advanced Internet Devel., 2000—; chmn. Argonne Zero Gradient Synchrotron Users Group, 1970—72; trustee Argonne Univs. Assn., 1971—74, 1977—80; physics adv. panel NSF, 1976—79, chmn. physics adv. panel, 1987—89; high energy physics adv. panel U.S. Dept. Energy, 1977—81. Contbr. articles to profl. jours. Mem. bd. regents Smithsonian Instn., 1989—2001; trustee Ctr. for Strategic and Internat. Studies, 1990—2000, Oak Ridge Nat. Lab., Tenn., 1993—99; mem. Smithsonian Coun. on the Nat. Mus. African Am. History and Culture, 2004—; mem. bd. overseers Superconducting Super Collider, 1989—93; trustee Environ. Rsch. Inst. of Mich., 1994—96, Lounsbery Found., 2005—, NY Sea Grant Inst., 1982—86. Recipient Stony Brook medal, 1986, Ind. U. Disting. Alumni award, 1994; fellow NSF, 1966—67, Sloan, 1968, Guggenheim, 1980—81. Fellow: AAAS, Am. Acad. Arts and Scis., Am. Phys. Soc.; mem.: Univs. Rsch. Assn. (trustee), Sigma Xi. Office: Dept Physics Rm 2477 Randall Lab 450 Church St Ann Arbor MI 48109-1040

NEAL, LANGDON D., lawyer; BA, Cornell U., 1978; JD, U. Ill., 1981. Bar: Supreme Ct. Ill., US Dist. Ct., No. Dist. Ill., Mem. of Trial Bar. Assoc. Neal, Murdock& Leroy LLC, Chgo. Lectr. Am. Inst. Real Estate Appraisers, Cook County Bar Assoc., Judicial Candidates Symposium. Mem. West DePaul Neighbors, Coordinated Advise and Referral Program for Legal Svcs., Chgo. Pub. Edn. Fund, Jane Addams Juvenile Ct. Found., Children's Place Assn., The Support Group; bd. dirs. Cole Taylor Bank; chmn. Ill. State Bd. Elections, 1991—93, Chgo. Bd. Election Commissioners, 1997—. Mem.: ABA, Ill. State Bar Assn., Chgo. Bar Assn., Cook County Bar Assn., Chgo. Hist. Soc. Office: Neal Murdock & Leroy LLC 203 N LaSalle St Ste 2300 Chicago IL 60601-1213 Office Phone: 312-641-7144.

NEAL, MO (P. MAUREEN NEAL), sculptor; b. Houston, Oct. 26, 1950; d. Gordon Taft and Mary Louise (O'Connor) N.; m. Thomas Alan Buttars, Jan. 2, 1984. BA cum laude, Wash. State U., 1988; MFA, Va. Commonwealth U., 1991. Assoc. prof. art and art history U. Nebr., Lincoln, 1994—. Adj. faculty dept. fine arts U. S.D., Vermillion, 1991-92. Grantee S.D. Arts Coun., 1992, 94, Nat. Endowment for Arts, 1994; fellow Nebr. Arts Coun., 1998. Mem. Mid Am. Coll. Art Assn. (bd. dirs. 1997, pres. 2000-02), Phi Beta Kappa. Democrat. Office: U Nebr Dept Art & Art History Rm 120 Richards Hall Lincoln NE 68588-0114 E-mail: moneal@unl.edu.

NEALE, GARY LEE, utilities executive; b. Lead, SD, Mar. 3, 1940; s. Vearl J. and Gladys M. (Trenkle) N.; m. Sandra C. Lovell, June 16, 1962; children: David G., Julie C. BA in Econs., U. Wash., 1962, MBA, 1965. Loan examiner Wells Fargo, 1966-69; sr. fin. analyst Kaiser Industries, 1969-70; chmn., pres., chief exec. officer Planmetrics, Chgo., 1970-89; pres., chief oper. officer No. Ind. Pub. Svc. Co., Hammond, 1989-93; chmn., pres., CEO NiSource Inc. (formerly o. Ind. Pub. Svc. Co.), Hammond, Ind., 1993—2005, chmn., 2005—06. Bd. dirs. Modine Mfg., Racine, Wis., Am. Gas Assn., Arlington, Va., Ind. Gas Assn./Ind. Electric Assn., Indpls., Nipsco Industries Inc., Hammond. Bd. dirs. N.W. Ind. Symphony, 1990; mem. Ind. Energy Policy Forum, 1991. Lt. (j.g.) USN, 1962-64. Mem. Econ. Club Chgo., Chgo. Univ. Club, NYU Club.

NEALE, HENRY WHITEHEAD, plastic surgery educator; b. Richmond, Va., July 18, 1940; s. Richard C. and Eva W. Neale; m. Margaret C. Neale, June 20, 1964; children: Leigh, Jennifer, Henry Whitehead Neale Jr., William. BS, Davidson Coll., 1960; MD, Med. Coll. Va., 1964. Diplomate Am. Bd. Surgery, Am. Bd. Plastic Surgery. Intern Mercy Med. Ctr., Springfield, Ohio, 1964—65; resident in gen. surgery U. Cin. Med. Ctr., 1965—71, dir. divsn. plastic, reconstructive and hand surgery, 1974—; resident in plastic surgery Duke U. Med. Ctr., Durham, NC, 1971—74; fellow in hand surgery, Christine Kleinert hand fellow U. Louisville, 1973; asst. prof. surgery U. Cin. Coll. Medicine, 1974—77, assoc. prof., 1977—82, prof., 1982—; active staff, dir. hand surgery and plastic surgery clinics U. Cin. Med. Ctr. Hosp. Group, 1974—, prof., chmn. divsn. plastic surgery, 1974—. Guest examiner Am. Bd. Plastic Surgery, 1986—90, dir., 1990—96, com. on plans and qualifying exam. com., liaison to Am. Bd. Surgery, 1993—96, exec. com., 1993—, chmn. certifying examing com., 1993—95, ethics com., 1993, chmn.-elect, 1995—96; dir. burn reconstructive and plastic surgery, co-dir. hand surgery svc. Shriners Burns Inst., Cin., 1983—; dir. divsn. plastic, reconstructive and hand surgery and plastic surgery clinic Childrens Hosp. Med. Ctr., Cin., 1983—; assoc. attending staff Good Samaritan Hosp.; courtesy staff Christ Hosp., Jewish Hosp.; presenter in field. Mem. editl. bd.: Jour. Plastic and Reconstructive Surgery, 1989—; contbr. articles to profl. jours. Grantee Rsch. grant, Eli Lilly Co., 1979—91. Fellow: ACS; mem.: AMA, Plastic Surgery Rsch. Coun., Ohio Valley Soc. Plaastic and Reconstructive Surgery (pres. 1985—86), Ohio Med. Assn., Greater Cin. Soc. Plastic and Reconstructive Surgeons (pres. 1988—89), Grad. Surg. Soc. Cin., Cin. Surg. Soc., Assn. Acad. Chairmen in Plastic Surgery, Acad. Medicine Cin., Am. Soc. for Surgery of Hand, Am. Soc. Plastic and Reconstructive Surgeons, Am. Soc. for Aesthetic Plastic Surgery, Am. Cleft Palate Assn., Am. Burn Assn., Am. Assn. Plastic Surgeons. Office: U Cin Coll Medicine Plastic Reconst and Hand Su 231 Bethesda Ave Cincinnati OH 45267-0001 Home: PO Box 1268 Montreat NC 28757-1268

NEAMAN, MARK ROBERT, hospital administrator; b. Buffalo, Oct. 22, 1950; married. B, Ohio State U., 1972, MHA, 1974. Adminstrv. asst. Evanston (Ill.) Hosp., 1974-76, asst. to v.p., 1976-78, asst. v.p., 1978-80, v.p., 1980-84, sr. v.p., 1984-85, pres., exec. v.p., 1985-90, pres., 1990-92, pres., CEO, 1992—. Chmn. Am. College of Healthcare Execs., 2002—; bd. trustees Healthcare Leadership Coun. Fellow Am. Coll. Healthcare Execs. (chmn., RS Hudgens award 1988). Office: Evanston Northwestern Healthcare 1301 Central St Evanston IL 60201-1781

NEARY, DANIEL P., insurance company executive; b. Carroll, Iowa, 1952; m. Shirley Neary; 4 children. Degree, U. Iowa, 1974. With Mut. of Omaha, 1975—, exec. v.p. group benefit svcs., 1999—2003; pres., bd. dirs. Mut. of Omaha and United of Omaha, 2003—05, CEO, chmn., 2005—. Bd. dir. Comml. Fed. Bank, Comml. Fed. Corp., America's Health Ins. Plans, Creighton U. Bd. dirs. United Way, Midlands and Am. Red Cross; mem. Boy Scouts Am. Mid-Am. Coun.; chmn. Walk to Cure Diabetes Juvenile Diabetes Rsch. Found., 2004; bd. trustees Strategic Air & Space Mus. Mem.: Soc. Actuaries. Office: Mut of Omaha Mutual of Omaha Plz Omaha NE 68175

NEAVES, WILLIAM BARLOW, cell biologist, educator; b. Spur, Tex., Dec. 25, 1943; s. William Fred and Revvie Lee (Hefner) N.; m. Priscilla Wood, Jan. 28, 1965; children: William Barlow, Clarissa D'laine. AB magna cum laude, Harvard U., 1966; postgrad., Med. Sch., 1966-67, PhD, 1969. Lectr. vet. anatomy U. Nairobi, 1970-71, vis. prof., 1978; lectr. anatomy Harvard U., 1972; asst. prof. cell biology U. Tex. Health Sci. Ctr., Dallas, 1972-74, assoc. prof., 1974-77, prof., 1977—, Doris and Brian Wildenthal Prof. of Biomed. Sci., 1993—, dean Grad. Sch. Biomed. Scis., 1980-88, interim dean Southwestern Med. Sch., 1986-88, dean Southwestern Med. Sch., 1989-98, exec. v.p. acad. affairs, 1998—2000; prof. medicine U. Mo., Kans. City, 1998—2000; pres., CEO, bd. dirs. Stowers Inst. Med. Rsch., Kans. City, 2000—. Dir. Cerner Corp., Midwest Rsch. Inst., Kans. City Area Life Scis. Inst.; trustee Wash. U.; mem. nat. coun. Wash. U. Sch. Medicine; rsch. assoc. herpetology Los Angeles County Mus., 1970-73; vis. lectr. U. Chgo., 1976-77. Assoc. editor Anat. Record, 1975-87; mem. editl. bd. Biology of Reprodn., 1983-86, Jour. Andrology, 1987-89; contbr. chpts. to books, articles to profl. jours. Bd. dirs. Dallas Zool. Soc., 1989-94, Dallas Mus. Natural History, 1993-95, Damon Runyan-Walter Winchell Cancer Fund, 1986-92, v.p., 1990-92, Sarnoff Endowment, 1998—. Rockefeller Found. fellow, 1970-71; Milton Fund grantee, 1970-71; Population Council grantee, 1973-75; NIH grantee, 1973-89; Ford. Found. grantee, 1976-78. Fellow AAAS; mem. Am. Assn. Anatomists, Am. Soc. Andrology (Young Andrologist award 1983), Dallas Assembly, N.Y. Acad. Scis., Soc. Study of Reprodn., Liaison Com. on Med. Edn. (joint com. of AMA and Assn. Am. Med. Colls.), Sigma Xi, Alpha Omega Alpha. Methodist. Office: Stowers Inst Med Rsch 1000 East 50th St Kansas City MO 64110 Office Phone: 816-926-4040. Business E-Mail: wbn@stowers-institute.org.

NECHEMIAS, STEPHEN MURRAY, lawyer; b. St. Louis, July 27, 1944; s. Herbert Bernard and Toby Helen (Wax) N.; m. Marcia Rosenstein, June 19, 1966 (div. Dec. 1981); children: Daniel Jay, Scott Michael; m. Linda Adams, Aug. 20, 1983. BS, Ohio State U., 1966; JD, U. Cin., 1969. Bar: Ohio 1969. Ptnr. Taft, Stettinius & Hollister, Cin., 1969—. Adj. prof. law No. Ky. U., Chase Coll. Law. Tax comment author: Couse's Ohio Form Book, 6th edit., 1984. Mem. Ohio State Bar Assn. (former chmn. taxation com.), Cin. Bar Assn. (former chmn. taxation sect. 1985), Legal Aid Soc. Cin. (former pres., trustee), Am. Bar Assn. (taxation sect.) Democrat. Jewish. Home: 2490 Royalview Ct Cincinnati OH 45244 Office: 1800 US Bank Tower 425 Walnut St Cincinnati OH 45202-3923 Office Phone: 513-357-9392.

NECHIN, HERBERT BENJAMIN, lawyer; b. Chgo., Oct. 25, 1935; s. Abraham and Zelda (Benjamin) Nechin; m. Susan Zimmerman (div.); 1 child, Jill Rebecca; m. Roberta Fishman, Oct. 24, 1976; 1 child, Stefan. BA with distinction and with honors in History, Northwestern U., Evanston, Ill., 1956; JD, Harvard U. Law Sch., Cambridge, Mass., 1959. Bar: Ill. 1960. From assoc. to ptnr. Brown Fox & Blumberg, Chgo., 1960-75; ptnr. Taussig Wexler & Shaw, Chgo., 1975-79, Fink Coff Stern, Chgo., 1979-81, Holleb & Coff, Chgo., 1981-2000; of counsel Levin & Schreder, Ltd., Chgo., 2000—04; assoc. dir. gift planning Northwestern U., Evanston, Ill., 2004—. Contbr. articles to profl. jours. Pres. Emanuel Congregation, Chgo., 1994—97. Staff sgt. USAR, 1960—66. Mem.: ABA, Am. Coll. Trust and Estate Counsel, Chgo. Bar Assn. (chmn. trust law com. 1990—91), Ill. Bar Assn., Cliff Dwellers Club, Phi Beta Kappa. Office: Northwestern U Office Alumini Rels and Devel 2020 Ridge Ave 3rd Fl Evanston IL 60208-4307 Home Phone: 773-929-5889; Office Phone: 847-491-7394. Business E-Mail: h-nechin@northwestern.edu.

NEEDHAM, GEORGE MICHAEL, association executive; b. Buffalo, July 3, 1955; s. Paul James and Dolores Ann (Duffy) N.; m. Joyce Elaine Leahy, Nov. 28, 1992; 1 stepchild, Katherine Callison. BA in English, SUNY, Buffalo, 1976, MLS, 1977. Various profl. positions Charleston (S.C.) County Libr., 1977-84; dir. Fairfield County Dist. Libr., Lancaster, Ohio, 1984-89; mem. svcs. dir. Ohio Libr. Assn., Columbus, 1990-92; exec. dir. Pub. Libr. Assn., Chgo., 1993-96; state librarian State of Mich., Lansing, 1996-99; v.p. mem. svcs. OCLC Online Computer libr. Ctr., Dublin, Ohio, 1999—. Trustee Learning Point Assocs, 2004-. Co-author: A Director's Checklist for Connecting Public Libraries to the Internet, 1995; author (book revs.) Booklist, 1994-2002 (video revs.), Libr. Jours., 1979-94. Bd. dirs. Fairfield County chpt. ARC, Lancaster, 1984-88, Mt. Prospect Theatre Soc., Mt. Prospect, Ill., 1993-96, Lib. Media Project, 1997-2007. Mem. ALA, Pub. Libr. Assn., Ohio Libr. Assn. Achievements include 2 time Jeopardy champion. Avocations: acting, traditional folk music, writing. Office: OCLC Online Computer Libr Ctr 6565 Kilgour Pl Dublin OH 43017-3395 Home Phone: 614-761-0372; Office Phone: 614-761-5173. E-mail: needhamg@oclc.org.

NEEDHAM, GLEN RAY, entomology and acarology educator, researcher; b. Lamar, Colo., Dec. 25, 1951; s. Robert Lee and Evor Elaine (Kern) N.; m. Karla Marie Lohr, May 28, 1983; children: Kathleen Marie, John Harrison, Elizabeth Anne. BS, S.W. Okla. State U., 1973; MS, Okla. State U., 1975, PhD, 1978. Grad. rsch. asst. Okla. State U., Stillwater, 1974-78; asst. prof. Ohio State U., Columbus, 1978-84, assoc. prof., 1984—, co-organizer and coord. acarology summer program. Co-editor: Africanized Honey Bees and Bee Mites, 1988, Acarology IX: Proceedings and Symposia. Donor ARC, Columbus. Recipient Dist. Alumnus award Okla. State U., 1992; Faculty Christian fellowship Ohio State U. Mem. Acarology Soc. Am. (pres. 1994), Ohio Acad. Sci., Ohio Asthma Coalition, Ctrl. Ohio Asthma Coalition, Gamma Sigma Delta. Methodist. Achievements include research in tick and dust mite biology and control. Office: Ohio State U 318 W 12th Ave Columbus OH 43210 Office Phone: 614-688-3026. Business E-Mail: needham.1@osu.edu.

NEEDLEMAN, BARBARA, newspaper executive; BS in Eng., Northwestern Univ., 1994. V.p. Tribune Media Svcs., Chgo., 1993—. Office: Tribune Media Svcs 435 N Michigan Ave Ste 1500 Chicago IL 60611-4012

NEEL, HARRY BRYAN, III, surgeon, scientist, educator; b. Rochester, Minn., Oct. 28, 1939; s. Harry Bryan and May Birgitta (Bjornsson) N.; m. Ingrid Helene Vaga, Aug. 29, 1964; children: Carlton Bryan, Harry Bryan IV, Roger Clifton. BS, Cornell U., 1962; MD, SUNY-Bklyn., 1966; PhD, U. Minn., 1976. Diplomate Am. Bd. Otolaryngology. Intern Kings County Hosp., Bklyn., 1966-67; resident in gen. surgery U. Minn. Hosps., Mpls., 1967-68; clin. assoc. NCI/NIH, 1968—70; resident in otolaryngology Mayo Grad. Sch. Medicine Mayo Clinic, Rochester, Minn., 1970-74, cons. in otorhinolaryngology, 1974—2005, cons. in cell biology, 1981—2005, assoc. prof. otolaryngology and microbiology Med. Sch., 1979-84, prof., 1984—, also chmn. dept. otolaryngology. Mem. sci. adv. com. Pitts. Eye and Ear Found.; lifetime vis. prof. Hunan U., China, 2003—. Author: Cryosurgery for Cancer, 1976; contbr. chpts. to books, articles to profl. jours. V.p. bd. dirs. Minn. Orch. in Rochester, Inc., 1982, pres., chmn., 1983—84; mem. devel. com. Minn. Orchestral Assn., 1983, Mayo Found., 1983—86; bd. dirs. Mayo Health Plan, 1986—92, chmn., 1990—92; mem. bd. Mayo Mgmt. Svcs., Inc., 1992—94; mem. Mayo Found. Academic Appointments and Formation Coir, 2005—07; mem. bd. regents U. Minn., 1991—2003, chair faculty staff, student affairs com., 1993—95, 1999, vice chmn. bd., 1995—97, chmn. fin. and ops. com., 1999, mem. audit com., 1995—2000, chair litigation review com., 2001—03, chair facilities com., 2001—03; bd. dirs. Greater Rochester Area Univ. Ctr., 1993—2003; trustee U. Minn. Found., 1996—2005, mem. fin. com., 1999—2005; chmn. U. Minn. Investment Adv. Com., 1999—2003; mem. U. Minn., Conflict Interest Coir, 2006—, State Commn. on U. Minn. Excellence, 2002; founder U. Minn.-Rochester Neel Scholarship Endowment Fund Health Scis., 2003. With USPHS, 1968—70. Recipient travel award Soc. Acad. Chmn. Otolaryngology, 1974, Ira J. Tresley rsch. award Am. Acad. Facial and Reconstructive Surgery, 1982, Master Tchr. award in surgery Alumni Assn. Coll. Medicine, SUNY, Health Sci. Ctr., Bklyn., 1991, Notable award Nat. Assn. Collegiate Women Athletic Adminstrs., 1992; name one of Best Drs. in Am., Good Housekeeping, 1991, Best Drs. in Am., Woodward/White, 1992—, Best Drs. in Minn., Minn. Monthly, 2003, Cmty. Leaders of World, Am.'s Top Physicians, Consumers' Rsch. Coun. Mem. AMA, ACS (bd. govs. 1985-90, devel. bd. 1988—, treas. 1990-98, sec.-treas. Minn. chpt. 1983-85, pres. 1988-89), Am. Acad. Otolaryngology-Head and Neck Surgery (prize for basic rsch. in otolaryngology 1972, bd. dirs. 1988-91, established Neel Disting. Rsch. Lectureship Endowment Fund 1994, audit com. 1998-2000, chair investment adv. com. 1995—, chmn. audit com. 1999-2000), Minn. Med. Assn. (com. on adminstrn. and fin. 2003—05, Cmty. Svc. award for outstanding cmty. svc. 2003, Pub. Svc. Achievement award 2003), Zumbro Valley Med. Soc., Am. Broncho-Esophagological Assn. (pres. 1989-90), Am. Laryngological, Rhinological and Oto. Sco. (Mosher award 1980, pres.-elect 1995-96, centennial pres. 1996-97, investment com. 1994—, historian, 2001—), Am. Laryngological Assn. (Casselberry award 1985, sec. 1988-93, v.p. 1994, pres. 1994—, Newcomb award 1996, Baker lectr. 1998), Assn. for Rsch. in Otolaryngology, Assn. Acad. Depts. in Otolaryngology (sec.-treas. 1984-86, pres.-elect 1986, pres. 1988-9), Alumni Assn. Cornell U. (Outstanding Alumni award 1985), Collegium ORL Amicitiae Sacrum (bd. dirs., 2d sec. 2000—), Am. Bd. Otolaryngology (bd. dirs. 1986-2005, treas. 1998-2004), Am Laryngol. Voice Rsch. and Edn. Found. (charter bd. dirs. 1996-2003), Rochester Golf and Country Club. Republican. Presbyterian. Home: 828 8th St SW Rochester MN 55902-6310 Office: Mayo Clinic 200 1st St SW Rochester MN 55905-0002 Home Phone: 507-282-0035. Personal E-mail: ivyneel@aol.com.

NEELY, ELLEN J., lawyer; b. 1964; BA in Govt. and History, U. Tex.; JD, U. Chgo. Assoc. Wildman, Harrold, Allen & Dixon; asst. gen. counsel Chgo. Mercantile Exchange, 1995—99; v.p., gen. counsel Chgo. Stock Exchange, 1999—2001, sr. v.p. legal and market regulation, gen. counsel, corp. sec., 2001—05, pres. & gen. counsel, 2005—. Office: Chgo Stock Exchange One Financial Pl 440 S LaSalle St Chicago IL 60605

NEESE, TIMOTHY, state representative; Grad., Ball State U. Adminstr. Solid Waste Mgmt. Dist. Elkhart County, Ind.; rep. dist. 48 Ind. Ho. of Reps., Indpls., 2002—. Mem. Ind. Recycling Coalition; bd. mem. Dollars for Scholars; bd. dirs. Elkhart YMCA. Republican. Office: Ind Ho of Reps 200 W Washington St Indianapolis IN 46204-2786

NEFF, DAVID M., lawyer; b. Allentown, Pa., Nov. 18, 1960; BSJ, Northwestern Univ., 1982; JD, DePaul Univ., 1985. Bar: Ill. 1985, US Dist. Ct. (no. Ill., ea. & we. Wis., we. Mich. dist.). Law clk. Judge Robert E. Ginsberg, US Bankruptcy Ct., no. dist. Ill., 1985—86; ptnr., co-chmn. Lodging & Timeshare practice group DLA Piper US LLP, Chgo. Contbr. articles to profl. jours. Mem.: Internat. Soc. Hospitality Consultants (chmn.), ABA (co-chmn. publications, Bankruptcy & Insolvency subcommittee.), Am. Bankruptcy Inst., 7th Cir. Bar Assn. (Ill. bankruptcy liason), Chgo. Bar Assn. (chmn. bankruptcy & reorganization com. 1998—99). Office: Perkins Coie LLP 131 S Dearborn St Ste 1700 Chicago IL 60603-5559 Office Phone: 312-324-8689. Business E-Mail: dneff@perkinscoie.com.

NEFF, ROBERT MATTHEW, lawyer, finance company executive; b. Huntington, Ind., Mar. 26, 1955; s. Robert Eugene and Ann (Bash) N.; m. Lee Ann Loving, Aug. 23, 1980; children: Alexandra, Graydon, Philip. BA in English, DePauw U., 1977; JD, Ind. U., Indpls., 1980. Bar: Ind. 1980, U.S. Dist. Ct. (so. dist.) Ind. 1980, U.S. Supreme Ct., 1993. Assoc. Krieg, DeVault, Alexander & Capehart, Indpls., 1980-85, ptnr., 1986-88, Baker & Daniels, Indpls., 1988-92; of counsel, 1993-96; dept. to chmn. Fed. Housing Fin. Bd., Washington, 1992-93; pres., CEO Circle Investors, Inc., Indpls., 1993-97, also bd. dirs.; chmn., CEO Senex Fin. Corp., Indpls., 1998—2007; pres., CEO Clarian Health Ventures, Inc., Indpls., 2007—. Mem. faculty Grad. Sch. of Banking of South, 1988—1990; chmn. Liberty Bankers Life Ins. Co., 1995—1998, Am. Founders Life Ins. Co., Laurel Life Ins. Co., Aztek Life Assurance Co., 1996—1997; bd. dirs. Quanta Specialty Lines Ins. Co., CH Assurance Ltd., Clarian Health RRG, Unified Fin. Svcs., Inc., Conseco Strategic Income Fund. Exec. editor Ind. Law Rev., 1979-80. Participant Lacy Exec. Leadership Conf., Indpls., 1985-86; trustee DePauw U., 1977-80; bd. govs. Riley Children's Found., 1999-; del. White House Conf. on Aging, 2005. Mem. ABA (chmn. bus. law com. young lawyers divsn. 1988-90, banking law com. 1990-92), Ind. Bar Assn. (chmn. corps. banking and bus. law sect. 1987-88), DePauw Alumni Assn. (bd. dirs. 1982-88), Phi Kappa Psi, Phi Beta Kappa. Avocations: golf, fishing. Home: 7202 Merriam Rd Indianapolis IN 46240 Office: Clarian Health Ventures 10 W Market St No 400 Indianapolis IN 46204 Office Phone: 317-656-8511. Business E-Mail: rmneff@clarian.org.

NEGISHI, EI-ICHI, chemistry professor; arrived in U.S., 1960; BS in Organic Chemistry, U. Tokyo, 1958; PhD in Organic Chemistry, U. Pa., 1963. Rsch. chemist Teijin Ltd., 1958-65; postdoctoral assoc. Purdue U., 1966-68, asst. to H.C. Brown, 1968-72; asst. prof. Syracuse (N.Y.) U., 1972-76, assoc. prof., 1976-79; prof. Purdue U., West Lafayette, Ind., 1979-99, Herbert C. Brown disting. prof., 1999—. Lectr. in field. Recipient A. von Humboldt Rschr. award 1998—; Fulbright scholar, 1960-63. Mem.: Royal Soc. Chemistry (Sir E. Frankland Prize lectureship 2000), Japan Chem. Soc. (award 1997), Am. Chem. Soc. (Organometallic Chemistry award 1998), Sigma Xi, Phi Lambda Epsilon. Office: Purdue U Chem Dept 560 Oval Dr West Lafayette IN 47907-2084 Home Phone: 765-463-4439; Office Phone: 765-494-5301. Business E-Mail: negishi@purdue.edu.

NEHRA, GERALD PETER, lawyer; b. Detroit, Mar. 25, 1940; s. Joseph P. and Jeanette M. (Bauer) N.; m. children: Teresa, Patricia; m. Peggy Jensen, Sept. 12, 1987. BIE, Gen. Motors Inst., Flint, Mich., 1962; JD, Detroit Coll. Law, 1970. Bar: Mich. 1970, N.Y. 1972, Colo. 1992, U.S. Dist. Ct. (ea. dist.) Mich. 1970, U.S. Dist. Ct. (so. dist.) N.Y. 1972, U.S. Dist. Ct. (no. dist.) N.Y. 1976, U.S. Ct. Appeals (6th cir.) 1978. Successively engr., supr., gen. supr. Gen. Motors Corp., 1958-67; mktg. rep. to regional counsel IBM Corp., 1967-79; v.p. gen. counsel Church & Dwight Co., Inc., 1979-82; dep. chief atty. Amway Corp., 1982-83; dep. gen. counsel, 1983-92; dir. legal div., 1989-91; sec., dir. corp. law, 1991-92; v.p. gen. cousnel Fuller Brush, Boulder, Colo., 1991-92; pvt. practice, 1992—. Adj. instr. Dale Carnegie Courses, 1983-91. Recipient Outstanding Contbn. award Am. Cancer Soc., 1976. Mem. ABA, Mich. Bar Assn., Colo. Bar Assn., N.Y. State Bar Assn. Home and Office: 1710 Beach St Muskegon MI 49441-1008 Home Phone: 231-755-3800; Office Phone: 231-755-3800. Business E-Mail: gnehra@mlmatty.com.

NEHS, (WILLIAM) SCOTT, lawyer; b. Janesville, Wis., Mar. 7, 1966; m. Jacqueline Nehs. BA, Northwestern U., 1988; JD, U. Wis., Madison, 1991. Bar: Ill. 1991, Wis. 1991, US Dist. Ct. No. Dist. Ill. 1991, US Dist. Ct. We. Dist. Wis. 1991, US Dist. Ct. Ea. Dist. Wis. 1993. Assoc. Wildman, Harrold, Allen & Dixon, Chgo., 1991—99; dep. gen. counsel Pepsi-Cola Gen. Bottlers Inc., Rolling Meadows, Ill., 2000—01; asst. gen. counsel PepsiAmericas Inc. (formerly Whitman Corp.), Rolling Meadows, Ill., 2000—01, v.p. legal, 2001—, chief compliance officer. Pro bono work Legal Clinic for the Disabled, 1992—, Les Turner ALS Found., 1995—. Named one of The Top 40 Lawyers Under 40 in Ill., Chgo. Daily Law Bulletin, 2004. Mem.: Assn. of Corp. Counsel, Wis. State Bar, Chgo. Bar Assn. Office: Pepsiamericas Caribbean Inc 1475 E Woodfield Rd Ste 1300 Schaumburg IL 60173-5482

NEIDHARDT, FREDERICK CARL, microbiologist, educator; b. Phila., May 12, 1931; s. Adam Fred and Carrie (Fry) N.; m. Elizabeth Robinson, June 9, 1956 (div. Sept. 1977); children: Richard Frederick, Jane Elizabeth; m. Germaine Chipault, Dec. 3, 1977; 1 son, Marc Frederick. BA, Kenyon Coll., 1952, DSc (hon.), 1976; PhD, Harvard U., 1956; DSc (hon.), Purdue U., 1988, Umea U., 1994. Research fellow Pasteur Inst., Paris, 1956-57; H.C. Ernst research fellow Harvard Med. Sch., 1957-58, instr., then assoc., 1958-61; mem. faculty Purdue U., 1961-70, assoc. prof, then prof., assoc. head dept. biol. scis., 1965-70; mem. faculty U. Mich., Ann Arbor, 1970—, chmn. dept. microbiology and immunology, 1970-82, F.G. Novy disting. univ. prof., 1989-99, F.G. Novy disting. univ. prof. emeritus, 2000—, assoc. dean faculty affairs, 1990-93, assoc. v.p. for rsch., 1993-96, acting v.p. for rsch., 1996-97, interim v.p. for rsch., 1997, v.p. for rsch., 1998. Cons. Dept. Agr., 1964-65; mem. grant study panel NIH, 1965-69, 88-92; mem. commn. scholars Ill. Bd. Higher Edn., 1973-79; mem. test com. for microbiology Nat. Bd. Med. Examiners, 1975-79, chmn., 1979-83; mem. sci. adv. com. Neogen Corp., 1982-92; mem. basic energy scis. adv. com. U.S. Dept. Energy, 1994-98; Wellcome vis. prof. in microbiology U. Ky., 1986. Author books and papers in field; mem. editorial bd. profl. jours. Recipient award bacteriology and immunology Eli Lilly and Co., 1966; Alexander von Humboldt Found. award for U.S. sr. scientist, 1979; NSF sr. fellow U. Copenhagen, 1968-69 Mem. Am. Soc. Microbiology (pres. 1981-82), Am. Acad. Arts and Scis., Am. Soc. Biochemistry and Molecular Biology, Am. Inst. Biol. Scis., Genetics Soc. Am., Bavarian Acad. Sci., Soc. Gen. Physiology, Waksman Found. for Microbiology (bd. dirs. 1996—, pres. 2001—), Phi Beta Kappa, Sigma Xi. Office: U Mich Med Sch Dept Microbiology and Immunology Ann Arbor MI 48109-0620 Home Phone: 734-995-2951; Office Phone: 734-763-1209. E-mail: fcneid@umich.edu.

NEIDIG, BRYCE P., farmer, farm association administrator; Pres. Nebr. Farm Bur.; owner, gen. farming operation Madison, Nebr. Office: 5225 S 16th St PO Box 80299 Lincoln NE 68512

NEIN, SCOTT R., state legislator; b. Hamilton, Ohio, Apr. 13, 1951; m. Janis Nein; children: Jason, Courtney, Beckett, Brody. BS, Bowling Green State U., 1974. Mem. Ohio Ho. of Reps from 58th dist., Columbus, 1991-95, Ohio Senate from 4th dist., Columbus, 1995—. Agt. Miller Ins.; mem. Butler County Rep. exec. com. Recipient Congl. appt. 8th Congl. Dist. Awards Coun., 1987. Mem. Prof. Ins. Agts. Assn., Ohio Ind. Ins. Agts. Assn., Middletown Ind. Ins. Agts. Assn. (past pres.), Rotary (past pres., Paul Harris Fellow), Middletown C. of C. (bd. dirs.), Farm Bur.

NEITHERCUT, DAVID J., real estate company officer; BA, St. Lawrence U.; MBA, Columbia U. With real estate dept. Continental Bank; with comml. mortgage banking div. Draper & Kramer, Inc.; sr. v.p. fin. Equity Group Investments; joined Equity Residential, 1993, CFO, 1995—2004, exec. v.p. corp. strategy, 2004—05, pres., 2005—, CEO, 2006—. Office: Equity Residential Properties Trust 2 N Riverside Plz Ste 450 Chicago IL 60606-2600

NELLEMANN, LYNNE O'SHEA, management consultant; b. Chgo., Oct. 18, 1955; d. Edward Fisk and Mildred Lessner O'Shea. BA, BJ in Polit. Sci. and Journalism, U. Mo., MA in Info. Theory, 1971; PhD in Consumer Cultures, Northwestern U., 1978; postgrad., Sch. Mgmt. and Strategic Studies, U. Calif., 1988. Congl. asst., Washington, 1968—70; brand mgr. Procter & Gamble Co., Cin., 1971-73; v.p. Foote, Cone & Belding, Inc., Chgo., 1973-79; v.p. corp. comms. Internat. Harvester Co., Chgo., 1979-82; dir. mktg. and comms. Arthur Andersen & Co., Chgo., 1983-86; v.p. bus. devel. Gannett Co., Inc., Chgo., 1987-94; pres., chief oper. officer Shalit Place L.L.C., 1995—98; exec. v.p. Mus. Broadcast Comm., Chgo., 1996-97; dir. A.T. Kearney, Chgo., 1998—2005; pres. Ill. Women's Forum, 2005—; head Women's Leadership Initiative, Dominican

U., 2007—. Prof. mktg. U. Chgo. Grad. Sch. Bus., 1979—80, Kellogg Grad. Sch. Mgmt., 1983—84, 1994—95; co-chair Fed. Glass Ceiling Commn., 1991—95; exec.-in-residence, prof. Kellstadt Grad. Sch. Bus., DePaul U., 2000—03; founder Women's Leadership Inst. Dominican U., 2006—; bd. dirs. AskRex.com, Clark/Bardes Inc., Motown Snacks, Robison Securities/Fleet Bank, Internat. Leadership Found. Co-chair Fed. Glass Ceiling Commn., 1991—95, Com. 21st Century, 1992—; bd. dirs. Internat. Forum Found., Off-the-St. Club, Chgo., 1977—86; adv. bd. U. Ill. Coll. Commerce, 1980—2000, Chgo. Crime Commn., 1987—90, DePaul U., 1989—95, Roosevelt U., 1994—2000, St. Mary's U., 1995—98. Named Advt. Women of the Yr., Chgo. Advt. Club, 1989; named one of Top 100 in Tech., 2003; recipient numerous Eagle Fin. Advt. awards, Silver medal, Am. Advt. Fedn., 1989; fellow, Internat. Leadership Forum, 2005—. Mem.: Chgo. Network, Social Venture Network, Women's Forum Chgo., Internat. Women's Forum (v.p. devel., v.p. comm., mem. exec. com., bd. dirs.), Women's Athletic Club Chgo., Mid-Am. Club (bd. govs. 1990—92). Office: 1703 Shoreline Dr Saint Charles IL 60174-5562 Home Phone: 630-587-6180; Office Phone: 847-778-8411. Personal E-mail: lynneoshea@juno.com.

NELLY, (CORNELL HAYNES JR.), rap artist; b. Austin, Tex., Nov. 2, 1974; s. Cornell Haynes and Rhonda Mack; children: Chanel, Cornell III. Formed St. Lunatics, 1993; co-owner, co-founder, spokesperson Vokal Clothing Co., St. Louis, 1997—; co-owner, founder Apple Bottoms, 2003—; co-owner Billy Ballew Motersports, NASCAR racing team, 2003—; CEO Derrty Entertainment, 2003—; co-owner Charlotte Bobcats, 2004—. Performer: (albums) Country Grammar, 2000 (Album of Yr., Source Hip-Hop Music awards, 2001), (with St. Lunatics) Free City, 2001, Nellyville, 2002 (Grammy award for best make rap solo performance, 2002, Grammy award best rap/sung collaboration for "Dilemma," featuring Kelly Rowland, 2002), Da Derrty Versions: The Reinvention, 2003, Iz U, 2004, Sweat, 2004, Suit, 2004, (singles) E.I., 2001, Ride With Me, 2001, (songs) Shake Ya Tailfeather (with P. Diddy and Murphy Lee), Bad Boys II soundtrack, 2003 (Grammy award best rap performance by a duo or group, 2003); actor: (films) Snipes, 2001, The Longest Yard, 2005. Founder 4sho4kids. Recipient New Artist of Yr., Source Hip-Hop Music Awards, 2001, Best New Artist, BET awards, 2001, Best R&B/Soul or Rap New Artist, Soul Train Music Awards, 2001, Favorite Artist-Rap/Hip-Hop, Am. Music Awards, 2002, Source Found. Image Award, Source Hip-Hop Music Awards, 2003, Artist of Yr., 2003, Sammy Davis Jr. Entertainer of Yr., Soul Train Music Awards. Office: Uptown/Universal Records 1755 Broadway New York NY 10019 also: The 4Sho4Kids Found Inc 9648 Olive Blvd Ste 230 Saint Louis MO 63132 also: Vokal Clothing 1835 Belt Way Dr Saint Louis MO 63114-5815 Office Phone: 314-531-3346.

NELSEN, WILLIAM CAMERON, educational consultant; b. Omaha, Oct. 18, 1941; s. William Peter and Ellen Lucella (Cameron) N.; m. Margaret Leone Rossow, May 30, 1981; children by previous marriage: William Norris, Shawna Lynn; 1 adopted dau., Sarah Ruth. BA, Midland Luth. Coll., Fremont, Nebr., 1963; MA, Columbia U., 1966; PhD, U. Pa., 1971; Fulbright scholar, U. Erlangen, W. Ger., 1964; D (hon.), Midland Luth. Coll., 1995. Program exec. Danforth Found., St. Louis, 1970-73; asst. dean, then v.p., dean coll. St. Olaf Coll., Northfield, Minn., 1973-80; dir. Project on Faculty Devel. Assn. of Am. Colls., 1979; pres. Augustana Coll., Sioux Falls, SD, 1980-86, Scholarship Am., St. Peter, Minn., 1986—2004; v.p. develop. NC Wesleyan Coll., Rocky Mount, NC, 2004—. Bd. dirs. 1st Nat. Bank and Bancommunity Svc. Corp., St. Peter, Minn., Learning Cmtys. Coalition, USA Funds. Author: Effective Approaches to Faculty Development, 1980, Renewal of the Teacher Scholar, 1981, also articles. Bd. dirs. S.D. Symphony, 1980-85, Sioux Falls YMCA, 1980-86, Luth. Ednl. Conf. .Am., 1982-86, Sioux Falls United Way, 1983-86; nat. bd. advisors Coun. Aid to Edn.; mem. nat. coun. Connect Am., Points of Light Found., 1998-2003; chmn. bd. U.S. Dream Acad., 1999-2004; mem. exec. bd. Nat. Assembly, 2001-2004; bd. dirs. Nat. Scholarship Providers Assn., 1999-2004, chmn. bd., 2003-04; dir. Learning Comtys. Coalition; mem. Registry of Coll. and Univ. Pres.; interim v.p. devel. N.C. Wesleyan Coll.; bd trustees Midland Luth. Coll. Recipient McKee award Nat. Assn. Ptnrs. in Edn., 1999, award Freedoms Found., 2003; Danforth Grad. fellow, 1963, Woodrow Wilson fellow, 1963. Mem. Assn. Am. Colls. (bd. dirs. 1984-86), Shoreland Country Club (pres. 1996-99), Consortium for Advancement of Pvt. Higher Edn., Coun. of Ind. Colls., Nat. Dollars for Scholars, Rotary Club. Republican. Lutheran.

NELSON, (EARL) BEN(JAMIN), senator, former governor, lawyer; b. McCook, Nebr., May 17, 1941; s. Benjamin Earl and Birdella Ruby (Henderson) N.; m. Diane C. Gleason, Feb. 22, 1980; children from a previous marriage: Sarah Jane, Patrick James; stepchildren: Kevin Michael Gleason, Christine Marie Gleason. BA in Philosophy, U. ebr., 1963, MA in Philosophy, 1966, JD, 1970; LLD (hon.), Creighton U., 1992, Peru State Coll., 1993. Bar: Nebr. 1970. Instr. dept. philosophy U. Nebr., Lincoln, 1963-65; supr. Dept. Ins. State of Nebr., Lincoln, 1965-72; dir. ins., 1975-76; asst. gen. counsel, gen. counsel, sec., v.p. The Ctrl. Nat. Ins. Group Omaha, 1972-75, exec. v.p., 1976-77, pres., 1978-81, CEO, 1980-81; of counsel Kennedy, Holland, DeLacy & Svoboda, Omaha, 1985-90, Lumson, Dugan and Murray, Omaha, 1999—2001; gov. State of Nebr., Lincoln, 1991—99; US Senator from Nebr., 2000—. Com. rules and adminstrn. US Senate, com. commerce, sci. and transp., com. armed services, com. agr., nutrition and forestry. Co-chmn. Carter/Mondale re-election campaign, Nebr., 1980; chair Nat. Edn. Goals Panel, 1992-94; co-founder Gov.'s Ethanol Coalition, chair, 1991, 94; pres. Coun. of State Govs., 1994; bd. trustee Wesley House Found., Omaha, 1970-76. Recipient Friends of Nebr. Broadcasters award Nebr. Broadcasters Assn., 1993, Disting. Eagle award Nat. Eagle Scout Assn., 1994; named Amb. Plenipotentiary, 1993. Mem. ABA, Nat. Assn. Independent Insurers, Nat. Assn. Ins. Commrs. (exec. v.p. 1982-85), Nebr. Bar Assn., Consumer Credit Ins. Assn., Midwestern Govs. Assn. (chair 1994), Western Govs. Assn. (vice chair 1994, chair 1995), Happy Hollow Club, Omaha Club, Hillcrest Country Club. Democrat. Methodist. Avocations: reading, hunting, fishing. Office: US Senate 720 Hart Office Bldg Washington DC 20510 also: District Office Ste 205 7602n Pacific St Omaha NE 68114 Office Phone: 202-224-6551, 402-391-3411. Office Fax: 202-224-0012, 402-391-4725.

NELSON, CAROLYN, state legislator; b. Madison, Wis., Oct. 8, 1937; m. Gilbert W. Nelson; children: Paul, John, Karla. BS, N.D. State U., 1959, MS, 1960. Sr. lectr. emeritus N.D. State U., 1968—; mem. N.D. Ho. of Reps., 1986-88, 92-94, N.D. Senate from 21st dist., 1994—; mem. judiciary com., vet. affairs com. .D. Senate, minority caucus leader, 2000—. Mem. N.D. State Investment Bd., 1989-92. Mem. Bd. Edn., Fargo, N.D., 1985-91, pres., 1989-90; trustee N.D. Tchrs. Fund for Retirement, 1985-92, pres., 1990-92; mem. N.D. PTA, pres., 1978-81, N.D. Women's and Children's Caucus. Recipient Merit Svc. award Gamma Phi Beta, 1978, 90, Legis. Voices award Children's Caucus, 1995; named Legislator of Yr., N.D. Bar Assn., 2000, N.D. Student Assn., 2001. Mem. LWV, Am. Guild English Handbell Ringers (area chmn. 1982-84, nat. bd. dirs. 1982-90), Nat. Fedn. Music Clubs (bd. dirs. 2003—, legis. chair 2003-07, regional v.p. 2005—07, 1st v.p. 2007-), N.D. Fedn. Music Clubs (life, pres. 1997-2001, nat. bd. mem. 2005—, legis. chair, Rose Fay Thomas fellow 2001), Gamma Phi Beta, Phi Kappa Phi, Sigma Alpha Iota. Office: ND Senate State Capitol Bismarck ND 58505 Address: One 2d St S 5 402 Fargo ND 58103-1959 Business E-Mail: cnelson@nd.gov.

NELSON, CHARLOTTE BOWERS, retired public administrator; b. Bristol, Va., June 28, 1931; d. Thaddeus Ray and Ruth Nelson (Moore) Bowers; m. Gustav Carl Nelson, June 1, 1957; children: Ruth Elizabeth, David Carl, Thomas Gustav. BA summa cum laude, Duke U., 1954; MA, Columbia U., 1961; MPA, Drake U., 1983. Instr. Beaver Coll., 1957-58, Drake U., Des Moines, 1975-82; office mgr. LWV of Iowa, Des Moines, 1975-82; exec. asst. Iowa Dept. Human Svcs., Des Moines, 1983-85; exec. dir. Iowa Commn. on Status of Women Dept. Human Rights, Des Moines, 1985—2007; pub. adminstr. State of Iowa, 1983—2007. Bd. dirs., pres. LWV, Beloit, Wis., 1960-74; bd. dirs. LWV, Des Moines, 1974-82, Westminster House, Des Moines, 1988-97, pres. 1996-97. Recipient Gov.'s Golden Dome award as Leader of the Yr., 2002; named Visionary Woman, Young Women's Resource Ctr., 1994. Mem. Am. Soc. Pub. Adminstrn. (mem. exec. coun. 1984-92, 98-99, past pres., Mem. of Yr. 1993), Phi Beta Kappa, Pi Alpha Alpha. Home: 1141 Cummins Cir Des Moines IA 50311-2113 E-mail: nelson514@aol.com.

NELSON, CHRIS A., state official; b. Mitchell, SD, Aug. 18, 1964; m. Penny Pfeifle; 1 child, Rebekah; 1 stepchild. BS in Animal Sci., SD State U., 1987. Self-employed farmer/rancher, 1981—; UCC supr. State of SD, Pierre, 1987—89, state election supr., 1989—2002, asst. sec. state, 2002—03, sec. state, 2003—. Nat. Govs. Assn. rep. US Election Assistance Commn. Bd. Advs., 2005. Recipient Excellence in SD Mcpl. Govt. award, SD Mcpl. League, 2003, Hazeltine/Taylor award, SD Kids Voting, 2004. Republican. Office: Office Sec State 500 E Capitol Ave Ste 204 Pierre SD 57501 Office Phone: 605-773-3537. Fax: 605-773-6580.

NELSON, DARRELL WAYNE, retired academic administrator, research scientist; b. Aledo, Ill., Nov. 28, 1939; s. Wayne Edward and Olive Elvina (Peterson) N.; m. Nancyann Hyer, Aug. 27, 1961; children: Christina Lynne, Craig Douglas. BS in Agriculture, U. Ill., 1961, MS in Agronomy, 1963; PhD in Agronomy, Iowa State U., 1967. Cert. profl. soil scientist. Div. chief U.S. Army Chem. Corps., Denver, 1967-68; asst. prof. Purdue U., West Lafayette, Ind., 1968-73, assoc. prof., 1973-77, prof. agronomy, 1977-84; dept. head U. Nebr., Lincoln, 1984-88, dean for agr. rsch. and dir. Nebr. Agrl. Experiment Sta., 1988—2005; ret., 2005. Cons. U.S. EPA, Washington, 1977-79, Ind. Bd. of Health, Indpls., 1977-83, Eli Lilly Co., Indpls., 1976. Editor: Chemical Mobility and Reactivity in Soils, 1983. Served to capt. U.S. Army, 1967-68. Fellow AAAS, Am. Soc. Agronomy (bd. dirs., pres.-elect, pres. 2001, past pres. 2002, CIBA-Geigy award 1975, Agronomic Achievement award 1983, Environ. Quality Rsch. award 1985), Soil Sci. Soc. Am. (bd. dirs., pres. elect 1992, pres. 1993, past. pres. 1994); mem. Internat. Soil Sci. Soc., Lions Lodge (treas. 1980-83, Lafayette, Ind. chpt.). Presbyterian. Avocations: fishing, skiing, jogging. Office: Univ of Nebr Agrl Rsch Divsn Lincoln NE 68583-0704 Business E-Mail: dnelson1@unl.edu.

NELSON, DAVID ALDRICH, former federal judge; b. Watertown, NY, 1932; s. Carlton Low and Irene Demetria (Aldrich) Nelson; m. Mary Dickson, 1956; 3 children. AB, Hamilton Coll., 1954; postgrad., Cambridge U., Eng., 1954—55; LLB, Harvard U., 1958. Bar: Ohio 1958, NY 1982. Atty.-advisor Office of the Gen. Counsel, Dept. of the Air Force, 1959—62; assoc. Squire, Sanders & Dempsey, Cleve., 1958—67, ptnr., 1967—69, 1972—85; judge US Ct. Appeals (6th cir.), Cin., 1985—99, sr. judge, 1999—2006. Gen. counsel US Post Office Dept., Washington, 1969—71; sr. asst. postmaster gen., gen. counsel US Postal Svc., Washington, 1971; nat. coun. Ohio State U. Coll. Law, 1988—98. Trustee Hamilton Coll., 1984—88. Served to maj. USAFR, 1959—73. Recipient Benjamin Franklin award, US Post Office Dept., 1969; Fulbright scholar, 1954—55. Fellow: Am. Coll. Trial Lawyers; mem.: Ohio Bar Assn., Fed. Bar Assn., Emerson Lit. Soc., Ct. of Nisi Prius (sgt. emeritus), Phi Beta Kappa.

NELSON, DAVID LEONARD, data processing executive; b. Omaha, May 8, 1930; s. Leonard A. and Cecelia (Steinert) N.; m. Jacqueline J. Zerbe, Dec. 26, 1952; 1 child, Nancy Jo. BS, Iowa State U., 1952. Mktg. adminstr. Ingersoll Rand, Chgo., 1954-56; with Accuray Corp., Columbus, Ohio, 1956-87, exec. v.p., gen. mgr., 1967, pres., 1967-87, chief exec. officer, 1970-87; pres. process automation bus. unit Combustion Engring., Inc., Columbus, 1987-90; pres. bus. area process automation Asea Brown Boveri, Stamford, Conn., 1990-91, v.p. customer satisfaction Ams. region, 1991-93, v.p. customer support Ams. region, 1994-95; chmn. bd. dirs. Herman Miller Inc., Zeeland, Mich., 1995-2000, counsel, 2000—04. Served to capt. USMCR, 1952-54. Mem. IEEE, Instrument Soc. Am., Newcomen Soc. .Am., Tau Beta Pi, Phi Kappa Phi, Phi Eta Sigma, Delta Upsilon. Achievements include patents in field. Home: 1113 Roundhouse Ln Alexandria VA 22314-5935 Office Phone: 703-299-4588. Business E-Mail: david-nelson@hermanmiller.com.

NELSON, DON JEROME, electrical engineering and computer science educator; b. Nebr., Aug. 17, 1930; s. Irvin Andrew and Agnes Emelia (Nissen) N. BSc, U. Nebr., 1953, MSc, 1958; PhD, Stanford U., 1962. Registered profl. engr., Nebr. Mem. tech. staff AT&T Bell Labs., Manhattan, N.Y., 1953, 55; instr. U. Nebr., Lincoln, 1955-58, from asst. to assoc. prof., 1960-63, dir. computer ctr., 1963-72, prof. electrical engring., 1967—, prof. computer sci., 1969—, co-dir. Ctr. Comm. & Info. Sci., 1988-91, dir. rsch. computing group, 1993-97; gen. mgr. Interactive Info. R&D, 1997—. Cons. Union Life Ins., Lincoln, 1973, Nebr. Pub. Power Dist., Columbus, 1972-83, Taiwan Power Co., Taipei, 1974. 1st lt. USAF, 1953-55. Mem. IEEE (sr., Outstanding Faculty award 1989), Assn. Computing Machinery. Republican. Home: 4911 Concord Rd Lincoln NE 68516-3330 Office: U Nebr Dept Elec Engring 209N WSEC Lincoln NE 68588-0511 E-mail: nelson@izrd.com, nelson@yoda.unl.edu.

NELSON, DONNIE, professional sports team executive; b. Sept. 10, 1962; s. Don Nelson; m. Lotta Nelson; children: Christie, D.J. Grad., Wheaton Coll., Ill., 1986. Regional scout Milw. Bucks, 1984—86; asst. coach Golden State Warriors, 1986—94, Phoenix Suns, 1994—97; asst. coach, dir. player pers. Dallas Mavericks, 1998—2002, acting head coach, 2001, 2002, pres. basketball ops., 2002—, gen. mgr., 2005—. Asst. coach Lithuanian Nat. Team, 1990—; scout at World Championships USA Basketball, Toronto, Canada, 1994; founder Global Games, Dallas; hon. amb. League of Industries; chief adv. Chinese Nat. Basketball Team. Founder Assist Youth Found. (now combined with Heroes), 2002. Named to Wheaton Coll. Hall of Honor, 1997; recipient Grand Cross of the Comdr., Pres. of Lithuania, 2004. Office: Dallas Mavericks The Pavilion 2909 Taylor St Dallas TX 75226 E-mail: dcn@dallasmavs.com.

NELSON, ERIC JOHN, lawyer; BA, Eastern U., St. Davids, Pa., 1996; JD, Hamline U. Sch. Law, 2001. Bar: Minn. 2001. Jud. law clk. First Jud. Dist.; founding ptnr. Halberg Criminal Def., Bloomington, Minn. Contbg. author: DWI Desk Book. Named a Rising Star, Minn. Super Lawyers mag., 2006. Mem.: Hennepin County Bar Assn., Minn. Bar Assn., Nat. Assn. Criminal Def. Lawyers. Office: Halberg Criminal Def Northland Plz Ste 1590 3800 American Blvd W Bloomington MN 55431 Office Phone: 952-224-4848. E-mail: enelson@halbergdefense.com.

NELSON, GARY J., state legislator; m. Linda; 3 children. Degree, Concordia Coll. Farmer; mem. N.D. Senate, 1977—; minority whip, 1991; majority whip. Past pres. Cent. Cass Sch. Bd.; farmer. Mem. Farm Bur., Crop Improvement Assn., Casselton Cmty. Club, Masons, N.D. Wildlife Fedn., Wildlife Club. Office: PO Box 945 Casselton ND 58012-0945 also: State Senate State Capital Bismarck ND 58505

NELSON, GARY MICHAEL, lawyer; b. Mpls., July 12, 1951; s. Emery Marshal and Henrietta Margaret (Flategraff) Nelson; m. Deb Snyder; 1 child, Courtney Snyder; children: Rachel Mary, Amy Margaret. BA, Gustavus Adolphus Coll., St. Peter, Minn., 1973; JD, Harvard U., 1976. Bar: Minn. 1976, U.S. Dist. Ct. Minn. 1976. With Oppenheimer Wolff & Donnelly, Mpls., 1976—97, mng. ptnr., 1987—89, mem. policy com., 1989—95, dep. chmn., 1991—93, chair, CEO, 1993—95; exec. v.p., gen. counsel, corp. sec. Ceridian Corp., Mpls., 1997—. Chair corp. practice inst. Minn. Inst. Legal Edn., Mpls., 1978-93. Recipient Significant Contbns. award Am. Girls' Clubs Am., 1982. Mem. ABA, Minn. State Bar Assn., Hennepin County Bar Assn., Corp. Legal Officers Group Lutheran. Avocations: fishing, hunting, hiking, reading. Home: 2685 Maplewood Rd Wayzata MN 55391 Office: Ceridian Corp 3311 E Old Shakopee Rd Minneapolis MN 55425-1640

NELSON, GLEN DAVID, health products executive, physician; b. Mpls., Mar. 28, 1937; s. Ralph and Edna S. Nelson; m. Marilyn Carlson, June 30, 1961; children: Diana, Curtis, Wendy. BA, Harvard U., Cambridge, Mass., 1959; MD, U. Minn., 1963. Diplomate Am. Bd. Surgery, also sub-bd. bariatric and peripheral vascular surgery; cert. Am. Bd. Surgery, 1970. Intern Hennepin County Gen. Hosp., Mpls., 1963—64, resident in gen. surgery, 1964—69; staff surgeon Park Nicollet Med. Ctr. (formerly St. Louis Park Med. Ctr.), Mpls.; practiced surgery, 1969—86; chmn., pres. and CEO Park Nicollet Med. Ctr., 1975—86; chmn. and CEO Am. MedCenters, Inc., 1984—86; dir. Medtronic, Inc., 1980—2002, exec. v.p., 1986—88, vice chmn., 1988—2002; chmn., prin. owner GDN Holdings, LLC, Minnetonka, Minn., 2002—. Bd. dirs. Arstasis, Inc., Harvard Bus. Sch. Healthcare Initiative Adv. Bd., Harvard U. Com. on U. Resources, Internal Med., Inc., Advanced BioSurfaces, Inc., Cardiovascular Systems, Inc., Carlson Holdings, Inc., Carlson Cos., Inc., DexCom, Inc., Evera Med., Inc., Guided Delivery Sys., Inc., Harvard U. Com. on Sci. and Engring., Johns Hopkins Medicine Bd. of Advisors, Inspire Med. Sys., LLC, Minute-Clinic, Inc. (wholly owned subs. CVS Pharmacy), chmn.; bd. dirs., trustee and chmn. Am. Pub. Media/Minn. Pub. Radio; sr. advisor CVS Pharmacy, RedBrick Health, Reliant Technologies, Inc., Stemedica Cell Technologies, Inc., Travelers Cos., Inc.; emeritus clin. prof. surgery, U. Minn. Trustee Am. Pub. Media/Minn. Pub. Radio, chmn.

NELSON, H. H. RED, insurance company executive; b. Herman, Nebr., June 2, 1912; m. Ruth Hansen; children: John, Steve. BA, U. Nebr., 1934, JD, 1937. Bar: Iowa, ebr. 1938; CLU, 1948. Asst. mgr. life accident group depts. Travelers Inc. Co., Omaha, 1939-44; chmn. bd. Redlands Ins. Co., Omaha, 1945—, Ins. Agts. Inc., Council Bluffs, Iowa, 1945—, Am. Agrisurance Co., Council Bluffs, 1969—, Am. Growers Ins., Council Bluffs, 1995—, Acceptance Ins., Tex., Council Bluffs, 1988—; chmn. Silverstone Group, Council Bluffs, 1997-2001, chmn. emeritus, 2001—. Chmn. Redland Group Cos. Pres. United Fund, Western Iowa council Boy Scouts Am.; bd. dirs. Nat. Scout Council; pres. Christian Home Orphanage, Council Bluffs Indsl. Found. Named to, Iowa Ins. Hall of Fame, 1997. Office: Silverstone Group 300 W Broadway Ste 200 Council Bluffs IA 51503-9099 E-mail: hhnelson@ssgi.com.

NELSON, HARRY DONALD, telecommunications executive; b. Chgo., Nov. 23, 1933; s. Harry E. and Elsie I. (Liljedahl) N.; m. Carol J. Stewart, Mar. 31, 1957; children: Donald S., David S., Sharon J. Arnold. BS, Northwestern U., Evanston, Ill., 1955, MBA, 1959. Sales rep., sales trainer Procter & Gamble, Chgo., 1955-58; sales adminstr. internat. products GE, N.Y., Ky., 1959-70, Md., Ohio, 1959-72, product mgr. Louisville, Ky., 1978-81; mgr. mktg. Tex. Instruments, Dallas, 1972-74; v.p. mktg. Rockwell Internat., Anaheim, Calif., 1975, HMW-Pulsar, Lancaster, Pa., 1976-78, Genesco, Nashville, 1981-83; v.p. cellular ops. Tel. and Data Systems, Chgo., 1983-85; pres., CEO U.S. Cellular, Chgo., 1985—. Mem. Dean's Adv. Bd. Kellogg Sch. Mgmt. Northwestern U., Evanston, 1994—, Alumni Adv. Bd., 1991—. With U.S. Army, 1956-57. Recipient Dean's Alumni award Kellogg Sch. Mgmt., 1996. Mem. Cellular Telecomm. Industry Assn. (treas., bd. dirs., exec. com. 1986—, Pres.'s award 1996). Republican. Baptist. Avocations: paperweight collecting, antique sales, stamp and coin collecting. Office: US Cellular 8410 W Bryn Mawr Ave Ste 700 Chicago IL 60631-3486

NELSON, HERBERT LEROY, psychiatrist; b. Eddyville, Iowa, June 15, 1922; s. Albert and Bessie Mae (Durham) Nelson; m. Carol Lorayne Hofert, Dec. 23, 1943; children: Richard Kent, Vicki Lurae, Thadeus Leroy, Cylda Vermae. BA, U. Iowa, 1943, MD, 1946. Diplomate Am Bd Psychiatry and Neurology. Intern Univ Hosps. of U. Iowa, Iowa City, 1946-47; resident Brooke Army Med. Ctr, Fort Sam Houston, Tex., 1947-49, U.S. VA Hosp., Knoxville, Iowa, 1949-51, Oreg. State Hosp., Salem, 1951-52, clin. dir., 1952-63; asst. prof. psychiatry U. Iowa, Iowa City, 1963-66, assoc. prof., 1966-73, prof., 1973-84, prof. emeritus, 1984—; dir. Iowa Mental Health Authority, Iowa City, 1968-82; med. dir. Mideast Iowa Community Mental Health Ctr., Iowa City, 1969-84. Adj prof Tulane Univ, New Orleans, 1974—77. Co-author: 4 monographs; contbr. articles to profl jours. Served as capt MC US Army, 1947—49. Fellow: Am Psychiat Asn; mem.: AMA, Am Col Mental Health Adminrs, Am Asn Psychiat Adminrs, Johnson County Med Soc, Iowa Psychiat Soc (pres 1970—71, chmn subcom psychiat care 1973—77). Republican. Methodist. Avocations: gardening, fishing, woodworking, painting, travel. Home and Office: Melrose Meadows #1009 350 Dublin Dr Iowa City IA 52246 E-mail: hlnelson@mchsi.com.

NELSON, JULIE LOFTUS, lawyer; b. Milw., Jan. 14, 1967; BA, U. Wis., Madison, 1996; JD cum laude, Hamline U., 2002. Bar: Minn. 2002, US Ct. Appeals (8th cir.) 2004, US Dist. Ct. (dist. Minn.) 2005. Jud. clk. to Judge R.A. Randall Minn. Ct. Appeals; jud. clk. to Judge P. Hunter Anderson Dist. Ct.; assoc. Frederic Bruno & Assocs., Mpls. Named a Rising Star, Minn. Super Lawyers mag., 2006. Mem.: Minn. Assn. Criminal Def. Attys., Minn. State Bar Assn. (sec. criminal law sect.). Office: Frederic Bruno & Assocs 5500 Wayzata Blvd Ste 1450 Minneapolis MN 55416 Office Phone: 763-545-7900. E-mail: julie@brunolaw.com.

NELSON, MARILYN CARLSON, hotel and travel company executive; b. Mpls. m. Glen Nelson; children: Diana, Curtis C., Wendy. Student, U. Sorbonne, Paris, Inst. Hautes Etudes Econ., Geneva; degree in internat. econs. with honors, Smith Coll., 1961; DBA (hon.), Johnson & Wales U.; DHL (hon.), Coll. St. Catherine, Gustavus Adolphus Coll. Securities analyst Paine Webber, Mpls.; pres., COO Carlson Companies, Inc., Minnetonka, 1998—2003, chmn., CEO, 1998—2008, chmn., 2008—. Co-chair Carlson Holdings, Inc., 2000—; co-chair Carlson Wagonlit Travel, 1994-2003; disting. vis. prof. Johnson & Wales U.; bd. dirs. Exxonmobil Corp., Mayo Clinic Found., Com. to Encourage Corp. Philanthropy; chmn. Nat. Women's Bus. Coun., 2002-05; vice chair U.S. Travel and Tourism Adv. Bd.; bd. mem. Singapore Tourism Bur. Pres. United Way Mpls., campaign chair, 1984; bd. dirs. United Way Am., 1984-90, U.S. Nat. Tourism Orgn., 1996-98, Ctr. for Internat. Leadership, 1989-2003; mem. disting. adv. coun. Coll. of St. Catherine, 1991-94; hon. bd. dirs. Svenska Inst., Stockholm, 1993—; mem. adv. bd. Hubert H. Humphrey Inst. Pub. Affairs, 1992-96; co-founder Minn. Women's Econ. Roundtable, 1974—; chair Minn. Super Bowl Task Force, 1984-92; chair, founder Midsummer Internat. Festival of Music, 1992; co-chair New Sweden '88; past bd. dirs. Guthrie Theatre, Greater Mpls. Girl Scout Coun., Jr. Achievement, Jr. League Mpls., KTCA Pub. TV, Minn. Econ. Assn., Minn. Congl. Award, Minn. Opera Co., Women's' Assn. Minn. Symphony Orch.; trustee Smith Coll., Northampton, Mass., 1980-85, Macalester Coll., St. Paul, 1974-80; mem. adv. bd. Minn. Women's Yearbook; trustee Curtis L. Carlson Family Found. amed Sales Exec. of Yr., Sales and Mktg. Exec. Mpls., Woman of Yr., Minn. Exec. Women in Tourism, 1991—92, Outstanding Individual in Tourism, Minn. Office Tourism, 1992, Woman of Yr., Roundtable Women in Food Svc., 1995, #1 Most Powerful Women in Travel, Travel Agent Mag., 1997—2003, Businesswoman of World, Bus. Women's Network, 2001, Swedish Am. of Yr., King and Queen of Sweden, 2003, Minnesotan of Yr., Minn. Monthly mag., 2003, Businesswoman of Yr., US Commerce Dept. Small Bus. Adminstrn., 2005, Life Dir., Minn. Orchestra, 2006; named one of Exec. Yr. Corp. Report Minn., 1999, Forbes Richest Americans, 2006, Am.'s Best Leaders, US News and World Report, 2006, 100 Most Powerful Women, Forbes mag., 2007; named to Hall of Fame, Sales and Mktg. Execs. Mpls., 2003; recipient Minn. Congl. award for initiative and svc. to cmty., Commendation cert., State of Minn., Cmty. Svc. award, YWCA, Independence award, Vinland Nat. Ctr., Cmty. Svc. award, Park-Nicollet Med. Ctr., Outstanding Mktg. Exec. of Yr. award, Minn. Distributive Edn. Club Am., Career Achievement award, Sales and Mktg. Execs. Mpls., Outstanding Achievement award, United Way Mpls., Extraordinary Leadership award, Greater Mpls. C. of C., Disting. Svc. award, United Way of Am., 1984—90, Nat. Caring award, Caring Inst., 1995, Outstanding Bus. Leader award, Northwood U., 1995, Disting. Svc. award (highest vol. honor), United Way Minn., 1998, Good Neighbor award, WCCO Radio, 1999, Caring Heart award, Larry King Cardiac Found., 1999, Svc. Above Self award, Rotary Club Downtown, Minn., 1999, Northwest Airlines Disting. World Traveler award, Hospitality Sales and Mktg. Assn. Internat., 2000, Responsible Capitalism award, FIRST mag., 2001, Glass Ceiling award, Minn. Women's Consortium, 2001, Great Swedish Heritage award, Swedish Coun. Am., 2002, Lifetime Achievement award, Internat. Investment Forum, 2002, Athena award, Athena Found., 2004, Lifetime Achievement award, Hospitality Sales and Mktg. Assn. Internat., 2004, 18th Ann. Lucia Travel award, 2005, Chevalier knight, French Legion Honor, 2006, Icon award, Nat. Bus. Travel Assn., 2006, Leadership award, Multicultural Devel. Ctr., 2006. Mem. World Econ. Forum, World Travel and Tourism Coun., Travel Industry Assn. Am. (bd. dirs.), Hennepin County Med. Soc. Aux., Bus. Roundtable, Smith Coll. Alumni Assn., Smith Club Mpls., Woodhill Country Club, Mpls. Club, N.W. Tennis Club, Nat. Ctr. Social Entrepreneurs, Com. of 200, Hospitality Sales and Mktg. Assn. Internat. (Lifetime Achievement award 2004), Minn. Orchestral Assn., Orphei Dranger, Alpha Kappa Psi. Office: Carlson Companies Inc 701 Carlson Pkwy Minnetonka MN 55305*

NELSON, MARY ELLEN DICKSON, retired actuary; b. Mpls., Mar. 24, 1933; d. William Alexander and Laura Winona (Baxter) Dickson; m. David Aldrich Nelson, Aug. 25, 1956; children: Frederick Dickson, Claudia Baxter, Caleb Edward. BA, Vassar Coll., 1954; postgrad., Cambridge U., Eng., 1954-55. Rsch. assoc. N.Am. Life & Casualty Co., Mpls., 1955-56; actuarial asst. John Hancock Mut. Life Ins. Co., Boston, 1956-58; actuary David R. Kass & Assocs., Cleve., 1973-74; pres. elson & Co., Cleve., 1975, Conrad, Nelson & Co., Cleve., 1975-81, Nelson & Co., Cleve./Cin., 1981-99; ret., 1999. Trustee Clovernook Ctr. for the Blind and Visually Impaired, Cin. Fulbright scholar, 1954—55. Fellow: Soc. Actuaries, Phi Beta Kappa; mem.: Am. Acad. Actuaries, Midwest Benefits Conf. (chair 1991), Cin. Actuaries Club. Republican.

NELSON, PAMELA A., state legislator; m. Vic Nelson; 2 children. Mem. S.D. State Ho. of Reps., 1986-88, S.D. State Senate, 1988-96; commr. SD pub. utilities commn., Pierre, 1997—. Democrat. Roman Catholic. Mem. Kiwanis W, mem. LWV. Home: 2505 S Marion Rd Sioux Falls SD 57106-0842 Office: Pub Utilities Commn Capitol Bldg 1st Fl 500 E Capitol Ave Pierre SD 57501-5070

NELSON, PHILIP EDWIN, food scientist, educator; b. Shelbyville, Ind., Nov. 12, 1934; s. Brainard R. and Alta E. (Pitts) N.; m. Sue Bayless, Dec. 27, 1955; children: Jennifer, Andrew, Bradley. BS, Purdue U., 1956, PhD, 1976. Plant mgr. Blue River Packing Co., Morristown, Ind., 1956-60; instr. Purdue U., West Lafayette, Ind., 1961-76, head dept. food sci., 1983—2003, Scholle chair prof., 2004—. Cons. PEN Cons., West Lafayette, 1974; chair Food Processors Inst., Washington, 1990-93; mem. adv. bd. USDA, 2002-06. Editor: Fruit Vegetable Juice Technology, 1980, Principles of Aseptic Processing and Packaging, 1992. Recipient Pers. Achievement award USDA, 1997, World Food Prize Laureate, 2007. Fellow Inst. Food Techs. (pres. 2001-02, Indsl. Achievement award 1976, icholas Appert award 1995, 49'er Svc. award 1995, Tanner lectr. 1999), Internat. Acad. Food Sci. and Tech. (USDA specialty crops com. 2005-07); mem. AAAS, Sigma Xi, Phi Tau Sigma (pres. 1976-77). Achievements include 11 U.S. and foreign patents. Office: Purdue U Dept Food Sci 745 Ag Mall Drive West Lafayette IN 47907-2009 E-mail: pen@purdue.edu.

NELSON, PRINCE ROGERS See **PRINCE**

NELSON, R. DAVID, electronics executive; Various mfg., quality control metallurgy, materials, sales and mktg., and purchasing pos. TRW Inc., 1957—87; v.p. purchasing to sr. v.p. purchasing and corp. affairs Honda of Am. Mfg., Marysville, Ohio, 1987—97, bd. dirs.; v.p. worldwide supply mgmt. Deere & Co., Moline, Ill., 1997—2001; v.p. global supply mgmt. Delphi Corp., Troy, Mich., 2002—. Founding mem. Nat. Initiative Supply Chain Integration, Ltd.; bd. dirs. Purchasing Round Table. Co-author: 2 books. Recipient medal of profl. excellence, Purchasing Mag., 2001. Mem.: CAPS Rsch. (bd. trustees), Inst. Supply Mgmt. (chmn.). Office: World Hdqrs Delphi Corp 5725 Delphi Dr Troy MI 58098-2815

NELSON, RALPH ALFRED, physician; b. Mpls., June 19, 1927; s. Alfred W. and Lydia (Johnson) N.; m. Rosemary Pokela, Aug. 7, 1954; children: Edward Ancher, Audrey Anne, Elizabeth Marie, Andrew William, Evan Robert. BA, U. Minn., 1949, MD, 1953, PhD, 1961. Diplomate Am. Bd. Internal Medicine. Intern Cook County (Ill.) Hosp., 1953-54; resident U. Minn. Hosps., Mpls., 1954-55, U. Minn., Mpls., 1955-56; fellow in physiology Mayo Grad. Sch., Rochester, Minn., 1957-60, resident in internal medicine, 1976-78; practice medicine specializing in internal medicine and clin. nutrition Sioux Falls, SD, 1978-79, Urbana, Ill., 1979—. Bd. dirs. Scott Research Lab., Fairview Park Hosp., Cleve., 1962-67; assoc. in physiology Western Res. U., Cleve., 1962-67; asst. prof. physiology Mayo Grad. Sch., 1967-73, Mayo Med. Sch., 1973, assoc. prof. nutrition, 1974; cons. in nutrition Mayo Clinic, 1967-76; assoc. prof. medicine U. S.D. Sch. Medicine, Sioux Falls, 1978-79; prof. nutrition U. Ill. Coll. Medicine, Urbana-Champaign, 1986—2002, chmn. dept. medicine prof. nutritional sci., physiology, biophysics dept. food sci. Sch. Agr., 1979-2002, also prof. medicine, exec. head dept. internal medicine, 1989-2002, exec. head four sites of Coll. Medicine, 2002, emeritus prof. internal medicine, emeritus prof. nutritional scis.; dir. med.research Carle Found. Hosp., Urbana, 1979—; cons. nutritional support service Danville (Ill.) VA Hosp., 1980—. Co-author: The Mayo Clinic Renal Diet Cookbook, 1974; contbr. articles on nutrition, physiology, and hibernation to sci. jours.; editor: Geriatrics, 1980—2002, The Physician and Sportsmedicine, 1980-88, Am. Jour. Clin. Nutrition, 1980-83. Cons. in nutrition Nat. Cancer Inst., 1976; cons. in nutrition HEW, 1976, 79, 89, Nat. Heart and Lung Inst., 1976. Served with USAF, 1945-47. Fulbright scholar, Morocco, 1988. Fellow ACP; mem. Am. Physiol. Soc., Am. Inst. Nutrition, Am. Soc. Clin. Nutrition, Central Soc. Clin. Research, Am. Gastroent. Assn. Lutheran. Home: 2 Illini Cir Urbana IL 61801-5813 Office: Carle Found Hosp Dir Med Rsch 611 W Park St Urbana IL 61801-2529 Office Phone: 217-344-4676. Personal E-mail: ralph.nelson@carle.com.

NELSON, RALPH STANLEY, lawyer; b. Mpls., Mar. 15, 1943; s. Stanley L. and Louise M. Nelson; m. Judy E. Nelson, July 8, 1867; children: Sara C., Amy E., David A. BS in Bus. Adminstrn., U. Minn., 1966; JD with honors, Drake U., 1972. Bar: Minn. 1973, Wash. 1982, Tex. 1985, Ga. 2003. Assoc. Wiese and Cox, Ltd., Mpls., 1973-76; atty. Burlington No. R.R., St. Paul, 1976-81; sr. corp. counsel Burlington No. Inc., Seattle, 1981-85; v.p. law and adminstrn. Burlington Motor Carriers Inc., Ft. Worth, 1985-88, exec. v.p. and gen. counsel, 1988-93, sr. v.p., gen. counsel Daleville (Indpls.), Ind., 1993-96, Trism Inc., Kennesaw, Ga., 1996-2001, exec. v.p., gen. counsel, 2001—03; sr. v.p., gen. counsel Tango Transport Inc., Shreveport, La., 2003—. Mem. law rev. Drake U. Mem. Order of the Coif. Office: 6009 Financial Plz Shreveport LA 71129-2615 Office Phone: 318-683-6605. Personal E-mail: ralphnelso@yahoo.com.

NELSON, RICHARD ARTHUR, lawyer; b. Fosston, Minn., Apr. 8, 1947; BS in Math., with distinction, U. Minn., 1969, JD magna cum laude, 1974. Bar: Minn. 1974, U.S. Ct. Appeals (D.C. cir.) 1975, U.S. Dist. Ct. Minn. 1975. Law clk. U.S. Ct. Appeals (D.C. cir.), Washington, 1974-75; ptnr. Faegre and Benson, Mpls., 1975—, group head employee benefits group, 2002—07. Seminar lectr. in employee benefits and labor laws, 1983—. Note and articles editor Minn. Law Rev., 1973-74. Active Dem.-Farmer-Labor Party State Cen. Com., Minn., 1976—, del. dist. and local coms. and convs., 1970—, state exec. com., 1990—; student rep. bd. regents U. Minn., Mpls., 1973-74; mem. IRS employee plans adv. couns., Mid-States Key Dist., 1996-2000, Ctrl. Mountains Region TE/GE, 2001-05, IRS Great Lakes Region TE/GE, 2006-; chair Mpls. Pension Coun., 1999-00; Minn. State Bd. Continuing Legal Edn., 2000-06, chair, 2005-06. With US Army, 1970—72. Mem. ABA, Minn. Bar Assn. (chair employee benefits sect. 1997-98), Order of Coif, Tau Beta Pi. Lutheran. Office: Faegre and Benson 90 S 7th St Ste 2200 Minneapolis MN 55402-3901 Office Phone: 612-766-7321. Business E-Mail: rnelson@faegre.com.

NELSON, RICHARD DAVID, lawyer; b. Chgo., Jan. 29, 1940; s. Irving E. and Dorothy (Apolsky) N.; m. Davida Distenfield, Dec. 17, 1960; children: Cheryl, Laurel. BS in Acctg., U. Ill., 1961, LLB, 1964. Bar: Ill. 1964. Ptnr. Defrees & Fiske Law Offices, Chgo., 1964-81; ptnr., counsel Heidrick & Struggles, Inc., Chgo., 1981—2001, chief fin. officer, 1981—97, chief adminstrv. officer, 1981—2001; pres. Galrk Sheridan, Inc., Highland Park, Ill., 2001—. Bd. dirs., exec. com. Heidrick & Struggles, Inc., Chgo., 1981-99. Pres. Jewish Cmty. Ctrs. of Chgo., 1987-89; chmn. Sign Graphics Task Force, Highland Park, Ill., 1986-88; mem. bus. and econ. devel. commn., Highland Park, 1993-96, 2000-, chmn. 2004-06, Ft. Sheridan Joint Plan Commn., 1997-2000. Mem. Ill. State Bar Assn., Chgo. Bar Assn., Standard Club, Northmoor Country Club. Office: Galrk Sheridan Inc 1896 Sheridan Rd Ste 200 Highland Park IL 60035-4635

NELSON, RICHARD LAWRENCE, JR., surgeon, educator; b. Evanston, Ill., Oct. 11, 1946; s. Richard Lawrence and Mary Jane Nelson; m. Susan Jane Berryman, June 17, 1972; children: Cicely Adams, Jospeh Lawrence, Moira Louise, Eric James, Patrick Matthew. BA, Stanford U., 1968; MD, U. Chgo., 1972. Diplomate Am. Bd. Surgery, Am. Bd. Colon and Rectal Surgery. Prof. surgery U. Ill., Chgo., 1980—; asst. prof., epidemiology and biometry U. Ill. Sch. Pub. Health, Chgo., 1987—. Cons. NIH, Bethesda, Md., 1991—2004; cons. consultation on incontinence WHO, 2001, 04; invited lectr. NAS, 1999. Author: Surgery of the Samll Intestine, 1998, 2d edit., 2000; musician: (albums) Championship Brass, 1998, Shaken Not Stirred, 2000; mem.: Champion Brass Band (Champions, NABBA, 1996, 1997, 1998, 2000, 2001, 2002). Past pres. Am. Bd. Colon & Rectal Surgery, past chair residency rev. com.; colorectal cancer collaborative rev. group mem. Cochrane Collaboration. Named one of Top 25 Cancer Rschrs. in U.S., Am. Cancer Soc., 1996; recipient Order of Brass Band World -New Years Honors List, Brass Band World, 2000. Fellow: ACS, Am. Soc. Colon and Rectal Surgery (pres. 2001—02). Roman Catholic. Achievements include patents for intestinal tubes. Avocations: music, bicycling, skiing, hiking, brass banding. Home: 2224 Lincolnwood Dr Evanston IL 60201-2020 Home Phone: 011 44 114 235 9854. Home Fax: 1 312 996 2704. Personal E-mail: rick.nelson@sth.nhs.uk.

NELSON, ROBERT EDDINGER, retired management consultant; b. Mentone, Ind., Mar. 2, 1928; s. Arthur Irven and Tural Cecile (Eddinger) N.; m. Carol J., Nov. 24, 1951; children: Janet K., Eric P. BA, Northwestern U., 1949; LHD, Iowa Wesleyan Coll., 1969, North Ctrl. Coll., 1987. Asst. dir. alumni rels. Northwestern U., Evanston, Ill., 1950-51; v.p., dir. pub. rels. Iowa Wesleyan Coll., Mt. Pleasant, 1955-58; vice chancellor for devel. U. Kansas City, 1959—61; v.p. instl. devel. Ill. Inst. Tech., Chgo., 1961-68; pres. Robert Johnston Corp., Oak Brook, Ill., 1968-69, Robert E. Nelson Assocs., Inc., Oak Brook, 1969—2004; ret., 2004. Bd. dirs. Chautauqua Workshop in Fund Raising and Instl. Relations, Continental Bank Oak Brook Terr., Sun Cos.; nat. conf. chmn. and program dir. Am. Coll. Pub. Relations Assn., 1961; trustee Iowa Wesleyan Coll., 1962-68, Have a Heart Found.; faculty mem. Ind. U. Workshops on Coll. and Univ. Devel., 1963-65, Lorretto Heights Summer Inst. for Fund Raising and Pub. Rels., 1964-68; pub. rev. panel for grants programs Lilly Endowment, Inc., 1975. Contbr. chpt. to Handbook of College and University Administration, 1970. With U.S. Army, 1951-54. Mem.: Chgo. Soc. Fundraising Execs., Nat. Small Bus. Assn., Nat. Soc. Fundraisers, Pub. Rels. Soc. Am., Coun. Fin. Aid to Edn. (bd. dirs. 1957—63), Union League, Internat. Club (Chgo.), Blue Key, Execs. Club, Club Internat., DuPage Club, Econ. Club, Masons, Delta Tau Delta. Methodist. Home: 5 Oakbrook Club Dr N101 Oak Brook IL 60523-1348

NELSON, ROY JAY, retired French educator; b. Pitts., July 27, 1929; s. Roy J. and Ruth Brown (Bainbridge) N.; m. Anita Lee Chandler, Aug. 16, 1954; children: Wendy Nelson Wilson, Barbara Nelson Videira. BA, U. Pitts., 1951; MA, Middlebury Coll., 1952; PhD, U. Ill., 1958. Instr. French, U. Mich., Ann Arbor, 1957-60, asst. prof., 1960-65, assoc. prof., 1965-72, prof., 1972-94, prof. emeritus, 1994—. Author: Péguy poète du sacré, 1960, Causality and Narrative in French Fiction from Zola to Robbe-Grillet, 1989; editor: 20e siècle: La Problématique du discours, 1986; contbr. articles to French Rev. Recipient Ruth Sinclair counseling award U. Mich., 1982, cert. for outstanding tchg., 1986; faculty tchg. award Amoco Found., 1992. Mem. MLA, Am. Assn. Tchrs. French Avocation: writing fiction. Office: U Mich Dept Romance Langs and Lits Ann Arbor MI 48109-1275 Personal E-mail: rnelson01@comcast.net.

NELSON, STEVEN CRAIG, lawyer; b. Oakland, Calif., May 11, 1944; s. Eskil Manfred and Florence Lucille (Boatman) N.; m. Kathryn Cassel Stoltz, Nov. 30, 1974 (div. Apr. 1997); children: Carleton Philip, Whitney Cassel. BA in Econs. with exceptional distinction, Yale U., 1966, LLB, 1969. Bar: DC 1969, Minn. Supreme Ct. 1975, U.S. Supreme Ct. 1973, Hong Kong 2000. From atty. adviser to asst. legal adviser U.S. Dept. State, Washington, 1969-74; from assoc. to ptnr. Oppenheimer, Wolff, Foster, Shepard & Donnelly, St. Paul and Mpls., 1975-85; ptnr., internat. practice group Dorsey & Whitney LLP, Mpls., 1985—, co-chmn., Asia practice Hong Kong & Mpls. Mem. bd. appeals NATO, Brussels, 1977-2003; adj. prof. law U. Minn, 1980-86; spkr. in field. Contbr. articles to profl. jours. Mem. ABA (chmn. internat. law and practice 1988-89), Minn. Bar Assn., Internat. Bar Assn. (mem. coun. 1996-2000, mem. WTO Working Group, 2000-present), Inter-Pacific Bar Assn., Minikahda Club. Avocations: golf, tennis, skiing, sailing. Office: Dorsey & Whitney 3008 One Pacific Pl 88 Queensway Hong Kong SAR China Office Phone: 852 2105 0211. Business E-Mail: nelson.steve@dorsey.com.

NELSON, THOMAS GEORGE, retired consulting actuary; b. Mason City, Iowa, Mar. 27, 1949; s. George Burton and Bonny Sue (Sharp) N.; m. Beverlee Joan Trindl, Sept. 28, 1974; children: Kristen Elizabeth, Joseph Charles. BA in Math., U. Iowa, 1971; MA in Math., U. Mich., 1972. Actuary CNA, Chgo., 1972-80; consulting actuary William M. Mercer, Inc., Chgo., 1980-82, A.S. Hansen, Inc., Chgo., 1982-83; sr. consulting actuary, prin., nat. dir. health, bd. dirs. Milliman USA, Chgo., 1983—2005. Mem. task force on acctg. for non-pension retiree benefits Fin. Acctg. Standards Bd., Norwalk, Conn., 1986-90. Contbr. articles to profl. jours. Fellow, 1972, teaching fellow, 1972, U. Mich. Fellow Soc. Actuaries; mem. Am. Acad. Actuaries (bd. dirs. 1989-92, chmn. com. on health and welfare plans 1984-89, com. on rels. with accts. 1987-89, budget and fin. com. 1987-89, chmn. audit subcom. 1991-92, task force on taxation employee benefits 1986), Conf. of Consulting Actuaries (bd. dirs. 1989-95, v.p. 1991-92, exec. com. 1991-95, treas. 1992-95, chmn. com. on recognition of continuing edn. 1989-92, com. on health issues 1985-91), Chgo. Actuarial Soc. Roman Catholic. Avocations: golf, music, reading, sports. Home: 11462 Ashley Woods Dr Westchester IL 60154 E-mail: picthon@hotmail.com.

NELSON, VIRGINIA SIMSON, pediatrician, educator, physiatrist; b. LA; d. Jerome and Virginia (Kuppler) Simson; children: Eric, Paul. AB, Stanford U., 1963, MD, 1970; MPH, U. Mich., 1974. Diplomate Am. Bd. Pediatrics, Am. Bd. Phys. Medicine and Rehab. Pediatrician Inst. Study Mental Retardation and Related Disabilities, U. Mich., Ann Arbor, 1973-80; mem. faculty phys. medicine and rehab. dept. U. Mich. Med. Ctr., Ann Arbor, 1980-83, 85—, resident in phys. medicine and rehab., 1983-85, chief pediatric phys. medicine and rehab. physician, 1985—, prof. phys. medicine and rehab., 2002—. Contbr. articles to profl. jours. Home Phone: 734-485-8638; Office Phone: 734-936-7200. Business E-Mail: pedsrehab@umich.edu.

NEMCEK, ADRIAN R., electronics executive; BSEE, Ill. Inst. Tech.; MBA, Loyola U., Chgo. Joined Motorola, Inc., 1970, with wireless infrastructure global sales and market ops. group, 1994—2000, sr. v.p., gen. mgr. Global Telecom Solutions Sector, exec. v.p., pres., CEO Global Telecom. Solutions Sector Arlington Heights, Ill., 2001—. Mem. bd. advisors HP Corp. Office: Motorola 1303 E Algonquin Rd Schaumburg IL 60196

NEMCOVA, EVA, professional basketball player; b. Czech Republic, Dec. 3, 1972; arrived in U.S., 1997; Guard A.S. Montferrand, France, 1993—96, Bourges, France, 1996—97, Cleveland Rockers, (WNBA), 1997—2003. Named Best Player European Championship, 1995, 1996. Avocations: volleyball, handball, football, mountain biking.

NEMMERS, JOSEPH M., JR., pharmaceutical executive; b. Dec. 22, 1954; B in History, Ariz. State U. Numerous positions in comml. ops., mfg. and materials mgmt. Abbott Labs., Abbott Park, Ill., 1980—99, v.p., exec. dir. Clara Abbott Found., 1999—2000, divisional v.p. Acquisition Integration Mgmt., 2001—02, corp. v.p., 2001—02, v.p. hosp. products bus. sector, 2002, v.p. global comml. ops., 2002—03, sr. v.p. diagnostic ops., 2003—06, exec. v.p. diagnostics & animal health, 2006—. Mem. supervisory bd. Abbott Mgmt. GmbH and Abbott Holding GmbH. Chmn. bd. dirs. United Way Lake County, Carmel H.S.; bd. dirs. Ct. Appointed Spl. Advs., Boys and Girls Club Waukegan. With USAR. Office: Abbott Labs 100 Abbott Park Rd Abbott Park IL 60064-6400

NEPPLE, JAMES ANTHONY, lawyer; b. Carroll, Iowa, Jan. 5, 1945; s. Herbert J. and Cecilia T. (Irlmeier) N.; m. Jeannine Ann Jennings, Sept. 9, 1967; children: Jeffrey B., Scott G., Carin J., Andrew J. BA, Creighton U., 1967; JD, U. Iowa, 1970; postgrad. in bus., Tex. Christian U., 1971; LLM in Taxation, NYU, 1982. Bar: Iowa 1970, Ill. 1973, U.S. Dist. Ct. (so. dist.) Iowa 1972, U.S. Dist. Ct. (cen. dist.) Ill. 1972, U.S. Dist. Ct.(no. dist.) Iowa 1975, U.S. Ct. Appeals (7th and 8th cirs.) 1975, U.S. Supreme Ct. 1975, U.S. Ct. Claims 1976, U.S. Tax Ct. 1976. Tax acct. Arthur Young & Co., Chgo., 1970; v.p., treas., bd. dirs. Stanley, Rehling, Lande & VanDerKamp, Muscatine, Iowa, 1972-92; pres. Nepple, VanDerKamp & Flynn, P.C., Rock Island, Ill., 1992-98, Nepple Law P.L.C., 1999—. Scoutmaster Boy Scouts Am., Muscatine, 1982—85, dist. chmn., 2005—; trustee State His. Soc. Iowa, 1986—92, vice-chmn., 1991—92; bd. dirs. Iowa Hist. Found., 1988—95, pres., 1991—93; trustee Musser Pub. Libr., 2000—04; pres. Muscatine Hist. Preservation Commn., 2001—07, chmn., 2001—04. Recipient Gov.'s Vol. award State of Iowa, 1988, 90, Jr. Achievement of the Quad Cities Bronze award, 1996, Silver award, 2000. Fellow: Ill. Bar Found., Iowa Bar Found., Am. Bar Found., Am. Coll. Trust and Estate Counsel; mem.: ABA (tax sect. 1972—, chair bus. coop. & agrl. tax com. 2001—03), Iowa Bar Assn. (mem. tax sect. 1978—91, chmn. tax sect. 1988—91), Quad City Estate Planning Coun. (pres. 1987), Iowa Assn. Bus. and Industry (tax com. 1978—, chmn. 1986—88), Rock Island County Bar Assn., Scott County Bar Assn., Muscatine Bar Assn. (pres. 1982—83), Ill. Bar Assn. (fed. tax. sect. coun. 1993—99, chair 1997—98, bus. advice and fin. planning sect. coun. 2000—, chair 2007), Fed Bar Assn., Muscatine C. of C. (pres. 1985), Geneva Golf and Country Club (pres. 1990—91), Elks, Kiwanis (pres. Muscatine chpt. 1978). Republican. Roman Catholic. Home: 2704 Mulberry Ave Muscatine IA 52761-2746 Office Phone: 563-264-6840. Office Fax: 563-264-6844. Personal E-mail: nepple@machlink.com. Business E-Mail: jim@nepplelaw.com.

NESBITT, JOHN ARTHUR, recreational therapist, writer, educator, researcher; b. Detroit, Mar. 29, 1933; s. John Jackson and Anna Maye (Hartley) N.; children: John Arthur, and Victoria Bowen. Attended, Howe Mil. Sch., 1945-51, Olivet Coll., 1952-53; BA, Mich. State U., 1955; MA, Columbia Univ., 1961, EdD, 1968. Registered hosp. recreation dir.; cert. therapeutic recreation splty. Program dir. Jaycees Internat., Miami, Fla., 1957-60; therapeutic recreation specialist Rusk Inst. Rehab. Medicine, N.Y.U., Bellevue Med. Ctr., 1960-61; dir. World Commn. on Vocat. Rehab., Rehab. Internat., NYC, 1963—65; dep. dir. gen. World Leisure and Recreation Assn., NYC, 1964—66; asst. sec. gen. Rehab. Internat., NYC, 1966-68; assoc. prof., coord. rehab. svc., leisure studies San Jose State U., Calif., 1968—72; prof., chmn. recreation edn. program U. Iowa, Iowa City, 1972-76, prof. therapeutic recreation, 1977—91, prof. emeritus, 1991—. Pres., CEO Spl. Recreation disABLED Internat., Inc., 1978—; dir., vice chair People to People Com. Disability, 1964-2000; chmn. sub com. recreation and leisure U.S. President's Com. on Employment of Handicapped, 1972-81; dir. Internat. Ctr. on Spl. Recreation, 1978—; webmaster Global Vision of Rehab. and Recreation for People with Disabilities in the 21st Century. Author, editor books in field; editor Alert Mag., 1956; Jaycees Internat. World, 1957-60; Internat. Rehab. of Disabled Rev., 1965-68; Therapeutic Recreation Jour., 1968-70; Jour. Iowa Parks and Recreation, 1974-76; Play, Recreation, and Leisure for People Who Are Disabled, 1977; Fed. Funding for Spl. Recreation, 1978; New Concepts and New Processes in Spl. Recreation, 1978; New Horizons in Profl. Tng. in Recreation Svc. for Handicapped Children and Youth, 1983; Nisbet, Nesbitt Family Surname Assn. Newsletter, 1983-86; Spl. Recreation for DisABLED Digest, 1983-89; U.S.A. Ban Fireworks and Fireworks Safety Campaign Bull., 1988—; UNAGRAM, 1997-99; sr. editor Recreation and Leisure Svc. for Disadvantaged, 1969 (Nat. Recreation Lit. award); editor, compiler Spl. Recreation Compendium of 1,500 Resources for Disabled People, 3d edit., 1989; Special Recreation for Disabled Press, Iowa, 1989; webmaster Global Vision Rehab. and Recreation for People with Disabilities Stop Fireworks Victimization Campaign. Bd. dirs. United Cerebral Palsy Assn., San Mateo and Santa Clara County, 1970-72; bd. dirs. Harold Russell Found., 1971-73; Goodwill Industries Santa Clara County, 1969-72; rehab. counselor, master therapeutic recreation specialist; bd. dir. Hawkeye Area Poverty Cmty. Action Program, Iowa; Iowa Pk. and Recreation Assn., Am. Leisure and Recreation Assn., Washington, others; bd. dirs., state v.p. Iowa Aging Coalition, Iowa; bd. dirs., founding pres. Santa Clara County Assn. on Recreation Handicapped, Iowa; bd. dirs., tech. adv. Disability Internat. Found., 1997—. Served in USAFR, 1955-57; maj. Ret. Recreation Svc. Ill. and Handicapped fellow; recipient numerous awards and citations for work with handicapped, including Torch of Gold Award, Nat. Boy Scouts Am.; Appreciation Award Philippines Found. Mem. Nat. Therapeutic Recreation Soc. (pres. 1970-71, Disting. Svc. Award), Nat. Rehab. Assn.; Am. Assn. Leisure and Recreation (bd. dir. 1977-80, Tommy Wilson svc. Handicapped Youth award); Nat. Consortium on Phys. Edn. and Recreation for Handicapped (pres. 1976-77, Nat. Scholarship award); Nat. Forum Comml. Recreation and Handicapped (chmn. 1979); Iowa Parks and Recreation Assn. (bd.dir. 1973-75, 89-90); Nat. Rehab. Counseling Assn.; Council Exceptional Children; Pi Sigma Epsilon. Presbyterian. Avocations: art, travel, genealogy, cmty. svc. Office Phone: 319-466-3192.

NESS, DAVID MICHAEL, lawyer; b. Mpls., July 9, 1969; BA, Gustavus Adolphus Coll., 1991; JD with distinction, Thomas M. Cooley Law Sch., 1998. Bar: Minn. 1998. Assoc. Bernick & Lifson, P.A., Mpls., 2001—. Assoc. editor: Thomas M. Cooley Jour. of Practical and Clin. Law. Named a Rising Star, Minn. Super Lawyers mag., 2006; recipient Am. Jurisprudence awards, Gaming Law, Computer Assisted Legal Rsch. and Estate Planning. Mem.: ABA, Minn. State Bar Assn., Hennepin County Bar Assn. Office: Bernick & Lifson PA Colonnade Ste 1200 5500 Wayzata Blvd Minneapolis MN 55416 Office Phone: 763-546-1200. E-mail: dness@bernick-lifson.com.

NESS, ROBERT, state legislator, educational consultant; b. 1935; m. Marianne Ness; four children. BS, Bemidji State U.; MA, U. Minn. Edn. cons.; constrn. mgr.; Dist. 20A rep. Minn. Ho. of Reps., St. Paul, 1993—. Home: 24966 729th Ave Dassel MN 55325-3436

NESTER, WILLIAM RAYMOND, JR., retired academic administrator; b. Cin., Feb. 19, 1928; s. William Raymond and Evelyn (Blettner) N.; m. Mary Jane (dec.); children: William Raymond, Mark Patrick, Brian Philip, Stephen Christopher. BS, U. Cin., 1950, EdM, 1953, PhD, 1965, DHL (hon.), 2005, No. Ky. U., 2001, U. Nebr., 2002, U. Cin., 2005. Dir. student union U. Cin., 1952-53, asst. dean of men, 1953-60, dean of men, 1960-67, assoc. prof. edn., 1965-70, dean of students, 1967-69, vice provost student and univ. affairs, 1969-76, prof. edn., 1970-78, assoc. sr. v.p., assoc. provost, 1976-78; v.p. student svcs. Ohio State U., Columbus, 1978-83, prof. edn., 1978-83; pres. Kearney State Coll., Nebr., 1983-91, prof. edn. Nebr., 1983-93; chancellor U. Nebr., Kearney, 1991-93, prof. emeritus, chancellor emeritus, 1993—; v.p. univ. rels. devel. No. Ky. U., 1996-99. Pres. emeritus Mus. Nebr. Art, 1991—; cons. on higher edn., 1993—. Pres. Metro-Six Athletic Conf., 1975-76. Mem. Am. Assn. State Colls. and Univs. (bd. dirs.), Ctrl. States Intercollegiate Conf. (pres. 1986-89), Nat. Assn. Student Pers. Adminstrs. (past regional v.p., mem. exec. com.), Am. Assn. Higher Edn., Ohio Assn. Student Pers. Adminstrs. (past pres.), Nat. Intrafrat. Conf. (pres. 1991-92), Frat. Scholarship Officers Assn. (past pres.), Mortar Bd., Pi Kappa Alpha (nat. pres. 1978-80, pres. nat. interfrat. conf. 1988-89, past pres. Pi Kappa Alpha Ednl. Found.), Omicron Delta Kappa, Phi Delta Kappa, Phi Alpha Theta, Phi Eta Sigma, Sigma Sigma. Episcopalian. Home: 299 Eden Ave Unit 2A Bellevue KY 41073 E-mail: wrnchanem@cs.com.

NETHERLAND, JOSEPH H., manufacturing executive; BS in Indsl. Engring., Ga. Inst. Tech.; MBA, U. Pa. Bus. planner machinery group FMC Technologies, 1973-78, ops. mgr. ordnance divsn., 1978-83, mgr. fluid control divsn., 1983-84, mgr. wellhead divsn., 1984-85, gen mgr. wellhead divsn., 1985-89, gen. mgr. specialized machinery group, 1989-99, pres., 1999—2006, chmn., CEO, 2001—06, chmn., 2006—. Bd. dirs. Am. Petroleum Inst. Mem. adv. bd. Dept. Engring. Tex. A&M Univ.; mem. Pres. Council Ga. Inst. Tech. Recipient Don E. Waggener Butch Griffin award, Spindletop Internat., 2002. Office: FMC Technologies 1803 Gears Rd Houston TX 77067

NETHING, DAVID E., state legislator; m. Marjorie; 3 children. Degree, Jamestown Coll., U. N.D. Attorney; mem. N.D. Senate, 1966—; majority whip, 1974-86; mem. appropriations com. Past pres. Nat. Conf. State Legislators, Found. State Legislators, Coun. State Govt.; past mem. adv. commn. Intergovt. Rels.; past adm. Conf. of U.S. Mem. ABA, Am. Legion, Masonic Bodies, Rotary (past pres.), Elks (past bd. dirs, past exalted ruler), N.D. Affiliate Diabetic Assn. Office: PO Box 1059 Jamestown ND 58402-1059 also: State Senate State Capital Bismarck ND 58505

NETTELS, GEORGE EDWARD, JR., retired mining executive; b. Pittsburg, Kans., Oct. 20, 1927; s. George Edward and Mathilde A. (Wulke) N.; m. Mary Joanne Myers, July 19, 1952; children: Christopher Bryan, Margaret Anne, Katherine Anne, Rebecca Jane. BSCE, U. Kans., Lawrence, 1950. With Black & Veatch Engrs., Kansas City, Mo., 1950-51, Spencer Chem. Co., Kansas City, Mo., 1951-55, Freeto Constrn. Co., Pittsburg, 1955-57; pres. Midwest Minerals, Inc., Pittsburg, 1957—; chmn. bd. McNally Pittsburg Mfg. Corp., 1970-76, pres., CEO, 1976-87, ret., 1987. Past chmn. bd. Nat. Limestone Inst.; bd. dirs. Pitts. Indsl. Devel. Com. Mem. bd. advisors U. Kans. Endowment Assn.; mem. Kans. U. Chancellor's Club, Kans., Inc.; past pres. Bd. Edn. 250, Pittsburg; past chmn. bd. trustees Mt. Carmel Hosp.; past mem. Kans. Commn. Civil Rights; chmn. Kans. Republican Com., 1966-68; Kans. del. Rep. Nat. Conv., 1968, Kans. Bus. and Industry Com. for Re-election of Pres., 1972. With AUS, 1946-47. Recipient Disting. Svc. citation U. Kans., 1980, Disting. Engring. citation U. Kans., 1985; named Kansan of Yr. Natives Sons and Daus. Kans., 1986. Mem. ASCE, NAM (past. dir.), Kans. C. of C. and Industry (dir., chmn. 1983-84), Kans. Right to Work (dir.), Pittsburg C. of C. (past dir.), Kans. U. Alumni Assn. (pres. 1977), Kans. Leadership Com., Crestwood Country Club, Wolf Creek Golf Club (Olathe), Tau Beta Pi, Omicron Delta Kappa, Beta Theta Pi. Office: Midwest Minerals Inc 509 W Quincy St Pittsburg KS 66762-5689 Business E-Mail: george@midwestminerals.com.

NETTL, BRUNO, anthropologist, musicologist, educator; b. Prague, Czechoslovakia, Mar. 14, 1930; s. Paul and Gertrud (Hutter) N.; m. Wanda Maria White, Sept. 15, 1952; children: Rebecca Nettl-Fiol, Gloria Roubal. AB, Ind. U., 1950, PhD, 1953; MA in L.S, U. Mich., 1960; LHD (hon.), U. Chgo., 1993; LHD (hon.), U. Ill., 1996, Carleton Coll., 2000, Kenyon Coll., 2002. Mem. faculty Wayne State U., Detroit, 1953-64, asst. prof., 1954-64, music librarian, 1958-64; mem. faculty U. Ill., Urbana, 1964—, prof. music and anthropology, 1967—, chmn. div. musicology, 1967-72, 75-77, 82-85. Vis. lectr., Fulbright grantee U. Kiel, Fed. Republic of Germany, 1956-58; cons. Ency. Brit., 1969—; cons. on ethnomusicology to various univs.; vis. prof. Williams Coll., 1971, Washington U., 1978, U. Louisville, 1983, U. Wash., 1985, 88, 89, 93, 95, 98, 2000, Fla.

State U., 1988, Harvard U., 1989, U. Alta., 1991, Colo. Coll., 1992, orthwestern U., 1993, U. Minn., 1994, U. Chgo., 1996, 2006, Carleton Coll., 1996, U. So. Calif., 2002, U. Denver, 2005. Author: Theory and Method in Ethnomusicology, 1964, Music in Primitive Culture, 1956, Folk and Traditional Music of the Western Continents, 1965, 2nd edit., 1973, Eight Urban Musical Cultures, 1978, The Study of Ethnomusicology, 1983, new edit., 2005, The Western Impact on World Music, 1985, The Radif of Persian Music, 1987, rev. edit., 1992, Blackfoot Musical Thought, 1989, Comparative Musicology and Anthropology of Music, 1991, Heartland Excursions, 1995, In the course of Performance, 1998, Encounters in Ethnomusicology, a Memoir, 2002; co-author Excursions in World Music, 1992, 3rd edit., 2000, 5th edit., 2007; editor Ethnomusicology, 1961-65, 98-2002, Yearbook of the International Folk Music Council, 1975-77; sr. adv. editor Garland Ency. of World Music; contbr. articles to profl. jours. Recipient Koizumi prize in ethnomusicology, Tokyo, 1994; named hon. prof. Ctrl. Conservatory Music, Beijing, 2007. Fellow Am. Acad. of Arts and Scis.; mem. Soc. Ethnomusicology (pres. 1969-71), Am., Internat. musicol. socs., Internat. Coun. for Traditional Music, Coll. Music Soc, Am. Musicological Soc. (hon.), Soc. for Ethnomusicology (hon.) Office: U Ill Sch Music Urbana IL 61801 Home: 1423 Cambridge Dr Champaign IL 61821-4958 Office Phone: 217-333-9613. Business E-Mail: b-nettl@uiuc.edu.

NETZLEY, ROBERT ELMER, state legislator; b. Laura, Ohio, Dec. 7, 1922; s. Elmer and Mary (Ingle) N.; m. Marjorie Lyons; children: Kathleen, Carol Anne, Robert. Grad. Midshipman Sch., Cornell U., 1944; BS, Miami U., 1947. State rep. 7th Dist. Ohio State Congress, 1961-82, state rep. Dist. 68, 1982—. Pres. Miami County Young Reps., Ohio, 1952-54; chmn. Miami County Rep. Ctrl. and Exec. com., 1958—; del. Rep. Nat. Conv., 1980, presdl. elector, 1980; sec.-treas., part owner Netzley Oil Co., 1947—; v.p. Romale Inc., 1961—. Recipient Purple Heart, Am. and Pacific Theaters. Mem. VFW, Miami County Heart Coun., Am. Legion, AmVets, Grange, Laura Lions; Phi Kappa Tau.

NEU, RICHARD W., credit agency executive; B of Acctg., Ea. Mich. U., 1977. Sr. audit mgr. KMPG Peat Marwick; sr. v.p., chief fin. officer FirstFed Mich. Corp., 1985—89, chief fin. officer, 1989—95; exec. v.p., chief fin. officer Charter One Fin., Inc., 1995—. Past chmn. Thrift Industry Acctg. Com. Office: Charter One Fin Inc 1215 Superior Ave Cleveland OH 44114

NEUBAUER, CHARLES FREDERICK, investigative reporter; b. Berkeley, Ill., Feb. 13, 1950; s. Fred Charles and Dolores Jeanne (Pries) N.; m. Sandra Carol Bergo, Oct. 4, 1975; 1 child, Michael Frederick. BSJ., Northwestern U., 1972, MSJ., 1973. Investigator Better Govt. Assn., Chgo., 1971-73; investigative reporter Chgo. Today, 1973-74, Chgo. Tribune, 1974-83, Chgo. Sun Times, 1983—2001; investigative reporter Washington bur. L.A. Times, 2001—. Recipient Pulitzer prize local reporting, 1976; Edward Scott Beck award for domestic reporting Chgo. Tribune, 1980 Office: 401 N Wabash Ave Chicago IL 60611-5642

NEUBAUER, LISA S., lawyer; b. Mpls., July 21, 1957; BA polit. sci., U. Wis., 1979; JD with honors, U. Chgo., 1987. Bar: Wis. 1987. Legis. aide to Fred Risser pres. Wis. State Senate, 1979—82; staff mem. U.S. Senate, 1982—84; law clk. to Hon. Barbara B. Crabb chief judge, U.S. Dist. Ct., We. Dist. Wis.; ptnr. Foley & Lardner LLP, Milw., chairperson recruiting com.-Milw. office, chairperson ins. dispute resolution practice group. Mem.: State Bar Wis., ABA, Racine Bar Assn., Milw. Bar Assn., Order Coif. Office: Foley & Lardner LLP 777 E Wisconsin Ave Milwaukee WI 53202-5306 Office Phone: 414-297-5507. Office Fax: 414-297-4900. Business E-Mail: lneubauer@foley.com.

NEUBAUER, NICKOLAS J., brokerage house executive; BA, U. Minn., 1967; JD, Stanford U. Law Sch.; MBA, Stanford U. Bus. Sch. Co-founder and pres. Tradelink Corp., 1979—87; mgmt. cons. McKinsey and Co.; corp. and tax lawyer Sidley & Austin, Chgo.; vice chmn. arbitration com. Chgo. Bd. Trade, 1993—97, chmn. bd. dirs., 2000—02, full mem. dir., 2003—; pres. Sano Corp., 1991—. Office: Chgo Bd Trade 141 W Jackson Blvd Chicago IL 60604-2994

NEUEFEIND, WILHELM, economics professor, university administrator; b. Viersen, Germany, Mar. 6, 1939; arrived in U.S., 1978; m. Ingrid Leuchtenberg, Mar. 30, 1966; children: Nicole, Bettina. MBA, U. Cologne, Germany, 1962, MA in Math., 1969; PhD in Econs., U. Bonn, 1972. Lectr. econs. U. Bonn, 1973—77; prof. econ. Wash. U., St. Louis, 1977, prof. emeritus, chmn. dept. econs., 1983—99. Contbr. articles to profl. jours. Mem. Econometric Soc., Am. Econ. Assn., Assn. for Advancement Econ. Theory. Office: Washington U Dept Econs 1 Brookings Dr # 1208 Saint Louis MO 63130-4899

NEUFELD, MELVIN J., state legislator; m. Maxine Neufeld. Student, Tabor Coll. Rep. dist. 115 State of Kans. Mem. NRA, Lions Club, Nat. Railroaders Club. Republican. Address: RR 1 Box 13 Ingalls KS 67853-9706

NEUHAUSER, DUNCAN VONBRIESEN, medical educator; b. Phila., June 20, 1939; s. Edward Blaine Duncan and Gernda (vonBriesen) Neuhauser; m. Elinor Toaz, Mar. 6, 1965; children: Steven, Ann. BA, Harvard U., 1961; MHA, U. Mich., 1963; MBA, U. Chgo., 1966, PhD, 1971. Rsch. assoc. U. Chgo., 1965—70; asst. prof. Sch. Pub. Health, Harvard U., Boston, 1970—74, assoc. prof., 1974—79; cons. in medicine Mass. Gen. Hosp., Boston, 1975—80; assoc. dir. Health Systems Mgmt. Ctr. Case Western Res. U., Cleve., 1979—85, prof. epidemiology, biostats., orgnl. behavior, 1979—, prof. medicine, 1981—, prof. family medicine, 1990—, Charles Elton Blanchard prof. health mgmt., 1995—, co-dir. Health Systems Mgmt. Ctr., 1985—. Mem. biomed. staff Metrohealth Med. Ctr., 1981—; adj. mem. med. staff Cleve. Clinic Found., 1984—99; vis. prof. Vanderbilt U. Sch. Nursing, 1998—, Karolinska Med. Sch., Stockholm, 2002—. Author: numerous books, sci. papers; editor (jours.): Health Matrix, 1982—90, Med. Care, 1983—97. Vice chmn. bd. dirs. Vis. Nurse Assn. Greater Cleve., 1983—84, chmn., 1984—85; bd. dirs. New Eng. Grenfell Assn., Boston, 1972—, Braintree Hosp., Mass., 1975—86; trustee Internat. Grenfell Assn., St. Anthony, Nfld., Canada, 1975—83, Blue Hill Hosp., Maine, 1983—94, Hough Norwood Health Ctr., 1983—94, chmn., 1993—94; mem. vis. com. Columbia U. Sch. Nursing, 2000—; founding bd. dirs. Acad. for Healthcare Improvement, 2004—. Recipient E.F. Meyers Trustee award, Cleve. Hosp. Assn., 1987, Hope award, Nat. Multiple Sclerosis Soc., 1992, Neuhauser lectr., Soc. Pediatric Radiology, 1982, Freedlander lectr., Ohio Permanente Med. Group, 1986, Univ. medal, Tohoku Med. U., Sendai, Japan, 2001, Arthur Shapiro Best Book of Yr. Hypnosis award, 2003, McAuley lectr., Georgetown U., 2007; scholar Keck Found., 1982—; Duncan Neuhauser Endowed chair in cmty. health improvement at Case Western Res. U. and MetroHealth Med. Ctr., 2003, Kellogg fellow, U. Chgo., 1963—65. Mem.: Soc. for Clin. Decision Making, Inst. Medicine NAS, Cleve. Skating Club, Kollegewidgwok Yacht Club (Blue Hill) (commodore 1991—93), St. Botolph Club (Boston), Beta Gamma Sigma. Home (Summer): PO Box 932 Blue Hill ME 04614-0932 Office: Case Western Reserve U Med Sch 10900 Euclid Ave Cleveland OH 44106-4945 Home: 2641 Idlewood Rd 1st Fl Cleveland OH 44118-4249 Home Phone: 216-321-1327; Office Phone: 216-368-3726. Office Fax: 216-368-3970. Business E-Mail: dvn@cwru.edu.

NEUMAN, LINDA KINNEY, retired state supreme court justice, lawyer; b. Chgo., June 18, 1948; d. Harold and Mary E. Kinney; m. Henry G. Neuman; children: Emily, Lindsey. BA, U. Colo., 1970, JD, 1973; LLM, U. Va., 1998. Ptnr. Betty, Neuman, McMahon, Hellstrom & Bittner, 1973-79; v.p., trust officer Bettendorf Bank & Trust Co., 1979-80; dist. ct. judge, 1982-86; supreme ct. justice State of Iowa, 1986—2003; ptnr. Betty Neuman & McMahon. L.L.P., Davenport, Iowa, 2003—05. Mem. adj. faculty U. Iowa Law Sch., 2003-; part-time jud. magistrate Scott County, 1980-82; mem. Supreme Ct. continuing legal edn. commn.; chair Iowa Supreme Ct. commn. planning 21st Century; mem. bd. counselors Drake Law Sch., time on appeal adv. com. Nat. Ctr. State Cts.; mem. Uniform State Laws Commn., 2004. Trustee St. Ambrose U.; commnr. Nat. Conf. Commr. on Uniform State Laws, 2004-. Recipient Regents scholarship, U. Colo. award for disting. svc. Fellow ABA (life; chair appellate judges conf. 1995); mem. Am. Judicature Soc., Iowa Bar Assn., Scott County Bar Assn., Dillon Am. Inn of Ct. (pres. 2003-04), Am. Acad. ADR Attys (pres. 2006-07). Office Phone: 563-289-3255. Office Fax: 563-289-3255. Business E-Mail: lkn@neumanadr.com.

NEUMANN, DONALD A., physical therapist, educator; BS in Phys. Therapy, U. Fla.; MS in Sci. Edn., U. Iowa, 1986, PhD in Exercise Sci. and Phys. Edn., 1986. Phys. therapist Woodrow Wilson Rehab. Ctr., Fishersville, Va., 1976, coord. clin. edn. Phys. Therapy Dept.; faculty mem. to prof. phys. therapy dept. Marquette U., Milw., 1986—. Tchr. kinesiology Kaunas Med. Sch., Lithuania, 2002; tchr. kinesiology Phys. Therapy Prog. Semmelweis U., Budapest, Hungary, 2005. Contbr. articles to profl. jours.; assoc. editor: Jour. Orthop. & Sports Phys. Therapy; author: Kinesiology of the Musculoskeletal System: Foundations for Physical Rehabilitation, 2002. Recipient Steven J. Rose Endowment award for Excellence in Orthop. Phys. Therapy Rsch., Am. Phys. Therapy Assn., Eugene Michels New Investigator award for Outstanding Rsch. by a Young Investigator, Dorothy J. Baethke -Eleanor J. Carlin award for Excellence in Acad. Tchg., Jack Walker award for Best Article on Clin. Rsch. Published in Phys. Therapy, 1999, Fulbright Sr. Specialist award, 2005, US Prof. of Yr. award, Carnegie Found. for Advancement of Tchg. and Coun. for Advancement and Support of Edn., 2006; grantee Fulbright scholarship, 2002. Office: Coll Health Scis Marquette U PO Box 1881 Milwaukee WI 53201-1881 Office Phone: 414-288-3319. E-mail: donald.neumann@marquette.edu.

NEUMANN, MARK W., former congressman, real estate developer; b. Waukesha, Wis., Feb. 27, 1954; m. Sue; 3 children. BS, U. Wis., Whtiewater, 1975; MS, U. Wis., River Falls, 1977. Real estate developer Neumann Devels. (now Neumann Corp.), 1980—; mem. 104th and 105th Congresses from 1st Wis. dist., 1994-97; candidate Wis. State Senate, 2004. Mem. appropriations, nat. security, vets. affairs, HUD and ind. agys., budget coms. Address: W330 N6233 Hasslinger Dr ashotah WI 53058-9432

NEUMANN, ROY COVERT, architect; b. Columbus, Nebr., Mar. 1, 1921; s. LeRoy Franklin and Clara Louise (Covert) N.; children: Tali, Scott; m. Donna Corwin, Oct. 11, 2003. Student, Midland Coll., 1939-40, U. Calif.-Berkeley Armed Forces Inst., overseas, 1942-43; AB, U. Nebr., 1948, BArch, 1949; MA, Harvard U., 1952; postgrad., U. Wis., Iowa State U. Registered profl. architect, Iowa, Nebr., Kans., Minn., SD, NY, Mass., Ohio, Pa., Tenn., Ky., Va., W.Va., Ga., Mich., Mo., Ill., Wis., Tex., Colo. Ptnr., architect R. Neumann Assocs., Lincoln, Nebr., 1952-55; officer mgr. Sargent, Webster, Crenshaw & Folley, Schenectady, Y, 1955-59; dir. architecture, ptnr. A.M. Kinney Assocs., Cin., 1959-65; officer mgr. Hunter, Campbell & Rea, Johnstown, Pa., 1965-66; dir. architecture, ptnr. Stanley Cons., Muscatine, Iowa, 1966-76; pres., chmn. bd. Neumann Monson P.C., Iowa City, 1976—. Ptnr. Clinton St. Ptnrs., Iowa City, 1983—, Iris City Devel. Co. Mt. Pleasant, Iowa, 1986, Linn Mar Elem./Mid. Sch., Marion, Iowa. Prin. works include Harbour Facilities, Antigua, W.I., SC Johnson Office Bldg., Racine, Wis., Iowa City Transit Facility Bldg., addition to Davenport Ctrl. High Sch., V.A. Adminstrv. Office Bldg., Iowa City, Johnson County Office Bldg., Iowa City Mercer Park Aquatic Ctr., Iowa City, Coll. Bus. U. Iowa, Iowa City, renovation Lawrence County Courthouse, Deadwood, SD, HS and Elem. Schs., Mt. Pleasant, Iowa, Riverview Ctr., Muscatine, Iowa, Muscatine County Adminstv. Bldg., Iowa. Mem. bd. edn. Muscatine Cmty. Sch. Dist., 1974-76. Served with USN, 1942-46, PTO. Recipient Honor award Portland Cement Assn., 1949, Lorraine D. Wright award for outstanding constrn. Camanche HS, Iowa, 1998-99. Mem. AIA (Honor award 1975), Constrn. Specifications Inst. (pres. 1974-76, Honor award 1983, 84, 85, 86), Soc. Archtl. Historians, Archtl. Assn. London, U. Nebr. Alumni Assn., Harvard U. Alumni Assn., Iowa City C. of C., Phi Kappa Psi, Univ. Athletic Club (Iowa City), Masons, Ea. Star, Elks Republican. Presbyterian. Avocations: golf, fishing, medieval history, big band music. Home: 312 Locust St Muscatine IA 52761-3510 Office: Neumann Monson Architects 221 E College St Iowa City IA 52240-4012 Office Phone: 319-338-7878. E-mail: roy@neumannmonson.com.

NEUMANN, THOMAS ALAN, educational administrator; b. Green Bay, Wis., Apr. 7, 1949; s. William and Elena (Peabody) N.; m. Carla Simonson, Aug. 17, 1974; children: athaniel, Amanda. BSN, U. Wis., 1977; MSN, U. Minn., 1982; BS in Edn., U. Wis., 1972. RN, Wis. Instr. diploma nursing program Mounds-Midway Sch. Nursing, St. Paul, 1980-83; staff devel. instr. Hennepin County Med. Ctr., Mpls., 1983-84; instr. in AD nursing Western Wis. Tech. Coll., LaCrosse, 1984-86; chair nursing practice and edn. com. Nat. Coun. of State Bds. of Nursing, Chgo., 1989-92; adminstrv. officer Wis. Dept. Regulation and Licensing; assoc. dean health, human and protective svcs. Madison (Wis.) Area Tech. Coll., 2000—. Cons. Wis. Bd. Nursing, 1986-99; v.p. Nat. Coun. State Bds. Nursing, 1994-96, pres., 1996-98. Mem. Sigma Theta Tau. Home: 652 Birch Ct Verona WI 53593-1660 Office: Madison Area Tech Coll 3550 Anderson St Madison WI 53704-2520

NEUMANN, WILLIAM ALLEN, retired state supreme court justice; b. Minot, ND, Feb. 11, 1944; s. Albert W. and Opal Olive (Whitlock) N.; m. Jaqueline Denise Buechler, Aug. 9, 1980; children: Andrew, Emily. BSBA, U. N.D., 1965; JD, Stanford U., 1968. Bar: N.D. 1969, U.S. Dist. Ct. N.D. 1969. Pvt. practice law, Williston, ND, 1969-70, Bottineau, ND, 1970-79; judge N.D. Judicial Dist. Ct., N.E. Judicial Dist., Rugby and Bottineau, 1979-92; justice N.D. Supreme Ct., Bismarck, 1993—2005; exec. dir. State Bar Assn., ND, 2005—. Chmn. elect N.D. Jud. Conf., 1985-87, chmn. 1987-89. Mem. ABA, State Bar Assn. N.D., Am. Judicature Soc. (bd. dirs. 1998-2004). Lutheran. Office: ND State Bar Assn 504 N Washington St Bismarck ND 58501 Office Phone: 701-255-1404.

NEUMER, STEPHEN M., lawyer; b. Grand Rapids, Mich., July 27, 1940; BBA magna cum laude, U. Mich., 1962; JD, Stanford U., 1965. Bar: Ill. 1966. Ptnr. Katten Muchin Zavis Rosenman, Chgo. Mem.: ABA, Internat. Bar Assn, Chgo. Bar Assn., The Joffrey Ballet of Chgo., Phi Kappa Phi, Beta Gamma Sigma, Beta Alpha Psi. Office: Katten Muchin Zavis Rosenman 525 W Monroe St Chicago IL 60661 Office Phone: 312-902-5269. Office Fax: 312-577-8866. E-mail: stephen.neumer@kmzr.com.

NEUVILLE, THOMAS M., state legislator, lawyer; b. Marinette, Wis., Jan. 31, 1950; s. Morris and Dallas (Thompson) N.; m. Marilynn Hamilton, Jan. 31, 1976; children: Mark, John, Anne, Luke, Maggie. BSChemE, Mich. Tech. U., 1972; JD, William Mitchell Law Sch., St. Paul, 1976. Bar: Minn. 1976, U.S. Dist. Ct. Minn. 1977. Ptnr. Grundhoefer & Neuville, Northfield, Minn., 1976-82, pres., atty., 1982—; delegate State Republican Party, 1988, 90, 92, 94; mem. Minn. Senate, Saint Paul, 1990—. Arbitrator Am. Arbitration Assn., 1988—; civil and family arbitrator Hennepin County Dist. Ct., Mpls., 1986—. Treas. Rice County Rep. Com., 1982—. Mem. ABA, Minn. Bar Assn., Northfield C. of C. (pres. 1986-87), Tau Beta Pi. Roman Catholic. Avocations: golf, guitar, basketball. Home: PO Box 7 515 Water St S Northfield MN 55057-2033 Office: Grundhoefer & Neuville PO Box 7 Northfield MN 55057-0007 Address: Minn Senate 123 State Capitol 100 Constitution Ave Saint Paul MN 55155-1232

NEVILLE, DALLAS S., protective services official; married; 1 child. Student, Chippewa Valley Tech. Coll. Deputy sheriff Clark County Sheriff's Dept., Neillsville, Wis., 1980-94; U.S. marshal U.S. Marshal's Svc., Madison, Wis., 1994—. Office: US Marshals Svc US Courthouse 120 N Henry St Ste 440 Madison WI 53703-2559

NEVILLE, JAMES MORTON, retired lawyer, consumer products company executive; b. Mpls., May 28, 1939; s. Philip and Maurene (Morton) N.; m. Judie Martha Proctor, Sept. 9, 1961; children: Stephen Warren, Martha Maurene Hereford. BA, U. Minn., JD magna cum laude, 1964. Bar: Minn. 1964, Mo. 1984. Assoc. Neville, Johnson & Thompson, Mpls., 1964-69, ptnr., 1969-70; assoc. counsel Gen. Mills, Inc., Mpls., 1970-77, sr. assoc. counsel, 1977-83, corp. sec., 1976-83; v.p., sec., asst. gen. counsel Ralston Purina Co., St. Louis, 1983-84, v.p., gen. counsel, sec., 1984-96, v.p., gen. counsel, 1996-2000, v.p., sr. counsel, 2000-01; ret., 2001. Lectr. bus. law. U. Minn., 1967-71; chmn. The Thompson Ctr., 2002. Bd. mem. Haven of Grace, 1997—2000. Named Man of Yr., Edina Jaycees, 1967. Mem. ABA, Mo. Bar Assn., U.S. Supreme Ct. Bar Assn., St. Louis Bar Assn., U. Minn. Law Sch. Alumni Assn., Old Warson Country Club, Ladue Racquet Club, Order of Coif, Phi Delta Phi, Psi Upsilon. Episcopalian. Avocation: bridge. Home: 9810 Log Cabin Ct Saint Louis MO 63124-1133 Home Phone: 314-993-6607. Personal E-mail: jnev57@aol.com.

NEVIN, JOHN ROBERT, business educator, consultant; b. Joliet, Ill., Jan. 27, 1943; s. Robert Charles and Rita Alice (Roder) N.; m. Jeanne M. Conroy, June 10, 1967; children: Erin, Michael. BS, So. Ill. U., 1965; MS, U. Ill., 1968, PhD, 1972. Asst. prof. bus. U. Wis., Madison, 1970—77, assoc. prof. bus., 1977—83, prof. bus., 1983—, Grainger Wis. disting. prof. bus., 1989—, exec. dir. Grainger Ctr. for Supply Chain Mgmt., 1992—, assoc. dean masters program, 1999—2002, exec. dir. Ctr. Brand and Product Mgmt., 2003—07. Mem. investment adv. com. Venture Investors of Wis., Inc., Madison, 1986-99. Author: International Marketing: An Annotated Bibliography, 1983; mem. editl. bd. Jour. of Mtg. Channels, The Haworth Press, Inc., 1991—; contbr. articles to profl. jours. Bd. dirs. Madison Civic Ctr., 1983—99. Mem. Am. Mktg. Assn. (bd. dirs. PhD consortium 1979, editorial bd. Jour. of Mktg. Chgo. chpt. 1983-97), Assn. for Consumer Rsch. Avocations: golf, skiing, running. Home: 7514 Red Fox Trl Madison WI 53717-1860 Office: U Wis Grainger Ctr Supply Chain Mgmt 975 University Ave Madison WI 53706-1324 Office Phone: 608-262-8912. E-mail: jnevin@bus.wisc.edu.

NEVIN, ROBERT CHARLES, information systems executive; b. Dayton, Ohio, Nov. 4, 1940; s. Robert Steely and Virginia (Boehme) N.; m. Linda Sharon Fox, Apr. 16, 1966; children: Heather, Andrew. BA, Williams Coll., 1962; MBA, U. Pa., 1970. Fin. planning mgr. Huffy Corp., Dayton, Ohio, 1971-72, asst. treas., 1972-73, treas., 1973-75, v.p. fin., 1975-79, exec. v.p., 1982-85; pres., gen. mgr. Frabill Sporting Good, Milw., 1979-82; exec. v.p. Reynolds & Reynolds, Dayton, Ohio, 1985-88, pres. bus. forms divsn., 1988-97; pres. automotive group, 1997—. Bd. dirs. Reynolds & Reynolds, Olympic Title Ins. Co. Bd. dirs., pres. Camp Fire Girls, Dayton, 1975; bd. dirs. ARC, 1977; participant, then trustee Leadership Dayton, 1986-95; vice chmn. Med. Am. Corp.; trustee, treas. Victory Theater Assn., 1985-91, Dayton Mus. Natural History, 1982-96; trustee, chmn. Alliance for Edn., Dayton Art Inst. 1st lt. USN, 1962-70. Mem. Beta Gamma Sigma, Racquet (Dayton), Dayton Country, Country Club of the North. Republican. Episcopalian.

NEVLING, LORIN IVES, JR., museum administrator; b. St. Louis, Sept. 23, 1930; s. Lorin I. and Rose Elizabeth (Meyer) N.; m. Janet Frances Sullivan, June 1, 1957; children— Lorin, Luara, Mark, James, John. BS, St. Mary's Coll., 1952; postgrad., U. Notre Dame, 1952-53; A.M., Washington U., St. Louis, 1957, PhD, 1959. Research asst. flora of Panama Mo. Bot. Garden, St. Louis, 1957-58, 59; asst. curator Gray Herbarium, 1963-69, curator herbarium, 1969-73, mem. faculty arts and scis., 1966-73; curator Arnold Arboretum, 1969-73, lectr. biology, 1969-73, coordinator bot. systematic collections, 1972-73; curator Field Mus. atural History, Chgo., 1973-80, chmn. dept. botany, 1973-77, asst. dir. sci. and edn., 1978-80, dir., 1980—. Cons. and lectr. in field. Contbr. articles to sci. jours.; assoc. editor Rhodora, 1964-70; mem. editorial bd. Anales del Instituto de Biologia, Mexico, 1970-74. Bd. dirs. Ill. Inst. Natural Resources, 1979—. Served with U.S. Army, 1953-55. Recipient Outstanding Vol. award United Way Met. Chgo., 1978; NSF grantee, 1970-81; Van Blarcom scholar, 1959. Fellow AAAS; mem. Am. Inst. Biol. Scis. (governing bd. 1974-77), Am. Assn. Museums, Bot. Soc. Am., Assn. for Tropical Biology (travel grantee 1966), Internat. Assn. Plant Taxonomy, Am. Soc. Plant Taxonomists (pres. 1977, council 1974-78, George R. Cooley award 1970), Linnean Soc. London, Sociedad Botanica de Mexico, Sigma Xi. Office: Ill Nat History Survey Nat Resources Bldg 607 E Peabody Dr Champaign IL 61820-6917

NEW, ROSETTA HOLBROCK, retired secondary school educator, retired department chairman, retired nutrition consultant; b. Aug. 26, 1921; d. Edward F. and Mabel (Kohler) Holbrock; m. John Lorton New, Sept. 3, 1943; 1 child, John Lorton Jr. BS, Miami U., Oxford, Ohio, 1943; MA, U. No. Colo., 1971; PhD, Ohio State U., 1974; student, Kantcentrum, Brugge, Belgium, 1992, Lesage Sch. Embroidery, Paris, 1995, Kent State U., 1998. Cert. tchr. Colo. Tchr. English and sci. Monahans (Tex.) H.S., 1943—44; emergency war food asst. USDA, College Station, Tex., 1945—46; dept. chmn. home econs., adult edn. Hamilton (Ohio) Pub. Schs., 1946—47; tchr., dept. chmn. home econs. East H.S., Denver, 1948—59, Thomas Jefferson H.S., Denver, 1959—83; ret., 1983. Exec. bd. Denver Pub. Schs.; lectr. in field; exec. dir. Ctr. Nutrition Info. U.S. Office Edn. Grantee, Ohio State U., 1971—73. Mem.: Internat. Platform Assn., Fairfield (Ohio) Hist. Soc., Ohio State Home Econs. Alumni Assn., Ohio State U. Assn., Hamilton Hist. Soc., Am. Vocat. Assn., Am. Home Econs. Assn., Nat. Trust for Hist. Preservation, Cin. Art Mus., Internat. Old Lacers, Embroiders Guild Am., Rep. Club Denver, Order White Shrine of Jerusalem, Daus. of the Nile, Masons, Order of Ea. Star, Phi Upsilon Omicron. Presbyterian.

NEWBLATT, STEWART ALBERT, federal judge; b. Detroit, Dec. 23, 1927; s. Robert Abraham and Fanny Ida (Grinberg) N.; m. Flora Irene Sandweiss, Mar. 5, 1965; children: David Jacob, Robert Abraham, Joshua Isaac. BA with distinction, U. Mich., 1950, JD with distinction, 1952. Bar: Mich. 1953. Ptnr. White & Newblatt, Flint, Mich., 1953-62; judge 7th Jud. Cir. Mich., 1962-70; ptnr. Newblatt & Grossman (and predecessor), Flint, 1970-79; judge U.S. Dist. Ct. (ea. dist.) Mich., Flint, 1979-93, sr. judge, 1993—. Adj. instr. U. Mich.-Flint, 1977-78, 86. Mem. Internat. Bridge Authority Mich., 1960-62. Served with AUS, 1946-47. Mem. Fed. Bar Assn., State Bar Mich., Dist. Judges Assn. 6th Circuit. Jewish.

NEWBORG, GERALD GORDON, retired state archives administrator; b. Ada, Minn., Dec. 13, 1942; s. George Harold and Olea (Halstad) N.; m. Jean Annette Gruhl, Aug. 14, 1964; children: Erica, Annette. BA, Concordia Coll., Moorhead, Minn., 1964; MA, U. N.D., 1969; MBA, Ohio State U., 1978. Cert. archivist. Tutor, preceptor Parsons Coll., Fairfield, Iowa, 1964-67; state archivist Ohio Hist. Soc., Columbus, 1968-76; v.p. Archival Systems Inc., Columbus, 1978-81; state archivist State Hist. Soc. of N.D., Bismarck, 1981—2007. Instr. Franklin U., Columbus, 1974; adj. prof. Bismarck State Coll., 1985-86. Co-author: North Dakota: A Pictorial History, 1988. Recipient Resolution of Commendation Ohio Ho. of Reps., Columbus, 1976; Governor's award. Mem. Acad. Cert. Archivists Home: 1327 N 18th St Bismarck ND 58501-2827 Office: State Hist Soc 612 E Boulevard Ave Bismarck ND 58505-0660

NEWCOMB, MARTIN EUGENE, JR., chemistry professor; b. Mishauaha, Ind., Nov. 17, 1946; s. Martin Eugene and Yolanda Frances (Saliani) N.; 1 child, Jennifer Ruth. BA, Wabash Coll., 1969; PhD in Chemistry, U. Ill., 1973. Asst. prof. Tex. A&M U., College Station, 1973-81, assoc. prof., 1981-85, prof. chemistry, 1985-91, Wayne State U., Detroit, 1991-2001; prof. U. Ill., Chgo., 2001—. Contbr. articles to Accounts of Chem. Rsch., 1988, Jour. Am. Chem. Soc. 1989— Named Dreyfus Tchr.-Scholar, Camille and Henry Dreyfus Found., 1980-85. Mem. AAAS, Am. Chem. Soc.(Arthur C. Cope Scholar award, 1994, James Flack Norris award in Physical Organic Chemistry, 2000). Office: U Ill Chgo Dept Chemistry Chicago IL 60607

NEWCOMER, KERMIT LEE, retired internist, kidney specialist; b. Bryan, Ohio, Nov. 15, 1930; MD, Case Western Res U., 1959. Intern Walter Reed Gen. Hosp., Washington, 1959—60, resident, 1960—63; internal medicine physician Gundersen /Luth. Hosp., LaCrosse, Wis., 1967—95; ret. Past pres. World Svc. La Crosse, Inc., med. cons., bd. mem., 1995—. Recipient Benjamin Rush award for citizenship and cmty. svc., AMA, 2003, Presdl. Citation award, Wis. Med. Soc., 2004. Achievements include development of specialized health ctr. in Russia, China, Ukraine. Office: World Svc La Crosse Inc 1601 Caledonia St Ste B La Crosse WI 54603 Home Phone: 608-788-2618; Office Phone: 608-781-4194. Office Fax: 608-781-4197. E-mail: knew3213@aol.com.

NEWLIN, CHARLES FREMONT, lawyer; b. Palestine, Ill., Nov. 18, 1953; s. Charles Norris and Regina Helen (Correll) N.; m. Jean Bolt, Jan. 6, 1975; children: Christian N., Charles W., Ethan A. BA in Polit. Sci. summa cum laude, Ill. Wesleyan U., 1975; JD cum laude, Harvard U., 1978. Bar: Ill. 1978, US Dist. Ct. (no. dist.) Ill. 1978, US Tax Ct. 1980. Law clk. Sugarman, Rogers, Barshak & Cohen, Boston, 1976-78; assoc. Mayer, Brown & Platt, Chgo., 1978-84, ptnr., 1985-94, Sonnenschein, Nath & Rosenthal, 1994—2002, McGuire Woods LLP, 2002—03, Harrison & Held LLP, Chgo. Research asst., Harvard Law Sch., Mass., 1976, adj. prof. law DePaul U., Chgo., 1986-90, adminstr. Wealth Mgmt.(trusts, estates and found. practice area), 1989-1994. Contbg. author: Am. Law of Property, 1975, Trust Adminstrn. Ill., 1983, 87, 92, 99, Bogert on Trusts, 1986-91, The Lawyer's Guide to Retirement, 1991, 94; contbr. articles to profl. jours. Scouting coord. DuPage area coun. Boy Scouts Am., Woodridge, Ill., 1984-86; bishop's counselor Mormon Ch., Woodridge, 1984-86; mem. planned giving com. Ill. divsn. Am. Cancer Soc., 1988—, chair, 1997—; active Boys and Girls Clubs of Chgo., 1993—; mem. bd. dirs. Suburban Chgo. Planned Giving Coun., 1997, Ill. Inst. for Continuing Legal Edn., 1999—, vol. legal cons. The Tower Chorale, Westner Springs, Ill., 1989-91. Listed in Who's Who in Am., Who's Who in Am. Law, Who's Who of Emerging Leaders in Am., Who's Who in Practicing Atty., Internat. Who's Who Profl., named Leading Ill. Atty., Am. Research Corp., 1997. Fellow Am. Coll. Trust and Estate Counsel; mem. Chgo. Bar Assn., 1982-, Chgo. Estate Planning Coun., Tech. Practice Com., 1991-2000, Elder Law Com., 1995-, Probate Practice Com., U Club Chgo., 1986-1992, Met. Club Chgo., 1994-2000. Democrat. Mem. Lds Ch. Office: Harrison & Held LLP 333 W Wacker Dr Ste 1700 Chicago IL 60606 Office Phone: 312-322-3940. Office Fax: 312-753-6191. Business E-Mail: mnewlin@harrisonheld.com.

NEWMAN, ANDREA FISCHER, air transportation executive; AB, U. Mich., Ann Arbor, 1979; JD, George Washington U., 1983. With Patton, Boggs, Washington; dept. asst. to V.P. George Bush The White House; spl. counsel to asst. sec. def. for acquisitions and logistics Dept. Def.; sr. ptnr Miller, Canfield, Paddock and Stone, Detroit; v.p. state and local affairs NW Airlines Corp., sr. v.p. govt. affairs Detroit, 2001—. Bd. regents U. Mich., Ann Arbor, 1994—; vice chmn. George W. Bush for Pres. Campaign, co-chmn. fin. com. Mich., 2000; bd. dirs. Mich. Econ. Devel. Corp. Found., Mich. Thanksgiving Day Parade Found., Isiah Thomas Found. Mem.: Detroit Econ. Club (v.p.). Office: NW Airlines Detroit Met Airport 2601 WorldGateway Pl Detroit MI 48242 E-mail: afnewman@umich.edu.

NEWMAN, ANDREW EDISON, restaurant manager; b. St. Louis, Aug. 14, 1944; s. Eric Pfeiffer and Evelyn Frances (Edison) N.; m. Peggy Gregory, Feb. 14, 1984; children: Daniel Mark, Anthony Edison. BA, Harvard U., 1966, MBA, 1968. With Office of Sec. Def., Washington, 1968-70; with Edison Bros. Stores, Inc., St. Louis, 1970-95, v.p. ops. and adminstrn., 1975-80, dir., 1978-96, exec. v.p., 1980-86, chmn., 1987-95; chmn., CEO Race Rock Internat., St. Louis, 1995—. Bd. dirs. Lee Enterprises, Davenport, Iowa. Trustee Washington U. Office: 8000 Maryland Ave Saint Louis MO 63105-3752

NEWMAN, CHARLES ANDREW, lawyer; b. LA, Mar. 18, 1949; s. Arthur and Gladys Newman; m. Elizabeth F.; children: Anne R., Elyse S. BA magna cum laude, U. Calif., 1970; JD, Washington U., 1973. Bar: Mo. 1973, DC 1981, Ill. 2001, Wis. 2003, NY 2006, US Dist. Ct. (ea. dist.) Mo. 1973, US Dist. Ct. (so. dist.) Ill. 2001, US Dist. Ct. (ctrl. dist.) Ill. 1996, US Dist. Ct. (ea. dist.) Mich. 2002, US Ct. Appeals (8th cir.) 1975, US Supreme Ct. 1976, US Tax Ct. 1981, US Claims Ct. 1981, US Ct. Appeals (11th cir.) 1994, US Ct. Appeals (9th cir.) 1995, US Ct. Appeals (3d, 5th, 7th and 10th cirs.) 1996, US Ct. Appeals (6th cir.) 1997, US Dist. Ct. (so. dist.) Ill. 2001, US Dist. Ct. (ea. dist.) Wis. 2003, US Ct. Appeals (1st & 4th cirs.) 2006, US Ct. Appeals (2d cir.) 2006, US Ct. Appeals (DC cir.) 2006. From assoc. to ptnr. Thompson & Mitchell, St. Louis, 1973-96; ptnr. Thompson Coburn, St. Louis, 1996-97, Bryan Cave LLP, St. Louis, 1997—. Lectr. law Washington U., St. Louis, 1976-78. Bd. dirs. Hawthorn Found., 1997-2000; trustee Mo. Bar Found., 1990-96, mem. Mo. Bar Bd. Govs, 1980-84; bd. dirs. United Israel Appeal, N.Y.C., 1990-93, Coun. Jewish Fedns., N.Y.C., 1992-95, United Jewish Appeal Young Leadership Cabinet, N.Y.C., 1985-88, Ctr. for Study of Dispute Resolution, 1985-88, Legal Svcs. Ea. Mo., 1985-94, St. Louis Community Found., 1992-2001, vice-chmn. 1997-99, St. Louis chpt. Young Audiences 1993-95, Planned Parenthood St. Louis, 1986-89, Jewish Fedn., St. Louis, 1986-98, asst. treas., 1989-90, v.p. fin. planning, 1990-93, asst. sec., 1994-95; v.p. Repertory Theatre, St. Louis, 1986-89, sr. v.p., 1990-91; pres. St. Louis Opportunity Clearinghouse, 1974-78. Recipient Lon O. Hocker Meml. Trial award Mo. Bar Found., 1984, What's Right with the Region award, FOCUS St. Louis, 2005. Mem. Bar Assn. Met. St. Louis (Merit award 1976). Democrat. Avocations: golf, reading, music, sailing. Office: Bryan Cave LLP One Metropolitan Square Saint Louis MO 63102-2750 Home Phone: 314-725-4199; Office Phone: 314-259-2000. Business E-Mail: canewman@bryancave.com.

NEWMAN, DANNY MERRIL, lawyer; BA, U. Ariz., 1997; JD, Capital U. Law Sch., 2002. Bar: Ohio 2002, US Dist. Ct. Southern Dist. Ohio 2002, Commonwealth Ky. 2003, US Dist. Ct. Western Dist. Ky. 2003, US Dist. Ct. Eastern Dist. Ky. 2003, US Ct. of Appeals, Sixth Cir. 2003. Jud. clerk Franklin County Probate Ct. Judge; atty. Reminger & Reminger Co., Cin. Named one of Ohio's Rising Stars, Super Lawyers, 2006. Mem.: Ohio Assn. Civil Trial Attorneys, Assn. Cert. Fraud Examiners, Ky. Bar Assn., Def. Rsch. Inst., FBA, Assn. Trial Lawyers Am., ABA, Ohio State Bar Assn., Clermont County Bar Assn., Cin. Bar Assn. Office: Reminger & Reminger Co 525 Vine St Ste 1700 Cincinnati OH 45202 Office Phone: 513-721-1311. Office Fax: 513-721-2553.

NEWMAN, DIANA S., foundation administrator, consultant, writer; d. Fred Andrew and Thelma Elizabeth (Hewitt) Smith; m. Dennis Ryan Newman, Feb. 15, 1964; children: Barbara Lynn Newman LaBine, John Ryan, Elizabeth Anne. Student, Oberlin Coll., Ohio, 1961—64. Cert. fund raising exec. Asst. treas. Marble Cliff Quarries Co., 1964-68; cmty. vol., 1968-83; dir. Ohio Hist. Found., Columbus, 1983-90; v.p. advancement The Columbus (Ohio) Found., 1990-95; pres. Philanthropic Resource Group, Columbus, 1995—. Author: Opening Doors: Pathways to Diverse Donors, 2002 (AFP/Skystone Ryan prize for rsch., 2003), onprofit Essentials: Endowment Building, 2005. Bd. dirs. Leader Inst., Inc., 2001-04; mem. governing bd. First Cmty. Ch., 1983-88, chair, 1987-88; bd. dirs. LWV Ctrl. Ohio, 1968-72, Ohio Mus. Assn., 1985-90, Crittenton Family Svcs., Columbus, 1992-95; founder Franklin County Com. on Criminal Justice, Columbus, 1972; pres. Jr. League Columbus, 1980-81. Mem. Assn. Fundraising Profls. (bd. dirs. Ctrl. Ohio chpt. 1985-88, 2004-, nat. rsch. coun. 2003—, Outstanding Profl. Fundraiser Ctrl. Ohio chpt., 2004), Ctrl. Ohio Planned Giving Coun. (bd. dirs. 1990-2001, pres. 1998), Columbus Female Benevolent Soc. (bd. dirs. 1984—). Office: Philanthropic Resource Group 926 Augusta Glen Dr Columbus OH 43235-5097 Home: 926 Augusta Glen Dr Columbus OH 43235 Business E-Mail: diana@diananewman.com.

NEWMAN, JOAN MESKIEL, lawyer; b. Youngstown, Ohio, Dec. 12, 1947; d. John F. and Rosemary (Scarmuzzi) Meskiel; children: Anne R., Elyse S. BA in Polit. Sci., Case-Western Reserve U., 1969; JD, Washington U., St. Louis, 1972, LLM in Taxation, 1973. Bar: Mo. 1972. Assoc. Lewis & Rice, St. Louis, 1973-80, ptnr., 1981-90, Thompson Coburn, St. Louis, 1990—2005. Adj. prof. law Washington U. Sch. Law, St. Louis, 1975-92; past pres. St. Louis chpt., mem. Midwest Pension Conf. Mem. nat. coun. Washington U., Sch. Law, 1988—91; chmn. bd. dir. Great St. Louis Coun. Girl Scouts USA, 1975—92, officer, 1978—92; mem. cmty. wide youth svcs. panel United Way Greater St. Louis, 1992—96; fin. futures task force Kiwanis Camp Wyman, 1992—93; chmn. staff blue ribbon fin. com. Sch. Dist., Clayton, 1986—87; vol. Women's Self Help Ctr.; bd. dirs. Parents as Teachers, 2001—04; bd. dir., exec. com. Girl Scouts USA, 1993—99, nat. treas., 1996—99; bd. dirs. Met. Employment and Rehab. Svcs., 1980—2001, chmn. bd. dir., 1994—96, Women of Achievement, 1993—96; bd. dirs. Jewish Ctr. Aged, 1990—92, bd. dir., 1999—2001, Jewish Fedn. St. Louis, 1991—96, City Mus., 1998—2001, United Way Greater St. Louis, 2000—, Oasis, 1999—2001; chair bd. dirs. MERS/Goodwill Industries, 2007—, chmn. bd. dirs., 2007—; bd. dirs. Walker Scottish Rite Ctr., 2002—. Named Woman of Achievement St. Louis, 1991. Mem. Mo. Bar Assn. (staff pension and benefits com. 1991—), Bar Met. St. Louis (past chmn. taxation sect.), St. Louis Forum, Order of Coif (hon.). Home Phone: 314-781-3002; Office Phone: 314-645-5001. Business E-Mail: joan@joannewmanassociates.com.

NEWMAN, JOHN KEVIN, classics educator; b. Bradford, Yorkshire, Eng., Aug. 17, 1928; arrived in US, 1969, naturalized, 1984; s. Willie and Agnes (Shee) N.; m. Frances M. Stickney, Sept. 8, 1970; children: Alexandra, John, Victoria. BA in Lit.-Humaniores, Exeter Coll., Oxford U., 1950, BA in Russian, 1952, MA, 1953; PhD, Bristol U., 1967. Classics master St. Francis Xavier Coll., Liverpool, Eng., 1952-54, Downside Sch., Somerset, Eng., 1955-69; mem. faculty U. Ill., Urbana, 1969—, prof. classics, 1980—, chmn. dept., 1981-85; emeritus, 2000. Author: Augustus and the New Poetry, 1967, Latin Compositions, 1976, The Concept of Vates, 1967, Pindar's Art, 1984, The Classical Epic Tradition, 1986, Roman Catullus, 1990, Lelio Guidiccioni, Latin Poems, 1992, Augustan Propertius, 1997, Troy's Children, 2005; co-author: (with A.V. Carozzi) Horace-Benedict de Saussure, 1995, De Saussure on Geography, 2003; editor: Ill. Classical Studies, 1982-87; contbr. The New Princeton Encyclopedia of Poetry and Poetics, 1993. Mem. sr. common room Corpus Christi Coll., Oxford U., 1985-86 Recipient silver medals Vatican, Rome, 1960, 62, 65, 97. Roman Catholic. Office: Dept Classics U Ill 703 W Delaware Ave Urbana IL 61801-4806 Office Phone: 217-333-1008. E-mail: j-newman@uiuc.edu.

NEWMAN, JOHN M., JR., lawyer; b. Youngstown, Ohio, Aug. 15, 1944; BA, Georgetown U., 1966; JD, Harvard U., 1969. BAr: Ill. 1970, Calif. 1972, Ohio 1976. Law clerk ctrl. dist. U.S. Dist. Ct., Calif., 1969-70, asst. U.S. Atty. ctrl. dist. Calif., 1970-75; ptnr. Jones, Day, Cleve. Fellow Am. Coll. Trial Lawyers; mem. Phi Beta Kappa. Office: Jones Day North Point 901 Lakeside Ave E Cleveland OH 44114-1190 Office Phone: 216-586-7207. Business E-Mail: jmnewman@jonesday.com.

NEWMAN, JOSEPH HERZL, advertising executive, consultant; b. NYC, Dec. 1, 1928; s. Max A. and Tillie C. (Weitzman) N.; m. Ruth Zita Marcus, Dec. 19, 1954 (div. Feb. 1987); children: Deborah Lynn, David Alan, Mark Jonathan; m. Nancy Rose Kramer Deutschman, Aug. 19, 1990 (dec. Feb. 2005); stepchildren: Pamela Sue Deutschman, Douglas Hayes Deutschman, Cindi Elaine Deutschman-Ruiz. AB, Bethany Coll., W.Va., 1949; MS Grad. Sch. Bus., Columbia U., NYC, 1956. With 20th Century Fox Film Corp., NYC, 1949—53; media supr. Fred Wittner Advt. Agy., NYC, 1953—56; media dir. O.S. Tyson & Co., NYC, 1956—64; v.p., media dir. Marsteller Inc., NYC, 1965—85; v.p., assoc. media dir. HBM/Creamer, NYC, 1985—87, Della Femina, McNamee, Inc., NYC, 1987—89; pres. Newman And Assocs., Cleve., 1989—. Mem. faculty Advt. Age Media Workshop, 1972; past chmn. media mgrs. adv. com. Bus. Publs. Audit of Circulation Inc., NYC; condr. profl. media planning seminars, 1989-99. Contbr. articles to profl. jours. Past chmn. bus.-to-bus. media com. Am. Assn. Advt. Agys.; vice chmn. tax incentive rev. coun. City of Mayfield Heights, Ohio, 1994-97, chmn., 1997-2005, co-vice chmn., 2005-06; mem. master plan adv. com. City of Mayfield Heights, 2003-04, mem. mayor's cmty. coun., 2006—; rep. Mayfield Heights to Euclid Creek Watershed Coun., 2003-. With US Army, 1950-52. Mem. Bus. Mktg. Assn. (past mem. media comparability coun., media data form com. and rsch. resource com., Agy. Exec. of Yr., NY chpt. 1960, 66, 71, 73, cert. bus. communicator). Home and Office: 6338 Woodhawk Dr Mayfield Heights OH 44124-4153 Office Phone: 440-449-1804. E-mail: nknewmansion@aol.com.

NEWMAN, LAWRENCE WILLIAM, financial executive; b. Chgo., Jan. 14, 1939; s. Eskil William and Adele Diane (Lawnicki) N.; m. Christine Harriet Jaronski, Sept. 22, 1962; children: Paul, Scott, Ron. BBS, U. Ill., 1965; MBA, Northwestern U., 1970. CPA, Ill. Auditor Price Waterhouse, Chgo., 1965-66; controller ECM Corp., Schaumburg, Ill., 1966-70, Nachman Corp., Des Plaines, Ill., 1970-76, v.p., treas., controller, 1976-79; v.p. fin. P & S Mgmt. Inc., Schiller Park, Ill., 1979-83; controller Underwriters Labs., Northbrook, Ill., 1983-86, asst. treas., 1986-89, v.p., 1990-98, treas., 1990-97; CFO, 1997—; sr. v.p. Underwriters Labs., Northbrook, 1998—. Mem. Fin. Execs. Inst., Am. Inst. CPA's. Clubs: Exec. of Chgo. Office: Underwriters Labs 333 Pfingsten Rd orthbrook IL 60062-2002

NEWMAN, TERRY E., lawyer; b. Chgo., Jan. 15, 1947; BA, Loyola U., Ill., 1969; JD, DePaul U., 1977. Bar: Ill. 1977, U.S. Dist. Ct. (no. dist.) Ill. 1977, D.C. 1991. Asst. states atty. Cook County, 1977-78; ptnr. Katten Muchin Zavis Rosenman, Chgo. Sec. bd. trustees City Coll. Chgo., 1989. Mem. ABA, Ill. State Bar, D.C. Bar, Chgo. Bar Assn. (real estate tax sect.). Office: Katten Muchin Zavis Rosenman 525 W Monroe St Ste 1600 Chicago IL 60661-3649 Office Fax: 317-577-8781.

NEWSOM, GERALD HIGLEY, astronomy educator; b. Albuquerque, Feb. 11, 1939; s. Carroll Vincent and Frances Jeanne (Higley) N.; m. Ann Catherine Bricker, June 17, 1972; children: Christine Ann, Elizabeth Ann. BA, U. Mich., 1961; MA, Harvard U., 1963, PhD, 1968. Research asst. McMath-Hulbert Obs., Pontiac, Mich., summers 1959, 61; research asst. astronomy dept. U. Mich., Ann Arbor, 1959-61; research asst. Shock Tube Lab. Harvard U., Cambridge, Mass., 1962, 64-68; research asst. dept. physics Imperial Coll., London, 1968-69; asst. prof. astronomy Ohio State U., Columbus, 1969-73, assoc. prof., 1973-82, prof., 1982—2004, acting chmn. dept. astronomy, 1991-93, vice chmn. dept. astronomy, 1993—2004, acting asst. dean, 1985-86; sr. post-doctoral research asst. Physikalisches Institut, Bonn, Fed. Republic of Germany, 1978. Author: Astronomy, 1976, Exploring the Universe, 1979; contbr. articles to profl. jours. Fellow Woodrow Wilson Found., 1961-62, NSF, 1961-63; grantee Noble Found., 1961-64. Mem.: Am. Astron. Soc., Internat. Astron. Union. Home: 46 W Weisheimer Rd Columbus OH 43214-2545 Office: Ohio State U Dept Astronomy 140 W 18th Ave Columbus OH 43210-1173 Home Phone: 614-263-8240; Office Phone: 614-292-2632. Business E-Mail: gnewsom@astronomy.ohio-state.edu.

NEWSOM, JAMES THOMAS, lawyer; b. Carrollton, Mo., Oct. 6, 1944; s. Thomas Edward and Hazel Love (Mitchell) N.; m. Sherry Elaine Retzloff, Aug. 9, 1986; stepchildren: Benjamin A. Bawden, Holly K. Bawden. AB, U. Mo., 1966, JD, 1968. Bar: Mo. 1968, US Supreme Ct. 1971. Assoc. Shook, Hardy & Bacon, London and Kansas City, Mo., 1972, ptnr., 1976—. Mem. Mo. Law Rev., 1966-68. Lt. comdr. JAGC, USNR, 1968-72. Mem. ABA, Kansas City Met. Bar Assn., U. Mo. Law Sch. Law Soc., U. Mo. Jefferson Club, Order of Coif, Perry (Kans.) Yacht Club, Stone Horse Yacht Club (Harwich Port, Mass.). Avocations: skiing, sailing, auto racing. Office: Shook Hardy & Bacon 2555 Grand Blvd Kansas City MO 64108-2613 Home Phone: 913-381-5605; Office Phone: 816-474-6550. Business E-Mail: jnewsom@shb.com.

NEWTON, FREDERICK J., III, utilities executive; married; 2 children. BBA in Human Resources, U. R.I.; MBA in Labor Rels. and Human Resources, San Diego State U. Mgr. human resource functions Pepsico, Tex., Kans. and Calif.; sr. dir. human resources Unilever, NYC; sr. v.p. human resources Venator Group, NYC; exec. v.p., chief adminstrv. officer Cinergy Corp., Cin., 2002—. Vis. lectr., prof. Bellarmine U. Bd. dirs. Kentuckiana Minority Supplier Devel. Coun., Greater Louisville, Inc., Louisville Orch., Lincoln Heritage coun. Boy Scouts Am., Pritchard Com. Officer USN. Mem.: Soc. Human Resource Mgmt., Human Resource Planning Soc., Conf. Bd. Office: Cynergy Corp 139 E 4th St Cincinnati OH 45202

NEWTON, JOHN MILTON, academic administrator, psychologist, educator; b. Schenectady, Feb. 25, 1929; s. Harry Hazleton and Bertha A. (Lehmann) N.; m. Elizabeth Ann Slattery, Sept. 11, 1954; children: Patricia, Peter, Christopher. BS, Union Coll., Schenectady, 1951; MA, Ohio State U., 1952, PhD, 1955. Lic. psychologist, Nebr. Rsch. psychologist Electric Boat divsn. Gen. Dynamics Corp., Groton, Conn., 1957-60; mem. faculty U. Nebr., Omaha, 1960—, prof. psychology, 1966-99, chmn. dept., 1967-74, acting vice chancellor acad. affairs, 1994-95, prof. emeritus, 1999—, dean Coll. Arts and Scis., 1974-94, dean emeritus, 1999—. Cons. in field, 1960-72 Author research papers in field. Served to 1st lt. Med. Service Corps, AUS, 1955-57. Mem. Am. Psychol. Assn., Psychonomic Soc., Midwestern Psychol. Assn. Home: 5611 Jones St Omaha NE 68106-1232 Office: Univ of Nebr-Omaha Dept Psychology Omaha NE 68182-0274 Business E-Mail: jnewton@mail.unomaha.edu.

NEWTON, WILLIAM ALLEN, JR., pediatrician, pathologist; b. Traverse City, Mich., May 19, 1923; s. William Allen and Florence Emma (Brown) N.; m. Helen Patricia Goodrich, Apr. 21, 1945; children: Katherine Germaine, Elizabeth Gale, William Allen, Nancy Anne. BSc cum laude, Alma Coll., Mich., 1943; MD, U. Mich., 1946. Diplomate: Am. Bd. Pathology, Am. Bd. Pediatrics. Intern Wayne County Gen. Hosp., Detroit, 1947; resident in pediatric pathology/oncology/hematology Children's Hosp. Mich., Detroit, 1948-50; resident in pediat. Children's Hosp. Phila., 1950; dir. labs. Children's Hosp. Columbus, Ohio, 1952-88, rsch. pathologist Ohio, 1989—; mem. faculty Coll. Medicine, Ohio State U., 1952—, prof., 1965—, chief pediatric pathology, 1952-89, chief divsn. pediatric hematology, 1952—82, prof. emeritus, 1989—. Chmn. pathology com. Children's Cancer Study Group, 1965-91; chmn. Pathology Com. Intergroup Rhabdomyosarcoma Study Group; chmn. pathology com. Late Effects Study Group. Contbr. articles to med. jours. Trustee, exec. com. Ohio divsn. Am. Cancer Soc., 1972-86; adv. com. on childhood cancer Am. Cancer Soc.; chmn. exec. com. Consortium for Cancer Control Ohio, 1982-86; sci. adv. com. Armed Forces Inst. Pathology; pres. Internat. Consortium for Cure of Childhood Cancer in China, 2000—. Served to capt. M.C. U.S. Army, 1950-52, brig. gen. Res. ret. Mem. Ohio State Med. Assn. (com. on cancer), Midwest Soc. Pediatric Research (mem. council 1960-63, pres. 1964-65), Soc. Pediatric Research, Am. Pediatric Soc., Pediatric Pathology Club (pres. 1968-69), Am. Soc. Clin. Oncology, Internat. Soc. Pediatric Oncology, Sigma Xi, Phi Sigma Pi. Republican. Baptist. Home: 2500 Harrison Rd Johnstown OH 43031-9540 Office: PO Box 6957 Columbus OH 43205 Office Phone: 614-722-3269. Business E-Mail: wnewton@chi.osu.edu.

NEYER, JEROME CHARLES, consulting civil engineer; b. Cin., July 15, 1938; s. Urban Charles and Marie Helen (Hemsteger) N.; m. Judy Ann Drolet, June 17, 1961; children: Janet, Karen. BCE, U. Detroit, 1961; MCE, U. Wash., 1963. Registered profl. engr. 16 states. Facilities engr. Boeing Co., Seattle, 1961-62; found. engr. Metro Engrs., Seattle, 1962-65; project engr. Hugo N. Helpert Assocs., Detroit, 1965-70; pres. NTH Cons. Ltd., Farmington Hills, Mich., 1970—. Adj. prof. U. Detroit, 1973-79. Contbr. articles to profl. jours. Mem. mineral well adv. bd., Lansing, Mich., 1975, mem. constrn. safety stds. bd., 1982; chmn. bldg. appeals bd. City of Farmington Hills, 1983. Mem. ASTM, ASCE (br. pres. 1973-74), Engring. Soc. Dtroit, Cons. Engrs. Mich. (pres. 1981), Mich. Soc. Profl. Engrs. (bd. dirs. 1980), Assn. Engring. Firms Practicing in the Geoscis. (pres. 1991). Roman Catholic. Avocations: golf, tennis. Home: 26478 Ballantrae Ct Farmington Hills MI 48331-3528 Office: NTH Consultants Ltd 38955 Hills Tech Dr Farmington MI 48331-3434 Home Phone: 734-459-5952; Office Phone: 248-553-6300. Business E-Mail: jneyer@nthconsultants.com, jneyer007@comcast.net.

NICASTRO, TRACEY A., lawyer; b. 1969; BA, U. Ill., 1991; JD, Valparaiso U., 1994. Bar: Ill. 1994. With Sidley Austin Brown & Wood, Chgo., 1996—, ptnr., 2002—. Mem.: ABA, Chgo. Bar Assn. Office: Sidley Austin Brown and Wood Bank One Plz 10 S Dearborn St Chicago IL 60603

NICE, DON, artist; b. Visalia, Calif., 1932; BFA, UCLA, 1954; MFA, Yale Univ., New Haven, 1964. Tchr. Mpls. Sch. of Art; tchr. to dean Sch. Visual Arts, YC; artist-in-residence Dartmouth Coll., Hanover, NH, 1982—. One-man shows: Gallery Moos, Toronto, 1980, Hood Mus. of Art, Dartmouth Coll, 1982, Images Gallery, Toledo, Ohio, 1983, Lincoln Ctr. Art Gallery, NYC, 1983, Nancy Hoffman Gallery, NYC, 1984, Univ. Okla.-Norman, 1985, Fine Arts Mus. Long Island, Y, 1985, Pace Editions, NYC, 1986, John Berggruen Gallery, San Francisco, 1987, 89, Lake Placid Ctr. for Arts, NY, 1987, Elaine Horwitch Galleries, Palm Springs. Calif., 1987, Sun Valley Ctr. for Arts and Humanities, Idaho, 1990; group exhbns.: Mus. Modern Art, NYC, 1984, Chrysler Mus., Norfolk, Va., 1984, Stamford Mus., Conn., 1984, Paine Art Ctr. and Arboretum, Wis., 1985, Sordoni Art Gallery, Wilkes Barre, Pa., 1985, Vassar Coll., NY, 1986, Contemporary Arts Ctr., New Orleans, 1986, Mus. of Art, RI Sch. Design, 1987, Rutgers Barclay Gallery, Santa Fe, 1988, Barbara Fendrick Gallery, NYC, 1989; principal works: wall of murals at Nat. Fine Arts Commn., Lake Placid, Art in Arch. Project, Veterans Adminstrn., White River Junction, NY; represented in permanent collections: Whitney Mus. Am. Art, Penn. Acad. of Fine Arts, Nat. Mus. of Art, Canberra, Australia, Hedendaagse Kunst, Utrecht, Holland, Del. Art Mus., Chase Manhattan Bank. Recipient Ford Found. Purchase award, 1963. Mem.: NAD (academician). Office: Tandem Press Univ Wisconsin 201 S Dickinson St Madison WI 53703 Office Phone: 608-263-3437.

NICHOLAS, ARTHUR SOTERIOS, manufacturing executive; b. Grand Rapids, Mich., Mar. 6, 1930; s. Samuel D. and Penelope A. (Kalapodes) N.; m. Bessie Zazanis, Aug. 25, 1957; children: Niki Stephanie, Arthur S., Thomas. BS in Chem. Engring, U. Mich., 1953; BA in Indsl. Mgmt, Wayne State U., 1957. Registered profl. engr., Mich. Project engr. B.F. Goodrich Co., 1953-54; plant mgr. Cadillac Plastics and Chem. Co., 1954-69; pres., chief exec. officer Leon Chem. and Plastics, Inc., Grand Rapids, 1960-69; with U.S. Industries, Inc., 1969-73, pres., chief operating officer, 1973; now pres. The Antech Group. Bd. dirs. ERO Industries, Inc. Patentee in field. Judge Jr. Achievement, Chgo. Served with USNR, 1948-49. Recipient Distinguished Alumni award Grand Rapids Jr. Coll., 1970 Mem. Young Pres. Orgn., Soc. Plastic Engrs., Mich. Acad. Sci., Arts and Letters, Chgo. Coun. on Fgn. Rels., Pres.' Assn. Mem. Greek Orthodox Ch. Clubs: Chgo. Athletic Assn. (Chgo.), Executives (Chgo.). Office: 2300 Barrington Rd # 411 Hoffman Estates IL 60195-2082 Home: 467 Park Barrington Barrington IL 60010 Personal E-mail: anicholas@aol.com.

NICHOLAS, RALPH WALLACE, anthropologist, educator; b. Dallas, Nov. 28, 1934; s. Ralph Wendell and Ruth Elizabeth (Oury) N.; m. Marta Ruth Weinstock, June 13, 1963. BA, Wayne U., 1957; MA, U. Chgo., 1958, PhD, 1962. From asst. prof. to prof. Mich. State U., East Lansing, 1964-71; prof. anthropology U. Chgo., 1971—2000, chmn. dept., 1981-82, dep. provost, 1982-87, dean of coll., 1987-92, dir. Ctr. Internat. Studies, 1984-95, William Rainey Harper prof. anthropology and social scis., 1992-2000, William Rainey Harper prof. emeritus, 2000—; pres. Internat. House of Chgo., 1993-2000. Cons. Ford Found., Dhaka, Bangladesh, 1973 Author: (with others) Kinship Bengali Culture, 1977, The Fruits of Worship, 2003, Rites of Spring, 2008; editor: Jour. Asian Studies, 1975-78. Sec. Coun. Am. Overseas Rsch. Ctrs., 2005—; v.p. Am. Inst. Indian Studies, 1974—76, treas., 1993—2001, pres.-elect, 2001—02, pres., 2002—; trustee Bangladesh Found., 1972—2005; dir. Indo-Am. Ctr., Chgo. Ford Found. fgn. area tng. fellow, India, 1960-61; Sch. Oriental and African Studies research fellow, London, 1962-63; sr. Fulbright fellow, West Bengal, India, 1968-69 Fellow AAAS, Am. Anthrop. Assn., Royal Anthrop. Inst. (Eng.); mem. Assn. Asian Studies, India League of Am. Found. (trustee). Office: U Chgo Dept Anthropology 1126 E 59th St Chicago IL 60637-1580 also: Am Inst Indian Studies 1130 E 59th St Chicago IL 60637

NICHOLS, DAVID EARL, pharmacy educator, researcher, consultant; b. Covington, Ky., Dec. 23, 1944; s. Earl and Edythe Lee (Brooker) N.; m. Kathy J. Nichols; children: Charles D., Daniel P. BS, U. Cin., 1969; PhD, U. Iowa, 1973. Asst. prof. medicinal chemistry Purdue U., West Lafayette, Ind., 1974-79, assoc. prof., 1979-85, prof., 1985—. Founder, pres. Heffter Rsch. Inst., Santa Fe, 1993—; co-founder Darpharma, Inc., Chapel Hill, NC, 2001. Contbr. articles to profl. jours. Recipient Provost's Outstanding Grad. Mentor award, 2006; grantee Nat. Inst. on Drug Abuse, 1978—, NIMH, 1978—. Fellow: Am. Assn. Pharm. Scientists, Am. Pharm. Assn. (Irwin H. Page lectr. 2004); mem.: Am. Coll. Neuropsychopharmacology. Achievements include patents in field. Office: Purdue U Sch Pharmacy West Lafayette IN 47907 Home Phone: 765-497-2320. Business E-Mail: drdave@pharmacy.purdue.edu.

NICHOLS, DONALD ARTHUR, economist, educator; b. Madison, Conn., Dec. 20, 1940; s. Edward Charles and Ruth (Nilson) Nichols; m. Linda Powley, Aug. 19, 1962 (dec. Oct. 1982); children: Charles Spencer, Elizabeth Clarke; m. Barbara Jakubowski Noel, May 22, 1983 (dec. Dec. 26, 2000); m. Jane Bartels, Sept. 26, 2001. BA, Yale U., 1962, MA, 1963, PhD, 1968. Mem. faculty dept. econs. U. Wis., Madison, 1966—2006, prof., 1977—2006, chmn. dept. econs., 1983-86, 88-90, mem. exec. com. faculty senate, 1987-90, chmn., 1989-90, dir. Robert M. LaFollette Sch. Pub. Affairs, 2002—06, Wis. Idea fellow, 2004—06, emeritus prof., 2006—; lectr. Yale U., 1970—71; sr. economist Senate Budget Com., Washington, 1975—76; dep. asst. sec. for econ. policy and rsch. Dept. Labor, Washington, 1977-79; dir. Ctr. for Rsch. on Wis. Economy. Econ. advisor to gov. State of Wis., 1983—86; exec. sec. Gov.'s Coun. Econ. Advisors, 1983—86; mem. Gov.'s Export Strategy Commn., 1994—95, Gov.'s Econ. Growth Coun., 2003—; mem. acad. adv. coun. Fed. Res. Bank of Chgo., 2004—; bd. dirs. Thompson, Plumb Funds, 1987—, Sustainable Woods Co-operative, 2001—03; dir. Ctr. for World Affairs and Global Economy, 1995—2000; affiliate Christensen Assocs., Madison, 1999—; cons. in field. Author: (with Clark Reynolds) Principles of Economics, 1970, Dollars and Sense, 1994; contbr. articles to profl. jours. Trustee U. Wis. Bookstore, 1990-95; bd. advisors Am. Players Theatre, Spring Green, Wis., 1993-2001, Taliesin Coun., 2001-04. NSF fellow, 1963-66, 70-72; Nat. Commn. Employment Policy rsch. grantee, 1980-82; recipient William H. Kiekhofer Meml. Teaching prize U. Wis., 1973 Mem. Am. Econ. Assn., Royal Econ. Soc. Office: Univ Wis 1180 Observatory Dr Madison WI 53706

NICHOLS, ELIZABETH GRACE, nursing educator, dean; b. Tehran, Iran, Feb. 1, 1943; d. Terence and Eleanor Denny (Payne) Quilliam; m. Gerald Ray Nichols, Nov. 20, 1965; children: Tina Lynn, Jeffrey David. BSN, San Francisco State U., 1969; MS, U. Calif., San Francisco, 1970, D of Nursing Sci., 1974; MA, Idaho State U., Pocatello, 1989. Staff nurse Peninsula Hosp., Burlingame, Calif., 1966-72; asst. prof. U. Calif.-San Francisco Sch. Nursing, 1974-82; chmn. dept. nursing Idaho State U., Pocatello, 1982-85; assoc. dean Coll. Health Scis. Sch. Nursing U. Wyo., Laramie, 1985-91, asst. to pres. for program revs., 1991-95; dean Coll. Nursing U. N.D., 1995—2004, Mont. State U., Bozeman, 2004—. Cons. U. Rochester, NY, 1979, Carroll Coll., Mont., 1980, divsn. Nursing Dept. HHS, Washington, U. Maine, Ft. Kent, 1992, Stanford Hosp. Nursing Svc., Calif., 1981—82, Ea. N.Mex. U., 1988, Met. State U., Minn., 1998, U. Nev.-Reno, 2003; cons. evaluator Higher Learning Commn., 1993—2004; site visitor CCNE, 1998—; mem. accreditation review com. The Higher Learning Commn., 2001—04, budget com. Contbr. articles to profl. jours. Mem. adv. bd. dir. U. Calif. Home Care Svc., San Francisco, 1975—82, Ombudsman Svc. of Contra Costa Calif., 1979—82, Free Clin. of Pocatello, 1984; mem. bd. of rev. coun. baccalaureate & higher degree programs, 1990—92; mem bd. dirs. United Way of Grand Forks/East Grand Forks, 2000—04. Recipient Jo Eleanor Elliott award, 1994; fellow ACE, U. Maine Sys., 1990—91. Fellow: Am. Acad. Nursing, Gerontol. Soc. Am. (chmn. clin. medicine sect. 1987, sec. 1990—93); mem.: ANA, Western Inst. Nursing (chmn. 1990—92, bd. govs., bd. dir. mid-west alliance), Idaho Nurses Assn. (dist. 51 adv. bd. dir. 1982—84), ND Nurses Assn. (pres. 2003—04), Oakland Ski Club. (1st v.p. 1981—82), Sigma Theta Tau. Democrat. Home Phone: 406-586-2298; Office Phone: 406-994-3784. Business E-Mail: egnichols@montana.edu.

NICHOLS, GRACE A., retired retail executive; b. 1946; m. John J. Nichols; 2 children. BS in Polit. Sci., UCLA, MA in History. With Weinstock's, Sacramento, 1971—78; mgr. gen. merchandise The Broadway, Calif., 1978—86; v.p., mgr. gen. merchandise Victoria's Secret Stores, 1986—88, exec. v.p., mgr. gen. merchandise, 1989—91, pres., CEO, 1991—2007. Bd. dirs. Pacific Sunwear Calif., Inc., 2007—, NY & Co., Inc., 2008—. Bd. govs. The World of Children.*

NICHOLS, KAREN J., dean; b. Ind. m. Jim Nichols. DO, U. Health Scis., Coll. Osteo. Medicine, Kansas City. Intern and resident in internal medicine Okla. Osteo. Hosp., Tulsa; asst. dean grad. med. edn. Ariz. Coll. Osteo. Medicine; dean Chgo. Coll. Osteo. Medicine, 2002—, prof. medicine. Contbr. articles to profl. jours. Bd. trustees Mut. Ins. Co. of Ariz.; with Mesa Symphony, Mesa United Way, Central Christian Ch. Recipient Physician of Yr., Ariz. Osteo. Med. Assn., 1996, Educator of Yr., Mesa Gen. Hosp. Mem.: Am. Osteo. Assn. (chair bur. state and govt. affairs, mem. health related and fed. health policies coms., chair adv. com. of end-of-life care). Office: Chgo Coll Osteo Medicine Midwestern U 555 31st St Downers Grove IL 60515

NICHOLS, RICHARD DALE, former congressman, banker; b. Ft. Scott, Kans., Apr. 29, 1926; s. Ralph Dale and Olive Marston (Kittell) N.; m. Constance Weinbrenner, Mar. 25, 1951 (dec. June 1994); children: Philip William, Ronald Dale, Anita Jane Nichols Bomberger; m. Linda Hupp, Apr. 21, 1996. BS in Agr. and BS in Journalism, Kans. State U., 1951. Info. counsel Kans. State Bd. Agr., Topeka, 1951-54; assoc. far. dir. Sta. WIBW, WIBW-TV, Topeka, 1954-57; agr. rep. to v.p. Hutchinson (Kans.) Nat. Bank and Trust, 1957-69; pres., CEO Home State Bank, McPherson, Kans., 1969-79, chmn., pres., CEO, 1979-91; chmn. Home State Bank & Trust, McPherson, Kans., 1985-91, 93—; mem. 102d Congress from 5th Kans. dist., 1991-92. Pres. Arts Coun., McPherson, 1979; 5th Dist. chmn. Kans. Rep. Party, 1986-89; bd. dirs. Camp Wood YMCA Camp, Elmdale, Kans., 1995; Meth. Ch. lay spkr., 1994—; bd. trustees Ctrl. Christian Coll., McPherson. Ensign USNR, 1944-47; ATO. Named Hon. Citizen N.Y.C., 1988. Mem. VFW, Kans. Bankers Assn. (pres. 1985-86), Am. Bankers Assn. (advisor 1986-88), Kans. Assn. Banking Ag. Reps. (pres. 1965), Am. Legion, McPherson C. of C. (pres. 1977), Kans. State U. Golden Key Alumni Assn. (pres.), Optimist (pres. Hutchinson club 1965), Rotary (pres. McPherson club 1978), Kans. Cavalry (cmdg. gen. 1986-89). Methodist. Home: 404 N Lakeside Dr Mcpherson KS 67460-3600 Office: Home State Bank and Trust PO Box 1266 Mcpherson KS 67460-1266 E-mail: dick@hsbt.com.

NICHOLS, ROBERT LEIGHTON, civil engineer; b. Amarillo, Tex., June 24, 1926; s. Marvin Curtis and Ethel Nichols; m. Frances Hardison, June 8, 1948; children: Eileen, William C., Michael L. BSCE, Tex. A&M U., Coll. Station, 1947, MSCE, 1948. Grad. asst., instr. Tex. A&M U., 1947-48; assoc. Freese & Nichols (and predecessors), Ft. Worth, 1948-50, ptnr., 1950-77, v.p., 1977-88, pres., 1988-91, vice chmn., 1991-92, pres. emeritus, 1992—. Mem. Bldg. Stds. Commn., 1956—62; pres. Tri-State Water Resource Coalition, 2003—. Chmn. Horn Frog dist. Boy Scouts Am., pres. Longhorn coun., 1990—93, Ozark Trails coun., 1998—99; mem. City Coun., Webb City, Mo., 2004—06. Mem.: NSPE (pres. 1977—78, pres. Ednl. Found.), ASCE, Environ. Task Force Jasper and Newton Counties (pres. 2003—), Tri-state Water Resource Coalition (pres. 2002—), Nat. Inst. Engring. Ethics (pres. 1995—97), Tex. Pub. Works Assn., Tex. Water Utilities Assn., Am. Pub. Works Assn., Water Environ. Assn. Tex. (pres. 1962—63), Water Environ. Fedn., Tex. Water Conservation Assn., Am. Water Works Assn., Tex. Soc. Profl. Engrs. (pres. 1965—66), C. of C. Webb City, Mo. (exec. dir. 1997—2001), Masons, Chi Epsilon, Tau Beta Pi. Methodist. Office Phone: 417-673-7151. Business E-Mail: rln@freese.com.

NICHOLS, ROCKY, state representative, non-profit consultant; b. Topeka, Sept. 4, 1969; s. Kenneth Leroy and Rita Ann Nichols. BA in Polit. Sci., Washburn U., 1993; M in Pub. Adminstrn., U. Kans., 2002. Lic. Nat. Soc. Fund Raising Execs. Legis. aide State of Kans., Topeka, 1991-92; state legislator 58th dist. State Ho. of Reps., Topeka, 1992—; owner P.M. Consulting, Topeka, 1993-97; dir. of devel. Family Svc. & Guidance Ctr., Topeka, 1995-98; owner Fund Consulting, Topeka, 1997—. Dir. Inst. for Cmty. Partnerships, Washburn U., Topeka, 1995-97; mem. adv. bd. Pres.'s Com. on Mental Retardation, Washington, 1997-99; mem. adv. com. Capper Found., Topeka, 1995—; bd. dirs. Kans. Film Commn.; com. mem. Coun. of State Govt., Washington, 1997—. Plenary lectr. Pres.'s Com. on Mental Retardation, Washington, 1997; bd. dirs. Friends of Topeka Zoo, 1995—; Big Brother, Big Bros./Big Sisters Topeka, 1993-2000. Named Outstanding Pub. Ofcl. of Yr., Kans. Assn. of Mental Health Ctrs., 1996, Frank A. Hines Legislator of Yr., Kans. Chiropractic Assn., 1996, Legislator of Yr., Kans. Assn. Pub. Employees, 1994, 96, 97; BILLD fellow La Follette Inst. Pub. Affairs, Wis., 1997. Mem. ETAP (bd. dirs.), Highland Park Optimist Club (pres. 1997-98), Shawnee Heights Optimists Club, Highland Park Alumni Assn. (bd. dirs.). Democrat. Baptist. Avocations: exercise, computers. Home: 2329 SE Virginia Ave Topeka KS 66605-1358 Office: State Ho of Reps State Capitol Topeka KS 66612

NICHOLS, RONALD, state legislator; m. Sue; 4 children. BS, MS, N.D. State U. Mem. N.D. Ho. of Reps., 1991-2000, N.D. Senate from 4th dist., 2001—. Past. mem. fin. and taxation com. N.D. Ho. Reps., Agr. com., edn.; agr. loan officer; farmer, rancher. Mem. Stanley Cmty. Hosp.; past pres. coun. Holy Rosary Cath. Ch. Recipient Outstanding Agriculturist award N.D. State U. Mem. KC, Stanley Am. Legion (past comdr.), N.D. Stockman's Assn., Vietman Vet. Am. Home: 5837 73rd Ave NW Palermo ND 58769-9515

NICHOLSON, BRUCE J., insurance company executive; BS, St. Olaf Coll., Northfield, Minn., 1968. With Ministers Life Ins. Co., Mpls., 1975-1984, Towers Perrin Co, Mpls., 1984-1990; exec. v.p., CFO Lutheran Brotherhood, Mpls., 1990—97, exec. v.p., COO, 1997—99, pres., COO, 1999—2000, pres., CEO, 2000—02, Thrivent Fin. for Lutherans, Mpls., 2002—05, chmn., pres., CEO, 2005—. Mem. bd. regents St. Olaf Coll.; bd. mem. Luther Sem., Minn. Orchestral Assn., Minn. Bus. Partnership, Fox Cities C. of C. Fellow: Soc. of Actuaries; mem.: Am. Acad. of Actuaries. Office: Thrivent Financial for Lutherans 625 4th Ave S Minneapolis MN 55415

NICHOLSON, JAMES M., chemicals executive; b. 1967; Worked for Amerisure Cos., Aon Corp.; v.p. PVS Chemicals Inc., Detroit, 1995—; mgr. Chantland Material Handling Solutions. Named one of 40 Under 40, Crain's Detroit Bus., 2006. Mem.: Mich. Mfg. Assn. (chmn. 2005). Office: PVS Chemicals Inc 10900 Harper Ave Detroit MI 48213 Office Phone: 313-921-1200. Office Fax: 313-921-1378.

NICHOLSON, RALPH LESTER, botanist, educator; b. Lynn, Mass., Aug. 25, 1942; s. Nathan Aaron and Muriel Spinney (Buxton) N. BA, U. Vt., 1964; MS, U. Maine, 1967; PhD, Purdue U., 1972. Prof. dept. botany and plant pathology Purdue U., West Lafayette, Ind., 1972—. Contbr. chpts. to books, more than 100 articles to profl. jours. Active Big Bros./Big Sisters, Lafayette, Ind., 1974—. Fellow Am. Phytopathol. Soc. Office: Purdue U Botany and Plant Pathology Lafayette IN 47907 E-mail: nicholson@btny.purdue.edu.

NICKELL, CECIL D., agronomy educator; BS, Purdue U., 1963; MS, Mich. State U., 1965, PhD, 1968. Asst. instr. crop sci. dept. Mich. State U., East Lansing, 1963-67; from asst. prof. to assoc. prof. soybean breeding Kans. State U., Manhattan, 1967-79; from assoc. prof. to prof. plant breeding U. Ill., Urbana, 1979-95, prof. plant breeding dept. crop scis., 1995—. Fellow Am. Soc. Agronomy (Achievement-Crops award for Crops 1995, Agron. Rsch. award 1998), Crop Sci. Soc. Am. Office: U Ill Dept Crop Scis 262 Nat Soybean Rsch Lab 1102 W Peabody Dr Urbana IL 61801

NICKELL, JAKE, internet retail executive, apparel designer; b. Crown Point, Ind., 1980; m. Shondi Nickell, 2004. Attended, Ill. Inst. Art, 1998—2001. Co-founder & pres. SkinnyCorp, Chgo., 2000—. Co-creator (SkinnyCorp websites) Threadless, 2000, Naked & Angry, OMG Clothing, Extra Tasty, Yay Hooray!, 15 Megs of Fame. Named one of 40 Under 40, Crain's Chgo. Bus., 2006. Home: Skinny Corp STE 206 4043 N Ravenswood Ave Chicago IL 60613-2435 Office Phone: 773-878-3557. Office Fax: 888-595-3258. E-mail: info@skinnycorp.com.

NICKELS, ELIZABETH ANNE, office furniture manufacturing executive; 2 children. BSBA in Acctg., Econs. and Bus. Admin., Aquinas Coll., 1983. CPA. CFO, mem. exec. and ops. coms. Universal Forest Products, Grand Rapids, Mich., 1993-2000; CFO Herman Miller, Inc., Zeeland, Mich., 2000—. Office: Herman Miller Inc 855 E Main Ave Zeeland MI 49464-0302

NICKELS, JOHN L., retired state supreme court justice; m. Merita Nickels; 7 children. Bachelor's degree, No. Ill. U.; law degree, DePaul U. Pvt. practice, 20 yrs; judge Appellate Ct.; cir. judge 16th Jud. Cir.; supreme ct. justice State of Ill., 1992-98; ret., 1998. Bd. dirs. Kane County Bank & Trust Co. Bd. trustees Waubonsee Coll.; mem. Kane County Planning Commn., Zoning Bd. Appeals; mem. St. Gall's Parish, Elburn. Home: 17901 Owens Rd Maple Park IL 60151

NICKERSON, DON C., lawyer, retired prosecutor, judge; married; 3 children. JD, Drake U., 1977. Bar: Iowa 1977, admitted to practice: US Ct. Appeals (8th Cir.) 1977, US Dist. Ct. (So. Dist.) Iowa 1977. US atty. US Dist. Ct. (So. Dist.), Iowa, 1993—2001; assoc. gen. counsel Wellmark Blue Cross & Blue Shield, Iowa, 2001—03; judge Dist. Ct. (5th Dist.), Iowa, 2003—. Bd. mem. Urban Dreams, United Way of Central Iowa, Cmty. Focus, Inc., Des Moines Enterprise Cmty. Recipient Medal of Honor, Drake U., Cmty. Svc. award, Iowa State Bar Assn. Mem.: Commn. on Planning for the 21st Century, Polk County Bar Assn., Iowa Nat. Bar Assn., Iowa State Bar Assn. Office: State of Iowa Dist Ct 5C Polk County Courthouse 500 Mulberry Rm 212 Des Moines IA 50309 Office Phone: 515-245-4500, 515-286-3391. Office Fax: 515-286-3858.

NICKERSON, GREG, public relations executive; b. Iowa, Nov. 3, 1958; BS in Agrl. Journalism, Iowa State U., 1981. Mkt. analyst, exec. editor Brock Assocs., Brookfield, Wis., 1981-85; with pub. rels. dept. Bader Rutter & Assocs., Brookfield, 1985-88, acctg. group supr., 1988-90, v.p., group supr., 1990-92, v.p., dir. pub. rels. group, 1992-98, exec. v.p., 1998—. Office: Bader Rutter & Associates 13845 Bishops Dr Brookfield WI 53005-6604

NICKERSON, JAMES FINDLEY, retired education educator; b. Gretna, Nebr., Dec. 16, 1910; s. Elmer Samuel and Lulu Perkins (Patterson) Nickerson; m. Juanita M. Bolin, Mar. 3, 1934; children: Ann Rogers Nickerson Lueck, Maria De Miranda. BS, Nebr. Wesleyan U., 1932; MA, Columbia Tchrs. Coll., 1940; PhD, U. Minn., 1948; ScD (hon.), Yankton Coll., SD, 1971. Tchr. pub. schs., Giltner, Nebr., 1932-35; sch. music supr. Gordon, Nebr., 1936-38, Bayshore, LI, 1939-41, Grand Island, ebr., 1941-42; instr. Coll. Edn., music supr. HS U. Minn., 1942-46, vis. prof. Coll. Edn., 1948; asst. prof. music edn. U. Kans., 1946-48, assoc. prof., 1948-53; prof. psychology, dean edn., dir. summer quar. Mont. State U., 1954—64, head dept. psychology, 1954—56; rsch. assoc. Electronics Rsch. Lab., 1958—64; v.p. acad. affairs N.D. State U., Fargo, 1964—66; pres. Minn. State U., Mankato, 1966—73, disting. svc. prof., pres. emeritus, 1973—76. Mem. vis. com. Schola Cantorum, NYC, 1938—39, Choral Arts Soc., Washington, 1969—71, Harvard Grad. Sch. Edn., 1970—76; rsch. assoc. dept. psychology U. So. Calif.; with human factors divsn. USN Electronics Lab., San Diego, 1953—54; bd. dirs. Svc. Mems. Opportunity Colls.; mem. steering com. Pacific N.W. Coun. Higher Edn., 1962; cons. pub. edn. Office Gov. Wash., 1964; exec. sec., study dir. interim com. edn. Wash. Legislature, 1959—60; chmn. regional conf. womanpower at. Manpower Coun. and Mont. State Coll., 1957; mem. adv. com. sci. edn. NSF, 1968—71, chmn., 1970—71. Stringbass Mont. State Coll. Symphonette, 1959—63, Mankato Symphony Orch., 1967—73, 1983—93, bd. dirs., 1987—90; author: Out of Chaos, 2006. Named Nicerkson Conf. Rm. in his honor, Student Union, Minn. State U., 2003; named to Internat. Adult and Continuing Edn. Hall of Fame, 1999; recipient Alumni award, Nebr. Wesleyan U., 1968, Sec. Def. medal for Outstanding Pub. Svc., 1981, citation, Am. Coun. Edn., 1981, James F. Nickerson medal of Merit for Outstanding Svc. to Mil. Edn., Am. Assn. Sr. Colls. and Univs., 1981; Danforth Found. Adminstrn. grantee, 1969. Mem.: Edn. Commn. States (commr. 1967—73, mem. task force coord., governance and structure postsecondary edn. 1973), Assn. Minn. Colls. (pres. 1972), Am. Assn. Higher Edn. (chmn. resolutions com. 1974), Am. Assn. Colls. Tchr. Edn. (bd. dirs. 1969—71), Am. Assn. State Colls. and State Univs. (bd. dirs. 1966—71), Nat. Assn. Student Univs. and Land Grant Colls. (senate, chmn. divsn. tchr. edn. 1962—65, sec. coun. acad. officers 1965), Sigma Xi, Phi Mu Alpha Sinfonia. Home and Office: 77 Stadium Rd Apt 23 Mankato MN 56001-1022

NICKLESS, RALPH WALTER, bishop; b. Denver, May 28, 1947; s. Walter and E. Margaret (McGovern) Nickless. BA, St. Thomas, 1969; MA in Pastoral Theology, Pontifical Gregotian U., Rome, 1973, STB in Sacred Theology, 1972. Ordained priest Archdiocese of Denver, Colo., 1973, vicar gen. Colo.; pastor Our Lady of Fatima Parish, Lakewood, Colo.; bishop Diocese of Sioux City, 2005—; ordained bishop, 2006. Roman Catholic. Office: Diocese of Sioux City 1821 Jackson St PO Box 3379 Sioux City IA 51102-3379 Office Phone: 712-233-7555. Office Fax: 712-233-7557. E-mail: bishopnickless@scdiocese.org.*

NICKLIN, EMILY, lawyer; b. Cooperstown, NY, June 24, 1953; d. George Leslie Jr. and Katherine Mildred (Aronson) N.; m. Jay Schleusener, Dec. 28, 1974; children: Max, Lucas, Anna. BA, U. Chgo., 1975, JD, 1977. Bar: Ill. 1977, US Dist. Ct. (no. dist. Ill.) 1979, US Ct. Appeals (7th cir.) 1979. Law clk. to judge US Dist. Ct. (no. dist. Ill.), Chgo., 1977-79; assoc. Kirkland & Ellis, Chgo., 1979-83, ptnr., 1983—, mem. firm mgmt. com., 1995—. Tchr. Ill. Continuing Legal Edn. Bar Prog., Chgo., 1983—; fellow Salzburg Seminar, Austria, 1983; dep. corp. counsel City of Chgo., 1989-91; mem. bd. trustees, U. Chgo., lectr. law, 2001. Named one of Am. Top 50 Women Litigators, Nat. Law. Jour., 2001, 30 Tough Lawyers, Chgo. Mag. Mem. Nat. Inst. Trial Advocacy (tchr., team leader 1982—), Order of Coif, Phi Beta Kappa. Office: Kirkland & Ellis LLP 200 E Randolph Dr Fl 54 Chicago IL 60601-6636 Office Phone: 312-861-2387. Office Fax: 312-861-2200. E-mail: enicklin@kirkland.com.

NICOL, BRIAN, publishing executive; Publisher Home & Away, Inc., Omaha. Office: Home & Away Inc 10703 J St Omaha NE 68127-1023

NICOLS, HOWARD J.C., lawyer; b. Woodhaven, NY, 1956; BA summa cum laude, SUNY, Albany, 1978; JD cum laude, Cornell U., 1981. Bar: Ohio 1981, NY 2000, US Ct. Appeals, 2nd, 6th, 9th, 10th Circuits 2003, US Dist. Ct. 2003, Northern Dist. Ohio 2003. Ptnr., litigation Squire, Sanders & Dempsey, LLP, Cleve., mem. mgmt. com. Master bencher Judge Anthony J. Celebrezze Am. Inn Ct.; chancellor Cornell Moot Ct. Bd.; presenter in field. Bd. editor Cornell Internat. Law Jour.; co-author: Taxes on Profits of Multinational Companies and Implications for Russia, 2004. Mem.: Cleve. Bar Assn. Office: Squire Sanders & Dempsey LLP 4900 Key Tower 122 Public Sq Cleveland OH 44114-1304 Office Phone: 216-479-8743. Office Fax: 216-479-8780. Business E-Mail: hnicols@ssd.com.

NIEBYL, JENNIFER ROBINSON, obstetrician, gynecologist, educator; BSc, McGill U., Mont., 1963; MD, Yale U., 1967. Diplomate Am. Bd. Ob-Gyn., Am. Bd. Maternal and Fetal Medicine. Intern in Internal Medicine N.Y. Hosp.-Cornell Med. Ctr., 1967-68, resident in ob-gyn., 1968-70, Johns Hopkins Hosp., Balt., 1970-73, fellow in maternal and fetal medicine, 1976-78, mem. staff, 1973—88, U. Iowa Hosps. and Clinics, Iowa City, 1988—; prof., head ob-gyn. dept. U. Iowa Sch. Medicine, Iowa City, 1988—. Mem. ACOG, Am. Gynecol. and Obstetrical Soc., Soc. Gynecol. Investigation, Soc. Maternal Fetal Medicine, Inst. Medicine of NAS. Office: U Iowa Hosps & Clinics 200 Hawkins Dr Iowa City IA 52242 Office Phone: 319-356-1976.

NIEDERBERGER, JANE, information technology executive; m. Mark Niederberger; children: Amy, Sarah. BS in nutrition, Simmons Coll., 1982; MBA in health care adminstrn., Northeastern U. Various mgmt. positions Harvard Pilgrim Health Care, Boston, 1983—96; with IT divsn. Anthem, Inc., Indpls., 1997, acting chief info. officer, 1998—99, sr. v.p., chief info. officer, 1999—. Bd. dir. Managed Care Exec. Group. Bd. mem. Jr. Achievement, Indpls. Recipient Women and Hi Tech Leading Light award, 2002.

NIEDERHUBER, JOHN EDWARD, federal agency administrator, oncologist, surgeon, immunologist; b. Steubenville, Ohio, June 21, 1938; s. William Henry and Helen (Smittle) N.; m. Tracey J. Williamson (dec. Dec. 2001); children: Elizabeth Ann, Matthew John. BS, Bethany Coll., 1960; MD, Ohio State U., 1964. Diplomate Am. Bd. Surgery. Internship, surgery Ohio State U. Hosp., Columbus, 1964-65; from resident surgery to prof. U. Mich. Med. Ctr., Ann Arbor, 1967—80, prof. surgery, prof. microbiology and immunology, 1980-87, chief divsn. surg. oncology sect. gen. surgery, 1983—86, assoc. dean rsch., 1982—85, sr. assoc. dean med. sch., 1983—85; cons. Wayne County Gen. Hosp., Mich., 1973-84; cons. surgery Ann Arbor VA Hosp., 1973-87; prof. surgery, oncology, molecular biology and genetics The Johns Hopkins U. Sch. Med., Balt., 1987-91; Emile Holman prof. surgery, chair, dept. surgery, head sect. surgical scis. Stanford U. Sch. Medicine., 1991-95, prof. microbiology and immunology, 1991-97; chief of surgery Stanford U. Hosp., 1991-95; dir. planning Comp. Cancer Ctr. Stanford Med. Ctr., 1991-95; prof. surgery and oncology Sch. Medicine U. Wis., Madison, 1997—2005, asst. dean oncology, dir. Comprehensive Cancer Ctr., 1997—2002; dep. dir. for translational & clin. sciences, COO Nat. Cancer. Inst., NIH, Bethesda, Md., 2005—, acting dir., 2006, dir., 2006—. Vis. prof. Howard Hughes Med. Inst. dept. molecular biology and genetics Howard Hughes Med. Inst., The Johns Hopkins U. Sch. Medicine, Balt., 1986-87; cons. in field. Author books on cancer and surgery; mem. editl. bd. Jour. Immunology, 1981-85, Jour. Surg. Res., 1989-95, Current Opinion in Oncology, 1989—95, Cure, 2002-04, Annals of Surgery, 1991—97, Surg. Oncology, 1991—, Jour. Clin. Oncology, 1993, Annals of Surg. Oncology, 1993—, Jour. ACS, 1994—, The Oncologist, 1995—, Surgery, 1999-2004; contbr. articles to profl. jours. Active bd. sci. councilors NCI divsn. Cancer Treatment, 1986-91, chmn., 1987-91, Gen. Motors Cancer Rsch. Found. Awards Assembly, 1988-92, 98-2003; chmn. nat. cancer adv. bd. NCI, 2002—05; mem. C-Change, 2001—, mem. planning and budget com., vice-chair cancer ctrs. constituency com., vice-chair rsch. com., 2005-, mem. CEO Roundtable, 2003—. Served to capt. U.S. Army, 1965-67 Recipient USPHS Rsch. Career Devel. award Nat. Inst. Allergy and Infectious Disease, 1974-79, Disting. Faculty Svc. award U. Mich., 1978, Alumni Achievement award Ohio State U. Coll. Medicine, 1989, Alumni Achievement award in Medicine Bethany Coll., 1995; vis. rsch. fellow divsn. immunobiology Karolinska Inst., Stockholm, 1970-71, Am. Cancer Soc. Jr. Faculty Clin. fellow, 1977-79. Fellow ACS; mem. Am. Soc. Transplant Surgeons, Transplantation Soc., Am. Surg. Assn., Am. Assn. Immunologists, Am. Assn. Cancer Insts. (v.p. 1999-2001, pres. 2001-03), Coller Surg. Soc., Soc. Univ. Surgeons, Assn. Acad. Surgeons, Soc. Surg. Oncology (v.p. 1999-2001, pres. 2001-02), Ctrl. Surg. Soc., Am. Assn. Cancer Rsch., Am. Soc. Clin. Oncology, Soc. Clin. Surgery, Biology Club II, Robert M. Zollinger-Ohio State U. Surg. Soc., Pacific Coast Surg. Assn., Soc. Surgery of the Alimentary Tract. Avocations: golf, gardening. Office: Nat Cancer Inst IH Bldg 31 Room 11A03 31 Center Dr MSC 2590 Bethesda MD 20892-2590 Office Phone: 301-496-6511. Business E-Mail: niederhj@mail.nih.gov.

NIEDERPRUEM, GARY J., metal company executive; Grad., Canisuis Coll.; MBA, U. Rochester. Sales/product mgmt. Ryerson Tull Inc., Buffalo, 1973-80, inside sales mgr. Mpls., 1980-85, gen. mgr. Buffalo, 1985-93, pres. Ryerson East, 1993-98, pres. Ryerson Ctrl. Chgo., 1998-99, exec. v.p., 1998—. Office: Ryerson Tull Inc 2621 W 15th Pl Chicago IL 60608-1712

NIEHAUS, MARY C., lawyer; b. 1961; BA with honors, Grinnell Coll., 1985; JD cum laude, Northwestern U., 1988. Bar: Ill. 1988, U.S. Dist. Ct. (no. dist.) Ill. 1988, U.S. Tax Ct. 1989. With Sidley & Austin, Chgo., 1988—, ptnr., 1996—. Mem. editl. staff Northwestern U. Law Rev., 1987-88. Mem. Order of Coif, Phi Beta Kappa. Office: Sidley & Austin Bank One Plz 10 S Dearborn St Chicago IL 60603 Fax: 312-83-7036. E-mail: mniehaus@sidley.com.

NIEHM, BERNARD FRANK, retired health facility administrator; b. Sandusky, Ohio, Feb. 7, 1923; s. Bernard Frank and Hedwick (Panzer) N.; m. Eunice M. Patterson, Oct. 4, 1924; children: Julie, Patti, Bernie. BA, Ohio State U., 1951, MA, 1955, PhD in Ednl. Exceptional Children, Guidance and Couseling, Psychology, 1968. Tchr. pub. schs., Sandusky, 1951-57; chief ednl., vocat. and occupational therapy svcs. Vineland Tng. Sch., NJ, 1957-61; exec. dir. Franklin County Coun. Retarded Children, Columbus, Ohio, 1962-64; dir. Ohio Sheltered Workshop Planning Project Mental Retardation, 1964-66, coordinator mental retardation planning, 1966-68; project dir. Ohio Gov.'s Citizen Com. on Mental Retardation Planning, 1966-68; adminstr. Franklin County Program for Mentally Retarded, 1968-70; supt. Gallipolis State Inst., Ohio, 1970-76; tchr. spl. edn. Ohio U., Columbus, 1975-77, dir. consultation and edn., 1977-79, dir., 1978-95; exec. dir. Woodland Ctrs. Inc., Gallipolis, 1995; ret. Woodland Farm, Gallipolis, 1995. Pres. Gallco, 1989-90. Contbr. articles to profl. jours. Active Foster Grandparents Adv. Coun., Gallia County, 1974-76, Gallipolis State Inst. Parent Vol. Assn., 1970-76, Franklin County Bd. Mental Retardation, 1967-68; chmn. MGM dist. Tri-State Boy Scout Coun.; chmn. Meigs, Gallia, Mason Counties Boy Scout Dist., 1972-94; pres. Gallipolis Girls Athletic Assn. Booster Club, 1976—, Gallia County Arthritis Unit, 1986-96, Galleo Industries Bd. to Serve Handicapped Adults, 1987-94; pres. bd. dirs. Outreach Ctr. Gallia County, 1997-99; mem. Ch. Coun., St. Paul Luth. Ch., 1994-99, pres.; bd. dirs. United Cerebral Palsy, Columbus, 1968-70, Gallco Sheltered Workshop for Mentally Handicapped, Outreach Inc., Tri-State coun. Boy Scouts of Am.; mem. gov. bd. Gallia County Coun. on Aging; bd. alcohol, drug addiction and mental health svcs. Gallia-Jackson, Meigs; pres. Gallia County Pub. Employment Retiree Inc.; mem. United Way Gallia County. With U.S. Army, 1943-46. Mem. Am. Assn. Mental Deficiency (past chmn. Ohio chpt., chmn. Great Lakes region), Am. Mental Health Adminstrs. (nat., Ohio chpts.), Nat. Rehab. Assn., Ohio Rehab. Assn., Ohio Assn. Retarded Children (2d v.p. 1974-76, dir.), Vocat. Rehab. Assn., Ohio Coun. Community Mental Health Ctrs., Gallia County Arthritis Assn. (pres. 1991—), Gallipolis Area C. of C., Gallipolis Rotary. Lutheran. Home: 1525 Mill Creek Rd Gallipolis OH 45631-8616 Office: Woodland Ctr Inc 3086 State Route 160 Gallipolis OH 45631-8418

NIEHOFF, ROBERT L., academic administrator; BA, U. Wash., 1972, MA in Theology, MBA; PhD, Gonzaga U. Ordained priest Roman Cath. Ch., 1982; treas. Jesuit Sch. of Theology; assoc. treas. Oreg. Province, Soc. Jesus; fin. officer Archdiocese of Nassau, The Bahamas; fin. analyst, v.p. student life, co-dir Mission and Identity Gonzaga U.; assoc. dean Sch. Edn. U. San Francisco, 1996—2000, assoc. provost, 2000—02, assoc. provost, v.p. planning and budget, 2002—05; pres. John Carroll U., University Heights, Ohio, 2005—. Bd. dirs. Wheeling Jesuit U.; trustee, mem. acad. affairs and fin. coms. St. Louis U.; trustee Regis U. Office: John Carroll U 20700 N Park Blvd University Heights OH 44118-4581 Office Phone: 216-397-4281. E-mail: president@jcu.edu.

NIELSEN, FORREST HAROLD, research nutritionist; b. Dancy, Wis., Oct. 26, 1941; s. George Adolph and Sylvia Viola (Blood) N.; m. Emily Joanne Currie, June 13, 1964; children: Forrest Erik, Kistin Emily. BS, U. Wis., 1963, MS, 1966, PhD, 1967. NIH grad. fellow, dept. biochemistry U. Wis., Madison, 1963-67; rsch. chemist, Human Nutrition Rsch. Inst. USDA, Beltsville, Md., 1969-70, rsch. chemist Human Nutrition Rsch. Ctr. Grand Forks, ND, 1970-86, ctr. dir. and rsch. nutritionist, 1986-2001, rsch. nutritionist, 2001—. Adj. prof. dept. biochemistry and molecular biology, U. N.D., Grand Forks, 1971—, speaker in field. Assoc. editor Magnesium and Trace Elements Jour., 1990-93; mem. editl. bd. Jour. Trace Elements in Exptl. Medicine, 1988—2004, Biol. Trace Element Rsch. Jour., 1979—, Jour. Nutrition, 1984-88, Biofactors, 1997—; contbr. articles to profl. jours. Capt. U.S. Army, 1967-69. Recipient Klaus Schwarz Commemorative medal and award Internat. Assn. of Bioinorganic Scientists; named Scientist of Yr. U.S. Dept. Agrl., 1993. Mem. Internat. Soc. Trace Element Rsch. in Humans (gov. bd. 1989—, pres. 1992-95), Soc. for Exptl. Biology and Medicine, Am. Soc. Nutrition (fellow), N.D. Acad. Sci. (pres. 1988-89), Internat. Bone and Mineral Soc., Sigma Xi (pres. U. N.D. chpt. 1976-77). Lutheran. Achievements include patent for use of Boron Supplements to Increase in Vivo Production of Hydroxylated Steroids; discovery of the nutritional essentiality of the trace elements boron and nickel. Office: USDA ARS GFHNRC 2420 2 Ave N Stop 9034 Grand Forks ND 58202-9034 Home Phone: 701-775-2798; Office Phone: 701-795-8455. Business E-Mail: forrest.nielsen@ars.usda.gov.

NIELSEN, GEORGE LEE, architect; b. Ames, Iowa, Dec. 12, 1937; s. Verner Henry and Verba Lucile (Smith) N.; m. Karen Wall, Feb. 28, 1959; children: David Stuart, Kristina, Melissa. B.Arch., Iowa State U., 1961; M.Arch., M.I.T., 1962. Registered arch., Mass., Ohio, N.Y., Ill., Ind., Ky., Miss., Kans., Colo., Mich., at. Coun. Archtl. Registration Bds. Designer Perry, Shaw, Hepburn & Dean, Boston, 1961-64, F.A. Stahl & Assos., Cambridge, Mass., 1964-65; project architect Peirce & Pierce, Boston, 1965-70; project mgr. A.M. Kinney Assos., Cin., 1970—, partner, 1978—; sec. A.M. Kinney Assocs., Inc., Ill., 1993—, also dir. Cin.; v.p. A.M. Kinney Inc., Cin., 1992-94, pres., 1994-99, also dir.; sr. prin. A.M. Kinney Inc. Assocs., 1999—. Architect prin. works include Avco Rsch. Lab., Cin. Children's Hosp. Med. Ctr., Square D. Corp., Nalco Chem. Co., Olin Corp., Mead Johnson/Bristol Myers Squib, Cin. Gas and Elec. Co., ovartis Pharm. Corp., Hoechst Celanese, Hoechst Marion Roussel, Martek Bioscis., Witco Corp., Sotheby's, Shell Chem. Co., Bayer Corp., U. Ky.

Biomed./Biol. Scis. Rsch. Bldg., U. Ky. Chandler Med. Ctr. Patient Care Facility, Wright Patterson Environ. Hazzards Bldg. and Edwards AFB Sci. Rsch. Bldg. With US Army, 1962—64. Mem.: AIA (design awards 1970—71, 1974, 1978, 1981, 1991, 1994, 1995, 2001, 2002). Episcopalian. Home: 5680 Windridge View Cincinnati OH 45243-2518 Office: A M Kinney Inc 150 E 4th St Fl 6 Cincinnati OH 45202-4131 Office Phone: 513-421-2265.

NIELSEN, NANCY H., health organization executive; m. Don Nielsen; 5 children. BA, W.Va. U., 1964; MS in Microbiology, Cath. U., 1967, PhD in Microbiology, 1969; MD, SUNY Medicine and Biomedical Scis., Buffalo, 1967. Past chief med. officer N.Y. State Dept. Health Western Region; former pres. med. staff Buffalo Gen. Hosp.; asst. dean med. edn., clin. prof. medicine U. Buffalo Sch. Medicine and Biomed. Sci., Buffalo; apptd. to serve US Dept. Health and Human Svcs. Adv. Com. on Regulatory Reform, 2002; assoc. med. dir. for quality, interim chief med. officer Independent Health Assn., NY, now chief med. officer NY; clin. prof. medicine, sr. assoc. dean med. edn. SUNY. Bd. dir. Med. Liability Mut. Ins. Co., Kaleida Health, Nat. Patient Safety Found.; former trustee SUNY; former mem. Commn. for the Prevention of Youth Violence, Task Force on Quality and Patient Safety. Bd. dirs. Nat. Patient Safety Found. Recipient Samuel P. Capen award, U. Buffalo Alumni Assn., 1996. Fellow: ACP; mem.: AMA (vice speaker Ho. of Dels. 2000—03, speaker Ho. of Dels. 2003—, pres.-elect 2007—, bd. trustee, former mem. Coun. on Sci. Affairs, del. med. sch. sect., liaison to the Coun. on Med. Edn.), Inst. Medicine (Consumer Empowerment Com. of America's Health Information Cmty., Roundtable on Evidence Based Medicine), NY State Soc. Internal Medicine (bd. dir.), Med. Soc. State of NY (spkr. ho. dels. 1995—2000), Erie County Med. Soc. (former pres.). Office: Independant Health Assn 511 Farber Lakes Dr Buffalo NY 14221 also: AMA 515 N State St Chicago IL 60610 Business E-Mail: nielse@buffalo.edu.

NIELSEN, PAUL DOUGLAS, engineering executive, retired military officer; s. Jack Alton and Shirley Mae (Gillette) N.; m. Dorothy Webb Spragins, May 3, 1975. BS in Physics and Math., USAF Acad., 1972; MS in Applied Sci., U. Calif., Davis, 1973, PhD in Plasma Physics, 1981; MBA, U. N.Mex., 1977; postgrad., Nat. War Coll., 1988-89. Physicist Nat. Security Agency Ft. George G. Meade, Md., 1973—75; space sys. procurement officer nuc. techs. Air Force Weapons Lab., Kirtland AFB, N.Mex., 1975—77; sys. programs mgmt. officer nuc. techs. Air Force Sys. Command, Andrews AFB, Md., 1977—78, aide to comdr., 1977—78; space sys. procurement mgmt. officer Hdqrs. AFSC, Andrews AFB, Md., 1978; mil. rsch. assoc. Dept. Energy Lawrence Livermore Nat. Libr., 1978—81; asst. chief advanced sys., chief Satellite Attitude Control br., Satellite Engring. divsn., sec. Air Force Office Spl. Projects, L.A. Air Force Sta., Calif., 1981—84; sys. program dir. electronics sys. divsn. Command Ctr. Processing and Display Sys. Replacement Program, Hanscom AFB, Mass., 1984—85; sys. program dir. Space Def. Ops Ctr., 1985—87; chief engr. Strat. Sys. Deputate, ESD, Hanscom AFB, Mass., 1987—88; mil. asst., col. Office of Asst. Sec. Def., Washington, 1989-92; comdr. Rome Lab., Griffiss AFB, 1992-95; command dir. Cheyenne Mountain Ops. Ctr., Cheyenne Mountain Air Sta, Colo., 1995—96, chief ops., 1996-97; brig. gen., dir. plans N.Am. Aerospace Def. Command, Peterson AFB, Colo., 1997-99; vice comdr. Aero. Systems Ctr., AFMC, Wright-Patterson AFB, Ohio, 1999-2000; comdr. Air Force Rsch. Lab., Wright-Patterson AFB, 2000—04; CEO, dir. Software Engring Inst. Carnegie Mellon U., Pitts., 2004—. With USAF, 1972, ret. USAF, 2004, 2d lt., 1972, 1st lt., 1974, capt., 1976, major, 1981, lt. col., 1986, col., 1989, brigadier gen., 1997, major gen., 2001. Decorated Def. Superior Svc. medal with oak leaf cluster, Meritorious Svc. medal with two oak leaf clusters, Disting. Svc. medal, Legion of Merit, Def. Meritorious Svc. medal; fellow Hertz Found., Livermore, Calif., 1972-73, 78-81. Fellow AIAA (Hap Arnold award 2002, pres.), IEEE; mem. Armed Forces Comm. and Electronics Assn., Air Force Assn. Office: Software Eng Inst Carnegie Mellon Univ 4500 Fifth Ave Pittsburgh PA 15213-3890 Home: 30 Wedgewood Ln Pittsburgh PA 15215-1560 Office Phone: 412-268-7740. Business E-Mail: nielsen@sei.cmu.edu.

NIEMANN, RICHARD HENRY, retail executive; b. Quincy, Ill., Feb. 18, 1931; s. Ferdinand Elmer and Antoinette E. (Heckenkamp) Niemann; m. Constance M. Volm, Oct. 6, 1951; children: Linda M., Connie A., Richard Henry, Daniel M., Ted M., Christopher J., Margaret M., Amy E. BS in Mktg., Quincy Coll., 1953. Warehouse mgr. iemann Bros., Quincy, 1953—69; pres., CEO Niemann Foods Inc., Quincy, 1969—. Ptnr. Niemann Farms, Quincy, 1953—; v.p. A'Village Land Corp., Quincy, 1969—82; mng. ptnr. FoodCo Land Trust, Quincy, 1973—; pres. Johannes Meats Inc., Quincy, 1979—83. Trustee Quincy Foods Profit Sharing Trust, 1971—; dir., exec. com. Great River Econ. Devel. Found.; trustee Culver Stockton Coll.; pres.'s bd. Adv. Quincy Coll.; past pres. bd. trustees St. Mary Hosp.; past pres. bd. edn. Quincy Pub. Sch.; Chmn. Ill. Food Distbrs. Polit. Action Com., Lombard, Ill., 1983—; past pres. Deanery Coun. Cath. Men; bd. dirs. State Street Bank & Trust, Quincy, Western Ill. U. Found., Quincy Area Project, Quincy Cath. Charities. Mem.: Ill. Retail Mchts. Assn. (bd. dirs. 1981—), Ill. Food Retailers Assn. (dir., exec. com. 1972—), Quincy Area C. of C. (bd. dirs.), Quincy Country Club, Rotary (past pres. Quincy chpt.), KC (past master). Democrat. Roman Catholic. Home: 2 Old Orchard Rd Quincy IL 62305-6545 Office: Niemann Foods Inc 1501 N 12th St Quincy IL 62301-1996

NIEMEYER, GLENN ALAN, academic administrator, history professor; b. Muskegon, Mich., Jan. 14, 1934; s. John T. and Johanna F. (Walhout) N.; m. Betty Sikkenga, July 8, 1955; children: Kristin, Alexis, Sander BA in History, Calvin Coll., 1955; MA in History, Mich. State U., 1959, PhD in History, 1962. Tchr. soc. sci. Grand Haven Christian Sch., Mich., 1955-58; teaching asst., asst. instr. Mich. State U., East Lansing, 1958-63; asst. prof. history Grand Valley State U., Allendale, Mich., 1963-66, assoc. prof., 1966-70, prof., 1970—, dean Coll. Arts and Scis., 1970-73, v.p. of colls., 1973-76, v.p. acad. affairs, 1976—, provost, 1980—. Evaluator commn. on instns. of higher edn. North Ctrl. Assn., Chgo., 1974—, vice chair, 1994, chair, 1995, v.p., 1996, pres., 1997; mem. Acad. Officers, Pres.'s Coun. State Univs. of Mich. Author: The Automotive Career of Ransom E. Olds, 1963; contbr. articles and book revs. to profl. publs. Trustee Calvin Coll., Grand Rapids, Mich., 1974-80; trustee Unity Christian High Sch., Hudsonville, Mich., 1978-80, pres. bd., 1979-80 Mem. Am. Coun. on Edn., Am. Assn. Higher Edn. Mem. Christian Ref. Ch. Office: Grand Valley State U Allendale MI 49401

NIENKE, STEVEN A., construction company executive; b. 1950; Carpenter Halsey Tevis, Wichita, Kans., 1970-72; pres. Midwest Drywall Co. Inc., Wichita, Kans., 1972—. Office: Midwest Drywall Co Inc PO Box 771170 1351 S Reca Ct Wichita KS 67277-1170 Office Phone: 316-722-9559. Office Fax: 316-722-9682. Business E-Mail: dennis@mwdw.com.

NIENSTEDT, JOHN CLAYTON, archbishop; b. Detroit, Mar. 18, 1947; s. John and Elizabeth S. (Kennedy) N. BA, Sacred Heart Sem., 1969; BST, Pontifical Gregorian U., 1972; Licentiate in Sacred Theology, Pontifical Inst. of St. Alphonsus, 1977, DST, 1985. Ordained deacon North Am. Coll., Rome, 1972, priest Sacred Heart Ch., Dearborn, Mich., 1974. Deacon intern Sacred Heart Parish, Dearborn, Mich., 1973-74; ordained priest Archdiocese of Detroit, Mich., 1974; assoc. pastor Guardian Angels Ch., Clawson, Mich., 1974-76; sec. to Cardinal John Dearden, 1977-80; prof. moral theol. St. John Provincial Sem., Plymouth, Mich., 1977—78; vicar gen. Archdiocese of Detroit, 1979—80; apptd. minor official of 2nd grade Vatican Secretariate of State, 1980-85; temporary assoc. pastor St. Regis Parish, Birmingham, Mich., 1986; pastor St. Patrick's Parish, Union Lake, Mich., 1986-87; rector Sacred Heart Major Sem., Detroit, 1988—94, asst. prof. moral theol., 1988—2000; pastor Shrine of the Little Flower parish, Royal Oak, Mich., 1994—96; ordained bishop, 1996; aux. bishop, so. region Archdiocese of Detroit, 1996—2001; bishop Diocese of New Ulm, Minn., 2001—07; coadjutor archbishop Archdiocese of Saint Paul & Mpls., 2007—. Weekend assoc. pastor St. Fabian's Parish, Farmington HIlls, Mich., 1977, Our Lady of Sorrow's Parish, Farmington, 1978-80; mem. med. moral com. Mich. Conf. for Cath. Health Facilities, 1977-80; asst. chaplain Baby Jesus Hosp., Rome, Italy 1980-83; chaplain Bros. of Holy Cross assigned to Notre Dame High Sch. for Boys, Rome, 1981-84; instr. religion First Eucharist Program Marymont Internat. Sch., 1980-83; adj. prof. moral theology Orchard Lake Schs., 1986; bd. trustees Madonna Coll., 1989-94, trustee com. acad. affairs, 1989—; mem. Midwest/Western Rector's Conf., 1987—, Wranglers, 1986-90, Archdiocesan Med. Moral Com., 1987; trustee, Cath. Relief Soc., 2005-. Contbr. articles to profl. jours. Apptd. a Chaplain to His Holiness by Pope John Paul II bearing title Monsignor, 1985, a Prelate of Honor by Pope John Paul II, 1990. Mem. Cath. Theol. Soc. Am., Assn. Gov. Bds. of U. and Colls. (workshop theol. sch. trustees, chief execs. Cin. chpt. 1989), Midwest Assn. Theol. Schs. (ann. participation 1988, 89, 90), Assn. Am. Colls. (ann. participation 1990). Roman Catholic. Office: Archdiocese of St Paul & Mpls 226 Summit Ave Saint Paul MN 55102-2197*

NIERSTE, JOSEPH PAUL, software engineer; b. Marion, Ind., Feb. 20, 1952; s. Louis Lemuel and Mary Catherine (Dragstrem) N.; m. Deborah Mae Goble, Sept. 20, 1986. BA Applied Piano, Bob Jones U., 1975; MM in Musical Performance, Ball State U., 1977, MS in Computer Sci., 1984. Instr. Marion Coll., 1983-84, Ball State U., Muncie, Ind., 1983-84; software engr. Tokheim Corp., Ft. Wayne, Ind., 1984, Delco Electronics, Kokomo, Ind., 1984-98, Delphi Delco Electronics Sys., Kokomo, 1998—2003, Delphi Electronics & Safety, Kokomo, 2003—. Mem. Pi Kappa Lambda. Republican. Baptist. Avocations: sports, music, computers. Home: 3508 Melody Ln W Kokomo IN 46902-7514 Office: Delphi Delco Electronics Systems MS 6044 PO Box 9005 Kokomo IN 46904-9005 E-mail: xz8wpb@eng.delcoelect.com.

NIGL, JEFFREY M., telecommunications company executive; b. 1958; CFO, v.p., treas. Electronic Telecomms. Inc., Waukesha, Wis. Office: Electronic Telecomms Inc 1915 MacArthur Rd Waukesha WI 53188

NIJMAN, JENNIFER T., lawyer; b. Aug. 27, 1962; BA, U. Ill., 1984; JD, U. Chgo., 1987. Bar: Ill. 1987, US Dist. Ct. (no. dist.) Ill. 1987. Ptnr. Nijman Franzetti LLP, Chgo., 2008—; assoc. to ptnr. Winston & Strawn LLP, Chgo., 1994—2007. Bd. dirs. Pub. Interest Law Initiative, Ctr. Conflict Resolution; chair Ill. Legal eeds Study, Ill. Coalition Equal Justice. Contbr. articles to profl. jours. Mem.: ABA (mem. environ. litigation com.), Economic Club Chgo., Ill. State Bar Assn., Chgo. Bar Assn. (pres. 2002—03). Office: Nijman Franzetti LLP 10 S Lasalle St Ste 3600 Chicago IL 60603 Office Phone: 312-251-5590. Office Fax: 312-251-4610. Business E-Mail: jn@nijmanfranzetti.com.

NIKOLAI, LOREN ALFRED, accounting educator; b. Northfield, Minn., Dec. 14, 1943; s. Roman Peter and Loyola (Gertrude) N.; m. Anita Carol Baker, Jan. 15, 1966; children: Trishia, Jay. BA, St. Cloud State U., 1966, MBA, 1967; PhD, U. Minn., 1973. CPA, Mo. Asst. prof. U. N.C., Chapel Hill, 1973-76; assoc. prof. U. Mo., Columbia, 1976-80, prof., 1980-82, Ernst & Young Disting. prof. Sch. Accountancy, 1982—, dir. masters programs, 2002—. Author: Financial Accounting: Concepts and Uses, 1988, 3d edit., 1995, Intermediate Accounting, 1980, 10th edit., 2007, Accounting Information for Business Decisions, 2000, updated 2d edit., 2007. Recipient Faculty award of merit Fedn. Schs. of Accountancy, 1989, Disting. Alumni award St. Cloud U., 1990, Coll. of Bus. Faculty Mem. of Yr. award, 1991, Mo. Outstanding Acctg. Educators award, 1993; Kemper fellow U. Mo., 1992, Alumni award MU Faculty, 1996, UM Presdl. awd. for Outstanding Teaching, 1999; Coll. of Bus. Teacher of the Yr., 1999. Mem. AICPA, Am. Acctg. Assn., Mo. Soc. CPAs, Fedn. Schs. of Acctg. (pres. 1994). Office: U Mo Sch Accountancy 303 Cornell Hall Columbia MO 65211-0001 Business E-Mail: nikolai@missouri.edu.

NINIVAGGI, DANIEL A., lawyer, manufacturing executive; b. NYC, June 27, 1964; m. Katie Ninivaggi; children: Caleb, Matthew, Jane, Jack. BA, Columbia U., 1986; MBA, U. Chgo., 1988; JD, Stanford U., 1991. Bar: Ill. 1991, NY 1995, Mich. 2003. Assoc. Skadden, Arps, Slate, Meagher & Flum, Winston & Strawn, LLP, NYC, 1992—98, ptnr., 1998—2003; v.p., sec., gen. counsel Lear Corp., Southfield, Mich., 2003—04, sr. v.p., sec., gen. counsel, 2004—06, exec. v.p., sec., gen. counsel, 2006—. Office: Lear Corp 21557 Telgraph Rd PO Box 5008 Southfield MI 48086-5008 Office Phone: 248-447-1500. Business E-Mail: dninivaggi@lear.com.

NIRO, CHERYL, lawyer; b. Feb. 19, 1950; d. Samuel James and Nancy (Canezaro) Ippolito; m. William Luciano Niro, July 1, 1979; children: Christopher William, Melissa Leigh. BS with highest honors, U. Ill., 1972; JD, No. Ill. U., 1980. Bar: Ill. 1981, U.S. Dist. Ct. (no. dist.) Ill. 1981, U.S. Ct. Appeals (7th cir.) 1990, U.S. Supreme Ct. 1999, cert.: negotiator, mediator, facilitator, arbitrator. Ptnr. Quinlan & Carroll, Chgo., 1999—2005; pres. Judicial Dispute Resolution, Inc., Chgo.; exec. dir. commn. on professionalism Ill. Supreme Ct., Chgo., 2006—. Spl. counsel to Atty. Gen., 1996—99; tchg. asst. program instrn. lawyers mediation and negotiation workshops and guest lectr. Harvard Law Sch. Program of Instrn. for Lawyers Harvard U.; mem. appt. panel U.S. Ct. Appeals (7th cir.); found. dir. Nat. Ctr. for Conflict Resolution Edn.; mem. copyright arbitration royalty panel U.S. Libr. of Congress, 2000—05; mem. London Ct. of Internat. Arbitration. Named 100 Women Making A Difference, Today's Chgo. Woman Found., 2001; named one of Ten Most Influential Women Lawyers in Ill, Am Lawyer Media, 2000; named to Today's Chgo. Woman Mag. Hall of Fame, 2002. Mem.: ATLA, ABA (comn multijurisdictional practice, standing comt bar servs, dispute resolution sect coun, house delegs), Nat. Caucus State Bar Assns. (pres.-elect), Internat. Ctr. for Healing the Law (mem. bd. adv.), Internat. Bar Assn., Ill. State Bar Assn. (mem assembly 1993, bd govs 1994—97, treas 1995—96, 2d vpres 1997—98, pres 1999—2000, standing comt legal-related educ pub), Ill Trial Lawyers Asn. Home: 633 N East Ave Oak Park IL 60302-1715 Office: Prudential Plz 180 N Stetson Ave Ste 1950 Chicago IL 60601 Office Phone: 312-363-6210. Office Fax: 312-365-6218. Business E-Mail: cheryl.niro@ilsccp.org.

NISBET, THOMAS K., architect; b. Richland Center, Wis., Jan. 9, 1931; s. Thomas Kenneth and Eva Louise (Klein) N.; m. Lynnette Patricia MacIntyre, Aug. 27, 1954; children: Bruce W., Jay T., Christopher W. Student, Columbia Coll., 1949-51; BArch, Columbia U., 1955. Registered arch., N.Y., Wis. Apprentice arch. Albert M. Skinner AIA, Watertown, N.Y., 1946-49; asst. editl. Archtl. Record, NYC, 1950-51; draftsman Weiler/Strang, Madison, Wis., 1952-55; arch. H.C. Montgomery AIA, Watertown, 1958-61; arch./assoc. Flad & Assocs., Madison, 1961-83; prin. Nisbet/Archs., Madison, 1983—. Mem. Wis. Examining Bd., 1982-83, at. Coun. Archs. Registration Bd., 1981-. Works include co-designer Sentry Ins. home office, 1975 (honor award 1975), Wis. Telephone/ASC/WARF, 1970-75 (merit awards 1970-75), U. Wis. Libr./Vilas Hall (merit award 1974); awarded commission for Tri State Vets. Meml. with Severson/Schultz Sculptors. Deacon Westminster Presbyn. Ch., Madison, 1964; v.p., bd. dirs. Nakoma Golf Club, Madison, 1976-82. Recipient Columbia U. traveling fellowship Europe, 1957-58. Mem. AIA (emeritus), Wis. Archs. Found. (pres. 1981-85). Avocations: art, photography. Office: Nisbet/Architects 4340 Hillcrest Cir Madison WI 53705-5017 Office Phone: 608-233-2320. Personal E-mail: tknisbet@charter.net.

NISBETT, RICHARD EUGENE, psychology professor; b. Littlefield, Tex., June 1, 1941; s. R. Wayne and Helen (King) N.; m. Susan Ellen Isaacs, June 29, 1969; children: Matthew, Sarah. AB summa cum laude, Tufts U., 1962; PhD, Columbia U., 1966. Asst. prof. psychology Yale U., New Haven, 1966-71; assoc. prof. psychology U. Mich., Ann Arbor, 1971-77, prof., 1977—, Theodore M. Newcomb prof. psychology, 1989-92, Theodore M. Newcomb disting. univ. prof. of psychology, 1992—. Author: (with others) Attribution: Perceiving the Causes of Behavior, 1972, Induction: Processes of Inference, Learning and Discovery, 1986, Rules for Reasoning, 1992, (with L. Ross) Human Inference: Strategies and Shortcomings of Social Judgment, 1980, The Person and the Situation, 1991, (with D. Cohen) Culture of Honor, 1996, The Geography of Thought, 2003. Recipient Donald T. Campbell award for disting. rsch. in social psychology APA, 1982, Disting. Sci. Contbn. award APA, 1991, Am. Acad. Arts & Sci., 1992, Disting. Sr. Scientist award Soc. Exptl. Social Psychology, 1995, J. McKeen Cattell award Am. Psychol. Assn., 1998; fellow Ctr. for Advanced Studies in Behavioral Scis., William James award Am. Psychol. Soc., 1995, John Simon Guggenheim fellow, 2001; Russell Sage Found. scholar, 2001, Nat. Acad. Sci., 2002. Office: U Mich 5261 ISR Rsch Ctr Group Dynamics Ann Arbor MI 48106 Office Phone: 734-761-5847. Business E-Mail: nisbett@umich.edu.

NISCHKE, ANN M., state legislator; b. Jan. 19, 1951; BS, U. Wis., Eau Claire, 1977. Real estate marketer; exec. dir. C. of C.; mem. Wis. State Assembly, Madison, 2002—, vice chair econ. devel. com., mem. aging and long-term care com., mem. edn. reform com., mem. energy and utilities com., mem. fin. instns. com., mem. small bus. com. Republican. Office: State Capitol Rm 8 N PO Box 8953 Madison WI 53708-8953 Home: 202 W College Ave Waukesha WI 53186-4931

NISSEN, STEVEN E., cardiologist, researcher; b. Toledo, 1949; m. Linda Butler. BS, U. Mich., Ann Arbor; MD, U. Mich. Sch. Medicine, Ann Arbor. Intern internal medicine Univ. Calif. Davis, Sacramento, resident internal medicine; fellowship in cardiology Chandler Med. Ctr. Univ. Ky., Lexington; cardiologist Cleveland Clinic, 1992—, dir. coronary ICU, 1992—97, sect. head clinical cardiology, 1992—2002, vice chmn. dept. cardiology, 1993—2002, interim chmn., dept. cardiovascular med., 2006, chmn., dept. cardiovascular med., 2006—, dir., Joseph J. Jacobs Ctr. for Thrombosis and Vascular Biology; prof. medicine Ohio State U. Mem. and chmn. CardioRenal adv. panel US FDA; spl. govt. employee US FDA Committees; mem. med. & sci. adv. bd. Forbes Medi-Tech Inc.; vis. prof. at med. colleges and universities internationally and nationally. Contbr. articles to profl. jours., chapters to books; mem. editl. bd. Internat. Jour. Cardiac Imaging, Cardiology Today, Clinical Cardiology; editor: Current Cardiology Reports, 2006—; sr. consulting editor Journal of American College of Cardiology, 2002—. Named one of The World's Most Influential People, TIME Mag., 2007; recipient Award for Outstanding Rsch. in Cardiovascular Rsch., Gill Heart Inst., U. Ky., 2004. Mem.: Am. Coll. Cardiology (pres., chmn. bd. trustees 2006—, ednl. products com., info. tech. com.). Achievements include development of intravascular ultrasound imaging; published rsch. on cardiovascular problems caused by Cox-2 inhibitor drugs, such as Vioxx & Celebrex. Avocation: bicycling. Office: Cleveland Clinic Mail Code F 15 9500 Euclid Ave Cleveland OH 44195 Office Phone: 216-445-6852. Business E-Mail: nissens@ccf.org.*

NISSEN, WILLIAM JOHN, lawyer; b. Chgo., July 28, 1947; s. William Gordon Jr. and Ruth Carolyn (Banas) N.; m. Patricia Jane Press, Jan. 16, 1971; children: Meredith Warner, Edward William. BA, Northwestern U., 1969; JD magna cum laude, Harvard U., 1976. Bar: Ill. 1976, U.S. Dist. Ct. (no. dist.) Ill. 1976, U.S. Ct. Appeals (7th cir.) 1981. Assoc. Sidley & Austin, Chgo., 1976-83, ptnr., 1983—. Gen. counsel Heinold Commodities, Inc., Chgo., 1982-84. Editor Harvard U. Internat. Law Jour., 1974-76. Served to lt. USN, 1969-73. Mem. ABA (co-chmn. futures regulation subcom. on pvt. litig. 1996-98), Chgo. Bar Assn. (chmn. futures regulation com. 1985-86), Am. Legion (comdr. union league post 758 1994-95), Union League Club Chgo. (dir. 1999-2002, sec. 2003-05). Home: 348 Foss Ct Lake Bluff IL 60044-2753

NISSL, COLLEEN KAYE, lawyer; b. McMinnville, Oreg., June 3, 1950; d. Anton Arthur and Luella Elaine (Kerr) N.; m. Roger Philip Sugarman; children: Jordan Elizabeth, Zachary Max. BA, Ohio Wesleyan U., 1972; JD, U. Toledo, 1975. Bar: Ohio 1975, U.S. Dist. Ct. (so. dist.) Ohio 1977, U.S. Supreme Ct. 1980. Litigation sect. chief Atty. Gen. Ohio, Columbus, 1976-82; sr. counsel Battelle Meml. Inst., Columbus, 1982-84; v.p., asst. gen. counsel Borden Chemical, Inc., Columbus, 1984—. Mem. ABA, Ohio Bar Assn., Columbus Bar Assn. (chmn. alt. dispute resolution com.). Democrat. Roman Catholic. Avocations: skiing, bicycling, antiques. Office: Borden Inc 180 E Broad St 27th Fl Columbus OH 43215

NITIKMAN, FRANKLIN W., lawyer; b. Davenport, Iowa, Oct. 26, 1940; s. David A. and Janette (Gordon) N.; m. Adrienne C. Drell, Nov. 28, 1972. BA, Northwestern U., 1963; LLB, Yale U., 1966. Bar: Ill. 1966, US Dist. Ct. (no. dist.) Ill. 1967, US Tax Ct. 1972, Fla. 1977, DC 1981. Assoc. McDermott, Will & Emery, Chgo., 1966-72, ptnr., 1973—2006, counsel, 2007—. Co-author: Drafting Wills and Trust Agreements, 1990. Bd. dirs. Owen Coon Found., Glenview, Ill., 1985—, Jewish Fedn. Met. Chgo., Jewish United Fund, 1994—2003, Spertus Inst. Jewish Studies, Chgo., 1991—, chmn. bd., 1999—2002. Fellow Am. Coll. Trust and Estate Coun., Am. Bar Found.; mem. Standard Club, Arts Club (Chgo.). Home: 365 Lakeside Pl Highland Park IL 60035-5371 Office: McDermott Will & Emery LLP 227 W Monroe St Ste 4700 Chicago IL 60606-5096 Office Phone: 312-984-7614. Business E-Mail: fnitikman@mwe.com.

NIX, EDMUND ALFRED, lawyer; b. Eau Claire, Wis., May 24, 1929; s. Sebastian and Kathryn (Keirnan) N.; m. Mary Kathryn Nagle Daley, Apr. 27, 1968; children: Kim, Mary Kay, Norbert, Edmund Alfred, Michael. BS, Wis. State U., 1951; LL.B., U. Wis., 1954, postgrad. in speech, 1956-57. Bar: Wis. 1954. Practice in, Eau Claire, 1954-65; dist. atty. Eau Claire County, 1958-64; U.S. atty. Western Dist. Wis., Eau Claire, 1965-69, U.S. magistrate, 1969-70; dist. atty. La Crosse County, Wis., 1975-77; mcpl. judge City of La Crosse, 1992—. Co-chmn. United Fund, Eau Claire, 1958; Pres. Young Democrats Wis., 1951-53; mem. adminstrv. bd. Wis. Dem. party, 1953-54; chmn. 10th Congl. dist., 1965; sec. Kennedy for Pres. Club Wis., 1959-60. Served with AUS, 1954-56. Mem. Fed. Bar Assn., Wis. Bar Assn. (state chmn. crime prevention and control com.), La Crosse County Bar Assn. (pres.), Nat. Dist. Attys. Assn., KC. Roman Catholic.

NIXON, CHARLES WILLIAM, retired acoustician; b. Wellsburg, W.Va., Aug. 15, 1929; s. William E. and Lenora S. (Treiber) Nixon; m. Barbara Irene Hunter, May 19, 1956; children: Timothy C., Tracy Scott. BS, Ohio State U., 1952, MS, 1953, PhD, 1960. Tchr. spl. edn. Ohio and W.Va. Pub. Schs., Wheeling, 1954—56; rsch. audiologist Aeromed Lab., Wright Patterson AFB, Ohio, 1956—67; supervisory rsch. audiologist Armstrong Lab., Wright Patterson AFB, 1967—96, Veridian, Dayton, 1996—2004. Chair W4 Am. Nat. Stds. Inst., NYC, 1968—96; U.S. rep. hearing protection Internat. Stds. Orgn., Geneva, 1968—96; USAF rep. NRC-NAS Hearing Com., Washington, 1976—94; chair robotics panel Joint Dirs. Labs., Washington, 1987—88. Author: reports and book chpts. Cpl. US Army, 1953—55. Recipient Meritorious Svc. medal, U.S. Dept. Def., Dayton, Ohio, 1986, Outstanding Civilian Svc. award, 1996. Fellow: Acoustical Soc. Am.; mem.: Rsch. Soc. Am. Achievements include research in noise exposure, voice communications, hearing protection, sonic boom, active noise reduction, 3-D audio displays, others. Home: 4316 Sillman Pl Dayton OH 45440-1141

NIXON, DAVID, dancer; b. Windsor, Ont., Can. Student, The Nat. Ballet Sch. Dancer Nat. Ballet Can., 1978—82, 1st soloist, 1982—84; prin. dancer Deutsche Opera Ballet, Berlin, 1985—90, Komische OperaBallet, Berlin, 1991—93; artistic dir. Ballet met., Columbus, Ohio, 1995—2001, No. Ballet Theatre, England, 2001—. Various guest appearance including Munich Ballet, 1990-91, Staatsoper, Berlin, 1990, Birmingham Royal Ballet, 1990-93. Dancer Bayerisches Staatsoper Ballet Munich, 1990—91, Alexander Godunov and Stars, 1982, Milw. Ballet, 1984, Sydney Ballet Australia, 1984, World Ballet Festival Tokyo, 1985, 1988, Hamburg Ballet, 1988, 1989, Staatsoper Berlin, 1988—91, Bayerisches Staatsballet, 1988—90, Komische Opera Berlin, 1990—93; prodr.: David Nixon's Dance Theatre, Hebbel Theatre Berlin, 1990, 1991; choreographer Butterfly, 1983, La Follia, 1984, Dangerous Liaisons, 1990, 1996, African Fantasy, 1990, Celebrate Mozart, 1991, Sudden Impulse, 1994, A Summer's Nights Reflections, 1995, Full-Length Nutcracker, 1995, Butterfly, 1996, Beauty and the Beast, 1997, Carmen, 1997, Romeo and Juliet, 1998, Swan Lake, 1998, Dracula, 1999, A Midsummer Nights Dream, 2000—03, A Celebration of Dance with Music by Gershwin, 2001, Wuthering Heights, 2002, Peter Pan, 2004, Undine, 2006. Recipient Ollivier award, 2005, Best Dir. award, 2004, 2006. Office: Northern Ballet Theatre West Park Centre Spen Ln Leeds LS16 5BE England

NIXON, JEREMIAH W. (JAY), state attorney general; b. DeSoto, Mo., Feb. 13, 1956; s. Jeremiah and Betty (Lea) Nixon; m. Georganne Nixon; children: Jeremiah, Will. BS in Polit. Sci., U. Mo., 1978, JD, 1981. Ptnr. Nixon, Nixon, Breeze & Roberts, Jefferson County, Mo., 1981—86; mem. Mo. State Senate from Dist. 22, 1986—93; atty. gen. State of Mo., 1993—. Chmn. select com. ins. reform; creator video internat. devel. and edn. opportunity prog. Named Outstanding Young Missourian, Jaycees, 1994, Outstanding Young Lawyer, Barrister's Mag., 1993; recipient Conservation Fedn. Mo award, 1992. Mem.: Mo. Assn. Trial Attys., Midwest Assn. Attys. Gen., Nat. Assn. Attys. Gen. Democrat. Methodist. Office: Office of Atty Gen Supreme Ct Bldg 207 W High St Jefferson City MO 65101

NIXON, JUDITH MAY, librarian; b. Gary, Ind., June 14, 1945; d. Louis Robert Sr. and Mable Sophia (Reiner) Vician; m. Cleon Robert Nixon III, Aug. 20, 1967; 1 child, Elizabeth Marie. BS in Edn., Valparaiso U., 1967; MA in LS, U. Iowa, 1974. Tchr. U.S. Peace Corps, Tonga, 1968—69; popular books libr. Lincoln Libr., Springfield, Ill., 1971—73; ref. libr. Cedar Rapids (Iowa) Pub. Libr., 1974—76; ref.coord. U. Wis., Platteville, 1976—82; bus. libr. U. Ariz., Tucson, 1982—84; consumer and family sci. libr. Purdue U., West Lafayette, La., 1984—93, Krannert mgmt. and econs. libr., 1993—2005, humanities, social sci. and edn. head libr., 2005—. Editor: Industry and Company Information, 1991, Organization Charts, 1992, 2d edit., 1996, Hotel and Restaurant Industries, 1993; editor quar. serial Lodging and Restaurant Index, 1985-93. Leader Girl Scouts U.S., Lafayette, 1985—2005. Recipient John H. Moriarty award Purdue

U. Librs., 1989. Mem. ALA (chair bus. reference and svcs. sect. 1995-96, GALE Rsch. award for excellence in bus. librarianship 1994). Home: 2375 N 23rd St Lafayette IN 47904-1242 Office: Purdue U Libraries Humanities Social Sci Edn Libr 504 W State St West Lafayette IN 47907-2058 Office Phone: 765-494-2834. Business E-Mail: jnixon@purdue.edu.

NOBACK, RICHARDSON KILBOURNE, medical educator; b. Richmond, Va., Nov. 7, 1923; s. Gustav Joseph and Hazel (Kilborn) N.; m. Nan Jean Gates, Apr. 5, 1947; children: Carl R., Robert K., Catherine E. MD, Cornell U., 1947; BA, Columbia U., 1993. Diplomate Am. Bd. Internal Medicine. Intern N.Y. Hosp., 1947-48; asst. resident Cornell Med. div. Bellevue Hosp., NYC, 1958-50, chief resident, 1950-52; instr. medicine Cornell U., NYC, 1950-53; asst. prof. medicine SUNY Upstate Med. Ctr., Syracuse, 1955-56; assoc. prof. medicine U. Ky. Med. Ctr., Lexington, 1956-64; exec. dir. Kansas City (Mo.) Gen. Hosp. and Med. Ctr., 1964-69; assoc. dean, prof. medicine U. Mo. Sch. Medicine, Columbia, 1964-69, founding dean Kansas City, 1969-78, prof. medicine, 1969-90, prof. and dean emeritus, 1990—. Cons. U. Tenn., U. Mich., U. Del., Northeastern Ohio Group, U. Mo., Eastern Va. Med. Sch., Tex. Tech. U. Author Realism, Standards, and Performances: Three Essentials in Assessment, Planning, and Action, 2005; contbr. numerous articles to profl. jours. Bd. dirs. Kansas City Gen. Hosp., Truman Med. Ctr., Wayne Miner Health Ctr., Jackson County Med. Soc., The Shepherd's Ctr., Am. Fedn. Aging Rsch., Mo. Gerontol. Inst., The Shepherd's Ctrs. of Am.; dir. Mo. Geriatric Edn. Ctr., 1985-88. With US Army, 1943—46, with USAF, 1953—55. Recipient medal of honor Avila Coll., Kansas City, 1968, merit award Met. Med. Soc., 1991, recognition award Mo. Soc. Internal Medicine, 1993. Mem. AMA, Mo. Med. Assn. (former mem. ho. of dels., v.p. 1992), Am. Geriatric Soc., Alpha Omega Alpha, Phi Kappa Phi. Avocations: photography, writing, travel. Home: 2912 Abercorn Dr Las Vegas NV 89134-7440 Personal E-mail: nanori@earthlink.net.

NOBLE, ROBERT B., advertising executive; b. 1945; BFA, Southwest Mo. State U. With Batz, Hodgson & Nevwoehner Advt. Agy., St. Louis, 1965-69, Noble & Assocs., Springfield, Mo., 1969—, now pres., CEO. Address: Noble & Assoc 2155 W Chesterfield Blvd Springfield MO 65807-8650

NOBLITT, NILES L., medical products executive; s. William S. and Genevieve Noblitt. Grad., Rose Hulman Inst. Tech., Terre Haute, Ind., 1974. Co-founder, chmn. Biomet, Inc., Warsaw, Ind., 1977—; CEO Biomet-Merck, joint venture, Darmstadt, Germany, 1997—. Bd. dir. Advanced Medical Tech. Assn., Washington. Trustee Rose Hulman Inst. Tech. Office: Biomet Inc 56 E Bell Dr Warsaw IN 46582 Office Phone: 574-267-6639. Office Fax: 574-267-8137.

NOCE, DAVID D., judge; AB, St. Louis U.; JD, U. Mo., Columbia. Bar: Mo. Law clk. to Hon. H. Kenneth Wangelin US Dist. Ct. (ea. and we. dists.) Mo.; law clk. to Hon. John F. Nangle US Dist. Ct. (ea. dist.) Mo.; asst. US atty. (ea. dist.) Mo US Dept. Justice, St. Louis; magistrate judge US Dist. Ct. (ea. dist.) Mo., St. Louis, 1976—. Adj. prof. law St. Louis U. Sch. Law, Washington U. Sch. Law, St. Louis. Author: Jury Instructions Drafting Workbook West, 1999. Lagal Officer, U.S. Army. Mem. ABA, Mo. Bar, Bar Assn. Met. St. Louis, Fed. Magistrate Judges Assn. Office: US Courthouse 17th Flr N 111 S 10th St Saint Louis MO 63102 Office Phone: 314-244-7630.

NODDLE, JEFFREY, retail and food distribution executive; BA, U. Iowa. Various positions, including pres. 2 food divsns. Supervalu Inc., Eden Prairie, Minn., 1976-92, exec. v.p. mktg., 1992-95, exec. v.p. mktg.; pres., COO wholesale food cos., 1995-99, pres., COO, 2000-01, pres., CEO, 2001—04, chmn., CEO, 2004—. Bd. mem. Ind. Grocers Alliance Inc., Food Industry Ctr., U. Minn., Acad. Food Mktg., St. Joseph's U., Pa.; corp. bd. Donaldson Co. Inc.; chmn. bd. Food Mktg. Inst. Bd. dir. Greater Twin Cities United Way; bd. overseers U. Minn. Carlson Sch. Mgmt.; exec. com. Minn. Bus. Partnership. Office: Supervalu Inc 11840 Valley View Rd Eden Prairie MN 55344-3691

NOE, CINDY J., state representative; b. St. Louis, Mo., Aug. 23, 1947; m. John Noe; 2 children. BS, Ind. U., 1969. Budget analyst Atlantic-Richfield, 1970—71; dir. recruiting and placement Louisville Vocat./Tech. Sch., 1971—72; former corp. sec.-treas., v.p. IHM Facility Svcs., Inc., Hamilton County, Ind., CEO, majority owner; state rep. dist. 87 Ind. Ho. of Reps., Indpls., 2001. Precinct committeeman Washington Twp. Dist. 87, Ind., 1996—; del. Ind. Rep. State Conv., 1998, 2000, 2001; v.p. bd. Character Coun. of Ind., late 1990s. Mem.: Sales and Mktg. Execs. (sec. 1994—96), Nat. Fedn. Ind. Bus. (leadership coun. 1990—), Ind. C. of C. (mem. com. 1998—2002). Republican. Office: Ind Ho of Reps 200 W Washington St Indianapolis IN 46204-2786

NOEL, EDWIN LAWRENCE, lawyer; b. St. Louis, July 11, 1946; s. Thomas Currie and Christine (Jones) N.; m. Nancy Carter Simpson, Feb. 7, 1970; children: Caroline, Edwin C. BA, Brown U., 1968; JD cum laude, St. Louis U., 1974. Bar: Mo. 1974, U.S. Dist. Ct. (ea. dist.) Mo. 1974, U.S. Ct. Appeals (8th cir.) 1974, U.S. Ct. Appeals (6th cir.) 1978, U.S. Ct. Appeals (7th cir.) 1994, U.S. Supreme Ct. 1986. Ptnr. Armstrong, Teasdale, LLP, St. Louis, 1974—, mng. ptnr., 1993-97. Bd. dirs. Corley Printing Co., St. Louis, Home Fed. Savs. Bank of Mo., 1988—93. Bd. dirs. Edgewood Children's Ctr., St. Louis, 1982-92, St. Louis Assn. for Retarded Citizens, 1984-87, Churchill Sch., 1988-94, Whitfield Sch., 1991-95; chmn. Mo. Clean Water Com., Jefferson City, 1982-88. Mem. Mo. Bar Assn., Bar Assn. Met. St. Louis, Attys. Liability Assurance Soc. (bd. dirs. 1995—, chmn. 2006—). Republican. Episcopalian. Home: 301 S Mcknight Rd Saint Louis MO 63124-1884 Office: Armstrong Teasdale LLP 1 Metropolitan Sq Ste 2600 Saint Louis MO 63102-2740 Office Phone: 314-621-5070. Business E-Mail: enoel@armstrongteasdale.com.

NOEL, FRANKLIN LINWOOD, judge; b. NYC, Dec. 7, 1951; s. Charles Alexander and Mayme (Loth) N.; m. Ellen Barbara Perl, Sept. 15, 1979; children: Kate Alexandra, Charles David. BA, SUNY, Binghamton, 1974; JD, Georgetown U., 1977. Bar: D.C. 1977, U. S. Dist. Ct. D.C. 1978, U.S. Ct. Appeals (D.C. cir.) 1978, Pa. 1979, Minn. 1983, U.S. Ct. Appeals (8th cir.) 1983, U.S. Dist. Ct. Minn. 1984. Assoc. Arnold & Porter, Washington, 1977-79; asst. dist. atty. Phila. Dist. Attys. Office, 1979-83; asst. U.S. atty. U.S. Attys. Office, Mpls., 1983-89; U.S. magistrate judge U.S. Dist. Ct., Mpls., 1989—. Legal writing instr. U. Minn., Mpls., 1989-92, adj. prof. Law Sch., 1996—. Mem. League Am. Bicyclists, Phi Beta Kappa. Episcopalian. Avocation: bicycling. Office: US Dist Ct 300 S 4th St Minneapolis MN 55415-1320

NOELKEN, MILTON EDWARD, biochemistry educator, researcher; b. St. Louis, Dec. 5, 1935; s. William Henry Noelken and Agnes (Westbrook) Burkemper; m. Carol Ann Agne, June 9, 1962. BA in Chemistry, Washington U., St. Louis, 1957, PhD in Chemistry, 1962. Rsch. chemist Ea. Regional Rsch., Dept. Agr., Phila., 1964-67; asst. prof. dept. biochemistry U. Kans. Med. Ctr., Kansas City, 1967-71, assoc. prof., 1971-81, acting chmn., 1973-74, prof., 1981—, interim chmn., 1993-94. Vis. prof. Fed. U. Minas Gerais, Brazil, 1978. Contbr. articles to profl. jours. Recipient Scholastic Achievement award Am. Inst. Chemists, Washington U., 1957; NSF fellow, Washington U., 1959. Mem. Am. Chem. Soc., Am. Soc. for Biochemistry and Molecular Biology, Biophysical Soc., Sigma Xi. Achievements include research in properties of antibody molecules related to antigen binding, stucture of collagen of basement membranes, and stability of proteins. Office: U Kans Med Ctr Dept Biochemistry 39th And Rainbow Blvd Kansas City KS 66160-7421 E-mail: mnoelken@kumc.edu.

NOER, RICHARD J., physics professor, researcher; b. Madison, Wis., July 3, 1937; s. Rudolf J. and Anita M. (Showerman) N.; m. Raymonde Tasset, Aug. 17, 1967; children— Geoffrey, Catherine BA, Amherst Coll., 1958; PhD, U. Calif., Berkeley, 1963. Physicist Atomic Energy Research, Harwell, Eng., 1963-64; asst. prof. physics Amherst Coll., Mass., 1964-66; from asst. prof. physics to prof. Carleton Coll., Northfield, Minn., 1966—98, Laurence McKinley Gould prof. natural scis., 1998—2004, emeritus, 2004—, chmn. dept. physics, 1974—77, 1989—92, 2001—02. Vis. prof. Cornell U., 2004; physicist Ames Lab., Iowa, summers 1977-80, 82-84; rsch. physicist U. Geneva, 1980-81, 84-85; vis. scientist U. Paris, Orsay, France, 1972-73, Cornell U., summers 1986, 88-91, Centre d'Etudes Nucléaires, Saclay, France, 1992-93, KEK High Energy Accelera, Tsukuba, Japan, 2000-01. Co-author: Revolutions in Physics, 1972; contbr. articles to profl. jours. Mem.: AAAS, Am. Assn. Physics Tchrs., Am. Phys. Soc., Sigma Xi, Phi Beta Kappa. Home: 101 Winona St Northfield MN 55057-2232 Office: Carleton Coll Dept Physics Northfield MN 55057 Business E-Mail: rnoer@carleton.edu.

NOLAN, ALAN TUCKER, lawyer, writer, arbitrator; b. Evansville, Ind., Jan. 19, 1923; s. Val and Jeannette (Covert) N.; m. Elizabeth Clare Titsworth, Aug. 26, 1947 (dec. Nov. 1967); children: Patrick A., Thomas C., Mary F., Elizabeth T., John V.; m. Jane Ransel DeVoe, Feb. 7, 1970; adopted children: John C. DeVoe, Ellen R. DeVoe, Thomas R. DeVoe. AB in Govt. with honors, Ind. U., Bloomington, 1944, LHD, 1993; LLB, Harvard U., Cambridge, Mass., 1947. Bar: Ind. 1947. Law clk. U.S. Ct. Appeals (7th Cir.), Chgo., 1947-48; assoc. Ice, Miller, Donadio & Ryan, Indpls., 1948-58, ptnr., 1958-93, ret., 1993—. Chmn. Disciplinary Commn. Supreme Ct. Ind., Indpls., 1966-73. Author: The Iron Brigade, 1961, As Sounding Brass, 1964, Lee Considered, 1991; editor (with S. Vipond) Giants in Tall Black Hats, 1998, (with Gary Gallagher) The Myth of the Lost Cause and Civil War History, 2000, Rally Once Again, 2000; contbg. editor The Civil War, 1985-89; contbr. numerous articles to profl. jours. Life mem. NAACP Indpls., v.p., 1950-54; bd. dirs., founder Ind. Civil Liberties Union, Indpls., 1953-60; bd. dirs. Indpls. Art League, 1981-87; chmn., bd. trustees Ind. Hist. Soc., Indpls., 1986-98; trustee Eiteljorg Mus., Indpls., 1987-93. Fellow Co. Mil. Historians, Am. Bar Found., State Hist. Soc. Wis.; mem. ABA, ACLU, Ind. Bar Assn., Indpls. Bar Assn. (bd. mgrs. 1958-60, chmn. Grievance Com. 1960-64), Indpls. Civil War Round Table, Ensemble Music Soc. (bd. dirs. 1999—), Phi Beta Kappa. Democrat. Roman Catholic. Avocations: travel, gardening, reading. Home and Office: 3307 Bay Road North Drive Indianapolis IN 46240 Office Phone: 317-585-1988. Personal E-mail: indynolan@sbcglobal.net.

NOLAN, VAL, JR., retired biologist, lawyer; b. Evansville, Ind., Apr. 28, 1920; s. Val and Jeannette (Covert) N.; m. Susanne Howe, Dec. 23, 1946 (div. Aug. 29, 1980); children: Val, Ann Clare, William Alan; m. Ellen D. Ketterson, Oct. 17, 1980. AB, Ind. U., 1941, JD, 1949. Bar: Ind. 1949. Dep. U.S. marshal, 1941; agt. White House Detail, U.S. Secret Service, 1942; asst. prof. law Ind. U., 1949-52, assoc. prof., 1952-56, prof., 1956-85, prof. emeritus, 1985—, research scholar in zoology, 1957-68, prof. zoology, 1968-77, prof. biology, 1977-85; prof. emeritus, 1985—; acting dean Sch. Law, 1976, 80. Author: (with F.E. Horack, Jr.) Land Use Controls, 1955, Ecology and Behavior of the Prairie Warbler, 1978; editor Ind. Law Jour., 1945-46, Jour. Avian Biology, 1998—2005, Current Ornithology, 1994-2004. Served with USNR, 1942-46. Guggenheim fellow, 1957; recipient Ind. U. Disting. Alumni Svc. award, 1987; named to Acad. Law Alumni Fellows, Ind. U., 1988. Fellow AAAS, Am. Ornithologists Union (v.p. 1989-90, Brewster Meml. award 1986), Animal Behavior Soc.; mem. Brit. Ornithologists Union, Cooper Ornithol. Soc., Wilson Ornithol. Soc. (co-recipient (with Ellen D. Ketterson) Margaret M. Nice award 1998), Assn. Field Ornithologists, Ecol. Soc. Am., Am. Soc. Naturalists, Deutsche Ornithologen-Gesellschaft, Nederlandse Ornithologische Unie, Soc. Study of Reprodn., Phi Beta Kappa, Sigma Xi. Democrat. Home: 4675 E Heritage Woods Rd Bloomington IN 47401-9312 E-mail: vnolan@indiana.edu.

NOLAND, MARIAM CHARL, foundation executive; b. Parkersburg, W.Va., Mar. 29, 1947; d. Lloyd Henry and Ethel May (Beare) Noland; m. James Arthur Kelly, June 13, 1981. BS, Case Western Res. U., 1969; M in Edn., Harvard U., 1975. Asst. dir admissions, fin. aid Baldwin-Wallace Coll., Berea, Ohio, 1969-72; asst. dir. admissions Davidson (N.C.) Coll., 1972-74; case writer Inst. Edn. Mgmt., Cambridge, Mass., 1975; sec., treas., program officer The Cleve. Found., 1975-81; v.p. The St. Paul Found., 1981-85; pres. Community Found. for S.E. Mich., 1985—. Trustee Coun. Mich. Founds., 1988-98, Coun. on Founds., 1994-99, Henry Ford Health System, 1994-2002, 2004— Alma Coll., 1994-2004, John S. and James L. Knight Found., 2002—, Detroit Riverfront Conservancy, 2003—; commr. Detroit 300, 2000-01. Office: Community Found SE Mich 333 W Fort St Ste 2010 Detroit MI 48226-3134 Office Phone: 313-961-6675. Business E-Mail: mnoland@cfsem.org.

NOLAND, N. DUANE, state legislator; b. Blue Mound, Ill., Sept. 12, 1956; m. Tina L. Beckett; children: Grant, Blake. BS with high honors, U. Ill., 1978. V.p. oland Farms, 1982—; mem. Ill. Ho. of Reps. from 102d dist., 1990-98, Ill. Senate from 51st dist., 1998—. Minority vice spokesman Agr., Counties and Twps. Coms. Ill. Ho. of Reps., mem. Econ. and Urban Devel., Ins., Pub. Safety and Infrastructure Appropriations Coms. Recipient Award of Excellence Nat. Corn Growers Assn., Ill. Young Leader award Am. Soybean Assn.; named Outstanding Young Farmer, Decatur-Mason (Ill.) Jaycees. Mem. Ill. Corn Growers Assn. (bd. dirs., treas.), Macon County Farm Bur. (bd. dirs.), Corn-Soy Commodity Orgn. (chmn.), Masons, Aircraft Owners and Pilots Assn. Republican. Home: RR 2 Box 206 Blue Mound IL 62513-9557

NOLD, CARL RICHARD, museum administrator; b. Mineola, NY, Nov. 26, 1955; s. Carl Frederick and Joan Catherine (Heine) N.; m. Mary Beth Krivoruchka (div.). BA in History magna cum laude, St. John's U., Jamaica, NY, 1977; MA in History Mus. Studies, SUNY, Oneonta, 1982. Pres. Gregory Mus., Hicksville, N.Y., 1977; registrar N.Y. State Hist. Assn., Cooperstown, 1978-80; dir., curator Gadsby's Tavern Mus., Alexandria, Va., 1980-84; dir. State Mus. Pa., Harrisburg, 1984-91; exec. dir. Mackinac State Hist. Parks, Lansing, Mackinac Island, Mich., 1992—2003; pres., CEO Historic New Eng. (Soc. Preservation New England Antiquities), Boston, 2003—. Grant reviewer Inst. Mus. Svcs., Washington, 1982-90, 95—, mus. assessment prog. reviewer, 1985—, panelist, 1992-94; panelist mus. grant program Nat. Endowment for Humanities, 1990-93, panelist challenge grant program, 1997. Co-author: Gadsby's Tavern Mus. Interpretive Master Plan, 1984; contbr. articles to profl. jours. Mem. adv. bd. for Grad. History George Mason U., Fairfax, Va., 1982-84, Ctr. for Great Lakes Culture, Mich. State U., 2000-2002; adv. com. Susquehanna Mus. Art, Harrisburg, 1989-91; bd. dirs. Harrisburg-Hershey-Carlisle Tourism and Visitor Bur., 1987-91, bd. sec., 1990-91; mem. mayor's adv. bd. city of Mackinac Island, 1993-2003; mem. task force Mich. Cultural Tourism, 1998—; mem. Essex Nat. Heritage Commn., 2003-06. Fellow Mass. Hist. Soc.; mem. Assn. of Midwest Mus. (treas. 1998-2000, pres. 2000-2002, Mich. Mus. Assn. (bd. dirs. 1995-98, bd. sec. 1999-2001, Dist. Svc. award, 2002, 06), Am. Assn. Mus. (vis. com. mus. accreditation 1989—, chmn. coun. of regions 2000-01, MAP adv. com. 2002-, bd. dirs. 2003—, chair fin. com., 2005—, bd. vice chmn., 2007—), Am. Assn. for State and Local History (elections chmn. 1990, mem. performance measurement program task force 2002-03), Colonial Soc. Mass. (audit com., 2007—), Cooperstown Grad. Assn. (bd. dirs. 1985-87), St. Botolph Club(Boston). Home: 21 Grove St Winchester MA 01890-3837 Office: Hist New Eng 141 Cambridge St Boston MA 02114-2702

NOLEN, WILFRED E., church administrator; Pres. Brethren Benefit Trust, 1983. Office: 1505 Dundee Ave Elgin IL 60120-1605

NOLL, MARK A., history professor; BA in English, Wheaton Coll.; MA, Trinity Evangelical Div. Sch., Ill.; PhD in History of Christianity, Vanderbilt Univ., 1975. Faculty Wheaton Coll., Ill., 1979—, McManis prof. Christian Thought Dept. History, 2006, co-founder and dir. Inst. Study Am. Evangs., 2006; Francis A. McAnaney prof. history U. Notre Dame, 2006—. Vis. lectr. Harvard Div. Sch., Chgo. Div. Sch., Westminster Theol. Sem., Regent Coll., Vancouver, BC. Contbr. articles to religious journals. Recipient Nat. Humanities Medal, NEH, 2006. Fellow: Am. Acad. Arts & Sci. Office: Dept History U Notre Dame 219 OShaughnessy Hall Notre Dame IN 46556 Office Phone: 574-631-7574. E-mail: Mark.Noll.8@nd.edu.

NOLPH, GEORGIA BOWER, physician; b. Appleton, Minn., Jan. 26, 1938; d. Clarence Walter and Gladys Mae (Hanson) Bower; m. Karl David Nolph, July 26, 1961; children: Erika Lynn, Kristoper Karl. BA, St. Olaf Coll., 1960; MD, Woman's Med. Coll. Pa., 1964. Pvt. practice with G.H. Ferguson MD, Bala-Cynwyd, Pa., 1965-67; civil service Walter Reed Army Med. Ctr., Washington, 1967-69; instr. community health and med. practice U. Mo., Columbia, 1969-70; asst. prof. U. Mo. Med. Sch., Columbia, 1970-77, assoc. prof. family and community medicine, 1977—. Acting med. dir. Family Med. Care Ctr., U. Mo. Hosp. and Clinics, Columbia, 1980—87; med. dir. NBA Lenoir Retirement Cmty., 1987—99, Lenoir bd. dirs., 2000—05, v.p., 2001—03, pres., 2003—05. Assoc. editor. (profl. jour.) Continuing Education for the Family Physician, 1972-73. V.p. Parents for Drug Free Youth, Columbia, Mo., 1985-86, 86-87, pres. 1987-88, 88-89; bd. dir. Columbia Civic Orch., 2003—, sec., 2004—. Mem.: Boone County Med. Soc., Mo. State Med. Assn., Am. Bus. Women's Assn. (pres. Boone Belles chpt. 2004—06), Am. Med. Women's Assn. (state dir. 1975—2003, region VII gov. 1996—2003), Am. Legion Aux. Republican. Methodist. Avocations: music, reading, travel, needlecrafts. Home: 908 Hickory Hill Dr Columbia MO 65203-2320 Office: U Mo Med Sch Dept Family and Cmty Medicine 1 Hospital Dr Columbia MO 65201-5276

NOLTE, HENRY R., JR., lawyer, former automobile company executive; b. NYC, Mar. 3, 1924; s. Henry R. and Emily A. (Eisele) Nolte; m. Frances Messner, May 19, 1951; children: Gwynne Conn, Henry Reed III, Jennifer Stevens, Suzanne Saunders. BA, Duke U., 1947; LLB, U. Pa., 1949. Bar: N.Y. 1950, Mich. 1967. Assoc. Cravath, Swaine & Moore, NYC, 1951-61; assoc. counsel Ford Motor Co., Dearborn, Mich., 1961, asst. gen. counsel, 1964-71, assoc. gen. counsel, 1971-74, v.p., gen. counsel, 1974-89, Philco-Ford Corp., Phila., 1961-64; v.p., gen. counsel, sec. Ford of Europe Inc., Warley, Essex, Eng., 1967-69; gen. counsel fin. and ins. subs. Ford Motor Co., 1974-89; sr. ptnr. Miller, Canfield, Paddock & Stone, Detroit, 1989-93, of counsel, 1993—. Formerly vice chmn. and trustee Cranbrook Ednl. Cmty.; mem. Internat. and Comparative Law Ctr. of Southwestern Legal Found.; trustee Beaumont Hosp. Lt. USNR, 1943-46, PTO. Mem. ABA (past chmn. corp. gen. counsel), Mich. Bar Assn., Assn. Bar City N.Y., Assn. Gen. Counsel, Orchard Lake Country Club, Bloomfield Hills Country Club, Everglades Club (Fla.), Gulfstream Golf Club (Fla.), Ocean Club (Fla.). Episcopalian. Office: Miller Canfield Paddock & Stone 840 W Long Lake Rd Troy MI 48098-6356

NOONAN, JACK, analytics software and solutions company executive; With field engring. and sys. devel. IBM Corp., 1967—77; from with software devel., mktg., customer svc. to v.p. corp. product support Amdahl Corp., Santa Clara, Calif., 1977—85; v.p. Product Group Candle Corp., 1985—90; pres., CEO Microrim Corp., 1990—91; pres. SPSS Inc., Chgo., 1992—, CEO, 1992—, bd. dir. Bd. dir. Morningstar, Inc., Repository Technologies, Inc., Fortel Inc.; adv. com. Geneva Tech. Ptnrs., Inc. Office: SPSS Inc 233 S Wacker Dr 11th Fl Chicago IL 60606

NOONAN, SHEILA M., energy consulting company executive; BA in Bus. Adminstrn., U. St. Thomas; postgrad., Harvard U., Boston U. Numerous positions including dir. security & fire alarm bus. Honeywell; v.p. sales Cadence Networks, Cin. Office: Cadence Networks 105 E 4th St Ste 250 Cincinnati OH 45202-4006

NORA, LOIS MARGARET, neurologist, educator, academic administrator, dean; BS in Biology with honors, U. Ill., 1976; MD, Rush Med. Coll., Chgo., 1979; JD, U. Chgo., 1987; MBA, U. Ky., 2002. Fellow Am. Bd. Neurology, Am. Bd. Electrodiagnostic Medicine; bar: Ill. 1988, D.C. 1988. Intern in family medicine Cmty. Meml. Gen. Hosp., LaGrange, Ill., 1980; resident in neurology Rush-Presbyn.-St. Luke's Med. Ctr., Chgo., 1981-84, chief resident in neurology, 1983-84, fellow electromyography and neuromuscular disease, 1984-85; asst. prof. dept. neurology, asst. dean clin. curriculum Rush Med. Coll., Chgo., 1987-94, assoc. prof. dept. neurology, 1994-95; fellow Ctr. for Clin. Med. Ethics U. Chgo., 1993-95; assoc. dean acad. affairs, assoc. prof. dept. neurology U. Ky. Coll. Medicine, 1995—2002; prof. neurology U. Ky. Coll. Law, 1996—2002; pres. Northeastern Ohio Univ. Coll. of Med., 2002—, dean, 2002—. Spkr. in field. Contbr. articles to profl. jours., chpts. to books. Vice chair Epilepsy Found. of Greater Chgo., 1988-90, chair, 1991, chair strategic planning com. 1990-91, bd. dirs., 1987-94; bd. dirs. Epilepsy Found. of Am., 1992-95, co-chair quality standards com. 1992-94; mem. needs assessment com. United Way of Chgo., 1989-90; camp physician children's summer camp program Muscular Dystrophy Assn., 1984-86; vol. tchr. Christ the King Elem. Sch., 1996—2002. Mem. AMA (mem. dean's com. on family violence curriculum 1993, mem. report and resolutions subcom. for reference com. C 1997), Am. Acad. Neurology (mem. ethics com. 1997—2002), Am. Assn. Electrodiagnostic Medicine (chair profl. practice com. 1991—97, sec., treas., 1999-2002, pres.-elect, 2002-03, pres. 2003-04), Soc. Clin. Neurologists. Office: Northeastern Ohio U Coll Med PO Box 95 4209 St Rt 44 Rootstown OH 44272

NORBERG, ARTHUR LAWRENCE, JR., historian, physicist, educator; b. Providence, Apr. 13, 1938; s. Arthur Lawrence Sr. and Margaret Helen (Riley) N.; children: Catherine E. orberg Morin, Patricia A. Norberg Fetta, Timothy E., Gregory T. BS in Physics, Providence Coll., 1959; MS in Physics, U. Vt., 1962; PhD in History of Sci., U. Wis., 1974. Asst. prof. physics St. Michael's Coll., Winooski, Vt., 1961-63, 64-68; assoc. scientist Westinghouse Electric Co., Pitts., 1963-64; instr. in physics U. Wis., Whitewater, 1968-71; rsch. historian U. Calif., Berkeley, 1973-79; program mgr. NSF, Washington, 1979-81; dir. Charles Babbage Inst. for History of Info. Processing U. Minn., Mpls., 1981—93, 1999—2006, prof. history of sci. and tech., 1995—2005, assoc. prof. computer sci., 1981-95, prof. computer sci., 1995—2005, prof. emeritus, 2005—, consulting historian, 2006—. Del. Am. Coun. Learned Socs., N.Y.C., 1981-87; mem. adv. coun. NASA, Washington, 1988-93; endowed ERA Land Grant chair U. Minn., 1989-93, 99—2006. Editor: Annals of the History of Computing, 1982-93; adv. editor Tech. and Culture, 1985-92, (books) Transforming Computer Technology: Information Processing for the Pentagon, 1996, Computers and Commerce, 2005; contbr. articles to profl. jours Founding pres. City Works-A Tech. Ctr., Mpls., 1987-90; exec. dir. Charles Babbage Found., 1984-94; trustee Charles Babbage Found., 1993-96. Fellow AAAS; mem. History of Sci. Soc. (treas. 1975-80), Brit. Soc. for History of Sci., Soc. for History of Tech., Sigma Xi. E-mail: norberg@cs.umn.edu.

NORBERG, RICHARD EDWIN, physicist, researcher; b. Newark, Dec. 28, 1922; s. Arthur Edwin and Melita (Roefer) N.; m. Patricia Ann Leach, Dec. 27, 1947 (dec. July 1977); children: Karen Elizabeth, Craig Alan, Peter Douglas; m. Jeanne C. O'Brien, Apr. 1, 1978. BA, DePauw U., 1943; MA, U. Ill., 1947, PhD, 1951. Research assoc., control sytems lab. U. Ill., 1951-53, asst. prof., 1953; vis. lectr. physics Washington U., St. Louis, 1954—, mem. faculty, 1955—, prof. physics, 1958—, chmn. dept., 1962-91. Mem. editl. bd. Magnetic Rsch. Rev. Served with USAAF, 1942-46. Co-recipient ISMAR prize, 2004. Fellow Am. Phys. Soc., Internat. Soc. Magnetic Research. Home: 7134 Princeton Ave Saint Louis MO 63130-2308 Office: Washington U Dept Physics PO Box 1105 Saint Louis MO 63188-1105 Business E-Mail: ren@wuphys.wustl.edu.

NORD, HENRY J., transportation executive; b. Berlin, May 1, 1917; came to U.S., 1937, naturalized, 1943; s. Walter and Herta (Riess) N.; children: Stephen, Philip. Student, U. Oxford, Eng., 1934, Northwestern U., 1938-40, Ill. Inst. Tech., 1942; JD, De Paul U., 1949. CPA, Ill. Apprentice in export, Hamburg, Germany, 1935-37; with GATX Corp., Chgo., 1938-85, comptroller, 1961-67, v.p., 1967-71, exec. v.p., 1971-78, sr. v.p., 1978-80, v.p., 1980-82, cons., 1982-84, fin. cons., 1982—, dir., 1964-78. Dir. Planned Lighting, Inc. to 1988. Trustee DePaul U. Served to 1st lt. AUS, 1943—46. Mem. Internat. Law Assn. Clubs: Tavern (Chgo.). Home: 1000 N Lake Shore Pl Chicago IL 60611-1308 Office: 111 N Wabash Ave Chicago IL 60602-1936

NORD, ROBERT EAMOR, lawyer; b. Ogden, Utah, Apr. 11, 1945; s. Eamor Carroll and Ella Carol (Winkler) N.; m. Sherryl Anne Smith, May 15, 1969; children: Kimberly, P. Ryan, Debra, Heather, Andrew, Elizabeth. BS, Brigham Young U., 1969; JD, U. Chgo., 1972. Bar: Ill. 1972, U.S. Dist. Ct. (no. dist.) Ill. 1972, U.S. Ct. Appeals (D.C. cir.) 1974, U.S. Dist. Ct. (mid. dist.) Fla. 1976, U.S. Ct. Appeals (7th cir.) 1977, U.S. Dist. Ct. (no. dist.) Ind. 1978, U.S. Dist. Ct. (no. dist.) Fla. 1979, U.S. Supreme Ct. 1981, U.S. Dist. Ct. (ea. dist.) Mich. 1984, U.S. Ct. Appeals (11th cir.) 1985, U.S. Ct. Appeals (3d cir.) 1996, U.S. Ct. Appeals (2d cir.) 2002. Assoc. Chadwell & Kayser, Chgo., 1972-75; from assoc. to ptnr. Hinshaw & Culbertson, Chgo., 1975—2002, of counsel, 2003—. Assoc. internat. legal counsel, Area Presidency LDS Ch., Moscow, 2005, Frankfurt, Germany, 2006. Republican. Home: 481 Woodlawn Ave Glencoe IL 60022-2175 Office: Hinshaw & Culbertson 222 N La Salle St Ste 300 Chicago IL 60601-1081 Office Phone: 312-704-3120. Personal E-mail: robertnord@gmail.com.

NORDBERG, JOHN ALBERT, federal judge; b. Evanston, Ill., June 18, 1926; s. Carl Albert and Judith Ranghild (Carlson) N.; m. Jane Spaulding, June 18, 1947; children: Carol, Mary, Janet, John. Student, Carleton Coll., 1943—44, student, 1946—47; JD, U. Mich., 1950. Bar: Ill. 1950, U.S. Dist. Ct. (no. dist.) Ill. 1957, U.S. Ct. Appeals (7th cir.) 1961. Assoc. Pope & Ballard, Chgo., 1950-57; ptnr. Pope, Ballard, Shepard & Fowle, Chgo., 1957-76; judge Cir. Ct. of Cook County, Ill., 1976-82, U.S. Dist. Ct. (no. dist.) Ill., Chgo., 1982-95, sr. judge, 1995—. Editor-in-chief, bd. editors Chgo. Bar Record, 1966-74 Magistrate of Cir. Ct. and justice of peace Ill., 1957-65. Served with USN, 1944-46; PTO Mem. ABA, Chgo. Bar Assn., Am. Judicature Soc., Law Club Chgo., Legal Club Chgo., Union League Club of Chgo., Order of Coif. Office: US Dist Ct #1886 219 S Dearborn St Chicago IL 60604-1706

NORDBY, EUGENE JORGEN, orthopedic surgeon; b. Abbotsford, Wis., Apr. 30, 1918; s. Herman Preus and Lucille Violet (Korsrud) N.; m. Olive Marie

Jensen, June 21, 1941; 1 child, Jon Jorgen BA, Luther Coll., Decorah, Iowa, 1939; MD, U. Wis., 1943. Diplomate Am. Bd. Orthopaedic Surgery. Intern Madison Gen. Hosp., Wis., 1943-44, asst. in orthopedic surgery Wis., 1944-48; practice medicine specializing in orthopedic surgery Madison, Wis., 1948—. Pres. Bone and Joint Surgery Assocs., S.C., 1969—91; chief staff Madison Gen. Hosp., 1957—63; assoc. clin. prof. U. Wis. Med. Sch., 1961—; bd. dirs. Wis. Physicians Svcs., 1958—, Norweguan Am. Geneal. Ctr., Naeseth Libr.; chmn. Wis. Physicians Svcs., 1979—; dir. Wis. Regional Med. Program, Chgo. Madison and No. R.R.; bd. govs. Wis. Health Care Liability Ins. Plan; chmn. trustees S.M.S. Realty Corp.; mem. bd. attys. Profl. Responsibility of Wis. Supreme Ct., 1992—. Mem. editl. bd. Clin. Orthopaedics and Related Research, 1964—, Spine, 1994-2000. Pres. Vesterheim Norwegian Am. Mus., Decorah, Iowa, 1968-97, pres. emeritus, 1997—. Served to capt. M.C., AUS, 1944-46 Decorated Knight 1st class Royal Norwegian Order St. Olav, 1979; named Notable Norwegian Dane County orwegian-Am. Fest, 1995; recipient Disting. Svc. award Internat. Rotary,1 987, Den Hoyeste Aere award Vesterheim, 1993, Lyman Smith, M.D. and Eugene J. ordby, M.D. award for minimally invasive spine surgery established N.Am. Spine Soc., 1998, The Nordby Bldg. designated Wis. Phys. Svc. Health Ins. Co., 1998, Internat. Therapy Soc. Lifetime Achievement award, 2006. Fellow Wisdom Hall of Fame; mem. Am. Acad. Orthop. Surgeons (bd. dirs. 1972-73, 1st chmn. bd. councilors 1972), Clin. Orthop. Soc., Assn. Bone and Joint Surgeons (pres. 1973), Internat. Soc. Study Lumbar Spine, State Med. Soc. Wis. (chmn. 1968-76, treas. 1976-97, Coun. award 1976), Am. Orthop. Assn., N.Am. Spine Soc., Internat. Intradiscal Therapy Soc. (sec. 1987-99, exec. dir. 1996-2006, exec. dir. emeritus 2006—. Eugene J. Nordby Rsch. award established in his honor 1993, Lifetime Achievement award 2006), Wis. Orthop. Soc., Dane County Med. Soc. (pres. 1957), Nat. Exch. Club, Madison Torske Klubben (founder, pres. 1978-98, pres. emeritus 1998—), Norwegian-Am. Orthop. Soc., Am. Acad. Orthop. Surgeons, Am. Orthop. Assn., Norwegian Am. Found., Norwegian-Am. Geneal. Ctr. (bd. mem. 2006), Phi Chi. Lutheran. Home: 7824 Courtyard Dr Madison WI 53719 Office: 304 S Whitney Way Madison WI 53705 Home Phone: 608-831-2356; Office Phone: 608-831-2356. Personal E-mail: ejnor@charter.net.

NORDLAND, GERALD, museum administrator, historian, consultant; b. LA; AB, JD, U. So. Calif. Dean of faculty Chouinard Art Sch., LA, 1960-64; dir. Washington Gallery of Modern Art, 1964-66, San Francisco Mus. Art, 1966-72, Frederick S. Wight Art Galleries, UCLA, 1973-77, Milw. Art Mus., 1977-85; ind. curator, author, editor Chgo., 1985—. Author: Paul Jenkins, 1972, Gaston Lachaise/The Man and His Work, 1974, Richard Diebenkorn, 1987, rev. edit., 2001, Frank Lloyd Wright: In the Realm of Ideas, 1988, Zhou Brothers, 1994, Ynez Johnston, 1996, Lev Syrkin, 1998, Twentieth Century American Drawings, 1999, Jon Schueler: To The North, 2002, In the Spirit of the Times, 2003, Emerson Woelffer: A Solo Flight, 2003, Richard Drebenkorn in New Mexico, 2007, Breaking the Mold, 2007. Gaston Lachaise Found. grantee, 1973-74; John Simon Guggenheim Found. fellow, 1985-86. Home and Office: 645 W Sheridan Rd Chicago IL 60613-3316 Office Phone: 773-348-5133. Personal E-mail: geraldnordland@sbcglobal.net.

NORDLIE, ROBERT CONRAD, biochemistry educator; b. Willmar, Minn., June 11, 1930; s. Peder Conrad and Myrtle (Spindler) N.; m. Sally Ann Christianson, Aug. 23, 1959; children: Margaret, Melissa, John. BS St. Cloud State Coll., Minn., 1952; MS, U. N.D., 1957, PhD, 1960. Tchg., rsch. asst. biochemistry U. N.D. Med. Sch., Grand Forks, 1955-60, James J. Hill rsch. prof. biochemistry, 1962-74, Chester Fritz disting. prof. biochemistry, 1974—, Cornatzer prof., chmn. dept. biochemistry and molecular biology, 1983-2000, Chester Fritz disting. emeritus prof., 2000—. Hon. prof. San Marcos U., Lima, Peru, 1981, 82—; emeritus prof., 2000-; NIH fellow Inst. Enzyme Rsch., U. Wis., 1960-61; mem. biochemistry study sect. NIH; merit rev. com. VA, 1994—; cons. enzymology Oak Ridge, 1961—; vis. prof. Tokyo Biomed. Inst., 1984; mem. predoctoral fellowship rev. group Howard Hughes Inst., 1990-93. Mem. editorial bd.: Jour. Biol. Chemistry, Biochimca et Biophysica Acta. Research publs. on enzymology relating to metabolism of various carbohydrates in mammalian livers, regulation blood sugar levels. Served with AUS, 1953-55. Recipient Disting. Alumnus award St. Cloud State U., 1983; recipient Sigma Xi Rsch. award, 1969, Golden Apple award U. N.D., 1968, Edgar Dale award U. N.D., 1983, Burlington No. Faculty Scholar award, 1987, Thomas J. Clifford Faculty Achievement award for excellence in rsch. U. N.D. Found., 1993, Hippocratic Dignity award, 2005. Mem. AAAS, Am. Soc. Biol. Chemistry and Molecular Biology, Am. Chem. Soc., Internat. Union Biochemists, Soc. Exptl. Biology and Medicine, Am. Inst. Nutrition, Sigma Xi, Alpha Omega Alpha. Home: 162 Columbia Ct Grand Forks ND 58203-2947 Office Phone: 701-777-2751. Business E-Mail: rnordlie@medicine.nodak.edu.

NORDLOH, DAVID JOSEPH, literature and language professor, dean; b. Cin., May 3, 1942; s. Joseph Westerman and Josephine (Fusz) N.; m. Barbara Jane Beddow, June 29, 1968; children: Geoffrey David, Jennifer Ellen Blum. AB in English, Coll. of Holy Cross, 1964; PhD in English, Ind. U., 1969. From asst. prof. to prof. emeritus English Ind. U., Bloomington, 1969—2007, prof. emeritus English, 2007—, assoc. dean faculties, 2003—06. Vis. assoc. prof. U. Va., Charlottesville, 1978; dir. Am. Studies Program, Ind. U., 1987-94. Gen. editor: A Selected Edition of W.D. Howells, 1974—; editor: Twayne's United States Author's Series, 1978-90; co-editor: American Literary Scholarship, 1986—; mem. editl. bd. Walter Scott Edition, 1984—; adv. bd. The Writings of James Fenimore Cooper, 1995—. Pres. Bloomington Symphony Orch., 1986-88, 93-94. Fulbright scholar, 1982-83. Mem. Am. Lit. Assn. Home: 1601 Morganton Rd L-3 Pinehurst NC 28374 Personal E-mail: nordloh@indiana.edu.

NORDLUND, JAMES JOHN, dermatologist; b. St. Paul, Aug. 11, 1939; m. Mary Flanagan, Sept. 28, 1963; children: Christa, Michael, Marguerite. BA, St. John's U., 1961; BS, U. Minn., 1963, MD, 1965. Diplomate Am. Bd. Internal Medicine, Am. Bd. Dermatology. Clin. investigator VA, West Haven, Conn., 1977-80; assoc. prof. dermatology Yale U., New Haven, 1978-82, prof. dermatology, 1982-83; prof., chmn. U. Cin., 1983—98, prof., 1998—2000, prof. emeritus, 2002—. Mem. nat. adv. com. St. John's U., Collegeville, Minn. Editor: Dermatology Resource Manual, 1988, Pigmentary Disorders, 1988, Cutaneous Aging, 1988. Lt. comdr. USPHS, 1967-69. Mem. Soc. Investigative Dermatology, Am. Dermatol. Assn., Pan Am. Soc. for Pigment Cell Rsch. (pres. 1986-91), Am. Acad. Dermatology (bd. dirs. 1987-91), N.Y. Acad. Sci., Assn. Profs. Dermatology, Internat. Fedn. Pigment Cell Socs. (sec.-treas. 1989-92), Sigma Xi. Avocations: scuba, hiking, woodworking, gardening. Office: GHA 7423 Mason Montgomery Rd Mason OH 45040 E-mail: jjnordlund@fuse.net.

NORDMAN, CHRISTER ERIC, chemistry professor; b. Helsinki, Finland, Jan. 23, 1925; came to U.S., 1948, naturalized, 1960; s. Eric Johan and Gertrud (Nordgren) N.; m. Barbara Lorraine Neal, Nov. 28, 1952 (div. 1993); children: Christina, Aleta, Eric, Carl; m. Outi Marttila, Dec. 28, 1994. Dipl. Ing., Finnish Inst. Tech., Helsinki, 1949; PhD, U. Minn., 1953. Research asso. Inst. Cancer Research, Phila., 1953-55; mem. faculty U. Mich., Ann Arbor, 1955—, prof. chemistry, 1964-95; prof. emeritus, 1995—. Mem. U.S. Nat. Com. Crystallography, 1970-72. Served with Finnish Army, 1943-44. NIH spl. fellow, 1971-72; recipient A.L. Patterson award, 1997. Fellow AAAS; mem. Am. Chem. Soc., Am. Phys. Soc., Am. Crystallographic Assn., Finnish Soc. Scis. and Letters. Home: 27 Haverhill Ct Ann Arbor MI 48105-1406 Office: Univ Mich Dept Chemistry Ann Arbor MI 48109 Business E-Mail: cnordman@umich.edu.

NORDWALD, CHARLES, state legislator; b. Aug. 25, 1955; m. Nina Hoelscher; 3 children. Mem. dist. 19 Mo. Ho. of Reps., 1992—; co-owner Allen & Nordwald Auction Svc., Warrenton, Mo. Mem. Warren County Fair Bd. Mem. NRA, Montgomery City C. of C., Elks Club. Office: 20 Hawthorne Warrenton MO 63383

NORGLE, CHARLES RONALD, SR., federal judge; b. Mar. 3, 1937; BBA, Northwestern U., Evanston, Ill., 1964; JD, John Marshall Law Sch., Chgo., 1969. Asst. state's atty. DuPage County, Ill., 1969-71, dep. pub. defender Ill., 1971-73, assoc. judge Ill., 1973-77, 78-81, cir. judge Ill., 1977-78, 81-84; judge U.S. Dist. Ct. (no. dist.) Ill., Chgo., 1984—2006, Criminal Law Com., Chgo., 2006—. Mem. exec. com. No. Dist. Ill.; mem. 7th Cir. Jud. Coun., 7th Cir. Jud. Conf. planning com., subcom. grant requests Fed. Defender Orgn., Fed. Defender Svcs. Com.; mem. Jud. Conf. Criminal Law Com.; adj. faculty Northwestern U. Sch. Law, John Marshall Law Sch., Chgo.; pres. Atticus Finch Inn Ct. Mem. ABA, Fed. Bar Assn., Fed. Circuit Bar Assn., Ill. Bar Assn., DuPage County (Ill.) Bar Assn., at. Attys. Assn., DuPage Assn. Women Attys., Chgo. Legal Club, Northwestern Club. Office: US Dist Ct 219 S Dearborn St Ste 2346 Chicago IL 60604-1802

NORINS, ARTHUR LEONARD, dermatologist, educator; b. Chgo., Dec. 2, 1928; s. Russell Joseph and Elsie (Lindemann) N.; m. Mona Lisa Wetzer, Sept. 12, 1954; children: Catherine, Nan, Jane, Arthur. BS in Chem. Engring, Northwestern U., 1951, MS in Physiology, 1953, MD, 1955. Diplomate: Am. Bd. Dermatology; subcert. in dermatopathology. Intern U. Mich., Ann Arbor, 1955-56; resident in dermatology Northwestern U., Chgo., 1956-59; asst. prof. Stanford U., 1961-64; prof., chmn. dept. dermatology, prof. pathology Ind. U. Sch. Medicine, Indpls., 1964-93, prof. emeritus, 1993—. Mem. staff Riley Children's Hosp., Univ. Hosp., Wishard Hosp.; cons. VA Hosp. Contbr. articles to profl. jours. Capt. M.C. U.S. Army, 1959-61. Recipient Pres.' award Ind. U., 1979 Fellow ACP; mem. Am. Acad. Dermatology (bd. dirs.), Am. Dermatol. Assn., Soc. Pediatric Dermatology (founder, past pres.), Am. Soc. Dermatopathology, Am. Soc. Photobiology (founder), Soc. Investigative Dermatology. Home: 10100 Torre Ave Apt 211 Cupertino CA 95014-2168 Office: 550 University Blvd Ste 3240 Indianapolis IN 46202-5149 E-mail: norinssr@ix.netcom.com.

NORLING, RAYBURN, food service executive; b. 1934; Pres. Willmar (Minn) Poultry Co., Inc.; with Norling Farms, Inc., Svea, Minn., 1979—. Office: Willmar Poultry Co Inc 3735 County Road 5 SW Willmar MN 56201-9712

NORMAN, ART, newscaster; married. BS Math and Physics, Johnson C. Smith U. Tv engr. Sta. WCCB-TV, Charlotte, NC, 1969; reporter Sta. WPCQ-TV, Charlotte, NC, Sta. WSOC-TV, Charlotte, NC; reporter, weekend anchor Sta. WMAR-TV, Balt., 1979—82; gen. assignment reporter NBC 5, Chgo., 1982, co-anchors weekday editions 5 pm, 5:30 pm, 6 pm and 11 am. Spokesman, on air host of telethon United Negro Coll. Fund. Recipient award, N.C. Radio and TV News Dirs. Assn., 1975, Sch. Bell award, Nat. Assn. Educators, 1978, award, Internat. Radio and TV News Dirs. Assn., 1984, Emmy award, 1986, Wilbur award, Religious Pub. Rels. Coun., 1987, Chgo. Emmy award, 1989, award for Best Investigative Reporting, AP, 1992—93. Mem.: Omega Psi Phi. Office: NBC 454 N Columbus Dr Chicago IL 60611

NORMAN, CHARLES HENRY, broadcast executive; b. St. Louis, June 13, 1920; s. Charles Henry and Grace Vincent (Francis) N. BS, U. So. Calif., LA, 1942. Announcer WIL, KSTL Radio Stas., St. Louis, 1948-55; owner Norman Broadcasting Co., St. Louis, 1961—. Lt. USN, 1943-45. Mem. St. Louis Ambassadros, Phi Kappa Phi. Episcopalian. Office: Portland Towers 265 Union Blvd Apt 1315 Saint Louis MO 63108-1240

NORMAN, JACK LEE, church administrator, consultant; b. Lancaster, Ohio, Aug. 5, 1938; s. Clearence Herbert and Jeanette Belle (Bennett) N.; m. Boneda Mae Coppock, June 30, 1957; children: Anthony Lee, Becky Lynn Norman Hux. Student, Circleville Bible Coll., Olivet U. Ordained min. Ch. of Christ, 1961. Pastor Chs. of Christ in Christian Union, Chillicothe, Ohio, 1959-62, 65-90, Winchester, Ohio, 1962-65, dist. supt. Circleville, Ohio, 1990—. Trustee Chs. of Christ in Christian Union, mem. dist. bd., mem. ch. ext. bd., mem. bd. exam. and ordination, mem. Evang. Christian Youth Bd. Trustee Circleville Bible Coll. Sgt. USNG, 1956-59. Avocations: fishing, boating, classic cars. Office: Ch of Christ in Christian Union PO Box 30 Circleville OH 43113-0030

NORMAN, LALANDER STADIG, retired insurance company executive; b. Binford, ND, Apr. 10, 1912; s. John and Corinne (Stadig) N.; m. Garnet Johnston, Nov. 8, 1941; children: Eric John, Martha Mary Norman Neely, Carol Jean Norman Wellborn, Shirley Ann Norman Cook. AB, U. Mich., 1935, MBA, 1937. Actuarial asst. Central Life Ins. Co. of Ill., Chgo., 1937-40, mgr. Eastern dept., 1940-41; actuary Mich. Life Ins. Co., Detroit, 1941-43; asst. actuary Guarantee Mut. Life Co., Omaha, 1946-49; asso. actuary Am. United Life Ins. Co., Indpls., 1949, actuary, 1950-77, dir., 1959-77, v.p., 1962-69, sr. v.p., 1969-77; ret., 1977. Bd. mgrs. AUL Fund B, 1969-84, chmn., 1973-84; actuary Ind. Dept. Ins., 1977-79 Bd. dirs. Cyprus Village Assn., 1981, 1983—85. With USNR, 1943—46. Recipient Navy Commendation award, 1946, Theta Xi Distinguished Service award, 1958. Fellow Soc. Actuaries; mem. Am. Acad. Actuaries, Indpls. Actuarial Club (past pres.), Woodland Country Club (Carmel), Sugarmill Woods Golf and Racquet Club, So. Woods Golf Club, Phi Beta Kappa, Theta Xi (regional dir. 1953-59), Phi Kappa Phi, Beta Gamma Sigma. Republican. Home: Sugarmill Woods 21 Graytwig Ct W Homosassa FL 34446-4727 Office: 1 American Sq Indianapolis IN 46282-0020

NORQUIST, JOHN OLAF, former mayor; b. Princeton, NJ, Oct. 22, 1949; s. Ernest O. and Jeannette (Nelson) N.; m. Susan R. Mudd, Dec. 1986; children: Benjamin Edward, Katherine Elisabeth. Student, Augustana Coll., Rock Island, Ill., 1967-69; BS, U. Wis., 1971, MPA, 1988. Assemblyman Wis. State Assembly, Madison, 1974-82, co-chmn. state joint com. fin., 1980-81; mem. Wis. State Senate, 82-88, asst. majority leader, 1984-85, 87; mayor City of Milw., 1988—2004. Adj. assoc. prof. Sch. Arch. U. Wis., Marquette U. Author: The Wealth of Cities, 1998. Bd. dirs. Congress for the New Urbanism. Sgt. USAR, 1971-77. Mem. Wis. Alliance of Cities, Congress for New Urbanism (bd. dirs.). Democrat. Presbyterian. Avocation: map collecting.

NORRIS, ALAN EUGENE, federal judge; b. Columbus, Ohio, Aug. 15, 1935; s. J. Russell and Dorothy A. (Shrader) N.; m. Nancy Jean Myers, Apr. 15, 1962 (dec. Jan. 1986); children: Tom Edward Jackson, Tracy Elaine; m. Carol Lynn Spohn, Nov. 10, 1990. BA, Otterbein Coll., 1957, HLD (hon.), 1991; cert., U. Paris, 1956; LLB, YU, 1960; LLM, U. Va., 1986; HLD (hon.), Capital U. Law Sch., 2001. Bar: Ohio 1960, US Dist. Ct. (so. dist) Ohio 1962, US Dist. Ct. (no. dist) Ohio 1964. Law clk. to judge Ohio Supreme Ct., Columbus, 1960-61; assoc. Vorys, Sater, Seymour & Pease, Columbus, 1961-62; ptnr. Metz, Bailey, Norris & Spicer, Westerville, Ohio, 1962-80; judge Ohio Ct. Appeals (10th dist.), Columbus, 1981-86, US Ct. Appeals (6th cir.), Columbus, 1986—. Contbr. articles to profl. jours. Mem. Ohio Ho. of Reps., Columbus, 1967—80. Named Outstanding Young Man, Westerville Jaycees, 1971; recipient Legislator of Yr. award Ohio Acad. Trial Lawyers, Columbus, 1972. Mem. Ohio Bar Assn., Columbus Bar Assn. Lodges: Masons (master 1966-67). Republican. Methodist. Office: US Ct Appeals 328 US Courthouse 85 Marconi Blvd Columbus OH 43215-2823

NORRIS, ALBERT STANLEY, psychiatrist, educator; b. Sudbury, Ont., Can., July 14, 1926; s. William and Mary (Zell) N.; m. Dorothy James, Sept. 2, 1950; children: Barbara Ellen, Robert Edward, Kimberly Ann. MD, U. Western Ont., 1951. Intern Ottawa (Ont.) Civic Hosp., 1951-52; resident in psychiatry U. Iowa, Psychopathic Hosp., Iowa City, 1953-55, Boston City Hosp., 1955-56; practice medicine Kingston, Ont., Canada, 1956-57; instr. Queen's U., Kingston, 1956-57; asst. prof. psychiatry U. Iowa, 1957-62, asso. prof., 1962-64, 1965-66, prof., 1966-72; asso. prof. U. Oreg., 1964-65; prof. So. Ill. U. Sch. Medicine, Springfield, 1972-84, chmn. dept. psychiatry, 1972-82; prof. emeritus, 1984—; practice medicine specializing in psychiatry Cedar Rapids, Iowa, 1984—. Vis. prof. U. Auckland, N.Z., U. Otago, New Zealand, U. Liverpool. Contbr. chpts. to books, articles to med. jours. Fellow Am. Psychiat. Soc. (life); mem. AMA, Am. Psychopath. Assn., Soc. Biol. Psychiatry, Can. Psychiat. Soc., Am. Soc. Psychosomatic Ob-Gyn, Royal Soc. Medicine. Republican. Presbyterian. Home: 5 Penfro Dr Iowa City IA 52246-4927 Office: PO Box 1408 Cedar Rapids IA 52406-1408 Personal E-mail: asnorris@msn.com.

NORRIS, ANDREA SPAULDING, art museum director; b. Apr. 2, 1945; d. Edwin Baker and Mary Gretchen (Brendle) Spaulding. BA, Wellesley Coll., 1967; MA, NYU, 1969, PhD, 1977. Intern dept. western European arts Met. Mus. Art, NYC, 1970, 72; rsch. and editorial asst. Inst. Fine Arts NYU, 1971, lectr. Washington Sq. Coll., 1976-77; lectr. Queens Coll. CUNY, 1973-74; asst. to dir. Art Gallery Yale U., New Haven, 1977-80, lectr. art history, 1979-80; chief curator Archer M. Huntington Art Gallery, Austin, Tex., 1980-88; lectr. art history Dept. Art U. Tex., Austin, 1984-88; dir. Spencer Mus. Art U. Kans., Lawrence, 1988—2004. Co-author: (catalogue) Medals and Plaquettes from the Molinari Collection at Bowdoin College, 1976; author: (exhbn. catalogues) Jackson Pollock: New-Found Works, 1978, Vanished Voices, The Legacy of the Northeast Kansas Indians, 2004; exhbn. The Sforza Court: Milan in the Renaissance 1450-1535, 1988-89, Am. Indian Traditions Transformed, 2000. Mem.: Mus. Loan Network (adv. bd. 2002—04), Assn. Art Mus. Dir., Coll. Art Assn. (bd. dir. 2000—05, v.p. for coms. 2002—04, v.p. for ann. conf. 2004—05), Renaissance Soc. Am., Phi Beta Kappa. Office: Spencer Mus Art U Kans 1301 Mississippi St Lawrence KS 66045-7500 Home Phone: 785-841-8436. E-mail: asnorris@earthlink.net.

NORRIS, CLARENCE W. (CLANCY NORRIS), former state agency administrator; Former pres., CEO, chmn. Kans. State Bank, Holton, Kans.; commr. Kans. State Banking Dept., 2003—06.

NORRIS, JAMES RUFUS, JR., chemist, educator; b. Anderson, SC, Dec. 29, 1941; s. James Rufus and Julia Lee (Walker) N.; m. Carol Anne Poetzsch, Dec. 28, 1963; children: Sharon Adele, David James. BS, U. N.C., 1963; PhD, Washington U., St. Louis, 1968. Postdoctoral appointee Argonne (Ill.) Nat. Lab., 1968-71, asst. chemist, 1971-74, chemist, 1974-79, photosynthesis group leader, 1979-95, sr. chemist, 1991-95; prof. dept. chemistry U. Chgo., 1995—. Prof. chemistry U. Chgo., 1984—; chmn. internat. organizing com. 7th Internat. Conf. on Photochemical Conversion and Storage of Solar Energy, Northwestern U., Evanston, Ill., 1988. Co-editor: Photochemical Energy Conversion, 1989; mem. editorial bd. Applied Magnetic Resonance Jour., 1989—. Recipient Disting. Peformance award U. Chgo., 1977, 2 R&D 100 awards R&D mag., 1988, E.O. Lawrence Meml. award Dept. of Energy, 1990, Rumford Premium AAAS, 1992, Humboldt Rsch. award for Sr. Scientists, 1992, Zavoisky award Am. Acad. Arts and Scis., 1994. Mem. Am. Chem. Soc., Biophysical Soc. Achievements include discovery that the primary donor of photosynthesis is a dimeric special pair of chlorophyll molecules. Office: U Chgo Dept Chemistry 5735 S Ellis Ave Chicago IL 60637-1403

NORRIS, JOHN HART, lawyer, director; b. New Bedford, Mass., Aug. 4, 1942; s. Edwin Arter and Harriet Joan (Winter) Norris; m. Anne Kiley Monaghan, June 10, 1967; children: Kiley Anne, Amy O'Shea. BA, Ind. U., 1964; JD, U. Mich., 1967. Bar: Mich. 1968, U.S. Ct. Mil. Appeals 1969, U.S. Supreme Ct. 1974, U.S. Ct. Claims 1975, U.S. Tax Ct. 1979. From assoc. to ptnr. Monaghan, Campbell, LoPrete, McDonald and Norris, 1970-83; of counsel Dickinson, Wright, Moon, Van Dusen & Freeman, 1983-84, ptnr., 1985—; dep. asst. atty. gen. State of Mich., 1997—. Natural gas law counsel to claims mediator Columbia Gas Transmission Corp.; chpt. 11 bankruptcy procs. Wilmington (Del.) Bankruptcy Ct., 1992—; dep. asst. atty. gen. State of Mich., 1997—; bd. dirs. Prime Securities Corp., Ray M. Whyte Co., Ward-Williston Drilling Co., One Stop Capital Shop. Contbr. articles to profl. jours. Trustee Boys and Girls Clubs Southeastern Mich., 1979—, Mich. Wildlife Habitat Found.; trustee, bd. dirs. African Wildlife Found.; mem. Rep. State Fin. Com.; founder, co-chmn. Rep. Majority Club; trustee Mercy Coll., Detroit, Detroit Hist. Soc., 1984—; trustee, 1st vice chmn. Salk Inst. Fellow: Mich. State Bar Found.; mem.: ABA (litig. and natural resources sects.), Def. Orientation Conf. Assn., Fin. and Estate Planning Coun. Detroit, Am. Arbitration Assn., Detroit Bar Assn. (mem. pub. adv. com.), Oakland County Bar Assn., State Bar Mich. (chmn. environ. law sect. 1982—83, probate and trust law sect., mem. energy conservation task force, mem. oil and gas com.), Mich. Oil and Gas Assn. (mem. legal and legis. com.), Detroit Zool. Soc., Yondotega Club, Bloomfield Hills Country Club, Turtle Lake Club, Prismatic Club, Hundred Club, Thomas M. Cooley Club, Detroit Athletic Econ. Club (Detroit), Blue Key, Phi Delta Phi. Home: 1325 Buckingham Ave Birmingham MI 48009-5881 Office: Dickinson Wright 38525 Woodward Ave Ste 2000 Bloomfield Hills MI 48304-2971 Home Phone: 248-646-7139; Office Phone: 248-433-7227. Business E-Mail: jnorris@dickinsonwright.com.

NORRIS, RICHARD PATRICK, museum director, historian, educator; b. Galveston, Tex., May 21, 1944; s. William Gerard and Iris Elsa (Allington) N.; m. Therese Louise Aalid, July 27, 1974; children: William Gerard, John Patrick. BA, Ohio State U., 1966; MA in Polit. Sci., SUNY, Binghamton, 1968; PhD in Am. Studies, U. Minn., 1976. Instr. U. Minn., Mpls., 1970-76; lectr. U. Md., Europe/Asia, 1976-78; dir. Chippewa Valley Mus., Eau Claire, Wis., 1978-80, Kalamazoo Valley Mus., 1985—; curator of history Mus. Sci. & Hist., Fort Worth, 1980-85. Lectr. Tex. Christian U., Fort Worth, Tex., 1981—85; cons. Am. Assn. Mus., Washington, 1979—, NEH, Washington, 1989; adj. prof. We. Mich. U., Kalamazoo, 1986—. Author: History by Design, 1984; book reviewer Mus. News, History News; contbr. articles to profl. jours. Mem.: Assn. Midwest Mus., Internat. Coun. Mus., Am. Assn. State and Local History, Am. Assn. Mus., Rotary (dir. Kalamazoo club 1991—93, pres. 1999—2000). Office: Kalamazoo Valley Museum PO Box 4070 Kalamazoo MI 49003-4070 Home Phone: 269-345-5295; Office Phone: 269-373-7988. Business E-Mail: rnorris@kvcc.edu.

NORRIS, TRACY HOPKINS, retired public relations executive; b. Ainsworth, Iowa, Nov. 1, 1927; s. Lee E. and Ruth C. (Simpson) N.; m. Emilie Lathrop, Nov. 11, 1956; 1 child, Shawn Tracy. BA, Cornell Coll., 1952; MA, U. Iowa, 1957. Admissions counselor Cornell Coll., Mt. Vernon, Iowa, 1952—54; dir. news bur. Wittenberg U., Springfield, Ohio, 1956—70; exec. dir. rels. and comm. Ball State U., Muncie, Ind., 1970—88; ret., 1988. Exec. United Way Springfield, Ohio, Muncie, 1965—. Served with USN, 1945-48. Recipient Silver Anvil award, Pub. Rels. Soc. Am., 1967. Mem.: Coun. for Advancement and Support Edn., Exch. Club. Lutheran. Avocations: golf, travel, gardening. Home: 3700 Allen Ct Muncie IN 47304 Personal E-mail: tnorris629@aol.com.

NORTH, DOUGLASS CECIL, economist, educator; b. Cambridge, Mass., Nov. 5, 1920; s. Henry Emerson and Edith (Saitta) North; m. Elisabeth Willard Case, Sept. 28, 1972; children from previous marriage: Douglas Alan, Christopher, Malcolm Peter. BA, U. Calif., Berkeley, 1942, PhD, 1952; D in Natural Scis. (hon.), U. of Cologne, Federal Republic of Germany, 1988, U. Zurich, Switzerland, 1993, Stockholm Sch. of Econs., Sweden, 1994, Prague Sch. Econs., 1995. Asst. prof. econs. U. Wash., 1950—56, assoc. prof., 1957—60, prof., 1960—83, chmn. dept., 1967—79, prof. emeritus, 1983—; dir. Inst. Econ. Research, 1960—66, Nat. Bur. Econ. Research, 1967—87; Spencer T. Olin prof. in arts and scis. Washington U., St. Louis, 1983—. Pitt prof. Am. history and instns. Cambridge U., 1981—82; fellow Ctr. for Advanced Study on Behavioral Scis., 1987—88; co-founder Internat. Soc. for the New Institutional Econ., 1997. Author: The Economic Growth of the U.S. 1790-1860, 1961, Growth and Welfare in the American Past, 1966; author: (with L. Davis) Institutional Change and American Economic Growth, 1971; author: (with R. Miller) The Economics of Public Issues, 1971, 1974, 1976, 1978, 1980; author: (with R. Thomas) The Rise of the Western World, 1973; author: Structure and Change in Economic History, 1981, Institutions, Institutional Change and Economic Performance, 1990. Recipient obel Prize in Econ. Sci., Nobel Found., 1993; fellow Guggenheim Found., 1972—73; grantee, Social Sci. Rsch. Coun., 1962, Rockefeller Found., 1960—63, Ford Found., 1961, 1966, NSF, 1967—73, Bradley Found., 1986—. Fellow: Am. Acad. Arts and Scis.; mem.: Econ. History Assn., The Brit. Acad. (corr.), Am. Econ. Assn. Office: Dept Econ Washington Univ Rm 305 Elliot Hall Box 1208 Saint Louis MO 63130

NORTH, JOHN E., JR., lawyer; b. Omaha, Feb. 26, 1952; s. John E. and Joyce (Zimmerman) N.; m. Pamela K. Black, Nov. 22, 1978; children: Stuart, Jeremy, Katherine, Jacqueline, Rebecca. BSBA, U. Nebr., 1974; JD, Creighton U., Nebr., 1977. Bar: Nebr. 1977, U.S. Dist Ct. Nebr. 1977, U.S. Ct. Appeals (8th cir.) Nebr. 1979, U.S. Tax Ct. Nebr. 1980, U.S. Dist Ct. (no. dist.) Texas, 1993. Assoc. McGrath, North, Dwyer, O'Leary & Martin, Omaha, 1977-78, Lathrop, Albright & Swenson, Omaha, 1978-80; ptnr. Fromkin, Herzog, Jabenis & North, Omaha, 1980-84; prin. North & Black, PC, Omaha, 1984-89, McGrath, North, Mullin & Kratz, PC, Omaha, 1989—. Mem. ABA, Nebraska State Bar Assn., Omaha Bar Assn., Nebraska Assn. Trial Attys.

NORTH, WALTER, state legislator; b. Jan. 31, 1933; Grad., Mich. State U. County commr.; mem. Mich. Senate from 37th dist., Lansing, 1995—. Chmn. agriculture & forestry com. Mich. State Senate, edn. com., transp. com., tourism com., joint com. on adminstrv. rules. Address: PO Box 30036 Lansing MI 48909-7536

NORTHRIP, ROBERT EARL, lawyer; b. Sleeper, Mo., May 8, 1939; s. Novel and Jessie (Burch) N.; m. Linda Kay Francis, June 15, 1968; children: Robert E. Jr., William F., Darryl F., David F. BA, Southwest Mo. State, 1960; MA, U. N.C., 1965; JD, U. Mo., 1968. Bar: Mo. 1968, U.S. Dist. Ct. (we. dist.) Mo. 1968, U.S. Ct. Appeals (10th cir.) 1976, U.S. Ct. Appeals (8th cir.) 1980, U.S. Ct. Appeals (9th cir.) 1983, U.S. Ct. Appeals (3d cir.) 1987, U.S. Supreme Ct. 1978. Ptnr. Shook, Hardy & Bacon, Kansas City, Mo., 1968—. Active Nelson Art Gallery, Soc. of Fellows, Kans. City, Mo. 1st lt. US Army, 1963-65. Mem. Mo. Bar Assn.,

Lawyers Assn. Kansas City, Mo. Orgn. Def. Lawyers, Kansas City Met. Bar Assn., U. Mo. Alumni Assn. (past pres. Kansas City chpt.), Nat. Soc. Arts and Letters. Republican. Avocations: baseball, football. Office: Shook Hardy & Bacon 2555 Grand Blvd Kansas City MO 64108-2613 Home: 6439 Wenonga Rd Mission Hills KS 66208 Office Phone: 816-474-6550. Business E-Mail: rnorthrip@shb.com.

NORTON, LLOYD DARRELL, research soil scientist; b. Batesville, Ind., Oct. 20, 1953; s. Milton Walker and Enamay (Doan) N.; children: Benjamin D., Amber J., Jon A. BS, Purdue U., 1975, MS, 1976; PhD, Ohio State U., 1981. Soil scientist Ind. Dept. Natural Resources, Indpls., 1974; rsch. assoc. Purdue U., West Lafayette, Ind., 1975-77, Ohio State U., Columbus, 1977-82; soil scientist and dir. Nat. Soil Erosion Rsch. Lab. USDA, West Lafayette, 1982—; prof. agronomy and earth and atmospheric scis. Purdue U., 1982—. Cons. AID, Washington, 1986, 87, FAO, Rome, 1991; vis. scientist div. soils Commonwealth Sci. and Indsl. Rsch. Orgn., Canberra, Australia, 1990. Contbd. over 140 articles to profl. jours. Mem. Internat. Soc. Soil Sci. (cert. of appreciation 1988), Soil Sci. Soc. Am. (cert. of appreciation 1988), World Assn. Soil Water Cons. Office: Purdue U USDA Nat Soil Erosion Lab 1196 Soils West Lafayette IN 47907-1196

NORTON, ROBERT R., JR., former food products executive; b. 1946; BS, Mo. Western State Coll., 1966; MBA, N.W. Mo. State U., 1968. Sec., treas. Dugdale Packing Co., St. Joseph, Mo., 1966-86; with BeefAmerica Operating Co., Inc., Omaha, 1986-96, pres., 1988-96. Office: Beef America Ste 216 3610 Dodge St Omaha NE 68131-3218

NOSBUSCH, KEITH D., multi-industry high-technology company executive; BS in Elec. and Computer Engring., U. Wis., Milw., 1974, MBA, 1976. Joined Allen-Bradley (subs. Rockwell Internat.), Milw., 1974; mktg. devel. specialist, indsl. control div. Rockwell Automation, 1978, sr. market planner, corp. planning, 1980, mgr. bus. planning, motion ctrl. div., 1982, devel. engring. mgr., motion ctrl. div., 1983, dir. prod. planning and devel., motion ctrl. div., 1985, v.p., presence sensing, automation group, 1988, v.p. control logix, automation group, 1994, pres. Automation Control Sys., 1998—2004, pres., CEO, 2004—, chmn., 2005—. Bd. dirs. Manitowoc Co., 2003—, Met. Milw. Assn. of Commerce. Advisory coun. U. Wis., Milw. Sch. Bus.; bd. trustees Boys & Girls Club of Milw. Mem.: Nat. Elec. Mfrs. Assn. (bd. govs.), Mfrs.' Alliance (bd. trustees). Office: Rockwell Automation 1201 2d St Milwaukee WI 53204

NOSOFSKY, ROBERT M., psychology educator; Prof. psychology Ind. U., Bloomington. Recipient Troland Rsch. NAS, 1995. Office: Ind U Dept Psychology Bloomington IN 47405

NOTTESTAD, DARRELL, state legislator; m. Ellen Nottestad; 2 children. Student, Mayville State Coll.; MEd, U. N.D.; postgrad., N.D. State U., Denver U., Ctrl. Mich. U. Sch. prin.; rep. Dist. 43 N.D. State U., mem. judiciary and natural resources com. Bd. dirs. Area Sch. Credit Union; mem. Grand Forks County Hist. Soc. Mem. Sons of Norway. Home: 2110 Westward Dr Grand Forks ND 58201-4167

NOTZ, JOHN KRANZ, JR., arbitrator, mediator, retired lawyer; b. Chgo., Jan. 5, 1932; s. John Kranz and Elinor (Trostel) N.; m. Janis Wellin, Apr. 23, 1966; children: Jane Elinor Notz, John Wellin. BA, Williams Coll., Williamstown, Mass., 1953; JD, Northwestern U., Chgo., 1956. Bar: Ill. 1956, Fla. 1957, Wis. 1989, U.S. Supreme Ct. 1960. Assoc. 1st Nat. Bank Chgo., 1954, 1956; from assoc. to ptnr. Gardner, Carton & Douglas, Chgo., 1960-95, of counsel, 1990-95; ret., 1996. Arbitrator, mediator Am. Arbitration Assn., Chgo. Internat. Dispute Resolution Assn., FINRA Dispute Resolution Inc., Nat. Futures Assn. Contbr. articles to profl. jours. Mem. Sec. of State Corp. Acts Adv. Com., 1982-95, chmn., 1987-89; pres. Chgo. Lit. Club, 1996-97; mem. Ill. Inst. Continuing Legal Edn., 1980-91, chmn., 1990-91; former pres. Black Point Historic Preserve, Inc.; trustee Graceland Cemetery; former treas. Soc. Archl. Historians; bd. dirs. Libr. Am. Landscape History. 1st lt. USAF, 1957-60. Recipient Svc. award Northwestern U., 1978 Fellow Am. Bar Found. (life), Ill. Bar Found. (life), Chgo. Bar Found. (life); mem. Am. Law Inst., Ill. State Bar Assn., Chgo. Bar Assn., Wis. State Bar, Lawyers Club City Chgo., Racquet Club Chgo., Lake Geneva (Wis.) Country Club, Tower Club (Chgo.), Literary Club (Chgo.), Caxton Club (Chgo.), Cliff Dwellers (Chgo.), The Antiquarian Soc., Asian Arts Coun., Art Inst. Chgo., Rsch. and Collections Comm., The Field Mus.(Chgo.). Office: 191 N Wacker Dr 3700 Chicago IL 60606-1698 Home Phone: 773-348-5196; Office Phone: 312-569-1088.

NOUSS, JAMES L., JR., lawyer; AB, U. Mo., 1976; JD, Georgetown U., 1979. Bar: Mo. 1979. Ptnr., group leader Audit Com. Counseling, group co-leader Corp. Fin. and Securities Bryan Cave LLP, St. Louis. Mem.: Phi Alpha Delta. Office: Bryan Cave LLP One Metropolitan Square 211 N Broadway, Ste 3600 Saint Louis MO 63102 Office Phone: 212-541-2275. E-mail: jlnouss@bryancave.com.

NOVAK, JOHN PHILIP, state legislator; b. Berwyn, Ill., Feb. 15, 1946; s. John Peter and Cordelia Ann (Moss) N.; (div.); 1 child, Todd Alexander. BS, Eastern Ill. U., Charleston, 1971, MA, 1973. Asst. pers. adminstr. Ill. Dept. Mental Health, 1973-76; pers. adminstr. Manville Corp., 1976-81; labor rels. adminstr. Am. Spring Wire, 1981-82; mem. Ill. Ho. of Reps. from 85th dist., 1987—. Mem. Agr., Edn. Appropriations, Environ. & Energy, Vet. Affairs Com. Ill. Ho. of Reps., vice chmn. Mcpl. and Conservation Laws Coms. Trustee Village of Bradley, Ill., 1975-82; treas. Kankakee County, Ill., 1982-86, 86-87, chmn., 1986-87, precinct committeeman, 1974-80, 86—; bd. dirs. Am. Cancer Soc., 1985-88. Decorated Unit Campaign Clusters; recipient Good Conduct medal, Agr. award, Ill. Farm Bur., 1987, 1988, Major Legislation Sponsorship award Northeastern Ill. Waterfowlers Assn., 1990, Friend of Edn. award Ill. Edn. Assn., 1990; named Outstanding Freshman Legislator, Ind. Cmty. Banks, 1987, Legislator of Yr., Ill. Assn. County Treas. Mem. Lions (treas. Bradley County chpt. 1982-83), Am. Legion (bd. dirs. Post No. 702 1981—), Vietnam Vets. Am. (bd. dirs. 1984—, Cert. of Recognition 1988), Moose, Pi Sigma Alpha. Democrat.

NOVAK, LESLIE HOWARD, lawyer; b. Chgo., May 10, 1944; s. Sidney and Sadie (Jensky) N.; m. Nancy Ruth Sherman, July 2, 1967; children: Heidi Ellen, Shani Beth. BS in Bus. with high distinction, U. Minn., 1966, JD cum laude, 1969. Bar: Minn. 1970, U.S. Dist. Ct. Minn. 1970, U.S. Ct. Appeals (8th cir.) 1974, U.S. Supreme Ct. 1995. Assoc. Robins, Kaplan, Miller & Ciresi, Mpls., 1969-77, ptnr., 1977-92, Mackall, Crounse & Moore, PLC., Mpls., 1992—, mng. ptnr., 1997-99. Bd. dirs. Am. Israel C. of C. and Industry of Minn., Mpls., 1981—, founding pres., 1981-91; founding sec., founding bd. dir. Assn. N.Am.-Israel Chambers Commerce, Inc., 1993—; bd. dirs. United Jewish Fund and Coun., St. Paul, 1986-2007; founding dir. Illusion Theater and Sch.; past bd. dirs., past pres. Jewish Family Svc. St. Paul; past bd. dirs. Mt. Zion Temple. Named Leading Am. Atty., Am.'s Registry Outstanding Profls. Mem. Oakridge Country Club, Gopher Golf Boosters Club, Phi Delta Phi, Beta Gamma Sigma. Avocations: biking, golf, tennis, skiing. Office: Mackall Crounse & Moore PLC 1400 AT&T Tower 901 Marquette Ave Minneapolis MN 55402-2859 Home Phone: 952-471-7575; Office Phone: 612-305-1460. Business E-Mail: lhn@mcmlaw.com.

NOVAK, RAYMOND FRANCIS, environmental services administrator, pharmacology educator; s. Joseph Raymond and Margaret A. (Cerutti) N.; m. Frances C. Holy, Apr. 12, 1969; children: Jennifer, Jessica, Janelle, Joanna. BS in Chemistry, U. Mo., St. Louis, 1968; PhD in Phys. Chemistry, Case Western Res. U., 1973. Assoc. in pharmacology Northwestern U. Med. Sch., Chgo., 1976-77, asst. prof. pharmacology, 1977-81, assoc. prof., 1981-86, prof., 1986-88; prof. pharmacology Wayne State U. Sch. Medicine, Detroit, 1988—; dir. Inst. Environ. Health Scis. Wayne State U., Detroit, 1988—, dir. EHS Ctr. in Molecular and Cellular Toxicology with Human Application, 1994—, dir. interdisciplinary grad. program in Molecular and Cellular Toxicology, 1994—. Mem. toxicology study sect. IH, Bethesda, Md., 1984-88, mem. and chair numerous grant review com.; adj. sci. Inhalation Toxicology Rsch. Inst., Lovelace Biomed. and Environ. Rsch. Inst., 1991-98; program leader Epidemiology and Environ. Carcinogenesis, Karmanos Cancer Inst. and Comprehensive Cancer Ctr., 1996-98. Assoc. editor Toxicol. Applied Pharmacology, 1992-96, Toxicol. Scis., 2004—; editor Drug Metabolism and Disposition, 1994-2000; mem. editorial bd. Jour. Toxicology and Environ. Health, 19 87-92, In Vivo, 1986—, Toxic Substances Jour., 1993-98; mem. bd. pub. trustees Am. Soc. Pharmacology and Experimental Therapeutics, 1994-2000; publr. over 125 sci. manuscripts, review articles and book chpt. in profl. jour. and books. Co. comdr., field grade officer (Major) USAR, 1968—99. Recipient Disting. Alumni award U. Mo., St. Louis, 1988; grantee Nat. Inst. Environ. Health Sci., 1979—, Gen. Medicine sect. NIH, 1979-82, 89-94. Mem. Am. Soc. for Biochem. and Molecular Biology, Soc. Toxicology (councilor 1996-98, chmn. cont. edn. com. 1995-96), Am. Assn. for Cancer Rsch., Am. Soc. for Pharmacology and Exptl. Therapeutics (bd. publ. trustees 1994-99), Am. Soc. Hematology, Internat. Soc. for Study Xenobiotics. Achievements include patents in field. Office: Wayne State U Inst Environ Health Scis 2727 2nd Ave Rm 4000 Detroit MI 48201-2671 Business E-Mail: R.Novak@wayne.edu.

NOVAK, STEVEN G., state legislator; b. May 26, 1949; m. Julie Novak; four children. BA, Hamline U.; postgrad., U. Minn., Duluth. Comm. coord. Minn. Mus. Art; v.p. devel. Ramsey Health Care, Inc., and Ramsey Found.; state rep. Minn. Ho. of Reps., St. Paul, 1975-82; Dist. 52 senator Minn. State Senate, St. Paul, 1982—. Chmn. jobs, energy and cmty. devel. com., mem. environ. and natural resources, jobs, energy and cmty. devel. (fin. divsn.), rules and adminstrn., taxes and tax laws, transp. and pub. transit, and fin. divsn. coms., Minn. State Senate. also: State Senate State Capital Building Saint Paul MN 55155-0001 Office: 1313 Brighton Sq Saint Paul MN 55112-2411

NOVAK, THEODORE J., lawyer; b. Dec. 8, 1940; BS, U. Ill., Urbana-Champaign, 1962; JD, Chgo.-Kent Coll. of Law, Ill. Inst. Tech., 1968. Bar: Ill. 1967, U.S. Dist. Ct. (no. dist.) Ill. 1967. Ptnr. Rudnick & Wolfe, Chgo.; ptnr., Real Estate, Land Use & Devel. practices, chmn. Land Use & Condemnation practice, mem. policy com. DLA Piper Rudnick Gray Cary, Chgo., 2005—. Adj. prof. Northwestern Univ. Sch. Law, 1998—; lectr. Univ. Chgo. Law Sch., 2000—. Co-author: Ill. Zoning, Eminent Domain & Land Use Manual, 1997; contbr. articles to profl. jours. Mem.: ABA, Am. Coll. Real Estate Lawyers, Ill. State Bar Assn., Chgo. Bar Assn., Lambda Alpha Internat., Ely chpt. Office: DLA Piper Rudnick Gray Cary Suite 1900 203 N La Salle St Chicago IL 60601-1293 Office Phone: 312-368-4037. Office Fax: 312-236-7516. Business E-Mail: theodore.novak@dlapiper.com.

NOVICH, NEIL S., metals distribution company executive; BA in Physics summa cum laude, Harvard U., 1974; MS in Nuclear Engring., MIT, 1979, MS in Mgmt., 1981. Former dir. Bain & Co.; COO Ryerson Inc., Chgo., 1994—99, chmn., pres., CEO, 1999—. Dir. W.W. Grainger, Inc. Trustee Field Mus. Natural History, Children's Home & Aid Soc. Ill.; mem. vis. com. Divsn. Phys. Scis., U. Chgo. Nat. Sci. Found. scholar, Ford scholar. Mem. Phi Beta Kappa. Office: Ryerson Inc 2621 W 15th Pl Chicago IL 60608

NOVICK, ANDREW CARL, urologist; b. Montreal, Apr. 5, 1948; came to U.S., 1974; s. David and Rose (Ortenberg) N.; m. Thelma Silver, June 29, 1969 (div. Dec. 1983); 1 child, Lorne J.; m. Linda Friedman, May 24, 1992; children: Rachel H., Eric D. BSc, McGill U., 1968, MD, CM, 1972. Diplomate Am. Bd. Urology. Resident in surgery Royal Victoria Hosp., Montreal, 1972—74; resident in urology Cleve. Clinic Found., 1974—77, staff dept. urology, 1977—, head sect. renal transplant, 1977—, chmn. Urol. Inst., 1985—, chmn. Organ Transplant Ctr., 1985—92. Trustee Am. Bd. Urology, 1995—2001, Urology Residence Rev. Com., 1997—2002. Editor: Vascular Problems in Urology, 1982, Stewart's Operative Urology, 1989, Renal Vascular Disease, 1995, Innovations in Urologic Surgery, 1997, Campbell's Urology, 2002, 2007, Operative Urology at the Cleveland Clinic, 2006; contbr. more than 500 articles to profl. jours. Fellow ACS, Med. Coun. Can.; mem. Am. Urol. Assn., Am. Assn. Genito-Urinary Surgeons, Clin. Soc. Genito-Urinary Surgeons. Office: Cleve Clinic Found 9500 Euclid Ave A100 Cleveland OH 44195-0001 Home: 24875 Woodside Ln Beachwood OH 44122 Office Phone: 216-444-5584. Business E-Mail: novicka@ccf.org.

NOVIK, STEVE, finance company executive; BSBA, U. Mo., 1972; MBA, Washington U., 1974. Ptnr. KPMG Peat Marwick; from gen. prin. to CFO Steve Novik, St. Louis, 1983-95; CFO Edward Jones, St. Louis, 1995—. Office: Edward Jones 12555 Manchester Road Saint Louis MO 63131

NOVOTNEY, DONALD FRANCIS, superintendent of schools; b. Streator, Ill., July 10, 1947; s. Andrew Stephen and Irene Marie (Lux) Novotney; m. Jane Francis Loeffelholz, June 3, 1972; children: Nicole, Tara, Thomas, Michael, Theresa. BA, Loras Coll., 1969; MS in Tchg., U. Wis., Platteville, 1973; MS, U. Dayton, 1985. Cert. tchr., Wis.; cert. tchr. and adminstr., Ohio. Prin. Holy Ghost Sch., Dickeyville, Wis., 1969-75, St. John Sch., Green Bay, Wis., 1975-76, Beaver Dam (Wis.) Cath. Schs., 1976-83; coord. Jordan Cath. Schs., Rock Island, Wis., 1983-85; supt. schs. Diocese of Fargo, ND, 1985—87, Diocese of La Crosse, Wis., 1987—2001, Diocese of Jefferson City, Mo., 2002—. Mem. Nat. Cath. Edn. Assn. (del. to nat. congress for Cath. schs.). Republican. Roman Catholic. Avocations: athletics, travel. Home: 4000 Terra Bella Jefferson City MO 65109 Office: Diocese of Jefferson City 402 N Clark Ave Jefferson City MO 65102 Personal E-mail: donnjanen@aol.com.

NOVOTNY, DONALD WAYNE, electrical engineer, educator; b. Chgo., Dec. 15, 1934; s. Adolph and Margaret Novotny; m. Louise J. Eenigenburg, June 26, 1954; children: Donna Jo Kopp, Cynthia Mason. BEE, Ill. Inst. Tech., 1956, MS, 1957; PhD, U. Wis., 1961. Registered profl. engr., Wis. Instr. Ill. Inst. Tech., 1957-58; mem. faculty U. Wis., Madison, 1958—, prof. elec. engring., 1969-96, Grainger prof. power electronics, 1990—96, prof. emeritus, 1996—, chmn. dept. elec. and computer engring., 1976-80. Vis. prof. Mont. State U., 1966, Eindhoven (The Netherlands) Tech. U., 1974, Tech. U. Louvain, Belgium, 1986; Fulbright lectr. Tech. U. Ghent, Belgium, 1981; diw. Wis. Elec. Machines and Power Electronics Consortium, 1981—96; assoc. dir. Univ.-Industry Rsch. Program, 1982—93; chmn. elec. engring. program Nat. Technol. U., 1989—2003; cons. to industry. Author: Introductory Electromechanics, 1965, Vector Control and Dynamics of AC Drives, 1996; contbr. scientific papers to profl. jours.; assoc. editor: Electric Machines and Power Systems, 1976—99. Named Disting. Lectr., IEEE-IAS, 1995; recipient Outstanding Paper award, Engring. Inst. Can., 1966, Outstanding Achievement award, IEEE-IAS, 1998; fellow, GE, 1956, Ford Found., 1960; grantee, numours industries and govt. agys. Fellow: IEEE (prize paper award 1983, 1984, 1986, 1987, 1990, 1991, 1993, 1994, 3d Millennium medal 2000); mem.: Am. Soc. Engring. Edn., Rotary, Sigma Xi, Eta Kappa Nu, Tau Beta Pi. Congregationalist. Home: 1421 E Skyline Dr Madison WI 53705-1132 Office: U Wis Dept Elec and Computer Engring 1415 Engineering Dr Madison WI 53706-1607 Office Phone: 608-262-6926. Business E-Mail: novotny@engr.wisc.edu.

NOVOTNY, MILOS VLASTISLAV, chemistry professor; b. Brno, Czechoslovakia, Apr. 19, 1942; came to U.S., 1969; BS, U. Brno, Czechoslovakia, 1962, PhD, 1965. Rsch. assoc. Inst. Analytical Chemistry Czechoslovak Acad. Scis., Brno, 1965-68; rsch. assoc. Royal Karolinska Inst., Stockholm, 1968-69; rsch. assoc. dept. chemistry U. Houston, 1969-71; from instr. to Rudy prof. of chemistry Ind. U., Bloomington, 1971—. Office: Ind U Dept of Chemistry Bloomington IN 47405

NOWACKI, JAMES NELSON, lawyer; b. Columbus, Ohio, Sept. 12, 1947; s. Louis James and Betty Jane (Nelson) N.; m. Catherine Ann Holden, Aug. 1, 1970; children: Carrie, Anastasia, Emma. AB, Princeton U., 1969; JD, Yale U., 1973. Bar: Ill. 1973, N.Y. 1982, U.S. dist. Ct. (no. dist.) Ill. 1973, U.S. Ct. Appeals (7th cir.) 1978, U.S. Ct. Appeals (6th cir.) 1987, U.S. Supreme Ct. 1992. Assoc. Isham, Lincoln & Beale, Chgo., 1976-79; ptnr. Kirkland & Ellis, Chgo., 1980—. Mem. Winnetka Sch. Bd. Dist. 36, Ill. 1983-91, bd. pres., 1989-91; mem. New Trier Sch. Bd., 1997-99, pres., 1997-98. Harlan Fiske Stone prize Yale U., 1972. Mem. ABA (forum com. on constrn. industry, litigation sect.), Mid-Am. Club, Skokie Country Club. Home: 708 Prospect Ave Winnetka IL 60093-2320 Office: Kirkland & Ellis LLP 200 E Randolph St Fl 60 Chicago IL 60601-6636 Business E-Mail: jnowacki@kirkland.com.

NOWAK, ROBERT MICHAEL, chemist; b. South Milwaukee, Wis., Oct. 28, 1930; s. Casimer M. and Anita Marie (Anderson) N.; m. Susan Lora Boyd, Oct. 12, 1957; children: Karen Sue Nowak Sapsford, Janet Lynn Nowak McMorris. Student, U. Wis., Racine, 1949-51; BS, U. Wis., Madison, 1953; PhD, U. Ill., 1956. Rsch. chemist Phys. Rsch. Lab., Dow Chem. Co., Midland, Mich., 1956-64, from group leader to asst. lab dir., 1964-72; dir. rsch. and devel. plastics dept. Dow Chem. Co., Midland, 1972-73, dir. rsch. and devel. Olefin and Styrene plastics depts., 1973-78, dir. rsch. and devel. plastics dept., 1978-83, dir. cen. rsch., 1983-90, chief scientist, dir. cen. rsch. and devel., 1990-94; pres., CEO Mich. Molecular Inst., Midland, 1994—. Contbr. articles to profl. jours.; patentee organic reaction mechanisms and reinforced plastics. Mem. NAE, AIChE, Am. Chem. Soc. Office: MI Molecular Inst 1910 W Saint Andrews Rd Midland MI 48640-2657 E-mail: nowak@mmi.org.

NOYES, RUSSELL, JR., psychiatrist; b. Indpls., Dec. 25, 1934; s. Russell and Margaret (Greenleaf) N.; m. Martha H. Carl, Nov. 13, 1960; children: Marjorie oyes-Aamot, Nancy Heifner, James R. BS, DePauw U., 1956; MD, Ind. U., 1959. Diplomate Am. Bd. Psychiatry and Neurology. Intern Phila. Gen. Hosp., 1959-60; residency U. Iowa, Iowa City, 1961-63, asst. prof. psychiatry, 1966-71, assoc. prof., 1971-78, prof., 1978—2002, prof. emeritus, 2002—. Co-author: The Anxiety Disorders, 1998; editor: Handbook of Anxiety, 1988-91; contbr. 250 articles to profl. jours. With USN, 1963-65. Fellow Am. Psychiat. Assn., Acad. Psychosomatic Medicine (pres. 1990-91); mem. Iowa Psychiat. Soc. (pres. 1986-87). Republican. Lutheran. Avocation: gardening. Home: 326 MacBride Rd Iowa City IA 52246-1716 Office: Psychiatry Rsch Med Edn Bldg Iowa City IA 52242-1009 Business E-Mail: russell-noyes@uiowa.edu.

NOZARI, MOE S., manufacturing executive; b. Iran; BS, Hope Coll., 1965; PhD in Organometallic Chemistry, U. Detroit; MS, U. Ill. Sr. rsch. chemist 3M Co., 1971, consumer products mgmt., group v.p., consumer and other markets group, 1996—99, exec. v.p., consumer and office bus. dept., 1999—. Bd. trustees Mpls. Inst. of the Arts. Recipient Acad. Award, Sci. and Engring. Award, Lab. Divsn., 1982. Office: 3M Co 3M Ctr Saint Paul MN 55144

NRIAGU, JEROME OKON, environmental geochemist; b. Ora-eri Town, Anambra, Nigeria, Oct. 24, 1942; arrived in U.S., 1993; s. Martin and Helena (Anaekwe) N.; children: Chinedu Delbert, Uzoma Vivian, Osita Jide. BSc with honors, U. Ibadan, Nigeria, 1965, DSc, 1987; MS, U. Wis., 1967; PhD, U. Toronto, Ont., 1970. Rsch. scientist Environment Can., Burlington, Ont., 1970-93; prof. environ. chem. sch. of pub. health U. Mich., Ann Arbor, 1993—; dir. environ. health scis. program, 1996-99; rsch. prof. Ctr. for Human Growth and Devel., U. Mich., 1997—. Adj. prof. U. Waterloo, Ont., 1985—96; vis. scientist NOAA, Ann Arbor, 1992; bd. dirs. Ecology Ctr. Mich., Alliance to End Childhood Lead Poisoning, Washington, 1998—. Author: Lead and Lead Poisoning in Antiquity, 1983; editor: (book series) Advances in Environmental Science and Technology, 1982—, Trace Metals in the Environment, 1996—, 29 books on various environ. topics, 1979—, Sci. of the Total Environment, 1983—; mem. editl. bds.: 9 jours.; contbr. articles to profl. jours. Recipient Rigler medal, Can. Soc. Limnologists, 1988; Fulbright sr. fellow, 2002. Fellow: Royal Soc. Can. (Romanowski medal 1999); mem.: AAAS, Am. Pub. Health Assn. Roman Catholic. Avocations: photography, reading (African authors), travel. Office: Univ Michigan Environ/Indsl Health 109 Observatory St Ann Arbor MI 48109-2029

NUGENT, DANIEL EUGENE, agricultural products executive, director; b. Chgo., Dec. 18, 1927; s. Daniel Edward and Pearl A. (Trieger) N.; m. Bonnie Lynn Weidman, July 1, 1950; children: Cynthia Lynn, Mark Alan, Dale Alan. BSME, Northwestern U., 1951. With U.S. Gypsum Co., Chgo., 1951-71, dir. corp. devel., to 1971; pres. Am. Louver Co., Chgo., 1971-72; v.p. ops. ITT Corp., Cleve., 1972-74, exec. v.p. St. Paul, 1974-75; v.p., ops. Pentair, Inc., St. Paul, 1975, pres., COO, 1975-81, pres., CEO, 1981-86, chmn., CEO, 1986-92, chmn. exec. com., 1992-97, chmn. nominating com., dir., 1990-99; dir. exec. com. Fiberstar, Inc., St. Paul, 1999—2004. Bd. dirs., audit, exec., compensation and corp. governance coms. Apogee Enterprises, Inc.; dir. Wavecrest, Inc., 1997-2001. Vice-chmn. local planning commn., 1968-72; co-chmn. Wellspring, 1989-92; trustee Harper Coll., Palatine, 1970-73; mem. adv. commn. McCormick Engring. and Kelloggg Schs. at Northwestern U., MBA Sch. of St. Thomas U., St. Paul; mem. exec. com. Indian Head coun. Boy Scouts Am. With AUS, 1946-47. Mem. North Oaks Golf Club, Quail Creek Country Club (Naples). Republican. Presbyterian. Home (Winter): 8960 Bay Colony Dr Apt 1501 Naples FL 34108-0767 Home (Summer): 4 Aopin Lane North Oaks MN 55127 E-mail: denugent4@aol.com.

NUGENT, DONALD CLARK, judge; b. Mpls., Mar. 7, 1948; s. Paul Donald and Kathleen June (Leasman) N. BA, Xavier U., 1970, Loyola U., Rome, 1969; JD, Cleve. State U., 1974. Bar: Ohio 1974. Prodn. supr. C. Schmidt & Sons, Inc., Cleve., 1971-75; pros. atty. Cuyahoga County, Ohio, 1975-85, judge Common Pleas Ct. Ohio, 1985—. Mem. Nat. Dist. Attys. Assn., Ohio Bar Assn., Greater Cleve. Bar Assn., Cuyahoga County Bar Assn. Roman Catholic. Avocations: marathon running, classical guitar. Home: 328 Cornwall Rd Cleveland OH 44116-1629

NUGENT, JOHNNY WESLEY, state legislator, tractor company executive; b. Cleve., July 18, 1939; s. Carl Howard and Velma (Holland) N.; m. Nancy Carol Whiteford, Dec. 16, 1960; 1 child, Suzette. Grad. high sch., Aurora, Ind. Owner, mgr. Nugent Tractor Sales, Lawrenceburg, Ind., 1960—; mem. Ind. Senate from 43rd dist., Indpls., 1978—. Bd. dirs. 1st Nat. Bank Aurora. Commr. Dearborn County, Lawrenceburg, 1966-74. With USAR, 1957-64. Republican. Baptist. Office: Ind Senate Dist 43 200 W Washington St Indianapolis IN 46204-2728

NUGENT, S. GEORGIA, academic administrator; m. Thomas J Scherer. B cum laude, Princeton U., 1973; PhD in classics, Cornell U. Instr. Swarthmore Coll.; assoc. prof. Brown U., 1985; asst. prof. Princeton U., 1979, dean, Harold McGraw Jr. Ctr. for tchg. and learning, asst. to pres., 1992—95, assoc. provost, 1995; pres. Kenyon Coll., 2003—. Author books. Recipient Wriston award for excellence in tchg. Office: Office of Pres Ransom Hall Kenyon Coll Gambier OH 43022 Office Phone: 740-427-5111. Office Fax: 740-427-2335. Business E-Mail: nugent@kenyon.edu.

NÜHN, ADRIAAN, food products executive; b. 1953; BA, Eindhoven Hogere Econ. Sch., Netherlands; MBA, U. Puget Sound, Tacoma, Wash. With Xerox Corp., Rochester, Y, Richardson Vicks/Procter & Gamble; mng. dir. Procter & Gamble, Vienna; gen. mgr., household and body care divsn. Sara Lee/DE, Netherlands, 1990—91, pres., Kortman Intradal, 1991—94, regional v.p., Beneleux countries, 1994, regional v.p., continental Europe, 1994—95, corp. v.p., CEO worldwide household and body care divsn., bd. mgmt., 1995—96, chmn., bd. mgmt., 2003—; corp. sr. v.p. Sara Lee Corp., 1996—99, pres., worldwide coffee & tea divsn., 1999—2003, exec. v.p., chmn. bd. mgmt. Sara Lee Internat., 2003—. Office: Sara Lee Corp Three First Nat Plaza Chicago IL 60602-4260

NURNBERGER, JOHN I., JR., psychiatrist, educator; b. NYC, July 18, 1946; married; 3 children. BS in Psychology magna cum laude, Fordham U., 1968; MD, Ind. U., 1975, PhD, 1983. Diplomate Am. Bd. Psychiatry and Neurology. Resident in psychiatry Columbia Presbyn. Med. Ctr., NYC, 1975-78, med. officer sect. psychogenetics, 1977-78; sr. staff fellow, outpatient clinic adminstr. sect. psychogenetics NIH, Bethesda, Md., 1978-83, staff psychiatrist, chief NIMH Outpatients Clinic, 1983-86, acting chief sect. clin. genetics, 1986; prof. psychiatry, dir. Inst. Psychiatric Rsch., rsch. coord. dept. psychiatry Ind. U. Med. Ctr., Indpls., 1986—; prof. med. psychiatry, neurobiology and med. genetics Ind. U. Grad. Sch., Indpls., 1987—; Joyce and Iver Small prof. psychiatry, dir. Inst. Psychiat. Rsch., Ind. U., Indpls. Clin. cons. Cold Spring VA Hosp., 1986—; cons., lectr. in field. Editor-in-chief: Psychiatric Genetics; field editor: Neuropsychiatric Genetics; contbr. articles to profl. jours. NSF fellow, 1968; recipient NAMI Exemplary Psychiatrist award Nat. Alliance Mentally Ill, 1992, 94. Fellow Am. Psychiatric Assn., Am. Psychpathological Assn.; mem. AAAS, Am. Soc. Human Genetics, Internat. Soc. Psychiatric Genetics (bd. dirs.), Am. Coll. Neuropsychopharmacology, Soc. Light Treatment and Biol. Rhythms, Soc. Neursci., Assn. Rsch. in Nervous and Mental Disease, Soc. Biol. Psychiatry, Sigma Xi. Office: Ind U Sch Medicine Psychiatric Rsch Inst 791 Union Dr Indianapolis IN 46202-2873

NUSS, LAWTON R., state supreme court justice; b. Salina, Kans., Dec. 30, 1952; m. Barbara Nuss; 5 children. BA in English and History, U. Kans., 1975, JD, 1982. Atty. Clark Mize & Linville, 1982—2002; special prosecutor City of Salina, 1994—96; justice Kans. Supreme Ct., Topeka, 2002—. Former mediator U.S. Dist. Ct., Kans. Combat engring. officer USMC. Mem.: Kans. Assn. Def. Counsel (pres.), Kans. Bar Assn. (chmn. bd. editors jour.). Office: Kans Jud Ctr 301 SW 10th Topeka KS 66612-1507

NUSSBAUM, A(DOLF) EDWARD, mathematician, educator; b. Rheydt, Fed. Republic Germany, Germany, Jan. 10, 1925; came to U.S., 1947; s. Karl and Franziska (Scheye) N.; m. Anne Ebbin, Sept. 1, 1957; children: Karl, Franziska. MA, Columbia U., 1950, PhD, 1957. Mem. staff electronic computer project Inst. Advanced Study, Princeton, N.J., 1952-53, mem., 1962-63; instr. math U. Conn., Storrs, 1953-55; asst. prof. Rensselaer Poly. Inst., Troy, N.Y., 1956-58; vis. scholar Stanford U., Calif., 1967-68; asst. prof., then assoc. prof. Washington U., St. Louis, 1958-66, prof., 1966-95, prof. emeritus, 1995—. Contbr. articles to profl. jours. Grantee NSF, 1960-79 Mem. Am. Math. Soc. Home: 8050 Watkins Dr Saint Louis MO 63105-2517 Office: Washington U Dept Math Saint Louis MO 63130 Business E-Mail: addi@math.wustl.edu.

NUSSBAUM, BERNARD J., lawyer; b. Berlin, Mar. 11, 1931; came to U.S., 1936; s. William and Lotte (Frankfurther) N.; m. Jean Beverly Enzer, Sept. 4, 1956; children: Charles, Peter, Andrew AB, Knox Coll., 1948-52; JD, U. Chgo., 1955. Assoc. Proskauer Rose Goetz & Mendelsohn, NYC, 1955-56, Sonnenschein Nath & Rosenthal LLP, Chgo., 1959-65; sr. ptnr. Sonnenschein Nath & Rosenthal, Chgo., 1965—. Master bencher Am. Inns of Ct., 1986—; appointed to com. on civility 7th cir. U.S. Ct. Appeals, 1989-92. Editor U. Chgo. Law Rev., 1954-55; mem. nat. adv. bd. BNA Civil Trial Man., 1985—; contbr. articles to profl. jours. Mem. vis. com. U. Chgo. Law Sch., 1977-83. Served to capt. U.S. Army, 1956-59 Fellow Am. Bar Found., Ill. Bar Found. (charter); mem. ABA, Chgo. Bar Assn. (chmn. com. on fed. civil procedure 1968-69, mem. com. on judiciary 1970-76), Ill. Bar Assn. (council Antitrust sect. 1971-73, assembly del. 1972-80), U. Chgo. Law Sch. Nat. Alumni Assn. (pres. 1981-83). Avocations: skiing, bicycling. Office: Sonnenschein Nath & Rosenthal LLP 7800 Sears Tower 233 S Wacker Dr Ste 8000 Chicago IL 60606-6491 Office Phone: 312-876-8039. Business E-Mail: bnussbaum@sonnenschein.com.

NUSSBAUM, MARTHA CRAVEN, philosophy and classics educator; b. NYC, May 6, 1947; d. George and Betty (Warren) Craven; m. Alan Jeffrey Nussbaum, Aug., 1969 (div. 1987); 1 child, Rachel Emily. BA, NYU, 1969; MA, Harvard U., 1971, PhD, 1975; LHD (hon.), Kalamazoo Coll., 1988, Grinnell Coll., 1993. Asst. prof. philosophy and classics Harvard U., Cambridge, 1975-80, assoc. prof., 1980-83; vis. prof. philosophy, Greek and Latin Wellesley (Mass.) Coll., 1983-84; assoc. prof. philosophy and classics Brown U., Providence, R.I., 1984-85, prof. philosophy, classics and comparative lit., 1985-87, David Benedict prof. philosophy, classics and comparative lit., 1987-89, prof., 1989-95; prof. law and ethics U. Chgo., 1995-96, prof. philosophy dept., 1995—, prof. Divinity Sch., 1995—, Ernst Freund prof. law and ethics Law Sch./Divinity Sch., 1996-99, assoc. mem. classics dept., 1996—. Rsch. advisor World Inst. Devel. Econs. Rsch., Helsinki, Finland, 1986-93; vis. prof. law U. Chgo., 1994. Author: Aristotle's De Motu Animalium, 1978, The Fragility of Goodness, 1986, Loe's Knowledge, 1990, The Therapy of Desire, 1994, Poetic Justice: The Literary Imagination and Public Life, 1996, For Love of Country, 1996, Liberty of Conscience: In Defense of America's Tradition of Religious Equality, 2008; editor: Language and Logos, 1983; (with A. Rorty) Essays on Aristotle's De Anima, 1992, (with A. Sen) The Quality of Life, 1993, (with J. Brunschwig) Passions & Perceptions, 1993, (with J. Glover) Women, Culture and Development, 1995, Poetic Justice, 1996, Cultivating Humanity, 1997, Sex and Social Justice, 1998. Soc. Fellows Harvard U. jr. fellow, 1972-75, Humanities fellow Princeton U., 1977-78, Guggenheim Found. fellow, 1983, NIH fellow, vis. fellow All Souls Coll., Oxford, Eng., 1986-87; recipient Brandeis Creative Arts award, 1990, Spielvogel-Diamondstein award, 1991; Gifford lectr. U. Edinburgh, 1993. Fellow Am. Acad. Arts and Scis. (membership com. 1991-93, coun. 1992-96), Am. Philos. Soc.; mem. Am. Philos. Assn. (exec. com. Ea. divsn. 1985-87, chair com. internat. coop., ex-officio mem. nat. bd. 1989-92, chair com. on status of women 1994-97), Am. Philol. Assn., PEN. Office: U Chicago The Law Sch 1111 E 60th St Chicago IL 60637-2776

NUTI, WILLIAM R., computer services company executive; married; 1 child. BS in Fin. and Economics, Long Island U., 1986. Various sales positions to sr. sales staff mem. IBM, 1982—88; sales mgr. Network Equipment Technologies, 1988—90, Netrix Corp., 1990—92; with Cisco Systems, 1992—2002, v.p. then pres. Greater Asia Pacific region, sr. v.p., pres. Europe, Middle East and Africa ops. London, 1999—2001, sr. v.p. worldwide service provider bus. and US theatre ops., 2001—02; pres., COO Symbol Tech., Holtsville, NY, 2002—03, pres., CEO, 2003—05; pres. & CEO NCR Corp., Dayton, Ohio, 2005—. Bd. dirs. Opus 360, 1999—. Bd. dir. Fair Media Council; trustee Long Island U. Office: NCR Corp 1700 S Patterson Blvd Dayton OH 45479

NUTTER, FORREST, plant pathologist; BS in Botany, U. Md., 1976; MS in Plant Physiology, U. N.H., 1978; PhD, N.D. State U., 1983. Assoc. prof. plant pathology Iowa State U. Recipient CIBA-GEIGY award Am. Phytopathological Soc., 1995. Office: Iowa State University Plant Pathology Dept Ames IA 50011-0001

NYBERG, LARS, former electronics company executive; b. Sweden; married; 4 children. BSBA, U. Stockholm, 1974. With Philips Electronics NV, chmn., CEO comm. sys. divsn.; chmn., CEO AT&T Global Info. Solutions, 1995—96; chmn., pres., CEO NCR Corp., 1997—2003, non-exec. chmn., 2003—05. Bd. mem. Snap-On Inc., Sandvik AB. Office: NCR Corp 1700 S Patterson Blvd Dayton OH 45479-0002

NYCKLEMOE, GLENN WINSTON, bishop; b. Fergus Falls, Minn., Dec. 8, 1936; s. Melvin and Bertha (Sumstad) N.; m. Ann Elizabeth Olson, May 28, 1960; children: Peter Glenn, John Winston, Daniel Thomas. BA, St. Olaf Coll., 1958; MDiv, Luther Theol. Sem., St. Paul, 1962; D of Ministry, Luth. Sch. Theology, Chgo., 1977. Ordained to ministry Am. Luth. Ch., 1962. Assoc. pastor Our Savior's Luth. Ch., Valley City, N.D., 1962-64, Milw., 1964-67, co-pastor, 1967-73, sr. pastor Beloit, Wis., 1973-82, St. Olaf Luth. Ch., Austin, Minn., 1982-88; bishop Southeastern Minn. Synod, Evang. Luth. Ch. in Am., Rochester, 1988—2001. Bd. dirs. Luth. Social Svcs. of Minn., Mpls., Bd. of Social Ministries, St. Paul, Minn. Coun. Chs., Mpls. Mem. bd. regents St. Olaf Coll., Northfield, Minn., 1988—. Lutheran. Avocations: skiing, trap shooting, golf.

NYE, MICHAEL EARL, former state legislator; b. Indpls., Aug. 3, 1946; s. Clair Zurmehly and Isabelle (Volk) N.; m. Marceline Leuzinger, 1974; children: Jessica E., Justin M. BS, Purdue U., 1968, JD, 1973. Rep. Mich. Dist. 58, Mich. Dist. 41, until 1998. Minority vice chmn. House Jud. Com. Mich. Ho. Reps., mem. conservation com., environ. com., recreation com., labor & tourism com., wildlife com., civil rights com., women's issues com. Farmer; pvt. practice law; adv. bd. State Bar Mich. Named environ. legis. of yr. Mich. Environ. Def. Assn., 1990, legis. of yr. Mich. Assn. Chiefs of Police. Mem. ABA, Am. Legion, Hillsdale County Bar Assn., Masons, Scottish Rite, Litchfield Exch. Clubs, Hillsdale Exch. Clubs, Mich. Farm Bur., Alpha Gamma Rho. Home: 7111 Anderson Rd Litchfield MI 49252-9772 Address: State Capitol PO Box 30014 Lansing MI 48909-7514

NYENHUIS, JACOB EUGENE, academic administrator; b. Mille Lacs County, Minn., Mar. 25, 1935; s. Egbert Peter and Rosa (Walburg) N.; m. Leona Mae Van Duyn, June 6, 1956; children: Karen J. Louwsma, Kathy J. Kurtze, Lorna J. Cook, Sarah Van Duyn N. AB in Greek, Calvin Coll., 1956; AM in Classics, Stanford U., 1961, PhD in Classics, 1963; LittD (hon.), Hope Coll., 2001. Asst. in classical langs. Calvin Coll., Grand Rapids, Mich., 1957-59; acting instr. Stanford (Calif.) U., 1962; from asst. prof. to prof. Wayne State U., Detroit, 1962-75, dir. honors program, 1964-75, chmn. Greek and Latin dept., 1965-75; prof. classics, dean for humanities Hope Coll., Holland, Mich., 1975-78, dean for arts and humanities, 1978-84, provost, 1984—2001, prof. and provost emeritus, 2001—; sr. rsch. fellow A.C. Van Raalte Inst., 2001—02, dir., 2002—. Cons. Mich. Dept. Edn., Lansing, 1971-72, Gustavus Adolphus Coll., St. Peter, Minn., 1974, orthwestern Coll., Orange City, Iowa, 1983, Whitworth Coll., Spokane, Wash., 1987, The Daedalus Project, 1988, Albion Coll., 2002-03, Kalamazoo Coll., 2003—04; reviewer NEH, Washington, 1986-87, panelist, 1991; reviewer Lilly Endowment, Indpls., 1987-89, U.S. Dept. Edn., 1993, Mich. Humanities Coun., 1999-2001, 2006; vis. assoc. prof. U. Calif., Santa Barbara, 1967-68, Ohio State U., Columbus, 1972; vis. rsch. prof. Am. Sch. Classical Studies, Athens, Greece, 1973-74, mng. com.; vis. scholar Green Coll. Oxford U., 1989; mem. editl. adv. bd. Christianity and The Arts, 1998-2001, chmn., 1999-2001. Co-author: Latin Via Ovid, 1977, rev. edit., 1982, A Dream Fulfilled: The Van Raalte Sculpture in Centennial Park, 1997; editor: Petronius: Cena Trimalchionis, 1970, Plautus: Amphitruo, 1970, A Goodly Heritage: Essays in Honor of the Reverend Dr. Elton J. Bruins at Eighty, 2007; author: Centennial History of 14th Street Christian Reformed Church, Holland, Michigan, 2002, Myth and the Creative Process: Michael Ayrton and the Myth of Daedalus, the Maze Maker, 2003; contbr. articles to profl. jours. Elder Christian Ref. Ch., Palo Alto, Calif., 1960—62, elder, clk. Grosse Pointe, Mich., 1964—67, Holland, Mich., 1976—85, v.p., 1988—91, exec. com., 1994—95; trustee Calvin Theol. Sem., 2001—07, mem. exec. com., 2002—07, v.p., 2003—07; chmn. human rels. coun. Open Housing Com., Grosse Pointe, 1971—73. Mem. Am. Philol. Assn., Danforth Assocs. (chmn. regional com. 1975-77), Mich. Classical Conf. (1st v.p. 1965-66, pres. 1966-67), Mich. Coun. Humanities (bd. dirs., 1976-84, 88-92, 96-99, chmn. 1980-82, Disting. Svc. award 1984), Nat. Fedn. State Humanities Couns. (bd. dirs. 1979-84, pres. 1981-83), Gt. Lakes Colls. Assn. (bd. dirs. 1991-93), Coun. on Undergrad. Rsch. (councilor-at-large 1993-99), Green Coll. Soc., Mortar Board, Phi Beta Kappa, Eta Sigma Phi. Democrat. Avocations: photography, carpentry. Office: Hope Coll Van Raalte Inst PO Box 9000 Holland MI 49422-9000 Office Phone: 616-395-7171. Business E-Mail: nyenhuis@hope.edu.

NYERGES, ALEXANDER LEE, museum director; b. Rochester, NY, Feb. 27, 1957; s. Sandor Elek and Lena (Angeline) N.; m. Kathryn Gray; 1 child, Robert Angeline. BA, George Washington U., 1979, MA, 1981. Intern The Octagon, Washington, 1976-79; archeol. asst. Smithsonian Instn., Washington, 1977; curatorial intern Nat. Mus. Am. History, 1978-79; adminstrv. asst. George Washington U., Washington, 1979-81; exec. dir. DeLand Mus. Art, Fla., 1981-85, Miss. Mus. Art, Jackson, 1985-92; dir. Dayton Art Inst., 1992—2006, Va. Mus. Fine Arts, Richmond, 2006—. Mem. grants panel Nat. Endowment for the Arts, 1988—; field surveyor Inst. Mus. Svcs., Washington, 1985-88, nat. review panel, 1990-92; treas., bd. dirs. Volusia County Arts Coun., Daytona Beach, Fla., 1983-85. Author: Selections from the Permanent Collection, 1999, In Praise of Nature: Ansel Adams and Photographers of the American West, The Harold W Shaw Collection: Pre Columbian Treasures, 2003, Edward Weston: A Photographer's Love of Life, 2004; contbr. articles to profl. jours. Bd. dirs. West Volusia Hist. Soc., 1984-85; pres. Miss. Inst. Arts and Letters, 1987-88; trustee Cultural Arts Ctr., DeLand, 1984-85, Miami Valley Cultural Alliance, 1993-95, Intermus. Conservation Lab., 1993-99, Montgomery County Arts and Culture Dist., 1994-2001; trustee, chmn. Dayton-Montgomery County Conv. and Visitors Bur.; bd. trustees Assn. Art Mus. Dirs., 2007—. U.S. Dept. Edn. scholar, 1973. Mem. DeLand Area C. of C. (bd. dirs., tourist adv. com. 1984-85), Assn. Art Mus. Dirs., Am. Assn. Mus. (S.E. regional rep. to non-print media com. 1983-85, nat. legis. com. 1986-93), Miss. Mus. Assn., Southeastern Mus. Conf. (bd. dirs. 1991-92), Fla. Mus. Assn., Fla. Art Mus. Dirs. Assn., Cultural Roundtable (pres. 1993-95), Ohio Mus. Assn. (trustee 1993-98), Phi Beta Kappa. Avocations: photography, music, writing, sports, scuba diving. Office: Virginia Mus Fine Arts 200 N Blvd Richmond VA 23220 E-mail: anyerges@aol.com.

NYHAN, LAWRENCE J. (LARRY), lawyer; b. Chgo., May 16, 1955; BA, U. Chgo., 1977; JD, Loyola U., Chgo., 1980. Bar: Ill. 1980. Extern to Hon. Robert Eisen US Bankruptcy Judge, no. dist. Ill., 1979—80; now ptnr. bankruptcy law Sidley Austin LLP, Chgo., chmn. nat. and internat. corp. reorgn. and bankruptcy group, mem. exec. com. Office: Sidley Austin LLP 1 S Dearborn St Chicago IL 60603 Office Phone: 312-853-7710. Office Fax: 312-853-7036. Business E-Mail: lnyhan@sidley.com.

NYHUS, LLOYD MILTON, retired surgeon, educator; b. Mt. Vernon, Wash., June 24, 1923; s. Lewis Guttorm and Mary (Shervem) N.; m. Margaret Goldie Sheldon, Nov. 25, 1949; children: Sheila Margaret, Leif Torger. BS, Pacific Luth. Coll., 1945; MD, Med. Coll. Ala., 1947; Doctor honoris causa, Aristotelian U., Thessalonika, Greece, 1968, Uppsala U., Sweden, 1974, U. Chihuahua, Mex., 1975, Jagallonian U., Cracow, Poland, 1980, U. Gama Filho, Rio de Janeiro, 1983, U. Louis Pasteur, Strasbourg, France, 1984, U. Athens, 1989. Diplomate Am. Bd. Surgery (chmn. 1974-76). Intern King County Hosp., Seattle, 1947-48, resident in surgery, 1948-55; practice medicine specializing in surgery Seattle, 1956-67, Chgo., 1967—; instr. surgery U. Wash., Seattle, 1954-56, asst. prof., 1956-59, assoc. prof., 1959-64, prof., 1964-67; Warren H. Cole prof., head dept. surgery U. Ill. Coll. Medicine, 1967-89, emeritus head, 1989—, prof. emeritus, 1993, established Lloyd M. Nyhus, MD chair of gen. surgery, dept. surgery Chgo., 2007; ret., 1993. Emeritus surgeon-in-chief U. Ill. Hosp.; sr. cons. surgeon Cook County, West Side VA, Hines VA hosps., Ill.; cons. to Surgeon Gen. NIH, 1965-69. Author: Surgery of the Stomach and Duodenum, 1962, 4th edit., 1986, named changed to Surgery of the Esophagus, Stomach and Small Intestine, 5th edit., 1995, Hernia, 1964, (book name change) yhus and Condon's Hernia, 5th edit., 2002, Chinese (Mandarin) edit., 2004, Abdominal Pain: A Guide to Rapid Diagnosis, 1969, 95, Spanish edit., 1996, Russian edit., 2001, Manual of Surgical Therapeutics, 1969, latest rev. edit., 1996, Mastery of Surgery, 1984, 3d edit., 1997, Spanish edit., 1999, Surgery Ann., 1970-95, Treatment of Shock, 1970, 2d rev. edit., 1986, Surgery of the Small Intestine, 1987; editor-in-chief Rev. of Surgery, 1967-77, Current Surgery, 1978-90, emeritus editor, 1991—; assoc. editor Quar. Rev. Surgery, 1958-61; editl. bd. Am. Jour. Digestive Diseases, 1961-67, Scandinavian Jour. Gastroenterology, 1966-97, Am. Surgeon, 1967-89, Jour. Surg. Oncology, 1969-99, Archives of Surgery, 1977-86, World Jour. Surgery, 1977-95; contbr. articles to profl. jours. Served to lt. M.C. USNR, 1943-46, 50-52. Decorated Order of Merit (Poland); postdoctoral fellow USPHS, 1952-53; recipient M. Shipley award So. Surg. Assn., 1967, Rovsing medal Danish Surg. Soc., 1973; Disting. Faculty award U. Ill Coll. Medicine, 1983, Disting. Alumnus award Med. Coll. Ala., 1984, Disting. Alumnus award U. Wash., 1993, 99; Guggenheim fellow, 1955-56. Fellow ACS (1st v.p. 1987-88), Assn. Surgeons Gt. Brit. and Ireland (hon.), Royal Coll. Surgeons Eng. (hon.), Royal Coll. Surgeons Ireland (hon.), Royal Coll. Surgeons Edinburgh (hon.), Royal Coll. Physicians and Surgeons Glasgow (hon.), Internat. Soc. Surgery Found. (hon., sec.-treas. 1992-2001); mem. Am. Gastroent. Assn., Am. Physiol. Soc., Pacific Coast Surg. Assn., Am. Surg. Assn. (recorder 1976-81, 1st v.p. 1989-90), Western Surg. Assn., Ctrl. Soc. Clin. Rsch., Chgo. Surg. Soc. (pres. 1974), Ctrl. Surg. Assn. (pres. 1984), Seattle Surg. Soc., St. Paul Surg. Soc. (hon.), Kansas City Surg. Soc. (hon.), Inst. Medicine Chgo., Internat. Soc. Surgery (hon. fellow 2001, pres. U.S. sect. 1986-88, pres. 34th World Congress 1991, internat. pres. 1991-93), Internat. Soc. for Digestive Surgery (pres. III world congress Chgo. 1974, internat. pres. 1978-84), Soc. for Surgery Alimentary Tract (sec. 1969-73, pres. 1974), Soc. Clin. Surgery, Soc. Surg. Chmn., Soc. U. Surgeons (pres. 1967), Duetschen Gesellschaft für Chirurgie (hon.), Polish Assn. Surgeons (hon.), L'Academie de Chirurgie (France) (corr.), at. Acad. of Medicine (France, Argentina and Brazil, hon.), Swiss Surg. Soc. (hon.), Brazilian Coll. Surgeons (hon.), Surg. Biology Club, Warren H. Cole Soc. (pres. 1981), Japan Surg. Soc. (hon.), Assn. Gen. Surgeons of Mex. (hon.), Columbian Surg. Soc. (hon.), Costa Rican Coll. Medicine & Surgery (hon.), Assn. Surgeons Costa Rica (hon.), Internat. Fedn. Surg. Colls. (hon. treas. 1992-99), Sigma Xi, Alpha Omega Alpha, Phi Beta Pi. Home: 310 Maple Row orthfield IL 60093-1036 Office: U Ill Coll Medicine Dept Surgery MC 958 840 S Wood St Chicago IL 60612-7322 Personal E-mail: lmn_23@msn.com.

OAKAR, MARY ROSE, congresswoman; b. Cleve., Mar. 5, 1940; d. Joseph M. and Margaret Mary (Ellison) O. BA in English, Speech and Drama, Ursuline Coll., Cleve., 1962, LHD (hon.); MA in Fine Arts, John Carroll U., Cleve., 1966; LLD (hon.), Ashland U., 1978, Ursuine Coll., 1984, St. Mary's Notre Dame, 1989, Baldwin Wallace Coll., 1988; LHD (hon.), Trinity Coll., 1987. Instr. English and drama Lourdes Acad., Cleve., 1963-70; asst. prof. English, speech and drama Cuyahoga Community Coll., Cleve., 1968-75; mem. Cleve. City Council from 8th Ward, 1973-76, 95th-102nd Congresses from 20th Dist. Ohio, 1977-92; mem. Pepper Commn. on Long Term Health Care, chair subcom. internat. devel., fin., trade and monetary policy; chair task force on social security, elderly, women; chair subcom. on personnel and police; mem. banking, fin. and urban affairs com., select com. on aging, post office and civil service com., com. on house adminstrn., also numerous subcoms.; ptnr. Mary Rose Oakar and Assocs. Apptd. to Sec. Conf. to Establish Nat. Action Plan on Breast Cancer, 1994, by Pres. Clinton to bd. dirs. Bldrs., For Peace, 1994, to policy to White House Conf. on Aging. Founder, vol.-dir. Near West Side Civic Arts Center, Cleve., 1970; ward leader Cuyahoga County Democratic Party, 1972-76; mem. Ohio Dem. Central Com. from 20th Dist., 1974; trustee Fedn. Community Planning, Cleve., Health and Planning Commn. Cleve., Community Info. Service Cleve., Cleve. Soc. Crippled Children, Public Services Occupational Group Adv. Com., Cuyahoga Community Coll., Cleve. Ballet, Cleve. YWCA. Recipient Outstanding Service awards OEO, 1973-78, Community Service award Am. Indian Center, Cleve., 1973, Community Service award Nationalities Service Center, 1974, Community Service award Club San Lorenzo, Cleve., 1976, Cuyahoga County Dem. Woman of Yr., 1977, Ursuline Coll. Alumna of Yr. award, 1977, awards Irish Nat. Caucus, awards West Side Community Mental Health Center, awards Am. Lebanese League, awards Cleve. Fedn. Am.-Syrian Lebanese Clubs, Breast Cancer Awareness award Nat. Women's Health Resource Ctr., 1989, 1st lay recipient Barbara Bohen-Pfeiffer award Italian-Am. Found. Cancer Rsch., 1989, Disting. Svc. award Am. Cancer Soc., 1989, Myrl H. Shoemaker award Ohio Dem. Party, 1992, Philip Hart award Consumer Fedn. Am., 1987; cert. appreciation City of Cleve.; Woman of Yr. award Cuyahoga County Women's Polit. Caucus, 1983; decorated Knight of Order of St. Ladislaus of Hungary, Women in Aerospace Outstanding Ach. award, Black Focus Woman of the Decade award. Office: 1888 W 30th St Cleveland OH 44113-3447

OAKES, LAURA, radio personality; Grad. Comms. and History, U. Minn.; postgrad., Brown Inst. With radio, Fergus Falls, Minn.; with radio and TV Duluth; news reporter, morning news anchor Sta. KDLH-TV; co-anchor 5 pm Sta. WCCO News Hour. Mem.: Minn. AP Broadcasters Assn. (bd. dirs.). Avocations: competitive figure skater, music, theater, sports. Office: WCCO 625 2nd Ave S Minneapolis MN 55402

OAKES, ROBERT JAMES, physics and astronomy professor; b. Mpls., Jan. 21, 1936; s. Sherman E. and Josephine J. (Olson) O.; children: Cindy L., Lisa A. BS, U. Minn., 1957, MS, 1959, PhD, 1962. NSF fellow Stanford U., 1962-64; asst. prof. physics, 1964-68; assoc. prof. physics Northwestern U., 1968-70, prof. physics, 1970-76, prof. physics and astronomy, 1976—. Vis. staff mem. Los Alamos Sci. Lab., 1971-92; vis. scientist, user Fermi Nat. Accelerator Lab., 1975-2006, CERN, 1966-67; mem. Inst. for Advanced Study, Princeton, 1967-68; vis. scientist DESY, 1971-72; faculty assoc. Argonne Nab. Lab., 1982—2002; U.S. scientist NSF-Yugoslav joint program, 1982-92; panelist Nat. Rsch. Coun., 1990-98. A.P. Sloan fellow 1965-68; Air Force Office Sci. Rsch. grantee, 1969-71, NSF grantee 1971-87, Dept. Energy grantee, 1987—; named Fulbright-Hays Disting. prof. U. Sarajevo, Yugoslavia, 1979-80; recipient Natural Sci. prize China, 1993. Fellow Am. Phys. Soc., AAAS; mem. N.Y. Acad. Sci., Ill. Acad. Sci., Sigma Xi, Tau Beta Pi. Office: Northwestern U Dept Physics 2145 Sheridan Rd Evanston IL 60208-0834

OAKLEY, DEBORAH JANE, public health service officer, nursing educator; b. Jan. 31, 1937; d. George F. and Kathryn (Willson) Hacker; m. Bruce Oakley, June 16, 1958; children: Ingrid Andrea, Brian Benjamin. BA, Swarthmore Coll., 1958; MA, Brown U., 1960; MPH, U. Mich., 1969, PhD, 1977. Dir. teenage and adult programs YWCA, Providence, 1959-63; editl. asst. Stockholm U., 1963-64; rsch. investigator, lectr. dept. population planning U. Mich., 1971-77, asst. prof. cmty. health programs Ann Arbor, 1977-79, asst. prof. nursing rsch., 1979-81, assoc. prof., 1981-89, prof., 1989—2002, interim dir. Ctr. Nursing Rsch., 1988-90, acting dir. Ctr. Nursing Rsch., 1998, prof. emeritus, 2002—, interim dir. Health Asian Ams. program, 2005. Vis. prof. Beijing Med. U., 1996-2002; prin. investigator NIH, CDC and pvt. found. funded rsch. grants and contracts on family planning, women's health and health care in China, nat. adv. com. nursing rsch., 1993-97; adv. workshop on Nat. Survey on Family Growth, 1994-97; co-chair Mich. Initiative for Women's Health, 1993-95. Author: (with Leslie Corsa) Population Planning, 1979; contbr. articles to profl. jours. Bd. dirs. Planned Parenthood Fedn. Am., 1975-80. Recipient Margaret Sanger award Washtenaw County Planned Parenthood, 1975, Outstanding Young Woman of Ann Arbor award Jaycees, 1970, Dist. Faculty award Mich. Assn. Gov. Bds., 1992, Blue Cross Blue Shield Found. of Mich. award for Excellence in Health Policy, 1996. Mem. APHA (chmn. population sect. coun.), Internat. Union Sci. Study Population, Midwest Nursing Rsch. Soc., Population Assn. Am., Delta Omega, Sigma Theta Tau (hon.). Democrat. Home: 5200 S Lake Dr Chelsea MI 48118-9481 Office: U Mich Sch Nursing Ann Arbor MI 48109-0482 Office Phone: 743-763-6730. E-mail: doakley@umich.edu.

OAKLEY, ROBERT ALAN, insurance executive; b. Columbus, Ohio, Nov. 1, 1946; s. Bernard Harmon and Mary Evelyn (Mosier) O.; m. Ann Lucille Liesenhoff, Aug. 3, 1968; children: Jeff, David. BS in Aero. Enging., Purdue U., 1968; MBA, Ohio State U., 1969, PhD in Fin., 1973. Mgr. fin. projects Nationwide Mut. Ins. Co., Columbus, 1976-79, regional controller, 1979-82, dir. ops. controls, 1982-83, v.p., corp. controller, 1983—, exec. v.p., CFO, 1993—2002. Exec.-in-res. The Ohio State Univ. Fisher School of Bus., 2003—. Author: Insurance Informations Systems, 1985. Capt. USAF, 1972-76. Mem. Fin. Mgmt. Assn., Fin. Execs. Inst., Am. Soc. CLU's. Avocations: golf, reading, teaching. Office: Fisher Sch Bus Fisher Hall 2100 Neil Ave Columbus OH 43210 Office Phone: 614-688-4625.

OATES, THOMAS R., former university executive; married; 4 children. BA in English and Philosophy, St. Louis U., 1964, MA in English, 1970; postgrad., Am. Film Inst. Ctr., Beverly Hills, Calif., 1971; PhD in Am. Lit., St. Louis U., 1979. Coord., dir. program assts. and counselors upward bound pgm. Webster Coll., 1970-71, dir. media/journalism degree program, 1974-81, coord. MA program in media comms., 1975-81; chair, assoc. prof. dept. journalism St. Michael's Coll., 1981-85; campus dean U. Wis. Ctr., Richland Center, 1985-89; dir. U.S. ops. and acad. programs Coop. Assn. of States for Scholarships, Georgetown U., Washington, 1989-94; pres. Spalding U., Louisville, 1994—2002, Rocky Mountain Coll., Billings, Mont., 2002—06. Mem. media adv. com. Mo. State Coun. of Arts, 1973-77; mem. planning commn. State Dept. of Higher Edn., Baton Rouge, 1979-80; mem., rep. Mo.'s ind. colls. and univs. Cen. Ednl. Network Mo., 1979-81; mem. adv. bd. Tri-State Bilingual Tng. Program, St. Michael's Coll., 1981-83; mem. Vt. Cath. Press Assn. Bd., 1984-85; mem., appointed chair Internat. Edn. Coun., U. Wis. Sys., 1987-88, designer, author Ctr. of Excellence project, 1988; mem. acad. staff adv. bd., U. Wis. Ctr. Sys., 1987-89, chair acad. staff grievance com., 1988; mem. 9-person state commn. to develop criteria for legal evaluations of devel. projects reviewed under Act 250 environ. law, Vt., 1984-85; presenter on internat. ednl. regional and nat. meetings of various orgns. Author, designer: (slide-tape program on history of early French and English explorers in mid-west) Old Land, New Land, 1985; author, designer: (book) Images, Values, and Development in Chittenden County, 1984; prodr.: (documentary photographic study on 5 rural Alaskan comtys.) Images of Continuity, Images of Change, 1977; prodr., dir.: (16mm documentary film) The Faces of British Honduras, 1974. Grantee Mo. Coun. on Arts, 1972, 76, NEH, 1975, U. Alaska, 1978, Mo. Coun. on Humanities, 1979, Vt. Coun. on Humanities, 1981, IBM, 1982, U. Wis. Ext., 1988, Wis. Coun. for Humanities, 1989, Orgn. for Petroleum Exporting Countries, 1992, C.C.'s for Internat. Devel., 1992. Home: 5010 Delawanda AVE Columbus OH 43214-1502

OATES, ZEHAVAH WHITNEY, data processing executive; b. Houston, Nov. 22, 1956; d. Alfred Peter and Sarah (Carsey) Whitney. AA, College of DuPage, 1988; BA, Nat. Louis U., 1989. Cert. quality analyst, cert. software test engr. Mgmt. analyst U. Ill., Abraham Lincoln Sch. Medicine, Chgo., 1976-83; sr. analyst quality assurance Ofcl. Airline Guides, Oak Brook, Ill., 1983-95; dir. application quality mgmt. U.S. Cellular, 1995—. Mem. Quality Assurance Inst., Am. Soc. for Quality Control, Chgo. Quality Assurance Assn., Chicagoland Handicapped Skiers (pres. 1986-87, 89-91), Profl. Ski Instrs. Am. Avocations: skiing, golf, birdwatching. Office: US Cellular 1101 Tower Ln Bensenville IL 60106

OBAMA, BARACK HUSSEIN, JR., senator, former state legislator; b. Honolulu, Aug. 4, 1961; s. Barack Obama Sr. and Shirley Ann (Dunham); m. Michelle Robinson, Oct. 18, 1992; children: Malia Ann, Natasha. Student, Occidental Coll., 1979—81; BA in Polit. Sci., Columbia U., 1983; JD magna cum laude, Harvard U., 1991. Editor-in-chief Harvard Law Review; writer, fin. analyst Bus. Internat. Corp., 1984—85; dir. Developing Communities Project, 1985—88; exec. dir. PROJECT VOTE!, Ill., 1992; assoc. Davis, Miner, Barnhill & Galland, P.C., 1993—96, of counsel, 1996—2004; mem. Ill. Senate Dist. 13, Springfield, 1997—2005; mem. judiciary & local govt. com. Ill. Senate, Springfield, chmn., pub. health & human svcs. com.; US Senator from Ill., 2005—. Sr. lecturer U. Chgo. Law Sch., 1993—2004; keynote speaker Dem. Nat. Convention, Boston, 2004; mem. com. environment and public works US Senate, com. fgn. relations, com. veterans affairs. Author: Dreams From My Father: A Story of Race and Inheritance, 1995 (Publishers Weekly paperback besteseller list, 2005, Grammy award for Best Spoken Word or Non-Musical Album, Recording Acad., 2006), Audacity of Hope: Thoughts on Reclaiming the American Dream, 2006 (Best Literary Work in onfiction, NAACP Image awards, 2007, Grammy award for Best Spoken Word Album, Recording Acad., 2008). Bd. dirs. Chgo. Lawyers Com. for Civil Rights Under the Law and Pub. Allies, Joyce Found., 1994—, Woods Fund Chgo., Ctr. for Neighborhood Tech., Chgo. Annenberg Challenge, Lugenia Burns Hope Ctr.; chmn. Chgo. Lawyers Com. for Civil Rights Under the Law. Named one of The World's Most Influential People, TIME mag., 2005—07, Most Influential Black Americans, Ebony mag.,

2006; recipient 40 Under 40 award, Crains Chgo. Bus., 1993, Monarch award for Outstanding Public Service, 1994, "Legal Eagle" award for Litigation, IVI-IPO, 1995, Freshman Legis. award, Ind. Voters of IL Ind. Precint Organizations, 1997, Outstanding Legis. award, Campaign for Better Health Care-IL Primary Health Care Assn., 1998, Legis. award, Associated Firefighters of IL, 2004, Chmn.'s award, NAACP, 2005, Harvard Law Sch. Assn. award, 2005, Howard Blake Walker award, Christopher House, 2005, Lifetime Achievement award, Detroit, Mich. chapter NAACP, 2005, Congl. Leadership award, Nat. Urban League, 2006. Mem.: vis. com., Irving B. Harris Grad. Sch. Pub. Policy Studies, U. Chgo., IL Bar Assn., Cook County Bar Assn. Democrat. Ch. Christ. Office: US Senate B40B Dirksen Senate Office Bldg Washington DC 20510 also: John C Kluczynski Fed Office Bldg Ste 3900 230 Sourth Dearborn St Chicago IL 60604-1480 Office Phone: 202-224-2854, 312-886-3506. Office Fax: 202-228-4260, 312-886-3514.

OBAMA, MICHELLE (MICHELLE LAVAUGHN ROBINSON OBAMA), hospital administrator, lawyer; b. Chgo., Jan. 17, 1964; d. Fraser and Marian Robinson; m. Barack Hussein Obama, Jr., Oct. 18, 1992; children: Malia Ann, Natasha. BA cum laude, Princeton U., 1985; JD, Harvard U., 1988. Assoc. mktg. and intellectual property Sidley and Austin LLP, Chgo., 1988—91; asst. to mayor, asst. commr. planning and devel. City of Chgo., 1991—93; founding exec. dir. Pub. Allies -Chgo., 1993—96; assoc. dean students, dir. cmty. svc. U. Chgo., 1997—2005; exec. dir. cmty. and external affairs U. Chgo. Med. Ctr., 2002—05, v.p. cmty. and external affairs, mgr. bus. diversity program, 2005—. Bd. dirs. TreeHouse Foods, Inc., 2005—07, Chgo. Coun. on Global Affairs. Former bd. mem. Commn. on Chgo. Landmarks; bd. mem. Otho S.A. Sprague Meml. Inst., Facing History and Ourselves, Muntu Dance Co. Named one of 25 of the World's Most Inspiring Women, Essence mag., 2006. Democrat. Protestant. Office: U Chgo Med Ctr 5841 S Maryland Ave Chicago IL 60637*

OBATA, GYO, architect; b. San Francisco, Feb. 28, 1923; s. Chiura and Haruko (Kohaski) O.; m. Majel Chance, 1947 (div. 1971); children: Kiku, Nori, Gen; m. Courtney Bean, Nov. 28, 1984; 1 child, Max. BArch, Washington U., St. Louis, 1945; MArch in Urban Design, Cranbrook Acad. Art, 1946. Registered architect 39 states, D.C. Sr. designer Skidmore, Owings, & Merrill, Chgo., 1947-51; designer Hellmuth, Yamasaki & Leinweber, Detroit, 1951-55; pres., chmn. bd. dirs. Hellmuth, Obata & Kassabaum, Inc., St. Louis, 1955-93, now design arch. Affiliate prof. Washington U., 1971; frequent lectr. design and urban environment; serves on competition juries on design throughout country. Projects include Nat. Air and Space Mus., King Saud U., Riyadh, Saudi Arabia, Dalls and Houston Gallerias, King Khaled Airport, Riyadh, hdqrs. Kellogg Co., hdqrs. BP America, World Bank, Washington, St. Louis Union Sta., Met. Sq., Dallas-Ft. Worth Airport, Squibb Corp. Rsch. Ctr., Lawrenceville, N.J., Burger King Corp. Hdqrs., numerous others. Recipient Lifetime Achievement award, Japanese Am. Nat. Mus., 2004. Fellow AIA; mem. Log Cabin Club, Noonday Club, St. Louis Club. Avocations: skiing, tennis. Office: Hellmuth Obata & Kassabaum Inc 211 N Broadway # 600 Saint Louis MO 63102-2733 Business E-Mail: gyo.obata@hok.com.

OBENBERGER, THOMAS E., lawyer; b. Milw., Nov. 29, 1942; AB, Marquette U., 1965, JD, 1967. Bar: Wis. 1967. Law clk. to Hon. E. Harold Hallows Wis. Supreme Ct., 1967-68; ptnr. Michael, Best & Friedrich, Milw., 1968—. Mem. editorial bd. Marquette Law Rev., 1966-67. Mem. ABA. Office: Michael Best & Friedrich 100 E Wisconsin Ave #3300 Milwaukee WI 53202-4108

OBERHAUS, GEOFFREY LUTHER, lawyer; b. Bowling Green, Ohio, Dec. 15, 1969; s. Luther and Cindy Oberhaus. BChemE, U. Detroit, 1992; JD, Rutgers U., 1998. Bar: Ohio 1998. Environ. engr. Occidental Chem. Corp., Burlington, NJ, 1992—98; ptnr. Dinsmore & Shohl LLP, Cin., 1998—. Named one of Ohio's Rising Stars, Super Lawyers, 2006. Mem.: Ohio State Bar Assn., Cin. Intellectual Property Law Assn., Cin. Bar Assn., ABA, Am. Intellectual Property Owners Assn., Am. Intellectual Property Lawyers Assn. Office: Dinsmore & Shohl LLP 255 East 5th St Cincinnati OH 45202 Home Phone: 513-826-0903; Office Phone: 513-977-8623. Office Fax: 513-977-8141. Business E-Mail: geof.oberhaus@dinslaw.com.

OBERHELMAN, DOUGLAS R., tractor company executive; Grad., Millikin Univ. With Caterpillar Inc., Peoria, Ill., 1975—, mng. dir., Shin Caterpillar Mitsubishi Tokyo, 1991—94, v.p., CFO Peoria, Ill., 1995—98, v.p., dir. engine products divsn., 1998—2001, group pres., 2001—, bd. dir., 2003—. Bd. dir. Nat. Assn. Manufacturers, Ameren Corp., South Side Bank. Trustee, past chmn. Millikin Univ.; bd. dir. Ill. chpt., Nature Conservancy, Forest Park Found., Cordell Hull Inst. Office: Caterpillar Inc 100 NE Adams St Peoria IL 61629-0002

OBERLANDER, MICHAEL I., lawyer, consumer products company executive; AB, U. Chgo.; JD, Vanderbilt U. Bar: Mo. 1993, Ill. 1994. Atty. Bryan Cave LLP, 1993—2000; v.p., gen. counsel Brown Shoe Co., Inc., St. Louis, 2000—01, 2001—06, sr. v.p., gen. counsel, corp. sec., 2006—. Office: Brown Shoe Co, Inc 8300 Maryland Ave Saint Louis MO 63105 Office Phone: 314-854-4119. E-mail: moberlander@brownshoe.com.

O'BERRY, PHILLIP AARON, retired veterinarian; b. Tampa, Fla., Feb. 1, 1933; s. Luther Lee and Marjorie Mae (Mahlum) O'B.; m. Terri Martin, July 31, 1960; children: Kelly, Eric, Holly, Danny, Andy, Toby. BS in Agr., U. Fla., Gainsville, 1955; DVM, Auburn U., Ala., 1960; PhD, Iowa State U., Ames, 1967. With Agrl. Rsch. Svc. USDA, 1956—2003, asst. to dir. vet. scis. rsch. div. Beltsville, Md., 1967-72; asst. dir. Nat. Animal Disease Ctr., Ames, Iowa, 1972-73, dir., 1973-88, tech. transfer coord., 1988—2003; prin. scientist Office Agr. Biotech., USDA, 1988-90; ret., 2003. Adj. prof. Coll. Vet. Medicine, Iowa State U., 1973—; expert panel livestock infertility FAO; sci. adv. com. Pan Am. Zoonosis Ctr., Buenos Aires; mem. Fed. Coun. Sci. and Tech.; com. animal health, world food and nutrition study NRC; cons. Govt. of Italy, Govt. of Mex., USDA, Govt. of Egypt; nat needs grad. fellowship rev. panel USDA, 1989-91, cons. agr. biotech. rsch. adv. com.; sci. adv. bd. Biotech. R&D Corp., 1992-2001, sci. review bd. Am. Jour. Vet. Rsch., 1990-92; mem. USDA Patent Review Com., 1988-2003. Author 27 rsch. publs.; mem. editl. adv. bd. Food Safety mag. Recipient Cert. Merit, Agrl. Rsch. Svc., 1972, 84, 2005, Alumni Merit award Iowa State Club Chgo., 1982, Cert. Appreciation, 1988, Tech. Transfer award 1989, 2004, USDA, Disting. Alumnus award Auburn U., 1991; named Hon. Diplomate Am. Coll. Vet. Microbiologists, 1995, Ames Citizen the Yr., 2000, Iowa Gov.'s Vol. award, 2001, Philanthropy award, 2006. Mem. APHA, AVMA, AAAS, Nat. Assn. Fed. Vets., Iowa Vet. Med. Assn., NY Acad. Scis., Conf. Rsch. Workers Animal Diseases, Am. Soc. Microbiology, Am. Assn. Lab. Animal Sci., US Animal Health Assn., Am. Assn. Bovine Practitioners, Livestock Cons. Inst., Sigma Xi, Phi Zeta, Phi Kappa Phi, Gamma Sigma Delta (Alumni award Merit 1976), Alpha Zeta, Spades, Blue Key. Democrat. Home: 1612 Woodhaven Cir Ames IA 50010-4130 Personal E-mail: terrioberry@mchsi.com.

OBERSTAR, JAMES L., congressman; b. Chisholm, Minn., Sept. 10, 1934; s. Louis and Mary (Grillo) O.; m. Jo Garlick, Oct. 12, 1963 (dec. July 1991); children: Thomas Edward, Katherine Noelle, Anne-Therese, Monica Rose; m. Jean Kurth, Nov. 1993; stepchildren: Corinne Quinlan Kurth, Charles Burke Kurth, Jr. BA summa cum laude, St. Thomas Coll., 1956; postgrad. in French, Laval U., Que., Can.; MS in Govt. (scholar), Coll. Europe, Bruges, Belgium, 1957; postgrad. in govt, Georgetown U. Adminstrv. asst. Congressman John A. Blatnik, 1963-74; adminstr. Pub. Works Com. US Ho. Reps., 1971-74; mem. US Congress from 8th Minn. Dist., 1975—, ranking minority mem. transp. and infrastructure com. Mem.: Am. Polit. Sci. Assn. Democrat. Office: US Ho Reps 2365 Rayburn Ho Office Bldg Washington DC 20515-2308

OBERT, PAUL RICHARD, lawyer, manufacturing executive; b. Pitts. s. Edgar F. and Elizabeth T. Obert. BS, Georgetown U., 1950; JD, U. Pitts., 1953. Bar: Pa. 1954, D.C. 1956, Ohio 1972, Ill. 1974, U.S. Supreme Ct. 1970. Sole practice, Pitts., 1954-60; asst. counsel H.K. Porter Co., Inc., Pitts., 1960—62, sec., gen. counsel, 1962-71, Addressograph-Multigraph Corp., Cleve., 1972-74; v.p. law Marshall Field & Co., Chgo., 1974-82, sec., 1976-82; v.p., gen. counsel, sec. CF Industries, Inc., Long Grove, Ill., 1982—, also officer, dir. various subs. Served to lt. col. USAF. Mem. ABA (corp. gen. counsel com.), Pa. Bar Assn., Allegheny County Bar Assn., Ill. Bar Assn., Chgo. Bar Assn., Am. Soc. Corp. Secs., Am. Retail Fedn. (bd. dirs. 1977-80), Georgetown U. Alumni Assn. (bd. govs.), Pitts. Athletic Assn., Univ. Club (Chgo.), Delta Theta Phi. Office: CF Industries Inc 1 Salem Lake Dr Long Grove IL 60047-8401

OBEY, DAVID ROSS, congressman; b. Okmulgee, Okla., Oct. 3, 1938; s. Orville John and Mary Jane (Chellis) Obey; m. Joan Therese Lepinski, June 9, 1962; children: Craig David, Douglas David. BS in Polit. Sci., U. Wis., Madison, 1960; MA in Soviet Politics, U. Wis., 1962. Mem. Wis. State Gen. Assembly, 1963-69, asst. minority leader, 1967-69; mem. US Congress from 7th Wis. dist., 1969—, ranking minority mem. appropriations com., ranking minority mem. labor, health and human svcs., edn. and related agencies subcommittee. Mem. adminstrv. com. Wis. Dem. Com., 1960-62 Named Edn. Legislator of Yr., Rural div. NEA, 1968; recipient Legis. Leadership award Eagelton Inst. Politics, 1964, award of merit Nat. Coun. Sr. Citizens, 1976, citation for legis. statesmanship Coun. Exceptional Children, 1976. Democrat. Office: US Ho Reps 2314 Rayburn Ho Office Bldg Washington DC 20515-4907 Office Phone: 202-225-3365.

O'BLOCK, ROBERT, association, publishing executive; BS in Sociology, Pitts. State U., Kans., 1972, MS in Sociology, 1973, EdS, 2001; PhD, Kans. State U., 1976; MA in Psychology, Newport U., 1998, PsyD in Psychology, 2000; MDiv, Trinity Coll., 2001, DMin, 2003; STD (hon.), St. Elins Sch. Orthodox Theology, 2003. Ordained deacon So. Episcopal Ch., 1999; ordained priest So. Episcopal Ch., 2002. Patrolman Frontenac (Kans.) Police Dept., 1971-73; probation officer Crawford County Juvenile Ct., 1973-74; supr. Children's Ct. Ctr., 1974; adminstrv. asst. to dean student affairs/cmty. svc. Labette Cmty. Jr. Coll., 1976; dir. night sch. Marymount Coll., 1976; asst. prof. dept. adminstrv. justice Wichita State U., 1977-79; assoc. prof. dept. criminal justice/polit. sci. Appalachian State U., Boone, NC, 1979-89; prof. and chair dept. adminstrn. justice Coll. Ozarks, Point Lookout, Mo., 1989—93; exec. dir. Am. Coll. Forensic Examiners, Springfield, Mo., 1994—. Founder Am. Bd. Forensic Medicine, Am. Bd. Forensic Examiners, Am. Bd. Forensic Psychol.; lectr., cons. in field. Author: Criminal Justice Research Sources, 1983, 4th edit., 1992, (with others) Security and Crime Prevention, 2d edit., 1990, The 7 Steps to the Cure of Souls, 2005; founder, pub. The Forensic Examiner, Annals of the Am. Psychotherapy Assn., contbr. articles to profl. jours., holder 25 U.S. fed. trademarks. Adv. bd. Larnard State Hosp. Named Knight Chevalier, Sovereign Military Order of Temple of Jerusalem, 2001; grantee, Gov.'s Commn. on Criminal Adminstrn., 1976—77. Mem.: Am. Assn. Integrative Medicine (co-founder, CEO), Am. Coll. Forensic Examiners (founder), Am. Psychotherapy Assn. (founder, chmn., CEO). Office: 2750 E Sunshine St Springfield MO 65804-2047 Home: 3686 E Kingswood Dr Springfield MO 65809-4635 Office Phone: 417-881-3818. Personal E-mail: rloblock@aol.com.

O'BRIEN, DANIEL WILLIAM, lawyer, lumber company executive; b. St. Paul, Jan. 6, 1926; s. Daniel W. and Kathryn (Zenk) O'B.; m. Sarah Ward Stoltze, June 20, 1952; children: Bridget Ann, Daniel William, Kevin Charles, Timothy John. Student, U. Dubuque, 1943, Ill. State U., 1944; BSL, U. Minn., 1948, JD, 1949. Bar: Minn. 1949. Practice in, St. Paul, 1950—; partner Randall, Smith & Blomquist, 1955-65; of counsel Doherty, Rumble & Butler, 1965-99; pres., chmn. bd. dirs. F.H. Stoltze Land & Lumber Co., 1964—; pres. Maple Island, Inc., 1968—. Served to ensign USNR, 1943-46. Mem. Minn., Ramsey County bar assns., World Pres's. Orgn., Chief Execs. Orgn. Office: 2497 7th Ave E Ste 105 North Saint Paul MN 55109-2902 Home (Winter): 3951 S Placita de la Moneda Green Valley AZ 85614-5063 Address: 4734 Bouleau Rd White Bear Lake MN 55110-3355 Business E-Mail: dwobrien@maple-island.com.

O'BRIEN, DONALD EUGENE, federal judge; b. Marcus, Iowa, Sept. 30, 1923; s. Michael John and Myrtle A. (Toomey) O'B.; m. Ruth Mahon, Apr. 15, 1950; children: Teresa, Brien, John, Shuivaun. LL.B., Creighton U., 1948. Bar: Iowa bar 1948, U.S. Supreme Ct. bar 1963. Pvt. practice law, Sioux City, 1948—61; asst. city atty., 1949—54; county atty. Woodbury County, Iowa, 1955—59; mcpl. judge Sioux City, Iowa, 1959-60; U.S. atty. No. Iowa, 1961-67; U.S. Dist. judge Sioux City, 1978—; chief judge U.S. Dist. Ct. (no. dist.) Iowa, Sioux City, 1985-92, sr. judge, 1992—; pvt. practice law Sioux City, 1967—78. Rep. 8th cir. dist. ct. judges to Jud. Conf. U.S., 1990-97. Served with USAAF, 1942-45. Decorated D.F.C., air medals. Mem. Woodbury County Bar Assn., Iowa State Bar Assn. Roman Catholic. Office: US Dist Ct PO Box 267 Sioux City IA 51102-0267 Office Phone: 712-233-3916. E-mail: Don_OBrian@iand.uscourts.gov.

O'BRIEN, GREGORY MICHAEL ST. LAWRENCE, academic administrator; b. NYC, Oct. 7, 1944; s. Henry Joseph and Mary Agnes (McGoldrick) O'B.; m. Mary K. McLaughlin, Dec. 28, 1968; children: Jennifer Jane, Meredith Kathleen. BA with honors, Lehigh U., 1966; MA, Boston U., 1968, PhD, 1969. Assoc. in psychology Lab. Community Psychology, Harvard Med. Sch., Boston; dir. Human Svcs. Design Lab., Sch. Applied Social Scis., Case Western Res. U., Cleve., 1970-74; dean, prof. Sch. Social Welfare, U. Wis., Milw., 1974-78; provost, prof. psychology U. Mich.-Flint, 1978-80; prof. social work and psychology, v.p. acad. affairs U. South Fla., Tampa, 1980-83, provost, 1983-87, prof. mgmt., 1986-87; chancellor U. New Orleans, 1987—2003; interim supr. New Orleans Paris Schs., 1999; pres. Argosy U. Sys., 2004—07, pres. emeritus, 2008—. Bd. dirs. WLAE-TV (PBS), Bank One New Orleans Region, Entergy New Orleans, Nat. Coalition for Advanced Mfg., Nat. Assn. State Univs. and Land-Grant Colls. Contbr. chpts. to books, articles to profl. jours. State of La. Econ. Devel. Coun., 1997—; vice chmn. State of La. Film and Video Commn., 1993-94, mem., 1993-2003; chmn. Metro. Coun. Govts. MetroVision, 1992-1994; adv. mem. Bus. Coun. New Orleans and the River Region; bd. dirs. The Chamber/New Orleans and the River Region, 1988-2003; mem. Kellogg Commn. on Future of Land Grant Colls. and State Univs., 1996-1998. NIMH fellow, 1968-69 Fellow Am. Coll. Mental Health Adminstrs. (founding fellow, pres. 1984-86); mem. NCAA (chair pres. commn. 1992-93), Nat. Assn. Social Workers, Nat. Conf. Social Welfare, Soc. Gen. Systems Research, Am. Psychol. Assn., Am. Public Health Assn., Metrovision Partnership Found. (1992-93), Council Social Work Edn. (presdl. task force on structure of assn.), Indsl. Relations Research Assn. Roman Catholic. Home: 512 N Mcclurg Ct Apt 5407 Chicago IL 60611-4185 Office: 900 Gulf Shore Dr # 1022 Destin FL 32541

O'BRIEN, JAMES ALOYSIUS, foreign language educator; b. Cin., Apr. 7, 1936; s. James Aloysius and Frieda (Schirmer) O'B.; m. Rumi Matsumoto, Aug. 26,1961. BA, St. Joseph's Coll., 1958; MA, U. Cin., 1960; PhD, Ind. U., 1969. Instr. English, St. Joseph's Coll., Rensselaer, Ind., 1960-62; asst. prof. Japanese, U. Wis., Madison, 1968-74, assoc. prof., 1974-81, prof., 1981—2003, prof. emeritus, 2003—, chmn. East Asian langs and lit., 1979-80, 82-85, 1996—2000. Author: Dazai Osamu, 1975, Akutagawa and Dazai: Instances of Literary Adaptation, 1988; translator: Selected Stories and Sketches (Dazai Osamu), 1983, Three Works (Muro Saisei), 1985, Crackling Mountain and Other Stories (Dazai Osamu), 1989. Mem. MIddleton City Common Coun., 1996-2004. Ford Found fellow, 1965-66; Fulbright-Hays and NDEA fellow, 1966-68; Social Sci. Research Council fellow, 1973-74; Japan Found. fellow, 1977-78 Mem. Assn. Asian Studies, Assn. Tchrs. of Japanese (exec. com. 1981-84, dir. devel. 1981-83, pres. 1984-90) Home: 2533 Branch St Middleton WI 53562-2812 Office Phone: 608-262-2291. Business E-Mail: jaobrie1@wisc.edu.

O'BRIEN, JAMES PHILLIP, lawyer; b. Monmouth, Ill., Jan. 6, 1949; s. John Matthew and Roberta Helen (Cavanaugh) O'B.; m. Laurene Reason, Aug. 30, 1969 (div. 1980); m. Lynn Florsheim, Sept. 5, 1987 (dec. May 2005). BA, Western Ill. U., 1971; JD, U. Ill., 1974. Bar: Ill. 1974. Asst. atty. gen. State Ill., Springfield, 1974-75; jud. clerk Ill. Appellate Ct., Springfield, 1975-76; assoc. Graham & Graham, Springfield, 1976-81; corp. counsel Am. Hosp. Assn., Chgo., 1981-84; ptnr., chmn. health care dept. Katten, Muchin Rosenman, Chgo., 1984—. Task force med. malpractice reform legislation Am. Hosp. Assn., 1983-84, tax adv. com., 1987-91, tax reporting and compliance com., 1990-91; spkr. in field. Contbr. numerous articles to profl. jours. Recipient cert. recognition Ill. Dept. Children and Family Svcs., 1981; Edward Arthur Mellinger Found. scholar, Western Ill. U. 1971. Mem.: Am. Arbitration Assn. (Task Force Health Care Dispute Resolution 1982—84), Am. Health Lawyers Assn. Office: Katten Muchin Rosenman 525 W Monroe St Ste 1900 Chicago IL 60661-3693 Home Phone: 312-943-9460; Office Phone: 312-902-5630. Business E-Mail: phillip.obrien@kattenlaw.com.

O'BRIEN, JOHN FEIGHAN, investment banker; b. Cleve., Aug. 8, 1936; s. Francis John and Ann (Feighan) O'B.; m. Regina Quaid Harahan, June 27, 1959 (div. 1976); children: Regina, Victoria, Julie, John Jr.; m. Marilyn E. Schreiner, 1977. BS, Georgetown U., 1958. Salesman Appliance Mart, Cleve., 1958-59, ptnr., 1960-66; investment broker McDonald & Co. Investments, Cleve., 1966-71, ptnr., 1971-83, exec. v.p., 1983-88, mng. dir., 1988-91, sr. mng. dir., 1993—2007; investment assoc. UBS, 2007—. Bd. dirs. Hitchcock House, Cleve., 1978-89, Recovery Resources; chmn. Alcoholism Svcs. of Cleve., 1989-92, Alcohol and Drug-Addiction Svcs. Bd. of Cuyahoga County, 1992-98; trustee St. Edward H.S., Lakewood, Ohio, Alumnus of Yr., 1997, chmn. capital campaign, 1993-95; grand jury foreman Cuyahoga County, 2000. Named Good Fellow of Yr., Irish Good Fellows Club Cleve., 1996, Benefactor of Yr., St. Edward HS, 2003. Mem. Leadership Cleve., Greater Cleve. Growth Assn., Georgetown U. Alumni Assn. (alumni bd. senator, John Carroll award 1999), Westwood Country Club, Cleve. Yacht Club, Catawba Island Club, Lago Mar Club. Home (Winter): 1800 S Ocean Dr Fort Lauderdale FL 33316-3704 Office: McDonald & Co Investments 18500 Lake Rd Ste 300 Rocky River OH 44116-1744 Personal E-mail: jfeighanob@aol.com.

O'BRIEN, MARY KATHLEEN, state legislator, lawyer; b. Kankakee, Ill., June 4, 1965; d. Donald Lawrence and Norma Margaret O'Brien. BS, Western Ill. U., 1986; JD, U. Ill., 1994. Bar: Ill. 1994. Asst., advocate Ill. Atty. Gens. Office, Kankakee, 1987-91; asst. state's atty. Grundy County State's Atty., Morris, Ill., 1993-94; lawyer Cortina, Mueller & O'Brien, Coal City, Ill., 1994-99; pvt. practice Coal City, 1999—; state rep. Ill. Gen. Assembly, Coal City, 1997—. Bd. dirs. Trailways Girl Scouts, Joliet, 1998—, Breaking Award Domestic Violence, Morris, 1997—, Ill. Valley Ctr. for Ind. Living, LaSalle, Ill., 1998—; precinct com. Kankakee County Dems., 1988-90, Grundy County Dems., Morris, 1996—. Named Legis. of Yr. Advocates United, 1999, Cmty. Behavioral Assn. of Ill., 1998; recipient William Morgan Meml. award Kankakee County Mental Health Coun., 1998, Activator award Ill. Farm Bur., 1998. Mem. Kiwanis Club of Ill. Roman Catholic. Avocations: gardening, reading, cooking. Office: 760 E Division St Coal City IL 60416-1367

O'BRIEN, NANCY LYNN, bank executive; b. Norfolk, Nebr., Sept. 6, 1951; d. Robert Sammie and Betty Ann (Petersen) Auten; m. Leo E. O'Brien, Aug. 3, 1984. BSE, U. ebr.-Lincoln, 1972, U. Nebr.-Omaha, 1975; PhD, U. Nebr.-Lincoln, 1979. Tchr. spl. edn. Omaha Pub. Schs., 1973—79; devel. studies specialist Metro Tech. Community Coll., Omaha, 1979—80; mgr. tng. Omaha Nat. Bank, 1981—84, mgr. employment and tng, 1984—. Area rep/travel cons. Am. Leadership Study Groups, Worcester, Mass., 1977—; grant mgr. Coun. Exceptional Children, 1978; adj. faculty Coll. St. Mary's, Omaha, 1983—. Active United Way, Omaha; pres. Child Abuse Coun., Omaha, 1982—83, Coun. for Exceptional Children, 1981. Grantee, Coun. for Exceptional Children, 1978. Mem.: ASTD (dir.). Democrat. Lutheran. Home: 22627 Wilson Ave Waterloo NE 68069-9797

O'BRIEN, NANCY PATRICIA, librarian, educator; b. Galesburg, Ill., Mar. 17, 1955; d. Leo Frederick O'Brien and Yvonne Blanche (Uhlmann) O'Brien Tabb; 1 child, Nicole Pamela. AB in English, U. Ill., 1976, MS in LS, 1977. Vis. instr. U. Ill., Urbana, 1977-78, asst. prof. libr. adminstrn., 1978-84, assoc. prof., 1984-91, prof., 1991—, serials bibliographer, 1977-78, social sci. bibliographer collection devel. div., 1979-81, project dir. Title II-C grant, 1987-88, acting libr. and info. sci. libr., 1989-90, head Edn. and Social Sci. Libr., 1994—, coord. social scis. divsn., 1996—2003, edn. subject specialist, 1981—. Discussion leader Ill. White House Conf. on Libr. and Info. svcs., 1990; mem. nat. adv. bd. Office Ednl. Rsch. and Improvement, US Dept. Edn., 1989-91; grant proposal reviewer NEH, 1991; mem. adv. bd. Ctr. for Children's Books, 1992-97; cons. Ark. Coll., 1989; chmn. rev. team Instrnl. Materials Ctr., U. Wis., Madison, 1989; chair exec. com. Nat. Edn. Network Nat. Libr. Edn. US Dept. Edn., 1998—2002; mem. ERIC Steering Com., Inst. Edn. Sci., US Dept. Edn., 2007-presenter in field. Author: Test Construction: A Bibliography of Resources, 1988, (with Emily Fabiano) Core List of Books and Journals in Education, 1991; Education: A Guide to Reference and Information Sources, 2d edit., 2000, (with Paul Fehrmann) Directory of Test Collections in Academic, Professional, and Research Libraries, 2001, (with John Collins III) Greenwood Dictionary of Edn., 2003; (with Kate Corby) Education in Resources in College Libraries, 2006; co-editor Media/Microforms column Serials Rev., 1979-82; mem. editl. bd. Bull. Bibliography, 1982-90; asst. editor Libr. Hi Tech., 1983-85; editor EBSS Newsletter, 1990-91; contbr. articles to profl. jours., chpts. to books. Mem. ALA (Whitney-Carnegie grantee 1990-91), Am. Ednl. Rsch. Assn. (mem. spl. interest group libr. resources and info. tech.), Assn. Coll. and Rsch. Librs. (mem. access policy guidelines task force 1990-95, vice chmn., chmn.-elect edn. and behavioral scis. sect. 1993-94, chmn. 1994-95, mem. acad. status com. 1996-2000, Disting. Edn. and Behavioral Scis. Libr. award 1997, mem. new pubs. adv. bd. 2004-07, chair disting. edn. and behavioral sci. libr. award com., 2004-07), Libr. Adminstrn. and Mgmt. Assn. (mem. edn. and tng. com. pub. rels. sect. 1990-95), Resources and Tech. Svcs. Divsn.(mem. micropub. com. 1982-85, chmn. 1983-85, cons. 1985-87). Office: U Ill Edn & Social Sci Libr 100 Main Libr 1408 W Gregory Dr Urbana IL 61801-3607 Office Phone: 217-333-2408. Business E-Mail: npobrien@uiuc.edu.

O'BRIEN, RICHARD L(EE), physician, educator, academic administrator; b. Shenandoah, Iowa, Aug. 30, 1934; s. Thomas Lee O'B. and Grace Ellen (Sims) Parish; m. Joan Frances Gurney, June 29, 1957; children: Sheila Marie, Kathleen Therese, Michael James, Patrick Kevin. MS in Physiology, Creighton U., 1958, MD, 1960. Diplomate Nat. Bd. Med. Examiners. Intern and resident Columbia med. divsn. Bellevue Hosp., NYC, 1960-62; postdoctoral fellow in biochemistry Inst. for Enzyme Rsch., U. Wis., 1962-64; asst. prof. to prof. pathology Sch. Medicine, U. So. Calif., LA, 1966-82, dep. dir. Cancer Ctr., 1975-80, dir. rsch. and edn. Cancer Ctr., 1980-81, dir. Cancer Ctr., 1981-82; dean Sch. Medicine Creighton U., Omaha, 1982-92, acting v.p. health scis., 1984-85, v.p. health scis., 1985-99, prof. health policy and ethics, Univ. prof., 2002—, dir. office of interprofl. edn., 2002—05. Vis. prof. molecular biology U. Geneva, 1973-74; mem. cancer control rsch. grants rev. com. NIH, Nat. Cancer Inst.; mem. Cancer Ctr. Support grant rev. com. Nat. Cancer Inst., 1984-88, chmn. 1987-88; co-chmn. United Way/CHAD Pacesetter campaign, 1988, 94; bd. dirs. Health Future Found., 2003—; cons. in field. Contbr. articles to profl. jours.; editor various profl. jours. Bd. dirs. Opera Omaha, 1994-2001, 04—, pres., 1998-2000, Opera Omaha Found., 2000—06, chmn., 2004—06; co-chair, Building Bright Futures Adolescent Behavioral Health Task Force, 2007-, NE Medical Assn. Health Care Reform Task Force, 2007-. Capt. US Army, 1964-66. Recipient Disting. Svc. award Met. Omaha Med. Soc., 1987, Silver Rose Opera Omaha, 2000; Spl. fellow Nat. Cancer Inst., 1967-69; named Citizen of Yr. Combined Health Agys. Drive-Health, 1986. Mem. ACP, Am. Assn. Pathologists, Am. Assn. Cancer Rsch., Am. Assn. Cancer Edn., AAAS, Am. Assn. Cancer Insts. (dir. 1982-83), Assn. Am. Med. Colls. (chmn. MCAT evaluation panel 1987-88, liaison com. on med. edn., 1988-93, co-chmn, 1989-93, adv. panel Strategic Planning Health Care Reform 1992-96), Assn. Acad. Health Ctrs. (long-range planning com. 1986, 2000, nominating com. 1987, 96, Task Force Health Care Delivery 1992, mem. task force on leadership and instl. values 1993-99, bd. dirs. 1998-99), Am. Cancer Soc. (adv. com. Inst. Rsch. Grants 1977-80, Outstanding Leadership award 1981, dir. Calif. divsn. 1980-82, dir. Nebr. divsn. 1992-96), Am. Hosp. Assn. (com. on med. edn. 1986-89), Alpha Omega Alpha. Home: 9927 Essex Dr Omaha NE 68114-3873 Office: Creighton Univ California At 24th Omaha NE 68178-0001 Home Phone: 402-392-0331; Office Phone: 402-280-2017. Business E-Mail: rlo@creighton.edu.

O'BRIEN, RONALD JOSEPH, lawyer; b. Columbus, Ohio, Nov. 7, 1948; BA, Ohio Dominican Coll., 1970; JD, Ohio State U., 1974. Bar: Ohio 1974, U.S. Dist. Ct. (so. dist.) Ohio 1974, U.S. Supreme Ct. 1978, U.S. Ct. Appeals (6th cir.) 1982. Asst. prosecutor Franklin County, Columbus, 1974-77; chief prosecutor City of Columbus, 1978-85, city atty., 1986-96; pros. atty. Franklin County, Columbus, 1996—. Mem. Ohio Bar Assn., Columbus Bar Assn., Nat. Dist. Atty. Assn. Republican. Roman Catholic. Home: 543 Yaronia Dr N Columbus OH 43214-3137 Office: Courthouse 373 S High St Columbus OH 43215-4516

O'BRIEN, TIMOTHY MICHAEL, lawyer; b. Kansas City, Mo., Aug. 5, 1958; s. Harry Joseph and Patricia Marie (McDonald) O'B.; m. Melinda L. Cadle, June 25, 1983; children: Kyle J., Evan M., Molly M. BA, U. Kans., 1980, JD, 1983. Bar: Kans. 1983, U.S. Dist. Ct. Kans. 1983, U.S. Ct. Appeals (10th cir.) 1985, U.S. Tax Ct. 1990, U.S. Supreme Ct. 1994. Law clk. to Hon. Earl I'Connor U.S. Dist. Ct., Kansas City, Kans., 1983-85; assoc. Logan & Martin, Overland Park, Kans., 1985, Shook, Hardy & Bacon LLP, Overland Park, Kans., 1985-90, ptnr., shareholder, 1990—. Assoc. editor Univ. of Kans. Law Rev., 1982-83; editor (newsletter) The Barletter, 1993-94; contbr. articles to profl. jours. Dir. Johnson County Mental Retardation Ctr., Lenexa, Kans., 1993—. Recipient Justice Lloyd B. Kagey award U. Kans., 1983. Mem. ABA, Kans. Bar Assn., Kans. Assn. Def. Counsel, Johnson County Bar Assn. (bd. dirs. 1993—), Johnson County Bar Found. (bd. dirs. 1994—), Johnson County Young Lawyers (pres. 1988), Internat. Assn. of Def. Counsel (state membership chmn.), U. Kans. Law Soc.

(bd. govs. 1998-2001), Earl E. O'Connor Am. Inns of Ct. Democrat. Roman Catholic. Home: 11512 Hemlock St Overland Park KS 66210-2444 Office: Shook Hardy & Bacon PC 84 Corporate Woods 10801 Mastin, Ste 1000 Overland Park KS 66210-1697 Office Phone: 913-663-8914, 913-451-8879. E-mail: tobrien@shb.com.

O'BRIEN, WILLIAM JOSEPH, materials engineer, educator, consultant; b. NYC, July 25, 1940; s. William P. O'Brien; divorced; children: Anne Marie, Matthew. BS, CCNY, 1960; MS, NYU, 1962; PhD, U. Mich., 1967. Assoc. dir. rsch. J.F. Jelenko Inc., NYC, 1956-61; from asst. to assoc. prof. Marquette U., Milw., 1961-67; mech. engr., dir. Biomaterials Rsch. Ctr., Milw., 1967-70; prof. biologic and materials scis. U. Mich., Ann Arbor, 1970—, dir. Biomaterials Rsch. Ctr., 1994—. Cons. WHO, N.Y.C., 1967-70, Johnson & Johnson, Inc., New Brunswick, N.J., 1970-83; chmn. rsch. com. Sch. Dentistry U. Mich., 1987-91. Editor: (book) Dental Materials, 1989; inventor Magnesia Ceramic, 1985. Recipient UN Cert., 1967, Disting. Contbn. award Mexican Prosthodontics Soc., 1991. Mem. Materials Rsch. Soc., Acad. Dental Materials, Adhesion Soc., Dental Materials Group (pres. 1985). Office: U Mich Biomaterials Rsch Ctr 1011 N University Ave Ann Arbor MI 48109-1078

O'CALLAGHAN, PATTI LOUISE, urban ministry administrator; b. Bklyn., Mar. 26, 1953; d. Cornelius Leo and Louise Patricia (Casey) O'C.; m. Mark A. Diekman, Dec. 17, 1977; children: Casey, Brian. BA in Biology, NYU, 1975; MS in Physiology, Colo. State U., 1983. Cert. in program adminstrn. Grad. asst. Colo. State U., Ft. Collins, 1975-78; rsch. technician Iowa State U., Ames, 1978-80; counselor trainer Tecumseh Planned Parenthood, Lafayette, Ind., 1985; program coord. Date-rape Awareness and Edn., Lafayette, 1986-89; dir. Tippecanoe Ct. Apptd. Spl. Advocates, Lafayette, 1989-2000; dir. social justice Lafayette (Ind.) Urban Ministry, 2001—. Mem. adv. commn. Ind. State Supreme Ct., Indpls., 1992-2000, chair, 1995-98; mem. Tippecanoe Child Abuse Prevention, 1992—, pres. 1996-98. Editor tng. manuals; contbr. articles to profl. jours. Mem. adv. com. Jour. and Courier, Lafayette, 1992-93; vol. adv. Urban Ministries Homeless Shelter, Lafayette, 1992-93; coach Tippecanoe Soccer Assn., West Lafayette, Ind., 1989-2001; coach girls soccer West Lafayette H.S., 1994-2004; sec., v.p., pres. West Lafayette Sch. Bd., 1988-96; mem. Tippecanoe County Child Protection Team, 1994-99; mentor Mothers Adv. Bd., 1994-2003; gov. apptd. Water Pollutions Control. Bd., legis. com. Ind. Assn. Cities and Towns, 2003—. Recipient Salute to Women award in Govt. and Politics, 1997, Sagamore of Wabash award Gov. of Ind., 2000; named Ind. Child Adv. of Yr., 1992, Nat. CASA Dir. of Yr. Nat. Assoc. Soc. Workers, 1995, Region 4 Citizen of Yr., 1998, Local Pub. Health Ofcl. of Yr. Ind. Pub. Health Assn., 2005. Mem. Ind. Chpt. for Prevention of Child Abuse, Ind. Advs. for Children (program com. 1991-92), Ind. Sch. Bd. Assn. (legis. com. 1991-92), Ctrl. Ind. Assn. Vol. Adminstrs., Assn. of Women in Sci., Nat. Ct. Apptd. Spl. Adv. Assn., West Lafayette Swim Club (v.p. 1989-92), West Lafayette City Coun. (pres. 2001, 04, 05). Democrat. Christian. Avocations: soccer, swimming, reading, camping, travel. Office: Lafayette Urban Ministry 525 N 4th St Lafayette IN 47901 Home Phone: 765-743-6473; Office Phone: 765-423-2691.

OCHS, SIDNEY, neurophysiology researcher, educator; b. Fall River, Mass., June 30, 1924; s. Nathan and Rose (Kniaz) O.; m. Bess Ratner; children: Rachel F., Raymond S. Susan B. PhD in Physiology, U. Chgo., 1952. Rsch. assoc. Ill. Neuropsychiat. Inst., Chgo., 1952-54; rsch. fellow Calif. Inst. Tech., Pasadena, 1954-56; asst. prof. dept. physiology U. Tex. Med. Br., Galveston, 1956-58; assoc. prof. dept. physiology Ind. U., Indpls., 1958-61, prof., 1961-94, prof. emeritus, 1994—. Author: Elements of Neurophysiology, 1965, Axoplasmic Transport and Its Relation to Other Nerve Functions, 1982, A History of Nerve Functions: From Animal Spirits to Molecular Mechanisms, 2004; founding editor, editor-in-chief: Devel. Neurobiology (formerly Jour. Neurobiology), 1969-76, assoc. editor, 1977-86. With US Army, 1943—45. Mem. Internat. Brain Rsch. Orgn., Internat. Soc. Neurochemistry, Internat. Soc. Hist. eurosciences, Am. Physiol. Soc., Soc. Neurosci., Am. Soc. Neurochemistry, Peripheral Nerve Soc., Hist. Sci. Soc. Democrat. Jewish. Avocations: amateur radio, history. Office: Ind U Med Ctr Dept Cellular & Integ Physiology 635 Barnhill Dr Indianapolis IN 46202-5126 Office Phone: 317-274-7940. Business E-Mail: sochs@iupui.edu.

OCKERMAN, HERBERT W., agricultural studies educator; b. Chaplin, Ky., Jan. 16, 1932; m. Frances Ockerman (dec.). BS with Distinction, U. Ky., 1954, MS, 1958; PhD, .C. State U., 1962; postgrad., Air U., 1964-70, Ohio State U., 1974, postgrad., 1983, postgrad., 1987, postgrad., 2001, postgrad., 2003—07; PhD (hon.), Wyzial U., Poland, 2004. Asst. prof. Ohio State U., Columbus, 1961-66, assoc. prof., 1966-71, prof., 1971—. Former mem. Inst. Nutrition and Food Tech.; judge regional and state h.s. sci. fairs, 1965—, Ham Contest, Ky. State Fair, Sausage and Ham Contest, Ohio Meat Processing Groups, 1965; cons. Am. Meat Inst., 1977-88, USDA, 1977-2003, CRC Press., Inc., 1988—; bd. examiners U. Calcutta, 1987-88; examiner U. Mysore, India, 1990-97, U. We. Sydney, Australia, 2005, U. Newcastle, Australia, 2005-07; expert witness, various firms, 1992—, UN expert 95; expert cons. com. FAO/WHO, 2003-; hon. mem. vet., med. faculty Assiut U., Egypt; adv. bd. Bull. Vet. Inst. Poland, 2004—; chmn. sci. bd. Egyptian Jour. Meat Sci. and Tech.; presenter, cons. in field. Chmn. sci. bd.: Egyptian Jour. Molecular Sci. and Tech., 2002; contbr. more than 222 articles to profl. jours., more than 135 chpts. to books. Comdr. pilot USAF, 1955-58. Fisher Packing scholar; named Highest Individual in Beef Grading, Kansas City Meat Judging Contest, 1952, Hall of Disting. Alumni, U. Ky., 1995; recipient Am. Soc. Animal Sci. Meat Rsch. award Lilly Rsch. Labs., 1987, Appreciation cert. Ohio Assn. Meat Processors, 1987-2006, Profl. Devel. award Cahill Faculty, commendation Ohio Ho. of Reps., Merit Svc. badge Polish Govt., plaque Argentina Nat. Meat Bd., Animal Sci. award Roussel UCALF, France, U. Assiuit, Egypt, Silver Platter award Nat. Meat Bd., Sec. Agr., Livestock and Fishery, Argentina, Svc. award Coun. Grad. Students, Pomerance Tchg. award, Outstanding Alumni award U. Ky., Outstanding Ednl. Achievements award Argentine Soc. Agr., Coop. award Vet. Faculty. U. Cordoba, Svc. award Panoma Legis. Br., Brazil; Vet. Faculty award U. Cordoba, Spain, 1982, 94, award Nat. Chung-Hsing U., 1982, 95, You Are The Best award INTA Sci., 1997, award Vet. Mus. Ciechanowcu, Poland, Internat. award Assn. Nat. Tech. en Alimentos de Mexico, Can. Indst. Food Sci. and Tech., 1998, Appreciation plaque Republic of Argentina, 1999, Candle Stick of Knowledge award Ludhiana U., Punjab, India, 1999, Internat. award Am. Meat Sci. Assn., 1999, 2000, Appreciation plaque Am. Coll. Commerce, Taiwan, 1999, plaque Selcuk U., Turkey, 1999, Folklore and Cultural memento Sudanese Socs., Sudan U., 1999, Homage and Acknowledgment award Argentine Sec. Agr., 2000, Internat. award Am. Most. Sci. Assn., 2000, Most Honored Guest award Weifang, China, 2001, World History award Jhadong U., China, 2001, plaque Congress of Ham, Cordoba, Spain, 2001, Michal Oczapowski award Polish Acad. Sci., 2002, Sausage Maker award Poland, 2001, Great Educator award China, 2001, Silver Medallion award INTA Argentina, 2001, Pub. award Taiwan, 2002, Animal Sci. plaque, China, 2002, Food award China, 2002, Publ. award Dayeh U., Taiwan, 2003, Coop. award Cath. U., Argentina, 2004, Lifetime Achievement award PAU India, 2005, Sci. award Argentina Nat. Acad., 2006, The World is your Classroom award DaYeh U., 2006, Lifetime Achivement Alumni award Ag & HES Alumni Assn., orth Ctrl. Reagan, U. Ky., Plaque of Recognition CIVIT U. Philippines, 2007, Ednl. (Producing Good Students) Tree award Da Yea U., Taiwan, 2007, Porcelain award, 2007, Embroidered Plaque for Presenting 7 Presentations Agrl. Conf. Changsha, China, 2007, Chinese Yoke for Caring Students, 2007, Appreciation Cert. CIVIT U., U. Philippines, 2007, numerous others; co-recipient 2 plaques Al Falat HS, India, 2006; plaque Tangai U., Taiwan; plaque for 36,000 books Da Yeh U., Yunnan U., China, Symobolism award U. Turkey, Presdl. plaque Chkurova, Turkey. Mem. NAS, NCR, ASTM, Am. Meat Sci. Assn., Am. Soc. Animal Sci. (Rsch. award 1987), Reciprocal Meat Conf., European Meeting of Meat Rsch. Workers, Polish Vet. Soc. (hon.), Inst. Food Technologists (nat. and OVS chpts.), Inst. Food Tech. (Internat. award 1998, 2000), Can. Meat Sci. Assn., Internat. Congress Meat Sci. and Tech., Rsch. in Basic Sci., Nat. Acad. Agronomy and Vet. Medicine Argentina(corr. academic), Phi Beta Delta (treas. 1987, pres. 1991, Internat. scholar award 1991, Internat. Faculty award 1991, Presdl. medallion award), Gamma Sigma Delta (Rsch. award 1977, Internat. award of merit 1988), Sigma Xi (outstanding advisor in coll. award 1995), Phi Beta Kappa (Outstanding Tchg. award 1997, Extension Diversity award 1997, Pomerene Tchg. Enhancement award 1997, Outstanding Internat. Faculty award 1997), Internat. Gamma Sigma Delta (Disting. Achievement Nat. award 1998), Phi Kappa Phi. Achievements include american coordinator for memorandum of understanding between OSU and Assiut University Egypt, 2007; dedication of Ockerman-Hansan Hall CIVIT University, Philippines. Only the 2nd international university building dedicated to an OSU professor, 2007; outstanding volunteer recognition from the United Nations and the International Voluntary Organizations, 2007. Office: Ohio State U Meat Lab Animal Sci 2029 Fyffe Rd Columbus OH 43210-1007 Office Phone: 614-292-2201. Business E-Mail: ockerman.2@osu.edu.

O'CONNELL, DANIEL CRAIG, retired psychologist, educator; b. Sand Springs, Okla., May 20, 1928; s. John Albert and Letitia Rutherford (McGinnis) O'C. BA, St. Louis U., 1951, Ph.L., 1952, MA, 1953, S.T.L., 1960; PhD, U. Ill., 1963. Joined Soc. of Jesus, 1945; asst. prof. psychology St. Louis U., 1964-66, asso. prof., 1966-72, prof., 1972-80, trustee, 1973-78, pres., 1974-78; prof. psychology Loyola U., Chgo., 1980-89, Georgetown U., Washington, 1990-98, emeritus, 1998—, chmn., 1991-96. Vis. prof. U. Melbourne, Australia, 1972, U. Kans., 1978-79, Georgetown U., 1986, Loyola U., Chgo., 1998-2003; Humboldt fellow Psychol. Inst. Free U. Berlin, 1968; sr. Fulbright lectr. Kassel U., W. Ger., 1979-80. Author: Critical Essays on Language Use and Psychology, 1988; contbr. articles to profl. jours. Recipient Nancy McNeir Ring award for outstanding teaching St. Louis U., 1969; NSF fellow, 1961, 63, 65, 68; Humboldt Found. grantee, 1973; Humboldt fellow Tech. U. of Berlin, 1987. Fellow: APA, Mo. Psychol. Assn.; mem.: AAAS, AAUP, Mo. Acad. Sci., N.Y. Acad. Sci., Psychonomic Soc., Eastern Psychol. Assn., Southwestern Psychol. Assn., Midwestern Psychol. Assn., Soc. Scientific Study of Religion, Psychologists Interested in Religious Issues, Phi Beta Kappa. Home and Office: 4517 W Pine Blvd Saint Louis MO 63108-2109 Office Phone: 314-758-7143. Business E-Mail: doconnell@jesuits-mis.org.

O'CONNELL, DAVID PAUL, state legislator; b. Bottineau County, ND, June 3, 1940; s. Basil and Dorothy (Zimny) O'C.; m. Anadine Picard, 1960; children: Russell, Patricia Hetland, Marlys. Student, N.D. U. Mem. N.D. Ho. of Reps., Bismark, 1983-88, N.D. Senate from 6th dist., Bismark, 1989—; chmn. joint constrn. revision com. .D. Senate, vice chmn. edn., transp. coms. Farmer. Mem. Lansford Fire & Ambulance Squad. Named Legislator of Yr., N.D. Vocat. Edn., 1990. Mem. KC, Farmers Union, Farm Bur., C. of C. Office: ND Senate State Capitol Bismarck ND 58501 Home: 2624 County Road 30 Lansford ND 58750-9736

O'CONNELL, EDWARD JOSEPH, III, financial executive, accountant; b. Evergreen Park, Ill., Aug. 9, 1952; s. Edward Joseph Jr. and Mary Jane O'C.; m. Mary M. Witt, May 30, 1976; children: Kelly, Edward IV, Molly, Kevin. BBA, U. Notre Dame, 1974. CPA, Ill. Mem. audit staff Coopers and Lybrand, Chgo., 1974-78, audit mgr., 1978-81; controller Union Spl. Corp., Chgo., 1981-83, v.p., CFO, 1983—89, exec. v.p. fin. and adminstrn., chief. fin. officer, 1989-91; sr. v.p. fin., CFO GenDerm Corp., Lincolnshire, Ill., 1991-95; COO Keck, Mahin & Cate, Chgo., 1995-98; sr. v.p. fin. and adminstrn., CFO Delphi Info. Sys., Inc., Rolling Meadows, Ill., 1998—99; CFO Hey Co. LLC, Chgo., 1999—2000, Gardner Carton & Douglas, LLC, Chgo., 2000—. Mem. Am. Inst. CPA's, Ill. Soc. CPA's, Fin. Execs. Inst., Machinery and Allied Products Inst. (fin. council II). Clubs: Notre Dame of Chgo. (bd. govs. 1984-86). Roman Catholic. Avocations: rugby, running, reading, golf. Home: 10420 Lamon Ave Oak Lawn IL 60453-4743 Office: Gardner Carton & Douglas LLC Ste 3700 191 N Wacker Dr Chicago IL 60606-1698 Home Phone: 708-857-7326; Office Phone: 312-569-1103. E-mail: coconnell@gcd.com.

O'CONNELL, JAMES JOSEPH, port official; b. Lockport, Ill., Feb. 7, 1933; m. Phyllis Ann Berard, Aug. 1, 1953; children: Lynn, Kathryn, Julia. BSBA, Lewis U., 1958. lic. pvt. pilot FAA. Recorder Will County, Joliet, Ill., 1976-88. Dir., treas., corp. sec., v.p. Joliet Regional Port Dist., 1972—; dir. Des Plaines Valley Enterprise Zone, Joliet; dir., sec. Joliet Land Clearance Commn.; reg. lobbyist Ill. Assn. Pt. Dists., Ill. Real Estate Broker, 1959—; real estate cons. O'Connell Enterprises. Nat. dir., nat. U.S. pres. Internat. O'Connell Clan, Kerry County, Ireland, 1996—; precinct committeeman Will County, Joliet, 1962-72, exec. cen. committeeman, 1965-70, dir. Will County Young Reps., Joliet, 1984, sec. Will County Econ. Affairs Commn., Joliet; GOP candidate for Ill. dist. 11, U.S. Congress, 1994.; treas. U.S. Jaycee Found., 1999; treas. Joliet Housing Authority, 2000-2001. With U.S. Army, 1953-54, Korea. Mem. Ill. Assn. Port Dists. (sec., treas. 1982-86), Ill. Jaycees (senate pres. 1972-73, named to Hall of Fame 1993, Disting. Svc. award 1977), Joliet Flying Club (sec.), Joliet Navy League (pres. 1996—), KC (past Grand Knight 1972, 91), Joliet Exch. Club, Three Rivers Mfg. Assn. (pub. affairs com.), Joliet Columbian Club (pres.), Am. Legion (life, former post officer), VFW (life), U.S. Jr. C. of C. (found. trustee 1997-2001). Roman Catholic. Office Phone: 815-405-6433.

O'CONNELL, LAURENCE J., bioethics research administrator; b. Chgo., May 12, 1945; s. Joseph J. and Eleanor (Coleman) O'C.; m. Angela M. Schneider; 1 child, Coleman Brian. BA in Theology, Cath. U. Leuven, Belgium, 1969, MA in Religious Studies, 1970, PhD, STD Religious Studies/Theology, 1976. Prof., dept. chair dept. theol. studies St. Louis U., 1979-82, 86-90; v.p. theology, mission and ethics Cath. Health Assn. U.S., St. Louis, 1985-89; pres., chief. Park Ridge Ctr. for the Study Health, Faith, Ethics, Chgo., 1989—. Adj. asst. prof. dept. medicine Stritch Sch. Medicine, Loyola U., Chgo., 1990—; bd. dirs. Am. Health Decisions, 1990—, SSM Health Care System, St. Louis, 1990—. Author: The Gospel Alive: The Care of Persons with AIDS and Other Diseases, 1988, Ethics Committees: A Practical Approach, 1986. Mem. Soc. for Bioethics Consultation (pres. 1989-91), Univ. Club Chgo. Home: 4520 Dietz Way Fair Oaks CA 95628-6011 Office: The Park Ridge Center 205 W Touhy Ave Ste 203 Park Ridge IL 60068-4201

O'CONNELL, MAURICE DANIEL, lawyer; b. Ticonderoga, NY, Nov. 9, 1929; s. Maurice Daniel and Leila (Geraghty) O'C.; m. Joan MacLure Landers, Aug. 2, 1952; children: Mark M., David L., Ann M., Leila K., Ellen A. Grad., Phillips Exeter Acad., 1946; AB, Williams Coll., 1950; LLB, Cornell U., 1956. Bar: Ohio 1956. Since practiced in, Toledo; assoc. Williams, Eversman & Black, 1956-60; ptnr. Robison, Curphey & O'Connell, 1961-95, of counsel, 1996—; spl. hearing officer in conscientious objector cases U.S. Dept. Justice, 1966-68. Mem. complaint rev. bd. Bd. Commrs. on Grievance and Discipline of Supreme Ct. Ohio, 1987. Mem. Ottawa Hills Bd. Edn., 1963-66, pres., 1967-69; former trustee Toledo Soc. for Handicapped; past trustee Woodlawn Cemetery; past trustee Toledo Hearing and Speech Center, Easter Seal Soc.; mem. alumni council Phillips Exeter Acad. Served to 1st lt. USMCR, 1950-53. Life fellow Ohio State Bar Found.; mem. W Ohio Alumni Assn. of Williams Coll. (past pres.), Ohio Bar Assn., Toledo Bar Assn. (chmn. grievance com. 1971-74), Kappa Alpha, Phi Delta Phi. Clubs: Toledo. Home: 3922 W Bancroft St Toledo OH 43606-2533 Office: 9th Flr Four SeaGate Toledo OH 43604

O'CONNOR, JAMES, JR., (JIM O'CONNOR), telecommunications industry executive; b. 1967; m. Julie O'Connor; 2 children. BA, JD, Georgetown Univ.; MBA, Northwestern Univ. Kellogg Sch. Bar: Ill. Mgmt. consultant AT Kearney; fell. White House, 1998; founder Motorola Ventures, Chgo., 1999; v.p., tech. incubation., commercialization Motorola, Chgo., 1999—. Adv. bd. mem. J.L. Kellogg Sch. Mgmt.; co-chmn. Chicagoland Entrepreneurial Ctr.; bd. mem. Chicagoland Chamber Commerce; founder Kellogg Corps, Field Mus. Assoc., Lyric Opera Aux. Bd.; mem. bd. Children's Home & Aid Soc., Chgo. Cities in Schools, Big Shoulders Bd. Recipient East Coast Athletic Conf. All-Star, GTE Academic All-American, CEO Volunteer award, Motorola, 2002, CEO outstanding Achievement award, 2004; grantee Leadership Greater Chgo., 2000, Japan Leadership, 2000, Henry Crown Leadership, Aspen Inst., 2004. Mem.: Econ. Club Chgo., ABA. Office: Motorola Inc 1303 E Algonquin Rd Schaumburg IL 60196 Office Fax: 847-576-5372.

O'CONNOR, KAY F., state legislator; b. Everett, Wash., Nov. 28, 1941; d. Ernest S. and Dena (Lampers) Wells; m. Arthur J. O'Connor, Sept. 1, 1959; 6 children. Diploma, Lathrop H.S., Fairbanks, Alaska, 1959. Office mgr. Blaylock Chemicals, Bucyrus, Kans., 1981-84; store mgr. Copies Plus, Olathe, Kans., 1984-86; acct. Advance Concrete Inc., Spring Hill, Kans., 1986-92; mem. Kans. Ho. of Reps. from 14th dist., 1993-2000, Kans. Senate from 9th dist., 2001—. Exec. dir. Parents in Control, Inc.; bd. dirs. Hometel Ltd.; author sch. voucher legis. State of Kans., 1994-2002; corrections and juvenile justice oversight com., judiciary com., fed. and state affairs com., vice chair elections and local govt. com. Kans. Senate, 2001—. Republican. Roman Catholic. Avocations: choir directing, statue renovations, speaking on school vouchers. Home: 1101 N Curtis St Olathe KS 66061-2709 Office: PO Box 2232 Olathe KS 66051-2232 E-mail: kayoisok@comcast.net.

O'CONNOR, KEVIN, construction materials manufacturing executive; b. 1969; JD, Calif. Western Sch. Law, San Diego, 1996; MBA, U. Chgo. Lic.: (before Supreme Ct.). Copy writer Foote Cone & Belding, Taipei, Taiwan; litigator LA, 1996—2000; corp. atty. Caterpillar Inc., Peoria, Ill., 2000—02, legal counsel Beijing, 2002—06, dir. China bus. devel., 2006—. Named one of 40 Under 40, Crain's Chgo. Bus., 2006. Office Phone: 480-345-7330. Business E-Mail: kevinro@cat.com.

O'CONNOR, MAUREEN, state supreme court justice; b. Washington, Aug. 7, 1951; d. Patrick and Mary E. O'Connor; children: Alex, Ed. BA, Seton Hill Coll., 1973; postgrad., SUNY, 1975-76; JD, Cleve. State U., 1980. Pvt. practice, 1981-85; magistrate Summit County Probate Ct., 1985-93; judge Summit County Ct. of Common Pleas, 1993-95; prosecuting atty. Summit County, 1995-99; lt. gov., dir. Dept. Pub. Safety State of Ohio, 1999—2003; justice Ohio Supreme Ct., Ohio, 2003—. Dir. Summit County Child Support Enforcement Agy.; former chair Ohio Security Task Force, Building Security Review Com.; spkr. in field. Parishioner St. Vincent's Ch.; vol. Comty. Drug Bd., Am. Cancer Soc., bd. dirs.; bd. dirs. Victim Assistance, St. Edward Home, Fairlawn, Furnace St. Mission. Recipient MADD Law Enforcement award, 1997, Cleve. State Disting. Alumnae award for Civic Achievement, 1997. Mem. MADD, Nat. Dist. Attys. Assn., at. Child Support Enforcement Assn., Nat. Coll. Dist. Attys. Assn., Ohio Prosecuting Attys. Assn. (exec. com.), Ohio Family Support Assn., Atty. Gen.'s Prosecutor Liaison Com., Summit County Police Chiefs Assn., Summit Forum, Summit County Child Mortality. Republican. Office: Ohio Supreme Ct 65 S Front St Columbus OH 43215

O'CONNOR, PATRICK J., state legislator; m. Susan Reckert; children: Patrick, Michael, Meghan. Student, U. Mo., St. Louis. Mem. Mo. State Ho. of Reps. Dist. 79, 1993—, mem. labor, higher edn., pub. health and safety coms., 1993—, mem. children, youth and family com., 1993—. Mem. Woodson Terrace Lion's Club, North County Labor Legis. Club, Pipefitters Local 562, N.W. Twp. Dem. Club (v.p.).

OCVIRK, OTTO GEORGE, artist; b. Detroit, Nov. 13, 1922; s. Joseph and Louise (Ekle) O.; m. Betty Josephine Lebie, June 11, 1949; children: Robert Joseph, Thomas Frederick, Carol Louise. B.F.A., State U. Iowa, 1949, M.F.A., 1950. Advt. artist apprentice Bass-Luckoff Advt. Agy., Detroit, 1941; engring. draftsman Curtiss-Wright Aircraft Corp., Buffalo, 1942; faculty Bowling Green (Ohio) State U., 1950—, assoc. prof., 1960-65, prof. art, 1965-85, prof. emeritus, 1985—. Exhibited in group shows at, Denver Mus. Art, 1949, 50, 53, Detroit Inst. Art, 71948, 49, 50, 53, 56, Dayton (Ohio) Art Inst., 1950, 51, 56, Ohio State U., 1953, Walker Art Center, Mpls., 1948, 49, Library of Congress, Washington, 1949, Bklyn. Mus., 1949, Joslyn Mus., Omaha, 1949, Colorado Springs Fine Arts Center, 1949; represented in permanent collections, Detroit Inst. Arts, Dayton Art Inst., Friends of Am. Art, Grand Rapids, Mich., State U. Iowa, Iowa City, Bowling Green State U.; (Recipient 24 nat., regional juried art exhbn. awards 1947-57, others.); Author: (with R. Stinson, P. Wigg, R. Bone and David Cayton) Art Fundamentals— Theory and Practice, 1960-97, 7th edit., 1994, 8th edit., 1997, 9th edit., 2001, 10th edit., 2005. Scoutmaster Toledo Area council Boy Scouts Am., 1960-63, asst. scoutmaster, 1963-74, dist. commr., 1978-80. Served with AUS, 1943-46. Recipient Silver Beaver award Boy Scouts Am., 1976, Magnifico award Medici Circle, Bowling Green State U., 1987. Mem. Delta Phi Delta (hon.) Methodist. Home and Office: 231 Haskins Rd Bowling Green OH 43402-2206

O'DANIEL, WILLIAM L., state legislator; b. Union County, Ky., Dec. 4, 1923; m. Norma Norris; 5 children. Student, Agr. Ext. Svc. Farmer, businessman; mem. Ill. Ho. of Reps., 1974-77; exec. dir. Agr. Stabilization and Conservation Svc. U.S. Dept. Agr., 1977-81; mem. Ill. State Senate from 54th dist. Vice chmn. Agr. Com. Ill. State Senate, mem. Revenue, Transp., Elec., Joint Com. on Adminstrv. Rules Coms. Decorated Purple Heart, Bronze Star. Home: RR 4 Mount Vernon IL 62864-9804

ODDEN, ALLAN ROBERT, education educator; b. Duluth, Minn., Sept. 16, 1943; s. Robert Norman and Mabel Eleanor (Bjornnes) Odden; m. Eleanor Ann Rubottom, May 28, 1966; children: Sarina, Robert. BS, Brown U., 1965; MDiv, Union Theol. Sem., 1969; MA, Columbia U., 1971, PhD, 1975. Tchr. N.Y.C. Pub. Schs., 1967-72; rsch. assoc. Teachers' Coll. Columbia U., NYC, 1972-75; dir. policy Edn. Commn. of the States, Denver, 1975-84; prof. U. So. Calif., LA, 1984-93, U. Wis., Madison, 1993—. Rsch. dir. Sch. Fin. Commns., Conn., 1974—75, SD, 1975—76, Mo., 1975—76, Mo., 1993, Mo., 94, NY, 1978—81, NJ, 1991—92, Ark., 2003, Ark., 2005—06, Wyo., 2005, Wyo., 05, Wyo., 06, Wash., 2005—06, Wis., 2005—07; co-dir. Consortium Policy Rsch. Edn., Strategic Mgmt. Human Capital Pub. Edn., 2008—; cons. Nat. Govs. Assn., Nat. Conf. State Legislatures, US Sec. Edn., US Senate, US Dept. Edn., many state legislatures and govs.; mem. task force sch. fin. equity adequacy and productivity NRC, 1996—99; ct. master Superior Ct. NJ in Abbott V. Burke Sch. Fin. Case, 1997—98. Author: (book) Education Leadership for America's Schools, 1995; co-author: (books) Financing Schools for High Performance, 1998, Paying Teachers for What They Know and Do, 1997, 2d edit., 2002, School Finance: A Policy Perspective, 1992, 4th edit., 2007, Reallocating Resources: How to Boost Student Achievement Without Spending More, 2001, How to Create World Class Teacher Compensation, 2007; editor: Education Policy Implementation, 1991, Rethinking School Finance, 1992, School-Based Financing, 1999; contbr. articles to profl. jours., chapters to books. Mem. L.A. Chamber Edn. and Human Resources Commn., 1986, Gov.'s Sch. Fin. Commn., Calif., 1987, Calif. Assessment Policy Com., Gov.'s Edn. Task Force, Wis., 1996, Carnegie Corp. Task Force Edn. in the Early Yrs., 1994—96; mem. nat. rsch. coun. com. sch. fin. equity, adequcy and productivity, 1996—99; mem. Gov.'s Blue Ribbon Commn. State and Local Partnerships 21st Century, Wis., 2000. Grantee, Dept. Edn., Carnegie Corp., Spencer Found., Ford Found., Atlantic Philanthropic Svcs., Mellon Found., Carnegie Corp., Pew Charitable Trusts, Rockefeller Found., Joyce Found. Mem.: Nat. Soc. Study Edn., Politics Edn. Assn., Am. Ednl. Fin. Assn. (pres. 1979—80), Am. Ednl. Rsch. Assn. Avocations: Lionel training collecting, youth soccer, baseball coach. Office: U Wis Sch Edn Wis Ctr Edn Rsch 1025 W Johnson St # 653E Madison WI 53706-1706 Home: 360 W Washington Ave Unit 1002 Madison WI 53703-2766 Home Phone: 608-233-8720. Business E-Mail: arodden@wisc.edu.

O'DEAR, CRAIG STEVEN, lawyer; b. Quincy, Ill., June 26, 1957; s. H.C. and Martha Lou (Holbert) O'D.; m. Stephanie Doolin Patterson, Feb. 11, 1995. BS in Engring. Mgmt., U. Mo., Rolla, 1979; JD, Vanderbilt U., 1982. Bar: Mo. 1982, U.S. Dist. Ct. (we. dist.) Mo. 1982, U.S. Ct. Appeals (8th cir.) 1984, U.S. Ct. Appeals (10th cir.) 1988, U.S. Ct. Appeals (11th cir.) 1994. Indsl. engr. IBM Corp., Endicott, N.Y., summer 1979; summer assoc. Bass, Berry & Sims, ashville, 1980, Stinson, Mag & Fizzell, Kansas City, Mo., 1981, Kirkland & Ellis, Chgo., 1981; assoc. Stinson, Mag & Fizzell, Kansas City, 1982-88, Bryan Cave LLP, Kansas City, 1988-89, ptnr., 1990—, mem. exec. com. Chmn. recruiting com. Bryan Cave, Kansas City, 1988-92, coord. litigation dept., 1994—, group leader product liability client svc., 1996—. Chmn. United Way Pacesetter Camp, Kansas City, 1985; mem. leadership devel. program Kansas City Tomorrow, Kansas City, 1990. Patrick Wilson scholar Vanderbilt U., 1979-82. Mem. Kansas City Club. Republican. Presbyterian. Avocations: flying, golf, running, motorcycling. Office: Bryan Cave LLP 3500 One Kansas City Pl 1200 Main St Kansas City MO 64105-2122 Office Phone: 816-374-3207. E-mail: csodear@bryancave.com.

ODELBO, CATHERINE G., publishing executive; BA in Am. History with gen. honors, U. Chgo., 1985, MBA with honors, 2000. Mut. fund analyst Morningstar, Inc., Chgo., 1988-91, editor closed-end funds, 1991-95, pub. equities group, 1995-97, v.p. retail markets, 1997-98, sr. v.p. content devel., 1998-99; pres. Morningstar.com., 2000—. Mem. Phi Beta Kappa. Avocations: bridge, movies, reading. Office: Morningstar Inc 225 W Wacker Dr Chicago IL 60606-1224

O'DELL, JAMES E., newspaper publishing executive; V.p. ops. and techs. Chgo. Tribune, 1993-97, Chgo. Tribune Pub., 1997—. Office: Chgo Tribune Pub 435 N Michigan Ave Chicago IL 60611-4066

O'DELL, JANE, automotive company executive; Co-owner Westfall GMC Truck Inc., Kansas City, Mo. Office: Westfall GMC Truck Inc 3915 Randolph Rd Kansas City MO 64161-9383

O'DELL, MICHAEL RAY, accountant, bank executive; b. Camden, Ohio, Sept. 27, 1951; s. Donald Lee and Donna Louise (Buell) O'D. BS in Bus., Miami U., 1977; MBA, Xavier U., 1979. CPA, Ohio. Asst. trust officer First Nat. Bank

Southwestern Ohio, Hamilton, Ohio, 1977-83, acctg. officer Middletown, Ohio, 1983-86, comptroller, 1986-87, v.p., comptroller, 1987-96; CFO, sr. v.p. and sec. First Fin. Bancorp, Hamilton, OH, 1996—. Instr. microecons. Am. Inst. Banking, Cin., 1980-82; pres., bd. dirs. Cmty. First Fin., 1996—; bd. dirs. Sand Ridge Bank, Ohio City Ins. Agy.; bd. dirs., treas. First Fin. Bancorp Svc. Corp., 1999—. Bus. cons. applied econs. program Jr. Achievement, Springboro, Ohio, 1985. Served with USN, 1969-73. Mem. Am. Inst. CPA's, Ohio Soc. CPA's (com. chmn. 1985-88, pres. 1988-89, state dir. 1989-90). Clubs: Liberty (Ind.) Country. Avocation: golf. Home: 85B S Lafayette St Camden OH 45311-1019 Office: First Fin Banncorp 300 High St Hamilton OH 45011-6078

ODEN, ROBERT A., JR., academic administrator; m. Teresa Oden; children: Robert, Katherine. BA in History and Lit., Harvard Coll.; MA in Religious Studies/Oriental Langs., Cambridge U.; MA in Theology, Harvard Divinity, 1972; PhD in Near Eastern Langs. and Lit., Harvard U., 1975; MA (hon.), Dartmouth Coll., 1987. Faculty Dartmouth Coll., 1975—89, prof., 1985—89, chair dept. of religion, 1983—89; dir., founder Dartmouth's Humanities Inst.; headmaster Hotchkiss Sch., Lakeville, Conn., 1989—95; pres. Kenyon Coll., Gambier, Ohio, 1995—2002, Carleton Coll., Northfield, Minn., 2002—. Chmn. com. on orgn. and policy Dartmouth Coll., com. on admissions and fin. aid; lectr. in field. Author: The Bible Without Theology, 1987. Mem.: Conn. Assn. Ind. Schs. (bd. dirs.). Avocations: fishing, running, religious studies, archaeology. Office: Carleton Coll 1 North College St Northfield MN 55057 Office Phone: 507-646-4305. E-mail: president@acs.carleton.edu.

ODLE, JOHN H., metal products executive; married; 2 children. BA in Pre-law, Miami U., Oxford, Ohio. Mgmt. trainee USX Corp., Cin., Pitts. and St. Paul, 1964-68; mktg. rep. RTI Internat. Metals, Inc., Niles, Ohio, 1968-73, gen. mgr. sales, 1978-81, v.p. sales, 1981-89, sr. v.p., 1989-96, exec. v.p. ops., mktg., purchasing, 1996—, also bd. dirs.; western regional mgr. Teledyne Allvac, 1973-78. Bd. dirs. Reamet S.A. Mem. Am. Soc. Metals, Internat. Titanium Assn. Office: RTI Internat Metals Inc 1000 Warren Ave Niles OH 44446-1168

ODOM, TERI WANG, chemist; BS in chemistry, Stanford U., 1996; AM in chemistry, Harvard U., 1999, PhD in chemical physics, 2001, postdoctoral rsch., 2001—02. Asst. prof. dept. chemistry Northwestern U. Contbr. articles in profl. jours. Named one of Top 100 Young Innovators, MIT Tech. Review, 2004; recipient Prize for Young Chemists, IUPAC, 2001, Top Prize, Australian Jour. Chemistry, 2001, Victor K. LaMer award, ACS, 2003, Career award, NSF, 2004, NUE award, 2004; fellow, David and Lucille Packard, 2003; postdoctoral fellowship, NIH NRSA, 2001, Searle fellow, 2003. Mem.: Phi Beta Kappa. Office: Northwestern U Dept Chemistry 2145 Sheridan Rd Evanston IL 60208 Business E-Mail: todom@northwestern.edu.

O'DONNELL, F. SCOTT, former state agency administrator; b. Brownsville, Pa., Sept. 20, 1940; s. Francis Horner and Rebecca (Warren) O'D.; m. Ann Bukmir, Dec. 30, 1976. BA, Grove City Coll., Pa., 1962; postgraduate student, U. Wis. Grad. Sch. Banking, 1970, Internat. Sch. Banking, U. Colo., 1972. Nat. bank examiner Comptr. Currency, Cleve., 1965—71; sr. v.p. First Nat. Bank, Steubenville, Ohio, 1971—75; supt. banks State of Ohio, Columbus, 1975-77; exec. v.p. Heritage Bancorp, Steubenville, 1977-80; from v.p. to exec. v.p. Soc. Corp., Cleve., 1980-95; dep. tax commr. State of Ohio, Columbus, 1996-99; supt. fin. instns. divsn. Ohio Dept. Commerce, 1999—2006. Mem. state banking bd. Div. of Banks, Columbus, 1979-85, govt. affairs com. Ohio Bankers Assn., 1982-84. Served with USCG, 1963-69. Mem. Columbus Athletic Club, Pitts. Univ. Club, Belmont Hills Country Club, Lakewood Country Club. Avocations: travel, politics, antiques.

O'DONNELL, GENE, retail executive; With Zayre, 1971-74; various Hills Dept. Stores, 1974-92; exec. v.p. True*Serve Corp. (formerly Hills Dept. Stores), 1992-99; exec. v.p. merchandising and mktg. Office Max, Inc., Shaker Heights, Ohio, 1999—. Office: Office Max Inc 3605 Warrensville Center Rd Shaker Heights OH 44122-5248

O'DONNELL, KEVIN, retired metal products executive; b. Cleve., June 9, 1925; s. Charles Richard and Ella (Kilbane) O'Donnell; m. Ellen Blydenburgh, Aug. 16, 1965; children: Kevin, Susan, Michael, John, Maura, Neil, Megan, Hugh. AB, Kenyon Coll., Gambier, Ohio, 1947, PhD (hon.) in Law, 1980; MBA, Harvard U., 1947; PhD in Econs. (hon.), Pusan Nat. U., Korea, 1970; PhD in Humanities (hon.), Ohio Wesleyan U., 1972. Gen. sales mgr. Steel Improvement & Forge Co., Cleve., 1947-60; mgmt. cons. Booz, Allen and Hamilton, Cleve., 1960-62; gen. mgr., dir. Atlas Alloys-Rio Algom Corp., Cleve., 1963-66; dir. Peace Corps, Seoul, Republic of Korea, 1966-70, dir. adminstrn. and fin., then acting dep. dir., 1970-71; assoc. dir. internat. ops. ACTION, 1971-72; exec. v.p. SIFCO Industries, Inc., Cleve., 1972-75, pres., chief oper. officer, 1976-83, pres., chief exec. officer, 1983-89, chief exec. officer, 1989-90, chmn., exec. comm., 1990-94; ret., 1994. Bd. dirs. Ctrl. Pk. Media Corp., NYC, Doyle Pacific Industries, Ltd., Hong Kong; adv. dir. Capital Strategies, Inc., Cleve. Mem. Washington Inst. Fgn. Affairs, Cleve. Com. Fgn. Rels., chmn., 1979—82, CCWA, 1982—89; pres. Guest Ho., Inc., 1990—92; trustee Alcohol Svcs., Cleve., 1993—, Cleve. Coun. World Affairs, Nat. Peace Corps. Assn. Decorated Order Civil Merit Republic of Korea; recipient Disting. Internationalist award, Cleve. Coun. World Affairs, 2007. Mem.: Harvard Bus. Sch. Alumni Assn. (dir. Boston 1991—94), Army-Navy Club (Washington), Westwood Country Club, Union Club, 50 Club, First Friday Club, Harvard Bus. Sch. Club Cleve., Knights of Malta (master knight). Republican. Roman Catholic. Avocations: golf, reading. Office Phone: 216-226-3505. Personal E-mail: kevodoncle@aol.com.

O'DONNELL, TERRENCE, state supreme court justice; b. Cleve., Feb. 11, 1946; m. Mary Beth O'Donnell; children: Terrence, Michael, Colleen, Nora. BA in Polit. Sci., Kent State U., 1968; JD, Cleve. State U., 1971. Bar: Ohio 1971. Instr. speech and debate Cuyahoga Cmty. Coll., 1968—70; instr. grades 7 & 8 St. Brendan Sch., North Olmstead, 1970; law clerk to Judge Justice J.J.P. Corrigan Supreme Ct. Ohio, 1971—72; law clerk to Judge John M. Manos and Judge V. Corrigan 8th Dist. Ct. Appeals, 1972—74; dir. program paralegal edn. David M. Myers Coll., 1974—76; atty. Marshman, Snyder & Corrigan, 1976—80; judge Cuyahoga County Ct. Common Pleas, 1980—95, 8th Dist. Ct. Appeals, 1995—2003; justice Ohio Supreme Ct., 2003—. Vis. judge counties throughout Ohio, 2003—; chmn. Ohio Legal Rights Svc. Commn.; instr. CPA bus. law rev. Cleve. State U.; instr. several continuing legal edn. programs; mem. Ohio Supreme Ct. Commn. on Professionalism. Past pres. Legal Eagles; former mem. bd. trustees Magnificat HS, Rocky River, past pres. Father's Club; exec. dir. emeritus St. Patrick's Day Parade, Cleve.; coach Little League Baseball, Rocky River; instr. pub. sch. religion program St. Bernadette Ch., Westlake; mem. St. Bernadette Parish, Westlake, Ohio; mem. bd. dirs. Our Lady Wayside. Mem.: Ohio Supreme Ct., Ohio State Bar Assn. (mem. pub. understanding law sect.), Cleve. Bar Assn. (chmn. law related edn. com., Pres.'s award 1989—99), Cath. Lawyer's Guild Cleve. (officer). Office: Ohio Supreme Ct 65 S Front St Columbus OH 43215-3431

O'DWYER, MARY ANN, automotive executive; BS, DePaul U.; MS, Benedictine U. CPA. With Ernst and Young, McDonald's Corp.; various positions CC Industries (a Henry Crown Co.); sr. v.p. fin. ops., CFO Wheels, 1991—; sr. v.p. fin & ops., CFO Frank Consol. Enterprises. Office: Frank Consol Enterprises 666 Garland Pl Des Plaines IL 60016

OEHME, FREDERICK WOLFGANG, medical researcher, educator; b. Leipzig, Germany, Oct. 14, 1933; arrived in U.S., 1934; s. Friedrich Oswald and Frieda Betha (Wohlgamuth) Oehme; m. Nancy Beth McAdam, Aug. 6, 1960 (div. June 1981); children: Stephen Frederick, Susan Lynn, Deborah Ann, Heidi Beth; m. Pamela Sheryl Ford, Oct. 2, 1981; 1 child, April Virginia. BS in Biol. Sci., Cornell U., 1957, DVM, 1958; MS in Toxicology and Medicine, Kans. State U., 1962; DMV in Pathology, Justus Liebig U., Giessen, Germany, 1964; PhD in Toxicology, U. Mo., 1969. Diplomate Am. Bd. Toxicology, Am. Bd. Vet. Toxicology, Acad. Toxicol. Scis. Resident intern, Large Animal and Ambulatory Clinic Cornell U., 1957-58; gen. practice vet. medicine, 1958-59; from asst. to assoc. prof. medicine Coll. Vet. Medicine Kans. State U., 1959-66, 69-73, dir. comparative toxicology labs., 1969—, prof. toxicology, medicine and physiology Coll. Vet. Medicine, 1974-96, prof. toxicology, pathobiology, medicine and physiology, 1996—; postdoctoral research fellow in toxicology, NIH U. Mo., 1966-69. Cons. FDA, Washington, Ctr. for Vet. Medicine, Rockville, Md.; cons. animal care com. U. Kans., Lawrence, 1969—76, Syntex Corp., Palo Alto, Calif., 1976—77; mem. sci. adv. panel on PBB Gov.'s Office, State of MIch., 1976—77; mem. Coun. for Agrl. Sci. and Tech. Task Force on Toxicity, Toxicology and Environ. Hazard, 1976—83; cons., mem. adv. group on pesticides EPA, Cin., 1977—; expert state and fed. witness; advisor WHO, Geneva; presenter numerous papers to profl. meetings. Reviewer: Toxicology and Applied Pharmacology, Spectroscopy, numerous others. Mem. adv. coun. Cub Scouts Am., Eagle Scouts; mgr., coach Little League Baseball; active PTA; mem. Manhattan Civic Theatre; trustee Manhattan Marlin Swim Team; dir. meet Little Apple Invitational Swim Meet, 1984; mem. coun. Luth. Ch. Am., mem. sr. choir, numerous coms. Recipient Disting. Grad. Faculty award, Kans. State U., 1977—79, Dir.'s Letter of Commendation, FDA, 1983, Kenneth P. DuBois award, Midwest Soc. Toxicology, 1991, Kenneth F. Lampe award, Am. Acad. Toxicology, 1993, John Doull award, Ctrl. States Soc. Toxicology, 1994, medal, Azabu U., 1994, Silver award, Aristotelian U., 1995, others; fellow, Morris Animal Found., 1967—69. Fellow: Am. Acad. Vet. and Comparative Toxicology (past sec.-treas., numerous coms.), Am. Acad. Toxicology (past pres., numerous coms.); mem.: NRC (subcom. on organic contaminants in drinking water, safe drinking water com., adv. ctr. on toxicology assembly life scis. 1976—77, panel on toxicology marine bd., assembly of engring. 1976—79), AVMA (com. on environmentology 1971—73, adv. com. coun. on biol. and therapeuric agts. 1971—74, Samuel Shiedy award 1999), Nat. Ctr. Toxicol. Rsch. (vet. toxicology rep. sci. adv. bd., sci. adv. bd. 1974—77), N.Y. Acad. Scis., Soc. Toxicologic Pathologists, World Fedn. Clin. Toxicology Ctrs. and Poison Control Ctrs. (past pres.), Soc. Toxicology (past pres., numerous coms., Edn. award 2003), Cornell U. Athletic Assn., Manhattan Square Dance Club, Cornell U. Crew Club, Sigma Xi, Phi Zeta, Omega Tau Sigma. Republican. Avocations: reading, writing, walking, travel. Home: 148 S Dartmouth Dr Manhattan KS 66503-3079 Office: Kans State Univ Comparative Toxicology Labs 1800 Denison Ave Manhattan KS 66506-5660 Office Phone: 785-532-4334. E-mail: oehme@vet.ksu.edu.

OEHME, REINHARD, physicist, researcher; b. Wiesbaden, Germany, Jan. 26, 1928; arrived in U.S., 1954, permanent resident, 1956; s. Reinhold and Katharina (Kraus) O.; m. Mafalda Pisani, Nov. 5, 1952. Diplom Physiker, U. Frankfurt am Main, Germany, 1948; doctoral student of Werner Heisenberg, Max Planck Inst. Physik and U. Goettingen, 1949—51; Dr. rer. nat., U. Goettingen, Germany, 1951. Asst. Max Planck Inst. Physics, Goettingen, 1949—54; research asso. Fermi Inst. uclear Studies, U. Chgo., 1954-56; mem. faculty dept. physics and Fermi Inst., 1958—, prof. physics, 1960—; mem. Inst. Advanced Studies, Princeton, 1956-58. Vis. prof. Inst. de Física Teórica, São Paulo, Brazil, 1952-53, U. Md., 1957, U. Vienna, Austria, 1961, Imperial Coll., London, Eng., 1963-64, U. Karlsruhe, Fed. Republic Germany, 1974, 75, 77, U. Tokyo, 1976, 88; vis. scientist Internat. Centre Theoretical Physics, Miramare-Trieste, Italy, Brookhaven Nat. Lab., Lawrence Radiation Lab., U. Calif., Berkeley, CERN, Geneva, Switzerland, Max Planck Inst., Munich, Fed. Republic Germany, Rsch. Inst. for Fundamental Physics, Kyoto (Japan) U. Author articles in field, chpts. in books. Guggenheim fellow, 1963-64; recipient Humboldt award, 1974, Japan Soc. for Promotion of Sci. Fellowship awards, 1976, 88. Fellow: Am. Phys. Soc. Achievements include discovery of charge-conjugation non-invariance; the fundumental importance of CP-transformations; formulation and proof of Edge of the Wedge theorem, and of hadronic dispersion relations and sum rules; reduction of quantum field theories using renormalization group methods, supersymmetric theories as particular solutions; superconvergence relations for propagators and their implications for the confinement of gluons and quarks. Office: U Chgo Enrico Fermi Inst 5640 S Ellis Ave Chicago IL 60637-1433 Home Phone: 773-684-7983; Office Phone: 773-702-7299. Business E-Mail: oehme@theory.uchicago.edu.

OELSLAGER, W. SCOTT, state legislator; b. Oct. 15, 1953; m. Elsie Price, 1994. BA, Mt. Union Coll., 1975; JD, Capitol U. Sch. Law, 2002. Aide to U.S. rep. Ralph Regula, 1973-78; asst. Sen. Thomas Walsh, 1981-84; mem. Ohio Senate from 29th dist., Columbus, 1985—. Mem. Hwy. & Transp. com.; chmn. com. on criminal justice Senate Judiciary, chmn. edn. com., chmn. rules com.; dir. pub. rels. Malone Coll., 1978—80; dir. svc. Ohio Auto Dealers Assn. Bd. dir. Akron & Canton Arthritis Found. Recipient Watchdog of Treas. award, 1986, 88, 90; Rep. Legis. of Yr. award Nat. Rep. Legis. Assn., 1986, Disting. Legis. award Assn. Ohio Health Commr., 1989, Lay Person of Yr. award Phi Delta Kappa, 1989, Pub. Officer of Yr. award Social Workers Assn., 1992, Legis. of Yr. award Common Cause of Ohio & Ohio Nurses Assn., 1993, Legis. of Yr. Ohio Acad. Trial Lawyers, Disting. Svc. award Ohio State Bar Assn. Office: State Senate State Capital Columbus OH 43215 Home: 1585 Yorkshire Trce Se Canton OH 44709-4855

OESTERLE, ERIC ADAM, lawyer; b. Lafayette, Ind., Dec. 2, 1948; s. Eric Clark and Germaine Dora (Seelye) Oesterle; m. Carolyn Anne Scherer, Sept. 16, 1973; children: Adam Clark, Allison Margaret. BS, U. Mich., 1970, JD, 1973. Bar: Ill. 1973, US Dist. Ct. (no. dist.) Ill. 1973, US Ct. Appeals (7th cir.) 1987, US Supreme Ct. 1986. Assoc. Sonnenschein, Carlin, Nath & Rosenthal, Chgo., 1973—80; ptnr. Sonnenschein Nath & Rosenthal, Chgo., 1980—2007, Miller Shakman & Beem, LLP, Chgo., 2007—. Major gifts com. U. Mich. Law Sch., 2002—. Fellow: Am. Bar Found.; mem.: ABA, Chgo. Bar Assn., Ill. Bar Assn. Home: 645 Lake Rd Glen Ellyn IL 60137-4249 Office: Miller Shakman and Beem LLP 180 N La Salle, Ste 3600 Chicago IL 60614 Business E-Mail: eoesterle@millershakman.com.

OESTERLING, THOMAS OVID, retired pharmaceutical executive; b. Butler, Pa., Mar. 6, 1938; s. Victor Kenneth and Marjorie Gertrude (Oswald) O.; m. Janet Westrick, Dec. 30, 1960 (div. 1983); children: Thomas, Jennifer, Daniel; m. Cynthia Adler, 1984 (div. 1987). BS, Ohio State U., 1962, MS, 1964, PhD, 1966. Rsch. assoc., rsch. head Upjohn Co., Kalamazoo, 1966-76; dir. R&D dermatol. divsn. Johnson & Johnson Corp., New Brunswick, N.J., 1976-78, dir. pharm. R&D, 1978-79; v.p. med. products R&D Mallinckrodt, Inc., St. Louis, 1979-83; sr. v.p. R&D Collaborative Rsch. Inc., Bedford, Mass., 1984-86, pres., 1986-89; chmn., pres., CEO Gliatech Inc., Cleve., 1989-2000; ret. Mem. faculty Arden House Conf. on Stability Evaluation Pharm. Dosage Forms, 1979 Contbr. numerous sci. articles to profl. jours.; patentee in field. Recipient Disting. Alumni award Ohio State U. Coll. Pharmacy, 1982; Parke Davis rsch. grantee, 1962-64; Am. Found. for Pharm. Edn. fellow, 1964-66 Mem. Am. Chem. Soc., Soc. Nuclear Medicine, Acad. Pharm. Scis., Soc. for Neurosci.

O'FLAHERTY, PAUL BENEDICT, lawyer; b. Chgo., Feb. 11, 1925; s. Benedict Joseph and Margaret Celestine (Harrington) O'F.; m. Catherine Margaret Bigley, Feb. 13, 1954; children: Paul, Michael, Kathleen, Ann, Neil. JD cum laude, Loyola U., Chgo., 1949. Bar: Ill. 1949, U.S. Dist. Ct. (no. dist.) Ill. 1949, U.S. Ct. Appeals (7th cir.) 1956, U.S. Supreme Ct. 1959. Ptnr. Madden, Meccia, O'Flaherty & Freeman, Chgo., 1949-56; ptnr. Groble, O'Flaherty & Hayes, Chgo., 1956-63, Schiff Hardin & Waite, Chgo., 1963—. Mem. adj. faculty Loyola U., 1959-65 Author: (with others) Illinois Estate Administration, 1983; contbr. articles to profl. jours. Bd. advisors Cath. Charities, Chgo., 1979-92; trustee Clarke Coll., Dubuque, Iowa, 1982—. Served to 2d lt. U.S. Army, 1943-46. Fellow Am. Coll. Trust and Estate Counsel; mem. ABA, Ill. Bar Assn. (past chmn. fed. taxation sect. council), Chgo. Bar Assn. (past chmn. trust law com.), Chgo. Estate Planning Council Clubs: Union League, Metropolitan (Chgo.).

OGATA, KATSUHIKO, engineering educator; b. Tokyo, Jan. 6, 1925; came to U.S., 1952; s. Fukuhei and Teruko (Yasaki) O.; m. Asako Nakamura, Sept. 6, 1961; 1 son, Takahiko. BS, U. Tokyo, 1947; MS, U. Ill., 1953; PhD, U. Calif., Berkeley, 1956. Research asst. Sci. Research Inst., Tokyo, 1948-51; fuel engr. Nippon Steel Tube Co., Tokyo, 1951-52; mem. faculty U. Minn., 1956—, prof. mech. engring., 1961—; prof. elec. engring. Yokohama Nat. U., 1960-61, 64-65, 68-69. Author: State Space Analysis of Control Systems, 1967, Modern Control Engineering, 1970, 2002, Dynamic Programming, 1973, Ingenieria de Control Moderna, 1974, 1998, Metody Przestrzeni Stanow w Teorii Sterowania, 1974, System Dynamics, 1978, 2003, Engenharia de Controle Moderno, 1982, 2003, Teknik Kontrol Automatik, 1985, Discrete-Time Control Systems, 1986, 1995, Gendai Seigyo Riron, 1986, Dinamica de Sistemas, 1987, Solving Control Engineering Problems with MATLAB, 1994, Gendai Seigyo Kogaku, 1994, Designing Linear Control Systems with MATLAB, 1994, Kejuruteraan Kawalan Moden, 1996, Sistemas de Control en Tiempo Discreto, 1996, Projeto de Sistemas Lineares de Controle com MATLAB, 1996, Solucao de Problemas de Engenharia de Controle com MATLAB, 1997, MATLAB for Control Engineers, 2007. Recipient Outstanding Adv. award Inst. of Tech., U. Minn., 1981, John R. Ragazzini Edn. award Am. Automatic Control Coun., 1999. Fellow ASME; mem. Sigma Xi, Pi Tau Sigma. Personal E-mail: kogata02@aol.com.

OGG, WILLIAM L., state legislator; m. Janice Ogg; children: Julie Lynne, William Kenneta, Shana Jo. Student, Ohio U. Commr. Scioto County, Ohio; vice mayor, mem. city coun. City of Portsmouth, Ohio, mayor; rep. dist. 92 Ohio Ho. Reps., Columbus. Chmn. Ohio Valley Regulation Devel. Commn., 1986-91. Named to Dem. Hall of Fame, Scioto County, 1990. Mem. Portsmouth C. of C. Home: 2700 Dogwood Ridge Rd Wheelersburg OH 45694-8800

O'GRADY, MICHAEL J., lawyer; b. Cin., 1970; BA, U. Mich., 1992; MBA, U. Cin., 1996, JD, 1995. Bar: Ohio 1995, US Dist. Ct. Southern Dist. Ohio 1996, US Ct. of Appeals Sixth Cir. 2002. Jud. clerk Hon. Burton Perlman, Southern Dist. Ohio, 1995—97; atty. Frost Brown Todd, LLC, Cin. Named one of Ohio's Rising Stars, Super Lawyers, 2006. Mem.: Am. Bankruptcy Inst., ABA, Ohio State Bar Assn., Cin. Bar Assn. Office: Frost Brown Todd LLC 2200 PNC Ctr 201 E Fifth St Cincinnati OH 45202-4182 Office Phone: 513-651-6800. Office Fax: 513-651-6981.

O'GUINN, M. DAVE, III, lawyer; b. Dec. 29, 1969; BS, DePauw U., 1992; MS in Polit. Sci., Ind. U., 1994; JD, Notre Dame Law Sch., 2001. Bar: Ohio 2001, US Dist. Ct. Southern Dist. Ohio 2002, US Dist. Ct. Northern Dist. Ohio, US Dist. Ct. Southern Dist. Ind., Ct. of Appeals Sixth Dist. Assoc. Dinsmore & Shohl LLP, Cin. Chair, Young Professionals Com. Am. Red Cross, Cin., mem., Personnel Com., mem., Ops. Com. Named one of Ohio's Rising Stars, Super Lawyers, 2006. Mem.: Ohio State Bar Assn., ABA, Cin. Bar Assn. Office: Dinsmore & Shohl LLP 255 E Fifth St Ste 1900 Cincinnati OH 45202-4700 Office Phone: 513-977-8200. Office Fax: 513-977-8141.

O'HAGAN, JAMES JOSEPH, lawyer; b. Chgo., Dec. 29, 1936; s. Francis James and Florence Agnes (Dowgialo) O'H.; m. Suzanne Elizabeth Wiegand, June 28, 1958; children: Timothy, Karen, Peggy, Kevin. B in Commerce, De Paul U., 1958, JD, 1962. Sr. ptnr. O'Hagan Spencer, Chgo., 2006—. Mem. Cook County Pres.'s Com. on the Cts. for the 21st Century, chmn. suburban subcom., 1998—2000; lawyer Chgo. Claim Mgrs. Assn., 1992—2006; chmn. USLaw Network, Inc., 2001—03, mem. exec. com., 2001—06; founding mem. Profl. Lines Atty. Network. Mem. ABA, Ill. Bar Assn. Chgo. Bar Assn., Am. Bd. Trial Advocates, Internat. Assn. Def. Coun., Def. Rsch. Inst., Profl. Liability Underwriters Soc. Roman Catholic. Avocations: golf, tennis, physical conditioning, painting, reading. Office: O'Hagan Spencer 1 East Wacker Dr Ste 3 Chicago IL 60601 Home Phone: 847-292-1266; Office Phone: 312-422-6121. Business E-Mail: johagan@ohaganspencer.com.

O'HAIR, JOHN D., lawyer; b. Detroit; m. Barbara Stanton. BA in Polit. Sci., DePauw U., 1951; JD, Detroit Coll. Law, 1954, LLD (hon.), 1992. Asst. corp. counsel City of Detroit; mem. Common Pleas Ct. Detroit, 1965-68; judge Wayne County Cir. Ct., 1968-83; corp. counsel Wayne County, 1983, prosecutor, 1983—. Assoc. prof., v.p., bd. trustees Detroit Coll. Law; chmn. Criminal Assessments Commn.; past vice-chmn., mem. adv. bd. Wayne County Comty. Corrections Bd.; mem. Housing and Pub. Safety Com., New Detroit, Inc., Prosecuting Attys. Coordinating Coun., Gun Violence Coalition; former instr. Mich. Jud. Inst.; former mem., vice-chmn. Mich. Jud. Tenure Commn. Mem. adv. bd. St. Ambrose Acad., Wayne County unit Am. Cancer Soc.; mem. Pres.'s Commn. on Model State Drug Laws; mem. adv. com. Drug Free Sch. Zones. With U.S. Army. Mem. Mich. State Bar (commn. on death and dying), Mich. Hospice Assn. (adv. bd.), Inc. Soc. Irish/Am. Lawyers (past pres.), Prosecuting Attys. of Mich. (past pres.), Prosecuting Attys. Assn. (chmn. legis. com.). Office: Office of Prosecuting Atty Frank Murphy Hall Justice 1441 Saint Antoine St Detroit MI 48226-2311

O'HARA, PATRICIA ANNE, dean, law educator; BA summa cum laude, Santa Clara U., 1971; JD summa cum laude, Notre Dame, 1974. Bar: Calif. 1974. Assoc. Brobeck, Phleger & Harrison, 1974—79, 1980—81; assoc. prof. law Notre Dame Law Sch., 1981, prof., 1990, v.p. student affairs, 1990—99, Joseph A. Matson dean, law educator, 1999—. Chair nominating com. Am. Assn. Law Schools, 2005—06, chair, sect. law sch. deans, 2007. Contbr. chapters to books, articles to law jours. Mem.: Law Sch. Admissions Coun. (bd. trustees). Office: U Notre Dame 203 Law Sch PO Box 780 Notre Dame IN 46556-0780 Office Phone: 574-631-6789. Office Fax: 574-631-8400. E-mail: Patricia.A.O'Hara.3@nd.edu.

OHM, HERBERT WILLIS, agronomy educator, agriculturist; b. Albert Lea, Minn., Jan. 28, 1945; s. Wilhelm Carl and Lena Ann (Finkbeiner) O.; m. Judy Ann Chrisinger, Aug. 8, 1964; children: Cari Lynn, David William. BS in Agrl. Edn., U. Minn., St. Paul, 1967; MS in Plant Breeding, N.D. State U., 1969; PhD in Plant Genetics and Breeding, Purdue U., 1972. Cert. agronomist. Asst. prof. Purdue U., West Lafayette, Ind., 1972-77, assoc. prof. agronomy, 1977-83, prof., 1983—2004, disting. prof., 2004—. Team leader Interdisciplinary Wheat and Oat Genetics and Breeding Program, West Lafayette, 1980—, Interdisciplinary Purdue/AID Devel. Program, Burkina Faso, West Africa, 1983-85; mgr. hard red winter wheat rsch. Pioneer Hi-Bred Internat., Inc., Hutchinson, Kans., 1980. Contbr. book chpts. Recipient Soils and Crops Merit award Ind. Crop Improvement Assn., 1988, Merit award Orgn. of African Unity, 1989, Meritorious Svc. award Sci., Tech. and Rsch. Commn., 1989, Agronomic Achievement award American Soc. of Agronomy, 1994, Sch. of Agr. Team award, 2000, Distinction cert. Purdue Agr. Alumni Assn., 2005. Fellow: AAAS, Crop Sci. Soc. Am. (chmn. divsn. 1991), Am. Soc. Agronomy; mem.: Am. Registry Cert. Profls. in Agrl. Crops and Soils (cert.), Coun. Agrl. Sci. and Tech., Nat. Oat Improvement Coun. (chmn.), Am. Oat Workers Conf. (chmn.). Avocations: woodworking, music. Office: Purdue U Dept Agronomy Lilly Hall Life Scis West Lafayette IN 47907-1150 Office Phone: 765-494-8072. Business E-Mail: hohm@purdue.edu.

OKA, TAKESHI, physicist, physical chemist, astronomer, educator; b. Tokyo, June 10, 1932; arrived in U.S., 1981, naturalized, 2004; s. Shumpei and Chiyoko O.; m. Keiko Nukui, Oct. 24, 1960; children: Ritsuko, Noriko, Kentaro, Yujiro. B.Sc., U. Tokyo, 1955, PhD, 1960; DSc (hon.), U. Waterloo, 2001, Univ. Coll., London, 2004. Rsch. assoc. U. Tokyo, 1960-63; fellow NRC Can., Ottawa, Ont., 1963-65, asst., 1965-68, assoc., 1968-71, sr. rsch. physicist, 1971-80; prof. U. Chgo., 1981—, Robert A. Millikan disting. prof., 1989—; prof. Enrico Fermi Inst., 1993—2004, emeritus, 2004—. Mem. editorial bd. Chem. Physics, 1972-92, Jour. Molecular Spectroscopy, 1973—, Jour. Chem. Physics, 1975-77. Recipient Steacie prize, 1972; Earle K. Plyler prize, 1982, Norman McLean award U. Chgo., 2004. Fellow Royal Soc. Can., Royal Soc. London (Davy medal 2004), Am. Phys. Soc., Optical Soc. Am. (William F. Meggers award 1997, Ellis R. Lippincott award 1998), Am. Acad. Scis. and Arts; mem. Am. Astron. Soc; Am. Chem. Soc. (E. Bright Wilson award, 2002). Home Phone: 773-753-5263; Office Phone: 773-702-7070. Business E-Mail: t-oka@uchicago.edu.

OKADA, RONALD SHIG, lawyer; b. Cleve., June 11, 1960; s. Shig and Mary Mariko (Machida) O.; m. Ann (Haugan) Aug. 18, 1984; children: Lauren Mariko, David Ryon, Julia Elise. BA, Carleton Coll., 1982; JD, U. Mich., 1985. Bar: Ohio 1985, U.S. Dist. Ct. (no. dist.) Ohio 1985, U.S. Ct. Appeals (6th cir.) 1988, (11th cir.), 1998, U.S. Supreme Ct., 1999. Assoc. Baker & Hostetler LLP, Cleve., 1985-92, ptnr., litigation dept., 1993—, mem. policy com., 2002—. Mem. ABA, Ohio Bar Assn., Cleve. Bar Assn., Carleton Coll. Alumni Club (no. Ohio). Office: Baker & Hostetler LLP 3200 National City Ctr Cleveland OH 44114-3485 Home Phone: 440-572-6514; Office Phone: 216-861-7645. Office Fax: 216-696-0740. Business E-Mail: rokada@bakerlaw.com.

OKARMA, JEROME D., lawyer, manufacturing executive; m. Pam Okarma; 2 children. BA, Western Ill. U., 1974; JD, Northwestern U., 1977. Bar: Ill. 1977, Wis. 1989. Atty. Inland Steel Co., 1977—82; sr. atty. Borg-Warner Corp., 1982—89; joined Johnson Controls, Inc., Milw., 1989, asst. sec., 1990—2004, dep. gen. counsel, 2000—04, corp. v.p., 2003—, gen. counsel, sec., 2004—. Office: Johnson Controls, Inc 5757 N Green Bay Ave Milwaukee WI 53209 Office Phone: 414-524-1200. E-mail: jerome.d.okarma@jci.com.

O'KEEFE, DANIEL P., lawyer; b. Superior, Wis., 1952; BA cum laude, Coll. St. Thomas, 1974; JD magna cum laude, William Mitchell Coll. Law, 1978. Bar: Minn. 1978. Law clerk U.S. Dist. Ct., Minn., 1978; ptnr. Dorsey & Whitney, Mpls., E.W. Blanch & Co., Bloomington. Adj. prof. William Mitchell Coll. Law. Exec. editor William Mitchell Law Review, 1977-78. Office: EW Blanch & Co 3500 W 80th St Ste 600 Bloomington MN 55431-4435

O'KEEFE, FRANCIS RONALD, lawyer; b. Oct. 7, 1950; AB, Georgetown U., 1972; JD, Cleve.-Marshall Coll., 1977. Bar: Ohio 1977, U.S. Dist. Ct. (no. dist.) Ohio 1978, U.S. Supreme Ct. 2002. Pvt. practice, 1977—86; sec. and gen. counsel Broadview Fin. Corp., 1986—89; ptnr. Hahn, Loeser & Parks LLP, 1989—. Named Ohio Super Lawyer, Cin. mag., 2004, 2005; named to Best Lawyers in Am. in corp. law, 2001—; recipient Sindell Tort Competition prize, Cleve.-Marshall Law Sch., 1977, Most Useful to Practicing Attys. Law Rev. Article award, 1977. Mem.: ABA, Soc. Corp. Governance Profls., Greater Cleve. Bar Assn., Ohio State Bar Assn. Office: Hahn Loeser & Parks LLP 200 Public Sq Ste 3300 Cleveland OH 44114-2301 Office Phone: 216-274-2396. E-mail: frokeefe@hahnlaw.com.

O'KEEFE, MICHAEL, academic administrator, physicist; b. Mc Cloud, Minn. BS in Physics, Mathematics & Philosophy, Marquette U.; MS in Nuclear Physics & Mathematics, U. Pitts.; LittD (hon.), Hamline U. Pres. Consortium for Advancement of Pvt. Higher Edn., Washington, 1983—89; exec. v.p. & CEO McKnight Found., Mpls.; asst. sec. Fed. Dept. Health, Edn. & Welfare; human svcs. commr. State of Minn., 1999—2002; pres. Mpls. Coll. Art & Design, 2002—. Co-chmn. -edn. program Aspen Inst., 1987—; bd. regents U. Minn., 1996—2002; bd. dirs. Minn. Pub. Radio. Office: Office of President Minneapolis College Art & Design 2501 Stevens Ave Minneapolis MN 55404 Office Phone: 612-874-3785.

O'KEEFE, MICHAEL DANIEL, lawyer; b. St. Louis, Jan. 3, 1938; s. Daniel Michael and Hanoria (Moriarty) O'K.; m. Bonnie Bowdern, July 11, 1964; children: Collen Coyne, Daniel Michael. AB, LLB, St. Louis U., 1961; postgrad., George Washington U., 1963. Bar: Mo. 1961, U.S. Ct. Appeals (8th cir.) 1961, U.S. Dist. Ct. (ea. dist.) Mo. 1961, Ill. 1975, U.S. Ct. (so. dist.) Ill. 1975, U.S. Ct. Appeals (5th and 7th cirs.) 1983, (10th cir.) 1995. Asst. cir. atty., St. Louis, 1961—62, 1964—65; pvt. practice, 1964-67; ptnr. Lucas, Murphy & O'Keefe, St. Louis, 1967-74, Thompson & Mitchell, St. Louis, 1974-96, Thompson Coburn, St. Louis, 1996—. Adj. prof. trial practice Sch. of Law, St. Louis U., 1992—. Editor: American Maritime Cases, 1985—. Trustee St. Louis U. Capt. USAF, 1962-64. Fellow Am. Coll. Trial Lawyers; mem. Internat. Assn. Def. Counsel, Fedn. Ins. and Corp. Counsel, Maritime Law Assn., Nat. Assn. Railroad Trial Counsel, Am. Law Inst. Democrat. Roman Catholic. Avocations: reading, tennis, fencing, archaeology, microbiology. Home: 372 Walton Row Saint Louis MO 63108-1909 Office: Thompson Coburn One US Bank Plz Saint Louis MO 63101-1643 Office Phone: 314-552-6092. Business E-Mail: mokeefe@thompsoncoburn.com.

O'KEEFE, THOMAS JOSEPH, metallurgical engineer; b. St. Louis, Oct. 2, 1935; s. Thomas and Hazel (Howard) O'K.; m. Jane Gilmartin, Aug. 31, 1957; children— Thomas, Kathleen, Matthew, Daniel, Margaret, Robert. BS, Mo. Sch. Mines, 1958; PhD, U. Mo., Rolla, 1965. Process control engr. Dow Metal Products Co., Madison, Ill., 1959-61; mem. faculty U. Mo., Rolla, 1965—, prof. metall. engring., 1972—, Curators prof. metall. engring., 1985-86, Curators Disting. prof., 1986—. Rsch. technologist NASA, Houston, summer 1965; rsch. metall. engr. Ames (Iowa) Lab., 1966-67; rsch. metall. engr., cons. Cominco Ltd., Trail, B.C., Can., 1970-71; Disting. lectr. hydrometallurgy U. B.C., 1992, U. Mo.-Rolla Sch. Mining and Metallurgy Acad. Recipient Alumni Merit award U. Mo., Rolla, 1971, Outstanding Tchg. award, 1979, Silver medal paper award AESF, 1994; Jefferson-Smurfit fellow, 1984-85. Mem. AIME (dir. 1976-77, 79-81, EMD lectr. 1991), Testing Materials Soc., The Metall. Soc., Sigma Xi, Alpha Sigma Mu, Tau Beta Pi, Phi Kappa Theta (dir. 1965-77, cert. commendation 1970, pres. citation 1986). Home: 905 Southview Dr Rolla MO 65401-4720 Office: Material Research Center Univ Mo Rolla MO 65409

O'KEEFE, THOMAS MICHAEL, academic administrator; b. St. Cloud, Minn., Mar. 25, 1940; s. Thomas William and Genevieve B. (McCormick) O'K.; m. Kathleen Marie Gnifkowski, Aug. 20, 1966; children: Steven Michael, Ann Catherine. Student, Marquette U., 1961-65, BS, 1965; MS in Nuclear Physics, U. Pitts., 1968; DHL, Hamline U., 1989. Dir. edn. planning HEW, Washington, 1969-70, dep. asst. sec., 1977-80; v.p. Carnegie Found. for Advancement of Teaching, Washington, 1980-83; pres. Consortium for Advancement Pvt. Higher Edn., Washington, 1983-89; exec. v.p. McKnight Found., Mpls., 1989-99; commr. Dept. Human Svcs., State Minn., St. Paul, 1999—2002; pres. Mpls. Coll. Art and Design, 2002—. Dir. Washington internships in edn. George Washington U., 1970-73; dir. policy analysis and evaluation U. Ill., Chgo., 1973-74, assoc. v.p. acad. affairs, 1974-77; head U.S. del. to Orgn. Econ. Coop. and Devel., 1979, 80; mem. Carnegie Forum on Edn. and the Economy, 1985-88; mem. N.J. Commn. on Ind. Higher Edn., 1986-88; mem. task force on ind. higher edn. Edn. Commn. States, 1987-89; co-chair Edn. Program, The Aspen Inst., 1987—. Contbr. articles to profl. jours.; contbg. editor: Change mag., 1985—2001; bd. dirs.: Editl. Project in Edn., 1984—93. Bd. dirs. The Edn. Resources Inst., Boston, 1987-94, Minn. Coun. on Founds., 1994-99, Minn. Pub. Radio, 1999—, Alliance Excellent Edn., 2004-; trustee Buena Vista Coll., Storm Lake, Iowa, 1984-90; mem. Coun. on Fgn. Rels., 1995-99; bd. regents U. Minn., 1996-02. Mem.: Mpls. Club. Democrat. Office: Mpls Coll Art and Design 2501 Stevens Ave S Minneapolis MN 55404 Business E-Mail: michael_okeefe@mcad.edu.

OKIISHI, THEODORE HISAO, mechanical engineering educator; b. Honolulu, Jan. 15, 1939; s. Clifford Muneo and Dorothy Asako (Tokushima) O.; m. Rae Wiemers, May 28, 1963; children: Christopher Gene, John Clifford, Mark William, Kenneth Edward. Student, U. Hawaii, 1956-57; BS, Iowa State U., 1960, MS, 1963, PhD, 1965. Registered profl. engr., Iowa, Ohio. From asst. prof. to prof., assoc. dean coll. engring. Iowa State U., Ames, 1967—2007. Cons. on fluid dynamics Contbr. articles to profl. jours. Served to capt. C.E., U.S. Army, 1965-67 Decorated Joint Services Commendation award; named Outstanding Prof., Iowa State U. student sect. ASME, 1983, Mech. Engring. Dept. Prof. of Yr., Iowa State U., 1977, 86, 90; recipient award for research NASA, 1975; Ralph R. Teetor award Soc. Automotive Engrs., 1976, Engring. Coll. Superior Teaching award Iowa State U., 1987, Cardinal Key Iowa State U., 1991. Fellow ASME (Melville medal 1989, 98, dedicated svc. award, 2001, R. Tom Sawyer award); mem. AIAA, Sigma Xi. Republican. Mem. Ch. of Jesus Christ of Latter-day Saints. Club: Osborn Research Home: 2940 Monroe Dr Ames IA 50010-4362 Office: Iowa State U 106 Nuclear Engineering Lab Ames IA 50011-0001 Office Phone: 515-294-4395. Business E-Mail: tedo@iastate.edu.

OKUN, MAURY, dance company executive; Exec. dir. Eisenhower Dance Ensemble, Troy, Mich., 1996—; co-founder, exec. dir. Detroit Chamber Winds & Strings; exec. dir. Great Lakes Chamber Music Festival. Office: Detroit Chamber Winds Strings 20300 Civic Center Dr Ste 100 Southfield MI 48076-4166

OLDFORD, FLOYD MARK, legal association administrator; b. Detroit, Mich., Apr. 29, 1932; s. William Augustus and Hazel (Davis) Oldford; m. Rosemarie Parzych, Jan. 15, 1955; children: Mark, Leslie, Rosanne, Karen, Marcianne, Matthew. BS, U. Detroit, 1954; JD, Detroit Coll. Law, 1974. Bar: Mich. 1975. Sr. auditor Arthur Andersen & Co., Detroit, 1954—58; contr.-treas. Burr, Patterson & Auld, Detroit, 1958—62; dir. proterty and tax Mich. Consolidated Gas Co., Detroit, 1963—75; contr. Am. Natural Resources Co., Detroit, 1975—83, dir. acctg. rsch., 1984—86; dir. adminstrn. Butzel, Long, Gust, Klein & Van Zile, Detroit, 1986—. Bd. dirs. Detroit br. YMCA. Mem.: Detroit Bar Assn., Mich. Bar Assn. Republican. Office: Butzel Long Gust Klein & Van Zile 1650 First National Bldg Detroit MI 48226

OLDMAN, TERRY L., museum director; BS, U. Kans., MA in Art Mus. Edn.; MS in Bus. Adminstrn., U. Hawaii. Interim asst. dir. Spencer Mus., Lawrence, Kans.; dir./curator edn. Mus. Art, Tallahassee; dir. Albrecht-Kemper Mus. Art, Saint Joseph, Mo., 1999—. Decorated Disting. Flying Cross, Bronze Star, Aerial Achievement Medal. Office: Albrecht-Kemper Mus Art 2818 Frederick Ave Saint Joseph MO 64506 E-mail: toldham@albrecht-kemper.org.

OLDS, JOHN WARD, internist; b. Apr. 25, 1935; s. Thayer Stevens and Dorris (La Venture) O.; m. Rosemary Burns, July 10, 1957; children: David, James, Miriam. BS, Iowa State U., 1956; MD, U. Tenn., 1967. Diplomate Am. Bd. Internal Medicine, Am. Bd. Infectious Diseases, cert. physician exec. Intern San Francisco Gen. Hosp., 1967—68; resident, fellow U. N.Mex., 1968—72; practice internal medicine Des Moines, 1972—2002; dir. continuing med. edn. Iowa Meth. Med. Ctr., 1983—93, cons. infectious diseases, 1972—2002, attending physician, 1972—2002; asst. clin. prof. U. Iowa, Iowa City, 1978—95; co-dir. infectious disease and epidemiology Iowa Meth. Med. Ctr., 1985—93, dir. med. affairs, 1989—93; Medicare med. dir. for Iowa, 1993—97; Part A Medicare med. dir. for Iowa and S.D., 1997—2004; med. dir. Medicare RHHI, 1997—2007. Mem. Iowa Bd. Med. Examiners, 1987—93, vice chmn., 1991—93, med. advisor, 2005—. Contbr. articles to med. jour. Lt. USNR, 1956—61. Recipient Roche award, U. Tenn., 1966. Fellow: ACP, Infectious Diseases Soc. Am., Am. Coll. Physician Execs.; mem.: AMA, Iowa Found. Med. Care (dist. chmn. 1981—83, bd. dirs. 1985—), Iowa Med. Soc. (councilor 1980—84), Med. Libr. Club (pres. 1985—86). Avocation: squash. Office: 400 E Court Ave Des Moines IA 50309 Business E-Mail: john.olds@iowa.gov.

OLDSON, JO, state representative, lawyer; b. Ft. Dodge, Iowa, May 15, 1956; BA, JD, Drake U. First dep. ins. commr., 1994—99; policy advisor to Gov. Tom Vilsack, 1999—2000; state rep. dist. 61 Iowa Ho. of Reps., 2003—; mem. commerce, regulation and labor com.; mem. govt. oversight com.; mem. state govt. com.; mem. ways and means com.; mem. oversight appropriations subcom. Vol. Young Women's Resource Ctr. Democrat. Office: State Capitol East 12th and Grand Des Moines IA 50319

O'LEARY, DANIEL VINCENT, JR., lawyer; b. Bklyn., May 26, 1942; s. Daniel Vincent and Mary (Maxwell) O'L.; m. Marilyn Irene Gavigan, June 1, 1968; children: Daniel, Katherine, Molly, James. AB cum laude, Georgetown U., 1963; LLB, Yale U., 1966. Bar: Ill. 1967. Assoc. Wilson & Mc Ilvaine, Chgo., 1967—75, ptnr., 1975—87, Peterson & Ross, Chgo., 1987—94, Schwartz & Freeman, Chgo., 1994—95; of counsel Mandell, Menkes & Surdyk, LLC, Chgo., 1995—. Pres., bd. dirs. Jim's Cayman Co., Ltd.; pres. TV and Radio Purchasing Group Inc.; asst. sec. L.M.C. Ins. Co. Bermuda, 1990—; pres. Wagering Ins. N.Am. Purchasing Group Inc., 1997—. Lt. comdr. USNR, ret. Roman Catholic. Avocations: fishing, scuba diving. Office: Mandel Menkes LLC Ste 300 333 W Wacker Dr Chicago IL 60606 Office Phone: 312-251-1000. E-mail: doleary@mandellmenkes.com.

O'LEARY, DENNIS SOPHIAN, accrediting body executive; b. Kansas City, Mo., Jan. 28, 1938; s. Theodore Morgan and Emily (Sophian) O'L.; m. Margaret Rose Wiedman, Mar. 29, 1980; children: Margaret Rose, Theodore Morgan. BA, Harvard U., 1960; MD, Cornell U., 1964. Diplomate Am. Bd. Internal Medicine, Am. Bd. Hematology. Intern U. Minn. Hosp., Mpls., 1964-65, resident, 1965-66, Strong Meml. Hosp., Rochester, NY, 1966—67, chief resident and hematology fellow, 1967—68; asst. prof. medicine and pathology George Washington U. Med. Ctr., Washington, 1971-73, assoc. prof., 1973-80, prof. medicine, 1980-86, assoc. dean grad. med. edn., 1973-77, dean clin. affairs, 1977-86; pres. Joint Commn., Oakbrook Terrace, Ill., 1986—2007. Med. dir. George Washington U. Hosp., 1974-85, v.p. Univ. Health Plan, 1977-85; pres. D.C. Med. Soc., 1983. Chmn. editl. bd. Med. Staff News, 1985-86; contbr. articles to profl. jours. Founding mem. Nat. Capital Area Health Care Coalition, Washington, 1982; trustee James S. Brady Found., Washington, 1982-87; bd. dirs. Nat. Quality Forum, 2001-07, Nat. Adv. Coun. Agy. for Healthcare Rsch. and Quality, 2002-04. Maj. U.S. Army, 1968-71. Recipient Community Service award D.C. Med. Soc., 1981, Key to the City, Mayor of Kansas City, Mo., 1982. Master ACP; fellow Am. Coll. Physician Execs.; mem. AMA (Resolution commendation 1981, Disting. Svc. award 2005), Am. Hosp. Assn. (del. 1984-86, Resolution commendation 1981), Internat. Club (Chgo.). Avocation: tennis.

O'LEARY, ROBERT J., retail executive; b. Bellefonte, Pa. m. Linda O'Leary; 2 children. BA in advt., Pa. State U., 1971. With advt. and pub. rels. divsns. United Techs. Corp., Hartford, Conn., IBM; v.p. pub. rels. and advt. Unisys, Blue Bell, Pa., 1988—94; gen. mgr. global pub. affairs Mobil Oil Corp., Fairfax, Va., 1995—2000; v.p. pub. affairs and comm. Bacardi Ltd., 2000; sr. v.p. global comm. Goodyear Tire & Rubber Co., Akron, Ohio, 2002—03; sr. v.p. pub. rels., comm., and govt. Sears, Roebuck & Co., Hoffman Estates, Ill., 2003—. Bd. visitors Pa. State U. Coll. Comm.; bd. trustees Found. Am. Comm. Alumni Fellow, Pa. State U. Office: Sears Roebuck & Co 3333 Beverly Rd Hoffman Estates IL 60179

OLEEN, LANA, state legislator; b. Kirksville, Mo., Apr. 26, 1949; d. Robert James and Frances (Primm) Scrimsher; m. Kent E. Oleen; children: Brooke, Bentson. BS in Edn., Ks. State Tchrs. Coll., 1972; MS in Curriculum, Emporia State U., 1977. Tchr., Council Grove, Kans., 1972-74, St. George, Kans., from 1978; communications coord. Woodward-Clyde Cons., San Francisco, 1974-75; dir. communication Kans. Dept. Human Resources; mem. Kans. State Senate, 1988—. Mem. Rep. Precinct Com., 1978—. Active Kans. Rep. Women, Riley County Rep. Women. Mem. NEA, Nat. Coun. Tchrs. of English. Lutheran. Office: Kansas Senate State Capitol Rm 136-N Topeka KS 66612 Address: 1619 Poyntz Ave Manhattan KS 66502-4148

OLEN, GARY, marketing company executive; b. Milw., Mar. 29, 1942; s. Norbert John and Irene (Rydlewicz) O.; m. Maryann Wozniak (div. May 1988); children: Wendy, Jeff. Grad. high sch., Milw. Rebuyer catalog div. J.C. Penney Co., Milw., 1960-67; buyer C&H Distbrs., Milw., 1967-70; mktg. dir. Fidelity Products, Mpls., 1970-77; owner, mgr. Sportsman's Guide, Mpls., 1977-89, exec. v.p., prin., 1989—. Republican. Roman Catholic. Avocations: hunting, fishing, travel. Office: Sportsmans Guide 411 Farwell Ave South Saint Paul MN 55075-2464 Home: 14529 High Eagle Drive SE Bemidji MN 56601

OLIAN, ROBERT MARTIN, lawyer; b. Cleve., June 14, 1953; s. Robert Meade and Doris Isa (Hessing) Olian; m. Terri Ellen Ruther, Aug. 10, 1980; children: Andrew Zachary, Alix Michelle, Joshua Brett. AB, Harvard U., 1973, JD, 1977, M in Pub. Policy, 1977. Bar: Ill. 1977, U.S. Dist. Ct. (no. dist.) Ill., U.S. Ct. Appeals (7th cir.) 1983, U.S. Dist. Ct. (no. dist. trial bar) Ill. 1992, U.S. Dist. Ct. (we. dist.) Mich. 1994, U.S. Dist. Ct. (cen. dist.) Ill. 2004. Assoc. Sidley & Austin, Chgo., 1977-84; ptnr. Sidley Austin LLP, Chgo., 1985—. Editor: (book) Illinois Environmental Law Handbook, 1988, 1997. Panel atty. Chgo. Vol. Legal Svcs., 1983—; bd. dirs. Friends IDF, 2003—07; trustee North Shore Congregation Israel, 1990—, sec., 1995—96, v.p., 1996—2003, first v.p., 2004—05, pres., 2005—; mem. regional strategic/mktg. com. Alexian Bros. Ill., Inc., Elk Grove, 1985—88; mem. dean's alumni leadership coun. JFK Sch. Govt. Harvard U., 2003—. Mem.: ABA, Chgo. Bar Assn., Harvard Club (Chgo.), Std. Club. Jewish. Home: 85 Oakmont Rd Highland Park IL 60035-4111 Office: Sidley Austin LLP One S Dearborn # 2800 Chicago IL 60603-2302 Home Phone: 847-432-5662; Office Phone: 312-853-7208. Business E-Mail: rolian@sidley.com.

OLIN, WILLIAM HAROLD, orthodontist, educator; b. Menominee, Mich., Mar. 7, 1924; s. Harold H. and Lillian (Hallgren) Olin; m. Bertha Spitters, May 6, 1950; children: William Harold, Paul Scott, Jon Edward. DDS, Marquette U., 1947; MS, U. Iowa, 1948. Asst. prof. orthodontics Univ. Hosps., U. Iowa, Iowa City, 1948, assoc. prof., 1963-70, prof., 1970-93, prof. emeritus, 1995—. Chmn. bd. dirs. Hills Bank. Author: (book) Cleft Lip and Palate Rehabilitation, 1960; contbr. articles to profl. jours. Fund raiser, participant Ops. Smile. Served to capt. US Army, 1952—54. Mem.: Am. Acad. Sports Dentistry (bd. dirs., sec./treas. 1989—95), Am. Cleft Palate Assn. (pres. 1970), Iowa Orthodontic Soc. (pres. 1959), Midwest Orthodontic Soc. (pres. 1968—69), Angle Orthodontic Soc. Midwest (pres. 1982), Univ. Athletic Club (bd. dirs.), Rotary (pres. Iowa City). Republican. Methodist. Avocations: collecting political memorabilia, music box collecting, sports, travel, politics, coin collecting/numismatics. Home: 426 Mahaska Dr Iowa City IA 52246-1610 Personal E-mail: w.olin@mchsi.com.

OLINGER, GORDON NORDELL, surgeon; b. Denver, 1942; MD, U. Rochester, 1968. Intern UCLA, 1968-69, resident, 1969-70, 72-74; resident in surgery NIH Clinic, Bethesda, Md., 1970-72; with Froedert Meml. Luth. Hosp.; prof. Med. Coll. Wis. Mem. ACS, Soc. Thoracic Surgery, Am. Assn. for Thoracic Surgery, Am. Surg. Assn. Office: Acad Faculty 9200 W Wisconsin Ave Milwaukee WI 53226-3522

OLINS, ROBERT ABBOT, communications research executive; b. Cambridge, Mass., Sept. 25, 1942; s. Harry and Janice Olins; m. Irma Westrich, June 16, 1967; 1 son, Matthew Abbot. Student, Hobart Coll., 1961-62, San Francisco Art Inst., 1962; BA, U. Mass., 1967; postgrad., U. Tampa, 1968; MA, U. Mo., 1969, PhD, 1972. With Marsteller, 1972, N.W. Ayer, 1972, Post, Keys & Gardner, Chgo., 1973, Young & Rubicam, Chgo., 1973-76, mng. dir. comm. rsch. divsn., 1976-77; pres., CEO, subs. Comm. Rsch. Inc., Chgo., 1978—, owner, chmn., 1979—. Pres., CEO Insights, Chgo., 1976—; assoc. prof. Howard Univ., 2004—. Contbr. articles to profl. jours. Recipient Chgo./4 award for creative excellence, 1974; winner Chgo. Mackinac race, 1981; Am. Assn. Advt. Agys. grantee, 1968-71 Mem.: Mid orth Assn. (bd. dirs., chmn. planning), Am. Mktg. Assn., Chgo. Yacht Club, Lake Mich. Yachting Assn., U.S. Sailing Club, Skyline Club. Avocations: skiing, sailing, power boating.

OLIPHANT, PATRICK, cartoonist; b. Adelaide, Australia, July 24, 1935; came to U.S., 1964; children: Laura, Grant, Susan. L.H.D. (hon.), Dartmouth Coll., 1981. Copyboy, press artist Adelaide Advertiser, 1953-55, editorial cartoonist, 1955-64; world tour to study cartooning techniques, 1959; editorial cartoonist Denver Post, 1964-75, Washington Star, 1975-81, L.A. Times Syndicate, 1965-80, Universal Press Syndicate, 1980—; represented by Susan Conway Gallery, Washington. Author: The Oliphant Book, 1969, Four More Years, 1973, An Informal Gathering, 1978, Oliphant! A Cartoon Collection, 1980, The Jellybean Society, 1981, Ban this Book, 1982, But Seriously Folks, 1983, The Year of Living Perilously, 1984, Make My Day, 1985, Between a Rock and a Hard Place, 1986, Up to There in Alligators, 1987, Nothing Basically Wrong, 1988, What Those People Need Is a Puppy, 1989, Fashions for the New World Order, 1991, Just Say No, 1992, Why do I Feel Uneasy?, 1993, Waiting for the Other Shoe to Drop, 1994, Off to the Revolution, 1995, Maintain The Status Quo, 1996, So That Where They Come From, 1997, Oliphant's Anthem, 1998, Are We There Yet?, 1999, Now We'll Have to Spray for Politicians, 2000, When We Can't See the Forest for the Bushes, 2001. Recipient 2d Place award as funniest cartoonist Internat. Fedn. Free Journalists in Fleet St., London, 1958, Profl. Journalism award Sigma Delta Chi, 1966, Pulitzer prize for editl. cartooning, 1967, Cartoonist of Yr. award Nat. Cartoonist Soc., 1968, 72, Best in Bus. award Washington Journalism Rev., 1985, 87, Premio Satira Politica award Forte de Marmi, 1992, Thomas Nast award, 1992. Office: Universal Press Syndicate 4520 Main St Ste 700 Kansas City MO 64111-7701

OLIVER, EDWARD CARL, retired state legislator, insurance company executive, small business owner; b. St. Paul, May 31, 1930; s. Charles Edmund and Esther Marie (Bjugstad) O.; m. Charlotte Severson, Sept. 15, 1956; children: Charles E., Andrew T., Peter A. BA, U. Minn., 1955. Sales rep. Armstrong Cork Co., NYC, 1955; registered rep. Piper, Jaffray & Hopwood, Mpls., 1958; mgr. Mut. Funds Inc., subs. Dayton's, Mpls., 1964, NWNL Mgmt. Corp. subs. Northwestern Nat. Life Ins. Co., Mpls., 1968-72, v.p., 1972-81, pres., dir., 1981-90; mem. Minn. State Senate, 1992—2003, asst. minority leader, 1998—2003; owner Oliver Fin., 2003—. Arbitrator/mediator, Nat. Assn. Securities Dealers Dispute Resolution, Inc., 1988—; bd. dir. 1st Minn. Bank, N.A. Mem. Gt. Lakes Commn., 1993—; bd. dirs. Minn. State Arts Bd., 2003—. Mem. Internat. Assn. Fin. Planners (past pres. Twin City chpt., nat. governing com.), Psi Upsilon, Mpls. Athletic Club. Home: 20230 Cottagewood Rd Excelsior MN 55331-9300 Office: 464 2d St Ste 203 Excelsior MN 55331 Office Phone: 952-380-0107. E-mail: oliverfinancial@earthlink.net.

OLIVER, JERRY ALTON, former police chief; 5 children. BS in Criminal Justice, Ariz. State U., MS in Pub. Adminstrn., 1988; postgrad., Police Exec. Rsch. Forum, Washington. From patrolman to supr. Phoenix Police Dept., from supr. to asst. chief of police, 1971-90; dir. drug policy Memphis Mayors Office; chief of police Pasadena (Calif.) Police Dept., 1991—94, Richmond (Va.) Police Dept., 1995—2002, Detroit, Mich., 2002—03; spl. policy advisor Ariz. Atty. Gen., 2004—05; dep. dir. Ariz. Dept. Admin., 2005—06; dir. Ariz. Dept. Liquor Lics. & Control. Founder Spl. Friends Project, Richmond, 1988—. Inductee Ariz. State U. Coll. Pub. Programs Hall of Fame, 1989; recipient Phoenix chpt. Image award NAACP, 1990, People of Yr. award Law Enforcement News, 1999, Richmonder of Yr. award Richmond Style Mag., 1999, U.S. Atty. Gen.'s award for outstanding contbns. to cmty. partnership for pub. safety, 2000, othrs. Home Phone: 480-840-1313; Office Phone: 602-542-1932. E-mail: jaoxfive@hotmail.com.

OLIVER, JOHN PRESTON, chemistry professor; b. Klamath Falls, Oreg., Aug. 7, 1934; s. Robert Preston and Agnes May (McCornack) O.; m. Elizabeth Ann Shaw, Aug. 12, 1956; children: Karen Sue Oliver Vernon, Roy John, Gordon Preston. BA, U. Oreg., 1956; PhD, U. Wash., 1959. Asst. prof. chemistry Wayne State U., Detroit, 1959-64, assoc. prof., 1964-67, prof., 1967—, assoc. dean R&D, Coll. Liberal Arts, 1987-91, acting dean, 1991-92, interim dean Coll. Sci., 1992-93, dep. provost, 1996—2003, v.p. for rsch., 2003—. Chmn. organizing com. XIV Internat. Conf. on Organometallic Chemistry. Mem. Ferndale (Mich.) Bd. Edn., 1984-88. Mem. Am. Chem. Soc., Detroit sect. Am. Chem. Soc., Sigma Xi. Office: Wayne State Univ 5057 Woodard Rm 6409 Detroit MI 48202-3489 Home Phone: 248-548-2320; Office Phone: 313-577-5600. Business E-Mail: jpo@wayne.edu.

OLIVER, SOLOMON, JR., judge; b. Bessemer, Ala., July 20, 1947; s. Solomon Sr. and Willie Lee (Davis) O.; married; 2 children. BA, Coll. of Wooster, 1969; JD, NYU, 1972; MA, Case Western Res. U., 1974. Bar: Ohio 1973, U.S. Dist. Ct. (no. dist.) Ohio 1977, U.S. Ct. Appeals (6th cir.) 1977, U.S. Supreme Ct. 1980. Asst. prof. dept. polit. sci. Coll. of Wooster, Ohio, 1972-75; sr. law clk. to Hon. William H. Hastie U.S. Ct. Appeals (3d cir.), Phila., 1975-76; asst. U.S. atty. U.S. Atty.'s Office, Cleve., 1976-82, chief civil divsn., 1978-82; spl. asst. U.S. atty., chief appellate divsn. Dept. Justice, Cleve., 1982, spl. asst. U.S. atty., 1982-85; prof. law Cleve. State U., 1982-94, assoc. dean faculty and adminstrn., 1991-94. Lectr. in law, trial practice Case Western Res. U., Cleve., 1979-82; vis. scholar Stanford U. Coll. Law, 1987; vis. prof. Comenius U., Bratislava, Czechoslovakia, 1991, Charles U., Prague, Czechoslovakia, 1991. Chair O.K. Hoover Scholarship com. Bapt. Ch., 1987-89; trustee Coll. of Wooster, Ohio, 1991-97, 2000—. Mem. ABA, Nat. Bar Assn. Office: 801 W Superior Ave Cleveland OH 44113-1838

OLIVER, THORNAL GOODLOE, retired health care executive; b. Memphis, Aug. 26, 1934; s. John Oliver and Evelyn Doris (Goodloe) Mitchell; m. Pauline Reid, Oct. 1, 1959. B.S., Tenn. State U., Nashville, 1956; M.H.A., Washington U., St. Louis, 1973. Cert. nursing home adminstr., Mo. Asst. dir., King Meml. Hosp., Kansas City, Mo., 1973-75; evening mgr. Truman Med. Ctr., Kansas City, Mo., 1975-77; asst. adminstr. Mid-Am. Radiation Ctr. U. Kans. Coll. Health Sci., Kansas City, Kans., 1977-81; dir. CHS, Inc., Leawood, Kans., 1981-82; adminstr. Poplar Bluff Hosp., Mo., 1982-83; adminstr. The Benjamin F. Lee Health Ctr., Wilberforce, Ohio, 1983-86; asst. clin. prof. Dept. Community Medicine, Wright State U., Dayton, 1986-89; asst. patent adminstr. Munson Army Hosp., Ft. Leavenworth, Kans., 1987-2004, ret., 2004; cons. Urban Health Assocs., Nashville, 1986-87, others. Contbr. articles to profl. jours. Served with U.S. Army, 1957-59, USAR, 1959-63. Fellow Am. Coll. Hosp. Adminstrs.; mem. Am. Hosp. Assn., at. Assn. Health Services Execs., Am. Med. Record Assn., Mo. League of Nursing Home Adminstrs. Home: 10641 N Grand Ave Kansas City MO 64155-1655

OLIVER, TIMOTHY ALLEN, lawyer; b. Lebanon, Ohio, July 13, 1950; s. George Wilbur and Ruthanna Mae (Ward) O.; m. Lois Anne Jacquemin, Oct. 28, 1972; children: Daniel, Matthew. BSBA, Ohio State U., 1971, JD, 1974. Bar: Ohio 1974, U.S. Dist. Ct. (so. dist.) Ohio 1975, U.S. Supreme Ct. 1978. Asst. pros. atty. County of Warren, Lebanon, 1974-76, 79-86, pros. atty., 1986—. Past ptnr. Oliver & Powell, Lebanon. Bd. dirs. Countryside YMCA, Lebanon, 1987-92, Warren/Clinton Drug and Alcohol Coun., Lebanon, 1987—; exec. com. Warren County Rep. Cen. Com., Lebanon, 1987—; trustee Coalition for Drug-Free Greater Cin., 1995—. Mem. ABA, Ohio Bar Assn., Warren County Bar Assn., Nat. Dist. Attys. Assn., Ohio Pros. Attys. Assn. (pres. 1998), Kiwanis (bd. dirs. Lebanon chpt. 1987-93, pres. 1991-92). Avocations: coaching, golf. Office: Warren County Prosecutor 500 Justice Dr Lebanon OH 45036-2379

OLIVIERI, JOSÉ ALBERTO, lawyer; b. San Juan, Aug. 28, 1957; s. José Juan Olivieri and Carmen Rivera; m. Jeanne Nikolai Olivieri, Aug. 12, 1978; children: Elisa, Lucas, Elena. BA in Polit. Sci. cum laude, Carroll Coll., 1978; JD, Marquette U., 1981. Bar: Wis. 1981. Lawyer Michael, Best & Friedrich, Milw., 1981. Asst. prof. law Marquette U., Milw., 1986-88, adj. prof., 1988—; bd. dirs. U.S. Bank, Milw. Articles editor Marquette Law Rev. Chmn. bd. dirs. Milw. Found., 1998; bd. dirs., pres. United Cmty. Ctr., Milw., 1987-92; mem. U. Wis. Bd. Regents, 1998—. Recipient Pro bono award Posner Found., Milw., 1985, Cmty. Svc. award Future Milw., 1987, Vol. Fundraiser award Nat. Assn. Fundraising Execs., 1993, Leadership award Milw. Civic Alliance, 1995; named Hispanic Man of Yr., United Migrant Opportunity Svcs., Milw., 1998. Mem. ABA, Wis. Hispanic Lawyers Assn. (pres. 1984), Wis. State Bar Assn. (chair labor and employment law sect. 1996), Milw. Bar Assn. Avocations: reading, sports. Office: Michael Best & Friedrich 100 E Wisconsin Ave Ste 3300 Milwaukee WI 53202-4108 Office Phone: 414-271-6560.

OLLINGER, W. JAMES, lawyer; b. Kittanning, Pa., Apr. 5, 1943; s. William James and Margaret Elizabeth (Reid) Ollinger; m. Susan Louise Gerspacher, Oct. 20, 1979; children: Mary Rebecca, David James. BA, Capital U., Columbus, Ohio, 1966; JD, Case Western Res. U., 1968. Bar: Ohio 1968, US Dist Ct (no dist) Ohio 1971. Ptnr. Baker & Hostetler, Cleve., 1968—. Mem. Bentleyville Village Coun., Ohio, 1990—93; mayor Bentleyville, 1997—99. Mem.: Order of Coif, Phi Delta Phi. Office: Baker & Hostetler 3200 Nat City Ctr 1900 E 9th St Ste 3200 Cleveland OH 44114-3475 Office Phone: 216-861-7473. Business E-Mail: jollinger@bakerlaw.com.

OLMAN, GLORIA G., secondary school educator; BA in English, minor in journalism, Mich. State U., 1963; MA in Reading, Oakland U., 1978. Tchr. journalism Utica High Sch., Mich., newspaper adviser, 1977—. Bd. mem. Mich. Interscholastic Press Assn., 1984—, pres., 1989—90, legis. chair. Named Nat. H.S. Journalism Tchr. of Yr., 1992, Spl. Recognition advisor, 1981, Disting. Advisor Dow Jones Newspaper Fund Inc., 1987; named to Mich. Journalism Hall of Fame, 1997. Mem.: Journalism Edn. Assn. (cert. master journalism educator). Office: Utica High Sch 47255 Shelby Rd Utica MI 48317-3156

OLMAN, LYNN, state legislator; Rep. dist. 51 Ohio Ho. of Reps., Columbus, 1995—. Office: 604 Ford St Maumee OH 43537-1948

OLMSTEAD, WILLIAM EDWARD, mathematics professor; b. San Antonio, June 2, 1936; s. William Harold and Gwendolyn (Littlefield) Olmstead; m. Adele Cross, Aug. 14, 1957 (div. 1967); children: William Harold, Randell Edward. BS, Rice U., 1959; MS, Northwestern U., 1962, PhD, 1963. Mem. rsch. staff S.W. Rsch. Inst., San Antonio, 1959—60; Sloan Found. postdoctoral fellow Johns Hopkins, 1963—64; prof. applied math. Northwestern U., Evanston, Ill., 1964—, chmn. dept. engring. scis. and applied math., 1991—93. Vis. mem. Courant Inst. Math. Scis. NYU, 1967—68; faculty visitor U. Coll. London, 1973, Calif. Inst. Tech., 1987, 90; editor Options Prof. Newsletter, Spear Capital Mgmt., 2003—07. Contbr. articles to profl. jours. Named Technol. Inst. Tchr. of Yr., 1980, Charles Deering McCormick prof., 1994—97; recipient Award for Tchg. Excellence, Northwestern Alumni Assn., 1993. Mem.: Am. Contract Bridge League (silver life master), Soc. Indsl. and Applied Math. (editl. bd. jour. 1998—), Am. Phys. Soc., Am. Math. Soc., Am. Acad. Mechanics, Soc. Engring. Sci. (bd. dirs. 1998—2000), John Evans Club, Sigma Tau, Tau Beta Pi, Sigma Xi. Episcopalian. Home: 153 E Laurel Ave #203 Lake Forest IL 60045 Office: Northwestern U Dept Engring Scis And Applie Evanston IL 60208-0001

OLNESS, KAREN NORMA, medical educator; b. Rushford, Minn., Aug. 28, 1936; d. Norman Theodore and Karen Agnes (Gunderson) O.; m. Hakon Daniel Torjesen, 1962. BA, U. Minn., 1958, BS, MD, 1961. Diplomate Am. Bd. Pediat., Am. Bd. Med. Hypnosis, Develop. & Behavioral Pediatrics. Intern Harbor Gen. Hosp., Torrance, Calif.; resident Nat. Children's Hosp. Med. Ctr., Washington; asst. prof. George Washington U., Washington, 1970-74; assoc. prof. U. Minn., Mpls., 1974-87; prof. pediat., family medicine and internat. health Case Western Res. U., Cleve., 1987—. Named Outstanding Woman Physician, Minn. Assn. Women Physicians, 1987; recipient Christopherson award Am. Acad. Pediat., 1998, Aldrich award, Am. Acad. Pediat., 1999, Ann. award Soc. Devel. and Behavioral Pediat., 2003, Outstanding Alumni award U. Minn., 2007; named to Cleve. Med. Hall of Fame, 2000. Fellow: Soc. Clin. and Exptl. Hypnosis (pres. 1991—93), Am. Soc. Clin. Hypnosis (pres. 1984—86), Am. Acad. Pediat. (chair internat. health sect. 2001), Am. Acad. Family Physicians; mem.: Internat. Hypnosis Soc. (pres. 2003—06), Northwestern Pediat. Soc. (pres. 1977), Soc. Devel. and Behavioral Pediat. Office: Case Western Res U 11100 Euclid Ave Cleveland OH 44106-6038 Office Phone: 216-368-4368. Business E-Mail: karen.olness@case.edu.

OLNEY, JOHN WILLIAM, psychiatry professor; b. Marathon, Iowa, Oct. 23, 1931; married, 1957; 3 children. BA, U. Iowa, 1957, MD, 1963. Diplomate Am. Bd. Psychiatry, Am. Bd. Neurology. Intern Kaiser Permanente Found., San Francisco, 1963-64; resident, 1964-68; from instr. to assoc. prof. psychiatry Washington U., St. Louis, 1968-77, prof. psychiatry and neuropathology Sch. Medicine, 1977—. NIMH biol. sci. trainee Washington U., 1966-68; asst. psychiatrist Barnes Hosp., 1968—; cons. psychiatrist Malcolm Bliss Mental Health Ctr., 1968—; elected to Inst. Medicine/NAS, 1996. Recipient Wakeman award Rsch. Neurosci., 1992; co-recipient Charles A. Dana award for Pioneering Achievements in Health, 1994. Mem. APA, Am. Assn Neuropathology, Soc. Neurosci. Assn. Rsch. Nervous & Mental Disorders, Psychiatric Rsch. Soc. Achievements include research in role of excitatory neurotoxins in disorders of the nervous system. Office: Washington U Dept Psychiatry Sch Med Saint Louis MO 63110

OLOPADE, OLUFUNMILAYO FALUSI (FUNMI OLOPADE), geneticist, educator, oncologist, hematologist; b. Nigeria, Apr. 29, 1957; m. Christopher Sola Olopade; 3 children. MD with distinction, U. Ibadan, Nigeria, 1980. Diplomate Am. Bd. Internal Medicine, Am. Bd. Med. Oncology, Am. Bd. Hematology; lic. MD Ill., Ind. Med. officer Nigerian Navy Hosp.; intern in medicine, surgery, pediatrics, ob-gyn. Univ. Coll. Hosp., Ibadan, 1980—81; intern in internal medicine Cook County Hosp., Chgo., 1983—84, resident in internal medicine, 1984—86, chief resident in medicine, 1986; clin. instr. U. Ill. Abraham Lincoln Sch. Medicine, Chgo., 1986—87; postdoctoral fellow jt. sect. hematology/oncology U. Chgo., 1987—91, asst. prof. hematology/oncology, Pritzker Sch. Medicine, 1991—2002, mem. Cancer Rsch. Ctr., 1991—, mem. Cancer Biology com., 1994—, mem. Genetics com., 1996—, assoc. prof. medicine, prof. medicine and human genetics Ill., 2002—, dir. Ctr. for Clinical Cancer Genetics, Cancer Risk Clinic Ill., 1992—, dir. Hematology/Oncology Fellowship Program Ill., 1998—. Attending physician Cook County Hosp., Chgo., 1987; mem. steering com., cooperative family registry for breast cancer studies, Nat. Cancer Inst., also mem. adv. com. Cancer Genetics Network and bd. scientific counselors; mem. adv. bd. Cancerandcareers.org; lectr. in field. Ad hoc reviewer Jour. AMA, Genes, Chromosomes and Cancer, Genomics, Human Molecular Genetics, Cancer Rsch., Blood, Molecular Carcinogenesis, Jour. Clin. Oncology, New Eng. Jour. Medicine; contbr. articles to profl. jours.; contbr. to book chpts. and abstracts on topics including genetics of cancer. Mem. med. adv. bd. Young Survival Coalition. Named a Top Doctor, Chicago Mag., 1997; recipient Sir Samuel Manuwa Gold medal for Excellence in Clin. Sciences, 1980, Scholar award, James S. McDonnell Found., 1992, Doris Duke Disting. Clin. Scientist award, 2000, Phenomenal Women award, 2003, People Are Today's Heroes (PATH), Gov. Rod R. Blagojevich, presented by First Lady Patti Blagojevich, State Ill., 2005, Heroes In Healthcare award, Access Cmty. Network, 2005, Am. Assn. Cancer Rsch. (AACR)-Minorities in Cancer Rsch. Jane Cooke Wright Lectureship, 2006; Ellen Ruth Lebow Fellowship, Assn. for Brain Tumor Rsch., 1990, MacArthur "Genius Grant" Fellow, John D. and Catherine T. MacArthur Found., 2005. Mem. AAAS, Am. Assn. Cancer Rsch. (membership credentialing com. 1994-95, program com. carcinogenesis subcom. 1993), Am. Soc. Clin. Oncology (mem. program com. subcom. tumor biology and genetics 1997, Young Investigator award, 1991), Am. Assn. Preventive Oncology, Women in Cancer Rsch., Am. Soc. Hematology, Am. Coll. Physicians, Am. Soc. Breast Disease, Am. Soc. Hematology, Assn. Am. Professors, Nigerian Med. Assn., Am. Cancer Soc. (adv. com. cancer control investigations, epidemiology, diagnosis, therapy 1994-97). Office: U Chgo Med Ctr 5841 S Maryland Ave # MC2115 Chicago IL 60637-1463 Office Phone: 773-702-1632, 773-702-6149. Office Fax: 773-702-0963. Business E-Mail: folopade@medicine.bsd.uchicago.edu.

OLOWOKANDI, MICHAEL, professional basketball player; b. Apr. 3, 1975; Student, U. Pacific, 1998. Guard, center L.A. Clippers, 1998—2002; player Min. Timberwolves, 2003—. Named to Schick All-Rookie Second Team, 1998—99. Achievements include recording 16 points and game-highs of 17 rebounds and 3 steals against the Vancouver Grizzlies; scored in double figures in six consecutive games; logged two double-doubles. Office: Min Timberwolves 600 First Ave N Minneapolis MN 55403

OLSEN, EDWARD JOHN, geologist, educator, curator; b. Chgo., Nov. 23, 1927; s. Edward John and Elizabeth (Bornemann) O.; children— Andrea, Ericka. AB, U. Chgo., 1951, MS, 1955, PhD, 1959. Geologist Geol. Survey Can., 1953, U.S. Geol. Survey, 1954—, Canadian Johns-Manville Co., Ltd., 1956, 57, 59; asst. prof. Case Inst. Tech., also Western Res. U., 1959-60; curator mineralogy Field Mus. Natural History, 1960-91, chmn. dept. geology, 1974-78; research assoc. prof. dept. geophys. scis. U. Chgo., 1977—. Adj. prof. U. Ill., Chgo. Circle, 1970-91. Assoc. editor Geochim. et Cosmochim. Acta., 1985-91. Fellow Mineral. Soc. Am.; mem. Mineral. Assn. Can., Geochem. Soc., Meteoritical Soc. Achievements include spl. research stability relations of minerals in earth's mantle and meteorites. Home: 437 Wild Indigo Ln Madison WI 53717-2148 Office: U Chgo Dept Geophys Sci Chicago IL 60637

OLSEN, LUTHER S., state legislator; b. Feb. 26, 1951; BA, U. Wis. Assemblyman Wis. State Dist. 41, 1994—. Owner (farm supply store) Omro. Mem. Berlin Area Bd. Edn., 1976-95. Home: 2021 Hwy 49 Berlin WI 54923 Office: PO Box 8952 Madison WI 53708-8952

OLSEN, REX NORMAN, trade association executive; b. Hazeltown, Idaho, Apr. 9, 1925; s. Adolph Lars and Pearl (Robbins) O. B.J., BA in English, U. Mo., 1950. Editor Clissold Pub. Co., Chgo., 1950-54; copy editor Am. Peoples Ency., Chgo., 1955; asst. editor Am. Hosp. Assn., Chgo., 1956-59, mng. editor, 1959-64, dir. jours. div., 1964-69, dir. publs. bur., 1969-75, exec. editor, asso. pub., 1975-79; v.p., treas. Am. Hosp. Pub., Inc., 1980-85; pres. Words Ltd., 1985—. Dir. publs. ETNA Comms., Chgo., 1997—. Served with USNR, 1943-46. Mem. Soc. Nat. Assn. Pubs. (sec. 1975-76, 2d v.p. 1976-77, 1st v.p. 1977-78, pres. 1978-79), Chgo. Bus. Publs. Assn. (dir. 1974-78, 4th v.p. 1978-79), Sigma Delta Chi. Home and Office: 5510 N Sheridan Rd Unit 12-A Chicago IL 60640-1630 Personal E-mail: rexorudy@aol.com.

OLSON, ALLEN INGVAR, former governor of North Dakota; b. Rolla, ND, Nov. 5, 1938; s. Elmer Martin and Olga (Sundin) O.; m. Barbara Starr Benner, Aug. 29, 1964; children: Kristin, Robin, Craig. BSBA, U. ND, 1960, JD, 1963. Bar: ND 1963, US Supreme Ct. 1967. Asst. dir. ND Legis. Council, 1967-69; ptnr. Conmy, Rosenberg, Lucas & Olson, Bismarck, ND, 1969-72; atty. gen. State of ND, 1972-80, gov., 1981-85; pvt. legal practice, bus. cons. Mpls., 1985—87; cons. Physicians of Minn. & affiliated cos., 1987—88; pres. & CEO Ind. Cmty. Bankers Minn., Eagan, 1988—2003; commr. Internat. Joint Commn., 2002—. Bd. dirs. Bank of ND, ND Mill & Elevator, Allina Health Sys., Red River Trade Corridor; chmn. Interstate Oil Compact Commn., WESTPO, 1983. Pres. Dakota Zool. Soc., 1977; bd. dirs. Missouri Valley YMCA. Served with JAG Corps US Army, 1963—67. Decorated Army commendation medal; named Am. of Year Am. Religious Town Hall Found., 1977, Man of Yr. Assoc. Gen. Contractors, 1981, Water Statesman of Year Nat. Water Resources Assn., 1983 Mem. Nat. Govs. Assn. (chmn. soil conservation task force, chmn. legal affairs com.), ND Bar Assn., Burleigh County Bar Assn., Ind. Cmty. Bankers Minn. (pres. & CEO 1988-2003) Citizens League, Lambda Chi Alpha, Am. Legion, Hazeltine Nat. Golf Club, Exchange Club, Masons, Elks, Sons of Norway. Republican. Presbyterian. Office: Internat Joint Commn Ste 100 1250 23rd St NW Washington DC 20440 Office Phone: 202-736-9000. Office Fax: 202-735-9015. E-mail: mnicbm@aol.com.*

OLSON, DAVID WENDELL, bishop; b. St. Paul, Apr. 4, 1938; s. Wendell Edwin and Eva Victoria (Edstrom) O.; m. Nancy Grace Evans, July 9, 1961; children: Kathryn, Jonathan, Justin. BA, St. Olaf Coll., 1960; MDiv, Luther Sem., St. Paul, 1964. Ordained to ministry Am. Luth. Ch.,1964. Pastor St. Paul's Ch., Balt., 1964-69; co-pastor St. James Ch., Crystal, Minn., 1969-78; dir. North Mpls. Luth. Coalition, 1978-82; asst. prof. Luther N.W. Sem., St. Paul, 1982-84; asst. to bishop S.E. Minn. dist. Am. Luth. Ch., St. Paul, 1984-87; bishop Mpls. area synod Evang. Luth. Ch. in Am., Mpls., 1987—. Chair Robbinsdale (Minn.) Sch. Bd., 1976-82; trustee Fairview Hosp., Mpls. Bush Found. fellow, 1975; Regents scholar St. Olaf Coll. Office: Evang Luth Ch in Am 122 W Franklin Ave Ste 600 Minneapolis MN 55404-2455

OLSON, DONOVAN, state representative; b. Boone, Iowa, June 12, 1965; Student, Des Moines Area C.C.; B of Art and Designs, Iowa State U., M of Cmty. and Regional Planning. Coord. distance edn. Iowa State U.; state rep. dist. 48 Iowa Ho. of Reps., 2003—; mem. econ. growth com.; mem. environ. protection com.; mem. local govt. com.; mem. adminstrn. and regulation appropriations subcom. Supr. Boone County, Iowa; chair Boone County Empowerment Bd.; mem. steering com. Family Resource Ctr.; mem. Wallace House Rural/Urban Leaders Discussion Group; vol. Boone County Tire Round-up and Household Hazardous Waste Collection; coach Boone Little League Tee Ball; mem. parish rels. com. First United Meth. Ch. Democrat. Office: State Capitol East 12th and Grand Des Moines IA 50319

OLSON, EDGAR, state legislator; b. Nov. 19, 1937; m. Phyllis Olson; 2 children. Degree, N.D. State U. Mem. Minn. Ho. of Reps., St. Paul, 1984-98. Mem. taxes, agr., local govt. and met. affairs coms., others; farmer. Democrat. Home: RR 3 Box 99 Fosston MN 56542-9546 Office: Minn Ho of Reps State Capitol Saint Paul MN 55155-0001

OLSON, GEN, state legislator; b. May 20, 1938; BS in Edn. with distinction, U. Minn., EdD. Mayor, Minnetrista, Minn., 1981-82; mem. Minn. Senate from 34th dist., St. Paul, 1983—. Former mem. Park and Recreation Commn., Planning and Zoning Commn., Police Commn., City Council. Republican. Office: Minn State Senate State Capitol Building Saint Paul MN 55155-0001

OLSON, GREGORY BRUCE, materials science and engineering educator, academic director; b. Bklyn., Apr. 10, 1947; s. Oscar Gustav Fritz and Elizabeth Rose (Dorner) Olson; m. Jane Ellen Black, May 10, 1980; 1 child, Elise Marie. BS, MS in Materials Sci. and Engring., MIT, 1970, ScD in Materials Sci. and Engring., 1974. Rsch. assoc. dept. materials sci. and engring. MIT, Cambridge, 1974-79, prin. rsch. assoc., 1979-85, sr. rsch. assoc., 1985-88; prof. materials sci. and engring. Northwestern U., Evanston, Ill., 1988—, Wilson-Cook prof. engring. design, 1999—. Cons. Army Materials Tech. Lab., Watertown, Mass., 1975-88, Lawrence Livermore (Calif.) Nat. Lab., 1983-89; Jacob Kurtz Exchange Scientist Technion-Israel Inst. Tech., 1979; SERC vis. prof. U. Cambridge, 1992; assoc. chmn. dept. materials sci. and engring. Northwestern U., 1992-98, dir. materials tech. lab.-steel rsch.group, 1985—; founding mem. Questek Innovations LLC, 1997—. Editor: Innovative UHS Steel Technology, 1990, Martensite, 1992; contbr. numerous papers and articles to jours., encys., and symposia; inventor hydrogen-res. UHS steels, stainless bearing steel, ultrahard carburizing steels. Fellow AMAX Found., 1972-74; named N.Mex. Disting. lectr. in Materials, 1983; recipient Creativity Extension award NSF, 1983-85; Wallenberg grantee Jacob Wallenberg Found., Sweden, 1993; recipient Tech. Recognition award NASA, 1994, Tech. of Yr. award Industry Week mag. 1998, Pollution Prevention Project of Yr. award, Strategic Environ. R & D Program, 2003, Innovation of Yr. award Sun-Times Chgo., 2003. Fellow ASM (chmn. phase transformation com. 1987-90, Boston chpt. Saveur Meml. lectr. 1986, Phila. chpt. 1998, Alpha Sigma Mu lectr. 1996), TMS-AIME (student affairs com., M.R. Tenebaum award 1993); mem. AAAS, Materials Rsch. Soc., Internat. Soc. Martensitic Transformation, Assn. Univ. Related Rsch. Parks (Tech. Transfer award 1998). Lutheran. Avocations: sports cars, jazz, trumpet. Office: orthwestern U Dept Materials Sci and Engring 2220 Campus Dr Evanston IL 60208-3108

OLSON, JACK CONRAD, JR., geriatrician; b. Muskegon, Mich., 1955; BS in Chemistry, Mich. State U., 1977, BA in English, 1977; MD, U. Mich., 1984. Bd. cert. internal medicine, bd. cert. geriatric medicine. Intern U. Wis. Hosps. and Clinics, Madison, 1984—85, resident internal medicine, 1985—87, fellow geriatrics, 1987—89; assoc. med. dir. Mendota Mental Health, U. Wis., 1989—92; dir. Windermere Sr. Health Ctr., U. Chgo., 1992—99; asst. clin. prof., fellowship dir. Rush U. Med. Ctr., Chgo., 1999—. Office: 1725 W Harrison St Ste 955 Chicago IL 60612 Office Phone: 312-942-7030. Business E-Mail: jolson@rush.edu.

OLSON, JOHN MICHAEL, lawyer; b. Grafton, ND, Feb. 9, 1947; s. Clifford Inguold and Alice M. (Schwandt) O.; children: Dana Michel, Kirsten Lee. BA, Concordia Coll., Moorhead, Minn., 1969; JD, U. N.D., 1972. Bar: N.D. 1972. Asst. atty. gen. N.D. Atty. Gen.'s Office, Bismarck, 1972-74; state's atty. Burleigh County, Bismarck, 1974-82; pvt. practice Bismarck, 1983-91; mem. 49th dist. N.D. Senate, Bismarck, 1983-91, minority leader, 1987-91; ptnr. Olson Cichy Bismarck, Bismarck, 1994—, Olson Cichy Attys., Bismarck, 1994—. Recipient Disting. Svc. award N.D. Peace Officers Assn., 1981, Outstanding Bismarcker award Bismarck Jaycees, 1981. Mem. N.D. Bar Assn. Republican. Lutheran. Office: 115 N 4th St Bismarck ND 58501-4002

OLSON, KEVIN MEL, state legislator; Mem. S.D. State Senate, 1993—2001, mem. edn. and state affairs coms.; tchr.; mem. S.D. Ho. Reps., Pierre, 2002—. Ho. minority leader S.D. Ho. Reps., Pierre, 2002—, consumer and state affairs com. mem., 2002—. Home: 600 W 3rd Ave Mitchell SD 57301-2434 Office: SD State Senate State Capitol Pierre SD 57501

OLSON, MARK, state legislator; b. July 1955; Mem. from dist. 19A Minn. Ho. of Reps., St. Paul, 1993—; mem. civil law com., edn. policy com., family and early childhood edn. com., fin. com., health and human svcs. policy com. Carpenter, log home builder, qualified neutral mediator. Republican. Home: 17085 142nd St SE Big Lake MN 55309-8925 Office: 501 State Office Bldg Saint Paul MN 55155 Home: 20945 County Road 43 N Big Lake MN 55309-9641

OLSON, NORMAN FREDRICK, not-for-profit developer, retired food science educator; b. Edmund, Wis., Feb. 8, 1931; s. Irving M. and Elva B. (Rhinerson) O.; m. Darlene Mary Thorson, Dec. 28, 1957; children: Kristin A., Eric R. BS, U. Wis., 1953, MS, 1957, PhD, 1959. Asst. prof. U. Wis.-Madison, 1959-63, assoc. prof., 1963-69, prof., 1969-93, dir. Walter V. Price Cheese Research Inst., 1976-93; dir. Ctr. Dairy Research, 1986-93; disting. prof. U. Wis.-Madison, 1993-97, prof. emeritus, 1997—; dir. outreach Shama, Inc., 2007—. Cons. to cheese industry, 1997—. Author: Semi-soft Cheeses; inventor enzyme microencapsulation; sr. editor Jour. Dairy Sci., 1996-2000. Lt. U.S. Army, 1953-55. Recipient Laureate award Nat. Cheese Inst., 1998, Disting. Svc. award Coll. Agrl. Life. Sci., U. Wis., 2002; named Highly Cited Rschr. ISI, 2002. Fellow Inst. Food Technologists (Macy award 1986), Am. Dairy Sci. Assn. (v.p. 1984-85, pres. 1985-86, Pfizer award 1971, Dairy Rsch. Inc. award 1978, Borden Found. award 1988, Hon. award 1997); mem. Inst. Food Technologists. Democrat. Lutheran. Avocation: cross country skiing. Home: 114 Green Lake Pass Madison WI 53705-4755 Office: U Wis Dept Food Sci Babcock Hall Madison WI 53706 Business E-Mail: nfolson@wisc.edu.

OLSON, ROBERT GRANT, lawyer; b. Ft. Dodge, Iowa, Mar. 29, 1952; s. Grant L. and R. June (Pohlmann) Olson; m. Cynthia Lynn Murray, Sept. 7, 1978; children: Brendon, Elisabeth, Jeffrey, Daniel. BS, Iowa State U., 1973; JD, U. Iowa, 1976. Bar: Mo. 1976, Ill. 1977. Ptnr. Thompson & Mitchell, St. Louis, 1976-92, Riezman & Blitz, P.C., St. Louis, 1992-2000, Stone, Leyton & Gershman, P.C., St. Louis, 2000—. Editor: Jour. Corp. Law, 1975—76. Vol. Habitat for Humanity, Gephardt for Pres. Campaign, 1988, Carnahan for Lt. Gov. Campaign, 1988, Carnahan for Gov. Campaign, 1992; arbitrator Better Bus. Bur., Taxpayer Assistance Program. Mem.: ABA, Met. St. Louis Bar Assn., Ill. Bar Assn., Mo. Bar Assn., Downtown St. Louis Lions Club (pres. 1990—91). Home: 424 E Jackson Rd Saint Louis MO 63119-4128 Office: Stone Leyton & Gershman 7733 Forsyth Blvd Ste 500 Saint Louis MO 63105-1817 Home Phone: 314-968-0570; Office Phone: 314-721-7011.

OLSON, ROBERT WYRICK, lawyer; b. Madison, Wis., Dec. 19, 1945; s. John Arthur and Mary Katherine (Wyrick) O.; m. Carol Jean Duane, June 12, 1971; children: John Hagan, Mary Catherine Duane. BA, Williams Coll., 1967; JD, U. Va., 1970. Assoc. Cravath, Swaine & Moore, NYC, 1970-79; asst. gen. counsel Penn Cen. Corp., Cin., 1979-80, assoc. gen. counsel, 1980-82, v.p., dep. gen. counsel, 1982-87; sr. v.p., gen. counsel, sec. Am. Premier Underwriters, Inc. (formerly Penn Cen. Corp.), Cin., 1987-95; sr. v.p., gen. counsel and sec. Chiquita Brands Internat., Inc., Cin., 1995—2006; ret., 2006. Mem. ABA.

OLSON, SANDRA, aerospace engineer; BSChE, U. Pitts.; MS in Mech. and Aerospace Engring., Case We. Res. U., PhD. Aerospace engr. Glenn Rsch. Ctr. NASA, Cleve. Avocations: Karate, horseback riding, ice skating, singing, scuba diving. Office: NASA Glenn Rsch Ctr MS 77-5 Cleveland OH 44135

OLSON, SANDRA FORBES, neurologist; b. East Chicago, Ind., Jan. 8, 1938; MD, Northwestern U., 1963. Diplomate Am. Bd. Psychiatry and Neurology. Intern Chgo. Wesley Meml. Hosp., 1963—64, resident in internal medicine, 1964—65; resident in neurology Northwestern Med. Sch., Chgo., 1965—68, fellow in electroencephalography, 1968—69; pvt. practice neurology Chgo., 1969—2003; assoc. attending physician Northwestern Meml. Hosp., Chgo., 1969—75; attending physician Northwestern Meml. Hosp., Chgo., 1975—; prof. clin. neurology Northwestern U., Chgo. Bd. dirs. Accreditation Coun. for Grad. Med. Edn., 2004. Bd. dirs. Northwestern Meml. Found., 2004. Mem.: AMA (past chair, Coun. on Med. Edn., del., Ill.), Ill. State Med. Soc. (past pres.), CNS, AE, Am. Acad. eurology (pres.-elect 2002—03, pres. 2003—). Office: Northwestern U Feinberg Sch Medicine Dept Neurology Abbott Hall 11th Fl Room 1419 710 N Lake Shore Dr Chicago IL 60611-3078 Office Phone: 312-503-4658. Fax: 312-503-4649. E-mail: sfolsonnw@aol.com.

OLSON, STEVEN, state representative, farmer; b. Jan. 1947; married. Farmer, Iowa; state rep. dist. 83 Iowa Ho. of Reps., 2003—; mem. econ. growth com.; mem. environ. protection com.; mem. transp. com.; vice chair agr. com. Republican. Office: State Capitol East 12th and Grand Des Moines IA 50319

OLSON, STEVEN R., lawyer; b. Baraboo, Wis., July 10, 1955; BS, Andrews U., 1978; JD, John Marshall Law Sch., 1982. Bar: Ill. 1982. Ptnr., chmn. Health Care Practice, mem. exec. com. Katten Muchin Zavis Rosenman, Chgo. Mem.: Am. Health Lawyers Assn. Office: Katten Muchin Rosenman LLP 525 W Monroe St Chicago IL 60661 Office Phone: 312-902-5640. Office Fax: 312-577-8954. E-mail: steven.olson@kattenlaw.com.

OLSON, THARLIE EARL, paper company executive; b. Birthold, ND, 1932; BS in Chemistry, Northland Coll. With Kimberly-Clark Corp., 1959—77; pres. Niagara of Wis. Paper Corp., 1977—82; sr. v.p. paper group Pentair, Inc., St. Paul, 1982—.

OLSSON, BJÖRN ESKIL, railroad supply company executive; b. Kristianstad, Sweden, Oct. 7, 1945; came to U.S., 1990; m. Cecilia Lindblad, July 6, 1968; children: Fredrik, Karin, Eva. M Bus. and Adminstrn., U. Lund, Sweden, 1968. Internal auditor Kockums Mek. Verkstad, Malmö, Sweden, 1969-71, mgr. acctg., 1971-74; v.p. fin. and adminstrn. Kockums Industri, Söderhamn, Sweden, 1974-76, Linden Alimak, Skellefteå, Sweden, 1976-81, Sonessons, Malmö, 1981-82; pres. Sab-Nife, Malmö, 1982-87; v.p. corp. devel. Investment AB Cardo, Malmö, 1987-90; pres., CEO Harmon Industries Inc., Blue Springs, Mo., 1990—. Bd. dirs. BJ Pappetrats, Malmo, Green & Co., Malmö; mem. adv. bd. Ctrl. Mo. State U. Bus. Sch., Warrensburg, 1991—. Staff sgt. Swedish Army, 1964-65. Avocations: golf, skiing. Office: Harmon Industries Inc PO Box 600 Grain Valley MO 64029-0600

OLTMAN, C. DWIGHT, conductor, educator; b. Imperial, Nebr., May 27, 1936; s. George L. and Lois Beryl (Wine) O.; m. Shirley Jean Studebaker, May 30, 1966; children— Michelle Leigh, Nicole Alicia BS, McPherson Coll., 1958; M.Mus., Wichita State U., 1963; postgrad., U. Cin., 1967-70; student, Nadia Boulanger, Paris, 1960, Pierre Monteux, 1963. Asst. prof. music Manchester Coll., North Manchester, Ind., 1963-67; prof. of conducting, music dir. symphony orch. and Bach Festival Baldwin-Wallace Coll., Berea, Ohio, 1970—; music dir. Ohio Chamber Orch., Cleve., 1972-92, laureate conductor, 1992—; music dir., prin. condr. Cleve. Ballet, 1976—; music dir. Cullowhee Music Festival, N.C., 1977-79; guest conductor Europe, Can., U.S.A. Mem. Am. Symphony Orch. League, Conductor's Guild. Democrat. Avocations: reading; walking; theater; spectator sports. Home and Office: 21631 Cedar Branch Trl Strongsville OH 44149-1287

O'MALLEY, JOHN DANIEL, lawyer, educator, banker; b. Chgo., Dec. 18, 1926; s. William D. and Paula A. (Skaugh) O'M.; m. Caroline Tyler Taylor, July 12, 1958; children: John Daniel, Taylor John. Grad., St. Thomas Mil. Acad., 1945; BS, Loyola U., Chgo., 1950, MA, 1952, JD, 1953; grad., U.S. Army Intelligence Sch., 1962, Command & Gen. Staff Coll., 1965. Bar: Ill. 1953, Mich. 1954, U.S. Supreme Ct. 1962. Asst. prof. law Loyola U., 1953-59, asso. prof., 1959-65; formerly spl. counsel and bond claims mgr. Fed. Ins. Co.; prof. law Loyola U. Grad. Sch. Bus., 1965—, chmn. dept. law, 1968-86. Trust officer, v.p. First Nat. Bank Highland Park (Ill.), Marina City Bank, Chgo., Hyde Park Bank & Trust Co., 1970-75; exec. v.p. Harris Bank Winnetka, Ill., 1975-95. Author: Subrogation Against Banks on Forged Checks, 1967, Common Check Frauds and the Uniform Commercial Code, 1969; Contbr. articles to profl. jours. and law revs. Served to maj. AUS, 1945-47, 61-62. Decorated Knight Grand Cross Papal Order of Holy Sepulchre, Knight Comdr. with star Constantinian

Order of St. George (Italy), Knight of Malta. Mem. ABA, Chgo., Ill., Mich. bar assns., Chgo. Crime Commn., French Nat. Hon. Soc., Am., Chgo. bus. law assns., Mil. Govt. Assn., Order of St. Maurice and St. Lazarus (Italy, officer). Home: 1630 Sheridan Rd 6-L Wilmette IL 60091-1830 Office: Loyola U Ste 530 820 N Michigan Ave Chicago IL 60611-2147

O'MALLEY, KATHLEEN M., federal judge; b. 1956; AB magna cum laude, Kenyon Coll., 1979; JD, Case Western Reserve, 1982. Law clk. to Hon. Nathaniel R. Jones U.S. Ct. of Appeals, 6th circuit, 1982-83; with Jones, Day, Reavis & Pogue, Cleve., 1983-84, Porter, Wright, Morris & Arthur, Cleve., 1985-91; chief counsel, first asst. atty. gen., chief of staff Office of Atty. Gen., Columbus, 1991-94; district judge U.S. Dist. Ct. (Ohio no. dist.), 6th circuit, Cleve., 1994—. Vis. prof. Sch. Law Case Western Res. U. Mem.: ABA, FBA, Fed. Cir. Bar Assn., Anthony J. Celebrezze Inn of Ct., Order of Coif, Phi Beta Kappa. Office: US District Ct 801 W Superior Ave Cleveland OH 44113-1840

O'MALLEY, KATHY, radio personality; b. July 22, 1945; children: Patrick, Colleen. Student, No. Ill. Univ. Sec. Chgo. Tribune, 1979—83, reporter to co-writer, Inc. column, 1983—94, features writer, 1994—95; radio talk show host with Judy Markey WGN-AM, Chgo., 1989—. Co-founder Aaron Gold Scholarship Fund, Theater Sch., DePaul Univ.; vol. Open Hand, Chgo.; tutor Fourth Presbyn. Ch. Chgo. Partners in Edn. Named Career Woman of Yr., Ill. Prairie Girl Scout Coun., 1987; named one of 100 Most Influential Women, Crain's Chicago Bus., 2004, 100 Most Important Talk Show Hosts in Am., Talkers Mag., 2005; named to 20th Anniversary Hall of Fame, Today's Chgo. Woman, 2002. Office: WGN Radio 435 N Michigan Ave Chicago IL 60611 Office Phone: 312-222-4700. Office Fax: 312-222-5165. Business E-Mail: kathyomalley@wgnradio.com.

O'MALLEY, KEVIN FRANCIS, lawyer, educator, writer; b. St. Louis, May 12, 1947; s. Peter Francis and Dorothy Margaret (Cradick) O'M.; m. Dena Hengen, Apr.2, 1971; children: Kevin Brendan, Ryan Michael. AB, St. Louis U., 1970, JD, 1973. Bar: Mo. 1973, U.S. Ct. Appeals D.C. 1974, U.S. Ct. Appeals (8th cir.) 1979, Ill. 1993. Trial lawyer U.S. Dept. Justice, Washington, 1973-74, Los Angeles, 1974-77, Phoenix, 1977-78, asst. U.S. atty. St. Louis, 1978-83. Adj. prof. law St. Louis U., 1979—85; lectr. Ctrl. and Ea. European Law Initiative, Russian Fedn., 1996, Poland, 99. Author: (with Devitt, Blackmar, O'Malley) Federal Jury Practice and Instruction, 1990, 92, (with O'Malley, Grenig & Lee), 1999, 2000, 01; contbr. articles to law books and jours. Cmty. amb. Expt. in Internat. Living, Prague, Czechoslovakia, 1968; bd. dirs. St. Louis-Galway (Ireland) Sister Cities. Capt. U.S. Army, 1973. Named one of Best Lawyers in Am., 2005—; recipient Atty. Gen.'s Disting. Svc. award, US Dept. Justice, 1977, John J. Dwyer Meml. Scholarship award, 1967—70, Best Lawyers in Am., 2006, 2007. Fellow Am. Coll. Trial Lawyers; mem. ABA (chmn. govt. litigation counsel com. 1982-86, chmn. jud. com. 1986-87, chmn. com. on ind. and small firms, chmn. trial practice com. 1991-94, health care litigation 1994-98, mem. task force on fed. practice 2005-06), Am. Law Inst., Met. Bar Assn. St. Louis (chmn. criminal law sect.), Nat. Inst. Trial Advocacy, Mo. Athletic Club. Roman Catholic. Office: Greensfelder Hemker & Gale PC 10 S Broadway Ste 2000 Saint Louis MO 63102-1747 Business E-Mail: kom@greensfelder.com.

O'MALLEY, KEVIN THOMAS, lawyer; b. St. Paul, May 1, 1951; s. Walter Thomas and Margret Patricia O'M.; m. Marcia Steyaert, June 21, 1974; children: Brian, Daniel. AB, Marquette U., Milw., 1973; JD, U. Minn., 1976. Bar: Minn. 1976, Ind. 1990, U.S. Dist. Ct. (so. dist.) Ind. 1990. Atty. Cardiac Pacemakers, Inc., St. Paul, 1976-78, mgr. legal and regulatory affairs, 1978-81, gen. counsel, 1981-86, Hybritech Inc., San Diego, 1986-89; asst. gen. counsel Eli Lilly & Co., Indpls., 1989-90, gen. counsel med. dir. diagnostic div., 1990—94; v.p., gen. counsel St. Jude Med., Inc., St. Paul, 1994, corp. sec., 1996. Mem. ABA. Republican. Roman Catholic. Home: 3037 Edgewater Pl Saint Paul MN 55125-8706 Office: St Jude Med, Inc One Lillehei Plaza Saint Paul MN 55117

O'MALLEY, PATRICK J., state legislator; b. Evergreen Park, Ill., Oct. 22, 1950; BS, MS, Purdue U.; JD, John Marshall Law Sch. Mem. Ill. State Senate from 18th dist. Trustee Moraine Valley C.C.; pres. Palos Fire Protection Dist., Ill.; active Am. Cancer Soc., Vietnam Vets. Leadership Program, Coletta's of Ill. Found. Mem. Southwest Bar Assn., Chgo. Bar Assn. Republican. Home: 12744 S 87th Ave Palos Park IL 60464-1868

O'MALLEY, ROBERT C., bank executive; b. Madison, Wis., Feb. 9, 1925; s. Robert Connor and Ursula Ann (Brennan) O'Malley; m. Mary Ellen Meuer, Dec. 28, 1946; children: Sally, Robert, Michael, Dennis, Colleen. BBA in Acctg., U. Wis., Madison, 1948, LLB, 1952. CPA; bar: Wis. 1952. Chmn., pres. United Bank, Madison, 1979—; pres. United Banks of Wis., Madison, 1980—.

O'MALLEY, THOMAS D., petroleum industry executive; b. NYC, 1941; Grad., Manhattan Coll., 1963. Vice chmn., dir. Salomon, Inc. (formerly Phibro-Salomon, Inc.), NYC; former chmn., CEO, pres. Phibro Energy, Inc., Greenwich, Conn.; chmn. Argus Investments (formerly Argus Resources), Stamford, Conn., 1987; chmn., CEO Tosco Corp., Conn., 1989—2001; vice chmn., dir. Phillips Petroleum, 2001; CEO, pres., chmn. Premcor Inc., St. Louis, 2002—. Bd. dirs. PETsMART, Inc., 2002.

OMAN, RICHARD HEER, retired lawyer; b. Columbus, Ohio, Jan. 4, 1926; s. B. R. Oman and Marguerite H. (Oman) Andrews; m. Jane Ellen Wert, Oct. 5, 1963; children: Sarah M., David W. BA, Ohio State U., 1948, JD, 1951; D in Cmty. Leadership (hon.), Franklin U., 2005. Bar: Ohio 1951. Atty. Ohio Nat. Bank, Columbus, 1951-55; ptnr. Isaac, Postlewaite, O'Brien & Oman, Columbus, 1955-71; dir. Columbus Found., 1955-77, counsel, 1955—2005; ptnr. Porter, Wright, Morris and Arthur (and predecessor firm), Columbus, 1972-89; of counsel Vorys, Sater, Seymour and Pease, Columbus, 1990, ptnr., 1991-96, of counsel, 1997—2004, ret., 2005. Mem. Columbus Airport Commn., 1960-64; trustee Reinberger Found., Cleve., 1980—, Columbus Acad., 1981-87, Grant Hosp., 1978-86, Harding Hosp., 1978-86; sr. warden Trinity Episc. Ch., 1985-88; counsel Columbus Jewish Found., 1985-2005, Wexner Ctr. Found., 1990-2005, Found. Cath. Diocese, Columbus, 2000-2005. Fellow Ohio State Bar Found.; mem. ABA, Am. Coll. Trust and Estate Counsel, Ohio State Bar Assn. (past mem. bd. govs. probate and trust law sect.), Columbus Bar Assn., Columbus Club, Rocky Fork Hunt and Country Club, Nantucket (Mass.) Yacht Club, Kit Kat Club. Republican. Episcopalian. Office: Vorys Sater Seymour & Pease LLP PO Box 1008 52 E Gay St Columbus OH 43215-3161 Home Phone: 614-755-4843; Office Phone: 614-464-6453. Fax: 614-714-4731. Business E-Mail: rhoman@vssp.com.

O'MARA, THOMAS PATRICK, manufacturing executive; b. St. Catharine's, Ont., Can., Jan. 17, 1937; s. Joseph Thomas and Rosanna Patricia (Riordan) O'M.; m. Nancy Irene Rosevear, Aug. 10, 1968; children: Patricia Catharine, Tracy Irene, Sara Megan. BS, Allegheny Coll., 1958; MS, Carnegie Inst. Tech., 1960. Mktg. analyst U.S. Steel Corp., Pitts., 1960-65; dir. info. systems AMPCO Pitts. (formerly Screw & Bolt Corp.), Pitts., 1965-68; v.p., gen. mgr. Toy div. Samsonite Corp., Denver, 1968-73; regional mgr. Mountain Zone, Hertz Corp., Denver, 1973-75; asst. to chmn. Allen Group, Melville, NY, 1975-76; group exec. v.p. fin. and adminstrn. Bell & Howell Co., Chgo., 1976-77, corp. controller, 1977-78, corp. v.p., 1978-85, pres. visual communications, 1978-85; pres., chief operating officer, dir. Bridge Product Inc., Northbrook, Ill., 1985-87; chmn., chief exec. officer Micro Metl Corp., Indpls., 1987-91; chmn. Omara Ptnrs., 1992—; CEO Engineered Materials Corp., 2002—. Bd. dirs. Loyola U. Press; chmn. Plastics Group, ABC Windows. Mem. Lake Forest H.S. Bd., 1989-96, pres. 1993-96. With USAR, 1961-66. Mem. Econs. Club Chgo., Newcomen Soc. U.S., Sigma Alpha Epsilon, Knollwood Club. Home: 1350 Inverleith Rd Lake Forest IL 60045-1540 Business E-Mail: tomara@omarapartners.com.

O'MEARA, JOHN CORBETT, federal judge; b. Hillsdale, Mich., Nov. 4, 1933; s. John Richard and Karolyn Louise (Corbett) O'M.; m. Penelope Reingier Appel, June 9, 1962 (div. Feb. 1975); children: Meghan Appel, John Richard, Corbett Edge, Patrick Fitzpatrick, Tighe Roberts; m. Julia Donovan Darlow, Sept. 20, 1975; 1 child, Gillian Darlow. AB, U. Notre Dame, 1955; LLB, Harvard U., 1962. Bar: Mich. 1962. Assoc. Dickinson, Wright, Moon, Van Dusen & Freeman, Detroit, 1962-70; mem. faculty U. Detroit, 1965-70; ptnr. Dickinson, Wright, Moon, Van Dusen & Freeman, Detroit, 1970-94, head of labor group, 1985-94; judge U.S. Dist. Ct., Detroit, 1994—. Bd. dirs. Mich. Opera Theatre, Detroit. Contr. articles to profl. jours. Fin. chmn. Dem. Party Mich., 1968-70; chmn. U.S. Cts. Com. State Bar Mich., 1984-94. Lt. USN, 1955-59. Fellow Am. Coll. Trial Lawyers, Am. Bar Found.; mem. ABA, U.S. Supreme Court Bar, Am. Judicature Soc., Mich. State Bar Assn., 6th Cir. Court Appeals Bar (life mem., 6th Cir. Jud. Conf. 1986). Office: US Dist Ct 200 E Liberty St Ann Arbor MI 48104 Office Phone: 734-741-2106. Personal E-mail: omearajomeara@sbcglobal.net.

O'MEARA, ONORATO TIMOTHY, academic administrator, mathematician; b. Cape Town, Republic of South Africa, Jan. 29, 1928; arrived in U.S., 1957; s. Daniel and Fiorina (Allorto) O'M.; m. Jean T. Fadden, Sept. 12, 1953; children: Maria, Timothy, Jean, Kathleen, Eileen. B.Sc., U. Cape Town, 1947, M.Sc., 1948; PhD, Princeton U., 1953; LLD (hon.), U. Notre Dame, 1987. Asst. lectr. U. Natal, Republic South Africa, 1949; lectr. U. Otago, New Zealand, 1954-56; mem. Inst. for Advanced Study, Princeton, NJ, 1957-58, 62; asst. prof. Princeton U., 1958-62; prof. math. U. Notre Dame, Ind., 1962-76, chmn. dept., 1965-66, 68-72, Kenna prof. math., 1976-98, provost, 1978-96, provost emeritus, 1996—, Kenna prof. emeritus, 1998—. Vis. prof. Calif. Inst. Tech., 1968; Gauss prof. Göttingen Acad. Sci., 1978; mem. adv. panel math. scis. NSF, 1974-77, cons., 1960—. Author: Introduction to Quadratic Forms, 1963, 71, 73, 2000, Lectures on Linear Groups, 1974, 2d edit., 1977, 3d edit., 1988, Russian translation, 1976, Symplectic Groups, 1978, 82, Russian translation, 1979, The Classical Groups and K-Theory (with A.J. Hahn), 1989; contbr. articles on arithmetic theory of quadratic forms and isomorphism theory of linear groups to Am. and European profl. jours. Mem. Cath. Commn. Intellectual and Cultural Affairs, 1962—, Commn. on Cath. Scholarship, 1997-99; life trustee U. of Notre Dame, 1996—. Recipient Marianist award U. Dayton, 1988; Alfred P. Sloan fellow, 1960-63. Mem. Am. Math. Soc., Am. Acad. Arts and Sci., Collegium (bd. dirs. 1992-96). Roman Catholic. Home: 1227 E Irvington Ave South Bend IN 46614-1417 Office: U Notre Dame Office of Provost Emeritus 255B Hurley Hall Notre Dame IN 46556 Personal E-mail: omeara1227@sbcglobal.net.

O'MEARA, PATRICK O., political science professor; b. Cape Town, South Africa, Jan. 7, 1938; came to U.S., 1964. s. Daniel and Fiorina (Allorto) O'M. BA, U. Capetown, 1960; MA, Ind. U., 1966, PhD, 1970; D (hon.), Nat. Inst. Devel. Adminstrn., Bangkok, 2005. Dep. dir. African studies program, asst. prof. polit. sci. Ind. U., Bloomington, 1970-72, dir. African studies program, 1972—, assoc. prof. polit. sci. and pub. and environ. affairs, 1972-81, prof. polit. sci. and pub. and environ. affairs, 1981—, dean office of internat. programs, 1993—97; v.p. Internat. Affair, 2007—. Mem. Ind. Gov.'s Asia Delegation, 2005; cons. in field. Author: Rhodesia: Racial Conflict or Coexistence?, 1975; editor (with Gwendolen M. Carter): Southern Africa in Crisis, 1977; editor: African Independence: The First Twenty-Five Years, 1985, Southern Africa: The Continuing Crisis, 1979, International Politics in Southern Africa, 1982; editor: (with Phyllis M. Martin) Africa, 1977, 3d edit., 1995; editor: (with C.R. Halisi and Brian Winchester) Revolutions of the Late Twentieth Century, 1991; editor: (with Howard D. Mehlinger and Matthew Krain) Globalization and the Challenges of a New Century, 2000; editor: (with Howard D. Mehlinger and Roxanna Ma Newman) Changing Perspectives on International Education, 2001; contbr. articles to profl. jours., chapters to books. Decorated Cross of St. George (Catalonia, Spain); recipient John D. Ryan award Ind. U., 1993, Thomas Hart Benton medallion Ind. U., 1994, Medal of Warsaw U., 2001, Amicus Poloniae, Embassy of Poland, 2003, Founders award Soc. Coll. and Univ. Planning, 2005, Gold Cross of Merit, Republic of Hungary, 2007. Mem. African Studies Assn., Pi Alpha Alpha. Roman Catholic. Office: Ind U Bryan Hall 205 Bloomington IN 47405 Business E-Mail: omeara@indiana.edu.

O'MEARA, THOMAS FRANKLIN, priest, educator; b. Des Moines, May 15, 1935; s. Joseph Matthew and Frances Claire (Rock) O'M. MA, Aquinas Inst, Dubuque, Iowa, 1963; PhD, U. Munich, Germany, 1967. Ordained priest Roman Cath. Ch., 1962. Assoc. prof. Aquinas Inst. of Theology, Dubuque, Iowa, 1967-79; prof. U. Notre Dame, South Bend, Ind., 1981-84, William K. Warren prof. of theology, 1985—. Author 14 books, including: Romantic Idealism and Roman Catholicism, 1983, Theology of Ministry, 1985, revised edit., 1999, Church and Culture, 1991, Thomas Aquinas: Theologian, 1997, Erich Przywara, S.J., His Theology and His World, 2002, A Theologian's Journey, 2002, God in the World: Karl Rahnen's Theology. Mem. Catholic Theol. Soc. Am. (pres. 1980). Roman Catholic. Office: St Thomas Aquinas Priory 7200 Division St River Forest IL 60305 Office Phone: 708-714-9155. Personal E-mail: tomeara@nd.edu.

OMENN, GILBERT STANLEY, academic administrator, internist, scientist; b. Chester, Pa., Aug. 30, 1941; s. Leonard and Leah (Miller) O.; m. Martha Darling; children: Rachel Andrea, Jason Montgomery, David Matthew. AB, Princeton U., 1961; MD, Harvard U., 1965; PhD in Genetics, U. Wash., 1972. Lic. Mass., Washington, Bd. Internal Medicine Part 1(1970), Part 2, (1972), Specialty Bd. Med. Genetics-Clin. Genetics, 1982. Intern Mass. Gen. Hosp., Boston, 1965-66; tchg. fellow in medicine Harvard U., 1966-67; rsch. assoc., Nat. Inst. Arthritis and Metabol Diseases NIH, Bethesda, Md., 1967-69; fellow, divsn. med. genetics U. Wash., 1969-71, asst. prof. medicine Seattle, 1971—74, assoc. prof. medicine, 1974—79, dir., Robert Wood Johnson Clin. Scholars Program, 1975—77, investigator Howard Hughes Med. Inst., 1976-77, prof. medicine, 1979-97, prof. environ. health, 1981—, chmn. dept. environ. health, 1981-83; dean U. Wash. Sch. Pub. Health and Cmty. Medicine, 1982-97, dean emeritus, 1997—; CEO health sys. U. Mich. Health Sys., Ann Arbor, 1997—2002; exec. v.p. med. affairs U. Mich., 1997—2002, prof. internal medicine, human genetics and pub. health, 1997—, dir. ctr. biomedical proteomics, 2002—, dir. ctr. computational medicine and biology, 2005—. Bd. dirs. Amgen, Rohm & Haas Co., CNAC, Population Svcs. Internat.; sci. adv. bd. 3M, Motorola, Divergence, Pac N.W. Nat. Lab.; attending staff, U. Hosp., Harborview Med. Ctr., VA Hosp, Providence Hosp., cons. staff, Children's Hosp. and Med. Ctr., Seattle, 1971-97, attending staff, U. Mich. Health Sys., 1997-; White House fellow/spl. asst. to chmn. AEC, 1973-74; asst. dir., 1977-78, assoc. dir., for Human Resources and Social and Economic Svcs, Office Sci. and Tech. Policy, The White House, 1977-80; assoc. dir. human resources Office Mgmt. and Budget, 1980-81; vis. sr. fellow Woodrow Wilson Sch. Pub. and Internat. Affairs, Princeton U., 1981; sci. and pub. policy fellow Brookings Instn., Washington, 1981-82; joint mem. Fed Hutchinson Cancer Rsch. Ctr., Seattle, 1983-; cons. govt. agys., Lifetime Cable Network; mem. Nat. Commn. on the Environment, Rene Dubos Ctr. for Human Environments, AFL-CIO Workplace Health Fund., Electric Power Rsch. Inst., Carnegie Commn. Task Force on Sci. and Tech. in Jud. and Regulatory Decision Making, adv. com. to dir., Ctrs. Disease Control, 1992-95, adv. com. Critical Technologies Inst., RAND; mem. Pres.'s Coun., U. Calif., 1992-97; chair, Pres. Congrl. Commn. on Risk Assessment and Risk Mgmt., 1994-97; mem. Nat. Enterprise for the Environment. Co-author: Clearing the Air, Reforming the Clean Air Act, 1981. Editor: (with others) Genetics, Environment and Behavior: Implications for Educational Policy, 1972; Genetic Control of Environmental Pollutants, 1984; Genetic Variability in Responses to Chemical Exposure, 1984, Environmental Biotechnology: Reducing Risks from Environmental Chemicals through Biotechnology, 1988, Biotechnology in Biodegradation, 1990, Biotechnology and Human Genetic Predisposition to Disease, 1990, Annual Review of Public Health, 1991-97, Clinics in Geriatric Medicine, 1992, Oxford Textbook of Public Health, 1997; editor: Exploring the Human Plasma Proteome, 2006; mem. bd. Jour. Proteome Research, Environ. Health Perspectives; contbr. articles on cancer prevention including proteomics for cancer biomarkers, human biochem. genetics, prenatal diagnosis of inherited disorders, susceptibility to environ. agts., clin. medicine and health policy to profl. publs. Mem. Pres. Coun. on Spinal Cord Injury; mem. Nat. Cancer Adv. Bd., Nat. Heart, Lung and Blood Adv. Coun., Wash. State Gov.'s Commn. on Social and Health Svcs., Ctr. for Excellence in Govt.; chmn. awards panel Gen. Motors Cancer Rsch. Found., 1985-86; chmn. bd. Environ. Studies and Toxicology, Nat. Rsch. Coun., 1988-91; mem. Bd. Health Promotion and Disease Prevention, Inst. Medicine; mem. adv. com. Woodrow Wilson Sch., Princeton U., 1978-84; mem., Report Review Com., NAS, 2001-; chair & mem., various com. of Nat. Rsch. Coun. Inst. Madiana; trustee Pacific Sci. Ctr., Fred Hutchinson Cancer Rsch. Ctr., Seattle Symphony Orch., Seattle Youth Symphony Orch., Seattle Chamber Music Festival, Santa Fe Chamber Music Festival, Univ. Mus. Soc., Ann Arbor, United Way Washtenaw County, Mich.; chmn. rules com. Dem. Conv., King County, Wash., 1972. Served with USPHS, 1967-69. U.S. Pub. Health Svc. Spl. Fellow, 1969-71, at. Genetics Found. Fellow, 1971-72, White House fellow, 1973-74; recipient Research Career Devel. award USPHS, 1972-76. Fellow ACP, AAAS (pres.-elect, pres., chmn. bd. dirs. 2004-07), Hastings Ctr. Inst. Soc., Ethics and Life Sciences, Collegium Ramazzini; mem. Nat. Acad. Social Ins., Western Assn. Physicians, Inst. Medicine of NAS, White House Fellows Assn., Am. Soc. Human Genetics, Western Soc. Clin. Rsch., Assn. Am. Physicians, Am. Acad. Arts and Scis., Am. Assn. for Advancement of Humanities, Am. Occupational Medicine Assn., Phi Beta Kappa, Sigma XiAlpha Omega Alpha. Jewish. Home: 3340 E Dobson Ann Arbor MI 48105-2583 Office: Univ Mich Med Sch 2017 F Palmer Commons 100 Washtenaw Ave Ann Arbor MI 48109-2218 E-mail: gomenn@umich.edu.

O'MORCHOE, CHARLES CHRISTOPHER CREAGH, anatomist, surgeon, educator; b. Quetta, India, May 7, 1931; came to U.S., 1968; s. Nial Francis C. and Jessie Elizabeth (Joly) O'M.; m. Patricia Jean Richardson, Sept. 15, 1955; children: Charles Eric Creagh, David James Creagh. BA, Trinity Coll., Dublin U., Ireland, 1953, MB, BCh, BAO, 1955, MA, 1959, MD, 1961, PhD, 1969, DSc, 1981. Resident Halifax Gen. Hosp., England, 1955-57; lectr. in anatomy Sch. Medicine Trinity Coll., Dublin (Ireland) U., 1957-61, 63-65, lectr. in physiology, 1966-67, assoc. prof. in physiology, 1967-68; instr. in anatomy Harvard Med. Sch., Boston, 1962-63; vis. prof. physiology U. Md. Sch. Medicine, Balt., 1961-62, assoc. prof. anatomy, 1968-71, prof. anatomy, 1971-74; chmn. anatomy bd. State of Md., 1971-73; prof., chmn. dept. anatomy Stritch Sch. Medicine Loyola U., Maywood, Ill., 1974-84; dean Coll. Medicine, U. Ill., Urbana-Champaign, 1984-98, prof. anat. scis. and surgery, 1984-98, emeritus dean and prof., 1998—. WHO cons., vis. prof. physiology Jaipur, India, 1967, S.M.S. Med. Coll., U. Rajasthan, vis. prof. anatomy, 1971; vis. scholar U. Wash. Sch. Medicine, 2003-06, affiliate prof., 2007-. Assoc. editor: Anatomical Record, 1978-98, Am. Jour. Anatomy, 1987-91, Lymphology, 2004—; contbr. articles to profl. jours. Elected fellow Trinity Coll., Dublin U., 1966; named faculty mem. of yr. Loyola U., Chgo., 1982. Mem. N.Am. Soc. Lymphology (v.p. 1982-84, pres. 1984-86, sec. 1993-98, Cecil K. Drinker award 1992), Am. Assn. Anatomy Chairmen (emeritus), Am. Assn. Anatomists (dir. placement svc. 1981-91), Internat. Soc. Lymphology (exec. com. 1987-97, pres. 1993-95, Presdl. award 2001), Alpha Omega Alpha. Mem. Church of Ireland. Home: 5645 NE Lincoln Rd East Poulsbo WA 98370-7756 Office: U Ill Coll Medicine 190 Med Sci Bldg 506 S Mathews Ave Urbana IL 61801-3618 Business E-Mail: cccom@uiuc.edu.

OMTVEDT, CRAIG P., consumer products executive; m. Jane Omtvedt. Degree, U. Minn. Dir. of audit Fortune Brands, Inc., Lincolnshire, Ill., 1989-92, dep. contr., 1992-97, v.p., chief acctg. officer, 1997-99, sr. v.p., CFO Deerfield, Ill., 1999—. Bd. dir. Gen. Cable. Mem. Fin. Exec. Inst., Inst. of Mgmt. Accts., Tax Exec. Inst. Office: Fortune Brands Inc 520 Lake Cook Rd Deerfield IL 60015

O'NEAL, JERMAINE, professional basketball player; b. Columbia, SC, Oct. 13, 1978; s. Angela Ocean. Basketball player Portland Trail Blazers, 1997—2000; forward ctr. Ind. Pacers, 2000—. Named to All-NBA 2nd Team, 2002—04, Ea. Conf. All-Star Team, NBA, 2002—04, 2007. Achievements include being the youngest person to play in an NBA game, 1996. Office: Ind Pacers 125 S Pennsylvania Ave Indianapolis IN 46204

O'NEAL, MICHAEL RALPH, state legislator, lawyer; b. Kansas City, Mo., Jan. 16, 1951; s. Ralph D. and Margaret E. (McEuen) O'N.; children from a previous marriage: children: Haley Anne, Austin Michael; m. Cindy Wulfkuhle, Apr. 9, 1999. BA in English, U. Kans., 1973, JD, 1976. Bar: Kans. 1976, U.S. Dist. Ct. Kans. 1976, U.S. Ct. Appeals (10th cir.) 1979. Intern Legis. Counsel State of Kans., Topeka, 1975-76; assoc. Hodge, Reynolds, Smith, Peirce & Forker, Hutchinson, Kans., 1976-77; ptnr. Reynolds, Peirce, Forker, Suter, O'Neal & Myers, Hutchinson, 1980-88; shareholder Gilliland & Hayes, P.A., Hutchinson, 1988—, mng. ptnr., 1999—2000; mem. Kans. Ho. of Reps., 1984, minority whip, 1991-92, majority whip, 1995-96; pres. Gilliland & Hayes, P.C., 1999-2000. Instr. Hutchinson CC, 1977-88; com. mem., chmn. jud. com. Kans. Ho. Reps., 1997—, fiscal oversight com., 1997-2001, tax, commerce, transp. and jud. budget com., 2003-06, vice-chmn. ho. select com. sch. fin., 2005-06, vice-chmn. ho. rules com., 2005-, vice chmn. ho. edn. budget sub-com., 2007-; vice-chmn. Kans. Jud. Performance Commn., 2006-. Vice chmn. Rep. Ctrl. Com., Reno County, Kans., 1982-86; bd. dirs. Reno County Mental Health Assn., Hutchinson, 1984-89, YMCA, 1984-86, Crime Stoppers (ex-officio), Hutchinson; chmn. adv. bd. dirs. Wesley Towers Retirement Cmty., 1984-96; mem. Kans. Travel and Tourism Commn., 1990-94; bd. govs. U. Kans. Law Sch., 1991-94; mem. Kans. Sentencing Commn., 1997-2000, Tax Transp. Jud. Budget subcom., 2003-06. Recipient Leadership award Kans. C. of C. and Industry, 1985; named one of Outstanding Young Men Am., 1986. Mem. ABA, Nat. Conf. State Legislatures (criminal justice com.), Kans. Assn. Def. Counsel, Def. Rsch. Inst., Kans. Bar Assn. (prospective legis. com., Outstanding Svc. award), Hutchinson C. of C. (ex-officio bd. dirs., Leadership award 1984), Am. Coun. Young Polit. Leaders (del. Atlantic conf. biennial assembly), Kans. Jud. Coun., Commn. Uniform State Laws. Avocations: basketball, tennis, golf. Home: 8 Windemere Ct Hutchinson KS 67502-2020 Office: Gilliland & Hayes PA 2d Flr Box 2977 20 W 2nd Ave Hutchinson KS 67504-2977 Home Phone: 620-663-9181; Office Phone: 620-662-0537. Business E-Mail: mike@gh-hutch.com.

O'NEAL, RODNEY, automotive company executive; b. Dayton, OH, Aug. 27, 1953; s. James H. and Ida B. O'Neal; m. Pamela Estell O'Neal, Aug. 20, 1983; children: Heather Marie, Damien Cain. B Indsl. Adminstrn., GM Inst., 1976; MBA (Sloan fellow), Stanford U., 1991. Various engring. and mfg. pos. GM Inland Divsn., Dayton, Portugal, and Can., 1976—91; dir. indsl. engring. Chevrolet-Pontiac-GM of Can. Group, 1991—92; dir. mfg. GM Automotive Components Group Worldwide, Troy, Mich., 1992—94; gen. dir. warehousing and distbn. GM Svc. Parts Ops., 1994—97; v.p. GM, 1997—98; pres. Delphi Interior Systems, Troy, Mich., 1998—2000, exec. v.p. Safety, Thermal and Elec. Arch. sector, 2000—03; pres. dynamics, propulsion and thermal Delphi Corp., Troy, Mich., 2003—05, pres., COO, 2005—06, pres., CEO, 2007—. Bd. dir. Goodyear Tire & Rubber Co., 2004—, Delphi Corp., 2005—, Sprint Nextel Corp., 2007—; mem. Exec. Leadership Coun. Adv. bd. Focus: HOPE. Recipient Lifetime Achievement in Industry award, Nat. Soc. Black Engineers, 2002. Office: World Hdqrs Delphi Corp 5725 Delphi Dr Troy MI 48098-2815

O'NEIL, J. PETER (JAMES PETER O'NEIL), elementary school educator, computer scientist; b. Rockville Center, NY, Apr. 2, 1946; s. Clement Lee and Frances Rita (Theis) O'N.; m. Carol Ann Sypniewski, June 8, 1968; children: Kelly Ann, Thomas Joseph. BA in Psychology, Loyola U., Chgo., 1968; MA in Sci. Edn., Webster Coll., St. Louis, 1972. Cert. elem. tchr. K-8, Mo., elem. tchr. K-8, Wis., dir. instruction, Wis. Tchr., student tchr. Sacred Heart Sch., Florissant, Mo., 1968-73; tchr. sci. Waunakee (Wis.) Mid. Sch., 1973-96, chmn. K-8 sci. dept., chmn. K-12 dept., 1984-92; learning coord. Deforest (Wis.) Area Sch. Dist., 1992—2000. Dir. Waunakee Summer Sci. Program, 1975-91; dir. instrn./tech. Brodhead Wis., 1996-99; designer sci. curriculum computer CD-ROM programs Sci. Curriculum Assistance Program and Elem. Sci. Curriculum Assistance Program, 1990—; dir. instrn. DeForest (Wis.) Area Sch. Dist., 2000—; adj. prof. Viterbo U., 2003—; rsch. cons. IDEAS Wis., 2002—. Feature editor: Science Scope, 1989-96; contbr. over 30 activities and articles to profl. jours. Group worker settlement houses Chgo., St. Louis; mem. Parish Coun.; dir. Waunakee Area Edn. Found. Named Master Tchr. NSF, Waunakee, 1986-96; recipient Tchr. of Yr. award Waunakee, 1984, 90, 92, Kohl Found. award, 1992, Mid. Sch. Tchr. of Yr. award Wis., 1992-93. Mem.: Wis. Soc. Curriculum Designers, Am. Soc. Curriculum Designers. Roman Catholic. Avocations: computers, sports, writing, walking. Home: 119 Simon Crestway Waunakee WI 53597-1721 Office: Deforest Area Sch Dist 520 E Holum St De Forest WI 53532-1316 Office Phone: 608-842-6531. Business E-Mail: jponeil@deforest.k12.wi.us.

O'NEIL, MICHAEL C., lawyer; b. Pitts., Nov. 21, 1961; BA with high honors, Bklyn. Coll., 1986; JD with honors, DePaul Univ., 1989. Bar: Ill. 1989. Ptnr., chmn. Privacy Litigation practice group DLA Piper Rudnick Gray Cary, Chgo. Editor (articles & notes): DePaul Law Rev., 1988—89. Office: DLA Piper Rudnick Gray Cary Suite 1900 203 N LaSalle St Chicago IL 60601-1293 Office Phone: 312-368-4098. Office Fax: 312-236-7516. Business E-Mail: michael.oneil@dlapiper.com.

O'NEIL, THOMAS J., mining company executive; BS in Mining Engring., Lehigh U.; MS, Pa. State U.; PhD, U. Ariz. Numerous sr. positions in minerals industry; head dept. mining and geol. engring. U. Ariz.; pres., COO Cleveland-Cliffs Inc., Cleve., 2000—. Mem. NAE, Am. Iron Ore Assn. (chmn.), Soc. Mining, Metallurgy and Exploration (dir., pres.-elect). Office: Cleveland-Cliffs Inc 1100 Superior Ave Cleveland OH 44114-2589

O'NEILL, BRIAN BORU, lawyer; b. Hancock, Mich., June 7, 1947; s. Brian Boru and Jean Anette (Rimpela) O'N.; m. Ruth Bohan, Sept. 18, 1991; children: Dru Groves, Brian Boru, Maggie Byrne, Phelan Boru, Ariel Margaret. BS, U.S. Mil. Acad., 1969; JD magna cum laude, U. Mich., 1974; D in Pub. Svc. (hon.), Northland Coll., 1999. Bar: Mich. 1974, U.S. Dist. Ct. Minn. 1977, U.S. Ct. Mil. Appeals 1975, U.S. Ct. Appeals (6th cir.) 1975, U.S. Ct. Appeals (8th cir.) 1977, U.S. Ct. Appeals (Fed. cir.) 1983, U.S. Ct. Appeals (7th cir.) 1985, U.S. Ct. Appeals (10th cir.) 1986, U.S. Ct. Appeals (9th cir.) 1990, U.S. Ct. Appeals (D.C. cir.) 2005, U.S. Ct. Claims 1981, U.S. Supreme Ct. 1981. Asst. to gen. counsel Dept. Army, Washington, 1974-77; assoc., ptnr. Faegre & Benson, Mpls., 1977—. Mem. com. vis. Mich. Law Sch., 1994—; counsel Defenders of Wildlife, Washington, 1977—, also bd. dirs; counsel Sierra Club, Audubon Soc. Mng. editor: Mich. Law Rev., 1973—74. Advocate Am. Bd. Trial Advocates, 2004—. Capt. US Army, 1969—77. Decorated Meritorious Svc. medal; named Environmentalist of Yr. Sierra Club North Star, 1982, 96, 97, 98; recipient William Douglas award Sierra Club, 1985, Trial Lawyer of Yr. award Trial Lawyers for Pub. Justice, 1995. Fellow Am. Coll. Trial Lawyers (regent 2003—), Internat. Acad. Trial Lawyers, Order of the Coif; mem. Am. Bd. Trial Advs. (adv. 2005—), Mpls. Golf Club, Mpls. Athletic Club (pres.) Office: Faegre & Benson 2200 Wells Fargo Tower 90 S 7th St Ste 2200 Minneapolis MN 55402-3901 Office Phone: 612-766-8318. E-mail: boneill@faegre.com.

O'NEILL, BRIDGET R., lawyer; b. 1963; BSBA, Georgetown U., 1985; JD, U. Wis., 1988. Bar: Wis. 1988, Ill. 1988, N.Y. 1992. With Sidley Austin Brown & Wood, Chgo., ptnr., 1996—. Office: Sidley Austin Brown & Wood Bank One Plz 10 S Dearborn St Chicago IL 60603

O'NEILL, JOHN JOSEPH, speech educator; b. De Pere, Wis., Dec. 6, 1920; s. John Joseph and Elizabeth (Murray) O'N.; m. Dorothy Jane Arnold, Dec. 28, 1943; children— Katherine, Thomas, John, Philip. BS, Ohio State U., 1947, PhD, 1951. From instr. to assoc. prof. speech Ohio State U., 1949-59; prof. speech U. Ill. at Champaign, 1959-91, prof. emeritus, 1991—; prof. audiology U. Ill. Coll. Medicine, Chgo., 1965-79, head speech and hearing sci. dept., 1973-79. Research assoc. U.S. Naval Sch. Aviation Medicine, summers 1953, 54; cons. in field. Co-author: Visual Communication, 1961, 81;, Hard of Hearing, 1964, Applied Audiometry, 1966. Pres. Columbus Hearing Soc., 1956-58; Bd. dirs. Champaign County Assn. Crippled-United Cerebral Palsy, 1961-63. Served with inf. AUS, 1942-46. Decorated Purple Heart, Bronze Star with oak leaf cluster, Jubilee of Liberty medal, France, 2000; recipient Disting. Alumnus award dept. speech Ohio State U., 1969, recipient honors, 1979. Fellow Am. Speech and Hearing Assn. (pres. 1969), Ohio Psychol. Assn.; mem. Am. Bd. Examiners Speech Pathology and Audiology (pres. 1967-68), Acad. Rehabilitative Audiology (pres. 1969) Home: 1203 W University Ave Champaign IL 61821-3224 E-mail: j-oneill@uiuc.edu.

O'NEILL, MARK E., military officer; b. St. Louis; married; 2 children. BS, US Mil. Acad., 1978; MA, Naval Postgrad. Sch.; grad., Def. Lang. Inst., Armed Forces Staff Coll., US Army War Coll. Commd. inf. officer US Army, 1978, advanced through grades to brig. gen.; asst. Army attaché Am. Embassy, Beijing; served in Operation Uphold Democracy, Haiti, Operation Enduring Freedom, Afghanistan, Operation Iraqi Freedom, Baghdad; dep. divsn. comdr. Multinational Divsn., Baghdad; dep. dir. US Army Dept. Strategy, Plans & Policy; dep. comdt. US Army Command & Gen. Staff Coll., Ft. Leavenworth, Kans.; acting comdr. Combined Arms Ctr., Ft. Leavenworth, Kans. Mem. Coun. Fgn. Rels. Decorated Legion of Merit with four oak leaf clusters, Bronze Star medal, Def. Meritorious Svc. medal, Meritorious Svc. medal with four oak leaf clusters, Army Commendation medal with oak leaf cluster, Army Achievement medal, Iraq Campaign medal, War on Terrorism Svc. medal, Nat. Def. Svc. medal with star, Armed Forces Expeditionary medal, Humanitarian Svc. medal, Army Svc. ribbon, Four Overseas Svc. ribbons. Office: US Army Command & Gen Staff Coll 100 Stimson Ave Fort Leavenworth KS 66027

O'NEILL, SHEILA, principal; Prin. Cor Jesu Acad., St. Louis. Recipient Blue Ribbon award U.S. Dept. Edn., 1990-91. Office: Cor Jesu Acad 10230 Gravois Rd Saint Louis MO 63123-4099

O'NEILL MORELAND, TAMARA, lawyer; b. 1972; BA in Polit. Sci. summa cum laude, Centenary Coll., Shreveport, La., 1994; JD cum laude, Hamline U. Sch. Law, St. Paul, 1997. Bar: Minn. 1997, US Dist. Ct. (dist. Minn.) 2001, US Ct. Appeals (7th cir.) 2002. Law clk. to Judge John J. Sommerville Hennepin County Dist. Ct., 1997—98; shareholder, mem. real estate litig. dept. Larkin, Hoffman, Daly & Lindgren, Ltd., Mpls., 1998—. Named a Rising Star, Minn. Super Lawyers mag., 2006. Mem.: Minn. State Bar Assn., Minn. Women Lawyers, Minn. Comml. Real Estate Women, Phi Alpha Delta. Office: Larkin Hoffman Daly & Lindgren Ltd 1500 Wells Fargo Plz 7900 Xerxes Ave S Minneapolis MN 55431 Office Phone: 952-896-6711. E-mail: toneill@larkinhoffman.com.

ONG, CHEE-MUN, engineering educator; b. Ipoh, Perak, Malaysia, Nov. 23, 1944; came to U.S., 1978; s. Chin-Kok Ong and Say-Choo Yeoh; m. Penelope Li-Lok, July 17, 1971; children: Yi-Ping, Yi-Ching, Chiew-Jen. BE with honors, U. Malaya, 1967; MS, Purdue U., 1968, PhD, 1974. Registered profl. engr. Ind., Eng. Plant engr. Guinness Brewery, Malaysia, 1967; asst. lectr. U. Malaysia, 1968-73, lectr., 1976-78; rsch. asst. Purdue U., West Lafayette, Ind., 1973-74, vis. asst. prof., 1975-76, asst. prof., 1978-81, assoc. prof., 1981-85, prof., 1985—. Cons. SIMTECH, West Lafayette, 1978-85, L.A. Water and Power Co., 1986-88, Caterpillar, 1993-94, Franklin Electric, 1997-98, P Plus Corp., 1999-, PPlus, 1999-, Unibus, 2002. Author: Dynamic Simulation of Electric Machinery, 1998; contbr. articles to profl. jours. Fulbright-Hayes scholar, 1967-68; UNESCO fellow, 1969-70. Avocations: gardening, fishing, reading. Office: Purdue U Dept Elec/Computer Engring West Lafayette IN 47907-1285 Business E-Mail: ong@purdue.edu.

ONG, JOHN DOYLE, former ambassador, retired manufacturing executive; b. Uhrichsville, Ohio, Sept. 29, 1933; s. Louis Brosee and Mary Ellen (Liggett) O.; m. Mary Lee Schupp, July 20, 1957; children: John Francis Harlan, Richard Penn Blackburn, Mary Katherine Caine. BA, MA, Ohio State U., 1954; LLB, Harvard, 1957; LHD, Kent State U., 1982; HHD (hon.), Ohio State U., 1996; LHD (hon.), U. Akron, 1996; D in pub. svc. (hon.), SD State U., 2002. Bar: Ohio 1958. Asst. counsel B.F. Goodrich Co., Akron, 1961-66, group v.p., 1972-73, exec. v.p., 1973-74, vice chmn., 1974-75, pres., dir., 1975-77, pres., COO, 1978-79, chmn. bd., pres., CEO, 1979-84, chmn. bd., CEO, 1984-96, chmn. bd., 1996-97, chmn. emeritus, 1997—; US amb. to Norway Oslo, 2002—05. V.p. exploring Great Trail coun. Boy Scouts Am., 1974-77; bd. dirs. Nat. Alliance of Bus., 1981-94, chmn., 1984-86, 91; trustee Mus. Arts Assn., Cleve., 1975-, chmn., 1995-2002; Bexley Hall Sem., 1974-81, Case Western Res. U., 1980-92, Ft. Ligonier Assn., 1997-, Kenyon Coll., 1983-85, Hudson Libr. and Hist. Soc., Ohio, trustee, 1967-80, pres., 1971-72, Western Res. Acad., Hudson, 1975-95, pres. bd. trustees, 1977-95; nat. trustee Nat. Symphony Orch., 1975-83, John S. and James L. Knight Found., 1995-2002; mem. bus. adv. com. Transp. Ctr. Northwestern U., 1975-78, Carnegie-Mellon U. Grad. Sch. Indsl. Adminstrn., 1978-83; life trustee U. Chgo., 1991—; chmn. Ohio Bus. Roundtable, 1994-97; trustee Ohio Hist. Soc., 1998-2002; dir. New Amn. Schs., 1991, chmn., 1998-2002. Mem. Ohio Bar Assn. (bd. govs. corp. counsel sect. 1962-74, chmn. 1970), Rubber Mfrs. Assn. (bd. dirs. 1974-84), Chem. Mfrs. Assn. (bd. dirs. 1988-91, 94-97), Conf. Bd., Coun. Ret. Chief Execs., Coun. Am. Ambs., RTI Internat. (sr. vis. fellow 2006-), Bohemian Club, Chagrin Valley Hunt Club, Portage Country Club, Rowfant Club, Union Club, Links, Union League, Ottawa Shooting Club, Met. Club, Rolling Rock Club, Castalia Trout Club, Phi Beta Kappa, Phi Alpha Theta. Episcopalian. Home Phone: 330-650-1649; Office Phone: 330-665-3830.

ONO, KEN, mathematician, educator; b. Phila., Mar. 20, 1968; s. Sachiko Ono; m. Erika Dawn Anderson; children: Aspen, Sage. PhD, UCLA, 1993. Mem. Sch. Math., Inst. for Advanced Study, Princeton, NJ, 1995—97; asst. prof. math. Pa. State U., University Park, 1997—99, Louis A. Martarano prof. math., 1999—2000; assoc. prof. U. Wis., Madison, 1999—2001, prof., 2001—03, Solle P. and Margaret Manasse prof., 2004—. Contbr. articles to profl. jours. Recipient Young Investigator award, Nat. Security Agy., 1997, Career award, NSF, 1998, Presdl. Early Career award, Pre Clinton, 2000; fellow David and Lucile Packard fellow, David and Lucile Packard Found., 1999, Alfred P. Sloan Rsch. fellow, Alfred P. Sloan Found., 1999, H. I. Romnes fellow, U. Wis., 2002. Office: U Wis Dept Math Van Vleck Hall 480 Lincoln Madison WI 53706 Office Phone: 608-263-2604. E-mail: ono@math.wisc.edu.

ONO, KENT ALAN, communications educator; b. Casper, Wyo., 1964; BA in English, DePauw U., 1987; MA in Comm., Miami U., 1988; PhD in Rhetoric, U. Iowa, 1992. Founder, Asian Am. cultural politics rsch. cluster U. Calif.-Davis, 1997, interim dir. MURALS undergrad. rsch. program, 1999—2000, co-founder & dir. cultural studies grad. program, 1999—2002; dir. & prof. Asian Am. studies and prof. comm. U. Ill., Urbana-Champaign, 2003—. Founder Comm. and Critical/Cultural Studies Jour.; former chair, critical and cultural studies Div. NCA, chair, Asian Pacific Am. Caucus, 1996—97, co-founder, Asian Am. studies, latino studies, and gay and lesbian studies div.; chair Asian Pacific Am. Caucus of Soc. for Cinema Studies, 1999—2001. Co-author: Shifting Borders: Rhetoric, Immigration, and California's Proposition 187, 2002; co-editor: Enterprise Zones: Critical Positions on Star Trek, 1996. Grantee Ford Found. Diversity of Edu. Grant, 1990—91. Office: U Ill Inst Comm Rsch 228 Gregory Hall 810 S Wright St Urbana IL 61801

ONSTEAD, R. RANDALL, JR., food products executive; m. Pam Onstead; 2 children. BA in mktg., Tex. Tech. U., 1978; attended mgmt. devel. program, Harvard U., 1986. Mng. dir. Chapman Ptnrs., LLC; CEO Garden Ridge Co., 2002—03; pres., CEO Randall's Food Markets, Inc., Houston. Bd. mem. Metro YMCA, York Christian Coll., York, Nebr., Randall's Food Markets, Topco Assoc., Inc., Mem. Care Sys. Office: Dominicks Finer Foods Inc 711 Jorie Blvd Oak Brook IL 60523

OPAT, MATTHEW JOHN, lawyer; b. Riceville, Iowa, Nov. 5, 1952; s. Wesley John and Dolores Genevieve (Ludwig) O.; m. Therese Ann Dusheck, Aug. 13, 1977; children: Michael, Kristin, Steven. BA in History, U. Iowa, 1974; JD, Hamline U., 1977. Bar: Iowa 1977, Minn. 1977. Prin. Opat Law Office, Chatfield, Minn., 1977—. Atty. Fillmore County, 1997-2003. Mem. Fillmore County Bar Assn. (pres. 1984-85), Minn. State Bar Assn. (bd. dirs. 1985-87), Tenth Dist. Bar Assn. (chmn. ethics com. 1989-96, pres. 2001-2002, 2004-2005) Office: 22 2nd St SE PO Box 455 Chatfield MN 55923-1203 Office Phone: 507-867-4080.

OPATZ, JOE, state legislator; BA, St. Cloud U.; MEd, Kent State U.; PhD in Edn., U. Minn. Mem. Minn. Ho. of Reps., St. Paul, 1993—. Univ. adminstr. Democrat. Home: 402 Riverside Dr SE Saint Cloud MN 56304-1032 Office: Minn Ho of Reps State Capitol Saint Paul MN 55155-0001

OPFER, DARRELL WILLIAMS, state representative, educator; b. Genoa, Ohio, June 17, 1941; s. Milton William and Iva Marie (Gleckler) O. BS in Edn., Bowling Green State U., 1963, MA, 1964. Cert. tchr., Ohio. Tchr. Peace Corps, Kenya, East Africa, 1965-68, Woodward High Sch., Toledo, 1969, Genoa High Sch., 1969-82; county commr. Ottawa County, Port Clinton, Ohio, 1983-92; state rep. State of Ohio, 1993-98. Sec. Dem. Party, Ottawa County, 1974-80; pres. Ottawa County Dem. Club, 1976-80. Named Outstanding Pub. Ofcl., Ohio Dirs.-Pvt. Industry Coun., 1992. Mem. Commodore Perry Fed. Credit Union (pres. 1982-92), Moose, Kiwanis. Mem. United Ch. of Christ. Home: 12342 W State Route 105 Oak Harbor OH 43449-9410

OPPEGAARD, GRANT E., water transportation executive; b. 1943; MBA, U. NH, 1968. With Dayton Hudson Corp., Mpls., 1969-71, Minstar Inc., Mpls., 1971-82, Cuyuna Engine Co., Mpls., 1982-83, Allstate Lawn Products Inc., Mpls., 1983-84, C.V.N. Cos. Inc., Mpls., 1984-89, Fingerhut Cos. Inc., Hopkins, Minn., 1989-96; CEO Genmar Holdings Inc., Mpls., 1997—. Office: Genmar Holdings Inc Ste 2900 80 S 8th St Minneapolis MN 55402-2250

OPPMANN, ANDREW JAMES, newspaper editor; b. Hopkinsville, Ky., Apr. 3, 1963; s. Patrick George Oppmann and Elizabeth Anne (Freeman) Peace; m. Emily Elise Wey, Oct. 8, 1988; children: Emily Katherine, Sarah Elizabeth. BA in Journalism, U. Ky., 1985. Staff writer The Orange County Register, Santa Ana, Calif., 1985-86; copy editor, staff writer Lexington (Ky.) Herald-Leader, 1986-87, bur. chief, asst. metro editor, 1988-91; urban affairs writer The Knoxville (Tenn.) ews-Sentinel, 1987-88; asst. city editor The Houston Post, 1991-92, dep. met. editor, 1992, asst. to mng. editor, 1992, met. editor, 1992-94; Ky. editor The Cin. (Ohio) Enquirer, 1994-97; supervising editor The Ky. Enquirer, Ft. Mitchell, 1994-97; mng. editor Montgomery (Ala.) Advertiser, 1998-2001; exec. editor The Post-Crescent, Appleton, Wis., 2001—. Bd. vis. U. Ky. Sch. Journalism, 1994-97. Fellow U. Ky., 1984; recipient Gannett Newsroom Supr. Recognition award, 1995, 2000. Mem. U. Ky. Journalism Alumni Assn. (v.p. 1997-2000, pres. 2001-03), Soc. Profl. Journalists (bd. dirs. Queen City chpt. 1995-97), Ala. AP Mng. Editors (bd. dirs. 1998—), U. Ky. Nat. Alumni Assn. (bd. dirs. 1998-2001). Office: The Post-Crescent PO Box 59 Appleton WI 54912 E-mail: oppedit@aol.com.

ORDONEZ, FRANCISCO A. (FRANK), automotive executive; b. Havana, Cuba; BBA, MBA, U. Detroit. Fin. mgr. GM Espana, 1981—84; fin. dir. worldwide purchasing function GM, 1984—88; various fin. and bus. planning pos., including dir. fin. Delphi Safety & Interior Systems Delphi Corp., 1988—99, gen. mgr. Product & Svc. Solutions, 1999—. Past bd. mem. U. Detroit Jesuit HS. Mem.: Motor Equipment Mfrs. Assn. (bd. mem.). Office: World Hdqrs Delphi 5725 Delphi Dr Troy MI 48098-2815 also: Delphi Product & Svc Solutions 408 Dana St PO Box 431 Warren OH 44486

ORDONEZ, MAGGLIO JOSE, professional baseball player; b. Caracas, Venezuela, Jan. 28, 1974; m. Dagly Ordonez; children: Magglio Jr., Maggliana, Sophia. Outfielder Chgo. White Sox, 1997—2004, Detroit Tigers, 2005—. Mem. Venezuela Team World Baseball Classic, 2006. Named MVP, Venezuelan Winter League, 1996, Tiger of Yr., 2007, Am. League Batting Champion, 2007; named to Winter League All-Star Team, Baseball Am., 1997, Am. League All-Star Team, 1999—2001, 2003, 2006—07; recipient Silver Slugger award, 2000, 2002, 2007. Achievements include becoming the second Venezuelan-born player ever to hit 1,000 RBI's, 2008. Mailing: c/o Detroit Tigers Comerica Pk 2100 Woodward Ave Detroit MI 48201*

ORDWAY, ELLEN, biologist, educator, entomologist, researcher; b. NYC, Nov. 8, 1927; d. Samuel Hanson and Anna (Wheatland) Ordway. BA, Wheaton Coll., Mass., 1950; MS, Cornell U., 1955; PhD, U. Kans., 1965. Field asst. N.Y. Zool. Soc., NYC, 1950-52; rsch. asst. Am. Mus. Natural History, NYC, 1955-57; tchg. asst. U. Kans., Lawrence, 1957-61, rsch. asst., 1959-65; asst. prof. U. Minn., Morris, 1965-70, assoc. prof. biology, 1970-85, prof., 1986-97, prof. emeritus, 1997, acad. advisor, 1997—. Cooperator, cons. USDA Bee Rsch. Lab., Tucson, 1971, Tucson, 83. Contbr. articles to profl. jours. Lectr. Morris area svc. clubs, 1972—2004; mgr. preserves Nature Conservancy, Mpls., 1975—; bd. dirs. county chpt. ARC, 1998—2003; vol. Stevens County Hist. Mus., 2005—; bd. dirs. U. Minn. Morris Retirees Assn., 1997—2003, sec., treas., 1998—2003. Mem.: AAAS, Ecol. Soc. Am., Internat. Bee Rsch. Assn., Kans. Entomol. Soc., Sigma Xi. Episcopalian. Avocations: travel, photography. Office: U Minn Div Sci And Math Morris MN 56267

O'REILLY, CHARLES TERRANCE, university dean; b. Chgo., May 30, 1921; s. William Patrick and Ann Elizabeth (Madden) O'R.; m. Rosella Catherine Neilland, June 4, 1955; children: Terrance, Gregory, Kevin, Joan Bridget, Kathleen Ann. BA, Loyola U., Chgo., 1942, MSW., 1948; postgrad., U. Cattolica, Milan, Italy, 1949-50; PhD, U. Notre Dame, 1954. Instr. DePaul U., Chgo., 1948-49; asst. in psychology U. Cattolica, 1949-50; caseworker Cath. Charities, NYC, 1953-54; exec. dir. Family Service, Long Branch, N.J., 1954-55; asst. prof. Loyola U., 1955-59; vis. lectr. Ensiss Sch. Social Work, Milan, 1959-60; asso. prof. U. Wis.-Milw., 1961-64; prof., asso. dir. U. Wis. Sch. Social Work, Madison, 1965-68; dean social welfare, v.p. acad. affairs SUNY-Albany, 1969-76; dean social work Loyola U., Chgo., 1976-92, dean emeritus, sr. prof., 1994—; vis. prof. sch. social work SS Maria Asunta, Rome, 1992-93. Author: OAA Profile, 1961, People of Inner Core North, 1965, Men in Jail, 1968, Italian Social Work Education 1946-1997, 1998, Italy's War of Liberation, 1998, The Enola Gay Controversy and the Smithsonian, 2004; contbr. articles to profl. jours. Pres. Community Action Commn. Dane County, Wis., 1967-68; bd. dirs. Council Community Services, Albany, Family and Children's Service, Albany; mem. adv. bd. Safer Found.; vice chmn. Ill. Pub. Aid Citizens Council. Served with AUS, 1942-46, 51-52. Fulbright scholar, 1949-50; fellow, 1959-60 Mem. AAUP, Nat. Assn. Social Workers. Roman Catholic. Home: 4073 Bunker Ln Wilmette IL 60091-1001 Office: Sch Social Work Loyola Univ Chicago IL 60611 E-mail: coreill@luc.edu.

O'REILLY, DAVID E., auto parts company executive; s. Charles Chub O'Reilly; 3 children. Grad., Drury Coll., 1971. With Southwestern Bell; joined O'Reilly Automotive, Springfield, Mo., 1972—, now co-chmn., CEO. Bd. dir. O'Reilly Automotive, 1993—; past chair Auto Value Inc. Mem. Springfield Catholic Schs. Devel. bd.; past pres. Drury Univ. Alumni Assn., Springfield YMCA. Mem.: Automotive Warehouse Distributors Assn. (past chmn.). Office: O'Reilly Automotive 233 S Patterson Springfield MO 65802 Office Phone: 417-862-6708.

O'REILLY, JAMES THOMAS, lawyer, educator, writer; b. NYC, Nov. 15, 1947; s. Matthew Richard and Regina (Casey) O'R.; children: Jean, Ann. BA cum laude, Boston Coll., 1969; JD, U. Va., 1974. Bar: Va. 1974, Ohio 1974, U.S. Supreme Ct. 1979, U.S. Ct. Appeals (6th cir.) 1980. Atty. Procter & Gamble Co., Cin., 1974-76, counsel, 1976-79, sr. counsel for food, drug and product safety, 1979-85, corp. counsel, 1985-93, assoc. gen. counsel, 1993-98; adj. prof. in adminstrv. law U. Cin., 1980-97, vis. prof. law, 1998—. Cons. Adminstrv. Conf. U.S., 1981-82, 89-90, Congl. Office of Compliance, 1995-96; arbitrator State Employee Rels. Bd.; mem. Ohio Bishops Adv. Coun., Mayor's Infrastructure Commn., Cin. Environ. Adv. Coun.; Vice Mayor, City Wyoming, Ohio. Author: Federal Information Disclosure, 1977, Food and Drug Administration Regulatory Manual, 1979, Unions' Rights to Company Information, 1980, Federal Regulation of the Chemical Industry, 1980, Administrative Rulemaking, 1983, Ohio Public Employee Collective Bargaining, 1984, Protecting Workplace Secrets, 1985, Emergency Response to Chemical Accidents, 1986, Product Defects and Hazards, 1987, Protecting Trade Secrets Under SARA, 1988, Toxic Torts Strategy Deskbook, 1989, Complying With Canada's New Labeling Law, 1989, Solid Waste Management, 1991, Ohio Products Liability Handbook, 1991, Toxic Torts Guide, 1991, ABA Product Liability Resource Manual, 1993, RCRA and Superfund Practice Guide, 1993, Clean Air Permits Manual, 1994, United States Environmental Liabilities, 1994, Elder Safety, 1995, Environmental and Workplace Safety for University and Hospital Managers, 1996, Indoor Environmental Health, 1997, Product Warnings, Defects & Hazards, 1999, Accident Prevention Manual, 2000, Food Crisis Management Manual, 2002, Police Racial Profiling, 2002, Homeland Security Deskbook, 2004, Ohio Tort Reform, 2005, Ohio Personal Injury Practice, 2006, Gangs and Law Enforcement, 2007; mem. editl. bd. Food and Drug Cosmetic Law Jour.; contbr. articles to profl. jours. Trustee Regional Coun. of Govts.; mem. Hamilton County Dem. Ctrl. Com. With US Army, 1970—72. Mem. ABA (chmn. AD law sect.), FBA, Food and Drug Law Inst. (chair program com.), Leadership Cin. Democrat. Roman Catholic. Office: 24 Jewett Dr Cincinnati OH 45215-2648 Office Phone: 513-556-0062. Personal E-mail: joreilly@fuse.net. Business E-Mail: james.oreilly@uc.edu.

O'REILLY, LAWRENCE P., auto parts company executive; s. Charles Chub O'Reilly; m. Nancy O'Reilly; 3 children. Grad., Drury Coll., 1968. Co-chmn., COO O'Reilly Automotive, Springfield, Mo. Dir. O'Reilly Automotive, 1993—. Big Brothers/Big Sisters; YPO; bd. trustees St. John's Regional. Health Ctr., Cath. Sch. Devel. bd. Mem.: Nat. Car Care Coun., Automotive Warehouse Distributors Assn. Office: O'Reilly Automotive 233 S Patterson Springfield MO 65802 Office Phone: 417-862-6708.

O'REILLY, WILLIAM M., lawyer, insurance company executive; BA, U. Ill., 1977; JD, Loyola U., 1980. Bar: Ill. 1980, Wis. 1987. Law clk. & assoc. William B. Handley & Assocs., 1979—80; assoc. Bell, Boyd & Lloyd, 1981—84, Ross & Hardies, 1984—86; assoc. counsel Sentry Insurance Group, Stevens Point, Wis., 1986—92, assoc. gen. counsel, corp. sec., 1992—94, v.p., gen. counsel, corp. sec., 1994—. Office: Sentry Insurance 1800 N Point Dr Stevens Point WI 54481 Office Phone: 715-346-6000. Fax: 715-346-7516.

OREN, DONALD G., transportation executive; Pres. Dart Transit Co., Eagan, Minn., 1979—. Office: Dart Transit Co 800 Lone Oak Rd Eagan MN 55121-2212

ORFIELD, MYRON WILLARD, JR., state legislator, educator; b. Mpls., July 27, 1961; BA summa cum laude, U. Minn., 1983; grad., Princeton U., 1983-84; JD, U. Chgo., 1987. Bar: Minn. 1988. Law clk. Judge Gerald W. Heaney, U.S. Ct. Appeals, 8th Cir., 1987-88; rsch. assoc. Ctr. for Studies in Criminal Justice, U. Chgo., 1988-89; assoc. Faegre & Benson, 1989; asst. atty. gen. Minn. Atty. Gen.'s Office, 1989—; Bradley fellow Ctr. for Studies in Criminal Justice, U. Chgo., 1990-91; mem. Minn. Ho. of Reps. from dist. 60B, St. Paul, 1991-2000, Minn. Senate from 60th dist., St. Paul, 2001—. Adj. prof. law U. Minn., 1991—, Hamline U., 1991—; dir. Met. Area Protram, Mpls.' mem. com. on improving future of U.S. cities through improved met. governance Nat. Acad. Scis., 1996—. Author: Metropolitics, 1997; contbr. articles to profl. jours. Mem. Assn. Pub. Policy Analysis and Mgmt. (bd. dirs. 1997).

ORIANI, RICHARD ANTHONY, metallurgical engineer, educator; b. El Salvador, July 19, 1920; arrived in U.S., 1929, naturalized, 1943; s. Americo and Berta (Siguenza) Oriani; m. Constance Amelia Gordon, June 26, 1949; children: Margaret, Steven, Julia, Amelia. B in Chem. Engring, CCNY, 1943; MS, Stevens Inst. Tech., 1946; MA, Princeton U., 1948, PhD, 1949. Lab. asst. CCNY, 1943; chemist Bakelite Corp., Bloomfield, NJ, 1943-46; instr. physics Miss Fine's Finishing Sch., Princeton, NJ, 1946-47; rsch. assoc. GE Rsch. Lab., Schenectady, 1949-59; asst. dir. U.S. Steel Corp. Rsch. Lab., Monroeville, Pa., 1959-80; prof. U. Minn., Mpls., 1980-89, dir. Corrosion Rsch. Ctr., 1980-87, prof. emeritus, dir. emeritus, 1989—. Cons. in field. Contbr. articles to profl. jours., chapters to books. Founder, mem. Foxwood Civic Assn., Monroeville, 1959—80; founder, v.p. Monroeville Pub. Libr., 1960—80. Recipient Alexander von Humboldt Sr. Scientist award, 1984, W. R. Whitney award, 1987. Fellow: Electrochemical Soc., Nat. Assn. Corrosion Engrs., N.Y. Acad. Scis., Am. Inst. Chemists, Am. Soc. Metals; mem.: AAAS, Am. Inst. Metall. Engrs., Am. Phys. Soc. Republican. Home: 7250 Lewis Ridge Pky # 305 Edina MN 55439 Office: U Minn 112 Amundson Hall 221 Church St SE Minneapolis MN 55455-0113 Office Phone: 612-625-5862. E-mail: orian001@umn.edu.

ORMESHER, DAVID T., advertising executive; married; 3 children. BA, Wheaton Coll.; MTS, Garrett-Evang. Theol. Sem. Producer, journalist; CEO, founder Closer Look Group, Inc., Chgo., 1987—. Producer (documentary series) A Closer Look. Bd. dirs. Lyric Opera Guild, Shelter Now Internat. Mem. Assn. Multimedia Communicators, Chgo. Software Assn. Office: Closer Look Creative 212 W Superior St Ste 300 Chicago IL 60610-3557

ORMOND, PAUL A., healthcare company executive; b. Aurora, Ill. B in economics with honors, Stanford U., 1971, MBA, 1973. Mem. corp. staff, positions with glass container divsn. Owens-Ill., Inc., 1973-77, nat. mktg. mgr. soft drinks, glass container divsn., 1977-78; mgr. Atlanta sales dist., glass container divsn. Owens-Ill. Inc., 1978-80, asst. gen. mgr. Gerresheimer Glas (internat. affiliate Owens-Ill. Inc.) Germany, 1980-82, v.p. glass container group, 1982-84, v.p. packaging ops., dir. market strategy and devel., 1984-91, corp. v.p., 1986-91; pres., CEO Health Care and Retirement Corp. (HCR) (subs. Owens-Ill. Inc.), Toledo, 1986-91; chmn., pres., CEO Health Care and Retirement Corp. (HCR) (now ind. co.), Toledo, 1991—98; pres., CEO HCR Manor Care Inc., Toledo, 1998—99, Manor Care, Inc., Toledo, 1999—2001, chmn., pres., CEO, 2001—. Office: Manor Care 333 N Summit St Toledo OH 43604-2617

O'ROURKE, WILLIAM ANDREW, literature and language professor, writer; b. Chgo., Dec. 4, 1945; s. William Andrew and Elizabeth (Kompare) O'R.; m. Marion Teresa Ghilarducci, July 9, 1986; 1 child, Joseph Ghilarducci. BA, U. Mo. at Kansas City, 1968; M.F.A., Columbia U., 1970. Instr. journalism Kean Coll., Union, NJ, 1973; asst. prof. English Rutgers U., 1975-78, Mount Holyoke Coll., 1978-81, U. Notre Dame, Ind., 1981-87, assoc. prof. Ind., 1987-94, prof. Ind., 1994—. Writer-in-residence Thurber House, Columbus, Ohio, fall 1984 Author: The Harrisburg 7 and the New Catholic Left, 1972, The Meekness of Isaac, 1974, Idle Hands, 1981, Criminal Tendencies, 1987, Signs of the Literary Times: Essays, Reviews, Profiles 1970-92, 1993, Notts, 1996,Campaign America '96: The View From the Couch, 1997, Campaign America 2000: The View From the Couch, 2001, On Having a Heart Attack: A Medical Memoir, 2006; editor: On the Job, 1977. Fine Arts Work Ctr. fellow, Provincetown, Mass., 1970-72; recipient Creative Artists Pub. Svc. award N.Y. State Coun. on Arts, 1975; Nat. Endowment for Arts creative writing fellow, 1981-82, 90-91. Mem. Authors Guild, PEN Am. Ctr., Nat. Book Critics Cir. Office: U Notre Dame Dept English 356 O'Shag Notre Dame IN 46556 Office Phone: 574-631-7377.

ORR, JAMES FRANCIS, retired business process outsourcing executive; b. Phila., Oct. 10, 1945; s. James F. Jr. and Dorothy (Gallagher) O.; m. Catherine Marie Reinholt; children: Kristin Leah, Lauren Beth, James Desmond. Student, Pa. State U., 1963-64, Rutgers U., Camden and New Brunswick, NJ, 1964-67. Various sales mgmt. positions Procter & Gamble, 1967-73, dist. mgr. White Plains, N.Y., 1973-76, nat. accounts mgr. Cin., 1976-78, sales div. mgr., 1978-81, sales merchandising mgr., 1981-82; sales dir. Procter & Gamble Ltd., Newcastle upon Tyne, Eng., 1982-85; v.p. sales Crush Internat. Inc., Cin., 1985-88; v.p. mkt. devel. Matrixx Mktg. Inc. subs. Cin. Bell Inc., Cin., 1989-92, pres., CEO, 1993; COO Cincinnati Bell Inc.; pres Convergys Corp., Cin., 2000—05, CEO, 2000—07, chmn., 2000—07. Mem. parents adv. coun. Hamilton Coll., Clinton, N.Y., 1989-91, vice chmn. Parents Fund, 1989-90, chmn., 1990-91; active Grad. Leadership Cin., class XVI, 1992-93. Mem. Direct Mktg. Assn., Soc. Consumer Affairs Profls., Greater Cin. C. of C., Coldstream Country Club (trustee), Melrose Club (Daufuskie Island, S.C.). Avocations: golf, theater, antiques, travel.

ORR, KAY A., former governor of Nebraska; b. Burlington, Iowa, Jan. 2, 1939; d. Ralph Robert and Sadie Lucille (Skoglund) Stark; m. William Dayton Orr, Sept. 26, 1957; children: John William, Suzanne. Student, U. Iowa, 1956-57. Exec. asst. to Gov. Charles Thone, Lincoln, Nebr., 1979-81; treas. State of Nebr., Lincoln, 1981-86, gov., 1987-91. Bd. dirs. Williams Group, Tulsa, ServiceMaster, Chgo., VanCorn, Ill. Del., mem. platform com. Rep. Nat. Conv., 1976, 80, 84, co-chmn. 1984, chmn. 1988; mem. Nat. Women's Coalition, Rep. Nat. Com., 1984-85; trustee Hastings (Nebr.) Coll., 1985-95, Freedom Forum, Arlington, Va., 1991-93; mem. Commn. on Presidential Debates, 1986, Hitchcock Ctr., U. Nebr. Sch. Journalism, 1991, Nebr. Agr. Leadership Coun., 1993; Nat. Adv. Coun. on Rural Devel., 1988; vice-chair, Pres.'s Coun. on Rural America, 1990-92; adv. com. First Amendment Ctr., Vanderbilt U., 1992-93, Lincoln Crisis Pregnancy Ctr., 1993. Named Outstanding Young Rep. Woman in Nebr., 1969, Nebr. Wildlife Fedn. Conservationist of Yr., 1989; recepient Sower award, Lincoln Found., Duncan Aviation award for Leadership, 1988. Mem. Women Execs. in State Govt., Nat. Govs. Assn. (vice-chmn., lead gov. Telecommunications subcom., chmn. Transportation, Commerce & Communications com., mem. Force on Fgn. Markets), Lincoln Gen. Hosp. Auxiliary (life), Omicron Delta Kappa. Republican. Lutheran.*

ORR, SAN WATTERSON, JR., lawyer; b. Madison, Wis., Sept. 22, 1941; s. San Watterson and Eleanor Augusta (Schalk) Orr; m. Joanne Marie Ruby, June 26, 1965; children: San Watterson III, Nancy Chapman. BBA, U. Wis., 1963, JD, 1966. CPA Wis.; bar: Wis. 1966. Sec., tres., bd. dirs. Yawkey Lumber Co., Wausau, Wis., 1971—; pres. Forewood, Inc., Wausau, 1979—, also bd. dirs.; dir. Marshall & Ilsley Bank, Wausau, 1988—, Marshall & Ilsley Corp., 1994—; chmn. bd. dirs. Wausau Paper Corp., 1997—. Editor: U. Wis. Law Rev., 1962—63. Bd. dirs. Aytchmonde Woodson Found., Inc., Wausau, 1966—2006, Leigh Yawkey Woodson Art Mus., Inc., Wausau, 1981—; pres. Woodson YMCA Found., Wausau, 2002, Nancy Woodson Spire Found., Inc., 2000, Aspirus Health Found., Inc., Wausau, 1998—; chmn. U. Wis. Found., Madison, 2003—05, chmn. emeritus; bd. dirs. Wis. Taxpayers Alliance, Madison, 1983—2006, Wis. Mfrs. and Commerce, 2001—04, Woodson YMCA Found., Wausau, 1979—, Nancy Woodson Spire Found., Inc., 1980—, Aspirus Health Found., Inc., Wausau, 1981—, U. Wis. Found., Madison, 1991—, Wis. Policy Rsch. Inst., Milw., 1995—2006; bd. regents U. Wis. Sys., Madison, 1993—2000, pres., 1998—2000; bd. dirs. Lynde and Harry Bradley Found., 2006—. Mem.: Am. Law Inst., Wis. Bar Assn., Ocean Club Fla., Country Club Fla., Minocqua Country Club. Office: Yawkey Lumber Co 500 3rd St Ste 602 Wausau WI 54403-4857

ORT, SHANNON, lawyer; b. Appleton, Wis. BA magna cum laude in Criminal Justice and Legal Studies, Hamline U., 1998; JD magna cum laude, William Mitchell Coll. Law, 2001. Bar: Minn. 2001, Wis. 2002. Assoc. Steffens & Rasmussen; assoc. atty. litig. dept. Rider Bennett, LLP, Mpls.; founder, ptnr. Terzich & Ort, LLP, Mpls., 2007—. Named a Rising Star, Minn. Super Lawyers mag., 2006; recipient, 2007, 2008. Mem.: Hennepin County Bar Assn., Minn. State Bar Assn. Office: Terzich and Ort LLP Ste # 5 8525 Edinbrook Crossing Minneapolis MN 55443 Office Phone: 763-391-7412. Business E-Mail: sort@tolawoffice.com.

ORTMAN, ELDON E., retired entomologist, educator; b. Marion, SD, Aug. 11, 1934; s. Emil and Kathryn (Tieszen) O.; m. Margene Adrian, June 27, 1957; children— Karen, Connie, Nancy. AB, Tabor Coll., 1956; MS, Kansas State U., 1957, PhD, 1963. Rsch. entomologist USDA, No. Grain Insects Rsch. Lab., Brookings, S.D., 1961-68, dir., leader investigations, 1968-72; asst. prof. entomology S.D. State U., Brookings, 1961-63, assoc. prof., 1963-68, prof., 1968-72; asst. Entomology Rsch. Divsn. Office, Beltsville, Md., 1971; prof. entomology Purdue U., West Lafayette, Ind., 1972-89, head dept. entomology, 1972-89; assoc. dir. Ind. Agrl. Rsch. Programs, 1989—2001; ret. Fellow AAAS; mem. Entomol. Soc. Am., Phi Kappa Phi, Gamma Sigma Delta, Sigma Xi. Achievements include research in plant resistance to insects and pest mgmt. Home: 3805 W Capilano Dr West Lafayette IN 47906-8881 E-mail: eortman@purdue.edu.

ORTMAN, GEORGE EARL, artist; b. Oakland, Calif., Oct. 17, 1926; s. William Thomas and Anna Katherine (Noll) O.; m. Conni Whidden, Aug. 5, 1960 (dec.); 1 stepson, Roger Graham Whidden. Student, Calif. Coll. Arts and Crafts, 1947-49, Atelier Stanley William Hayter, 1949, Acad. Andre L'Hote, Paris, 1949-50, Hans Hoffman Sch. Art, 1949-50. Co-founder Tempo Playhouse, NYC, 1954; Instr. painting and drawing NYU, 1962-65; co-chmn. fine arts Sch. Visual Arts NYC, 1963-65; artist-in-residence Princeton U., 1966-69, Honolulu Acad. Art, 1969; head painting dept. Cranbrook Acad. Art, Bloomfield Hills, Mich., 1970-92. One-man exhbns. include Tanager Gallery, 1954, Wittenborn Gallery, 1955, Stable Gallery, 1957, 60, Howard Wise Gallery, 1962, 63, 64, 66, 69, Gimpel-Weitzenhoffer Gallery, 1972 (all N.Y.C.), Swetzoff Gallery, Boston, 1961-62, Fairleigh Dickinson U., 1962, Mirvish Gallery, Toronto, Can., 1964, Walker Art Center, Mpls., 1965, Milw. Art Center, 1966, Dallas Mus. Art, 1966, Portland Mus. Art, 1966, Akron Inst. Art, 1966, U. Chgo., 1967, Princeton U. Art Mus., 1967, Honolulu Acad. Art, 1969, Reed Coll., 1970, Cranbrook Acad. Art, 1970, 92, Indpls. Mus. Art, 1971, J.L. Hudson Gallery, Detroit, 1971, Gimpel-Weitzenhoffer, N.Y.C., 1972, 73, Gertrude Kasle Gallery, Detroit, 1976, Lee Hoffman Gallery, Detroit, 1977, Flint (Mich.) Mus. Art, 1977; other one-man exhbns. include Cranbrook Mus. Art, 1982; exhibited numerous group shows including Whitney Mus. Am. Art Annual, 1962, 63, 64, 65, 67, 73, Carnegie Internat., Pitts., 1964, 67, 70, Jewish Mus., N.Y.C., 1964, Corcoran Mus., Washington, 1964, Mitchell Algos Gallery, N.Y.C., 2002, 07, others; represented permanent collections, Walker Art Center, Mpls., Mus. Modern Art, Whitney Mus. Am. Art, (both N.Y.C.), Guggenheim Mus., N.Y.C., Albright-Knox Mus., Buffalo, NYU, Christian Theol. Sem., Indpls., Indpls. Mus. Art, Cleve. Mus. Art, Mus. Am. Art, Washington, Honolulu Acad. Art, Newark Mus. Art, Container Corp. Am., Chgo. Ind. U. Music Bldg., Wausau (Wis.) Hosp. Center, Unitarian Ch., Princeton, Mfr. Hanover Trust Bldg., Albert Kahn & Assos., Detroit, Renaissance Center, Detroit, Mich. State Univ. Performing Arts Ctr., East Lansing, Detroit Inst. Arts. Guggenheim fellow, 1965-66; Ford Found. grantee, 1966, Lee Krasner Found. grantee; One of five Am. artists selected for 1965 Japanese Bi-ann.; recipient Gov. NJ's Purchase award 2d ann. exhbn. art, 1967, Krasner Found. award, 2003, Lifetime Achievement award; Best of Show Religion in Art Exhbn., Birmingham, Ala., 1966. Mem. Nat. Acad. of Design. Office Phone: 212-794-6551.

ORTON, COLIN GEORGE, medical physicist; b. London, June 4, 1938; came to U.S., 1966; s. Frederick G. and Audrey V. (Sewell) O.; m. Barbara G. Scholes, July 25, 1964; children: Nigel, Susanne, Philip. BS in Physics with honors, Bristol U., 1959; MS in Radiation Physics, London U., 1961, PhD in Radiation Physics, 1965; MA (hon.), Brown U., 1976. Diplomate Am. Bd. Radiology, Am. Bd. Med. Physics. Instr. London U. St. Barts' Hosp., 1961-66; assoc. prof. NYU Med. Ctr., 1966-75, Brown U., RI, 1975-81; prof., chief physicist Wayne State U., Harper Hosp., Detroit, 1981—2003. Dir. grad. program Wayne State U., 1981-2003. Author: Radiation Physics Review Books I, 1971, II, 1978; editor: Electron Treatment Planning, 1978, Progress in Medical Physics I, 1982, II, 1985, Radiation Dosimetry, 1986; editor Medical Physics, 1997-2004. Recipient Marie Curie Gold medal Health Physics Soc., 1987. Fellow Am. Assn. Physicists in Am. (pres. 1981, William D. Coolidge award 1993), Am. Coll. Med. Physics (chmn. 1985, Marvin M. D. Williams award, 1997), Inst. Physics London, Am. Coll. Radiology; mem. Internat. Orgn. for Med. Physics (sec. gen. 1988-94, pres. 1997-2000), Am. Brachytherapy Soc. (pres. 2001-02), Internat. Union Physics and Engring. Sci. in Medicine (pres. 2003-06, Merit award 2003). Avocations: golf, badminton, tennis, running, squash. Home: 15810 Lakeview Ct Grosse Pointe Park MI 48230-1806 Office Phone: 313-823-8079. E-mail: ortonc@comcast.net.

ORVICK, GEORGE MYRON, religious organization administrator, minister; b. Hanlontown, Iowa, Jan. 9, 1929; s. George and Mabel Olina (Mandsager) O.; m. Ruth Elaine Hoel, Aug. 25, 1951; children: Daniel, Emily, Mark, Kirsten. AA, Bethany Luth. Coll., Mankato, Minn., 1948, candidate of theology, 1953; BA, Northwestern Coll., Watertown, Wis., 1950; postgrad., U. Wis. Ordained to ministry Evang. Luth. Synod, 1953. Pastor Our Saviour Luth. Ch., Amherst Junction, Wis., 1953-54, Holy Cross Luth. Ch., Madison, Wis., 1954-86; cir. visitor Evang. Luth. Synod, Mankato, 1964-69, v.p., 1969—70, pres., 1970—76, 1980—2002, dir. dept. archives and history, 2002—; bd. regents Bethany Luth. Coll., 1957—69. Author: Our Great Heritage, 1966, Forget Not All His Benefits, 2003; columnist: The Luth. Sentinel, 1982-2002. Lutheran. Home: 224 Terrace Dr Mankato MN 56001-4728 Office: Evang Luth Synod 6 Browns Ct Mankato MN 56001-6121 Home Phone: 507-387-1498; Office Phone: 507-344-7308. Business E-Mail: gorvick@blc.edu.

ORWOLL, GREGG S.K., lawyer; b. Austin, Minn., Mar. 23, 1926; s. Gilbert M. and Kleonora (Kleven) O.; m. Laverne M. Flentie, Sept. 15, 1951; children: Kimball G., Kent A., Vikki A., Tristen A., Erik G. BS, Northwestern U., Evanston, Ill., 1950; JD, U. Minn., Mpls., 1953. Bar: Minn. 1953, US Supreme Ct. 1973. Assoc. Dorsey & Whitney, Mpls., 1953-59, ptnr., 1959-60; assoc. counsel Mayo Clinic, Rochester, Minn., 1960-63, gen. counsel, 1963-87, sr. legal counsel, 1987-91, sr. counsel, 1991-92. Gen. counsel, dir. Rochester Airport Co., 1962-84, v.p., 1981-84; gen. counsel Mayo Med. Svcs., Ltd., 1972-90; bd. dirs., sec. and gen. counsel Mayo Found. for Med. Edn. and Rsch., 1984-90; gen. counsel Mid-Am. Orthop. Assn., 1984—, Minn. Orthop. Soc., 1985-95; counsel orwegian Am. Orthopaedic Soc., 1999—, Intl. Soc. of Amyloidosis 2002—; asst. sec./sec. Mayo Found., Rochester, 1972-91; sec. Mayo Emeritus Staff, 1998-99, vice chair, 1999-2000, chair, 2000-2001; bd. dirs. Charter House, 1986-90; dir., officer Travelure Motel Corp., 1968-86; dir., v.p. Echo Too Ent., Inc.; dir., v.p. Oberhamer Inc., 1989-99; bd. dirs. Am. Decal and Mfg. Co., 1989-93, sec., 1992-93; adj. prof. William Mitchell Coll. Law, 1978-84. Contbr. articles to profl. jours., chpts. to books; mem. editl. bd. Minn. Law Rev., 1952-53, HealthSpan, 1984-93 Trustee Minn. Coun. on Founds., 1977-82, Mayo Found., 1982-86; trustee William Mitchell Coll. Law, 1982-88, 89-98, mem. exec. com. 1990-98; bd. visitors U. Minn. Law Sch., 1974-76, 85-91; mem. U. Minn. Regent Candidate Adv. Coun., 1988-99, Minn. State Compensation Coun., 1991-97. With USAF, 1944-45. Recipient Outstanding Svc. medal, US Govt., 1991. Mem. ABA, AMA (affiliate), Am. Corp. Counsel Assn., Minn. Soc. Hosp. Attys. (bd. dirs. 1981-86), Minn. State Bar Assn. (chmn. legal/med. com. 1977-81), Olmsted County Bar Assn. (v.p., pres. 1977-79), Rochester C. of C., U. Minn. Law Alumni Assn. (bd. dirs. 1973-76, 85-91), Rochester U. Club (pres. 1977), The Doctors Mayo Soc., Mid Am. Orthop. Assn. (hon.), Mayo Alumni Assn. (hon.), Phi Delta Phi, Phi Delta Theta. Republican. Home: 2233 5th Ave NE Rochester MN 55906-4017 Office: Mayo Clinic 200 1st St SW Rochester MN 55905-0002 Office Phone: 507-284-2691.

OSBORN, GERALD GUY, dean, psychiatrist, educator; b. Cin., Nov. 6, 1947; s. Guy Henry and Doris Irene (Taylor) Osborn; m. Sue Ellen Granger, July 9, 1983; children: Erica Tyrell, Eric Gerald, Ellen Stephanie. BA, Wilmington Coll., 1969; student, Schiller U., Klein-Ingersheim, Germany, 1968—69; DO, Kirksville Coll. Osteo. Medicine, 1973; postgrad. in Psychiatry, U. Sheffield, Eng., 1973; MPhil, Cambridge U., 1986. Diplomate Am. Osteo. Bd. Neurology and Psychiatry, 1982, Am. Bd. Psychiatry and Neurology. Rotating intern Lansing Gen. Hosp., Mich., 1973—74; resident, postdoctoral fellow Dept. Psychiatry Mich. State U., East Lansing, 1974—77, chief resident in psychiatry, 1976—77, instr. in psychiatry, 1974—77, asst. prof., 1977—82, assoc. prof., 1982, dir. residency tng. osteo divsn., 1979—81, assoc. dean acad. affairs Coll. Osteo. Medicine, 1981—83, assoc. adj. prof. Dept. History, 1986, prof. psychiatry, acting chmn. Dept. Psychiatry; chmn. Dept. Psychiatry St. Lawrence Hosp., Lansing, 1986; dean Kirksville Coll. Osteo. Medicine A.T. Still U., 2002—04. Psychiat. reviewer Mich. Dept. Social Services; chmn. Lansing Area Psychiatry Coun., 1983; cons. in field. Contbr. articles to profl. jours. Med. dir. Catholic Social Services, Family and Child Services of Lansing; active Physicians for Social Responsibility, East Lansing. Recipient Med. Writing award, Mich. Osteo. Coll. Found., 1976, Prof. of Yr. award, Mich. State U., 1981; Kettering scholar, 1968. Mem.: Am. Assn. Directors Psychiat. Residency Tng., Mich. Osteo. Neuropsychiat. Soc., Am. Coll. Neuropsychiatrists (bd. govs. 1982, pres.-elect 1986, pres. 1987), Mich. Psychiat. Soc., Am. Psychiat. Assn., Ingham County Osteo. Soc., Mich. Assn. Osteo. Physicians and Surgeons, Am. Osteo. Assn., Osteo. Physicians and Surgeons Calif. (assoc.), US Internat. Sailing Assn., Aircraft Owners and Pilots Assn., Sigma Sigma Phi. Democrat. Mem. Soc. Of Friends.

OSBORN, SHANE, state official; b. SD, 1974; m. Teri Osborn, 2003; 2 children. BS in Math., Statistics, Univ. Nebr., 1996. State treas. State of Nebr., 2007—. Pilot, World Watchers Fleet Air Reconnaissance Squadron One USN, 1996—2005, Iraq, Iran, Afghanistan, S. Am., Asian Pacific. Decorated Disting. Flying Cross for heroism and extraordinary achievement in flight. Mem.: CAP. Office: State Treas Rm 2005 State Capitol Bldg PO Box 94788 Lincoln NE 68509-4788 Office Phone: 402-471-2455. Office Fax: 402-471-4390. Business E-Mail: info@treasurer.org.

OSBORN, WILLIAM A., investment company executive; b. Culver, Ind., Oct. 14, 1947; married; 2 children. BA, Northwestern U., 1969, MBA, 1973. Joined No. Trust Corp., 1970, sr. exec. v.p., commercial banking Chgo., pres., COO, 1993—95, chmn., pres., CEO, 1995—2007, chmn., 2008—. Bd. dirs. No. Trust Corp., 1994—, Nicor, Inc., 1999—2006, Caterpillar Inc., 2000—, The Tribune Co., 2001—; Class A dir. Fed. Reserve Bank Chgo. Bd. trustees Mus. Sci. and Industry, Chgo., orthwestern U., Chgo.; bd. dirs. Chgo. Symphony Orch., Northwestern Meml. HealthCare, Chgo. Urban League, Chgo. Horticultural Society, Lyric Opera Chgo., United Way Metropolitan Chgo.; bd. mgrs. YMCA Metropolitan Chgo.; advisory bd. J.L. Kellogg Grad. Sch. Mgmt., Northwestern. Mem.: Commercial Club of Chgo. (chmn., vice chmn. civic com.), Chgo. United (bd. dirs.), Chgo. Coun. Foreign Relations (bd. dirs.), Financial Services Roundtable, Chgo. Club, Executives' Club (bd. dirs.), Economic Club (bd. dirs.). Office: No Trust Co 50 S Lasalle St Chicago IL 60675-0001

OSBORNE, TOM (THOMAS WILLIAM OSBORNE), college athletic director, former congressman, retired college football coach; b. Hastings, Nebr., Feb. 22, 1937; m. Nancy Tederman; children: Mike, Ann, Susie. BA in Hist., Hastings Coll., Nebr., 1959; MA in Ednl. Psych., U. Nebr., 1963, PhD in Ednl. Psych., 1965. Flanker Washington Redskins, 1959-61, San Francisco 49ers, 1961-62; asst. football coach U. Nebr., 1962—67, receivers coach, 1967—71, asst. head coach, 1972, head football coach, 1973-97, prof. emeritus, 1998-2000, interim athletic dir., 2007—, interim head football coach, 2007—08; mem. US Congress from 3rd Nebr. dist., 2001—07, mem. agr. com., mem. edn. and the workforce com., mem. transp. and infrastructure com. Bd. dirs. Corp. Nat. & Community Svc., 2007—. Co-founder Osborne Endowment for Youth. Sgt. in US Army Nat. Guard and USAR, 1960—66. Named Big Eight Coach of Yr., 1975, 1978, 1980, Bobby Dodds Nat. Coach of Yr., 1978; recipient Amos Alonzo Stagg award, Am. Football Coaches Assn., 2000, Policy Maker of Yr., Assn. Career and Tech. Edn., 2005, Paul "Bear" Bryant Lifetime Achievement award, Nat. Sportscasters & Sportswriters Assn., 2008. Mem.: Fellowship Christian Athletes. Republican. Meth. Achievements include coaching the U. Nebr. football team in several bowl games including the Sugar Bowl, 1971, Cotton Bowl, 1974, Astro-Bluebonnet Bowl, 1976, Liberty Bowl, 1977, Orange Bowl, 1979, 83, 84,89, 92-95, Sun Bowl, 1980; coached team to NCAA Divsn. IA Nat. Championship, 1994, 1995, 1997. Office: U Nebr Athletics One Memorial Stadium PO Box 880120 Lincoln NE 68588-0120 Office Phone: 202-225-6435, 402-472-3011.

OSGOOD, CHRIS, professional hockey player; b. Peace River, Alta., Canada, Nov. 26, 1972; Goalie Detroit Red Wings, 1991—2001, 2005—, NY Islanders, 2001—05. Co-recipient William M. Jennings Trophy, NHL, 1996; named to WHL East All-Star 2d Team, 1990—91, Sporting News All-Star Team, 1996, Second All-Star Team, HL, 1996, NHL All-Star Game, 1996, 2008. Achievements include being a member of Stanely Cup Champion Detroit Red Wings, 1997, 1998. Office: c/o Detroit Red Wings Joe Louis Arena 600 Civic Center Dr Detroit MI 48226-4408*

OSGOOD, RUSSELL KING, academic administrator; b. Fairborn, Ohio, Oct. 25, 1947; s. Richard M. and Mary Russell Osgood; m. Paula Haley, June 6, 1970; children: Mary, Josiah, Micah, Iain. BA, Yale U., 1969, JD, 1974. Bar: Mass. 1974, U.S. Dist. Ct. Mass. (admitted to) 1976. Assoc. Hill & Barlow, Boston, 1974—78; assoc. prof. Boston U., 1978—80; prof. Cornell U., Ithaca, NY, 1980—88, dean law sch., 1988—98; pres. Grinnell Coll., Iowa, 1998—. Lt. USNR, 1969—71. Mem.: Selden Soc., Stair Soc., Mass. Hist. Soc. Office: Grinnell Coll 1121 Park St Grinnell IA 50112-1640 Office Phone: 641-269-3000. E-mail: osgood@grinnell.edu.

O'SHAUGHNESSY, JAMES PATRICK, lawyer, consultant; b. Rochester, NY, Mar. 3, 1947; s. John Andrew and Margaret May (Yaxley) O'S.; m. Terry Lee Wood. BS cum laude, Rensselaer Poly. Inst., 1972; JD, Georgetown U., 1977. Bar: Va. 1977, Ohio 1979, Wis. 1987. Assoc. Squire, Sanders & Dempsey, Cleve., 1978-81; ptnr. Hughes & Cassidy, Sumas, Wash., 1981-84; patent counsel Kimberly-Clark Corp., Neenah, Wis., 1984-85; ptnr. Foley & Lardner, Milw., 1986-96; v.p., chief intellectual property counsel Rockwell Automation, Inc., Milw., 1996—2004; ind. cons. Mequon, Wis., 2004—. Founder Innovatech Co., 1996-2000, Lake Street Holdings, LLC 2006-, Donges Bay Group, LLC 2007-; mem. tech. adv. coun. Ideation Internat., Inc., 1999-2004; mem. adv. bd. Licensing Econs. Rev., 1998-2002; co-founder Intellectual Property Bus. Internat., 2002-04; mem. bd. visitors Georgetown U. Sch. Nursing, 1996-2000; bd. dir. Gemstar TV Guide Internat. Inc., comp. com., 2004—; mem. coun. of advisors Nat. Inst. Play, 2006-; chmn. bd. dirs. ICmty. Svcs., Inc. 2007-; lectr. in field. Contbg. author: Technology Licensing: Corporate Strategies for Maximizing Value, 1996, Profiting From Intellectual Capital: Extracting Value From Innovation, 1998; mem. editl. bd. Am. Criminal Law Rev., 1976-77; contbr. articles to profl. jours. Bd. dirs. Skylight Opera Theatre, 1991-92, Milw. Florentine Opera Co., 1999—, pres., 2002-03. With USN, 1964—68, USS Boxer. Recipient Matthew Albert Hunter prize, Rensselaer Poly. Inst., 1972. Mem. CPR Inst. for Dispute Resolution (mediation/arbitration panel), Lic. Execs. Soc., Am. Intellectual Property Law Assn., Assn. Chief Patent Coun. (emeritus), Innovation Practitioners Network, Disabled Am. Vets., Tau Beta Pi, Alpha Sigma Mu. Avocations: golf, fly fishing, curling, bridge. Home and Office: 3207 W Donges Bay Rd Mequon WI 53092-5119 Office Phone: 262-512-9883. Business E-Mail: jim@jposhaughnessy.com.

O'SHONEY, GLENN, church administrator; Exec. dir. Mission Svcs. of Luth. Ch. Mo. Synod Internat. Ctr., St. Louis. Office: Luth Ch Mo Synod Inter Ctr 1333 S Kirkwood Rd Saint Louis MO 63122-7226

OSNES, LARRY G., academic administrator; b. Scottsbluff, Nebr., Oct. 30, 1941; s. Earl E. and Rose (DeRock) O.; m. Susan C.; 1 child, Justin. BA in History, Anderson Coll., 1963; MA in History, Wayne State Coll., 1965; PhD in History, U. Cin., 1970. Asst. prof. history and govt. U. Cin., 1967-69; dir. Am. studies Anderson (Ind.) Coll., 1970-75, chmn. dept. history, 1975-76, dean acadmeic devel., 1975-78, asst. corp. sec., dean academic devel. and pub. affairs, 1978-83; pres. Minn. Pvt. Coll. Coun., St. Paul, 1983-88, Hamline U., St. Paul, 1988—. Mem. Assoc. Colls. Twin Cities (chmn. 1988-90), Mpls. Club, St. Paul Athletic Club. Office: Hamline Univ 1536 Hewitt Ave Saint Paul MN 55104-1284

OSSKOPP, MIKE, state legislator; b. Oct. 3, 1951; m. Monica Osskopp; 2 children. BA, Inst. Broadcast Arts; MA, Moody Bible Inst. Minn. state rep. Dist. 29B, 1994—. Radio broadcast journalist. Office: Minn Ho of Reps State Capitol Saint Paul MN 55155-0001 Home: 17385 Halifax Path Lakeville MN 55044-9566

OSTER, LEWIS HENRY, manufacturing executive, industrial engineer, consultant; b. Mitchell, SD, Jan. 18, 1923; s. Peter W. and Lucy (Goetsch) Oster; m. Mary Mills, Aug. 17, 1948; children: David, Lewis, Nancy, Susan. BS in Engring., Iowa State U., 1948; MBA, Syracuse U., 1968. Registered profl. engr., Iowa. Mgr. Maytag Co., Newton, Iowa, 1953—59; sr. staff engr., mgr. Philco-Ford Corp., Phila., 1959—62; mgr. mech. and indsl. engring. Carrier Corp., Syracuse, NY, 1962—75; v.p. Superior Industries Internat., Van Nuys, Calif., 1981—. V.p., gen. mgr. Superior/Ideal, Inc., Oskaloosa, Iowa, 1975—; cons. in field. Author: MTM Application Manual, 1957. Leader Boy Scouts Am., Syracuse, NY, 1965—73; fund chmn. United Fund, Syracuse, 1965—73. Lt. col. USAFR, ETO. Decorated Purple Heart, DFC, Air medal with four oak leaf clusters. Mem.: Am. Inst. Indsl. Engrs. (pres. 1951—53), Ret. Officers Assn., Oskaloosa Country Club, Am. Legion, Elks.

OSTERGREN, GREGORY VICTOR, insurance company executive; b. Mpls., May 27, 1955; s. Theodora Carl and Donna Marie Ostergren; m. Diane Jane Schaller, Oct. 12, 1985; children: Patrick, Cynthia. BS in Math., BA in Econs., U. Minn., 1977. Actuarial analyst Allstate Ins. Co., Northbrook, Ill., 1977-79; actuary MSI Ins. Co., Arden Hills, Minn., 1979-84, dir. actuarial dept., 1984-86, v.p. ops., 1986-90; chmn., pres., CEO Am. Nat. Property and Casualty Ins. Co., Springfield, Mo., 1990—, also bd. dirs. Chmn., Farm Family Ins. Cos., Albany, N.Y., 2001—; mem. governing bd. Minn., S.D. and N.D. Auto Assigned Risk, Mpls., 1984-90; bd. dirs. Guaranty Fed. Bank. Bd. dirs. United Way of Ozarks, Springfield, 1990-98, Springfield Pub. Sch. Found., 1994—; mem. cert. com. S.W. Mo. State U., Springfield, 1992-93; mem. steering com. Salvation Army, Springfield, 1992-93; chmn. adv. bd. Coll. Natural and Applied Scis. S.W. Mo. State U. Mem. Casualty Actuarial Soc., Am. Acad. Actuaries, Internat. Actuarial Assn., Midwest Actuarial Forum, Ins. Fraternity. Baptist. Avocations: golf, boating, scuba diving, reading, travel. Home: 1951 E Buena Vista St Springfield MO 65804-4326 Office: Am Nat Property Casualty 1949 E Sunshine St Springfield MO 65899-0001 E-mail: gostergren@anpac.com.

OSTERHAUS, ROBERT, state representative, pharmacist; b. Dyersville, Iowa, Jan. 1931; m. Ann Osterhaus. BS, U. Iowa. Pharmacist, Iowa; state rep. dist. 25 Iowa Ho. of Reps., 1997—; mem. commerce and regulation com.; mem. transp. com.; mem. ways and means com.; ranking mem. human svcs. appropriations com. Mem. Sacred Heart Ch. With US Army, 1952—54. Mem.: Iowa Pharmacists Assn., Am. Pharm. Assn. (past pres.), Maquoketa Area Found. (co-founder). Democrat.

OSTFIELD, ALAN, professional sports team executive; m. Jennifer Ostfield; children: Benjamin, Hannah. B in Econs., U. Pa.; JD magna cum laude, Boston U., MBA. Atty. Wilmer, Cutler & Pickering, Washington; sr. v.p., gen. counsel San Diego Padres Baseball Club; sr. v.p. bus. & legal affairs Palace Sports & Entertainment/Detroit Pistons, 2000—02, COO, asst. gen. mgr., 2002—. Tchr. sport mgmt. masters prog. U. Mich.; tchr. U. San Diego Sch. Law; bd. dirs. Mich. Sports Hall of Fame; bd. advs. Nat. Sports Law Inst. Contbr. articles to profl. pubis. Named one of Forty Under 40, St. & Smith SportsBusiness Jour., 2000, 2001, 2002; named to Forty Under 40 Hall of Fame, St. & Smith, 2002. Office: Detroit Pistons 5 Championship Dr Auburn Hills MI 48326

OSTMANN, CINDY, state legislator; BS, Lindenwood Coll. Tchr. Ft. Zumwalt Sch. Dist., 1958-62, 64-67, Fayetteville Sch. Sys., 1963-64; owner, mgr. residential property; mem. Mo. State Ho. of Reps. Dist. 14, 1992—, mem. children, youth and families com., mem. energy and environ. com., mem. local govt. and related matters com. Recipient Outstanding Contbr. to Edn. award Phi Delta Kappa, 1988. Mem. Coun. of Chambers Charter Govt. Com., St. Charles County Arts Coun., Grand Order of Pachyderm, Friends of St. Louis Symphony, Mo. Fedn. Rep. Women, First Capitol Rep. Club. Home: 445 Knaust Rd Saint Peters MO 63376-1713

OSTRACH, SIMON, engineering educator; b. Providence, Dec. 26, 1923; s. Samuel and Bella (Sackman) O.; m. Gloria Selma Ostrov., Dec. 31, 1944 (div. Jan. 1973); children: Stefan Alan, Louis Hayman, Naomi Ruth, David Jonathan, Judith Cele; m. Margaret E. Stern, Oct. 29, 1975. BS in Mech. Engring, U. R.I., 1944, ME, 1949; MS, Brown U., 1949, PhD in Applied Math, 1950; DS (h.c.) Technion, Israel Inst. Tech., 1986; D of Eng. (hon.), Fla. State U., 1994; DS (hon.), U. R.I., 1995; ScD (hon.), Brown U., 1997. Aeronautical rsch. scientist NACA, 1944-47; rsch. assoc. Brown U., 1947-50; chief fluid physics br. Lewis Rsch. Ctr. NASA, 1950-60; prof. engring., head div. fluid, thermal and aerospace scis. Case Western Res. U., Cleve., 1960-70. Wilbert J. Austin Distinguished prof. engring., 1970—; home sec. Nat. Acad. Engring., 1992—2000; dir. Nat. Ctr. for Microgravity Rsch. on Fluids and Combustion, 1997—. Disting. vis. prof. City Coll. CUNY, 1966-67, Fla. A&M U., Fla. State U. Coll. Engring., 1990; Lady Davis fellow, vis. prof. Technion-Israel Inst. Tech., 1983-84; cons.

to industry, 1960—; mem. rsch. adv. com. fluid mechanics NASA, 1963-68, mem. space applications adv. com., 1985—; hon. prof. Beijing U. Aeronautics and Astronautics, 1991; mem. space studies bd. Nat. Rsch. Coun., 1992, bd. govs., 1993—. Contbr. papers to profl. lit. Fellow Japan Soc. for the Promotion of Sci., 1987; recipient Conf. award for best paper Nat. Heat Transfer Conf., 1963, Richards Meml. award Pi Tau Sigma, 1964, Disting. Svc. award Cleve. Tech. Socs. Coun., 1987, Disting. pub. svc. medal NASA, 1993, Space Processing award Am. Inst. of Aeronautics and Astronautics, 1994 Fellow AIAA (Space Processing award 1993), ASME (hon., Heat Transfer Meml. award 1975, Freeman scholar 1982, Thurston lectr. 1987, Max Jacob meml. award 1983, Heat Transfer divsn. 50th Anniversary award 1988), Am. Acad. Arts and Sciences, Am. Acad. Mechanics; mem. NAE (chmn. com. on membership 1986, chmn. nominating com. 1989, chmn. awards com. 1990, sec., mem. space studies bd. 1992), Univs. Space Rsch. Assn. (trustee 1990), Soc. Natural Philosophy, Sigma Xi (nat. lectr. 1978-79), Tau Beta Pi. Home: 28176 Belcourt Rd Cleveland OH 44124-5618 Office: Case Western Res U Dept of Engineering Cleveland OH 44106 Office Phone: 216-368-0749. Business E-Mail: sostrach@mcmr.org.

OSTROM, DON, political science professor; b. Chgo., Mar. 9, 1939; s. Irving and Margaret (Hedberg) O.; m. Florence Horan, Jan. 13, 1972; children: Erik, Rebecca, Katherine. BA, St. Olaf Coll., Northfield, Minn., 1960; MA, Washington U., 1970, PhD, 1972. Prof. polit. sci. Gustavus Adolphus Coll., St. Peter, Minn., 1972—2004; state rep. Minn. Ho. of Reps., St. Paul, 1988-96; vis. prof. polit. sci. St. Olaf Coll., Northfield, 2004—. Co-editor: Perspectives on Minnesota Government and Politics, 1998. Democrat. Home: 2737 Ewing Ave S Minneapolis MN 55416 E-mail: dostrom@gac.edu.

OSTROM, ELINOR, political science professor, researcher; b. LA, Aug. 7, 1933; d. Adrian and Leah (Hopkins) Awan; m. Charles Scott, Aug. 8, 1954 (div. 1961); m. Vincent Ostrom, Nov. 23, 1963. AB with honors, UCLA, 1954, MA, 1962, PhD, 1965; D in Econs. (hon.), U. Zurich, 1999; D (hon.), Inst. Social Studies, The Hague, 2002, Luleå U. Tech., Sweden, 2005, Uppsala U., 2007, Humboldt U., Berlin, 2007; DHL (hon.), U. Mich., Ann Arbor, 2006. Vis. asst. prof. dept. gov. Ind. U., Bloomington, 1965-66, asst. prof., grad. advisor, dept. gov., 1966-69, assoc. prof. dept. polit. sci., 1969-74, prof. polit. sci., 1974-91, Arthur F. Bentley prof. polit. sci., 1991—, prof., chmn. dept. polit. sci., 1980—84, acting chair dept. polit. sci., 1989—90, co-dir. workshop in polit. theory and policy analysis, 1973—, co-dir. Ctr. Study Instns., Population and Environ. Change, 1996—2006, prof. part-time Sch. Pub. and Environ. Affairs; founding dir. Ctr. for Study Instl. Diversity, Ariz. State U., 2007—. Employment interviewer, asst. employee relations mgr., Godfrey L. Cabot, Inc., Boston, 1955-57; personnel analyst III, U. Calif., LA, 1957-61; bd. cons., Internat. Assn. Chiefs Police: Police Discipline Project, 1974-75; adv. bd. at. Evaluation Program Law Enforcement Assistance (Adminstrn.), Washington, 1975-76; mem. Nat. Adv. Panel, Nat. Acad. Pub, Adminstrn.; eighborhood-Oriented Metropolitan Gov., 1975-76, task force on criminal justice rsch. and devel. Nat. Adv. Com. on Criminal Justice Standards and Goals, 1975-76, Nat. Sheriffs Assn.: Study of Contract Law Enforcement, 1975-76; adv. panel Div. Policy Rsch. and Analysis, NSF, Washington, 1977-78, panel on Instl. Develop., 1985; rev. panel Polit. Sci. div. NSF, 1983-84; Interuniversity Consortium for Polit. and Social Rsch. Coun., 1983-85; adv. com. nat. urban policy NAS/NRC, 1985-88, panel on Common Property Resources Mgmt., 1985-86, Scientific Com. on Problems of the Environ., 1995-98; rsch. adv. com. U.S. AID, 1989-91; local gov. rsch. adv. bd., US Adv. Commn. on Intergovernmental Rels., 1985-88; adv. bd., Inst. for Policy Reform, 1993-96; bd. dirs., Beijer Internat. Inst. Ecol. Econs., Royal Swedish Acad. Scis., 1997-; academic adv. bd., Max-Planck-Inst. für Gesellschaftsforschung, 2000-; cons. in field. Co-author: Policing Metropolitan America, 1978, Local Government in the United States, 1988, Institutional Incentives and Sustainable Development: Infrastructure Policies in Perspective, 1993, Rules, Games, and Common-Pool Resources, 1994, The Samaritan's Dilemma, 2005, Seeing the Forest and the Trees, 2005; author: Governing the Commons, 1990, Crafting Institutions for Self-Governing Irrigation Systems, 1992, Understanding Institutional Diversity, 2005; editor: Strategies of Political Inquiry, 1982; co-editor: The Commons in the New Millennium: Challenges and Adaptations, 2003, Trust and Reciprocity: Interdisciplinary Lessons from Experimental Research, 2003, Jour. Theoretical Politics, 1987-95, People and Forests: Communities, Institutions, and Governance, 2000, Protecting the Commons: A Framework for Resource Management in the Americas, 2001, Foundations of Social Capital, 2003; mem. editl. bd. Am. Jour. Polit. Sci., Am. Polit. Sci. Review, Criminal Justice Review, Pub. Productivity Review, Publius, Quarterly Jour. Adminstrn., Sage Urban Affairs Ann. Review, Social Sci. Quarterly, Urban Affairs Quarterly, Ecol. Economics; contbr. articles to profl. jours. Grantee SF, 1974-85, 87—, NIMH, 1977-81, U.S. Dept. Justice, 1978-82, AID, 1984-94, U.S. Geol. Survey, 1987-89, Ford Found., 1991—, FAO, 1992—, MacArthur Found., 1996-; recipient Frank E. Seidman Disting. award in Polit. Economy, 1997, Johan Skytte prize in Polit. Sci., Upsala University, 1999, Aaron Wildavsky Enduring Contbn. award for Governing the Commons, APSA, Pub. Policy Sect., 2000, John J. Carty award for the Advancement Sci., NAS, 2004, Sustainability Sci. award Ecol. Soc. Am., 2005, James Madison award Am. Polit. Sci. Assn., 2005, Cozzarelli prize Proceeding Nat. Acad. Scis., NAS, 2006. Fellow AAAS, Am. Acad. Arts and Scis. (lifetime achievement award Atlas Econ. Rsch. Found. 2003); mem. NAS, Am. Philos. Soc., Assn. for Politics and the Life Scis., Pub. Choice Soc. (pres. 1982-84, co-chair Duncan Black award com. 1986-87, chair Duncan Black award com. 1990, exec. coun. 1982-), Am. Polit. Sci. Assn. (v.p. 1975-76, pres.-elect 1995-96, pres. 1996-97, chmn. several coms. 1978-88, mem. several coms. 1970-2002), Midwest Polit. Sci. Assn. (pres. 1984-85), Internat. Polit. Sci. Assn., Am. Econ. Assn., Internat. Assn. for Study Common Property (pres. 1990-91, program co-chair 2000), Policy Studies Orgn., (nominating com. 1986-87, Miriam Mills award 1996, Thomas R. Dye Svc. award 1997). Democrat. Home: 5883 E Lampkins Ridge Rd Bloomington IN 47401-9726 Office: Ind Univ Workshop in Polit Theory & Policy Analys 513 N Park Ave Bloomington IN 47408-3895 Home Phone: 812-332-9821; Office Phone: 812-855-0441. Office Fax: 812-855-3150. Business E-Mail: ostrom@indiana.edu.

OSTROM, VINCENT A(LFRED), political science professor; b. Nooksack, Wash., Sept. 25, 1919; s. Alfred and Alma (Knudson) Ostrom; m. Isabell Bender, May 20, 1942 (div. 1963); m. Elinor Awan, Nov. 23, 1963. BA in Polit. Sci., UCLA, 1942, MA in Polit. Sci., 1945, PhD in Polit. Sci., 1950. Tchr. Chaffey Union H.S., Ontario, Calif., 1943-45; asst. prof. polit. sci. U. Wyo., Laramie, 1945-48, U. Oreg., Eugene, 1949-54, assoc. prof. polit. sci., 1954-58, UCLA, 1958-64; prof. polit. sci. Ind. U., Bloomington, 1964-90, Arthur F. Bentley prof emeritus polit. sci., 1990—. Hooker disting. vis. scholar McMaster U., 1984-85; rsch. assoc. Bur. Mcpl. Rsch., 1950, Resources for Future, Inc., 1962-64; assoc. dir. Pacific NW Coop. Program in Ednl. Adminstrn., 1951-58; founding dir. Workshop in Polit. Theory and Policy Analysis, Ind. U., Bloomington, 1973—; cons. and lectr. in field. Author: Water and Politics, 1953, The Political Theory of a Compound Republic, 1971, 2nd rev. edit., 1987, The Intellectual Crisis in American Public Administration, 1974, 2nd edit., 1989, The Meaning of American Federalism, 1991, The Meaning of Democracy and the Vulnerability of Democracies, 1997; co-author: Understanding Urban Government, 1973, Local Government in the United States, 1988; co-editor: Comparing Urban Service Delivery Systems, 1977, Guidance, Control and Evaluation in the Public Sector, 1986, Rethinking Institutional Analysis and Development, 1988, 2d. edit. 1993; mem. bd. editors Publius, 1972—; mem. editl. bd. Constnl. Polit. Economy, 1989—, Nigerian Jour. Fin. and Human Resources Mgmt., 1996—, Internat. Jour. Orgn. Theory and Behavior, 1997—; contbr. articles to profl. jours. Program coord. Wyo. Assessors' Sch., 1946-48, Budget Officer's Sch., 1947-48; exec. sec. Wyo. League of Municipalities, 1947-48; cons. Wyo. Legis. Interim Com., 1947-48, Nat. Resources, Alaska Constitutional Convention, 1955-56, Tenn. Water Policy Commn., 1956; mem. founding bd. Com. on Polit. Economy of the Good Soc., 1990—. Grantee and fellowships Social Sci. Rsch. Coun., 1954-55, Ctr. Advanced Study in Behavioral Scis., 1955-56, Ctr. Interdisciplinary Rsch., 1981-82; co-recipient (with Elinor Ostrom) Lifetime Achievement award Atlas Economic Rsch. Found. Fund, 2003, Robert O. Anderson Sustainable Arctic award Inst. of the North 2003. Mem. AAAS, Am. Polit. Sci. Assn. (Spl. Achievement award for Significant Contbns. to Study of Federalism, 1991, Best Book on Federalism and Intergovtl. Rels. award 1999, John Gaus Disting. lecturer award 2005), Am. Econ. Assn., Am. Soc. Pub. Adminstrn., Pub. Choice Soc., Internat. Polit. Sci. Assn. Home: 5883 E Lampkins Ridge Rd Bloomington IN 47401-9726 Office: Ind U Workshop in Polit Theory 513 N Park Ave Bloomington IN 47408-3895 Home Phone: 812-332-9821; Office Phone: 812-855-0441. Business E-Mail: ghiggins@indiana.edu, workshop@indiana.edu.

OSUCH, DEBRA K., environmental engineer; b. 1969; married; 3 children. BS in Med. Physics, Oakland U.; MS in Hazardous Waste Mgmt., Wayne State U. Mgr., Devel. Services Soil and Materials Engineers Inc., Shelby Twp. Named one of 40 Under 40, Crain's Detroit Bus., 2006. Mem.: Comml. Real Estate Women (pres., Detroit Chpt.). Office: Soil and Materials Engineers Inc 13019 Pauline Dr Shelby Township MI 48315 Office Phone: 586-731-3100. Office Fax: 586-731-3582.

OTIS, JAMES, JR., architect; b. Chgo., July 8, 1931; s. James and Edwina (Love) O.; m. Diane Cleveland, Apr. 9, 1955; children: James III, Julie C., David C. BArch cum laude, Princeton U., 1953; postgrad., U. Chgo., 1955-57. Registered architect, Ill., Ariz., Colo., Ind., Iowa, Wis., N.Mex., Mo. Designer Irvin A. Blietz Co., Wilmette, Ill., 1955-57; pres. Homefinders Constrn. Corp., Wilmette, 1957-59, O & F Constrn. Co., Northbrook, Ill., 1959-61; chmn. bd., chief exec. officer Otis Assocs., Inc., Northbrook, Ill., 1960-89; chmn., CEO Otis Co., 1981—. Bd. dirs. Banco Popular, Chgo., Trout & Grouse, Inc., OCO, Inc., Ranch Ptnrs., LLC, Lane Fin., Inc.; ptnr. Good Otis, LLC. Prin. works include GBC Corp. Hdqrs., Northbrook, Ill., AON Ins. Co. Corp. Hdqrs., Performing Arts Ctr., Northbrook, All State Regional Hdqrs., Skokie, Ill., Zurich Nat. Hdqrs.-Zurich Towers, Schaumburg, Ill. Trustee Evanston Hosp., Ill., 1971-93, Better Govt. Assn., Chgo., Graham Found., 1984-86; chmn. bd. trustees Ill. Nature Conservancy, North Suburban YMCA, Northbrook, 1990-97; governing mem. Shedd Aquarium; bd. govs. Chgo. Zool. Soc.; mem. adv. bd. Cook County Forest Preserve Dist.; mem. founder's coun. Field Mus., Chgo. Lt. USNR, 1953—55. Mem. AIA, Nat. Coun. Archtl. Registration Bds., Urban Land Inst., Northwestern U. Assocs., Princeton Club (pres. 1971-72), Econ. Club, Commonwealth Club, Chgo. Club, Comml. Club, Glen View Golf Club, Old Elm Club, Coleman Lake Club, Angler's Club. Republican. Episcopalian. Office: Otisco 1450 American Ln Ste 1750 Schaumburg IL 60173-6010 Office Phone: 847-969-9000. Business E-Mail: jotisjr@otiscompany.com.

O'TOOLE, JAMES, state legislator; Mem. Mo. State Ho. of Reps. Dist. 68. Home: 5445 Finkman St Saint Louis MO 63109-3540

O'TOOLE, ROBERT JOSEPH, retired manufacturing executive; b. Chgo., Feb. 22, 1941; s. Francis John O'Toole; children: William, Patricia, Timothy, Kathleen, John. BS in Acctg., Loyola U., Chgo., 1961. Fin. analyst A.O. Smith Corp., Milw., 1963-66, mgr. corp. fin. analysis and planning, 1966-68, contr. electric motor div. Tipp City, Ohio, 1968-71; mng. dir. Bull Motors, Ipswich, England, 1971-74; gen. plant mgr. electric motor div. A.O. Smith Corp., Tipp City, 1974-79, v.p., gen. mgr., 1979-83, sr. v.p. Milw., 1984-85, pres., chief oper. officer, 1986-89, pres., 1989—2004, CEO, 1989—2005, also bd. dirs. Milw., and chmn. bd. dirs., 1992—2005. Bd. dirs. Briggs & Stratton Corp., Factory Mutual Ins. Co., Marshall & Ilsley Corp., Manufacturers Alliance/MAPI Inc.; mem. exec. com. TEC XIV, Milw., Mfrs. Alliance for Productivity and Innovation, Bus. Roundtable, Greater Milw. Com., Competitive Wis., Inc. Mem. Wis. Mgrs. and Commerce Assn. (exec. com.), Met. Milw. Assn. Commerce (bd. dirs.), Milw. Country Club, Univ. Club. Office: A O Smith Corp Ste 1001 11270 W Park Pl Milwaukee WI 53224-3690

OTREMBA, KEN, state legislator; b. Oct. 29, 1948; m. Mary Ellen Otremba; 4 children. Minn. state rep. Dist. 11B, 1994—. Farmer. Home: RR 2 Box 17 Long Prairie MN 56347-9561 Office: Minn Ho of Reps State Capitol Saint Paul MN 55155-0001

OTT, ALVIN R., state legislator; Mem. Wis. Assembly from 3rd assembly dist. Republican. Home: PO Box 112 N8855 Church St Forest Junction WI 54123

OTT, BELVA JOLEEN, former state legislator; b. Wichita, Kans., June 5, 1940; d. Kenneth Theodore and Vera Esther (Harvey) Massey; m. Harold Arthur Ott, 1959; children: Teresa Dawn, Bruce Kenton. Mem. from dist. 92 Kans. State Ho. of Reps., 1977-82, 95-97, chmn. ho. election com., 1979-82. Mem. Women's Polit. Caucus; med. sec. Mid-Am. Heart Assn., Pa., 1977-81; mem. Kans. Fedn. Rep. Women; precinct committeewoman Sedgwick County Rep. Party, 1972—, ward chmn., 1973—; del. 4th Dist. Rep. Party Conv., 1976—; alt. del. Kans. State Rep. Conv., 1976. Mem. LWV, Am. Coun. Young Polit. Leaders, Sedgwick County Rep. Women's Club. Address: 821 Litchfield St Wichita KS 67203-3106

OTT, DAVID T., insurance company executive; BS in Mktg. and Bus. Mgmt., U. Mo., St. Louis, 1977. Dir., mktg. HealthLink, Inc., 1986, v.p., sales & mktg., exec. v.p., 1991—99, pres., 1999—. Office: HealthLink Hqrs 12443 Olive Blvd Saint Louis MO 63141

OTT, DORIS ANN, librarian; b. Elgin, ND, Sept. 24, 1942; d. Oscar Edward Hirning and Lorraine Wilhelmina Gruebele; m. Richard Donald Ott, Nov. 21, 1998; m. Bennett Gordon Reinke, Sept. 1961 (div.); 1 child, Scott Bernnett Reinke; m. James Lee Daugherty, June 1974 (div.). BS, Dickinson State U., 1964; MLS, George Peabody Coll., 1965. Lic. Ind. life tchr. Elem. tchr. Mott Pub. Schs., ND, 1963-64; asst. prof. Dickinson State U., ND, 1965-73; media specialist Minot Pub. Schs., ND, 1973-74; head tech. svcs. Bartholomew County Libr., Columbus, Ind., 1974-75; media specialist Rushville Pub. Schs., Ind., 1975-86; head interlibr. loan ND State Libr., Bismarck, 1986-87, asst. state libr., 1987—2001, state libr., 2001—. Image cons. Beauty For All Seasons, 1984—. Mem. Humane Soc. Mem.: ALA, Mountain Plains Libr. Assn., ND Libr. Assn. Avocation: image consulting. Office: ND State Libr 604 E Boulevard Ave Dept 250 Bismarck ND 58505-0800 Office Phone: 701-328-2492. Business E-Mail: dott@nd.gov.

OTT, KARL OTTO, nuclear engineer, consultant; b. Hanau, Germany, Dec. 24, 1925; arrived in U.S., 1967, naturalized, 1987; s. Johann Josef and Eva (Bergmann) Ott; m. Gunhild G. Göring, Sept. 18, 1958 (div. 1986); children: Martina, Monika; m. Birgit Fehse, May 1, 1995. BS, J. W. von Goethe U., Frankfurt, Germany, 1948; MS, G. August U., Göttingen, Fed. Republic Germany, 1953, PhD, 1958. Physicist Nuc. Rsch. Ctr., Karlsruhe, Germany, 1958-67, sect. head, 1962-67; prof. Sch. Nuc. Engring. Purdue U., West Lafayette, Ind., 1967-2001, prof. emeritus, 2000—. Cons. Argonne Nat. Lab., 1967—2001. Author: (book) uclear Reactor Statics, 1983, 2d edit., 1989, Nuclear Reactor Dynamics, 1985, Chinese edit., 1991. Recipient Disting. Appointment award, Argonne Universities Assn., 1973. Fellow: Am. Nuc. Soc. (Arthur Holly Compton award 1993). Office Phone: 765-494-5739. E-mail: kobott@sbcglobal.net.

OTTE, FRANK J., federal judge; b. 1938; BS, Ind. U., 1960, JD, 1966. Pvt. practice law, Indpls., 1966-86; bankruptcy judge U.S. Dist. Ct. (so. dist.) Ind., Indpls., 1986—. 1st lt. U.S. Army, 1960-63. Mem. Ind. Bar Assn., Indpls. Bar Assn., Nat. Conf. Bankruptcy Judges. Office: 335 US Courthouse 46 E Ohio St Indianapolis IN 46204-1903

OTTE, PAUL JOHN, academic administrator, consultant; b. Detroit, July 10, 1943; s. Melvin John Otte and Anne Marie (Meyers) Hirsch; children: Deanna Kropf, John. BS, Wayne State U., 1968, MBA, 1969; EdD, Western Mich. U., 1983. With Detroit Bank and Trust Co., 1965-68; teaching fellow Wayne State U., Detroit, 1968-69; auditor, mgr. Arthur Young & Co., Detroit, 1969-75; contr., dir. Macomb Community Coll., Warren, Mich., 1975-79, v.p. bus., 1979-86; pres. Franklin U., Columbus, Ohio, 1986—, prof. undergrad. and grad. programs, 1986—. Author various tng. manuals, 1982. Cpl. USMC, 1961-65. Teaching fellow Wayne State U., 1968-69. Mem. AICPA, Mich. Assn. CPAs (chmn. continuing profl. edn. com. 1980-82, leadership com. 1981-83), Nat. Assn. Coll. and Univ. Bus. Officers (acctg. prins. com. 1986), Assn. Ind. Colls. and Univs. Ohio (bd. dirs.), Greater Detroit C. of C. (leadership award 1983), Columbus C. of C. (info. svc. com.). Roman Catholic. Avocation: travel. Office: Franklin U 201 S Grant Ave Columbus OH 43215-5399

OTTERMAN, ROBERT J., state representative; b. Akron, Ohio, July 29, 1932; widowed; 2 children. BA, U. Akron, 1958, MA, 1964. Ret. h.s. counselor; state rep. dist. 45 Ohio Ho. of Reps., Columbus, ranking minority mem., homeland security engring. and archtl. design com., mem. banking pensions and securities, human svcs. and aging, and rules and reference coms. Sgt. USMC, 1950—54. Mem.: NEA, Akron Counselor's Assn. (past pres.), Magic City Dems., Barberton Kiwanis, Lambda Chi Alpha. Democrat. Roman Catholic. Office: 77 S High St 10th fl Columbus OH 43215-6111

OTTINO, JULIO MARIO, engineering educator; b. La Plata, Buenos Aires, Argentina, May 22, 1951; came to U.S., 1976; naturalized, 1990; s. Julio Francisco and Nydia Judit (Zufriategui) O.; m. Alicia I. Löffler, Aug. 20, 1976; children: Jules Alessandro, Bertrand Julien. Diploma in Chem. Engring., U. La Plata, 1974; PhD in Chem. Engring., U. Minn., 1979; exec. program Kellogg Sch. Mgmt., Northwestern U., 1995. Instr. in chem. engring. U. Minn., Mpls., 1978-79; asst. prof. U. Mass., Amherst, 1979-83, adj. prof. polymer sci., 1979-91, assoc. prof. chem. engring., 1983-86, prof., 1986-91; Chevron vis. prof. chem. engring. Calif. Inst. Tech., Pasadena, 1985-86; sr. rsch. fellow Ctr. for Turbulence Rsch. Stanford (Calif.) U., 1989-90; Walter P. Murphy prof. chem. engring. Northwestern U., Evanston, Ill., 1991-2000, chmn. dept. chem. engring., 1992-2000; McCormick Inst. prof., 2000—; George T. Piercy Disting. prof. U. Minn., 1998, adj. prof. mech. engring., 2001—; dir. Northwestern Inst. Complex Sys., 2004—, dean Sch. Engring. and Applied Sci. Cons. to U.S. and European corps.; mem. tech. adv. bd. Dow Chem.; mem. bd. dirs. Coun. Chem. Rsch.; prof. U. Minn.; Reily lectr. Notre Dame U., 2006; lectr. in field. Author: The Kinematics of Mixing: Stretching, Chaos and Transport, 1989; contbr. articles to profl. jours.; assoc. editor Physics Fluids A, 1991—; mem. editl. bd. Internat. Jour. Bifurc. Chaos, 1991—; assoc. editor Am. Inst. Chem. Engring. Jour., 1991-95, assoc. editor., 1995—; one man art exhibit, La Plata, 1974. Recipient Presdl. Young Investigator award NSF, 1984, Alpha Chi Sigma award AIChE, 1994, W.H. Walker award AIChE, 2001, E.W. Thiele award AIChE, Chgo., 2002; Univ. fellow U. Mass., 1988, J.S. Guggenheim fellow, 2001; Lacey lectureship, Calif. Inst. Tech., 1994, Danckwerts lectureship Royal Instn., 1999, Robb lectr. Pa. State U., 2002, Reily lectr., U. Notre Dame, 2006. Fellow Am. Phys. Soc.; mem. AAAS, NAE, Am. Acad. Arts and Scis., Am. Chem. Soc., Am. Phys. Soc., Am. Soc. Engring. Edn., Sigma Xi (disting. lectr. 1997-99), Coun. for Chem. Rsch.(gov. bd. coun. 1999-2001). Achievements include research in granular dynamics, chaos, complex systems and mixing. Avocations: visual arts, painting. Home: 1092 Crescent Ln Winnetka IL 60093-1501 Office: Northwestern U Dept Chem Engring 2145 Sheridan Rd Evanston IL 60208-0834 Office Phone: 847-491-5221. Business E-Mail: jm-ottino@northwestern.edu.

OTTO, CHARLOTTE R., consumer products company executive; b. Duluth, Minn., Aug. 15, 1953; BS, Purdue U., 1974, MS in Mgmt., 1976. With Procter & Gamble, 1976—, from asst. brand mgr. to brand mgr. various products, 1977-83, assoc. advt. mgr. paper products divsn., 1984-87, assoc. advt. mgr. toilet tissue/towels, paper products div., 1987-89, dir. issues mgmt., pub. affairs divsn., 1989-90, dir. pub. rels., pub. affairs divsn., 1990-91; v.p. pub. rels. Procter & Gamble USA, 1991-93; v.p. corp. comms. Procter & Gamble Worldwide, 1993-95, v.p. pub. affairs, 1995-96; sr. v.p. pub. affairs The Procter & Gamble Co., 1996-99, global pub. affairs officer, 1999—2000, global external rels. officer, 2000—. Dir. Royal Bank Fin. Grou, Canada; adv. bd. Jour. Corp. Pub. Rels., The Medill Sch. Journalism, Northwestern Univ. Mem. nat. bd. Boys & Girls Club Am.; mem. YWCA Acad. Career Women of Acheivement; chair (past pres.) Cin. Playhouse in the Park; chair exec. com. Downtown Cin., Inc.; mem. Riverfront Advisors Commn.; v.p. exec. com. Joy Outdoor Edn. Ctr.; trustee Arts & Cultural Coun. Greater Loveland; bd. mem. Am. Red Cross, Cin. Chpt.; bd. selectors, The Jefferson Awards Am. Inst. Pub. Svc.; vice-chmn. exec. com. Greater Cin. C. of C.; bd. mem. The Port of Greater Cin. Devel. Authority, Good Samaritan Hosp., Cin. Fire Mus.; mem. Leadership Cin. -Class XIV. Recipient YWCA Career Woman of Achievement award, 1993, Woman of Distinction award Gt. Rivers Girl Scouts Coun., Inc., 1998, Purdue "Old Master", 1996; recipient Disting. Alumni, Purdue U., Krannert Sch. Mgmt.; named Cincinnatian of the Yr., 2003, Juvenile Diabetes Rsch. Found., Cin. Enquirer Woman of the Yr., 2005; recipient Human Rels. award, Am. Jewish Com., 2004, Matrix award for public rels., NY Women in Comm., 2005. Mem. Ctr. Quality Leadership Founders, Vice Pres.'s Forum, Commonwealth Club, Women's Capital Club, Queen City Club (bd. govs.), Club at Harper's Point, Arthur Page Soc., PR Seminar Com., Kenwood Country Club. Office: Procter & Gamble Co 1 Procter And Gamble Plz Cincinnati OH 45202-3393

OURADA, MARK, state legislator; b. Apr. 28, 1956; m. Christi Ourada. Student, St. John's U. Mem. Minn. Senate from 19th dist., St. Paul, 1994—. Former lab. technician. Address: 1110 Innsbrook Ln Buffalo MN 55313-1295 Office: Mem Senate State Capitol Saint Paul MN 55155-0001

OURADA, THOMAS D., former state legislator; b. Antigo, Wis., Dec. 17, 1958; BA, Marquette U., 1981; grad. studies, U. Ky. Assemblyman, Dist. 35 State of Wis., 1984—99; exec. asst. Wis. Revenue Dept., 1999. Republican. Office Phone: 608-226-7622. Office Fax: 608-266-5718.

OUZTS, DALE KEITH, broadcast executive; b. Miami, Fla., Aug. 26, 1941; s. Jacob C. and Edna P. (Sloan) O.; m. Susan Ouzts; children: Dale Keith Jr., Karen, Ryan Keith. BJ, U. Ga., 1965, MA, 1966; postgrad. advanced mgmt. seminar, Harvard U., 1977. Mgr. Sta. WSJK-TV, Knoxville, Tenn., 1966-69; exec. v.p., gen. mgr. Sta. KPTS-TV, Wichita, Kans., 1969-72; gen. mgr. Sta. WSSR-FM, Springfield, Ill., 1972-77; sr. v.p. Nat. Pub. Radio, Washington, 1977-79; gen. mgr. Sta. WOSU-AM-FM and Sta. WOSU-TV, Ohio State U., Columbus, Ohio, 1979—; gen. mgr. Sta. WPBO-TV, Portsmouth, Ohio, 1979—; Sta. WOSE-FM, Coshocton, 1996—; gen. mgr. Sta. WOSV-FM, Mansfield, Ohio, 1988—, Sta. WOSP-FM, Portsmouth, 1993—; assoc. prof. comm. Ohio State U., Columbus, Ohio, 1979—, assoc. prof. journalism, 1983—; pres. Sta. WOSU-AN-FM, Columbus. Adminstrv. dir. Ohio State Awards, 1979-94; mem. Ohio Ednl. TV Stas., v.p., 1983-84, pres., 1988-90; pres. Ohio Pub. Radio, 1995—, Ohio Alliance for Pub. Telecom., 1996—; chmn. Nat. Pub. Radio, 1990-92; pres. Pub. Radio in Mid-Am., 1976-77, 85-87. Bd. dirs. Ctr. of Vocat. Alts. in Mental Health, 1985-93, 96—, sec.-treas., 1986-88, chmn., 1988-90, Pub. Radio Expansion Task Force, 1989-90; bd. dirs. Brule Conservation Trust, 1985-94, Columbus Zoo, 1984—, Mental Health Assn., Franklin County, 1987-93, Ohio China Coun., 1982-93, v.p., 1984-85, pres., 1987-89; advisor Chinese Student and Scholar Soc. at Ohio State U., 1987-91; program rev. panel Nat. Telecomms., 1988; mgmt. cons. Corp. for Pub. Broadcasting, 1975-95. Recipient Disting. Service award Nat. Pub. Radio, 1986, Disting. Service award Nat. Black Program Consortium, 1985, Disting. Service award PRIMA, 1977, 87, award for fundraising and promotion Corp. Pub. Broadcasting, 1971, Outstanding Broadcaster award Wichita (Kans.) Chpt. of Kappa Mu Psi, 1970, OEBIE award Ohio Ednl. Broadcasting Network Commn., 1987, Emmy award nomination Acad. TV Arts and Scis., 1987. Mem. Nat. Assn. Broadcasters, Ohio Alliance for Pub. Telecom. (pres. 1995-97), Ohio Assn. Broadcasters, Nat. Assn. State Univs. and Land Grant Colls. (mem. telecomms. com. 1980-93), Columbus Ducks Unltd. (bd. dirs. 1982-93), Scioto Valley Skeet Club (bd. dirs. 1982-92), Grand Hotel Hunt Club, Sawmill Athletic Club, Ohio-Rocky Mountain Elk Found., Rotary (Dublin-Worthington, v.p. 1988-89, pres. 1990-91). Avocations: racquetball, softball, golf, hunting, tennis. Office: Sta WOSU 2400 Olentangy River Rd Columbus OH 43210-1027 Home: 5825 Willow Lake Dr Grove City OH 43123-8842

OVAERT, TIMOTHY CHRISTOPHER, mechanical engineering educator; b. Chgo., Apr. 30, 1959; s. Walter Allen and Joyce Ann (Collins) O.; m. Valerie Mora, July 16, 1988; children: Teresa Noel, Christina Lynn. BSME, U. Ill., 1981; MEM, Northwestern U., 1985, PhD, 1989. Plant engr. Wells Mfg. Co.-Dura Bar Div., Woodstock, Ill., 1981-85; mech. engr. Nat. Inst. of Standards and Tech., Gaithersburg, Md., 1986; asst. prof. Penn State U., 1989-95; assoc. prof. Pa. State U., 1995-2000, prof., 2000, U. Notre Dame, Ind., 2000—. Assoc. editor ASME Trans., Jour. Tribology, 1998—2003. Traffic safety com. Borough of State College, Pa., 1992. amed Nat. Young Investigator, NSF, 1992. Office: U Notre Dame 374 Fitzpatrick Hall Notre Dame IN 46556 Office Phone: 574-631-9371.

OVERBY, OSMUND RUDOLF, art historian, educator; b. Mpls., Nov. 8, 1931; s. Oscar Rudolph and Gertrude Christine (Boe) O.; m. Barbara Ruth Spande, Mar. 20, 1954; children: Paul, Katherine, Charlotte. BA, St. Olaf Coll., 1953; B.Arch., U. Wash., 1958; MA, Yale U., 1960, PhD, 1963. Asst. in instruction dept. of history of art Yale U., 1959-60, 61-62; architect Hist. Am. Bldgs. Survey, U.S. Nat. Park Service, 1960-61, summers 1959, 62, 63, 65, 68, 69, 70, 73, 85; lectr. dept. fine arts U. Toronto, Ont., Canada, 1963-64; faculty dept. art history and archaeology U. Mo., Columbia, 1964—, dept. chmn., 1967-70, 75-77, prof. art history, 1979-98, prof. emeritus, 1998—, dir. Mus. of Art and Archaeology, 1977-83. Vis. prof. dept. architecture U. Calif., Berkeley, 1980; Morgan prof. U. Louisville, 1989; vis. prof. dept. art history and archaeology Washington U., St. Louis, 1996; bd. advisors Nat. Trust for Hist. Preservation, 1974-83; cons., panelist Nat. Endowment for Humanities, 1974—; bd. Mo. Mansion Preservation Commn., 1974-87; advisor Heritage/St. Louis

Survey, 1974-76; counsellor to St. Louis Landmarks Assn., 1977—; chmn. Task Force on Hist. Preservation City of Columbia, 1977-78; cons. on hist. preservation; active Mo. Adv. Council on Hist. Preservation, 1967-82; lectr., exhibitor profl. confs. in field Author: Historic American Buildings Survey, Rhode Island Catalog, 1972, William Adair Bernoudy, Architect, Bringing the Legacy of Frank Lloyd Wright to St. Louis, 1999; co-author: Laclede's Landing, a History and Architectural Guide, 1977, The Saint Louis Old Post Office, A History and Architectural Guide to the Building and Its Neighborhood, 1979; co-author, editor: Illustrated Museum Handbook, A Guide to the Collections in the Museum of Art and Archaeology, University of Missouri-Columbia, 1982; editor in chief Buildings of the United States series, 1990-96; contbr. sects. to books, articles to profl. publs. in field. Served with U.S. Army, 1953-55. Recipient various fellowships and grants in field. Fellow Soc. Arctl. Historians (bd. dirs. 1968-73, 78-81, Jour. editor 1968-73, dir. Mo. Valley chpt., session chmn. ann. meeting 1976, v.p. 1982-86, pres. 1986-88, chmn. coms.), Historic Am. Bldgs. Survey; mem. Mid-Continent Am. Studies Assn. (editorial bd. American Studies 1965-70), Midwest Art History Soc. (bd. 1975-78, gen. chmn. annual meeting 1977), Mid-Am. Coll. Art Assn. (session chmn. annual meeting 1975), Mo. Heritage Trust (pres. 1976-79, 81-83, bd. dirs. 1979—), Coll. Art Assn., Landmarks Assn. St. Louis. Lutheran. Home: 1118 W Rollins Rd Columbia MO 65203-2221 Office: U Mo Dept Art History & Archaeolo Columbia MO 65211-0001 Office Phone: 573-442-7882. Business E-Mail: overbyo@missouri.edu.

OVERGAARD, ROBERT MILTON, retired religious organization administrator; b. Ashby, Minn., Nov. 6, 1929; s. Gust and Ella (Johnson) O.; m. Sally Lee Stephenson, Dec. 29, 1949; children: Catherine Jean Overgaard Thuleen, Robert Milton, Elizabeth Dianne Overgaard Almendinger, Barbara, Craig, David (dec.), Lori Overgaard oack. Cert., Luth. Brethren Sem., 1954; BS, Mayville State U., ND, 1959; MS, U. Oreg., 1970. Ordained to ministry Ch. Luth. Brethren Am., 1954. Pastor Elim Luth. Ch., Frontier, Sask., Can., 1954-57, Ebenezer Luth. Ch., Mayville, 1957-60, Immanuel Luth. Ch., Eugene, Oreg., 1960-63, 59th Street Luth. Ch., Bklyn., 1963-68, Immanuel Luth. Ch., Pasadena, Calif., 1969-73; exec. dir. world missions Ch. Luth. Brethren Am., Fergus Falls, Minn., 1973-86, pres., 1986—2001, ret., 2001. Editor Faith and Fellowship, 1967-75. Lutheran. Home: 806 W Channing Ave Fergus Falls MN 56537-3221 Office: Ch Luth Brethren Am PO Box 655 Fergus Falls MN 56538-0655 E-mail: rmo@clba.org.

OVERHAUSER, ALBERT WARNER, physicist; b. San Diego, Aug. 17, 1925; s. Clarence Albert and Gertrude Irene (Pehrson) Overhauser; m. Margaret Mary Casey, Aug. 25, 1951; children: Teresa, Catherine, Joan, Paul, John, David, Susan, Steven. AB, U. Calif., Berkeley, 1948, PhD, 1951; DSc (hon.), U. Chgo., 1979; LLD (hon.), Simon Fraser U., 1998; DSc (hon.), Purdue U., 2005. Rsch. assoc. U. Ill., 1951—53; asst. prof. physics Cornell U., 1953—56, assoc. prof., 1956—58; supr. solid state physics Ford Motor Co., Dearborn, Mich., 1958—62, mgr. theoret. scis., 1962—69, asst. dir. phys. scis., 1969—72, dir. phys. scis., 1972—73; prof. physics Purdue U., West Lafayette, Ind., 1973—74, Stuart disting. prof. physics, 1974—2004, Stuart disting. prof. emeritus, 2004—. With USNR, 1944—46. Recipient Alexander von Humboldt sr. U.S. scientist award, 1979, Nat. medal of Sci., Pres. of U.S., 1994. Fellow: Am. Acad. Arts and Scis., Am. Phys. Soc. (Oliver E. Buckley Solid State Physics prize 1975); mem.: NAS. Home: 236 Pawnee Dr West Lafayette IN 47906-2115 Office: Purdue U Dept Of Physics West Lafayette IN 47907 Home Phone: 765-463-4662; Office Phone: 765-494-3037. Business E-Mail: awo@physics.purdue.edu.

OVERSCHMIDT, FRANCIS S., state legislator; Mem. Mo. State Ho. of Reps. Dist. 110. Home: 151 N Outer Rd Union MO 63084-4400

OVERTON, BO, professional basketball coach; b. Ada, Okla., July 9, 1960; s. Claudell and Sue Overton. BS in Comm., U. Okla., 1983; BA in Phys. Edn., Southwestern Okla. State U., 1987. Draft pick Phoenix Suns, 1983; grad. asst. men's basketball U. Okla., Norman, 1983—84; asst. coach women's basketball U. Okla, 1998—2004; basketball player Continental Basketball Assn. Pensacola Tornadoes, Fla., 1984—85; asst. coach Continental Basketball Assn. Pensacola Tornados, Fla., 1985-86, Oral Roberts U., Tulsa, Okla., 1986—87, 1991—93, S.W. Tex. State U., 1993—94, La. Tech U., 1994—98; head coach, athletic dir. Murray State Jr. Coll., Tishomingo, Okla., 1989—91; head coach women's basketball U. Mo., Kans. City, 2004—06; head coach WNBA Chgo. Sky, 2006—. Office: Chgo Sky 20 W Kinzie St Ste 1010 Chicago IL 60610

OVERTON-ADKINS, BETTY JEAN, foundation administrator; b. Jacksonville, Fla., Oct. 10, 1949; d. Henry and Miriam (Gordon) Crawford; children from previous marriage: Joseph Alonzo III, Jermaine Lamar; m. Eugene Adkins, Apr. 24, 1992. BA in English, Tenn. State U., 1970, MA in English, 1974; PhD in English, Vanderbilt U., 1980; student Inst. Ednl. Mgmt., Harvard U., 1990. Reporter Race Rels. Reporter Mag., Nashville, 1970-71; tchr. Met. Nashville Sch. System, 1971-72; instr., project dir. Tenn. State U., Nashville, 1972-76; asst. prof. Nashville State Tech. Inst., 1976-78, Fisk U., Nashville, 1978-83; assoc. dean. grad. sch. U. Ark., Little Rock, 1983-85, dean grad. sch., 1985-91; program dir. Kellogg Found., Battle Creek, Mich., 1991—; asst. dir. Kellogg Nat. Fellowship Program, Battle Creek, Mich., 1991-94; coord. higher edn. programs Kellogg Found., Battle Creek, 1994—. Instr. U. Tenn., Nashville, 1976-82; dir. rsch. sponsored programs U. Ark., 1986-88; bd. dirs. Ark. Sci. and Info. Liaison Office, 1984-91. Bd. dirs. Ark. Sci. and Tech. Authority, Little Rock, 1989—, Women's Project, 1986—, Ark. Pub. Policy Panel, 1988-91, No. Bank Women's Adv. Bd., 1988-91, Nashville Panel, 1974-83, Ctrl. Ark. Libr. Sys., 1990-91, Ark. coun. NCCJ, 1990-92, Bread for World, 1990-95; mem. Commn. on Edn. Credits and Credentials, Am. Coun. on Edn., 1989-95; chmn. bi-racial adv. com. Little Rock Sch. Dist., 1987— Fellow Am. Coun. Edn., 1981-82, W.K. Kellogg Found., 1988-93. Mem. Nat. Coun. Tchrs. of English, Coun. Grad. Schs., Coun. So. Grad. Schs., Women Color United Against Domestic Violence (pres.), An. Assn. High Edn., Rotary, Alpha Kappa Alpha. Democrat. Roman Catholic. Office: W K Kellogg Found One Michigan Ave E Battle Creek MI 49017

OVSHINSKY, STANFORD ROBERT, physicist, inventor, energy executive, information company executive; b. Akron, Ohio, Nov. 24, 1922; s. Benjamin and Bertha T. (Munitz) O.; m. Iris L. Miroy, Nov. 24, 1959 (dec. Aug. 16, 2006); children— Benjamin, Harvey, Dale, Robin Dibner, Steven Dibner. Student public schs., Akron; DSc (hon.), Lawrence Inst. Tech., 1980; DEng (hon.), Bowling Green State U., 1981; DSc (hon.), Jordan Coll., Cedar Springs, Mich., 1989. Pres. Stanford Roberts Mfg. Co., Akron, 1946-50; mgr. centre drive dept. New Britain Machine Co., Conn., 1950-52; dir. research Hupp Corp., Detroit, 1952-55; pres. Gen. Automation, Inc., Detroit, 1955-58, Ovitron Corp., Detroit, 1958—2004; pres., CTO, chief scientist Energy Conversion Devices, Inc., Rochester Hills, Mich., 2004—. Adj. prof. engring. scis. Coll. Engring., Wayne State U.; hon. advisor for sci. and tech. Beijing (China) Inst. Aeronautics and Astronautics (name changed to Beijing U. Aeros. and Astronautics); chmn. Inst. for Amorphous Studies. Contbr. articles on physics of amorphous materials, neurophysiology and neuropsychiatry to profl. jours. Recipient Diesel Gold medal German Inventors Assn., 1968, Coors Am. Ingenuity award, 1988, Karl W. Böer solar energy medal of merit U. Del. and Interna. Solar Energy Soc., 1999; named to Mich. Chem. Engring. Hall of Fame, 1983, Mich. Scientist of Yr., Impression 5 Sci. Mus., 1987, Hero for the Planet, Time mag., 1999, Hero of Chemistry, Am. Chem. Soc., 2000, Sir William Grove award IAHE, 2000. Fellow AAAS, Am. Phys. Soc.; mem. IEEE (sr.), Soc. Automotive Engrs., N.Y. Acad. Scis., Electrochem. Soc., Engring. Soc. Detroit, Cranbrook Inst. Sci. (bd. govs. 1981). Office: Energy Conversion Devices Inc 2956 Waterview Dr Rochester MI 48309

OWEN, CLARENCE B., construction materials manufacturing executive; BS in mech. engring., La. Tech. U., 1972. Joined US Gypsum Co., Chgo., 1972, plant mgr., dir. tech. svcs.; v.p. oper. US Gypsum Co. Interiors; v.p. tech. svcs. US Gypsum Co.; pres. mng. dir. US Gypsum Co. Europe; sr. v.p. US Gypsum Internat.; v.p., internat. tech. US Gypsum Co., v.p., chief tech. officer Chgo., 2003—. Office: United States Gypsum Industrial Products PO Box 803871 Chicago IL 60680-3871

OWEN, DAVE A., finance executive; B in Acctg., Ind. U. CPA. Sr. acct., auditor Price Waterhouse; with Essex Group, Inc., 1976, contr. magnet wire and insulation divsn., 1983-85, contr. wire and cable divsn., 1985-88, dir. treasury and fin. svcs., 1988-93, treas., 1992-94, v.p. fin., CFO, 1993-94, exec. v.p., CFO, 1994—99; exec. v.p. Superior Essex (formerly Essex Group, Inc.), 1999—. Bd. dir. Cmty. Harvest Food Bank. Office: Essex Express 1601 Wall St Fort Wayne IN 46802-4352

OWEN, LYNN, state legislator; b. Lawrence County, Ala., Feb. 22, 1946; m. Diana; children: Amy, Andrew. Student, Washtenaw C.C., Cerritos Jr. Coll. Supervisor, assessor London Twp., Mich., 1978-84; rep. Mich. State 56, 1986-98; exec. asst. legal affairs Office of Atty. Gen., Lansing, Mich., 1998—. House appropriations com. Mich. Ho. Reps. Gov. bd. dirs. Monroe County Opportunity Program; pres. Milan Area Fire Dept.; chmn. London-Maybee-Raisinville Fire Dept. Named pub. servant of yr. Mich. chpt. Paralyzed Vet. Am., state legis. yr. Vientam Vets. Am.; recipient star award Dep. Sheriff's Assn. Mem. Am. Legion, Disabled Am. Vets., Purple Heart Assn., West County Ambulance Assn. (former vice chair). Home: 2520 York Rd Lansing MI 48911-1237 Address: Olds Plz Bldg Rm 925 Lansing MI 48913-0001

OWEN, MICHEAL, agronomist, educator; Prof. dept. agronomy Iowa State U., Ames. Recipient CIBA-GEIGY/Weed Sci. Soc. Am. award CIBA-GEIGY Corp., 1992. Mem. Weed Sci. Soc. Am. (Outstanding Paper in Weed Tech. 1996), North Ctrl. Weed Soc. (Disting. Achievement award 1995). Office: Iowa State U Dept Agronomy 2104 Agronomy Hl Ames IA 50011-0001

OWENDOFF, STEPHEN PETER, lawyer; b. Morristown, NJ, Aug. 1, 1943; m.; 4 children. Student, Bowdoin Coll., 1966; BA, Kent State U., 1966; JD, Georgetown U., 1969. Bar: Ohio 1969. Assoc. Hahn Loeser & Parks and predecessor firms, Cleve., 1969-77; ptnr. Hahn Loeser & Parks (formerly Hahn, Loeser, Freedheim, Dean and Wellman), 1977—; mgmt. com. Hahn Loeser & Parks (formerly Hahn, Loeser, Freedheim Dean). Lectr. in field. Active Gesu Ch., University Heights, Ohio; mem. adv. bd. Learning About Bus., Inc.; past pres. Parmadale (Ohio) Adv. Bd.; bd. trustees, cmty. svcs. panel Fedn. Cath. Cmty. Svcs.; rep. United Way Assembly, Parmadale; bd. trustees LeBlond Housing Corp., Health Hill Hosp. Mem. Nat. Assn. Bond Lawyers, Nat. Assn. Coll. and Univ. Attys., Shaker Heights (Ohio) Country Club. Office: 3300 Bp Tower 200 Public Sq Cleveland OH 44114-2316

OWENS, CAROL, state legislator; b. Aug. 8, 1931; Town clk, Nekimi, 1977—93; bd supvr Winnebago Cty, 1980—92; State assemblywoman, Dist 53 Wis., 1992—. Recipient Friend of Agri, 1994 & 1996. Republican. Lutheran. Office: Wis Assembly PO Box 8952 Madison WI 53708-8952

OWENS, JAMES W., manufacturing executive; b. Elizabeth City, NC; PhD in Econs., NC State U., 1973. Corp. economist Caterpillar Inc., Peoria, Ill., 1972—75; chief economist Caterpillar Overseas S.A., Geneva, 1975—80; mgmt. positions, Acctg., Product Source Planning Depts. Caterpillar Inc., Peoria, 1980—87, mng. dir., P.T. Natra Raya Indonesia, 1987—90, pres., Solar Turbines Inc., 1990—93, v.p. group svcs. divsn. Peoria, Ill., 1993-94, group pres., 1995—2003, vice chmn., 2003—04, chmn., CEO, 2004—. Dir. Inst. Internat. Econ., Washington, Alcoa Inc., Pitts., FM Global Ins. Co., RI; bd. dir. IBM. Mem. cmty. adv. bd. St. Francis Med. Ctr.; mem. Civic Fedn. Bd., Peoria. Mem.: Conf. Bd. NY (mem. global adv. coun.), Bus. Roundtable, Bus. Coun., Mfg. Coun., Coun. Fgn. Rels. Office: Caterpillar Inc 100 NE Adams St Peoria IL 61629 Office Phone: 309-675-1000. Office Fax: 309-675-1182.

OWENS, JEFFREY J., electronics executive; BS in Engring., Kettering U., 1978; MBA, Ball State U., 1983; grad. Global Exec. Program, Duke U., 1997. Assoc. mfg. engr. Delco Electronics Divsn., GM, Kokomo, Ind., 1978—82, 1984—90; mng. dir. HE Microwave, Tucson, 1990—94; dir. advanced engring. and systems integration Delco Electronics, 1994—95, exec. dir. emerging products and systems, 1995—97, dir. systems and software engring., 1997—98, product line exec. for Integrated Body, 1998—2000, gen. dir. engring., 2000—01, gen. dir. Bus. Line Mgmt., 2000—01; pres. Delphi Delco Electronics Systems, 2001—; v.p. Delphi Corp., 2001—. Office: World Hdqrs Delphi Delco 5725 Delphi Dr Troy MI 48098-2815 also: Delphi Delco Electronic Sys One Corporate Ctr PO Box 9005 Kokomo IN 46904-9005

OWENS, JOHN C., academic administrator; BS, W. Texas State U.; MS, Texas Tech U; PhD, Iowa State U. Chief acad. officer N.Mex. State U., Las Cruces, 1999—2001; Vice Chancellor U. Nebr.-Lincoln, Nebr., 2001—. Office: U Nebr-Lincoln Varner Hall 3835 Holdrege Lincoln NE 68583

OWENS, JUDITH L(YNN), lawyer; b. Benkelman, Nebr., Oct. 17, 1942; d. Daniel E. and Estelle M. (Carlin) O. BA in History, MA in History, Creighton U., 1967, JD, 1978. Bar: Nebr. 1978. Adminstrv. asst. Creighton U., Omaha, 1968; grad. asst. Am. U., Washington, 1972; tchr. Omaha Pub. Schs., 1972-75; atty. Owens and Owens, Benkelman, 1979-82; legal counsel Nebr. Legislature, Lincoln, 1982-87; pvt. practice Benkelman, 1987—. Mem. delinquency prevention bd. City of Benkelman, 1995—; mem. juvenile delinquency prevention com. State of Nebr., Nebr. Crime Commn., Lincoln, 1994—; mem. cert. of need bd. State of Nebr. Health Dept., Lincoln, 1993—. Elected county atty. Dundy County, Benkelman, 1995—; del. Dem. Nat. Conv., San Francisci, 1984; bd. dirs., chair Cmty. Family Ctr., Benkelman, 1991-95. Mem. Internat. PEO (local pres. 1982—), Nebr. State Bar Assn. Avocations: reading, politics, theater, singing. Office: Box 316 508 Chief St Benkelman NE 69021

OWENS, SCOTT ANDREW, sales executive; b. Waconia, Minn., Jan. 6, 1958; s. John Herbert and Amy Lou (Anderson) O.; m. Cheri Lynn Anderson, Sept. 22, 1988 (div. Sept. 1995); m. Jennifer Lee Lumsden, Sept. 7, 2002. BSBA magna cum laude, U. Nebr., Omaha, 1986. Adminstrv. asst. Hodne Stageberg Ptnrs., Mpls., 1978-80; pres. Orange Triangle Co., Mpls., 1980; asst. mgr. Wendy's, Mpls., 1980; pres. We Deliver, Mpls., 1980-81; asst. mgr. Color Tile, Roseville, Minn., 1982-83; v.p. mktg. 20/20 Minn., St. Louis Pk., 1983; account rep. Unisys Corp., Minnetonka, 1986-88, sr. account rep. Eagan, 1988-89, third party sales mgr., 1990-91; v.p. mktg. TEP Systems, Bloomington, 1991-93; v.p. Benchmark Comms. Svc., Mpls., 1992—; strategic alliance regional mgr. Dataserv, a BellSouth Co., Eden Prairie, Minn., 1994-96; strategic alliance mgr. MAI Systems, Boston, 1996-97; mktg. dir. Triangle Fin. Svcs. & Internet Mktg. Group, Mpls., 1997—; area mgr. Sunrise Solutions, Inc., Edina, Minn., 1997-98; prof. ProCon Solutions, Inc., Plymouth, Minn., 1998—2000; area mgr. Internet Fin. Solutions, 2000—01, Coldwell Banker Burnet, 2003—04; nat. sales mgr. Penchant Software, 2004—06; bus. devel. RSM McGladrey, 2007—. Classroom cons. Jr. Achievement, Bloomington, Minn., 1990. Mem. Am. Mktg. Assn., Am. Prdn. Inventory Control Soc., Profl. Sales Assn., Sales and Mktg. Execs. Avocations: reading, writing, painting, architecture, photography, golf, travel. Home and Office: Benchmark Comm PO Box 582299 Minneapolis MN 55458-2299 Office Phone: 612-747-3653. Personal E-mail: somsgs@gmail.com.

OWENS, STEPHEN J., lawyer; b. Kansas City, Mo., June 4, 1955; BSPA, U. Mo., 1977; JD, Wake Forest U., 1980. Bar: Mo. 1980, U.S. Dist. Ct. (we. dist.) Mo. 1980, U.S. Ct. Appeals (8th cir.) 1981, U.S. Ct. Appeals (10th cir.) 1982, U.S. Ct. Appeals (5th cir.) 1988, U.S. Ct. Appeals (4th cir.) 1992. Law clerk to Hon. William R. Collinson U.S. Dist. Ct. (we. dist.) Mo., 1980-81; ptnr. Stinson, Mag & Fizzell, Kansas City, Mo., 1981—. Mem. ABA (litigation and natural resources divsns.), Mo. Bar, Kansas City Met. Bar Assn. Office: Stinson Mag & Fizzell PO Box 419251 Kansas City MO 64141-6251

OWENS, WILLIAM DON, anesthesiology educator; b. St. Louis, Dec. 12, 1939; s. Don and Caroline Wilhemena (Raaf) Owens; m. Patricia Gail Brown, Dec. 12, 1964; children: Pamela, David, Susan. AB, Westminster Coll., 1961; MD, U. Mich., 1965. Diplomate Am. Bd. Anesthesiology. Resident and fellow Mass. Gen. Hosp. and Harvard Med. Sch., Boston, 1969—72; instr. Harvard Med. Sch., Boston, 1972—73; asst. prof. anesthesiology Washington U. Sch. Medicine, St. Louis, 1973—76, assoc. prof., 1976—82, prof., 1982—2004, prof. emeritus, 2004—, chmn. dept., 1982—92. Trustee Barnes Hosp., St. Louis, 1987—89; bd. dirs. Anesthesia Found., 1994—, pres., 1999—; sec.-treas. Am. Bd. Anesthesiology, 1991—94, pres., 1995—96, bd. dirs., 1984—96, Found. Anesthesia Edn. and Rsch., 1990—95, pres., 1994—95; mem. Mo. State Bd. Healing Arts, 2003—04. Assoc. editor Survey of Anesthesiology, 1977—92; contbr. numerous articles to profl. jours. and chpts. to books. Served to lt. comdr. USN, 1966—69. Fellow: Am. Coll. Anesthesiology; mem.: Assn. Univ. Anesthesiologists, Acad. Anesthesiology, Internat. Anesthesia Rsch. Soc., Am. Soc. Anesthesiologists (bd. dirs. 1989—99, 1st v.p. 1995—96, pres. 1997—98). Office: Washington U Sch Med Dept Anesthesiology 660 S Euclid Ave Saint Louis MO 63110-1010

OWNBY, JERRY STEVE, landscape architect, educator; b. Shawnee, Okla., Jan. 25, 1939; s. Hugh H. and N. Lorraine (Hopkins) O.; children by previous marriage: Gregory Steve, Mitchell Hugh; m. Arnola Colson, Dec. 19, 1971; 1 child Steven Cory. BS, Okla. State U., 1961; MS in Landscape Architecture, Kans. State U., 1964, M in Landscape Architecture, 1970. Coun. Landscape Archtl. Registration Bds. cert. and registered landscape architect, Ariz., Kans., Mo. Extension landscape architect Kans. State U., Manhattan, 1963-64, instr., 1969-70; landscape architect Beardsley & Talley, Seattle, 1964-65; extension specialist Okla. State U., Stillwater, 1965-69, from asst. prof. to prof. landscape architecture and coordinator landscape architecture, 1970-85; pvt. practice, 1985—. Chmn. Okla. Landscape Architect Registration Bd., 1980-85; mem. 1985 Expert Panel for Uniform Nat. Exam., 1984-85; gov.'s appointee Mo. Coun. Landscape Architects, 1991-97 Designs include Las Laderas residence, 1978 (Merit award 1981), Student Union courtyard Okla. State U., 1981 (Honor award 1983). Chmn. Oklahomans for Landscape Architecture, 1979-80; chmn., vice chmn. Stillwater Park and Recreation Adv. Bd., Okla., 1971-79. Recipient Outstanding Prof. award, Okla. State U. chpt. Alpha Zeta, 1975, Svc. award, Stillwater City Commn., 1980, design awards, Springfield Planning and Zoning Commn., 1988, 1989, 1990, 1999, design award, Springfield Environ. Adv. Bd., 1990, Gov.'s Landscape Design award for Andy Williams's Moon River Theatre, Branson, Mo., 1992, for Charley Pride Theater, Branson, 1995, design award, Watershed Com., 1993, Disting. Alumnus award, dept. horticulture and landscape architecture Okla. State U., 2005; alumni fellow, Kans. State U., 1995, Paul Harris fellow, Rotary Internat., 2006. Fellow Am. Soc. Landscape Architects (v.p. 1983-85, Okla. chpt. Svc. award 1980); mem. Nat. Coun. State Garden Clubs (accredited instr. 1964—), Nat. Coun. of Educators in Landscape Architecture, Mo. Assn. of Landscape Architects, Coun. Landscape Archtl. Registration Bds. (cert.), Phi Kappa Phi, Sigma Lambda Alpha. Republican. Baptist. Avocations: travel, photography, fishing. Home: 234 Sunset Cove # 108 Branson MO 65616-3604 Home Phone: 417-338-8432. E-mail: jsownby@aol.com.

OWYANG, CHUNG, gastroenterologist, researcher; b. Chung King, China, Nov. 20, 1945; arrived in Can., 1965; s. Chi and Ching-Ying (Fung) O.; m. Jeannette Lim; children: Stephanie, Christopher. BS with honors, McGill U., Montreal, Can., 1968, MD, 1972. Diplomate Am. Bd. Internal Medicine, Gastroenterology; lic. Gen. Med. Coun., U.K., Que., Can., Min. Med. lic., Mich. med. lic. Intern in internal medicine Montreal Gen. Hosp./McGill U., 1972-73, resident in internal medicine, 1973-75; clin. teaching fellow in internal medicine McGill U., 1974-75; fellow in gastroenterology Mayo Clinic and Found., Rochester, Minn., 1975-78; instr. internal medicine Mayo Med. Sch., Rochester, 1977-78; asst. prof. U. Mich., 1978-84, assoc. prof., 1984-88, assoc. chief divsn. gastroenterology, 1984-90, prof., 1988—, chief divsn. gastroenterology, 1991—, dir. med. procedures unit, 1992—. Assoc. dir. Gastrointestinal Peptide Rsch. Ctr., U. Mich., 1984-95, dir. 1996—; cons. Rsch. Coun. Janssen Pharmaceutica Inc., 1985—, Ann Arbor VA Med. Ctr., 1978—, NIH, Bethesda, Md., 1989-94, FDA, Bethesda, 1995—; H. Marvin Pollard chair in gastroenterology, U. Mich., 1996—; speaker, presenter in field. Co-author: Textbook of Gastroenterology, 1991, 2d edit. 1995, Atlas of Gastroenterology, 1992; mem. edit. bd. Pancreas, 1986—, Am. Jour. Physiology, 1988—, Regulatory Peptide Letter, 1988—, Gastroenterology, 1990—, guest editor, 1991—, Digestive Diseases, 1993—; contbr. numerous chpts. to books, articles to profl. jours., jours. refereed. Grantee in field. Fellow ACP; mem. Am. Assn. Physicians, Am. Soc. Clin. Investigation, Am. Gastroenterological Assn., Am. Pancreatic Assn., Am. Diabetes Assn., Am. Fedn. Clin. Rsch., Am. Motility Soc., Ctrl. Soc. Clin. Rsch., Internat. Assn. Pancreatology, Midwest Gut Club. Office: U Mich Med Ctr Divsn Gastroenterology PO Box 362 Ann Arbor MI 48106-0362

OXENDER, GLENN S., state legislator; b. Three Rivers, Mich., Aug. 8, 1943; s. Harry Bryan and Myrtle (Sherck) O.; m. F. Dianne Ellis, 1966; children: Xanne, Katrina, Robert, Kalynn, Melinda. BS, Manchester Coll., 1965; MA, Western Mich. U., 1969; postgrad., U. Mo., 1971. Math. tchr. Livonia (Mich.) Pub. Schs., 1965-66, Sturgis (Mich.) Pub. Schs., 1966-69, Sturgis H.S., 1969-82; rep. Mich. State Dist. 42, Mich. State Dist. 59, 1982-98. Farmer, 1974—; appropriations standing com. Mich. Ho. Reps., cmty. coll. subcom., mental health subcom., joint capital outlay subcom., state police subcom., mil. affairs subcom., ad hoc edn. com., chmn. K-12 Dept. Edn. subcom. Trustee Libr. Mich. Named outstanding legis. of yr., 1989, 94, Mich. Occupl. Edn. Assn.; recipient pres.'s award Mich. Assn. Sch. Bd., 1995. Mem. Sturgis Exch. Club, NEA, Mich. Edn. Assn., Sturgis Edn. Assn., Rotary, Nat. Rep. Legis. Assn., Am. Legis. Exch. Coun., Ctrl. Regional Edn. Lab. Home: 27221 Wait Rd Sturgis MI 49091-9154

OXLEY, DENNIE R., II, state representative; b. Huntingburg, Ind., Dec. 22, 1970; married; 1 child. Grad., Ind. U. Southeast, 1993, MS, 1996. Project mgr. Sam Oxley and Co., 1990—94; math tchr. Crawford County H.S., Ind., 1994—; state rep. dist. 73 Ind. Ho. of Reps., Indpls., 1998—, vice chmn., fin. instns. com., mem. appointments and claims, interstate and internat. cooperation, and rules and legis. procedures coms., Dem. whip. Mem. Valley Creek Boys Gospel Quartet. Mem.: Farm Bur., Crawford County Classroom Tchrs. Assn. (pres.), Ind. State Tchrs. Assn., Fairview Gen. Bapt. Ch., Milltown (Ind.) Vol. Fire Dept., Crawford County C. of C., Crawford County Optimists, Milltown Masonic Lodge. Democrat. Baptist. Office: Ind Ho of Reps 200 W Washington St Indianapolis IN 46204-2786

OXLEY, DWIGHT K(AHALA), pathologist; b. Wichita, Kans., Dec. 2, 1936; s. Dwight K. Jr. and Ruth Erdene (Warner) O.; m. Patricia Warren, June 18, 1961; children: Alice DeBlois, Thomas Oxley. AB, Harvard U., 1958; MD, U. Kans., 1962. Diplomate Am. Bd. Pathology (trustee 1992—, pres. 1999), Am. Bd. Nuclear Medici ne. Pathologist Wesley Med. Ctr., Wichita, 1969-74, Eisenhower Med. Ctr., Rancho Mirage, Calif., 1974-78, St. Joseph Health Ctr., Kansas City, Mo., 1978-88; chmn. dept. pathology Wesley Med. Ctr., 1988—. Bd. editors Archives of Pathology and Lab. MEdicine, Chgo., 1984-95, Clinica Chimica Acta, Amsterdam, 1980-86, Am. Jour. Clin. Pathology, Chgo., 1974-80. Sr. warden St. Stephens Episcopal Ch., Wichita, 1994. Lt. commdr. USN, 1964-69. Fellow: Coll. Am. Pathologists (various offices), Am. Soc. Clin. Pathologists (various offices); mem.: Kans. Soc. Pathologists (pres. 1993—94), Am. Pathology Found. (bd. dirs. 1979—89). Republican. Avocations: music, athletics. Office: Wesley Med Ctr 550 N Hillside St Wichita KS 67214-4910

OXLEY, MARGARET CAROLYN STEWART, elementary school educator; b. Petaluma, Calif., Apr. 1, 1930; d. James Calhoun Stewart and Clara Thornton (Whiting) Bomboy; m. Joseph Hubbard Oxley, Aug. 25, 1951; children: Linda Margaret, Carolyn Blair Oxley Greiner, Joan Claire Oxley Willis, Joseph Stewart, James Harmon, Laura Marie Oxley Brechbill. Student, U. Calif., Berkeley, 1949—51; BS summa cum laude, Ohio State U., 1973, MA, 1984, student, 1985, student, 1988, student, 1992, student, 2003—08. Cert. tchr., Ohio. 2d grade tchr. St. Paul Sch., Westerville, Ohio, 1973—. Mem. editl. bd. Reading Tchr., vol. 47-48, 1993—94, Jour. Children's Lit., 1996—2007; mem. adv. bd. Lang. Arts, 2006—07; presenter in field. Co-author: Reading and Writing, Where it All Begins, 1991, Teaching with Children's Books: Path to Literature-Based Instruction, 1995, Adventuring With Books, vol. 12, 2000, vol. 13, 2002, Children's Literature Remembered: Issues, Trends, and Favorite Books, 2004. Active Akita Child Conservation League, Columbus, Ohio, 1968-70. Named Columbus Diocesan Tchr. of Yr., 1988; Phoebe A. Hearst scholar, 1951, Rose Sterheim Meml. scholar, 1951; recipient Mary Karrer award Ohio State U., 1994. Mem. Nat. Coun. Tchrs. English (Notable Children's Books in the Lang. Arts com. 1993-94, chair 1995-96, treas. Children's Literature Assembly bd. dirs. 1996-99, co-chair fall breakfast children's lit. assembly, 2000-03, co-chair excellence in poetry for children com. 2003-06), Internat. Reading Assn. (Exemplary Svc. in Promotion of Literacy award 1991), Ohio Coun. Internat. Reading Assn., Literacy Connection (pres.), Children's Lit. Assembly, Ohio Coun. Tchrs. English Lang. Arts (Outstanding Educator 1990), Phi Kappa Phi, Pi Lambda Theta (hon., Outstanding Work in Literacy Edn. citation 2004, v.p. local chpt.). Democrat. Roman Catholic. Avocations: reading, writing, travel, gardening, working with children. Home: 298 Brevoort Rd Columbus OH 43214-3826

OZANNE, DOMINIC LAURANT, lawyer, construction company executive; b. Cleve., Apr. 10, 1953; s. Leroy and Betty Jean (Peyton) O. B.S./B.A., Boston U., 1975; J.D., Harvard U., 1978. Bar: Ohio 1979. Assoc. Thompson, Hine & Flory, Cleve., 1978-80; gen. counsel Ozanne Constrn. Co. Inc., Cleve. Trustee Ctr. for Venture Devel., Cleve., 1983—. Mem. Nat. Assn. Minority Contractors (sec. 1983). Roman Catholic. Office: Ozanne Constrn Co Inc 1635 E 25th St Cleveland OH 44114-4214

OZAWA, MARTHA NAOKO, social work educator; b. Ashikaga, Tochigi, Japan, Sept. 30, 1933; arrived in US, 1963; d. Tokuichi and Fumi (Kawashima) O.; m. May 1959 (div. May 1966). BA in Econs., Aoyama Gakuin U., 1956; MS in Social Work, U. Wis., 1966, PhD in Social Welfare, 1969. Asst. prof. social work Portland State U., Oreg., 1969-70, assoc. prof. social work, 1970-72, 1975-76; assoc. rsch. prof. social work NYU, 1972-75; prof. social work Washington U., St. Louis, 1976-85, Bettie Bofinger Brown prof. social policy, 1985—2003, Bettie Bofinger Brown Disting. prof. social policy, 2003—; dir. Martha N. Ozawa Ctr. Social Policy Studies, 2005—. Author: Income Maintenance and Work Incentives, 1982; editor: Women's Life Cycle: Japan-U.S. Comparison in Income Maintenance, 1989, Women's Life Cycle and Economic Insecurity: Problems and Proposals, 1989; editl. bd. Social Work, Silver Spring, Md., 1972-75, 85-88, New Eng. Jour. Human Svcs., Boston, 1987-95, Ency. of Social Work, Silver Spring, 1974-77, 91-95, 99-2003, Jour. Social Svc. Rsch., 1977-97, Children and Youth Svcs. Rev., 1991—, Social Work Rsch., 1994-97, Jour. Poverty, 1997-2004; co-editor-in-chief Asian Social Work and Policy Rev., 2005—. Grantee Adminstrn. on Aging, Washington, 1979, 84, NIMH, 1990-93. Mem. Nat. Assn. Social Workers (presdl. award 1999), Nat. Acad. Social Ins., Nat. Conf. on Social Welfare (bd. dirs. 1981-87), The Gerontol. Soc. Am., Soc. for Social Work and Rsch., Washington U. Faculty Club (bd. dirs. 1986-91). Avocations: photography, tennis, swimming, gardening. Home: 13018 Tiger Lily Ct Saint Louis MO 63146-4339 Office: PO Box 1196 Saint Louis MO 63130-4899 Office Phone: 314-935-6615. Business E-Mail: ozawa@wustl.edu.

OZKAN, UMIT SIVRIOGLU, chemical engineering professor; b. Manisa, Turkey, Apr. 11, 1954; came to U.S., 1980; d. Alim and Emine (Ilgaz) Sivrioglu; m. H. Erdal Ozkan, Aug. 13, 1983. BS, Mid. East Tech. U., Ankara, Turkey, 1978, MS, 1980; PhD, Iowa State U., 1984. Registered profl. engr., Ohio. Grad. rsch. assoc. Ames Lab. U.S. Dept. Energy, 1980-84; asst. prof. Ohio State U., Columbus, 1985-90, assoc. prof. chem. engring., 1990-94, prof., 1994—, assoc. dean for rsch. Coll. Engring., 2000—05. Contbr. articles to profl. jours. French Ctr. NAt. Rsch. Sci. fellow, 1994-95; recipient Women of Achievement award YWCA, Columbus, 1991, Outstanding Engring. Educator Ohio award Soc. Profl. Engrs., 1991, Union Carbide Innovation Recognition award, 1991-92, NSF Woman Faculty award in sci. and engring., 1991, Engring. Tchg. Excellence award Keck Found., 1994, Ctrl. Ohio Outstanding Woman in Sci. & Tech., 1996, Pitts.-Cleve. Catalysis Soc. Outstanding Rsch. award, 1998, Achievement award Soc. Women Engring., 2002, Columbus Outstanding Rsch. award ACS, 2002, Fulbright award, 2006. Fellow Am. Inst. Chemists; mem. NSPE, N.Am. Catalysis Soc., Am. Inst. Chem. Engring., Am. Soc. Engring. Edn., Am. Chem. Soc., Combustion Inst., Sigma Xi. Achievements include research in selective oxidation; electrocatalysis; in-situ spectroscopy; fuel reformulation; hydrodenitrogenation; hydrodeoxygenation; hydrodesulfurization; NO reduction; hydrogenation. Office: Ohio State U Chem Engring 140 W 19th Ave Columbus OH 43210-1110 Office Phone: 614-292-6623. E-mail: ozkan.1@usa.edu.

OZMENT, DENNIS DEAN, state legislator; b. Farmington, Minn., May 2, 1945; s. Clyde Lee and Dolores (Bell) O.; m. Gayle Farrior, 1967; children: Wanda Kaye, Dennis Eugene. Student, U. Minn., Met. Cmty. Coll., Minn. Mem. Minn. Ho. of Reps., St. Paul, 1984—. Mem. edn. com., environ. and natural resources com., regulated industry com.; fire capt. Republican. Home: 3275 145th St E Rosemount MN 55068-5909 Office: Minn Ho of Reps State Capitol Saint Paul MN 55155-0001

OZOG, DIANE L., allergist; b. Chgo., July 28, 1955; MD, U. Health Scis., Chgo. Med. Sch., 1982. Cert. allergy and immunology 1987, pediat. 1987. Resident Cook County Hosp., Ill., 1982—85; fellowship Children's Meml. Hosp., Ill., 1985—87; allergist Good Samaritan Hosp. Mem.: Children's Comm. Physicians Assn. Address: 636 Raymond Naperville IL 60563

PAANANEN, VICTOR NILES, language educator; b. Ashtabula, Ohio, Jan. 31, 1938; s. Niles Henry and Anni Margaret (Iloranta) P.; m. Donna Mae Jones, Aug. 15, 1964; children: Karl, Neil. AB magna cum laude, Harvard U., 1960; MA, U. Wis., 1964, PhD, 1967. Instr. English Wofford Coll., Spartanburg, SC, 1962-63; asst. prof. Williams Coll., Williamstown, Mass., 1966-68, Mich. State U., East Lansing, 1968-73, assoc. prof., 1973—82, prof., 1982—2002, asst. dean Grad. Sch., 1977-82, chmn. dept. English, 1986-94, prof. emeritus, 2002—. Vis. prof. Roehampton U., London, 1982, 96, hon. fellow, 92; mem. Harvard Inst. Learning Ret., 2006. Author: William Blake, 1977, 2d edit., 1996, British Marxist Criticism, 2000; contbr. articles to profl. and scholarly jours. Univ. fellow U. Wis., 1962, 63-64, Roehampton Inst. hon. fellow, London, 1992—; Harvard Nat. scholar, 1956-60. Home: 350 Revere Beach Blvd 5-5W Revere MA 02151-4851 E-mail: paananen@msu.edu.

PAAR, CHRISTOPHER R., lawyer; b. 1971; m. Martha Paar; 2 children. BA, JD, U. Iowa. Bar: Minn. 1997. Atty. Zelle, Hofmann, Voelbel, Mason & Gette, L.L.P., Mpls. Named a Rising Star, Minn. Super Lawyers mag., 2006. Mem.: ABA, Minn. Bar Assn., Iowa Bar Assn. Office: Zelle Hofmann Voelbel Mason & Gette LLP 500 Washington Ave S Ste 4000 Minneapolis MN 55415 Office Phone: 612-336-9113. E-mail: cpaar@zelle.com.

PAAVO, JARVI, conductor; b. Tallinn, Estonia; Studied under Leonard Bernstein; student in percussion and conducting, Tallinn Sch. Music; student under Otto-Werner, Max Rudolf, Curtis Inst. Music; student under Leonard Bernstein, L.A. Philharmonic Inst. Music dir. Cin. Symphony Orch., 2001—. Prin. guest conductor Royal Stockholm Philharmonic, City of Birmingham (Eng.) Symphony Orch., guest conductor N.Y. Philharmonic, Berlin Philharmonic, Munich Philharmonic, London Philharmonic, San Francisco Symphony, Phila. Orch. (Carnegie Hall debut), NHK Symphony, Tokyo Symphony, Israel Philharmonic, St. Petersburg Philharmonic, Orch. Filarmonica della Scala, L.A. Philharmonic, Philharmonic orch. and many others, (works by Bernstein) City of Birmingham Symphony Orch., Royal Stockholm Philharmonic Orch., (recordings with Estonian composers Part, Tuur, and Tubin) Searching for Roots, Sibelius' Kullervo, Lemminkainen Suite, (concerts with cellist Turls Mork); condr.: recs. with Cin. Symphony Orch. Office: Cin Symphony Orch 1241 Elm St Cincinnati OH 45210

PACE, OLE BLY, III, lawyer; b. 1939; AB, Ill. Wesleyan Univ., 1963; JD, Univ. Ill. Coll. of Law, 1966. Bar: 1966, US Dist. Ct., No. and Ctrl. Dist. Ill. Law clerk Appellate Ct. Justice A. J. Scheineman; spl. asst. atty. gen., 1968—80; ptnr. Ward, Murray, Pace & Johnson. Bd. dir. Northwestern Steel & Wire Co., First at. Bank, Sterling-Rock Falls, Ill., Mercantile Bank, Sterling-Rock Falls, Ill. Past pres. Sterling C. of C., Sinnissippi Mental Health Ctr. US Army, 1958—60. Named Illinois Super Lawyer, 2005—08; named one of the Best Lawyers in Am., 2003—08. Fellow: Ill. Bar Found.; mem.: ABA, Ill. Cmty. Coll. Attorneys Assn. (bd. mem., vice chair), Ill. Acad. of Lawyers (bd. regents, chancellor), Nat. Assn. of Coll. and Univ. Attorneys, Whiteside County Bar Assn. (past pres.), Ill. State Bar Assn. (bd. gov. 1995—2001, third v.p. 2001, pres. 2004, Bd. of Gov. award 1989), Order of Coif, Phi Delta Phi. Office: Ward Murray Pace & Johnson PC PO Box 400 202 E Fifth St Sterling IL 61081 Office Phone: 812-625-8200. Office Fax: 815-625-8363. Business E-Mail: pace@wmpj.com.

PACE, ORLANDO LAMAR, professional football player; b. Sandusky, Ohio, Nov. 4, 1975; Attended, Ohio State Univ. Lineman St. Louis Rams, 1997—. Donater Disadvantaged Kids; participant Spearheads Annual Offensive Line Thanksgiving Project, Chesterfield, Mo. Named to NFL Pro-Bowl, 1999—2005. Achievements include first to being the first player in college history to win two consecutive Lombardi awards, 1995, 1996; being the overall first pick in NFL Draft, 1997; being a member of Super Bowl XXXIV Champion St. Louis Rams, 2000. Office: 1 Rams Way Saint Louis MO 63045

PACHECO, BRYAN E., lawyer; b. Akron, Ohio, Mar. 21, 1969; BA, U. Akron, 1992; JD, U. Cin., 1997. Bar: Ohio 1997, US Dist. Ct. Southern Dist. Ohio 1998, US Ct. of Appeals Sixth Cir. 2001. Ptnr. Dinsmore & Shohl LLP, Cin. Dep. solicitor City of Blue Ash, Ohio; city solicitor City of Silverton, Ohio; mem. Hope Evang. Free Ch. Named one of Ohio's Rising Stars, Super Lawyers, 2006. Mem.: ABA, Ohio State Bar Assn., Cin. Bar Assn., Order of Coif. Office: Dinsmore & Shohl LLP 255 E Fifth St Ste 1900 Cincinnati OH 45202-4700 Office Phone: 513-977-8200. Office Fax: 513-977-8141.

PACHECO, MANUEL TRINIDAD, retired academic administrator; b. Rocky Ford, Colo., May 30, 1941; s. Manuel J. and Elizabeth (Lopez) Pacheco; m. Karen M. King, Aug. 27, 1966; children: Daniel Mark, Andrew Charles, Sylvia Lois Elizabeth. BA, N.Mex. Highlands U., 1962; MA, Ohio State U., 1966, PhD, 1969. Mem. faculty Fla. State U., 1968—71, U. Colo., 1971; prof. edn., univ. dean Tex. A&I U., Laredo, 1972—77; prof. multicultural edn., chmn. dept. San Diego State U., 1977—78; prof. Spanish and edn. Laredo State U., 1978—80; exec. dir. Bilingual Edn. Ctr., Kingsville Tex. A&I U., 1980—82; assoc. dean Coll. Edn. U. Tex., El Paso, 1982—86, exec. dir. for planning, 1984; pres. Laredo State U., 1984—88, U. Houston-Downtown, 1986—97, U. Ariz., Tucson, 1991—97, U. Mo. Sys., Columbia, 1997—2002; ret., 2002. Cons. lang. divsn. Ency. Britannica, 1965—72; bd. dirs. Valley Nat. Bank Corp., Nat. Security Edn. Program, ASARCO, PNM Resources, Inc.; mem. exec. com. Bus.-Higher Edn. Forum. Co-editor: Handbook for Planning and Managing Instruction in Basic Skills for Limited English Proficient Students, 1983; prodr.: (videotapes) Teacher Training, 1976. Named, Most Prominent Am.-Hispanics Spanish Tchr. Mag., 1984, one of 100 Outstanding Hispanics Hispanis Bus., 1988, Man of Yr., Hispanic Profl. Action Com., 1991; recipient Disting. Alumnus award, Ohio State U., Columbus, 1984, Disting. Leadership in Higher Edn. award, Sec. of Edn. Richard Riley, 1997; Fulbright fellow, U. de Montepellier, France, 1962. Mem.: Tex. Assn. Chicanos in Higher Edn., Hispanic Assn. Colls. and Univs., Nat. Acad. Pub. Adminstrn., Am. Assn. State Colls. and Univs., Rotary, Phi Delta Kappa.

PACHER, NANCY A., real estate company executive; Grad. cum laude, Georgetown U.; JD, Northwestern U. Atty. Katten Muchin Rosenman LLP, Chgo., 1975; sr. v.p., prin. Howard Ecker & Co.; pres., COO US Equities Realty, Chgo., 1993—. Commr. City of Chgo. Plan Commn. Mem. editl. adv. bd.: Ill. Real Estate Jour. Named Broker of the Yr., Chgo. Sun-Times, 1986, 2004; named one of 100 Most Influential Women in Chgo., Crain's Chgo. Bus., 1996; named to Who's Who in Chgo. Bus., 2002, 20th Ann. Hall of Fame, Today's Chgo. Women. Mem.: ABA, Comml. Real Estate Orgn., Comml. Real Estate Exec. Women, The Chgo. Network (bd. chair 2005—06), Chgo. Bar Assn., Econ. Club Chgo., Phi Beta Kappa. Office: US Equities Realty Ste 400 20 N Michigan Ave Chicago IL 60602

PACKARD, SANDRA PODOLIN, education educator, consultant; b. Buffalo, Sept. 13, 1942; d. Mathew and Ethel (Zolte) P.; m. Martin Packard, Aug. 2, 1964; children: Dawn Esther, Shana Fanny BFA, Syracuse U., 1964; MSEd, Ind. U., 1966, EdD, 1973. Cert. tchr. art K-12, N.Y. Asst. prof. art SUNY-Buffalo, 1972-74; assoc. prof. art Miami U., Oxford, Ohio, 1974-81, spl. asst. to provost, 1979-80, assoc. provost, spl. programs, 1980-81; dean Coll. Edn. Bowling Green State U., Ohio, 1981-85; provost and vice chancellor for acad. affairs U. Tenn., Chattanooga, 1985-92; pres. Oakland U., Rochester, Mich., 1992-95, prof. edn., 1995—, dir. higher edn. doc. cognate; sr. fellow, dir. tech. in edn. Am. Assn. State Colls. and Univs., 1995; acting dir. PhD program in ednl. leadership Oakland U., 2003—04. Cons. Butler County Health Ctr., Hamilton, Ohio, 1976-78, Univ. of the North, South Africa Project of the Am. Coun. on Edn., 1995; vis. prof. art therapy Simmons Coll., 1979, Mary Mount Coll., Milw., 1981; corp. adv. com. Corp. Detroit Mag., 1994-95. Sr. editor Studies in Art Edn. jour., 1979-81; mem. editl. adv. bd. Jour. Aesthetic Edn., 1984-90; editor: The Leading Edge, 1986; contbr. articles to profl. jours., chpts. to conf. papers Chmn. com. Commn. on Edn. Excellence, Ohio, 1982-83, Tenn. State Peformance Funding Task Force, 1988, Tenn. State Task Force on Minority Tchrs., 1988; reviewer art curriculum NY Bd. Edn., 1985; supt. search com. Chattanooga Pub. Schs., 1987-88; mem. Chattanooga Met. Coun., 1987-88, Chattanooga Ballet Bd., 1986-88, Fund for Excellence in Pub. Edn., 1986-90, Tenn. Aquarium Bd. Advisors, 1989-92, Team Evaluation Ctr. Bd., 1988-90; strategic planning action team Chattanooga City Schs., 1987-88, Siskin Hosp. Bd., 1989-92, Blue Ribbon Task Force Pontiac 2010: A New Reality, City of Pontiac Planning Divsn., 1992—; steering com., cultural action bd. Chattanooga, planning com United Way, 1987; Jewish Fedn. Bd., 1986-91; mem. coun. for policy studies Art Edn. Adv. Bd., 1982-91; ex-officio mem. Meadow Brook Theatre Guild, 1992-95; bd. chair Meadow Brook Performing Arts Co., 1992-95; chair World Cup Soccer Edn. Com./Mich. Host Com. 1993-95; bd. dirs. Ptnrs. for Preferred Future, Rochester Cmty. Schs., 1992-95, Traffic Improvement Assn. Oakland County, 1992-95, Oakland County Bus. Roundtable, 1993-95; Rochester C. of C. host com. chair on edn. World Cup, 1992-95; fin. adv. com. Jewish Fedn. Detroit, 1995-97; bd. dirs. United Way Southeastern Mich., 1992-95: bd. dirs. United Way Oakland County, 1992-95, Pontiac 2010: A New Reality, mayor's transition team city/sch. rels. task force: team evaluation leader Dept. of State Am. U. Bulgaria, 1995; bd. trustees Cohn's & Colitis Found., 1996-97; trustee Nat. Art Edn. Found., 2004—, chair fin. com.; steering com. Nat. Forum Access to Democracy Project, 2004. Am. Coun. on Edn. and Mellon fellow Miami U., 1978-79; recipient Cracking the Glass Ceiling award Pontiac Area Urban League, 1992. Fellow Nat. Art Edn. Assn. (disting.); mem. Nat. Coun. Profs. of Ednl. Adminstrn. (technology com., 2000-03), Am. Assn. Colls. for Tchr. Edn. (com. chair 1982-85), Am. Art Therapy Assn. (registered), Nat. Art Edn. Assn. Women's Caucus (founder, pres. 1976-78, McFee award 1986), Am. Assn. State Colls. and Univs. (com. profl. devel. 1993-95, state rep. 1994-95), Econ. Club Detroit (bd. dirs. 1992-95), Rotary Club, Great Lakes Yacht Club (social chmn. 1996-97, ground chmn., bd. dirs. 1997-98), Phi Delta Kappa (Leadership award 1985), Nat. Assn. Profs. of Edn. Adminstrn. (com. chair 1998-), Great Lakes Yacht Club, 1995 (bd. dir. 1996-1998). Avocation: sailing. Home: 10471 Scout Trail White Lake MI 48386 Office: Oakland U 475 Education Bldg Rochester MI 48309-4423 Office Phone: 248-370-3059. Business E-Mail: packard@oakland.edu.

PADILLA, JAMES JEROME (JIM PADILLA), retired automotive executive; b. Detroit, June 13, 1946; s. David J. and Irene C. (Clos) P.; m. Alice M., Dec. 27, 1968; children: James Jr., Kathryn, Daniel. BSChemE, MS in Engring., U. Detroit, 1969, MA in Econ., 1970. Fuel econ. planning mgr. Ford Motor Co., Dearborn, Mich., 1977-78, engine planning engring. mgr. Detroit, 1979-80, engine controls dept. mgr., 1980-83, exec. engr., powertrain-electronics, 1983-85, chief engr., trim-chassis-elect-emissions, 1985, programs operations mgr., 1990, dir., small cars unit, 1991, exec. dir., engring. and mfg., Jaguar Cars, Ltd., 1992—94, dir., performance luxury vehicle lines, 1994—96, pres., Argentina and Brazil operations, 1996—98, pres. S. Am. operations, group v.p., mfg. and quality, 1999—2001, group v.p., N. Am., 2001—02, exec. v.p. Detroit, 2002, pres. Americas, 2002—04, pres., COO, 2004—06, chmn. worldwide automotive operations, 2004—06. Spl. asst to sec., US Dept. Commerce, 1978-79; bd. dirs. Am. Supplier Inst., Dearborn. Pres. Civic Assn., Canton, Mich., 1972-74, Plymouth (Mich.) Sch. Bd., 1981-84; mem. Plymouth Parish Council, 1980-84, Plymouth Edn. Commn., 1980-85. Served to 2d Lt. USNG, 1970-76. White House fellow U.S. Govt., Washington, 1978-79, fellow, Nat. Acad. Engring., 2001-; rsch. grantee Dow Chem. Co., Detroit, 1968-69; recipient Engr. of the Year, Hispanic Engr. Nat. Achievement Awards Conf., 2000, Ohtli medal from Mexican President Vincente Fox, 2004; named one of 50 Most Important Hispanics in Tech. & Bus., Hispanic Engr. & Info. Tech. mag., 2005. Mem. Soc. Automotive Engrs., Engring. Soc. Detroit. (selection com. U.S. Senate fellows 1982-84, named Outstanding Young Engr. 1980). Roman Catholic.

PADRON, D. LORENZO, state agency administrator; B in Mgmt., U. Ill., Chgo. Positions in comml. and internat. divsns. First Nat. Bank Chgo.; asst. v.p. Banco Popular; sr. v.p. Met. Bank, Chgo.; owner Nat. Facility and Supply Co./Chgo. Contract Cleaning and Supply Co., 1998—2001; dir. divsn. banking Ill. Office Fin. and Profl. Regulation, 2003—. Bd. dirs. Latin Am. C. of C., chmn. emeritus. Office: Ill Office Fin and Profl Regulation Divsn Banking 122 S Michigan Ave Ste 1900 Chicago IL 60603 Office Phone: 312-793-3000.

PAGAC, GERALD J., state agency administrator; Dir. Out Recreation, Ind.; divsn. dir. Ind. Dept. Natural Resources Divsn. State Pks., Indpls., 1993—. Office: Ind Dept Natural Resources Divsn State Pks 402 W Washington St Rm W298 Indianapolis IN 46204-2739 Fax: 317-232-4132.

PAGANO, RICHARD C., lawyer, trucking executive; b. Waukesha, Wis., May 5, 1953; BA magna cum laude, St. Norbert Coll., 1974; JD, Northwestern U., 1978. Bar: Ill. 1978, US Dist. Ct., Ill. 1978. Atty. Centel Corp., Chicago, Ill., 1978—90; asst. gen. counsel, asst. sec. USF Corp., Chicago, Ill., 1990—92, v.p., assoc. gen. counsel, sec., 1992—93, sr. v.p., gen. counsel, sec., 1993—. Mem.: ABA, Assn. of Corp. Counsel, Am. Soc. of Corp. Secretaries, Chicago Bar Assn. Office: USF Corp 8550 W Bryn Mawr Ave Ste 700 Chicago IL 60631

PAGE, ALAN C., state supreme court justice; b. Canton, Ohio, Aug. 7, 1945; s. Howard F. and Georgianna (Umbles) P.; m. Diane Sims, June 5, 1973; children: ina, Georgianna, Justin, Khamsin. BA, U. Notre Dame, 1967; JD, U. Minn., 1978; LLD (hon), U. Notre Dame, 1993, St. John's U., 1994, Westfield State Coll., 1994, Luther Coll., 1995, U. New Haven, 1999; LHD (hon), Winston-Salem State U., 2000, Gustavus Adolphus Coll., 2003, U. Notre Dame, 2004. Bar: Minn. 1979, U.S. Dist. Ct. Minn. 1979, U.S. Supreme Ct. 1988. Profl. football player Minn. Vikings, Mpls., 1967-78, Chgo. Bears, 1978-81; assoc. Lindquist & Vennum, Mpls., 1979-85; special asst. atty. gen. employment law Minn. Atty. Gen.'s Office, St. Paul, 1985—87, asst. atty. gen., 1987—93; assoc. justice Minn. Supreme Ct., St. Paul, 1993—. Cons. NFL Players Assn., Washington, 1979-84. Commentator Nat. Pub. Radio, 1982-83. Founder Page Edn. Found., 1988. amed NFL's Most Valuable Player, 1971, one of 10 Outstanding Young Men Am., U.S. Jaycees, 1981; named to NFL Hall of Fame, 1988, Coll. Football Hall of Fame, 1993, Internat. Scholar-Athlete Hall of Fame, 2002; named one of 50 Greatest Sports Figures from Ohio Sports Illustrated, 1999; recipient NCAA Theodore Roosevelt award, 2004, Disting. Am. award Nat. Football Found. and Coll. Hall Fame, 2005, Honoree Trumpet awards Found., 2007. Mem. ABA, Minn. Bar Assn., Nat. Bar Assn., Hennepin County Bar Assn., Minn. Assn. Black Lawyers, Am. Law Inst. Avocations: running, biking. Office: 423 Minnesota Judicial Ctr 25 Rev Dr Martin Luther King Jr Blvd Saint Paul MN 55155-1500

PAGE, DAVID RANDALL, hospital administrator; b. Plainfield, NJ, Oct. 30, 1940; married BA, Davidson Coll., NC, 1962; MA, Duke U., Durham, NC, 1964. Administrv. resident Durham County Gen. Hosp., NC, 1964, Duke U. Hosp., 1963-64, administrv. asst., 1964-65; asst. dir. Children's Mercy Hosp., Kansas City, 1968-69, Meml. Mission Hosp., Asheville, NC, 1969-71, assoc. dir., 1971-81; exec. v.p., dir. Ochsner Fedn. Hosp., New Orleans, 1981-93; pres., ceo Hermann Hosp., Houston, 1993—; CEO Fairview Hosp., Mpls. Fellow ACHE; mem. AHA. Address: Fairview Hosp 2450 Riverside Ave Minneapolis MN 55454-1450

PAGE, GREGORY R., agricultural products and diversified services company executive; b. Bottineau, ND, 1951; m. Cynthia M. Page. BA in Economics, U. ND, 1973. Joined as trainee in Feed divsn., various positions in the US animal nutrition bus. in merchandising, prod. services and admin. Cargill, Inc., Kansas City, Kan.; Fort Worth, Texas; Stockton, Calif.; Minneapolis, 1974—85, head animal nutrition operations in Asia, Cargill Southeast Asia Ltd Singapore, 1985, head poultry processing bus., Sun Valley Thailand Saraburi Province, Thailand, 1989—92, returned to US to work with the U.S. beef operations of Cargills Excel subs. Mpls., 1992, pres. red meat group, 1995—98, corp. v.p., sect. pres., 1998—2000, exec. v.p., 1999—2000, pres., COO, 2000—07, chmn., pres., CEO, 2007—. Bd. dirs. Eaton Corp. Mem.: Am. Meat Inst. (chmn. 2000). Office: Cargill Inc PO Box 9300 Minneapolis MN 55440

PAGE, LINDA KAY, bank executive; b. Wadsworth, Ohio, Oct. 4, 1943; d. Frederick Meredith and Martha Irene (Vance) P. Student, Ohio U., 1976-77; grad. banking program, U. Wis., 1982-84; BA, Capital U. Asst. v.p., gen. mgr. Bancohio Corp., Columbus, 1975-78, v.p., dist. mgr., 1979-80, v.p., mgr. employee rels., 1980-81, v.p., divsn. mgr., 1982-83; commr. of banks State of Ohio, Columbus, 1983-87, dir. Dept. Commerce, 1988-90; pres., CEO Star Bank Ctrl. Ohio, Columbus, 1990—92; state dir. Rural Devel/USDA, 1993-2000; pub. svc. dir. City of Columbus, 2000—04; mgr. Nationwide Fed. Credit Union, 2004—. Bd. dirs. Clark County Mental Health Bd., Springfield, Ohio, 1982-83, Springfield Met. Housing, 1982-83, Pvt. Industry Coun. Franklin County, 1990-2000—, Ohio Higher Edn. Facilities Commn., 1990-93, Ohio Devel. Corp., 1995—; bd. advisers Orgn. Indsl. Standards, Springfield, 1982-83; trustee League Against Child Abuse, 1986-90; treas. Ohio Housing Fin. Agy., 1980-90; vice chair Fed. Res. Bd. Consumer Adv. Coun., 1989-91; trustee, treas. Columbus State C.C. Found., 1990-00, pres., 1997-99; bd. dirs. Columbus Urban League, 1992-98; mem. CompDrug Bd., 1998-00; mem. Mid Ohio Regional Planning Commn., 2000-04; devel. chair Ohio Coun. Econ. Edn., 2003-. Recipient Leadership Columbus award Sta. WTVN and Columbus Leadership Program, 1975, 82, Outstanding Svc. award Clark County Mental Health Bd., 1983, Giles Mitchell Housing award, 1996. Mem.: LWV (treas. edn. fund 1992—2000), Ohio Coun. Econ. Edn. (devel. chair 2004—), Womens Fund Ctrl. Ohio (grant reader 2003—05), Risk Mgmt. Assn., Women in Transp. (bd. trustees Ohio chpt. 2000, bd. dirs. 2002), Internat. Womens Forum, Am. Pub. Works Assn. (treas. Ohio chpt. 2000—04, govt. affairs com. 2002—03, treas. 2002—04), Ohio Mortgage Bankers Assn. (legis. commn. 1998), Ohio Devel. Assn., Ohio Bankers Assn. (bd. dirs. 1982—83, 1991—92), Conf. State Bank Suprs. (dist. chmn. 1984—85, sec.-treas. 1985—90, bd. dirs.), Women Execs. in State Govt., Am. Bankers Assn. (govt. rels. coun. 1990—92, cert.), Nat. Assn. Bank Women (pres. 1980—81), Rotary. Democrat. Avocations: reading, cultural arts, travel. Home: 1477 Sedgefield Dr New Albany OH 43054-9431 Personal E-mail: lpage@insight.rr.com.

PAIGE, JEFFERY MAYLAND, sociologist, educator; b. Providence, June 15, 1942; s. Charles Warren and Dorothy Frances (Rice) P.; m. Karen Ericksen, Apr. 30, 1966 (div. 1980). AB summa cum laude, Harvard U., 1964; PhD, U. Mich., 1968. Asst. prof. U. Calif., Berkeley, 1968-76; assoc. prof. U. Mich., Ann Arbor, 1976-82, prof., 1982—, dir. ctr. for rsch. on social orgn., 1992-97; vis. scholar MIT, Cambridge, Mass., 1998. Vis. lectr. U. Ctrl. Am., San Salvador, El Salvador, 1990, Fla. Internat. U., Miami, 1992; internat. observer Nicaraguan Nat. Adv. Commn. on Atlantic Coast, Managua, 1986. Author: Agrarian Revolution, 1975 (Sorokin award 1976), Coffee and Power, 1997; co-author: The Politics of Reproductive Ritual, 1981. Fulbright fellow, 1990, Kellog fellow, 1991; rsch. grantee NSF, 1990-92. Mem. Am. Sociol. Assn. (coun. chair polit. econ. of world sys. sect. 1987-89), Latin Am. Studies Assn., Sociol. Rsch. Assn. Democrat. Avocations: hiking, skiing, sailing. Office: U Mich Dept Sociology Ann Arbor MI 48109

PAINE, ANDREW J., JR., bank executive; b. Chgo., Oct. 18, 1937; s. Andrew J. and Louise (Kelly) P.; m. Jane Medaris, June 25, 1960; children: Linda, Stephanie, Andrew. BA, DePauw U., 1959; MBA, Ind. U., 1967; grad., Stonier Grad. Sch. Banking, 1969. Asst. cashier Ind. Nat. Bank, Indpls., 1964-66, asst. v.p., 1966-68, v.p., 1968-72, sr. v.p., 1972-76, exec. v.p. corp. devel., 1976-77, exec. v.p. corp. banking, 1977-79, pres., 1979—, chief oper. officer; also vice chmn. Ind. Nat. Corp. (now NBD Bank, N.A.); now pres., ceo. Vice chmn. Ind. Nat. Corp., 1981—; dir. Indpls. Life Ins. Co., Hammond Co., Newport Beach, Calif. Mem. past pres.'s council Jr. Achievement Central Ind.; nat. bd. dirs. Jr. Achievement Inc.; trustee Children's Mus., DePauw U.; bd. dirs. Community Service Council Met. Indpls.; bd. govs. United Way, chmn. campaign, 1983. Recipient Key Man award Indpls. Jaycees, 1972; Alumni citation DePauw U., 1978 Mem. Am. Bankers Assn. (chmn. govt. relations council), Young Presidents Orgn., Ind. U. Sch. Bus. Alumni Assn. (past pres.) Clubs: Columbia, Meridian Hills Country. Methodist. Office: NBD Bank NA 1 Indiana Sq # 501 Indianapolis IN 46204-2004

PAIROLERO, PETER CHARLES, surgeon, educator; b. Bessemer, Mich., 1938; MD, U. Mich., 1963. Diplomate Am. Bd. Surgeons, Am. Bd. Thoracic Surgeons, Am. Bd. Gen. Vascular Surgeons. Intern St. Mary's Hosp., Duluth, Minn., 1963-64; resident gen. surgery Mayo Grad. Sch. Medicine, Rochester, Minn., 1966-71, fellow cerebral vascular resch., 1968-69, resident thoracic-cardio surgery, 1971-73; fellow cerebral vascular surgery Baylor U., Houston, 1973; chmn. American Board of Thorasic Surgery, 2001—; staff surgeon Mayo Clinic, Rochester, Minn., 1974—, chair vascular surgery, 1987—90, chair gen. thoracic surgery, 1989—93, chair cardiothoracic surgery, 1992—93, chair dept. of surgery, 1993—. Served in US Army, 1964—66. Mem. AMA, Am. Bd. Thorasic Surgery (chmn., 2001-). Office: 200 1st St SW Rochester MN 55905-0001

PALAHNIUK, RICHARD JOHN, anesthesiology educator, researcher; b. Winnipeg, Man., Can., Dec. 5, 1944; s. George and Teenie (Lukinchuk) P.; m. Patricia June Smando, July 15, 1967; children: Christopher, Daniel, Andrew. BS in Medicine, U. Man., 1968, MD, 1968. Head obstetric anaesthesia Health Scis. Ctr., Winnipeg, 1973-79; prof. and chmn. of anaesthesia U. Man., Winnipeg, 1979-89; prof. anesthesiology, head dept., dir. dept. anesthesiology U. Minn., Mpls., 1989—. Contbr. papers and book chpts. to profl. publs.; mem. editorial bd. Can. Jour. Anaesthesia, Toronto, 1985-89. Fellow Med. Rsch. Coun. Can., 1972, rsch. grantee, 1974-79. Fellow Royal Coll. Physicians of Can.; mem. Can. Anaesthetists' Soc., Am. Soc. Anesthesiology, Internat. Anesthesia Rsch. Soc. (editorial bd. Cleve. chpt. 1987—). Roman Catholic. Avocations: running, fishing, carpentry. Office: U Minn Med Sch Box 294 420 Delaware St SE Minneapolis MN 55455-0374

PALAMARA, JOSEPH, state legislator; s. Sam and Eleanor P.; m. Aline; children: Lauren Grace, Lance Joseph. BA, Mich. State U., 1975; JD, Detroit Coll. Law, 1985. Rep. Mich. State Dist. 30, 1985-94, Mich. State Dist. 24, 1995-98; county commr. Wayne County, Mich., 1998—. Majority whip Mich. Ho. Reps., chmn. election com., mem. corp. & fin. com., pub. health com., ins. com., jud. com.; pvt. practice law, Mich., 1986—. Home: 8963 Marquette Dr Grosse Ile MI 48138-1581

PALANS, LLOYD ALEX, lawyer; b. St. Louis, Aug. 6, 1946; s. Hyman Robert and Mae (Sherman) P.; m. Deborah Regn, Aug. 5, 1972; children: Emily Rebecca, Samantha Jane. BS, Tulane U., 1968; JD, U. Mo., 1972. Bar: Mo. 1972, US Dist. Ct. (ea. and we. dists.) Mo. 1972, US Ct. Appeals (8th cir.) 1972, US Ct. Appeals (5th cir.) 1974, US Supreme Ct. 1975, US Ct. Appeals (9th cir.) 1992. Ptnr. Kramer, Chused, Kramer, Shostak & Kohn, St. Louis, 1972-77, Blumenfeld, Marx & Tureen, P.C., St. Louis, 1978-81, Gallop, Johnson & Neuman, St. Louis, 1981-90, Bryan Cave, LLP, St. Louis, 1990—. Adj. prof. Washington U. Sch. Law, St. Louis, 1989—. Bd. dirs. St. Louis Chpt. ARC, 1987—, St. Louis Chpt. Leukemia Soc., 1988—, Combined Health Appeal Greater St. Louis, 1988—, Combined Health Appeal of Am., 1990. Fellow Am. Coll. Bankruptcy; mem. ABA, Mo. Bar, St. Louis Met. Bar Assn. Office: Bryan Cave LLP 1 Metro Sq 211 N Broadway Saint Louis MO 63102-2733 Office Phone: 314-259-2301.

PALCHICK, BERNARD S., academic administrator, painter, educator; b. Chgo., Sept. 24, 1945; m. Lisa Palchick; children: Linnea, Benjamin. BA in Painting, Purdue U., 1967; MFA in Sculpture, RISD, 1971. Instr. art Kalamazoo Coll., 1972—74, asst. prof. art, 1974—79, assoc. prof. art, 1979—87, prof. art, 1987—, chair art dept., 1977—85, chair divsn. fine arts, 1982—95, dir. endowed artist-in-residence program, 1984—, assoc. provost, 1987—89, spl. asst. to pres. for comm., 1990, acting chair theatre dept., 1994—95, acting provost, 1996—97, v.p. coll. advancement, 1997—2006, interim pres., 2004—05. Bd. mem. Kalamazoo Inst. of Arts, 1994—99, Plz. Arts Cir., Western Mich. U., 1999—2003, Kalamazoo Cmty. in Schs., 2005—, Greater Kalamazoo Arts Coun., 2005—. Mem.: Mich. Watercolor Soc., Watercolor USA Honor Soc., Coun. for Advancement and Support of Edn. Office: Kalamazoo Coll 1200 Academy St Kalamazoo MI 49006 E-mail: palchick@kzoo.edu.

PALENSKY, FREDERICK J., manufacturing executive; Joined 3M Co., 1968, v.p., dental products divsn., 1997—2001, v.p., gen. mgr., 3M ESPE, 2001, exec. v.p., specialty material mkts. & corp. svcs., 2001—02, exec. v.p., safety, security & protection svcs. bus., 2002—. Office: 3M Co 3M Ctr Saint Paul MN 55144

PALERMO, GREGORY SEBASTIAN, architect; b. Westfield, NY, Oct. 28, 1946; s. Sebastian and Frances Joan (Ciminella) P.;m. Olivia Madison; children: Mark Sebastian, Christopher Anthony. BArch, Carnegie Mellon U., 1969; MArch in Urban Design, Wash. U., 1976. Registered architect, Mo., Calif., N.Y., Iowa. Architect PGAV Inc., St. Louis, 1976-79; sr. v.p. HOK, Inc., St. Louis, 1980-87; sr. assoc. Mackey Assocs., St. Louis, 1987-89; v.p., prin. Stone Marraccini Patterson, St. Louis, 1989-91. Affiliate asst. prof. Washington U. Sch. Arch., 1984-90; vis. assoc. prof. Iowa State U. Dept. Arch., 1992-95, assoc. prof., 1995-2001, prof., 2001—, undergrad. program coord., 1996-98, assoc. chair undergrad. program, 1999—; chair Des Moines Archtl. Adv. Com., 1996-97; mem. Des Moines Gateway Planning Com., 1996. Mem. editl. bd. Iowa Architect mag., 1992—, assoc. ed., 1995—; mem. editl. bd. Jour. Archtl. Edn., 2001-04. Mem. Light Rail Transit Rev. Com., 1985, St. Louis Mayoral Task Force, 1986; exec/coun. Arts in Transit Com., St. Louis, 1987—; chmn. design rev. com.,St. Louis Metrolink Transit System, 1989-91; chair Nat. AIA Edn. Task Force, 1990; mem. Leadership St. Louis, 1990-91, Archtl. Adv. Commn. city of Des Moines, 1992-2000. Fellow AIA (bd. dirs., nat. v.p., pres. St. Louis chpt. 1984, pres. Iowa chpt. 2004, pres. Iowa State Faculty Senate 2006-07, Iowa Edn. award, 2007); mem. Nat. Archtl. Accreditation Bd (pres. 1993-94, Disting. Prof., 2008). Home: 2048 Pinehurst Dr Ames IA 50010-4561

PALERMO, JAMES W., artistic director; b. Cleve. BMus, MMus, Ind. U. Gen. mgr. Evansville (Ind.) Philharmonic Orch., 1989-92; orch. mgr. Louisville Orch., 1992-95; artistic and gen. dir. Grant Park Orch., Chgo., 1995—. Musician Spoleo Festival Orch., Orquesta Sinfonica Del Valle, Cali, Columbia; intern Chgo. Office Fine Arts. Active Grant Park Cultural and Ednl. Cmty., program planning com. Sherwood Conservatory, search com. Chgo. Youth Symphony Orch., 25th anniversary com. Chgo. Opera Theater. Orch. Mgmt. fellow Am. Symphony Orch. League.

PALIZZI, ANTHONY N., retired lawyer, retail corporation executive; b. Wyandotte, Mich., Oct. 27, 1942; s. Vincenzo and Nunziata (Dagostini) P.; children: A. Michael, icholas A. PhB, Wayne State U., 1964, JD, 1966; LLM, Yale U., 1967. Bar: Mich. 1967. Prof. law Fla. State U., Tallahassee, 1967-69; prof. law Tex. Tech U., Lubbock, 1969-71; atty. Kmart Corp., Troy, Mich., 1971-74, asst. sec., 1974-77, asst. gen. counsel, 1977-85, v.p., assoc. gen. counsel, 1985-91, sr. v.p., gen. counsel, 1991-92, exec. v.p., gen. counsel, 1992—2000. Editor law rev. Wayne State U., 1964-66 Chmn. Brandon Police and Fire Bd., Mich., 1982-87. Mem. ABA, Am. Corp. Counsel Assn., Mich. State Bar Assn. Roman Catholic.

PALLASCH, B. MICHAEL, lawyer, director; b. Chgo., Mar. 30, 1933; s. Bernhard Michael and Magdalena Helena (Fixari) P.; m. Josephine Catherine O'Leary, Aug. 15, 1981; children: Bernhard Michael III and Madeleine Josephine (twins). BSS, Georgetown U., 1954; JD, Harvard U., 1957; postgrad., John Marshall Law Sch., 1974. Bar: Ill. 1957, U.S. Dist. Ct. (no. dist.) Ill. 1958, U.S. Tax Ct. 1961, U.S. Ct. Claims 1961, U.S. Ct. Appeals (7th cir.) 1962. Assoc. Winston & Strawn, Chgo., 1958-66, resident mgr. br. office Paris, 1963-65, ptnr. Chgo., 1966-70, sr. capital ptnr., 1971-91; sr. ptnr. B. Michael Pallasch & Assocs., 1991—. Corp. sec. Tanis, Inc., Calumet, Mich., 1972-2000, Greenbank Engring. Corp., Dover, Del., 1976-91, C.B.P. Engring. Corp., Chgo., 1976-91, Arthur Andersen Assocs., Inc., Chgo., 1976-98, Chgo. Cutting Svcs. Corp., 1977-88, L'hotel de France of Ill., Inc., Chgo., 1980-85, Water & Effluent Screening Co., Chgo., 1988-91. Bd. dirs. Martin D'Arcy Mus. Medieval and Renaissance Art, Chgo., 1975—; bd. dirs. Katherine M. Bosch Found., 1978—; asst. sec. Hundred Club of Cook County, Chgo., 1966-73, bd. dirs., sec., 1974—. Served with USAFR, 1957-63. Decorated Knight of Merit with silver star Sacred Mil. Constantinian Order of St. George of Royal House of Bourbon of Two Sicilies, Grand Officer with gold and silver stars Sovereign Mil. Order of Temple of Jerusalem; named Youth Mayor, City of Chgo., 1950; recipient Outstanding Woodland Mgmt. Forestry award, Monroe County (Wis.) Soil and Water Conservation Dist., 1975. Mem. Ill. Bar Assn. (tax lectr. 1961), Advs. Soc., Field Mus. Natural History (life), Max McGraw Wildlife Found., English Speaking Union. Clubs: Travellers (Paris); Saddle and Cycle (Chgo.). Roman Catholic. Home: 737 W Hutchinson St Chicago IL 60613-1519 Office: 35 W Wacker Dr Ste 4700 Chicago IL 60601-1614

PALLMEYER, REBECCA RUTH, judge; b. Tokyo, Sept. 13, 1954; arrived in U.S., 1957; d. Paul Henry and Ruth (Schrieber) Pallmeyer; m. Dan P. McAdams, Aug. 20, 1977; 2 children. BA, Valparaiso U., Ind., 1976; JD, U. Ill., Chgo., 1979. Bar: Ill. 1980, U.S. Ct. Appeals (7th cir.) 1980, U.S. Ct. Appeals (11th and 5th cir.) 1982. Judge clk. Minn. Supreme Ct., St. Paul, 1979-80; assoc. Hopkins and Sutter, Chgo., 1980-85; judge, administrv. law Ill. Human Rights Commn., Chgo., 1985-91; magistrate judge U.S. Dist. Ct. (No. Dist.), Chgo., 1991-98, dist. judge, 1998—. Mem. jud. resources com. Jud. Conf. U.S., 1994—2000. Nat. adv. coun. Christ Coll., Valparaiso U., 2001—; bd. dirs. Augustana Ctr., 1990—91; mem. vis. com. U. Chgo. Div. Sch., 2006—. Recipient Profl. Achievement award, Chgo.-Kent Coll. of Law, 2002, Alumni Achievement award, Valparaiso U., 2002, President's Award for Disting. Svc., N.W. Suburban Bar Assn., 2003. Mem.: FBA (bd. mgrs. Chgo. chpt. 1995—2004), Alliance Women Chgo. Bar Assn. (exec. bd. 2007—), Chgo. Bar Assn. (chair devel. law com. 1992—93, bd. mgrs. 2004—06, David C. Hilliard award 1990—91), Fed. Magistrate Judges Assn. (bd. dirs. 1994—97), Womens Bar Assn. Ill. (bd. mgrs. 1995—98), Valparaiso U. Alumni Assn. (bd. dirs. 1992—94). Lutheran. Avocations: choral music, sewing, running. Office: US Dist Ct 219 S Dearborn St Ste 2178 Chicago IL 60604-1877 Office Phone: 312-435-5636.

PALMBERG, PAUL W., retired electronics executive; Dir. R&D, gen. mgr. Phys. Electronics, Inc. (divsn. of Perkin-Elmer), Eden Prairie, Minn.; pres., CEO Phys. Electronics, Inc., Eden Prairie, 1994-97; ret., 1997. Mem. Am. Vacuum Soc. (Gaede-Langmuir award 1998). also: Am Vacuum Soc 120 Wall St Fl 32 New York NY 10005-4001 Office: Physical Electronics Inc 18725 Lake Dr E Chanhassen MN 55317-9384

PALMER, BRADLEY BERAN, sportscaster; b. Madison, Wis., July 21, 1940; s. Robert and Cerise (Beran) P.; m. Patricia Carey, Oct. 19, 1974; two children. BS in Comms., U. Ill., 1963. Officer USN, U.S.S. Shangri-La, 1963-65; news anchor, reporter KGLO-AM/TV, Mason City, Iowa, 1965; news reporter WTVO-TV, Rockford, Ill., 1965-66; news writer, prodr. WGN-AM/TV, Chgo., 1966-68; sports dir. WBBM-AM, Chgo., 1968-85; sports anchor, reporter WLS-TV, Chgo., 1985—. Named Ill. Sportscaster of Yr., Nat. Sportscaster & Sportwriters Assn., 1980, 82, 86, 87, 88, 93, 95, 98, 02.

PALMER, BRIAN EUGENE, retired lawyer; b. Mpls., May 16, 1948; s. Eugene Philip and Virginia Breeze (Rolfshus) P.; m. Julia Washburn Morrison, Dec. 29, 1972; 1 child, Julia Hunter. AB, Brown U., 1970; JD, William Mitchell Coll. of Law, 1974. Bar: Minn. 1974, U.S. Dist. Ct. Minn. 1975, U.S. Dist. Ct. (ea. dist.) Wis. 2001, U.S. Ct. Appeals (8th cir.) 1980, U.S. Ct. Fed. Claims 1984, U.S. Supreme Ct. 1980. Asst. pub. defender Hennepin County Pub. Defender, Mpls., 1974-78; assoc. Dorsey & Whitney LLP, Mpls., 1978-82, ptnr., 1983—2004, of counsel, 2005—06, ret., 2006. Home: 1190 Lyman Ave Wayzata MN 55391-9671 Office Phone: 612-340-2797. E-mail: palmer.brian@dorsey.com.

PALMER, CARSON, professional football player; b. Fresno, Calif., Dec. 27, 1979; s. Bill and Danna Palmer; m. Shaelyn Fernandes, July 5, 2003. BA in Pub. Policy, U. So. Calif., 2002. Quarterback Cin. Bengals, 2003—. Co-founder Carson Palmer Found., 2004—. Named NFL Pro Bowl MVP, 2007; named to Am. Football Conf. Pro Bowl Team, 2005—06; recipient Heisman Meml. Trophy, Heisman Trophy Trust, 2002. Achievements include being the first overall selection in the 2003 NFL Draft. Office: c/o Cincinnati Bengals 1 Paul Brown Stadium Dr Cincinnati OH 45202

PALMER, CHARLES A., lawyer, educator; b. Jackson, Mich., Jan. 25, 1945; s. Robert E. and Gertrude (Caldwell) P.; m. Barbara Ann DiTiberio, May 10, 1975; children: Robert, Joseph, Christopher. BBA, U. Mich., 1967, JD, 1970. Bar: Mich. 1970, U.S. Dist. Ct. (we. and ea. dists.) Mich. 1970, U.S. Tax Ct., U.S. Ct. Appeals (6th cir.). Jud. clk. Ingham County Cir. Ct., Lansing, Mich., 1971; assoc. Cummins, Butter & Thorburn, Lansing, 1971-72; prin. Charles A. Palmer, P.C., Lansing, 1973-88; prof. law Thomas M. Cooley Law Sch., Lansing, 1988—. Mayor, JAG, Mich. N.G., Jackson, 1978—; chmn. bd. dirs. Ind. Bank of South Mich., Leslie, 1989—. Pres. Legal Aid of Cen. Mich., Lansing. Mem. ABA, Mich. Bar Assn., Ingham County Bar Assn. Office: Independent Bank Corp 230 W Main St PO Box 491 Ionia MI 48846

PALMER, CRUISE, newspaper editor; b. Kansas City, Kans., Apr. 9, 1917; s. Thomas Potter and Margaret Scroggs (McFadden) P.; m. Dorraine Humphreys, Sept. 7, 1946; children: Thomas Cruise, Martha D. Sprague. BS in Journalism, Kans. State U., 1938. With Kansas City (Mo.) Star, 1938—, news editor, 1963-64, mng. editor, 1965-66; exec. editor, bd. dirs. Star and Times, 1967—78, cons., 1978—. Bd. dirs. Purtec Systems, Inc. Author: Bosses of the News Room, 1927-2006, 2003. Mem. bd. govs. Am. Royal Live Stock and Horse Show Assn., 1967-91; bd. dirs. ARC, 1978-91, Kansas City Mayor's Corps Progress, 1978-91; found. trustee Kans. State U.; trustee Kansas City Sister Cities Commn., 1978-91. Served to lt. (j.g.) USNR, 1943-46. Recipient Distinguished Service award Kans. State U., 1967; First Place award Pro-Am. Southgate Open Golf Tournament, 1973; Second Place award Pro-Am. Hawaiian Open, 1973, 85; Third Place, 1981; First Place award Jim Colbert Celebrity Tournament, 1981, First Place Team award Kansas City area Am. Cancer Soc. Golf Tournament, 1986. Mem. Am. Soc. Newspaper Editors, Soc. Profl. Journalists, Kansas City Sr. Golf Assn., Kansas City Press Club (pres. 1953-54, 64-65, permanent trustee, pres. scholarship found. 1989), Kansas City Club, Chiefs Red Coat Club, Milburn Golf and Country Club, Beta Theta Pi (Greater Kansas City Beta of Yr. 1980). Episcopalian (former vestryman and lay reader). Home: Lakeview Retirement Village 14100 W 90th Ter Apt 504 Lenexa KS 66215-5430 Office: 1729 Grand Ave Kansas City MO 64108-1413

PALMER, DAVE RICHARD, retired military officer, academic administrator; b. Ada, Okla., May 31, 1934; s. David Furman and Lorena Marie (Clardy) P.; m. LuDelia Clemmer, Apr. 13, 1957; children: Allison, J. Kersten. BS, U.S. Military Acad., 1956; MA in History, Duke U., 1966; postgrad., Army War Coll., 1972-73; PhD (hon.), Duke U., 1990. Commd. U.S. Army, 1956, advanced through grades to lt. gen.; mem. faculty dept. history U.S. Mil. Acad., 1966-69; mem. staff (Pentagon), 1973-76, Joint Chiefs of Staff, 1979-81; comdr. Baumholder Mil. Community, W. Ger., 1981-83; dep. comdt. Command and Gen. Staff Coll., Ft. Leavenworth, Kans., 1983-85; comdg. gen. 1st Armored Div., W.Ger., 1985-86; supt. U.S. Mil. Acad., 1986-91, ret., 1991; pres. Walden U., 1995-99; CEO Walden Corp., 1999-2000. Author: The River and the Rock, 1969, The Way of the Fox, 1975, Summons of the Trumpet, 1978, 1794-America, Its Army, and The Birth of the ation, 1994, First in War, 2000, Provide for the Common Defense, 2001, Washington and Arnold, 2006. Bd. dirs. Walden U., 1992-2001. Decorated Legion of Merit (3); Bronze Star (2), D.S.M.(2); named Disting. Grad., U.S. Mil. Acad., 2005. Mem. Assn. U.S. Army, Armor Assn., Mil. History, Soc. Cin. Office Phone: 254-933-0554. Personal E-mail: davepalmer@clearwire.net.

PALMER, DEBORAH JEAN, lawyer; b. Williston, ND, Oct. 25, 1947; d. Everett Edwin and Doris Irene (Harberg) P.; m. Kenneth L. Rich, Mar. 29, 1980; children: Andrew, Stephanie. BA, Carleton Coll., 1969; JD cum laude, Northwestern U., 1973. Bar: Minn. 1973, U.S. Dist. Ct. Minn. 1973, U.S. Ct. Appeals (8th cir.) 1975, U.S. Supreme Ct. 1978, U.S. Ct. Appeals (11th cir.) 1999. Econ. analyst Harris Trust & Savs. Bank, Chgo., 1969-70; assoc. Robins, Kaplan, Miller & Ciresi LLP, Mpls., 1973-79, ptnr., 1979—. Trustee Carleton Coll., 1984-88; mem. bd. religious edn. Plymouth Congl. Ch., 1992-95; bd. dirs. Mpls. YWCA, 1996-99; mem. Dist. Minn. Civil Justice Reform Act Adv. Group, 1990-93; bd. dirs. RKM&C Found. Edn., Pub. Health & Social Justice, 1999—. Mem. ABA, Minn. Bar Assn., Minn. Women Lawyers Assn. (sec. 1976-78), Minn. Fed. Bar Assn. (chpt. bd. dirs. 1996-98), Hennepin County Bar Assn., Hennepin County Bar Found. (bd. dirs. 1978-81), Carleton Coll. Alumni Assn. (bd. dirs. 1978-82, sec. 1980-82), Women's Assn. of Minn. Orch. (bd. dirs. 1980-85, treas. 1981-83). Home: 1787 Colfax Ave S Minneapolis MN 55403-3008 E-mail: djpalmer@rkmc.com.

PALMER, DENNIS DALE, lawyer; b. Alliance, Nebr., Apr. 30, 1945; s. Vernon D. Palmer and Marie E. (Nelson) Fellers; m. Rebecca Ann Turner, Mar. 23, 1979; children: Lisa Marie, Jonathan Paul. BA, U. Mo., 1967, JD, 1970. Bar: Mo. 1970, U.S. Dist. Ct. (we. dist.) Mo. 1970, U.S. Ct. Appeals (8th and 10th cirs.) 1973, U.S. Supreme Ct. 1980. Staff atty. Legal Aid Soc. Western Mo., Kansas City, 1970-73; assoc. Shughart, Thomson & Kilroy, P.C., Kansas City, 1973-76, ptnr., bd. dirs., 1976—. Contbr. articles on franchise and employment law to legal jours. Bd. dirs., chmn. legal assts. adv. bd. Avila Coll., Kansas City, 1984-87. 2d lt. U.S. Army, 1970. Mem. ABA (litigation com. 1980, forum com. on franchising 1987), Mo. Bar Assn. (antitrust com. 1975—, civil practice com. 1975—), Kansas City Bar Assn. (chmn. franchise law com. 1987—), Univ. Club. Avocations: jogging, golf, tennis, outdoor activities, reading. Home: 13100 Canterbury Rd Leawood KS 66209-1700 Office: Shughart Thomson & Kilroy 12 Wyandotte Plz 120 W 12th St Fl 17 Kansas City MO 64105-1902

PALMER, FREDRICK D., lawyer, energy executive; b. Ariz., 1945; BA, JD, U. Ariz. CEO, gen. counsel Western Fuels Assn., Inc., Westminster, Colo., 1986—2000; counsel Shook Hardy & Bacon, Wash., DC, 2001; exec. v.p. legal & external affairs Peabody Energy, Saint Louis, Mo., 2001—05, sr. v.p. govt. rels., 2005—. Chmn. Environ. Info Council; bd. pres. Greening Earth Soc.; chmn. legal com. & climate change task force Nat. Mining Assn. Recipient Erskine Ramsay medal, Soc. for Mining, Metallurgy & Exploration, 2004. Mem.: DC Bar Assn., Calif. Bar Assn. Office: Peabody Energy 701 Market St Saint Louis MO 63101

PALMER, J. CRISMAN, lawyer; BA, SD State U., 1971; JD, U. SD, 1974. Bar: SD 1974. Ptnr. Gunderson Palmer Goodsell Nelson LLP, Rapid City, SD. Mem. SD Bd. Pardons and Parole, 1991—97, chmn., 1993—97; mem. SD Judicial Qualifications Commn., 2004—08; adj. prof. U. SD. Mem.: Am. Bd. Trial Advocates (sec.-treas. 2005—06, v.p. 2006—07), Fedn. Def. and Corp. Counsel, Def. Rsch. Inst., SD Coun. Sch. Attys., SD Def. Lawyers Assn. (bd. dirs. 1995—98, sec. 1998), SD Trial Lawyers Assn., State Bar SD (commr. 1983—86, mem. disciplinary bd. 1996—2002, pres. 2006—07), ABA, Pennington County Bar Assn. (pres. 1985). Office: Gunderson Palmer Goodsell & Nelson LLP PO Box 8045 Rapid City SD 57709-8045

PALMER, JAMES F., aerospace transportation executive; BS, Southeast Mo. State, 1971. Sr. v.p., CFO McDonnell Douglas Corp., 1995—97; pres., Boeing Shared Services Group The Boeing Co., 1997—2000, sr. v.p.; pres. Boeing Capital Corp., 2000—04; exec. v.p., CFO Visteon Corp., 2004—07; corp. v.p., CFO Northrop Grumman Corp., LA, 2007—. Office: Northrop Grumman Corp 1840 Century Park E Los Angeles CA 90067-2199 Office Phone: 734-710-2020.

PALMER, JOHN BERNARD, III, lawyer; b. Ft. Wayne, Ind., May 18, 1952; s. John Bernard and Dorothy Alma (Lauer) P. BA, Mich. State U., 1974; JD, U. Mich., 1977. Bar: Ill. 1977, US Dist. Ct. (no. dist.) Ill. 1977, US Ct. Appeals 2002, US Tax Ct. 1979, US Ct. Claims 2001. Assoc. Mayer Brown & Platt, Chgo., 1977-80, Hopkins & Sutter, Chgo., 1980-83, ptnr., 1983-2001, Foley & Lardner LLP, Chgo., 2001—, chmn. taxation practice group. Adj. prof. Ill. Inst. Tech.-Kent Coll. of Law, Chgo., 1984—. Mem. ABA (tax sect.). Office: Foley & Lardner LLP 321 N Clark St Chicago IL 60610 Office Phone: 312-832-4575. Business E-Mail: jpalmer@foley.com.

PALMER, PATRICK EDWARD, radio astronomer, educator; b. St. Johns, Mich., Dec. 6, 1940; s. Don Edward and Nina Louise (Kyes) P.; m. Joan Claire Merlin, June 9, 1963; children: Laura Katherine, Aidan Edward, David Elijah. SB, U. Chgo., 1963; MA, Harvard U., 1965, PhD, 1968. Radio astronomer Harvard U., Cambridge, Mass., 1968; asst. prof. astronomy and astrophysics U. Chgo., 1968-70, assoc. prof., 1970-75, prof., 1975—2006, prof. emeritus, 2006—. Vis. assoc. prof. astronomy Calif. Inst. Tech., Pasadena, 1972; vis. radio astronomer Cambridge (Eng.) U., 1973; vis. rsch. astronomer U. Calif., Berkeley, 1977, 86; vis. scientist Nat. Radio Astronomer Obs., 1980-2006. Contbr. articles on radio astron. investigations of comets and interstellar medium to tech. jours. Recipient Bart J. Bok prize for contbns. to galactic astronomy, 1969, Alfred P. Sloan Found. fellow, 1970-72, Helen B. Warner prize, 1975. Fellow AAAS (chmn. sect. D astronomy 1984); mem. AAUP, Am. Astron. Soc. (chmn. nominating com. 1981, mem. publs. bd. 1985-86, mem. Warner Prize selection com. 1977-78), Royal Astron. Soc., Internat. Astron. Union, U. Chgo. Track Club. Home: 5549 S Dorchester Ave Chicago IL 60637-1720 Office: Univ Chgo Astronomy & Astrophysics Ctr 5640 S Ellis Ave Chicago IL 60637-1433 Home Phone: 773-955-2223; Office Phone: 773-702-7972. E-mail: ppalmer@oskar.uchicago.edu.

PALMER, RAYMOND ALFRED, administrator, librarian, consultant; b. Louisville, May 8, 1939; BA in Biology, U. Louisville, 1961; MLS, U. Ky., 1966. Adminstrv. asst. Johns Hopkins Med. Libr., Balt., 1966-69; asst. librarian Harvard Med. Libr., Boston, 1969-74; health scis. librarian Wright State U., Dayton, Ohio, 1974-82, assoc. prof. library adminstrn., 1974-82; exec. dir. Med. Libr. Assn., Chgo., 1982-92, Am. Assn. Immunologists, Bethesda, Md., 1992-95; dir. info.-edn. svcs. Nat. Ctr. Edn. Maternal-Child Health Georgetown U., Arlington, Va., 1995-97—. Cons. Acad. Mil. Med. Scis. Libr., Beijing, 1990, Alzheimer's Assn., Chgo., 1991. Author: Management of Library Associations; mng. editor: Jour. Immunology, 1992-95; contbr. articles to profl. jours. Mem. ALA, Am. Soc. Assn. Execs., Greater Washington Soc. Assn. Execs., Spl. Librs. Assn., Biomed. Communication Network (chmn. 1980-82), Am. Mgmt. Assn. (strategic planning adv. coun. 1987-91), Coun. Biology Editors, Friends of Nat. Libr. Medicine (bd. dirs. 1989-92, 94-97), Internat. Fedn. Libr. Assns. and Instns. (exec. com. Round Table for Mgmt. of Libr. Orgns. 1989-92), Med. Libr. Assn. E-mail: rap539@aol.com.

PALMER, ROBERT ERWIN, association executive; b. Texarkana, Ark., Feb. 6, 1934; s. Burgess Prince and Ruth (Erwin) P. BJ, U. Tex., 1961. Reporter Texarkana Gazette, 1961; editor Southwestern Bell Telephone, Houston, 1961, info. specialist St. Louis, 1961-63; editor Shell Oil Co., Houston and Chgo., head office pub. relations NYC; dir. pub. relations Nat. PTA, Chgo., 1969-74; program dir. Nat. Assn. Realtors, Chgo., 1974-76; corp. communications mgr. The Milw. Rd., Chgo., 1976-78; staff v.p. Soc. Real Estate Appraisers, Chgo., 1978-83, exec. v.p., 1983-90; sr. v.p. communications, 1991—; co. exec., v.p. Appraisal Inst., Chgo., 1992-93, v.p. mem. svcs., 1993-98. Bd. dirs. Tower Advt., Chgo., Costumes Unltd. ltd., Chgo. Founding mem. Chgo. Crime Commn., 1967. Served to staff sgt. USAF, 1953-57. Recipient Award of Merit, Chgo. Internat. Film Festival, 1970, 71, Spl. Corrs. Pring Feature award, 1971, 72, Golden Trumpet award Realtor Week promotion, 1975, Golden Trumpet award Pvt. Property Week promotion, 1977, Golden Trumpet award Realtor bicentennial program, 1977, Gold Circle award Chpt.-by-Chpt. program, 1982. Mem. Pub. Relations Soc. Am., Am. Soc. Assn. Execs., Sigma Delta Chi. Clubs: Chgo. Headline. Methodist.

PALMER, ROGER RAYMOND, finance educator; b. NYC, Dec. 31, 1926; s. Archibald and Sophie (Jarnow) P.; m. Martha West Hopkins, June 7, 1986; children by previous marriage: Kathryn Sue, Daniel Stephen, Susan Jo. BS, U. Wis., 1949; MBA, Cornell U., 1951; postgrad., NYU, 1951-54. Auditor, Ernst and Ernst, CPA's, NYC, 1953-54; auditor Gen. Dynamics Corp., 1956-60; mgr. corp. audits Tex. Instruments, 1960-64; auditor 1st Nat. Bank, St. Paul, 1964-68, v.p. planning, 1968-69, v.p., comptr., 1969-75, sr. v.p., contr., 1975-82; chmn. dept. fin. Coll. of St. Thomas (now U. St. Thomas), St. Paul, 1996—; prof. emeritus U. St. Thomas, 2005—. Dir. First Met. Travel, Inc.; guest lectr. U. Minn., 1966; conf. leader, speaker, 1959— Contbr. articles to publs. Bd. dir. Waterford (Conn.) Civic Assn., 1959-60, Friends of St. Paul Pub. Library, 1967, Mpls. Citizens League; chmn. bd. dirs. Film in the Cities, 1983-85; mem. acctg. adv. council U. Minn.; trustee, chmn. fin. com. Hazelton Found. With U.S. Maritime Svc., 1945-47; with U.S. Army, 1954-56. Mem. Inst. Internal Auditors (pres. So. New Eng chpt. 1957-60, edn. chmn. Dallas 1961, Twin City chpt. 1965-66), Nat. Assn. Accts. (dir. Norwich, Conn. chpt. 1958-60), Nat. Assn. Accountants (St. Paul chpt. 1967), Assn. Bank Audit, Control and Operation, Am. Inst. Banking, Fin. Execs. Inst., Planning Forum (pres. Twin Cities chpt. 1984-85), Univ. Club (St. Paul). Clubs: St. Paul Athletic. Home: 415 Oak Ridge Dr San Marcos TX 78666 Business E-Mail: rrpalmer@stthomas.edu.

PALMISANO, DONALD J., surgeon, medical educator; b. New Orleans, 1939; m. Robin Palmisano; 3 children. MD, Tulane U., 1963; JD, Loyola U., 1982. Diplomate Am. Bd. Surgery; bar: La. Intern Charity Hosp., New Orleans, 1963-64, resident in surgery, 1964-68, Lallie Kemp Charity Hosp., Independence, 1967-68; pvt. practice; clin. prof. surgery, clin. prof. med. jurisprudence Tulane U.; pres. Intrepid Resources. Mem. Gov.'s Commn. on organ donations; chair La. Med. Disclosure Panel; founding mem. La. Med. Mutual Ins. Co.; lectr. in field; commr. Joint Com. on Accreditation of Healthcare Organizations, 1999-. Contbr. articles to profl. publs. With USAF. Named one of top doctors in New Orleans, 2001; recipient Air Force Commendation medal. Fellow ACS, AMSUS, SAFCS; mem. AMA (bd. trustees 1996-2004, chair devel. com., Physician Outreach awards, exec com. mem. 1999-, sec-treas. 2001, pres-elect 2002, pres. bd trustees 2003-04), La. State Med. Soc. (pres. 1984-85); bd. dirs. Nat. Patient Safety Found., Nat. Advisory Council, Annenberg Ctr. Health Sci. Avocation: photography. Office: AMA 515 N State St Chicago IL 60610-4325

PALMORE, RICK (RODERICK A. PALMORE), consumer products company executive, lawyer; b. Pitts., Feb. 14, 1952; s. Jefferson and Sophie (Spencer) Palmore; m. Lynne Avril Janifer, June 3, 1978; children: Jordan, Adam. BA in Econs., Yale U., 1974; JD, U. Chgo., 1977. Bar: Pa. 1977, Ill. 1982. Assoc. atty. Berkman, Ruslander, Pohl, Lieber & Engel, Pitts., 1977-79; asst. US atty. (no. dist.) Ill. US Dept. Justice, Chgo., 1979-82; assoc. atty. Wildman, Harrold, Allen & Dixon, Chgo., 1982-86, ptnr., 1986-93, Sonnenschein, Nath & Rosenthal, Chgo., 1993-96; v.p., dep. gen. counsel Sara Lee Corp., Chgo., 1996-99, sr. v.p., gen. counsel, sec., 1999—2004, exec. v.p., gen. counsel, sec., 2004—08; exec. v.p., gen. counsel, chief compliance & risk mgmt. officer Gen. Mills, Inc., Mpls., 2008—. Commr. Oak Park Plan Commn., 1988—, chair, 1994—; lectr. Youth Motivation Prog. Chgo. Coun. Commerce & Industry, 1989—; chair Oak Pk. Pub. Art Adv. Com., 2002—; bd. dirs. Pub. Interest Law Initiative, Legal Assistance Found. Chgo., Chgo. Bd. Options Exch., 2002—,

Nuveen Investments, 2003—, United Way Met. Chgo., 2003-07; trustee Chgo. Symphony Orch., 2006—. Named one of Outstanding African-Am. Businessmen, Dollars & Sense mag., Chgo., 1991, The 50 Most Influential Gen. Counsels, Inside Counsel, 2006; recipient ACC Excellence in Corp. Practice award, 2003, MCCA Employers of Choice award ACC Diversity award, 2005, Equal Justice Works Acales of Justice award, 2005, ABA Spirit of Excellence award, 2006, Corp. Exemplar award Nat. Legal Aid & Defender Assn., 2007 Mem. ABA (monirity ptnrs. conf. 1991—), Nat. Bar Assn., Cook County Bar Assn., Chgo. Bar Assn. (bd. dirs. 1992-94, co-chmn. minority clerkshop prog. 1991-92), Chgo. Com. on Minorities in Law Firms (bd. dirs. 1990-92), Chgo. Bar Found. (bd. dirs. 1993-94). Mem. Trinity United Ch. Of Christ. Avocations: running, biking, tennis, reading. Office: General Mills Inc 1 General Mills Blvd Minneapolis MN 55426*

PALMORE, RODERICK A. See PALMORE, RICK

PALMQUIST, MARK L., energy and food products executive; Grad., Gustavus Adolphus Coll., St. Peter, Minn., 1979; student, U. Minn. Grain buyer Harvest States, Inver Grove Heights, Minn., 1979, v.p., dir. grain mktg. divsn., 1990-93, sr. v.p., 1993; exec. v.p., COO Ag. Bus. CHS Inc. (merger of Cenex and Harvest States), Inver Grove Heights, Minn., 2005—. Bd. dirs. Agriliance LLC, Ventura Foods, LLC, InTrade, Nat. Coop. Refinery Assn., Schnitzer Steel Industries, Inc., Portland, Oreg. Office: CHS Inc PO Box 64089 Saint Paul MN 55164-0089 Office Phone: 651-355-6000.

PALO, NICHOLAS EDWIN, professional society administrator; b. Waukegan, Ill., Nov. 18, 1945; s. Edwin Arnold and Eevi Kustaava (Hukkala) P.; m. Lauren M. Reynolds, Aug. 18, 1990 (dec.). BA, U. Wis., Eau Claire, 1971; MS, U. Mo., 1975. Instr., coordinator U. Mo. Extension, Columbia, 1974-85; exec. officer Am. Bd. Profl. Psychology, Columbia, 1984—. Pres. Columbia Community Band, 1987; chmn. Arts Resources Coun., Columbia, 1988; adv. bd. Columbia Art League. Mem. Am. Soc. Assn. Execs., Psychology Execs. Roundtable, Intertel, Mensa, Windjammers Unltd. Club, Am. Assn. Concert Bands Club, Internat. Trombone Assn., .Am. Brass Band Assn., Phi Delta Kappa (hon.), Phi Mu Alpha (hon.). Democrat. Lutheran. Avocation: music. Home: 608 Spring Valley Rd Columbia MO 65203-2261

PALUMBO, MICHAEL, investment company executive; b. 1966; Ptnr. Third Millenium Investment Firm, Chgo., 1996—. Named one of Top 100 Fin. Traders in the World, Trader Monthly, 2004, 40 Under Forty, Crain's Bus. Chgo., 2005.

PAMPUSCH, ANITA MARIE, foundation administrator; b. St. Paul, Aug. 28, 1938; d. Robert William and Lucille Elizabeth (Whaley) P. BA, Coll. of St. Catherine, St. Paul, 1962; MA, U. Notre Dame, 1970, PhD, 1972. Tchr. St. Joseph's Acad., St. Paul, 1962-66; instr. philosophy Coll. of St. Catherine, St. Paul, 1970-76, assoc. acad. dean, 1979, acad. dean, 1979-84, pres., 1984-97; Am. Council Edn. fellow Goucher Coll., Balt., 1976-77; pres. Bush Found., St. Paul, 1997—. Bd. dirs. St. Paul Cos.; head Women's Coll. Coalition, 1988-91. Author: (book rev.) Philological Quarterly, 1976; contbr. articles to profl. jours. Mem. adv. com. Instl. Leadership project, Columbia U., 1986—; dist. chmn. Rhodes Scholarship Selection com., Mo., Neb., Minn., Kans., N.D., S.D., 1987—; exec. com. Women's Coll. Coalition, Washington, 1985—. Mem. Coun. for Ind. Colls. (bd. dirs. 1987—, chair 1991—), Am. Philos. Assn., St. Paul C. of C. (bd. dirs. 1986—), St. Paul's Athletic Club, Mpls. Club, Phi Beta Kappa. Roman Catholic. Avocations: swimming, camping, reading, music. Home: 161 Stonebridge Rd Saint Paul MN 55118

PANICH, DANUTA BEMBENISTA, lawyer; b. East Chicago, Ind., Apr. 9, 1954; d. Fred and Ann Stephanie (Grabowski) B.; m. Nikola Panich, July 30, 1977; children: Jennifer Anne, Michael Alexei. AB, Ind. U., 1975, JD, 1978. Bar: Ill. 1978, U.S. Dist. Ct. (no. dist.) Ill. 1978, U.S. Dist. Ct. (ctrl. dist.) Ill. 1987, U.S. Ct. Appeals (7th cir.) 1987, U.S. Dist. Ct. (no. dist.) Ind. 2001, U.S. Dist. Ct. (ea. dist.) Mich. 2003, U.S. Ct. Appeals (6th cir.) 2003, U.S. Dist. Ct. (so. dist.) Ill., 2004. Assoc. Mayer Brown & Platt, Chgo., 1978-86, ptnr., 1986—2001, Mayer Brown Rowe & Maw, LLP, Chgo., 2002—. Bd. dirs. Munster (Ind.) Med. Rsch. Found., 1990—, Pub. Interest Law Initiative, 2003—. Mem. ABA, Fed. Bar Assn., Ill. Bar Assn. Republican. Roman Catholic. Office: Mayer Brown Rowe & Maw LLP 71 S Wacker Dr Chicago IL 60606 Office Phone: 312-701-7198. Business E-Mail: dpanich@mayerbrownrowe.com.

PANKAU, CAROLE, state senator; b. Aug. 13, 1947; m. Anthony John Pankau Jr.; 4 children. BS, U. Ill., 1981. Mem. Ill. House of Rep., 1993—2004, Ill. Senate from 23th dist., 2004—. Mem. DuPage County (Ill.) Bd., 1984-92; committeeman Bloomingdale Twp. Rep. Precinct 70; mem. Keeneyville (Ill.) Sch. Dist. 20; vice chair Bloomingdale Twp. Rep. Orgn. also: One Tiffany Pointe Bloomingdale IL 60108 Office: 105-K State House Springfield IL 62706 E-mail: carole@pankau.org.

PANKO, JESSIE SYMINGTON, education educator; b. Jan. 19, 1935; Student, Hunter Coll., NYC, 1959-62; BA, MS, SUNY, 1969; PhD, Syracuse U., 1974. Tchr. Anderson Elem. Sch., Mariana Islands, Guam, 1964-65; tchr. Herman Ave. Elem. Sch., Auburn, NY, 1969-71; asst. prof. edn. dept. SUNY, Cortland, NY, 1971-76, Utica, Rome, Y, 1974-76; asst. prof. applied scis. dept. Loop Coll., Chgo., 1976-77; assoc. prof. social scis. dept. Truman Coll., Chgo., 1977-81; dir. student teaching St. Xavier Coll., Chgo., 1976—94, dir. undergrad. edn., 1977-79, dir. grad. edn., 1979-81, prof. edn. ctr., 1981-83, dir. grad. prog. in edn., 1983-86, dir. edn. ctr., 1986-89, dean sch. edn., 1989-92. Bd. dirs. Queen of Peace, Acad. of Our Lady; mem. com. grad. programs St. Xavier Coll., 1986-89, tchr. edn. coun., 1976-94, early childhood adv. bd., 1976-92. Moffett SUNY scholar, 1969. Mem. AAUP, ASCD, Am. Assn. Colls. of Tchr. Edn. (instnl. rep. 1987-92), Assn. Ind. Liberal Arts Colls. of Tchr. Edn. (instl. rep. 1986-92), Ill. Assn. of Tchr. Edn. in Pvt. Colls. (instnl. rep. 1985-98), Ill. Assn. Colls. Tchr. Edn. (coll. rep. 1981-98, sec. 1990-92), Assn. Tchr. Educators, Nat. Assn. Educatos Young Children, Ill. Dirs. Student Tchg., Chgo. Consortium Dirs. Student Tchg. (chairperson 1976-79), Ill. Assn. Tchr. Educators, Chgo. Area Dir. Student Tchg. (chmn. 2002-04), Pi Lambda Theta, Kappa Delta Pi. Office: St Xavier U 3700 W 103rd St Chicago IL 60655-3105 Office Phone: 773-298-3215. Business E-Mail: panko@sxu.edu.

PANKRATZ, TODD ALAN, obstetrician, gynecologist; b. Henderson, NC, Dec. 10, 1965; MD, U. Nebr. Coll. Medicine, 1992. Diplomate Am. Bd. Obstetrics and Gynecology. Intern Truman Med. Ctr., Kansas City, Mo., 1992—96; staff Mercy Hosp., Iowa City, 1996—98, Mary Lanning Hosp., Hastings, Nebr., 1998; pvt. practice in ob-gyn. Obstetrics and Gynecologists, PC, Hastings, Nebr. Recipient Excellence in Medicine Leadership award, AMA Found., 2004. Mem.: AMA (state del. Young Physicians Section), Nebr. Med. Soc. Office: Obstetrics and Gynecology PC 2115 N Kansas Ave Ste 204 Hastings NE 68901 Office Phone: 402-463-6793. Office Fax: 402-463-6894.

PANZER, MARY E., state legislator; b. Waupun, Wis., Sept. 19, 1951; d. Frank E. and Verna L. P.; 1 adopted child, Melissa. BA, U. Wis., 1974; mem., Wis. State Ho. Reps. from 53rd dist. Rep. State of Wis., Madison, 1980-93; mem. Wis. Senate from 20th dist., Madison, 1993—. Home: 635 W Tamarack Dr West Bend WI 53095-3653

PAPAI, BEVERLY DAFFERN, retired library director; b. Amarillo, Tex., Aug. 31, 1949; d. Clarence Wilbur and Dora Mae (Henderson) Daffern; m. Joseph Andrew Papai, Apr. 3, 1976. BS in Polit. Sci., West Tex. State U., Canyon, 1972; MSLS, Wayne State U., 1973. Head extension dept. and Oakland County Subregional Libr. The Farmington Cmty. Libr., Farmington Hills, Mich., 1973-79, coord. adult svcs., br. head, 1980-83, asst. dir., 1983-85, dir., 1985—2005; ret., 2005. Cons. U.S. Office of Edn., 1978, Battelle Meml. Inst., Columbus, Ohio, 1980; presenter in field; libr. cons. 2005-. Contbr. articles to profl. jours. Bd. dirs. Mich. Consortium, 1987-91; bd. dirs. Oakland Literacy Coun., 1998—, vice chair, 2000-01, chair, 2001—; trustee Libr. of Mich., 1989-92, vice chair, 1991, 97-98, chair, 1992; del. White House Conf. on Librs. and Info. Svcs., 1991; founder, treas., fiscal agt. METRO NET Libr. Consortium, 1993—; mem. edn. com. Child Abuse and Neglect Coun. of Oakland County, 1998-2000; mem. Commn. on Children, Youth and Families, 1996—, Multiracial Cmty. Coun., 1995—; chair Edn. and Tng. Com., 2000—04. Recipient Athena award Farmington/Farmington Hills C. of C. and Gen. Motors, 1994, Chairperson's Rainbow award, 2001, Spl. Recognition award Oakland County, 2004; Amarillo Pub. Libr. Friends Group fellow, 1972, Wayne State U. Inst. Gerontology fellow, 1972. Mem. ALA (officer), Mich. Libr. Assn. (chair specialized libr. svcs. roundtable 1975, chair conf. program 1982, chair pub. policy com. 1988-89, chair devel. com. 1994-95, chair ann. conf. and program coms. 1995-96, pres. 1996-97, Loleta D. Fyan award 1975, Libr. of Yr. award 2004), LWV of Mich., Farmington Exch. Club, Coun. on Resource Devel. Democrat. Roman Catholic. Home: 6805 Wing Lake Rd Bloomfield Hills MI 48301-2959 Personal E-mail: papaibev@farmlib.org.

PAPAZIAN, DENNIS RICHARD, retired historian, educator, commentator; b. Augusta, Ga., Dec. 15, 1931; s. Nahabed Charles and Armanouhe Marie (Pehlevanian) P.; m. Mary Arshagouni. BA, Wayne State U., 1954; MA, U. Mich., 1958; NDG, Moscow State U., 1962; PhD, U. Mich., 1966. Head dept. social and behavioral scis. U. Mich., Dearborn, 1966-69, head div. lit., sci. and the arts, 1969-73, assoc. dean acad. affairs, 1973-74, dir. grad. studies, 1979-85, prof. history, dir. Armenian Rsch. Ctr., 1985—2006, prof., dir. emeritus, 2006—; dir. Armenian Assembly Am., Washington, 1975-79. Fellow Ctr. for Russian and East-European Studies, U. Mich., Ann Arbor, 1982-92; chmn. bd. dirs. Mich. Ethnic Heritage Studies Ctr., U. Mich., 1987-92. Author: St. John's Armenian Church, 1974; editor: The Armenian Church, 1983, Out of Turkey, 1994; editor Jour. of Soc. Armenian Studies, 1994—. Bd. dirs. Armenian Apostolic Soc., Southfield, Mich., 1968-78; chmn. bd. dirs. Alex Manoogian Found., Taylor, Mich., 1969-77; mem. evaluation team Ind. Schs. Assn. Ctrl. States, Chgo., 1985; polit. commentator WXYZ-TV, ABC, Detroit, Southfield, 1984—, WWJ-Radio, Detroit, 1984—; bd. dirs. Southeastern Mich. chpt. ARC, 1988-98, chmn. internat. svcs. com., 1988-98, disaster and mil. family svcs. com., 1988-98; mem. NJ Commn. on Holocaust Edn., 2005—. Scholar/diplomat U.S. Dept. State, Washington, 1976; grantee NEH, Washington, 1977, AID, Washington, 1978. Mem. AAUP (chpt. pres. 1962-65), Nat. Assn. Armenian Studies and Rsch. (bd. dirs. 1961-91), Nat. Ethnic Studies Assn. (bd. dirs. 1976-85), Am. Hist. Assn., Soc. Armenian Studies (pres. exec. com. 1988-91, 97—, sec./treas. exec. com. 1991-97), Am. Assn. Advancement of Slavic Studies, Am. Acad. Polit. Sci., Armenian Students Assn. (Arthur S. Dadian Armenian Heritage award 1993), Knights of Vartan. Armenian Orthodox. Avocations: reading, travel. Home: 9 Blueberry Dr Woodcliff Lake NJ 07677 Office: U Mich 4901 Evergreen Rd Dearborn MI 48128-1491 Office Phone: 313-593-5181. Business E-Mail: papazian@umich.edu.

PAPPAGEORGE, JOHN, state official; b. Detroit, July 19, 1931; married; 3 children. BS, U.S. Mil. Acad., 1954; MA, U. Md., 1971; postgrad., U.S. Army War Coll., 1972-73. Active Oakland County Bd. Commrs., 1989-93; Rep. candidate U.S. House, 1992, 96. With U.S. Army, 1954-84. Greek Orthodox. Home: 6655 John R Rd Troy MI 48085-1010

PAPPANO, ROBERT DANIEL, financial company executive; b. Chgo., Apr. 8, 1942; s. John Robert and Lucille Carmelita (Metallo) P.; m. Karen Marie Muellner, July 2, 1966; children: John, Kimberly, Robert, William. BS in Commerce, DePaul U., Chgo., 1964; MBA, Roosevelt U., Chgo., 1982. CPA, Ill. Audit supr. Alexander Grant & Co., Chgo., 1964-73; with W.W. Grainger, Inc., Lake Forest, Ill., 1973—, asst. to contr., 1973-75, contr., corp. acct., 1975-78, contr., asst. treas., 1978-84, v.p., contr., asst. treas., 1984-85, v.p., treas., asst sec., 1985-95; v.p. financial reporting and investor rels., 1995-99; v.p. fin. reporting W.W. Grainger, Inc., Lake Forest, 1999—. 1st lt. U.S. Army, 1965-67. Mem. AICPA, Ill. CPA Soc., Fin. Execs. Inst. Roman Catholic. Office: W W Grainger Inc 100 Grainger Pkwy Lake Forest IL 60045-5201

PAPPAS, GEORGE DEMETRIOS, anatomist, cell biologist, educator; b. Portland, Maine, Nov. 26, 1926; s. James and Anna (Dracopoulos) Pappatheodoros; m. Bernice Levine, Jan. 14, 1952; children: Zoe Alexandra, Clio Nicollette. BA, Bowdoin Coll., Brunswick, Maine, 1947; MS, Ohio State U., Columbus, 1948, PhD, 1952; DSc (hon.), U. Athens, Greece, 1988. Vis. investigator Rockefeller Inst., NYC, 1952-54; assoc. in anatomy Coll. Physicians and Surgeons, Columbia U., NYC, 1956-57, asst. prof. anatomy, 1957-63, assoc. prof., 1963-66; prof. anatomy Albert Einstein Coll. Medicine, Yeshiva U., NYC, 1967-77, prof. neurosci., 1974-77, vis. prof. neurosci., 1977-97; prof., head dept. anatomy and cell biology U. Ill. Coll. Medicine, Chgo., 1977-96, prof. cell biology and psychiatry, 1996—. Trustee Marine Biol. Lab., Woods Hole, Mass., 1975-81. Author: (with others) The Structure of the Eye, 1961, Growth and Maturation of the Brain, vol. IV, 1964, Nerve as a Tissue, 1966, The Thalmus, 1966, Pathology of the Nervous System, vol. 1, 1968, Structure and Function of Synapses, 1972, Methodological Approaches to the Study of Brain Maturation and Its Abnormalities, 1974, Advances in Neurology, vol.12, 1975, The Nervous System, vol. 1 The Basic Neurosciences, 1975, Cellular and Molecular Basis of Synaptic Transmission, 1988; contbr. over 250 articles to profl. jours.; former mem. editl. bd. Anatomical Record, Biol. Bull., Brain Rsch., Jour. Neurocytology, Microstructure, Neurol. Rsch. Arthritis and Rheumatism Found. fellow, 1954-56; recipient Career Devel. award Columbia U., 1964-66; Rsch. grant NIH. Fellow AAAS, NY Acad. Scis., Inst. Medicine Chgo.; mem. Am. Soc. Cell Biology (pres. 1974-75), Am. Assn. Anatomists (chmn. pub. policy com. 1981-82, Henry Gray award 2003), Assn. Anatomy Chmn. (exec. com. 1978-80, pres. 1981-82), Electron Microscopy Soc. Am. (program chmn. 1984-85), NY Soc. Electron Microscopy (pres. 1967-68), Soc. for Neurosci. (pres. Chgo. chpt. 1985-86), Harvey Soc., Internat. Brain Rsch. Orgn., Cajal Club, Sigma Xi. Achievements include patents for method inducing analgesia by implantation of cells releasing neuroactive substances. Home: Apt 512 S 680 N Lake Shore Dr Chicago IL 60611 Office: U Ill Psychiat Inst MC 912 1601 W Taylor St Chicago IL 60612-4310 Office Phone: 312-413-4562. Business E-Mail: gdpappas@uic.edu.

PAPPAS, SANDRA LEE, state senator; b. Hibbing, Minn., June 15, 1949; m. Neal Gosman, 1976; 3 children. BA, Met. State U., 1986; MPA, Harvard U., 1994. Mem. Minn. Ho. of Reps., St. Paul, 1984-90, Minn. Senate, St. Paul, 1990—. Part-time coll. instr. Mem. Dem. Farmer Labor Party. Home: 182 Prospect Blvd Saint Paul MN 55107-2136 Office: Minn State Senate 120 State Capitol 75 Martin Luther King Jr Blvd Saint Paul MN 55155-1601 Office Phone: 651-296-1802. E-mail: sen.sendra.pappas@senate.mn.

PAQUETTE, JACK KENNETH, management consultant, author, historian; b. Toledo, Ohio, Aug. 14, 1925; s. Hector J. and Nellie (McCormick) P.; m. Jane Russell, Sept. 13, 1947; children: Jan Eriksen, Mark Russell, Mary Beth, John Eric. Student, Baldwin-Wallace Coll., 1943-44, Marquette U., 1944; BA, Ohio State U., 1949, MA, 1951; postgrad., Wayne State U., 1966. Editor monthly pub. Bur. Motor Vehicles, Ohio, 1947-49; asst. city editor, copy editor Ohio State Jour., 1949-51; copywriter Owens-Ill., Inc., Toledo, 1951-53, copy chief mktg. dept., 1953-55, asst. advt. mgr. mktg. dept., 1955-59; advt. mgr. Owens-Ill., Inc. (Libbey div.), 1959-61; mgr. advt. and sales promotion Owens-Ill., Inc. (Libbey products), 1961-64, mgr. customer mktg. services glass container div., 1964-67, dir. corporate orgn. planning, 1967-69, v.p. adminstrv. div., dir. corp. relations, 1969-70, corporate v.p., dir. corp. relations, 1970-80, corp. v.p., asst. to chmn. bd., 1980-84, cons., 1984-86; pres. Paquette Enterprises, 1984—; owner The Trumpeting Angel, antiques, 1985—. Mem. adv. bd. Cresset Chem. Co., 1987—. Author: A History of Owens-Illinois Inc., (1818-1984), 1985, The Glassmakers, 1994, Blowpipes, 2002, A Boy's Journey Through the Great Depression, 2005. Bd. dirs. Toledo YMCA, 1970-74, Vis. Nurse Svc., 1970-73, Children's Svcs., Lucas County, 1973-80, Toledo coun. Boy Scouts Am., trustee, v.p. fin., 1978-84; trustee Owens Tech. Coll. Found, 1978-81; mem. Advt. Club Toledo, 1951-75, trustee, 1960-62; hon. bd. dirs. Greater Toledo area chpt. ARC, 1970—; mem. adv. bd. Mercy Hosp., Toledo, 1981-84, Mary's Adult Day Care Ctr., 1989-93, St. Anthony's Children's Ctr., 1993, Mid-Coast Hosp., Brunswick, Maine, 1998—; mem. pub. rels. com. Cath. U. Am., 1979-82; chmn. U.S. Savs. Bonds, Lucas County, 1977-79; trustee Bowling Green State U. Found., 1976-83, pres., 1980-82; mem. Nat. Commn. on a Free and Responsible Press, 1980-83; v.p. trustee, Toledo Repertoire Theatre, 1984-88; trustee Crosby Gardens, 1983-89, chmn. 1987-88; trustee Toledo Bot. Gardens, 1989-90, chmn. emeritus and hon. lifetime trustee, 1990—; mem. pres.'s coun. Toledo Mus. Art, Bowling Green State U.; trustee Riverside Hosp. Found., 1984-94, chmn. 1986-89; mem. Juvenile Justice Adv. Bd., 1986-87; advisor R.B. Hayes Presdl. Ctr., 1990-92. With USNR, 1943-46, PTO. Recipient Gold Key award Pub. Rel. News, 1970, Silver Anvil award Pub. Rel. Soc., 1971, 72; named to Toledo Clean Hall of Fame, 1983. Mem. Soc. Profl. Journalists (co-founder Columbus and Toledo chpts.), Ohio Mfrs. Assn. (v.p., trustee 1969-84), Keep Am. Beautiful, Inc. (nat. chmn., exec. com., 1978-84, chmn. emeritus, mem. nat. adv. coun. 1984—), Bus. Com. for the Arts (corp. liaison 1980-84), U.S. C. of C. (cons. affairs com. 1980-84), Western Lake Erie Hist. Soc. (life, trustee 1998-2003), USN Armed Guard Assn., Sampson WWII Navy Vets. Assn., OSU Alumni Assn. (life), Maine Maritime Mus., Toy Soldier Collectors of Am. Soc., Toledo Glass Club, Fostoria Glass Club, Toledo Press Club (founding trustee), Toledo Club, Torch Club (trustee), Rotary (Paul Harris fellow), U.S. Navy League, Am. Legion (Toledo post), Pi Sigma Alpha. Home and Office: 2355 Parliament Sq Toledo OH 43617-1256

PARAGAS, ROLANDO G., physician; b. Philippines, Apr. 15, 1935; came to U.S., 1959; s. Epifanio Y. and Ester (Guiang) P.; m. Liwayway Galvey, May 5, 1963; children: Suzanne, Richard, Esther, Dawn. AA, U. Philippines, 1953; MD, Far Eastern U., 1958. Physician pvt. practice, Burlington, Iowa, 1968—. Fellow Am. Acad. Pediatrics; mem. AMA, Assn. Philippine Physicians in Am., Iowa Med. Soc. Office: 828 N 7th St Burlington IA 52601-4921 Office Phone: 319-754-5761.

PARDUE, HARRY L., chemist, educator; b. Big Creek, W.Va., May 3, 1934; m. Mary Schultz; 1 child, Jonathan. BS, Marshall U., 1956, MS, 1957; PhD in Chemistry, U. Ill., 1961. From asst. to assoc. prof. Purdue U., West Lafayette, Ind., 1961-70, prof. chemistry, 1970—, head dept. chemistry, 1983-87. Recipient Am. Chem Soc. award in Analytical Chemistry, 1995. Mem. Am. Chem. Soc. (Chem. Instrumentation award Analytical Chem. divsn. 1982, Analytical Chemistry award 1995), Am. Assn. Clin. Chemists (award 1979, Samuel Natelson award 1982, Anachem award 1990). Achievements include research in instrumentation for chemical research, chemical kinetics. Office: Purdue U Dept Chem 1393 Brown Bldg Lafayette IN 47907-1393

PARETSKY, SARA N., writer; b. Ames, Iowa, June 8, 1947; d. David Paretsky and Mary E. Edwards; m. S. Courtenay Wright, June 19, 1976; children: Kimball Courtenay, Timothy Charles, Philip William. BA, U. Kans., 1967; MBA, PhD, U. Chgo., 1977. Mgr. Urban Rsch Ctr., Chgo., 1971-74, CNA Ins. Co., Chgo., 1977-85; writer, 1985—. Author: (novels) Indemnity Only, 1982, Deadlock, 1984 (Friends of Am. Writers award 1985), Killing Orders, 1985, Bitter Medicine, 1987, Blood Shot, 1988 (Silver Dagger award Crime Writers Assn., 1988), Burn Marks, 1990, Guardian Angel, 1992, Tunnel Vision, 1994, Ghost Country, 1998, Hard Time: A V.I. Warshawski Novel, 1999, Total Recall, 2001, Blacklist, 2003 (Gold Dagger, Brit. Crime Writers Assn.), Fire Sale, 2005 (Publishers Weekly Bestseller hardcover fiction list, 2005), also numerous articles and short stories. Pres. Sisters in Crime, Chgo., 1986-88; dir. Nat. Abortion Rights Action League Ill., 1987—; mentor Chgo. inner-city schs. Named Woman of Yr. Ms mag., NYC, 1987; recipient Mark Twain award for disting. contbns. to Midwestern lit., 1996, Lifetime Achievement award, Private Eye Writers Am., 2005, Cartier Diamond Dagger for Lifetime Achievement, Brit. Crime Writers Assn., 2005. Mem. Crime Writers Assn. (Silver Dagger award 1988), Mystery Writers Am. (v.p. 1989), Authors Guild, Chgo. Network Achievements include being the founder of two scholarships at U. Kans. Office: c/o Dominick Abel Lit Agy #1B 146 West 82nd St New York NY 10024 Business E-Mail: viwarshawski@mindspring.com.

PARHAM, ELLEN SPEIDEN, nutrition educator; b. Mitchells, Va., July 15, 1938; d. Marion Coote and Rebecca Virginia (McNiel) Speiden; m. Arthur Robert Parham, Jr., Dec. 16, 1961; children: Katharine Alma, Cordelia Alyx. BS in Nutrition, Va. Poly. Inst., 1960; PhD in Nutrition, U. Tenn., 1967; MSEd in Counseling, No. Ill. U., 1994. Registered dietitian; lic. clin. profl. counselor. Asst. prof. to prof. nutrition No. Ill. U., DeKalb, Ill., 1966—2003, coord. programs in dietetics, 1981—86, 1990—2003, coord. grad. faculty sch. family, consumer, nutrition scis., 1985-87, interim chair Sch. Applied Health Professions, 2005—06; state coord. Ill. Homeland Security Ednl. Alliance, 2006—. Cons. on nutrition various hosps., clins. and bus., Ill., 1980-88; founder, dir. Horizons Weight Control Program, DeKalb, 1983-91; founder, leader "Escaping the Tyranny of the Scale" Group, 1994—; co-chair Nutrition Coalition for Ill., 1989-90; ptnr., mgr. Blue Chicory Arts, 1986—; adj. counselor Ctr. for Counsel, Family Svc. Agy. of DeKalb County. Bd. editors Jour. Nutrition Edn., 1985-90, 97—2005, Jour. Am. Dietetic Assn., 1991-97; contbr. articles to profl. jours. Recipient Fisher award, No. Ill. U. Coll. Health and Human Svcs., 2001, Sullivan award, 2002, No. Ill. Amazing Woman award, 2006. Mem. Am. Inst. Nutrition, Soc. Nutrition Edn., Am. Dietetic Assn. (named Ill. Outstanding Dietetics Educator 2001, Excellence in Dietetics Edn. award 2001), Soc. Nutrition Edn. (treas. 1991-94, chair divsn. nutrition and weight realities 1995-96, chair jour. com. 2002—05, Weight Realities Cert. of Achievement 1999), N.Am. Assn. Study Obesity. Democrat. Avocations: painting in watercolor, gardening, reading. Business E-Mail: eparham@niu.edu.

PARINS, ROBERT JAMES, professional football team executive, judge; b. Green Bay, Wis., Aug. 23, 1918; s. Frank and Nettie (Denissen) P.; m. Elizabeth L. Carroll, Feb. 8, 1941; children: Claire, Andrée, Richard, Teresa, Lu Ann. BA, U. Wis., 1940, LLB, 1942. Bar: Wis. Supreme Ct. 1942. Pvt. practice, Green Bay, Wis., 1942-68; dist. atty. Brown County, Wis., 1949-50, cir. judge Wis., 1968-82, res. judge Wis., 1982—; pres. Green Bay Packers, Inc., 1982-90, chmn. bd., 1990-92; hon. chmn. bd., 1992-94. Mem.: Wis. State Bar Assn. Roman Catholic.

PARISEAU, PATRICIA, state legislator; b. St. Paul, Aug. 10, 1936; d. James Martin and Mary Margaret (May) Wright; m. Kenneth Edward Pariseau, July 9, 1960; children: Susan M., Douglas C., Penny A., Linda D., Barbara J., Jacqueline. RN, Ravenswood Hosp. Sch. Nursing, Chgo., 1957. Staff nurse Ravenswood Hosp., Chgo., 1957-58, St. Joseph's Hosp., St. Paul, 1958-59, Office of Drs. Roy & Hilker, St. Paul, 1959-60; aide to U.S. Senator Rudy Boschwitz, St. Paul, 1982-88; mem. Minn. Senate from 37th dist., St. Paul, 1989—2002, Minn. Senate from 36th Dist., St. Paul, 2003—. Mem. adv. bd. St. Paul chpt. ARC, 1986-88; vol., officer Minn. Ind. Rep. Com., 1972-83; bd. dirs. Ind. Sch. Dist. 192, Farmington, Minn., 1976-79. Mem. Farmington C. of C., Dakota Arts Coun., Ducks Unltd., Eagles Aux., Am. Legion Aux. (sec. Farmington chpt., v.p. Igton chpt.), Nat. Alliance Spontaneous Caucuses (v.p.), VFW Aux., So. Dakota County Sportsmen Club. Avocations: needlecrafts, knitting, drawing, painting, travel. Office: Minn Senate 117 Stat Office Bldg Saint Paul MN 55155-1232

PARISI, JOSEPH (ANTHONY), magazine editor, writer, consultant, educator; b. Duluth, Minn., Nov. 18, 1944; s. Joseph Carl Parisi and Phyllis Susan (Quaranta) Schlecht BA with honors, Coll. St. Thomas, 1966; MA, U. Chgo., 1967, PhD with honors, 1973. Asst. prof. Roosevelt U., Chgo., 1969-78; assoc. editor POETRY Mag., Chgo., 1976-83, acting editor, 1983-85, editor, 1985—2003; exec. dir. Modern Poetry Assn. (The Poetry Found.), 1995—2003. Vis. prof. U. Ill., Chgo., 1978-87; cons., writer ALA, Chgo., 1980—; cons. NEH, 1983—. Author: The Poetry Anthology, 1912-1977, 1978, Voices and Visions Reader's Guide, 1987, Marianne Moore: The Art of a Modernist, 1990, (listener's guide) Poets in Person, 1992, 97, Dear Editor: A History of Poetry in Letters, 2002, The Poetry Anthology, 1912-2002, 2002; contbr. articles and reviews to profl. jours.; producer, dir. (audio series on NPR) Poets in Person, 1991. Recipient Alvin Bentley award, Duns Scotus Coll., 1963; fellow, U. Chgo., 1966—69, Guggenheim, 2000, Churchill Coll., Cambridge, 2001. Mem. Arts Club of Chgo., Cliff Dwellers Club, Delta Epsilon Sigma Avocations: piano, photography, book collecting. Office: Poetry Mag 60 W Walton St Chicago IL 60610-7324

PARIZEK, ELDON JOSEPH, geologist, educator, dean; b. Iowa City, Apr. 30, 1920; s. William Joseph and Libbie S. P.; m. Mildred Marie Burger, Aug. 9, 1944; children: Richard, Marianne, Elizabeth, Amy. BS, U. Iowa, 1942, MS, 1946, PhD, 1949. Instr. U. Iowa, 1947-49; asst. prof. geology U. Ga., 1949-54, asso. prof., 1954-56, U. Kansas City, 1956-63; prof. U. Mo., Kansas City, 1963—, chmn. dept. geoscis., 1968-78; dean U. Mo. (Coll. Arts and Scis.), 1979-86. Served with USN, 1942-45. Fellow Geol. Soc. Am.; mem. AAUP, Assn. Mo. Geologists, AAAS, Sigma Xi. Roman Catholic. Achievements include research, numerous publs. on mass wasting, slope failure, underground space, geology of West Mo. Home: 6913 W 100th Shawnee Mission KS 66212 Office: 5100 Rockhill Rd Kansas City MO 64110-2481

PARK, JOHN THORNTON, retired academic administrator; b. Phillipsburg, NJ, Jan. 3, 1935; s. Dawson J. and Margaret M. (Thornton) P.; m. Dorcas M Marshall; June 1, 1956; children: Janet Ernst, Karen Daily. BA in Physics with distinction, Nebr. Wesleyan U., 1956; PhD, U. Nebr., 1963. NSF postdoctoral fellow Univ. Coll., London, 1963-64; asst. prof. physics U. Mo., Rolla, 1964-68, assoc. prof. physics, 1968-71, prof., 1971-2000, prof. emeritus, 2000—, chmn. dept. physics, 1977-83, vice chancellor acad. affairs, 1983-85, 86-91, interim chancellor, 1985-86, 91-92, chancellor, 1992-2000, chancellor emeritus,

2000—; ret., 2000. Vis. assoc. prof. NYU, 1970-71; pres. Talema Electronics, Inc., St. James, Mo., 1983-99, Tortran Corp., 1990—; prin. investigator NSF Rsch. Grants, 1966-92; bd. dirs. Mo. Tech. Corp., Jefferson City, Mo., 1994—, Mo. Enterprise, 1990—, Phelps County Bank, 1997—, Phelps County Regional Med. Ctr. Contbr. articles to profl. jours. Recipient Most Disting. Scientist award Mo. Acad. Sci., 1994. Fellow Am. Phys. Soc. (mem. divsn. elec. and atomic physics); mem. Am. Assn. Physics Tchrs., Rotary. Methodist. Personal E-mail: parkj@umr.edu.

PARKE, TERRY RICHARD, state legislator; b. Pittsfield, Ill., Feb. 21, 1944; m. Joanne Toombs; 2 children. BS, 1970. Mem. Ill. Ho. of Reps. from 44th dist., 1985—. Rep. spokesman ins. com., mem. telcom. com.; mem. labor com.; mem. consumer protection, mem. environment and energy com., mem. environ. health com.; co-chmn. Ill. Commn. on Govt. Forecasting and Accountability; mem. Employee Suggestion Award Bd.; past pres. Elgin Area Life Underwriters. Exec. comm. Bus. and Labor Am. Legis. Exch. Coun. Past Pres. and Nat. Coun. of Ins. Legis.; past pres. N.W. Schaumburg Assn. Commerce and Industry; bd. dirs., Boy Scouts Northwest Suburban Coun.; past mem. Girl Scouts Crossroads Coun. Mem. Rotary (past pres. Schaumburg club). Republican. Office: 220 State House Springfield IL 62706-0001 also: 837 W Higgins Rd Schaumburg IL 60195 Home: 6098 Delaney Dr Hoffman Estates IL 60192-4811 Office Phone: 847-882-0270. Personal E-mail: cityparkxx@yahoo.com.

PARKER, ALAN JOHN, veterinary neurologist, educator, researcher; b. Portsmouth, Eng., Oct. 28, 1944; arrived in U.S., 1969, naturalized, 2002; s. William Barton and Emily (Begley) P.; m. Heather Margaret Nicholson, Oct. 30, 1971; children: Alyxander John, Robert William. BSc with honors, Bristol U., 1966, BVSc with honors, 1968; MS, U. Ill., 1973, PhD, 1976. Diplomate Am. Coll. Vet. Internal Medicine-Neurology, European Coll. Vet. Neurology. Intern Vet. Coll., U. Calif.-Davis, 1969—70; instr. vet. clin. medicine U. Ill., Urbana, 1970—71, 1972—76, asst. prof., 1976—77, assoc. prof., 1977—82, prof., 1982—2000, prof. emeritus, 2001—. Cons. pharm. cos., seminar presenter; cons. in neurology Berwyn Vet. Hosp., Chgo., 1973—. Lake Shore Animal Hosp., Chgo., 1978-03. Contbr. numerous articles to sci. jours., chpts. to books. Active Boy Scouts Am., Champaign, Ill., 1982—; active Presbyn. Ch., Monticello, Ill., 1979-2006. Recipient Vigil Honor and Founder's award Order of the Arrow, Silver Beaver award Boy Scouts Am.; sci. grantee various orgns., 1972-2000. Mem. AVMA, Am. Animal Hosp. Assn., Brit. Vet. Assn., Ill. State Vet. Assn. Republican. Office: 2845 S Harlem Ave Berwyn IL 60402 Office Phone: 708-749-4200.

PARKER, BONITA M., civil rights organization executive; b. Jan. 23, 1968; married; 2 children. Degree in Fin., DePaul U. Several positions with Urban Fin. Services, Am. Bankers Assn.; intern Northern Trust Co., second v.p.; co-owner Skills For Life Tng. Co.; dir., Investments and Econ. Empowerment Salem Bapt. Ch., Chgo.; COO Rainbow/Push Coalition, Chgo. Fin. specialist USAR. Mem.: Nat. Assn. County Officials. Office: RainbowPush Coaltion 930 E 50th St Chicago IL 60615-2702 Home Phone: 708-331-5473; Office Phone: 773-551-8661. Personal E-mail: bp5225@aol.com.

PARKER, CHARLES WALTER, JR., retired manufacturing executive; b. nr. Ahoskie, NC, Nov. 22, 1922; s. Charles Walter and Minnie Louise (Williamson) P.; m. Sophie Nash Riddick, ov. 26, 1949; children: Mary Parker Hutto, Caroline Parker Robertson, Charles Walter III, Thomas Williamson. BS in Elec. Engring, Va. Mil. Inst., 1947; Dr. Engring. (hon.), Milw. Sch. Engring., 1980. With Allis-Chalmers Corp., 1947-87, dist. mgr. Richmond, Va., 1955-57, Phila., 1957-58, dir. sales promotion industries group Milw., 1958-61, gen. mktg. mgr. new products, 1961-62, mgr. mktg. services, 1962-66, v.p. mktg. and public relations services, 1966-70, v.p., dep. group exec., 1970-72, staff group exec. communications and public affairs, 1972-87, ret., 1987; prin. Charles Parker & Assocs., Ltd., Milw., 1987—. Founding mem. World Mktg. Contact Group, London; bd. dirs. Internat. Gen. Ins. Corp., Dinermite Corp. Gen. chmn. United Fund Greater Milw. Area, 1975; trustee Boy Scouts Am. Trust Fund, Milw.; bd. dirs., pres. Jr. Achievement; pres. bd. trustees Univ. Sch. Milw., 1978-80; trustee Carroll Coll., Waukesha, Wis.; bd. dirs. Milw. Children's Hosp.; bd. regents Milw. Sch. Engring.; mem. Greater Milw. Com.; chmn. bd. dirs. Milw. Found., 1987-89. Served to capt. AUS, 1943-46, ETO. Decorated Bronze Star. Mem. NAM (dir.), Wis. C. of C. (pres. 1974-76), Sales and Mktg. Execs. Internat. (pres., CEO 1974, 75, Eduardo Rihan Internat. Mktg. Exec. of Yr. award 1979), Wis. Mfrs. and Commerce Assn. (exec. com.), Pi Sigma Epsilon (pres. 1976-77, trustee and chmn. nat. edn. found. 1979-86), Kappa Alpha. Office: 828 N Broadway Ste 100 Milwaukee WI 53202-3611 Home: St Johns on the Lake 1840 N Prospect Ave 604 Milwaukee WI 53202

PARKER, DAN J., political organization administrator; Chair Ind. Dem. Party; mem. Dem. Nat. Com. Democrat. Office: Ind Dem Party Ste 200 One North Capitol Indianapolis IN 46204 Office Phone: 317-231-7100. Office Fax: 317-231-7129. E-mail: dparker@indems.org.*

PARKER, GARY DEAN, manufacturing executive; b. Omaha, Mar. 27, 1945; s. Norman and Dolores (Pierce) P.; m. Joanne Baker, Aug. 27, 1966; children: Jason E., Rodney R. BS in BA, Nebr. Wesleyan U., BS in Econs. Dir. sales Lindsay Mfg. Co., Nebr., 1971-73, v.p. sales-mktg. Nebr., 1973-76, sr. v.p. Nebr., 1976-78, exec. v.p. Nebr., 1978-83, pres., 1983—, dir., 1977—. Pres. Irrigation Assocs., Silver Springs, Md., 1981-82, dir., 1978-83; dir. Irrigation Found. & Research, Silver Springs, 1978— Mem. Nebr. Mfg. Assn. (pres. 1982-83), Delta Omicron Epsilon Lodges: Elks. Office: Lindsay Mfg Co PO Box 156 Lindsay NE 68644-0156

PARKER, GEORGE EDWARD, III, lawyer; b. Detroit, Sept. 26, 1934; s. George Edward and Lucia Helen (Muir) P.; m. Margaret G. Koehler; children—George, David, Benjamin AB, Princeton U., 1956; JD, U. Mich., 1959. Bar: Mich. 1959, D.C. 1981, Fla. 1982. Assoc. Miller, Canfield, Paddock & Stone, Detroit, 1959-68, ptnr., 1968-96, of counsel, 1996—; gen. counsel, sec. Republic Bancorp Inc., Ann Arbor, Mich. Bd. dirs. Univ. Liggett Sch.; trustee David Whitney Fund, Grayling Fund. Republican. Office: Miller Canfield Paddock et al 150 W Jefferson Ave Ste 2500 Detroit MI 48226-4416 E-mail: gparkerrbi@earthlink.net.

PARKER, KATHLEEN KAPPEL, state legislator; b. Pitts., Sept. 21, 1943; m. Keith Parker; 2 children. BA, U. Miami, 1968. Tax assessor Northfield Twp., 1979-83; mem. Regional Transp. Authority Bd., 1983-95; del. Ill. and Nat. Rep. Convs., 1988; Northfield Twp. coord. George Bush's Presdl. Campaign, 1988; mem. U.S. Archtl. and Transp. Barriers Compliance Bd., 1991-94; Ill. state sen., 1995—. Mem. Fin. Inst., vice chair Pub. Health and Welfare Comms., Transp. Com., 1995—, chair; co-owner Keith Parker and Assocs., 1985—; pres., bd. dirs. Chgo. divsn. Busch Jewelry Co., 1988-93. Chair Mental Health Task Force. Mem. ortheastern Ill. Planning Coun., Met. Planning Coun. Office: 4104 Timberlane Dr Northbrook IL 60062-6123

PARKER, LEE FISCHER, sales executive; b. Chgo., Nov. 28, 1932; d. Meyer Louis and Lena (Raphael) Fischer; m. Joseph Schwartz, Mar. 18, 1950 (div. Jan. 1986); 1 child, Steven Darryl; m. Robert K. Parker, Jan. 13, 1991. Student, Mallinkroudt Coll., Wilmette, Ill., 1976. Freelance fashion model, Chgo., 1958-78; sales assoc. Neiman-Marcus, Northbrook, Ill., 1978-79; owner Keystone Svcs., Woodale, Ill., 1969-82; sales assoc. Marshall Field's, Skokie, Ill., 1986-94, Jacobson's, Boca Raton, Fla., 1996-99. Fashion coord. Arnie's Restaurant, Chgo., 1964-68, Blackhawk Restaurant, Chgo., 1964-66, Jim Conway TV Show, Chgo., 1968-70; commentator dog fashion show, Ft. Pierce, Fla., 2003—. Appeared in movie, 2000. Commentator Charity Fashion Show, Ft. Pierce, Fla., 2003; mem. Hadassah. Mem. Brandeis Women's Aux., Holocaust Mus. Democrat. Jewish. Avocations: golf, dance, reading.

PARKER, LEONARD S., architect, educator; b. Warsaw, Jan. 16, 1923; came to U.S. 1923; s. Rueben and Sarah (Kollica) Popuch; m. Betty Mae Buegen, Sept. 1, 1948 (dec. 1983); children— Bruce Aaron, Jonathan Arthur, Nancy Anne, Andrew David BArch., U. Minn., 1948; MArch., MIT, 1950. Sr. designer Eero Saarinen Assocs., Bloomfield Hills, Mich., 1950-56; CEO, chmn. bd., pres., dir. design The Leonard Parker Assocs., Mpls., 1957-97; pres., dir. design The Alliance Southwest, Phoenix, 1981-91; chmn. bd. dirs. The Leonard Parker Assn., Minn., 1997—. Prof. grad. program Sch. Architecture, U. Minn., Mpls., 1959—; pres. Minn. Archtl. Found., 1991. Author: Abandoning the Catalogs, 1979, Rivers of Modernism, 1986, Collaboration-Same Bed, Different Dream? Panel mem. Mpls. City Hall Restoration Com., Am. Arbitration Assn., USAF bd. visitors (chmn.). Served with U.S. Army, 1943-46; ETO Firm has received 84 nat. and regional awards for design excellence. Fellow AIA; mem. Minn. Soc. Architects (pres. 1981, Gold medal 1986, pres. Mpls. chpt. 1979), Tau Sigma Delta. Home: 3936 Willmatt Hl Hopkins MN 55305-5142 Office: The Leonard Parker Assocs 430 Oak Grove St Ste 300 Minneapolis MN 55403-3234

PARKER, LINDA BATES, professional development organization administrator; Grad., U. Dayton, U. Cin., Harvard U., 1991. Pres., founder Black Career Women, Cin. Dir. Career Devel. Ctr., mgmt. prof. U. Cin. Author: Career Portfolio; columnist for Nat. Black Collegian Mag.; presenter in field. Office: Black Career Women PO Box 19332 Cincinnati OH 45219-0332

PARKER, R. JOSEPH, lawyer; b. St. Louis, June 29, 1944; s. George Joseph and Ann Rosalie Parker; m. Theresa Gaynor, Aug. 26, 1967; children: Christa Michele, Kevin Blake. AB, Georgetown U., 1966; JD, Boston Coll., 1969. Bar: Ohio 1969. Law clk. to judge U.S. Ct. Appeals (6th Cir.), Akron, Ohio, 1969-70; assoc. Taft, Stettinius & Hollister, Cin., 1970-78, ptnr. Arbitrator Am. Arbitration Assn., Cin., 1980—; faculty Nat. Inst. for Trial Advocacy, 1990—; faculty advanced trial advocacy program IRS, 1993. Editor Law Rev. Ann. Survey Mass. Law, 1967-69; contbg. author: Fed. Civil Procedure Before Trial-6th Circuit. Bd. dirs. West End Health Ctr., Inc., Cin., 1972-76, Legal Aid Soc. Cin., 1982-85; chmn. bd. dirs. Vol. Lawyers for Poor Found., Cin., 1986-88; master Am. Inn of Court, 1984—. Fellow Am. Coll. Trial Lawyers; mem. Ohio State Bar Assn., Cin. Bar Assn., Cin. Country Club, Order of Coif. Democrat. Roman Catholic. Office: 425 Walnut St Ste 1800 Cincinnati OH 45202-3759 E-mail: parker18002000@yahoo.com.

PARKER, ROBERT FREDERIC, university dean emeritus; b. St. Louis, Oct. 29, 1907; s. Charles T. and Lydia (Gronemeyer) P.; m. Mary L. Warner, June 20, 1934; children: David Frederic, Jane Eleanor (Mrs. Howard H. Hush, Jr.). BS, Washington U., St. Louis, 1925, MD, 1929. Diplomate: Am. Bd. Microbiology. Asst. radiology Washington U. Med. Sch., 1929-30, instr. medicine, 1932-33; asst. Rockefeller Inst., 1933-36; mem. faculty Case Western Res. U., 1936—, prof. microbiology, 1954-77, prof. emeritus, 1977—, assoc. dean, 1965-73, dean, 1973-76, dean emeritus, 1976—. Mem. Cleve. Acad. Medicine (past bd. dirs.), Am. Soc. Clin. Investigation, Central Soc. Clin. Research, Am. Acad. Microbiology, Sigma Xi, Alpha Omega Alpha. Achievements include spl. research virus immunology, quantitative aspects virus infection, tissue culture, action of antibiotics. Home: 2181 Ambleside Dr Apt 404 Cleveland OH 44106-7603

PARKER, SARA ANN, librarian, consultant; b. Cassville, Mo., Feb. 19, 1939; d. Howard Franklin and Vera Irene (Thomas) P. BA, Okla. State U., 1961; M.L.S., Emporia State U., Kans., 1968. Adult svcs. librarian Springfield Pub. Libr., Mo., 1972-75, bookmobile dir. Mo., 1975-76; coord. S.W. Mo. Libr. Network, Springfield, 1976-78; libr. developer Colo. State Libr., Denver, 1978-82; state librarian Mont. State Libr., Helena, 1982-88, State Libr. Pa., Harrisburg, 1988-90; Pa. commr. librs., dep. sec. edn. State of Pa., Harrisburg, 1990-95; state libr. State of Mo., Jefferson City, 1995—2005. Cons. and lectr. in field. Author, editor, compiler in field; contbr. articles to profl. jours. Sec. Western Coun. State Librs., Reno, 1984—88; mem. Mont. State Data Adv. Coun., 1983—88, Mont. Telecomm. Coun., 1985—88, WLN Network Coun., 1984—87, Kellogg ICLIS Project Mgmt. Bd., 1986—88; mem. adv. com. Gates Libr. Initiative, 1998—2005; mem. OCLC Strategic Directions and Governance Study Adv. Coun., 2000—01, webjunction adv. coun., 2003—05. Recipient Pres.'s award, ature Conservancy, 1989, Friends award, Pa. Assn. Ednl. Comms. and Techs., 1989, Friend of Sch. Librs. award, Mo. Sch. Librs. Assn., 2000, Bohley Libr. Cooperation award, 2001; fellow Inst. Ednl. Leadership, 1982. Mem.: ALA, Mountain Plains Libr. Assn. (sec. chmn. 1980, pres. 1987—88, chair MOREnet adv. coun. 2004—05), Mont. Libr. Assn. (bd. dirs. 1982—88), Chief Officers State Libr. Agys. (pres. 1996—98).

PARKHURST, BEVERLY SUSLER, lawyer, judge; b. Decatur, Ill. d. Sewell and Marion Susler; m. Todd S. Parkhurst, Aug. 15, 1976. BA with honors, U. Ill., 1966, JD, 1969. Bar: Ill. 1969, U.S. Dist. Ct. (no. dist.) Ill. 1969, U.S. Ct. Appeals (7th cir.) 1975, U.S. Supreme Ct. 1980. Asst. U.S. atty. U.S. Atty.'s Office U.S. Dist. Ct. (no. dist.) Ill., Chgo., 1974-78, exec. asst. U.S. atty., 1978-81; pvt. practice law Offices of Beverly Susler Parkhurst, Chgo., 1982-86; trial judge Cir. Ct. Cook County, 1996-98; of counsel Witwer, Poltrock & Giampietro, Chgo., 1997—2003, Hedlund & Hanley LLC, 2003—04; appt. fed. adminstr. law judge, 2004—. Faculty Nat. Inst. of Trial Advocacy; bd. dirs. Internat. Forum Travel and Tourism Advs., vice chmn. 2d Internat. Conf., Jerusalem, 1986, regional chmn. 3d Internat. Conf., San Francisco, 1987; chmn. inquiry bd. Ill. Atty. Registration and Disciplinary Commn., 1985-87; guest lectr. legal ethics Washington U., St. Louis, 1986; lectr. on travel law, fed. civic procedures and med. malpractice; adj. prof. John Marshall Law Sch., 1999-2002; mediator Jud. Disput Resolution. Contbr. articles to profl. jours.; spkr. in field. Mem. Ill. Toll Hwy. Adv. Com., 1985-90; bd. dirs. Ill. Soc. for Prevention of Blindness, Cook County Ct. Watchers, Chgo. State U. Found., 1997—2003. James scholar U. Ill., 1962-66; recipient Spl. Achievement award U.S. Dept. Justice, 1978, Dir.'s award, 1981, Cert. of Profl. Achievement in Mediation, DePaul U. Dispute Resolution Ctr.; U.S. Utility Patent grantee 1984. Mem. ABA (chmn. subcom. alternatives to discovery litigation sect. 1985-87), Ill. Bar Assn. (com. profl. responsibility), Women's Bar Assn., Fed. Bar Assn., Chgo. Bar Assn. (chmn. judiciary commn. 1988-90, bench bar symposium 1988-91, exec. com. Alliance for Women), Nat. Inst. Trial Advocacy (faculty N.E. region), Lincoln Inn of Ct. (pres.), Legal Club of Chgo. Avocations: scuba diving, swimming, cooking. Office: Fed Adminstr Law Judge Chicago IL 60603

PARKHURST, TODD SHELDON, lawyer; b. Evanston, Ill., Mar. 8, 1941; s. Don A. and Ruth Ellen (Sheldon) P.; m. Karen Judy Huckleberry, Sept. 2, 1968 (dec. Sept. 1969); m. Beverly Ann Susler, Aug. 15, 1976. BS in Gen. Engring., U. Ill., 1963; JD, U. Pa., 1966. Bar: Ill. 1968, U.S. Dist. Ct. (no. dist.) Ill. 1968, U.S. Dist. Ct. (ea. dist.) Wis. 1989, U.S. Ct. Appeals (7th cir.) 1977, U.S. Ct. Appeals Fed. Cir. 1978, U.S. Ct. Mil. Appeals, 1968, U.S. Patent and Trademark Office, 1973, U.S. Supreme Ct. 1973. Assoc. Wolfe, Hubbard, Voit & Osann, 1968-72; assoc. and ptnr. Trexler, Wolters, Bushnell & Fosse, Chgo., 1972-84; ptnr. Jenner & Block, Chgo., 1984-87, Gardner, Carton & Douglas, 1996-98, Hill & Simpson, Chgo., 1998-2000; ptnr., mgr. intellectual property practice Schiff Hardin & Waite, Chgo., 1987-96, Holland & Knight, Chgo., 2000—07, Wildman Harrold Allen & Dixon LLP, 2007—. Adj. prof. John Marshall Law Sch., Chgo., 1980-84, Ill. Inst. Tech.-Chgo. Kent Law Sch., 1989—. Contbr. articles to profl. jours. Mem. Lifeline Pilots, Inc., pres. 1994-96; hearing officer Ill. Pollution Control Bd., 1972-96. Capt. Corps of Engrs. US Army, 1966—68. Mem. Am. Intellectual Property Law Assn., Licensing Execs. Soc., Chgo. Bar Assn., Patent Law Assn. Chgo., Chgo. Lit. Club (pres. 1989-90), Adventurers Club Chgo. (sec. 1988). Methodist. Avocations: flying, scuba diving, photography, theatrical acting. Office: Wildman Harrold Allen & Dixon LLP 233 W Wacker Dr Ste 3000 Chicago IL 60606 Office Phone: 312-201-2000. Personal E-mail: todd.parkhurst@hklaw.com.

PARKINSON, MARK VINCENT, lieutenant governor, former state legislator; b. Wichita, Kans., June 24, 1957; s. Henry Filson and Barbara Ann (Gilbert) Horton; m. Stacy Abbott Parkinson, Mar. 7, 1983; children: Alex Atticus, Sam Filson, Kit Harlan. BA in Edn., Wichita State U., 1980; JD, Kans. U., 1984. Assoc. Payne and Jones Law Firm, Olathe, Kans., 1984-86; ptnr. Parkinson, Foth & Reynolds, Lenexa, Kans., 1986—96; mem. Kans. Ho. Reps., 1990-92, Kans. State Senate, 1993-97; chmn. Kans. Rep. Party, 1999—2003; lt. gov. State of Kans., Topeka, 2007—. Mem. ABA, Johnson County Bar Found. (pres. 1993—), Kans. Bar Assn. Democrat. Avocations: travel, running, movies. Office: Lieutenant Governor State Capitol 300 SW 10th Ave Ste 2225 Topeka KS 66612 Office Phone: 785-296-2213. Office Fax: 785-296-5669.

PARKINSON, ROBERT L., JR., medical products executive, health facility administrator; BBA, MBA, Loyola U., Chgo. With Abbott Labs., Abbott Park, Ill., 1976, v.p. European ops., 1990-93, sr. v.p. chem. and agrl. products, 1993-95, pres. internat. divsn., 1995-98, bd. dirs., 1998, pres., COO, 1999-2001; dean Loyola U. Chgo.'s Sch. of Bus. Adminstrn. and Grad. Sch. of Bus., 2002—04; chmn., CEO Baxter Internat., Inc., 2004—. Chmn. Geneva (Switzerland) Proteomics, 2001; bd. trustees Healthcare Leadership Coun. Bd. dirs. Northwestern Mem. Hosp., Northwestern Mem. Found. Office: Baxter Internat Inc One Baxter Pkwy Deerfield IL 60015 Office Phone: 847-948-2000.

PARKINSON, WILLIAM CHARLES, physics professor, researcher; b. Jarvis, Ont., Can., Feb. 11, 1918; came to U.S., 1925, naturalized, 1941; s. Charles Franklin and Euphemia Alice (Johnston) P.; m. Martha Bennett Capron, Aug. 2, 1944; children: Martha Reed, William Reid. BSE, U. Mich., 1940, MS, 1941, PhD, 1948. Physicist Applied Physics Lab., Johns Hopkins U., 1942-46, OSRD, 1943-44; mem. faculty U. Mich., 1947—, prof. physics, 1958-88, prof. emeritus physics, 1988—, dir. cyclotron lab., 1962-77; mem. subcom. nuclear structure NRC, 1959-68; mem. nuclear physics sub panel mgmt. and costs nuclear program, 1969-70; adv. panel physics NSF, 1966-69. Cons. grad. sci. facilities, 1968, chmn. postdoctoral fellowship evaluation panel, 1969, cons. to govt. and industry, 1955— Quondam mem. Trinity Coll., Cambridge, Eng. Recipient Ordnance Devel. award Navy Dept., 1946; Fulbright research scholar Cavendish Lab., Cambridge U., 1952-53 Fellow Am. Phys. Soc.; mem. N.Y. Acad. Scis., Biophys. Soc., Grad. "M" Club (awarded hon. "M" 1991), Flounders Water Polo, Sigma Xi, Phi Kappa Phi, Kappa Kappa Psi. Achievements include invention of automatic judging and timing for swim meets, fast neutron spectroscopy using cyclotrons; development of high resolution nuclear spectroscopy with cyclotrons. Home: 1600 Sheridan Dr Ann Arbor MI 48104-4052 Office: Univ Mich Dept Physics Ann Arbor MI 48109 Office Phone: 734-764-3458. Business E-Mail: wcpark@umich.edu.

PARKS, BLANCHE CECILE, public administrator; b. Leavenworth, Kans., Feb. 2, 1949; d. Nile Eugene Sr. and Fern (Dickinson) Williams; m. Sherman A. Parks Jr.; children: Michael A., Stacy M. BEd, Washburn U., 1971, MEd, 1976, postgrad., 1983-84. Tchr. Topeka Pub. Schs., 1971-76, reading specialist, 1979-84; ins. regulator Kans. Ins. Dept., Topeka, 1984-88; spl. asst. to sec. Kans. Dept. Human Resources, Topeka, 1988-92; real estate lease adminstr. State of Kans., Topeka, 1992—. Pres. Kans. Children's Svc. League, 1990-94, YWCA, Topeka, 1992-94; chmn. Topeka Human Rels. Commn., 1991-93; mem. Topeka Pub. Schs. Found., 1993-94; participant Leadership Topeka, 1994, Leadership Kans., 1994 Named The Outstanding Young Woman of Kans. Jaycee Women, 1984, 85, one of Outstanding Young Women Am., 1985. Mem. Jr. League of Topeka (Gold Rose award 1993), Jack and Jill Am., Kans. C. of C. (leadership award 1985), Links, Phi Kappa Phi, Phi Delta Kappa, Alpha Delta Kappa, Delta Kappa Gamma, (life) Delta Sigma Theta (v.p. 1980-82). Republican. Mem. A.M.E. Ch. Home: 1727 SE 36th Terrace Topeka KS 66605

PARKS, LINDA S., lawyer; b. Oneida, NY, Aug. 19, 1957; BA summa cum laude, Washburn U., 1979, JD cum laude, 1983. Bar: Kans. 1983, Kans. Supreme Ct., US Ct. Appeals (10th Cir.), US Dist. Ct. (Dist. Kans.). Ptnr. Hite Fanning & Honeyman LLP, Wichita, Kans. Bd. mem. YWCA. Fellow: ABA (Kans. Bar Assn. del. 1999—2005); mem.: Kans. Bar Found. (trustee 2000—02), Am. Bar Found., Nat. Assn. Women Bar Assoc. (bd. mem. 2005—), Wichita Women Attys. Assn., Kans. Women Attys. Assn. (pres. 1994—96), Kans. Bar Assn. (mem. bd. gov. 1999—, chair law related edn. com. 2000—02, exec. com. 2000—, v.p. 2005—06, pres.-elect 2006—07, pres. 2007—08), Wichita Bar Assn. Office: Hite Fanning & Honeyman LLP Ste 950 100 N Broadway Wichita KS 67202-2209 Office Phone: 316-265-7741. Office Fax: 316-267-7803. E-mail: parks@hitefanning.com.

PARKS, PATRICK, English language educator, humanities educator; BA in Lit. and Mass Comms., Southwest State U., 1975; BS in English Edn. and Journalism, Bemidji State U., 1977; MFA in English, U. Iowa, 1982. Instr. English and journalism, newspaper advisor Harris-Lake Park H.S., Lake Park, Iowa, 1977-78, Ely (Minn.) H.S., 1978-79; tchg. asst. in rhetoric and lit. U. Iowa, Iowa City, 1981-82; instr. English and Journalism, pubs. advisor Muscatine (Ill.) C. C., 1982-86; prof. English and Humanities, dir. writers ctr. Elgin (Ill.) C. C., 1986-98, disting. prof. English and Humanities, 1998—. Instr. creative writing and composition evening program Southeastern C. C., Burlington, Iowa, 1979-80, creative writing Arts Outreach program U. Iowa, Iowa City, 1981, fiction writing The Writer's Workshop weekend program, 1982; facilitator No. Ill. Network Stff Devel., Lake Geneva, Wis., 1992, 1994; co-coord. ALA and Lila Wallace/Reader's Digest pilot program, Elgin, Ill., 1993; faculty adv. The Sarajevo Project, Elgin C. C., 1992—; presenter, lectr. in field. Editor, adv. (literary jour.) Farmer's Market; contbr. numerous stories, poems to literary jours., articles to profl. jours. Artist fellow Ill. Arts Coun. 1988; recipient Outstanding C. C. Professor of the Year award Carnegie Foun. Advancement of Tchg. and Coun. Advancement an Support of Edn. 1994, Outstanding Faculty award Ill. Cmty. Coll. Trustees Assn. 1994, Honorable Mention Fla. State U. World's Best Short Story Contest 1992, writing contest Rambunctious Review 1991, Excellence in Tchg. award Nat. Inst. Staf and Orgnl. Devel. 1991, First Place fiction writing contest Roselle Pub. Lib. 1988. Mem. Ill. Writers, Inc. (chair, bd. dirs.), Assoc. Writing Programs, C. C. Humanities Assn., Nat. Coun. Tchrs. English, Campus Compact Ctr. Cmty. Coll., Tchrs. and Writers Collaborative. Office: Elgin Comm Coll English Dept 1700 Spartan Dr Elgin IL 60123-7189 Office Phone: 847-214-7265. E-mail: pparks@elgin.edu.

PARKS, ROBERT D., real estate company executive; Chmn. Inland Real Estate Investment Corp., Oak Brook, Ill., 1969—. Office: Inland Real Estate Investment Corp 2901 Butterfield Rd Ste 1 Oak Brook IL 60523-1190

PARLOW, CYNTHIA MARIA, professional soccer player; b. Memphis, May 8, 1978; BS in Nutrition, U. N.C., 1998. Profl. soccer player Atlanta Beat, 2001—03. Mem. U.S. Women's Nat. Soccer Team, 1996—, U.S. Under-20 Nat. Team, Nordic Cup championships, Denmark, 1997, U-16 Nat. Team pool. Named All-ACC and ACC Rookie of Yr., 1995, Soccer Am. Freshman of Yr., 1995, Most Valuable Player, 1995 Under-17 U.S. Youth Soccer nat. tournament, World Cup Champion, 1999; recipient Gold medal, Centennial Olympic Games, 1996, Herman Trophy, Mo. Athletic Club Player of Yr. award, 1997, Silver medal, Sydney Olympic Games, 2000. Achievements include helped U. N.C. to NCAA Championship 1996, 97; 1st-Team All-ACC selection in 1997; named to 1997 NCAA All-Tournament Team. Office: US Soccer Fedn 1801-1811 S Prairie Ave Chicago IL 60616

PARMELEE, WALKER MICHAEL, psychologist; b. Grand Haven, Mich., Apr. 26, 1952; s. Walker Michael and Evelyn Mae (Essenberg) P.; m. Gayle Ann Klempel, Jan. 11, 1975; children: Morgan Christine, Kathryn Ann, Elizabeth Mae. BS, Ctrl. Mich. U., 1974, MA, cert. specialist in psychology, 1977; D in Counseling Psychology, Western Mich. U., 1986. Lic. psychologist, Mich. Sch. psychologist Oakridge Pub. Schs., Muskegon, Mich., 1977—82, Ravenna (Mich.) Schs., Muskegon Heights (Mich.) Schs., 1982—84; sr. staff therapist Steelcase Counseling Svcs., Grand Rapids, Mich., 1984—90; prin., psychologist Parmelee and Assocs. Psychol. Cons., Grand Haven, 1989—. Consulting psychologist Cross Rds. Family Ctr., Grand Haven, 1989—2000. Contbr. articles to profl. jours. Bd. dirs. Planned Parenthood, Muskegon, 1979-82, Harbinger Inc., Grand Rapids, 1986-90, Tri Cities Ministries Counseling, 2003-07; elder 2d Ref. Ch., Grand Haven, 1989-92, 2006—; mem. women and families adv. group Allegan, Muskegon, Ottawa Substance Abuse Agy., 1992-95; mem. support team ARC, 2005-07. Mem. Nat. Assn. Child Alcoholics, Mich. Psychol. Assn., Mich. Sch. Psychologists. Avocations: woodworking, skiing, running, tennis, camping. Home: 215 Howard St Grand Haven MI 49417-1806 Office: Parmelee and Assocs Psychol Cons 321 Fulton Ave Grand Haven MI 49417-1231 Office Phone: 616-842-4772. Personal E-mail: parmeleenet@netscape.net.

PARMENTER, CHARLES STEDMAN, chemistry professor; b. Phila., Oct. 12, 1933; s. Charles Leroy and Hazeltene Lois (Stedman) P.; m. Patricia Jean Patton, Mar. 31, 1956; children: Tighe Stedman, Kyle Kirkland, Leigh Patton. BA, U. Pa., 1955; PhD in Phys. Chemistry, U. Rochester, 1963. Tech. rep. photo products E.I. du Pont de Nemours & Co., 1958; NSF fellow chemistry Harvard U., Boston, 1962-63, NIH rsch. fellow, 1963-64, from asst. prof. to prof., 1964-88; Disting. prof. chemistry Ind. U., Bloomington, 1988—. Simon H. Guggenheim fellow U. Cambridge, 1971-72; vis. fellow Joint Inst. Lab. Astrophysics, Nat. Bur. Standards and U. Colo., 1977-78, 92, Exeter Coll. Oxford U., 1999. Lt. USAF, 1956-58. Recipient Humboldt Sr. Scientist award Tech. U. Munchen, 1986; Fulbright Sr. Scholar Griffith U., Australia, 1980. Earle K. Plyler Prize, Am. Physical Soc., 1996. Fellow AAAS, Am. Phys. Soc. (Earle K. Plyler prize 1996); mem. NAS, Am. Acad. Arts and Scis., Am. Chem. Soc. (chmn. div. phys. chemistry 1986-87). Achievements include research in photochemistry, laser spectroscopy, energy transfer. Office: Ind U Dept of Chemistry Bloomington IN 47405

PARRETTE, LESLIE JACKSON, lawyer; b. Mt Pleasant, Mo., Aug. 25, 1961; s. Leslie Jackson and Janet Parrette. AB, Harvard Coll., 1983; JD, Harvard Law Sch., 1986. Assoc. Hale & Dorr, Boston, 1986-89, Watson Ess Marshall &

Enggas, Kansas City, Mo., 1989-91, Bryan Cave, Kansas City, Mo., 1991-92; ptnr. Blackwell Sanders Peper Martin, Kansas City, Mo., 1992-2000; gen. coun., sr. v.p., corp. sec. Aquila Inc., Kansas City, Mo., 2000—05. Mem. Sister City Commn. of Kansas City, Mo., 1999—; bd. dirs. Am. Jazz Mus., 2002—03. E-mail: les.parrette@aquila.com.

PARRINO, CHERYL LYNN, federal agency administrator; b. Wisconsin Rapids, Wis., Jan. 21, 1954; m. Jack J. Parrino, Sept. 1, 1990; 1 child, George. BBA in Acctg., U. Wis., 1976. Auditor Pub. Svc. Commn. Wis., Madison, 1976-82, dir. utility audits, 1982-86, exec. asst. to chmn., 1986-91, commr., 1991-98, chmn., 1992-98; chmn., CEO Universal Svc. Adminstrv. Co., Madison, 1998—. Mem. adv. bd. Bellcore, 1991; vice chmn. bd. dirs. Wis. Ctr. Demand Side Rsch., Madison, 1991-92; chmn. bd. dirs. Wis. Pub. Utility Inst., Madison, 1992-95 Mem. Gov.'s Task Force Gross Receipts Tax, Madison, 1991-92, Gov.'s Task Force Alternative Fuels, Madison, 1992-98, Gov.'s Task Force Clean Air, Madison, 1992-98, Gov.'s Task Force Telecom., Madison, 1993-94. Mem. Nat. Assn. Pub. Utility Commrs. (exec. com. 1991, chmn. comm. com. 1992-98, pres. 1995-96, pres. Gt. Lakes conf. 1996). Republican. Lutheran. Avocations: skiing, tennis, travel. Fax: (608) 827-8893.

PARRISH, MAURICE DRUE, museum executive; b. Chgo., Mar. 5, 1950; s. Maurice and Ione Yvonne (Culumns) P.; m. Gail Marie Sims, Sept. 2, 1978; children: Theodore, Andrew, Brandon, Cara. BA in Arch., U. Pa., 1972; MArch, Yale U., 1975. City planner City of Chgo., 1975-81; architect John Hiltscher & Assocs., Chgo., 1981-83, Barnett, Jones & Smith, Chgo., 1983-84; zoning adminstr. City of Chgo., 1984-87, bldg. commr., 1987-89; dep. dir. Detroit Inst. of Arts, 1989-97, interim dir., 1997-99, exec. v.p., 1999—. Bd. dirs. Arts League of Mich., Detroit, 1994-97, Mosaic Youth Theatre Detroit, 2000—, chmn., 2002—; co-chmn. Mayor's Affordable Housing Task Force, Chgo., 1984-89; chmn. Chgo. Elec. Commn., 1988-89; mem. Chgo. Econ. devel. Commn., 1987-89; pres. St. Philip Neri Sch. Bd., Chgo., 1981-85, South Shore Commn., Chgo., 1982-84. King Chavez Parks fellow U. Mich., 1991, H.I. Feldman fellow Yale U., 1972; Franklin W. Gregory scholar Yale U., 1974, Nat. Achievement scholar U. Pa., 1968. Mem. Am. Assn. Mus., Am. Assn. Mus. Adminstrs., Constrn. Specifications Inst., Lambda Alpha. Avocations: sailing, chess, reading, astronomy. Office: Detroit Inst of Arts 5200 Woodward Ave Detroit MI 48202-4094 E-mail: mparrish@dia.org.

PARRISH, OVERTON BURGIN, JR., pharmaceutical corporation executive; b. Cin., May 26, 1933; s. Overton Burgin and Geneva Opal (Shinn) P. BS, Lawrence U., 1955; MBA, U. Chgo., 1959. With Pfizer Inc., 1959-74; salesman Pfizer Labs., Chgo., 1959-62, asst. mktg. product mgr. NYC, 1962-63, product mgr., 1964-66, group product mgr., 1966-67, mktg. mgr., 1967-68, v.p. mktg., 1969-70, v.p., dir. ops., 1970-71; exec. v.p. domestic pharm. div. Pfizer Pharms., 1971-72; exec. v.p., dir. Pfizer Internat. Divsn., 1972-74; pres., chief operating officer G.D. Searle Internat., Skokie, Ill., 1974-75, pres., chief exec. officer, 1975-77; pres. Worldwide Pharm./Consumer Products Group, 1977-86; pres., chief exec. officer Phoenix Health Care, Chgo., 1987—; chmn., CEO, bd. dirs. Wis. Pharmiacal Co., Inc., 1990-96; co-chmn. Inhalon Pharms., 1991-95, also bd. dirs.; chmn. ViatiCare Fin. Svcs. LLC, 1993—, also bd. dirs.; chmn., CEO, bd. dirs. The Female Health Co., 1996—. Bd. dirs., chair Abiant Inc. Author: The Future Pharmaceutical Marketing; International Drug Pricing, 1971. Trustee Mktg. Sci. Inst.; trustee Food and Drug Law Inst., 1979-86, Lawrence U., 1983-87, 98—. Served to 1st lt. USAF, 1955-57. Mem. Beta Gamma Sigma, Phi Kappa Tau. Office: Phoenix Health Care 515 N State St Chicago IL 60610 Home Phone: 312-822-0790; Office Phone: 312-595-9833. Personal E-mail: oparrish@aol.com.

PARRY, DALE D., publisher, editor; BS in Journalism cum laude, Ball State U., Muncie, Ind., 1981. Feature writer Richmond (Ind.) Palladium-Item, 1981-84, Cin. Enquirer, 1984-86; editor Today section The Dallas Morning News, 1987-90; assignment editor The Way We Live sect. Detroit Free Press, 1990-92, dep. features editor, 1992-94, features editor, 1993-96, asst. mng. editor, 1997-2000, dep. mng. editor, 2001—06; pub. Signature Media, Detroit, 2007—. Mem. Am. Assn. Sun. and Feature Editors. Office: Signature Media 615 W Lafayette Blvd Detroit MI 48226

PARRY-JONES, RICHARD, automotive executive; b. Wales, 1951; Mech. engring. (hon.), Univ. Salford, Manchester, 1973; D (hon.), Loughborough Univ., 1995. Apprentice Ford's European Product Devel. Group, 1969; leading role in devel. of the 1981 European Escort Ford Motor Co., 1981, apptd. mgr. small car programs, 1982, v.p. European vehicle ctr. Dearborn, Mich., 1994—98, group v.p. global product devel. and quality, 1998—2001, group v.p., chief tech. officer, 2001—. Vis. prof. Dept. of Aero. and Automotive Engring. at England's Loughborough U., 2001. Named Exec. Engr.of Ford's Technol. Rsch. in Europe, 1985, Chief Engr. for Vehicle Rngring., 1991, Man of the Yr., Bit. publ. Autocar, 1994, U.S. mag. Automobile, 1997, sr. exec. for Mazda oversight on Nov. 15, 2001; recipient Golden Gear Award, Wash. Motor Press Assn., 2001, Mktg. Statesman of the Yr., Sales and Mktg. Executives of Detroit. Fellow: Inst. of Mech. Engineers, Royal Acad. Engineers. Office: Ford Motor Co One American Rd Dearborn MI 48126-1899

PARSONS, CHARLES ALLAN, JR., lawyer; b. Mpls., July 16, 1943; s. Charles Allan and Grace Adelaide (Covert) P.; m. JoAnne Ruth Russell, Oct. 16, 1965; children: Charles, Daniel, Nancy. BS, U. Minn., 1965, JD cum laude, 1972. Bar: Minn. 1972, U.S. Dist. Ct. Minn. 1972, U.S. Supreme Ct. 1995. Ptnr. Moss & Barnett, P.A., 1972—. Bd. dirs. Legal Advice Clinics Ltd., Mpls., 1975-93, Legal Aid Soc. Mpls., 1999-2004, first v.p., 2000-02, pres., 2002-04; bd. dirs. Mid-Minn. Legal Assistance, 2001-04; chair steering com. S.E. Asian Legal Assistance Project, Mpls., 1988-93. Capt. USMCR, 1968—69, Vietnam. Named Vol. Atty. of Yr., Legal Advice Clinics, Ltd., Mpls., 1990, Top 100 Super Lawyers in Minn., 2004, 05, 06, 07. Mem. ABA, Am. Coll. Real Estate Lawyers, Am. Coll. Mortgage Attys., Minn. State Bar Assn. (co-chair legis. com. real property sect. 1986-06, coun. mem. 1986-06, chair real property sect. 1993-94), Hennepin County Bar Assn. (chair real property sect. 1988-89, Van Valkenburg award for pub. svc. 2002). Roman Catholic. Avocations: reading, walking, biking, hiking. Office: Moss & Barnett PA 4800 Wells Fargo Ctr 90 S 7th Minneapolis MN 55402-4129 Office Phone: 612-877-5276. Business E-Mail: parsonsc@moss-barnett.com.

PARSONS, JEFFREY ROBINSON, anthropologist, educator; b. Washington, Oct. 9, 1939; s. Merton Stanley and Elisabeth (Oldenburg) P.; m. Mary Thomson Hrones, Apr. 27, 1968; 1 child, Apphia Hrones. BS, Pa. State U., 1961; PhD, U. Mich., 1966. Asst. prof. anthropology U. Mich., Ann Arbor, 1966-71, assoc. prof., 1971-76, prof., 1976—2006, dir. mus. anthropology, 1983-86, emeritus prof., 2006—. Vis. prof. Universidad Nacional Autonoma de Mexico, 1987; vis. prof. Universidad Buenos Aires, 1994, Univ. Nac de Catamarca, Argentina, 1996, Univ. Nac de Tucuman, Argentina, 1996, Univ. Mayor de San Andres, Bolivia, 1999. Author: Prehistoric Settlement Patterns in the Texcoco Region, Mexico, 1971; (with William T. Sanders and Robert Santley) The Basin of Mexico: The Cultural Ecology of a Civilization, 1979; (with E. Brumfiel) Prehispanic Settlement Patterns in the Southern Valley of Mexico, 1982; (with M. Parsons) Chinampa Agriculture and Aztec Urbanization in the Valley of Mexico, 1985; (with Mary H. Parsons) Maguey Utilization in Highland Central Mexico, 1990; The Production and Consumption of Salt During Postclassic Times in the Valley of Mexico, 1994; (with E. Brumfiel and M. Hodge) The Developmental Implications of Earlier Dates for Early Aztec in the Basin of Mexico, 1996; (with C. Hastings and R. Matos) Rebuilding the State in Highland Peru, 1997; A Regional Perspective on Inca Impact in the Sierra Central, Peru, 1998; (with C. Hastings and R. Matos) Prehispanic Settlement Patterns in the Upper Mantaro-Tarma Drainage, Peru, 2000; The Last Saltmakers of Nexquipayac, Mexico, 2001; (with Luis Morett) Recursos aquaticos en la subsistancia Azteca; 2004, The Last Pescadores of Chimalhuacan, Mexico, 2006. Rsch. grantee NSF, 1967, 70, 72-73, 75-76, 81, Nat. Geog. Soc., 1984, 86, 88, 2003. Mem. Am. Anthrop. Assn. (Alfred V. Kidder award 1998), Soc. Am. Archaeology, AAAS, Inst. Andean Rsch., Inst. Andean Studies, Sociedad Mexicana de Antropologia, Sociedad Argentina de Antropologia. Office: Museum of Anthropology U Mich Ann Arbor MI 48109 Business E-Mail: jpar@umich.edu.

PART, HOWARD MITCHELL, dean; b. NYC, Apr. 26, 1949; m. Kristine Kunesh-Part. BS, Ohio U.; MD, Ohio State U., 1982. Cert. Am. Bd. Internal Medicine. Intern Ohio State U. Hospitals, Columbus, 1982—83, resident in internal medicine, 1983—85; voluntary faculty mem. Wright State U. Sch. Medicine, Dayton, Ohio, 1986—88, mem. faculty, 1988—, chief of gen. medicine consult svc., dir. internal medicine residency program Dayton VA Med. Ctr., assoc. dean faculty and clin. affairs, 1995—98, acting dean, 1998—99, dean, 1999—. Recipient Dean's Award for Excellence in Med. Edn., Wright State U. Sch. Medicine, 1992, Disting. Teaching award, 1996, Master Teacher of Medicine award, Am. Coll. of Physicians, 2000. Fellow: Am. Coll. Physicians (Gov.'s Award -Ohio Chpt.); mem.: Am. Bd. of Internal Medicine. Office: 115 Med Scis Bldg Wright State U 3640 Colonel Glenn Hwy Dayton OH 45435-0001 Office Phone: 937-775-3010. Office Fax: 937-775-2211.

PARTLOW, MADELINE, principal; married; 4 children. Degree in Early and Mid. Childhood Edn., Ohio State U., M in Early and Mid. Childhood, 1995, PhD in Ednl. Adminstrn., 1997. Tchr. New Albany Mid. Sch., Ohio, 1979—83, 1985—88, prin., 2001—06; from tchr. to prin. Blacklick Elem., Gahanna, 1992—2000; dir. tchg. and learning New Albany Local Schs., 2006—. Office: New Albany Mid Sch 6600 E Dublin-Granville Rd New Albany OH 43054-8740

PARTRIDGE, MARK VAN BUREN, lawyer, educator, mediator, writer; b. Rochester, Minn., Oct. 16, 1954; s. John V.B. and Constance (Brainerd) P.; m. Mary Roberta Moffitt, Apr. 30, 1983; children: Caitlin, Lindsay, Christopher. BA, U. Nebr., 1978; JD, Harvard U., 1981. Bar: Ill. 1981, U.S. Dist. Ct. (no. dist.) Ill. 1981, U.S. Dist. Ct. (ea. dist.) Mich. 1983, U.S. Ct. Appeals (1st. cir) 2003, U.S. Ct. Appeals (4th cir.) 1986, U.S. Ct. Appeals (7th cir.), 1992, U.S. Ct. Appeals (5th cir.) 1993, U.S. Ct. Appeals (3rd cir.) 1998. Assoc. Pattishall, McAuliffe, Newbury, Hilliard & Geraldson, LLP, Chgo., 1981-88, ptnr., 1988—, exec. com., 2003—. Adj. prof. John Marshall Law Sch., Chgo., 1987—; arbitrator Cook County Mandatory Arbitration Program, 1989-2003; v.p. Harvard Legal Aid Bur., 1980-81; mediator no. dist. Ill. Voluntary Mediation Program, 1997—; panelist World Intellectual Property Orgn., Domain Name Dispute Resolution Svc., 1999—; neutral Nat. Arbitration Forum, Intellectual Property Mediation and Arbitration Panel, 2004—; mediator Internat. Trademark Assn. Panel of eutrals, 2005—; bd. adv. N.W. Law Sch., Jour. Tech. and Intellectual Property. Author, Guilding Rights Trademarks, Copyright and the Internet, iUniverse, 2003, Contbr. articles to profl. jours.; mem. editl. bd. The Trademark Reporter, 1994-97; adv. bd. IP Litigator, 1995—. Vol. Chgo. Vol. Legal Svcs., 1983—. Fellow Am. Intellectual Property Law Assn. (com. chmn. 1989-91, 96-98, bd. dirs. 1998-2001); mem. ABA (com. chmn. 1989-91, 94-99, rep. 2006—), Internat. Trademark Assn. (com. vice chmn. 1996), World Intellectual Property Orgn. (experts panel internet domain name process 1998-99), Intellectual Property Law Assn. Chgo. (com. chmn. 1993-96), Brand Names Ednl. Found. (moot ct. regional chmn. 1994-96, nat. vice-chmn. 1997-98, nat. chmn. 1998-99), at. Spkrs. Assn. (Ill. chpt. pres.-elect 2006), Legal Club (v.p. 1998, pres. 1999), Lawyers Club Chgo. (pres. 2000, bd. dirs. 2000-01), Execs. Club, Union League Club, Harvard Club Chgo., Bagatelle Club. Avocations: writing, music, genealogy, travel, internet. Office: Pattishall McAuliffe Newbury Hilliard & Geraldson LLP 311 S Wacker Dr Ste 5000 Chicago IL 60606-6631 Office Phone: 312-554-8000. Business E-Mail: mpartridge@pattishall.com.

PARZEN, STANLEY JULIUS, lawyer; b. NYC, Feb. 6, 1952; BA, Earlham Coll., 1973; LLB cum laude, Harvard U., 1976. Bar: Ill. 1978, U.S. Dist. Ct. (no. dist.) Ill. 1978, U.S. Dist. Ct. (no. dist.) Calif. 1989, U.s. Dist. Ct. (we. dist.) Mich. 1995, U.S. Ct. Appeals (7th cir.) 1981, U.S. Ct. Appeals (8th cir.) 1983, U.S. Ct. Appeals (5th cir.) 1992, U.S. Ct. appeals (D.C. cir.) 1992, U.S. Ct. Appeals (2d cir.) 1990, U.S. Ct. Appeals (9th cir.) 1996, U.S. Ct. Appeals (6th cir.) 2003. Law clk. to judge U.S. Ct. Appeals 4th cir., 1976-77; ptnr. Mayer, Brown Rowed Maw LLP, Chgo. Mem. Phi Beta Kappa. Office: Mayer Brown Rowe Maw LLP 71 S Wacker Dr Chicago IL 60603-4637 Office Phone: 312-701-7326. E-mail: sparzen@mayerbrownrowe.com.

PASCAL, ROGER, lawyer; b. Chgo., Mar. 16, 1941; s. Samuel A. and Harriet E. (Hartman) P.; m. Martha Hecht, June 16, 1963; children: Deborah, Diane, David AB with distinction, U. Mich, 1962; JD cum laude, Harvard U., 1965. Bar: Ill. 1965, US Dist. Ct. (no. dist. Ill.) 1965, US Ct. Appeals (7th cir.) 1969, US Supreme Ct. 1976, Wis. 1985, US Ct. Appeals (2nd, 6th, 9th and 10th cirs.) 1986. Lic. pilot, FAA, 1977, instrument rating, 1979. Assoc. Schiff Hardin, LLP, Chgo., 1965-71, ptnr., 1972—. Adj. prof. law Northwestern U. Law Sch., 1994—; bd. dirs. Evanston Cmty. Defender; instr. Nat. Inst. for Trial Advocacy, 1989-. Bd. dirs., mem. exec. com. Chgo. Law Enforcement Study Grp., 1975-80, pres., 1978-80; pres. Harvard Law Soc. Ill., 1976-78; bd. dirs. ACLU of Ill., 1984—, gen. counsel, 1986—. Recipient Roger Baldwin Lifetime Achievement award, 2003. Fellow Am. Bar Found.; mem. ABA (antitrust, intellectual property, and litig. sects.), Pub. Interest Law Initiative (bd. dirs. 1989—, v.p. 1995-97, pres. 1997-98), Fund for Justice (v.p., bd. dirs. 1986-97), Chgo. Coun. Lawyers (bd. dirs. 1970-74, 80-84, 2004—), Chgo. Legal Assistance Found. (bd. dirs. 1985-88), Chgo. Bar Found.(recipient Edward Lewis II Pro Bono Svc. award, 2003), Univ. Club, Met. Club, Phi Beta Kappa. Avocation: flying. Office: Schiff Hardin LLP 6600 Sears Tower Chicago IL 60606-6473 Office Fax: 312-258-5600. E-mail: rpascal@schiffhardin.com.

PASCUAL, MERCEDES, biology professor; PhD in Joint Program, Woods Hole Oceanographic Inst. and MIT, 1995. Asst. prof. dept. ecology and evolutionary biology U. Mich., 2001—. Mem. Ctr. for the Study of Complex Systems U. Mich. Named one of 50 Most Important Women in Sci., Discover mag., 2002; Alexander Hollaender Disting. Postdoctoral Fellow, U.S. Dept. of Energy, Centennial Fellowship, Global and Complex Systems from the James S. McDonnell Found. Office: U Mich Kraus 2045 Ann Arbor MI 48109-1048

PASKACH, DAVID M., lawyer, food products executive; BS in Acctg., Iowa State U., 1980; JD, U. Ill., 1983. Bar: Iowa 1983, Ill. 1983, Minn. 1989. Atty., Iowa; corp. atty. Schwan Food, Marshall, Minn., 1989—93, sr. atty., 1993—97, gen. counsel, 1997, v.p. adminstrn., exec. v.p., gen. counsel, sec., 1997—2004; pres. Schwan's Venture Group, Marshall, 2005—. Lt. col. USAFR, ret. Office: Schwan Food 115 W College Dr Marshall MN 56258

PASTORE, DONNA LEE, physical education educator; BA in Phys. Edn., U. Fla., 1981, MA in Phys. Edn., 1983; PhD, U. So. Calif., 1988. Instr. Pa. State U., Beaver, Pa.; asst. prof. Sch. Health Ohio State U., assoc. prof. Advisor Sports Mgmt. Club. Editl. bd. Jour. Sport Mgmt.; rev. Strategies. State coord. Nat. Girls and Women in Sport Day, 1992. Recipient NAGWS Linds to to Leadership award, 1982, NAGWS Rsch. award, 1983, Mabel Lee award, 1995. Mem. Ohio AHPERD (chair rsch. sect. higher edn., v.p.-elect sports sci. divsn., eastern dist. bylaws & oper. code com.), N. Am. Soc. Sports Mgmt. Office: Ohio State U Sch Phys Activity and Ednl Svcs 455 Larkins Hall 337 W 17th Ave Columbus OH 43210 E-mail: pastore.3@osu.edu.

PASULA, ANGELA MARIE, lawyer; b. Michigan City, Ind., Oct. 2, 1956; d. Edward Joseph Pasula and Theresa Jeanette (Stella) Hack; m. David Mark Prusa, June 19, 1982. BA in Polit. Sci. cum laude, Western Mich. U., 1977; JD, Valparaiso U., 1980. Bar: Mich. 1980. Asst. pros. atty. Kalamazoo (Mich.) Prosecutors Office, 1980-82, Berrien County Prosecutors Office, Niles, Mich., 1982—. Office: Berrien County Prosecutors Office 1205 Front St Niles MI 49120-1627

PATE, PAUL DANNY, mayor; b. Ottumwa, Iowa, May 1, 1958; s. Paul Devern and Velma Marie (McConnell) P.; m. Jane Ann Wacker, July 15, 1978; children: Jennifer Ann, Paul Daniel III, Amber Lynn. AA in Bus., Kirkwood Coll., 1978; cert. fin. mgmt. program, U. Pa., 1990. Exec. dir. Jr. Achievement, Cedar Rapids, Iowa, 1978-82; pres. PM Systems Corp., Cedar Rapids, 1982—; senator Iowa State Senate, Des Moines, 1989-93; Sec. of State State of Iowa, 1994-98; mayor City of Cedar Rapids, 2002—06. Chmn. Iowa Young Reps., Des Moines, 1989-93. Recipient Guardian Small Bus. award Nat. Fedn. Independent Bus., 1990; named Young Entrepreneur of Yr. U.S. Small Bus. Adminstrn., Iowa, 1988, Alumnus of Yr. Kirkwood Coll., Cedar Rapids, 1990. Republican. Methodist. Avocation: water-skiing. Home: 6801 Bowman Ln NE Cedar Rapids IA 52402-1575 Office: Pate Group 3285 3rd Ave Marion IA 52302-3928

PATEL, HOMI BURJOR, apparel executive; b. Bombay, June 28, 1949; s. Burjor Ratan and Roshen Burjor (Marfatia) P.; married; children: Neville H., Cyrus H., Natasha E. BS in Stats., U. Bombay, 1973; MBA in Fin. and Mktg., Columbia U., 1975. Exec. asst. to pres. Corbin Ltd., NYC, 1976, dir. mktg., 1978; with subs. Hartmarx Corp., Chgo., 1979—; v.p., gen. mgr. Fashionaire Apparel Inc., Chgo., 1979-81; exec. v.p. Austin Reed of Regent St., Chgo., 1981-82, M. Wile and Co., Buffalo, 1982-84; pres., chief exec. officer M. Wile & Co., Johnny Carson Apparel, Intercontinental Apparel, Buffalo, 1984—; group exec. v.p. Hartmarx Mens Apparel Group Corp., Buffalo, 1987-91, chmn., ceo Chgo., 1991-92; pres., COO Hartmarx Corp., Chgo., 1992—, bd. dirs., 1994—2001, CEO, 2002—. Mem. Clothing Mfrs. Assn. Am. (bd. dirs. 1984—, chief labor negotiator for U.S. tailored clothing industry), Univ. Club N.Y., Chgo. Club. Office: Hartmarx Corp 101 N Wacker Dr Fl 23 Chicago IL 60606-1718

PATEL, VIRENDRA CHATURBHAI, mechanical engineer, educator; b. Mombasa, Kenya, Nov. 9, 1938; arrived in US, 1969, naturalized, 1975; s. Chaturbhai S. and Kantaben N. (Rai) Patel; m. Manjula Patel, May 29, 1966; children: Sanjay, Bindiya. BSc with honors, Imperial Coll., London, 1962; PhD, Cambridge U., Eng., 1965; Dr. honoris causa, Tech. U. Civil Engring., Bucharest, Romania, 1994. Sr. asst. in rsch. Cambridge U., 1965-69; vis. prof. Indian Inst. Tech., Kharagpur, 1966; cons. Lockheed Ga. Co., Marietta, 1969-70; from mem. faculty to disting. prof. U. Iowa, Iowa City, 1971—90, disting. prof., 1990—, Edwin B. Green chair in hydraulics, 2000—; rsch. engr. Iowa Inst. Hydraulic Rsch., 1971—, dir., 1994—2004, hon. prof. Dharamsinh Desai Inst. Tech., 2002—, dir. Ctr. Computer Aided Design, 2003—05. Mem. Iowa Gov. Sci. Adv. Coun., 1977—83; mem. resistance com. Internat. Towing Tank Conf., 1978—87; vis. prof. U. Karlsruhe, Germany, 1980—81, Ecole Nationale Superieure de Mechanique, Nantes, France, 1984, Nantes, 96; jubilee prof. Chalmers Inst. Tech., Goteborg, Sweden, 1988; dir. Ctr. for Computer Aided Design, 2003—; cons. in field. Author: (book) Three Dimensional Turbulent Boundary Layers, 1972; contbr. articles to profl. jours.; assoc. editor: AIAA Jour., 1987—90. V.p. internat. com. Anooram Mission, Mogri, India. Recipient Sr. Scientist award, Alexander von Humboldt Found., 1980, 1993. Fellow: ASME (Fluids Engring. award 1997), AIAA (assoc.); mem.: Soc. Naval Archtl. Marine Engrs., Am. Soc. Engring. Edn., Pi Tau Sigma, Sigma Xi. Home: 60 Kennedy Pkwy Iowa City IA 52246-2780 Office: IIHR Hyrdoscience and Engring U Iowa 302 Hydraulics Laboratory Iowa City IA 52242-1585 Business E-Mail: v-c-patel@uiowa.edu.

PATIENT, WILLIAM F., chemicals executive; V.p. sales and mktg. Borg-Warner Chemicals, v.p. mfg.; pres. Borg-Warner Chemicals Europe; sr. v.p. BF Goodrich Company, pres. Geon Vinyl divsn.; CEO Geon (now PolyOne Corp.), 1993—99; chmn. PolyOne, Corp., 2003—06, lead dir., 2006—. Bd. dir. Navistar Internat. Corp. Bd. dir. Wash. U.; chmn. of bd. Cleve. State U. Found. Office: 33587 Walker RD Avon Lake OH 44012-1145

PATRICK, DANICA SUE, race car driver; b. Beloit, Wis., Mar. 25, 1982; d. T.J. and Bev Patrick; m. Paul Edward Hospenthal, Nov. 19, 2005. Race car driver Indy Racing League Rahal Letterman Racing, 2005—06, Andretti Green Racing, 2007—. 4th pl. Indy Japan 300 Twin Ring Motegi, 2005, 1st pl. Indy Japan 300, 08; 4th pl. Indpls. 500 Indpls. Motor Speedway, 2005; 4th pl. Firestone Indy 200 Nashville Superspeedway, 2006, 3rd pl. Firestone Indy 200, 07; 4th pl. ABC Supply Co. A.J. Foyt 225 Milw. Mile, 2006; 3rd pl. Bombardier Learjet 550 Tex. Motor Speedway, 2007; 2nd pl. Detroit Indy Grand Prix Raceway on Belle Isle, 2007. Co-author (with Laura Morton): Danica: Crossing the Line, 2006. Named Rookie of Yr., Indy 500, 2005, Indy Racing League, 2005. Roman Catholic. Achievements include being the first female driver to win pole position at the Toyota Atlantic, Portland, 2004; being the fourth woman ever to qualify for the Indianapolis 500, 2005; becoming the first female driver in the Indy Racing League's history to place first, 2008. Mailing: c/o Andretti Green Racing 7615 Zionsville Rd Indianapolis IN 46268*

PATRICK, JOHN JOSEPH, social sciences educator; b. East Chicago, Ind., Apr. 14, 1935; s. John W. and Elizabeth (Lazar) P.; m. Patricia Grant, Aug. 17, 1963; children: Rebecca, Barbara AB, Dartmouth Coll., 1957; Ed.D., Ind. U., 1969. Social studies tchr. Roosevelt High Sch., East Chicago, 1957-62; social studies tchr. Lab. High Sch., U. Chgo., 1962-65; research assoc. Sch. Edn., Ind. U., Bloomington, 1965-69, asst. prof., 1969-74, assoc. prof., 1974-77, prof. edn., 1977—2004, prof. emeritus edn., 2004—, dir. social studies devel. ctr., 1986—2004, dir. ERIC clearinghouse for social studies, social sci. edn., 1986—2003. Bd. dirs. Biol. Scis. Curriculum Study, 1980-83; ednl. cons. Author: Progress of the Afro-American, 1968, The Young Voter, 1974; (with L. Ehman, Howard Mehlinger) Toward Effective Instruction in Secondary Social Studies, 1974, Lessons on the Northwest Ordinance, 1987; (with R. Remy) Civics for Americans, 1980, rev. edit. 1986; (with Mehlinger) American Political Behavior, 1972, rev. edit. 1980, (with C. Keller) Lessons on the Federalist Papers, 1987; America Past and Present, 1983; (with Carol Berkin) History of the American Nation, 1984, rev. edit., 1987; Lessons on the Constitution, 1985, James Madison and the Federalist Papers, 1990, How to Teach the Bill of Rights, 1991, Ideas of the Founders on Constitutional Government: Resources for Teachers of History and Government, 1991, Young Oxford Companion to the Supreme Court of the United States, 1994, Founding the Republic: A Documentary History, 1995, (with Gerald Long) Constitutional Debates on Freedom of Religion: A Documentary History, 1999, (with Richard M. Pious and Donald A. Ritchie) The Oxford Essential Guide to the U.S. Government, 2000, The Bill of Rights: A History in Documents, 2002, Understanding Democracy, 2006, (with Kermit L. Hall) The Pursuit of Justice: Supreme Court Decisions That Shaped America, 2006. Bd. dirs. Law in Am. Soc. Found., 1984-88, Social Sci. Edn. consortium, 1984—; mem. Gov.'s Task Force on Citizenship Edn., Ind., 1982-87; active Ind. Commn. on Bicentennial of U.S. Constn., 1986-92; bd. dirs. Coun. for the Advancement of Citizenship, Nat. History Edn. Network, 1994-96; mem. Natr. Coun. for History Standards, 1991-94. Recipient John W. Ryan award for disting. svc. in internat. programs and studies, Ind. U., 2002, Civic Edn. award, Ind. State Bar Assn., 2005. Mem. ASCD, Nat. Coun. Social Studies, Social Sci. Edn. Consortium (v.p. 1985-87), Coun. for Basic Edn., Am. Polit. Sci. Assn., Am. Hist. Assn., Orgn. Am. Historians, Ind. State Bar Assn. (recipient Civic Edn. award 2005), Phi Delta Kappa. Home: 1209 E University St Bloomington IN 47401-5045 Office: Ind U 2805 E 10th St Bloomington IN 47408-2601 Business E-Mail: patrick@indiana.edu.

PATTEN, RONALD JAMES, university dean; b. Iron Mountain, Mich., July 17, 1935; s. Rudolph Joseph and Cecelia (Fuse) Pataconi; m. Shirley Ann Bierman, Sept. 5, 1959; children: Christine Marie, Cheryl Ann, Charlene Denise. BA, Mich. State U., East Lansing, 1957, MA, 1959; PhD, U. Ala., Tuscaloosa, 1963. Acct. Price Waterhouse & Co., Detroit, 1958; instr. No. Ill. U., 1959-60; asst. prof. U. Colo., 1963-65; assoc. prof. Va. Poly. Inst. and State U., 1965-67, prof., 1967-73, head dept. accounting, 1966-73; dir. research Financial Accounting Standards Bd., Conn., 1973-74; dean Sch. Bus. Adminstrn., U. Conn., Storrs, 1974-88; chief of party-Eastern Caribbean Arthur D. Little Internat., 1988-89; dean Coll. Commerce and Kellstadt Grad. Sch. Bus. De Paul U., Chgo., 1989-99; dean Ritsumeikan Asia Pacific U. Grad. Sch. Mgmt., Beppu, Japan, 2003—06. Individual investors adv. com. NY Stock Exch., 1993—98; cons. in field. Contbr. chapters to books, articles to profl. jours. Bd. dirs. US com. UNICEF, Chgo., 1996—99. Recipient Nat. Quartermaster award Nat. Quartermaster, Assn., 1956; Earhart Found. fellow, 1962-63. Mem. AICPA, Am. Acctg. Assn., Inst. Mgmt. Accts., Acad. Internat. Bus. (Internat. Dean of Yr. award 1987), Internat. Assn. for Acctg. Edn. and Rsch., Ill. Coun. Econ. Edn. (Chgo., trustee 1989-2006, chmn. bd. trustees 1997-2000), Pacioli Soc., Internat. Trade and Fin. Assn., dir. 1998-2000, Heidelberg Club Internat., Scabbard and Blade, Golden Key, Beta Gamma Sigma (mem. bd. govs. 1975-90, nat. sec.-treas. 1980-82, nat. v.p. 1982-84, nat. pres. 1984-86), Beta Alpha Psi (bd. dirs. 1992-94), Delta Sigma Pi, World Assn. for Case Method Rsch. and Application, Adv Bd., 1998-, Phi Kappa Phi, Delta Mu Delta. Avocations: hiking, softball, golf, travel, singing. Home: PO Box 190 Newfield ME 04056 Business E-Mail: rpatten@depaul.edu.

PATTERSON, DEB, women's college basketball coach; Grad., Rockford Coll., 1979. Coach Hononegah HS, Ill., 1982—86; asst. coach No. Ill. U., 1986—87, asst. coach, recruiting coord., 1987—91, Vanderbilt U., 1992-96; asst. coach So. Ill. U., 1991-92; head coach Kans. State U., 1996—. Asst. coach World U. Games, 1997, World Championships, 1998, Jr. World Championship Qualifying Team, 2000; asst. coach Women's Sr. Nat. Team USA Invitational Tournament of Champions, 1997. amed Coach of Yr. Ill. HS Assn., 1985, Conf. Coach of Yr., 1985, 86, Women's Coll. Basketball Coach of Yr. Kans. Basketball Coaches Assn., 1997, 2002, ESPN The Mag. Coach of Yr., 2002, Big 12 Coach of Yr., 2002, Women's Basketball Coaches Assn. Dist. V Coach of Yr., 2002, Dallas Morning News, Austin-Am. Statesman and San Antonio Express News Big 12 Coach of Yr., 2002. Achievements include leading Kansas State to Women's

National Invitational Tournament Championship as head coach, 2006. Office: Kansas State U Womens Basketball 1800 College Ave Manhattan KS 66502-3308 Office Phone: 785-532-6970. E-mail: dlpip@k-state.edu.

PATTERSON, JAMES MILTON, marketing specialist, educator; b. DeQueen, Ark., Oct. 15, 1927; s. Charles Edward and Phoebe Allene (Steel) P.; m. Della Jeanne Hays, July 3, 1964; children— J. Marshall, Julia M.; children by previous marriage— Robert T., Donald A. BS, U.S. Mcht. Marine Acad., 1948; MBA (Teagle Found. fellow), Cornell U., 1954, PhD (Ford Found. dissertation fellow), 1961. Third mate Esso Shipping Co., 1948-52; instr. in bus. adminstrn. Northwestern U., 1957-60; lectr. Center for Programs in Govt. Adminstrn., U. Chgo., 1959; asst. prof. mktg. Ind. U., 1960-63, asso. prof., 1963-69, prof., 1969—, chmn. dept. mktg., 1972-78, asso. dir. Poynter Ctr., 1980, acting dir., 1981, co-sec. U. Faculty Coun., pres. Bloomington Faculty Coun.; dir. Ind. U. Inst. for Advanced Study, 1994-97. Bd. dirs. Inst. Advanced Study; cons. petroleum mktg.; expert witness on antitrust and mktg. Author: Marketing: The Firm's Viewpoint, 1964, Highway Robbery: An Analysis of the Gasoline Crisis, 1974, Competition Ltd.: The Marketing of Gasoline, 1972. With USNR, 1945-48. Mem. Assn. for Practical & Profl. Ethics. Democrat. Office: Ind U Inst Advanced Study Bloomington IN 47405 E-mail: tartan33@aol.com.

PATTERSON, MARIA JEVITZ, microbiology/pediatric infectious disease professor; b. Berwyn, Ill., Oct. 23, 1944; d. Frank Jacob and Edna Frances (Costabile) Jevitz; m. Ronald James Patterson, Aug. 22, 1970; children: Kristin Lara, Kier Nicole. BS in Med. Tech. summa cum laude, Coll. St. Francis, Joliet, Ill., 1966; PhD in Microbiology, Northwestern U., Chgo., 1970; MD, Mich. State U., 1984. Diplomate Am. Bd. Med. Examiners, Am. Bd. Pediatrics Gen. Pediatrics, Am. Bd. Pediatrics Infectious Diseases. Lab. asst., instr. med. microbiology for student nurses Med. Sch. Northwestern U., Chgo., 1966-70; postdoctoral fellow in clin. microbiology affiliated hosps. U. Wash., Seattle, 1971-72; asst. prof. microbiology and pub. health Mich. State U., East Lansing, 1972-77, assoc. prof., 1977-82, assoc. prof. pathology, 1979-82, lectr. dept. microbiology and pub. health, 1982-87, resident in pediatrics affiliated hosps., 1984-85, 86-87, clin. instr. dept. pediatrics and human devel., 1984-87, assoc. prof. microbiology-pub. health-pediatrics-human devel., 1987-90, prof., 1990—. Staff microbiologist dept. pathology Lansing Gen. Hosp., 1972-75; dir. clin. microbiology grad. program. Mich. State U., 1974-81, staff microbiologist, 1978-81; postdoctoral fellow in infectious diseases U. Mass. Med. Ctr., Worcester, 1985-86; asst. dir. pediatrics residency Grad. Med. Edn. Inc., Lansing, 1987-90; med. dir. Pediatrics Health Ctr. St. Lawrence Hosp., Lansing, Mich., 1987-90, Ingham Med. Ctr., 1990-94; cons. clin. microbiology Lansing Gen. Hosp., 1972-75, Mich. State U., 1976-82, Mich. Dept. Pub. Health, 1976—, Ingham County Health Dept., 1988—, Am. Health Cons., 1993, State of Mich. Atty. Gen. Office, 1994-98, Lansing Sch. Dist., 1998—, Mich. Antibiotic Resistance Reduction, 1998—; cons. to editl. bd. Infection and Immunity, 1977; cons. Mich. State U. AIDS Edn. Tng. Ctr, 2001—; presenter seminars. Contbg. author: Microbiology: Principles and Concepts, 1982, 4th edit., 1995, Pediatric Emergency Medicine, 1992, Principles and Practice of Emergency Medicine, 1997, Rudolph's Pediatrics, 2002; item writer certifying bd. examination Bd. Am. Acad. Pediats., 1990—, Am. Bd. Osteopathy, 1997—; contbr. articles to profl. jours. and publs. Mem. hon. com. Lansing AIDS Meml. Quilt, 1993. Recipient award for tchg. excellence Mich. State U. Coll. Osteo. Medicine, 1977, 78, 79, 80, 83, Disting. Faculty award Mich. State U., 1980, Woman Achiever award, 1985, excellence in pediatric residency tchg. award, 1988, 2001, 03, 05, Alumni Profl. Achievement award Coll. of St. Francis, 1991, excellence in diversity award Mich. State U., 2000, Weil Endowed Disting. Pediat. Faculty award, 2001; grantee renal disease divsn. Mich. Dept. Pub. Health 1976-82. Fellow Pediatric Infectious Diseases Soc., Infectious Diseases Soc. Am., Am. Acad. Pediatrics; mem. Am. Coll. Physician Execs., Am. Soc. Microbiology, Am. Soc. Clin. Pathologists (affiliate, bd. registrant), South Ctrl. Assn. Clin. Microbiology, Mich. Infectious Diseases Soc., N.Y. Acad. Scis., Kappa Gamma Pi, Lambda Iota Tau. Roman Catholic. Home: 1520 River Ter East Lansing MI 48823-5314 Office: Mich State Univ Microbiology/Molecular Genetics/Pediat East Lansing MI 48824-4320

PATTERSON, NEAL L., information systems company executive; BS in Fin., Okla. State U., MBA. Sys. cons., mgr. Arthur Andersen & Co., Kansas City, Mo.; co-founder, CEO, chmn. bd. dirs. Cerner Corp., Kansas City, Mo., 1979—. Trustee Midwest Rsch. Inst.; mem. steering com. Coun. Growing Cos. Named Entrepreneur of Yr., Ernst & Young, 1991. Mem. Health Execs. Network. Office: Cerner Corp 2800 Rockcreek Pkwy Ste 601 Kansas City MO 64117-2521

PATTIS, MARK R., publishing company executive; b. Chgo., Mar. 15, 1953; BS in Econs. with hons., Swarthmore Coll.; postgrad. studies, U. Chgo., London Sch. Econs., Sorbonne, Paris. Banker Chase Manhattan Bank, Am. Nat. Bank, Chgo.; staff Marmon Group; exec. NTC/ Contemporary Publ. Co., Lincolnwood, Ill., 1977—, pres., CEO, 1996-2000, Next Chpt. Holdings, Highland Park, Ill., 2000—. Recipient Palmes Academiques award Govt. of France, 1993, Electronic Book award of excellence, Sony, 1994; nominated for Watson fellowship. Mem. Chgo. Book Clinic, U.S. Electronic Book Publ. Com. (co-chmn 1991-95), Multimedia and Electronic Book Internat. Com. (vice chmn.). Office: Next Chpt Holdings Ste 205 600 Center Ave Highland Park IL 60035

PATTON, SYLVESTER, state representative; b. Youngstown, Ohio, June 12, 1949; 2 children. State rep. dist. 60 Ohio Ho. of Reps., Columbus, 1997—, ranking minority mem., transp. and justice subcom., mem. fin. and appropriations, human svcs. and aging, state govt., and transp. and pub. safety coms. V.p. family svcs. agy. Mahoning County, Ohio; mem. strategic planning commn. Youngstown (Ohio) Bd. Edn.; chmn. Gov.'s Commn. of African Am. Males; 1st vice chmn. Mahoning Dem. Party; Youngstown committeeman 5th Ward. Recipient Friends of Family Planning award, Planning Parenthood of Mahoning Valley, 2000, award, Black Knights Police Assn. Office: 77 S High St 10th fl Columbus OH 43215-6111

PATTON, THOMAS, state representative; Co-founder Cleve. Bus. Systems; mktg. cons. Meritech Blue, Cleve.; state rep. dist. 18 Ohio Ho. of Reps., Columbus, 2002—, vice chair, transp. and justice subcom., mem. banking pensions and securities, fin. and appropriations, ins., pub. utilities, and rules and reference coms. Del. Cleve. AFL-CIO; fin. chmn. St. Colman's Ch.; mem. Holy Name Endowment Bd. Mem.: Treasurers and Ticket Sellers Union (pres., 18 yrs.), Cleve. Police Hist. Soc. (trustee). Office: 77 S High St 11th fl Columbus OH 43215-6111

PAUL, ALLEN E., state legislator; b. Ind., Mar. 30, 1945; m. Terri Mann; 1 child, Allen H.L. BS in Polit. Sci. and History, Parsons Coll., 1967. Del. Rep. State Conv., 1972-88; mem. from dist. 27 Ind. Senate from 27th dist., 1986—; majority whip Senate Leadership, 1992—; mem. govt. and regulatory affairs, natural resources, rules and legislative procedures coms. Ind. Senate; pres. Innovative Industries, Inc., Richmond, Ind. Author: Vietnam Letters. Exec. bd. dirs. Richmond YMCA; past v.p. Civic Theatre, bd. dirs; past. pres. Wayne County Hist. Soc. and Mus.; past comdr. Sons of Vets. Hist. Group. Sgt. U.S. Army, 1967-70, Viet Nam. Decorated Bronze Star; recipient Sagamore of the Wabash Gov. Orr, 1988. Mem. VFW, AMVETS, Am. Legion, Marine Corps League (hon. life), Richmond and Wayne County C. of C. (free enterprise com., legis. com., small bus. com., Outstanding Svc. of Month award), Howe Mil. Acad. Alumni (bd. dirs.), Ind. Football Hall of Fame (past bd. mem.), Jaycees of Richmond, Rotary, Yorkfellow Luncheon Group, Tau Kappa Epsilon (past pres.). Republican. Methodist. Office: Ind Senate Dist 27 200 W Washington St Indianapolis IN 46204-2728

PAUL, ANNEGRET, mathematics professor; PhD, Univ. Md., College Park, 1996. Adj. asst. prof. Univ. Calif., Berkeley, 1996—99; now assoc. prof. math. We. Mich. Univ., Kalamazoo. Mem.: Assn. Women in Math., Am. Math. Soc., Pi Mu Epsilon. Achievements include being one of 18 top mathematicians and computer scientists (Atlas of Lie Groups Project) from the US to successfully map E8, one of the largest and most complicated structures in mathematics. Office: Dept Math 6619 Everett Tower Western Mich Univ Kalamazoo MI 49008-5248 Business E-Mail: annegret.paul@wmich.edu, paul@wmich.edu.

PAUL, ARA GARO, university dean; b. New Castle, Pa., Mar. 1, 1929; s. John Hagop and Mary (Injejikian) P.; m. Shirley Elaine Waterman, Dec. 21, 1962; children: John Bartlett, Richard Goyan. BS in Pharmacy, Idaho State U., 1950; MS, U. Conn., 1953, PhD in Pharmacognosy, 1956. Cons. plant physiology Argonne Nat. Lab., Ill., 1955; asst. prof. pharmacognosy Butler U., Indpls., 1956-57; faculty U. Mich., Ann Arbor, 1957—, prof. pharmacognosy, 1969—; dean U. Mich. Coll. Pharmacy, 1975-96, dean emeritus, Hans W. Vahlteich prof. pharmacognosy, 2001—04, prof. emeritus, 2005—. Vis. prof. microbiology Tokyo U., 1965-66; mem. vis. chemistry faculty U. Calif., Berkeley, 1972-73; del. U.S. Pharmacopeial Conv., 1980, 90; scholar-in-residence Am. Assn. Colls. Pharmacy, 1996; bd. grants Am. Found. Pharm. Edn., 1997—, chmn., 1999, 2007, co-chmn. endowment com., 2002—, bd. dirs., 2003—; mem. organizing com. Millennial World Congress Pharm. Scis., 1996-2000; mem. FIP Found., 2000—05, chmn. bd. trustees, 2001—05. Contbr. articles to profl. jours. Recipient Outstanding Tchr. award Coll. Pharmacy, U. Mich., 1969, Outstanding Alumnus award Idaho State U., 1976, Profl. Achievement award Coll. Pharmacy, Idaho State U., 1990; G. Pfeiffer Meml. fellow Am. Found. Pharm. Edn., 1965-66, Disting. Svc. Profile award Am. Found Pharm. Edn., 1992; fellow Eli Lily Found., 1951-53, Am. Found. Pharm. Edn., 1954-56, NIH, 1972-73. Fellow AAAS; mem. Am. Pharm. Assn., Am. Soc. Pharmacognosy, Acad. Pharm. Scis., Am. Assn. Colls. Pharmacy, Am. Assn. Pharm. Scientists, Phi Lambda Upsilon, Sigma Xi, Phi Delta Chi, Phi Sigma Kappa, Rho Chi. Home: 1415 Brooklyn Ave Ann Arbor MI 48104-4496 Office: U Mich Coll Pharmacy Ann Arbor MI 48109-1065 Office Phone: 734-763-4267. Business E-Mail: arapaul@umich.edu.

PAUL, ELDOR ALVIN, agriculture, ecology educator; b. Lamont, Alta., Can., Nov. 23, 1931; s. Reinhold and Ida (Mohr) P.; m. Phyllis Ellen Furhop, Aug. 3, 1955; children: Lynette, Linda. BSc, U. Alta., 1954, MSc, 1956; PhD, U. Minn., 1958. Asst. prof. U. Saskatchewan, Saskatoon, Can., 1959-64, assoc. prof., 1964-70, prof., 1970-80; mem. faculty, chmn. dept. plant and soil biology U. Calif., Berkeley, 1980-85; mem. faculty, chairperson dept. of crop and soil sciences Mich. State U., East Lansing, 1985-94, prof. crop and soil sci., 1994—2000; rsch. scientist Nat. Resource Ecology Lab., Colo. Sate U., Ft. Collins, 2000—. Vis. prof. U. Ga., Athens, 1972-73, USDA, Ft. Collins, 1992-93. Author: Soil Microbiology and Biochemistry, 1988, 1996; editor: Soil Biochemistry, vols. 3-5, 1973-81; Soil Organic Matter in Temperate Agro Ecosystems, 1997; contbr. over 260 articles on microbial ecology, soil microbiology and soil organic matter to sci. publs. Fellow AAAS, Soil Sci. Soc. Am., Can. Soc. Soil Sci., Am. Soc. Agronomy (Soil Sci. Rsch. award 1995); mem. Internat. Soc. Soil Sci. Soil Biology (chmn. 1978-82), Am. Ecol. Soc. Home: 843 Rossum Dr Loveland CO 80537-7944 Office: Natural Resource Ecology Lab Colo State Univ Fort Collins CO 80521 Home Phone: 970-461-3034; Office Phone: 970-491-1990. E-mail: eldor@nrel.colostate.edu.

PAUL, JACK DAVIS, retired state official, addictions consultant; b. Bismarck, ND, Mar. 16, 1927; s. Harry Ernest and Bernice Ambert (Davis) P.; m. Mary Ann Langness, Aug. 23, 1955; children: Steven, William. BSc in Law, U. N.D., 1956, LLB, 1957, JD, 1969. Bar: N.D. 1957; cert. master addiction counselor, addictions clin. supr., profl. educator; lic. social worker, N.D.; diplomate Internat. Orgn. for Treatment of Sex Offenders, 1986. Pvt. practice law, Bismarck, 1957-71; exec. sec., gen. counsel N.D. Trade Commn., 1965-69; master addiction counselor N.D. Corrections Dept., Bismarck, 1972-79, dir. programs, 1980-89; ret., 1989; acting warden, 1986, 88. Instr. alcohol and drug edn. St. Mary's Ctrl. High Sch., Bismarck, 1977-87; dir. penal family treatment N.D. State Penitentiary, 1976-89; lectr. psychology, sociology Bismarck State Coll., 1992-2000; cons. additions, sex therapist and sex offender rehab. programs, prison treatment programs, Mandan, N.D., 1974—; lectr. on addictions, 1974—; mem. faculty N.D. Internat. Alcohol Studies, Grand Forks, 1980-83; cons. Internat. Orgn. for Treatment of Sex Offenders and Violence, 1979—, Johnson Inst., 1978-83. Mem. Mandan City Citizens Planning Com. for Law Enforcement, 1984; del. Nat. Conf. on Corrections Policy, Washington, 1986. With USN, 1945-46, PTO; capt. U.S. Army, 1949-53. Recipient citation for nat. flood relief Govt. of Netherlands, 1953. Mem. N.D. Social Workers Assn., N.D. Lic. Addiction Counselors (v.p. 1980). Democrat. Congregationalist. Avocations: volleyball, racquetball, golf, volunteering, reading. Home: 701 3rd Ave NW Mandan ND 58554-2810

PAUL, RONALD NEALE, management consultant; b. Chgo., July 22, 1934; s. David Edward and Frances (Kusel) P.; m. Nona Maria Moore, Dec. 27, 1964 (div. Oct. 1981); children: Lisa, Karen, Brenda; m. Georgeann Elizabeth Lapkoff, Apr. 10, 1982. BS in Indsl. Engring., Northwestern U., 1957, MBA, 1958. Asst. to pres. Victor Comptometer Co., Chgo., 1958-64; cons. Corplan, Chgo., 1964-66; pres. Technomic Inc., Chgo., 1966—. Mng. ptnr. L/P Ptnrs., Chgo., 1978-84; bd. dirs. Summit Restaurants, Salt Lake City, 1990-96. Co-author: The 101 Best Performing Companies in America, 1986, Winning the Chain Restaurant Game, 1994. Mem. Am. Mktg. Assn., Am. Mgmt. Assn., Planners Forum, Pres.'s Assn., Product Devel. Mgmt. Assn., Beta Gamma Sigma. Avocations: reading, racquetball. Office: Technomic Inc 300 S Riverside Plz Ste 1200 Chicago IL 60606-6613 Office Phone: 312-876-0004. Business E-Mail: rpaul@technomic.com.

PAUL, STEPHEN HOWARD, lawyer; b. Indpls., June 28, 1947; s. Alfred and Sophia (Nahmias) P.; m. Deborah Lynn Dorman, Jan. 22, 1969; children: Gabriel, Jonathan. AB, Ind. U., 1969, JD, 1972. Bar: Ind. 1972, US Dist. Ct. (so. dist.) Ind. 1972. Assoc. Baker & Daniels, Indpls., 1972-78, ptnr., 1979—, chmn. mgmt. com., 2004. Mem. bd. visitors Ind. U. Sch. Law, Bloomington, adj. prof. Editor in chief Ind. U. Law Jour., 1971. Pres. Belle Meade Neighborhood Assn., Indpls., 1974-78; v.p., counsel Brentwood Neighborhood Assn., Carmel, Ind., 1985-88, pres., 1988-91. Mem. ABA (state and local tax com. 1985—, sports and entertainment law com.), Am. Property Tax Counsel (founding mem.), Counsellors to Real Estate, Ind. State Bar Assn., Order of Coif. Office: Baker & Daniels 300 N Meridian St Ste 2700 Indianapolis IN 46204-1782 Office Phone: 317-237-0300. Business E-Mail: stephen.paul@bakerd.com.

PAULEY, EDWARD E., museum administrator; b. Huntington, W.Va. BFA, Marshall U.; MFA in painting, Ohio U. Dir. edn. Huntington Mus. Art, W.Va.; exec. dir. Black Mountain-Swannanoa Ctr. for Arts, NC, Cultural Ctr. Fine Arts, Parkersburg, W.Va.; pres., CEO Plains Art Mus., Fargo, ND, 2003—. Tchr. Marshall U., Huntington, U. NC, Asheville. Office: Plains Art Mus 704 1st Ave N Fargo ND 58102 E-mail: epauley@plainsart.org.

PAULL, MATTHEW H., food service executive; BA, U. Ill., M in Acctg. Ptnr. Ernst & Young; with McDonald's Corp., 1993—, v.p. corp. tax, sr. v.p., fin. Oak Brook, Ill., 1999—2001, exec. v.p., CFO, 2001—04, sr. exec. v.p., CFO, 2004—. Adv. dir. bd. dirs. McDonalds Corp., 1999—2000, mem. chmns. coun., mem. Japan Bd., 2002—03; mem. adv. coun. Fed. Res. Bank, Chgo.; bd. dirs. Best Buy Co., Inc. Active Kohl Children's Mus., Chgo. Symphony Orch.; trustee Ravinia Festival Assn.; bd. mem. Loyola Ronald McDonald House. Office: McDonalds Corp McDonalds Plaza Oak Brook IL 60523

PAULOSE, RACHEL KUNJUMMEN, federal agency administrator, former prosecutor; b. Kerala, India, Mar. 12, 1973; d. Joseph and Rachel Paulose. BA, U. Minn., 1994; JD, Yale Law Sch., 1997. Law clk. to Hon. James B. Loken US Ct. Appeals (8th Cir.), 1997—98; trial atty. Civil Rights Divsn. US Dept. Justice, Washington, 1998—99, asst. US atty. Dist. Minn. Mpls., 1999—2002; atty. Williams & Connolly LLP, Washington; atty Dorsey & Whitney LLP, Mpls.; sr. counsel to atty. gen. US Dept. Justice, Washington, 2006, interim US atty. Dist. Minn. Mpls., 2006, US atty., 2006—07, counselor to acting asst. atty. gen. for legal policy Washington, 2007—. Mem.: Nat. Asian-Am. Bar Assn. (bd. mem.), Fed. Bar Assn. (bd. mem.). Office: US Dept Justice Rm 4234 Main Justice Bldg 950 Pennsylvania Ave NW Washington DC 20530

PAULS, JANICE LONG, state legislator; m. Ron Pauls. BS, Sterling Coll., Kans., 1973; JD, U. Kans., 1976. Rep. dist. 102 Kans. Ho. of Reps., mem. Judiciary, rules and regulations, transp., corrections and juvenile justice coms. Democrat. Home: 1634 N Baker St Hutchinson KS 67501-5621 Office: Kans Ho of Reps State Capitol Topeka KS 66612

PAULSEN, ERIK, state legislator; b. Bakersfield, Calif., May 14, 1965; s. Gerald and Janet (Lindfors) P.; m. Kelly Spowls, 1989; 1 child, Cassandra. BA, Olaf Coll., Norfield, Minn., 1987. Mktg. mgr. CVN Co., 1987-89; field dir. U.S. Sen. Rudy Baschwitz, 1989-90; legis. asst. U.S. Congressman Jim Ramstad, 1991-92, dist. dir., 1994; Minn. state rep. Dist. 42B, 1995—. Mem. C. of C. Address: 9158 E Staring Ln Eden Prairie MN 55347-2518

PAULSEN, KRAIG, state representative, military officer; b. Monticello, Iowa, Sept. 9, 1964; m. Cathy Paulsen, Mar. 16, 1985; children: Kassandra, Kylere, Kale, Keith. BBA, Iowa State U., 1987; MBA, Embry-Riddle Aero. U.; JD, U. Iowa. Commd. USAF, 2d lt., 1988—90, first lt., 1990—92, capt., 1992—98, minuteman missile operator and maintainer, tng. squadron ops. officer; state rep. dist. 35 Iowa Ho. of Reps., 2003—; mem. edn. com.; mem. ways and means com.; mem. adminstrn. and regulation subcom.; vice chair judiciary com. Republican. Office: State Capitol East 12th and Grand Des Moines IA 50319

PAUPORE, JEFFREY GEORGE, lawyer; b. Iron Mountain, Mich., Feb. 22, 1949; s. John Cyril and Marion Maybelle (Plante) P.; m. Patricia Barbara Byzcek, Oct. 26, 1974; children: Kristin Leigh, Eric Jeffrey. BS, No. Mich. U., 1973; JD, Thomas M. Cooley Coll., 1982. Bar: Ariz. 1983, U.S. Dist. Ct. Ariz. 1985, Mich. 1990, Wis. 1994. Assoc. John Payant Attys., Iron Mountain, 1982, Sylvester & Assocs., Tucson, 1983-89; pvt. practice Tucson, 1989-90, Iron Mountain, Mich., 1990-96; elected prosecutor Dickinson County, Iron Mountain, Mich., 1997—. Bd. dirs. ARC, Iron Mountain, 1975-77; tribunal advocate Diocese Tucson, 1986, Ariz. Coll. Trial Advocacy. Mem. Mich. Bar Assn., Ariz. Bar Assn., ABA, Pima County Bar Assn. (vol. radio program 1985-89), Dickinson County Bar Assn., Iron Mountain Jaycees (v.p. 1974-76). Lodges: Elks (trustee Tucson club 1985-89). Republican. Roman Catholic. Avocations: jewelry making, hiking, swimming. Office: Dickonson County Prosecutor Correctional Ctr Iron Mountain MI 49801 Home: N3840 Grand Oak Dr Iron Mountain MI 49801-9467

PAUWELS, COLLEEN KRISTL, library director, educator; AB, Barat Coll., 1968; MLS, Ind. U., 1975, JD, 1986. Pub. svcs. libr. Ind. U. Sch. Law, Bloomington, 1975—78, acting dir. Law Libr., 1978—80, interim dir., 1980—83, dir., 1983—, assoc. prof. Office: Ind U Sch Law Indiana U Sch Law Bloomington IN 47405-7001 Office Phone: 812-855-9666. E-mail: pauwels@indiana.edu.

PAVALON, EUGENE IRVING, lawyer; b. Chgo., Jan. 5, 1933; m. Lois M. Frenzel, Jan. 15, 1961; children: Betsy, Bruce, Lynn. BSL, Northwestern U., 1954, JD, 1956. Bar: Ill. 1956. Sr. ptnr. Pavalon, Gifford & Laatsch, Chgo., 1970—. Adj. prof. Northwestern U. Sch. Law; mem. com. on discovery rules Ill. Supreme Ct., 1981—; lectr., mem. faculty various law schs. Author: Human Rights and Health Care Law, 1980, Your Medical Rights, 1990; contbr. articles to profl. jours., chpts. in books. Mem. bd. overseers Inst. Civil Justice, Rand Corp., 1993-99; mem. vis. com. Northwestern U. Law Sch., 1990-96. Capt. USAF, 1956-59. Fellow Am. Coll. Trial Lawyers, Internat. Soc. Barristers, Internat. Acad. Trial Lawyers, Am. Bd. Trial Advs., Inner Cir. Advs., Roscoe Pound Found. (life mem., pres. 1988-90); mem. ABA, Chgo. Bar Assn. (bd. mgrs. 1978-79), Ill. Bar Assn., Ill. State Bar Assn., Ill. Trial Lawyers Assn. (pres. 1980-81, Lifetime Achievement award 1996), Trial Lawyers for Pub. Justice (founding mem., v.p. 1991-92, pres.-elect 1992-93, pres. 1993-94, Champion of Justice award 2000), ATLA (parliamentarian 1983-84, sec. 1984-85, v.p. 1985-86, pres.-elect 1986-87, pres. 1987, pres., bd. trustees 2003-05, Champion of Justice award 2003), Am. Bd. Profl. Liability Attys. (diplomate), Laureate, Ill. Acad. Lawyers, Chgo. Athletic Assn., Std. Club, Union League Club. Home: 1540 N Lake Shore Dr Chicago IL 60610-6684 Office: Pavalon Gifford et al 2 N La Salle St Chicago IL 60602-3702 Home Phone: 312-280-2331; Office Phone: 312-419-7400. Business E-Mail: pavalon@pglmlaw.com.

PAVE, ANGELA, newscaster; b. Columbus, Ohio; B, Capital U., 1977. News dir., reporter Sta. WCLT, Newark, Ohio; reporter Sta. WCMH-TV, Columbus, anchor; cmty. rels. specialist Sta. WBNS-TV, anchor, 1993—. Recipient Outstanding Alumni award, Capital U., Martin Luther King Jr. Humanitarian award, Columbus Edn. Assn., Pi Lamba Educators award, Wink Hess Journalism award, 1983, Golden Rule award, Columbus Sch. Dist., Govs. award Journalism and Cmty. Svc., 1992, Women Acheivement award, WYCA Ctrl. Ohio, 1994. Office: WBNS-TV 770 Twin Rivers Dr Columbus OH 43215

PAVELICH, DANIEL L., retired account and tax management consulting executive; CEO BDO Seidman LLP, Chgo.; ret., 1999. Office: BDO Seidman LLP Two Prudential Plaza 130 E Randolph St Fl 2800 Chicago IL 60601-6300

PAVSEK, DANIEL ALLAN, banker, educator; b. Cleve., Jan. 18, 1945; s. Daniel L. and Helen A. (Femec) P. AB, Maryknoll Coll., Glen Ellyn, Ill., 1966; MA, Maryknoll Sch. Theology, Ossining, NY, 1971, Cleve. State U., 1972; PhD, Case Western Res. U., 1981; MS, George Washington U., 2000. Pres. Coun. Richmond Heights, Ohio, 1972-75; lectr. econs. Cleve. State U., 1972-75; asst. prof. Baldwin-Wallace Coll., Berea, Ohio, 1975-81; v.p., economist Ameritrust Co., Cleve., 1981-91; dean, prof. econs. Harry F. Byrd Jr. Sch. Bus. Shenandoah U., Winchester, Va., 1992-99, Durell prof. money and banking H.F. Byrd Jr. Sch. Bus., 1999—2007, prof. emeritus, econs., 2007—. Adj. prof. bus. adminstrn. Baldwin-Wallace Coll., Berea, Ohio, 1981-91 Mem. Am. Econ. Assn., Nat. Assn. Bus. Econs. Democrat. Home: 21343 Sawyer Sq Ashburn VA 20147-4728 E-mail: dpavsek@dkdp.net.

PAWLAK, ANDRZEJ M., electrical engineer; b. Poland; m. Ewa; 1 child, Patricia. MS in Electrical Engring., Posnan U. Tech., 1971; PhD, Silesian U. Tech., Gliwice, 1981. Staff rsch. engr. GM, 1981, sr. staff rsch. engr. electrical and electronics dept. Speaker in field. Recipient Achievement award Indsl. Rsch. Inst. Patentee in field. Office: GM R&D Ctr 30500 Mound Rd Warren MI 48092-2031

PAWLENTY, TIMOTHY JAMES, governor; b. South St. Paul, Minn., Nov. 27, 1960; m. Mary Elizabeth Anderson, 1987; children: Anna, Mara BA, U. Minn., 1983; JD, U. Minn.Law Sch., 1986. Chmn. Eagan Planning Commn., 1988-89; mem. Minn. Ho. of Reps. from Dist. 38, St. Paul, 1993—2002, majority leader, 1999—2002; gov. State of Minn., St. Paul, 2003—. Active Eagan city coun., 1990-92. Fannie Gilbertson Coll. scholar. Republican. Lutheran. Office: Office of the Gov 130 State Capitol 75 Rev Dr Martin Luther King Jr Blvd Saint Paul MN 55155 Office Phone: 651-296-3391. Office Fax: 651-296-2089. E-mail: tim.pawlenty@state.mn.us.

PAXSON, JOHN, professional sports team executive, retired professional basketball player; b. Dayton, Ohio, Sept. 29, 1960; s. Jim Paxson; m. Carolyn Paxson; children: Ryan, Drew. Grad., U. Notre Dame, 1983. Player San Antonio Spurs, 1983—85, Chgo. Bulls, 1985—94, radio and TV color analyst, asst. coach, 1995—96, exec. v.p. basketball ops., 2003—. Achievements include winning NBA Championships as a member of the Bulls, 1991, 92, 93. Office: Chgo Bulls United Ctr 1901 W Madison St Chicago IL 60612-2459

PAYNE, THOMAS H., market research company executive; Pres., CEO Market Facts, Inc., Arlington Heights, Ill., 1996—. Office: Market Facts Inc 222 S Riverside Plz Ste 350 Chicago IL 60606-5809

PAYNE, THOMAS L., university official; b. Bakersfield, Calif., Oct. 17, 1941; s. Harry LeRoy and Opal Irene (Ansel) P.; m. S. Alice Lewis, Feb. 1, 1963; children: Jacob, Joanna. AA in Liberal Arts, Bakersfield Coll., Calif., 1962; BA in Zoology, U. Calif., Riverside, 1965, MS in Entomology, 1967, PhD in Entomology, 1969. Asst. prof. entomology and forest sci. Tex. A&M U., College Station, 1969-73, assoc. prof., 1973-78, prof., 1978-87, rsch. coord. USDA so. pine beetle program, 1974-78; prof. entomology, head dept. Va. Poly. and State U., Blacksburg, 1987-92; dir. Ohio Agrl. R & D Ctr., Wooster; assoc. dean rsch., assoc. v.p. agrl. adminstrn. Ohio State U. Coll. Agr., Wooster, 1993—99; vice chancellor, dean agr., food and natural resources. U. Mo. Coll. Agr., Columbia, 1999—. Sec. protection sect. Nat. Planning Conf. for Rsch. in Forestry and assoc. Rangelands, 1977; bd. dirs. Urban Pest Control Rsch. Ctr. Endowment Fund, 1988—; dean's rep., ex officio mem. Va. Pesticide Control Bd., 1989—; vis. prof. Forest Zoology Inst., U. Freiburg, Germany, 1978. Editor: (with Birch and Kennedy) Mechanisms in Insect Olfaction, 1986; mem. editorial bd. Jour. Ga. Entomol. Soc., 1979-83; co-editor Jour. Insect Behavior, 1987—; contbr. chpts. to books. Pres., co-founder Brazos County Firefighters Assn., 1979-81; v.p., co-founder Precinct 2 Vol. Fire Dept., 1979-80, pres., 1982-86; author grant to build Edge Tex. Sr. Citizens Ctr., 1979; mem. Friends of Blacksburg Master Chorale. Recipient numerous awards, 1976—, including cert. of appreciation for svc. as rsch. coord. expanded so. pine beetle rsch. USDA, 1976, 78, 80, rsch. award Tex. Forestry Assn., 1977, awards Am. Registry Profl. Entomologists, 1979, Alexander von Humboldt Stiftung sr. U.S. scientist award, 1982, Faculty Disting. Achievement award in rsch. Assn. Former Students Tex. A&M U., 1985,

A.D. Hopkins award for outstanding rsch.-adminstrn. in forest entomology, 1991; Volkswagenwerk fellow U. Freiburg, 1978. Mem. AAAS, Entomol. Soc. Am. (CIBA-GEIGY agrl. recognition award 1982), Internat. Soc. Chem. Ecology, Internat. Chemoreception Workshop on Insects, Internat. Union Forest Rsch. Orgns., Nat. Corn Growers Assn., So. Forest Insect Work Conf., Va. Agribus. Coun., Va. Agrl. Chem. and Soil Fertility Assn., Va. Hort. Soc. (exec. coun. 1989), Va. Corn Growers Assn., Va. Soybean Assn., Va. Pest Control Assn, Western Forest Insect Work Conf., Coll. Agr. and Life Scis. Agr. Faculty Assn., Sigma Xi, Gamma Sigma Delta. Office: Univ Missouri Coll Agr Food/Nat Resource 2-69 Agrl Bldg Columbia MO 65211-0001 E-mail: cafnr@missouri.edu.

PAYNE, WILLIAM BRUCE, lawyer, director; b. Tulsa, Apr. 18, 1943; s. Marvin Ream and Audrey Arlene (Jones) P.; m. Suzanne Cooper, June 4, 1966; children: Allison, Stephanie. BS, U. Okla., 1965, JD, 1968. Bar: Minn. 1968, U.S. Dist. Ct. Minn. 1968, U.S. Ct. Appeals (8th cir.) 1968. Ptnr. Dorsey & Whitney LLP, Mpls., 1968—, head M&A group, 1992—. 1st lt. USAR, 1968—74. Mem. ABA, Minn. Bar Assn. Office: Dorsey & Whitney LLP 50 S 6th St Minneapolis MN 55402-1498 Office Phone: 612-340-2722. Office Fax: 612-340-2868. Business E-Mail: payne.bill@dorsey.com.

PAYTON, SALLYANNE, law educator; b. 1943; BA, Stanford U., 1964, LLB, 1968. Bar: Calif. 1969, DC 1969. Staff asst. to Pres. of U.S. White House Domestic Coun., Washington, 1971-73; chief counsel urban mass transp. adminstrn. U.S. Dept. Transp., Washington, 1973-76; assoc. prof. U. Mich. Law Sch., Ann Arbor, 1976-85, prof., 1985—; William W. Cook Prof. Law. Trustee Stanford U., 1972-82; mem. Adminstrn. Conf. U.S., 1980—; bd. dirs. Roosevelt Ctr. Am. Policy Studies, 1982—. Fellow: Nat. Acad. of Pub. Adminstrn. Office: U Mich Law Sch 336 Hutchins Hall 625 S State St Ann Arbor MI 48109-1215 Office Phone: 734-763-0220. Office Fax: 734-763-9375. E-mail: spayton@umich.edu.

PAZ, GEORGE, health products executive; b. St. Louis, Aug. 27, 1955; s. Geronimo and Collen May (Hart) P.; m. Georgene Marie Wade, July 27, 1974; children: Stacy, Kelly, Rebecca. BSBA, U. Mo., St. Louis, 1982. CPA, Mo. Jr. acct. Gen. Am., St. Louis, 1980-82, sr. acct., 1982-83, acctg. adminstr., 1983-85, tax planning analyst, 1985-87, dir. tax planning, 1987; ptnr. Coopers & Lybrand, 1988—93, 1996—98; exec. v.p., CFO Life Ptnrs. Group, 1993—95; sr. v.p., CFO Express Scripts Inc., St. Louis, 1998—2003, pres., 2003—, bd. dirs., 2004—, CEO, 2005—, chmn., 2006—. Bd. dirs. Gen. Am. Employees Fed. Credit Union, 1985. Fellow Life Office Mgmt. Assn.; mem. AICPA, Mo. Soc. CPA, Pharm. Care Mgmt. Assn. Lutheran. Avocations: golf, running, softball. Office: Express Scripts Inc 13900 Riverport Dr Maryland Heights MO 63043 Office Phone: 314-770-1666. Office Fax: 314-702-7037.

PAZANDAK, CAROL HENDRICKSON, liberal arts educator; b. Mpls. d. Norman Everard and Ruth (Buckley) Hendrickson; m. Bruce B. Pazandak (dec. 1986); children: David, Bradford, Chris, Eric, Paul, Ann; m. Joseph P. O'Shaughnessy, May 1991 (dec. Feb. 2000). PhD, U. Minn., 1970. Asst. dir. admissions U. Minn., Mpls., 1970-72, asst. dean liberal arts, 1972-79, asst. to pres., 1979-85, office of internat. edn., acting dir., 1985-87, asst. prof. to assoc. to prof. liberal arts, 1970-96, prof. emerita, 1996—; ptnr. Hollrad-Pers. Consulting, Reykjavik, Iceland, 1999—. Vis. prof. U. Iceland, Reykjavik, 1984, periods in 1983, 86-99; vis. rsch. prof. U. Oulu, Finland, 1993; exec. sec. Minn.-Iceland Adv. Com., U. Minn., 1984—; cons. U. Iceland, 1983-98; co-chair Reunion of Sisters-Minn. and Finland Confs., 1986-98; sec. Icelandic Assn. of Minn., 1995-97. Editor: Improving Undergraduate Education in Large Universities, 1989. Past pres. Minn. Mrs. Jaycees, Mpls. Mrs. Jaycees; formerly bd. govs. St. John's Preparatory Sch., Collegeville, Minn.; former bd. trustees Coll. of St. Teresa, Winona, Minn. Recipient Partnership award for contbn. to advancing shared interests of Iceland and Am., 1994, Recognition award U. Iceland, 2002, Recognition award yrs. collaboration Iceland and U. Minn., 2002; named to Order of the Falcon, Govt. of Iceland, 1990, Coll. Liberal Arts Alumna Notable Achievement, 1995, Pres.'s Club, U. Minn., 1996. Mem. APA, Waikoloa Village Outdoor Cir. Home: 4505 Harry's Ln Dallas TX 75229 Office: U Minn N 218 Elliott Hall 75 E River Rd Minneapolis MN 55455-0280 E-mail: carolpz@umn.edu.

PEACOCK, CHRISTOPHER A., former real estate company executive; b. 1946; Student, Wellington Coll., Berkshire, Eng. With Jones Lang Wooten (now Jones Lang LaSalle Inc.), 1972—2004, ptnr. Eng., 1974, former mem. exec. bd. continent of Europe, mng. ptnr. continent of Europe, chmn. leasing agy., 1992-96, European CEO, 1996-97, internat. CEO, 1997-99, pres., dep. CEO, COO, chmn. mgmt. exec. com., dir., 1999—2002, CEO, 2002—04. Fellow Royal Instn. Chartered Surveyors.

PEARLMAN, JERRY KENT, electronics company executive; b. Des Moines, Mar. 27, 1939; s. Leo R. Pearlman; married; children: Gregory, Neal. BA cum laude, Princeton U., 1960; MBA, Harvard U., 1962. With Ford Motor Co., 1962-70; v.p. fin. dir. Behring Corp., 1970-71; from contr. to chmn. Zenith Electronics Corp., Glenview, Ill., 1971-95. Bd. dirs. Smurfit-Stone Container Corp., Nanophase Techs., Evanston Northwestern Healthcare, chmn., Transp. Com. Bd. dirs. Northwestern U. Office: 225 Barton Ave Palm Beach FL 33480 E-mail: jpearl@northwestern.edu.

PEARLSTEIN, ROBERT M., physics educator; b. NYC, Oct. 16, 1937; s. Joseph and Sylvia (Leibow) P.; m. Linda Ellen Schecter, June 19, 1960; children: Daniel A., Deborah . AB in Physics, Harvard U., 1960; PhD in Physics, U. Md., 1966. Physicist Inst. Muscle Rsch. Marine Biol. Lab., Woods Hole, Mass., 1962-63; rsch. asst., pub. health svc. fellow U. Md., College Park, 1963-66; NSF postdoctoral fellow biology divsn. Oak Ridge (Tenn.) Nat. Lab., 1966-67, mem. rsch. staff biology divsn., 1967-76, leader photosynthesis group biology divsn., 1972-75, coord. solar energy rsch., 1975-77, mem. rsch. staff chemistry divsn., 1975-78; lectr. Oak Ridge Grad. Sch. Biomed. Scis. U. Tenn., 1969-78; sr. rsch. scientist Battelle Columbus (Ohio) Labs., 1978-82; prof., chmn. physics Ind. U.-Purdue U., Indpls., 1983-90, prof. physics, 1983—; Argonne fellow Argonne (Ill.) Nat. Lab., 1994—. Scholar Harvard Club Washington, 1955-56; jr. engr. Baird-Atomic, Inc., Cambridge, Mass., 1958-60; physicist Nat. Bureau Standards, Washington, 1960-61; teaching asst. U. Md., Colleg Park, 1962; predoctoral fellow Pub. Health Svc., 1965-66; postdoctoral fellow NSF, 1966-67; chmn. organizing com. Internat. Conf. on Photosynthetic Unit, Gatlinburg, Tenn., 1969-70; sec., treas. photochemistry and photobiology group Biophys. Soc., 1970-71; vis. scientist Swiss Fed. Inst. Tech., Zurich, summers, 1984, 85; lectr. Bat-Sheva summer sch. on photosynthesis Weizmann Inst., Rehovot, Israel, 1988; faculty rsch. participant Argonne Nat. Labs., summers, 1992, 93. Author: (with others) Excited States of Biological Molecules, 1976, Excitons, 1982, Photosynthesis: Energy Conversion by Plants and Bacteria, 1982, Advances in Photosynthesis Research, 1984, Antennas and Reaction Centers of Photosynthetic Bacteria—Structure, Interactions, and Dynamics, 1985, Photosynthesis, 1987, Photosynthetic Light-Harvesting Systems, 1988, The Photsynthetic Bacterial Reaction Center, 1988, Chlorophylls, 1991; assoc. editor Biophys. Jour., 1981-84; guest editor Photochemistry and Photobiology, 1971; mem. hon. editorial bd. Photochemistry and Photobiology, 1971-73; contbr. articles to profl. jours. Recipient Biological Physics prize Am. Physical Society, 1994 Fellow AAAS, Am. Phys. Soc. (chem. divsn., biol. physics divsn., biophys. lectr. Ohio State sect. Fall meeting 1969, publs. com. divsn. biol. physics 1975-78, program com. divsn. biol. physics 1975-76, exec. com. divsn. biol. physics 1982-85, fellowship com. divsn. biol. physics 1990—, Biol. Physics prize 1994); mem. Biophys. Soc., Am. Soc. Photobiology, Sigma Xi. Office: Ind U-Purdue U Dept Physics 402 N Blackford St Indianapolis IN 46202-3217

PEARSON, ANDREW R., lawyer; married; 2 children. BA in Govt., St. John's U., Collegeville, Minn., 1992; JD cum laude, William Mitchell Coll. Law, St. Paul, 1998. Bar: Minn. 1998. Assoc. counsel Bradshaw & Bryant, P.L.L.C., St. Cloud, Minn. Vol. Peace Corps. Named a Rising Star, Minn. Super Lawyers mag., 2006. Mem.: Benton/Stearns County Bar Assn., Assn. Trial Lawyers of Am., Minn. Trial Lawyers Assn., Minn. Criminal Def. Lawyers (Spl. Achievement award 2005), Nat. Assn. Criminal Def. Lawyers, Minn. State Bar Assn. Office: Bradshaw & Bryant PLLC 1505 Division St Waite Park MN 56387 Office Phone: 320-251-6889.

PEARSON, FORD G., manufacturing executive; BS, Univ. Minn.; MBA, Univ. Chgo. Comml. lender Continental Bank; CFO Frank Consolidated Enterprises Inc., Des Plaines, Ill., exec. v.p., COO, Wheels Inc.; CEO Herbst LaZar Bell, Inc., Chgo., 2005—. Bd. dir. Priority Am., Fleet Logistics Inc, AAA, Fleet Synergy Inc., Dynascan, Inc. Office: Herbst LaZar Bell Inc 355 N Canal St Chicago IL 60606 Office Phone: 312-454-1116.

PEARSON, GERALD LEON, food products executive; b. Mpls., June 24, 1925; s. Perry and Lillian (Peterson) P.; m. Beverly Mary Schultz, Nov. 10, 1946; children: Steven, Perry, Liecia. Treas. Trimont Packing Co., 1946-52; v.p. Spencer Foods, Iowa, 1952-68, pres., chief exec. officer Iowa, 1969-80, chmn. bd., chief exec. officer Iowa, 1972-80; chmn. Beef Specialists of Iowa Inc., 1983-94. Bd. dirs. Graffaloy, Inc.; chmn., CEO World Champions of Golf Inc.; owner Brooks Golf Club, Okoboji, Iowa. Pres. Pearson Art Found.; bd. dirs. Bethany Coll., Lindsborg; commr. Nat. Mus. Am. Art-Smithsonian Instn., 1995-99; founder Internat. Ctr. for Jazz Found. With USN, 1943-46. Mem. Swedish Royal Roundtable, Swedish Council Am. (bd. dirs.). Office: Brooks Golf Club PO Box 948 Okoboji IA 51355-0948 Home: 5209 Lake Shore Dr Okoboji IA 51355-2597 Home Phone: 712-382-5571; Office Phone: 712-332-7873. E-mail: bud.pearson@worldnet.att.net, bpearson@iowaone.net.

PEARSON, LOUISE S., lawyer; b. 1955; BS in Chemistry, U. Wash.; MS in Chemistry, U. Tex.; JD, U. Houston. Bar: 1984. Pvt. practice Kirkland & Ellis, Vinson & Elkins; with Baxter Internat., 1991—2000; v.p., gen. counsel, sec. Dade Behring, Inc., Deerfield, Ill., 2000—. Mem.: ABA. Office: Dade Behring Inc 1717 Deerfield Rd Deerfield IL 60015 Office Phone: 847-267-5300.

PEARSON, MARK, radio personality; Radio host midday weekday show Sta. WHO-AM, Des Moines. Office: WHO Radio 1801 Grand Ave Des Moines IA 50309

PEARSON, PAUL HAMMOND, physician; b. Bolenge, Belgian Congo; s. Ernest B. and Evelyn (Utter) P. BS, Northwestern, 1944, B.Medicine, 1946, MD, 1947; M.P.H., UCLA, 1963. Diplomate: Am. Bd. Pediatrics. Intern Los Angeles County Gen. Hosp., 1946-47; resident Cin. Children's Hosp., 1949-51; fellow convulsive disorders and electroencephalography Johns Hopkins Hosp., Balt., 1951-53; resident in child psychiatry U. B.C., Can., Vancouver, 1976-77; practice medicine specializing in pediatrics LA, 1953-62; chief mental retardation br. USPHS div. chronic disease, 1963-65; asst. dir. mental retardation program Nat. Inst. Child Health and Human Devel., NIH, 1965-66; spl. asst. to surgeon gen. USPHS, 1966-67; C.L. Meyer prof. child health, prof. pub. health and preventive medicine, dir. Meyer Children's Rehab. Inst., 1967-81, McGaw prof. adolescent medicine, dir. adolescent medicine, 1982-89, prof. emeritus dept. pediatrics, 1989—; mem. grad. faculty U. Nebr. Coll. Medicine, Omaha, 1967—, med. dir. Univ. Hosp. Eating Disorder Program, 1983-89, sr. cons. Univ. Hosp. Eating Disorder Program, 1989—. From instr. to asst. clin. prof. U. So. Calif. Med. Sch., 1953-62; from assoc. clin. prof. pediatrics to clin. prof. pediatrics Georgetown U. Sch. Medicine, Washington, 1963-67; Cons., mem. profl. services program com. United Cerebral Palsy Assn., 1969-72, mem. nat. awards com., 1971; Am. Acad. Pediatrics liaison rep. to Am. Acad. Orthopedic Surgery, 1969-73; apptd. to Nat. Adv. Council Services and Facilities for Developmentally Disabled Dept. Health. Edn. and Welfare, 1971-75; councilor Accreditation Council Facilities for Mentally Retarded, Joint Commn. on Accreditation Hosps., 1973-74; fellow adolescent medicine Boston Children's Hosp. Med. Center, 1981 Cons. editor: Am. Jour. Mental Deficiency, 1970-72; Contbr. articles to profl. jours. Mem. com. on accessible environments Nat. Acad. Scis., 1974-77. Served to capt. MC AUS, 1947-49. Mem. Am. Acad. Pediatrcs (com. on children with handicaps 1969-75, com. sect. on child devel. 1974—), Am. Assn. Mental Deficiency, Nat. Assn. for Retarded Children, Greater Omaha Assn. for Retarded Children (dir.), Am. Pub. Health Assn., Am. Acad. Cerebral Palsy and Developmental Medicine (exec. com. 1971-76, chmn. sci. program com. 1972-74, sec. 1974-77, mem. research and awards com. 1977-78, pres. 1981-82, bd. dirs. 1982-84), Assn. Univ.-Affiliated Facilities (exec. com. 1973—, v.p. 1974-75, pres. 1975-76, dir. 1971-78), Soc. Adolescent MedicineAlpha Omega Alpha.

PEARSON, RONALD DALE, retail food stores corporation executive; b. Des Moines, 1940; married. BS in Bus. Adminstrn., Drake U., 1962. With Hy-Vee Food Stores, Inc. (name changed to Hy-Vee, Inc. in 1996), Chariton, Iowa, 1962—; pres. Hy-Vee, Inc., Chariton, Iowa, 1983—, chmn., pres., & CEO, 1989—2001, chmn., CEO, COO West Des Moines, Iowa, 2001—. Dir. Beverage Mfrs., Inc., Civic Ctr. Cts., Inc.; chmn. Food Marketing Inst. Found., Washington. Bd. dir. Keep Iowa Beautiful Inc., Greater Des Moines Partnership. Office: Hy-Vee Inc 5820 Westown Pkwy West Des Moines IA 50266-8223

PEARSON, WILBERT D., career officer; BS in Aerospace Engring., Tex. A&M U., 1969; postgrad., Ball State U., 1975. Commd. 2d lt. USAF, 1970, advanced through grades to brig. gen., 1997; F-4 combat pilot Korat Royal Thai AFB, Thailand, 1972-73; instr. pilot, standardization/evaluation pilot 22nd Tactical Fighter Squadron, Bitburg AB, West Germany, 1973-76; instr. pilot, wing weapons and tactics officer 53rd Tactical Fighter Squadron, Bitburg AB, West Germany, 1976-78; F-15 operational test pilot 422nd Fighter Weapons Squadron, Nellis AFB, Nev., 1978-81; F-4 and F-5 test pilot 6512 Test Squadron, Edward AFB, Calif., 1983-84, F-20 test pilot, 1984-85, dir. F-15 anti-satelite combined test force, 1985-87, comdr., 1987-89; dir. ops. mgmt. Hdqrs. AF Systems Command, Andrews AFB, Md., 1989-91; dep. for aeronautical systems Office of the Undersec. of Def. for Acquisition and Tech., Washington, 1992-96; vice comdr. Electronic Systems Ctr., Hanscom AFB, Mass., 1996-97; dir. ops., brig. gen. Hdqrs. Air Force Material Command, Wright-Patterson AFB, 1997—. Decorated DFC with two oak leaf clusters, Air medal with nine oak leaf clusters, Republic of Vietnam Gallantry Cross with palm, Republic of Vietnam campaign medal, Air Force Systems Command Primus award; Ira Eaker fellowship Air Force Assn., 1985. Office: HQ AFMC/DO 4375 Chidlaw Rd Ste 143 Wright Patterson AFB OH 45433-5066

PECANO, DONALD CARL, automotive manufacturing executive; b. LA, Dec. 2, 1948; s. Domenick Lawrence and Carlotta Noble (Martello) P.; m. Sandra Ann Tuminello, Apr. 26, 1969; children: Julia Ann, Melissa Ann, Donald Carl. BS in Acctg, Pa. State U., 1970; MBA in Mktg., Youngstown State U., 1981. CPA, Pa.; cert. mgmt. acct., cert. fin. mgr. Contr. Atlas Guard Svc. subs. SERVISCO, East Orange, NJ, 1974-76; asst. to pres. SERVISCO, Hillside, NJ, 1976-77; v.p. fin. Columbus Svcs., Inc. subs. SERVISCO, New Castle, Pa., 1977-82; dir. fin. East Mfg. Corp. and subs. cos., 1982-88, v.p. fin. and adminstrn., 1988-99, also mem. exec. com., exec. v.p., CFO, 1999—; v.p. fin. Intermodal Techs. Inc., 1991—. Bd. dirs. Intermodal Techs. Inc. Weatherhead fellow Case Western Res. U., 1995. Republican. Roman Catholic. Office: 1871 State Route 44 Randolph OH 44265

PECK, ABRAHAM, editor, writer, educator, media consultant; b. NYC, Jan. 18, 1945; s. Jacob and Lottie (Bell) Peckolick; m. Suzanne Wexler, Mar. 19, 1977; children: Douglas Benjamin, Robert Wexler. BA, NYU, 1965; postgrad., CUNY, 1965-67; cert. in advanced exec. program, Northwestern U., 1997. Engaged in cmty. organizing and tutoring, 1962-64; with NYC Welfare Dept., 1965—67; free-lance writer, 1967—; writer, organizer Chgo. Action Youth Internat. Party, 1968; editor Chgo. Seed, 1968-70; treas. Seed Pub., Inc., 1968-70; mem. coordinating com. Underground Press Syndicate, 1969; assoc. editor Rolling Stone mag., San Francisco, 1975-76, contbg. editor, 1976-2001; feature writer Chgo. Daily News, 1977-78; with features dept. Chgo. Sun-Times, 1978-81; from asst. prof. to prof. Northwestern U., Evanston, Ill., 1981—2001, Sills prof. journalism, 2001—06, Helen Gurley Brown prof. journalism, 2006—, chair mag. dept., 1981—2006, dir. mag. programs Media Mgmt. Ctr., 2002—, chair journalism and cross-media storytelling, 2006—. Editor, co-founder Sidetracks, alt. newspaper supplement, Chgo. Daily News, 1977—78; critic at large Sta. WBBM, 1979—82; mem. exec. com. mag. divsn. Assn. Edn. Journalism and Mass Communication, 1987—89, 1992—96, 2003—04, pres., 1994—95; mem. adv. bd. Academe mag., AAUP, 1990—2000, Heartland Jour., 1990—2002, Technos, 1992—; editl. co-auditor Advanstar Comm., 1999—; mem. adv. bd. Chgo. chpt. Asian Am. Journalists Assn., 2002—; chair ethics subcom. Am. Bus. Media, 2002; cons., lectr. in field. Editor: Dancing Madness, 1976; author: Uncovering the Sixties: The Life and Times of the Underground Press, 1985, 1991; contbg. editor: Satisfaction Mag., 2005—06, consulting editor, contbr.: The Sixties, 1977; contbr. chapters to books. With US Army, 1967. Named to Chgo. Journalism Hall of Fame, 2006; recipient Mag. Divsn. Educator of Yr., Assn. Edn. Journalism and Mass Comm., 2003—04. Office: Northwestern U Medill Sch Journalism 1845 Sheridan Rd Evanston IL 60208-0815 Office Phone: 847-491-2068. Business E-Mail: a.peck@northwestern.edu.

PECK, GARNET EDWARD, pharmacist, educator; b. Windsor, Ont., Can., Feb. 4, 1930; s. William Crozier and Dorothy (Marentette) P.; m. Mary Ellen Hoffman, Aug. 24, 1957; children: Monique Elizabeth, Denise Anne, Philip Warren, John Edward. BS in Pharmacy with Distinction, Ohio No. U., 1957; MS in Indsl. Pharmacy, Purdue U., 1959, PhD, 1962. Sr. scientist Mead Johnson Research Center, 1962-65, group leader, 1965-67; assoc. prof. indsl. and phys. pharmacy Purdue U., West Lafayette, 1967—73, prof., 1973—2003, dir. indsl. pharmacy lab., 1975—, assoc. dept. head, 1989-96, prof. emeritus, 2003—. Cons. in field. Contbr. articles to profl. jours. Mem. West Lafayette Mayor's Advisory Com. on Community Devel., 1973-; mem. West Lafayette Citizen's Safety Com., 1974-81; mem. West Lafayette Park Bd., 1981-, pres., 1983-96. Served with U.S. Army, 1951-53. Recipient Lederle Faculty award Purdue U., 1976 Fellow APHA, AAAS, Am. Inst. Chem., Am. Assn. Pharm. Scientists; mem. Am. Chem. Soc., Acad. Rsch. and Sci. (Sidney Riegelman award 1994), Am. Assn. Colls. Pharmacy, Cath. Acad. Sci. (founding mem.), KC, Knight of Holy Sepulchre, Sigma Xi, Rho Chi, Phi Lambda Upsilon, Phi Kappa Phi, Phi Sigma Lambda, Phi Lambda Sigma. Roman Catholic. Office: Purdue U Sch Pharmacy & Pharm Scis Dept Industrial & Physical Pharm West Lafayette IN 47907 Office Phone: 765-494-1400. Business E-Mail: gepeck@pharmacy.purdue.edu.

PECK, WILLIAM ARNO, internist, educator, dean, academic administrator; b. New Britain, Conn., Sept. 28, 1933; m. Patricia Hearn, July 10, 1982; children by previous marriage: Catherine, Edward Pershall, David Nathaniel; stepchildren: Andrea, Elizabeth, Katherine. AB, Harvard U., 1955; MD, U. Rochester, NYC, 1960; DSc (hon.), U. Rochester, 2000. Intern, then resident in internal medicine Barnes Hosp., St. Louis, 1960-62; fellow in metabolism Washington U. Sch. Medicine, St. Louis, 1963; mem. faculty U. Rochester Med. Sch., 1965-76, prof. medicine and biochemistry, 1973-76, head divsn. endocrinology and metabolism, 1969-76; John E. and Adaline Simon prof. medicine, co-chmn. dept. medicine Washington U. Sch. Medicine, St. Louis, 1976-89; physician in chief Jewish Hosp., St. Louis, 1976-89; prof. medicine and exec. vice chancellor med. affairs, dean sch. medicine, pres. univ. med. ctr. Washington U., St. Louis, 1989—2003, Wolff disting. prof., dean emeritus and dir. ctr. for health policy, 2003—. Chmn. endocrinology and metabolism adv. com. FDA, 1976-78; chmn. gen. medicine study sect. NIH, 1979-81; chmn. Gordon Conf. Chemistry, Physiology and Structure of Bones and Teeth, 1977, Consensus Devel. Conf. on Osteoporosis, NIH, 1984; co-chmn. Workshop on Future Directions in Osteoporosis, 1987; chmn. Spl. Topic Conf. on Osteoporosis, U.S. FDA, 1987; bd. dirs. Allied Healthcare Products, Rsch! Am., St. Louis Regional Chamber and Growth Assn., TIAA-CREF Trust Co., Centene Health Policy Adv. Coun. Editor Bone and Mineral Rsch. Anns., 1982-88. Pres. Nat. Osteoporosis Found., 1985-90. Served as med. officer USPHS, 1963-65. Paul Harris fellow Rotary Found., 2001; recipient Lederle Med. Faculty award, 1967, Career Program award NIH, 1970-75, Commr.'s Spl. citation FDA, 1988, Humanitarian award Arthritis Found. Ea. Mo., 1995, Crohn's and Colitis Fedn. Am., 1999, Founders award Nat. Osteoporosis Found., 1996, Huntington Disease Soc. Am. award, 2002, Juvenile Diabetes Rsch. Found. Lifetime Achievement award, 2003, Internat. Brotherhood award Bikur Cholim Hosp., Jerusalem, 2003, Nat. Children's Cancer Soc. Legacy award, Disting. Svc. award Washington U. Sch. Medicine, Lifetime Achievement award health care. Fellow AAAS, ACP; mem. Internat. Bone & Mineral Soc., Royal Soc. Medicine, Am. Assn. Clin. Endocrinologists, Am. Geriatrics Soc., Am. Soc. Biochemistry & Molecular Biophysics, Am. Soc. Bone and Mineral Rsch. (councilor 1978-81, pres.-elect 1982-83, pres. 1983-84), Am. Soc. Clin. Investigation, Am. Soc. Internal Medicine, Assn. Am. Med. Colls. (coun. deans adminstrv. bd. 1992—, chmn. 1996-97, chair elect 1997-98, chair 1998—, immediate past chair 1999), Assn. Am. Physicians, Endocrine Soc., Orthopaedic Rsch. Soc., Soc. Med. Adminstrs., St. Louis Metro. Med. Soc., St. Louis Soc. Internal Medicine (pres. 1986), Inst. Medicine Nat. Acad. Sci., Washington U. Health Adminstrn. Program Alumni Assn. (hon.), Research! Am. (vice chair 1999—), Pi Theta Epsilon (hon.), Sigma Xi, Alpha Omega Alpha (bd. dirs 1992-95). Home: 32 Huntleigh Downs Saint Louis MO 63131 Office: Washington U Sch Medicine #1 Brookings Dr Box 1133 Saint Louis MO 63130

PECK, WILLIAM HENRY, curator, archaeologist, educator, art historian; b. Savannah, Ga., Oct. 2, 1932; s. William Henry Peck and Mildred (Bass) Peck Tuten; m. Ann Amelia Keller, Feb. 2, 1957 (dec. 1965); children: Alice Ann, Sarah Louise; m. Elsie Holmes, July 8, 1967; 1 child, William Henry IV. Student, Ohio State U., 1950-53; BFA, Wayne State U., 1960, MA, 1961. Jr.curator Detroit Inst. Arts, 1960-62, asst. curator, 1962-64, assoc. curator, 1964-68, curator ancient art, 1968—2004, acting chief curator, 1984-88, sr. curator, 1988—2004; lectr. art history Coll. Creative Studies, 2004—. Lectr. art history Cranbrook Acad. Art, Bloomfield Hills, Mich., 1963-65; vis. lectr. U. Mich., Ann Arbor, 1970, U. Mich., Dearborn, 2005—; adj. prof. art history Wayne State U., Detroit, 1966—; excavations in Egypt, Mendes, 1964-66, Precinct of Mut, Karnak, 1978—; adj. faculty art history Coll. Creative Studies, Detroit, 2004—, U. Mich., Dearborn, 2005—; sessional instr. U. Windsor, Ont., 2006. Author: Drawings from Ancient Egypt, 1978, The Detroit Institute of Arts: A Brief History, 1991, Splendors of Ancient Egypt, 1978; co-author: Ancient Egypt: Discovering its Splendors, 1978, Mummies, Diseases and Ancient Cultures, 1980, Arts and Humanities Through the Ages: Ancient Greece and Rome, 2005; contbr. articles to profl. publs. With U.S. Army, 1953-55. Recipient award in the arts Wayne State U., 1985; Ford Motor Co. travel grantee, 1962; Am. Rsch. Ctr. Egypt fellow, 1971; Smithsonian Instn. travel grantee, 1975. Mem. Archaeol. Inst. Am., Am. Rsch. Ctr. Egypt, Internat. Assn. Egyptologists, Soc. Study Egyptian Antiquities, Assn. Study Travel in Egypt and the Near East, Am. Assn. Mus., Oriental Inst.-U. Chgo. Democrat. Episcopalian. Avocations: oragami, early music performance, collecting T.E. Lawrence material. Office: 1901 Orleans Detroit MI 48207-2718 Personal E-mail: whpeck@yahoo.com.

PECKENPAUGH, ROBERT EARL, investment advisor; b. Potomac, Ill., July 17, 1926; s. Hilery and Zella (Stodgel) P.; m. Margaret J. Dixon, Sept. 21, 1945; children: Nancy Lynn, Carol Sue, David Robert, Daniel Mark, Jeanne Beth, Douglas John. Student, Ind. U., 1946—47; BS, Northwestern U., 1949, MBA with distinction, 1952. Chartered fin. analyst. With First Nat. Bank Chgo., 1949—52; pres. Security Suprs., Inc., Chgo., 1952—73; v.p. Chgo. Title & Trust Co., 1973—77; pres. Hotchkiss & Peckenpaugh, Inc., Chgo., 1977—84; v.p. Morgan Stanley Asset Mgmt. Inc., Chgo., 1984—86, Morgan Stanley & Co., Inc., Chgo., 1986—91; pres. Peckenpaugh Asset Mgmt. Inc., Chgo., 1991—2006; sr. v.p. Whitnell & Co., Oak Brook, 2006—. Chmn., Evang. Covenant Ch. of Hinsdale, Ill., 1981-84. Served with USN, 1944-46. Mem. CFA Soc. Chgo. (pres. 1963-64), Mid-Day Club, Hinsdale Golf Club. Home: 429 S County Line Rd Hinsdale IL 60521-4724 Office: Whitnell & Co 701 Harger Rd Oak Brook IL 60523

PECOULAS, GEORGE A., lawyer; b. Chgo., Ill., Oct. 30, 1949; BA, So. Ill. Univ., 1971; JD summa cum laude, John Marshall Law Sch., 1987. Bar: Ill. 1987. Assoc. Schiff Hardin & Waite, Chgo., 1987—90, Mayer Brown Rowe & Maw, Chgo., 1990—96, ptnr., fin. & securitization, 1996—. Office: Mayer Brown Rowe Maw Llp 230 S La Salle St Ste 400 Chicago IL 60604-1407 Office Phone: 312-701-7956. Office Fax: 312-706-8186. Business E-Mail: gpecoulas@mayerbrownrowe.com.

PEDERSEN, DWITE A., state legislator; b. Chamberlain, SD, Oct. 20, 1941; m. Priscilla Dougherty, Apr. 3, 1970; children: Andrew, Michaela, Megan. Undergrad., S.D. State U., S.D. So. State Tchrs. Coll.; B in human rels., Doane Coll., 1995. Cert. Gambling counselor Nebr. Nat. Assns. Alcoholism and Drug Abuse. Substance abuse counselor; acct., bus. adminstr. Internat. Harvester Co.; owner; counselor, adminstr. Boys Town; tchr.; mem. Nebr. Legislature from 39th dist., Lincoln, 1992—. Mem. Western Douglas Cty. C. of C., Elkhorn Eagles Club, Elkhorn Lions Club, St. Patrick's Cath. Ch. Men's Club. Mem. Nebr. and at. Assns. Alcoholism and Drug Abuse Counselors, Elkhorn Optimist Club (charter mem.), Nebr. Child Care Workers' Assn. (pres.). Roman Catholic. Office: State Capitol (Dist 39) Room 1018 PO Box 94604 Lincoln NE 68509-4604

PEDERSEN, KAREN SUE, electrical engineer; b. Indianola, Iowa, Apr. 27, 1942; d. Donald Cecil and Dorothy Darlene (Frazier) Kading; m. Wendell Dean Pedersen, May 6, 1961; children: Debra Ann Pedersen Schwickerath, Michael Dean. AA in Math., Grand View Coll., Des Moines, 1975; BSEE, Iowa State U., 2007; MBA in Econ., Bentley Coll., Waltham, Mass., 1989. Registered profl. engr., Iowa, Mass., Ill. Engr. Iowa Power & Light Co., Des Moines, 1978—80, rate engr., 1980—84; sr. rsch. engr. Boston Edison Co., Boston, 1984—87, sr.

engr., 1987—94, prin. rsch. analyst, 1994—98; sr. engr. MidAmerican Energy Co., Davenport, Iowa, 1998—2006; prin. Pedersen Power Solutions, Davenport, 2006—. Ops. chmn. Old South Ch., Boston, 1989-98. Recipient Disting. Svc. award, Iowa Engring. Soc., 2004. Mem. IEEE (chmn. Iowa ctrl. sect. 1983-84, sec. Iowa-Ill. sect. 2003), NSPE (v.p. 1999-2000, v.p. North Ctrl. region 2001-03, Outstanding Svc. award), Mass. Soc. Profl. Engrs. (pres. 1992-93), Eta Kappa Nu. Independent. Congregationalist. Avocations: golf, gardening. Office Phone: 563-340-2139. Personal E-mail: kspedersen@mchsi.com.

PEDERSEN, PEER, lawyer; BS, U. Ill., 1947, JD, 1948. Bar: Ill. 1949. Assoc. Arrington & Healy; founding ptnr. Pedersen & Houpt, 1957—. Bd. dirs. Delray Farms, Inc., Fla. Office Property Co., Inc., Home Access Health Corp., Martin Brower Co., River East Devel., Spraying Systems Co., Tempel Steel Co., Tennis Corp. Am. Pres. Robert R. McCormick Boys and Girls Club; bd. dirs. Boys and Girls Club Chgo., Children's Meml. Hosp., Children's Meml. Found., Rehabilitation Inst. Chgo., Lyric Opera Chgo., U. Ill. Law Sch. Served USN, WWII. Mem.: ABA, Ill. State Bar Assn., Chgo. Bar Assn., Law Club. Office: Pedersen & Houpt 161 N Clark Ste 3100 Chicago IL 60601-3242

PEDERSON, DONALD W., state legislator; b. Hasting, Nebr., Dec. 23, 1928; m. Virginia L. Cummings, Dec. 28, 1953; children: David, Steven, Scott, Jeff. Student, U. ebr., Omaha, U. Nebr., Lincoln, Grinnell Coll. Lawyer; mem. Nebr. Legislature from 42nd dist., Lincoln, 1996—. Former mem., pres. N. Platte Bd. Edn., N. Platte Jr. Coll.; mem. Presbyn. Ch. N. Platte. Mem. Nebr. State Bar Assn., Lincoln County Bar Assn., Mid-Nebr. Cmty. Found. (former pres., bd. dirs.), Rotary. Office: State Capitol Dist 42 PO Box 94604 Rm 1016 Lincoln NE 68509-4604 Home: 4501 Dryden Place #LL Lincoln NE 68516

PEDERSON, GORDON ROY, state legislator, retired military officer; b. Gayville, SD, Aug. 8, 1927; s. Roy E. and Gladys F. (Masker) P.; m. Betty L. Ballard, Mar. 8, 1955; children: James D., Carol A. Pederson Niemann, Nancy G. Pederson Holub, Gary W. Student, Yankton Coll., 1948-50, Fla. State U., 1963; advanced course, Infantry Sch., 1958-59. Drafted U.S. Army, 1945-47, commd. 2nd lt., 1952, advanced through grades to lt. col., 1967, served CONUS World War II, platoon leader 17th infantry regiment, 7th infantry divsn. Korea, 1953-54, served Korean War, 1950-54, rifle co. commdr. 10th mountain divsn. Germany, 1955-58, instr., dir. instrn. U.S. Army Jungle Warfare Tng. Ctr. Ft. Sherman, Canal Zone, 1961-63, comdr. post, 1963-64, 1st brig., 1st infantry divsn. Vietnam, 1965—66, dir. tng. hdqs. G3, Ft. Leonard Wood, 1966—68; advisor Ministry of Nat. Def., Rep. China on Taiwan, 1969-70; retired U.S. Army, 1970; operator Elkton Restaurant Post, 1971—78; rep. S.D. Ho. Reps., Pierre, 1977-99, 2001—; operator Dairy Queen, Wall, SD, 1990-95. Chmn. transp. com. S.D. Ho. Reps., 1979-93, vice chair state affairs com., 1994-98, vice chair commerce com., 1998, chmn. budget audit com., 2001-2002, chmn. transp. com., 2002—; exec. bd. Legis. Rsch. Coun., 2002—. Del. S.D. Rep. Conv., 1974-78, 80, 82, 84, 87-98, 2002-04; del. Nat. Rep. Conv., 1976, 80, 84, 88, 92, 96, 2000, 04; bd. dirs. Legis. Rsch. Coun., 1988, 90, 92, 96, 98, 2001-02, 05-06, vice chair, 2004-06. Decorated Bronze Star, Medal of Merit, U.S. Presdl. Unit Citation, Rep. Korea Presdl. Unit Citation, Rep. Vietnam Presdl. Unit Citation, Combat Infantry Badge with Star, Legion of Merit, Air Medal with 2 Oak Leaf Clusters, Army Accomodation medal with 2 oak leaf clusters, Cross of Gallantry with Palm, Republic Vietnam. Mem. VFW, DAV, Am. Legion, Retired Officers Assn., Wall C. of C., Internat. Lions Club, Sons of Norway. Lutheran. Home: PO Box 312 116 W 7th St Wall SD 57790 Office: SD Ho of Reps State Capitol Bldg Pierre SD 57501 Office Phone: 605-279-2610. Office Fax: 605-279-2609. Business E-Mail: bpers@gwtc.net, rep.gordonpederson@state.ussd.

PEDERSON, SALLY J., former lieutenant governor; b. Muscatine, Iowa, Jan. 13, 1951; d. Gerald and Wineva Pederson; m. James A. Autry, Feb. 6, 1982; children: Rick, Jim Jr., Ronald. Grad., Iowa State U., 1973. With Meredith Corp., 1973-84; sr. food editor Better Homes & Gardens mag.; lt. gov. State of Iowa, Des Moines, 1999—2007. Pres. Polk County Health Svcs.; bast bd. trustees Nat. Alliance for Autism Rsch.; pres. bd. trustees Autism Soc. Iowa; founding pres. The Homestead Living and Learning Ctr. for Adults with Autism; past cmty. bd. svcs. includes Des Moines Cmty. Playhouse, Very Spl. Arts Iowa, YWCA Aliber Child Care Ctr., YMCA Ctr. Br.; parent rep. Heartland AEA Autism Steering Com.; mem. Iowa State Spl. Edn. Adv. Bd; bd. dirs. Blank Children's Hosp., Mid-Iowa Health Found.; gov.'s appointee State Spl. Edn. Adv. Panel. Democrat.

PEDLEY, JOHN GRIFFITHS, archaeologist, educator; b. Burnley, Eng., July 19, 1931; arrived in U.S., 1959, naturalized, 2002; s. George and Anne (Whitaker) Pedley; m. Mary Grace Sponberg, Aug. 30, 1969. BA, Cambridge U., Eng., 1953, MA, 1959; postgrad. (Norton fellow), Am. Sch. Classical Studies, Greece, 1963-64; PhD, Harvard U., 1965. Loeb rsch. fellow in classical archaeology Harvard U., Cambridge, Mass., 1969-70; asst. prof. classical archaeology and Greek U. Mich., Ann Arbor, 1965-68, assoc. prof., 1968-74, acting chmn. dept. classical studies, 1971-72, 75-76; dir. Kelsey Mus. Archaeology, 1973-86, prof., 1974—2002, prof. emeritus, 2002—. Guest scholar J. Paul Getty Mus.; mem. staff excavations, Sardis, Turkey, 1962—64, Pylos, Greece, 1964; co-dir. excavations, Apollonia, Libya, 1966—68; field dir. Corpus Ancient Mosaics, Tunisia, 1972—73; co-prin. investigator excavations, Carthage, North Africa, 1975—79; dir. excavations, Paestum, Italy, 1982—85, Paestum, 1993, Paestum, 95; vis. scholar UCLA, 1989; resident in archaeology Am. Acad., Rome, 1990. Author: (book) Sardis in the Age of Croesus, 1968, Sardis in the Age of Croesus, reprint, 1999, Ancient Literary Sources on Sardis, 1972, Greek Sculpture of the Archaic Period: The Island Workshops, 1976, Paestum: Greeks and Romans in Southern Italy, 1990, Greek Art and Archaeology, 1992, Greek Art and Archaeology, 3d edit., 2002, Greek Art and Archaeology, 4th edit., 2007, Sanctuaries and the Sacred in the Ancient Greek World, 2005; co-author: Apollonia, the Port of Cyrene, 1977, The Sanctuary of Santa Venera at Paestum, Vol. 1, 1993, Corpus des Mosaiques de Tunisie, Vol. III, 1996; editor: New Light on Ancient Carthage, 1980; co-editor: Studies Presented to GMA Hanfmann, 1971. Fellow Am. Coun. Learned Socs., 1972—73, NEH, 1986; grantee, Am. Philol. Soc., 1979, at. Endowment Arts Mus., 1974, 1977, 1979, 1980, NEH, 1967, 1975, 1983, 1984. Home: 1720 Morton Ave Ann Arbor MI 48104-4522 Office: Dept Classical Studies Univ Mich Ann Arbor MI 48109 E-mail: jpedley@umich.edu.

PEEBLES, CHRISTOPHER SPALDING, anthropologist, educator, dean, academic administrator; b. Clearwater, Fla., May 26, 1939; s. Frederick Thomas and Corinne deGarmendia (Stephens) P.; m. Laura Ann Wisen, Oct. 6, 1993. AB, U. Chgo., 1963; PhD, U. Calif., Santa Barbara, 1974. Asst. prof. U. Windsor, Ont., Canada, 1970-74; asst. curator U. Mich., Ann Arbor, 1974-81; prof. prehistory U. Amsterdam, Netherlands, 1981-82; prof. Ind. U., Bloomington, 1983—, dean acad. computing, assoc. v.p., 1992—. Author: Excavations at Moundville, 1974, Representations in Archaeology, 1992. With USAF, 1956-60. Mem. Cosmos Club. Avocation: flying. Office: Ind U Glenn A Black Lab 423 N Fess Bloomington IN 47408-3800 Home Phone: 812-334-7823; Office Phone: 812-855-9544. Business E-Mail: peebles@indiana.edu.

PEEKEL, ARTHUR K., secondary school educator; Tchr. social scis. Rolling Meadows (Ill.) High Sch. Recipient State Tchr. of Yr. Social Scis. award Ill., 1992. Office: Rolling Meadows High Sch 2901 W Central Rd Rolling Meadows IL 60008-2536

PEERCY, PAUL STUART, engineering educator; s. Robert L. and Ernest (Bell) P.; m. Catherine B. Christen, July 17, 1965; children: Michael, Mark. BS in physics, Berea Coll., 1961; MS in physics, U. Wis., Madison, 1963, PhD in physics, 1966. Postdoctoral fellow Bell Labs., Murray Hill, NJ, 1966-68; mem. tech. staff Sandia Nat. Labs., Albuquerque, 1968-76, divsn. supr., 1976-82, mgr. ion-solid rsch. dept., 1982-86, mgr. compound semicondr. and device rsch. dept., 1986-91, dir. microelectronics and photonics, 1991-95; pres. SEMI/SEMATECH, 1995—99; dean Coll. Engring. U. Wis., Madison, 1999—, prof. dept. materials sci. and engring., 1999—. Mem. solid state sciences com. NRC, Washington, 1989-91; mem. external adv. bd. U. Ill. elec. engring. dept.; mem. microelectronics sci. bd. Jet Propulsion Lab., Calif. Inst. Tech., Pasadena, Calif., 1992—; mem. indsl. adv. coun. U. Ariz. Coll. Engring., Tucson, 1992—; mem. external rev. bd. Carnegie Mellon Rsch. Inst., Pitts., 1992-97; mem. Roadmap Coordinating Group for the Nat. Tech. Roadmap for Semiconductors Semiconductor Industry Assn., 1994; mem. policy bd. NSF Engring. Rsch. Ctr. in Semiconductor Environment and Safety, 1997-99, Nat. Nanofabrication Users etwork, 1998-; chair U. Wis. Tech. Enterprise Coop., 1999-; mem Wis. Tech. and Entrepreneurship Coun., 2000-; bd. dirs. Meriter Hosp. and Health Services, Madison, Wis., 2000-, Mason-Wells, Milw., 2003-. Editor 3 books; prin. editor: Jour. Materials Rsch., 1986-91; contbr. more than 175 articles to profl. jours. Recipient Sandia Award for Excellence, Woody award for Exceptional Svc., Materials Rsch. Soc. Fellow IEEE, AAAS (councilor, 1998-, Am. Phys. Soc. (chair divsn. material physics 1994, councilor 1998—, mem. exec. com. 1999—2000); mem. NAE, The Minerals, Metall., and Materials Soc. (chair electronics materials com. 1991-92), Materials Rsch. Soc. (v.p. 1987, councilor and mem. exec. com., 2001-; Woody Award for Exceptional Svc.), Phi Kappa Phi, Sigma Pi, Tau Peta Pi (disting. mem.); Nat. Acad. Engineers. Achievements include 2 patents in field. Office: U Wis 2610 Engring Hall 1415 Engineering Dr Madison WI 53706-1691 Home Phone: 608-833-0370; Office Phone: 608-262-3482.

PEERMAN, DEAN GORDON, magazine editor; b. Mattoon, Ill., Apr. 25, 1931; s. Staley Jacob and Irene (Monen) P. BS with highest distinction, Northwestern U., 1953; postgrad., Cornell U., 1953-54; B.D., Yale, 1959; D.D., Kalamazoo Coll., 1967. With Christian Century Found., 1959—; copy editor Christian Century mag., 1959-61, assoc. editor, 1961-64, mng. editor, 1964-81, exec. editor, 1981-85, sr. editor, 1985-98, contbg. editor, 1998—. Author: (with M.E. Marty) Pen-ultimates, 1963, (with Marty, L.M. Delloff, J.M. Wall) A Century of The Century, 1987; editor: Frontline Theology, 1967; co-editor: (with Marty) New Theology 1-10, 1964-73, A Handbook of Christian Theologians, 1965, enlarged edit., 1984, (with Alan Geyer) Theological Crossings, 1971; contbg. author: Chile: Under Military Rule, 1974; editor, contbr. Faithful Witness, 2002. Active Chgo. cmty. theater groups. Recipient award for distinction in lay ministry within the church Yale Div. Sch., 1995. Mem. ACLU, Fellowship of Reconciliation, Amnesty Internat., Chgo. Religious Leadership Network on Latin Am., Phi Beta Kappa. Democrat. Baptist. Office: Christian Century Mag 104 S Michigan Ave Ste 700 Chicago IL 60603-5901 Office Phone: 312-263-7510 ext. 236. E-mail: dpeerman@christiancentury.org.

PEHLKE, ROBERT DONALD, materials and metallurgical engineering educator; b. Ferndale, Mich., Feb. 11, 1933; s. Robert William and Florence Jennie (McLaren) P.; m. Julie Anne Kehoe, June 2, 1956; children: Robert Donald, Elizabeth Anne, David Richard. BS in Engring, U. Mich., 1955; S.M., Mass. Inst. Tech., 1958, Sc.D., 1960; postgrad., Tech. Inst., Aachen, Ger., 1956-57. Registered profl. engr., Mich. Mem. faculty U. Mich., 1960—, prof. materials sci. and engring., 1968—2002, prof. emeritus materials sci. and engring., 2003—, chmn. dept., 1973-84. Cons. to metall. industry; vis. prof. Tohoku U., Sendai, Japan, 1994; Campbell Meml. lectr., 2001. Author: Unit Processes of Extractive Metallurgy, 1973; editor, contbr. more than 300 articles to profl. jours. Pres. Ann Arbor Amateur Hockey Assn., 1977-79. NSF fellow, 1955-56; Fulbright fellow, 1956-57 Fellow Am. Soc. Metals (tech. divsn. bd. 1982-84, sec. metals acad. com. 1977), Minerals, Metals and Materials Soc. of AIME (Gold Medal award extractive metallurgy divsn. 1976), Alpha Sigma Mu (disting. life, pres. 1977-78); mem. Iron and Steel Soc. of AIME (Disting. life mem., chmn. process tech. divsn. 1976-77, dir. 1976-79, Howe meml. lectr. 1980), Germany, London, Japan Socs. Iron and Steel, Am. Foundry Soc., Am. Soc. Engring. Edn., Sigma Xi, Tau Beta Pi. Home: 1035 Young Pl Ann Arbor MI 48105-2587 Office: U Mich Materials Sci & Engring Dow Bldg 2300 Hayward St Rm 2006 Ann Arbor MI 48109-2136 Office Phone: 734-764-7489. E-mail: rdpehlke@umich.edu.

PELATH, SCOTT D., state representative; b. Michigan City, Ind. m. Kim Pelath; children: Israel, Isabella. BS in Pub. Affairs, Ind. U., 1992, grad. ROTC program; grad., Armor Officer Basic Course, Ft. Knox, Ky. Sales rep. Correlated Products, Inc.; human resources dir. Swanson Ctr., Michigan City, Ind.; state rep. dist. 9 Ind. Ho. of Reps., Indpls., 1998—, chmn., rules and legis. procedures com., mem. commerce and econ. devel., elections and ins. corps. and small bus. coms. Aide U.S. Rep. Tim Roemer, 1992—97; del. Dem. Nat. Conv., 2000. Served to 1st lt. USAR. Democrat. Office: Ind Ho of Reps 200 W Washington Indianapolis IN 46204-2786

PELHAM, JUDITH, health system administrator; b. Bristol, Conn., July 23, 1945; d. Marvin Curtis and Muriel (Chodos) Pelham; m. Jon N. Coffee, Dec. 30, 1992; children: Rachel Welch, Molly, Edward. BA, Smith Coll., 1967; MPA, Harvard U., 1975. Various govt. postions, 1968-72; prin. analyst Urban Systems, Cambridge, Mass., 1972-73; dir. devel. and planning Roxbury Dental and Med. Group, Boston, 1975-76; asst. to dir. for gen. medicine and ambulatory care Peter B. Brigham Hosp., Boston, 1976-77, asst. dir. ambulatory care, 1977-79; asst. v.p. Brigham and Women's Hosp., Boston, 1980-81; dir. planning and mktg. Seton Med. Ctr., Austin, Tex., 1980-82, pres., 1982-92, CEO, 1987-92; pres., CEO Daughters of Charity Health Svcs., Austin, 1987-92, Mercy Health Svcs., Farmington Hills, Mich., 1993—2000, Trinity Health (merger of Mercy Health Svcs. and Holy Cross Health Sys.), Novi, Mich., 2000—04, pres. emeritus, 2005—. Bd. dirs. Amgen, 1995—, Cath. CEO Healthcare Connection, 1998—2004; cons. Robert W. Johnson Found., 1979—80; mem. mgmt. bd. Inst. for Diversity in Health Mgmt., 1994—97; chair Coalition for Non-Profit Healthcare, 1997—2000, exec. com., 1997—2002; mem. Healthcare Rsch. and Devel. Inst., 1998—2005, bd., 2003—05; mem. adv. com. RAND Health Compare Strategic Policy, 2005—; mem. strategic adv. bd. Shattuck Hammond, 2005—; mem. strategic adv. com. for comprehensive assessment of reform efforts RAND Corp., 2006—. Contbr. articles to profl. jours. Trustee A. Shivers Radiation Therapy Ctr., Austin, 1982—92, Marywood Maternity and Adoption Agy., 1982—86; bd. dirs. Quality of Life Found., Austin, 1985, Austin Rape Crisis Ctr., adv. bd. mem., 1986—88; bd. dirs., trustee League House, 1992—93, Seton Fund, 1982—93, Greater Detroit Area Health Coun.; mem. Gov.'s Job Tng. Coordinating Coun., 1983—85; mem. adv. coun. U. Tex. Social Work Found., 1983—85; charter mem. Leadership Tex., Austin, 1983—93. Named one of Detroit's 100 Most Influential Women, Crain's Detroit Bus., 1997, 2002; recipient Leadership award, YWCA Austin, 1986, CEO IT Achievement award, Modern Healthcare, Healthcare Info. Mgmt. Sys. Soc., 2004. Fellow: Am. Hosp. Assn., Am. Coll. Healthcare Execs. (bd. dirs. 1987—95); mem.: Cath. Health Assn. (sec., treas. 1982—95, com. on govt. rels. 1984—91, chair fin. com. 1992—95, bd. dirs. 1987—95), Tex. Conf. Health Facilities (bd. dirs. 1985—89, pres. 1988), Austin Area Rsch. Orgn., Tex. Hosp. Assn. (various couns. 1982—87). Home (Winter): 9939 E Celtic Dr Scottsdale AZ 85260

PELINI, BO, college football coach; b. Youngstown, Ohio, Dec. 13, 1967; m. Mary Pat Pelini; children: Patrick, Kate, Caralyn. B Bus. Mktg., Ohio State U., 1990. Grad. asst. Iowa U., 1991; quarterbacks coach Cardinal Mooney HS, 1993; defensive backs coach San Francisco 49ers, 1994—96; linebackers coach New England Patriots, 1997—99, Green Bay Packers, 2000—02; defensive coord., interim coach U. Nebr., 2003, head coach, 2008—; co-defensive coord., def. backs coach Okla. U., 2004; defensive coord. La. State U., 2005—07. Mailing: U Nebr Nebr Football Office One Meml Stadium PO Box 880125 Lincoln NE 68588*

PELLEGRENE, THOMAS JAMES, JR., editor, researcher; b. Wilmington, Del., Dec. 26, 1959; s. Thomas J. and MaryBelle (McGowan) P.; m. Pamela Heinecke, Apr. 5, 1986. BS in Journalism, Northwestern U., 1981, MS in Journalism, 1982. Staff writer Ft. Wayne (Ind.) Journal-Gazette, 1982-87, bus. editor, 1987-95, asst. metro editor, 1995-98, mgr. news techs., 1998—. Mem. Soc. Profl. Journalists, Spl. Librs. Assn. Office: Fort Wayne Journal-Gazette 600 W Main St Fort Wayne IN 46802-1408 E-mail: tpellegrene@jg.net.

PELLOW, RICHARD MAURICE, former state legislator; b. Mpls., 1931; m. Jean Schwaab; 5 children. Grad. h.s. Mem. Minn. Ho. of Reps., 1988-92, 95-97. Former mem. commerce, econ. devel., edn., transp. coms.; currently self-employed. Address: 1354 Jackson St Saint Paul MN 55117-4614

PELOFSKY, JOEL, lawyer; b. June 23, 1937; s. Louis J. and Naomi (Hecht) Pelofsky; m. Brenda L. Greenblatt, June 19, 1960; children: Mark, Lisa, Carl. AB, Harvard U., 1959; LLB, Harvard Law Sch., 1962. Bar: Mo. 62, U.S. Dist. Ct. (we. dist.) Mo. 62, U.S. Ct. Appeals (8th cir.) 68, U.S. Ct. Appeals (10th cir.) 70. Law clk. to judge U.S. Dist. Ct. (we. dist.) Mo., 1962—63; mem. Miniace & Pelofsky, Kansas City, Mo., 1965—80; asst. pros. atty. Jackson County, Mo., 1967—71; mem. Kansas City (Mo.) City Coun., 1971—79; judge U.S. Bankruptcy Ct. Western Dist. Mo., Kansas City, 1980—85; ptnr. Shughart, Thomson & Kilroy P.C., Kansas City, 1986—95; U.S. Trustee Ark., Mo., Nebr., 1995—2003; of counsel Spencer, Fane, Britt and Browne, LLP, Kansas City, Mo., 2003—. Intermittent lectr. in law U. Mo. Bd. dirs., mem. exec. com. Truman Med. Ctr., Kansas City, Mo., pres. bd., 1988—90, chmn. bd., 1990—92; pres., trustee JVS, 2000—04; mem. Kansas City (Mo.) Sch. Bd., 2002—. Lt. US Army, 1963—65. Mem.: ABA, Am. Coll. Bankruptcy, Kansas City Met. Bar Assn., Mo. Bar. Office: 1000 Walnut Ste 1400 Kansas City MO 64106-2140 Office Phone: 816-292-8189. E-mail: jpelofsky@spencerfane.com.

PELOWSKI, GENE P., JR., state legislator; b. Feb. 1952; m. Deborah Pelowski; 2 children. BS, Winona State U. Mem. Minn. Ho. of Reps., St. Paul, 1986—. Mem. econ. devel. com., gen. legis. com., gaming com., edn. com., others, vicechmn. vet affairs and elec. coms.; educator; golf profl. Democrat. Home: 257 Wilson St Winona MN 55987-5238 Office: Minn Ho of Reps State Capitol Saint Paul MN 55155-0001

PELTZMAN, SAM, economics professor; b. Bklyn., Jan. 24, 1940; s. Benjamin Raphael and Ceil (Heller) P.; m. Nancy Virginia Bradney, Sept. 7, 1952; children: Shira Malka, Talya Rose. BBA, CCNY, 1960; PhD, U. Chgo., 1965. Prof. econs. UCLA, 1964-73; sr. staff economist Coun. Econ. Advisers, Washington, 1970-71; prof. econs. grad. sch. bus. U. Chgo., 1973-87, Sears, Roebuck prof., 1987-2001, dir. George J. Stigler Ctr. Study of Economy and the State, 1992—2005, Ralph and Dorothy Keller disting. svc. prof., 2001—05, Ralph and Dorothy Keller prof. emeritus, 2005—. Vis. fellow Inst. for Advanced Study Hebrew U., Jerusalem, 1978; dir. CMP Industries LLC, 1995—; mem. coun. acad. advisers Am. Enterprise Inst., 1995—. Author: Political Participation and Government Regulation, 1998; co-author: Public Policy Toward Mergers, 1967; editor Jour. Law and Econs.; contbr. articles to profl. jours. Mem. Am. Econ. Assn., Mt. Pelerin Soc. Jewish. Office: U Chgo Grad Sch Bus 5807 S Woodlawn Ave Chicago IL 60637-1620 Home Phone: 773-752-4246; Office Phone: 773-702-7457. Business E-Mail: samp@uchicago.edu.

PEÑA, TONY (ANTONIO FRANCISCO PEÑA), professional baseball coach, retired professional baseball player; b. Monte Cristi, Dominican Republic, June 4, 1957; m. Amaris Peña; children: Tony Peña, Jr., Jennifer Amaris, Francisco Antonio. Catcher Pitts. Pirates, 1980-86, St. Louis Cardinals, 1987—89, Boston Red Sox, 1990—93, Cleve. Indians, 1994—96, Chgo. White Sox, 1997, Houston Astros, 1997; coord., Dominican ops. Chgo. White Sox, 1998; mgr. New Orleans Triple-A, 1999—2001, Kans. City Royals, 2002—05; bench coach Houston Astros, 2002; first base coach NY Yankees, 2005—. Named Am. League Mgr. of Yr., 2003; named to Nat. League All-Star Team, 1982, 1984, 1985, 1986, 1989; recipient Golden Glove award, 1983, 1984, 1985, 1991. Achievements include being only the third Major League Baseball manger born in the Dominican Republic. Office: NY Yankees 161st St and River Ave Bronx NY 10451

PENCE, MICHAEL RICHARD, congressman; b. Columbus, Ind., June 7, 1959; m. Karen; 3 children. Grad., Hanover Coll., 1981; JD, Ind. U. Sch. Law, 1986. Atty., 1986—91; pres. Ind. Policy Rev. Found., 1991; mem. US Congress from 2nd Ind. dist., 2001—, mem. judiciary com., internat. relations com., agr. com., chmn. Ho. Rep. Study Com., 2004—. Host (radio shows) The Mike Pence Show, 1992—99. Republican. Office: US Ho Reps 426 Cannon Ho Office Bldg Washington DC 20515-1406 Office Phone: 202-225-3021. Office Fax: 202-225-3382.

PENCE, THOMAS C., lawyer; b. Muncie, Ind., Sept. 4, 1955; BA, Ind. U., 1977, JD magna cum laude, 1980. Bar: Wis. 1985, Ind. 1980, U.S. Dist. Ct., So. Dist. Ind. 1980, U.S. Dist. Ct., Ea. Dist. Wis. 1985, U.S. Dist. Ct., We. Dist. Wis. 1985, U.S. Ct. Appeals, third cir., U.S. Ct. Appeals, seventh cir., U.S. Supreme Ct. Law clk. to Hon. William I. Garrara Ind. Ct. Appeals, 1980—81; ptnr. Foley & Lardner LLP, Milw., chmn. labor & employment practice group. Mem.: ABA, State Bar Wis., Ind. State Bar Assn., Order Coif. Office: Foley & Lardner LLP 777 E Wisconsin Ave Milwaukee WI 53202-5306 Office Phone: 414-297-5809. Office Fax: 414-297-4900. Business E-Mail: tpence@foley.com.

PENDER, NANCY, newscaster; b. Concord, Calif., 1960; BBus in mktg. with honors, Sacramento State U. Freelance reporter, LA and San Francisco; dep. press sec. Calif. Assembly Spkr. Willie J. Brown, Jr.; with KCRL-TV, Reno, Orange County Newschannel, Calif., KMST-TV, Monterey, KJEO-TV, Fresno, KCOY-TV, Santa Maria; morning news anchor KUSI-TV, San Diego; weekend news anchor and reporter WFLD-TV, Chgo., 1997—. Office: WFLD-TV 205 N Mich Ave Chicago IL 60601

PENGRA, R. RENE, lawyer; b. 1967; BA, U. Wyo., 1988; JD, NYU, 1993. Bar: Ill. 1995, N.Y. 2000. Law clk. to Hon. David B. Sentelle U.S. Ct. Appeals, D.C. Cir., 1993; with Sidley Austin Brown & Wood, Chgo., 1993—, ptnr., 2002—. Office: Sidley Austin Brown and Wood Bank One Plz 10 S Dearborn St Chicago IL 60603

PENISTEN, GARY DEAN, entrepreneur; b. Lincoln, Nebr., May 14, 1931; s. Martin C. and Jayne (O'Dell) P.; m. Nancy Margaret Golding, June 3, 1951; children: Kris D., Janet L., Carol E., Noel M. BS in Bus. Adminstrn., U. Nebr., Omaha, 1953; LLD (hon.), Concordia Coll., 1993. With Gen. Electric Co., 1953-74, mgr. group fin. ops. power generation group NYC, 1973-74; asst. sec. navy fin. mgmt., 1974-77; sr. v.p. fin., chief fin. officer, dir. Sterling Drug Inc., NYC, 1977-89; sr. v.p. fin., health group Eastman Kodak Co., NYC, 1989-90. Chmn. bd. dirs. Acme United Corp., 1996—2006, chmn. emeritus, 2007—. Mem. corp. adv. bd. U. Nebr. Coll. Bus., Omaha. Recipient Disting. Public Service award Navy Dept., 1977; Alumni Achievement citation U. Nebr., Omaha, 1975. Mem. Fin. Execs. Inst., Navy League of U.S., Army and Navy Club (Washington), Rotary, Union League (N.Y.), Ft. Lauderdale (Fla.) Country Club, White Eagle Golf Club (Naperville). Republican. Unitarian Universalist. Home and Office: 1409 Aberdeen Ct Naperville IL 60564-9787 Home Phone: 630-978-7092; Office Phone: 630-978-7093. Personal E-mail: asnfm@aol.com.

PENKAVA, ROBERT RAY, radiologist, educator; b. Virginia, Nebr., Jan. 30, 1942; s. Joseph Evert and Velta Mae (Oviatt) P.; m. Kathy Bennett Secrest, Apr. 6, 1973; children: Ashley Secrest, J. Carson Bennett. AB BS, Peru State Coll., Nebr., 1963; MD, U. Nebr., Omaha, 1967. Intern Lincoln Gen. Hosp., Nebr., 1967-68; resident Menorah Med. Ctr., Kansas City, 1968—71, chief resident, 1970-71; adj. faculty U. Mo., Kansas City, 1970-71; staff radiologist Ireland Army Hosp., Ft. Knox, Ky., 1971-72, chief, dept. radiology & nuclear med., 1972-73; staff radiologist Deaconess Hosp., Evansville, Ind., 1973-99; mem. faculty U. So. Ind., Evansville, 1973—; assoc. faculty Ind. U. Coll. Med., Bloomington, 1973—; med. dir. Sch. Radiol. Tech. U. So. Ind., Evansville, 1978; dep. coroner Vanderburgh County, 1991—; med. dir. Deaconess Breast Ctr., 1999—. Chmn. So. Ind. Health Sys., 1980-83; pres. Vanderburgh County Med. Soc. Svc. Bur., 1979—; mem. roentgen soc. liaison com. Ind. Bd. Health, 1968. Author numerous articles on med. ultrasound, nuclear med., angiography, and computed tomography. Chmn. profl. div. United Way of So. Ind., 1983; bd. dirs. S.W. Ind. Pub. Broadcasting, 1978-84, S.W. Ind. PSRO, 1982; v.p. Mesker Zoo Found., bd. dirs., 1991-95; mem. Evansville Pub. Safety Bd., 2000—. Maj. U.S. Army, 1971-73. Named Sci. Tchr. of Year, Lewis & Clark Jr. High Sch., 1963. Mem. AMA, Evansville Med. Radiol. Assn. (treas. 1987-98), Am. Soc. Breast Disease, Internat. Soc. Clin. Dosimetry, Tri-State Radiology Assn. (pres.), Vanderburgh County Med. Soc. (pres.), Physicians Svc. Bur. (treas.), Magnetic Resonance Imaging, Inc. (treas. 1995-98), Am. Coll. Radiology, Radiol. Soc. .Am., Am. Roentgen Ray Soc., Am. Inst. Ultrasound in Medicine, Soc. Cardiovascular and Interventional Radiology. Avocations: golf, boating, flying.

PENLAND, JAMES GRANVILLE, psychologist; b. Dallas, Mar. 1, 1951; s. James Marr and Katherine (Lindsley) P.; m. Michelle Elizabeth Stahl, Aug. 13, 1977; children: Abraham Christopher, Simon Peter, Zachary James. BA summa cum laude, Met. State Coll., 1977; MA, U. N.D., 1979, PhD, 1984. Instr. U. N.D., Grand Forks, 1978-83, statistician, 1981-84, psychologist, 1984-85; rsch. psychologist USDA, Agrl. Rsch. Svc., Grand Forks, 1985—. Adj. prof. U. N.D., 1984—; mem. panel on micronutrients Food and Nutrition Bd. Inst. of Medicine; mem. Commn. Mil. Nutrition Rsch.; cons. in field. Mem. editl. bd. Nutritional Neurosci.; contbr. articles to profl. jours. Met. State Coll. scholar, 1977. Mem. APA, Am. Inst. Nutrition, Midwestern Psychol. Assn., N.D. Acad. Sci., Am. Statis. Assn., Sigma Xi. Home: 1804 S 36th St Grand Forks ND 58201-5740 Office: USDA Agrl Rsch Svc GFHNRC Box 9034 2420 2nd Ave N Grand Forks ND 58202-9034 E-mail: jpenland@gfhnrc.ars.usda.gov.

PENN, J. B., economist, former federal agency administrator; b. Lynn, Ark., Dec. 18, 1944; s. Jacob Bernard and Virginia Lucille (Martin) P.; m. Martha Ann Brannon (div.); children: Penny Alane, Kristin J. Rens. BS, Ark. State U., 1965; MS, La. State U., Baton Rouge, 1967; PhD, Purdue U., 1973. Rsch. economist

Econ. Rsch Svc., USDA, Baton Rouge, W. Lafayette, Ind., 1967-75, leader policy group Washington, 1975-76, dep. adminstr. for econs., 1979-81; mem. sr. staff, Coun. Econ. Advisers Exec. Office of the Pres., Washington, 1977-78; pres. Econ. Perspectives, Inc., Washington, 1981-88; sr. v.p. Sparks Commodities, Inc., Washington, 1988—2001; under sec. for farm & foreign agr. services USDA, Washington, 2001—06; chief economist Deere & Co., Moline, Ill., 2006—. Co-author: (textbook) Agriculture and Food Policy, 3d edit., 1995. Mem. adv. bd. Ctr. for Nat. Policy, Washington, 1990; bd. dirs. Found. for Devel. of Polish Agr., Warsaw, 1990, Farm Found., 1995. Mem. Am. Agrl. Econs. Assn., Am. Econs. Assn. Office: Deere & Co 1 John Deere Rd Moline IL 61265-8098

PENNIMAN, NICHOLAS GRIFFITH, IV, retired newspaper publisher; b. Balt., Mar. 7, 1938; s. Nicholas Griffith Penniman III and Esther Cox Lony (Wight) Keeney; m. Linda Jane Simmons, Feb. 4, 1967; children: Rebecca Helmle, Nicholas G. V. AB, Princeton U., 1960; MA, Washington U., 1999. Asst. bus. mgr. Ill. State Jour. Register, Springfield, 1964-69, bus. mgr., 1969-75; asst. gen. mgr. St. Louis Post-Dispatch, 1975-84, gen. mgr., 1984-86, pub., 1986-99; sr. v.p. newspapers ops. Pulitzer Pub. Co., 1986-99; pres., CEO Pulitzer Comm. Newspapers Inc., 1997-99; chmn. bd. Penniman & Browne, Inc., Balt., 2001—. Chmn. Downtown St. Louis, Inc., 1988-90, Mo. Health and Ednl. Facilities Adminstrn., 1982-85, Ill. State Fair Bd., Springfield, 1973-75, Forest Pk. Forever, 1991-93, Pks. and Open Space Task Force St. Louis 2004, 1996-00, St. Louis Sports Com., 1992-93, Gateway Pks. and Trls. 2004, 1999-04; pres. Caring Found. Children, 1988-91; trustee St. Louis Country Day Sch., 1983-86, Nat. Recreation Found., 2003—, Merc. Libr. St. Louis, 1997-00; bd. dirs. Mo. Coalition for Environment, 1997-2000, Randall Rsch. Ctr., Pineland, Fla., 2001—, Friends of Rookery Bay, 2004—; chmn. bd. Am. Rivers, 2004-06, Conservancy of SW Fla., 2007—; mem. Collier County Environ. Adv. Coun., Fla., 2005—. With US Army, 1962—67. Mem.: Rolling Rock Club, Elkridge Club, Noonday Club (pres. 1994), Grey Oaks Country Club. Home: 611 Portside Dr Naples FL 34103-4118 E-mail: ngpiv@aol.com.

PENTELOVITCH, WILLIAM ZANE, lawyer; b. Mpls., Sept. 6, 1949; s. Norman Oscar and Esther (Misel) Pentelovitch; m. Barbara Susan Ziman, Aug. 21, 1971 (dec. Oct. 1994); m. Vivian Gail Fischer, June 14, 1998; children: Norman Henry, Tovah Elana, Noah Ziman, Ari Benjamin Fischer, Miriam Esther Fischer. BA summa cum laude, U. Minn., 1971; JD, U. Chgo., 1974. Ptnr., bus. & appellate litig. Maslon, Edelman, Borman & Brand, Mpls., 1974—. Contbr. articles to profl. jours. Trustee Blake Sch., 1998—2004; dir. & gen. counsel Planned Parenthood Minn. & S.D., 1997—2001. Named a Minn. Super Lawyer, Minn. Law & Politics, 2001—05. Mem.: Hennepin County Bar Assn., Minn. State Bar Assn., Phi Beta Kappa. Home: 6 Park Ln Minneapolis MN 55416-4340 Office: Maslon Edelman Borman et al 3300 Wells Fargo Ctr Minneapolis MN 55402 Home Phone: 612-920-8780; Office Phone: 612-672-8338. Office Fax: 612-642-8338. Business E-Mail: bill.pentelovitch@maslon.com.

PEOPLES, JOHN, JR., physicist, researcher; b. S.I., NY, Jan. 22, 1933; s. John and Annie Alice (Wall) P.; m. Brooke Detweiler, Dec. 16, 1955; children—Jennet, Vanessa BS in Elec. Engring., Carnegie Inst. Tech., 1955; MA in Physics, Columbia U., 1961, PhD in Physics, 1966. Engr. Martin Marietta Co., Middle River, Md., 1955-60; asst. prof. physics Columbia U., NYC, 1966-69; asst. prof. Cornell U., Ithaca, N.Y., 1969-71, assoc. prof., 1972; scientist Fermilab, Batavia, Ill., 1972—, dir., 1989—; prof. physics Northwestern U., 1989—. Mem. high energy physics adv. panel Dept. Energy, Washington, 1976-80, 84-85 Contbr. articles to profl. jours. Alfred Sloan Found. fellow, 1970 Fellow AAAS, Am. Phys. Soc. (chmn. div. particles and fields 1984), Internat. Com. for Future Accelarators (chair). Home: 201 Ford St Geneva IL 60134-1449 Office: Fermi Nat Accelerator Lab MS 127 PO Box 500 Batavia IL 60510-0500 also: Fermilab Directors Office PO Box 500 Batavia IL 60510-0500

PEPE, STEVEN DOUGLAS, federal magistrate judge; b. Indpls., Jan. 29, 1943; s. Wilfrid Julius and Roselda (Gehring) P.; m. Janet L. Pepe. BA cum laude, U. Notre Dame, 1965; JD magna cum laude, U. Mich., 1968; postgrad., London Sch. Econs. and Polit. Sci., 1970-72; LLM, Harvard U., 1974. Bar: Ind. 1968, U.S. Dist. Ct. Ind. 1968, D.C. 1969, U.S. Dist. Ct. D.C. 1969, Mass. 1973, Mich. 1974, U.S. Dist. Ct. (ea. dist.) Mich., 1983. Law clk. Hon. Harold Leventhal U.S. Cir. Ct. Appeals, Washington, 1968-69; staff atty. Neighborhood Legal Svcs. Program, 1969-70; cons. Office of Svcs. to Aging, Lansing, Mich., 1976-77, Adminstrn. Aging, Dept. Health and Human Svcs., 1976-78; U.S. magistrate judge Eastern Dist., Ann Arbor, Mich., 1983—. Mem. Biregional Older Am. Advocacy Assistance Resource and Support Ctr., 1979-81; cons., bd. dirs. Ctr. Social Gerontology (1988-93); clin. prof. law, dir. Mich. Clin. Law Program, U. Mich. Law Sch., 1974-83; adj. prof. law Detroit Mercy Sch. Law, 1985; lectr. U. Mich. Law Sch., 1985-97. Editor Mich. Law Rev.; contbr. articles to profl. jours. Recipient Reginald Heber Smith Cmty. Lawyer fellowship, 1969-70; Mich.-Ford Internat. Studies fellow, 1970-72, Harvard Law Sch. Clin. Teaching fellow, 1972-73. Mem. State Bar Mich., State Bar Ind., Fed. Bar Assn., Washtenaw County Bar Assn., Am. Inn Court XI, U. Detroit Mercy, Pi Sigma Alpha, Order of Coif. Office: US District Court PO Box 7150 Ann Arbor MI 48107-7150 E-mail: Steven_Pepe@mied.uscourts.gov.

PEPPEL, MICHAEL E., computer company executive; BA, U. Notre Dame. Money desk mgr. Edward J. DeBartolo Corp., 1987-90; dir., CFO Diversified Data Products, Inc., 1990-96; v.p., CFO Miami Computer Supply Corp., Dayton, Ohio, 1996—.

PEPPER, JOHN ENNIS, JR., former consumer products company, historical museum executive; b. Pottsville, Pa., Aug. 2, 1938; s. John Ennis Sr. and Irma Elizabeth (O'Connor) P.; m. Frances Graham Garber, Sept. 9, 1967; children: John, David, Douglas, Susan BA, Yale U., 1960; PhD (hon.), Mt. St. Joseph Coll., St. Petersburg U., Russia, Xavier U. Staff asst. Procter & Gamble Co., Cin., 1963-64, asst. brand mgr., 1964-66, brand mgr., 1966-68, copy supr., 1968-69, brand promotion mgr., 1969-72, advt. mgr. bar soap and household cleaning products divsn., 1972-74, gen. mgr. Italy subs., 1974-77, divsn. mgr. internat., 1977-78, v.p. packaged soap and detergent divsn., 1978-80, group v.p. bar soap and household cleaning products divsn., 1980-81, group v.p. Europe, 1981-84, exec. v.p. U.S. bus., 1984-86, pres. U.S. Bus., 1986-90, pres. internat. bus., 1990-95, chmn., CEO, 1995-99, chmn., 1999—2002, mem. exec. com. of bd., 2000—03; v.p. fin. & adminstrn. Yale U., New Haven, 2004—05. Bd. dirs. Xerox Corp., 1990-2005, Motorola, Inc., 1994-2005, Boston Scientific Corp., 1999-2001, The Walt Disney Co., 2006-, non-exec chmn. 2007-. Chmn. U.S. Advisory Com. for Trade Policy and Negotiations; group chmn. Cin. United Appeal Campaign, 1980; bd. trustees Xavier U., 1985-89, mem. exec. com., 1989; trustee Cin. Coun. World Affairs, Cin. Art Mus., Ctr. Strategic & Internat. Studies, Christ Ch. Endowment Fund; fellow Yale Corp.; gen. chmn. United Way Campaign, 1994; mem. Gov.'s Edn. and Bus. Advisory Group, State of Ohio; mem. adv. coun. Yale Sch. Mgmt.; mem. schs. com. Cin. Bus. Com.; co-chmn., mem. exec. com. Cin. Youth Collaborative; mem. Total Quality Leadership steering com.; mem., bd. dirs. United Negro Coll. Fund; former v.p. Am. C. of C., Brussels, Belgium (1981-84); former mem. Cin. Symphony Bd. (1979-81), Cin. Art Mus; bd. mem. Population Services Internat.; honorary co-chair, Nat. Underground Railroad Freedom Ctr, CEO 2006-. Served to lt. USN, 1960—63. Mem. Am. Soc. Corp. Execs., Grocery Mfrs. Am., Nat. Alliance Businessmen (chmn. communication com.), Partnership for a Drug-Free Am., Soap and Detergent Assn. (bd. dirs.), The Bus. Coun., Bus. Roundtable, Yale Club, Queen City Club, Commonwealth Club, Comml. Club (former pres.). Office: Nat Underground Railroad Freedom Ctr 50 E Freedom Way Cincinnati OH 45202

PEPPER, JONATHON L., media executive; b. Dearborn, Mich., Aug. 23, 1955; s. Joseph Daniel and Norma (McIntyre) P.; m. Diane Sharon Garelis, May 12, 1984; children: Jonathon Jay, Lauren Claire, Scott Joseph. BA, Mich. State U., 1977. Copywriter Detroit Free Press, 1977-84, reporter, 1984-87; nat. corr. Detroit News, 1987-91, bus. columnist, 1991-2000; host talk show Sta. WXYT, 1995-96; assoc. bus. editor Detroit News, 1997-2000; pres. Small Times Media LLC, Ann Arbor, Mich., 2000—. Mem. Writers Guild Am., The Fairlane Club (vice chmn.). E-mail: jonpepper@ardesta.com.

PERELMAN, DAVID S., federal judge; b. 1934; Law clk. to Hon. Paul C. Weick U.S. Dist. Ct. No. Dist. Ohio and Sixth Cir. Ct. Appeals, 1958-60; law clk. to Hon. Ben C. Green U.S. Dist. Ct. (no. dist.) Ohio, 1962-79, magistrate judge Cleve., 1979—; pvt. practice, 1960. Office: US District Courts 801 W Superior Ave Cleveland OH 44113-1029 Fax: 216-357-7145.

PERES, FRANK J., healthcare administrator; b. Havanna, Cuba, Oct. 4, 1943; arrived in U.S., 1962; s. Julian N. and Silvia N. (Hernandez) P.; m. Carmen Rosario Perez, Apr. 10, 1966; children: Shelley, Vanessa, Karen. BS, Columbia Union Coll., 1970; M in Health Care Adminstrn., George Washington U., 1974. Exec. v.p. Christ Hosp., Jersey City, 1974-79; exec. dir. Bella Vista Hosp., Mayaquez, PR, 1979-85, Caribe Hosp. Affiliates, Bayamon, PR, 1985-88; pres. Atlantic Adventist Healthcare, Stoneham, Mass., 1988-94, Cmty. Hosps. of Ea. Middlesex, Stoneham, 1992-94, New England Meml. Hosp., Stoneham, 1988-94; pres., CEO Kettering (Ohio) Med. Ctr., 1994—. Pres. State Health Facilities Com., Mayaquez, 1985-90; bd. dirs. New Am. Hosp. Assn. Co-author: The Conference Board, 1995; contbr. articles to profl. jours. Trustee Hospice of Dayton, Ohio, 1995-96, Dayton Ballet, 1995-96; bd. dirs. Ohio Quality Cardiac Care Found., Columbus, 1996. Recipient Presdl. Citation for Sustained Bus. Leadership Atlantic Union Coll., 1993; named one of Top 10 Latino Leaders LatinoLeaders mag., 2004 Fellow Am. Coll. of Healthcare Execs., Am. Hosp. Assn., Kettering Coll. of Med. Arts (bd. dirs. 1994-96), Greater Dayton Area Hosp. Assn. (bd. dirs. 1994-96), Dayton Area C. of C. (trustee 1996), PPS State Hosp. Assn. (bd. dirs., v.p., chmn. 1985-88) Office: Kettering Med Ctr 3535 Southern Blvd Kettering OH 45429-1221

PERES, JUDITH MAY, journalist; b. Chgo., June 30, 1946; d. Leonard H. and Eleanor (Seltzer) Zurakov; m. Michael Peres, June 27, 1972 (div. 2004); children: Dana, Avital. BA, U. Ill., 1967; M Studies in Law, Yale U., 1997. Acct. exec. Daniel J. Edelman Inc., Chgo., 1967-68; copy editor Jerusalem (Israel) Post, 1968-71, news editor, 1971-75, chief night editor, 1975-80, editor, style book, 1978-80; copy editor Chgo. Tribune, 1980-82, rewriter, 1982-84, assoc. fgn. editor, 1984-90, nat. editor, 1990-95, nat./fgn. editor, 1995-96, specialist writer, 1997—; Yale Law fellow, 1996-97. Recipient Media award, U. Mich., 2000, Soc. Women's Health Rsch., 2004. Office: Chicago Tribune 435 N Michigan Ave Chicago IL 60611-4066 Office Phone: 312-222-4330. Business E-Mail: jperes@tribune.com.

PEREZ, CARLOS A., radiation oncologist, educator; b. Colombia, Nov. 10, 1934; came to U.S., 1960, naturalized, 1969; children: Carlos S., Bernardo, Edward P. BS, U. de Antioquia, Medellin, 1952, MD, 1960. Diplomate: Am. Bd. Radiology (trustee 1985-97). Rotating intern Hosp. U. St. Vincente de Paul, Medellin and Caldas, 1958-59; resident Mallinckrodt Inst. Radiology Barnes Hosp., St. Louis, 1960-63, mem. faculty, 1964—; prof. radiation oncology Mallinckrodt Inst. Radiology Washington U., St. Louis, 1972—, dir. radiation oncology ctr., 1976—. Fellow radiotherapy M.D. Anderson Hosp. and Tumor Inst., U. Tex., Houston, 1963-64. Co-editor: Principles and Clinical Practice of Radiation Oncology, Principles and Practice of Gynecologic Oncology; mem. editl. bd. Internat. Jour. Radiation and Physics, 1975—, Cancer, 1993—; contbr. articles to med. jours. Recipient Am. Coll. of Radiology Gold Medal award, 1997. Fellow Am. Coll. Radiology; mem. AAAS, AMA, Am. Soc. Clin. Oncology, Am. Soc. Therapeutic Radiologists (pres. 1981-82, Gold medal 1992), Am. Radium Soc., Am. Assn. Cancer Rsch., Am. Assn. Cancer Edn., Radiol. Soc. N.Am., Mo. Radiol. Soc., Mo. Acad. Sci., Mo. Med. Soc., St. Louis Med. Soc., Greater St. Louis Soc. Radiologists, Radiation Rsch. Soc. Office: Washington U Radiation Oncology Ctr 4511 Forest Park Ave Ste 200 Saint Louis MO 63108-2190 E-mail: perez@radonc.wustl.edu, caperez2@mehsi.com.

PEREZ, DAVID, utilities executive; b. Mexico, 1970; arrived in US, 1976; Grad., U. Ill., Chgo. Tech. investigations mgr. Commonwealth Edison Co., Chgo., maintenance mgr., regional dir. distbn. ops., 2005—. Named one of 40 Under 40, Crain's Chgo. Bus., 2006. Office: ComEd PO Box 805379 Chicago IL 60680-5379 also: Exelon Corp PO Box 805398 Chicago IL 60680 Office Phone: 800-334-7661.

PEREZ, DIANNE M., medical researcher; b. Cleve., Dec. 13, 1959; BA in Chemistry and Biology with honors, Coll. of Wooster, 1982; PhD in Chemistry, Calif. Inst. Tech., 1988. Grad. rsch. asst. dept. chemistry Calif. Inst. Tech., Pasadena, 1982—87, grad. tchg. asst. introductory chemistry and biochemistry, 1982—87; sr. rsch. scientist Specialty Labs., Inc., Santa Monica, Calif., 1987—88; fellow dept. eye rsch. Doheny Eye Inst., LA, 1988—89; fellow dept. heart and hypertension rsch. Cleve. Clinic Found., 1989—91, rsch. assoc. dept. cardiovasc. biology, 1992—93, project scientist dept. molecular cardiology, 1993—95, mem. asst. staff dept. molecular cardiology, 1996—. Coord. Molecular Cardiology's Protein Group Seminar Series Cleve. Clinic Found., 1994—95, supr. DNA Synthesis Core Facility Rsch. Inst., fellow's rep. Dept. Heart and Hypertension Rsch. to Divsn. Com.; adj. asst. prof. dept. pharmacology U. Ky., Lexington, 1994—; manuscript referee Molecular Pharmacology, Circulation Rsch., Cardiovasc. Rsch., Jour. Pharmacology and Exptl. Therapeutics, Gene, Biochemistry; lectr. in field. Contbr. articles to profl. jours.; patentee in field. Recipient Nat. Rsch. Svc. award, NIH, 1991; grantee Glaxo, 1994—; scholar Lubrizol, Coll. of Wooster, 1980. Mem.: AAAS, Am. Soc. Biochemistry and Molecular Biology, Am. Chem. Soc. (cert.), Am. Heart Assn. (Established Investigator award 1996), Am. Soc. Pharmacology and Therapeutics, Sigma Xi, Iota Sigma Pi, Phi Beta Kappa.

PEREZ, SYLVIA, newscaster, reporter; married; 2 children. B, U. Okla. Sch. of Journalism. Reporter KRPC-TV, Houston, Denver, Lawton, Okla.; weekend anchor and reporter WLS-TV, Chgo., 1989—, med. reporter, anchor 11am news. TV journalist with prodr. Holly Grisham HealthBeat, WLS-TV (Silver Dome award, 2001), TV journalist with prodr. Christine Tressel Desktop Doctors (Peter Lisagor award, 2002). Office: WLS-TV 190 N State St Chicago IL 60601

PEREZ, WILLIAM D. (BILL PEREZ), candy company executive, former sports apparel company executive; b. Akron, Ohio, 1947; s. Dorothy Perez; m. Catherine A. Perez; 2 children. BA in Govt., Cornell U., 1969; BIM, American Grad. Sch. of Internat. Mgmt., 1970. Joined Johnson Wax SC Johnson & Son, Inc., 1970, gen. mgr. Spanish Johnson, v.p., regional dir. Americas, v.p. home care bus., exec. v.p. N. American consumer products, pres., COO worldwide consumer products Racine, Wis., 1993-97, pres., CEO, 1997—2004, Nike, Inc., Beaverton, Oreg., 2004—06, William Wrigley Jr. Co., Chgo., 2006—. Bd. dirs. May Dept. Stores Co., 1998—2004, Kellogg Co., 1999—, Hallmark Cards, Inc., Grocery Mfr. Am. Mem. Cornell U. Council; advisory bd. Racine Youth Leadership Acad.; bd. dirs. Sustainable Racine. Recipient Out & Equal Champion for Workplace Equality award, Out & Equal Workplace Advocates, 2002. Mem.: Grocery Manufacturers of Am. (bd. dirs.). Achievements include 11 marathons. Avocations: running, golf. Office: William Wrigley Jr Co 410 N Michigan Ave Chicago IL 60611

PERGAMENT, EUGENE, medical geneticist; b. NYC, Aug. 11, 1933; BS, Yale U., 1955; MS, Purdue U., 1957, PhD, 1959; MD, U. Chgo., 1970. Diplomate Am. Bd. Med. Genetics. Prof. ob-gyn. Northwestern U., Chgo., 1988—2001. Bd. dirs. Reprogenetic Rsch., Inc., Chgo., 2001. Editor: Prenatal Genetics; spl. editor: Prenatal Diagnosis. Mem.: Am. Coll. Med. Genetics (founding), Am. Soc. Human Genetics. Home: 680 N Lake Shore Dr Ste 1428 Chicago IL 60611-8700

PERKINS, HUEL, newscaster; m. Priscilla Perkins. B in Comm., Ctrl. State U., Wilberforce, Ohio. Anchor, reporter WRBT-TV, Baton Rouge, 1982—86, WSDK-TV, St. Louis, 1986—89; anchor morning and noon WJBK-TV, Detroit, 1989—93, anchor 6 and 11pm news, 1993—97, anchor 5, 6 and 11pm news, 1997—. Recipient Emmy award, NATAS. Office: WJBK-TV FOX 2 PO Box 2000 Southfield MI 48037-2000

PERKINS, STEPHEN J., manufacturing executive; b. 1947; BS in Indsl. Engring., U. Pitts.; MBA, U. Chgo. Indsl. engr. U.S. Steel, 1968-71; with Copperweld Corp., 1971-79, Sr. Flexonics Inc., Bartlett, Ill., 1979-96, pres., CEO, 1983-96, Aftermarket Tech. Corp., Westmont, Ill., 1996-99; pres., COO, CEO-designate Comml. Intertech Corp., Youngstown, Ohio, 1999-2000; pres., CEO DT Industries, Inc., Springfield, Mo., 2000—. Office: Dt Industries Inc 313 Mound St Dayton OH 45402-8370

PERKINS, WILLIAM H., JR., retired finance company executive; b. Rushville, Ill., Aug. 4, 1921; s. William H. and Sarah Elizabeth (Logsdon) P.; m. Eileen Nelson, Jan. 14, 1949; 1 child, Gary Douglas. Degree, Ill. Coll., Jacksonville, 1939. Pres. Howlett-Perkins Assos., Chgo. Mem. Ill. AEC, 1963-84, sec., 1970-84; apptd. by Pres. to adv. bd. Nat. Armed Forces Mus., Smithsonian Instn., 1964-82; army aide to Anthony Eden and Lord Halifax of Great Britain, UN Conf., 1945. Sgt.-at-arms Democratic Nat. Conv., 1952, 56, del.-at-large, 1964, 68, 72; spl. asst. to chmn. Dem. Nat. Com., 1960; mem. Presdl. Inaugural Com., 1961, 65, 69, 73, ins. policy agent, 1961. With US Army, 1944-46 Mem. Ill. Ins. Fedn. (pres. 1965-84), Ill. C. of C. (chmn. legis. com. 1971), Chgo. Assn. Commerce and Industry (legis. com., Raoul Wallenberg Humanitarian award 1993), Sangamo Club, Masons, Shriners. Methodist. Home: 726 Community Dr La Grange Park IL 60526-1555

PERKOFF, GERALD THOMAS, physician, educator; b. St. Louis, Sept. 22, 1926; s. Nat and Ann (Schwartz) Perkoff; m. Marion Helen Maizner, June 7, 1947; children: David Alan, Judith Ilene, Susan Gail. MD cum laude, Washington U., 1948. Intern Salt Lake City Gen. Hosp., 1948—49, resident, 1949—53; fellow in metabolism and endocrinology, dept. medicine U. Utah Sch. Medicine, 1950—53; from instr. to asso. prof. medicine U. Utah, 1954—63; chief med. service Salt Lake VA Hosp., 1961—63; from instr. to prof. medicine Washington U. Sch. Medicine, St. Louis, 1954—79; chief Med. Svc., St. Louis City Hosp., 1963—68; prof. preventive medicine and pub. health, dir. divsn. health care rsch. Med. Svc. St. Louis City Hosp., 1968—79; Curators prof. and assoc. chmn. dept. family and cmty. medicine and prof. medicine U. Mo., Columbia, 1979—91, Curators prof. emeritus, 1991—, co-dir. program health care and human values, 1984—85. Chmn. nat. adv. com. Robert Wood Johnson Clin. Scholars Program, 1989—96; founder, dir. Med. Care Group Washington U., 1968—70. Contbr. articles to profl. jours. Career rsch. prof. neuromuscular diseases Nat. Found. Neuromuscular Diseases, 1961; dep. dir. Robert Wood Johnson Found. Generalist Physician Initiative, 1991—. Jr. asst. surgeon USPHS, 1953—54. Fellow Henry J. Kaiser Sr. fellow, Ctr. Advanced Studies in Behavioral Sci., 1976—77, 1985—86; scholar John and Mary R. Markle scholar med. sci., 1955—60. Mem.: Inst. Medicine (Nat. Acad. Scis.), Assn. Am. Physicians, Soc. Tchrs. Family Medicine, Am. Soc. Clin. Investigation. Office: U Mo Sch Medicine Dept Family & Community Medicine M228 Med Scis Columbia MO 65212-0001

PERKOVIC, ROBERT BRANKO, retired international management consultant; b. Belgrade, Yugoslavia, Aug. 27, 1925; came to U.S., 1958, naturalized, 1961; s. Slavoljub and Ruza (Pantelic) P.; m. Jacquelyn Lee Lipscomb, Dec. 14, 1957; children: Bonnie Kathryn, Jennifer Lee. MS in Econs, U. Belgrade, 1954; B.F.T., Am. Grad. Sch. Internat. Mgmt., 1960; grad. Stanford exec. program, Stanford U., 1970. Auditor Gen. Foods Corp., White Plains, NY, 1960-62, controller Mexico City, 1962-64; dir. planning Monsanto Co., Barcelona, 1964-67, dir. fin. Europe, Brussels, 1967-70, dir. fin. planning-internat. St. Louis, 1970-71, asst. treas., 1971-72, Brussels, 1972-74; corp. treas. Fiat-Allis Inc. & BV, Deerfield, Ill., 1974-78; v.p., treas. TRW Inc., Cleve., 1978-88; pres. RBP Internat. Cons., Cleve., 1988—. Former dir. U.S. Bus. Coun. for Southeastern Europe, Inc. Active Cleve. Commn. on Fgn. Relations. Inc. Served with Yugoslavian Army, 1944-47. Mem. Fin. Execs. Inst., Cleve. Treas. Club (past bd. dirs., pres.), Latin Am. Bus. Assn. (co-founder), Mayfield Village (Ohio) Racquet Club. Office: RBP Internat Cons 26 Pepper Creek Dr Cleveland OH 44124-5248

PERLMAN, BURTON, judge; b. Dec. 17, 1924; s. Phillip and Minnie Perlman; m. Alice Weihl, May 20, 1956; children: Elizabeth, Sarah, Nancy, Daniel. BE, Yale U., 1945, ME, 1947; LLB, U. Mich., 1952. Bar: Ohio 1959, N.Y. 1953, Conn. 1952, U.S. Dist. Ct. (so. and ea. dists.) N.Y. 1954, U.S. Dist. Ct. (so. dist.) Ohio 1959, U.S. Ct. Appeals (2d cir.) 1953, U.S. Ct. Appeals (6th cir.) 1959. Assoc. Armand Lackenbach, NYC, 1952—58; pvt. practice Cin., 1958—61; assoc. Paxton and Seasongood, Cin., 1961—67; ptnr. Schmidt, Effton, Josselson and Weber, Cin., 1968—71; U.S. magistrate U.S. Dist. Ct. (so. dist.) Ohio, 1971—76, U.S. bankruptcy judge, 1976—. Chief bankruptcy judge so. dist. Ohio, 1986—93; adj. prof. U. Cin. Law Sch., 1976—. With US Army, 1944—46. Mem.: ABA, Cin. Bar Assn., Am. Judicature Soc., Fed. Bar Assn. Office: US Bankruptcy Ct Atrium 2 8th Fl 221 E 4th St Cincinnati OH 45202-4124

PERLMAN, HARVEY STUART, academic administrator; b. Lincoln, Nebr., Jan. 17, 1942; s. Floyd Ted and Rosalyn (Lashinsky) P.; m. Susan G. Unthank, Aug. 27, 1966; children: Anne, Amy. BA, U. Nebr., 1963, JD, 1966. Bar: Nebr. 1966, Va. 1980. Teaching fellow U. Chgo. Law Sch., 1966-67; mem. faculty U. Nebr. Sch. Law, 1967-74, prof., 1972-74; prof. law U. Va., Charlottesville, 1974-83; dean law sch. U. Nebr., Lincoln, 1983—98, interim sr. vice chancellor, 1995—96, interim chancellor, 2000—01, chancellor, 2001—; exec. dir. Nebr. Commn. on Law Enforcement. Author: (with Edmund Kitch) Legal Regulation of the Competitive Process, 1972, 79, 86; assoc. editor: Jour. Law and Human Behavior, 1974-86. Named Ida Beam Distinguished Vis. Prof. Law, U. Iowa, 1981-86. Mem. Am. Bar Assn., Nebr. Bar Assn., Law-Psychology Assn., Am. Law Inst. Office: U Nebr Office of the Chancellor 201 ADM UNL Lincoln NE 68588 E-mail: hperlman1@unl.edu.

PERLMAN, LAWRENCE, retired information technology executive; BA, Carleton Coll., 1960; JD, Harvard U., 1963. Bar: Minn. 1963. Law. clk. for fed. judge, 1963; assoc., ptnr. Fredrikson & Byron, Mpls., 1964-75; gen. counsel, exec. v.p. U.S. pacing ops. Medtronic, Inc., Mpls., 1975-78; sr. ptnr. Oppenheimer, Wolff & Donnelly, Mpls., 1978-80; exec. Control Data Corp. (now Ceridian Corp.), 1980—2000, CEO, 1990—92, chmn., CEO, 1992—2000; ret., 2000. Dir., chmn. Seagate Tech., 1989-2000; bd. dirs. Carlson Cos., Inc., The Valspar Corp.; chmn. Arbitron Inc.; trustee Carleton Coll. Bd. dirs. Walker Art Ctr.; regent Univ. of Minn., 1993-95; chmn. 21st Century Workforce Commn., 1999-2000. Address: 818 W 46th St 201 Minneapolis MN 55419

PERLMUTTER, DAVID H., physician, educator; b. Bklyn., May 11, 1952; s. Herman Arthur and Ruth (Jacobs) P.; m. Barbara Ann Cohlan, Feb. 7, 1981; children: Andrew, Lisa. BA, U. Rochester, 1974; MD, St. Louis U., 1978. Intern then resident in pediatrics U. Pa. Sch. Medicine, Phila., 1978-81; fellow in pediatric gastroenterology Harvard U. Sch. Medicine, Boston, 1981-84, instr. pediatrics, 1983-85, asst. prof. pediatrics, 1985-86; Donald Strominger prof. of pediatrics Washington U. Sch. Medicine, St. Louis, 1986-89, prof. cell biology, physiology, 1989—. Editor: Pediatric Rsch., 1990—; editl. bd. Gastroenterology, 1990—; dir. divsn. gastrology and nutrition and pediatrics; contbr. articles to profl. jours. Recipient Established Investigator award Am. Heart Assn., 1987, Rsch. Scholar award Am. Gastroent. Assn., 1985, RJR Nabisco Co., 1986. Mem. Soc. Pediatric Rsch. (coun. rep. 1990—), Am. Soc. Cell Biology, Am. Soc. Clin. Investigation.

PERLMUTTER, ROBERT, land company executive; Chmn., CEO David Street Land Co., Evanston, Ill., 1999—. Office: 630 David St Evanston IL 60602

PERNICK, MARTIN STEVEN, history professor; b. NYC, June 2, 1948; s. Louis W. and Florence P. (Goldberg) P. m. Marie R. Deveney, July 8, 1983; 1 child, Benjamin William. BA, Brandeis U., 1968; MA, Columbia U., 1969, PhD, 1979. Lectr. Coll. Medicine Pa. State U., Hershey, 1972-79; from asst. prof. to prof. U. Mich., Ann Arbor, 1979—. Vis. lectr. Harvard U., Cambridge, Mass., 1975-76; creator, dir. Hist. Health Film Collection, Ann Arbor, 1986—. Author: A Calculus of Suffering, 1985, The Black Stork, 1996; contbr. chpt. to Death: Beyond Whole-Brain Criteria, 1988. Nat. Libr. Medicine fellow, 1984-85, NEH fellow, 1985-88. Mem. Am. Assn. History Medicine (exec. coun. 1992-95). Office: U Mich Dept History Ann Arbor MI 48109-1003

PERO, PERRY R., investment company executive; CFO Northern Trust Corp., Chgo., 1988—, sr. exec. v.p., vice chmn., 1999—. Office: Northern Trust Corp 50 S Lasalle St Chicago IL 60675-1006

PERRELLI, THOMAS J., lawyer; b. Falls Church, Va., Mar. 12, 1966; AB magna cum laude, Brown U., 1988; JD magna cum laude, Harvard U., 1991. Bar: Va. 1991, DC 1993, Supreme Ct. Va. 1991, U.S. Dist. Ct. DC 1994, U.S. Ct. Appeals (Fed. cir.) 2002, U.S. Supreme Ct. 1996. Law clerk to Hon. Royce C. Lamberth U.S. Dist. Ct. DC, 1991—92; assoc. Jenner & Block, Washington, 1992—97; counsel to atty. gen. U.S. Dept. Justice, Washington, 1997—99, dep. asst. atty. gen., 1999—2001; ptnr. Jenner & Block, Washington, 2001—, co-chair entertainment and new media practice. Contbr. articles to profl. jours. Named one of Top 40 Lawyers Under 40, Nat. Law Jour., 2005. Mem.: Brown U. Club Washington (pres.). Office: Jenner & Block LLP One IBM Plz Chicago IL 60611 Office Phone: 202-639-6004. Office Fax: 202-639-6066. E-mail: tperrelli@jenner.com.

PERRICONE, CHARLES, former state legislator; b. Oct. 10, 1960; Student, Kalamazoo Coll., Western Mich. U.; DPS (hon.), W. Mich. U. Rep. Mich. State Dist. 61, 1995—2001; spkr. of the house Lansing, 1999—2001; pres., CEO New Era Consulting. Vice chair tax policy com.; mem. corrections com., house oversight and ethics com., legis. coun.; asst. Rep. leader. Recipient Champion of Commerce, Mich. Chamber of Commerce, Guardian of Small Business, Nat. Fed. of Ind. Bus. Republican.

PERRIN, KENNETH LYNN, university chancellor; b. LA, July 29, 1937; s. Freeman Whitaker and Lois Eileen (Bowen) P.; m. Shirley Anne Cupp, Apr. 2, 1960; children: Steven, Lynne. BA, Occidental Coll., 1959; MA, Calif. State U., Long Beach, 1964; PhD, Stanford U., 1969. Lic. in speech pathology, Calif. Chmn. dept. communicative disorders U. Pacific, Stockton, Calif., 1969-77; dir. edn. and sci. programs Am. Speech-Lang.-Hearing Assn., Rockville, Md., 1977-80; dean faculty profl. studies West Chester U., Pa., 1980-82, acting acad. v.p., 1982, pres., 1983-91, Coun. on Postsecondary Edn., Washington, 1991-93; chancellor, system sr. v.p. U. Hawaii, Hilo and West Oahu, 1993-97; chancellor Ind. U., South Bend, 1997—. Bd. vis. C.C. Airforce, 1997—. Contbr. articles to profl. jours.; editor: Guide to Graduate Education Speech Pathology and Audiology, 1980. Bd. dirs. South Bend Meml. Hosp., 1997—, Pub. TV Sta., 1997—; trainee Vocat. Rehab. Adminstrn., 1965-69. Named Disting. Alumnus Sch. Humanities Calif. State U., Long Beach, 1988. Fellow Am. Speech-Lang.-Hearing Assn. Office: Indiana U South Bend PO Box 7111 South Bend IN 46634-7111 Home: 2935 Winters Chase Way Annapolis MD 21401-7285

PERRIS, TERRENCE GEORGE, lawyer; b. LA, Oct. 18, 1947; s. Theodore John Grivas and Penny (Sfakianos) Perris. BA magna cum laude, U. Toledo, 1969; JD summa cum laude, U. Mich., 1972. Bar: Ohio 1972, U.S. Tax Ct. 1982, U.S. Ct. Fed. Claims 1983, U.S. Supreme Ct. 1983. Law clk. to judge U.S. Ct. Appeals (2d cir.), NYC, 1972-73; law clk. to Justice Potter Stewart U.S. Supreme Ct., Washington, 1973-74; assoc. Squire, Sanders & Dempsey LLP, Cleve., 1974-80; ptnr., taxation practice group Squire, Sanders & Dempsey, Cleve., 1980—. V.p., trustee SS&D Found., Cleve., 1984—; nat. coord. Taxation Practice Area, 1987—, mgmt. com., 1996—2000; chmn. Cleve. Tax Inst., 1993; vis. prof. law U. Mich., 1996; adj. prof. Case Western Res. U., Cleve., 2001—; lectr. in field. Vis. com. U. Mich. Law Sch., 1986—. Capt. US Army, 1974. Mem.: ABA, Tax. Club Cleve., Supreme Ct. Hist. Soc., Cleve. Bar Assn., Ohio Bar Assn. (subchtp. C of internal revenue code task force), Pres.'s Club, Union Club Cleve., Club Cleve., U. Mich. Club Cleve., Order of Coif, Phi Kappa Phi. Republican. Eastern Orthodox. Avocation: landscape gardening. Office: Squire Sanders & Dempsey LLP 4900 Key Tower 127 Public Sq Cleveland OH 44114-1216 Office Phone: 216-479-8647. Office Fax: 216-479-8780. E-mail: tperris@ssd.com.

PERRUCCI, ROBERT, sociologist, educator; b. NYC, Nov. 11, 1931; s. Dominic and Inez (Mucci) P.; m. Carolyn Land Cummings, Aug. 4, 1965; children: Mark Robert, Celeste Ann, Christopher Robert, Alissa Cummings, Martin Cummings. BS, SUNY, Cortland, 1958; MS, Purdue U., West Lafayette, Ind., 1959, PhD, 1962. Asst. prof. sociology Purdue U., West Lafayette, Ind., 1962-65, asso. prof., 1965-67, prof., 1967—, head dept., 1978-87. Vis. Simon prof. U. Manchester (Eng.), 1968-69; Bd. dirs. Ind. Center on Law and Poverty, 1973-76 Author: Sociology, 1983, Circle of Madness, 1974, Divided Loyalties, 1980, The Triple Revolution, 1971, Profession Without Community, 1968, The Engineers and the Social System, 1968, Mental Patients and Social Networks, 1982, Plant Closings: International Context and Local Consequences, 1988, Networks of Power, 1989, Japanese Auto Transplants in the Heartland: Corporatism and Community, 1994, The New Class Society, 1999, Science Under Siege?, 2000, The New Class Society: Goodbye American Dream, 2008, The Transformation of Work in the New Economy,2007; editor: The American Sociologist, 1982—84, Social Problems, 1993-96, Contemporary Sociology, 2000-2005; contbr. articles to profl. jours. Served with USMC, 1951-53. Recipient grants, NSF, 1966—68, 1976—78, NIMH, 1969—72, Sloan Found., 2002—05; fellow, Sociol. Rsch. Coun., 1962. Mem. Am. Sociol. Assn., Soc. Study Social Problems (dir. 1980-83, v.p. 1996-97, pres. 1999-2000), N. Central Sociol. Assn. (pres. 1973-74) Home: 305 Leslie Ave West Lafayette IN 47906-2411 Office: Dept Sociology Purdue U West Lafayette IN 47907

PERRY, BURTON LARS, retired pediatrician; b. Midland, Mich., Dec. 8, 1931; s. Willard Russell and Myrl Alice (Jacobsen) P.; m. Nancy Fawn Towsley, Aug. 24, 1956; children: Ellen, Willard. BS, U. Mich., 1953, MD, 1960. Diplomate Am. Bd. Pediats.; sub-bd. pediat. cardiology. Physician U. Mich., Ann Arbor, 1960-78, Childrens Hosp. Mich., Detroit, 1978-97. 1st lt. infantry, U.S. Army, 1954-56.

PERRY, CHRIS NICHOLAS, retired advertising executive; b. Pitts., Dec. 25, 1945; s. Nicholas and Georgia (Demas) P.; Kathleen Clarke, June 19, 1971; children: Damien, Adam, Dana. BA, U. Pitts., 1968. With Youngstown (Ohio) Steel, 1968-70; creative supr. Ketchum Communications, Pitts., 1970-74; pres., creative dir. Hedding, Perry, Davis Inc., Charlotte, N.C., 1974-76; v.p., creative dir. Fahlgren & Swink Advt., Marion, Ohio, 1976-79, Meldrum and Fewsmith Communications, Inc., Cleve., 1979-82, sr. v.p. creative services, 1982-85, exec. v.p. creative services, 1985-86, pres., chief operating officer, 1986-87, chmn., chief exec. officer, creative dir., 1987-98, also bd. dirs. Mem. bd. disting. judges and advisors The N.Y. Festivals, 1988—. Recipient numerous awards for creative excellence. Mem. Am. Assn. Advt. Agys. (sec.-treas. cen. region 1990-91, chmn. 1992-93), Cleve. Advt. Club, Cleve. Soc. Communicating Arts (pres. 1985-87, Disting. Communicator award 1991), The Hermit Club, Columbia Hills Country Club, The Union Club, Firestone Country Club.

PERRY, EDWIN CHARLES, lawyer; b. Lincoln, Nebr., Sept. 29, 1931; s. Arthur Edwin and Charlotte C. (Peterson) P.; m. Joan Mary Hanson, June 5, 1954; children: Mary Mills, Judy Phipps, James Perry, Greg Perry, Jack Perry, Priscilla Hefferfinger. BS, U. Nebr., 1953, JD, 1955. Bar: Nebr. 1955; U.S. Dist. Ct. Nebr., 1955; U.S. Ct. Appeals Nebr., 1968. Of counsel Perry, Guthery, Haase & Gessford, P.C., Lincoln, 1957—. Chmn. Lincoln Lancaster County Planning Com., Madonna Rehab. Hosp. Fellow Am. Bar Found., Nebr. Bar Found.; mem. Nebr. State Bar Assn. (chair ho. dels. 1987-88, pres. 1991-92), Nebr. Coun. Sch. Attys. (pres. 1978-79), Lincoln Bar Assn. (pres. 1982-83). Republican. Roman Catholic. Office: Perry Guthery Haase & Gessford PC 233 S 13th St Ste 1400 Lincoln E 68508-2005 Office Phone: 402-476-9200. Personal E-mail: perryzport@alltel.net.

PERRY, ESTON LEE, real estate and equipment leasing company executive; b. Wartburg, Tenn., June 16, 1936; s. Eston Lee and Willimae (Heidle) P.; m. Alice Anne Schmidt, Oct. 21, 1961; children: Julie Anne, Jeffrey John, Jennifer Lee. BS, Ind. State U., 1961. With Oakley Corp., 1961—, dir., 1965—. Corp. officer Ind. State Bank, Terre Haute, 1975-80; pres. One Twenty Four Madison Corp., Terre Haute, 1979—, also bd. dirs., chmn. bd., 1981—; bd. dirs. Fifth Third Bank of Ind. Bd. dirs. Salvation Army, Terre Haute, 1975-91, mem. exec. adv. bd., 1979-87; bd. dirs. Vigo County Dept. Pub. Welfare, 1979-82, Jr. Achievement Wabash Valley, 1980-86; bd. dirs. United Way of Wabash Valley, 1984-89, chmn. fund campaign, 1984, bd. dirs. United Way of Ind., 1984-90, v.p., 1986, pres., 1988-89; trustee Oakley Found., 1970—; bd. dirs. Terre Haute Symphony Orch., 1984-87, Ind. State U. Found., 1988—, Goodwill Industries of Terre Haute, 1984-97, Leadership Terre Haute, 1984-88, Cen. Eastside Assocs., 1984-88, pres., 1984-85; mem. exec. com. Ind. State U. Found., 1990-94; bd. dirs. City of Terre Haute Hulman Links Commn., pres., 1986-91; mem. President's Assocs., Ind. State U., adv. bd.; bd. overseers Sheldon Swope Art Gallery of Terre Haute, 1984-87; bd. assocs. Rose Hulman Inst. Tech., 1986—. Served with U.S. Army, 1955-57. Mem.: Sycamore Athletic Scholarship Fund (Ind. State U.), C. of C. Terre Haute (bd. dirs. 1984—93, vice chmn. 1986—88, chmn. 1990), Jaycees Terre Haute (v.p. 1967—69), ESPFL of Terre Haute (hon.), Aviation Trades Assn., Air Safety Found., Aircraft Owners and Pilots Assn., Wabash Valley Pilots Assn., Strawberry Hill Cannoneers, Aero Club of Terre Haute, Country Club of Terre Haute (bd. dirs.), Elks, Lions (pres. Terre Haute 1983—84), Lambda Chi Alpha. Home: 25 Bogart Dr Terre Haute IN 47803-2401 Office: 8 S 16th St Terre Haute IN 47807-4102 E-mail: bperry@oakleyusa.com.

PERRY, GEORGE, neuroscientist, educator; s. George Richard and Mary Arlene (George) P.; m. Paloma Aguilar, May 21, 1983; children: Anne, Elizabeth. AA in Liberal Arts, Allan Hancock Coll., Santa Maria, Calif., 1973; BA in Zoology with honors, U. Calif., Santa Barbara, 1974; PhD in Marine Biology, U. Calif., San Diego, 1979; PhD (hon.), Arturo Prat, Iquique, Chile, 2007. Postdoctoral fellow Baylor Coll. Medicine, Houston, 1979-82; from asst. prof. to prof. pathology Case Western Res. U., Cleve., 1982-94, prof., 1994—2005, interim chair dept., 2001—05; affiliated prof. chemistry and biochemistry U. Alaska, Fairbanks, 2001—; dean Coll. of Scis. U. Tex., San Antonio, 2006—. Tchg. asst. U. Calif., San Diego, 1977, Stanford U., 1978—79; memory task force on Alzheimer's disease Ohio Gov., 1987, 90; mem. sci. adv. bd. Familial Alzheimer's Disease Rsch. Found., 1988—; mem., chair neurology scis. study sect. NIH, Bethesda, Md., 1989—95; cons. Nymox, Inc., Panacea Pharms., Inc., Prion Devel. Labs., Voyager, Takada Pharms., Alzheimer Rsch. Disease and Regeneration Forum; mem. Faculty of 1000 Biology, Neurobiology Sect., 2004—; spkr. in field; mem. numerous rev. bds. nationally/internationally. Author: The Neuronal Cytoskeleton, 1992, numerous publs. in field; co-author: Frontiers in Biosciences, 2002, Neurosignals, 2002, Brain Pathology, 2004, Microscopy Rsch. and Technique, 2005, Internat. Jour. Exptl. Pathology, 2005; assoc. editor: Am. Jour. Pathology, 1994-2000, Jour. Biomedicine and Biotechnology, 2004—; sr. assoc. editor: Microscopy Rsch. and Technique, 2002—; mem. editl. bd. Am. Jour. Pathology, 1992—, Alzheimer Disease and Associated Disorders, 1994—, Alzheimer's Disease Rev., 1995-98, Jour. Alzheimer's Disease, 1997—, Jour. Exptl. Neurol., 1997-99, Molecular Chem. Neuropathology, 1997-99, Jour. Neural Transmission, 1998-2003, Investigational Drugs Jour., 1998—, Brain Pathology, 1999—, Jour. Molecular Neurosci., 1999-2001, Antioxidant and Redox Signaling, 2000—, Research Signpost, 2000, Lab. Investigation, 2000—06, Brain Rsch., 2002—, Current Medicinal Chemistry, 2002—, Neurobiology of Lipids, 2003—, Jour. Biomed. Biotech., 2002—, Pathology, 2003—, Pharm. Devel. Regime, 2003—, Med. Chemistry Rev.-Online, 2003-05, Current Alzheimer Rsch., 2003—, euroSignals, 2003—, Disease Markers, 2003—, Neurobiology Disease, 2004—, Lett Drug Design Discovery, 2004—; reviewer: Expert Review of Neurotherapeutics, 2004—, Mini-Reviews in Medicinal Chemistry, 2005—, Future Neurology, 2005—, Jour. Biological Chemistry, 2006—, Developmental Microbiology and Molecular Biology, 2006—, CNS Agents in Medicinal Chemistry, 2006—, Jour. Clin. Pathology, 2007—, Molecular Neurodegeneration, 2007—, Open Medicinal Chemistry Jour., 2007—, Acta Neuropathol., Alan Liss Publ. Co., Am. Jour. Pathol., Ann Neurol, others; contbr. articles to Exptl. Cell Rsch., Jour Cell Biology, Devel. Biology, Brain Rsch., Am. Jour. Pathology, Jour. Neurosci., European Jour. Cell Biology, Nature, Annals Neurology, Lancet, Acta Neuropathology, Jour. Neurochemistry, Neurosci. Letters, Neuroreport, Med. Hypotheses, Nature Medicine, Neurodegeneration, Sci., others. Pres. Serra Club, 1995-97. Tng. corps. USAR, 1972—74, U. Calif. Santa Barbara. Recipient Bausch and Lomb medal, 1971, Rsch. Career Devel. award, NIH, 1988—93, Career Devel. award, 1988, Temple award, Alzheimer's Assn., 1999, Disting. Am. Portuguese Ancestry award, Portuguese-Am. Hist. Found., Inc., 2001, Mensch award, Alzheimer Rsch. Forum, 2003, Cmty. Svc. award, Cleve. Area Chpt. Alzheimer's Assn., 2004, Zenith award, Alzheimer Assn., 2007; fellow, Kennecott Copper, 1974—75, Muscular Dystrophy Assn., 1980—82, Philip Morris, USA, 2003—06; grantee, NIH, 1985—, Am. Health Assistance Found., 1988—90, 1997—99, Alzheimer's Assn., 1989—90, 1998—2002, 2004—, United Mitochondrial Disease Fund, 2000—02. Fellow AAAS; mem. AAUP (case chapter exec. com. 1996—2006, membership chair 1996-98, v.p. 1998-99, pres. 1999—2006), Am. Soc. Cell Biology, Electron Microscopy Soc. N.E. Ohio (treas. 1986-88, trustee 1988-90, pres. 1990-91), Soc. Neurosci., Am. Assn. Neuropathologists (awards com. 1992-93, 95-2002, chmn. 2001-02, internat. congress neuropathology concilator 1995-2000, sec.-treas. 2003-08, pres. elect. 2007-08, pres. 2008-), Am. Soc. Investigative Pathology (program com. 1998-2001), Am. Soc. Neurochemistry, U.S. and Can. Acad. of Pathology, Hispanic Med. Assn. (com. on status of Portuguese in medicine and sci.), Soc. for Neurosci., Sigma Xi (pres. chpt. 2004-06). Democrat. Roman Catholic. Avocation: genealogy. Office: U Tex San Antonio Coll Scis One UTSA Circle San Antonio TX 78249-0661 Office Phone: 210-458-4450. Business E-Mail: george.perry@utsa.edu.

PERRY, HAROLD OTTO, dermatologist; b. Rochester, Minn., Nov. 18, 1921; s. Oliver and Hedwig Clara (Tornow) P.; m. Loraine Thelma Moehnke, Aug. 27, 1944; children— Preston, Oliver, Ann, John. AA, Rochester Jr. Coll., 1942; BS, U. Minn., 1944, MB, 1946, MD, 1947; MS, Mayo Grad. Sch. Medicine, 1953. Diplomate Am. Bd. Dermatology with spl. competence in dermatopathology. Intern Naval Hosp., Oakland, Calif., 1946-47; resident in dermatology Mayo Grad. Sch. Medicine, 1949-52; practice medicine specializing in dermatology Rochester, 1953-86; mem. staff Mayo Clinic, 1953-86, mem. emeritus staff, 1987—; instr., asst. prof., assoc. prof. Mayo Med. Sch., 1953-86, prof., 1978-83, Robert H. Kieckhefer prof. dermatology, 1978-83, head dept. dermatology, 1975-83, emeritus prof. dermatology, 1987—. Civilian cons. dermatology to surgeon gen. USAF, 1973-84. Contbr. articles to med. jours. and, chpts. to books. With USNR, 1943-45, 46-49. Inducted into Rochester (Minn.) C.C. Alumni Hall of Fame, 1993; recipient Disting. Alumnus award Mayo Found., 1995. Mem. AMA, Am. Acad. Dermatology (pres. 1981, Sulzberger internat. lectr. 1986, Gold Medal for visionary leadership 1998), Am. Dermatol. Assn. (bd. dirs. 1985-89, pres. 1989-90), Am. Bd. Dermatology (bd. dirs. 1979-90, v.p. 1989, pres. 1990), Noah Worcester Dermatol. Soc. (pres. 1969), Minn. Dermatol. Soc. (pres. 1967), Chgo. Dermatol. Soc., Internat. Soc. Tropical Dermatology, Minn. Med. Assn.; hon. mem. French Dermatol. Soc., Spanish Acad. Dermatology, Brazilian Dermatol. Soc., Ga. Dermatol. Soc., Iowa Dermatol. Soc., Korean Dermatol. Soc., Bolivar Soc. Dermatology, Jacksonville Dermatol. Soc., N.Am. Clin. Dermatol. Soc., Pacific Dermatol. Assn. Office: Mayo Clinic Emeritus Staff Ctr 10th Fl Plummer Bldg Ctr Rochester MN 55905-0001 Office Phone: 507-284-2691.

PERRY, JAMES ALFRED, environmental scientist, academic administrator, educator, consultant; b. Dallas, Sept. 27, 1945; BA in Fisheries, Colo. State U., 1968; MA, Western State Coll., 1973; PhD, Idaho State U., 1981. Sr. water quality specialist Idaho Div. Environ., Pocatello, 1974-82; area mgr. Centrac Assocs., Salt Lake City, 1982; H.T. Morse disting. prof. water quality U. Minn., 1982—, head dept. fisheries, wildlife, conservation biol., 2000—06, dir. natural resources policy and mgmt., 1985—2002, spl. asst. to dean grad. sch., 1996-2000, interim assoc. v.p., dean internat. programs, 2006. Vis. scholar Oxford U., Green Coll., England, 1990—91; dep. dir. AID-funded Environ. Tng. Project for Ctrl. and Ea. Europe, 1992—96; assoc. Internat. Inst. Sustainable Devel., 2007—; cons. in field. Author: Water Quality Management of a Natural Resource, 1996, Ecosystem Management for Central and Eastern Europe, 2001; editor: Jour. Natural Resources and Life Scis. Edn., 1996—2004; mem. editl. bd. Mitigation and Adaptation Strategies for Global Change, 1998—2005. Charter mem. Leadership Devel. Acad., Lakewood, Minn., 1988; bd. dirs. Minn. Ctr. for Environ. Advocacy, 1995-2006, vice chmn., 2005. Fellow Pres.'s Academic Leadership Initiative, 2003-05; recipient Richard C. Newman Art of Tchg. award, 1998, Morse-Alumni award, 1999, Outstanding Svc. award U. Minn., 2001, Ctr. Integrative Study Writing award interdisciplinary tchg. of writing, 2003, Juror Brock Internat. Edn. prize, 2006; ACOP/ESCOP nat. leadership fellow, 1995-96, CIC acad. leadership fellow, 2000-01, Gordon L. Starr Leadership award, 2003-05. Fellow: Am. Inst. Fish Resource Biology; mem.: Acad. Disting. Tchrs., Nat. Assn. Univ. Fish and Wildlife Programs (sec./treas. 2001—), Soc. for Conservation Biology, Wildlife Soc., Am. Fisheries Soc., N.Am. Benthol. Soc. (exec. bd. Albuquerque 1990—91), Internat. Soc. Theoretical and Applied Limnology, Internat. Water Resources Assn., Am. Water Resources Assn., Minn. Acad. Scis. (bd. dirs. 1987—90), Gamma Sigma Delta (merit award 2001), Xi Sigma Pi, Sigma Xi. Office: Univ Minn Dept Fisheries Wildlife and Conservation Biology 320 Hodson Hall 1980 Folwell Ave Saint Paul MN 55108-1037 Office Phone: 612-625-4717. Business E-Mail: jperry@umn.edu.

PERRY, JEANINE, state representative; b. Apr. 3, 1942; married; 2 children. BEd, U. Toledo. State rep. dist. 49 Ohio Ho. of Reps., Columbus, 1998—, ranking minority mem., transp. and pub. safety com., mem. agr. and natural resources, econ. devel. and tech., homeland security engring. and archtl. design, and human svcs. and aging coms., mem. natural resources, parks and recreation subcom. Councilwoman Toledo City Coun., 1993—98. Named Legislator of Yr., Point Place Bus. Assn., 1999; recipient Outstanding Svc. award, Toledo PTA Pub. Schs. Mem.: U. Toledo Alumni Assn., Friends of the Libr., Fraternal Order of Police Aux., Toledo Power Squadron (hon.), Ohio PTA (life). Democrat. Office: 77 S High St 10th fl Columbus OH 43215-6111

PERRY, JOSEPH NATHANIEL, bishop; b. Chgo., Apr. 18, 1948; Attended, Capuchin Sem. of St. Mary, Crown Point, Ind., 1967—71; BA in Philosophy, St. Joseph Coll., Rensselaer, Ind., 1971, BA in Theology, 1971; MDiv, St. Francis de Sales Major Sem., Milw., 1975; JCL, Cath. U. Am., Washington, DC, 1981. Ordained priest Archdiocese of Milw., 1975, priest, 1975—98, with Tribunal, 1976—95, chief judicial officer with Tribunal, 1983—95; assoc. pastor St. Nicholas Parish, Milw., 1975—76; instr. canon law studies Sacred Heart Sch. Theology, Hales Corners, Wis., 1983—98, Marquette U. Sch. Law, Milw., 1996—98, St. Mary of the Lake Sem., Mundelein, Ill., 1997—; pastor All Sts. Parish, Milw., 1995—98; episcopal vicar, Vicariate VI Archdiocese of Chgo., 1998—, aux. bishop, 1998—; ordained bishop, 1998. Mem. adv. bd. Archbishop Quigley Prep. Sem., 1998—, bd. mem., 1999—; liaison liturgy and liturgical tng. publs. Archdiocese of Chgo., 1999—, Episcopal liaison for Catechetics, 2003—; judge US Ct. Appeals, Province Chgo., 1999—. Mem.: Black Cath. Congress (v.p. bd. 2004—), Knights of St. Peter Claver and Ladies Auxiliary, US Conf. Cath. Bishops (mem. ad hoc com. for pienary coun. 2002—, secretariat for family, laity, women and youth 2002—, mem. ad hoc com. on Catholics' Use of Holy Scripture 2003—, mem. com. on edn. 2003—, chmn. com. on African Am. Catholics 2004—), Canon Law Soc. Roman Catholic. Office: PO Box 733 South Holland IL 60473-0733*

PERRY, KENNETH WILBUR, finance educator; b. Lawrenceburg, Ky., May 21, 1919; s. Ollie Townsend and Minnie (Monroe) P.; m. Shirley Jane Kimball, Sept. 5, 1942; 1 dau., Constance June (Mrs. Linden Warfel). BS, Eastern Ky. U., 1942; MS, Ohio U., 1949; PhD, U. Ill., 1953; LL.D., Eastern Ky. U., 1983. C.P.A., Ill. Instr. Berea Coll., 1949-50, U. Ky., summer 1950; teaching asst. U. Ill. at Champaign, 1950-53, asst. prof. accounting, 1953-55, asso. prof., 1955-58, prof., 1958—, Alexander Grant prof., 1975—. Vis. prof. Northeastern U., summer 1966, Parsons Coll., 1966-67, Fla. A. and M. U., fall 1971; Carman G. Blough prof. U. Va., fall 1975; dir. Illini Pub. Co. Author: Accounting: An Introduction, 1971, Passing the C.P.A. Examination, 1964, (with N. Bedford and A. Wyatt) Advanced Accounting, 1960; contbg. author: Complete Guide to a Profitable Accounting Practice, 1965, C.P.A. Review Manual, 1971; Editor: The Ill. C.P.A, 1968-70; contbg. editor: Accountants' Cost Handbook, 1960. Served to maj. AUS, 1942-46; col. Res. ret. Named outstanding alumnus Eastern Ky. U., 1969 Mem. Am. Accounting Assn. (v.p. 1963, Outstanding Educator award 1974), Am. Inst. C.P.A.'s, Am. Statis. Assn., Nat. Assn. Accountants (dir. 1969-71), Ill. Soc. C.P.A.s (chair in accountancy), Beta Alpha Psi, Beta Gamma Sigma (Distinguished scholar 1977-78), Omicron Delta Kappa. Methodist. Home: 2314 Fields South Dr Champaign IL 61822-9302 Office: Commerce W U Ill Champaign IL 61822

PERRY, LEWIS CURTIS, historian, educator; b. Somerville, Mass., Nov. 21, 1938; s. Albert Quillen and Irene (Lewis) P.; m. Ruth Opler, June 5, 1962 (div. 1970); 1 child, Curtis Alan; m. Elisabeth Israels, Nov. 26, 1970; children: Susanna Irene, David Mordecai. AB, Oberlin Coll., 1960; MS, Cornell U., Ithaca, NY, 1964; PhD, Cornell U., 1967. Asst. prof. history SUNY, Buffalo, 1966-72, assoc. prof., 1972-78; prof. Ind. U. Bloomington, 1978-84; Andrew Jackson prof. history Vanderbilt U., 1984-99, dir. Am. Studies, 1992-95; John Francis Bannon prof. history St. Louis U., 1999—. Ampart lectr. U.S. Info. Service, India and Nepal, 1986, France, 1989; vis. prof. U. Leeds, 1988-89; vis. Raoul Wallenberg fellow Rutgers U., 1991-92; chair Frederick Douglass prize jury, Gilder Lehrman Ctr., 2003-04. Author: Radical Abolitionism, 1973, reissue, 1995, Childhood, Marriage, and Reform, 1980, Intellectual Life in America, 1984, 2nd edit. 1989, Boats Against the Current, 1993, 2nd edit., 2002; co-author: Patterns of Anarchy, 1966, Antislavery Reconsidered, 1979; co-editor Moral Problems in American Life, 1998; editor: Jour. Am. History, 1978-84, American Thought and Culture Series, 1985—. Pres. Unitarian-Universalist Ch., Bloomington, Ind., 1983-84; mem. Ralph Waldo Emerson prize com. Phi Beta Kappa, 1997-99, chair, 1999. N.Y. State Regents fellow, 1965-66, Am. Coun. Learned Socs. fellow, 1972-73, Nat. Humanities Inst. fellow, 1975-76, John Simon Guggenheim Found. fellow, 1982, NEH fellow, 1987-88. Mem.: Soc. Historians Early Am. Republic, Am. Hist. Assn., Orgn. Am. Historians (editor 1978—84, exec. bd. 1996—99). Office: St Louis U Dept History 3800 Lindell Blvd Saint Louis MO 63108 Home Phone: 314-772-6536; Office Phone: 314-977-7140. Business E-Mail: perryl@slu.edu.

PERRY, MICHAEL CLINTON, internist, academic administrator, educator; b. Wyandotte, Mich., Jan. 27, 1945; s. Clarence Clinton and Hilda Grace (Wigginton) P.; m. Nancy Ann Kaluzny, June 22, 1968; children: Rebecca Carolyn, Katherine Grace. BA, Wayne State U., 1966, MD, 1970; MS in Medicine, U. Minn., 1975. Diplomate Am. Bd. Internal Medicine, Am. Bd. Hematology, Am. Bd. Oncology. Intern in internal medicine Mayo Grad. Sch. Medicine, Rochester, Minn., 1970-71, resident, 1971-72, fellow, 1972-75; instr. Mayo Med. Sch., Rochester, 1974-75; asst. prof. U. Mo., Columbia, 1975-80, assoc. prof., 1980-85, prof., 1985—, chmn. dept. medicine, 1983-91, sr. assoc. dean, 1991-94, Nellie A Smith chair oncology, dir. div. hematology/oncology, 1994—. Prin. investigator Cancer and Leukemia Group B, Nat. Cancer Inst., Chgo., 1982—, exec. com., 1982-84, 1987-90. Author, co-author 30 book chpts.; editor: Toxicity of Chemotherapy, 1984, The Chemotherapy Source Book, 1992, 96, 2001, Comprehensive Textbook of Thoracic Oncology, 1996; contbr. articles to profl. jours. Recipient Faculty Alumni award U. Mo., Columbia, 1985, Disting. Alumnus award Wayne State U., 1995, Disting. Oncologist of Yr. award So. Assn. Oncology, 2000. Fellow ACP; mem. Am. Soc. Hematology, Am. Soc. Clin. Oncology, Cen. Soc. Clin. Research, Am. Soc. Internal Medicine (Young Internist of Yr. 1981), Sigma Xi, Alpha Omega Alpha. Office: U Mo-Columbia 516 Ellis Fischel Cancer Ctr 115 Business Loop 70 W Columbia MO 65203-3244 Home: 3111 S Bobcat CT Columbia MO 65201-3141 E-mail: perrym@health.missouri.edu.

PERRY, NANCY, foundation administrator; m. Ken Perry; 1 child, Brad. BS in Elem. Edn., U. Kans. Kindergarten tchr. Avondale East Elem. Sch.; host local Romper Room TV program; variety/talk show host; pres., CEO United Way of Greater Topeka. Mem. fin. and outreach coms., mem. altar guild Grace Episcopal Cathedral. Mem.: Rotary Club. Office: United Way of Greater Topeka 1315 SW Arrowhead Rd Topeka KS 66604

PERSAUD, TRIVEDI VIDHYA NANDAN, anatomy educator, researcher, consultant; b. Port Mourant, Berbice, Guyana, Feb. 19, 1940; arrived in Canada, 1972; s. Ram Nandan and Deen (Raggy) P.; m. Gisela Gerda Zehden, Jan. 29, 1966; children: Indrani Uta and Sunita Heidi (twins), Rainer Narendra. MD, Rostock U., Germany, 1965, DSc, 1974; PhD in Anatomy, U. West Indies, Kingston, Jamaica, 1970. Intern, Berlin, Germany, 1965-66; govtl. med. officer Guyana, 1966-67; lectr., sr. lectr. anatomy dept. U. West Indies, 1967-72; assoc. prof. anatomy dept. U. Man., Winnipeg, 1972-75, prof., 1975—, prof. ob-gyn., reproductive scis., 1979-99, prof. emeritus, 1999—, prof. pediatrics and child health, 1989—, prof., chmn./head dept. human anatomy & cell sci., 1977-93, dir. Teratology Rsch. Lab., 1972-97. Cons. in teratology, Children's Centre, Winnipeg, 1973—; mem. sci. staff Health Scis. Centre, Winnipeg, 1973—. Author, editor 22 med. textbooks, including: Early History of Human Anatomy: From Antiquity to the Beginning of the Modern Era, 1984, (with others) Basic Concepts in Teratology, 1985, Environmental Causes of Human Birth Defects, 1991, History of Human Anatomy: The Post-Vesalian Era, 1997, (with K.L. Moore) The Developing Human, 8th edit., 2007, Before We Are Born, 7th edit., 2007; rev. Medical Embryology, 6th edit., 2003; contbr. numerous chpts. to books, over 200 articles to profl. jours. Recipient Carveth Jr. Scientist award Can. Assn. Pathologists, 1974, Albert Einstein Centennial medal German Acad. Scis., 1975, Dr. & Mrs. H.H. Saunderson award U. Manitoba, 1985, 12th Raymond Truex Disting. Lectureship award Hahnemann U., 1990, Queen Elizabeth II Golden Jubilee medal Govt. Can., 2003. Fellow Royal Coll. Pathologists of London; mem. Can. Assn. Anatomists (pres. 1981-83, J.C.B. Grant award 1991), Am. Assn. Anatomists, Teratology Soc., European Teratology Soc. Office: U Man Dept Anatomy & Cell Sci 730 William Ave Winnipeg MB Canada R3E OW3 Office Phone: 204-789-3333. Business E-Mail: persaud@cc.umanitoba.ca.

PERSICO, VINCENT ANTHONY, state legislator; b. Oak Pk., Ill., Dec. 9, 1948; s. Vincent Michael and Lavergne (Gehrke) P.; (div.); 1 child, Derek. BA, U. Ill., 1971; MA, o. Ill. U., 1986. Tchr.; mem. Ill. Ho. of Reps. from 39th dist., 1991—. Mem. Edn. Appropriations, Elem. and Secondary Edn., Energy & Environ., Transp. & Motor Vehicles Coms. Ill. Ho. of Reps., vice spokesman Edn. Fin. Com. Trustee Milton Twp., Ill., 1988-91. Mem. Ill. Edn. Assn. Republican. Office: Ill Ho of Reps State Capitol Springfield IL 62706-0001 Home: 1310 N Ritchie Ct Apt 10c Chicago IL 60610-4956

PERSKY, MARLA SUSAN, lawyer; b. Pitts., Feb. 15, 1956; d. Bernard and Elaine (Matus) P.; m. Craig Heberton IV, May 20, 1984. BS, Northwestern U., 1977; JD, Washington U., St. Louis, 1982. Bar: Ill. 1982. Asst. dir. med. records Chgo. Lake Shore Hosp., 1978; sales/mktg. rep. Colgate-Palmolive Co., Chgo.,

1978-79; mem. Lurie Sklar & Simon, Chgo., 1982-86; corp. counsel Baxter Healthcare Corp., Deerfield, Ill., 1986-91; lead litigation counsel Baxter Internat. Inc., 1991-94; assoc. gen. counsel Baxter Healthcare Corp., Deerfield, 1994—98, dep. gen. counsel, 1998—2004, gen. counsel, corp. sec., 2004—. Dir. Cytyc Corp. Sr. editor Urban Law Ann., 1981-82; contbr. articles to profl. jours. Mem. Chgo. Bar Assn., Ill. Bar Assn. (writing contest award 1983), ABA (vice chmn. medicine and law com. 1984-86), Am. Soc. Law and Medicine, Am. Acad. Hosp. Attys. Democrat. Office: Baxter Internat Inc One Baxter Pkwy Deerfield IL 60015-5281

PERSSON, ERLAND KARL, electrical engineer, executive; b. Soderala, Sweden, Oct. 9, 1923; arrived in U.S., 1949, naturalized, 1953; m. Elaine Darm; children: Ann Monn, Eric. BSEE, U. Minn., 1955. Registered profl. engr., Minn. Prin. engr. Gen. Mills, Mpls., 1956-61; v.p. engring. Electro-Craft Corp., Hopkins, Minn., 1961-72, v.p. R & D, 1972-83, sr. v.p., chief tech. officer, 1983-86; pres. Erland Persson Co., Mpls., 1987—. Contbr. articles to profl., chapters to books. Mem. mech. engring. adv. com. U. Minn.; bd. dirs. Minn. High Tech. Coun., 1984—86, mem., 1987. Fellow: IEEE (life; mem. indsl. drives com.), Audio Engring. Soc. (life; founder midwest chpt. 1974); mem.: Eta Kappa Nu. Achievements include patents in field. Office: 216 Janalyn Cir Minneapolis MN 55416-3321 Home Phone: 763-377-2531.

PERSYN, MARY GERALDINE, law librarian, educator; b. Elizabeth, NJ, Feb. 25, 1945; d. Henry Anthony and Geraldine (Sumption) P. AB, Creighton U., 1967; MLS, U. Oreg., 1969; JD, Notre Dame U., 1982. Bar: Ind. 1982, U.S. Dist. Ct. (no. and so. dists.) Ind. 1982, U.S. Supreme Ct. 1995. Social scis. libr. Miami U., Oxford, Ohio, 1969-78; staff law libr. Notre Dame (Ind.) Law Sch., 1982-84; dir. law libr. Valparaiso (Ind.) U., 1984-87, law libr., assoc. prof. law, 1987—. Editor Journal of Legislation, 1981-82; mng. editor Third World Legal Studies, 1986—. V.p. Ind. Coop. Libr. Svcs. Auth., 1997-98, pres., 1998-99. Mem. ABA, Ind. State Bar Assn., Am. Assn. Law Librs. Ohio Regional Assn. Law Librs. (pres. 1990-91), Ind. State Quilt Guild (pres. 1996-2000). Roman Catholic. Home: 1308 Tuckahoe Park Dr Valparaiso IN 46383-4032 Office: Valparaiso U Law Libr Sch Law Valparaiso IN 46383 E-mail: mary.persyn@valpo.edu.

PESCH, ELLEN P., lawyer; BA, Barat Coll., 1986; JD, John Marshall Law Sch., 1989; LLM, DePaul U., 1991. Bar: Ill. 1989, U.S. Dist. Ct. (no. dist.) Ill. With Sidley Austin Brown & Wood, Chgo., 1989—, ptnr., 2001—. Mem.: ABA, Internat. Swaps and Derivatives Assn., Stable Value Investment Assn.

PESHKIN, MURRAY, physicist; b. Bklyn., May 17, 1925; s. Jacob and Bella Ruth (Zuckerman) P.; m. Frances Julie Ehrlich, June 12, 1955; children—Michael, Sharon, Joel. BA, Cornell U., 1947, PhD, 1951. Instr., then asst. prof. physics Northwestern U., 1951-59; physicist, then sr. scientist Argonne (Ill.) Nat. Lab., 1959—, assoc. dir. physics div., 1972-83. Fellow Weizmann Inst. Sci., Rehovoth, Israel, 1959-60, 68-69. Served with AUS, 1944-46. Home: 838 Parkside Ave Elmhurst IL 60126-4813 Office: Argonne Natl Lab Argonne IL 60439 Business E-Mail: peshkin@anl.gov.

PESSIN, JEFFREY E., physiology educator; b. NYC, Jan. 2, 1953; s. Al Pessin; m. Rene Debra Bronner, June 23, 1975; children: Jacob, Lauren, Melanie. BA in Chemistry, MA in Chemistry, CUNY, 1975; PhD in Biochemistry, U. Ill., 1980; postgrad., U. Mass., 1980. Grad. rsch. asst. U. Ill., Urbana, 1975-80; asst. prof. physiology U. Iowa, Iowa City, 1983-88, assoc. prof., 1988-91, prof., 1991—, assoc. dir. Diabetes and Endocrinology Rsch. Ctr., 1991—. Contbr. articles to Molecular and Cellular Biology, Endocrinology. Basil O'Connor rsch. scholar March of Dimes Birth Defects Found., 1987-90; grantee NIH, 1988-93. Mem. AAAS, NIH (mem. metabolism study sect. 1989-93), Am. Chem. Soc., Am. Diabetes Assn. (R & D award 1985-87, rsch. award 1995), Sigma Xi. Office: U Iowa Dept Physiology and Biophysics Bowman Sci Bldg 5-530 Iowa City IA 52242 Home: 51 Woodchuck Hollow Ct Port Jefferson NY 11777-2093

PESTELLO, FRED P., academic administrator; BA in Sociology, John Carroll U.; MA in Sociology, PhD in Sociology, U. Akron. Joined U. Dayton, Ohio, 1984, prof. sociology, assoc. dean, 1997—2001, sr. v.p. for ednl. affairs and provost, 2001—. Office: Office of the Provost Univ Dayton 300 College Park St Marys Hall 212 Dayton OH 45469-1634

PESTILLO, PETER JOHN, auto parts company executive, lawyer; b. Bristol, Conn., Mar. 22, 1938; s. Peter and Ruth (Hayes) P.; m. BettyAnn Barraclough, Aug. 29, 1959; children: Kathleen, Karen, Kerry. BSS, Fairfield U., Conn., 1960; LLB, Georgetown U., 1963. Bar: D.C. 1964. Mgr. union relations planning Gen. Electric Co., NYC, 1968-74; v.p. employee relations B.F. Goodrich Co., Akron, Ohio, 1974-80; v.p. labor relations Ford Motor Co., Dearborn, Mich., 1980-85, v.p. employee relations, 1985-86, v.p. employee and external affairs, 1986—90, v.p. corp. rels. and diversified businesses, 1990—93, exec. v.p. corp. rels., 1993, vice chmn., chief of staff; chmn. Visteon Corp., Dearborn, 2000—, CEO, 2000—04. Mem. adv. bd. United Found., Detroit. Mem. Am. Arbitration Assn. (dir.), U.S. C. of C. (labor relation com.), D.C. Bar, Bus. Roundtable, Labor Policy Assn., Nat. Assn. Mfgs., UBA. Office: Visteon Corp 17000 Rotunda Corp Dearborn MI 48120

PETERLE, TONY JOHN, zoologist, educator; b. Cleve., July 7, 1925; s. Anton and Anna (Katic) P.; m. Thelma Josephine Coleman, July 30, 1949; children: Ann Faulkner, Tony Scott. BS, Utah State U., 1949; MS, U. Mich., 1950, PhD (univ. scholar), 1954; Fulbright scholar, U. Aberdeen, Scotland, 1954-55; postgrad., Oak Ridge Inst. Nuclear Studies, 1961. With Niederhauser Lumber Co., 1947—49, Macfarland Tree Svc., 1949—51; rsch. biologist Mich. Dept. Conservation, 1951—54; asst. dir. Rose Lake Expt. Sta., 1955—59; leader Ohio Coop. Wildlife Rsch. unit U.S. Fish and Wildlife Svc., Dept. Interior, 1959—63; asso. prof., then prof. zoology Ohio State U., Columbus, 1959—89, prof. emeritus, 1989, chmn. faculty population and environ. biology, 1968—69, chmn. dept. zoology, 1969—81, dir. program in environ. biology, 1970—71; liaison officer Internat. Union Game Biologists, 1965—93; chmn. internat. affairs com., mem. com., ecotoxicology co-organizer XIII Internat. Congress Game Biology, 1979—80; propr. The Iron Works, 1989—. Pvt. cons., 1989—; mem. com. rev. EPA pesticide decision making Nat. Acad. Scis.-NRC; mem. vis. scientists program Am. Inst. Biol. Scis.-ERDA, 1971-77; mem. com. pesticides Nat. Acad. Scis., com. on emerging trends in agr. and effects on fish and wildlife; mem. ecology com. of sci. adv. council EPA, 1979-87; mem. research units coordinating com. Ohio Coop. Wildlife and Fisheries, 1963-89; vis. scientist EPA, Corvallis, 1987. Author: Wildlife Toxicology, 1991; editor: Jour. of Wildlife Mgmt., 1969-70, 84-85, 2020 Vision Meeting the Fish and Wildlife Conservation Challenges of the 21st Century, 1992. Served with AUS, 1943-46. Named Internat. Scientists of Yr., 2002. Fellow AAAS, Am. Inst. Biol. Scis., Ohio Acad. Sci.; mem. Wildlife Disease Assn., Wildlife Soc. (regional rep. 1962-67, v.p. 1968, pres. 1972, Leopold award 1990, hon. mem. 1990, Profl. award of merit North Ctrl. sect. 1993), Nat. Audubon Soc. (bd. dirs. 1985-87), Ecol. Soc., INTECOL-NSF panel U.S.-Japan Program, Xi Sigma Pi, Phi Kappa Phi. Home: 4072 Klondike Rd Delaware OH 43015-9513 Office: Ohio State U Dept Evolution Ecology Organismal Bi 318 W 12th Ave Columbus OH 43210

PETERS, CHARLES H.R., lawyer; BS magna cum laude, Miami U., 1982; JD cum laude, Northwestern U., 1986. Bar: Ill. 1986, US Dist. Ct. (no. dist. Ill.) 1986, US Ct. Appeals (7th cir.) 1992, US Supreme Ct. 2001. Ptnr. Schiff Hardin, LLP, Chgo. Mem.: ABA, Chgo. Coun. Lawyers. Office: Schiff Hardin LLP 6600 Sears Tower Chicago IL 60606-6473 Office Phone: 312-258-5683. Office Fax: 312-258-5600. E-mail: cpeters@schiffhardin.com.

PETERS, DAVID ALLEN, mechanical engineering educator, consultant; b. East St. Louis, Ill., Jan. 31, 1947; s. Bernell Louis and Marian Louise (Blum) P.; children: Michael H., Laura A., Nathan C. BS in Applied Mechanics, Washington U., St. Louis, 1969, MS in Applied Mechanics, 1970; PhD in Aeros. and Astronautics, Stanford U., 1974. Assoc. engr. McDonnell Astronautics, 1969-70; rsch. scientist Army Aeronautics Lab., 1970-74; asst. prof. Washington U., 1975-77, assoc. prof., 1977-80, prof. mech. engring., 1980-85, chmn. dept., 1982-85; prof. aerospace engring. Ga. Inst Tech., Atlanta, 1985-91; dir. NASA Space Grant Consortium Ga. Inst. Tech., Atlanta, 1989-91; dir. Ctr. for Computational Mechanics Washington U., 1992—, prof. dept. mech. engring. St. Louis, 1991—, chmn. dept. mech. engring., 1997—2007, McDonnell Douglas prof. engring., 1999. Contbr. 150 articles to profl. jours. Recipient sci. contbn. award ASA, 1975, 76, Disting. Faculty award Washington U., 2006. Fellow AIAA, ASME, Am. Acad. Mechanics, Am. Helicopter Soc. (jour. editor 1987-90, Alexander ikolsky award, 2008); mem. Am. Soc. for Engring. Edn., Internat. Assn. for Computational Mechanics (charter), Pi Tau Sigma (gold medal 1978). Baptist. Home: 7629 Balson Ave Saint Louis MO 63130-2150 Office: Wash U Dept Mech Engr Campus Box 1185 Saint Louis MO 63130 Office Phone: 314-935-4337. Business E-Mail: dap@me.wustl.edu.

PETERS, DENNIS GAIL, chemist; b. LA, Apr. 17, 1937; s. Samuel and Phyllis Dorothy (Pope) P. BS cum laude, Calif. Inst. Tech., 1958; PhD, Harvard U., 1962. Mem. faculty Ind. U., 1962—, prof. chemistry, 1974—, Herman T. Briscoe prof., 1975—. Co-author textbooks, contbr. articles profl. jours. Woodrow Wilson fellow, 1958-59; NIH predoctoral fellow, 1959-62; vis. fellow Japan Soc. for Promotion Sci., 1980; recipient Ulysses G. Weatherly award disting. teaching Ind. U., 1969, Disting. Teaching award Coll. Arts and Scis. Grad. Alumni Assn. Ind. U., 1984, Nat. Catalyst award for Disting. Teaching Chem. Mfrs. Assn., 1988, Henry B. Linford award The Electrochem. Soc., 2002; grantee NSF. Fellow Ind. Acad. Sci., Am. Inst. Chemists, Electrochem. Soc. 2007; mem. ACS (grantee, Div. of Analytical Chemistry award for excellence in teaching 1990, James Flack Norris award 2001). Home: 1401 S Nancy St Bloomington IN 47401-6051 Office: Dept Chemistry Ind U Bloomington IN 47405 Home Phone: 812-334-2487; Office Phone: 812-855-9671. Business E-Mail: peters@indiana.edu.

PETERS, GARY CHARLES, state legislator, lawyer, educator; b. Pontiac, Mich., Dec. 1, 1958; s. Herbert Garrett and Madeleine (Vignier) P.; m. Colleen Ochoa; children: Gary Jr., Madeleine, Alana. BA, Alma Coll., 1980; MBA, U. Detroit, 1984; JD, Wayne State U., 1989. Bar: Mich. 1990. Fin. cons., resident mgr., asst. v.p. Merrill Lynch, Pierce, Fenner & Smith, Inc., Rochester, Mich., 1980-89; br. mgr., v.p. Paine Webber, Inc., Rochester, Mich., 1989—; mem. Mich. Snenate from dist. 14, Lansing, 1994—. Securities arbitrator, mediator Nat. Assn. Securities Dealers, N.Y. Stock Exchange, Am. Arbitration Assn., 1990—; adj. prof. Oakland U., Rochester, 1991-93, instr. Wayne State U., 1992-94; vice chair Mich. Senate Dem. Whip fin. com.; mem. edn. com., judiciary com., families, mental health and human svcs. com., econ. devel. & econ. trade com., law revision com. Mich. Sentencing Commn. Councilman City of Rochester Hills, 1992-94, mem. zoning bd. appeals and Paint Creek Trailways Commn., 1992-94; officer-at-large Mich. Dem. Party, 1996. Officer USNR, 1993—. Mem. Mich. State Bar Assn., Sierra Club, Phi Beta Kappa. Avocations: hiking, motorcycling, world travel, soaring, scuba diving. Home: 2645 Bloomfield Xing Bloomfield Hills MI 48304-1710 Office: PaineWebber Inc PO Box 80730 Rochester MI 48308-0730

PETERS, GORDON BENES, retired musician; b. Oak Park, Ill., Jan. 4, 1931; s. Arthur George and Julia Anne (Benes) P.; children: Rénee Kemper, Erica Kemper. Student, orthwestern U., 1949-50; studied with Pierre Monteux, 1952—63; MusB, Eastman Sch. Music, 1956, MusM, 1962. Founder, dir. Marimba Masters, 1954—59; percussionist Rochester (NY) Philharm. Orch., 1954—59; prin. percussionist, asst. timpanist Grant Park Symphony Orch., Chgo., 1954—58; mem. faculty Rochester Bd. Edn., 1956-57, Geneseo State Tchrs. Coll., 1957-58; acting prin. percussionist Rochester Philharm., NY, 1958-59; prin. percussionist and assoc. prin. timpanist Chgo. Symphony Orch., 1959—2001; condr., adminstr. Civic Orch. Chgo., 1966-87; condr. Elmhurst Symphony Orch., 1968-73. Instr. percussion instruments Northwestern U., 1963-68, lectr., 1991; guest condr. Bangor Symphony, Maine, 1993; lectr. Winthrop U., SC, 2006. Author, pub. Treatise on Percussion, 1962, rev., 1975 as The Drummer: Man, 1975, rev., 2003 (CD); arranger-pub. Marimba Ensemble arrangements; composer-pub.: Swords of Moda-Ling; editor: percussion column Instrumentalist mag, 1963-69; contbr. articles to profl. jours. Bd. dirs. Pierre Monteux Sch., Hancock, Maine, 1965-95. With U.S. Mil. Acad. Band, 1950-53. Recipient Pierre Monteux Disciple Conducting award, 1962; named Prin. Timpani chair GBP, Chgo. Youth Symphony Orch., 2000. Mem. Percussive Arts Soc. (pres. 1964-67, bd. dirs. Hall of Fame 2004), Am. Symphony Orch. League, Condrs. Guild (treas., exec. com. 1979-82, 86-90), Japan Xylophone Assn., Phi Mu Alpha Sinfonia (life). Home (Winter): 824 Hinman Ave Evanston IL 60202-5906 Home (Summer): PO Box 403 Hancock ME 04640-0403

PETERS, HENRY AUGUSTUS, neurologist; b. Oconomowoc, Wis., Dec. 21, 1920; s. Henry Augustus and Emma N. P.; m. Jean McWilliams, 1950; children— Henry, Kurt, Eric, Mark. BA, MD, U. Wis. Prof. dept. neurology and rehab. medicine U. Wis. Med. Sch., Madison, emeritus prof., 1996—. Mem. med. adv. bd. Muscular Dystrophy Assn. Served to lt. M.C. U.S. Navy. Fellow A.C.P.; mem. Wis. Med. Assn., Am. Acad. Neurology, Am. Psychiatric Assn. Clubs: Rotary. Office: 600 Highland Ave Madison WI 53792-0001 Office Phone: 608-233-1568. Business E-Mail: hapeters@hosp.wisc.edu.

PETERS, HOWARD NEVIN, foreign language educator; b. Hazleton, Pa., June 29, 1938; s. Howard Eugene and Verna P.; m. Judith Anne Griessel, Aug. 24, 1963; children: Elisabeth Anne, Nevin Edward. BA, Gettysburg Coll., 1960; PhD, U. Colo., 1965. Asst. prof. fgn. langs. Valparaiso (Ind.) U., 1965-69, assoc. prof., 1969-75, dir. grad. divsn., 1967-70, acting dean Coll. Arts and Scis., 1970-71, assoc. dean Coll. Arts and Scis., 1971-74, dean Coll. Arts and Scis., 1974-81, prof. fgn. langs., 1975—, prof. fgn. langs. and lits., chair dept. fgn. langs. and lits., 1994—95, prof. emeritus fgn. langs. and lits., 1995—. Author (poetry) Espejo De Son, 1997. NDEA fellow, 1960-63 Mem. Midwest MLA, Phi Beta Kappa, Sigma Delta Pi, Phi Sigma Iota. Lutheran. Home: 860 N Cr 500 E Valparaiso IN 46383 Office: Meier Hall Rm 113 Valparaiso U Valparaiso IN 46383 Business E-Mail: Howard.Peters@valpo.edu.

PETERS, JOHN G., academic administrator, political scientist; m. Barbara Cole Peters; 1 child, Russell. BA, John Carroll U.; MA in Govt., Ohio U.; PhD in Polit. Sci., U. Ill., Urbana-Champaign, 1974. Adminstr. U. Nebr.-Lincoln; provost, COO U. Tenn., Knoxville; pres. No. Ill. U., DeKalb, 2000—. Chair Mid Am. Conf. Coun. of Pres., 2003—04; bd. dirs. Ill. Coalition, East-West Corp. Corridor Assn., Castle Bank, N.A., Ill. Coun. on Econ. Edn.; co-chair Ctr. for Child Welfare and Edn.; polit. adviser Nat. Cattlemens Assn. Assoc. editor Great Plains Quarterly, 1986—93; contbr. articles to profl. jours. Recipient No. Leadership Inst. Award, 2001. Fellow: Ctr. for Great Plains Studies; mem.: Nat. Assn. Telecommunications Officers, Nat. Assn. State Land Grant Colls. and Univs., Nat. Fedn. Local Cable Programmers, Policy Studies Orgn., Coun. Colls. of Arts and Scis., Western Polit. Sci. Assn., Internat. Polit. Sci. Assn., Midwest Polit. Sci. Assn., Am. Polit. Sci. Assn., Pi Alpha Alpha (hon.), Phi Beta Kappa (hon.), Phi Kappa Phi (hon.). Office: Office of Pres No Ill U 1425 W Lincoln Hwy Dekalb IL 60115-2825 Office Phone: 815-753-9500. E-mail: b40jgp1@wpo.cso.niu.edu.*

PETERS, LEON, JR., retired engineering educator; b. Columbus, Ohio, May 28, 1923; s. Leon P. and Ethel (Howland) Pierce; m. Mabel Marie Johnson, June 6, 1953; children: Amy T. Peters Thomas, Melinda A. Peters Todaro, Maria C. Cohee, Patricia D., Lee A., Roberta J. Peters Cameruca, Karen E. Peters Ellingson. BSE.E., Ohio State U., 1950, MS, 1954, PhD, 1959. Asst. prof. elec. engring. Ohio State U., Columbus, 1959-63, assoc. prof., 1963-67, prof., 1967-93, prof. emeritus, 1993—, assoc. dept. chmn. for rsch. Columbus, 1990-92, dir. electro sci. lab., 1983-94. Contbr. articles to profl. jours. Served to 2d lt. U.S. Army, 1942-46, ETO. Fellow: IEEE. Home: 2087 Ellington Rd Columbus OH 43221-4138 Office: Ohio State U Electrosci Lab 1320 Kinnear Rd Columbus OH 43221-1156 Business E-Mail: peters.6@osu.edu.

PETERS, THOMAS M., lawyer; b. Saginaw, Mich., Apr. 10, 1943; s. Donald James and Jean Eleanor (Kelly) P.; m. Jane Caryl Fetters, Jan. 6, 1968; children: Jenifer Caryl, Thomas Jr. Grad., Syracuse East European Language Sch., NY, 1966; BA, Mich. State U., 1969; JD, Wayne State U., 1973. Assoc. Vandeveer, Garzia, Tonkin, Kerr, Heaphy, Moore, & Sills, Detroit, 1973-80, prin., ptnr., 1980—. Mem. local and state bar coms. U.S. Dist. Ct. and U.S. Ct. Appeals. Served to staff sgt. USAF, 1965-69. Mem. ABA, Def. Research Inst., Mich. Def. Trial Counsel, Assn. Def. Trial Counsel (bd. dirs. 1978—, pres. 1985-86, award for valuable service 1986), Mediation Tribunal Assn., Am. Arbitration Assn. Clubs: Port Huron (Mich.) Golf, Otsego Ski (Gaylord, Mich.), Beachwood Swim and tennis (Troy, Mich.), Tournament Players (Jacksonville, Fla.). Lodges: Elks. Home: 4906 Rivers Edge Dr Troy MI 48098-4137 Office: Vandeveer Garzia, PC Ste 100 1450 W Long Lake Rd Troy MI 48098-6330 Office Phone: 248-312-2900. E-mail: tpeters@VGpcLAW.com.

PETERS, WILLIAM P., oncologist, science administrator, dean, educator; b. Buffalo, Aug. 26, 1950; m. Elizabeth Zentai; children: Emily, Abigail, James. BS, BS, BA, Pa. State U., 1972; MPhil, PhD, Columbia U., 1976, MD, 1978; postgrad., Harvard U., 1984; MBA, Duke U., 1990. Diplomate Am. Bd. Internal Medicine, Am. Bd. Med. Oncology. Prof. medicine Duke U. Med. Ctr., Durham, N.C., 1993-95, assoc. dir. for clin. ops. Duke Comprehensive Cancer Ctr., 1994-95, dir. bone marrow transplant program, 1984-95; pres., CEO, Mich. Cancer Found., Detroit, 1995—2001; pres., dir., CEO Karmanos Cancer Inst., Detroit, 1995—2001; assoc. dean for cancer programs Wayne State U., Detroit, 1995—2001, prof. oncology, medicine, surgery and radiation oncology, 1995—; disting. chair of oncology Wayne State U., Detroit, 2002—; pres., dir., CEO CETAID, Karmanos Cancer Inst., 2001—; pres. Inst. for Strategic Analysis and Innovation, Detroit Med. Ctr., 2001—. Sr. v.p. for cancer svcs. Detroit Med. Ctr., 1995-2001.

PETERSEN, ANNE C. (CHERYL PETERSEN), foundation administrator, educator; b. Little Falls, Minn., Sept. 11, 1944; d. Franklin Hanks and Rhoda Pauline (Sandwick) Studley; m. Douglas Lee Petersen, Dec. 27, 1967; children: Christine Anne, Benjamin Bradfield. BA, U. Chgo., 1966, MS, 1972, PhD, 1973. Asst. prof., rsch. assoc. Dept. Psychiatry U. Chgo., 1972-80, assoc. prof., rsch. assoc., 1980-82; prof. human devel., head Dept. Individual and Family Studies Pa. State U., University Park, 1982-87, dean Coll. Health and Human Devel., 1987-92, prof. health and human devel., 1987-92; dean grad. sch., v.p. for rsch. throughout state U. Minn., Mpls., 1992-94, prof. adolescent devel. and pediatrics, 1992-96; dep. dir., COO NSF, Arlington, Va., 1994-96; sr. v.p. programs W.K. Kellogg Found., 1996—2005; dep. dir. Ctr. Advanced Study Behavioral Scis. Stanford U., 2006—, prof. Dept. Psychology, 2006—. Vis. prof., fellow Coll. Edn., R&D Psychology, Roosevelt U., Chgo., 1973-74; cons. Ctr. for Health Adminstrn. Studies U. Chgo., 1976-78, Ctr. for New Schs., Chgo., 1974-78, Robert Wood Johnson Found. Mathtech, Inc., 1987-89; coord. clin. rsch. tng. program Michael Reese Hosp. and Med. Ctr., Chgo., 1976-80, dir. Lab. for Study of Adolescence, 1975-82; faculty Ill. Sch. for Profl. Psychology, 1978-79; statis. cons. Coll. Nursing U. Ill. Med. Ctr., 1975-83; assoc. dir. health program MacArthur Found., 1980-82, also cons. health program, 1982-88; chair sr. adv. bd. NIMH, 1987-88; nat. adv. mental health coun. NIH, 1997-2003; trustee at. Inst. Statis. Scis., 1998-2004. Author: Sex Related Differences in Cognition Functioning: Developmental Issues, 1979, Promoting Adolescent Health: A Diolog on Research and Practice, 1982, Firls at Puberty: Biological and psychosocial Perspectives, 1983, Brain Maturation and Cognitive Development: Comparative and Cross Cultural Perspectives, 1991, Narrowing the Margins: Adolescent Unemployment and the lack of a social role, 1991, Grofit: A Fortran Program for the Estimation of Parameters of a Human Growth Curve, 1972, Girls at Puberty: Biological and Psychosocial Perspectives, 1983, Adolescence and Youth: Psychological Development in a Changing World, 1984, Youth Unemployment and Society, 1994, Transitions Through Adolescence: Interpersonal Domains and Context, 1996; reviewer Jour. Youth and Adolescence, 1975-80, Devel. Psychology, 1979—, Sci., 1979—, Jour. Edn. Psychology, 1979—, Child Devel., 1980—, Jour. Edn. Measurement, 1980, Ednl. Rschr., 1980, Am. Ednl. Rsch. Jour., 1981—, Jour. Mental Imagery, 1982-92, Sex Roles, 1984—; cons. editor Psychology of Women Quar., 1978-82, assoc. editor, 1983-86; adv. editor Contemporary Psychology, 1985-86; mem. editl. bd. various profl. jours.; contbr. chpts. to books and articles to profl. jours. Bd. overseers Lewis Coll., Ill. Inst. Tech., 1980-82; mem. adv. bd. longitudinal data archive project Murray Ctr., Radcliffe Coll., 1985-91, mem. sci. adv. bd., 1983-91 Fellow: APA (chmn. task force on reproductive freedom 1979—81, program chmn. 1981—82, chmn. task force on long range planning 1986—89, pres. divsn. 7 1992—93), AAAS; mem.: NAS (nat. forum on future children and their families 1987—91, chmn. panel on child abuse and neglect 1991—93, mem. forum on adolescence Inst. of Medicine 1997—2000, chair bd. on behavioral, cognitive and sensory scis. 1997—, mem. nat. academics com. sci., engring., and policy 2003—), Global Phys. Therapy Alliance (pres. 2005—), Soc. for Rsch. on Adolescence (pres. 1990—92, past pres. 1992—94, chmn. nominations com. 1992—94, mem. fin. com. 2004—), Acad. Europaea, Psychometric Soc., Behavior Genetics Assn., Assn. Women in Sci. (bd. dirs. 1996—2000), Am. Ednl. Rsch. Assn. (various offices), Internat. Soc. for the Study of Behavioral Devel. (coun. mem. 1995—, pres.-elect 2002—06, pres. 2006—), Inst. for Medicine. Home: 3715 Blackberry Ln Kalamazoo MI 49008-3333 Office Phone: 650-321-2052. E-mail: globalphilliance@yahoo.com.

PETERSEN, DONALD SONDERGAARD, lawyer; b. Pontiac, Ill., May 14, 1929; s. Clarence Marius and Esther (Sondergaard) P.; m. Alice Thorup, June 5, 1954; children: Stephen, Susan Petersen Schuh, Sally Petersen Riordan. Student, Grand View Coll., 1946—48; BA, Augustana Coll., Rock Island, Ill., 1951; JD, Northwestern U., 1956. Bar: Ill. 1957. Assoc. Norman & Billick and predecessors, Chgo., 1956-64, ptnr., 1965-78; counsel Sidley & Austin, Chgo., 1978-80, ptnr., 1980-93, ret., 1993. Pres. Chgo. Exhibitors Corp., Chgo., 1972-85. Bd. dirs. Mount Olive Cemetery Co. Inc., Chgo., 1972-90; bd. dirs. Augustana Hosp., 1983-87, The Danish Home, 1976—; bd. dirs. Luth. Gen. Hosp., Park Ridge, Ill., 1968-2005, chmn., 1979-81, 89-91; bd. dirs. Luth. Gen. Health System and predecessors, Park Ridge, 1980-95, chmn., 1980-81, 83-85; bd. dirs., chmn. Parkside Health Mgmt. Corp., Parkside Home Health Svcs., 1985-88. With U.S. Army, 1951-53. Mem. Chgo. Bar Assn., Ill. State Bar Assn. Clubs: Union League (Chgo.). Home: 241 N Aldine Ave Park Ridge IL 60068-3009 Office: 9th Fl One S Dearborn St Chicago IL 60603 Office Phone: 312-853-7232.

PETERSEN, DOUGLAS ARNDT, financial consultant; b. Albert Lea, Minn., Sept. 18, 1944; s. Arndt H. and Helen L. (Slater) Petersen; m. Winnifred K. Taylor, Aug. 14, 1964 (div. July 1970); children: Scott, Jennifer; m. Cynthia L. Schnabel, June 14, 1975; 1 child, Christopher. BS in Edn., Mankato State U., 1966, postgrad., 1966—68. Youth dir. Mankato (Minn.) YMCA, 1965—68; tchr. Mankato State U., 1965—68; exec. dir. YMCA Camp Christmas Tree, Mound, Minn., 1968—72, Eastside YMCA, Mpls., 1972—75; asst. exec. dir. West Suburban YMCA, Minnetonka, Minn., 1968—72, Mpls. Red Cross, 1979—89; program/fin. devel. dir. Eastside eighborhood Svc., Mpls., 1975—79; dir. major/planned gifts ARC Nat. Staff, Mpls., 1989—91; pres., CEO, cons. D.A. Petersen Assocs., Mpls., 1992—. Pres. APD YMCA Am., 1974; chair St. Anthony/New Brighton Found., 1988—92; pres. MFDDC ARC, 1988—89. Lutheran. Avocations: travel, community service, scuba diving, canoeing, backpacking. Home: 3216 Skycroft Dr Minneapolis MN 55418-2552 Office: PO Box 18415 Minneapolis MN 55418-0415 Office Phone: 612-782-0604. Personal E-mail: dapa2@comcast.net.

PETERSEN, JAMES L., lawyer; b. Bloomington, Ill., Feb. 3, 1947; s. Eugene and Cathryn Theresa (Hemmele) P.; m. Helen Louise Moser, Nov. 20, 1971; children: Christine Louise, Margaret Theresa. BA, Ill. State U., 1970; MA, U. Ill., Springfield, 1973; JD magna cum laude, Ind. U., 1976. Bar: Ind. 1976, Fla. 1980, U.S. Dist. Cts. (no. and so. Ind.), U.S. Ct. Appeals (7th cir.), U.S. Supreme Ct. Admissions officer U. Ill., Springfield, 1970-71, asst. to v.p., 1971-72, registrar, 1972-73; assoc. Ice Miller, Indpls., 1976-83, ptnr., 1983—. Pres. United Cerebral Palsy of Ctrl. Ind., 1981-83, pres. Found., 1988-90, Stanley K. Lacy Leadership Series participant. Mem. ABA, Fla. Bar Assn., Ind. Bar Assn., Am. Coll. Trial Lawyers, Intl. Franchise Assn. (bd. mem. Symposium Organizing Cmte., 2003-04), Defense Trial Coun. Ind. (past co-chair, Prods. Liability Cmte; elected 1997 Diplomat), The Business Council, Inc., Ill. State U. Alumni Assn. (pres. 1990-92), Ind. U. Law Alumni Assn. (bd. dirs. 1992—, pres. 1998-99), Ind. U. Bd. Visitors 1998-99, Order of Coif. Home: 11827 Sea Star Dr Indianapolis IN 46256-9400 Office: Ice Miller LLP PO Box 82001 One American Sq Indianapolis IN 46282 Office Phone: 317-236-2308.

PETERSEN, JANET, state representative; b. Des Moines, Aug. 1, 1970; BA, U. No. Iowa; MA, Drake U. Constituency coord. 1992 Clinton-Gore Campaign; comm. specialist Am. Heart Assn.; sr. account exec. Strategic Am.; mem. Iowa Ho. Reps., DesMoines, 2001—, mem. commerce and regulation com., mem. econ. devel. com., mem. appropriations com., mem. edn. com., mem. local govt. com. Active Beaverdale Neighborhood Assn., Walnut Hills Meth. Ch.; bd. mem. DesMoines Arts Festival, United Way Ctrl. Iowa, Women in Pub. Policy, Polk County Housing Trust Fund. Democrat. Office: State Capitol East 12th and Grand Des Moines IA 50319 Home: 4300 Beaver Hills Dr Des Moines IA 50310-6300

PETERSEN, MAUREEN JEANETTE MILLER, management information technology director, retired nurse; b. Evanston, Ill., Sept. 4, 1956; d. Maurice James and M. Joyce (Mielke) Miller; m. Gregory Eugene Petersen, July 7, 1984; children: Trevor James, Tatyana Brianne. BS in Nursing cum laude, Vanderbilt U., 1978; MS in Biometry and Health Info. Systems, U. Minn., 1984. Nurse U. Iowa Hosps. and Clinics, Iowa City, 1978—82; research asst. Sch. Nursing, U.

Minn., Mpls., 1982—83; mgr. Accenture, Mpls., 1984—2001; dir. health info. tech. Park Nicollet, Eden Prairie, Minn., 2003—. Mem.: Project Mgmt. Inst. (proj. mgmt. profl.), Mensa. Methodist. Avocation: travel. Home: 1050 County Rd C2 W Roseville MN 55113-1945 Office: Park Nicollet 7905 Golden Triangle Dr Eden Prairie MN 55344 Office Phone: 952-993-9893. E-mail: peters1050@aol.com, petema@parknicollet.com.

PETERSEN, ROBERT R., brokerage house executive; b. Nebr. m. Doris Petersen. Pres. Nat. Grain Trade Coun., Washington, 1983—2000; CEO and pres. Kans. City Bd. Trade, Mo., 2000—04. Office: Kans City Bd Trade 4800 Main St Ste 303 Kansas City MO 64112

PETERSEN, STEVEN E., neuroscientist, health facility administrator, educator; BA in Anthropology, U. Mont., Missoula, 1974; PhD in Biology, Calif. Inst. Tech., 1982. Prof. neurology, psychology and radiology, chief neuropsychology Washington U. Sch. Medicine, St. Louis, 1985—; postdoctoral position Nat. Eye Inst. Office: Washington U Sch Medicine Campus Box 8111 660 S Euclid Saint Louis MO 63110

PETERSON, ADRIAN LEWIS, professional football player; b. Palestine, Tex., Mar. 21, 1985; s. Nelson Peterson and Bonita Jackson; 1 child, Adeja. Attended, U. Okla. Running back Minn. Vikings, 2007—. Named NFL Offensive Rookie of Yr., AP, 2007, NFL Rookie of Yr., 2007, NFL Pro Bowl MVP, 2008; named to Nat. Football Conf. Pro Bowl Team, 2008; recipient Ball Park Nat. HS Player of Yr. award, 2003. Achievements include setting a new NFL single-game rushing record with 296 yards on November 4, 2007. Mailing: c/o Minn Vikings Metrodome 34 Kirby Puckett Pl Minneapolis MN 55415*

PETERSON, ANN SULLIVAN, physician, consultant; b. Rhinebeck, NY, Oct. 11, 1928; AB, Cornell U., 1950, MD, 1954; MS, MIT, 1980. Diplomate Am. Bd. Internal Medicine. Intern Cornell Med. Divsn.-Bellevue Hosp., NYC, 1954—55, resident, 1955—57; fellow in medicine and physiology Meml.-Sloan Kettering Cancer Ctr., Cornell Med. Coll., NYC, 1957—60; instr. medicine Georgetown U. Sch. Medicine, Washington, 1962—65, asst. prof., 1965—69, asst. dir. clin. rsch. unit, 1962—69; assoc. prof. medicine U. Ill., Chgo., 1969—72, asst. dean, 1969—71, assoc. dean, 1971—72; assoc. prof. medicine, assoc. dean Coll. Physicians and Surgeons, Columbia U., NYC, 1972—80, Cornell U. Med. Coll., NYC, 1980—83; assoc. dir. divsn. med. edn. AMA, Chgo., 1983—86, dir. div. grad. med. edn., 1986—89, v.p. mgmt. cons. corp., 1989—93; ind. cons. Chgo., 1993—2005. Contbr. articles to med. jours. Mem. bd. regents Uniformed Svcs. U. of Health Scis., 1984—90. John and Mary R. Markle scholar, 1965—70, Alfred P. Sloan fellow, MIT, 1979—80. Fellow: ACP; mem.: Mortar Bd., Alpha Omega Alpha, Alpha Epsilon Delta.

PETERSON, BART (BARTON R. PETERSON), former mayor; b. Indpls., June 15, 1958; m. Amy Minick; 1 child, Meg. Grad., Purdue U., 1980; JD, U. Mich., 1983. Atty. Ice Miller Donadio & Ryan, Indpls.; from exec. asst. for environ. affairs to chief of staff Ind. Gov. Evan Bayh, 1989-95; pres., co-founder Precedent Cos., 1995; mayor City of Indpls., 2000—08. Bd. mem. Ind. Nature Conservancy, Regenstrief Found. Democrat.

PETERSON, BRADLEY LAURITS, lawyer; b. Mpls. m. Christine Elizabeth Stoutner, Sept. 16, 1989; 4 children. MBA, U. Chgo., 1982; JD, Harvard U., 1988. Bar: Ill. 1988. Mktg. rep. IBM, Chgo., 1982-85; assoc. Kirkland & Ellis, Chgo., 1988-93, Wildman & Harrold, Chgo., 1993-95; ptnr. Mayer Brown Rowe & Maw LLP, Chgo., 1995—. Author: The Smart Way to Buy Information Technology: How to Maximize Value and Avoid Costly Pitfalls, 1998. Office: Mayer Brown Rowe & Maw LLP 71 S Wacker Dr Chicago IL 60606-4637 Office Phone: 312-701-8568. Business E-Mail: bpeterson@mayerbrownrowe.com.

PETERSON, BRUCE D., lawyer, energy executive; b. Chgo., Nov. 1956; BA, North Park Coll., 1978; JD, U. Notre Dame Law Sch., 1982. Fgn. svc. officer US State Dept., Washington, 1982; ptnr. Hunton & Williams, Washington, 1989—2002; sr. v.p., gen. counsel DTE Energy Co., Detroit, 2002—05. Mem. legal com. Am. Gas Assn., Edison Electric Inst. Bd. dirs. Detroit Symphony Orch.; trustee Cranbrook Ednl. Cmty.; bd. govs. Cranbrook Inst. Sci.

PETERSON, CARL V., professional football team executive; b. Mpls. 1 child, Dawn. BS in Kinesiology, UCLA, 1966, MS in Kinesiology, 1967, EdD in Adminstrn. in Higher Edn., 1970. Asst. coach Wilson High Sch., Calif., 1966, Loyola High Sch., 1967-68, Calif. State U., Somona, 1969-70, head coach, 1970-72; receivers coach UCLA, 1972-74, receivers coach, adminstrv. asst., 1974-76; coach recievers and tight ends Phila. Eagles, 1976, dir. player personnel, 1977-82; pres., gen. mgr. Phila. Stars, 1982-86; pres., gen. mgr., CEO, Kansas City Chiefs, Mo., 1988—. Pres., CEO, PhillySport Mag., Phila., 1987; mem. nat. bd. Maxwell Football Club and Pop Warner Little Scholar Orgn. Recipient USFL Exec. of Yr. award Sporting News, 1983, 84. Mem. Young Pres. Orgn. (Kansas City chpt.), World Press Orgn. Office: Kansas City Chiefs 1 Arrowhead Dr Kansas City MO 64129-1651

PETERSON, COLLIN C., congressman; b. Fargo, ND, June 29, 1944; children: Sean, Jason, Elliott. BA in Bus. Adminstrn. and Acctg., Moorhead State U., 1966. CPA Minn. Senator State of Minn., 1976-86; mem. US Congress from 7th Minn. dist., 1991—; mem. agrl. com., subcoms. gen. farm commodities, specialty crops and natural resources, livestock, environ. credit and rural devel.; mem. permanent select Com. Intelligence, 2001—; mem. govt. ops. com., chmn. subcom. employment housing and aviation; mem. resource conservation com., rsch. and forestry subcom., livestock, dairy and poultry subcom., govt. reform and oversight com.; nat. econ. growth com., nat. resources and regulatory affairs com.-ranking minority mem., vet. affairs com. With U.S. Army N.G., 1963-69. Mem. Am. Legion, Ducks Unltd., Elks, Sportsmen's Club, Rural Caucus, Mainstream Forum, Cormorant Lakes Sportsmen Club, Congl. Sportsmen's Caucus, Mainstream Forum, Congl. Rural Caucus. Democrat. Office: US Ho Reps 2159 Rayburn Ho Office Bldg Washington DC 20515-2307 also: Lake Ave Plaza Bldg Ste 107 714 Lake Ave Detroit Lakes MN 56501

PETERSON, DAVID C., lawyer; b. 1970; BS in Materials Sci. and Engring., U. Minn. Inst. Tech., 1993; JD, U. Minn., 2000. Bar: Minn. 2000. With intellectual property dept. Toro Co.; engr. Hutchinson Tech., Inc.; lawyer Schwegman, Lundberg, Woessner & Kluth, P.A., Mpls. Named a Rising Star, Minn. Super Lawyers mag., 2006. Mem.: Minn. Intellectual Property Law Assn. (chair by-laws com.), Am. Intellectual Property Law Assn. Office: Schwegman Lundberg Woessner & Kluth PA 1600 TCF Tower 121 S 8th St Minneapolis MN 55402 Office Phone: 612-373-6944. E-mail: dpeterson@slwk.com.

PETERSON, DAVID CHARLES, photojournalist; b. Kansas City, Mo., Oct. 22, 1949; s. John Edward and Florence Athene (Hobbs) P.; m. Adele Mae Johnson, Dec. 31, 1952; children: Brian David, Scott Ryun, Anna Victoria. BS in Edn., Kansas State U., 1971; BS in Journalism, U. Kans., 1973, BS in Journalism, 1974. Staff photographer Topeka Capital-Jour., 1975-77, Des Moines Register, 1977—. Photographer (photo essay) Shattered Dreams-Iowa's Rural Crisis, 1986 (Pulitzer prize 1987); exhibited at Creative Ctr. Photography, Tucson, 1989. Mem. Nat. Press Photographers Assn. (Nikon sabbatical 1986). Democrat. Office: Des Moines Register News Dept 715 Locust St Des Moines IA 50309-3767 Home: 4805 Pinehurst Ct Pleasant Hill IA 50327-0959

PETERSON, DAVID MAURICE, retired physiologist; b. Woodward, Okla., July 3, 1940; s. Maurice Llewellyn and Katharine Anne (Jones) P.; m. Margaret Ingegerd Sundberg, June 18, 1965; children: Mark David, Elise Marie. BS, U. Calif., Davis, 1962; MS, U. Ill., 1964; PhD, Harvard U., 1968. Rsch. biologist Allied Chem. Corp., Morristown, NJ, 1970-71; plant physiologist U.S. Dept. Agr.-Agrl. Rsch. Svc., Madison, Wis., 1971—2004; from asst. prof. to prof. U. Wis., Madison, 1971—2004; ret., 2004. Capt. U.S. Army, 1968-70. Capt. US Army, 1968—70. Fellow AAAS; mem. Am. Soc. Plant Biologists (editorial bd. 1984-86), Am. Assn. Cereal Chemists (assoc. editor 1988-91), Crop Sci. Soc. Am. (assoc. editor 1975-78).

PETERSON, DONALD MATTHEW, insurance company executive; b. Mt. Vernon, NY, Dec. 22, 1936; s. Cornelius J. and Catherine M. (Carney) P.; m. Patricia A. Frusciante, Sept. 10, 1960; children: Daniel, Linda, David, Debra, James. BA in Econs., LaSalle U., 1958. CLU; ChFC; FSA, MAAA, EA, RHU. Actuarial analyst Met. Life, NYC, 1958-63; actuarial assoc. N.Am. Co. for Life and Health, Chgo., 1963-66; chmn. bd. dirs. Trustmark Ins. Co., Lake Forest, Ill., 1966—. Bd. dirs. Trustmark Ins. Co., Trustmark Life Ins. Co., Star Mktg. and Adminstrs., InfoTrust Coresource. Bd. dirs. Glenview (Ill.) Pub. Schs., 1973-76, Lake County (Ill.) United Way, 1989-96, Glenview Dist. 34 Found., 1990-93, Lake Forest Hosp., 1992-2001, Ill. Life Ins. Coun., 1990-94, Barat Coll., 1994-2001, Lake Forest Grad. Sch. Mgmt., 1995-2001. Mem. NALU, Nat. Assn. Health Underwriters, Am. Acad. Actuaries, Health Ins. Assn. Am. (bd. dirs. 1992-99), Am. Coun. Life Ins. (bd. dirs. 1995-98), Econ. Club Chgo., North Shore Country Club, Conway Farms Golf Club, Pelican Nest Golf Club, Exec. Club. Republican. Roman Catholic. Avocations: golf, curling, swimming, running. Office: Trustmark Ins Co 400 N Field Dr Lake Forest IL 60045-4809

PETERSON, DOUG, state legislator; b. 1948; m. Elly Peterson; 2 children. BS, Augustana Coll., Sioux Falls, SD. Mem. Minn. Ho. of Reps., St Paul, 1990—. Mem. agrl. com., environ. and natural resources com., met. affairs com., others; tchr., farmer. Democrat. Home: RR 3 Box 90 Madison MN 56256-9452

PETERSON, ERIK CHARLES, prosecutor; BA, Drake U., 1992; JD, Marquette U. Law Sch., 1995. Asst. dist. atty. Richland County, 1995—98; dist. atty. Iowa County, 1999—2006; US atty. (we. dist.) Wis. US Dept. Justice, Madison, 2006—. Office: US Atty PO Box 1585 Madison WI 53701

PETERSON, FRANCIS, retired physicist, educator; BEE, Rensselaer U., 1964; PhD, Cornell U., 1968. Prof. physics dept. Iowa State U., Ames, prof. emeritus, 2003—. Recipient Disting. Svc. Citation award, 1993. Mem. Am. Assn. Physics Tchrs. Address: 669 El Tango La Casa Venice FL 34287-2501

PETERSON, GALE EUGENE, historian; b. Sioux Rapids, Iowa, May 23, 1944; s. George Edmund and Vergene Elizabeth (Wilson) P. BS, Iowa State U., 1965; MA, U. Md., 1968, PhD, 1973. Instr. dept. history U. Md., College Park, 1971-72, Cath. U. Am., Washington, 1972-73; prin. investigator Gregory Directory project Orgn. Am. Historians, Bloomington, Ind., 1973-75; instr. dept. history Purdue U., West Lafayette, Ind., 1975-76; dir. U.S. Newspaper Project, Orgn. Am. Historians, Bloomington, Ind., 1976-78; exec. dir. Cin. Hist. Soc., 1978-96, exec. dir. emeritus, 1996—; exec. dir. Ohio Humanities Coun., 1998—. Author: (with John T. Schlebecker) Living Historical Farms Handbook, 1970, Harry S Truman and the Independent Regulatory Commissions 1945-52, 1985. Mem. Cin. Bicentennial Commn., 1983-88. Mem. Orgn. Am. Historians (treas. 1993-2003), Am. Assn. State and Local History, Am. Hist. Assn., Am. Assn. Mus., Assn. Midwest Museums (v.p.-at-large 1993-95, exec. v.p. 1995-96, pres. 1996-98), Nat. Coun. on Pub. History (bd. dirs. 1992-95). Office: Ohio Humanities Coun Ste 1620 471 E Broad St Columbus OH 43215-3857 Office Phone: 614-461-7802. Personal E-mail: galep@one.net.

PETERSON, GARY J, retail executive; Gen. mgr. WalMart, 1984—85; dir. of distbn. and transp. systems, 1985—88; sr. v.p. Carter, Hawley, Hale Stores, 1988—91; sr. v.p. of operation svcs. Thrifty Drug Stores, 1991—93; COO Southeast Frozen Foods, LP, 1993—96; exec. officer, COO Blockbuster Entertainment, 1996—2000; pres., COO OfficeMax, 2000—.

PETERSON, JON M., state representative; b. Prescott, Wis., Oct. 25, 1953; married; 2 children. BA, Ohio Wesleyan U.; MPA, Fla. Atlantic U.; JD, Capital U. State rep. dist. 2 Ohio Ho. of Reps., Columbus, 1999—, vice chair, ethics and elections subcom., mem. fin. and appropriations, rules and reference, and state govt. coms., and human svcs. subcom., asst. majority whip. Former Delaware County auditor, Franklin County fin. dir., budget/mgmt. analyst in Ohio Office Budget and Mgmt. Mem. Delaware County Rep. Ctrl. Com., Delaware/Morrow County Mental Health Bd. Mem.: Govt. Fin. Officer's Assn. (Cert. Excellence in Fin. Reporting), County Auditor's Assn. Ohio, Farm Bur., Zion United Ch. of Christ, Touchstone Group Home, Inc., Delaware County United Way, Delaware Area Recovery Resources, Andrews House, Delaware Kiwinis, Hiram Masonic Lodge. Republican. Office: 77 S High St 14th fl Columbus OH 43215-6111

PETERSON, LANCE ROBERT, physician; b. Mpls., Sept. 2, 1947; s. Alvin Robert and Norma Lorraine (Soderlin) P.; m. LoAnn Charlotte Liukonen, Aug. 24, 1968; children: Anja Kristine, Kari Elizabeth. BS, U. Minn., 1970, MD, 1972. Diplomate Am. Bd. Internal Medicine, Am. Bd. Infectious Diseases, Am. Bd. Med. Microbiology. Intern U. Minn., 1972—73, resident, 1973—75; med. dir. home care VA Med. Ctr., Mpls., 1975—77, staff infectious diseases, 1977—92; dir. clin. microbiology orthwestern Meml. Hosp., Chgo., 1992—2002; dir. microbiology and infectious diseases rsch. Evanston Northwestern Healthcare, 2002—. Prof. medicine U. Minn., Mpls., 1990—92, prof. lab. medicine, 1990—92; prof. pathology and medicine Northwestern U., Chgo., 1992—; healthcare epidemiologist Evanston orthwestern Healthcare, 2005—; chief microbiology VA Med. Ctr., Mpls., 1979—92, assoc. chief molecular biology, 1987—89; staff infectious diseases orthwestern Meml. Hosp., Chgo., 1992—2002, dir. prevention epicenter, 1999—2002. Co-editor: Diagnostic Microbiology, 9th edit.; editor: The Biologic and Clinical Basis of Infectious Diseases, 5th edit.; contbr. chpts. to books and articles to profl. jours. Pres. Greater Mpls. Day Care Assn., 1985-86; bd. dir. Cmty. Child Care Ctr., Mpls., 1986-89, VA Employees Child Care Ctr., Mpls., 1987-92, chair fundraising com., 1987-92. Grantee, VA Dept., 1978—88, Bayer, Inc., 1985—2006, R.W. Johnson Rsch. Instn., 1990—2004, Ctrs. Disease Control, 1999—2004, Wyeth, Inc., 2003—, Wash. Sq. Health Found., 2003—04, 2006—, Gene Ohm Scis., 2006—, Cepheid, Inc., 2006—, Nanosphere, Inc., 2006—, others. Fellow: Ctrl. Soc. Clin. Rsch. (chair. infectious diseases sect. 1995—97), Am. Soc. Clin. Pathologists, Infectious Diseases Soc. Am. (regional bd. 1991—92, sec.-treas. Chgo. area 2003—), Am. Acad. Microbiology; mem.: Brit. Soc. Antimicrobial Chemotherapy, Am. Soc. Microbiology (BD Rsch. Clin. Microbiology award 2005, NQF Eisenberg award 2007). Avocations: travel, jogging, dining, gardening. Office: Evanston Northwestern Healthcare 2650 Ridge Ave Evanston IL 60201 Home Phone: 847-835-2971; Office Phone: 847-570-1637. Business E-Mail: lpeterson@enh.org.

PETERSON, M. JEANNE, historian, educator; b. Minn., Nov. 26, 1937; d. Clifford Woodrow and Mildred Amelia (Kukas) P.; divorced. BA, U. Calif., 1966, PhD, 1972. Lectr., asst., assoc. prof. Ind. U., Bloomington, 1971-87, prof. history, 1987—, chairperson dept. history, 1987—93, exec. assoc. dean Coll. Arts and Scis., 1993—99, acting chair gender studies dept., 1999—2000, prof. emerita history, found. prof. emerita gender studies, 2001—. Cons. Jour. Women's History, Bull. Hist. Medicine, U. Mich. Press, Butler U., Indpls., Harvard U. Press, Princeton U. Press, Columbia U. Press, Ind. U. Press, SUNY Press, Food and Foodways, Med. History, ACLS, Am. Hist. Rev., Victorian Studies, NEH, NIH, Can. Coun., Adam Matthew Ltd., Johns Hopkins U. Press, U. Va. Press, U. Toronto Press, Ligature, Inc., Am. Philos. Soc., Wellcome Trust (U.K.); external review com. U. Nebr., Lincoln, 1992, U. Iowa, Iowa City, 1995; MA review com. U. N.C., Greensboro, 1993. Author: The Medical Profession in Mid-Victorian London, 1978, Family, Love, and Work in the Lives of Victorian Gentlewomen, 1989; assoc. editor: Oxford Dictionary of National Biography; co-editor: Lizzie Borden: A Case Book of Family and Crime in the 1890s, 1980; contbr. articles to profl. jours. NEH fellow, 1978-79, Guggenheim Found. fellow, 1984-85, Inst. for Advanced Study fellow Ind. U., 1984-85. Mem. Am. Hist. Assn., Soc. for the Social History Medicine, N.Am. Conf. Brit. Studies, Am. Assn. History Medicine, N.Am. Victorian Studies Assn. Home: 1311 S Rechter Ct Bloomington IN 47401-6173 Office: Ind U Dept Gender Studies 742 Ballantine Rd Bloomington IN 47401-5022 Home Phone: 812-332-0458; Office Phone: 812-855-0101. Business E-Mail: petersom@indiana.edu.

PETERSON, MICHAEL K., political organization administrator; b. Ft. Dodge, Iowa, Feb. 13, 1960; s. Earl and LaVonne P. Peterson; m. Julie Kraft; children: Gabrielle, Keenan. BA, JD, U. Iowa. State rep. Dist. 95, Iowa, 1985-93, Dist. 80, Iowa, 1993-94; chmn. Iowa State Dem. Party, 1995—; atty. Polking Law Office, Carroll. Mem. Iowa Bar Assn., Carroll County Optimists Club. Methodist. Home: 1713 NW Pine Rd Apt 8 Ankeny IA 50021-1241 Office: 5661 Fleur Dr Des Moines IA 50321-2841

PETERSON, NANCY, special education educator; AS, Webster State Coll., 1963; BS in Elem. Edn. magna cum laude, Brigham Young U., 1964, MS in Ednl. Psychology, 1966, PhD in Ednl. Psychology, 1969. Instr. in tchr. edn. Brigham Young U., Provo, Utah, 1966-69; asst. prof. edn. dept. spl. edn. U. Kans., Lawrence, 1969-74, dir. spl. edn. classes for handicapped children Clin. Tng. Ctr., 1969-89, project dir. head start tng., 1973-74, coord. edn. univ. affiliated facility Clin. Tng. Ctr., 1969-74, coord. pers. tng. programs in mental retardation, 1973-76, assoc. prof. edn., 1974-88, project dir. pers. tng. programs, 1986-93, prof. edn. dept. spl. edn., 1988—, dept. chair, 1994—. Rsch. sci. Bur. Child Rsch., U. Kans., 1969—; prin. investigator for Kans. U. Kans. Early Childhood Rsch. Inst., 1977-82; Matthew Guglielmo Endowed Chair, Charter Sch. Edn., Calif. State U., LA, 1998-2000; Mary Ann Alia lectureship Charter Sch. Edn. Calif. State U. LA, 1999; prof. spl. edn. U. Kans., 2000—. Recipient J.E. Wallace Wallin award Internat. Coun. Exceptional Children, 1993. Office: U Kans Dept Spl Edn 521 Pearson Hall Lawrence KS 66045-3101

PETERSON, NEAL N., lawyer; b. 1968; BA summa cum laude, St. Olaf Coll., 1990; JD, Cornell Univ., 1993. Bar: Conn. 1993, Minn. 1996. Assoc., health law dept. Murtha, Cullina, Richter and Pinney, 1993—96; assoc. Dorsey & Whitney LLP, Mpls., 1996—2000, ptnr., health care practice group, 2001—, head, health care practice group. Writer, lectr. in field. Named a Rising Star, Minn. Law & Politics Mag. Mem.: Minn. State Bar Assn. (governing coun., health sect.), Am. Health Lawyers Assn. Office: Dorsey & Whitney LLP Ste 1500 50 S Sixth St Minneapolis MN 55402-1498 Office Phone: 612-343-7943. Office Fax: 612-340-2868. Business E-Mail: peterson.neal@dorsey.com.

PETERSON, PATTY, radio personality; d. Willie and Jeanne Arland Peterson; m. Stuart Paster; 4 children. Radio show host Sta. WCCO Radio, Mpls., 1997—. Singer: (albums) The More I See You. Recipient 7 time Minn. Music award winner for Best Female Vocalist and Best Group. Office: WCCO 625 2nd Ave S Minneapolis MN 55402 Mailing: PO Box 390697 Minneapolis MN 55439-0697

PETERSON, PENELOPE LORAINE, dean, education educator; b. Moline, Ill., Nov. 25, 1949; d. Leroy P.; m. W. Patrick Dickson; children: Andrew, Joshua, Elissa. BS, Iowa State U., 1971; MS, PhD, Stanford U., 1976. Asst. prof. dept. ednl. psychology U. Wis., Madison, 1976-80, assoc. prof., 1980-81, prof. ednl. psychology, 1982-85, Sears-Bascom Prof., 1985-87; prof. ednl. psychology & tchr. edn. Mich. State U., East Lansing, 1987—97, co-dir. Inst. Rsch. on Teaching, 1987—97, co-dir. Elem. Subjects Ctr., 1987-92, co-dir. Ednl. Policy Practice Study, 1992—97; dean Northwestern U. Sch. Edn. & Social Policy, Evanston, Ill., 1997—, Eleanor R. Baldwin prof. edn., 1997—. Author chpts. to books; editor: Rev. Ednl. Rsch, 1984-90; contbr. articles to profl. jours. Recipient Palmer O. Johnson award Am. Edn. Rsch. Assn., 1980, Raymond B. Cattell Early Career award Am. Ednl. Rsch. Assn., 1986, Disting. Rsch. award Assn. Tchr. Edn., 1992. Fellow Am. Psychol. Soc. Office: Northwestern U Sch Edn & Social Policy Annenberg Hall Rm 252 2120 Campus Dr Evanston IL 60208 E-mail: p-peterson@northwestern.edu.

PETERSON, RANDALL THEODORE, law librarian, educator; b. Sioux City, Iowa, Aug. 27, 1944; s. Theodore Melvin and Ileann Grace (Wendrich) Peterson; m. Judith Ashcroft, Aug. 24, 1967; children: Kristin, Randall, Heidi, Travis, Robert, Quinn. Student, Dixie Coll., 1962—63; BS, Brigham Young U., Provo, Utah, 1968, MLS, 1974; JD, U. Utah, 1972. Asst. law libr. Brigham Young U., Provo, Utah, 1972—74, assoc. law libr., 1974—77; asst. prof. law and dir. libr. svcs. John Marshall Law Sch., Chgo., 1977—86, assoc. prof. law and dir. libr. svcs., 1986—90, assoc. prof. law, 1990—. Mem.: ABA. Mem. Lds Ch. Office: John Marshall Law Sch 315 S Plymouth Ct Chicago IL 60604-3968 Home Phone: 630-505-0874; Office Phone: 312-978-2372. Business E-Mail: 7rtp@jmls.edu.

PETERSON, RICHARD WILLIAM, retired judge, lawyer; b. Council Bluffs, Iowa, Sept. 29, 1925; s. Henry K. and Laura May (Robinson) Peterson; m. Patricia Mae Fox, Aug. 14, 1949; children: Katherine Ilene Peterson Sherbondy, Jon Eric, Timothy Richard. BA, U. Iowa, 1949, JD with distinction, 1951; postgrad., U. Nebr.-Omaha, 1972-80, 86. Bar: Iowa 1951, U.S. Dist. Ct. (so. dist.) Iowa 1951, U.S. Supreme Ct. 1991, U.S. Ct. Appeals (8th cir.) 1997. Pvt. practice law, Council Bluffs, 1951—; U.S. commr. U.S. Dist. Ct. (so. dist.) Iowa, 1958-70, U.S. magistrate judge, 1970—99; ret., 2005. Nat. faculty Fed. Jud. Ctr., Washington, 1972—82; emeritus trustee Children's Sq., U.S.A., 1969—; verifying ofcl. Internat. Prisoner Transfer Treaties, Mexico City, 1977, La Paz, Bolivia, 1980—81, Lima, Peru, 1981. Author: The Court Moves West: A Study of the United States Court Decision of Appeals from the United States Circuit and District Court of Iowa, 1846-1882, 1988, West of the Nishnabotna: The Experience of Forty Years of a Part-Time Judicial Officer as United States Commissioner, Magistrate and Magistrate Judge, 1958-1998, 1998; author: (with George Mills) No One is Above the Law: The Story of Southern Iowa's Federal Court, 1994; contbr. articles to legal publs. Bd. dirs. Pottawattamie County chpt. ARC, Iowa, state fund chmn. Iowa, 1957—58; dist. chmn. Trailblazer dist. Boy Scouts Am., 1952—55; state chmn. Radio Free Europe, 1960—61; mem. exec. coun. Mid-Am. Ct., 1976—; pres. St. John Found., 1986; Sunday sch. tchr. St. John Luth. Ch., Council Bluffs, 1952—72, coun. mem., 1955—75. With US Army, 1943—46. Decorated Purple Heart, Bronze Star; named Outstanding Young Man, Council Bluffs C. of C., 1959; recipient Jason award, Children's Sq., 2005. Fellow: Am. Bar Found. (life); mem.: ABA, Hist. Soc. U.S. Cts. 8th Jud. Cir. (pres. 1989—99, ct. historian U.S. Dist. Ct. S.D. and Iowa 2000—), Iowa Conf. Bar Assn. (pres. 1985—87), Fed. Magistrate Judges Assn. (pres. 1978—79), Inter-Am. Bar Assn., Fed. Bar Assn., Pottawattamie County Bar Assn. (pres. 1979—80), Iowa Bar Assn. (chmn. com. fed. practice 1978—80, probate and trust coun. and sect. 1997—), Am. Judicature Soc., Supreme Ct. Hist. Soc., Masons, Kiwanis (pres. Coun. Bluffs), Omicron Delta Kappa, Delta Sigma Rho, Phi Delta Phi. Republican. Lutheran. Home: 1007 Arbor Ridge Cir Council Bluffs IA 51503-5000 Office: PO Box 248 25 Main Pl Ste 200 Council Bluffs IA 51503-0790

PETERSON, ROBERT L., meat processing executive; b. Nebr., July 14, 1932; married; children: Mark R., Susan P. Student, U. Nebr., 1950. With Wilson & Co., Jim Boyle Order Buying Co.; cattle buyer R&C Packing Co., 1956—61; cattle buyer, plant mgr., v.p. carcass prodn. Iowa Beef Processors, 1961—69; exec. v.p. ops. Spencer Foods, 1969—71; founder, pres., chmn., CEO Madison (Nebr.) Foods, 1971—76; group v.p. carcass divsn. Iowa Beef Processors, Inc. (name now IBP, Inc.), Dakota City, Nebr., 1976—77, pres., COO, 1977—80, CEO, 1980—81, co-chmn. bd. dirs., 1981—82, CEO, CFO, 1980—2001, chmn., CEO; bd. dir. Tyson Foods, Inc., 2001—03; ret. Served with Q.M.C. US Army, 1952—54. Mem.: Sioux City Country Club. Office: IBP Inc 800 Stevens Port Dr Dakota Dunes SD 57049-5005

PETERSON, RONALD ROGER, lawyer; b. Chgo., July 27, 1948; married; children: Elizabeth G., Ronald W. AB, Ripon, 1970; JD, U. Chgo., 1973. Bar: Ill. 1974, US Dist. Ct. (no. dist.) Ill. 1974, US Ct. Appeals (7th cir.) 1974, US Dist. Ct. (ea. dist.) Wis. 1975, US Dist. Ct. (no. dist.) Ind. 1978, US Dist. Ct. (ctrl. dist.) Ill. 1980, US Ct. Appeals (8th cir.) 1984, US Ct. Appeals (6th cir.) 1990, US Ct. Appeals (9th cir.) 1996, US Dist. Ct. (we. dist.) Mich. 1999, US Ct. Appeals (3d cir.) 2001, US Dist. Ct. (ea. dist.) Mich. 2004. Commd. 2d lt. US Army, 1968, advanced through grades to 1st lt., 1973, with mil. intelligence, 1968-78; ptnr. Jenner & Block, Chgo., 1974—. Editor: Consumer Bankruptcy in Illinois; contbr., articles to profl. jours. Trustee Ripon Coll.; mem. exec. bd. Northeast Ill. Coun. Boy Scouts of Am. Named to, Best Lawyers in Am., Chambers USA: Ill. Super Lawyer. Mem.: ABA, Fed. Bar Assn., Am. Coll. Bankruptcy Lawyers, Am. Bankruptcy Inst., Comml. Law League, Internat. Soc. Insolvency Practitioners, Chgo. Bar Assn., US Supreme Ct. Hist. Soc. Avocation: skiing. Office: Jenner & Block 330 North Wabash Fl 4000 Chicago IL 60611-7603 Office Phone: 312-923-2981. Business E-Mail: rpeterson@jenner.com.

PETERSON, RUTH D., sociologist; BA, Cleve. State U., 1969, MA, 1973; PhD, U. Wis., Madison, 1993. Asst. prof. U. Iowa, 1982—85, Ohio State U., 1985—89, assoc. prof., 1989—96, prof., 1996—, dir. Criminal Justice Rsch. Ctr., 1999—. Mem. editl. bd. Race and Society, 1998—2002. Co-editor: Crime and Inequality, 1995; editor (assoc.): Criminology, 1997—2000; contbr. articles to prof. jour. Fellow: Am. Soc. Criminology (v.p. 1999—2000, Herbert Bloch award 1995); mem.: Am. Sociol. Assn. Office: Ohio State U Sociology Dept 300 Bricker Hall 190 N Oval Mall Columbus OH 43210 Office Phone: 614-247-6379. Business E-Mail: peterson.5@osu.edu.

PETERSON, VOLEEN BRIANNE, chemical engineer; b. Sault St. Marie, Mich., July 24, 1956; d. Robert and Eleanor Boyes; m. Bob Martin Peterson; children: Thomas, Ella. BSChemE, U. Mich., Ann Arbor, 1978, MSChemE, 1980, PhD in Chem. Engring., 1982. Jr. rschr. Meriks Chems. Inc., Southfield, Mich., 1982—83, sr. rschr., 1983—85, chem. engr., 1985—97, project mgr., 1997—. Cons. in field, 2000—. Contbr. articles to profl. jours. Recipient Outstanding Rsch. award, Meriks Chems. Inc., 1985; fellow, NSF, 1980—82.

Mem.: AIChE, Electrochem. Soc., Rotary. Libertarian. Presbyterian. Avocations: travel, art, music, dance. Office: Meriks Chems Inc 29209 Northwestern Hwy #501 Southfield MI 48034-1023

PETERSON, WILLIAM E., state legislator; b. Chgo., Feb. 2, 1936; m. Patricia Guiffre; 3 children. BA, North Pk. Coll.; MS, No. Ill. U.; postgrad., Loyola U., Chgo. Tchr.; prin.; mem. Ill. Ho. of Reps. from 60th dist., 1983-93, Ill. State Senate from 26th dist., 1993—. Mem. Consumer Protection, Aging, Aeronauticsm, Counties and Twps. Coms. Ill. Ho. of Reps., Minority Spokesman, mem. Energy, Environ and Natural Resources, Ins. and Revenue Coms. Trustee, supr. Vernon Twp. (Ill.); active Lake County (Ill.) United Way. With U.S. Army Reserve. Mem. LWV, Lions. Republican. Home: 1480 Meadowlark Dr Long Grove IL 60047-9549 Office: Ill Senate State Capitol Springfield IL 62706-0001

PETKA, ED (EDWARD F.), state legislator; b. Chgo., Mar. 10, 1943; m. Phyllis Petka; children: Jennifer, Edward, Tanya, Melinda. AB, So. Ill. U., 1966; JD, John Marshall Law Sch., 1971. State's atty. Will County, Ill., 1976-86; mem. Ill. Ho. of Reps. from 82d dist., 1987-93, Ill. State Senate from 42d dist., 1993—, majority whip. Mem. Judiciary II, Exec. and Vet. Affairs, Cities and Villages, Election Law, Consumer Protection Coms, Ill. Ho. of Reps.; chair com. on exec. appts., vice chair exec. com., mem. ins. and pensions com., judiciary com. Ill. Senate Mem. Ill. State Attys. Assn. (past pres.). Republican. Home: 15210 Eyre Cir Plainfield IL 60544-1499 Office: 122 Capitol Bldg Springfield IL 62706

PETOSA, JASON JOSEPH, publisher; b. Des Moines, Apr. 26, 1939; s. Joseph John and Mildred Margaret (Cardamon) P.; m. Theodora Anne Doleski, Aug. 12, 1972; 1 son, Justin James. Student, Marquette U., 1957-59, St. Paul Sem., 1959-63, 65-67, Colegio Paolino Internationale, Rome, 1963-65. Asso. editor Cath. Home Mag., Canfield, Ohio, 1965-67, editor, 1968; dir. Alba House Communications, Canfield, 1968-71; with Office of Radio and TV, Diocese of Youngstown, Ohio, 1969-71; dir. pub. relations, instr. Alice Lloyd Coll., Pippa Passes, Ky., 1971-76; writer, cons. Bethesda, Ohio, 1976-79; pres., pub. Nat. Cath. Reporter, Kansas City, Mo., 1979-85; v.p., gen. mgr. Towsend-Kraft Pub. Co., Liberty, Mo., 1985-86; pres., pub. Steadfast Pub. Co., Kansas City, 1986—. Bd. dirs. David (Ky.) Sch., 1973-79; mem. Mayor's UN Day Com., Kansas City. Mem. Kansas City Direct Mktg. Assn., UN Assn. (bd. dirs. Met. Kansas City chpt., pres. 2000). Roman Catholic. Office: 19 W Linwood Blvd PO Box 410265 Kansas City MO 64141-0265

PETRI, THOMAS EVERT, congressman; b. Marinette, Wis., May 28, 1940; s. Robert and Marian (Humleker) Petri; m. Anne Neal, Mar. 26, 1983; 1 child, Alexandra. BA in Govt., Harvard U., 1962, JD, 1965. Bar: Wis. 1965. Law clk. to US Judge James Doyle US Dist. Ct. (we. dist.) Wis., Madison, 1965-66; vol. Peace Corps, Somalia, 1966-67; aide White House, Washington, 1969-70; dir. crime and drug studies Pres.'s Nat. Adv. Coun. on Exec. Orgn., 1969; lawyer pvt. practice, Fond du Lac, Wis., 1970-79; mem. Wis. State Senate, Madison, 1973-79, US Congress from 6th Wis. dist., 1979—, sr. mem. edn. and labor com., transp. and infrastructure com., ranking mem. on aviation subcom. Editor: Nat. Indsl. Policy: Solution or Illusion, 1984. Republican. Lutheran. Avocations: reading, swimming, hiking, bicycling, skiing. Office: US Ho Reps 2462 Rayburn Ho Office Bldg Washington DC 20515-0001 Office Phone: 202-225-2476.

PETRICK, ERNEST NICHOLAS, mechanical engineer, researcher; b. Pa., Apr. 9, 1922; s. Aurelius and Anna (Kaschak) P.; m. Magdalene Simcoe, June 13, 1946; children: Deborah Petrick Healey, Katherine, Denise, Victoria Petrick Kropp. BS in Mech. Engring, Carnegie Inst. Tech., 1943; MS, Purdue U., 1948, PhD, 1955. Registered profl. engr., Mich. Faculty Purdue U., 1946-53; dir. heat transfer research Curtiss-Wright Corp., Woodridge, NJ, 1953-56; chief advanced propulson systems Curtiss-Wright Research divsn., Quehanna, Pa., 1957-60; chief research engr. Kelsey-Hayes Co., Detroit, 1960-65; chief scientist, tech. dir. U.S. Army Tank-Automotive Command, Warren, Mich., 1965-82; chief scientist, dir. engring. labs. Gen. Dynamics, 1982-87; engring. cons., 1987—; panel mem. combat vehicles NATO, 1973-82; mem. adv. bd. on basic combustion research NSF, 1973; chmn. advanced transp. systems com. White House Energy Project, 1973; mem. adv. com. NSF-RANN research program Drexel U. Coll. Engring., 1976-78; mem. Army Sci. Bd., 1983-89; cons. Air Force Studies Bd. NRC, 1991-93, cons. Def. Sci. Bd., 1994-95; cons. NAS, 1997—99, US Army Tank Automotive Rsch., Devel. & Engring. Ctr., 2001—03, Bd. Army Sci. and Tech. Rev. NAS Naval Studies Bd., 2003; adj. prof. engring. Wayne State U., Detroit, 1972-82, U. Mich., Ann Arbor, 1982-83; con. Coun. Environ. Quality, White House, 1973. Contbr. articles on transp., ground vehicles, propulsion and project mgmt. to profl. jours. Lt., chief engr. destroyer USNR, 1942—46, WWII. Recipient certificate of achievement U.S. Army, 1967, Outstanding Performance awards, 1970, 71, 76, 82, Outstanding Mech. Engring. award Purdue U., 1991; named Disting. Engring. Alumnus Purdue U., 1966. Mem. Soc. Automotive Engrs. (nat. dir. 1978-80), Am. Def. Preparedness Assn. (chmn. land warfare survivability divsn. 1990-95, Silver medal 1992, Recognition award 1992), Assn. U.S. Army, Sigma Xi, Pi Tau Sigma. Home: 1540 Stonehaven Rd Ann Arbor MI 48104-4150 Office: ENP Cons 1540 Stonehaven Rd Ann Arbor MI 48104

PETRICOFF, M. HOWARD, lawyer, educator; b. Cin., Dec. 22, 1949; s. Herman and Neoma P.; m. Hanna Sue, Aug. 11, 1974; children: Nicholas, Eve. BS, Am. U., 1967-71; JD, U. Cin., 1971-74; M in Pub. Adminstrn., Harvard U., 1980-81. Bar: Ohio, U.S. Ct. Appeals (D.C. cir.) 1977, U.S. Ct. Appeals (10th cir.) 1985, U.S. Ct. Appeals (6th cir.) 1989, U.S. Supreme Ct. 1989. Asst. city law dir. City of Toledo (Ohio), 1975-77; asst. atty. gen. Ohio Atty. Gen. Office, Columbus, 1977-82; ptnr. Vorys, Sater, Seymour & Pease, Columbus, 1982—. Adj. prof. law Capital U. Law Sch., Columbus, 1991—. Contbr. articles to profl. jours. Reginald Heber Smith Found. fellow Washnigton, 1974-75. Mem. Ohio Bar Assn., Columbus Bar Assn., Ohio Oil and Gas Assn. Office: Vorys Sater Seymour & Pease PO Box 1008 52 E Gay St Columbus OH 43215-3161 Office Phone: 614-464-6400. Business E-Mail: mhpetricoff@ussp.com.

PETRIDES, GEORGE ATHAN, ecologist, educator; b. NYC, Aug. 1, 1916; s. George Athan and Grace Emeline (Ladd) P.; m. Miriam Clarissa Pasma, Nov. 30, 1940; children: George H., Olivia L., Lisa B. BS, George Washington U., 1938; MS, Cornell U., 1940; PhD, Ohio State U., 1948; postdoctoral fellow, U. Ga., 1963-64. aturalist Nat. Park Service, Washington and Yosemite, Calif., 1938-43, Glacier Nat. Park, Mont., 1947, Mt. McKinley Nat. Park, Alaska, 1959; game technician W.Va. Conservation Commn., Charleston, 1941; instr. Am. U., 1942-43, Ohio State U., 1946-48; leader Tex. Coop. Wildlife Unit; assoc. prof. wildlife mgmt. Tex. A. and M. Coll., 1948-50; assoc. prof. wildlife mgmt., zool. and African studies Mich. State U., 1950-58, prof., 1958—; research prof. U. Pretoria, S. Africa, 1965; vis. prof. U. Kiel, Germany, 1967; vis. prof. wildlife mgmt. Kanha Nat. Park, India, 1983; del. sci. confs. Warsaw, 1960, airobi and Salisbury, 1963, Sao Paulo, Aberdeen, 1965, Lucerne, 1966, Varanasi, India, Nairobi, 1967, Oxford, Eng., Paris, 1968, Durban, 1971, Mexico City, 1971, 73, Banff, 1972, Nairobi, Moscow, The Hague, 1974, Johannesburg, 1977, Sydney, 1978, Kuala Lumpur, 1979, Cairns, Australia, Mogadishu, Somalia, Peshawar, Pakistan, 1980. Participant NSF Expdn., Antarctic, 1972, FAO mission to, Afghanistan, 1972, World Bank mission to, Malaysia, 1975 Author: Field Guide to Trees and Shrubs, 1958, 2d edit., 1972, Field Guide to Eastern Trees, 1988, 98, Field Guide to Western Trees, 1992, 98, First Guide to Trees, 1993, Trees of the California Sierra Nevada, 1996, Trees of the Pacific Northwest, 1998, Trees of the Rocky Mountains and Intermountain West, 2000, Trees of the American Southwest, 2000; editor wildlife mgmt. terrestrial sect. Biol. Abstracts, 1947-72; contbr. articles to biol. publs. Served to lt. USNR, 1943-46. Fulbright research awards in E. Africa Nat. Parks Kenya, 1953-54; Fulbright research awards in E. Africa Nat. Parks Kenya, Uganda, 1956-57; N.Y. Zool. Soc. grantee Ethiopia, Sudan, 1957; N.Y. Zool. Soc. grantee Thailand, 1977; Mich. State U. grantee Nigeria, 1962; Mich. State U. grantee Zambia, 1966; Mich. State U. grantee Kenya, 1969; Mich. State U. grantee Africa, 1970, 71, 73, 81; Mich. State U. grantee Greece, 1974, 83; Mich. State U. grantee Iran, 1974; Mich. State U. grantee Botswana, 1977; Mich. State U. grantee Papua New Guinea, Thailand, 1979; Iran Dept. Environment grantee, 1977; Smithsonian Instn. grantee India and Nepal, 1967, 68, 75, 77, 83, 85; World Wildlife Fund grantee W. Africa, 1968 Mem. Am. Ornithologists Union, Am. Soc. Mammalogists, Wildlife Soc. (exec. sec. 1953), Wilderness Soc., Am. Comm. Internat. Wildlife Protection, Ecol. Soc., Fauna Preservation Soc., E. African Wildlife Soc., Internat. Union Conservation Nature, Zool. Soc. So. Africa, Sigma Xi. Presbyterian. Home: 4895 Barton Rd Williamston MI 48895-9305 Office: Mich State U Dept Botany East Lansing MI 48824 E-mail: petrides@msu.edu.

PETRIE, BRUCE INGLIS, lawyer; b. Washington, Nov. 8, 1926; s. Robert Inglis and Marion (Douglas) P.; m. Beverly Ann Stevens, Nov. 3, 1950 (dec. Oct. 1993); children: Laurie Ann Roche, Bruce Inglis, Karen Elizabeth Medsger. BBA, U. Cin., 1948, JD, 1950. Bar: Ohio 1950, U.S. Dist. Ct. (so. dist.) Ohio 1951, U.S. Ct. Appeals (6th cir.) 1960, U.S. Supreme Ct. Assoc. Kunkel & Kunkel, Cin., 1950-51, Graydon, Head & Ritchey, 1951-57, ptnr., 1957—. Exec. prodr. (sch. video) Classical Quest, 2000; author: How To Get the Most Out of Your Lawyer, 2002; contbr. articles to legal jours. Pres. Charter Rsch. Inst., 2000—03; bd. edn. Indian Hill Exempted Village Sch. Dist., 1965—67, pres., 1967; adv. bd. William A. Mitchell Ctr., 1969—86; Green Areas adv. com. Village of Indian Hill, Ohio, 1969—80, chmn., 1976—80; active Ohio Ethics Com., 1974—75; founder Parents as Tchrs. Metro Housing Authority Commn., 1991—; a prin. advocate merit selection judges Ohio; trustee, mem. bd. Seven Hills Neighborhood Houses' Inst. for Learning in Retirement; organizer Late Gt. Lakes Book Distbn. project, global vol. tchr. China, 2003—07; elder, trustee, deacon Knox Presbyn. Ch.; bd. dirs. Charter Com. Greater Cin., 1952—, Hamilton County Good Govt. League, Murray Seasongood Good Govt. Fund, 1975—, chmn., 1989—; bd. dirs. Nat. Civic League, Cin. Vol. Lawyers for Poor Found., Linton Music Series, Amernet Chamber Music Soc.; co-founder Sta. WGUC-FM; mem. WGUC-FM Cmty. Bd., 1974—, chmn., 1974—76. Recipient Pres.'s award U. Cin., 1976, Disting. Alumnus award, 1995. Fellow: Am. Bar Found.; mem.: ABA, Ohio State Bar Assn. Found. (Outstanding Rsch. in Law and Govt. award 1986, Charles P. Taft Civic Gumption award 1988, Ohio Bar medal 1988), Am. Law Inst., Nat. Civic League (coun. 1984—, Disting. Citizen award 1985), Am. Judicature Soc. (dir., Herbert Lincoln Harley award 1973), Cin. Bar Assn. (pres. 1981, Trustee's award 2000), Ohio Bar Assn., Cin. Country Club, Univ. Club, Cincinnatus Assn., Lit. Club, Order of Coif. Avocations: tennis, squash, woodworking, writing, horticulture. Home: 2787 Walsh Rd Cincinnati OH 45208-3428 Office: Graydon Head & Ritchey 1900 Fifth 3d Ctr 511 Walnut St Ste 1900 Cincinnati OH 45202-3157

PETRILLO, NANCY, public relations executive; CFO, exec. v.p. Edelman Pub. Rels. Worldwide, Chgo. Office: Edelman Pub Rels Worldwide 200 E Randolph St Fl 63D Chicago IL 60601-6436

PETRO, JIM (JAMES MICHAEL), former state attorney general; b. Cleve., Oct. 25, 1948; s. William John and Lila Helen (Janca) P.; m. Nancy Ellen Bero, Dec. 16, 1972; children: John Bero, Corbin Marie. BA, Denison U., 1970; JD, Case Western Res., 1973. Bar: Ohio 1973, U.S. Dist. Ct. (no. dist.) Ohio 1974, U.S. Ct. Appeals (6th cir.), U.S. Supreme Ct. Spl. asst. U.S. senator W.B. Saxbe, Cleve., 1972-73; asst. pros. atty. Franklin County, Ohio, 1973-74; asst. dir. law City of Cleve., 1974; ptnr. Petro & Troia, Cleve., 1974-84; dir. govt. affairs Standard Oil Co., Cleve., 1984-86; ptnr. Petro, Rademaker, Matty & McClelland, Cleve., 1986-93, Buckingham, Doolittle & Burroughs, Cleve., 1993-95; auditor State of Ohio, Columbus, 1995—2003, atty. gen., 2003—07. Mem. city coun. Rocky River, Ohio, 1977-79, dir. law, 1980; mem. Ohio Ho. of Reps., Columbus, 1981-84, 86-90; commr. Cuyahoga County, Ohio, 1991-95. Mem.: ABA, Ohio State Bar Assn., Cleve. Bar Assn. Republican. Methodist.

PETROWSKI, JERRY J., state legislator; b. Wansan, Wis., June 16, 1950; Student, U. Wis., North Ctrl. Tech. Coll. Mem. Wis. State Assembly, Madison, 1998—, mem. agr. com., chair hwy. safety com.; mem. state affiars and transp. coms. Mem. Farm Bur.; Merrill Toastmasters. With USAR, 1968—74. Republican. Roman Catholic. Office: State Capitol Rm 4 W PO Box 8953 Madison WI 53708-8953 Address: Town of Stettin 720 N 136th Ave Marathon WI 54448-6193

PETTIS, MARK L., state legislator; b. Osceola, Wis., Dec. 18, 1950; m. Juzel Pettis; children: Mark Jr., Mystie. Student, Wis. Indianhead Tech. Coll. Mem. Wis. State Assembly, 1998—, mem. aging and long-term care coms., chair info. policy and tech. com., mem. joint com. on info. policy and tech., mem. ins. and natural resources com. With USN. Republican. Lutheran. Office: State Capitol Rm 20 N PO Box 8953 Madison WI 53708-8953 Address: 3830 State Rd 70 Hertel WI 54845

PETTITT, JAY S., architect, consultant; b. Redford, Mich., Jan. 6, 1926; s. Jay S. and Florence Marian (Newman) P.; m. Ruth Elizabeth Voigt, June 21, 1947; children— J. Stuart, Laura Ellen, Patricia Lynn, Carol Ann B.Arch., U. Mich., 1951. Registered architect, Mich. Draftsman Frank J. Stepnoski and Son, Fond du Lac, Wis., 1951; project architect Albert Kahn Assocs., Inc., Detroit, 1951-62, chief archtl. devel., 1962-67, v.p., 1967-88, dir. architecture, 1975-88; archtl. cons. Beulah, Mich., 1988—. Active Jr. Athletic Assn., Redford, Mich., 1959-63; com. chmn. Boy Scouts Am., 1960-65; supr. Benzonia Twp. Served with U.S. Army. 1943-46, ETO. Fellow AIA; mem. Mich. Soc. Architects (pres. 1967), Am. Arbitration Assn., Am. Assn. Hosp. Planning, Engring. Soc. Detroit, U. Mich. Pres.' Club Avocations: sailing, skiing. Office Phone: 231-882-4040. Personal E-mail: jaypettitt@bignetnorth.net.

PETTY, ELIZABETH MARIE, geneticist; b. Chgo., July 13, 1959; d. Ralph David and Joyce Elizabeth (Carlson) P.; life ptnr. Karen Kay Milner, Dec. 15, 1985. BA, Clarke Coll., 1981; MD, U. Wis., 1986. Diplomate Nat. Bd. Med. Examiners, Am. Bd. Pediats., Am. Bd. Med. Genetics, Molecular Genetics and Clin. Genetics. Pediat. intern and resident U. Wis., Madison, 1986-89; genetics fellow Yale U., New Haven, 1989-93; assoc. prof. U. Mich., Ann Arbor, 1994—, med. dir. genetic counseling program, 1996—, dir. med. genetics outpatient clinic, 1996—2006, assoc. dean student programs Med. Sch., 2006—. Expert witness DNA testing in State of Ohio and Mich., 1995—; presenter regional, nat. and internat. confs. on genetics, 1991—. Contbr. chpt. to books, articles, editls. to profl. jours.; peer reviewer various jours., 1994—. Participant Gay and Lesbian Health Group, Ann Arbor, 1994—; apptd. to State of Mich.'s Gov.'s Commn. on Genetic Privacy and Progress, 1997-98. Recipient Clin. Investigator award NIH-NCI, 1995-2000, RO1 award, 1997—, Am. Cancer Rsch. Fund award, 1997-98, U. Mich. award for Disting. Pub. Svc., 2000, Breast Cancer award Dept. Def., 2001, 06. Fellow Am. Soc. Human Genetics, Am. Coll. Med. Genetics; mem. AMA, Am. Acad. Scis., European Soc. Human Genetics, Human Genome Orgn., Alpha Omega Alpha. Democrat. Roman Catholic. Avocations: flute, photography. Office: U Mich 5220 MSRB III Ann Arbor MI 48109-0640

PETTY, MARGE D., state senator; b. Ft. Wayne, Ind., Feb. 26, 1946; children: Brandon, Megan. BS, Tex. Christian U., 1968; MEd, Kans. U., 1978; JD, Washburn U. Sch. Law, 1990. Tchr., 1968-69; mgmt. consultant, 1981—94; health educator, 1978-81; mem. City Council of Topeka, 1985-89; dep. mayor Topeka, 1986; mem. Kans. Senate, 1989—2000; dir. pub. affairs and consumer protection Kans. Corp. Commn., 2003—. Mem. Topeka Metro. Ballet, Chamber of Commerce, Mulvane Art Ctr. Episcopalian. Home: PO Box 4262 Topeka KS 66604 Address: 1500 SW Arrowhead Rd Topeka KS 66604-4027

PETYO, MICHAEL EDWARD, construction company owner; b. East Chicago, Ind., Mar. 29, 1949; m. Janet Lynn; 2 children. Candidate for Lake County Sheriff, 1994; Rep. candidate for U.S. House, 1st Dist., Ind., 1996.

PETZOLD, JOHN PAUL, judge; b. 1938; BA, U. Maine, 1961; LLB, Washington & Lee U., 1962. Bar: Ohio 1962, Va. 1962. Pvt. practice law, Ohio, 1962-91; asst. atty. gen. State of Ohio, 1964-71; law dir. City of Miamisburg, Ohio, 1979-91; judge Montgomery County Common Pleas Ct., Dayton, Ohio, 1991—. Bd. tax appeals City of Kettering, Ohio, 1971-91. Mem. ABA, Ohio State Bar Assn. (bd. govs., former chairperson young lawyers sect., chairperson pub. rels. com., vice chairperson lawyers assistance com., eminent domain com., banking, comml., and bankruptcy law com., pres. 1998-99), Dayton Bar Assn. (pres. 1989-90), Common Pleas Judge Assn. (mem. bd. commrs. on grievances and discipline 1995-97). Avocations: golf, swimming, writing, teaching, reading, genealogy. Office: Montgomery County Common Pleas Ct 41 N Perry St Dayton OH 45402-1431

PEVEC, ANTHONY EDWARD, bishop emeritus; b. Cleve., Apr. 16, 1925; s. Anton and Frances Darovec P. MA, John Carroll U., Cleve., 1956; PhD, Western Res. U., Cleve., 1964. Ordained priest Diocese of Cleve., Ohio, 1950; assoc. pastor St. Mary Church, Elyria, Ohio, 1950—52, St. Lawrence Ch., Cleve., 1952—53; rector-prin. Borromeo Sem. HS, Wickliffe, Ohio, 1953—75; adminstrv. bd. Nat. Cath. Edn. Assn., 1972—75; pastor St. Vitus Ch., Cleve., 1975—79; rector-pres. Borromeo Coll., Wickliffe, 1979—82; ordained bishop, 1982; aux. bishop Diocese of Cleve., 1982—2001, aux. bishop emeritus, 2001—. Mem. v.p. Slovenian-Am. Heritage Found., Cleve., 1975—. Named Man of Yr., Fedn. Slovenian Nat. Homes, Cleve., 1985, Cath. Man of Yr., KC, 1998, Man of Yr., Pioneer Assn., 2001, Cathedral Latin Alumni Assn., 2003; named to Hall of Fame, St. Vitus Alumni Assn., 1989, Wickliffe Hall of Fame, 2000; recipient honoree, Heritage Found., Cleve., 1982, Alumni medal, John Carroll U., 2004. Mem.: KC (state chaplain 2003—05), Cath. Order Foresters (state chaplain 2000—04), U.S. Cath. Conf. (nat. adv. coun. 1996—97), Nat. Conf. Cath. Bishops (com. on vocations 1984—86, com. on pro-life activities 1990—92, com. on priestly formation 1993—95, com. on sci. and human values 1993—96). Democrat. Roman Catholic. Avocations: reading, music. Home and Office: Diocese of Cleveland 28700 Euclid Ave Wickliffe OH 44092-2527 Home Phone: 440-944-1400. Business E-Mail: bpaepevec@dioceseofcleveland.org.*

PFEIFER, PAUL E., state supreme court justice; b. Bucyrus, Ohio, Oct. 15, 1942; m. Julia Pfeifer; 3 children. BA, Ohio State U., 1963, JD, 1966. Asst. atty. gen. State of Ohio, 1967-70; mem. Ohio Ho. of Reps., 1971-72; asst. prosecuting atty. Crawford County, 1973-76; mem. Ohio Senate, 1976-92, minority floor leader, 1983-84, asst. pres. pro-tempore, 1985-86; ptnr. Cory, Brown & Pfeifer, 1973-92; justice Ohio Supreme Ct., 1992—. Chmn. jud. com. Ohio Senate, 10 yrs. Mem. Grace United Meth. Ch., Bucyrus. Office: Supreme Court of Ohio 65 S Front St Columbus OH 43215-3431 Office Phone: 614-387-9020.

PFENDER, EMIL, mechanical engineering educator; b. Stuttgart, Germany, May 25, 1925; came to U.S., 1964, naturalized, 1969; s. Vinzenz and Anna Maria (Dreher) P.; m. Maria Katharina Staiger, Oct. 22, 1954; children: Roland, Norbert, Corinne. Student, U. Tuebingen, Germany, 1947-49; diploma in physics, U. Stuttgart, Germany, 1953, D Ing. in Elec. Engring., 1959. Assoc. prof. mech. engring. U. Minn., Mpls., 1964-67, prof., 1967—2000, prof. emeritus, 2000—. Contbr. articles to profl. jours.; patentee in field. Fellow: ASME; mem.: NAE. Home: 1947 Bidwell St Saint Paul MN 55118-4417 Office: U Minn Dept Mech Engring 111 Church St SE Minneapolis MN 55455-0150 Office Phone: 612-625-6012. Business E-Mail: pfender@tc.umn.edu.

PFENING, FREDERIC DENVER, III, manufacturing executive; b. Columbus, Ohio, July 28, 1949; s. Frederic Denver Jr. and Lelia (Bucher) P.; m. Cynthia Gordon, July 1, 1978 (div. 1999); children: Lesley, Frederic Denver IV; m. Janet Evans, 1999. BA, Ohio Wesleyan U., 1971; MA, Ohio State U., Columbus, 1976. Various positions Fred. D. Pfening Co., Columbus, 1976-88, pres., 1988—. Bd. dirs. Friends of Ohio State U. Librs., 1988-94, 1998-2008, pres. 2004-06, Columbus State C.C. Devel. Found., 1991-99, Hist. Sites Found., Baraboo, Wis., 1984-2004, 2008-, pres., 1987-91. Mem. Am. Soc. Bakery Engrs., Orgn. Am. Historians, Bakery Equipment Mfrs. Assn. (bd. dirs. 1985-91), Young Pres.'s Orgn., World's Pres.'s Orgn., Circus Hist. Soc. (pres. 1986-89, mng. editor Bandwagon Jour.), Rotary. Office: 1075 W 5th Ave Columbus OH 43212-2629 Home Phone: 614-451-2939; Office Phone: 614-294-5361 ext 102. Business E-Mail: fpfening@pfening.com.

PFLUM, BARBARA ANN, retired allergist; b. Cin., Jan. 10, 1943; d. James Frederick and Betty Mae (Doherty) P.; m. Makram I. Gobrail, Oct. 20, 1973; children: Christina, James. BS, Coll. Mt. St. Vincent, 1967; MD, Georgetown U., 1971; MS, Coll. Mt. St. Joseph, 1993. Cons. Children's Med. Ctr., Dayton, Ohio, 1975—2006, dir. allergy clinic, 1983-89; dir. allergy divsn. Hopeland Splty. Clinic, Dayton, 1998-2000; ret., 2006. Fellow Am. Acad. Pediatrics, Am. Acad. Allergy and Immunology, Am. Coll. Allergy and Immunology; mem. Ohio Soc. Allergy and Immunology, Western Ohio Pediatric Soc. (pres. 1985-86) Roman Catholic. Home Phone: 937-293-2079. Personal E-mail: bapflum@hotmail.com.

PFLUM, PHILLIP, state representative; m. Diana Pflum; 2 children. Grad., Alquina H.S., 1962. Farmer; ret. mfg. mgr.; state rep. dist. 56 Ind. Ho. of Reps., Indpls., 2002—, vice chmn., labor and employment com., mem. edn., rds. and transp., and ways and means coms. Served Ind. NG, 1965—71. Democrat. Roman Catholic. Office: Ind Ho of Reps 200 W Washington St Indianapolis IN 46204-2786

PHARES, E. JERRY, retired psychology professor; b. Glendale, Ohio, July 21, 1928; s. Bruce and Gladys (West) P.; m. Betty L. Knost, Aug. 6, 1955; 1 dau., Lisa M. BA, U. Cin., 1951; MA, Ohio State U., 1953, PhD, 1955. Faculty Kans. State U., Manhattan, 1955—, prof. psychology, 1964-91, head dept., 1967-89, prof. emeritus, 1991—. Vis. asso. prof. Ohio State U., Columbus, Ohio Wesleyan U., 1961-62 Author, co-author books.; Contbr. articles to profl. jours. Research grantee NIMH, 1960, 80; Research grantee NSF, 1964-76; Research grantee Population Council, 1971 Fellow Am. Psychol. Assn., Am. Psychol. Soc. Office: 2812 evada St Manhattan KS 66502-2330 E-mail: ephares@ksu.edu.

PHARES, LYNN LEVISAY, public relations communications executive; b. Brownwood, Tex., Aug. 6, 1947; m. C. Kirk Phares, Aug. 22, 1971; children: Laura, Margaret, Adele, Jessica. BA, La. State U., 1970; MA, U. Nebr., 1987. Asst. to advt. mgr. La. Nat. Bank, 1970-71; writer, producer, asst. v.p., account exec. Smith, Kaplan, Allen & Reynolds, Inc., Omaha, 1971-80; assoc. dir. pub. affairs U. Nebr. Med. Ctr., 1980-83; dir. pub. rels. ConAgra Inc., Omaha, 1985-87, v.p. pub. rels., 1987-90, v.p. pub. rels. and cmty. affairs, 1990-97, v.p., corp. rels., 1997-2000. Pres. ConAgra Found., Feeding Children Better Found. Office: ConAgra Inc 1 ConAgra Dr Omaha NE 68102-5001

PHELPS, DAVID DWAIN, state agency administrator, former congressman; b. Eldorado, Ill., Oct. 26, 1947; m. Leslie Phelps; 4 children. BS, So. Ill. U. Mem. Ill. Ho. of Reps. from 118th dist., 1985-98; mem., 106th Congress from 19th Ill. dist., 1999—2003; mem. agr. com.; mem. small bus.; asst. sec. Ill. Dept. Transp., Springfield, Ill., 2003—. Mem. Transp. and Motor Vehicles, Appropriations I, Energy, Environ. and Natural Resources, Edn. Appropriations, Human Svcs., Elem. and Secondary Edn., Counties and Twp., Econ. Devel. Coms. Ill. Ho. of Reps., vice chmn. Coal Devel. and Mktg., Econ. and Urban Devel. Coms., chmn. Health Care Com. Democrat. Office: Ill Dept Transp 2300 S Dirksen Pkwy Rm 300 Springfield IL 62764

PHENIS-BOURKE, NANCY SUE, educational administrator; b. Anderson, Ind., Oct. 29, 1943; d. Wilma (Anderson) Baker; m. Richard W. Phenis, June 11, 1966; 1 child, Heidi L. BA, Ind. State U., 1965; MA, Ball State U., 1974, postgrad., 1985. Elem. tchr. Highland Park (N.J.) Schs., 1966-68, Anderson City Schs., 1969-71; elem. tchr., tchr. gifted and talented South Madison Schs., Pendleton, Ind., 1974-85, elem. prin., 1985—. K-12 curriculum dir. South Madison Schs., 1984; mem. CAPE grant com. Eli Lilly Found., 2000. Bd. dirs. South Madison Community Found., Pendleton, 1991, First Am. Bank First-Grant; devel. bd. St. John's Health Care Systems; mem. Prin.'s Leadership Summit, U.S. Dept. Edn., 2000. Recipient Outstanding Contbn. award Internat. Reading Assn., 1991; grantee Eli Lilly Found., 1993. Mem. NAESP (Ind. state rep. 1998—, membership adv. com. 1999), AAUW (pres. 1985-87), Ind. Assn. Sch. Prins. (bd. dirs. 1994—), First Am. (bd. dirs. 1992-95), Phi Delta Kappa (historian 1987, Leadership award 1994), Delta Kappa Gamma (sec. 1990-92, pres. 1992-94, Leadership/Adminstr. award 1993). Office: East Elem Sch 893 E Us Highway 36 Pendleton IN 46064-9580

PHIBBS, CLIFFORD MATTHEW, surgeon, educator; b. Bemidji, Minn., Feb. 20, 1930; s. Clifford Matthew and Dorothy Jean (Wright) P.; m. Patricia Jean Palmer, June 27, 1953; children— Wayne Robert, Marc Stuart, Nancy Louise BS, Wash. State U., Pullman, 1952; MD, U. Wash., Seattle, 1955; MS, U. Minn., 1960. Diplomate Am. Bd. Surgery. Intern Ancker Hosp., St. Paul, 1955—56; resident in surgery U. Minn. Hosps., 1956—60; practice medicine specializing in surgery Oxboro Clinic, Mpls., 1962—, pres., 1985—; cons. to health risk mgmt. corps., 1994—. Mem. Children's Hosp. Ctr., Northwestern-Abbott Hosp., Fairview-Southdale Hosp., Fairview Ridges Hosp.; clin. asst. prof. U. Minn., Mpls., 1975-78, clin. assoc. prof. surgery, 1978—; med. dir. Minn. Protective Life Ins. Co. Contbr. articles to med. jours. Bd. dirs. Bloomington Bd. Edn., Minn., 1974—, treas., 1976, sec., 1977-78, chmn., 1981-83; mem. adv. com. jr. coll. study City of Bloomington, 1964-66, mem. cmty. facilities com., 1966-67, advisor youth study commn., 1966-68; vice chmn. bd. Hillcrest Meth. Ch., 1970-71; mem. Bloomington Adv. and Rsch. Coun., 1969-71; bd. dirs. Bloomington Symphony Orch., 1976—, Wash. State U. Found., trustee, 1990—; dir. bd. mgmt. Minnesota Valley YMCA, 1970-75; bd. govs. Mpls. Met. YMCA, 1970—; bd. dirs. Bloomington Heart-Health Found., 1989—, Martin Luther Manor, 1989; pres. Oxboro Clinics, 1985—; bd. dirs. Bloomington History Clock Tower Assn., 1990—; bd. dirs. Fairview Hosp. Clinic, 1994—, Bloomington Sister city Orgn., 1999-, Bloomington Cmty. Found., 1997-, v.p., Bloomington Health Adv. Bd., 2000-, MMA Minority and

Cross-Cult. Affairs Com., 2000-, Com. on Cult. Competence Minnesota Med. Assn., 1986. Capt. MC, US Army, 1960-62; mem. Minn. Med. Assn. Minority and Cultural Affairs Com., 2007. Mem. ACS, AMA (Physician Recognition awards 1969, 73, 76, 79, 82, 85, 88, 91, 94), Assn. Surg. Edn., Royal Soc. Medicine, Am. Coll. Sports Medicine, Minn. Med. Assn. (del. 1991-94), Minn. Surg. Soc., Mpls. Surg. Soc., Hennepin County Med. Soc., Pan-Pacific Surg. Assn., Jaycees, Bloomington C. of C. (chmn. bd. 1984, chmn. 1985-86), Bloomington Adv. Bd. health, Bloomington Sister City Bd., Bloomington Cmty. Found. (bd. dirs. 1996-). Home: 9613 Upton Rd Minneapolis MN 55431-2454 Office: 600 W 98th St Minneapolis MN 55420-4773 Personal E-mail: kphiibs@aol.com.

PHILBIN, JACK, communications executive; b. 1976; m. Lindsay Philbin; 1 child, Sierra. BA, Boston Coll.; student, Northwestern U. Kellogg Sch. Mgmgt. Co-founder & pres. Vibes Media, Chgo., 1998—. Named one of 40 Under 40, Crain's Chgo. Bus., 2006. Office: Vibes Media 19th Fl 205 W Wacker Dr Chicago IL 60606 Office Phone: 312-753-6330. Office Fax: 312-753-6332. E-mail: contact@vibes.com.

PHILIP, JAMES (PATE PHILIP), retired state legislator; b. Elmhurst, Ill., May 26, 1930; married; 4 children. Student, Kansas City Jr. Coll., Kans. State Coll. Ret. dist. sales mgr. Pepperidge Farm, Inc.; rep. State of Ill., 1967-74, senator, 1975—2002. Asst. senate minority leader, 1979, senate minority leader, 1981-93, senate pres., 1993-2002; chmn. DuPage County Rep. Ctrl. Com.; committeeman Addison Twp. Precinct 52; past Jr. Nat. Rep. Committeeman. Past dir. Nat. Found. March of Dimes; past gen. chmn. Elmhurst March of Dimes; spl. events chmn. DuPage Heart Assn.; mem. DuPage Meml. Hosp. Century Club; dir. Ray Graham Assn. Handicapped Children; mem. bd. sponsors Easter Seal Treatment Ctr.; active Lombard YMCA; bd. dirs. Danada Sculpture Garden. With USMC, 1950-53. Recipient Ill. Coun. on Aging award, 1989, Leaders of 90's award Downers Grove Twp., 1989, Man of Yr. award United Hellenic Voters Am., 1989, Legis. of Yr. award Ill. County Treas.'s Assn., 1990, TaxSavers award Ill. Assn. County Auditors, 1990, Statesman of Yr. award Internat. Union of Operating Engrs. Local 150, 1991, Friend of Youth award Assn. Ill. Twp. Com. on Youth, 1991, Spl. Svc. award Serenity House, 1991, Recognition award DuPage Ctr. Independent Living, 1991. Mem. Am. Legion, Ill. Young Reps. (past pres.), DuPage County Young Rep. Fedn. (past chmn.), DuPage County Marine Corps League (life), DuPage Indsl. and Mfg. Assn. (past dir.), Suburban Bus. Mgmt. Coun. (past v.p.), Mil. Order Devil Dogs, Gocery Mgmt. and Sales Exec. Club Chgo., Exec. Club DuPage County, Shriners, Elks, Masons, Order of DeMolay (life), Moose. Republican.

PHILLIPS, BARRY L., manufacturing executive; Pres., CEO Gradall Industries, Inc., New Philadelphia, Ohio. Office: Gradall Industries Inc 406 Mill Ave New Philadelphia OH 44663

PHILLIPS, CARL, poet, educator; b. 1959; BA magna cum laude, Harvard U., 1981; MA in Latin and Classical Humanities, U. Mass., Amherst, 1983; MA in Creative Writing, Boston U., 1993. Latin tchr., 1983—91; asst. prof. English Washington U., St. Louis, 1993—95, assoc. prof., 1995—, dir. creative writing prog., 1996—98, 2000—02. Author: In the Blood, 1992 (Samuel French Morse Poetry Prize, 1992), Cortege, 1995 (Nat. Book Critics Cir. Award finalist, Lambda Lit. Award finalist), From the Devotions, 1998 (Nat. Book Award finalist), Pastoral, 2000 (Lambda Lit. Award), The Tether, 2001 (Kingsley Tufts Poetry Award), Rock Harbor, 2002, The Rest of Love: Poems, 2004 (Nat. Book Award finalist, 2004). Recipient Lit. Award, AAAL, Pushcart Prize, Acad. Am. Poets Prize; grantee Witter Bynner Found. Fellowship, Libr. Congress, 1997, Guggenheim Fellowship. Fellow: Am. Acad. Arts & Sci. Office: Washington U Campus Box 1122 One Brookings Dr Saint Louis MO 63130 Office Phone: 314-935-7133. E-mail: cphillips@wustl.edu.

PHILLIPS, CHARLES W., state agency administrator; BS in Indsl. Mgmt., U. Ky., 1950. Asst. examiner St. Louis dist. FDIC, 1950-54, examiner St. Louis dist., 1954-57; exec. v.p. Floyd County Bank, New Albany, Ind., 1958-62, pres., 1962-85; ret.; dir. Ind. Dept. Fin. Instns., 1989—. Mem. Ind. Bank Law Study Commn., 1963-64; mem. state banking law steering com. Am. Bankers Assn., 1965-66, mem. leadership coun., 1980-82; chmn. mems. Ind. Dept. Fin. Instns., 1965-68; chmn. sr. mgmt. com. Ind. Bankers Assn., 1972, chmn. legis. com., 1973. Mem. bd. advisors Ind. U. S.E., 1973-78, chmn. bd. escot, 1976-82; charter dir. Leadership Louisville, 1978-81; dir. WKPC Ch. 15 PBS, Louisville, 1980-85, mem. bd. overseers, 1985-88; active Metro United Way. Recipient Chancellor's medallion for disting. svc. Ind. U. S.E., 1994. Mem.: Conf. State Bank Suprs. (vice chmn. dist. 2 1992—99, bd. dirs., chmn. dist. 2 1999—). Office: Fin Instn Dept 30 S Meridian St Ste 300 Indianapolis IN 46204

PHILLIPS, EDWARD JOHN, consulting firm executive; s. Harold E. and Mary C. P.; m. Kathleen A. Everett, July 23, 1960; children: Elizabeth J., Edward J. B of Mech. Engring., Villanova U., 1973; MBA, Widener U., 1975. Registered profl. engr., Ill., Pa., Ohio; chartered engr., U.K. Tech. ops. mgr. Motorola, Inc., Franklin Park, Ill., 1976-81; v.p. engring. Rival Mfg. Co., Kansas City, Mo., 1981-82; prin., sr. cons. Richard Muther & Assocs., Kansas City, 1982-85; chmn. KANDE, Inc., Overland Park, Kans., 1983-86; pres., CEO Sims Cons. Group Inc., Lancaster, Ohio, 1986—; chmn. bd. dirs., pres. Sims Consulting Group, Lancaster, Ohio. Bd. dirs. KANDE, Inc., Wilmington, Del. Author: Manufacturing Plant Layout, 1997; contbr. articles to profl. jours. Recipient Profl. Achievement award, Villanova U., 2006. Mem. NSPE, ASME (chmn. material handling divsn. 1989-91, internat. mgmt. com. 1977), MIMechE, Soc. Mfg. Engrs., Tau Beta Pi, Pi Tau Sigma. Office: Sims Cons Group Inc PO Box 968 Lancaster OH 43130-0968

PHILLIPS, FREDERICK FALLEY, architect; b. Evanston, Ill., June 18, 1946; s. David Cook and Katharine Edith (Falley) P.; m. Gay Fraker, 1983 (div. 1993); m. Linda Gardner, 2002; children: Daniel Gardner, Alice Katharine. BA, Lake Forest Coll., 1969; MArch, U. Pa., 1973. Registered architect, Ill., Wis. Intern Harry Weese & Assocs., 1974, 75; architect pvt. practice, Chgo., 1976-81; pres. Frederick Phillips and Assocs., Chgo., 1981—. Bd. dirs. Landmarks Preservation Coun., 1981-85, Chgo. Acad. Sci., 1988-97, Friends of Ceuros de Escazu, Costa Rica, 1992-95, Project Rush Chgo., 2001-; mem. aux. bd. Chgo. Architecture Found., 1975-89. Recipient award Townhouse for Logan Sq. Competition, AIA and Econ. Redevel. Corp. Logan Sq., 1980, Gold medal award Willow St. Houses, Ill. Ind. Masonry Coun., 1981, Silver award for pvt. residence, 1989, Gold medal award pvt. residence, 1994, Three Record Houses awards Archtl. Record, 1990, 95, award 2d Compact House Design Competition, 1990, award of exellence for pvt. residence AIA/Nat. Concrete Masonry Assn., 1992, 98, award pvt. residence Am. Wood Coun., 1993, Honorable mention-Best in Am. Living award Profl. Builders Mag., 1995, Builder's Choice award pvt. residence, Builder Mag., 1996, Jury's Choice award pvt. residence Chgo. Athenaeum, 1996, 2001, Am. Architecture award Chgo. Athenaeum, 2001, Grand award Residential Architecture Mag., 2003, award Custom Builder Mag., 2003, award Am. Inst. Steel Construction, 2004. Fellow AIA (chmn. task group mfg. housing Nat. Com. Design 1994-96, mem. awards task group 1998-01, chmn. 2000-01, Disting. Bldg. award for Willow St. Houses, Chgo. chpt. 1982, for Pinewood Farm 1983, for Pvt. Residences 1990, 92, 98, for Tower House, 2001, Housing Com. award 2006); mem. Chgo. Archtl. Club, Racquet Club (bd. govs. 1983-89), Arts Club, Cliff Dwellers Club (bd. govs. 1985-88). Office: Frederick F Phillips & Assocs 1456 N Dayton St Ste 200 Chicago IL 60622-2636

PHILLIPS, HARVEY G., musician, performing arts educator; b. Aurora, Mo., Dec. 2, 1929; s. Jesse E. and Lottie A. (Chapman) P.; m. Carol A. Dorvel, Feb. 22, 1954; children: Jesse E., Harvey G., Thomas A. Student, U. Mo., 1947-48, Juilliard Sch. Music, 1950-54, Manhattan Sch. Music, 1956-58; MusD (hon.), New England Conservatory of Mu, 1971; HHD (hon.), U. Mo., Columbia, 1987. Founder, v.p. Mentor Music, Inc., NYC, 1958—79; v.p. Wilder Music, Inc., NYC, 1964-77, Magellan Music, Inc., NYC, 1971—, Peaslee Music Inc., 1971—; established faculty position Aspen Sch. Music, summer 1962, U. Wis., summer 1963, Hartt Sch. Music, Hartford, Conn., 1962-64, Mannes Sch. Music, NYC, 1964-65; exec. v.p. Orch. USA, NYC, 1962-65; exec. v.p., pers. mgr., tubist Symphony of the Air .Y.C., 1957-66; v.p. Brass Artists, Inc., NYC, 1964—; adminstrv. asst. to Julius Bloom, Rutgers U., New Brunswick, NJ, 1966-67; v.p. fin. affairs New Eng. Conservatory of Music, Boston, 1967-71; mem. faculty Sch. Music, Ind. U., Bloomington, 1971-94, disting. prof. music, trustee, 1979, disting. prof. emeritus, 1994. Adv. bd. Am. Brass Chamber Music, Inc., 1971—; chmn. bd. Summit Brass/Keystone Brass Inst., 1985—92, Rafael Mendez Brass Inst., 1993—; cons. Margun Music, Inc., 1977—; bd. dirs. Summit Brass. Brass coach Festival at Sandpoint, Idaho, 1986-94; mem. faculty Joven Orch., Spain, 1987-94, Festival Casal Orch., San Juan, P.R., 1964-76; dir. 1st Internat. Tuba Symposium Workshop, Ind. U., 1973, Brass-Wind Music Studios, Carnegie Hall, N.Y.C., 1961-67; tubist, King Bros. Circus Band, 1947, Ringling Bros. & Barnum & Bailey Circus Band, 1948-50, N.Y.C. Ballet Orch., 1951-71, N.Y.C. Opera Orch., 1951-62, Voice of Firestone Orch., 1951-53, Sauter-Finegan Orch., 1952-53, Band of Am., 1952-54, NBC Opera Orch., 1956-65, Bell Tel. Hour Orch., 1956-66, Goldman Band, 1957-62; founding mem., tubist N.Y. Brass Quintet, 1954-67; condr., co-prodr. Burke-Phillips All Star Concert Band, 1960-62; co-founder, tubist Matteson-Phillips Tubajazz Consort, 1976—; founding mem. TubaShop Quartet, 1996—; rec. artist Crest Records, 1958-78—; originator Octubafest, TubaChristmas, Tubasantas, Tubajazz, TubaEaster, Tubacompany, Summertubafest; exec. editor Instrumentalist mag., 1986-96, bd. advisors, 1996—. Founder, pres. Harvey Phillips Found., Inc., N.Y.C., 1977—; bd. dirs. Mid-Am. Festival of the Arts, 1982-90, Bloomington Area Arts Coun., 1983-90; judge 1st Internt. tuba competition of CIEM Internat. Competition for Musical Performers, Geneva, 1991. Served with U.S. Army Field Band, 1955-56. Recipient Disting. Svc. to Music award Kappa Kappa Psi, 1978, Cmty. Svc. award City of Bloomington, 1978, Nat. Assn. Jazz Educators award, 1977, 78, Nat. Music Conf. award, 1977, T.U.B.A. award, 1978, MI Hummel The Tuba Player award, 1990, Disting. Achievement award Ednl. Press Assn. Am., 1991, Mentor Ideal award Assn. Concert Bands, 1994, Lifetime Achievement award United Music Instruments, 1995, Sudler award medal of the Order of Merit Sousa Found., 1995, Summit Brass Outstanding Svc. and Support Internat. Brassfest, 1995, Orpheus award Phi Mu Alpha Sinfonia, 1997; elected to Acad. Wind and Percussion Arts Nat. Band Assn., 1995; recipient Edwin Franko Goldman citation Am. Bandmasters Assn., 1996, Devel. of Mus. Artistry and Opportunities for Future Generations award Colonial Euphonium Tuba Inst., 1998, Lifetime Achievement award Rafael Mendez Brass Inst., 1998, Platinum Piston Lifetime Achievement award, U. Ga., 1999; Legion of Hon., Goldman Meml. Band, 2002; Harvey Phillips Day proclaimed New England Conservatory Music, 1971, Harvey Phillips Day proclaimed Marionville, Mo. Bicentennial, 1976, Harvey Phillips Weekend Gov. of Mo., 1982; named hon. mem. U.S. Army Band Pershings Own, 1984. Mem. Am. Fedn. Musicians, Tubists Universal Brotherhood Assn. (bd. advs. 1973—, pres. 1984-87, hon.), Hoagy Carmichael Jazz Soc. (founder, acting pres. 1983—), Tau Beta Sigma, Phi Mu Alpha Sinfonia (Orpheus award 1997), Kappa Gamma Psi. Home and Office: Tubaranch 4769 S Harrell Rd Bloomington IN 47401-9028 Office: Sch of Music Ind U Bloomington IN 47405 Business E-Mail: philliph@indiana.edu.

PHILLIPS, JAMES EDGAR, lawyer; b. NYC, Aug. 30, 1949; s. Jack Louis Phillips and Jacqueline (Kasper) Ehrman; children: Zachary J., Mark H. BA, Boston U., 1971; JD, Case Western Reserve U., 1975. Bar: Ohio 1975, US Supreme Ct. 1977, US Dist. Ct. (so. dist.) 1978, US Ct. Appeals (6th cir.) 1981, US Dist. Ct. (no. dist.) 1982, US Ct. Appeals (7th cir.) 2001. Asst. prosecutor Franklin County Prosecutor Office, Columbus, Ohio, 1975-77, sr. asst. prosecutor, 1977-79; assoc. Vorys, Sater, Seymour & Pease, Columbus, 1979-84, ptnr., 1984—; spl. prosecutor State of Ohio, 1993—. Gen. counsel Nat. Fraternal Order of Police, Washington, 1987-2002, Conrail Police #1, US Postal Police #2; mem. Bd. Profl. Law Enforcement Certification; mem. Wong Sun Soc., 1997—; adj. prof. Ohio State U. Moritz Sch. Law, 2005—. Author: Civil Recovery in Ohio, 1986, Collective Bargaining in the Pub. Sector, 1988; editor Bar Briefs; contbr. articles Jours., 1987-89. Pres. bd. dir. Ohio Ctr. for Law-Related Edn., 1985—95; bd. dirs. Schottenstein Stores Corp., 2002—, Alvis House, 2005—06. Fellow Ohio Bar Found., Columbus Bar Found., Ohio Bar Assn. (chmn. com. law-related edn. 1982-86), Columbus Bar Assn., Sixth Cir. Jud. Conf. (life); Ohio Assn. Criminal Defense Lawyers (bd. dirs., treas.). Avocations: travel, photography. Office: Vorys Sater Seymour & Pease PO Box 1008 52 E Gay St Columbus OH 43216-1008 Office Phone: 614-464-5610. Business E-Mail: phillips@vssp.com.

PHILLIPS, RONALD LEWIS, plant geneticist, educator; b. Huntington County, Ind., Jan. 1, 1940; s. Philemon Lewis and Louise Alpha (Walker) P.; m. Judith Lee Lind, Aug. 19, 1962; children: Brett, Angela. BS in Crop Sci., Purdue U., 1961, MS in Plant Breeding and Genetics, 1963, Doctorate (hon.), 2000; PhD in Genetics, U. Minn., 1966; postgrad., Cornell U., 1966-67. Rsch. and tchg. asst. Purdue U., 1961—62; rsch. asst. U. Minn., St. Paul, 1962—66, rsch. assoc., 1967—68, asst. prof., 1968—72, assoc. prof., 1972—76, prof. genetics and plant breeding, 1976—93, Regents prof., 1993—, McKnight presdl. chair in genomics, 2000—. Vis. prof., Italy, 1981, Canada, 83, China, 86, Japan, 90, Morocco, 96; program dir. Competetive Rsch. Grants Office USDA, Washington, 1979, chief scientist, 1996—98, mem. adv. grant panels, NSF, DOE; chmn. Gordon Conf. on Plant Cell and Tissue Culture, 1985; mem. sci. adv. coun. U. Calif. Plant Gene Expression Ctr., Berkeley, 1986—93, chair, 1992—93; program adv. com. Palm Oil Rsch. Inst. Malaysia, 1992—2001; non-resident fellow Noble Found., 2001—06; sci. adv. bd. Donald Danforth Plant Sci. Ctr., St. Louis, 2000—; sci. liaison officer Internat. Rice Rsch. Inst. USAID, 2000—03, bd. trustees, 2004—, mem. adv. grant panels; dir. Plant Molecular Genetics Inst., 1991—94; trustee Biol. Stain Commn.; mem. Nat. Plant Genetic Resources Bd.; dir. Ctr. Microbial and Plant Genomics U. Minn., 2000—05. Co-editor: Cytogenetics, 1977, Molecular Genetic Modification of Eucaryotes, 1977, Molecular Biology of Plants, 1979, The Plant Seed: Development, Preservation and Germination, 1979, Genetic Improvement of Crops: Emergent Techniques, 1980, DNA-Based Markers in Plants, 1994, 2d edit., 2001; assoc. editor Genetics, 1978—81, Can. Jour. Genetics and Cytology and Genome, 1985—90, mem. editl. bd. Maydica, 1978—, In Vitro Cellular and Devel. Biology, 1988—92, Cell Culture and Somatic Cell Genetics of Plants, 1983—91, Jour. of the Oil Palm, 1994—, Proc. NAS, 1996—98; contbr. chpts. to Maize Beeding and Genetics, 1978, Staining Procedures, 1981, Chromosome Structure and Function, 1987, Corn and Corn Improvement, 1988, Plant Transposable Elements, 1988, Chromosome Engring. in Plants, 1991, Maize Handbook, 1994, sci. articles to profl. jours. Mem. chmn. coun. on ministries, lay leader United Meth. Ch., 1968, dir. Project AgGrad, 1983—; Cub Scout Pack co-chmn. Boy Scouts Am., 1976-77; judge Minn. Regional and State Sci. Fair, 1970-80. Recipient Purdue Agrl. Alumni Achievement award, 1961, Purdue Disting. Agrl. Alumni award, 1993; NSF fellow, 1961; NIH fellow, 1966-67; recipient Northrup King Oustanding Faculty Performance award, 1985, DeKalb Genetics Crop Sci. Disting. Career award, 1997. Fellow: AAAS (program com. 2003—06, chair sect. O, Wolf Agr. prize 2007), Crop Sci. Soc. Am. (awards com., divsn. chmn., bd. rep. 1988—91, pres.-elect 1998—99, pres. 1999—2000, past pres. 2000—01, Rsch. award 1988), Am. Soc. Agronomy (Caleb-Dorr award); mem.: NAS (chair sect. 62 1999—2002, nominating com. 2002), Coun. Sci. Soc. (presidents chair 2006), Am. Soc. Agronomy (award student sect.), Genetics Soc. Am., Sigma Xi, Alpha Zeta, Gamma Sigma Delta (award of merit 1994), Gamma Alpha (nat. treas.). Office: U Minn Dpt Agronomy-Plant Genetics Saint Paul MN 55108 Business E-Mail: phill005@umn.edu.

PHILLIPS, SIDNEY FREDERICK, gastroenterologist, educator; b. Melbourne, Australia, Sept. 4, 1933; s. Clifford and Eileen Frances (Fitch) P.; m. Decima Honora Jones, Mar. 29, 1957; children: Penelope Jane, Nichola Margaret, David Sidney. M.B.BS, U. Melbourne, 1956, MD, 1961. Resident med. officer Royal Melbourne Hosp., 1957-61, asst. sub-dean clin. sch., 1961-62; research asso. Central Middlesex Hosp., London, 1962-63; rsch. assoc. Mayo Clinic, Rochester, Minn., 1963-66, cons. in gastroenterology, 1966-2000; prof. medicine Mayo Med. Sch., 1976-2000, prof. medicine emeritus, 2000—, dir. gastroenterology rsch. unit, 1977-94; program dir. Mayo Gen. Clin. Rsch. Ctr., 1974-87; dir. Mayo Digestive Diseases Core Ctr., 1984-90; Karl F. and Marjory Hasselman prof. rsch., 1994-2000. Editor: Digestive Diseases and Sciences, 1977-82, Gastroenterology International, 1990-95; sr. assoc. editor: Gastroenterology, 1991-96; contbr. chpts. to books, articles to profl. jours. Fellow ACP, Royal Coll. Physicians, Royal Australian Coll. Physicians; mem. Am. Motility Soc. (pres. 1994-96), Am. Soc. Clin. Investigation (emeritus), Gastroenterology Soc. Australia (hon.), Am. Gastroenterology Assn. Assn. Am. Physicians, Brit. Soc. Gastroenterology (hon.). Office: St Mary's Hosp Gastroenterology Unit 200 1st St SW Rochester MN 55905-0001 Home: Dakota on the Park 209 8th St E #411 Saint Paul MN 55101-3389 Personal E-mail: decimasidney@aol.com.

PHILLIPS, T. STEPHEN, lawyer; b. Tennyson, Ind., Oct. 1, 1941; AB, DePauw U., 1963; LLB, Duke U., 1966. Bar: Ohio 1966. Assoc. Frost & Jacobs, Cin., 1966-72; ptnr. Frost & Jacobs (now Frost Brown Todd LLC), Cin., 1972—. Adj. prof. North Ky. U. Chase Coll. Law, Highland Hights, 1983—. Contbg. editor: Ohio Probate Practice (Addams and Hosford), Page on Wills. Trustee Spring Grove Cemetery, Cin., Bethesda Found. Methodist. Office: Frost Brown Todd LLC 2500 PNC Ctr 201 E 5th St Ste 2500 Cincinnati OH 45202-4182 Office Phone: 513-651-6835.

PHILLIPS, TED, professional sports team executive; b. Oneida, NY, June 27, 1957; m. Katie Phillips; children: Matthew, Max, Frank. BBA in Acctg., U. Notre Dame, 1983; M Mtkg. and Mgmt., Northwestern U., 1989. Auditor, tax acct. Ernst & Whinney (now Ernst & Young), 1979—83; contr. Chgo. Bears, 1983—87, dir. fin., 1993, v.p. ops., 1993, CEO. Office: 100 Football Dr Lake Forest IL 60045

PHILLIPS, THOMAS JOHN, lawyer; b. Mpls., Nov. 24, 1948; BA, U. Minn., 1970; JD, U. Utah, 1973; LLM in Taxation, NYU, 1974. Bar: Wis. 1974. Ptnr. Quarles & Brady, Milw., 1991—. Co-author: Wisconsin Limited Liability Company Forms and Practice Manual, 1999. Mem. ABA (corp. tax com. tax sect.), Wis. Bar Assn., Profl. Inst. Taxation, Mil. Tax Club, North Shore Country Club, Order of Coif. Avocations: gardening, golf, hockey, jogging, racquetball. Office: 411 E Wisconsin Ave Ste 2040 Milwaukee WI 53202-4497 Home Phone: 262-241-5314; Office Phone: 414-277-5831. Business E-Mail: tjp@quarles.com.

PHINNEY, WILLIAM CHARLES, retired geologist; b. South Portland, Maine, Nov. 16, 1930; s. Clement Woodbridge and Margaret Florence (Foster) P.; m. Colleen Dorothy Murphy, May 31, 1953; children— Glenn, Duane, John, Marla. BS, MIT, 1953, MS, 1956, PhD, 1959. Faculty geology U. Minn., 1959-70; chief geology br. NASA Lyndon B. Johnson Space Center, Houston, 1970-82, chief planetology br., 1982-89, ret., 1994. NASA prin. investigator lunar samples. Contbr. articles to profl. jours. Served with C.E. AUS, 1953-55. Recipient NASA Exceptional Sci. Achievement medal, 1972, NASA Cert. of Commendation, 1987; NASA rsch. grantee, 1972-94, NSF rsch. grantee, 1960-70. Mem. Am. Geophys. Union, AAAS, Mineral. Soc. Am., Geol. Soc. Am., Minn. Acad. Sci. (dir.), Sigma Xi. Home: 18063 Judicial Way S Lakeville MN 55044-8895

PHIPPS, JOHN RANDOLPH, retired army officer; b. Kansas, Ill, May 16, 1919; s. Charles Winslow and Kelsey Ethel (Torrence) P.; m. Pauline M. Prunty, Feb. 8, 1946; children: Charles W., Kelsey J. Phipps-Selander. BS in Econs. with honors, U. Ill., 1941; M.P.A., Sangamon State U., 1976; A course, Command and Gen. Staff Coll., 1959, nuclear weapons employment course, 1962; course, U.S. Army War Coll., 1973, U.S. Nat. Def. U., 1978. Owner, operator chain shoe stores in, Ill., 1946-70; commd. 2d lt. F.A. U.S. Army, 1941, advanced through grades to capt., 1943; service in Philippines and Japan; discharged as maj., 1946; organizer, comdr. Co. E, 130th Inf., Ill.; N.G., Mattoon, 1947, comdg. officer 2d Bn., 130th Inf., 1951, lt. col. 2d Bn., 130th Inf., 1951; called to fed. service, 1952; adv. (29th Regt., 9th Republic of Korea Div.), 1952-53; comdr. officer 1st Bn., 130th Inf., Ill. N.G., 1954, col., 1959; comdg. officer 2d Brigade, 33d Div., 1963-67; asst. div. comdr. 33d Inf. Div., 1967, brig. gen., 1967; comdr. 33d Inf. Brigade, Chgo., 1967-70, Ill. Emergency Ops. Hdqrs., 1970, asst. adj. gen. Ill., 1970-77, acting adj. gen., 1977-78, adj. gen., 1978, promoted to maj. gen., 1978, now maj. gen. ret. Decorated Silver Star, Bronze Star, Disting. Service medal, Combat Infantry Badge, Army Disting. Service medal Ill., various Philippine and Korean decorations; State of Ill. Long and Honorable Service medal. Mem. VFW, Adj. Gens. Assn. U.S., N.G. Assn. U.S., N.G. Assn. Ill., Am. Legion, Amvets. Home: 100 Wabash Ave Mattoon IL 61938-4524

PHOENIX, G. KEITH, lawyer; b. Centralia, Ill., Aug. 13, 1946; BA in Liberal Arts, So. Ill. U., 1968; JD, St. Louis U., 1973. Bar: Mo. 74, U.S. Dist. Ct. (so. dist.) Ill. 75, U.S. Ct. Appeals (7th and 8th cirs.) 82. Assoc. Coburn, Croft & Shepherd & Putzell, St. Louis, 1974—79; sr. counsel, pres. Sandberg, Phoenix & von Gontard, St. Louis, 1979—. Legal cons. Am. Acad. Pedist. Contbr. articles on med./legal topics to profl. jours. Mem. bd. trustees St. Louis U., 2005—. 1st lt. US Army, 1968—71, Vietnam. Decorated Bronze Star with cluster, Air medal with cluster, Vietnam medal; named one of Mo. and Kans. Civil Litig. Super Lawyers, 2005; named to Best Lawyers in Am., 2003, 2004, 2005, 2006. Mem.: Product Liability Adv. Coun., Am. Bd. Trial Advocacy (past pres.), Lawyer's Assn. (past pres.), St. Louis Bar Assn., Mo. Bar Assn., Ill. Bar Assn. (Named One of the Top Trial Lawyers in Am. 2002, 2003). Office: Sandberg Phoenix & von Gontard One City Centre 1500 Saint Louis MO 63101-1880 Office Phone: 314-231-3332. Business E-Mail: kphoenix@spvg.com.

PIANALTO, SANDRA, bank executive; b. Valli del Pasubio, Italy, Aug. 4, 1954; B in Economics, U. Akron, 1976; M in Economics, George Washington U., 1985; LHD (hon.), U. Akron, Baldwin-Wallace Coll., Kent State U., Ursuline Coll.; D of Bus. Adminstrn. (hon.), Cleve. State U. Economist bd. govs. Fed. Reserve Sys.; staff mem. budget com. U.S. Ho. of Reps.; economist rsch. dept. Fed. Res. Bank Cleve., 1983—84, asst. v.p. pub. affairs, 1984—88, v.p., sec. bd. dirs., 1988—93, first v.p., COO, 1993—2003, pres., 2003—. Bd. dirs. Cleve. Found., Gr. Cleve. Partnership, U. Hosp. Health Sys., United Way Svcs. Cleve., Rock and Roll Hall of Fame and Mus., N.E. Ohio Coun. Higher Edn., Cath. Diocese Cleve. Found., Ohio Bus. Alliance for Higher Edn. and Economy. Office: Fed Res Bank Cleve PO Box 6387 Cleveland OH 44101-1387 Office Phone: 216-579-2000.

PIASECKI, DAVID ALAN, social studies educator; b. Marquette, Mich., Sept. 14, 1956; s. Vincent Jerome and Irene Beatrice (Tousinant) P.; m. Linda Marie Anderson Piasecki, Aug. 2, 1985; children: Andrew Jacob, Zachary David. BA, No. Mich. U., 1978, MA, 1982, MA, 1984. Cert. 7-12 Social Studies, Sch. Adminstrn. and Prin. Supt., Alaska. Social studies tchr. Galena City Sch., Alaska, 1978-80, Tanana H.S., Alaska, 1980-85, activities dir. Alaska, 1984-85; social studies tchr. Denali Borough Sch. Dist., Healy, Alaska, 1985-99; prin. Upsala H.S., Minn., 1999—. Student Taft Seminar For Tchrs., U. Alaska. Named Alaska Tchr. of Yr., Dept. Edn., Juneau and Anchorage, 1992, Railbelt Sch. Dist. Tchr. of Yr., NEA, Healy, 1992; recipient Secondary Econ. award Alaska Coun. on Econ. Edn., Fairbanks, Alaska, 1988, 91-92. Mem. NEA, Holy Mary of Guadalupe Cath. Ch., Nat. Alaska Coun. on Social Studies, Alaska Geographic Alliance, Nat. Coun. for Geographic Edn. Democrat. Roman catholic. Avocations: cross county skiing, basketball, tennis, hunting, travel. Home: PO Box 11 Upsala MN 56384-0011 Office: Upsala HS 415 S Main St PO Box 190 Upsala MN 56384-0190

PICHLER, JOSEPH ANTON, food products executive; b. St. Louis, Oct. 3, 1939; s. Anton Dominick and Anita Marie (Hughes) Pichler; m. Susan Ellen Eyerly, Dec. 27, 1962; children: Gretchen, Christopher, Rebecca, Josh. BBA, U. Notre Dame, 1961; MBA, U. Chgo., 1963, PhD, 1966. Asst. prof. bus. U. Kans., 1964—68, assoc. prof., 1968—73, prof., 1973—80; dean U. Kans. Sch. Bus., 1974—80; exec. v.p. Dillon Cos. Inc., 1980—82, pres., 1982—86; exec. v.p. Kroger Co., Cin., 1985—86, pres., COO, 1986—90, pres., CEO, 1990, chmn., CEO, 1990—2003, chmn., 2003—, also bd. dirs. Spl. asst. to asst. sec. for manpower U.S. Dept. Labor, 1968—70; chmn. Kans. Manpower Svcs. Coun., 1974—78; bd. dirs. Cin. Milacron Inc., Federated Dept. Stores, Inc., Catalyst. Author (with Joseph McGuire): The Poor and the Rich in America, 1969; co-author: Creativity and Innovation in Manpower Research and Action Programs, 1970, Contemporary Management: Issues and Viewpoints, 1973, Institutional Issues in Public Accounting, 1974, Co-Creation and Capitalism: John Paul II's Laborem Exercens, 1983; co-editor (contbg. author): Ethics, Free Enterprise, and Public Policy, 1978; contbr. articles to profl. jours. Nat. bd. dirs. Boys Hope, 1983—96; mem. Nat. Alliance of Bus. Bd., 1988—95, chmn., 1991—93; mem. fellow adv. com. Woodrow Wilson Found., 1990—93; mem. adv. bd. Salvation Army Sch. for Officers Tng., 1994—2000; bd. dirs. Cin. Opera, 1987—96, adv. mem., 1996—; bd. dirs. Tougaloo Coll., 1986—; mem. Cin. Bus. Com., 1991—, chmn., 1997—98. amed Disting. Alumnus U. Chgo., 1994; recipient Disting. Svc. award, Nat. Conf. Cmty. Justice, 2000, William Booth award, Salvation Army, 1998, Horatio Alger award, 1999, Hall of Fame, Greater Cin. and No. Ky. Bus., 2001; Woodrow Wilson fellow, Ford Found. fellow, Standard Oil Indsl. Rels. fellow, 1966. Mem.: Greater Cin. C. of C. (trustee), Catalyst Bd., Bus. Roundtable, Comml. Club of Cin., Queen City Club. Office: Kroger Co 1014 Vine St Cincinnati OH 45202-1100

PICK, HEATHER, newscaster; b. Platteville, Wis. m. Joe Pick; 1 child. Reporter, anchor Sta. WREX-TV, Rockford, Ill.; anchor Sta. WBNS-TV, Columbus, Ohio, 2002—. Office: WBNS-TV 770 Twin Rivers Dr Columbus OH 43215

PICKARD, WILLIAM FRANK, plastics company executive; b. LaGrange, Ga., Jan. 28, 1941; s. William H. and Victoria (Woodward) P. AS, Mott Community Coll., 1962; BS, Western Mich. U., 1964; MSW, U. Mich., 1965; PhD, Ohio State U., 1971; PhD in Bus. Adminstrn. (hon.), Cleary Coll., 1980. Dir. employment and edn. Urban League Cleve., 1965-67; exec. dir. NAACP, Cleve., 1967-69; assoc. dir. dept. urban studies Cleve. State U., 1971-72; assoc. prof. Wayne State U., Detroit, 1972-74; owner, operator McDonald's Restaurants, Detroit, 1971—; chmn., chief exec. officer Regal Plastics, Roseville, Mich., 1985—. Vis. lectr. Cleve. State U., U. Chgo., Hiram Coll., U. Toledo, U. Mich., Case Western Res. U., Ohio State U., Wayne County Community Coll., McDonald's Hamburger U.; participant mgmt. seminar Case Western Res. U., Greater Cleve. Associated Found. and Rockefeller Found., 1968; chmn. Gov.'s adv. com. on minority bus., pres. 1976; bd. dirs. First Ind. Nat. Bank, Mich. Nat. Bank Corp., Farmington Hills. Mem. Pres.-elect Ronald Regan's transition team to SBA; chmn. econ. devel. com. Nat. Black Rep. Council, 1978, bd. dirs. com. to elect Gov. Ronald Reagan Pres., 1980, chmn. congl. liaison com., 1982; chmn. Mich. Reps. Urban Campaign to elect Gov. Reagan Pres., 1980; vice chmn. Mich. Rep. State Com., 1981; bd. control Grand Valley State Coll., Allendale, Mich.; bd. dirs. Oakwood Hosp., Kirkwood Gen. Hosp., Detroit, Detroit Black Causes, Detroit Econ. Devel. Corp., 1977, Nat. Minority Purchasing Council, Washington, Detroit Urban League, vice chmn.; appointed by Pres. Ronald Regan, and confirmed by U.S. Senate Chmn. of African Devel. Found., 1983. Named one of Ten Outstanding Young Men Cleve., Jaycees, 1969; Alice W. Gault schlor, 1962-63; Nat. Urban League fellow, 1964. Mem. Booker T. Washington Bus. Assn., NAACP, Jaycees, Alpha Phi Alpha. Home: 335 Pine Ridge Dr Bloomfield Hills MI 48304-2140

PICKETT, JAMES V., food service executive; Chmn. Pickett Realty Advisors, Inc., Dublin, Ohio; pres., CEO of various companies generally known as Pickett Companies, 1969—; vice-chmn. Banc On Capital Corp., 1993—99; prin. Stonehedge Fin. Holding, Inc., 1999—2004. Bd. dir. Wendy's Internat., Inc., Dublin, 1982—2006, chmn. bd. dirs., 2006—. Mailing: Wendy's Internat Inc One Dave Thomas Blvd Dublin OH 43017

PICKHARDT, PERRY J., radiology educator, researcher; BS in Physics, U. Wis., Madison, 1991; MD, U. Mich. Med. Sch., 1995. Resident, diagnostic radiology Mallinckrodt Inst. Radiology, Wash. U., St. Louis, 1995—99; dept. head, radiology US Naval Hosp., Guantanamo Bay, Cuba, 1999—2000; head, GI-GU imaging Nat. Naval Med. Ctr., Bethesda, Md., 2000—03; asst. prof., radiology Uniformed Svcs. U. Health Scis., Bethesda, Md.; assoc. prof., radiology U. Wis. Med. Sch., Madison, Wis., 2003, assoc. prof., abdominal imaging. Co-editor textbook on body CT; pub. a number of scientific papers; contbr. chapters to books. Figley Fellowship, AJR Editl. Office, Winston-Salem, NC, 2002. Office: U Wis Sch Medicine and Pub Health E3/366 Clinical Sciences Ctr 600 Highland Ave Madison WI 53792-3252 Office Phone: 608-263-9028. Business E-Mail: ppickhardt2@uwhealth.org.*

PICKLE, ROBERT DOUGLAS, lawyer, apparel executive; b. Knoxville, Tenn., May 22, 1937; s. Robert Lee and Beatrice Jewel (Douglas) P.; m. Rosemary Elaine Noser, May 9, 1964. AA summa cum laude, Schreiner Mil. Coll., Kerrville, Tex., 1957; BSBA magna cum laude, U. Tenn., 1959, JD, 1961; graduate (hon.), Nat. Def. U., 1979, US Army JAG Sch., US Army Logistics Mgmt. Sch.; graduate, US Army Inf. Sch., Army Command-Gen. Staff Coll. Bar: Tenn. 1961, Mo. 1964, U.S. Ct. Mil. Appeals 1962, U.S. Supreme Ct. 1970. Atty. Brown Shoe Co., Inc., St. Louis, 1963-69, asst. sec., atty., 1969-74, sec., gen. counsel, 1974-85; v.p., gen. counsel, corp. sec. Brown Shoe Co., Inc. (formerly Brown Group, Inc.), St. Louis, 1985—. Indiv. mobilization augmentee, asst. army judge adv. gen. civil law The Pentagon, Washington, 1984-89. Provisional judge Municipal Ct., Clayton, Mo., summer 1972; chmn. Clayton Region attys. sect., profl. div. United Fund Greater St. Louis Campaign, 1972-73, team capt., 1974-78; chmn. City of Clayton Parks and Recreation Commn., 1985-87; liaison admissions officer, regional and state coordinator U.S. Mil. Acad., 1980—. Col. JAGC, U.S. Army, 1961-63. Decorated Meritorious Svc. medal; 1st U. Tenn. Law Coll. John W Green law scholar; recipient Cold War Recognition cert. Sec. Def. Fellow Harry S. Truman Meml. Library; mem. ABA, Tenn. Bar Assn., Mo. Bar Assn., St. Louis County Bar Assn., Bar Assn. Met. St. Louis, St. Louis Bar Found. (bd. dirs. 1979-81), Am. Corp. Counsel Assn., Am. Soc. Corp. Secs. (treas. St. Louis regional group 1976-77, sec. 1977-78, v.p. 1978-79, pres., mem. Quarter-Century Club 1979-80), U. Tenn. Gen. Alumni Assn. (pres., bd. dirs. St. Louis chpt. 1974-76, 80-84, bd. govs. 1982-89), U.S. Trademark Assn. (bd. dirs. 1978-82), Tenn. Soc. St. Louis (bd. dirs. 1980-88, treas., sec., v.p. 1984-87, pres. 1987-88), Smithsonian Nat. Assocs., World Affairs Coun. St. Louis, Inc., Am. Legion, University Club (v.p., sec. St. Louis chpt. 1976-81, bd. dirs. 1976-81), Stadium Club, West Point Soc. St. Louis (hon. mem., bd. dirs. 1992—), Conf. Bd. (coun. chief legal officers), Fontbonne Coll. Pres.'s Assocs. (O'Hara and Tower Socs), St. Louis U. Billiken Club, St. Louis U. DuBourg Soc. (hon. v.p.). Republican. Presbyterian. Avocations: reading, sports. Home: 214 Topton Way Saint Louis MO 63105-3638 Office: Brown Shoe Co Inc 8300 Maryland Ave Saint Louis MO 63105-3645 E-mail: rpickle@brownshoe.com.

PICKLEMAN, JACK R., surgeon; MD, McGill U., Montreal, Que., Can., 1964. Intern Royal Victoria Hosp., Montreal, Que., Can., 1964-65; resident in surgery U. Chgo. Med. Ctr., 1967-73; asst. prof. surgery Loyola U., Chgo., 1973-77, assoc. prof. surgery, 1977-81, prof., chief gen. surgery, 1981—. Attending physician Loyola Med. Ctr., Maywood, Ill. Mem. ACS. Office: Loyola U Med Ctr 2160 S 1st Ave Maywood IL 60153-3304

PIDERIT, JOHN J., university educator; b. NYC, Feb. 26, 1944; BA in Math. and Philosophy magna cum laude, Fordham U., 1967; Lic. in Sacred Theology cum laude, Philosophische und Theologische Hochschule Sankt Georgen, Frankfurt, West Germany, 1971; MPhil, Oxford U., 1974; MA, PhD in Econ., Princeton U., 1979. Ordained Jesuit priest Roman Cath. Ch., 1971. Tchr. math. Regis H.S., NYC, 1967-68; asst. campus minister Fordham U., 1971-72, Princeton U., 1975-78, preceptor, 1976-77; asst. chairperson grad. studies Fordham U., 1984-88, dir. program internat. polit. econ. and devel., 1981-83, 87-88, asst. chairperson dept. econs., 1979-82, 88-89, asst. prof. econs., 1978-89, assoc. prof. econs., 1989-90; corp. v.p. Marquette U., 1990-93; pres. Loyola U. Chgo., 1993—. Vis. fellow Woodstock Theol. Ctr., Washington, summer 1982; sabbatical Santa Clara U., 1989-90; master Queen's Ct. Residential Coll., 1987-90; chmn. responsible investment com. N.Y. province SJ, 1986-88, mem. fin. com., 1986-88; mem. joint commn. govtl. rels. of Am. Coun. Edn., 1994—; mem. exec. com. at. Planning Com. Jesuit Assembly '89, 1988-90. Contbr. articles to profl. jours. Founder, moderator Friends of Loyola, 1987-90; pres. Univ. Neighborhood Housing Corp., 1986-90, Maroon Enterprises, Inc., 1986-90; trustee Canisius Coll., Buffalo, 1983-88, 89-94, Loyola Marymount U., L.A., 1996—, John Carroll U., University Heights, Ohio, 1996—; bd. dirs. Corp. Cmty. Schs. of Am., 1993—; promoter PIVOT H.S. and Middle Sch. with Milw. Pub. Schs., 1990-93; mem. Greater Milw. Edn. Trust, 1990-93; mem. steering com., chair edn. task force Milw. Cmty. Traffic Safety Com., 1991-93; mem. steering com. Libr. Literacy Soc. Milw., 1991-93; mem. scholarship com. Knitworkers Union Local 155, N.Y.C., 1982-90; mem. Princeton Schs. Com. N.Y. Region, 1985-88, chmn. Federation of Indp. Colls. and Univs., 1999—. Mellon grantee Fordham U., summer 1983, summer grantee Fordham U., 1979, Princeton U. fellow, 1974-78. Office: Loyola U Chgo 820 N Michigan Ave Chicago IL 60611-2147

PIEKARSKI, VICTOR J., lawyer; b. Lawrence, Mass., Feb. 20, 1950; BA cum laude, Boston Coll., 1971; MBA, U. Chgo., 1978; JD cum laude, Northwestern U., 1974. Bar: Ill. 1974, U.S. Ct. Appeals (7th cir.) 1977, U.S. Supreme Ct. 1978. Ptnr. Querrey & Harrow Ltd., Chgo., to 1997, O'Hagan, Smith and Amundsen, LLC, Chgo., 1997—. Mem. ABA, Def. Rsch. Inst. Office: O'Hagan Smith and Amundsen LLC 150 N Michigan Ave Ste 3300 Chicago IL 60601-7586 E-mail: vpiekarski@osalaw.com.

PIEPGRAS, DAVID G., neurosurgeon, educator; b. Luverne, Minn., 1940; MD, U. Minn., 1965. Diplomate Am. Bd. Neurol. Surgery. Intern Mary Hitchcock Hosp., Hanover, Minn., 1965—66; resident in surgery Hennepin County Gen. Hosp., Mpls., 1969—70; resident in neurol. surgery Mayo Grad. Sch. Medicine, Rochester, 1970—74; staff St. Mary's Hosp., Rochester, 1974—, Rochester Meth. Hosp., 1974—; staff cons. dept. neurosurgery Mayo Clinic, Rochester, 1974—, prof. neurol. surgery. Bd. dirs. Am. Bd. Neurol. Surgery, 2002—. Fellow: ACS; mem.: AMA, Congress of Neurol. Surgeons, Am. Acad. Neurol. Surgeons. Office: Mayo Clinic Dept Neurol Surgery Rochester MN 55905-0001

PIEPHO, ROBERT WALTER, pharmacy educator, researcher; b. Chgo., July 31, 1942; s. Walter August and Irene Elizabeth (Huybrecht) Apfel; m. Mary Lee Wilson, Dec. 10, 1981. BS in Pharmacy, U. Ill.-Chgo., 1965; PhD in Pharmacology, Loyola U., Maywood, Ill., 1972. Registered pharmacist, Ill., Mo. Assoc. prof. U. Nebr. Med. Ctr., Omaha, 1970-78; prof. pharmacy, assoc. dean Sch. Pharmacy U. Colo., Denver, 1978-86; prof. pharmacol., dean U. Mo. Sch. Pharmacy, Kansas City, 1986—. Contbr. articles to profl. jours., chpts. to books. Pres. Club Monaco Homeowners Assn., Denver, 1980-82. Named Outstanding Tchr. U. Nebr. Coll. Pharmacy, 1975; recipient Arthur Hassan Colo. Pharmacal Assn., 1983, Excellence in Teaching U. Colo. Med. Sch., 1983 Fellow Am. Coll. Clin. Pharmacology (regent 1983-88, 91-96, pres. 1998-2000); mem. Am. Soc. Hosp. Pharmacists, Am. Soc. Pharmacology and Exptl. Therapeutics, Rho Chi Roman Catholic. Office: U Mo Sch Pharmacy 2464 Charlotte St Kansas City MO 64108-2718 Office Phone: 816-235-1609. Business E-Mail: piephor@umkc.edu.

PIERCE, HARVEY R., retired insurance company executive; m. Delores Pierce. Agt. Am. Family Ins. Group, 1963, exec. v.p. field ops., regional v.p., state dir., dist. sales mgr., pres., COO, 1990—99, chmn., CEO Madison, Wis., 1999—2006; ret., 2006. Adv. bd. U. Wis. Children's Hosp.; mem. Founders' Club S.W. Mo. State U. Ins. Chair. Mem.: Ins. Inst. Hwy. Safety (chmn. 2004—05), Property Casualty Insurers Assn. Am. (chmn. bd. govs. 2005).

PIERCE, MATT, state representative; b. Newton County, Ind. BA in Telecomm., Ind. U., 1984, JD, 1987. Bar: Ind., Colo., Pa., D.C. Atty.; intern U.S. Ho. of Reps. Subcom. on Telecomm., Consumer Protection and Fin., Washington; legal clk. Nat. Assn. Broadcasters; chief of staff Congressman Baron Hill, 9th Dist. Ind., Washington, 1999—2001; prin. clk. Ind. Ho. of Reps., Indpls., 1996—98; legis. asst., rsch. and policy analyst, majority and minority atty. Ind. Gen. Assembly, Indpls., 1988—2002; state rep. dist. 61 Ind. Ho. of Reps., Indpls., 2002—, vice chmn., environ. affairs com., mem. cts. and criminal code, judiciary, and tech. R & D coms. Consumer watchdog Bloomington (Ind.) Telecomm. Coun.; rep. 3d dist. Bloomington City Coun., 1995—2002. Democrat. Office: Ind Ho of Reps 200 W Washington St Indianapolis IN 46204-2786

PIERRE, PERCY ANTHONY, engineering educator; b. Donaldsville, La., Jan. 3, 1939; s. Percy John and Rosa (Villavaso) P.; m. Olga A. Markham, Aug. 8, 1965; children: Kristin Clare, Allison Celeste. BSEE, U. Notre Dame, 1961, MSEE, 1963, D of Engring. (hon.), 1977; PhD in Elec. Engring, Johns Hopkins U., 1967; postgrad., U. Mich., 1968; DSc (hon.), Rensselear Poly. Inst. Asst. prof. elec. engring. So. U., 1963; instr. Johns Hopkins U., Balt., 1963-64; instr. physics Morgan State Coll., 1964-66; instr. info. and control engring. U. Mich., Ann Arbor, 1967-68; instr. systems engring. UCLA, 1968-69; research engr. in communications RAND Corp., 1968-71; White House fellow, spl. asst. Office of Pres., 1969-70; dean Sch. Engring., Howard U., Washington, 1971-77; program officer for engring. edn. Alfred P. Sloan Found., 1973-75; asst. sec. for research, devel. and acquisition U.S. Dept. Army, 1977-81; engring. mgmt. cons., 1981-83; pres. Prairie View (Tex.) Agrl. and Mech. U. System, 1983-89, Honeywell prof. elec. engring., 1989-90; v.p. rsch. and grad. studies Mich. State U., East Lansing, 1990-95, prof. elec. engring., 1995—. Dir. engring. coll. council Am. Soc. for Engring. Edn., 1973-75; mem. sci. adv. group Def. Communications Agy., 1974-75; mem. adv. panel Office Exptl. Research and Devel. Incentives, NSF, 1973-74; mem. Commn. Scholars To Rev. Grad. Programs, Ill. Bd. Higher Edn., 1972-74; mem. panel on role U.S. engring. sch. in fgn. tech. assistance, 1972, co-chmn. symposium on minorities in engring., 1973; mem. rev. panel for Inst. for Applied Tech., Nat. Bur. Standards, 1973-77; chmn. com. on minorities Nat. Acad. Engring., 1976-77; cons. to dir. Energy Rsch. and Devel. Adminstrn., 1976-77; mem. Army Sci. Bd., 1984; mem. adv. bd. Sch. Engring., Johns Hopkins U., 1981-84; cons. Office Sec. Def., 1981-84; mem. adv. bd. Lincoln Labs., MIT. Contbr. articles on communications theory to profl. publs. Trustee U. Notre Dame, 1974-77, 81—; trustee, mem. exec. com. Nat. Fund for Minority Engring. Students, 1976-77; bd. dirs. The Hitachi Found., 1987, Ctr. for Naval Analysis, 1986, Assn. Tex. Colls. and Univs.; pres. Southwest Athletic Conf., 1985-87, bd. dirs. CMS Corp., 1990—, Defense Sci., 1992-94, Old Kent Fin. Corp., 1993—, bd. trustee Aerospace Corp., 1991—. Recipient Disting. Civilian Service award Dept. Army, 1981; award of merit from Senator Proxmire, 1979. Mem. IEEE (sr. mem.; Edison award com. 1978-80), Sigma Xi, Tau Beta Pi. Home: 2445 Emerald Lake Dr East Lansing MI 48823-7256 Office: Mich State U 3224 Engineering East Lansing MI 48824-1226 Business E-Mail: pierre@msu.edu.

PIERREHUMBERT, JANET BRECKENRIDGE, language educator; AB in Linguistics, Harvard Univ., 1975; Rotary Found. grad. fellow, Univ. of Turku, Finland, 1975—76; PhD in Linguistics, MIT, 1980. Cons., dept. linguistics and speech analysis AT&T Bell Labs, 1980—82, technical staff mem., dept. linguistics and artificial intelligence rsch., 1982—89; rsch. assoc., Ctr. for Cognitive Sci. MIT, 1980—82; cons. asst. prof., dept. linguistics Stanford Univ., 1984—85; faculty Linguistic Soc. of Am. Summer Inst., 1986, 1993; visitor, dept. speech transmission and music acoustics Royal Inst. of Tech., Stockholm, 1987—88; assoc prof., dept. linguistics Northwestern Univ., 1989—93, chair, 1993—96, prof., 1993—; faculty, LOT (Dutch post-grad. sch. of linguistics Univ. Nijmegen, 1997; visitor Ecole National Superieure des Telecommunications, Paris, 1996—97; poste rouge Centre Nat. de la Recherche Scientifique, 1997. Assoc. editor Jour. Phonetics, 1989—, adv. editor Oxford Surveys in Generative Phonology, 2000—; co-author (with M. Beckman): (monograph) Japanese Tone Structure, Linguistic Inquiry Monograph, 1988; co-author: (with M. Broe) (books) Papers in Laboratory Phonology V, 2000; contbr. articles to profl. journals, chapters to books. Fellow John Simon Guggenheim Mem. Found., 1996—; grantee NSF Grad. Fellowhip, 1976—79. Fellow: Am. Acad. Arts & Sci. Office: Dept Linguistics Northwestern Univ 2016 Sheridan Rd Evanston IL 60208 Office Phone: 847-467-1570. Office Fax: 847-491-3770. Business E-Mail: jbp@northwestern.edu.

PIERSOL, LAWRENCE L., federal judge; b. Spirit Mound Township, SD, Oct. 21, 1940; s. Ralph Nelson and Mildred Alice (Millette) P.; m. Catherine Anne Vogt, June 30, 1962; children: Leah C., William M., Elizabeth J. BA, U. S.D., 1962, JD summa cum laude, 1965. Bar: S.D. 1965, U.S. Ct. Mil. Appeals, 1965, U.S. Dist. Ct. S.D. 1968, U.S. Supreme Ct. 1972, U.S. Dist. Ct. Wyo. 1980, U.S. Dist. Ct. Nebr. 1986, U.S. Dist. Ct. Mont. 1988. Ptnr. Davenport, Evans, Hurwitz & Smith, Sioux Falls, SD, 1968-93; judge U.S. Dist. Ct. SD, Sioux Falls, 1993—, chief judge, 1999—2005. Mem. budget com. Jud. Conf. U.S., 1996-2003, chair economy subcom., 2001-03; chmn. tribal ct. com., security com. 8th Cir. Jud. Coun.; editor-in-chief Law Rev.; mem. Judl. Conf. US, 2005-, exec. com., 2006-. Majority leader S.D. Ho. of Reps., Pierre, 1973-74, minority whip, 1971-72; del. Dem. Nat. Conv., 1972, 76, 80; S.D. mem. del. select commn. Dem. Nat. Com., 1971-75. Mem. ABA, State Bar S.D., Fed. Judges Assn. (bd. dirs., pres.). Avocations: reading, running, painting, sailing. Office: US Dist Ct 400 S Phillips Ave Sioux Falls SD 57104-6824 Home Phone: 605-338-7245; Office Phone: 605-330-6640.

PIERSON, EDWARD SAMUEL, engineering educator, consultant; b. Syracuse, NY, June 27, 1937; s. Theodore and Marjorie O. (Bronner) P.; m. Elaine M. Grauer, June 6, 1971; 1 child, Alan. BS in Elec. Engring., Syracuse U., 1958; SM, MIT, 1960, ScD, 1964. Asst. prof., fellow MIT, 1965-66; assoc. prof., assoc. dept. head U. Ill., Chgo., 1966-75; program mgr. Argonne Nat. Labs., Ill., 1975-82; head dept. engring. Purdue U. Calumet, Hammond, Ind., 1982-95, spl. asst. to chancellor for environ. programs, 1995—2005. Cons. Argonne Nat. Lab., 1972-75, 82-93, Solmecs Corp., 1982-88, HMJ Corp., Washington, 1983-88, LM Mfg., 1994—. Contbr. articles to profl. jours. NSF fellow, 1958-60 Mem. IEEE, ASME, Am. Soc. Engring. Edn. Office: Purdue Univ Calumet Hammond IN 46323 Home Phone: 773-327-9188; Office Phone: 219-989-2467. E-mail: pierson@calumet.purdue.edu.

PIERSON, JOHN THEODORE, JR., manufacturing executive; b. Kansas City, Mo., Oct. 13, 1931; s. John Theodore and Helen Marguerite (Sherman) P.; m. Susan K. Chadwick, Apr. 16, 1977; children by previous marriage— Merrill Sherman, Karen Louise, Kimberly Ann. BSE, Princeton U., 1953; MBA, Harvard U., 1958. With Vendo Co., Kansas City, Mo., 1960—, gen. automatic products salesman, 1960-61, mgr. new products, 1961-63; v.p. sales equipment for Coca-Cola, 1963-66; pres. Vendo Internat., 1966-69, exec. v.p., chief operating officer, 1969-71, pres., chief exec. officer, 1971-74; chmn. Preco Industries, Inc., 1976—. Chmn. Internat. Trade and Exhbn. Ctr. Co-author: Linear Polyethylene and Polypropylene: Problems and Opportunities, 1958. Trustee Midwest Rsch. Inst.; bd. dirs. and chmn. MidAm. Mfg. Tech. Ctr.; bd. dirs. Johnson County Bus. Tech. Ctr., Youth Symphony Kansas City, 1965-69; past trustee Pembroke-Country Day Sch., Barstow Sch.; past mem. adv. coun. U.S.-Japan Econ. Rels. Coun.; mem. coun. chmn. for exploring Boy Scouts Am., mem. Nat. coun. Lt. ONI USNR, 1953-56. Mem. Kansas City C. of C., U.S.C.of C. (dir. 1970-74), River Club (pres. 1994-96), Kansas City Country Club. Office: 9705 Commerce Pkwy Lenexa KS 66219-2403

PIESHOSKI, MICHAEL J., construction executive; V.p., CFO Peter Kiewit Sons', Inc., Omaha, 2000—. Office: Peter Kiewit Sons Inc Kiewit Plz Omaha NE 68131

PIESTER, DAVID L(EE), magistrate judge; b. Lincoln City, Nebr., Nov. 18, 1947; s. George Piester; married; children. BS, U. Nebr., 1969, JD, 1972. Bar: Nebr. 1972, U.S. Dist. Ct. Nebr. 1972, U.S. Ct. Appeals (8th cir.) 1976, U.S. Supreme Ct. 1979. Staff atty. Legal Svcs. S.E. Nebr., Lincoln, 1972-73, exec. dir., 1973-79; asst. U.S. atty. Dept. Justice, Lincoln, 1979-81; magistrate judge U.S. Dist. Ct. Nebr., Lincoln, 1981—. Cons. Legal Services Corp., Nat. Legal Aid and Defender Assn., 1974-77. Mem. Lincoln Human rights commn., 1978-79. Mem. Nebr. State Bar Assn., Fed. Magistrate Judges Assn., Lincoln Bar Assn., Eighth Cir. Jud. Coun. (ex officio 1993-96). Office: US Dist Ct 100 Centennial Mall North 566 Fed Bldg Lincoln NE 68508

PIETROFESA, JOHN JOSEPH, psychologist, educator; b. NYC, Sept. 12, 1940; s. Louis John and Margaret P.; m. Cathy Marks, June 22, 1985; children: John, Paul, Maria, Dolores. EdB cum laude, U. Miami, 1961; MEd, 1963, Ed.D., 1967. Diplomate Am. Bd. Sexology; cert. cognitive behavior therapist, forensic counselor, sex therapist; lic. psychologist, social worker. Counselor Dade County (Fla.) pub. schs., 1965-67; prof. edn. Wayne State U., Detroit, 1967—; div. head theoret. and behavioral founds., 1977-83; dept. chair counselor edn., 1999—. Cons. Nat. Football League, 2003—; cons. to various schs., hosps. and univs. Author: The Authentic Counselor, 1971, 2nd edit., 1980, School Counselor as Professional, 1971, Counseling and Guidance in the Twentieth Century, 1971, Elementary School Guidance and Counseling, 1973, Career Development, 1975, Career Education, 1976, College Student Development, 1977, Counseling: Theory Research and Practice, 1978, Guidance: An Introduction, 1980, Counseling: An Introduction, 1984; mem. editl. bd. Counseling and Values, 1972-75. 1st lt. Mil. Police Corps, AUS, 1963-65. Mem. APA, ACA, Mich. Counseling ASsn., Assn. Counselor Edn. and Supervision, Phi Delta Kappa. Home: PO Box 99 Bloomfield Hills MI 48303-0099 Office: Wayne State U 321 Education Detroit MI 48202 Home Phone: 248-646-0821; Office Phone: 248-642-6066.

PIETROWSKI, ANTHONY, research and development company executive; Founder, pres., CEO RDA Group, Inc., Bloomfield Hill, Mich., 1969—. Office: RDA Group Inc 450 Enterprise Ct Bloomfield Hills MI 48302-0386

PIGMAN, JACK RICHARD, lawyer; b. Fostoria, Ohio, June 5, 1944; s. Jack R. and A. Ada (McDevitt) P.; m. Judy Lynn Price, June 19, 1968 (div. 1983); m. Carolyn Ruth Parker, May 31, 1986; children: Shaeney E. Pigman Craig, J. Ryan Pigman, Adam Parker. BA, U. Notre Dame, 1966; JD cum laude, Ohio State U., 1969. Bar: Ohio 1969, U.S. Ct. Mil. Appeals 1970. Law clk. Ohio Supreme Ct., Columbus, 1969-70; assoc. Wright, Harlor, Morris & Arnold, Columbus, 1970, 74-76; ptnr. Porter, Wright, Morris & Arthur and predecessor firms, Columbus, 1977—. Spkr. in field. Trustee Dublin Arts Coun., 2001—06, pres., 2005, 06; trustee Ctr. for New Directions, 1990-96, treas., 1996; trustee United Cerebral Palsy of Columbus and Franklin County, 1976-82, pres., 1980; trustee Columbus Met. Club, 1980-87, pres., 1985-86; trustee Brass Band of Columbus. 2007-. Capt. JAG US Army, 1970—74. Named to Best Lawyers in Am., Ohio Super Lawyers, 2004—07, Chambers USA, 2004—07. Mem. Ohio State Bar Assn., Columbus Bar Assn. (chmn. bankruptcy com. 1982-84). Republican. Avocations: tennis, reading, cooking, photography. Office: Porter Wright Morris & Arthur LLP 41 S High St Ste 2800 Columbus OH 43215-6194 Office Phone: 614-227-2119. Business E-Mail: jpigman@porterwright.com.

PIIRMA, IRJA, chemist, educator; b. Tallinn, Estonia, Feb. 4, 1920; came to U.S., 1949; d. Voldemar Juri and Meta Wilhelmine (Lister) Tiits; m. Aleksander Piirma, Mar. 10, 1943; children: Margit Ene, Silvia Ann. Diploma in Chemistry, Tech. U., Darmstadt, Fed. Republic of Germany, 1949; MS, U. Akron, 1957, PhD, 1960. Rsch. chemist U. Akron, Ohio, 1952-67, asst. prof., 1967-76, assoc. prof., 1976-81, prof., 1981-90, prof. emerita, 1990—, dept. head, 1982-85. Author: Polymeric Surfactants, 1992; editor: Emulsion Polymerization, 1982; contbr. articles to profl. jours. Recipient Extra Mural Rsch. award BP Am., Inc., 1989. Mem. Am. Chem. Soc. Avocations: swimming, skiing. Home: 3528 Adaline Dr Cuyahoga Falls OH 44224-3929 Office: U Akron Inst Polymer Sci Akron OH 44325-3909 Home Phone: 330-688-4834. Personal E-mail: irjapiirma@cs.com, irjapiirma@sbcglobal.net.

PIKE, KERMIT JEROME, cultural organization administrator; b. East Cleveland, June 19, 1941; s. Frank James and Pauline Frances (Prijatel) P.; m. Joyce Rita Massillo, June 27, 1964; children: Christopher James, Laura Elizabeth. BA, Case Western Res. U., 1963, MA, 1965. Rsch. asst. Western Res. Hist. Soc., Cleve., 1965-66, curator manuscripts, 1966-72, chief libr., 1969-75, dir. libr., 1976—2002, COO, 1997—2007, capital campaign mgr., 2006—07, sr. v.p., 2007—. Adj. prof. history, libr. sci. Case Western Res. U., 1975-84. Author: Guide to the Manuscripts and Archives, 1972, Guide to Shaker Manuscripts, 1974; editor: Guide to Jewish History Sources, 1983; Compiler: Guide to Major Manuscript Collections, 1987. Mem. Super Sesquicentennial Com., Cleve., 1971, Cleve. Bicentennial History Com., 1992—96, Ohio Preservation Coun., 1997—, Ohio Hist. Records Adv. Bd., 2002—; chmn. Family Heritage Adv. Bd., Numa Corp., 1995—99; chmn. vis. com. on humanities and arts Cleve. State U., 1980—82; trustee Nationalities Svc. Ctr., Cleve., 1978—86. Recipient Achievement award o. Ohio Live, Cleve., 1987; Spl. Recognition award Gov. Richard F. Celeste of Ohio, 1990. Mem. Soc. Ohio Archivists (co-founder 1968, pres. 1971-72), Black History Archives (founder 1970), Orgn. Am. Historians, Soc. Am. Archivists, Manuscripts Soc., Midwest Archives Conf., Ohio Geneal. Soc., Early Settlers Assn. of the Western Res., Rowfant Club, Lake County Farmers' Conservation Club, Lambda Chi Alpha. Roman Catholic. Office: Western Res Hist Soc 10825 East Blvd Cleveland OH 44106-1777 Office Phone: 216-721-5722. Business E-Mail: kermit@wrhs.org.

PIKE, ROBERT WILLIAM, insurance company executive, lawyer; b. Lorain, Ohio, July 25, 1941; s. Edward and Catherine (Stack) P.; m. Linda L. Feitz, Dec. 26, 1964; children: Catherine, Robert, Richard. BA, Bowling Green State U., 1963; JD, U. Toledo, 1966. Bar: Ohio 1966, Ill. 1973. Ptnr. Cubbon & Rice Law Firm, Toledo, 1968-72; asst. counsel Allstate Ins. Co., Northbrook, Ill., 1972-74, assoc. counsel, 1974-76, asst. sec., asst. gen. counsel, 1976-77, asst. v.p., asst. gen. counsel, 1977-78, v.p., asst. gen. counsel, 1978-86, sr. v.p., sec., gen. counsel, bd. dirs., 1987-99, exec. v.p., 1999—. Bd. dirs. Allstate subs. Mem. bd. overseers Inst. for Civil Justice. Served to capt. inf. U.S. Army, 1966-68. Mem. ABA, Ill. Bar Assn., Ohio Bar Assn., Property Casualty Insurers Assn. Am. (bd. dirs., exec. com.), Ivanhoe (Ill.) Club. Roman Catholic. Home: 1795 W North Pond Ln Lake Forest IL 60045-Office: Allstate Ins Co 2775 Sanders Rd Ste F8 Northbrook IL 60062-6127

PILAND, JOHN CHARLES, lawyer; b. Paxton, Ill., Dec. 6, 1961; s. Joseph C. and Jo Anne (Hortin) P.; m. Debra Ann Stewart, July 28, 1984; children: Jacqueline Prince, David Lincoln. BSBA, U. Ill., 1984, JD, 1987. Bar: Ill. 1987, U.S. Dist. Ct. (cen. dist.) 1988, U.S. Ct. Appeals (7th cir.) 1988, U.S. Supreme Ct. 1991. Atty. Heyl, Royster, Voelker & Allen, Urbana, Ill., 1987-95; spl. legal counsel to Ill. House Rep. Leader, 1993-94; state's atty. Champaign County, 1995—. Mem. nat. adv. coun. SBA, Washington, 1988-89; mem. gov.'s adv. bd., Springfield, Ill., 1988-90; mem. Ill. Truth-in-Sentencing Commn., 1995-98. Fl. page U.S. Ho. of Reps., Washington, 1979-80; legis. aide Ill. Ho. of Reps., Springfield, 1981-82. Harry S. Truman Found. scholar, 1982. Fellow Am. Bar Found.; mem. ABA, SAR, Ill. State Bar Assn. (bd. govs. 1995-2001), Champaign County Bar Assn., Nat. Dist. Attys. Assn., Ill. States Attys. Assn. (exec. com. 1995—), Lions, Masons, Rotary, Phi Alpha Delta. Republican. Office: Champaign County States Atty PO Box 785 Urbana IL 61803-0785

PILARCZYK, DANIEL EDWARD, archbishop; b. Dayton, Ohio, Aug. 12, 1934; s. Daniel Joseph and Frieda S. (Hilgefort) Pilarczyk. Student, St. Gregory Sem., Cin., 1948—53; PhB, Pontifical Urban U., Rome, 1955, PhL, 1956, STB, 1958, STL, 1960, STD, 1961; MA, Xavier U., 1965; PhD, U. Cin., 1969; LLD (hon.), Xavier U., 1975, Calumet Coll., 1982, U. Dayton, 1990, Marquette U.,

1990, Thomas More Coll., 1991, Coll. Mt. St. Joseph, 1994, Hebrew Union Coll., 1997. Ordained priest Archdiocese of Cin., Ohio, 1959, asst. chancellor, 1961—63; synodal judge Archdiocesan Tribunal, 1971—82; faculty Athenaeum of Ohio, St. Gregory Sem., 1963—74; v.p. Athenaeum of Ohio, 1968—74, trustee, 1974—; rector St. Gregory Sem., 1968—74; ordained bishop, 1974; aux. bishop Archdiocese of Cin., 1974—82, vicar gen. Ohio, 1974—82, dir. ednl. services Ohio, 1974—82, archbishop, 1982—. V.p. Nat. Conf. Cath. Bishops, 1986—89, pres., 1989—92, chmn. com. on doctrine, 1996—2000; U.S. rep. Episc. bd. Internat. Commn. on English in Liturgy, 1987—97, chmn., 1991—97; jt. com. Orthodox and Cath. Bishops, 2002. Author: Praepositini Cancellarii de Sacramentis et de Novissimis, 1964—65, Twelve Tough Issues, 1988, We Believe, 1989, Living in the Lord, 1990, The Parish: Where God's People Live, 1991, Forgiveness, 1992, What Must I Do?, 1993, Our Priests: Who They Are and What They Do, 1994, Sacraments, 1994, Bringing Forth Justice, 1996, 1999, Thinking Catholic, 1998, Practicing Catholic, 1999, Believing Catholic, 2000, Live Letters, 2001, Twelve Tough Issues and More, 2002, Being Catholic, 2006, When God Speaks, 2006. Trustee Cath. Health Assn., 1982—85, Cath. U. Am., 1983—91, 1997—2000, Pontifical Coll. Josephinum, 1983—92. Ohio Classical Conf. scholar, Athens, 1966. Mem.: Am. Philol. Assn. Roman Catholic. Home and Office: 100 E Eighth St Cincinnati OH 45202-2129 Office Phone: 513-421-3131.

PILCH, SAMUEL H., controller, corporate financial executive; B in Acctg., Bryant Coll. COO Travelers Ins. Co., Hartford, Conn.; controller promoted to group v.p. Allstate Ins. Co., 1999; mem. sr. mgmt. team Allstate Corp., controller, divisional v.p., 2001—, acting CFO, 2001. Served US Army, 1968—70. Office: Allstate Corp 2775 Sanders Rd Northbrook IL 60062

PILCHEN, IRA A., editor; b. Chgo., Jan. 17, 1964; s. Bernard J. and Erna (Lee) P. BA in History, U. Ill., 1986. Assoc. editor Judicature jour., Chgo., 1991-98; dir. comms. Am. Judicature Soc., Chgo., 1991-98; editor Student Lawyer mag. ABA Publishing, Chgo., 1999—. Mem. adv. coun. Ill. State Justice Commn., 1995. Vol. interpretive guide Friends of the Chicago River, 1991—. Named Vol. of Yr., Friends of Chicago River, 1993. Avocations: swimming, bicycling, history. Office: ABA Publishing 750 N Lake Shore Dr Fl 8 Chicago IL 60611-4403

PILCHER, JAMES ERIC, physicist; b. Toronto, Ont., Can., Apr. 23, 1942; came to US 1965; s. Francis Eric and Isabel (Brand) P.; m. Carla Grosso, Aug. 31, 1970; children: Marc R., Daniel E., Erica M. BASc, U. Toronto, 1964, MSc, 1966; PhD, Princeton U., 1968. Rsch. assc. Princeton U., Princeton, NJ, 1968-69; vis. scientist CERN, Geneva, 1969-70, sci. assoc., 1979—80; asst. prof. Harvard U., Cambridge, Mass., 1970-72; asst./assoc. prof. U. Chgo., 1972-79, prof., 1979—, dir. Enrico Fermi Inst., 2001—. Member Physics Adv. Com., SSC, Dallas, 1990-. Author numerous articles to profl. jours. Fellow Alfred P. Sloan Found., 1972—76. Fellow Am. Phys. Soc. Achievements include discovery that there are exactly 3 families of light neutrinos. Office: University of Chicago EFI Box 47 5640 S Ellis Ave Chicago IL 60637 Office Phone: 773-702-7443. Office Fax: 773-702-1914. E-mail: j-pilcher@uchicago.edu.

PILGRIM, JILL, lawyer, consultant; b. London, Nov. 26, 1958; came to U.S., 1969; d. Winslow and Florence L. (Hardy) P. BA, Princeton U., 1980; JD, Columbia U., 1984. Bar: N.Y. 1985. Assoc. Willkie Far & Gallagher, NYC, 1984-86, Cowan Liebowitz & Latman, NYC, 1986-88; of counsel Kurzman Karelsen & Frank, NYC, 1988-89; pvt. practice Pilgrim & Assocs., NYC, 1990—98; gen. counsel, dir. bus. affairs USA Track & Field, Inc., Indpls., 1998—. Examiner in guardianship matters, 1991—; bd. arbitrators Nat. Assn. Securities Delers, Inc.; guest speaker to law students, numerous N.Y. area law schs. Bd. editors The Partnership Handbook, 1986. Mem. Temp. N.Y. State Commn. on Bklyn. Recreation Facilities, 1994—; founder, pres. Ctr. for Protection Athletes' Rights Inc.; bd. dirs., mem. exec. com. Bklyn. Sports Found.; v.p. Friends of Princeton Track; mem. alumni coun. exec. com. Princeton U., 1993-95; bd. dirs. Griffith-Sandiford Family Assistance Fund, Inc.; mem. adv. bd. Bond Street Theater Coalition, Ltd., New Federal Theater. Recipient Essence award Essence Comm., Inc. and Colgate-Palmolive Co., 1990; named Woman of Yr., West Side Residents, 1993. Mem. ABA, Practicing Law Inst., Met. Black Bar Assn., Assn. Bar City N.Y., Assn. Black Women Attys., Sports Lawyers Assn. (bd. mem.), Indpls. Nat. Jr. Tennis Team (bd. mem.), Indpls. Bar Assn. (chairperson sports law sec.), U.S. Olympic Com. (mem. disabled sports com.) Avocations: tennis, field hockey, badminton, volleyball, basketball, track & field. Office: USA Track & Field 1 RCA Dome, Ste 140 Indianapolis IN 46225

PILLAERT, E(DNA) ELIZABETH, museum director; b. Baytown, Tex., Nov. 19, 1931; d. Albert Jacob and Nettie Roseline (Kelley) P. BA, U. St. Thomas, 1953; MA, U. Okla., 1963; postgrad., U. Wis., 1962-67, 70-73. Asst. curator archaeology Stovall Mus., Norman, Okla., 1959-60, ednl. liaison officer, 1960-62; research asst. U. Okla., Norman, Okla., 1962, U. Wis., Madison, 1962-65, cons. archaeol. faunal analysis, 1965—; curator osteology Zool. Mus., Madison, 1965—, chief curator, 1967-92, assoc. dir., 1992—2007, disting. rschr., 2000—, dir., 2007—. Bd. dirs. Lysistrata Feminist Coop., Madison, 1977-81, Univ. YMCA, Madison, 1974-77 Mem. Wis. Archaeol. Soc., Okla. Anthrop. Soc., Am. Assn. Mus., NOW, Stoughton Hist. Soc., Am. Ornithological Union, Friends of Stoughton Libr., Friends of Stoughton Auditorium. Home: 216 N Prairie St Stoughton WI 53589-1647 Office: U Wis Zool Mus 434 Noland Bldg 250 N Mills St Madison WI 53706-1708 Office Phone: 608-262-3766. Business E-Mail: pillaert@facstaff.wisc.edu.

PILLAI, PRAGASH, communications executive; b. 1973; BSEE, U. Mo., Columbia. V.p., Advanced Engring. Digital Video Charter Comm. Named one of 40 Executives Under 40, Multichannel News, 2006; recipient Young Engr. award, Soc. Cable Telecomm. Engineers, 2003, Cable's Next Generation of Innovators award, Multichannel ews, 2004, Pacesetter award, Comm. Engring. & Design, 2004. Mem.: Inst. Elec. Electronics Engineers (vice chmn. 2003, young Engr. award for St. Louis 2002). Office: Charter Communications Inc 12405 Powerscourt Dr Ste 100 Saint Louis MO 63131-3660 Office Phone: 314-965-0555. Office Fax: 314-965-9745.

PILNICK, GARY H., food products executive, lawyer; b. Forest Hills, NY, Sept. 17, 1964; m. Helen Pilnick. Grad., Lafayette Coll., 1986; law degree with honors, Duke U., 1989. Atty. Jenner and Block, Chgo., 1989—95; v.p., chief corp. counsel Specialty Foods Corp., 1995—97; chief counsel corp. devel. and fin. Sara Lee Corp., 1997—99; v.p., chief counsel Sara Lee Branded Apparel, 1999—2000; v.p., dep. gen. counsel, asst. sec. Kellogg Co., 2000—03, sr. v.p., gen. counsel corp. devel., sec., 2003—. Office: Kellogg Co Box 3599 1 Kellogg Sq Battle Creek MI 49016-3599 E-mail: gary.pilnick@kellogg.com.

PINCUS, THEODORE HENRY, public relations executive; b. Chgo., Sept. 15, 1933; s. Jacob T. and J. (Engel) Pincus; m. Sharon Barr, Jan. 16, 1988; children: Laura, Mark, Susan, Anne, Jennifer. BS in Journalism, Ind. U., 1955. Free-lance bus. writer, 1955—58; sr. exec. Harshe Rotman & Druck, Chgo., 1958—62; owner Theodore Pincus & Assocs., Chgo., 1962—, prin., owner, 2003—; chmn., CEO Fin. Rels. Bd., Inc., Chgo., 1965—98; vice chmn. BSMG Worldwide divsn. Interpub. Group, YC, 1998—2001; fin. columnist Chgo. Sun Times, 2002—; mng. ptnr. Stevens Gould & Pincus, 2007—. Pub. affairs advisor to Nelson Rockefeller, NYC, 1960, YC, 68; advisor U.S. Info. Agy., 1993—; adj. prof. fin. MBA Sch., DePaul U., 2002—; former mem. adv. bd. NASDAQ, USIA; ind. comm. cons., 2003—. Author: Giveaway Day, 1977, On the Offensive, 2001; contbr. artcles to profl. jours. including Wall St. Jour., Fortune and N.Y. Times; author: Read at Your Own Risk, 2007. Active presdl. nomination campaigns; vice-chmn. Midwest Region Am. Jewish Com.; mem. adv. bd. Ind. U. Bus. Sch., The Ill. Coalition. With USAF, 1955—57. Named Entrepreneur of Yr., Ernst and Young Merrill Lynch, 1998; recipient numerous nat. awards for profl. excellence in investor rels. and corp. pub. rels., including Silver Anvil award, Pub. Rels. Soc. Am., 1966, Civic Achievement award, Am. Jewish Com., 1993, Pub. Rels. Profl. of Yr., Pub. Rels. Soc. Am., 2002. Mem.: Nat. Investor Rels. Inst. (founding), Young Pres.'s Orgn., Union League, Standard Club. Office: 400 E Ohio St Chicago IL 60611-3322 Office Phone: 312-321-1202.

PINDYCK, BRUCE EBEN, lawyer, corporate financial executive; b. NYC, Sept. 21, 1945; s. Sylvester and Lillian (Breslow) P.; m. Mary Ellen Schwartz, Aug. 18, 1968; children: Ashley Beth, Eben Spencer, Blake Michael Lawrence. AB, Columbia U., 1967, JD, 1970, MBA, 1971. Bar: N.Y. 1971, Wis. 1987. Assoc. Olwine, Connelly, Chase, O'Donnell & Weyher, NYC, 1971-80; asst. gen. counsel Peat, Marwick, Mitchell & Co., NYC, 1980-82; ptnr. Hollyer, Jones, Pindyck, Brady & Chira, NYC, 1983-87; pres., CEO Meridian Industries, Inc., Milw., 1985—, also chmn. bd. dirs.; CEO Majilite Corp., Dracut, Mass., 1987—, also chmn. bd. dirs. Mem. capital campaign com. Columbia U., 1984-87. Mem. bd. visitors Columbia Coll., 2001—; bd. dirs. Harambee Cmty. Sch., 1991—96, Milw. Ballet Co., 1993—97, Milw. Pub. Mus., 1994—98, The Private Bank, Milw., 2005—, Jr. Achievement, 2005—. Mem. Columbia Coll. Alumni Assn. (regional dir. 1988-94, v.p. 1994-98, exec. com., 1994-98), World Pres.'s Orgn. Office: 100 E Wisconsin Ave Milwaukee WI 53202-4107 Home Phone: 414-352-9196; Office Phone: 414-224-0610. E-mail: bpindyck@meridiancompanies.com.

PING, CHARLES JACKSON, philosophy educator, retired university president; b. Phila., June 15, 1930; s. Cloudy J. and Mary M. (Marion) P.; m. Claire Oates, June 5, 1951; children: Andrew, Ann Shelton. BA, Rhodes Coll., 1951; B.D., Louisville Presbyn. Theol. Sem., 1954; PhD, Duke, 1961. Assoc. prof. philosophy Alma Coll., 1962-66; prof. philosophy Tusculum Coll., 1966-69, v.p., dean faculty, 1967-68, acting pres., 1968-69; provost Central Mich. U., Mt. Pleasant, 1969-75; pres. Ohio U., Athens, 1975-94, pres. emeritus, Trustee prof. philosophy and edn., 1994—, co.-dir. Manasseh Cutler Scholars Program, dir. Ping Inst. for Tchg. Humanities, 1994-99, dir. emeritus, 1999—. Bd. dirs. Wing Lung Bank Internat. Inst. for Bus. Devel., Hong Kong; trustee Louisville Presbyn. Theol. Sem., Muskingum Coll., Ohio; mem. adv. bd. Inst. Ednl. Mgmt. of Harvard U.; chair Commn. Planning for Future of Higher Edn., Kingdom of Swaziland; mem. Commn. on Higher Edn. Republic of Namibia. Author: Ohio University in Perspective, 1985, Meaningful Nonsense, 1966, also articles. Fulbright Sr. Rsch. scholar for So. Africa, 1995. Mem. Coun. on Internat. Ednl. Exch. (chair bd.), David C. Lam Inst. for East-West Studies (bd. dirs.), Coun. Internat. Exch. Scholars (bd. dirs., chair Africa com.). Office: Ohio U Office of Pres Emeritus Athens OH 45701 E-mail: ping@ohio.edu.

PINIELLA, LOU (LOUIS VICTOR PINIELLA), professional baseball team manager; b. Tampa, Fla., Aug. 28, 1943; m. Anita Garcia, Apr. 12, 1967; children: Lou, Kristi, Derrick. Student, U. Tampa. Outfielder various minor-league teams, 1962-68, Cleve. Indians, 1968, Kans. City Royals, 1969-73, NY Yankees, 1974-84, coach, 1984-85, mgr., 1985-87, 1988, gen. mgr., 1987-88, spl. adv., TV announcer, 1989; mgr. Cin. Reds, 1990-92, Seattle Mariners, 1992—2002, Tampa Bay Devil Rays, 2003—05, Chgo. Cubs, 2006—; baseball analyst ESPN, 2005—06. Named Am. League Rookie of the Yr Baseball Writers Assoc of Amer, 1969; Named to Am. League All-Star Team, 1972; Named Am. League Mgr. of the Yr, 1995, 2001; recipient Ellis Island Medal of Honor, 1990 Achievements include winning two World Series while playing for the NY Yankees, 1977-78. Office: Chgo Cubs Wrigley Field 1060 W Addison St Chicago IL 60613

PINK, MICHAEL, performing company executive; b. York, Eng. Trained as classical dancer, Royal Ballet Sch. Dancer English Nat. Ballet, 1975—85; founding dir. Ballet Ctrl., London, 1987—91; assoc. dir. Northern Ballet, 1988; artistic dir. Milw. Ballet. Internat. tchr. Norwegian Nat. Ballet, Aterballetto, Balleto di Toscanna Italy, The Hartford Ballet, Rozas Dance Co., London Contemporary Dance Co., White Oaks Dance Project, Ballet Rambert, English Nat. Ballet, Phoenix Dance Co., London Ballet. Recipient First Pl. in inaugural, Ursula Moreton Choreographic Competition, First Pl., Royal Soc. of Arts Competition. Office: Milwaukee Ballet 504 W National Ave Milwaukee WI 53204 E-mail: michael@milwaukeeballet.org.

PINKEL, GARY, college football coach; b. Akron, Ohio, Apr. 27, 1952; m. Vicki Pinkel; children: Erin, Geoff, Blake. BS in Edn., Kent St. Univ., 1973, grad. studies, Bowling Green. Grad. asst. Kent State U. Golden Flashes, 1974—75; tight ends coach Washington U. Huskies, 1976, wide receivers coach, 1979—83, offensive coord., 1984—90; wide receivers coach Bowling Green St. U. Falcons, 1977—78; head coach U. Toledo Rockets, 1991—2000, U. Mo. Tigers, 2001—. amed to Kent State Hall of Fame, 1997. Office: Univ Mo c/o Tigers Athletics Columbia MO 65211*

PINSKY, MICHAEL S., lawyer; b. Chgo., July 25, 1945; s. Joseph and Irene (Sodakoff) P.; m. Judy R. Rabin, Sept. 29, 1974; children: David, Susie, Jodie. BS, U. Ill., 1967; JD, DePaul U., 1971. Bar: Ill. 1971. Conferee, revenue agt. IRS, Chgo., 1967-72; ptnr. Levenfeld & Kanter, Chgo., 1972-80, Levenfeld, Eisenberg Janger, Chgo., 1980-84, Vedder Price, Kaufman & Kammholz, Chgo., 1984-88, Gottlieb & Schwartz, Chgo., 1989-92, Levin & Schreder, Chgo., 1993-97, Altheimer & Gray, Chgo., 1997-2000, Schain, Burney, Ross & Citron, Ltd., 2000—. Bd. dirs. Better Boys Found., Chgo., 1989-94; mem. planned giving com. Am. Soc. for Technion, 1997—. Mem. Am. Bar Assn., Assn. of Bar of State of Ill., Assn. of Bar of City of Chgo. (com. chmn. 1984-86). Office: 222 N La Salle St Ste 1910 Chicago IL 60601-1102 Home: 1212 Carol Ln Glencoe IL 60022-1105 Office Phone: 312-332-0200. Business E-Mail: mpinsky@Schainlaw.com.

PIPER, ADDISON LEWIS, securities executive; b. Mpls., Oct. 10, 1946; s. Harry Cushing and Virginia (Lewis) P.; m. Louise Wakefield (div.); children: Gretchen, Tad, William; m. Cynthia Schuneman, Nov. 14, 1979; children: Elisabeth LaBelle, Richard LaBelle. BA in Econs., Williams Coll., 1968; MBA, Stanford U., 1972. Mktg. cons. Earl Savage and Co., Mpls., 1968-69; mem. capital market dept. Piper and Jaffray, Mpls., 1969-70; asst. syndicate mgr. Piper, Jaffray and Hopwood, Mpls., 1972-73, v.p., 1973-79, dir. trading, 1973-77, dir. sales, 1977-79, exec. v.p., dir. mktg., 1979-83, chief exec. officer, chmn. mgmt. com., 1983—, chmn. bd. dirs., 1988—2003; vice chmn., dir. Piper Jaffray Cos. (spun off from U.S. Bancorp), Mpls., 2003—. Adv. com. N.Y. Stock Exch., 1966-90; bd. dirs. Allina Health Systems, Greenspring Corp., Mpls., Minn. Bus. Partnership, Mpls., Abbott Northwestern Hosp., Mpls.; trustee CARE Found., Mpls. Fin. chmn. Senator Durenberger Fin. Com., Mpls., 1980-88; chmn. Minn. Pub. Radio, 1985-95. Mem. Securities Industry Assn. (bd. govs. 1986-90, tax policy com.), Country Club of the Rockies (Colo.), Mpls. Club, Ventana Canyon (Tucson), Woodhill Country Club (Wayzata). Republican. Episcopalian. Avocations: skiing, golf, hunting, tennis, horseback riding. Office: Piper Jaffray Cos J1012058 800 Nicollet Mall Ste 800 Minneapolis MN 55402-7020

PIPER, KATHLEEN, former political organization administrator; b. Ida County, Iowa; d. Pat and Rita Donahey McGuire; m. James Carl Piper, 1971; 2 children. Student, U. Iowa, Morningside Coll., Mt. Marty Coll. Co-owner Pied Piper Flower Shop, Yankton, S.D., 1986; vice chair Yankton County Dem. Com., 1980-95, state ctrl. committeewoman, 1995—; commr. Yankton County, 1986—, chair, 1996; state ctrl. com. S.D. Dem. Party, 1989-99, exec. bd., 1992-99, chairwoman, 1996-99. Mem. health care adv. com. Senator Tom Daschle, 1991—. Del. Nat. Dem. Conv., N.Y.C., 1992; mem. Gold adv. coun. appointed by Gov., 1993-95; participant Pres. Clinton and Hillary Rodham-Clinton's Health Care Initiative Rev., White House, 1993, Gt. Plains Rural Health Summit, 1994, Pres., Clinton and SBA Chief Roundtable Discussion Small Bus. and Health Care Reform, Washington, 1994; appointed del. White House Conf. Small Bus., 1994. Recipient Woman of Yr. award Ed Yankton Daily Press and Dakota, 1986, Emerging Leader for S.D. award Sioux Falls Argus Leader, 1990. Mem. S.D. County Commr. Assn. (exec. bd. 1992-94). Roman Catholic. Home: PO Box 737 Sioux Falls SD 57101-0737 also: 4412 Woolworth Ave Omaha NE 68105-1757

PIPER, ODESSA, chef; m. Terry Theise. Chef L'Etoile Restaurant, Madison, Wis., 1976—. Contbr. Wis. Pub. Radio, NPR; cons. Ctr. for Integrated Agrl. Sys., U. Wis., Madison. Contbr. Fine Cooking, Food & Wine, Bon Appetit, Eating Well, Wine Spectator, Sierra. Recipient award, James Beard Found., 2001. Mem.: Women Chefs and Restauranteurs (mem. scholarship com.), Chefs Collaborative 2000 (bd. dirs.). Office: L'Etoile Restaurant 25 N Pinckney Madison WI 53711

PIPPIN, M. LENNY, food products executive; m. Judy Pippin. BA, Fla. Atlantic U. CEO Albert Fischer, N.A., Dallas; pres., CEO Lykes Bros. Inc., Tampa, Fla., 1997-99, The Schwan Food Co., Marshall, Minn., 1999—. Office: The Schwan Food Co 115 W College Dr Marshall MN 56258 Office Fax: 507-537-8226.

PIRAINO, THOMAS ANTHONY, JR., lawyer; b. Cleve., July 12, 1949; s. Thomas Anthony and Margaret (Stephens) P.; m. Barbara McWilliams, Sept. 4, 1976; children: Margaret, Ann, Mary. BA in History, magna cum laude, Allegheny Coll., 1971; JD, Cornell U., 1974. Bar: Ohio 1974. Assoc. counsel Parker-Hannifin Corp., Cleve., 1981-84, asst. gen. counsel, 1984-98, v.p., gen. counsel, sec., 1998—. Contbr. articles to legal jours. Mem. ABA, Ohio Bar Assn., Am. Corp. Counsel (sec. 1985—), Am. Soc. Corp. Secs. (past pres., Ohio chapter.) Avocations: tennis, jogging. Office: Parker Hannifin Corp 6035 Parkland Blvd Cleveland OH 44124-4141

PIRKLE, WILLIAM H., chemistry professor; b. Shreveport, La., May 2, 1934; married, 1956; 4 children. BS, U. Calif., Berkeley, 1959; PhD in Chemistry, U. Rochester, 1963. NSF fellow Harvard U., 1963-64; asst. prof., 1964-69; assoc. prof. chemistry U. Ill., Urbana, 1969-80, prof. chemistry, 1980—. Vis. prof. U. Wis., Madison, 1971. Assoc. editor Enantiomer; mem. editl. bd. Jour. Liquid Chromatogrpahy, Chirality, HRC, Supramolecular Chemistry. Recipient A.J.P. Martin medal Chromatographic Soc. Gt. Britain, 1990, Merit award Chgo. Chromatography Discussion Group, 1991, Chirality medal Swedish Assn. Pharm. Scis., 1994, Robert Boyle Gold medal Royal Soc. of Chemistry, 1998, ISCO award U. Nebr., 1998, Ea. Analytical award in Separation Sci., 1998, Dal Nogare award Del. Valley Chromatography Forum, 2000; Alfred P. Sloan fellow, 1971-72. Mem. Am. Chem. Soc. (Chromatography award 1994), Am. Chem. Soc. Office: U Illinois 161 Roger Adam Lab 505 S Mathews Ave Urbana IL 61801-3617

PIRSCH, CAROL MCBRIDE, retired county official, state senator, community relations manager; b. Omaha, Dec. 27, 1936; d. Lyle Erwin and Hilfrie Louise (Lebeck) McBride; m. Allen I. Pirsch, Mar. 28, 1954 (dec.); children: Pennie Elizabeth, Pamela Elaine, Patrice Eileen, Phyllis Erika, Peter Allen, Perry Andrew. Student, U. Miami, Oxford, Ohio, U. Nebr., Omaha. Former mem. data processing staff Omaha (Nebr.) Pub. Schs.; former mem. wage practices dept. Western Electric Co., Omaha; former legal sec. Omaha; former office mgr. Pirsch Food Brokerage Co., Inc., Omaha; former employment supr., mgr. pub. policy U.S. West Comm., Omaha; mem. Nebr. Senate, 1979-97; commr. Douglas County, 1997—2005, chair, 1999, 2004, vice chair, 2001, 2003. Founder, 1st pres., bd. dirs. Nebr. Coalition for Victims of Crime (Lifetime award 2002); bd. dirs. Centris Fed. Credit Union, 1st v.p., 2003—. Mem. Omaha Douglas County Bldg. Commn., 1997—2003, sec., 2000—03; cmty. cons. Omaha Jr. League, 2002—. Recipient Golden Elephant award, Kuhle award, 1986, Nebr. Coalition for Victims of Crime, Outstanding Legis. Efforts award YWCA, 1989, Breaking the Rule of Thumb award Nebr. Domestic Violence Sexual Assault Coalition, 1989, Cert. of Appreciation award U.S. Dept. Justice, 1988, Partnership award N.E. Credit Union League, 1995, Wings award LWV Greater Omaha, 1995, N.E. VFW Spl. Recognition award for Exceptional Svc., 1995, Victim Rights Week Recognition award, 1995, Victim Adv. Lifetime Achievement award, 2002; Crime Victims Adv. award Nebr. Atty. Gen., 1995. Mem. VASA, Nat. Orgn. Victim Assistance (Outstanding Legis. Leadership award 1981), Freedom Found., Douglas County Hist. Soc., Nebr. Taxpayers Assn., Keystone Citizen Patrol (Comm. Network of Citizen Patrols award, 1995), Audubon Soc., N.W. Cmty. Club, Keystone Task Force (Keystoner of the month, 1987, Queen Keystone, 2002), Omaha Bus. and Profl. Rep. Women.

PIRTLE, LAURIE LEE, retired women's college basketball coach; b. Columbus, Ohio, Jan. 1, 1958; BS in Phys. Edn., Ohio State U., 1980. Asst. coach girl's basketball William Fisher HS, Lancaster, Ohio, 1981—82; head coach Capital U., Columbus, Ohio, 1982—86, U. Cin., 1986—2007. Named Coach of Yr. Dist.III Ohio Athletic Commn. and Converse III, 1985-86, Ohio Intercollegiate Coaches Assn., 1985, Metro Conf., 1989, Conf. USA, 1999, Leading Woman in Cin., 2000. Mem. Women's Basketball Coaches Assn., Greater Cin. and No. Ky., Women's Sports Assn. (mem. com.).

PISKORSKI, THOMAS JAMES, lawyer; b. Chgo., Oct. 30, 1955; m. Susan P. Piskorski, July 5, 1986. BS, Marquette U., 1977; MBA, JD, Notre Dame U., 1981. Bar: Ill. 1981, US Dist. Ct. (no. dist.) Ill. 1981, US Ct. Appeals (7th cir.) 1982, US Ct. Appeals (10th cir.) 1986, US Dist. Ct. (no. dist.) Ill. 1986, US Dist. Ct. (no. dist.) Calif. 1994, US Dist. Ct. (ea. dist.) Wis. 1995, US Ct. Appeals (5th cir.) 1996, US Ct. Appeals DC cir. 1997, US Ct. Appeals (ea. dist.) Mich. 1998, US Ct. Appeals (6th cir.) 1998, US Supreme Ct. 1998, US Dist. Ct., (ctrl. dist.) Ill. 1999, US Ct. Appeals (8th cir.) 2000, US Dist. Ct. (we. dist.) Mich. 2002, US Ct. Appeals (1st cir.) 2002, US Dist. Ct. (ea. dist.) Tex. 2004, US Ct. Appeals (4th cir.) 2004. Law clk. to hon. sr. dist. judge Robert A. Grant U.S. Dist. Ct. (no. dist.) Ind., South Bend, 1980-82; assoc. Seyfarth, Shaw, Fairweather & Geraldson, Chgo., 1982-89, ptnr., 1989—, Seyfarth Shaw LLP, chmn. lawyer devel. com. Instr. Loyola U. Coll. Law, Chgo., 1985—88. Contbr. articles to profl. jours. Mem.: Chgo. Bar Assn. (labor and employment law sect.), Ill. Bar Assn. (labor and employment law sect.), ABA (labor and employment law sect., litig. sect.). Office: Seyfarth Shaw LLP 55 E Monroe St Ste 4200 Chicago IL 60603-5863 Office Phone: 312-346-8000. Office Fax: 312-269-8869. Business E-Mail: tpiskorski@seyfarth.com.

PITONIAK, GREGORY EDWARD, mayor; b. Detroit, Aug. 12, 1954; s. Anthony Edward and Constance Elizabeth (Matuszak) P.; m. Denise Ruth Kadi, Apr. 21, 1979; children: Gregory, Mallory. BA, U. Mich., 1976; Masters, U. N.C., 1980. Adminstrv. asst. Taylor (Mich.) Neighborhood Devel. Com., 1977-78; pers. analyst Downriver Community Conf., Southgate, Mich., 1978-79; dir. client svcs. Econ. Devel. Corp. Wayne County, Dearborn, Mich., 1979-84, exec. dir. Livonia, Mich., 1984-88; dir. econ. dev. Downriver Community Conf., Southgate, Mich., 1988; state rep. Mich. Ho. Reps., Lansing, 1989-97; mayor City of Taylor, 1997—. Councilman Taylor City Coun., 1981-88, chmn., 1983-85, 87-88; pres. Mich. Young Dems., 1982-84; treas. 15th Congl. Dist. Dem. Orgn., Taylor, 1988-90. amed Outstanding Young Person, Taylor Jaycees, 1987, State Legislator of Yr., Mich. Credit Union League, 1993. Mem. Am. Econ. Devel. Coun. (cert. econ. developer 1984), Am. Soc. Pub. Adminstrn., Polish Am. Congress, Dem. Club Taylor, KC. Roman Catholic. Home: 9686 Rose St Taylor MI 48180-3046 Office: City of Taylor 23555 Goddard Rd Taylor MI 48180-4116

PITOT, HENRY CLEMENT, III, pathologist, educator; b. NYC, May 12, 1930; s. Henry Clement and Bertha (Lowe) Pitot; m. Julie S. Schutten, July 29, 1954; children: Bertha, Anita, Jeanne, Catherine, Henry, Michelle, Lisa, Patrice. BS in Chemistry, Va. Mil. Inst., 1951; MD, Tulane U., 1955, PhD in Biochemistry, 1959, DSc (hon.), 1995. Instr. pathology Med. Sch. Tulane U., New Orleans, 1955-59; postdoctoral fellow McArdle Lab. U. Wis., Madison, 1959-60, mem. faculty Med. Sch., 1960—, prof. pathology and oncology, 1966-99, prof. emeritus, 1999—, chmn. dept. pathology, 1968-71, acting dean Med. Sch., 1971-73, dir. McArdle Lab., 1973-91. Recipient Borden Undergrad. Rsch. award, 1955, Leaderle Faculty award, 1962, Career Devel. award, Nat. Cancer Inst., NIH, 1965, Parke-Davis award, 1968, Noble Found. Rsch. award, 1984, Esther Langer award, U. Chgo., 1984, Hilldale award, U. Wis., 1991, Founders award, Chem. Industry Inst. Toxicology, 1993, Midwest Regional chpt. Soc. Toxicology award, 1996, Emeritus Faculty award, U. Wis. Med. Sch., 2001, Disting. Lifetime Toxicology award, Soc. Toxicology, 2003, Gold-headed Cane award, Am. Soc. Investigative Pathology, 2005, Lifetime Disting. Alumnus award, Tulane Med. Sch., 2005, Disting. Svc. award, Assn. Pathology Chairs, 2005. Fellow: AAAS, N.Y. Acad. Scis.; mem.: Soc. Toxicologic Pathologists, Soc. Toxicology, Soc. Surg. Oncology (Lucy J. Wortham award 1981), Soc. Exptl. Biology and Medicine (pres. 1991—93), Am. Soc. Investigative Pathology (pres. 1976—77), Am. Cancer Soc. (life), Japanese Cancer Soc. (hon.), Am. Chem. Soc., Am. Soc. Biochemistry and Molecular Biology, Am. Assn. Cancer Rsch., Am. Soc. Cell Biology. Roman Catholic. Home: 314 Robin Pkwy Madison WI 53705-4931 Office: U Wis McArdle Lab Cancer Rsch 1400 University Ave Madison WI 53706-1599 Office Phone: 608-262-3247. Business E-Mail: pitot@oncology.wisc.edu.

PITT, BERTRAM, cardiologist, educator, consultant; b. Kew Gardens, NY, Apr. 27, 1932; s. David and Shirley (Blum) P., m. Elaine Liberstein, Aug. 10, 1962; children: Geoffrey, Jessica, Jillian BA, Cornell U., 1953; MD, U. Basel, Switzerland, 1959. Diplomate Am. Bd. Internal Medicine, Am. Bd. Cardiology. Intern Beth Israel Hosp., NYC, 1959-60, resident Boston, 1960-63; fellow in cardiology Johns Hopkins U., Balt., 1966-67, from instr. to assoc. prof., 1967-77; prof. medicine, dir. div. cardiology U. Mich., Ann Arbor, 1977-91, prof. medicine Sch. Medicine, 1991—2005, prof. medicine emeritus Sch. Medicine, 2005—. Author: Atlas of Cardiovascular Nuclear Medicine, 1977; editor: Cardiovascular Nuclear Medicine, 1974; co-editor: Clinical Trials in

Cardiology, 1997, Current Controlled Trials in Cardiovascular Medicine, 1999—. Served to capt. U.S. Army, 1963-65. Mem. ACP, Am. Coll. Cardiology, Am. Soc. Clin. Investigation, Assn. Am. Physicians, Am. Physiol. Soc., Am. Heart Assn. (James. B. Herrick award 2005), Assn. Univ. Cardiologists, Am. Coll. Chest Physicians, Johns Hopkins U. Soc. Scholars. Home: 24 Ridgeway St Ann Arbor MI 48104-1739 Office: U Mich Divsn Cardiology 1500 E Medical Center Dr Ann Arbor MI 48109-0005 Office Phone: 734-709-9894. Business E-Mail: bpitt@umich.edu.

PITTELKO, ROGER DEAN, clergyman, theology studies educator; b. Elk Reno, Okla., Aug. 18, 1932; s. Elmer Henry and Lydia Caroline (Nieman) Pittelko. AA, Concordia Coll., 1952; BA, Concordia Sem., St. Louis, 1954, MDiv, 1957, STM, 1958; postgrad., Chgo. Luth. Theol. Sem., 1959-61; ThD, Am. Div. Sch., Pineland, Fla., 1968; DMin, Faith Evang. Luth. Sem., Tacoma, 1983. Ordained to ministry Luth. Ch., 1958. Vicar St. John Luth. Ch., SI, NY, 1955—56, asst. pastor New Orleans, 1958-59; pastor Concordia Luth. Ch., Berwyn, Ill., 1959-63, Luth. Ch. Holy Spirit, Elk Grove Village, Ill., 1962—87; chmn. Commn. on Worship, Luth. Ch.-Mo. Synod, 1982—92, chmn. commn. worship, 1994—98, asst. bishop Midwest region English dist., 1983, pres., bishop English dist., 1987-97, 3d v.p., 1997—2001; prof. pastoral theology Concordia Theol. Sem., Ft. Wayne, Ind., 1997—2003; pastor Trinity Luth. Ch., Villa Park, Ill., 2003—05, Grace English Luth. Ch., Chgo., 2005—06. Author: Guide to Introducing Lutheran Worship; contbr. articles to jours. Mem.: Luth. Acad. for Scholarship, Concordia Hist. Inst., Itasca Country Club (Ill.), Maywood Sportsmans Club (Ill.). Republican. Lutheran. Office: Trinity Luth Ch 300 S Ardmore Ave Villa Park IL 60181-2699 Office Phone: 630-834-3440. Personal E-mail: emep@juno.com.

PITTELKOW, MARK ROBERT, physician, dermatologist, educator, researcher; b. Milw., Dec. 16, 1952; s. Robert Bernard and Barbara Jean (Thomas) P.; m. Gail L. Gamble, Nov. 26, 1977; children: Thomas, Cameron, Robert. BA, Northwestern U., 1975; MD, Mayo Med. Sch., 1979. Intern then resident Mayo Grad. Sch., 1979-84, post-doctoral exptl. pathology, 1981-83; from asst. to assoc. prof. dermatology Mayo Med. Sch., Rochester, Minn., 1984-95, prof. dermatology, 1995—, assoc. prof. biochemistry and molecular biology, 1992—. Cons. Mayo Clinic/Found., Rochester, 1984— Fellow Am. Acad. Dermatology; mem. AAAS, Am. Dermatol. Assn., Soc. Investigative Dermatology, Am. Burn Assn., Am. Soc. Cell Biology, N.Y. Acad. Scis., Chi Psi. Achievements include discovery of skin and epidermal growth control; autocrine growth factor production; growth and differentiation of keratinocytes. Home: 721 12th Ave SW Rochester MN 55902-2027 Office: Mayo Clinic 200 1st St SW Rochester MN 55905-0002 Office Phone: 507-284-2555. Business E-Mail: pittelkow.mark@mayo.edu.

PITTS, BEVERLEY J., academic administrator; m. William Pitts; 2 children. BA in English, Anderson U., 1968; MA in Journalism, Ball State U., 1971, EdD in Higher Edn., 1981. Chair, dept. comm. Anderson U., 1980—85; coord., News Editl. Sequence Ball State U., 1985—88, dir. grad. studies in journalism, 1985—88, dir. gen. studies, 1988—90, dir. academic assessment and general studies, 1990, asst. provost, exec. dir. rsch. and undergraduate curriculum, 1990—92, acting provost, 1994, 2001, acting supr. for information technology, 2000—01, assoc. provost, 1993—2002, provost, v.p. for academic affairs, 2002, acting pres., 2004; pres. U. Indpls., 2005—. Instr. english Anderson U., 1977—80, advisor student publs., 1977—85, asst. prof. comm., 1980—85; assoc. prof. journalism Ball State U., 1985—90, prof. journalism, 1991—. Staff writer, researcher, comm. cons. Nat. Football League Players Assn., Washington, DC (Nat. Football League Players Assn. award of Excellence, 2000); contbr. articles to profl. jours. and newspapers; book review editor College Media Review, 1982—85; design editor College Media Review, 1985—86; reviewer Journalism Educator, 1990—99, grant reviewer Nat. Endowment for the Humanities, 1990, co-publisher (textbook) The Process of Media Writing, 1997, editl. bd. mem. Perspectives, Journal of the Association of General and Liberal Studies, 1997—2001, co-founder Ind. Teachers of Writing, 1981, pres., 1982—83, program chair, fall conf., 1982. Bd. dir. Family Svcs. of Delaware County, 1999—2002, Lyn St. James Found., 2000—02, Cmty. Alliance to Promote Edn., 2001—03, Delaware County CofC, 2003—, Sagamore Inst., 2004—, Ind. Youth Inst., 2000—, chair, 2005; bd. dir. Muncie Rotary Club, 2000—04, sec., 2000—01, pres.-elect, 2001—02, pres., 2002—03; mem. Cmty. Found. Muncie, Ind. Humanities Coun.; bd. dir. pres. Prof. Garfield Found., 2004—; bd. dir. Delaware County Cmty. Found., 2000—, vice-chair, 2003—04, chair-elect, 2005; and several others. Recipient Anderson U. Outstanding Alumni award, 1999, Ball State U. Alumni award, 2000, Woman of Acheivement in Edn. award, Women in Communication; Ottoway Fellowship for Advanced Study, Am. Press Inst., Reston, Va., Ottoway Newspaper Found., 1986, Am. Press Inst. Fellowship for Advanced Study for Journalism Educators, 1987, Fellowship, Think Tank, Coll. of Scis. and Humanities, Ball State U., 1988, Fulbright Scholarship to study in Germany, 1994. Mem.: Assn. for General and Liberal Studies (nat. bd. dir. 1989—94, pres. 1993—94), Assn. for Edn. in Journalism and Mass Comm., Am. Conf. Academic Deans, Am. Assn. U. Adminstrators, Am. Assn. Higher Edn., Nat. Football League Players Assn. (cons. 1984—), Profl. Atheletes Found. (bd. dir. 1990—2004), Sigma Delta Chi. Office: U Indpls 1400 East Hanna Ave Indianapolis IN 46227-3697 Office Phone: 317-788-3211.

PITTS, TERENCE RANDOLPH, museum director, consultant; b. St. Louis, Feb. 5, 1950; s. Benjamin Randolph and Barbara Avalon (Gilliam) P.; children: Jacob Richard, Rebecca Suzanne. BA, U. Ill., 1972, MLS, 1974; MA in Art History, U. Ariz., 1986. Registrar Ctr. for Creative Photography, Tucson, 1976-77, curator, 1978-88, dir., 1989-2000; exec. dir. Cedar Rapids (Iowa) Mus. Art, 2000—. Cons. Art and Architecture Thesaurus, Getty Mus., 1984—. Author: (with others) George Fiske: Yosemite Photographer, 1981, Edward Weston: Color Photography; author exhbn. catalogs Four Spanish Photographers, 100 Years of Photography in the American West, Photography in the American Grain, Reframing America. Fellow Nat. Endowment Arts, 1983; travel grantee Nat. Mus. Act, 1979, rsch. grantee U. Ariz., 1983. Office: Cedar Rapids Mus Art 410 3d Ave SE Cedar Rapids IA 52401 E-mail: pitts@crma.org.

PIVERONUS, PETER JOHN, JR., education educator; b. Boston, Nov. 29, 1941; s. Peter John Sr. and Rose Camella (Pasciuto) P.; m. Bonnie Jean Kennedy, June 7, 1969 (div. 1981); children: Elizabeth Schaeffler, William Schaeffler, Michelle Montesano; m. Elisabeth Doris Roth, Nov. 21, 1988; children: Shannon Roth, Sara Roth. BA, Boston U., 1964, MA, 1966; PhD, Mich. State U., 1972. Asst. prof. SUNY, Buffalo, 1967-69, Claflin Coll., Orangeburg, SC, 1969-70; adj. prof. Lansing CC, Mich., 1972—, Montcalm CC, Sidney, 1973—2000, Jackson CC, 1979—2006, Baker Coll., Owosso, 2002—06. Vis. prof. Mich. State U., East Lansing, 1986, Alma (Mich.) Coll., 1987. Editor, contbr.: Conflict in Ireland, 1976; contbr. articles to profl. jours. Precinct del. Ingham County Dems., Lansing, 1980-81; trustee Southland Complex Condo Assn., Lansing, 1987-90; pres. Gaelic League of Lansing, 1981-82. HEW fellow Claflin Coll., 1969-70; postdoctoral rsch. grantee U. Mich. Ctr. for Russian and East European Studies, 1985. Mem. Am. Com. for Irish Studies, Ohio Employee Ownership Ctr., Capital Ownership Group, at. Ctr. for Employee Ownership, Irish-Am. Cultural Inst., Soc. for History of Discoveries, Mich. Assn. Higher Edn. (faculty senator 1978-79), Mich. Edn. Assn., Econ. and Bus. Hist. Soc. Roman Catholic. Avocations: reading, travel, camping, boating. Office: Lansing Community Coll 419 N Capitol Ave Lansing MI 48933-1207 Office Phone: 517-483-1028. Business E-Mail: pivetop@lcc.edu.

PIZER, HOWARD CHARLES, sports and entertainment executive; b. Chgo., Oct. 23, 1941; s. Edwin and Estyr (Seeder) P.; m. Sheila Graff, June 14, 1964; children: Jacqueline, Rachel. BBA, U. Wis., 1963; JD magna cum laude, Northwestern U., 1966. Assoc. McDermott, Will & Emery, Chgo., 1966-72; ptnr. Katten, Muchin, Zavis, Chgo., 1972-74; exec. v.p., gen. counsel Balcor Co., Skokie, Ill., 1975-80; exec. v.p. Chgo. White Sox, Chgo., 1981—. Exec. v.p. United Ctr. Joint Venture. Past pres. Chgo. Spl. Olympics; bd. dirs. Chgo. Conv. and Tourism Bur., Inc., 1983—, Spl. Children's Charities, 1984—, Chgo. Baseball Cancer Charities, 1983—, Near West Side Cmty. Devel. Corp. Mem. Chgo. Bar Assn., Standard Club Chgo., Briarwood County. Home: 300 Euclid Ave Winnetka IL 60093-3606 Office: Chgo White Sox 333 W 35th St Chicago IL 60616-3651

PIZZUTI, RONALD A., real estate developer; m. Ann Pizzuti; 3 children. BS, Kent State U., 1962. Chmn., CEO Pizzuti Cos., Columbus, Ohio, 1976—. Mem. Ohio Arts & Sports Facilities Commn.; bd. trustees Kenyon Coll.; chair bd. trustees Kent State U.; bd. dir. Kent State Found. Named one of Top 200 Collectors, ARTnews Mag., 2003—06; recipient Shining Stars of Seminole County. Lifetime Achievement award, 2002. Mem.: Columbus C. of C. (exec. com.). Avocation: Collecting modern and contemporary art. Office: Pizzuti Cos Ste 800 Two Miranova Pl Columbus OH 43215 Business E-Mail: rpizzuti@pizzuti.com.

PLACE, MICHAEL D., priest, former health association administrator; b. 1944; MA in Ecclesiastical History, D in Sacred Theology, Cath. U. Am.; MDiv, lic. in sacred theology, St. Mary of the Lake Sem. Ordained priest Roman Cath. Ch., 1970. Assoc. pastor Most Holy Redeemer Parish, Evergreen, Ill., 1970—74; mem. faculty, adminstr. St. Mary of the Lake Sem., Mundelein, Ill., 1977—81; dean Athenaeum of Ohio, 1981—84; acad. dean Mt. St. Mary's Sem. of the West, 1981—84; consul for policy devel. Archdiocese of Chgo., 1984—98; pres., CEO Cath. Health Assn., St. Louis, 1998—2005. Named one of 100 Most Powerful People in Healthcare, Modern Healthcare mag., 2002, 2003.

PLACHE, KIMBERLY MARIE, state legislator; b. Racine, Wis., Jan. 4, 1961; Student, U. Wis., Whitewater, 1978-81; BS, U. Wis., Parkside-Kenosha, 1984. Legis. asst. to state rep. Jeff Neubauer, 1984-88; mem. Wis. Assembly from 21st dist., madison, 1988-96, Wis. Senate from 21st dist., Madison, 1996—. Mem. NOW, AAUW, Wis. Action Coalition. Office: Wis State Assembly State Capital Madison WI 53702-0001 Home: 110 Emerald Dr Racine WI 53406-3422

PLAGMAN, RALPH, principal; Prin. George Washington High Sch., Cedar Rapids, Iowa, 1981—. Recipient Blue Ribbon Sch. award Dept. Edn., 1983, 91, 2000. Office: George Washington High Sch 2205 Forest Dr SE Cedar Rapids IA 52403-1653

PLAKMEYER, STEVE, food service executive; CFO Gordon Food Svc. Inc., Grand Rapids, Mich.

PLALE, JEFFREY T., state legislator; b. South Milwaukee, Wis., May 31, 1968; m. Elizabeth Plale; 2 children. BA in Comms. and Pub. Rels., Marquette U., Milw., 1990; MA in Comms. and Pub. Rels., Marquette U., 1992. Shareholder ops. specialist Strong Capital Mgmt., 1988—96; mem. Wis. State Assembly, Madison, 1996—, mem. bldg. commn., mem. com. on energy and utilities, fin. instns. com., mem. joint survey com. on retirement systems, transp. com. Alderman Town of South Milwaukee, 1993—96; mem. Milw. Irish Fest; chair cmty. fundraising Boy Scouts Am.; mem. Am. Legis. Exch. Coun., South Shore Christian Men's Fellowship, Dem. Leadership Coun. Recipient Freshman Legislator of the Session award, Ind. Bus. Assn. Wis., 1996. Mem.: NASD, Marquette U. Alumni Assn., Lions, Rotary. Democrat. Roman Catholic. Office: State Capitol Rm 107 N PO Box 8953 Madison WI 53708-8953 Address: 1404 18th Ave South Milwaukee WI 53172

PLANK, BETSY (MRS. SHERMAN V. ROSENFIELD), public relations counsel; b. Tuscaloosa, Ala., Apr. 3, 1924; d. Richard Jeremiah and Bettye (Hood) P.; m. Sherman V. Rosenfield, Apr. 10, 1954. Student, Bethany Coll., W.Va., 1940-43; AB, U. Ala., 1944. Continuity dir. radio sta. KQV, Pitts., 1944-47; account exec. Mitchell McKeown Orgn., Chgo., 1947-54; pub. rels. counsel Chgo. chpt. A.R.C., 1954-57; dir. pub. rels. Chgo. Coun. on Fgn. Rels., 1957-58; v.p. Ronald Goodman Pub. Rels. Counsel, Chgo., 1958-61; exec. v.p., treas., dir. Daniel J. Edelman, Inc., Chgo., 1961-73; dir. pub. rels. planning AT&T, NYC, 1973-74; dir. external rels. Ill. Bell, Chgo., 1974-90; prin. Betsy Plank Pub. Rels., Chgo., 1990—. Dep. chmn. VII World Congress on Pub. Rels., 1976; co-chmn. nat. commn. on Pub. Rels. Edn., 1984-87; mem. adv. bd. Ill. Issues, 1975—. Bd. dirs. United Way Chgo., 1986-90; chmn. Citizenship Coun. Met. Chgo., 1990-96, Betsy Plank chpt. Pub. Rels. Student Soc. Am., No. Ill. U.; trustee Found. for Pub. Rels. Rsch. and Edn., 1975-80; nat. bd. dirs. Girl Scouts U.S., 1975-85. Recipient Millennium award Coll. Journalism, U. Fla., 2000, Alexander Hamilton award, Inst. Pub. Rels., 2000, Plank Ctr. Pub. Rels. Studies, U. Ala., 2005; named one of World's 40 Leading Pub. Rels. Profls., Pub. Rels. News, 1984, Pub. Rels. Hall of Fame Rowan U., 2005. Fellow Pub. Rels. Soc. Am. (accredited, nat. pres. 1973, Outstanding Profl. award 1977, Outstanding Cmty. Svc. award 1989, Disting. Svc. award 2001, Plank Nat. Scholarships); mem. Ill. Coun. on Econ. Edn. (past chmn., trustee 1974—, Extraordinary Leadership award 2001), Internat. Pub. Rels. Assn., Chgo. Network (chmn. 1980-81), Arthur W. Page Soc. (lifetime achievement award 2000), Union League Club of Chgo., Econ. Club Chgo., Zeta Tau Alpha. Presbyterian.

PLANT, JOHN CHARLES, automotive executive; b. West Bromwich, West Midlands, Eng., Aug. 1, 1953; s. John and Florence (Harrison) P.; m. Christine Ann; children: Alexa Jayne, John Alexander. B in Commerce, Econs., Acctg. and Law, Birmingham U., Eng., 1974. Auditor Touche Ross, Birmingham, 1974-77; financier Lucas Auto Ltd., Birmingham, 1977—, Burnley, England, 1983—; mng. dir. Lucas Varity Elec. and Electronics, 1991—97; pres. Lucas Varity Automotive, 1999; pres., CEO TRW Chassis; gen. mgr. TRW Automotive, exec. v.p., 1999—2001, co-CEO, pres., CEO Livonia, Mich., 2001—. Bd. dirs. Martin Currie Portfolio Investment Trust PLC. Fellow Inst. Chartered Accts. in Eng. and Wales (mng. dir., FCA award 1981). Avocation: tennis. Office: TRW Automotive 12025 Tech Center Dr Livonia MI 48150

PLANT, THOMAS A., lawyer; b. 1948; Bar: Ohio, 1974. BA, Alfred U.; JD, Akron U. Sr. v.p., asst. gen. counsel Nat. City Corp., Cleve. Office: National City Corp 1900 E 9th St Fl 17 Cleveland OH 44114-3401

PLAPP, BRYCE VERNON, biochemistry educator; b. DeKalb, Ill., Sept. 11, 1939; s. Vernon Edgar and Eleanor Barbara (Kautz) P.; m. Rosemary Kuhn, June 13, 1962; children— Brendan Bryce, Laurel Andrea BS, Mich. State U., East Lansing, 1961; PhD, U. Calif.-Berkeley, 1966. Research assoc. J.W. Goethe U., Frankfurt/Main, Germany, 1966-68; research assoc. Rockefeller U., NYC, 1968-70; faculty U. Iowa, Iowa City, 1970—, prof. biochemistry, 1979—. Contbr. articles to profl. jours.; mem. editorial bd. Archives Biochemistry and Biophysics. Am. Cancer Soc. fellow, 1966-68 Mem. Am. Soc. for Biochemistry and Molecular Biology, Am. Chem. Soc., Sigma Xi Avocations: travel, sports. Office: Univ Iowa Dept Biochemistry 4-712 Iowa City IA 52242 Office Phone: 319-335-7909. E-mail: bv-plapp@uiowa.edu.

PLATT, JEFFREY LOUIS, experimental surgeon, immunologist, pediatric nephrologist, educator; b. New Rochelle, NY, Mar. 21, 1949; s. Charles Alfred and Paula Platt. BA in Politics with honors, NYU, 1971; postgrad., Columbia U., 1971-73; MD, U. Southern Calif., 1977. Diplomate Am. Bd. Pediatrics, Nat. Bd. Med. Examiners. Pediatrics intern Children's Hosp. LA, 1977-78, resident, 1978-79, Della M. Mudd resident, 1979-80; med. fellow in pediatric nephrology U. Minn., Mpls., 1980-85, instr. dept. pediatrics, 1985-86, asst. prof., 1986-88, assoc. prof. pediatrics and cell biology and neuroanatomy, 1988-92; prof. surgery, pediatrics and immunology depts. Duke U., Durham, NC, 1992—98, Dorothy W. and Joseph W. Beard prof. exptl. surgery, 1994—98; prof. surgery immunology and pediatrics Mayo Clinic, Rochester, Minn., 1998—2008, dir. transplantation biology, 2006—; prof. surgery U. Mich., 2008—, prof. microbiology and immunology, 2008—. Mem. editl. bd.: Transplantation, Transplant Immunology, Xenotransplantation, Jour. Immunology, Cellular Immunology; mem. editl. bd. Human Immunology, editor Innate Immunity; contbr. over 500 articles to med. jours.; author: 4 books. Recipient Clinician-Scientist award Am. Heart Assn., 1983-88, Established Investigator award Am. Heart Assn., 1988-93, Inst. Medicine of NAS. Mem. AAAS, NIH (Merit award), Assn. Am. Physicians, Fellow Am. Heart Assn (coun. kidney in cardiovasc. disease, coun. basic sci.), Internat. Soc. Nephrology, Am. Assn. Immunologists, Am. Fedn. Clin. Rsch., Am. Soc. ephrology, Am. Assn. Pathologists, Soc. for Devel. Biology, Clin. Immunology Soc., Soc. Pediatric Rsch., Soc. Glycobiology, Soc. Exptl. Biology and Medicine, Alpha Omega Alpha. Office: Dept Surgery Univ Mich Biomedical Sciences Res Bldg Ann Arbor MI 48109 Business E-Mail: platt.jeffrey@mayo.edu, plattjl@umich.edu.

PLAUT, JONATHAN VICTOR, rabbi; b. Chgo., Oct. 7, 1942; s. W. Gunther and Elizabeth (Strauss) P.; m. Carol Ann Fainstein, July 5, 1965; children: Daniel Abraham, Deborah Maxine. BA, Macalester Coll., St. Paul, Minn., 1964; postgrad., Hebrew Union Coll., Jerusalem, 1967-68; BHL, Hebrew Union Coll., Cin., 1968, MA, 1970, DHL, 1977, DD (hon.), 1995. Ordained rabbi, 1970. Rabbi Congregation Beth-El, Windsor, Ont., Canada, 1970-84; sr. rabbi Temple Emanu-El, San Jose, Calif., 1985-93; dir. comty. outreach and involvement Jewish Fed. of Met. Detroit, 1993-95; pres. JVP Fund Raising Cons., Inc., Farmington Hills, Mich., 1994—. Lectr. Assumption Coll. Sch., 1972-84, St. Clair Coll., 1982-84, U. Windsor, Ont., Can., 1984; adj. asst. prof. Santa Clara U., 1985-93; adj. prof. U. Detroit Mercy, 2002—; vis. Rabbinic scholar Temple Beth El, 1993—95; pres. JVP Fund Raising Cons., 1994—; rabbi emeritus Congregation Beth El, Traverse City, Mich., 1999—2004; rabbi Temple Beth Israel, Jackson, Mich., 2000—. Contbg. author: Reform Judaism in America: A Biographical Dictionary and Sourcebook, 1993; editor: Through the Sound of Many Voices, 1982, Jour. Can. Jewish Hist. Soc., 1976-83, The Jews of Windsor 1790-1990: A Historical Chronicle, 2007, One Voice: The Selected Sermons of W. Gunther Plaut, 2007, The Plaut Family Tracing the Legacy, 2007, also articles; host weekly program Religious Scope, Sta. CBET-TV, Religion in News, Sta. CKWW, 1971-84. Pres. Jewish Nat. Fund Windsor, 1978-81, chmn. bd. dirs., 1981-84; chmn. United Jewish Appeal Windsor, 1981-83, State of Israel Bonds, Windsor, 1980; nat. bd. dirs. Jewish Nat. Fund Can., 1972-84; pres. Reform Rabbis of Can., 1982-84; bd. dirs. Can. Jewish Congress, 1978-84, Jewish Family Svc. Santa Clara County, 1987-90, Jewish Fedn. Greater San Jose, 1986-93; chaplain San Jose Fire Dept., 1987-93; mem. exec. cabinet United Jewish Appeal, Windsor, 1971-84, mem. nat. rabbinic cabinet, 1993-95; mem. exec. com. Windsor Jewish Community Coun., 1970-84, chmn. 1975-84; mem. adv. coun. Riverview unit Windsor Hosp. Ctr., 1972-81; pres. Credit Counselling Svc. Met. Windsor, 1977-79. Honoree Jewish Nat. Fund, 1985. Mem. NCCJ, Can. Jewish Congress (nat. exec. bd. 1978-84), Can. Jewish Hist. Soc. (nat. v.p. 1974-84), Calif. Bd. Rabbis, Rabbinic Assn. Greater San Jose (chmn. 1986-87), Ctrl. Conf. Am. Rabbis, Nat. Assn. Temple Educators. Home and Office: 30208 Kingsway Dr Farmington Hills MI 48331-1648 Office Phone: 248-505-8888. Fax: 248-788-4144. Personal E-mail: jvplaut@earthlink.net.

PLEAU, LARRY (LAWRENCE WINSLOW PLEAU), professional sports team executive; b. Boston, June 29, 1947; s. Ernest and Norma (Knowles) Pl.; m. Wendy Sargent MacDougall, May 3, 1969; children, Steven Lawrence, Shannon Lynn. Grad. high sch. Player Montreal Canadiens, 1969-72, N.Eng. Whalers, Hartford, Conn., 1972-79; asst. coach Hartford Whalers, 1979-80, coach, gen. mgr., 1980-83, asst. gen. mgr., 1983-84, coach, 1988-89; coach, gen. mgr. Binghamton Whalers, NY, 1984-88; asst. gen. mgr. player devel. NY Rangers, 1989, asst. gen. mgr., v.p. player personnel; gen. mgr. St. Louis Blues, 1997—. Player U.S. Olympic Hockey Team, Grenoble, France, 1968, U.S. Nat. Hockey Team, Stockholm, 1969, U.S.A. Hockey Team, Providence, 1976; radio, TV commentator, ESPN, Hartford, 1979-80; owner Bridge Marina Inc. With U.S. Army, 1967-69. Mem. All-Star Teams, 1973, 74, 75; named Coach of Yr. Am. Hockey League, 1986-87, Exec. of Yr., The Sporting News, 1999-2000. Democrat. Achievements include being a member of Stanley Cup Champion Montreal Canadiens, 1971. Avocations: deep sea fishing, golf, tennis. Office: St Louis Blues Hockey Club Savvis Ctr 1401 Clark Ave Saint Louis MO 63103

PLEHAL, JAMES BURTON, career officer; m. Sandra Plehal; 1 child, Andrew. BA in Polit. Sci. with hons, U. Utah, 1969; Diploma, U.S. Naval Submarine Sch. Ensign USN, 1969; advanced through ranks to rear adm. USNR; various assignments to Res. Cryptologic Area Coord., Ctrl., Naval Res. Security Group Program, 1995-99; comdr. Naval Res. Security Group Command, Ft. Worth, 1998—; asst. v.p. and fin. cons. Merrill Lynch, St. Paul; active duty dep. dir. Nat. Infrastructure Protection Ctr., Washington, 2001—. Mem., mental health provider Red Wing Charter Commn., Minn.; former city coun., Dist. Legal Ethics Com. Office: 1015 W 4th St Red Wing MN 55066-2421

PLESTED, WILLIAM G., III, surgeon; b. Wichita, Kans., June 1, 1936; m. Carolyn Plested. BS, U. Colo.; MD, U. Kans., 1962. Diplomate Am. Bd. Surgery, Am. Bd. Thoracic Surgery. Intern UCLA, 1962-63, resident, 1963-68, asst. clin. prof. surgery; resident Mayo Clinic, Rochester, 1964; pvt. practice, thoracic and cardiovascular surgeon Los Angeles, 1970—. Bd. dirs. Santa Monica-UCLA Hosp., IPA, Blue Shield of Calif., Unihealth, Auto Digest Found. Mem. ACP, AMA (chair AMA bd. of trustees, 2003-, pres.-elect 2005-), Calif. Med. Assn. (pres.), L.A. County Med. Assn., Soc. of Thoracic Surgeons, Western Thoracic Surg. Assn.Soc. for Clin. Vascular Surgery, Pacific Coast Surg. Assn., Am. Soc. of Gen. Surgery, Am. Coll. of Surgeons. Office: AMA 515 N State St Chicago IL 60610-4325

PLETZ, THOMAS GREGORY, lawyer; b. Toledo, Oct. 3, 1943; s. Francis G. and Virginia (Connell) P.; m. Carol Elizabeth Connolly, June 27, 1969; children: Anne M., John F. BA, U. Notre Dame, 1965; JD, U. Toledo, 1971. Bar: Ohio 1971, U.S. Ct. Appeals (6th cir.) 1978, U.S. Supreme Ct. 1985. Ct. bailiff Lucas County Common Pleas Ct., Toledo, 1967-71; jud. clk. U.S. Dist. Ct. (no. dist.) Ohio, Toledo, 1971-72; assoc. Shumaker, Loop & Kendrick, Toledo, 1972-76, litigation ptnr., 1976—. Acting judge Sylvania (Ohio) Mcpl. Ct., 1990—; mem. Ohio Bar Bd. Examiners, 1993-2003, chmn., 1996-99. Active Toledo Parish Coun., 1987-2003; mem. Nat. Conf. Bar Examiners Com., 1996-2001. With USNR, 1965-92; ret. CDR. Recipient Toledo Jr. Bar award, 1995. Mem. ABA, Ohio State Bar Assn., Toledo Bar Assn. (trustee 1981-93), Diocesan Attys. Bar Assn., 6th Cir. Jud. Conf. (life). Roman Catholic. Office: Shumaker Loop & Kendrick 1000 Jackson St Toledo OH 43604-1573 Office Phone: 419-321-1231. Business E-Mail: tpletz@slk-law.com.

PLONUS, MARTIN ALGIRDAS, electrical engineering educator; b. Trumpininken, Lithuania, Dec. 21, 1933; came to U.S. 1949, naturalized, 1955; s. Christopher and Anna (Sliupas) P.; m. Martina Rauer, Feb. 20, 1965; children— Sabine, Jacqueline, Marcus, Michelle BS, U. Ill., 1956, MS, 1957; PhD, U. Mich., 1961. Asst. prof. elec. engring. Northwestern U., Evanston, Ill., 1961-64, assoc. prof., 1964-69, prof., 1969—, dir. grad. program, 1989—; rsch. mathematician U. Mich., summers 1964-66. Bd. dirs. Ctr. Integrated Microelectronic Systems. Author: Applied Electromagnetics, 1978; contbr. articles to profl. jours. Grantee OSRD, 1964, NSF, 1967, 75-77, 94—, U.S. Air Force, 1980-85. Fellow IEEE (chmn. group antennas and propagation Chgo. sect. 1966-67, spl. recognition award 1971); mem. Internat. Sci. Radio Union, AAUP, U. Mich. Rsch. Club, Electromagnetics Acad., Sigma Xi, Eta Kappa Nu, Sigma Tau, Tau Beta Pi. Nat. sailing champion Shields class. Home: 2525 Orrington Ave Evanston IL 60201-2427 Office: Northwestern U Dept Elec Engring & Comp Sci Evanston IL 60208-3118 Office Phone: 708-491-3445. E-mail: plonus@northwestern.edu.

PLOTKIN, MANUEL D., management consultant, educator, former corporate executive, government official; s. Jacob and Bella (Katz) P.; m. Diane Fern Weiss, Dec. 17, 1967; 1 child, Lori Ann. BS with honors, Northwestern U., 1948; MBA, U. Chgo., 1949. Price economist, survey coordinator U.S. Bur. Labor Statistics, Washington, 1949-51, Chgo., 1951-53; sr. economist Sears Roebuck & Co., Chgo., 1953-61, mgr. market research, 1961-66, chief economist, mgr. mktg. rsch., 1966-73, dir. corp. planning and research, 1973-77, exec. corp. planner, 1979-80; dir. U.S. Bur. Census, Washington, 1977-79; v.p., dir. group practice Divsn. Mgmt. Cons. Austin Co., Evanston, Ill., 1981-85; pres. M.D. Plotkin Research & Planning Co., Chgo., 1985—. Tchr. statistics Ind. U., 1953-54; tchr. econs. Wilson Jr. Coll., Chgo., 1954-55; tchr. quantitative methods and managerial econs. Northwestern U., 1955-63; tchr. mktg. rsch. and mktg. mgmt. DePaul U., Chgo., 1992-95; mem. Conf. Bd. Mktg. Rsch. Adv. Coun., 1968-77, chmn.-elect, 1977; chmn. adv. com. U.S. Census Bur., 1974-75; trustee Mktg. Sci. Inst., 1968-77; mem. Nat. Commn. Employment and Unemployment Stats., 1978-79, Adv. Coun. Edn. Stats., 1977-79, Interagy. Com. Population Rsch., 1977-79; mem. adv. coun. Kellstadt Ctr., DePaul U., 1987-92; trustee U.S. Travel Data Ctr., 1977-79. Contbr. articles to profl. jours. Served with AUS, 1943-46, ETO. Decorated Bronze Star medal with oak leaf cluster. Mem. Am. Mktg. Assn. (pres. Chgo. 1968-69, nat. dir. 1969-70, nat. v.p. mktg. rsch. 1970-72, nat. v.p. mktg. mgmt. 1981-83, pres., CEO 1985-86), Am. Statis. Assn. (pres. Chgo. 1966-67, Forecasting award 1963), Am. Econ. Assn., Nat. Assn. Bus. Economists, Planning Execs. Inst., World Future Soc., Midwest Planning Assn., U. Ill. Businessmen Rsch. Adv. Group, Chgo. Assn. Commerce and Industry, Beta Gamma Sigma, Alpha Sigma Lambda, Delta Mu Delta. Home and Office: 2650 N Lakeview Ste 3910 Chicago IL 60614-1831

PLOTNICK, HARVEY BARRY, publishing executive; b. Detroit, Aug. 5, 1941; s. Isadore and Esther (Sher) Plotnick; m. Susan Regnery, Aug. 16, 1964 (div. Apr. 1977); children: Andrew, Alice; m. Elizabeth Allen, May 2, 1982; children: Teresa, Samuel. BA, U. Chgo., 1963. Editor Contemporary Books, Inc., Chgo., 1964-66, pres., pub., 1966—94; pres., CEO Paradigm Holdings, Inc., Chgo., 1994—. CEO Molecular Electronics Corpn., 2000. Trustee U. Chgo., 1994—, bd. gov., Argonne at. Lab., 2001—. Named one of Top 200 Collectors, ARTnews mag., 2005—06. Avocations: collecting old master prints, collecting Islamic ceramics. E-mail: harvey1844@aol.com.

PLOTNIK, ARTHUR, writer, columnist; b. White Plains, NY, Oct. 1, 1937; s. Michael and Annabelle P.; m. Meta Von Borstel, Sept. 6, 1960 (div. 1979); children: Julia Nicole, Katya Michelle.; m. Mary Phelan, Dec. 2, 1983. BA, State U. N.Y., Binghamton, 1960; MA, U. Iowa, 1961; MS in L.S, Columbia U., 1966. Gen. reporter, reviewer Albany (N.Y.) Times Union, 1963-64; freelance writer, 1964-66; editor Librarians Office, Library of Congress, 1966-69; assoc. editor Wilson Library Bull., Bronx, NY, 1969-74; editor-in-chief Am. Libraries, Chgo., 1975-89; assoc. pub. ALA, 1989-97; editl. dir. ALA Editions, 1993-97; writer, 1997—. Adj. instr. journalism Columbia Coll., Chgo., 1988-89; speaker in field. Author: The Elements of Editing: A Modern Guide for Editors and Journalists, 1982, Jacob Shallus, Calligrapher of the Constitution, 1987, Honk If You're a Writer, 1992, The Elements of Expression, 1996, 2d edit., 2006, The Urban Tree Book, 2000, The Elements of Authorship (reprint of Honk if You're a Writer), 2000, Spunk & Bite: A Writer's Guild to Punchier, More Engaging Language and Style, 2005, Paperback, 2007, Subtitled A Writers Guide to Bold Contemporary Style, gen. articles, fiction and poetry; contbg. editor: The Writer, 2000—07; mem. editl. bd.:, 2007—; exec. prodr.: Libr. Video mag., 1986—91; columnist: Editorial Eye, 1995—2001; contbr. articles to profl. jours. Bd. dirs. Am. Book Awards, 1979-82; bd. advs. Univ. Press of Am., 1982—1997. Served with USAR, 1962-67. Fellow Iowa Writers Workshop Creative Writing, 1961; recipient award Ednl. Press Assn. Am., 1973 (3), 77, 82, 83; cert. of excellence Internat. Reading Assn., 1970, First Pl. award Verbatim essay competition, 1986, award Am. Soc. Bus. Press Editors, 1987, First Pl. award poetry competition Irish-Am. Heritage Ctr., Chgo., 2005. Mem. ALA, ACLU, Treekeepers (Openlands Project). Home and Office: 2120 W Pensacola Ave Chicago IL 60618-1718 also: N E Pub Assocs Literary Agents PO Box 5 Chester CT 06412-0005

PLOUFF, JOE, state legislator; b. De Pere, Wis., Feb. 8, 1950; married; 2 children. BS, U. Wis., Eau Claire, 1976; MS, U. Wis., Stout, 1986. Sales cons.; mem. Wis. State Assembly, Madison, 1996—, mem. agr. com., mem. fin. instns. and ins. coms., mem. rural econ. devel. bd., mem. transp. com. Mem. Menomonie City Coun., 1995—96; former chair Menomonie Mkt. Natural Food Co-op; mem. Tainer/Meenomin Lake Assn., Wis. Farmers Union, Wis. Farmland Conservancy, Wis. Citizen Action, Friends of Wis. Pub. TV, Citizens Advocates for Children, Dunn County Hist. Soc., Friends of the Menomonie Pub. Libr.; active Dunn County Dem. Party. With US Army, 1970—72. Mem.: Wis. Pub. Radio Assn., Nat. Wildlife Fedn., Sierra Club. Democrat. Address: 1421 Messenger St Menomonie WI 54751

PLOWDEN, DAVID, photographer; b. Boston, Oct. 9, 1932; s. Roger and Mary Russell (Butler) P.; m. Pleasance Coggeshall, June 20, 1962 (div. 1976); children: John, Daniel; m. Sandra Oakes Schoellkopf, July 8th, 1977; children: Philip, Karen. BA Econs., Yale U., 1955; pvt. studies with Minor White and Nathon Lyons, Rochester, NY, 1959-60. Asst. O. Winston Link Studio, NYC, 1958-59, George Meluso Studio, NYC, 1960-62; photographer, writer, 1962—. Assoc. prof. Inst. Design, Ill. Inst. Tech., Chgo., 1978-86; lectr. U. Iowa Sch. Journalism, 1985-88; vis. prof. Grand Valley State Univ., 1988-90, 91-2007; artist-in-residence U. Balt., 1990-91. Author and photographer: Farewell to Steam, 1968, Lincoln and His America, 1970 (Benjamin Barondess award 1971), The Hand of Man on America, 1971, 2d edit, 1974, The Floor of the Sky: the Great Plains, 1972, Bridges: the Spans of North America, 1974, 2d edit. 1984, 3d edit., 2002, Commonplace, 1974, Tugboat, 1976 (notable Children's books ALA 1976, Children's Book Showcase 1976), Steel, 1981, An American Chronology, 1982 (Notable Books ALA 1982, Booklist's Best of the 80s 1989), Industrial Landscape, 1985, A Time of Trains, 1987, A Sense of Place, 1988, End of an Era: The Last of the Great Lakes Steamboats, 1992, Small Town America, 1994, Imprints: The Photographs of David Plowden, 1997, David Plowden: The American Barn, 2003, A Handful of Dust, 2006, David Plowden: Vanishing Point Fifty Years of Photography, 2007; co-author, photographer, Nantucket, 1970, Cape May to Montauk, 1973, Desert and Plains, the Mountains and the River, 1975, The Iron Road, 1978 (notable children's books 1978, Honor list Horn Books 1979), Wayne County: the Aesthetic Heritage of a Rural Area, 1979; introduction The Gallery of World Photography/the Country, 1983; commd. illustrator Gems, 1967, The Freeway in the City, 1968, America the Vanishing, 1969, New Jersey, 1977, North Dakota, 1977, Vermont, 1979, New York, 1981, A Place of Sense, 1988; contbr. articles to numerous jours. including Time, Newsweek, Life, Audubon, Fortune, Smithsonian, Camera Arts, Lenswork; one-man shows include Columbia U., 1965, Smithsonian Instn., 1970-71, 75-76, 81, 89, Internat. Ctr. Photography, NY, 1976, Witkin Gallery, NYC, 1979, Cin. Art Acad., 1979, Gilbert Gallery, Chgo., 1980-81, Chgo. Ctr. Contemporary Photography, 1982, Fed. Hall Mus., NYC, 1982, Calif. Mus. Photography, Riverside, 1982-83, Chgo. Hist. Soc., 1985, Martin Gallery, Washington, 1987, Kunstmuseum, Luzern, Switzerland, 1987, Burchfield Ctr., Buffalo, 1987-88, Iowa State Mus., Des Moines, 1988-89, Catherine Edelman Gallery, Chgo., 1990, Grand Valley State U., 1993, Ewing Gallery, Washington, 1994, Beinecke Rare Book and Manuscript Lib. Yale U., 1997, Albright-Knox Art Gallery, 1997, Mus. Contemporary Photography, Chgo., 1998, Albin O. Kuhn Libr. & Gallery, U. Md., Balt., 1998, Tatar/Alexander Photogallery, Toronto, 1999, Lawrence Miller Gallery, NYC, 2000, The Chgo. Cultural Ctr., 2002, Peter Fetterman Gallery Photog. Works of Art, Santa Monica, Calif., 2004-05, Copia, Napa, Calif., 2004, Catherine Edelman Gallery, Chgo., 2007; exhibited in group shows at Met. Mus. Art, NYC, 1967, Kodak Gallery, NYC, 1976, Currier Gallery Art, Manchester, NH, 1978, Whitney Mus., 1979, Art Inst. Chgo., 1983-87, Witkin Gallery, NYC, 1988, Davenport (Iowa) Mus. Art, 1992, Mus. Contemporary Photography, Chgo., 1996, 98-99, City, 2000, Fay Gold Gallery, Atlanta, 2003-04, Catherine Edelman Gallery, Chgo., 2007; represented in permanent collections Albright-Knox Gallery, Art Inst. Chgo., Calif. Mus. Photography, Ctr. Creative Photography, Chgo. Hist. Soc., Libr. Congress, Smithsonian Instn., U. Md., J.B. Speed Mus., Iowa Humanities Bd., Iowa State Hist. Dept., Burchfield Art Ctr., Buffalo and Erie County Hist. Soc., Internat. Mus. Photography George Eastman House, Internat. Ctr. Photography, Ekstrom Libr. U. Louisville, Beinecke Rare Book and Mauscript Libr., Yale U., 1995—, Mus. Contemporary Photography, Chicy, Bayly Mus. U. Va., Charlottesville. John Simon Guggenheim fellow, 1968; grantee .Y. State Coun. Arts, 1966, 87, Smithsonian Inst., 1970-71, Dept. Transp. and Smithsonian Inst., 1975-76, H. E. Butt Found., 1977, United Bd. Homeland Ministries, 1976, Chgo. Hist. Soc., 1980-84, Seymour H. Knox Found., 1987, Baird Found., 1987, State Hist. Soc. Iowa, 1987-88, Iowa Humanities Bd., 1987-88; recipient R.R. History award, 1989, Honored Image-maker, Soc. for Photographic Edn., 2002; subjectof PBS documentary: David Plowden: Light, Shadow & Form, 2000. Mem. Am. Soc. Media Photographers. Home and Office: 609 Cherry St Winnetka IL 60093-2614 Office Phone: 847-446-2793. Home Fax: 847-446-2795. Personal E-mail: david@davidplowden.com.

PLUIMER, EDWARD J., lawyer; b. Rapid City, SD, 1949; BA cum laude, U. S.D., 1971; JD cum laude, NYU, 1974. Bar: Minn. 1975. Law clk. to Hon. Robert A. Ainsworth, Jr. U.S. Ct. Appeals (5th cir.), 1974-75; ptnr. Dorsey & Whitney, Mpls., 1975—. Mem. Minn. Supreme Ct. ADR Task Force, 1988-92. Editor N.Y. U. Law Rev. Mem. Order of the Coif. Office: Dorsey & Whitney LLP Ste 1500 50 S 6th St Minneapolis MN 55402-1498 E-mail: pluimer.ed@dorseylaw.com.

PLUMLEY, S. PATRIC, retail executive; b. West Hamlin, W.Va., Jan. 2, 1949; s. Caudle and Nellie Brook (Honaker) P.; m. Rose M. McBee, Jan. 16, 1970. BA in Acctg. cum laude, U. South Fla., 1980, M Accountancy, 1986. CPA, Fla., Calif. Mem. acctg. staff Lucky Stores, Inc., Tampa, Fla., 1973-82, acctg. mgr., 1982-84, contr., 1984-86, v.p., contr. Buena Park, Calif., 1986-90, sr. v.p. adminstrn. Dublin, Calif., 1990-94; with Am. Stores, Inc., Salt Lake City, 1994—. Vice chmn. bd. dirs. Olive Crest, homes for abused children, Anaheim, Calif., 1988-90; bd. dirs. Jr. Achievement of Bay Area, 1992-94. With USN, 1967-71. Mem. AICPA, Inst. Mgmt. Accts. (cert.). Baptist. Avocations: golf, coin collecting/numismatics. Office: Eagle Food Ctr 801 E First St Rte 67 & Knoxville Rd Milan IL 61264-6700

PLUMMER, ALFRED HARVEY, III, lawyer; b. Wabash, Ind., June 10, 1943; s. Alfred H. and Aileen (Kester) P.; m. Patricia Ann Hughes, June 5, 1966; children: Alfred H. IV, Ann H., Alexander J. BS, Ind. U., 1965, JD, 1968. Bar: Ind. 1968, U.S. Dist. Ct. (so. dist.) Ind. 1968, U.S. Dist. Ct. (no. dist.) Ind. 1980, U.S. Ct. Appeals (7th cir.) 1968. City atty. City of Wabash, Ind., 1968—72; atty. Town of LaFontaine, Ind., 1969—; pros. atty. Wabash County, Wabash, Ind., 1983—2002. Mem. Wabash (Ind.) C. of C. (pres. 1970), Rotary, Elks, Shriners (pres. 1988). Republican. Presbyterian. Office: Alfred H Plummer III 21-27 W Canal PO Box 421 Wabash IN 46992-0421

PLUMMER, PATRICIA LYNNE MOORE, chemist, educator; b. Tyler, Tex., Feb. 26; d. Robert Lee and Jewell Ovelia (Jones) Moore; m. Otho Raymond Plummer, Apr. 10, 1965; children: Patrick William Otho, Christina Elisa Lynne. BA, Tex. Christian U., Ft. Worth, Tex., 1960; postgrad., U. N.C., 1960-61; PhD, U. Tex., Austin, 1964; grad., Bryn Mawr Summer Inst., 1992. Instr., Welch postdoctoral fellow U. Tex., Austin, 1964-66; postdoctoral fellow Dept. Chemistry, U. Ark., Fayetteville, 1966-68; rsch. assoc. Grad. Ctr., Cloud Phys. Rsch., Rolla, Mo., 1968-73; asst. prof. physics U. Mo., Rolla, 1973-77; assoc. dir. Grad. Ctr. Cloud Phys. Rsch., 1977-79, sr. investigator, 1980-85; assoc. prof. physics U. Mo., 1977-85, prof. dept. chemistry and physics Columbia, 1986—. Mem. internat. sci. com. Symposium on Chemistry and Physics of Ice, 1982—, vice chair, 1996—; nat. judge Siemens-Westinghouse Sci. Projects, 1999—. Assoc. editor Jour. of Colloid and Interface Sci., 1980-83; contbr. articles to profl. jours., chpts. to books. Rsch. grantee IBM, 1990-92, Air Force Office Rsch., 1989-91, NSF, 1976-86, NASA, 1973-78; Air Force Office Rsch. summer fellow, 1988, Bryn Mawr Summer Inst., 1992, Faculty fellow Cherry Emerson Ctr. for Sci. Computation, Emory U., 1998-99. Mem. Am. Chem. Soc., Am. Phys. Soc., Am. Geophys. Union, Sigma Xi (past pres., UM-Rolla chptr.). Democrat. Baptist. Avocations: sailing, gardening, tennis, photography. Office: U Mo 201 Physics Bldg Columbia MO 65211-0001 Fax: (573) 882-4195. E-mail: plummerp@missouri.edu.

PLUNKETT, PAUL EDMUND, federal judge; b. Boston, July 9, 1935; s. Paul M. and Mary Cecilia (Erbacher) P.; m. Martha Milan, Sept. 30, 1958; children: Paul Scott, Steven, Andrew, Kevin BA, Harvard U., 1957, JD, 1960. Ptnr. Mayer Brown & Platt, Chgo., 1960-63, 78-83; asst. atty. U.S. Atty.'s Office, Chgo., 1963-66; ptnr. Plunkett Nisin et al, Chgo., 1966-78; sr. judge U.S. Dist. Ct. (no. dist.) Ill., Chgo., 1983—. Adj. faculty John Marshall Law Sch., Chgo., 1964-76, 82—, Loyola U. Law Sch., Chgo., 1977-82. Mem. Fed. Bar Assn. Clubs: Legal, Law, Union League (Chgo.). Office: US Dist Ct Everett McKinley Dirksen Bldg 219 S Dearborn St Ste 1446 Chicago IL 60604-1705

PLUSH, MARK J., finance company executive; With Keithley Instruments, Inc., 1982, corp. officer, 1989, corp. contr., CFO, 1998—. Office: 28775 Aurora Rd Solon OH 44139-1837

PLUSQUELLIC, DONALD L., mayor; b. Akron, Ohio, July 3, 1949; m. Mary Plusquellic; children: Dave, Michelle. BS, Bowling Green State U., 1972; JD, U. Akron, 1981. Councilman Akron City Council, 1973-81, councilman-at-large, 1982-86, council pres., 1984-86; mayor City of Akron, 1987—. Trustee U.S. Conf. of Mayors; mem task force for funding homeland security in US cities US Dept Homeland Security, 2006—. Office: Office of the Mayor 200 Municipal Bldg 166 S High St Akron OH 44308-1626

POCAN, MARK, state legislator; b. Kenosha, Wis., Aug. 14, 1964; BA, U. Wis., 1986. Owner Budget Signs and Specialties, 1988—; mem. Wis. State Assembly, Madison, 1998—, mem. campaigns and elections com., mem. corrections and the cts. com., mem. environment com., mem. ways and means com. Chair Midwest Progressive Elected Ofcls. Network, 2000; supr. Dane County Bd. Suprs., 1991—96; bd. dirs. Wis. Citizen Action, 1999—2000. Democrat. Office: State Capitol Rm 322 W PO Box 8953 Madison WI 53708-8953 Home: 309 N Baldwin St Madison WI 53703-1701

POCHYLY, DONALD FREDERICK, physician, hospital administrator; b. Chgo., June 3, 1934; s. Frank J. and Vlasta (Bezdek) P.; m. Diane Dilelio, May 11, 1957; children: Christopher, Jonathan, David. MD, Loyola U., 1959; M.Ed., U. Ill., 1971. Diplomate Am. Bd. Internal Medicine, Am. Bd. Geriatrics. Fellow ACP, 1966-67; asst. prof. med. edn. U. Ill., 1967-72, asso. prof., 1972-74; chmn. dept. health scis. edn. U. of Health Scis., Chgo. Med. Sch., 1975-77, provost, acting pres., 1977-79; prof. clin. medicine Loyola U., Chgo., 1980—; v.p. med. affairs N.W. Community Hosp., Arlington Heights, Ill. Chmn. com. rev. and recognition Am. Coun. Continuing Med. Edn., 1993; cons. Nat. Libr. Medicine, WHO. Contbr. articles to med. jours. Mem. AMA, Ill. Geriatrics Soc. (pres. Chgo. chpt. 1988-89), Ill. Med. Soc., Chgo. Med. Soc., Alpha Omega Alpha. Roman Catholic. Office: Northwest Community Hosp 800 W Central Rd Arlington Heights IL 60005-2392

POE, DONALD RAYMOND, state legislator; m. Carol Henrikson; children: Collette Schultz, Cherrilyn Mayfield, Lance. Grad., DeVry Inst. Tech., Chgo., 1963, Agriculture Leaders of Tomorrow, 1983. Farmer, Sherman, Ill., 1964—; mem. Ill. State Ho. of Reps. Dist. 99, 1995—. Mem. agriculture & conservation, appropriations-edn., elem. & secondary edn., higher edn., pers. & pensions coms. 99th Legis. Dist., Ill. Gen. Assembly; rep. Ill. Farm Bur., mem. state coun. bus.-edn. partnership Ill. State Bd. Edn., 1990—; mem., exec. bd. dirs. Ill. Farm Bur., past. pres., past mem. pub. rels. com. Bd. mem. Williamsvill Cmty. H.S., 1970-91, past pres.; fundraiser supr. Sherman United Meth. Ch., youth group leader, 1980-90, past chmn. bd., past chmn. bd. trustees com., pastor parish com.; active Sangamon County Sheriff's DUI Taskforce, 1995-96.

POEHLMANN, CARL JOHN, agricultural researcher; b. Jamestown, Mo., Jan. 29, 1950; s. Edwin and Lucille P.; m. Linda Kay Garner, Dec. 29, 1973; children: Anthony, Kimberly. BS, U. Mo., 1972, MS, 1978. Farmer, Jamestown, Mo., 1972-73; vocat. agrl. tchr. Linn (Mo.) Pub. Schs., 1973-75, Columbia (Mo.) Pub. Schs., 1975-78; dir., mgr. agronomy rsch. ctr. U. Mo., Columbia, 1978-2000; dir. MOAES Field Ops., 2000—06; asst. dir. Mo. Agrl. Rsch. Sta., 2006—. Mem. Am. Soc. Agronomy (div. A-7 chair 1985-86, bd. mem. 1991-94, cert. crop advisor 1993—), Crop Sci. Soc. Am., Soil Sci. Soc. Am., Internat. Assn. Mechanization Field Experiments, Users and Screeners Assn. (fed. excess personal property). Mem. Christian Ch. (Disciples Of Christ). Office: MU Field Ops 3600 New Haven Rd Columbia MO 65201-9608 Business E-Mail: poehlmannc@missouri.edu.

POEL, ROBERT WALTER, military officer, physician; b. Muskegon, Mich., July 24, 1934; s. Abel John and Fannie M. (Vanderwall) P.; m. Carol Anne Noordeloos, June 24, 1960; children: Kathryn Anne Poel Engle, James Robert, Sharon Kay Poel Thompson. BS, Calvin Coll., 1957; MD, U. Mich., 1959. Diplomate Am. Bd. Surgery. Commd. capt. USAF, 1962, advanced through grades to brig. gen., 1988, ret., 1993; comdr. Hosp. Malmstrom AFB, Great Falls, Mont., 1971-73; dir. profl. svcs. Hdqrs. Tactical Air Command Command Surgeon's Office, Langley AFB, Va., 1973-74; div. chief, med. plans Office of Air Force Surgeon Gen., Wash., 1974-78; comdr. regional hosp. Sheppard AFB, Wichita Falls, Tex., 1978-83; dir. profl. svcs. Office of Air Force Logistics Command Surgeon, Wright-Patterson AFB, Ohio, 1983-85; vice-comdr. Wilford Hall USAF Med. Ctr., San Antonio, 1985-87; chief, quality assurance, dir. plans and resources Air Force Surgeon Gen., Bolling AFB, Wash., 1987-89; hosp. comdr. Malcolm Grow Med. Ctr., Andrews AFB, 1989-93; med. dir. near south office Meth. Occupational Healthctrs. Inc., Indpls., 1995—. Dir. Andrews Fed. Credit Union, 1991-95, vice chmn. bd. dirs., 1992-95. Advisor, bd. regents Uniformed Svcs. U. the Health Scis., Bethesda, Md., 1989-93; mem. pres. coun. Calvin Coll., 1990. Named Disting. alumnus, Calvin Coll., 1990; Paul Harris fellow Rotary Club of Wichita Falls, 1982. Mem. AMA, Am. Coll. Occupl. and Environ. Medicine, Assn. Mil. Surgeons of U.S. (life), Ret. Officers Assn. (life). Republican. Home: 12085 Waterford Ln Carmel IN 46033-5501 Office: 1101 Southeastern Ave Indianapolis IN 46202-3946 Office Phone: 317-955-2020. Personal E-mail: poelrc@indy.rr.com.

POGEMILLER, LAWRENCE J., state legislator; b. Sept. 18, 1951; BS, U. Minn., 1974; MPA, Harvard U., 1988. Mem. Minn. Ho. of Reps., St. Paul, 1980—82, Minn. Senate from 59th dist., St. Paul, 1983—. Mem. various ho. coms. including most recently; chmn. tax. com. Minn. Ho. Reps., mem. higher edn. funding com., mem. commerce pensions com., mem. rules and adminstrn. com. Democrat. Home: 201 University Ave NE Minneapolis MN 55413-2250 Office: State Senate 235 State Capital Building Saint Paul MN 55155-0001 Office Phone: 651-296-7809.

POHL, KATHLEEN SHARON, editor; b. Sandusky, Mich., Apr. 7, 1951; d. Gerald Arthur and Elizabeth Louise (Neukamm) P.; m. Bruce Mark Allen Reynolds, June 11, 1982. BA in Spanish, Valparaiso U., 1973; MA in English, No. Mich. U., 1975. Producer, dir. fine arts Sta. WNMU-FM, Marquette, Mich., 1981-82; instr. communications Waukesha County (Wis.) Tech. Inst., 1983; editor Ideals mag., Milw., 1983-85; editor, mng. editor Raintree Pubs., Milw., 1985-87; mng. editor, now exec. editor Country Woman mag., Greendale, Wis., 1987—; exec. editor Country Handcrafts mag., Greendale, 1990-93, Taste of Home Mag., Greendale, Wis., 1993—; editor Talk About Pets, Greendale, 1994-95. Author nature book series, 1985-87; sr. editor: Country Woman Christmas Book, 1996—; mng. editor: Irwin the Sock (Chgo. Book Clinic award 1988); exec. editor Taste of Home's Quick Cooking Mag., 1998—, Down the Aisle Countr Style, 2000, Taste of Home's Light & Tasty Mag., 2000—. Mem. Nat. Mus. of Women in Arts, Alpha Lambda Delta (hon.). Home: N54 W26326 Lisbon Rd Sussex WI 53089-4249 Office: Country Woman Mag 5400 S 60th St Greendale WI 53129-1404

POHLAD, CARL R., bank and professional sports team executive; b. West Des Moines, Iowa, Aug. 23, 1915; m. Eloise Pohlad (dec. 2003); 3 children. Student, Gonzaga U. With MEI Diversified, Inc., Mpls., 1959—, chmn. bd., 1976—94; pres. Marquette Bank Mpls., N.A., pres., dir., Bank Shares, Inc.; owner Minn. Twins, 1985—. Bd. dirs. Meth. Hosp. Adminstrv. Group, T.G.I. Friday's, Tex. Air Corp., Ea. Airlines, Continental Airlines, Inc., Carlson Cos. Inc. Named one of Forbes' Richest Americans, 2006. Address: MN Twins Hubert H Humphrey Metrodome 34 Kirby Puckett Pl Minneapolis MN 55415-1523

POHLAD, ROBERT C., consumer products company executive; Dir. Mesaba Holdings Inc.; v.p. N.W. area Pepsi-Cola Bottling Group; pres. Pohlad Cos., 1987—2000; CEO PepsiAmericas, 2000—, vice chmn., 2001—02, chmn., 2002—. Office: PepsiAmericas 4000 Dain Rauscher Plaza 60 S Sixth St Minneapolis MN 55402

POHLMAN, LYNETTE, museum director, curator; BA, Iowa State U., 1972, MA in applied art, 1976. Dir., chief curator Univ. Mus. at Iowa State U. Adj. prof. art & design Iowa State U.; organizer Art in State Bldgs. Prog. Curator Emperors, Shoguns and Kings, 1981, Fiber to Glass, 1987, Land of Fragile Giants: Landscapes, Environments and Peoples of the Loess Hills, 1994—96, The Golden Age of Glass: 1875-1939, 1999. Recipient Christian Petersen Design Award, 2004. Mem.: Assn. Coll. and Univ. Mus. and Galleries (founding mem.). Office: Univ Mus 290 Scheman Bldg Ames IA 50011-1110 Office Phone: 515-294-3342. E-mail: lpohlma@iastate.edu.

POINTER, PETER LEON, investment executive; b. Erie, Pa., Aug. 3, 1934; s. Leon Royce and Katherine (Hermen) P.; m. Linda Milla Jensen, Sept. 21, 1957; children: Philip Leon, David Andrew. BS in Econs., U. Pa., 1956; MBA, U. Mo., 1968. V.p. Roose-Wade & Co. Inc., Toledo, 1976-78; br. mgr. Wm. C. Roney & Co., Detroit, 1978-79; v.p. Lowe & Assocs., Columbus, Ohio, 1979-88; pres. Pointer Investment Co., Columbus, 1988—2004. Arbitrator Nat. Assn. Security Dealers, Washington, 1987—. Trustee, sec.-treas. Univ. Urology Ednl. and Rsch. Found., 1993-2004. Lt. col. USAF, 1956-76. Mem. Brookside Golf and Country Club (treas., trustee 1991-94), Sigma Nu (treas. 1955-56). Republican. Methodist. Avocations: aviation, golf, gardening. Home: 2290 Haverford Rd Columbus OH 43220

POINTS, ROY WILSON, municipal official; b. Quincy, Ill., Oct. 21, 1940; s. Jess C. and Gladys (Wilson) P.; m. Karen Lee Olsen, July 23, 1966; children: Eric, Holly. BBA, Culver Stockton Coll., 1968. Tchr., coach Lewis County C-1, Ewing, Mo., 1968-69, Community Unit 3, Camp Point, Ill., 1969-78; real estate salesman Landmark, Quincy, 1978-80; supr. of assessment County of Adams, Quincy, 1980-90; assessor City Twp. of Quincy, 1990—. Chmn. Adams County Bd. Rev., 1977—80. Bd. dirs., 1st v.p., sec. Quincy Jaycees, 1970-76, Quincy Rotary East, 1980. Mem. Cert. Ill. Assessing Officers, Internat. Assn. Assessing Officers (cert. ednl. recognition 1988), Ill. Assessors Assn. (bd. dirs. 1992-2008), Twp. Ofcls. Ill. (bd. dirs. 1995-2001), North Ctrl. Regional Assn. Assessing Officers (bd. dirs. 1997—). Democrat. Avocations: fishing, hunting, jogging, raising cattle. Office: Quincy Twp Assessor City Hall Annex 706 Maine St Quincy IL 62301-4013 Office Phone: 217-228-4505.

POLAKIEWICZ, LEONARD ANTHONY, foreign language and literature educator; b. Kiev, Ukraine, Mar. 30, 1938; came to the U.S., 1950; s. Wladyslaw and Aniela (Ossowska) P.; m. Marianne Helen Swanson, Sept. 7, 1963; children: Barbara, Kathryn, Janet. BS in Russian with distinction, U. Minn., 1964, BA in Internat. Rels., 1964; MA in Russian, U. Wis., 1968; cert. Russian area studies, 1969; PhD in Slavic Langs./Lit., U. Wis., 1978; diploma in Polish Curriculum and Instrn., Curie-Sklodowska U., Lublin, Poland, 1981. Instr. U. Minn., Mpls., 1970-78, asst. prof., 1978—90, assoc. prof., 1990—, Morse Alumni disting. teaching assoc. prof. Slavic langs. and literatures, dir. Inst. Langs., 1991-93, chair Slavic dept., 1993—97, 1999—2000, 2006—. Vis. asst. prof. U. London, 1984; dir. U. Minn. Polish Lang. Program, Curie-Sklodowska U., Lublin, Poland, summers 1984-89, dir. Russian Faculty Exch., Herzen Pedagogical U., St. Petersburg, Russia, 1993—; mem. selection com. Fulbright Tchr. Exch. Program, USIA, 1989, Title VI Dept. Edn., 1990, NEH Tchr.-Scholar Program, 1994; reviewer divn. ednl. programs NEH, 1990, translation program, 1993, 94; mem. rev. bd. Ctr. Applied Linguistics Polish Proficiency Test, 1990; mem. exec. com. Coun. on Internat. Edn., N.Y.C., 1991-94; mem. Russian Lang. Program Acad. Policy Com. CIEE, N.Y.C., 1994-2002; mem. nat. task force Polish Studies in Am., Ind. U., 1995-96; project dir. Nat. Coun. Orgns. of Less Commonly Taught Langs. Polish Lang. Learning Framework, 1995-2001; Polish examiner Yale U. Ctr. Lang. Study, 2006—; dir. U. Minn. Curie Sklodowska U. Faculty Exch., 1988—, U. Minn. Cath. U. of Lublin Faculty Exch., 1995-2001; coord. Def. Lang. Inst. Polish Proficiency Testing, 1998; apptd. adv. bd. Am. U. Poland, 2004—; mem. nat. screening com. Fulbright-Hays Program, US Dept. State, 2006; mem. rev. panel Boren fellowship, Nat. Security Edn. Program, 2007-08. Author: Supplemental Materials for First Year Polish, 1991, Supplemental Materials for Fifteen Modern Polish Short Stories, 1994, Directory of US Institutions of Higher Education and Faculty Offering Instruction in Polish Language, Literature and Culture, 1996-97, Intermediate Polish: A Cultural Reader with Exercises, 1999, (with Joanna Radwanska Williams and Waldemar Walczynski) Polish Language Learning Framework, 2002; assoc. editor Slavic and East European Jour., 1988-94; complier, editor, contbr. Can.-Am. Slavic Studies, Vol. 48, 2008; mem. editl. bd. The Learning and Tchg. of Slavic Langs. and Cultures: Toward the 21st Century, 1996-2000; reviewer Choice Mag., Modern Lang. Jour., Canadian Slavonic Papers, Slavic and East European Jour., Soviet and Post-Soviet Rev. Bd. dirs. Immigration Hist. Rsch. Ctr., Mpls., 1984-89, Am. Univ. in Poland, 2004—; co-founder Polish-Am. Cultural Inst., Mpls., 1986; vice-chair Polish Am. Congress' Commn. Edn., 1987; mem. gov.'s Commn. on Ea. Europe, St. Paul, 1991. With U.S. Army, 1961-63. Ford Found. fellow, 1964-65, NDEA fellow, Title IV, 1966-68; grantee Kościuszko Found., 1981, Coun. for European Studies grantee Columbia U., 1981, 84, 86, Rsch. Assoc. grantee Russian and East European Ctr., U. Ill., 1982, 83, 84, Wasie Found. grantee, 1983, IREX Collaborative Activities and New Exchs. grantee, 1984, Ireland Travel grantee Trinity Coll., Dublin, 1984, Bush Found. Rsch. grantee, 1986-87, grantee U.S. Dept. Edn., 1988-91; Fulbright-Hays Group Projects Abroad grantee for Poland, 1989, USIA U. Linkage grantee for Poland, 1989-93, IREX Short Term Travel grantee, 1995, USIA Coll. and Univ. Affiliations grantee for Poland, 1995-2000; recipient Polanie Club of the Twin Cities Merit award, 1982, Curie-Sklodowska U. medal for acad. linkage devel., 1992, Cavalier's Cross of Order of Merit of Republic of Poland, 1999, Disting Svc. award Herzen Pedagogical U., St. Petersburg, Russia, 2002, Pres.'s Outstanding Svc. award, 2003, A. Ronald Walton award Nat. Coun. Less Commonly Taught Langs., 2006. Mem. AAUP, Am. Assn. for the Advancement Slavic Studies, Am. Assn. Tchrs. Slavic and East European Langs. and Lits. (com. on testing and profl. devel. 1997—, Excellence in Tchg. in U.S. award 1994), Internat. Czeslaw Milosz Soc. (pres. 1984-85), N.Am. Chekhov Soc., Am. Coun. Tchrs. of Russian, Polish Inst. Arts & Scis. Am. (N.Y.C., Waclaw Lednicki Humanities award com. 1996), Assn. Literary Scholars & Critics, Soc. of Lovers of the Russian Book, Irish Assn. of Russian and East European Studies, Polish Tchrs. Assn. of Am., Polish Studies Assn. (mem. biannual prize jury 1998), Bristol Group Internat. Assn. Tchrs. Polish, U. Minn. Acad. Disting. Tchrs., The Australia and New Zealand Slavists' Assn. Roman Catholic. Avocations: reading, philatelics, genealogy, touring, gardening. Home: 466 Oak Creek Dr S Vadnais Heights MN 55127-7008 Office Phone: 612-625-1384. Business E-Mail: polak001@tc.umn.edu.

POLANCO, PLACIDO ENRIQUE, professional baseball player; b. Santo Domingo, Dominican Republic, Oct. 10, 1975; m. Lily Polanco; children: Aide Rose, Ishmael. Student, Miami-Dade Wolfson CC, Fla. Draft pick St. Louis Cardinals, 1994, player, 1998—2002, Phila. Phillies, 2002—05, Detroit Tigers, 2005—. Mem. Dominican Republic Team World Baseball Classic, 2006. Named Am. League Championship Series MVP, 2006; named to Am. League All-Star Team, 2007; recipient Stockton/Broeg award, Baseball Writers' Assn. of Am., St. Louis chpt., 2000—01, Gold Glove award, 2007, Silver Slugger award, 2007,

MLB.com's Defensive Player of Yr. award, 2007. Achievements include setting a Major League Baseball record for second basemen by playing 144 straight games without an error, August 13, 2007. Avocation: golf. Mailing: Detroit Tigers Comerica Park 2100 Woodward Ave Detroit MI 48201*

POLASKI, ANNE SPENCER, lawyer; b. Pittsfield, Mass., Nov. 13, 1952; d. John Harold and Marjorie Ruth (Hackett) Spencer; m. James Joseph Polaski, Sept. 14, 1985. BA in Psychology, Allegheny Coll., 1974; MSW, U. Pa., 1976; JD, George Washington U., 1979. Bar: DC 1979, US Ct. Appeals (DC cir.) 1980, Ill. 1982, US Dist. Ct. (no. dist.) Ill. 1982, US Ct. Appeals (7th cir.) 1982. Law clk. to assoc. judge D.C. Ct., Washington, 1979-80; trial atty. Commodity Futures Trading Commn., Chgo., 1980-84, sr. trial atty., 1984, dep. regional counsel, 1984-88; assoc. Gottlieb and Schwartz, Chgo., 1988-91; staff atty. Chgo. Bd. of Trade, 1991-92, sr. atty., 1992-94, asst. gen. counsel, 1994—. Mem. ABA, Chgo. Bar Assn. Office: Chgo Bd of Trade 141 W Jackson Blvd Chicago IL 60604-2992 E-mail: apolaski@cbot.com.

POLAY, BRUCE, musician, conductor, educator; b. Bklyn., Mar. 22, 1949; s. Benjamin and Joan Polay; m. Louise Phillips, Dec. 17, 1983; children: Elizabeth, Adam, Rachel, Jacob, Julia. MusB, U. So. Calif., 1971; MA, Calif. State U., 1977; DMA, Ariz. State U., 1989. Music dir. So. Calif. Philharm., Long Beach, 1971-81; grad. asst. in theory and orch., asst. condr. univ. symphony Ariz. State U., Tempe, 1981-83; condr. Phoenix Symphony Guild Youth Orch., 1981-83; music dir. Knox-Galesburg (Ill.) Symphony, 1983—; prof. music Knox Coll., Galesburg, 1983—, chair music dept., 2001—05. Guest condr. in Belarus, Italy, Eng., Mexico, Romania, Russia, Ukraine, Spain; bd. dirs. Ill. Coun. of Orchs., 1992—; mem. adv. bd. Found. for New Music, 1996—; bd. advisors Barlow Endowment for Music Composition, 1999-2004; mem. music program adv. panel Ill. Arts Coun., 2004—. Orchestral compositions include Enconium, 1986, Perspectives, 1989, Concerto for Tenor Trombone, 1990, Tranquil Cycle for Tenor and Orch., 1992, Cathedral Images, 1993, Bondi's Journey: An Orchestral Rhapsody on Jewish Themes, 1994, Pictures For an Exhibition Piano, 1995, Anniversary Mourning for a cappella choir, 1996, Sandburg Cycle for Soprano, Tenor and Piano, 2000, Semi-Suite for Vin, Cello and Piano, 2001, Golden Oldie for Orchestra, 2001, Elegy for Violin and Small Orchestra, 2002, Suite of Preludes for Organ, 2002, Illumination for Orchestra, 2003, Suite on Catalonian Folksongs for String Orchestra, 2004, 3 Violin Duets on Catalonian Folksongs, 2005, 5 novelettes for harp and string orchestra, 2006, Sparkle for Orchestra, 2007. Recipient Ill. Condr. of Yr. award Ill. Coun. Orchs., 1997, 2004, Exceptional Achievement award Knox Coll., 1999, 2004, Programming of the Yr. award, 2006; named Ill. Orchestra of Yr. Knox-Galesburg Symphony, 1986, 2003. Mem. ASCAP, Am. Music Ctr., Phi Kappa Phi. Mem. Lds Ch. Avocations: body surfing, reading, American history. Home: 1577 N Cherry St Galesburg IL 61401-1820 Office: Knox Coll Campus Box 5 Galesburg IL 61401-4999 Home Phone: 309-337-3720; Office Phone: 309-341-7208. Business E-Mail: bpolay@knox.edu.

POLIAN, BILL, professional football team executive; b. NYC, Dec. 8, 1942; m. Eileen Polian; children: Lynn, Chris, Brian, Dennis. Grad., NYU. Asst. coach Manhattan Coll., 1965-67; asst. coach football U.S. Mcht. Marine Acad., 1968-70, head coach baseball, 1971-75; scout Kansas City Chiefs, 1978-82; dir. player personnel Winnipeg (Can.) Blue Bombers, 1983; dir. personnel Buffalo Bills, 1984-85, gen. mgr., v.p. adminstrn., 1985—. Mem. competition com. NFL, 1989—. Named NFL Exec. of Yr., 1991. Office: Indianapolis Colts 7001 W 56th St Indianapolis IN 46254

POLICANO, ANDREW J., dean, finance educator; b. July 4, 1949; m. Pamela Z. Policano; children: Emily, Keith. BS in math., SUNY, Stony Brook, 1971; MA in economics, Brown U., 1973, PhD in economics, 1976. Asst. prof. U. Iowa, Iowa City, 1975-79, assoc. prof. dept. economics, 1979-81, prof., chair dept. economics, 1984-87, sr. assoc. dean academic affairs, 1987-88; prof. dept. economics Fordham U., NYC, 1981-84, asst. chair, dir. grad. studies, 1982-83; rsch. assoc. Ctr. for Study of Futures Markets Columbia U., NYC, 1982-86; dean divsn. social & behavioral sci. SUNY, Stony Brook, 1988-91; dean Sch. Bus., U. Wis., Madison, 1991—2001, Kuechenmeister Prof. Bus., 2001—04; dean Pual Merage Sch. Bus., U. Calif., Irvine, 2004—, prof. economics/pub. policy, 2004—. Guest prof. Inst. Advanced Studies, Vienna, Austria, 1985; dir. Nat. Guardian Life, Madison, 1991-2004, PIC Wis., 1995-2002, Badger Meter, 1997—; mem. Wis. Glass Ceiling Commn., 1995-2000. Recipient Disting. Alumnus award SUNY, Stony Brook, 1994. Mem. Assn. to Advance Collegiate Schools of Bus. (bd. dirs., 1997-98). Office: U Calif Paul Merage Sch Bus 350 SB Irvine CA 92697-3125 Office Phone: 949-824-8470. Business E-Mail: dean@merage.uci.edu.

POLICY, CARMEN A., professional sports team executive; b. Youngstown, Ohio, Jan. 26, 1943; s. Albert and Ruby (Tisone) P.; m. Aug. 8, 1964 (div. Mar. 1989); children: James, Daniel, Edward, Kerry, Kathy; m. Gail Marie Moretti, June 27, 1991. Grad., Youngstown State U., 1963; JD, Georgetown U., 1966. Bar: Ohio 1966, Va. 1966, D.C. 1966. Assoc. Nadler & Nadler, Youngstown, 1966-68; asst. prosecutor City of Youngstown, 1968-69; ptnr. Flask & Policy, Weimer & White, Youngstown, 1969-90; spl. counsel to atty. gen. State of Ohio, 1970-91; v.p., gen. counsel San Francisco 49ers, NFL, 1983-90, pres., 1990-99; pres., CEO & co-owner Cleve. Browns, 1998—2004, consultant, 2004—. Mem. various coms. NFL, 1990—; bd. dirs. World League Am. Football, N.Y.C., 1991—. Com. mem. various charities, Youngstown, 1969-90, San Francisco, 1990—. Mem. Va. Bar Assn., Ohio Bar Assn., D.C. Bar Assn. Roman Catholic. Avocations: scuba diving, hiking. Home and Office: 1330 Jones St Apt 503 San Francisco CA 94109

POLIS, MICHAEL PHILIP, engineering educator; b. NYC, Oct. 24, 1943; s. Max and Sylvia (Goldner) P.; m. Claudette Martin, May 28, 1966; children: Melanie Bobby, Martin Pascal, Karine Melissa. BSEE, U. Fla., 1966; MSEE, Purdue U., West Lafayette, Ind., 1968, PhD, 1972. Grad. instr. elec. engring. Purdue U., West Lafayette, 1966-71; postdoctoral fellow Ecole Polytechnique, Montreal, 1972-73, asst. prof. elec. engring., 1973-74, assoc. prof., 1974-82, prof., 1982-83; program dir. sys. theory NSF, Washington, 1983-87; chmn. dept. elec. and computer engring. Wayne State U., Detroit, 1987-93; dean Sch. Engring. and Computer Sci. Oakland U., Rochester, Mich., 1993-2001, prof. elec. and systems engring., 2001—. Expert witness various law firms, 1989—; cons. Mich. Bell-Ameritech, Detroit, 1989-95, ICAM Technologies, Inc., Montreal, 1981-83; vis. rsch. assoc. LAAS, Toulouse, France, 1978. Contbr. articles to profl. jours. Mem. IEEE (sr.), IEEE Control Sys. Soc. (bd. govs. 1993-95, 98-2000, Best Paper Trans. on Automatic Control 1974-75, Disting. Mem. 1993, v.p. mem. activities 1990-91, assoc. editor 1981-82). Office: Oakland Univ Sch Engring & Computer Sci Rochester MI 48309-4778 Home Phone: 313-886-5089; Office Phone: 248-370-2743.

POLLACK, GERALD LESLIE, physicist, researcher, educator; b. Bklyn., July 8, 1933; s. Herman and Jennie (Tenenbaum) P.; m. Antoinette Amparo Velasquez, Dec. 22, 1958; children: Harvey Anton, Samuela Juliet, Margolita Mia, Violet Amata. BS, Bklyn. Coll., 1954; Fulbright scholar, U. Gottingen, 1954-55; MS, Calif. Inst. Tech., 1957, PhD, 1962. Physics student trainee Nat. Bur. Standards, Washington, 1954-58, solid state physicist, 1961-65, cons. Boulder, Colo., 1965-70; assoc. prof. dept. physics Mich. State U., East Lansing, 1965-69, prof., 1969—2005, prof. emeritus, 2005—; cons. NRC, Ill. Dept. Nuclear Safety; physicist aval Med. Rsch. Inst., Bethesda, Md., summer 1979. Physicist USAF Sch. Aerospace Medicine, San Antonio, Tex., summer 1987; adj. prof. Dept. Physics, Colo. Sch. Mines, Golden, 2005-06. Co-author (with D.R. Stump): Electromagnetism, 2002; contbr. articles to profl. jours. Fellow Am. Phys. Soc.; mem. Am. Assn. Physics Tchrs. Business E-Mail: pollack@msu.edu.

POLLACK, HENRY NATHAN, geophysics educator; b. Omaha, July 13, 1936; s. Harold Myron and Sylvia (Chait) P.; m. Lana Beth Schoenberger, Jan. 29, 1963; children: Sara Beth (dec.), John David. AB, Cornell U., 1958; MS, U. Nebr., 1960; PhD, U. Mich., 1963. Lectr. U. Mich., 1962, asst. prof., assoc. prof., prof. geophysics, 1964—, assoc. dean for research, 1982-85, chmn. dept. geol. scis., 1988-91. Rsch. fellow Harvard U., 1963-64; sr. lectr. U. Zambia, 1970-71; vis. scientist U. Durham, U. Newcastle-on-Tyne, Eng., 1977-78, U. Western Ont., 1985-86; chmn. Internat. Heat Flow Commn., 1991-95. Author: Uncertain Science.Uncertain World, 2003. Fellow: AAAS, Geol. Soc. Am.; mem.: Am. Geophys. Union. Achievements include research on thermal evolution of the earth, recent climate change. Office: U Mich Dept Geol Scis Ann Arbor MI 48109

POLLACK, MARK BRIAN, investment company executive; b. Milw., June 20, 1941; s. Jack and Florence (Sosnay) P.; m. Barbara Eisendrath, Aug. 18, 1963; children: Deborah Lynn, Suzanne Renee. BBA, U. Wis., 1963, JD, 1966. Bar: Wis. 1966, N.Y. 1983. Assoc. atty. Godfrey & Kahn, Milw., 1966—70; legal counselor Comml. Loan Ins. Corp., Milw., 1971—72, v.p., sec., 1972—75, sr. v.p., 1975—76; v.p. MGIC Investment Corp., Milw., 1977—81, sr. v.p., 1981—84, exec. v.p., 1984—. Trustee Village of Fox Point, Wis., 1977—82. Mem.: Order of Coif, State Bar Wis., N.Y. State Bar Assn. Office: MGIG Investment Corp MGIC Plaza Milwaukee WI 53201

POLLACK, SEYMOUR VICTOR, computer science educator; b. Bklyn., Aug. 3, 1933; s. Max and Sylvia (Harrison) P.; m. Sydell Altman, Jan. 23, 1955; children: Mark, Sherie. BChemE, Pratt Inst., 1954; MChemE, Bklyn. Poly. Inst., 1960. Lic. chem. engr., Ohio. Engr. Schwarz Labs., Mt. Vernon, NY, 1954-55; design engr. Curtiss-Wright, Wood-Ridge, NJ, 1955-57, Fairchild Engines, Deer Park, NY, 1957-59, GE, Evendale, Ohio, 1959-62; rsch. assoc. U. Cin., 1962-66; prof. computer sci. Washington U., St. Louis, 1966-95, prof. emeritus, 1995—. Cons. Mo. Auto Club, St. Louis, 1969-82, United Van Lines, Fenton, Mo., 1984-86, Computer Sci. Accreditation Bd., N.Y.C., 1985-93. Author: Structured Fortran, 1982, UCSD Pascal, 1984, Studies in Computer Science, 1983, The DOS Book, 1985, Turbo Pascal Programming, 1991; cons. editor Holt Rinehart & Winston, N.Y.C., 1979-86. Bd. dirs. Hillel orgn., Washington U., 1983-84. Recipient Alumni Achievement award Pratt Inst., 1966, Outstanding Teaching award Burlington Northern Found., 1987. Mem. Assn. for Computing Machinery, Am. Assn. for Engring. Edn. Jewish. Avocations: trombone, walking, classical and jazz piano, jogging. Office: Washington U PO Box 1045 Saint Louis MO 63188-1045 Business E-Mail: svp@cse.wustl.edu.

POLLAK, BARTH, mathematics professor; b. Chgo., Aug. 14, 1928; s. Samuel and Esther (Hirschberg) P.; m. Helen Charlotte Schiller, Aug. 22, 1954; children: Martin Russell, Eleanor Susan. BS, Ill. Inst. Tech., 1950, MS, 1951; PhD, Princeton U., 1957. Instr. math. Ill. Inst. Tech., Chgo., 1956-58; asst. prof. Syracuse (N.Y.) U., 1958-63; assoc. prof. U. Notre Dame, Ind., 1963-67, prof. Ind., 1967-2000, prof. emeritus, 2000—. Office: U Notre Dame Dept Math 173 Hurley Notre Dame IN 46556 E-mail: barth.pollak.1@nd.edu.

POLLAK, RAYMOND, general and transplant surgeon; b. Johannesburg, Nov. 12, 1950; came to U.S., 1977; MB BCh, U. Witwatersrand, Johannesburg, 1973. Diplomate Am. Bd. Surgery. Rotating intern Gen. Hosp., Johannesburg, 1974; intern in surgery U. Ill. Hosps. and Clinics, Chgo., 1977-78, resident in surgery; immunology and transplant fellow U. Ill., Chgo., 1982-84, assoc. prof. surgery, chief divsn. transplant dept. surgery, 1988-98, prof. surgery dept., surgeon, 1995—, chief divsn. transplant Peoria, 2000—05; dir. Clinical Trials Dept. Edward Hosp., Naperville, Ill., 2005—. Fellow ACS, Royal Coll. Surgeons Edinburgh. Office: Edward Hosp Clinical Trials Dept 801 S Washington St Naperville IL 60540 Office Phone: 630-527-5672. Business E-Mail: rpollak@edward.org.

POLLARD, C. WILLIAM, environmental services executive; b. Chgo., June 8, 1938; m. Judy Pollard; four children. Grad., Wheaton Coll.; JD, Northwestern U. of Law. Lawyer, 1963-72; v.p., faculty Wheaton (Ill.) Coll., 1972-77; CEO The ServiceMaster Co., Downers Grove, Ill., 1983-93, chmn., 1993-99, chmn., CEO, 1999—2002, chmn. emeritus, 2002—; bd. chmn. UnumProvident Corp., Chattanooga, 2004—06. Bd. dirs. Herman Miller, Inc., Coro, Inc., UnumProvident Corp., Inst. for Diversity in Health Mgmt.; chmn. bd. trustees Wheaton Coll.; chmn. bd. dirs. Hosp. Rsch. and Ednl. Trust; mem. adv. bd. Drucker Found. for onprofit Mgmt.; bd. visitors Drucker Grad. Mgmt. Ctr. at Claremont. Author: The Soul of the Firm; contbr. author books and mags.

POLLARD, MORRIS, microbiologist, educator; b. Hartford, Conn., May 24, 1916; s. Harry and Sarah (Hoffman) P.; m. Mildred Klein, Dec. 29, 1938 (dec. 2001); children: Harvey, Carol, Jonathan. D.V.M., Ohio State U., 1938; MS, Va. Poly. Inst., 1939; PhD (Nat. Found. Infantile Paralysis fellow), U. Calif.-Berkeley, 1950; DSc (hon.), Miami U., Ohio, 1981. Mem. staff Animal Disease Sta., Nat. Agrl. Research Center, Beltsville, Md., 1939-42; asst. prof. preventive medicine Med. br. U. Tex., Galveston, 1946-48, assoc. prof., 1948-50, prof., 1950-61; prof. biology U. Notre Dame, Ind., 1961-66, prof., chmn. microbiology, 1966-81, prof. emeritus, 1981—, 2001—, dir. Lobund Lab., 1961-85, Coleman dir. Lobund Lab., 1985—, Coleman Found. prof., 1985—2001. Vis. prof. Fed. U. Rio de Janeiro, Brazil, 1977; vis. prof. Katholicke U., Leuven, Belgium, 1981; mem. tng. grant com. NIH, 1965-70; mem. adv. bd. Inst. Lab. Animal Resources NRC, 1965-68; mem. adv. com. microbiology Office Naval Research, 1966-68, chmn., 1968-70; cons. U. Tex., M.D. Anderson Hosp. and Tumor Inst., 1958-66; mem. colon cancer com. Nat. Cancer Inst., 1972-76, chmn. tumor immunology com., 1976-79; mem. com. cancer cause and prevention NIH, 1979-81; program rev. com. Argonne Nat. Lab, 1979-85, chmn., 1983-85; lectr. Found. Microbiology, 1978 Editor: Perspectives in Virology Vol. I to XI, 1959-80; contbr. articles to profl. jours. Served from 1st lt. to lt. col. Vet. Corps, AUS, 1942-46. Recipient Disting. Alumnus award Ohio State U., 1979, Army Commendation medal, Presdl. citation, Hope award Am. Cancer Soc., 2000; named Hon. Alumnus U. Notre Dame, 1989; McLaughlin Faculty fellow Cambridge U., 1956; Raine Found. prof. U. Western Australia, 1975; vis. scientist Chinese Acad. Med. Scis., 1979, 81; hon. prof. Chinese Acad. Med. Scis., 1982. Mem. Am. Acad. Microbiology (charter), Brazilian Acad. Scis., Soc. Exptl. Biology and Medicine, Am. Soc. Microbiology (Acad. Sci. Achievement award 1990), Am. Soc. Investigative Pathology, Am. Assn. Cancer Rsch., Am. Soc. Lab. Animal Sci., Am. Soc. Virology, Assn. Gnotobiotics (pres.), Internat. Commn. Lab. Animal Sci., AAAS, Internat. Assn. Gnotobiology (pres.), Internat. Assn. Gnotobiotics (hon. pres. 1987), Sigma Xi, Phi Delta Epsilon (hon.), Phi Zeta (hon.). Office: Lobund Lab U Notre Dame Notre Dame IN 46556 Home: 1025 Park Pl Apt 137 Mishawaka IN 46545-3537 Office Phone: 574-631-7564.

POLLIHAN, THOMAS HENRY, lawyer; b. St. Louis, Nov. 15, 1949; s. C.H. and Patricia Ann (O'Brien) P.; m. Donna M. Bickhaus, Aug. 25, 1973; 1 child, Emily Christine. BA in Sociology, Quincy U., 1972; JD, U. Notre Dame, 1975; Exec. Masters in Internat. Bus., St. Louis U., 1992. Bar: Mo. 1975, Ill. 1976. Jud. law clk. to judge Mo. Ct. of Appeals, St. Louis, 1975-76; from assoc. to ptnr. Greenfield, Davidson, Mandelstamm & Voorhees, St. Louis, 1976-82; asst. gen. counsel Kellwood Co., St. Louis, 1982-89, gen. counsel, sec., 1989—, v.p., 1993—2002, sr. v.p., 2002—05, exec. v.p., 2005—. Adj. prof. St. Louis U. Cook Sch. Bus., 2001—04. Trustee Quincy (Ill.) U., 1987-93, 97-2004, pres. alumni bd., 1986-87, Quincy (Ill.) U. Found., 1993-94, 97-; dir., sec. New Piasa Chautauqua, Ill., 1996-97. Named Quincy U. Alumnus of Yr., 1997. Mem. Bar Assn. Met. St. Louis. Roman Catholic. Avocations: soccer, bicycling. Office: Kellwood Co 600 Kellwood Pkwy Ste 300 Chesterfield MO 63017-5897 Home: 2080 Key Harbour Dr Lake Saint Louis MO 63367 Office Phone: 314-576-3312. Business E-Mail: tom.pollihan@kellwood.com.

POLLNER, JULIA A., financial executive; BBA, Miami U., Oxford, Ohio. CPA, Ohio. With Red Roof Inns Inc., Columbus, Ohio, 1987; v.p., contr., asst. treas. Metatec Internat. Inc., Columbus, v.p. fin., sec., treas., 1997—. Mem. AICPA, Ohio Soc. CPAs, Fin. Execs. Inst. Office: Metatec Internat Inc 7001 Metatec Blvd Dublin OH 43017-3219

POLLOCK, EARL EDWARD, lawyer; b. Decatur, Nebr., Feb. 24, 1928; s. Herman and Della (Rosenthal) P.; m. Betty Sokol, Sept. 8, 1951; children: Stephen, Della, Naomi. BA, U. Minn., 1948; JD, Northwestern U., 1953; LLD (hon.), Morningside Coll., 1995. Bar: D.C. 1955, Va. 1955, Ill. 1959, U.S. Supreme Ct. 1960. Law clk., chief justices Vinson and Warren, U.S. Supreme Ct. Washington, 1953-55; atty. antitrust div. Dept. Justice, Washington, 1955-56, asst. to solicitor gen., 1956-59; ptnr. Sonnenschein Nath & Rosenthal, Chgo., 1959—. Life trustee Loyola U., Chgo., Northwestern Meml. Hosp.; pres. Fla. West Coast Symphony, Sarasota, 2004-05. Mem. Chgo. Bar Assn. (chmn. antitrust law com. 1967-68), ABA (chmn. antitrust law sect. 1979-80), Alumni Assn. Northwestern U. Sch. Law (pres. 1974-75, svc. award 1976). Office: Sonnenschein Nath 233 S Wacker Dr Ste 8000 Chicago IL 60606-6491

POLLOCK, KAREN ANNE, computer analyst; b. Elmhurst, Ill., Sept. 6, 1961; d. Michael Paul and Dorothy Rosella (Foskett) Pollock. BS, Elmhurst Coll., 1984; MS, North Ctrl. Coll., 1993. Formatter Nat. Data Corp., Lombard, Ill., 1985; computer specialist Dept. VA, Hines, Ill., 1985—. Lutheran. Avocations: cross-stitch, mystery books, bowling, bicycling, softball.

POLLOCK, R. JEFFREY, lawyer; b. San Francisco, Jan. 5, 1946; BA, DePauw U., 1968; MT, Harvard U., 1971; JD, Northeastern U., 1976. Bar: Ohio 1976, Mich. 2002. Asst. sec. dept. community devel. Commonwealth of Mass., 1972—73; assoc. Burke, Haber & Berick, Cleve., 1976—84, ptnr., 1984—90; atty. McDonald, Hopkins LLC, prin., 1990—; gen. counsel Metaldyne Corp., 2001—05. Mem. ABA, Ohio State Bar Assn., Cleve. Bar Assn. Office: McDonald Hopkins LLC 600 Superior Ave E Ste 2100 Cleveland OH 44114-2653 Home Phone: 216-321-2565; Office Phone: 216-348-5400. E-mail: jpollock@mcdonaldhopkins.com.

POLLOCK, ROBERT ELWOOD, nuclear scientist; b. Regina, Sask., Can., Mar. 2, 1936; s. Elwood Thomas and Harriet Lillian (Rooney) Pollock; m. Jean Elizabeth Virtue, Sept. 12, 1959; children: Bryan Thomas, Heather Lynn, Jeffrey Parker, Jennifer Lee. BSc (hon.), U. Man., Can., 1957; MA, Princeton U., 1959, PhD, 1963. Instr. Princeton (N.J.) U., 1961—63, asst. prof., 1964—69, rsch. physicist, 1969—70; Nat. Rsch. Coun. Can. postdoctoral fellow Harwell, England, 1963—64; assoc. prof. Ind. U., Bloomington, 1970—73, prof., 1973—84, disting. prof., 1984—2001, prof. emeritus, 2001—, dir. Cyclotron Facility, 1973—79, mem. nuc. sci. adv. com., 1977—80. Recipient Alexander von Humboldt Sr. U.S. Scientist award, 1985—88. Fellow: Am. Phys. Soc. (Bonner prize 1992). Home: 2811 Dale Ct Bloomington IN 47401-2414 Office: Ind U Swain Hall Dept Physics Bloomington IN 47405

POLLOCK, SHELDON IVAN, language educator; b. Cleve., Feb. 16, 1948; s. Abraham and Elsie (Russ) P.; m. Estera Milman, Dec. 21, 1968 (div. May 1985); children: Nira, Mica; m. Ute Gregorius, 1991. AB, Harvard U., 1971, AM, 1973, PhD, 1975. Instr. Harvard U., Cambridge, Mass., 1974-75; asst. prof. U. Iowa, Iowa City, 1975-79, assoc. prof., 1979-85, prof., 1985-89; George V. Bobrinskoy prof. Sanskrit and Indic Studies U. Chgo., 1989—, chmn. Dept. S. Asian Langs. and Civilizations, 1991. Vis. prof. Collège de France, Paris, 1991; prin. investigator NEH collaborative rsch. project Literay Cultures in History, 1995-98. Author: Aspects of Versification in Sanskrit Lyric Poetry, 1977, Ramayana of Valmiki, Vol. II, 1986, Vol. III, 1991; regional editor: Harper Collins World Reader; contbr. articles to profl. jours. Am. Inst. Indian Studies sr. and short-term fellow, 1979, 84, 87, 94; Maharaja of Cochin Meml. lectr., Sanskrit Coll., Tripunithura, Kerala, 1989. Mem. Am. Oriental Soc., Assn. Asian Studies, Social Sci. Rsch. Coun. (Joint Com. on South Asia 1990-96). Office: U Chgo Dept South Asian Langs 1130 E 59th St Chicago IL 60637-1539

POLLOCK, STEPHEN MICHAEL, operations research engineer, educator, consultant; b. NYC, Feb. 15, 1936; s. Meyer and Frances R. Pollock; m. Bettina Dorn, Nov. 22, 1962; children: Joshua, Aaron, Ethan. B in Engring. Physics, Cornell U., 1958; SM, MIT, 1960, PhD in Physics and Ops. Research, 1964. Mem. tech. staff Arthur D. Little Inc., Cambridge, Mass., 1964-65; asst. prof. Naval Postgrad. Sch., Monterey, Calif., 1965-68, assoc. prof., 1968-69, U. Mich., Ann Arbor, 1969-73, prof., dept. indsl. and ops. engring., 1974—, chmn. dept., 1980-90. Cons. to over 40 orgns. Area editor Ops. Rsch. Jour., 1977-82; sr. editor Inst. Indsl. Engrs. Trans., 1985-89, Army Sci. Bd., 1994-99; contbr. more than 60 tech. papers to profl. jours. Fellow, Space Tech. Labs., 1960, Inst. Ops. Rsch. Mgmt. Sci.; sr. fellow NSF, 1975. Fellow: AAAS; mem.: Nat. Acad. Engring., Ops. Rsch. Soc. Am. (pres. 1986—87), Inst. Mgmt. Sci. Office: U of Mich Dept Indsl Ops Engring Ann Arbor MI 48109-2117

POLOVITZ, MICHAEL, state legislator; m. Barbara Polovitz; 4 children. MusM, U. Mich. Mem. N.D. Senate from 42d dist., Bismark, 2001—. With USN, 1944-46. Democrat. Office: 2529 9th Ave N Grand Forks ND 58203 E-mail: mpolovit@state.nd.us.

POLSKY, DONALD PERRY, architect; b. Milw., Sept. 30, 1928; s. Lew and Dorothy (Geisenfeld) P.; m. Corinne Shirley Neer, Aug. 25, 1957; children: Jeffrey David, Debra Lynn. BArch, U. Nebr., Lincoln, 1951; postgrad., U. So. Calif., 1956, U. Calif., Los Angeles, 1957, U. Nebr., Omaha, 1964, U. Ill., 1965. Project architect Richard Neutra, Architect, Los Angeles, 1953-56, Daniel Dworsky, Architect, Los Angeles, 1956; prin. Polsky, AIA & Assocs., Los Angeles, 1956-62, Omaha, 1964—; dir. dept. architecture MCA, Inc., Universal City, Calif., 1962-64. Adj. prof. Coll. Arch., U. Nebr., 1998—99. Prin. works include Mills residence, 1958, apt. bldgs., 1960, Polsky residence, 1961, Milder residence, 1965. Chmn. Design Control 1480 Study Mayor's Riverfront Devel., Omaha, 1969, 71; pres. Swanson Sch. Community Club, Omaha, 1972; mem. Mayor's Adv. Panel Design Services, Omaha, 1974; vice chmn. Omaha Zoning Bd. Appeals, 1976; dir. Siena/Francis House. Recipient archtl. awards Canyon Crier Newspaper, Los Angeles, 1960, House and Home Mag., Life Mag., AIA, Santa Barbara, Calif., 1962. Fellow AIA (pres. Omaha chpt. 1968); mem. Nebr. Soc. Archs. (pres. 1975, awards 1964, 68, 87, 91, 93, 94, 95, 97, 01, Firm of Yr. 1997, Harry F. Cunningham Gold medal 2002). Home: 10010 Frederick St Omaha NE 68124-2651 Office Phone: 402-391-7176 ext. 15.

POLSTER, DAN AARON, judge; b. Cleve., Dec. 6, 1951; s. Lewis H. and Elinor Ruth (Guren) P.; m. Deborah Ann Coleman, May 29, 1977; children: Joshua, Shira, Ilana. AB, Harvard U., 1972, JD, 1976; PhD (hon.), Cleve. Coll. Jewish Studies, 1988. Bar: Ohio 1976, U.S. Dist. Ct. (no. dist.) Ohio 1981, U.S. Ct. Appeals (6th cir.) 1982. Atty. Dept. Justice, Cleve., 1976-82, asst. U.S. atty., 1982-98; U.S. dist. judge U.S. Dist. Ct., Cleve., 1998—. Pres. bd. trustees Agnon Sch., Beachwood, Ohio, 1993-96; chmn. bd. govs. Cleve. Coll. Jewish Studies, Beachwood, 1984-88; bd. dirs. Jewish Cmty. Fedn. Cleve., 1989-2001, 03—. Recipient Special Achievement award U.S. Dept. Justice, 1980, 84, Special Commendation, 1988, ORT Jurisprudence award, 2005. Mem. Fed. Bar Assn., Cleve. Bar Assn. Jewish. Office Phone: 216-357-7190. Business E-Mail: dan_polster@ohnd.uscourts.gov.

POLSTON, MARK FRANKLIN, minister; b. Indpls., Feb. 9, 1960; s. Albert Franklin and Mildred (Wiggington) P.; m. Lisa Kaye Polston, July 21, 1984; children: Jordan Franklin, Jonathan Mark. AS, Somerset CC, Ky., 1981; BS, Campbellsville Coll., 1984; JD, Ind. Sch. Law, 1995. Real estate agt. Homestead Real Estate, Somerset, 1978-89; pastor Trace Fork Separate Bapt. Ch., Liberty, Ky., 1979-81, Calvary Separate Bapt. Ch., Nancy, Ky., 1980-84, Harmony Separate Bapt. Ch., Jacksonville, Fla., 1984-85, Fairview Separate Bapt. Ch., Russell Springs, Ky., 1985-89, Calvary Separate Bapt. Ch., Nancy, Ky., 1989-91, Edinburgh (Ind.) Separate Bapt. Ch., 1991; sales rep. Sentry Ins., Somerset, 1989-91; dep. atty. gen. Ind. Atty. Gen., Indpls., 1992—. Clk. Gen. Assn. Separate Bapt., 1988-96; bd. dirs. Separate Bapt. Missions., Inc., 1988-92; adj. prof. Ind. Vocat. Tech. Coll., Indpls., 1993-95. Office: Ind Atty Gen 402 W Washington St Indianapolis IN 46204-2739 Address: Edinburgh Separate Bapt Ch 905 S Main St Edinburgh IN 46124-1311

POLVERINI, PETER J., dean, dental educator; m. Carol Polverini. B in Biology, Marquette U., 1969, DDS in Dental-Oral Pathology, 1973; DMS, Harvard U. Cert. in oral and maxillofacial pathology Harvard U. Asst. prof. dept. diagnostic and surgical sciences U. Pittsburgh Sch. Dental Medicine, 1977—81; various positions orthwestern U. Med. and Dental Sch., 1981—92; prof. dentistry and chief oral and maxillofacial pathology U. Mich. Sch. Dentistry, 1992—95, chair dept. oral medicine, pathology, and surgery, 1995—96, chair dept. oral medicine, pathology, and oncology, 1996—2000, Donald A. Kerr Endowed Collegiate Prof., 1996—2000; dean U. Minn. Sch. Dentistry, 2000—03, U. Mich. Sch. Dentistry, 2003—. Mem. editl. bd. Lab. Investigation, Jour. Oral Pathology and Medicine; assoc. editor Angiogenesis. Address: U Mich Sch Dentistry 1011 N Univ Ave Ann Arbor MI 48109-1078

POLZIN, CHARLES HENRY, lawyer; b. Saginaw, Mich., June 9, 1954; s. James William and Dorothy Marie (Koski) P.; m. Roberta Anne Zaremba, May 26, 1984; children: Alexander James, Matthew Robert, Madelyn Marie. BA magna cum laude, Western Mich. U., 1975; JD cum laude, U. Mich., 1979. Bar: Mich. 1979. Assoc. Hill, Lewis, Adams, Goodrich & Tait, Detroit, 1979-81, Martin, Axe, Buhl & Schwartz, Bloomfield Hills, Mich., 1981-83, Hill, Lewis, Adams, Goodrich & Tait, Birmingham, Mich., 1983-86; ptnr. Hill Lewis, Birmingham, 1986-96; mem. Clark Hill P.L.C., Birmingham, 1996—. Mem. founders jr. coun. bd. Detroit Inst. Arts, 1986-92, treas., 1988-89, pres., 1989-91; bd. dirs. Coalition on Temporary Shelter, 1992—, pres., 1997—. Waldo Sangren scholar Western Mich. U., 1974. Mem. ABA, Oakland County Bar Assn. (chmn. continuing legal edn. com. 1986-88). Office: Clark Hill PLC 255 S Old Woodward Ave Fl 3D Birmingham MI 48009-6182

POMERANTZ, MARVIN ALVIN, manufacturing executive; b. Des Moines, Aug. 6, 1930; s. Alex and Minnie (Landy) P.; m. Rose Lee Lipsey, Nov. 12, 1950; children: Sandy Pomerantz, Marcie Morrison, Vickie Ginsberg, Lori Long. BS in Commerce, U. Iowa, 1952. Exec. v.p. Midwest Bag Co., Des Moines, 1952-60; founder, pres., gen. mgr. Gt. Plains Bag Corp., Des Moines, 1961-75; v.p. Continental Can Co. Inc., Greenwich, Conn., 1971-75; v.p., gen. mgr. Forest Products Brown Systems Operation (div. Continental Can Co. Inc.), Greenwich, Conn., 1975-77; pres. Diversified Group Internat. Harvester, Chgo., 1980-81, ex. v.p., 1981-82; pres., chmn., chief exec. officer The Mid-Am. Group, Des Moines, 1981—; chmn., chief exec. officer Gaylord Container Corp., Deerfield, Ill., 1986—2002. Mem. Greater Des Moines Commn.; trustee Drake U., 1978—; pres. Iowa State Bd. Regents, 1987-93, 95-96; mem. US Olympic Budget and Audit Commn., Colorado Springs., Colo., 1989-92. Republican. Office: The Mid-Am Group 4700 Westown Pkwy Ste 303 West Des Moines IA 50266-6718 Office Phone: 515-224-3600.

POMEROY, EARL RALPH, congressman, retired commissioner; b. Valley City, ND, Sept. 2, 1952; s. Ralph and Myrtle Pomeroy; 2 children. Student, Valley City State U.; BA in Polit. Sci., U. ND, 1974, JD, 1979. Bar: ND 1979. Atty. Sproul, Lenaburg, Fitzner and Walker, Valley City, 1979-84; mem. ND State Ho. Reps., 1980—84; ins. commr. State of ND, Valley City, 1984-92; mem. US Congress from ND (at large), 1993—, mem. ways and means com., mem. agr. com., co-chair Ho. Dem. Social Security Task Force, co-chair Rural Health Care Coalition. Recipient Found. award Rotary, 1975, Rural Health Champions Legis. award Nat. Rural Health Assn. 2004; named Outstanding Young North Dakotan ND Jaycees, 1982. Mem. Nat. Assn. of Ins. Commrs. (chmn. midwest zone 1987-88, exec. com. 1987-88), Phi Beta Kappa. Democrat. Presbyterian. Office: US House Reps 1501 Longworth House Office Bldg Washington DC 20515 Office Phone: 202-225-2611. Office Fax: 202-226-0893.

POND, BYRON O., JR., retired manufacturing executive; b. 1936; BSBA, Wayne State U., 1961. With Fed. Mogul Corp., Detroit, 1958-68, Maremont Corp., Chgo., 1968—86, dir. sales exhaust systems div., 1970-74, corp. v.p., 1974-76, sr. v.p. nat. accounts, 1976-78, exec. v.p., 1978-79, pres., CEO, 1979—86; exec. v.p. Arvin Industries, Columbus, Ind., 1991—93, pres., CEO, 1993—96, chmn., 1996—99; pres. Amcast Industrial Corp., 2001—02, chmn., 2002—05, pres., CEO, 2004—05; interim CEO Cooper Tire & Rubber Co., Findlay, Ohio, 2006. Bd. dirs. Cooper Tire & Rubber Co., 1998—. Recipient Disting. Alumni award, Wayne St. U.

POND, PHYLLIS JOAN RUBLE, state legislator, educator; b. Warren, Ind., Oct. 25, 1930; d. Clifford E. and Rosa E. (Hunnicutt) Ruble; m. George W. Pond, June 10, 1951; children: William, Douglas, Jean Ann. BS, Ball State U., Muncie, Ind., 1951; MS, Ind. U., 1963. Tchr. home econs., 1951-54; kindergarten tchr., 1961-98; mem. Ind. Ho. of Reps., Inpdls., 1978—, majority asst. caucus chmn., vice chmn. ways and means com., 1995. Active Rep. Precinct Com., 1976—; del. Ind. Rep. Conv., 1976, 80, 84, 86, 88, 90, 92, 96, 2000; alt. del. Rep. Nat. Conv., 1980, del., 1996; alt. del. to Rep. Nat. conv., 2000. Mem. AAUW, Regional Red Cross Bio-Med. Bd., New Haven Am. Legion Aux., New Haven Woman's Club. Lutheran.

PONDER, ANITA J., lawyer; BA, Fisk U.; JD, U. Fla. Bar: Ill. 1985, U.S. Dist. Ct. (No. Dist. Ill.) 1985. Dir. contract compliance Chgo. Dept. Procurement Svcs., 1983—88; ptnr. Holstein, Mack & Klein, Chgo., 1992—94, Altheimer & Gray, 1994—2002, Quarles & Brady LLP, 2002—04, Gardner, Carton & Douglas LLP, 2004—. Spkr. in field. Recipient Cert. of Appreciation, Aurora C. of C., Chgo. N.P. Constrn. Com., Inc., City of Chgo. and Turn Constrn. Co. Constrn. Mgmt. Tng. Program, Mem. of Yr., Cosmopolitan C. of C., Women Bus. Advocate of Yr., U.S. Small Bus. Adminstrn., others. Office: Gardiner Carton & Douglas LLP 191 N Wacker Dr Ste 3700 Chicago IL 60606-1698 Office Phone: 312-569-1153. Office Fax: 312-569-3153. E-mail: aponder@gcd.com.

PONDER, DAN, public relations executive; MBA, BA, Mich. State U.; grad., Leadership Detroit X. Mem. pvt. co. adv. svc. Deloitte & Touche, Detroit; CFO Franco Pub. Rels. Group, 1985, CEO Detroit, 1985—93. Mem.: Henry Ford Estate Adv. Bd., Mich. Coun. Econ. Edn. (bd. trustees), Alliance for a Safer, Greater Detroit (mem. bd. dirs.), Mich. State Chamber (mem. bd. dirs.), Detroit Regional Chamber (mem. bd. dirs., past chmn. small bus. exec. com., Svc. award 1996—97). Office: Franco Pub Rels Group 400 Renaissance Ctr Ste 1050 Detroit MI 48243 Business E-Mail: ponder@franco.com.

PONDROM, LEE GIRARD, physicist, researcher; b. Dallas, Dec. 26, 1933; s. Levi Girard and Guinevere (Miller) P.; m. Cyrena Jo Norman, Aug. 25, 1961. BS, So. Meth. U., 1953; MS, U. Chgo., 1956, PhD, 1958. Instr., dept. physics Columbia U., NYC, 1960-63; assoc. prof. dept. physics U. Wis., Madison, 1963-69, prof. physics, 1969—, Robert Williams Wood prof., 1992—. Dept. chmn. U. Wis., 1997-2000; mem. high energy adv. com. Brookhaven Nat. Lab., 1973-75, chmn. Associated Universities, Inc., vis. com., 1987; mem. physics adv. com. Fermi Nat. Accelerator Lab., 1979-82, chmn., 1981-82; adv. com. for physics NSF, 1981-84; mem. high energy adv. panel (physics) U.S. Dept. Energy, 1981-84, 87-88, chmn. subcom. on detectors, 1987-88, mem. subpanel on future facilities, high energy physics, 1983, mem. subpanel on future modes of exptl. research in high energy physics, 1987; trustee Univs. Research Assn., 1973-76, 82-85; mem. sci. policy com. Stanford Linear Accelerator Ctr., 1984-88; mem. Internat. Com. Future Accelerators, 1984-90; chmn. Snowmass 1986 Summer Study on the SSC.; chmn. User's Orgn. for the SSC, 1987-89, mem. sci. policy com. SSC Lab., 1992; mem. CDRF awards com. to scientists in former Soviet Union, 1996. Contbr. articles to profl. jours. Served to 1st lt. USAF, 1958-60. J.S. Guggenheim Meml. fellow, 1971-72, Japan Soc. for Promotion of Sci. fellow; recipient Disting. Alumni award So. Meth. U., 1983, W.K.H. Panofsky award Am. Phys. Soc., 1994. Fellow Am. Phys. Soc. (chmn. div. particles and fields 1987, com. on status of women in physics 1989—, chmn. com. to award the Panofsky prize 1991); mem. AAAS, Phi Beta Kappa (pres. Wis. Alpha chpt. 1996-97). Episcopalian. Home: 210 Princeton Ave Madison WI 53726-4077 Office: U Wis Dept Physics Madison WI 53706 E-mail: pondrom@hep.wisc.edu.

PONITZ, DAVID H., former academic administrator; b. Royal Oak, Mich., Jan. 21, 1931; s. Henry John and Jeanette (Bouwman) P.; m. Doris Jean Humes, Aug. 5, 1956; children: Catherine Anne, David Robinson. BA, U. Mich., 1952, MA, 1954; EdD, Harvard U., 1964; PhD (hon.), U. Dayton, 1996. Prin. Waldron (Mich.) Area Schs., 1956-58, supt., 1958-60; cons. Harvard U., Boston Sch. Survey, 1961-63; supt. Freeport (Ill.) Pub. Schs., 1962-65; pres. Freeport C.C., 1962-65, Washtenaw C.C., 1965-75, Sinclair C.C., 1975-97, pres. emeritus, 1997—. Cons. to cmty. colls.; chmn., pres. Ohi Advanced Tech. Ctr.; ednl. cons., 1997—. Mem. editl. adv. bd. Nations Schs., 1963-70; chmn. adv. bd. C.C. Rev., 1978-89. Past chmn. Dayton Mayor's Coun. on Econ. Devel., 1977-85; mem. Nat. Adv. Coun. on Nursing; former co-chair Performing Arts Edn. Task Force; bd. dirs. Alliance for Edn.; former campaign chmn. Ann Arbor and Dayton United Way; past vice chmn. Dayton Citizens Adv. Coun. for Desegregation Implementation; v.p. Miami Valley Rsch. Park; mem., past chmn. Area Progress Coun., Dayton; bd. dirs. Dayton Devel. Coun.; mem. F.S.B. bd. Citizens Fed. Banks, Universal Energy Systems Bd.; past chmn. Miami Valley Joint Labor/Mgmt. Profls., Area Progress Coun.; chmn. bd. dirs Ctr. Occupational R&D; bd. chair Wright Tech. Network; bd. dirs. Dean Family Funds; trustee Thomas B. Fordham Found., pres., 2006—; mem. Midwestern Higher Edn. Commn.; vice chair Miami Valley Rsch. Found.; past chmn. bd. dirs. League Innovation C.C.; bd. dirs. Miami Valley Regional Planning Commn.; chair found. bd. Mus. of USAF. Served with U.S. Army, 1954-56. Named Outstanding Alumnus, U. Mich., One of Top 100 Pres. in U.S. Coun. for Advancement and Support of Edn., Exec. of Yr., Bd. Realtors; named to Hall of Fame, Nat. Mgmt. Assn., 2001; recipient Presdl. medallion, Patron emeritus Horry-Georgetown Tech. Coll., Bogie Buster Red Jacket award, 1987, Thomas J. Peters award for Excellence, Assn. Cmty. and Jr. Colls., 1988, Marie N. Martin Chief Exec. Officer award, ACCT, 1989, The Living Legend award, Martin Luther King Jr. Holiday Celebration Com., 1991, Hon. Alumnus award, Sinclair, 1991, honor, India Found., 1992, Disting. Eagle Scout award, Nat. Eagle Scout Assn., 1993, Smitty award, Anti-Defamation award, Anti-Defamation League, 1996, Citizen Legion of Honor award, 1997, hon. award, Citizen Legion, 1997, Edn. award, Gov., 1999. Mem. Am. Assn. Cmty. and Jr. Colls. (nat. future comm., bd. dirs., chmn. 1988-89, Nat. Leadership award 2002), Ohio Tech. and C.C. Assn. (pres. 1979-80), Nat. Mgmt. Assn. (Hall of Fame award 2001), Rotary. Methodist. Business E-Mail: dponitzsinclair@woh.rr.com.

PONITZ, JOHN ALLAN, lawyer; b. Battle Creek, Mich., Sept. 7, 1949; m. Nancy J. Roberts, Aug. 14, 1971; children: Amy, Matthew, Julie. BA, Albion Coll., 1971; JD, Wayne State U., 1974. Bar: Mich. 1974, U.S. Dist. Ct. (ea. dist.) Mich. 1975, (we. dist.) Mich. 1986, U.S. Ct. Appeals (6th cir.) Mich. 1981, U.S. Supreme Ct. 1992. Assoc. McMachan & Kaichen, Birmingham, Mich., 1974—75; atty. Grand Trunk Western R.R., Detroit, 1975-80, sr. trial atty., 1980-89, gen. counsel, 1990-95; ptnr. Hopkins & Sutter, Detroit, 1995-2000, Maxwell, Ponitz & Sclawy, Troy, Mich., 2000—01; of counsel Fabrizio & Brook, P.C., Troy, 2002—03; gen. counsel A&M Hospitality, Southfield, Mich., 2002—. Served to capt. USAR, 1974-82. Mem.: Mich. Bar Assn., Oakland County Bar Assn. Lutheran. Avocation: golf. Office: A&M Hospitality 24725 Greenfield Rd Southfield MI 48075 Office Phone: 248-395-5250. Business E-Mail: jponitz@ponitzlaw.com.

PONKO, WILLIAM REUBEN, architect; b. Wausau, Wis., Apr. 4, 1948; s. Reuben Harrison and Ora Marie (Ranke) P.; m. Kathleen Ann Hilt, May 5, 1973; children: William Benjamin, Sarah Elizabeth. BArch magna cum laude, U. Notre Dame, 1971. Cert. Nat. Coun. Archtl. Registration Bds. V.p., arch., dir. ednl., instl. specialty Le Roy Troyer & Assocs. (now the Troyer Group), Mishawaka, Ind., 1971—; design instr. dept. arch. U. Notre Dame, 1976. Mem. Ind. State Bd. Registration for Architects, 1990—; mem. registration exam com. Nat. Coun. Archtl. Registration Bds., 1992—, vice chair 1996, chair 1997. Prin. archtl. works include: St. Peter Luth. Ch., Mishawaka, Ind., 1979, 4 brs. for South Bend Pub. Libr., 1983, Edward J. Funk & Sons office bldg. Taylor U., Upland, Ind., 1982, Taylor U. Lbir., carillon tower, 1985, Early Childhood Devel. Ctr. U. Notre Dame, 1994, Convents for Sisters of Holy Cross St. Mary's, Notre Dame, Ind., 1995. Mem. AIA (gold medal for exellence in archtl. edn. 1971), Ind. Soc. Archs. (Design Excellence award 1978, chpt. pres. 1985, Juliet Peddle award 2000). Office: The Troyer Group Inc 550 Union St Mishawaka IN 46544-2346

PONSETI, IGNACIO VIVES, orthopaedic surgery educator; b. Cuidadela, Balearic Islands, Spain, June 3, 1914; s. Miguel and Margarita (Vives) P.; 1 child, William Edward; m. Helena Percas, 1961. BS, U. Barcelona, 1930, MD, 1936, D honoris causa, 1984. Instr. dept. orthopaedic surgery State U. Iowa, 1944-57, prof., 1957—. Author papers and a book on cogenital and developmental skeletal deformities. Capt. M.C. Spanish Army, 1936-39. Recipient Kappa Delta award for orthopaedic rsch., 1955. Mem. Assn. Bone and Joint Surgeons, Am. Acad. Cerebral Palsy, Soc. Exptl. Biology and Medicine, Internat. Coll. Surgeons, N.Y. Acad. Sci., AMA (Ketoen gold medal 1960), Am. Acad. Orthopedic Surgeons, ACS, Am. Orthopedic Assn., Pediatric Orthopaedic Soc. (hon.), Iowa Med. Soc., Orthopedic Rsch. Soc. (Shands award 1975), Sigma Xi, Asociacion Argentina de Cirugia (hon.), Asociacion Balear de Cirugia (hon.), Sociedad de Cirujanos de Chile (hon.), Sociedad Espanola de Cirugia Ortopedica (hon.), Sociedad Brasilera de Ortopedia e Traumatologia (hon.). Home: 110 Oakridge Ave Iowa City IA 52246-2935 Office: Carver Pavilion U Iowa Hosps Iowa City IA 52242 Business E-Mail: ignacio-Ponseti@uiowa.edu.

PONTIUS, STANLEY N., bank holding company executive; b. Auburn, Ind., Aug. 26, 1946; s. Clayton and Frances (Beuret) P.; m. Cheryl Ann Dawson, Aug. 3, 1968; children: Jarrod B., Dorian K. BS, Ind. U., 1968; grad., Stonier Grad. Sch. of Banking, 1979. Bank One, 1968-91; dir., pres., COO 1st Fin. Bancorp, Hamilton, Ohio, 1991, dir., pres., CEO, 1992—2003, 1st Nat. Bank of Southwestern Ohio, Hamilton, 1991-97, chmn., CEO, 1997-98, chmn., 1998—2003. Bd. dirs. Health Alliance Greater Cin., Ohio Casualty Corp. (chmn., 1994-), Fort Hamilton Health Network (chmn.), Hamilton Cmty. Found. With U.S. Army, 1968-70. Mem. Am. Bankers Coun., Hamilton-Fairfield Arts Assn. Leadership Hamilton, Metropolitan Growth Alliance, "The Community Banker" magazine (adv. bd.).

POOLE, WILLIAM, retired bank executive; b. Wilmington, Del., June 19, 1937; s. William and Louise (Hiller) P.; m. Mary Lynne Ahroon, June 26, 1960 (div. May 1997); children: William, Lester Allen, Jonathan Carl; m. Geraldine S. Stroud, July 12, 1997. AB, Swarthmore Coll., 1959, LLD (hon.), 1989; MBA, U. Chgo., 1963, PhD, 1966. Asst. prof. polit. economy Johns Hopkins U., Balt., 1963-69; professorial lectr. Am. U., Washington, 1970-71; assoc. professorial lectr. George Washington U., Washington, 1971-73; professorial lectr. Georgetown U., Washington, 1972; vis. lectr. Harvard U., Cambridge, Mass., 1973, MIT, Cambridge, 1974, 77; Bank Mees and Hope vis. prof. econs. Erasmus U. Rotterdam, 1991; prof. econs. Brown U., Providence, 1974-98, dir. ctr. for study fin. markets and insts., 1987-92, chmn. econs. dept., 1981-82, 85-86; economist Fed. Res. Sys., Washington, 1964, 69-70, sr. economist, 1970-74; pres., CEO Fed. Res. Bank St. Louis, 1998—2008; sr. fellow The Cato Inst., 2008—; Disting. fellow in residence U. Del., 2008—. Adviser Fed. Res. Bank, Boston, 1973-74, cons., 1974-81; vis. economist Res. Bank of Australia, 1980-81; mem. Coun. Econ. Advisers, 1982-85; adj. scholar Cato Inst., 1985-98. Author: (book) Principles of Economics, 1991; contbr. articles to profl. jours. Dir. United Way Gr. St. Louis; bd. trustees Webster U. Recipient Adam Smith award, at. Assn. Bus. Econs., 2006. Mem. Am. Econ. Assn., Western Econ. Assn. (mem. internat. exec. com. 1986-89, mem. nominating com. 1995). Office: The Cato Inst 1000 Massachusetts Ave NW Washington DC 20001

POOLMAN, JIM, commissioner; b. Fargo, ND, May 15, 1970; s. Robert Francis and Susan Faye (Brown) Poolman; m. Nicole Poolman; 3 children. BBA, U. N.D., 1992. Sales cons. Straus Co., Grand Forks, ND, 1987-95; state representative ND State Ho. of Reps., 1992—2001; trust officer First Am. Bank, 1995—; ins. commr. State of ND, 2001—. Task force State of N.D., Grand Forks, 1992; mem. United Hosp. Corp. United Health, Grand Forks, 1992—, Presdl. Search Com., U. N.D., 1992; bd. dirs. Red River Red Cross, 1995, Big Brothers Big Sisters of Bismarck-Mandan. Mem. Toastmasters Internat. (sec.), Phi Delta Theta Alumni (varsity bachelors club scholarship ednl. found. 1992). Republican. Lutheran. Avocations: fishing, water sports, golf. Home: 505 Portage Dr Bismarck ND 58503-0266

POOR, J. STEPHEN, lawyer; b. 1955; BA with honors, Ind. U., 1977; JD with honors, U. Va., 1980. Bar: Ill. 1980, US Supreme Ct., US Dist. Ct. (no. dist.) Ill., US Dist. Ct. (ctrl. dist.) Ill., US Ct. Appeals (4th cir.), US Ct. Appeals (6th cir.), US Ct. Appeals (7th cir.), US Ct. Appeals (8th cir.). Ptnr. Seyfarth Shaw LLP, Chgo., chmn. exec. com. Mem.: Computer Law Assn., Chgo. Bar Assn., ABA, Order of Coif, Phi Beta Kappa. Office: Seyfarth Shaw LLP 55 E Monroe St Ste 4200 Chicago IL 60603 Office Phone: 312-269-8893. Office Fax: 312-269-8869. Business E-Mail: spoor@seyfarth.com.

POOR, JANET MEAKIN, III, landscape designer; b. Cin., Nov. 27, 1929; d. Cyrus Lee and Helen Keats (Meakin) Lee-Hofer; m. Edward King Poor III, June 23, 1951; children: Edward King IV, Thomas Meakin. Student, Stephens Coll., 1947-48, U. Cinn., 1949-51, Triton Coll., 1973-76. Pres. Janet Meakin Poor Landscape Design, Winnetka, Ill., 1975—. Chmn. bd. dirs. Chgo. Botanic Garden. Author, editor: Plants That Merit Attention Vol. I: Trees, 1984, Vol. II: Shrubs; contbr. articles to profl. jours. Participant in long range planning City of Winnetka, 1978-82, archtl. and environ. bd., 1980-84, beautification commn., 1978-84, garden coun., 1978-82; adv. coun., Sec. of Agr. Nat. Arboretum, Washington; nat. adv. bd. Filoli, San Francisco; trustee Ctr. Plant Conservation at Mo. Bot. Garden, St. Louis, also mem. exec. com.; mem. adv. coun. The Garden Conservancy, 1989—, chmn. Open Days Program Garden Conservancy; trustee Winnetka Congl. Ch., 1978-80; bd. dirs. Lady Bird Johnson Wildflower Ctr., Austin, Tex., McKee Bot. Garden, Vero Beach, Fla. Recipient merit award Hadley Sch. Blind, 1972; named Vol. of Yr. Hadley Sch. Blind. Mem. Chgo. Hort. Soc. (chmn. bd. dirs. 1987-93, medal 1984, gold medal garden design, exec. com., chmn. rsch. com., women's bd., designer herb garden Farwell Gardens at Chgo. Botanic Garden, Hutchinson medal 1994), Am. Hort. Soc. (bd. dirs., Catherine H. Sweeney award 1985), Garden Club Am. (chmn. nat. plant exchange 1980-81, chmn. hort. com. 1981-83, bd. dirs., 1983-85, corresponding sec. 1985-87, Horticulture award Zone XI 1981, Creative Leadership award 1986), Fortnightly Club, Garden Guild (bd. dirs.), Garden Club Am. (v.p. 1987-89, medal awards chmn. 1991-93, Medal of Honor 1994). Republican. Avocations: gardening, writing, music, lecturing, horticulture research. Office Phone: 847-446-2898.

POORMAN, ROBERT LEWIS, retired academic administrator; b. Germantown, Ohio, Dec. 9, 1926; s. Dale Lowell and Bernice Velma (Krick) P.; m. Lois May Romer, Dec. 26, 1949; children: Paula Beth, Janice Marie, Mark Leon, John Alex, Lisa Ann, Daniel Romer. Student, Ohio Wesleyan U., 1944-45, U. Va., 1945-46; BSEd., Ohio State U., 1948, MA, 1950; postgrad., U. So. Calif., 1951-53; Ed.D. (Kellogg fellow 1960-62, Disting. Scholar Tuition grantee 1960-62), UCLA, 1964. Tchr., counselor, adminstr., secondary schs., Colo., Mo., Ariz., 1948-57; registrar Phoenix Coll., 1957-60; intern Bakersfield Coll., 1960-63, asst. to pres., 1963-64, asso. dean instrn., 1964-65, dean students, 1965-67; founding pres. Lincoln Land C.C., 1967-88, pres. emeritus; edn. cons. MARA of Malaysia, 1983; higher edn. cons. Springfield, Ill., 1988—; interim pres. Parkland Coll., Champaign, Ill., 1989-90. Vis. assoc. prof. Fla. Internat. U., 1994-95, Fulbright Sr. Specialist peer reviewer, 2007-; lectr. in field; cons. in field. Contbr. articles to profl. jours. Bd. dirs. (past) United Way of Springfield, bd. dirs. Urban League of Springfield, Good Will Industries of Springfield, Springfield (Ill.) Symphony, Catholic Youth Orgn., Springfield, Gov.'s Prayer Breakfast, Springfield Mental Health, Griffin H.S. Bd., Diocesan Sem.; mem. adv. bd. Sacred Heart Acad., Springfield Commn. on Internat. Visitors, Sister Cities Assn. With USNR, 1944—46. Recipient Midwest region CEO of Yr. Assn. C.C. Trustees, 1988, recognition Ill. C.C. Trustees Assn., 1988; named an Outstanding CEO for Ill. Cmty. Colls. U. Tex. Leadership Program, 1987; named a leader in shaping the century State Jour. Register, 1999; Phi Theta Kappa fellow, 1981; Fulbright Sr. scholar, Lithuania, 1993, Ukraine, 1996, China, 2000; Fulbright sr. specialist, Tanzania, 2003. Mem. Am. Assn. Cmty. and Jr. Colls., Ill. Coun. Pub. C.C. Pres. (sec. 1973-74, vice chmn. 1974-75, chmn. 1975-76), Coun. North Ctrl. Cmty. and Jr. Colls. (exec. bd. 1979-81), North Ctrl. Assn. (cons., evaluator 1984-88) Republican. Roman Catholic. Home and Office: 2324 Willemoore Ave Springfield IL 62704-4362 Home Phone: 217-546-1936. Home Fax: 217-793-6939. E-mail: rpoorman@att.net.

POPE, DANIEL JAMES, lawyer; b. Chgo., Nov. 22, 1948; BA, Loyola U., Chgo., 1972; JD cum laude, John Marshall Law Sch., 1975; postgrad., U. Chgo., 1977-78. Bar: U.S. Merchant Marines 1966, Ill. 1975, U.S. Dist. Ct. (no. dist.) Ill. 1982, N.Y. 1983, U.S. Tax Ct. 1985, Tex. 1995, U.S. Supreme Ct. 1995. Corp. trust adminstr. Continental Bank, Chgo., 1972-74; assoc. Haskell & Perrin, Chgo., 1975-77, Coffield, Ungaretti, Harris & Slavin, Chgo., 1977-81, ptnr., 1981-90, head litigation dept., 1988-90; ptnr. Seyfarth Shaw Fairweather & Geraldson, Chgo., 1990-95, Bell, Boyd & Lloyd, 1996—; lead felony prosecutor Champaign County, 2001—02; gen. counsel CCPC, 2002—03; of counsel Phoebus & Koester, 2004—. Adj. prof. John Marshall Law Sch., Chgo., 1978-79; appointed panel atty. Fed. Defender Program, Chgo., 1983. Mem. ABA, Pub. Interest Law Initiative (dir. 1989-91), Champaign Country Club. Home: 3506 Cypress Creek Rd Champaign IL 61822-7948 Business E-Mail: dpope@phebuslaw.com.

POPE, KERIG RODGERS, retired magazine executive; b. Waukesha, Wis., Sept. 30, 1935; s. Kerig James Pope and Mildred (Offerman) Troemel; m. Claudia T. Koralewski, ov. 1961 (div. 1975); children— Kerig William, Giles Thomas; m. Beth Leslie Kasik, May 24, 1980; children: Kolin Jared, Zoe Alissa. Grad., Art Inst. Chgo., 1958. Designer Jack Denst Wallpaper Designs, Chgo., 1958-60; designer Continental Casualty Ins. Co., Chgo., 1960-62, Leo Burnett Advt. Agy., Chgo., 1962-63; art dir. Mercury Records Corp., Chgo., 1963-66; mng. art dir. Playboy mag., Chgo., 1966—. Exhibited in group shows Whitney Mus. Am. Art, N.Y.C., 1969, Mus. Contemporary Art, Chgo., 1972, Bienal de Sao Paulo, Brazil, 1973, Museo de Arte Moderno, Mexico City, 1974, Nat. Collection Fine Arts, Washington, 1979, Moderno, Mexico City, 1974, Mus. Contemporary Art, Chgo., 1996; represented in permanent collections Nat. Collection Fine Arts, Washington, Mus. Contemporary Art, Chgo., Smart Mus., U. Chgo. Recipient silver medal Communigraphics, N.Y.C., 1971, gold medal, 1971, 72; award of excellence Soc. Publ. Designers, 1979, 4 awards of excellence Design Ann., 1984, Silver medal Illustrators 29, 1986, Silver medal Soc. of Illustrators, 1988. Mem.: Soc. Publ. Arts (3 Silver awards 1987), Soc. Typog. Arts (Silver medal 1998, Gold medal 1999, 2001), Art Dirs. Club N.Y., Soc. Illustrators (Gold medal 1981, 1984, Silver medal 1988, Gold medal 1991, Silver medal 1998, Gold medal 1999), Arts (Chgo.), Arts Club (Chgo.). Office: Playboy Enterprises Inc 680 N Lake Shore Dr Fl 15 Chicago IL 60611-4455

POPE, MARK ANDREW, lawyer, academic administrator; b. Munster, Ind., May 22, 1952; s. Thomas A. and Eleanor E. (Miklos) P.; m. Julia Risk Pope, June 15, 1974; children: Brent Andrew, Bradley James. BA, Purdue U., 1974; JD cum laude, Ind. U., 1977. Bar: Ind. 1977, U.S. Dist. Ct. (so. dist.) Ind. 1977, U.S. Ct. Appeals (7th cir.) 1984. Assoc. Johnson & Weaver, Indpls., 1977-79, Rocap, Rocap, Reese & Young, Indpls., 1980-82, Dutton & Overman, Indpls., 1982-88, ptnr., 1988-89; asst. gen. counsel Lincoln Nat. Corp., Fort Wayne, Ind., 1989-91, sr. counsel, 1991-95, v.p. govt. rels., 1995-2001; dir. athletics Ind. U.-Purdue U., Ft. Wayne, 2001—07, U. St. Francis, 2007—. Bd. dirs. Ft. Wayne Bicentennial Coun.; pres., bd. dirs. ARCH, Inc., 1994-97. Bd. editors, devel. editor Ind. U. Law Rev., 1976-77 Mem. pres.'s coun. Purdue U., 1977—; applied econs. cons. Jr. Achievement, 1989—95; bd. dirs. Jr. Achievement of No. Ind., 1992—94; grad. Leadership Ft. Wayne, 1992; adv. coun. Ind. U. Bus. Sch., Purdue U., Ft. Wayne, 2000—02; trustee Allen County War Meml. Coliseum, 2002—; bd. mem. Ft. Wayne Urban League, 2006—; mem. parish coun. St. Elizabeth Ann Seton Ch., 1993—96, pres., 1993—95; bd. edn. mem. Bishop Luers HS, 2000—03, pres., 2002—03; mem. bd. trustees Allen County War Meml. Coliseum, 2002—; mem. bd. dirs. Ft. Wayne Urban League, 2006—. Named Disting. Hoosier, Gov. of Ind., 1974. Fellow Ind. Bar Found., Indpls. Bar Found. (disting.); mem. ABA (dist. rep. young lawyers divsn. 1981-83, dir. 1983-84, liaison coord. 1985-86, 87-88, exec. coun. 1981-88, cabinet 1982-88, gen. practice sect. coun. mem. 1986—, membership chmn. 1987-89, chmn. career and family com. 1990-92, dir. 1991-93), Indpls. Bar Assn. (v.p. 1983, chmn. young lawyers divsn. 1981), 500 Festival Assocs. (vice-chmn. of 500 festival parade 1985-89), Orchard Ridge Country Club (bd. dirs. 1995-2001, sec. 1996-97, pres. 1999-2001). Avocations: tennis, golf, running. Office: Univ of St Francis 2701 Spring St Fort Wayne IN 46808 Office Phone: 260-399-7700 Ext. 6202. Business E-Mail: mpope@sf.edu.

POPE, MICHAEL ARTHUR, lawyer; b. Chgo., June 27, 1944; s. Arthur Wellington and Phyllis Anne (O'Connor) P.; m. Christine Collins, Nov. 19, 1966; children: Jennifer, Amy, Katherine. BS, Loyola U., Chgo., 1966; JD cum laude, Northwestern U., 1969. Bar: Ill. 1969, N.Y. 1985, U.S. Dist. Ct. (no. dist.) Ill. 1969, U.S. Ct. Appeals (7th cir.) 1970, U.S. Supreme Ct. 1980. Tchg. asst. U. Ill. Coll. Law, Champaign, 1969-70; assoc. Isham, Lincoln & Beale, Chgo., 1970-76; ptnr. Phelan, Pope & John, Ltd., Chgo., prin., 1976—95; capital ptnr. McDermott, Will & Emery, Chgo., 1995—. Adj. prof. law Chgo.-Kent Law Sch. Ill. Inst. Tech., 1982-85; chair bd. trustees Nat. Jud. Coll., 2002-03. Mem. ABA, Ill. Bar Assn., Chgo. Bar Assn., Am. Bd. Profl. Liability Attys. (pres. 1985-87), 7th Cir. Bar Assn. (pres. 2003-04), Internat. Assn. Def. Counsel (pres. 1993-94), Internat. Soc. Barristers, Am. Coll. Trial Lawyers, Internat. Acad. Trial Lawyers (bd. dirs. 1999-2004), Am. Law Inst., Econ. Club Chgo., The Chgo. Club, Skokie Country Club (Glencoe Ill.), East Bank Club (Chgo.). Office: McDermott Will & Emery 227 W Monroe St Chicago IL 60606-5096 Home Phone: 847-835-5340; Office Phone: 312-984-7780. E-mail: mpope@mwe.com.

POPE, RICHARD M., rheumatologist; b. Chgo., Jan. 10, 1946; Student, Procopius Coll., 1963-65, U. Ill., 1965-66; MD, Loyola U., 1970. Diplomate Am. Bd. Internal Medicine. Intern in medicine Med. Ctr. Michael Reese Hosp., Chgo., 1970-71, resident in internal medicine, 1971-72; fellow in rheumatology U. Wash., Seattle, 1972-74; asst. clin. prof. medicine U. Hawaii, 1974-77; asst. prof. medicine U. Tex. Health Sci. Ctr., San Antonio, 1976-81, assoc. prof. medicine, 1981-85, Northwestern U. Med. Sch., 1985-88, prof. medicine, 1988—; attending physician Northwestern Meml. Hosp., Chgo., 1985—, VA Lakeside Med. Ctr., Chgo., 1985—, Rehab. Inst. Chgo., 1985—; divsn. chief rheumatology divsn. Northwestern U., Chgo., 1992—. Chief divsn. rheumatology VA Lakeside Med. Ctr., 1985-91, divsn. arthritis-connective tissue diseases Northwestern U. and Northwestern Meml. Hosp., 1989—, Northwestern Med. Faculty Found., 1989—; mem. program com. Cen. Soc. Clin. Rsch., 1987, cen. region Am. Rheumatism Assn., 1987; mem. sci. com. Ill. chpt. Arthritis Found., 1988-92, bd. dirs., 1990—, mem. chpt. rev. grants subcom., 1983-88, chmn. chpt. rsch. grant subcom., 1986-88, mem. rsch. com., 1986-88; mem. site visit teams NIH, 1986, 87, 89, 96, 97; cons. reviewer VA Merit Rev. Bd., 1984, 87, 91; cons. reviewer Arthritis Soc. Can., 1986, 87; mem. editl. adv. bd. Arthritis and Rheumatism Jour. Lab. and Clin. Medicine, 1992—. Author: (with others) The Science and Practice of Clinical Medicine, 1979, Proceedings of the University of South Florida International Symposium in the Biomedical Sciences, 1984, Concepts in Immunopathology, 1985, Biology Based Immunomodulators in the Therapy of Rheumatic Diseases, 1986, Primer on the Rheumatic Diseases, 1988; contbr. numerous articles to profl. jours. With U.S. Army, 1974-76. Anglo-Am. Rheumatology fellow, 1983. Mem. ACP, Am. Coll. Rheumatology (councillor cen. region coun. 1990-93, program com. 1983-86, 91), Am. Assn. Immunologists, Am. Fedn. Clin. Rsch., Am. Soc. Clin. Investigation, Lupus Found. Ill. (mem. adv. bd. 1990-93), Chgo. Rheumatism

Assn. (pres. 1991-93), Cen. Soc. Clin. Investigation, Soc. Irish and Am. Rheumatologists (sec., treas. 1989-93), Univ. Rheumatology Coun. Chgo., Alpha Omega Alpha. Achievements include research in pathophysiology of rheumatoid arthritis, T cell activation, T cell receptor, macrophage gene expression. Office: Northwestern U Dept Divsn Rheumatology Ward 3-315 303 E Chicago Ave Chicago IL 60611-3093

POPE, ROBERT E(UGENE), fraternal organization administrator; b. Wellington, Kans., Sept. 10, 1931; s. Samuel E. and Opal Irene (Davis) P. BSChemE with honors, U. Kans., 1952, MS, 1958. Registered profl. engr., Kans. Asst. instr. U. Kans., Lawrence, 1952-56; lab. technician Monsanto Co., St. Louis, 1952; project engr. Mallinckrodt, Inc., St. Louis, 1953-59; traveling sec. Theta Tau, St. Louis, 1959-62, exec. sec., 1963-84, exec. dir., 1984-96, exec. dir. emeritus, 1996—. Carillonneur, Grace United Meth. Ch., St. Louis, 1985—, chmn. adminstrv. coun., 1991-95, trustee, 1997-99; lay mem. Mo. Conf., United Meth. Ch., 2000-06; trustee Theta Tau Ednl. Found., 1997-2002; bd. dirs. St. Louis Cmty. Tower Bells, 2000—. Mem. Am. Soc. Assn. Execs. (life), Profl. Fraternity Execs. Assn. (charter), Profl. Fraternity Assn. (exec. sec. 1977-86, Disting. Svc. award 1995), Theta Tau (Alumni Hall of Fame 1988, mem. bd. editors The Gear of Theta Tau 1993—2001, editor-in-chief 1996—2001), Tau Beta Pi, Phi Lambda Upsilon, Omicron Delta Kappa. Democrat. United Methodist. Avocations: physical fitness, sports, photography, stamp collecting, writing. Home: 13 Sona Ln Saint Louis MO 63141-7742

POPE-ROBERTS, SONDY, state legislator; b. Apr. 27, 1950; Student, Edgewood Coll. Mem. Wis. State Assembly, Madison, 2002—, mem. aging and long-term care com., mem. edn. com., mem. rural affairs com., mem. small bus. com. Democrat. Office: State Capitol Bldg Rm 420 W PO Box 8953 Madison WI 53708 Address: 3426 Valley Woods Dr Verona WI 53593

POPP, NATHANIEL, archbishop; b. Aurora, Ill., June 12, 1940; s. Joseph and Vera (Boytor) P. BA, St. Propcopius Coll., 1962; MDiv, Pontifical Gregorian U., Rome, 1966; PhD, U. Oradea, Romania, 2003. Ordained priest Romanian Greek Cath. Ch., 1966; consecrated bishop Romanian Orthodox Episcopate of Am., 1980; elevated to archbishop, 1999. Asst. pastor St. Michael Byz Ch., Aurora, 1967; parish priest Holy Cross Romanian Orthodox Ch., Hermitage, Pa., 1975-80; aux. bishop Romanian Orthodox Episcopate of Am., Orthodox Ch. in Am., Jackson, Mich., 1980-84, ruling bishop Detroit, 1984—; mem. Holy Snyod Orthodox Ch. in Am., Syosset, NY, 1980—; Episcopal moderator Pastoral Life Ministries, O.C.A., 1991—2000. Bd. dirs. Moldovita Romanian Orthodox Ch., Hayward, Calif, 1982; tchr. summer youth programs Romanian Diocese; confessor to sisterhood Holy Transfiguration Monastery; rep. Conf. on Monasticism, Cairo, 1978; participant Monastic Consultation, Cairo, 1979, Seventh Assembly, Vancouver, Can., 1983; active mem. diocesan liturgical commn.; spkr., lectr. in field. Author: Holy Icons, 1969; editor newspaper Solia; contbr. numerous articles to profl. jours. Chmn. Romanian-Am. Heritage Ctr., Grass Lake, Mich.; organizer, chmn. Help for Romania Nat. Relief Fund and Help the Children of Romania Relief Fund; chmn. Congress of Romanian Ams., 1991—; mem. adv. bd. Orthodox Christian Laity, 1999—; pres. Ctr. for Orthodox Christian Studies, St. Andrew, Detroit, 2000; Dr. Honoris Causa, U. Oradea, Romania, 2003; chmn. bd Orthodox Witness, 2003-. Romanian Orthodox. Home and Office: Romanian Orthodox Episcopate Am 2535 Grey Tower Rd Jackson MI 49201-9120 also: PO Box 305 Grass Lake MI 49240-0309 Office Phone: 517-522-4800. E-mail: hgbnpopp@aol.com, nathaniel@roea.org.

POPPEN, STEVE, professional sports team executive; m. Christy Poppen; children: Natalie, Andrew, Nathan, Avery. BA in Acctg., Evangel U., Springfield, Mo., 1991. CPA Mo. With bus. assurance grop PricewaterhouseCoopers LLP, Kansas City, Mo., 1991—99; dir. fin. Minn. Vikings Football Club Inc., Eden Prairie, 1999, v.p. fin. Office: 9520 Vikings Dr Eden Prairie MN 55344

PORCH, ROGER A., former state legislator; m. Lois Porch; 2 children. Grad., U. S.D. Mem. S.D. Ho. of Reps., 1985-90; mem. agr. and natural resources com., edn. com.; mem. S.D. State Senate, 1990-97, mem. agr. and natural resources coms., mem. edn., legis. procedure and state affairs coms.; rancher; loan officer. Address: PO Box 317 Philip SD 57567-0317

PORCHER, ROBERT, III, entrepreneur, retired professional football player; b. 1969; BA in Criminal Justice, South Carolina State U., 1992; grad., Nat. Automotive Dealers Acad., 2007. Cert. in bus. course Stanford Sch. Bus., 1999. Former profl. football player Detroit Lions, 1992—2004; pres. Southern Hospitality Restaurant Grp., Detroit Football Classic L.L.C., 2002—; founder Porcher Cancer Relief Fund; apprentice Honda Bloomfield, Mich., 2007—. Bd. mem. Super Bowl XL Host Com., NFL Players Assn. Exec. Bd., 2000—06, Detroit Econ. Growth Corp.; NFL bd. players rep., 1997—2000; mem. NFL Players Assn. Diversity Com., 2003—06, NFL Agent Disciplinary Com., 2005—; chmn. Cmty. Rels. Action Team, 2006; steering com. NAACP, 2006. Hon. chairperson Detroit Tribute to Local Initiatives Support Corp. Silver Anniversary event; involved with The Heat and Warmth Fun, Police Athletic League, Skillman Found., Focus: HOPE. amed Detroit News Michigander of Yr., 2006, Nat. Father of Yr., Nat. Fatherhood Initiative, 2000; named one of 40 Under 40, Crain's Detroit Bus., 2006; recipient NFL Extra Effort award, NFL Walter Payton Man of Yr. Office: RP3 Inc 243 W Congress ste 330 Detroit MI 48226 Office Phone: 313-963-1940, 313-962-4277. Office Fax: 313-963-1947, 313-962-4380.

PORILE, NORBERT THOMAS, chemistry professor; BA, U. Chgo., 1952, MS, 1954, PhD, 1957. Rsch. assoc. Brookhaven Nat. Lab., Upton, NY, 1957-59, assoc. chemist, 1959-63, chemist, 1963-64; vis. prof. chemistry McGill U., 1963-65; assoc. prof. chemistry Purdue U., West Lafayette, Ind., 1965-69, prof. chemistry, 1969—. Rsch. collaborator Brookhaven Nat. Lab., Argonne Nat. Lab., Los Alamos Sci. Lab., Lawrence Berkeley Lab.; vis. prof. Facultes des Scis., Orsay, France; fellow Soc. Promotion of Sci. in Japan, Inst. Nuclear Study, U. Kyoto, 1961. Editor: Radiochemistry of the Elements and Radiochemical Techniques, 1986-90. John Simon Guggenheim meml. fellow Institut de Physique Nucleaire Orsay, 1971-72; recipient F.D. Martin Undergrad. Teaching award, 1977; Von Humboldt Sr. U.S. Scientist award Philipps U., Marburg, W. Ger., 1982 Mem. Am. Chem. Soc., Am. Phys. Soc. Office: Purdue U Dept Chemistry Brown Lab Lafayette IN 47907 Office Phone: 765-494-5329.

POROTSKY, RICHARD D., JR., lawyer; b. Cin., Oct. 10, 1970; BS, Vanderbilt U., 1993, JD, 1996. Bar: Ohio 1996, US Dist. Ct. Southern Dist. Ohio 1996, US Ct. of Appeals Sixth Cir. 2000, Ky. 2004. Assoc. Dinsmore & Shohl LLP, Cin. Mentor, HOSTS Prog. Cin. Youth Collaborative; head coach, Youth Baseball White Oak Athletic Assn.; co-chair, Red Mass 2005 St. Thomas More Soc.; mem., pastoral coun., lector St. James Ch.; co-chair, coord. Holiday Giving Basket; mem. Western Econ. Coun. Named one of Ohio's Rising Stars, Super Lawyers, 2006. Mem.: ABA, Ohio State Bar Assn., Cin. Bar Assn. (Cmty. Svc. Com.). Office: Dinsmore & Shohl LLP 255 E Fifth St Ste 1900 Cincinnati OH 45202-4700 Office Phone: 513-977-8200. Office Fax: 513-977-8141.

PORTER, CHRIS, food products executive; With Burlington Industries, Greensboro, NC; head electronic bus. unit Sara Lee Corp., CFO European food divsn., v.p. bakery market expansion Chgo., 2004—. Named one of Top 40 Under 40, Crain's Chgo. Bus., 2006. Office: Sara Lee Corp 3500 Lacey Rd Downers Grove IL 60515 E-mail: cporter@saralee.com.

PORTER, CLOYD ALLEN, former state representative; b. Huntley, Ill., May 22, 1935; s. Cecil and Myrtle (Fisher) P.; m. Joan Hawkins, July 25, 1959; children: Ellen, LeeAnn, Jay, Joli. Grad. high sch., Burlington, Wis. Ptnr. Cecil W. Porter & Son Trucking, 1955-70; treas. Burlington Sand and Gravel, 1964-70; owner Cloyd A. Porter Trucking, Burlington, 1970-72; state rep. 43d dist. Wis. State Assembly, Madison, 1972-82, state rep. 66th dist., 1982-2001; ret., 2001. Mem. coun. on recycling, Wis., 1991-94, fire svc. legis. adv. com., 1987-94, legis. coun. com. on fire inspections and fire dues, 1991, legis. coun. spl. com. on emergency med. svcs., 1992-93, joint com. fins., 1995—, Am. Legislature Exch. Coun. Task Force on Fiscal Policy, 1995—, Nat. Coun. State Legislators com. sci., energy and environ. resources, v. chmn. joint fin. com., 1999-2000, budget conf. com., 1999-2000, nat. conf. state legis., 1999-2000, assembly on issues sci., energy, environ. resources com., 1999-2000, am. legis. exchange coun., 1999-2000, task force on tax and fiscal policy, 1999-2000, assembly com. on rules, 1999-2000. Contbr. articles to profl. jours. Chmn. Town of Burlington, 1971-75; state and met. affairs chmn. Jaycees, Wis., 1963, state v.p., 1969, adminstrv. asst., 1970, exec. v.p., 1971; mem. Wis. Conservation Congress for Natural Resources Leadership and Support in the State Assembly, 1994; hon. chair Walkathon for Healthier Babies, March of Dimes, Burlington, 1998. Recipient many awards and honors including being named hon. mem. State Fire Chiefs Assn., Wis., 1992, Guardian of Small Bus., NFIB, Wis., 1991, Friend of Agr., Farm Bur. of Wis., 1992, 94, Friend of Edn. Fair Aid Coalition, 1995, Cert. of Appreciation, Wis. Counties Assn., 1993, award Wis. State Fire Chiefs Assn., 1995, Inn Appreciation award Wis. Bed and Breakfast Assn., 1998, Bethel Baptist Ch. award Burlington, 1998, Svc. award Town of Salem, 1998, Mem. Appreciation award Tavern League of Wis., 1999; named Outstanding Legislator Wis. Counties Assn., 1996, 97-98; named to Vietnam Vets. Am. Legis. All-Star Team Wis. Coun. Vietnam Vets. Am., 1995-97. Mem. Wis. Alliance for Fire Safety. Republican. Roman Catholic. Home: 28322 Durand Ave Burlington WI 53105-9408

PORTER, DAVID LINDSEY, history and political science professor, writer; b. Holyoke, Mass., Feb. 18, 1941; s. Willis Hubert and Lora Frances (Bowen) P.; m. Marilyn Esther Platt, Nov. 28, 1970; children: Kevin, Andrea. BA magna cum laude, Franklin Coll., 1963; MA, Ohio U., 1965; PhD, Pa. State U., 1970. Asst. prof. history Rensselaer Poly. Inst., Troy, NY, 1970-75, co-dir. Am. studies program, 1972-74; ednl. adminstrv. asst. Civil Svc. Office State of N.Y., Troy, 1975-76; asst. prof. history William Penn U., Oskaloosa, Iowa, 1976-77, assoc. prof. history, 1977-82, prof. history and polit. sci., 1982-86, Louis Tuttle Shangle prof. history and polit. sci., 1986—, chmn. Sperry & Hutchinson Found. lectureship series, 1980-82, acting chair social and behavioral scis. divsn., 2000—01. Supr. legis. internship program Iowa Gen. Assembly, 1978—, records inventory project Mahaska County, 1978-79, internship program Washington Ctr., 1985—; active Franklin D. Roosevelt Meml. Commn.; chpt. adviser Phi Alpha Theta, 1977—. Author: The Seventy-sixth Congress and World War II, 1939-40, 1979, Congress and the Waning of the New Deal, 1980, Michael Jordan: A Biography, 2007; co-author: The San Diego Padres Encyclopedia, 2002; contbr. Dictionary of American Biography, 1981, 1988, 1994, 1995, Directory of Teaching Innovations in History, 1981, The Book of Lists #3, 1983, Biographical Dictionary of Internationalists, 1983, The Hero in Transition, 1983, Herbert Hoover and the Republican Era: A Reconsideration, 1984, The History of Mahaska County, Iowa, 1984, Franklin D. Roosevelt, His Life and Times: An Encyclopedic View, 1985, The Rating Game in American Politics: An Interdisciplinary Approach, 1987, Sport History, 1987, Book of Days, 1988, Sports Encyclopedia North America, 1988, The Harry S. Truman Encyclopedia, 1989, Encyclopedia of Major League Baseball Team Histories: The National League, 1991, Twentieth Century Sports Champions, 1992, Statesmen Who Changed the World, 1993, Ency. Modern Social Issues, 1996, Advanced Placement U.S. History 2, 1996, Encyclopedia of United States Popular Culture, 1997, Encyclopedia of Civil Rights, 1997, Encyclopedia of Propaganda, 1997, Total Padres, 1997, The Scribner Encyclopedia of American Lives, 1998, 1999, 2001, 2004, 2007, American National Biography, 1999, The Sixties in America, 1999, Racial and Ethnic Relations in America, 1999, History of Mahaska County, Iowa, 2000, Great Athletes, rev. edit., 2001, The Scribner Encyclopedia of American Lives, Sports Figures, 2002, Great Events: 1900-2001, rev. edit., 2002, The Scribner Encyclopedia of American Lives, The 1960's, 2003, Encyclopedia of US History, 2003, American: The Development of the Industrial United States, 1870—99, Dictionary of American History, 3rd. edit., 2003, Encyclopedia of the Great Depression, 2003, Native Americans in Sports, 2004, The Fifties in America, 2005; contbr.: The Seventies in America, 2006; editor, contbr. Biographical Dictionary of American Sports: vols. Baseball, 1987, Football, 1987, Outdoor Sports, 1988, Basketball and Other Indoor Sports, 1989, 1989-92 Supplement for Baseball, Football, Basketball and Other Sports, 1992, 1992-95 Supplement for Baseball, Football, Basketball and Other Sports, 1995, African-American Sports Greats, 1995, Baseball, revised and expanded edit., 3 vols., 2000, Latino and African American Athletes Today, 2004, Basketball: A Biographical Dictionary, 2005, compiler A Cumulative Index to the Biographical Dictionary of American Sports, 1993, assoc. editor (with others) American National Biography, 24 vols., 1999; contbr. articles to profl. jours., local newspapers. Mem. Franklin D. Roosevelt Meml. Commn.; participant Green Bay Packers Project, 1992; historian United Meth. Ch.; official scorer Babe Ruth State Tournament, 2000, 03. Grantee NSF, 1967, NEH, 1974, Rensselaer Poly. Inst., 1974, Eleanor Roosevelt Inst., 1981, William Penn Univ., 1986, 89, 92; recipient Choice Outstanding Acad. Book awards, 1989. Mem. AAUP, Am. Hist. Assn., Orgn. Am. Historians, N.Am. Soc. for Sport History, Soc. History Am. Fgn. Rels., Ctr. for Study of the Presidency, Soc. Am. Baseball Rsch., Friends of the Nat. Baseball Hall of Fame, Popular Culture Assn., Profl. Football Rschrs. Assn., Coll. Football Rschrs. Assn., Coll. Football Hist. Soc., State Hist. Soc. Iowa, Mahaska County Hist. Soc. (v.p.), Iowa State UN Assn. (chmn. ann. assembly 1982, nat. soc. Disting. Svc. award 1981), Mahaska County UN Assn. (v.p.), Oskaloosa Babe Ruth League (bd. dirs.), Oskaloosa Cmty. Choir, Friends of Oskaloosa Pub. Libr. (mem. nominating com.), Friends of the Nat. Baseball Hall of Fame, Phi Alpha Theta, Kappa Delta Pi. Home: 2314 Ridgeway Ave Oskaloosa IA 52577-9109 Office: William Penn Univ Dept Social and Behavioral Scis Divsn Oskaloosa IA 52577-1757

PORTER, GREGORY W., state legislator; m. Yvette Brewster. BA, Earlham Coll. Property mgr. Cmty. Action of Greater Indpls.; mem. from 96th dist. Ind. State Ho. of Reps., 1992—. Mem. cts. and criminal code com., edn. com., pub. safety com., vice chmn. urban affairs com. Bd. dirs., pres. Near Eastside Fed. Credit Union, Friends of Urban League; bd. dirs. Indpls. Urban League; mem. Ch. Fedn. Greater Indpls.; mem. United N.W. Area Devel. Corp.; bd. dirs. Martin Ctr. Home: 3614 N Pennsylvania St Indianapolis IN 46205-3436 Office: Ind Ho of Reps State Capitol Indianapolis IN 46204

PORTER, JIM, human resources specialist; m. Deb Porter; 4 children. Grad., Northwest Mo. State U. Various human resources positions Trane Co., La Crosse, Wis., Hoechst-Roussell Pharmaceuticals, Inc., Somerville, NJ, ELBA Corp., Denver; recruiter to sr. v.p. and chief adminstrn. officer Honeywell Internat., 1982—2003; sr. v.p. human resources Carlson Cos., Inc., Minnetonka, Minn., 2003—05, exec. v.p. human resources, 2005—. Office: Carlson Cos Inc 701 Carlson Pkwy Minnetonka MN 55305 Office Phone: 763-212-1000. Office Fax: 763-212-2219.

PORTER, JOHN WILSON, educational association administrator, director; b. Ft. Wayne, Ind., Aug. 13, 1931; BA, Albion Coll., Mich., 1953, D (hon.) in Pub. Adminstrn., 1973; MA, Mich. State U., East Lansing, 1957, PhD, 1962, LLD (hon.), 1977, Cleary Coll., Howell, Mich., 1987, LLD, 1989; LHD, Adrian Coll., Mich., 1970, U. Detroit, 1979; LLD, Western Mich. U., Kalamazoo, 1971, Ea. Mich. U., Ypsilanti, 1975; HHD, Kalamazoo Coll., 1973, Detroit Coll. Bus., 1975, Madonna Coll., Livonia, Mich., 1977; DEd, Detroit Inst. Tech., 1978; AA, Schoolcraft Coll., Livonia, Mich., 1979; DBA, Lawrence Inst. Tech., 1988. Counselor Lansing Pub. Schs., Mich., 1953-58; cons. Mich. Dept. Pub. Instrn., 1958-61; dir. Mich. Higher Edn. Assistance Authority, 1961-65; assoc. supt. for higher edn. Mich. Dept. Edn., 1966-69, state supt. schs., 1969-79; pres. Ea. Mich. U., Ypsilanti, 1979-89; v.p. Nat. Bd. for Profl. Teaching Standards, 1989; gen. supt. Detroit Pub. Schs., 1989-91; CEO Urban Edn. Alliance, Inc., Ypsilanti, Mich., 1991—2003. Mem. numerous profl. commns. and bds., 1959—, including Commn. on Financing Postsecondary Edn., 1972-74, Commn. for Reform Secondary Edn., Kettering Found., 1972-75, Edn. Commn. of States, 1973-79, at. Commn. on Performance-Based Edn., 1974-76, Nat. Commn. on Manpower Policy, 1974-79, Mich. Employment and Tng. Svcs. Coun., 1976-79, Nat. Adv. Coun. on Social Security, 1977-79, Commn. on Ednl. Credit, Am. Coun. on Edn., 1977-80; task panel on mental health of family Commn. on Mental Health, 1977-80; mem. Nat. Coun. for Career Edn. (HEW), 1974-76; pres. bd. dirs. Chief State Sch. Officers, 1974-79; pres. Coun. Chief State Sch. Officers, 1977-78; bd. dirs. Comerica Bank, 1986-2002; former chmn. bd. Coll. Entrance Exam. Bd., 1984-86; apptd. by Gov. John Engler, Mich. Sch. Dist. Accountability Bd., 1999, Gov. Jennifer M. Granholm, Lt. Gov.'s Commn. on Higher Edn. and Econ. Growth, 2004. Author: Mich. Internat. Student Problem Inventory, 1962, Educational Leadership for the 21st Century, 2006. Mem. East Lansing Human Relations Commn., 1965-69, Mich. Martin Luther King, Jr. Holiday Commn., 1986-90, Gov. James Blanchard's Blue Ribbon Commn. on Welfare Reform, Nat. Measurement Coun., 1972-78, Mich. Sch. Dist. Accountability Bd., 1999, Catherine McAuley Health Systems Bd., 1990-2000, Lt. Gov.'s Commn. Higher Edn. and Econ. Growth, 2004; trustee East Lansing Edgewood United Ch., 1963-79, Nat. Urban League, 1973-79, Charles Stewart Mott Found., 1981—, Albion Coll., 1989-; bd. dirs. Mich. Congress Parents and Tchrs., 1958-68, Mich. Internat. Council, 1977—; chmn. Am. Assn. State Colls. and US Task Force on Excellence in Edn., 1983; mem. bd. overseers com. for Grad. Sch., Harvard U., 1980-88; mem. edn. com. AACP; convener goal 6 Nat. Edn. Goals Panel, 1990-2000. Recipient numerous awards including Disting. Svc. award Mich. Congress Parents and Tchrs., 1963, Disting. Svc. award NAACP, Lansing, 1968; cert. of outstanding achievement Delta Kappa chpt. Phi Beta Sigma, 1970; award for disting. svc. Assn. Ind. Colls. and Univs. Mich., 1974; Disting. Alumni award Coll. Edn., Mich. State U., 1974; award for disting. svc. to edn Mich. State U., 1974; Disting. Alumni award, 1979; award for disting. svc. to edn. in Mich. Mich. Assn. Secondary Sch. Prins., 1974; Pres.'s award as disting. educator Nat. Alliance Black Sch. Educators, 1977; Marcus Foster Disting. Educator award, 1979; recognition award Mich. Ednl. Rsch. Assn., 1978; recognition award Mich. Assn. Secondary Sch. Prins., 1978; recognition award Mich. Assn. Intermediate Sch. Adminstrs., 1979; recognition award Mich. Assn. Sch. Adminstrs., 1979; Mich. Sch. Bus. Ofcls., 1979; resolution Mich. State Legislature, 1978; Anthony Wayne award Coll. Edn., Wayne State U., 1979; Educator of Decade award Mich. Assn. State and Fed. Program Specialists, 1979; Spirit of Detroit award Detroit City Coun., 1981; Disting. Svc. award Ypsilanti Area C. of C., 1988; Philip A. Hart award Mich. Women's Hall of Fame, 1988; Summit award Greater Detroit C. of C., 1991; Mich. State C. of C. award 1991; Olivet Coll. award for Leadership and Social Responsibility, 2001; Lifetime Achievement award Albion Coll., 2003; inducted Mich. Edn. Hall of Fame, 1992; John W. Porter Disting. Chair endowed at Eastern Mich. U., 1999; Coll. of Edn. bldg. at Ea. Mich. U. named for him, 1999; bestowed 1st ever John W. Porter Leadership award Detroit Pub. TV, 2006. Mem.: NAACP (life), East Mich. U. (Martin Luther King Jr. Honor award 2007), Am. Assn. Sch. Adminstrs., Am. Assn. State Colls. and Univs. (pres.'s coun., chmn. task force on excellence in edn. 1983), Greater Detroit C. of C. (Summit award 1991), Tuskeegee Airmen (Disting. Svc. award 1991), Ea. Mich. U. Alumni Assn. (disting. svc. award 1997), Mich. PTA (hon. life), Mich. State C. of C. (Disting. Svc. and Leadership award 1991), Econ. Club (dir. 1979), Sigma Pi Phi, Phi Delta Kappa.

PORTER, PHILIP WAYLAND, geography educator; b. Hanover, NH, July 9, 1928; s. Wayland Robinson and Bertha Maria (LaPlante) P.; m. Patricia Elizabeth Garrigus, Sept. 5, 1950; children: Janet Elizabeth, Sara Louise, Alice Catherine. AB, Middlebury Coll., 1950; MA, Syracuse U., 1955; PhD, U. London, 1957. Instr. geography U. Minn., Mpls., 1957-58, asst. prof., 1958-64, assoc. prof., 1964-66, prof., 1966-2000, prof. emeritus, 2000—; assoc. to v.p. acad. affairs, also dir. Office Internat. Programs, 1979-83. Geography panel Com. on Space Programs for Earth Observations Nat. Acad. Scis., 1967-71; liaison officer Midwest Univs. Consortium for Internat. Activities, 1979-83 Author: (with Eric S. Sheppard) A World of Difference: Society, Nature, Development, 1998, Challenging ature: Local Knowledge, Agroscience and Food Security in Tanga Region, Tanzania, 2006; contbr. articles to profl. jours. With AUS, 1952-54. Grantee Ctrl. Rsch. Fund, 1955-56, NSF, 1961-62, 78-80, 92-93, Social Sci. Rsch. Coun., 1966-67, Rockfeller Found., 1969, 71-73, Gen. Svc. Found., 1981-83, Exxon Edn. Found., 1983-84, Fulbright, 1992-93; Bush Sabbatical fellow, 1985-86. Mem. Assn. Am. Geographers (Lifetime Achievement award 2004), Phi Beta Kappa (alumni mem.). Home: 10 Burkehaven Terr Sunapee NH 03782-2402 Office: U Minn Dept Geography Minneapolis MN 55455 Personal E-mail: pwporter@verizon.net.

PORTER, ROBERT HUGH, economics educator; b. London, Ont., Can., Jan. 25, 1955; came to U.S., 1976; s. Hugh Donald and Olive Marie (Anderson) P.; m. Therese Jane McGuire, June 20, 1981. BA with honors, U. Western Ont., London, 1976; PhD, Princeton U., 1981. Asst. prof. econs. U. Minn., Mpls., 1980-84; post doctoral fellow Bell Labs., Murray Hill, N.J., 1982-83; assoc. prof. SUNY, Stony Brook, 1984-87; mem. tech. staff Bell Communications Rsch., Morristown, N.J., 1986-88; prof. Northwestern U., Evanston, Ill., 1987—. Mem. bd. editors Am. Econ. Rev., 1987-88, 94-96; assoc. editor Internat. Jour. Indsl. Orgn., 1989-95; co-editor Econometrica, 1988-93, Rand Jour. Econs., 1995—; contbr. articles to profl. jours. NSF grantee, 1985, 88, 93, 97. Fellow Econometric Soc.; mem. Am. Econ. Assn., Can. Econs. Assn., Am. Acad. Arts and Scis. Office: Northwestern U Dept Econs 2003 Sheridan Rd Evanston IL 60208-0826 Home: 1318 Hinman Ave Evanston IL 60201-4732

PORTNOY, ELLIOTT IVAN, lobbyist, lawyer; b. Morgantown, W.Va., Nov. 1, 1965; s. Donald Charles and Enid Joan (Pallant) Portnoy; m. Estee Renee Mermelstein, Sept. 6, 1992; children: Joshua Brandon, Noah Abraham, Daniela Faye. BA, Syracuse U., 1986; PhD in Politics, Oxford U., Eng., 1989; JD, Harvard U., 1992. Bar: Md. 1992, DC 1993. Staff asst., cons. dem. policy com. US Senate, Washington, 1985-88; ptnr. Arent Fox Kintner Plotkin & Kahn, Washington, 1992—2002, past head lobbying practice; ptnr. Sonnenschein Nath & Rosenthal LLP, Washington, 2002—, chair firm pub. law & policy strategies group, 2002—06, chmn., 2007—, mem. firm policy & planning com. Atty. Clinton-Gore presdl. transition, Washington, 1992-93. Author: Guide to Congress, 1991. Founder, pres. bd. dirs. Kids Enjoy Exercise Now Found., Washington, Oxford, 1987—; bd. dirs. Jewish Social Services Agy., Washington, 1996—; exec. com. Dem. Young Lawyers Com., Washington, 1996—. Named Washingtonian of Yr., Washingtonian mag., 1999; named one of 50 Top Lobbyists, 2007; recipient Rhodes scholar, Oxford U., 1986—89. Mem.: ABA (vice chair legis. process & lobbying com.). Office: Sonnenschein Nath & Rosenthal LLP Ste 600, East Tower 1301 K St NW Washington DC 20015 Office Phone: 202-408-6433. Office Fax: 202-408-6399. Business E-Mail: eportnoy@sonnenschein.com.

PORTOGHESE, PHILIP SALVATORE, medicinal chemist, educator; b. NYC, June 4, 1931; s. Philip A. and Constance (Antonelli) P.; m. Christine L. Phillips, June 11, 1960; children— Stephen, Stuart, Philip. BS, Columbia U., 1953, MS, 1958; PhD, U. Wis., 1961; Dr. honoris causa, U. Catania, Italy, 1986, Royal Danish Sch. Pharmacy, Copenhagen, 1992. Asst. prof. Coll. Pharmacy, U. Minn., Mpls., 1961-64, assoc. prof., 1964-69, prof. medicinal chemistry, 1969—, prof. pharmacology, 1987—, dir. grad. study in medicinal chemistry, 1974-86, head dept., 1974-83; disting. prof. medicinal chemistry, 2000; medicinal Chemistry hall of fame, 2006; div. medicinal Chemistry Am. Chem. Soc. Cons. NIMH., 1971-72; mem. med. chemistry B sect. NIH, 1972-76; mem. pharmacology, substance abuse and environ. toxicology interdisciplinary cluster President's Biomed. Research Panel, 1975; mem. expert panel of Flavor and Extract Mfrs. Assn. of U.S., 1984—. Mem. editorial adv. bd. Jour. Med. Chemistry, 1969-71; editor-in-chief, 1972—; mem. editorial adv. bd. Med. Chem. series, 1972-77. US Army, 1954—56. Named Highly Cited Rschr., Inst. for Sci. Info., 2001; recipient Ernest H. Volwiler award (oustanding contbns. to pharm. scis., Am. Assn. Colls. Pharmacy, 1984, N.B. Eddy Meml. award, Coll. on Problems of Drug Dependency-NAS NRC, 1991, Recognition award, U. Wis., 1996, Merit award, NIH, 1997, Oak and the Tulip award, European Fedn. Medicinal Chemistry, 1999, Nauta award, Internat. Fedn. Medicinal Chemistry, 2006. Fellow AAAS, Acad. Pharm. Scis., Am. Assn. Pharm. Scientists (Rsch. Achievement award 1990); mem. Am. Chem. Soc. (Medicinal Chemistry award 1990, E.E. Smissman-Bristol-Meyers-Squibb award 1991, Alfred Burger award 2000, named to Hall of Fame 2007), Am. Soc. Pharm. Exptl. Therapeutics, Internat. Union Pure and Applied Chemistry (commn. on medicinal chemistry 1978-82, internat. com. med. chemistry 1982-85), Soc. Neurosci., Sigma Xi, Rho Chi (Lectr. award 1999), Phi Lambda Upsilon. Home: 17 Oriole Ln Saint Paul MN 55127-6334 Office: U Minn Coll of Pharmacy 308 Harvard St SE Minneapolis MN 55455-0353 Office Phone: 612-624-9174. Business E-Mail: porto001@umn.edu.

PORZIG, ULLRICH E., retail executive; m. Linda K. Porzig. With May Co., 1982—93, sr. v.p. fin., CFO Foley's, 1988—93; sr. v.p., CFO, treas. Payless ShoeSource, Inc., Topeka, 1986—88, 1996—, Petro Stopping Ctrs. L.P., 1993—96. Office: Payless ShoeSource Inc 3231 SE 6th Ave Topeka KS 66607-2207

POSCOVER, MAURY B., lawyer; b. St. Louis, Jan. 13, 1944; s. Edward and Ann (Chapnick) P.; m. Lorraine Wexler, Aug. 14, 1966; children: Michael, Daniel, Joanna. BA, Lehigh U., 1966; JD, Washington U., 1969. Bar: Mo. 1969. Assoc. Husch & Eppenberger LLC, St. Louis, 1969-75, ptnr., mem., 1975—. Lectr. Washington U., St. Louis, 1972—79. Editor-in-chief: The Business Lawyer, 1995-96; contbr. articles to profl. jours. Bd. dirs. Childhaven, St. Louis, 1978-92, pres. 1986; pres. Jewish Community Rels. Coun., 1990-92. Mem.: Am.-Israel C. of C. (pres. 2000—02, chair 2002—), Wash. U. Alumni Law Assn. (pres. 1980—81), Am. Judicature Soc. (dir. 1981—87), Mo. Bar Assn. (bd. govs. 1979—81), Bar Assn. Met. St. Louis (pres. 1983—84), ABA (chair bus. law sect. 1997—98, bd. govs. 1999—2002, mem. exec. com. bd. govs. 2001—02, chair ops. and comms. com. 2001—02, chmn. comml. fin. svcs. com. bus. law sect. coun., editor-in-chief jour.). Jewish. Office: Husch & Eppenberger LLC 190 Carondelet Plz Ste 600 Saint Louis MO 63105-3441 E-mail: maury.poscover@husch.com.

POSHARD, GLENN (GLENDAL W. POSHARD), academic administrator, former congressman; b. Herald, Ill., Oct. 31, 1945; BA, Southern Ill. U., 1970, MS, 1974, PhD, 1984. Tchr. high sch., 1970—74; asst. dir. then dir. Ill. State Regional Edn. Svc. Ctr., 1974—84; mem. Ill. State Senate, 1984-88, 101st-105th Congresses from 22nd (now 19th) Ill. Dist., 1989-98; tchr., adminstr. John A. Logan Coll., Carterville, Ill.; vice chancellor for adminstrn. So. Ill. U., Carbondale, Ill., 1999—2003, chmn. bd. trustees, 2004—05, pres., 2006—. Founder Poshard Found. for Abused Children. Served in US Army, 1962—65. Democrat. Office: So Ill U 1400 Douglas Dr Carbondale IL 62901 E-mail: poshard@notes.siu.edu.

POSLER, GERRY LYNN, agronomist, educator; b. Cainsville, Mo., July 24, 1942; s. Glen L. and Helen R. Posler; m. O. Shirley Weeda, June 23, 1963; children: Mark L., Steven C., Brian D. BS, U. Mo., 1964, MS, 1966; PhD, Iowa State U., 1969. Asst. prof. Western (Macomb) Ill. U., 1969-74; assoc. prof. Kans. State U., Manhattan, 1974-80, prof., 1980—, asst. dept. head, 1982-90, dept. head, 1990-98. Contbr. articles to profl. jours. and popular publs., abstracts, book reviews. Fellow Am. Soc. Agronomy, Crop Sci. Soc. Am.; mem. Am. Forage Grassland Coun., Crop Science Soc. Am. (C-3 div. chmn. 1991), Coun. Agrl. Science Tech. (Cornerstone club), Nat. Assn. Colls. Tchrs. Agr. (tchr. fellow award 1978, ensminger interstate dist. teaching award, 1987, north cen. region dir. 1989, v.p. 1990, pres. 1991; life mem.), Kans. Assn. Colls. Tchrs. Agr. (pres. 1983-85), Kans. Forage Grassland Coun. (bd. dirs. 1989-92), Gamma Sigma Delta (Outstanding Faculty award 1991, pres. 1987). Home: 3001 Montana Ct Manhattan KS 66502-2300 Office: Kans State U Dept Agronomy Throckmorton Plant Sci Ctr Manhattan KS 66506 E-mail: gposler@oznet.ksu.edu.

POSNER, KATHY ROBIN, retired communications executive; b. Oceanside, NY, Nov. 3, 1952; d. Melvyn and Davonne Hope (Hansen) P. BA in Journalism, Econs., Manhattanville Coll., 1974. Corp. liaison Gulf States Mortgage, Atlanta, 1980-82; dir. promotion Gammon's of Chgo., 1982-83; coordinator trade show mktg. Destron, Chgo., 1983-84; pres. Postronics, Chgo., 1984-87; v.p. Martin E. Janis & Co., Inc., Chgo., 1987-90; chmn. Comm 2 Inc., Chgo., 1990—2005, ret., 2005. Editor: How to Maximize Your Profits, 1983; contbg. editor Internat. Backgammon Guide, 1974-84, Backgammon Times, 1981-84, Chgo. Advt. and Media; columnist Food Industry News. Bd. dirs. Chgo. Beautification Com., 1987, Concerned Citizens for Action, Chgo., 1987, Midwest Bd. Shaare Zedek, Med. Ctr. Jerusalem; mem. steering com. Better Boys Found.; campaign mgr. Brown for Alderman, Chgo., 1987; mem. bd. cons. Little City Found.; mem. benefit bd. C.A.U.S.E.S. Mem. NATAS, Soc. Profl. Journalists, Mensa, Chgo. Acad. for Arts (bd. mem.), Chgo. Area Pub. Affairs Group, City Club Chgo. (bd. dirs.), Chgo. Legal Clinic (bd. dirs.), Kup Purple Heart Found. (bd. dirs.). Republican. Jewish. Avocations: politics, reading. Home: 100 E Huron # 3505 Chicago IL 60611 Personal E-mail: kathyposner@aol.com.

POSNER, KENNETH ROBERT, former hotel corporation executive; b. Chgo., Sept. 2, 1947; m. Arlene Lynn Robinson, June 21, 1970; children: Zachary, Brennan BS in Acctg., So. Ill. U., 1970. C.P.A., Ill. Acctg. mgr. Jewel Cos., Inc., Melrose Park, Ill., 1970-72; audit ptnr. Laventhol & Horwath, Chgo., 1972-81; v.p. fin. Hyatt Corp., Chgo., 1981-99; bd. dirs. Ill. CPA Soc., Chgo., 2000—. also: Lodigan Inc 3445 Peachtree N E, Ste 700 Atlanta GA 30326 Office: Illinois CPA Society 550 W Jackson Blvd #900 Chicago IL 60661-5741

POSNER, RICHARD ALLEN, federal judge; b. NYC, Jan. 11, 1939; s. Max and Blanche Posner; m. Charlene Ruth Horn, Aug. 13, 1962; children: Kenneth A., Eric A. AB, Yale U., 1959, LLD (hon.), 1996; LLB, Harvard U., 1962; LLD (hon.), Syracuse U., 1986; LLD (hon.), Georgetown U., 1992, U. Pa., 1997; LLD (hon.), Northwestern, 2001, Aristotle Univ. Thessaloniki, 2002; PhD (hon.), U. Ghent, 1995, Univ. Athens, 2002. Bar: NY 1963, US Supreme Ct. 1966. Law clk. to Hon. William J. Brennan Jr. US Supreme Ct., Washington, 1962—63; asst. to commr. FTC, Washington, 1963—65; asst. to solicitor gen. US Dept. Justice, Washington, 1965—67; gen. counsel Pres.'s Task Force on Comm. Policy, Washington, 1967—68; assoc. prof. Stanford U. Law Sch., Calif., 1968—69; prof. U. Chgo. Law Sch., 1969—78, Lee and Brena Freeman prof., 1978—81, sr. lectr., 1981—; judge US Ct. Appeals (7th cir.), Chgo., 1981—, chief judge, 1993—2000. Rsch. assoc. Nat. Bur. Econ. Rsch., Cambridge, Mass., 1971—81; pres. Lexecon Inc., Chgo., 1977—81. Author: Antitrust Law: An Economic Perspective, 1976, The Economics of Justice, 1981, The Problems of Jurisprudence, 1990, Cardozo: A Study in Reputation, 1990, Sex and Reason, 1992, The Essential Holmes, 1992, Overcoming Law, 1995, Aging and Old Age, 1995, The Federal Courts: Challenge and Reform, 1996, Law and Legal Theory in England and America, 1996, Law and Literature, revised and enlarged edit., 1998, The Problematics of Moral and Legal Theory, 1999, An Affair of State: The Investigation, Impeachment, and Trial of President Clinton, 1999, Frontiers of Legal Theory, 2001, Breaking the Deadlock: The 2000 Election, The Constitution, and the Courts, 2001, Antitrust Law, 2d edit., 2001, Public Intellectuals, 2001, Law, Pragmatism and Democracy, 2003, Catastrophe: Risk and Response, 2004, Preventing Surprise Attacks: Intelligence Reform in the Wake of 9/11, 2005, Uncertain Shield: The U.S. Intelligence System in the Throes of Reform, 2006—, Not a Suicide Pact: The Constitution in a Time of National Emergency, 2006—; author: (with William M. Landes) The Economic Structure of Tort Law, 1987, Little Book of Plagiarism, 2007, The Economic Structure of Intellectual Property Law, 2003; author: (with Tomas J. Philipson) Private Choices and Public Health: The AIDS Epidemic in an Economic Perspective, 1993; pres. Harvard Law Rev., 1961—62; editor: Jour. Legal Studies, 1972—81, Am. Law and Econs. Rev., 1999—2005. Fellow: AAAS, Brit. Acad., Am. Law Inst.; mem.: Am. Law and Econ. Assn. (pres. 1995—96), Am. Econ. Assn., Century Assn. Office: US Ct Appeals 7th Cir 219 S Dearborn St Chicago IL 60604-1702

POST, JEFFREY H., insurance company executive; BBA, Univ. Wis., Madison. Chief actuary Fireman's Fund Ins. Co., 1994—96, CFO, 1996—2001, pres., CEO, 2001—04; pres., CEO, dir. CUNA Mutual Group, Madison, Wis., 2005—. Dir. Am. Ins. Assn. Fellow: Casualty Actuarial Soc.; mem.: Am. Acad. Actuaries. Office: CUNA Mutual Group 5910 Mineral Point Rd Madison WI 53705

POSTHUMUS, RICHARD EARL, former lieutenant governor, farmer; b. Hastings, Mich., July 19, 1950; s. Earl Martin and Lola Marie (Wieland) Posthumus; m. Pamela Ann Bartz, June 23, 1972; children: Krista, Lisa, Heather, Bryan. BS in Agrl. Econs. and Pub. Affairs Mgmt., Mich. State U., 1972. Exec. v.p. Farmers and Mfrs. Beet Sugar Assn., Saginaw, Mich., 1972—74, Mich. Beef Commn., Lansing, 1974—78; dir. constituent rels. Rep. caucus Mich. House Reps., 1979—82; senator State of Mich., 1983—98, senate maj. leader, 1991—98, lt. gov., 1999—2002. Self-employed farmer, 1974—. Third vice chmn. Mich. Rep. Com., 1971—73; mem. hope Ch. of Brethren. Mem.: Alpha Gamma Rho. Republican. Office: Varnum Riddering Schmidt and Howlett Bridgewater Pl 333 Bridge St NW PO Box 352 Grand Rapids MI 49501-0352

POSTIGLIONE, COREY M., artist, critic, educator; b. Chgo., July 25, 1942; BA, U. Ill. Circle Campus; also with Martin Hurtig & Roland Ginzel; MA in 20th Century Art History, Sch. Art Inst. Chgo. Instr. painting Evanston Art Ctr., Ill., 1971—79, Ill. Inst. Tech., 1975—83, Columbia Coll., Chgo., 1979—89, Art Inst. Chgo., 1981—83, U. Ill., Chgo., 1983; instr. art history and criticism Columbia Coll., Chgo., 1990—, tenured prof., 1996—, instr., 2D design studio, 1999—. Asst. dir. Jan Cicero Gallery, Chgo., 1975—76; juror 38th Ann. Old Orchard Art Festival, 1995, 19th Elkhardt Regional, Midwest Mus. Am. Art, Elkhardt, Ind., 1997; judge Riverside Artfair '97, Riverside Art Ctr., Riverside, Ill., 1997; bd. dir. White Walls, 1992. Contbr. editor of reviews and articles The New Art Examiner, 1976—83, Dialogue mag., 1989—, Contbr. reviews and articles New Art Assn., 1975—76, C mag., contbr. editor ArtForum, 2003; contbr. catalogue essay for Liz Langer Retrospective, Artemisia Gallery, Chgo., catalogue essay for Alexandra Domowska for the Pougialis Exhbn., Columbia Coll. Chgo. Hokin Annex Gallery, catalogue essay for Karen Lebergott one-person exhbn., Columbia Gallery, catalogue essay for John Pillips, 2005; collections arranged, Art in Chgo., 1996, 1998, 2000, 2002, one-man shows include Evanston Art Ctr., Ill., 1972, Mayer Kaplan JCC, Skokie, Ill., 1973, Jan Cicero Gallery, Chgo., Ill., 1976, 1978, 1983, 1985, 1995, 1997, Columbia Coll. Gallery, Chgo., 1981, 1997—98, Passages, Oakton Cmty. Coll., 1998, A&D Gallery, Columbia Coll., Rivereast Art Ctr., Chgo., 2005, exhibitions include New Works on Paper, Jan Cicero Gallery, 1993, Labyrinth Series, Jan Cicero Gallery, 1993, Exquisite Corpse, Transmission Gallery, Glasgow, Scotland, 1994, Lakeside Views, Evanston Art Ctr., 1994, Brad Cooper Gallery, Tampa, Fla., 2003, and others, installation work, Blink, No. Ill. U. Gallery, Chgo., 2000. Recipient Third Prize (all show), Italian Am. Exhibit, 1981, Merit award, Evanston & Vicinity Exhbn., 1998. Mem.: Am. Abstracts Artists, NY, Chgo. Art Critics Assn. Home: 4508 N Monticello Chicago IL 60625 Office: Columbia Coll Dept Art & Design 623 S Wabash Rm 1004 Chicago IL 60625 Office Phone: 312-344-7190. Business E-Mail: cpostiglione@colum.edu, cpostiglione@popmail.colum.edu.

POSTON, WALKER SEWARD, II, medical educator, researcher; BA in Biol. Scis., U. Calif., Davis, 1983; PhD in Psychology, U. Calif., Santa Barbara, 1990; MPH, U. Tex., Houston, Health Sci. Ctr. Clin. psychology resident USAF Med. Ctr., Wright-PAtterson AFB, Ohio, 1989-90; dir. psychology svcs., asst. chief mental health svcs. 9th Med. Group, Beale AFB, 1990-92; fellow in behavioral medicine Wilford Hall Med. Ctr., 1992-93; chief health and rehab. psychology svc. Malcolm Grow Med. Ctr., 1993-95, faculty, 1993-95; clin. asst. prof. dept. med. and clin. psychology F. Edward Herbert Sch. Medicine, Bethesda, Md., 1993-95; asst. prof. medicine Baylor Coll. Medicine, Houston, 1995-99; assoc. prof. U. Mo., Kansas City, 1999—. Rsch. exch. scientist Karolinska Inst., Stockholm, Sweden, 1997, 98. Contbr. articles to profl. jours. Recipient Minority Scientist Devel. award Am. Heart Assn., 1995; U. Calif. Doctoral scholars fellow, 1984-85, 85-86, 86-87, 88-89, Clin. fellow Wilford Hall Med. Ctr., Lackland AFB, 1992-93; Nat. Merit scholar, 1979-80. Fellow, Am. Heart Assn., North Am. Assoc. for the Study of Obesity. Office: Univ Mo 5319 Holmes St Kansas City MO 64110-2437

POTCHEN, E. JAMES, radiology educator; b. Queens County, NY, Dec. 12, 1932; s. Joseph Anton and Eleanore Joyce P.; children: Michelle, Kathleen, Michael, Joseph. BS, Mich. State U., East Lansing, 1954; MD, Wayne State U., 1958; MS, MIT, 1973; JD, U. Mich., 1984. Diplomate Am. Bd. Nuclear Medicine, Am. Bd. Radiology (examiner 1968-78). Intern Butterworth Hosp., Grand Rapids, Mich., 1958-59; resident Peter Bent Brigham Hosp., Boston, 1961-64; jr. assoc. radiology, 1965; dir. dept. radiology, 1965-66; gen. practice medicine Grand Rapids, Mich., 1959-61; chief resident radiology Peter Bent Brigham Hosp., Children's Hosp., Pondville State Cancer Hosp., 1964; dir. div. nuclear medicine Med. Sch. Harvard U., 1965-66; dir. nuclear medicine divsn. Mallinckrodt Inst. Radiology Wash. U. Sch. Medicine, 1966-73; chief diagnostic radiology, 1971-72; asst. prof. radiology Washington U., St. Louis, 1966; assoc. prof. radiology, 1967-70; prof. radiology, 1970-73; prof. radiology, dean mgmt. resources Johns Hopkins U., Balt., 1973-75; mem. faculty Mich. State U., East Lansing, Mich., 1975—, prof. radiology Coll. Human Medicine, prof. mgmt. Coll. Bus., Univ. Disting. Prof., 1990, chmn. radiology, chmn. family group practice, chmn. anatomy. Chmn. Liason Com. Med. Edn., 1980-86; mem. Bur. Radiologic Health-Med. Radiation Adv. Com. FDA, 1982-85; mem. med. necessity in diagnostic imaging adv. com. Nat. Blue Cross/Blue Shield, 1981. Assoc. editor: Investigative RAdiology, 1968-72, Jour. Nuclear Medicine, 1969-74, Jour. Microvascular Rsch., 1970-78, Radiology, 1970-90, Internat. Jour. Radiation Ocnology, 1977-86, Biology and Physics, Cont. Edn. Radiolgy; mem. editl. bd. Radilogy, 1970-71; editor-in-chief The Radiology Resident, 1992-94; contbr. articles to various publs. Recipient awards including Dist. Alumni award Wayne State U., 1970, John J. Larkin award for basic med. rsch., 1963;; Scholar in Radiologic Rsch. James Picker Found., 1967-68; advanced fellow Academic Radiology James Picker Found., Nat. Acad. Scis.-NRC, 1965-66, Disting. Alumnus award Brigham Women's Hosp., 1993, Gosta Forsell medal Swedish Acad. Medicine, 1996. Fellow ACP, Am. Coll. Chest Physicians; mem. Acad. Mgmt. (div. sec. 1977-78), Am. Cancer Soc. (div. sec. 1977-78), Am. Cancer Soc. (div. bd. trustees 1977-78), ABA, Am. Physiologic Soc., Am. Radium Soc., Am. Roentgen Ray Soc., Am. Soc. Clin. Investigation, Assn. Am. Med. Colls., Assn. U. Radiologists (mem. exec. com. 1970-72, mem. com. 1971-72), Ctrl. Soc. Clin. Rsch., Fleischner Soc. (pres. 1993), Interam. Coll. Radiology, Ingham County Med. Soc. (mem. com. 1977—), Mich. State Med. Soc. (mem. adv. com. mem. edn. 1980—), Nat. Inst. Health Found. Advanced Edn. Scis., Radiologic Soc. N.Am., Acad. Radiology Depts. (soc. chmn., mem. exec. com.), Soc. Nuclear Medicine (nat. pres. 1975-76), Soc. Health and Human Values, Soc. Med. Decision Making (founding mem. 1979), Soc. Thoracis Radiology (founding mem. 1982—), Sigma Xi, Alpha Omega Alpha. Office: Mich State U Dept Radiology Rm 160 Radiology Bldg East Lansing MI 48824-1313 Office Phone: 517-355-0120. Office Fax: 517-353-9893. E-mail: jim.potchen@radiology.msu.edu.

POTTER, CALVIN J., retired library director; b. Sheboygan, Wis., Nov. 3, 1945; married. Student, U. Wis., Sheboygan; BA, Lakeland Coll., 1968; postgrad., U. Wis. Past Wis. state assemblyman dist. 26; with dist. 9 Wis. State Senate, 1990-98, chmn. edn. com.; asst. supt. Dept. Pub. Instrn., Madison, Wis., 1998—2003. Former tchr. Mem. Sheboygan County Hist. Soc. Mem. NEA, Wis. Edn. Assn., Izaak Walton League. Address: N6266 Rio Rd Sheboygan Falls WI 53085-2203

POTTER, DAVID B., lawyer; b. Nov. 1, 1954; BA, Southwest State U., 1977; JD magna cum laude, U. Minn., 1980. Bar: Minn. 1980. Ptnr., bus. litig. Oppenheimer Wolff & Donnelly LLP, Mpls., chmn., 2007—. Editor (note & comment): Minn. Law Rev.; contbr. articles to profl. jours. Mem.: Order of the Coif. Office: Oppenheimer Wolff & Donnelly LLP Plaza VII Ste 3300 45 S 7th St Minneapolis MN 55402 Office Phone: 612-607-7412. Office Fax: 612-607-7100. E-mail: dpotter@oppenheimer.com.

POTTER, JOHN WILLIAM, federal judge; b. Toledo, Ohio, Oct. 25, 1918; s. Charles and Mary Elizabeth (Baker) P.; m. Phyllis May Bihn, Apr. 14, 1944; children: John William, Carolyn Diane, Kathryn Susan. PhB cum laude, U. Toledo, 1940; JD, U. Mich., 1946. Bar: Ohio 1947. Assoc. Zachman, Boxell, Schroeder & Torbet, Toledo, 1946-51; ptnr. Boxell, Bebout, Torbet & Potter, Toledo, 1951-69; mayor City of Toledo, 1961-67; asst. atty. gen. State of Ohio, 1968-69; judge 6th Dist. Ct. Appeals, 1969-82, U.S. Dist. Ct., Toledo, 1982—, sr. judge, 1992—. Presenter in field. Sr. editor U. Mich. Law Rev., 1946. Pres. Ohio Mcpl. League, 1965; past assoc. pub. mem. Toledo Labor Mgmt. Commn.; past pres., bd. dirs. Commn. on Rels. with Toledo (Spain); past bd. dirs. Cummings Sch. Toledo Opera Assn., Conlon Ctr.; past trustee Epworth United Meth. Ch.; hon. chmn. Toledo Festival Arts, 1980. Capt. F.A., U.S. Army, 1942-46. Decorated Bronze Star; recipient Leadership award Toledo Bldg. Congress, 1965, Merit award Toledo Bd. Realtors, 1967, Resolution of Recognition award Ohio Ho. of Reps., 1982, Outstanding Alumnus award U. Toledo, 1966, conf. rm. named in his honor, U.S. Courthouse, Toledo, 1998; named to Field Arty. Officer Candidate Sch. Hall of Fame, 1999. Fellow Am. Bar Found., Am. Judicature Soc., 6th Jud. Cir. Dist. Judges Assn., Fed. Judges Assn.; mem. ABA, Ohio Bar Assn. (Found. Outstanding Rsch. award 1995), Toledo Bar Assn. (exec. com. 1962-64, award 1992), Lucas County Bar Assn., U. Toledo Alumni Assn. (past pres.), Toledo Zool. Soc. (past bd. dirs.), Old Newsboys Club, Toledo Club, Kiwanis (past pres.), Phi Kappa Phi. Home: 2418 Middlesex Dr Toledo OH 43606-3114 Office: US Dist Ct 307 US Courthouse 1716 Spielbusch Ave Toledo OH 43624-1363

POTTER, KEVIN, lawyer; Former dist. atty., Wood County, Wis.; former chmn. Wis. Tax Appeals Commn., Wis. Labor and Indsl. Review Commn.; U.S. Atty. We. Dist. Wis., Madison, 1991-93; mem. Brennan Steil Basting and MacDougall S.C., Madison, 1993—2001; chief legal counsel Wis. Dept. Corrections, 2001—. Office: Wis Dept Corrections 3099 E Washington Ave PO Box 7925 Madison WI 53707-7925 Office Phone: 608-240-5035.

POTTER, MICHAEL J., retail stores executive; b. Oreg., 1960; BS, U. Oreg., 1983; MBA, Capital U., Ohio. CFO, sr. v.p. Consolidated Stores Corp. (now Big Lots), Columbus, Ohio, 1991—2000; pres., CEO Big Lots, Columbus, Ohio, 2000—. Office: Big Lots 300 Phillipi Rd Columbus OH 43228-5311

POTTER, ROSEMARY, state legislator; b. Apr. 15, 1952; m. Steve Nichols, 1994. BA, U. Wis., Milw., 1974, MA, 1983. Former dist. dir. Combined Health Appeal Wis. Ho. of Reps.; chairwoman Dem. Caucus; Wis. state assemblywoman Dist. 20, 1989-98; pub. polit. advocate Foley & Lardner, Milw., 1998—. Former tchr. Office: Doley & Lardner 1st Star Center 777 E Wisconsin Ave Ste 3800 Milwaukee WI 53202-5367 Home: W314n8709 Winchester Trl Hartland WI 53029-9525

POTTER, SUSAN KUNIHOLM, bank executive; BA, Cornell U., 1988; MBA, U. Pa. Sr. mgr. Sotheby's, 1992—94; bus. analyst McKinsey & Co., Cleve., 1994—98, engagement mgr., 1998—2002; exec. v.p. product mgmt. consumer banking group KeyCorp, Cleve., 2002—04, exec. v.p. retail bus. devel., 2004—. Named One of 25 Women to Watch, U.S. Banker Mag., 2003. Office: KeyCorp 127 Public Square Cleveland OH 44114-1306

POTTORFF, JO ANN, state legislator; b. Wichita, Kans., Mar. 7, 1936; d. John Edward McCluggage and Helen Elizabeth (Alexander) Ryan; m. Gary Nial Pottorff; children: Michael Lee, Gregory Nial. BA, Kansas State U., 1957; MA, St. Louis U., 1969. Elem. tchr. Pub. Sch., Keats and St. George, 1957-59; cons., elem. specialist Mid Continent Regional Edn. Lab., Kansas City, Mo., 1971-73; cons. Poindexter Assocs., Wichita, 1975; campaign mgr. Garner Shriver Congl. Camp, Wichita, 1976; interim dir. Wichita Area Rape Ctr., 1977; conf. coord. Biomedical Synergistics Inst., Wichita, 1977-79; real estate sales asst. Chester Kappelman Group, Wichita, 1979-98, J.P. Weigard & Sons, Wichita, 1998—; state rep. State of Kans., Topeka, 1985—; regional dir. Women in Govt. Mem. exec. com. Nat. Conf. State Legis. Com. Mem. sch. bd. Wichita Pub. Schs., 1977-85; bd. dirs. Edn. Consol. and Improvement Act Adv. com., Kans. Found. for the Handicapped; mem. Children and Youth Adv. com. (bd. dirs.); active Leadership Kans.; chairperson women's network Nat. Conf., State Legislators; mem. Wichita Children's Home Bd.; vice chmn. Nat. Assessment Governing Bd.; chair edn. com. assembly on state issues Nat. Conf. State legislators. Recipient Disting. Svc. award Kans. Assn. Sch. Bds., 1983, Outstanding Svc. to Sch. Children of Nation award Coun. Urban Bds., 1984, awards Gov.'s Conf. for Prevention of Child Abuse and Neglect, Kans. Assn. Reading. Mem. Leadership Am. Alumnae (bd. dirs., sec) Found. for Agr. in Classroom (bd. dirs.), Jr. League, Vet. Aux. (pres.), Bd. Nat. State Art Agys., Rotary, Ky. Assn. Rehab. Facilities (Ann. award), Nat. Order Women in Legislature (past bd. dirs.), at. Conf. State Legislatures (chmn. edn. assembly state issues, exec. com.), Rotary, Chi Omega (pres.). Avocations: politics, travel. Office: Weigard 6530 E 13th St N Wichita KS 67206-1247

POTTS, ANTHONY VINCENT, optometrist, orthokeratologist; b. Detroit, Aug. 10, 1945; m. Susan Claire, July 1, 1967; 1 child, Anthony Christian. Student, Henry Ford Community Coll., 1964—65, Eastern Mich. U., 1965—66; OD, So. Coll. Optometry, 1970; MS in Health Svcs. Mgmt., LaSalle U., 1995. Practice orthokeratology and contact lenses, Troy, Mich., 1975—; head of optometry Nat. Naval Med. Ctr., Bethesda, Md. Adj. prof. optometry So.Calif. Coll. Optometry, Pa. Coll. Optometry; lectr., author orthokeratology, contact lenses and astigmatism; head optometry Nat. Naval Med. Ctr. Bethesda Md. Comdr. MSC, USN, 1992—. Fellow Internat. Orthokeratology Soc. (membership chmn. 1976-83, bd. dirs. local chpt. 1976-83, chmn. Internat. Eye Rsch. Found. sect. 1981-83, bd. dirs. nat. chpt. 1985—, adminstrv. dir. nat. chpt. 1985—, chmn. nat. chpt. 1987-1992), Fellow Am. Acad. Optometry, Am. Optometric Assn.; mem. Am. Assn. Healthcare Execs., Armed Forces Optometric Soc., Nat. Eye Rsch. Found., Naval Order Am., Assn. of Mil. Surgeons of U.S., Naval Hosp. Am. Care Ctr., Am. Coll. Healthcare Execs. Roman Catholic. Office: Med Sq Troy 1575 W Big Beaver Rd Ste 11C Troy MI 48084-3525

POTTS, ROBERT LESLIE, academic administrator; b. Jan. 30, 1944; s. Frank Vines and Helen Ruth (Butler) Potts; m. Irene Elisabeth Johansson, Aug. 22, 1965; children: Julia Anna, Robert Leslie. BA, So. Coll., 1966; JD, U. Ala., 1969; LLM, Harvard U., 1971. Law clk. to chief judge U.S. Dist. Ct. (no. dist.) Ala., 1969—70; rschr. Herrick, Smith, Donald, Farley & Ketchum, Boston, 1970—71; lectr. Boston U., 1971, U. Ala., 1973—75, 1988; ptnr. Potts & Young, Florence, Ala., 1971—84; gen. counsel U. Ala. Sys., 1984—89; pres. U. North Ala., 1990—2004; chancellor ND Univ. Sys., 2004—. Mem. Nat. Adv. Com. on Instnl. Quality and Integrity, 1994—2001; com. on colls. So. Assn. Colls. and Schs., 2001—04; chmn. Nat. ROTC subcom. for Sec. of Army, 1999—2001; adv. com. rules of civil procedure Ala. Supreme Ct., 1973—88; chmn. Ala. Bd. Bar Examiners, 1983—86, Ala. Coun. Coll. and Univ. Pres., 2001—03, Nat. Conf. Bar Examiners, 1994—95. Contbr. numerous articles to profl. jours., edn. and schs. Trustee Ala. State U., 1976—79, Oakwood Coll., 1978—81; pres. Ala. Higher Edn. Loan Corp., 1988—93. Mem.: ABA (ho. of dels. 2001—03), ND State Bd. Career Technical Edn., Western Interstate commn. Higher Edn., Midwestern Higher Edn. Compact (commr.), Am. Assn. State Colls. and Univs. (bd. dirs. 2002—04), Ala. Bar Assn. (pres. young lawyers sect. 1979—80). Office: ND Univ Sys 600 E Blvd Ave Dept 215 Bismarck ND 58505-0230 Home Phone: 701-255-3054; Office Phone: 701-328-2963. Business E-Mail: robert.potts@ndus.nodak.edu.

POUCHE, FREDRICK, state legislator; b. Independence, Mo., Aug. 3, 1945; m. Martha M. Pouche; children: Sean R., Ash Thomas. BA in Bus. Adminstrn. summa cum laude, Park Coll., Parkville, Mo., 1980; MA in Bus. Adminstrn. and Mgmt. magna cum laude, Webster U., 1982. Prin. Pouche Corp.; adminstr. labor rels., sr. fin. analyst Trans World Airlines, 1965-84; fee agt. Mo. Dept. Revenue, 1985-89; auditor Platte County, 1989-91; state rep. 30th dist. Mo. Ho. of Reps., 1995-97. Candidate Mo. Ho. of Reps., 1982, 86, 88, 94; committeeman Platte County Rep. Com., 1983-84; staff rep. Ashcroft for Gov. Com., 1984; fin. chmn. Platte Rep. Com., 1984-85; dist. chmn. Dole for Pres. Com., 1987-88; Mo. del. Rep. Nat. Conv., 1988; Platte County coord. Roy Blunt for Gov. Com., 1994 Decorated Army Commendation medal with oak leaf cluster (2), others. Mem. KC (# 3430), Northland C. of C., South Platte Rotary Club (Paul Harris fellow), Platte Rep. Assn. Roman Catholic.

POUR-EL, MARIAN BOYKAN, mathematician, educator; b. NYC; d. Joseph and Mattie (Caspe) Boykan; m. Akiva Pour-El; 1 child. AB, Hunter Coll.; A.M., Harvard U., 1951, PhD, 1958. Prof. math. U. Minn., Mpls., 1968—2000, prof. emeritus, 2000—. Mem. Inst. Advanced Study, Princeton, N.J., 1962-64; mem. coun. Conf. Bd. Math. Scis., 1977-82, lectr. internat. congresses in math. logic and computer sci., Eng., 1971, Hungary, 1967, Czech Republic, 1973, 1998, Germany, 1983, 96-97, Japan, 1985, 88, China, 1987; lectr. Polish Acad. Sci., 1974; lectr. Fed. Republic of Germany, 1980, 1983, 87, 89, 91, 96 Japan, 1985, 87, 90, 93, China, 1987, Sweden, 1983, 94, Finland, 1991, Estonia, 1991, Moscow, 1992, Amsterdam, 1992; mem. Fulbright Com. on Maths., 1986-89; invited spkr. Internat. Congress on Computability and Complexity Theory, Kazan U., Russia, 1997, Workshop on Computability and Complexity in Analysis, held in conjunction with 23rd Internat. Symposium on Math. Founds. of Computer Sci. and Computer Sci. Logic, Brno, Czech Republic, 1998, IEEE Workshop on Real Number Computation, 1998 Author: (with I. Richards) Computability in Analysis and Physics, 1989; contbr. articles to profl. jours. Named to Hunter Coll. Hall of Fame, 1975; AS grantee, 1966. Fellow AAAS, Japan Soc. for Promotion of Sci.; mem. Am. Math. Soc. (coun. 1980-88, numerous com., spkr., orgn. spl. sessions on math. logic), Assn. Symbolic Logic, Math. Assn. Am. (nat. panel vis. lectr.), Phi Beta Kappa, Sigma Xi, Pi Mu Epsilon (mathematics), Sigma Pi Sigma (physics). Achievements include research in mathematical logic (theoretical computer science) and in computability and noncomputability in physical theory—wave, heat, potential equations, eigenvalues, eigenvectors. Office: U Minn Sch Math Vincent Hall Minneapolis MN 55455-0488 E-mail: pour-el@math.umn.edu.

POVINELLI, LOUIS A., aeronautical engineer; b. NYC, June 10, 1931; With Bell Aircraft Corp., 1951-56; chief scientist turbomachinery and propulsion sys. NASA Glenn Rsch. Ctr., Cleve., 1960—. Program dir. Inst. for Computational Mechanics in Propulsion, 1987—. Contbr. over 110 articles to profl. jours. Recipient Aircraft Engine Tech. award IGTI, 1999. Fellow AIAA (Air Breathing Propulsion award 1997), ASME. Office: NASA Lewis Rsch Ctr Cleveland OH 44135-3191

POWELL, ANTHONY J., state legislator, lawyer; m. Betty Powell. Atty., Wichita, Kans.; mem. from dist. 85 Kans. State Ho. of Reps., Topeka. Office: Kans Ho of Reps State House Topeka KS 66612 Home: 10313 E Ayesbury Ct Wichita KS 67226-3653

POWELL, BARRY BRUCE, classicist, educator; b. Sacramento, Apr. 30, 1942; s. Barrett Robert and Anita Louise (Burns) Powell; m. Patricia Ann Cox; children: Elena Melissa, Adam Vincent. BA in Classics, U. Calif., Berkeley, 1963, PhD, 1971; MA, Harvard U., 1965. Asst. prof. Northern Ariz. U., Flagstaff, 1970-73; from asst. prof. to prof. U. Wis., Madison, 1973—, chmn. dept. classics, 1985-92, chmn. program integrated liberal studies. Author: Composition by Theme in the Odyssey, 1973, Homer and the Origin of the Greek Alphabet, 1991, Classical Myth, 1995, 6th edit., 2008, New Companion to Homer, 1997, A Short Introduction to Classical Myth, 2001, Writing and the

Origins of Greek Literature, 2002, Homer, 2003, 2d edit., 2007, Ramses in Nighttown, 2006, The War at Troy: A True History, 2006; author: (with Ian Morris) The Greeks: Society, Culture, History, 2004, numerous poems; writer screenplays; contbr. articles to profl. jours.; author (writing): Theory and History: The Technology of Civilization. Woodrow Wilson fellow, 1965. Mem.: Am. Acad. in Rome, Classical Assn. Midwest and South, Archeol. Inst. Am., Am. Sch. Classical Studies at Athens (mng. com.), Am. Philol. Assn., Phi Beta Kappa (former pres. Madison chpt.). Home: 1210 Sweetbriar Rd Madison WI 53705-2228 Office: Univ Wis Dept Classics Madison WI 53707 Home Phone: 608-233-5991; Office Phone: 608-262-2041. E-mail: bbpowell@wisc.edu.

POWELL, DAVID W., manufacturing executive; V.p., stationary and office supplies 3M Co., sr. v.p., mktg., 1999—. Mem., bd. overseers Carlson Sch. Mgmt., U. Minn., 2003—04. Pres. 3M Found. Office: 3M Co 3M Ctr Saint Paul MN 55144

POWELL, DEBORAH ELIZABETH, pathologist, dean; b. Lynn, Mass., Nov. 28, 1939; MD, Tufts U., 1965. Diplomate Am. Bd. Pathology. Intern Georgetown Med. Ctr., Washington, 1965-66; resident in pathology NIH, Bethesda, Md., 1966-69; exec. dean, vice-chancellor clin. affairs U. Kans. Sch. Medicine, Kansas City, 1997—2002; dean, asst. v.p. for clin. scis. U. Minn. Med. Sch., Mpls., 2002—. Past pres. U.S. & Can. Acad. Pathology, Inc.; trustee Am. Bd. Pathology. Mem.: Am. Soc. Investigative Pathologists, Inst. Medicine, Coll. Am. Pathologists. Office: U Minn Med Sch Dean's Office MMC 293 Mayo 8293 420 Delaware St SE Minneapolis MN 55455 Home Phone: 952-546-1215. Business E-Mail: dpowell@umn.edu.

POWELL, KEN (KENDALL J. POWELL), consumer products company executive; b. 1954; BA, Harvard U., 1976; MBA, Stanford U., 1979. Mktg. & mgmt. positions Gen. Mills, Inc., Mpls., 1979—90; v.p. mktg. dir. Cereal Partners Worldwide, 1990—96; pres. Yoplait USA divsn. Gen. Mills, Inc., Mpls., 1996—97, pres. Big G Cereals divsn., 1997—99, sr. v.p., 1998—2004; CEO CPW, S.A. (Cereal Partners Worldwide), Morges, Switzerland, 1999—2004; exec. v.p. Meals, Pillsbury USA, Bakeries & Foodservice Gen. Mills, Inc., Mpls., 2004—05, exec. v.p., COO U.S. retail, 2005—06, pres., COO, 2006—07, CEO, 2007—. Bd. mem. Cereal Partners Worldwide. Bd. mem. Twin Cities United Way. Office: General Mills Inc 1 General Mills Blvd Minneapolis MN 55426*

POWELL, KENNETH GRANT, aerospace engineering educator; b. Euclid, Ohio, July 3, 1960; s. Thomas Edward and Mary Catherine (Byrum) P.; m. Susanne Maria Krummel, Aug. 31, 1991; children: Jasmine Tara, Ryan Grant, Nicole Maia. SB in Math., MIT, 1982, SB in Aeronautics, 1982, SM in Aeronautics, 1984, ScD in Aeronautics, 1987. Asst. prof. dept. aerospace engring. U. Mich., Ann Arbor, 1987-93, assoc. prof. dept. aerospace engring., 1993-2000, prof. dept. aerospace engring., 2000—02, Arthur F. Thurnau prof., 2002—. Lectr. Von Karman Inst. for Fluid Dynamics, Brussels, 1990, 96; cons. Ford Motors, Dearborn, Mich., 1992-95; cons. Detroit Edison, 1996-98; exec. dir. Francois-Xavier Bagnoud Prize Bd., 1998-2000. Named Presdl. Young investigator NSF, 1988; recipient Tchg. Excellence award U. Mich. Coll. Engring., 1992, Outstanding Tchg. award Tau Beta Pi, 1988, 99, 2005, Tchg. Excellence award Sigma Gamma Tau, 1989, 95. Fellow AIAA (assoc.); mem. Tau Beta Pi, Sigma Xi, Sigma Gamma Tau. Home: 5531 Spring Hill Dr Ann Arbor MI 48105-9552 Office: U Mich Dept of Aerospace Engring Ann Arbor MI 48109

POWELL, MICHAEL N., metal products executive; V.p., gen. mgr. Superior Valve divsn. Amcast Indsl. Corp., 1994-96, pres. Amcast Flow Control, 1996—. Office: PO Box 1008 Elkhart IN 46515-1008

POWER, JOSEPH EDWARD, lawyer; b. Peoria, Ill., Dec. 2, 1938; s. Joseph Edward and Margaret Elizabeth (Birkett) P.; m. Camille June Repass, Aug. 1, 1964; children— Joseph Edward, David William, James Repass Student, Knox Coll., Galesburg, Ill., 1956-58; BA, U. Iowa, 1960, JD, 1964; CAP, The Am. Coll., Bryn Mawr, Pa., 2004. Bar: Iowa 1964. Law clk. to judge U.S. Dist. Ct., 1964-65; mem. Bradshaw, Fowler, Proctor & Fairgrave, P.C., Des Moines, 1965—2005, of counsel, 2005—. Trustee Am. Inst. Bus., 1987-2002, chmn., 1992-2002; bd. dir. Iowa Law Sch. Found., 1992-2004, Plymouth Ch. Found., 1991-99; bd. dir. Des Moines Cmty. Found., 1996-2007, sec.-treas., 2001-07; bd. dir. Iowa Natural Heritage Found., 1995—, chmn., 2003-05; mem. Des Moines Civil War Roundtable. Fellow Am. Coll. Trust and Estate Counsel (state chair 1994-2000); mem. Iowa Bar Assn. (chmn. probate, property and trust law com. 1983-87), Polk County Bar Assn., Des Moines Estate Planners Forum (pres. 1982-83), Wakonda Club, Rotary Club. Mem.United Ch. Of Christ. Home: 1928 Elm Cr West Des Moines IA 50265 E-mail: jedwardpower@aol.com.

POWERS, BRUCE THEODORE (TED POWERS), state legislator; b. Plymouth, Ind., June 24, 1934; s. Theodore Roosevelt and Mary (McKee) P.; m. Betty Mae Wehling; children: Cindy Jo (Mrs. John G.K. Kennedy), Shari Lynn (Mrs. Peter Bonneson), Charles Theodore. BMF, Phillips U., 1956; MME, Wichita State U., 1960; postgrad., Kans. U., 1963. Music tchr. Unified Sch. Dist. 263, 1956-92; band and vocal tchr. Mulvane, Kans., 1992—; mem. from dist. 81 Kans. State Ho. of Reps., 1993—. Mem. NRA, AARP, Numismatic Assn., Optimists, Lions, Phi Mu Alpha. Office: Capitol Bldg Rm 155E Topeka KS 67110

POWERS, DAVID RICHARD, educational administrator; b. Cambridge Springs, Pa., Apr. 5, 1939; s. William Herman and Elouise Fancheon (Fink) Powers; m. Mary Julia Ferguson, June 11, 1960. Student, Pa. State U., 1957-60; BA, U. Pitts., 1963, MA, 1965, PhD, 1971. Dir. CAS advising ctr. U. Pitts., 1966-68, asst. dean faculty, 1968-70, asst. to chancellor, 1970-76, assoc. provost, 1976-78, vice provost, 1978-79; v.p. for acad. affairs George Mason U., Fairfax, Va., 1979-82; vice chancellor for acad. affairs W.Va. Bd. Regents, Charleston, 1982-88; exec. dir. Minn. Higher Edn. Coord. Bd., St. Paul, 1989-94, Nebr. Coord. Commn. Post-secondary Edn., Lincoln, 1994—2005, exec. dir. emeritus, 2005. Prin. author: Making Participatory Management Work, 1983, Higher Education in Partnership with Industry, 1988; contbr. articles to Ednl. Record, Adult Learning, Forum for Applied Rsch. on Pub. Policy. Founder mem. bd. trustees Western Govs. U. Grantee USOE Faculty Seminar, Taiwan, 1967, ARC Ctr. for Edn. & Rsch. with Industry Appalachian Regional Commn., 1983, Republic of China Sino-Am. Seminar, 1985; recipient Award for Acad. Quality W.Va. Coun. Faculty, 1986. Mem. State Higher Edn. Exec. Officers, Western Coop. Ednl. Telecomm., Civil Air Patrol, Pi Sigma Alpha. Avocation: boating. Home: 6513 Spencer Ln Clinton WA 98236 Office Phone: 360-341-1533. Personal E-mail: davidpowers@whidbey.com.

POWERS, JAMES G., corporate financial executive; With Arthur Andersen & Co., 1983—91; controller Moog Automotive, Inc., 1991—93; v.p., controller Berg Elec. Corp., 1993—95; v.p. fin. Crain Industries, Inc.; exec. v.p. Viasystems, 1997—2001, sr. v.p., cheif fin. officer, 2001; chief fin. officer UniGroup, 2002—. Office: UniGroup 1 Premier Dr Fenton MO 63026

POWERS, LINDA S., art association administrator; Degree in Sales and Mktg., Davenport U. With Amway Corp., Digital Equipment Corp., IBM Corp.; mktg. dir. private country club; founder, pres. Arts and Crafts Assn. Am., 1999—. Office: Arts and Crafts Assn Am 4888 Cannon Woods Ct Belmont MI 49306 Office Phone: 616-874-1721. Office Fax: 616-874-1771. Business E-Mail: powers@triton.net.

POWERS, MARIAN, finance educator; PhD in Acctg., U. Ill. Acctg. faculty Kellogg Grad. Sch. Mgmt. Northwestern U., Evanston, Ill., 1980-88; dept. acctg. U. Ill., Chgo., 1989-92; prof. acctg. Allen Ctr. Exec. Edn., 1987; vis. assoc. prof. acctg. Kellogg Grad. Sch. Mgmt. Northwestern U., 1993—. Rschr. in field. Contbr. articles to profl. jours.; co-author software. Mem. Am. Acctg. Assn., Ill. CPA Assn., European Acctg. Assn., Internat. Assn. Acctg., Edn. and Rsch., Am. Soc. Women Accts. (past pres. Chgo. chpt.), Edn. Found. Women in Acctg. (trustee 1999). Office: The Allen Ctr Northwestern U 633 Clark St Evanston IL 60208-0001

POWERS, MIKE, state legislator; b. Madison, Wis., Mar. 31, 1962; married; 1 child. Student, Ealing Poly., London, 1982; BS in Land Reclamation, U. Wis., Platteville, 1984; postgrad., Pittsburg State U., 1985. Land conservationist Green County, Wis.; mem. Wis. State Assembly, Madison, 1994—, mem. energy and utilities com., mem. environment and natural resources coms., chair personal privacy com. Mem. Farm Bur.; vol. Big Bros. and Big Sisters, Albany Vol. Firefighters. Mem.: Moose. Republican. Address: N6772 Attica Rd Albany WI 53502

POWERS, PAUL J., manufacturing executive; b. Boston, Feb. 5, 1935; s. Joseph W. and Mary T. Powers; m. Barbara Ross, June 3, 1961; children: Briana, Gregory, Jeffrey. BA in Econs., Merrimack Coll., 1956; MBA, George Washington U., 1962. Various mfg. and fin. positions with Chrysler Corp., Detroit and overseas, 1963-69; v.p., gen. mgr. Am. Standard, Dearborn, Mich., 1970-78; pres. Abex-Dennison, Columbus, Ohio, 1978-82; group v.p. Comml. Intertech Corp., Youngstown, Ohio, 1982-84, pres., chief ops. officer, 1984-87, chmn., pres., CEO, 1987-00, Chairman of the Compensation Committee Chairman of the Compensation Committee and member of the Executive Committee., Chairman of the Compensation Committee and member of the Executive Committee and Nominating and Governance Committee. Bd. dirs. 1st Energy Corp., Twin Disc, Inc., Global Marine Inc., CUNO, Inc., 19 96—. Bd. dirs. Youngstown Symphony, 1984-88. Lt. USNR, 1957-63. Mem. NAM (bd. dirs. 1986-93, 95—), Nat. Fluid Power Assn. (bd. dirs. 1984-87), Mfrs. Alliance (bd. dirs. 1995—), Youngstown Area C. of C. (bd. dirs. 1990—). Office: Commercial Intertech Corp PO Box 239 Youngstown OH 44501-0239

POWERS, RAMON SIDNEY, historian, society administrator; b. Gove County, Kans., Sept. 24, 1939; s. Sanford and Gladys Fern (Williams) P.; m. Eva Redin, Apr. 11, 1963; children: Elisabeth, Christina. AB, Ft. Hays State U., Kans., 1961, MA, 1963; PhD, U. Kans., 1971. Instr. western civilization U. Kans., Lawrence, 1963-67; asst. prof. history U. Mo., Kansas City, 1967-71; instr. Haskell Indian Jr. Coll., Lawrence, 1971-73; rsch. asst. Kans. Legis. Rsch. Dept., Topeka, 1973-77, rsch. analyst, 1977-78, prin. analyst, 1978-88; asst. exec. dir. Kansas State Hist. Soc., Topeka, 1988, exec. dir., 1988—. Contbr. articles to various jours. Chair Eisenhower Centennial Adv. Com., Topeka, 1988-90, Kans. Antiquities Commn., 1988—, State Records Bd., 1988—, Sante Fe atl. Hist. Trail Adv. Coun., 1988-96; mem. bd. review Kans. Hist. Sites, 1988—; mem. State Hist. Records Adv. Bd., 1988—, Gov.'s Commn. on Travel and Tourism, 1988—, mem. bd. dirs. Nat. Conf. of State Historic Preservation Officers, 1991-95. Recipient regional award Col. Dames Am., 1965, Disting. Alumni award Ft. Hays State U., 2000, Hays Rotary Club, 1978; travel grantee N.J. Hist. Commn., 1971, summer grantee NEH, 1973; elected to Kans. Bus. Hall of Fame (bd. dirs.), 1988. Mem. SAR (Thomas Jefferson chpt.), Am. Assn. State and Local History, Kans. Corral of the Westerns, Kans. History Tchrs. Assn., Western History Assn., Travel Industry Assn. (bd. dirs. 1988-92, 97—), Natural and Scientific Area Adv. Bd., 1998—, Santa Fe Trail Assn. Vice Pres., 1996-97; Greater Topeka C. of C., Topeka Heritage League, Sat. Night Literary Club. Office: Kans History Ctr 6425 SW 6th Ave Topeka KS 66615-1099 E-mail: ramonpowers@aol.com, rpowers@kshs.org.

POWERS, ROBERT P., electric power industry executive; B in Biology, Tufts U., Medford, Mass., 1975; M in Radiol. Hygiene, U. NC, 1976. Cert. sr. reactor operator 1991. Radiation protection engr. Pacific Gas & Electric Co., San Francisco, 1982; sr. engr. radiation protection Diablo Canyon Nuc. Generating Sta., 1984, radiation protection mgr., 1987, dir. mech. maintenance, 1991, mgr. site svcs., 1992, mgr. quality svcs., 1993, mgr. ops. svcs., 1996, v.p., 1996; sr. v.p. nuc. generation Am. Electric Power Svc. Corp., 1998, exec. v.p. nuc. and tech. svcs., 2001—03, exec. v.p. generation, 2003, exec. v.p. AEP Utilities -East. Office: Am Electric Power Svc Corp 1 Riverside Plz Columbus OH 43215-2373 Office Phone: 614-716-1000.

POWSNER, EDWARD RAPHAEL, physician; b. NYC, Mar. 17, 1926; m. Rhoda Lee Moscovitz, June 8, 1950; children: Seth, Rachel, Ethan, David. SB in Elec. Engring., MIT, 1948, SM in Biology, 1949; MD, Yale U., 1953; MS in Internal Medicine, Wayne State U., 1957; MHSA, U. Mich. Diplomate Am. Bd. Nuclear Medicine, Am. Bd. Pathology in clin. pathology and anatomic pathology, Am. Bd. Internal Medicine; lic. physician, Mich. Intern Wayne County Gen. Hosp., Eloise, Mich., 1953-54, resident internal medicine, 1954-55, Detroit Receiving Hosp., 1955-56; fellow in hematology Wayne State U. and Detroit Receiving Hosp., 1957-58; clin. investigator VA Hosp., Allen Park, Mich., 1958-61, chief nuclear medicine svc., 1961-78; dir. clin. labs. Mich. State U., East Lansing, 1978-81; staff pathologist Ingham Med. Ctr., Lansing, Mich., 1978-81; dir. nuclear medicine St. John Hosp., Detroit, 1982-95. Rsch. asst. biology MIT, 1948-49, 50; asst. instr. medicine Wayne State U. Coll. Medicine, 1954-56, instr., 1959-61; assoc. prof. pathology Wayne State U. Sch. Medicine, 1961-68, assoc. medicine, 1961, prof. pathology, 1968-78; prof. pathology Mich. State U., 1978-81, assoc. chairperson, 1980-81, clin. prof., 1981-82; chief clin. labs. Detroit Gen. Hosp., 1969-73; chief lab. svcs. Health Care Inst., Wayne State U., 1976-78; mem. adv. coun. Nuclear Medicine Tech. Cert. Bd., 1990-91. Bd. editors Am. Jour. Clin. Pathology, 1963-76, 83-88; author 2 textbooks, 11 chpts., 50 peer reviewed papers, 17 abstracts and other publs. With U.S. Army, 1944-47. Mem. AMA (sect. coun. on pathology), Am. Soc. Clin. Pathologists (rep. 1987-89, 93-2000, govt. rels. com. 1993-95, mem. coun. nuclear medicine 1978-82, chmn. 1982-84), Am. Coll. Nuclear Physicians, Am. Soc. Nuclear Cardiology, Coll. Am. Pathologists, Detroit Acad. Medicine, Mich. Soc. Pathologists, Mich. State Med. Soc., Soc. Nuclear Medicine, Washtenaw County Med. Soc., Sigma Xi, Tau Beta Pi. Office: Eastside Nuclear Medicine 2370 E Stadium Blvd #315 Ann Arbor MI 48104-4810

POZNANSKI, ANDREW KAROL, pediatric radiologist; b. Czestochowa, Poland, Oct. 11, 1931; came to U.S., 1957, naturalized, 1964; s. Edmund Maurycy and Hanna Maria (Ceranka) P.; children: Diana Jean, Suzanne Christine. BSc, McGill U., 1952, MD CM, 1956. Diplomate: Am. Bd. Radiology, Royal Coll. Physicians and Surgeons Can. Intern Montreal (Que., Can.) Hosp., 1956-57; resident Henry Ford Hosp., Detroit, 1957-60, staff radiologist, 1960-68, U. Mich. Med. Center, Ann Arbor, 1968-79; co.-dir. pediatric radiology C.S. Mott Children's Hosp., Ann Arbor, 1971-79; radiologist-in-chief Children's Meml. Hosp., Chgo., 1979-99; prof. radiology U. Mich., 1971-79, Northwestern U. Med. Sch., 1979—. Bd. dirs. Nat. Coun. on Radiation Protection, 1983-90; mem. Internat. Commn. on Radiologic Protection, 1981-89; mem. adv. panel on radiologic devices FDA, 1975-77, chmn., 1976-77; trustee Am. Bd. Radiology, 1993-2003. Author: The Hand in Radiologic Diagnosis, 1974, 2d edit., 1983, Practical Approaches to Pediatric Radiology, 1976; co-author: Bone Displasias, An Atlas of Genetic Disorders of Skeletal Development, 2002 bd. editors: Skeletal Radiology, 1975-95, Radiographics, 1980-84, Pediatric Radiology, 1986-91. Mem.: AMA, Internat. Skeletal Soc. (founder, pres. 1992—94), John Caffey Soc., Radiol. Soc. N.Am., Soc. Pediatric Radiology (pres. 1980—81), Am. Roentgen Ray Soc. (pres. 1993—94), Polish Radiol. Soc. (hon.), Can. Assn. Radiologists (hon.), European Soc. Radiology (hon.), Alpha Omega Alpha. Home: 2400 N Lakeview Ave Chicago IL 60614-2747 Office: Childrens Meml Hosp 2300 N Childrens Plz Chicago IL 60614-3394 Office Phone: 773-880-3521. Business E-Mail: apoznanski@ameritech.net.

PRABHU, KRISH ANANT, former telecommunications industry executive, educator; b. Ankola, India, Aug. 2, 1954; came to U.S., 1975; s. Anant K. and Indira (Mahale) P.; m. Shuba George, June 14, 1980; 3 children. BSc with honors, Bangalore U., India, 1973; MSc, Indian Inst. Tech., Bombay, 1975; MSEE, U. Pitts., 1977, PhD, 1980. Mem. tech. staff Bell Labs., Holmdel, NJ, 1980-84; mem. tech. staff, also mgmt. positions Rockwell Internat., Richardson, Tex., 1984-92; v.p. R & D, Alcatel Network Systems, Richardson, 1992—95; pres. Alcatel Broadband Products, 1995—97; CEO Alcatel USA, Inc., 1997—99; COO Alcatel S.A., 1999—2001; venture ptnr. Morgenthaler Ventures, 2001—04; pres., CEO Tellabs, Inc., Naperville, Ill., 2004—08. Adj. prof. U. Tex. at Dallas, Richardson, 1988—; mem. adv. coun. U. Tex., Arlington, 1992—. Contbr. articles to tech. jours. Mem. IEEE (sr.), NMA. Avocations: tennis, chess, reading.*

PRABHUDESAI, MUKUND M., pathology educator, health facility and academic administrator, researcher; b. Lolyem, Goa, India, Mar. 17, 1942; came to U.S., 1967; s. Madhav R. and Kusum M. Prabhudesai; m. Sarita Mukund Usha, Feb. 1, 1972; 1 child, Nitin M. MB, BS (MD), G.S. Med., Bombay, 1967, postgrad., 1973-75. Diplomate Am. Bd. Pathology. Asst. pathologist Fordham Hosp., Bronx, NY, 1973-74, assoc. pathologist, 1974-76; assoc. dir. clin. pathology Lincoln Med., Bronx, 1976, dep. dir. pathology, 1977-79; chief pathology and lab. medicine svc., coord. R&D VA Med. Ctr., Danville, Ill., 1979—, dir. electron microscopy lab., 1987—. Senator U. Ill. Chgo.; co-investigator U. Ill. Coll. Medicine, Urbana-Champaign, clin. prof. pathology and internal medicine, 1982—. Contbr. articles to Am. Jour. Clin. Nutrition, Jour. AMA, Am. Jour. Clin. Pathology. Member Gifted Student Adv. Bd., Danville, 1984-86; v.p. Am. Cancer Soc. Vermilion County chpt., 1982, pres., 1986-88. VA rsch. grantee, 1980-82, 82-85, 83. Fellow Coll. Am. Pathology (inspector 1981-, Ill. state del. to C.A.P. Ho. Dels. 1992-, mem. reference com. 1993, chair, standard and integration com., 2000-); mem. AAAS, Am. Coll. Physician Execs., Ill. State Soc. Pathologists (bd. dirs. 1990-, chmn. membership com. 1990-). Achievements include development of cancer of bladder following portocarval shunting; research in adverse effects of alcohol on lung structure and metabolism; on effects of soy and bran on cholesterol, fish and coronary artery disease, endocrine response to soy protein, in induction and reversibility of atherosclerosis in trout, effects of ethanol on Vitamin A, lymphatics in atherosclerosis, iron in atherosclerosis, development of dermofluorometer for detection of P.V.D. Office: PO Box 3583 Placida FL 33946 Office Phone: 217-748-6272. E-mail: sarita@soltec.net, mdesaih@aol.com.

PRAEGER, SANDY, state legislator; b. Oct. 21, 1944; m. Mark A. Praeger. Student, U. Kans., 1966. V.p. Douglas County Bank; mem. Kans. Senate from 2nd dist., Topeka, 1992—. Vice chmn. Douglas County Rep. Cent. Com.; chmn. Leadership Kans.; pres. bd. dirs. United Way. Home: 3601 Quail Creek Ct Lawrence KS 66047-2134

PRAGER, MARK L., lawyer; BA magna cum laude, U. Ill., 1973; JD, Washington U., Mo., 1976. Bar: Ill. 1976, cert.: US Dist. Ct. (no. dist.) Ill. 1978, US Ct. Appeals (7th cir.) 1980, US Tax Ct. 1985, US Supreme Ct. 1982. Clk. to Hon. Robert L. Eisen Bankruptcy Ct., No. Dist. Ill., Ea. Div., 1975; mng. ptnr.-Chgo. office Foley & Lardner LLP, Chgo., mem. mgmt. com., chmn. bus. reorganizations practice group. Author: Growing Use Liquidating Trusts Chpt 11 Cases Practical Considerations, 2002. Mem.: Am. Bankruptcy Inst., Chgo. Coun. Lawyers (chmn. legis. com. 1988—90, sec. bd. gov. 1989—90), ABA, Ill. State Bar Assn., Chgo. Bar Assn., Private Panel, No. Dist. Ill., Ea. Div. (U.S. trustee 1990, 1992, 1993), Nat. Assn. Securities Dealers (arbitrator 1985—88), Village Glencoe Nominating Com. (chmn. 1995—96). Office: Foley & Lardner LLP 321 N Clark St Ste 2800 Chicago IL 60610-4764 Office Phone: 312-832-4503. Office Fax: 312-832-4700. Business E-Mail: mprager@foley.com.

PRAGER, STEPHEN, chemistry professor; b. Darmstadt, Germany, July 20, 1928; came to U.S., 1941, naturalized, 1950; s. William and Gertrude Ann (Heyer) P.; m. Julianne Heller, June 7, 1948. B.Sc., Brown, 1947; PhD, Cornell, 1951. Mem. faculty U. Minn., Mpls., 1952—, assoc. prof. chemistry, 1956-62, prof., 1962-90, prof. emeritus, 1990—. Cons. Union Carbide Corp., Oak Ridge, 1954-74 Asso. editor: Jour. Phys. Chemistry, 1970-79. Fulbright scholar and Guggenheim fellow, 1958, 59; Fulbright lectr. and Guggenheim fellow, 1966-67 Mem.: Am. Phys. Soc., Am. Chem. Soc. Home: 3320 Dunlap St N Saint Paul MN 55112-3709 E-mail: psprager@cs.com.

PRAHL, JOSEPH MARKEL, mechanical engineering educator; b. Beverly, Mass., Mar. 30, 1943; s. Frederick Adolph and Dorothy (Markel) P.; m. Rena Elizabeth Wadt, July 11, 1964 (div. June 1970); m. Lawanda McDuffie, July 15, 1977; children: Erika Elise, Meagan Michelle. BA, Harvard U., 1963, SM, PhD, Harvard U., 1968. Reg. profl. engr., Ohio. Asst. prof. Case Western Res. U., 1968-74, assoc. prof., 1974-85, prof., 1985—, chmn. dept. mech. and aerospace engring., 1992—. Payload specialist NASA-JSC, Houston, 1990-92. Contbr. articles to sci. jours. Recipient Abe Zarem Educator award, AIAA, 2006. Office: Dept Mech & Aerospace Engring Case Western Res U 10900 Euclid Ave Cleveland OH 44106-7222 Office Phone: 216-368-2941. E-mail: joseph.prahl@case.edu.

PRAKASH, UDAYA B.S., internist, educator; b. Bangalore, Mysore, India, July 22, 1945; s. Putta Honnappa, Lakshmidevamma Sanjivappa; m. Pushpa Iyengar; children: Apurva, Anna, Amita. MB BS, Bangalore Med. Coll., 1970. Diplomate Am. Bd. Internal Medicine, Pulmonary Disease Am. Bd. Internal Medicine. Edward W. and Betty Knight Scripps prof. medicine Mayo Med. Sch./Mayo Grad. Sch. Medicine, Rochester, Minn. Cons. pulmonary, critical care and internal medicine, dir. bronchoscopy Mayo Clinic/Mayo Med. Ctr., Rochester. Author: Bronchoscopy, 1994. Recipient Shigeto Ikeda award, World Assn. for Bronchology, 1998. Fellow: RCPC, Am. Coll. Chest Physicians (pres.-elect 2002—, chair nominations com., chair program com., editl. bd., dept. editor, regent at large, continuing edn. com.). Office: Mayo Clinic Rochester MN 55905-0001

PRANGE, MICHAEL J., finance company executive; V.p., gen. merchandise mgr. Prange Dept. Stores, 1985—87, the id, 1987—89; pres., gen. merchandising mgr. Am. Specialty Stores, 1989—94; v.p., gen. merchandising mgr. Christopher & Banks, 1994—95, sr. v.p., gen. merchandising mgr., 1995—97, pres., chief merchandising mgr., 1997—98, pres., CEO, 1998—99, chmn., CEO, 1999—. Office: 2400 Xenium Ln N Minneapolis MN 55441 Office Phone: 763-551-5000. Office Fax: 763-551-5198.

PRANGE, ROY LEONARD, JR., lawyer; b. Chgo., Sept. 12, 1945; s. Roy Leonard and Marjorie Rose P.; m. Carol Lynn Poels, June 5, 1971; children: David, Ellen, Susan. BA, U. Iowa, 1967; MA, Ohio State U., 1968; JD, U. Wis.-Madison, 1975. Bar: Wis. 1975, U.S. Dist. Ct. (we. and ea. dists.) Wis. 1975, U.S. Ct. Appeals (7th cir.) 1978, U.S. Supreme Ct. 1978. Assoc. Ross & Stevens, S.C., Madison, Wis., 1975—79, ptnr., 1979—90, Quarles & Brady, LLP, Madison, 1990—. Lectr. bankruptcy, debtor-creditor rights, U. Wis., Madison, 1982--. Contbr. Wis. Lawyer's Desk Reference Manual, 1987, Comml. Litigation in Wis. Practice Handbook, 1995, West's Bankruptcy Exemption Manual, 1997—. 1st lt. U.S. Army, 1969-72. Fellow Am. Coll. Bankruptcy; mem. ABA, Wis. State Bar (dir. bankruptcy, insolvency, creditors rights sect. 1985-91, chair 1990-92, mem. continuing legal edn. com. 1990-95), Am. Bankruptcy Inst., Dickens Fellowship (v.p. 1980-84). Avocations: swimming, bicycling, scuba diving. Office: Quarles & Brady LLP PO Box 2113 33 E Main St Ste 900 Madison WI 53701-2113 Office Phone: 608-283-2485. Business E-Mail: rlp@quarles.com.

PRASAD, ANANDA SHIVA, medical educator; b. Buxar, Bihar, India, Jan. 1, 1928; came to U.S., 1952, naturalized, 1968. s. Radha Krishna and Mahesha (Kaur) Lall; m. Aryabala Ray, Jan. 6, 1952; children: Rita, Sheila, Ashok, Audrey. BSc, Patna Sci. Coll., India, 1946, MB, BChir, 1951; PhD, U. Minn., 1957; doctorate honoris causa, U. Claude Bernard of Lyon, 1999. Intern Patna Med. Coll. Hosp., 1951-52; resident St. Paul's Hosp., Dallas, 1952-53, U. Minn., 1953-56, VA Hosp., Mpls., 1956; instr. dept. medicine Univ. Hosp., U. Minn., Mpls., 1957-58; vis. assoc. prof. medicine Shiraz Med. Faculty, Nemazee Hosp., Shiraz, Iran, 1960; asst. prof. medicine and nutrition Vanderbilt U., 1961-63; mem. faculty, dir. div. hematology dept. medicine Wayne State U., Detroit, 1963-84, assoc. prof., 1964-68, prof., 1968-2000, dir. research dept. medicine, 1984-97, disting. prof., 2000—. Mem. staff Harper-Grace Hosp., VA Hosp., Allen Park, Mich.; mem. trace elements subcom. Food and Nutrition Bd., NRC-Nat. Acad. Scis., 1965-68; chmn. trace elements com. Internat. Union Nutritional Scis.; mem. Am. Bd. Nutrition; pres. Am. Coll. Nutrition, 1991-93. Author: Zinc Metabolism, 1966, Trace Elements in Human Health and Disease, 1976, Trace Elements and Iron in Human Metabolism, 1978, Zinc in Human Nutrition, 1979, Biochemistry of Zinc, 1993; editor: Clinical, Biochemical and Nutritional Aspects of Trace Elements, 1982, Am. Jour. Hematology, Jour. Trace Elements in Exptl. Medicine; editor: Zinc Metabolism, Current Aspects in Health and Disease, 1977; co-editor: Clinical Applications of Recent Advances in Zinc Metabolism, 1982, Zinc Deficiency in Human Subjects, 1983, Essential and Toxic Trace Elements in Human Health and Disease, 1988, Essential and Toxic Trace Elements in Human Health and Disease: An Update, 1993; Jour. Am. Coll. utrition; contbr. articles to profl. jours., also reviewer. Trustee Detroit Internat. Inst., Detroit Gen. Hosp. Rsch. Corp., 1969—72. Recipient Rsch. Recognition award Wayne State U., 1964, award Am. Coll. Nutrition, 1976, Disting. Faculty Fellowship award Wayne State U., 1986, Medal of Honor, City of Lyon, France, 1989, Pioneer in Sickle Cell Disease Rsch. award Nat. Heart Lung Blood Inst./NIH, 1997; Pfizer scholar, 1955-56, WCMS Spl. Recognition award for Profl. Ach., 1998, Klaus Schwartz medal Internat. Assn. Bioinorganic Scientists, 2001, Spl. Recognition award Am. Assn. Physicians India, 2001; inducted Heritage Hall Fame, Mich., 2003, Asian Acad. Hall Fame, 2007. Master ACP (Outstanding Rsch. Related to Medicine award 2007), Am. Coll. Nutrition; fellow AAAS, Am. Inst. Nutrition (trace elements panel), Internat. Soc. Hematology; mem. AMA (Goldberger award 1975), Internat. Soc. Trace Element Rsch. in Humans (pres. 1986-92, chmn. steering com. 1985-86, Raulin award 1989), Am. Soc. Clin. Nutrition (awards com. 1969-70), Am. Fedn. Clin. Rsch. (pres. Mich. 1969-70), Am. Physiol. Soc., Am. Soc. Clin. Investigation,

Am. Soc. Hematology, Assn. Am. Physicians, European Acad. Scis., Arts and Humanities (corr.), Ctrl. Soc. Clin. Rsch., Soc. Exptl. Biology and Medicine (councillor Mich. 1967-71), Wayne State U. Acad. Scholars (pres.-elect 1997-98, pres. 1998-99), Wayne County Med. Soc., Internat. Soc. Internal Medicine, Am. Soc. Clin. Nutrition (Robert H. Herman award 1984), Nutrition Soc. India (Gopalan oration award 1988), Nat. Heart, Lung, Blood Inst. NIH (mem. coun. 2002-2004), Cosmos Club (Washington), Sigma Xi. Home: 4710 Cove Rd Orchard Lake MI 48323-3604 Office: Univ Health Ctr 5-C 4201 Saint Antoine St Detroit MI 48201-2153 Office Phone: 313-577-1597. Business E-Mail: prasada@karmanos.org.

PRATHER, SUSAN LYNN, public relations executive; b. Melrose Park, Ill. d. Horace Charles and Ruth Anna Paula (Backus) P.; divorced. BS, Ind. U., 1973, MS, 1975. Arts administr. Lyric Opera Chgo., 1975; jr. account exec. Morton H. Kaplan Assocs., Chgo., 1976-78, sr. account exec., 1978-81; account supr. Ketchum Pub. Relations, Chgo., 1981-83, v.p., 1983-87, v.p., group mgr., 1985-87; v.p., dir. pub. relations Cramer-Krasselt, Chgo., 1987-95, sr. v.p., dir. pub. rels., 1996—. Cons. Velamints, Foster Wheeler, Kellogg Co., Battle Creek, Mich., 1985—, Village of Rosemont, Ill., PrincCo Personal Comm., Sr. Friendlys, Anti-Cruelty Soc. Chgo., Ill. State Toll Hwy. Authority; founder, prin. pratherpr, 2003-. Singer various recitals; founder, dir. Chgo. Sports Hall of Fame, 1978-81. Mem. archives com. Chgo. Symphony Orch., 1986—, mem. long term planning com., 1987-89; mem. press advance team Papal Visit to Chgo., 1978; mem. White House Press Advance Team, Chgo., 1976-80. Mem. Pub. Rels. Soc. Am. (bd. dirs. Chgo. chpt. 1987—), Internat. Pub. Rels. Assn., Publicity Club (bd. dirs. 1986—, Merit award 1982, Golden Trumpet awards, Silver Trumpet awards), Bus. and Profl. Assn. Lutheran. Avocation: figure skating. Home: 155 N Harbor Dr Apt 2212 Chicago IL 60601-7321

PRATT, ROBERT WINDSOR, lawyer; b. Findlay, Ohio, Mar. 6, 1950; s. John Windsor and Isabelle (Vance) P.; m. Catherine Camak Baker, Sept. 3, 1977; children: Andrew Windsor, David Camak, James Robert. AB, Wittenberg U., Springfield, Ohio, 1972; JD, Yale U., 1975. Bar: Ill. 1975, U.S. Dist. Ct. (no. dist.) Ill. 1976, U.S. Dist. Ct. (we. dist.) Mich. 1995, U.S. Ct. Appeals (fed. cir.) 1984, U.S. Ct. Appeals (7th cir.) 1996, U.S. Ct. Appeals (D.C. cir.) 2004. Assoc. Keck, Mahin & Cate, Chgo., 1975—81, ptnr., 1981—97; pvt. practice Wilmette, Ill., 1998—99; sr. asst. atty. gen. Office Ill. Atty. Gen., 1999—2001, chief antitrust bur., 2001—. Bd. dirs. Chgo. region ARC, 1985-96, vice chmn., 1988-92, chmn., 1992-96, bd. dirs. Mid-Am. chpt., 1992-96. Mem. ABA, Yale Club (Chgo.). Office Phone: 312-814-3722. Business E-Mail: rpratt@atg.state.il.us.

PRATTE, ROBERT JOHN, lawyer; b. Victoria, BC, Can., Feb. 14, 1948; s. Arthur Louis Jr. and Marie Bertha (Latremouille) P.; children: Merie Elise, Jessica Louise, Allison Adele, Chelsea Nicole. BA, Northwestern U., 1970; JD, Tulane U., 1976. Bar: Minn. 1976, Ariz. 1997. Ptnr. Best & Flanagan, Mpls., 1976-84, Briggs & Morgan, Mpls., 1985—2007, head mortgage banking group; ptnr. DLA Piper US LLP, Mpls., 2007—. Editor: Mortgage Lending in Minnesota—A Desktop Reference Guide, 1990. Ex-officio mem. Wilderness Inquiry, Minn.; pres. Twin Cities Northwestern U. Alumni Assn., 1978; active Wayzata Cmty. Ch., Mpls. With US Coast Guard, 1971—73. Fellow Am. Coll. Mortgage Attys. (regent); mem. ABA, Minn. State Bar Assn., Hennepin County Bar Assn., Mortgage Bankers Assn. (mem. Legal Issues and Regulatory Compliance Com.) Avocations: fly fishing, wine collecting, cooking. Office: DLA Piper US LLP 90 S Seventh St Minneapolis MN 55402-3903 Office Phone: 612-524-3030. Business E-Mail: robert.pratte@dlapiper.co.

PRAY, LLOYD CHARLES, geologist, educator; b. Chgo., June 25, 1919; s. Allan Theron and Helen (Palmer) P.; m. Carrel Myers, Sept. 14, 1946; children: Lawrence Myers, John Allan, Kenneth Palmer, Douglas Carrel. BA magna cum laude, Carleton Coll., 1941; MS, Calif. Inst. Tech., 1943, PhD (NRC fellow 1946-49), 1952. Geologist Magnolia Petroleum Co., summer 1942, U.S. Geol. Survey, 1943-44; hydrographic officer USN, 1944-46; Geologist U.S. Geol. Survey, 1946-56 part time; instr. to assoc. prof. geology Calif. Inst. Tech., 1949-56; sr. research geologist Denver Research Ctr., Marathon Oil Co., 1956-62, research assoc., 1962-68; prof. geology U. Wis., Madison, 1968-88; emeritus prof. geology, 1989—. Short course vis. prof. U. Tex., Austin, 1964, U. Colo., 1967, U. Miami, 1971, U. Alta., 1969, Colo. Sch. Mines, 1985; vis. scientist Imperial Coll. Sci. and Tech., London, 1977, U. Calif. Santa Cruz, 1987, Nat. Park Svc. Geology panel, 1993. Author articles sedimentary carbonates, the Permian Reef complex, stratigraphy and structural geology So. N.M. and W. Tex., porosity of carbonate facies, Calif. rare earth mineral deposits. Pres. Colo. Diabetes Assn., 1963-67, v.p., 1968; mem. adv. panel earth scis. NSF, 1973-76. Served as hydrographic officer USNR, 1944-46. Named Layman of Year Am. Diabetes Assn., 1968; recipient Disting. Teaching award U. Wis. Madison, 1988, Disting. Achievement citation Carleton Coll., 1991, Wallace Pratt Resources Stewardship award Guadalupe Mountains Nat. Pk., 1998. Fellow Geol. Soc. Am. (rsch. grants com. 1965-67, com. on nominations 1973, com.Penrose medal 1979-81); mem. Am. Assn. Petroleum Geologists (rsch. com. 1958-61, lectr. continuing edn. program 1966-69, continuing edn. com. 1978-80, Levorsen award 1966, Matson trophy 1967, Disting. lectr. 1986-87, 87-88, Disting. Educator award 1998), Soc. Sedimentary Geologists (hon. life mem. Permian Basin sect. 1977, hon. mem. internat. soc. 1982, sec.-treas. 1961-63, v.p. 1966-67, pres. 1969-70, Twenhofel award 1999), Am. Geol. Inst. (edn. com. 1966-68, ho. bd. dels. 1970-72), West Tex. Geol. Soc. (Disting. Svc. award 2005, Pioneer award 2006), Phi Beta Kappa. Office: Univ Wis Dept Geology Madison WI 53706

PREECE, LYNN SYLVIA, lawyer; b. Birmingham, Eng., June 13, 1955; d. Norman and Sylvia Florence (James) Preece. LLB, Leeds U., Eng., 1976; postgrad., Washington U., St. Louis, 1978-79; JD, Loyola U., 1981. Bar: Ill., 1981. Assoc. Barnes Richardson, Chgo., 1980-86; from assoc. to ptnr. Burditt & Radzius, Chgo., 1986-88; ptnr. Katten Muchin & Zavis, Chgo., 1988-96, Baker & McKenzie, Chgo., 1996—. Adj. prof. John Marshall Law Sch., 1998—. Contbr. articles to profl. jours. Chair customs com. Chgo. Bar Assn., 1986-87, Am. Bar Sect. Internat. Law, Washington, 1993-95, practitioners workshop bd., 1995-97; sec., dir. Women in Internat. Trade, Chgo., 1986-89, British Am. C. of C., Chgo., 1990; dir. Chgo. Internat. Sch., 1994-96. Recipient Gold medal Duke of Edinburghs award Scheme, London, 1973. Mem.: ABA (program officer, coun. mem., newsletter editor 1996—98), Internat. Bar Assn., Ct. Internat. Trade Bar Assn. Avocation: gardening. Office: Baker & McKenzie Ste 3500 130 E Randolph Dr Chicago IL 60601-6342 Home Phone: 773-665-0243; Office Phone: 312-861-8022. E-mail: Lynn.S.Preece@Bakernet.com.

PREER, JOHN RANDOLPH, JR., biology professor; b. Ocala, Fla., Apr. 4, 1918; s. John Randolph Sr. and Ruth (Williams) P.; m. Louise Bertha Brandau; children: James Randolph, Robert William. BS with highest honors, U. Fla., 1939; PhD, Ind. U., 1947; D in Math. and Natural Scis., West Fäölische Wilhelms U., 1993. From asst. prof. to assoc. prof. to prof. depts. zoology and biology U. Pa., Phila., 1947-67, chmn. grad. group depts. zoology and biology, 1958-67, admissions officer grad. sch. arts and scis., 1960-61; prof. depts. zoology and biology Ind. U., Bloomington, 1968-77, chmn. dept. biology, 1977-79, disting. prof. depts. zoology and biology, 1977—, disting. prof. emeritus, 1988—. Contbr. 85 articles to profl. jours. and chpts. to books. Served to 1st lt. USAF, 1942-45, ETO. NSF sr. postdoctoral fellow, 1967-68, Guggenheim fellow 1976-77. Mem. AAAS, Nat. Acad. Scis. (elected 1976), Am. Inst. Biol. Scis., Am. Soc. Cell Biology, Am. Soc. Protozoology (pres. 1986-87), Phi Beta Kappa. Democrat. Methodist. Home: 1414 E Maxwell Ln Bloomington IN 47401-5143 Office: Ind Univ care Dept of Biology Bloomington IN 47405

PREISER, WOLFGANG FRIEDRICH ERNST, architect, educator, consultant, researcher; b. Freiburg, Germany, June 26, 1941; came to U.S., 1967; s. Gerhard Friedrich and Ursula Helene (von Huelsen) P.; m. Cecilia M. Fenoglio, Feb. 16, 1985; children: Johanna, Timothy, Andreas, Nicholas. Student, Vienna Tech. U., 1963; diploma in Engring., Architecture, Inst. of Tech., 1967; M.Arch., Va. Poly. Inst. and State U., 1969; PhD in Man-Environ. Relations, Pa. State U., 1973. Architect, Germany, Austria, Eng., 1960-66; prof. architecture Va. Poly. Inst. and State U., Pa. State U., U. Ill., U. N.Mex., U. Cin., 1970—2008; research architect constrn. engring. research lab. U.S. Army, 1973-76; co-dir. Inst. Environ. Edn., U. N.Mex., 1976-86; dir. Ctr. for R & D, U. N.Mex., Albuquerque, 1986-90; dir. research Archtl. Research Cons. Inc., 1976—2008; pres. Planning Rsch. Inst., Albuquerque, 1980—90; prin. Preiser Cons., Cin., 1990—2008. Lectr. ednl., profl. and civic groups worldwide; v.p. faculty club U. N.Mex., 1976-78; pres. Internat. Club, Va. Poly. Inst. and State U., 1968-69; rschr. in field. Author: Improving Building Performance, 2003; co-author: Post-Occupancy Evaluation, 1988; contbr. articles to profl. jours., chapters to books; editor: Facility Programming, 1982, Programming the Built Environment, 1985, Building Evaluation, 1989, Pueblo Style and Regional Architecture, 1989, Design Intervention: Toward A More Humane Architecture, 1991, Professional Practice in Facility Programming, 1993, Design Review: Challenging Urban Aesthetic Control, 1994, New Direction in Urban Public Housing, 1998, Directions in Person-Environment Research and Practice, 1999, Universal Design Handbook, 2001, Japanese transl., 2001, Assessing Building Performance, 2005, Designing for Designers: Learning From Sch. of Architecture, 2007. Trustee Cin. Chamber Orch., 1992-98, v.p., 1995-98. Recipient Outstanding Svc. award Coll. Design, Arch., Art, and Planning U. Cinn., 2005, Career award Environ. Design Rsch. Assn., 1999, Ann. Rieveschl award, U. Cin., 1999, MCB Univ. Press (UK) award excellence, 1998, Faculty Devel. award rsch. U. Cin., 1992, Faculty Achievement award, 1995, Pogue/Wheeler Traveling award, 1993, Dean's Spl. award, 1994, Finland's Inst. Tech. award, 1966, awards Am. Iron and Steel Inst., 1968, Progressive Arch. Ann., 1985, 89, undergrad. teaching award U. Ill., 1976, hon. mention 1st Kyoto award Internat. Coun. of Soc. Indsl. Design, 1979; Fulbright fellow, 1967, 87, Ford Found. fellow, 1968, Nat. Endowment Arts fellow, 1979, 82; grad. fellow U. Cin., 1996 Mem.: NAS (bldg. rsch. bd. 1985—86, chmn. com. on programming and post-occupancy evaluation), Environ. Design Rsch. Assn. (vice chmn. 1974—76, Lifetime Achievement award 2007), Soc. Human Ecology (pres. 1980—86), Prof. Emeritus of Architecture (life), U. Cin. Grad. Fellows (sec. 1973—74), Phi Kappa Phi. Office Phone: 513-556-6743. Business E-Mail: wolfgang.preiser@uc.edu.

PREISS, JACK, biochemistry professor; b. Bklyn., June 2, 1932; s. Erool and Gilda (Friedman) P.; m. Karen Sue; children: Jennifer Ellen, Jeremy Oscar, Jessica Michelle. BS in Chemistry, CCNY, 1953; PhD in Biochemistry, Duke U., 1957. Scientist NIH, Bethesda, Md., 1960-62; asst. prof. dept. biochemistry, biophysics U. Calif., Davis, 1962-65, assoc. prof., 1965-68, prof., 1968-85, chair dept. biochemistry, 1971-74, 77-81; prof. dept. biochemistry Mich. State U., East Lansing, 1985-2000, chair dept., 1985-89, Univ. Disting. Prof., 2001—. 16th loomis lectr. Iowa State U., 1997—98. Mem. editl. bd.: Jour. Bacteriology, 1969—74, Arch. Biochem. Biophysics, 1969—, Plant Physiology, 1969—74, 1977—80, assoc. editor:, 1980—92; editor, 1993—95, Jour. Biol. Chemistry, 1971—76, 1978—83, 1994—99, 2000—05, Plant Physiol. Biochemistry, 1997—2003. Recipient Camille and Henry Dreyfus Disting. scholar award Calif. State U., 1983, Alexander von Humboldt Stiftung Sr. US Scientist award, 1984, Merit award, Japanese Soc. Starch Sci., 1992, Disting. Faculty Mem. award Mich. Assn. Governing Bds. State Univ., 1997, Mich. Sci. of Yr. award Impressions 5 Mus., 1997, Pan-Am. Biochemistry and Molecular Biology award lectr. Spanish Biochem. Soc., 2000; Alsberg-Schoch Meml. lectr. Am. Assn. Cereal Chemists, 1990, Nat. Sci. Coun. lectr. Republic of China, 1988; Guggenheim Meml. fellow, 1969-70, Japan Soc. for Promotion of Sci. fellow, 1992-93; grantee NIH, 1963-97, NSF, 1978-89, Dept. Energy, 1993-2005, USDA, 1988—, US-Isreal Binat. Agrl. R & D Fund., 2005—. Mem. AAAS (elected fellow 2007), Am. Chem. Soc. (Charles Pfizer award in enzyme chemistry 1971), Biochem. Soc., Am. Soc. Biol. Chemists and Molecular Biology, Am. Soc. Microbiologists, Am. Soc. Plant Physiologists, Soc. for Complex Carbohydrates, Protein Soc., Pan Am. Soc. Biochemistry and Molecular Biology (sec. gen., 1994-96, vice chmn. 1997-99, chmn. 2000-02, past chmn. 2003-05). Office: Mich State Univ Dept Of Biochemistry & Molecular Biology East Lansing MI 48824 Office Phone: 517-353-3137. Business E-Mail: preiss@msu.edu.

PREISTER, DONALD GEORGE, state legislator, greeting card manufacturer; b. Columbus, Nebr., Dec. 23, 1946; s. Maurice J. Preister and Leona T. (Dusel) Chereck. BS in Edn., U. Nebr., 1977. Unit dir. Boys' Clubs of Omaha, 1973-83; dep. city clk. City of Omaha, 1984-85; tchr. The Great Peace March, U.S., 1986; founder, owner Joy Creations, Co., Omaha, 1988—; mem. Nebr. Legislature from 5th dist., Lincoln, 1992—. Instr. Metro C.C., Omaha, 1979-80. Author: (sect.) Drug Abuse Prevention, 1977. Troop leader Boy Scouts Am., Omaha, 1973-83. Served with U.S. Army, 1966-68, Vietnam. Decorated Bronze Star. Mem. Vets. for Peace, Nebr. Sustainable Agr. Soc., Optimist. Democrat. Roman Catholic. Avocations: gardening, running, horses. Home: 4522 Borman St Omaha NE 68157-2318 Office: State Capitol Dist 5 Lincoln NE 68509

PRENDERGAST, FRANKLYN G., health facility administrator, medical educator; b. Linstead, Jamaica, 1945; MD, U. West Indies, 1968; PhD in biochemistry, U. Minn., 1977; BA in physiology, Oxford U., 1971, MA in physiology, 1979; DSc (hon.), Purdue U., 1994. With Mayo Clinic, Rochester, Minn., 1975—; instr. Mayo Med. Sch., Rochester, Minn., 1975—77, asst. prof. in pharmacology, 1977—81, assoc. prof. pharmacology, 1981—86, prof. in pharmacology, biochemistry, and molecular biology, 1986—, Edmond and Marion Guggenheim Prof. of Biochemistry and Molecular Biology, 1987—; named Mayo Disting. Investigator, 1988; assoc. cons. pharmacology Mayo Found., Rochester, Minn., 1977—81, cons. pharmacology, 1981—85, named cons. and chair dept. biochemistry and molecular biology, 1985, bd. trustees; named dir. rsch. Mayo Clinic, Rochester, Minn., 1992; dir. Mayo Clinic Comprehensive Cancer Ctr, Rochester, Minn., 1995—. Bd. dirs. Eli Lilly & Co., 1995—; mem. Bd. on Radiation Effects Rsch. NAS. Contbr. articles to profl. jours. Named a Disting. Alumnus, U. West Indies, 1991; recipient E.E. Just Award, Am. Soc. Exptl. Biology, 1997, Musgrave Gold Medal, Inst. Jamaica, 2003; Rhodes Scholar, 1969, Minnesota Heart Postdoctoral Fellow, 1975—77, Searle Foundation Fellow, 1980—83. Mem.: Sigma Xi, Am. Soc. Biochemistry and Molecular Biology, Biophysical Soc., AAAS, Am. Soc. Photobiology, Am. Chem. Soc. Office: Mayo Cancer Ctr 200 1st St SW Rochester MN 55905-0001

PRENSKY, ARTHUR LAWRENCE, pediatric neurologist, educator; b. NYC, Aug. 31, 1930; s. Herman and Pearl (Newman) P.; m. Sheila Carr, Nov. 13, 1969. AB, Cornell U., 1951; MD, N.Y. U., 1955. Diplomate: Am. Bd. Psychiatry and Neurology. Intern Barnes Hosp., St. Louis, 1955-56; resident and research fellow in neurology Harvard U., Mass. Gen. Hosp., Boston, 1959-66; instr. neurology Harvard Med. Sch., 1966-67; mem. faculty Washington U. Sch. Medicine, St. Louis, 1967—, prof. pediatrics and neurology, to 1975, Allen P. and Josephine B. Green prof. pediatric neurology, 1975-2000, prof. emeritus of neurology, 2000—; pediatrician St. Louis Children's Hosp.; neurologist Barnes and Allied Hosps., Jewish Hosp., St. Louis. Author: (with others) Nutrition and the Developing Nervous System, 1975; editor: (with others) Neurological Pathophysiology, 2d edit, 1978, Advances in Neurology, 1976; mem. editorial bd. Pediatric Neurology, 1984-90, Jour. Child Neurology, 1985—. Served with USAF, 1957-59. Fellow Am. Acad. Neurology; mem. Am. Neurol. Assn., Am. Soc. Neurochemistry (mem. council 1973-77), Central Soc. Neurol. Rsch. (pres. 1977-78), Child Neurology Soc. (pres. 1979-80, Hower award 2000), Am. Pediatric Soc., Internat. Child eurology Assn., Japanese Soc. Child Neurology, Profs. Child Neurology (pres. 1984-86) Office: 1 Children's Pl Saint Louis MO 63110-1014 Home: 40 North Kinshigway Apt 12F Saint Louis MO 63108 Office Phone: 314-454-6120. Business E-Mail: prenskya@neuro.wustl.edu.

PRENTICE, MATTHEW, food service executive; b. Detroit, Dec. 1, 1958; married; four children. Student, Culinary Inst. Am. Pres. Unique Restaurant Corp., Franklin, Mich. Lectr. Wayne State U. Avocation: reading. Office: Unique Restaurant Corp 30100 Telegraph Rd Franklin MI 48025-4514

PRENTISS, C. J., state legislator; BA in Edn., Cleve. State U., 1969, MEd, 1975; cert., Kent State U., 1976; grad. Weatherhead Sch. Mgmt., Case Western Res. U., 1978. Mem. Ohio Ho. of Reps. from 8th dist., Columbus, 1990-98, Ohio Senate from 21st dist., Columbus, 1999—, majority leader. Chair edn. policy Ohio legislative Black Caucus and Black elected Democrats of Cleve., vice-chair edn. com. Nat. Conf. State Legislatures; past vice-chair HouseEdn. com., ways and means, ins.; mem. State Bd. Edn., 1984-90, chair lit. and youth-at-risk com., legis. stds. com., past chair joint select com. on infant health and family support; chair elem. and secondary edn. com. Nat. Black Caucus of State Legislators; mem. rules, ref. legis. svc. com. Joint Legis. Ethics; pres. Ohio Legislative Black Caucus Found. Past Vice-chair Black Leadership Cleve. Alumni; past mem. gov.'s com. Socially Disadvantaged Black Males. Office: Statehouse Rm 303 Columbus OH 43215

PRESCOTT, EDWARD C., economist, educator; b. 1940; BA in Math., Swarthmore Coll., 1962; MS in Ops. Rsch., Case Western Res. U., 1963; PhD in Econs., Carnegie Mellon U., 1967. Lectr. U. Penn, 1966—67; asst. prof. econs. dept. U. Penn., 1967—71; asst. prof. Grad. Sch. Indsl. Admin., Carnegie Mellon U., 1971—72, assoc. prof., 1972—75, prof. econs., 1975—80, U. Minn., 1980—98, 1999—2003; vis. prof. econs. Norweigan Sch. Bus. and Econs., 1974—75, Northwestern U., 1979—80, vis. prof. fin., Kellogg Grad. Sch. Mgmt., 1980—82; Ford vis. rsch. prof. U. Chgo., 1978—79, prof. econs., 1998—99; sr. advisor rsch. dept. Fed. Reserve Bank, Mpls., 1980—2003; prof. dept. econs. Ariz. State U., 2003—; sr. monetary advisor Fed. Res. Bank, Mpls., 2003—. Leader NBER/NSF Workshop in Indsl. Orgn., 1977—84; rsch. assoc. Nat. Bureau of Economic Rsch., 1988—; spkr. in field. Author (with S.L. Parente): Barriers to Riches, 2000; co-editor: Economic Theory, 1991; assoc. editor: Jour. Econometrics, 1976—82, Internat. Economic Review, 1980—90, Jour. Economic Theory, 1990—92; contbr. articles to profl. jours. Named Regents' Prof., U. Minn., 1996, McKnight Presidential Chair in Economics, 2003, W.P. Carey Chair, U. Ariz., 2003; recipient Erwin Plein Nemmers prize in Econ., Northwestern U., 2002, Laurea Honoris Causa in Economica, U. Rome, 2002, Nobel Prize for Econ. Sciences, 2004; fellow, Econometric Society, 1980, Am. Acad. Arts & Scis., 1992; Brookings Economic Policy Fellow, 1969—70, Guggenheim Fellow, 1974—75. Mem.: Soc. Advancement of Econ. Theory (pres. 1992—94), Soc. Econ. Dynamics and Control (pres. 1992—95). Office: Ariz State U Dept Econs Tempe AZ 85287-3806

PRESKA, MARGARET LOUISE ROBINSON, historian, educational association administrator; b. Parma, NY, Jan. 23, 1938; d. Ralph Craven and Ellen Elvira (Niemi) Robinson; m. Daniel C. Preska, Jan. 24, 1959; children: Robert, William, Ellen Preska Steck. BS summa cum laude, SUNY, 1957; MA, Pa. State U., 1961; PhD, Claremont Grad. Sch., 1969. Instr. LaVerne (Calif.) Coll., 1968-75, asst. prof., asso. prof., acad. dean, 1972-75; instr. Starr King Sch. for Ministry, Berkeley, Calif., summer, 1975; v.p. acad. affairs, equal opportunity officer Minn. State U., Mankato, 1975-79, pres., 1979-92; project dir. Kalinin-grad (Russia) Mil. Re-Tng., 1992-96; disting. svc. prof. Minn. State U. Sys., 1993—; pres. Inst. for Effective Tchg. Minn. State U., Winona, 1993—98; owner BuildaBikeInc.com, 2000—. Bd. dirs. XCEL Energy Co., Milkweed Edits.; pres. emerita Minn. State U., Mankato, 1992—; provost, CEO AbuDhabi Campus, Zayed U., United Arab Emirates, 1997-99. Pres. Pomona Valley chpt. UN Assn., 1968-69, Unitarian Soc. Pomona Valley, 1968-69, PTA Lincoln Elem. Sch., Pomona, 1973-74; pres., chmn. bd. Nat. Camp Fire Boys and Girls, 1984-88; mem. Pomona City Charter Revision Commn., 1972; chmn. The Fielding Inst., Santa Barbara, 1983-86; bd. dirs. Elderhostel Internat., 1983-87, Minn. Agrl. Interpretive Ctr. (Farmam.), 1983-92, Am. Assn. State Colls. and Univs., Moscow on the Mississippi -Minn. Meets the Soviet Union; nat. pres. Campfire, Inc., 1985-87; chmn. Gov.'s Coun. on Youth, Minn., 1983-86, Minn. Edn. Forum, 1984; mem. Gov.'s Commn. on Econ. Future of Minn., 1985—, NCAA Pres. Commn., 1986-92, NCAA Cost Cutting Commn., Minn. Brainpower Compact, 1985; commr. Great Lakes Govs.' Econ. Devel. Coun., 1986, Minn Gov.'s Commn. on Forestry. Carnegie Found. grantee Am. Coun. Edn. Deans Inst., 1974; recipient Outstanding Alumni award Pa. State, Outstanding Alumni award Claremont Grad. Sch., YWCA Leader award 1982, Exch. Club Book of Golden Deeds award, 1987; named One of top 100 alumni, SUNY, 1895-1985, 1985, Hall of Heritage award, 1988, Wohelo Camp Fire award, 1989. Fellow Fielding Inst.; mem. AAUW (pres. Mankato 1990-92), LWV, Women's Econ. Roundtable, St. Paul/Mpls. Com. on Fgn. Rels., Am. Assn. Univ. Adminstrs., Rotary, Horizon 100. Unitarian Universalist. Home: 10 Sumner Hls Mankato MN 56001-3931 E-mail: mpreska@hickorytech.net.

PRESLEY, JOHN WOODROW, educator, dean; b. Jonesboro, Ark., Mar. 24, 1948; s. Marvin Woodrow and Willa Louise (Taylor) P.; m. Katherine Bailey Harrison, Oct. 17, 1978. BSE, Ark. State U., 1970; MA, So. Ill. U., 1972, PhD, 1975; postgrad., Johns Hopkins U., 1976, U. Tex., 1980. From asst. prof. to prof., asst. v.p. acad. affairs Augusta State U., 1974—89; assoc. provost Lafayette Coll., 1989—92; dean Coll. of Arts, Scis. and Letters U. Mich., Dearborn, 1992-99; provost, v.p. acad. affairs SUNY at Oswego, 1999—2003; v.p. acad. affairs, provost Ill. State U., 2003—08. Author, tchr. and presenter in fields of modern lit. and higher edn. adminstrn. Author: The Robert Graves Letters and Manuscripts at Southern Illinois University, 1976. NDEA fellow, 1972. Office: Ill State Univ 330 De Garmo Hall Normal IL 61790 Office Phone: 309-438-2351. E-mail: jwpresl@ilstu.edu.

PRESS, CHARLES, retired political science professor; b. St. Louis, Sept. 12, 1922; s. Otto Ernst and Laura (Irion) P.; m. Nancy Miller, June 10, 1950; children: Edward Paul, William David, Thomas Leigh, Laura Mary. Student, Elmhurst Coll., Ill.; B of Journalism, U. Mo., 1948; MA, U. Minn., 1951, PhD, 1953. Faculty .D. Agrl. Coll., 1954-56; dir. Grand Rapids Area Study, 1956-57; with Bur. Govt., U. Wis., 1957-58; faculty Mich. State U., East Lansing, 1958-91, prof. polit. sci., 1964-91; emeritus, 1991—; chmn. dept. Mich. State U., 1966-73. Cons. Mich. Constl. Conv., 1962-63; supr. Ingham County, 1966-72; tchr. summers, London; tchr. U. N.S.W., Sydney, Mich. State U. Author: Main Street Politics, 1962, (with Charles Adrian) The American Government Process, 1965, Governing Urban America, 1968, 5th edit., 1977, American Politics Reappraised, 1974, (with Kenneth VerBurg) States and Community Governments in a Federal System, 1979, 3d edit., 1991, American Policy Studies, 1981, The Political Cartoon, 1982, (with others) Michigan Political Atlas 1984, (with Kenneth VerBurg) American Politicians and Journalists, 1988, (with Kenneth VerBurg) Looking Over Sir Arthur's Shoulder, How Doyle Turned the Trick, 2004, Parodies and Pastiches Buzzing Around Sir Arthur Conan Doyle, 2006; (weekly newspaper column) The Pros and Cons of Politics. Sec. Ingham County Bd. Health, 1983-93; chmn., mem. East Lansing Bd. Rev., 1966-86; bd. dirs. Urban League, 1971-73; mem. East Lansing Housing and Urban Devel. Commn., 1988-93. Served with AUS, 1943-45. Recipient Disting. Prof. award Mich. State U., 1980, Alumni Merit award Elmhurst (Ill.) Coll., 1995; grantee, Ford Foundation, 1953-54. Mem. Am. Polit. Sci. Assn., Midwest Polit. Sci. Assn. (pres. 1974-75), So. Polit. Sci. Assn., Mich. Conf. Polit. Scientists (pres. 1972-73), Nat. Municipal League, B.S.I. Democrat. Home: 987 Lantern Hill Dr East Lansing MI 48823-2831 Personal E-mail: pressc@msu.edu.

PRESS, JIM (JAMES E. PRESS), automotive executive; b. L.A., Oct. 4, 1946; m. Linda Press; 4 children. BA in Bus. Adminstrn., Kans. State U., 1968. With Ford Motor Co., 1968—70; joined Toyota Motor Corp., Torrance, Calif., 1970; exec. v.p. Toyota Motor Sales, U.S.A., Inc., 1999—2005, COO, 1999—2005, pres., 2005—07; mng. officer Toyota Motor Corp., 2003—07, pres. Toyota N. Am., 2006—07; vice chmn., pres., sales, mktg. & product strategy Chrysler LLC, Auburn Hills, Mich., 2007—; vice chmn. Cerberus Operating & Advisory Co. LLC, 2007—. Bd. dirs. Toyota Motor Corp., 2007, Chrysler LLC, 2007—, Assn. Internat. Automobile Manufacturers. Bd. dirs. Automotive Youth Ednl. Systems, Detroit Area Coun. Boy Scouts America; mem. advisory bd. Pitts. State U.; bd. trustees Coll. Creative Studies, Detroit, Chadwick Sch., Rolling Hills, Calif. Recipient Disting. Svc. Citation award, Automotive Hall of Fame, 2004. Avocations: boating, motorcycling, auto racing, skiing, scuba diving. Office: Chrysler LLC 1000 Chrysler LLC Auburn Hills MI 48326*

PRESSER, STEPHEN BRUCE, lawyer, educator; b. Chattanooga, Aug. 10, 1946; s. Sidney and Estelle (Shapiro) P.; m. Carole Smith, June 18, 1968 (div. 1987); children: David Carter, Elisabeth Catherine; m. ArLynn Leiber, Dec. 13, 1987; children: Joseph Leiber, Eastman Leiber. AB, Harvard U., 1968, JD, 1971. Bar: Mass. 1971, DC 1972. Law clk. to Judge Malcolm Richard Wilkey U.S. Ct. Appeals (D.C. cir.), 1971-72; assoc. Wilmer, Cutler & Pickering, Washington, 1972-74; asst. prof. law Rutgers U., Camden, NJ, 1974-76; vis. assoc. prof. U. Va., 1976-77; prof. Northwestern U., Chgo., 1977—, class 1940 rsch. prof., 1992-93, Raoul Berger prof. legal history, 1992—, assoc. dean acad. affairs Sch. Law, 1982-85. Prof. bus. law Kellogg Sch. Mgmt., Northwestern U., Chgo., 1992—. Author: (with Jamil S. Zainaldin) Law and Jurisprudence in American History, 1980, 6th edit., 2006, Studies in the History of the United States Courts of the Third Circuit, 1983, The Original Misunderstanding: The English, The Americans and the Dialectic of Federalist Jurisprudence, 1991, Piercing the Corporate Veil, 1991, revised ann., (with Ralph Ferrara and Meredith Brown) Takeovers: A Strategist's Manual, 2d edit., 1993, Recapturing the Constitution, 1994, (with Douglas W. Kmiec, John Eastman and Raymond Marcin) The American Constitutional Order: History, Cases, and Philosophy, 1998, 2d edit., 2004, An Introduction to the Law of Business Organizations, 2005, 2nd edit., 2008; assoc. articles editor Guide to American Law, 1985. Trustee Village Winnetka, Ill., 2000-04, police and fire commr., 2004-; mem. acad. adv. bd. Washington Legal Found. Recipient summer stipend NEH, 1975; Fulbright Sr. scholar Univ. Coll., London Sch. Econs. and Polit. Sci., 1983-84, Inst. Advanced Legal Studies, 1996; Adams fellow Inst. U.S. Studies, London, 1996; assoc. rsch. fellow Inst. U.S. Studies, 1999—. Mem. Am. Soc. Legal History (bd. dirs.

1979-82), Am. Law Inst., Univ. Club Chgo. (bd. dirs. 1997-99, sec. 1999), Legal Club Chgo., Reform Club (London), Mich. Shores Club (Wilmette). Office: Northwestern U Law Sch 357 E Chicago Ave Chicago IL 60611-3069 E-mail: s-presser@law.northwestern.edu.

PRESSLEY, FRED G., JR., lawyer; b. NYC, June 19, 1953; s. Fred G. Sr. and Frances (Sanders) P.; m. Cynthia Denise Hill, Sept. 5, 1981. BA cum laude, Union Coll., 1975; JD, Northwestern U., 1978. Bar: Ohio 1978, U.S. Dist. Ct. (so. dist.) Ohio 1979, U.S. Dist. Ct. (no. dist.) Ohio 1985, U.S. Dist. Ct. (ea. dist.) Wis. 1980, U.S. Ct. Appeals (6th cir.). Assoc. Porter, Wright, Morris & Arthur, Columbus, Ohio, 1978-85, ptnr., 1985—. Bd. dirs. Columbus Area Leadership Program, 1981-84, Franklin County Bd. Mental Retardation and Devel. Disabilities, Columbus, 1989-97, Union Coll., Schenectady, N.Y., 1992—. Recipient Civic Achievement award Ohio Ho. of Reps., 1988. Mem. ABA. Avocations: jogging, golf, basketball, history. Office: Porter Wright Morris & Arthur 41 S High St Ste 2800 Columbus OH 43215-6194

PRESSMAN, RONALD R., utilities executive; b. NYC, Apr. 11, 1958; m. Mary Pressman; 3 children. Grad., Hamilton College, NY, 1980. Gen. mgr. ctr. and ea. Europe GE, London, 1990—92; CEO GE Power Sys. Europe, 1992—95, CEO Power Sys. global mktg., 1995—96; pres., CEO GE Capital Real Estate, 1997; sr. v.p. GE Co., 2000—; pres., CEO G.E. Employers Reinsurance Co., 2000—. Bd. dirs. A Better Chance, Kansas City Civic Coun.; mem. exec. bd. Nat. Realty Com., Wharton Real Estate Bus. Sch. Recipient Crown American Golden Crown award, 1998, Fin. Svcs. Exec. of Yr., Comml. Property News. Office: GE Employers Reinsurance Co PO Box 2991 Shawnee Mission KS 66201-1391

PRESZLER, GARY, state commissioner; Commr. N.D. Banking and Fin. Instns. Dept., Bismarck, 1975—2001, N.D. State Land Dept., 2001—. Office: ND State Land Dept PO Box 5523 Bismarck ND 58506

PRETLOW, THOMAS GARRETT, physician, pathology educator, researcher; b. Warrenton, Va., Dec. 11, 1939; s. William Ribble and May (Tiffany) P.; m. Theresa Pace, June 29, 1963; children: James Michael, Joseph Peter, David Mark. AB, Oberlin Coll., 1960; MD, U. Rochester, 1965. Intern U. Hosps., Madison, Wis., 1965-66; fellow McArdle Lab., 1966-67; rsch. assoc. Nat. Cancer Inst., Bethesda, Md., 1967-69; asst. prof. pathology Rutgers Med. Sch., Piscataway, N.J., 1969-70; assoc. prof. pathology U. Ala., Birmingham, 1971-73, prof. pathology, 1974-83, prof. biochemistry, 1982-83; vis. prof. pathology Harvard Med. Sch., Boston, 1983-84; prof. pathology Case Western Res. U., Cleve., 1983—, prof. oncology, 1987—, prof. environ. health scis., 1991—, prof. urology, 1994—. Cons. NIH, Bethesda, 1976-2000, Am. Inst. Cancer Rsch., 1995-98; chmn. pathobiolog y 2 prostate cancer grant reviewer U.S. Army, 1998, 99. Mem. editl. bd. Cell Biophysics, Cambridge, Mass., 1978-82; editor: Cell Separation: Methods and Selected Applications, 5 vols., 1982, 83, 84, 87, Biochemical and Molecular Aspects of Selected Cancers, 2 vols., 1991, 94. Mem. exec. bd. Birmingham coun. Boy Scouts Am., 1979-83, Greater Cleve. coun. Boy Scouts Am., 1984-90. Served to lt. comdr. USPHS, 1967-69. Recipient Rsch. Career Devel. award Nat. Cancer Inst., 1973-78; grantee for cancer rsch. Mem. Am. Assn. Pathologists, Am. Assn. Immunologists, Internat. Acad. Pathology, Am. Soc. Clin. Oncology, Am. Assn. Cancer Rsch., Serra Club (pres. Birmingham chpt. 1982-83). Avocations: camping, fishing, boy scouts, classical music, biking. Home: 3061 Chadbourne Rd Cleveland OH 44120-2446 Office: Inst Pathology Case Western Reserve U Cleveland OH 44106 Business E-Mail: tgp3@cwru.edu.

PREUS, DAVID WALTER, bishop, minister; b. Madison, Wis., May 28, 1922; s. Ove Jacob Hjort and Magdalene (Forde) P.; m. Ann Madsen, June 26, 1951; children: Martha, David, Stephen, Louise, Laura. BA, Luther Coll., Decorah, Iowa, 1943, DD (hon.), 1969; postgrad., U. Minn., 1946-47; BTh, Luther Sem., St. Paul, 1950; postgrad., Union Sem., 1951, Edinburgh U., 1951-52; LLD (hon.), Wagner Coll., 1973, Gettysburg Coll., 1976; DD (hon.), Pacific Luth. Coll., 1974, St. Olaf Coll., 1974, Dana Coll., 1979, Tex. Luth. Coll., 1994; LHD (hon.), Macalester Coll., 1976; DD (hon.), Luther Coll., 1969. Ordained to ministry Luth. Ch., 1950; asst. pastor First Luth. Ch., Brookings, SD, 1950-51; pastor Trinity Luth. Ch., Vermillion, SD, 1952-57; campus pastor U. Minn., Mpls., 1957-58; pastor Univ. Luth. Ch. of Hope, Mpls., 1958-73; v.p. Am. Luth. Ch., 1968-73, pres., presiding bishop, 1973-87; exec. dir. Global Mission Inst. Luther orthwestern Theol. Sem., St. Paul. Disting. vis. prof. Luther-Northwestern Sem., St. Paul, 1988-94; Luccock vis. pastor Yale Div. Sch., 1969; chmn. bd. youth activity Am. Luth. Ch., 1960-68; mem. exec. com. Luth. Council U.S.A.; v.p. Luth. World Fedn., 1977-90; mem. cen. com. World Council Chs., 1973-75, 80-90; Luth. del. White House Conf. on Equal Opportunity Chmn. Greater Mpls. Fair Housing Com., Mpls. Council Chs., 1960-64; Mem. Mpls. Planning Commn., 1965-67; mem. Mpls. Sch. Bd., 1965-74, chmn., 1967-69; mem. Mpls. Bd. Estimate and Taxation, 1968-73, Mpls. Urban Coalition; sr. public adv. U.S. del. Madrid Conf. of Conf. on Security and Cooperation in Europe, 1980-81; bd. dirs. Mpls. Inst. Art, Walker Art Center, Hennepin County United Fund, Ams. for Childrens Relief, Luth. Student Found., Research Council of Gt. City Schs., Urban League, NAACP; bd. regents Augsburg Coll., Mpls. Served with Signal Corps AUS, 1943-46, PTO. Decorated comdr.'s cross Royal Norwegian Order St. Olav, Order of St. George 1st deg. Orthodox Ch. of Georgia (USSR), 1989; recipient Regents medal Augustana Coll., Sioux Falls, S.D., 1973, Torch of Liberty award Anti-Defamation League, 1973, St. Thomas Aquinas award St. Thomas U., Pax Christi award St. John's Univ/. Collegeville, Minn., 1997. Lutheran.

PREUSS, DAPHNE, geneticist, biology professor; BS in Chemistry, U. Denver, 1985, BS in Natural Scis., 1985; PhD in Genetics, MIT, 1990. Albert D. Lasker prof. molecular genetics & cell biology U. Chgo., 1995—; prin. investigator Howard Hughes Med. Inst., Chgo., 2000—06; co-founder Chromatin, Inc., Chgo., 2000, sr. v.p., 2007, chief sci. officer, 2007—, pres., 2007—. Bd. gov. Argonne Nat. Lab. Contbr. articles to profl. jours. Bd. govs. Argonne Nat. Labs., Chgo., 2003—. Named one of Discover 20 (List of 20 Promising Young Scientists), Discover Mag., 2000, 40 under 40, Chgo. Crain's Bus. Review, 2001; recipient Ammi Hyde award for Young Alumni Achievement, U. Denver, Women in Cell Biology Jr. award, Am. Soc. Cell Biology, Promega Early Career Life Scientist award, 2001; David and Lucille Packard fellow, Packard Found., 1997-2004, Searle Scholar. Mem.: NAS (lifetime nat. assoc.). Achievements include invention of chromosomes for plants; Chromatin's patented mini-chromosome technology. Office: Dept Molecular Genetics and Cell Biology U Chgo Ctr for Integrative Sci 929 E 57th St CIS W519 Chicago IL 60637 also: Chromatin Inc 2201 W Campbell Park Dr Ste #10 Chicago IL 60612 Office Phone: 773-702-1605, 312-455-1935. Office Fax: 773-702-6648, 312-563-9120. E-mail: dpreuss@midway.uchicago.edu.

PREUSSER, JOSEPH WILLIAM, academic administrator; b. Petersburg, Nebr., June 18, 1941; s. Louis Henry and Elizabeth Sophia (Oberbrocking) P.; m. Therese Marie Mahoney, Aug. 12, 1967; children: Scott, Michelle, Denise. BA in Social Scis., Wayne State Coll., 1965; MA in Geography, U. Nebr., Omaha, 1971; PhD in Adminstrn., U. Nebr., 1978. Coord. social studies Lewis Ctrl. Cmty. Sch. Dist., Council Bluffs, Iowa, 1967-71; chmn. social sci. divsn., instr. Platte Jr. Coll., Columbus, Nebr., 1972-73; dean instrn./Platte campus Ctrl. C.C., Columbus, 1973-82, v.p. ednl. planning cmty. edn., pres. Platte campus, 1982-84, pres. Grand Island, Nebr., 2004—. Mem. devel. com. Nebr. Tech. C.C., 1973-75, sec., dean instrn., 1974-76, chmn. pres.'s coun., 1990-91; mem. Archdiocese Omaha Bd. Edn., 1980-84; chmn. St. Bonaventure Bd. Edn., 1976-80; bd. dirs. Edgerton Edn. Found.; spkr. in field. Contbr. articles to profl. jours. Bd. dirs. Ctrl. Nebr. Goodwill Industries, Grand Island, 1987-95, treas., 1990-91, chmn. 1992; chmn. sustaining membership enrollment campaign Overland Trails Boy Scouts Am., 1990; mem. Columbus City Planning Commn., 1979-84, chmn., 1981, 82. With U.S. Army, 1959-61. Named one of Outstanding Young Mem of Am., 1976; recipient Nat. Leadership award U. Tex., 1988-89, Pres. of Yr. award Am. Assn. Women in Comm., 1996, award Nebr. Tech. C.C. Assn., Vision for Future award, 1999; named to Ctrl. Cath. H.S. Booster Club Hall of Fame, 1995. Mem. Am. Assn. Cmty. and Jr. Colls., Am. Voct. Assn., Nebr. Vocat. Assn. (Outstanding Svc. award 1986), Nebr. C.C. Assn. (coun. of pres. 1984—, pres. 1987, 93, 99), Rotary (Grand Island Noon Club bd. dirs. 1999-2000, pres. 1999, lt. gov. dist. 5630 1999—, Svc. award 1999), KC, Phi Delta Kappa. Democrat. Roman Catholic. Avocations: golf, gardening, woodworking.

PRICE, CHARLES H., II, former ambassador; b. Kansas City, Mo., Apr. 1, 1931; s. Charles Harry and Virginia (Ogden) P.; m. Carol Ann Swanson, Jan. 10, 1969; children: Caroline Lee, Melissa Marie, Charles H., C. B., Pickette. Student, U. Mo., 1951-53; LLD (hon.), Westminster Coll., 1984, U. Mo., 1988; LHD (hon.), Baker U., 1991; DSc (hon.), U. Buckingham, Eng., 1993. Chmn. bd., dir. Price Candy Co., Kansas City, 1969-81, Am. Bancorp., Kansas City, 1973-81; chmn., chief exec. officer Am. Bank & Trust Co., Kansas City, 1973-81; Am. ambassador to Belgium Brussels, 1981-83; Am. ambassador to U.K. London, 1983-89. Chmn. bd. Americanc, Inc., St. Joseph, Mo., 1989—92, pres., CEO, 1990—92; chmn. bd. Merc. Bank Kansas City, Mo., 1992—96; bd. dirs. Palmer Capital Assocs., Ltd., London. Trustee Midwest Rsch. Inst., Kansas City, chmn., 1990-93. Hon. fellow Regent's Coll., London, 1986; recipient William Booth award Salvation Army, 1985, World Citizen of Yr. award Mayor of Kansas City, 1985, Trustee Citation award Midwest Rsch. Inst., 1987, Disting. Svc. award Internat. Rels. Coun., 1989, Mankind award Cystic Fibrosis Found., 1990, Gold Good Citizenship award SAR, 1991, Chancellor's medal U. Mo. Kansas City, 1992, William F. Yates medallion William Jewell Coll., 1996. Mem.: The Vintage Country Club, White's Club, Swinley Forest Club, Kansas City Country Club, Eldorado Country Club, Brook Club, Cypress Point Club, Los Angeles County Club, River Club, Sigma Alpha Epsilon. Republican. Episcopalian. Office: 1 W Armour Blvd Ste 300 Kansas City MO 64111-2087 Office Phone: 816-360-6175.

PRICE, CHARLES T., lawyer; b. Lansing, Mich., Feb. 11, 1944; BA, Ohio Wesleyan U., 1966; JD, Harvard U., 1969. Bar: Ohio 1969, U.S. Dist. Ct. (no. dist.) Ohio 1974, U.S. Ct. Appeals (6th cir) 1981, U.S. Supreme Ct. 1982, Ill. 1989. Former ptnr. Baker & Hostetler, Cleve.; pres., pub. Chgo. Sun-Times, 1978-88; exec. v.p. Sun-Times Co., 1989-92; ptnr. Foley & Lardner, Chgo., 2000—04, Bell, Boyd & Lloyd LLC, Chgo., 2004—. Mem. bd. govs. Sch. of Art Inst. of Chgo., former chmn.; mem. bd. trustees LaRabida Children;s Hosp. Mem.: Econ. Club, Phi Beta Kappa. Office: Bell Boyd & Lloyd 70 W Madison St Chicago IL 60602 Home Phone: 847-256-3640; Office Phone: 312-807-4431. E-mail: cprice@bellboyd.com.

PRICE, CLARA SUE, state legislator; b. Sept. 10, 1953; m. Gary Price; 1 child. BA in Bus. Adminstrn., Minot State U., 1977. Mem. N.D. Ho. of Reps., 1991—, chmn. Rep. caucaus, 1993-94, vice chair human svcs. com., 1995, mem. transp. com., chmn. human svcs., 1997—. Employee benefit specialist BCBS of N.D., 1982-87; stockbroker INVEST, 1988-90; sec. Cal-Dak Cabinets, 1975—; owner, operator Dakota Gardens & Herbs, 1993—. Past mem. Minot Commn. Status of Women; bd. dirs. Trinity Health. Mem. Internat. Peace Garden, C. of C. Republican. Lutheran. Home: 3520 30th St NW Minot ND 58703-0312 Office: ND Ho of Reps State Capitol Bismarck ND 58505 E-mail: cprice@state.nd.us.

PRICE, HENRY ESCOE, broadcast executive; b. Jackson, Miss., Oct. 13, 1947; s. Henry E. Price Sr. and Alma Kate (Merrill) Noto; m. Maria Diane Harper, Apr. 8, 1972; children: Henry E. III, Norman Harper. BS in Radio, TV, Film, Journalism, U. So. Miss., 1972. Announcer, news dir. Sta. WROA Radio, Gulfport, Miss., 1967-69; comml. producer Sta. WJTV-TV, Jackson, Miss., 1969-73; prodn. mgr. Sta. WAAY-TV, Huntsville, Ala., 1973-77, Sta. WPEC-TV, West Palm Beach, Fla., 1977-79; dir. promotion Sta. WPTV-TV, Palm Beach, Fla., 1979-81; TV cons. Frank Magid Assoc., Marion, Iowa, 1981-83; dir. advt. and promotion Sta. WJLA-TV, Washington, 1983-84; v.p., dir. programming Sta. WUSA-TV, Gannett TV, Washington, 1984-88; pres., gen. mgr. Sta. WFMY-TV, Gannett TV, Greensboro, .C., 1988-91, Sta. KARE-TV, Mpls., 1991-96; v.p., gen. mgr. Sta. WBBM-TV, CBS TV Stas., Chgo., 1996—2000; pres., gen. mgr. Sta. WXUU-TV, Winston-Salem, C, 2000—; sr. fellow in TV, Northwestern U. Media Mgmt. Ctr. Pres. Carolina News Network, 1988-91; sr. dir. media mgmt. Ctr. Northwestern U., 2000—. Vice chair, bd. dirs. The Courage Ctr., Mpls.; regional dir. Nat. Conf.; mem. exec. com., bd. dirs. The Minn. Orch.; Pacesetter program chair Mpls. United Way Campaign; active Twin Cities Dunkers, Twin Cities Comm. Coun., 11 Who Care. Mem. Chgo. C. of C. (bd. dirs.), Ill. Broadcasters Assn. (bd. dirs.). Avocations: furniture design and construction, reading, walking, bicycling. Address: 700 Coliseum Dr Winston Salem NC 27106

PRICE, JAMES TUCKER, lawyer; b. Springfield, Mo., June 22, 1955; s. Billy L. and Jeanne Adele Price; m. Francine Beth Warkow, June 8, 1980; children: Rachel Leah, Ashley Elizabeth. BJ, U. Mo., 1977; JD, Harvard U., 1980. Bar: Mo. 1980. Assoc. firm Spencer Fane Britt & Browne, Kansas City, 1980-86; ptnr. Spencer Fane Britt & Browne LLP, Kansas City, 1987—, chair environ. practice group, 1994—, mem. exec. com., 1997—. Mem. Brownfields Commn., Kansas City, 1999—; mem. steering com. Kansas City Bi-State Brownfields Initiative, 1997—. Contbr. to monographs, other legal publs. Mem. ABA (coun. sect. environ, energy and resources 1992-95, vice chmn. solid and hazardous waste com. 1985-90, chmn. 1990-92, chmn. brownfields task force 1995-97, vice chmn. environ. transactions and brownfield com. 1998-2000), Mo. Bar Assn., Kansas City Met. Bar Assn. (chmn. environ. law com. 1985-86), Greater Kansas City C. of C. (co-chair Brownfields Working Group, 1996-98, chmn. energy and environ. com. 1987-89). Office: Spencer Fane Britt & Browne LLP 1000 Walnut St Ste 1400 Kansas City MO 64106-2140 Office Phone: 816-292-8228. Business E-Mail: jprice@spencerfane.com.

PRICE, JOSEPH MICHAEL, lawyer; b. St. Paul, Dec. 2, 1947; s. Leon and Rose (Kaufman) P.; m. Louise Rebecca Braunstein, Dec. 19, 1971; children: Lisa, Laurie, Julie. BA, U. Minn., 1969, JD, 1972. Bar: Minn. 1972, U.S. Dist. Ct. Minn. 1974. Ptnr. Faegre & Benson, Mpls., 1972—. Mem. Minn. Bar Assn., Hennepin County Bar Assn. Home: 4407 Country Club Rd Minneapolis MN 55424-1148 Office: Faegre & Benson 2200 Wells Fargo Ctr 90 S 7th St Ste 2200 Minneapolis MN 55402-3901 Office Phone: 612-766-8617. Business E-Mail: Jprice@faegre.com.

PRICE, LARRY, state representative; Spl. asst., cmty. affairs coord. Mayor Michael B. Coleman, Columbus, Ohio, 2000—02; state rep. dist. 26 Ohio Ho. of Reps., Columbus, 2002—, mem. county and twp. govt., econ. devel. and tech., human svcs. and aging, mcpl. govt. and urban revitalization, and transp. and pub. safety coms. Message clk. Ohio Dem. Caucus, 1970s; staff U.S. Rep. Bob Shamansky, 1980s; asst. sgt.-at-arms Ohio Statehouse. Democrat.

PRICE, LEONARD RUSSELL (LEN PRICE), state legislator; b. Sept. 21, 1942; m. Stephanie Wright; 3 children. BS, MS, U. Wis., River Falls. Mem. Minn. Ho. of Reps., St. Paul, 1982-90; vicechmn. gen. legis. com., vet. affairs com., gaming com.; mem. appropriations com., environ. and natural resource com.; mem. Minn. Senate from 57th dist., St. Paul, 1990—. Co-vice chmn. edn. com., mem. commerce and comsumer protection com., taxes com., others; tchr. Mem. NEA (life), Minn. Edn. Assn. Democrat. Home: 6264 Applewood Rd Woodbury MN 55125-1105 Office: Minn Senate State Capitol Saint Paul MN 55155-0001

PRICE, MARIAN L., state legislator; b. Page, Nebr., Aug. 6, 1938; children: Mark Reed Price, Penni Lou Price Godemann, Randall Joseph Price, Ronald Noble Price. Student, Wesleyan U., 1955-56; grad., Bryan Meml. Hosp. Sch., 1959. RN, Nebr. With Bryan Meml. Hosp., 1959—63; co-owner family restaurants, Lincoln, ebr., 1971—90; mem. Nebr. Legislature from 26th dist., Lincoln, 1998—. Bd. dirs. Home Health Svcs. for Independent Living, Inc., VITAL Inc. Mem. Lincoln Bd. Edn., 1985-98, pres., 1994-97, chair legis. subcom., 1997-98; chair Lancaster County Reorgn. Com., 1990-98; pres. Ednl. Svc. Unit No. 18, 1991-96; del. Nat. Sch. Bds. Assns. Fed. Rels. Network, 1989-98; mem. Bethany Christian Ch., Lincoln, past pres., mem. Christian women's fellowship, past ch. wedding coord.; past bd. dirs. Lincoln Cmty. Playhouse Guild. Mem. Bryan Meml. Sch. Nursing Alumnae Assn. (past bd. dirs.), Bethany Women's Club, Alpha Gamma Delta Alumnae Assn. (past bd. dirs.), Phi Sigma Alpha (past pres., bd. dirs.). Home: 6735 Lexington Cir Lincoln NE 68505-1338 Office: State Capitol Dist 26 PO Box 94604 Rm 1117 Lincoln NE 68509-4604

PRICE, PAUL L., lawyer; b. Chgo., Apr. 21, 1945; s. Walter S. and Lillian (Czerepkowski) L.; m. Dianne L. Olech, June 3, 1967; children: Kristen, Kathryn. BBA, Loyola U., Chgo., 1967; JD with honors, Chgo. Kent IIT, 1971. Bar: Ill. 1971, U.S. Dist. Ct. (no. dist.) Ill., U.S. Ct. Appeals (7th cir.). Tax acct. Arthur Anderson & Co., Chgo., 1970—71; assoc. Doyle & Tarpey, Chgo., 1971—75, Gordon & Assocs., Chgo., 1975—76; from assoc. to ptnr. Pretzel & Stouffer, Chartered, Chgo., 1976—96; ptnr. Price, Tunney, Reiter, Chgo., 1996—2007, Hepler Broom LLC, 2007—. With USMC, 1969—70. Fellow: Am. Coll. Trial Lawyers; mem.: ABA, Ill. Inst. Tech.-Chgo. Kent Coll. Law Alumni Assn. (pres. 1989—90), Assn. Def. Trial Attys., Lawyers for Civil Justice (bd. dirs. 1999—2001), Def. Rsch. Inst. (bd. dirs. 1999—2001), Fedn. Def. and Corp. Counsel (pres. 1999—2000), Ill. Assn. Def. Trial Counsel (pres. 1990—91), Soc. Trial Lawyers, Ill. Bar Assn. Roman Catholic. Office: Hepler Broom LLC 150 N Wacker Dr Ste 3100 Chicago IL 60606 Home Phone: 847-253-3896; Office Phone: 312-230-9100. Business E-Mail: plprice@heplerbroom.com.

PRICE, THEODORA HADZISTELIOU, mental health services professional; b. Athens, Greece, Oct. 1, 1938; arrived in U.S., 1967; d. Ioannis and Evangelia (Emmanuel) Hadzisteliou; m. David C. Long Price, Dec. 26, 1966 (div. 1989); children: Morgan N., Alkes D. L. Diploma in piano tchg., Nat. Conservatory, Athens, 1958; BA in History/Archaeology, U. Athens, 1961; DPhil, U. Oxford, Eng., 1966; MA in Clin. Social Work, U. Chgo., 1988. LCSW, bd. cert. diplomate in clin. social work. Mus. asst., resident tutor U. Sydney, Australia, 1966-67; instr. anthropology Adelphi U., NYC, 1967-68; archaeologist Hebrew Union Coll., Gezer, Israel, 1968; asst. prof. classical archaeology/art U. Chgo., 1968-70; jr. rsch. fellow Harvard Ctr. Hellenic Studies, Washington, 1970-71; clin. social worker Harbor Light Ctr., Salvation Army, Chgo., 1988-89; therapist Inst. Motivational Devel., Lombard, Ill., 1989-90; caseworker Jewish Family & Cmty. Svc., Chgo., 1989-90; staff therapist Family Svc. Ctrs. of South Cook County, Chicago Heights, 1990-91; pvt. practice child, adolescent, family therapy Bolingbrook, Ill., 1991—; dir. counseling svcs., clin. supr., psychotherapist Family Link, Inc., Chgo., 1993; staff therapist Cen. Bapt. Family Svcs., Gracell Rehab., Chgo., 1991, 91-92; casework supr., counselor Epilepsy Found. Greater Chgo., Chgo., 1992-93; therapist children, adolescents and families dept. foster care Cath. Charities, Chgo., 1993-94; individual and family therapist South Ctrl. Cmty. Svcs. Individual-Family Counseling Svcs., Chgo., 1994-97. Bd. dirs., counselor Naperville Sch. Gifted and Talented, 1982—84; lectr. in field. Author: (monograph) Kourotrophos, Cults and Representations of the Greek Nursing Deities, 1978; contbr. articles to profl. jours. Eleutherios Venizelos scholar, 1962—65, Meyerstein Traveling grantee, Oxford, Eng., 1963, 1964. Mem.: NASW, Am. Bd. Clin. Soc. Workers, Ill. Clin. Social Workers, Nat. Acad. Clin. Social Workers. Avocations: piano, Byzantine chanting, writing. Home and Office: 10 Pebble Ct Bolingbrook IL 60440-1557 Office Phone: 630-378-1187.

PRICE, WILLIAM RAY, JR., state supreme court justice; b. Fairfield, Iowa, Jan. 30, 1952; s. William Ray and Evelyn Jean (Darnell) P.; m. Susan Marie Trainor, Jan. 4, 1975; children: Emily Margret, William Joseph Dodds. BA with distinction, U. Iowa, 1974; postgrad., Yale U., 1974-75; JD cum laude, Washington and Lee U., 1978. Bar: Mo. 1978, U.S. Dist. Ct. (we. dist.) Mo. 1978, U.S. Ct. Claims 1978, U.S. Ct. Appeals (8th cir.) 1985. Assoc. Lathrop & Norquist, Kansas City, Mo., 1978-84, ptnr., 1984-92, chmn. bus. litigation sect., 1987-88, 90-92, exec. com., 1989-92; judge Mo. Supreme Ct., Jefferson City, 1992—, chief justice, 1999—2001. G.L.V. Zumwalt monitoring com. U.S. Dist. Ct. (we. dist.) Mo., Kansas City. Pres. Kansas City Bd. Police Commrs.; mem. Together Ctr. & Family Devel. Ctr., Kansas City; chmn. merit selection com. U.S. marshal Western Dist. of Mo., Kansas City; bd. dirs. Truman Med. Ctr., Kansas City. Rockefeller fellow, 1974-75; Burks scholar Washington & Lee U., 1976. Mem. Christian Ch. Office: Supreme Ct Mo PO Box 150 207 W High St Jefferson City MO 65102-0150

PRICE, WILLIAM S., lawyer; b. Evanston, Ill., May 9, 1942; BSBA, Denver U., 1965; JD cum laude, Northwestern U., 1968. Bar: Ill. 1968. With Bell, Boyd & Lloyd, Chgo., 1968—. Mem. ABA, Nat. Assn. Bond Lawyers. Office: Bell Boyd & Lloyd Three First National Plz 70 W Madison St Ste 3300 Chicago IL 60602-4284

PRIDE, MIRIAM R., college president; b. Canton, China, June 6, 1948; d. Richard E. and Martha W. Pride; divorced. Grad., Berea College Found. Sch., 1966, Coll. of Wooster, 1970; MBA, U. Ky., 1989. Intern in administrn. in higher edn., head resident Coll. of Wooster, Ohio, 1970-72; accounts payable clk., dir. Boone Tavern Hotel, head resident, dir. student activities Berea Coll., 1972-88; eligibility worker dept. human resources State of Ky., 1975-76; asst. in undergrad. advising Coll. Bus., U. Ky., 1987-89; asst. to pres. for campus life, v.p. for administrn., pres. Blackburn Coll., Carlinville, Ill., 1989—. Chmn. United Way Berea, Carlinville, 1989—92; fin. chmn. Carlinville Hosp., 1995—97; mem. Ill. Commn. on Status of Women; bd. dirs. Land of Lincoln Girl Scouts, 1993—2000, fin. chmn., 1995—2000, mem. nominating com., 2000—; bd. dirs. Carlinville Area Hosp., 1993—97, Assn. Presbyn. Colls. and Univs., Fedn. Ill. Colls. and Univs., 1993—, Federated Ch. Bd., 1998—2001. Mem. Carlinville C. of C. (bd. dirs.), Rotary (bd. dirs. 1996—). Mem. Federated Ch. Avocations: reading, walking, knitting. Office: Blackburn Coll Office of the President Carlinville IL 62626

PRIEBUS, REINCE, lawyer, political organization administrator; BS cum laude, U. Wis., Whitewater, 1994; JD cum laude, U. Miami, 1998. Bar: Wis. 1998, US Dist. Ct. (we. dist.) Wis., US Dist. Ct. (ea. dist.) Wis. Ptnr. Litig. Practice Group Michael Best & Griedrich LLP. Co-chair Southeastern Wis. Am. Heart Assn. Heart Ball, 2007, chair, 2008; vice chmn. 1st dist. Rep. Party of Wis., chmn. 1st dist., treas., vice chmn., 2006—07, chmn., 2007—; exec. com. mem. Rep. at. Com. Named one of Milwaukee's 40 Under 40, Milw. Bus. Jour., 2008. Office: Michael Best & Griedrich LLP Ste 3300 100 E Wisconsin Ave Milwaukee WI 53202-4108 also: Rep Party of Wis 148 E Johnson St Madison WI 53703 Office Phone: 414-225-2746. Office Fax: 414-227-0656. E-mail: rrpriebus@michaelbest.com, Reince@wisgop.org.*

PRIMM, EARL RUSSELL, III, publishing executive; b. Rhinelander, Wis., Oct. 24, 1958; s. Earl Russell and Betty Joan (Dennis) P. AB in Classics (hon.), Loyola U. Chgo., 1980; MA in Libr. Sci., U. Chgo., 1990. Asst. to edn. dir. J.G. Ferguson Pub. Co., Chgo., 1981-84; prodn. mgr. Joint Commn. on Accreditation of Hosps., Chgo., 1984-85; sr. editor J.G. Ferguson Pub. Co., Chgo., 1985-87; asst. editor U. Chgo. Press., 1987-88; editorial dir. J.G. Ferguson Pub. Co., Chgo., 1988-89; project mgr. Children's Press, Chgo., 1989-92; exec. editor Franklin Watts, Inc., Chgo., NYC, 1992-95; editl. dir. Grolier Children's Pub., Danbury, Conn., 1995-97; pres. Editl. Directions, Inc., Chgo., 1997—. Mem. adv. bd. U. Chgo. Pub. Program, 1990-2000; judge Lambda Lit. awards, Washington, 1994-2000; guest lectr. Sch. Edn. Harvard U., 2004. Editl. chief: Career Discovery Encyclopedia, 1990, Favorite Children's Authors and Illustrators, 2002, 2nd edit. 2006; editor: Civil Rights Movement in America, 2nd edit., 1991, Extraordinary Hispanic Americans, 1991; editl. dir. The Child's World, 2002-05, Tradition Books, 2002. Mem. crisis counselor Nat. Runaway Switchboard, Chgo., 1985-88; Horizon's hotline counselor, Chgo., 1987-88; bd. dirs. Gerber/Hart Libr. and Archives, Chgo., 1992-94. Named Honors Sr. of Yr., Loyola U. Chgo., 1980; recipient Mertz Latin Scholarship key Loyola U. Chgo., 1980. Mem. Am. Libr. Assn. Democrat. Home: 1000 W Washington Blvd #147 Chicago IL 60607-2148 Office: 1000 W Washington Blvd # 203 Chicago IL 60607 Office Phone: 312-829-5456. E-mail: russell@editorialdirections.com.

PRIMO, QUINTIN E., III, real estate company executive; b. 1955; BS in Fin. with honors, Ind. U.; MBA, Harvard U. Mng. dir. Q. Primo & Co., Inc.; co-founder, chmn., CEO Capri Capital Advisors, LLC, Chgo., 1992. Chmn. Urban Family and Cmty. Ctrs.; chmn. Com. of 100 Ill. Pub. Policy Caucus. Mem.: Urban Land Inst., Pension Real Estate Assn., Real Estate Roundtable (dir.). Office: Capri Capital Advisors LLC Ste 3430 875 N Michigan Ave Chicago IL 60611 E-mail: qprimo@capricapital.com.*

PRINCE, THOMAS RICHARD, accountant, educator; b. New Albany, Miss., Dec. 7, 1934; s. James Thompson and Callie Florence (Howell) P.; m. Eleanor Carol Polkoff, July 14, 1962; children: Thomas Andrew, John Michael, Adrienne Carol. BS, Miss. State U., 1956, MS, 1957; PhD in Accountancy, U. Ill., 1962. CPA, Ill. Instr. U. Ill., 1960—62; mem. faculty Northwestern U. Kellogg Sch. Mgmt., Evanston, Ill., 1962—, prof. acctg. info. and mgmt., 1969—, chmn. dept. acctg. info. and mgmt., 1968—75, prof. health industry mgmt., 1990—; cons. in field. Dir. Applied Rsch. Sys., Inc. Author: Extension of the Boundaries of Accounting Theory, 1962, Information Systems for Management Planning and Control, 3d edit, 1975, Financial Reporting and Cost Control for Health Care Entities, 1992, Product Life-Cycle Costing and Management of Large-Scale Medical Systems Investments, 1997, Strategic Management for Health Care Entities: Creative Frameworks for Financial and Operational Analysis, 1998. 1st lt. US Army Fin. Corps, 1957—60. Mem. AICPA, INFORMS, AHA, HFMA, HIMMS, AUPHA, Am. Accounting Assn., Am. Econ. Assn., Fin. Execs. Inst., AAAS, Ill. Soc. CPA, Inst. Mgmt. Acct., Alpha Tau Omega, Phi Kappa Phi,

Omicron Delta Kappa, Delta Sigma Pi, Beta Alpha Psi. Congregationalist. Home: 303 Richmond Rd Kenilworth IL 60043-1138 Office: Northwestern U Leverone Hl Evanston IL 60208-2002 Office Phone: 847-491-2669. Business E-Mail: t-prince@kellogg.northwestern.edu.

PRINCE, (PRINCE ROGERS NELSON), musician, actor; b. Mpls., June 7, 1958; s. John L. and Mattie D. (Shaw) Nelson; m. Mayte Garcia, 1996 (div., 2000); 1 son (dec.); m. Manuela Testolini, Dec. 31, 2001 (separated, 2006) Singer, songwriter, actor. Albums include For You, 1978, Dirty Mind, 1979, Controversy, 1981, 1999, 1983, film star and soundtrack Purple Rain, 1984 (Academy Award for best original score, 1984), Around the World in a Day, 1985 (Best Soul/Rhythm and Blues Album of the Yr., Downbeat readers poll, 1985), Parade, 1986, Chaos and Disorder, 1996, Sign O' the Times, 1987, Lovesexy, 1988, Batman: Motion Picture Soundtrack, 1989 (Soundtrack of Yr. award Playboy mag. readers' poll, Best Pop/Rock album Downbeat mag. readers' poll), (with the New Power Generation) Diamonds and Pearls, 1991, (symbol as title), 1992, Come, 1995, The Greatest Romance Ever Sold, 1999, 94 East, 2000, The Very Best of Prince, 2001, Beautiful Experience, 2001, The Rainbow Children, 2001, One Night Alone.Live!, 2002, N.E.W.S., 2003, Musicology, 2004, 3121, 2006, Planet Earth, 2007 (Grammy award for Best Male R&B Vocal Performance, 2008); films include Purple Rain, 1984, film star and soundtrack Under the Cherry Moon, 1986, film star and soundtrack Sign O' the Times, 1987; film appearance and soundtrack Graffiti Bridge, 1990 (ASCAP award for most performed songs from a motion picture, 1991); formerly mem. group Prince and the Revolution (Best Soul/Rhythm and Blues Group of Yr. Downbeat mag. readers poll 1985); composer Showgirls, 1995, Girl 6, 1996, The Gold Experience, 1995, Crystal Ball, 1998, Rave Un2 the Joy Fantastic, 1999, Bamboozled, 2000, Happy Feet, 2006 (The Song of the Heart, Best Original Song-Motion Picture, Golden Globe award, Hollywood Fgn. Press Assn., 2007). Recipient 3 Grammy awards, 1985, Am. Music Achievement award for infuence on look and sound of the 80's, NAACP Spl. Achievement award, 1997, Webby Lifetime Achievement award, Internat. Acad. Digital Arts and Sciences, 2006, Best Male R&B award, Black Entertainment TV (BET), 2006, Male Artist award, NAACP Image Awards, 2007; named Rhythm and Blues Musician of Yr. Down Beat mag. readers' poll, 1984, 1992; inducted Rock and Roll Hall of Fame, 2004. Office: Paisley Park Studios 7801 Audubon Rd Chanhassen MN 55317-8201

PRINGLE, BARBARA CARROLL, state legislator; b. NYC, Apr. 4, 1939; d. Nicholas Robert and Anna Joan (Woloshinovich) Terlesky; m. Richard D. Pringle, Nov. 28, 1959; children: Christopher, Rhonda. Student, Cuyahoga C.C. With Dunn & Bradstreet, 1957-60; precinct committeewoman City of Cleve., 1976-77; elected mem. Cleve. City Coun., 1977-81; mem. Ohio Ho. of Reps., Columbus, 1982—. 20th dist. state ctrl. commetteewoman, 1982-92; asst. minority leader econ. devel. & small bus. com., pub. utilities com.; mem. Children & Family Svcs. com.; mem. Ohio Legis. Svc. Commn.; mem. Ohio Children's Trust Fund, Midwestern Legis. Conf. Coun. State Govts.' Com. Status Children. Vol. Cleve. Lupus Steering Com., various community orgns.; charter mem. Statue of Liberty Ellis Island Found. Recipient cert. of appreciation Cleve. Mcpl. Ct., 1977, Exch. Club Bklyn., 1978, Cmty. Recreation Appreciation award City of Cleve., 1978, Key to City of Cleve., 1979, Cleve. Area Soapbox Derby cert., 1976, 77, 81, cert. of appreciation Ward 9 Youth League, 1979-82, No. Ohio Patrolman's Benevolent Assn. award, 1983, Cuyahoga County Firefighters award, 1983, Outstanding Pub. Servant award for Outstanding Svc. to Hispanic Cmty., 1985, Nat. Sr. Citizen Hall of Fame award, 1987, cert. of appreciation Cleve. Coun. Unemployed Workers, 1987, Ohio Farmers Union award, 1990, award of appreciation United Labor Agy., 1993, Susan B. Anthony award, 1995. Mem. Nat. Order Women Legislators, Fedn. Dem. Women of Ohio, Nat. Alliance Czech Catholics, St. Michael Ch. Altar and Rosary Soc., Ward 15 Dem. Club, Polish Falcons. Democrat. Home: 708 Timothy Ln Cleveland OH 44109-3733

PRINGLE, LEWIS GORDON, marketing professional, educator; b. Lansing, Mich., Feb. 13, 1941; s. Gordon Henry and Lucile Roxana (Drake) P.; children: Lewis Gordon Jr., William Davis, Thomas Benjamin. BA, Harvard U., 1963; MS, MIT, 1965, PhD, 1969. V.p., dir. mktg. sci. BBDO, Inc., NYC, 1968—73; asst. prof. mktg. Carnegie-Mellon U., Pitts., 1973—74; exec. v.p., dir. rsch. svcs., corp. dir. BBDO, Inc., NYC, 1978—91; exec. v.p. BBDO Worldwide, 1986—91; chmn., CEO BBDO Europe, 1986—91, LG Pringle and Assocs., 1992—95; Joseph C. Seibert prof. mktg. Farmer Sch. Bus. Adminstrn., Miami U., Oxford, Ohio, 1995—2000. Bd. dirs. Yorktown U., prof.; mem. vis com. Sloan Sch. Mgmt., MIT. Assoc. editor Jour. Advt. Rsch.; mem. editl. bd. Jour. Mktg. Sci.; mem. editl. bd. Jour. Market Rsch.; contbr. numerous articles to Harvard Bus. Rev., Mktg. Scis., others. Active local Boy Scouts Am. Ford Found. fellow, 1967 Fellow Royal Statis. Soc.; mem. INFORMS (chmn. mktg. strategy com.), Market Rsch. Coun., Am. Psychol. Assn., European Soc. Mktg. and Opinion Rsch., Am. Mktg. Assn., Inst. Ops. Rsch. and Mgmt. Sci. Office: Mind / Matter 2858 N Stout Rd Liberty IN 47353 Personal E-mail: lewpring@ruraltek.com. Business E-Mail: lewpring@hughes.net.

PRINGLE, ORAN ALLAN, mechanical and aerospace engineering educator; b. Lawrence, Kans., Sept. 14, 1923; s. Oran Allan and Mae (McClell) Pringle; m. Billie Hansen, June 25, 1947; children: Allan, Billie, James, Rebecca. BSME, U. Kan., 1947; MS, U. Wis., 1948, PhD, 1967. Registered profl. engr., Mo. Mech. engr. Black and Veatch (cons. engrs.), Kansas City, Mo., 1947-48; engr. Boeing Airplane Co., Wichita, 1952—; prof. U. Mo., Columbia, 1948—90, prof. emeritus, 1991—. Co-author: Engineering Metallurgy, 1957; contbr. articles to profl. lit. Bd. dirs. Untied Cerebral Palsy Boone County, Mo. With US Army, 1943—45. Ford Found. grantee. Mem.: ASME (chmn. fastening and joining com. design engring. divsn.), Sigma Xi. Home: 1820 University Ave Columbia MO 65201-6004 Office: Dept Mech and Aerospace Engring U Mo Columbia MO 65201

PRINS, HARALD EDWARD LAMBERT, anthropologist, educator; b. Alphen aan de Rijn, The Netherlands, Sept. 7, 1951; came to US, 1978; s. Adriaan Hendrik Johan and Pietertje Anna Catharina (Poorter) P.; m. Bunny McBride, Sept. 29, 1985. Doctorandus, Radboud U. Nijmegen, The Netherlands, 1976; cert. in advanced 16 mm filmmaking, Parsons Sch., NYC, 1980; PhD, New Sch. Social Rsch., NYC, 1988. Asst. prof. comparative hist. Radboud U. Nijmegen, 1976—78; dir. R & D Assn. Aroostook Indians, Houlton, Maine, 1981—82; staff anthropologist Aroostook Band of Micmacs, Presque Isle, Maine, 1982—90; mem. grad. faculty Kans State U., Manhattan, 1990—, prof. anthropology, 1996—, Coffman chair Univ. Disting. Tchg. Scholars, 2004—05, Univ. Disting. prof., 2005—. Vis. lectr. anthropology Bowdoin Coll., Brunswick, Maine, 1986—88; vis. asst. prof. Colby Coll., Waterville, Maine, 1988—89; adj. prof. U. Maine, Orono, 1989; expert witness on Indian rights US Congress, Washington, 1990; faculty adv. AISES, 1992—97, Native Am. Student Body, 1997—2001; internat. observer presdl. elections, Paraguay, 1993; expert witness Nfld. aboriginal landclaims Nfld. Fed. and Provincial Ct., Canada, 1998—; disting. lectr. U. Maine, Presque Isle, 2002; keynote spkr. High Plains Soc. Applied Anthropology, 2002, Northeastern Anthrop. Assn., 2003; plenary spkr. U. Nijmegen, Netherlands, 2003; prin. investigator Acadia Nat. Pk. Ethnohistory Project, Nat. Pks. Svc., 2003—07; invited speaker UNESCO Symposium, Paris, 2005; guest curator mus. exhibit Smithsonian Instn., 2003—07. Co-prodr.: (documentaries) Our Lives in Our Hands, 1986, Oh, What a Blow that Phantom Gave Me!, 2003; mem. editl. bd. Maine Hist., 1992—, Am. Anthropologist, 1998—2002, Explorations in Media Ecology, 2005—; co-editor: American Beginnings, 1994; author: The Mi'kmaq: Resistance, Accommodation and Cultural Survival, 1996; editor: Am. Anthropologist, 1998—2002, Visual Anthropology Rev., 2000—04; co-author: Cultural Anthropology: The Human Challenge, 2005, Asticou's Island Domain: Wabanaki Peoples at Mount Desert Island, 1500-2000, 12th edit., 2007, Evolution and Prehistory: The Human Challenge, 2005; co-editor: 8th edit., 2007; co-author: The Essence of Anthropology, 2006; contbr. chapters to books, articles to profl. jours. Mem adv. bd. Salt Inst. Documentary Field Studies, Maine, 1990—; adv./rschr. land claims Miawpukek Band of Mikmaq, Conne River, Nfld., 1996—; cultural preservation adv. Plains Apache Tribe, Anadarko, Okla., 1993-97; fed. recognition and landclaims adv./rschr. Aroostook Band of Micmacs, Presque Isle, 1981-91. Named Kans. Prof. of Yr., Carnegie Found. for Advancement of Tchg. and Coun. for Advancement and Support of Edn., 2006; recipient Conoco Prize Outstanding Tchg., Kans. State U., 1993, Presdl. award Outstanding Tchg., 1999, John Culkin award Outstanding Practice in Media, 2004; grantee, NEH, 1989; Vera List fellow, 1978. Mem.: NY Acad. Scis., Soc. Anthropology of Lowland S.Am., Maine Hist. Soc., Soc. L.Am. Anthropology, Soc. Visual Anthropology (prog. editor 1995, bd. dirs. 1995—, pres. 2000—), Am. Anthrop. Assn. (jury Ethnographic Film Festival 1998). Avocations: hiking, sailing, drawing, photography, wildlife. Office: Dept Anthropology Kans State U 207 Waters Hall Manhattan KS 66506 Office Phone: 785-532-4966. E-mail: prins@ksu.edu.

PRINZ, RICHARD ALLEN, surgeon; MD, Loyola U., Chgo., 1972. Diplomate Am. Bd. Surgery, bd. dirs., 1994—. Intern Barnes Hosp., St. Louis, 1972-73, resident in surgery, 1973-74, Loyola U., Chgo., 1974-77, attending surgeon, 1980-93; staff Rush Presbyn.-St. Luke's Med. Ctr., Chgo., 1993—; Helen Shedd Keith prof., chmn. dept. gen. surgery Rush U., Chgo., 1993—. Mem. Am. Surg. Assn., Am. Assn. Endocrine Surgeons (pres. 1996), Midwest Surg. Assn. (pres. 1997), Western Surg. Assn. (treas. 1993-97, pres. 2002-), Chgo. Surg. Soc. (pres.-elect 2002-, pres. 2003). Office: Rush U 818 Profl Bldg 1725 W Harrison St Chicago IL 60612-3828 Office Phone: 312-942-6511. Business E-Mail: rprinz@rush.edu.

PRIOR, DAVID JAMES, college dean; b. Anniston, Ala., Dec. 13, 1943; m. Merry Lucille; children: Andrea Suzanne, Christopher Sutton. AB, Olivet Coll., Mich., 1965; MS, Ctrl. Mich. U., 1968; PhD, U. Va., 1972. Postdoctoral fellow-neurobiology Princeton (N.J.) U., 1972-73; asst. prof. biolg. scis. U. Ky., Lexington, 1973-78, prof. biology, 1985-87, assoc. prof. physiology and biophysics, 1984-87, prof. physiology and biophysics Coll. Medicine, 1987; prof., chair biology No. Ariz. U., Flagstaff, 1987-92, dean Coll. Arts and Scis., 1992—. Office: U Wisconsin-Whitewater Office Provost 800 W Main St Whitewater WI 53190

PRIOR, GARY L., lawyer; b. Niagara Falls, NY, June 26, 1943; s. Harold D. and Adeline Thelma (Lee) Prior; m. Nancy O'Shaughnessy, Aug. 23, 1975; children: Joseph Lee, Julia Elizabeth. BS, Tulane U., 1965; JD, U. Chgo., 1968. Bar: Ill. 1968, U.S. Dist. Ct. (no. dist.), Ill. 1968, U.S. Ct. Appeals (7th cir.) 1973, U.S. Ct. Appeals (3d cir.) 1974, U.S. Trial Bar 1983, U.S. Supreme Ct. 1989, U.S. Dist. Ct. (we. dist.) Wis. 1992, U.S. Dist. Ct. (ea. dist.) Wis. 1993, U.S. Dist. Ct. Minn. 1994, U.S. Ct. Appeals (fed. cir.) 2002. Assoc. Rooks, Pitts, and Poust, Chgo., 1968-71, McDermott, Will, and Emery, Chgo., 1971-74, ptnr., 1974—2002, dir. trial dept. tng., 1980-85, mem. securities approval com., 1986—94, mem. nominating com., chmn., 1988-89, partnership com., 1989-92, mem mgmt. com., 1991-93; of counsel Tabet, DiVito, and Rothstein, LLC, Chgo., 2002—03, ptnr., 2004—. Trustee Prior Family Charitable Found., Furry Friends Found. Mem.: Fed. Cir. Bar Assn., Ill. State Bar Assn., Ill. Appellate Lawyers Assn. Avocations: history, farming, scuba diving. Home: 2512 Burling St Chicago IL 60614-2510 Office: Tabet DiVito & Rothstein The Rookery 209 S LaSalle Ste 700 Chicago IL 60604 Office Phone: 312-762-9472. Business E-Mail: gprior@tdrlawfirm.com.

PRITCHARD, JONATHAN K., geneticist, educator; BSc in Biology and Math., Pa. State U., 1994; PhD in Biol. Scis., Stanford U., Calif., 1998. Postdoctoral fellow dept. stats. U. Oxford, England, 1998—2001; asst. prof. dept. human genetics U. Chgo., 2001—05, prof., 2006—. Contbr. articles to sci. jours. Co-recipient Paper of Yr. award, Lancet, 2003; recipient Mitchell prize, Am. Statis. Assn. and Internat. Soc. Bayesian Analysis, 2002; Packard fellow, 2004, Alfred P. Sloan fellow, 2004. Office: Dept Human Genetics U Chgo 920 E 58th St CLSC 507 Chicago IL 60637 Office Phone: 773-834-5248. Office Fax: 773-834-0505. E-mail: pritch@uchicago.edu.

PRITCHARD, SARAH MARGARET, library director; b. Boston, Feb. 8, 1955; d. Wilbur Louis and Kathleen Hunton (Moss) P.; m. Timothy John Brennan, Aug. 20, 1977 (div. 1993); m. eal Edward Blair, July 15, 2005. BA, U. Md., 1975; MA in French, U. Wis., 1976, MLS, 1977. Intern Libr. Congress, Washington, 1977-78, reference specialist in women's studies, 1978-88, head microform reading rm., 1988-90; sr. program officer Assn. Rsch. Librs., Washington, 1990-91, assoc. exec. dir., 1991-92; acad. libr. mgmt. intern Coun on Libr. Resources Princeton U., NJ, 1988-89; dir. librs. Smith Coll., Northampton, Mass., 1992-99; univ. libr. U. Calif., Santa Barbara, 1999—2006, Northwestern U., Evanston, Ill., 2006—. Editl. advisor Women's Rsch. and Edn. Inst., Washington, 1987-92; bd. dirs. Western Mass. Regional Libr. Sys., 1997-98; bd. dirs. U. Calif. So. Regional Libr. Facility, Gold Coast Libr. Network, Libr. Calif.; mem. steering com. Scholarly Pub. and Academic Resources Coalition, 2006—; Charles Deering McCormick disting. chair rsch. libr. U. Wis., 2006. Editor: The Women's Annual, 1984; compiler ARL Stats., 1990-92; contbr. articles to profl. jours.; mem. editl. bd. Jour. Acad. Librarianship, 1993-99, Portal: Librs. and the Acad., 2000—; contbg. editor Libr. Issues, 1994-99. Trustee Leroy C. Merritt Humanitarian Fund, 1991-94. Named Wis. Alumni Rsch. Found. fellow, 1975-77, Outstanding Alumna U. Wis. Sch. of Libr. and Info. Studies, 1997. Mem. ALA (chair machine assisted reference sect. 1986-87, chair women's studies sect. 1989-90, coun. 1990-98, 2000-04, chair stds. com. 1998-2002, chair ethics com. 2002-06, Equality award 1997), Nat. Women's Studies Assn., Cosmos Club, Phi Beta Kappa. Democrat. Office: Northwestern Univ Libr Evanston IL 60208

PRITCHETT, KELVIN, professional football player; b. Atlanta, Oct. 24, 1969; Student, U. Miss. Football player Detroit Lions, 1991-94, 99—, Jacksonville (Fla.) Jaguars, 1995-98. Office: Detroit Lions Inc 222 Republic Dr Allen Park MI 48101-3650

PRITIKIN, DAVID T., lawyer; b. Freeport, Ill., May 2, 1949; BA summa cum laude, Cornell U., 1971; JD magna cum laude, Harvard U., 1974. Bar: Ill. 1974, US Ct. Appeals (9th cir.) 1975, US Ct. Appeals (7th cir.) 1976, U.S. Supreme Ct. 1977, US Ct. Appeals (fed. cir.) 1993. Ptnr. Sidley Austin LLP, Chgo., chair, nat. intellectual property practice. Fellow: Am. Coll. of Trial Lawyers. Office: Sidley Austin LLP 1 S Dearborn St Chicago IL 60603 Office Phone: 312-853-7359. Office Fax: 312-853-7036. Business E-Mail: dpritikin@sidley.com.

PRITZKER, NICHOLAS J., diversified financial services company executive; BA, Lake Forest Coll.; JD, Univ. Chgo. Bar: Ill. 1975. Joined Hyatt Corp., 1978, formerly exec. v.p. devel. Chgo.; pres. Hyatt Devel. Corp., Chgo., 1981—99, chmn., 1999—; and vice chmn. Hyatt Internat. and Hyatt Corp., Chgo.; also ptnr. Pritkzer & Pritzker law, Chgo. Chmn. bd. Eos Biotechnology, San Francisco, 2000—. Named one of Forbes' Richest Americans, 2006. Office: Hyatt Devel Corp 200 W Madison St Chicago IL 60606-3414

PRITZKER, PENNY, investor; b. Chgo., May 2, 1959; d. Donald N. and Sue Ann (Sandel) Pritzker; m. Bryan Traubert, Sept. 10, 1988; children: Donald Pritzker Traubert, Rose Pritzker Traubert. B in Econs., Harvard U., 1981; JD, MBA, Stanford U., 1985. Bar: Ill. 1985. Mgr. Hyatt Devel. Corp., Chgo., 1985-87; pres. Classic Residence by Hyatt, Chgo., 1987—; ptnr. Pritzker & Pritzker, Chgo., 1987—; pres. Pritzker Realty Grp. (formerly Penguin Group, L.P.), Chgo., 1990—; chmn. TransUnion Corp., 2005—. Chmn. exec. com. Encore Sr. Living, Portland, Oreg.; corp. adv. bd. mem. Mayor Daley's Exec. Fellows Prog., Chgo.; mem. Mayor Daley's fin. com.; bd. dirs. William Wrigley, Jr. Co., Chgo., Coast-to-Coast Fin. Corp., NYC, Nat. Investment Conf., Washington.; Nat. Fin. chmn., Obama for Pres. Chair Mus. Contemporary Art, Chgo.; adv. bd. dirs. Chgo. Cares; mem. dean's coun. Harvard U.; mem. Women's Issues Network, Chgo., 1991—, The Chgo. Network, 1992—, Internat. Women's Forum, Chgo., Coun. Fgn. Rels., NY. Named a Woman to Watch, Crain's Chgo. Bus., 2007; named one of 50 Women to Watch, Wall St. Jour., 2005, 100 Most Powerful Women in World, Forbes mag., 2005, 400 Richest Ams., 2006; recipient Brick & Mortar award, Chgo. Equity Fund, 1991, Disting. Svc. award, REIA Kellogg, 1995. Mem. Nat. Assn. Sr. Living Industry Execs. (bd. dirs. 1989-91), Urban Land Inst., Young Pres.'s Orgn. Office: Classic Residence By Hyatt 71 S Wacker Dr Ste 900 Chicago IL 60606-4637

PRITZKER, THOMAS JAY, hotel executive; b. Chgo., June 6, 1950; s. Jay Arthur and Marian (Friend) P.; m. Margot Lyn Barrow-Sicree, Sept. 4, 1977; 3 children. BA, Claremont Men's Coll., Calif., 1971; MBA, U. Chgo., 1976, JD, 1976. Assoc. Katten, Muchin, Zavis, Pearl and Galler, Chgo., 1976-77; exec. v.p. Hyatt Corp., Chgo., 1977-80, pres., 1980—2002, chmn., CEO, 1999—2004; chmn. Hyatt Hotels Corp., 1980—2002, Hyatt Internat. Corp., 1999—2004; ptnr. Pritzker & Pritzker, Chgo., 1980—; CEO Global Hyatt Corp., Chgo., 2005—06, chmn., 2005—. Chmn. bd. dirs. The Pritzker Orgn., 1998—; bd. dirs. Royal Caribbean Cruises Ltd. Bd. trustees, chmn. Art Inst. Chgo., 1988—; bd. trustees U. Chgo. Named one of Forbes' Richest Americans, 2006. Mem. ABA, Ill. Bar Assn., Chgo. Bar Assn., Standard Club, Lake Shore Country Club. Office: Hyatt Ctr 71 S Wacker Dr Ste 4700 Chicago IL 60606 Office Phone: 312-873-4901.

PROCHNOW, DOUGLAS LEE, lawyer; b. Omaha, Jan. 9, 1952; s. Albert Delmer and Betty Jean (Wood) Prochnow. BA with high distinction, U. Nebr., 1974; JD, Northwestern U., 1977. Bar: Ill. 1977, U.S. Dist. Ct. (no. dist.) Ill. 1977, U.S. Ct. Appeals (7th cir.) 1989, U.S. Supreme Ct. 2000. Assoc. Wildman, Harrold, Allen & Dixon, Chgo., 1977-84, ptnr., 1985—. Spl. asst. corp. counsel City of Chgo., 1986—87; adj. prof. law Northwestern U. Sch. Law, 2005—. Pres. Chgo. bd. Prevent Child Abuse Am. Mem. ABA, ATLA (assoc.), Ill. Bar Assn., Chgo. Bar Assn., Soc. Trial Lawyers, Def. Rsch. Inst., Am. Health Lawyers Assn., Phi Beta Kappa, Phi Eta Sigma. Office: Wildman Harrold Allen & Dixon 225 W Wacker Dr Ste 2700 Chicago IL 60606-1224 Home: 159 E Walton St Unit 12B Chicago IL 60611 Home Phone: 312-951-8975; Office Phone: 312-201-2526. Business E-Mail: prochnow@wildman.com.

PROCTOR, BARBARA GARDNER, advertising agency executive, writer; b. Ashville, NC; d. William and Bernice (Baxter) Gardner; m. Carl L. Proctor, July 20, 1961 (div. Nov. 1963); 1 son, Morgan Eugene. BA, Talladega Coll., Ala., 1954. Music critic, contbg. editor Down Beat Mag., Chgo., 1958—; internat. dir. Vee Jay Records, Chgo., 1961-64; copy supr. Post-Keyes-Gardner Advt., Inc., Chgo., 1965-68, Gene Taylor Assos., Chgo., 1968-69, North Advt. Agt., Chgo., 1969-70; contbr. to gen. periodicals, 1952—; founder Proctor & Gardner Advt. (divsn. Proctor Comm. Network), Chgo., 1970—, pres., CEO. Pres., CEO Proctor Comm. Network, Chgo.; Mem. Chgo. Urban League, Chgo. Econ. Devel. Corp.; cons. pub. rels. and promotion, record industry; bd. dir. Window to the World Comm., Inc.; bd. trustee 98.7WFMT, WTTW11. Author: (TV documentary) Blues for a Gardenia, 1963. Bd. dirs. People United to Save Humanity, Better Bus. Bur., Window to the World Comm., Inc., Ill. Bell Telephone Co., Northwestern Hosp., Mid-City Nat. Bank, Coun. Chgo. Better Bus. Bur., Louisville Courier-Jour., United Way, Econ. Club; Mem. NARAS, USIA, Chgo. Media Women, Women's Advt. Club, NY Art Dirs. Club, Woman's Day Club, Cosmopolitan C. of C. (dir.); bd. trustee 98.7WFMT, WTTW11; co-chair, State Ill. Gannon-Proctor Commn.; governing coun. mem. Ill. State Bar Assn. Inst. for Pub. Affairs. Recipient Armstrong Creative Writing award, 1954; awards Chgo. Fedn. Advt., Frederick Douglas Humanitarian award, 1975, Headliner award, Assn. for Women in Comm., 1978; named Chgo. Advt. Woman of Yr., 1974; named to Smithsonian Instn. "Black Women Achievements Against the Odds" Hall of Fame and the series' poster-calendar traveling exhbn. Mem. Female Execs. Assn., Internat. Platform Assn., Smithsonian Instn. Assn.

PROFFITT, KEVIN, archivist; b. Hamilton, Ohio, Dec. 24, 1956; s. Henry C. and Marjorie O. (Elam) P.; m. Joan Moriarity, May 17, 1986. BA, Miami U., Oxford, Ohio, 1979; MA, Wright State U., 1980; MLS, U. Ky., 1998. Archivist Am. Jewish Archives, Cin., 1981—. Contbr. articles to profl. jours. Mem. Soc. Am. Archivists, Acad. Cert. Archivists (cert.), Midwest Archives Conf., Soc. Ohio Archivists (pres. 1987-89). Office: Am Jewish Archives 3101 Clifton Ave Cincinnati OH 45220-2404

PROFIT, KIRK A., former state legislator; b. Mt. Pleasant, Mich., Sept. 12, 1952; s. Lewis Edwin and Maxine (Merritt) P.; m. Sharon Grace Langen; children: Jennifer, Kristine, Kirk. BS, Ea. Mich. U.; JD, U. Detroit; DSc (hon.), Cleary Coll. Bar: Mich. Pvt. practice law, 1979-80; legal adv., undersheriff Washington County Sheriff's Dept., Mich., 1981-84; rep. Mich. Dist. 54, 1989-98; account exec. Govt. Cons. Svcs., Inc., Lansing, Mich., 1998—. Chmn. higher edn. com. Mich. Ho. Reps., ethics & oversight com., judiciary com., taxation com., bus. com., fin. com. Mem. Dem. Leadership Coun. Named legis. of yr. Police Officers Assn. Mich., 1991, Mich. Assn. Chiefs of Police, 1993; recipient disting. svc. award Ind. Colls. and Univs. Mich., 1994. Mem. Sierra Club, Optimists Internat. Home: 205 Valley Dr Ypsilanti MI 48197-4460 Office: Govt Cons Svcs Inc 530 W Ionia St Lansing MI 48933-1062

PROHOFSKY, DENNIS E., lawyer, insurance company executive; BA, U. Minn., 1965; JD, William Mitchell Coll. Law, 1972. Bar: Minn. 1972. Sr. underwriter Minn. Life Ins. Co., St. Paul, 1962—72, second v.p., 1982—94, sr. v.p., gen. counsel, sec., 1994—2002, exec. v.p., gen. counsel, sec., 2002—. Office: Minn Life Ins Co 400 Robert St N Saint Paul MN 55101 Office Phone: 651-665-3500. Business E-Mail: dennis.prohofsky@minnesotamutual.com.

PROKOP, KEVIN, investment company executive; b. 1968; BBA, Georgetown U., 1990; MBA, U. Chgo. Investment profl. First Chgo.-NBD Capital Markets; assoc. Kleinwort Benson, Ltd.; assoc., engagement mgr. McKinsey & Co., 1994—97; dir. Questor Mgmt. Co., Southfield, Mich., 1998—. Former bd. mem. GeoLogistics Corp.; bd. mem. Internet Ops. Ctr., U. Cancer Found., New Detroit. Named one of 40 Under 40, Crain's Detroit Bus., 2006; recipient Turnaround of Yr. award, Buyouts mag., 2006. Office: Questor Management Co 2000 Town Ctr Ste 2450 Southfield MI 48075 Office Phone: 248-213-2200. Office Fax: 248-213-2215.

PROKOPANKO, JAMES T., agricultural products executive; b. 1953; BS, U. Manitoba; MBA, U. We. Ontario. With Cargill Inc., 1978—2006, v.p. N.Am. crop inputs bus., corp. v.p. procurement, 2002—06; exec. v.p., CEO The Mosaic Co., Plymouth, Minn., 2006—07, pres., CEO, 2007—. Office: The Mosaic Co Atria Corp Ctr 3033 Campus Dr Ste E490 Plymouth MN 55441 Office Phone: 800-918-8270. Office Fax: 763-559-2960.

PROSSER, DAVID THOMAS, JR., state supreme court justice and former legislator; b. Chgo., Dec. 24, 1942; s. David Thomas, Sr. and Elizabeth Averell (Patterson) Prosser. BA, DePauw U., 1965; JD, U. Wis., 1968. Bar: Wis. 1968. Lectr. Ind. U., Indpls., 1968-69; advisor U.S. Dept. Justice, Washington, 1969-72; adminstrv. asst. to U.S. Rep. Harold V. Froehlich, Washington, 1973-74; pvt. practice Washington, 1975, Appleton, Wis., 1976; dist. atty. Outagamie County Wis., Appleton, 1977-78; state rep. State of Wis., Madison, 1979-96; commr. Tax Appeals Commn., 1997-98; justice Supreme Ct. Wis., 1998—. Jud. Coun., 2002—06. Commr. Nat. Conf. Commrs. Uniform State Laws, 1982—96, 2005—07; mem. Wis. Sesquicentennial Commn., Madison, 1993—99; minority leader Wis. Assembly, 1989—94, spkr., 1995—96. Mem.: Outagamie Bar Assn., Milw. Bar Assn., Dane Bar Assn., Wis. Bar Assn. Presbyterian. Avocation: art collector of American prints. Office: Supreme Ct Wis PO Box 1688 Madison WI 53701-1688

PROSSER, FRANKLIN PIERCE, computer scientist; b. Atlanta, July 4, 1935; s. Edward Theron and Eunice (McDaniel) P.; m. Brenda Mary Lau, June 16, 1960; children: Edward, Andrea. BS, Ga. Inst. Tech., 1956, MS, 1958; PhD, Pa. State U., 1961. Prof. computer sci. Ind. U., Bloomington, 1969-99; asso. dir. Wrubel Computing Center, 1969-81, chmn. dept. computer sci., 1971-77, 87-93, spl. asst. for acad. computing, 1979-81; v.p. Logic Design, Inc., 1982-92. Cons. Lockheed Theoretical Physics Lab., Palo Alto, Calif., 1967 Home: 1200 S Longwood Dr Bloomington IN 47401-6072 Office: Ind U Dept Computer Sci Bloomington IN 47405

PROST, DONALD, former state legislator; Mem. Mo. State Ho. of Reps. Dist. 162, 1993-97; dir. joint com. on legis. rsch. State of Mo., 1997—. Office: Rm 117-A Mo State Capitol Jefferson City MO 65101

PROTSCH, ELIOT G., utilities and corporate financial executive; BBA in Econs. and Fin., U. SD, Vermillion, 1975, MBA, 1976. Cert. Fin. Analyst 1981. With Mut. of Omaha Ins. Co., 1976—78; asst. treas. treasury dept. Wis. Power & Light Co. (now Alliant Energy Corp.), Madison, Wis., 1978—85, dist. mgr. Dane County, 1985—89, v.p. and gen. mgr. energy svc., 1989—92, v.p. customer sales and svc., 1992—93, sr. v.p., 1993—98; exec. v.p. energy delivery Interstate Power & Light (now Alliant Energy Corp.), Cedar Rapids, Iowa, 1998—2003, pres., 1998—; sr. exec. v.p. and CFO Alliant Energy Corp., Madison, Wis., 2004—. Bd. dir. uclear Mgmt. Co, Am. Family Ins., chair audit com., 2000—; bd. dir. Capstone MicroTurbine Corp., Alliant Energy Found. Mem. Iowa Bus. Coun., 2000—, chair, 2004—; bd. dir. Mercy Med. Ctr., Cedar Rapids, 1997—, Cedar Rapids C. of C., 2002—; bd. dirs. Iowa Natural Heritage Found., Des Moines, 2000—. Office: Alliant Energy Corp 4902 N Biltmore Ln Madison WI 53718

PROVUS, BARBARA LEE, retired executive search consultant; b. Washington, Nov. 20, 1949; d. Severn and Birdell (Eck) P.; m. Frederick W. Wackerle, Mar. 29, 1985. Student, NYU, 1969-70; BA in Sociology, Russell Sage Coll., 1971; MS in Indsl. Rels., Loyola U., Chgo., 1978; postgrad., Smith Coll., 1971. Sec. Booz, Allen & Hamilton, Chgo., 1973-74, mgr. tng., 1974-77, dir. rsch., 1977-79, cons. search, 1979-80; mgr. mgmt. devel. Federated Dept. Stores, Cin.,

1980-82; v.p. Lamalie Assocs., Chgo., 1982-86; prin., founder Sweeney, Shepherd, Bueschel, Provus, Harbert & Mummert, Inc., Chgo., 1986-91; founder Shepherd Bueschel & Provus Inc., Chgo., 1992—2005; ret., 2005. Bd. dirs. Anti-Cruelty Soc., Chgo., 1990—, pres., 1996-97; trustee Sage Colls., Troy, N.Y., 1999-2000. Mem. Assn. Exec. Search Cons. (dir. 1989-92), The Chgo. Network (bd. dirs. 1993—, chair 2002-03), Econ. Club Chgo. Avocations: collecting rubber bands, modern art, baseball. Home: 3750 N Lake Shore Dr Chicago IL 60613-4238 Home Phone: 773-935-0141.

PRUGH, WILLIAM BYRON, lawyer; b. Kansas City, Mo., Jan. 3, 1945; s. Byron E. and Helen Prugh; m. Linda Stuart, Aug. 12, 1968; 1 child, K. Niccole. BA, U. Mo., Kansas City, 1966, JD, 1969, LLM in Taxation, 1971. Bar: Mo. 1969, U.S. Tax Ct. 1975, U.S. Supreme Ct. 1975, Kans. 1982. Mem. Shughart Thomson & Kilroy, P.C., Kansas City, 1969—. Author, editor: Missouri Corporation Law and Practice, 1985, Missouri Taxation Law and Practice, 1987, 3d edit., 1996. Mem.: ABA, Kansas City Met. Bar Assn. (chmn. tax com. 1989—90, chmn. computer law com. 1989—91, Pres. award 1988), Mo. Bar Assn. (chmn. taxation com. 1988—90, chmn. computer tech. com. 1989—90). Republican. Methodist. Office: Shughart Thomson & Kilroy 12 Wyandotte Plz 120 W 12th St Fl 18 Kansas City MO 64105-1902 Office Phone: 816-421-3355 ext 3570. Business E-Mail: wprugh@stklaw.com.

PRUSSING, LAUREL LUNT, mayor, economist; b. NYC, Feb. 21, 1941; d. Richard Valentine and Maria (Rinaldi) Lunt; m. John Edward Prussing, May 29, 1965; children: Heidi Elizabeth, Erica Stephanie, Victoria Nicole Johanna. AB, Wellesley Coll., 1962; MA, Boston U., 1964; postgrad., U. Calif., San Diego, 1968-69, U. Ill., 1970-76. Economist Arthur D. Little, Cambridge, Mass., 1963-67, U. Ill., Urbana, 1971-72; mem. county bd. Champaign County, Urbana, 1972-76, county auditor, 1976-92; legis. dir. ERA Ill., 2002—03; founder ERA Yes!, 2003. Mem. local audit adv. bd. Office Ill. Compt., Chgo., 1984-92. Contbr. to Illinois Local Government: A Handbook, 1990. Founding mem. Citizens Forum on Gambling and Campaign Fin. Reform, 1999; downstate program dir. Citizen Action/Ill., 1999; legis. dir. AAUW, Ill., Inc., 2001; with Champaign-Urbana Mass Transit Dist. Bd., 2004—05; state rep. 103d dist. Ill. Gen. Assembly, 1993—95; Dem. nominee Ill. 15th dist. U.S. Congress, 1996—98; mayor Urbana, 2005—. Named Best Freshman Legislator Ind. Voters Ill., 1994; recipient Friend of Agriculture award Ill. Farm Bur., 1994; named to Legis. Honor Roll Ill. Environ. Coun., 1994. Mem. AAUW, NAACP, LWV, Govt. Fin. Officers Assn., U.S. and Can. (com. on acctg., auditing and fin. reporting 1980-88, Fin. Reporting award 1981-91, Disting. Budget award 1986), Nat. Assn. Local Govt. Auditors (charter), Ill. Assn. County Auditors (pres. 1984-85), US Conf. Mayors, Mayors Water Council. Democrat. Home: 2106 Grange Dr Urbana IL 61801-6609 Office Phone: 217-328-2071.

PRYCE, DEBORAH DENINE, congresswoman; b. Warren, Ohio, July 29, 1951; m. Randy Walker (div.); 1 child. BA cum laude, Ohio State U., 1973; JD with honors, Capital U. Law Sch., 1976. Bar: Ohio 1976. Adminstrv. law judge Ohio State Dept. Ins., 1976—78; first asst. city prosecutor, sr. asst. city atty., asst. city mgr. Columbus City Atty.'s Office, Ohio, 1978—85; judge Franklin County Mcpl. Ct., Columbus, 1989, 1990, 1992; mem. US Congress from 15th Ohio dist., 1993—, chair Ho. Rep. Conf., 2003—, mem. fin. svcs. com., ranking mem. subcommittee on capital markets, ins. and govt. sponsored enterprises, 2007—, dep. whip, co-chair cancer caucus. Republican. Presbyterian. Avocation: skiing. Office: 500 S Front St Ste 1130 Columbus OH 43215 Office Phone: 202-225-2015, 614-469-5614.

PRYOR, CHUCK, state legislator; m. Louella Pryor; children: Dustin, Ryan, Devon. Rep. dist. 116 State of Mo., Versailles, 1993—. Mem. agriculture com., commerce com., judiciary com., rules, joint rules, bills perfected and printed com., transp. com., tourism, recreation and cultural affairs com., iterim com. on agriculture, iterim joint com. on asset forfeitures, drug seizure and asset forfeiture com., joint com. on transp. oversight com. Chmn. bd. Versailles Christ. Ch.; bd. govs. Capitol Region Med. Ctr. Office: 410 Newton Rm 109-h Versailles MO 65084

PTAK, FRANK STANLEY, manufacturing executive; b. Chgo., Apr. 23, 1943; s. Frank J. and Stella R. (Los) P.; m. Karen M. Novoselsky, May 2, 1971; children: Jeffrey B., Jacquelyn F., Russell E. BSc, De Paul U., 1965. CPA, Ill. Sr. auditor Arthur Young & Co., Chgo., 1965-69; sr. rsch. cons. Kemper Fin. Svcs., Chgo., 1969-71; asst. sec., mgr. acquisitions Sara Lee Corp., Chgo., 1971-73, asst. treas., 1973-74, asst. to chmn., 1974, v.p. planning, 1974-75; bus. devel. mgr. ITW Conex, Des Plaines, Ill., 1975-77; mktg. mgr. ITW Shakeproof, Elgin, Ill., 1977-78, group pres., 1977-78, ITW Metal Components Cos., Glenview, Ill., 1978-91; exec. v.p. Global Automotive Components ITW Corp., Glenview, 1991-95, vice-chmn., 1996—2005; pres., CEO, The Marmon Group, Inc., Chgo., 2006—. Bd. dir. The Marmon Group, Morningstar Inc.; adv. coun. DePaul U. Coll. Commerce, Chgo., 1998. Patentee in field. Mem. AICPA, Assn. Corp. Growth, ITW Patent Soc., Econ. Club Chgo., Comml. Club Chgo., Executives CLub Chgo. Jewish. Home: 1415 Waverly Rd Highland Park IL 60035-3714 Office: The Marmon Group 181 W Madison Chicago IL 60602 Business E-Mail: fptak@itw.com.

PUCKO, DIANE BOWLES, public relations executive; b. Wyndotte, Mich., Aug. 15, 1940; d. Mervin Arthur and Bernice Letitia (Shelly) Bowles; m. Raymond J. Pucko, May 22, 1965; children: Todd Anthony, Gregory Bowles. BA in Sociology, Bucknell U., Lewisburg, Pa., 1962. Accredited in pub. rels. Asst. to pub. rels. dir. Edward C. Michener Assocs., Inc., Harrisburg, Pa., 1962-65; advt./pub. rels. coord. Superior Switchboard & Devices, Canton, Ohio, 1965-66; editorial dir. women's svc. Hutchins Advt. Co., Inc., Rochester, N.Y., 1966-71; pres. Editorial Communications, Rochester and Elyria, Ohio, 1971-77; mgr. advt. and sales promotion Tappan Air Conditioning, Elyria, 1977-80; mgr. pub. affairs Kaiser Permanente Med. Care Program, Cleve., 1980-85; corp. dir. pub. affairs Keystone Health Plans, Inc., Camp Hill, Pa., 1985-86; v.p., dir. client planning Young-Liggett-Stashower, Cleve., 1986; v.p., dir. pub. rels. Marcus Pub. Rels., Cleve., 1987-91; sr. v.p. Proconsul, Cleve., 1991-95, also bd. dirs.; sr. ptnr. pub. rels. Poppe Tyson, Cleve., 1995-96; managing dir. Bozell Pub. Rels., Cleve., 1996-97; sr. counsel Pub. Rels. Ptnrs., Inc., Cleve., 1997—2002. Mgr., role model Women in Mgmt. Field Placement program, Cleve. State U., 1983-92; pub. rels. adv. bd. profl. adviser, Pub. Rels. Student Soc. Am., Kent State U., 1988-2003 Bd. trustees, mem. exec. com., chmn. pub. rels. adv. com. Ronald MacDonald House of Cleve., 1993—2000; bd. dirs., chmn. pub. rels. com. Assn. Retarded Citizens, Cleve., 1987-91; mem. pub. rels.-mktg. com. Beech Brook, 1996—2000; mem. journalism comm. adv. bd. Elon Coll., 1998—2001. Recipient Woman Profl. Excellence award YMCA, 1984, MacEachern award Acad. Hosp. Pub. Rels., 1985, Bell Ringer award Cmty. Rels. Report, 1985, Bronze Quill Excellence award Internat. Assn. Bus. Communicators, 1992, 93, Cleve. Comms. award Women in Comms. Internat., 1993, 95, Tower award Bus./Profl. Advt. Assn., 1993, 95, Creativity in Pub. Rels. award, 1994, Silver Screen award U.S. Internat. Film & Video Festival, 1995, Silver Quill Excellence award Internat. Assn. Bus. Communicators, 1995, 2001, Internat. Assn. Bus. Communicators. Fellow Pub. Rels. Soc. Am. (bd. dirs. 1983-85, 86-94, officer 1991-95, mem. counselors acad. 1986—, Silver Anvil award 1985, Mktg./Consumer Rels. award East Ctrl. dist. 1992, 95, Lighthouse award 1995); mem. Press Club Cleve. (bd. dirs. 1989-96, v.p. 1990-96), Cleve. Advt. Club, Women's City Club Cleve., Nat. Agri-Mktg. Assn. (Nat. Merit award 2000). Republican. Methodist. Avocation: soccer. Home: 656 University Ave Elyria OH 44035-7278

PUFFER, RICHARD JUDSON, retired college chancellor; b. Chgo., Aug. 20, 1931; s. Noble Judson and Lillian Katherine (Olson) P.; m. Alison Foster Cope, June 28, 1952; children— Lynn, Mark, Andrew. Ph.B., Ill. Wesleyan U., 1953; MS in Edn, Ill. State U., 1962; PhD (Roy Clark Meml. scholar), Northwestern U., 1967. Asst. plant supt. J.A. Olson Co., Winona, Miss., 1957-59; tchr. Leroy Community Unit Dist. (Ill.), 1959-60; tchr., prin. Community Unit, Dist. 7, Lexington, Ill., 1960-62; asst. county supt. schs. Cook County, Ill., 1962-65; dean arts and scis. Kirkwood Community Coll., Cedar Rapids, Iowa, 1967-69; v.p. Black Hawk Coll., Moline, Ill., 1969-77, pres., 1977-82, chancellor, 1982-87; pres. The Ark Computer Ctr., 1989-92. Dir. W. Ctrl. Ill. Ednl. TV Corp., Springfield, Ill., 1977-87; cons. examiner North Central Assn., 1978-87. Editor: Cook County Ednl. Digest, 1962-65. Bd. dirs. Cedar Rapids Symphony, 1967-69, United Way of Rock Island and Scott Counties, Ill., 1978-80, Unitarian Universalist Dist. of Mich., 1995-98; bd. dirs., sec. West Shore Unitarian Universalist Congregation, 1996-99; sec., treas. Ill. Ednl. Retirement Cts., 1987-91; vice-chmn. Illini Hosp. Bd., 1988-93, chmn., 1993-95; bd. dirs. Illowa coun. Boy Scouts Am., 1979-83, v.p., 1981-83. With USNR, 1953-57. Mem. Rotary (pres. 1975-76, East Moline, Ill.), Green Medallion, Blue Key, Phi Delta Kappa, Pi Gamma Mu. Home and Office: 6191 Grace Ave Ludington MI 49431-8629

PUGH, COY, state legislator; b. Chgo., Feb. 27, 1952; s. Willie James and Martha (Nelson) P.; m. Laura L. Williams; children: Courtney, Leshawn. BA, ortheastern Ill. U., 1992. Adminstrv. asst. to State Rep. Ill. Ho. of Reps., 1984-86; owner Wescor Contracting, 1991-93; mem. Ill. Ho. of Reps., 1993—. Democrat. Home: 1748 N Mason Ave # 2 Chicago IL 60639-4011 Office: Mem Ho of Reps State Capitol Springfield IL 62706-0001

PUGH, DAVID L., manufacturing executive; b. Lynchburg, Va. m. Barbara Pugh; 2 children. BSEE, Duke U. Former chief mktg. officer, v.p. and gen. mgr. power equipment bus. unit Square D Co.; former plant mgr., v.p. constrn. sales Westinghouse Electric Corp.; sr. v.p. indsl control group Rockwell Automation, 1994-99; pres., COO Applied Indsl. Technologies, Cleve., 1999-2000, chmn., CEO, 2000—. Bd. dir. J.L.G. Industries, R.W. Beckett Corp. Office: Applied Indsl Technologies 1 Applied Plz 3301 Euclid Ave Cleveland OH 44115

PUGH, EDWARD W., state legislator; Atty.; mem. from dist. 61 Kans. State Ho. of Reps., Topeka, 1994-97; mem. Kans. Senate from 1st dist., Topeka, 1998—. Address: 16705 Mil Trail Rd Wamego KS 66547

PUGH, RODERICK WELLINGTON, retired psychologist; b. Richmond, Ky., June 1, 1919; s. George Wilmer and Lena Bernetta (White) P.; m. Harriet Elizabeth Rogers, Aug. 29, 1953 (div. 1955). BA, Fisk U., 1940; MA, Ohio State U., 1941; PhD, U. Chgo., 1949. Diplomate: Am. Bd. Profl. Psychology. Instr. Albany (Ga.) State Coll., 1941-43; psychology trainee VA, Chgo., 1947-49; lectr. Roosevelt U., Chgo., 1951-54; staff clin. psychologist VA Hosp., Hines, Ill., 1950-54, asst. chief psychologist for psychotherapy, 1954-58, chief clin. psychology sect., 1958-60, supervising psychologist, coord. psychol. internship tng., 1960-66; pvt. practice clin. psychology Chgo., 1958—99; assoc. prof. psychology Loyola U., Chgo., 1966-73, prof., 1973-88, emeritus prof. psychology, 1989—. Cons. St. Mary of the Lake Sem., Niles, Ill., 1965-66, Ill. Div. Vocational Rehab., 1965-82, Center for Inner City Studies, Northeastern State U., Chgo., 1966-67, VA Psychology Tng. Program, 1966—, Am. Psychol. Assn. and Nat. Inst. Mental Health Vis. Psychologists Program, 1966-89; juvenile problems research rev. com. NIMH, 1970-74; cons. Center for Minority Group Mental Health Programs, 1975-77, cons. psychology edn. br., 1978-82; lectr. U. Ibadan, Nigeria, 1978; Mem. profl. adv. com. Div. Mental Health, City of Chgo., 1979-82; mem. adv. com. U.S. Army Command and Gen. Staff Coll., 1981-83 Author: Psychology and the Black Experience, 1972; Contbr.: chpt. in Black Psychology, 1972; Cons. editor: Contemporary Psychology, 1975-79; contbr. articles to profl. jours. Sec. bd. trustees Fisk U., 1968-78. Served to 2d lt. AUS, 1943-46, ETO. Vis. scholar Fisk U., 1966, vis. prof. in psychology, 1994. Fellow Am. Psychol. Soc., Am. Psychol. Assn. (nat. adv. panel to Civilian Health and Med. Program of Uniformed Services 1980-83, joint coun. on profl. edn. in psychology 1988-90); mem. Midwestern Psychol. Assn., Ill. Psychol. Assn. (chmn. legis. com. 1961, council mem. 1960-62, Disting. Psychologist award 1988, Outstanding Contbn. to Profession of Psychology award 2001), Soc. for Psychol. Study Social Issues, Assn. Behavior Analysis, AAUP, Sigma Xi, Alpha Phi Alpha, Psi Chi. Home: Unit 25C 5201 S Cornell Ave Chicago IL 60615-4204 Office: Loyola U 6525 N Sheridan Rd Chicago IL 60626-5344 Business E-Mail: 72752.47@compuserve.com.

PUGH, THOMAS WILFRED, lawyer; b. St. Paul, Aug. 3, 1949; s. Thomas Leslie and Joann Marie (Tauer) P.; m. Susan Elizabeth Beattie, Sept. 12, 1971; children: Aimee Elizabeth, Douglas Thomas. AB cum laude, Dartmouth Coll., 1971; JD cum laude, U. Minn., 1976. Assoc. Thuet & Lynch, South St. Paul, 1976-79; ptnr. Thuet, Lynch & Pugh, South St. Paul, 1980-85; atty., pres. Thuet, Pugh, Rogosheske & Atkins, Ltd., South St. Paul, 1986—2007; mem. Minn. Ho. of Reps., St. Paul, 1989—2004, Dem. leader, 1999—2002; commr. Minn. Pub. Utilities Commn., 2004—. Mem. Supreme Ct. Task Force Conciliation Ct., St. Paul, 1992, Dakota County Tech. Coll. Adv. Bd., 1991-96. Bd. dirs. Wakota Arena, South St. Paul, 1984-87; pres. Luther Meml. Ch., South St. Paul, 1983-84. Daniel Webster scholar Dartmouth Coll., 1970, Rufus Choate scholar, 1971. Mem. Minn. State Bar Assn., 1st Dist. Bar Assn., Ducks Unltd., Pheasants Forever, South St. Paul C. of C. (local issues chair 1982, Dedicated Svc. award 1983), South St. Paul Jaycees (pres. 1978-79, Key award 1979), Lions. Lutheran. Avocations: tennis, golf, hunting, fishing, reading. Office: 121-7th Place E Saint Paul MN 55101

PUJANA, MARIA JOSE, neurologist; MD, Universidad Complutense, Madrid. Former chief resident, neurophysiology dept. Veteran Hosp., Madrid; adj. instructor Ctr. for Global Hlth. and Diseases, Sch. of Med., Case Western Reserve U., 1994—. Pres., designer Marise Jewelry Designs. Former v.p. of council Cleve. Ballet; adv. bd. mem. Cleve. Inst. of Art; trustee Cleve. Found., 2002—; mem. cmty. adv. bd. Rock and Roll Hall of Fame and Museum; bd. mem. Cuyahoga Cmty. Coll. Found., MetroHealth Found., Beck Ctr. for Arts, Cleve. Red Cross.

PUJOLS, ALBERT (JOSE ALBERTO PUJOLS), professional baseball player; b. Santo Domingo, Dominican Republic, Jan. 16, 1980; naturalized, US, 2007; m. Deidre Pujols, Jan. 1, 2000; children: Isabella, Albert Jr., Sophia. Attended, Maple Woods CC, Kansas City, Mo., 1999. First baseman St. Louis Cardinals, 2001—. First baseman Dominican Republic Team World Baseball Classic, 2006; co-owner Patrick's Restaurant, Maryland Heights, Mo. Founder Pujols Family Found., 2005. Named Nat. League Rookie of Yr., 2001, Maj. League Player of Yr., 2003, Nat. League Championship Series MVP, 2004, Nat. League MVP, 2005, Best Maj. League Baseball Player, ESPY awards, 2005, 2006, Best Internat. Player, 2006, Man of Yr., Players Choice awards, 2006; named to Nat. League All-Star Team, 2001, 2003—07; recipient Silver Slugger award, 2001, 2003—04, Hank Aaron award, 2003, Gold Glove award, 2006. Achievements include winning the National League batting title (.359 average), 2003; leading the National League in runs (137), 2003; being fourth player in MLB history to start career with 4 straight 100 RBI season's, 2004; being first player in MLB history to hit 30 HR and 100 RBI's in first 5 seasons, 2005; tying consecutive record for at-bats resulting in a HR, 2006; being a member of the World Series Champion St. Louis Cardinals, 2006. Mailing: c/o St Louis Cardinals Busch Stadium 250 Stadium Plz Saint Louis MO 63102*

PULIDO, JOSE S., physician; b. Apr. 29, 1956; BA with hons., U. Chgo., 1976, MS, 1977; MD, Tulane U., New Orleans, 1981; MBA, U. Iowa, 1993; MPH, U. Ill., 2005. Diplomate Am. Bd. Ophthalmology. Intern Tulane Affil. Hosps.-Charity Hosp., New Orleans, 1981-82; resident in ophthalmology U. Ill., Chgo., 1982-85, chief resident in ophthalmology, 1985-86; fellow vitreoretinal surgery Bascome Palmer Eye Inst./U. Miami Sch. Medicine, 1986-87, fellow retina rsch., 1987; fellow ocular oncology Wills Eye Hosp./Thomas Jefferson U. Sch. Medicine, Phila., 1998; head and prof. dept. ophthalmology and visual scis. U. Ill., Chgo., 1998—. Instr. organic chemistry U. Chgo., 1976-77; asst. prof. ophthalmology Coll. of Medicine, U. Iowa, Iowa City, 1987-92, assoc. prof., 1992-97, prof. 1997-98; prof. and chmn. U. Ill., 1998-2004; prof. Mayo Clinic, 2005. Reviewer numerous jours., including: Archives of Ophthalmology, 1985—, Ophthalmology, 1987—, Am. Jour. of Ophthalmology, 1992—, others; abstract editor: Diabetes 2000 Newsletter, 1992—, Ophthalmology World News, 1994-96, others; editor: Evidence-Based Eye Care, 1998—; contbr. articles to profl. jours. Mem. Am. Diabetes Assn. (del.), Am. Acad. Ophthalmology, Pan-Am. Acad. Ophthalmology, Retina Soc., Vitreous Soc., Fluorescein Reading and Macular Evaluation, Assn. for Rsch. in Vision and Ophthalmology, Am. Coll. Surgeons, Schepens Internat. Soc., Am. Ophthal. Soc., Macula Soc. Office: Mayo Clinic 200 First St SW Rochester MN 55905

PULITZER, MICHAEL EDGAR, publishing executive; b. St. Louis, Feb. 23, 1930; s. Joseph and Elizabeth (Edgar) P.; m. Cecille Stell Eisenbeis, Apr. 28, 1970; children: Michael Edgar, Elizabeth E. Voges, Robert S., Frederick D., Catherine D. Culver, Christina H. Eisenbeis, Mark C. Eisenbeis, William H. Eisenbeis. Grad., St. Mark's Sch., Southborough, Mass., 1947; AB, Harvard U., 1951, LLB, 1954. Bar: Mass. 1954. Assoc. Warner, Stackpole, Stetson & Bradlee, Boston, 1954-56; reporter Louisville Courier Jour., 1956-60; reporter, news editor, asst. mng. editor St. Louis Post-Dispatch, 1960-71, assoc. editor, 1978-79; pub. Ariz. Daily Star, Tucson, 1971—; pres. chief operating officer Pulitzer Pub. Co. (and subs.), 1979-84, vice chmn., 1984-86, pres., 1986-99, also bd. dirs., CEO, 1988-99, chmn., 1993-99, Pulitzer Inc., 1999. Trustee St. Louis U., 1989—. Mem.: St. Louis Country; Mountain Oyster (Tucson). Office: Pulitzer Pub Co 900 N Tucker Blvd Saint Louis MO 63101-1069

PULLEN, PENNY LYNNE, non-profit organization administrator, retired state legislator; b. Buffalo, Mar. 2, 1947; d. John William and Alice Nettie (McConkey) P. BA in Speech, U. Ill., 1969. Tv technician Office Instnl. Resources, U. Ill., 1966-68; cmty. newspaper reporter Des Plaines (Ill.) Pub. Co., 1967-72; legis. asst. to Ill. legislators, 1968-77; mem. Ill. Ho. of Reps., 1977-93, chmn. ho. exec. com., 1981-82, minority whip, 1983-87, asst. minority leader, 1987-93; pres., founder Life Advocacy Resource Project, Arlington Heights, Ill., 1992—. Exec. dir. Ill. Family Inst., 1993-94; dir. Legal Svcs. Corp., 1989-93; mem. Pres.'s Commn. on AIDS Epidemic, 1987-88; mem. Ill. Goodwill Del. to Republic of China, 1987. Summit conf. observer as mem. adhoc Women for SDI, Geneva, 1985; active Nat. Coun. Ednl. Rsch., 1983—88; dir. Eagle Forum of Ill., 1999—2003, pres., 2003—; del. Rep. Nat. Conv., 1984; mem. Rep. Nat. Com., 1984—88; del. Atlantic Alliance Young Polit. Leaders, Brussels, 1977; pres. Maine Twp. Rep. Women's Club, 1997—99, Rep. Women of Park Ridge, Ill., 2001—03, Rep. Women of Wheeling Twp., Ill., 2004—. Recipient George Washington Honor medal Freedoms Found., 1978, Dwight Eisenhower Freedom medal Chgo. Captive Nations Com., 1977, Outstanding Legislator awards Ill. Press Assn., Ill. Podiatry Soc., Ill. Coroners Assn., Ill. County Clks. Assn., Ill. Hosp. Assn., Ill. Health Care Assn.; named Ill. Young Republican, 1968, Outstanding Young Person, Park Ridge Jaycees, 1981, One of 10 Outstanding Young Persons, Ill. Jaycees, 1981. Mem. DAR, Am. Legis. Exch. Coun. (dir. 1977-91, exec. com. 1978-83, 2d vice chmn. 1980-83), Com. on the Status of Women (sec. 1997—).

PULLEN, ROBERT W., telecommunications industry executive; BSEE, BS, U. Ill.; MBA, Northwestern U. Elec. engr. Tallabs, Inc., Naperville, Ill., 1985, dir. product mgmt. and mktg. Digital Sys. Divsn., 1993—97, v.p., 1997—2000, sr. v.p. optical networking group, 2000—02, sr. v.p. N.Am. mktg. and sales, 2002—05, sr. v.p. global svcs., 2005—08, pres., CEO, dir., 2008—. Mem.: Electronics Industries Alliance (bd. govs.), Telecom. Industry Assn. (TIA) (chmn. exec. bd.). Office: Tellabs Inc One Tellabs Ctr 1415 W Diehl Rd Naperville IL 60563 Office Phone: 630-798-8800.*

PULTE, WILLIAM J., construction executive; married; 14 children. Founder, pres. William J. Pulte, Inc., 1950—69; pres. Pulte Homes Corp. (formerly William J. Pulte, Inc.), 1969—, chmn. of exec. com. of bd., 1972—90, chmn., 1991—99, 2001—. Named one of Forbes' Richest Ams., 2005—06. Avocations: golf, art. Office: Pulte Homes 100 Bloomfield Hills Pky Ste 300 Bloomfield Hills MI 48304

PUMA, GRACE M., air transportation executive; b. 1963; BA in Bus. Adminstrn. Econs., Ill. Benedictine U. Lead procurement Gillette Co., BASF Corp.; lead internat. strategic sourcing team Motorola, Inc.; v.p., global indirect materials and svcs. procurement Kraft Foods; sr. v.p. strategic sourcing, chief procurement officer United Air Lines Inc., Elk Grove Village, Ill., 2007—. Bd. mem. Inst. for Supply Mgmt. Office: United Air Lines Inc 1200 E Algonquin Rd Elk Grove Village IL 60007*

PUMPER, ROBERT WILLIAM, microbiologist, educator; b. Clinton, Iowa, Sept. 12, 1921; s. William R. and Kathrine M. (Anderson) P.; m. Ruth J. Larkin, June 24, 1951; 1 son, Mark. BA, U. Iowa, 1951, MS, 1953, PhD, 1955. Diplomate: Am. Soc. Microbiology. Asst. prof. Hahnemann Med. Coll., Phila., 1955-57; prof. microbiology U. Ill. Med. Sch., Chgo., 1957-92, prof. emeritus, 1992—, Raymond B. Allen Med. lectr., 1970, 74, 76, 87. Co-author: Essentials of Medical Virology; contbr. articles to profl. jours. Served with USAAF, 1942-46. Recipient Chancellors' award U. Ill., Bombeck award, 1992 Mem. Tissue Culture Assn., Sigma Xi, Phi Rho Sigma. Lutheran. Home: 18417 Argyle Ave Homewood IL 60430-3007

PUOTINEN, ARTHUR EDWIN, college president, minister; b. Crystal Falls, Mich., Sept. 7, 1941; s. Kaleva Weikko and Ines Pauline (Maki) P.; m. Judith Cathleen Kapoun, Aug. 8, 1964; children: Anne, Marjetta, Sara. AA, Suomi Coll., 1961; BA, Augustana Coll., Rock Island, Ill., 1963; MDiv, Luth. Sch. Theology, Chgo., 1967; MA, U. Chgo., 1969, PhD, 1973; MBA, Wake Forest U., 1984. Pastor Trinity Luth. Ch., Chgo., 1968-70; asst. prof. religion Cen. Mich. U., Mt. Pleasant, 1971-74; dean faculty Suomi Coll., Hancock, Mich., 1974-78; v.p. acad. affairs Lenoir-Rhyne Coll., Hickory, N.C., 1978-83; assoc. dean acad. affairs Roanoke Coll., Salem, Va., 1983-84; exec. dir. Luth. Ednl. Conf. of N.Am., Washington, 1984-88; pres. Grand View Coll., Des Moines, 1988-96; v.p., provost Finlandia U., Hancock, Mich., 1996—2002; pastor Bethlehem Luth. Ch., Elgin, Ill., 2004—. Pastor ELCA Met. Chgo. Synod, Evang.-Luth. Ch. Am. Author: Finnish Radicals., 1979; contbr. articles to books and jours. Grantee NEH, U.S. Dept. Edn. Democrat. Avocations: jogging, reading, travel. Home: 2885 Weld Rd Elgin IL 60124 Office Phone: 847-741-8434. E-mail: artpuotinen@sbcglobal.net.

PURCELL, JAMES FRANCIS, former utility executive, consultant; b. Miles City, Mont., May 13, 1920; s. Robert E. and Mary A. (Hickey) P.; m. Dorothy Marie Abel, Nov. 4, 1944; children— Angela, Ann, Alicia, Anita, Alanna, James Francis, Andrea, Adria, Michael, Gregory, Amara. AB magna cum laude, U. Notre Dame, 1942; MBA, Harvard U., 1943. With McGraw-Hill Pub. Co., NYC, 1946-48; dir. public relations Am. Maize Products Co., NYC, 1948-51; public relations cons. Selvage & Lee, Chgo., 1951-53; with No. Ind. Public Service Co., Hammond, 1953—, v.p. public relations, 1961-75, sr. v.p., 1975-84, bd. dirs., chmn. environ. and consumer affairs com.; owner, pres. James F. Purcell and Assocs., 1984—. Chmn. bd. govs. Our Lady of Mercy Hosp., Dyer, Ind., 1979-83; past chmn. Hammond Community Chest drive; past mem. nat. president's council St. Mary's (Ind.) Coll.; bd. dirs. Catholic Charities, 1965-85; chmn. bd. dirs. Bishop Noll Found., 1988-90. Served to lt. USNR, 1943-46. Named Man of Year Notre Dame U., 1967 Mem. Pub. Rels. Soc. Am. (past pres. Hoosier chpt.), N.W. Ind. Assn. Commerce and Industry (v.p., dir. 1979-83), Newcomen Soc. N. Am., Briar Ridge Country Club (Schererville), Serra Club (past pres. Calumet region), Notre Dame Club, Harvard U. Bus. Sch. Club of Chgo. Office: 2842 45th St Highland IN 46322-2905

PURDOM, PAUL WALTON, JR., computer scientist; b. Atlanta, Apr. 5, 1940; s. Paul Walton and Bettie (Miller) P.; m. Donna Armstrong; children: Barbara, Linda, Paul BS, Calif. Inst. Tech., 1961, MS, 1962, PhD, 1966. Asst. prof. computer sci. U. Wis.-Madison, 1965-70, asst. prof., 1970-71; mem. tech. staff Bell Telephone Labs., Naperville, Ill., 1970-71; assoc. prof., chmn. computer sci. dept. Ind. U., Bloomington, 1977-82, prof. computer sci., 1982—. Grant researcher FAW, Ulm, Germany. Author: (with Cynthia Brown) The Analysis of Algorithms; assoc. editor: Computer Surveys; contbr. articles to profl. jours. NSF grantee, 1979, 81, 83, 92, 94. Mem. AAAS, Soc. for Indsl. and Applied Math., Assn. Computing Machinery, Sigma Xi. Democrat. Methodist. Home: 2212 S Belhaven Ct Bloomington IN 47401-6803 Office: Ind U Dept Computer Science 215 Lindley Hall Bloomington IN 47405-4101 Office Phone: 812-855-1501. Business E-Mail: pwp@cs.indiana.edu.

PURDY, JAMES AARON, medical physics professor; b. Tyler, Tex., July 16, 1941; s. Walter Bethel and Florence (Hardy) P.; m. Marilyn Janette Coers, Jan. 29, 1965; children: Katherine, Laura. BS, Lamar U., 1967; MA, U. Tex., 1968, PhD, 1971. Asst. rsch. scientist U. Tex., Austin, 1969-71; rsch. asst. M.D. Anderson Hosp. and Tumor Inst., Houston, 1968-69, fellow in med. physics, 1972-73; from instr. physics to prof. Sch. of Medicine, Washington U., St. Louis, 1973—83, chief physics sect., 1976—2004, prof., 1983—2004, assoc. dir. Radiation Oncology Ctr., 1987—2004; prof., vice chmn. Med. Ctr. Dept. Radiology Oncology U. Calif., Davis, 2004—. Mem. NIH Radiaton Study sect. Divsn. Rsch. Grantes, 1991-95; Landauer lectr., Oakland, Calif., 1991. Editor: Three Dimensional Treatment Planning, 1991, Advances in Radiation Oncology, 1992, 3D Radiation Treatment Planning and Conformal Therapy, 1995, A Practical Guide to 3D Planning and Conformal Radiation Therapy, 1999, 3-D Conformal and Intensity Modulated Radiation Therapy: Physics and Clinical Applications, 2001; sr. physics editor: Internat. Jour. Radiation Oncology, Biology, and Physics, 1996—2003. With USMC, 1961-64. Fellow Am. Assn. Physicists in Medicine (pres. 1985, William D. Coolidge award 1997), Am. Coll. Radiology (ACR Gold Medal 2002), Am. Coll. Med. Physics (chmn. bd. chancellors 1990, Marvin M.D. Williams award 1996); mem. Am. Inst. Physics, Am. Bd. Med. Physics (vice chmn. 1988-92), Am. Bd. Radiology, Am. Soc. Therapeutic Radiology and Oncology (ASTRO Gold medal 2000). Methodist. Avocation: travel. Home: 918 Eucalyptus St Davis CA 95616 Office: Univ Calif

Davis Med Ctr Dept Rad Oncology 4501 X St Ste G126 Sacramento CA 95817 Home Phone: 530-758-9149; Office Phone: 916-734-3932. Business E-Mail: james.purdy@ucdmc.ucdavis.edu.

PURI, MADAN LAL, mathematics professor; b. Sialkot, Feb. 20, 1929; came to U.S., 1957, naturalized, 1973; s. Ganesh Das and S. W. P.; m. Uma Kapur, Aug. 24, 1962; 3 children. BA, Punjab U., India, 1948, MA, 1950, DSc, 1975; PhD, U. Calif., Berkeley, 1962. Head dept. math. D.A.V. Coll., Punjab U., 1955-57; instr. U. Colo., 1957-58; tchg. asst., rsch. asst., jr. rsch. statistician U. Calif. at Berkeley, 1958-62; asst. prof., assoc. prof. math. Courant Inst., YU, 1962-68; prof. math. Ind. U., Bloomington, 1968—, Coll. Arts and Scis. Disting. Rsch. scholar, 2004—. Vis. rsch. assoc. prof. U. NC., 1966, 1967; guest prof. stats. U. Gottingen, West Germany, 1972, Alexander von Humboldt guest prof., 1974-75; guest prof. U. Dortmund, West Germany, 1972, Technische Hochschule Aachen, West Germany, 1973, U. Goteborg, Chalmers U. Tech., both Sweden, 1976; vis. prof. U. Auckland, N.Z., 1977, U. Calif., Irvine, 1978, U. Wash., Seattle, 1978-79, U. Bern, Switzerland, 1982, Va. Poly. Inst., 1988; disting. vis. London Sch. Econs. and Polit. Sci., 1991; vis. prof. U. Göttingen, Germany, 1991-92; rsch. fellow Katholieke U., Nijmegen, The Netherlands, 1992; vis. prof. U. Des Scis. et Tech. de Lille, France, 1994, U. Basel, Switzerland, 1995—, U. NSW, Australia, 1996; vis. fellow Australian Nat. U., Canberra, Australia, 1999; guest prof. U. Konstanz, Germany, 2000, U. Gottingen, 2001. Co-author: Non Parametric Methods in Multivariate Analysis, 1971, Non Parametric Methods in General Linear Models, 1985. Editor Stochastic Process and Related Topics, 1975, Statistical Inference and Related Topics, 1975, Non Parametric Techniques in Statistical Inference, 1970; co-editor: Nonparametric Statistical Inference, Vols. I and II, 1982, New Perspectives in Theoretical and Applied Statistics, 1987, Mathematical Statistics and Probability Theory, Vol. A, 1987, Statistical Sciences and Data Analysis, 1993, Recent Advances in Statistics and Probability, 1994, Asymptotics in Statistics and Probability, 2000, Probability, Statistics and their Applications, 2003. Recipient Sr. U.S. Scientist award, Humboldt Preis, 1974-75, 83, Rsch. award Humboldt Found., U. Göttingen, 2001; disting. vis. scholar Inst. for Advanced Study, Ind. U., 2007. Fellow Royal Statis. Soc. (adv. editor statistics book series Taylor and Francis Book Group Inc., 2005), Inst. Math. Statistics, Am. Statis. Assn., Internat. Indian Statis. Assn. (hon.); mem. Internat. Statis. Inst. Office: Ind U Dept Math Rawles Hall Bloomington IN 47405 Office Phone: 812-855-9537. Business E-Mail: puri@indiana.edu.

PURKERSON, MABEL LOUISE, physician, physiologist, educator; b. Goldville, SC, Apr. 3, 1931; d. James Clifton and Louise (Smith) P. AB, Erskine Coll., 1951; MD, M.U.S.C., Charleston, 1956. Diplomate Am. Bd. Pediat. Instr. pediat. Washington U. Sch. Medicine, St. Louis, 1961-67, instr. medicine, 1966-67, asst. prof. pediat., 1967-98, asst. prof. medicine, 1967-76, assoc. prof. medicine, 1976-89, prof., 1989-98, prof. emerita, 1998—, assoc. dean curriculum, 1976-94, assoc. dean acad. projects, 1994-98. Cons. in field. Editl. bd. Am. Jour. Kidney Diseases, 1981-87; contbr. articles to profl. jours. Mem. bd. counselors Erskine Coll., 1971—87, trustee, 2000—06, The Mabel Dorn Reeder Found., 2007—; historian St. Louis Symphony Orch., trustee; bd. dirs. Trailnet, 2008—, St. Louis Acad. Sci., 2008—. USPHS spl. fellow, 1971-72. Mem. Am. Heart Assn. Coun. on the Kidney (exec. com. 1973-81), Am. Physiol. Soc., Am. Soc. Nephrology, Internat. Soc. Nephrology, Ctrl. Soc. Clin. Rsch., Am. Soc. Renal Biochemistry and Metabolism, Internat. Assn. History Nephrology, Am. Osler Soc., Explorer's Club (exec. com. 1973-81), Alpha Omega Alpha. Home: 20 Haven View Dr Saint Louis MO 63141-7902 Office: Wash Univ Sch Medicine Bernard Becker Med Libr PO Box 8132 Saint Louis MO 63110-1093 Home Phone: 314-994-1649; Office Phone: 314-362-4234. Business E-Mail: purkerm@wustl.edu.

PURSELL, CARROLL WIRTH, history educator; b. Visalia, Calif., Sept. 4, 1932; s. Carroll Wirth and Ruth Irene (Crowell) P.; m. Joan Young, Jan. 28, 1956 (dec. 1985); children: Rebecca Elizabeth, Matthew Carroll; m. Angela Woollacott, Dec. 20, 1986. BA, U. Calif., Berkeley, 1956, PhD, 1962; MA, U. Del., 1958. Asst. prof. history Case Inst. Tech., Cleve., 1963-65; asst. prof. U. Calif., Santa Barbara, 1965-69, asso. prof., 1969-76, prof., 1976-88; Adeline Barry Davee Disting. prof. history Case Western Res. U., Cleve., 1988—, chair history dept., 1998—. Mellon prof. Lehigh U., Bethlehem, Pa., 1974-76; vis. research scholar Smithsonian Instn., 1970 Author: Early Stationary Stem Engines in America, 1969, Military Industrial Complex, 1972, From Conservation to Ecology, 1973, White Heat, 1994, The Machine in America, 1995, American Technology, 2001. Fellow: AAAS; mem.: Am. Hist. Assn., Orgn. Am. Historians, Soc. History of Tech. (pres. 1990—92, pres. internat. com.for history of tech. 1998—2001, Leonardo da Vinci medal 1991), Phi Beta Kappa. Democrat.

PURTAN, JOANNE, announcer; d. Dick Purtan; m. Eric Purtan; children: Lauren, Adam. B of Telecom., Mich. State U. Morning anchor/reporter WGRB-TV, Albany, NY, 1991—98, co-anchor 5pm, 6pm and 11 pm news, 1994—98; co-anchor Action News This Morning, WXYZ-TV, Detroit, 1998—, reporter Healthy Living, 2002—. Recipient 3 Emmy nominations. Office: WXYZ-TV 20777 W Ten Mile Rd Southfield MI 48037

PUSATERI, JAMES ANTHONY, judge; b. Kansas City, Mo., May 20, 1938; s. James A. and Madeline (LaSalle) P.; m. Jacqueline D. Ashburne, Sept. 1, 1962; children: James A., Mark C., Danielle L. BA, U. Kans., 1960, LLB, 1963. Bar: Kans. 1963, U.S. Dist. Ct. Kans. 1963, U.S. Ct. Appeals (10th cir.) 1964. Assoc. Payne, Jones, Chartered, Olathe, Kans., 1963-65, James Cashin, Prairie Village, Kans., 1965-69; asst. U.S. atty. Dept. Justice, Kansas City, Kans., 1969-76; judge U.S. Bankruptcy Ct. Dist. Kans., Topeka, 1976—. Active Prairie Village City Coun., 1967-69. Mem. Kans. Bar Assn., Topeka Bar Assn., Nat. Conf. Bankruptcy Judges, Am. Bankruptcy Inst., Sam A. Crow Am. Inn of Ct.

PUTATUNDA, SUSIL KUMAR, metallurgy educator; b. Santipur, W. Bengal, India, Jan. 31, 1948; came to U.S., 1983; s. Provat Chandra and Santi Kana Putatunda; m. Ivy M. George, June 7, 1984; children: Sujata, Shibani. BS, Instn. Engrs., Calcutta, 1975; MS, U. Mysore, India, 1979; PhD, Indian Inst. Tech., Bombay, 1983. Metallurgist Hindustan Copper Ltd., Khetri, Rajsthan, 1973-77; grad. rsch. asst. U. Mysore, Mangalore, India, 1977-79; R & D engr. Hindustan Electrographites, Bhopal, India, 1979-80; grad. rsch. asst. Indian Inst. Tech., Bombay, 1980-83; Fulbright scholar U. Ill., Urbana, 1983-84; assoc. prof. metallurgy Wayne State U., Detroit, 1985—2001, prof., 2001—. Govt. India scholar, New Delhi, 1977, 80; Fulbright fellow USIA, Washington, 1982. Mem. Am. Soc. Metals, The Metall. Soc., ASTM (editor spl. tech. pub. on fractography 1989), Iron and Steel Soc., Engring. Soc. Detroit. Home: 2732 Brady Dr Bloomfield Hills MI 48304-1725 Office: Wayne State U Coll Engring 5050 Anthony Wayne Dr Detroit MI 48202-3902 Home Phone: 248-333-7784. Office Fax: 313-577-3810. Business E-Mail: sputa@chem1.eng.wayne.edu.

PUTH, JOHN WELLS, manufacturing executive, consultant; b. Orange, NJ, Mar. 14, 1929; s. Leonard G. and Elizabeth R. (Wells) P.; m. Betsey Leeds Tait, Mar.1, 1952; children: David Wells, Jonathan Craig, Alison Leeds. BS cum laude, Lehigh U., 1952. Dir. mktg. Purolator Products, Rahway, NJ, 1955-61; pres., chief exec. officer Bridgeport (Conn.) Hardware Mfg. Co. subs. Purolator, 1962-65; group v.p. H.K. Porter Co., Pitts., 1965-72; pres., CEO Disston Inc., Pitts., 1972-75, Vapor Corp., Niles, Ill., 1975-83; chmn., pres., CEO Clevite Industries Inc., Glenview, Ill., 1983-89; pres. JW Puth Assocs., Skokie, Ill., 1989—. Bd. dir. Adam Street Ptnrs., L.B. Foster, Pitts., A.M. Castle & Co., Franklin Park, Ill., V.J. Growers Inc., Apopka, Fla., George W. Schmidt Inc., iles, Ill.; advisor GTCR Funds. Chmn. bd. trustees Hadley Sch. for Blind, Winnetka, Ill., 1982-84; former trustee Lehigh U., Kenilworth Union Ch.; bd. dirs. Iaccoca Inst. With US Army, 1946—47. Mem.: Loblolly Pines Club, Old Elm Club, Indian Hill Country Club, Comml. Club, Chgo. Club. Republican. Presbyterian. Home: 180 De Windt Rd Winnetka IL 60093-3744 Office Phone: 847-967-4390. Personal E-mail: jwputh@aol.com.

PUTKA, ANDREW CHARLES, lawyer; b. Cleve., Nov. 14, 1926; s. Andrew George and Lillian M. (Koryta) Putka. Student, John Carroll U., 1944, U.S. Naval Acad., 1945-46; AB, Adelbert Coll., Western Res. U., 1949, JD, 1952. Bar: Ohio 1952. Practice law, Cleve.; instr. govt. Notre Dame Coll.; v.p. Koryta Bros. Coal Co., Cleve., 1952-56; supt. divsn. bldg. and loan assns. Ohio Dept. Commerce, 1959-63; pres., chmn. bd., CEO Am. Nat. Bank, Parma, Ohio, 1963-69; dir. fin. City of Cleve., 1971-74; dir. port control, 1974-78; dir. Cleve. Hopkins Internat. Airport, 1974-78. Mem. Ohio Ho. of Reps., 1953-56, Ohio Senate, 1957-58; dep. auditor, acting sec. Cuyahoga County Bd. Revision, 1970-71; mem. exec. com. Cuyahoga County Democratic Com., 1973-81, Assn. Ind. Colls. and Univs. Ohio, 1983-89; bd. govs. Sch. Law, Western Res. U., 1953-56; mem. exec. com. World Service Student Fund, 1950-52; U.S. rep. Internat. Pax Romana Congress, Amsterdam, 1950, Toronto, 1952; mem. lay adv. bd. Notre Dame Coll., 1968-90, trustee, 1990-93, hon. trustee, 1993—, life mem., 1993—; mem. adv. bd. St. Andrew's Abbey, 1976-88; trustee Case-Western Res. U., Newman Found. No. Ohio, 1980-93, hon. trustee, life mem., 1993—; 1st v.p. First Cath. Slovak Union of U.S., 1977-80; pres. USO Council of Cuyahoga County, 1980-83. Voted an outstanding legislator Ohio Press Corrs., 1953; named to All-Star Legislative team Ohio Newspaper Corrs., 1955; named one of Fabulous Clevelanders Cleve. Plain Dealer, John Henry Newman honor Soc. Mem. DAV (life), KC (4th degree), CCJ, Cuyahoga County, Cleve. Bar Assn., Nat. Assn. State Savs. and Loan Suprs. (past. nat. pres.), US Savs. and Loan League (mem. legis com, 1960-63), Am. Legion, Ohio Mcpl. League (bd. trustees 1973), Parma C. of C. (bd. dir., treas. 1965-67), Newman Fedn. (past nat. pres.), Cath. Lawyers Guild (treas.), Am. Ohio Bankers Assn., Am. Inst. Banking, Adelbert Alumni Assn. (exec. com.), Cathedral Latin Alumni Assn. (trustee 1952—), Internat. Order Alhambra (internat. parliamentarian 1971—, past grand comdr., supreme advocate 1973), Amvets, Pi Kappa Alpha, Delta Theta Phi (past. pres. Cleve. alumni senate, master inspector 1975). Office: 28 Pond Dr Cleveland OH 44116-1062

PUTNAM, J. E. (JIM), state legislator; b. Armour, SD, Apr. 18, 1940; Grad. high sch., Armour, SD. Mem. S.D. Ho. of Reps. from 19th dist., Pierre, 1993-2000; Ho. Asst. Majority Whip S. D. Ho. of Reps., Pierre, 1993-2000; farmer; mem. S.D. Senate from 19th dist., Pierre, 2001—. Mem. appropriations com. (vice chair), legis. procedure com. Home: Rte 1 Box 98 Armour SD 57313-9749

PUTNEY, JOHN, state senator, farmer; b. Gladbrook, Iowa, Mar. 6, 1944; s. Lawrence and Geneva Putney; m. Emily Putney; children: Leah, Carolyn, Mark. Student, U. Nebr.; degree in Farm Ops., Iowa State U. Farmer; spl. asst. to U.S. Senator Charles Grassley, 1989—93; state senator dist. 20 Iowa Senate, 2003—; mem. agr. com.; mem. econ. growth com.; mem. judiciary com.; mem. rules and adminstrn. com.; mem. econ. devel. appropriations subcom.; vice chair transp. com. Active Tama County Farm Bur.; mem. Gladbrook Meth. Ch.; exec. dir. Iowa State Fair Blue Ribbon Found., 1993—; pres. Tama County Fair Bd., Iowa Beef Breeds Coun./Iowa Beef Expo, Iowa Found. Agr. Advancement/Sale of Champions; chmn. Tama County Friends of Ext.; beef supt. Iowa State Fair. Officer Iowa NG. Mem.: Iowa Cattlemen's Assn., Tama County Cyclone Club (pres.), Rotary, Shriners, Scottish Rite, Olivet Lodge, Am. Legion. Republican. Office: State Capitol East 12th and Grand Des Moines IA 50319

PUTNEY, MARK WILLIAM, lawyer, utilities executive; b. Marshalltown, Iowa, Jan. 25, 1929; s. Lawrence Charles and Geneva (Eldridge) P.; m. Ray Ann Bartnek, May 25, 1962 (dec. Feb. 2000); children: Andi Bartnek, William Bradford, Blake Reinhart; m. Linda Phelps, July 21, 2003. BA, U. Iowa, 1951, JD, 1957. Bar: Iowa 1957, U.S. Supreme Ct. 1960. Ptnr. Bradshaw, Fowler, Proctor & Fairgrave, Des Moines, 1961-72, of counsel, 1992-94; chmn., CEO. Bradford & Blake Ltd., Dakota Dunes, SD, 1992—; pres., chmn., chief exec. officer Iowa Resources, Inc., 1984-90; chmn., chief exec. officer Iowa Power & Light Co., 1984-90, Iowa Gas Co., 1984-85, Midwest Resources Inc., 1990-92. Civilian aide to Sec. Army Iowa, 1975-77; bd. dirs. Greater Des Moines YMCA, 1976-86, Boys' Home Iowa, 1982-86, Hoover Presdl. Libr. Assn., 1983—, U. Iowa Found., 1984—, Edison Electric Inst., 1986-89, Greater Des Moines Com., 1984—, pres. 1988; bd. dirs. Assoc. Edison Illuminating Cos., 1988-93, pres., 1991-92; chmn. Iowa Com. Employer Support of Guard and Res., 1979-86; bd. dirs. Des Moines Devel. Corp., 1984-92, chmn., 1989-90; bd. dirs. Iowa Law Sch. Found., 2006-. With USAF, 1951-53. Recipient Disting. Alumnus award U. Iowa, 1995. Mem. Iowa Utility Assn. (chmn. 1989, dir.), Des Moines Club (pres. 1977), Desert Forest Golf Club (Carefree, Ariz.), Masons, Shriners, Delta Chi, Phi Delta Phi. Republican. Episcopalian. Home: PO Box 1126 Carefree AZ 85377 Office Phone: 602-549-7731. Personal E-mail: markwputney@aol.com.

PYKE, JOHN SECREST, JR., lawyer, polymers company executive; b. Cleve., July 11, 1938; s. John S. and Elma B. P.; m. Judith A., Dec. 26, 1970; 1 child: John Secrest, III. Attended, Haverford Coll., 1956—58; BA, Columbia Coll., 1960; postgrad., Columbia Sch. Grad. Faculties, 1960—61; JD, Columbia Law Sch., 1964. Bar: .Y. 1965. Assoc. firm Townsend & Lewis (now Thatcher, Proffit & Wood), NYC, 1964—68; atty. M.A. Hanna Co., Cleve., 1968—, sec., 1973—, v.p., gen. counsel, 1979—. Author: Landmark Preservation, 1969, Landmark Preservation, 2d edit, 1972. Trustee Western Res. Acad., Hudson, Ohio, 1976—. Mem.: Am. Corp. Counsel Assn., Am. Soc. Corp. Secs., Assn. Bar City N.Y., ABA, Cleve. Yachting Club, Clifton Club, Union Club. Office: MA Hanna Co Mexico Div 33587 Walker Rd Avon Lake OH 44012-1145

PYLE, DAVE, newspaper editor; Bur. chief AP, Mpls., 1980—. Home: 511 11th Ave S Ste 460 Minneapolis MN 55415-1568

PYLE, THOMAS F., JR., consumer products company executive; b. Phila., 1941; Diploma, La Salle U., 1962, U. Wis., 1963. Chmn., pres., CEO Rayovac Corp., Madison, Wis. Dir. Johnson Worldwide Assocs., Kewaunee Sci. Corp., Riverside Paper Corp. Office: Rayovac Corp 601 Ray O Vac Dr Madison WI 53711-2497 also: Johnson Worldwide Assoc 555 Main St Ste 20 Racine WI 53403-1035

PYTELL, ROBERT HENRY, retired lawyer, judge; b. Detroit, Sept. 27, 1926; s. Henry Carl and Helen (Zielinski) P.; m. Laurie Mazur, June 2, 1956; children: Mary Beth, Mark Henry, Robert Michael. JD, U. Detroit, 1951. Bar: Mich. 1952. Of counsel Pytell & Varchetti, P.C., Detroit, 1952-2001; asst. U.S. atty. Ea. Dist. Mich., 1962-65; judge Mcpl. Ct., Grosse Pointe Farms, Mich., 1967-85. With USNR, 1945-46. Mem. Am. Coll. Trust and Estate Counsel, State Bar Mich. (mem. probate coun. probate sect. 1998-2000), Crescent Sail Yacht Club (Grosse Pointe), Delta Theta Phi. Roman Catholic. Avocations: gardening, bicycling, photography.

PYTTE, AGNAR, physicist, retired academic administrator; b. Kongsberg, Norway, Dec. 23, 1932; arrived in U.S., 1949, naturalized, 1965; s. Ole and Edith (Christiansen) Pytte; m. Anah Currie Loeb, June 18, 1955; children: Anders H., Anthony M., Alyson C. AB, Princeton U., 1953; AM, Harvard U., 1954, PhD, 1958. Faculty Dartmouth Coll., 1958—87, prof. physics, 1967—87, chmn. dept. physics and astronomy, 1971—75, assoc. dean faculty, 1975—78, dean grad. studies, 1975—78, provost, 1982—87; pres. Case Western Res. U., Cleve., 1987—99; adj. prof. physics Dartmouth Coll., 1999—. Rschr. in plasma physics; mem. Project Matterhorn Princeton U., 1959—60, 1978—79, U. Brussels, 1966—67. Bd. dirs. Goodyear Tire and Rubber Co., 1988—2004, Accreditation Coun. for Grad. Med. Edn., 2000—04, A.O. Smith Corp., 1991—2003, Sherman Fairchild Found., Inc., 1987—2006. Mem.: Am. Phys. Soc., Sigma Xi, Phi Beta Kappa. Personal E-mail: agnar.x.pytte@dartmouth.edu.

QASIM, IMAD ISA, lawyer; b. Tripoli, Libya, Sept. 14, 1957; came to US, 1973; s. Isa and Nawal Q.; m. Nancy Meloy Qasim, May 19, 1990. AB with honors, Hamilton Coll., 1979; JD, Georgetown U., 1982. Bar: NY 1983, Ill. 1987, DC 1989. Assoc. Sidley & Austin, Chgo., 1983, 85-88, Muscat, Oman, 1983-85, Washington, 1988-91, ptnr., 1991—2001, Sidley, Austin, Brown & Wood, Chgo., 2001—. Mem. ABA (mem. securities law sect.), DC Bar Assn. Office: Sidley Austin Brown & Wood 1 S Dearborn Chicago IL 60603 Office Phone: 312-853-7000, 312-853-7094. Office Fax: 312-853-7036.

QUAAL, WARD LOUIS, broadcast executive; b. Ishpeming, Mich., Apr. 7, 1919; s. Sigfred Emil and Alma Charlotte (Larson) Q.; m. Dorothy J. Graham, Mar. 9, 1944; children: Graham Ward, Jennifer Anne. AB, U. Mich., 1941; LL.D. (hon.), Mundelein Coll., 1962, No. Mich. U., 1967; D.Pub.Svc., Elmhurst Coll., 1967; D.H.L. (hon.), Lincoln Coll., 1968, DePaul U., 1974. Announcer-writer Sta. WBEO (now sta. WDMJ), Marquette, Mich., 1936—37; announcer, writer, producer Sta. WJR, Detroit, 1937—41; spl. events announcer-producer WGN, Chgo., 1941—42, asst. to gen. mgr., 1945—49; exec. dir. Clear Channel Broadcasting Service, Washington, 1949—52, pres., chief exec. officer, 1964—74; v.p., asst. gen. mgr. Crosley Broadcasting Corp., Cin., 1952—56; v.p., gen. mgr., mem. bd. WGN Inc., Chgo., 1956; exec. v.p., then pres. WGN Continental Broadcasting Co. (now Tribune Broadcasting Co.), 1960—75; pres. Ward L. Quaal Co., 1975—; dir. Tribune Co., 1961—75; dir., mem. exec. com. U.S. Satellite Broadcasting Co., 1982—2000. Bd. dirs. Christine Valmy Inc.; chmn. exec. com., dir. WLW Radio Inc., Cin., 1975-81; co-founder, dir. Universal Resources Inc., 1961-86; mem. FCC Adv. Com. on Advanced TV Sys., 1988-96. Author: (with others) Broadcast Management, 1968, rev. edit., 1979, new edit. 1997; co-prodr. (Broadway play) Teddy and Alice, 1988. Mem., Hoover Commn. Exec. Br. Task Force, 1949-59; mem. U.S.-Japan Cultural Exchange Commn., 1960-70; mem. Pres.'s Council Phys. Fitness and Sports, 1983-93; bd. dirs. Farm Found., 1963-73; bd. trustees Hollywood (Calif.) Mus., 1964-78, MacCormac Jr. Coll., Chgo., 1974-80; chmn. exec. com. Council for TV Devel., 1969-72; mem. bus. adv. coun. Chgo. Urban League, 1964-74; bd. dirs. Broadcasters Found., Internat. Radio and TV Found., Sears Roebuck Found., 1970-73; trustee Mundelein Coll., 1962-72, Hillsdale Coll., 1966-72. Served as lt. USNR, 1942-45. Named Radio Man of Yr., Am. Coll. Radio, Arts, Crafts & Scis., 1961, Laureate in Order of Lincoln, Lincoln Acad. Ill., 1965, Communicator of Yr., Jewish United Fund, 1969, Advt. Club Man of Yr., 1973; named one of Top 100 Mems., Delta Tau Delta, 1999, 1st 100 5th Estaters, Broadcasting 20th Century, 1999, First 50 Giants of Broadcasting, Libr. Am. Broadcasting, 2003; named to Delta Tau Delta Disting. Svc. Chpt., 1970, Broadcasting Mag. Hall of Fame, 1991, Mgmt. Hall of Fame, NATAS/TV Bur. Advt., 2003; recipient Disting. Bd. Gov.'s award, ATAS, 1966, 1987, Inaugural Inductee Mgmt. Hall of Fame, 2003, Freedoms Found. award, Valley Forge, 1966, 1968, 1970, Disting. Alumnus award, U. Mich., 1967, Loyola U. Key, 1970, Advt. Man of Yr. Gold medallion, Chgo. Advt. Club, 1968, Disting. Svc. award, Nat. Assn. Broadcasters, 1973, Ill. Broadcaster of Yr. award, 1973, Press Vet. of Yr. award, 1973, Comm. award of distinction, Brandeis U., 1973, Founder & Leadership award, Broadcast Pioneers Libr., 1991, 1st recipient Sterling medal, Barren Found., 1985, Lifetime Achievement award in broadcasting, Ill. Broadcasters Assn., 1989, Lifetime Achievement award, WGN TV, 1998, 1st person named to Better Bus. Bur. Hall of Fame, Coun. on Better Bus. Burs., Inc., 1975. Mem. NATAS (bd. govs. 1966-76, Silver Circle award 1993), Nat. Press Found. (bd. dirs. 1991-99), Nat. Assn. Broadcasters (bd. dirs. 1952-56), Fed. Comm. Bar Assn., Broadcast Music Inc. (bd. dirs. 1953-70), Assn. Maximum Svc. Telecasters Inc. (bd. dirs. 1952-72), Broadcast Pioneers (pres., bd. dirs. 1962-73), Broadcast Pioneers Libr. (pres. 1981-84), Broadcast Pioneers Ednl. Fund Inc., Broadcasters Found. (chmn. bd. 1996-99). Office: Ward L Quaal Co PO Box 336 Winnetka IL 60093

QUADE, VICKI, editor, writer, playwright, theater producer; b. Chgo., Aug. 15, 1953; d. Victor and Virginia (Uryasz) Q.; m. Charles J. White III, Feb. 15, 1986 (div. Aug. 1996); children: Michael, David, Catherine. BS in Journalism, No. Ill. U., 1974. Staff reporter news divsn. The News-Tribune, LaSalle, Ill., 1975-77; staff writer news divsn. The News-Sun, Waukegan, Ill., 1977-81; staff writer ABA Jour., Chgo., 1981-85; mng. editor ABA Press, Chgo., 1985-90, editor, 1990-2000, sr. editor, 1994-2000. Author: (poetry) Rain and Other Poems, 1976, Laughing Eyes, 1979, Two Under the Covers, 1981, (biography) I Remember Bob Collins, 2000; playwright Late Nite Catechism, 1993, Room for Advancement, 1994, Mr. Nanny, 1997, (musical) Lost in Wonderland, 1998, (musical) Here Come the Famous Brothers, 2001, Put the Nuns in Charge!, 2005, Sunday School Cinema, 2007; prodr. Late Nite Catechism, Mr. Nanny, Here Come the Famous Brothers, Christopher Carter Messes With Your Mind, Forever Plaid, Cast on a Hot Tin Roof, Verbatim Verboten, Put the Nuns in Charge; U.S. premiere of Drapes, 2005; contbr. to numerous anthologies and publs.; contbd. to: 20th Century Chicago: 100 Years, 100 Voices (contbd. the year 1953), owner/operator Crossroads Theater, Naperville, Ill Recipient numerous awards from Soc. Nat. Assn. Publs., AP, UPI, Spirit of Benedict award Benedictine Sisters Chgo., 2003, Partners in Mission award Sisters of the Living Word, 2005 Mem. Am. Soc. Bus. Press Editors (award), Chgo. Newspaper Guild (award), Am. Soc. Assn. Execs. (Gold Circle award 1989, 90). Avocations: travel, photography.

QUAINI, DUANE C., lawyer; b. Napa, Calif., Mar. 30, 1945; BA summa cum laude, Claremont Men's Coll., 1967; JD, Stanford U., 1970. Bar: Ill. 1970. Assoc. Sonnenschein Nath & Rosenthal LLP, Chgo., 1970—76, ptnr., 1976—, chmn., 1997—2007. Note editor Stanford Law Rev., 1969-70. Mem. exec. com. bd. visitors Stanford Law Sch., 1995—, chmn.; vice chmn. bd. Jane Addams Juvenile Ct. Found.; dir. emeritus Les Turner ALS Found. Office: Sonnenschein Nath & Rosenthal LLP 8000 Sears Tower 233 S Wacker Dr Chicago IL 60606 Office Phone: 312-876-8051. Office Fax: 312-876-7934. Business E-Mail: dquaini@sonnenschein.com.

QUALLS, ROXANNE, mayor; D (hon.), Cin. State Tech. and C.C., 1996. Former exec. dir. Women Helping Women; former dir. No. Ky. Rape Crisis Ctr.; former dir. Cin. office Ohio Citizen Action; councilwoman City of Cin., 1991-93, mayor, 1993-98, founder youth summer jobs program Artworks, Cin. Homeownership Partnership. Former chairperson Cin. City Council's Intergovtl. Affairs and Environment Com.; former vice chairperson Community Devel., Housing and Zoning Com.; mem. Gov.'s Commn. on Storage and Use of Toxic and Hazardous Materials, Solid Waste Adv. Com. of State of Ohio, Gov.'s Waste Minimization Task Force; former chair bd. commrs. Cin. Met. Housing Authority; bd. dirs. Shuttlesworth Housing Found. Hon. chair Friends of Women's Studies; mem. Jr. League Adv. Coun.; bd. dirs. Nat. Underground Railroad Freedom Ctr., Ctr. Voting and Democracy; past bd. didrs. No. Ky. Cath. Commn. Soc. Jusitice. Recipient Woman of Distinction award Girl Scouts U.S., 1992, Woman of Distinction award Soroptimists, 1993, Outstanding Achievement award Cin. Woman's Polit. Caucus, 1993, Women of Achievement award YWCA, 1994, Outstanding Svc. award Ohio Pub. Employees Lawyers Assn., 1996, Pub. Offcl. of Yr. award State of Cinn., 1996, Nat. Assn. Soc. Workers, 1996, Nat. Homebuilders Assn., 1997. Mem. Nat. Assn. Regional Couns. (former pres., 1st v.p., 2d v.p.), Ohio Ky. Ind. Regional Coun. Govts. (1st v.p., 2d v.p.). Fax: 513-352-5201.

QUAM, LOIS, investment company executive, former health insurance company executive; b. June 12, 1961; m. Matt Entenza; children: Ben, Steve. BA magna cum laude, Macalaster Coll., Minn.; MA in Philos., Politics, Econs., U. Oxford, 1985. Dir. rsch. and eval. UnitedHealth Group, 1989-93, v.p. pub. sector svcs., 1993, CEO AARP/United divsn. Mpls., 1996-98, exec. v.p., CEO Ovations, 2002—06, exec. v.p., pres. public & sr. markets group, 2006—07; mng. dir. alternative investments Piper Jaffray & Co., Mpls., 2007—. Bd. dirs. General Mills, 2007—, George C. Marshall Found., Coun. Fgn. Rels.; adv. com. Am. Democracy Inst.; sr. adv. The White House Task Force Nat. Health Care Reform, 1993—96. Mem. editl. bd.: British Med. Jour.; contbr. articles to profl. jours. Bd. trustees Macalester Coll. Named one of Next 20 Female CEOs, Pink Mag. & Forté Found., 2006, 50 Most Powerful Women in Bus., Fortune mag., 2006; recipient America-Norway Heritage Fund award, Nordmann-Forbundett Norway-Am. Assn. Office: Piper Jaffray & Co 800 Nicollet Mall Ste 800 Minneapolis MN 55402

QUANDAHL, MARK C., former state legislator, lawyer, political organization administrator; b. Omaha, Oct. 10, 1961; m. Stacey Quandahl, May 24, 1986; children: Sarah, Scott, R.J. Grad., U. Nebr., 1984, grad., 1987. Cert. Consumer Credit Exec.; bar: US Dist. Ct. Nebr. 1987, US Dist. Ct. Iowa 1988. Atty. Brumbaugh & Quandahl, Omaha; mem. Nebr. Legislature from 31st dist., Lincoln, 1999—2005; chmn. Nebr. Rep. Party, 2005—. Del. Rep. Nat. Conv., 2004. Mem.: Phi Delta Phi, Comml. Law League Nebr., Nat. Assn. Retail Collection Attorneys, Iowa State Bar Assn., Nebr. State Bar Assn. Office: Nebr Rep Party 4885 S 118th St Ste 100 Omaha NE 68137 Office Phone: 402-861-4702.*

QUARLES, BETH, civil rights administrator; Commr. Civil Rights Commn., Indpls. With presdl. task force, Mits task force, Muncie task force ADA; with Pecso CEO Learning Ctr.; active in youth leadership, employment opportunities and law enforcement ADA; hearing impaired cons.; condr. sign lang. classes. Bd. dirs. Open Door Comty., Muncie (Ind.) Pub. Libr., United Way, County Commty. Partnership on Disability, Muncie Civic Theater; vol. interpreter for deaf; mentor numerous minority bus. Recipient Frieda Dawkins award, Presdl. Points of Light award, also state, nat., and internat. awards for theatrical prodns. Office: Civil Rights Commn 100 N Senate Ave Rm W103 Indianapolis IN 46204-2273

QUAST, LARRY WAYNE, lawyer; b. Beulah, ND, Aug. 13, 1945; s. Clarence and Lorraine (Meske) Q.; m. Linda Mae Borth, June 18, 1971; children: Tiffany, Phillip. BA cum laude, Dickinson Coll., 1968; JD, U. N.D., 1973. Bar: N.D. 1973, U.S. Dist. Ct. N.D. 1973. Small claims ct. referee, magistrate Grand Forks (N.D.) County, 1973-74; justice Mercer County, Stanton, N.D., 1974-78; assoc. Hagen, Quast & Alexander, Beulah, 1974—. Atty. City of Stanton, N.D.,

1976—. Served to corpsman 4th class USN, 1968-70. Mem. ABA, N.D. Bar Assn. Lutheran. Avocation: raising and racing thoroughbred race horses. Home: 1050 Elbowoods Dr Hazen D 58545-4912 Office: Hagen Quast Alexander PO Box 340 Beulah ND 58523-0340

QUEBE, JERRY LEE, retired architect; b. Indpls., Nov. 7, 1942; s. Charlie Christopher and Katheryn Rosella (Hankins) Q.; m. Mary Lee Darby (div.); children: Chad, Tara; m. Julie Ann Gordon (div.); 1 child, Dana Ann; m. Lisbeth Jane Gray, Mar. 16, 1986. BArch, Iowa State U., 1965. Registered arch., Wis. Mem. staff Hansen Lind Meyer, Iowa City, 1965-70, assoc., 1970-74, prin., 1975-77, prin., v.p. Chgo., 1977-86; exec. v.p. VVKR, Inc., Alexandria, Va., 1986-93; prin., sr. v.p. Perkins & Will, Chgo., 1994-96, also bd. dirs.; sr. v.p. RTKL Assocs. Inc., Chgo., 1996—2002, ret., 2002. Chmn. Cedar Rapids/Iowa City Architects Council, 1974. Author: Drafting Practices Manual, 1978; contbr. articles to profl. jours. Pres. bd. dirs. Mental Health Assn. of Greater Chgo., 1990-95. Fellow AIA, Am. Coll. Healthcare Archs.(founder); mem. Forum for Health Care Planning (bd. dirs. 1992-99). Avocations: photography, woodworking, gardening. Home: 43495 Trout Creek Rd Soldiers Grove WI 54655-7090 E-mail: jlquebe@mwt.net.

QUEEN, JOYCE, elementary school educator; b. Cleve., Mar. 17, 1945; d. Wilbur and Mae Closterhouse; m. Robert Graham Queen, Mar. 17, 1973. BA in Biology, Macalester Coll., 1966; MS in Conservation and Natural Resource Mgmt., U. Mich., 1968. Cert. tchr. biol. and earth scis., Ohio. Exhibitor, docent, coord. Grand Rapids (Mich.) Pub. Mus., 1967-68; tchr., naturalist Rose Tree-Media (Pa.) Outdoor Edn., 1967, Willoughby-Eastlake (Ohio) Schs., 1969-70, Independence (Ohio) Schs., 1970-78; sci. tchr. Hathaway Brown Sch., Cleve., 1970—, chmn. dept. primary sci., 1998—. Designer Courtland Woods nature trail, 1986, designer sci. greenhouse, 1990-92; designer sci. classroom Van Dyke Architects/Hathaway Brown Sch., 1990-92; designer, coord. Dampeer Primary sci. courtyard, 1993, Oliva Herb Garden, 1998, Colini Landscape Design/Hathaway Brown Sch., Shaker Hts., Ohio; edn. adv. com. William G. Mather Vessel Mus., Cleve., 1992, Holden Arboretum, Kirtland, Ohio, 1992-97, Shaker Lakes Nature Ctr., 2005-06, Squire Valleyvue Farm, 2006; youth divsn. judge Cleve. Botanic Garden Show, 1999, 2000, 02, 05, 07, NOAA Live From Antarctica, 2003; presenter in field. Contbr. articles to profl. jours. Active Belize (Ctrl. Am.) Tchrs. Workshop, 1994; Sagamore Adirondack Great Camps Workshop, 2003; vol. PARI Radio Telescope, 2005; task force, agrl. edn. commn. HB Engring., 2005-06. Catalyst grant Hathaway Brown Sch. Gt. Lks. Curriculum, 1991; recipient Ohio Alliance for Environment, 1986, Presdl. Excellence in Elem. Sci. Tchg. award NSF, 1992, Sheldon Exemplary Equipment and Facilities award, 1992, Garden Club Am. Hull award, 2005; Great Lakes Lighthouse Keepers Assn. scholar, Marine Ecology scholar Marine Resources, Inc., 1989, Internat. Space Sta. Conf. scholar, 2000, Maine Salt Marsh Ecology Curriculum scholar, 2001, Calif. Coastal Wetlands and Desert Study scholar, 2002, NASA Mars Mission Scholar, 2006, Hong Kong-Sci./Tech. China scholar, 2006., Great Lakes Scholar's Tchr. the Yr. award, 2007. Mem. NSTA, Cleve. Regional Coun. Sci. Tchrs., Cleve. Natural Hist. Mus., Cleve. Zool. Park, Ind. Sch. Assn. Ctrl. Sts., Internat. Pen Pal Exch. Progam, Great Lakes Sci. Ctr. Holden Arboretum (mem. profl. women's adv. bd. 2007). Presbyterian. Avocations: orchardist, naturalist, horticulturist. Office: Hathaway Brown Sch 19600 N Park Blvd Cleveland OH 44122-1899

QUENON, ROBERT HAGERTY, retired mining consultant and holding company executive; b. Clarksburg, W.Va., Aug. 2, 1928; s. Ernest Leonard and Josephine (Hagerty) Q.; m. Jean Bowling, Aug. 8, 1953; children: Evan, Ann, Richard. BS in Mining Engring., W.Va. U., 1951; LL.B., George Washington U., 1964; PhD (hon.), U. Mo., 1979, Blackburn Coll., 1983, W.Va. U., 1988. Mine supt. Consol. Coal Co., Fairmont, W.Va., 1956-61; mgr. deep mines Pittston Co., Dante, Va., 1964-66; gen. mgr. Riverton Coal Co., Crown Hill, W.Va., 1966-67; mgr. ops. coal and shale oil dept. Exxon Co., Houston, 1967; pres. Monterey Coal Co., Houston, 1969-76; sr. v.p. Carter Oil Co., Houston, 1976-77; exec. v.p. Peabody Coal Co., St. Louis, 1977-78, pres., chief exec. officer, 1978-83, Peabody Holding Co., Inc., St. Louis, 1983-90, chmn., 1990-91. Bd. dirs. Newmont Mining Co., Denver, Ameren Corp., St. Louis, Laclede Steel Co., St. Louis, Miss. Lime Co., Alton, Ill.; bd. dirs., chmn. Fed. Res. Bank St. Louis, 1993-95, dep. chmn., 1990-92; mem. coal industry adv. bd. Internat. Energy Agy., 1980-97, bd. chmn., 1984-90; chmn. Bituminous Coal Operator's Assn., 1980-83, 89-91. Trustee Blackburn Coll., Carlinville, Ill., 1975-83, St. Louis U., 1981-91; pres. St. Louis Art Mus., 1985-88. Served with AUS, 1946-47. Recipient Eavenson award Soc. Mining, Metallurgy, and Exploration, 1994, Erskine Ramsay award Am. Inst. Mining, Metallurg. and Petroleum Engrs., 1985. Mem. Am. Mining Congress (vice-chmn. 1980-91), Nat. Coal Assn. (chmn. bd. 1978-80), U.S. C. of C. (dir. 1982-88). Office: PO Box 11328 Saint Louis MO 63105-0128

QUICK, ALBERT THOMAS, lawyer, educator; b. Battle Creek, Mich., June 28, 1939; s. Robert and Vera Quick; m. Brenda Jones; children: Lori, Traci, Becki, Breton, Regan, Leigh. BA, U. Ariz., 1962; MA, Cen. Mich. U., 1964; JD, Wayne State U., 1967; LLM, Tulane U., 1974. Bar: Mich. 1968. Asst. prosecutor Calhoun County, Marshall, Mich., 1968-69; assoc. Hatch & Hatch, Marshall, 1969-70; asst. prof. U. Maine, Augusta, 1970-73; prof. law U. Louisville, 1974-87, spl. asst. to univ. provost, 1983-87; dean, prof. law Ohio No. U., Ada, 1987-95; prof. law, dean U. Toledo, 1995-99, dean and prof. emeritus, 1999—; of counsel Smith Haughey Rice & Roegge, Traverse City, Mich., 2002—. Vis. prof. Mich. State U. Law Sch., 2000, Barry U. Law Sch., 2004, Jilin U. Law Sch., Chiua, 2005. Co-author: Update Federal Rules of Criminal Procedure; contbr. articles to profl. jours. V.p. bd. Human Rights Commn., co-chair; bd. visitors Wayne State U., 2003—. Recipient Medallion of Justice Nat. Bar Assn., 1995. Mem. ABA, ACLU, Mich. State Bar Assn. (justice initiatives standing com. 2003-04), Willis Soc., Ohio State Bar Assn., Phi Kappa Phi, Coif. Episcopalian. Avocations: golf, art, reading. Office: 202 E State St Traverse City MI 49685-0848 Office Phone: 231-929-4878. Personal E-mail: atquick@charter.net.

QUICK, EDWARD E., state legislator; b. Rich Hill, Mo., Feb. 16, 1935; City councilman, Kansas City, Mo., 1975-85; mem. Mo. Senate Dist. 17, 1985—. Office: 13004 County Road A Liberty MO 64068-8127 also: State Senate State Capitol Building Jefferson City MO 65101-1556 Address: 13004 County Rd A Liberty MO 64068-8127

QUIE, PAUL GERHARDT, pediatrician, educator; b. Dennison, Minn., Feb. 3, 1925; s. Albert Knute and Nettie Marie (Jacobson) Quie; m. Elizabeth Holmes, Aug. 10, 1951; children: Katie, Bill, Paul, David. BA, St. Olaf Coll., 1949; MD, Yale U., 1953; PhD (hon.), U. Lund, 1993. Diplomate Am. Bd. Pediat., Nat. Bd. Med. Examiners (mem.). Intern Hennepin County Hosp., 1953—54; pediatric resident U. Minn. Hosps., 1957—59; mem. faculty U. Minn. Med. Sch., 1959—, prof. pediatrics, 1968—99, prof. microbiology, 1974—99, assoc. dean of students, 1992—, Am. Legion meml. heart research prof., 1974—91, Regents prof., 1991; Regent's prof. emeritus, 1999—; interim dir. Ctr. for Biomed. Ethics U. Minn. Med. Sch., 1985—86; attending physician Hennepin County Hosp., 1959—91. Cons. U. Minn. Nursery Sch., 1959—91; chief of staff U. Minn. Hosp., 1979—84; vis. physician Radcliffe Infirmary, Oxford, England, 1971—72; mem. Adv. Allergy and Infectious Disease Coun., 1976—80; mem. pediat. com. NRC, 1978; mem. bd. sci. counselors Gamble Inst., 1985—90; vis. prof. U. Bergen, 1991; hon. prof. U. Hong Kong Med. Sch., 1995; vis. prof. pediat. Chubu Hosp., Nagasaki, Japan, 1996; co-dir. internat. med. edn. and rsch. program U. Minn. Med. Sch., 1998—. Editl. bd. Pediat., 1970—76, Rev. Infectious Diseases, 1989—92. Pres. Fairview Found., 1998—2007; bd. dirs. Ctr. for Victims of Torture, Elizabeth Glaser Pediat. AIDS Found., 1998—2005. Med. officer USNR, 1954—57. Recipient E. Mead-Johnson award, Am. Acad. Pediat., 1971, Shotwell award, Hennipen Med. Soc., 2001, Gold Headed Cane award in Pediatrics, 2005; fellow Guggenheim, 1971—72, Alexander von Humboldt, 1986; scholar John and Mary R. Markle, 1960—65. Mem.: Minn. Acad. Medicine (pres. 1993—94), Assn. Am. Physicians, Am. Acad. Pediat., Minn. Acad. Pediat., Am. Soc. Clin. Investigation, Am. Pediatric Soc. (coun. 1976—83, pres. 1987—88), Soc. Pediatric Rsch., Infectious Diseases Soc. Am. (coun. 1977—82, pres. 1985, Bristol award 1994), Am. Soc. Microbiology, Am. Fedn. Clin. Rsch., Minn. Med. Found. (pres. 1986—88), N.W. Pediat. Soc., Inst. Medicine of NAS. Achievements include research in function of human leukocytes and international medical education and research. Home: 2154 Commonwealth Ave Saint Paul MN 55108 Office: PO Box 293 Minneapolis MN 55455-0374 Office Phone: 612-626-2558. Business E-Mail: quiex001@umn.edu.

QUIGLEY, HERBERT JOSEPH, JR., pathologist, educator; b. Phila., Mar. 6, 1937; s. Herbert Joseph and Mary Kathleen (Carney) G.; m. Jacqueline Jean Stocksdale, Nov. 28, 1965 (div. 1974); 1 child, Amelia Anne. BS in Chemistry, Franklin and Marshall Coll., 1958; MD, U. Pa., 1962. Diplomate Am. Bd. Pathology. Intern Presbyterias Hosp., NYC, 1962—66, resident, 1962—66; chief pathology Monroe County Hosp., Key West, Fla., 1966-68; from asst. prof. to assoc. prof. pathology Creighton U., Omaha, 1968-72, prof., 1972—2003, prof. emeritus, 2003; chief pathology svc. VA Med. Cr., Omaha, 1968-88. Bd. dirs. Triton-Chito Inc., Omaha. Contbr. articles to profl. jours.; patentee in field. Bd. dirs., former pres., chmn. Nebr. Assn. Earth Sci. Clubs, Omaha, 1972—. Lt. comdr. USNR, 1966-68. Recipient career devel. award NIH, 1962-66, Borden prize for med. rsch. Borden Co., Inc., 1962; fellow NIH, Nat. Cancer Inst., 1958-62. Fellow Coll. Am. Pathologists, Am. Soc. Clin. Pathologists, Am. Inst. Chemists; mem. Nebr. Assn. Pathologists, N.Y. Acad. Scis. Republican. Roman Catholic. Avocations: paleontology, geology. Home: 9511 Mockingbird Dr Omaha NE 68127-2423 Office: VA Med Ctr 4101 Woolworth Ave Omaha NE 68105-1850

QUIGLEY, JOHN BERNARD, law educator; b. St. Louis, Oct. 1, 1940; s. John Bernard and Ruth Rosina (Schieber) Q. BA, Harvard U., 1962, MA, LLB, 1966. Bar: Ohio 1973, Mass. 1967, U.S. Dist. Ct. (so. dist.) Ohio 1976, U.S. Ct. Appeals (6th cir.) 1986, U.S. Supreme Ct. 1989. Research assoc. Harvard U. Law Sch., Cambridge, Mass., 1967-69; prof. law Ohio State U., Columbus, 1969—. Author: Basic Laws on the Structure of the Soviet State, 1969, The Soviet Foreign Trade Monopoly, 1974, Palestine and Israel: A Challenge to Justice, 1990, The Ruses for War: American Interventionism since World War II, 1992, 2nd edit., 2007, Flight into the Maelstrom: Soviet Immigration to Israel and Middle East Peace, 1997, Genocide in Cambodia, 2000, The Case for Palestine: An International Law Perspective, 2005, The Genocide Convention: An International Law Analysis, 2006, Soviet Legal Innovation and the Law of the Western World, 2007. Mem. at. Lawyers Guild (v.p. 1977-79), Am. Soc. Internat. Law, AAUP. Avocations: tennis, speed skating, violin. Office: Ohio State U Coll of Law Coll of Law 55 W 12th Ave Columbus OH 43210-1338

QUINLAN, MARK, credit agency executive; BA in Bus. Adminstrn, U. Rochester, MBA. V.p. First Fidelity Bancorp; sr. v.p. Star Bancorp; v.p. info. and human svcs. Union Ctrl. Ins. and Investments; sr. v.p., chief info. officer Charter One Fin. Inc., 2003—. Office: Charter One Fin Inc 1215 Superior Ave Cleveland OH 44114

QUINLAN, MICHAEL ROBERT, retired fast food franchise company executive; b. Chgo., Dec. 9, 1944; s. Robert Joseph and Kathryn (Koerner) Q.; m. Marilyn DeLashmutt, Apr. 23, 1966; children: Kevin, Michael. BS, Loyola U., Chgo., 1967, MBA, 1970. With McDonald's Corp., Oak Brook, Ill., 1966—, v.p., 1974-76, sr. v.p., 1976-78, exec. v.p., 1978-79, chief ops. officer, 1979-80, pres. McDonald's U.S.A., 1980-82, pres., 1982-89, COO, 1982-87, CEO, 1987-97, chmn., 1989-97, bd. dirs., 1992—2002. Dir. Dun & Bradstreet Corp, Short Hills, NJ, 1989—. Mem.: Butterfield Country, Oakbrook Handball-Racquetball. Republican. Roman Catholic. Office: Dun & Bradstreet Corp 103 JFK Parkway Short Hills NJ 07078

QUINLAN, THOMAS J., III, printing company executive; b. Feb. 3, 1963; m. Diane Quinlan; 4 children. BS, Pace U. Sr. v.p., treas. World Color Press Inc.; exec. v.p., treas. Walter Industries, Inc., 2000, Moore Wallace Inc., 2000—02, exec. v.p., bus. integration, 2003—04; exec. v.p. ops. R.R. Donnelley & Sons Co., Chgo., 2004—06, group pres. glob. services, CFO, 2006—07, pres., CEO, 2007. Office: RR Donnelley & Sons Co 111 S Wacker Dr Chicago IL 60606-4301

QUINLAN, WILLIAM J., lawyer; b. 1976; s. William R. and Jane Quinlan. Grad., U. Ill., Georgetown U. Law Sch. Atty. Gardner Carton & Douglas, Chgo., Quinlan & Carroll, Ltd., Chgo.; gen. counsel Ill. Gov.'s Office, Springfield, 2004—. Mem.: Ill. Bar Assn. Office: Office of the Gov 207 State House Springfield IL 62706 Office Phone: 312-814-8974. Office Fax: 217-782-1853.

QUINN, ALEXANDER JAMES, bishop; b. Cleve., Apr. 8, 1932; Attended, St. Charles Coll., Catonsville, Md., St. Mary Sem., Cleve., Lateran Sem., Rome, Cleve. State U. Ordained priest Diocese of Cleve., 1958, aux. bishop, 1983—, vicar western region; ordained bishop, 1983. Roman Catholic. Office: 2500 Elyria Ave Lorain OH 44055-1367 E-mail: ajquinn@dioceseofcleveland.org.*

QUINN, DENNIS B., English language and literature educator; b. Bklyn., Oct. 3, 1928; s. Herbert John and Thelma Leona (Warren) Q.; m. Eva M. Jensen, Aug. 13, 1952; children— Timothy, Monica, Alison. Student, Creighton U., 1948-50; BA in English, U. Wis., 1951, MA in English, 1952, PhD in English, 1958. Instr. English U. Kans., Lawrence, 1956-60, asst. prof. English, 1960-64, assoc. prof. English, 1964-68, prof. English, 1968—, dir. Pearson Coll., 1968-75, dir. integrated humanities program, 1971-79. Author: Iris Exiled: A Synoptic History of Wonder, 2002; contbr. articles Medieval and Renaissance literature and children's literature to profl. jours. Served with U.S. Army, 1946-48, Japan. Recipient student Fulbright award, Leiden, The Netherlands, 1955-56, research Fulbright award, Salamanca, Spain, 1962-63; H. Bernard Fink Outstanding Tchr. award U. Kans., 1965, H.O.P.E. Teaching award, 1969; NEH grantee, 1971; Kemper Tchg. fellow, 1997. Roman Catholic. Avocations: gardening, travel. Home: 1102 W 25th St Lawrence KS 66046-4441 Office: Univ Kansas Dept English Lawrence KS 66045-0001 Home Phone: 785-842-4598; Office Phone: 785-864-2513.

QUINN, DONAL, diagnostic equipment company executive; BS in Econs., Cork U., Ireland. Exec. positions with Mallinckrodt Med., Abbott Labs.; group pres. Biology products divsn. Dade Behring, Deerfield, Ill., 1998-99, pres. Europe, Mid. East and Africa divsn., 1999—.

QUINN, JEFFRY N., chemicals executive, lawyer; BS, Univ. Ky., 1981, JD, 1984. Sr. v.p. sec., gen. counsel Arch Coal Inc.; exec. v.p., chief adminstrv. officer, sec., gen. counsel Premcor Inc.; sr. v.p., gen. counsel, chief restructuring officer Solutia Inc., St. Louis, 2004—04, pres., CEO, 2004—06, chmn., pres., CEO, 2006—. Office: Solutia Inc 575 Maryville Centre Dr Saint Louis MO 63166 Business E-Mail: jnquin@solutia.com.

QUINN, JOHN MICHAEL, bishop; b. Detroit, Dec. 17, 1945; s. George and Mary Quinn. BA, Sacred Heart Sem., Detroit; MDiv, St. John's Provincial Sem., Plymouth; M in Religious Studies, U. Detroit/Mercy, M in Systemic Theology. Ordained priest Archdiocese of Detroit, 1972, assoc. dir. justice & peace, assoc. dir. religious edn., dir. edn. dept., 1990—2003; ordained bishop, 2003; aux. bishop for ctrl. region Archdiocese of Detroit, 2003—. Cardinal's del. Sacred Heart Major Sem., Detroit, adj. faculty, also bd. trustees; bd. trustees Madonna U., Livonia, Mich., Loyola HS, Detroit. Bd. mem. New Detroit, Salvation Army, Habitat for Humanity. Mem.: Internat. Order of Alhambra, Equestrian Order of the Holy Sepulchre of Jerusalem (chaplain), US Conf. Cath. Bishops (African Am. Catholics com., Cath. Campus Ministry com., episcopal advisor Commn. on Accreditation & Certification). Roman Catholic. Office: Archdiocese of Detroit 305 Michigan Ave Detroit MI 48226-2605 Office Phone: 313-237-5800.*

QUINN, PATRICK, lieutenant governor; b. Chgo., Sept. 22, 1948; 2 children. BS, Georgetown U., 1971; JD Northwestern U. Sch. of Law. Commr. Cook County Bd. of Tax Appeal, 1982; treas. State of Ill., 1990—94, lt. gov., 2003—. Chmn. Ill. River Coordinating Counc., Ill. Rural Affairs Counc., Ill. Rural Bond Bank. Democrat. Catholic. Office: Office Lt Governor James R Thompson Ctr 100 W Randolph Ste 15-200 Chicago IL 60601 also: Office Lt Governor State Capitol 214 State House Springfield IL 62706 Office Phone: 312-814-5220, 217-782-7884. Office Fax: 312-814-4862, 217-524-6262.

QUINN, R. JOSEPH, district judge; m. Carole Quinn. BA, St. John's U.; JD, Hamline U. Minn. State rep., 1983-90; formerly judge Minn. Supreme Ct., 1991-99; now. judge Dist. Ct., 1999; chief judge 10th judicial dist., Minn. Office: Anoka County Court 325 E Main St Anoka MN 55303-2483

QUINNELL, BRUCE ANDREW, retail book chain executive; b. Washington, Jan. 6, 1949; s. Robert Kay and Marion Louise (Moseley) Q.; m. Aug. 31, 1972 (div. June 1986); children: Paul David, Andrea Carolyn; m. Marcia Melodie Mundie. BS in Acctg., Va. Poly. Inst. and State U., 1971, MA in Acctg., 1972. CPA, Ohio, Mo., Tex., Tenn. Sr. auditor Ernst & Whinney, Columbus, Ohio, 1972-75; treas., chief fin. officer Midway Ford Truck Ctr., Kansas City, Mo., 1975-82; sr. v.p., chief fin. officer Rsch. Health Svcs., Kansas City, 1982-85; sr. v.p. VHA Enterprises Inc., Irving, Tex., 1985-87; v.p., treas., chief fin. officer Dollar Gen. Corp., Nashville, 1987-92; exec. v.p. Pace Membership Warehouse, Englewood, Colo., 1992-93; exec. v.p., COO Walden Book Co., Stamford, Conn., 1993, pres., 1994-97, Borders Group, Inc., Ann Arbor, Mich., 1997-99; vice chmn. Borders Group Inc., 1999—. Bd. dirs. Advs. Tenn. State U. Coll. Bus., ashville, 1991-92, Jr. Achievement Mid. Tenn., 1992, Hot Topic, Inc., 1998—; mem. adv. coun. Reading Is Fundamental, 1998—, chmn. adv. coun., 1999—. Mem. Fin. Execs. Inst., Am. Inst. CPA'S, Nat. Investor Rels. Inst. Republican. Lutheran. Avocations: racquetball, golf, scuba diving. E-mail: coobaq@bordersgroupinc.com.

QUINT, DOUGLAS JOSEPH, neuroradiology educator; b. NYC, Apr. 25, 1956; s. George and Barbara (Gilder) Q.; m. Leslie Eisenbud, May 23, 1982; children: Mark Harry, Jason Meyer. BA, Wesleyan U., Middletown, Conn., 1978; MD, Cornell U., 1982. Diplomate Nat. Bd. Med. Examiners, Am. Bd. Radiology. Med. intern U. Mich. Hosps., Ann Arbor, 1982-83, resident in radiology, 1983-86; fellow in neuroradiology, mem. assoc. staff Henry Ford Hosp., Detroit, 1986-88; prof. neuroradiology and MRI U. Mich. Med. Sch., Ann Arbor, 1988—. Contbr. articles to med. jour. Mem. Am. Soc. Neuroradiology (sr.), Radiol. Soc. N.Am., Am. Roentgen Ray Soc., Am. Coll. Radiology, AMA. Avocations: softball, tennis, model trains, photography, baseball. Office: U Mich Hosp Radiology Dept 1500 E Medical Ctr Dr Ann Arbor MI 48109-0030 Office Phone: 734-936-4460. Business E-Mail: djquint@umich.edu.

QUIRING, PATTI LEE, human resource consulting company executive; b. Indpls. d. Harold Woodrow and Flora Lee (Hoffman) Dulin; m. David Allen Niederhaus, June 1972; (div. May 1974); m. David Jonathon Quiring, Dec. 7, 1976; 1 child: Erin Ashley. AA, Ball State U., Muncie, 1972, BS, 1975; MBA, Ind. Wesleyan U., 1990. Profl. Sec. Summer employee P. R. Mallory and Co., Inc., Indpls., 1970, 1971; student asst. Ball State U., Muncie, Ind., 1970-72; adminstrv. asst. Ball Corp., Muncie, 1972-74; student asst. Ball State U., Muncie, 1975; adminstrv. asst. P. R. Mallory and Co., Inc., 1975-76; various mgmt. level positions Blue Cross and Blue Shield of Ind., Indpls., 1976-87; exec. recruiter Tech. Resource Group, Indpls., 1988-91; pres. Quiring Assocs., Inc., Indpls., 1991—. Co-facilitator Corp. Bd. Task Force, 1993—94; bd. dirs. Mega Sys, Inc. Co-chmn. venture com. United Way, 1991-93, mem. adv. com. women's divsn., 1991-94, bd. dirs., mem. exec. com., 1993-99, mem. goals and priorities com., 1993, vice chmn. agy. rels. cabinet 1993-94, chmn., 1995-98, co-chmn. campaign cluster, 1994-95, mem. campaign cabinet, 1995, N.E. area team leader, 1995; vol. Pan. Am. Games, Indpls., 1987; dir. alumni rels. Ball State U. Coll. Bus., Muncie, 1988-97, mem. alumni coun., 1994-97; bd. dirs. Heritage Place Sr. Citizens Ctr., Indpls., 1988-90, Indpls. YWCA, 1988-90, Feathercove Homeowners Assn., 1990-97, Geist Harbors Property Owner's Assn., 1994-97, Lawrence Twp. Found., 2000-01; corp. capt. Humane Soc., 1990-91; mem. mktg. com. Children's Mus., 1992-97, mem. bd. advisors, 1995—; mem. Equal Opportunity Adv. Bd., 1992-95, Indpls. BBB; bd. dirs. Lawrence Twp. Found., 2000—. Recipient Blue Cross award of Excellence, Indpls., 1985, City Ctr Vol. award, Indpls., 1985, Salute to Women of Achievement Individual award YWCA, 1993, etwork of Women in Business Networker of Yr. award, 1993; named Blue Cross Bus. Women of Yr., Indpls. 1982, 86, Humane Soc. Outstanding Vol., Indpls., 1985. Mem. Ind. Assn. Pers. Svc. Bd., Network Women in Bus. (pres. 1993), Ind. C. of C. (small bus. coun. bd.), Nat. Assn. Pers. Svcs. (mem. bd.), Indpls. and Ind. C. of C. (bd. dirs.), Better Bus. Bur. Avocations: fishing, boating, arts, tennis. Office: Quiring Assocs Inc 7267 C Jessman Rd West Dr Indianapolis IN 46256 Office Phone: 317-841-7575.

QUIRK, BRIAN, state representative; b. July 1968; State rep. dist. 15 Iowa Ho. of Reps., 2001—; mem. agr. and natural resources com.; mem. appropriations com.; mem. commerce and regulation com.; mem. econ. devel. com.; mem. transp. com. Democrat. Office: State Capitol East 12th and Grand Des Moines IA 50319 Home: 1011 Sunset St New Hampton IA 50659-1826

QUIST, GORDON JAY, federal judge; b. Grand Rapids, Mich., Nov. 12, 1937; s. George J. and Ida F. (Hoekstra) Q.; m. Martha Jane Capito, Mar. 10, 1962; children: Scot D., George J., Susan E., Martha J., Peter K. BA, Mich. State U., 1959; JD with honors, George Washington U., 1962. Bar: DC 1962, Ill. 1964, US Dist. Ct. (no. dist.) Ill. 1964, US Supreme Ct. 1965, Mich. 1967, US Dist. Ct. (we. dist.) Mich. 1967, US Ct. Appeals (6th cir.) 1967. Assoc. Hollabaugh & Jacobs, Washington, 1962-64, Sonnenschein, Levinson, Carlin, Nath & Rosenthal, Chgo., 1964-66, Miller, Johnson, Snell & Cummiskey, Grand Rapids, 1967-72, ptnr., 1972-92, mng. ptnr., 1986-92; judge US Dist. Ct. (we. dist.) Mich., Grand Rapids, 1992—2006, sr. judge, 2006—. Mem. Code of Conduct com. U.S. Cts., 2000—, chmn., 2004—. Bd. dirs. Wedgewood Acres-Ch. Youth Home, 1968-74, Mary Free Bed Hosp., 1979-88, Christian Ref. Publs., 1968-78, 82-88, Opera Grand Rapids, 1986-92, Mary Free Bed Brace Shop, 1988-92, Better Bus. Bur., 1972-80, Calvin Theol. Sem., 1992-93; bd. dirs. Indian Trails Camp, 1970-78, 82-88, pres., 1978, 88. Recipient Disting. Alumnus award George Washington U. Law Sch. 1998 Mem. Fed. Bar Assn., Am. Judicature Soc., Mich. State Bar Found., Univ. Club Grand Rapids, Order of Coif. Avocations: reading, travel. Office: 482 Ford Fed Courthouse 110 Michigan St NW Grand Rapids MI 49503-2313 Business E-Mail: Gordon_J_Quist@miwd.uscourts.gov.

QUTUB, MUSA YACUB, hydrogeologist, educator, consultant; b. Jerusalem, June 2, 1940; came to U.S., 1960; s. Yacub and Sarah Qutub; married; children: Hanhia, Jennan, Sarmad, Muntaser, Aya, Saif, Tasneem. BA in Geology, Simpson Coll., Indianola, Iowa, 1964; MS in Hydrogeology, Colo. State U., 1966; PhD in Water Resources, Iowa State U. Sci. and Tech., 1969. Instr. earth sci. Iowa State U., Ames, 1966-69; from asst. prof. to prof. Northeastern Ill., Chgo., 1969-80, prof. geography and environ. studies, 1980—. Cons. hydrogeology, Des Plaines, Ill., 1970—; sr. adviser Saudi Arabian Ministry Planning, Riyadh, 1977-78; leader U.S. environ. sci. del. to People's Republic of China, 1984; pres., founder Islamic Info. Ctr. Am. Author: Secondarty Environmental Science Methods, 1973; contbr. numerous articles to profl. jours.; editor Environ. Resource, Directory Environ. Educators and Cons. World. NSF grantee, 1970-71, 71-72, 72-73, 75, 76, Hew grantee, 1974, grantee Ill. Dept. Edn., 1970. Mem. AAAS, NSF (cons.), Am. Waterworks Assn., Am. Men and Women Sci., at. Assn. Geology Tchrs. (pres. central sect. 1974), Environ. Sci. Inst. (edn. com.), Internat. Assn. Advancement of Earth and Environ Sci. (pres. 1975—, founder), Ill. Earth Sci. Edn. (pres. 1971-73, founder), Phi Delta Kappa. Muslim. Avocations: tennis, track, cross country, soccer.

RAABE, WILLIAM ALAN, tax writer, business educator; b. Milw., Dec. 14, 1953; s. William Arthur and Shirley R.; m. Nancy Elizabeth Miller, Mar. 1989; children: Margaret Elisabeth, Martin William. BS, Carroll Coll., 1975; MAS, U. Ill., Urbana, 1976, PhD, 1979. Wis. Disting. prof. U. Wis., Milw., 1979-96; tax edn. cons. Price Waterhouse Coopers, NYC, 1985—; prof., dir. acctg. programs Samford U., Birmingham, Ala., 1997-2001; founding dean Sch. Mgmt., disting. prof. Capital U., Columbus, Ohio, 2001—02; tax faculty Fisher Coll. Bus. Ohio State U., Columbus, 2002—. Vis. assoc. prof. Ariz. State U., Tempe, 1985; vis. faculty Ernst & Young, NYC, 1990—, Deloitte & Touche, NYC, 1998—, Calif. CPA Found., 1986, AICPA, 1984-94, Wis. Bar Assn., 1992, Capital U. Law Sch., 2002—; developer Estate Tax Planner, McGraw Hill Software, NYC, 1980-88; expert witness, 1985—; cons. corp. income tax State Ala., 1997-01, State of Wis., 1995, 99; dir. Fisher/Ohio State U. Tax Clinic, 2003—. Author West's Federal Taxation, 1985—, Federal Tax Research, 1986—, Income Shifting After Tax Reform, 1987, Multistate Corporate Tax Guide, 1985-96, California Income Taxation, 1999-2006, Schedule M-3, 2006; editor CCH, 2005, Price Waterhouse Coopers Tax Case Studies, 2005-; contbr. articles to profl. jours. Bd. dirs., Luth. High Sch. Assn. Milw., 1991-96, pres., 1993-96, Bethesda Luth. Home and Found., Watertown, Wis., 1989-91, Luth. Counseling and Family Svcs., 1982-88, Concord Chamber Orch., Milw., 1983-88; mem. Econ. Devel. Com., Wauwatosa, Wis., 1986-89; faculty athletic rep. to NCAA from U. Wis. Milw., 1990-96; mem. Milw. Symphony Chorus, Master Singers of Milw., Samford Master Singers; vice chair faculty senate Samford U., 2000-01. Named to Alumni Hall Fame, Milw. Luth. H.S., 1995, Carroll Coll., 2005; fellow, U. Ill., 1978, at. Ctr. Tax Edn. and Rsch., 1977. Mem. Am. Acctg. Assn., Wis. Inst. CPAs (Educator of Yr. 1987), Ala. Acctg. Educators Assn. (pres. 1999-2000). Office: Fisher Coll Bus 2100 Neil Ave Columbus OH 43210-1144 Office Phone: 614-292-4023. Business E-Mail: raabe.12@osu.edu.

RABB, GEORGE BERNARD, zoologist, conservationist; b. Charleston, SC, Jan. 2, 1930; s. Joseph and Teresa C. (Redmond) R.; m. Mary Sughrue, June 10, 1953. BS, Coll. Charleston, 1951, LHD (hon.), 1995; MA, U. Mich., 1952, PhD, 1957. Teaching fellow zoology U. Mich., 1954-56; curator, coord. rsch. Chgo. Zool. Park, Brookfield., Ill., 1956-64, assoc. dir. rsch. and edn., 1964-75, dep. dir., 1969-75, dir., 1976—2003, dir. emeritus, 2003—. Rsch. assoc. Field Mus., 1965—; lectr. dept. biology U. Chgo., 1965-89; mem. Com. on Evolutionary Biology, 1969—; pres. Chgo. Zool. Soc., 1976-2003, pres. emeritus, 2004—; mem. steering com. Species Survival Commn., Internat. Union Conservation of Nature/World Conservation Union, 1983-2003, vice-chmn. N.Am., 1986-88, dep. chmn., 1987-89, chmn., 1989-96, vice-chmn. comms., 1997-2003; chmn. policy adv. group Internat. Species Info. System, 1974-89, chmn. bd., 1989-92; pres. bd. dirs. Chgo. Wilderness Mag., 1999—; v.p. Fauna and Flora Internat., 1998—; chmn. bd. Ill. State Mus., 1999—; bd. dirs. Ctr. Humans and Nature. Bd. dirs. Defenders of Wildlife, 2002—. Fellow AAAS; mem. Am. Soc. Ichthyologists and Herpetologists (pres. 1978), Herpetologists League, Soc. Systematic Zoology, Soc. Mammalogists, Soc. Study Evolution, Ecol. Soc. Am., Soc. Conservation Biology (council mem. 1986), Soc. for Integrative and Comparative Zoology, Soc. Study Animal Behavior, Am. Assn. Museums (named to Centennial Honor Roll, 2006), Am. Soc. Naturalists, Am. Assn. Zool. Parks and Aquariums (dir. 1979-80), World Assn. Zoos and Aquariums, World Conservation Union (hon. mem.), Sigma Xi. Office: 9236 Broadway Brookfield IL 60513 Personal E-mail: georgerabb@sbcglobal.net.

RABIN, JOSEPH HARRY, marketing research company executive; b. Chgo., Dec. 12, 1927; s. Morris and Libby (Broder) Rabinovitz; m. Barbara E. Leader, Oct. 31, 1954; children: Marc Jay, Michelle Ann, Deborah Susan. BSc, Roosevelt U., 1950; MBA, DePaul U., 1951. Account exec. Gould, Gleiss & Benn, 1951-56; asst. dir. mktg. rsch. Paper Mate Co., Chgo., 1956-63; pres. Rabin Rsch. Co., Chgo., 1963—. Pres. Mather HS Coun., 1972-74; mem. adv. coun. U. Toledo, 1976-77, Kellstadt Ctr. DePaul U., 1986-93; mem. adv. com. Bur. of the Census, 1978-83; bd. dirs. Market Rsch. Inst., 1973-75, Ner Tamid Synagogue, 1976-2007, Jewish Vocat. Svc., 1977-80. With AUS, 1946-47. Mem. Am. Mktg. Assn. (pres. Chgo. chpt. 1961-62, nat. dir. 1973-75, nat. v.p. mktg. rsch. 1978-79, nat. pres. 1981-82), Assn. Consumer Rsch., Am. Statis. Assn. (pres. Chgo. chpt. 1962-63), Am. Assn. Pub. Opinion Rsch. Home: 7061 N Kedzie Ave Chicago IL 60645-2846 Office: Rabin Rsch Co 150 E Huron St Chicago IL 60611-2999 Home Phone: 773-465-6661; Office Phone: 312-482-8500. Business E-Mail: jrabin@rabin-research.com.

RABINEAU, PHYLLIS, museum administrator; AB in Anthropology, Cornell U., 1970, MA in Anthropology, 1973. Collections mgr., dept. anthropology Field Mus., 1974—85, project direction staff, 1986—96; sr. mgmt., v.p. interpretation and edn. Chgo. Hist. Soc., 1997—. Exhibit curator Field Mus., 1981—85, dep. chair, program devel., 1991—94; cons. in field. Contbr. articles to profl. jours. Mem.: Am. Assn. Mus. (mem. nat. program com. 2005, 2006, 2008, mem. nominations com. 2007, Curators' Com. award 1991), QM2 Dep. Dirs. Roundtable, Nat. Assn. Mus. Exhbn. (bd. dirs. 1994—96, pres. 2004—, mem. standing profl. com. for exhbns. 2005—). Office: Chgo History Mus 1601 N Clark Chicago IL 60614 Office Phone: 312-799-2130. Office Fax: 312-799-2430. Business E-Mail: rabineau@chicagohistory.org.*

RABINOVICH, SERGIO, physician, educator; b. Lima, Peru, Apr. 8, 1928; m. Nelly; children— Gina, Sergio, Norca, Egla. MD, San Fernando Med. Sch., U. San Marcos, Lima, Peru, 1953. Intern San Fernando Med. Sch., U. San Marcos, Lima, 1947-54; resident in medicine Grasslands Hosp., Valhalla, NY, 1954-57, Henry Ford Hosp., Detroit; prof., head dept. internal medicine U. Arequipa Med. Sch., 1960-61; asst. prof. dept. internal medicine U. Iowa, Iowa City, 1963-65, asst. prof., 1965-69; attending physician and cons. VA Hosp., Iowa City, 1965-73; assoc. prof. U. Iowa, 1969-73; prof., chief dept. medicine div. infectious disease So. Ill. U. Sch. Medicine, Springfield, 1973-96, prof., chmn. dept. medicine, 1974-88, pres. Faculty Coun., 1992-93, prof. emeritus, 1996. Author: (with I.M. Smith, S.T. Donta) Antibiotics and Infection, 1974. Fellow ACP, Infectious Disease Soc. Am.; mem. AMA, Am. Soc. Microbiology, N.Y. Acad. Sci., Am. Fedn. Clin. Research, AAAS, Am. Thoracic Soc., Ill. Thoracic Soc. (pres. 1978-79), Central Soc. Clin. Research, Sigma Xi. Office: So Ill U Sch Medicine 800 N Rutledge St Springfield IL 62794-9636 Home Phone: 217-787-5984; Office Phone: 217-545-0181. Personal E-mail: sergiorabinovich@aol.com.

RABINOWITZ, PAUL H., mathematics educator; b. Newark, Nov. 15, 1939; BA, NYU, 1961, PhD, 1966. Prof. math. U. Wis., Madison. Mem. Am. Math. Soc., Soc. Indsl. & Applied Math. Office: U Wis Dept Math 450 Lincoln Dr Van Vleck Hall EB813 Madison WI 53706

RACCAH, DOMINIQUE MARCELLE, publisher; b. Paris, Aug. 24, 1956; arrived in U.S., 1964; d. Paul and Colette Raccah; m. Raymond W. Bennett, Aug. 20, 1980; 3 children. BA, U. Ill., Chgo., 1978; MS, U. Ill., Champaign-Urbana, 1981. Rsch. analyst Leo Burnett Advt., Chgo., 1980-81, rsch. supr., 1981-84, assoc. rsch. dir., 1984-87; pres., pub., owner Sourcebooks, Inc., Naperville, Ill., 1987—; co-CEO Login Pubs. Consortium, Chgo., 1990-99. Author: Financial Sourcebooks' Sources, 1987; editor: Poetry Speaks, 2001, Poetry Speaks to Children, 2005, The Sourcebooks Shakespeare, 2005. Bd. dirs. Com. of 200, Book Industry Study Group. Recipient Blue Chip Enterprise award, 2000, Ernst & Young Entrepreneur of Yr. Ill. and N.W. Ind., 2000; named to Inc. 500 list; inducted into Univ. Ill. Entrepreneurship Hall of Fame, 2001. Mem. Pubs. Mktg. Assn., Am. Booksellers Assn., Am. Assn. Pubs. Office: Sourcebooks Inc 1935 Brookdale Rd # 139 aperville IL 60563-9245 Office Phone: 630-961-3900. Business E-Mail: dominique.raccah@sourcebooks.com.

RACLIN, GRIER C., lawyer; BA, JD, Northwestern U. Vice chmn., mng. ptnr. Gardner, Carton & Douglas; exec. v.p., chief adminstrv. office, gen. counsel, corp. sec. Global TeleSystems, Inc.; chief legal officer, corp. sec. SAVVIS, Inc., St. Louis; exec. v.p., gen. counsel, corp. sec. Charter Comms., St. Louis, 2005—. Office: Charter Comms 12405 Powerscourt Dr Saint Louis MO 63131 Office Phone: 314-543-2308. Office Fax: 314-965-0555.

RACTLIFFE, ROBERT EDWARD GEORGE, management executive; b. Hertfordshire, Eng., July 25, 1943; came to U.S., 1965; s. Augustus David John and Veronica Phyllis (Jones) R.; m. ancy Jane Brumbaugh, June 29, 1968; children: Richard Alban, Tiffany Elizabeth, Courtney Veronica. BS with honors, U. London, 1965; MSEE, U. Pitts., 1969, MBA with honors, 1972; PMD, Harvard U., 1975. Engr. Westinghouse Electric Corp., Pitts., 1965-69, sales mgr. LRA Div., 1969-73, mfg. engr. mgr. LRA Div., 1974-76, dept. mgr. Hydrogenerator Dept., 1976-78, mgr. product mktg. Steam Turbine Generator Div. Phila., 1979-81, mgr. strategic planning Power Generation Bus. Unit, 1981-84, gen. mgr. Power Generation Comml. Div. Orlando, Fla., 1984-86; pres., North Am. Ops. United Tech. Carrier Corp., Syracuse, .Y., 1986-88; pres., chief exec. officer NORDYNE Inc., St. Louis, 1989—. Patentee in field; contbr. articles to profl. jours. Mem. AAIM (bd. dirs.), Gas Appliance Mfrs. Assn. (co. rep.), Manufactured Housing Inst. (co. rep.), Air Conditioning and Refrigeration Inst. (bd. dirs., v.p. exec. com., com. chmn., co. rep.). Republican. Episcopalian. Avocations: golf, tennis, skiing. Office: NORDYNE Inc PO Box 8809 O Fallon MO 63366-8809

RADER, RALPH TERRANCE, lawyer; b. Clarksburg, W.Va., Dec. 5, 1947; s. Ralph Coolidge and Jeanne (Cover) R.; m. Rebecca Jo Vorderman, Mar. 22, 1969; children: Melissa Michelle, Allison Suzanne. BSME, Va. Poly. Inst., 1970; JD, Am. U., 1974. Bar: Va. 1975, U.S. Ct. Customs and Patent Appeals, 1977, U.S. Dist. Ct. (ea. dist.) Mich. 1978, Mich. 1979, U.S. Ct. Appeals (6th cir.) 1979, U.S. Dist. Ct. (we. dist.) Mich. 1981, U.S. Ct. Appeals (fed. cir.) 1983. Supervisory patent examiner U.S. Patent Office, Washington, 1970-77; patent atty., ptnr. Cullen, Sloman, Cantor, Grauer, Scott & Rutherford, Detroit, 1977-88; ptnr. Dykema, Gossett, Detroit, 1989-96; founder, ptnr. Rader, Fishman & Grauer, Bloomfield Hills, Mich., 1996—. Contbr. articles to profl. jours. Mem. adminstrv. bd. 1st United Meth. Ch., Birmingham, Mich., 1980—. With U.S. Army, 1970-76. Mem. ABA, Am. Patent Law Assn., Mich. Patent Law Assn., Mich. Bar (governing coun. patent, trademark and copyright law sect. 1981-84), Engring. Soc. Detroit, Masons, Tau Beta Pi, Pi Tau Sigma, Phi Kappa Phi. Methodist. Home: 4713 Riverchase Dr Troy MI 48098-4186 Office: Rader Fishman & Grauer 39533 Woodward Ave Ste 140 Bloomfield Hills MI 48304-5098 Office Phone: 248-594-0620. Business E-Mail: rtr@raderfishman.com.

RADKE, RODNEY OWEN, agricultural research executive, consultant; b. Ripon, Wis., Feb. 5, 1942; s. Edward Ludwig and Vera Ione (Phillips) R.; m. Jean Marie Rutsch, Sept. 1, 1963; children: Cheryl Lynn, Lisa Diane, Daniel E. BS, U. Wis., 1963, MS, 1965, PhD, 1967. Rsch. scientist Monsanto Agrl. Co., St. Louis, 1969-75, sr. rsch. group leader, 1975-79, rsch. mgr., 1979-81, mgr. rsch., 1981-93; pvt. practice cons., 1993—2002; ret., 2002—. Contbr. articles to profl. jours.; patentee in field. Served to capt. U.S. Army, 1967-69. Mem. North Ctrl. Weed Sci. Soc. Lutheran. Avocations: power boating, soccer, gardening, woodshop. Home and Office: 1119 Grand Prix Dr Saint Charles MO 63303-6313

RADKOSKI, DONALD J., food products company executive; V.p., dir. fin., asst. tres. Bob Evans Farms, Columbus, Ohio, 1980-88, CFO, group v.p. fin., treas., 1988—. Office: Bob Evans Farms Inc 3776 S High St Columbus OH 43207-0863

RADMER, MICHAEL JOHN, lawyer, educator; b. Wisconsin Rapids, Apr. 28, 1945; s. Donald Richard and Thelma Loretta (Donahue) R.; children from previous marriage: Christina Nicole, Ryan Michael; m. Laurie J. Anshus, Dec. 22, 1983; 1 child, Michael John BS, Northwestern U., 1967; JD, Harvard U., 1970. Bar: Minn. 1970. Assoc. Dorsey & Whitney, Mpls., 1970-75, ptnr., corp. practice group, 1976—, chmn., funds practice. Lectr. law Hamline U. Law Sch., St. Paul, 1981-84; gen. counsel, rep., sec. 58 federally registered investment cos., Mpls. and St. Paul, 1977—. Contbr. articles to legal jours. Active legal work Hennepin County Legal Advice Clinic, Mpls., 1971—. Mem. ABA, Minn. Bar Assn., Hennepin County Bar Assn., Mpls. Athletic Club. Office: Dorsey & Whitney 50 South 6th St Ste 1500 Minneapolis MN 55402 Home Phone: 612-824-6919; Office Phone: 612-340-2724. Office Fax: 612-340-8738. Business E-Mail: radmer.michael@dorsey.com.

RADNOR, ALAN T., lawyer; b. Cleve., Mar. 10, 1946; s. Robert Clark and Rose (Chester) R.; m. Carol Sue Hirsch, June 22, 1969; children: Melanie, Joshua, Joanna. BA, Kenyon Coll., 1967; MS in Anatomy, Ohio State U., 1969, JD, 1972. Bar: Ohio 1972. Ptnr. Vorys, Sater, Seymour & Pease, Columbus, Ohio, 1972—. Adj. prof. law Ohio State U., Columbus, 1979-99. Author: Cross-Examining Doctors: A Practical Guide, 1999; contbr. articles to profl. jours. Bd. dirs., trustee Congregation Tifereth Israel, Columbus, 1975—, pres., 1985-87; trustee Columbus Mus. Art, 1995-98; pres. The Thurber House., 2004. Named Boss of Yr., Columbus Assn. Legal Secs., 1983. Fellow Am. Coll. Trial Lawyers; mem. ABA, Ohio State Bar Assn., Columbus Bar Assn., Def. Rsch. Inst., Internat. Assn. Def. Counsel. Avocations: reading, sculpture. Home: 400 S Columbia Ave Columbus OH 43209-1629 Office: Vorys Sater Seymour & Pease 52 E Gay St PO Box 1008 Columbus OH 43216-1008

RADOGNO, CHRISTINE, state legislator; b. Oak Park, Ill., Dec. 21, 1952; BA, MSW, Loyola U. Mem. Ill. Senate, Springfield, 1997—, mem. appropriations, commerce & industry & pub. health coms. Republican. Office: State Capitol Capitol Bldg M-121 Springfield IL 62706-0001 also: 521 S LaGrance Rd Ste 104 La Grange IL 60525

RADOMSKI, ROBYN L., marketing executive; b. Pitts., 1956; d. Robert G. and Helen L. Moses; m. A. David Radomski; children: Lauren E., Kristen L. BA in Journalism, Pa. State U., 1975; MBA in Mktg., DePaul U., 1989. Dir. Sedgwick-James, Inc., Chgo., 1977-81; v.p. Edelman Worldwide, Chgo., 1981-84, Playboy Enterprises, Inc., Chgo., 1984-91; sr. v.p. Bozell Worldwide, Chgo., 1991-92; v.p. mktg. Fluid Mgmt., L.P., Wheeling, Ill., 1992-96; v.p. mktg., CMO Wace, The Imaging etwork, Chgo., 1996—98; v.p. mktg., pub. rels. and physician svcs. Northwestern Meml. Hosp., 1998—99; chief mktg. officer Sonnenschein Nath & Rosenthal, Chgo., 1999—; chmn. worldwide mktg. N.Am. Lex Mundi, 2003—. Bd. dirs. Playboy Found., Chgo. Mem.: Internat. Assn. Bus. Communicators (bd. dirs.), Pub. Rels. Clinic, Pub. Rels. Soc. Am., Nat. Investor Rels. Assn., Am. Mktg. Assn., Sigma Delta Chi. Avocation: yacht sailing. Office: Sonnenschein Nath & Rosenthal 8000 Sears Tower Chicago IL 60606

RADUNZ, PAUL A., transportation executive; BA, St. Olaf Coll. Sr. v.p., chief info. officer GE Card Svcs., GE Capital Fleet Svcs.; v.p., chief info. officer CH Robinson, Eden Prairie, Minn., 2001—. Office: CH Robinson 8100 Mitchell Rd Eden Prairie MN 55344-2248

RAE, NANCY A., human resources specialist, automotive executive; 1 child. Diploma in Bus. Adminstrn., Ea. Mich. U., M in Indsl. Rels. Interviewer Chrysler Corp., Warren, Mich., 1978; various positions DaimlerChrysler Corp., Auburn Hills, Mich., 1978—92, group personnel exec., procurement and supply and product strategy and regulatory affairs, 1992—94, mgr. workforce diversity and econ. equality, 1994, group personnel mgr., Chrysler Tech. Ctr., 1994—96, group human resources mgr. tech. ops., 1996—98, mgr. health ins. and disability, 1998, v.p. compensation and benefits, 1998—2000, sr. v.p. human resources, 2000—. Office: DaimlerChrysler Corp 1000 Chrysler Dr Auburn Hills MI 48326-2766 Office Phone: 248-576-5741. Office Fax: 248-576-4742.

RAEBURN, JOHN HAY, language educator; b. Indpls., July 18, 1941; s. Gordon Maurice and Katherine (Calwell) R.; m. Gillian Kimble, Aug. 18, 1963 (div. July 1979); children— Daniel Kennedy, Nicholas Kimble; m. Kathleen Kamerick, July 5, 1986. AB with honors, Ind. U., 1963; A.M., U. Pa., 1964, PhD, 1969. Asst. prof. U. Mich., Ann Arbor, 1967-74; vis. lectr. U. Iowa, Iowa City, 1974-75, assoc. prof., 1976-83, prof. English, 1983—; chmn. Am. Studies dept., 1983-85, 94-2000; chmn. English dept. U. Iowa, Iowa City, 1985-91; assoc. prof. U. Louisville, 1975-76. Author: Fame Became of Him: Hemingway as Public Writer, 1984, A Staggering Revolution: A Cultural History of Thirties Photography, 2006; editor: (with others) Frank Capra: The Man and His Films, 1975. Mem.: Am. Studies Assn., Orgn. Am. Historians. Democrat. Home: 321 Hutchinson Ave Iowa City IA 52246-2407 Office: U Iowa Dept Am Studies 210 Jefferson Bldg Iowa City IA 52242-1418 Home Phone: 319-338-5590; Office Phone: 319-335-0320. Business E-Mail: john-raeburn@iowa.edu.

RAECKER, SCOTT, state representative, educational association administrator; b. Waterloo, Iowa, Aug. 30, 1961; m. Martha Raecker; children: Emily, Max. BA, Grinnell Coll., 1984. V.p. First Nat. Bank of Vail, 1986—88, Vail Valley Found., 1988—92; exec. dir. Iowa Student Sesquicentennial Commn., 1992—97, Inst. Character Devel., 1997—; state rep. dist. 63 Iowa Ho. of Reps., 2003—; mem. adminstrn. and regulation com.; mem. appropriations com.; mem. commerce and regulation com.; mem. judiciary com.; mem. labor and indsl. rels. com. Active 21st Century Workforce Coun., 1999, Govs. 2010 Strategic Planning Coun., 2000; bd. dirs. Adv. Network for Aging Iowans, 1999—, Iowa Natural Heritage Found., 1997—. Mem.: Drake Bus. Assn. (bd. dirs. 1997—), Rotary (bd. dirs. 1997—). Republican. Lutheran. Address: 9011 Iltis Dr Urbandale IA 50322 Office: State Capitol East 12th and Grand Des Moines IA 50319

RAFF, RUDOLF A., science educator, researcher; BS, Pa. State U., 1963; PhD, Duke U., 1967. Instructor-in-chief, summer embryology course Marine Biol. Lab. at Woods Hole; founder Ind. Molecular Biology Inst., 1993; dir., Inst. for Molecular and Cellular Biology, Office of Rsch. and U. Grad. Sch. Ind. U, Bloomington, Ind., disting. prof., James H. Rudy prof. biology, adj. prof. History and Philosophy Sci., Coll. Arts and Scis. Invited lectr. for several universities and coll.; vis. scholar U. Sydney, Australia. Author four books on evolutionary developmental biology.; contbr. articles to profl. jours.; served as assoc. editor for several other jours.; mem. editl. bds. History of Biology; mem. editl. bds. Biology and Philosophy, co-founder, editor-in-chief Evolution & Development. Lt. Navy. Recipient Kowalevsky medal, 2000; scholar Nat. Naval Med. Ctr., 1967—69; NIH Fellowship, Am. Cancer Soc. Fellowship, Guggenheim Found. Fellowship. Mem.: Am. Acad. of Arts and Scis. Office: Inst for Molecular Biology Rsch 800 E Third St Bloomington IN 47405 Office Phone: 812-855-2791. Office Fax: 812-855-6082. Business E-Mail: rraff@bio.indiana.edu.

RAGA, TOM, state representative; b. Cin., Oct. 5, 1965; married; 2 children. BS in Agrl. Econs., Cornell U. State rep. dist. 67 Ohio Ho. of Reps., Columbus, 2000—, mem. fin. and appropriations, human svcs. and aging, and judiciary coms., and human svcs. subcom. Trustee Deerfield Twp., Ohio, 1998—2000; exec. com. Rep. Party. Named one of Tri-State's 21 to Watch, Cin. Enquirer, 2000. Mem.: Ohio Twp. Assn., Farm Bur., Moeller Alumni Assn., Young Rep. Club (chair). Republican. Office: 77 S High St 12th fl Columbus OH 43215-6111

RAGAN, AMANDA, state senator; b. Mason City, Sept. 1954; m. James Ragan; children: Edith, Charles. AA, N. Iowa Area CC; BA in Human Svcs., cum laude, Buena Vista U. Legis. asst. to Rep. Ed Parker; co-chair Ho. Majority Leader John Groninga, 1987—89; dist. rep. Iowa Dem. State Ctrl. Com., 1992—2002; legis. page Iowa State Senate, 1973, mem. DesMoines, 2002—, asst. leader, co-chair human resources com., mem. agr. com., mem. econ. growth com., mem. rules and adminstrn. com., mem. appropriations com., mem. health & human svcs. com., mem. budget com.; co-chair Senate Human Resources Com. Active Mason City Sesquicentennial Com., Sesquicentennial Com.; mem. Birth Defects Adv. Bd., HAWK-I Bd.; exec. dir. Meals on Wheels, Mason City, Cmty. Kitchen North Iowa, Inc., Mason City; mem. N. Iowa Band Festival Planning Com., Buena Vista Alumni Found., Coun. Social Agencies, Maternal Health Adv. Coun.; active Iowa Dem. Party State Ctrl. Com.; asst. leader Dem. Caucus; mem. Cerro Gordo County Dem. Ctrl. Com.; past chair. Cerro Gordo Re-Elect Clinton-Gore Com.; bd. dirs. Charles City C. of C., Osage C. of C., Francis Lauer Youth Svc. Mem.: N Iowa Fund-Raising Profls. Assn., Mason City C. of C., Mason City Sunrise Rotary (bd. dirs.). Office: State Capitol Bldg East 12th and Grand Des Moines IA 50319 Home: 20 Granite Ct Mason City IA 50401

RAGATZ, THOMAS GEORGE, lawyer; b. Madison, Wis., Feb. 18, 1934; s. Wilmer Leroy and Rosanna (Kindschi) Ragatz; m. Karen Christensen, Dec. 19, 1965; children: Thomas Rolf, William Leslie, Erik Douglas. BBA, U. Wis., 1957, LLB, 1961. CPA Wis.; bar: Wis. 1961, U.S. Dist. Ct. (ea. and we. dists.) Wis. 1961, U.S. Tax Ct. 1963, U.S. Ct. Appeals (7th cir.) 1965, U.S. Supreme Ct. 1968. Staff acct. Peat, Marwick, Mitchell & Co., Mpls., 1958; instr. Sch. Bus., U. Wis., Madison, 1958-60; formerly lectr. in acctg. and law Law Sch. U. Wis.; law clk. Wis. Supreme Ct., 1961-62; assoc. Boardman Suhr Curry & Field, Madison, 1962-64, ptnr., 1965-78, Foley & Lardner, Madison, 1978—2002, mng. ptnr., 1984-93, chmn. budget com., 1994-99. Bd. dirs. Wolf Appliance Co., LLC, Sub-Zero Freezer Co., Inc., Norman Bassett Found., Wis. Sports Found., United Way Found.; pres. Courtier Found.; bd. dirs., pres. Wis. Sports Devel. Corp.; lectr. seminars on tax subjects. Editor-in-chief Wis. Law Rev., 1960—61, chmn. Nat. Conf. Law Revs., 1960—61; author: The Ragatz History, 1989; contbr. articles to profl. jours. Formerly dir. United Way, Meth. Hosp. Found; mem. U. Wis. Found.; chmn. site selection com. U. Wis. Hosp. Com.; past pres., past moderator 1st Congl. Ch.; bd. dirs. Found. for Madison Pub. Schs.; pres. Bus. and Edn. Partnership, 1983—89, bd. dirs.; past pres., vice pres. Hospice-Care Found.; bd. regents U. Wis., panel provision of legal svcs.; bd. dirs. Met. YMCA, Madison, 1983—90. Fellow: Am. Bar Found.; mem.: ABA, Dane County Bar Assn. (pres. 1978—79, chmn. jud. qualification com., sec.), Wis. Inst. CPA, State Bar Wis. (sec. 1969—70, bd. govs. 1971—75, chmn. fin. com. 1975—80, chmn. tax sect., chmn. spl. com. on econs., chmn. svcs. for lawyers com.), Wis. Bar Found., Seventh Cir. Bar Assn., Am. Judicature Soc., Order of Constantine, Bascom Hill Soc., Order of Coif, Madison Club (pres. 1980—81), Madison Club House Corp. (pres. 1999—, bd. dirs.), Sigma Chi, Beta Gamma Sigma. Republican. Home: 3334 Lake Mendota Dr Madison WI 53705-1469 Office: Foley & Lardner LLP PO Box 1497 Madison WI 53701-1497 also: Foley & Lardner LLP 1st Wisconsin Ctr 777 E Wisconsin Ave Ste 3800 Milwaukee WI 53202-5302 E-mail: tgragatz@yahoo.com.

RAGGIO, ROBERT FRANK, career officer; BEE, Mont. State U., 1966; MSc in Indsl. Engring., Purdue U., 1967. Commd. 2d. lt. USAF, 1966, advanced through grades to lt. gen., 1998; pilot McGuire AFB, N.J., 1968-70; rescue helicopter pilot Bergstrom AFB, Tex., 1970-71, Bien Hoa Air Base, South Vietnam, 1971, Udorn Royal Thai AFB, Thailand, 1971-72; instr. pilot Hill AFB, Utah, 1972-74; various assignments Aeronautical Sys. Ctr. Wright-Patterson AFB, Ohio, 1975-82, 88-96; comdr. Aeronautical Sys. Ctr. Wright-Patterson AFB, 1998—; various assignments The Pentagon, Washington, 1983-87, 96-98; exec. officer to comdr. Air Force Sys. Ctr. Andrews AFB, Md., 1987-88. Decorated D.S.M., Legion of Merit with oak leaf cluster, Air medal with oak leaf cluster, Meritorious Svc. medal with two oak leaf clusters, Vietnam Svc. medal with three svc. stars, Rep. of Vietnam Gallantry Cross with Palm. Home: 9401 David Andrew Way Dayton OH 45458-3644

RAGLAND, TERRY EUGENE, emergency physician; b. Greensboro, NC, June 14, 1944; s. Terry Porter and Virginia Lucile (Stowe) R.; m. Marguerite Elizabeth Morton, May 15, 1976; children: Kenneth John McConnell, Ryan Lee Ragland. BS, Cen. Mich. U., 1966; MD, U. Mich., 1970. Diplomate Am. Bd. Internal Medicine. Intern St. Joseph Mercy Hosp., Ann Arbor, Mich., 1970-71, internal medicine resident, 1974-77, chief resident internal medicine, 1975-76, emergency physician, 1977-2001, med. dir. emergency ctr., 1985-97, chief of staff, 1996-97, assoc. dir. dept. emergency svcs., 1997-2000; CEO Secure Care, Inc., 1992—2003; pres. Huron Valley Phys. Assn., 1997-2000. Clin. asst. prof. U. Mich., Ann Arbor, 1981—2002; examiner Am. Bd. Emergency Medicine, 1983—2001; med. dir. Life Support Svcs., Ann Arbor, 1983—92; mem. Mercy Health Plans Bd., 1999—2000; mem. sci. adv. com. Ecology Ctr./Mich. Environ. Coun., 2001—03; chmn. adv. bd. Coll. Health Professions Ctrl. Mich. U., 2001—04. Contbr. chapters to books. Trustee Ann Arbor Twp. Bd., 2002—. Lt. USN, 1972—74. Nat. Assn. Emergency Med. Technicians, Mich. State Med. Soc. (alt. del. 1982-84, 89-90, del. 1991-94, mem. jud. commn. 1999—), Mich. Emergency Med. Technicians Assn., Washtenaw County Med. Soc. (pres. 1993). Democrat. Avocations: trout fishing, gardening, skiing.

RAHMAN, YUEH-ERH, biologist; b. Kwangtung, China, June 10, 1928; came to U.S., 1960; d. Khon and Kwei-Phan (Chan) Li; m. Aneesur Rahman, Nov. 3, 1956; 1 dau., Aneesa. BS, U. Paris, 1950; MD magna cum laude, U. Louvain, Belgium, 1956. Clin. and postdoctoral research fellow Louvain U., 1956-60; mem. staff Argonne (Ill.) Nat. Lab., 1960-72, biologist, 1972-81, sr. biologist, 1981-85; prof. pharmaceutics Coll. Pharmacy, U. Minn., Mpls., 1985—2002, prof. emeritus, 2002—, dir. grad. studies, pharmaceutics, 1989-92, head dept. pharmaceutics, 1991-96, 97-98. Vis. scientist State U. Utrecht, Netherlands, 1968-69; adj. prof. No. Ill. U., DeKalb, 1971-85; cons. NIH.; Mem. com. of rev. group, div. research grants NIH, 1979-83 Author; patentee in field. Recipient IR-100 award, 1976; grantee Nat. Cancer Inst., Nat. Inst. Arthritis, Metabolic and Digestive Diseases. Fellow Am. Assn. Pharm. Scientists; mem. AAAS, Am. Soc. Cell Biology, N.Y. Acad. Scis., Radiation Rsch. Soc., Assn. for Women in Sci. (1st pres. Chgo. area chpt. 1978-79). Unitarian Universalist. Home: 939 Coast Blvd Unit 6G La Jolla CA 92037-4115

RAICHLE, MARCUS EDWARD, radiology and neurology educator; b. Hoquiam, Wash., Mar. 15, 1937; m. Mary Elizabeth Rupert, 1964; children: Marcus Edward, Timothy Stephen, Sarah Elizabeth, Katherine Ann. BS, U. Wash., 1960, MD, 1964. Diplomate Am. Bd. Psychiatry and Neurology. Intern Balt. City Hosps., 1964—65, resident, 1965—66; asst. neurologist N.Y. Hosp. Cornell Med. Ctr., NYC, 1966—68, neurologist, chief resident, 1968—69; clin. instr. dept. medicine divsn. neurosci. U. Tex. Med. Sch., San Antonio, 1969—70; rsch. instr. Washington U. Sch. Med., St. Louis, 1971—72, from asst. prof. neurology to assoc. prof. neurology, 1972—78, from asst. prof. radiology (radiation scis.) to assoc. prof. radiology Edward Mallinckrodt Inst. Radiology, 1972—79, from asst. prof. to assoc. prof. biomedical engring., 1974-79, prof. neurology, 1978—, prof. radiology Edward Mallinckrodt Inst. Radiology, 1979—, prof. biomedical engring., 1979—; and prof. psychology Washington Univ., St. Louis, 2000—. Instr. dept. neurology Cornell U. Med. Coll., NYC, 1968—69; asst. neurologist Barnes Hosp., St. Louis, 1971—75, assoc. neurologist, 1975—78, neurologist, 1978—; cons. neurologist St. Louis Children's Hosp., 1975—; neurologist Jewish Hosp., St. Louis, 1984—, St. Louis Regional Hosp., St. Louis, 1984—; mem. neurology study sect. A NIH, 1975—79; mem. com. cerebrovascular diseases Nat. Inst. Neurol. Diseases and Stroke, long range planning effort, 1978, basic sci. task force, 78; mem ad hoc adv. panel Nat. Inst. Neurol. Diseases and Stroke, 1983, chmn. PET grants spl. rev. com., 83, chmn. brain imaging ctrs. spl. rev. com., 85; mem. adv. bd. McDonnell-Pew Program cognitive neuroscience, 1989; other coms. Mem. editl. bd.: Stroke, 1982, Neurology, 1976—82, Annals of Neurology, 1979—86, Brain, 1985—90, Journal Cerebral Blood Flow and Metabolism, 1983—86, dep. chief editor:, 1981—83, mem. editl. bd.: Human Neurobiology, 1985—87, Brain Rsch., 1985—90, Synapse, 1987—90, Jour. Neurosci., 1989—95, Jour. Cognitive Neurosci., 1989—, Cerebral Cortex, 1990—, Jour. Nuclear Medicine, 1990—96. Maj. USAF, 1969—71. Recipient umerous awards, lectrs., fellows including Charles A. Dana award for pioneering achievements in health and edn., Dana Found., 1996. Fellow: Am. Assn. Advancement of Sci.; mem.: NAS, Inst. Medicine of NAS.

RAIKES, RONALD E., state legislator; b. Lincoln, Mar. 11, 1943; m. Helen Holz, Dec. 26, 1966; children: Heather, Abbie, Justin. BS in Farm Operation, Iowa State U.; MS in Agr. Bus., U. Calif., Davis, PhD in Agr. Econ. Former assoc. prof. dept. econs. Iowa State U.; farmer, cattle feeder, soil conservation contractor; mem. Nebr. Legislature from 25th dist., Lincoln, 1997, 98—. Mem. Nebr. Econ. Forecasting Adv. Bd., 1983-87. Mem. Nebr. Farm Bus. Assn., Nebr. Land Improvement Contractors Assn., Nebr. Agr. Rels. Coun., Agr. Builders Nebr. Home: 3221 S 76th St Lincoln NE 68506-4612 Office: State Capitol Dist 25 PO Box 94604 Rm 1008 Lincoln NE 68509-4604

RAILSBACK, MIKE, radio personality; b. St. Joseph, Mo., Mar. 16, 1958; m. Linda Railsback; children: Paul, Don. BS Agrl. Bus., Northwest Mo. State U. Radio host WDAF/61 Country, Westwood, Kans., 1989—. Office: WDAF/61 Country 4935 Belinder Rd Westwood KS 66205

RAILTON, PETER ALBERT, philosophy educator; b. Elgin, Ill., May 23, 1950; s. Arthur Roy and Marjorie Elizabeth Marks Railton; m. Rebecca Jarvis Scott, Apr. 21, 1978; children: John Scott-Railton, Thomas Scott-Railton. AB magna cum laude, Harvard U., 1971; PhD, Princeton U., 1980. From asst. prof. philosophy to assoc. prof. U. Mich., Ann Arbor, 1979—90, prof. philosophy, 1990—, Nelson prof., 1999—2001, Perrin Collegiate prof., 2001—, dept. chair, 2002—05. Vis. prof. U. Calif., Berkeley, 1984-85, Princeton (N.J.) U., 1990; mem. Coun. for Philos. Studies, N.Y.C., 1992-94; rsch. assoc. Ecole Poly., Paris, 1995—, CSMN, U. Oslo. Co-editor, author: Moral Discourse and Practice, 1997; author: Facts, Values and Norms, 2003; mem. editl. bd.: Ethics, Utilitas; contbr. articles to profl. jours. Am. Coun. Learned Socs. fellow, 1988-89, 2000, NEH fellow, 1999, Guggenheim fellow, 2001-2002, Am. Acad. Arts and Scis. fellow, 2004—. Mem. Am. Philos. Assn. (various coms. 1978—), Am. Soc. for Polit. and Legal Philosophy, Philosophy of Scis. Assn. (com. mem. 1978—), Soc. for Philosophy and Psychology, Mich. Soc. Fellows (jr. fellow 1979-82, sr. fellow 2005-). Office: U Mich Dept Philosophy 2215 Angell Hall Ann Arbor MI 48109 Office Phone: 734-764-6285.

RAINS, M. NEAL, lawyer; b. Burlington, Iowa, July 26, 1943; s. Merritt and Lucille Rains; children: Robert Baldwin, Kathleen Kellogg. BA in Polit. Sci. with honors, U. Iowa, 1965; JD, Northwestern U., 1968. Bar: Ohio 1968. Assoc. Arter & Hadden, Cleve., 1968-76, ptnr., 1976—2001, mem. exec. com., 1981-90, Cleve. mng. ptnr., 1990-92; ptnr. Frantz Ward LLP, Cleve., 2001—. Lectr. on profl. topics, including alternative dispute resolution, distbn. law, litigation practice and procedure, and antitrust. Contbr. articles to profl. jours. With U.S. Army, 1968-70 Fellow: Am. Bar Found.; mem.: ABA, William K. Thomas Am. Inn Ct. (pres. 1999—2000), Cleve. Bar Found. (pres. 2005—07), Cleve. Bar Assn. (v.p. 2007—), Ohio State Bar Assn., Rowfant Club, Union Club, City Club, Print Club, Phi Delta Phi, Omicron Delta Kappa, Phi Beta Kappa. Office: Frantz Ward LLP 2500 Key Ctr 127 Public Sq Cleveland OH 44114 Home: 29409 Hummingbird Circle Westlake OH 44145 Office Phone: 216-515-1660. Business E-Mail: nrains@frantzward.com.

RAINSON, RONALD LEE, engineering executive, consultant; b. NYC, May 20, 1940; s. E.G. and D.E. (Burke) R.; m. Patricia J. Zugay, Aug. 29; children: Athena, Felicia, Erica. BSEE, Lawrence Inst. Tech., 1966, BS in Indsl. Mgmt., 1969. Registered profl. engr., Mich., Ohio, Vt., Ill. Project chief Bendix Corp., Southfield, Mich., 1970—72; gen. mgr. Holland PBW, Mich., 1972—75; pres. E. Ky. Power, Lexington, 1975—80; v.p. Ctrl. Ill. Light Co., Peoria, 1980—88; pres., CEO, chmn. bd. dirs. Environ. Sci. & Engring., Peoria, 1988—. Dir. Breeder Reactor Corp., Ky. Ctr. for Energy Rsch., NERC. Mem. Gov.'s Ill. Econ. Tech. Adv. Com., Gov.'s Task Force on Utility Regulation. Recipient Ann. Alumni award, Lawrence Tech., 1977. Mem.: IEEE (sr.), Freemasons, Tau Beta Pi. Republican. Office: Environ Sci & Engring Inc 8901 N Industrial Rd Peoria IL 61615-1509

RAINWATER, GARY L., electric power industry executive; BSEE, U. Mo., Columbia; M of Systems Mgmt., U. So. Calif. Engr. electric transmission and distbn. Union Electric Co. (now Ameren Corp.), v.p. corp. planning, 1993—97; exec. v.p. Ameren CIPS, 1997, pres., CEO, 1997—2001, Ameren CILCO, 2000—01; pres., COO Ameren Corp., St. Louis, 2001—04, chmn., pres., CEO, 2004—. Mem. dean's adv. coun. U. Mo. Sch. Engring.; mem. adv. coun. engring. mgmt. and engring. tech. Washington U.; bd. dirs. AmerenUE, Ameren CILCO, Ameren CIPS and other Ameren subs., Mo. Hist. Soc., St. Louis USO, Ill. Energy Assn., Urban League Met. St. Louis, US Bank. Recipient Mo. Honor award for disting. svc. in engring., U. Mo.-Columbia Coll. Engring., 2000. Mem.: Engrs.' Club (Knight of St. Patrick 2000). Office: Ameren 1901 Chouteau Saint Louis MO 63166-6149

RAJAN, FRED E. N., clergy member, church administrator; Exec. dir. Commn. for Multicultural Ministries of the Evangelical Lutheran Church in America, Chicago, Ill., 1992. Office: Evangelical Lutheran Church Am 8765 W Higgins Rd Chicago IL 60631-4101

RAJURKAR, KAMLAKAR PURUSHOTTAM, mechanical engineering educator; b. India, Jan. 6, 1942; came to U.S., 1975; s. Purushottam S. and Indira P. Rajurkar; m. Sanjivani K. Natu, Feb. 3, 1972; children: Piyush, Suneela. B.Sc., Vikram U., India, 1962, B.Engring. with honors, 1966; M.S., Mich. Tech. U., 1978, Ph.D., 1982. Lectr. mech. engring. Govt. Poly., Bhopal, India, 1966-75; grad. teaching and research asst. Mich. Tech. U., Houghton, 1975-81, asst. prof., 1981-83; assoc. prof. U. Nebr., Lincoln, 1983-88; Mohr prof. engring. and dir. ontraditional Mfg. Rsch. Ctr., 1988-2002, disting. prof. engring., 2003—; Contbr. to profl. jours. Fellow ASME (Blackall Machine Tool and Gage award 1995), Soc. Mfg. Engrs.; mem. Internat. Inst. Prodn. Rsch., Tau Beta Pi. Home: 7308 Skyhawk Cir Lincoln NE 68506-4659 Office: University of Nebraska 175 ebraska Hall Lincoln NE 68588-0158 E-mail: krajurkar1@unl.edu.

RAKOLTA, JOHN, JR., construction executive; b. Detroit, May 26, 1947; BSCE, Marquette U. Design engr. Bendix Machine Tool; mem. sr. staff aerospace sector engring. Allied Signal; chmn., CEO Walbridge Aldinger Co., Detroit. Mem. NAACP, Automotive Industry Action Group (bd. dirs.), Detroit Urban League, Engring. Soc. Detroit. Office: Walbridge Aldinger 613 Abbott St Ste 300 Detroit MI 48226-2521

RALPH, DAMANI, professional soccer player; b. Kingston, Jamaica, Nov. 6, 1980; Attended, Merdian Cmty. Coll., Miss., 1999—2001, U. Conn., 2001—03. Forward, men's soccer Meridian Cmty. Coll., 1999—2001, U. Conn., 2001—03; forward DC United Major League Soccer, Washington, 2004—. Named MVP, Nat. Junior Coll. Athletic Assn. Tournament, 2000, Offensive Player of Yr., Big East, 2002; named to First Team, Big East, 2002; recipient Finalist, Hermann Trophy, MO Athletic Commn., 2002. Achievements include team leader in goals scored (10) and points (26) for men's soccer at the U. Conn. in 2001. Office: Soldier Stadium 425 E McFetridge Dr Chicago IL 60605

RALSTON, RICHARD H., lawyer; b. LA, Sept. 28, 1942; BA, U. Kans., 1965; JD, U. Mo., Kansas City, 1969. Bar: Mo. 1969, U.S. Dist. Ct. (we. dist.) Mo., U.S. Ct. Appeals (8th cir.). Law clerk to Hon. Elmo B. Hunter U.S. Dist. Ct. (we. dist.) Mo., 1968-72, U.S. magistrate judge, 1976-88; prof. law Creighton U., 1972-76; mem. Polsinelli, White, Vardeman & Shalton, Kansas City, Mo., 1976—. Adj. prof. law U. Mo. Kansas City, 1977-79; chmn. subcom. on patterned civil jury instructions U.S. Ct. Appeals (8th cir.), 1986—. Editor-in-chief U. Mo. Kansas City Law Rev., 1968-69; contbr. articles to profl. jours. Mem. ABA (chmn. state membership com. 1988—), Mo. Bar (chmn. fed. practice com. 1988-92), Kansas City Met. Bar Assn. (exec. com. 1991-95), Ross T. Roberts Inn Ct. (master 1986-91), Phi Delta Phi.

RAMALINGAM, SUBBIAH, mechanical engineer, educator; MS in Mech. Engring., U. Ill., Urbana-Champaign, 1961, PhD, 1967. Prof. mech. engring. U. Minn., Mpls. Contbr. articles to profl. jours. Mem. NAE. Achievements include research in modeling thin films for tribological applications, intelligent sensors, real-time sensing for manufacturing automation, tribology, thin-film deposition processes and coating technology, machining theory, metal forming and manufacturing automation. Office: U Minn Engring Inst Tech 111 Church St SE Minneapolis MN 55455-0111

RAMDAS, ANANT KRISHNA, physicist, optics scientist; b. Poona, India, May 19, 1930; married, 1956. BSc, U. Poona, India, 1950, MSc, 1953, PhD in Physics, 1956. Rsch. assoc. physics, 1956-60; from asst. prof. to assoc. prof., 1960-67; prof. physics Purdue U., Lafayette, Ind., 1967—2002, Lark-Horovitz disting. prof. physics, 2002—. Alexander von Humboldt U.S. sr. scientist, 1977-78. Fellow Am. Physical Soc. (Frank Isakson prize 1994), Indian Acad. Sci., Optical Soc. Am., Third World Acad. Scis., Am. Vaccuum Soc. Achievements include research in spectroscopy; application of spectroscopic techniques to solid state physics; electronic and vibrational spectra of solids studied by absorption and emission spectra in the visible and the infrared and by Raman and Brillouin spectroscopy. Office: Purdue U Dept Physics West Lafayette IN 47907 Office Phone: 765-494-3028. Business E-Mail: akr@physics.purdue.edu.

RAMER, JAMES LEROY, civil engineer; b. Marshalltown, Iowa, Dec. 7, 1935; s. LeRoy Frederick and Irene (Wengert) Ramer; m. Jacqueline L. Orr, Dec. 15, 1957; children: Sarah T., Robert H., Eric A., Susan L. Student, U. Iowa, Iowa City, 1953-57; MCE, Washington U., St. Louis, 1976, MA in Polit. Sci., 1978; postgrad., U. Mo., Columbia, 1984—. Registered profl. engr., land surveyor. Civil and constrn. engr. US Army C.E., Tulsa, 1960-63; civil and relocations engr. US State Dept., Del Rio, Tex., 1964; project engr. H.B. Zachary Co., San Antonio, 1965-66; civil and constrn. engr. US Army C.E., St. Louis, 1967-76, tech. advisor for planning and nat. hydropower coord., 1976-78; project mgr. for EPA constrn. grants Milw., 1978-80; chief arch. and engring. HUD, Indpls., 1980-81; civil design and pavements engr. Whiteman AFB, Mo., 1982-86; project mgr. maintenance, 1993—; soil and pavements engr. Hdqrs. Mil. Airlift Command, Scott AFB, Ill., 1986-88. Project mgr. AF-1 maintenance hangar; cattle and grain farmer, 1982—; pvt. practice civil-mech. engr., constrn. mgmt., estimating, cost analysis, cash flow, project scheduling, expert witness, profl. land surveying, Fortuna, Mo., 1988—2001; chief constrn. inspector divsn. design and constrn. State of Mo., 1992—93; project engr. Mil. Housing, 2001—; adj. faculty civil engring. Washington U., 1968—78, U. Wis., Milw., 1978—80, Ga. Mil. Coll., Whiteman AFB, Longview Coll., Kansas City; adj. rsch. engr. U. Mo., Columbia, 1985—86; project engr., quality control officer Korte Constrn. Co. Mem.: AAUP, NSPE, ASCE, Soc. Am. Mil. Engrs., Optimists Internat. Lutheran. Achievements include patents for in diverse art, 9 copyrights; development of solar waterstill, deep shaft hydropower concept. Office Phone: 660-882-9444. Business E-Mail: jlramer@iland.net.

RAMEY, DENNY L., bar association executive director; b. Portsmouth, Ohio, Feb. 22, 1947; s. Howard Leroy and Norma Wylodine (Richards) R.; m. Jeannine Gayle Dunmyer, Sept. 24, 1971 (div. Nov. 1991); children: Elizabeth Michelle, Brian Michael. BBA, Ohio U., 1970; MBA, Capital U., 1976. Cert. assn. exec. Adminstrv. mgr. Transit Warehouse div. Elston Richards Storage Co., Columbus, Ohio, 1970-73; mgr. continuing profl. edn. Ohio Soc. CPA's, Columbus, 1973-79; exec. dir. Engrs. Found. of Ohio, Columbus, 1979-80; asst. exec. Ohio State Bar Assn., Columbus, 1980-86, exec. dir., sec., treas., 1986—. Treas., exec. com., bd. dirs. Ohio Bar Liability Ins. Co., Columbus, 1986—; treas. Ohio State Bar Found., 1986—; treas. Ohio Legal Ctr. Ins., Columbus, 1988-91; sec. Ohio Printing Co., Ltd., 1991; v.p. Osbanet, Inc., 1993—; chmn. Lawriter LLC, 2000—; bd. dirs. OSBA.com, LLC. Mem.: Ohio Soc. Assn. Execs., Am. Soc. Assn. Execs., Nat. Assn. Bar Execs., Scioto Country Club. Methodist. Avocations: golf, sports, music, art. Office: Ohio State Bar Assn 1700 Lake Shore Dr PO Box 16562 Columbus OH 43216-6562 Office Phone: 614-487-4405. Business E-Mail: dramey@ohiobar.org.

RAMIREZ, ARAMIS, professional baseball player; b. Santo Domingo, Dominican Republic, June 25, 1978; Third baseman Pittsburgh Pirates, 1998—2003, Chicago Cubs, 2003—. Named to Nat. League All-Star Team, 2005. Office: Chicago Cubs 1060 W Addison St Chicago IL 60613

RAMMES, LISA M., lawyer; b. Dayton, Ohio, Mar. 4, 1969; BA, Miami U., 1991; JD, U. Cin., 1996. Bar: Ohio 1996, US Dist. Ct. Southern Dist. Ohio 1997. Atty. Wood & Lamping LLP, Cin., 1996—. Mem., Bd. Dirs. CancerFree Kids Pediatric Cancer Rsch. Alliance, mem., Bd. Advisors. Named one of Ohio's Rising Stars, Super Lawyers, 2006. Mem.: Ohio State Bar Assn., Cin. Bar Assn. Office: Wood & Lamping LLP 600 Vine St Ste 2500 Cincinnati OH 45202-2491 Office Phone: 513-852-6000. Office Fax: 513-852-6087.

RAMPERSAD, PEGGY A. SNELLINGS, sociologist, consultant; b. Fredericksburg, Va., Jan. 12, 1933; d. George Daniel and Virginia Riley (Bowler) Snellings; m. Oliver Ronald Rampersad, Mar. 19, 1955; 1 child, Gita. BA, Mary Washington Coll., Fredericksburg, 1953; student, Sch. Art Inst. Chgo., 1953—55; MA, U. Chgo., 1965, PhD, 1978. Grad. admissions counselor U. Chgo., 1954—57, adviser fgn. students, 1958, dir. admissions Grad. Sch. Bus., 1958—63, rsch. project specialist, 1970—78, pers. mgr., 1979—80, mgr. orgnl. devel., 1980—82, adminstr. dept. econs., 1983—95; cons. PSR Consulting, Chgo., 1995—. Cons. North Ctrl. Assn. Colls. and Secondary Schs., Chgo., 1964—70, Orchestral Assn. Chgo. Symphony Orch., 1982, Chgo. Ctr. Decision Rsch., 1982, Harvard U., 1993—97. Exhibitions include Va. Mus. Fine Arts, Art Inst. Chgo., others; editor: North Ctrl. Assn. Quar., 1972; contbr. articles to profl. jours. Grad. fellow, U. Chgo., 1963—67. Mem.: AAUW, Am. Acad. Polit. and Social Sci., Am. Econ. Assn., Art Inst. Chgo. (assoc.), Pi Lambda Theta (past pres.). Episcopalian. Avocations: painting, drawing, opera, reading, walking. Home and Office: 28 Seneca Ter Fredericksburg VA 22401-1115

RAMPONE, CHRISTIE P., professional soccer player; b. Broward County, Fla., June 24, 1975; m. Chris Rampone, Nov. 9, 2001. BS in spl. edn., Monmouth U., NJ, 1997. Mem. .Y. Power, WUSA, 2001—; soccer player, defender U.S. Women's Nat. Team, 1997, mem. World Cup championship team, 1999. Founding player N.Y. Power, WUSA, 2001. Named First Team All-Mid-Atlantic Region, 1995, 1996, Player of Yr., N.E. Conf., 1995, 1996.

RAMSEY, JAMIE M., lawyer; b. Ft. Thomas, Ky., Mar. 14, 1974; BS, Northern Ky. U., 1996; JD, Salmon P. Chase Coll. Law, Northern Ky. U., 1999. Bar: Ohio 1999, US Dist. Ct. Southern Dist. Ohio 1999, Ky. 2000, US Dist. Ct. Eastern Dist. Ky. 2000, US Ct. of Appeals Sixth Cir. 2001, US Dist. Ct. Western Dist. Ky. 2003, US Tax Ct. 2004, US Supreme Ct. 2005. Ptnr. Keating Muething & Klekamp PLL, Cin. Former sec., treasurer Kenton County Dem. Party; mem., bd. dirs. Children's Law Ctr. Named one of Ohio's Rising Stars, Super Lawyers, 2005, 2006. Mem.: Northern Ky. U. Alumni Assn. (bd. mem., former pres.), Northern Ky. Bar Assn., Ohio State Bar Assn., Ky. Bar Assn., Cin. Bar Assn., ABA. Office: Keating Muething & Klekamp PLL One E Fourth St Ste 1400 Cincinnati OH 45202 Office Phone: 513-639-3928. Office Fax: 513-579-6457.

RAMSEY-GOLDMAN, ROSALIND, physician; b. NYC, Mar. 22, 1954; d. Abraham L. and Miriam (Colen) Goldman; m. Glenn Ramsey, June 29,1 975; children: Ethan Ramsey, Caitlin Ramsey. BA, Case We. Res. U., 1975, MD, 1978; MPH, U. Pitts., 1988, DPH, 1992. Med. resident U. Rochester, NY, 1978—81; chief resident Rochester Gen. Hosp., 1981—82; staff physician U. Health Svc., Rochester, 1982—83; rheumatology fellow U. Pitts., 1983—86, instr. medicine, 1986—87, asst. prof., 1987—91, co-dir. Lupus Treatment and Diagnostic Ctr., 1987—91; asst. prof. medicine Northwestern U., Chgo., 1991—96, assoc. prof. medicine, 1996—2001, prof. medicine, 2001—. Dir. Chgo. Lupus Registry, Northwestern U., Chgo., 1991—, chairperson Systemic Lupus Internat. Collaborating Clinics Group, 2003—; program dir. Gen. Clin. Rsch. Ctr. at NCRR/NIH, 2005— Contbr. rsch. articles to profl. jours. Recipient Finkelstein award Hershey (Pa.) Med. Ctr., 1986. Fellow ACP, Am. Coll. Rheumatology; mem. Soc. for Epidemiologic Rsch., Ctrl. Soc. Clin. Rsch. Office: Northwestern U Feinberg Sch Medicine McGaw Pavilion 240 E Huron Ste M-300 Chicago IL 60611 Office Phone: 312-503-8003. Business E-Mail: rgramsey@northwestern.edu.

RAMSTAD, JAMES, congressman, lawyer; b. Jamestown, ND, May 6, 1946; s. Marvin Joseph and Della Mae (Fode) Ramstad. BA, U. Minn., 1968; JD with honors, George Washington U., 1973. Bar: ND 1973, DC 1973, Minn. 1979, admitted to practice: US Supreme Ct. 1976. Adminstrv. asst. to Lt. Duxbury Minn. Ho. Reps., 1969, spl. asst. to Congressman Tom Kleppe, 1970; pvt. practice law Jamestown, 1973, Washington, 1974—78, Mpls., 1978—90; asst. campaign mgr. for Congressman William E. Frenzel US Ho. Reps., 1978; mem. Minn. Senate, 1981—90, asst. minority leader, 1983—87; mem. US Congress from 3rd Minn. dist., 1991—. Adj. prof. Am. U., Washington, 1975—78. Bd. dir. D.A.R.E., Minn., Children's Heart Fund, Lake Country Food Bank; mem. C. of C., Twin West, Wayzata, North Metro. 1st lt. USAR, 1968—74. Named Representative of Yr., Nat. Assn. of Police Organizations, 1997, 2000, Legislator of Yr., Nat. Assn. of Alcoholism and Drug Addiction Counselors, 1998, Nat. Mental Health Assn., 1999; recipient Fulbright Disting. Pub. Service award. Mem.: Hennepin County Bar Assn., ND Bar Assn., DC Bar Assn., Minn. Bar Assn., Minn. Prayer Breakfast Com., Plymouth Lions Club, U. Minn. Alumni Assn., Am. Legion, Phi Delta Theta, Phi Beta Kappa. Republican. Office: US Ho Reps 103 Cannon Ho Office Bldg Washington DC 20515-2303

RAMUNDO, KIMBERLY E., lawyer; b. Covington, Ky., Dec. 23, 1971; BA, Miami U., 1993; JD, U. Cin., 1996. Bar: Ohio 1996, US Dist. Ct. Southern Dist. Ohio 1998, US Ct. of Appeals Sixth Cir. 2001, Ky. 2002, US Dist. Ct. Eastern Dist. Ky. 2002; cert. Constrn. Industry Technician. Ptnr. Thompson Hine LLP, Cin. Mem., Bd. Dirs., sec. Tallstacks Music Arts & Heritage Festival. Named Rising Star, YWCA, 2003; named one of Ohio's Rising Stars, Super Lawyers, 2006. Mem.: Ky. Bar Assn., Ohio Bar Assn., Cin. Bar Assn., ABA, Nat. Assn. Women in Constrn., Cin. Acad. Leadership for Lawyers. Office: Thompson Hine LLP 312 Walnut St 14th Fl Cincinnati OH 45202-4089 Office Phone: 513-352-6656. Office Fax: 513-241-4771.

RAN, SHULAMIT, composer; b. Tel Aviv, Oct. 21, 1949; U.S. m. Abraham Lotan, 1986. Studied composition with, Paul Ben-Haim, Norman Dello, Joio, Ralph Shapey; student, Mannes Coll. Music, NYC, 1963—67. With dept. music U. Chgo., 1973—, William H. Colvin prof. music; composer-in-residence Chgo. Symphony Orch., 1990—97, Lyric Opera of Chgo., 1994—97. Compositions include 10 Children's Scenes, 1967, Structures, 1968, 7 Japanese Love Poems, 1968, Hatzvi Israel Eulogy, 1969, O the Chimneys, 1969, Concert Piece for piano and orch., 1970, 3 Fantasy Pieces for Cello and Piano, 1972, Ensembles for 17, 1975, Double Vision, 1976, Hyperbolae for Piano, 1976, For an Actor: Monologue for Clarinet, 1978, Apprehensions, 1979, Private Game, 1979, Fantasy-Variations for Cello, 1980, A Prayer, 1982, Verticals for piano, 1982, String Quartet No. 1, 1984, (for woodwind quintet) Concerto da Camera I, 1985, Amichai Songs, 1985, Concerto for Orchestra, 1986, (for clarinet, string quartet and piano) Concerto da Camera II, 1987, East Wind, 1987, String Quartet No. 2, 1988—89, Symphony, 1989—90, Mirage, 1990, Inscriptions for solo violin, 1991, Chicago Skyline for brass and percussion, 1991, Legends for orch., 1992—93, Invocation, 1994, Yearning for violin and string orch., 1995, (opera) Between Two Worlds (The Dybbuk), 1995—97, Soliloquy, 1997, Vessels of Courage and Hope for orch., 1998, (flute concerto) Voices, 2000, Three Scenes for solo clarinet, 2000, Supplications for chorus and orch., 2002, Violin Concerto, 2003, commd. pieces include for Am. Composers Orch., Phila. Orch., Chgo. Symphony, Balt. Symphony, Chamber Soc. of Lincoln Ctr., Mendelssohn String quartet, Da Capo Chamber Players, Sta. WFMT, Lyric Opera Chgo., composer and soloist for 1st performances Capariccio, 1963, Symphonic Poem, 1967, Concert Piece, 1971. Named Guggenheim fellow, 1977, 1990; recipient Acad. Inst. Arts and Letters award, 1989, Pulitzer prize for music, 1991, Friedheim award for orchestral music, Kennedy Ctr., 1992. Office: U Chgo Dept Music 1010 E 59th St Chicago IL 60637-1512

RANCOURT, JAMES DANIEL, optical engineer; b. Maine; BA in Physics, Bowdoin Coll., 1963; MS in Physics, Carnegie Tech., 1965; PhD in Optical Scis., U. Ariz., 1974. Engr. Itek Corp., Lexington, Mass., 1965-69; rsch. assoc. U. Ariz., Tucson, 1969-74; engr. OCLI, Santa Rosa, Calif., 1974-95, chief scientist, 1996-97; dir. product devel. Guardian Industries Corp., Carleton, Mich., 1997—. Author: Optical Thin Films Users Handbook, 1987; patentee in field. Fellow Optical Soc. Am. Achievements include 13 patents. Office: Guardian Industries 14511 Romine Rd Carleton MI 48117-9706

RAND, KATHY SUE, public relations executive, consultant; b. Miami Beach, Fla., Feb. 24, 1945; d. William R. and Rose (Lasser) R.; m. Peter C. Ritsos, Feb. 19, 1982. BA, Mich. State U., 1965; MBA, Northwestern U., 1980. Asst. editor Lyons & Carnahan, Chgo., 1967-68; mng. editor Cahners Pub. Co., Chgo., 1968-71; pub. rels. writer Super Market Inst., Chgo., 1972-73; account supr. Pub. Communications Inc., Chgo., 1973-77; divisional mgr. pub. rels. Quaker Oats Co., Chgo., 1977-82; exec. v.p., dep. gen. mgr. Golin/Harris Communications, Chgo., 1982-90; exec. v.p. Lesnik Pub. Rels., Northbrook, Ill., 1990-91; mng. dir. Manning, Selvage & Lee, Chgo., 1991—2002; public rels. cons., 2002—. Dir. midwest region NOW, 1972-74; mem. Kellogg Alumni Adv. Bd.; bd. dirs. Jr. Achievement of Chgo. Mem. Pub. Rels. Soc. Am. (Silver Anvil award 1986, 87), Pub. Club Chgo. (Golden Trumpet awards 1982-87, 90, 94, 95, 97, 98, 99, 00), Vet. Feminists of Am. (bd. dirs., v.p. pub. rels.), Northwestern Club Chgo., Kellogg Alumni Club, Beta Gamma Sigma. Home: 400 Riverwoods Rd Lake Forest IL 60045-2547 Personal E-mail: ksrand@aol.com.

RAND, LEON, academic administrator; b. Boston, Oct. 8, 1930; s. Max B. and Ricka (Muscanto) Rakisky; m. Marian L. Newton, Aug. 29, 1959; children: Debra Ruth, Paul Martin, Marta Leah. BS, Northeastern U., 1953; MA, U. Tex., 1956, PhD, 1958. Postdoctoral fellow Purdue U., 1958-59; asst. prof. to prof. U. Detroit, 1959-68; prof., chmn. dept. chemistry Youngstown (Ohio) State U., 1968-74, dean grad. studies and research, 1974-81, acting acad. v.p., 1980; vice chancellor acad. affairs U. N.C., Pembroke, 1981—85; chancellor Ind. U.-S.E., New Albany, 1986-96; chancellor emeritus Ind. U., 1996—, prof. emeritus, 1999—; spl. asst. to chancellor IUPUI, 1996-98. Bd. dirs. Floyd Meml. Hosp., New Albany, 1987—90, Jewish Hosp., Louisville, 1991—96. Bd. dirs., mem. exec. com. Louisville (Ind.) area chpt. ARC; docent Indpls. Mus. Art, 1998—. Mem.: Metroversity (bd. dirs.), Am. Inst. Chemists, Am. Chem. Soc., Sigma Xi, Phi Kappa Phi. Home: 1785 Arrowwood Dr Carmel IN 46033-9019 E-mail: LRand7658@sbcglobal.net.

RAND, PETER ANDERS, architect; b. Hibbing, Minn., Jan. 8, 1944; s. Sidney Anders and Dorothy Alice (Holm) R.; m. Nancy Ann Straus, Oct. 21, 1967; children: Amy, Dorothy. BA, St. Olaf Coll., 1966; cert., Oslo Internat. Summer Sch., Norway, 1964, U. Minn. Sch. Architecture, 1969-72. Registered architect, Minn. Designer, architect, dir. pub. rels. Setter, Leach & Lindstrom, Inc., Mpls., 1972-78; dir. bus. devel, head Eden Prairie (Minn.) office Archtl. Design Group, Inc., 1979-80; dir. mktg. and publs. Minn. Soc. AIA, 1981-82, exec. dir., 1982-85, exec. v.p., CEO, 1986-98, v.p., 1999; exec. v.p. Minnesota Arch. Found. Pub. Architecture Minn. mag.; bd. dirs. MSAADA Architects & Engrs.; cons., archtl. designer. Bd. dirs. Project for Pride in Living, 1979-88, chmn., 1980-86; trustee Bethlehem Luth. Ch., 1980-86, chmn. bd. trustees, 1985, chmn. com. on worship, 1993-96, mem. ch. coun., 1993-96; mem. Minn. Ch. Ctr. Commn., 1981-89, chmn., 1985-88; sec. Coun. Archtl. Component Execs. of AIA, 1987, 92, pres., 1997-98; bd. dirs. Minn. Coun. Chs., 1985-89, sec., 1989; bd. dirs. Mpls. Coun. Chs., 1985-88; bd. dirs. Arts Midwest, 1987-96, treas., 1989, v.p., 1990-91, chmn., 1992-93; bd. dirs. Nordic Ctr., Preservation Alliance Minn., 1995. Served with U.S. Army, 1966-69. Fellow AIA (jour. honor awrd 1981, Nat. Svc. award 1993); mem. Minn. Soc. AIA, Nat. Trust Hist. Preservation, Torske Klubben. Home: 1728 Humboldt Ave S Minneapolis MN 55403-2809

RANDA, RUDOLPH THOMAS, federal judge; b. Milw., July 25, 1940; s. Rudolph Frank and Clara Paula (Kojis) R.; m. Melinda Nancy Matera, Jan. 15, 1977; children: Rudolph Daniel, Daniel Anthony. BS, U. Wis.-Milw., 1963; JD, U. Wis.-Madison, 1966. Bar: Wis. 1966, U.S. Dist. Ct. (ea. and we. dists.) Wis. 1966, U.S. Ct. Appeals (7th cir.) 1973, U.S. Supreme Ct. 1973. Pvt. practice, Milw., 1966-67; prin. city atty. Office Milw. City Atty., 1970-75; judge Milw. Mcpl. Ct., 1975-79, Milw. County Cir. Ct., 1979—92, Appellate Ct., Madison, 1981—84; fed. judge U.S. Dist. Ct. (ea. dist.) Wis., 1992—, chief judge, 2002—. Chmn. Wis. Impact, Milw., 1980—; lectr. Marquette U. Law Sch., Milw., 1980—. Capt. U.S. Army, 1967-69, Vietnam. Decorated Bronze Star. Mem. Milw. Bar Assn., Wis. Bar Assn., Trial Judges Wis., Am. Legion (adjutant Milw. 1980), Thomas More Lawyers Soc. (former pres. Milw. chpt.), Milw. Hist. Soc., Phi Alpha Theta. Roman Catholic. Office: US Dist Ct 362 US Courthouse 517 E Wisconsin Ave Milwaukee WI 53202-4504

RANDALL, CHANDLER CORYDON, theologian; b. Ann Arbor, Mich., Jan. 22, 1935; s. Frederick Stewart and Madeline Leta (Snow) R.; m. Marian Archias Montgomery, July 2, 1960; children: Sarah Archias, Elizabeth Leggett, Rebekah Stewart. AB in History, U. Mich., 1957; S.T.B. in Theology, Berkeley Div. at Yale, 1960, D.D. (honoris causa), 1985; PhD in Hebraic Studies, Hebrew Union Coll., 1969. Rector St. Paul's Episcopal Ch., Richmond, Ind., 1967-71; rector Trinity Episcopal Ch., Ft. Wayne, Ind., 1971-88, St. Peter's Episcopal Ch., Del Mar, Calif., 1988—2000; theologian-in-residence Christ Ch. Cranbrook, Bloomfield Hills, Mich., 2000—08. Bd. dirs. Living Ch. Found., Milw.; bibl. theologian Episcopal Ch. Stewardship, N.Y.C., 1985; alumni coun. Berkeley Divinity at Yale, New Haven, Conn., 1981-87; bishop's cabinet Diocese of No. Ind., South Bend, 1983-87. Author: Satire in the Bible, 1969, An Approach to Biblical Satire, 1990; contbr. articles to profl. jours. Founder Canterbury Sch., Ft. Wayne, 1977; commr. Ind. Jud. Qualifications Commn., Indpls., 1981-87;

pres. Ft. Wayne Plan Commn., 1977; bd. dirs. Ft. Wayne Park Found., 1983-88; platform com. Ind. Republican Party, Indpls., 1974. Recipient Disting. Svc. medal U. Mich., 1981, Scheuer scholar Hebrew Union Coll., 1963-66, Liberty Bell award Ft. Wayne Bar Assn., 1988; named Sagamore of the Wabash, Gov. Ind., 1987. Mem. Am. Schs. Oriental Research, Yale U. Alumni Club (pres. 1982-88), Quest Club (pres.), Mayflower Soc. in Mich. (historian 2001-, gov. 2007-), Detroit Soc. Geneal. Rsch. (pres. 2000-), Oakland County Geneal. Soc. (pres.), Rotary Club, Chi Psi (nat. chaplain 1982). Republican. Episcopalian. Avocation: genealogy. Office: Christ Ch Cranbrook 470 Ch Rd Bloomfield Hills MI 48304 Office Fax: 248-644-0148. Personal E-mail: umpadre@aol.com.*

RANDALL, DOUGLAS D., biochemist, educator; b. Cheyenne, Wyo. BS, SD State U., 1965; PhD, Mich. State U., 1970. With U. Mo.-Columbia, 1971—, prof. emeritus biochemistry, dir. interdisciplinary program on plant biochemistry-physiology, 1981—. Bd. dirs. Nat. Sci. Bd., 2002—; mem. Great Barrier Reef Photorespiration Expdn. Nat. Sci. Found., 1973. Mem. editl. bd. Plant Physiology, Annual Reviews Plant Physiology and Plant Molecular Biology, Protein Expression and Purification, Biochemical Archives, Current Topics in Plant Biochemistry and Physiology; contbr. articles to profl. jours. Recipient William H. Byler Disting. Prof. Award, U. Mo.-Columbia, Faculty/Alumni Award, Gold Chalk Teaching Award, Disting. Alumni Award, SD State U., Biochemistry Dept.'s Alumni Award, Mich. State. Fellow: Am. Soc. Plant Biologists (chmn. bd. trustees 1996—99); mem.: Am. Soc. of Plant Physiologists (sec. 1991—93, chmn. bd. trustees), Am. Chemical Soc., Am. Soc. Biol. Chemistry. Achievements include research in plant metabolism, signal transduction, regulation of plant enzymes and understanding the metabolic interations between photosynthesis, photorespiration and respiration. Office: U Mo Columbia Biochemistry Dept 117 Schweitzer Hall Office 213 Columbia MO 65211 Office Phone: 573-882-4847. Office Fax: 573-882-5635. Business E-Mail: randalld@missouri.edu.

RANDALL, GARY LEE, former state legislator; b. Ithaca, Mich., June 18, 1943; s. Clifton Peet and Elsie Mae (Martyn) R.; m. Brenda Faye Martin, 1973; children: Amy Kathryn, Clifton Lee. BA, Mich. State U., 1970; MA, Ctrl. Mich. U., 1972. Program dir. WFYC Radio, Alma, Mich., 1965-70; dir. pub. affairs WCMU TV/WCML TV, Mt. Pleasant, Mich., 1970-79; rep. Mich. Dist. 89, Mich. Dist. 93; clk. Mich. Ho. of Reps. Asst. Rep. leader Mich. Ho. Reps., former chair bus. & fin. com., mem. agriculture com., fin. com., edn. com., adminstrn. rules & capitol restoration coms. Trustee Libr. Mich. Mem. Assn. Edn. Broadcasters, Mich. Farm Bur., Lions, Jaycees, Elks, Sigma Delta Chi. Home: 1210 E Pickard Mount Pleasant MI 48858 Address: PO Box 30014 Lansing MI 48909-7514

RANDALL, GERARD, foundation administrator; Grad., Marquette U. Former social studies tchr. Dominican H.S., Milw.; former tchr. Milw. Pub. Schs.; pres., adminstr. Pvt. Industry Coun. Milwaukee County, Milw. V.p. bd. regents U. Wis., 1994—; bd. dirs. Milw. Pub. Mus., Milw. Symphony Orch., Marcus Ctr. for Performing Arts, Rosalie Manor. Recipient 2 bronze tchr. awards, Ameritech. Mem.: Phi Delta Kappa. Office: Private Industry Council of Milwaukee County 2338 N 27th St Milwaukee WI 53210-3100

RANDALL, KARL W., air transportation executive, lawyer; b. Mount Pleasant, Mich., Feb. 12, 1951; s. Herbert J. and Wilma E. (Worstell) R.; m. Natalie Kilmer Randall, Dec. 17, 1971; children: Adam B., Kara J. AA, Mich. Christian Coll., Rochester, 1971; BA, Oakland U., Rochester, 1977; JD, Wayne State U. Law Sch., Detroit, 1981. Bar: Mich., 1981, U.S. Dist. Ct., 1981, U.S. Ct. Appeals, 1983; cert. airport mgr., Mich., 1993. Quality contr. Staley SNO BOL Corp., Pontiac, Mich., 1971-72; engring. tech. Oakland Co. Drain Comm., Pontiac, 1972-83; sr. asst. corp. counsel Oakland County Corp. Counsel, Pontiac, 1983-93; mgr. aviation Oakland County Internat. Airport, Waterford, Mich., 1993—. Dir. Integrity Jour., Mt. Pleasant, 1980-98, Oakland County Coord. Child Care Coun., Waterford, 1992-97. Author, editor: (religious jour.) Integrity, 1982, 94-95. Mem. Rep. Com. Oakland County, 1988—, Exec. Club Oakland County, 1993—. Mem. Mich. Assn. Airport Execs. (exec., pres., 2005-2006), Langsford Men's Chorus. Republican. Mem. Ch. of Christ. Avocations: physical fitness, motorcycling, jogging, golf, piano. Office: Oakland County Internat Airport 6500 Highland Rd Waterford MI 48327-1607 Office Phone: 248-666-3900. E-mail: randallk@co.oakland.mi.us.

RANDALL, LINDA LEA, biochemist, educator; b. Montclair, NJ, Aug. 7, 1946; d. Lowell Neal and Helen (Watts) Randall; m. Gerald Lee Hazelbauer, Aug. 29, 1970. BS, Colo. State U., 1968; PhD, U. Wis., 1971. Postdoctoral fellow Inst. Pasteur, Paris, 1971—73; asst. prof. Uppsala (Sweden) U., 1975—81; assoc. prof. Wash. State U., Pullman, 1981—83, prof. biochemistry, 1983—2000; Wurdock prof. biochemistry U. Mo., Columbia, 2000—. Guest scientist Wallenberg Lab. Uppsala U., 1973—75; mem. study sect. NIH, 1984—88. Contbr. articles to profl. jours.; co-editor: (book) Virus Receptors Part I, 1980; mem. editl. bd.: Jour. Bacteriology, 1982—96. Recipient Eli Lilly award in Microbiology and Immunology, 1984, Faculty Excellence Award in Rsch., Wash. State U., 1988, Parke-Davis award, 1995. Fellow: AAAS, Am. Acad. Arts and Scis., Am. Acad. Microbiology; mem.: NAS, Protein Soc., Am. Soc. Biol. Chemists, Am. Microbiological Soc. Avocation: dance. Office: Univ Mo Dept Biochemistry 117 Schweitzer Hall Columbia MO 65211 Home Phone: 573-449-2042; Office Phone: 573-884-4160.

RANDALL, WILLIAM SEYMOUR, leasing company executive; b. Champaign, Ill., July 5, 1933; s. Glenn S. and Audrey H. (Honnold) R.; m. Sharon Larsen; children: Steve, Cathy, Mike, Jennifer. BS, Ind. State U., 1959. Controller Amana Refrigeration Co., Iowa, 1966-70; div. controller Trane Co., Clarksville, Tenn., 1970-74, corporate controller La Crosse, Wis., 1974-79; v.p., chief fin. officer Sta-Rite Industries, Milw., 1979-82; pres., owner Profl. Staff Resources, Inc., Milw., 1982—. Served with AUS, 1953-55. Mem. Financial Execs. Inst. Lodges: Rotary. Home: 13365 Tulane St Brookfield WI 53005-7141 Office: 14430 W Bluemound Rd Ste 103 Milwaukee WI 53226 Office Phone: 414-778-5100. E-mail: wmrandall@msn.com.

RANDAZZO, RICHARD P., human resources professional; BSBA, Rochester Inst. Technology, 1965; MBA, Ind. U., 1967. Former various human resource mgmt. positions Xerox Corp.; former sr. v.p. human resources Asea Brown Boveri, Inc. Amerias Region, Conn.; sr. v.p. human resources Nextel Comms., Inc., 1994-97; v.p. human resources to sr. v.p. human resources Federal-Mogul Corp., Southfield, Mich., 1997-99, 99—. Office: Federal-Mogul Corp 26555 Northwestern Hwy Southfield MI 48034-2146

RANDOLPH, JACKSON HAROLD, utility company executive; b. Cin., Nov. 17, 1930; s. Dward Bradley and Cora Belle (Puckett) R.; m. Angelina Losito, June 20, 1958; children: Terri, Patti, Todd, Craig. BBA, U. Cin., 1958, MBA, 1968. C.P.A., Ohio. Acct. Arthur Andersen & Co., Cin., 1958-59; with Cin. Gas & Electric Co., 1959—, v.p. fin. and corp. affairs, 1981-85, exec. v.p., 1985-86, chmn., pres., CEO, from 1986, now chmn., also dir.; chmn. CINergy Corp., 1994—, now chmn.; former pres., now chmn. Union Light Heat and Power Co., Covington, Ky. Bd. dirs. Cen. Trust Bank, N.A., Cin. Fin. Corp., PNC Corp.; CEO CINergy Corp., 1994-95, chmn., 1995—. V.p., bd. dirs. Gen. Protestant Orphan Home, Cin., 1981-86; treas., bd. dirs. Cin. chpt. ARC, 1975—; mem. adv. com. Catherine Booth Home, 1980—, Dan Beard council Boy Scouts Am., 1985. Served with USN, 1951-55. Mem. Cin. Country Club, Queen City Club, Met. Club, Bankers Club, Delta Sigma Pi, Phi Eta Sigma, Beta Gamma Sigma. Office: CINergy Corp 139 E 4th St Cincinnati OH 45202-4003 Home: 392 Cameron Rd Cincinnati OH 45246-4131 Office: Union Light Heat Power 1697 Monmouth St # A Newport KY 41071-2634

RANDOLPH, JENNINGS, JR., (JAY RANDOLPH), sportscaster; b. Cumberland, Md., Sept. 19, 1934; s. Jennings and Mary Katherine (Babb) R.; m. Sue Henderson, May 28, 1966; children: Jennings, Brian Robert, Rebecca Sue. Student, George Washington U., 1952—54, student, 1957—58; BA, Salem Coll., W.Va., 1963. Sports and promotion dir. Sta. WHAR, Clarksburg, W.Va., 1958-61; sportscaster Sta. KLIF, Dallas, 1963-66; Sta. KMOX, St. Louis, 1966-68; with Sta. KSDK-TV, St. Louis, 1968—, sports dir., 1968-88, spl. sports corr., 1988—, also on nationally televised broadcasts for various sports events including Sr. PGA tour; TV announcer Fla. Marlins Baseball Club, Ft. Lauderdale, 1993—2002; announcer PGA Tour Classic on Golf Channel, 2002—06; staff KFNS Radio, St. Louis, 2002—06; St. Louis Cardinals announcer Sta. KSDK-TV, 2007—. Interviewer analyst Champions Tour on Golf Channel and CNBC; broadcaster coll. basketball ESPN regional TV; TV announcer St. Louis Cardinals, 1970-87, Cin. Reds., 1988; mem. NBC's broadcast staff for 1988 Olympics, Seoul, Korea and 1992 Summer Games, Barcelona, Spain; host The Golf Show. Trustee Salem Coll., 1976-89. With U.S. Army, 1954-56. Named to Boys and Girls Clubs of Am. Hall of Fame, 1990, Tex. Radio Hall Fame, 2005, Mo. Sports Hall of Fame, 2007; named Champion, So. Conf. Golf, 1958 Mem. Nat. Assn. Sportscasters, Delta Tau Delta (Disting. Alumni award 2006) Achievements include being an amateur golf champion. Home: 12021 Charter Oakpky Saint Louis MO 63146

RANKIN, ALFRED MARSHALL, JR., manufacturing executive; b. Cleve., Oct. 8, 1941; s. Alfred Marshall and Clara Louise (Taplin) R.; m. Victoire Conley Griffin, June 3, 1967; children: Helen P., Clara T. BA in Econs. magna cum laude, Yale U., 1963, JD, 1966. Mgmt. cons. McKinsey & Co., Inc., Cleve., 1970-73; with Eaton Corp., Cleve., 1974-81, pres. materials handling group, 1981-83, pres. indsl. group, 1984-86, exec. v.p., 1986, vice chmn., chief oper. officer, 1986-89; pres., COO NACCO Industries, Inc., Cleve., 1989-91, pres., CEO, 1991-94, also bd. dirs., chmn., pres., CEO, 1994—. Bd. dir. Goodrich Corp., Vanguard Group. Former pres., trustee Hathaway Brown Sch.; trustee U. Hosps. Health Sys., Cleve., Mus. Arts Assn., Univ. Circle, Inc., Cleve. Mus. Art, John Huntington Art Trust, Greater Cleve. Partnership; dir., exec. com. mem. Nat. Assn. Manufacturers; past chairperson The Cleve. Found. Mem. Ohio Bar Assn. Clubs: Chagrin Valley Hunt, Union, Tavern, Pepper Pike, Kirtland Country (Cleve.); Rolling Rock (Ligonier, Pa.); Met. (Washington). Republican. Office: NACCO Industries Inc 5875 Landerbrook Dr Ste 300 Mayfield Heights OH 44124 Office Phone: 440-449-9600. Office Fax: 440-449-9607.

RANKIN, JAMES WINTON, lawyer; b. Norfolk, Va., Sept. 9, 1943; s. Winton Blair and Edith (Griffin) R.; m. Donna Lee Carpenter, June 25, 1966 (dec.); children— Thomas James, William Joseph, Elizabeth Jeanne; m. JoAnne Katherine Murray, Feb. 11, 1978. AB magna cum laude, Oberlin Coll., 1965; JD cum laude, U. Chgo., 1968. Bar: Ill. 1968, U.S. Dist. Ct. (no. dist.) Ill. 1969, U.S. Ct. Appeals (7th cir.) 1971, U.S. Ct. Appeals (5th cir.) 1979, U.S. Supreme Ct. 1975, Calif. 1986. Law clk. U.S. Dist. Ct. (no. dist.) Ill., 1968-69; assoc. Kirkland & Ellis, Chgo., 1969-73, ptnr., 1973—. Fellow Am. Bar Found.; mem. ABA, Order of Coif, Mid-Am. Club, Univ. Club, Mich. Shores Club, Kenilworth Club, Ephriam Yacht Club. Presbyterian. Home: 633 Kenilworth Ave Kenilworth IL 60043-1070 Office: Kirkland & Ellis 200 E Randolph St Fl 54 Chicago IL 60601-6636

RANKIN, SCOTT DAVID, artist, educator; b. Newark, Mar. 21, 1954; s. Clymont J. and Jean L. (Lane) R.; m. Linda K. Piemonte, Sept. 3, 1989 (div. Apr. 2000); m. Stephanie Volz, Apr. 23, 2005. BFA, Tyler Sch. of Art, Phila., 1976; MFA, UCLA, 1980. Asst. prof. U. Iowa, Iowa City, 1985-86, U. Chgo., 1986-94; assoc. prof. Ill. State U., Normal, 1994—2005, prof., 2005—. Video cons. Math. Edn. Rsch. Project, LA, 1991—93, 3d internat. math. and sci. study UCLA dept. psychology, 1994—95, 1998—99. Prodr., dir.: (videotapes) Fugue, 1985, This and that (version 1), 1987, (version 2), 1990, The Pure, 1993, Wire, 1998, Flow, 2000, Central, 2001, Path, 2003, Piccadilly, 2004. Regional media arts fellow, Nat. Endowment for Arts, 1984, visual artists fellow, Ill. Arts Coun., 1989, 1990, Nat. Endowment for Arts, 1990, 1993. Office Phone: 309-438-8090. Business E-Mail: sdranki@ilstu.edu.

RANSEL, DAVID LORIMER, history professor; b. Gary, Ind., Feb. 20, 1939; s. Joseph A. and Patricia (Lorimer) R.; m. Therese Holma; children: Shairstin, Annaliisa. BA, Coe Coll., 1961; MA, Northwestern U., 1962; PhD, Yale U., 1969. Instr. Tollare Folkhogskola, Boo, Sweden, 1959-60; asst. instr. Yale U., New Haven, 1966-67; instr. U. Ill., Urbana, 1967-69, asst. prof., 1969-73, assoc. prof., 1973-81, prof., 1981-85, Ind. U., Bloomington, 1985—, Robert F. Byrnes prof. history, 2001—, dir. Russian and East European Inst., 1995—; co-dir. European Union Ctr., 2005—. Author: The Politics of Catherinian Russia, 1975, Mothers of Misery, 1988, Village Mothers: Three Generations of Change in Russia and Tataria, 2000; editor: The Family in Imperial Russia, 1978, Imperial Russia: ew Histories for the Empire, 1998, Polish Encounters, Russian Identity, 2005; editor/translator: Village Life in Late Tsarist Russia, 1993; editor Slavic Rev., Urbana, 1980-85, Am. Hist. Rev., Bloomington, 1985-95; bd. editors The History of the Family: An International Quarterly, Historisk Tidskrift, Forum for Anthropology and Culture, Kritika: Explorations in Russian and Eurasian History, Jour. Modern History, 2005—. Fellow Guggenheim Found., 1989-90, Wilson Nat. Fellowship Found., 1989-90, NEH, 1998-99, Bogliasco Found., 2007; Fulbright-Hays grantee, 1979, 90, Irex grantee, 1990, 93. Mem. Am. Hist. Assn. (gov. coun. 1985-95, fin. com. 1989-95), Am. Assn. for Advancement of Slavic Studies (bd. dirs. 1979-85, mem. fin. com. 1980-85, chmn. com. on status of women 1991-93, v.p., pres.-elect 2003, pres. 2004-05, immediate past pres. 2005), Irex (program com. 1995-99). Avocations: classical guitar, sailing, swimming. Office: Ind Univ Russian/East European Inst 565 Ballantine Hall Bloomington IN 47401-5017 Office Phone: 812-855-7309. Business E-Mail: ransel@indiana.edu.

RANSOM, RANDY, marketing executive; BA, U. Calif., Berkeley; MBA, UCLA. Dir. internat. bus. devel. FEMSA Corp.; chief mktg. officer FEMSA Cerveza; sr. v.p. portfolio strategy Coca-Cola N.Am.; pres. ConvergencePoint Group; exec. v.p., chief mktg. officer Miller Brewing Co., Milw., 2006—. Office: Miller Brewing Co 3939 W Highland Blvd Milwaukee WI 53208

RANTS, CAROLYN JEAN, academic administrator, educator; b. Hastings, Nebr., Oct. 3, 1936; d. John Leon and Christine (Helzer) Halloran; m. Marvin L. Rants, June 1, 1957 (div. July 1984); children: Christopher Charles, Douglas John. Student, Hastings Coll., 1954—56; BS, U. Omaha, 1960; EdM, U. Nebr., 1968; EdD, U. S.D., 1982. Elem. sch. tchr. Ogallala (Nebr.) Cmty. Sch., 1956-58, Omaha Pub. Schs., 1958-60, Hastings Pub. Schs., 1960-64, Grosse Pointe (Mich.) Cmty. Schs., 1964-67; asst. prof., instr. Morningside Coll., Sioux City, Iowa, 1974-82, dean for student devel., 1982-84, v.p. for student affairs, 1984-94, interim v.p. for acad. affairs, 1992-94, v.p. enrollment and student svcs., 1994-96, v.p. adminstrn., 1996-99; exec. dir. enrollment svcs. Western Iowa Tech C.C., 1999—, dean of students, 2000—06, interim v.p. instrn. and student svcs. Iowa, 2006—. Pres. New Perspectives, Inc., 1999—2000. New agy. com., chmn. fund distbn. and resource deployment com. United Way, Sioux City, 1987-94, co-chair, United Way Day of Caring, 1996; active Iowa Civil Rights Commn., 1989-97; bd. dirs. Leadership Sioux City, 1988-93, pres., 1992-93; bd. dirs. Siouxland Y, Sioux City, 1985-90, pres., 1988; bd. dirs. Girls, Inc., 1995-2000, Sioux City Symphony, 2001—, Red Cross, 2002—; mem. Vision 2020 Cmty. Planning Task Force, 1990-92; pres. bd. dirs. Siouxland Youth Chorus, 2001—, treas., 2002—; mem. Vision Iowa Bd., 2005—. Mem. Iowa Women in Ednl. Leadership (pres. Sioux City chpt. 1986), Nat. Assn. Student Pers. Adminstrs.(region IV-E adv. bd.), Nat. Assn. for Women Deans, Adminstrs. and Counselors, Iowa Student Pers. Adminstr. (chmn. profl. devel. Iowa chpt. 1988-89, pres. 1991-92, Outstanding Svc. award 1992, Disting. Svc. award 1994), AAUW (corp. rep., coll./univ. rep. 1994-96), P.E.O. (pres. Sioux City chpt., Tri-State Women's Bus. Conf. (treas., planning com. Sioux City chpt. 1987-89), Quota Club (com. chmn. Sioux City 1987-89, v.p. 1992-94, pres. 1994-95, Siouxland Woman of Yr. award 1988), Sertoma (officer, bd. govs., regional dir.), Omicron Delta Kappa (faculty dir. province X 1996-99), Delta Kappa Gamma (state 1st v.p. 1993-95, state pres. 1995-97, internat. com. 1998-2000, 2002-04, N.W. regional dir. 2004-06, 1st v.p. 2006—), Phi Delta Kappa (pres. 1988-89, Excellence in Leadership award 1998, Spl. Commendation Bessie Gabbard award 2001). Republican. Methodist. Avocations: handbells, cross-stitching. Home: 2904 S Cedar St # 4 Sioux City IA 51106-4246 Office: Western Iowa Tech Comm Coll PO Box 5199 4647 Stone Ave Sioux City IA 51102-5199 E-mail: rantsc@witcc.com, cjrants@willinet.net.

RANTS, CHRISTOPHER C., state representative; b. Grosse Point, Mich., Sept. 16, 1967; m. Trudy Rants; 2 children. BA, Morningside Coll., 1989. Coord. Metz Baking Co., 1990—98; cons. Susan Pierce & Assocs., 1998—; mem. Iowa Ho. Reps., Des Moines, 1993—, mem. adminstrn. and rules com., asst. majority leader, 1997—98, majority leader, 1999—, spkr. pro tempore, 1999, spkr., 2003—. Active United Way Loaned Exec. Program, Grace United Meth. Ch. Mem.: Nat. Fedn. Ind. Bus. (Iowa affiliate), Omicron Delta Kappa. Republican. Methodist. Office: State Capitol East 12th and Grade Des Moines IA 50319 also: 2740 S Glass St Sioux City IA 51106

RANUM, JANE BARNHARDT, state senator, lawyer; b. Charlotte, NC, Aug. 21, 1947; d. John Robert and Gladys Rose (Swift) B.; m. James Harry Ranum, Mar. 29, 1972; 1 child, Elizabeth McBride. BS, East Carolina U., 1969; JD, Hamline U., 1979. Bar: Minn. 1979, U.S. Dist. Ct. Minn. 1979. Tchr. elem. sch. Durham County, Durham, .C., 1960-70; tchr. Dept. Def., Baumholder, Germany, 1970-72, Dist. 196, Rosemount, Minn., 1972-76; law cclk. Hennepin County Dist. Ct., Mpls., 1982; asst. county atty. Hennepin County, Mpls., 1982—; mem. Minn. Senate, St. Paul, 1991—. Chmn. legislature commn. on children, youth and their families, 1993—, mem. rep. chem. abuse and prevention resource coun., 1993. Mem. exec. com., lobbying coord. Dem. Farmer Labor Feminist Caucus, St. Paul, 1980-84; bd. dirs. Project 13 for Reproductive Rights, Mpls., 1981-82; state del. Minn. Dem. Farmer Labor Party Conv., 1982, 84, precinct del., 1974—. Named Feminist of Yr., Minn. NOW, 1994, Legislator of Yr., Minn. Assn. for Retarded Citizens, 1994. Mem. Minn. Bar Assn., Minn. Women Lawyers, Minn. Family Support and Recovery Coun., Hennepin County Bar assn. Democrat. Home: 5045 Aldrich Ave S Minneapolis MN 55419-1207 Office: Minn Senate State Capitol Saint Paul MN 55155-0001

RAO, DABEERU C. (D.C. RAO), epidemiologist, educator; b. Apr. 6, 1946; came to U.S., 1972; naturalized. s. Ramarao Patnaik and Venkataratnam (Raghupatruni) R.; m. Sarada Patnaik, 1974; children: Ravi, Lakshmi. BS in Stats., Indian Statis. Inst., Calcutta, 1967, MS, 1968, PhD, 1971. Rsch. fellow U. Sheffield, England, 1971-72; asst. geneticist U. Hawaii, Honolulu, 1972-78, assoc. geneticist, 1978-80; dir. divsn. biostats. Washington U. Med. Sch., 1980—, assoc. prof. St. Louis, 1980-82, prof. depts. biostats., psychiatry and genetics, 1982—. Adj. prof. math., 1982—. Author: A Source Book for Linkage in Man, 1979, Methods in Genetic Epidemiology, 1983, Genetic Epidemiology of Coronary Heart Disease, 1984; editor-in-chief Genetic Epidemiology jour., 1984-91; contbr. over 400 articles to profl. jours. Grantee NIH, 1978—; Telugu Assn. N.Am. Mem. Am. Statis. Assn., Am. Soc. Human Genetics, Internat. Genetic Epidemiology Soc. (pres. 1996), Behavior Genetics Assn., Soc. Epidemiol. Rsch., Biomed. soc. Office: Washington U Sch Medicine Divsn Biostats Box 8067 660 S Euclid Ave Saint Louis MO 63110-1010 E-mail: rao@wubios.wustl.edu.

RAO, NANNAPANENI NARAYANA, electrical engineer; b. Kakumanu, Andhra Pradesh, India; m. Sarojini Jonnalagadda, June 10, 1955; children: Vanaja, Durgaprasad, Hariprasad. BSc in Physics, U. Madras, India, 1952; DMIT in Electronics, Madras Inst. Tech., 1955; MSEE, U. Wash., Seattle, 1960, PhD in Elec. Engring, 1965. Acting instr. elec. engring. U. Wash., 1960-64, acting asst. prof., 1964-65; asst. prof. elec. engring. U. Ill., Urbana, 1965-69, asso. prof., 1969-75, prof., 1975—2007, Edward C. Jordan prof., 2003—07, Edward C. Jordan prof. emeritus, 2007—, assoc. head elec. and computer engring., 1987—2007; disting. prof. Amrita U., India, 2006—. Cons. Fakultas Teknik, Univ. Indonesia, Jakarta, 1985-86, 87. Author: Basic Electromagnetics with Applications, 1972, Elements of Engineering Electromagnetics, 6th edit., 2004; contbr. numerous articles to profl. jours. Recipient Engring. award Telugu Assn. N.Am., 1983, Excellence in Edn. award, 1999, Fakultas Teknik award Universitas Indonesia, 1986. Fellow IEEE (life) (Undergrad. Teaching award 1994); mem. Am. Soc. Engring. Edn. (life) (AT&T Found. award for excellence in instrn. engring. students 1991), Internat. Union Radio Sci. (US Commn. G). Achievements include contributions to engineering education in the United States and abroad. Home: 2509 S Lynn St Urbana IL 61801-6841 E-mail: rao@ece.uiuc.edu.

RAO, PALAKURTHI S.C., soil science educator; b. Warangal, India, Feb. 15, 1947; came to U.S., 1967; s. Seshagiri and Arya (Kondapalli) R.; m. Keiko Yohena, June 7, 1970; 1 child, Masaru. BSc, A.P. Agrl. U., Hyderabad, India, 1967; MS, Colo. State U., 1970; PhD, U. Hawaii, 1974. Research assoc. U. Fla., Gainesville, 1975-77, asst. research scientist, 1977-79, asst. prof. soil sci., 1979-82, assoc. prof., 1982-85, prof. of soil and water sci., 1985-99; Lee A. Reith disting. prof. Perdue U, W. Lafayette, IN, 1999—. Vis. prof. U. Hawaii, Honolulu, 1986—. Assoc. editor Jour. Environ. Quality, 1980-83; co-editor: Role of Unsaturated Zone in Hazardous Waste Disposal, 1983; co-editor Jour. Contaminant Hydrology, 1986. Mem. Internat. Soil Sci. Soc., Soil Sci. Soc. Am., Am. Geophys. Union, Am. Chem. Soc., Am. Soc. Agronomy. Avocations: outdoor sports, anthropology, history of sci. Office: Perdue U Civil Engineering 1284 Civil Engineering Bldg Lafayette IN 47907-1284

RAO, PRASAD, electronics executive; Pres., CEO, Cybertech Sys., Inc., Oak Brook, Ill. Office: Cybertech Systems Inc 1250 E Diehl Rd Ste 403 Naperville IL 60563-9389

RAO, VITTAL SRIRANGAM, electrical engineering educator; b. Inumpamula, India, June 8, 1944; came to U.S., 1981; s. Rangaiah Srirangam and Lakshmamma (Immadi) R.; m. Vijaya Morishetti, Feb. 28, 1965; children: Asha, Ajay. M of Tech., Indian Inst. Tech., 1972, PhD, 1975. Asst. prof. Indian Inst. of Tech., New Delhi, India, 1975-79; vis. prof. T.U., Halifax, N.S., Can., 1980-81; assoc. prof. U. Mo., Rolla, 1981-88, prof., 1988—; dir. Intelligent Systems Ctr., Rolla, 1991—. Cons. Delco Remy, Anderson, Ind., 1985-87, Allison Gas Turbines, Indpls., 1986-87, U.S. Army Picatinny Arsenal, N.J., 1988-91. Contbr. articles to profl. jours. including Suboptimal/Near Optimal Control, Reduced Order Modeling Techniques, Robust Control, Large Space Structures, Smart Structures. Fellow AIAA (assoc.); mem. IEEE (sr., subsect. 1981-88, Centennial medal 1984). Achievements include devel. of reduced order modeling techniques for large space structures, interdisciplinary approach for control of smart structures and structural health monitoring. Home: 501 Oak Knoll Rd Rolla MO 65401-4727 Office: U Mo Intelligent Systems Ctr Rolla MO 65401

RAPOPORT, ROBERT MORTON, medical educator; b. Oakland, Calif., Nov. 20, 1952; married; 2 children. BA in Biological Scis., U. Calif., Santa Barbara, 1974; PhD in Pharmacology, U. Calif., LA, 1980; postdoc. studies in Pharmacology, U. Va., 1980-81, Stanford U., 1981-83. Rsch. pharmacologist VA Med. Ctr., Palo Alto, Calif., 1983-84, Cin., 1984—. Asst. prof. dept. pharmacology and cell biophysics U. Cin., 1984-91, assoc. prof., 1991—; asst. dir. med. pharmacology, 1994; spkr. in field. Reviewer manuscripts. various jours., grants various assns.; contbr. over 100 articles to profl. publs. Grantee U. Calif., 1977, VA, 1983-86, 85-86, 87-90, NIH, 1985-87, 88-93, Am. Heart Assn. S.W. Ohio, 1985-86, 86-87, 88-89, 89-91, 91-92, U. Cin., 1985-86, Am. Heart Assn., 1987-90, 1995—, Veterans Affairs, 1994-95, 95—, Univ. Rsch. Coun., 1994-95, Parke-Davis, 1994, 95; recipient Rsch. Career Devel. award, 1986-91. Office: Dept Pharmacology Univ Cincinnati 231 Bethesda Ave Cincinnati OH 45267-0001

RAPP, GEORGE ROBERT (RIP), geology and archeology educator; b. Toledo, Sept. 19, 1930; s. George Robert and Gladys Mae (Warner) R.; m. Jeannette Messner, June 15, 1956; children: Kathryn, Karen. BA, U. Minn., 1952; PhD, Pa. State U., 1960. Asst. then assoc. prof. S.D. Sch. Mines, Rapid City, 1957-65; assoc. prof. U. Minn., Mpls., 1965-75, prof. geology and archeology Duluth, 1975-95, dean Coll. Letters and Sci., 1975-84, dean Coll. Sci. and Engring., 1984-89, dir. Archeometry Lab., 1975—2004, Regents' prof. geoarchaeology, 1995—2003, emeritus, 2003—. Prof. Ctr. for Ancient Studies, U. Minn., Mpls., 1970-93, prof. interdisciplinary archaeol. studies, 1993—; cons. USIA, Westinghouse Corp., Exxon Corp., Ford Found. Author, editor: Excavations at Nichoria, 1978, Troy: Archeological Geology, 1982, Archeological Geology, 1985, Excavations at Tel Michal, 1989, Encyclopedia of Minerals, 1989, Phytolith Systematics, 1992, Geoarchaeology, 1998, Artifact Copper Sources, 2000, Archaeomineralogy, 2002; mem. editl. bd. Jour. Field Archeology, 1976-85, Jour. Archeol. Sci., 1977-79, Geoarcheology Jour., 1984-92, Am. Jour. Archeology, 1985-92. NSF postdoctoral fellow, 1963-64, Fulbright-Hayes sr. rsch. fellow, 1972-73. Fellow AAAS (chmn. sect. E, 1987-88, nat. coun. 1992-95), Geol. Soc. Am. (Archeol. Geology award 1983), Mineral. Soc. Am.; mem. Nat. Assn. Geology Tchrs. (pres. 1986-89), Soc. for Archeol. Sci. (pres. 1983-84), Assn. Field Archeology (pres. 1979-81), Archaeol. Inst. Am. (Pomerance medal 1988), Sigma Xi (bd. dirs. 1990-98). Avocations: classical music, exercise, nutrition. Office: U Minn-Duluth Dept Geol Scis Duluth MN 55812 Business E-Mail: grapp@d.umn.edu.

RAPP, ROBERT ANTHONY, metallurgical engineering educator; s. Frank J. and Goldie M. (Royer) R.; m. Heidi B. Sartorius, June 3, 1960; children: Kathleen Rapp Raynaud, Thomas, Stephen, Stephanie Rapp Surface. BSMetE, Purdue U., 1956; MSMetE, Carnegie Inst. Tech., 1959, PhDMetE, 1960; D (hon.), Inst. Polytech., Toulouse, France, 1995. Asst. prof. metall. engring. Ohio State U., Columbus, 1963—66, 1966—69, prof., 1969—, M.G. Fontana prof., 1988—95, prof., 1989—95, disting. univ. prof. emeritus, 1995—. Vis. prof. Ecole Nat. Superior d'Electrochimie, Grenoble, France, 1972-73, U. Paris-Sud, Orsay, 1985-86, Ecole Nat. Superior de Chimie, Toulouse, France, 1985-86, U. New South Wales, Australia, 1987; Acta/Scripta Metallurgica lectr., 1991; rsch.

metallurgist WPAFB, Ohio, 1960-63. Editor: Techniques of Metals Research, vol. IV, 1982, High Temperature Corrosion, 1984; translator Metallic Corrosion (Kaesche), 1986; bd. rev. jour. Oxid. Metals; contbr. 265 publs. and numerous articles to profl. jours. First lt. USAF, 1960—63, Wright-Patterson AFB. Decorated chevalier des Palmes Academiques; recipient Disting. Engring. Alumnus award Purdue U., 1988, B.F. Goodrich Collegiate Inventor's award, 1991, 92, Ulrick Evans award Brit. Inst. Corrosion, 1992; Guggenheim fellow, 1972; Fulbright scholar Max Planck Inst. Phys. Chemistry, 1959-60, Linford award for Disting. Tchg.,The Electrochem. Soc., 1998. Fellow: Nat. Assn. Corrosion Engrs. (W.R. Whitney award 1986), Electrochem. Soc. (HTM Divsn. Outstanding Achievement award 1992, Linford Tchr. award 1998, Olin Palladium award 2005), Mining Metals and Materials Soc. (R.F. Mehl medal 2000, Educator award 2003), Am. Soc. Metals Internat. (Zay Jeffries lectr. 2006, B. Stoughton award 1968, Howe gold medal 1974, Gold medal 2000); mem.: Nat. Acad. Engring., French Soc. Metals and Materials (hon.). Lutheran. Achievements include about twenty patents. Avocations: gardening, golf, travel. Home: 1379 Southport Dr Columbus OH 43235-7649 Office Phone: 614-292-6178. E-mail: rrapp001@columbus.rr.com, rapp.4@osu.edu.

RAPP, ROBERT NEIL, lawyer; b. Erie, Pa., Sept. 10, 1947; m. Sally K. Meder; 1 child: Jeffrey David. BA, Case Western Res. U., 1969, JD, 1972; MBA, Cleve. State U., 1989. Bar: Ohio 1972, U.S. dist. Ct. (no. dist.) Ohio 1973, U.S. Ct. Appeals (6th crct.) 1981, U.S. Supreme Ct. 1980. Assoc. Metzenbaum, Gaines & Stern, Co., L.P.A., Cleve., 1972-75; ptnr. Calfee, Halter & Griswold, Cleve., 1975—. Adj. prof. law Case Western Res. U., 1975—78, 1994—98, Cleve. Marshall Coll. Law, Cleve. State U., 1976—82; practitioner-in-residence Cornell U. Law Sch., 1993; mem. legal adv. bd. Nat. Assn. Securities Dealers, 1992—96; mem. market ops. rev. com. Nasdaq Stock Market, 1996—; arbitrator, practitioner mediator Nat. Futures Assn. Author: Blue Sky Regulation, 2d edit., 2003; contbr. numerous articles to law jours. Mem. ABA (sect. bus. law: mem. com. fed. regulation of securities, subcom. broker-dealer regulation, sect. litigation: mem. com. securities litigation), Am. Arbitration Assn. (securities arbitrator, mem. comml. adv. coun. Cleve. region), Ohio State Bar Assn. (elected mem. coun. dels. 1976-82, corp. law com. 1980—), Cleve. Bar Assn. (chmn. young lawyers sect. 1976-77), assoc. mem. cert. grievance com., sect. securities law: exec. coun. 1980-85, chmn. govt. liaison com. 1980-81). Office: Calfee Halter & Griswold LLP 1400 McDonald Investment Ct Cleveland OH 44114-2688

RAPPAPORT, GARY BURTON, defense equipment executive; b. Mpls., Apr. 27, 1937; s. Max and Beatrice (Berkinsky) R.; m. Susan Heller, Nov. 26, 1961; children: Debra Lynn, Melissa Ellen. BS, U. Pa., 1959. Asst. to pres. Napco Industries, Inc., Hopkins, Minn., 1959-61, v.p., 1961-65, exec. v.p., 1964-65, pres., 1965-74, CEO, 1974-84, Venturian Corp., Hopkins, 1984—, also chmn. bd. dirs. Dir. La Maur, Inc., Mpls., 1980-87. Chmn. bd. govs. Mt. Sinai Hosp., Mpls., 1979-81. Served with Air N.G., 1960-64. Jewish. Office: Venturian Corp 11111 Excelsior Blvd Hopkins MN 55343-3434

RAPPAPORT, RICHARD J., lawyer; b. Chgo., Aug. 13, 1943; m. Roberta Rappaport; children: Michael, Barbara. BS, Loyola U., 1965, JD cum laude, 1967. Bar: Ill. 1967, Fla. 1993, US Dist. Ct. No. Dist. Ill. 1967, US Ct. Appeals 7th Cir. 1978, 10th Cir. 1978, 6th Cir. 1986, 4th Cir. 1988, 11th Cir. 1997, 8th Cir. 2000, 2d Cir. 2006, US Tax Ct. 1988, US Supreme Ct. 1979. Trial atty. antitrust divsn. US Dept. Justice, Washington, 1967-69; ptnr. Ross & Hardies (merged with McGuireWoods LLP in 2003), Chgo., McGuireWoods LLP, Chgo., 2003—, co-mng. ptnr. Chgo. office, 2003—04. Bd. dirs. Am. Assn. for Klinefelter Syndrome Info. & Support; bd. mem. Loyola U. Sch. Law Inst. Consumer Antitrust Studies. Fellow: Am. Bar Found.; mem.: ABA, Lawyers Club of Chgo., Chgo. Bar Assn. Office: McGuireWoods LLP Ste 4100 77 W Wacker Dr Chicago IL 60601-1818 Office Phone: 312-750-8618. Office Fax: 312-920-3696. Business E-Mail: rrappaport@mcguirewoods.com.

RAPPLEYE, RICHARD KENT, financial executive, consultant, educator; b. Oswego, NY, Aug. 10, 1940; s. Robert Edward and Evelyn Margaret (Hammond) R.; m. Karen Tobe Greenberg, Sept. 7, 1963; children: Matthew Walker, Elizabeth Marion. AB, Miami U., Oxford, Ohio, 1962; postgrad., Boston U., 1962-63; MBA, U. Pa., 1964; postgrad., DePaul U., 1965-66; MRA, U. Detroit Mercy, Mich., 1997. CPA, Ill. Auditor DeLoitte Haskins & Sells, Chgo., 1962-67, mgmt. cons., 1967-71; controller United Dairy Industry Assn., Rosemont, Ill., 1971, dir. fin. and adminstrn., 1971-73, exec. v.p., 1973-74; asst. to exec. v.p. Florists' Transworld Delivery, Southfield, Mich., 1974-75, group dir. fin. and adminstrn., 1975-80; asst. treas. Erb Lumber Co., Birmingham, Mich., 1980, v.p. fin., chief fin. officer, 1981-83; v.p., sec.-treas. C.S. Mott Found., Flint, Mich., 1983-2000, v.p. field svcs., 2000—03; program officer The Kresge Found., Troy, Md., 2003—. Lectr. U. Mich., Flint, 1987-91, 98-99; cons. in field; instr. Oakland U., Rochester, Mich., 1981-83; bd. dirs. Treas. Coun. Mich. Fedn., 1986-92, 96-2002. Trustee Mich. State Bar Fedn., 2001—, Mich. Masonic Home Charitable Fedn., 2004—. Mem. AICPA, Mich. Assn. CPAs, Theosophical Soc., Masons, Rotary. Unitarian Universalist. Home: 503 Arlington St Birmingham MI 48009-1639 Office: The Kresge Foundation 2701 Troy Center Dr Ste 150 Troy MI 48084-4755 E-mail: RKRappleye@NPOperations.com.

RARICK, PHILIP JOSEPH, lawyer, retired state supreme court justice; b. Troy, Ill., Nov. 10, 1940; s. Philip J. and Mary (Buckman) R.; m. Janet N. Arnovitz, Feb. 1, 1963; 1 child, Philip J. IV. BA, So. Ill. U., 1962; JD, St. Louis U., 1966. Bar: Ill. 1966, U.S. Dist. Ct. Ill. 1966. Twp. atty. Collinsville & Jarvis, Collinsville, Ill., 1966-75; asst. state's atty. Madison County, Edwardsville, Ill., 1966-75; city atty. City of Collinsville, 1967-75; cir. judge Third Jud. Cir., Edwardsville, 1975-88; presiding judge Criminal Div. in Madison County, Ill., 1982—85; chief cir. judge Third Jud. Cir., Edwardsville, 1985-87; presiding judge Criminal Div. in Madison County, Ill., 1987—88; elected judge Appellate Ct., Fifth Dist., Ill., 1988; judge indsl. commn. divsn. Ill. Appellate Ct., 1988—2002; elected judge, retained Appellate Ct., Fifth Dist., Ill., 1998; justice Ill. Supreme Ct., 2002—04; with Callis, Papa, Hale, Szewczyk, Rongey & Danzinger, PC, Granite City, Ill., 2004—. Mem. exec. com. Ill. Jud. Conf., Springfield, 1985—2000, chmn. complex litigation com., 1988—2000, mem. Industrial Comm. Div. of the Appellate Ct., 1992-2002, Ill. Cts. Commn. State of Ill., Springfield, 1992—99. Chmn. (manual) Illinois Manual for Complex Litigation. Mem. Ill. State Bar Assn., Ill. Judges Assn. (dir. 1977—82), Madison County Bar Assn., Tri-City Bar Assn. Office: Callis Papa Hale Szewczyk Rongey & Danzinger PC 1326 Niedringhaus Ave Granite City IL 62040 Office Phone: 618-452-1323.

RASCHE, ROBERT HAROLD, banker, retired economics educator; b. New Haven, June 29, 1941; s. Harold A. and Elsa (Bloomquist) R.; m. Dorothy Anita Bensen, Dec. 28, 1963; children: Jeanette Dorothy, Karl Robert. BA, Yale U., 1963; A.M., U. Mich., 1965, PhD, 1966. Asst. prof. U. Pa., Phila., 1966-72; assoc. prof. econs. Mich. State U., East Lansing, 1972-75, prof., 1975-98, prof. emeritus, 1999—; sr. v.p., dir. rsch. St. Louis Fed. Res. Bank, 1999—. Vis. scholar St. Louis Fed. Res., 1971-72, 76-77, 94-98, San Francisco Fed. Rsch. Bank, 1985, Bank of Japan, Tokyo, 1990; disting. vis. prof. econs. Ariz. State U., Tempe, 1986; rsch. assoc. Nat. Bur. Econ. Rsch., Cambridge, Mass., 1982-91; mem. Mich. Gov. Coun. Econ. Advisers, 1992-96; mem. Shadow Open Market Com., 1973-98. Mem. Am. Econs. Assn. Lutheran. Home: 14531 Radcliffborough Ct Chesterfield MO 63017-5626 Office: Fed Res Bank St Louis Rsch Divsn PO Box 442 Saint Louis MO 63166-0442 Home Phone: 636-728-1918. Business E-Mail: rasche@msu.edu.

RASHKIN, MITCHELL CARL, internist, pulmonary medicine specialist; b. NYC, June 1, 1951; m. Karen B. Ohlbaum, Aug. 8, 1982. BS in Computer Sci., U. Mich., 1973, MD, 1977. Diplomate Am. Bd. Internal Medicine, subspecialty Pulmonary Disease, Nat. Bd. Med. Examiners; cert. in critical care medicine Am. Bd. Internal Medicine; insr. Advanced Cardiac Life Support. Intern U. Cin. Med. Ctr., 1977-78, resident, 1978-80, fellowship in pulmonary medicine, 1980-82, dir. med. intensive care unit, 1982—, program dir. critical care medicine, 1989-95, co-dir. pulmonary care unit, 1990-93, dir. respiratory therapy, 1993—, dir med. stepdown unit, 1993—, asst. prof. medicine, 1982-89, assoc. prof. medicine, 1989—. Asst. prof. clin. emergency medicine U. Cin. Hosps., 1988-90, assoc. prof. 1990—; fellowship dir. Pulmonary/Critical Care U. Cin. Med. Ctr., 1995—; mem. numerous hosp. coms. Fellow ACP, Am. Coll. Chest Physicians; mem. Am. Thoracic Soc., Ohio Thoracic Soc. Office: U Cin Med Ctr PO Box 670564 231 Bethesda Ave Rm 6004 Cincinnati OH 45229-2827 E-mail: mitchell.rashkin@uc.edu.

RASIN, RUDOLPH STEPHEN, corporate financial executive; b. Newark, July 5, 1930; m. Joy Kennedy Peterkin, Apr. 11, 1959; children: Rudolph Stephen, James Stenning, Jennifer Shaw Denniston. BA, Rutgers U., 1953; postgrad., Columbia U., 1958-59. Mgr. Miles Labs., Inc., 1959-61; devel. mgr. Gen. Foods Corp., White Plains, NY, 1961-62; asst. to pres., chmn. Morton Internat. Inc., Chgo., 1962-72; pres. Rasin Corp., Chgo., 1971—, Alliance Brands, LLC. Bd. dirs. Facets Media. Bd. dirs. Geneva Lakes Conservancy, Gatherings Waters Land Trust, Poetry Found. With USAF, 1954—56. Mem. Hinsdale Golf Club, Mid Am. Club (Chgo.), Lake Geneva Country Club, Williams Coll. Club (N.Y.C.), Casino Club (Chgo.), Chgo. Club. Mem. United Ch. of Christ. Office: Alliance Brands LLC 30 W Monroe St Chicago IL 60603 Office Phone: 312-236-8453.

RASKIND, LEO JOSEPH, law educator; b. Newark, Nov. 2, 1919; s. Isaac and Fannie (Michelson) R.; m. Mollie Gordon, June 14, 1948; children— Carol Inge, John Richard. AB, UCLA, 1942; MA, U. Wash., 1949; PhD, London Sch. Econs., 1952; LLB, Yale U., 1955. Faculty Stanford Law Sch., 1955-56; lectr., research asso. Yale Law Sch., 1956-58; faculty Vanderbilt Law Sch., 1958-64, Ohio State U. Coll. of Law, 1964-70, U. Minn., 1970-90, emeritus, 1991—. Counsel Am. Econ. Assn., 1979—88; vis. tchr. NYU, 1964, 83, U. Tex., 1964, U. Utah, 1967, So. Meth. U., 1973, U. N.C., 1978, Lyon III, 1984, Kiel U., 1988; vis. prof. Coll. Law, U. Tenn., Knoxville, 1994, Law Sch., U. Calif., Davis, 1995, U. Minn., 1998, Bklyn. Law Sch., 1998—2004. Co-author: Casebook Corporate Taxation, 1978, Casebook Antitrust Law, 2001; mem. adv. bd. BNA jour. Served to capt. AUS, 1942-46. Fulbright fellow, London Sch. Econs., 1952. Mem. Am. Law Inst. Office: U Minn Law Ctr 229 19th Ave S Minneapolis MN 55455 Personal E-mail: ljraskind@aol.com.

RASMUSSEN, DAN, state representative, contractor; b. Independence, Iowa, Aug. 12, 1947; BA, Iowa State U. Land improvement contractor; state rep. dist. 23 Iowa Ho. of Reps., 2003—; mem. state govt. com.; mem. transp. com.; mem. agr. and natural resources subcom.; vice chair natural resources com. Active Independence Cmty. Sch. Bd. Mem.: Iowa Land Improvement Contractors Assn. (exec. dir.). Republican. Address: 1310 8th Ave NE Independence IA 50644 Office: State Capitol East 12th and Grand Ave Des Moines IA 50319

RASMUSSEN, EARL R., lumber company and home improvement retail executive; Treas., DFO Menard Inc., Eau Claire, Wis. Office: Menard Inc 4777 Menard Dr Eau Claire WI 54703-9625

RASMUSSEN, STEPHEN S., insurance company executive; BS in Bus. Adminstrn., U. Iowa. Underwriting & mktg. Allied, 1974—82, regional v.p., pacific coast regional office, 1982—86, v.p., underwriting, 1986—98, exec. v.p., product mgmt., 1998—2001; pres., COO CalFarm Ins., 2001—03; pres., COO, property casualty ins. ops. ationwide Mutual Ins. Co., Columbus, Ohio, 2003—. Trustee Grand View Coll.; 2002 Walk corp. chair, ctrl. Iowa chpt. Juvenile Diabetes Rsch. Found. Office: Nationwide One Nationwide Pl Columbus OH 43215-2220

RASSEL, RICHARD EDWARD, lawyer; b. Toledo, Jan. 10, 1942; s. Richard Edward and Madonna Mary (Tuohy) R.; m. Elizabeth Ann Frederick, Dec. 5, 1967 (dec. June 1977); children: Richard III, Elizabeth; m. Dawn Ann Lynch, Sept. 17, 1983; children: Lauren, Brian. BA, U. Notre Dame, 1964; JD, U. Mich., 1966; cert. judge advocate, USN Judge Advocate Sch., 1967. Law clk. Mich. Ct. Appeals, Detroit, 1966-70; shareholder, v.p. Butzel Long, Detroit, 1970-94, chmn., CEO, 1994—2006, dir. global client rels., 2006—. Bd. dirs. Robertson-Jamieson Corp., Birmingham, Mich., WTVS-Channel 56. Pres. Birmingham Cmty. House; bd. advisors U. Detroit Mercy Grad. Sch. Bus.; bd. dirs. Detroit Legal News, Detroit Police Athletic League, Internat. Visitors Coun., William Beaumont Hosp.; chair meta. affairs coalition Oakland U. Coll. Arts and Scis.; past pres., past bd. dirs. Rosa Parks Scholarship Found.; trustee Seed Found. Lt. USNR, 1967-69. Mem. ABA (vice chmn. media and law com.), State Bar of Mich. (chmn. multidisciplinary practice law com.), Am. Coll. Trial Lawyers, Birmingham Athletic Club, Detroit Athletic Club, Otsego Ski Club, Village Club. Office: Butzel Long 150 W Jefferson Ave Ste 900 Detroit MI 48226-4416 E-mail: rassel@butzel.com.

RATAJ, EDWARD WILLIAM, lawyer; b. St. Louis, Oct. 14, 1947; m. Elizabeth Spalding, July 4, 1970; children: Edward, Suzanne, Anne, Thomas, Charles. BS in Acctg., St. Louis U., 1969, JD, 1972. Assoc. Bryan, Cave, McPheeters & McRoberts, St. Louis, 1972-82, ptnr., 1983—. Office: Bryan Cave McPheeters & McRoberts 211 N Broadway Saint Louis MO 63102-2733

RATCHYE, BOYD HAVENS, lawyer; b. Helena, Mont., June 10, 1938; s. John Frederick and Leanora (Boyd) R.; m. Jean P. Cunningham, Sept. 1, 1962 (div. Oct. 1985); children: Ellen C., Stephen B.; m. Susan Light, May 21, 1994. BA cum laude, Harvard U., 1960, JD, 1963. Bar: Minn. 1964, U.S. Dist. Ct. (Minn. 1964, ND 1993), U.S. Ct. Appeals (8th cir.) 1967, U.S. Supreme Ct. 1972, U.S. Ct. Appeals (fed. cir.) 1983. Law clk. to justice J.C. Otis Supreme Ct. Minn., St. Paul, 1963-64; assoc. Erickson, Popham, Haik & Schnobrich, Mpls., 1964-65; assoc. to ptnr. Doherty, Rumble & Butler, P.A., St. Paul, 1966—99; shareholder, civil litig. Bassford Remele, Mpls., 1999—. Adj. prof. William Mitchell Coll. of Law, 1975-94. Chmn., bd. dir. Yellowstone Assn., Animal Human Soc. Named a Minn. Super Lawyer, Mpls.-St. Paul Mag. and Minn. Law and Politics mag., 2000—07; named one of Best Lawyers in Am., 1986—2007. Mem. ABA, Am. Bd. Trial Advocates (pres. Minn. chpt. 1990-91), Minn. State Bar Assn., Minn. Def. Lawyers Assn., Hennepin County Bar Assn., Harvard Radcliffe Club Minn., Inns of Ct. (Warren Burger chpt., pres. 1999-2000, counselor 2000-01). Episcopalian. Avocations: rowing, running, cross country skiing, scuba diving, snorkeling. Office: Bassford Remele Ste 3800 33 S 6th St Minneapolis MN 55402 Office Phone: 612-376-1604. Office Fax: 612-333-8829. Business E-Mail: boydr@bassford.com.

RATHBUN, RANDALL KEITH, lawyer; b. Miami Beach, Fla., Aug. 24, 1953; s. Ronald K. and Betty L. (Stockstill) R.; m. Janet Sue Meyer, Oct. 8, 1983; children: Zachary Keith, Joshua George, Kelsea Rebecca. BS, Kans. State U., 1975; JD, Washburn U., 1978. Bar: Kans. 1978, U.S. Dist. Ct. Kans. 1978, U.S. Ct. Appeals (10th cir.) 1985. Assoc. Curfman, Harris, Bell, Weigand & Depew, Wichita, Kans., 1978-80; ptnr. Depew, Gillen & Rathbun, Wichita, 1980-93; U.S. atty. U.S. Dept. of Justice, Wichita, Kans., 1993-96; ptnr. Depew & Gillen, Wichita, Kans., 1996—. Bd. dirs. Washburn Law Jour., 1977-78. Chair 4th Congressional Dist. Democrats, Kans., 1986-88; exec. com. State Dem. Party, Topeka, 1986-88; del. Dem. Nat. Conv., Atlanta, 1988; treas. State Dem. Party, 1991—; officer, bd. dirs. Sedgwick County unit Am. Cancer Soc.-Wichita, 1984-90; bd. dirs. Kans. div. Am. Cancer Soc., Wichita, 1987-90. Mem. Wichita Bar Assn. (sec.-treas. 1991-92), Wichita Young Lawyers (pres. 1983-84), Kans. Bar Assn. Democrat. Methodist. Office: Depew Gillen Llc 8301 E 21st St N Ste 450 Wichita KS 67206-2936

RATHI, MANOHAR LAL, pediatrician, neonatologist; b. Beawar, Rajasthan, India, Dec. 25, 1933; came to U.S. 1969; s. Bagtawarmal and Sitadevi (Laddha) R.; m. Kamla Jajoo, Feb. 21, 1960; children: Sanjeev A., Rajeev. MBBS, Rajasthan U., 1961. Diplomate Am. Bd. Pediats., sub-bd. Neonatal Perinatal Medicine; lic. physician, N.Y., Ill., Calif. Resident house physician internal medicine Meml. Hosp., Darlington, U.K., 1963-64; resident sr. house physician pediatrics Gen. Hosp., Oldham, U.K., 1964-65; dir. perinatal medicine Christ Hosp. Perinatal Ctr., Oak Lawn, Ill., 1974-98, attending physician, 1974—2002; assoc. prof. pediatrics Rush Med. Coll., Chgo., 1979—; cons. obstetrician Christ Hosp., Oak Lawn, 1974—2000; cons. neonatologist Little Company of Mary Hosp., Evergreen Park, Ill., 1972—2002, Palos Cmty. Hosp., Palos Heights, Ill., 1978—2002; chmn. Midwest Neoped Assocs., Oak Brook, Ill., 1997—. Cons./lectr. in field. Contbr. articles to profl. jours.; editor: Clinical Aspects of Perinatal Medicine, 1984, Vol. I, 1985, Vol. II, 1986, Current Perinatology, 1989, Vol. II, 1990; editor with others: Perinatal Medicine Vol. I, 1978, Vol. I, 1980, Vol. II, 1982. Hummell Found. grantee, 1976-77, WyethLab grantee, 1977-78; recipient Physicians Recognition award AMA, 1971-74, 91-92, Outstanding New Citizen's award State of Ill., 1978, Asian Human Svcs. of Chgo., 1988, Nitric Oxide Study by Ohmeda, 1994-95. Fellow Am. Acad. Pediats. (perinatal sect., Ill. chpt. treas. 1994-96); mem. AMA, Chgo. Med. Soc., Ill. Med. Soc., Chgo. Pediat. Soc., Med. Soc. County of Kings Bklyn., N.Y. Acad. Scis., Am. Thoracic Soc., Soc. Critical Care Medicine. Republican. Hindu. Office: Midwest Neoped Assocs Ltd 900 Jorie Blvd Ste 186 Oak Brook IL 60523-3808 Office Phone: 630-954-6700.

RATHOD, MULCHAND, mechanical engineering educator; b. Pathri, India, Mar. 3, 1945; came to U.S., 1970, naturalized, 1981; s. Shamjibhai Laljibhai and Ramaben Rathod; m. Damayanti Thakor, Aug. 15, 1970; children: Prerana, Falgun, Sejal. BS in Mech. Engring., Sardar Patel U., India, 1970; MS, Miss. State U., 1972, PhD, 1975. Rsch. grad. asst. Miss. State U., 1970-75; cons. engr. Bowron & Butler, Jackson, Miss., 1975-76; asst. prof. Tuskegee Inst., Ala., 1976-78; assoc. prof., coord. MET program SUNY, Binghamton, 1979-87; prof. Wayne State U., Detroit, 1987—, dir. engring. tech. divsn., 1987—2003. Cons. Interpine, Hattiesburg, Miss., 1977-79, Jet Propulsion Lab., 1980-83, IBM Corp., 1982-85; pres. Shiv-Parvati, Inc. 1982—. Contbr. articles to profl. jours.; patentee in field. Den leader Susquahanna coun. Boy Scouts Am., Vestal, N.Y., 1983-84. Recipient award NASA, 1981; grantee SUNY Found., 1984, Dept. Energy, 1978, GM, 1988-92, UAW Chrysler, 1990-91, Hudson-Webber Found., 1991-92, Ford, 1992-93, Kellogg Found., 1993-94, SME Found., 1994, Mich. Dept. Edn., 1994, NSF, 1995-2001. Fellow: ASME (cert. of appreciation 1982—89, 1991—2005, Dedicated Svc. award 1995, Ben C. Sparks medal 1998, BMW award 2001); mem.: ASHRAE, Profl. Order Engring. Tech., N.Y. State Engring. Tech. Assn., Am. Soc. Engring. Edn. (reviewer), India Assn. Miss. State U. (pres. 1972—73), Tau Beta Pi, Tau Alpha Phi (founder, faculty advisor 1989—), Pi Tau Sigma. Home: 1042 Woods Ln Grosse Pointe Woods MI 48236-1157 Office: Wayne State U Div Engring Tech Detroit MI 48202

RATNER, ALBERT B., building products company executive, land developer; b. Cleve., 1927; Grad., Mich. State U., 1951. With Forest City Enterprises, Inc., Cleve., 1964—, sec., 1960-68, exec. v.p., from 1968, now pres., chief exec. officer, dir., also co-chmn brd. Mem. exec. com., dir. Univ. Circle Devel. Corp.; dir. Am. Greetings Corp. Mem. Internat. Council Shopping Ctrs. Office: Forest City Enterprises Inc 1100 Terminal Tower 50 Public Sq # 1170 Cleveland OH 44113-2202

RATNER, CARL JOSEPH, opera stage director, baritone; b. Memphis, Sept. 17, 1957; MusB, Oberlin Conservatory of Music, 1980; MA, Northeastern Ill. U., 1999; DM, orthwestern U., 2005. Intern Juilliard Sch., NYC, 1980-81, N.Y.C. Opera, 1981-82; asst. dir. Lyric Opera Chgo., 1982-84; prodn. asst. San Francisco Opera, 1985-86; asst. dir. Metropolitan Opera, NYC, 1989-90; artistic dir. Chamber Opera Chgo., 1985-93, Chgo. Opera Theater, 1994-99; opera dir. Western Mich. U., 2001—. Cons. in field. Home: 3440 N Lake Shore Dr Apt 9D Chicago IL 60657-2848 Office: Western Michigan Univ Sch Music Dalton Ctr 1903 W Michigan Ave Kalamazoo MI 49008-5434 Office Phone: 269-387-4706, 773-454-4919. Personal E-mail: carlratner@aol.com.

RATNER, CHARLES A., real estate executive; Pres., CEO Forest City Enterprises, Inc., Cleve. Office: Forest City Enterprises Inc 50 Public Sq Ste 1100 Cleveland OH 44113-2267

RATNER, GERALD, lawyer; b. Chgo., Dec. 17, 1913; s. Peter I. and Sarah (Soreson) R.; m. Eunice Payton, June 18, 1948. PhB, U. Chgo., 1935, JD cum laude, 1937. Bar: Ill. 1937. Since practiced in, Chgo.; sr. ptnr. Gould & Ratner and predecessor firm, 1949—. Officer Henry Crown & Co., CC Industries, Inc., Material Svc. Corp., Freeman United Coal Mining Co., Mineral and Land Resources Corp.; lectr., writer on real estate law. Capt. US Army, 1942—46. Gerald Ratner Athletics Ctr. named in his honor, U. Chgo.; recipient Disting. Svc. medal U. Chgo., 2005 Mem. ABA, Ill. Bar Assn., Chgo. Bar Assn., Order of Coif, Phi Beta Kappa. Home: 180 E Pearson St Apt 6205 Chicago IL 60611-2191 Office: 222 N La Salle St Ste 800 Chicago IL 60601-1086 Office Phone: 312-236-3003. Business E-Mail: gratner@gouldratner.com.

RATNER, JAMES, real estate developer; m. Susan Ratner; 2 children. BA, Columbia U.; MBA, Harvard U. Former loan officer Citibank, NYC; with Nasher Co., Dallas, 1971—76; chmn., CEO Forest City Commercial Group, Cleve., 1976—; pres. devel. divsn. Forest City Enterprises, Cleve., 1978—. Bd. mem. Cleve. Museum of Art, Urban Land Inst., Playhouse Square Found. Office: Forest City Mgmt Terminal Tower 50 Public Sq Ste 1100 Cleveland OH 44113-2267

RAUENHORST, GERALD, architectural engineer, construction executive; b. Mpls., Dec. 8, 1927; s. Henry and Margaret (Keltgen) R.; m. Henrietta Schmoll, Sept. 2, 1950; children: Judith, Mark, Neil, Joseph, Michael, Susan, Amy. BA, U. St. Thomas, 1948, LLD, 1971; BSCE, Marquette U., 1951, LLD (hon.), 2001. Instr. civil engring. Marquette U., Milw., 1950-51; engr. Peter Rasmussen & Son, Oshkosh, Wis., 1951-52, Viking Constrn., Mpls., 1952-53; pres., founder Rauenhorst Corp. (name changed to Opus Corp.), Mpls., 1953—, chmn. bd., CEO, 1982—, founding chmn., 2000—. Chmn. and CEO Opus Nat., L.L.C., 1997—; dep. chmn. 1991-93, chmn. bd. dirs. Fed. Res. Bank, Mpls., 94-95, dir., chmn. human resources com. ConAgra, Omaha, 1982-98; bd. dirs. Cornerstone Properties, Inc., .Y., 1993-98. Treas., mem. devel. com. Papal Found.; trustee U. St. Thomas; chmn. bd. trustees Marquette U., 1985—87, trustee emeritus; dir. emeritus Cath. Cmty. Found. Recipient Disting. Engring. award Marquette U., 1974, Ernst & Young Lifetime Achievement award/Entrepreneur of Yr., 1997; named Alumnus of Yr., Marquette U., 1969, Coll. of St. Thomas, 1978, Minn. Exec. of Yr., Corp. Report mag., 1983, Developer of Yr., NAIOP, 1992, No. 1 Developer in Country, Nat. Real Estate Investor mag., 1995; named to Minn. Bus. Hall of Fame, 1980. Mem. ASCE, NSPE, World Pres. Orgn., Minn. Soc. Profl. Engrs., Mpls. Club, Interlachen Club, Naples Yacht Club, Port Royal Club, Royal Poinciana Golf Club, Serra Club (past gov. dist. 7, past pres. Mpls.), Knight of Holy Sepulchre, Knight of St. Gregory, Triangle. Roman Catholic. Avocations: fishing, golf, pottery. Office: Opus Corp PO Box 59110 Minneapolis MN 55459-0110

RAUSCHENBERGER, STEVEN J., state legislator; b. Elgin, Ill., Aug. 29, 1956; BBA, Coll. of William and Mary. Mem. Ill. State Senate, Dist. 33, Elgin Downtown Adv. Commn.; owner Rauschenberger Furniture Co.; gen. mgr. Ackerman Bros. Corp., Elgin, Ill. Active Boy Scouts Am. Office: Ill Senate Mem State Capitol Springfield IL 62706-0001 Home: 422 N Worth Ave Elgin IL 60123-3451

RAUSSEN, JIM, state representative; b. Cin., Dec. 19, 1970; m. Tara Murphy, 1998. BA in Polit. Sci., Xavier U., 1993; student, Oxford U., Eng. Sr. claims rep. Great Am. Ins. Co., Blue Ash, Ohio; state rep. dist. 28 Ohio Ho. of Reps., Columbus, vice chair, ins. com., mem. human svcs. and aging, mcpl. govt. and urban revitalization, and ways and means coms. Elected town trustee Hamilton Twp., Ohio, 1994—97. Mem.: Blue Chip Reps., Ams. for Tax Reform. Republican. Office: 77 S High Sch 11th fl Columbus OH 43215-6111

RAVEN, FRANCIS HARVEY, mechanical engineer, educator; b. Erie, Pa., July 29, 1928; s. Frederick James and Eleanor Elizabeth (Sopp) R.; m. Therese Mary Strobel, June 21, 1952; children: Betty, Ann Raven McCarthy, Paul, John, Mary Raven Mansmann, Cathy, Linda. BS in Math., Gannon U., Erie, Pa., 1948; BSME, Pa. State U., University Park, 1950, MSME, 1951; PhD, Cornell U., Ithaca, NY, 1958. Design engr. Hamilton Standard div. United Techs., Hartford, Conn., 1951-54; instr. Cornell U., Ithaca, N.Y., 1954-58; asst. prof. mech. engring. U. Notre Dame, 1958-62, assoc. prof., 1962-66, prof., 1966—. Cons. microprocessor and computer control of robots and mech. systems; devel. Vector Loop Method (first analytical method for the design of mechanisms and cam systems.). Author: Automatic Control Engineering, 1961, 5th edit., 1995, Mathematics of Engineering Systems, 1966, Engineering Mechanics, 1973; pub. McGraw-Hill Book Co. Mem. ASME, Am. Soc. for Engring. Edn. (AT&T Teaching award 1968-69), Sigma Xi. Roman Catholic. Office Phone: 574-631-7381. Business E-Mail: fraven@nd.edu.

RAVEN, PETER HAMILTON, botanist, director; b. Shanghai, June 13, 1936; s. Walter Francis and Isabelle Marion (Breen) R.; children— Alice Catherine, Elizabeth Marie, Francis Clark, Kathryn Amelia. AB with highest honors, U. Calif.-Berkeley, 1957; PhD, UCLA, 1960; DSc (hon.), St. Louis U., 1982, Knox Coll., 1983, So. Ill. U., 1983, Miami U., 1986, U. Goteborg, 1987, Rutgers U., 1988, U. Mass., 1988, Leiden U., The Netherlands, 1990; HHD (hon.), Webster U., 1989; D.Sc. (hon.), Universidad Nacional de La Plata, Argentina, 1991, Westminster Coll., 1992, U. Mo., 1992, Washington U., 1993, U. Conn., 1993; DSc (hon.), U. Cordoba, Argentina, 1993. Taxonomist, curator Rancho Santa Ana Botanic Garden, Claremont, Calif., 1961-62; asst. prof., then assoc. prof. biol. scis. Stanford U., Calif., 1962-71; dir. Mo. Bot. Garden, St. Louis, 1971—; adj. prof. biology St. Louis U., 1973—; Engelmann prof. botany Washington U., St. Louis, 1971—; adj. prof. biology U. Mo., St. Louis, 1976—. Sr. rsch. fellow

New Zealand Dept. Sci. and Indsl. Rsch., 1969-70; v.p. XIII Internat. Bot. Congress, Sydney, 1981; Home Sec. Nat. Acad. Scis., 1987—; chmn. report rev. com. NRC, 1989—; mem. pres. com. Adv. on Sci. and Tech., 1994—; hon. vice-chair 27th Internat. Geographical Cong., 1992; hon. v.p. XV Internt. Bot. Cong., Tokyo, 1993; mem. Nat. Sci. Bd., 1990-94; mem. jury Internat. St. Francis Prize for Environment, 1990-93; mem. exec. com. Joint Appeal by Religion and Sci. for Environment, 1991—; mem. external adv. bd. Com. on Peabody Mus., Yale U., 1992-94; mem. coun. World Resources Inst., 1992—; mem. adv. com. Africa Ctr. for Resources and Environment, 1992—, Third World Found. .Am., 1993; mem. adv. com. to biodiversity com. Chinese Acad. Scis., 1993—; mem. Exec. Com. Round Table, St. Louis, 1993—; mem. hon. fgn. adv. bd. Botanical Garden Orgn. Thailand, 1993—. Author: Native Shrubs of Southern California, 1966, (with P.R. Ehrlich, R.W. Holm) Papers on Evolution, 1969, (with H. Curtis) Biology of Plants, 1971, 4th edit., 1986, (with R.F. Evert and S.E. Eichhorn) 5th edit., 1992, (with B. Berlin and D. Breedlove) Principles of Tzeltal Plant Classification, 1974, (with G.B. Johnson) Biology, 1986, 3d edit., 1992, Understanding Biology, 1988, 3d edit., 1995; editor: (with L.E. Gilbert) Coevolution of Animals and Plants, 1981, (with F.J. Radovsky & S.H. Sohmer) Biogeography of the Tropical Pacific, 1984, (with others) Topics in Plant Population Biology, 1979, (with K. Iwatsuki and W.J. Bock) Modern Aspects of Species, 1986; editor-in-chief Brittonia, 1963-66; mme. editorial bd. Flora Neotropica, 1965-84; editor (with D.E. Osterbrock) Origins and Extinctions, 1988, paperback, 1992, (with R.M. Polhill) Advances in Legume Systematics, 1981 (with L. Berg and G.B. Johnson) Environment, 1995; mem. editorial bd. Evolution, 1963-65, 76-79, Memoirs of N.Y. Botanical Garden, 1966-84, N.Am. Flora, 1966-84, Am. Naturalist, 1967-70, Annual Rev. Ecology and Systematics, 1971-75, Flora of Ecuador, 1974—, Evolutionary Theory, 1975—, Adansonia, 1976—, Jour. Biogeography, 1978—, Science, 1979-82, Proceedings of U.S. Nat. Acad. Scis., 1980-87, World Book, Inc., 1982-86, Diversity, 1985-90, Bothalia, 1985—, Serie Botánica of the Anales del Instituto de Biología UNAM, 1989, Ecol. Applications, 1989-92, others; mem. adv. bd. Applied Botany Abstracts, 1981—, Tropical Plant Sci. Research, 1982—, Darwiniana, 1985—; mem. internat. editl. com. Acta Botánica Mexicana, 1987—; mem. internat. editl. adv. bd. Candollea, 1995—; mem. editl. bd. Botanical Bulletin Academia Sinica, 1988—, Botanical Mag., 1988-92, Chinese Jour. of Botany, 1991—, Edinburgh Jour. of Botany, 1994—; co-chmn. editl. com. Flora of China, 1988—; advisor Plants Today, 1988-89; contbr. over 400 articles to profl. jours. Bd. curators U. Mo., 1985-90; commr. Tower Grove Park, St. Louis, 1971—; mem. Arnold Arboretum Vis. Com., 1974-81, chmn. 1976-81; bd. overseers Morris Arboretum, 1977-81; mem. sci. adv. bd. Nat. Tropical Botanical Garden, 1975—; mem. Smithsonian Council, 1985-90; chmn. St. Louis Area Mus. Collaborative, 1985-91, Commn. for Flora Neotropica, 1985—; mem. Commn. on Mus. for New Century, 1981-84; mem. sci. and engring. panel Com. on Scholarly Communication with People's Republic China, 1981-85; chmn. com. to visit dept. organismic and evolutionary biology Harvard U., 1982-84, mem. 84-85; ednl. adv. bd. John Simon Guggenheim Meml. Found., 1986—; research assoc. botany Bernice P. Bishop Mus., 1985—; hon. trustee Acad. Sci. of St. Louis, 1986—; chmn. Internat. Union for the Conservation of Nature, World Wildlife Fund, 1984-87, hon. chmn. 1987-90; mem. adv. and tech. bd. Fundación de Parques acionales and Fundación Neotrópica, Costa Rica, 1988—; mem. Nat. Coun. World Wildlife Fund and Conservation Foun., 1989—, U.S. bd. dirs. 1983-88, bd. dirs. Conservation Found., 1985-88, sci. adv. com. Conservation Internat., 1988—, chmn's. coun., 1989, World Wildlife Fund, 1987-90, Conservation Found., 1989—, Found. Flora Malesianna, 1992—, Sci. Svc., 1993—; hon. scientific adv. com. XVII Pacific Sci. Congress, 1990-91; adv. bd. The Winslow Found., 1993—, The Internat. Sci. Camp The Earth We Share, 1993—; exec. bd. Internat. Sci. Found. for the Former Soviet Union, 1992—; internat. adv. bd. Fifth ICSEB Congress, Hungary, 1994—. Commn. mem. U.S. MAB, 1994-95. Recipient A.P. DeCandolle prize, Geneva, 1970; Disting. Service award Japan Am. Soc. So. Calif., 1977; award of Merit, Bot. Soc. Am., 1977; Achievement medal Garden Club Am., 1978; Willdenow medal Berlin Bot. Garden, 1979; Disting. Service award Am. Inst. Biol. Scis., 1981; Joseph Priestly medal, Dickinson Coll., 1982; Gold Seal medal Nat. Council of State Garden Clubs, 1982; Internat. Environ. Leadership medal UN Environ. Program, 1982; Spl. citiation Doña Doris Yankelewitz de Monge, 1985, Internat. Prize for Biology, Govt. Japan, 1986, Hutchinson medal Chgo. Hort. Soc., 1986, Archie F. Carr medal, 1987, Global 500 Honor Roll UN Environ. Program, 1987, Am. Fuchsia Soc. Achievement Medal, 1987, George Robert White Medal of Honor Mass. Horticultural Soc., 1987, Robert Allerton Medal Nat. Tropical Bot. Garden, 1988, Nat. Conservation Achievement award Nat. Wildlife Fedn., 1989, Delmer S. Fahrney medal Franklin Inst., Phila., 1989, (with E.O. Wilson) Environ. prize Institut de la Vie (Paris), 1990, Order of Golden Ark (officer), The Netherlands, 1990, award for Support of Sci. Coun. Sci. Soc. Pres., 1990, (with Norman Myers) Volvo Environ. prize, 1992, Pres.'s Conservation Achievement Awd., 1993, Nature Conservancyvement award TNC, 1993, Internat. award Internat. Inst. of St. Louis, 1994, Founder's Coun. Centennial Merit award The Field Mus. of Natural History, 1994, Sword of St. Ignatius Loyola award St. Louis U., 1994, Tyler Environ. Achievement prize, 1994, and numerous other botanical awards and honors; Guggenheim fellow, 1969-70; John D. and Catherine T. MacArthur Found. fellow, 1985-90, NSF postdoctoral fellow, Brit. Mus. London, 1960-61. Fellow Am. Acad. Arts and Scis. (com. on membership 1980-82), Linnean Soc. London (fgn. mem.), Calif. Acad. Scis. (CAS Fellow, Fellows' medal 1988), AAAS, Indian Nat. Sci. Acad., Third World Acad. Scis., World Acad. Art & Sci.; mem. NSF (systematic biology panel 1973-76, chmn. adv. com. for biol. behavioral and social scis. 1984-90), NAS (com. on human rights 1984-87, home sec. 1987—), Royal Danish Acad. Scis. and Letters (fgn. hon.), Royal Swedish Acad. Scis. (fgn.), Royal Soc. New Zealand (hon.), NRC (gov. bd. 1983-86, 87-88, chmn. com. on research priorities in tropical biology 1977-79, assembly life scis. 1979-81, com. on selected research problems in humid tropics 1980-82, commn. internat. relations 1981-82), Calif. Bot. Soc. (v.p. 1968-69), Am. Soc. Plant Taxonomists (pres. 1972), Assn. Systematics Collections (pres. 1980-82, Fed. Council Arts and Humanities, Nat. Geographic Soc. (com. on research and exploration 1982—), Internat. Orgn. Plant Biosystematists (v.p. 1989-92, pres. 92-95), Internat. Assn. for Plant Taxonomy (council 1981—), Orgn. Tropical Studies (treas. 1981-84, v.p. devel. 1984-85, pres. 1985-88, past pres. 1988-90, bd. dirs. 1981-91), Am. Soc. Naturalists (pres. 1983), Miller Inst. Basic Research in Sci. (adv. bd. 1983-89), Am. Inst. Biol. Scis. (pres. 1983-84), Mo. Acad. Scis., Geol. Soc. Am., Bot. Soc. Am. (pres. 1975, chmn. com. on sci. exchange with People's Republic China 1978-84), Assn. Tropical Biology (bd. dirs. 1981-85), Am. Assn. Mus. (exec. com. 1980-83, named to Centennial Honor Roll, 2006), Assn. Sci. Mus. Dirs., Assn. Pacific Systematists, Sociedad Argentina de Botanica (socio honorario), Fundación Miguel Lillo (hon.), Soc. Systematic Zool., Sociedad Botánica de México (life), Assn. pour l'Etude Taxonomique de la Flore d'Afrique Tropicale, Orgn. for Phyto-Taxonomic Investigation of Mediterranean Area (council 1975-89), All-Union Botanical Soc. USSR (hon. fgn. mem.), Accademia Nazionale delle Scienze detta dei XL (fgn.), Am. Philosophical Soc, Russian Acad. Scis. (fgn. mem.), Nat. Acad. Scis. India (fgn. fellow 1990—), Academia de Ciencias Exactas, Físicas y Naturales, Austrian Acad. Scis., Academia Chilena de Ciencias, Academia Nacional de Ciencias, Academy Scis. Ukraine, Chinese Acad. Scis., Nature Conservancy (Pres. Conservation Achievement Awd., 1993), Phi Beta Kappa, Sigma Xi Office: Missouri Botanical Garden PO Box 299 Saint Louis MO 63166-0299 Office Phone: 314-577-5111. Office Fax: 314-577-9595. E-mail: peter.raven@mobot.org.

RAVENCROFT, THOMAS A., food company executive; V.p. corp. planning Dean Foods Co., Franklin Park, Ill., 1979-88, group v.p., 1988-89, pres. dairy divsn., 1994-98, sr. v.p., 1989—, also bd. dirs. Office: 3600 River Rd Franklin Park IL 60131-2152

RAWDEN, DAVID, financial services company executive; CFO, Peregine, Southfield, Mich., until 1999; prin. Jay Alix & Assocs., Southfield, 1999—. Office: Jay Alix and Associates 2000 Town Ctr Ste 2400 Southfield MI 48075-1250

RAWLINS, RANDA, lawyer; Grad., Truman State U., 1979; JD, U. Mo., 1982. Bar: Mo., Kans., U.S. Dist. Ct. (ea. and we. dists.) Mo., U.S. Ct. Appeals (8th and 10th cirs.). Shareholder Niewald Waldeck & Brown, Kansas City, Kans. Bd. govs. Truman State U., 1997—; mem. Assn. of Governing Bds. of Univs. and Coll. Coun. of Bd. Chairs; vol. atty. CASA, Project Consent; mem. adv. bd. Inst. for Women in Pub. Life; lay leader St. John's United Meth. Ch., 1997—. Named one of 12 most disting. attys., Mo. Lawyers Weekly, 2001; recipient Pershing scholarship, Truman State U., Lon O. Hocke award, Mo. Bar Found., 1994. Mem.: Assn. Women Lawyers Greater Kansas City (2000 Woman of Yr.), Women Lawyers Greater Kansas City, Am. Bd. Trial Advocates, Kansas City Met. Bar Assn., Kans. Bar Assn.

RAWSON, RACHEL L., lawyer; BA magna cum laude, Kenyon Coll., 1987; JD, Columbia U., 1990. Bar: N.Y. 1991, Ohio 1995. With Jones Day, Cleve., 1992—, ptnr., 2003—. Mem.: ABA (bus. law sect.), Cleve. Bar Assn. (banking and bus. law sect.). Office: Jones Day North Point 901 Lakeside Ave Cleveland OH 44114-1190

RAWSON, ROBERT H., JR., lawyer; b. Washington, Oct. 18, 1944; AB, Princeton U., 1966; MA, Oxford U., Eng., 1968; JD, Harvard U., 1971. Bar: Ohio 1971, D.C. 1972. Ptnr. Jones, Day, Cleve.; ptnr.-in-charge Jones Day, Cleve. Rhodes scholar. Mem.: ABA, Bar Assn. of DC, Cleve. Bar Assn., Ohio State Bar Assn., Phi Beta Kappa. Office: Jones Day North Point 901 Lakeside Ave E Cleveland OH 44114-1190 Office Phone: 216-586-3939. Office Fax: 216-579-0212. Business E-Mail: rrawson@jonesday.com.

RAY, DOUGLAS KENT, newspaper executive; Pres., CEO Daily Herald/Sunday Herald, Arlington Heights, Ill., 1970—. Named Pubisher of Yr., Editor & Publisher, 2006. Office: Daily Herald/Sunday Herald Paddock Publs PO Box 280 Arlington Heights IL 60006-0280

RAY, FRANK ALLEN, lawyer; b. Lafayette, Ind., Jan. 30, 1949; s. Dale Allen and Merry Ann (Fleming) R.; m. Carol Ann Olmutz, Oct. 1, 1982; children: Erica Fleming, Robert Allen. BA, Ohio State U., 1970, JD, 1973. Bar: Ohio 1973, U.S. Dist. Ct. (so. dist.) Ohio 1975, U.S. Supreme Ct. 1976, U.S. Tax Ct. 1977, U.S. Ct. Appeals (6th cir.) 1977, U.S. Dist. Ct. (no. dist.) Ohio 1980, U.S. Dist. Ct. (ea. dist.) Mich. 1983, U.S. Ct. Appeals (1st cir.) 1986; cert. civil trial adv. Nat. Bd. Trial Advocacy. Asst. pros. atty. Franklin County, Ohio, 1973-75, chief civil counsel, 1976-78; dir. econ. crime project Nat. Dist. Attys. Assn., Washington, 1975-76; assoc. Brownfield, Kosydar, Bowen, Bally & Sturtz, Columbus, Ohio, 1978, Michael F. Colley Co., L.P.A., Columbus, 1979-83; pres. Frank A. Ray Co., L.P.A., Columbus, 1983—93, 2000—05, Ray & Todaro Co., LPA, Columbus, 1993-94, Ray, Todaro & Alton Co., L.P.A., Columbus, 1994-96, Ray, Todaro, Alton & Kirstein Co., L.P.A., Columbus, 1996, Ray, Alton & Kirstein Co., L.P.A., Columbus, 1996—98; sr. ptnr. Ray & Alton, L.L.P., Columbus, 1998—2000; ptnr. Chester, Willcox & Saxbe, LLP, 2006—; adj. prof. Moritz Coll. of Law, Ohio State U., 2003—. Mem. seminar faculty Nat. Coll. Dist. Attys., Houston, 1975-77; mem. nat. conf. faculty Fed. Jud. Ctr., Washington, 1976-77; bd. editors Man. for Complex Litigation, Fed. Jud. Ctr., 1999—2004; bd. mem. bar examiners Ohio Supreme Ct., 1992-95, mem. rules adv. com., 1995-99. Editor: Economic Crime Digest, 1975-76; co-author: Personal Injury Litigation Practice in Ohio, 1988, 91. Fin. com. Franklin County Rep. Orgn., Columbus, 1979-84, 2005—; trustee Ohio State U. Coll. Humanities Alumni Soc., 1991-93, at. Coun. Ohio State U., Moritz Coll. Law Alumni Soc., 1998—; capital campaign fund cabinet Legal Aid Soc. of Columbus, 1998. Capt. inf. U.S. Army, 1976. Named to Ten Outstanding Young Citizens of Columbus, Columbus Jaycees, 1976; recipient Nat. award of Distinctive Svc., Nat. Dist. Attys. Assn., 1977, Worthy Adversary award Ohio Assn. Civil Trial Attys., 2005, Disting. Alumnus award Ohio State U. Moritz Coll. Law, 2006. Fellow: Ohio Acad. Trial Lawyers (pres. 1989—90, Pres.'s award 1986), Ohio State Bar Found., Roscoe Pound Found., Am. Coll. Trial Lawyers, Internat. Soc. Barristers, Columbus Bar Found. (v.p. 2008—); mem.: ATLA (state del. 1990—92), Franklin County Trial Lawyers Assn. (pres. 1987—88, Pres.'s award 1990), Ohio State Bar Assn. (com. negligence law 1990—97, mem. com. jury instrns. 2002—06, coun. del. 2008—, Friend of Legal Edn. award 2005), Million Dollar Advs. Forum, Columbus Bar Assn. (pres. 2001—02, Profl. award 1987), Am. Bd. Trial Advs. (pres., Ohio Chpt. 2004), Inns of Ct. (pres. Judge Robert M. Duncan chpt. 1993—94). Presbyterian. Home: 2030 Tremont Rd Columbus OH 43221-4330 Office: 65 E State St Ste 1000 Columbus OH 43215-4216 Office Phone: 614-221-4000. Business E-Mail: fray@cwslaw.com.

RAY, GARY J., food products executive; Chmn. bd. dirs. Rochelle (Ill.) Foods Inc.; exec. v.p. ops. Hormel Foods, Austin, Minn. Office: Hormel Foods 1 Hormel Pl Austin MN 55912-3680

RAY, GLENN, art association administrator; Exec. dir. Assn. for the Advancement of Arts Edn., Cin. Office: Assoc For The Advancement Of Arts Edu 1223 Central Pkwy # 100 Cincinnati OH 45214-2812 Office Phone: 513-721-2223.

RAY, ROY LEE, state legislator, public finance consultant; b. Akron, Ohio, July 16, 1939; s. Charles Henry Ray and Geneva Lee (Edwards) Kendall; m. Frances Margaret Jordan, Aug. 24, 1968; children: Christopher Lee, Brian Edward. BS, Akron U., 1962. Sales rep. internat. div. Goodyear Tire & Rubber Co., Akron, 1962-68; stockbroker Francis I. DuPont & Co., Akron, 1968-69; rsch. analyst City of Akron, 1969-72, dep. dir. pub. svc., 1972-73, commr. pub. utilities, 1973-74, budget dir., 1974-79, fin. dir., 1977-79, mayor, mgr., safety dir., 1980-83; pres. Albrecht, Inc., Akron, 1983-85; cons. Ohio Co., Akron, 1988—; mem. Ohio Senate from 27th dist., Columbus, 1986—; fin. chmn. Ohio Senate, Columbus, 1996—. State sen. Ohio Senate, 1986—. Pres. Ohio Mcpl. League, 1982-83; chmn. Conf. Ohio Big-City Mayors, 1981-83, N.E. Ohio Four-County Coord. Orgn., 1981-82; bd. trustees local United Way, Akron Gen. Med. Ctr., Am. Cancer Soc. Recipient Alumni Honor award U. Akron, 1987, Freshman of Yr. award Columbus Monthly mag., 1988. Mem. Kiwanis, Phi Kappa Tau (Ray C. Bliss award 1983), Omicron Delta Kappa. also: Ohio Senate 1st Fl Rm 127 Senate Bldg Columbus OH 43215

RAY, WILLIS HARMON, chemical engineer; b. Washington, Apr. 4, 1940; BA, Rice Univ., 1962, BSChE, 1963; PhD, Univ. Minn., 1966. Asst. prof. chem. engring. Univ. Waterloo, 1966-69, assoc. prof., 1969-70; assoc. prof. to prof. State Univ. N.Y., Buffalo, 1970-76; prof. chem. engring. U. Wis., Madison, 1976-86, chmn. chem. engring., 1981-83, Steenbock prof. engring., 1986-96, Vilas prof., 1996—. Cons. 1967—; vis. prof. Rijksuniversiteit Gent & Univ. Leuven, 1973-74, Tech. Univ. Stuttgart, West Germany, 1974, dept. chem. engring. Univ. Minn., 1986, Cornell Univ., 1991; dist. vis. lectr. Univ. Alta, Can., 1982, McMaster Univ., Ont., 1985; lectr. Calif. Inst. Tech., 1988. Recipient Eckman award Am. Automatic Control Coun., 1969, A.K. Doolittle award Am. Chem. Soc., 1981, Prof. Progress award Am. Inst. Chem. Engring., 1982, Disn Reilly Lect. award Univ. Notre Dame, 1984, Edn. award Am. Automatic Control Coun., 1989; Guggenheim fellow 1973-74. Fellow Am. Inst. Chem. Engrs.; mem. IEEE, Nat. Acad. Engring., Am. Chem. Soc., Am. Soc. Engring. Edn., Soc. Industrial & Applied Math., Chem. Inst. Can., Sigma Xi. Office: Univ Wis Dept Chem Engring Madison WI 53706

RAYBURN, DAVID B., retired manufacturing executive; b. Gallipolis, Ohio, May 24, 1948; BS, Pa. State Univ., 1970; MBA, Xavier Univ., 1979. Mgmt. positions through dir. mfg. Rockwell Internat., 1970—91; v.p., gen. mgr. heavy duty & indsl. div. Modine Mfg. Co., Racine, Wis., 1991—93, v.p., gen. mgr. automotive div., 1993—94, group v.p. highway products, 1994—98, exec. v.p., 1998—2002, pres., COO, 2002—03, pres., CEO, 2003—08. Bd. dirs. Marshall & Illsley Bank, Twin Disc, Jason Holdings Inc., RAMAC, Modine Mfg. Co., 2003—08. Mem.: Soc. Automotive Engineers.*

RAYHONS, HENRY V., state representative; b. Garner, Iowa, May 8, 1936; m. Marvalyn Rayhons; children: Carol, Dale, Sara, Gary. Student, Farmers Night Sch., 1954—58. Farmer; state treas. Iowa Cath. Workman, 1982—; state dir. Iowa Farm Bur., 1987—96; mem. soil commn. Hancock Soil Constrn. Dist., 1980—96; state rep. dist. 11 Iowa Ho. of Reps., 1997—; mem. agr. com.; mem. natural resources com.; vice chair transp. com.; mem. transp., infrastructure, and capitals appropriations com. Mem.: Iowa Soybean Assn., Am. Dairy Assn., Iowa Corn Growers, Iowa Beef Prodrs., Farm Bur., Hancock County Soil Conservation Commnrs., Iowa Cath. Workman, Garner Lions. Republican. Roman Catholic. Office: State Capital East 12th and Grand Des Moines IA 50319 Address: 2820 Oak Ave Garner IA 50438

RAYMOND, BRUCE ALLEN, retired surgeon, medical association administrator; b. Aberdeen, SD, Dec. 8, 1924; s. Samuel A. and Pearl (Blackstone) R.; m. Virginia Stratton, Apr. 2, 1948 (div. 1969); children: Judith Ann, Jaqueline Marie, Bruce Allen Jr., Brian Andrew; m. Jane Molnar, Nov. 15, 1969; children: Douglas A., Andrew D., Colin K. BS, Leland Stanford U., U. S.D., 1945; MD, Washington U., St. Louis, 1949. Diplomate Am. Bd. Surgery, Am. Bd. Thoracic Surgery. Intern U. Ored. Med. Sch. Hosps., Portland, 1949-50; resident Walter Reed Gen. Hosp., Washington, 1953—60, asst. chief thoracic surgery, 1959-60; chief thoracic and cardiovascular surgery Letterman Gen. Hosp., San Francisco, 1960-64, Fitzsimmons Gen. Hosp., Denver, 1967-69, chief dept. surgery, 1969-71; pvt. practice surgery Warwick, RI, 1975-86; sr. med. dir. various insurance co.; med. dir. The Health Plan of the Upper Ohio Valley, 1996—2003. Asst. clin. prof. U. Colo., 1967-71; assoc. clin. prof. surgery Northwestern U., Chgo., 1973-80; mem. staff Kent County Med. Mem. Hosp., Warwick, 1975-86, Miriam hosp., Providence, 1975-86; cons. in field. Contbr. articles to profl. jours. Col. MC US Army, 1949—72. Decorated Legion of Merit. Fellow ACS, Am. Coll. Cardiology, Am. Coll. Chest Physicians; mem. Soc. Thoracic Surgeons. Avocation: downhill skiing. Home: 218 Salem Dr Upper Saint Clair PA 15241-2226 Personal E-mail: braymond66@adelphia.net.

RAYMOND, RICHARD GERARD, JR., lawyer; b. Detroit, Jan. 1, 1959; s. Richard G. Raymond Sr. and Mary Jo (Bradley) Raymond; m. Holly Lyn Russell, Aug. 4, 1984; 3 children. BS in chemistry, U. Mich., 1981; JD, U. Detroit, 1986. Bar: Mich. 1986, US Dist. Ct. Ea. Dist. Mich. 1986. Indsl. chemist Product-Sol Inc., Birmingham, Mich., 1982-83; assoc. Johnson & Valentine, Detroit, 1986—89; asst. gen. counsel Fruehauf Trailer Corp., 1989; assoc. gen. counsel, asst. sec. Gen. Automotive Corp.; corp. counsel Am. Axle & Mfg. Holdings Inc., 1995—2000, gen. counsel, 2000—. Mem. ABA, Mich. Bar Assn., Detroit Bar Assn., Am. Chem. Soc. Roman Catholic. Office: Am Axle & Mfg Holdings Inc 1840 Holbrook Ave Detroit MI 48212

RAYNAL, LAZAR POL, lawyer; b. 1963; BS, U. Wis., 1985; JD cum laude, U. Notre Dame, 1988. Bar: Ill. 1988, US Dist. Ct. (no. dist. Ill.), US Ct. Appeals (7th & 10th cirs.), US Supreme Ct. Ptnr. McDermott, Will & Emery, Chgo., co-chair Trust & Estate Controversy practice. Named one of Litig.'s Rising Stars, The Am. Lawyer, 2007. Mem.: Def. Rsch. Inst., Fed. Defender Prog. Panel No. Ill. Office: McDermott Will & Emery 227 W Monroe St Chicago IL 60606-5096 Office Phone: 312-984-3653. Office Fax: 312-984-7700. E-mail: lraynal@mwe.com.

RAYWARD, WARDEN BOYD, librarian, educator; b. Inverell, NSW, Australia, June 24, 1939; s. Warden and Ellie Rayward. BA, U. Sydney, 1960; diploma in libr., U. NSW, 1964; MS in L.S, U. Ill., 1965; PhD, U. Chgo., 1973. Asst. state library, NSW, 1961-64; research librarian planning and devel. NSW, 1970; lectr. Sch. Librarianship U. NSW, Sydney, 1971-72, head sch. Info., Libr. and Archive Studies, 1986-92, prof., 1986-00, dean Faculty Profl. Studies, 1993-96, prof. emeritus, 2000—; asst. prof. U. Western Ont., 1973-74, Grad. Library Sch. U. Chgo., 1975-77, assoc. prof., 1978-80, prof., 1980-86; dean U. Chgo. Grad. Library Sch., 1980-86; rsch. prof. U. Ill., Champaign, 2000—, prof., 2004—, prof. emeritus, 2008—. Cons. NEH, 1976-79, U.S. Dept. Edn., 1981; bd. govs. Charles Stuart U., 1994-96; bd. dirs. Internat. House-U. NSW, 1992-97; George A. Miller vis. prof. U. Ill., 1997-98; Leverhulme Trust vis. prof. Leed Met. U., 2002; vis. prof. Leeds Met. U., 2004—. Author: The Universe of Information: The Work of Paul Otlet for Documentation and International Organization, 1975 (also transl. Russian and Spanish), Hasta la documentacion electronica, 2002; editor: The Variety of Librarianship: Essays in Honour of John Wallace Metcalfe, 1976, The Public Library: Circumstances and Prospects, 1978, Library Quar., 1975-79, Library History in Context, 1988, Libraries and Life in a Changing World: the Metcalfe Years 1920-1970, 1993; editor, translator: International Organization and the Dissemination of Knowledge: Selected Papers of Paul Otlet, 1990; editor Confronting the Future, University Libraries in the Next Decade, 1992, Developing a Profession in Librarianship in Australia: Travel Diaries and Other Papers of John Wallace Metcalfe, 1996, Aware and Responsible: Papers of The Nordic-International Colloquium (Scarlid), 2004, Pioneers in Library Info Science, 2005; (with Christine Jenkins) Libraries in Time of War Revolution and Social Change,; mem. editl. bd. European Modernism & Re-Information Society, 2008,World Book of Encyclopedia, 1990-97; co-editor: History and Heritage of Scientiful and Technological Information Systems, 2004; contbr. articles to profl. jours. Coun. on Library Resources fellow, 1978, vis. fellow U. Coll. London, 1986, 90, Mortenson fellow U. Ill., 1992-93, Garfield fellow in hist. sci. lit., 2000. Mem.: ALA, Union Interant. Assns., Am. Soc. Info. Sci. (Rsch. award 2004), Australian Libr. and Info. Assn. (hon.). Office Phone: 217-244-9741. Business E-Mail: wrayward@uiuc.edu.

RAZ, HILDA, editor-in-chief, educator; b. Rochester, NY, May 4, 1938; d. Franklyn Emmanuel and Dolly (Horwich) R.; m. Frederick M. Link, June 9, 1957 (div. 1969); children: John Franklin Link, Aaron Link; m. Dale Nordyke, Oct. 4, 1980. BA, Boston U., 1960. Asst. dir. Planned Parenthood League of Mass., Boston, 1960-62; edit. asst. Prairie Schooner, Lincoln, Nebr., 1970-74, contbg. editor, 1974-77, assoc. editor, 1977-87, acting editor, 1981-83, 85, poetry editor, 1980-87, editor-in-chief, 1987—; prof. dept English U. Nebr., Lincoln, 1990—. Luschei endowed lectr., reader, panelist in field; participant many workshops, symposia, confs.; panelist creativity arts com. NEA, 2000, PEN, 2004; judge Kenyon Rev., 1990, Ill. Art Coun./NEA fellowships, 1987; bd. govs. Ctr. for Great Plains Studies, U. Nebr., 1989-95. Author: The Bone Dish, 1997, What Is Good, 1997, Divine Honors, 1998, Trans, 2001, What Becomes You, 2007; editor: Best of Prairie Schooner: Fiction and Poetry, 2001, Best of Prairie Schooner: Essays, 2000, Living on the Margins, 1999, other books; editor Nebr. Humanist, 1990. Pres. Assoc. Writing Programs, bd. dirs., 1988-89, ex-officio pres., 1989-90, v.p., 1987-88; bd. dirs. Nebr. Libr. Heritage Assn., 1988-91; mem. Mayor's Blue Ribbon Com. on Arts, 1985-88; bd. dirs. Planned Parenthood League Nebr., 1978-83, sec. bd. dirs., 1979-80, chair long-term planning com., 1980-81, 81-82. Recipient Literary Heritage award, Mayor's Art award, Lincoln, 1988, 2002, ORCA award, 2002, May Sartm award, NE Poetry Club, 2004; Bread Loaf scholar editors, 1974, poetry, 1985; Robert Frost fellow, 1988, 89, Mag. Panel fellow, 1993, 94. Avocation: gardening. Home: 960 S Cotner Blvd Lincoln NE 68510-4926 Office: Univ of Nebraska Lincoln Prairie Schooner 201 Andrews Hall Lincoln NE 68588-0334 Office Phone: 402-472-1812. E-mail: HRaz1@unl.edu.

RAZEK, EDWARD G., retail executive; Exec. v.p., creative dir. Shelly Berman Communicators; v.p. mktg. Ltd. Stores, 1983—87, exec. v.p., 1987—92; v.p., dir. mktg. Ltd., Inc., Columbus, Ohio, 1993—97, pres. creative svcs., 1997—. Office: Ltd Brands Three Ltd Pkwy Columbus OH 43230

RAZOV, ANTE, professional soccer player; b. LA, Mar. 2, 1974; Student, UCLA, 1992-95. Forward L.A. Galaxy, 1996-97, Chgo. Fire, 1998-2000, team leading scorer, 1999; forward U.S. Nat. Team, 1999—. Avocations: reading mystery books, listening to reggae/hip hop music. Address: 12635 Heflin Dr La Mirada CA 90638

REA, ANNE E., lawyer; b. 1959; AB, Brown U., 1981; JD, U. Cgho., 1984. Bar: Ill. 1984. With Sidley Austin Brown & Wood, Chgo., 1984—, ptnr., 1992—. Selected as one of 15 Rising Stars You Won't Want to Oppose in Ct., Ill. Legal Times. Mem.: ABA, Leadership Greater Chgo., Chgo. Bar Assn., Ill. State Bar Assn.

REA, CABOT, newscaster; m. Heather Leach; children: Joshua, Meredith, Cassie. Degree in music, Ottervein Coll., 1978; postgrad., Ohio State U. Prof. singer, actor; tchr. music Newark City Schs.; reporter Sta. WCMH-TV, Columbus, Ohio, 1985, anchor, 1985—. Recipient Emmy award, The Westerville Sertoma Svc. to Humanity award, 2002. Office: WCMH-TV 3165 Olentangy River Rd PO Box 4 Columbus OH 43202

READ, SISTER JOEL, retired academic administrator; BS in Edn., Alverno Coll., 1948; MA in History, Fordham U., 1951; degree (hon.), Lakeland Coll., 1972, Wittenburg U., 1976, Marymount Manhattan Coll., 1978, DePaul U., 1985, Northland Coll., 1986, SUNY, 1986, Lawrence U., 1997, Marquette U., 2003. Former prof., dept. chmn. history dept. Alverno Coll., Milw., pres., 1968—2003. Past pres. Am. Assn. for Higher Edn., 1976-77; mem. coun. NEH, 1977-84; bd. dirs. Ednl. Testing Svc., 1987-93, Neylan Commn., 1985-90; past pres. Wis. Assn. Ind. Colls. and Univs.; mem. Commn. on Status of Edn. for Women, 1971-76, Am. Assn. Colls., 1971-77. Bd. dirs. Jr. Achievement, 1991-2003, State of Wis. Coll. Savs. Bd., 2000-03, Greater Milw. Com., Wis. Found. Ind. Colls., 1990-99, Women's Philanthropy Inst., 1997-2000, Wis. Women Higher Edn. Leadership, 1997-2000; bd. dirs. YMCA, 1989-2003, trustee, 2003-; mem. Profl. Dimensions. First recipient Anne Roe award Harvard U. Grad. Sch. Edn., 1980; recipient Morris T. Keaton award, Coun. for Adult and Experiential Learning, 1992; recipient Jean B. Harris award, Rotary; Paul Harris fellow, Rotary. Fellow Am. Acad. Arts and Scis., Wis. Acad. Arts and Scis. Personal E-mail: joel.read@alverno.edu.

READ, SARAH J., lawyer; BA cum laude, Yale U., 1978; JD, U. Wis., 1981; postgrad., Ctr. for Conflict Resolution, Chgo., MIT-Harvard U. Bar: Wis. 1981, Ill. 1981, U.S. Dist. (we. dist.) Wis. 1981, U.S. Dist. Ct. (no. dist.) Ill. 1981. Ptnr. Sidley & Austin, Chgo., also mem. telecom., energy and petrochems. practice goup, mem. alternative dispute resolution resource group. Mem. Ohio Telecom. Adv. Bd., 1984. Mem. ABA, Wis. Bar Assn., Chgo. Bar Assn., Order of Coif. Office: Sidley & Austin 1 S First National Plz Chicago IL 60603-2000 Fax: 312-853-7036.

READING, ANTHONY JOHN, accountant; b. London, Aug. 8, 1943; came to U.S., 1993; m. Myra Elizabeth Steer, Aug. 27, 1966; 1 child, Jason. Chartered acct. Mng. dir., dir. mfg., dir. fin. Donaldson Co. Inc., Brussels, 1970-80; group exec. Thomas Tilling Plc, London, 1980-83; divisional group chief exec. BTR Plc, London, 1983-87; group mng. dir. Polly Peck Internat., London, 1987-89, Pepe Group Plc, London, 1989-90; divisional dir. Tomkins Plc, London, 1990-92, also bd. dirs.; chmn., CEO Tomkins Corp., Dayton, Ohio, 1992—. Chmn. Orgn. Internat. Investment, Washington, 2002. Named Mem. of Most Excellent Order of Brit. Empire, Her Majesty Queen Elizabeth II, 1978. Fellow Inst. Chartered Accts. Eng. and Wales; mem. Naval and Mil. Club London. Avocations: music, golf, water sports. Office: Tomkins Corp 6450 Poe Ave Ste 109 Dayton OH 45414-2646 E-mail: areading@tomkins-industries.com.

REAGAN, PAUL V., lawyer; b. 1947; m. Jane Reagan; 3 children. BA in History, Rutgers U., 1969; JD, U. Notre Dame, 1973. Bar: NY 1974, admitted to practice: US Dist. Ct. (Ea. Dist.) NY 1976, US Dist. Ct. (So. Dist.) NY 1976, US Dist. Ct. (No. Dist.) NY 1976, US Dist. Ct. (We. Dist.) NY 1976. Assoc. Dewey Ballantine, NY, 1973—80; various positions, Legal Dept. Bankers Trust Co., 1980, mng. dir. and counsel, Real Estate Finance Group; gen. counsel Harris Bank, Chgo.; sr. v.p., US gen. counsel Bank of Montreal. Bd. mem. Ill. State Banking Bd., Assn. for the Advancement of Black Accts. Office: Harris Bank 111 West Monroe St Chicago IL 60603 Office Phone: 213-461-3167.

REAME, NANCY KING, nursing educator; BSN, Mich. State U., 1969; MSN, Wayne State U., Detroit, 1974, PhD in Physiology, 1977. RN. Postdoctoral fellow U. Mich., Ann Arbor, prof. dept. nursing, 1980—; Rhetaugh Graves Dumas Endowed Chair, Nursing Rsch. U. Mich. Health Sys., rsch. scientist, Reproductive Sciences Program, 1990—, dir., Nat. Ctr. for Infertility Rsch., 1990—95. Co-author: Our Bodies, Ourselves; actress The Vagina Monologues, U. Mich., 2002. Bd. dir. .Am. Menopause Soc. Fellow: AAAS; mem.: Am. Acad. Nursing, Inst. Medicine. Achievements include research in in brain aging and menopause; long-term satisfaction and outcomes after surrogate pregnancy; bioethics of assisted reproduction; gender and health. Office: Univ Mich Sch Nursing 400 N Ingalls Bldg Rm 2238 Ann Arbor MI 48109-0482 Office Phone: 734-647-0134. Office Fax: 734-936-3591. E-mail: nreame@umich.edu.

REAMS, MICHAEL THOMAS, director, singer, actor; b. Peoria, Ill., Jan. 4, 1966; s. Thomas Clyde and Carol Ann (Wiltz) R. BA, Bradley U., 1988. Asst. mgr. Cabaret Music Theatre, Peoria, 1985-86; dir. park players Peoria Park Dist., 1987-88; mgr. Strawmill Playhouse, Peoria, 1989. Actor (mus.) Follies, 1985, Company, 1986, Do Black Patent Leather Shoes Really Reflect Up?, 1988, Sweeney Todd, 1989, Baby, 1989, A Funny Thing Happened on the Way to the Forum, 1990, Guys and Dolls, 1993, Damn Yankees, 1995, Into the Woods, 1995, Ruthless, 1996, It's A Bird, It's A Plane, It's Superman, 1996, The Fantasticks, 1997, (plays) Amadeus, 1987, The Nerd, 1988, 95, Noises Off, 1989, Bleacher Bums, 1992, Rumors, 1992, Lend Me A Tenor, 1993, (opera) Amahl and the Night Visitors, 1990; dir. (plays) The Dining Room, 1989, Social Security, 1990, Broadway Bound, 1991, A Day in Hollywood/A Night in the Ukraine, 1994, Nunsense, 1994, Nunsense II, 1995, Do Black Patent Leather Shoes Really Reflect Up?, 1996. Mem. Peoria Players Theatre, Cornstock Theatre. Avocations: cast recordings collector, writing.

REARDON, JOHN E., broadcast executive; b. Chgo., Jan. 26, 1954; BA in Bus. Adminstrn. and Fin., Loyola U., 1977. Account exec. WGN-TV, Chgo., 1985—86, regional sales mgr., 1986—87, local sales mgr., 1979—89, dir. sales, 1989—92; sta. mgr. KTLA-TV, LA, 1992—96, v.p. & gen. mgr., 1996—2004; group v.p. Tribune Broadcasting Co., 2004—05, pres. & CEO Chgo., 2005—. Bd. dirs. Lincoln Park Zoo, Chgo. Mem.: Nat. Assn. Broadcasters (TV bd. dirs.), TV Bur. Advt. (bd. dirs.). Office: Tribune Co 435 N Michigan Ave Chicago IL 60611 Office Phone: 312-222-9100.

REARDON, MARK, radio personality; b. Chgo. married; 2 children. B Journalism, U. Mo. News anchor, co-host morning show KPLA-FM, Columbia, Mo., news dir.; radio host KFRU-AM, 1992—96, KSD-AM, St. Louis, 1996, WTMJ, Milw., 1997—. Avocations: hunting, fishing, music, movies, thoroughbred racing, golf. Office: WTMJ 720 E Capital Dr Milwaukee WI 53212

REARDON, MICHAEL EDWARD, lawyer; b. Independence, Mo., Apr. 15, 1948; s. Neil Willison and Marjorie (Winters) R.; m. Gloria Kay Nelson, Jan. 31, 1970; children— Darin Thomas, Laura Michelle. B.A. magna cum laude, William Jewell Coll., 1970; J.D. with distinction, U. Mo.-Kansas City, 1973, LL.M. in Criminal Law, 1978. Bar: Mo. 1973, U.S. Dist. Ct. (we. dist.) Mo. 1974, U.S. Supreme Ct. 1978. Assoc. Morris, Larson, King, Stamper-Bold, Kansas City, Mo., 1973-74, M. Randall Vanet, North Kansas City, Mo., 1974-75; ptnr. Duncan, Russell & Reardon, Kansas City, 1975-82, Michael E. Reardon & Assocs., Kansas City, 1982-86; Clay County Pros. Atty., Liberty, Mo., 1987-98; pvt. practice, 1999—. Bd. dirs. Clay County Sheltered Facilities, 1982-84; chmn. Clay County Dem. Com., Kansas City, 1982-84; treas. Mo. 6th Congl. Dist. Dem. Com., 1982-86; bd. dirs. Clay County Investigative Squad, Liberty, 1987-98. Mem. Mo. Bar Assn., Mo. Assn. Trial Attys., Clay County Bar Assn., Kansas City Bar Assn., ATLA, Gladstone C. of C. Office: 5716 N Broadway St Kansas City MO 64118-3962

REARDON, NANCY ANNE, food products executive; b. Little Falls, NY, Sept. 19, 1952; d. Warren Joseph and Elizabeth Owen (Tiel) Reardon; m. Steven Jonathan Sayer, Aug. 28, 1976; children: Scott Jason, Kathryn Anne. BS in Psychology, Union Coll., 1974; MS in Social Psychology, Syracuse U., 1978. With GE Co., NYC, 1979-85, Avon Products Inc., NYC, 1985-89, Am. Express, NYC, 1989-91; sr. v.p. human resources Duracell Internat., Inc., Bethel, Conn., 1991-97; sr. v.p. corp. affairs & human resources Borden Inc., Columbus, Ohio, 1997—2004; sr. v.p., chief human resources and comm. officer Campbell Soup Co., Camden, NJ, 2004—. Bd. dir. Warnaco Group Inc. 2006-; adv. bd. mem. Catalyst, 1995. Mem. Human Resource Planning Soc. (bd. dirs. 1991-94, treas. 1992-93), N.Y. Human Resource Planners (bd. dirs., pres. 1989-91), Sr. Pers. Execs. Forum, Nat. Fgn. Trade Coun. (bd. dirs. 1995), Soc. Human Resource Mgmt., Phila. Women's Forum. Avocation: skiing. Office: Campbell Soup Co 1 Campbell Pl Camden NJ 08103-1799

REARDON, THOMAS R., physician, medical association administrator; m. Elizabeth Reardon. MD, U. Colo., 1959. Intern Balt. City Hosp.; pvt. practice Portland, Oreg. Apptd. Congrl. Physician Payment Rev. Commn., 1986-94; mem. Pres. Commn. on Patient Rights and Quality Care. Chair of judges Portland Rose Festival Parade. With USAF, 1960-63. Mem. AMA (pres., chair bd. trustees 1997, mem. 1990—, exec. com. 1994—, sec. treas. 1994-95, vice chair bd. trustees 1995-97, hosp. med. staff sect. in ho. of dels. 1983-90, steering com.), Am. Rose Soc., Portland Rose Soc. (past pres.), Multnomah County Med. Soc. (pres. 1980-81, Disting. Svc. award 1982), Oreg. Med. Assn. (pres. 1983-84). Avocation: horticulture. Office: AMA 515 N State St Chicago IL 60610-4325

REASONER, MICHAEL J., state representative, small business owner; b. Davenport, Iowa, Aug. 17, 1960; m. Margaret Reasoner. BA, Creighton U., 1983, JD, 1986. Owner bus., 1989—; state rep. dist. 95 Iowa Ho. of Reps., 2003—. Supr. Union County, 1995—. Mem.: Petroleum Marketers Iowa, Creston C. of C. Democrat. Address: 702 New York Ave Creston IA 50801 Office: State Capitol East 12th and Grand Des Moines IA 50319

REASONER, WILLIS IRL, III, lawyer; b. Hamilton, Ohio, Dec. 24, 1951; s. W. Irl Jr. and Nancy Jane (Mitchell) R.; m. Lana Jean Mayes, Apr. 19, 1975 (div. Sept. 1985); 1 child, Erick; m. Joan Marie Mogil, Dec. 30, 1985; children: Scott, Sally. BA in History, Ind. U., 1974; JD cum laude, U. S.C., 1978. Bar: Ohio 1978, U.S. Dist. Ct. (so. dist.) Ohio 1978, U.S. Dist. Ct. (no. dist.) Ohio 1979, U.S. Ct. Appeals (6th cir.) 1988, U.S. Ct. Appeals (1st cir.) 1991, U.S. Ct. Appeals (7th cir.) 1999. Assoc. Porter, Wright, Morris & Arthur, Columbus, Ohio, 1978-83; ptnr. Baker & Hostetler, Columbus, 1983-94, Habash, Reasoner & Frazier, 1994—. Mem. ABA, Ohio Bar Assn., Columbus Bar Assn. Home: 4005 Redford Ct New Albany OH 43054-9500 Office: Habash, Reasoner & Frazier 471 E Broad St Ste 800 Columbus OH 43215-3854 Office Phone: 614-221-9400. E-mail: jreasoner@hrf-law.com.

REATEGUI, LISA J., lawyer; b. 1966; BA magna cum laude, Princeton U., 1988; MA in Latin Am. Studies, Stanford U., 1990; JD magna cum laude, Northwestern U., 1995. Atty. Sidley Austin Brown & Wood, Chgo., 1995—2003, ptnr., 2003—. Chmn. major gifts fund raising Princeton U.; mem. women's bd. The Field Mus., mem. young profl.'s bd. Mem.: ABA, Chgo. (Ill.) Bar Assn. Office: Sidley Austin Brown & Wood Bank One Plz 10 South Dearborn St Chicago IL 60603

REBAR, ALAN H., dean; b. Stillwater, Okla. DVM, Purdue U., 1973, PhD, 1975; diplomate, Am. Coll. Veterinary Pathologists. Diplomate Am. Coll. Vet. Pathologists. Asst. prof. clin. pathology Purdue U., West Lafayette, Ind., 1976; assoc. dean for rsch. Purdue U. Sch. Vet. Medicine, West Lafayette, Ind., 1989—, head dept. vet. pathology, 1995—, dean, 1996—, prof. vet. clin. pathology. Recipient Award of Merit, Am. Animal Hosp. Assn., Gaines Cycle Fido award. Mem.: Am. Coll. Vet. Pathologists (diplomate). Office: Purdue U Sch Vet Medicine 1240 Lynn Hall Purdue U West Lafayette IN 47907-1240 Office Phone: 765-494-7608. Office Fax: 765-496-1261. Business E-Mail: rebara@vet.purdue.edu.

REBEIN, JOSEPH M., lawyer; b. Dodge City, Kans. BS, U. Kans., 1982, JD, 1985. Bar: Mo. 1985. Ptnr., chair Gen. Litig. Div. Shook, Hardy & Bacon LLP, Kansas City, Mo. Mem.: ABA, Order of the Coif. Office: Shook, Hardy & Bacon LLP 2555 Grand Blvd Kansas City MO 64108 Office Phone: 816-559-2227. Office Fax: 816-421-5547. E-mail: jrebein@shb.com.

REBEIZ, CONSTANTIN ANIS, plant biochemist, lab and foundation administrator, educator; b. Beirut, July 11, 1936; arrived in U.S., 1959, naturalized, 1975; s. Anis C. and Valentine A. (Choueyri) Rebeiz; m. Conness Carole Louise, Aug. 18, 1962; children: Paul A., Natalie, Mark J. BS, Am. U., Beirut, 1959; MS, U. Calif., Davis, 1960, PhD, 1965. Dir. dept. biol. scis. Agrl. Rsch. Inst., Beirut, 1965—69; rsch. assoc. biology U. Calif., Davis, 1969—71; assoc. prof. biochem. plant physiology U. Ill., Urbana-Champaign, 1972—76, prof., 1976—2005, dir. Lab. Plant Biochemistry and Photobiology, 1973—2005, prof. emeritus, 2005—; pres. Rebeiz Found. for Basic Rsch., Champaign, 2005—. Adj. prof. U. Limerick, Ireland, 2003. Contbr. articles to profl. jours. Bd. dirs. Rebeiz Found. for Basic Rsch. Named one of 100 Outstanding Innovators, Sci. Digest, 1984—85; recipient Beckman Rsch. award, 1982, 1985, Funk award, 1985, Sr. Rsch. award, U. Ill., 1994, Presdl. Green Chemistry Challenge award, 1999, Outstanding Sci. Achievement award, Faculty of Agrl. and Food Sci., Am. U. Beirut, 2002; grantee John P. Trebellas Rsch. Endowment, 1986, C.A. and C.C. Rebeiz Endowment for basic rsch., 2000. Mem.: AAAS, Lebanese Assn. Advancement Scis. (exec. com. 1967—69). Achievements include research in pathway of chlorophyll biosynthesis; chloroplast development; bioengineering of photosynthetic reactors; first to biosynthesis of chlorophyll in vitro; duplication of greening process of plants in test tube; development of demonstration of operation of multibranched chlorophyll biosynthetic pathway in nature; formulation of a blue-print chloroplast bioengineering in green plants aimed at improving plant productivity; formulation and design of laser herbicides, insecticides and cancer chemotherapeutic agents. Home: 2209 Edgewater Pl Champaign IL 61822 Office: Rebeiz Found Basic Rsch 2209 Edgewater Pl Champaign IL 61822 Office Phone: 217-377-9148. Business E-Mail: crebeiz@uiuc.edu.

RECHTZIGEL, SUE MARIE (SUZANNE RECHTZIGEL), child care center executive; b. St. Paul, May 27, 1947; d. Carl Stinson and Muriel Agnes (Oestrich) Miller; m. Gary Elmer Rechtzigel, Aug. 20, 1968 (div. Feb. 1982); children: Brian Carl, Lori Ann. BA in Psychology, Sociology, Mankato State U., Minn., 1969. Lic. in child care, Minn. Rep. ins. State Farm Ins. Co., Albert Lea, Minn., 1969-73; free-lance child caretaker Albert Lea, Minn., 1973-78; owner, dir. Lakeside Day Care, Albert Lea, Minn., 1983—. Asst. Hawthorne Sch. Learning Ctr., Albert Lea, 1978-83. Mem. New Residents and Newcomers Orgn., Albert Lea, 1970—, past. pres.; asst. pre-sch. United Meth. Ch., Albert Lea, 1975-78, tchr. Sunday sch., 1976-80, tchr. Bible sch., 1980-85; active Ascension Luth. Ch., 1976-80. Mem. Freeborn Lic. Day Care Assn. (v.p. 1986, pres. 1987), AAUW (home tour 1977, treas. 1980-81), Bus. and Profl. Women, YMCA, Albert Lea Art Ctr. Clubs: 3M Families. Republican. Avocations: ceramics, calligraphy, painting, art, sewing. Home and Office: 1919 Brookside Dr Albert Lea MN 56007-2142

RECKER, THOMAS EDWARD, fraternal organization executive; b. Livonia, Mich., Feb. 28, 1960; s. Peter Edward and Patricia Ann (Heidenwolf) R. BA in Ednl. Psychology, U. Mich., 1982; MA in Coll. Student Personnel, Bowling Green State U., 1985. Asst. exec. dir. Grand Chpt. of Phi Sigma Kappa, Indpls., 1985-87, exec. dir., 1987-90; exec. v.p. Grand Chpt. of Phi Sigma Kappa and Phi Sigma Kappa Found., Indpls., 1990—. Mem. Am. Soc. Assn. Execs., Assn. Frat. Advisers, Frat. Execs. Assn. Office: Phi Sigma Kappa Frat 2925 E 96th St Indianapolis IN 46240-1368

REDBURN, AMBER LYNNE, nursing educator; b. West Plains, Mo., Jan. 4, 1963; d. Norris Bert and Chlora Ivene (Brickey) Cozort; m. Timothy Mark Redburn, Apr. 26, 1997; 1 child, Corby Lee. BSN, Rockhurst Coll. and Rsch. Coll. of Nursing, Kansas City, Mo., 1985. RN Mo. Psychiat. staff nurse Cox Med. Ctr. North, Springfield, Mo., 1985; psychiat. technician Park Cen. Hosp., Springfield, 1985-86; orthop. staff nurse St. John's Regional Health Ctr., Springfield, 1986-97; comprehensive care nurse Ozarks Med. Ctr., West Plains, 1997-98, nurse educator, 1998, also former instr. BLS, 1998; short term BLS instr. South Ctrl. Area Vocat.-Tech. Sch., West Plains, 1998; spl. edn. aide West Plains H.S., 2005—. Mem. com. St. John's Med. Explorer Post 339, 1989-90, pres., 1990-91; mem. Greene County Rep. Party-TARGET, 1993-97; mem. Rep. Nat. Com., 1995-98; mem. com. S.W. Mo. Nurses Recognition Dinner, 1992-97, chair, 1994-97; mem. West Plains Adult Day Svcs., 1997; reading vol. West Plaine Elem. Sch., 2004-2005. Mem. Mo. Nurses Assn. (corr. sec., past bd. dirs., 4th dist., mem. nominating com., med.-surg. spl. interest group 1993-98, sec. 1996-98, regional dir. region F 1994-96, mem. nominating com. 2004—, Mo. Nurses Assn.-PAC com. 1996—, comm. com. 1995-99, state bd. dirs. 1997-99, membership and mktg. com. 1997-99, nursing practice com. 1999, regional dir. region F 2002-2004), at. Assn. Orthopedic Nurses, Rsch. Coll. Alumni Assn., Rsch. Coll. Honor Soc. Personal E-mail: amberredburn7@hotmail.com.

REDD, CHARLES APPLETON, lawyer; b. Quincy, Ill., Aug. 13, 1954; s. Charles Lambert and Julia (Harrell) R.; m. Susan Backer, June 2, 1978; children: Elizabeth Appleton, Christopher O'Leary, Thomas Charles, Daniel Louis. BA, St. Louis U., 1976, JD, 1979. Bar: Wis. 1979, U.S. Dist. Ct. (ea. and we. dists.) Wis. 1979, Mo. 1980, Ill. 1991, U.S. Dist. Ct. (ea. dist.) Mo. 2007. Trust adminstr. First Wis. Trust Co., Milw., 1979-80; asst. counsel Centerre Trust Co. of St. Louis (now Bank of Am., N.A.), 1980-83; assoc. Armstrong, Teasdale, Schlafly & Davis, St. Louis, 1983-85; ptnr. Armstrong, Teasdale LLP and predecesssor firm, St. Louis, 1986-94; chmn. trust and estates dept., 1993-94. Adj. prof. law in fed. estate tax and estate planning Northwestern U. Mem. Estate Planning Coun. of St. Louis; bd. dirs. Make-A-Wish Found. of Metro. St. Louis. Recipient Pres.'s award, Mo. Bar, 1991. Fellow Am. Coll. of Trust and Estate Counsel (mem. fiduciary litig. com., estate and gift tax com.); mem. ABA (real property, probate and trust law sect.), Wis. Bar Assn., Mo. Bar Assn. (probate and trust com.), Ill. State Bar Assn., Bar Assn. Met. St. Louis (past chmn. probate and trust sect.). Home: 7245 Maryland Ave University City MO 63130-4419 Office: Sonnenschein Nath & Rosenthal LLP Ste 3000 1 Metropolitan Sq Saint Louis MO 63102-2711 Home Phone: 314-725-2122; Office Phone: 314-259-5819. Business E-Mail: credd@sonnenschein.com.

REDDICK, CATHERINE ANNE (CAT REDDICK), Olympic athlete; b. Richmond, Va., Feb. 10, 1982; Majoring in comm., U. N.C., 2000—. Mem. Under-16 Nat. Team, 1998, Under-18 Nat. Team, 1998—99, capt., 2000; mem. Under-21 Nat. Team, 2003; soccer player, defender U.S. Women's Nat. Team, 2000—; mem. U.S. Olympic Soccer Team, Athens, 2004. Co-recipient U-18 Soccer Gold medal, Pan Am. Games, 1999, Nordic Cup, Denmark, 2000, 2001, 2002, 2003; named Defensive MVP, NCAA Final Four, 2000, Freshman All-Am. Team, NSCAA, 2000, Second Team All-Am., 2001, First Team All-Am., 2002; named to First Team All-ACC, 2002. Achievements include being a member of gold medal winning US Women's Soccer Team, Athens Olympic Games, 2004. Office: US Soccer Fedn 1801 S Prairie Ave Chicago IL 60616

REDDY, JANARDAN K., medical educator; b. Moolasaal, India, Oct. 7, 1938; MB, BS, Osmania U., Hyderabad, India, 1961; MD in Pathology, All India Inst. Med. Scis., 1965. Lic. physicain, Mo., Kans., Ill.; diplomate Am. Bd. Pathology. Rotating house officer Osmania Gen. Hosp., 1961-62; instr. pathology Kakatiya Med. Coll., Warangal, India, 1962-63, asst. prof., 1965-66; resident fellow pathology U. Kans. Med. Ctr., 1966-68, rsch. fellow pathology, 1968-70, asst. prof., 1970-73, assoc. prof., 1973-76, prof., 1976; prof. pathology Northwestern U. Med. Sch., Chgo., 1976—, dir. med. scientist tng. program, 1990-93, chmn. pathology, 1993—. Dir. anatomic pathology Northwestern Meml. Hosp., 1978-81, mem. med. staff, 1976—; mem. Northwestern U. Cancer Ctr., 1976—; mem. med. staff VA Lakeside Hosp., 1990—; group leader Chem.Carcinogenesis Rsch. Group, Northwestern U. Cancer Ctr., 1990—, assoc. dir. cancer edn., 1991—; mem. Task Force on an Environ. Sci./Policy Initiative, Northwestern U., 1991—; chmn. NIH clin. scis. study sect., 1990-91; mem. NIH spl. study sect., 1992; mem. com. on comparative toxicity of naturally occurring carcinogens, 1993—; mem. Nat. Toxicology Program Rev. Com., 1992—; mem. monograph com. WHO, Internat. Agy. on Cancer Rsch., Lyon, France, 1994. Mem. editl. bds. Jour. Histochemistry and Cytochemistry, 1973-76, Exptl. Pathology, 1982—, Toxicologic Pathology, 1983—, Internat. Jour. Pancreatology, 1986—, Lab. Investigation, 1988—, Carcinogenesis, 1989—, The Jour. Northwestern U. Cancer Ctr., 1990—, Gene Expression, 1990—, Internat. Jour. Toxicology, Occupational and Environ. Health, 1992—, Life Sci. Advanced, Oncology, 1991—; assoc. editor Jour. Toxicology and Environ. Health, 1984—, Cancer Rsch., 1985-90. Grantee Joseph Mayberry Endowment Fund, Cancer Rsch. Found., 1991-93, NIEHS, 1995—, NIGMS, 1992-2001, NIDDK, 1995—, NIGMS, 1992-97; merit scholar Osmania U., 1954-61, Govt. of Andhra Pradesh merit scholar, 1963-65; WHO Yamagiwa-Yoshida Internat. Cancer fellow in Japan, 1985; recipient NIH merit award, 1987, UN Devel. Programme-Tokten award, 1988, Fletscher scholar award, 1991; named George H. Joost Outstanding Basic Sci. Tchr., 1995, 97. Fellow AAAS, Assn. Scientists of Indian Origin in Am. (pres. 1983-84, sr. scientist award 1991), Soc. Toxicology (v.p. molecular toxicology speciality sect. 1990-91, pres. 1991-92, pres. carcinogenesis specialty sect. 1990-91, Kenneth P. Dubois award 1990), Am. Pancreatic Assn., Am. Assn. Pathologists (mem. program com. 1989-93), Am. Assn. Cancer Rsch. (mem. program com. 1990-91), Internat. Acad. Pathology, Am. Soc. Cell Biology, Histochem. Soc., Soc. Exptl. Biology and Medicine, Biochem. Soc. London, Soc. Toxicology Pathologists, Internat. Assn. Pancreatology, N.Y. Acad. Scis. Office: Northwestern U Med Sch Dept Pathology Ward 6-204 303 E Chicago Ave Chicago IL 60611-3072

REDDY, VENKAT NARSIMHA, ophthalmologist, researcher; b. Hyderabad, India, Nov. 4, 1922; came to U.S., 1947; s. Malla and Manik (Devi) R.; m. Alvira M. DeMello, Dec. 10, 1955; children: Vinay Neville, Marlita Alvira. BSc, U. Madras, 1945; MS, PhD, Fordham U., 1952. Rsch. assoc. Coll. of Physicians and Surgeons Columbia U., YC, 1952-56, Banting and Best Inst., Toronto, Can., 1956; ass. and assoc. prof. ophthalmology Kresge Eye Inst. Wayne State U., Detroit, 1957-68; prof., biomed. scis., asst. dir. Eye Rsch. Inst. Oakland U., Rochester, Mich., 1968-75, prof., dir., 1975-98, Disting. prof. biomed. scis., dir., 1996-98; prof. ophthalmology Kellogg Eye Ctr. U. Mich., Ann Arbor, 1998—. Mem. study sect. NIH, Bethesda, 1966-70, nat. adv. eye coun., 1982-87, mem. bd. sci. counselors at. Eye Inst., 1977-81 Mem. editl. bd. Investigative Ophthalmology and Visual Scis., 1969-72, 78-88, Ophthalmic Research, 1978-90, Experimental Eye Research, 1985-2000; contbr. articles to profl. jours. Recipient Friendenwald award Assn. Rsch. in Ophthalmology, 1979, Rsch. award Cataract Rsch. Found., 1987, Merit award Nat. Eye Inst., 1989; named Scientist of Yr. State of Mich., 1991, Disting. Faculty Mem. Mich. Assn. Governing Bds. State Univs., 1994. Mem. AAAS, Internat. Soc. Eye Rsch., The Biochem. Soc., Assn. Rsch. in Vision and Ophthalmology (pres. 1985), Am. Soc. for Biochemistry and Molecular Biology, Soc. Free Radicals, Oxygen Soc. Sigma Xi. Achievements include research on cataract etiology, intraocular fluids dynamics relating to glaucoma, cell biology of lens, ciliary body and retinal pigment epithelium, cell differentiation. Office: U Mich Kellogg Eye Ctr 1000 Wall St Ann Arbor MI 48105-1912 Home Phone: 248-334-9339; Office Phone: 734-763-7246. Business E-Mail: venreddy@med.umich.edu.

REDFERN, CHRIS, political organization administrator, former state representative; b. 1964; m. Kim Redfern. BA in Polit. Sci., Bowling Green State U., MA in State and Local Govt. State rep. Ohio State Ho. of Reps., 1999—, caucus chmn., 2002—03, minority leader, 2003—06; chmn. Ohio Dem. Party, 2005—. Exec. com. mem. Dem. Nat. Com. (DNC); v.p. Midwestern Region Assn. of State Dem. Chairs. Named Citizen of Yr., Port Clinton Area C. of C., 2004; recipient Builders award, Wood County Dem. Party, Pub. Official award, Ottawa County Sr. Fair Bd., Vol. award, Port Clinton Pks. and Recreation Dept., Pres. award, Friends of Camp Perry, Myrl H. Shoemaker Award, 2003. Mem.: Ohio Employee Ownership Assn., Farm Bur., Lake Erie Charter Boat Assn., Port Clinton City Schs. Champions for Children, Farmers Union Nature Conservancy, Put-in-Bay C. of C., Pheasants Forever, Ducks Unlimited, Friends of Edison Woods, Woodmore HS FFA, Ottawa County Dem. Club, Elks, Kiwanis. Office: 727 Brentwood Ave Youngstown OH 44511 also: Ohio Dem Party 340 East Fulton St Columbus OH 43215 Office Phone: 614-221-6563.*

REDFERN, DONALD B., state legislator, lawyer; b. Nebraska City, Nebr., June 9, 1945; BA, Carleton Coll., 1967; JD, Columbia U., 1973. Ptnr. Redfern, Mason, Dieter, Larsen and Moore; mem. Iowa Senate from 12th dist., Des Moines, 1993—; mem. commerce com., mem. jud. com.; chair edn. com.; mem. rules and adminstrn. com. Adj. instr. U. No. Iowa. Bd. dirs. Cedar Valley Econ. Devel. Corp.; mem. Western Home, 1983-90, Friends of Sta. KHKE/KUNI Pub. Radio, 1985-87, Cedar Falls Pub. Libr., 1985-87; vol. Lawyers Project; mem. First United Meth. Ch.; mem. Cedar Valley Lakes Assn., 1987-90. Mem. Iowa Bar Assn., Hudson C. of C., Cedar Falls C. of C., Rotary (Cedar Falls), Waterloo C. of C. Republican. E-mail: don_redfern@legis.state.ia.us.

REDFIELD, PAMELA A., state legislator; b. Chgo., Aug. 11, 1948; m. Jerry Redfield; 6 children. BS in Edn., U. Nebr., 1969. Mem. Nebr. Legislature 12th dist., Lincoln, 1998—. Mem. Ralston Bd. Edn. 1992-1998. Coun. State Govt.; Nat. Conf. State Legislatures; Am. Legis. Exch. Conf.; Nat. Coun. Ins. Legislators Mem.: Am. Legis. Exch. conf., Nat. Conf. State Legis., Nat. Coun. Ins. State Legis.

REDGRAVE, MARTYN ROBERT, retail executive; BA in Econs., Princeton U.; MBA in Finance, NYU. CPA Minn. Various fin. and gen. mgmt. positions PepsiCo, 1980—90; exec. v.p. fin., CFO Kentucky Fried Chicken Corp., 1990—94; CFO, exec. v.p Carlson Cos. Inc., Mpls., 1994—2005; exec. v.p., chief admin. officer Limited Brands, Inc., Columbus, Ohio, 2005—; CFO Limited Brands., Inc., Columbus, Ohio, 2006—07. Vol. United Way. Office: Limited Brands Inc 3 Limited Pkwy Columbus OH 43216

REDISH, MARTIN HARRIS, law educator; b. Lynbrook, NY, Aug. 16, 1945; m. Caren Beverly Redish; 1 child, Jessica. AB, U. Pa., 1967; JD magna cum laude, Harvard U., 1970. Bar: NY 1971, US Dist. Ct. (so. dist.) NY 1971, US Ct. Appeals (2d cir.) 1971, US Ct. Appeals (7th cir.) 1973. Law clk. Honorable J. Joseph Smith US Ct. Appeals (2d cir.), 1970—71; assoc. Proskauer, Rose, Goetz & Mendelsohn, NYC, 1971—73; asst. prof. Northwestern U. Sch. Law, Chgo., 1973—76, assoc. prof., 1976—78, prof., 1978—90, Louis and Harriet Ancel prof. law and pub. policy, 1990—. Vis. assoc. prof. law Cornell U., 1977, Stanford U., 1977; vis. prof. law U. Mich., 1987—88; mem. 7th Cir. Rules Adv. Com.; cons. U.S. Senate Jud. Com. Author: Federal Jurisdiction: Tensions in the Allocation of Judicial Power, 1980, Federal Courts: Cases, Comments and Questions, 1983, Freedom of Expression: A Critical Analysis, 1984, The Constitution as Political Structure, 1995, Money Talks: Speech, Economic Power and the Values of Democracy, 2001; co-author: Constitutional Law: Principles and Policy, 1987, Civil Procedure: A Modern Approach, 1989, Understanding Federal Court Jurisdiction, 1999; contbr. articles to profl. jours. Mem.: Am. Coll. Trial Lawyers, Am. Law Inst. Office: Northwestern U Sch Law 357 E Chicago Ave Chicago IL 60611-3059 Office Phone: 312-503-8545. E-mail: m-redish@law.northwestern.edu.

REDLIN, ROLLAND W., state legislator; b. Lambert, Mont., Feb. 29, 1920; m. Christine Nesje; children: Ilene, Jeannette, Lisa, Daniel, Steven. Student, U. Wash., .D. State Coll. Mem. N.D. Senate, 1958-64, mem. appropriations com.; mem. Congress, 1965-66; agr. cons. U.S. Dept. State, 1967; mem. N.D. Ho. of Reps. Cons. Bank of Agr. and Pub. Rels.; owner farm, past operator. Dem. candidate from N.D., Ho. of Reps., 1966, 68; pres. Minot Vocat. Workshop; trustee ature Conservancy. Recipient Friend of Edn. award Minot Edn. Assn., 1988, Laura award for Dising. Svc. to Edn., 1991, Legis. award Libr. Assn. Mem. N.D. Bankers Assn., Farmers Union, Minot C. of C. Democrat. Office: 1005 21st St NW Minot ND 58703-1724 also: State Senate State Capitol Bismarck ND 58505

REDMAN, BARBARA KLUG, nursing educator; b. Mitchell, SD; d. Harlan Lyle and Darlien Grace (Bock) Klug; m. Robert S. Redman, Sept. 14, 1958; 1 child, Melissa Darlien. BS, S.D. State U., 1958; MEd, U. Minn., 1959, PhD, 1964; LHD (hon.), Georgetown U., 1988; DSc (hon.), U. Colo., 1991; M in Bioethics, U. Pa., 2004, MBE, 2004. RN. Asst. prof. U. Wash., Seattle, 1964-69; assoc. dean U. Minn., Mpls., 1969-75; dean Sch. Nursing U. Colo., Denver, 1975-78; VA scholar VA Ctr. Office, Washington, 1978-81; postdoctoral fellow Johns Hopkins U., Balt., 1982-83; exec. dir. Am. Assn. Colls. Nursing, Washington, 1983-89, ANA, Washington, 1989-93; prof. nursing Johns Hopkins U., Balt., 1993-95; dean, prof. Sch. Nursing U. Conn., Storrs, 1995-98; dean Coll. Nursing Wayne State U., Detroit. Vis. fellow Kennedy Inst. Ethics, Georgetown U., 1993-94; fellow in med. ethics Harvard Med. Sch., 1994-95, 2004—; vis. scholar U. Pa. Ctr. for Bioethics, 2004—. Author: Practice of Patient Education, 1968—; contbr. articles to profl. jours. Bd. dirs. Friends of Nat. Libr. of Medicine, Washington, 1987—. Recipient Disting. Alumnus award S.D. State U., 1975, Outstanding Achievement award U. Minn., 1989. Fellow Am. Acad. Nursing. Home: 12425 Bobbink Ct Potomac MD 20854-3005 Office: Wayne State U 5557 Cass Ave Detroit MI 48202-3615

REDMAN, CLARENCE OWEN, lawyer; b. Joliet, Ill., Nov. 23, 1942; s. Harold F. and Edith L. (Read) R.; m. Barbara Ann Pawlan, Jan. 26, 1964 (div.); children: Scott, Steven; m. 2d, Carla J. Rozycki, Sept. 24, 1983. BS, U. Ill., 1964, JD, 1966, MA, 1967. Bar: Ill. 1966, US Dist. Ct. (ea. dist.) Ill. 1967, US Ct. Appeals (7th cir.) 1973, US Ct. Appeals (4th cir.) 1982, US Supreme Ct. 1975. Assoc. Keck, Mahin & Cate, Chgo., 1969-73, ptnr., corp. ptnr., 1973—, CEO, 1986-97; of counsel Lord, Bissell & Brook, Chgo., 1997—2007. Spl. asst. atty. gen. Ill., 1975-8; bd. dirs. AMCOL Internat. Corp. Mem. bd. visitors U. Ill. Coll. of Law, 1991-95. Capt. U.S. Army, 1967-69. Decorated Bronze Star. Mem. Ill. State Bar Assn. (chmn. young lawyers sect. 1977-78, del. assembly 1978-81, 84-87), Seventh Cir. Bar Assn.

REDMAN, PETER, finance company executive; b. Phila., Feb. 9, 1935; s. Hamilton Matthew and Martha (Lawson) R.; m. Julie Anne Burr, June 9, 1984; children: Kristen, Heidi, Gretchen, Britt. BA in Econs., Middlebury Coll., 1958. Sr. group ins. rep. Conn. Gen. Life Ins. Co., Hartford, 1962—65; v.p. Conn. Bank & Trust Co., Hartford, 1965—73, Midlantic Nat. Bank, Newark, 1973—75, 4th Nat. Bank, Wichita, Kans., 1975—78; v.p., gen. mgr. Cessna Internat. Fin. Corp. subs. Cessna Aircraft Co., Wichita, 1978—82, pres., dir.; pres., gen. mgr., dir. Cessna Fin. Corp., Wichita, 1982—. 1st lt. US Army, 1958—62. Republican. Episcopalian. Office: Cessna Fin Corp PO Box 308 Wichita KS 67201-0308 Home: 649 N Crest Ridge Ct Wichita KS 67230-1621

REDMOND, ANDREA, executive recruiter; b. Glen Ellyn, Ill., Feb. 21, 1956; m. Bill Ferguson; 1 child, Duke. BS, No. Ill. Univ.; MBA, George Williams Coll. Asst. v.p. First Nat. Bank of Chgo., 1981—86; with Russell Reynolds Assoc., Chgo., 1986—, mng. dir., co-head, CEO/bd. services practice, 1994—. Mutual fund bd. mem. Fischer, Francis, Trees & Watts. Co-author (with Charles A. Tribbett III): Business Evolves, Leadership Endures, 2004. Bd. dir. Y-Me Breast Cancer Orgn., Chgo. Children's Meml. Hosp. Named one of 100 Most Influential Women, Crain's Chgo. Bus., 2004. Mem.: Chgo. Econ. Forum, Chgo. Club, Executives Club. Office: Russell Reynolds Assoc Inc Ste 2900 200 S Wacker Dr Chicago IL 60606-5802 Office Phone: 312-993-0704. Office Fax: 312-876-1919. Business E-Mail: aredmond@russellreynolds.com.

REDMOND, ROBERT FRANCIS, nuclear engineering educator; b. Indpls., July 15, 1927; s. John Felix and Marguerite Catherine (Breinig) R.; m. Mary Catherine Cangany, Oct. 18, 1952 (dec. May 1988); children: Catherine, Robert, Kevin, Thomas, John; m. Carole Moon Jacobs, Apr. 9, 1994. BS in Chem. Engring, Purdue U., 1950; MS in Math, U. Tenn., 1955; PhD in Physics, Ohio State U., 1961. Engr. Oak Ridge Nat. Lab., 1950-53; scientist, adviser-cons. Battelle Meml. Inst., Columbus, Ohio, 1953-70; prof. nuclear engring. Ohio State U., Columbus, 1970-92, assoc. dean Coll. Engring., dir. Engring. Experiment Sta., 1977-92, acting dean, 1990-92, prof. emeritus mech. engring., assoc. dean emeritus, 1992—. Contbr. articles to profl. jours. V.p. Argonne Univs. Assn., 1976-77, trustee, 1972-80; mem. Ohio Power Siting Commn., 1978-82; trustee Edison Welding Inst., 1988-92. With AUS, 1945-46. Mem. Am. Nuclear Soc. (chmn. Southwestern Ohio sect.), AAAS, Nat. Regulatory Rsch. Inst. (bd. dirs. 1988-92), Trans. Rsch. Ctr., Am. Soc. Engring. Edn., Sigma Xi, Tau Beta Pi. Home: 4621 Nugent Dr Columbus OH 43220-3047 Office: Ohio State U Coll Engring Columbus OH 43220

REDWINE, JOHN NEWLAND, state legislator, physician; b. Pratt, Kans., Oct. 28, 1950; s. Albert Herold and Joyce Nadean (Durall R.; m. Barbara Ann Bomgaars, Dec. 27, 1975; children: John Newland II, William Merritt, Adam Boone. BA with honors, U. Kans., 1972; cert. med. technology, U. Tex. at Houston, 1974; DO, U. Health Scis., Kansas City, Mo., 1978. Diplomate Am. Bd. of Family Practice. Intern U. Hosp., Ctr. for Health Scis., Kansas City, Mo., 1978-79; family practice resident Siouxland Med. Edn. Found., Sioux City, Iowa, 1979-81; med. dir. Morningside Family Practice, Sioux City, Iowa, 1981-95; v.p. St. Luke's Health Sys., Inc., Sioux City, Iowa, 1995-2001; primary care physician Cmty. Based Outpatient Clinic Dept. Veterans Affairs, 2001—04; mem. Iowa Senate from 2nd dist., Des Moines, 1996—2003; mem. med. staff Sioux Falls (S.D.) VA Med. Ctr.; chmn. Siouxland Instnl. Rev. Bd., 2002—04; mem. med. staff Fayetteville (Ark.) VA Med. Ctr., 2004—. Sr. aviation med. examiner FAA, 1979—95; clin. lectr. Iowa U. Coll. Medicine, Iowa City, 1983—95; pres. Siouxland Med. Edn. Found., 1982—2001; past chmn. family practice St. Luke's Regional Med. Ctr., Sioux City, Iowa, pres.-elect, 1993—95; chmn. Siouxland Instnl. Rev. Bd., 2002—. Contbr. articles to profl. jours. Past v.p. Prairie Gold Area coun. Boy Scouts Am., Sioux City, bd. dirs. Mid.Am. coun., 1984-2004; bd. dirs. New Perspectives, Inc., 1996-2002, Sioux City Cmty. Sch. Dist., 1994-97, Crittenton Ctr., 2000-04, Morningside Coll., 2000-04; elected 2d dist. Iowa Senate, 1996-2003, asst. majority leader, 1998-2002. Recipient achievement award Upjohn Pharm. Co., Kansas City, 1978, Silver Beaver award Prairie Gold Area Coun., Boy Scouts Am., 1997, Pub. Ofcl. award Siouxland Dist. Health Dept., 1998, Leadership award Iowans for LIFE, 2000, Guardian of Small Bus. award Nat. Fedn. Ind. Bus., 2001, Iowa Friend of the Family award Christian Coalition Iowa, 2001, 02, Legis. award Iowa Acad. Family Practice, 2002. Fellow Am. Acad. Family Physicians; mem. AMA, Am. Osteo. Assn., Iowa Med. Soc., Woodbury Med. Soc. (past pres.), Flying Physicians Assn. Republican. Avocation: politics. Office Phone: 479-443-4301. E-mail: john@redwine.org.

REECE, MAYNARD FRED, artist, writer; b. Arnolds Park, Iowa, Apr. 26, 1920; s. Waldo H. and Inez V. (Latson) R.; m. June Carman, Apr. 7, 1946; children: Mark A., Brad D. Privately educated. Artist Meredith Pub. Co., Des Moines, 1938-40; artist, asst., mus. dir. Iowa Dept. History and Archives, Des Moines, 1940-50. Artist: Fish and Fishing, 1963, Waterfowl of Iowa, 1943; watercolor Trout, Saturday Evening Post (award of Distinctive Merit 1962); watercolors 73 Fish, Life mag. (cert. of merit 1955); print of Water's Edge Canada Geese for Am. Artist Collection, Am. Artist Mag., 1985; author, artist: The Waterfowl Art of Maynard Reece, 1985, The Upland Bird Art of Maynard Reece, 1997. Chmn. Gov.'s Com. Conservation of Outdoor Resource, 1963-64; trustee Iowa Natural Heritage Found., Des Moines, 1979—; hon. trustee Ducks Unltd., Inc., 1983—; trustee J.N. "Ding" Darling Conservation Found., Inc., Des Moines, 1962—. Served with AUS, 1943-45. Recipient awards for duck stamps and others Dept. Interior, 1948, 51, 59, 69, 71; recipient award Govt. Bermuda, 1963, award Iowa Conservation Commn., 1972, 77, 80, 81, award Fish and Game Commn., Little Rock, 1982, 88, award Tex. Parks and Wild Life Dept., 1983, award Nat. Fish & Wildlife Found., 1988, award Wash. State Dept. Wildlife, 1989, award Idaho Dept. Fish & Game, 1998, 4 awards Ill. Dept. of Natural Resources, 1997-2000; named Artist of Yr. Ducks Unltd. Inc., 1973; chosen Master Artist 1989, Leigh Yawkey Woodson Art Mus., Wausau, Wis., 1989. Mem. Nat. Audubon Soc., Nat. Wildlife Fedn., Izaak Walton League Am. (hon. pres. 1974-75). Home and Office: 5315 Robertson Dr Des Moines IA 50312-2133 Office Phone: 515-277-3623.

REECE, ROBERT WILLIAM, zoological park administrator; b. Saginaw, Mich., Jan. 21, 1942; s. William Andrews and Mary Barbara (Murphy) R.; m. Jill Whetstone, Aug. 21, 1965; children: William Clayton, Gregory Scott, Mark Andrews. BS, Mich. State U., 1964; postgrad., U. West Fla., 1969-71, U. South Fla., 1974-76. Dir. orthwest Fla. Zool. Gardens, Pensacola, Fla., 1970-72; zool. dir. Lion Country Ga., Stockbridge, 1972-73; asst. dir. Salisbury Zoo, Md., 1976-77; dir. zoology Wild Animal Habitat, Kings Island, Ohio, 1977-92; exec. dir., then pres. The Wilds Internat. Ctr. for Preservation of Wild Animals, Cumberland, Ohio, 1992—. Assoc. editor: Sci. Jour. Zoo Biology, 1982—. Lt. USN, 1964-69, Korea. Profl. fellow Am. Assn. Zool. Parks and Aqariums; mem. Cin. Wildlife Rsch. Fedn., Am. Soc. Mammalogists, Animal Behavior Soc., Captive Breeding Specialist Group, Species Survival Commn., Internat. Union for Conservation of ature and Natural Resources. Republican. Episcopalian. Office: The Wilds 14000 International Rd Cumberland OH 43732-9500 Home: 8200 Lakeshore Dr Apt 306 Lantana FL 33462-6056

REED, JAN STERN, lawyer; Asst. corp. sec., legal counsel Wheelabrator Technologies Inc., 1995—97; asst. corp. sec., asst. gen. counsel Baxter Internat., 1997—98, corp. sec., assoc. gen. counsel, 1998—2004, chief governance officer, 2003—04; sr. v.p., gen. counsel, sec. Solo Cup Co., Highland Park, Ill., 2004—05, exec. v.p., gen. counsel, sec., 2005—. Office: Solo Cup Co 1700 Old Deerfield Rd Highland Park IL 60035

REED, JOHN WESLEY, lawyer, educator; b. Independence, Mo., Dec. 11, 1918; s. Novus H. and Lilian (Houchens) R.; m. Imogene Fay Vonada, Oct. 5, 1946 (div. 1958); m. Dorothy Elaine Floyd, Mar. 5, 1961; children: Alison A., John M. (dec.), Mary V., Randolph F., Suzanne M. AB, William Jewell Coll., 1939, LLD, 1995; LLB, Cornell U., 1942; LLM, Columbia U., 1949, JSD, 1957. Bar: Mo. 1942, Mich. 1953. Assoc. Stinson, Mag, Thomson, McEvers & Fizzell, Kansas City, Mo., 1942-46; assoc. prof. law U. Okla., 1946-49; assoc. prof. U. Mich., 1949-53, prof., 1953-64, 68-85, Thomas M. Cooley prof., 1985-87, Thomas M. Cooley prof. emeritus, 1987—; dean, prof. U. Colo., 1964-68, Wayne State U., Detroit, 1987-92, prof. emeritus, 1992—. Vis. prof. NYU, 1949, U. Chgo., 1960, Yale U., 1963-64, Harvard U., 1982, U. San Diego, 1993; dir. Inst. Continuing Legal Edn., 1968-73; reporter Mich. Rules of Evidence Com., 1975-78, 83-84; mem. faculty Salzburg Sem., 1962, chmn., 1964. Author: (with W.W. Blume) Pleading and Joinder, 1952; (with others) Introduction to Law and Equity, 1953, Advocacy Course Handbook series, 1963-81; editor in chief Cornell Law Quar., 1941-42; contbr. articles to profl. jours. Pres. bd. mgrs. of mins. and missionaries benefit bd. Am. Bapt. Chs. U.S.A., 1967-74, 82-85, 88-94; mem. com. visitors JAG Sch., 1971-76; trustee Kalamazoo Coll., 1954-64, 68-70; bd. dirs., Ann Arbor Area Cmty. Found., 2004-. Recipient Harrison Tweed award Assn. Continuing Legal Edn. Adminstrs., 1983, Samuel E. Gates award Am. Coll. Trial Lawyers, 1985, Roberts P. Hudson award State Bar Mich., 1989. Fellow Internat. Soc. Barristers (editor jour. 1980—); mem. ABA (mem. coun. litigation sect.), Assn. Am. Law Schs. (mem. exec. com. 1965-67), Am. Acad. Jud. Edn. (v.p. 1978-80), Colo. Bar Assn. (mem. bd. govs. 1964-68), Mich. Supreme Ct. Hist. Soc. (bd. dirs. 1991—), Sci. Club Mich., Order of Coif. Office: U Mich Sch Law Ann Arbor MI 48109-1215 Office Phone: 734-763-0165. Business E-Mail: reedj@umich.edu.

REED, KEITH ALLEN, lawyer; b. Anamosa, Iowa, Mar. 5, 1939; s. John Ivan and Florence Lorine (Larson) R.; m. Beth Illana Kesterson, June 22, 1963; children: Melissa Beth, Matthew Keith. BBA, U. Iowa, 1960, JD, 1963. Bar: Ill. 1963, Iowa 1963. Ptnr. Seyfarth Shaw, Chgo., 1963—. Co-author: Labor Arbitration in Healthcare, 1981; co-editor: Chicagoland Employment Law Manual, 1994, Employment and Discrimination, 1996, Federal Employment Law and Regulations, 1989-99, 2001-; co-contbr. articles to Am. Hosp. Assn. publs., 1986-89. Trustee Meth. Hosp. Chgo., 1985—; mem. ad hoc labor adv. com. Am. Hosp. Assn., Chgo., 1980—; bd. dirs. Lyric Opera Chgo. Ctr. for Am. Artists, pres., 1983-86. Mem. ABA (dir. health law forum 1979-82), Chgo. Bar Assn. (chair labor and employment law com. 1996-), Union League Club Chgo. (bd. dirs. 1985-88), Sunset Ridge Country Club (Northfield, Ill.). Republican. Methodist. Avocations: music, theater, tennis, golf. Office: Seyfarth Shaw 55 E Monroe St Ste 4200 Chicago IL 60603-5863

REED, M. SCOTT, accounting company executive; CFO Grant Thornton LLP, Chgo., 1997-99, CEO, 1999-2000. Office: Grant Thornton LLP 175 W Jackson Blvd #20 Chicago IL 60604-3033

REED, MICHAEL JOHN, dentist, dean, educator; b. Wednesbury, Eng., Dec. 25, 1940; came to U.S., 1967, naturalized, 1972; s. Harry Ernest and Ida Veva (Heywood) R.; m. Pamela Twycross, July 4, 1965 (div. Feb. 1976); children: Justine Marianne, Helena Clare; m. Ingrid Liepins, Sept. 8, 1978; children: Kathryn Anne, Matthew Harrison. BS with honors, U. Durham, Eng., 1963; B in Dental Surgery, U. Newcastle-Upon-Tyne, Eng., 1967; PhD, SUNY, Buffalo, 1971. Lic. dentist U.K., N.Y., Miss. Instr. oral biology SUNY, Buffalo, 1971-72, asst. prof. oral biology, 1972-77, assoc. prof., 1977-79; asst. dean Sch. Dentistry, U. Miss., Jackson, 1980-85, assoc. dean, 1985; dean, prof. oral biology Sch. Dentistry, U. Mo., Kansas City, 1985—. Cons. Nat. Inst. Dental Rsch., Washington, 1975-85. Contbr. numerous articles to profl. jours. Recipient rsch. career devel. award NIH, 1975-80. Fellow Acad. Dentistry Internat., Internat. Coll. Dentists, Am. Coll. Dentists; mem. ADA (cons. 1982—, joint com. on nat. dental exam., 1988-93, chair 1992-93), Am. Assn. Dental Schs. (sect. chair 1985-86. chmn. schs. coun. of deans, 1992-93, pres. 1997-98), Am. Assn. Dental Rsch. (councillor 1974-76), Fedn. Dentaire Internat., Am. Assn. for Microbiology, Mid-Am. Masters Club, Omicron Kappa Upsilon. Episcopalian. Avocations: running, European current affairs. Office: U Mo-Kansas City Sch Dentistry 650 E 25th St Kansas City MO 64108-2716 Office Phone: 816-235-2010. Office Fax: 816-235-2157. Business E-Mail: reedm@umkc.edu.

REED, SCOTT, automotive parts company executive; With Chrysler Corp., 1983-98; CFO Donnelly Corp., Holland, Mich., 1998, pres. Electronic Sys. Group, 2001—. Office: Electric Sys Group Donnelly Corp 49 W 3d St Holland MI 49423

REED, SUELLEN KINDER, school system administrator; BA in History, Polit. Sci. and Secondary Edn., Hanover Coll., 1967; MA in Elem. Edn. and History, Ball State U., 1970, EdD in Adminstrn. and Supervision, LLD (hon.), 1997; EdD (hon.), Vincennes U., 1996; LittD (hon.), U. Indpls., 1997; LHD (hon.), St. Joseph Coll., 1999, Hanover Coll., 2003; postgrad., Fla. Atlantic U., U. Scranton, Purdue U., Earlham Coll., Ind. U., Ind. State U., U. So. Ind., Butler U., U. Alaska, Edinburgh U., Scotland, Oxford U., Eng. Lic. supt., life lic. in elem. edn., U.S. history, world history, govt., adminstrn. and supervision and endorsement in edn. for gifted and talented K-12, Ind.; lic. adminstr., U.S. history, world history, govt., middle sch. lang. arts, social studies, elem. edn., gifted edn., Fla. Tchr. 5th and 6th grades Rushville Consol. Sch. Corp., Ind., 1967-70; tchr., world history and coll. prep Latin Am. history Shelbyville HS, Ind., 1970-71; tchr. 6th, 7th and 8th grade social studies and civic, curriculum coord., dir. gifted programs, homebase guidance dir., & handwriting inservice coord. Broward County Sch. Corp., Fla., 1971-76; reading tchr. Rushville Jr. HS, Ind., 1976-77; asst. prin. Rushville Elem. Sch., Ind., 1977-79; prin. Frazee Elem. Sch., Connersville, Ind., 1979-87; asst. supt. Rushville Consolidated Schs., Ind., 1987—91, supt. Ind., 1991-93; supt. pub. instrn., chairperson bd. edn., CEO dept. edn. State of Indiana, Indpls., 1993—. Pres. N. Ctrl. Regional Edn. Lab., Oak Brook, Ill., 1993—97, Oak Brook, 2002; mem. The Ctr. on Congress Outstanding Tchr. Award Selection Com., Task Force on Strengthening Profl. Practice, Western Interstate Commn. for Higher Edn., State Scholar Initiative Adv. Coun., 2005; co-chair Ind. Commn. for Early Learning and School Readiness, Ind. Edn. Roundtable, 1998—; visited schools & addresses administrators, teachers, parents, and students; prepared units of study on Japan, China, Singapore, Taiwan, former Union Soviet Socialist Republics, UK, Germany, France, Australia, Italy, The Netherlands, Austria, Hong Kong, & Spain. Contbr. articles to profl. jours.; regular contbr. Ind. Reading Assn. Jour., Ind. Principal's Assn. Indianagram. Bd. trustees Hanover Coll., Commn. Drug-Free Ind., Ind. Commn. Cmty. Svc., Ind. Higher Edn. Telecom. Sys., Ctr. Agrl. Sci. Heritage; hon. bd. mem. Rush County Cmty. Found.; alumni bd. Ball State U. Tchrs. Coll., 1999-; bd. dirs. Nat. Children's Film Festival; trustee, mem. New Salem United Meth. Ch.; bd. dirs. Ind. Historic Landmarks Found., Agy. for Instrnl. Tech., Project Lead the Way, Virtual H.S., 2003-; bd. visitors Ind. U.; mem. Commn. for Drug-Free Ind., Ind. Commn. on Cmty. Svc., Ind. Higher Edn. Telecommunication System, Ind. Commn. on the Social Status of Black Males, Ind. State Mus. Performing Arts and Edn. Adv. Com., Ctr. for Agr. Sci. and Heritage, Indpls. Art Mus., Indpls. Zoo; mem. adv. coun., Ball State U. Sch. Continuing Studies and Pub. Svc.; hon. bd. mem. Indpls. Zool. Soc.; hon. chair, Young Audiences Ind. Fundraising Campaign, 1994-95. Named Outstanding Sch. Edn. Alumnus, Ball State U., 1994, Govt. Leader Yr., Ind. C. of C., 2001, Exemplary Friend, Butler U., Coll. Edn., 2005; recipient Certificate of Appreciation, Fayette-Rush County NAACP, 1993, Certificate of Appreciation in Helping to Reduce Crime and to Improve Communities, Nat. Crime Prevention Coun., Partnership with the Bur. Justice Assistance, Office of Justice Programs, US Dept. of Justice, 1994, Pres. award, Ind. Assn. Sch. Prins., 1996, Achievement award, Ind. Network Women Adminstrs., 1996, Alumni award, Hanover Coll., 1997, Legis. award, Ind. Assn. for the Edn. Young Children, 1998, Pres. award, Ind. Middle Level Edn. Assn., 2001, Elizabeth Heywood Wyman award for alumnae, Alpha Omicron Pi, 2001, Friend Youth award, Ind. Sch. Counselors, 2001, Hoosier Heritage Civic Leadership award, 2002, Turn Off the Violence award, Ind. Crime Prevention Coalition, 2002, Ind. Sch. Safety Leadership award, 2002, Citizen's award, Ind. Libr. Fedn., Counselor's award, Assn. for Ind. Media Educators, Spl. Contributions to Edn. award, Ind. U. Sch. Adminstr. Assn., 2004, Disting. Alumni award, Ind. 4-H Found.-Ind. 4-H Centennial, 2004, Friend Fgn. Languages award, Ind. Fgn. Language Teachers Assn., 2004, Sagamore of the Wabash award, 1997, 2005, Leadership award for Continuing Advocacy for Gifted Children, Ind. Assn. for the Gifted, 2005, Indian Trails Career Cooperative for Continued Support to Career and Tech. Edn., 2005, Citation for Courage, Ind. Assn. for Adult and Continuing Edn., 2005. Mem. ASCD (nat. and Ind. chpts.), Internat. Reading Assn., Internat. Edn. Com., Nat. Coun. for Accreditation Tchr. Edn. (mem. exec. bd.), Nat. Assn. Elem. and Mid. Sch. Prins. (assoc.), Nat. Assn. Gifted Children (nat. adv. bd.), Internat. Tech. Edn. Assn. (mem. adv. com.), Ind. Assn. Pub. Sch. Supts.(Outstanding Educator award, 2004), Ind. Assn. Elem. and Mid. Sch. Prins. (assoc.), Women's Coun. on Literacy for the Ind. Literacy Found., Indpls. Bd. Associates, Rose Hulman Inst. Tech., Network Woman Adminstrs., Indpls. Bd. Assocs., Bus. and Profl. Women of Rushville, Connersville Area Reading Coun., Smithsonian, Rushville Rotary Club, Monday Cir., K-12 Compact Learning and Citizenship (first nat. chairwoman), Edn. Commn. States (commr., mem. exec. com., steering com. 1994-98, 2002-, treas., chair policy and priorities com.), Coun. Chief State Sch. Officers (v.p. 1999-2000, pres.-elect., 2000-01, pres., 2001-02), ex-officio bd. dir., North Ctrl. Assn., Ind. Hist. Soc., Ind. State Mus., Conner Prairie Farm, Order of Ea. Star (Andersonville chpt.), Delta Kappa Gamma (past pres.), Phi Lambda Theta, Phi Delta Kappa (Conner Prairie), Kappa Delta Pi, Altrusa Club Connersville (chmn. internat. rels., 1979-87), The Gathering. Office: Superintendent Edn Dept Room 229 State House Indianapolis IN 46204-2798 Office Phone: 317-232-6665. Office Fax: 317-232-8004. Business E-Mail: sureed@doe.state.in.us.

REED, WILLIAM T., broadcast executive; b. 1938; With Pub. TV, Reading, Calif., 1967-74, Pub. Broadcasting Sys., Washington, 1974-92; pres., gen. mgr. Sta. KCPT-TV, Kansas City, Mo., 1992—. Office: Sta KCPT-TV 125 E 31st St Kansas City MO 64108-3216

REEDY, JOHN J., state legislator; b. Midland, SD, Aug. 23, 1927; Grad. high sch., Vermillion, SD. Mem. S.D. Ho. of Reps., Pierre, 1990-96, mem. agr. and natural resources and edn. coms.; owner Our Own Hardware, 1960-85; ins. salesman Mutual of Omaha, 1985—; mem. S.D. Senate from 17th dist., Pierre, 1996—. Home: 314 E Main St Vermillion SD 57069-2728 Office: SD Senate Members State Capitol Pierre SD 57501

REESE, HOWARD FRED, wholesale distribution executive; b. Newark, Oct. 12, 1947; s. Howard Fred Sr. and Rose Eleanor (Heintjes) R.; m. Pamela Mae Pearce, June 19, 1971; children: Bethany Lauren, Douglas Howard. BS in Acctg., Fairleigh Dickinson U., 1972, MBA, 1974. Acctg. supr. Thomas Edison Industries, West Orange, .J., 1967-69; acctg. mgr. Artistic Mfg., Carlstadt, N.J., 1969-71; contr., gen. mgr., then exec. v.p. Rousana Cards, Hillside, N.J., 1971-86; exec. dir. Am. Greetings, Cleve., 1986-87; pres. Acme Frame Products (subs. Am. Greetings), Chgo., 1987-92; v.p. sales and mktg. Vitco, Plainview, N.Y., 1993-94; v.p., gen. mgr. Levy Home Entertainment, Hillside, Ill., 1994-95, pres, COO; pres., CEO Chas. Levy circulating Co., Lisle, Ill., 2005—. Coach Hudson (Ohio) Athletic Assn., 1990-96. Mem. White Eagle Golf Club. Republican. Avocations: golf, chess, skiing, tennis. Office: Chas Levy Circ 815 Ogden Lisle IL 60532

REETZ, HAROLD FRANK, JR., agronomist; b. Wat., Ill. s. Harold Frank and Evelyn Evedeen (Russell) R.; m. Christine Lee Kaiser, Aug. 25, 1973; children: Carrie, Wesley, Anthony. BS in Agrl. Sci., U. Ill., 1970; MS in Agronomy, Purdue U., 1972, PhD in Agronomy, 1976. Extension and rsch. specialist Purdue U., West Lafayette, Ind., 1974-82; regional dir. Potash & Phosphate Inst., Monticello, Ill., 1982—2003; v.p. Found. for Agronomic Rsch., 1996—2003, pres., 2004—. Cons. Control Data Corp., Mpls., 1978-82, Internat. Harvester Co., Chgo., 1979-82, Monsanto Agrl. Chem. Co., St. Louis, 1981-82; adj. prof. Crop Scis. U., Ill., 1999—. Author: Crop Simulation Model, CORNCROPS, 1976, several crops mgmt. computer programs; contbr. articles to profl. jours. Chmn. Ill. Com. for Agrl. Edn., 1987-89; mem. Ill. Groundwater Adv. Coun., 1988-2002; mem. Ill. Fertilizer Rsch. and Edn. Coun., Ill. Dept. Agr., 1989-98, 2003-2005, Ill. Dept. Agr. Nutrient Mgmt. Com.; bd. dirs. Fluid Fertilizer Found., 2004—. Recipient Hon. mem. Hon. State Farmer Ill. Assn. FFA, Urbana, 1987; IFCA Spl. Recognition award Ill. Fertilizer and Chem. Assn., 1988, Site-Liner award Farm Chems., 1997, Alumni award of merit U. Ill., 2000, Alumni Acheivement award Purdue U. Agronomy Dept., 2003. Fellow Crop Sci. Soc. Am., Am. Soc. Agronomy (Agronomic Industry award 2000); mem. Soil Sci. Soc. Am. (divsn. chmn. editl. bd., chmn. internat. cert. crop adviser exec. com. 1996-2003, chmn. internat. CCA bd.), Ill. Assn. Vocat. Agrl. Tchrs. (hon. life 1989—), Gamma Sigma Delta (Merit award 2001). Methodist. Avocations: photography, travel, computers. Office Phone: 217-762-2074.

REEVE, JOHN NEWTON, molecular biology and microbiology educator; b. Wakefield, W. Yorkshire, Eng., June 21, 1947; came to U.S., 1979; s. Arthur Newton and Lilian Elsworth (Tallant) R.; m. Patricia Margaret Watson, Sept. 21, 1967; children: Simon Arthur, Daniel John. BS with 1st class honors, U. Birmingham, Eng., 1968; PhD, U. B.C., Vancouver, Can., 1971. Rsch. scientist U. Ariz., Tucson, 1971-73, Nat. Inst. Med. Rsch., Mill Hill, London, 1973-74; rsch. dir. Max-Planck Inst., Berlin, 1974-79; prof. microbiology Ohio State U., Columbus, 1979—, chmn. dept., 1985—, Rod Sharp prof. microbiology, 1999—. Cons. Battelle Rsch. Lab., Columbus, 1982-87, Govt. of Bulgaria, Sofia, 1987, Promega Corp., Madison, Wis., 1990, Procter and Gamble Co., Cin., 1990; mem. sci. adv. bd. BioTrol. Inc., Chaska, Minn., 1986-90; Disting. vis. prof. U. Adelaide, Australia, 1984, U. Wyo., Laramie, 1988, U. Calcutta, India, 1989, Frei U., Berlin, 1991, U. Karachi, Pakistan, 1995, U. Concepcion, Chile, 1995; governing coun. So. Petrochems. Corp., Chennai, India, 1999—2001; chmn. biosci. coun. Dept. of Energy, 2001—; mng. editor Extremophiles, 2003—. Named Disting. Rsch. Scholar Ohio State U., 1989. Fellow Am. Soc. Microbiology (lectr. Found. for Microbiology 1987-88, 94-96. chmn. divsn. K, microbial physiol. 1998-99, coun. 2000-02, US nat. organizing com. for 2005 Internat. Congress of Microbiology Socs., 2002—). Office: Ohio State U Dept of Microbiology 484 W 12th Ave Columbus OH 43210-1214 Office Phone: 614-292-2301. Office Fax: 614-292-8120. Business E-Mail: reeve.2@osu.edu.

REEVE, LEE M., farmer; married; 3 children. BS in Agr. Econs., Kans. State U. Group mgr., owner Reeve Cattle Co., Garden City, Kans. Bd. dirs. Fidelity State Bank, Garden City, Garden City C. of C., Beef Empire Days, Garden City Fed. Land Bank. Mem. Agr. Value Added Processing Leadership Coun.; bd. dirs. Agrl. non-Food Use Task Force; mem. Kans. Coun. Vocat. Edn., Alt. Agr. Rsch. & Commercialization bd. Recipient Innovator of Yr. award State Bd. Agr., Environ. Achievement award Nat. Environ. Awards Coun., Wheeler McMillan award New Uses Coun., Disting. Agrl. Econs. Alumnus Kans. State U. Office: Reeve Cattle Co PO Box 1036 Garden City KS 67846-1036

REEVES, BRUCE, social worker; b. Centerville, Utah, Jan. 8, 1955; s. Leon W. and Maxine (Hodson) R. BA, U. Utah, 1979, MSW, 1983. Mental health caseworker Traveler's Aid Soc. Salt Lake, Salt Lake City, 1983-86; socialwork cons. Home Health Utah, Bountiful, 1985-86; victim svcs. counselor Salt Lake County Atty's. Office, Salt Lake City, 1986-87; mgr., cons. AIDS and employee assistance program Aetna and Human Affairs Internat., Salt Lake City, 1987-96;

dir. social work and therapies Paracelsus Home Care & Hospice, Salt Lake City, 1996-98; registrar, bus. mgr. Awakening Spirit Massage Sch., L.C., Salt Lake City, 1998-99; mgr. Christus St. Joseph Villa, Salt Lake City, 1999-2001; med. social worker Harmony Home Care and Hospice, Salt Lake City, 1999-2001; owner, operator Satori Pers. Coaching and Cons., 1999—; exec. dir. Violence Intervention Project, Thief River Falls, Minn., 2001—04. Health educator Health Horizons, L.C., 1996-98; adj. faculty U. Utah Dept. Social Work, 1998-2001, Dept. Social Work, U. N.D., 2001-; presenter in field. Bd. dirs. Walk-ons, Inc., Salt Lake City, 1989-98, Gay and Lesbian Cmty. Ctr. Utah, Salt Lake City, 1998-99, Utah chpt. Gay Lesbian Straight Edn. Network, 1996-99, Minn. Coalition for Battered Women, 2002-04, Crossroads Displaced Homemakers's Program, 2002-2003, The Day One Ctr., Inc., 2003-05; mem. appropriations com. United Way Greater Salt Lake, Salt Lake City, 1990-99, bd. assocs. Ririe-Woodbury Dance Co., Salt Lake City, 1991-95, human svcs. com. Utah Stonewall Ctr., Salt Lake City, 1992-95; mem. Minn. Dept. Health's Cmty. Cooperative Coun. on HIV/AIDS Prevention, 2004—. Mem.: NASW. Democrat. Avocations: theater, dance, theater, music, literature.

REEVES, KATHLEEN WALKER, English language educator; b. Mt. Pleasant, Mich., Dec. 7, 1950; d. John J. and Gladys M. W.; m. Daniel H. Reeves, Mar. 10, 1972; children: Sheila, Michael. BA, Ctrl. Mich. U., 1973, MA, 1984. English tchr. Shepherd (Mich.) High Sch., 1973-76, Chippewa Hills High Sch., Remus, Mich., 1978-79, Onekama (Mich.) Pub. Sch., 1983-86, Seaholm High Sch., Birmingham, Mich., 1986—. Bd. dirs. Nat. Bd. Profl. Tchg. Stds.

REGAN, GILBERT J., retired career officer; BA in Econs., St. Michael's Coll., 1966; LLD, Harvard U., 1969. Commd. 2d lt. USAF, 1969, advanced through grades to brig. gen., 1996; asst. staff judge advocate 313th Combat Support Group, Forbes AFB, 1970-72; mil. judge Clark AB, Republic of the Philippines, 1972-74, 85-87, MacDill AFB, Fla., 1974-76; assoc. appellate govt. counsel Hdqrs. USAF, Washington, 1976-78, spl. counsel to judge advocate gen., 1978-81; staff judge advocate 836th Combat Support Group, Davis-Monthan AFB, Ariz., 1981-85, 13th Air Force, Clark AB, 1987-89; mil. asst. and spl. counsel to the gen. counsel of the AF Washington, 1989-91; staff judge advocate 22nd Air Force, Travis AFB, Calif., 1991-93, 15th Air Force, Travis AFB, 1993-94, Hdqrs. Pacific Air Forces, Hickam AFB, Hawaii, 1994-96; chief counsel Hdqrs. US Transp. Command, Scott AFB, Ill., 1996—; staff judge advocate Hdqrs. Air Mobility Command, Scott AFB, 1996-2000. Ret., 2000. Contbr. articles to profl. publs. Decorated Legion of Merit with oak leaf cluster. Office: HQ AMC/JA 402 Scott Dr Unit 3l2 Scott Air Force Base IL 62225-5300

REGAN, TIMOTHY JAMES, grain company executive; b. Atchison, Kans., July 31, 1956; s. Vincent James and Phyllis (Brull) R.; m. Veronica Sue Kasten, June 25, 1977; children: Katrina Sue, Brian James. BS, Kans. State U., 1978. Corp. acct. Lincoln Grain Co., Atchison, 1978-80; acctg. supr. Pillsbury Co., St. Joseph, Mo., 1980, br. account mgr., 1980-82, Omaha, 1982, internal auditor Mpls., 1983, regional account mgr. Huron, Ohio, 1983-84, Scoular Grain Co., Omaha, 1984-87, controller, 1987-91, v.p., mem. exec. com., 1990-99, CFO, 1991—2000; ex-v.p., CFO J.D. Heiskell & Co., Tulare, Calif., 2000—06, sr. v.p., CFO Elkhorn, Nebr., 2006—. Fin. adviser Grace Abbott Sch. PTO, Omaha, 1987, treas., 1990-91; bd. dirs. Cath. Charities, 1994-2000, treas., 1997-99; coach Little League Baseball and Soccer. Mem. KC, Elks. Republican. Roman Catholic. Avocations: jogging, basketball, coaching little league baseball and soccer. Office: 20010 Manderson Elkhorn NE 68022 Business E-Mail: tregan@heiskell.com.

REGNELL, BARBARA CARAMELLA, retired media educator; b. Paterson, NJ, May 5, 1935; d. William Joseph and Mafalda Erminia (Benedetto) Caramella; m. Joseph C. Tirre, July 12, 1958 (div. June 1977); children: Conrad J., William C.; m. John Albin Regnell, Apr. 2, 1983. BS, Syracuse U., 1957, MA, 1966; postgrad., Washington U., St. Louis, 1972. Editor, continuity dir. Sta. WWBZ-AM, Vineland, N.J., 1958; dir. publicity Conti Adv., Ridgewood, N.J., 1958; copywriter Sta. KCNY, San Marcos, Tex., 1959; tchr. Henninger High Sch., Syracuse, N.Y., 1966-67; instr. Belleville (Ill.) Area Jr. Coll., 1968; from instr. to assoc. prof. mass comm. So. Ill. U., Edwardsville, 1967-97, chmn. mass communications, 1985-95, prof. emerita, 1997—; comms. cons., 1997—. Trainer Nat. Iranian Radio, TV, Tehran, Iran, 1974—75; cons. in field. Mem. grant com. Ronald McDonald Ho. Charities, St. Louis, 2004—. Mem. Nat. TV Acad. (Silver Cir., mem. bd. govs. St. Louis chpt., 2d v.p., pres. 2002-03), Delta Sigma Rho, Alpha Chi Omega. Republican. Home: 6 Hawthorne Ct Saint Louis MO 63122-4512

REGULA, RALPH STRAUS, congressman, lawyer; b. Beach City, Ohio, Dec. 3, 1924; s. O.F. and Orpha (Walter) Regula; m. Mary Rogusky, Aug. 5, 1950; children: Martha, David, Richard. BA, Mt. Union Coll., 1948, LLD, 1981; LLB, William McKinley Sch. Law, 1952; LLD, Malone Coll., 1976. Bar: Ohio 1952. Sch. adminstr. Stark County Bd. Edn., 1948-55; lawyer Navarre, 1952—; mem. Ohio State Ho. Reps., 1965-66, Ohio State Senate, 1967-72, US Congress from 16th Ohio dist., 1973—, mem. appropriations com.; ptnr. Regula Bros. Mem. Pres.'s Commn. Fin. Structures and Regulation, 1970-71. Mem. Ohio Bd. Edn., 1960-64; hon. mem. adv. bd. Walsh Coll., Canton, Ohio; trustee Mt. Union Coll., Alliance, Ohio, Stark County Hist. Soc., Stark County Wilderness Soc. With USNR, 1944—46. Named Outstanding Young Man of Yr. Canton Jr. C. of C., 1957, Legis. Conservationist of Yr. Ohio League Sportsmen, 1969; recipient Cmty. Svc. award Navarre Kiwanis Club, 1963, Meritorious Svc. in Conservation award Canton Audubon Soc., 1965, Ohio Conservation award Gov. James Rhodes, 1969, J. Sterling Morton award Nat. Arbor Day Found., 2000, Sheldon Colemon Great Outdoors award Am. Recreation Coaltion, 2000, Award for Legis. Excellence, Nat. Assn. Mfrs., 2001, Legislator of Yr., Assn. Home Appliances Mfrs., 2001, Pick and Gavel award, Assn. Am. State Geologists, 2001, Spirit of Enterprise award, US C.of C., 2001, Vanguard award North Country Trail Assn., 2001, Thomas Jefferson award, Food Distributors Internat., 2002, Disting. Cmty. Health Champion award, at. Assn. Cmty. Health Ctrs., 2002, Nat. Ednl. Svc. award Am. Assn. CC, 2002, Policy Maker of Yr. award, Assn. Corp. Travel Execs., 2002-03, Pub. Svc. award Creutzfeldt-Jacob Disease Found., 2003, Benjamin Franklin Pub.Policy award Nat. Assn. Mutual Ins. Cos., 2003, Crystal Apple award Affiliate Assembly of the Am. Assn. Sch. Librarians, 2003, Disting. Legis. award, Nat. Devel. & Rsch. Insts., Inc. 2003, Congl. Am. Spirit Medallion, Nat. D-Day Mus., 2004 Republican. Episcopalian. Office: US House Reps 2306 Rayburn House Office Bldg Washington DC 20515-3516 Office Phone: 202-225-3876. Office Fax: 202-225-3059.

REH, THOMAS EDWARD, radiologist, educator; b. St. Louis, Sept. 12, 1943; s. Edward Paul and Ceil Anne (Golden) R.; m. Benedette Texada Gieselman, June 22, 1968; children: Matthew J., Benedette T., Elizabeth W. BA, St. Louis U., 1965, MD, 1969. Diplomate Am. Bd. Radiology, Nat. Bd. Med. Examiners. Intern St. John's Mercy Med. Ctr., St. Louis, 1969-70; resident St. Louis VA Hosp., 1970-73; fellow in vascular radiology Beth Israel Hosp., Boston, 1973-74; radiologist St. Mary's Health Ctr., St. Louis, 1974—, chmn. dept. radiology, 1986—; clin. asst. prof. radiology St. Louis U. Sch. Medicine, 1978-98, clin. prof. radiology, 1998—; clin. assoc. prof. radiology, 1989—. Fellow Am. Coll. Radiology; mem. AMA, Radiol. Soc. N.Am., St. Louis Met. Med. Soc., Alpha Omega Alpha, Alpha Sigma Nu, Delta Sigma Phi. Republican. Roman Catholic. Clubs: St. Louis, Confrerie des Chevaliers du Tastevin. Home: 9850 Waterbury Dr Saint Louis MO 63124-1046 Office: Bellevue Radiology Inc 4 Sunnen Bus Park Saint Louis MO 63143

REHBERG, KITTY, state legislator; b. Cedar Rapids, Iowa, Oct. 16, 1938; m. Franklin Rehberg; 3 children. Student, Rowly C.C. Mem. Iowa Senate from 14th dist., Des Moines, 1996—; mem. appropriations com., mem. rules and adminstrn. com.; vice chair edn. com. Des Moines; mem. natural resources and environment com. Republican. E-mail: kitty_rehberg@legis.state.ia.us.

REHERMAN, RONALD GILBERT, gas and electric company executive; b. Evansville, Ind., Aug. 14, 1935; s. Gilbert and Anna (Lawrence) R.; m. Rosalynn Reherman, Oct. 25, 1959; children: Robin, Chris, David. BS, U. Evansville, 1958; MBA, Ind. State U., 1971. Registered profl. engr., Ind. With So. Ind. Gas and Electric Co., Evansville, 1960—, v.p., dir. gas ops., 1982-84, exec. v.p., gen. mgr. ops., 1985-88; pres., COO So. Ind. Gas and Elec. Co., Evansville, 1988-90, pres., CEO, 1990-92, pres., chmn., CEO, 1992—. Bd. dirs. Evansville Indsl. Found., Evansville Coun. Boy Scouts Am., Vision 2000, Deaconess Hosp., Evansville United Way, campaign chmn. 1986-87; bd. trustees Evansville Mus. With U.S. Army, 1958-60. Mem. Met. Evansville C. of C. (bd. dirs. 1987), Ind. C. of C. (exec. com.)/ Avocations: camping, reading, golf, skiing. Office: So Ind Gas & Electric Co 20 NW 4th St Evansville IN 47708-1724

REHM, JACK DANIEL, publishing executive; b. Yonkers, NY, Oct. 10, 1932; s. Jack and Ann (McCarthy) R.; m. Cynthia Fenning, Oct. 18, 1958; children: Lisabeth R., Ann M., Cynthia A., Jack D. Jr. BSBA, Coll. of the Holy Cross, 1954. Advt. sales trainee, asst. account exec. Batten, Barton, Durstine & Osborne, NYC, 1954-59; mgr. Suburbia Today, NYC, 1959-62; with advt. sales dept. Better Homes and Gardens Meredith Corp., NYC, 1962-66, mgr. advt. sales Phila., 1966-67, NYC, 1967-69, advt. sales dir. Better Homes and Garden mag., 1969-73, v.p., pub. dir. mag. divsn., 1973-75, v.p., pub. Better Homes and Gardens, pub. dir. mag. divsn., 1975-76, v.p. pub. group, gen. mgr., mag. pub., 1976-80, pres. pub. group Des Moines, 1980-86, exec. v.p. corp. svcs., 1986-88, pres., COO, 1988—, pres., CEO, 1989—, chmn., pres., CEO, 1992—, also bd. dirs. Bd. dirs. Norwest Bank Iowa, N.A., Vernon Co., Newton, Iowa, Internat. Multifoods, Mpls., Equitable of Iowa Cos., Am. Coun. for Capital Formation. Bd. govs. Drake U., 1988—; trustee Coll. Holy Cross, Worcester, Mass.; mem. bus. com. Mus. Modern Art, N.Y.C., Greater Des Moines Com., Inc.; chmn. Des Moines Devel. Corp., 1993-94; active Iowa Bus. Coun.; mem. mag. and print com. USIA. With U.S. Army, 1956-57. Mem. Mag. Pubs. Am. (bd. dirs. 1981—, chmn. 1983-85, Publisher of Yr. 1988), Pine Valley Golf Club, Scarsdale Golf Club, Wakonda Golf Club. Roman Catholic. Avocation: golf. Office: Meredith Corp 1716 Locust St Des Moines IA 50309-3023 Home: 7116 SE Greenview Pl Hobe Sound FL 33455-8041

REHM, SUSAN, physician; BS, U. Nebr., 1975; MD, U. Nebr., Omaha, 1978. Diplomate Am. Bd. Internal Medicine with subspecialty in infectious disease. Resident in internal medicine The Cleve. Clinic Found., 1978—81, fellow in infectious diseases, 1981—83, assoc. chief of staff, 1997—. Clin. assoc. prof. Ohio State U., Columbus. Mem.: AMA, ACP, Am. Coll. Physician Execs., Infectious Diseases Soc. Am., Am. Soc. Microbiology, Nat. Found. for Infectious Diseases (med. dir.). Office: The Cleveland Clinic 9500 Euclid Ave Cleveland OH 44195

REIBEL, KURT, physicist, researcher; b. Vienna, May 23, 1926; came to U.S., 1938; s. Michael and Regina (Pak) R.; m. Eleanor Elvira Mannino, June 10, 1954; children— Leah, Michael, David BA, Temple U., 1954; MS, U. Pa., 1956, PhD, 1959. Jr. research assoc. in physics Brookhaven Nat. Lab., 1957-59; research assoc. U. Pa., Phila., 1959-61; asst. prof. Ohio State U., Columbus, 1961-64, assoc. prof., 1964-70, prof. physics, 1970-92, prof. emeritus, 1992—. Vis. scientist CERN, Geneva, Switzerland, 1968-69, 75-76 Author research papers on nuclear and elementary particle physics NSF fellow, 1954-56 Mem. Am. Phys. Soc., AAUP, Fedn. Am. Scientists, Union Concerned Scientists, Sigma Xi Jewish. Office: Ohio State U Dept Physics 191 W Woodruff Ave Columbus OH 43210-1117

REICH, ALLAN J., lawyer; b. Chgo., July 9, 1948; s. H. Robert and Sonya (Minsky) R.; m. Lynne Susan Roth, May 23, 1971; children: Allison, Marissa, Scott. BA, Cornell U., 1970; JD cum laude, U. Mich., 1973. Bar: Ill. 1973, U.S. Dist. Ct. (no. dist.) Ill. 1973. Ptnr. McDermott, Will & Emery, Chgo., 1973-93; vice chmn. D'Ancona & Pflaum LLC, Chgo., 1993—2003; ptnr., chair nat. corp. practice group Seyfarth Shaw LLP, Chgo., 2003—. Trustee Oakmark Family of Mutual Funds, 1994—. V.p., mem. exec. com. Coun. for Jewish Elderly, 1989—97; mem. men's coun. Mus. Contemporary Art, Chgo., 1988—89; mem. Chgo. exec. bd. Am. Jewish Com., 1989—, nat. bd. govs., pres., 2007; mem. met. Chgo. bd. Am. Heart Assn.; bd. dirs. Young Men's Jewish Coun., Chgo., 1974—84, Coun. for Jewish Elderly, 1986—97. Fellow: Am. Bar Found.; mem.: ABA, Chgo. Bar Assn., Econ. Club Chgo., Northmoor Country Club (Highland Park, Ill.), Standard Club (Chgo.). Home: 936 Skokie Ridge Dr Glencoe IL 60022-1434 Office: Seyfarth Shaw LLP 131 S Dearborn St Ste 2400 Chicago IL 60603 Home Phone: 847-835-3225; Office Phone: 312-460-5650. Business E-Mail: areich@seyfarth.com.

REICH, CHARLES, manufacturing executive, research scientist; b. Mpls., Aug. 2, 1942; BS in Chemistry, U. Minn.; PhD in Organic Chemistry, U. Wis. Rsch. chemist 3M Co., 1968—73, various tech. mgmt. positions, 1973—82, mng. dir., Switzerland opers., 1982—89, v.p., dental products divsn., 1989—97, v.p., occupl. health and environ. safety divsn., 1997—98, group v.p., chem. markets group, 1998, group v.p., specialty material markets group, 1999, exec. v.p., specialty material markets and corp. svcs., 1999—2001, exec. v.p., elec. and comm. markets, 2001—02, exec. v.p., health care bus., 2002—. Office: 3M Co 3M Ctr Saint Paul MN 55144

REICH, VICTORIA J., consumer products company executive; b. Southborough, Mass., Sept. 24, 1957; BS in Applied Math. & Econs., Brown U. With GE Co., 1979—96; v.p., contr. Brunswick Corp., Lake Forest, Ill., 1996-2000, sr. v.p., CFO, 2000—03, pres. Brunswick European Group, 2003—06; sr. v.p., CFO United Stationers Inc., Deerfield, Ill., 2007—. Office: United Stationers Inc One Pkwy N Blvd Ste 100 Deerfield IL 60015

REICHERT, DAVID, lawyer; b. Cin., Nov. 23, 1929; s. Victor E. and Louise F. Reichert; m. Marilyn Frankel, May 31, 1959; children— James G., Steven F., William M. BA, Bowling Green State U., Ohio, 1951; JD, U. Cin., 1954. Bar: Ohio 1954, US Supreme Ct. 1963. Of counsel Porter, Wright, Morris & Arthur, formerly sr. ptnr. Reichert, Strauss & Reed and predecessors, Cin. Dir. numerous corps. Monthly columnist: Scrap Age mag, 1966-74; bd. editors: U. Cin. Law Rev, 1953-54. Pres. brotherhood Rockdale Temple, Cin., 1960-61, temple treas., 1973-75, v.p., 1975-79, pres., 1979-81; mem. Amberley Village Planning Commn. & Zoning Bd. Appeals, 1972-79, Ohio Solid Waste Adv. Group, 1974; treas. Contemporary Arts Ctr., Cin., 1973-75, pres., 1976-77, trustee, 1982-88; trustee Cin. Art Mus., 1978-93, v.p., 1992-93, chmn. vis. com. for contemporary art, 1990-92; trustee Jewish Publ. Soc., 1980-86, Cin. Sculpture Coun., 1984-87; mem. acquisitions com. Miami U. Art Mus., 1982-85. Mem. Cin. Print and Drawing Cir. (pres. 1974-76), The Literary Club (sec. 1988-91, v.p. 1991-92, pres. 1992-93, hon. mem. 2007), Losantiville Country Club (bd. govs. 1985-92, sec. 1986-90, pres. 1990-92), ISRI 20th Century Club (hon. 1998), Omicron Delta Kappa, Sigma Tau Delta, Phi Delta Phi, Zeta Beta Tau. Office: Porter Wright Morris & Arthur 250 E 5th St Ste 2200 Cincinnati OH 45202-5118

REICHGOTT JUNGE, EMBER DARLENE, broadcast commentator, retired state senator, lawyer, writer, radio personality, communications executive; b. Detroit, Aug. 22, 1953; d. Norbert Arnold and Diane (Pincich) Reichgott; m. Michael Junge. BA summa cum laude, St. Olaf Coll., Minn., 1974; JD, Duke U., 1977; MBA, U. St. Thomas, 1991. Bar: Minn. 1977, D.C. 1978. Assoc. Larkin, Hoffman, Daly & Lindgren, Bloomington, Minn., 1977-84; counsel Control Data Corp., Bloomington, Minn., 1984-86; ptnr. The Gen. Counsel, Ltd., 1987—2007; mem. Minn. State Senate, 1983-2000, chmn. legis. com. on econ. status of women, 1984-86, vice chmn. senate edn. com., 1987-88, senate majority whip, 1990-94, chmn. property tax divsn. senate tax com., 1991-92, chmn. senate judiciary com., 1993-94, senate asst. majority leader, 1995-2000, chmn. spl. subcom. on ethical conduct; pres. Ember Comm., Inc., 2005—. Dem. endorsed candidate Minn. Atty. Gen., 1998; instr. polit. sci. St. Olaf Coll., Northfield, Minn., 1993; bd. dirs. Citizens Ind. Bank, St. Louis Park, Minn. 1993-. Host cable TV monthly series Legis. Report, 1985-92. Cand. US Congress, 2006; state co-chair Clinton/Gore Presdl. Campaign, Minn. Dem. Farmer-Labor Party, 1992, 1996; del. Nat. Dem. Conv., 1984, 1992, 1996; pres. Minn. Women's Polit. Caucus, 2002—04; trustee, bd. dirs. N.W. YMCA, New Hope, Minn., 1983—88, United Way Mpls., 1989—, Greater Mpls. ARC, 1988—2004, chair, 2001—03. Recipient Woman of Yr. award North Hennepin Bus. and Profl. Women, 1983, award for contbn. to human svcs. Minn. Social Svcs. Assn., 1983, Clean Air award Minn. Lung Assn., 1988, Disting. Svc. award Mpls. Jaycees, 1984, Minn. Dept. Human Rights award, 1989, Myra Bradwell award Minn. Women Lawyers, 1993, Disting. Alumnae award Lake Conf. Schs., 1993, Disting. Alumnae award St. Olaf Coll., 1998, awards for leadership Am. Lung Assn., 1999, Am. Heart Assn., 1997, Everyday Hero award Up with People, 1995, Unsung Hero award United Way of Mpls., 1999, 2000 Innovations in Am. Govt. award Harvard U. and Ford Found., others; 1st recipient of award named in her honor for prevention of sexual assault, 2000; charter inductee Robbinsdale H.S. Hall of Fame, 2000; named One of ten Outstanding Young Minnesotans, Minn. Jaycees, 1984, Policy Adv. of Yr., NAWBO, 1988, Woman of Achievement, Twin West C. of C., 1989, Marvelous Minn. Woman, 1993. Mem. Minn. Bar Assn. (bd. govs. 1992-96, Pro Bono Publico Atty. award 1990), Hennepin County Bar Assn., Corp. Counsel Assn. (v.p. 1989-96). Home: 500 E Grant St #1308 Minneapolis MN 55404 Personal E-mail: ember@visi.com.

REICIN, RONALD IAN, lawyer; b. Chgo., Dec. 11, 1942; s. Frank Edward and Abranita (Rome) R.; m. Alyta Friedland, May 23, 1965; children: Eric, Kael. BBA, U. Mich., 1964, MBA, 1967, JD cum laude, 1967. Bar: Ill. 1967, U.S. Tax Ct. 1967; CPA, Ill. Mem. staff Price Waterhouse & Co., Chgo., 1966; ptnr. Jenner & Block, Chgo., 1967—. Bd. dirs. Nat. Kidney Found., Ill., 1978-2003, v.p., 1992-95, pres., 1995-98, life trustee, 2004—; bd. dirs. Ruth Page Found., 1985—, v.p., 1990—; bd. dirs. Scoliosis Assn. Chgo., 1981-90, Kohl Children's Mus., 1991-95, River North Chgo. Dance Co., 1999—. Mem.: Ill. State Bar Assn., Chgo. Mortgage Attys. Assn., Chgo. Bar Assn., ABA, Lawyers Club (Chgo.), Exec. Club, Beta Alpha Psi, Beta Gamma Sigma, Phi Kappa Phi. Office: Jenner & Block LLP 330 N Wabash Ave Fl 40 Chicago IL 60611-3586 Home Phone: 847-831-5969; Office Phone: 312-923-2687. Personal E-mail: rreicin@jenner.com.

REID, DANIEL JAMES, public relations executive; b. Grand Rapids, Mich., Sept. 7, 1960; s. Robert Alexander and Janette Helen (Hickey) R.; m. Meredith Christine Ryan, Apr. 30, 1994; children: Ryan Paul, Katherine Baxter, Charles William Edward. BA, Mich. State U., 1983. Sr. account exec. Burson-Marsteller, Chgo., 1983-88; group dir. Ogilvy & Mather, Chgo., 1988-90; sr. ptnr. FRB/BSMG Worldwide (subs. True North Comms.), Chgo., 1990-98; sr. nat. mng. ptnr. BSMG Worldwide, Chgo., 1998-2000, pres. fin. svcs., 2000—; exec. v.p. Weber Shandwick Worldwide, Chgo., 2001—. Contbr. articles to profl. publs. and newspapers. Bd. dirs. Prospect Fin., L.A., Opportunity, Inc., Chgo., LEC Ltd. Mem. Pub. Rels. Soc. Am., Union League Club Chgo., Excec.'s Club Chgo. Republican. Roman Catholic. Office: Weber Shandwick 676 St Clair Chicago IL 60611

REID, IRVIN D., academic administrator; m. Pamela Trotman, Aug. 27, 1966; children: Nicole, Dexter. BS, Howard U., MS in Exptl. Psychology; MA, PhD, U. Pa.; PhD (hon.), Montclair State U., 2003. Head dept. mktg. & bus. law U. Tenn., Chattanooga, 1979-83, dean Sch. Bus. Adminstrn., John Stagmaier prof. econs. and bus. adminstrn., Alan Lorberbaum prof. mktg.; assoc. prof. mktg. Howard U., Washington, 1978-79; cons. U.S. Consumer Product Safety Commn., 1977-78; sr. staff specialist mktg. & econ. rsch. NASA, 1976-77, 78-79; asst. prof. mktg. coll. bus. Drexel U., 1970-78; pres. Montclair State U., Upper Montclair, NJ, 1989—97, Wayne State U., Detroit, 1997—. Bd. mem. Detroit Renaissance, Handleman Co., Fed. Reserve Bank of Chgo., Mack-Cali Real Estate Trust. Bd. dirs. Detroit 300 Com., 1998—; exec. com. Detroit Med. Ctr., 1997—, Karmanos Cancer Inst., 1997—, New Detroit, 1998—, NJ/Israel Trade Commn., 1994-97, NCAA Pres.'s Commn., 1994-99, Nat. Conf. Christians and Jews, 1992-97, Mich. Econ. Devel. Corp., 1999—, Detroit Urban League, 1999—, Mich. Opera Theater, 1998—; steering com. Mich. Life Sci. Initiative, 2000—. Mem. Econ. Club Detroit, Univ. Cultural Ctr. Assn., Upper Montclair (N.J.) Country Club. Office: Wayne State U Office of the Pres 4200 Faculty/Adminstrn Bldg Detroit MI 48202 Office Phone: 313-577-2230. Office Fax: 313-577-3200. E-mail: president@wayne.edu.*

REID, JAMES SIMS, JR., former automobile parts manufacturer; b. Cleve., Jan. 15, 1926; s. James Sims and Felice (Crowl) R.; m. Donna Smith, Sept. 2, 1950; children: Sally, Susan, Anne (dec.), Jeanne. AB cum laude, Harvard U., 1948, JD, 1951. Bar: Mich., Ohio 1951. Pvt. practice law, Detroit, 1951-52, Cleve., 1953-56; with Standard Products Co., Cleve., 1956-99, dir., 1959, pres., 1962-89, chmn., chief exec. officer, 1989-99; ret., 1999. Trustee John Carroll U., 1967—, chmn., 1987-91, Musical Arts Assn. of Cleve. Orch., 1973—. Office: Hanna Bldg Ste 545 1422 Euclid Ave Cleveland OH 44115-1901

REID, MARILYN JOANNE, state legislator, lawyer; b. Chgo., Aug. 14, 1941; d. Kermit and Newell Azile (Hahn) N.; m. M. David Reid, Nov. 26, 1966 (div. Mar. 1983); children: David, Nelson. Student, Miami U., Oxford, Ohio, 1959-61; BA, U. Ill, 1963; JD, Ohio No. U., 1966. Bar: Ohio 1966, Ark. 1967, U.S. Dist. Ct. 1967. Trust adminstr. First Nat. Bank, Dayton, Ohio, 1966-67; assoc. Sloan & Ragsdale, Little Rock, 1967-69; ptnr. Reid and Reid, Dayton, 1969-76, Reid & Assocs., Dayton, 1975—; mem. Ohio Ho. of Reps., 1993-98. Mem. health ins. and HMO's com., chmn. ins. com., vets. com., pub. utilities com. Mem. Ohio adv. bd. U.S. Commn. Civil Rights; trustee Friends Libr. Beavercreek, Ohio; bd. dirs. Beavercreek YMCA, 1985—88; pres. Greene County Commn., 2005; chair Miami Valley Regional Planning Commn.; bd. mem. County Commn. of Ohio; chmn., treas. various polit. campaigns, 1975—; chmn. Greene County Rep. Party; active Mt. Zion United Ch. of Christ. Mem. ABA, Ohio Bar Assn., Greene County Bar Assn., Beavercreek C. of C. (pres. 1986-87), Dayton Panhellenic Assn. (pres. 1982), Altrusa (v.p. Greene County 1978-79, pres. 1979-80), Lions (pres. Beavercreek 1975), Greene County Rep. Party (chmn.), Rotary, Kappa Beta Pi, Gamma Phi Beta (v.p. 1974-75). Mem. Ch. Christ. Avocations: tennis, skiing, boating, bridge. Office: Reid & Assocs 3866 Indian Ripple Rd Dayton OH 45440-3448

REID, ORIEN, former medical association administrator; b. Oct. 1945; BA, Clark Coll., Atlanta. MSW. Anchor WCAU-TV, Phila., 1979—98; chmn., bd. dirs. Alzheimer's Assn.'s Nat. Bd. Dirs., 1999—2002. Former mem. bd. govs. Nat. Acad. Television Arts and Scis.; former pres. Phila. Consumer Coun. Recipient Best Investigative Reporting, Phila. Press Assn., Excellence in Journalism award, Inst. Food Technologists.

REID, ROBERT LELON, engineering educator, dean; b. Detroit, May 20, 1942; s. Lelon Reid and Verna Beulah (Custer) Menkes; m. Judy Elaine Nestell, July 21, 1962; children: Robert James, Bonnie Kay, Matthew Lelon. ASE, Mott C.C., Flint, Mich., 1961; BChemE, U. Mich., 1963; MME, So. Meth. U., 1966, PhDME, 1969. Registered profl. engr., Tenn., Tex., Wis. Asst. rsch. engr. Atlantic Richfield Co., Dallas, 1964-65; assoc. staff engr. Linde Divsn., Union Carbide Corp., Tonawanda, NY, 1966-68; from asst. to assoc. prof. U. Tenn., Knoxville, 1969-75; assoc. prof. Cleve. State U., 1975-77; from assoc. to full prof. U. Tenn., Knoxville, 1977-82; prof., chmn. U. Tex., El Paso, 1982-87; dean Coll. Engring., Marquette U., Milw., 1987-98, prof. mech. engring., 1998-2001; dean emeritus, 2001. Summer prof. NASA Marshall Space Ctr., Huntsville, Ala., 1970, EXXON Prodn. Rsch., Houston, 1972, 73, NASA Lewis Space Ctr., Cleve., 1986; cons. Oak Ridge Nat. Lab., 1974-75, TVA, 1978, 79, State of Calif., Sacramento, 1985, Tex. Higher Edn. Coordinating Bd., Austin, 1987. Contbr. articles 100 articles on heat transfer and solar energy. Grantee NSF, DOE, TVA, NASA, DOI, 1976-87; named Engr. of Yr. Engring. Socs. El Paso, 1986. Fellow ASME (Centennial medallion 1980, chmn. cryogenics com. 1977-81, chmn. solar energy divsn. 1983-84, chmn. Rio Grande sect. 1985-87, John Yellott award, 1997, Dedicated Svc. award 1998); mem. ASHRAE, Engrs. and Scientists Milw. (bd. dirs. 1988-93, v.p. 1989-90, pres. 1991-92), Wis. Assn. Rsch. Mgmt. (pres. 1996-97). Lutheran. Avocations: travel, classic car restoration. Business E-Mail: bobreid@umich.edu.

REID, S.W., language educator; b. Neptune, NJ, Nov. 24, 1943; s. Sidney Webb and Mary Cook (Bennett) R.; m. Judith Wright, Aug. 22, 1969; 1 child, Laura. BA, Duke U., 1965; MA, U. Va., 1966, PhD, 1972. Grad. tchg. fellow U. Va., Charlottesville, 1968-70; asst. prof. English, Kent (Ohio) State U., 1970-75, assoc. prof., 1975-84, prof., 1984—, dir. Inst. Bibliography and Editing, 1985—. Vis. fellow Clare Hall, Cambridge (Eng.) U., 1992-93, life mem., 1993—. Textual editor Bicentennial Edition of Charles Brockden Brown, 6 vols., 1977-87; editor-in-chief: (Cambridge edits. of Joseph Conrad) The Secret Agent, 1990, Almayer's Folly, 1994, Notes on Life and Letters, 2004. NDEA fellow U. Va., 1965-68; Rsch. grantee NEH, 1977-84. Office: Kent State University Inst Bibliography-Editing 1118 Library Kent OH 44242-0001 Office Phone: 330-672-2092.

REID, WILLIAM HILL, mathematics professor; b. Oakland, Calif., Sept. 10, 1926; s. William Macdonald and Edna Caroline (Hill) R.; m. Elizabeth Mary Kidner, May 26, 1962; 1 child, Margaret Frances. BS, U. Calif., Berkeley, 1949, MS, 1951; PhD, Cambridge U., Eng., 1955, ScD (hon.), 1968; AM (hon.), Brown U., 1961. Lectr. Johns Hopkins U., Balt., 1955-56; NSF fellow Yerkes Observatory, Williams Bay, Wis., 1957-58; asst. prof. Brown U., Providence, 1958-61, assoc. prof., 1961-63, U. Chgo., 1963-65, prof., 1965-89, prof. emeritus, 1989—; prof. Ind. U.-Purdue U., Indianapolis, 1989—2007. Cons. research labs. Gen. Motors Corp., Warren, Mich., 1960-73. Author (with P.G. Drazin): Hydrodynamic Stability, 1981; author: 2d edit., 2004; contbr. articles to profl. jours. Served with U.S. Mcht. Marine, 1945-47, with AUS, 1954-56.

Fulbright Rsch. scholar, Australian Nat. U., 1964—65. Fellow Am. Phys. Soc., Cambridge Philos. Soc.; mem. Am. Math. Soc., Am. Meteorol. Soc., Sigma Xi. Office: Ind U-Purdue U Dept Math Scis 402 N Blackford St Indianapolis IN 46202-3216 Home: 115 Lake of the Woods Ln #407 Jacksonville FL 32259 Business E-Mail: wreid@math.iupui.edu.

REID-ANDERSON, JAMES, diagnostic equipment company executive; BS in Commerce with honors, U. Birmingham, Eng.; MBA, Rutgers U. Exec. level positions with Pepsico Inc., Grand Met. PLC, Mobil Oil Corp.; COO, chief adminstrv. officer Wilson Sporting Goods, Chgo., 1994-96; exec. v.p., CFO Dade Behring, Deerfield, Ill., 1996-97, exec. v.p., CFO, chief adminstrv. officer, 1997-99, pres., COO, 1999—2000, pres., CEO, 2000—02, chmn., pres., CEO, 2002—. Fellow Chartered Assn. Cert. Accts. Office: Dade Behring Corp Hdqrs 1717 Deerfield Rd Deerfield IL 60015-3977

REIDELBACH, LINDA, state representative; b. Cin., Apr. 1, 1949; BS, Miami U. Ohio. Exec. v.p. MJR Enterprises, Inc.; state rep. dist. 21 Ohio Ho. of Reps., Columbus, vice chair, banking pensions and securities com., chair, children's healthcare and family svcs. subcom., mem. edn., health, human svcs. and aging, and juvenile and family law coms., and fed. grant rev. and edn. oversight subcom. Mem. Columbus team Abstinence Educators Network; mem. Franklin County Rep. Ctrl. Com., Ohio; bd. dirs. Destiny Training Camp. Mem.: Worthington Christian Ch., Worthington League for Decency. Office: 77 S High St 12th fl Columbus OH 44321-6111

REIDINGER, RUSSELL FREDERICK, JR., fish and wildlife scientist; b. Reading, Pa., June 19, 1945; BS, Albright Coll., 1967; PhD in Zoology, U. Ariz., 1972. Asst. prof. biology Augustana Coll., 1971-74; rsch. physiologist The Philippines, 1974-78; asst. mem., wildlife biologist Monell Chem. Senses Ctr., 1978-86; dir. Denver Wildlife Rsch. Ctr. U.S. Dept. Agr., Denver, 1987-93; dir. Ctr. Excellence Wildlife Mgmt. Lincoln U., Jefferson City, Mo., 1993—. Vis. prof. dept. zoology U. Philippines, 1975-78; cons. Bangladesh Agr. Rsch. Coun., USAID, 1977, Ministry Agrl. Devel. & Agrarian Reform, Nicaragua, 1981, CID, Uganda, 1996. Mem. Am. Soc. Mammalogists, Wildlife Soc., Nat. Animal Damage Control Assn. Office: Lincoln U Dept Ag Nat & Home Econ Jefferson City MO 65102-0029

REIDY, DANIEL EDWARD, lawyer; b. Chgo., Nov. 21, 1949; s. Francis W. and Ann E. (Harrington) R.; m. Elizabeth Gamble, Aug. 21, 1971; children: David, Patrick, Kevin, Jean. BA in Polit. sci., cm laude, Loyola U., 1971; JD magna cum laude, U. Mich., 1974. Bar: Ill. 1974, US Dist. Ct. (no. dist.) Ill. 1974, Supreme Ct., Ill., 1974, US Ct. Appeals (7th cir.) 1975, US Ct. Appeals (11th cir.) 1992, US Ct. Appeals (fed. cir.) 1994, US Dist. Ct. (ctrl. dist.) Ill. 1995, US Dist. Ct. (so. dist.) Ill. 2002, US Ct. Appeals (1st cir.), 2004. Law clk. to Hon. Walter J. Cummings U.S. Ct. Appeals (7th cir.), Chgo., 1974-75; asst. US atty. US Atty.'s Office, Chgo., 1975—85; first asst. US atty. No. Dist. of Ill., Chgo., 1985—87; ptnr. Jones Day, Chgo., 1987—. Litig. group coord., Chgo. & nat. chair, Corp. Criminal Investigation Practice; mem. commn. adminstrn. justice Ill. Supreme Ct., Chgo., 1992-93. Fellow Internat. Acad. Trial Lawyers, Am. Coll. Trial Lawyers; mem. ABA, Chgo. Bar Assn.(sec. 2001-2005), Fed. Bar Assn., Chgo. Coun. Lawyers, Chgo. Inn Ct. Office: Jones Day 77 W Wacker Ste 3500 Chicago IL 60601-1692 Office Phone: 312-782-3939. Business E-Mail: dereidy@jonesday.com.

REIDY, THOMAS ANTHONY, lawyer; b. Bronx, NY, Sept. 30, 1952; s. John Alexander and Elinor Ann (Tracey) R.; m. Victoria Mary Moxham, Mar. 12, 1977; children: J. Benjamin, Jacob T., Thomas A. II. BA with honors, Lehigh U., 1974; JD, U. Va., 1978. Bar: Ohio 1978, U.S. Dist. Ct. (so. dist.) Ohio 1980. Assoc. Moritz, McClure, Hughes, Kerscher & Price, Columbus, Ohio, 1978-80, Porter, Wright, Morris & Arthur, Columbus, 1980-87, ptnr., 1987-92; v.p. human resources and employment counsel The Longaberger Co., Dresden, Ohio, 1993-94, gen. counsel, 1994—. Mem.: Direct Selling Assn. (chmn. ethics and self-regulation com. 2001—). Office: Longaberger Co PO Box 3400 Newark OH 43058-3400

REILLY, KEVIN P., academic administrator; BA, U. Notre Dame, 1971; MA, U. Minn., 1974, PhD in English, 1979. Teaching asst. dept. English U. Minn., Mpls., 1974-79, asst. to dir. undergrad. study dept. English, 1976-77; coord. project on ednl. advisement in the work setting N.Y. State Bd. Regents, 1979-80, dir. Teaching and Beyond project, 1983-84, dir. nat. program non-coll. sponsored instrn., 1979-84, dir. div. coll. and univ. evaluation, 1984-92; assoc. provost for acad. programs, sec. of the univ. SUNY Sys., Albany, 1992—96; also sr. fellow in univ./sch. rels. SUNY Systems, Albany, 1992—96; provost, vice-chancellor U. Wis.-ext., 1996—2000, chancellor, 2000—04, U. Wis. System, Madison, 2004—. Mem. vis. del. Am. educators to rev. sch. system in No. Ireland, 1990; lectr. and presenter in field. Editor: (with Carol Wolfe) A Guide to Educational Programs in Noncollegiate Organizations, 1983, (with Sheila Murdick) Teaching and Beyond: Nonacademic Career Programs for Ph.D.'s, 1984; contbr. numerous articles to profl. jours. Tutor, Literacy Vols. of Am., Schenectady, 1988-90. Recipient Mgmt. Performance awards N.Y. State, 1989, 90; recipient fellowships at U. Minn. Mem. MLA, Am. Assn. for Higher Edn., Am. Conf. for Irish Studies, Am. Ednl. Rsch. Assn., Assn. for Continuing Higher Edn., Irish Am. Cultural Inst. Office: U Wis System 1720 Van Hise Hall 1220 Linden Dr Madison WI 53706-1557 E-mail: kreilly@uwsa.edu.

REILLY, ROBERT FREDERICK, investment banker; b. NYC, Oct. 3, 1953; s. James J. and Marie (Griebel) Reilly; m. Janet H. Steiner, Apr. 16, 1975; children: Ashley Lauren, Brandon Christopher, Cameron Courtney. BA in Econs., Columbia U., 1975, MBA in Fin., 1976. CPA Ohio, Ill., cert. mgmt. acct.; CFA, cert. real estate appraiser, rev. appraiser, gen. appraiser Ill., Va., Utah, Oreg., NY, bus. appraiser, accredited bus. valuator, valuation cons. Sr. cons. Booz, Allen & Hamilton, Cin., 1975-76; dir. corp. planning Huffy Corp., Dayton, Ohio, 1976-81; v.p. Arthur D. Little Valuation, Inc., Chgo., 1981-85; ptnr., nat. dir. valuation svcs. Deloitte & Touche, Chgo., 1985-91; mng. dir. Willamette Mgmt. Assocs., Chgo., 1991—. Adj. prof. acctg. U. Dayton Grad. Sch. Bus., 1977—81; adj. prof. econs. Elmhurst Coll., Ill., 1982—87; adj. prof. fin. Ill. Inst. Tech. Grad. Sch. Bus., Chgo., 1985—91; adj. prof. taxation U. Chgo. Grad. Sch. Bus., 1985—87. Co-author: (book) Valuing Small Businesses and Professional Practices, 1993, Business Valuation Video Course, 1993, Valuing a Business, 1995;: 4th edit., 2000, Valuing Accounting Practices, 1997, Valuing Professional Practices--A Practitioner's Approach, 1997, Valuing Intangible Assets, 1998, Handbook of Advanced Business Valuation, 1999, Handbook of Business Valuation and Intellectual Property Analysis, 2004, Guide to ESOP Valuation, 2007, Guide to Property Tax Valuation, 2008; editor, columnist: Ohio CPA Jour., 1984—86, Ill. Bus. Rev., 1991—2001, Small Bus. Taxation, 1989—90, Bus. Valuation Rev., 1989—90, Jour. Real Estate Acctg. and Taxation, 1991—93, Jour. Property Taxation Mgmt., 1993—, Jour. Am. Bankruptcy Inst., 1993—, Valuation Strategies, 2003—; co-editor: (book) Financial Valuation-Valuation of Business and Business Interests, 1997; contbr. articles to profl. jours. Mem.: AICPA (mem. ABV exam. com. 2002—06, mem. bus. valuation com. 2006—), Appraisal Inst., Nat. Assn. Bus. Economists, Am. Econ. Assn., Am. Bankruptcy Inst., Inst. CFAs, Chgo. Soc. Investment Analysts, Bus. Valuation Assn., Accreditation Coun. Accountancy (accredited fed. income taxation), Ohio Soc. CPAs (chpt. dir. 1978—81), Ill. Soc. CPAs, Inst. Property Taxation, Inst. Cert. Mgmt. Accts. (chpt. dir. 1976—), Nat. Assn. Real Estate Appraisers, Am. Soc. Appraisers (mem. bd. examiners 1985—89), Inst. Bus. Appraisers (life). Home: 310 Algonquin Rd Barrington IL 60010-6109 Office: 8600 W Bryn Mawr Ave Chicago IL 60631-3579 Office Phone: 773-399-4300.

REIMAN, ROY J., publishing executive; Pub., founder Reiman Publs., Greendale, Wis., 1964—. Office: Reiman Publs 5400 S 60th St Greendale WI 53129-1404

REIMER, BENNETT, music educator, writer; b. NYC, June 19, 1932; s. George and Sarah (Talkofsky) R.; children: Jan Ellen, Terry. BM, State Tchr.'s Coll. (now SUNY-Fredonia), 1954; MM, U. Ill., 1955, EdD, 1963. Asst. prof. music edn. U. Ill., Urbana, 1960-65; Kulas prof., chmn. dept. music edn. Case Western Res. U., Cleve., 1965-78; John W. Beattie prof. emeritus Northwestern U., Evanston, Ill., 1978-97. Author: A Philosophy of Music Education, 1970, 2d edit., 1989, Developing the Experience of Music, 1985; editor: Toward an Aesthetic Education, 1971, The Arts, Education and Aesthetic Knowing, 1992, On the ature of Musical Experience, 1992; co-author: The Experience of Music, 1972, Silver Burdett Music Grades 1-8, 1974, 4th edit., 1985; contbr. over 100 articles on music and arts edn. to profl. jours. Mem. Music Educators Nat. Conf., Music Edn. Research Council, Edn. Aesthetic Awareness (bd. dirs.). Office: Northwestern U Sch Music Evanston IL 60208-0001

REIMER, JUDY MILLS, pastor, religious executive; m. George G. Reimer, 1964; children: Todd, Troy. BA, Emory and Henry Coll., 1962; MDiv, Bethany Theol. Sem., 1994. Ordained into Set Apart Ministry, Ch. of the Brethren, 1994. Vol. Brethren Vol. Svc. NIH, Bethesda, Md., 1962-64, Hessish Lichtenau, Germany, 1964-65; elem. sch. tchr. Pub. and Private Schs., various cities, 1965-76; deacon Ch. of the Brethren, 1966—; mem Virlina Dist. Bd., 1978-90; chair of nurture com. Ch. of the Brethren Virlina Dist., 1979-82, chair of outdoor ministry, 1983-84, conf. speaker, 1992; founding pastor Ch. of the Brethren, Smith Mountain Lake, Va., 1996-98, gen. bd. exec. dir., 1998—2003; owner, sr. v.p. Harris Office Furniture Co., Roanoke, Va., 1976—. Co-chair and vice-chair of two Virlina Fin. Campaigns, Ch. of the Brethren, 1980s, mem. Gen. Bd., Ch. of Brethren, 1977-90; mem. PTA, United Way Allocation Com., Roanoke Valley Women Owners Assn. (charter mem.); adult advisor Nat. Youth Cabinet. 1991, 92; worship coord. Nat. Youth Conf. 1994 numerous other coms. for Ch. of Brethren; official observer for Nat. Coun. of Chs. at Nicaraguan Election, Feb., 1990; rep. of Ch. of the Brethren, 1989, Atlanta, The Torch of Conscience Campaign to sensitize congregation to the campaign to abolish death penalty; workshop leader across the denomination on leadership devel., pastor/spouse retreats, women's rallies, etc.; ann. conf. moderator elect, 1993-94. Mem. Inst. Indsl. Comml. Chaplains (chmn. bd. dirs. local unit, asst. treas. nat. bd.). Office: Church of the Brethren General Offices 1451 Dundee Ave Elgin IL 60120-1694

REIN, JEFFREY A., retail executive; b. New Orleans, Feb. 28, 1952; m. Susan Naber; 2 children. BS in Acctg., U. Ariz., 1974, BS in Pharmacy, 1980. Pharmacist Long Drugs, Calif.; asst. store mgr. Walgreen Co., Tucson, 1982—84, store mgr. Tex., 1984—90, dist. mgr. N.Mex., 1990—96, divisional v.p., treas. Ill., 1996—2000, v.p. mktg. systems svcs., 2000—01, exec. v.p. mktg., 2001—03, COO, 2003—06, pres., 2003—07, CEO, 2006—, chmn., 2007—. Office: Walgreen Co 200 Wilmot Rd Deerfield IL 60015

REINDL, JAMES, newspaper editor; Bur. chief AP, Chgo., 2000—. Office: 10 S Wacker Dr Ste 2500 Chicago IL 60606-7491

REINHARD, JOAO PEDRO, chemicals company executive; b. Sao Paulo, Brazil, Aug. 4, 1945; BA, MBA, Escola de Administração de Empresas, da Fundação Getulio Vargas, São Paulo, Brazil, 1967; completed postgraduate studies at the U. Cologne, Germany and Stanford U. Fin. planning supr. Squibb do Brazil, Sao Paulo, 1968; credit mgr. Dow Quimica, Sao Paulo, 1970-72; fin. asst. Dow Latin Am., Miami, Fla., 1973; treas. Latin Am. Dow Lepetit Latin Am., Miami, Fla., 1974-76; corp. fin. planning mgr. Dow Chem. Co., Midland, Mich., 1976-77, treas., 1988—96, v.p., 1990—95, fin. v.p., 1995—96, CFO, 1995—2005, exec. v.p., 1996—2005, sr. advisor, 2005; fin. dir. Dow Quimica S.Am., Sao Paulo, Brazil, 1978-80, Dow Europe, Horgen, Switzerland, 1981-85, asst. treas., 1984, v.p., 1985-87; mng. dir. Dow Italy, Milan, 1985—88. Bd. dirs. Royal Bank of Canada, 2000-, Dow Corning Corp., 1995-2007, Sigma-Aldrich Corp., 2001-, Coca-Cola Co., 2003-06, Colgate-Palmolive Co., 2006-, Liana Ltd., Midland, Mich., Dorinco Reinsurance Co., Midland, Dow Chem. Internat. BV, Midland, DCOMCO Inc., Midland, Dow Chm. Inter-Am. Ltd., Midland, Dow Chem. Internat. Inc. (Panama), Midland,, Dow Chem. Internat. Ltd., Midland, Midland Pipeline Corp., Dow Chem. Overseas Capital NV, Midland, Bank Mendes Gans NV, Amsterdam, The Netherlands; mem. Environment Health & Safety Com., Dow Chemical Co. Mem. Fin. Execs. Inst., Fin. Mgmt. Assn., Nat. Assn. Corp. Treasurers, Corp. Fin. Inst.

REINHARD, PHILIP GODFREY, federal judge; b. LaSalle, Ill., Jan. 12, 1941; s. Godfrey and Ruth R.; m. Virginia Reinhard; children: Bruce, Brian, David, Philip. BA, U. Ill., Champaign, 1962, JD, 1964. Asst. state atty. Winnebago County, 1964-67; atty. Hyer, Gill & Brown, 1967-68; state atty. Winnebago County, 1968-76; judge 17th Jud. Cir., Ill., 1976-80, 2nd Dist. Ct. Appeals, Ill., 1980-92, US Dist. Ct. (no. dist.) Ill., 1992—2007, sr. judge, 2007—. Mem. Am. Acad. Jud. Edn., Winnebago County Bar Assn. Office: US Courthouse 211 S Court St Rockford IL 61101-1219 Office Phone: 815-987-4480.

REINHARD, STEVE, state representative; b. Bucyrus, Ohio, Sept. 12, 1967; BS in Agrl. Econs. and Agrl. Edn., Ohio State U. Tchr.; farmer; state rep. dist. 82 Ohio Ho. of Reps., Columbus, 2000—, vice chair, state govt. com., mem. agr. and natural resources, econ. devel. and tech., and edn. coms., and fed. grant rev. and edn. oversight and ethics and elections subcoms., chair transp., pub. safety and homeland security coms, mem. edn. com., mem. agrl. and natural resources com., mem. econ. devel. and environment com. Mem.: Bucyrus Twp. Fire Dept., Ohio Farm Bur., Ohio Assn. Agrl. Educators. Office: 77 S High St 12th fl Columbus OH 43215-6111

REINHARDT, JOHN W., dean, dental educator; b. Nashville, Ill. m. Claudia Reinhardt. B in biology, Ill. Wesleyan U., 1971; DDS, Loyola U., 1975; MS in operative dentistry, U. Iowa, 1979; MPH in health services rsch., Harvard U., 1988. Diplomate Am. Bd. Operative Dentistry. With US Army Dental Corps; asst. prof. U. Iowa Coll. Dentistry, 1980—84, assoc. prof., 1984—90, head dept. operative dentistry, 1988—2000, prof., 1990—2000; dean U. Nebr. Med. Ctr. Coll. Dentistry, 2000—, prof. dept. adult restorative dentistry, 2000—. Rschr. in field; cons. NIH, ADA, US Navy, Am. Dental Edn. Assn., Consortium Operative Dentistry Educators, Internat. Assn. Dental Rsch., others.; chair Children's Amalgam Trial Data and Safety Monitoring Bd. Nat. Inst. Dental and Craniofacial Rsch., 1997—; mem. bd. dirs. Friends of the Nat. Inst. of Dental and Craniofacial Rsch., 2005—. Contbr. articles to profl. pubs., scientific papers, chapters to books. Fellow: Internat. Coll. Dentists, Am. Coll. Dentists; mem.: ADA, Am. Bd. Operative Dentistry, Acad. Operative Dentistry (pres. 1997, chair. bd. dirs. founder's fund 2000—, Award of Excellence 2002). Office: U Nebr Med Ctr Coll Dentistry 40th and Holdrege Streets Box 830740 Lincoln E 68583-1301 Office Phone: 402-472-1344. Office Fax: 402-472-6681. Business E-Mail: jreinhardt@unmc.edu.

REINHART, DIETRICH THOMAS, academic administrator, social studies educator; b. Mpls., May 17, 1949; s. Donald Irving and Eleanor Therese (Noonan) R. BA in History, St. John's U., Collegeville, Minn., 1971; AM in History, Brown U., 1976, PhD in History, 1984. Benedictine monk St. John's Abbey, 1971—; prof. history St. John's U., 1981—, dean of the coll., 1988-91, pres., 1991—. Dir. liturgy St. John's Abbey, 1983-88. Bd. dirs. Minn. Pvt. Coll. Coun., 1991—, George A. MacPherson Fund, 1991—, Hill Monastic Manuscript Library, 1991—, Inst. for Ecumenical and Cultural Rsch., 1991—, First Am. Nat. Bank St. Cloud., 1992—; bd. overseers St. John's Prep. Sch., 1990—. Home: St Johns Abbey Collegeville MN 56321 Office: St John's U Office of Pres Collegeville MN 56321

REINHART, ROBERT ROUNTREE, JR., lawyer; b. Chgo., Oct. 21, 1947; s. Robert Rountree and Ruth (Duncan) R.; m. Elizabeth Aileen Plews, July 26, 1969; children: Andrea Jean, Jessica Elizabeth, Rebecca Jill. BA, Northwestern U., 1968; JD, U. Mich., 1971. Bar: Ill. 1971, Mich. 1972, Minn. 1973, U.S. Supreme Ct. 1976. Law clk. to judge U.S. Dist. Ct. (we. dist.) Mich., Grand Rapids, 1971-73; assoc. Oppenheimer Wolff & Donnelly, Mpls., 1973-77, ptnr., 1978-96, chair labor and employment bus. group, 1985-92; ptnr. Dorsey & Whitney, Mpls., 1996—, chair labor and employment practice group, 2000—. Co-chmn. Upper Midwest Employment Law Inst., Mpls., 1984—; gen. counsel Minn. Empoyment Law Coun., 1990—. Mem. ABA (labor and employment, civil litigation sects.), Minn. Bar Assn. Office: Dorsey & Whitney Ste 1500 50 S 6th St Minneapolis MN 55402-1498 Office Phone: 612-340-7835. Office Fax: 612-340-2868. E-mail: reinhart.robert@dorseylaw.com.

REINKE, WILLIAM JOHN, lawyer; b. South Bend, Ind., Aug. 7, 1930; s. William August and Eva Marie (Hein) R.; m. Sue Carol Colvin, 1951 (div. 1988); children: Sally Sue Taelman, William A., Andrew J.; m. Elizabeth Beck Lockwood, 1991. AB cum laude, Wabash Coll., 1952; JD, U. Chgo., 1955. Bar: Ind. 1955. Assoc. Barnes & Thornburg and predecessors, South Bend, Ind., 1957-61, ptnr., 1961—96, of counsel, 1996—, former chmn. compensation com. Mem. mgmt. com. Barnes & Thornburg and predecessors. Trustee Stanley Clark Sch., 1969-80, pres., 1977-80; life mem. adv. bd. Salvation Army, 1973—, pres., 1990-92; bd. dirs. NABE Mich. chpt., 1990-94, pres. 1993-94, Isaac Walton League, 1970-81; bd. dirs. United Way, 1979-81; pres. South Bend Round Table, 1963-65; trustee First Meth. Ch., 1976-70, 2005-07; bd. dirs. So. Bend Civic Theatre, 1997-2003. With U.S. Army, 1955-57. Recipient Outstanding Local Pres. award Ind. Jaycees, 1960-61, Boss of Yr. award, 1979, South Bend Outstanding Young Man award, 1961. Mem. ABA, Ind. State Bar Assn., St. Joseph County Bar Assn., Ind. Bar Found. (patron fellow), Am. Judicature Soc., Summit Club (founders com.), Rotary (bd. dirs. 1970-73, 94-97). Home: 51795 Waterton Square Cir Granger IN 46530-8317 Office: Barnes & Thornburg 1st Source Bank Ctr 100 N Michigan St Ste 600 South Bend IN 46601-1632 Office Phone: 574-233-1171.

REINOEHL, RICHARD LOUIS, artist, scholar; b. Omaha, Oct. 11, 1944; s. Louis Lawrence and Frances Margaret (Robinson) R.; 1 child, Joy Margaret Iroff-Reinoehl. BS in Sociology, Portland State U., 1970; MSW, U. Minn., Duluth, 1977; postgrad., Cornell U., 1984-88. Acting dir. Vanguard Group Homes, Virginia, Minn., 1976-77; dir. Minn. Chippewa Tribe Group Home, Duluth, 1978, Human Devel. Consortium, Minn., N.Y., Ohio, 1978—; coord. NE Ohio Green Libertarian Partys' Vote Recount Observation Teams, 2004. Faculty Social Work Program U. Wis., Superior, 1981-84, Bohecker Coll., 2005—; adv. bd. Computers in Social Svcs. etwork, 1982-85; mem. Com. on Internat. Social Welfare Edn., 1982-86, Am. Evaluation Assn., 1986-89; affiliate scholar Oberlin Coll., 1991—; artist-in-residence Ohio Arts Coun., 1996-97. Editor: Computer Literacy in Human Services Education, 1990, Computer Literacy in Human Services, 1990, Men of Achievement, 16th edit., 1993; mem. editl. bd. Computers in Human Svcs., 1983-96, 99, Jour. Technology in Human Svcs., 1999—; assoc. editor book rev., 1996-99; contbr. numerous articles to profl. jours. Mem. Legis. Task Force Regional Alcoholism Bd., 1972-73, Assn. Drug Abuse, Prevention and Treatment, 1973-74, Minn. Pub. Health Assn., 1976-78, Minn. Social Svc. Assn., 1976-83, Wis. Coun. Social Work Edn., 1983-84, N.Y. State Coun. Family Rels., 1986-89, at. Coun. Family Rels., 1986-89; exec. bd. Duluth Community Action Program, 1982-83; Dem. precinct chair, Portland, Oreg., 1972-74; precinct vice-chair Dem. Farmer-Labor Party, Duluth, 1979-81, chair, 1981-83, 2d vice-chair exec. bd., 1981-83; mem. Zoning Appeals Bd., New Russia Twp., Ohio, 1996—; mem. art edn. com. Fireland Assn. Visual Arts, 1996-99; mem. land use planning com. New Russia Twp., Ohio, 1998—; chair Lorain County Comprehensive Plan Growth Mgmt. Com., 1999—; mem. Smart Devel. Coalition of Lorain County, 1998—, Lorain County Multi-Modal Transp. Planning Steering Com., 2000—, airport subcom., 2000—, roadways sub-com., 2000—, transit subcom., 2000—, info. tech. sub-com., 2000—; field spl. projects field coord., nat. coord. rural issues Kucinich for Pres. campaign, 2003-; chmn. Smart Devel. Coalition Lorain County, 1996-98, Lorain County Growth Mgmt. Com., mem. Environ. Sub.-Com., 1997-98; mem. Lorain County Multi-Modal Transp. Plan Steering Com., sub-coms. transit, roadways, airports, rail, and info. tech., 1999-2001, New Russia Township Zoning Bd. Appeals, 1995-2000, New Russia Township Land Use Planning Com., 1996-98; coord. Ohio Voters Reform, 2005—. Mem. NASW (exec. com., chair program com. Arrowhead Region Minn. chpt., 1980-81, co-chair task force on computers in social work, 1981-82), Acad. Cert. Social Workers, Cornell U. Sailing Club (pres. 1990). Avocations: canoeing, antique volkswagens, wilderness hiking.

REINSDORF, JERRY MICHAEL, professional sports team owner, real estate company executive, accountant, lawyer; b. Bklyn., Feb. 25, 1936; s. Max and Marion (Smith) Reinsdorf; m. Martyl F. Rifkin, Dec. 29, 1956; children: David Jason, Susan Janeen, Michael Andrew, Jonathan Milton. BA, George Washington U., 1957; JD, orthwestern U., 1960. CPA Ill., registered mortgage underwriter; bar: DC, Ill. 60; cert. specialist real estate securities, rev. appraiser. Atty. staff regional counsel IRS, Chgo., 1960—64; assoc. law firm Chapman & Cutler, 1964—68; ptnr. Altman, Kurlander & Weiss, 1968—74; of counsel Katten, Muchin, Gitles, Zavis, Pearl & Galler, 1974—79; gen. ptnr. Carlyle Real Estate Ltd. Partnerships, 1971—72; chmn. bd. Balcor Co., 1973—87; mng. ptnr. TBC Films, 1975—83; chmn. Chgo. White Sox, 1981—, Chgo. Bulls, 1985—; ptnr. Bojer Fin., 1987—. Lectr. John Marshall Law Sch., 1966—68; bd. overseers Inst. Civil Justice, 1996—98; lectr. real estate, sports and taxation. Author (with L. Herbert Schneider): Uses of Life Insurance in Qualified Employee Benefit Plans, 1970. Mem. Chgo. region bd. Anti-Defamation League, 1986—2001; mem., trustee Ill. Inst. Tech., 1991—96; mem. Ill. Commn. on African-Am. Males, 1992—; bd. dirs. Chgo. Youth Success Found., 1992—, Corp. for Supportive Housing, 1995—; nat. trustee Northwestern U., 1993—2005, bd. govs., 1993—2005, Hugh O'Brian Youth Found.; mem. internat. adv. bd. Barrow Neurol. Found., 1996—97; active Chgo. Baseball Cancer Charities, 1994, 1998; bd. trustees Equity Office Properties, 1997—2004. Named Sportsman of Yr., Nat. Italian-Am. Sports Hall of Fame, 2006; named one of The Most Influential People in the World of Sports, Bus. Week, 2007; named to B'nai B'rith Nat. Jewish Am. Sports Hall of Fame, 1994, Chgo. Sports Hall of Fame, 1997; recipient Hallmark award, Chgo. Baseball Cancer Charities, 1986, Corp. Superstar award, Ill. chpt. Cystic Fibrosis Found., 1988, Chicagoan of Yr. award, Chgo. Park Dist., 1990, Kellogg Excellence award, 1991, Cmty. Hero award, Interfaith Organizing Project, 1991, Operation Push Bridgebuilder award, 1992, Alumni Merit award, Northwestern U., 1992, Ellis Island Medal of Honor award, Nat. Ethnic Coalition of Orgns., 1993, Sportsman of Yr. award, 1994, Lifetime Achievement award, March of Dimes, 1994, Hallmark Hall of Fame Civic award, Ind. Sports Charities, 1994, Am. Spirit award, USAF, 1995, Alpha Epsilon Pi Arthur and Simiteich Outstanding Alumnus award, 1995, Order of Lincoln, 1997, Mayor's medal Hon., 1997, Bklyn. Businessman of Yr., 1997, Guardian of Children award, Jewish Coun. for Youth Svc., 1998, Amb. award, Keshet, 2005, Nat. Humanitarian award, Nat. Conf. Cmty. and Justice, 2006, Merit award, Decalogue Soc., 2007, History Maker award, Chgo. Hist. Soc., 2007. Mem.: FBA, ABA, Nat. Sports Lawyers Assn., Chgo. Bar Assn., Ill. Bar Assn., Northwestern U. Law Sch. Alumni Assn. (bd. dirs.), Order of Coif, Comml. Club Chgo., Omega Tau Rho. Achievements include owner, MLB World Series Champions, 2005. Office: Chgo White Sox 333 W 35th St Chicago IL 60616-3651 Office Phone: 312-674-5200.

REIS, LESLIE ANN, lawyer, educator; b. Plainfield, NJ, Apr. 21, 1958; BS cum laude, Syracuse Univ., 1981; JD, John Marshall Law Sch., Chgo., 1996. Bar: Ill. 1996. Broadcast journalist, 1981—96; legal fellow Reporters Com. for Freedom of the Press, 1996—97; adj. prof. John Marshall Law Sch., 1997—, dir. Ctr. for Info. Tech. & Privacy Law, 1997—. Supr. Jour. of Computer and Info. Law; contbr. articles to prof. jours. Mem. Fed. Info. Security & Privacy Adv. Bd. Mem.: Am. Judicature Soc. (past dir., Ctr. for Judicial Independence). Office: Ctr Info Tech and Privacy Law John Marshall Law Sch 315 S Plymouth Ct Chicago IL 60604 Office Phone: 312-987-1425. Business E-Mail: 7reis@jmls.edu.

REISER, RICHARD SCOTT, lawyer; b. Chester, SD, Apr. 8, 1946; s. Kinney S. and Edna E. (Sweet) R.; m. Mary Lynn Durrie, Aug. 24, 1968; children: Todd S., Sally A. BS, U. Nebr., 1968, JD, 1972. Bar: Iowa 1972, Nebr. 1972, U.S. Dist. Ct. Nebr. 1972, U.S. Ct. Appeals (8th cir.) 1989. Assoc. Nelson & Harding, Omaha, 1972-75, ptnr., 1975-84; dir. Gross & Welch, P.C., Omaha, 1984-92; v.p., gen. counsel Werner Enterprises, Inc., Omaha, 1993—96, exec. v.p., gen. counsel, 1996—. Com. mem. Nebr. Transp. Efficiency Task Force, Lincoln, 1995. Bd. dirs., treas. Fontenelle Forest Assn., Omaha, 1988-94; pres. 2d lt. USAR, 1968-74. Mem. Am. Corp. Counsel Assn., Transp. Lawyers Assn., Omaha Bar Assn. (bd. dirs., exec. com.), Nebr. State Bar Assn. (mem. task force on civil justice sys. 1994-95), Iowa State Bar Assn, Nebr. State Hwy. (comm Dist.2, 2001-), Nebr. Trucking Assn. (bd. dir., sec., 2003-), Am. Trucking Assn. (bd. dir., 1999-). Democrat. Presbyterian. Avocations: hunting, skiing, motorcycling. Office: Werner Enterprises Inc PO Box 45308 Omaha NE 68145-0308

REISING, RICHARD P., lawyer; BA, Stanford U.; JD, U. Mo. Bar: Ill. 1970. Asst. gen. counsel, sec. Archer-Daniels-Midland Co., Decatur, Ill., v.p., sec., gen. counsel, 1991-97, sr. v.p., 1997—. Office: Archer-Daniels-Midland Co 4666 E Faries Pky Decatur IL 62526-5666

REITER, MICHAEL A., lawyer, educator; b. Pitts., Nov. 15, 1941; BS, U. Wis., 1963, MS, 1964, JD, 1967, PhD, 1969. Bar: Wis. 1967, Ill. 1975, U.S. Supreme Ct. 1975. Ptnr. Holleb & Coff, Chgo., 1987-99, Duane Morris LLP, Chgo., 1999—. Adj. prof. law Northwestern U., Chgo., 1977—99; mem. faculty Nat. Inst. Trial Advocacy, 1980—. Office: Duane Morris LLP 227 W Monroe St Ste 3400 Chicago IL 60606-5098 Office Phone: 312-499-6718.

REITER, ROBERT EDWARD, banker; b. Kansas City, Mo., Dec. 27, 1943; s. Robert Vincent and Helen Margaret (Petrus) R.; m. Mary J. Darby, June 20, 1964; children: Mollie K., Jennifer M., Ellen R., Robert E. Jr. BA, Rockhurst Coll., 1964; JD, St. Louis U., 1967; LLM, U. Mo., Kansas City, 1969. Bar: Mo. 1967. Assoc. atty. Burke, Jackson & Millin, Kansas City, 1967-69; personal trust adminstr. City Nat. Bank and Trust Co., Kansas City, 1969-71; estate planning officer United Mo. Bank of Kansas City, 1971-73, v.p., 1973-80, sr. v.p., 1980-85; exec. v.p. UMB Bank, N.A., 1985—. Pres., corp. bd. Seton Ctr., Kansas City, 1992-95. Contbr. articles to profl. jours. Bd. of Counselors St. Joseph Health Ctr., Kansas City, 1977-85; pres. St. Joseph Health Ctr. Adv. Coun., Kansas City, 1985-86; treas., bd. trustees Endowment Trust Fund for Cath. Edn., 1989—; bd. regents Rockhurst U., 1999—, mem. planned giving coun., 1999—. Grantee St. Louis U. Sch. of Law, 1964-67. Mem. Mo. Bar Assn., Kansas City Bar Assn. (chmn. employee benefits com. 1989-90), Employee Benefit Inst. (adv. bd. 1986—, chmn. 1989), Inst. Cert. Bankers (cert. retirement svcs. profl. 1995—), Estate Planning Soc. Kansas City (pres. 1985-86), Serra Club of Kansas City (v.p. 1987-89). Home: 1024 W 70th St Kansas City MO 64113-2004 Office: UMB Bank NA 1010 Grand Blvd PO Box 419692 Kansas City MO 64141-6692

REITER, STANLEY, economist, educator; b. NYC, Apr. 26, 1925; s. Frank and Fanny (Rosenberg) R.; m. Nina Sarah Breger, June 13, 1944; children: Carla Frances, Frank Joseph. AB, Queens Coll., 1947; MA, U. Chgo., 1950, PhD, 1955. Rsch. assoc. Cowles Commn., U. Chgo., 1948-50; mem. faculty Stanford U., 1950-54, Purdue U., 1954-67; prof. econs. and math. Northwestern U., 1967—, now Morrison prof. econs. and math. Weinberg Coll. Arts and Scis., Morrison prof. managerial econs. and decision scis. Kellogg Sch. Mgmt. Dir. Ctr. for Math. Studies in Econs. and Mgmt. Sci.; cons. in field. Trustee Roycemore Sch., Evanston, Ill., 1969-71, treas., 1970-71. Served with inf. AUS, 1943-45. Decorated Purple Heart. Fellow Econometric Soc., AAAS; mem. Soc. Indsl. and Applied Math., Inst. Mgmt. Scis., Ops. Rsch. Soc. Am., Am. Math. Soc., Math. Assn. Am., Am. Acad. of Arts and Scis. Home: Apt 4B 838 Michigan Ave Evanston IL 60202 Office: Northwestern U Ctr for Math Studies 2001 Sheridan Rd Evanston IL 60208-0814 Office Phone: 847-491-3527. Business E-Mail: s-reiter@northwestern.edu.

REITMAN, JERRY IRVING, advertising agency executive; b. Phila., Jan. 9, 1938; s. Benjamin and Ruth (Eisenberg) R.; m. Monica Birgitta Hall, Oct. 27, 1968; children: Jennifer Sharon, Sarah Beth. BS in Fin., Pa. State U., 1961. Exec. v.p., CEO Brit. Pubs., NYC and London, 1965-69; pres., pub. Acad. Media, Sherman Oaks, Calif., 1969-73; v.p. Pubs. Clearing House, Port Washington, NY, 1973-78; exec. v.p. Ogilvy & Mather, NYC, 1978-81; with Scali, McCabe, Sloves, Inc., NYC, 1981-86; pres. Scali, McCabe, Sloves Direct, NYC; chmn. bd. dirs. The Reitman Group, 1986; exec. v.p. The Leo Burnett Co., Chgo., 1986-96; pres., CEO, vice chair Internat. Data Response Corp., Chgo., 1996—. Dir. Scandinavian Airlines Sys. Pub./Distbn. Svcs.; mem. adv. bd. Ill. Dept. Trade and Tourism, 1988—; internat. awards chmn., bd. dirs. John Caples Internat., 1989—; mem. Internat. Direct Mktg. Symposium, Zürich, Switzerland; dir. Catylst Direct, Goliath Solutions, LLC. Author: A Common Sense Approach to Small Business, 1968, Beyond 2000: The Future of Direct Marketing, 1994; contbr. articles to profl. jours. Trustee Locust Valley Libr. Assn., NY, 1982—; exec. com. mem. Pub. Hall of Fame, 1987—; bd. govs. Children's Miracle Network, 1992-, vice chmn., chmn. bd. govs., 1998—, 1999-2001, chmn. 2002-04, dir.; bd. dirs. Children's Meml. Found. Telethon, The Direct Mktg. Ednl. Found., exec, dir., 1996—. Anderson scholar, 1960; recipient Key to City, New Orleans, 1959, Silver Apple award N.Y. Direct Mktg. Club, 1989, Ed Mayer award Ednl. Found., 1996, Charles S. Downs award, 1997, Direct Marketer of Yr. award. Fellow Psychiat. Re-Edn. Assn.; mem. Am. Mktg. Assn. (at-large mem., 2000, bd. dirs.), Direct Mktg. Assn. (bd. mem. ethics com. 1984), Creative Guild (dir. 1984), Internat. Direct Mktg. Assn. (bd. dirs. 1981-82), Publ. Hall of Fame (exec. com. 1988—), Direct Mktg. Club N.Y. (pres. 1983-84), Beta Gamma Sigma. Avocations: tennis, auto restoration, woodworking. Home and Office: Callahan Group LLC 2204 N Leavitt St Chicago IL 60647-3204 Home (Summer): Ringso 237 Nasbyviken 64061 Stallanholmen Sweden Office Phone: 773-342-1973. Personal E-mail: jireitman@aol.com.

REITMAN, ROBERT STANLEY, management consultant, not-for-profit advisor; b. Fairmont, W.Va., Nov. 18, 1933; s. Isadore and Freda A. (Layman) R.; m. Sylvia K. Golden, Dec. 24, 1955; children: Scott Alan, Alayne Louise. BS in Acctg., W.Va. U., 1955; JD, Case Western Res. U., 1958. Bar: Ohio 1958. Mem. firm Burke, Haber & Berick, Cleve., 1958-60, ptnr., 1960-68; exec. v.p., vice chmn. Tranzonic Cos. (formerly AAV Cos.), Pepper Pike, Ohio, 1968-70, pres., vice-chmn., 1970-73, chief exec. officer, pres., vice chmn., 1973-82, pres., chmn., CEO, 1982-98, chmn. emeritus, bd. dirs., 1998—; prin. Riverbend Advisors, 1998—. Bus. adv. com. Mandel Ctr. for non-profit Orgn. Case We. Res. U., 1995-99, vis. com. Weatherhead Sch. of Bus., 1995-03, vis. com. Sch. of Law, 1998-03, chmn. dean's nat. adv. com., Sch. of Law, 1997-98; pvt. banking adv. bd. Key Bank, N.A., 1997-2007; dean's adv. com. Sch. Medicine, 2004-06. Mem. Rep. fin. com., Cuyahoga County, 1968-78; mem. Com. for Econ. Growth for Israel, Cleve., 1977-80, pres., 1978-80; adv. coun. Cleve. Mus. Nat. History, 1982-85, Cleve. Opera, 1977—; del. Coun. of Jewish Fedns., NYC, 1981-97; gen. co-chmn. Jewish Welfare Fund, Cleve., 1975-78, 81-85, gen. vice chmn., 1985-89, gen. chmn., 1989-91; sect. and divsn. chmn., team capt. United Way Svcs., 1974-97, del. assembly, 1976-85, trustee, 1977-2000, v.p., 1985-88, chmn. nominating. com., 1988-90, campaign chmn., 1993, chair fund raising planning com., 1994-97, chair bd. trustees, 1997-2000, life trustee, 2000—; employment com. Jewish Vocat. Svc., Cleve., 1974-83; bd. dirs. Capital for Israel, Inc., NYC, 1986-87; nat. vice chmn. United Jewish Appeal, 1987-92, nat. allocations chmn., 1987-90, trustee, 1988-94, chair retirement fund com., 1994-97; trustee B'nai B'rith Hillel Found., 1975-81, Cleve. Jewish News, 1976-79, Ideastream, Cleve., 1976-99, vice chmn. 1986-90, chmn. bd., 1990-97, immediate past chair, 1997-99, chair emeritus, 1999—; trustee, pres. Bus. Volunteerism Coun., 1994-96, chmn. 1996-97; trustee Jewish Cmty. Fedn. Cleve., 1983-98, 1999-03, treas., 1991-94, v.p., 1995-97, life trustee, 2003—, Jewish Edn. Ctr. of Cleve., 1993-96, Cleve. Zool. Soc., 1972—, pres., 1979-87, chmn., 1987-92, chmn. emeritus, 1992—, chmn. JDC-Brookdale Inst. of Gerontology and Human Devel., Israel, 1995; trustee Am. Jewish Joint Distbn. Com., 1988—, United Israel Appeal, 1987-94, Mt. Sinai Med. Ctr., Cleve., 1976-96, chmn., 1982-85; trustee Cleve. State U. Devel. Found., 1988-91, Greater Cleve. Roundtable, 1991-04, The Wilds, 1995-99, adv. bd., 1999-02, trustee Mt. Sinai Health Care Found., 1995-04, life trustee, 2004—, vice chair 1998-2001, chair, 2001-04; trustee Univ. Hosps. Health Sys., 1999-04, 05-, Univ. Hosps. Cleve., 1999-2007; trustee, chair Heather Hill, Inc., 2001—; coun. mem. Village of Gates Mills, Ohio, 1997-00, clk., 2000-07. Mem. The 50 Club Cleve., Case We. Res. Univ. Sch. of Law Soc. Benchers, Am. Kennel Club (regional del. 1960-75), We. Res. Kennel Club (officer, trustee 1959-75), Beechmont Club (fin. com. 1972-80, house com. 1974), Pepper Pike Club, Union Club, Carambola Golf Club, Masons, Zeta Beta Tau, Tau Epsilon Rho. Avocations: golf, swimming. Office: Riverbend Advisors 2087 Chagrin River Rd Gates Mills OH 44040-9740 Home Phone: 440-423-1515. Business E-Mail: rsrform@core.com.

REITZ, CHRISTOPHER M., lawyer, gas industry executive; Corp. counsel Blackwell Sanders Peper Martin LLP, Sprint Corp., Cerner Corp.; joined Aquila, Inc., Kansas City, Mo., 2000, asst. gen. counsel, interim gen. counsel, corp. sec., 2005, sr. v.p., gen. counsel, corp. sec., 2005—. Office: Aquila, Inc 20 W Ninth St Kansas City MO 64105 Office Phone: 816-467-3611. E-mail: christopher.reitz@aquila.com.

REJAI, MOSTAFA, political science professor; b. Tehran, Iran, Mar. 11, 1931; came to U.S., 1954; s. Taghi and Forough (Lashgari) R. AA, Pasadena City Coll., 1957; BA, Calif. State U., LA, 1959, MS, 1961; PhD, UCLA, 1964. Teaching fellow UCLA, 1963-64; asst. prof. polit. sci. Miami U., Oxford, Ohio, 1964-67, assoc. prof., 1967-70, prof., 1970-83, Disting. prof., 1983—. Vis. scholar Ctr. for Internat. Affairs, Harvard U., 1972, Hoover Instn. on War, Revolution and Peace, Stanford U., 1973, Inst. Internat. Studies, Iran, 1974-75; vis. prof. Western Coll., Oxford, 1971, 72. Author: World Military Leaders: A Collective and Comparative Analysis, 1996, The Strategy of Political Revolution, 1973, The Comparative Study of Revolutionary Strategy, 1977, Comparative Political Ideologies, 1984; (with Kay Phillips) Leaders of Revolution, 1979, World Revolutionary Leaders, 1983, Loyalists and Revolutionaries: Political Leaders Compared, 1988, Political Ideologies: A Comparative Approach, 1991, 2d edit., 1995, Demythogizing an Elite: American Presidents in Empirical, Comparative, and Historical Perspectives, 1993, World Military Leaders: A Collective and Comparative Analysis, 1996, Leaders and Leadership: An Appraisal of Theory and Research, 1997, The Young George Washington in Psychobiographical Perspective, 2000, Concepts of Leadership in Western Political Thought, 2002; editor, contbr.: Democracy: The Contemporary Theories, 1967, Decline of Ideology?, 1971; editor: Mao Tse-Tung on Revolution and War, 1969, rev. edit., 1970; assoc. editor Jour. Polit. and Mil. Sociology, 1973—; contbr. articles to profl. jours., book chpts. Recipient Outstanding Teaching award Miami U., 1970. Mem. Am. Polit. Sci. Assn. (polit. psychology sect.), Am. Sociol. Assn. (polit. soc. sect.), Internat. Polit. Sci. Assn., Internat. Soc. Polit. Psychology, Internat. Studies Assn., Inter-Univ. Seminar on Armed Forces and Soc., Conf. for Study Polit. Thought, Midwest Polit. Sci. Assn., So. Polit. Sci. Assn., Wesetern Polit. Sci. Assn., Pi Gamma Mu, Pi Sigma Alpha. Office: Miami U Dept of Political Science Oxford OH 45056

REKLAITIS, GINTARAS VICTOR, chemical engineer, educator; b. Oct. 20, 1942; BS, Ill. Inst. Tech., 1965; MS, PhD, Stanford U., Calif., 1969. Edward W. Comings prof. chem. engring. Purdue U., West Lafayette, Ind., 1970—; co-dir. Pharm. Tech. & Edn. Ctr., 2006—; dep. dir. NSF Engring. Rsch. Ctr. Structured Organic Composites, 2006—. Contbr. articles to sci. jours. Mem.: NAE. Office: Purdue U Sch Chem Engring Forney Hall Chem Engring 480 Stadium Mall Dr West Lafayette IN 47907-2100 Office Phone: 765-494-9662. Office Fax: 765-494-0805. E-mail: reklaiti@purdue.edu.

REKSTIS, WALTER J., III, lawyer; b. San Diego, 1945; BBA, U. Cin., 1968, JD, 1972. Bar: Ohio 1972. Ptnr. Squire, Sanders & Dempsey, Cleve. Office: Squire Sanders & Dempsey 4900 Key Tower 127 Public Sq Cleveland OH 44114-1304

RELIAS, JOHN ALEXIS, lawyer; b. Chgo., Apr. 2, 1946; s. Alexis John and Marie Helen (Metos) R.; m. Linda Ann Pontious, Nov. 27, 1971; children: Anne, Alexandra. BA, orthwestern U., Evanston, 1968; LLB, Northwestern U., Chgo., 1972. Bar: Ill., 1972, U.S. Dist. Ct. (no. dist.) Ill. 1972, U.S. Ct. Appeals (9th cir.) 1981, U.S. Ct. Appeals (7th cir.) 1983, U.S. Supreme Ct. 1997. Assoc. Vedder, Price, Kaufman & Kammholz, Chgo., 1972-78, ptnr., 1979-94, Franczek, Sullivan, Mann, Crement, Hein & Relias, Chgo., 1994—. Mem. bd. edn. Wilmette (Ill.) Sch. Dist. 39, 1989-97, 2001—, pres., 1992-93, 1995-96. Mem. Nat. Assn. Sch. Attys., Ill. Assn. Sch. Attys., Order of the Coif, Phi Beta Kappa. Greek Orthodox. Home: 2500 Kenilworth Ave Wilmette IL 60091-1337 Office: Franczek Sulian Mann Crement Hein & Relias 300 S Wacker Dr Chicago IL 60606-6680 Office Phone: 312-786-6160. Business E-Mail: jar@franczek.com.

RELLE, ATTILA TIBOR, dentist, geriatrics services professional; b. Columbus, Ohio, Aug. 31, 1959; s. Ferenc Matyas and Trudi (Tubach) Relle; m. Kim Ann McDonald, Apr. 26, 1986; 1 child, Ilona. DDS, Case We. Res. U., 1985; BS, Ohio State U., 1985, postgrad., 1985—88, postgrad., 1993, Wright State U. Sch. Medicine, 1988-93; DMD, Case We. Reserve U., 2004—. Dentist Mobile Care Corp., Dublin, Ohio, 1985; assoc. dentist Richard P. Deeds, DDS and Assocs., Columbus, 1985-86; dentist Family Dental and Denture Ctr. II, Dayton, Ohio, 1986-87; gen. dentist Midwest Mobile Dental Care, Inc., Hamilton, Ohio, 1988-91, Mobile Dental Care, Inc., Hamilton, Ohio, 1991-92; gen. dentist, owner Attila T. Relle, DDS & Assocs., Columbus, 1985—, Hilliard, 1995—, Attila T. Relle, DMD & Assocs., Upper Arlington, Ohio, 2004—; dentist Jerry Owens, D.D.S. and Assocs., Lancaster, Ohio, 1989-92; state dir. Ohio Resident-care dental geriatric program Meridian Svc. Care Corp. of Ohio, 1992-94, gen. dentist, 1992-94; dentist Mercy Meml. Hosp., 2002—, Meml. Hosp. of Union County, 2003—06. Co-chmn. Ohio Dental Careers Day, Columbus, 1980—81; regional dir. Midwest Mobile Dental Care, Inc., 1988—89; mem. adv. com. N.Am. Health Corp., 1989—92; sci. judge Ohio Acad. Sci., Delaware, 1985—92. Mem. Columbus Maennerchor, 1986—88, Hungarian Cultural Assn., Hungarian Reformed Ch., 1999—; benefactor Columbus Zoo and Aquarium, 1998—2000, mem., 1996—, Franklin Count Farm Bur., 1999—, Brookwood Presbyn. Ch., 1974—. Mem.: ADA, AMA, Am. Acad. Implant Dentistry, Hoverclub of Am., Inc., U.S. Figure Skating Assn., Columbus Dental Soc., Ohio Dental Assn., Am. Student Dental Assn., U.S. Tennis Assn. (Midwest/Ohio Valley), Ohio State U. Alumni Assn. (life), Hungarian Assn. Magyar Tarsasag Hungarian Congress Arpad Acad., Alumni Case Western Res. Univ. Sch. Dentistry, Civitan Internat. (pres. Ea. Columbus club 1986—87). Presbyterian. Avocations: tennis, skiing, boating, hovercraft, ice skating. Home and Office: Attila T Relle DMD & Assocs 2818 Swansea Rd Upper Arlington OH 43221-1754 Office: Ste 100 4984A Scioto Darby Rd Hilliard OH 43026-1550 also: 5203 Carifa Ct Hilliard OH 43026-9589 Office Phone: 614-527-9797. Business E-Mail: relle.core@core.com.

RELLE, FERENC MATYAS, chemist; b. Gyor, Hungary, June 13, 1922; came to U.S., 1951, naturalized, 1956; s. Ferenc and Elizabeth (Netratics) R.; m. Gertrud B. Tubach, Oct. 9, 1946; children: Ferenc, Ava, Attila. BSChemE, MS, Jozsef Nador Poly. U., Budapest, Hungary, 1944. Lab. mgr. Karl Kohn Ltd. Co., Landshut, Germany, 1947-48; resettlement officer Internat. Refugee Orgn., Munich, 1948-51; chemist Farm Bur. Coop. Assn., Columbus, Ohio, 1951-56; indsl. engr. N.Am. Aviation, Inc., Columbus, 1956-57; rsch. chemist Keever Starch Co., Columbus, 1957-65, Ross Labs. divsn. Abbott Labs., Columbus, 1965-70, rsch. scientist, 1970-89; cons. in field. Congl. sci. counselor, 1971—81. Chmn. Columbus and Ctrl. Ohio UNWeek, 1963; pres. Berwick Manor Civic Assn., 1968; trustee Stelios Stelson Found., 1968-69; deacon Brookwood Presbyn. Ch., 1963-65, 92-93, trustee, 1990-91. Decorated knight St. Ladislaus Order. Mem. Am. Chem. Soc. (emeritus; alt. councilor 1973, chmn. long range planning com. Columbus sect. 1972-76, 78-80), Am. Assn. Cereal Chemists (life; chmn. Cin. sect. 1974-75), Ohio Acad. Sci., Arpad Acad. (gold medal mem.), Internat. Tech. Inst. (adv. dir. 1977-82), Nat. Intercollegiate Soccer Ofcls. Assn., Am. Hungarian Assn., Hungrian Cultural Assn. (pres. 1978-81), Ohio Soccer Ofcls. Assn., Columbus Mannerchor, Germania Singing and Sport Soc., Civitan (gov. Ohio dist. 1970-71, dist. treas. 1982-83, pres. Ea. Columbus 1963-64, 72-73, gen. sec. for Hungary 1991-92, Ea. European growth mgr. 1993-94, amb. at large 1994—, established 1st Civitan club in Hungary 1991, Ukraine, 1992, Slovakia 1994, Internat. Gov. of Yr. award 1971, Internat. Honor Key 1992, Internat. Found. fellow 2000, master club builder award 1992, various other awards), World Fedn. Hungarian Engrs. Home and Office: 2983 Melford Rd Upper Arlington OH 43221-2822

RELWANI, NIRMAL MURLIDHAR (NICK RELWANI), mechanical engineer; b. Bombay, Aug. 9, 1954; came to the U.S., 1976; m. Prema Vasandani; children: Karuna, Daksh. BS in Mech. Engring., U. Baroda, 1976; student, U. Nebr., 1977-78; MS in Mech. Engring., U. Wis., Milw., 1980. Registered profl engr., Wis., Ill. Rsch. asst. dept. mech. engring. U. Nebr., Lincoln, 1978; design engr. Allis Chalmers Corp., Milw., 1978-80; engring. cons. Bombay, 1980-86; assoc. engr. IIT Rsch. Inst., Chgo., 1986; mech. engr. Gen. Energy Corp., Oak Park, Ill., 1987-89, Arrowhead Environ. Control, Chgo., 1989-90; environ. engr. Ill. Dept. Pub. Health, Bellwood, 1990-92; sr. environ. protection engr. field ops. sect. bur. air Ill. EPA, Maywood, 1992—. Recipient Cert. of appreciation Ill. EPA, 1993, 94. Mem. ASME, ASHRAE (energy conservation award 1991), Assn. Energy Engrs. (sr.). Home: 1806 Marne Rd (River Bend) Bolingbrook IL 60490-4589 Office: Ill EPA 9511 W Harrison St Des Plaines IL 60016 Office Phone: 847-294-4030.

REMBOLT, JAMES EARL, lawyer; b. Nov. 13, 1943; s. Earl Lester and Dorothy Elouise (Mehring) Rembolt; m. Marilyn Sue Schmadeke, July 16, 1972; children: Tami Anne, Michelle Sue. BBA, U. Nebr., 1965; MA in Bus. Orgn. and Mgmt., 1967, JD with distinction, 1972. Bar: Nebr. 1972, U.S. Dist. Ct. Nebr. 1972, U.S. Tax Ct. 1978, U.S. Ct. Claims 1978. Pres. Nebr. Moot Ct. Bd., 1972; pilot Nebr. Air Nat. Guard, Lincoln, 1969-74; lecr. legal writing U. Nebr. Coll. Law, 1973-74; ptnr. Rembolt, Ludtke LLP, Lincoln, 1976—. Chmn. bd. trustees YWCA, Lincoln, 1982—83; mem., past pres. Lincoln/Lancaster Sr. Ctrs. Found., Inc., bd. dirs., 1988—90; mem., past chair bd. dirs. Madonna Found., Inc., 1989—91; trustee, past bd. dirs. U.Nebr. Found.; past bd. dirs., pres. Nebr. Continuing Legal Edn., Inc.; bd. elders Eastridge Presbyn. Ch., Lincoln, 1979—82. Fellow: ABA, Nebr. State Bar Found., Am. Coll. Trust and Estate Counsel; mem.: Lincoln Estate Planning Coun. (past pres.), Lincoln Probate Discussion Group (charter mem.), Nebr. State Bar Assn. (pres. 2002—03), Lincoln Bar Assn., U. ebr. Lincoln Coll. Bus. Adminstrn. Alumni Assn. (past pres.). Office: Rembolt Ludtke LLP 1201 Lincoln Mall Ste 102 Lincoln NE 68508-2839 Office Phone: 402-475-5100. Business E-Mail: jrembolt@remboltludtke.com.

RENDER, LORNE, museum director; Formerly dir. C.M. Russell Mus., Gt. Falls, Mont.; dir. Marianna Kistler Beach Mus. of Art, Manhattan, Kans., 1999—. Address: Marianna Kistler Beach Art Mus Kansas State U 701 Beach Ln Manhattan KS 66506 E-mail: lrender@ksu.edu.

RENNER, ROBERT GEORGE, federal judge; b. Nevis, Minn., Apr. 2, 1923; s. Henry J. and Beatrice M. (Fuller) R.; m. Catherine L. Clark, Nov. 12, 1949; children: Robert, Anne, Richard, David. BA, St. John's U., Collegeville, Minn., 1947; JD, Georgetown U., 1949. Bar: Minn. 1949. Pvt. practice, Walker, 1949-69; U.S. atty. Dist. of Minn., 1969-77, U.S. magistrate, 1977-80, U.S. dist. judge, 1980-92, assumed sr. status, 1992—. Mem. Minn. Ho. of Reps., 1957-69. Served with AUS, 1943-46. Mem. FBA. Roman Catholic.

RENNERFELDT, EARL RONALD, state legislator, farmer, rancher; b. Epping, ND, July 10, 1938; s. Carl John and Margaret E. (Long) R.; m. Lois Ann Thune, Sept. 12, 1959; children: Charysse Renee, Carter Ryan. Student, NDSSS, Wahpeton, ND, 1958. Farmer/rancher, Williston, N.D.; mem. N.D. Ho. of Reps., Bismarck, 1991—, chmn. nat. resources com., 2001. Bd. dirs. Am. State Bank., Ho. Appropriations Com., 2003—. Mem. Lake Sacajawea Planning Bd., Williston, 1992, First Luth. Ch.; mem. Am. Legis. Exch. Coun., 1991-92; mem. adv. bd. N.D. State U. Exptl. Sta.; bd. dirs. Mercy Med. Found., 1990-96. With U.S. Army, 1962-64. Recipient Harvest Bowl award N.D. State U., 1988; named Outstanding Young Farmer C. of C., 1972. Mem.: ND Durum Growers, Williston C. of C. (agrl. com., energy com., transp. com.), Elks, Moose, Am. Legion. Republican. Avocations: antiques, golf. Home and Office: 1704 Rose Ln Williston ND 58801-4362

RENO, ROGER, lawyer; b. Rockford, Ill., May 16, 1924; s. Guy B. and Hazel (Kinnear) R.; m. Janice Marie Odelius, May 17, 1952 (dec. Aug. 2005); children: Susan Marie, Sheri Jan Reno-Rudolph, Michael Guy. Student, Kenyon Coll., 1943-44, Yale U., 1944, U. Wis., 1946; AB, Carleton Coll., 1947; LL.B., Yale U., 1950. Bar: Ill. 1950. Practiced in Rockford, 1950; assoc. firm Reno, Zahm, Folgate, Lindberg & Powell, 1950-56, partner, 1956-84; of counsel Reno & Zahm LLC, 1984—. Chmn. Amcore Fin. Inc., 1982-95; atty. Rockford Bd. Edn., 1955-64. Past pres., bd. dirs. Childrens Home Rockford; trustee Swedish-Am. Hosp. Assn., 1967-77, Keith Country Day Sch. Served to 1st lt. USAAF, 1943-46. Mem. ABA, Ill. Bar Assn., Winnebago County Bar Assn. (pres. 1979-80) Clubs: Forest Hills Country (Rockford). Methodist. Home: 2515 Chickadee Trl Rockford IL 61107 Office: 2902 McFarland Rd #400 Rockford IL 61107 Home Phone: 815-877-0810. Office Fax: 815-961-4092.

RENWICK, GLENN M., insurance company executive; b. May 22, 1955; B in Math. & Econs., U. Canterbury, Christchurch, New Zealand; MS in Engring., U. Fla., Gainesville, 1978. With Progressive Corp., 1986—, chief info. officer, 1998—2000, CEO ins. ops., 2000, pres., CEO, 2001—; CEO, ins. ops. and bus. tech. process leader Progressive Casualty Ins. Co., 1998—2000, pres., chmn., CEO, 2000—04. Bd. dirs. Fiserv Inc. Office: Progressive Corp 6300 Wilson Mills Rd Cleveland OH 44143-2109 Office Phone: 440-461-5000.

RENWICK, SCOTT, lawyer; BA, Purdue U., 1974; JD, Northwestern U., 1977. Corp. sec., counsel Unitrin, Inc., 1991—95, gen. counsel, corp. sec., 1995—2002, sr. v.p., sec., gen. counsel, 2002—. Office: Unitrin Services Co One E Wacker Dr Chicago IL 60601

RENZ, CHRISTOPHER P., lawyer; BA, St. Olaf Coll., 1998; JD, U. Minn. Law Sch., 2001. Bar: Minn. 2001, US Dist. Ct. (dist. Minn.) 2002. Pros. atty. City of Edina and the Met. Airports Commn.; atty. Thomsen & Nybeck, P.A., Edina, Minn. Legal writing instr. U. Minn. Law Sch., 2003—. Contbr. articles to profl. publs. amed a Rising Star, Minn. Super Lawyers mag., 2006. Mem.: Assn. Trial Lawyers of Am., Hennepin County Bar Assn., Minn. State Bar Assn., ABA. Office: Thomsen & Nybeck PA 3300 Edinborough Way Ste 600 Edina MN 55435 Office Phone: 952-835-7000. E-mail: crenz@tn-law.com.

RENZ, GREG W., lawyer; b. Huntington, Ind., Sept. 4, 1950; BA summa cum laude, Marquette U., 1972; JD cum laude, U. Chgo., 1975. Bar: Wis. 1975. Ptnr. Foley & Lardner LLP, Milw., chmn. employee benefits practice group. Mem.: State Bar Wis., Order Coif. Office: Foley & Lardner LLP 777 E Wisconsin Ave Milwaukee WI 53202-5306 Office Phone: 414-297-5806. Office Fax: 414-297-4900. Business E-Mail: grenz@foley.com.

RENZAGLIA, KAREN A., biologist, educator; PhD, Southern Ill. U. Vis. prof. dept. plant biology So. Ill. U., Carbondale. Recipient Edgar T. Wherry award Bot. Soc. Am., 1993, Michael Cichan award Bot. Soc. Am., 1999. Office: So Ill U Dept Plant Biology Mail Code 6509 Carbondale IL 62901-6509

REPPERT, RICHARD LEVI, lawyer; b. Phila., Nov. 6, 1948; s. William Downing and Angela R. (Schmid) R.; m. Faith Simpson, Dec. 30, 1972 (div. Aug. 1992); 1 child, Richard Jacob; m. Jeanette T. deHaven, Apr. 10, 1994. BA, Lehigh U., 1970; JD, Villanova U., 1974. Bar: Ohio 1974, U.S. Dist. Ct. (no. dist.) Ohio 1974, Pa. 1993. Assoc. Thompson, Hine and Flory, Cleve., 1974-82, ptnr., 1982-89, Jones Day, Cleve., 1989—. Mem. ABA, Am. Coll. Real Estate Lawyers, Ohio State Bar Assn., Cleve. Bar Assn. Office: Jones Day North Point 901 Lakeside Ave Cleveland OH 44114-1190 E-mail: rreppert@jonesday.com.

REQUARTH, WILLIAM HENRY, surgeon; b. Charlotte, NC, Jan. 23, 1913; s. Charles William and Amelia (George) R.; m. Nancy Charlton, 1948 (div. 1966); children— Kurt, Betsy, Jeff, Jan, Tim, Suzanna; m. Connie Harper, 1977. AB, Millikin U., 1934, LLD, 1996; MD, U. Ill., 1938, MS, 1939. Diplomate: Am. Bd. Surgery. Intern St. Luke's Hosp., Chgo., 1938-39; resident Cook County Hosp., Chgo., 1940-42, 46-48; pvt. practice medicine, specializing in surgery Decatur, Ill., 1950—. Clin. prof. surgery U. Ill. Med. Sch., from 1962, now emeritus; Mem. Chgo. Bd. Trade. Author: Diagnosis of Abdominal Pain, 1953, The Acute Abdomen, 1958; also contbg. author chpts. books. Chmn. trustees Millikin U.; chmn. James Millikin Found.; bd. dirs. Decatur Meml. Hosp. Served to comdr. USNR, 1941-46. Mem. ACS, Cen. Surg. Assn., Western Surg. Assn., Chgo. Surg. Soc., Ill. Surg. Soc. (founder, pres. 1970-71), Am. Soc. Surgery Hand (founder), Am. Soc. Surgery Trauma, Soc. Surgery Alimentary Tract, Warren Cole Soc. (founder), Societe Internationale Chirurgie, Nat. Pilots Assn. (pres. 1960-61), Soaring Soc. Am., Sportsman Pilot Assn. (pres. 1966-67), Aerobatic Club Am., Internat. Aerobatic Club. Home: 1860 S Spitler Dr Decatur IL 62521-4417 Office: 158 W Prairie Ave Decatur IL 62523-1230 E-mail: bilreq@fginet.com.

RESCHKE, MICHAEL W., real estate company officer; b. Chgo., Nov. 29, 1955; s. Don J. and Vera R. (Helmer) R.; children: Michael W. Jr., Tiffanie G., Taylor N. BS summa cum laude with univ. honors, No. Ill. U., 1977; JD summa cum laude, U. Ill., 1980. Bar: Ill. 1980; CPA, Ill. Assoc. Winston & Strawn, Chgo., 1980-82; pres., CEO The Prime Group, Inc., Chgo., 1981, chmn. bd. dirs., CEO, 1981—. Mem. Chgo. Devel. Coun., 1987—. Mem. ABA, Ill. Bar Assn., Urban Land Inst., Chgo. Econ. Club, Real Estate Roundtable (dir.), Order of Coif, Phi Delta Phi, Beta Alpha Psi. Business E-Mail: mreschke@primegroupinc.com.

RESEK, ROBERT WILLIAM, economist; b. Berwyn, Ill., July 2, 1935; s. Ephraim Frederick and Ruth Elizabeth (Rummele) R.; m. Lois Doll, July 9, 1960; 1 child, Richard Alden. BA, U. Ill., 1957; AM, Harvard U., 1960, PhD, 1961. Asst. prof. econs. U. Ill., Urbana, 1961-65, assoc. prof., 1965-70, prof., 1970—2005, prof. emeritus, 2005—; vis. scholar MIT, Cambridge, 1967-68; dir. Bur. Econ. and Bus. Rsch., 1977-89, acting v.p. for acad. affairs, 1987-89, v.p. for acad. affairs, 1989—94, v.p. emeritus, 1995—; prof. Inst. Govt. and Pub. Affairs, 1994—2005, prof. emeritus, 2005—. Tchg. fellow Harvard U., 1959-61; vis. prof. U. Colo., 1967, 74-76, 82, Kyoto (Japan) U., 1976; cons. GM, 1964-66, U.S. Congress Joint Econ. Com., 1978-80, ABA, 1980-82; vis. scholar UCLA, 1994-95; co-dir. Midwest Economy: Issues and Policy, Midwest Govs. Conf., 1981; bd. dirs. Midwest U. Consortium Internat. Activities, 1989-94, v.p., 1991-94; mem. Ill. Gov.'s Econ. Policy Coun., 1999-2003. Co-author: Environmental Contamination by Lead and Other Heavy Metals--Synthesis and Modeling, 1978, Special Topics in Mathematics for Economists, 1976, A Comparative Cost Study of Staff Panel and Participating Attorney Panel Prepaid Legal Service Plans, 1981, Illinois Higher Education: Building the Economy, Shaping Society, 2000; editor: Illinois Economic Outlook, 1982-87, Illinois Economic Statistics, 1981, Economic Edge, 1996-2004; co-editor: The Midwest Economy: Issues and Policy, 1982, Frontiers of Business and Economic Research Management, 1983, Illinois Statistical Abstract, 1987, 2002-04. Mem. exec. com. Assn. Univ. Bus. and Econ. Rsch., 1977-89, v.p., 1978-82, pres., 1982-83. Woodrow Wilson fellow, 1957; Social Sci. Rsch. Coun. grantee, 1964; NSF fellow, 1967-69, grantee, 1974-77; U.S. Dept. State scholar, Japan, 1976; grantee Ill. Bd. Higher Edn., 1998-99. Mem. Econometric Soc., Beta Gamma Sigma, Phi Kappa Phi. Home: 201 E Holmes St Urbana IL 61801-6612 Office: Univ Ill 211 IGPA 1007 W Nevada St Urbana IL 61801-3812 Business E-Mail: resek@uiuc.edu.

RESER, ELIZABETH MAY (BETTY RESER), bookkeeper; b. Le Roy, Kans., Sept. 4, 1939; d. William David II and Vera Hazel (Dreyer) Meats; m. William Joseph Reser, Sept. 26, 1958; children: Dee Anna Reser, Donna Sue Reser. Diploma in computer programming, Control Data Inst., St. Louis, 1980; student, Washburn U., 1991. Cert. computer programmer, Mo. Computer programmer Regional Justice Info. Sys., St. Louis, 1980; sec. Shawnee Heights H.S., Tecumseh, Kans., 1973-78, bookkeeper, 1984-90. Treas. Secs. Assn. Shawnee Heights Unified Sch. Dist. 450, 1975-76, 86-87; vol. March of Dimes, Topeka, 1995-2001; mem. bd. trustees Susanna Wesley United Meth. Ch., Topeka, 1992-94, mem. prayer chain, 1993-94. Republican. Avocations: computers, shopping, crocheting, quilting. Home: 2849 SW Dukeries Rd Topeka KS 66614-4726

RESHOTKO, ELI, aerospace engineer, educator; b. NYC, Nov. 18, 1930; s. Max and Sarah (Kalisky) R.; m. Adina Venit, June 7, 1953; children: Deborah, Naomi, Miriam Ruth. BS, Cooper Union, 1950; MS, Cornell U., 1951; PhD, Calif. Inst. Tech., 1960. Aero. research engr. NASA-Lewis Flight Propulsion Lab., Cleve., 1951-56, head fluid mechanics sect., 1956-57; head high temperature plasma sect. NASA-Lewis Research Center, 1960-61, chief plasma physics br., 1961-64; asso. prof. engring. Case Inst. Tech., Cleve., 1964-66, dean, 1986-87; prof. engring. Case Western Res. U., Cleve., 1966-88, chmn. dept. fluid thermal and aerospace scis., 1970-76, chmn. dept. mech. and aerospace engring., 1976-79, Kent H. Smith prof. engring., 1989-98, Kent H. Smith prof. emeritus, 1999—. Susman vis. prof. dept. aero. engring. Technion-Israel Inst. Tech., Haifa, Israel, 1969-70; cons. Inst. Def. Analyses, Dynamics Tech. Inc., Wyle Labs., Rockwell Sci. Ctr.; adv. com. fluid dynamics NASA, 1961-64; aero. adv. com. NASA, 1980-87, chmn. adv. subcom. on aerodynamics, 1983-85; chmn. U.S. Boundary Layer Transition Study Group, NASA/USAF, 1970—2001, steering com., 2001-; U.S. mem. fluid dynamics panel AGARD-NATO, 1981-88; chmn. steering com. Symposium on Engring. Aspects of Magneto-hydro-dynamics, 1966, Case-NASA Inst. for Computational Mechanics in Propulsion, 1985-92, USRA/NASA ICASE Sci. Coun., 1992; Joseph Wunsch lectr. Technion-Israel Inst. Tech., 1990 Contbr. articles to tech. jours. Chmn. bd. govs. Cleve. Coll. Jewish Studies, 1981-84 (life trustee); bd. govs. Technion-Israel Inst. Tech., Haifa, Israel, 1999-2005; mem. NRC Air Force Studies bd., 2000-06. Guggenheim fellow Calif. Inst. Tech., 1957-59. Fellow ASME, AAAS, AIAA (Fluid and Plasma Dynamics award 1980, Dryden lectr. in rsch. 1994), Am. Phys. Soc. (vice-chmn. divsn. fluid dynamics 1998, chair-elect 1999, chair 2000, Otto Laporte award in fluid dynamics 1999), Am. Acad. Mechanics (pres. 1986-87); mem. NAE, Ohio Sci. and Engring. Roundtable, Sigma Xi, Tau Beta Pi, Pi Tau Sigma. Home: 1200 Humboldt St Apt 601 Denver CO 80218-2454

RESKE, SCOTT E., state representative; BS in Civil Engring., Purdue U., 1983; MPA, City U. Seattle, 1990; grad., USMC Command and Staff Coll., 2001. V.p. Beam, Longest and Neff, LLC; state rep. dist. 37 Ind. Ho. of Reps., Indpls., 2001—, chmn., rds. and transp. com., mem. commerce and econ. devel., ins. corps. and small bus., and pub. health coms. Firefighter, both vol. and paid. Active duty, marine aviator USMC, 10 yrs., lt. col., USMC Reserves. Democrat. Office: Ind Ho of Reps 200 W Washington St Indianapolis IN 46204-2786

RESNICK, ALICE ROBIE, retired state supreme court justice; b. Erie, Pa., Aug. 21, 1939; d. Adam Joseph and Alice Suzanne (Spizarny) Robie; m. Melvin L. Resnick, Mar. 20, 1970 PhB, Siena Heights Coll., 1961; JD, U. Detroit, 1964; LLD (hon.), Heidelberg Coll., 1999, U. Akron, 1994. Bar: Ohio 1964, Mich. 1965, U.S. Supreme Ct. 1970. Atty. priv. practice, 1964—75; asst. county prosecutor Lucas County Prosecutor's Office, Toledo, 1964-75, trial atty., 1965-75; judge Toledo Mcpl. Ct., 1976-83, 6th Dist. Ct. Appeals, State of Ohio, Toledo, 1983-88; instr. U. Toledo, 1968-69; justice Ohio Supreme Ct., 1988—2006. Co-chairperson Ohio State Gender Fairness Task Force. Trustee Siena Heights Coll., Adrian, Mich., 1982—; organizer Crime Stopper Inc., Toledo, 1981—; mem. Mayor's Drug Coun.; bd. dirs. Guest House Inc. Named to Ohio Women's Hall of Fame, 1995; recipient Gertrude W. Donahey award, Ohio Democratic Party, 1999, Woman of Toledo award, St. Vincent Mercy Medical Ctr., 1999. Mem. ABA, Toledo Bar Assn., Lucas County Bar Assn., Ohio State Bar Assn. (Nettie Cronise Lutes award 1995), Nat. Assn. Women Judges (Making A Difference award 1996), Am. Judicature Soc., Toledo Women's Bar Assn., Ohio State Women's Bar Assn. (Alice Robie Resnick Outstanding Lawyer award 1998), Toledo Mus. Art, Internat. Inst. Toledo. Roman Catholic. Personal E-mail: icenick@aol.com.

RESNICK, DONALD IRA, lawyer; b. Chgo., July 19, 1950; s. Roland S. and Marilyn B. (Weiss) R.; m. Jill Allison White, July 3, 1977; children: Daniel, Allison. BS with high honors, U. Ill., 1972; JD, Harvard U., 1975. Bar: Ill. 1975, U.S. Dist. Ct. (no. dist.) Ill. 1975. Assoc. Arvey, Hodes, Costello & Burman, Chgo., 1975-80, ptnr., 1981-83; sr. ptnr. Nagelberg & Resnick, Chgo., 1983-89, Levenstein & Resnick, Chgo., 1989-91; chmn. real estate dept. Jenner & Block, Chgo., 1992—. Mem. mgmt. com. Jenner & Block, Chgo. Mem. ABA, Birchwood (Highland Park, Ill.) Club. Office: Jenner & Block 1 E Ibm Plz Fl 4000 Chicago IL 60611-7603 E-mail: dresnick@jenner.com.

REST, ANN H., state legislator; b. Apr. 24, 1942; 1 child. BA, Northwestern U.; MA, U. Chgo.; MAT, MPA, Harvard U.; MBT, U. Minn. Mem. Minn. Ho. of Reps. dist. 46A, St. Paul, 1985-2000, Minn. Senate from 46th dist., St. Paul, 2001—. Chmn. taxes com., rules and legis. adminstrv. com., mem. ways and means com.; CPA. Recipient Women of Achievment award North Hennepin Bus. and Profl. Women, 1988; named Legislator of Yr., Politics in Minn., 1990. Mem. Resources for Adoptive Parents, Libr. Found. of Hennepin County, YMCA. Democrat.

RESTIVO, CHARLES L., academic administrator; BS, Rutgers U.; MS, Steven Inst. Tech.; MBA, Rutgers U. Pres. DeVry Inst. Tech., Dallas; exec. v.p. & dir. Wade Coll.; pres. Ill. Inst. Art-Chgo., 2002—. Office: Office of Pres Illinois Institute Art 350 North Orleans St Ste 136 Chicago IL 60654-1593

REUM, JAMES MICHAEL, lawyer; b. Oak Park, Ill., Nov. 1, 1946; s. Walter John and Lucy (Bellegay) R. BA cum laude, Harvard U., Cambridge, Mass., 1968, JD cum laude, 1972. Bar: NY 1973, DC 1974, US Dist. Ct. (so. dist.) NY 1974, Ill. 1979, US Dist. Ct. (no. dist.) Ill. 1982. Assoc. Davis Polk & Wardwell, NYC, 1973-78; assoc. Minority Counsel Com. on Judiciary US Ho. of Reps., Washington, 1974; ptnr. Hopkins & Sutter, Chgo., 1979-93, Winston & Strawn, Chgo., 1994—. Dir. Great Books Found., 2007—; Midwest advance rep. Nat. Reagan Bush Com., 1980; nominee commr. Securities and Exchange Comm., Pres. Bush, 1992; mem. fin. com. G.W. Bush, 2000; mem. US Coun. for Internat. Bus., 2007—. Served to SP4 USAR, 1969—75. Recipient Harvard U. Honorary Nat. Scholarship, 1964-72. Mem.: Monte Carlo Country Club (Monaco), Univ. Club (NYC), Racquet Club Chgo. Republican. Home: 12 E Scott St Chicago IL 60610-2320 Office: Winston & Strawn 35 W Wacker Dr Ste 4200 Chicago IL 60601-1695 Office Phone: 312-558-5644. Business E-Mail: jreum@winston.com.

REUM, W. ROBERT, manufacturing executive; b. Oak Park, Ill., July 22, 1942; m. Sharon Milliken. BA, Yale U., 1964; JD, U. Mich., 1967; MBA, Harvard U., 1969. Dir. investment analysis City Investing Co., NYC, 1969-72; v.p. corp fin. Mich. Nat. Corp., Bloomfield Hills, Mich., 1972-78; v.p., treas. White Motor Corp., Cleve., 1978-79; v.p. fin., CFO, Lamson & Sessions, Cleve., 1980-82, The Interlake Corp., Oak Brook, Ill., 1982-88, exec. v.p., 1988-90, chmn., pres., CEO, 1991-99, Amsted Industries Inc., Chgo., 2001—, also bd. dirs. Bd. dirs. Lindberg Corp. Contbr. articles to Harvard Bus. Rev. Bd. dirs. Morton Arboretum, Lisle, Ill.; trustee Elgin (Ill.) Acad. Mem. Chgo. Golf Club, Chgo. Club, Rolling Rock Club (Ligonier, Pa.). Office: AMSTED Industries Inc 205 Michigan Ave 44th Fl Chicago IL 60601

REUTER, JAMES WILLIAM, lawyer; b. Bemidji, Minn., Sept. 30, 1948; s. John Renee and Monica (Dugas) R.; m. Patricia Carol Creelman, Mar. 30, 1968; children: Kristine, Suzanne, Natalee. BA, St. John's U., 1970; JD, William Mitchell Coll. Law, 1974. Bar: Minn. 1974, U.S. Dist. Minn. 1975, U.S. Ct. Appeals (8th cir.) 1985; cert. civil trial specialist. Editor West Pub. Co., St. Paul, 1970-73; assoc. Terpstra & Merrill, Mpls., 1974-77; ptnr. Barna, Guzy, Merrill, Hynes & Giancola, Ltd., Mpls., 1977-89, Lindquist & Vennum, Mpls., 1989—. Recipient Cert. award Nat. Inst. Trial Advocacy, 1978. Mem. ABA (torts and ins. practice, and civil litigation sects.), ATLA, Minn. Bar Assn. (civil litigation and computer sects.), Hennepin County Bar Assn. (ins. com.), Anoka County Bar Assn. (pres. 1981-82). Avocations: skiing, golf, reading. Office: Lindquist & Vennum 4200 IDS Ctr 80 S 8th St Ste 4200 Minneapolis MN 55402-2274 Office Phone: 612-371-3519.

REUTER, MARK F., lawyer; b. South Bend, Ind., Sept. 13, 1971; BA, U. Notre Dame, 1992; JD, U. Notre Dame Law Sch., 1996. Bar: Ohio 1996. Ptnr. Keating Muething & Klekamp PLL, Cin. Mem., Bd. Trustees Summit County Day Sch.; mem., Deal Maker Awards Nomination Com. Greater Cin. Assn. for Corp. Growth. Named one of Ohio's Rising Stars, Super Lawyers, 2005, 2006, 2007. Fellow: Cin. Acad. Leadership for Lawyers; mem.: Ohio State Bar Assn. (mem., Corp. Law Com.), Cin. Bar Assn. Office: Keating Muething & Klekamp PLL One E Fourth St Ste 1400 Cincinnati OH 45202 Office Phone: 513-579-6400. Office Fax: 513-579-6457. Business E-Mail: mreuter@kumklaw.com.

REVELLE, DONALD GENE, manufacturing and health care company executive, consultant; b. Cape Girardeau, Mo., July 16, 1930; s. Lewis W. and Dorothy R.; m. Jo M. Revelle, Aug. 1, 1954; children— Douglas, David, Daniel, Dianne BA, U. Mo., 1952; JD, U. Colo., 1957; grad., Harvard U. Bus. Sch., 1971. Dir. employee relations Westinghouse Corp., Pitts., 1957-65; asst. to v.p. Diebold Corp., 1966; v.p. human resources TRW Corp., Cleve., 1967-84; sr. v.p. human resources Black and Decker Co., Towson, Md., 1984-86; exec. v.p. corp. rels. Montefiore Acad. Med. Ctr., Bronx, 1987-98; pres., CEO Syzygy, Inc., 1998—. Univ. lectr.; cons. Duerba Ship, Blue Cross N.Y., Windsor Hosp., Salvation Army Contbr. articles to profl. jours. Mem. sch. bd. State of N.Y. Lt. USNR, 1952-54 Mem.: ABA (labor law com.), Human Resource Planning Soc., Fed. Bar Assn., Colo. Bar Assn., MBA Assn., Rotary. Methodist. Home and Office: Syzygy Inc 29903 Baywood Ln Wesley Chapel FL 33543-9744 Home Phone: 813-994-3403; Office Phone: 813-994-3403.

REVISH, JERRY, newscaster, reporter; m. Danielle Revish; children: Nicole, Jerome. Student, Youngstown State U., Chapman Coll. Reporter Sta. WBBW, Youngstown, Ohio, 1972, Sta. WBNS-TV, Columbus, anchor, reporter, 1980—. Nominee Emmy awards (16); recipient Emmy awards (5), Best Feature award, Associated Press and United Press Internat., Best Documentary award, Best Spot News, Achievement in Journalism award, Ohio Chpt. Profl. Journalists, Blue Chip award in Comm., Carl Day award Outstanding Achievement, Best Internat. Reporting award, Nat. Assn. Black Journalists. Office: WBNS-TV 770 Twin Rivers Dr Columbus OH 43215

REVNEW, THOMAS RICHARD, lawyer; b. 1968; BBA with distinction, U. Mich., Ann Arbor, 1991; JD, Marquette U. Law Sch., 1994. Bar: Wis. 1994, Minn. 1999. Shareholder Seaton, Beck & Peters, P.A., Mpls. Contbr. articles to profl. publs.; assoc. editor: Marquette Law Rev. Named a Rising Star, Minn. Super Lawyers mag., 2006. Mem.: ABA, Minn. State Bar Assn., Milw. Bar Assn. Office: Seaton Beck & Peters PA 7300 Metro Blvd Ste 500 Minneapolis MN 55439 Office Phone: 952-921-4622. E-mail: trevnew@seatonlaw.com.

REVZEN, JOEL, conductor; BS, MS, Juilliard Sch. Music; studied with Jorge Master, Jean Martinon,Margaret Hills, Abraham Kaplan. Mem. Fargo-Moorhead Symphony, Fargo, N.D., Berkshire Opera Co.; former dean St. Louis Conservatory Music. Recipient Grammy award for recording with Soprano Arleen Anger, 1993; named guest conductor of Kirov Opera, St. Petersburg, Russia, 1994, 95. Office: Fargo Moorhead Symphony 810 4th Ave S Moorhead MN 56560-2844

REX, DOUGLAS KEVIN, gastroenterologist, educator; b. Ft. Wayne, Ind., Aug. 21, 1954; Grad. with highest distinction (summa cum laude), Harvard Coll., 1976; MD, Ind. U. Sch. Medicine, 1980. Cert. Internal Medicine, 1985, Pediatric Gastroenterology, 1987. Intern, internal medicine Ind. U. Med. Ctr., Indpls., 1980—81, resident, internal medicine, 1981—82, fellow, 1982—84; chief med. resident, gastroenterology Ind. U. Hosp., Indpls., 1984—85, clin. gastroenterologist, dir., endoscopy; joined Ind. U. Sch. Medicine, Indpls., 1985, hosp. appt., medicine, prof., dept. medicine, divsn. gastroenterology and hepatology, chancellor's prof. Chmn. US Multisociety. Task Force on Colorectal Cancer, 1999—2006. Contbr. articles to profl. jours., chapters to books; assoc. editor Jour. Watch Gastroenterology, Reviews on Gastroenterological Disorders, mem. editl. bd. Clin. Gastroenterology and Hepatology, Jour. Clin. Gastroenterology, World Jour. Gastroenterology, Gastroenterology and Hepatology. Mem.: Am. Coll. Gastroenterology (rep. to Nat. Colorectal Cancer Round, chmn. bd. govs., past sec., past treas., past pres.). Office: Ind U Dept Medicine 550 University Blvd Rm 4100 Indianapolis IN 46202-5149 Office Phone: 317-274-0912. Office Fax: 317-274-5449. Business E-Mail: drex@iupui.edu.*

REXROTH, NANCY LOUISE, photographer; b. Washington, June 27, 1946; d. John Augustus and Florence Bertha (Young) R. B.F.A., Am. U., 1969; M.F.A. in Photography, Ohio U., Athens, 1971. Asst. prof. photography Antioch Coll., Yellow Springs, Ohio, 1977-79, Wright State U., Dayton, Ohio, 1979-82. Author: Iowa, 1976, The Platinotype, 1977, 1976; exhibited photography at Weinstein Gallery, Mpls. Nat. Endowment Arts grantee, 1973; Ohio Arts Coun., 1981. Mem. Am. Massage Therapy Assn. Democrat. Home and Office: 255 Hosea Ave Apt 1 Cincinnati OH 45220-1736 E-mail: rexnex@cinci.rr.com.

REYELTS, PAUL C., chemical company executive; MBA, Harvard U. V.p. corp. fin. dept. Piper, Jaffray & Hopwood; sr. v.p. fin., CFO Valspar Corp., Mpls. Office: Valspar Corp 1101 Third St South Minneapolis MN 55415

REYES, J. CHRISTOPHER, food products distribution executive; BS in Fin., U. Md., 1975. Co-founder, CEO Reyes Holdings, Lake Forest, Ill., 1976—. Bd. dirs. Fortune Brands Inc., Wintrust Financial Corp., 1991—, Allstate Corp., Tribune Co., 2005—. Bd. dirs. Lyric Opera of Chgo., Mus. Sci. and Industry, Northwestern Meml. Found., U. Notre Dame. Mem.: Old Elm, Onwentsia. Office: Reyes Holdings LLC 9500 W Bryn Mawr Ave Ste 700 Rosemont IL 60018 Office Fax: (847) 604-9972.

REYES, VICTOR H., lawyer; b. Mex., Apr. 28, 1964; BA Polit. Sci., Loyola Univ., 1987; JD, DePaul Univ., 1990. Bar: Ill. 1990. Asst. to Mayor City of Chgo., 1989—95, dir. Mayor's Off. Intergovernmental Affairs, 1995—2002; shareholder, governmental and adminstrv. law dept. Greenberg Traurig LLP, Chgo., 2002—. Bd. dir. Park Fed. Savings. Bd. dir. Rehabilitation Inst. Chgo.; bd. overseers Chgo.-Kent Coll. of Law. Mem.: Ill. Inst. Technology (bd. trustees). Office: Greenberg Traurig LLP Ste 2500 77 W Wacker Dr Chicago IL 60601-1732 Office Phone: 312-456-8400. Office Fax: 312-456-8435. Business E-Mail: reyesv@gtlaw.com.

REYNA, CLAUDIO, professional soccer player; b. Springfield, NJ, July 20, 1973; m. Danielle Egan, 1997; 2 children. Student, U. Va. Midfielder Bayer Leverkusen, Germany, 1994—97, VfL Wolfsburg, Germany, 1997—99, Glasgow Rangers, Scotland, 1999—2000, Sunderland FC, England, 2001—03, Manchester City FC, England, 2003—. 109 caps, 8 goals U.S. Nat. Soccer Team, 1994—, capt., 1999—; mem. U.S. World Cup Team, 1994, 98, 2002, 06. Named Nat. H.S. Player of the Yr., Parade Mag., 1989—90, N.J. H.S. Player of the Yr., 1990, Gatorade H.S. Player of the Yr., 1990, Freshman of Yr., Soccer Am., 1991, 3-time first-team All-Am., Nat. Soccer Coaches Assn. Am., 1991—93; recipient Player of Yr. award, Mo. Athletic Club, 1992, 1993. Office: US Soccer Fedn 1801 S Prairie Ave Chicago IL 60616-1319

REYNARD, CHARLES G., lawyer, educator; b. Indpls., Apr. 13, 1946; s. Granville G. R. and Helen (Rizzoli) Phoebus; m. Judith Valente; children: Rachel, Meghan. BA in English, St. Joseph's Coll., 1968; JD, Loyola U., 1974. Bar: Ill. 1974, U.S. Dist. Ct. (cen. dist.) Ill. 1985. Asst. state's atty. McLean County, Bloomington, Ill., 1975-78, state's atty., 1987—; pvt. practice Bloomington, 1978-82; partner Reynard & Robb, Bloomington, 1982-87; cir. judge Bloomington, 2002—. Tchr., Chgo., 1968—; pres. McLean Child Protection Network, Bloomington, 1990-94; sec. McLean County Child Protection Network, 1994—. Author: Voir Dire in Child Sex Abuse Trials, 1996, The Violence Stops Here: Prosecuting Domestic Violence, 1999. Mem. Ill. Violence Prevention Authority, 1996—. Recipient Friend of Children award Youth Svcs. of Mid.-Ill., Bloomington, 1991-92, Human Dignity award Ill. Coalition Against Domestic Violence, 1998. Mem. Ill. State Bar Assn., Ill. State's Atty's. Assn. (bd. govs. 1991—), McLean County Bar Assn. Republican. Roman Catholic. Avocations: reading, writing, music. Office: McLean County State's Attys Office 104 W Front Rm 522 Bloomington IL 61701 Business E-Mail: judge.reynard@mcleancountyil.gov.

REYNOLDS, A. WILLIAM, retired manufacturing company executive; b. Columbus, Ohio, June 21, 1933; s. William Morgan and Helen Hibbard (McCray) R.; m. Joanne D. McCormick, June 12, 1953; children: Timothy M., Morgan Reynolds Brigham, Mary Reynolds Miller. AB in Econs., Harvard U., 1955; MBA, Stanford U., 1957. Pres. Crawford Door Co., Detroit, 1959-66; staff asst. to treas TRW Inc., Cleve., 1957-59, asst. to exec. v.p. automotive group, 1966-67, v.p. automotive aftermarket group, 1967-70, exec. v.p. indsl. and replacement sector, 1971-81, exec. v.p. automotive worldwide sector, 1981-84; pres. GenCorp, Akron, Ohio, 1984-85, pres., chief exec. officer, 1985-87, chmn., CEO, 1987-94, chmn., 1994-95. Bd. dirs. Eaton Corp., Cleve., Boise (Idaho) Cascade Corp., Boise Cascade Office Products Corp., Itasca, Ill., Stant Corp., Richmond, Ind., Fed. Res. Bank Cleve., now chmn.; mem. dean's adv. coun. Stanford (Calif.) U. Grad. Sch. Bus., 1981-88. Chmn. United Way-Red Cross of Summit County, Ohio, 1987; trustee Univ. Hosps. of Cleve., 1984—, chmn., 1987-94. Mem. SAE, Bus. Roundtable (policy com.), Coun. on Fgn. Rels., Kirtland Country Club, Union Club, Rolling Rock Club, John's Island Club, Pepper Pike Club. Episcopalian. Avocations: hunting, fly fishing, skiing, golf. Office: Old Mill Investments Old Mill Group 1696 Georgetown Rd Ste E Hudson OH 44236-4094

REYNOLDS, ERNEST WEST, retired internist, educator; b. Bristow, Okla., May 11, 1920; s. Ernest West and Florence (Brown) R. BS, U. Okla., 1942, MD, 1946, MS, 1952. Diplomate: Am. Bd. Internal Medicine. Intern Boston City Hosp., 1946-47; resident Grady Meml. Hosp., Atlanta, 1949-50; practice medicine Tulsa, Okla., 1953-54; prof. medicine U Mich., 1965-72; prof. medicine, dir. cardiology U. Wis., 1972-90, prof. emeritus, 1991—. Dir. Kellogg Found. Comprehensive Coronary Care Project, 1967-72; chmn. NIH Cardiovascular Study Sect. A, 1972-73 Mem. editorial bd.: Am. Heart Jour; Contbr. articles to profl. jours. Served to capt. AUS, 1947-49. Mem. Am. Heart Assn. (fellow coun. clin. cardiology), Ctrl. Soc. Clin. Rsch. Home: 17 Red Maple Trl Madison WI 53717-1515 Personal E-mail: ernest_reynolds@yahoo.com.

REYNOLDS, JOHN FRANCIS, insurance company executive; b. Escanaba, Mich., Mar. 29, 1921; s. Edward Peter and Lillian (Harris) R.; m. Dorothy Gustafson, May 1, 1946; children: Lois, Margaret, Michael. BS, Mich. State U., 1942. Claims and assoc. surety mgr. Hartford Ins. Co., Escanaba, Mich. and Chgo., 1946-55; asst. v.p., bond mgr. Wolverine Ins. Co., Battle Creek, Mich., 1955-64, v.p. underwriting, 1964-69; Midwest zone underwriting mgr. Transamerica Ins. Co. (Wolverine Ins. Co.), Battle Creek, Mich., 1969-74; pres., gen. mgr. Can. Surety Co. subs. Transamerica Ins. Co., Toronto, Ont., Canada, 1974-75; v.p. midwestern zone mgr. Transamerica Ins. Group, Battle Creek, Mich., 1975-83, pres., chief operating officer Los Angeles, 1983-84, chmn., chief exec. officer, 1984-85; apptd. spl. dep. ins. commr., dep. conservator Cadillac Inc. Co., 1989. Pres. Underwriting Exec. Council Midwest, 1967; dir. Underwriters Adjustment Bur., Toronto, 1974, Underwriters Labs. of Canada, Montreal, 1974; chmn. Mich. Assn. Ins. Cos., Lansing, 1976, Mich. Basic Property Ins. Assn., Detroit, 1973. Commr. City of Battle Creek, 1967-69; dir. Urban League, Battle Creek, 1969, 70, dir. Mich. Ins. Fedn., Lansing, 1975-83. Served to sgt. U.S. Army, 1942-45; New Guinea Roman Catholic. Avocations: golf, fishing. Home: 14037 N Cameo Dr Sun City AZ 85351-2903 Personal E-mail: reynolds213@yahoo.com.

REYNOLDS, MARTIN L., state legislator; b. Feb. 8, 1950; Mayor, Ladysmith, Wis., 1986-92; Wis. state assemblyman Dist. 87, 1990—. Plumbing and heating contractor. Mem. VFW, NRA, Am. Legion. Address: 101 Lake Ave E Ladysmith WI 54848-1304

REYNOLDS, PAUL L., lawyer, bank executive; b. Covington, Ky., May 29, 1961; BS cum laude, No. Ky. U., Highland Heights, 1983; JD, U. Ky. Coll. Law, Lexington, KY., 1986. Bar: Ohio 1986, US Dist. Ct. (so. dist. Ohio) 1986, Ky. 1987. Gen. counsel, asst. sec. Fifth Third Bank, 1995, asst. sec., 1995, sr. v.p., 1997; exec. v.p. Fifth Third Bancorp, Cin., 1999—, gen. counsel, sec., 2002—. Recipient Am. Jurisprudence award, Constl. Law, Am. Jurisprudence award, Corp. Fin. Law. Mem.: Ky. Bar Assn., Cin. Bar Assn., Ohio State Bar Assn. Office: Fifth Third Bancorp 38 Fountain Square Plz Cincinnati OH 45263

REYNOLDS, R. JOHN, academic administrator, educator; b. Milw., Dec. 3, 1936; s. Edward R. and Elizabeth (Wickenhauser) R.; m. Carol G. Lucas, Dec. 15, 1956; children: John D., Katherine A. BEd, U. Wis., Whitewater, 1961; MA, No. Mich. U., 1967; PhD, So. Ill. U., 1971. Bus. instr. Green Bay (Wis.) Tech. Inst., 1964-65; dir. vocat. tng. No. Mich. U., Marquette, 1965-68; v.p. Tech. Edn. Corp., St. Louis, 1968-69, prof., 1969-71; acting dean, chmn dept. So. Ill. U., Carbondale, 1969-71, 74-80, 81-82; assoc. acad. dean N.H. Coll., Manchester, 1971-74; head. bus. and econs. dept. Lake Superior State U., Sault Ste. Marie, Mich., 1981-82; pres. Nat. Coll., Rapid City, S.D., 1982-84, Huron (S.D.) U., 1984-93, Tri-State U., Angola, Ind., 1993—. Cons. in field. Contbr. articles to profl. jours. Pres. Dakotaland Mus., Huron, 1986-91. Named Researcher of Yr. Ill. Bus. Edn. Assn., 1971. Office: Tri State Univ 1 University Ave Angola IN 46703-1764

REYNOLDS, RICHARD I., food products company executive; With Libbey Inc., Toledo, Ohio, 1970—, v.p., CFO, now exec. v.p., COO, 1995—. Office: Libbey Inc 300 Madison Ave Fl 4 Toledo OH 43604-2634

REYNOLDS, ROBERT A., JR., electric distributor executive; Degree in bus., Stonehill Coll., 1972. Joined Graybar Electric Co., St. Louis, 1972, various mgmt. positions, v.p. commn./data divsn., 1991, pres., CEO, 2000—, chmn., 2001—. Mem.: Nat. Assn. Wholesaler-Distributors (sec., vice chmn. 2002—05, chmn. elect 2005—). Office: Graybar Electric 34 N Meramec Ave Saint Louis MO 63105

REYNOLDS, ROBERT HUGH, lawyer; b. St. Louis, Jan. 3, 1937; s. Leslie A. and Rebecca (McWaters) R.; m. Carol Jemison, Apr. 8, 1961; children: Stephen H., Cynthia C., Laura M. BA, Yale U., 1958; JD, Harvard U., 1964. Assoc. Barnes & Thornburg, Indpls., 1964—70, ptnr., 1970—2004, chmn. bus. dept., 1983—91, chmn. internat. practice group, 1992—2004, of counsel, 2005—; vice-chmn. TerraLex, 1996—2003, chmn., 2003—06, chmn. emeritus, 2007—. Co-chmn., editor Comml. Real Estate Financing for Ind. Attys., 1968; vice-chmn., co-editor Advising Ind. Businesses, 1974; chmn., editor Counseling Ind. Businesses, 1981, The Purchase and Sale of a Business, 1987. Bd. dir. Crossroads Am. Coun. Boy Scouts Am., v.p., 1971—75, pres., 1987—89, v.p. Area 4 Ctrl. Region, 1989—92, pres., 1992—93, pres. Ctrl. Region, 1993—96, nat. exec. bd., 1993—; bd. dir. Family Svc. Assn. Indpls., 1974—81, pres., 1978—80; bd. dir. Family Svc. Am., 1979—88, Greater Indpls. Fgn. Trade Zone, 1987—2000, Indpls. Conv. and Visitors Assn., 1989—2000, Indpls. Econ. Devel. Corp., 1983—99, Greater Indpls. Progress Com., 1986—2000, exec. com., vice chmn.; trustee Children's Mus. Indpls., 1988—96, chmn., 1992—94; bd. dirs. Indpls. Downtown Inc., chmn., 1996—99; bd. govs. Legacy Fund, 1992—2007, vice chmn., 2000—03, chmn., 2004—06; bd. dir. Noyes Meml. Found., pres., 2004—; bd. dir. Japan-Am. Soc. Ind., pres., 1994—2005, pres. emeritus, 2005—; bd. dir. Ctrl. Ind. Cmty. Found., 2003—07; bd. dirs. Indpls. Symphony Orch. Found., 2004—. With USN, 1958—61, lt. comdr. USNR, 1961—78. Named hon. Consul Gen. of Japan, 1999—, hon. trustee, Children's Mus. Indpls., 1997—; recipient Silver Buffalo award, Boy Scouts Am., Charles L. Whistler award, Greater Indpls. Progress Com., Sagamore of the Wabash award, Gov. Ind. Fellow Ind. Bar Found., Indpls. Bar Found.; mem. ABA, Ind. Bar Assn. (chmn. corp., banking and bus. law sect. 1981-82, chmn. internat. sect. 1994-96), Internat. Bar Assn., Indpls. Bar Assn., Greater Indpls. C. of C. (bd. dirs., sec. 2000-05, dir. emeritus 2005—), Econ. Club Indpls. (bd. dirs. 1995-2004), Kiwanis. Republican. Office: Barnes & Thornburg LLP 11 S Meridian St Indianapolis IN 46204-3535 Office Phone: 317-231-7227. Business E-Mail: rreynolds@btlaw.com.

REYNOLDS, THOMAS A., III, lawyer; b. Evanston, Ill., May 12, 1952; BSBA, Georgetown U., 1974; JD, Emory U., 1977. Bar: Ill. 1977, U.S. Dist. Ct. (no. dist.) Ill. 1978, U.S. Ct. Appeals (7th cir.) 1979, U.S. Dist. Ct. (no. dist. trial bar) Ill. 1983. Asst. pub. defender, Cook County, Ill., 1977—78; asst. atty. gen. Ill., 1981—83; assoc. to ptnr. litigation Winston & Strawn, Chgo., 1983—. Dir.

Smurfit-Stone Container Corp. Dir., v.p. Lyric Opera; dir. LINK Unlimited; pres. Brain Rsch. Found.; dir. U. Chgo. Hospitals; prin. Chgo. United. Mem.: Comml. Club Chgo. Office: Winston & Strawn LLP 35 W Wacker Dr Ste 4200 Chicago IL 60601-9703 Office Phone: 312-558-5895. Fax: 312-558-5700. E-mail: treynolds@winston.com.

REYNOLDS, TOM G., state senator; b. Milw., Dec. 16, 1956; m. Sandy Reynolds; 4 children. Grad., Nathan Hale H.S., 1975. Owner, oper. Endeavor Press, 1984—; state sen. Wis. State Senate, Madison, 2002—. Winner Rep. primary, Wis., 1996. Republican. Office: State Capitol Rm 306 S PO Box 7882 Madison WI 53707-7882

REYNOLDS, TOMMY, secondary school educator; b. Dec. 23, 1956; BSE ind. tech., CMSU, 1979, MS ind. voc. tech. edu., 1983. Secondary tchr. Lee's Summit (Mo.) North High Sch., 1979; tchr. PLJH, 1979-80, Lee's Summit High Sch., 1980—, Lee's Summit North High Sch., 1995-98; ind. tech. dept. coord., 1992-96. Recipient Tchr. Excellence award Internat. Tech. Edn. Assn., 1992. Office: Lee's Summit North High Sch 901 NE Douglas St Lees Summit MO 64086-4505

REYNOLDS, ZACKERY E., lawyer; b. Eureka, Kans., Dec. 19, 1957; BA, U. Kans., 1979; JD with honors, Washburn U., 1982. Bar: Kans. 1982, Mo. 1992. Pvt. practice, Fort Scott, Kans. Mem. ABA (exec. coun., young lawyers divsn. 1991-92), ATLA, Kans. Bar Assn. (pres.-elect 1998-99, v.p. 1997-98, sec.-treas. 1996-97, chair profl. ethics grievance com. 1993-95, pres. young lawyers sect. 1986-87, Outstanding Svc. award 1992), Mo. Bar Assn., Kans. Trial Lawyers Assn., Phi Delta Phi. Office: Reynolds Law Firm PA PO Box 32 102 S Jordan Fort Scott KS 66701

REYNOLDSON, WALTER WARD, retired judge, lawyer; b. St. Edward, Nebr., May 17, 1920; s. Walter Scorer and Mabel Matilda (Sallach) Reynoldson; m. Janet Aline Mills, Dec. 24, 1942 (dec. 1986); children: Vicki, Robert; m. Patricia A. Frey, June 3, 1989. BA, State Tchrs. Coll., 1942; JD, U. Iowa, Iowa City, 1948; LLD (hon.), Simpson Coll., Indianola, Iowa, 1983, Drake U., Des Moines, 1987. Bar: Iowa 1948. Justice Iowa Supreme Ct., 1971-78, chief justice, 1978-87, sr. judge, 1989-93; of counsel Reynoldson Law Firm, Osceola, Iowa, 1993—. County atty. Clark County, Iowa, 1953—57; adj. prof. law Drake U., 1989—93. Co-author: (book) Trial Handbook, 1969. Pres. Nat. Ctr. State Cts.; trustee Drake U., 1987—2000. With USNR, 1942—46. Recipient Osceola Cmty. Svc. award, 1968. Fellow: Am. Bar Found.; mem.: Am. Coll. Trial Lawyers, Conf. Chief Justices (pres. 1984—85), Acad. Trial Lawyers, Am. Judicature Soc. (bd. dirs. 1983—87, Herbert Harley award 1990), Iowa Bar Assn. (chmn. com. legal edn. and admission to bar 1964—71). Office: Reynoldson Law Firm 200 W Jefferson St Osceola IA 50213-1413 Home Phone: 515-242-0231.

RHEIN, ARTHUR, computer company executive; V.p. mktg. Harvey Electronics, 1983—86; sr. v.p. mktg. Pioneer, 1986; from v.p. mktg. to pres., CEO Agilysys, Inc., Boca Raton, Fla., 1986—2002, pres., CEO, 2002—03, chmn., pres., CEO, 2003—. Office: Agilysys Inc Ste 301E 2255 Glades Rd Boca Raton FL 33431

RHEIN, DAVE, newspaper editor; b. Chgo., Mar. 9, 1949; BE, Drake U., 1970. Deputy mng. editor Des Moines Register, 1995-99, asst. metro editor 1999—. Office: Des Moines Register 715 Locust St Des Moines IA 50309-3767

RHIND, JAMES THOMAS, lawyer; b. Chgo., July 21, 1922; s. John Gray and Eleanor (Bradley) R.; m. Laura Haney Campbell, Apr. 19, 1958; children: Constance Rhind Robey, James Campbell, David Scott. Student, Hamilton Coll., 1940-42; AB cum laude, Ohio State U., 1944; LL.B. cum laude, Harvard U., 1950. Bar: Ill. bar 1950. Japanese translator U.S. War Dept., Tokyo, 1946-47; congl. liaison Fgn. Operations Adminstrn., Washington, 1954; atty. Bell, Boyd & Lloyd, Chgo., 1950-53, 55—, ptnr., 1958-92, chmn. exec. com., 1976—88, of counsel, 1993—. Bd. dirs. Kewaunee Scientific Corp., Statesville, NC. Commr. Gen. Assembly United Presbyn. Ch., 1963; life trustee Ravinia Festival Assn., Hamilton Coll., Clinton, N.Y., U. Chgo.; Northwestern Univ. Assocs.; chmn. Cook County Young Republican Orgn., 1957; Ill. Young Rep. nat. committeeman, 1957-58; v.p., mem. bd. govs. United Rep. Fund Ill., 1965-84; pres. Ill. Childrens Home and Aid Soc., 1971-73, life trustee; bd. dirs. E.J. Dalton Youth Center, 1966-69; governing mem. Chgo. Symphony Orch., Chgo.; mem. Ill. Arts Council, 1971-75; mem. exec. com. div. Met. Mission and Ch. Extension Bd., Chgo. Presbytery, 1966-68; trustee Presbyn. Homes, W. Clement and Jessie V. Stone Found., U. Chgo. Hosps. Served with M.I. AUS, 1943-46. Mem. ABA, Ill. Bar Assn., Chgo. Bar Assn. (bd. mgrs. 1967-69), Fed. Bar Assn., Chgo. Coun. on Fgn. Rels., Japan Am. Soc. Chgo., Lawyers Club Chgo., Phi Beta Kappa, Sigma Phi. Clubs: Chicago, Glen View (Ill.), Commercial (Chgo.), Mid-Day Club (Chgo.), Economic (Chgo.). Home: 830 Normandy Ln Glenview IL 60025-3210 Office: Bell Boyd & Lloyd 3 First National Plz 70 W Madison St Ste 3200 Chicago IL 60602-4244 Office Phone: 312-372-1121. Business E-Mail: jrhind@bellboyd.com.

RHOADES, KITTY, state legislator; b. Hudson, Wis., Apr. 7, 1951; m. Frank Rhoades; 3 children. BA, U. Wis., River Falls, 1973; MA, Ill. State U., 1978. Exec. dir. Hudson C. of C., 1991—96; pres. Suburban C. of C., 1996—; sml. bus. owner; classroom tchr.; mem. Wis. State Assembly, Madison, 1998—, chair aging and long-term care com., mem. colls. and univs. com., mem. edn. com., mem. fin. instns. com., mem. joint legis. coun. Mem. U. Wis. River Falls Alumni Found.; mem. pres.'s adv. coun. Century Coll.; mem. pastoral coun. St. Patrick's Ch.; bd. dirs. Minn. C. of C. Exec. Assn., United Way. Mem.: Rotary. Republican. Roman Catholic. Office: State Capitol Bldg Rm 321 E PO Box 8953 Madison WI 53708-8953 Address: 708 4th St Hudson WI 54016

RHOADES, RODNEY ALLEN, physiologist, educator; b. Greenville, Ohio, Jan. 5, 1939; s. John H. and Floris L. Rhoades; m. Judith Ann Brown, Aug. 6, 1961; children: Annelisa, Kirsten. BS, Miami U., 1961; MS, 1963; PhD, Ohio State U., 1966. Asst. prof. Pa. State U., State College, 1966-72, assoc. prof., 1972-75; rsch. scientist NIH, Bethesda, Md., 1975-76; prof. Ind. U. Sch. Medicine, Indpls., 1976-81, 81—, chmn., 1981—2003. Dir. Indpls. Ctr. for Advanced Rsch. Author: Physiology, 1984; contbr. articles to profl. jours. Fellow NASA, 1964-66; recipient Rsch. Career Devel. award NIH, 1975-80. Mem. Am. Physiol. Soc, AHA, Am. Thoracic Soc., Biophysics Soc., Sigma Xi. Home: 1768 Spruce Dr Carmel IN 46033-9025 Office: Ind U Sch Medicine 635 Barnhill Dr Indianapolis IN 46202-5126

RHOADS, PAUL KELLY, lawyer; b. La Grange, Ill., Sept. 4, 1940; s. Herbert Graves and Mary Margaret (Gurrie) R.; m. Katheryn Virginia Reissaus, Sept. 14, 1963; children: Elizabeth S. R. Saline, Katheryn B.R. Meek, Julia C. Rhoads Brenneman. BA, Washington & Lee U., 1962; JD, Loyola U., Chgo., 1967. Bar: Ill. 1967, U.S. Dist. Ct. (no. dist.) Ill. 1967, U.S. Tax Ct. 1980. Trust officer 1st Nat. Bank Chgo., 1963-69; with Schiff Hardin & Waite, Chgo., 1969-98, ptnr., 1973-98; sole practitioner Western Springs, Ill., 1999—. Author: Starting a Private Foundation, 1993, Managing a Private Foundation, 1997; contbr. articles to profl. jours. and chpts. to books. Trustee Ill. Inst. Tech., 1985-95, Western Springs (Ill.) Hist. Soc., 1983-92, Philanthropy Roundtable, Washington, 1992-2000; bd. dirs. Cyrus Tang Scholarship Found., 1984-91, McKay Enterprises, Chgo., 1981-2002; bd. overseers Ill. Inst. Tech. Chgo.-Kent Coll. Law, 1985-95; pres., bd. dirs. Grover Hermann Found., Chgo., 1984—; sec., bd. dirs. Western Springs Svc. Club, 1976-86; sec. Vandivort Properties, Inc., Cape Girardeau, Mo., 1990-2002; mem. adv. com. estate, tax and fin. planning Loyola U., 1986-92; adv. com. Thomas A. Roe Inst. for Econ. Policy Studies, Heritage Found., 1989—. Fellow Am. Coll. Trust and Estate Coun.; mem. Ill. State Bar Assn., Chgo. Bar Assn., Portage Lake Yacht Club (Onekama, Mich.) (commodore 1988, bd. dirs. 1985-89), Heathlands Golf Club (Onekama). Republican. Avocations: sailing, golf, tennis. Office: 1000 Hillgrove Ave Western Springs IL 60558-1420 Home Phone: 708-246-6769; Office Phone: 708-246-8200. E-mail: paulkrhoads@ameritech.net.

RHODES, CHARLES HARKER, JR., lawyer; b. Chgo., May 24, 1930; s. Charles Harker and Claire (Hepner) R.; m. Mae Ellen Svoboda, Apr. 19, 1952; children: Charles Harker, James Albert, Edward Joseph. BA, U. Chgo., 1948, JD, 1951. Bar: Ill. 1951. Assoc. Schatz & Busch, Chgo., 1951-53; assoc. Sonnenschein Nath & Rosenthal, Chgo., 1953-60, ptnr., 1961-92, ret. ptnr., 1992—. Dir. Ill. Inst. for Continuing Legal Edn., Springfield, 1977-84, 86-88; pres. Ill. Bar Automated Rsch., 1975-85. Trustee Nat. Ctr. for Automated Info. Rsch., N.Y.C., 1976-94; pres. B.R. Ryall YMCA, Glen Ellyn, Ill., 1967. Fellow Am. Bar Found., Chgo. Bar Found. (pres. 1977-80), Ill. Bar Found. (fellows chmn. 1990-91); mem. ABA (long range planning com. 1991-92, mem. pub. editorial bd. com. 1993-94), Ill. State Bar Assn. (bd. govs. 1975-79, chmn. liaison com. Atty. Registration and Disciplinary Commn. 1992-93), Chgo. Bar Assn. (libr., bd. mgrs. 1969-72), Am. Arbitration Assn. (arbitrator), Nat. Conf. Bar Founds. (trustee, pres. 1987-88), Met. Club Chgo. Republican. Presbyterian. Avocations: travel, photography. Home: 267 N Montclair Ave Glen Ellyn IL 60137-5508 Office: Sonnenschein Nath & Rosenthal 233 S Wacker Dr Ste 8000 Chicago IL 60606-6491

RHODES, JIM, state legislator; b. Apr. 1942; m. Judy Rhodes. AA, U. Minn. Minn. state rep. Dist. 44B, 1993—, chair govt. ops. and vets. affairs com. Retail gen. mgr.

RIBBINS, MARK, radio personality; Radio host WNWV, Elyria, Ohio. Office: WNWV 538 W Broad St PO Box 4006 Elyria OH 44036

RIBEAU, SIDNEY A., academic administrator; M in Interpersonal Comm., U. Ill., 1973, D in Interpersonal Comm., 1979. Prof. comm. studies Calif. State U., LA, 1976, chair Pan African studies dept., 1987; dean Coll. Liberal Arts Calif. Poly., San Luis Obispo, 1990, v.p. for acad. affairs Pomona, 1992; pres. Bowling Green (Ohio) U., 1995—. Bd. dirs. The Andersons Inc., Maumee, Ohio; lectr., spkr. and presenter in field. Co-author: African American Communication: Ethnic Identity and Cultural Interpretations, 1994 (Disting. Scholarship award Speech Comm. Assn.); contbr. papers to scholarly jours. Mem. Ohio Bd. Regent's Higher Edn. Funding Commn., Am. Coun. on Edn.'s Leadership and Instnl. Change Commn., Higher Edn. Bus. Coun., Urban League Toledo; bd. dirs. Toledo Symphony Orch. Mem. Bowling Green C. of C., Toledo C. of C. Office: Bowling Green State U Bowling Green OH 43403-0001

RICART, FRED, automotive company executive; Owner Ricart Automotive, Columbus, Ohio. Office: Ricart Automotive Rte 33 and Hamilton Rd Columbus OH 43227-1342

RICART, RHETT C., retail automotive executive; b. 1956; Grad., Ohio State U., 1977. Prin. Ricart Ford, Groveport, Ohio, 1977—, pres., CEO, 1988—; ceo Ricart Automotive, Columbus, Ohio. Office: Ricart Automotive PO Box 27130 Columbus OH 43227-0130 also: Ricart Automotive 4255 S Hamilton Rd Groveport OH 43125-9332

RICE, CHARLES MARCUS, II, lawyer; b. June 20, 1946; s. Jay Goldman and Bonna (Lafferty) Rice; m. Marian Clifford Jones, June 16, 1979; children: Charles Marcus III, Rebecca Wells. AB magna cum laude, Princeton U., 1968; MPub. Policy, U. Mich., 1973, JD cum laude, 1974. Bar: N.Y. 1975, Mo. 1978. Mem. adv. coun. Sch. Forestry, U. Mo., Columbia, Mo., 1982—92; pres. Rice Money Mgrs., Inc., 1992—. Sec. Anglican Inst., St. Louis, 1984—87. Home: 8510 Colonial Ln Saint Louis MO 63124-2007 Office: Rice Money Managers Inc 231 South Bemiston Ave Ste 800 Saint Louis MO 63105 Office Phone: 314-854-1388. Office Fax: 314-854-9118.

RICE, DAVID LEE, university president emeritus; b. New Market, Ind., Apr. 1, 1929; s. Elmer J. and Katie (Tate) R.; m. Betty Jane Fordice, Sept. 10, 1950; children: Patricia Denise Rice Dawson, Michael Alan. BS, Purdue U., 1951, MS, 1956, PhD, 1958; degree (hon.), U. Evansville, 1994, U. So. Ind., 1995; LHD, U. Evansville, 1994; LLD, U. So. Ind., 1995. Dir. prof. research Ball State U., Muncie, Ind., 1958-66; v.p. Coop. Ednl. Research Lab., Inc., Indpls., 1965-67; research coordinator, bur. research HEW, Washington; dean campus Ind. State U., Evansville, 1967-71, pres. campus, 1971-85; pres. U. So. Ind., Evansville, 1985-94, pres. emeritus, 1994—. Adminstrv. asst. Gov.'s Com. on Post High Sch. Orgn. Contbr. articles to profl. jours. Past mem. State Citizens Adv. Bd. Title XX Social Security Act; bd. dirs., past pres. bd. commrs. Evansville Housing Auth.; pres. Leadership Evansville, 1978-79; bd. dirs., past pres. S.W. Ind. Pub. TV, 1972—; chair Indian Pub. Broadcasting Sts., 1990-93; bd. dirs. Villages Inc.; mem. Buffalo Trace Coun. Boy Scouts Am., 1963—, New Harmony Commn., 1989-94; chair So. Ind. Rural Devel. Project., Inc.; bd. trustees Rapp Granary-Owen Found.; bd. dirs. So. Ind. Higher Edn. Inc., U. So. Ind. Found. With inf. U.S. Army, 1951-53. Decorated Bronze Star, Combat Infantryman's Badge; recipient Svc. to Others award Salvation Army, 1974, Citizen of Yr. award Westside Civitan Club, 1972, Boss of Yr. award Am. Bus. Women's Assn., 1976, Disting. Citizen of Yr. award Ivy Tech State Coll., 1994; David L. Rice Libr./U. So. Ind. named in his honor, 1994. Mem. DAR (medal of honor for cmty. svc. 1998), Am. Assn. Higher Edn., Am. Ednl. Rsch. Assn., Am. Assn. State Colls. and Univs., Nat. Soc. Study Edn., Met. Evansville C. of C. (dir.), Evansville Kennel Club, Rotary (civic award Evansville club 1985, life), Alpha Kappa Psi, Alpha Zeta, Phi Delta Kappa. Methodist. Home: 335 W Church St Box 400 New Harmony IN 47631 Office: Neef Lesueur House 404 Church St New Harmony IN 47631

RICE, DERICA W., pharmaceutical executive; b. Decatur, Ala., 1965; m. Robin Rice; 3 children. BSEE, Kettering U. (formerly GMI Engring. and Mgmt. Inst.), Flint, Mich., 1988; MBA, Ind. U., 1990. Internat. treasury assoc. Eli Lilly and Co., 1990—92, various positions including sales rep., mgr. global fin. planning and analysis for med. devices divsn., global planning mgr. pharms., fin. dir., CFO Can., 1995—97, exec. dir., CFO European ops. London, 1997—2000, gen. mgr. UK and Republic of Ireland, 2000—03, mem. Diversity Leadership Coun., v.p., contr. Indpls., 2003—06, sr. v.p., CFO, 2006—, mem. policy and strategy and ops. coms. Bd. dirs. Clarian Health North. Bd. govs. Indpls. Mus. Art. Office: Eli Lilly and Co Lilly Corp Ctr Indianapolis IN 46285 Office Phone: 317-276-2000.

RICE, JOHN RISCHARD, computer scientist, researcher, educator; b. Tulsa, June 6, 1934; s. John Coykendal Kirk and Margaret Lucille (Rischard) R.; m. Nancy Ann Bradfield, Dec. 19, 1954; children: Amy Lynn, Jenna Margaret. BS, Okla. State U., 1954, MS, 1956; PhD, Calif. Inst. Tech., 1959. Postdoctoral fellow Nat. Bur. Standards, Washington, 1959-60; rsch. mathematician GM Rsch. Labs., Warren, Mich., 1960-64; prof. Purdue U., West Lafayette, Ind., 1964-89, head dept. computer sci., 1983-96, disting. prof., 1989—. Editor-in-chief ACM Trans. Math. Software, N.Y.C., 1975-93; chmn. ACM-Signum, N.Y.C., 1977-79; dir. Computing Rsch. Bd., Washington, 1987-94; chair Computing Rsch. Assn., Washington, 1991-93. Author: The Approximation of Functions, 1964, Vol. 2, 1969, umerical Methods, Software and Analysis, 1983; author and editor: Mathematical Software, 1971; editor: Intelligent Scientific Software Systems, 1991. Fellow AAAS, ACM (George Forsythe Meml. lectr. 1975); mem. IFIP (working group 2.5, vice chmn. 1977-91), Soc. Indsl. and Applied Math., Nat. Acad. Engring., Phi Kappa Phi. Home: 112 E Navajo St West Lafayette IN 47906-2153 Office: Purdue U Computer Sci Dept West Lafayette IN 47907

RICE, JON RICHARD, health facility administrator, physician; b. Grand Forks, ND, July 10, 1946; s. Harry Frazer and Marian (Lund) R.; m. Roberta Jane Lindbergh, June 7, 1969; children: Kristen, Jennifer. BA, U. N.D., 1969, BS, 1970; MD, U. Tex., San Antonio, 1972; MS in Health Adminstrn., U. Colo., 1991. Intern U.S. Naval Hosp., San Diego, 1972-73; resident U. N.D. Sch. Medicine, Minot, 1975-77; physician Valley Med., Grand Forks, 1977-93; state health officer .D. Dept. Health, Bismarck, 1993-97; dir. managed care Blue Cross Blue Shield of N.D., Fargo, 1997—. Contbg. author: Pilots, Personality and Performance. Lt. USN, 1972-75. Recipient Outstanding Vol. award Dakota Heart Assn., 1989, YMCA, 1992, Outstanding Health Care Provider Grand Forks C. of C., 1992, Award of Excellence N.D. Hosp. Assn., 1995. Mem. AMA, Am. Acad. Family Physicians, Am. Coll. Physician Execs., Alpha Omega Alpha. Office: Blue Cross Blue Shield ND 4510 13th Ave S Fargo ND 58121-0002 E-mail: jon_rice_1999@yahoo.com, jon.rice@noridian.com.

RICE, JOY KATHARINE, psychologist, education educator; d. Joseph Theodore and Margaret Sophia (Bednarik) Straka; m. David Gordon Rice, Sept. 1, 1962; children: Scott Alan, Andrew David. BFA with high honors, U. Ill., 1960; MS, U. Wis., 1962, MS, 1964, PhD, 1967. Lic. clin. psychologist. USPHS predoctoral fellow dept. psychiatry Med. Sch. U. Wis., Madison, 1964-65, asst. dir. Counseling Ctr., 1966-74, dir. Office Continuing Edn. Svcs., 1972-78, prof. ednl. policy studies and women's studies, 1974-95, clin. prof. psychiatry, 1995—; pvt. practice psychology Psychiat. Svcs., S.C., Madison, 1967—. Mem. State Wis. Ednl. Approval Bd., Madison, 1972—73; mem. Adult Edn. Commn. U.S. Office Career Edn., Washington, 1978; co-chmn. Wis. Lt. Gov.'s Task Force on Women and Depression, 2005—. Author: Living Through Divorce, A Developmental Approach to Divorce Therapy, 1985, 2d edit., 1989, Transforming Leaderships Diverse Visions and Women's Voices, 2007; mem. editl. bd. Lifelong Learning, 1979—86; cons. editor: Psychology Women Quar., 1986—88, assoc. editor:, 1989—94, cons. editor: Handbook of Adult and Continuing Education, 1989, Encyclopedia of Women and Gender, 2001, Handbook of Girls' and Women's Psychological Health, 2005; contbr. articles to profl. jours. Pres. Big Bros. Big Sisters Dane County, 2002, bd. dirs.; co-chair Wis. Lt. Gov.'s Task Force on Women and Depression, 2005—06. Recipient Disting. Achievement award, Ednl. Press Assn. Am., 1992, John Fritschler Jr. award for Disting. Achievement, 2004; Knapp fellow, U. Wis., Madison, 1960—62, Tchg. fellow, 1962—63. Fellow: APA (exec. bd. psychology women divsn. 1994—, internat. psychology divsn. 1998—, exec. bd. 1998—, chair internat. com. women 2000—02, chair com. internat. rels. psychology 2005, divsn. pres. 2006, Disting. Leadership award 2000—02, Woman of Yr. award, Sect. for Advancement of Women in Counseling Psychology 2007); mem.: Am. Assn. Continuing and Adult Edn. (Meritorious Svc. award 1978—80, 1982), Internat. Coun. Psychologists (bd. dir. 1998—2001, sec. 2002—04, bd. dir. 2004—), Nat. Assn. Women Edn. (editl. bd. jour. 1984—88, cons. editor Initiatives 1988—91), TEMPO Internat. (bd. dir., sec. 2000—03, 2006—), Rotary, Phi Delta Kappa. Avocations: interior decorating, painting, gardening, travel. Home: 4230 Waban Hl Madison WI 53711-3711 Office: 2727 Marshall Ct Madison WI 53705-2255 Office Phone: 608-238-9354.

RICE, LEONARD S., lawyer; b. 1950; AB, Ripon Coll., 1972; JD, William Mitchell Coll., 1981. Bar: Minn. 1981. Ptnr., chair, public fin. group Dorsey & Whitney LLP, Mpls. Editor: Law Rev. Served to 1st lt. Airborne-Ranger US Army, 1972—75. Mem.: ABA, Hennepin Co. Bar Assn., Minn. State Bar Assn.

RICE, LINDA JOHNSON, publishing executive; b. Chgo., Mar. 22, 1958; d. John J. and Eunice Johnson; m. Andre Rice, 1984, 1 child, Alexa Christine; m. Mel Farr Sr. BA Journalism, Univ. Southern Calif., LA, 1980; MBA, Northwestern Univ., Evanston, Ill., 1987. With Johnson Pub. Co., 1980—, past v.p. and asst. to pub., COO, 1987—2002; pres. Johnson Pub. Co., Inc., Chgo., 1987—, CEO, 2002—; pres. Fashion Fair Cosmetics, Ill., 1987—. Named one of 100 Most Powerful Women in Chgo., Chgo. Sun-Times, Chicago's 40 Under 40, Crain's Chgo. Bus.; recipient Women of Power award, Nat. Urban League, Trumpet award, Turner Broadcasting, Alumni Merit award, Univ. So. Calif., Alumni of the Year award, Kellogg Grad. Sch. Mgmt., stern University. Mem.: Exec. Club Chgo., Econ. Club Chgo., Young Presidents Orgn., Nat. Assn. Black Journalists, Fashion Group Internat., Comml. Club Chgo. Office: Johnson Pub Co Inc 820 S Michigan Ave Chicago IL 60605-2191 Business E-Mail: ljr@ebony.com.

RICE, WALTER HERBERT, federal judge; b. Pitts., May 27, 1937; s. Harry D. and Elizabeth L. (Braemer) R.; m. Bonnie Rice; children: Michael, Hilary, Harry, Courtney Elizabeth. BA, Northwestern U., 1958; JD, MBA, Columbia U., 1962; LLD (hon.), U. Dayton, 1991; DHL (hon.), Wright State U., 2000. Bar: Ohio 1963. Asst. county prosecutor, Montgomery County, Ohio, 1964-66; assoc. Gallon & Miller, Dayton, Ohio, 1966-69; 1st asst. Montgomery County Prosecutor's Office, 1969; judge Dayton Mcpl. Ct., 1970-71, Montgomery County Ct. Common Pleas, 1971-80, U.S. Dist. Ct. (so. dist.) Ohio, 1980—, chief judge, 1996—2003. Adj. prof. U. Dayton Law Sch., 1976—, bd. visitors, 1976—; chmn. Montgomery County Supervisory Coun. on Crime and Delinquency, 1972-74; vice chmn. bd. dirs. Pretrial Release, Inc., 1975-79; trustee Wright Dunbar, Inc. Author papers in field. Pres. Dayton Area Coun. on Alcoholism and Drug Abuse, 1971-73; chmn. bd. trustees Stillwater Health Ctr., Dayton, 1976-79, Family Svc. Assn. Dayton, 1978-80; chmn. RTA in 2000 Com., 2003 Com. Designed To Bring Nat. Park to Dayton To Honor Wright Bros. and Birth of Aviation; chmn. Martin Luther King Jr. Meml. Com., Dayton Aviation Heritage Commn.; trustee Montgomery County Vol. Lawyers Project, Miami Valley Cultural Alliance, Barbara Jordan Com. Racial Justice; co-chmn., Dayton Dialogue on Race Rels.; founding trustee Aviation Heritage Found., Inc.; former bd. mem. Sinclair C.C., U.S. Air & Trade Show. Recipient Excellent Jud. Service award Ohio Supreme Ct., 1976, 77, Outstanding Jud. Service award, 1973, 74, 76, Man of Yr. award Disting. Service Awards Council, Dayton, 1977, Outstanding Jurist in Ohio award Ohio Acad. Trial Lawyers, 1986, Pub. Ofcl. of Yr. award Ohio region of Nat. Assn. Social Workers, 1992, Humanitarian award NCCJ, 1993, City Mgr.'s Cmty. Svc. award City of Dayton, 1994, Paul Laurence Dunbar Humanitarian award, 1996, Pres.' award NAACP, 1996, greater Dayton Peace Bridge (civil rights) Hall of Fame, Mark of Excellence award Nat. Forum Black Pub. Adminstrs., 2001, Conservation Svc. award U.S. Dept. Interior, 2002, Marie Kendrick Fair Housing award Dayton Area Bd. Realtors, 2003, Tom Joyner Hardest Workin Civil Rights Activist award Wilberforce U., 2003. Mem. Dayton Bar Assn., Fed. Judges Assn., Carl D. Kessler Inn of Ct. (founder, former chmn.).

RICE, WILLIAM EDWARD, journalist; b. Albany, NY, July 26, 1938; s. Harry Edward, Jr. and Elizabeth (Lally) R.; m. Carol Timmon, June 3, 1978 (div.); m. Jill Van Cleave, Aug. 20, 1983. BA in History, U. Va., 1960; MS with honors, Columbia U., 1963. Reporter, editorial writer, critic Washington Post, 1963-69; student LeCordon Bleu, Paris, 1969-70; dir. L'Ecole de Cuisine, Bethesda, Md., 1971-72; freelance writer, restaurant critic Washingtonian Mag., 1971-72; exec. food editor Washington Post, 1972-80; editor-in-chief Food and Wine Mag., NYC, 1980-85; food and wine columnist Chgo. Tribune, 1986—2003. Dining In columnist Gentlemen's Quarterly, 1987-89; chmn. restaurant awards com. James Beard Found., 1993-2003, chmn. who's who food and beverage in Am. com., 2005—. Author: Feasts of Wine and Food, 1986, Steak Lovers Cookbook, 1997; editor: (with others) Where to Eat in America, 1978, 2d edit., 1980, 3d edit., 1987. Served with USN, 1960-62. Recipient Vesta award as outstanding newspaper food editor, 1979, Ordre du Merite Agricole (France), 1983 Home: 655 W Buena Ave Chicago IL 60613-2201 Office Phone: 773-975-6685. Personal E-mail: wricechicago@yahoo.com.

RICH, DANIEL HULBERT, retired chemistry professor; b. Fairmont, Minn., Dec. 12, 1942; married, 1964; 2 children. BS, U. Minn., 1964; PhD in Organic Chemistry, Cornell U., 1968. Rsch. assoc. organic chemist Cornell U., Ithaca, NY, 1968; rsch. chemist Dow Chem. Co., 1968—69; rsch. assoc., organic chemist Stanford U., Palo Alto, Calif., 1969—70; asst. prof. pharm. chemistry U. Wis., Madison, 1970—75, assoc. prof., 1975—81, prof. dept. med. chemistry, 1981—2006, prof. dept. organic chemistry, 1988—2006, Ralph F. Hirschmann prof. medicinal and organic chemistry, 1994—2006, emeritus prof. chemistry and organic chemistry, 2006—. Cons. biorganic natural product study sect., NIH, 1981-85, chmn., 1985. Recipient H.I. Romnes award, 1980, Vincent du Vigneaud award, 1990, Hitchings award for innovative methods in drug design, 1992, Alexander von Humboldt award, 1993, E. Volwiler award Am. Assn. Colls. Pharmacy, 1995, Outstanding Achievement award U. Minn., 2004; fellow NIH, 1968. Fellow AAAS, Am. Chem. Soc. (Ralph F. Hirschmann award in peptide chemistry 1993, divsn. medicinal chemistry award 1991, A.C. Cope scholar 1999, E. Smissman award, 2005), Am. Assn. Pharm. Sci. (rsch. achievement award 1992), Am. Assn. Coll. Pharmacy (Volwiler award 1995). Am. Peptide Soc. (R.B. Merrifield award 1999). Achievements include research in synthesis in peptides and hormones, inhibition of peptide receptors and proteases, characterization, synthesis and mechanisms of action of peptide natural products. Office: U Wis Dept Med Chemistry 7109 Rennebohm Hall 777 Highland Ave Madison WI 53705-2222

RICH, HARRY EARL, corporate financial executive; b. Wichita, Kans., Mar. 5, 1940; s. Hubert E. and Lorene (Sadler) R.; m. Elfreda Elizabeth Babcock, Aug. 8, 1964; children: Lisa G., Carey E., Ashley H. BA, Harvard U., 1962, MBA, 1968. Pres. instrumentation divsn. Baxter Travenol, Deerfield, Ill., 1977-78; group v.p. Mallinckrodt, Inc., St. Louis, 1978-83; sr. v.p., chief fin. officer Brown Group, Inc., St. Louis, 1983-88, exec. v.p., chief fin. officer, 1988-00, also bd. dirs. Bd. dirs. Gen. Am. Capital Co. divsn. GenAm. Bd. dirs. Repertory Theatre, 1984-90, 1998—, pres. bd. dirs.,1988-90; treas., v.p. Fair Found., 1985-88; bd. trustees Mary Inst., 1986-90, Mary Inst./St. Louis Country Day Sch., 1990-97, chmn., 1995-97. Lt. USN, 1962-66. Avocations: tennis, jogging, sailing. Home: 101 Fair Oaks Saint Louis MO 63124-1579

RICH, NANCY JEAN, lawyer; b. Chgo., June 11, 1959; d. John Keith and Phyllis Vallerie (Delaney) R. AB with honors, Loyola U., Chgo., 1981, JD, 1984. Bar: Ill. 1984, U.S. Dist. Ct. (no. dist.) Ill. 1984. Asst. atty. gen. environ. control div. Ill. Atty. Gen.'s Office, Chgo., 1984-87; assoc. Isham, Lincoln & Beale,

Chgo., 1987-88, Sidley & Austin, Chgo., 1988-89, Bell, Boyd & Lloyd, Chgo., 1989-91, ptnr., 1992, Katten Muchin Zavis Rosenman, Chgo. Bd. dirs. Pub. Interest Law Initiative. Contbr. to Loyola Consumer Law Reporter, 1991. Adminstrv. asst. Hartigan for Atty. Gen. Campaign, Chgo., 1982; bd. dirs. Suburban Area Agy. on Aging, 1990-2004, pres. bd. dirs., 1999-2001, chmn. resource devel. com., 1991—. Mem. ABA, Ill. Bar Assn., Chgo. Bar Assn. (environ. law com.). Office: Katten Muchin Zavis Rosenman 525 W Monroe St Chicago IL 60661 Home Phone: 708-749-8130; Office Phone: 312-902-5536. Office Fax: 312-577-8676. Business E-Mail: nancy.rich@kattenlaw.com. E-mail: nancy.rich@kmzr.com.

RICH, ROBERT EDWARD, lawyer; b. Corbin, Ky., Feb. 4, 1944; s. Edward Bluch and Marjorie Brooks (Wentworth) R.; m. Janet Sue Shearer, May 14, 1966; children: Susan M., Christopher R., David E., Sarah M. AB, U. Ky., 1966; JD, Harvard U., 1969. Bar: Ohio 1970. Jud. clk. U.S. Ct. Appeals for 6th Cir., Louisville, 1969-70; assoc. Taft, Stettinius & Hollister, Cin., 1970, ptnr., 1978—. Pres. Lighthouse Youth Svcs., Inc., Cin., 1985, Ky. YMCA Youth Assn., Frankfort, 2001; mem. exec. bd. Ky. Hist. Soc.; pres. Cin. Bar Found., 1991. Mem. ABA, Cin. Bar Assn. Republican. Presbyterian. Home: 215 Hilltop Ln Wyoming OH 45215-4121 Office: 1800 US Bank Tower 425 Walnut St Cincinnati OH 45202-3923 Office Phone: 513-357-9355. E-mail: rich@taftlaw.com.

RICH, S. JUDITH, public relations executive; b. Chgo., Apr. 14; d. Irwin M. and Sarah I. (Sandock) R. BA, U. Ill., 1960. Staff writer, reporter Economist ewspapers, Chgo., 1960—61; asst. dir. pub. rels. and communications Coun. Profit Sharing Industries, Chgo., 1961—62; dir. advt. and pub. rels. Chgo. Indsl. Dist., 1962—63; account exec., account supr., v.p., sr. v.p., exec. v.p. and nat. creative dir. Edelman Pub. Rels. Worldwide, Chgo., 1963—85; exec. v.p., dir. Ketchum Pub. Rels. Worldwide, Chgo., 1985—89, exec. v.p., exec. creative dir. USA, 1990—97, exec. v.p., chief creative officer worldwide, 1998—2001; pres. Rich Rels. A Creativity Consultancy, Chgo., 2002—. Frequent spkr. on creativity and brainstorming; workshop facilitator. Contbr. articles to popular mags. Mem. pub. rels. adv. bd. U. Chgo. Grad Sch. Bus., Roosevelt U., Chgo., DePaul U., Chgo., Gov.'s State U. Recipient Pub. Rels. All-Star award for Creativity, Inside PR mag., 1999. Mem. Pub. Rels. Soc. Am. (Silver Anvil award, judge Silver Anvil awards), Counselors Acad. of Pub. Rels. Soc. Am. (exec. bd.), Chgo. Publicity Club (8 Golden Trumpet awards). Avocations: theater, swimming, bicycling, racquetball. Office: Rich Rels A Creative Consultancy Ste 2603 2500 N Lakeview Ave Chicago IL 60614

RICHARD, HOWARD M., lawyer; b. Oak Park, Ill., Sept. 20, 1944; BA, Cornell U., 1965; LLB, Harvard U., 1968. Bar: Ill. 1968. Ptnr. Katten Muchin Rosenman, Chgo. Bd. editors Harvard Law Rev., 1967-68. Mem. ABA (sect. real property, probate and trust law), Chgo. Bar Assn. Office: Katten Muchin Rosenman 525 W Monroe St Ste 1900 Chicago IL 60661-3693 Home Phone: 847-432-7924; Office Phone: 312-902-5219. Office Fax: 312-577-8670. E-mail: howard.richard@kattenlaw.com.

RICHARD, PATRICK, science research administrator, nuclear scientist; b. Crowley, La., Apr. 28, 1938; married; two children. BS, U. Southwestern La., 1961; PhD, Fla. State U., 1964. Rsch. assoc. prof. nuclear physics U. Wash., 1965-68; from asst. prof. to prof. physics U. Tex., Austin, 1968-72; dir. J.R. MacDonald Lab. physics dept., disting. prof. Kansas State U., 1972—. Cons. Columbia Sci. Rsch. Inst., 1969-71. Mem. Am. Phys. Soc. Office: Kans State U J R MacDonald Lab Physic Dept Cardwell Hall Manhattan KS 66506 also: Kans State U Physics Dept Cardwell Hall Manhattan KS 66506

RICHARDS, BRIAN F., lawyer; b. Oaklawn, Ill., Jan. 23, 1967; BS in Finance with highest honors, U. Ill., 1989; JD, U. Va., 1992. Bar: Ill. 1992. Atty. Winston & Strawn, Chgo.; v.p., gen. counsel sofware devel. co.; ptnr., co-chair Mergers and Acquisitions Practice Katten Muchin Zavis Rosenman, Chgo. Mem. Children's Inner City Edn. Fund, Chgo., Holy Angels Adv. Bd., Chgo.; mem. bd. trustees Cristo Rey Jesuit High Sch.; mem. adv. coun. to bd. trustees Holy Trinity High Sch.; active Philo J. Carpenter Elem. Sch., Chgo. Recipient Armour Scholar, U. Va. Sch. Law. Mem.: Order of the Coif. Office: Katten Muchin Zavis Rosenman 525 W Monroe St Chicago IL 60661-3693 Office Phone: 312-902-5234. Office Fax: 312-577-8764. E-mail: brian.richards@kattenlaw.com.

RICHARDS, CARLYLE EDWARD, lawyer; b. Deadwood, SD, July 21, 1935; BA, Northwestern U., 1957; LLB, U. S.D., 1960. Bar: S.D. 1960. Law clk. to judge U.S. Dist. Ct., 1960-61; pvt. practice Aberdeen, SD, 1961—; U.S. magistrate, 1971-2000. Mem. S.D. Bar Assn., Brown County Bar Assn. Office: 222 Midwest Bldg Aberdeen SD 57401 Address: PO Box 114 Aberdeen SD 57402-0114

RICHARDS, DANIEL WELLS, manufacturing executive; b. Taylor, Pa., Dec. 16, 1928; s. Daniel Wells and Bernice (Robling) R.; m. Helen Reilly, Feb. 10, 1979; children: Kenneth, Deborah, Thomas. BA, Dickinson Coll., 1950; postgrad., U. Pitts., 1953-54. Mgr. advt. prodn. Miller Machine Co., Pitts., 1954-55; mgr. sales promotion Gen. Paper Co., Pitts., 1955-57; advt. and product mgr. Harris Seybold Co., Cleve., 1957-67; v.p. mktg. Colwell Systems Inc., Champaign, Ill., 1967-86, pres., 1986-91; Disting. lectr., exec. in residence Ill. State U., 1991-93; pres. D.W. Richards & Assocs., Champaign, 1994—. Mem. Urbana (Ill.) City Council, 1975-77; budget dir. Ill. Humanities Council, 1980-84; bd. dirs. United Way Champaign County, 1987-92, Sinfonia da Camert, 1987-95. Served to lt. U.S. Army, 1950-53. Unitarian Universalist. Home and Office: 3407 Mill Creek Ct Unit 8 Champaign IL 61822-8201

RICHARDS, JERRY LEE, academic administrator, religious studies educator; b. Lawrenceville, Ill., Nov. 4, 1939; s. Russell O. and Elvessa A. (Goodman) R.; m. Lee Ann, Apr. 25, 1986; children: Mark, Renee, Teresa, Angela. BA, Lycoming Coll., 1965; BD, Evang. Congregational Sch. Theology, 1967; MDiv, Garrett Theol. Sem., 1968; D in Ministry, St. Paul Sch. Theology, 1975. Ordained to ministry Meth. Ch., 1968. Pastor chs., Pa., 1960-65, Williamsport, Iowa, 1965-70; mem. faculty Iowa Wesleyan U., Mt Pleasant, 1970-85, prof. religion, dir. responsible social involvement Mt. Pleasant, 1975-85, v.p. for acad. affairs, 1975-82, pres., 1982-85; dir. gift planning U. Wis., Eau Claire, 1985—. Pres. Mental Health Inst. Aux., Mt. Pleasant, 1976. Mem. Phi Alpha Theta Office: U Wis Office of Devel 215 Schofield Hall Eau Claire WI 54702-4004

RICHARDS, JON, state legislator; b. Waukesha, Wis., Sept. 5, 1963; BA, Lawrence U., 1986; JD, U. Wis., 1994. Pvt. practice law; mem. Wis. State Assembly, Madison, 1998—, mem. fin. instns. and ins. coms., mem. tax and spending limitations com., mem. transp. projects commn. Tchr. English, Japan. Mem. Friends of WOWR, Milw., Wis. Women's Bus. Initiative Corp., New Brady St. Area Orgn.; mem. election staff Sen. Herb Kohl, 1994. Mem.: Milw. Bar Assn. Democrat. Presbyterian. Office: State Capitol Rm 6 N PO Box 8953 Madison WI 53708-8953 Address: 1823 N Oakland Ave Milwaukee WI 53202

RICHARDSON, BRENT EARL, otolaryngologist; BA in Biology and Anthropology, Washington U., St. Louis, 1986; MD with honors, U. Wash., Seattle, 1990; MS in Otolaryngology, U. Minn., Mpls., 1996. Cert. Am. Bd. Otolaryngology, 1997. Fellow, laryngology and voice Loyola U. Med. Ctr., Maywood, Ill., 1996—97; intern, dept. surgery Hennepin County Med. Ctr., Minneapolis, Minn., 1990—91, resident, dept. surgery, 1991—92; resident, dept. otolaryngology U. Minn., Minneapolis, 1992—96; attending physician, surgical svc., divsn. otolaryngology Hines VA Med. Ctr., Ill., 1997—2002; attending physician Foster McGaw Hosp., Loyola U. Med. Ctr., Maywood, Ill., 1997—2003; asst. prof., otolaryngology Stritch Sch. Medicine, Loyola U. Chgo., Maywood, Ill., 1997—2003; attending physician Advocate Good Samaritan Hosp., Downers Grove, Ill., 2003—; laryngologist Bastian Voice Inst., Downers Grove, Ill., 2003—. Cons., surgical svc., divsn. otolaryngology Hines VA Med. Ctr., Ill., 2002—03; invited presenter in the field. Contbr. articles to profl. jours. Named to Guide to America's Top Physicians, Consumers' Research Coun. Am., 2003. Mem.: Nat. Assn. Teachers of Singing, Am. Speech-Language-Hearing Assn., Dysphagia Rsch. Soc., Christian Soc. Otolaryngology/Head and Neck Surgery, Christian Med. Assn., Chgo. Laryngological and Otological Soc., Am. Acad. Otolaryngology/Head and Neck Surgery, Am. Acad. Med. Ethics, Phi Kappa Phi, Alpha Omega Alpha. Office: Bastian Voice Inst 3010 Highland Pkwy Ste 550 Downers Grove IL 60515 Office Phone: 630-724-1100. Office Fax: 630-724-0084.*

RICHARDSON, ERIC W., lawyer; b. Ft. Thomas, Ky., 1973; BA, Thomas More Coll., 1993; JD, U. Cin., 1996. Bar: Ohio 1996, Ky. 1997, US Supreme Ct., US Ct. of Appeals Sixth Cir., US Ct. of Appeals Fed. Cir., US Dist. Ct. Southern Dist. Ohio, US Dist. Ct. Eastern Dist. Ky., US Dist. Ct. Western Dist. Ky. Law clerk Hon. R. Guy Cole, Jr., US Ct. of Appeals Sixth Cir., 1996—97; ptnr. Vorys, Sater, Seymour and Pease LLp, Cin. Named one of Ohio's Rising Stars, Super Lawyers, 2006. Mem.: Ky. Bar Assn., Cin. Bar Assn., Order of Coif, Delta Epsilon Sigma. Office: Vorys Sater Seymur and Pease LLP Atrium Two Ste 2000 221 E Fourth St PO Box 0236 Cincinnati OH 45202-0236 Office Phone: 513-723-4019. Office Fax: 513-852-7885. E-mail: ewrichardson@ussp.com.

RICHARDSON, JOHN THOMAS, academic administrator, clergyman; b. Dallas, Dec. 20, 1923; s. Patrick and Mary (Walsh) R. BA, St. Mary's Sem., Perryville, Mo., 1946; S.T.D., Angelicum U., Rome, Italy, 1951; MA, St. Louis U., 1954. Prof. theology, dean studies Kenrick Sem., St. Louis, 1951-54; lectr. Webster Coll., 1954; dean Grad. Sch. DePaul U., Chgo., 1954-60, exec. v.p., dean faculties, 1960-81, pres., 1981-93; prof. DePaul U. Coll. Law, Chgo., 1955; chancellor DePaul U., Chgo., 1993—. Vis. mem. theology faculty Christ the King Major Sem., Nyeri, Kenya, East Africa, 1997—. Trustee DePaul U., Chgo., 1954-93, life trustee, 1993-. Office: De Paul U 1 E Jackson Blvd Chicago IL 60604-2287

RICHARDSON, KATHY KREAG, state legislator; Student, Purdue U. Clk. Hamilton County Circuit Ct., 1984-91; mem. from 29th dist. Ind. State Ho. of Reps., 1992—. Mem. cts. and criminal code com., judiciary com., local govt., cityies and towns, county and twp. com., election and apportionment com., family and children com. Mem. Hamilton County Bd. Election Surps. Mem. Assn. Clks. Circuit Cts., Assn. Ind. Counties, Noblesville C. of C. (bd. dirs.), Noblesville H.S. Alumni Assn. (sec.), Kiwanis, Soroptimist, Republican Woman, Hamilton County Hist. Soc. Home: 1363 Grant St Noblesville IN 46060-1925 Office: Ind Ho of Reps State Capitol Indianapolis IN 46204

RICHARDSON, LAUREL WALUM, sociology educator; b. Chgo., July 15, 1938; d. Tyrrell Alexander and Rose (Foreman) R.; m. Herb Walum, Dec. 27, 1959 (div. 1972); children: Benjamin, Joshua; m. Ernest Lockridge, Dec. 12, 1981. AB, U. Chgo., 1955, BA, 1956; PhD, U. Colo., 1963. Asst. prof. Calif. State U., Los Angeles, 1962-64; postdoctoral fellow Sch. Medicine Ohio State U., Columbus, 1964-65, asst. prof. sociology, 1970-75, assoc. prof., 1975-79; prof. sociology Sch. Medicine Ohio State U., Columbus, 1979—, prof. cultural studies, edn. policy and leadership; asst. prof. sociology Denison U., Granville, Ohio, 1965-69. Mem. editl. bd. Jour. Contemporary Ethnography, Symbolic Interaction, Gender and Soc., Qualitative Sociology, The Sociol. Quar.; disting. lectr. Acad. Creative Writing, U. Iceland, 2005; Miegunyah disting. fellow U. Melbourne, 2006. Author: Dynamics of Sex and Gender, 1977, 3d edit. 1988, The New Other Woman, 1985, Die Neve Andere, 1987, A Nova Outra Mulher, 1987, Writing Strategies: Reaching Diverse Audiences, 1990, Gender and University Teaching: A egotiated Difference, 1995; editor: Feminist Frontiers, 1983, 5th edit., 2000, Fields of Play Constructing an Academic Life, 1997 (Charles H. Cooley award for best sociology book 1998), (with Ernest Lockridge) Travels with Ernest: Crossing the Literary/Sociological Divide, 2004, Last Writes: A Daybook for a Dying Friend, 2007; assoc. editor Symbolic Interaction; author more than 100 rsch. articles and papers. Ford Found. fellow, 1954-56; NSF dissertation fellow, 1960-62; post doctoral fellow Vocat. Rehab., Columbus, 1964; grantee Ohio Dept. Health, 1986-87, Nat. Inst. Edn., 1981-82, NIMH, 1972-74, NSF, 1963-64, NEH, 1992; internat. fellow Copenhagen, 2000, Iceland, 2005, Miengalow Fellow, Melbourne, 2006; recipient Disting. Affirmative Action award Ohio State U., 1983, Feminist Mentor award, 1998. Mem. Am. Sociol. Assn. (com. on coms. 1980-81, com. on pub. info. 1987—), North Ctrl. Sociol. Assn. (pres. 1986-87), Sociologists for Women in Soc. (coun. mem. 1978-80), Ctrl. Ohio Sociologists for Women in Soc. (past pres.), Women's Poetry Workshop, Soc. for Study of Symbolic Interaction (publs. com.). Avocations: hiking, poetry, book arts. E-mail: richardson.9@osu.edu.

RICHARDSON, RALPH C., dean; BS, Kans. State U., 1969, DVM, 1970. Intern Purdue U.; resident small animal internal medicine dept. U. Mo., Columbia, 1973; asst. prof. medicine dept. small animal clinics Purdue U., West Lafayette, Ind., 1976—80, assoc. prof. medicine dept. small animal clinics, 1980—84, prof. internal medicine and comparative oncology, 1984—98, head dept., 1987—98; dean Kans. State U. Coll. Vet. Medicine, Manhattan, 1998—. Capt. Vet. Corps US Army. amed Paws Vet. of Yr., Ind. Divsn. Am. Cancer Soc., 1996. Mem.: Am. Assn. Vet. Clinicians, Am. Assn. Vet. Med. Colls., Am. Animal Hosp. Assn., Am. Coll. Vet. Internal Medicine (diplomate internal medicine, diplomate oncology), Am. Vet. Medicine Assn. Office: Kans State U Coll Vet Medicine 101 Trotter Hall Manhattan KS 66506-5601

RICHARDSON, RUDY JAMES, toxicology and neurosciences educator; b. May 13, 1945; BS magna cum laude, Wichita State U., 1967; Sc.M., Harvard U., 1973, Sc.D., 1974. Diplomate Am. Bd. Toxicology. Rsch. geochemist Columbia U., NYC, summer 1966; NASA trainee SUNY, Stony Brook, 1967-70; rsch. biochemist Med. Research Council, Carshalton, England, 1974-75; asst. prof. U. Mich., Ann Arbor, 1975-79, assoc. prof., 1979-84, prof. toxicology, 1984—, assoc. prof. neurotoxicology neurology dept., 1987—, Dow prof. toxicology, 1998—, acting dir. toxicology program, 1993, dir., 1994-99, dir. toxicology tng. program, 2003—. Vis. scientist Warner-Lambert Co., Ann Arbor, 1982-83; vis. prof. U. Padua, Italy, 1991; cons. NAS, Washington, 1978-79, 84, Office Tech. Assessment U.S. Congress, 1988-90, Nat. Toxic Substance Disease Registry, 1990—; mem. sci. adv. panel on neurotoxicology EPA, 1987-89; chmn. work group on neurotoxicity guidelines Orgn. for Econ. Coop. and Devel., 1990, Nat. Inst. Orgnl. Safety and Health, 1990, 94; mem. acute cholinesterase risk assessement expert panel Internat. Life Scis. Inst., 1996; mem. steering com., working group Risk Sci. Inst., 1997; presenter sci. adv. panel U.S. EPA, 1998-99, WHO, Geneva, 1998; chair expert panel on dichlorvos neurotoxicity and cholinesterase inhibition SRA Internat., Washington, 1998-99, guest panel mem. Mich. Environ. Sci. Bd., 2003—; invited spkr. in field. Mem. editorial bd. Neurotoxicology, 1980—, Toxicology and Indsl. Health, 1986—, Toxicology and Applied Pharmacology, 1989-97, Jour. Toxicology and Environ. Health, 1997—; contbr. articles to profl. jours., chpts. to books. Mem. Mich. Lupus Found., Ann Arbor, 1979—. Grantee NIH, 1977-86, 95—, EPA, 1977-86, U.S. Civilian R & D Found., 1996—, U.S. Army Rsch. Office, 2002—. Mem. AAAS, Am. Coll. Toxicology, Soc. Toxicology (pres. neurotoxicology sect. 1987-88, councillor 1988-89, co-recipient Best Paper award 2003), Soc. for Neurosci., Am. Diabetes Assn., Am. Chem. Soc., Internat. Soc. Neurochemistry, Internat. Brain Rsch. Orgn. Achievements include co-discoverer (with B.R. Dudek) of lymphocyte neuropathy target esterase (NTE); development of lymphocyte NTE as biomarker of exposure to neuropathic organophosphates; refinement of NTE assay for use in neurotoxicity testing; use of protein mass spectrometry in mechanistic toxicology and sensor development.

RICHARDSON, SHIRLEY MAXINE, editor; b. Rising Sun, Ind., May 3, 1931; d. William Fenton and Mary (Phillips) Keith; m. Arthur Lee Richardson, Feb. 11, 1950; children: Mary Jane Hunt, JoDee Mayfield, Steven Lee Richardson. Pers. mgr. Mayhill Pubs., Knightstown, Ind., 1967-87, prodn. mgr., 1975-87, editor, 1967-87; info. staff, assoc. editor Ind. Farm Bur., Inc., 1987-89, dir. info. and pub. rels., 1989-94; genealogy editor AntiqueWeek, 1996-2001; exec. editor Knightstown Banner, 2001—. Avocations: travel, reading, boating, quilting. Home: 366 E Carey St Knightstown IN 46148-1208 Office: 24 N Washington St Knightstown IN 46148-1242 Office Phone: 765-345-2292.

RICHARDSON, WILLIAM CHASE, retired foundation executive; b. Passaic, NJ, May 11, 1940; s. Henry Burtt and Frances (Chase) R.; m. Nancy Freeland, June 18, 1966; children: Elizabeth, Jennifer. BA, Trinity Coll., 1962; MBA, U. Chgo., 1964, PhD, 1971; PhD (hon.), from 11 Univs. including, U. Mich., 2006. Rsch. assoc., instr. U. Chgo., 1967-70; asst. prof. health services U. Wash., 1971-73, assoc. prof., 1973-76, prof., 1976-84, chmn. dept. health services, 1973-76, assoc. dean Sch. Pub. Health, 1976-81, acting dean, 1977, 78, dean Grad. Sch., vice provost, 1981-84; exec. v.p., provost, prof. dept. family and community medicine Pa. State U., 1984-90; pres. Johns Hopkins U., Balt., 1990-95, pres., prof. emeritus, 1995, prof. dept. health policy, mgmt., 1990-95, prof. emeritus, 1995—; pres., CEO W.K. Kellogg Found, Battle Creek, Mich., 1995—2005; prof. policy Kalamazoo Coll., 2005—. Cons. in field; bd. dir. CSX Corp., Bank of NY, Exelon Corp.; chmn., bd. dir. Coun. on Founds.; chmn. Kellogg Trust, 1996-2006. Author: books, including Ambulatory Use of Physicians Services, 1971, Health Program Evaluation, 1978; contbr. articles to profl. jours. Mem. adv. com. Rand Corp. Kellogg Coll. fellow, Oxford U., 1965—. Mem.: Nat. Acad. Arts and Scis., Nat. Acad. Scis., Inst. Medicine, Am. Public Health Assn.

RICHARDSON-LOWRY, MARY, lawyer; b. June 26, 1957; BA, U. San Francisco State, 1981; JD, Tex. So. U., 1984. Bar: U.S. Dist. Ct. (No. Dist. Ill.) 1986, Ill. Supreme Ct. 1986. Asst. corp. counsel Dept. Law City of Chgo., 1987—92, sr. supervising atty., 1992—94; asst. to Mayor Richard M. Daley City of Chgo., 1994—98, commr. dept. bldgs., 1998—2002; ptnr. Mayer, Brown, Rowe & Maw LLP, Chgo., 2002—. Chmn. Cmty. Devel. Commn. City of Chgo., 2004—. Office: Mayer Brown Rowe Maw Llp 230 S La Salle St Ste 400 Chicago IL 60604-1407 Office Phone: 312-701-8442. Office Fax: 312-706-8427. E-mail: mbrl@mayerbrown.com.

RICHERSON, HAL BATES, internist, allergist, immunologist, educator; b. Phoenix, Feb. 16, 1929; s. George Edward and Eva Louise (Steere) R.; m. Julia Suzanne Bradley (dec. 1996), Sept. 5, 1953; children: Anne, George, Miriam, Julia, Susan. BS with distinction, U. Ariz., 1950; MD, Northwestern U., 1954. Diplomate Am. Bd. Internal Medicine, Am. Bd. Allergy and Immunology, Bd. Diagnostic Lab. Immunology; lic. physician, Iowa. Intern Kansas City (Mo.) Gen. Hosp., 1954-55; resident in pathology St. Luke's Hosp., Kansas City, 1955-56; trainee in neuropsychiatry Brooke Army Hosp., San Antonio, 1956; resident in medicine U. Iowa Hosps., Iowa City, 1961-64, fellow in allergy and immunology, 1964-66; fellow in immunology Mass. Gen. Hosp., Boston, 1968-69; instr. internal medicine U. Iowa Coll. Medicine, Iowa City, 1964-66, asst. prof., 1966-70, assoc. prof., 1970-74, prof., 1974-98, prof. emeritus, 1998—; acting dir. divsn. allergy/applied immunology U. Iowa Hosps. and Clinics, Iowa City, 1970-72, dir. allergy and clin. immunology sect., 1972-78, dir. divsn. allergy and immunology, 1978-91; gen. practice, asst. to Gen. Surgeon Ukiah, Calif., 1958; gen. practice medicine Holbrook, Ariz., 1958-61. Vis. lectr. medicine Harvard U. Sch. Medicine, Boston, 1968-69; vis. prof., rsch. scientist U. London and Brompton Hosp., 1984; prin. investigator Nat. Heart, Lung and Blood Inst., 1971-94, mem. pulmonary diseases adv. com., 1983-87; prin. investigator Nat. Inst. Allergy and Infectious Diseases, 1983-94; dir. Nat. Inst. Allergy and Infectious Diseases' Asthma and Allergic Diseases Ctr., U. Iowa, 1983-94; mem. VA Merit Rev. Bd. in Respiration, 1981-84; mem. com. NIH Gen. Clin. Rsch. Ctrs., 1989-93; mem. rev. reserve NIH, 1993-98; mem. bd. sci. advisors Merck Inst., 1990-94; presenter lectures, seminars, continuing edn. courses; mem. numerous univ., coll. and hosp. coms., 1970—; cons. Merck Manual, 1982, 87, 92, 96-97. Contbr. numerous articles and revs. to profl. jours., chpts. to books; reviewer Sci., Jour. Immunology, Jour. Allergy and Clin. Immunology, Am. Rev. Respiratory Disease, New Eng. Jour. Medicine, Ann. Internal Medicine. Served to capt. U.S. Army, 1956-58. NIH fellow 1968-69. Fellow ACP (Laureate award 1996), Am. Acad. Allergy Asthma & Immunology (Disting. Clinician award 1998); mem. AMA (mem. residency and rev. com. for allergy and immunology; mem. accreditation coun. for grad. med. edn. 1980-85, vice-chmn. 1984-85), AAAS, Iowa Med. Soc., Iowa Thoracic Soc. (chmn. program com. 1964-65, 69-71, pres. 1972-73, mem. exec. com. 1972-74), Am. Thoracic Soc. (bd. dirs. 1981-82, councilor assembly on allergy and immunology 1980-81, mem. nominating com. 1988-90), Iowa Clin. Med. Soc., Am. Fedn. Clin. Rsch., Am. Assn. Immunologists, Ctrl. Soc. Clin. Rsch. (chmn. sect. on allergy-immunology 1980-81, mem. coun. 1981-84), Alpha Omega Alpha. Avocations: reading, trombonist, swimming, scuba diving. Home: 331 Lucon Dr Iowa City IA 52246-3300 Office: U Iowa Health Care Dept Internal Medicine 200 Hawkins Dr Iowa City IA 52242-1009 Personal E-mail: richersonh@mchsi.com. Business E-Mail: hal-richerson@uiowa.edu.

RICHERT, PAUL, law educator; b. Elwood, Ind., Aug. 31, 1948; m. Catherine George Stanton, June 24, 1972; children: John, William. AB, U. Ill., Urbana, 1970, MS, 1971; JD, Tulane U., New Orleans, 1977. Bar: Ohio 1977. Asst. law libr. U. Akron, 1977-78, law libr., 1978-83, assoc. prof., 1983-87, prof. law, 1987—. Local bd. dirs. Selective Svc. sys. Co-author: Searching the Law, 3d edit., 2005. Mem. United Chs. of Christ. With U.S. Army, 1971-74. Mem. Am. Assn. Law Librs., Akron Bar Assn., ABA. Home: 2030 Ganyard Rd Akron OH 44313-6050 Office: Univ Akron Sch Law Library 302 Buchtel Common Akron OH 44325-2902 Home Phone: 330-867-8272; Office Phone: 330-972-7330. Business E-Mail: richert@uakron.edu.

RICHMAN, HAROLD ALAN, social welfare policy educator; b. Chgo., May 15, 1937; s. Leon H. and Rebecca (Klieman) R.; m. Marlene M. Forland, Apr. 25, 1965; children: Andrew, Robert. AB, Harvard U., 1959; MA, U. Chgo., 1961, PhD, 1969. Asst. prof., dir. Ctr. for Study Welfare Policy, Sch. Social Svc., U. Chgo., 1967-69, dean, prof. social welfare policy, 1969-78, Hermon Dunlap Smith prof., 1978—, dir. of ctr., 1978-81, dir. Children's Policy Rsch. Project, 1978-84, dir. Chapin Hall Ctr. for Children, 1985—2002, faculty assoc. Chapin Hall Ctr. for Children, 2002—, chmn. univ. com. on pub. policy studies, 1974-77. Chmn. Univ. Lab. Schs., 1985-88; cons. to gov. State of Ill., Edna McConnell Clark Found., 1984-95, Lilly Endowment, 1987-90, Ford Found., 1987-89; co-chair Aspen Roundtable on Cmty. Change, 1993—. Chmn. editl. bd. Social Svcs. Rev., 1970-79; contbr. articles to profl. jours. Bd. dirs. Chgo. Com. Fgn. and Domestic Policy, 1969-78, S.E. Chgo. Commn., 1970—, Jewish Fedn. Met. Chgo., 1970-75, Ill. Facilities Fund, 1989-94, Welfare Coun. Met. Chgo., 1970-72, Erikson Inst. Early Childhood Edn., 1972-79, Nat. Urban Coalition, 1975-86, Family Focus, 1980-89, Jewish Coun. Urban Affairs, 1982-87, Ctr. for Study Social Policy, 1983-92, chmn., 2003—; bd. dirs. Nat. Family Resource Coalition, 1990-93, Pub./Pvt. Ventures, 1992-98, Benton Found., 1994-2004; bd. dirs. Israel Ctr. on Children, chmn., 1995-04; bd. dirs. Info. and Rsch Ctr., Amman, Jordan, 2001—, Michael Reese Health Trust, 2002—, bd. dirs. U. Capetown Childen's Inst., dep. chair, 2002—; mem. adv bd. John Gardner Ctr., Stanford U., 2003—; bd. dirs. Brookdale Inst., Jerusalem, 2004—, Interfaith Youth Core, 2005—, SEED Found., 2005-, Bull. Atomic Scientists, 2006—. White House fellow, Washington, 1965-66; recipient Disting. Svc. citation U.S. Dept. Health, Edn. & Welfare, 1970, Quantrell award U. Chgo., 1990. Mem. White House Fellows Assn. (v.p. 1976-77), Am. Pub. Welfare Assn. (bd. dirs. 1989-92). Home: 5715 S Dorchester Ave Chicago IL 60637-1726 Office: U Chgo Chapin Hall Ctr for Children 1313 E 60th St Chicago IL 60637-2830 Office Phone: 773-256-5176. Business E-Mail: hrichman@chapinhall.org.

RICHMAN, JOAN M., lawyer; b. Chgo., Dec. 15, 1965; Diploma in Internat. Bus., The Netherlands Sch. Bus., 1989; B of Commerce with distinction, McGill U., 1988; JD, Georgetown U., 1992. Bar: Ill. 1992. Summer assoc. Baker & McKenzie, Chgo., 1991, assoc., 1992—99, ptnr., 1999—. Office: Baker and McKenzie One Prudential Plz 130 E Randolph Dr Chicago IL 60601

RICHMAN, JOHN MARSHALL, lawyer, food products executive; b. NYC, Nov. 9, 1927; s. Arthur and Madeleine (Marshall) R.; m. Priscilla Frary, Sept. 3, 1951; children: Catherine Richman Wallace, Diana H. BA, Yale U., 1949; LLB, Harvard U., 1952. Bar: N.Y. 1953, Ill. 1973. Assoc. Leve, Hecht, Hadfield & McAlpin, NYC, 1952-54; mem. law dept. Kraft, Inc., Glenview, Ill., 1954-63, gen. counsel Sealtest Foods div., 1963-67, asst. gen. counsel, 1967-70, v.p., gen. counsel, 1970-73, sr. v.p., gen. counsel, 1973-75, sr. v.p. adminstrn., gen. counsel, 1975-79, chmn. bd., chief exec. officer, 1979, Dart & Kraft, Inc. (name changed to Kraft, Inc. 1986), Glenview, 1980; chmn. Kraft Gen. Foods, Glenview, Ill., 1988-89; counsel Wachtell, Lipton, Rosen & Katz, Chgo., 1990-98. Life bd. dirs. Evanston Northwestern Healthcare. Life trustee Chgo. Symphony Orch., Northwestern U.; bd. dirs. Chgo. Coun. Global Affairs, Lyric Opera Chgo., Norton Mus. Art, West Palm Beach. Fla. Mem. Coun. Ret. Chief Exec., Comml. Club, Chgo. Club, Casino Club (Chgo.), Westmoreland Country Club (Wilmette, Ill.), Old Elm Club (Highland Park, Ill.), Lost Tree Club (N. Palm Beach, Fla.), Racquet Club of Chgo. Congregationalist. Office: 179 E Lake Shore Dr Chicago IL 60611-1306 E-mail: johnrichman@att.net.

RICHMAN, LAWRENCE I., lawyer; b. Chgo., Aug. 8, 1954; s. Jack and Reggie (Heller) R. BA magna cum laude, Columbia U., 1974; JD, U. Chgo., 1977. Bar: Ill. 1977. Atty. McDermott Will & Emery, Chgo., 1977-80, Neal Gerber & Eisenberg, Chgo., 1980—. Named one of Top 100 Attys., Worth mag., 2006—07. Mem. ABA (generation shipping transfer tax com. 1990, recipient cert. of appreciation 1989), Chgo. Bar Assn. (chmn. trust law com. 1988-89), Am. Technion Soc. (bd. dirs. 1987), Phi Beta Kappa. Avocation: skiing. Office: Neal Gerber & Eisenberg LLP 2 N LaSalle St Ste 2200 Chicago IL 60602-3801 Office Phone: 312-269-8070. Office Fax: 312-750-6460. E-mail: lrichman@ngelaw.com.

RICHMAN, STEPHEN ERIK, retired lawyer, consultant; b. Austin, Tex., Mar. 10, 1945; s. Allen A. and Erika (Zimmerman) Richman; m. Frances Ellen Sharpe, Aug. 29, 1971; children: Joshua Eric, Wendy Michelle. BA magna cum laude, Amherst Coll., Mass., 1967; JD cum laude, Harvard U., Cambridge, Mass., 1970. Bar: Wis. 1972. Assoc. Webster Sheffield, NYC, 1970-72, Quarles & Brady, Milw., 1972-78, ptnr., 1978—2006; ret., 2006. With Richman Nonprofit Strategies, LLC, 2005—. Pres. Milw. Youth Symphony Orch., 1985—87; bd. dirs. Milw. Symphony Orch., 1995—2004, chmn., 2000—02; chmn. steering com. Milw. Youth Arts Ctr., 2003—05; pres. Milw. Jewish Fedn., 1996—98; bd. dirs. United Performing Arts Fund, Milw., 2007—. Mem.: Phi Beta Kappa. Home and Office: 1611 W Eastbrook Ct Mequon WI 53092

RICHMOND, JAMES GLIDDEN, lawyer; b. Sacramento, Feb. 20, 1944; s. James Gibbs and Martha Ellen (Glidden) R.; m. Lois Marie Bennett, Oct. 22, 1988; 1 child, Mark R. BS in Mgmt., Ind. U., 1966, postgrad., 1966-69, JD, 1969. Bar: Ind. 1969, Ill. 1991, U.S. Dist. Ct. (no. dist.) Ind. 1971, U.S. Dist. Ct. (so. dist.) Ind., 1969, U.S. Ct. Appeals (7th cir.) 1975, U.S. Tax Ct. 1980. Spl. agent FBI, 1970-74; spl. agent Criminal Investigation Divsn. IRS, 1974-76; asst. U.S. atty. no. dist. U.S. Atty. Office, Ind., 1976-80; assoc. Galvin, Stalmack & Kirschner, Hammond, Ind., 1980-81; pvt. practice Highland, Ind., 1981-83; ptnr. Goodman, Ball & Van Bokkelen, Highland, Ind., 1983-85; U.S. atty. no. dist. State of Ind., Hammond, 1985-91; spl. counsel to dep. atty. gen. of the U.S. U.S. Dept. Justice, Washington, 1990-91; mng. ptnr. Ungaretti and Harris, Chgo., 1991-92, ptnr., 1995—2002; exec. v.p., gen. counsel Nat. Health Labs., 1992-95; shareholder Greenberg Traurig, Chgo., 2002—. Practitioner-in-residence Ind. U. Sch. Law, Bloomington, 1989, 2003. Minority counsel senate republicans October Surprise Hearings, 1992. Named one of Best Lawyers Am., 2006—07. Fellow Am. Coll. Trial Lawyers; mem. Chgo. Inn of Ct. (pres., 2007—). Avocation: fly fishing. Office: Greenberg Traurig 77 W Wacker Dr Ste 2500 Chicago IL 60601 Home Phone: 630-910-8191; Office Phone: 312-456-5204. Business E-Mail: richmondj@gtlaw.com.

RICHMOND, RICHARD THOMAS, journalist; b. Parma, Ohio, May 16, 1933; s. Arthur James and Frances Marie (Visosky) R.; m. Charlotte Jean Schwoebel, Dec. 19, 1933; children: Kris Elaine, Leigh Alison, Paul Evan. AB, Washington U., St. Louis, 1961. Bur. mgr. UPI News Pictures, St. Louis, 1957-62; from asst. picture editor to editor color sect. Post-Dispatch, St. Louis, 1962-80, columnist, 1971—2002, editor calendar sect., 1983-94, asst. entertainment editor, 1995-96, prodn. coord. Get Out Mag. Clayton, Mo., 1996—2000; v.p. Golden Royal Enterprises, St. Louis, 1976-78; pres. Oroquest Press, St. Louis, 1977-80; dir. U.S. Mortgage & Investment Corp., Hilton Head Island, NC, 1977-81; pres. Magalar Mining, Texarkana, Ark., 1979-83. Co-author: Treasure Under Your Feet, 1974, In the Wake of the Golden Galleons, 1976, Diabetes: The Facts That Will Let You Regain Control of Your Life, 1986, Produced By Comtemporary, 2008; editor: You Can Be Rich By Thursday, 1997, Male Homemaker's Handbook, 1997. Bd. dirs. Coll. Fine Arts and Comm. U. Mo., St. Louis, 2003—07. Avocation: undersea treasure hunting. Home: 307 Lebanon Ave Belleville IL 62220-4126

RICHMOND, WILLIAM PATRICK, lawyer; b. Cicero, Ill., Apr. 5, 1932; s. Edwin and Mary (Allgier) R.; m. Elizabeth A., Jan. 9, 1954 (div.); children: Stephen, Janet, Timothy; m. Magda, June 8, 1992. AB, Albion Coll., 1954; JD, U. Chgo., 1959. Bar: Ill. 1959, N.Y. 1985. Assoc. Sidley & Austin, Chgo., 1960-67, ptnr., 1967-98, counsel, 1998—. Served with U.S. Army, 1954-56. Fellow Am. Coll. Trial Lawyers; mem. ABA, Soc. Trial Lawyers, Chgo. Bar Assn., Desert Forest Golf Club (Carefree, Ariz.), Ruth Lake Country Club (Hinsdale, Ill.). Republican. Methodist. Home: 4 Tartan Ridge Rd Burr Ridge IL 60527-8904

RICHTER, GLENN, retail executive; BBA, George Washington U.; MBA, Duke U. Various exec. level positions with Frito-Lay Co., McKinsey and Co.; pres., CEO Specialty Foods Corp., 1994—97; sr. v.p., corp. contr. Dade Behring, Deerfield, Ill., 1997-99, CFO, 1998—99; exec. v.p., CFO St. Paul Companies Inc., 1997—2000; v.p., controller Sears Roebuck, Hoffman Estates, Ill., 2000—02, senior v.p., CFO, 2002—05, exec. v.p., CFO, 2005—. Office: Sears Roebuck 3333 Beverly Rd Schaumburg IL 60179

RICHTER, JUDITH ANNE, pharmacologist, educator; b. Wilmington, Del., Mar. 4, 1942; d. Henry John and Dorothy Madelyn (Schroeder) R. BA, U. Colo., 1964; PhD, Stanford U., 1969. Postdoctoral fellow Cambridge (Eng.) U., 1969-70, U. London, 1970-71; asst. prof. pharmacology Sch. Medicine Ind. U., Indpls., 1971-78, assoc. prof. pharmacology and neurobiology, 1978-84, prof., 1984—. Vis. assoc. prof. U. Ariz. Health Sci. Ctr., Tucson, 1983; mem. biomed. rsch. rev. com. Nat. Inst. on Drug Abuse, 1983-87. Mem. edtl. bd. Jour. Neurochemistry, 1982-87; contbr. numerous articles to sci. jours. Fellow, Wellcome Trust, 1969—71; scholar, Boettcher Found., 1960—64. Mem. AAAS, Am. Soc. for Pharmacology and Exptl. Therapeutics (exec. com. neuropharmacology div. 1989-91), Am. Soc. for eurochemistry, Internat. Soc. for Neurochemistry, Soc. for Neurosci., Women in Neurosci., Assn. Women in Sci., Phi Beta Kappa, Sigma Xi. Achievements include research in neuropharmacology, especially barbiturates, neurobiology of mutant mice and dopaminergic systems, and regulation of sensory neuron glutamate release. Office: Ind U Sch Medicine 635 Barnhill Dr Indianapolis IN 46202-5126 Home Phone: 317-291-9222; Office Phone: 317-274-7593. Business E-Mail: jrichter@iupui.edu.

RICHTER, MITCH, state legislator; b. Suffrin, NY, Sept. 5, 1960; m. Julie Fee. BA Business, Black Hills State U., 1981. Rep. S.D. State Dist. 11, 1994—; Owner & operator Dairy Queen. Appropriations com. S.D. Ho. Reps. Address: 5801 W King Arthur Dr Sioux Falls SD 57106-0676 Office: SD Mem Ho of Reps State Captiol Pierre SD 57501

RICHTER, ROBERT C., retired automotive executive; V.p.-admin. Dana Corp., Toledo, 1997—98, v.p.-fin. and admin., 1998—99, v.p., CFO, 1999—2006; chmn. Dana Credit Corp., 2002.

RICKER, JON, retail executive; V.p. corp. sys. devel. Fed. Express; v.p., CIO BellSouth, Ltd., Inc., Columbus, Ohio, 1996—99; pres., CEO, cIO Ltd. Tech. Svcs., Columbus, 1999—. Office: Ltd Brands Three Ltd Pkwy Columbus OH 43230

RICKERT, JEANNE MARTIN M., lawyer; b. Cambridge, Mass., May 13, 1953; d. Robert Torrence and Margaret (Mutchler) Martin; m. Scott Edwin Rickert, Aug. 19, 1978. BA, Cornell U., 1975; JD, Case Western U., 1978. Bar: Ohio 1980, admitted to practice: US Dist. Ct. (No. Dist.) Ohio 1980. Law clk. to Judge Leroy J. Contie Jr. U.S. Dist. Ct. Ohio, Akron, 1978-80; assoc. Jones, Day, Reavis & Pogue, Cleve., 1980-86; ptnr. Jones & Day, Cleve., 1987—. Author: The Limited Liability Company in Ohio: 1994 Senate Bill 74, with Commentary and Practice Pointers, 1994; co-author (with John Currivan): Ohio Limited Liability Companies, 1999. Mem.: ABA, Ohio State Bar Assn. (corp. law com. 1985—), Cleve. Bar Assn., Order of the Coif. Office: Jones Day Reavis & Pogue N Point 901 Lakeside Ave E Cleveland OH 44114-1190 Office Phone: 216-586-7220. Office Fax: 216-579-0212. Business E-Mail: jmrickert@jonesday.com.

RICKETTS, JOHN JOE, brokerage house executive; b. Nebraska City, Nebr., July 16, 1941; s. Donovan Platte and Florence Marie (Erhart) R.; m. Marlene Margaret Volkmer, June 15, 1963; children: J. Peter, Thomas, Laura. BA in Econ., Creighton U., 1969. Counselor Father Flannagan's Boys Home, Boys Town, Nebr., 1967—68; with sales dept. Dean Witter & Co., Omaha, 1968—74; investment counselor Ricketts & Co., Omaha, 1974—75; pres. Ameritrade Inc., Omaha, 1975—82, CEO, 1981—99, 2000—01, co-CEO, 1999—2000; chmn. TD Ameritrade Holding Corp. (formerly Ameritrade Inc.), Omaha, 2001—. Bd. dirs. TD Ameritrade Holding Corp. (formerly Ameritrade Inc.), 1981—. Named one of Forbes' Richest Americans, 2006. Republican. Roman Catholic. Office: TD Ameritrade Holding Corp 4211 S 102d St Omaha NE 68127*

RICORD, KATHY, diversified financial services company executive; Grad., Denison U.; degree in City and Regional Planning and Bus. Adminstrn., Ohio State U. With Nationwide Mutual Ins. Co., 1986—, asst. to CEO, 1997—99, sr. v.p. mktg. and strategy, 2002—03, exec. v.p., chief mktg. officer, 2003—. Office: ationwide Mutual Ins Co One Nationwide Plaza Columbus OH 43215-2220

RIDENOUR, JOEY, medical association administrator, operations research specialist; BSc in Nursing, Ariz. State U.; MN, U. Phoenix. RN Ariz. COO Maricopa Health Sys., Phoenix, 1975—95; exec. dir. Ariz. State Bd. Nursing, 1995—98; pres. Nat. Coun. State Bds. of Nursing, Chgo., 1998; exec dir Ariz State bd of nursing. Pres. Ariz. State Bd. Nursing, Phoenix, 1986—89, 1994—95; adj. faculty Ariz. State U. Recipient Disting. Achievement award, Am. Soc. Pub. Adminstrn., Ariz. State U. Coll. Nursing, U. Phoenix; fellow, Wharton. Office: Boards of Nursing Natl Coun of State 111 E Wacker Dr Ste 2900 Chicago IL 60601-4277

RIDGEWAY, LUANN, state legislator; m. Richard Ridgeway. Student, Am. U., 1977; BA in History and Polit. Sci., William Woods and Westminster Coll., 1978; student, Oxford U., Eng., 1978; JD, U. Mo., 1981. Mem. Mo. State Ho. of Reps. Dist. 35, 1992—2002, Mo. State Senate, Mo., 2004—. Mem. criminal law com., judiciary com., urban affairs com., chldn., youth and families com., civil and administrv. law com., joint com. on administrv. rules. Mem. Mo. Bar Assn. Home: 19405 Platte County Line Rd Smithville MO 64089-8798

RIDGLEY, THOMAS BRENNAN, lawyer; b. Columbus, Ohio, Apr. 29, 1940; s. Arthur G. and Elizabeth (Tracy) R.;); children: Elizabeth, Jennifer, Kathryn; m. Lisa Lester, Nov. 27, 1999. BA, Princeton U., NJ, 1962; JD with honors, U. Mich., 1965. Bar: Pa. 1965, Ohio 1968, U.S. Dist. Ct. (so. and no. dists.) Ohio, U.S. Dist. Ct. (ea. dist.) Pa., U.S. Ct. Appeals (6th, 3d and 10th cirs.), U.S. Supreme Ct. Assoc. Dechert, Price and Rhoades, Phila., 1965-67; ptnr. Vorys, Sater, Seymour and Pease LLP, Columbus, 1967—. Author: Interstate Conflicts and Cooperation, 1986, (with others) Fending Off Corporate Raiders, 1987. Bd. dirs., mem. exec. com. United Way of Franklin County, Columbus, 1986-98; bd. dirs. Cmty. Shelter Bd., 1992-98, pres. 1997-98; bd. dirs. Columbus Bar Found., 1992-99, pres., 1998. Fellow Am. Coll. Trial Lawyers. Office: Vorys Sater Seymour and Pease LLP 52 E Gay St Columbus OH 43215-3161 Office Phone: 614-464-6229. Business E-Mail: tbridgley@vssp.com.

RIEDL, JOHN ORTH, retired university dean; b. Milw., Dec. 9, 1937; s. John O. and Clare C. (Quirk) R.; m. Mary Lucille Priestap, Feb. 4, 1961; children: John T., Ann E., James W., Steven E., Daniel J. BS in Math. magna cum laude, Marquette U., Milw., 1958; MS in Math., U. Notre Dame, 1960, PhD in Math., 1963; postgrad., Northwestern U., 1963; degree (hon.), MedCentral Coll. Nursing, 2003. Asst. prof. math. Ohio State U., Columbus, 1966-70, assoc. prof., 1970—2003, asst. dean Coll. Math. and Phys. Sci., 1969-74, assoc. dean, 1974-87, acting dean, 1984-86, spl. asst. to provost, 1987—2003, dean, dir. Mansfield (Ohio) Campus, 1988—2003, exec. dean regional campus, 1988—2003, assoc. prof. emeritus, 2003—; ret., 2003; interim pres. MedCentral Coll. ursing, 2007—. Panelist sci. edn. NSF, 1980-91; cons. Ohio Dept. Edn., 1989, Ohio bd. regents subsidy cons., 1991, 95, 97, 99, 2001, 03; bd. dirs. Richland County Univ. and Coll. Access Network, 2001—, pres. Richland County bus. adv. coun., 2004—; trustee Mansfield Meml. Homes, 2007—. Pres., v.p. exec. com. Univ. Cmty. Assn., Columbus, 1970-78; mem. edn. commn. St. Peter's Schs., Mansfield, 1989-95; trustee Rehab. Svc. N. Ctrl. Ohio, Mansfield, 1990-99, v.p., 1993-94, pres., 1995-97; pres. Ohio Assn. Regional Campuses, 1993-94; co-chair capital campaign St. Peter's Schs., 1998. Recipient Faculty Svc. award, Nat. U. Continuing Edn. Assn., 1988, Creative Programming award, 1988; NSF grad. fellow, 1960—62. Mem. Math. Assn. Am. (chair com. on minicourse 1981-87), Downs Am. Chestnut Found. of Ohio (bd. dirs. 2001-04), Rotary Internat. (bd. dirs., pres.-elect, pres.) C. of C. (bd. dirs.). Democrat. Roman Catholic. Avocations: fishing, woodworking, gardening. Home: 789 Clifton Blvd Mansfield OH 44907-2284 Office: Ohio State U 1680 University Dr Mansfield OH 44906-1547 Business E-Mail: riedl.1@osu.edu.

RIEDTHALER, WILLIAM ALLEN, risk management professional; b. Cleve., May 13, 1948; s. Robert Wilbert and Jean Margaret (Trojanowski) R.; m. Janet Louise Clark, Nov. 10, 1973; children: Jennifer Margaret, Valerie Gretchen. AS in Law Enforcement, Cuyahoga C.C., 1968; BA in Pub. Safety Adminstrn., Kent State, 1974, BA in Criminal Justice Studies, 1974; EMBA in Healthcare, Baldwin-Wallace Coll., 2000; PhD in Internat. Police Studies (hon.), Baghdad Police Coll., Iraq, 2006. Cert. instr. and peace officer; cert. tchr., Ohio, Fla., Tex., Mich.; accredited healthcare fraud investigator. Police cadet Cleve. Police Dept., 1967-69, patrolman, 1969-74, detective, 1974-81, sgt. police, 1981-84; assoc. security advisor Cleve. Electric Illuminating Co., 1984-87, investigator, 1987-90; security advisor Centerior Energy Corp., Cleve., 1990-93, supr. claims Independence, 1993-96, mgr. risk mgmt., 1996-98; dir. spl. risk programs N.Am. Benefits Network, Inc., Rocky River, Ohio, 1998—2003; dir. mktg. and audit investigations Watermark Audit Group, Cleve., 2003—05; investigator Lorain County Prosecutor's Office, 2005—. Instr. gambling and vice Case Western Res. U., Cleve., 1979—90, Cleve. Police Acad., Cleve., 1974—, Ohio Peace Officers Tng. Acad., 1976—2004, Cuyahoga County Sheriffs Officers Acad., Cleve., 1981—98, Shaker Heights (Ohio) Police Acad., 1990—98; prof. Criminal Justice and Bus. Programs Tiffin U., 2002—; internat. polic trainer Iraq-MPRI, 2005—06; momey laundering analyst Key Bank, 2007—. Author: An Enforcement Guide to Carnival Games Gambling and Fraud, 1981, An Enforcement Guide to Monetary Operated Gambling Devices or Slot Machines, 2002; contbr. articles to profl. jours. Spl. dep. sheriff Cuyahoga County Sheriff's Office, Cleve., 1985—2004; past pres. Metrop. Crime Bur; trustee, 2d v.p. Metrop. Crime Clinic, 2d v.p., 2002—04, 1st v.p., 2005—; trustee, 2d v.p. Cleve. Crime Clinic, 1999—2003; bd. govs. Nat. Healthcare Antifraud Assn., 1999—2003. Recipient Patrolman of Yr. award Cleve. Exchange Club, 1979. Mem. Am. Soc. Indsl. Security, Met. Crime Clinic (v.p. 1992-93, 2001-04, pres. 1994-95), German Am. Police Assn., Fraternal Order of Police, Cleve. Claims Assn. Republican. Avocations: photography, hiking, swimming. Home: 8525 Olde Eight Rd # 4 Northfield OH 44067 Office: Watermark Audit Group 20325 Center Ridge Rd Ste 330 Rocky River OH 44116 Personal E-mail: larsonegames@yahoo.com. Business E-Mail: wriedthaler@enforcementguide.com.

RIEGER, MITCHELL SHERIDAN, lawyer; b. Chgo., Sept. 5, 1922; s. Louis and Evelyn (Sampson) Rieger; m. Rena White Abelmann, May 17, 1949 (div. 1957); 1 child, Karen Gross Cooper; m. Nancy Horner, May 30, 1961 (div. 1972); stepchildren: Jill Levi, Linda Hanan, Susan Perlstein, James Geoffrey Felsenthal; m. Pearl Handelsman, June 10, 1973; stepchildren: Steven Newman, Mary Ann Moseley, Nancy Halbeck. AB, Northwestern U., 1944; JD, Harvard U., 1949. Bar: Ill. 1950, U.S. Dist. Ct. (no. dist.) Ill. 1950, U.S. Supreme Ct. 1953, U.S. Ct. Mil. Appeals 1953, U.S. Ct. Appeals (7th cir.) 1954. Legal asst. Rieger & Rieger, Chgo., 1949-50, assoc., 1950-54; asst. U.S. atty. No. Dist Ill., Chgo., 1954-60, 1st asst., 1958-60; assoc. gen. counsel SEC, Washington, 1960-61; ptnr. Schiff Hardin & Waite, Chgo., 1961—, sr. counsel, 1998—. Instr. John Marshall Law Sch., Chgo., 1952—54. Contbr. articles to profl. jours. Mem. Chgo. Crime Commn., 1964—, bd. dirs., 1998—; pres. Park View Home Aged, 1969—71; bd. dirs. Spertus Mus. Judaica, 1987—91, mem. vis. com., 1991—2005; Rep. precinct committeeman Highland Park, Ill., 1964—68. Served to lt. (j.g.) USNR, 1943—46, PTO. Fellow: Am. Coll. Trial Lawyers; mem.: FBA (pres. Chgo. chpt. 1959—60, nat. v.p. 1960—61), ABA, 7th Cir. Bar Assn., Am. Judicature Soc., Ill. Bar Assn., Chgo. Bar Assn., Vail Racquet Club, Lawyers Club Chgo., Standard Club, Phi Beta Kappa. Jewish. Avocations: photography, skiing, sailing. Office: SchiffHardin LLP 6600 Sears Tower Chicago IL 60606 Office Phone: 312-258-5644. Personal E-mail: msheridanr@aol.com. Business E-Mail: mrieger@schiffhardin.com.

RIEGSECKER, MARVIN DEAN, pharmacist, state senator; b. Goshen, Ind., July 5, 1937; s. Levi and Mayme (Kauffman) R.; m. Norma Jane Shrock, Aug. 3, 1958; children: Steven Scott, Michael Dean. BA in Pharmacy, U. Colo., 1967. Pharmacist Parkside Pharmacy, Goshen, Ind., 1967-73, Walgreens, Goshen, 1994-96, Meijer, Goshen, 1998—2004; pharmacist, mgr. Hooks Drugs, Inc., Goshen, 1973-94; coroner Elkhart County, Goshen, 1977-84; mem. Ind. Senate from 12th dist., Indpls., 1988—; pharmacy cons., 2003—07. Bus. affairs cons. Goshen Health Sys., 1997-98. Rep. commr. Elkhart County, 1985-88; bd. commrs. pres., 1987-88; past adv. bd. dirs. Oaklawn Hosp.; past chmn. Michiana Area Coun. of Govts. Mem. Ind. Pharm. Assn. Republican. Mennonite. Avocation: jogging. Home: 1814 Kentfield Way Goshen IN 46526-5610 Office: Ind Senate Statehouse 200 W Washington St Indianapolis IN 46204-2728

RIELLY, JOHN EDWARD, educational association administrator; b. Rapid City, SD, Dec. 28, 1932; s. Thomas J. and Mary A. (Dowd) R.; m. Elizabeth Downs, Dec. 28, 1957 (marriage annulled 1976); children: Mary Ellen, Catherine Ann, Thomas Patrick, John Downs; m. Irene Diedrich, Aug. 1, 1987. BA, St. John's U., Collegeville, Minn., 1954; postgrad. (Fulbright scholar), London Sch. Econs. and Polit. Sci., 1955-56; PhD, Harvard U., 1961. Faculty dept. govt. Harvard U., 1958-61; with Alliance for Progress programs Dept. State, Washington, 1961-62; fgn. policy asst. to Sen. then Vice Pres. Hubert Humphrey, Washington, 1963-69; cons. office European and internat. affairs Ford Found., NYC, 1969-70; sr. fellow Overseas Devel. Council, Washington, 1970-71; exec. dir. Chgo. Council on Fgn. Relations, 1971-74, pres., 1974—2001. Adj. prof. Northwestern U., 2001—; vis. prof. Grad. Sch. Internat. Rels. U. Calif., San Diego, 2003-; cons. NSC; adv. bd. Grad. Sch. Arts and Scis., Harvard U. Alumni Assn.; bd. dirs. Am. Coun. on Germany, Nat. Com. on U.S.-China Rels., China Coun. of Asia Soc., Am. Ditchley Found., Trilateral Commn., commn. on U.S.-Brazilian Rels.; past pres. Nat. Coun. Comty. World Affairs Orgns. Contbr. articles to profl. jours.; editor: American Public Opinion and U.S. Foreign Policy, 1975, 2d edit., 1979, 83, 87, 91, 95, 99; editl. bd. Fgn. Policy Quar., 1974—. Former trustee St. John's U. Recipient Legion d'Honneur, France, Distinguished Service Cross, Germany, Commendatore of the Italian Republic, Bernardo O'Higgins Award, Chile, The Golden Decoration, Austria, European Friendship Award, European Union, Order of Leopold (Belgium), Nat. Hon. Southern Cross, Brazil. Mem.: Council on Fgn. Relations, N.Y.C. Home: 2021 Kenilworth Ave Wilmette IL 60091-1519 Office: Ctr for Internat & Comparative Studies 1902 Sheridan Rd Evanston IL 60208 Office Phone: 847-467-4409.

RIENDEAU, DIANE, secondary school educator; Teacher Barrington (Ill.) H.S., Barrington, Ill., 1985—. Recipient Innovative Teaching Grants Program, Am. Assn. of Physics Teachers, 1992.

RIES, THOMAS G. (TORCHY), former state legislator; m. Janet Ries; 7 children. Student, U. S.D. Cir. ct. judge; mem. S.D. Ho. Reps., 1984-88, 93-97, mem. judiciary com. and local govt. com.; mem. judiciary and transp. coms. Home: 1617 3rd Ave NE Watertown SD 57201-2001

RIESEBERG, LOREN, botanist, educator; BA, Southern Coll., Tenn., 1981; MS, U. of Tenn., Knoxville, 1984; PhD., Wash. State. u., 1987. Rsch. scientist Rancho Santa Ana Botanic Garden, Claremont, Calif., 1987—93; asst. prof. Claremont Grad. Sch., 1987—93; assoc. prof. biology Ind. U., Bloomington, Ind., 1993—97; dir. Plant Sci. Program, 1996—; prof. biology Ind. U., Bloomington, Ind., 1997—. Contbr. scientific papers more than 150 articles; editor (chief): (text book) Molecular Ecology, 1999. Recipient George R Cooley award in Plant Systematics, 1990, David Starr Jordan award in Evolution, Ecology, and Organismal Biology, 1998; grantee MacArthur Found. Fellowship, 2003. Fellow: Am. Acad. Arts & Sciences; mem.: Am. Genetics Assn. Office: Ind U dept of Biology 1001 E 3rd St Jordan Hall Bloomington IN 47405

RIESZ, PETER CHARLES, marketing educator, consultant; b. Orange, NJ, Apr. 30, 1937; s. Kolman and Ellen (Wachs) R.; m. Elizabeth Strider Dunkman, Dec. 28, 1968; children: Sarah Kathleen BS, Rutgers U., 1958; MBA, Columbia U., 1963, PhD, 1971. From asst. prof. to assoc. prof. U. Iowa, Iowa City, 1968-80, prof. mktg., 1980—2007, chmn. dept. mktg., 1981-87, Williams prof. tchg., 1994-97, prof emeritus, 2007—. Vis. prof. Boston U., 1974-75, Duke U., Durham, N.C., 1984-85; guest prof. Meiji U., Japan, summer 2004; cons. in field. Contbr. articles to profl. jours. Recipient Teaching Excellence award HON Industries, 1989; named MBA Prof. of Yr., 1990; Old Gold fellow U. Iowa, 1972. Mem. Am. Chem. Soc. Democrat. Presbyterian. Avocation: photography. Home: 2411 Tudor Dr Iowa City IA 52245-3638 Office: U Iowa Dept Mktg Tippie Coll Bus Adminstrn Iowa City IA 52242 Business E-Mail: peter-riesz@uiowa.edu.

RIFE, JACK, state legislator; b. Muscatine, Iowa, Apr. 10, 1943; m. Sharon Cooper. AA, Muscatine CC, Iowa, 1963; BS, Iowa State U., 1966. Agrl. advisor Liberty Trust Bank, 1968-73; farmer, 1973—; mem. Iowa Senate, Des Moines, 1982—, minority leader 74th, 75th and 76th Gen. Assembly, senate minority leader, mem. legis. coun., chair health and human rights com., mem. appropriations com., mem. bus. and labor rels. com., mem. local govt. com., mem. natural resources and environment com. Mem. United Meth. Ch.; past pres. Ext. Coun.; mem. legis. contact Bi-Sttae Econ. Devel. Adv. Com. With U.S. Army, 1966-68. Mem. Cattlemen's Assn., Am. Legion (polit. liaison), Pork Prodrs. (past pres.), Wilton Farm Bur., Muscatine Farm Bur., Cedar County Farm Bur., Alpha Gamma Rho. Republican. E-mail: jack_rife@legis.state.ia.us.

RIFKIN, LEONARD, metals company executive; b. NYC, Apr. 10, 1931; s. Irving W. and May (Goldin) Rifkin; m. Norma Jean Smith, Aug. 22, 1954 (dec. Jan. 1983); children: Daniel Mark, Richard Sheldon, Martin Stuart; m. Ariel Kalisky, Jan. 14, 1984. BS, Ind. U., Bloomington, 1952. Pres., CEO Omni Source Corp., Ft. Wayne, Ind., 1960—98, chmn., CEO, 1998—. Bd. dirs. Steel Dynamics, Butler, Ind., Qualitech Steel, Indpls. With US Army, 1956—58. Office: Omni Source Corp 1610 N Calhoun St Fort Wayne IN 46808-2762

RIGAUD, EDWIN JOSEPH, museum administrator; b. New Orleans, June 25, 1943; m. Carole Rigaud; children: Simone, Edwin, Eric. BS in Chemistry, Xavier U., Louisiana, 1965; MA in BioChemistry, U. Cincinnati, Ohio, 1972; LHD (hon.), Saint Joseph Coll., N. Kentucky U. Joined Procter & Gamble, 1965, v.p., gen. mgr. food and beverage products, 1992—95, v.p. govt. relations, 1996—2001; exec. dir. Nat. Underground Railroad Freedom Ctr., Cincinnati, 1996—2001, pres., 2001—; pres., CEO Enova Tech., LLC. Trustee emeritus Nat. Conference for Community & Justice, Cincinnati; bd. mem. Amistad Rsch. Ctr., Tulane U.; bd. dirs. Hebrew Union Coll., Tofa Bus. Consulting. Bd mem. Internat. Youth Inst.; adv. coun. Ohio River Way; bd. dirs. Knowledge Funding Ohio. Recipient Annual YMCA Black Achiever award, 1980. Mem.: Queen City Club (bd. dirs.), Jr. League Cin. (mentor). Office Phone: 513-557-5311.

RIGGINS, WILLIAM G., electric power industry executive; b. 1958; BS, JD, U. Kans.; MS, U. Mo., Kansas City. Bar: Mo. 1984. Atty. Great Plains Energy, Inc., Kansas City, Mo., 1991—92, staff atty., 1992—94, sr. atty., 1994—96, mng. atty., 1996, asst. gen. counsel, 1996—98, asst. chief legal officer, 1998—2000, gen. counsel, corp. sec., 2000—. Bd. mem. vice chmn. Swope Health Found. Office: Great Plains Energy Inc PO Box 418679 1201 Walnut St Kansas City MO 64141

RIGGLE, PATRICIA CAROL, special education educator; b. Gallipolis, Ohio, May 28, 1965; d. Pat and Freadith Fay Price; m. Richard Allan Riggle; children: Alana, Emily. BS, U. Rio Grande, 1989. Sub. tchr. Gallia County Local Schs., Gallipolis, Ohio, 1989—92, Gallipolis City Schs., Gallipolis, Ohio, 1989—92; tchr. Wellston City Sch., Wellston, Ohio, 1992—; child care provider Rio Grande Child Devel. Ctr., Rio Grande, Ohio, 1992—93. Vol. asst. dir. drama club Wellston HS, Wellston, Ohio, 1998—; career assessment adv. com. Gallia-Jackson-Vinton Joint Vocats. Sch. Dist., Rio Grande, Ohio, 2001—03. Youth Sunday sch. tchr. Okey Chapel, Scottown, Ohio, 1985—2000. Mem.: NEA, Ohio Farm Bur., Wellston Tchrs. Assn., Ohio Edn. Assn. Avocations: camping, travel, crafts. Home: 4767 Hannan Trace Rd Patriot OH 45658 Personal E-mail: star1@aceinter.net.

RIGGLEMAN, JAMES DAVID, former professional baseball team manager; b. Ft. Dix, NJ, Dec. 9, 1952; Degree in Physical Edn., Frostburg State U. Minor league baseball player, 1974-81; minor league baseball mgr., 1982-88, 91-92; dir. player devel., then coach St. Louis Cardinals, 1988-90; mgr. San Diego Padres, 1993-94, Chicago Cubs, 1995-99; bench coach Cleve. Indians, 1999—. Office: Cleve Indians 2401 Ontario St Cleveland OH 44115-4003

RIKLI, DONALD CARL, lawyer; b. Highland, Ill., June 16, 1927; s. Carl and Gertrude Louise (Stoecklin) R.; m. Joan Tate, Oct. 10, 1953; children: Kristine, David. AB, Ill. Coll., 1951; JD, U. Ill., 1953. Bar: Ill. 1953, U.S. Dist. Ct. (so. dist.) Ill. 1961, U.S. Ct. Appeals (7th cir.) 1968, U.S. Supreme Ct. 1974. Pvt. practice law, Highland, 1953-97. Atty. City of Highland, 1956-59; lectr. in field. Author: The Illinois Probate System, 1974, 75, 77, 78; bd. editors Illinois Real Property I, 1966, 71, Lawyers World, 1970-72, Law Notes, 1981-83, The Compleat Lawyer, 1985-87; contbr. over 60 articles to profl. jours. Mem. consistory United Ch. of Christ, 1960-62, 93-95. With U.S. Army, 1945-47. Fellow Am. Coll. Trust and Estate Counsel, Ill. Bar Found., Am. Bar Found.; mem. ABA (sec. chairperson gen. practice sect. 1990-91, Ho. of Dels. 1991-93, mem. coun. gen. practice sect. 1981-93, Sole Practitioner of Yr. 1990, posthumous Donald C. Rikli Solo Lifetime Achievement award gen. practice, solo practice and small firms sect.), Ill. Bar Assn. (chmn. Bill of Rights com. 1967-68, coun. estate planning probate and trust sect. 1976-81, sec. 1980-81), Madison County Bar Assn. (pres. 1966-67), Am. Acad. Estate Planning Attys. (bd. govs. 1994-95). Address: PO Box 366 Edwardsville IL 62025-0366

RILEY, ANTONIO, state legislator; b. Aug. 22, 1963; BA, Carroll Coll. Former staff asst. to Milw. mayor City of Milw., 1990-92; Wis. state rep. Dist. 18, 1992—. Mem. Midtown Neighborhood Assn. Office: State Capitol PO Box 8953 Madison WI 53708-8953

RILEY, JAMES B., JR., lawyer; b. Evanston, Ill., 1954; BA magna cum laude, U. Ill., 1976; JD cum laude, George Wash. U., 1979. CPA; bar: Ill. 1979, US Dist. Ct. No. Dist. Ill. 1979, US. Ct. Fed. Claims. Ptnr. Ross & Hardies (merged with McGuireWoods LLP in 2003), Chgo., 1985—2003, McGuireWoods LLP, Chgo., 2003—, co-chair firm health care dept., 2003—. Bd. dirs., past pres. Rebuilding Together North Suburban Chgo. Mem.: ABA (health law sect.), Ill. Assn. Hosp. Attorneys, Am. Health Lawyers Assn. Office: McGuireWoods LLP Ste 4100 77 W Wacker Dr Chicago IL 60601-1815 Office Phone: 312-750-8665. Office Fax: 312-920-6133. Business E-Mail: jriley@mcguirewoods.com.

RILEY, MICHAEL ROBERT, marketing and business development executive; b. Wisconsin Rapids, Wis., Apr. 17, 1938; s. Robert William and Anne Bates (Clark) R.; m. Judith Wood, Aug. 12, 1961; children: David T., Christopher W. BS, Hampton U., 1974; MS, Indsl. Coll. of Armed Forces, Washington, 1975; MPA, Golden Gate U., 1976, MBA, 1977. Commd. 2d lt. USAF, 1958, advanced through grades to lt. col., 1977, ret., 1979; mktg. exec. McDonnell Douglas Corp., St. Louis, 1979-90; pres. MRR Assocs., St. Louis, 1990—. Cons. Regional Commerce and Growth Assn., St. Louis, 1980-85, 90—. Pres. trustees Lake of the Woods Subdiv., St. Louis, 1980-85; pres. bd. dirs. St. Louis Chamber Chorus, 1986-88; mem. St. Louis Ambassadors, 1990—. Decorated D.F.C. with 2 oakleaf cluster, Bronze Star, Air medal with 23 oakleaf clusters; named Swimmer of the Yr., U.S. Amateur Athletic Union/NCAA, Portland, Oreg., 1956; recipient USAF Navigator Wings, Harlingen, Tex., 1959, USAF Pilot Wings, Chandler, Ariz., 1964, USN Wings, Beeville, Tex., 1971. Mem. Air Force Assn., Assn. Naval Aviation, Am. Mgmt. Assn., Internat. City Mgrs. Assn., Army Aviation Assn. Am., Am. Helicopter Soc., Navy League, River Rats. Avocations: sailing, golf, flying. Office: MRR Assocs 5846 Mango Dr Saint Louis MO 63129-2243

RILEY, ROBERT BARTLETT, landscape architect; b. Chgo., Jan. 28, 1931; s. Robert James and Ruth (Collins) R.; m. Nancy Rebecca Mills, Oct. 5, 1956; children: Rebecca Hill, Kimber Bartlett. PhB, U. Chgo., 1949; BArch, MIT, 1954. Chief designer Kea, Shaw, Grimm & Crichton, Hyattsville, Md., 1959-64; prin. partner Robert B. Riley (A.I.A.), Albuquerque, 1964-70; campus planner, asso. prof. architecture, dir. Center Environ. Research and Devel., U. N.Mex., 1966-70; prof. landscape architecture and architecture U. Ill., Urbana-Champaign, 1970—, head dept. landscape architecture, 1970-85, dir. PhD program, 1999—; vis. prof. Harvard U., 1996-97; prof. emeritus, dir. joint PhD program U. Ill., 1997—. Sr. fellow landscape architecture studies Dumbarton Oaks/Harvard U., 1992—, chmn. fellows, 1996—; mem. rev. panel landscape architects Fed. Civil Service-Nat. Endowment Arts. Assoc. editor Landscape mag., 1967-70; editor Landscape Jour., 1987—. Served with USAF, 1954-58. Nell Norris fellow U. Melbourne, Australia, 1977; project fellow Nat. Endowment Arts, 1985 Fellow Am. Soc. Landscape Architects (Nat. Honor award 1979); mem. Coun. of Educators in Landscape Architecture, pres. 1984-85, chmn. bd. dirs. 1985-86, Outstanding Educator award 1992, Pres.'s award 1994, chmn. editl. adv. bd. Landscape Architecture 1996-99), AIA (Design award Md. 1962, N.Mex. 1968, Environ. Svc. award N.Mex. 1970), Environ. Design Rsch. Assn. (chmn. bd. 1990-91, Career award 2003), Phi Beta Epsilon. Unitarian Universalist. Office: Univ Ill 101 Temple Buell Hall 611 E Lorado Taft Dr Champaign IL 61820-6921 Home: 407 E George Huff Dr Urbana IL 61801-6703 Business E-Mail: rbriley@uiuc.edu.

RILEY, ROBERT H., lawyer; BA, Denison U., 1975; JD, U. Chgo., 1978. Bar: Ill., Wis., U.S. Ct. Appeals (3d and 7th cir.), U.S. Dist. Ct. (no. and ctrl. dist.) Ill. Ptnr., chmn. Schiff Hardin LLP, Chgo. Mem.: ABA, State Bar Wis., Chgo. Bar Assn. Office: Schiff Hardin LLP 233 S Wacker Dr Ste 6600 Chicago IL 60606 Office Phone: 312-258-5664. Office Fax: 312-258-5600. E-mail: rriley@schiffhardin.com.

RILEY, SUSAN JEAN, retail executive; b. NYC, Apr. 6, 1958; d. Donald E. and Regina A. (Alt) R.; m. Clive D. Conley, June 22, 1985 (dec. 1994); 1 child, Emily Claire. BS, Rochester Inst. Tech., 1981; MBA, Pace U., 1987. CPA, N.Y. Acct. Goldstein & Viele, Rochester, NY, 1979-81; auditor Arthur Andersen & Co., Rochester, 1981-82; internal auditor Bristol Myers Squibb, NYC, 1982-83, sr. fin. analyst, 1983-84, mgr. finance, 1984-85, mgr. treas. ops., 1985-87; internat. fin. mgr. Tambrands Inc., Lake Success, N.Y., 1987-90, dir. fin. White Plains, N.Y., 1990-92, v.p. fin. Ams. divsn., 1992-94, v.p. corp. fin., 1994-95, CFO, 1995—97; sr. v.p., CFO Dial Corp., 1997—2000; CFO Mt. Sinai Med. Ctr., NY, 2002—04, Abercrombie & Fitch Co., 2004—05. Named Fin. Exec. of Yr. Inst. Mgmt. Accts., 1995, one of Acad. of Women Achievers YWCA of N.Y., 1994. Mem. Fin. Execs. Inst. Avocations: youth soccer coach, needlepoint, collecting doll house furniture. Office: Abercrombie & Fitch 6301 Fitch Path New Albany OH 43054

RILEY, WILLIAM JAY, federal judge; b. Lincoln, Nebr., Mar. 11, 1947; s. Don Paul and Marian Frances (Munn) R.; m. Norma Jean Mason, Dec. 27, 1965; children: Brian, Kevin, Erin. BA, U. Nebr., 1969, JD with distinction, 1972. Bar: Nebr. 1972, US Dist. Ct. Nebr. 1972, US Ct. Appeals (8th cir.) 1974; cert. civil trial specialist Nat. Bd. Trial Advocacy, 1994-2004. Law clk. US Ct. Appeals (8th cir.), Omaha, 1972-73; assoc. Fitzgerald, Schorr Law Firm, P.C., LLO, Omaha, 1973-79; shareholder Fitzgerald, Schorr Law Firm, Omaha, 1979—2001; judge US Ct. Appeals (8th cir.), 2001—. Adj. prof. trial practice Creighton U. Coll. Law, Omaha, 1991—, Nebr. Law Sch., Lincoln, 2006-; chmn. fed. practice com. Fed. Ct., 1992-94; mme. criminal law com. Jud. Conf. US, 2005—. Scoutmaster Boy Scouts Am., Omaha, 1979—89, scout membership chair Mid. Am. coun., 1995—98, trustee, 2001—. Recipient Silver Beaver award Boy Scouts Am., 1991. Fellow Am. Coll. Trial Lawyers (chair state com. 1997-99), Nebr. State Bar Found.; mem. Am. Bd. Trial Advs. (Nebr. chpt. pres. 2000), Nebr. State Bar Assn. (chmn. ethics com. 1996-98, ho. of dels. 1998—, profl. com. 2002—), Omaha Bar Assn. (treas. 1997-98, pres. 2000-01), Robert M. Spire Inns of Ct. (master 1994—2001, counselor 1997-98, 2007-, jud. mem. 2001-07), Order of Coif, Phi Beta Kappa. Republican. Methodist. Avocations: reading, hiking, bicycling. Office: Roman L Hruska US Courthouse 111 S 18th Plaza Ste 4303 Omaha NE 68102-1325 Office Phone: 402-661-7575.

RINDEN, DAVID LEE, clergyman; b. Lake Mills, Iowa, Aug. 1, 1941; s. Oscar Henry and Iva (Stensrud) R.; m. Gracia Elizabeth Carlson, Sept. 11, 1966; children: Jonathan, Elizabeth, Amy. BA, Moorhead State U., 1964; diploma, Luth. Brethren Sem., 1966; postgrad., Seattle Pacific U., 1973. Ordained to ministry Luth. Ch., 1967. Pastor Bethesda Luth. Ch., Eau Claire, Wis., 1968-72, Maple Pk. Luth. Ch., Lynnwood, Wash., 1972-79; v.p. Ch. of the Luth. Brethren of Am., Fergus Falls, Minn., 1991—; editor Faith & Fellowship, Fergus Falls, Minn., 1979-2000; exec. dir. Faith and Fellowship Press Ch. of the Luth. Brethren of Am., Fergus Falls, 1979-2000; pastor Gethsemane Lutheran Ch., Rochester, Minn., 2000—. Chmn. com. on commitment Ch. of Luth. Brethren, Fergus Falls, 1981-82, com. on role of women in ch., 1984-86, chmn. com. on 90th anniversary, chmn. bd. publs., 1968-78. Editor: Explanation of Luther's Small Catechism, 1988; author: Biblical Foundations, 1981. Founding com. JAIL, Inc., Fergus Falls, 1991; pres. bd. dirs. Fergus Falls Fed. Community Credit Union, 1987-2000. Mem. Fergus Falls Ministerial Assn. (sec. 1989-90, v.p. 1991-92, pres. 1992-93), Kiwanis (pres. 1994-95, lt. gov. 1996-97). Home: 1925 Century Valley Rd NE Rochester MN 55906-7705 Office: Gethsemane Lutheran Ch 2204 22d St NW Rochester MN 55901

RINDLER, ROBERT, academic administrator; b. NYC, May 21, 1948; BArch, The Cooper Union, 1970; M in Environ. Design, Yale U., 1972; Mgmt. Devel. Program, Harvard U., 1993-95. Chair art dept. U. Vt., Burlington, 1975-79; dean of students Boston Arch. Ctr., 1980-86; assoc. provost R.I. Sch. Design, Providence, 1986-94; dean Sch. Art The Cooper Union, NYC, 1994—2004; pres. Milw. Inst. of Art & Design, 2005—. One man shows include Pace U., N.Y., 1972, U. Vt., 1980, Harvard U., 1985, R.I. Sch. Design, 1990, Richard DeMarco Gallery, Edinborough, Scotland, Boston Archtl. Ctr., Yale U. Art Gallery. Mem. art steering com. R.I. State Coun. Arts, Providence, 1992-94. Grantee NEA, 1973, 74, Vt. Coun. Arts, 1977, Mass. Counc. Arts, 1980. Mem. Nat. Assn. Schs. Art and Design, Coll. Art Assn., Internat. Coun. Fine Arts Deans, Assn. Ind. Schs. Art and Design (bd. dirs. 1994—). Office: Milw Inst Art & Design 273 E Erie St Milwaukee WI 53202 E-mail: rindler@niad.edu.

RING, ALVIN MANUEL, pathologist, educator; s. Julius and Helen (Krolik) R.; m. Cynthia Joan Jacobson, Sept. 29, 1963; children— Jeffrey, Melinda, Heather. BS, Wayne State U., 1954; MD, U. Mich., 1958. Intern Mt. Carmel Hosp., Detroit, 1958-59; resident in pathology Michael Reese Hosp., Chgo., 1960-62; asst. pathologist Kings County Hosp., Bklyn., 1962-63; assoc. pathologist El Camino Hosp., Mountain View, Calif., 1963-65; chief pathologist, dir. labs. St. Elizabeth's Hosp., Chgo., 1965-72, Holy Cross Hosp., Chgo., 1972-87, Silver Cross Hosp., Joliet, Ill., 1990—. Instr. SUNY, 1962-63, Stanford U., 1963-65; asst. prof. pathology U. Ill., Chgo., 1966-69, assoc. prof., 1969-78, prof., 1978—; adj. clin. prof. No. Ill. U., 1981-87; adj. prof. med. edn. U. Ill. Coll. Medicine, 1988—; chmn. histotech. Nat. Accrediting Agy. for Clin. Lab Scis., 1977-81; mem. spl. adv. com. Health Manpower, 1966-71; pres. Spear Computer Users Group, 1981-82; mem. adv. com. Mid-Am. chpt. ARC, 1979-85; pres. Pathology and Lab Cons., Inc., 1985—; adj. prof., med. dir. Med. Tech., Moraine Valley C.C., 1994—; originator, coord. pathology, med. decision-making courses Nat. Ctr. for Advanced Med. Edn., 1981—, others; co-coord. computer courses Midwest Clin. Conf., 2000—. Author: Laboratory Correlation Manual, 1968, 82, 86, Laboratory Assistant Examination Review Book, 1971, Review Book in Pathology, Anatomic, 1986, Review Book in Pathology, Clinical, 1986; mem. editorial bd. Lab. Medicine, 1975-87; contbr. articles to med. jours. Fellow: Am. Soc. Clin. Pathology, Coll. Am. Pathology (insp. 1973—, ins. com. 2002—06, membership com. 2005—06, PathPac bd. dirs. 2007—, adv. com. on health care delivery); mem.: AMA, Assn. Brain Tumor Rsch. (cons.), Am. Assn. Blood Banks, Chgo. Pathol. Soc. (censor 1980—88, exec. com. 1985—89, program com. 1987—), Ill. Pathol. Soc. (trustee 1997—), Chgo. Med. Soc. (alt. councilor 1980—85), Ill. Med. Soc., Exec. Svc. Corps (exec. cons. 1988—), Phi Lambda Kappa (chpt. pres.). Home: 100 Graymoor Ln Olympia Fields IL 60461-1213 Office: Silver Cross Hosp 1200 Maple Rd Joliet IL 60432-1497

RING, GERALD J., real estate developer, insurance company executive; b. Madison, Wis., Oct. 6, 1928; s. John George and Mabel Sarah (Rau) R.; m. Armella Marie Dohm, Aug. 20, 1949; children: Michael J., James J., Joseph W. Student public schs., Madison. With Sub-Zero Freezer Co., Madison, 1948-70, mfr.'s rep., 1954-70; founder, chmn. bd. Parkwood Hills Corp., Madison, from 1965; founder, pres. Park Towne Devel. Corp., Madison, from 1969, Ring Devel. Co., 1992—. Bd. dirs. CUNA Mut. Ins. Soc., CUNA Mut. Ins. Group, CUNA Mut. Investment Corp., CUDIS Ins. Soc., all Madison, 1968-98, exec. com., 1973-83, chmn. bd., 1979-81; bd. dirs. CUMIS Ins. Soc., mem. exec. com., 1973-83, chmn. bd., 1977-79; bd. dirs. CMCI Corp., mem. exec. com., 1974-83, chmn. bd., 1981-83; treas. CUNADATA Corp., 1974-81; bd. dirs. Wis. Credit Union League, 1958-79, pres., 1965-67; mem. Wis. Credit Union Rev. Bd., 1967-83, chmn., 1973-76, 82-83; bd. dirs. CUNA Credit Union Nat. Assn., Inc., 1964-81, League Life Ins. Co., League Gen. Ins. Co., Southfield, Mich., CUNA Mut. Fin. Svcs. Corp., Century Ins. Co. Am., Waverly., Iowa. Chmn. Greater Madison C. of C., 1980, bd. dirs., 1976-89, v.p. econ. devel., 1983-85, v.p. govtl. affairs, 1985-89, mem. capital fund raising com., 1983—, chmn. 1983-86; mem. Mayor's Emergency Housing Com., 1984-85; chmn. fin. com. St. Patrick's Congregation, 1983-89; bd. dirs. Cath. Charities of Madison, 1995—, pres., 1996-99; bd. dirs. Future Madison Housing Fund, 1997—, pres, 2005—. Served with USMC, 1951-53. Mem. Aircraft Owners and Pilots Assn. Lodges: Rotary. (bd. dirs. 1981-83). Roman Catholic. Home: 607 Farwell Dr Madison WI 53704-6029 Office: 402 S Gammon Rd Madison WI 53719-1002

RING, HERBERT EVERETT, retired management executive; b. Norwich, Conn., Dec. 19, 1925; s. Herbert Everett and Catherine (Riordan) R.; m. Marilyn Elizabeth Dursin, May 21, 1955 (dec. Jan. 1994); children: Nancy Marie, Herbert Everett. BA, Ind. No. U., 1971, MBA, 1973; AMP, Harvard U., 1981. V.p. ops. Ogden Foods, Inc., Toledo, 1963-74, sr. v.p. Boston, 1974-75; v.p. concessions SportSvc. Corp., Buffalo, 1976-78, sr. v.p., 1978-80, pres., 1980-83, bd. dir.; pres. Universal Mgmt. Concept Counseling, Sylvania, Ohio, 1983—2003; prin. Hysen Group II, Livonia, Mich., 1991-95. Counselor L.A. Olympic Concessions Food Svc., 1984, Phila. Meml. Stadium, 1985, Del. North Cos. Internat. London Eng., 1985-86, Chgo. Stadium Corp., 1989-92, Buffalo Sabres N.Y., 1992, Fine Host Inc. Greenwich Ct., 1993, Delaware North of Australia Ltd., 1994, Temp DNC Health Support Ltd., Wellington, New Zealand, 1995, Fanfare Enterprises, 1997, Geneva Lakes Kennel Club, Delavan, Wis., 1997, St. Francis Health Care Ctr., Greenspring, Ohio, 1998, Detroit Opera House, 2000; bd. dirs. Greenfield Restaurant Co., Inc., Letheby and Christopher Ltd., Reading, Berkshire, Eng., Air Terminal Svcs., Inc., The Aud Club, Inc., Bluegrass Turf Svc., Inc., Concession Suppliers, Inc., Cosel Drive-In Theatre, Inc., G&H Sports Concessions, Inc., Hazel Park Parking, Inc. Mem. Toledo Mus. Art., 1985-92. Sgt. Air Corps U.S. Army, 1944-46, ETO, USAF, 1950-51. Mem.: N.W. Ohio Restaurant Assn. (bd. dirs. 1990—93), Internat. Assn. Auditorium Mgrs., Am. Culinary Fedn. Inc. Roman Catholic. Home and Office: 5540 Radcliffe Rd Sylvania OH 43560-3740

RING, LEONARD M., lawyer, writer; b. Taurage, Lithuania, May 11, 1923; came to U.S., 1930, naturalized, 1930; s. Abe and Rose (Kahn) R.; m. Donna R. Cecrle, June 29, 1959; children: Robert Steven, Susan Ruth Student, N.Mex. Sch. Mines, 1943-44; LLB, DePaul U., 1949, JD; LLD (hon.), Suffolk U., 1990. Bar Ill. 1949. Spl. asst. atty. gen. State Ill., Chgo., 1967-72; spl. atty. Ill. Dept. Ins., Chgo., 1967-73; spl. trial atty. Met. San. Dist. Greater Chgo., 1967-77; lectr. civil trial, appellate practice, tort law Nat. Coll. Advocacy, San Francisco, 1971, 72; chmn. and spl. atty. com. jury instrns. Ill. Supreme Ct., 1967—. Nat. chmn. Attys. Congl. Campaign Trust, Washington, 1975-79. Author: (with Harold A. Baker) Jury Instructions and Forms of Verdict, 1972. Editorial bd. Belli Law Jour., 1983—; adv. bd. So. Ill. U. Law Jour., 1983—. Contbr. chpts. to books including Callaghan's Illinois Practice Guide, Personal Injury, 1988 and chpt. 6 (Jury Selection and Persuasion) for Masters of Trial Practice, also numerous articles to profl. jours. Trustee, Roscoe Pound-Am. Trial Lawyers Found., Washington, 1978-80; chmn. bd. trustees Avery Coonley Sch., Downers Grove, Ill., 1974-75. Served with U.S. Army, 1943-46 Decorated Purple Heart. Fellow Am. Coll. Trial Lawyers, Internat. Acad. Trial Lawyers, Internat. Soc. Barristers, Inner Circle Advs.; mem. Soc. Trial Lawyers, Am. Judicature Soc., Appellate Lawyers Assn. (pres. 1974-75), Assn. Trial Lawyers Assn. (nat. pres. 1973-74), Ill. Trial Lawyers Assn. (pres. 1966-68), Trial Lawyers for Pub. Justice (founder, pres. 1990-91), Chgo. Bar Assn. (bd. mgrs. 1971-73, 2d v.p. 1993), ABA (coun. 1983—, chair tort and ins. sect. 1989—, fed. jud. standing com. 7th cir. 1991—), Ill. Bar Assn., Kans. Bar Assn. (hon., life), Lex Legion Bar Assn. (pres. 1976-78), Met. Club, Plaza Club, Meadow Club, River Club, Monroe Club. Home: Ginger Creek 6 Royal Vale Dr Oak Brook IL 60523-1648 Office: Ill Supreme Ct PO Box 4987 Oak Brook IL 60522-4987

RING, TWYLA L., state legislator, newspaper editor; b. Sept. 15, 1937; m. Ardell Ring; 4 children. Student, Cambridge C.C. Mem. Minn. Senate from 18th dist., St. Paul, 1999—. Home: 8500 285th Ave NE North Branch MN 55056-6406

RINGEN, CATHERINE OLESON, linguistics educator; b. Bklyn., June 3, 1943; d. Prince Eric and Geneva Muriel (Leigh) Oleson; m. Jon David Ringen, Nov. 22, 1969; children: Kai Mathias, Whitney Leigh. Student, Cornell U., 1961-63; BA, Indiana U., 1970, MA, 1972, PhD, 1975. Vis. lectr. U. Minn., Mpls., 1973-74; asst. prof. U. Iowa, Iowa City, 1975-79, assoc. prof., 1980—, prof., chair linguistics, 1987—93, 2003—. Author: Vowel Harmony: Theoretical Implications, 1988; co-editor ordic Jour. Linguistics, 2001—; contbr. articles to profl. jours. Sr. Fulbright prof. Trondheim, Norway, 1980, Poznan, Poland, 1994-95. Mem. AAAS, Linguistic Soc. Am., Nordic Assn. Linguists, Phi Beta Kappa. Office: U Iowa Dept Linguistics Iowa City IA 52242 Office Phone: 319-335-0212. Business E-Mail: catherine-ringen@uiowa.edu.

RINGLER, JAMES M., computer services company executive; b. 1945; BS, U. Buffalo, 1967, MBA, 1968. Mgr., cons. Arthur Andersen & Co., 1968-76; v.p. appliance group Tappan Co., Mansfield, Ohio, 1976-78, gen. v.p., mgr. appliance div., 1978-87, pres., COO, 1987-90, also bd. dirs., 1987-90; exec. v.p. Premark Internat., Inc., Deerfield, Ill., 1990-92, pres., COO, 1992-96, pres., CEO, 1996—99, chmn., 1997—99; vice chmn. Ill. Tool Works, Inc., Glenview, 1999—2004; interim CEO NCR Corp., Dayton, Ohio, 2005, chmn., 2005—. Bd. dir. Union Carbide Corp., 1996—2001, Dow Chemical Co., 2001—, Corn Products Internat., 2001—, FMC Tech., 2001—, Autoliv Lic., 2002—, NCR Corp., 2003—. Bd. mem. Lyric Opera Chgo.; trustee Boys & Girls Club of No. Am., Midwest region. Office: NCR Corp 1700 S Patterson Blvd Dayton OH 45479

RINK, LAWRENCE DONALD, cardiologist; b. Indpls., Oct. 14, 1940; s. Joe Donald and Mary Ellen (Rand) R.; m. Eleanor Jane Zimmerly, Aug. 10, 1963; children: Scott, Virginia. BS, DePauw U., 1962; MD, Ind. U., 1966. Diplomate Am. Bd. Internal Medicine, Am. Bd. Cardiology, Critical Care Medicine. Clin. asst. prof. Ind. U. Med. Sch., Indpls., 1973-79, clin. assoc. prof., 1979-85, clin. prof. medicine, 1985—; cardiologist IMA, Inc., Bloomington, Ind., 1974—; med. dir. Ind. U. Human Performance Lab., 1994—; dir. cardiac rehab. Bloomington Hosp., 1976—, dir. cardiology, 1983—; CEO, chmn. bd. dirs. IMA Inc., 1995—. Physician Ind. U. Basketball Team, 1979—; dir. med. edn. Bloomington Hosp., 1976—; med. dir. Track and Field Pan Am. Games, 1987; U.S. Olympic Physician Olympic Sports Festival, 1989, World Univ. Games, 1990, Olympic Games, Barcelona, 1992, World Univ. Games, Daegu, Korea, 1993, Fukuoka, Japan, 1995, Korea, 1997, Majorca, Spain, 1999, Beijing, 2001, Korea, 2003, Innsbruck, 2005; N.Am. continent rep. Fed. Internat. Student Univ. Sports, pres., 2004—, pres. med. commn. Bd. dirs. J.O. Ritchie Soc., Ind. U. Med. Sch. Bd. dirs., dean's coun. Ind. U. Med. Sch., 1992—. Recipient Quality of Life award Major Bloomington, 1978; named Most Outstanding Flight Surgeon, USN, 1968, Most Outstanding Alumnus, Ind. U. Med. Sch., 1998. Fellow Am. Coll. Cardiology, Am. Heart Assn. (Corvitae award 2003), Am. Soc. Critical Care, Am. Coll. Sports Medicine; mem. AMA, Ind. U. Med. Alumnae Assn. (pres. 1986-87, exec. alumna coun.). Avocations: reading, writing, golf, tennis. Office: IMA Inc 550 Landmark Ave Bloomington IN 47403 E-mail: lrink@ima-md.com.

RINTAMAKI, JOHN M., automotive executive; BBA, U. Mich., 1964, JD, 1967. Bar: Mich. 1968, Pa. 1973. Sr. atty. internat. Ford Motor Co., 1978-84, assoc. counsel corp. and financings, 1984-86, asst. sec., assoc. counsel, 1986-92, sec., asst. gen. counsel, 1993-98, v.p., gen. counsel, sec., 1999-00, chief staff, 2000—. Office: Ford Motor Co One American Rd Dearborn MI 48126-1899

RION, JOHN HAYES, lawyer; b. Dayton, Ohio, Aug. 4, 1943; s. Paul West and Vera E. (Spitler) R.; m. Barbara Smith, July 31, 1965; children: Stacey, Jennifer, Jon Paul. BA, Ohio State U., 1965; JD, U. Toledo, 1969. Bar: Ohio 1970, U.S. Dist. Ct. (so. dist.) Ohio 1970, U.S. Ct. Appeals (6th cir.) 1983, U.S. Supreme Ct. 1977; cert. Criminal Trial Advocate, Nat. Bd. Trial Advocacy. Ptnr., Rion, Rion & Rion, Dayton, Ohio, 1969-78; v.p. Rion, Rion & Rion, L.P.A., 1978-88; pres. John H. Rion & Assocs., 1988-97; ptnr., chmn. Rion, Rion & Rion, L.P.A., Inc., Dayton, 1997—; lectr. in field. Contbr. articles to profl. jours. Mem. jud. selection com. Republican Com., 1974. Mem. NACDL (life), ABA, Ohio State Bar Assn. (faculty 1983, chmn. criminal justice com. 1989-91, mem. setting standards for bd. cert. com. 1999), Dayton Bar Assn. (Outstanding Service award 1977, 80, chmn. bar briefs 1975), Ohio Assn. Criminal Def. Lawyers (life, pres. 1989, chmn. 1990), Montgomery County Trial Lawyers (v.p. 1989-90, mem. bd. trustees 1990), Calif. Def. Lawyers Assn., Ohio Trial Lawyers Assn. Republican. Methodist (pres. Grace United Ch. Ushers Club 1982-84). Clubs: Dayton Racquet, Comos (pres. 1982-84), Briarwood Sportsman. Lodges: Masons (32 degree), Shriners. Avocations: fly fishing, tennis. Office: Rion Rion and Rion Ste 2150 (21st Fl) 130 W Second St Ltd Dayton OH 45402 Office Phone: 937-223-9133. E-mail: info@rionlaw.com.

RIORDAN, MICHAEL C., hospital administrator; b. NJ, 1959; BA in Liberal Arts and English, Columbia U., 1980, MA in Edn. and Psychology, 1981; M in Health Sys., Ga. Inst. Tech., 1986. Various positions Crawford Long Hosp., Atlanta; COO Emory U. Hosp. Sys., 1995—2000; exec. v.p. and COO U. Chgo. Hospitals, 2000—01, pres. and CEO, 2001—. With USMC, 1981—85. Office: U Chgo Hosps and Health Sys 5841 S Maryland Ave Chicago IL 60637

RIPLEY, JUDITH G., state agency administrator; Student, U. Cin.; LLB, Ind. U., Indpls., 1981. Mem. Ind. Utility Regulatory Commn., 1998—2005; dir. Ind. Dept. Fin. Instns., 2005—. Mem. fed.-state joint bd. jurisdictional separations FCC, 2003. Adv. coun. N.Mex. State U. Ctr. Pub. Utilities. Mem.: Conf. State Bank Suprs. (vice chmn. dist II, vice chmn. legis. com.). Office: Dept Fin Instns Ste 300 30 S Meridian St Indianapolis IN 46204 Office Phone: 317-232-3955.

RIPLEY, MICHAEL A., state representative; b. Ft. Wayne, Ind., Dec. 1, 1956; married. BA, Ball State U. Adams County (Ind.) Econ. Devel. Dir.; Adams County Commr., 1987—96; state rep. dist. 79 Ind. Ho. of Reps., Indpls., 1996—, ranking Rep. mem. corps. and small bus. com., mem. local govt. and tech., R & D coms. Ex officio mem. Adams County Child Protection Team; assoc. mem. Ind. Farm Bur. Mem.: Ft. Wayne Assn. Life Underwriters, Decatur C. of C. (bd. dirs.). Office: Ind Ho of Reps 200 W Washington St Indianapolis IN 46204-2786

RIPPLE, KENNETH FRANCIS, federal judge; b. Pitts., May 19, 1943; s. Raymond John and Rita (Holden) Ripple; m. Mary Andrea DeWeese, July 27, 1968; children: Gregory, Raymond, Christopher. AB, Fordham U., 1965; JD, U. Va., 1968; LLM, George Washington U., 1972, LLD (hon.), 1992. Bar: Va. 1968, NY 1969, US Supreme Ct. 1972, US Supreme Ct. 1972, DC 1976, Ind. 1984, US Ct. Appeals (7th cir.), US Ct. Mil. Appeals, US Dist. Ct. (no. dist.) Ind. Atty. IBM Corp., Armonk, NY, 1968; legal officer US Supreme Ct., Washington, 1972—73, spl. asst. to chief justice Warren E. Burger, 1973—77; prof. law U. Notre Dame, 1977—; judge US Ct. Appeals (7th cir.), South Bend, 1985—. Reporter Appellate Rules Com., Washington, 1978—85; commn. on mil. justice US Dept. Def., Washington, 1984—85; cons. Supreme Ct. Ala., 1983, Calif. Bd. Bar Examiners, 1981, Anglo-Am. Jud. Exch., 1977; adv. com. Bill of Rights to Bicentennial Constn. Commn., 1989; adv. com. on appellate rules Jud. Conf. US, 1985—90, chmn., 1990—93; chmn. adv. com. on appellate judge edn. Fed. Jud. Ctr., 1996—2003; mem. jud. conf. adminstrv. office US Cts. Com., 2003—06; mem. faculty Law Clerkship Inst., Pepperdine U., 2001—04; mem. vis. com. U. Chgo. Sch. Divinity, 2005—, U. Chgo. Sch. Law, 2005—; mem. com. on jud. resources Jud. Conf. U.S., 2006—. Author: Constitutional Litigation, 1984. With JAGC USN, 1968—72. Mem.: ABA, Am. Law Inst., Phi Beta Kappa. Office: US Ct of Appeals 208 US Courthouse 204 S Main St South Bend IN 46601-2122 also: Fed Bldg 219 S Dearborn St Ste 2660 Chicago IL 60604-1803

RIPPLINGER, GEORGE RAYMOND, JR., lawyer; b. East St. Louis, Apr. 19, 1945; s. George Raymond and Virginia Lee (Toupnot) R. AB, U. Ill., 1967, JD, 1970. Bar: Ill. 1970, U.S. Dist. Ct. (so. dist.) Ill. 1970, U.S. Ct. Appeals (7th cir.) 1970, U.S. Dist. Ct. (ctrl. dist.) Ill. 1972, U.S. Tax Ct. 1971, U.S. Claims Ct. 1973, U.S. Ct. Mil. Appeals 1985, U.S. Supreme Ct. 1973, U.S. Ct. Internat. Trade 1973, U.S. Dist. Ct. (ea. dist.) Mo. 1977, U.S. Ct. Appeals (8th cir.) 1977. Assoc. Meyer & Meyer, Belleville and Greenville, Ill., 1970-72; assoc. Meyer & Kaucher, 1972—73; sole practice Belleville, 1974; ptnr. Ripplinger & Walsh, Clayton, Mo., 1974-76, Ripplinger, Dixon & Johnston, Belleville, Ill., St. Louis, Scott AFB, and Bellvue, Neb., 1976-94; prin. George Ripplinger & Assocs., Belleville, 1994—2005; mng. mem. Ripplinger & Zimmer LLC, Belleville, 2006—. Mem. com. minimum continuing legal edn. Ill. Supreme Ct., 2005—. Bd. visitors Coll. Law U. Ill., 1979-86, pres., 1983-84; pres., bd. dirs. Ill. Legal Aid on Line, 2006-2008, bd. dirs. 2005-2008. Col. USAR, 1970-2001. Recipient Disting. Alumnus award, U. Ill., Coll. Law, 2006, BF Fellows award. Fellow Am. Bar Found., Ill. Bar Found. (bd. dirs. 1988-2004, treas. 1998-2004); mem. ABA (ho. of dels. 1989-93, 95-99, chmn. workers compensation com. 1985-88, divsn. dir. 1988-89, 95-99, mem. coun. 1989-93, 99-2003, sec. 1999-2000, vice-chmn. 2000-2001, chmn. 2001-02, gen. practice/solo and small firm divsn.), ATLA, Lawyers Trust Fund Ill. (bd. dirs. 1988-94), Ill. Bar Assn. (bd. govs. 1981-83, 87-93, sec. 1991-92), St. Clair County Bar Assn., Bar Assn. Met. St. Louis, Mo. Bar Assn., Ill. Trial Lawyers Assn. (bd. advs. 1993—), Land of Lincoln Legal Assistance Found. (bd. dirs. 1982-88, vice-chmn. 1987-88), Res. Officers Assn. Democrat. Office: Ripplinger and Zimmer LLC 2215 W Main St Belleville IL 62226-6668 Home Phone: 618-398-6112; Office Phone: 800-733-8333. Business E-Mail: george@ripplingerlaw.com.

RISK, RICHARD ROBERT, health care executive; b. Chgo., Sept. 15, 1946; s. Clement Albert and Mary Catherine (Clarke) R.; m. Rebecca Ann Sandquist, Jan. 11, 1969 (div. Sept. 1984); children: Michael, Daniel, Laura; m. Louise L. Lawson, Dec. 1, 1984; stepchildren: Carrie Lawson, Valerie Lawson. BS in Econs., U. Ill., 1968; MBA in Health Adminstrn., U. Chgo., 1971. Asst. adminstr. U. Ill. Hosp., Chgo., 1969-72, Ctrl. DuPage Hosp., Winfield, Ill., 1972-74; mgmt. cons., v.p. Tribrook Group, Inc., Oak Brook, Ill., 1974-81; v.p. cons. svcs. Parkside Med. Svcs., Park Ridge, Ill., 1981-83; prin. health and med. divsn.

Booz, Allen, & Hamilton, Inc., Chgo., 1983-84; exec. v.p. EHS Health Care, Oak Brook, 1984-92, pres., CEO, 1992-95, Advocate Health Care, Oak Brook, 1995—. Bd. dirs. Landauer Corp.; mem. faculty Healthcare Fin. Mgmt. Assn., 1978-86, Am. Assn. Hosps. Cons., 1978-84; bd. dirs., mem. ad hoc ins. com., fin. com. Premier; lectr. grad. program social scis. No. Ill. U., 1982-88; lectr., adv. bd. multi-hosp. system study Kellogg Sch. Health Mgmt. Program Northwestern U., 1985—; lectr. Grad. Program in Health Adminstrn. U. Chgo., 1982-94. Mem. access com. Gov.'s Task Force on Health Reform, 1992-94; mem. chancellor's adv. bd. U. Ill. at Chgo.; chair South Cook county region United Way. Fellow Am. Assn. Hosp. Cons. (bd. dirs., treas., chmn. govt. rels. com., chmn. membership task force, liaison Nat. Coun. Cmty. Hosps.); mem. Am. Hosp. Assn. (chair healthcare systems sect.), Ill. Hosp. Assn. (chmn. coun. on health fin., mem. strategic plan com., bd. dirs., treas.), U. Chgo. Hosp. Adminstrn. Alumni Assn. (pres. exec. com. alumni coun., chmn. 50th ann. com.), Chgo. Health Policy Rsch. Coun. Office: Advocate Health Care 2025 Windsor Dr Oak Brook IL 60523-1586 Home: PO Box 179 Mancos CO 81328-0179

RISON, ANDRE, retired professional football player; b. Flint, Mich., Mar. 18, 1967; Student, Mich. State U. Wide receiver Indpls. Colts, 1989, Atlanta Falcons, 1990-95, Cleve. Browns, 1995-97, Kansas City Chiefs, 1997—99, Oakland Raiders, 2000. Named to Pro-Bowl, 1990, 91, 92, 93, 97, All-Pro 1990, 91, 92, 93, Sporting News All-Pro team, 1990.

RISSER, FRED A., state legislator; b. Madison, Wis., May 5, 1927; married; 3 children. BA, U. Oreg., LLB, 1952. Bar: Wis. Sole practice, Madison, 1952—; mem. Wis. Senate from 26th dist., Madison, 1962—; asst. minority leader Wis. State Senate, 1965-67, minority leader, 1967-75, pres. pro tem, 1975-79, pres., 1979-93, asst. minority leader, 1993-96, pres., 1996—. Mem. Wis. State Assembley, 1956-62; del. Democratic Conv., 1960, 64; presdl. elector-chmn. Wis. Electoral Coll., 1964; vice chmn. Bldg. Commn., Wis. Democrat. also: 5008 Risser Rd Madison WI 53705-1365 Office: Madison Office State Capitol Rm 220 S PO Box 7882 Madison WI 53707-7882 E-mail: sen.risser@legis.state.wi.us.

RISSMAN, BURTON RICHARD, lawyer; b. Chgo., Nov. 13, 1927; s. Louis and Eva (Lyons) R.; m. Francine Greenberg, June 15, 1952; children: Lawrence E., Thomas W., Michael P. BS, U. Ill., 1947, JD, 1951; LLM, NYU, 1952. Bar: Ill. 1951, U.S. Dist. Ct. (no. dist.) Ill. 1954, U.S. Ct. Appeals (7th cir.) 1978, U.S. Supreme Ct. 1982. Assoc. Schiff, Hardin & Waite, Chgo., 1953-59, ptnr., 1959—2003, mem. mgmt. com., 1984-92, chmn. mgmt. com., 1986-90; ret., 2003. Mem. faculty Practicing Law Inst. Bd. editor U. Ill. Law Forum, 1949-51; contbr. articles to profl. jours. 1st lt. JAGC USAF, 1952—53. Food Law fellow, 1951. Mem. ABA, Ill. Bar Assn., Chgo. Bar Assn., Chgo. Coun. Lawyers, Carlton Club.

RISTOW, GEORGE EDWARD, neurologist, educator; b. Albion, Mich., Dec. 15, 1943; s. George Julius and Margaret (Beattie) R.; 1 child, George Andrew Martin. BA, Albion Coll., 1965; DO, Coll. Osteo. Medicine/Surgery, Des Moines, 1969. Diplomate Am. Bd. Psychiatry and Neurology. Intern Garden City Hosp., 1969-70; resident Wayne State U., 1970-74; fellow U. Newcastle Upon Tyne, 1974-75; asst. prof. dept. neurology Wayne State U., Detroit, 1975-77; assoc. prof. Mich. State U., East Lansing, 1977-83, prof., 1983-84, 95—, prof., chmn., 1984-95, prof. emeritus, 2001—. Fellow Am. Acad. Neurology, Royal Soc. Medicine; mem. AMA, Am. Osteo. Assn., Pan Am. Med. Assn., World Fedn. Neurology, Am. Coll. Neuropsychiatrists (sr.). Home: 6149 Bridgewater Cir East Lansing MI 48823 Office Phone: 517-374-7600. Personal E-mail: gristow@cimamed.com.

RITCHIE, MARK, state official; b. 1951; m. Nancy Gaschott; 1 child, Rachel (dec.). Grad., Iowa State U., 1971. Founder League of Rural Voters, 1986—2005; founder, pres. Inst. Agr. and Trade Policy, Mpls., 1986—2005; founder, nat. coord. Nat. Voice NOVEMBER 2 Campaign, 2003—04; founder, coord. Internet Resources on Election Protection, 2003—; founder, vol. leader Ctr. Civic Participation, 2004—05; sec. state State of Minn., St. Paul, 2007—. Named a Patriotic Employer, Employers Support the Guard and Res., 2007; recipient Activist of Yr. award, Minn. Alliance for Progressive Action, 2004, Progressive Campaign award to Voting Rights Coalition, 2005, Nat. Progressive Leadership award, US Action, 2005, Carl King Disting. Svc. award, Am. Corn Growers Assn., Civic Engagement award, Minn. Commn. Serving Deaf and Hard of Hearing People. Office: Office Sec State 180 State Office Bldg 100 Rev Dr Martin Luther King Jr Blvd Saint Paul MN 55155-1299 Office Phone: 651-201-1328.

RITCHIE, WILLIAM PAUL, lawyer; b. Columbus, Ohio, June 3, 1946; s. Austin Everett and Helen (Drake) Ritchie; m. Diane Smith, Aug. 2, 1969; 1 child, Elizabeth Drake. BS in Bus. Adminstrn., Ohio State U., 1968; JD, U. Va., 1971. Bar: Ohio 1971, Calif. 1973, Ill. 1987. Assoc. Jones, Day, Reavis & Pogue, Cleve., 1971—77, ptnr., 1977—, ptnr.-in-charge Chgo., 1987—. Served to lt. USAR, 1972. Mem.: ABA, Chgo. Bar Assn., Calif. Bar Assn., Ohio Bar Assn., Chgo. Club, Mayfield Country Club Cleve. Republican. Office: Jones Day 77 W Wacker Dr Fl 35 Chicago IL 60601-1662 Office Phone: 312-782-3939. Office Fax: 312-782-8585. Business E-Mail: wpritchie@jonesday.com.

RITER, ROBERT C., JR., lawyer; b. Pierre, SD, July 8, 1948; BS, U. SD, 1970, JD, 1973. Bar: SD 1973. Asst. city atty., 1973—; with Riter, Rogers, Wattier & Brown, LLP, Pierre, SD, 1973—, ptnr. Lectr. in field. Contbr. articles to profl. jours. Fellow: Am. Bar Found., Am. Bd. Trial Advocates, Am. Coll. Trial Lawyers; mem.: ABA, Def. Rsch. Inst. (state rep. 1994—99, bd. dirs. 1999—2003), Am. Counsel Assn., SD Def. Lawyers Assn. (pres. 1994—95), State Bar SD (chmn. adminstrv. law com. 1979—81, continuing legal edn. com. 1981—84, ethics com. 1986—89, commr. 1992—95, pres. 2005—06), Phi Delta Phi. Office: Riter Rogers Wattier & Brown LLP Profl and Exec Bldg 319 S Coteau St PO Box 280 Pierre SD 57501 Office Phone: 605-224-5825. Office Fax: 605-224-7102. E-mail: r.riter@riterlaw.com.

RITTER, ROBERT FORCIER, lawyer; b. St. Louis, Apr. 7, 1943; s. Tom Marshall and Jane Elizabeth (Forcier) R.; m. Karen Gray, Dec. 28, 1966; children: Allison Gray Campione, Laura Thompson Capstick, Elisabeth Forcier Schoenecker. BA, U. Kans., 1965; JD, St. Louis U., 1968. Bar: Mo. 1968, U.S. Dist. Ct. (ea. and we. dists.) Mo. 1968. U.S. Ct. Mil. Appeals 1972, U.S. Supreme Ct. 1972, U.S. Ct. Appeals (8th cir.) 1980, U.S. Dist. Ct. (so. dist.) Ill. 1982. Assoc. Gray & Sommers, St. Louis, 1968-71; ptnr. Gray Ritter & Graham, P.C., St. Louis, 1974—; chmn., pres. Gray & Ritter, St. Louis, 1983—. Adv. com. 22nd cir. Supreme Ct., 1985—92; mem. Supreme Ct. com. civil jury instrns., 1988—2003; adv. com. U.S. Dist. Ct., 1993—95; mem. exec. planning com. Mo. Inst. for Justice, 2002—; mem. nat. adv. bd. Ctr. for Perinatal Medicine and Law, U. Calif., Davis, 2002—; lectr. in field. Contbr. articles to profl. jours. Mem. nat. adv. bd. Ctr. for Perinatal Medicine and Law, U. Calif., Davis, 2002—; bd. dirs. Cystic Fibrosis Found., Gateway chpt., pres., 1991; mem. exec. planning com. Mo. Inst. Justice, 2002—. Recipient Law Week award, Bur. Nat. Affairs, 1968, award of merit, Nat. Conf. Met. Cts., 1995, Lawyers Assn. award of honor, 2003, Best Lawyers, Am., Super Lawyer Mo. and Kansas, Top 100 Attys. and the Top 50 St. Louis Attys., by Mo./Kansas Super Lawyers Magazine. Fellow: Internat. Acad. Trial Lawyers, Am. Coll. Trial Lawyers, Internat. Soc. Barristers (bd. govs. 1994); mem.: Mo. Assn. Trial Attys. (bd. govs. 1984—), Lawyers Assn. St. Louis (exec. com. 1976—81, pres. 1977—78, award of honor 2003, 2003), Mo. Bar Found. (outstanding trial lawyer award 1978), Mo. Bar Assn. (coun. practice and procedure com. 1972—, coun. tort law com. 1982—, bd. govs. 1984—91, fin. com. 1984—91), Bar Assn. Met. St. Louis (chmn. trial sect. 1978—79, exec. com. 1980—82, chmn. bench bar conf. 1983, award merit 1976, award achievement 1982), Am. Bd. Trial Advocates (advocate), Assn. Trial Lawyers Am., Am. Judicature Soc., ABA, Windsor Club (founding mem.), Roaring Fork Club, Red Stick Golf Club (founding mem.), Racquet Club (bd. govs. 1988—93, pres. 1991—92), John's Is. Club (bd. dirs. 1998—), Bellerive Country Club, Noonday Club. Presbyterian. Home: 11 Gem Island Dr Vero Beach FL 32963 Office: Gray Ritter & Graham PC Ste 800 701 Market St Saint Louis MO 63101-1850 Office Phone: 314-241-5620. Office Fax: 314-241-4140. E-mail: rritter@grgpc.com.

RITTERSKAMP, DOUGLAS DOLVIN, lawyer; b. St. Louis, July 7, 1948; s. James Johnstone Jr. and Linn M. (Dolvin) R.; m. Linda S. Vansant, Mar. 23, 1974; 1 child, Tammy. AB, Washington U., 1970, JD, 1973; LLM in Taxation, NYU, 1978. Bar: N.Y. 1974, Mo. 1979. Assoc. Patterson, Belknap, Webb & Tyler, NYC, 1974-78; jr. ptnr. Bryan Cave LLP (and predecessors), St. Louis, 1978-82; ptnr. Bryan Cave LLP, St. Louis, 1983—2004, of counsel, 2005—. Trustee Scottish Rite Clinic for Childhood Lang. Disorders of St. Louis, Inc., 1987-97, St. Louis Mission and Ch. Ext. Soc., United Meth. Ch., 1987-97, Mo. United Meth. Found., 1994—2003, pres., 2000—03; trustee The Coll. Sch., 1995-2001. Served to capt. USAR, 1970—79. Mem. ABA (employee benefits com. sect. taxation 1987-91, 96—), Bar Assn. Met. St. Louis (steering com. employee benefits 1989—), Masons (32d degree, knight comdr. ct. of honor), Shriner. Methodist. Home: 5223 Sutherland Ave Saint Louis MO 63109-2338

RITTMER, SHELDON, state senator, farmer; b. Clinton, Iowa, Sept. 5, 1928; s. Elmer and Lois (Hass) R.; m. Elaine Heneke, June 11, 1950; children: Kenneth S., Lynnette Rittmer Jones, Robyn Jon (dec.), Paul (dec.). County supr. Clinton (Iowa) County Bd. Suprs., 1978, 1982, 1985, 1988, 1990, chair, 1978, 1982, 1985, 1988, 1990; chmn. Clinton County Title III Com., 1987-90; v.p. Iowa Assn. County Suprs., Des Moines, 1989-90; mem. Iowa Senate from 19th dist., 1990—2002. Bd. dirs. Iowa Pub. Employees Retirement System, 1990-2002; mem. Iowa Pub. Retirement Investment Bd., 2001-02, Elderly Affairs Com., 1999-2002, Iowa Mental Health/Retardation Devel./Disabilites Com., 1988-90. Chmn. 1st Luth. Ch., Maquoketa, Iowa, 1964-68; active Clinton County Hist. Soc., 1980—; mem. Elvira Luth. Ch. Recipient Spl. Recognition award Nat. Fedn. Ind. Bus., 1991-92, Spl. Recognition Iowa Soil Conservation award, 1994, Iowa Nurses Assn. Legis. award, 2002. Mem. Clinton County Farm Bureau (chair 1965-68), C&J Farm Svc. Bd. (1969-75), Izaak Walton League Iowa, DeWitt Lions, Ducks Unlimited U.S.A, Clinton County Pork Prodr's. Assn., Clinton County Cattlemen's Assn., Pheasants Forever, City of Clinton C. of C., DeWitt C. of C., Bettendorf C. of C. Republican. Avocations: public speaking, Iowa Legis. issues rsch., reading, agriculture. Home: 3539 230th St De Witt IA 52742-9208 Office: State Senate of Iowa State Capital Des Moines IA 50319-0001 E-mail: sheldon.rittmer@legis.state.ia.us, shelaine@gmtel.net.

RIVARD, JEROME G., engineering executive; b. Hudson, Wis., Nov. 21, 1932; BSME, U. Wis., 1955. Dir. engring. Bendix, 1962-76; chief engr. Ford Motor Co., 1976-86; vice pres., group exec. Bendix Electronics Group, 1986—88; pres. Global Tech. & Bus. Devel., Harrison Twp., Mich., 1988—. Fellow IEEE, Soc. Automotive Engrs.; mem. NAE. Acheivements include research in the application of electronics to automotive systems. Office: 29401 S Seaway Ct Harrison Township MI 48045

RIVENESS, PHILLIP J., city manager, retired state legislator; b. Karlstad, Minn., Dec. 14, 1947; s. John Anders and Ruth (Olson) R.; m. Gail Elaine Coffin, 1968; 3 children. BA, U. Minn., 1969. Former mem. Minn. Ho. of Reps., St. Paul; senator Minn. Senate, 1991-97; mem. Mpls. St. Paul Met. Coun. Vicechmn. govt. ops. and reform com., mem. environ. and natural resources com., health care com., others.; exec dir. South Hennyson Svc. Coun., 1974-78; health care adminstr. Chmn. Bloomington Dem-Farmer-Labor Club, 1979-80. Democrat. Office: Met Coun Mears Park Ctr 230 E 5th St Saint Paul MN 55101 Home: 2900 Thomas Ave S Apt 2010 Minneapolis MN 55416-4584

RIVERS, LYNN N., former congresswoman; b. Augres, Mich., Dec. 19, 1956; 2 children. BA, U. Mich., 1987; JD, Wayne State U., 1992. Mem. sch. bd. City of Ann Arbor, Mich., 1984-92; mem. Mich. House of Reps., 1992-94, U.S. Congress from 13th Mich. dist., 1994—2002; mem. edn. and workforce com., sci. com., 1994. Mem.: Nat. Adv. Bd., Univ. Mich. Depression Center, 2003-. Democrat.

RIVES, STANLEY GENE, retired academic administrator; b. Decatur, Ill., Sept. 27, 1930; s. James A. and Frances (Bunker) R.; m. Sandra Lou Belt, Dec. 28, 1957; children: Jacqueline Ann, Joseph Alan. BS, Ill. State U., 1952, MS, 1955; PhD, Northwestern U., 1963; EdD (hon.), Lincoln Coll., 1998. Instr. W.Va. U., 1955-56, Northwestern U., 1956-58; prof. Ill. State U., Normal, 1958-80, Am. Coun. on Edn. Fellows Program, 1969-70, assoc. dean faculties, 1970-72, dean undergrad. instrn., 1972-80, assoc. provost, 1976-80, acting provost, 1979-80; provost, v.p. acad. affairs, prof. Eastern Ill. U., Charleston, 1981-83, pres., 1983-92, pres. emeritus, 1992—. Vis. prof. U. Hawaii, 1963—64. Author: (with Donald Klopf) Individual Speaking Contests: Preparation for Participation, 1967, (with Gene Budig) Academic Quicksand: Trends and Issues in Higher Education, 1973, (with others) Academic Innovation: Faculty and Instructional Development at Illinois State University, 1979, The Fundamentals of Oral Interpretation, 1981; contbr. articles to profl. jours. Bd. dirs. Ill. State Univs. Ret. Sys., 1992-2005, treas., 1995-2001, pres., 2001-05; bd. dirs. Ea. Ill. Univ. Found., 1993-98, also pres., 1996-98, East Ctrl. Ill. Devel. Corp., 1983-92, Charleston Area Econ. Devel. Found., 1986-92, Coles Together, 1988-92; mem. pres. commn. NCAA, 1986-91; trustee Nat. Debate Tournament, 1967-75. With U.S. Army, 1952-54. Named to Co. of Edn. Hall of Fame; recipient Alumni Achievement award, Ill. State U., 1998. Mem. Am. Assn. State Colls. and Univs., Ill. State C. of C. (bd. dirs. 1990-92), Charleston C. of C. (bd. dirs. 1985-88), Theta Alpha Phi, Phi Kappa Delta, Pi Gamma Mu, Alpha Phi Omega, Alpha Zeta, Sigma Phi Epsilon (hon.). Home: 2231 Andover Pl Charleston IL 61920-3807 Personal E-mail: srives@consolidated.net.

RIVET, JEANNINE M., health insurance company executive; BS in Nursing, Boston Coll.; MPH, Boston U. Sch. Public Health. V.p. grp. ops. Prudential Ins. Co. Am.; v.p. health svc. ops. to CEO United HealthCare, Minnetonka, Minn., 1990-98, CEO, 1998—2000, Ingenix; exec. v.p. UnitedHealth Grp., 2000—. Office: UnitedHealth Group 9900 Bren Rd E Minnetonka MN 55343-9664*

RIZAI, MATTHEW M., marketing and finance professional; b. Istanbul, Turkey, Apr. 6, 1956; came to U.S. 1973; s. Andrew and Muriel (Wilson) Teneyck; m. Tonja M. Anstead, Mar. 14, 1987; 1 child, Aliyea Tiffany. BS, Mich. State U., 1978, MS, 1980, PhD, 1983; MBA Mktg. Fin., U. Chgo., 1990. Mgr. Modal Analysis Lab., Mich. State U., East Lansing, Mich., 1980-83; v.p. Computer Aided Design Software Inc., Oakdale, Iowa, 1983-84; cons. engr. NUTech Testing Corp., San Jose, Calif., 1984-85; sr. rsch. engr. GMC, Troy, Mich., 1985-90; assoc. Arch Devel. Corp., Chgo., 1989-90; pres., chief exec. officer Engring. Animation Inc., Ames, Iowa, 1990—. Office: Engring Animation Inc Isu Research Park 2625 Ames IA 50010

RIZZO, HENRY, state legislator; m. Silvia Rizzo; children: Tomy Mike, Johnny Joe. Mem. Mo. State Ho. of Reps. Dist. 40, 1985—. Mem. appropriations-gen. adminstrn. com., budget com., commerce com. (chmn.), local govt. and related matters com., urban affairs com., utilities regulation com. Home: 575 Harrison St Kansas City MO 64106-1265 Office: Mo Ho of Reps State Capitol Jefferson City MO 65101 Fax: 573-526-1947. E-mail: hrizzo@services.state.mo.us.

ROACH, ADRIENNE J., lawyer; b. London, Ohio, Nov. 30, 1971; BA, U. Richmond, 1993; JD, U. Cin. Coll. Law, 1996. Bar: Ohio 1996, Ky. 1998. Ptnr. Keating Muething & Klekamp PLL, Cin. Mentor Oyler Elem. Sch., Help One Student to Succeed Prog.; mem., Bd. Dirs. Art Machine, Inc. Named one of Ohio's Rising Stars, Super Lawyers, 2005, 2006. Fellow: Cin. Acad. Leadership for Lawyers; mem.: Ohio State Bar Assn. (Family Law Sect.), Northern Ky. Bar Assn., Northern Ky. Collaborative Grp., Inc., Ky. Bar Assn. (Family. Law Sect.), Collaborative Family Lawyers Cin., Cin. Bar Found. (trustee 2006—), Cin. Bar Assn. (sec. 2002—04, CLE chair 2004—06, vice chair, Domestice Rels. Com. 2004—06, chairperson, Domestic Rels. Com. 2006—), ABA (Family Law Sect.). Office: Keating Muething & Klekamp PLL One E Fourth St Ste 1400 Cincinnati OH 45202 Office Phone: 513-579-6400. Office Fax: 513-579-6457.

ROACH, THOMAS ADAIR, lawyer, mediator; b. Akron, Ohio, May 1, 1929; s. Edward Thomas and Mayme Bernice (Turner) R.; m. Sally Jane Bennett, July 11, 1953; children: Thomas, David, James, Dorothy, Steven, Patrick. AB, U. Mich., 1951, JD with distinction, 1953. Bar: Mich. 1953. Assoc. McClintock, Fulton, Donovan & Waterman (and successor firms), Detroit, 1956-62, ptnr., 1962-87; counsel Bodman, Longley & Dahling, Detroit and Ann Arbor, Mich., 1988-90, ptnr. Detroit and Ann Arbor, Mich., 1990-2000, sr. lawyer, 2001—. Bd. dirs. Ferndale Labs, Inc., Canterbury Health Care, Inc. Contbr. articles to profl. jours. Vice chmn. 14th Congl. Dist. Democratic Orgn., 1971-75; chmn. platform and resolution com. Mich. Dem. Party, 1971-74, treas., 1975-87; permanent chmn. Dem. State Conv., 1976; mem. platform com. and drafting subcom. Dem. Nat. Conv., 1972, mem. rules com., 1980, alt. del., 1984; Bd. regents U. Mich., 1975-90; bd. dirs. Mich. Tech. Coun., 1983-92, vice chmn. 1984-86, south-ctrl. region 1992-95; pres. 9th Dist. Res. Policy Bd. 1976-77; nat. chmn. Ann. Giving, U., Mich., 1987-97; mem. history and traditions com. U. Mich., 1998—; mem. Mich. Higher Edn. Assistance Authority, Mich. Higher Edn. Student Loan Authority, 1990-94, bd. dirs. Legal Counsel, 1999—, Great Sauk Trail Coun. Boy Scouts Am., 1993—; bd. dirs. Wolverine Coun. Boy Scouts Am., 1991-93; officer Compensation Commn. Pittsfield Twp., 1991-93. Served to capt. USCGR, 1953-56; res. group comdr., 1974-77. Mem. ABA, Fed. Bar Assn., Mich. Bar Assn. (chmn. constrn. law com. 1983-85), Detroit Bar Assn., Washtenaw County Bar Assn., Res. Officers Assn., Order of Coif (Disting. Alumni Achievement award, Spirit of Mich. award, Disting. Citizen of Yr., Washington Ct.), Thomas M. Cooley Club, U. Mich. Club (gov. 1970-74), U. Mich. Alumni Assn. (bd. dirs. 1991-94, 95—, pres. 1995-97, pres. Emeritus Club 2001-02), Rotary Club of Ann Arbor (bd. dirs. 1991-96, pres. 1994-95, chair Dist. Permanent Fund 1999-2001), Sigma Alpha Iota. Anglican. Office: Bodman Longley & Dahling 110 Miller Ave Ste 300 Ann Arbor MI 48104-1339 Home: 4001 Glacier Hills Dr Unit 144 Ann Arbor MI 48105-3656 E-mail: thomasa.roach@worldnet.att.net.

ROBAK, KIM M., lawyer; b. Columbus, Nebr., Oct. 4, 1955; m. William J. Mueller; children: Katherine, Claire. BS with distinction, U. Nebr., 1977, JD with highest distinction, 1985. Tchr. Lincoln Pub. Schs., Nebr., 1978—82; clerk Cline Williams Wright Johnson & Oldfather, 1983; summer assoc. Cooley Godward Castro Huddleson & Tatum, San Francisco, 1984, Steptoe & Johnson, Washington, 1985; ptnr. Rembolt Ludtke Parker & Berger, Lincoln, 1985—91; legal counsel Gov. E. Benjamin Nelson/State of Nebr., 1991—92, chief of staff, 1992—93; lt. gov. State of Nebr., 1993—98; v.p. external affairs, corp. sec. U. Nebr., 1999—2004; with Ruth Mueller Robak, LLC, Lincoln, Nebr., 2004—. Chair Prairie Fire Internat. Symposium on Edn., 1986; bd. dirs. Fiserv, Inc., First Ameritas Life Ins. Corp. NY, Union Bank & Trust Co. Program com. Leadership Lincoln, 1987—90; chair program com. Leadership Lincoln Alumni Assn., 1987, selection com., 1990; mem. Toll Fellowship Program, 1995; chair Nat. Conf. Lt. Govs., 1996; hon. chair Daffodil Day Campaign An, Cancer Soc.; hon chair Walktoberfest Am. Diabetes Assn.; hon. chair Prevent Blindness Campaign, Nebr.; hon. mem. Red Ribbon Campaign Mothers Against Drunk Driving, 1994—95; active Groundwater Found., 1997, Medicaid Managed Care Commn., 1993—98; bd. dirs. Nebr. Health Sys., 1997—2004, Nat. Found. Women Legislators Found., 1997—98; chair Nebr. Info. Tech. Commn., 1997—98; hon. Christmas chair Salvation Army, 1997; cert. program chair Nat. Order Women Legislators, 1997; mem. Martin Luther Home Soc., 1999—2001, Dem. Gen. Counsel, Nebr., 1985—92; bd. dirs. women's ministries First Congl. Ch., 1988—91, trustee, 1991—99, asst. moderator, 1999—; trustee Plymouth Congl. Ch., 1998—; bd. dirs. Doane Coll., 1997—, Lincoln Pub. Sch. Found., 1998—2004, Lincoln Partnership for Econ. Devel. Bd., 2000—, Nebr. Found. for the Humanities, 2003—, Lincoln Cmty. Found., 2004—, United Way of Lincoln and Lancaster County, 2000—, Strategic Air and Space Mus., 2006—, Exec. Women's Golf Assn., 2005—. Named Notable Woman, First Plymouth Congl. Ch.'s Bd. Women's Ministries, 1996; fellow, Leadership Lincoln, 1986—87. Mem.: ABA (steering com. 1997—), Lincoln Bar Assn., Nebr. State Bar Assn. (ethics com. 1987—92, chair com. yellow pages advt. 1988, vice chair com. pub. rels. 1988—92, ho. of dels. 1988—95), Nat. Inst. Trial Advocaty, Alzheimers Assn. (hon. chair Lincoln-Greater Nebr. chpt. 1996—98), Updowntowners, Exec. Women's Golf Assn. (trustee 2005—), Order of Coif, U. Nebr. Coll. Alumni Assn. (bd. dirs. 1986—89). Office: Ruth Mueller Robak LLC 530 S 13th St Ste 110 Lincoln NE 68508 Business E-Mail: robak@ruthmueller.com.

ROBBINS, ARNIE, editor; m. Terrie Robbins. Grad., Northwestern U. Medill Sch. Journalism, 1975. Sports reporter & editor Suburban Tribune, 1975—78; copy editor, dep. sports editor Chgo. Sun-Times, 1978—84; exec. sports editor, asst. mng. editor, features & change editor Mpls. Star Tribune, 1984—97; dir. news staff & orgnl. devel. St. Louis Post-Dispatch, 1997, dep. editor, 1997—99, mng. editor, 1999—2005, editor, 2005—. Office: St Louis Post-Dispatch 900 N Tucker Blvd Saint Louis MO 63101 Office Phone: 314-340-8130. E-mail: arobbins@post-dispatch.com.*

ROBBINS, DARRYL ANDREW, pediatrician; b. Modesto, Calif., Sept. 16, 1945; s. Jerome and Grace (Bass) Robbins; m. Harriette Lee Eisenberg, June 12, 1971; children: Jennifer Lynn, Julie Ellen, Alison Beth. BS, Dickinson Coll., 1967; DO, Phila. Coll. Osteo. Medicine, 1971. Diplomate Am. Bd. Pediat. Intern Doctor's Hosp., Columbus, Ohio, 1971-72; resident in pediatrics Children's Hosp. Med. Ctr., Cin., 1972-75; pvt. practice specializing in pediat. Columbus, 1975—. Mem. genetics svcs. adv. com. Ohio Dept. Health, 1978—86; bd. dirs. Diocesan Child Guidance Ctr., Columbus, 1983—88, vice-chmn., 1986; pres. med. staff Columbus Children's Hosp., 1996. Trustee Columbus Children's Hosp., 2001—; bd. dirs. Children's Practicing Pediatricians, Columbus, 1991—94, 1998—, pres., 2001—. Named Pediatrician of the Yr., Columbus Children's Hosp., 1982, 1990; recipient Samuel Dalinsky Meml. award for Outstanding Graduating Resident, Cin. Children's Hosp., 1975, Lifetime Achievement award, Ohio State Coll. Medicine, 2004, Career Contbn. award, Columbus Children's Hosp., 2004. Fellow: Am. Acad. Pediat.; mem.: Ctrl. Ohio Pediatric Soc. (pres. elect 1988, pres. 1989—90). Jewish. Office: 453 Waterbury Ct Gahanna OH 43230-5309 Home: 6388 Portrait Cir Westerville OH 43081 Home Phone: 614-245-8542; Office Phone: 614-471-0652. E-mail: drobbins@insightb.rr.com.

ROBBINS, HENRY ZANE, public relations and marketing executive; b. Winston-Salem, NC, Jan. 17, 1930; s. Romulus Mayfield and Vera Ethel (Daniel) R.; m. Barbara Anne Brown, Jan. 19, 1955; children: Zane Scott, Jill Stewart, Gail Ruth. AB, U. N.C., 1952; student, Emory U., 1952. Reporter Atlanta Constn., 1952; exhibit specialist Gen. Electric Co., Schenectady, 1952, employee relations specialist Cin., 1955, editor Schenectady, 1955, account supr. Winston-Salem, 1956-58, group supr. Schenectady, 1958-60; v.p., gen. mgr. Burson-Marsteller, Pitts. and Chgo., 1960-70, sr. v.p., 1970; pres., chief exec. officer SL&H-Robbins Inc., Chgo., 1970-72; also dir.; pres., chief exec. officer Beveridge Kraus Robbins & Manning, Chgo., 1973-75; also dir.; pres., dir., chief exec. officer Beveridge and Robbins Inc., Chgo., 1975-77; pres., chief exec. officer Financial Advt. of Ill., Inc., Chgo.; mng. dir. Sports Mgmt. Group, Chgo., 1975-77; dir. communications Arthur Andersen & Co., Chgo. and Geneva, Switzerland, 1977-81, dir. mktg. support services, 1981-89, dir. mktg. and comms., 1989-91; mem. Worldwide Alpha Group, 1991-96, exec. dir. global markets program, 1995—2000; prin. Arthur Andersen & Co., 1980—2000; cons. Exec. Svc. Corps, 2004—. Mem. journalism adv. com. Harper Coll., Palatine, Ill., exec. svc. corp.; dir. Evanston Environ. Assn.; mem. Ladd Arboretum Commn., Evanston, Ill.; pub. rels. com. Chgo. Met. Crusade Mercy; mem. Nat. Task Force on Environment; cons. sec. Dept. Health, Edn. and Welfare, 1970; chmn. pub. rels. com. Honor Am. Day Com., 1970. Author: Vision of Grandeur, 1988, Globalizing the Enterprise, 2000, Tradition of Excellence, 2001; contbr. articles to profl. jours. Counselor Council of Mojave, 1972-74; gen. chmn. Chgo. Children's Classic Golf Tournament, 1974-77; chmn. Chgo. fin. com. Am.'s Freedom Train, 1976; chmn. fund devel. com. Presbytery of Chgo., 1977-83, maj. mission fund, 1977-79; dist. commr. Boy Scouts Am., 1976-79, chmn. Wildcat dist., 1980-83; mem. exec. bd. N.E. Ill. council, 1980-85; mem. Republican Citizens Com. Ill., 1960-61, Allegheny County (Pa.) Rep. Com., 1962-65; Trustee Roycemore Sch., Evanston, 1971-74; trustee, v.p. devel. Child and Family Services Chgo.; bd. dirs. Fellowship of Christian Athletes, U. N.C. Alumni Ill., Stockbrokers Assn. Chgo.; chmn. devel. com. Potawotamie Dist., 2000, chmn. fin. com., 2001; bd. dirs. Evanston Environ. Ctr., Ladd Arboretum, North Shore Nature Ctr., 2001-; mem. Ctr. for the Rehab. of Wildlife; bd. visitors U. N.C., 2004-. Served to 1st lt. AUS, 1952-54. Elected to N.C. Pub. Rels. Hall of Fame, 1994. Mem.: Chgo. Assn. Commerce and Industry, Environ. Writers Assn. Am., Am. Mgmt. Assn., Pub. Rels. Counselors Roundtable, Chgo. Ednl. TV Assn., Midwest Travel Writers Assn., Nat. Investor Rels. Inst., Pub. Rels. Soc. Am., Art Inst. Chgo., Sunset Ridge Country Club, OptimistClub of Wilmette (pres. 2005—), Univ. Club, Chi Psi. Republican. Presbyterian. Home: 2759 Broadway Ave Evanston IL 60201-1556 Personal E-mail: hzrobbins@sbcglobal.net.

ROBBINS, JERRY HAL, educational administration educator; b. DeQueen, Ark., Feb. 28, 1939; s. James Hal and Barbara I. (Rogers) R. BA in Math, Hendrix Coll., 1960; M.Ed., U. Ark., 1963, Ed.D., 1966. Tchr. math. and music Clinton (Ark.) pub. schs., 1960-61; prin. Adrian (Mo.) High Sch., 1961-63; exec. sec. Ark. Sch. Study Council, Fayetteville, 1963-65; mem. faculty U. Miss., University, 1965-74, prof. ednl. adminstrn., 1970-74, chmn. dept. ednl. adminstrn., 1970-74; dean Coll. Edn., U. Ark., Little Rock, 1974-79; asso. v.p. for acad. affairs Ga. State U., Atlanta, 1979-84, dean Coll. Edn., 1984-90, prof. ednl. adminstrn., 1990-91; dean. Coll. Edn. Ea. Mich. U., Ypsilanti, 1991—2004, prof. ednl. leadership, 2004—05. Co-author: (with S. B. Williams Jr.) Student Activities in the Innovative School, 1969, School Custodian's Handbook, 1970,

Administrator's Manual of School Plant Administration, 1970. Mem. NEA, Am. Assn. Sch. Adminstrs., Am. Assn. Colls. Tchr. Edn. (dir. 1979-82, 2000-04), Nat. Assn. Secondary Sch. Prins., So. Regional Council Ednl. Adminstrn. (pres. 1970-71), Tchr. Edn. Coun. State Colls. and Univs. (pres. 1998-99), Phi Delta Kappa, Kappa Delta Pi (v.p. chpt. devel. 1978-80, pres. elect 1980-82, pres. 1982-84, past pres. 1984-86) Mem. United Meth. Ch. Home and Office: 3384 Bent Trail Dr Ann Arbor MI 48108-9316 E-mail: jerry.robbins@emich.edu.

ROBBINS, LAWRENCE HARRY, anthropologist, educator; b. Washington, Nov. 22, 1938; s. Maurice and Edith R.; m. Martha Ann Edwards, Dec. 16, 1967; children: Daniel, Brian, Michael, Mark. AB, U. Mich., 1961, A.M., 1962; PhD, U. Calif., Berkeley, 1968. Asst. prof. U. Utah, 1967; mem. faculty Mich. State U., East Lansing, 1968—, prof. anthropology and African studies, 1977—, chairperson ANP dept., 1992-95. Vis. rsch. assoc. U. Nairobi, Kenya, 1969-70, Nat. Mus. Kenya, 1975-76; Fulbright vis. prof. U. Botswana, 1982-83; vis. archaeologist Nat. Mus. and Art Gallery, Botswana, 1982-83 Author: Stones, Bones and Ancient Cities, 1990; contbr. articles to profl. jours. Grantee NSF, 1965-66, 69-70, 75-77, 91-2000, 03, Nat. Geographic Soc., 1987, 89. Mem. Registry Profl. Archaeologists, Soc. Africanist Archeologists in Am., So. African Archeol. Soc., Botswana Soc. Office: Mich State U Dept Anthropology E23 E Mcdonel Hall East Lansing MI 48824

ROBBINS, N. CLAY, foundation administrator; b. Indpls., May 30, 1957; m. Amy Robbins; 3 children. BA, Wabash Coll., Crawfordsville, Ind., 1979; JD, Vanderbilt U., 1982; LLD (hon.), Ind. State U., 2004; LHD (hon.), Rose-Hulman Inst. Tech., 2006. Exch. assoc. European Econ. Cmty. law dept. Rycken Burlion Bolle & Houben, Brussels, 1985-86; assoc. Baker & Daniels, 1982-85, ptnr., 1988—92; v.p. cmty. devel. Lilly Endowment Inc., Indpls., 1993-94, pres., 1994—. Mem. drafting com. Ind. Nonprofit Corp. Act 1991. Past dir., pres. Indpls. Chamber Orch.; past dir. Damar Homes, Inc.; bd. dirs., exec. com. Ctrl. Ind. Corp. Partnership; bd. dirs. United Way Ctrl. Ind. Mem. Ind. State Bar Assn., Indpls. C. of C. Methodist. Office: Lilly Endowment Inc 2801 N Meridian St PO Box 88068 Indianapolis IN 46208-0068

ROBBINS, OREM OLFORD, insurance company executive; b. Mpls., Feb. 5, 1915; s. Douglas Ford and Grace (Rorem) R.; m. Annette Strand Scherer, May 17, 1992; children: Ford M., Ross S., Gail R. Tomei, Cynthia R. Rothbard. BBA with distinction, U. Minn., 1936; BS in Law, William Mitchell Coll. Law, 1946, JD, 1948. Comml. rep. NW Bell Telephone Co., Mpls., 1936-48; dep. dir. US Treas. Dept., Mpls., 1948-49; sales rep. Conn. Gen. Life Ins. Co., Mpls., 1949-56; founder, chmn. Security Life Ins. Co. Am., Mpls., 1956—. Bd. dirs., past pres. Family and Children's Svcs., Mpls., 1968—; bd. govs., past chmn. Meth. Hosp., Mpls., 1960-90; past treas., bd. dirs. Goodwill/Easter Seals, St. Paul, 1958-68, 75-88; life trustee Hamline U., St. Paul, 1979—, chmn. bd. trustees, 1990-91. Col. US Army, 1941-46. Decorated Legion of Merit; recipient Outstanding Achievement award U. Minn., 2001; named Disting. Eagle Scout, 2000. Fellow Life Mgmt. Assn.; mem. Am. Soc. CLU (pres. Mpls. chpt. 1959), Health Underwriters Assn., Chartered Fin. Cons., Am. Legion, Skylight Club (Mpls.), Naples Yacht Club, Mpls. Club, Officer's Club, Masons. Republican. Methodist. Office: Security Life Ins Co Am 10901 Red Circle Dr Minnetonka MN 55343-9304 Home Phone: 239-261-4295. E-mail: oorobbins@securitylife.com.

ROBE, THURLOW RICHARD, retired engineering educator, dean; s. Thrulow Scott and Mary Alice (McKibben) R.; m. Eleanora C. Komyati, Aug. 27, 1955; children: Julia, Kevin, Stephen, Edward. BSC.E., Ohio U., 1955, MS in Mech. Engring., 1962; PhD in Applied Mechanics, Stanford U., 1966. Engr. Gen. Electric Co., Niles, Ohio, Cleve., Erie, Pa., Evendale,Ohio, 1954-60; acting instr. to instr. Ohio U., Athens, 1960-63, dean Russ Coll. Engring. and Tech., 1980-96, Cruse W. Moss prof. Engring. Edn., 1992-96, founding dir. T. Richard and Eleanora K. Robe Leadership Inst., 1997—2005, dir. Innovation Ctr. Authority, 1983-96; asst. prof to prof., assoc. dean, spl. asst. to pres. U. Ky., Lexington, 1965-80; rsch. fellow Postgrad. Sch. Applied Dynamics U. Edinburgh, Scotland, 1973; dean emeritus, Moss prof. emeritus Russ Coll. Engring. and Tech., Ohio U., Athens, 1996—; pres., chmn. bd. Q.E.D. Assocs., Inc., Lexington, 1975-83. Trustee Engring. Found. Ohio, 1988-94; bd. trustees Ohio Aerospace Inst. 1990-96, bd. govs. Edison Materials Tech. Ctr., 1987-96; mem. adv. bd. Robe Leadership Inst., 2005—; liaison engring. accreditation commn. Accreditation Bd. Engring. and Tech., 1989-91; mem. Russ Prize Selection Com., NAE, 2000—. Contbr. articles to profl. jours.; patentee trailer hitch. Bd. dirs. Athens County Cmty. Redevel. Corp., 1980-86; treas. South Lexington Little League, 1976-80; vice chmn. Thoroughbred dist., Boy Scouts Am., 1975-77; mem.-at-large Oconee Dist. Boy Scouts Am., 2007—; pres. Tates Creek H.S. PTA, Lexington, 1975-76; bd. dirs. U. Ky. Athletics Ass.n, 1975-80; bd. trustees Assn. Ohio Commodores, 1995-97; trustee Ohio U. Found., 1998-2007, trustee emeritus, 2007—. Maj. USAFR, 1955—85, officer, jet fighter pilot USAF, 1956—59. Recipient Alumni medal of merit Ohio U., 1993; named Am. Coun. on Edn. Adminstrn. fellow, 1970-71, Ohio U. Alumnus of Yr., 1996, inductee Acad. Disting. Grads., Russ Coll. Engring. & Tech., 2001. Mem. ASME, NSPE (profl. engring. in edn. exec. bd., ctrl. region vice-chmn. 1987-89), Am. Soc. Engring. Edn. (Outstanding Contbn. in Rsch. award 1966), Athens Reading Club, Athens Symposiarchs, Rotary, Sigma Xi, Tau Beta Pi, Omicron Delta Kappa, Alpha Lambda Delta Personal E-mail: robe@ohio.edu.

ROBEL, LAUREN, dean, law educator; b. Dec. 1953; BA with high honors, Auburn U., 1978; JD summa cum laude, Ind. U., 1983, postgrad., 1985. Bar: US Supreme Ct., Ind., Ill. Law clk. to Hon. Jesse Eschbach, U.S. Ct. Appeals (7th cir.), 1983—85; assoc. dean Ind. U. Sch. Law, Bloomington, Ind., 1991—2002, Val Nolan prof. law, 1999—, acting dean, 2002—03, dean, 2003—. Vis. faculty U. Panthenon-Assas, Paris; reporter rules com. U.S. Dist. Ct. (so. dist.) Ind.; mem. rules com. Ind. Supreme Ct. Author: Les États des Noirs: Federalisme et question raciale aux États-unis, 2000, Federal Courts: Cases and Materials on Judicial Federalism and The Lawyering Process, 2005; contbr. articles to profl. jours. Recipient Leon Wallace Teaching Award, 1997, Teaching Excellence Recognition Award, Ind. U. Sch. Law, 1997, 1999, Leonard D. Fromm Public Interest Award, 1999, 2002. Mem.: Ind. State Bar Women (Law Recognition award 2000), Ind. Bar Found. (Pro Bono Publico award 1997), Order of Coif. Office: Ind Univ Sch Law 211 S Indiana Ave Bloomington IN 47405 Home Phone: 812-334-8844; Office Phone: 812-855-8885. Business E-Mail: lrobel@indiana.edu.

ROBERSON, ROGER T., transportation executive; Chmn. Roberson Transp. Svcs., Mahomet, Ill., 1989—. Office: Roberson Transp Svcs 1100 S Roberson Dr Mahomet IL 61853-8532 also: PO Box 9800 Champaign IL 61826-8800

ROBERTS, A(RTHUR) WAYNE, organization administrator; b. Burlington, Vt., Feb. 25, 1944; s. Arthur William and Phyllis (Stockwell) R.; children: Arthur Weber, Morgan Wayne, Ethan Duvall. BS in Bus. Adminstrn., Babson Coll., 1964; MBA, U. Mass., 1967. IBM fin. analyst Space Guidance Ctr., 1965—; IBM fin. adviser Govt. Edn. Med. Region, Washington, 1965-66; advt. mktg. rep. IBM, Cin., 1966-72, account mgr. Albany, N.Y., 1972-75; pres., owner AWR Corp., 1973-80; asst. prof. econs. and mgmt. Johnson State Coll., 1974-80; sr. cons., regional polit. dir. Reagan-Bush Campaign Com. in Northeast, 1980; asst. dir. personnel for presdl. transition The White House, 1980-81, dep. dir. White House personnel, 1981; acting project mgr. U.S. Synthetic Fuel Corp., Washington, 1981; sec.'s regional rep. U.S. Dept. Edn., Washington, 1981-83, dep. under sec., 1983-86; pres. Lake Champlain Regional C. of C., Burlington, Vt., 1986—. Mem. Gov.'s Bd. on Small Bus., 1979; mem. Johnson State Small Bus. Adv. Bd. Vermont, 1982; del. Rep. Nat. Conv., 1980, 84, 88; mem. Chittenden County Rep. Com., South Burlington Rep. Com., Vt. Bush for Pres. Com., Bus. Roundtable, Vt. Bus. Forum; mem. bd. Vt./Can. Free Trade; mem. Small Bus. Adminstrn. Adv. Coun.; commr. Nat. Commn. Employment Policy, 1990-91. Recipient Commitment to Excellence in Edn. award Johnson State Coll. Found., 1985. Mem. Vt. State C. of C. (bd. dirs.). Office: Macalester College Saint Paul MN 55105 Home: 124 Fairway Dr South Burlington VT 05403-5844

ROBERTS, CHARLES PATRICK (PAT ROBERTS), senator; b. Topeka, Kans., Apr. 20, 1936; m. Frankie Fann, 1969; children: David, Ashleigh, Anne-Wesley. BA in Journalism, Kans. State U., 1958. Pub. Litchfield Park, Ariz., 1962-67; adminstrv. asst. to U.S. Senator Frank Carlson, U.S. Senate, Washington, 1967-68; adminstrv. asst. to U.S. Congressman Keith Sebelius U.S. Ho. of Reps., Washington, 1968-80; mem. 97th to 104th Congresses from Kans. 1st Dist., Washington, 1980-96; US Senator from Kansas, 1997—. Com. agr. US Senate, com. armed services, com. health, edn., labor and pensions, select com. ethics, chmn. select com. intelligence. Served with USMC, 1958—62. Recipient Am. Farmer award, Future Farmers of Am., 1986, Disting. Leadership award, Prodn. Credit Assn., Disting. Svc. award, Kans. Farm Bur., Wheat Man of Yr., Assn. Wheat Growers, 1993, Public Svc. award, Am. Chem. Soc., 2001, John H. Chafee award public svc., Rep. Main Street Partnership, 2003. Republican. Methodist. Office: US Senate 109 Hart Senate Off Bldg Washington DC 20510-1605 also: District Office Ste 203 100 Military Plz Dodge City KS 67801 Office Phone: 202-224-4774, 620-227-2244. Office Fax: 202-224-3514, 620-227-2264. E-mail: pat_roberts@roberts.senate.gov.

ROBERTS, DAVID, airport executive; Dir. Indpls. Internat. Airport. Office: Indpls Internat Airport Indpls Airport Authority 2500 S High School Rd Indianapolis IN 46241-4943

ROBERTS, DOUGLAS B., state official; Treas. State of Mich., Lansing, 1991-98, 2001—; v.p. best practices Lockhead Martin, 1998—2001. Office: Mich Dept Treasury Lansing MI 48922

ROBERTS, JOHN, radio personality; b. St. Louis; married; 2 children. Student, Meramec C.C., Lindenwood Coll. Music dir., announcer Classic 99, St. Louis. Office: Classic 99 85 Founders Ln Saint Louis MO 63105

ROBERTS, JOHN CHARLES, law educator; b. Aberdeen, SD, Feb. 29, 1940; s. Jacob John Schmitt and Leona (Blethen) Blake; m. Kathleen Kelly (div. 1985); children: Katherine, John Charles Jr.; m. Lynn Dale Friedman, Dec. 22, 1985; 1 child, Emily Sara. BS, Northwestern U., 1961; LL.B., Yale U., 1968. Bar: U.S. Dist. Ct. D.C. 1969, Mich. 1981. Assoc. Covington & Burling, Washington, 1968-71; assoc. dean, lectr. Yale U. Law Sch., New Haven, 1971-77; gen. counsel U.S. Senate Com. on Armed Services, 1977-80; adj. prof. law Washington Coll. Law, Am. U., 1978-80; dean, prof. law Wayne State U. Law Sch., Detroit, 1980-86; prof., dean Law Sch. DePaul U., Chgo., 1986-96, v.p. for univ. advancement, 1996-97, prof. law, 1997—. Mem. exec. com. Inst. for Continuing Legal Edn., Chgo., 1988-91. Mem. adv. com. Mich. Psychiat. Soc., 1980-86; bd. dirs. Constl. Rights Found., 1992-96. Lt. USN, 1961-65. Mem. ABA, Assn. Am. Law Schs. (mem. exec. com., chmn. sect. instn. advancement 1987-88, chmn., sec. adminstrn. law schs. 1993-94), Order of Coif. Democrat. Avocation: collecting modern first editions. Office: DePaul U Coll Law 25 E Jackson Blvd Chicago IL 60604-2289 Office Phone: 312-362-8776. Business E-Mail: jroberts@depaul.edu.

ROBERTS, MICHAEL J., former food products executive; b. Chgo., Oct. 20, 1950; m. Maureen Long; children: Lauren, Lindsey, Michelle. BA in Sociology, Loyola U. V.p., supply chain mgmt. McDonald's Corp, 1990—95; asst. v.p., district mgr., McDonald's LA region McDonald's Corp., 1989—90, regional v.p., Chgo. north region, 1995—96, v.p., field ops.; pres. West div. McDonald's USA, pres., 2001—04, CEO, 2004; pres., COO McDonald's Corp., 2004—06. Adv. dir. McDonald's Corp., bd. dirs., 2004—06.

ROBERTS, PATRICK KENT, lawyer; b. Waynesville, Mo., Feb. 9, 1948; s. J. Kent and Winona (Clark) R.; m. Jeanne Billings, April 17, 1976; children: Christopher, Kimberly, Courtney. Student, U. Ill., Urbana, 1970; AB, U. Mo., 1970, JD, 1973. Bar: Mo. 1974, U.S. Dist. Ct. (we. dist.) Mo. 1974, U.S. Ct. Appeals (8th cir.) 1979. Lawyer U.S. Senator Stuart Symington, Columbia, Mo., 1973-76; ptnr. Daniel, Clampett, Powell & Cunningham, Springfield, Mo., 1976—2001; of counsel Cunningham, Harpool & Cordonnier, Springfield, 2002—03, Patrick K. Roberts LLC, Springfield, 2004—. Adj. prof. Webster U., 2000—, Kaplan U., 2004—. Mem. ctrl. com. Greene County Dems., Springfield, 1982-84, 88-90. Mem. ABA, Mo. Bar Assn., Springfield Met. Bar Assn. Lodges: Rotary. Democrat. Methodist. Office: 3561 E Eastwood Blvd Springfield MO 65809-2120 Home Phone: 417-887-5567; Office Phone: 417-849-1239. E-mail: patrickkroberts@abanet.org.

ROBERTS, R. MICHAEL, animal scientist, biochemist, educator; b. U.K., 1941; BA in Botany, Oxford U., PhD in Plant Physiology and Biochemistry; doctorate (hon.), U. Liege, Belgium, 1998. Prof. animal scis. and biochemistry U. Mo., Columbia, 1985—, curators' prof., 1996—, dir. Life Scis. Ctr., 2004—. Vice-chmn. Gordon Conf. on Mammalian Genital Tract Plymouth State Coll., 1986; chmn. Gordon Conf. on Reproductive Tract Biology Brewster Acad., 1988; fgn. specialist Nat. Inst. Animal Industry, Japan, 1998; chief scientist Nat. Rsch. Initiative Competitive Grants Program/Coop. State Rsch., Edn., Extension Svc./USDA, 1998—2000. Contbr. articles to profl. jours. Named Disting. Scientist, USDA, 1992; recipient Rsch. award, Soc. for Study of Reproduction, 1990, Merit award, NIH, 1990—2000, Milstein award, Internat. Soc. Interferon and Cytokine Rsch., 1995, Alexander von Humboldt award for agr., 1996, Wolf prize in agr., Wolf Found., Israel, 2003. Mem.: NAS. Office: U Mo Columbia Divsn Animal Scis 158 Animal Sci Rsch Ctr Columbia MO 65211

ROBERTS, RANDY W., history professor; PhD, La. State U., 1978. Prof. hist. and Am. studies Purdue U., West Lafayette, Ind. Contbr. chapters to books, articles to profl. publs.; author: Jack Dempsey: The Manassa Mauler, 1979, Papa Jack: Jack Johnson and the Era of White Hopes, 1983, "But They Can't Beat Us:" Oscar Robertson and the Crispus Attucks Tigers, 1999; co-author (with James S. Olson): Winning is the Only Thing: Sports in America since 1945, 1989, Where the Domino Fell: America in Vietnam, 1990, John Wayne American, 1995, A Line in the Sand: The Alamo in Blood and Memory, 2000, American Experiences: Readings in American History, 2005; co-author: (with J. Gregory Harrison) Heavy Justice: The State of Indiana v. Michael G. Tyson, 1994; co-author: (with David Welky) The Steelers Reader, 2001, One for the Thumb: The New Steelers Reader, 2006; co-author: America and Its People: A Mosaic in the Making, 2003; co-author: (with Elliott J. Gorn and Terry D. Bilhartz) Constructing the American Past: A Source Book of a People's History, 2005; co-editor (with James S. Olson): My Lai: A Brief History with Documents, 1998; co-editor: (with David Welky) Charles Lindbergh: The Power and Peril of Celebrity, 1927-1941, 2003; editor: Pittsburgh Sports: Stories from the Steel City, 2000, The Rock, the Curse and the Hub: A Random History of Boston Sports, 2005. Recipient US Prof. of Yr. award, Carnegie Found. for Advancement of Tchg. and Coun. for Advancement and Support of Edn., 2006. Office: Dept Hist Purdue U University Hall 672 Oval Dr West Lafayette IN 47907-2087 Office Phone: 765-494-0040. Office Fax: 765-496-1755. E-mail: rroberts@purdue.edu.

ROBERTS, ROD, state representative; b. Waverly, Iowa, Oct. 22, 1957; BA, Iowa Christian Coll. Devel. dir. The Christian Chs./Chs. of Christ in Iowa; mem. Iowa Ho. Reps., DesMoines, 2001—, vice chair edn. appropriations com., mem. econ. devel. com., mem. edn. com., mem. human resources com. Dir. Carroll Cmty. Sch. Bd.; active Carroll Cmty. Christmas Chorus; bd. mem., found. trustee New Hope Fillage, Carroll. Mem.: Rotary Club. Republican. Office: State Capitol East 12th and Grand Des Moines IA 50319 also: 732 San Salvador Ave Carroll IA 51401

ROBERTS, THEODORE HARRIS, banker; b. Gillett, Ark., May 14, 1929; s. Edward and Gertrude (Harris) R.; m. Elisabeth Law, July 17, 1953; children: Susan, William(dec.), Julia, John. BA in Govt., Northwestern State U., 1949; MA in Polit. Sci., Okla. State U., 1950; postgrad., U. Chgo. Grad. Sch. Bus., 1956. With Harris Trust and Savs. Bank, Chgo., 1953-82; exec. v.p., sec., treas. Harris Bank and Harris Bankcorp Inc., 1971-82, dir., exec. com., 1975-82; pres. Fed. Res. Bank St. Louis, 1983-85; chmn. bd., chief exec. officer Talman Home Fed. Savs. & Loan, Chgo., 1985-92; pres. LaSalle Nat. Corp., 1992-95, retired. Sr. cons. ABN AMRO, 1995—. Mem. Chgo. Club, Comml. Club Chgo., Econ. Club Chgo., Exmoor Country Club (Highland Park, Ill.). Office: 135 S La Salle St Ste 260 Chicago IL 60603-4500 E-mail: ted.roberts@abnamro.com.

ROBERTS, THOMAS MICHAEL, state legislator; b. Mar. 3, 1952; s. Harold Leonard and Susie (Williams) R.; m. Regina Michele Walker; children: Edward, Erienne. Student, Sinclair Cmty. Coll.; BA, Univ. Dayton, 1977. Clerk Montgomery County Clerk's Civil Divsn., 1972-77; supr. Montgomery County Auto Title Divsn., 1977; bailiff Montgomery County Common Pleas Ct., 1977-86; mem. Montgomery County Dem. Com., 1984; mem. congress adv. coun. U.S. Rep. Tony Hall, 1985; Ohio State rep. Dist. 37, 1986-92, Dist. 39, 1993—; mem. adv com. Dayton Job Corp., 1993—. Chmn. Aging & Housing Com., mem. agrl. & Natural resources, Children & Youth, Energy & Environ. com., Zone oversights & Policy adv. group Dept. Youth Svc., chmn. Select Com. Homeless & Affordable Housing, mem. Judiciary & Criminal Justice Com., Child Abuse and Juvenile Justice. Active Boy Scouts, 1986; co-chmn. pub. affairs com. Montgomery County Mental Health Assn., 1979-84, pres., 1986-87. Recipient Outstanding Young Man of Yr. award Montgomery Coun. Young Dem., 1982, Outstanding Achievement award, 1986, Ohio Homeless Coalition award, Spl. Contbr. award Ohio Housing Coalition, Pres.'s award Ohio Youth Svc., Men & Women Courage award Cmty. Outreach. Mem. Dem. Voters League, Black Dem. of Ohio. Office: Ohio Ho of Reps State House Columbus OH 43215

ROBERTS, TOM, state senator; Student, Sinclair C.C.; BA, U. Dayton. Educator; state rep. Ohio Ho. of Reps., Columbus, 1986—2000; state sen., dist. 5 Ohio State Senate, Columbus, 2001—, ranking minority m em. agr. and ways and means and eocn. devel. coms., mem. energy, natural resources and environment, pub. utilities, and state and local govt. and vets. affairs coms. Chair, Domestic violence task force City of Dayton, Ohio; chair Home Based for Arts Coun.; former chmn. Alliance for Work Base Edn.; mem. Parity 2000; former chmn. Ohio Legis. Black Caucus; mem. Legal Assistance Found. Bd. Named Legislator of Yr., Ohio Manufactured Homes; recipient Al Clayton Svc. award, Trotwood Dem. Club, 2001. Democrat. Office: Senate Bldg Rm # 48 ground fl Columbus OH 43215

ROBERTS, WILLIAM EVERETT, lawyer; b. Pierre, SD, May 12, 1926; s. Everett David and Bonnie (Martin) R.; m. Cynthia Cline, July 18, 1953; children: Catherine C. Roberts-Martin, Laura M., Nancy F., David H. BS, U. Minn., 1947; LLB, Yale U., 1950. Bar: Ind. 1950, U.S. Supreme Ct. 1964. Employee, ptnr. Duck and eighbours, Indpls., 1950-58; ptnr. Cadick, Burns, Duck & Neighbours, Indpls., 1958-60, Roberts, Ryder, Rogers & Scism, Indpls., 1960-85, Barnes & Thornburg, Indpls., 1986-93, of counsel, 1994—. Pres., bd. dirs. Park-Tudor Sch., Indpls., 1982-83; elder Second Presbyn. Ch., Indpls., 1962—; trustee Indpls. Mus. Art, 1978—; pres. New Hope of Ind., Indpls., 1986-87. Fellow Am. Bar Found.; mem. ABA, Ind. Bar Assn., Indpls. Bar Assn., Rotary Club, Meridian Hills Country Club (pres. 1983-84). Republican. Home: 10466 Spring Highland Dr Indianapolis IN 46290-1101 Office: Barnes & Thornburg 11 S Meridian St Ste 1313 Indianapolis IN 46204-3535 Office Phone: 317-231-7520.

ROBERTS-MAMONE, LISA A., lawyer; BA magna cum laude, Grove City Coll., 1985; JD magna cum laude, Case Wester Res. U., 1988. Bar: Ohio 1988. With Jones Day, Cleve., 1988—, ptnr., 2000—. Trustee The Laub Found.; mem. Estate Planning Coun. of Cleve., Estate Planning Discussion Group, Cleve., Case Western Reserve U. Estate Planning Adv. Coun., Hathaway Brown Sch. Profl. Advisors Com.; mem. diamond adv. group U. Hosps. Cleve.; mem. nominating com. Girl Scouts NE Ohio. Mem.: Cleve. Bar Assn. (estate planning, probate and trust law sect.), Ohio State Bar Assn. (estate planning, trust and probate sect.). Office: Jones Day orth Point 901 Lakeside Ave Cleveland OH 44114-1190 Office Phone: 216-586-7172.

ROBERTSON, DAVID ALAN, museum director, educator; b. Jefferson City, Mo., Oct. 10, 1950; s. Roy Victor and Mary Jane (Buford-Threlkeld) R. BA in English, U. Mo., 1973, MA in Art History, 1976; PhD in Art History, U. Pa., 1983. Mus. asst. U. Mo. Mus., Columbia, 1975-76; rsch. asst. Victoria and Albert Museum, London, 1976; curatorial asst. Yale Ctr. for Brit. Art, New Haven, 1977-78; tchg. fellow U. Pa., Phila., 1978-81; staff supr. Rosenbach Mus. and Libr., Phila., 1980-82; dir. Dickinson Coll., Carlisle, Pa., 1982—2002, U. Oregon, Mus. Art, 1996—2000, Loyola U., D'Aray Gallery, 1992—96; assoc. dir. Smart Mus., U. Chgo., 2000—02; dir. Mary and Leigh Block Mus Art Northwestern U., Evanston, Ill., 2002—, lectr. art history dept., 2003—. Fulbright prof. U. Munich, Germany, 1989-90; mem. selection com. Fulbright Commn., Bonn, Germany, 1989; grant reviewer Inst. Mus. Svcs., Washington, 1989-91. Penfield fellow U. Pa., Vienna, Austria, 1981-82, Kress fellow Kress Found., London, 1976, Vienna, 1980. Mem. Am. Assn. Mus., Coll. Art Assn., Assn. Coll. and U. Mus. and Galleries. Office: Mary and Leigh Block Mus Art Northwestern U 40 Arts Circle Dr Evanston IL 60208 Office Phone: 847-491-2562. Business E-Mail: d-robertson@northwestern.edu.

ROBERTSON, DAVID WAYNE, pharmaceutical executive; b. Dumas, Tex., July 30, 1955; s. R.L. and N.C. R. BS, Stephen F. Austin State U., 1977; MS, U. Ill., 1978, PhD, 1981. Sr. medicinal chemist Eli Lilly and Co., Indpls., 1981-84, rsch. scientist, 1985-87, sr. rsch. scientist, 1988-89, rsch. group leader, 1988-89, dir. cen. nervous system rsch., 1990-91; v.p. medicinal chemistry Ligand Pharms., Inc., San Diego, 1991-92, v.p. rsch., 1992-93, v.p. discovery rsch., 1993-96; exec. dir. R & D DuPont Pharm. Co., Wilmington, 1996-99; v.p. rsch. Pharmacia & Upjohn, Kalamazoo, 1999—2001; exec. dir. global rsch. and devel. Pfizer, Ann Arbor, Mich., 2002—. Contbr. articles to profl. jours. Mem. Soc. for Neurosci., Am. Soc. Pharmacology and Exptl. Therapeutics, Am. Chem. Soc. Office: Pfizer Global Rsch & Devel 2800 Plymouth Rd Ann Arbor MI 48105

ROBERTSON, JAMES MAGRUDER, geological research administrator; b. Port Clinton, Ohio, Sept. 24, 1943; married. BA, Carleton Coll., 1965; MS, U. Mich., 1968, PhD in Econ. Geology, 1972. Asst. prof. geology Mich. Technol. U., 1972-74; mining geologist N.Mex. Bur. Mines and Mineral Resources, 1974-86, sr. econ. geologist, 1986-88, assoc. dir., 1988-92; dir. and state geologist Wis. Geol. Survey, Madison, 1992—. Mem. Geochem. Soc., Geol. Soc. Am., Soc. Econ. Geology, Sigma Xi. Office: Univ Wisconsin Geol & Natural History Survey 3817 Mineral Point Rd Madison WI 53705-5121 also: Wis Geol Survey 3817 Mineral Point Rd Madison WI 53705-5121

ROBERTSON, JERRY EARL, retired manufacturing company executive; b. Detroit, Oct. 25, 1932; s. Earl Howard and Nellie (Wright) R.; m. Joanne Alice Wesner, Sept. 3, 1955; children: Scott Clark, Lisa Kay, Stuart Todd. BS, Miami U., Oxford, Ohio, 1954; MS, U. Mich., 1956, PhD, 1959. With Minn. Mining & Mfg. Co., St. Paul, 1963-94, tech. dir. med. products div., 1973-74, dept. mgr. surg. products dept., 1974-75, gen. mgr. surg. products div., 1975-79, div. v.p. surg. products div., 1979-80, group v.p. health care products and services, 1980-84, exec. v.p. life scis. sector, 1984-86, exec. v.p. life scis. sector and corp. svcs., 1986-94; ret., 1994. Bd. dirs. Coherent, Inc., Choice Hotels Internat., Steris Corp. Bd. reference MAP Internat., Brunswick, Ga., 1986-94; bd. dirs. Project HOPE, 1988-98, Manor Care Inc., 1989-98, Cardinal Health Distbn., Inc., 1991-99. Mem. Pharm. Mfrs. Assn. (bd. dirs. 1984-89), Health Industry Mfrs. Assn. (bd. dirs. 1982-91, chmn. 1990-91). Unitarian Universalist. Office: Minn World Trade Ctr 30 7th St E Ste 3050 Saint Paul MN 55101-4921

ROBERTSON, LEON H., management consultant, educator; b. Atlanta; s. Grady Jospeh and Pearline (Chandler) R. BS in Indsl. Mgmt., Ga. Inst. Tech., 1957, MS, 1959; postgrad., U. Okla.-Norman, 1958, U. Mich., 1961; PhD in Bus. Adminstrn., Ga. State U., 1968. Mgr. mgmt. cons. divsn. Arthur Andersen & Co., Atlanta, 1960-65; prof. bus. adminstrn. Ga. State U., 1965-75; corp. v.p. Tex. Gas Corp., Owensboro, Ky., 1975-78, sr. v.p., 1982-83; chmn., CEO Am. Carriers, Inc., Overland Park, Kans., 1978-88; chmn. bd. dirs. Midwest Coast Transport, Overland Park, 1988-89; prof. mgmt., dir. divsn. bus. adminstrn. U. Mo., Kansas City, 1990-96, prof. Internat. Acad. Programs, 1996-98, dir. Ctr. for Internat. Bus., 1999—. Office: Univ of Mo-Kansas City Henry W Bloch Sch Bus & Pub Admn 5110 Cherry St Kansas City MO 64110-2426 Business E-Mail: robertsonl@umkc.edu.

ROBERTSON, MARTHA RAPPAPORT, state legislator, consultant; b. Boston, Sept. 14, 1952; d. Jerome Lyle and Nancy (Vahey) Rappaport; divorced; 1 child, Colby. BA, Franklin & Marshall Coll., 1974; MBA, U. Pa., 1976. Mktg. and new bus. devel. exec. Gen. Mills, Inc., Mpls., 1976-91; mem. Minn. Senate from 45th dist., St. Paul, 1993—. Republican.

ROBERTSON, MICHAEL SWING, minister; b. Boston, July 20, 1935; s. Charles Stuart and Elizabeth (Swing) R.; m. Margaret Filoon, Sept. 17, 1960 (dec. Oct. 1996); children: Michael Swing, Ashlee Whipple, Christopher Filoon, Andrew Stuart; m. Emily Erickson, Feb. 22, 1998. AB, Harvard U., 1957, grad. Advanced Mgmt. Program, 1979. With Robertson Factories, Inc., 1957-80, exec. v.p., 1968-73, pres., 1973-79, chmn. bd., 1979-80; dir. Robertson-Swing Co., 1980—; pres. The Berkley Co. Inc., 1981-90, Reactions Inc., 1985-90; treas. Falmouth Marine Inc., 1981-88; pres., treas. Orchard Computer Inc., 1984-91, chmn., treas., 1991-93; exec. sec. Nat. Assn. Congl. Christian Chs., Oak Creek, Wis., 1991-97; minister Pilgrim Congl. Ch., Taunton, Mass., 2000—02; ch. coord. Cmty. Faith Alliance, Milw., 1997-2000; exec. dir. Cmty. Village, Ltd., 1998-2000, 2003—; pastor Pilgrim Congrl. Ch., Taunton, 2001—02, Urban

Ministry Cmty. Bapt. Ch., Milw., 2003, Union Congl. Ch., Braintree, Mass., 2004—06, First Ch. of Squantum, Quincy, Mass., 2006—. V.p. adv. coun. Coll. of Bus. and Industry, Southeastern Mass. U., North Dartmouth, Mass., 1979-91; selectman, Town of Berkley, Mass., 1974-80, chmn. 1979-80; mem. Pres.'s Adv. Com. for Trade egotiations, 1983-86; bd. dirs. Mass. Easter Seal Soc., 1977-91, pres. 1982-83; bd. dirs. Nat. Easter Seal Soc., 1985-91, Wis. Easter Seal Soc., 1994-95; bd. dirs. Trips for Kids, New Bedford, 2005-, treas., 2007, chmn., pres., 2008; chmn. Berkley Rep. Town com., 1977-91; Rep. nominee U.S. Senate from Mass., 1976, nominee for Mass. state auditor, 1982; co-chmn. Mass Reagan for Pres. Com., 1980; Bristol County coord. Reagan/Bush campaign; co-chmn. Mass. Dole for Pres. Commn., 1987; chmn. Southeastern Mass. campaign Harvard Coll., 1981; chmn. Friends of Harvard Track, 1986-91; trustee Barnstable County Hosp., 1985-90, chmn., 1988. Mem. Harvard Varsity Club, Harvard Club of Boston, Harvard Bus. Sch. Assn. Boston, Squantum Yacht Club. Congregationalist. Home: 176 Bellevue Rd Squantum MA 02171 Office: 164 Bellevue Rd Squantum MA 02171 Office Phone: 617-328-6649. Office Fax: 617-328-3391. Personal E-mail: emmyandmike@verizon.net.

ROBERTSON, OSCAR PALMER (BIG O ROBERTSON), chemical company executive, former professional basketball player; b. Charlotte, Tenn., Nov. 24, 1938; BBBA, U. Cin., 1960. Player U.S. Olympic Basketball Team, 1960; basketball player Cin. Royals, 1960-70, Milw. Bucks, 1970-74; founder, pres., CEO, Orchem, Inc., Cin., 1981-1996, Orpack-Stone Corp., Herrin, Ill., 1990—, Orflex Ltd., Cin., 1995—, ORDMS, Marlton, N.J., 1997—. Player NBA Championship Team, 1971. Named Sporting News Coll. Player of Yr., 1958, 59, 60, Sporting News All-Star First Team, 1958, 59, 60, NBA Rookie of Yr., 1961, All NBA First Team, 1961-69; player NBA All Star Games, 1961-72; named MVP, NBA, 1964, MVP in NBA All-Star Games, 1961, 64, 69; named to NBA 35th Anniversary All-Star Team, 1980; elected to Naismith Meml. Basketball Hall of Fame, 1979, Nat. Collegiate Basketball Hall of Fame, 2006. Office: Orchem Corp 4293 Mulhauser Rd Fairfield OH 45014-5450

ROBERTSON, PAUL JOSEPH, state legislator; b. Depauw, Ind., Apr. 25, 1946; s. William Edward and Mary Rita (Sieg) R.; m. Jill Ann Moss, 1971; children: Jennifer Lynn, Chad Alan, Heather Leigh, Jessica Moss. Student, Vincennes U., 1964-66; BS, Ind. State U., 1968, MS, 1970. Tchr., coach North Ctrl. H.S., 1968-69, Eng H.S., 1969-71, Vincennes H.S., 1971-73, Corydon H.S., 1973-85; mem. from 70th dist. Ind. State Ho. of Reps., 1978—. Del. Ind. State Dem. Conv., 1976-78; mem. Dem. Youth for Hamilton Campaign, 1974. Recipient Legis. award Ind. Alliance for Better Child Care, Legis. award UnitedWay. Mem. NEA, Ind. Tchrs. Assn., Lions, KC. Home: 8990 Bird Trail Rd NW Depauw IN 47115-8923 Office: Ind Ho of Reps State Capitol Indianapolis IN 46204

ROBERTSON, RICHARD EARL, physical chemist, educator; b. Long Beach, Calif., Nov. 12, 1933; s. Earl Austin and A. Isobel (Roberts) R.; m. Joyce W. Conger, Sept. 4, 1955 (div. 1972); children: Christopher, Jill; m. Patricia L. Richmond, Apr. 20, 1974. BA, Occidental Coll., LA, 1955; student, UCLA, 1955-56; PhD, Calif. Inst. Tech., 1960. Phys. chemist rsch. lab. GE, Schenectady, NY, 1960-70; staff scientist Ford Motor Co., Dearborn, Mich., 1970-86; prof. materials sci. and engring. U. Mich., Ann Arbor, 1986—, dir. Macromolecular Sci. and Engring. Ctr., 1995—2000. Contbr. articles to profl. jours. Postdoctoral fellow Washington U., St. Louis, 1959-60. Fellow Am. Phys. Soc.; mem. Am. Chem. Soc., Sigma Xi. Office: U Mich Dept Materials Sci Eng Ann Arbor MI 48109-2136 E-mail: rer@umich.edu.

ROBERTSON, RICHARD STUART, insurance holding company executive; b. Spokane, Wash., June 14, 1942; s. Stuart A. and Marjory (Moch) R.; m. Trudy Ann Prendergast, July 31, 1976; children: Thomas Stuart, Richard Andrew. BS, Calif. Inst. Tech., 1963. Chief reinsurance actuary Lincoln Nat. Life Ins. Co., Ft. Wayne, Ind., 1963-74; sr. v.p., chief fin. officer Lincoln Nat. Corp., Ft. Wayne, 1974-86, exec. v.p., CFO, 1986-92, exec. v.p., corp. risk officer, 1992-98; sr. v.p. Lincoln Nat. Reassurance Co., 1999—. Bd. dirs. Lincoln Re S.A., Lincoln China, Kyoei Lincoln Reins. Svc. Co., Linsco Reins. Co.; chmn. Actuarial Stds. Bd., 1996-97. Fellow Soc. Actuaries (pres. 1985-86); mem. Am. Acad. Actuaries (v.p. 1980-81, pres. elect 1998, pres. 1999). Episcopalian. Home: 12618 Aboite Center Rd Fort Wayne IN 46814-9725 Fax: 219-455-1036. E-mail: rrobertson@lnc.com.

ROBERTSON, TIMOTHY JOEL, statistician, educator; b. Denver, Oct. 4, 1937; s. Flavel P. and Helen C. (Oliver) Girdner; m. Joan K. Slater, Aug. 18, 1959; children— Kelly, Jana, Doug, Mike BA in Math., U. Mo., 1959, MS in Math., 1961, PhD in Stats., 1966. Asst. prof. Cornell Coll., Mt. Vernon, Iowa, 1961-63; prof. stats. U. Iowa, Iowa City, 1965—2004, prof. emeritus, 2004—. Vis. prof. U. N.C., Chapel Hill, 1974-75, U. Calif.-Davis, 1983-84; Eugene Lukacs Disting. vis. prof. Bowling Green State U., 1991-92; vis. lectr. Com. Pres. Statis. Soc., 1971-74. Author: (with F.T. Wright and R.L. Dykstra) Order Restricted Statistical Inference; assoc. editor Am. Math. Monthly, 1977-81; mem. editl. bd. Comms. in Stats., 1981-92; assoc. editor Jour. Am. Statis. Assn., 1990-96; contbr. numerous articles to profl. jours. Recipient Collegiate Teaching award U. Iowa, 1990. Fellow Am. Statis. Assn. (council 1974-75), Inst. Math. Stats., Internat. Statis. Inst.; mem. Math. Assn. Am., Sigma Xi, Sierra Club Democrat. Avocations: canoeing, camping, bicycling, walking. Home: 673 Garfield Rd West Branch IA 52358-8574 Office: Univ Iowa Dept Stats/Actuarial Sci Iowa City IA 52242 Home Phone: 319-643-3118; Office Phone: 319-335-2019. Personal E-mail: rttincity@aol.com.

ROBERTSON, WILLIAM RICHARD, diversified financial services company executive, retired banker; b. Schenectady, NY, July 26, 1941; s. Bruce Manson and Mary Jo (Gillam) R.; m. Sarah Reed Parker, June 20, 1964; children: Deborah Graham, John William, Julie Elizabeth AB, Colgate U., 1964; MBA, Case Western Res. U., 1967. Nat. City Bank/Nat. City Corp., 1964-97; exec. v.p., chief fin. officer Nat. City Corp., Cleve., 1982-89, dep. chmn. bd. dirs., 1986-95; pres., 1995-97; mng. ptnr. Kirtland Capital Corp., 1997—. Bd. dirs. Kirtland Capital Corp. Trustee Coll. of Wooster, Ohio, 1982-91, Fairmount Presbyn. Ch., Cleve., 1983-86, St. Luke's Hosp., Cleve., 1984-97, Cleve. Ballet, 1985-89, United Way, 1986-97, Karamu House, 1988-95, Western Res. Hist. Soc., 1990—, Cleve. Mus. Art, 1991—, Salvation Army, 1985—, chmn. adv. bd., 1991-93; pres., trustee Big Bros. and Big Sisters, Cleve., 1973-80; chmn., bd. trustees United Way of Cleve., 1995-97, trustee Musical Arts Assn., 1994-97, chmn. vis. com. of Case Western Res. U. Weatherhead Sch. Mgmt., 1995-97. Mem. Fin. Execs. Inst., Cleve. Skating Club (pres. 1980-82), Union Club, Country Club, Pepper Pike Club, Ottawa Club, Desert Mountain Club. Republican. Avocations: travel, skiing, shooting, golf, history. Home: 13705 Shaker Blvd Cleveland OH 44120-5604

ROBERTSON, WILLIAM WRIGHT, JR., orthopedist, educator; b. Mayfield, Ky., Dec. 26, 1946; m. Karel Virginia Dierks, Jan. 26, 1974. BA, Rhodes Coll., 1968; MD, Vanderbilt U., 1972; MBA, Geo Washington U., 2000. Intern U. Calif., San Diego, 1972-73, resident in orthop. surgery, 1975-76, Vanderbilt U., Nashville, 1976-79; asst. prof. orthop. Tex. Tech U., Lubbock, 1979-86; assoc. prof. U. Pa., Phila., 1986-90; prof. orthop. surgery George Washington U., Washington, 1990-2000; chmn. pediat. orthop. Children's Nat. Med. Ctr., Washington, 1990-99. Field rep. accreditation coun. grad. med. edn. Fellow Am. Acad. Orthop. Surgeons, Am. Orthop. Assn., Pediat. Orthop. Soc. (bd. dirs. 1993-96—). Avocations: gardening, music. Office: Accreditation Coun Grad Med Edn 515 N State St Chicago IL 60610 Home Phone: 301-718-7867. Business E-Mail: wrobertson@acgme.org.

ROBIE, JOAN, elementary school principal; Prin. Monteith Elem. Sch., Grosse Pointe, Mich., 1989—. Recipient Elem. Sch. Recognition award U.S. Dept. Edn., 1989-90 Office: Monteith Elem Sch 1275 Cook Rd Grosse Pointe Woods MI 48236-2511

ROBILLARD, JEAN EUGENE, dean, educator; b. Montreal, 1943; m. Renee Robillard. BA, U. Montreal, 1964, MD, 1968. Pediat. residency Saint Justine Hosp., Montreal, 1969—72; pediat. nephrology fellowship UCLA Med. Ctr., Los Angeles, 1972—73, U. Iowa Med. Ctr., Iowa City, 1973—74; asst. prof., dept. pediat. U. Montreal Coll. Med., 1975—76; asst. prof. Dept. Pediat., Coll. Med., U. Iowa, 1974—75, 1976—78, assoc. prof., 1978—82, dir. nephrology div., 1976—96, prof., 1982—96, vice chmn.; chief pediat. U. Mich., Ann Arbor, 1996—2003; physician-in-chief C.S. Mott Children's Hosp., 1996—2003; dean Roy J. and Lucille A. Carver Coll Medicine, U. Iowa, 2003—; v.p. medico affairs U. Iowa, 2007—. Editl. bd. Jour. Pediat., 2001—; bd. dirs. Am. Bd. Pediat., 2001—, chmn. bd. dirs., 2006—. Author of over 220 sci. papers. Recipient Disting. Alumni Award for Achievement, U. Iowa, 2002. Fellow: Coun. for High Blood Pressure Rsch., Am. Heart Assn., Royal Coll. Physicians & Surgeons; mem.: Assn. Med. Sch. Pediat. Dept. Chairs, Inc., Am. Soc. Transplant Physicians, The Perinatal Rsch. Soc, Soc. for Gynecologic Investigation, Am. Physiol. Soc., Am. Assn. for Advancement Sci. (fellow 1999), Am. Soc. Pediat. Nephrology (pres. 1994—95), Soc. Pediat. Rsch., Am. Heart Assn., Am. Soc. Nephrology, Internat. Soc. Nephrology, Internat. Pediat. Nephrology Assn., Midwest Soc. Pediat. Rsch. (Founder's Award 2002), Am. Acad. Pediat., Am Pediat. Soc. Office: Roy J & Lucille A Carver Coll Med 312 CMAB Iowa City IA 52242

ROBIN, RICHARD C., lawyer; b. Brownwood, Tex., July 12, 1945; s. Milton and Bernice F. (Fine) R.; children: Gregory, Max. B.A., Tulane U.; J.D., DePaul U. Bar: Ill. 1970, U.S. Dist. Ct. (no. dist.) Ill. 1971, U.S. Ct. Appeals (6th cir.), U.S. Ct. Appeals (7th cir.), Trial Bar (no. dist.) Ill. 1982. With civil trial div. Ill. Atty. Gen. Office, Chgo., 1970-74; assoc. firm Vedder Price Kaufman & Kammholz, Chgo., 1974-76, ptnr., 1976—. Mem. ABA, (com. on litigation), Chgo. Bar Assn. Office: Vedder Price Kaufman & Kammholz 222 N La Salle St Ste 2600 Chicago IL 60601-1100

ROBINS, H(ENRY) IAN, medical oncologist; b. NYC, Feb. 17, 1945; AB in Biology, Boston U., 1966, AM in Biochemistry, 1968, PhD in Molecular Biology, 1971, MD, 1976. Diplomate Am. Bd. Internal Medicine, Am. Bd. Med. Oncology, Am. Bd. Forensic Medicine, Am. Bd. Forensic Examiners. Intern in internal medicine Univ. Hosps., Madison, Wis., 1976-77, resident in internal medicine, 1977-79; fellow in clin. oncology Wis. Clin. Cancer Ctr., Madison, 1979-81, fellow in rsch. oncology, 1981-82; instr. dept. human oncology, dept. medicine Dept. Human Oncology, Dept. Medicine U. Wis. Sch. Medicine, Madison, 1982-83, asst. prof., 1983-86, assoc. prof., 1986—; chief sect. med. oncology, dir. U. Wis. Sch. Medicine, Madison, 1990-95, prof. dept. human oncology, medicine and neurology, 1992—. Chmn. Systemic Hyperthermia Oncology Working Group. Contbr. numerous articles to profl. jours.; reviewer numerous sci. jours. including Biochem. Pharmacology, Internat. Jour. Radiation Biology, Jour. Clin. Oncology, New Eng. Jour. Medicine, others. Mem. N.Y. Acad. Scis., AAAS, ACP, Internat. Clin. Hyperthermia Soc., Radiation Rsch. Soc., N.am. Hyperthermia Group, Oncology Group, Am. Fedn. clin. Rsch., Ea. Coop. Oncology Group, European Soc. Hyperthermic Oncology, Vet. Cancer Soc., Transplantation Soc., Collaborative Ocular Melanoma Study Group, N.Am. Brain Tumor Consortium, Am. Soc. Clin. Hypnosis, Minn. Soc. Clin. Hypnosis, Sigma Xi. Office: Clin Sci Ctr K4/662 U Wis Sch Med 600 Highland Ave Madison WI 53792-0001

ROBINS, JOEL, import/export company executive; Pres. Robbins Trading Co., Chgo., 1983—. Office: Robbins Trading Co 8700 W Bryn Mawr Ave Ste 760 Chicago IL 60631-3512

ROBINS, LEE NELKEN, medical educator; b. New Orleans, Aug. 29, 1922; d. Abe and Leona (Reiman) Nelken; m. Eli Robins, Feb. 22, 1946 (dec. Dec. 1994); children: Paul, James, Thomas, Nicholas; m. Hugh Chaplin, Aug. 5, 1998. Student, Newcomb Coll., 1938-40; BA, Radcliffe Coll., 1942, MA, 1943; PhD, Harvard U., Cambridge, Mass., 1951. Mem. faculty Washington U., St. Louis, 1954—, prof. sociology in psychiatry, 1968-91, prof. sociology, 1969-91, prof. social sci. and social sci. in psychiatry, 1991-2000, prof. emeritus, 2001—. Past mem. Nat. Adv. Coun. on Drug Abuse; past mem. task panels Pres.'s Commn. on Mental Health; mem. expert adv. panel on mental health WHO; Salmon lectr. NY Acad. Medicine, 1983; Cutter lectr. Harvard U., 1997. Author: Deviant Children Grown Up, 1966; editor 11 books; mem. editl. bd. Psychol. Medicine, Jour. Studies on Alcohol, Social Psychiatry and Psychiatric Epidemiology, Epidemiol. e Psichiat. Sociale; contbr. articles to profl. jours. Recipient Rsch. Scientist award USPHS, 1970-90, Pacesetter Rsch. award Nat. Inst. Drug Abuse, 1978, Radcliffe Coll. Grad. Soc. medal, 1979, Sutherland award Am. Soc. Criminology, 1991, Nathan B. Eddy award Com. on Problems of Drug Dependence, 1993, Spl. Presdl. Commendation Am. Psychiat. Assn., 1999, Am. Acad. Arts and Scis., 1999, Commendation and Appreciation award Harvard Inst. Psychiat. Epidemiology and Genetics, 2000, Disting. Sci. Devel. award Soc. Rsch. in Child Devel., 2003, Peter Raven Lifetime award Acad. Sci. St. Louis, 2006; rsch. grantee IMH, Nat. Inst. on Drug Abuse, Nat. Inst. on Alcohol Abuse and Alcoholism. Fellow Am. Coll. Epidemiology, Royal Coll. Psychiatrists (hon.), Am. Soc. Psychiatrists (hon.), Soc. Study of Addiction (hon.); mem. APHA (Rema Lapouse award 1979, Lifetime Achievement award sect. on alcohol and drug abuse 1994), Internat. Fedn. Psychiat. Epidemiology (com.1992-2002), World Psychiat. Assn. (sect. com. on epidemiology and cmty. psychiatry, 1985-2002, co-chmn. sect. on rsch. instruments in psychiatry), Soc. Life History Rsch. in Psychopathology, Am. Coll. Neuropsychopharmacology, Inst. Medicine, Am. Psychopath. Assn. (pres. 1987-88, Paul Hoch award 1978), World Innovation Found. (hon. mem. 2004). Office: Washington U Med Sch Dept Psychiatry Saint Louis MO 63110 Business E-Mail: robinsl@psychiatry.wustl.edu.

ROBINSON, BARRY R., lawyer; b. Dover, Ohio, Dec. 8, 1946; AB, Princeton U., 1969; JD cum laude, Ohio State U., 1972. Bar: Ohio 1972. Ptnr. Baker & Hostetler, Columbus, Ohio. Fellow Am. Coll. Trust and Estate Counsel; mem. ABA, Ohio State Bar Assn., Columbus Bar Assn. Office: Baker & Hostetler Capital Sq 65 E State St Ste 2100 Columbus OH 43215-4260

ROBINSON, GENE EZIA, biologist, educator; b. Buffalo, Jan. 9, 1955; s. Jack and Sonja (Rubin) R.; m. Julia O. Robinson, Aug. 29, 1982; children: Aaron, Daniel, Sol. BS in Life Sciences, Cornell U., 1977, MS, 1982, PhD, 1986. Postdoctoral assoc. Ohio State U., Columbus, 1986-89; asst. prof. biology U. Ill., Urbana, 1989-93, assoc. prof. biology, 1993-98, prof. biology, 1998—2003, dir. neuroscience prog., 2001—, G. William Arends prof. of integrative biology, 2003—; team leader Inst. for Genomic Biology, 2004—. Cons. Songbird Genomic Initiative, 2003—. Assoc. editor Ann. Rev. Entomology, 1998—, editl. bd. Jour. Insect Physiology, 1992—, Genes, Brain, and Behavior, 2002—, Jour. Insect Biology, 2002—. Recipient Fulbright Sr. Rsch. Fellowship, Hebrew U., 1995-96, Guggenheim Fellowship, 2003. Fellow AAAS, Am. Acad. Arts & Sciences; mem. Am. Assn. Behavioral Neuroendocrinology, Animal Behavior Soc., Entomol. Soc. Am. (Founders Meml. award, 2003, Recognition award in insect physiology, 2004), Internat. Bee Rsch. Assn., Internat. Soc. Neuroethology, Soc. Neurosci., Internat. Union Study of Social Insects, Internat. Behavioural and Neural Genetics Soc., NAS, Sigma Xi. Achievements include discovery of hormone, neural and genetic factors that regulate behavioral plasticity and division of labor in honeybee colonies. Office: The Robinson Lab--Univ Ill 320 Morrill Hall 505 S Goodwin Ave Urbana IL 61801-3707 E-mail: generobi@uiuc.edu.

ROBINSON, JACK ALBERT, retail executive; b. Detroit, Feb. 26, 1930; s. Julius and Fannie (Aizkowitz) Robinson; m. Aviva Freedman, Dec. 21, 1952; children: Shelby, Beth, Abigail. B in Pharmacy, Wayne State U., 1952. Founder, chief exec. officer, chmn. bd. Perry Drug Stores, Inc., Pontiac, Mich., 1957-95; founder, chmn., pres. JAR Group LLC, Bloomfield Hills, Mich., 1996—. Chmn. Wayne State U. Fund, Detroit, 1986, Concerned Citizens for Arts Mich., 1990, 1991—; chmn. ann. fund Detroit Symphony Orch.; bd. dirs. United Way Pontiac, Mich., 1986, United Found. Detroit, 1986, Pontiac Area Urban League, Cmty. Found., S.E. Mich., Detroit Svc. Group, Save Orch. Hall, Inc., Cranbrook Inst. Sci., Jewish Fedn. Apts., Wetzman Inst. Sci., Holocaust Meml. Ctr., Harper-Grace Hosp., Detroit; past dir. Pontiac Symphony, Boys Club, Detroit Osteo. Hosp.; pres. United Jewish Found. Met. Detroit, 1992—94; co-chmn. Greater Detroit Interfaith Round Table NCCJ, 1986—92, v.p., 1994—95; pres. Jewish Fedn. Met. Detroit, 1992—94. Named Entrepreneur of the Yr., Harvard Bus. Sch., Detroit, 1982; named to Heritage Hall of Fame Inductee, Internat. Inst. Found., 2007; recipient Disting. Alumni award, Wayne State U. Coll. Pharmacy, 1975, Eleanor Roosevelt Humanities award, State of Israel, 1978, Youth Svcs. Am. Tradition award, B'nai B'rith, 1982, Gt. Am. Traditions award, 1991, Disting. Alumni award, Wayne State U., 1985, Corp. Leadership award, 1985, Tree of Life award, Jewish Nat. Fund, 1985, Disting. Citizen award, Pontiac Boy Scouts Am., 1985, Brotherhood award, Booker T. Washington Bus. Assn., 1986, Humanitarian award, March of Dimes, 1987, Variety Club, 1988, award, Weizmann Rsch. Inst., 1987, Fred M. Butzel award, Jewish Fedn. Met. Detroit, 1991, Cmty. Svc. award, Am. Arabic and Jewish Friends, 1995, Outstanding Philanthropic award, Nat. Soc. Fundraising Execs., 1999, Mich. Hall of Fame award in Real Estate and Retailing, Internat. Coun. Shopping Ctrs., 2001, Gov.'s Arts award Spl. Recognition, 2003. Mem.: Econ. Club (bd. dirs. Detroit chpt.), Am. Found. for Pharm. Edn. (bd. dirs.), Am. Pharm. Assn., Nat. Assn. Chain Drug Stores (chmn. 1987, Lifetime Achievement award 1995, Robert B. Begley award 1995). Avocations: skiing, jogging, photography, classical music, glass collecting. Office: JAR Group LLC Ste 3100 4190 Telegraph Rd Bloomfield Hills MI 48302-2082

ROBINSON, JOEL D., manufacturing executive; 3 children. Dir. Body-in-White assembly Chrysler; dir. vehicle assembly Am. Motors; Ford personnel devel. program Ford Motor Co.; dir. mfg. planning Am. Axle & Mfg., Detroit, 1994, dir. GMT800 program, exec. dir. mfg., v.p. mfg., exec. v.p., COO, 1998—2001, pres., COO, 2001—. Office: Am Axle and Mfg 1840 Holbrook Detroit MI 48212-3488

ROBINSON, JOHN HAMILTON, civil engineer; b. Kansas City, Mo., Feb. 14, 1927; s. David Beach and Aileen March (Weaver) R.; m. Patricia Ann Odell, June 17, 1949; children: John Hamilton, Patricia Ann, Donna Marie, Clinton Odell. BS, U. Kans., 1949. Registered profl. engr., Kans. With Black & Veatch (cons. engrs.), Kansas City, Mo., 1949—, ptnr., 1956—, exec. ptnr., 1971-92, mng. ptnr., 1983-92, chmn. emeritus, 1993. Trustee Johnson County Community Coll.; deacon, elder 2d Presbyterian Ch., Kansas City, Mo. Served with USNR, 1945-46. Fellow ASCE (hon. mem.); mem. Am. Cons. Engrs. Coun. (chmn. com. of fellows), Cons. Engrs. Coun. Mo. (dir. 1972—, pres. 1976-77), Mo. Soc. Profl. Engrs., Kans. Engring. Soc. (Kans. Engr. of Yr. award 1983), Am. Water Works Assn. (v.p. 1985, pres. 1987, Fuller award 1983), U. Kans. Alumni Assn. (pres.), Water Pollution Control Fedn., Mission Hills Country Club, Vanguard Club, Mercury Club, Rotary, Tau Beta Pi, Sigma Tau, Omicron Delta Kappa, Beta Theta Pi. Home: 3223 W 67th St Shawnee Mission KS 66208-1846 Office: Black Veatch Engrs 8400 Ward Pky Kansas City MO 64114-2031

ROBINSON, JOHN HAYES, law educator; b. Providence, Apr. 4, 1943; s. William Philip and Dorothy Frances (Hayes) R.; m. Deborah Ann Deery, Aug. 15, 1981; children: Gena, John. BA, Boston Coll., 1967; MA, Notre Dame U., Ind., 1972, PhD, 1975; JD, U. Calif., Berkeley, 1979. Bar: RI 1980. Asst. prof. U. San Francisco, 1973-76; instr. law U. Miami, Coral Gables, Fla., 1979-80; jud. clk. US Dist. Ct., Hartford, Conn., 1980-81; asst. prof. law and philosophy U. Notre Dame, 1981-96, assoc. prof. law, 1996—, assoc. dean acad. affairs, 2002—04, exec. assoc. dean, 2005—. Office: U Notre Dame Law Sch Box 780 Notre Dame IN 46556 Office Phone: 574-631-6980. Business E-Mail: robinson.1@nd.edu.

ROBINSON, JULIE ANN, judge; b. 1957; BS, U. Kans., 1978, JD, 1981. Bar: Kans. 1981. Asst. U.S. atty. for dist. Kans. U.S. Dept. Justice, Kansas City, Kans., 1983—94, sr. litigation counsel, 1991—94; law clk. to hon. Benjamin E. Franklin, U.S. Bankruptcy Ct. for Dist. Kans., Kansas City, Kans., 1981—83, bankruptcy judge, 1994—2001; judge bankruptcy appellate panel U.S. Ct. Appeals (10th cir.), Topeka, 1996—2001; U.S. dist. judge State of Kans., 2001—. Instr. trial practice U. Kans. Sch. Law, 1989—90. Fellow: Am. Bar Found.; mem.: ABA, Kans. Bar Assn. Office: US Dist Ct 405 US Courthouse 444 SE Quincy Topeka KS 66683

ROBINSON, JUNE KERSWELL, dermatologist, educator; b. Phila., Jan. 26, 1950; d. George and Helen S. (Kerswell) R.; m. William T. Barker, Jan. 31, 1981. BA cum laude, U. Pa., 1970; MD, U. Md., 1974. Diplomate Am. Bd. Dermatology, Nat. Bd. Med. Examiners, Am. Bd. Mohs Micrographic Surgery and Cutaneous Oncology. Intern Greater Balt. Med. Ctr., Hanover, NH, 1974, resident in medicine, 1974—75; resident in dermatology Dartmouth-Hitchcock Med. Ctr., Hanover, 1975—78, chief resident, clin. instr., 1977—78, instr. in dermatology, 1978; fellow Mohs; chemosurgery and dermatologic surgery NYU Skin and Cancer Clinic, NYC, 1978—79; instr. in dermatology NYU, NYC, 1979; asst. prof. dermatology Northwestern U. Med. Sch., Chgo., 1979, asst. prof. surgery, 1980—85, assoc. prof. dermatology and surgery, 1985—91, prof. dermatology and surgery, 1991—98; prof. medicine and pathology, dir. divsn. dermatology Cardinal Bernardin Cancer Ctr., Loyola U. Med. Ctr., 1998—2004, program leader skin cancer clin. program, 1998—2004; prof. medicine Med. Sch. Dartmouth U., 2004—05, chief Dermatology Sect. Hitchcock Med. Ctr., 2004—05; prof. clin. dermatology Feinberg Sch. Medicine, Northwestern U., Chgo., 2006—. Mem. consensus devel. conf. IH, 1992; mem. panel on use of sunscreens Internat. Agy. for Rsch. on Cancer, WHO, 2000; lectr. in field. Author: Fundamentals of Skin Biopsy, 1985, also audiovisual materials; editor: (textbooks) Atlas of Cutaneous Surgery, 1996, Cutaneous Medicine and Surgery: An Integrated Program in Dermatology, 1996, Surgery of the Skin, 2005; mem. editl. bd. Archives of Dermatology, 1988-97; sect. editor The Cutting Edge: Challenges in Med. and Surg. Therapeutics, 1989-97, editor, 2004—; contbg. editor Jour. Dermatol. Surgery and Oncology, 1985-88; mem. editl. com. 18th World Congress of Dermatology, 1982; contbr. numerous articles, abstracts to profl. publs., chpts. to books. Bd. dirs. Northwestern Med. Faculty Found., 1982-84, chmn. com. on benefits and leaves, 1984, nominating com. 1988. Grantee Nat. Cancer Inst., 1985-91, 2004—, Am. Cancer Soc., 1986-89, Skin Cancer Found., 1984-85, Dermatology Found., 1981-83, orthwestern U. Biomed. Rsch., 1981, Syntex, 1984. Fellow: Am. Coll. Chemosurgery (chmn. sci. program ann. meeting 1983, chmn. publs. com. 1986—87, chmn. task force on ednl. needs 1989—90, co-editor bull. 1984—87); mem.: Chgo. Dermatol. Soc., Women's Dermatol. Soc. (pres. 1990—92, Wilma Bergeld, MD Visionary and Leadership award 2002), Soc. Investigative Dermatology, Am. Soc. Dermatol. Surgery (pres. 1994—95, Samuel J. Stegman award disting. svc. 2006), Dermatology Found. (trustee 1995—98), Am. Acad. Dermatology (asst. sec.-treas. 1995—98, sec.-treas. 1998—2001, bd. dirs. 1993—95, Stephen Rothman Lectr. award 1992, Presdl. citation 1992, 2000), Am. Dermatol. Assn., Am. Cancer Soc. (pres. Ill. divsn. 1996—98, St. George Disting. Svc. medal 2004). Office: Northwestern U Feinberg Sch Med Dept Dermatology 132 E Delaware Pl #5806 Chicago IL 60611

ROBINSON, KEITH, newspaper editor; Bur. chief AP, Indpls., 2000—. Office: 251 N Illinois St Ste 1600 Indianapolis IN 46204-1943

ROBINSON, LARRY J., state legislator; m. Mary Lee; 2 children. BS, Valley City State U.; MS, N.D. State U. Mem. N.D. Senate from 24th dist., Bismark, 1989—; mem. appropriations com. N.D. Senate, Bismark. Mem. Gov.'s Coun. on Human Resources, Com. on Status of Women; aux. svc. dir. Valley City State U. Bd. dirs., adv. com. Mercy Hosp.; mem. adv. com. Barnes County, Extension Adv. Coun., Hi Soaring Eagle Ranch. Mem. KC, Elks, Eagles, Kiwanis, C. of C. (past pres.), Masons, Phi Delta Kappa. Office: State Senate State Capitol Bismarck ND 58505 Home: 3584 Sheyenne Cir Valley City ND 58072-9545

ROBINSON, LARRY ROBERT, insurance company executive; b. Indpls., Feb. 7, 1936; s. Manuel H. Robinson and Barbara Dawson Robinson Trees; m. Sharon Moore, Aug. 3, 1957; children: Christopher, Lizbeth, Lara, Jeremy. BA, DePauw U., Greencastle, Ind., 1957. Actuarial trainee State Life Ins. Co., Indpls., 1957-63, asst. actuary, 1963-66, actuary, 1966-67, asst. v.p., actuary, 1967-70, v.p., actuary, 1970-80, sr. v.p., actuary, 1980-83, exec. v.p., 1983-99, pres., 1999—, also bd. dirs. Chmn. cost disclosure com. Am. Coun. Life Ins., Washington, 1985-87, chmn. actuarial com., 1990-91. Bd. dirs. Marion County Assn. Retarded Citizens, Indpls., 1980-86. With U.S. Army, 1961-62. Fellow Soc. Actuaries; mem. Am. Acad. Actuaries, Indpls. Actuarial Club (past pres.), Actuarial Club Ind., Ky. and Ohio (past pres.), Phi Beta Kappa. Office: State Life Ins Co Ste 368 1 American Sq Indianapolis IN 46282-0002 E-mail: Larry_Robinson@statelife.com.

ROBINSON, LESTER W., airport executive; B in Bus. Adminstrn., Mich. State U., 1973. CPA. With Coopers & Lybrand; CFO 1st Independence Corp., Detroit, 1980-83, pres., CEO, 1989-91; auditor gen. Wayne County, Detroit, 1988-89, dept. dir. airports fin. & adminstrn. dept. airports, 1991-93, CFO dept. budget, 1993-95, dir. dept. airports, 2000—; corp. fin. rep. 1st Mich. Corp., 1995-2000. Office: Dept Aviation Detroit Met Airport Williams Rogell Dr Detroit MI 48242

ROBINSON, LOGAN GILMORE, lawyer; b. Cin., Dec. 26, 1949; s. Landon Graves and Alis (Rule) R.; m. Edrie Baker Sowell, Sept. 22, 1983; children: Leyland G., Landon G., Linden G., Lane G. BA in Econ. and History magna cum laude, Cornell U., 1972; JD, Harvard U., 1976; Cert. Competence in German, Goethe Inst., Freiburg, Germany, 1978. Bar: Ohio 1977, N.Y. 1979, Mich. 1989, U.S. Ct. Internat. Trade 1983. Rsch. faculty Leningrad State U., Russia, 1976-77; rsch. officer U. Leiden, Netherlands, 1977-78; assoc. Wender, Murase & White,

NYC, 1978-81, Coudert Bros., NYC, 1981-83; sr. counsel TRW Inc., Cleve., 1983-87; asst. gen. counsel Chrysler Corp., Highland Park, 1987—96; sec., v.p., gen. counsel ITT Automotive, Auburn Hills, Mich., 1996—98; v.p., gen. counsel Delphi Corp., Troy, Mich., 1998—2006; exec. v.p., gen. counsel, govt. rels. Metaldyne Corp., Plymouth, Mich., 2006—. Author: An American in Leningrad, 1982, paperback, 1984, Evil Star, 1986, paperback, 1987. Mem. Assoc. Gen. Counsels, Internat. Bar Assn. (co-chair corp. counsel forum), Mich. State Bar (former chmn. internat. sect., Outstanding Contbn. award), German Am. C. of C. Mich. (bd. dirs.), Coun. US and Italy, Phi Beta Kappa. Office: Metaldyne Corp 47603 Halyard Dr Plymouth MI 48170-2429

ROBINSON, REGINALD R., musician; b. Chgo., Oct. 19, 1972; Pianist and composer of classical ragtime music; signed by Delmark Records, 1992. Composer: (albums) The Strongman, 1993, Sounds in Silhouette, 1994, Euphonic Sounds, 1998, Man Out of Time, 2003. Named MacArthur Fellow, John D. and Catherine T. MacArthur Found., 2004. Office: c/o Delmark Records 4121 N Rockwell Chicago IL 60618

ROBINSON, ROBERT GEORGE, psychiatry educator; b. Pitts., May 22, 1945; s. Robert Campbell and Rosetta M. (Martindale) R.; m. Gretchen Priscilla Smith, Jan. 5, 1974; children: Christopher, Jonathan. BS in Engring. Physics, Cornell U., 1967, MD, 1971. Intern Montefiore Hosp. and Albert Einstein Med. Ctr., 1971-72; resident Cornell U., White Plains, N.Y., 1972-73; rsch. assoc. NIMH, Washington, 1973-75; resident Johns Hopkins U., 1975-77, asst. prof. to assoc. prof., 1977-85, prof., 1985—; prof., head of dept. U. Iowa Coll. Medicine, Iowa City, 1990—, Paul W. Penningroth prof., 1996—. Mem. editorial bds. Jour. europsychiatry & Clinical Neurosciences, Int. Jour. Psychiatry in Medicine, Psychiatry, J. Nervous and Mental Diseases. Author: The Clinical europsychiatry of Stroke, 1998; editor: Depression and Coexisting Disease, 1989, Depression in Neurologic Disease, 1993; mem. editl. bd. Jour. europsychiatry and Clin. Neuroscis., Internat. Jour. Psychiatry in Medicine, Psychiatry, Jour. Nervous and Mental Diseases; contbr. more than 300 articles and chpts. to publs. Rsch. Scientist award, NIMH, 1989; Mellon fellow Johns Hopkins U., 1977; recipient Rsch. prize Am. Psychiat. Assn., 1999, Acad. Pscyosomatic Medicine, 1999. Fellow APA, Am. Coll. Neuropsychopharmacology, Soc. for Neurosci.; mem. AAAS, Soc. Biol. Psychiatry, Johns Hopkins Soc. Scholars, Am. Neuropsychiat. Assn. (pres., 1998-99). Office: U Iowa Coll Med 200 Hawkins Dr Iowa City IA 52242-1009 E-mail: robert-robinson@uiowa.edu.

ROBINSON, ROBIN, newscaster; b. Chgo. m. Terrence Brantley, 1986 (div. 1989). B, San Diego State U., 1980. Reporter KGTV, San Diego, 1979—81; consumer reporter CBS affiliate, Denver, 1981—84; reporter WBBM-TV, Chgo., 1984—87; co-anchor Fox News at 9 WFLD-TV, Chgo., 1987—. Co-recipient Emmy awards. Office: WFLD-TV 205 N Mich Ave Chicago IL 60601

ROBINSON, SPENCER T. (HERK ROBINSON), professional baseball team executive; b. June 25, 1940; m. Kathy Robinson; children: Ashley, Amanda. Student, U. Miami, Washington U., St. Louis. With Cin. Reds., 1962-67; asst. Baltimore Orioles, 1968; asst. scouting dir. Kansas City Royals, 1969-72, dir. stadium ops., 1973-74, v.p., 1975-85, exec. v.p. adminstrn., 1985-90, v.p., 1975-85, exec. v.p., gen. mgr., 1990—, former mem. bd. dirs. Office: Kansas City Royals PO Box 419969 Kansas City MO 64141-6969

ROBINSON, STEPHEN MICHAEL, mathematician, educator; b. Columbus, Ohio, Apr. 12, 1942; s. Arthur Howard and Mary Elizabeth (Coffin) R.; m. Chong-Suk Han, May 10, 1968; children: Diana Marie Oestreich, James Andrew. BA, U. Wis., 1962, PhD, 1971; MS, NYU, 1963; Diploma, U.S. Army War Coll., 1986; Dr. honoris causa, Univ. Zürich, 1996. Adminstr. U. Wis., Madison, 1969-72, asst. prof., 1972-75, assoc. prof., 1975-79, prof. indsl. and sys. engring. and computer scis., 1979—2007, prof. emeritus indsl. sys. engring. and computer scis., 2008—, chmn. dept. indsl. engring., 1981-84. Cons. to various agys. Dept. Def., 1971—. Author: (with Jagdish Chandra) An Uneasy Alliance: The Mathematics Research Center at the University of Wisconsin, 1956-1987, 2005; editor: Math. of Ops. Rsch., 1981-86, assoc. editor, 1975-80, Jour. Ops. Rsch., 1974-86, Math. Programming, 1986-91; mem. bd. editors Annals Ops. Rsch., 1984-99, Set-Valued Analysis, 1992-99, Jour. Convex Analysis, 1994—2002; adv. editor Math. of Ops. Rsch., 1987—, Ops. Rsch. Letters, 2002-; mem. editl. bd. Springer Series in Ops. Rsch. and Fin. Engring., 1996—; contbr. numerous articles to profl. jours. Trustee Village of Shorewood Hills, Wis., 1974-76, mem. fin. com., 1973-87; bd. on math. scis. and their applications NRC, 2001-07, bd. overseers Simon's Rock Coll., Great Barrington, Mass., 1991-02. Served to capt. US Army, 1963—69, Korea, Vietnam, col. AUS, ret. Decorated Legion of Merit, Bronze star, Air medal, Army Commendation medal with 2 oak leaf clusters; recipient John K. Walker Jr. award, Mil. Ops. Rsch. Soc., 2001. Fellow Inst. Ops. Rsch. and Mgmt. Scis. (mem. Ops. Rsch. Soc. Am. coun. 1991-94, sec. 2000-03, treas. 2007—); mem. Inst. Indsl. Engrs., Soc. Indsl. and Applied Math., Math. Programming Soc. (mem.-at-large of coun. 1991-94, George B. Dantzig prize 1997), Madison Club. Home: 1014 University Bay Dr Madison WI 53705-2251 Office: U Wis Dept Indsl and Sys Engring 1513 University Ave Madison WI 53706-1539 Home Phone: 608-231-3065; Office Phone: 608-263-6862. Business E-Mail: smrobins@wisc.edu.

ROBINSON, STEVE, real estate company executive; b. 1967; BS in Civil Engring., Mich. Technol. U. V.p. Silverman Devel. Co., Bingham Farms, Mich., 1995—99, pres.; regional v.p. Toll Bros. Inc., 1999—2001. Named one of 40 Under 40, Crain's Detroit Bus., 2006. Mem.: Mich. Assn Planning (exec. bd. 2005), Am. Soc. Civil Engineers. Office: Silverman Development Co 32100 Telegraph Rd Ste 220 Bingham Farms MI 48025 Office Phone: 248-540-6400. Office Fax: 248-932-9131.

ROBINSON, WENDY Y., school system administrator; Attended, DePauw U., Ind. U.-Purdue U., Ball State U. Tchr. Ward Elem., 1973—86; asst. prin. Meml. Pk. Mid. Sch., 1986—87, Weisser Pk. Elem., 1987—89; prin. Price Elem., 1989—91; area admin., asst. supt. Wayne HS, 1991—95; dep. supt. Fort Wayne Comm. Schs., 1995—2003, supt. Fort Wayne, Ind., 2003—. Office: Fort Wayne Comm Sch 1200 S Clinton St Fort Wayne IN 46802

ROBIRDS, ESTEL, state legislator; Mem. Mo. State Ho. of Reps. Dist. 143, 1993—. Home: Rte 2 Box 2919 Theodosia MO 65761

ROBLING, CLAIRE A., state legislator; b. Oct. 22, 1956; m. Tony Robling; 2 children. Student, Coll. St. Catherine. Mem. dist. 35 Minn. Senate, St. Paul, 1996—. Office: 100 Constitution Ave Saint Paul MN 55155-1232 Home: 1169 Butterfly Ln Jordan MN 55352-9476

ROBOL, RICHARD THOMAS, lawyer; b. Norfolk, Va., Feb. 8, 1952; s. Harry James and Lucy Henley (Johnson) R. BA, U. Va., 1974; JD, Harvard U., 1978. Bar: Va. 1979, Ohio 1996, U.S. Dist. Ct. (ea. dist.) Va. 1979, U.S. Ct. Appeals (4th cir.) 1979, U.S. Dist. Ct. (we. dist.) Va. 1981, U.S. Supreme Ct. 1982, D.C. 1991, U.S. Ct. Appeals (4th, 6th and 9th cirs.) 1995. Law clk. to presiding justice U.S. Dist. Ct. (ea. dist.) Va., 1978-79; ptnr. Seawell, Dalton, Hughes & Timms, orfolk, 1979-87, Hunton and Williams, Norfolk, 1987-92; exec. v.p., gen. counsel Columbus Am. Discovery Group, Inc., 1992—. Adj. prof. U. Dayton Law Sch.; asst. prof. mil. sci. Capital U.; pro bono counsel Nat. Commn. for Prevention Child Abuse, Norfolk, 1983, Tidewater Profl. Assn. on Child Abuse, 1983, Parents United Va., 1981-82, Sexual Abuse Help Line, 1983-86; mem. Boyd-Graves Conf. on Civil Procedure in Va., 1981-87. Contbr. articles to law revs.; contbg. editor: International Law for General Practitioners, 1981. Bd. dirs. Va. Opera Assn. Guild, Norfolk, 1983-87, Tidewater br. NCCJ, 1991-92; deacon Ctrl. Bapt. Ch., Norfolk, 1980-83. Maj. USAR, 1992—. Fulbright scholar, 1974. Mem. Va. State Bar Assn. (bd. dirs. internat. law sect. 1984-87, chmn. 1982-83), Va. Young Lawyers Assn. (cir. rep. 1984-88), Va. Assn. Def. Attys., Maritime Law Assn., Norfolk-Portsmouth Bar assn. (chmn. speakers bur. 1987-88), Assn. Def. Trial Attys. (chmn. Va. 1987), Def. Rsch. Inst., 1982-88. Avocations: camping, rowing, scuba diving. Home: 60 Kenyon Brook Dr Worthington OH 43085-3629 Office: Robol Law Office LPA 433 W Sixth Ave Columbus OH 43201 Office Phone: 614-737-3739. Business E-Mail: rrobol@robollaw.com.

ROBSON, JUDITH BIROS, state legislator; b. Cleve., Nov. 21, 1939; d. George John and Mary Grace (Millen) Biros; m. Arthur Robson, Sept. 2, 1961; children: Marybeth, Marc, Matthew. BSN, St. John Coll., Cleve., 1961; MS, U. Wis., 1976. RN. Staff nurse Beloit (Wis.) Hosp., 1967-73; nurse practitioner Dr. Ken Gold, Beloit, 1976-78; instr. Blackhawk Tech. Coll., Jonesville, Wis., 1978-87; mem. Wis. Assembly, 1987-98; mem Wis. Senate from 15th dist., Madison, 1998—. Mem. bd. Bedcore, Beloit, 1990, YWCA, Beloit, 1992; sec. Majority Party Caucus, 1990—. Recipient Clean 16 award Environ. Decade. Avocations: biking, skiing, gardening, photography. Office: State Legislature State Capital PO Box 7882 Madison WI 53707-7882

ROBY, BRIAN L., bank executive; b. Kansas City, Mo., Apr. 16, 1960; s. F. Alan Roby and Mimi Jean (Halliburton) King; m. M. Elizabeth Santander, June 6, 1987. BSBA, U. Mo., 1982, MBA, 1983. V.p. Commerce Bank of Kansas City, 1983-90; sr. v.p. First Nat. Bank of Olathe, Kans., 1990—98, exec. v.p., 1998—2001, pres., CEO, 2001—. Mem. U. Mo. Bus. and Pub. Adminstrn. Alumni Assn. (v.p. 1989-92), Overland Park C. of C. (dir. 1993—). Republican. Roman Catholic. Avocations: tennis, bicycling. Office: First Nat Bank Olathe PO Box 1500 Olathe KS 66051-1500

ROCCA, SUE, state legislator; b. May 12, 1949; AS, Ctrl. Mich. Coll. Commr. Macomb County, Mich.; rep. Mich. Dist. 30, 1995-2000. Vice chmn. health policy com. Mich. Ho. Reps., joint com. on adminstrv. rules & regulatory affairs. Office: Office Bd Commrs Macomb County Court Bldg 2nd Fl 40 Gratiot Ct Mount Clemens MI 48043-5719 Address: Mich State Capitol PO Box 30014 Lansing MI 48909-7514

ROCHA, CATHERINE TOMASA, municipal official; BA, U. Mo., 1977, MA, 1979. Cert. mcpl. clk. U. Mo., 1991. Student svc. coord., academic advisor U. Mo., Kansas City, 1979-84; dir. records records dept. Jackson County Courthouse, Kansas City, 1984-87; city clk. Office of the City Clk. City of Kansas City, 1988—. Mem. human rels. adv. commn., 1982-84; mem. bd. zoning commn., 1978-79. Author: (oral history) Black Baseball-The Kansas City Monarch Experience, 1978; editor: newsletter CCFOA, 1991-95. Bd. dirs. Trinity Luth. Hosp. Found., 1996, Women's Found. Gtr. Kansas City; chmn. Westside Fountain Com., 1995-97; former trustee, chmn. auction benefit Westport Alien Ctr.; bd. dirs. Trinity Hosp., 1998-99. Harvard U. fellow, 1990; named 25 Most Influential Hispanic Leaders in Kansas City Dos Mundos newspaper, 1994. Mem. Internat. Inst. Mcpl. Clks. (chmn. big cities com. 1991-94, Harvard grant allocation com. 1994-95, profl. status com. 1995-96), Mexican-Am. Women's Nat. Assn., Friends of Art Coun. (mem. exec. bd.), Southwest Blvd. Merchants Assn. (bd. dirs.), Westside Bus. Assn. (pres. 1996-97). Home: 4545 Wornall Rd Kansas City MO 64111-3270 Office: City of Kansas City Mo Office of the City Clk City Hall 25th Fl 414 E 12th St Kansas City MO 64106-2702

ROCHE, JAMES MCMILLAN, lawyer; b. Detroit, Apr. 16, 1934; s. James Michael and Louise Cullen (McMillan) R.; m. Laura Jane McMillion, Oct. 27, 1962; children: James, Laura, David, Elizabeth. AB, Holy Cross Coll., 1956; LLB, Harvard U., 1959; LLM, Georgetown U., 1962. Bar: Mich. 1959, Ill. 1962. Ptnr., mem. mgmt. com. McDermott, Will & Emery, Chgo., 1962-98, of counsel, 1998—. Bd. dirs. Time Med Labeling, Inc., Burr Ridge, Ill. Contbr. articles to profl. jours. Chmn. Chgo. Econ. Devel. Corp., 1979-81; pres. Village of Kenilworth, Ill., 1982-85; bd. dirs. St. Francis Hosp., Evanston, 1987-97. Served to capt. USAF, 1959-62. Mem. ABA, Ill. Bar Assn., Chgo. Bar Assn., Mich. Bar Assn., Glen View (Ill.) Golf Club, Monroe Club (Chgo.), The Boulders Club (Ariz.), Desert Forest Club. Roman Catholic. Avocations: golf, indian art, wine. Office: McDermott Will & Emery 227 W Monroe St Ste 3100 Chicago IL 60606-5096

ROCHE, MARK A., lawyer, consumer products company executive; b. 1954; m. Barbara Roche. BA, U. Va.; JD, Cornell U. Bar: NY 1980. Assoc. to counsel Chadbourne & Park, LLP, NYC, 1981-88; group gen. counsel Fortune Brands Inc., Deerfield, Ill., 1988-91, Lincolnshire, Ill., 1991-96, v.p., assoc. gen. counsel, 1996-98, v.p., gen. counsel, 1998-99, sr. v.p., gen. counsel, 1999—2000, sr. v.p., sec., gen. counsel Deerfield, Ill., 2002—. Office: Fortune Brands Inc 520 Lake Cook Rd Deerfield IL 60015-5611 Office Phone: 847-484-4400.

ROCHKIND, LOUIS PHILIPP, lawyer; b. Miami, Fla., June 25, 1948; s. Reuben and Sarah R.; m. Rosalind H. Rochkind, July 4, 1971. BA in Psychology cum laude, U. Mich., 1970, JD cum laude, 1974. Bar: Mich. 1974, U.S. Dist. Ct. (ea. dist.) Mich. 1974. Ptnr. Jaffe, Raitt, Heuer & Weiss, Detroit, 1974—. Adj. prof. law Wayne St. U. Law Sch.; lectr. various profl. assns. and orgns. Assoc. editor U. Mich. Law Rev.; contbr. articles to profl. jours. publs. Mem. Am. Coll. Bankruptcy Lawyers, Detroit Bar Assn. (local rules in bankruptcy subcom. creditor-debtor law sect. 1980—), Phi Kappa Phi. Office: Jaffe Raitt Heuer Weiss 27777 Franklin Rd Ste 2500 Southfield MI 48034-8222 E-mail: larrol@jafferaitt.com.

ROCHON, THOMAS RICHARD, academic administrator; b. Wash., DC, July 29, 1952; s. Lawrence Charles and Elizabeth Rochon; m. Amber Rochon. BA, U. Mich., 1973, MA, 1976, PhD, 1980. Asst. prof. Princeton U., 1980—87; assoc. prof. Claremont Grad. U., Calif., 1987—96, prof., dean, 1996—2000, interim provost, 1997—98; fulbright scholar Kobe U., Japan, 1992—93; exec. dir., grad. record examination Ednl. Testing Svc., Princeton, 2000—03; exec. v.p., chief academic officer U. St. Thomas, St. Paul, 2003—. Author: Mobilizing For Peace, 1988 (Choice award, 1988), Culture Moves, 1998 (Sociology award, 2000), The Netherlands, 1999. Roman Cath. Avocation: tennis. Office: U St Thomas 2115 Summit Ave Saint Paul MN 55105 Office Phone: 651-962-6720. Office Fax: 651-962-6702. Business E-Mail: trrochon1@stthomas.edu.*

ROCK, HAROLD L., lawyer; b. Sioux City, Iowa, Mar. 13, 1932; s. Harold L. and Helen J. (Gormally) R.; m. Marilyn Beth Clark Rock, Dec. 28, 1954; children: Michael, Susan, John, Patrick, Michele, Thomas. BS, Creighton U., 1954, JD, 1959. Bar: Nebr., N.Y., Wyo. Law clk. to judge Woodrough U.S. Ct. Appeals 8th Circuit, Omaha, 1959-60; assoc. law clk. Fitzgerald Hamer Brown & Leahy, Omaha, 1960—65; of counsel Kutak Rock, Omaha, 1965—. Chmn. Nebr. Bd. Bar Examiners, 1989-96; bd. dirs. Mid City Bank, Omaha. Bd. dirs. Douglas County Hist. Soc., 1992-99, Nat. Equal Justice Libr., 1995—, Nebr. Nebr. Humanities Coun., 1996-2002. Served to 1st lt. U.S. Army, 1954-56. Recipient Alumni Achievement award Creighton U., 1995. Mem. ABA (ho. of dels. 1970-96, bd. govs. 1992-95), Nebr. Bar Assn. (ho. of dels., bd. dirs. 1985—, pres. 1988, Nebr. Bar found. bd. dirs., 1982-2003), Omaha Bar Assn. (pres. 1972-73), Omaha Legal Aid Soc. (pres. 1969-72), Nebr. State Bd. Pub. Accts. (bd. dirs. 1981-85). Roman Catholic. Office: Kutak Rock The Omaha Bldg 1650 Farnam St Omaha NE 68102-2186

ROCK, RICHARD RAND, lawyer, former state senator; b. Wichita Falls, Tex., Sept. 27, 1924; s. Parker Francis and Ruth Ann (Phillips) R.; m. Rosalee Deardorff, Aug. 23, 1947; children: Richard R. II, Darci Lee, Devon Ray, Robert Regan. BA, Washburn U., 1948, LLB, 1950, JD, 1970. Bar: Kans., U.S. Dist. Ct. Kans., U.S. Ct. Appeals (4th and 10th cirs.). Dir. indsl. rels. Maurer-Neuer Packers, Arkansas City, Kans., 1950-52, plant supt., 1952-54; atty. Rock, Smith & Mason, Arkansas City, Kans., 1955-95; pres., owner Shreveport (La.) Packing Co., 1972-83, Amarillo (Tex.) Beef Processors, 1977-82, Lubbock (Tex.) Beef Processors, 1978-81, Montgomery (Ala.) Food Processors, 1978-91, Humboldt (Iowa) Sausage Co., 1985-92, Great Bend (Kans.) Packing Co., 1984-95; state senator, asst. minority leader State of Kans., 1988-96; chmn. Rockgate Mgmt. Co., Overland Park, Kans., 1997—. Chmn. bd. dirs. Rockgate Mgmt. Co., Overland Park, Kans. Judge Cowley County, Kans., 1952-56; state rep. State of Kans., 1957-61; authority mem. Kans. Turnpike Authority, 1980-83, chmn., 1993-97; commr. Children with Spl. Health Care Needs, Kans., 1993-95. Served USN Air Corps, 1943-45. Mem. Kans. Bar Assn., Nat. Counsel State Legislatures, Kans. C. of C., VFW. Democrat. Mem. Christian Ch. (Disciples Of Christ). Avocations: golf, yard work. Address: US Marshal Kansas Federal Bldg 444 SE Quincy St Ste 456 Topeka KS 66683-3510

ROCK, RICHARD RAND, II, protective services official; b. 1949; BS, U. Kans, 1978; JD, Washburn U., 1988. Police officer U.S. Marshal's Svc., Lawrence, Kans., 1973-80; police lt. Largo Fla., 1980-85; atty. Mo., 1985-89, Kans., 1989-94; state rep. Kans. State Legislature 79th Dist., 1990-94; U.S. Marshall Dist. Kans., Topeka, 1994—. Office: US Marshals Svc Fed Bldg 444 SE Quincy St Ste 456 Topeka KS 66683-3576

ROCKENSTEIN, WALTER HARRISON, II, lawyer; b. Pittsburgh, SC, Jan. 2, 1943; s. Walter Harrison and Martha Lee (Morris) R.; m. Jodell Lynn Steinke, July 29, 1972; children: Martha Liv, Andrew Harrison. BA cum laude, Coll. of Wooster, 1965; LLB, Yale U., 1968. Bar: Minn. 1968, U.S. Dist. Ct. Minn. 1968, U.S. Ct. Appeals (8th crct.) 1977. Spl. asst. atty. gen., chief antitrust divsn. Office of Minn. Atty. Gen., 1970-72; assoc. Head & Truhn, 1972-73; alderman 11th ward Mpls. City Coun., 1974-83; assoc. Faegre & Benson, Mpls., 1984-85, ptnr., 1986—. Mem. Capital Long-Range Improvements Com., 1974-82, Gov.'s Econ. Roundtable, 1980-82, Hennepin County Waste Disposal & Energy Recovery Adv. Com., 1976-77; chmn. devel. strategies com. League of Minn. Cities, 1979-80, bd. dirs., 1980-83; Mpls. del. Metro. Aircraft Sound Abatement Coun., 1977-90, chmn., 1982-90; mem. aviation subcom. of transp. tech. adv. com. Metro. Coun., 1977-83; mem. airport noise adv. bd. Minn. Pollution Control Agy., bd. dirs. noise com., 1982-85, mem. tech. adv. com., 1990; adv. com. Nat. League of Cities, steering com. Environmental Quality, 1975-79, vice chmn., 1976, chmn., 1978, steering com. Energy, Environment and Natural Resources, 1980-83, Energy Task Force, 1977-79, Nat. Urban Policy Com., 1978; mem. Noise Task Force, Nat. League of Cities/Nat. Assn. of Counties, 1977-80; regional dir. Nat. Org. to Insure a Sound-Controlled Environment, 1976-90, v.p. legal affairs, 1983-90; cons. group nuclear waste mgt., U.S. Dept. Energy, 1978. Elder Westminster Presbyn. Ch., 1975-80, 95-2001, trustee, 1982-87, chair stewardship com., 1989, chair pastor nominating com., 1992-94, co-chair bldg. centennial com.; bd. dirs. Loring Nicollet-Bethlehem Cmty. Ctrs., Inc., 1984—, pres., 1988-92; bd. dirs. U. Minn. Underground Space Ctr. Adv. Bd., 1985-95, chair, 1988-95; bd. dirs. Minn. Ctr. for Book Arts, 1988-93; com. mem. Cub Scout pact 196, Diamond Lake Luth Ch., 1988-91, com. chair, 1990-91; alumni trustee, alumni bd. dirs. The Coll. of Wooster, 1990-96; com. mem. Boy Scout Troop 187, 1994-97; bd. dirs. Minn. Safety Coun., 1997-2002, v.p., 2001-2002, chair, 2003-04, immediate past chair, 2005-06. Served to sgt. USMC, 1968—70. Recipient Cert. of Appreciation, Upper Midwest chpt. Acoustical Soc. Am., 1977, Resolution of Appreciation, City of Mpls., 1983, Citation of Honor, Hennepin County, 1983, Cert. of Recognition, League of Minn. Cities, 1983, Hope of Rotary award City of Lakes Rotary Club, 1989, WCCO Good Neighbor award, 1992; named Best Lawyers in Am., Land Use & Zoning, 2006-. Mem. Minn. State Bar Assn. (coun. mem. environ. and natural resources law sect. 1997-98, 2000-2001), Hennepin County Bar Assn., Delta Sigma Rho-Tau Kappa Alpha, Phi Sigma Alpha. Republican. Presbyterian. Avocations: reading, backpacking, cross country skiing, woodworking. Office: Faegre & Benson LLP 2200 Wells Fargo Ctr 90 S 7th St Minneapolis MN 55402-3901 E-mail: wrockenstein@faegre.com.

ROCKWELL, WINTHROP ADAMS, lawyer; b. Pittsfield, Mass., May 7, 1948; s. Landon Gale Rockwell and Ruth (Adams) Lonsdale; m. Barbara Washburn Wood, June 20, 1970; children: Samuel Adams, Madeleine McCord. AB, Dartmouth Coll., 1970; JD, NYU, 1975. Bar: Minn. 1975, U.S. Dist. Ct. Minn. 1975. Asst. newsman fgn. desk N.Y. Times, YC, 1970-71; asst. to pres. Dartmouth Coll., Hanover, NH, 1971-72; assoc. Faegre & Benson, Mpls., 1975-79; assoc. chief counsel Pres.'s Commn. on Accident at Three Mile Island, Washington, 1979; assoc. Faegre & Benson, Mpls., 1979-82, ptnr., 1983—. Chmn. diversity com. Faegre & Benson, 1990—95, head gen. litig. group, 1995—2004, mem. mgmt. com., 2004—, head internat. ops., 2004—. Bd. dirs., v.p. Children's Theatre, Mpls., 1982-83; bd. dirs. Actors Theatre St. Paul, 1975-79, Trinity Films, Mpls., 1978-82, Minn. Ctr. for Book Arts, 1996-2003; adv. bd. U. Minn. Joint Degree Program in Law, Health and the Life Scis. Brit.-Am. Project fellow, 1987. Mem. ABA, Minn. Bar Assn., Hennepin County Bar Assn., Am. Agrl. Law Assn., Adirondack 46ers, Adirondack Mountain Club. Avocations: writing, tennis, mountain climbing, gardening. Home: 1901 Knox Ave S Minneapolis MN 55403-2840 Office: Faegre & Benson 2200 Wells Fargo Ctr 90 S 7th St Ste 2200 Minneapolis MN 55402-3901 Office Phone: 612-766-6901. E-mail: wrockwell@faegre.com.

ROCKWOOD, FREDERICK WHITNEY, insurance company executive; b. Salt Lake City, Dec. 18, 1947; s. Lewis Frederick and Muriel (Whitney) R.; m. Alyce Jolene Edmunds, Aug. 26, 1970; children: Justin, Melissa, Jennifer, Katherine, Elizabeth, David. Student, U. Utah, 1966-67, Columbia U., NYC, 1970; AB in Anthropology, Stanford U., 1972; JD, Harvard U., 1975. Bar: Mass. Corp. strategy cons. Boston Cons., 1975-77; corp. strategy cons. Bain & Co., Boston, 1977; dir. corp. strategy Hillenbrand Industries, Inc., Batesville, Ind., 1977-78, sr. v.p., 1978-85; pres. The Forethought Group, Batesville, 1985—. Mem. adj. faculty U. Mich. Grad. Sch. Bus., 1980; pres., bd. dirs. Rockwood Furniture, Inc., Salt Lake City, 1985—; chmn. curriculum adv. coun. Ind. State Bd. Edn., 1987-92. Rep. Ch. of Jesus Christ of Latter-day Saints, Hong Kong, 1967-69; unit scouting coord. Dan Beard coun. Boy Scouts Am., Cin., 1982-91; bishop Ch. of Jesus Christ, Batesville, 1986-90. Mem. ABA, Fellow Life Mgmt. Inst. (chartered life underwriter 1990, chartered fin. cons. 1992), Am. Mgmt. Assn., Phi Beta Kappa. Republican. Avocations: philatey, genealogy.

RODAMAKER, MARTI TOMSON, bank executive; m. Bill Rodamaker; children: Mackenzie, Meeghan. BA in Econs., U. No. Iowa; MBA in Fin., U. St. Thomas. Credit analyst Marquette Bank, Mpls., 1984—87; field examiner Norwest Bank, 1987—93; from mem. staff to pres. First Citizens Nat. Bank, Mason City, Iowa, 1993—2000, pres., 2000—. Mem. adv. coun. Fed. Res. Iowa. Chmn. Hosp. Found.; treas. campaign YMCA; bd. regents Luther Coll., 2003—. Named One of 25 Women to Watch, U.S. Banker Mag., 2003. Mem.: Iowa Ind. Bankers Assn. (pres. 2001), Mason City C. of C. (bd. dir.). Office: First Citizens National Bank 2601 Fourth St SW Mason City IA 50401-1708

RODEMAN, FREDERICK ERNEST, accountant; b. Chgo., Jan. 29, 1938; s. Ernest August and Elizabeth Mae (Penrod) R.; m. Marilyn Kay Paul, June 17, 1967. BBA, Ind. U., 1959; cert. bank controllership, U. Wis., 1975; MBA, De Paul U., 1976; ThD, La. Baptist Theol. Seminary, 2005. CPA, Ind., Wis. Auditor Arthur Andersen & Co., Chgo., 1959-67; acct. mgr. A.B. Dick & Co., Chgo., 1967-72; controller Beloit (Wis.) State Bank, 1972-77; pvt. practice Beloit, 1977—. Mem.: Internat. Soc. Poets (Poet of Merit award 2005, Editor's Choice award 2007), Am. Inst. CPA's. Independent. Baptist. Home and Office: 2372 Tara Ct Beloit WI 53511-1938

RODENHUIS, DAVID ROY, meteorologist, educator; b. Michigan City, Ind., Oct. 5, 1936; married; 2 children. BS, U. Calif., Berkeley, 1959, Pa. State U., 1960; PhD in Atmospheric Sci., U. Wash., 1967. From asst. prof. to assoc. prof. dept. meteorology U. Md., College Park, 1968-75, assoc. prof. meteorology, 1976-84, dir. Climate Analysis Ctr., 1985-95, dir. Aviation Weather Ctr., 1996—. Exec. scientist U.S. com. global atmospheric rsch. program NAS, 1972; sci. officer World Meteorol. Orgn., 1975—; U.S.-U.S.S.R. exchange scientist, 1980. Mem. Am. Geophys. Union, Am. Meteorol. Soc. Achievements include research in tropical meteorology, convection models, dynamic climate models. Office: Aviation Weather Ctr 7220 NW 101st Terr Rm 101 Kansas City MO 64153-2371

RODGERS, CYNTHIA, anchor, correspondent; Anchor Sta. WIFR-TV, Rockford, Ill.; Chgo. bur. chief Knight-Ridder Fin. News; corr. CNN Fin. News, Chgo., Washington, anchor, corr. Chgo. Adj. prof. Northwestern U. Sch. Journalism, Evanston, Ill. Office: CNN 435 N Michigan Ave Chicago IL 60611-4066

RODGERS, JAMES FOSTER, insurance research executive, economist; b. Columbus, Ga., Jan. 15, 1951; s. Laban Jackson and Martha (Jackson) R.; m. Cynthia Lynne Bathurst, Aug. 20, 1975. BA, U. Ala., Tuscaloosa, 1973; PhD, U. Iowa, 1980. Fed. intern Office Rsch. and Stats., Social Security Adminstrn., Washington, 1976-77; rsch. assoc. Ctr. Health Policy Rsch., AMA, Chgo., 1979-80, rsch. dir., 1980-82, asst. to dep. exec. v.p. AMA, 1982-85; dir. AMA Ctr. Health Policy Rsch., Chgo., 1985-96, v.p. health policy, 1996—2003; sr. rsch. exec. Blue Cross Blue Shield Assn., Chgo., 2003—. Contbr. articles on health econs. to profl. jours. Pharm. Mfrs. Assn. grantee, 1978; NSF grantee, 1978; Hohenberg fellow, 1969-70 Mem. Am. Econ. Assn., Am. Statis. Assn. Home: 2233 N Orchard St Chicago IL 60614-3713 Office: Blue Cross Blue Shield Assn 225 N Michigan Ave Chicago IL 60601 Office Phone: 312-297-6535.

RODMAN, LEONARD C., engineering and construction executive; BS in Civil Engring., Iowa State U., 1971; MS in Environ. Engring., U. Mo., 1978. Joined Black & Veatch, Kansas City, Mo., 1971, various project mgmt. positions environ. divsn., named head N.Am. divsn. infrastructure bus., 1992, CEO, pres., 1998—, also chmn., 2000—. Bd. trustees, cmty./legis. affairs com. U. Mo., Kansas City; bd. advisors U. Kans. -Edward Campus; mem. Iowa State Engring

Coll. Indsl. Adv. Consul. Recipient Profl. Achievement Citation in Engring., U. Iowa Coll. Engring., 2003. Mem.: Am. Acad. Environ. Engineers, Water Environment Fedn., Nat. Soc. Profl. Engineers, Mo. Soc. Profl. Engineers, Am. Water Works Assn., Am. Soc. Civil Engineers. Office: Black & Veatch 11401 Lamar Ave Overland Park KS 66211

RODNEY, JOEL MORRIS, university chancellor; b. Bklyn., Nov. 9, 1937; s. Samuel Seymour and Jane (Loorya) R.; m. Judith DeStefano, July 22, 1994; children from previous marriage: Jonathan, Adam, Benjamin. BA cum laude, Brandeis U., 1959; PhD, Cornell U., 1965; attended, Inst. Ednl. Mgmt. Harvard U., 1976. From instr. to assoc. prof. Wash. State U., Pullman, 1963-70; chmn. div. social scis., assoc. prof. history Elmira (N.Y.) Coll., 1970-72, coordinator flood relief and community planning, 1973; dean arts and sci., prof. history Widener Coll., Chester, Pa., 1973-76, acting chief acad. officer, dean, 1976-77, chief acad. officer, dean, 1977-81, dir. univ. grad. programs, 1979-81; v.p. acad. affairs Salisbury (Md.) State Coll., 1981-86; provost Rockford (Ill.) Coll., 1986-90; CEO, dean U. Wis. -Washington County, West Bend, 1990—2003; CEO Pa. State U., York, 2003, chancellor, 2005—. Editor Albion, 1967-78; contbr. articles to profl. jours. Vice chmn. Md. Gov.'s Com. on Employment of Handicapped, 1985-86, chmn. Lower Shore divsn., 1983-86; chmn. adv. bd., Crozer-Chester Med. Health Ctr., Chester, 1974-77; project evaluator NEH, 1986, RSA, 1993; mem., sec. Delaware County Mental Health/Mental Retardation Bd., 1975-81; adv. bd. Rehab. Inst. of Chgo., 1988-94; mem. coun. Ct. of Gov.'s Regents Coll., London, 1986-90, Rock Valley Coll. Indsl. Coun., Rockford, 1989-90; bd. dirs. Moraine Symphony Orch., 1990-93, Welcome Home, Inc., 1990—, pres., 1992—; citizens adv. bd. West Bend Bank One, 1991, Washington County Vol. Ctr., 1991-92; bd. dirs. The Threshold, 1992—2003, vice chair, 1990-2000, chair, 2000-2003; apptd. to State Wis. Coun. Phys. Disabilities, 1994, vice chmn., 1995, chmn., 1996-2000; exec. com. Moraine area Tech. Prep. Coun., 1994—; mem. Wis. Gov.'s Com. on Persons with Disabilities, 1994-97, vice chmn., 1996-2003; adv. bd. S.E. Wis. Area Health Edn. Coun., 1995-96, West Bend Art Mus., 1996-2001, chair, 1999-2001; active West Bend C. of C. Ambs., 1995-2002, Washington County Growth Mgmt. Task Force, 1996-2003, chair, 1999-2003; del. Washington County Reps., 1997-2003; bd. dirs. Kettle Moraine YMCA, 1999-2003, bd. dirs. York County Blind Ctr., 2003—, Easter Seals South Central Pa., 2003-, Crispus Attucks, 2004—, United Way York County, 2004-, York County Econ. Devel. Cosp., 2003-, Advanced Skills Ctr., 2003-; mem. adv. com. City of York, 2003—; mem. York Counts Task Force on Workforce Devel., 2003-04; transition team York County Commrs., 2004; dir. York County C. of C., 2003-; chair Probusiness Coun., 2005. Recipient Disting. Svc. award Widener Meml. Sch., 1978, Award of Merit, Md. Gov.'s Com. on Employment of Handicapped, 1984; named to Legion of Honor, Chapel of Four Chaplains, 1978; honoree West Phila. Vets. and Handicapped Employment Com., 1977. Mem. Am. Assn. Acad. Deans, Conf. on Brit. Studies, Am. Assn. Univ. Adminstrs., Nat. Spinal Cord Injury Assn. (bd. dirs. Ill. chpt. 1988-90), Rotary (youth exch. com.), Phi Alpha Theta. Republican. Office: Pa State U York 1031 Edgecomb Ave York PA 17403 Home Phone: 717-767-4257; Office Phone: 717-771-4121. Business E-Mail: jmr45@psu.edu.

RODOVICH, ANDREW PAUL, magistrate judge; b. Hammond, Indiana, Feb. 24, 1948; s. Andrew H. and Julia (Makar) R.; m. Gail Linda (Patrick), May 27, 1972; children: Caroline Anja, Mary Katherine, James Patrick. BA, Valparaiso U., Ind., 1970, JD, 1973. Bar: Ind., 1973. Ptnr. Hand, Muenich, and Rodovich, Hammond, Ind., 1973-78; chief dep. prosecutor Lake County Prosecutor's Office, Crown Point, Ind., 1979-82; U.S. magistrate U.S. Dist. Ct., Hammond, Ind., 1982—. Referee Hammond City Ct., 1978; adj. prof. Valparaiso Law Sch.,Ind., 1985—. Fellow Ind. Bar Found.; mem. Nat. Coun. U.S. Magistrates, Delta Theta Phi. Republican. Avocation: sports. Home: 7207 Baring Pkwy Hammond IN 46324-2218 Office: US Dist Ct 5400 Federal Plz Ste 3700 Hammond IN 46320-1529 Office Phone: 219-852-6600. Business E-Mail: andrew_rodovich@innd.uscourts.gov.

RODRIGUEZ, EDGAR, chef; b. Durango, Mex. Student, Cooking and Hospitality Inst. Chgo. Waiter, mgr., exec. chef Linda's Margaritas, Chgo.; exec. chef, co-owner Salbute, Hinsdale, Ill., 1997—. Active March of Dimes, Make A Wish Found., Share Our Strength, Meals on Wheels, Operation Frontline. Named One of Top 20 ew Restaurants, Chgo. mag., 1998; recipient Four Forks rev., Chgo. Tribune. Office: Salbute 20 E 1st St Hinsdale IL 60521

RODRIGUEZ, IVAN TORRES, professional baseball player; b. Vega Baja, PR, Nov. 30, 1971; m. Maribel Rivera, June 20, 1991; 3 children. Catcher Tex. Rangers, 1991—2002, Fla. Marlins, 2003, Detroit Tigers, 2004—. Co-founder Ivan Pudge Rodriguez Found., 1993. Named Am. League MVP, 1999, Nat. League Championship Series MVP, 2003; named to Am. League All-Star Team, 1992—2001, 2004—07, Am. League Silver Slugger Team, The Sporting News, 1994—99, 2004; recipient Gold Glove award, 1992—2001, 2004, 2006—07. Achievements include being a member of the World Series Championship Marlins, 2003; becoming the 87th player in Major League history to reach 2,500 hits, 2008. Office: c/o Detroit Tigers 2100 Woodward Ave Detroit MI 48201

RODRIGUEZ, MANUEL ALVAREZ, pathologist; b. Guantanamo, Cuba, Nov. 12, 1946; came to U.S., 1961, naturalized, 1970; s. Manuel and Maria Teresa (Alvarez) R.; children: Austin B., Matthew J. BSc in Biology, U. Nev., 1966; MT, St. Alexius Hosp., Bismarck, ND, 1969; BSc in Medicine, U. N.D., 1971; MD, U. Tex., Galveston, 1973; flight surgeon training, Brooks AFB, San Antonio, 1992. Diplomate Am. Bd. Pathology. Rotating intern Meml. Med. Ctr., Corpus Christi, Tex., 1973-74; commd. USPHS, 1974, advanced through grades to comdr., 1993; gen. surgery resident USPHS Hosp., New Orleans, 1974-75, anatomic/clin. pathology resident, 1975-76, U. N.D. Sch. Medicine, Grand Forks, 1976-77, Touro Infirmary Hosp., New Orleans, 1977-79; pvt. practice Houston, 1979-89; sr. med. officer USPHS-USCG Med. Clinic, New Orleans, 1990-92; flight surgeon, sr. med. officer USPHS-Brooks AFB, San Antonio, 1992, USPHS-USCG Air Sta. Med. Clinic, Sitka, Alaska, 1992-96; clin. dir. USPHS, El Centro, Calif., 1997-98; sr. med. officer PHS Indian Health Ctr., White Earth, Minn., 1998—. Instr. pathology La. State U. Med. Sch., Baton Rouge, 1979-80; tchg. fellow pathology U. N.D. Med. Sch., Grand Forks, 1976-77. Contbr. articles to profl. jours. Dir. charitable donations mil. ann. drive USPHS-USCG, New Orleans, Sitka, 1990-96, Miami Lakes, Fla., 1996. Fellow Am. Acad. Family Practice, Coll. Am. Pathologists. Avocation: writing professional articles.

RODRIGUEZ, RAMIRO, chef; b. Guanajuato, Mex. Chef Carlos' Restaurant, Highland Park, Ill. Active James Beard Found., Share Our Strength, Meals on Wheels. Office: Carlos' Restaurant 429 Temple Ave Highland Park IL 60035

RODRIGUEZ, RICH, college football coach; b. Grant Town, W.Va., May 24, 1963; m. Rita Rodriguez; children: Rhett, Raquel. BS in Phys. Edn., W.Va. U., 1986. Secondary coach, spl. teams coord. Salem Coll., 1986—87, asst. head coach, defensive coord., 1987—88, head coach, 1988; asst. coach W.Va. U., 1989; head coach Glenville State Coll., 1990—96; offensive coord., quarterbacks coach Tulane U., 1997—98; offensive coord., assoc. head coach Clemson U., 1999—2000; head coach W.Va. U., 2001—07, U. Mich., 2008—. Athletic dir. Glenville State Coll., 1995—95; mem. bd. trustees Am. Football Coaches Assn., 2005—. Named WVIAC Coach of Yr., 1993—94, NAIA Coach of Yr., 1993, W.Va. State Coll. Coach of Yr., 1993, Big East Coach of Yr., 2003, 2005, Dist. I Coach of Yr., Am. Football Coaches Assn., 2003, AFCA Region I Co-Coach of Yr., 2007; named to Glenville Sports Hall of Fame, 2003. Achievements include winning 4 Big East Conf. Championships with W.Va. U., 2003, 2004, 2005, 2007. Office: U Mich Football Athletic Dept 1000 S State St Ann Arbor MI 48109-2201*

ROE, BYRON PAUL, physics professor; b. St. Louis, Apr. 4, 1934; s. Sam S. and Gertrude Harriet (Claris) R.; m. Alice Susan Krauss, Aug. 27, 1961; children: Kenneth David, Diana Carol. BA, Washington U., St. Louis, 1954; PhD, Cornell U., 1959. Instr. physics U. Mich., Ann Arbor, 1959-61, asst. prof., 1961-64, assoc. prof., 1964-69, prof., 1969—. Guest physicist SSC Lab., 1991. Author: Probability and Statistics in Experimental Physics, 1992, 2d edit., 2001, Particle Physics at the New Millennium, 1996 (Libr. Sci. Book Club selection). CERN vis. scientist Geneva, 1967, 89; Brit. Sci. Rsch. Coun. fellow, Oxford, 1979; recipient inventor's prize CDC Worldtech, Edina, Minn., 1982, 83. Fellow Am. Phys. Soc. Home: 3610 Charter Pl Ann Arbor MI 48105-2825 Office: U Mich Physics Dept 500 E University Ave Ann Arbor MI 48109-1040 E-mail: byronroe@umich.edu.

ROE, JOHN H., manufacturing executive; b. 1939; BA, Williams Coll., 1962; MBA, Harvard U., 1964. With Bemis Co. Inc., Mpls., 1964—, plant supt., 1964-67, sales rep., 1967-68, sales mgr., 1968-70, plant mgr., 1970-73, gen. mgr. film div., 1973-76, exec. v.p. ops., 1976-87, pres., chief oper. officer, from 1987, chief exec. officer, 1990—, also bd. dirs., chmn. Office: Bemis Co Inc 222 S 9th St Ste 2300 Minneapolis MN 55402-4099

ROE, ROBERT A., state legislator; b. Hayti, SD, Mar. 3, 1954; BS, S.D. State U., 1976; postgrad., Northwestern U., 1979. Mem. S.D. Ho. of Reps., 1988—, Ho. Majority Whip, 1995—, mem. judiciary and state affairs coms.; stockbroker Piper, Jeffrey & Hopwood, 1984—. Home: 1820 Skyview Ln Brookings SD 57006-3535 Office: SD Ho of Reps State Capitol Pierre SD 57501

ROE, ROGER ROLLAND, JR., lawyer; b. Mpls., Dec. 31, 1947; s. Roger Rolland Roe Jr.; m. Paula Speltz, 1974; children: Elena, Madeline. BA, Grinnell Coll., 1970; JD, U. Minn., 1973. Bar: Minn. 1973, U.S. Dist. Ct. Minn. 1974, U.S. Ct. Appeals (8th cir.) 1977, U.S. Supreme Ct. 1978, Wis. 1988, U.S. Dist. Ct. Nebr. 1995, U.S. Dist. Ct. (ea. and we. dists.) Wis. Law clk. to Hon. Judge Amdahl Hennepin County Dist. Ct., Mpls., 1973-74; from assoc. to ptnr. Rider, Bennett, Egan & Arundel, Mpls., 1974-91; mng. ptnr. Yaeger, Jungbauer, Barczak, Roe & Vucinovich, PLC, Mpls., 1992-2000; ptnr. Best & Flanagan LLP, Mpls., 2000—. Mem. nat. panel arbitrators Am. Arbitration Assn.; judge trial practice class and moot ct. competitions law sch. U. Minn.; guest lectr. Minn. Continuing Legal Edn. courses. Fellow Internat. Soc. Barristers; mem. ATLA (guest lectr.), Am. Bd. Trial Advs. (diplomat, Minn. chpt. pres. 1996-97), Million Dollar Round Table. Avocations: golf, skiing. Office: Best & Flanagan LLP 225 S 6th St # 4000 Minneapolis MN 55402 Home Phone: 612-377-6964; Office Phone: 612-349-5683. Business E-Mail: rroe@bestlaw.com.

ROEHL, EVERETT, transportation executive; Owner Roehl Transport, Inc., Marshfield, Wis., 1963—. Office: Roehl Transport Inc PO Box 750 1916 E 29th St Marshfield WI 54449-0750

ROEHLING, CARL DAVID, architect; b. Detroit, June 25, 1951; m. Barbara K. Jeffries; children: Carl Robert, Kristin Virginia. BS in Architecture, U. Mich., 1973, MArch, 1975. Registered arch., Mich.; cert. Nat. Coun. Archtl. Registration Bds. Arch. Minoru Yamasaki and Assocs., Inc., Troy, Mich., 1976-77, TMP Assocs., 1977-81, Harley Ellington Pierce Yee Assocs., Inc., Southfield, Mich., 1981-83, Giffels/Hoyem Basso Assocs., Troy, 1983-87, Smith, Hinchman & Grylls Assocs., Inc., Detroit, 1987; pres., CEO SmithGroup, Detroit. With Chrysler World Hdqs., 1994. Prin. works include CBS/Fox Video Hdqs., Livonia, Mich. (Honor award Mich. Masonry Inst., 1985), First Ctr. Office Bldg., Southfield, Mich. (Honor award FAIA Mich., 1988), Ind. U. Chemistry Bldg., Bloomington (Honor award AIA Detroit, 1990, AIA Mich., 1990), U. Mich. Aerospace Lab. Bldg., Ann Arbor, 1993, Los Alamos Materials Sci. Lab., N.Mex., 1993, others. Fellow AIA (Mich. chpt. pres. bd. dirs. 1989, mem. nat. com. on environ. 1991, Detroit chpt. pres. 1994, Young Arch. of Yr., AIA Detroit, 1986, AIA Mich., 1991, regional dir. 1996, nat. bd. dirs.); mem. Am. Archtl. Found. (bd. dirs. 1997), Mich. Archtl. Found. (chmn. pres. scholarship program 1990). Office: Smith Group 500 Griswold St Ste 1700 Detroit MI 48226-3802 Office Phone: 313-983-3600. Office Fax: 313-983-3636.

ROELL, STEPHEN A., manufacturing executive; Mgmt. positions Johnson Controls, Inc., Milw., 1982—91, v.p., CFO, 1991—98, sr. v.p., CFO, 1998—2004, exec. v.p., CFO, 2004—05, bd. dir., 2004—, exec. v.p., vice chmn., 2005—07, CEO, 2007, chmn., CEO, 2008—. Bd. dir. Covenant Healthcare Sys., Inc., Interstate Battery Svc. of Am., Inc. Office: Johnson Controls Inc 5757 W Green Bay Ave Milwaukee WI 53201

ROEMER, JAMES PAUL, data processing executive, writer; b. Cin., June 6, 1947; s. Charles William and Lillian (Vollman) R.; m. Patricia Pipenger; children: Kimberly, Michelle. Student, U. Cin., 1965-68; A.M.P., U. Va., 1978. Systems analyst Union Central Life Ins. Co., Cin., 1965-70; program and systems mgr. Computer Systems, Inc., Florence, Ky., 1970-72; mgr. data processing Mead Products, Dayton, Ohio, 1972-77; dir. ops. Mead Data Central, Dayton, 1977-78, v.p. ops., 1978-80, acting pres., 1980-81, v.p. product devel., 1981-82, sr. v.p. legal, govt., acctg., sr. v.p. with responsibility for lexis, 1982-89; pres. Michie Group, Charlottesville, Va., 1989-91; pres., COO Bell and Howell Publs. Systems Co., 1991-93; pres., CEO Univ. Microfilms Internat., Ann Arbor, 1994-95; chmn., pres., CEO Bell & Howell, Skokie, Ill., 1995—. Active Harvard, 1989. Mem. Info. Industry Assn., Assn. for Info. and Image Mgmt. Republican. Roman Catholic.

ROEPER, RICHARD, columnist; b. Chgo., Oct. 17, 1959; s. Robert and Margaret R. BA, Ill. State U., 1982. Freelance writer, 1982-87; syndicated columnist Chgo.-Sun Times, 1987—, NY Times; regular contbr., film crtic WBBM-CBS 2, Chgo., 2002—; and co-host Ebert & Roeper, 2000—. Talk show host Sta. WLS-FM, Chgo.; commentator Fox Thing in the Morning, Sta. WFLD-TV, Fox TV, Chgo.; contbr., film critic WLS-Channel 7. Author: Ten Sure Signs a Movie Character is Doomed and Other Surprising Movie Lists, 2002, Schlock Value: Hollywood at Its Worst, 2005; contbr. monthly essays on film in Esquire. Recipient Outstanding Columnist Ill. Press Assn., 1992, Nat. Headliner award for top columnist Atlantic City Press Club, 1992, Emmy award, 1994. Mem. Am. Fedn. TV & Radio Artists, Chgo. Newspaper Guild. Office: Chicago Sun Times 350 N Orleans St Ste 1270 Chicago IL 60654-2148

ROESCH, ROBERT EUGENE, dentist; b. July 10, 1951; s. Wilber H. and Vivian (Reese) R.; m. Susan M. Tuttle, Aug. 25, 1973. BA, Midland Luth. Coll., 1973; DDS, U. Nebr., 1976. Pvt. practice, Fremont, Nebr., 1979—; mem. bd. Three Rivers Pub. Health Dept., 2002—, pres., 2006—. Dental cons. Dodge County Am. Cancer Soc., Fremont, 1984—98. Campaign chmn. Fremont United Way, 1987, v.p., 1988; mem. orgn. com. Main St. Fremont, 1995—, chmn. orgn. com., 1998—2000, 2nd v.p., 1998, 1st v.p., 1999, pres., 2000, bd. dirs., 1997—2001; pres. Sinai Luth. Ch. Coun., Fremont, 1983—84, bd. dirs., 1987—90; mem. endowment com. Sinai Luth. Ch., 1990—94. Master: Acad. Gen. Dentistry (v.p. region 10 1990—91, dir. 1991—93, trustee 1993—94, chmn. budget and fin. com., spkr. of house 1999—2005); fellow: Pierre Fauchard Acad., Am. Coll. Dentristry, Internat. Acad. Dentistry, Internat. Coll. Dentistry (pres. Nebr. chpt. 2006—); mem.: ADA (del. 2002, 2005—06), Acad. Gen. Dentistry Found. (bd. dirs. 2005—), Fremont Indsl. Found., Fremont C. of C. (diplomate 1985—94, vice-chmn. memberships and membership svcs. 1989—90, bd. dirs. 1991—94, vice-chmn. pub. affairs 1992—94), Fremont Wellness Coun. (bd. dirs. 1996—98), Omaha Dist. Dental Soc. (bd. dirs.), Am. Equilibration Soc., Am. Assn. Functional Orthodontists, Am. Orthodontic Soc., Nebr. Dental Assn. (v.p. 2000—02, pres. 2002), Nebr. Acad. Gen. Dentistry (pub. info. officer 1983—85, sec., treas. 1985—88, pres. 1990—92, exec. dir. 1992—94, legis. chmn. 1997—), Acad. Operative Dentistry, Midland Coll. Alumni (bd. dirs. 1981—87, pres. 1983—84), Dodge County Hist. Soc., Salmon Soc., Fremont Tennis Assn., Fremont Cmty. Players, R.V. Tucker ebr. Study Club (treas. 2005), Tri Valley Dental Study Club (sec.-treas. 1983, v.p. 1984, pres. 1985, v.p. 1989), Midland Luth. Coll. Boosters Club (bd. dirs. 1988—94), Main St. Ambs. (co-chmn. 1997—98, chmn. 1998—2000, pres. 2000), Optimists (bd. dirs. 1981—83, 1984—88, pres. 1987, bd. dirs. Fremont club 1991—93), Am. Legion. Avocations: tennis, travel. Home: 2137 Nye Dr Fremont NE 68025-2210 Office: 553 N Broad St Fremont NE 68025-4930 E-mail: broesch@agd.org.

ROESSLER, CAROL ANN, state legislator; b. Madison, Wis., Jan. 16, 1948; m. Paul Roessler. BS, U. Wis., Oshkosh, 1972. Dir. nutrition program for older adults County of Winnebago, Wis., 1973-82; instr. pre-retirement planning Fox Valley Tech. Inst., 1978—81; elected to assembly, 1982—86; mem. Wis. Assembly, Madison, 1983-87; elected to senate in spl. election, 1987; mem. Wis. Senate from 18th dist., Madison, 1987—. Home: 1506 Jackson St Oshkosh WI 54901-2942 Office: PO Box 7882 Madison WI 53707-7882 E-mail: Sen.Roessler@legis.state.wi.us.

ROG, JOSEPH W., engineering company executive; BS, Kent State U. Pres. Corrpro Cos., Inc., Medina, Ohio, 1984—93, chmn., 1993—2004, CEO, 1984—2004, bd. dirs., 2004—. Office: Corrpro Cos Inc 1090 Enterprise Dr Medina OH 44256-1328 Office Phone: 330-723-5082.

ROGALSKI, EDWARD J., university administrator; b. Manville, NJ, Feb. 16, 1942; s. Joseph Stanley and Wladyslawa (Kraszewski) R.; m. Barbara Ann Bogk, June 01, 1968; children: Edward, James, Daniel, David, Christopher. BA, Parsons Coll., 1965; MA, U. Iowa, 1968, PhD, 1985; LittD (hon.), Loras Coll., 1990. Dean of men, asst. dean of students Parsons Coll., Fairfield, Iowa, 1965-67; dean of students St. Ambrose Coll., Davenport, Iowa, 1968-74, v.p. adminstrn., 1974-80, sr. v.p., 1980-86, exec. v.p., 1986-87; pres. St. Ambrose U., Davenport, 1987—. Bd. dirs., past chmn. Genesis Med. Ctr.; bd. dirs. Genesis Health Sys., Genesis Health Svcs. Found., Firstar Bank Davenport N.A.; cons. ednl. divsn. Marriott Corp., 1988—. Past vice chairperson Civil Rights Commn., Davenport, 1975; bd. dirs. Handicapped Devel. Ctr., Davenport, 1987, Jr. Achievement, 1988, Big Brothers-Big Sisters, 1988, Iowa Coll. Found., 1992—. Grantee Kettering Found., 1968. Mem. Iowa Assn. Ind. Colls. and Univs. (exec. com. and past chmn., treas. 1992—), Nat. Assn. Ind. Colls. and Univs. (bd. dirs., past exec. sec.), Am. Assn. Higher Edn., Davenport One (bd. dirs. 1992, exec. com., past chair-elect), Rotary, Phi Delta Kappa. Roman Catholic. Home: 806 W Rusholme St Davenport IA 52804-1928 Office: St Ambrose U 518 W Locust St Davenport IA 52803-2898 E-mail: erogalsi@sau.edu.

ROGAN, ELEANOR GROENIGER, oncologist, educator; b. Nov. 25, 1942; d. Louis Martin and Esther (Levinson) G.; m. William John Robert Rogan, June 12, 1965 (div. 1970); 1 child, Elizabeth Rebecca. AB, Mt. Holyoke Coll., 1963; PhD, Johns Hopkins U., 1968. Lectr. Goucher Coll., Towson, Md., 1968-69; rsch. assoc. U. Tenn., Knoxville, 1969-73, U. Nebr. Med. Ctr., Omaha, 1973-76, asst. prof., 1976-80, assoc. prof. Eppley Inst., dept. pharm. scis., 1980-90, prof. dept. pharm. scis. and dept. biochem. & molecular biol, 1990—2007, chair, dept. environ. agrl. and occupl. health, 2007—. Contbr. articles to profl. jours. Predoctoral fellow USPHS, Johns Hopkins U., 1965-68; recipient Linus Pauling Functional Medicine award, 2006. Mem. AAAS, Am. Assn. Cancer Rsch., Soc. Toxicology. Democrat. Roman Catholic. Home: 8210 Bowie Dr Omaha NE 68114-1526 Office: U Nebr Med Ctr Eppley Inst 986805 Nebr Med Ctr Omaha NE 68198-6805 Home Phone: 402-397-7342; Office Phone: 402-559-4095. Business E-Mail: egrogan@unmc.edu.

ROGEN, MARK ENDRE, former state senator, farmer; b. Sioux Falls, SD, Dec. 29, 1956; s. E. Ordell and Ruth Alice (Hess) R.; m. Kristen M. Halvorson, Aug. 30, 1985; children: Ariana, Melysa, Zachary. BS in Animal Sci., S.D. State U., 1979. Farmer, Sherman, S.D., 1979—; state senator State of S.D., Pierre, 1992-97. Bd. dirs. Hermanson (S.D.) Sch. Bd., S.D. Cattleman's Assn., 1985-88; pres. S.D. Corn Growers Assn., 1986-88; sec. Nat. Corn Growers Assn., St. Louis, 1987-89. Democrat. Lutheran. Home and Office: 48790 246th St Garretson SD 57030-5519

ROGERS, BRIE S., lawyer; b. Cin., May 26, 1978; BA, Auburn U., 1998; JD, U. Cin., 2002. Bar: Ohio 2002. Assoc. Taft, Stettinius & Hollister LLP, Cin., mem., Intellectual Property Practice Grp., mem., Profl. Women's Resource Grp. Fundraising dir. Give Back Cin., mem., Operational Bd., 2005. Named one of Ohio's Rising Stars, Super Lawyers, 2006. Mem.: Order of Coif. Office: Taft Stettinius & Hollister LLP 425 Walnut St Ste 1800 Cincinnati OH 45202 Office Phone: 513-381-2838. Office Fax: 513-381-0205.

ROGERS, BRYAN L., dean; Chmn. Sch. Art Carnegie Mellon U., 1988—99; Dean Sch. Art & Design U. Mich., 1999—. Office: Office of the Dean U Mich Sch Art & Design 2055 Art & Arch Bldg Ann Arbor MI 48109 Office Phone: 734-763-4093. E-mail: blrogers@umich.edu.

ROGERS, BRYAN LEIGH, dean, artist, educator; b. Amarillo, Tex., Jan. 7, 1941; s. Bryan Austin and Virginia Leigh (Bull) R.; m. Cynthia Louise Rice; 1 child, Kyle Austin Rogers. BE, Yale U., 1963; MS, U. Calif., Berkeley, 1966, MA, 1969, PhD, 1971. Design engr. Monsanto Co., Texas City, Tex., 1962; research engr. Rocketdyne, Canoga Park, Calif., 1963-64; research scientist Lawrence Livermore (Calif.) Lab., 1966; lectr. U. Calif., Berkeley, 1972-73; fellow Akademie der Bildenden Künste, Munich, 1974-75; prof. art San Francisco State U., 1975-88; head, prof. sch. art Carnegie Mellon U., Pitts., 1988-99, dir. Studio for Creative Inquiry, 1989-99; dean, prof. Sch. of Art and Design U. Mich., Ann Arbor, 2000—. Fellow Ctr. Advanced Visual Studies MIT, Cambridge, Mass, 1981. Editor Leonardo Jour., San Francisco, 1982-85. One-man shows include: Laguna Beach (Calif.) Mus. Art, 1974, DeSaisset Art Gallery U. Santa Clara, Calif., 1974, San Francisco Mus. Modern Art, 1974, Baxter Art Gallery Calif. Inst. Tech., Pasadena, 1979, Contemporary Crafts gallery, Portland, Oreg., 1987; group exhbns. include: Berkeley (Calif.) Art Ctr., 1969, Hansen-Fuller Gallery, San Francisco, 1970, San Francisco Arts Commn. Gallery, 1984, Clocktower Gallery, N.Y.C., 1984, Otis-Parsons Gallery, L.A., 1985, P.P.O.W. Gallery, N.Y.C., 1985, 18th Internat. Bienal, São Paulo, Brazil, 1985, MIT, Cambridge, 1990, Objects Gallery, Chgo., 1992, ARTEC 93 Internat Biennale, Nagoya, Japan, 1993, Chgo. Cultural Ctr., 1993, Am. Iron and Steel Expo., Pitts., 1993, Pitts. Ctr. for Arts, 1994, Allegheny Coll. Gallery, Meadville, Pa., 1997, Aichi Art Ctr., Nagoya, Japan, 1997. Fellow NEA, Washington, 1981, 82, Deutscher Akademischer Austauschdienst, Fed. Republic of Germany, 1974, NSF, Washington, 1965-69; recipient SECA award San Francisco Mus. Modern Art, 1974. Office: Sch Art & Design Univ Michigan Ann Arbor MI 48109 Office Phone: 734-763-4093. Business E-Mail: blrogers@umich.edu.

ROGERS, CHARLES EDWIN, physical chemistry and polymer science professor; b. Rochester, NY, Dec. 29, 1929; s. Charles Harold and Maybelle (Johnson) R.; m. Barbara June Depuy, June 12, 1954; children: Gregory Newton, Linda Frances, Diana Suzanne. BS in Chemistry, Syracuse U., 1954; PhD in Phys. Chemistry, SUNY at Syracuse U., 1957. Rsch. assoc. dept. chemistry Princeton U., 1957-59, Goodyear fellow, 1957-59; mem. tech. staff Bell Telephone Labs., Murray Hill, NJ, 1959-65; assoc. prof. macromolecular sci. Case Western Res. U., Cleve., 1965-74, prof., 1974-98, prof. emeritus, 1998—. Sr. vis. fellow Imperial Coll., U. London, 1971; assoc. dir. Ctr. for Adhesives Sealants Coatings, Case Western Res. U., 1984-88, dir., 1988-91; co-dir. Edison Polymer Innovation Corp., Ctr. for Adhesives, Sealants and Coatings, 1991-97; cons. to polymer and chem. industries; devel. overseas ednl. instns. Editor: Permselective Membranes, 1971, Structure and Properties of Block Copolymers, 1977; contbr. numerous articles to profl. jours.; patentee in field. Staff sgt. 82nd airborne divsn. US Army, 1946—49, staff sgt. USAR, 1949—53, commd. officer USAR, 1953—63. Mem.: Adhesion Soc., N.Am. Membrane Soc., Am. Phys. Soc., Am. Chem. Soc. Home: 8400 Rockspring Dr Chagrin Falls OH 44023-4645 Office: Case Western Reserve U Dept Macromolecular Sc Cleveland OH 44106-7202 Office Phone: 216-368-6376. Business E-Mail: cer@case.edu.

ROGERS, DARLA POLLMAN, lawyer; b. 1952; BA, Wheaton Coll.; JD, U. S.D. Bar: S.D. 1979. Ptnr. Meyer & Rogers, Pierre, SD, Riter, Rogers, Wattier & Brown LLP, Pierre, SD, 2003—. Mem. ABA, S.D. Bar Assn. (pres., 1998-99); fellow, Am. Bar Found. Office: Riter Rogers Wattier & Brown PO Box 280 Pierre SD 57501-0280

ROGERS, DAVID, apparel executive; With Pickwick Internat., Mpls.; pres. Wilson's The Leather Experts, Inc., Brooklyn Park, Minn., 1979—. Office: Wilsons The Leather Experts Inc 7401 Boone Ave N Brooklyn Park MN 55428-1080

ROGERS, DAVID HUGHES, banking and financial service professor, dean, real estate company executive; b. Chgo., May 21, 1947; s. Joseph Gordon and Viola Winifred (Hughes) R.; Bonnie Hope Sinai, 1997; children: Kirsten Morgan, Loren Avery, Daniel Jay. BA, U. Mich., 1968; PhD, Columbia U., 1975. Economist Fed. Res. Bank of Cleve., 1974-75; asst. treas. B.F. Goodrich Co., Akron, Ohio, 1975-82; exec. v.p., chief fin. officer First Tex. Savs. Assn., Dallas, 1982-83; sr. exec. v.p., chief operating officer PriMerit Bank, Las Vegas, 1984-87, pres., dir., 1987-91, vice chmn., 1991-92; COO, The Baird Cos., Las Vegas, 1992-99; v.p., chief fin. officer Norall Labs., Las Vegas, 1999—2001; v.p., relationship mgr. Wells Fargo Bank, Las Vegas, Nev., 2001—04; CFO Lloyd Cos., Sioux Falls, SD, 2004—06; prof. banking and fin. svcs., asst. dean external programs No. State U., 2006—. Adj. prof. econs. C.C. So. Nev., 1998-2004. Author: Consumer Banking in New York, 1975; also articles. Bd. dirs. Boulder Dam Area coun. Boy Scouts Am., 1986—2004; bd. dirs. Nev. Sch. Arts, 1988-98; chmn. Las Vegas Bus. Bank, 1995-99. Office: No State U 2205 Career Ave Rm 268 D Sioux Falls SD 57107 Home Phone: 605-271-1103; Office Phone: 605-782-3236. Personal E-mail: dhrogers14@aol.com. Business E-Mail: dhrogers@northern.edu.*

ROGERS, DESIREE GLAPION, utilities executive; b. New, June 16, 1959; d. Roy and Joyce Glapion; 1 child, Victoria. B in Polit. Sci., Wellesley Coll., 1981; MBA, Harvard U., 1985. Customer svc. mktg. mgr. AT&T, N.J., 1985-87; dir.

devel. Levy Orgn., Chgo., 1987-89; founder, pres. Mus. Ops. Consulting Assocs., Chgo., 1989-91; dir. Ill. State Lottery, Chgo., 1991-97; chief mktg. officer Peoples Energy, Chgo., 1997—; pres. Peoples Gas and North Shore Gas, 2004—. Bd. dirs. Equity Residential, Blue Cross Blue Shield Ill. Bd. dirs. Mus. Sci. and Industry, Ravinia; trustee Lincoln Park Zoo. Named a Woman to Watch, Crain's Chgo. Bus., 2007. Mem. Com. of 200, Young Pres.' Orgn., The Econ. Club, Execs. Club, Comml. Club Chgo. Office: Peoples Energy 130 E Randolph Dr Fl 18 Chicago IL 60601-6207

ROGERS, EARLINE S., state legislator; b. Gary, Ind., Dec. 20, 1934; d. Earl and Robbie (Hicks) Smith; m. Louis C. Rogers, Dec. 24, 1956; children: Keith, Dana. d. Earl and Robbie (Hicks) Smith; m. Louis C. Rogers, Dec.24, 1956; children: Keith, Dana. BS, Ind. U., 1957, MS, 1971. Mem. Ind. State Ho. Reps, 1982-90, Ind. State Senate from 14th dist., 1990—, asst. minority whip, 1995—96. Mem. appointment and claims com. (ranking minority mem.), edn. com., health and provider svcs. com., rules and legis. procedure com. Mem. NAACP, Nat. Coun. Negro Women, League Women Voters, Urban League, Black Prfl. Women, Am. Fedn. Tchrs., Ind. State Tchrs. Assn. Democrat. Avocations: reading, sewing. Office: Ind State Senate Dist 3 200 W Washington St Indianapolis IN 46204-2728 also: 3636 W 15th Ave Gary IN 46404

ROGERS, EUGENE JACK, retired medical educator; b. Vienna, June 13, 1921; came to U.S., 1937; s. Louis and Malvina (Haller) R.; m. Joyce M. Lighter, Feb. 9, 1952; children: Jay A., Robert J. BS, CCNY; M.B., Chgo. Med. Sch., 1946, MD, 1947. Diplomate Am. Bd. Phys. Medicine and Rehab. Intern Our Lady of Mercy Med. Ctr. and Cabrini Meml. Hosps., NYC, 1946-48; resident Madigan Hosp., Tacoma, 1951, Mayo Clinic, Rochester, Minn., 1951, N.Y. Med. Coll. Met. Med. Ctr., 1953-55; USPHS fellow, 1955-56; ship's surgeon U.S. Lines, Grace Lines, NYC, 1948-49; indsl. physician Abraham & Strauss Stores, Bklyn., 1949-51; practice medicine specializing in phys. medicine and rehab. Bklyn., 1956-73; dir. rehab. service, attending physician N.Y. City Hosp. Dept., 1955-73; prof., chmn. dept. rehab. medicine Chgo. Med. Sch., North Chicago, Ill., 1973—2005, prof. emeritus dept. rehab. medicine, 2005—, Rosalind Franklin U. Medicine & Sci., 2005. Cons. N.Y.C. Mayor's Adv. Com. for Aged, 1957; asst. prof. SUNY Downstate Med. Sch., Bklyn., 1958-73; med. dir. Schwab Rehab. Hosp., Chgo., 1973-75; acting chief rehab. service VA Center, North Chicgo, 1975-77; chmn. Ill. Phys. Therapy Exam. Com., 1977-78; examiner Am. Bd. Phys. Medicine and Rehab., 1983; sec., dir. Microtherapeutics, Inc., 1972 Editor: Total Cancer Care, 1975; contbr. articles to med. jours.; contbg. editor Ill. Med. Jour., 1983-89 Served to capt. US Army, 1951—53. Recipient Bronze medal Am. Congress Rehab. Medicine, 1974 Fellow: ACP, Am. Acad. Phys. Medicine and Rehab. (Cert. Appreciation 1993); mem.: Chgo. Med. Sch. Alumni Assn. (asst. treas. 1983—93, treas. 1993—95, sec. 1995—97, 1st v.p. 1999, pres. 2001—03, exec. com., Disting. Alumnus award 1980, Presdl. plaque Greater N.Y. chpt.), Chgo. Med. Sch. Faculty Assembly (spkr. 1978—80), Ill. Soc. Phys. Medicine and Rehab. (pres. 1983—84), Ill. Med. Soc. (chmn. workmen's compensation com. 1980—83), Odd Fellows (pres. 1961—62), Phi Lambda Kappa (trustee 1980), Alpha Omega Alpha. Home: 1110 N Lake Shore Dr Chicago IL 60611-5248 Personal E-mail: eugenerogers@att.com.

ROGERS, JAMES DEVITT, judge; b. Mpls., May 5, 1929; s. Harold Neil and Dorothy (Devitt) R.; m. Leanna Morrison, Oct. 19, 1968. AB, Dartmouth Coll., 1951; JD, U. Minn., 1954. Bar: Minn. 1954, U.S. Supreme Ct. 1983. Assoc. Johnson & Sands, Mpls., 1956-60; sole practice Mpls., 1960-62; judge Mpls. Municipal and Dist. Ct., 1959-91. Mem. faculty Nat. Judicial Coll. Bd. dirs. Mpls. chpt. Am. Red Cross, chmn. service to mil. families and vets. com.; bd. dirs. Minn. Safety Coun., St. Paul, 1988-91; founding dir., sec. Forest Landowners Tax Coun. Served sgt. U.S. Army, 1954-56. Mem. ABA (chmn. nat. conf. spl. ct. judge, spl. com. housing and urban devel. law, traffic ct. program com., chmn. criminal justice sect., jud. adminstrn. div.), Nat. Jud. Coll. (bd. dirs.), Nat. Christmas Tree Grower's Assn. (pres. 1976-78), Mpls. Athletic Club. Congregationalist. Office: 14110 Prince Pl Minnetonka MN 55345-3027

ROGERS, JAMES EUGENE, energy executive; b. Birmingham, Ala., Sept. 20, 1947; s. James E. and Margaret (Whatley) R.; m. Robyn McGill (div.); children: Chrissi, Kara, Ben; m. Mary Anne Boldrick, Oct. 28, 1977. BBA, U. Ky., 1970, JD, 1974; LLD (hon.), Ind. State U.; DHL (hon.), Queens Univ., Charlotte NC. Reporter Lexington (Ky.) Herald Leader, 1967—70; asst. atty. gen. Commonwealth Ky., Louisville; asst. chief trial atty. Fed. Energy Regulation Commn., Washington, dep. gen. counsel litigation and enforcement; law clk. to presiding justice Supreme Ct Ky., Louisville; ptnr. Akin, Gump, Strauss, Hauer & Feld LLP, Dallas, Akin Gump Strauss Hauer & Feld LLP, Houston, 1985-86; exec. v.p. Enron Gas Pipeline Group, 1986—88; pres., CEO, chmn. PSI Resources, Inc, 1988—94, Cinergy Corp. (formerly PSI Resources, Inc.), Cin., 1994—2006; pres., CEO Duke Energy Corp., Charlotte, NC, 2006—07, chmn., pres., CEO, 2007—. 2nd vice chmn. Edison Electric Inst., 2004—05, vice chmn., 2005—06, chmn., 2006—; bd. dirs. Chesapeake Corp., 1999—2004, Duke Energy Corp., 2006—, Fifth Third Bancorp, Fifth Third Bank, Am. Gas Assn., US C. of C., Bus. Roundtable, Nat. Coal Coun.; bd. dir., mem. exec. com. Nuclear Energy Inst. Trustee Nat. Symphony Orch.; bd. dirs. Cin. Mus. Assn., The Nature Conservancy-Ind. chpt., U. Ky. Bus. Partnership Found. Named CEO of Yr., Platts Global Energy awards, 2007; named to Hall of Fame Gatton Coll. Bus. & Econ., Univ. Ky., Hall of Fame Coll. Law, Univ. Ky.; recipient Disting. Svc. Citation, NCCJ, 2004, Keystone Ctr. in Leadership in Industry award, 2005, Ronald McDonald House Lifetime Achievement award, 2005, Human Rels. award, Am. Jewish Com., 2006, Ellis Island Medal of Honor, Nat. Ethnic Coalition of Org., 2007. Mem. Ky. Bar Assn., D.C. Bar Assn., Meridian Hills Country Club, Crooked Stick Golf Club, Queen City Club, Met. Club. Baptist. Avocations: tennis, bicycling, skiing, golf. Office: Duke Energy Corp 526 S Church St Charlotte NC 28202 also: Edison Electric Inst 701 Pennsylvania Ave NW Washington DC 20004

ROGERS, JOHN MARSHALL, judge, educator; b. Rochester, NY, June 26, 1948; s. Harry Lovejoy III and Virginia Kathryn (Meyers) R.; m. Ying Juan Xiong, 1990. BA, Stanford U., 1970; JD, U. Mich., 1974. Bar: DC 1975, Ky. 1980, US Ct. Appeals, US Supreme Ct. Commd. USAR, 1970; appellate atty. civil div. US Dept. Justice, Washington, 1974-78; asst. prof. U. Ky., Lexington, 1978-81, assoc. prof., 1981-86, prof., 1986—2002, prof. emeritus, 2002—; cir. judge US Ct. Appeals (6th cir.), 2002—. Vis. prof. Civil Divsn. US Dept. Justice, Washington, 1983-85; Fulbright lectr. Fgn. Affairs Coll., Beijing, 1987-88, Zhongshan U., Guangzhou, People's Republic of China, 1994-95; spl. counsel impeachment com. Ky. Ho. of Reps., 1991. Author: Internat. Law and U.S. Law, 1999; contbr. articles to profl. jours. Mem. Coun. on Fgn. Rels., Am. Law Inst., Order of Coif, Phi Beta Kappa. Office: 532 Potter Stewart US Courthouse 100 E 5th St Cincinnati OH 45202-3988 also: Cmty Trust Bank Bldg 100 E Vine St Lexington KY 40507

ROGERS, JOHN W., JR., investment company executive; s. John W. Sr. and Jewel (Mankarious) R.; m. Sharon Fairley. AB in Econs., Princeton U., NJ, 1980. Broker William Blair & Co.; founder, chmn., CEO Ariel Capital Mgmt., LLC, Chgo., 1983—. Bd. dirs. Aon Corp., Exelon Corp., McDonald's Corp., Ariel Capital Mgmt., LLC, and Ariel Mutual Funds. Columnist: Forbes mag. Trustee U. Chgo.; dir. Chgo. Urban League; alumnus Leadership Greater Chgo. Named one of 50 for the Future, Time mag., 1994; recipient Disting. Fellow award, Leadership Greater Chgo., 2000, Most Influential Black Americans, Ebony mag., 2005. Office: Ariel Capital Mgmt # 2900 200 E Randolph St Chicago IL 60601-6436

ROGERS, JUSTIN TOWNER, JR., retired utility company executive; b. Sandusky, Ohio, Aug. 4, 1929; s. Justin Towner and Barbara Eloise (Larkin) R. AB cum laude, Princeton U., 1951; JD, U. Mich., 1954. Bar: Ohio 1954. Assoc. Wright, Harlor, Purpus, Morris & Arnold, Columbus, 1956-58; with Ohio Edison Co., Akron, 1958-93, v.p., then exec. v.p., 1970-79, pres., 1980-91, chmn. bd., 1991-93; ret., 1993. Past mem. coal adv. bd. Internat. Energy Agy. Past pres., trustee Akron Cmty. Trusts, Akron Child Guidance Ctr.; past chmn. Akron Assoc. Health Agys., U. Akron Assocs., Ohio Electric Utility Inst.; past chmn., trustee, Akron Gen. Health Sys.; trustee Sisler McFawn Found.; former trustee Stan Hywet Hall & Gardens, VNS-Hospice Found.; past dir. Edison Elec. Inst., Elec. Power Rsch. Inst., Assn. of Edison Illuminating Co.'s. Mem. Portage Country Club, Mayflower Club, Rockwell Springs Trout Club (Castalia, Ohio), Columbus Beach Club, Phi Delta Phi, Beta Gamma Sigma.

ROGERS, KENNY (KENNETH SCOTT ROGERS), professional baseball player; b. Savannah, Ga., Nov. 10, 1964; m. Rebecca Lewis; children: Jessica Lynn, Trevor. Pitcher Tex. Rangers, 1989-95, 2000—02, 2004—05, NY Yankees, 1996—97, Oakland A's, 1998—99, NY Mets, 1999, Minn. Twins, 2003, Detroit Tigers, 2006—. Active Habitat for Humanity. Recipient Am. League Gold Glove award, 2000, 2002, 2004-06; named to Am. League All-Star Team, 1995, 2004-06. Achievements include becoming the 14th pitcher in Major League history to pitch a perfect game, 1994; winning his 200th game against the Chicago Cubs, 2006; becoming the oldest starting pitcher (41 years old) to earn his first career postseason win, 2006. Avocations: golf, fishing. Office: c/o Detroit Tigers Comerica Pk 2100 Woodward Ave Detroit MI 48201*

ROGERS, MIKE (MICHAEL J. ROGERS), congressman; b. Livonia, Mich., June 2, 1963; m. Diane Rogers; 1 child. BA in Sociology and Criminal Justice, Adrian Coll., 1985. Spl. agt. FBI, 1989—94; small bus. owner; mem. Mich. Senate from 26th dist., 1995-2000; vice chmn. judiciary com. Mich. Senate, mem. fin. svc., human resources, labor and vet affairs coms., mem. reappropriations com., mem. tech. and energy commn., mem. banking and fin. com.; mem. US Congress from Mich. 8th dist., Washington, 2001—; mem. fin. svcs. and transp. coms.; mem. Com. on Energy and Commerce. Bd. trustees Cleary Coll., Mich. Served as 2nd Lt. rapid deployment US Army, 1985—88. Recipient Nextel Prepared award, Nextel Comm. Inc., 2004, ITS Congl. Champion awrad, Intelligent Transp. Systems Am., 2005, Joseph M. Magliochetti Industry Champion award, Motor and Equipment Manufacturers Assn., 2005. Mem.: Soc. Former Spl. Agents for FBI, Home Builders Assn., Livingston County, Mich., Am. Heart Assn. Republican. Meth. Office: US Congress 133 Cannon HOB Washington DC 20515-2208 also: District Office 1327 E Michigan Ave Lansing MI 48912 Office Phone: 202-225-4872, 517-702-8000. Office Fax: 202-225-5820, 517-702-8642.

ROGERS, NANCY HARDIN, dean, law educator; b. Lansing, Mich., Sept. 18, 1948; d. Clifford Morris and Martha (Wood) Hardin; m. Douglas Langston Rogers, Jan. 30, 1970; children: Lynne, Jill, Kim. BA with highest distinction, U. Kans., 1969; JD, Yale U., 1972. Bar: D.C. 1975, Ohio 1972, U.S. Ct. Appeals (6th cir.) 1973, U.S. Dist. Ct. (no. dist.) Ohio 1974, U.S. Dist. Ct. (so. dist.) Ohio 1975. Law clk. U.S. Dist. Judge Thomas D. Lambros, Cleve., 1972-74; staff atty. Cleve. Legal Aid Soc., 1974-75; vis. asst. prof. Coll. of Law Ohio State U., Columbus, 1975-76, asst. prof., 1976-78, 83-89, assoc. prof., 1989-92, prof., assoc. dean acad. affairs, 1992-97, prof., 1992—, Joseph S. Platt, Porter, Wright, Morris & Arthur prof. law Columbus, 1995—2001, vice provost acad. adminstrn., 1999—2001, dean, Michael E. Moritz chair in alternative dispute resolution Michael E. Moritz Coll. Law, 2001—. Adj. prof. Ohio State Coll., 1981-83; vis. prof. law Harvard Law Sch., 2000. Author (with Frank E.A. Sander, Sarah R. Cole, Stephen B. Goldberg): (Book) Dispute Resolution: egotiation, Mediation and Other Processes), 2007; author: (book with Craig A. McEwen and Sarah R. Cole) Mediation: Law, Policy, Practice, 2nd edit., 1994; mem. (adv. bd.) World Arbitration and Mediation Report, 1991—, Alternatives, 1992—, co-chair (editl. bd. with Frank E.A. Sander) Dispute Resolution mag., 1994—2002; contbr. chapters to books, articles to profl. jours. Bd. dirs. Assn. for Developmentally Disabled, Columbus, 1980-85; Legal Svcs. Corp. 1995-2003. Named Outstanding Prof., Ohio State U. Coll. Law Alumni Assn., 1996; recipient Book prize, Ctr. Pub. Resources for A Student's Guide to Mediation and the Law, 1987, Ctr. Pub. Resources for Mediation: Law, Policy, Practice, 1989, Peacemaker of Yr. award, Cmty. Mediation Svcs. Ctrl. Ohio, 1990, Disting. Svc. Recognition, Soc. Profls. in Dispute Resolution, 1990, Whitney North Seymour sr. medal, Am. Arbitration Assn., 1990, Svc. Recognition award, Legal Aid Soc. Columbus, 1996, Ritter award, Ohio State Bar Found for outstanding contbns. to adminstrn. of justice, 1998; grantee Exxon Edn. Found., 1986, William and Flora Hewlett Found., 1990, Ohio State U. Interdisciplinary Seed, 1990, Ohio State U. Symposium, 1992, William and Flora Hewlett Found., 1992—96, Nat. Sci. Found., 1993—95, State Justice Instn., 1994, Fund for Improvement Post-Secondary Edn., U. Mo., 1996—97, William and Flora Hewlett Found., 1997—2003. Mem. ABA (chair, standing com. dispute resolution 1988-91, D'Alemberte-Raven award sect. on dispute resolution 2002), Assn. Am. Law Schs. (pres. 2007), Phi Beta Kappa. Office: Ohio State U Coll Law 55 W 12th Ave Columbus OH 43210-1306 Office Phone: 614-292-0574. Business E-Mail: rogers.23@osu.edu.

ROGERS, PHIL, reporter; married; 1 child. BS in Journalism, Okla. State U., 1977. News dir. Sta. KVRO-FM, Stillwater, Okla.; reporter Sta. KOMA-AM, Oklahoma City, 1977—79; news writer then afternoon news prodr. Sta. WBBM-AM, 1979—84, mng. editor, asst. news dir., on-air anchor, reporter; gen. assignment reporter Sta. WMAQ-TV, Chgo., 1993—. Recipient award, AP, awards for Best Radio Reporting, UPI, 3 Peter Lisagor awards, Chgo. Headline Club, Edward R. Murrow award, Radio and TV News Dirs. Assn. Avocation: lic. pilot. Office: NBC 454 N Columbus Dr Chicago IL 60611

ROGERS, RICHARD DEAN, federal judge; b. Oberlin, Kans., Dec. 29, 1921; s. William Clark and Evelyn May (Christian) R.; m. Helen Elizabeth Stewart, June 6, 1947; children— Letitia Ann, Cappi Christian, Richard Kurt. BS, Kans. State U., 1943; JD, Kans. U., 1947. Bar: Kans. 1947. Ptnr. firm Springer and Rogers (Attys.), Manhattan, Kans., 1947-58; instr. bus. law Kans. State U., 1948-52; partner firm Rogers, Stites & Hill, Manhattan, 1959-75; gen. counsel Kans. Farm Bur. & Service Cos., Manhattan, 1960-75; judge U.S. Dist. Ct., Topeka, Kans., 1975—. City commr., Manhattan, 1950-52, 60-64, mayor, 1952, 64, county atty., Riley County, Kans., 1954-58, state rep., 1964-68, state senator, 1968-75; pres. Kans. Senate, 1975. Served with USAAF, 1943-45. Decorated Air medal, Dfc. Mem. Kans., Am. bar assns., Beta Theta Pi. Clubs: Masons. Republican. Presbyterian. Office: US Dist Ct 444 SE Quincy St Topeka KS 66683 Office Phone: 785-295-2735.

ROGERS, RICHARD F., construction company executive, architect, engineer; b. Chgo., July 25, 1942; s. Frank S. and Emily H. (Novak) R.; m. Christina L. Rogers, June 30, 1963; children: Mitchell, Cynthia. B in Architectural Engineering, U. Ill., Chgo., 1964. Registered architect, Ill., Wis., Mich., profl. engr., Ill. Architect Einstein Assocs. Inc., Skokie, Ill., 1963-69; v.p. Land Am. Corp., Chgo., 1969-70; project architect M.A. Lombard Constrn. Co., Alsip, Ill., 1970-73; sr. project mgr. W.E. O'Neil Constrn. Co., Chgo., 1973-78; pres. A.C.M. Assocs. Inc., Mt. Prospect, Ill., 1978—. Mem.: AIA. Office: 1306 S Wolf Rd Wheeling IL 60090-6444

ROGERS, RICHARD HUNTER, lawyer; b. Flushing, NY, Sept. 11, 1939; s. Royden Harrison and Frances Wilma (Hunter) R.; children: Gregory P., Lynne A., Reade H. BS in Bus. Adminstrn, Miami U., 1961; JD, Duke, 1964. Bar: Ill. 1964, Ohio 1973. Atty. Continental Ill. Nat. Bank, Chgo., 1964-65; sr. atty. Brunswick Corp., Chgo., 1965-70; corporate counsel The A. Epstein Cos., Inc. (real estate developers), Chgo., 1970-73; v.p., gen. counsel, sec. Price Bros. Co., Dayton, Ohio, 1973-82; v.p., divsn. mgr. Water Systems Tech. div. Price Bros. Co., Dayton, Ohio, 1982-85; pres. Internat. divsn. Price Bros. Co., Dayton, Ohio, 1986—88; pvt. practice law Dayton, 1988—; pres. Richard H. Rogers & Assocs. LPA. Pres. adv. coun. Miami U. Bus. Sch.; bd. dirs. Red and White Club, Miami U.; mem. Washington Twp. Task Force on Future Govt.; trustee Woodhaven, Inc.; mem. Washington Twp. Zoning Commn., 1990—, chmn., 1999—. Mem. ABA (forum com. on constrn.), Ill. Bar Assn., Ohio Bar Assn., Dayton Bar Assn. (chmn. corp. law dept. com. 1983-84, exec. com. 1986-87, editor Bar Briefs 1990-91), Miami U. Alumni Assn. (pres.), Miami U. Pres.'s Club. Office: 7333 Paragon Rd Ste 200 Dayton OH 45459-4157 Address: PO Box 751144 Dayton OH 45475-1144 Home Phone: 437-885-2335; Office Phone: 937-438-0555. Personal E-mail: rhrlawoffice@aol.com.

ROGERS, RICHARD LEE, academic administrator, educator; b. NYC, Sept. 17, 1949; s. Leonard J. and Beverly (Simon) R.; m. Susan Jane Thornton, Aug. 14, 1976; children: Caroline, Meredith. BA, Yale U., 1971, MA in Religion, 1973; postgrad., U. Chgo., 1977-80; MS in Edn., Bank St. Coll. Edn., NYC, 1989. Tchr. Foote Sch., ew Haven, 1974-77; devel. assoc. U. Chgo., 1980-81, spl. asst. to v.p. planning, 1981-82; spl. asst. to pres. New Sch. Social Rsch., NYC, 1982-83, sec. of corp., then v.p., sec., 1983-94; pres. Coll. for Creative Studies, Detroit, 1994—. Office: Coll for Creative Studies 201 E Kirby St Detroit MI 48202-4048 Office Phone: 313-664-7474. Business E-Mail: rrogers@collegeforcreativestudies.edu.

ROGERS, ROBERT ERNEST, medical educator; s. Jessie H. and Willie L. (Bahr) Rogers; m. Barbara Ann Hill, May 16, 1950; children: Robert E., Jr., Stephanie Ann Thompson, Cheri Lee Heck. BS in Biology, John B. Stetson U., 1949; MD, U. Miami, 1957. Diplomate Am. Bd. Ob-Gyn. Commd. 1st lt. M.C., U.S. Army, 1952, advanced through grades to col., 1971—74; ret. U.S. Army, 1974; intern Brooke Gen. Hosp., San Antonio, 1957-58, chief resident ob-gyn, 1960-61; resident in ob-gyn Jackson Meml. Hosp., Miami, Fla., 1958-60; fellow gynecology M.D. Anderson Hosp., Houston, 1965-66; asst. chief ob-gyn Tripler Army Med. Ctr., Honolulu, 1966-69; chmn. ob-gyn Walter Reed Med. Ctr., Washington, 1969-70, Madigan Army Med. Ctr., Tacoma, 1970-74; prof. Ind. U. Sch. Medicine, Indpls., 1974—, also chief gynecol. div., 1974—; chief ob-gyn svd. Wishard Meml. Hosp., Indpls., 1983-87. Contbr. articles to profl. jours.; editl. bd. Jour. Am. Coll. Surgeons, 2003—. Bd. dirs. Lake Stonebridge Homeowner's Assn., 2000—03, sec., 2000—03. Recipient Army Commendation medal, 1969, Army Meritorious Service Medal, 1971, Army Legion of Merit, 1974, Army Surgeon General's "A" Prefix for Profl. Excellence, 1974. Mem.: ACS, ACOG (chmn. gynecol. practice com., commr. practice, Sci. Exhibit award Armed Forces dist. 1971, Zimmerman Cons. award Armed Forces dist.), AMA (Certificate Merit for Sci. Exhibit 1971), Felix Rutledge Soc. (pres. 1981, historian), Internat. Soc. Advancement Humanistic Studies Medicine (pres. 1997—98), Soc. Gynecol. Oncologists, Soc. Gynecol. Surgeons (pres. 1983—84). Avocations: gardening, photography. Office: Ind U Sch Medicine 550 University Blvd Indianapolis IN 46202-5149 Home Phone: 317-849-4330; Office Phone: 317-849-4026. Personal E-mail: Bobberogers@hotmail.com. Business E-Mail: reroger@iupui.edu.

ROGERS, RODDY JACK, civil, geotechnical and water engineer; b. Springfield, Mo. BSCE cum laude, U. Mo., 1981, MSCE, 1983, MS in Engring. Mgmt., 1990. Registered profl. engr., Mo. Asst. and staff engr. Dames and Moore Consulting Firm, Phoenix, Ariz., 1983-85; project mgr. City Utilities, Springfield, 1985-90, sr. engr. civil engring. sect. system engring., 1990-97, dir. water engring., 1997—. Teaching asst. soil mechanics U. Mo., 1981-83, rsch. asst. soil mechanics lab., 1982-83; 5 time gov. appointee to Mo. Dam and Reservoir Safety Coun.; presented numerous papers. Contbr. articles to profl. jours. Trustee missions com. 1st Bapt. Ch., Springfield, 1989-94; judge sci. fair Springfield Pub. Schs., 1988-89; bd. dirs. Jr. Achievement, 1986-87; vol. Engring. Ministries Internat., 1988, 90-93. Needles scholar, Curators scholar; Recipient Young Engr. Awd., 1991, Nat. Soc. Profl. Engr. Mem. NSPE (chpt. treas. 1988-89, chpt. sec. mem. various coms., chpt. pres.-elect 1990-91, pres. 1991-92, Young Engr. of Yr. award Ozark chpt. 1990, Young Engr. of Yr. award 1991, Edmund Friedmund Young Engr. award for svc. to global cmty. 1991), ASCE, Am. Water Works Assn., Nat. Water Well Assn. (chair), Assn. State Dam Safety Ofcls. (award of excellence in dam safety), Mo. Soc. Profl. Engrs. (ethics task force chmn., Young Engr. of Yr. award 1990, Extra Mile Resolution award, nat. Ethics award), Mid-Mo. Soc. Civil Engrs. (3d v.p. 1989-90, 2d v.p. 1990-91, 1st v.p. 1991-92, pres. 1992-93), U. Mo.-Rolla Civil Engrs. Alumni Assn. (pres. Springfield chpt.), U. Mo.-Rolla Civil Engrs. Alumni Adv. Coun., Tau Beta Pi, Chi Epsilon. Home: 2241 E Powell St Springfield MO 65804-4692 Office: City Utilities Springfield PO Box 551 Springfield MO 65801-0551

ROGERS, ROY STEELE, III, dermatologist, educator, dean; b. Hillsboro, Ohio, Mar. 3, 1940; s. Roy S. Jr. and Anna Mary (Murray) R.; m. Susan Camille Hudson, Aug. 22, 1964; children: Roy Steele IV, Katherine Hudson. BA, Denison U., 1962; MD, Ohio State U., 1966; MS, U. Minn., 1974. Cert. dermatologist, dermatopathologist and immunodermatologist. Intern Strong Meml. Hosp., Rochester, NY, 1966—67; resident Duke U. Med. Ctr., Durham, NC, 1969—71, Mayo Clinic, Rochester, Minn., 1972—73, cons., 1973—, prof. dermatology, 1983—, dean Sch. Health Related Scis., 1991—99. Adv. coun. Rochester Community Coll., 1991-2000; citator of appreciation Internat. League Dermatologic Soc., 2007. Contbr. over 250 sci. articles to publs. Mem. Rochester Planning and Zoning Comm., 1980—88; bd. dir. Casabella Assn., 2006—. Capt., flight surgeon USAF, 1967—69. Recipient Alumni Achievement award Ohio State U. Coll. Medicine, 1991, Alumni citation Denison U., 1993, Faculty Svc. award Mayo Med. Sch., 1993, Gold medal 2d Med. Sch., Charles U., Prague, 2002; named Disting. Educator, Mayo Clinic, 2004, Thomas G. Pearson Meml. Edn. award, 2004, Everett J. Fox Lectureship, 2005, Paul A. O'Leary Lectureship, 2005. Mem. Am. Acad. Dermatology (hon., bd. dirs. 1987-91, v.p. 1999, Everett C. Fox lectureship 2005, Gold Triangle award 2004, Thomas G. Pearson Meml. Edn. award 2005), Am. Soc. Dermatologic Allergy and Immunology (sec.-treas. 1988-2000), Am. Dermatologic Assn. (v.p. 2002-03), Soc. Investigative Dermatology, Assn. Schs. Allied Health Professions, Dermatology Found. (Annenberg Circle 2002). Avocations: travel, reading, walking. Office: Mayo Clinic 200 1st St SW Rochester MN 55905-0002 Home: 10101 N Arabian Tail No 1006 Scottsdale AZ 85258 Home Phone: 480-991-4197; Office Phone: 507-284-2555. Business E-Mail: rogers.roy@mayo.edu.

ROGGENSACK, PATIENCE DRAKE, state supreme court justice; b. Joliet, Ill., 1941; BA, Drake U., 1962; JD, U. Wis. Law Sch., 1980. Atty. Dewitt Ross and Stevens, 1980—96; judge Wis. Ct. of Appeals, 1996—2003; justice Wis. Supreme Ct., 2003—. Mem.: ABA, Wis. Bar Assn. Office: Wis Supreme Ct PO Box 1688 Madison WI 53701-1688

ROHNER, NICHOLAS K., lawyer; b. Cin., Sept. 14, 1974; BA, Miami U., 1997; JD, U. Cin. Coll. Law, 2001. Bar: Ohio 2001, US Dist. Ct. Southern Dist. Ohio 2001, Ind. 2002, US Dist. Ct. Southern Dist. Ind. 2002, US Dist. Ct. Northern Dist. Ind. 2002. Assoc. Weltman, Weinburg & Reis Co., L.P.A., Cin. Named one of Ohio's Rising Stars, Super Lawyers, 2006. Mem.: Cin. Bar Assn., Ohio State Bar Assn., Ind. State Bar Assn., Alpha Phi Omega. Office: Weltman Weinberg & Reis Co LPA 525 Vine St Ste 800 Cincinnati OH 45202 Office Phone: 513-723-2200. Office Fax: 513-723-2239.

ROHRBACH, LARRY, state legislator; b. California, Mo., Nov. 12, 1946; s. Emmet H. and Ruth (Bieri) R.; m. Beth Ann Connell, 1974; 1 child, Eva Beth. BS, Ctrl. Mo. State U., 1968. Mem. Mo. State Ho. of Reps. from 115th dist., Jefferson City, 1982-93; former asst. minority floor leader Mo. State Ho. of Reps., 1982-93; mem. Mo. Senate Dist. 6, Jefferson City, 1993—. Pres. Ctrl. Mo. State Rep. Club, 1968, Moniteau County Rep. Club, Mo., 1974-76; chmn. Moniteau County Rep. Com., 23rd Senate Dist. Rep. Com. Recipient Taxpayers Watchdog award, 1988. Mem. Mo. Farmers Assn., Moniteau County Farm Bur., Moniteau County Pork Prodrs. (pres. 1973). Home: 25420 Highway D California MO 65018-2707 Office: Rm 433 State Capitol Jefferson City MO 65101

ROISMAN, PETER SCOTT, lawyer; b. Hartford, Conn., June 15, 1960; s. Gerald Asher and Ellen Brenda (Yush) R.; m. Emily Beth Neisloss, Dec. 21, 1985; children: Alexandra Kate, Victoria Brooke. BA, Amherst Coll., 1982; JD, U. Conn., Hartford, 1986. Bar: Conn. 1986, U.S. Dist. Ct. Conn. 1987. Prin. Roisman & Assocs., Hartford, 1986-94, Advantage Internat. Mgmt., McLean, Va., 1994—97, dir. golf div., 1994—2004; pres. The Ticket Reserve, Inc., Deerfield, Ill., 2004—. Pres. and founder U. Conn. Sports Law Soc., Hartford, 1985-86; agent NCAA, Mission, Kans., 1986, NBA Player Assn., N.Y.C., 1987; adv. com. mem. Conn. Sec. of PGA Am.; chmn. bd. dirs. Conn. Sports Mus. and Hall of Fame. Panelist The Sports Group. Mem. Greater Hartford Jaycess Chpt., 1987; bd. dirs. Greater Hartford Am. Red Cross, 1987. Inducted into the Greater Hartford Jewish Fedn. Sports Hall-of-Fame, 2003. Mem. ABA (mem. sports and entertainment section), Hartford County Bar Assn., Sports Lawyers Assn. (nat. sec. 1993—, bd. dirs.). Democrat. Jewish. Avocations: tournament golf, basketball, skiing, raquetball. Office: The Ticket Reserve Corp 510 Ctr 540 Lake Cook Rd Ste 400 Deerfield IL 60015 Office Phone: 703-481-5100. E-mail: psroisman@theticketreserve.com.

ROITMAN, JUDITH, mathematician, educator; b. NYC, Nov. 12, 1945; d. Leo and Ethel (Gottesman) R.; m. Stanley Lombardo, Sept. 26, 1978; 1 child, Ben Lombardo. BA in English, Sarah Lawrence Coll., 1966; MA in Math., U. Calif., Berkeley, 1971, PhD in Math., 1974. Asst. prof. math. Wellesley (Mass.) Coll., 1974-77; from asst. prof. to prof. math. U. Kans., Lawrence, 1977—. Author: Introduction to Modern Set Theory, 1990; contbr. articles to profl. jours. Grantee, SF, 1975—87, 1992—95. Mem. Assn. Symbolic Logic, Am. Math. Soc., Assn. Women in Math. (pres. 1979-81, Louise Hay award 1996), Kans. Assn. Tchrs. Math., at. Assn. Tchrs. Math. Avocation: poetry. Business E-Mail: roitman@math.ku.edu.

ROIZEN, MICHAEL F., anesthesiologist, medical educator, writer; b. NY, Jan. 7, 1946; m. Nancy J. Roizen; children: Jeffery, Jennifer. AB in Chemistry with honors, Williams Coll., Williamstown, Mass., 1967; MD, U. Calif. Sch. Medicine, San Francisco, 1971. Cert. Am. Bd. Internal Medicine, Am. Bd. Anesthesiology. Intern. medicine Beth Israel Hosp., Boston, 1971—72, resident, medicine, 1972—73; rsch. assoc. in pharmacology NIH, Bethesda, Md.,

1973-75; resident, anesthesia U. Calif., San Francisco, 1975—77, asst. prof., 1977-81, assoc. prof., 1981-85; prof. internal medicine U. Chgo., 1985, prof. and chair dept. anesthesia and critical care, 1985; prof., anesthesiology SUNY Upstate Med. Ctr. and Univ., Syracuse, NY; chmn., divsn. anesthiology, critical care medicine and comprehensive pain mgmt. Cleve. Clinic. Panel mem. FDA, past chmn. adv. com.; co-founder RealAge,Inc., chmn. scientific adv. bd; invited lectr. in field. Author: Essence of Anesthesia Practice, 1997, RealAge: Are You As Young as You Can Be?, 1999(NY Times #1 Best-Seller, Best Wellness Book, Books for a Better Life awards, 1999); co-author (with John La Puma) The RealAge Diet: Make Yourself Younger with What You Eat (NY Times Best-Seller, 2001), RealAge Way, The RealAge Makeover, 2004, (with Tracy Hafen) The RealAge Workout, (with Mehmet C. Oz) YOU: The Owner's Manual: An Insider's Guide to the Body That Will Make You Healthier and Younger (#1 Publishers Weekly Hardcover Bestseller list, NY Times Bestseller List), 2005, YOU: The Smart Patient: An Insider's Handbook for Getting the Best Treatment, 2006, YOU: On a Diet-The Owner's Manual for Waist Management, 2006, YOU: Staying Young: The Owner's Manual for Extending Your Warranty, 2007, (compact disc) YOU: On a Walk, 2007; former editor of several med. jours.; reviewer numerous anesthesia and med. jours.; contbr. of articles to peer-reviewed jours., chpt. to books, med. books; guest appearances on Oprah Winfrey Show, Today Show, 20/20, CBN, CNN, CBS, Good Morning America, Montel Williams Show and PBS; featured in magazines including Fortune, Glamourm Cosmopolitan, Good Housekeeping, Ladies' Home Journal, Reader's Digest, Men's Health and Prevention. Named an Best Doctors in Am., 1989—. Mem. Am. Bd. Anesthesiology (assoc.), Am. Bd. Internal Medicine (assoc.), Am. Soc. Anesthesiologists, Soc. of Cardiovascular Anesthesiologists (pres. 1995-97), U.S. Squash Racquets Assn., Alpha Omega Alpha, Phi Beta Kappa. 12 US patents and several fgn. patents. Office: RealAge Inc 10675 Sorrento Valley Rd Ste 200 San Diego CA 92121 also: RealAge Inc 555 Fifth Ave 14th Fl New York NY 10017 Office Phone: 858-812-3800. Office Fax: 858-812-3801. Business E-Mail: roizenm@upstate.edu. E-mail: mrzz@airway2.bsd.uchicago.edu.

ROIZEN, NANCY J., physician, educator; b. Hartford, Conn. m. Michael F. Roizen; children: Jeffrey, Jennifer. BS, Tufts U., 1968, MD, 1972. Diplomate Am. Bd. Pediats. Staff physician Oakland (Calif.) Children's Hosp., 1976-84; asst. prof. clin. pediats. Johns Hopkins Hosp., Balt., 1984-85; assoc. prof. pediat. and psychiatry U. Chgo., 1985—. Fellow Am. Acad. Pediats.; mem. Soc. for Devel. Pediats. (pres. 1996-98). Office: U Chgo Hosps MC 900 5841 S Maryland Ave Chicago IL 60637-1463

ROIZMAN, BERNARD, virologist, educator; b. Chisinau, Rumania, Apr. 17, 1929; arrived in US, 1947, naturalized, 1954; s. Abram and Liudmilla (Seinberg) Roizman; m. Betty Cohen, Aug. 26, 1950; children: Arthur, Niels. BA, Temple U., Phila., 1952, MS, 1954; ScD in Microbiology, Johns Hopkins U., Balt., 1956; DHL (hon.), Gov.'s State U., 1984; MD (hon.), U. Ferrara, Italy, 1991; DSc (hon.), U. Paris, 1997, U. Valladolid, Spain, 2001. From instr. microbiology to asst. prof. Johns Hopkins Med. Sch., 1956—65; from mem. faculty Divsn. Biol. Scis. to prof. U. Chgo., 1965—69, prof., 1969—, chmn. dept. molecular genetics and cell biology, 1985—88, Joseph Regoustein Disting. Svc. prof., 1984—. Co-founder Aviron, Inc., 1992; convener herpes virus workshop, Cold Spring Harbor, NY, 72; lectr. Am. Found. for Microbiology, 1974—75; mem. spl. virus cancer program devel. rsch. working group Nat. Cancer Inst., 1967—71; mem. steering com. human cell biology program NSF, 1971—74; mem. adv. com. cell biology and virology Am. Cancer Soc., 1970—74; chmn. herpes virus study group Internat. Commn. Taxonomy of Viruses, 1971—73; mem. Internat. Microbiol. Genetics Commn. Internat. Assn. Microbiol. Scis., 1974—81; mem. sci. adv. coun. NY Cancer Inst., 1971—88; mem. adv. bd. Leukemia Rsch. Found., 1972—77; mem. herpes-virus working team WHO/FDA, 1978—81; mem. bd. sci. cons. Sloan Kettering Inst., NYC, 1975—81; mem. study sect. exptl. virology NIH, 1976—80; mem. task force on virology Nat. Inst. Allergy and Infectious Disease, 1976—77; mem. com. to establish vaccine priorities Nat. Inst. Medicine, 1983—85; chmn. sci. adv. bd. Tampa Bay Rsch. Inst., 1983—, chmn. bd. trustees, 1991—97; cons. in field. Editor: (book) Herpes Viruses, Vol. 1, 1982, Herpes Viruses, Vol. 2, 1983, Herpes Viruses, Vols. 3 and 4, 1985, The Human Herpesviruses, 1993, Infectious Diseases in an Age of Change, 1995; editor-in-chief: Jour. Infectious Agts. and Disease, 1992—96, mem. editl. bd.: Infectious Diseases, 1965—69, Jour. Virology, 1970—, Jour. Intervirology, 1972—85, Archives of Virology, 1975—81, Virology, 1976—78, Microbiologica, 1978—, Cell, 1979—80, Virology, 1983—, Jour. Hygiene, 1985—91, Gene Therapy, 1994, Wiley Encyclopedia of Molecular Medicine, 2002; contbr. scientific papers, chapters to books. Trustee Goodwin Inst. Cancer Rsch., 1977—. Named hon. prof., Shandong Acad. Med. Scis., China, 1985; recipient Lederle Med. Faculty award, 1960—61, Career Devel. award, USPHS, 1963—65, Pasteur award, Ill. Soc. Microbiology, 1972, Esther Langer award for Achievement in Cancer Rsch., 1974, Outstanding Alumnus in Pub. Health award, Johns Hopkins U., 1984, ICN Internat. prize in Virology, 1988, J. Allyn Taylor Internat. prize in Medicine, 1997, Bristol-Myers Squibb award for Disting. Infectious Disease Rsch., 1998, Abbott-ASM lifetime achievement award, 2008; fellow Travelling, Internat. Agy. Rsch. Against Cancer, Karolinska Inst., Stockholm, 1970; grantee Facutly Rsch. Assoc., Am. Cancer Soc., 1966—71, USPHS/NIH, 1958—, Am. Cancer Soc., 1962—90, NSF, 1962—79; scholar Am. Cancer Soc., Pasteur Inst. Paris, 1961—62. Fellow: AAAS, Japanese Soc. for Promotion of Sci., Am. Acad. Arts and Scis.; mem.: NAS, Johns Hopkins U. Soc. Scholars, Chinese Acad. Engring. (fgn.), Hungarian Acad. Scis. (fgn.), Brit. Soc. Gen. Microbiology, Am. Soc. Molecular Biology and Biochemistry, Am. Soc. Virology, Am. Soc. Microbiology, Am. Assn. Immunologists, Am. Acad. Microbiology, Inst. Medicine, Quadrangle Club (Chgo.). Home: 5555 S Everett Ave Chicago IL 60637-1968 Office Phone: 773-702-1898. Business E-Mail: bernard.roizman@bsd.uchicago.edu.

ROJEK, KENNETH JOHN, health facility administrator; b. Chgo., Aug. 6, 1953; m. Carol Rojek; 2 children. BS with honors, U. Ill., 1975; MBA with honors, Roosevelt U., 1980. Diplomate Am. Coll. Healthcare Execs. Lab. mgr., tech. dir. Rush-Presbyn.-St. Lukes Med. Ctr., Chgo., 1977-80; adminstr. Wyler Children's Hosp., dept. pediatrics U. Chgo., 1980-86; v.p. Parkside Human Svcs., 1986-89, Luth. Gen. Med. Group, S.C., Chgo., 1989-92; sr. v.p. Luth. Gen. Hosp., Park Ridge, Ill., 1992-94, CEO, 1994-2000, Advocate North Side Health Network, 2000—. Adj. faculty U. Minn., St. Francis Coll., Joliet, Ill. Active numerous cmty. and civic orgns., cmty. devel. couns. Fellow Am. Coll. Med. Practice Execs. Med. Group Mgmt. Assn. Office: Ill Masonic Med Ctr 836 W Wellington Chicago IL 60657 E-mail: kenaojek@advocatehealth.com.

ROKITA, TODD, state official; b. Chgo., Feb. 9, 1970; m. Kathy Rokita. BA in Polit. Sci., Wabash Coll., 1992; JD, Ind. U. Sch. Law, 1995. Atty.; gen. counsel to sec. state State of Ind., Indpls., 1997, dep. sec. state, 1997—2003, sec. state, 2003—. Mem.: Indiana Coun. for Economic Edn. (Director's Circle), St. Thomas More Parish, Indiana State Bar Association's Aviation Law Com. (past chair). Republican. Catholic. Office: Office Sec of State 201 State House Indianapolis IN 46204 Office Phone: 317-232-6531, 317-232-6536. Office Fax: 317-233-3283. Business E-Mail: aa@sos.state.in.us.

ROLEN, SCOTT BRUCE, professional baseball player; b. Jasper, Ind., Apr. 4, 1975; m. Niki Warner, Feb. 2, 2002; 1 child, Raine Tyler. Third baseman Phila. Phillies, 1996—2002, St. Louis Cardinals, 2002—07, Toronto Blue Jays, 2008—. Founder Enis Furley Found. Named Nat. League Rookie Player of Yr., The Sporting News, 1997, Baseball Writers Assn. of Am., 1997; named to Nat. League All-Star Team, 2002—06; recipient Nat. League Gold Glove award, 1998, 2000—04, 2006, Nat. League Silver Slugger award, 2002. Mailing: c/o Toronto Blue Jays Rogers Centre 1 Blue Jays Way Ste 3200 Toronto M5V1J1 Canada

ROLEWICZ, ROBERT JOHN, estimating engineer; b. Chgo., Sept. 16, 1954; s. Frank Joseph and Margaret Mary (Ahlbach) R.; m. Vicki Lynn Heggeland, Sept. 1, 1985; children: Heather Margaret, Jeremy Robert. Diploma, Washburne Trade Sch., 1977. Level II inspector Kropp Forge Co., Chgo., 1974-77, chief cost estimator, 1978-88, mgr. estimating, chief estimating engr., 1989—2003; developer graphic design bus., 2003—. Pres. Kropp Employees Fed. Credit Union, 1986-88; founding mem. Metalworking Industry Adv. Coun., 1990. Mem. Nat. Arbor Day Found., 2000—; vol. instr. Boys Club, Cicero, 1975—84; coach local area children's soccer; vol. cmty. based holiday baskets for needy families, 1979—; vol. cmty. based drug awareness forum, 1985—; committeeman Citizens to Reelect Judy Baar Topinka, Cicero, Ill., 1984—96, Citizens to Reelect Jack Kubik, Cicero, 1984—96; mem. Missionary Oblates of Mary Immaculate, 2002—; bd. dirs. Cicero Family Svc. and Mental Health Ctr., 1979—87; supporter Misericordia Home Developmentally Disabled, 1974—, Seguin Sch. for Retarded Citizens Assn., Inc., 1985—, Berwyn Libr. Bldg. Fund., Lagrange Libr. Fund, Nat. Parks and Conservation Assn., 1990—. Recipient Hold My Hand award Children's Ctr. Cicero, 1982, Golden Anvil award Kropp Forge, 1989, 2001. Mem.: NRA, VFW (life), Metalworking Industry Adv. Coun. (founding mem.), Smithsonian Inst., U.S. Judo Fedn., at. Police & Trooper Assn., Western Springs Hist. Soc., Past Exalted Rulers Assn. (pres. 2004—06), Czechoslovak Soc. Am., Vets. Vietnam War Inc., Vietnam Vets. Am. Inc., Vietnow, Nat. Audubon Soc., Brookfield Zoo, Cicero Hist. Soc., History Channel Club (charter), No. Am. Fishing Club, Nat. Health and Wellness Club, Nat. St. Machine Club (charter), Home Arts Club, N.Am. Hunting Club, Nat. Home Gardening Club (charter mem.), Handyman Club Am., Kropp Key Club (pres. 1984—2003), St. Patrick HS Alumni Club, Moose, Elks (mag. editor 1976—, exalted ruler 1981—82, 1994—95, 2000—01, v.p. N.E. dist., P.E.R. plaque 1982, Elk of Yr. award Cicero-Berwyn 1989, Govt. Rels. award 1989, Elk of Yr. award Cicero-Berwyn 1993, Grand Exalted Rulers Commendation award 1998—99, Grand Lodge Order of Elks Disting. Citizenship award 1999, Grand Lodge Trail Blazer award 2000—01, Elk of Yr. award Cicero-Berwyn 2005, 2007), St. Jude League, Sacred Heart League. Republican. Roman Catholic. Avocations: jogging, swimming, camping, canoeing, hiking. E-mail: rjrper@sbc.global.net.

ROLFE, STANLEY THEODORE, civil engineer, educator; b. Chgo., July 7, 1934; s. Stanley T. and Eunice (Fike) R.; m. Phyllis Williams, Aug. 11, 1956; children: David Stanley, Pamela Kay, Kathleen Ann. BS, U. Ill., 1956, MS, 1958, PhD, 1962. Registered profl. engr., Pa., Kans. Supr. structural-evaluation sect. ordnance products divsn. U.S. Steel Corp., 1962-69, divsn. chief mech. behavior of metals divsn., 1969; A.P. Learned prof. civil engring. U. Kans., 1969—, chmn. civil engring. dept., 1975-98, Charles E. Spahr prof., 1999. Chmn. metall. studies panel ship rsch. com. Nat. Acad. Scis., 1967-70 Co-author: Fracture and Fatigue Control in Structures— Applications of Fracture Mechanics; co-author: textbook Strength of Materials; contbr. numerous articles to profl. jours. T.R. Higgins lectr., 1980; Recipient Sam Tour award Am. Soc. Testing Materials, 1971, H.E. Gould Distinguished Teaching award U. Kans., 1972, 75, AWS Adams Meml. Educator award, 1974; U. Ill. Civil Engring. Disting. Service award, 1985, U. Ill. Coll. Engring. Alumni Honor award Disting. Service in Engring., 1987; U. Kans. Irvin E. Youngberg research award, 1985. Mem. ASME, ASTM, ASCE (hon.; chmn. task force on fracture, State of Art award 1983, Ernest E. Howard award 2001), Nat. Acad. Engring., Soc. Exptl. Stress Analysis, Am. Soc. Engring. Edn., Chi Psi. Presbyterian. Office: Univ Kansas CEAE Dept 2150 Learned Hall 1530 W 15th St Lawrence KS 66045-7609

ROLLINS, ARLEN JEFFERY, osteopathic physician; b. Cleve., June 30, 1946; s. Lee Roy and Celia (Madorsky) R.; m. Deborah Joyce Gross, Dec. 18, 1971 (div.); children: Aaron Jason, Howard Philip, Lee Craig; m. Miriam Frankel, Dec. 29, 2003. AB, Miami U., Ohio, 1968; DO, Chgo. Coll. Osteo. Medicine, 1973; MS in Occupl. Medicine Environ. Health, U. Cin., 1984. Diplomate Am. Bd. Preventive Medicine. Intern Phoenix Gen. Hosp., 1973-74; resident in environ. health/occupl. medicine Cin. Gen. Hosp.-U. Cin., 1974-77; plant physician Ford Motor Co., Cin., 1974-77, Walton Hills, Stamping Plant Divsn., Cleve., 1987—; with primary and specialty care practices Univ. Hosps., 2006—. Assoc. med. dir. East Side Occupl. Health Ctr., Cleve., 1977-79; med. dir. Ferro Corp., Cleve., 1979—, S.K. Wellman Corp., Cleve., 1979-87, Morgan Matroc, 1979—; pres. Occupl. Health Mgmt. Cons.; cons. occupl. health Ohio Bell Tel. Co., Cleve., 1981-87; cons. Occupl. Health Ctr., Univ. Hosps. of Cleve.; dir. occupl. health program Bedford Med. Ctr. Univ. Hosps. Cleve., 1990-99; corp. med. cons. Cleve.-Cliffs Inc., 1998—; v.p. Internat. Toxic Inhalation Rsch. Group, 2005. Fellow Am. Acad. Occupl. Medicine, Am. Occupl. Med. Assn., Am. Coll. Preventive Medicine; mem. Ohio State Med. Assn., Cleve. Acad. Medicine (pub. health and immunization com., med.-legal com.), Western Res. Med. Dirs. Assn., Am. Osteo. Assn., Am. Osteo. Acad. Pub. Health and Preventive Medicine (past bd. dirs.). Home Phone: 216-292-6263; Office Phone: 440-232-0061. Personal E-mail: arlenrollins@att.net, arlenrollins@gmail.com.

ROLOFF, MARVIN L., publishing executive; m. Shirley Sekas, June 27, 1959; children: Reed, Ross, Robyn. BA, Wartburg Coll., 1955; postgrad., U. Iowa, 1956; BD, Wartburg Theol. Sem., 1960, DD (hon.), 1997; ThM, Princeton Theol. Sem., 1961. Ordained to ministry Luth. Ch., 1961. Pastor youth and edn. Grace Luth. Ch., Green Bay, Wis., 1961-65; editor Augsburg Pub. Ho., Mpls., 1965-70, sr. editor children's curriculum divsn. parish edn., 1970-71, curriculum editl. dir. divsn. parish edn., 1971-74, dir. media resources divsn. life and mission in congregation, 1974-76, dir. edn. resources bd. of publ., 1976-87; dir. ednl. resources pub. Pub. Ho. of Evangelical Luth. Ch. Am., 1988-91; v.p. mktg. Augsburg Fortress, Pubs., 1991-93, v.p. customer resources and relationships, 1993-95, acting pres., CEO, 1995-96, pres., CEO, 1996—. Vis. prof. Christian edn. Luther Northwestern Theol. Sem., 1981, 83, 89, instr. Christian Edn. Inst., summers 1976-90; cons., chairperson youth/adult and children's coms. Curriculum Selection Conf. of Armed Forces, 1971-91; mem. resource planning groups Evangelical Luth. Ch. Am.; mem. publ. com. Augsburg Fortress, Pubs. Mem. Assn. Profs. and Rschrs. in Religious Edn., Protestant Ch.-Owned Pubs. Assn. (mem. edn. com., chair armed forces com. 1993—, mem. exec. com., bd. dirs. 1993—), Nat. Coun. Chs. (Augsburg Fortress, Pubs. rep. to ministries in Christian edn. com., mem. unit com. 1988—, mem. budget and fin. com. 1992—, mem. Bible translation and utilization com. 1994—). Protestant Ch.-Owned Pubs. Assn. (pres. 1998—). Office: Augsburg Fortress Publishers 100 S 5th St Ste 600 Minneapolis MN 55402-1242 Fax: 612-330-3583.

ROLSHOVEN, ROSS WILLIAM, legal investigator, artist; b. Mandan, ND, Oct. 20, 1954; s. Raymond Paul and Bernice June (Mastel) R.; divorced; children: Ashley Anna, Carsen Ross. BA in Bus. Adminstrn., U. N.D., 1976. Lic. pvt. investigator, N.D., Minn. Claims adjuster, investigator Border Area Adjustments, Grand Forks, N.D., 1976-84; owner, mgr. Great Plains Claims, Inc., Grand Forks, N.D., 1984—. Chmn. N.D. Claims Seminar, Grand Forks, 1988; guest lectr. U. N.D. Law Sch., 1993-96. One-man shows include Minot State U., ND, 2005, Janks Meml. Ctr. Visual Arts, Williston, ND, 2005, ARts Ctr., Jamestown, ND, 2006; group shows include Artifacts, 1992 (1st pl. award 1992), Spirit of the Buffalo, 1992 (1st pl. award 1992), Grey Morn' on the Red, 1991 (Merit award 1991); featured artist Custer County Art Show, Miles City, Mont., 1995, Empire Art Ctr., 2000, American Artists, Ruidoso, N.Mex., 2000; sculpture How the West Was Won, 1992 (2d pl. award 1992); one-man shows include ND Mus. Art Inventions & Imagination, 2002, Spirit Rm. Gallery, Fargo, ND, 2003, Untitled Gallery, Fargo, 2004; Grand City Art Fest Juror, 2003. Mem. N.D. Mus. Art; patron Grand Forks Fire Hall Theater, 1988-92; mem. Fargo/Moorhead Art Assn., 1992; mem. bldg. restoration com. North Valley Arts Coun.; trustee, chmn. N.D. Cowboy Hall of Fame, 1998—, bd. dir., 2006-; chmn. Ctrl. Bus. Dist. Authority, Grand Forks, 1998-2000. Recipient Svc. Recognition award United Way, 1984, Hist. Preservation award N.D. Hist. Soc., 1990, Buckskinner award Roughrider Internat. Art Show Com., 1994, 2d Pl. award Fargo Regional Art Show, 1994-95. Mem. Nat. Assn. Legal Investigators, Minn. Assn. Detectives, Red River Valley Claims Assn. (pres. 1986-87), Upper Red River Valley Claims Assn. (pres. 1988-89), Dakota Masters Club Swim Club, Am. Power Boat Assn. (4th in nation, Nat. Tournament Sport Class, 8th in nation, Region 8 Sport C champion, 2006). Avocations: photography, painting, horseback riding, swimming, archaeology. Office: Great Plains Claims Inc 220 S 3d St Grand Forks ND 58201-6345

ROMAN, RAY, communications executive; BS in Fin., U. Ill., Chgo.; MBA in Fin. and Mktg., U. Chgo. Gen. mgr., sales and service Ameritech Small Business Services; corp. controller, v.p. of financial planning and analysis Alliant Foodservice, pres. N.E. div.; v.p. sales AT&T Wireless, 2001—03; corp v.p., gen. mgr. of No. Am., mobile devices Motorola Inc, 2003—03, sr. v.p. worldwide sales, mobile devices, 2005—. Coach youth soccer team, youth basketball team. Named one of the best 40 under 40 in business, Crain's Chicago Business, 2005. Office: c/o Motorola Inc 1303 E Algonquin Rd Schaumburg IL 60196

ROMAN, TWYLA I., state legislator; m. John Roman; children: Lisa, Sheryl. Student, U. Akron, 1977-78. Trustee Springfield Twp., 1981-94; mem. Ohio State Ho. Reps., Columbus, 1994—. Mem. Summit County Emergency Mgmt. Planning and Exec. Commn. Mem. MADD, S.E. Bd. of Trade, Ohio Twp. Assn., Summit County Twp. Assn., Brimfield Meml. House Assn.

ROMANI, JOHN HENRY, health science association administrator, educator; b. Milan, Mar. 6, 1925; s. Henry Arthur and Hazel (Pettengill) R.; m. Barbara A. Anderson; children: David John, Paul Nichols, Theresa A. Anderson. BA, MA, U. N.H., 1949; PhD, U. Mich., 1955. Instr. U. N.H., 1950-51; instr. U. Mich., Ann Arbor, 1954-55, assoc. prof., asst. to assoc. dean Sch. Pub. Health, 1961-69, assoc. v.p., 1971-75, chmn. health planning and adminstrn., 1975-80, prof., 1971-93, prof. emeritus pub. health adminstrn., 1993—, faculty assoc. program on the environment, 2004—; interim chair Pub. Health Policy and Adminstrn., 1991-92. Asst. prof. We. Mich. U., 1956-57; assoc. dir. Cleve. Met. Svcs. Commn., 1957-59; assoc. prof. U. Pitts., 1959-61; vice chancellor, prof. U. Wis.-Milw., 1969-71; rsch. fellow Brookings Instn., 1955-56; mem. task force Nat. Commn. on Orgn. Cmty. Health Svcs., 1963-66; dir. staff Sec.'s Com. on Orgn. Health Activities, HEW, 1965-66; dir. Govtl. Affairs Inst., 1969-75, chmn., 1970-72; trustee Pub. Adminstrn. Svc., 1969-75, chmn., 1973-75; mem. Delta Dental Plan Mich., 1972-78, bd. dirs. 1972-78, chmn. consumers' adv. coun., 1975-77; bd. dirs. Ctr. for Population Activities, 1975-81, chmn., 1975-81; lifetime vis. prof. Capital U. Economics and Bus., Beijing, 1996—; vis. rschr. Human Scis. Rsch. Coun., Pretoria, South Africa, 1999—. Author: The Philippine Presidency, 1956; editor: Changing Dimensions in Public Administration, 1962; contbr. articles to profl. jours. Mem. Citizens League, Cleve., 1957-59; mem. Ann Arbor Citizens Coun., 1965-69; bd. dirs. Southeastern Mich. Family Planning Project, 1975-77; trustee Congregational Summer Assembly, 1982-85; commr. Accrediting Commn. on Edn. for Health Svcs. Adminstrn., 1989-95. Served with AUS, 1943-46, ETO. Fellow Am. Pub. Health Assn. (chmn. program devel. bd. 1975-77, exec. bd. 1975-80, governing coun. 1975—, pres. 1979, chmn. publs. bd. 1984-88), Royal Soc. Health (hon.), Am. Polit. Sci. Assn. (life); mem. ASPA (past mem. coun.), Population Assn. Am., Phi Kappa Phi, Pi Sigma Alpha, Pi Gamma Mu, Delta Omega. Home and Office: 2125 ature Cove Apt 108 Ann Arbor MI 48104

ROMANOFF, MILFORD MARTIN, retired building contractor; b. Cleve., Aug. 21, 1921; s. Barney Sanford and Edythe Stolpher (Bort) R.; m. Marjorie Reinwald, Nov. 6, 1945; children: Bennett S., Lawrence M., Janet Beth (dec.). Student, U. Mich. Coll. Arch., 1939-42; BBA, U. Toledo, 1943. Pres. Glass City Constrn. Co., Toledo, 1951-55, Milford Romanoff, Inc., Toledo, 1956—2003. Co-founder Neighborhood Improvement Found. Toledo, 1960; active Lucas County Econ. Devel. Com., 1979—, Childrens Svcs. Bd. Lucas County, 1981—97, Arthritis Bd. Dirs., Crosby Gardens Bd. Advisors, 1983—96, Toledo Met. Area Govt. Exec. Com., 1996—; citizens adv. bd. Recreation Commn. Toledo, 1973—86; campus adv. com. Med. Coll. Ohio, 1980—; trustee Cummings Treatment Ctr. for Adolescents, 1981—; pres. Toledo B'nai Brith Lodge, 1958—59, Cherry Hill Nursing Home, 1964—85; bd. dirs. Anti-Defamation League, 1955—60, Ohio Hillel Orgns., Lucas County Dept. Human Svcs., Arthritis Assn., 1995—, Comprehensive Addiction Svc. Sys., 1998, Kidney Found. Northwestern Ohio, 1986—, sec., 1989; chmn. Comprehensive Addiction Svc. Sys., 1999, Toledo Amateur Baseball and Softball Com., 1979—81; cons. U.S. Care Corp., 1985—; bd. govs. Toledo Housing for Elderly, 1982—84, sec., 1989, pres. bd. govs., 1990—, pres., 1991—; bd. adv. Ret. Sr. Vol. Program, 1987—89, chmn., 1988—90, 1993—, sec. adv. bd., 1990—, bd. dirs., 2000—; vice chmn. adv. bd. Salvation Army, 1986—87, chmn. adv. bd., 1988—90, ct. apptd. spl. advocate adv., bd. treas., 1988—; chmn. Mental Health Adv. Bd., 1983—84, sec., 1989; bd. dirs. Toledo Urban Forestry Commn., 1991—, pres., 1993, 1995, Lucas County Dept. Human Svcs. Bd.; adv. coun. Renaissance Sr. Apts., 1997, chmn. adv. coun., 1999; adv. bd. Lucas Co. Correctional Facility, 1999—; chmn. Compass Bd., 2002—; bd. dirs. Area Office on Aging of Northwest Ohio, 2001, Lucas County Mental Health, 2001; chair Compass Corp. for Recovery Svcs., 2002—; mem. Lucas County Mental Health Bd., 2002, Juvenile Correction Bd. Lucas County, 2004—; bd. dirs. Mental Health Lucas Co.; mem. Juvenile Correction Bd. Lucas County, 2003—; mem. adv. bd. ACLU, 2005—, 2005—; active Dem. Precinct Com., 1975—78; trustee Temple Brotherhood, 1956—58, bd. dirs., 1981—; pres. Ohio B'nai Brith, 1959—60; bd. mem. ACLU, 2005—. Mem.: Friends Libr. Bd., Mental Health Bd. of Lucas County, U. Mich. Alumni Assn., Juvenile Justice (adv. bd.), Toledo Zool. Soc., Econ. Opportunity Planning Assn. Greater Toledo (adv. bd.), Nat. Coun. on Alcoholism & Drug Dependence, Toledo Mus. Art (assoc.), U. Toledo Alumni Assn., Am. Legion, Hadassah (assoc. Toledo chpt.), Masons (Outstanding Cmty. Svc. award of Lucas County 2001), Zeta Beta Tau. Home: Stratford in the Hills 4343 W Bancroft St Apt 4B Toledo OH 43615-3956

ROMOSER, W. DAVID, lawyer; b. Oak Park, Ill., July 12, 1943; BA, U. Ill., 1965; JD, Ill. Inst. Tech., 1970. Bar: Ill. 1970. Mem. Witwer, Moran and Burlage, Chgo., 1970—75; v.p., gen. counsel, sec. Amsted Industries, Inc., Chgo., 1975—92, A.O. Smith Corp., Milw., 1992—. Bd. dirs., dir. emeritus Siebert Lutheran Found.; bd. dirs. Wis. Equal Justice Fund, Inc.; mem. pres. coun. U. Ill.; sec. Next Door Found. Mem.: Am. Corp. Counsel Assn., Ill. State Bar Assn., Chgo. Bar Assn. Office: AO Smith Corp 11270 West Park Pl PO Box 245008 Milwaukee WI 53224-9508 Office Phone: 414-359-4137. Office Fax: 414-359-4198.

ROMPALA, RICHARD M., chemical company executive; B in Liberal Arts and Chem. Engring., Columbia U.; MBA, Harvard U. Bus. mgr. Olin Corp.; sr. v.p. ops. Mueller Brass Co.; joined PPG Industries, 1985, v.p. corp. devel., group v.p. chems., group v.p. coatings and resins; pres. Valspar Corp., Mpls., 1994, CEO, 1995—, chmn., 1998. Office: The Valspar Corp 1101 Third St S Minneapolis MN 55415

RONEN, CAROL, state legislator; b. Chgo., Mar. 28, 1945; BS, Bradley U.; MA, Roosevelt U. Dir. legis. and cmty. affairs Chgo. Dept. Human Svcs., 1985-89; exec. dir. Chgo. Commn. on Women, 1989-90; dir. planning and rsch. Chgo.-Cook County Criminal Justice Commn.; asst. commn. Chgo. Dept. Planning, 1991, Chgo. Dept. Housing; mem. Ill. Ho. of Reps., 1993-99, Ill. Senate from dist. 9, 2001—. Former pres. Ill. Task Force on Child Support; bd. dirs. Cook County Dem. Women, St. Martin De Porres Shelter for Women and Children, Alternatives Youth Orgn., Citizen Action Consumer Rights Orgn.; governing coun. Am. Jewish Congress Midwest Region; mem. Coun. Jewish Women. Democrat. Home: 6033 N Sheridan Rd Chicago IL 60660-3003 Office: Capitol Bldg Rm 413 Springfield IL 62706

ROODMAN, DAVID A., lawyer; b. St. Louis, Apr. 17, 1962; BSME, U. Mo., 1984, JD, 1990. Bar: Mo., Ill., U.s. Dist. Ct. (ea. dist.) Mo., U.S. Patent and Trademark Office, U.s. Ct. Appeals (fed. cir.), U.S. Dist. Ct. (so. dist.) Ill. Mech. design engr. Unidynamics Corp., St. Louis, 1985; sales engr. Reliance Elec. Co., Kansas City, Mo., 1985-87; assoc. Bryan Cave LLP, St. Louis, 1990, ptnr., group co-leader Intellectual Property. Assoc. editor-in-chief Mo. Law Rev. Mem. ABA (intellectual property law sect., patent legislation com., litigation sect.), Mo. Bar Assn. (civil practice and procedure com., tech. and computer law com., patent, trademark and copyright law com.), Order of Coif, Order of Barristers. Office: Bryan Cave One Metropolitan Sq 211 N Broadway Saint Louis MO 63102-2733 Office Phone: 314-259-2000. Business E-Mail: daroodman@bryancave.com.

ROONEY, JOHN EDWARD, communications company executive; b. Evergreen Park, Ill., Apr. 24, 1942; s. John Edward and Margaret Wilma (Stolte) R.; m. Germaine Rose Dettloff, June 26, 1965; children: Kathleen, John, Colleen, 7 grandchildren. BS, John Carroll U., 1964; MBA, Loyola U., 1969. Credit analyst Fed. Res. Bank, Chgo., 1964-69, adminstrv. asst., 1969-70; asst. treas. Pullman Inc., 1970-73, asst. contr., 1973-78; v.p. fin. Pullman Standard, 1978-79; sr. v.p. fin. Trailmobile, Chgo., 1979-81; treas. Firestone Tire & Rubber Co., Akron, Ohio, 1981-87, v.p. retail fin. services, 1987-88, sr. v.p. MasterCare Svc. Ctrs., 1988-90; v.p., treas. Ameritech Corp., Chgo., 1990-92; pres. Ameritech Cellular Services, Chgo., 1992—97, Ameritech Consumer Services, Chgo., 1997—99; pres., CEO U.S. Cellular, Chgo., 2000—. Instr. fin. Ill. Benedictine Coll., 1975-80; bd. dir. First midwest Bancorp, Cellular Telecommunications & Internet Assn. Trustee Loyola Univ.; mem. adv. bd. Sch. Bus. Adminstrn. Loyola Univ.; mem. presidents' bd. Uhlich Children's Advantage Network; bd. dir. Chgo. Children's Advocacy Ctr.; mem. Mayor's Council of Tech. Adv., Chgo.; bd. mem. World Bus. Chgo. Mem. Ohio Mfrs. Assn. (trustee 1983-87), Ohio Pub. Expenditure Coun. (trustee 1986-87), Glen Oak Country Club (Glen Ellyn, Ill.), Boulders Club (Carefree, Ariz.), The Tavern Club (Chgo.). Office: US Cellular 8410 W Bryn Mawr Chicago IL 60631

ROONEY, MATTHEW A., lawyer; b. Jersey City, May 19, 1949; s. Charles John and Eileen (Dunphy) R.; m. Jean M. Alletag, June 20, 1973 (div. Dec. 1979); 1 child, Jessica Margaret; m. Diane S. Kaplan, July 6, 1981; children: Kathryn Olivia, S. Benjamin. AB magna cum laude, Georgetown U., 1971; JD with honors, U. Chgo., 1974. Bar: Ill. 1975, U.S. Dist. Ct. (no. dist.) Ill. 1975, U.S. Ct. Appeals (7th cir.). 1990. Law clk. to cir. judge US Ct. Appeals (7th cir.), Chgo., 1974-75; assoc. Mayer, Brown, Chgo., 1975-80, ptnr., 1981—. Assoc. editor U. Chgo. Law Rev., 1973. Fellow Am. Coll. Trial Lawyers; mem. ABA, 7th Cir. Bar Assn., Order of Coif, Phi Beta Kappa. Democrat. Roman Catholic. Avocations: jogging, golf. Home: 2718 Sheridan Rd Evanston IL 60201-1754 Office: Mayer Brown LLP 71 S Wacker Dr Chicago IL 60606-4637 Office Phone: 312-702-7279. Business E-Mail: mrooney@mayerbrownrowe.com.

ROONEY, PHILLIP BERNARD, service company executive; b. Chgo., July 8, 1944; BA magna cum laude, St. Bernard Coll., 1966. With Waste Mgmt., 1969-97, Service Master Co., Downers Grove, Ill., 1997—2003; chmn. Claddaugh Investments LLC, 2004—. Trustee U. Notre Dame. Capt. USMC, 1966—69. Decorated Bronze Star USMC, 1966-69; recipient Semper Fidelis award Marine Corps Scholarship Found., El Valor's Corp. Visionary award, Man of Yr. award Ill. Viet Nam Vets. Mem.: Econ. Club Chgo. (past chmn.). Roman Catholic. Office: 1301 W 35th St Chicago IL 60609 Office Phone: 773-579-2474. Personal E-mail: pbrooney78@aol.com.

ROOP, JAMES JOHN, public relations executive; b. Parkersburg, W.Va., Oct. 29, 1949; s. J. Vaun and Mary Louise (McGinnis) R.; m. Margaret Mary Kuneck (div. 1982); m. Susan Lynn Hoell (div. 1989); m. Daisy P. Billue, 1990 (div. 1999); m. Constance E. West, 2005. BS in Journalism, W. Va. U., 1971. Various account mgmt. postions Ketchum Pub. Rels., Pitts., 1972-77, v.p., 1977-79, Burson-Marsteller, Chgo., 1979-81; sr. v.p. Hesselbart & Mitten/Watt, Cleve., 1981-84, exec. v.p., 1984-86, pres., 1986-87, Watt, Roop & Co. (formerly Hesselbart & Mitten/Watt), Cleve., 1987-96; chmn., pres., CEO Roop & Co., Cleve., 1996—. Contbr. articles to profl. jours. Mem. Leadership Clevel.; bd. dirs. Malachi House, Home Repair Resource Ctr., Animal Protective League. Fellow Pub. Rels. Soc. Am. (chmn. investor rels. sect. 1984-85, chmn. honors and awards com. 1995); mem. Nat. Investor Rels. Inst. (pres. Cleve./Akron/Pitts. chpt., sr. investor rels. roundtable), Cleve. Skating Club, Mayfield Country Club, Hermit Club. Republican. Home: 2697 Scarborough Rd Cleveland Heights OH 44106-3241 Office: Roop & Co 650 Huntington Bldg 925 Euclid Ave Cleveland OH 44115-1408

ROOT-BERNSTEIN, ROBERT SCOTT, biologist, educator; b. Washington, Aug. 7, 1953; s. Morton Ira and Maurine (Berkstresser) Bernstein; m. Michèle Marie Root-Bernstein, Sept. 2, 1978; children: Meredith Marie, Brian Robert. AB, Princeton U., 1975, PhD, 1980. Postdoctoral fellow Salk Inst. for Biol. Studies, La Jolla, Calif., 1981-82, rsch. assoc., 1983-84; from asst. to assoc. prof. Mich. State U., East Lansing, 1987-96, prof., 1996—. Cons. Parke-Davis Pharm. Rsch. Divsn., Ann Arbor, 1990-96, Chiron Corp., 1992-96; mem. adv. bd. Soc. for Advancement Gifted Edn., Chgo., 1987-92; Sigma Xi nat. lectr., 1994-96. Author: Discovering, 1989, Rethinking AIDS, 1993, Honey, Mud, Maggots and Other Medical Marvels, 1997, Sparks of Genius, 1999; columnist The Scis. mag., 1989-92, The Leonardo mag., 2004—; contbr. numerous articles to profl. jours. MacArthur Found. fellow, 1981-86; recipient D.J. Ingle Meml. Writing prize, 1988. Mem. Phi Beta Kappa (hon.), Sigma Xi. Avocations: painting, photography, cello, drawing, model building. Office: Mich State U Dept Physiology Biomed & Phys Scis Bldg East Lansing MI 48824 Office Phone: 517-355-6475 ext. 1101. Business E-Mail: rootbern@msu.edu.

ROPER, DONNA C., archaeologist; Rsch. assoc. prof. dept. Sociology & anthrop. Kans. State U., Manhattan. Mem.: Kans. State Hist. Soc., Nebr. Assn. Profl. Archeologists (pres.). Home: 1924 Bluehills Rd Manhattan KS 66502-4503 Office: Kans State U Dept Sociology Anthrop & Social Work 204 Waters Hill Manhattan KS 66506

ROPSKI, GARY MELCHIOR, lawyer; b. Erie, Pa., Apr. 19, 1952; s. Joseph Albert and Irene Stefania (Mszanowski) R.; m. Barbara Mary Schleck, May 15, 1982. BS in Physics, Carnegie-Mellon U., 1972; JD cum laude, Northwestern U. Sch. Law, 1976. Bar: Ill. 1976, U.S. Patent and Trademark Office 1976, U.S. Dist. Ct. (no. dist.) Ill. 1976, U.S. Ct. Appeals (7th cir.) 1977, U.S. Dist. Ct. (ea. dist.) Wis. 1977, U.S. Ct. Appeals (3d cir.) 1981, Pa. 1982, U.S. Ct. Claims 1982, U.S. Ct. Appeals (fed. cir.) 1982, U.S. Supreme Ct. 1982, U.S. Dist. Ct. (ea. dist.) Mich. 1984, U.S. Dist. Ct. (no. dist.) Calif. 1986. Assoc. Brinks Hofer Gilson & Lione, Chgo., 1976-81, shareholder, 1981—, pres., 2006—. Adj. prof. patents and copyrights Northwestern U. Sch. Law, Chgo., 1982-97. Contbr. numerous articles to profl. jours. Mem. ABA, Internat. Bar Assn., Internat. Trademark Assn., Am. Intellectual Property Law Assn., Ill. Bar Assn., Intellectual Property Law Assn. Chgo., Chgo. Bar Assn., Univ. Club, Chgo. Yacht Club. Roman Catholic. Office: Brinks Hofer Gilson & Lione Ste 3600 455 N Cityfront Plaza Dr Chicago IL 60611-5599 Office Phone: 312-321-4216. Business E-Mail: gropski@brinkshofer.com.

RORIG, KURT JOACHIM, chemist, science association director; b. Bremerhaven, Germany, Dec. 1, 1920; came to U.S., 1924, naturalized, 1929; s. Robert Herman and Martha (Grundke) R.; m. Helen Yonan, Mar. 20, 1949; children: James, Elizabeth, Miriam. BS, U. Chgo., 1942; MA, Carleton Coll., 1944; PhD, U. Wis., 1947. Lectr. Loyola U., Chgo., 1950-62; chemist to dir. Chem. Research G.D. Searle & Co., Chgo., 1947-87; pres. Chemo-Delphic Cons. Ltd., Chgo., 1987—. Adj. prof. chemistry U. Ill., Chgo., 1989—. Patentee in field. Mem. Sch. Bd., Wilmette, Ill., 1969-71. Mem. Am. Chem. Soc. (dir. Chgo. sect.), Am. Soc. Pharm. and Exptl. Therapeutics, N.Y. Acad. Scis., AAAS, Chgo. Chemists Club (past pres.) Presbyterian. Home and Office: 337 Hager Ln Glenview IL 60025-3329 Home Phone: 847-724-2808; Office Phone: 847-724-2808.

ROSATI, ALLISON, newscaster; b. Dover, Del., 1963; married; 4 children. Grad. Speech and Comms. cum laude, Gustavus Adolphus Coll., 1985. Gen. assignment reporter Sta. KTTC-TV, Rochester, Minn., 1985, prodr., co-anchor of 6 pm and 10 pm newscasts, 1986—87; gen. assignment reporter Sta. WGRZ-TV, Buffalo, 1987, anchor 6 pm and 10 pm newscasts; anchor, reporter NBC 5, Chgo., 1990—97, co-anchor 10 pm newscast, 1997—, co-anchor weekday 6 pm newscast. Active Big Brothers/Big Sisters; bd. dirs., organizer Bowl for Kids and Celebrity Golf Outing; active Greater Chgo. Food Depository, March of Dimes, Salvation Army, Ronald McDonald House. Recipient 1st Decade award for Most Accomplished Alumna of the Decade, Gustavus Adolphus Coll., Nat. Emmy award, Excellence in Comms. award, Justinian Soc. Chgo., David award for Achievement in Broadcasting, Joint Civic Com. Italian Ams., Dante award, 2001. Office: NBC 454 N Columbus Dr Chicago IL 60611

ROSE, ALBERT SCHOENBURG, lawyer, educator; b. Nov. 9, 1945; s. Albert Schoenberg Sr. and Karleen (Klein) Rose; m. Nancy K. Rose; children: Claudia, Micah Daniel. BSBA, U. Ala., 1967; JD, Washington U., St. Louis, 1970; LLM in Taxation, George Washington U., 1974. Bar: Mo. 1970, U.S. Dist. Ct. (ea. dist.) Mo. 1970, U.S. Tax Ct. 1970, U.S. Ct. Mil. Appeals 1970, U.S. Supreme Ct. 1970. Ptnr. Lewis Rice & Fingersh, St. Louis, 2001—. Adj. prof. law Washington U., 1979-98, Fontbonne Coll., 1993-96. Co-author: Missouri Taxation Law and Practice, 1986, supplement, 1989. Capt. U.S. Army, 1970-74, Korea. Mem.: Civic Entrepreneurs Orgn. (Bd. dirs., sec.), Tax Lawyers Club, Mid.Am. Tax Conf. (chmn.). Office: Lewis Rice & Fingersh 500 North Broadway Ste 2000 Saint Louis MO 63102 Office Phone: 314-444-1300. E-mail: arose@lewisrice.com.

ROSE, DONALD MCGREGOR, retired lawyer; b. Cin., Feb. 6, 1933; s. John Kreimer and Helen (Morris) R.; m. Constance Ruth Lanner, Nov. 29, 1958; children: Barbara Rose Burgess, Ann Rose Weston. AB in Econs., U. Cin., 1955; JD, Harvard U., Cambridge, Mass., 1958. Bar: Ohio 1958, U.S. Supreme Ct. 1962. Asst. legal officer USNR, Subic Bay, The Philippines, 1959-62, with Office of JAG The Pentagon, Va., 1962-63; assoc. Frost & Jacobs, LLP, Cin., 1963-70, ptnr., 1970-93, sr. ptnr., 1993-97, ret. ptnr., 1997. Co-chmn. 6th Cir. Appellate Practice Inst., Cin., 1983, 90, 6th Cir. adv. com., 1990-98, chmn. subcom. on rules, 1990-94, chmn., 1994-96. Trustee Friends of Cin. Pks., Inc., 1980-89, 93-98, pres. 1980-86; trustee Am. Music Scholarship Assn., Cin., 1985-88; pres. Social Health Assn. Greater Cin. Area Inc., 1969-72; co-chmn. Harvard Law Sch. Fund for So. Ohio, Cin., 1985-87; pres. Meth. Union, Cin., 1983-85; chmn. trustees Hyde Pk. Cmty. United Meth. Ch., Cin., 1974-76, chmn. coun. on ministries, 1979-81, chmn. adminstrv. bd., 1982-84, chmn. mem. canvass, 1985, chmn. staff parish rels. com., 1988-90, chmn. commn. missions, 1993-95; trustee Meth. Theol. Sch. Ohio, vice chmn. devel. com., 1990-94, sec. 1992-94, chmn. devel. com., 1994-98, vice chmn., 1998, chmn., 1999—2004; loaned exec. United Way, Cin., 1999. Lt. USNR, 1959-63. Mem.: 6th Cir. Judicial Conf. (sr.), Boothbay Country Club, Boothbay Harbor Yacht Club (bd. dirs. 2005—), Cin. Country Club. Republican. Avocations: sailing, golf. Home: 8 Walsh Ln Cincinnati OH 45208-3435 also: 11 Blackstone Rd Boothbay Harbor ME 04538-1943 Business E-Mail: dmrose@fbtlaw.com.

ROSE, JOSEPH HUGH, clergyman; b. Jewett, Ohio, Nov. 21, 1934; s. Joseph Harper and Lottie Louella (VanAllen) R.; m. Nila Jayne Habig, Feb. 14, 1958; children: J. Hugh II, Stephanie Jayne, David William, Dawnella Jayne. ThB, Apostolic Bible Inst., St. Paul, 1955, DD, 1990. Ordained United Pentecostal Ch. Assoc. min. Calvary Tabernacle, Indpls., 1956-73; Ind. youth sec. United Pentecostal Ch., 1958-60, Ind. youth pres., 1960-72, bd. edn. Hazelwood, Mo., 1974—, presbyter Ohio dist., 1975-97, hon. life presbyter Ohio, 1997; pastor Harrison Hills Ch., Jewett, Ohio, 1973—. Editor, Ind. Dist. News, 1959-70; narrator radio svc. Harvestime, 1961—. Republican. Mem. United Pentecostal Ch. Avocation: travel. Office: United Pentecostal Ch 8855 Dunn Rd Hazelwood MO 63042-2212 E-mail: jhrhhupc@eohio.net, jhrose@upci.org.

ROSE, (M.) LYNN, history professor; BA in History, U. Minn., Mpls., 1985, PhD in History, 1995. Asst. prof. history Truman State U., Kirksville, Mo., 1995—2000, assoc. prof., 2000—. Guest lectr. Institut für Klassische Altertumswissenschaften Martin Luther Universität Halle-Wittenberg, 2003—04. Author: The Staff of Oedipus: Transforming Disability in Ancient Greece, 2003; contbr. articles to profl. publs., chapters to books. Named Outstanding Tchr. of Yr., Mo. Coun. Pub. Higher Edn., 2006; recipient US Prof. of Yr. award, Carnegie Found. for Advancement of Tchg. and Coun. for Advancement and Support of Edn., 2006. Mem.: Women's Classical Caucus, Soc. Disability Studies, Internat. Assn. for Sci. Study of Intellectual Disabilities, Classical Assn. of Midwest and South, Am. Classical League, Assn. Ancient Historians. Office: Divsn Social Sci Truman State U Kirksville MO 63501 E-mail: lynnrose@truman.edu.

ROSE, MARYA MERNITZ, lawyer; b. Sept. 1962; m. Anthony J Rose. BA, Williams College, Williamstown, Mass.; JD, Ind. U. Corp. counsel Cummins Inc, 1997—98, corp. counsel & dir. public relations, 1998—99, corp. counsel & dir. public relations & comm. strategy, 1999—2000, v.p., gen. counsel, 2001—, also corp. sec. Office: Cummins Inc 500 Jackson St Columbus IN 47202

ROSE, MICHAEL DEAN, retired lawyer, educator; b. Johnstown, Pa., Oct. 22, 1937; BA, Ohio Wesleyan U., 1959; JD, Case Western Res. U., 1963; LLM, Columbia U., 1967. Bar: Ohio 1963. Assoc. firm Porter, Stanley, Treffinger & Platt, Columbus, Ohio, 1963-66; asst. prof. law Ohio State U., Columbus, 1967-69, assoc. prof., 1969-72, prof., 1972-99, Lawrence D. Stanley prof. law, 1987-99, prof. emeritus, 1999—. Staff asst. to chief counsel IRS, Washington, 1970-71. Author: (with Leo J. Raskind) Advanced Federal Income Taxation: Corporate Transactions, 1978, (with Joseph S. Platt) A Federal Taxation Primer, 1973, Hornbook on Federal Income Taxation, 3d edit., 1988; editor Selected Federal Taxation Statutes and Regulations, 1973-99, Ohio Will Manual, 1986-2002. Mem.: Am. Law Inst.

ROSE, ROBERT JOHN, bishop emeritus; b. Grand Rapids, Mich., Feb. 28, 1930; s. Urban H. and Maida A. (Glerum) R. Student, St. Joseph Sem., 1944-50; BA, Seminaire de Philosophie, Montreal, Que., Can., 1952; S.T.L., Pontifical Urban U., Rome, 1956; MA, U. Mich., 1962. Ordained priest Roman Catholic Ch., 1955; dean St. Joseph Sem., Grand Rapids, 1966-69; dir. Christopher House, Grand Rapids, 1969-71; rector St. John's Sem., Plymouth, Mich., 1971-77; pastor Sacred Heart Parish, Muskegon Heights, Mich., 1977-81; ordained bishop, 1981; bishop Diocese of Gaylord, Mich., 1981-89, Diocese of Grand Rapids, Mich., 1989—2003, bishop emeritus, 2003—. Mem. Nat. Conf. Cath. Bishops Roman Catholic.*

ROSE, SHELDON, property manager; Pres., CEO Edward Rose Bldg. Enterprise, Farmington Hills, Mich., 1995—. Office: Edward Rose Bldg Enterprise PO Box 9070 30057 Orchard Lake Rd Farmington Hills MI 48333 Fax: 248-539-2125.

ROSE, STUART, retail executive; Chmn., CEO REX Stores Corp., Dayton, Ohio, 1981—. Office: REX Stores Corp 2875 Needmore Rd Dayton OH 45414-4301

ROSE, THOMAS ALBERT, artist, educator; b. Washington, Oct. 15, 1942; s. Francis John and Ann Elizabeth (Voelkel) R.; m. Mary Melinda Moyer, Aug. 21, 1965; children: Sarah, Jessica. BFA, U. Ill., 1965; MA, U. Calif., Berkeley, 1967; postgrad., Lund U., Sweden, 1967-68. Instr. U. Calif., Berkeley, 1968-69, N.Mex. State U., Las Cruces, 1969-72; faculty mem. U. Minn., Mpls., 1972—, prof. art, 1983—, Fesler-Lampert chair in humanities, 2001—. Author: Winter Book, 1995, Where Do We Start?, 2003, 1018 W. Scott St., 2005, Time Frames, 2008; one-man shows include Clock Tower, N.Y.C., 1977, Truman Gallery, N.Y.C., 1977-78, Rosa Esman Gallery, N.Y.C., 1979, 81, 82, Marianne Deson Gallery, Chgo., 1984-86, Robert Thomson Gallery, Mpls., 1986, 91, 92, 95, Deson Saunders Gallery, Chgo., 1989, Mpls. Inst. Art, 1992, Weisman Art Mus., Mpls., 1994, Tweed Mus., Duluth, Minn., 1995, Steinbaum/Krauss Gallery, N.Y.C., 1996, 99, Brevard Mus. Art, Melbourne, Fla., 1997, Gensler Arch., Washington, 1999, 2004, Flanders Gallery, Mpls., 2000, 05, Bernice Steinbaum Gallery, Miami, Fla., 2001, 03, 05, Intermedia Arts, Mpls., 2003, Flanders Gallery, Mpls., 2005, Kent Mueller Gallery, Milw., 2005; exhibited in group shows at Walker Art Ctr., Mpls., 1974, 76, 77, Whitney Mus. Downtown, N.Y.C., P.S. #1, N.Y.C., 1978, Wave Hill, Bronx, N.Y., 1981, Hirshhorne Mus., Washington, 1981, Am. Ctr. in Paris, 1982, Harvard U. Sch. Architecture, 1983, Cultural Ctr., Chgo., 1983, Hal Bromm Gallery, N.Y.C., Sheldon Mus., Lincoln, Nebr., 1989, Tampa (Fla.) Mus., 1988, MCAD, Mpls., 1996, Minn. Mus. Art, 1996, Socrates Sculpture Park, N.Y.C., Fla. Internat. U., Miami, 1997, Gallerie Lipanjepuntin, Trieste, Italy, 2006, Luxan Acad. Art, Shenyang, China, 2006, Beijing Film Acad., 2006; represented in permanent collections Whitney Mus., N.Y.C., Getty Inst. L.A., Walker Art Ctr., Joslyn Mus., Omaha, Park St. Lofts, Springfield, Mass., U. Minn., Mpls., Am. Lung Assn. Target Ctr., Mpls., St. Lukes Episcopal Ch., Mpls., Wonkwang U., Republic of Korea, Mpls. Inst. Art, Weisman Mus. Art, Mpls., Stanford U. Libr., Sch. of the Art Inst., Chgo., Milw. Pub. Libr.; set designer: Fool for Love, Cricket Theater, Mpls., 1985, Circus, Theater de Jeune Lune, 1986; project dir. Works of Art in Pub. Places for Humphrey Inst. Pub. Affairs, Mpls., 1988; prin. works include Minn. Zoo, Marine Edn. Ctr., Sacred Heart U., Fairfield, Conn., Berniece Steinbaum Gallery, Miami, 1999, Steinbaum residence, 2002, Bennett Meml., Mpls., 2002. Named Rockefeller resident, Bellagio, Italy, 1993; recipient McKnight Artist fellow, 1995, travel fellow, Dayton-Hudson/Jerome, 1990, 1995, Jerome Found. Arts, 1993—94, Mellon Found., 1993, Fesler-Lampert Chair in Humanities, 2002; fellow, Nat. Endowment for Arts, 1977, 1981, Bush Found., 1979, Minn. State Arts Bd., 1979, 1984, McKnight Found., 1981, McKnight Found. Rsch., 1993—96, McKnight Photography, 2002; grantee, Arts Bd. Opportunities, 1993. Home: 91 Nicollet St Minneapolis MN 55401-1513 Office: Univ Minn 208 Studio Arts 23D S Avenue Minneapolis MN 55425 Office Phone: 612-889-9871. Personal E-mail: rosex001@umn.edu.

ROSEMARIN, CAREY STEPHEN, lawyer; b. Englewood, NJ, Aug. 19, 1950; s. Jack L. and Muriel Ruth (Gordon) R.; m. Joan Maxine Lafer, June 17, 1973; children: Benjamin Joseph, Meryl Ruth. BS, U. Mich., 1972; MS, Pa. State U., 1974; JD, U. Tenn., 1978. Bar: Tenn. 1978, Ill. 1982, U.S. Dist. Ct. (ea. dist.) Tenn. 1978, U.S. Dist. Ct. (no. dist.) Ill. 1982. Rsch. assoc. Union Carbide Corp., Oak Ridge Nat. Lab., 1974-80; asst. regional counsel U.S. EPA, Chgo., 1980-86; ptnr. Katten, Muchin, & Zavis, Chgo., 1986-90, Jenner & Block, Chgo., 1990-99; prin. Law Offices of Carey S. Rosemarin, P.C., Northbrook, Ill., 1999—. Mem. ABA, Tenn. Bar Assn., Chgo. Bar Assn. (chmn. environ. law com. 1985-86), Environ. Law Inst. (assoc.), North Suburban Bar Assn. (v.p.). Jewish. Avocations: licensed glider pilot, bicycling. Office: Law Offices of Carey S Rosemarin PC 500 Skokie Blvd Ste 510 Northbrook IL 60062-2893 Office Phone: 847-897-8000. Fax: 312-896-5786. Business E-Mail: csr@rosemarinlaw.com.

ROSEN, BARRY S., lawyer; BS magna cum laude, U. Ill., 1974; JD, Harvard U., 1977. Bar: Mass. 1977, Ill. 1978. Asst. atty. gen. Antitrust Divsn. Commonwealth of Mass., 1977—79; ptnr. Sachnoff & Weaver, Chgo., 1979—2007, Reed Smith LLP, Chgo., 2007—. Named Charles Merriam Scholar, U. Ill.; recipient Bronze Tablet. Mem.: Phi Beta Kappa. Office: Reed Smith LLP 40th Fl 10 S Wacker Dr Chicago IL 60606 Office Phone: 312-207-6483. Business E-Mail: brosen@areedsmith.com.

ROSEN, ERIC S., state supreme court justice; b. Topeka, May 25, 1953; BA, MA, U. Kansas; JD, Washburn U., 1984. Former social worker Topeka Public Sch.; former ptnr. Hein, Ebert and Rosen; former asst. dist. atty. & asst. public defender Shawnee County; judge domestic div. U.S. Dist. Ct., Third Dist., Shawnee County, Kans., 1993—95, judge Kans., 1993—2005; justice Kansas Supreme Ct., 2005—. Former assoc. gen. counsel Kans. Securities Commn.; former adjunct prof. Washburn U. Sch. of Law; mem. Koch Crime Commn., 1994; lecturer Menninger Sch. of Law and Psychiatry; mem. Kans. Sentencing Commn., 2004—. Recipient Atty. General's Victim's Svc. award, 2000, Martin Luther King Living the Dream Humanitarian award, 2002. Mem.: ABA, Kans. Bar Assn., Kans. Dist. Judges Assn., Am. Judicature Soc., Am. Judges Assn. Office: Kans Supreme Ct 301 W 10th Topeka KS 66612 Office Phone: 785-233-8200 ext. 4303. Office Fax: 785-296-1028.

ROSEN, GEORGE, economist, educator; b. St. Petersburg, Russia, Feb. 7, 1920; s. Leon and Rebecca (Rosenoer) Rosen; m. Sylvia Vatuk; 1 child, Mark. BA, Bklyn. Coll., 1940; MA, Princeton U., NJ, 1942, PhD, 1949. Prof. econs. Bard Coll., Annandale-on-Hudson, NY, 1946-50; economist Dept. State, Washington, 1951-54, Council Econ. Indsl. Research, Washington, 1954-55, MIT, CENIS, Cambridge, 1955-59, UN, NYC, 1959-60, Ford Found., NYC, Nepal and India, 1960-62, Rand Corp., Santa Monica, Calif., 1962-67; chief economist Asian Devel. Bank, Manila, Philippines, 1967-71; prof. econs. U. Ill.-Chgo., 1972-85, prof. econs. emeritus, 1985—, head dept., 1972-77; fellow Woodrow Wilson Internat. Ctr., Washington, 1989-90. Adj. prof. Johns Hopkins U.-Nanjing U. Ctr. Chinese-Am. Studies, 1986—87; cons. USAID, Egypt, 1994; treas. Am. Com. Asian Econ. Studies, 1990—2000; Golden Jubilee spkr. dept. commerce Osmania U., Hyderabad, India, 1999; disting. spkr. Ctr. Advanced Study Internat. Devel., Mich. State U., East Lansing, 1999. Author: Industrial Change in India, 1958, Some Aspects of Industrial Finance in India, 1962, Democracy and Economic Change in India, 1966, 1967, Peasant Society in a Changing Economy, 1975, Decision-Making Chicago-Style, 1980, Western Economists and Eastern Societies, 1985, Industrial Change in India 1970-2000, 1988, Contrasting Styles of Industrial Reform: China and India in the 1980s, 1992, Economic Development in Asia, 1996; co-author: The India Handbook, 1997, Globalization and Some of Its Contents: The Autobiography of a Russian Immigrant, 2005; book rev. editor: Econ. Devel. and Cultural Change, 1988—2004. Grantee, U. Ill., 1977—78, Social Sci. Rsch. Coun. and Am. Inst. Indian Studies, 1980—81, Am. Inst. Indian Studies, 1983—84, 1987—88, Rockefeller Found. Bellagio Study Ctr., 1984; Ford Found. fellow, NYU, 1971—72. Office: U Ill Dept Econs M/C 144 601 S Morgan St Chicago IL 60607-7121 Home: 5830 S Stony Island Ave Apt 11a Chicago IL 60637-2024

ROSEN, GERALD ELLIS, federal judge; b. Chandler, Ariz., Oct. 26, 1951; s. Stanley Rosen and Marjorie (Sherman) Cahn; m. Laurie DeMond; 1 child, Jacob DeMond. BA, Kalamazoo Coll., 1973; JD, George Washington U., 1979. Researchist Swedish Inst., Stockholm, 1973; legis. asst. U.S. Senator Robert P. Griffin, Washington, 1974-79; law clk. Seyfarth, Shaw, Fairweather & Gerardson, Wash., 1979; from assoc. to sr. ptnr. Miller, Canfield, Paddock and Stone, Detroit, 1979-90; judge U.S. Dist Ct. (ea. dist.) Mich., Detroit, 1990—. Mem. Jud. Evaluation Com., Detroit, co-chmn. 1983-88; adj. prof. law Wayne State U., 1992—, U. Detroit Law Sch., 1994-98, Cooley Law Sch., 2005-; mem. U. Mich. Law Sch., 2008-, U.S. Jud. Conf. Com. on Criminal Law; lectr. CLE confs., 1996-05, others. Co-author: Federal Civil Trials and Evidence, 1999, Michigan Civil Trials and Evidence, 2001, Federal Employment Litigation, 2006; contbr. articles to profl. jours. Rep. candidate for U.S. Congress, Mich., 1982; chmn. 17th Congl. Dist. Rep. Com., 1983-85; mem. Mich. Criminal Justice Commn., 1985-87; mem. Birmingham Athletic Club; bd. visitors George Washington U. Law Sch., 2000—; bd. dirs. Focus Hope, 2000—. Fellow Kalamazoo Coll. (sr. 1972); recipient Career Achievement award Rolex/Intercollegiate Tennis Assn. Mem. Fed. Judges Assn. (bd. dirs.). Jewish. Office: US Courthouse 231 W Lafayette Blvd Rm 730 Detroit MI 48226-2707 Office Phone: 313-234-5135.

ROSEN, MATTHEW STEPHEN, retired botanist; b. NYC, Oct. 7, 1943; s. Norman and Lucille (Cass) R.; m. Deborah Louise Mackay, June 16, 1974 (div. Feb. 1983); children: Gabriel Mackay, Rebecca Mackay; m. Kay Eloise Williams, July 11, 1987. MFSc, Yale U., New Haven, Conn., 1972; BS, Cornell U., Ithaca, NY, 1967. Instr. ornamental horticulture SUNY-Farmingdale, 1968-69; landscape designer Manhattan Gardener, NYC, 1969-70; instr. ornamental horticulture McHenry County Coll., Crystal Lake, Ill., 1972-74; coord. agrl. studies, asst. prof. biology, chemistry Mercer County Community Coll., West Windsor, NJ, 1974-79; adminstr. Des Moines Botanical Ctr., 1979—96; horticulture divsn. mgr. City of DeMoines, 1996—2007; ret., 2007. Cons. dir. West Mich. Hort. Soc., 1993; nat. judge Communities in Bloom, 2001-, Winter Lights, 2002-04, Am. in Bloom, 2002, sr. nat. judge, 2004-05, 2007-08; cons. in field. Contbr. articles to profl. jours. Com. chmn. United Way Cen. Iowa, 1982, divsn. chmn. 1983-86, 88-89, 91, 2000, group chmn. 1987, chmn. arts adv. com. 1985-86, pres. 1986, bd. dirs. Arts and Recreation Coun., 1985-86, com. chmn., 1992; career vocat. com. Des Moines Indsl. Sch. Dist., 1986, co-chmn., 1987, ptnrs. for progress com., 1988-90, sci. monitoring program, 1991-92; chmn. Two Rivers Festival, 1987-88; active Des Moines Sister City Program, Kofu, Japan, 1984, delegation, 1989, Naucalpan, Mexico, 1986, 87, Shijiazhuang, China, 1986, 90, 92, 95, 97; vice-chmn. Greater Des Moines Sister City Commn., 2004-05, chmn., 2005—; mem. edn. com. Am. Assn. Bot. Gardens and Arboretum, membership com., conservation com., bd. dirs. 1997-2001. Mem. Am. Assn. Bot. Gardens and Arboreta (edn. com.), Greater Des Moines C. of C. (team leader 1984—, chmn. new mem. sales, chmn. 8 O'clock new, Pres. Cabinet award 1983-85, bd. dirs., exec. com. 1995—, Achievement award C. of C. Fedn. 1986, exec. com. 1995-97), East Des Moines C. of C. (bd. dirs. 1992—, v.p., sec. 1993—, pres.-elect 1994, pres. 1995-96, sister cities commn. 1994, china chair 1995—, treas. 1995—, vice chair 2003, 04, chair 2005—), Greater Des Moines Conv. and Visitors Bur. (chmn. new mem. sales com. 1988-89), Iowa Advt. Rev. Coun., Affiliate Pres.'s Coun. of Chambers (chair 1995, 97), bd. dirs. DM Gen. Hosp., 1994-97, Bd. Coun. Internat. Trade, Latinos Unidos (bd. dirs. 1996-97), Rotary, Phi Kappa Phi, Pi Alpha Xi. Democrat. Jewish. Avocations: photography, reading, model trains, collecting old books, writing. Home: 1042 22nd St West Des Moines IA 50265-2219 E-mail: m.rosen@mchsi.com.

ROSEN, STEVEN TERRY, oncologist, hematologist; b. Bklyn., Feb. 18, 1952; married, 1976; 4 children. MB, Northwestern U., Evanston, Ill., 1972, MD, 1976. Genevieve Teuton prof., med. sch. Northwestern U., 1989—, dir. Robert H. Lurie Comprehensive Cancer Ctr., 1989—. Dir. clin. programs Northwestern Meml. Hosp., 1989—. Editor-in-chief Jour. Northwestern U. Cancer Center, 1989—, Contemporary Oncology, 1990-95, Cancer Treatment and Rsch., 1995—, In Touch, 1998-02. Mem. AAAS, ACP, AMA, Am. Soc. Hematology, Am. Soc. Clin. Oncology, Ctrl. Soc. Clin. Rsch. Achievements include research in hematologic malignancies, lung cancer, breast cancer, biologic and hormonal therapies. Office: Northwestern U Lurie 3-125 303 E Chicago Ave Chicago IL 60611-3093 Office Phone: 312-908-5250. Business E-Mail: s-rosen@northwestern.edu.

ROSEN, THOMAS J., food and agricultural products executive; 3 children. CEO Rosen's Diversified, Fairmont, Minn., 1986—. Bd. dirs. Morningside Coll., Danish Immigrants Coun. Minn. Mem. Minn. Agro-Growth Coun. Office: Rosen's Diversified 1120 Lake Ave Fairmont MN 56031-1939

ROSENAU, PETE, public relations executive; Owner, powersports franchises, import/export parts and accessories retail and wholesale operation; owner 6 new car franchises Honda, Hyundai, Mazda, Volkswagon, Toyota, Subaru, Mich.; chmn. Franco Pub. Rels. Group, 2002—. Bd. trustees YWCA Western Wayne County. Recipient Quality Dealer award, Time Mag., All-Star Dealer award (twice nominated), Sports Illustrated. Mem.: Henry Ford Cmty. Coll. (mem. found. bd.), BBB (serves exec. com.), Detroit Auto Dealers Assn. (past pres., exec. com., bd. dirs., co-chmn. 1997 and 1998 N.Am. Internat. Auto Shows, mem. bd. dirs. adv. ethics stds.). Office: Franco Pub Rels Group 400 Renaissance Ctr Ste 1050 Detroit MI 48243

ROSENBAUM, JACOB I., retired lawyer; b. Cleve., Oct. 4, 1927; s. Lionel C. and Dora (Heldman) R.; m. Marjorie Jean Arnold, Apr. 20, 1952; children: Laura Rosenbaum, Alexander, Judith Bartell. JD, U. N.Mex., 1951. Bar: N.Mex. 1951, Ohio 1952. Pres. Ohio Savs. Bank., Cleve., 1955—60, sr. v.p., 1960—92, also dir., 1995—; ptnr. Burke, Haber & Berick, 1955-79, Arter & Hadden, 1979-94, of counsel, 1994—2003, Tucker Ellis & West, 2003—05; ret., 2005. Active Judson Retirement Cmty., Cleve. Heights, Ohio, 1990—, trustee, 1994—2003,

2006—, pres., 1992, Cleve. Nat. Air Show, 1987—90, 1994—, pres. Found., 1995—2003, trustee, 1981—, Cleve. Zool. Soc., 1983—, Golden Age Ctrs. of Cleve., 1996—, RSVP, Inc., 2006—; pres. Temple Emanu El, University Heights, Ohio, 1965—67, 1995—. Mem.: Cleve. Execs. Assn. (pres. 1989, chmn. 1990, pres. 2003), Greater Cleve. Bar Assn., Ohio Bar Assn. (chmn. aviation law com. 1981—84), Lawyer-Pilots Bar Assn. (pres. 1981—82, editor jour. 1982—97), Kiwanis Club of Cleve. (pres. 1970—71, pres. found. 1999—). Democrat. Jewish. Home: 28050 N Woodland Rd Cleveland OH 44124-4521 Office: Tucker Ellis & West 1150 Huntington Bldg 925 Euclid Ave Cleveland OH 44115-1475 Office Phone: 216-696-2480. Business E-Mail: jrosenbaum@tuckerellis.com.

ROSENBAUM, JAMES MICHAEL, federal judge; b. Ft. Snelling, Minn., Oct. 12, 1944; s. Sam H. and Ilene D. (Bernstein) Rosenbaum; m. Marilyn Brown, July 30, 1972. BA, U. Minn., 1966, JD, 1969. Bar: (Minn) 1969, (Ill.) 1970, (U.S. Supreme Ct.) 1979. Atty. VISTA, 1969—70, staff atty., leadership coun. met. open communities Chgo., 1970—72; assoc. Katz, Taube, Lange & Frommelt, Mpls., 1972-77; ptnr. Rosenbaum & Rosenbaum, Mpls., 1977-79, Gainsley, Squier & Korsh, Mpls., 1979-81; US dist. atty. US Dept. Justice, Mpls., 1981-85; judge US Dist. Ct., Minn., 1985—, chief judge Minn., 2001—. 8th cir. rep. Jud. Conf. U.S., 1997—2005, mem. exec. com., 1999—2001. Author: (booklet) Guide to Practice Civil Rights Housing, 1972; co-author: U.S. Courts Design Guide, 1991—96; contbr. In Defense of the Hard Drive. Campaign chmn. People for Boschwitz, Minn., 1978; bd. vis. U. Minn. Law Sch. (pres. 1996-97). Mem.: FBA (bd. dirs.). Jewish. Office: US Courthouse 300 S 4th St Minneapolis MN 55415-1320

ROSENBAUM, ROBERT A., lawyer; s. Irwin L. and Marilyn E. Rosenbaum; m. Maggie A. Gilbert, May 1, 1994; m. Peggy A. Daly, Nov. 1982 (div. May 1991); children: Jacob A., Samuel A., Benjamin P. BA, Princeton U., 1978; JD, Harvard Law Sch., 1981. Bar: Calif. 1982, Minn. 1987. Assoc. atty. Latham & Watkins, LA, 1982—87; law clk. to chief justice Minn. Supreme Ct., St. Paul, 1981—82; ptnr., corp. securities law, corp. governance and compliance, and mergers and acquisitions groups Dorsey & Whitney LLP, Mpls., 1987—, and group head, corp., mem., mgmt. com. Mem., bd. dirs. Guthrie Theatre, Mpls., 2001—04. Named Am.'s Leading Bus. Lawyers, Chambers USA, 2003-2004, Minn. Superlawyer in M&A, Minn. Law and Politics, 1998-2004. Mem.: ABA, Minn. State Bar Assn. (ch. 302a subcommittee), Calif. Bar Assn., Hennepin Bar Assn., Mpls. Club. Office: Dorsey & Whitney LLP 50 South Sixth St Minneapolis MN 55402-1553 Office Phone: 612-340-5681. Office Fax: 612-340-2868. E-mail: rosenbaum.robert@dorsey.com.

ROSENBERG, BRIAN C, academic administrator; BA in English, Cornell U.; MA in English, PhD in English, Columbia U. Tchg. asst. Columbia U., NYC, 1979—80; English instr. Queens Coll., NY, 1980—82; asst. prof. The Cooper Union, NYC, 1982—83; asst. prof. to assoc. prof. to prof. to chmn., dept. of English Allegheny Coll., Meadville, Pa., 1983—98; chief acad. officer to dean of faculty and prof. English Lawrence U., Appleton, Wis., 1998—2003; pres. Macalester Coll., 2003—. Pres. fellowship Columbia U., 1977—78, 1980—81; bd. trustees The Dickens Soc., 2000—. Author: (book) Mary Lee Settle's Beulah Quintet: The Price of Freedom, 1991, Little Dorrit's Shadow's: Character and Contradiction in Dickens, 1996. Mem.: Phi Beta Kappa. Office: Office of the Pres, Macalester Coll 208 Weyerhaeuser Hall 62 Macalester St Saint Paul MN 55105 Office Phone: 651-696-6207.

ROSENBERG, CHARLES MICHAEL, art historian, educator; b. Chgo., Aug. 3, 1945; s. Sandor and Laura (Fried) R.; m. Carol Ann Weiss, June 25, 1967; children: Jessica Rachel, Jasper Matthew. BA, Swarthmore Coll., 1967; MA, U. Mich., 1969, PhD, 1974. Asst. prof. SUNY, Brockport, 1973-80; assoc. prof. U. Notre Dame, Ind., 1980-96, prof. Ind., 1996—. Author: 15th Century North Italian Painting and Drawing: Bibliography, 1986, Art and Politics in Late Medieval and Early Renaissance Italy, 1990, Este Monuments and Urban Development in Renaissance Ferrara, 1997; contbr. articles to Art Bull., Renaissance Quar., others. Kress Found. fellow Kunsthistorisches Inst., Florence, Italy, 1971-73, Am. Coun. Learned Socs. fellow, 1977-78, NEH fellow, Brown U., 1979-80, Villa i Tatti, Florence, 1985-86, Rome prize Am. Acad. Rome, 2000-01. Mem. Coll. Art Assn., Renaissance Soc. Am., Centro di Studi Europa Della Corti, Italian Art Soc. Office: Notre Dame U Dept Art Art History & Design Notre Dame IN 46556 E-mail: rosenberg.1@nd.edu.

ROSENBERG, GARY ARON, real estate development executive, lawyer; b. Green Bay, Wis., June 18, 1940; s. Ben J. and Joyce Sarah (Nemzin) R.; m. Gloria Davis, Nov. 1967 (div. 1975); children: Myra, Meredith; m. Bridgit A. Maile, Apr. 9, 1983. BS, Northwestern U., 1962, MBA, 1963; JD, U. Wis., 1966. Bar: Wis. 1966, Ill. 1967. Chmn., dir. The Rosenberg Found., 1960—; atty. U.S. SEC, Washington, 1966-67; pvt. practice Chgo., 1967-74; founder, chmn. bd., CEO UDC Homes, Inc. (formerly UDC-Universal Devel., L.P.), Chgo., 1968-1995; chmn., CEO, dir. Canterbury Devel. Corp., Chgo., 1986—; dir. Olympic Cascade Fin. Corp., Chgo., 1996-98, Nat. Securities, Chgo., 1996—; chair, pres., CEO, dir. OneStop Shop, Inc., Chgo., 1998—; dir. hometouch Ctrs., Inc., Chgo. Mem. adv. bd. Kellogg Grad. Sch. Mgmt. Northwestern U., Evanston, Ill., 1985—, founder, chmn. adv. bd. Kellogg Real Estate Rsch. Ctr., 1986—, adj. prof., 1982—; founder Shadow Hill Entertainment Corp., Beverly Hills, Calif., 1990. Recipient Arts Edn. Svc. award Ill. Alliance for Arts Edn., Chgo., 1988, Kellogg Schaffner Disting. Alumni award Kellogg Grad. Sch. Mgmt., 1993. Mem. Nat. Assn. Home Builders (coun. 1989-90), John Evans Club. Avocations: skiing, hiking, climbing, tennis, golf, reading. Office: Gary Rosenberg 1427 N State Pkwy Chicago IL 60610-1503 E-mail: bamgar@interaccess.com.

ROSENBERG, RALPH, retired state legislator, lawyer, non-profit administrator, educator; b. Chgo., Oct. 7, 1949; s. Nathan Benjamin and Rhea (Matlow) R.; m. Teresa Marie Sturm, July 11, 1989; children: Jacob Louis, Joel Patrick. BS in Commerce and Bus. Adminstrn., U. Ill., 1972; JD, Drake Law Sch., 1974. Bar: Iowa 1974. Sole practice Rosenberg Law Firm, Ames, Iowa, 1974—; mem. Iowa Ho. of Reps., Des Moines, 1981-90, Iowa Senate, Des Moines, 1990-94. Adj. faculty Des. Moines Area C.C., 1980—, Drake Law Sch., 1992, Upper Iowa U., 1993, Iowa State U., 1994—; dir. Environ. Planning Rsch. Group, Ames, 1976-77; exec. dir. Story County Legal Aid Soc., Nevada, Iowa, 1977-78; asst. Story County atty. County Attys. Office, Nevada, 1979-81; exec. dir., mng. atty. Youth Law Ctr., Des Moines, 1989-92; chair adv. bd. Inst. Pub. Leadership, 1994—; exec. dir. Coalition for Family and Childrens Svcs., 1995-2002; co-chair Iowans United for a Healthy Future; exec. dir. Heartland Sr. Svcs., 2003-04; exec. dir. Iowa Civil Rights Commn., 2004—. Author, editor: Public Interest Law, 1992; author: Family Theory, Law, Policy and Practice, 1994; editor: Descriptive Analysis of Iowa Environmental Agencies, 1977. Past chair Midwest Leadership Inst. of Coun. of State Govt.; bd. dirs. Emergency Residence Project Jewish Cmty. Rels. Commn., Iowa Protection and Advocacy, regional adv. bd. Legal Svcs. Corp. Iowa, Child and Family Policy Ctr.; past bd. dirs. Co-op. Child Care Svcs., Cmty. Action Rsch. Group, Rural Iowa. Recipient Outstanding Contbn. to Well-being of Children award Youth and Shelter Svcs., 1992, Excellence in Svc. award Legal Svcs. Group, 1993, Iowa LWV Cornerstone award, 1994, Iowa Farmers' Union Friend of the Farmer award, 1994, Iowa Consumer Action Network Citizen Svc. award, 1994; named LEgislator of Yr., Sierra Club, 1988, Isaak Walton League, 1993, Common Ground award Inst. of Public Leadership, 1997; named Legis. Conservationist of Yr., Wildlife Soc., 1988, Elected Ofcl. of Yr., Iowa Corrections Assn., 1984. Mem.: Nat. Conf. State Legislators (criminal justice com. 1986—94), Iowa State Bar Assn. Home: 811 Ridgewood Ave Ames IA 50010-5823 Office Phone: 515-242-6537. Personal E-mail: rosenberg_ralph@yahoo.com.

ROSENBERG, ROBERT BRINKMANN, information technology executive; b. Chgo., Mar. 19, 1937; s. Sidney and Gertrude (Brinkmann) Rosenberg; m. Patricia Margaret Kane, Aug. 1, 1959 (dec. Feb. 1988); children: John Richard, Debra Ann; m. Maryann Bartoli Manrot, June 25, 1989. BSChemE with distinction, Ill. Inst. Tech., 1958, MS in Gas Tech, 1961, PhD in Gas Tech, 1964. Registered profl. engr., Ill. Adj. asst. prof. Ill. Inst. Tech., 1965-69; mem. staff Inst. Gas Tech., Chgo., 1962-77, v.p. engring. rsch., 1973-77; v.p. R & D Gas Rsch. Inst., Chgo., 1977-78, exec. v.p., sr. v.p., 1978-84, v.p., 1984-96; pres. RBR Vision, Burr Ridge, Ill., 1996—; bd. dirs. IEA Internat. Ctr. Gas Tech. Info. Tech. program dir. World Energy Congress, 1996—98. Pres. Triangle Frat. Edn. Found., 1974—96, bd. dirs., 1996—2001, dir. emeritus; bd. dirs. Hinsdale Arts Coun., 1977—85, dir. emeritus, 1985—95; mem. adv. coun. U. Tex. Coll. Natural Scis. Found., 1990—95; mem. giving com. Morton Arboretum, 2004—; mem. Hinsdale Home Rule Ad Hoc Com., Ill., 1975—77; mem. vis. com. dept. chemistry U. Tex.; bd. advisors Chgo. 502, 2004—07; pres. Lake Ridge Club Homeowners Assn., 2001—. Recipient Gas Industry Rsch. award, 1985, Energy Exec. of the Yr. award, 1987, Profl. Achievement award, Ill. Inst. Tech. Alumni Assn., 1991. Mem.: AIChE, Triangle (Svc. Key and Outstanding Alumnus award 1987), Air Pollution Control Assn. (past sect. com. residential pollution sources), Gas Appliance Engrs. Soc. (past trustee), Internat. Gas Union, Atlantic Gas Rsch. Exch., Combustion Inst. (past treas. bd. dirs. ctrl. states sect.), Inst. Gas Engrs., Am. Gas Assn. (oper. sect. award of merit 1989). Achievements include patents for 13 patents in field. Avocations: cooking, gardening, travel. Home: 28 Lake Ridge Club Dr Burr Ridge IL 60527-7937 Office: RBR @ Vision 28 Lake Ridge Club Dr Burr Ridge IL 60527-7937 Office Phone: 630-654-3213. Personal E-mail: RBR3@comcast.net.

ROSENBERG, ROBIN, executive chef; b. Sausalito, Calif., Mar. 25, 1958; div.; 1 child. AA, Columbia Coll. Banquet chef, exec. chef Hilton Hotels, 1985-95; chef de cuisine Levy Restaurant, Chgo. Caterer Fire and Ice Charity Ball, L.A., 1989, Golden Globe Awards, 1991. Avocations: exploring current food trends, taking road trips, skiing, going to horse races, photography. Office: Levy Restaurants 980 N Michigan Ave Chicago IL 60611-4501

ROSENBERG, SAMUEL NATHAN, French and Italian language educator; b. NYC, Jan. 19, 1936; s. Israel and Etta (Friedland) R. AB, Columbia U., 1957; PhD, Johns Hopkins U., 1965. Instr. Columbia U., NYC, 1960-61; lectr. Ind. U., Bloomington, Ind., 1962-65, asst. prof., 1965-69, assoc. prof., 1969-81, prof. dept. French and Italian, 1981-99, prof. emeritus, 2000—. Chmn. dept. French and Italian Ind. U., Bloomington, 1977—84; editor ENCOMIA jour. of Internat. Courtly Lit. Soc., 2005—. Author: Modern French CE, 1970, (with others) Harper's Grammar of French, 1983, (with W. Apel) French Secular Compositions of the 14th Century, 3 vols., 1970-72, (with H. Tischler) Chanter m'estuet: Songs of the Trouveres, 1981; translator: (with S. Danon) Ami and Amile, 1981, rev. edit., 1996, Lyrics and Melodies of Gace Brulé, 1985; (with H. Tischler) The Monophonic Songs in the Roman de Fauvel, 1991, Lancelot-Grail Cycle, vol. 2, 1993, Chansons des trouvères, 1995, Songs of the Troubadours and Trouvères, 1997; (with others) Early French Tristan Poems, 2 vols., 1998; (with C. Callahan) Les Chansons de Colin Muset, 2005, (with E. Doss-Quinby) The Old French Ballette, 2006; (with Patricia Terry) Lancelot and the Lord of the Distant Isles, 2007. Pres. Mid-Am. Festival of the Arts, Inc., Bloomington, Ind., 1984-85. Woodrow Wilson Found. fellow, 1959-60; Fulbright fellow, 1960-61; Lilly Faculty fellow, 1986-87. Mem MLA, Am. Assn. Tchrs. French; mem. Medieval Acad. Am., Internat. Courtly Lit. Soc. (editor Encomia 2005—), Am. Lit. Translators Assn. (bd. dirs. 2002-06), Romance Philology Adv. Bd., Phi Beta Kappa. Home: PO Box 1164 Bloomington IN 47402-1164 Business E-Mail: srosenbe@indiana.edu.

ROSENBERG, SHELI ZYSMAN, retired finance company executive; b. NYC, Feb. 2, 1942; d. Stephen B. and Charlotte (Laufer) Zysman; m. Burton X. Rosenberg, Aug. 30, 1964; children: Leonard, Marcy. BA, Tufts U., 1963; JD, Northwestern U., 1966. Bar: Ill. 1966. Ptnr. Schiff, Hardin & Waite, Chgo., 1973-80; exec. v.p., gen. counsel Equity Fin. Mgmt., Chgo., 1980-90, Equity Group Investments, Inc., Chgo., 1988-94, pres., CEO, 1994—99, Equity Group Investments, LLC, Chgo., 1999—2000, vice chmn., 2000—03; prin. Rosenberg & Liebentritt, P.C., Chgo., 1980—97. Adj. prof. Northwestern U., 2000—03, J.L. Kellogg Grad. Sch. Bus., 2003—; bd. dirs. CVS/Caremark Corp., Capital Trust, Cendant Corp., Manufactured Home Communities, Inc., Equity Residential Properties Trust, Equity Office Properties Trust, Ventas, Inc.; adv. bd. J.L. Kellogg Grad. Sch. Bus. N.W. Univ.; trustee Equity Residential, 1993—, lead trustee, 2002—. Trustee Rush Presbyn. St. Luke's Med. Ctr., exec. com.; co-founder, pres. Ctr. for Exec. Women, J.L. Kellogg Grad. Sch. Bus., 2001—.

ROSENBERG, THOMAS B., film producer, real estate company executive; BA, Univ. Wis.; JD, Univ. Calif., Berkeley. Atty pvt. pratice; co-founder Capital Assoc. Group real estate, Chgo., 1977—; founder, co-chair, CEO Lakeshore Entertainment Corp, Chgo., 1994—. Investment com. Capri Capital Adv., Chgo. Films: (exec. prodr.) The Commitments, 1991, A Midnight Clear, 1992, Princess Caraboo, 1994, The Road to Wellville, 1994, Kids in the Hall: Brain Candy, 1996, Box of Moon Light, 1996, Prince Valiant, 1997, Homegrown, 1998, Phoenix, 1998, 200 Cigarettes, 1999, Arlington Road, 1999, The Hurricane, 1999, Madhouse, 2004, Suspect Zero, 2004; (prodr.) 'Til There Was You, 1997, The Real Blonde, 1997, Polish Wedding, 1998, Passion of Mind, 2000, The Next Best Thing, 2000, Autumn in New York, 2000, The Gift, 2000, The Mothman Prophecies, 2002, The Human Stain, 2003, Underworld, 2003, Cantado dietro i paraventi, 2003, Wicker Park, 2004, Million Dollar Baby, 2004 (Academy of Motion Picture Arts and Sciences award for Best Picture, 2005). Home: 875 N Michigan Ave Ste 3430 Chicago IL 60611-1958 Office Phone: 312-335-2600. E-mail: info@lakeshoreentertainment.com.

ROSENBLATT, KARIN ANN, cancer epidemiologist; b. Chgo., Apr. 22, 1954; d. Murray and Adylin Rosenblatt. BA, U. Calif., Santa Cruz, 1975; MPH, U. Mich., 1977; PhD, Johns Hopkins U., 1988. Postdoctoral fellow U. Wash., Seattle, 1987-89; staff scientist Fred Hutchinson Cancer Rsch. Ctr., Seattle, 1989-91; asst. prof. U. Ill., Champaign, 1991-97, assoc. prof., 1997—. Vis. scientist Fred Hutchinson Cancer Rsch. Ctr., 1999-2000; vis. scholar U. Wash., 1999-2000. Fellow Am. Coll. Epidemiology; mem. APHA (governing councilor epidemiology sect. 1988-2000), Internat. Epidemiologic Assn., Internat. Genetic Epidemiology Soc., Soc. for Epidemiologic Rsch. Office: Dept Cmty Health 120 Huff Hall MC 588 1206 S 4th St Champaign IL 61820-6920

ROSENBLOOM, LEWIS STANLEY, lawyer; b. Ft. Riley, Kans., Feb. 28, 1953; s. Donald and Sally Ann (Warsawsky) R.; children: Micah, Shaina. BA, Lake Forest Coll., 1974; JD with high honors, DePaul U., 1977. Bar: Ill. 1977, US Dist. Ct. (no. dist.) Ill, 1977, US Ct. Appeals (7th cir.) 1979, US Supreme Ct. 1983, US Ct. Appeals (9th cir.) 1987, US Ct. Appeals (3rd cir.) 1993. Sr. acct. Gale, Takahasi & Channon (now Ernst & Young), Chgo., 1973-74; law clk. to Hon. Robert L. Eisen U.S. Bankruptcy Ct. (no. dist.) Ill., Chgo., 1976; assoc. Nachman, Munitz & Sweig, Ltd., Chgo., 1976-82, prin., 1982-87; ptnr., co-chmn. involvency, bankruptcy & bus. reorgn. dept. Winston & Strawn, Chgo., 1987-93; ptnr., sr. corp. reorgn. counsel, practice group head McDermott, Will & Emery, Chgo., 1993—2006; ptnr., chmn. dept. bankruptcy and reorganization LeBoeuf, Lamb, Green & MacRae, LLP, Chgo., 2006—. Mem. bd. advisors to bankruptcy, comml. law advisor Bus. Laws, Inc., 1988—; lectr. in field. Contbr. articles to profl. jours. Mem. adv. com. and fin. subcom. Ill. Bd. Higher Edn., Springfield; mem. state edn. and legal aid subcom. Ill. Coun. on Children and Youth Welfare. Coll. Scholar Lake Forest Coll., 1973-74. Fellow Am. Coll. Bankruptcy (dir.); mem. ABA (bus. bankruptcy com. 1982—, chmn. new and pending bankruptcy legis. com. 1982-85, chmn. transp. reorganizations com. 1985-88), Chgo. Bar Assn. (bankrupcy reorganization com., co-chmn. subcom. on retention and fees 1987-88). Office: LeBoeuf Lamb Greene & MacRae LLP Two Prudential Plaza 180 N Stetson Ste 3700 Chicago IL 60601 Home Phone: 847-630-6943; Office Phone: 312-794-8090. Business E-Mail: lrosenbloom@llgm.com.

ROSENFELD, IRENE B., food products company executive; b. Bklyn., 1953; m. Richard Illgen; 2 children. BA in Psychology, Cornell U, 1975, MS in Bus., 1977, PhD in Mktg. & Statistics, 1980. With Dancer, Fitzgerald Sample Advertising (now Saatchi and Saatchi), 1979—81, Kraft Foods Inc., 1981—2004, exec. v.p., gen. mgr., beverages divsn., 1991—94, exec. v.p., gen. mgr. desserts & snacks divsn., 1994—96; pres. Kraft Foods Canada, 1996—2004; group v.p. Kraft Foods Inc., 2000—04; pres. Kraft Food N. Am., 2003—04; chmn., CEO Frito-Lay Inc. (divsn. of PepsiCo Inc.), Plano, Tex., 2004—06; CEO Kraft Foods Inc., orthfield, Ill., 2006—07, chmn., CEO, 2007—. Bd. dirs. AutoNation, Inc. Mem. YWCA Acad. Women Achievers; bd. trustees Cornell U. Named one of 100 Most Powerful Women, Forbes mag., 2006—07, 50 Most Powerful Women in Bus., Fortune mag., 2006, 50 Women to Watch, Wall St. Jour., 2006, Next 20 Female CEOs, Pink Mag. & Forté Found., 2006; recipient The Masters in Excellence award, Jewish Student Cmty. at Cornell Univ., 2005. Office: Kraft Foods Inc 3 Lakes Dr orthfield IL 60093

ROSENFIELD, ANDREW M., lawyer, educator; b. Chgo., Sept. 20, 1951; s. Maurice and Lois (Fried) R.; m. Betsy Bergman, Sept. 10, 1978; children: Zachary William, Edwin Alexander, Betty Alana, Jake Leonard. BA with honors, Kenyon Coll., 1973; MA, Harvard U., 1978; JD cum laude, U. Chgo., 1978. Bar: Ill. 1978. Pres., founder Lexecon Inc., Chgo., 1977; adj. prof. Northwestern U. Law Sch., Chgo., 1985-86; lectr. in law U. Chgo., 1986—; founder, chmn UNext, 2000—; mng. ptnr. Gleacher & Co. LLC. Lectr. numerous law and bus. seminars. Mem. bd. trustees U. Chgo., 1996—; vice chmn. bd. trustees Art Inst. Chgo. Mem. Order of Coif. Clubs: Chicago, Standard (bd. dirs.1985—). Jewish. Home: 10 W Deerpath Rd Lake Forest IL 60045-2111 Office: U Chgo Law Sch 1111 E 60th St Chicago IL 60637 also: UNext Ste 455 111 N Canal St Chicago IL 60606 Office Phone: 773-702-9597. E-mail: rosenfield@unext.com.

ROSENFIELD, ROBERT LEE, pediatric endocrinologist, educator; b. Robinson, Ill., Dec. 16, 1934; s. Irving and Sadie (Ospide) R.; m. Sandra L. McVicker, Apr. 14, 1973. BS, Northwestern U., 1956; MD, 1960. Diplomate Am. Bd. Pediat. Endocrinology. Intern Phila. Gen. Hosp. and Children's Hosp., Phila., 1960-63, 65-68; practice specializing in pediat. endocrinology; prof. pediats., medicine U. Chgo., 1968—. Vis. prof. U. Dundee, 1986-87. Contbr. articles to profl. jours. Capt. USMC, 1963-65. Fogarty Sr. Internat. fellow, USPHS, Weizmann Inst., Israel, 1977-78. Mem. Am. Bd. Pediat. (sub.-bd. pediatric endocrinology 1983-86), Am. Pediat. Soc., Lawson Wilkins Pediatric Endocrinology Soc. (pres.-elect, 2006), Endocrine Soc., Soc. Gynecol. Invetigation, Soc. Dermatol. Investigation, Chgo. Pediat. Soc. (pres. 1981). Democrat. Jewish. Avocation: photography. Home: 1700 E 56th St Apt 3502 Chicago IL 60637-5099 Office: U Chgo Med Ctr 5841 S Maryland Ave Chicago IL 60637-1463 Home Phone: 773-684-6528; Office Phone: 773-702-6432. Business E-Mail: robros@peds.bsd.uchicago.edu.

ROSENGREN, CHRISTOPHER PAUL, lawyer; b. 1968; BS, SUNY, 1995; JD, U. Minn. Law Sch., 1998. Bar: Minn. 1998, US Dist. Ct. Minn., US Ct. Appeals (8th cir.). Pros. atty.; assoc. Gislason & Hunter, L.L.P., Mankato, Minn. Paratrooper, Russian translator US Army. Named a Rising Star, Minn. Super Lawyers mag., 2006; recipient Pro Bono Atty. of Yr. award, 5th Jud. Dist., 2004. Office: Gislason & Hunter LLP Landkamer Bldg Ste 200 124 E Walnut St Mankato MN 56001 Office Phone: 507-382-6529. E-mail: crosengren@gislason.com.

ROSENGREN, JOHN CHARLES, lawyer; b. Ft. Benning, Ga., Apr. 23, 1946; s. Warren John Rosengren and Ann Mary (Burton) Paddock; m. Theresa Mary Koch, July 31, 1971; children: John, Elizabeth, Philip. BA, Loras Coll., 1968; JD, Boston Coll., 1971. Bar: N.Y. 1972, U.S. Dist. Ct. (ea. and so. dists.) N.Y. 1972. Assoc. Ide & Haigney, NYC, 1971-73, Alexander & Green, NYC, 1973-78; counsel Frank B. Hall & Co., Briarcliff, N.Y., 1978-79; ptnr. Marks & Murase, NYC, 1980-95; v.p., gen. counsel Arthur J. Gallagher & Co., Itasca, Ill., 1995—. Mem. ABA (subcom. on fgn. investment in the U.S.). Home: 26345 W Glenbarr Ln Barrington IL 60010-2864 Office: Arthur J Gallagher & Co The Gallagher Ctr 2 Pierce Pl Ste 100 Itasca IL 60143-1293

ROSENHEIM, MARGARET KEENEY, social welfare policy educator; b. Grand Rapids, Mich., Sept. 5, 1926; d. Morton and Nancy (Billings) Keeney; m. Edward W. Rosenheim, June 20, 1947; children: Daniel, James, Andrew. Student, Wellesley Coll., 1943-45; JD, U. Chgo., 1949. Bar: Ill. 1949. Mem. faculty Sch. Social Svc. Adminstrn. U. Chgo., Chgo., 1950—, assoc. prof., 1961—66, prof., 1966—, Helen Ross prof. social welfare policy, 1975—96, dean, 1978—83; lectr. in law U. Chgo., 1980—97. Vis. prof. U. Wash., 1965, Duke U., 1984; Helen Ross prof. emerita U. Chgo., 1996—; acad. visitor London Sch. Econs., 1973; cons. Pres.'s Commn. Law Enforcement and Adminstrn. Justice, 1966-67, Nat. Adv. Commn. Criminal Justice Stds. and Goals, 1972; mem. Juvenile Justice Stds. Commn., 1973-78; trustee Carnegie Corp. N.Y., 1979-87; trustee Children's Home and Aid Soc. of Ill., 1981—, chair, 1996-98; chair CHASI Sys. Inc., 1998-2001; dir. Nat. Inst. Dispute Resolution, 1981-89, Nuveen Bond Funds, 1982-97; mem. Chgo. Network, 1983—. Editor: Justice for the Child, 1962; contbr. 2d edit., 1977; editor: Pursuing Justice for the Child, 1976; editor: (with F.E. Zimring, D.S. Tanenhaus, B. Dohrn) A Century of Juvenile Justice, 2002; editor: (with Mark Testa) Early Parenthood and Coming of Age in the 1990s, 1992; contbr. articles to profl. jours. Home: Apt 303 1 Thomas Moore Way San Francisco CA 94130-2942

ROSENMAN, KENNETH D., medical educator; b. NYC, Feb. 25, 1951; AB, Cornell U., 1972; MD, NY Med. Coll., 1975. Bd. cert. internal medicine; bd. cert. occupational and preventive medicine. Asst. prof. U. Mass., Amherst, 1979-81; dir. occupational and environ. health N.J. Dept. Health, Trenton, 1981-86; pvt. practice Plainsboro, NJ, 1986-88; assoc. prof. Mich. State U., East Lansing, 1988-93, prof., 1993—. Office: Mich State U 117 W Fee Hall East Lansing MI 48824-1316 Office Phone: 517-353-1846. E-mail: rosenman@msu.edu.

ROSENOW, EDWARD CARL, III, medical educator; b. Columbus, Ohio, Nov. 2, 1934; s. Oscar Ferdinand and Mildred Irene (Eichelberger) R.; m. Constance Donna Grahame, Sept. 7, 1957; children: Sheryl Lynn, Scott Edward. BS, Ohio State U., 1955, MD, 1959; MS in Medicine, U. Minn., 1969. Diplomate Am. Bd. Internal Medicine, Am. Bd. Pulmonary Diseases. Intern Riverside Meth. Hosp., Columbus, Ohio, 1959-60; resident in internal medicine Mayo Grad. Sch. Medicine, Rochester, Minn., 1960-65, clin. fellow in thoracic diseases, 1965-66; cons. in internal medicine (pulmonary diseases) Mayo Clinic, Rochester, 1966; instr. in medicine Mayo Grad. Sch. Medicine, Rochester, 1969-73; asst. prof. medicine Mayo Med. Sch., Rochester, 1973-77, assoc. prof. medicine, 1977-80, prof. medicine, 1980; chmn. divsn. pulmonary and critical care medicine, 1987-94; assoc. dir. internal medicine residency program Mayo Clinic, Rochester, 1977-79, program dir. internal medicine residency program, 1979-84, sec. Mayo staff, 1979; pres. Mayo staff, 1986; Arthur M. and Gladys D. Gray prof. medicine Mayo Clinic, Rochester, 1987-96, prof. emeritus, 1996—. Cons. NASA, Houston. Capt. M.C., U.S. Army, 1962-64. Recipient Alumni Achievement award Coll. Medicine Ohio State U., 1989, Disting. Mayo Clinician award, 1994, Henry S. Plummer Disting. Internist award, 1994, Karis award Mayo Clinic, 1996, Disting. Alumnus award Mayo Found., 1998; Edward W. and Betty Knight Scripps Professorship named in his honor Mayo Med. Sch., 1994, Edward C. Rosenow, III, Outstanding Subsplty. fellow award established in his honor; inductee Sigma Chi Hall of Fame, 2005 Fellow ACP (gov. Minn. chpt. 1987-91, Ralph S. Claypoole Sr. award for Lifetime Dedication to Patient Care 1995, Minn. chpt. Laureate award 1994, Disting. Lectr. award 1996), Am. Coll. Chest Physicians (master fellow, editl. bd. CHEST 1973-78, editor spl. case reports 1975-90, com. on postgrad. med. edn. 1978-84, sci. program com. 1982, com. on undergrad. med. edn. 1981-82, co-chmn. sci. program com. Internat. Coll. Chest Physicians meeting, Sydney, Australia, 1985, regent 1984-88, pres. elect 1988-89, pres. 1989-90, pres. Chest Found. 1998—, Endowed Hon. Lectr. in name 2004—); mem. AMA, So. Minn. Med. Assn., Minn. Thoracic Soc., Am. Thoracic Soc., Sigma Xi. Office: Mayo Clinic Div Pulmonary Diseases 200 1st St SW Rochester MN 55905-0002 Office Phone: 507-284-2511. Business E-Mail: rosenow.edward@mayo.edu.

ROSENOW, JOHN EDWARD, foundation executive; b. Lincoln, Nebr., Sept. 15, 1949; s. Lester Edward and Lucille Louise (Koehler) R.; m. Nancy Kay Hadley; children: Matthew, Stacy. BS in Agrl. Engring., U. Nebr., 1971. Dir. of tourism Nebr. Dept. Econ. Devel., Lincoln, 1971-79, interim dept. dir., 1985; founder Nat. Arbor Day Found., 1972, exec. dir. million-mem. Lincoln and Nebraska City, 1979-94, pres., 1994—. Co-author: (book) Tourism: the good, the bad, and the ugly, 1979. Democrat. Mem. United Ch. of Christ. Office: Nat Arbor Day Found 211 N 12th St Lincoln NE 68508-1422 Office Phone: 888-448-7337.

ROSENSTOCK, SUSAN LYNN, orchestra administrator; b. Bklyn., Nov. 2, 1947; BS, SUNY, Cortland, 1969; MBA, So. Meth. U., 1977, MFA, 1978. Neval mgr. Columbus (Ohio) Symphony Orch., 1978—82; grants program dir., info. officer Greater Columbus Arts Coun., 1982-83, asst. dir. grants and adminstrn., 1983-84; dir. ann. giving and spl. events Columbus Symphony Orch., 1984-86, dir. devel., 1986-90, orch. mgr., 1990-98, gen. mgr., 1998—. Panelist Ohio Arts Coun. Music Panel, 1986, 87, NEA, 2002, Challenge Grants Panel, 1991, J.C. Penney Gold Rule Award Judges Panel, 1993, 94. Mem. Am. Symphony Orch. League (devel. dirs. steering com. nat. conf. 1987, 88), Nat. Soc. Fund Raising Execs. (program com. Ctrl. Ohio chpt. 1988-94, chmn. program com. 1993, 94, bd. dirs. 1993-95, treas. 1995). Office: Columbus Symphony Orch 55 E State St Columbus OH 43215-4203 E-mail: susanr@columbussymphony.com.

ROSENTHAL, AMNON, pediatric cardiologist; b. Gedera, Israel, July 14, 1934; came to U.S., 1949, naturalized, 1959; s. Joseph and Rivka Rosenthal; m. Prudence Lloyd, July 22, 1962; children: Jonathan, Eben, Nathaniel. MD, Albany Med. Coll., 1959. Intern Buffalo Children's Hosp., 1959-60; resident in pediatrics Children's Hosp. Med. Center, Boston, 1960-62, resident in pediatric cardiology, 1965-68; asso. prof. pediatrics Children's Hosp. Med. Center and Harvard U. Med. Sch., Boston, 1975-77; prof. pediatrics C.S. Mott Children's

Hosp., U. Mich., Ann Arbor, 1977—2006, assoc. dir. dept. pediatrics, 1989-92, dir. pediatric cardiology, 1977-97, prof. emeritus pediatrics, 2006—. Served to capt. M.C. USAF, 1962-65. Recipient Outstanding Clinician award (Pediat.), U. Mich., 2002, Disting. Svc. award, 2003, Founders award, Am. Acad. Pediat., 2003, Humanitarian award, Jewish Fedn.; Amnon Rosenthal endowed professorship, U. Mich., 1994. Mem. Am. Acad. Pediatrics, Soc. for Pediatric Rsch., Am. Pediatric Soc., Am. Heart Assn., Am. Coll. Cardiology, Am. Bd. Pediatrics, Am. Bd. Pediatric Cardiology (chmn. 1987-88). Office: CS Mott Children's Hosp Ann Arbor MI 48109-0204 Office Phone: 734-936-6703. Business E-Mail: amnonr@umich.edu.

ROSENTHAL, ARNOLD H., film director, producer, writer, graphic designer, calligrapher; b. Chgo., Jan. 31, 1933; s. Gus and Sara (Ariel) R.; children: Michel, Jason, Anthony. BA, U. Ill., 1954. Graphic designer Whitaker-Guernsey Studios, Chgo., 1954-55; art dir. Edward H. Weiss Advt., Chgo., 1956-60; owner Arnold H. Rosenthal & Assos., Chgo., 1960-70; partner, creative dir., pres. Meyer & Rosenthal Inc. (mktg. communications), Chgo., 1970-75; sr. v.p., creative dir. Garfield-Linn & Co. (Advt.), Chgo., 1975-81; pres., exec. prodr./dir. Film Chgo., 1981—. TV comml. jury chmn. Chgo. Internat. Film Festival, 1977, 78, 79, 87, mem. governing bd., 1984—; represented at Moscow Film Fest, 1990; TV jury chmn. U.S. Festival, 1980; lectr. Columbia Coll., Purdue U., U. Ill., Ohio State U. Contbr. articles to profl. publs. Bd. dirs. Jewish United Fund. Served with AUS, 1955-56. Recipient creative awards Communication Clubs Chgo., .Y.C., 1960—, Silver medal N.Y. Film Festival, 1986, Clio award, 1981. Mem. Soc. Typographic Arts (design awards 1958—, pres. 1971-72), Am. Inst. Graphic Arts (spl. award 1974), Dirs. Guild Am., Jazz Inst. Chgo. (charter, jazz drummer), Tau Epsilon Phi, Alpha Delta Sigma.

ROSENTHAL, JOEL, manufacturing executive; b. Ft. Worth, Oct. 25, 1946; s. Melvin and Jane (Hertzman) R.; m. Susan Ellman, Nov. 15, 1970; children: Jackie Ilene, Harold Joseph. BBA, No. Tex. State U., 1969. V.p. First Street Corp., Ft. Worth, 1969-72; mgr. Edison Jewelers & Distbrs., Ft. Worth, 1972-73; v.p. Yankton Sioux Industries, Wagner, S.D., 1973-81, pres., 1981-85; cons., Canton, S.D., 1985—; pres. Ctrl. Plains Tractor Parts, Sioux Falls, S.D., 1986—. Cons. econ. devel. State of S.D., Pierre, 1985-86; guest lectr. U. S.D., 2003. Chmn. S.D. Rep. Com., 1995-2003; mem. Electoral Coll., 1996, 2000; pres. City Coun., Wagner, 1978-83; trustee Carnegie Libr., Wagner, 1978-83; active Rep. Nat. Com., Washington, 1985-2003, S.D. Jud. Qualifications Commn., 1983-86, Pvt. Industry Coun., Pierre, 1985-86, SD Coun. of Econ. Advs., 2003. Named S.D. Vol. of Yr. Office of Gov., 1983. Republican. Jewish. Home: 6001 S Tomar Rd Sioux Falls SD 57013 Office: PO Box 1818 Sioux Falls SD 57101-1818 Office Phone: 605-334-0021.

ROSENZWEIG, PEGGY A., state legislator; b. Detroit, Nov. 5, 1936; married; 5 children. BS, U. Wis., Milw., 1978; postgrad., Wayne State U. Wis. state assemblyman Dist. 98, 1982-92, Dist. 14, 1993; mem. Wis. Senate from 5th dist, Madison, 1993—. Former ranking minority mem. Health Com. Former dir. comty. rels. Milw. Regional Med. Ctr.; former pres. Med. Coll. Wis. Mem. LWV. Address: 6236 Upper Pkwy N Wauwatosa WI 53213-2430 Office: Wis State Senate State Capitol PO Box 7882 Madison WI 53707-7882

ROSICA, GABRIEL ADAM, retired manufacturing executive, electrical engineer; b. NYC, Jan. 9, 1940; s. Gabriel J. and Elma (P.) R.; m. Bettina R. Nardozzi, Sept. 8, 1962; children: Gregory A., Julie Ann, Mark A. BA in Math. and Physics, Columbia U., 1962, BSEE, 1963; MSEE, Rensselaer Poly. Inst., 1966; MBA, Boston U., 1971. Registered profl. engr., Mass. Rsch. engr. United Aircraft Research Labs., East Hartford, Conn., 1963-67; mgr. electronic devel. The Foxboro (Mass.) Co., 1967-75, gen. mgr. U.S. div., 1975-77, v.p., 1977-80; pres., COO Modular Computer Sys., Inc., Ft. Lauderdale, Fla., 1980-82, pres., chmn., CEO, 1982-88; pvt. practice bus. cons. Boca Raton, Fla., 1988-91; sr. v.p. Elsag Bailey Corp., Pepper Pike, Ohio, 1991-92; exec. v.p. Bailey Controls Co., Wickliffe, Ohio, 1993-94; COO Bailey Control Co., Wickliffe, Ohio, 1994-96; sr. v.p. Keithley Instruments, Solon, Ohio, 1996-2001, exec. v.p., 2001—05, ret., 2005—. Chmn. engring. adv. coun. U. Fla., Gainesville, 1987-90; chmn. hi tech adv. coun. Coll. Boca Raton, Fla., 1987-90. Mem. Pres.'s Coun. Fla. Atlantic U., Boca Raton, 1987-91; trustee Nova U., Ft. Lauderdale, Fla., 1987-94. Recipient Boston U. Chair, 1971, Outstanding Young Engr. of Year award Mass. Soc. Profl. Engrs., 1974. Mem. IEEE (sr. mem.), Am. Electronics Assn. (bd. dirs. 1987, chmn Fla. bd. dirs. 1987-88), Fla. High Tech. and Industry Coun. Home: 35640 Spicebush Ln Solon OH 44139-5063 E-mail: gabe.rosica@att.net.

ROSIN, WALTER L., retired religious organization administrator; Sec. Luth. Ch.-Mo. Synod, St. Louis. Office: The Lutheran Ch-Missouri Synod 1333 S Kirkwood Rd Saint Louis MO 63122-7226

ROSKAM, JAN, aerospace engineer; b. The Hague, The Netherlands, Feb. 22, 1930; arrived in U.S., 1957; s. Kommer Jan and Agatha (Bosman) Roskam; m. Janice Louise Thomas-Barron, Dec. 21, 1994. MA in Aerospace Engring., Tech. U. Delft, 1954; PhD in Aeros. and Astronautics, U. Wash., 1965. Asst. chief designer Aviolanda Aircraft Co., Netherlands, 1954-57; sr. aerodynamics engr. Cessna Aircraft Co., Wichita, Kans., 1957-59; sr. group engr. Boeing Co., Wichita and Seattle, 1959-67; prof. emeritus aerospace engring. U. Kans., Lawrence, 1967—; cons. Design, Analysis and Rsch. Corp., 1991—. Cons. to govt. and industry. Author: Airplane Flight Dynamics and Automatic Flight Controls, 2 vols., 1979; co-author: Airplane Aerodynamics and Performance, 1981, Airplane Design, Part I-VIII, 1986, Roskam's Airplane War Stories, 2002. Served to 1st lt. Royal Netherlands Air Force, 1954—56. Fellow: AIAA, Soc. Automotive Engrs.; mem.: Exptl. Aircraft Assn., U.S. Chess Fedn., Koninklijk Instituut van Ingenieurs, Royal Aero. Soc., Air Force Assn., Aircraft Owners and Pilots Assn., Omicron Delta Kappa, Sigma Gamma Tau, Tau Beta Pi, Sigma Xi. Office: U Kans 2004 Lea Hl Lawrence KS 66045-0001 Personal E-mail: roskam@sunflower.com. Business E-Mail: roskam@darcorp.com.

ROSKAM, PETER JAMES, congressman, former state legislator, lawyer; b. Hinsdale, Ill., Sept. 13, 1961; s. Verlyn Ronald and Martha (Jacobsen) R.; m. Elizabeth Andrea Gracey, June 18, 1988; children: Gracey, James (dec.), Frances, Stephen, Alec. BA, U. Ill., 1983; JD, Ill. Inst. Tech., 1989. Bar: Ill. 1989. Tchr. All Saints H.S., St. Thomas, VI, 1984-85; legis. asst. to Rep. Tom Delay US Congress, Washington, 1985-86, legal asst. to Rep. Henry Hyde, 1986-87; exec. dir. Ednl. Assistance Ltd., Glen Ellyn, Ill., 1987-93; ptnr. Salvi & Roskam, Wheaton, Ill., 1994—2006; mem. Ill. Gen. Assembly from Dist. 40, Springfield, 1993—99, Ill. State Senate from Dist. 20, 2000—06, US Congress from 6th Ill. dist., 2007—, mem. fin. svcs. com. Legis. chmn. Ill. State Crime Commn. Named Hero of the Taxpayer, Americans for Tax Reform, 2005. Republican. Mem. Evangelical Covenant Ch. Presbyterian. Office: 150 S Bloomingdale Rd Bloomingdale IL 60108 also: 507 House Office Bldg Washington DC 20515

ROSKENS, RONALD WILLIAM, management consultant, retired academic administrator; b. Spencer, Iowa, Dec. 11, 1932; s. William E. and Delores A.L. (Beving) R.; m. Lois Grace Lister, Aug. 22, 1954; children: Elizabeth, Barbara, Brenda, William. BA, U. No. Iowa, 1953, MA, 1955, LHD (hon.), 1985; PhD, U. Iowa, 1958; LLD (hon.), Creighton U., 1978, Huston-Tillotson Coll., 1981, Midland Luth. Coll., 1984, Hastings Coll., 1981; LittD (hon.), Nebr. Wesleyan U., 1981; PhD (hon.), Ataturk U., Turkey, 1987; DSc (hon.), Jayewardenepura U., Sri Lanka, 1991; LHD (hon.), U. Akron, 1987, Am. Coll. Greece, Athens, 1994, Kent State U., 2005. Lic. min. United Ch. of Christ (Congl. and E&R). Tchr. Minburn (Iowa) High Sch., 1954, Woodward (Iowa) State Hosp., summer 1954; asst. counselor to men State U. Iowa, 1956-59; dean of men, asst. prof. spl. edn. Kent (Ohio) State U., 1959-63, assoc. prof., then prof., 1963-72, asst. to pres., 1963-66, dean for adminstrn., 1968-71, exec. v.p., prof. ednl. adminstrn., 1971-72; chancellor, prof. ednl. adminstrn. U. Nebr., Omaha, 1972-76; pres. U. ebr. System, 1977-89, pres. emeritus, 1989; hon. prof. East China Normal U., Shanghai, 1985; adminstr. USAID, Washington, 1990-92; pres. Action Internat., Inc., Omaha, 1993-96, Global Connections, Inc., Omaha, 1996—. Interim exec. officer Omaha Pub. Libr., 1996-98; mem. Bus.-Higher Edn. Forum, 1979-89, exec. com., 1984-87; mem. govtl. relations com. Am. Council Edn., 1979-83, bd. dirs., 1981-86, vice chair, 1983-84, chair, 1984-85; chmn. com. on financing higher edn. Nat. Assn. State Univs. and Land Grant Colls., 1978-83, vice chmn. com. on financing higher edn., 1983-84, chmn. com. on fed. student fin. assistance, 1981-87; mem. nat. adv. com. on accreditation and instl. eligibility U.S. Dept. Edn., 1983-86, chmn., bd. dirs., 1986; exec. bd. orth Cen. Assn., 1979-84, chmn. exec. bd., 1982-84, pres., 1989-90; active Environ. Ams. Bd., 1991-92, Strategic Command Consultation Commn., 1993-96, at. Exec. Res. Corps, Fed. Office Emergency Preparedness, 1968-88; chmn. Omaha/Douglas Pub. Bldg. Commn., 1996—. Co-editor: Paradox, Process and Progress, 1968; contbr. articles profl. jours. Mem. Kent City Planning Commn., 1962-66; bd. dirs. United Ch. of Christ Bd. Homeland Ministries, 1968-74, Met. YMCA, Omaha, 1973-77, Mid-Am. council Boy Scouts Am., 1973-77, Midlands United Community Services, 1972-77, NCCJ, 1974-77, Omaha Rotary Club, 1974-77, 93—, Found. Study Presdl. and Congl. Terms, 1977-89, First Plymouth Congl. Ch., 1989-90, Midland Luth. Coll., 1993-2000, Coun. Aid to Edn., 1985-89, ConAgra Foods, Inc., 1993—, Russian Farm Cmty. Project, Capitol Fed. Found., Topeka, Kans., 1999—, The Silverstone Group, 2004—; trustee Huston Tillotson Coll., Austin, Tex., 1968-81, chmn., 1976-78, Joslyn Art Mus., 1973-77, Nebr. Meth. Hosp., 1974-77, 1st Ctrl. Congregational Ch., Brownell-Talbott Sch., 1974-77, Harry S. Truman Inst., 1977-89, Willa Cather Pioneer Meml. and Ednl. Found., 1979-87; pres. Kent Area C. of C., 1966; mem. Met. Commn. Coll. Found., 1993-96; min.-in-residence Countryside Cmty. United Ch. Christ, Omaha, 2003—. Decorated comdr.'s cross Order of Merit (Germany); recipient Disting. Svc. award Kent, Ohio, 1967, Brotherhood award NCCJ, 1977, Americanism citation B'nai B'rith, 1978, Legion of Honor, Order of DeMolay, 1980, gold medal Nat. Interfrat. Coun., 1987, Agr. award Triumph Agr. Expn., Omaha, 1989, Disting. Alumni Achievement award U. Iowa, 2004; named Nat. 4-H Alumnus, 1967, Outstanding Alumnus, U. No. Iowa, 1974, Midlander of Yr., Omaha World Herald, 1977, King Ak-Sar-Ben LXXXVI, 1980; named to DeMolay Hall of Fame, 1993; named Hon. Consul Gen. of Japan, 1999. Mem. AAAS, APA, AAUP, Am. Coll. Pers. Assn., Assn. Urban Univs. (pres. 1976-77), Am. Ednl. Rsch. Assn., Coun. on Fgn. Rels., Chief Execs. Orgn., Young Pres. Orgn., Scottish Rite (bd. dirs. Omaha coun. 1999-), Lincoln C. of C. (bd. dirs. 1989-90), Masons (33 deg.), Rotary (bd. dirs. Omaha 1974-77, pres. Kent, Ohio chpt., 1970-71), Phi Delta Kappa, Phi Eta Sigma, Sigma Tau Gamma (pres. grand coun. 1968-70, Disting. Achievement award 1980, Disting. scholar 1981), Omicron Delta Kappa (nat. pres. 1986-90, Found. pres. 1986-96). Home: 10849 N 58th Plz Omaha NE 68152 Office Phone: 402-399-0928.

ROSKEY, CAROL BOYD, social studies educator, dean, director; b. Columbus, Ohio, Mar. 9, 1946; d. Clarence Eugene and Clara Johanna (Schwartz) B.; m. Joseph Meeks, Aug. 17, 1968 (div. 1981) m. William A. Roskey, Nov. 16, 2003; children: Catherine Rachael, Tiffany Johannah. BS, Ohio State U., Mex., 1968; MS, Ohio State U., 1969, PhD, 1972. Rsch. asst., assoc. Ohio State U., Columbus, 1968-71; internship Columbus Area C. of C., Ohio, 1970; lectr. Ohio State U., Columbus, 1970, 72; asst. prof. U. Mass., Amherst, 1972-74, Cornell U., Ithaca, N.Y., 1974-78, assoc. prof., 1978-80; legis. fellow Senate Com. Banking, 1984; supr. economist, head housing section USDA, Washington, 1980-85; assoc. prof. housing and consumer econs. U. Ga., Athens, 1985-90, prof., 1990-97, head housing and consumer econs., 1992-97; dean Coll. Family and Consumer Scis. Iowa State U., Ames, 1997—2003, dir. Family Policy Ctr., 2003—. Rsch. fellow Nat. Inst. for Consumer Rsch., Oslo, Norway, 1992; cons. Yale U., 1976-77, HUD, Cambridge, Mass., 1978, MIT Ctr. for Real Estate Devel. Ford Found. Project on Housing Policy; del. N.E. Ctr. for Rural Devel. Housing Policy Conf. Reviewer Home Econ. Rsch. Jour., 1987—01, ACCI conf., 1987—; contbr. articles to profl. mags. Mem. panel town of Amherst Landlord Tenant Bd.; bd. dirs. Am. Coun. Consumer Interests; mem. adv. coun. HUD Nat. Mfg. Housing, 1978-80, 91-93; chair Housing Mfg. Inst. Consensus Commn. on Fed. Standards. Recipient Leader award AAFCS, 1996, Disting. Alumni award Ohio State U., 1999; named one of Outstanding Young Women of Am., 1979; Columbus Womens Chpt. Nat. Assn. Real Estate Bds. scholar, Gen. Foods fellow, 1971-72, HEW grantee, 1978, travel grantee NSF bldg. rsch. bd., AID grantee, USDA Challenge grant, 1995-98. Mem. Am. Assn. Housing Educators (pres. 1983-84), Nat. Inst. Bldg. Sci. (bd. sec. 1984, 85, 89-92, bd. dirs. 1981-83, 85, 87-93), Internat. Assn. Housing Sci., Com. on Status on Women in Econs., Nat. Assn. Home Builders (Smart House contract 1989, treas. bd. human sci. 2001-03), Epsilon Sigma Phi, Phi Upsilon Omicron, Gamma Sigma Delta, Phi Beta Delta, Kappa Omicron Nu (v.p. of programs 1995-96), Phi Kappa Phi, others. Office: Iowa State U 2354 Palmer Ames IA 50011-0001 Office Phone: 515-294-3028. Business E-Mail: cbroskey@iastate.edu.

ROSNER, JONATHAN LINCOLN, physicist, researcher; b. NYC, July 23, 1941; s. Albert Aaron and Elsie Augustine (Lincoln) R.; m. Joy Elaine Fox, June 13, 1965; children: Hannah, Benjamin. BA, Swarthmore Coll., 1962; MA, Princeton U., 1963, PhD, 1965. Research asst. prof. U. Wash., Seattle, 1965-67; vis. lectr. Tel Aviv U., Ramat Aviv, Israel, 1967-69; asst. prof. physics U. Minn., Mpls., 1969-71, assoc. prof., 1971-75, prof., 1975-82, U. Chgo., 1982—. Contbr. numerous articles to profl. and scholarly jours. Alfred P. Sloan fellow, 1971-73, Guggenheim fellow, 2002. Fellow Am. Phys. Soc. Democrat. Jewish. Avocations: fishing, hiking, skiing, amateur radio. Office: U Chgo Enrico Fermi Inst 5640 S Ellis Ave Chicago IL 60637-1433 Business E-Mail: rosner@hep.uchicago.edu.

ROSNER, ROBERT, astrophysicist, educator; b. Garmisch-Partenkirchen, Bavaria, Germany, June 26, 1947; came to U.S., 1959; s. Heinz and Faina (Brodsky) R.; m. Marsha Ellen Rich, Sept. 5, 1971; children: Daniela Karin, Nicole Elise. BA, Brandeis U., 1969; PhD, Harvard U., 1976; PhD (hon.), Ill. Inst. Tech., 2006, o. Ill. U. Asst. prof. Harvard U., Cambridge, Mass., 1978-83, assoc. prof., 1983-86; astrophysicist Smithsonian Astrophys. Observatory, Cambridge, 1986-87; prof. U. Chgo., 1987—, William E. Wrather prof., 1998—; chief scientist Argonne Nat. Lab., 2002—05, dir., 2005—; pres. UChicago/Argonne LLC, 2006—. Trustee Adler Planetarium, Chgo., 1989-98, chmn. dept. astronomy and astrophysics, 1991-97. Contbr. more than 190 articles to profl. jours. Woodrow Wilson fellow, 1969. Fellow Am. Phys. Soc., Am. Acad. Arts and Scis. (elected); mem. Am. Astron. Soc., Soc. Indsl. and Applied Math., Am. Geophys. Union, orwegian Acad. Sci. and Letters (fgn. mem.). Home: 4950 S Greenwood Ave Chicago IL 60615-2816 Office: U Chicago Astrophysics 5640 S Ellis Ave Chicago IL 60637-1433 Business E-Mail: r-rosner@uchicago.edu.

ROSOWSKI, ROBERT BERNARD, manufacturing executive; b. Detroit, July 23, 1940; s. Bernard and Anna (Maciag) R.; m. Kathleen Patricia Bates, Aug. 26, 1961; children: John, Paul, Mary, Judith. BS, U. Detroit, 1962; MBA, Mich. State U., 1974. CPA Mich. Auditor, staff supr. Coopers and Lybrand, Detroit, 1962-71; fin. analyst Masco Corp., Taylor, Mich., 1971-73, controller, 1973-85, v.p., controller, 1985-96, v.p., controller and treas., 1996—2001, v.p., treas., 2001—. Bd. dirs. Detroit Cath. Ctrl. HS, 1999—, Detroit Cath. Ctrl. Alumni Assn., pres. 1999-2002; chmn. Oakwood Hosp. Found., 1990—; trustee Oakwood Healthcare System, 1997—. Mem. Am. Inst. CPA's, Mich. Assn. CPA's, Fin. Execs. Inst. Avocations: golf, fishing, boating, photography. Office: Masco Corp 21001 Van Born Rd Taylor MI 48180-1300 Office Phone: 313-792-6258. Business E-Mail: robert_rosowski@mascohq.com.

ROSS, CARSON, state legislator; b. Warren, Ark., Dec. 15, 1946; m. Eloise E. Ross; children: Shelely, Carla, Diane. BS, BA, Rockhurst Coll., 1977. Mem. Mo. State Ho. of Reps. Dist. 55, 1988—, former minority whip, former mem. various coms. With Corp. Diversity, Hallmark Cards. Recipient Black Achievement in Industry award SCLC, 1985, Spirit of Enterprise award Chamber, 1991. Home: 3305 SW Park Ln Blue Springs MO 64015-7146 Office: Mo Ho of Reps State Capitol Jefferson City MO 65101

ROSS, DENNIS E., retired automotive executive, lawyer; b. 1951; B, JD, U. Mich. Tax legis. counsel, dep. asst. sec. Office Tax Policy U.S. Treasury Dept., 1986—89; tax ptnr. Davis Polk and Wardwell, NY, 1989—95; chief tax officer Ford Motor Co., Dearborn, Mich., 1995—2000, v.p., gen. counsel, 2000—05, ret., 2005.

ROSS, DONALD, JR., language educator, academic administrator; b. NYC, Oct. 18, 1941; s. Donald and Lea (Meyer) R.; m. Sylvia Berger (div.); 1 child, Jessica; m. 2d, Diane Redfern, Aug. 27, 1971; children— Owen, Gillian BA, Lehigh U., 1963, MA, 1964; PhD, U. Mich., 1967. Asst. prof. English U. Pa., Phila., 1967—70; prof. writing, studies and English U. Minn., Mpls., 1970—, dir. composition program, 1982—86, 2002—03, dir. Univ. Coll., 1984—89. Author: American History and Culture from the Explorers to Cable TV, 2000; co-author: Word Processor and Writing Process, 1984, Revising Mythologies: The Composition of Thoreau's Major Works, 1988; co-editor, contbr.: American Travel Writers, 1776-1865, 1997, American Travel Writers, 1850-1915, 1998; contbr. articles to profl. jours. Grantee Am. Coun. Learned Socs., 1976, 90, NSF, 1974, Fund for Improvement of Postsecondary Edn., 1982-85; recipient Disting. Teaching award U. Minn., 1992. Mem. MLA, Assn. for Computers and Humanities (exec. sec. 1978-88), Internat. Soc. for Travel Writing (exec. sec. 2001—). Office: U Minn Dept English 207 Lind Hall 207 Church St SE Minneapolis MN 55455-0152 Business E-Mail: rossj001@umn.edu.

ROSS, DONALD ROE, federal judge; b. Orleans, Nebr., June 8, 1922; s. Roe M. and Leila H. (Reed) Ross; m. Janice S. Cook, Aug. 29, 1943; children: Susan Jane, Sharon Kay, Rebecca Lynn, Joan Christine, Donald Dean. JD, U. Nebr., 1948, LLD (hon.), 1990. Bar: Nebr. 1948. Practice law, Lexington, Nebr., 1948—53; mayor City of Lexington, 1953; ptnr. Swarr, May, Royce, Smith, Andersen & Ross, 1956—70; U.S. atty. Dist. Nebr. US Dept. Justice, 1953—56; gen. counsel Rep. Nat. Com., 1956—58; mem. Rep. Exec. Com. for Nebr., 1952—53; com. mem. Rep. Nat. Com., 1958—70, vice-chmn., 1965—70; judge US Ct. Appeals (8th cir.), 1970—87, sr. judge, 1987—. Office: 5815 N 148th Plaza Omaha NE 68116 Office Phone: 402-493-2129.

ROSS, EDWARD, cardiologist; b. Fairfield, Ala., Oct. 10, 1937; s. Horace and Carrie Lee (Griggs) R.; m. Catherine I. Webster, Jan. 19, 1974; children: Edward, Ronald, Cheryl, Anthony. BS, Clark Coll., 1959; MD, Ind. U., 1963. Diplomate Am. Bd. Internal Medicine; cert. specialist in clin. hypertension Am. Soc. Hypertension. Intern Marion County Gen. Hosp., Indpls., 1963; resident in internal medicine Ind. U., 1964-66, 68, cardiology rsch. fellow, 1968-70, clin. asst. prof. medicine, 1970; cardiologist Capitol Med. Assn., Indpls., 1970-74; pvt. practice medicine, specializing in cardiology Indpls., 1974—. Staff cardiologist Winona Meml. Hosp., Indpls., chief cardiovascular disease, 2000-04, med. dir. cardiovascular svcs., 2000—, med. dir. cardiac cath lab, 2000—, chief interventional cardiology, 2000-04; staff Meth. Hosp., Indpls., chmn. cardiovasc. sect., 1989-96; chmn. cardiovasc. sect., dir. cardiovasc. ctr. Meth. Hosp., 1990-92; bd. dirs. Meth. Hosp. Heart-Lung Ctr., med. dir. cardiovasc. svcs., 1991-98; med. dir. cardiovascular svcs. Methodist Hosp., Indpls., Ind., 2000—, cardiac catheterization lab., 2000—, cardiovascular programs, Clarian Health Indpls., 2000—, cardiovascular svcs., Cardicac Cath. Lab., cardiovascular programs, Clarian Health Ptnrs., 2000-. Assoc. editor Angiology, Jour. Vascular Disease; sr. editor Jour. Vascular Medicine, 1983—. Mem. Ctrl. Ind. Health Planning Coun., 1972-73; bd. dirs. Ind. chpt. Am. Heart Assn., 1973-74, multiphasic screening East Side Clinic, Flanner Ho. of Indpls., 1968-71; med. dir. Nat. Ctr. for Health Svc. R&D, HEW, 1970; consumer rep. radiologic device panel health FDA, 1988-92; dir. hypertensive screening State of Ind., 1974; J.B. Johnson Cardiovasc. lectr. Nat. Med. Assn., 1991. Capt. MC, USAF, 1966-68. Recipient Lifetime Achievement award, Ctr. Leadership Devel., 2003, Leadership award, Indpls. Police Dept., 2005; scholar, Nat. Found. Health, 1955, Gorges Found., 1956; Woodrow Wilson fellow, 1959. Fellow Royal Soc. Promotion of Health (Eng.), Am. Coll. Angiology (v.p. fgn. affairs, sec. 1993—), Internat. Coll. Angiology, Am. Soc. of Angiology, Am. Coll. Cardiology, Assn. Black Cardiologists (mem. bd. dirs. 1990-94); mem. NAACP, AMA, Am. Soc. Contemporary Medicine and Surgery, Nat. Med. Assn. (coun. sci. assembly 1985-89), Ind. Med. Soc., Marion County Med. Soc., Am. Coll. Physicians, Am. Heart Assn., Ind. Soc. Internal Medicine (pres. 1987-89), Ind. State Med. Assn. (chmn. internal medicine sect. 1987-89), Ind. Med. Soc., Aesculapean Med. Soc., Hoosier State Med. Assn. (pres. 1980-84, 90-95), Urban League, Alpha Omega Alpha, Alpha Kappa Mu, Beta Kappa Chi, Omega Psi Phi. Methodist. Office: 1801 N Senate Blvd #310 Indianapolis IN 46202 Home Phone: 317-966-4848; Office Phone: 317-962-2500. Business E-Mail: eross@clarian.org.

ROSS, FRANK HOWARD, III, management consultant; b. Charlotte, NC, Aug. 28, 1946; s. Frank Howard Jr. (dec.) and Alma (Richardson) R. (dec.); m. Beverly Hazel Ross, June 30, 1973 (dec.); children: Martha McCausland, Frank Howard IV; m. Barbara Rydz-Roth, July 9, 2005; children: Ingrid Rydz, Veronica Anne, Karl Vincent. BS in Engring., NC State U., Raleigh, 1968. Cons. Fails & Assocs., Inc., Raleigh, NC, 1968-73; ptnr. Ross-Payne & Assocs., Inc., Barrington, Ill., 1973—. Bd. dirs. Gilldorn Savs., Chgo., 1982-85, Brickman Industries, Inc., Chgo., 1980-90; CFO WRT, Inc., Chgo., 1993-95; pres., chmn. bd. dirs. Emerald Capital Investments, Inc., Barrington, 1993-97; adviser, spkr. on constrn. and fin.; bd. dirs. Sherman Plumbing, 1975-95. Author: More $ Through $ Management, 1975, MIS and You, 1978, Planning and Budgeting, 1979, Profit by Design, 1981, Pricing for Profit, 1983, Wealthbuilding, 1984, Equipment Cost Analysis, 1988, Survivial in a Tight Economy, 1988, Associated Landscape Contractors of America Operating Cost Survey, 1989, 91, Cash Flow, 1989, Dealing with the Competition of the 90's, 1990, Designing Your Accounting System, 1991, Bidding in a Tight Market, 1992, Industry's Wage and Benefit Study, 1992, Financing Your Business, 1993, Pricing, 1994, 2d edit., 1997, How Low Can You Go?, 1995, Valuing Your Business, 1998, Posturing for Growth and Prosperity, 1999, My Executive Dashboard, 2004, If You Can't Track It, You Can't Control It!, 2007. Active Presbyn. Ch. Barrington. Named to Anla Contractors Hall of Fame, 2007. Mem. Inst. Mgmt. Cons., Barrington Hills Country Club, Haig Point Country Club, Sigma Alpha Epsilon. Home and Office: Ross Payne Assocs Inc 190 Kimberly Rd Barrington IL 60010-2017 Office Phone: 847-381-8939.

ROSS, LORI, radio personality; b. Delta, Ohio, May 14; Radio host Sta. WMBI-AM, Chgo. Avocations: photography, being outside, travel. Office: WMBI 820 LaSalle Blvd Chicago IL 60610

ROSS, LORI A., lawyer; b. Cin., Apr. 14, 1975; BA in Psychology, Miami U., 1997, BA in Sociology, 1997; JD, U. Cin., 2000. Bar: Ohio 2000, US Dist. Ct. Southern Dist. Ohio 2000, Ky. 2001. Assoc. Strauss & Troy, Cin. Named one of Ohio's Rising Stars, Super Lawyers, 2006. Mem.: Ohio State Bar Assn., Ky. Bar Assn., Cin. Bar Assn., Order of Coif, Phi Beta Kappa, Phi Kappa Phi. Office: Strauss & Troy Federal Reserve Bldg 150 E Fourth St Cincinnati OH 45202-4018 Office Phone: 513-621-2120. Office Fax: 513-241-8259.

ROSS, MONTE, electrical engineer, researcher; b. Chgo., May 26, 1932; s. Jacob Henry and Mildred Amelia (Feller) R.; m. Harriet Jean Katz, Feb. 10, 1957; children— Karyn, Dianne, Ethan BS in Elec. Engring., U. Ill., 1953; MS, Northwestern U., 1962. Devel. engr. Chance Vought, Dallas, 1953-54; sr. electronics engr. Motorola, Chgo., 1955-56, project engr., 1957-59, assoc. dir. rsch., 1960-63; dir. rsch. Hallicrafters Co., Chgo., 1964-65; mgr. laser tech. McDonnell Douglas Astronautics Co., St. Louis, 1966-70, dir. laser comms.; program mgr. Laser Space Comms., 1971-87; pres. Ultradata Sys., Inc. (formerly Laser Data Tech.), St. Louis, 1987—2001, CEO, 2001—07; cons., 2007—. Mem. alumni bd. dept. elec. and computer engring. U. Ill., 1985-90; guest lectr. various univs.; cons. NSF. Author: Laser Receivers, 1966; tech. editor Laser Applications Series, vol. 1, 1971, vol. 2, 1974, vol. 3, 1977, vol. 4, 1980; patentee in field. Chmn. Laser Mus. and Space Signal Obs., 1997—. Recipient St. Louis High Tech. Entrepreneur of Yr. award, 1995; McDonnell Douglas Corp. fellow, 1985. Fellow IEEE; mem. Internat. Laser Comms. Soc. (pres. 1988-89), Sigma Xi. Home: 19 Beaver Dr Saint Louis MO 63141-7901 Business E-Mail: mross@ultradatasystems.com.

ROSS, NANCY G., lawyer; b. 1956; BA, U. Colo., 1978; JD, Loyola U., Chgo., 1985. Bar: Ill., US Dist. Ct. (no. dist.) Ill., US Dist. Ct. (ea. dist.) Wis., US Dist. Ct. (ea. dist.) Mich., US Ct. Appeals (1st, 2nd, 5th. 6th, 7th, 8th, 9th, 10th cirs.), US Supreme Ct. Ptnr., Trial Dept. McDermott Will & Emery, Chgo. Editor: Women's Law Reporter. Fellow: Am. Coll. Employee Benefits Counsel. Office: McDermott Will & Emery 227 West Monroe Chicago IL 60606 Office Phone: 312-984-7743. Office Fax: 312-984-7700. E-mail: nross@mwe.com.

ROSS, RICHARD FRANCIS, veterinarian, microbiologist, dean, educator; b. Washington, Iowa, Apr. 30, 1935; s. Milton Edward and Olive Marie (Berggren) R.; m. Karen Mae Paulsen, Sept. 1, 1957; children: Scott, Susan D.V.M., Iowa State U., 1959, MS, 1961, PhD, 1965. Rsch. assoc. Iowa State U., Ames, 1959—61, asst. prof., 1962—65, assoc. prof., 1966—72, prof., 1972—, assoc. dir., assoc. dean Coll. Vet. Medicine, 1990—92, interim dean, 1992—93, dean Coll. Vet. Medicine, 1993—2000, interim dean, dean Coll. Agr., dir. Agrl. Expt. Sta., 2000—02, prof. emeritus, 2004; oper. mgr. Vet. Lab. Inc., Remsen, Iowa, 1961—62; postdoctoral fellow NIAID, Hamilton, Mont., 1965—66. Sr. U.S. scientist Alexander von Humboldt Found., Bonn, Fed. Republic Germany, 1975-76; chmn. Internat. Rsch. Program on Comparative Mycoplasmology, 1982-86; pres. Iowa State U. Rsch. Found., Ames, 1984-86; Howard Dunne meml. lectr. Am. Assn. Swine Practitioners, 1984; mem. adv. bd. Sec. Agr., 1996-99; mem. strategic planning task force USDA, 1997-99, mem. safeguarding task force, 2001-02, mem. implementation team, 2003-04; bd. govs. ISU Found., 2004—. Contbr. numerous articles to profl. publs., 1963— Vol. Union Sta. Homeless Shelter, Pasadena, Calif., 2007—. Named Disting. Prof., Iowa

State U., 1982, Hon. Master Pork Producer, Iowa Pork Producers Assn., 1985; recipient faculty citation Iowa State U. Alumni Assn., 1984, Beecham award for rsch. excellence, 1985, Howard Dunne Meml. award Am. Assn. Swine Practitioners, 1988, Am. Feed Mfg. award for rsch., 1995, Sec. of Agr. award for personal and profl. accomplishment, 1996, Gamma Sigma Delta Merit award for disting. achievement in agr. 2002. Mem. Am. Coll. Vet. Microbiologists (diplomate, vice chmn. 1974-75, sec.-treas. 1977-83), Am. Soc. Microbiology (chmn. div. 1985-86), Internat. Orgn. Mycoplasmology (chair 1990-92, Bd. Dirs. award 2002), AVMA, AAAS, Osborn Research Club, Conf. Rsch. Workers in Animal Diseases (coun. mem., pres. 1992, Dedicatee, 2007), Assn. Am. Vet. Med. Colls. (pres. 1997-98), Rotary Club. Republican. Lutheran. Avocations: fishing, gardening, walking, reading, history. Home: 4022 Stone Brooke Rd Ames IA 50010-2900 Personal E-mail: rfross@iastate.edu.

ROSS, RICHARD LEE, lawyer; b. Columbus, Ohio, Sept. 23, 1951; s. Richard Earl and Dorothy Mae (Fitch) R.; m. Diana E. Gifford, Aug. 17, 1974; children: Rebecca, Jeremiah. B.S., Centre Coll., 1973; J.D., Capital U., 1976. Bar: Ohio, U.S. Tax Ct., U.S. Supreme Ct., U.S. Dist. Ct. (so. dist.) Ohio. Law librarian Morgan County, McConnelsville, Ohio, 1977-80; solicitor Stockport, Ohio, 1977-80; pros. atty. Morgan County, 1981—. Chmn. various Rep. coms. Mem. Ohio Pros. Attys. Assn., Morgan County Bar Assn., Nat. Dist. Attys. Assn., Nat. Sch. Attys. Assn., Rotary, Kiwanis (sec. 1977-79). Mem. Ch. of Christ. Avocations: golf, reading. Home: 1800 N Pleasant Valley Rd NW Malta OH 43758-9646 Office: 109 E Main St Mc Connelsville OH 43756-1125

ROSS, ROBERT EVAN, bank executive; b. Alliance, Ohio, Sept. 22, 1947; s. James Jacob Ross and Eva Mae (Forsha) Bodo; m. Susan Margaret Burd, June 20, 1970; children: Margaret Mae, James William. BBA, Kent State U., 1970; MBA, U. Chgo., 1977. Advisor to fraternities, dean of men's office Kent (Ohio) State U., 1970-71; trainee, supr. of trainees Northern Trust Co., Chgo., 1971-73, jr. analyst, 1973-74, trust rep., 1974-77, trust officer, 1977-81, v.p., div. head for personal fin. planning, 1981-85; portfolio mgr., investment rep. Morgan Stanley, Chgo., 1985-89; pres. Northern Trust Bank in Winnetka, Ill., 1989-92; exec. v.p. Northern Trust Bank/Lake Forest, Ill., 1992-95, vice chmn., 1995-97, pres., CEO, 1997—2001; pres., CEO Northern Trust Bank-Ohio, 2001—04; sr. v.p. wealth strategies group No. Trust Co., 2004—06; mng. dir. pvt. banking Harris Bank, Chgo., 2006—. Bd. dirs. No. Trust Bank, Lake Forest, O'Hare, Ill., DuPage, Ill. Bd. dirs. The Camerata Singers of Lake Forest, Lake Forest Symphony, 1992-2001, Ragdale Found., 1999-2000, Cleve. Zool. Soc., 2003; bd. govs. Ill. St. Andrew Soc., 1998-2001; suburban chair United Way North Region, 1993—; mem. centennial commn. on identity, values and comm. Kent State U., 1998; trustee DePaul U., Chgo., Barat Coll. Edn. Found., Kent State U. Found., 2003. Avocations: sports, reading, stock market, painting. Office: No Trust Bank Lake Forest Deerpath And Bank Ln Lake Forest IL 60045

ROSSI, ANTHONY GERALD, lawyer; b. Warren, Ohio, July 20, 1935; s. Anthony Gerald and Lena (Guarnieri) R.; m. Marilyn J. Fuller, June 22, 1957; children: Diana L., Maribeth, Anthony Gerald III. BS, John Carroll U., 1957; JD, Cath. U. Am., 1961. Bar: Ohio 1961. Ptnr. Guarnieri & Secrest, Warren, 1961—; former acting judge Warren Municipal Ct. Mem. Mahoning-Shenango Estate Planning Coun., 1968—, past sec.; past pres. Warren Olympic Club; past bd. govs. Cath. U. Am. Law Sch. Coun.; past trustee Trumbull Art Guild, Warren Civic Music Assn. Capt. Transp. Corps, AUS, 1957-65. Mem. ABA, Ohio Bar Assn., Trumbull County Bar Assn. (exec. com. 1975—, pres. 1976-77), Am. Arbitration Assn., Ohio State Bar Found., Ohio Motorist Assn. (corp. mem., trustee 1980-86, 92-98), Wolf's Club, KC, Elks, Ohio Acad. of Trial Lawyers. Home: 2500 Hidden Lakes Dr NE Warren OH 44484-4159 Office: 151 E Market St Warren OH 44481-1102 Home Phone: 330-856-3774; Office Phone: 330-393-1584. E-mail: ganslaw@netdotcom.com.

ROSSITER, ROBERT E., manufacturing executive; b. Detroit, 1946; BBA, Northwood U. With Lear Siegler Inc., 1971-87, pres. seating divsn.; pres. Lear Corp., 1984—2002, COO, 1988—97, 1998—2000, bd. dirs. Southfield, Mich., 1988—, COO internat. ops., 1997—98, CEO Southfield, Mich., 2000—, chmn., 2003—. Bd. dirs. Detroit Renaissance, Focus: HOPE, Detroit. Office: Lear Seating Corp 21557 Telegraph Rd Southfield MI 48034

ROSSMANN, JACK EUGENE, psychologist, educator; b. Walnut, Iowa, Dec. 4, 1936; s. Wilbert C. Rossmann and Claire L. (Mickel) Walter; m. Marilyn Martin, June 14, 1958; children: Ann, Charles, Sarah. BS, Iowa State U., 1958, MS, 1960; PhD, U. Minn., 1963; MA (hon.), Macalester Coll., St. Paul, 2007. Lic. psychologist Minn., 2007. Asst. prof. Macalester Coll., St. Paul, 1964-68, assoc. prof., 1968-73, prof., 1973—2007, prof. emeritus, 2007—, v.p. acad. affairs, 1978-86, chair dept. psychology, 1990-2000. Cons.-evaluator North Ctrl. Assn., 1975—; cons. Pers. Decisions Internat., Mpls., 1989—2000, Bush Found., 1993—2006; sr. advisor Spencer Found., 2004—. Author: (with others) Open Admissions at CUNY, 1975; contbr. articles to profl. jours. Bd. dirs. Twin City Inst. for Talented Youth, St. Paul, 1978-91; trustee United Theol. Sem., New Brighton, Minn., 1984-96; pres. Minn. Intercollegiate Athletic Conf., 2003-06. 2d lt. US Army, 1959. Recipient Thomas Jefferson award, Macalester Coll., 1990, Outstanding Svc. award, Minn. Intercollegiate Athletic Conf., 2007; Adminstrv. fellow, Am. Coun. on Edn., 1977—78. Mem.: AAUP (pres. Minn. conf. 1993—95, Robert Sloan award, Minn. Conf. 2003), APA, Minn. Psychol. Assn. (treas. 2001, pres. 2003), Assn. Instl. Rsch., Am. Psychol. Soc., Phi Kappa Phi, Phi Beta Kappa (hon.). Home: 99 Cambridge St Saint Paul MN 55105-1947 Office: Macalester Coll 1600 Grand Ave Saint Paul MN 55105-1801 Home Phone: 651-690-4370; Office Phone: 651-696-6110. Business E-Mail: rossmann@macalester.edu.

ROSSMANN, MICHAEL GEORGE, biochemist, educator; b. Frankfurt, Germany, July 30, 1930; s. Alexander and Nelly (Schwabacher) R.; m. Audrey Pearson, July 24, 1954; children: Martin, Alice, Heather. BSc with honors, Polytechnic, London, 1951, MSc in Physics, 1953; PhD in Chemistry, U. Glasgow, 1956; PhD (hon.), U. Uppsala, Sweden, 1983, U. Strasbourg, France, 1984, Vrije U., Brussels, 1990, U. Glasgow, 1993, U. York, Eng., 1994, U. Quebec, 1998. Fulbright scholar U. Minn., 1956-58; research scientist MRC Lab. Molecular Biology, Cambridge, Eng., 1958-64; assoc. prof. biol. scis. Purdue U., West Lafayette, Ind., 1964-67, prof., 1967-78, Hanley Disting. prof. biol. scis., 1978—, prof. biochemistry, 1975—. Mem. Nat. Sci. Bd., 2000—06. Editor: The Molecular Replacement Method, 1972; contbr. more than 400 articles to profl. jours. Grantee NIH, NSF, HFSP; recipient Fankuchen award Am. Crystallographic Assn., 1986, Horwitz prize Columbia U., 1990, Gregori Aminoff prize Royal Swedish Acad. Sci., 1994, Stein & Moore award Protein Soc., 1994, Ewald prize Internat. Union Crystallography, 1996, Cole award Biophys. Soc., 1998, Elion award Internat. Soc. for Antiviral Rsch., 2000, Ehrlich and Darmstaedter prize Paul Erhlich-Fedn., 2001, Seed for Success Award, 2004, Paul Janssen Prize in Advanced Biotech. and Medicine, Ctr. for Advanced Biotech. and Medicine and Rutgers U., 2004, 3rd NIH Merit award, 2006; edited fellow, Am. Acad. Microbiology, 2007. Mem. Am. Soc. Biol. Chemists, Am. Chem. Soc., Biophys. Soc. (Cole award 1998), Am. Crystallographic Assn. (Fankuchen award 1986), Brit. Biophys. Soc., Inst. Physics., Chem. Soc. (U.K.), AAAS, NAS, Indian Nat. Sci. Acad., Royal Soc., Lafayette Sailing Club. Democrat. Home: 1208 Wiley Dr West Lafayette IN 47906-2434 Office: Purdue U Dept Biol Scis 915 W State St West Lafayette IN 47907-2054 Office Phone: 765-494-4911. Business E-Mail: mr@purdue.edu.

ROSSO, JEAN-PIERRE, electronics executive; b. Aix-les Bains, Savoie, France, July 11, 1940; Diploma in civil engring., Ecole Polytechnique, Lausanne, Switzerland, 1964; MBA, U. Pa., 1967. Mgr. fin. and adminstrn. Honeywell, Paris, 1969—70, dir. African divsn., 1970—71, sales dir., 1971—75; pres., CEO Rossignol Ski, Burlington, Vt., 1975—81; dir. gen. Rossignol SA, Voiron, France, 1980—81; v.p. bus. devel. Honeywell Europe SA, Brussels, 1981—83, pres., 1981—94; v.p., gen. mgr. Honeywell Med. Electronics, NYC, 1983—85; group v.p. Honeywell Info. Systems, Mpls., 1985—87; pres., CEO Case Corp., Racine, Wis., 1994—99, chmn., 1996—99; former chmn., CEO CNH Global, 1999—. Mem. adv. com. Trade Policy and Negotiations, 2002—02; bd. overseers Wharton Sch.; bd. dirs. ADC Telecoms., Inc., Medtronic, Inc. Mem.: Bus. Roundtable. Avocations: golf, skiing. Office: Case Corp 700 State St Racine WI 53404-3392

ROST, WILLIAM JOSEPH, chemist; b. Fargo, ND, Dec. 8, 1926; s. William Melvin and Christine Ruth (Hamerlik) R.; m. Rita Cincoski, Sept. 15, 1951; children— Kathryn, Patricia, Carol. BS, U. Minn., 1948, PhD, 1952. From asst. prof. to prof. pharm. chemistry Sch. Pharmacy U. Kansas City, Mo., 1952-63; prof. pharm. chemistry Sch. Pharmacy U. Mo., Kansas City, 1963—. Co-author: Principles of Medicinal Chemistry, 1974, 3d rev. edit., 1988; contbr. articles profl. jours. Mem. Am. Pharm. Assn., Am. Chem. Soc., Sigma Xi, Kappa Psi, Rho Chi, Phi Lambda Upsilon. Office: U Mo Sch of Pharmacy Kansas City MO 64110 Home: 709 W 100th Ct Kansas City MO 64114

ROSTBERT, JIM, state legislator; b. May 28, 1956; m. Kathy Rostbert; 2 children. AA, Cambridge C.C.; postgrad., Met. State U. Minn. state rep. Dist. 18A, 1994—. Former vet. svc. officer. Address: 26450 Terrace Rd NE Isanti MN 55040-6143 Office: Minn Ho of Reps State Capitol Saint Paul MN 55155-0001

ROSTON, DAVID CHARLES, lawyer; b. Evanston, Ill., Oct. 15, 1943; BA cum laude, Brandeis U., 1964; JD cum laude, Harvard U., 1967. Bar: Ill. 1967. Ptnr. Altheimer & Gray, Chgo. Mem. pres. coun. Brandeis U. Mem. ABA, Ill. State Bar Assn., Chgo. Bar Assn. (chmn. com., on profl. responsibility 1997-98).

ROTH, DANIEL BENJAMIN, lawyer, company executive; b. Youngstown, Ohio, Sept. 17, 1929; s. Benjamin F. and Marion (Benjamin) R.; m. Joann M. Roth; children: William M., Jennifer A., Rochelle. BS in Fin., Miami U., Oxford, Ohio, 1951; JD, Case-Western Res. U., 1956. Bar: Ohio 1956, U.S. Supreme Ct. 1960, D.C. 1983. Chmn. Roth, Blair, Roberts, Strasfeld & Lodge, LPA, Youngstown, 1969—; co-founder, vice chmn. Nat. Data Processing Corp., Cin., 1961-69; chmn., pres., CEO Torent, Inc., Youngstown, 1971—; chmn. McDonald Steel Corp., 1980—; vice chmn. Torent Oil & Gas Co., 1979—2002, Vaughn Indsl. Car & Equipment Co., 1988—2002. Bd. dirs. Gasser Chair Co. Profl. singer: appearances including Steve Allen Show, 1952. Bd. dirs. Youngstown Symphony, Stambaugh Auditorium; bd. dirs. Youngstown Playhouse, v.p., 1991-93; pres. Rodef Sholom Temple, Youngstown, 1982-84. 1st lt. USAF, 1951-53, lt. col. Res., ret. Recipient Mgr. of Yr. award Mahoning Valley Mgmt. Assn., 1989, Man of Yr. award Youngstown YWCA, 1995. Mem. ABA, D.C. Bar Assn., Ohio Bar Assn., Mahoning County Bar Assn., Lawyer-Pilots Bar Assn., Soc. Benchers of Case Western Res. U. Law Sch., Youngstown Club, Pelican Marsh Club (Naples, Fla.), Zeta Beta Tau (nat. v.p. 1964-66), Omicron Delta Kappa, Phi Eta Sigma, Tau Epsilon Rho. Jewish. Office: Roth Blair Roberts Strasfeld & Lodge 600 City Centre One Youngstown OH 44503-1514 Office Phone: 330-744-5211.

ROTH, JAMES R., lawyer; Degree in Bus., Emporia State U.; JD, Washburn U. Ptnr. Woodard, Blaylock, Hernandez, Roth and Day, Wichita, Kans., 1979—. Mem. bd. govs. Washburn U., 1992—, chmn. bd., 1996—97. Office: Woodard Hernandez Roty & Day Emprise Bank Bldg 257 N Broadway Wichita KS 67202

ROTH, LAWRENCE MAX, pathologist, educator; b. McAlester, Okla., June 25, 1936; s. Herman Moe and Blanche (Brown) R.; m. Anna Berit Katarina Sundstrom, Apr. 3, 1965; children: Karen Roth Hart, David Josef. BA, Vanderbilt U., 1957; MD, Harvard U., 1960. Diplomate Am. Bd. Pathology. Rotating intern U. Ill. Research and Ednl. Hosps., Chgo., 1960—61; resident in anat. pathology Washington U. Sch. Medicine, St. Louis, 1961—64; resident in clin. pathology U. Calif. Med. Ctr., San Francisco, 1967—68; asst. prof. pathology Tulane U. Sch. Medicine, New Orleans, 1968—71; assoc. prof. pathology Ind. U. Sch. Medicine, Indpls., 1971—75, dir. divsn. surg. pathology, 1971—2001, prof., 1975—2001, prof. emeritus pathology, 2001—. Series editor: Contemporary Issues in Surgical Pathology; mem. editl. bd. Am. Jour. Surg. Pathology, Human Pathology, Seminars in Diagnostic Pathology, Internat. Jour. Gynecol. Pathology, Endocrine Pathology; contbr. articles to med. jours. Served to capt. US Army, 1965—67. Recipient James Harshman award, Ind. Assn. Pathologists, 1989. Mem. Am. Assn. Investigative Pathologists, U.S. and Can. Acad. Pathology, Am. Soc. Clin. Pathologists, Coll. Am. Pathologists, Internat. Soc. Gynecol. Pathologists, Arthur Purdy Stout Soc. Surg. Pathologists, Assn. Dirs. Anatomic and Surg. Pathology. Home: 7898 Ridge Rd Indianapolis IN 46240-2538 Office: 635 Barnhill Dr Indianapolis IN 46202-5120 Business E-Mail: lroth@iupui.edu.

ROTH, PHILIP R., manufacturing executive; BS in Bus. Adminstrn., U. Mo.; MBA, Washington U. CPA. With Price Waterhouse Co., Valley Industries, Inc.; v.p. fin., CFO Wiegand Indsl. divsn. Emerson Electric Co.; v.p. fin., CFO Gardner Denver, Inc., Quincy, Ill., 1995—. Office: 1800 Gardner Expy Quincy IL 62305-9364

ROTH, ROBERT EARL, ecologist, educator; b. Wauseon, Ohio, Mar. 30, 1937; s. Earl Jonas and Florence Lena (Mahler) R.; m. Carol Sue Yackee, Aug. 8, 1959; children; Robin Earl, Bruce Robert. BS, Ohio State U., 1959, BS in Secondary Sci. Edn., 1960, MS in Conservation Edn., 1960; PhD in Environ. Edn., U. Wis., 1969. Supr. conservation edn. Ethical Culture Schs., NYC, 1961-63; naturalist, sci. tchr. Lakeside Sch., Spring Valley, NY, 1963-65; instr. No. Ill. U., Oregon, 1965-67; asst. prof. Ohio State U., Columbus, 1969-73, assoc. prof., 1973-78, prof. environ. edn. and sci. edn., 1978-2001, prof. emeritus, 2001—, chmn. divsn., 1973-84, coord. office internat. affairs, 1985-89, asst. dir., sch. sec. Sch. Natural Resources, 1989-93, acting dir. Sch. Natural Resources, 1993-94, assoc. dir., 1994-2001, state extension specialist Environ. Edn., 1993-2001. Rsch. & devel. assoc. Mosely & Assocs., Columbus, 1986-89; project cons. NARMA project, U.S. Agy. internat. Devel., Santo Domingo, Dominican Rep., 1982-87; cons. Richard Trott & Assocs., 1988-90, Kinzelman & Kline, 1990-2001, Midwest consortium Internat. Activity, 1995; evaluator Montclair State U., N.J. Sch. Conservation, 1999; workshop leader Carribean Conservation Assn., Bridgetown, Barbados, 1981-83; vis. scholar Indonesian Second U. Devel. project, Jakarta, 1988; AID lectr., Thesolonika, Greece, 1992; bd. supr. Franklin Soil & Water Conservation Dist., 2003-05. Exec. editor Jour. Environ. Edn., 1974-91 (Pub.'s prize 1970); contbr. articles to profl. jours. Committeeman Boy Scouts Am., 1983-86; adv. coun. McKeever Environ. Learning Ctr., Pa., 1977-83. Named vis. scholar, Uganda Makerere U., 1989, Pacific Cultural Found., Taipei, Taiwan, 1989, 1999, 2001; recipient Pomerene Tchg. Enhancement award, Ohio State U., 1986, 1995, Environ. Edn. award, Ohio Alliance for the Enrivon., 1992, Outstanding Advising award, Coll. Food Agrl. and Environ. Scis., 1996. Mem.: Sch. Nat. Resource Alumni Assn. (inducted hon. 100), Nat. Sci. Tchrs. Assn. (life), N.Am. Assn. Environ. Edn. (life; bd. dirs. 1972—82, pres. 1977—78, Walt Jeske award 1988, Outstanding Contbns. to Rsch. award 2000). Avocations: swimming, canoeing, camping, fishing, travel. Home: 570 Morning St Columbus OH 43085-3775 E-mail: roth.3@osu.edu.

ROTH, THOMAS, marketing executive; Grad., Western Mich. U. With Tarkenton and Co., Atlanta; founder HR Skills divsn. Nat. Edn. Tng. Group, 1988-92; dir. product devel. Wilson Learning Corp., Eden Prairie, Minn., 1981-88, v.p. product mgmt. in global R & D, 1992-94, v.p. product mgmt. and tng. group, 1994-99, v.p. global cons., 1999—. Cons. IBM, AT&T, Ford Motor Co., Pfizer, E.I. DuPont, Gen. Electric, Oracle, Dow Chem., Lucent, Tex. Instruments, Colgate-Palmolive, Honeywell, others; spkr. in field. Co-author: Creating the High Performance Team, 1987. Office: Wilson Learning Corp Warehouse 8000 W 78th St #175 Minneapolis MN 55439-2536

ROTHAL, MAX, city manager, lawyer; b. Norwalk, Ohio, Jan. 2, 1932; Student, Kent State U., 1951-53; LLB, U. Akron, 1957. Bar: Ohio, 1958, U.S. Dist. Ct. Ohio. Chief prosecutor Law Dept. City of Akron, Ohio, 1959-60, dir. Ohio, 1987—. Mem. ABA, Ohio Defense Inst. Office: City of Akron Law Dept 161 S High St Akron OH 44308-1602 E-mail: rothama@ci.akron.oh.us.

ROTHENBERG, ELLIOT CALVIN, lawyer, writer; b. Mpls., Nov. 12, 1939; s. Sam S. and Claire Sylvia (Feller) R.; m. Sally Smalying; children: Sarah, Rebecca, Sam. BA summa cum laude, U. Minn., 1961; JD, Harvard U., Cambridge, 1964. Bar: Minn. 1966, U.S. Dist. Ct. Minn. 1966, D.C. 1968, U.S. Supreme Ct. 1972, N.Y. 1974, U.S. Ct. Appeals (2d cir.) 1974, U.S. Ct. Appeals (8th cir.) 1975. Assoc. project dir. Brookings Inst., Washington, 1966-67; fgn. svc. officer, legal advisor U.S. Dept. State, Washington, 1968-73; Am. Embassy, Saigon; U.S. Mission to the UN; nat. law dir. Anti-Defamation League, NYC, 1973-74; legal dir. Minn. Pub. Interest Rsch. Group, Mpls., 1974-77; pvt. practice law Mpls., 1977—. Adj. prof. William Mitchell Coll. Law, St. Paul, 1983—; faculty mem. several nat. comm. law and First Amendment seminars. Author: (with Zelman Cowen) Sir John Latham and Other Papers, 1965, The Taming of the Press: Cohen v. Cowles Media Co., 1999, The Taming of the Press, 1999; co-author: Defending the First, 2005, Whose First Amendment?, 2005; contbr. articles to profl. and scholarly jours. and books, newspapers, popular mags. State bd. dirs. YMCA Youth in Govt. Program, 1981-84; v.p. Twin Cities chpt. Am. Jewish Com., 1980-84; mem. Minn. Ho. of Reps., 1978-82, asst. floor leader (whip), 1981-82; pres., dir. North Star Legal Found., 1983—; legal affairs editor Pub. Rsch. Syndicated, 1986—; briefs and oral arguments published in full Landmark Briefs and Arguments of the Supreme Ct. of the U.S., Vol. 200, 1992; mem. citizens adv. com. Voyageurs Nat. Pk., 1979-81. Recipient Legis. Evaluation Assembly Legis. Excellence award, 1980, Vietnam Civilian Svc. medal U.S. Dept. State, 1970, North Star award U. Minn., 1961; Fulbright fellow, 1964-65. Mem. ABA, Minn. Bar Assn., Harvard Law Sch. Assn., Am. Legion, Mensa, Phi Beta Kappa. Jewish. Office: 2751 Hennepin Ave S Ste 231 Minneapolis MN 55408-2614 Personal E-mail: ecrothenberg@gmail.com.

ROTHENBERGER, DAVID ALBERT, surgeon; b. Sioux Falls, SD, 1947; MD, Tufts U., 1973. Cert. colon and rectal surgery. Intern St. Paul-Ramsey Med. Ctr., 1973-74, resident gen. surgery, 1974-78; fellow colon rectal surgery U. Minn., Mpls., 1978-79; mem. staff Fairview Univ. Med. Ctr., Mpls.; cln. prof. surgery U. Minn., Mpls., chief divsn. colon and rectal surgery, divsn. surg. oncology; dir. U. Minn. Cancer Ctr., Mpls.; former pres. Am. Bd. Colon & Rectal Surgery, Taylor, Mich., mem. advisory council. Fellow ACS, Am. Soc. Colon and Rectal Surgeons (exec. coun., past pres. 1997—), Am. Surg. Assn., Soc. for Surgery of the Alimentary Tract, Western Surg. Assn. also: Mayo Mail Code 806 420 Delaware St SE Minneapolis MN 55455-0374

ROTHERHAM, THOMAS G., diversified financial services company executive; BA, U. Iowa. CPA. From mem. staff to exec. ptnr. McGladrey & Pullen LLP, Davenport, Iowa, 1971-88, exec. ptnr., 1988—97, COO, 1997—2000; pres., CEO RSM McGladrey Inc., 2000—03. Bd. dirs. Peerless Systems Corp., 2004—. Mem. AICPA (SEC regulations com., SEC practice section exec. com.), Minn. Soc. CPAs. Mailing: Peerless Systems Corp Bd Directors 2381 Rosecrans Ave El Segundo CA 90245

ROTHERT, MARILYN L., dean, nursing educator; b. June 4, 1939; married; 3 children. BSN cum laude, Ohio State U., 1961; MA in Ednl. Psychol., Mich. State U., 1979, PhD in Ednl. Psychol., 1980. RN, Mich. Staff nurse Univ. Hosp., Columbus, Ohio, 1961; instr. sch. nursing Hurley Hosp., Flint, Mich., 1961-66; asst. instr. sch. nursing Mich. State U., East Lansing, 1967-77, grad. asst. dept. community health sci., 1977-80, asst. prof. Coll. Human Medicine, 1980-82, asst. prof., dir. lifelong edn. Coll. Nursing, 1982-84, asst. prof. Coll. Human Medicine, 1982-84, assoc. prof., dir. lifelong edn. Coll. Nursing, 1984-88, assoc. prof. Coll. Human Medicine, 1984-86, prof., dir. lifelong edn. Coll. Nursing, 1988-92, prof., assoc. dean outreach and profl. devel., 1992-96, prof., dean Coll. Nursing, 1996—. Cons. No. Ill. U., Ohio State U., Mich. State Dept. Natural Resources, Can. Nurses Assn., Mich. Judicial Inst., Med. Coll. Va., U. Wash., Kirtland Coll., Anderson Coll. Contbr. articles to profl. jours. Co-chmn. Capitol Health Event, 1987-88; mem. worksite health subcom. Mich. Dept. Pub. Health; mem. State 4-H Health Com. Coop. Extension Svc., 1972-75, 82—; mem. med. adv. com. Mich. Civil Svc. Health Screening Unit, 1984. Mem. ANA (mem. coun. continuing edn., nurse researchers), Mich. Nurses Assn. (chmn. continuing edn. adv. com. 1989), Soc. for Med. Decision Making, The Brunswik Soc., Soc. for Judgment and Decision Making, Soc. for Rsch. in Nursing Edn., Midwest Nursing Rsch. Soc., Am. Pub. Health Assn., Nat. Ctr. for Health Edn., Nat. League for Nursing, Mich. State U. Faculty/Profl. Women's Assn. (bd. dirs. 1989—), Capitol Area Dist. Nurses Assn. (mem. nom. com. 1984-86, continuing edn. com. 1984), Phi Kappa Phi. Office: Mich State U Coll Nursing A-230 Life Sci Bldg East Lansing MI 48824

ROTHMAN, JAY O., lawyer; BA summa cum laude, Marquette U., 1982; JD cum laude, Harvard U. Law Sch., 1985. Bar: Wis. 1985, cert.: U.S. Dist. Ct. Ea. & We. Dist. Wis. 1985, U.S. Dist. Ct., Ctrl. Dist. Ill. 1985, U.S. Ct. Appeals, seventh cir. 1986, bar: Minn. 1988. Law clk. to Hon. Harlington Wood Fr. U.S. Ct. Appeals, seventh cir., 1985—86; ptnr. Foley & Lardner LLP, Milw., 1986—, mem. mgmt. com., chmn. transactional & securities practice group. Mem.: ABA, State Bar Wis., Milw. Bar Assn. Office: Foley & Lardner LLP 777 E Wisconsin Ave Milwaukee WI 53202-5306 Office Phone: 414-297-5644. Business E-Mail: jrothman@foley.com.

ROTHMAN-DENES, LUCIA BEATRIZ, biology educator; b. Buenos Aires, Feb. 17, 1943; came to U.S., 1967; d. Boris and Carmen (Couto) Rothman; m. Pablo Denes, May 24, 1968; children: Christian Andrew, Anne Elizabeth. Lic. in Chemistry, Sch. Scis., U. Buenos Aires, 1964, PhD in Biochemistry, 1967. Vis. fellow NIH, Bethesda, Md., 1967-70; postdoctoral fellow biophysics U. Chgo., 1970-73, rsch. assoc., 1973-74, from asst. prof. to assoc. prof., 1974-83, prof. molecular genetics and cell biology, 1983—. Mem. microbial genetics study sect. NIH, 1980—83, 1993—96, chair, 1994—96, mem. genetic basis of disease study sect., 1985—89, mem. coun. Ctr. for Sci. Rev, 2000—04; sci. adv. com. Damon Runyon and Walter Winchell, NYC, 1989—93; biochemistry panel NSF, 1990—92. Contbr. articles to profl. jours. Fellow AAAS, Am. Acad. Microbiology (bd. govs. 2000-03); mem. Am. Acad. Arts and Scis., Am. Soc. Microbiology (divsn. chair 1985, divsn. group II rep. 1990-92, vice chair GMPC 1995-99, chair GMPC 1999-2001, chair meetings. bd. 2003-), Am. Soc. Virology (councilor 1987-90), Am. Soc. Biochemistry and Molecular Biology. Office: Univ Chgo 920 E 58th St Chicago IL 60637-5415 Office Phone: 773-702-1083. E-mail: lbrd@midway.uchicago.edu.

ROTHMEIER, STEVEN GEORGE, investment company executive; b. Mankato, Minn., Oct. 4, 1946; s. Edwin George and Alice Joan (Johnson) R. BBA, U. Notre Dame, 1968; MBA, U. Chgo., 1972. Corp. fin. analyst Northwest Airlines, Inc., St. Paul, 1973, mgr. econ. analysis, 1973-78, dir. econ. planning, 1978, v.p. fin., treas., 1978-82, exec. v.p., treas., dir., 1982-83, exec. v.p. fin. and adminstrn., treas., dir., 1983, pres., chief operating officer, 1984, pres., chief exec. officer, 1985-86, chmn., chief exec. officer, 1986-89, also bd. dirs.; pres. IAI Capital Group, Mpls., 1989-93; chmn., CEO Great No. Capital, St. Paul, 1993—. Bd. dirs. Arvin Meriter Inc., Precision Castparts, Waste Mgmt., Inc. Chmn. St. Agnes Found. Decorated Bronze Star. Mem. Mpls. Club, Chgo. Club. Republican. Roman Catholic. Office: Great Northern Capital 332 Minnesota St Ste W2900 Saint Paul MN 55101-1377

ROTHSCHILD, MATTHEW, editor; Grad, Harvard Univ. Past editor Multinational Monitor; assoc & mng editor The Progressive, 1983—94, editor, 1994—. Host Progressive Radio; co-founder & Dir The Progressive Media Project. Author: You Have No Rights: Stories of America in an Age of Repression, 2007. Office: The Progressive 409 E Main St Madison WI 53703

ROTHSTEIN, FRED C., health facility administrator; b. Cleve. m. Jackie Rothstein; 2 children. BA, Miami U., Oxford, Ohio; MD, Chgo. Med. Sch. U. Health Scis., 1976. Bd. cert. pediatrics and pedatric gastroenterology. Pediat. intern Cleve. Metro Gen. Hosp., Ohio, 1976—77, Rainbow Babies & Children's Hosp., Ohio, 1976—77, pediat. resident Ohio, 1977—79, pediat. gastroenterology fellow Ohio, 1979—81, chief divsn. pediat. gastroenterology Ohio, practicing physician, pediat. gastroenterologist Ohio, pres., CEO; dir. dept. pediatrics, sr. v.p. med. affairs Mt. Sinai Med. Ctr., Cleve., 1989; sr. v.p. clin. integration U. Hosps. Health System, Cleve., 1990—96, acting pres., CEO, 2002—03; pres., CEO U. Hosps. Cleve., 2003—. Asst. prof. pediatrics Case Western Reserve U., Cleve., 1981—86; prof. pediatrics Case Western Res. U., Cleve., 2004—; bd. trustees Ctr. Health Affairs (CHA), 2004, Geauga Regional Hosp., Chardon, Ohio, 1997; bd. dirs. BioEnterprise. Contbr. more than 60 peer-reviewed abstracts, articles, and book chapters on issues concerning pediatric gastroenterology. Mem.: N.Am. Soc. Pediat. Gastroenterology and Nutrition, Am. Gastroenterological Assn., Am. Acad. Pediatrics, Am. Coll. Gastroenterology. Office: Univ Hosps Cleve 11100 Euclid Ave Cleveland OH 44106 Office Phone: 216-844-6217.

ROTHSTEIN, RUTH M., county health official; Dir. Cook County Hosp., Chgo., to 1999; chief Cook County Bur. of Health Svcs., Chgo., 1999—. Office: Cook County Bur Hlth Svcs 1900 W Polk St Ste 220 Chicago IL 60612-3736

ROTI, THOMAS DAVID, judge; s. Sam N. and Theresa S. (Salerno) R.; m. Donna Sumichrast, 1972; children: Thomas S., Kyle D., Rebecca D., Gregory J. BS, Loyola U., Chgo., 1967, JD cum laude, 1970. Bar: Ill. 1970, U.S. Dist. Ct. (no. dist.) Ill. 1971, U.S. Ct. Appeals (7th cir.) 1971. Sr. law clk. to Judge Frank McGarr, U.S. Dist. Ct. No. Dist. Ill., 1971-72; assoc. Arnstein, Gluck & Lehr, Chgo., 1972-73, Boodell, Sears et al, Chgo., 1973-75; asst. gen. counsel Dominick's Finer Foods, Inc., Northlake, Ill., 1975-77, v.p., gen. counsel,

1977-97; judge Cir. Ct. Cook County, 2000—. Mem. nat. conf. lawyers and econs. com. Food Mktg. Inst., Washington, 1987—97; trustee Nat. Conf. Cmty. and Justice, 1995—2000; legis. com. Ill. Retail Mchts. Assn., Chgo., 1987—97. Trustee Joint Civic Com. Italian Ams., Chgo., 1986-95; mem. Chgo. Coun. EDU-CARE Scholarship Program, 1988; dir. Chgo. Clean Streak, 1990-97. Maj., Qartermaster Corps, USAR, 1967-83 Recipient Am. Jurisprudence award, 1970, Alumni Assn. award Loyola U., 1970. Mem. ABA, Ill. Bar Assn., Ill. Judges Assn. (bd. dirs. 2005-), Chgo. Bar Assn., N.W. Suburban Bar Assn. (bd. govs. 2006-, co-chair civil practice com.), Justinian Soc. Lawyers, Cath. Lawyers Guild Chgo. (bd. govs., dir. 2004—), Phi Alpha Delta, Alpha Signa Nu. Roman Catholic. Office: 2121 Euclid Ave Rolling Meadows IL 60008 Business E-Mail: tdroti@cookcountygov.com.

ROTMAN, CARLOTTA H., physician; b. Chgo., Apr. 8, 1958; d. Clarence Kenneth and Vlasta (Cizek) Hayes; m. Chester James Hill III, June 10, 1967 (div. 1974); m. Carlos A. Rotman, July 31, 1980; children: Robin Mercedes. BA magna cum laude, Knox Coll., 1969; MD with honors, U. Ill., 1973. Diplomate Nat. Bd. Med. Examiners, Am. Bd. Dermatology. Intern Mayo Sch. Medicine, Rochester, Minn., 1973-74; resident U. Ill., Chgo., 1975-78, asst. prof. clin. dermatology Coll. Medicine, 1978-93, assoc. prof. clin. dermatology Coll. Medicine, 1993—. Mem. U. Ill. Senate, Chgo., 1986-91, 99-2002; councilor Chgo. Med. Soc., 1990-96, 1999-2006. Contbr. articles to profl. jours. Bd. dirs. Summerfest St. James Cathedral, Chgo., 1986-91, YWCA, Lake Forest, Ill., 1995-, pres., 1998-2000; master gardner Chgo. Bot. Garden, Glencoe, Ill., 1994-98; bd. dirs. Lake Bluff Open Lands Assn., 1997-2006, Friends of Ryerson Woods, 2005—, Lake Forest/Lake Bluff Hist. Soc., 2006—; mem. Lake Bluff Libr. Bd., 2001-05. Recipient Janet Glascow award Am. Women's Med. Assn., 1973. Mem. Am. Acad. Dermatology, Herb Soc. Am. (ways and means No. Ill. unit 1992-94, treas. N. Ill. unit 1996-00, vice chair 2000-02, chair 2002-04, ctrl. dist. steering com. 2004-06, nat. herb garden com. 2006—), Chgo. Dermatol. Care Soc., Ill. Dermatologic Soc., Phi Beta Kappa, Alpha Omega Alpha. Avocations: travel, cooking, gardening, reading. Office: Dept Dermatology 808 S Wood St Chicago IL 60612-7300 Office Phone: 312-996-6966. Business E-Mail: chhill@uic.edu.

ROTNER, PHILIP R., lawyer; b. Chgo., Feb. 6, 1947; m. Janet Rotner. AB, U. Calif., 1969; JD, Harvard U., 1972. Bar: Ill. 1972, Mass. 1973, Calif. 1975, N.Y. 1996. Litig. assoc. Gaston, Snow, Motley & Holt, Boston, 1973—74, assoc., 1974—80; ptnr. McCutchen, Doyle, Brown & Enersen, San Francisco, 1981—95; gen. counsel Deloitte & Touche USA LLP, Broadway, NY, 1995—2005; ptnr. Mayer, Brown, Rowe & Maw LLP, Chgo., 2005—. Vis. faculty Law Sch. Trial Advocacy Program Harvard U., 1990, 93; spkr. in field. Office: Mayer Brown Rowe & Maw LLP 71 S Wacker Dr Chicago IL 60606 Home: 1040 North Lake Shore Dr Apt 33C Chicago IL 60611 E-mail: protner@mayerbrownrowe.com.

ROUGIER-CHAPMAN, ALWYN SPENCER DOUGLAS, furniture manufacturing company executive; b. Ostende, Belgium, Feb. 19, 1939; arrived in US, 1970; s. Douglas Alwyn and Simone (Stiernet) Rougier-C.; m. Christine Hayes, Mar. 14, 1964; children: Andrew Douglas, Duncan Peter Chartered Acct., City of London Coll., 1963. Chartered acct., Eng. and Wales; CPA, Mich. Articled clk. Spain Bros., London, 1958-64; mgr. Deloitte & Co., Brussels, 1964-70; ptnr. Seidman & Seidman, Grand Rapids, Mich., 1970-81; v.p. planning Steelcase Inc., Grand Rapids, Mich., 1981-83, sr. v.p., CFO, 1983. Dir. Meijer, Inc. Pres. French Soc., Grand Rapids, Mich., 1974-75; treas., vice chmn. Opera Grand Rapids, 1981-86, pres., 1987-89; treas. Grand Rapids Symphony, 1991-96; bd. trustees Blodgett Meml. Hosp., 1989-98; bd. dirs. Fin. Execs. Inst., Western Mich., 1988-94, pres., 1991-92; mem. fin. com. Spectrum Health, 1998—. Fellow Inst. Chartered Accts. Eng. and Wales; mem. Am. Inst. CPAs (computer exec. com. 1977-81), Mich. Assn. CPAs (auditing standards com. 1973-78) Clubs: Cascade Country, Peninsular (Grand Rapids). Roman Catholic. Avocations: golf, tennis, squash, travel, music.

ROUNDS, MIKE (MARION MICHAEL ROUNDS), governor; b. Huron, SD, Oct. 24, 1954; m. Jean Vedvei, 1978; children: Christopher, Lindsay, Brian, Carrie, John. BS in Polit. Sci., SD State U., Brookings, 1977. Ptnr. Fischer, Rounds & Assocs., Inc.; mem. SD State Senate from Dist. 24, 1991—2002, minority whip, 1993—94, majority leader, 1995—2002; gov. State of S.D., Pierre, 2003—. Bd. pres. Oahe YMCA; v.p. Home and Sch. Assn. St. Joseph Sch.; pres. Pierre-Ft. Pierre Exch. Club. Mem.: Midwestern Governors Assn. (chmn. 2008—), Ducks Unlimited, Knights of Columbus, Pierre Elks Lodge. Republican. Roman Catholic. Avocations: racquetball, hunting, boating, camping. Office: Office of Gov 500 E Capitol Ave Pierre SD 57501 Office Phone: 605-773-3212. Office Fax: 605-773-5844.

ROUSH, NANCY SCHMIDT, lawyer; b. Ottawa, Kans., Sept. 17, 1951; d. Raymond Stanley and Caroline Jeanne (Ward) Schmidt: m. John Mark Roush, Aug. 25, 1973; 1 child, Jessica Lynn. BA, Taylor U., Upland, Ind., 1973; JD, U. Kans., 1979. Bar: Kans. 1979, U.S. Dist. Ct. Kans. 1979, U.S. Ct. Appeals (10th cir.) 1980, U.S. Tax Ct. 1982. Jud. clk. U.S. Ct. Appeals (10th cir.), Olathe, Kans., 1979-80; lawyer Logan & Martin, Overland Park, Kans., 1980-85; ptnr. bus. planning and estate planning Shook, Hardy & Bacon LLP, Overland Park, 1986—. Editor and author: Kansas Estate Administration, 1986; contbr. articles to profl. jours. Mem. bd. govs. Kans. U. Law Sch., Lawrence, 1984-87; participant Midwest Bioethics Ctr., Kansas City, Mo., 1989-90. Fellow Am. Coll. of Trust and Estate Coun. (mem. Bus. Planning Com.); mem. ABA, Kans. Bar Assn. (pres. real estate probate and trust sect. 1984-86, pres. elect tax law sect. 1990-91, pres. 1991—, editor bd. edn. jour. 1982, Outstanding Svc. award 1985, 1991, 2001), Kansas City Met. Bar Assn., Mo. Bar Assn., Order of Coif. Office: Shook, Hardy & Bacon LLP 2555 Grand Blvd Kansas City MO 64108 Office Fax: 816-559-2501, 816-421-5547. E-mail: nroush@shb.com.

ROUSH, SUE, newspaper editor; b. Mason City, Iowa., Dec. 26, 1957; BS in Journalism, Northwestern U., 1980. Mng. editor Universal Press Syndicate, Kansas City, Mo., 1995—. Office: Universal Press Syndicate 4520 Main St Ste 700 Kansas City MO 64111-7701

ROUSH, WILLIAM R., chemistry professor; BS in Chemistry, UCLA, 1974; PhD in Chemistry, Harvard U., 1977. Disting. prof. chemistry dept. Ind. U., Bloomington; Warner Lambert Park Davis prof. chemistry, chair chemistry U. Mich., Ann Arbor, 1997—. Recipient Arthur C. Cope Scholar award Am. Chem. Soc., 1994, Alan R. Day award Phila. Organic Chemist's Club, 1992. Office: U Mich Dept Chemistry Ann Arbor MI 48109

ROUSSEAU, EUGENE ELLSWORTH, musician, educator, consultant; b. Blue Island, Ill., Aug. 23, 1932; s. Joseph E. and Laura M. (Schindler) R.; m. Norma J. Rigel, Aug. 15, 1959; children: Lisa-Marie, Joseph. B of Mus Edn., Chgo. Mus. Coll., 1953; MusM, Northwestern U., 1954; student, Paris Conservatory of Music, 1960-61; PhD in Music Lit. and Performance, U. Iowa, 1962. Instr. Luther Coll., 1956-59; asst. prof. Cen. Mo. State Coll., 1962-64; prof. music Ind. U., Bloomington, 1964-88, disting. prof. music, 1988—; prof. U. Minn., 2000—. Guest prof. U. Iowa, 1964, Hochschule fur Musik, Vienna, Austria, 1981-82, Ariz. State U., 1984, Prague Conservatory Music, 1985, Showa Coll. Music, 1996, 98, Tokyo Coll. Music, 1997, Paris Conservatory, 1997, Munshino Acad. Music, Tokyo, 2000; tchr. U. Wis.-Ext., 1969—; R&D of saxophone mouthpieces; music arranger; svc. on numerous acad. coms.; tchr. 1st course in saxophone Mozarteum in Salzburg, Austria, 1991—; mem. jury Munich Internat. competitions, 1987, 90, 2001, pres. of juries, 1991-92; first solo saxophonist to perform on Prague Spring Festival, 1993; mem. jury Can. Nat. Music competition, 1994; juror Japan Wind and Percussion Competition, 1997; v.p. jury Adolphe Sax Internat. Competition, Belgium, 1998; guest artist prof. Villa Musica, Mainz, 1998, 2000; faculty saxophone Ticino Music, Lugano, 2001, 02, 03; chief cons. saxophone R&D Yamaha corp., 1972-92; soloist Hamamatsu Wind Instrument Festival; faculty ann. master class Vancouver C.C.; host World Saxophone Congress XIII, U. Minn., Mpls., 2003; recorded for Deutsche Grammophon, 1971; guest faculty Am. Band Coll., 2000, 03, 06; adjudicator Thailand Internat. Composition Competition, 2006; artist-in-residence U. Ga., 2007. Worldwide concert saxophonist; Carnegie Hall debut, 1965; author: Marcel Mule: His Life and the Saxophone, 1982, Saxophone High Tones, 1978, revised 2d edit., 2003, Method for Saxophone (2 vols.), 1975; performer 1st solo saxophone recitals, several European cities, 1st Am. solo saxophone performance in Japan, 1984; 1st to record concert saxophone on compact disc (Delos); radio broadcasts in Berlin, Bremen, London, Montreal, Ostrava, Paris, Prague, Toronto, Vienna; saxophone recs. for Deutsche Gramophon, Golden Crest, Coronet, Delos, Liscio, ALM, McGill, RIAX, and Jeanné; CD rec. with Belgian RAF Band; numerous world premieres of composition written for him. Instr., asst. band leader 25th Infantry Div. U.S. Army, 1954-56. Named Hon. Prof. Music, Prague Conservatory, 1993, Braga Inst., Italy, 2001; recipient Edwin Franko Goldman award, Am. Bandmasters Assn., 1995, Disting. Alumni award, U. Iowa, 1996; grantee, Fulbright Found., 1960—61, Rsch. and Exchange Bd., 1985, NEA, 1986. Mem. N.Am. Saxophone Alliance (pres. 1978-80), Comite Internat. de Saxophone (pres. 1982-85), Coll. Music Soc., Clarinet and Saxophone Soc. (U.K.), Music Tchrs. Nat. Assn. (Tchr. of Yr. award for Ind. 1993), Fulbright Assn. (life), World Saxophone Congress (co-founder 1969, pres. organizing com. 2000--). Home Phone: 812-332-3284; Office Phone: 612-624-3875. E-mail: rouss007@umn.edu.

ROVNER, ILANA KARA DIAMOND, federal judge; b. Riga, Latvia, 1938; arrived in U.S., 1939; d. Stanley and Ronny (Medalje) Diamond. AB, Bryn Mawr Coll., 1960; postgrad., U. London King's Coll., 1961, Georgetown U., 1961—63; JD, Ill. Inst. Tech., 1966; LittD (hon.), Rosary Coll., 1989, Mundelein Coll., 1989; DHL (hon.), Spertus Coll. of Judaica, 1992. Bar: Ill. 1972, US Dist. (no. dist.) Ill. 1972, US Ct. Appeals (7th cir.) 1977, US Supreme Ct. 1981, Fed. Trial Bar (no. dist.) Ill. 1982. Jud. clk. US Dist. Ct. (no. dist.) Ill., Chgo., 1972—73; asst. US atty. US Atty.'s Office, Chgo., 1973—77, dep. chief of pub. protection, 1975—76, chief pub. protection, 1976—77; dep. gov., legal counsel Gov. James R. Thompson, Chgo., 1977—84; dist. judge US Dist. Ct. (no. dist.) Ill., Chgo., 1984—92; cir. judge US Ct. Appeals (7th cir.), Chgo., 1992—. Mem. Gannon-Proctor Commn. on the Status of Women in Ill., 1982—84; mem. civil justice reform act adv. com. 7th Cir. Ct., Chgo., 1991—95, mem. race and gender fairness com., 1993—; mem. fairness com. US Ct. Appeals (7th cir.), 1996—, mem. gender study task force, 1995—96; mem. jud. conf. US Com. Ct. Adminstrn. Case Mgmt., 2000—. Ctrl. and East European law initiative vol. ABA, 1997—; trustee Bryn Mawr Coll., Pa., 1983—89; mem. bd. overseers Ill. Inst. Tech./Kent Coll. Law, 1983—; trustee Ill. Inst. Tech., 1989—; mem. adv. coun. Rush Ctr. for Sports Medicine, Chgo., 1991—96; bd. dirs. Rehab. Inst. Chgo., 1998—; bd. visitors No. Ill. U. Coll. Law, 1992—94; vis. com. Northwestern U. Sch. Law, 1993—98, U. Chgo. Law Sch., 1993—96, 2000—03; chair Ill. state selection com. Rhodes Scholarship Trust, 1998—2000. Named Today's Chgo. Woman of the Yr., 1985, Woman of Achievement, Chgo. Women's Club, 1986, Inaugural Spkr., Disting. Judge Series CLE Program Ill. Atty. Gen. Office, 2007; named one of 15 Chgo. Women of the Century, Chgo. Sun Times, 1999; named to Today's Chgo. Women Hall of Fame, 2002; recipient Spl. Commendation award, US Dept. Justice, 1975, Spl. Achievement award, 1976, Ann. Nat. Law and Social Justice Leadership award, League to Improve the Cmty., 1975, Ann. Guardian Police award, 1977, Profl. Achievement award, Ill. Inst. Tech., 1986, ORT Women's Am. Cmty. Svc. award, 1987—88, commendation def. of prisoners com., Chgo. Bar Assn., 1987, Svc. award, Spertus Coll. of Judaica, 1987, Ann. award, Chgo. Found. for Women, 1990, Louis Dembitz Brandeis medal for Disting. Legal Svc., Brandeis U., 1993, 1st Woman award, Valparaiso U. Sch. Law, 1993, Hebrew Immigrant Aid Soc. Chgo. 85th Anniversary honoree, 1996, Arabella Babb Mansfield award, Nat. Assn. Women Lawyers, 1998, award, Chgo. Attys. Coun. of Hadassah, 1999, First Woman award, Chgo. Bar Assn. Alliance for Women and Women's Bar Assn. Ill., 2000, Georgetown U. Law Ctr., 2001, Chgo. Hist. Soc. Trailblazers Award, 2003, Lifetime Achievement award, Decalogue Soc. Lawyers, 2004, Vanguard award, Chgo. Bar Assn. and Lesbian and Gay Bar Assn. Chgo., 2004, Thurgood Marshall Career Achievement award, Assn. Corp. Counsel Chgo. chpt., 2005, Hero of Liberty award, Nat. Liberty Mus., 2005, Inaugural Judge Abraham Lincoln Marovitz Mentoring award, Chgo. Bar Assn. and Found. Lend-a-Hand Program, 2005. Mem.: Chgo. Bar Assn. (Justice John Paul Stevens award 2005), Jewish Judges Assn. Ill. (Lifetime Achievement award 2004), Decalogue Soc. of Lawyers (citation of honor 1991, Merit award 1997), Chgo. Coun. Lawyers, Women's Bar Assn. Ill. (ann. award 1989, 1st Myra Bradwell Woman of Achievement award 1994, 1st Woman Award (in conjunction with Chicago Bar Assn. Alliance for Women) 2000), Fed. Judges Assn., Fed. Bar Assn. (mem. selection com. Chgo. chpt. 1977—80, treas. 1978—79, sec. 1979—80, 2d v.p. 1980—81, 1st v.p. 1981—82, pres. 1982—83, 2d v.p. 7th cir. 1983—84, v.p. 7th cir. 1984—85), Kappa Beta Pi, Phi Alpha Delta (hon.). Office: 219 S Dearborn St Ste 2774 Chicago IL 60604-1803

ROWARK, MAUREEN, fine arts photographer; b. Edinburgh, Midlothian, Scotland, Feb. 28, 1933; came to U.S., 1960, naturalized, 1970; d. Alexander Pennycook and Margaret (Gorman) Prezdpelski; m. Robert Rowark, May 3, 1952 (dec. 1974). 1 child, Mark Steven. Student, Warmington Bus. Coll., Royal Leamington Spa, Eng., 1950-51, Royal Leamington Spa Art Sch.; diploma, Speedwriting Inst., NYC, 1961; AS in Edn., St. Clair County C.C., Port Huron, Mich., 1977, AA, 1978. Supr. proof reading Nevin D. Hirst Advt., Ltd., Leeds, England, 1952-55; publicity asst. Alvis Aero Engines, Ltd., Coventry, England, 1955-57; adminstrv. asst. Port Huron Motor Inn, 1964-66; adminstrv. asst. pub. rels. dept. Geophysics and Computer Svcs., Inc., New Orleans, 1966-68; sales mgr. Holiday Inn, Port Huron, 1968-70; adminstrv. asst. Howard Corp., Port Huron, 1971-73; sales and systems coord. Am. Wood Products, Ann Arbor, Mich., 1973-74; systems coord. Daniels & Zermack Architects, Ann Arbor, 1974; systems coord., cataloger fine arts dept. St. Clair County Community Coll., Port Huron, 1976-79; freelance fine arts photographer Port Huron, 1978—. Photographer Patterns mag. front cover, 1978, Erie Sq. Gazette, 1979, Bluewater Area Tourism Bur. brochure, 1989, 92, 95, 97, 2000, 01, Corits Castle, Lexington, 2002, Port Huron, Can. Legion, Wyo., Ont. Br., 1987, 88—, Grace Episcopal Ch. Mariner's Day, Port Huron, 1987, 92-2001, Homes mag., 1989. Photographer (one-woman shows) Grace Episcopal Ch., 1995, Port Huron Mus., 1995, St. Clair River Remedial Action Plan, 1995 (Best in Landscape Category), Mich. Waterways Coun. Girl Scouts Exhibit, 1996; Exhibited in group shows at Ea. Mich. Internat. Juried Exhbn., 2000, 1981—98 (Award of Excellence, 1982, 1983, Best Photography award, 1995, 1996, 1997), Our Town Juried Exhbn., 1997, St. Clair County C.C., 1983, 1986 (Award of Excellence, 1986), Gallery Lambton, Sarnia, Ont., Can., 1983—92 (Best Photography, 1988), 1994, 1996—97, 2000, Bluewater Bridge, 1988, Kaskilaaksontie, Finland, 1991 (Par Excellence award), Swann Gallery, Detroit, 1996, St. Clair (Mich.) Art Gallery, Genesis Gallery, Lexington, Mich., others, Studio 1219, Port Huron, Mich., Represented in permanent collections Royal Can. Legion, Wyo. Br. Centaph, Capac State Bank, Grace Episcopal Ch., Thomas Edison Inn, Port Huron Hosp., Front Cover Good Health News; costume design, manufacture and modelling Bluewater Art Assn., 2000—01, photographer Bluewater Percussion Brochure, 2001;, author short stories. Cons., buyer interior decor Grace Episcopal Ch., 1994; active Port Huron Mus., 1978; founder Bluewater les Chapeaux Rouge chpt. Red Hat Soc., 2000—; prodr., dir. calendar We Can Still Make Waves, 2005, Waiting for Our Ship to Come In, 2007; prodr., designer parade float Rotary Internat., 2005 (1st pl. award). Recipient hon. mention Gallery Lambton, Sarnia, 1981, 2d pl. memoir writing women's history month St. Clair County C.C., 1999; winner 2d and 3d place awards Times Herald Newspaper, 1988, 1st place juried photography award Port Huron Art Festival, 1997, 1st place St. Patrick's Day Parade Float, 2006, 1st place Rotary Internat. Day Parade Float, 2005. Mem. St. Clair County CC Alumni Assn., Red Hat Soc., Internat. Club, Moose, Phi Theta Kappa, Lambda Mu. Democrat. Episcopalian. Avocations: interior decorating, travel, theater, writing. Home and Office: 521 Holland Ave Port Huron MI 48060 Home Phone: 810-989-9192. Personal E-mail: ha-penerth-of-tar@prodigy.net.

ROWE, JOHN WILLIAM, utilities executive; b. Dodgeville, Wis., May 18, 1945; s. William J. and Lola R. (Rule) Rowe; m. Jeanne M. Rowe; 1 child, William John. BS, U. Wis., 1967, JD, 1970; D (hon.), DePaul U., Ill. Inst. Tech., Drexel U., U. Mass., Dartmouth, Bryant Coll. Bar: Wis. 1970, Ill. 1970, US Supreme Ct. 1979, Pa. 1982. Assoc. Isham, Lincoln & Beale, Chgo., 1970-77, ptnr., 1978-80; counsel to trustee Chgo. Milw. St. Paul & Pacific RR, Chgo., 1979-80; v.p. law Consol. Rail Corp., Phila., 1980-82, sr. v.p. law, 1982-84; pres., CEO Ctrl. Maine Power Co., Augusta, 1984-89, New Eng. Elecric Sys., Westboro, Mass., 1989-98, bd. dirs.; chmn., pres., CEO Unicom Corp. & Commonwealth Edison Co., 1998-2000; pres., co-CEO Exelon Corp., Chgo., 2000—03, chmn., pres., CEO, 2003—. Vice-chmn. Nuc. Energy Inst., 2006—07, chmn., 2007—; bd. dirs. Sunoco, No. Trust Co. Former pres. USS Constn. Mus., 1993—95; former chmn. Edison Electric Inst.; pres. Field Mus. Natural History; trustee Mechanics Hall, Pioneer Inst.; bd. trustees Art Inst. Chgo., Chgo. Hist. Soc., Wis. Alumni Rsch. Found., Am. Enterprise Inst.; bd. trustees Ill. chpt. Nature Conservancy; nat. trustee Northwestern U. Recipient World of Difference award, Anti-Defamation League, 2000, Citizen of Yr. award, City Club of Chgo., 2002, Corp. Leadership award, Spanish Coalition for Jobs, 2002, Civic Leadership award, Am. Jewish Com., 2004, Founder's award for Bus. Leadership, Union League Phila., 2005. Mem.: Comml. Club Chgo., Econ. Club Chgo., Order of the Coif, Phi Beta Kappa. Office: Exelon Corp 10 S Dearborn St 37th Fl PO Box 805398 Chicago IL 60680-5398 Office Phone: 800-483-3220.

ROWE, LISA DAWN, computer programmer, analyst, consultant; b. Kenton, Ohio, Feb. 2, 1966; d. Daniel Lee and Frances Elaine (Johnson) Edelblute; m. Jeffrey Mark Rowe, Feb. 13, 1982; children: Anthony David, Samantha Paige Elizabeth, Zane Thomas, Zachary Tyler. Student, Inst. of Lit., 1988-90, Acad. Ct. Reporting, 1988, Marion Tech. Coll., 1991-92; postgrad., Ohio State U., 1993—. Writer, model Newslife, Marion, Ohio, 1982-83; bookkeeper Nat. Ch. Residences, Columbus, Ohio, 1985, Insty-Prints, Columbus, 1985; asst. editor Columbus Entertainment, 1984-85; book reviewer, writer Columbus Dispatch, 1989-91; writer Consumer News, Delaware, Ohio, 1989-90; computer programmer, supr. Dyserv, Inc., Columbus, 1986-92; bookkeeper, acct., office mgr. Marion Music Ctr., Inc., 1990; computer programmer EBCO Mfg., Columbus, 1992-93; sr. programmer/analyst Borden, Inc., Columbus, 1993-94; computer cons. System X, Columbus, 1994-95, LDA Systems, Dublin, Ohio, 1995-96; pres. Rowe Techs. Inc., Marion, Ohio, 1996—. Editor newsletter Assn. System Users, 1989-90; contbr. articles and revs. to profl. jours. Mem. NAFE, MADD, DAV (chaplain 1990), Heart of Ohio Am. Cat Fanciers Assn. Cat Club (pres. 2002), Ragamuffin Cat Lovers Soc., Inc. (v.p. 2003). Republican. Mem. Lds Ch. Avocations: horseback riding, swimming, camping, fishing, reading. Home: 1150 Toulon Ave Marion OH 43302-6610 Office: Rowe Techs Inc 1150 Toulon Ave Marion OH 43302-6610 E-mail: Lisarowe@rowetech.com.

ROWE, RACHAEL A., lawyer; b. Cin., July 7, 1971; BA, Miami U., 1993; JD, U. Cin. Coll. Law, 1996. Bar: Ohio 1996, Ky. 1997, US Dist. Ct. Southern Dist. Ohio, US Dist. Ct. Eastern Dist. Ky., US Dist. Ct. Western Dist. Ky., US Ct. of Appeals Sixth Cir., US Dist. Ct. Eastern Dist. Mich. 2006. Ptnr. Keating Muething & Klekamp PLL, Cin. Juvenile ct. magistrate Hamilton County, Ohio; mem., Bd. Trustees Cin. Classic Hammer Soccer Club; bd. mem. Dress for Success. Named one of Ohio's Rising Stars, Super Lawyers, 2005, 2006. Mem.: Cin. Acad. Leadership for Lawyers (mem., Class VI), Ohio State Bar Assn., Ky. Bar Assn., Cin. Bar Assn. (mem., Adminstrn. & Fin. Com., mem., Jud. Endorsement Com.), ABA. Office: Keating Muething & Kleklamp PLL One E Fourth St Ste 1400 Cincinnati OH 45202 Office Phone: 513-579-6400. Office Fax: 513-579-6457.

ROWELL, KATHERINE RENEE, sociologist, educator; b. Lebanon, Ky., Nov. 24, 1964; d. Cronley Jr. and Betty Katharine (Rose) Teater; m. Kurt Edward Rowell, June 30, 1984; children: John Kyle, Jack Tyler. BA, Wright State U., 1987, MA in Applied Behavioral Sci., 1989; PhD, Ohio State U., 1994. Instr. sociology Wright State U., 1987-89, 92, mem. faculty dept. sociology, 1993-94; instr. sociology Ohio State U., Columbus, 1989-91, Presdl. fellow, 1991-93; mem. faculty Ctrl. State U., Wilburforce, Ohio, 1993-96; asst. prof. to prof. sociology Sinclair CC, Dayton, Ohio, 1996—. Permanency planner Salvation Army, Dayton, 1991; cons. Springfield Homelessness Group, 1992. Contbr. articles to profl. jours. Vol. liaison Senator Dave Hobson, Columbus, 1987; vol. Salvation Army, Dayton, also other orgns., 1987—. Named Outstanding Sociology Instr., Ohio State U., 1991; recipient US Professors of Yr. Award for Outstanding CC Prof., Carnegie Found. for Advancement of Tchg. and Coun. for Advancement and Support of Edn., 2005. Mem. Am. Sociol. Assn., North Ctrl. Sociol. Assn. (social policy chairperson 1994-95). Democrat. Home: 485 Lamplighter Pl Xenia OH 45385-1420 Office: Sinclair CC Dept Sociology 444 W 3rd St Dayton OH 45402-1421 Office Phone: 937-512-4598. Office Fax: 937-512-4331. E-mail: katherine.rowell@sinclair.edu.

ROWLAND, JAMES RICHARD, electrical engineering educator; b. Muldrow, Okla., Jan. 24, 1940; s. Richard Cleveland and Imogene Beatrice (Angel) R.; m. Jonell Condren, Aug. 24, 1963 (dec. May 1991); children: Jennifer Lynn, Angela Janel; m. Mary Anderson, Jan. 2, 1995. BSEE, Okla. State U., 1962; MSEE, Purdue U., 1964, PhD in Elec. Engring., 1966. Registered profl. engr., Okla. Instr. Purdue U., West Lafayette, Ind., 1964-65; from asst. to assoc. prof. Ga. Inst. Tech., Atlanta, 1966-71; from assoc. to full prof. Okla. State U., Stillwater, 1971-85; prof., chmn. dept. elec. and computer engring. U. Kans., Lawrence, 1985-89, prof., 1985—. Cons. Lockheed-Ga. Co., Marietta, 1966-71, U.S. Army Missile Command, Huntsville, Ala., 1969-79, Sandia Nat. Labs., Albuquerque, 1979, Puritan-Bennett, Lenexa, Kans., 1992. Author: Linear Control Systems, 1986; mem. editorial adv. bd. Computer and Elec. Engring., 1971-98; co-contbr. 60 articles to profl. jours. Fellow IEEE (edn. soc. pres. 1982-83, Centennial medal 1984, edn. soc. Achievement award 1986, edn. conf. award 1988, Region 5 Oustanding Educator award 1995, Svc. award 2002), Am. Soc. Engring. Edn. (dir. grad. div. 1987-89, Midwest sec. chair 2001-02), Eta Kappa Nu (dir. 1989-91), Kiwanis. Republican. Baptist. Avocations: golf, gardening. Home: 2424 Free State Ct Lawrence KS 66047-2831 Office: U Kans Dept Elec Engring & Computer Sci 2001 Eaton Hall Lawrence KS 66045 Home Phone: 785-842-5959; Office Phone: 785-864-8822. E-mail: jrowland@eecs.ku.edu.

ROWLAND, THEODORE JUSTIN, physicist, researcher; b. Cleve., May 15, 1927; s. Thurston Justin and Lillian (Nesser) R.; m. Janet Claire Millar, June 28, 1952 (div. 1967); children: Theodore Justin, Dawson Ann, Claire Millar; m. Patsy Marie Beard, Aug. 21, 1968 (div. 2007). BS, Western Res. U., 1948; MA, Harvard U., 1949, PhD, 1954. Rsch. physicist Union Carbide Metals Co., Niagara Falls, NY, 1954-61; prof. phys. metallurgy U. Ill., 1961-92, asst. dean Coll. Engring., acting assoc. dean Grad. Coll., 1990-91, prof. emeritus, 1992—; pres., dir. Materials Cons., Inc. Cons. physicist, 1961—; cons. metallurgist, 1976—. Editor 2 books; author monograph; contbr. articles to profl. jours. Fellow Am. Phys. Soc.; mem. AIME, AAAS, AAUP, Phi Beta Kappa, Sigma Xi. Achievements include initial verification of charge density waves in dilute alloys; original contributions to theory and experiment in nuclear magnetic resonance in pure metals and alloy. Home: 805 Park Lane Dr Champaign IL 61820-7613 Office: U Ill Dept Materials Sci and Engring 1304 W Green St Urbana IL 61801-2920 Business E-Mail: trowland@uiuc.edu.

ROWLETT, RALPH MORGAN, archaeologist, educator; b. Richmond, Ky., Sept. 11, 1934; s. Robert Kenny and Daisy (Mullikin) R.; m. Elsebet Sander-Jorgensen, Aug. 25, 1963 (div. Jan. 1986); children: Rolf R. Arvid, Erik Kenneth; m. Elizabeth Helen Dinan, Apr. 21, 1989 (div. Oct. 1995); 1 child, Helen Holly; m. Magda Mircea, 2005. Student, U. Ky., 1952-53; BA summa cum laude, Marshall U., 1956; postgrad., U. London, 1962-63; PhD, Harvard U., 1968. Instr. anthropology U. Mo., Columbia, 1965-67, asst. prof., 1967-69, assoc. prof., 1969-75, prof., 1975—. Postdoctoral fellow Ghent U., 1969; vis. prof. Bucuresti U., 2005. Co-author: Neolithic Levels on the Titelberg, Luxembourg, 1981, Meeting Anthropology Phase to Phase, 2000; anthropology editor Random House Unabridged Dictionary of English, 1980—; editor: Horizons and Styles, 1993, Horizons and Styles in West Eurasiatic Archaeology; developer thermoluminescence dating of flint, 1972; co-developer electron spin resonance dating of flint, 1981. 1st lt. arty., U.S. Army, 1956-58. Decorated officer Legion de Merit (Luxembourg); named Ky. col., 1976; grantee NSF, 1973-75, 76-79, 82-83, Earthwatch, 1985-88, Svc. Archeologique de Neuchatel, 1989, British Coun., 1993, Acad. of Romania, 1996, Internat. Rsch. and Exch. Bd., 1997. Fellow Am. Anthrop. Assn.; mem. AAAS, Archaeol. Inst. Am., Soc. Am. Archaeology, Societe Prehistorique de Luxembourg, Societe Archeologique Champenoise, English Heritage, Palomino Horse Breeders Assn., Sigma Xi. Green Party. Mem. Christian Ch. (Disciples Of Christ). Home: Hollywell Hill 1197 State Road Ww Fulton MO 65251-5106 Office: Univ Mo Dept Anthropology Columbia MO 65211-0001 Office Phone: 573-882-4731. Business E-Mail: rowlettR@missouri.edu.

ROWLEY, JANET DAVISON, physician; b. NYC, Apr. 5, 1925; d. Hurford Henry and Ethel Mary (Ballantyne) Davison; m. Donald A. Rowley, Dec. 18, 1948; children: Donald, David, Robert, Roger. PhB, U. Chgo., 1944, BS, 1946, MD, 1948; DSc (hon.), U. Ariz., 1989, U. Pa., 1989, Knox Coll., 1991, U. So. Calif., 1992, St. Louis U., 1997, St. Xavier U., 1999, Oxford U., Eng., 2000, Lund U., Sweden, 2003, Dartmouth U., 2004. Diplomate Am. Bd. Med. Genetics. Rsch. asst. U. Chgo., 1949—50; intern Marine Hosp., USPHS, Chgo., 1950—51; attending physician Infant Welfare and Prenatal Clinics Dept. Pub. Health, Montgomery County, Md., 1953—54; rsch. fellow Levinson Found., Cook County Hosp., Chgo., 1955—61; clin. instr. neurology U. Ill., Chgo., 1957—61; USPHS spl. trainee Radiobiology Lab. The Churchill Hosp., Oxford, England, 1961—62; rsch. assoc. dept. medicine and Argonne Cancer Rsch. Hosp. U. Chgo., 1962—69, assoc. prof. dept. medicine and Argonne Cancer

Rsch. Hosp., 1969—77, prof. dept. medicine and Franklin McLean Meml. Rsch. Inst., 1977—84, Blum-Riese Disting. Svc. prof., dept. medicine and dept. molecular genetics and cell biology, 1984—, Blum-Riese Disting. Svc. prof. dept. human genetics, 1997—, interim dep. dean for sci. biol. scis. divsn., 2001—02. Bd. sci. counsellors Nat. Inst. Dental Rsch., NIH, 1972—76, chmn., 1974—76; mem. Nat. Cancer Adv. Bd., Nat. Cancer Inst., 1979—84, Nat. Adv. Coun. for Human Genome Rsch. Inst., 1999—2004; adv. com. Frederick Cancer Rsch. Facility, 1983—84; bd. sci. counsellors Nat. Human Genome Rsch. Inst., NIH, 1994—99, chmn., 1994—97; adv. bd. Howard Hughes Med. Inst., 1989—94, MD Anderson Cancer Ctr., 1998—2005; vis. com. dept. applied biol. scis. MIT Corp., 1983—86; bd. sci. cons. Meml. Sloan-Kettering Cancer Ctr., 1988—90; adv. com. Ency. Britannica U. Chgo., 1988—96; Presdl. Symposium Am. Soc. Pediatric Hematology/Oncology, 1995; chmn. sci. adv. com. Translational Genomics Rsch. Inst., Phoenix., 2004—; med. adv. bd. Calif. Inst. Regenerative Medicine, 2005—; mem. sci. adv. coun. Children's Hosp., Boston, 2005—. Co-founder, co-editor: Genes, Chromosomes and Cancer, mem. editl. bd.: Oncology Rsch., Cancer Genetics and Cytogenetics, Internat. Jour. Hematology, Genomics, Leukemia; past mem. editl. bd. Internat. Jour. Cancer, Blood, Cancer Rsch., Hematol. Oncology, Leukemia Rsch.; contbr. chapters to books, articles to profl. jours. Adv. com. for career awards in biomed. scis. Burroughs Wellcome Fund, 1994—98; selection panel for Clin. Sci. award Doris Duke Charitable Found., 2000—02, 2006; mem. Pres.'s Adv. Coun. on Bioethics, 2001—; mem. med. rsch. material command leukemia program U.S. Army, 2002—04; mem. selection com. Rosalind Franklin young investigator award, 2004, 2007; nat. adv. com. McDonnell Found. Program for Molecular Medicine in Cancer Rsch., 1988—98; adv. bd. Leukemia Soc. Am., 1979—84; selection com. scholar award in biomed. sci. Lucille P. Markey Charitable Trust, 1984—87; trustee Adler Planetarium, Chgo., 1978—; med. adv. bd. G&P Charitable Found., 1999—. Co-recipient King Faisal Internat. prize in medicine, 1988, Charles Mott prize, GM Cancer Rsch. Found., 1989; named Chicagoan of Yr., Chgo. mag., 1998; recipient Esther Langer award, Ann Langer Cancer Rsch. Found., 1983, First Kuwait Cancer prize, 1984, A. Cressy Morrison award in natural scis., NY Acad. Scis., 1985, Past State Pres. award, Tex. Fedn. Bus. and Profl. Women's Clubs, 1986, Karnofsky award and lecture, Am. Soc. Clin. Oncology, 1987, Antoine Lacassagne Lique prize, Nat. Francaise Contre le Cancer prize, 1987, Katherine Berkan Judd award, Meml. Sloan-Kettering Cancer Ctr., 1989, Steven C. Beering award, U. Ind. Med. Sch, 1992, Robert de Villiers award, Leukemia Lymphoma Soc., 1993, Return of the Child award., Kaplan Family prize for cancer rsch. excellence, Oncology Soc. Dayton, 1995, Cotlove award and lecture, Acad. Clin. Lab. Physicians and Scientists, 1995, Nilsson-Ehle lecture, Mendelian Soc. and Royal Physiographic Soc., 1995, Gairdner Found. award, 1996, medal of honor, Basic Sci. Am. Cancer Soc., 1996, Nat. Medal of Sci., 1998, Lasker award for clin. scis., 1998, Woman Extraordinaire award, Internat. Women's Assocs., 1999, Golden Plate award, Am. Acad. Achievement, 1999, Women Achieving Excellence award, YWCA of Met. Chgo., 2000, Philip Levine award, Am. Soc. Clin. Pathology, 2001, Emile M Chamot award, State Microscopy Soc. Ill., 2001, Mendel medal, Villanova U., 2003, Benjamin Franklin medal, Am. Philos. Soc., 2003, Dist. Alumni Award, U. Chgo., 2003. Fellow: AAAS (nominating com. 1998); mem.: NAS (chmn. sect. 41 1995—99, mem. com. 2004), Chgo. Network, Inst. Medicine (coun. 1988—90), Cancer Rsch. (lectr. 2003, G.H.A. Clowes Meml. award 1989, Charlotte Friend award 2003, Dorothy P. Landon award 2005), Am. Soc. Hematology (lectr. Millenium Symposium 1999, Presdl. Symposium 1982, Dameshek prize 1982, Ham-Wasserman award 1995, Henry M. Stratton medal 2003), Genetical Soc., Am. Soc. Human Genetics (pres.-elect 1992, pres. 1993, Allen award and lectr. 1991, Disting. Sci. lectr. 2003), Am. Philos. Soc., Am. Acad. Arts and Scis. (nominating com. 1998), Phi Beta Kappa (hon.), Alpha Omega Alpha, Sigma Xi (William Proctor prize for sci. achievement 1989). Episcopalian. Home: 5310 S University Ave Chicago IL 60615-5106 Office: U Chgo 5841 S Maryland Ave MC 2115 Chicago IL 60637-1463 Office Phone: 773-702-6117. Business E-Mail: jrowley@medicine.bsd.uchicago.edu.

ROY, DAVID TOD, literature educator; b. Nanking, China, Apr. 5, 1933; s. Andrew Tod and Margaret (Crutchfield) R.; m. Barbara Jean Chew, Feb. 4, 1967. AB, Harvard U., 1958, AM, 1960, PhD, 1965. Asst. prof. Princeton U., 1963-67; assoc. prof. U. Chgo., 1967-73, prof., 1973—99, prof. emeritus, 1999—, chmn. com. on Far Eastern Studies, 1968-70, chmn. dept. Far Eastern Langs. and Civilizations, 1972-75. Author: Kuo Mo-jo: The Early Years, 1971; contbr.: How to Read the Chinese Novel, 1990, Minds and Mentalities in Traditional Chinese Literature, 1999; co-editor: Ancient China: Studies in Early Civilization, 1978; translator: The Plum in the Golden Vase or Chin P'ing Mei, vol. 1, 1993, vol. 2, 2001, vol. 3, 2006. Served with U.S. Army, 1954-56. Ford Found. fellow, 1958-60, Jr. fellow Harvard Soc. Fellows, 1960-63, fellow Fulbright-Hays Commn., 1967, Chgo. Humanities Inst. fellow, 1994-95; grantee Am. Coun. Learned Socs., 1976-77, NEH, 1983-86, 95-96. Mem. Am. Oriental Soc., Assn. for Asian Studies. Clubs: Quadrangle (Chgo.). Democrat. Office: U Chgo 1050 E 59th St Chicago IL 60637-1559 Home: 5443 S Cornell Ave Chicago IL 60615-5603 Business E-Mail: davidroy@uchicago.edu.

ROY, KEVIN, newscaster; b. Chgo. BA in Broadcast Journalism summa cum laude, U. Mo., Columbia, 1990. Anchor and reporter KCRG-TV, Cedar Rapids, Iowa, 1990—92; weekend anchor and reporter WHAS-TV, Louisville, 1992—93; Washington corr. Belo Broadcasting Bur., 1993—95; weekend anchor and investigative reporter KGW-TV, Portland, Oreg., 1995—98; reporter WLS-TV, Chgo., 1998—, co-anchor Weekend Morning News, 2002—. TV journalist Son of Suicide, 2001 (Best ews Series Emmy, 2001, Silver Dome award Best Series, 2001, nat. media award of Mental Health Assn. of Mentally Ill in Ill., 2001, Gold Bell Media award, Mental Health Assn. of Ill., 2001, Rosalynn Ctr. fellowship for Mental Health Journalism, 2007), AIDS in Africa: The Lost Generation, 2002 (Best Hard News Feature Emmy, 2002), (news segment) Frank Lloyd Wright, 2001 (AP Ill. honors, 2001). Vol. Loving Outreach to Survivors of Suicide Cath. Charities, Chgo.; bd. mem. Mental Health Assn. of Ill. Recipient Best Reporter Individual Excellence on Camera Emmy, NATAS, 2001, Individual Excellence in News Writing Emmy, 2002. Mem.: AFTRA, NATAS. Office: WLS-TV 190 N State St Chicago IL 60601 Home Phone: 773-928-5543; Office Phone: 312-750-7577. E-mail: krroy7@yahoo.com.

ROY, PAUL J.N., lawyer; b. Biddeford, Maine; BA, Colby Coll., 1978; MBA, Northwestern U., 1981; JD, Loyola U., 1985. Bar: Ill. 1985. Mgr. personal computer software devel., bus. sys. analyst Assocs. Comml. Corp., 1982—85; ptnr. Mayer, Brown, Rowe & Maw LLP, Chgo., 1985—. Mem.: ABA. Office: Mayer Brown Rowe Maw Llp 230 S La Salle St Ste 400 Chicago IL 60604-1407 Office Phone: 312-701-7370. Office Fax: 312-706-8196. E-mail: proy@mayerbrownrowe.com.

ROY, ROBERT RUSSELL, toxicologist; b. Mpls., Sept. 14, 1957; s. Rudolph Russell and Arlene Charlotte (Miller) R.; m. Barbara Jane Richie, Oct. 10, 1987; children: Andrew, Katherine. BA cum laude, Augsburg Coll., 1980; MS, U. Minn., 1986, PhD, 1989. Bd. cert. in toxicology. Toxicologist, project mgr. Pace Labs., Inc., Mpls., 1989-90; toxicologist Minn. Dept. Health, Mpls., 1990-93, Minn. Regional Poison Ctr., St. Paul, 1990-97; team leader, toxicology specialist 3M, St. Paul, 1997—, sr. toxicology specialist, 2000—. Lectr. U. Minn., Mpls., 1986-90, Midwest Ctr. Occupl. Health and Safety, St. Paul, 1990—, instr., 1989; adj. assoc. prof. U. Minn., 1993—; grad. faculty toxicology and pub. health U. Minn.; adj. asst. prof. emergency medicine Oreg. Health Sci. U., Portland. Active Mt. Carmel Luth. Ch. Coun., Mpls., 1983-85. Mem. Soc. Toxicology, Am. Indsl. Hygiene Assn., Delta Omega. Home: 6301 Oxbow Bend Chanhassen MN 55317-9110 Office: Corp Toxicology 3 M Ctr Bldg 220-6E-03 Saint Paul MN 55144-1000 Business E-Mail: rroy@mmm.com.

ROYAL, HENRY DUVAL, nuclear medicine physician, educator, director; b. Norwich, Conn., May 14, 1948; BS, Providence Coll., 1970; MD, St. Louis U., 1974. Diplomate Am. Bd. Internal Medicine; Am. Bd. Nuclear Medicine. Intern R.I. Hosp., Providence, 1974, resident in internal medicine, 1975-76; resident in nuclear medicine Harvard Med. Sch., Boston, 1977-79; from assoc. to staff physician Barnes Hosp., St. Louis, 1987—; from assoc. to cons. staff physician Children's Hosp., St. Louis, 1987—; prof. nuclear medicine Washington U., St. Louis, 1993—; exec. dir. Am. Bd. Nuc. Medicine, St. Louis, 2004—. Co-team leader health effects sect. Internat. Atomic Energy Agy. Internat. Chernobyl Project, 1990; mem. com. on assessment of CDC radiation studies NRC/NAS, 1993-98; mem. sci. com. 1 and 4 Nat. Coun. on Radiation Protection and Measurements, 1993—; mem. coun. Nat. Coun. on Radiation Protection, 1996—, bd. dirs., 2000-05; adv. com. environ. hazards Vets., 1997—; bd. dirs. Am. Bd. Med. Specialties, 2005—. Contbr. articles to profl. jours. Mem.: Soc. Nuc. Medicine (v.p. 2002, pres. 2003), Alpha Omega Alpha. Office: W Pavilion B Rm 961 Box 8223 Washington Univ 660 S Euclid Ave Saint Louis MO 63110 Home Phone: 314-454-1312; Office Phone: 314-362-2809. Business E-Mail: royalh@mir.wustl.edu.

ROYHAB, RONALD, journalist, editor; b. Lorain, Ohio, Oct. 6, 1942; s. Halim Farah and Elizabeth Della (Naiser) R.; m. Roberta Lee Libb, Apr. 20, 1969; children: David Libb, Aaron Nicholas. Reporter Lorain Jour., 1966—69; reporter spl. assignment Scripps Howard Cin. Post, 1971—72; investigative reporter Scripps Howard Cleve. Press, 1972—75; chief bur. Scripps Howard Ohio Bur., Columbus, 1975—78; asst. mng. editor Scripps Howard News Svc., Washington, 1978—81; mng. editor Scripps Howard El Paso Herald Post, 1981—83; asst. mng. editor Scripps Howard Pitts. Press, 1983—92; assoc. editor Pitts. Post Gazette, 1992—93; mng. editor Toledo Blade, 1993—97, exec. editor, 1997—; v.p. Toledo Blade Co., 2004—. Bd. dirs. Toledo Blade Co. With USAR, 1964-70. Decorated Knight Order St. Ignatius of Antioch; recipient 7 awards for Excellence Cleve. Newspaper Guild, 1972-75, Spl. Sect. awards Pa. Newspaper Pubs. Assn., 1985, 86, 88, Benjamin C. Bradlee Editor of the Yr. award Nat. Press Found. 2005; named to DeMolay Legion of Honor, 1997; Am. Polit. Sci. Assn. fellow, 1970-71. Mem. Am. Soc. Newspaper Editors, AP Soc. Ohio (pres. 2000-01), Ohio Newspaper Assn., Toledo Press Club (pres. 2002-03). Eastern Orthodox. Home: 27262 Fort Meigs Rd Perrysburg OH 43551-1230 Office: Toledo Blade 541 N Superior St Toledo OH 43660-0002 Home Phone: 419-874-3142; Office Phone: 419-724-6161. Personal E-mail: royhab@theblade.com.

ROZEBOOM, JOHN A., religious organization administrator; Dir. Christian Ref. Home Missions, 1983. Office: Christian Ref Ch in N Am 2850 Kalamazoo Ave SE Grand Rapids MI 49560-0001

ROZELL, JOSEPH GERARD, accountant; b. Kansas City, Kans., Mar. 20, 1959; s. Joseph Frank and Frances Elizabeth (Gojmeric) R. BSBA, Rockhurst Coll., 1981; MBA, U. Mo., Kansas City, 1992. Staff acct. Donnelly, Meiners & Jordan, Kansas City, Mo., 1981-82, Francis A. Wright & Co., Kansas City, Mo., 1982-88, Libby Corp., Kansas City, 1988-90, Sprint Corp., Overland Park, Kans., 1990—. Mem. Greater Kansas City Young Reps., pres. 1988-89; treas. Jackson County Rep. Com., 1989-97. Mem. AICPAs, Mo. Soc. CPAs (legis. com., liaison com.), Greater Kans. Jaycees (treas. 1988-89). Republican. Roman Catholic. Avocations: basketball, soccer, volleyball. Home: 12112 Madison Ct Kansas City MO 64145-1023

ROZELLE, LEE THEODORE, physical chemist, researcher; b. Rhinelander, Wis., Mar. 9, 1933; s. Theodore and Alice (Omholt) R.; m. Barbara J. Ingli, June 21, 1955; children— David, Steven, Carolyn, Ann, Kenneth BS, U. Wis., 1955, PhD, 1960. Rsch. chemist DuPont Corp., Circleville, Ohio, 1960-63; prin. scientist-tech. coord. Honeywell Corp., Mpls., 1963-67; dir. chemistry div. North Star Rsch. Inst., Mpls., 1967-74; v.p. R&D USCI div. C.R. Bard, Billerica, Mass., 1974-77; dir. engring. tech. div. Mellon Inst., Pitts., 1977-78; dir. rsch. and devel. Permutit Co., Monmouth Junction, NJ, 1978-80; v.p. rsch. and devel. Gelman Scis., Inc., Ann Arbor, Mich., 1980-82; v.p. sci. and tech. Culligan Internat. Co., Northbrook, Ill., 1982-87; assoc. dir. rsch. Olin Chems. Rsch. div. Olin Corp., Cheshire, Conn., 1987-92; cons. in water treatment tech., mktg. and mgmt., 1992—; pres., cons. Water Solutions, Inc., 1995—; exec. v.p. Puraq Water Systems, Inc., 1996—. Cons. in field; mem. Nat. Drinking Water Adv. Council EPA, 1987-90; mem. small bus. inovative rsch. com. U.S. EPA, 1999—. Contbr. chpts. to books, numerous articles to profl. jours. Bd. dirs. Unitarian Ch., Andover, Mass., 1974—77. NIH fellow, 1958-60; recipient Spl. Hominum award Nat. Sanitation Found., 1988. Fellow Am. Inst. Chemists; mem. AAAS, Am. Chem. Soc., Am. Soc. Artificial Internal Organs, Health Industry Mfrs. Assn. (chmn. spl. activities com.), Water Pollution Control Fedn., Water Quality Assn. (chmn. sci. adv. com., Award of Merit 1989), Am. Water Works Assn., Assn. Met. Water Agencies, Filtration Soc., Pacific Water Quality Assn. (bd. dirs. 1987-90, Robert Gans award 1988), Am. Soc. Agrl. Engring., Internat. Water Supply Assn., European Membrane Soc., N.Am. Membrane Soc., Asociacion Interamericano De Ingenieria Sanaitaria y Ambiental, Sigma Xi, Eta Phi Alpha, Phi Lambda Upsilon.

ROZOF, PHYLLIS CLAIRE, lawyer; b. Flint, Mich., Aug. 3, 1948; d. Eugene Robert and Loveta Lucille Greenwood; m. Robert James Rozof, July 17, 1970 (dec. Oct. 1995); children: Nathan, Zachary. AB with high distinction, U. Mich., 1970, JD magna cum laude, 1977. Bar: Mich. 1977, Fla. 1978. Assoc. Honigman Miller Schwartz and Cohn, Detroit, 1977-81, ptnr., 1982—. Mem. Comml. Real Estate Women Detroit (pres. 1992-93). Office: Honigman Miller Schwartz & Cohn LLP 2290 1st ational Bldg Detroit MI 48226 Office Phone: 313-465-7532. Business E-Mail: prozof@honigman.com.

RUAN, JOHN, transportation executive; b. Beacon, Iowa, Feb. 11, 1914; s. John Arthur and Rachel Anthony (Llewellyn) R.; m. Rose Duffy, July 10, 1941 (dec. May 1943); 1 child, John III; m. Elizabeth J. Adams, Sept. 6, 1946; children: Elizabeth Jayne Ruan Fletcher, Thomas Heyliger. Student, Iowa State U., 1931-32. Pres. The Ruan Cos., Des Moines, 1932-86, chmn., 1986—. Chmn. Ruan Transp. Corp., Ruan Leasing Co., Ruan Aviation Corp., Ruan Fin. Corp., Ruan Ctr. Corp.; pres. and treas. City Ctr. Corp.; chmn. bd. dirs. and chmn. exec. com. Bankers Trust Co.; bd. dirs. Heritage Communications, Inc., orthwestern States Portland Cement Co. Mem. Des Moines Devel. Corp.; past pres. Greater Des Moines Com., Iowa State Engring. Coll. Adv. Council; fin. chmn., exec. com. Northwestern U. Transp. Ctr.; bd. govs. Iowa State U. Found.; bd. dirs. Des Moines Area Council on Alcoholism, Living History Farms; trustee Hoover Presidential Library Assns., Inc. Named Des Moines Citizen Yr., Des Moines City Council, 1981; elected to Iowa Bus. Hall of Fame, 1982; recipient Disting. Iowa Citizen award Mid-Iowa Council Boy Scouts Am., 1985, Humanitarian award Variety Club of Iowa, 1986, People With Vision award Iowa Soc. Prevent Blindness, 1986. Mem. Am. Trucking Assns., Inc. (treas., exec. com., chmn. fin. com.), Am. Trucking Assns. Found. (trustee), Iowa Assn. Bus. and Industry (bd. dirs.), Des Moines C. of C. (bd. dirs.). Clubs: Wakonda, Des Moines; Lost Tree, Old Port Yacht (North Palm Beach, Fla.); Rancho LaCosta (Carlsbad, Calif.). Republican. Methodist. Avocations: golf, mushroom hunting. Home: 23 34th St Davenport IA 52806 Office: Ruan Fin Corp 666 Grand Ave Des Moines IA 50309-2506 also: Ruan Cos 3200 Ruan Ctr Des Moines IA 50309-2535

RUB, TIMOTHY F., museum director; b. NYC, Mar. 9, 1952; s. Louis Rub and Marguerite (Gustafson); m. Sally Rub; children: Peter, Katharine. BA in Art History, Middlebury Coll., 1974; MA in Art History, NYU, 1979; MBA, Yale U., 1987; postgrad., Harvard U., 1998. Curatorial intern Met. Mus. Art, 1983; lectr. art and archtl. history Cooper-Hewitt Mus./Parsons Sch. Design, Stevens Inst. Tech., 1979-84; guest curator Bronx Mus. Arts, NY, 1985-86; curator Cooper-Hewitt Mus., NYC, 1983-87; assoc. dir. Hood Mus. Dartmouth Coll., Hanover, NH, 1987-91, dir., COO, 1991-2000; dir. Cin. Art Mus., 2000—06; dir., CEO, Cleve. Mus. Art, 2006—. Avocation: gardening. Office: Cleveland Mus Art 11150 East Blvd Cleveland OH 44106 Office Phone: 216-421-7340, 216-707-2250. E-mail: info@clevelandart.org.

RUBEL, MATTHEW EVAN, retail executive; b. Ft. Lauderdale, Fla., Nov. 29, 1957; s. Stanley Bernard and Isabell Rubel. BS in Journalism, Ohio U., 1979; MBA, U. Miami, 1980. Pres. splty. store div. Revlon Inc., NYC, 1988; pres., CEO Pepe Jeans USA; exec. v.p. J. Crew Group, 1994—99, CEO Popular Club Plan, 1994—99; chmn., CEO Cole Haan, 1999—2005; pres., CEO Payless ShoeSource, Inc., 2005—. Bd. dirs. Furniture Brands Internat., Inc., 2006—. Trustee Ballet Theatre Found., Inc./Am. Ballet Theatre. Avocations: tennis, boating. Office: Payless ShoeSource Inc 3231 SE 6th Ave Topeka KS 66607

RUBEN, ALAN MILES, law educator; b. Phila., May 13, 1931; s. Maurice Robert and Ruth (Blatt) R.; m. Betty Jane Willis, May 23, 1965. AB, U. Pa., 1953, MA, JD, U. Pa., 1956. Bar: Pa. 1957, Ohio 1972. Law clk. Supreme Ct. Pa., 1956-58; pvt. practice Phila., 1958-65; assoc. counsel Aetna Life & Casualty Co., Hartford, Conn., 1965-69; corp. counsel Lubrizol Corp., Cleve., 1969-70; prof. Cleve.-Marshall Coll. Law, Cleve. State U., 1970—2003, prof. emeritus, 2003—; adv. prof. law Fudan U., Shanghai, People's Republic of China, 1993—; dep. to city solicitor Phila., 1958-61; dep. atty. gen. State of Pa., 1961-65; spl. counsel to U.S. Senate Subcom. on Nat. Stockpile, 1962; commentator Higher Edn. Issues Sta. WCLV-FM, Cleve., 1975-87. Mem. nat. panel labor arbitrators at. Acad. Arbitrators, Fed. Mediation and Conciliation Svc. and Am. Arbitration Assn., Ohio State Employment Rels. Bd.; lectr. law U. Conn. Law Sch., 1968; vis. prof. law FuDan U., Shanghai, Peoples Republic of China, 1988-89; cons. Shanghai Law Office for Fgn. Economy and Trade, Peoples Republic of China, 1991-94. Author: The Constitutionality of Basic Protection for the Automobile Accident Victim, 1968, Unauthorized Insurance: The Regulation of the Unregulated, 1968, Arbitration in Public Employee Labor Disputes: Myth, Shibboleth and Reality, 1971, Illicit Sex of Campus: Federal Remedies for Employment Discrimination, 1971, Model Public Employees Labor Relations Act, 1972, Sentencing the Corporate Criminal, 1972, Modern Corporation Law, supp. edit., 1978, An American Lawyer's Observations on the Inauguration of the Shanghai Stock Exchange, 1989, Ohio Limited Partnership Law, 1992-2002, Practice Guides, Ohio Limited Liability Company, Law, 1995; co-editor: How Arbitration Works, 1997, editor-in-chief 6th edit., 2003; contbr.: With an Eye to Tomorrow: The Future Outlook of the Life Insurance Industry, 1968, The Urban Transportation Crisis: The Philadelphia Plan, 1961, Philadelphia's Union Shop Contract, 1961, The Administrative Agency Law: Reform of Adjudicative Procedure and the Revised Model Act, 1963, The Computer in Court: Computer Simulation and the robinson Patman Act, 1964. Bd. dirs. U.S. Olympic Com., 1968-73; chmn. U.S. Olympic Fencing Sport Com., 1969-73; pres. U.S. Fencing Assn., 1968-73; capt. U.S. Pan-Am. Fencing Team, 1971, U.S. Olympic Fencing Team, 1972; bd. dirs. Legal Aid Soc. Cleve., 1973-77; trustee Cleve.-San Jose Ballet, 1999-2001. Winner Internat. Inst. Edn. Internat. Debate Championship, 1953; recipient Harrison Tweed Bowl and Am. Law Inst. prizes Nat. Moot Ct. Competition, 1955; named Guggenheim scholar, 1949-53, Fulbright scholar FuDan U., Shanghai, 1993-94. Fellow Coll. Labor and Employment Lawyers, Inc.; mem. ABA, Ohio Bar Assn. (corp. law and profl. responsibility com.), Cleve. Bar Assn. (Securities Law Inst. 1995-2002), Assn. Am. Law Schs. (chmn. sect. law and edn. 1976-78), Internat. Indsl. Rels. Rsch. Assn., Internat. Soc. Labor Law, Internat. Bar Assn., Union Internat. Des Avocats, Internat. Law Assn., AAUP (pres. Ohio conf. 1974-75), Rowfant Club, Phi Beta Kappa, Pi Gamma Mu. Home: 9925 Lake Shore Blvd Bratenahl OH 44108-1052 Office: Cleveland Marshall Coll Law Cleve State U 1801 Euclid Ave Cleveland OH 44115 Office Phone: 216-687-2310. Business E-Mail: alan.ruben@law.csuohio.edu.

RUBEN, GARY A., marketing and communications consultant; b. Cochem, Germany, Jan. 1, 1924; came to U.S., 1939, naturalized, 1943; s. Jules and Erna (Hirsch) R.; m. Irene Jehle, Aug. 12, 1962; 1 child, Monique L. Student, Acad. Comml. Art, Indpls., 1940-41. With advt. dept. Indpls. News, 1940-41; advt. mgr. Greater Indpls. Amusement Corp., 1941-42; pres. Ruben Advt. Agy., Indpls., 1948-68; chmn. bd. Ruben, Montgomery & Assos., 1968-76; pres. Prestige Program Sales Inc., 1973-76, Gary A. Ruben Inc. (advt. and mktg. cons.), Indpls., 1976—. Past lectr. advt. and bd. fellows Northwood Inst.; past pres. Nat. Fedn. Advt. Agys., 1971. Hon. trustee Indpls. Children's Mus. With Combat Engrs. AUS, 1943-46. Paul Harris fellow Rotary Internat. Mem.: Ind. Broadcast Pioneers. Office: 7370-D Lions Head Dr Indianapolis IN 46260

RUBENS, SIDNEY MICHEL, physicist, consultant; b. Spokane, Wash., Mar. 21, 1910; s. Max Zvoln and Jennie Golda (Rubinovich) R.; m. Julienne Rose Fridner, May 11, 1944; 1 child, Deborah Janet. BS, U. Wash., 1934, PhD, 1939. Instr. U. So. Calif., LA, 1939—40; rsch. assoc. UCLA, 1940—41; physicist Naval Ordnance Lab., Washington, 1941—46, Engring. Rsch. Assocs., St. Paul, 1946—52; mgr. physics Univac divsn. Sperry Rand, St. Paul, 1958—61, dir. rsch., 1961-66, staff scientist, 1969—71, dir. spl. projects, 1971—75, cons., 1975—81; tech. advisor Vertimag Sys. Corp., 1981—, Advanced Rsch. Corp., Mpls., 1986—. Lectr. U. Pa., 1960-61; mem. adv. subcom. on instrumentation and data processing NASA, 1967-69; mem. panel on computer tech. NAS, 1969. Author: Amplifier and Memory Devices, 1965; contbg. author: Magnetic Recording—The First Hundred Years, 1999. Hon. fellow U. Minn., 1977—. Fellow IEEE (Magnetic Soc. info. storage award 1987, Millennium medal 2000); mem. AAAS, N.Y. Acad. Scis., Am. Phys. Soc., Am. Geophys. Union, Acad. Applied Sci., Minn. Acad. Sci., Am. Optical Soc., Phi Beta Kappa, Sigma Xi, Pi Mu Esilon. Achievements include patents in magnetic material and devices. Office: Advanced Research Corporation 4459 White Bear Pkwy Saint Paul MN 55110-7626

RUBENSTEIN, JEROME MAX, lawyer; b. St. Louis, Feb. 16, 1927; s. Jacob J. and Anne (Frankel) R.; m. Judith Hope Grand, July 31, 1954; children—Edward J., Emily Rubenstein Muslin, Daniel H. AB, Harvard U., 1950, LLB, 1955. Bar: Mo. 1956, U.S. Dist. Ct. (ea. dist.) Mo. 1956, U.S. Ct. Appeals (8th cir.) 1956. Mem. English lit. faculty U. So. Philippines, Cebu, 1950-51; law clk U.S. Dist. Ct., St. Louis, 1955-56; assoc. Lewis, Rice, Tucker, Allen & Chubb, St. Louis, 1956-64, Grand, Peper & Martin, St. Louis, 1964-65, ptnr., 1965-66; jr. ptnr. Bryan Cave, St. Louis, 1966-67, ptnr., 1968-97, of counsel, 1998—. Dir. Commerce Bank, N.A. Bd. dirs. Independence Ctr., St. Louis, 1985-88, The Arts and Edn. Coun. Greater St. Louis, 1991-99. Served with USN, 1945-46. Bd. dirs. Independence Ctr., St. Louis, 1985. Served with USN, 1945-46 Mem. ABA, Mo. Bar Assn., St. Louis Bar Assn., Mo. Athletic Club, Harvard Club of St. Louis (pres. 1982-83, bd. dirs. 1983-90). Jewish. Avocations: jogging, tennis. Home: 7394 Westmoreland Dr Saint Louis MO 63130-4240 Office: Bryan Cave 1 Metropolitan Sq Ste 3600 Saint Louis MO 63102-2750

RUBENSTEIN, PAMELA SILVER, manufacturing executive; b. Lansing, Mich., May 12, 1953; d. Neil M. and Leah Rebecca (Coffman) Silver; m. Alec Robert Rubenstein. BA in Linguistics, U. Mich., 1974; MA in teaching English to spkrs. of other langs., Columbia U. Tchrs. Coll., 1976; MA in Linguistics, U. Ill., 1978, doctoral studies in linguistics, 1978-80. Instr. Columbia U. Tchrs. Coll., NYC, 1976, U. Ill., Urbana, 1978, libr. Linguistic Dept., 1978-79; asst. libr. Ill. State Geol. Survey, 1979-80; tchr. Congregation Temple Israel, Springfield, Ill., 1980-81; adminstr., tchr. Springfield Bd. Jewish Edn., 1981-82; instr. Comm. Divsn. Lincoln Land C.C., Springfield, 1981-82; tchr. Cmty. Hebrew Sch., Charleston, SC, 1982-83; instr. The Citadel and Coll. of Charleston, 1983; legal sec. Gibbs & Holmes, Charleston, 1984, May, Oberfell & Lorber, South Bend, Ind., 1984-88; instr. U. Notre Dame, Ind., 1987; tchr. Triton Sch. Corp., Bourbon, Ind., 1988-89; v.p., asst. treas. Allied Splty. Precision, Inc., Mishawaka, Ind., 1989—2005, CEO, owner, 2005—. Contbr. articles to profl. jours. Mem. Temple Beth-El Sisterhood, South Bend, Ind., 1987—. Mem.: Nat. Tooling and Machining Assn. (mem. edn. team, audit team 2005—, bd. mem., Mich. chpt. 2004—), Hadassah (life). Office: Allied Splty Precision Inc 815 E Lowell Ave Mishawaka IN 46545-6480 Office Phone: 574-255-4718. Business E-Mail: pam.rubenstein@aspi-nc.com.

RUBERG, ROBERT LIONEL, surgery educator; b. Phila., July 22, 1941; s. Norman and Yetta (Wolfman) R.; m. Cynthia Lief, June 26, 1966; children: Frederick, Mark, Joshua. BA, Haverford Coll., Pa., 1963; MD, Harvard U., 1967. Diplomate Am. Bd. Surgery, Am. Bd. Plastic Surgery. Instr. surgery U. Pa., Phila., 1972-75; asst. prof. Ohio State U., Columbus, 1975-81, assoc. prof., 1981-88, prof., 1988—. Bd. dirs. Am. Bd. Plastic Surgery, 1991-97, vice-chair, 1996-97; chmn. curriculum com. Coll. Medicine, Ohio State U., 1984-97; chief plastic surgery Ohio State U. Hosps., 1985—. Plastic Surgery Ednl. Found. research grantee, 1976, 78. Fellow ACS; mem. Am. Assn. Plastic Surgeons, Assn. Acad. Chairmen of Plastic Surgery (pres. 1994-95), Plastic Surgery Edn. Found. (pres. 2000-01). Avocation: bicycling. Home: 100 Walnut Woods Ct Gahanna OH 43230-6200 Office: N325-B Means Hall 1654 Upham Dr Columbus OH 43210

RUBIN, ALAN J., engineering educator; b. Yonkers, NY, Mar. 20, 1934; s. Jerome and Lydia R.; m. Ann Kopyt, June 17, 1962; 1 dau., Sara. BS in Civil Engring, U. Miami, 1959; MS in San. Engring, U. NC, Chapel Hill, 1962, PhD in Environ. Chemistry, 1966. Civil engr. FAA, Ft. Worth, 1959-60; asst. prof. U. Cin., 1965-68; prof. civil engring. Ohio State U., Columbus, 1968-91, prof. emeritus, 1991—; with U.S. Geol. Survey, Columbus, 1991-93. Vis. prof. Technion, Haifa, 1984. Editor 4 books on environ. chemistry; contbr. articles profl. jours. Served with AUS, 1953-55. Mem. Am. Water Works Assn., Water Pollution Control Fedn., Internat. Assn. Water Pollution Research. Achievements include research on giardia cysts, metal ion chemistry, flotation techniques, disinfection, flocculation, coagulation, adsorption, and other physical-chemical treatment processes. Home: 1438 Sherbrooke Pl Columbus OH 43209-3113 Office: Ohio State Univ Dept Civil and Environtl Engring Columbus OH 43210-1058 E-mail: arubin@columbus.rr.com.

RUBIN, PATRICIA, internist; b. Apr. 27, 1962; MD, Wright State U., 1988. Cert. internal medicine. Resident in internal medicine U. Cin., 1988-91; fellow in cardiology U. Hosp., Cleve., 1991; rsch. fellow in cardiology U. Wash. Sch.

Medicine, Seattle, 1993—; pvt. practice Cardiology One, Kent, Ohio. Recipient Clinician Scientist award Am. Heart Assn., 1995-96. Mem. ACP, AMA, ACC. Office: Cardiology One Box 8086 1330 Mercy Dr NW Ste 200 Canton OH 44708-2624

RUBIN, STANLEY GERALD, aerospace engineering educator; b. Bklyn., May 11, 1938; s. Harry Jack and Cele (Sake) R.; m. Carol Ruth Kalvin, Sept. 29, 1963; children— Stephany, Elizabeth, Barbara B.Ae.E., Poly Inst. Bklyn., 1959; PhD, Cornell U., 1963. Asst. prof. to prof. dept. aerospace engring. Poly. Inst. N.Y., Farmingdale, 1964-79, Assoc. dir. aerodynamic labs., 1977-79; prof. aerospace engring. and engring. mechanics U. Cin., 1979—2000, head dept., 1979-89, dir. NASA Univ. Space Engring. Ctr. on Health Monitoring Space Propulsion Systems, U. Cin., 1988-91, prof. emeritus, 2000—; sci. coun. Inst. for Computer Application in Sci./Engring. NASA Langley Rsch. Ctr., Hampton, Va., 1998—2002. Cons. Aerospace Corp., NASA AAC/ARTS, Allison (GM), others; mem. adv. com. Inst. for Computational Methods in Propulsion, NASA; keynote spkr. 9th Internat. Conf. Numerical Methods in Fluid Mechanics, Saclay, France Editor-in-chief Internat. Jour. Computers and Fluids, Elsevier Sci. Ltd., 1978—; contbr. articles to profl. jours. and Ann. Rev. Fluid Mechanics, 1992. SF fellow, 1963-64; grantee Office Naval Research, 1978-88, AFOSR 1968-92, NASA, 1973—96, others Fellow AIAA (assoc.), ASME; mem. Am. Soc. Engring. Edn., Sigma Xi, Sigma Gamma Tau, Tau Beta Pi Office: U Cin ML 070 611B Rhodes Hall Cincinnati OH 45221-0070 E-mail: srubin@sgr.ase.uc.edu.

RUBIN, STEPHEN D., food products executive; BBA, JD, U. Wis. Pres. Vita Food Products, Inc., Chgo., 1982—, dir., 1982—, chmn. bd. Office: Vita Food Products Inc 2222 W Lake St Chicago IL 60612

RUBNITZ, MYRON ETHAN, pathologist, educator; b. Omaha, Mar. 2, 1924; s. Abraham Srol and Esther Molly (Jonich) R.; m. Susan Belle Block, Feb. 9, 1952; children: Mary Lu Rubnitz Roffe, Peter, Thomas (dec.), Robert. BSc, U. Nebr., 1945; MD, U. Nebr., Omaha, 1947. Diplomate Am. Bd. Pathology. Intern Mt. Sinai Hosp., Cleve., 1947-48, fellow NYC, 1948-49; resident in pathology Michael Reese Hosp., Chgo., 1949-51; pathologist VA Hosp., Hines, Ill., 1953-56, chief labs., 1956-93, cons., 1993—; assoc. prof. pathology Loyola U. Med. Sch., Maywood, Ill., 1963-70, prof., 1970-99, prof. emeritus, 1999—. Adj. prof. Ill. State U., Normal, 1979-96, 2003—, U. St. Francis, Joliet, Ill., 1989—, Ea. Ill. U. Charleston, 1991—, Western Ill. U., Macomb, 1991—; clin. instr. Augustana Coll., Rock Island, Ill., 1991—. Chmn. candidates com. Village Caucus, Winnteka, Ill., 1969-70; bd. dirs. Chgo. Commons Assn., 1968—, North Shore Sr. Ctr., 1998—; mem. New Trier High Sch. Caucus, Winnetka, 1972-74. With AUS, 1943-46, PTO; Ist lt. M.C., U.S. Army, 1951-53. Fellow Am. Soc. Clin. Pathologists, Coll. Am. Pathologists; mem. Internat. Acad. Pathology, Assn. VA Pathologists (pres. 1982-84), Chgo. Pathology Soc., Lake Shore Country Club (Glencoe, Ill.), Mich. Shores Club (Wilmette, Ill.). Avocations: electronics, tennis, travel. Home: 979 Sheridan Rd Winnetka IL 60093 Personal E-mail: northfieldoc@juno.com.

RUCH, RICHARD HURLEY, manufacturing executive; b. Plymouth, Ind., Apr. 15, 1930; s. Dallas Claude and Mabel (Hurley) R.; m. Patricia Lou Overbeek, June 27, 1931; children: Richard, Michael, Christine, Douglas. BA, Mich. State U., 1952. Stores acctg. supr. Kroger Inc., Grand Rapids, Mich., 1954-55; chief acct. Herman Miller Inc., Zeeland, Mich., 1955-58, controller, 1958-63, dir. mfg., 1963-67, v.p. mfg., 1967-77, v.p. adminstrn., 1978, v.p. corp. resources, 1979-85, chief fin. officer, sr. v.p., 1985-87, chief exec. officer, 1988-92, pres, chief exec. officer, 1990-92, also vice chair bd. dirs., 1992-95; chmn. of bd., 1995—. Active Hope Coll., Twentieth Century Club, Holland, Mich.; formerly active Holland C. of C., Zeeland Planning Com.; bd. dirs. Words of Hope, 1997. Mem. Scanlon Plan Assocs. (bd. dirs., past pres.). Avocations: tennis, running. Office: Herman Miller Inc 855 E Main Ave Zeeland MI 49464-1372

RUCKER, FANON A., lawyer; b. Gary, Ind., Oct. 19, 1971; BA, Hampton U., 1993; JD, U. Cin., 1996. Bar: Ohio 1996, US Dist. Ct. (no. and so. dists.) Ohio 2000, US Ct. Appeals (6th cir.). Assoc. Santen & Hughes, Cin. Named one of Ohio's Rising Stars, Super Lawyers, 2006. Mem.: Ohio Mcpl. Attorney's Assn., Ohio Assn. Trial Attorneys, Black Lawyers Assn. Cin. (pres. 2001—03, trustee 2003—), Nat. Bar Assn., ABA, Ohio State Bar Assn., Cin. Bar Assn. (trustee 2002—), Lawyers Club. Office: Santen & Huges Ste 3100 312 Walnut St Cincinnati OH 45202 Office Phone: 513-721-4450. Office Fax: 513-721-0109.

RUCKER, RICHARD S., information systems executive; b. Dayton, Ohio, Sept. 4, 1947; s. Wilbert Hunter and Estelle Janet Rucker. BBA, Wright State U., Dayton, 1976; MBA, Cen. Mich. U., 1987; PhD in Mgmt. Info. Systems, Kennedy-Western U., 1990. Asst. program mgr. Synergy, Inc., Dayton, 1968-78; mgr. data processing Ledex, Inc., Vandalia, Ohio, 1978-83; cons. analyst NCR Corp., Dayton, 1983-85; mgr. info. systems SelectTech Corp., Dayton, 1985; dir. computing and tech. svcs. Dayton Bd. Edn., 1985-91, asst. supt. bus. and tech. svcs., 1991-92; v.p. Midwest region Metters Industries, Inc., 1992-97; CEO, pres. The Rucker Group, Dayton, 1997—. Pres. Richard S. Rucker & Assocs., Dayton, 1982-97. Bd. dirs. Dakota Youth Ctr., Dayton, 1983, Dayton Urban League, 1986—; mem. exec. council Congl. Adv. Council to U.S. Congressman Tony Hall, 1986. Named one of Outstanding Young Men Am., 1984, Man of Achievement, 1988. Mem. Kappa Alpha Psi. Democrat. Avocations: painting, reading, swimming, astro-physics, basketball. Home: 2914 Forest Grove Ave Dayton OH 45406-4039 Personal E-mail: rsrucker777@msn.com.

RUCKER, ROBERT D., state supreme court justice; b. Canton, Ga. married; 3 children. BA, Ind. U., 1974; JD, Valparaiso Sch. of Law, 1976; LLM, U. Va., 1998. Dep. prosecuting atty., Lake County, Ind.; city atty. City of Gary, Ind.; pvt. practice East Chicago; judge Ind. Ct. of Appeals, 1991—99; justice Ind. Supreme Ct., Indpls., 1999—. Former vice chmn. Ind. Commn. for Continuing Legal Edn. Bd. dirs. Legal Svcs. of N.W. Ind. Decorated Vietnam Vet. Fellow: Indianapolis Bar Foundation; mem.: ABA, Nat. Bar Assn. (exec. com. mem. Judicial Council), Ind. Judges Assn., Am. Judicature Soc. Office: Ind Supreme Ct State House Rm 312 200 W Washington St Indianapolis IN 46204-2798

RUDE, BRIAN DAVID, utilities executive; b. Viroqua, Wis., Aug. 25, 1955; s. Raymond and Conelee (Johnson) R.; m. Karen Thulin; children: Erik, Nels. BA magna cum laude, Luther Coll., 1977; MA, U. Wis., Madison, 1994. Mem. Wis. Assembly, Madison, 1982-84, Wis. Senate, Madison, 1984-2000; pres. Wis. State Sen., 1993-96, 98. With corp. comms. Trane Co., La Crosse, Wis., 1981-85; dir. external rels. Dairyland Power Coop.; bd. dirs. Fortress Bank of Westby, Riverfront, Inc. Mem. Lions, Sons of Norway, Norwegian-Am. Hist. Assn. (vice-chmn.), WWTC Found., Rotary. Republican. Lutheran. Avocations: reading, gardening, travel, fishing. Home: 307 Babcock St PO Box 367 Coon Valley WI 54623-0367 Office: 3200 East Ave S PO Box 817 La Crosse WI 54602 Office Phone: 608-788-4000. Personal E-mail: bdr@dairynet.com.

RUDELIUS, WILLIAM, marketing educator; b. Rockford, Ill., Sept. 2, 1931; s. Carl William and Clarissa Euclid (Davis) R.; m. Jacqueline Urch Dunham, July 3, 1954; children: Robert, Jeanne, Katherine, Kristi. BS in Mech. Engring., U. Wis., 1953; MBA, U. Pa., 1959, PhD in Econs., 1964. Program engr., missile and space vehicle dept. Gen. Electric Co., Phila., 1956-57, 59-61; sr. research economist North Star Research Inst., Mpls., 1964-66; lectr. U. Minn., Mpls., 1961-64, asst. prof. mktg. Coll. Bus. Adminstrn., 1964, assoc. prof., 1966-72, prof., 1972—. Co-author: (with W. Bruce Erickson) An Introduction to Contemporary Business, 1973, rev. 4th edit., 1985; (with Eric N. Berkowitz, Roger A. Kerin and Steven W. Hartley) Marketing, 1986, rev. 8th edit., 2006; (with Roger A. Kerin and Steven W. Hartley) Marketing: The Core, 2004, rev. 2d edit., 2007; (with Krzysztof Przybytowski, Roger A. Kerin and Steven W. Hartley) Marketing na Przykładach, 1998; (with others) Mapketkht, 1st Russian edit., 2001; contbr. articles to profl. jours. Served USAF, 1954—55. Home: 1425 Alpine Pass Minneapolis MN 55416-3560 Business E-Mail: rudelius@umn.edu.

RUDELL, MILTON WESLEY, aerospace engineer; b. Rice Lake, Wis., July 9, 1920; s. George C. and Edna (Bjoraa) R.; m. Doris Lorraine Shella, Nov. 30, 1941; children: Helen, Geoffrey, Lynn, Deborah, Leah, Andrea, Kessea, Eric, Erin. B in Aerospace Engring., U. Minn., 1946. Registered profl. engr. Chief tool engr. Boeing Aircraft Corp., Wichita, Kans. and Seattle, 1941-43, stateside and overseas field engr., 1943-45; chief fueling systems engr. N.W. Airlines, Mpls., 1946-50; pres. Rumoco Co., Frederic, Wis., 1950-68; registrar ECPI-Nat. IBM computer sch., Mpls., 1968-69; pres. Life Engring. Co., Milw. and Frederic, Wis., 1969—. Designer original med. surg. suture tape, 1951; designer 1st match-book cover with strike plate on rear side for safety, 1942; pioneered high-speed underwing fueling sys. for comml. aircraft and 1st hydrant ground fueling sys. for comml. aircraft; co-author Ops. & Maintenance Manual for B-29 aircraft, 1943. Founder Frederic Found. for Advanced Edn.; bd. dirs. Frederic Area Hist. Soc. Recipient WWII Aeronautical Engring. Citation from Pres. Eisenhower, 1944. Mem. Exptl. Aircraft Assn., Wis. Aviation Hall of Fame, Northwestern Wis. Mycol. Soc. (charter). Lutheran. Home and Office: PO Box 400 501 Wisconsin Ave N Frederic WI 54837-0400

RUDER, DAVID STURTEVANT, government official, lawyer, educator; b. Wausau, Wis., May 25, 1929; s. George Louis and Josephine (Sturtevant) R.; m. Susan M. Small; children: Victoria Chesley, Julia Larson, David Sturtevant II, John Coulter; stepchildren: Elizabeth Frankel, Rebecca Wilkinson. BA cum laude, Williams Coll., 1951; JD with honors, U. Wis., 1957, LLD, 2002. Bar: Wis. 1957, Ill. 1962. Of counsel Schiff Hardin & Waite, Chgo., 1971—76; assoc. Quarles & Brady, Milw., 1957—61; asst. prof. law Northwestern U., Chgo., 1961—63, assoc. prof., 1963—65, prof., 1965—2005, William W. Gurley meml. prof. of law, 1994—2005; emeritus, 2005—; assoc. dean Law Sch. Northwestern U., Chgo., 1965—66, dean Law Sch., 1977—85; chmn. Securities and Exch. Commn., Washington, 1987—89; ptnr. Baker & McKenzie, Chgo., 1990—94, sr. counsel, 1994—99. Cons. Am. Law Inst. Fed. Securities Code; planning dir. Corp. Counsel Inst., 1962-66, 76-77, com. mem., 1962-87, 90—; adv. bd. Ray Garrett Jr. Corp. and Securities Law Inst., 1980-87, 90—; vis. lectr. U. de Liege, 1967; vis. prof. law U. Pa., Phila., 1971; faculty Salzburg Seminar, 1976; mem. legal adv. com. bd. dirs. N.Y. Stock Exch., 1978-82; mem. com. profl. responsibility Ill. Supreme Ct., 1978-87; adv. bd. Securities Regulation Inst., 1978—, chmn., 1994-97; bd. govs. Nat. Assn. Securities Dealers, 1990-93, chmn. Legal Adv. Bd., 1993-96, Arbitration Policy Task Force, 1994-97; trustee Fin. Acctg. Found., 1996-2002, Internat. Acctg. Stds. Com. Found., 2000-05; mem. Internat. Acctg. Stds. Com. Strategy Working Party, 1997-99; chmn. Securities and Exch. Commn. Hist. Soc., 1999-04; chmn. Mut. Fund Dirs. Forum, 1999—. Editor-in-chief: Williams Coll. Record, 1950-51, U. Wis. Law Rev, 1957; editor: Proc. Corp. Counsel Inst, 1962-66; contbr. articles to legal periodicals. Dir. Glen View Club Scholarship Found., 2000-07. Ist lt. US Army, 1951-54. Recipient William O. Douglass award, Assn. Securities and Exchange Comm. Alumni, 2007. Fellow Am. Bar Found.; ABA (sec. bus. law 1970—, coun. 1970-94, com. chmn., mem. various coms.), Chgo. Bar Assn., Wis. Bar Assn., Am. Law Inst., Order of Coif, Comml. Club of Chgo., Lawyers Club Chgo., Gargoyle Soc., Phi Beta Kappa, Phi Delta Phi, Zeta Psi. Home: 325 Orchard Ln Highland Park IL 60035-1939 Office: orthwestern U Sch Law 357 E Chicago Ave Chicago IL 60611 Office Phone: 312-503-8444.

RUDNICK, ELLEN AVA, health facility administrator; b. New Haven; d. Harold and C. Vivian (Soybel) R.; children from previous marriage: Sarah, Noah; m. Paul W. Earle. BA, Vassar Coll., 1972; MBA, U. Chgo., 1973. Sr. fin. analyst Quaker Oats, Chgo., 1973-75; from with to pres. Baxter Internat., Deerfield, Ill., 1975—83; pres. Baxter Mgmt. Svcs., 1983-1990, HCIA, Balt., 1990-92, CEO Advs., Northbrook, Ill., 1992—; prin., chmn. Pacific Biometrics, Lake Forest, Calif., 1993-99; exec. dir., clin. prof. Polsky Ctr. for Entrepreneurship U. Chgo., 1999—. Bd. dirs. Liberty Mut. Ins., Pattrson Dental Co., First Midwest Bank. Chief crusader Met. Chgo. United Way, 1982—85; mem. cir. friends Chgo. YMCA, 1985—89; bd. dirs. Evanston Northwestern-Highland Park Hosp., 1990—99, 2003—, Health Mgmt. Sys., 1997—, Evanston-Northwestern Hosp., 2000—02; pres. coun. Nat. Coll. Edn., Evanston, Ill., 1983—93. Office: Univ Chgo Grad Sch Bus 5807 S Woodlawn Chicago IL 60637

RUDNICK, LEWIS G., lawyer; b. May 31, 1935; AB with honors, Univ. Ill., Urbana-Champaign, 1957; MBA, Columbia Univ., 1960; JD, Northwestern Univ., 1964. Bar: Ill. 1964, US Dist. Ct. (no. dist. Ill.) 1964. Of Councel, Franchise & Distribution practice group DLA Piper US LLP, Chgo. Former gen. counsel Internat. Franchise Assn. and Internat. Franchise Assn. Edn. Found.; mem., councel Ill. Franchise Adv. Bd.; mem. gov. com. ABA Forum on Franchising, 1977—84, chmn., 1981—83. Editor: Former Jour. of Internat. Franchising & Distribution Law; contbr. articles to profl. jours. Mem.: ABA, Internat. Franchise Assn. (counsel). Office: DLA Piper US LLP Suite 1900 203 N LaSalle St Chicago IL 60601-1293 Office Phone: 312-368-4055. Office Fax: 312-630-7312. Business E-Mail: lewis.rudnick@dlapiper.com.

RUDNICK, PAUL DAVID, lawyer; b. Chgo., May 15, 1940; s. Harry Louis and Cele (Gordon) R.; m. Hope Korshak, June 13, 1963; children: William A., Carolyn. BS, Tulane U., 1962; JD cum laude, Northwestern U., 1965. Bar: Ill. 1965, Colo. 1994, U.S. Dist. Ct. (no. dist.) Ill. Assoc. Schiff, Hardin & Waite, Chgo., 1965-66; ptnr. Piper Rudnick, Chgo., 1966-99, sr. counsel, 2000—04; sr. counsel, Real Estate practice DLA Piper Rudnick Gray Cary, Chgo., 2005—. Editor orthwestern U. Law Rev., 1964-65; co-editor, author: Illinois Real Estate Forms, 1989. Mem. Pitkin County Colo. Planning and Zoning Commn. Mem. Am. Coll. Real Estate Lawyers, Internat. Found. for Employee Benefit Plans, Order of Coif. Office: DLA Piper Rudnick Gray Cary Suite 1900 203 N La Salle St Chicago IL 60601-1293 Office Phone: 312-368-4060. Office Fax: 312-630-7353. Business E-Mail: paul.rudnick@dlapiper.com.

RUDNICK, WILLIAM ALAN, lawyer; b. Chgo., Apr. 22, 1964; s. Paul David and Hope Korshak Rudnick; m. Katherine Stuart Bergman, Apr. 13, 1991; children: Spencer Ford, William Stuart, Phoebe Elizabeth. BA cum laude, Tufts U., 1986; JD, Northwestern U., 1989; MBA with honors, U. Chgo., 1997. Bar: Ill. 1989. Assoc. Piper Marbury Rudnick & Wolfe, Chgo., 1989-96, ptnr., 1997—2004; ptnr., co-chmn. Nonprofit & Philanthropy practice group, mem. exec. com., policy com. DLA Piper Rudnick Gray Cary, Chgo., 2005—. Lead advance Dukakis for Pres., 1988; chmn. Perlee for State Rep., Chgo., 1992; bd. mem. & past chmn. Am. Second Harvest; chmn. emeritus Greater Chgo. Food Depository. Recipient Tommorow's Leaders Today award Pub. Allies, Chgo., 1995, Hunger's Hope-Bd. Leadership award Second Harvest, 1998. Mem. ABA. Avocations: reading, skiing, exercising, cooking, hiking. Office: DLA Piper Rudnick Gray Cary Suite 1900 203 N LaSalle St Chicago IL 60601-1293 Office Phone: 312-368-7078. Office Fax: 312-236-7516. Business E-Mail: william.rudnick@dlapiper.com.

RUDOLPH, CARL J., insurance company executive; Chartered life underwriter; cert. mgmt. acct.; CPA; cert. cash mgr. Dir. fin. planning & control sys. Thrivent Fin. for Lutherans, Appleton, Wis., 1971-86, v.p., controller, 1986-97, v.p., controller, treas. corp. fin. svcs., 1997-99, sr. v.p., CFO, 1999—2004. Bd. dir. Jewelers Mutual Ins. Co., 2004—. Mem. Fin. Execs. Inst., Treasury Mgmt. Assn., AICPAs. Mailing: Jewelers Mutual Ins Co 24 Jewelers Park Dr PO Box 458 eenah WI 54957-0468

RUDOLPH, LAVERE CHRISTIAN, library director; b. Jasper, Ind., Dec. 24, 1921; s. Joseph Frank and Rose (Stradtner) R. AB, DePauw U., 1948; B.D., Louisville Presbyn. Sem., 1951; PhD, Yale, 1958; student, U. Zurich, Switzerland, 1960; M.L.S., Ind. U., 1968. Ordained to Ministry Presbyn. Ch., 1950; pastor in Ind. and Conn., 1950-54; mem. faculty Louisville Presbyn. Sem., 1954-69, prof. ch. history, 1960-69; lectr. history U. Louisville, 1965-69; rare books bibliographer Van Pelt Library U. Pa.; head tech. services Lilly Library, Ind. U., 1970-78, curator of books, 1978-86, librarian emeritus, 1987—. Author: Hoosier Zion, 1963 (Thomas Kuch award Ind. U. Writers Conf. 1964), Story of the Church, 1966, Francis Asbury, 1966, Indiana Letters, 1979, Religion in Indiana, 1986, Hoosier Faiths, 1995. Served to capt. USAAF, 1940-46. Mem.: Am. Soc. Ch. History, Phi Beta Kappa. Democrat. Home: 2455 Tamarack Trail apt 211 Bloomington IN 47408 Office: Ind U Library Bloomington IN 47405

RUDOLPHSEN, WILLIAM M., retail executive; BS in Acctg., Marquette U.; MBA, DePaul U. With Walgreen Co., Deerfield, Ill., 1977—, dir. 3d party acctg., 1995—98, divisional v.p. acctg., contr., 1998—2004, sr. v.p., CFO, 2004—. Office: Walgreen Co 200 Wilmot Rd Deerfield IL 60015

RUDOY, HERBERT L., lawyer; b. 1942; m. Carole Rudoy; children: Jennifer, Michael. BA, Duke U., 1964; JD, Northwestern U., 1967. Atty. Interperformances Inc., Chgo. Bd. dirs. Sports Lawyers Assn. Mem.: Ill. Bar Assn. Office: Herbert L Rudoy Ltd 230 W Superior #510 Chicago IL 60610 also: Interperformances Inc 230 W Superior #510 Chicago IL 60610 Office Phone: 312-266-2525, 312-654-1717. Business E-Mail: chisport@aol.com.

RUDSTEIN, DAVID STEWART, law educator; b. Leeds, Eng., Sept. 27, 1946; BS, U. Ill., 1968, LL.M., 1975; JD, Northwestern U., 1971. Bar: Ill. 1971, U.S. Supreme Ct. 1977. Teaching asst. U. Ill. Coll. Law, 1971-72; law clk. to Justice Walter V. Schaefer Supreme Ct. Ill., Chgo., 1972-73; asst. prof. law Ill. Inst. Tech.-Chgo. Kent Coll., 1973-76, assoc. prof., 1976-79, prof., 1979—, assoc. dean, 1983-87. Author: Double Jeopardy, 2004, Criminal Constitutional Law, 1990, Criminal Law: Cases, Materials and Problem, 2007. Mem. ABA, Chgo. Coun. Lawyers, Order of Coif, Adv. Bd. First Defence Legal Aid. Office: Ill Inst Tech-Chgo 565 W Adams St Chicago IL 60661-3613 Home Phone: 773-281-4961; Office Phone: 312-906-5354. E-mail: drudstei@kentlaw.edu.

RUEBEL, MARION A., university president; b. Manson, Iowa; B in Biol. Scis., U. No. Iowa, 1958, M in Sch. Adminstrn., 1962; PhD in Ednl. Adminstrn., Iowa State U., 1969. Asst. prof. secondary edn. U. Akron, 1970—73, dept. chmn., assoc. prof., 1973, asst. dean Coll. Edn., dean Univ. Coll., exec. asst. to pres., interim sr. v.p., dir. alumni affairs and govtl. rels., prof. edn.; pres. St. Vincent-St. Mary H.S., 1994—96, U. Akron, 1996—99, trustee prof., 1999—. Bd. dirs. Ohio Aerospace Inst., Northeastern Ohio Univs. Coll. Medicine; mem. Ohio Scis. and Tech. Coun. Contbr. articles to profl. jours. Office: Univ of Akron Stitzleis Alumni Ctr Buchtel Common Akron OH 44325-2602

RUECK, JON MICHAEL, manufacturing executive; b. Riley, Kans., Oct. 23, 1940; s. G.M. Karl and Esther Margaret (Jones) R.; m. Connie Lee Dick Rueck, Apr. 14, 1962; children: Michael Jon, Robin Renee. BS in Nuclear Engring., Kans. State U., 1964, MS in Mech. Engring., 1971. Registered profl. engr., KS, Ohio. Radiation safety trainee Argonne Nat. Lab., Lemont, Ill., 1962; tech. sales trainee Owens-Corning Fiberglas Corp., Granville, Ohio, 1964-65, tech. sales Mpls., 1965-66, customer svc. engr. Granville, Ohio, 1966-67, environ. engr. Toledo, 1971-75; dir. plant ops. Leila Y. Post Montgomery Hosp., Battle Creek, Mich., 1975; environ. engr. Thompson Dehydrating Co., Topeka, 1976, Kans. Dept. Health Environ., Topeka, 1976-77; v.p. Hosp. Instrument Svc. Co., Silver Lake, Kans., 1977-80; supr. air pollution source monitoring Kans. Dept. of Health and Environ., 1979-85; chmn. Rueck Assocs., Silver Lake, Kans., 1985—; pres. Computers Et Cetera, Silver Lake, 1995—. Cons. to Nat. Coun. Examiners for Engring. and Surveying, 1993—; fin. cons. Telecomms. Rsch. Assocs., 1999—. Co-author: Environmental Engineering Examination Guide & Handbook, 1996. Res. police officer St. Mary's (Kans.) Police Dept., 1981-86; lay spkr. Kans. East Conf., United Meth. Ch., 1979—, vol. coord. Topeka dist. disaster response, 1993, coord. Kans. East Conf. United Meth. Disaster Relief, 1994-2000; merit badge counselor Boy Scouts Am., Silver Lake, 1988—; del. candidate for Robertson for Pres., Shawnee County, Kans., 1988; coord. Kans. Interfaith Disaster Recovery, 1993; rural mail carrier, 1999-2000. Mem. Am. Acad. Environ. Engrs. (diplomate, chmn. admissions com. Annapolis, Md. 1986-90, state rep. Kans. 1990-99, chmn. air pollution exam sub-com. 1999—), Midwest Air and Waste Mgmt. Assn. (officer 1987-90), Kaw Valley Bicycle Touring Club (Topeka), Lions. Republican. United Methodist. Avocations: bicycling, vocalist, amateur radio, computers. Office: Rueck Assocs 617 Walnut St Silver Lake KS 66539-9467 E-mail: jrueck@ejmark.org.

RUEDEN, HENRY ANTHONY, accountant; b. Green Bay, Wis., Dec. 25, 1949; s. Bernard M. and Audrey Virgin R. BS, U. Wis., Green Bay, 1971; MBA, U. Wis., Oshkosh, 1973; postgrad., Internat. Grad. Sch., St. Louis, 1984—. CPA, Ill., Wis.; cert. mgmt. acct.; cert. internal auditor; cert. info. systems auditor. Auditor U.S. Customs Svc., Chgo., 1974-86; systems acct. U.S. R.R. Retirement Bd., Chgo., 1986—. With USAR, 1972-2000 (ret.), Desert Storm, 1991, Operation Joint Endeavor, Bosnia, 1996, active duty, 2004-05, Iraq. Mem. CPAs For The Pub. Interest, Nat. Wildlife Fedn., Nat. Audubon Soc., Wis. Farm Bur., Wis. State Hist. Soc., Wis. Farm Bur. Fedn., Future Farmers Am., Am. Inst. CPAs, Wis. Inst. CPAs, Nat. Assn. Accts., Assn. Govt. Accts. Roman Catholic. Achievements include completed marathons in all 50 states and DC six times. Home: 2661 S Pine Tree Rd De Pere WI 54115-9028

RUEDENBERG, KLAUS, theoretical chemist, educator; b. Bielefeld, Germany, Aug. 25, 1920; came to U.S., 1948, naturalized, 1955; s. Otto and Meta (Wertheimer) R.; m. Veronika Kutter, Apr. 8, 1948 (dec. Jan. 2004); children: Lucia Meta, Ursula Hedwig, Annette Veronika, Emanuel Klaus. Student, Montana Coll., Zugerberg, Switzerland, 1938-39; licence es Scis., U. Fribourg, Switzerland, 1944; postgrad., U. Chgo., 1948-50; PhD, U. Zurich, Switzerland, 1950; PhD (hon.), U. Basel, Switzerland, 1975, U. Bielefeld, Germany, 1991, U. Siegen, 1994. Research assoc. physics U. Chgo., 1950-55; asst. prof. chemistry, physics Iowa State U., Ames, 1955-60, assoc. prof., 1960-62, prof., 1964-78, disting. prof. in sci. and humanities, 1978-91, disting. prof. emeritus, 1991—, sr. chemist Ames Lab., U.S. Dept. Energy, 1964-91, assoc., 1991—. Prof. chemistry Johns Hopkins, Balt., 1962-64; vis. prof. U. Naples, Italy, 1961, Fed. Inst. Tech., Zurich, 1966-67, Wash State U. at Pullman, 1970, U. Calif. at Santa Cruz, 1973, U. Bonn, Germany, 1974, Monash U. and CSIRO, Clayton, Victoria, Australia, 1982, U. Kaiserlautern, Germany, 1987; lectr. univs., rsch. instns. and sci. symposia, 1953—. Contbr. articles to profl. jours.; assoc. editor: Jour. Chem. Physics, 1964-67, Internat. Jour. Quantum Chemistry; Chem. Physics Letters, 1967-81, Lecture Notes in Chemistry, 1976-2003, Advances in Quantum Chemistry, 1987-2004; editor-in-chief Theoretica Chimica Acta, 1985-97; hon. editor Theoretical Chemistry Accounts, 1997—. Co-founder Octagon Center for the Arts, Ames, 1966, treas., 1966-71, also bd. dirs. Guggenheim fellow, 1966-67; Fulbright sr. scholar, 1982. Fellow: AAAS, Internat. Acad. Mathematical Chemistry, Internat. Acad. Quantum Molecular Scis., Am. Inst. Chemists, Am. Phys. Soc.; mem.: AAUP, Am. Chem. Soc. (Midwest award 1982, Nat. Award in Theoretical Chemistry 2002), Phi Lambda Upsilon, Sigma Xi. Office: Dept Chemistry Iowa State Univ Ames IA 50011-0001

RUEGSEGGER, DONALD RAY, JR., radiological physicist, educator; b. Detroit, May 29, 1942; s. Donald Ray and Margaret Arlene (Elliot) R.; m. Judith Ann Merrill, Aug. 20, 1965 (div.); children: Steven, Susan, Mark, Ann; m. Patricia Ann Mitchell, Oct. 16, 1999. BS, Wheaton Coll., 1964; MS, Ariz. State U., 1966, PhD (NDEA fellow), 1969. Diplomate Am. Bd. Radiology. Radiol. physicist Miami Valley Hosp., Dayton, Ohio, 1969—, chief med. physics sect., 1983—. Physics cons. X-ray dept. VA Hosp., Dayton, 1970-73; adj. asst. prof. physics Wright State U., Fairborn, Ohio, 1973-74, clin. asst. prof. radiology, 1976-81, clin. assoc. prof. radiology, 1981—, group leader in med. physics, dept. radiol. scis. Med. Sch., 1978-85. Mem. AAAS, Am. Assn. Physicists in Medicine (pres. Ohio River Valley chpt. 1982-83, co-chmn. local summer sch. arrangements com. 1986), Am. Coll. Radiology, Am. Coll. Med. Physics (founding chancellor), Am. Phys. Soc., Ohio Radiol. Soc. Home: 6252 Donnybrook Dr Centerville OH 45459-1837 Office: Radiation Therapy Miami Valley Hosp 1 Wyoming St Dayton OH 45409-2722 Home Phone: 937-433-6668; Office Phone: 937-208-4058. E-mail: drruegsegger@mvh.org.

RUEHLMANN, MARK JOHN, lawyer; b. Cin., Dec. 31, 1961; s. Eugene P. Ruehlmann and Virginia Mary (Juergens) Reuhlmann; m. S. Beth Myers; children: Abby Christine, Sydney Virginia, Richard Carl, Courtney Julia. BA in Acctg., U. Notre Dame, 1984; JD, Vanderbilt U., 1987. Bar: Ohio 1987, registered: US Dist. Ct. (So. Dist.) Ohio 1988, US Ct. Appeals (6th cir.) 1994. Assoc. litigation dept. Taft, Stettinius & Hollister, Cin., 1987-94, ptnr. litigation dept., 1995-99; mng. ptnr.-Cin. Office Squire, Sanders & Dempsey LLP, 1999—. Trustee Cin. Zoo., 1994—; chmn. Sisters of Charity Sr. Care, Cin., 1994—. Office: Squire, Sanders & Dempsey, LLP 312 Walnut St, Suite 3500 Cincinnati OH 45202 Office Phone: 513-361-1210. Office Fax: 513-361-1201. Business E-Mail: mruehlmann@ssd.com.

RUESINK, ALBERT WILLIAM, biologist, plant sciences educator; b. Adrian, Mich., Apr. 16, 1940; s. Lloyd William and Alberta May (Foltz) R.; m. Kathleen Joy Cramer, June 8, 1963; children: Jennifer Li, Adriana Eleanor. BA, U. Mich., 1962; MA, Harvard U., 1965, PhD, 1966. Postdoctoral fellow Swiss Fed. Inst. Tech., Zurich, 1966-67; prof. biology Ind. U., Bloomington, 1967—, spl. asst. to Pres. for Faculty Rels., 1999—2005. Recipient Amoco Teaching award Ind. U., 1980 Mem. AAUP (pres. chpt. 1978-79, 90-91), Am. Soc. Plant Physiologists, Bot. Soc. Am. Democrat. Mem. United Ch. of Christ. Home: 2605 E 5th St Bloomington IN 47408-4286 Office: Ind U Dept Biology 1001 E 3d St Bloomington IN 47405 Home Phone: 812-336-8366; Office Phone: 812-855-5555. Business E-Mail: ruesink@indiana.edu.

RUFF, L. CANDY, state legislator; m. Gregory W. Ruff. Student, U. Kans. Rep. dist. 40 State of Kans., 1993—. Democrat. Home: 321 Arch St Leavenworth KS 66048-3421 Office: Kans Ho of Reps State Capitol Topeka KS 66612

RUFFER, DAVID GRAY, museum director, former college president; b. Archbold, Ohio, Aug. 25, 1937; s. Lawrence A. and Florence A. (Newcomer) R.; m. Marilyn Elaine Taylor, Aug. 23, 1958; children: Rochelle Lynne, Robyn Lynne, David Geoffrey. BS, Defiance Coll., 1959; MA, Bowling Green State U., 1960; PhD, U. Okla., 1964. Spl. instr. U. Okla., 1963-64; asst. prof. biology Defiance Coll., 1964-68, asso. prof., 1968-73, faculty dean, 1969-73; provost Elmira (N.Y.) Coll., 1973-78; pres. Albright Coll., Reading, Pa., 1978-91, U. Tampa, Fla., 1991-94; exec. dir. Dayton (Ohio) Soc. Natural History, 1995-99; pres., exec. dir. Children's Mus. of the Valley, Youngstown, Ohio, 2001—. Author: Exploring and Understanding Mammals, 1971; contbr. articles to profl. jours. NSF grantee, 1965, 67; Ohio Biol. Survey grantee, 1968-69 Fellow AAAS; mem. Am. Assn. Museums, Rotary, Sigma Xi. Presbyterian. Home: 167 Mill Creek Rd Youngstown OH 44512-1402 E-mail: mdruffer@aol.com.

RUGLAND, WALTER S., fraternal benefit society executive; b. Appleton, Wis. BA, Luther Coll., 1959; MBA, U. Mich., 1961. With Conn. Gen. Life Ins. Co., until 1975; cons. actuary, equity prin. Milliman & Robertson, Inc., Hartford, Conn., 1975—98; exec. v.p., chief operating officer Aid Assn. Lutherans, Appleton, Wis., 1998—2001; exec. v.p Thrivent Fin. Luths., 2002—. Fellow Conf. Cons. Actuaries, Soc. Actuaries; mem. Inst. Actuaries. Office: Thrivent Fin Luths 4321 N Ballard Rd Appleton WI 54919-0001 E-mail: walt_rugland@aal.org.

RUH, MICHAEL A., JR., lawyer; b. Ft. Mitchell, Ky., May 27, 1968; BBA, U. Ky., 1990, MBA, 1991; JD, U. Cin., 1996. Bar: Ohio 1996, Ky. 1997. Ptnr. Strauss & Troy, Cin. Named one of Ohio's Rising Stars, Super Lawyers, 2006. Mem.: ABA, Ky. Bar Assn., Ohio State Bar Assn., Cin. Bar Assn. Office: Strauss & Troy Federal Reserve Bldg 150 E Fourth St Cincinnati OH 45202-4018 Office Phone: 513-621-2120. Office Fax: 513-241-8259.

RUKAVINA, TOM, state legislator; b. Aug. 1950; m. Lenore Rukavina; 2 children. BA, U. Minn. Mem. Minn. Ho. of Reps., St. Paul. Mem. govt. ops. com., econ. devel. com., taxes com., environ. and natural resources com., vice chair labor mgmt. rels. com.; legal asst. Democrat. Home: 6930 Highway 169 Virginia MN 55792-8040 Office: Minn Ho of Reps House Standing Com State Capitol Cmn Saint Paul MN 55155-0001

RULAND, RICHARD EUGENE, literature educator, critic, historian; b. Detroit, May 1, 1932; s. Eugene John and Irene (Janette) R.; m. Mary Ann Monaghan; children: Joseph, Michael, Paul, Susan; m. Birgit Noll. BA, Assumption Coll. U. Western Ont., Can., 1953; MA, U. Detroit, 1955; PhD, U. Mich., 1960. Instr., then asst. prof. English and Am. studies Yale U., New Haven, 1960-67, Morse rsch. fellow, 1966-67; prof. English and Am. lit. Washington U., St. Louis, 1967—, chmn. dept. English, 1969-74; chmn. comparative lit. program, 1993-94. Vis. Bruern prof. Am. lit. Leeds (Eng.) U., 1964-65; vis. Fulbright prof. U. Groningen, The Netherlands, 1975, Sch. of English and Am. Studies U. East Anglia, Eng., 1978-79; vis. disting. prof. Am. lit. Coll. of William and Mary, 1980-81. Author: The Rediscovery of American Literature: Premises of Critical Taste, 1900-1940, 1967, America in Modern European Literature: From Image to Metaphor, 1976, (with Malcolm Bradbury) From Puritanism to Postmodernism: A History of American Literature, 1991 (paperback 1992), translation into Czech and Hungarian, 1997; editor: Walden: A Collection of Critical Essays, 1967, The Native Muse: Theories of American Literature, Vol. I, 1972, 76, A Storied Land: Theories of American Literature, Vol. II, 1976; contbr. articles to profl. jours. Guggenheim Rsch. fellow, 1982-83. Mem. Assn. Depts. English (pres. 1974). Avocation: jazz musician. Office: Washington U Dept English Saint Louis MO 63130

RULE, JOHN CORWIN, history professor; b. Evanston, Ill., Mar. 2, 1929; s. Corwin V. and Elaine (Simons) R. AB, Stanford U., 1951, MA, 1952, Harvard U., 1955, PhD, 1958. Tutor and fellow Harvard U., Cambridge, Mass., 1956-58; instr. Northeastern U., Boston, 1955-56; from instr. to prof. history Ohio State U., Columbus, 1958—; vis. asst. prof. Western Res. U., Cleve., 1961; vis. prof. Johns Hopkins U., Balt., 1968. Editor and contbg. author: Louis XIV and the Craft of Kingship, 1970; editor: Louis XIV, 1974, Letters from the Hague and Utrecht, 1711-1712, 1979, The Reign of Louis XIV, 1990. Folger Shakespeare Library fellow, 1968, 1970; Huntington Library fellow, 1978; Am. Council Learned Socs. fellow, 1981 Fellow Royal Hist. Soc. (London); mem. Soc. for French Hist. Studies (sec. 1963-70, assoc. editor jour. 1975-86, co-pres. 1989-91), Signet Soc., Crichton Club. Democrat. Home: 118 E Beck St Columbus OH 43206-1110 Office: Dept History Ohio State U 230 W 17th Ave Rm 106 Columbus OH 43210-1367 Home Phone: 614-228-0787; Office Phone: 614-292-2674.

RUMMAN, WADI (SALIBA RUMMAN), civil engineer, consultant; b. Beit-Jala, Palestine, Sept. 7, 1926; came to U.S., 1948, naturalized, 1959; s. Saliba Y. and Miladeh (Nasrallah) R.; m. Doris E. Reed, Sept. 6, 1955; children— Mary Elaine, Linda Jean. BSE, U. Mich., 1949, MSE, 1953, PhD, 1959. Field engr. Finkbeiner Pettis and Strout, Toledo, 1949; structural engr. Vogt, Ivers, Seaman and Assos., Cin., 1950-51, Giffels and Vallet, Inc., Detroit, 1951-52; instr. U. Mich., 1952-59, asst. prof. civil engring., 1959-64, assoc. prof., 1964-75, prof., 1975-88, prof. emeritus, 1988—. Cons. on design of reinforced concrete chimneys and other tower structures to industry and other agys. Author: Engineering, 1974, 3d edit., 1991. Fellow Am. Concrete Inst.; mem. ASCE (life), Am. Soc. Engring. Edn. (life), Internat. Assn. Bridge and Structural Engring., Sigma Xi, Chi Epsilon, Phi Kappa Phi. Office: U Mich Dept Civil Engring Ann Arbor MI 48109 E-mail: wsrumman@umich.edu.

RUNBECK, LINDA C., state legislator; b. June 11, 1946; m. Richard Runbeck; 1 child. BA, Bethel Coll., 1968. Former mem. Minn. Ho. of Reps., St. Paul; mem. various coms.; U.S. senator from Minn., 1993—. Mem. govt. ops. and reform com., mem. jobs, energy and cmty. devel com., others; advt. exec. Mem. League Women's Voters. Home: 48 E Golden Lake Rd Circle Pines MN 55014-1725

RUND, DOUGLAS ANDREW, emergency physician; b. Columbus, Ohio, July 20, 1945; s. Carl Andrew and Caroline Amelia (Row) Rund; m. Sue E. Padavana, 1980; children: Carie, Emily, Ashley. BA, Yale U., 1967; MD, Stanford U., 1971. Lic. physician Ohio, diplomate Nat. Bd. Med. Examiners, Am. Bd. Family Practice, Am. Bd. Emergency Medicine. Intern U. Calif. San Francisco-Moffett Hosp., 1971—72; resident in gen. surgery Stanford U., 1972—74, Robert Wood Johnson Found. clin. scholar in medicine, 1974—76; med. dir. Mid-Peninsula Health Svc., Palo Alto, Calif., 1975—76; clin. instr. dept. medicine and preventive medicine Stanford U. Med. Sch., 1975—76; assoc. prof., dir. divsn. emergency medicine Ohio State Coll. Medicine, 1982—87, dir. emergency medicine residency program, assoc. prof. dept, 1976—87, prof., chmn. dept. preventive medicine, 1988—90, prof., chmn. dept. emergency medicine, 1990—, prof., interim chmn. dept. family medicine, 1994—95, assoc. dean, 2001—; pres. Ohio State Univ. Physicians, 2002—. Attending staff Ohio State U. Hosps., 1976—; med. dir. CSCC, Emergency Med. Svcs. Dept.; pres. Internat. Rsch. Inst. Emergency Medicine; sr. rsch. fellow NATO: Health and Med. Aspects of Disaster Preparedness, 1985—87; vis. epidemiology and injury control U. Edinburgh, Scotland, 1987; working group, emergency and critical care in space NASA, 2001—; bd. dirs. Am. Bd. Emergency Medicine, 1988—97, sr. editor in tng. exam., 1989—, pres., 1995—; pres., chmn. bd. dirs. Physicians of the Ohio State U. (POSU), 2002—; med. dir. Worthington Fire Dept. Author: Triage, 1981, Essentials of Emergency Medicine, 1982, 2d edit., 1986, Emergency Radiology, 1982, Emergency Psychiatry, 1983, Environmental Emergencies, 1985; editor: Emergency Medicine Ann., 1983—84, Emergency Medicine Survey, Annals of Emergency Medicine, Annals of Emergency Medicine Symposium, 1986; editor: (in chief) Ohio State Series on Emergency Medicine, Emergency Medicine Observer, 1986—87; mem. editl. bd.: Physician, Sports Medicine, Emergency Med. Svcs., Jour. Urgent Care Medicine; co-author: Family Medicine Priciples and Practice, 1978, 2d edit., 1983; contbr. articles to profl. jours. Recipient Faculty Tchg. award, Ohio State U., 1999, Douglas A. Rund Disting. Faculty award, Dept. Emergency Medicine, 2003. Fellow: Am. Coll. Emergency Physicians (task force on substance abuse and injury control, Outstanding Contbn. to Edn. award 1992); mem.: IAAA, Columbus Med. Review, Internat. Soc. for Emergency Med. Svcs. (med. dir.), Columbus Med. Forum (pres. 1993—), Soc. Acad. Emergency Medicine (chmn. internat. com. 1991—), Assn. Acad. Chairs Emergency Medicine (pres. 1992—93), Nat. Inst. on Alcohol Abuse and Alcoholism, Alpha Omega Alpha. Office: Ohio State U 146 Means Hall 1654 Upham Dr Columbus OH 43210-1240

RUNDIO, LOUIS MICHAEL, JR., lawyer; b. Chgo., Sept. 13, 1943; s. Louis Michael Sr. and Germaine Matilda (Pasternack) R.; m. Ann Marie Bartlett, July 10, 1971; children: Matthew, Melissa. BS in Physics, Loyola U., Chgo., 1965, JD, 1972. Bar: Ill. 1972, U.S. Dist. Ct. (no. dist.) Ill. 1972, U.S. Ct. Appeals (7th cir.) 1974, U.S. Dist. Ct. (ea. dist.) Mich. 1983. Assoc. McDermott, Will & Emery, Chgo., 1972-77, ptnr., 1978—. Served to 1st lt. U.S. Army, 1965-68, Vietnam. Mem. ABA, Chgo. Bar Assn. Home: 676 Skye Ln Barrington IL 60010-5506 Office: McDermott Will & Emery 227 W Monroe St Ste 3100 Chicago IL 60606-5096

RUNGE, KAY KRETSCHMAR, library consultant; b. Davenport, Iowa, Dec. 9, 1946; d. Alfred Edwin and Ina (Paul) Kretschmar; children: Peter Jr., Katherine. BS in History Edn., Iowa State U., Ames, 1969; MLS, U. Iowa, Iowa City, 1970. Pub. svc. libr. Anoka County Libr., Blaine, Minn., 1971-72; cataloger Augustana Coll., Rock Island, Ill., 1972-74; dir. Scott County Libr. Sys., Eldridge, Iowa, 1974-85, Davenport (Iowa) Pub. Libr., 1985—2001, Des Moines Pub. Libr., 2001—07, KKRunge Assoc., 2007—. V.p. Quad-Cities Conv. and Visitors Bur., 1992—97, Quad-Cities Grad. Study Ctr., 1992—2001, Downtown Davenport Devel. Corp., 1992—2000, Hall of Honor Bd., Davenport Ctrl. H.S., 1992—95, Brenton Bank Bd., 1995—2001, Wells Fargo Bank Bd., 2001; steering com. Quad-Cities Vision for the Future, 1987—91, Humanities Iowa, 1993—2000, chair, 1998—99; bd. govs. Iowa State U. Found., 1991—; dean's adv. bd. Liberal Arts and Sci. Coll. Iowa State U., 2004—, citizens adv. coun., 1998—2000, Leadership Iowa, 1998—99; adv. bd. U. Iowa Sch. Libr. Sci., 1999—, chair, 2006—, adj. prof., 2000—01; devel. bd. Iowa State U. Found., 2000—, Greater Des Moines Leadership, 2002—03; bd. regents Iowa Pub. Radio Exec. Coun., 2005—; bd. dirs. River Ctr. for Performing Arts, Davenport, 1983—97, Iowa State U. Rsch. Pk., 1998—2000, Davenport One, Downtown Devel., 2000—01, Des Moines Operation Downtown, 2004—; chmn. bd. dirs. Am. Inst. Commerce, 1989—98; mem. Qwest Coll. Bd., 1998—2000, Kaplan U. Bd., 2000—. Recipient Svc. Key award Iowa State U. Alumni Assn., 1979, ALA/ALTA Nat. Advocacy Honor Roll award, 2000, Des Moines Women of Influence award, 2004, Carrie Chapman Catt Pub. Advancement award Iowa State U. Alumni Assn., 2006; named Quad City Panhellenic Woman of Yr., 1998. Mem. ALA (chmn. libr. adminstrs. and mgrs. div., fundraising sect. 1988, bd. dirs., Exhibits Round Table 2003-, councilor 2007-), Iowa Libr. Assn. (pres. 1983, Mem. of Yr. award 2000), Pub. Libr. Assn. (bd. dirs. 1990-99, pres. 2000-01), Iowa Edn. Media Assn. (Intellectual Freedom award 1984), Alpha Delta Pi (alumni state pres. 1978). Lutheran. Home and Office: KKRunge Assoc 126 Forest Rd Davenport IA 52803 Office Phone: 515-669-1610. Business E-Mail: kkrunge@libraryconsulting.org.

RUNK, FRED J., retired insurance company executive; CFO Am. Fin. Group, Inc., Cin. Office: American Financial Group Inc 1 E 4th St Cincinnati OH 45202 Office Fax: (513) 579-2113.

RUNKLE, DONALD L., electronics executive; BSME, MSME, U. Mich.; M in Mgmt. Sci. (Sloan fellow, MIT. Various pos., including chief engr. powertrain and racing, dir. advanced vehicle engring., others GM; v.p., gen. mgr. Delphi Saginaw Steering Systems, 1993—96; gen. mgr. Delphi Energy and Engine Mgmt. Systems, 1996—2000; exec. v.p. Delphi Corp., Troy, Mich., 2000—03, pres., Dynamics and Propulsion sector, 2000—03; vice chmn. Delphi Corp. Enterprise Techs., Troy, Mich., 2003—. Mem.: Soc. Mfg. Engrs., Soc. Automotive Engrs., Shingo Prize Acad. (Wu Mfg. Leadership award 2003), Pi Tau Sigma, Tau Beta Pi. Achievements include patents for rotary engine mounting. Office: World Hdqrs Adelphi Corp 5725 Delphi Dr Troy MI 48098-2815

RUNKLE, MARTIN DAVEY, library director; b. Cin., Oct. 18, 1937; s. Newton and Ilo (Neal) R.; m. Nancy Force, Aug. 7, 1965; children: Seth, Elizabeth. BA, Muskingum Coll., 1959; MA, U. Pitts., 1964, U. Chgo., 1973. Library systems analyst U. Chgo., 1970-75, head cataloging librarian, 1975-79, asst. dir. tech. services, 1979-80, dir. library, 1980—2004. Sr. lectr. grad. library sch. U. Chgo., 1977-90. Fulbright grantee, 1965-67. Mem. ALA. E-mail: mrunkle183@comcast.net.

RUOHO, ARNOLD EINO, pharmacology educator; b. Thunder Bay, Ont., Can., Nov. 26, 1941; s. Eino Armas and Toini Helen (Kuusisto) R.; m. Marjorie Denise Anderson, Aug. 21, 1965; children— David, Daniel, Jonathon BS in Pharmacy, U. Toronto, Ont., Can., 1964; PhD in Physiol. Chemistry, U. Wis.-Madison, 1970. Helen Hay Whitney postdoctoral fellow U. Calif.-San Diego, 1971-74; asst. prof. pharmacology U Wis.-Madison, 1974-80, assoc. prof., 1980-84, prof., 1984—, acting chair dept. pharmacology Med. Sch., 1994-95, chair, 1995—, S. Jonathan Singer prof. and chair pharmacology, 1997—. Cons. NIH, Bethesda, Md., 1984—. Contbr. articles to profl. jours., chpts. to books Den leader local council Boy Scouts Am., Madison, 1975-77, mem. at large, 1979—; hockey coach, 1983—. Grantee March of Dimes, 1975-78, Pharm. Mfrs., 1975-76, NIH, 1975— Mem. AAAS. Lutheran.

RUPERT, TIMOTHY G., metal products executive; BS in Math., Indiana U. of Pa. Mgmt. trainee in acctg. USX Corp., 1968, various analytical positions Pitts., 1968-79, asst. dist. mgr. Saddlebrook, N.J., 1979-81, sr. investment analyst N.Y., 1981-83, mgr. N.Y. treasury ops. N.Y., 1983-84, gen. mgr. treasury coord. Pitts., 1984-86, dir. corp. treasury adminstrn., 1986-88, dir. corp. fin., 1988-90, dir. corp. staff, 1990-91; exec. v.p., CFO RTI Internat. Metals, Inc., iles, Ohio, 1991-99, pres., CEO, 1999—. Active United Way of Allegheny County, Boy Scouts Am.; grad. Leadership Pitts. Mem. Am. Inst. Mgmt. Accts., Fin. Execs. Inst., Youngstown/Warren Regional C. of C. (exec. mem.). Office: RTI Internat Metals Inc 1000 Warren Ave Niles OH 44446-1168

RUPNOR, JENNIFER, journalist; BA in Broadcast Journalism, U. Wis., Eau Claire, 2000. Mem. radio news staff WAXX-WAYY, 1997—2000; reporter, prodr. WEAU-TV, Eau Claire, Wis., 2000, anchor NewsCenter 13 sunrise and noon, 2000—. Avocations: baseball, mysteries. Office: WEAU-TV P oBox 47 Eau Claire WI 54702

RUPP, JOSEPH D., metal products executive; BS in Metallurgical Engring., U. Mo. With Olin Corp., 1972—, v.p., manufacturing and engineering, 1985—96; pres. Olin Brass, Olin Corp., 1996—2001; v.p. Olin Corp., 1996—2001, exec. v.p., operations, 2001—02, pres. CEO, 2002—, chmn., 2005—. Office: c/o Olin 190 Carondelet Plaza Clayton MO 63105

RUPPEL, WILLIAM J., state legislator; m. Miriam ruppel. BS, Butler U.; MS, Manchester Coll. Tchr., coach Tippecanoe Valley Sch. Corp.; mem. from 22d dist. Ind. State Ho. of Reps., 1992—. Mem. aged and acing com., fin. instns. com., local govt., county and twp. coms., human affairs com., vice chmn. pub. safety com. Mem. North Manchester (Ind.) Vol. Fire Dept.; mem. North Manchester Police Res.; mem. Butler U. Alumni Bd. Mem. Ind. Vol. Fireman Assn., Farm Bu., Rotary. Home: 909 State Road 13 W North Manchester IN 46962-9127 Office: Ind Ho of Reps State Capitol Indianapolis IN 46204

RUSCH, THOMAS WILLIAM, manufacturing executive; b. Alliance, Nebr., Oct. 3, 1946; s. Oscar William and Gwen Falerne (Middleswart) R.; m. Gloria Ann Sutton, June 20, 1968 (div. Oct. 1979); children: Alicia Catherine, Colin William; m. Lynn Biebighauser, Jan. 17, 1981. BEE, U. of Minn., 1968, MSEE, 1970, PhD, 1973; MS in Mgmt. of Tech., U. Minn., 1993. Sr. physicist cen. rsch. 3M Co., St. Paul, 1973-77, rsch. specialist cen. rsch., 1977-79; project scientist phys. electronics div. Perkin Elmer Corp., Eden Prairie, Minn., 1979-83, sr. project scientist phys. electronics div., 1983-85, lab mgr. phys. electronics div., 1985-87, product mgr. phys. electronics div., 1987-88, sr. product mgr. phys. electronics div., 1988-93; v.p. product devel. Chorus Corp., St. Paul, 1993-94; pres. Creekside Techs. Corp., Plymouth, Minn., 1994—; co-founder Xoft MicroTube, Inc., Plymouth, 1998, chief tech. officer Fremont, Calif., 2001—02; prin. engr. Xoft, Inc., 2002—07, chair, advanced tech., 2007—. Editor: X-rays in Materials Analysis, 1986; co-author: Oscillatory Ion Yields, 1977; patentee in field. Recipient IR100 award for transfer vessel Rsch. and Devel. mag., 1981, IR100 award for energy analyser, 1985. Office: 49000 Milmont Dr Fremont CA 94538

RUSH, BOBBY L., congressman; b. Albany, Ga., Nov. 23, 1946; m. Carolyn Rush; 5 children. BA in Polit. Sci., Roosevelt U., 1974; MA in Polit. Sci., U. Ill., 1992; MA in Theology, McCormick Theolocal Seminary, 1998. Fin. planner Sanmar Fin. Planning Corp.; assoc. dean Daniel Hale Williams U.; ins. agent Prudential Ins. Co.; city alderman Chgo., 1984-93; dem. committeeman Chgo. 2nd ward, 1984, 88, Central Ill., 1990; dep. chmn. Ill. Dem. Party, 1990; mem. US Congress from 1st Ill. Dist., 1993—. Chmn. Environ. Protection, Energy and Pub. Utilities com., Budget and Govt. Operations com., Capitol Devel. com., Hist. Landmark Preservation Com.; mem. Commerce com. Former mem. Student Non-Violent Coordinating com.; founder Ill. Black Panther Party; past coord. Free Breakfast for Children, Free Med. Clinic. With US Army, 1963-68. Recipient Ill. Enterprise Zone award Dept. Commerce and Community, Operation PUSH Outstanding Young Man award, Henry Booth House Outstanding Community Svc. award, Outstanding Bus. and Profl. Achievement award South End Jaycees, Chgo. Black United Communities Disting. Polit. Leadership award; named one of Most Influential Black Americans, Ebony mag., 2006. Democrat. Office: US Ho Reps 2416 Rayburn Ho Office Bldg Washington DC 20515-1301 Office Phone: 202-225-4372. Office Fax: 202-226-0333.

RUSHFELT, GERALD LLOYD, magistrate judge; b. Kansas City, Kans., Aug. 4, 1929; s. Henry Lawrence and Marie Ernestine (Heinrich) R.; m. Joy Marie Jungferman, May 28, 1960. AA, Graceland Coll., 1949; BA, U. Kans., 1953, LLB, 1958. Bar: Kans. 1958, U.S. Dist. Ct. Kans. 1958, U.S. Ct. Appeals (10th cir.) 1969. From assoc. to ptnr. Sullivant and Smith and successor firms, Kans. City, Overland Park, Kans., 1958-75; sr. ptnr. Rushfelt, Mueller, Lamar and Druten and successors, Overland Park, 1975-85; U.S. magistrate judge U.S. Dist. Ct. Kans., Kansas City, 1985—. Mcpl. judge pro tem City of Leawood (Kans.) 1977-85; critique instr. U. Kans. Law Sch., Lawrence, 1981-92. Active Roeland Park (Kans.) City Council, 1964-69. With U.S. Army, 1953-55. Fellow Am. Coll. Trial Lawyers, Internat. Soc. Barristers; mem. ABA, Kans. Bar Assn., Johnson County Bar Assn. (pres. 1986-87), Am. Bd. Trial Advocates, Earl E. O'Connor Am. Inn of Ct. Democrat. Mem. Cmty. Of Christ. Avocations: swimming, baseball, stamp collecting/philately. Office: 500 State Ave Rm 628 Kansas City KS 66101-2400

RUSSELL, DOUG, manufacturing executive, political organization administrator; BS in Bus. Adminstrn., U. Mo., Columbia. Pres. Durham Co., Lebanon, Mo., GEC Durham Industries, Inc., New Bedford, Mass.; chmn. Mo. Rep. Party, 2005—. Mem. U. Mo. Bd. Curators, Columbia, 1982—87, 2005—, v.p., pres., chair fin. and audit com., mem. exec. com., mem. academic and student affairs com., mem. external affairs com.; founding bd. mem., pres. Lebanon Edn. Found.; mem. bd. dirs. Am. Heartland Econ. Partnership; mem. bd. trustees Lifeway, Nashville. Sch. bd. mem. Lebanon R3; mem. Lebanon Ambassadors. Republican. Office: Durham Co PO Box 908 Lebanon MO 65536 also: Mo Rep Party 204 E Dunklin Jefferson City MO 65101 Office Phone: 417-532-7121.*

RUSSELL, FRANK ELI, retired newspaper publishing executive; b. Kokomo, Ind., Dec. 6, 1920; s. Frank E. and Maude (Wiggins) R.; children: Linda Carole Russell Atkins, Richard Lee, Frank E. III, Rita Jane Russell Eagle, Julie Beth Russell; m. Nancy M. Shover, Oct. 5, 1991 AB, Evansville Coll., 1942; JD, Ind. U., 1951; LLD (hon.), U. Evansville, 1985; HHD (hon.), Franklin Coll., 1989. Bar: Ind. 1951; CPA, Ind. Ptnr. George S. Olive & Co., Indpls., 1947—53; exec. v.p. Spickelmier Industries, Inc., Indpls., 1953—59; bus. mgr. Indpls. Star & News, 1959—77; v.p., gen. mgr. Ctrl. Newspapers, Inc., Indpls., 1977—79, pres., 1979—95, chmn., bd. dirs., 1996—98; ret., 1998; also bd. dirs. Ctrl. Newsprint; pres. Bradley Paper Co., also bd. dirs. Past chmn. adv. bd. Met. Indpls. TV Assn., Inc.; trustee retirement trust Ctrl. Newspapers, Inc.; chmn. retirement com. Hoosier State Press. Bd. dirs. Ariz. Cmty. Found., 1992-96, Eiteljorg Mus., 1994—; trustee, chmn. bd. Nina Mason Pulliam Charitable Trust, 1997— Recipient Disting. Alumni award Ind. U. Sch. Law, 1989, Life Trustee award U. Evansville, 1991, Ralph D. Casey award, 1997 Mem. ABA, AICPA, Ind. Bar. Assn., Indpls. Bar Assn. (past bd. dirs., past treas.), Ind. Assn. CPA (past dir.), Tax Execs. Inst. (past pres.), Ind. Assn. Credit Mgmt. (dir., v.p.), Inst. Newspaper Controllers and Fin. Officers (dir., past pres.), Ind. Acad. Ind. Assn. Colls., Midwest Pension Conf. (Ind. chpt.), Newspaper Advt. Bur. (bd. dirs.), Salvation Army (life, award 1989), Columbia Club, Meridian Hills Country Club, Masons, Shriners, Order of Coif, Phi Delta Phi, Sigma Alpha Epsilon Methodist. Office: Nina Mason Pulliam Charitable Trust 135 N Pennsylvania St Ste 1200 Indianapolis IN 46204-1956

RUSSELL, JEFFREY SCOTT, engineering educator; b. Alliance, Ohio, June 14, 1962; s. Ronald Francis Russell and Georgia Ann (Charleston) Holmes; m. Vicki Carolina Radford, Aug. 17, 1985; children: Nicole Lynne, Jacob Thomas, Matthew David, Rachel Marie. BS, U. Cin., 1985; MS, Purdue U., 1986, PhD, 1988. Grad. tchg. asst. Purdue U., West Lafayette, Ind., 1985-87, grad. rsch. asst., 1987-88, postdoctoral rsch. assoc., 1988-89; from asst. to assoc. prof. civil engring. U. Wis., Madison, 1989—. Lectr. Tex. A&M U., College Station, 1988—, U. Tex., Austin, 1992—, U. Wis., Madison Ext., 1990—. Editor Jour. Mgmt. in Engring., 1996—. Mem. Wis. Right to Life, Madison, 1989-94; project coord. U. Wis. Coll. Testament Distbn., Gideon's Internat., Madison West Camp, 1990—; dir. evangelistic ministries First Ch. of Nazarene, Madison, 1992-93. Recipient Presdl. Young Investigator award NSF, 1990, Edmund Friedman Young Engr. award for profl. achievement, 1993. Mem. ASCE (assoc., sec. constrn. div. 1989-92, Collingwood Prize 1991, Outstanding Profl. Civil and Environ. Engring. 1991, Walter L. Huber Civil Engring. Rsch. prize 1996, bd. dirs. 1998—), Am. Assn. Cost Engrs. (assoc.), Am. Soc. Engring. Edn., Constrn. Mgmt. Assn. Am., Sigma Xi, Tau Beta Pi. Achievements include identification of causes of constrn. contractor failure; devel. of analytical models to assist in predicting contractor failure prior to contract award. Office: U Wis-Madison 2304 Engring Hall 1415 Johnson Dr Madison WI 53706-1607

RUSSELL, JOHN THOMAS, state legislator; b. Lebanon, Mo., Sept. 22, 1931; s. Aubrey F. and Velma F. (Johnson) R.; m. Margaret Ann Carr, 1951; children: John Douglas, Georgia Jeanette, Sarah Melissa. Student, Drury Coll. Mem. Mo. Ho. of Reps., Laclede County, 1963-66, Mo. Ho. of Reps. Dist. 125, 1967-72, Mo. Ho. of Reps. Dist. 150, 1973-76, Mo. Senate from 33rd dist., Jefferson City, 1976—. Dir., officer Laclede Metal Product Co. and Detroit Tool & Engring. Co., Lebanon, 1957-89, now cons.; Gen. Alumni Supply Co., Kansas City, 1959—; with Mo. Transp. Co., Lebanon, 1960; ptnr. Faith Leasing Co., Lebanon, 1969—. Del. Rep. Nat. Conv., 1972. Mem. Kiwanis, Am. Legion, Mason (32 degree), Scottish Rite, Lebanon C. of C. Republican. Home: PO Box 93 Lebanon MO 65536-0093 Office: State Senate State Capitol Building Jefferson City MO 65101-1556 Fax: 573-751-2745. E-mail: jrusse01@services.state.mo.us.

RUSSELL, PAUL FREDERICK, lawyer; b. Kansas City, Mo., Feb. 3, 1948; s. Walter Edward and Dorothy Marie (Sickels) R.; m. Kerry Diann Anderson, June 2, 1973; children: Philip, Erin, Shannon, Kelsey, Scott. BA, Northwestern, 1970; JD cum laude, U. Mich., 1973. Bar: Ill. 1973, U.S. Dist. Ct. (no. dist.) Ill. 1973. Assoc. Vedder, Price, Kaufman & Kammholz, Chgo., 1973-79, ptnr., 1980—. Mem. ABA, Chgo. Bar Assn., Ill. State Bar Assn., Univ. Club (Chgo.), Mich. Shores Club. Office: Vedder Price 222 N La Salle St Chicago IL 60601-1003 Office Phone: 312-609-7740. Business E-Mail: prussell@vedderprice.com.

RUSSELL, TIM, radio personality; m. Judy Penly. Radio host Sta. WCCO Radio, Mpls., 1973—; actor Garrison Keillor's A Prairie Home Companion, 1994—. Actor: (films) Robert Altman's A Prairie Home Companion, Detective Fiction, Little Big League; voice over (nat. broadcast, regional radio, and TV commls.); writer, prodr., performer: Tim Russell's Comedy Christmas Carol; and numerous others. Recipient Outstanding Broadcast Personality of Yr. award, Minn. Broadcasters Assn., 1996, Best Radio Host award, Mpls./St. Paul Mag., 1996. Avocations: travel, antiques. Office: WCCO 625 2nd Ave S Minneapolis MN 55402 Business E-Mail: trussell@cbs.com.

RUSSELL, WILLIAM STEVEN, finance executive; b. Evanston, Ill., Aug. 5, 1948; s. John W. and Lillian H. Russell; m. Susan M. Hanson, Aug. 20, 1972. BS, So. Ill. U., 1970. CPA, Ill. Sr. staff auditor Arthur Andersen & Co., Chgo., 1972-76; acctg. mgr., controller, asst. sec. and treas. Lawter Internat., Inc., Northbrook, Ill., 1976-86, treas., sec., 1986-87, v.p. fin., treas. and sec., 1987-96, pvt. investor, 1996—. Served with U.S. Army, 1970-72. Mem. Am. Inst. CPA's, Beta Alpha Psi, Beta Gamma Sigma. Roman Catholic. Home and Office: 51 Park Lane Park Ridge IL 60068-2834

RUSSI, GARY D., academic administrator; BSc, Southwestern Oklahoma State U., 1969; PhD, U. Kansas, 1972. With U.S. Army various mgmt. positions, 1969—92; tchr., rsch. asst. Kansas U., 1969; various positions such as project coord. and v.p., rsch. and strategic planning et al. Drake U., 1973—93; v.p. acad. affairs Oakland U., 1993—95, interim pres., 1995—96, pres. Rochester, Mich.,

1996—. Contbr. articles to profl. jours;, author book reviews. Mem. bd. Automation Alley, Oakland County Bus. Roundtable; bd. trustees Citizens Rsch. Coun. of Mich., Crittenton Hosp.; chair, bd. dirs. Rochester Hills Strategic Planning Process; pres. coun. Mid-Continent Athletics Conf.; chair, bd. dir. Mich. Virtual U. Recipient Rho Ci Soc. undergrad. rsch. award, Southwestern Oklahoma State U., 1969, Merck Rsch. award, 1996, Disting. Alumni award, 1998, George Wibby Athletic award, Oakland U., 2002. Office: Oakland U 204 Wilson Hall Rochester MI 48309-4401 E-mail: russi@oakland.edu.

RUST, EDWARD BARRY, JR., insurance company executive, lawyer; b. Chgo., Aug. 3, 1950; s. Edward Barry Sr. and Harriett B. (Fuller) R.; m. Sally Buckler, Feb. 28, 1976; 1 child, Edward Barry III. Student, Lawrence U., 1968-69; BS, Ill. Wesleyan U., 1972; JD, MBA, So. Meth. U., 1975. Bar: Tex. 1975, Ill. 1976. Mgmt. trainee State Farm Ins. Cos., Dallas, 1975-76, atty. Bloomington, Ill., 1976, sr. atty., 1976-78, asst. v.p., 1978-81, v.p., 1981-83, exec. v.p., 1983-85, pres., CEO, 1985—87, CEO, chmn., 1987—. Pres. and bd. dirs. State Farm Investment Mgmt. Corp., State Farm Internat. Services, Inc., State Farm Cos. Found.; bd. dirs. exec. and investment coms. State Farm Annuity and Life Ins. Co., State Farm Mut. Automobile Ins. Co., State Farm Life Ins. Co., State Farm Fire and Casualty, State Farm Gen. Trustee Ill. Wesleyan U., 1985—; mem. adv. coun. Grad. Sch. Bus. Stanford U., 1987-94; mem. bus. adv. coun. Coll. Commerce and Bus. Adminstrn. U. Ill. Mem. Am. Enterprise Inst., Bus. Roundtable (chmn. edn. task force), Tex. State Bar Assn., Ill. Bar Assn., Am. Inst. Property and Liability Underwriters (trustee 1986-96), Ins. Inst. Am. (trustee 1986-96), Ins. Inst. for Highway Safety (vice chmn.), Nat. Alliance of Bus. (chmn. 1998—), Ill. Bus. Roundtable (chmn. 1998—). Bus. Advisory Coun. Univ. Ill. Coll. Commerce and Bus. Admin. Office: State Farm Ins Cos 1 State Farm Plz E-12 Bloomington IL 61710-0001

RUST, LOIS, food company executive; Pres. Rose Acre Farms, Seymour, Ind., 1989—. Office: Rose Acre Farms PO Box 1250 Seymour IN 47274-3850

RUSTHOVEN, PETER JAMES, lawyer; b. Indpls., Aug. 12, 1951; s. Richard and Henrietta (Iwema) R.; children: Julia Faith, David James, Mark Bennett, Matthew Boyd. AB magna cum laude, Harvard U., 1973, JD magna cum laude, 1976. Bar: Ind., 1976. Assoc. Barnes, Hickam, Pantzer & Boyd, Indpls., 1976-81; assoc. counsel to Pres. of U.S., White House, Washington, 1981-85; of counsel Barnes & Thornburg, Indpls., 1985-86; ptnr. Barnes & Thornburg LLP, Indpls., 1987—. Counsel Presdl. Commn. on Space Shuttle Challenger Accident, 1986; spl. cons. U.S. Atty. Gen.'s Adv. Bd. on Missing Children, 1988; with Transition Counsel's Office, Bush-Cheney Presdl. Transition, 2001. Contbr. monthly column The Am. Spectator mag., 1973-79; mem. bd. editors Harvard Law Rev., 1974-76, case editor, 1975-76; contbr. articles to nat. mags. Bd. dirs. Ednl. Choice Charitable Trust, 1994—, Legal Svcs. Orgn. Indpls., 1977-79; precinct committeeman Marion County Rep. Ctrl. Com., Indpls., 1978-81; state media dir. Ind. Reagan for Pres. Com., 1979-80, Ind. Reagan-Bush Com., 1980; speechwriter nat. Reagan for Pres. Campaign, 1980; mem. legal policy adv. bd. Washington Legal Found., 1989—; candidate for Rep. nomination for US Senate, Ind., 1998; Republican analyst, Indpls. NBC affiliate, 2000-; mem. merit selection com. for US Naval Acad., US Senator Richard G. Lugar, 2000-; mem. bd. dir. Indpls. Lawyers Chpt. of Federalist Soc., 2007-. Lt. cmdr. JAG corps. USNR, 1982—96. Grantee Inst. Politics, Harvard U., 1972. Mem.: Phi Beta Kappa. Republican. Roman Catholic. Avocations: golf, contract bridge. Office: Barnes & Thornburg LLP 11 S Meridian St Indianapolis IN 46204-3535 Home Phone: 317-341-0143; Office Phone: 317-231-7299. Business E-Mail: peter.rusthoven@btlaw.com.

RUTENBERG-ROSENBERG, SHARON LESLIE, retired journalist; b. Chgo., May 23, 1951; d. Arthur and Bernice (Berman) Rutenberg; m. Michael J. Rosenberg, Feb. 3, 1980; children: David Kaifel and Jonathan Reuben (twins), Emily Mara. Student, Harvard U., 1972; BA, Northwestern U., 1973, MSJ, 1975; cert. student pilot. Reporter-photographer Lerner Home Newspapers, Chgo., 1973—74; corr. Medill News Svc., Washington, 1975; reporter-newsperson, sci. writer UPI, Chgo., 1975—84; ret., 1984. Interviewer: exclusives White House chief of staff, nation's only mother and son on death row; others. Vol. Chgo.-Read Mental Health Ctr. Recipient Peter Lisagor award for exemplary journalism in features category, 1980, 81; Golden Key Nat. Adv. Bd. of Children's Oncology Svc. Inc., 1981; Media awards for wire svc. feature stories, 1983, 84, wire svc. news stories, 1983, 84, all from Chgo. Hosp. Pub. Rels. Soc. Mem. Profl. Assn. Diving Instrs., Nat. Assn. Underwater Instrs., Hon. Order Ky. Cols., Hadassah, Sigma Delta Chi, Sigma Delta Tau Home: 745 Marion Ave Highland Park IL 60035-5123

RUTHERFORD, DAN, state legislator; Degree, Ill. State U., 1978. Legis. asst. for State Rep. Tom Ewing, Ill., 1978-80; exec. dir. Ill. Reagan/Bush Com., 1980; asst. dir. Gov.'s Office of Pers., Ill., 1981; mem. adv. com. on internat. trade U.S. Govt. and Adv. Com. on Sports Medicine; mem. Livingston County Coun. for Econ. Devel., Ill.; Ill. State rep. Named One of the People to Watch in 1986 Chgo. Tribune. Mem. Livingston County Farm Bur., Ill. Corn Growers Assn., Pontiac C. of C., Pheasants Forever, Japan-Am. Soc. Republican. Home: 13266 E 950 North Rd Chenoa IL 61726-9049 Office: Ill Ho of Reps State Capitol Springfield IL 62706-0001

RUTHVEN, JOHN A., wildlife artist; b. Cin., 1924; m. Judy Ruthven; 1 child, Kevin. Student, Cin. Art Acad., Jack Storey Ctrl. Acad. Comml. Art. Opened comml. art studio, 1946; founder Wildlife Internationale Inc., 1971; major exhibits include Famous Figureheads Series, Nat. Mariner Mus., Washington, Cin. Mus. atural History, 1994, Artist of Am. exhbn., Denver, Leigh Yawkey Woodson Mus., Wausau, Wis., Soc. Animal Artists nat. tours, 1992—2000, Hiram Blauvelt Art Mus., Oradell, NJ, Rory Tory Peterson Inst. Natural History, Jamestown, NY, 1998, 2004—05, The Smithsonian Instn.'s Preservation and Rsch. Ctr., 1998; major commissions include Proctor & Gamble, Cin. Bengals, John Deere & Co., WILDS Internat. Ctr. for the Preservation of Wild Animals, Armco Steel Corp., Bankers Life & Casualty, Mead Corp., Colonial Williamsburg, Classical Music Hall of Fame. Co-author, illustrator (with William Zimmerman) Top Flight Speed Index to Waterfowl of N.Am., 1965, paintings featured in (books) An Instrument of Your Peace, Eyes of Tenderness, John A. Ruthven, In the Audubon Tradition. Served USN, WWII. Named Winner of Fed. Duck Stamp competition for "Redhead Ducks", 1960, Artist of Yr., Ducks Unlimited, 1972, First Ohio Duck Stamp/Print Artist, 1982, 25th Anniversary Artist, Trout Unlimited, 1984, First Ohio Animal Stamp/Print Artist, 1988, Pacific Flyaway Artist, Ducks Unlimited, 1989; recipient Irma Lazarus Award for sustained arts excellence, Ohio Gov.'s Awards for the Arts, 2001, Nat. Medal of Arts, 2004. Mem.: Soc. Animal Artists (past pres.), Nat. Audubon Soc., Am. Ornithological Assn., Cin. Bird Club, Outdoors Writers Assn. Achievements include painting unveilings at The White House, Hermitage Mus., St. Petersburg, Russia, Pres.'s Palace, Philippines, for Crown Prince Henri, Luxemborg, Neil Armstrong Space Mus., Ohio State Capital Rotunda. Office: Wildlife Internationale Inc 202 E Grant Ave PO Box 59 Georgetown OH 45121

RUTKOFF, ALAN STUART, lawyer; b. Chgo., May 31, 1952; s. Roy and Harriet (Ruskin) R.; m. Mally Zoberman, Dec. 22, 1974; children: Aaron Samuel, Jordana Michal, Robert athaniel. BA with high distinction, U. Mich., 1973; JD magna cum laude, Northwestern U., 1976. Bar: Ill. 1976, U.S. Dist. Ct. (no. dist.) Ill. 1976, U.S. Ct. Appeals (7th cir.) 1977, U.S. Ct. Appeals (3d cir.) 1978, U.S. Supreme Ct. 1981, U.S. Ct. Appeals (5th cir.) 1983, U.S. Ct. Appeals (8th cir.) 1990, U.S. Dist. Ct. (we. dist.) Wis. 1996, U.S. Ct. Appeals (6th cir.) 2003. Assoc. Altheimer & Gray, Chgo., 1976-80; ptnr. Kastel & Rutkoff, Chgo., 1980-83, Holleb & Coff Ltd., Chgo., 1983-84, McDermott Will & Emery LLP, Chgo., 1984—, gen. coun., 2005—. Pres. N. Suburban Synagogue Beth El, Highland Pk., Ill., 1999-2001. Mem. ABA, Chgo. Bar Assn., Order of Coif. Home: 801 Timberhill Rd Highland Park IL 60035-5148 Office: McDermott Will & Emery LLP 227 W Monroe St Ste 4400 Chicago IL 60606-5096 Home Phone: 847-432-2242; Office Phone: 312-984-7751. Business E-Mail: arutkoff@mwe.com.

RUTKOWSKI, JAMES ANTHONY, former state legislator; b. Milw., Apr. 6, 1942; BS in Bus., Marquette U., 1964, JD, 1966. Former instr. Marquette U., Milw.; asst. instr. U. Wis., Milw.; state legis. State of Wis., Madison, 1970-98. With USAR, 1966-72. Recipient Clean 16 award, 1982, 88, 90, 94, Wis. Man of Achievement award, 1976. Mem. KC, Greendale Jaycee Roosters. Home: 4550 S 117th St Greenfield WI 53228-2451

RUTLEDGE, CHARLES OZWIN, pharmacologist, educator; b. Topeka, Oct. 1, 1937; s. Charles Ozwin and Alta (Seaman) R.; m. Jane Ellen Crow, Aug. 13, 1961; children: David Ozwin, Susan Harriett, Elizabeth Jane, Karen Ann. BS in Pharmacy, U. Kans., 1959, MS in Pharmacology, 1961; PhD in Pharmacology, Harvard U., 1966. NATO postdoctoral fellow Gothenburg (Sweden) U., 1966-67; asst. prof. U. Colo. Med. Ctr., Denver, 1967-74, assoc. prof., 1974-75; prof., chmn. dept. pharmacology U. Kans., Lawrence, 1975-87; dean, prof. pharmacology Purdue U., West Lafayette, Ind., 1987—2002, exec. dir. Discovery Park, 2001—05, interim vice provost rsch., 2002—05, v.p. rsch., 2005—07. Contbr. articles on neuropharmacology to profl. jours. Grantee NIH, 1970-87. Mem. AAAS, Am. Soc. Pharmacology and Exptl. Therapeutics (councillor 1982 84, sec.-treas. 1990-93, pres. 1996-97), Am. Assn. Coll. Pharmacy (chmn. biol. scis. sect. 1983-84, chmn. coun. faculties 1986-87, chmn. coun. deans 1993-94, com. implement change pharm. edn. 1989-92, pres. 1996-97), Soc. for Neurosci., Am. Pharm. Assn. Avocations: gardening, skiing. Home: 40 Brynteg Est West Lafayette IN 47906-5643 Office: Purdue U Hovde Hall Rm 338 610 Purdue Mall West Lafayette IN 47907-2040 Office Phone: 765-494-6209. Business E-Mail: chipr@purdue.edu.

RUTTAN, VERNON WESLEY, agricultural economist, educator; b. Alden, Mich., Aug. 16, 1924; s. Ward W. and Marjorie Ann (Chaney) R.; m. Marilyn M. Barone, July 30, 1945; children: Lia Marie, Christopher, Alison Elaine, Lore Megan. BA, Yale U., 1948; MA, U. Chgo., 1950, PhD, 1952; LLD (hon.), Rutgers U., 1978; D Agrl. Sci. ((hon.), U. Kiel, Germany, 1986, Purdue U., 1991. Economist TVA, 1951-54; prof. agrl. econs. Purdue U., 1954-63; staff economist President's Council Econ. Advisers, 1961-63; economist Rockefeller Found., 1963-65; head dept. agrl. econs. U. Minn., St. Paul, 1965-70, Regent's prof., 1986-99, Regent's prof. emeritus, 2000—. Pres. Agrl. Devel. Council, N.Y.C., 1973-77 Author (with Y. Hayami): Agricultural Development: An International Perspective, 1971, 1985; author: U.S. Development Assistance Policy, 1996, Technology, Growth and Development, 2001, Social Science Knowledge and Economic Development, 2003, Is War Necessary for Economic Growth, 2006. Recipient Alexander von Humboldt award, 1985. Fellow AAAS, Am. Acad. Arts and Scis., Am. Agrl. Econs. Assn. (pres. 1971-72, Publ. award 1956, 57, 62, 66, 67, 71, 79, 85, 97); mem. NAS. Home: 1666 Coffman St Apt 112 Saint Paul MN 55108-1326 Office: Dept Applied Econs U Minn Saint Paul MN 55108 Business E-Mail: vruttan@umn.edu.

RUXIN, PAUL THEODORE, lawyer; b. Cleve., Apr. 14, 1943; s. Charles and Olyn Judith (Koller) R.; m. Joanne Camy, May 25, 1965; children; Marc J., Sarah. BA, Amherst Coll., 1965; LLB, U. Va., 1968. Bar: Ill. 1968, U.S. Dist. Ct. (no. dist.) Ill. 1968, U.S. Ct. Appeals D.C. 1972. Assoc. Isham, Lincoln & Beale, Chgo., 1968—73, ptnr., 1974—77; ptnr., chmn. energy utilities sect. Jones Day, Cleve., 1977—2005, of counsel, 2006—. Mem. editl. com. Yale U. edit. Boswell Papers, 2003—. Mem. Hudson Archtl. and Hist. Bd. Rev., 1981-81; chmn. bd. govs. Folger Shakespeare Libr., 2007—; exec. bd. Greater Cleve. Boy Scouts Am., 1978-90; bd. dirs. Cleve. chpt. ARC, 1991-97. Recipient Eminent Svc. medal, Amherst Coll., 2007. Mem. ABA, Chgo. Bar Assn., Internat. Assn. Bibliophiles, Rowfant Club, Chgo. Club, Caxton Club, Grolier Club, Chgo. Lit. Club. Office: Jones Day 77 W Wacker Dr Fl 35 Chicago IL 60601-1662 also: 901 Lakeside Ave Cleveland OH 44114-1116 Home Phone: 312-915-0533; Office Phone: 312-782-3939. E-mail: paultruxin@jonesday.com.

RYALL, JO-ELLYN M., psychiatrist; b. Newark, May 25, 1949; d. Joseph P. and Tekla (Paraszczuk) R. BA in Chemistry with gen. honors, Rutgers U., 1971; MD, Washington U., St. Louis, 1975. Diplomate Am. Bd. Psychiatry and Neurology. Resident in psychiatry Washington U., St. Louis, 1975-78, psychiatrist Student Health, 1978-83, asst. prof. clin. psychiatry, 1983—2003, assoc. prof. clin. psychiatry, 2003—. Inpatient supr. Malcolm Bliss Mental Health Ctr., St. Louis, 1978-80, pvt. practtice medicine specializing in psychiatry, St. Louis, 1980—. Bd. dirs. Women's Self Help Ctr., St. Louis, 1980. Fellow: APA (pres. ea. Mo. dist. br. 1983—85, sect. coun. AMA 1986—99, dep. rep. to assembly 1994—97, rep. 1997—2001, chair bylaws com. 2000—03, dep. rep. area 4 2001—06, rep. area 4 2006); mem.: AMA (alt. del. Mo. 1988—90, 1993—94, del. 1995—, mem. coun. on constn. bylaws 1998—2006, vice chair 2002—04, chair 2004—06), Manic Depressive Assn. St. Louis (chmn. bd. dirs. 1985—89), Mo. State Med. Assn. (vice spkr. ho. of dels. 1986—89, spkr. 1989—92), St. Louis Met. Med. Soc. (del. to state conv. 1981—86, councilor 1985—87, v.p. 1989, del. to state conv. 1993—), Am. Med. Women's Assn. (pres. St. Louis dist. br. 1981—82, regional gov. VIII 1986—89, pres. St. Louis dist. br. 1992, spkr. ho. of dels. 1993—96), Washington U. Faculty Club. Office: 12166 Old Big Bend Rd Ste 210 Saint Louis MO 63122 Office Phone: 314-909-0121.

RYAN, BO (WILLIAM F. RYAN JR.), men's college basketball coach; b. Chester, Pa., Dec. 20, 1947; s. Butch Ryan; m. Kelly Ryan; children: Megan, Will, Matt, Brenna, Mairin. BBA, Wilkes U., Pa., 1969; grad. student, Villanova U. Asst. coach Coll. Racine, Wis.; head coach Sun Valley HS, Phila.; asst. coach U. Wis., Madison, 1976—84, head coach, 2001—, Platteville, 1984—99, Milw., 1999—2001. Mem. Divsn. 1 Men's Basketball Issues Com. NCAA. Author: Passing and Catching: A Lost Art, How to Run the Swing Offense, Applying and Attacking Pressure. Named Delaware County Coach of Yr., Coach of Yr. (6 times), Wis. Intercollegiate Athletic Conf., Divsn. III Coach of Yr. (4 times), Nat. Assn. Basketball Coaches, Big Ten Coach of Yr., 2002, 2003; named to Wilkes Athletic Hall of Fame, 2003; recipient Guardians of the Game award for Svc., Nat. Assn. Basketball Coaches, 2004. Office: U Wis Men's Basketball Kohl Ctr 601 W Dayton St Madison WI 53715 Office Phone: 608-262-4597. E-mail: bfr@athletics.wisc.edu.

RYAN, CARL RAY, electrical engineer, educator; b. Gateway, Ark., Mar. 3, 1938; s. Clarence and Stella (Schnitzer) R.; m. Arline Walker; children: Carline, Julie. BSEE, U. Ark., 1962; MSEE, Iowa State U., 1963; PhD in Elec. Engring., U. Mo.-Rolla, 1969, profl. degree Elec. Engring., 1994. Instr. U. Mo.-Rolla, 1968-69; sr. engr. Govt. Electronics Group, Motorola Inc., Scottsdale, Ariz., 1969-72, mem. tech. staff, 1972-76, sr. mem. tech. staff, chief engr., 1979-89, v.p. tech. staff, 1989-90, dir. communication systems tech., 1990-98; pres. CRF, LLC, Cassvile, Mo., 1998—. Prof. Mich. Tech. U., 1976-79; adj. prof. Ariz. State U., Tempe, 1980-89; panel mem. Internat. Solid States Circuits Conf., Phila., 1977; session chmn. Future Space Communications Tech. Workshop, Pasadena, Calif., 1980; external advisor Mich. Technol. U. Contbr. articles to profl. jours.; patentee in field Assoc. Motorola Sci. Adv. Bd. Served with USAF, 1956-60 Fellow IEEE (communications tech., solid state circuits, accreditation com., Dan Nobel fellow, chmn. Phoenix chpt. 1981-82, program chmn. 1989, gen. chmn. Phoenix Conf. on computers and communication 1988)

RYAN, DANIEL LEO, bishop emeritus; b. Mankato, Minn., Sept. 28, 1930; s. Leonard Bennett and Irene Ruth (Larson) R. BA, Benedictine U., 1952; JCL, Pontificia Università Lateranense, Rome, 1960. Ordained priest Diocese of Joliet, Ill., 1956, parish priest, 1956—82, chancellor, 1965—78, vicar gen., 1977—79, aux. bishop, 1981—84; ordained bishop, 1981; bishop Diocese of Springfield, 1984—99, bishop emeritus, 1999—. Roman Catholic. Office: Diocese of Springfield PO Box 3187 1615 W Washington St Springfield IL 62708-3187 Office Phone: 217-698-8500. Office Fax: 217-698-0802. E-mail: dlryan@dio.org.*

RYAN, EDWARD F., lawyer; b. Chgo., Sept. 14, 1943; BA magna cum laude, U. St. Thomas, 1965; JD, Georgetown U. Law Ctr., 1968. Bar: Ill. 1968, Fla. 1984, US Dist. Ct. (No. Dist. Ill.), US Ct. Appeals (7th, 8th, 11th cirs.), US Supreme Ct. Ptnr. Holland & Knight LLP, Chgo., mem. dir. com. Lectr. in the field. Fellow: Am. Bar Found.; mem.: Fla. Bar, ABA, Chgo. Bar Assn. Office: Holland & Knight LLP 131 S Dearborn St 30th Fl Chicago IL 60603 Office Phone: 312-578-6552. Business E-Mail: edward.ryan@hklaw.com.

RYAN, JACK, physician, retired hospital corporation executive; b. Benton Harbor, Mich., Aug. 26, 1925; s. Leonard Joseph and Beulah (Southworth) R.; m. Lois Patricia Patterson; children: Michele, Kevin, Timothy, Sarah, Daniel. AB, Western Mich. U., 1948; postgrad., U. Mich. Law Sch., 1949-50, Emory U., 1950-51; MD, Wayne State U., 1955. Intern St. Luke's Hosp., Saginaw, Mich., 1955-56; pres. Meml. Med. Ctr., Warren, Mich., 1956-77; v.p. med. affairs Detroit-Macomb Hosps. Corp., 1976-77, pres. and chief exec. officer, 1977-96; ret., 1996. Assoc. prof. medicine Wayne State U., Detroit, 1974—; bd. chmn. Mich. Hosp. Ins. Co., 1990—. Recipient Disting. Alumnus award Wayne State U. Med. Sch., 1974, Wayne State U., 1979, Western Mich. U., 1989, Disting. Key award Mich. Hosp. Assn., 1986, Tree of Life award Jewish Nat. Fund, 1996. Fellow Am. Coll. Family Physicians, Am. Coll. Physician Execs., Detroit Acad. Medicine; mem. Internat. Health Econs. and Mgmt. Inst. (charter), Econ. Club Detroit, Detroit Athletic Club, Renaissance Club, Red Run Club. Avocations: civil war, history, golf, tennis. Home: 175 Hendrie Blvd Royal Oak MI 48067-2412

RYAN, JAMES E., former state attorney general; b. Chgo., Feb. 21, 1946; m. Marie Ryan; children: John, Jim, Matt, Amy, Patrick, Anne Marie(dec.). BA in Polit. Sci., Ill. Benedictine Coll., 1968; JD, Ill. Inst. Tech., 1971. Bar: Ill. 1971. Asst. state's atty. criminal divsn. DuPage County State's Atty.'s Office, 1971—74, 1st. asst. state's atty., 1974—76; founder Ryan & Darrah; state's atty. DuPage County State's Atty.'s Office, 1984—94; atty. gen. State of Ill., 1994—2002. Disting. fellow Benedictine U., Lisle, Ill., 2003—. Named Lawyer of Yr., DuPage County Bar Assn., 1997; recipient numerous awards from various orgns. including, Nat. Assn. Counties, Alliance Against Intoxicated Motorists. Mem.: Ill. State's Attys. Assn. (past pres., Ezzard Charles award). Republican. Roman Catholic.

RYAN, JAMES LEO, federal judge; b. Detroit, Nov. 19, 1932; s. Leo Francis and Irene Agnes Ryan; m. Mary Elizabeth Rogers, Oct. 12, 1957; children: Daniel P., James R., Colleen M. Hansen, Kathleen A. LLB, U. Detroit, 1956, LLD (hon.), 1986, BA, 1992; LLD (hon.), Madonna Coll., 1976, Detroit Coll., 1978, Thomas M. Cooley Law Sch., Lansing, Mich., 1986. Atty. Waldron, Brennan & Maher, 1960—62; pvt. practice Redford Twp., Mich., 1962—66; Justice of peace, 1963—66; judge 3d Cir. Ct. of Mich., 1966—75; justice Mich. Supreme Ct., 1975—86; judge US Ct. Appeals (6th cir.), 1985—2000, sr. judge, 2000—. Faculty Nat. Jud. Coll., Reno; adj. faculty, bd. dirs. Ave Maria Sch. Law; adj. prof. Thomas M. Cooley Law Sch., 1979—85, U. Detroit, 1974—. Contbr. articles to profl. jours. Capt. JAGC USNR, 1957—92, ret. mil. judge USNR. Mem.: USNR Lawyers Assn., Detroit Bar Assn., Fed. Bar Assn., State Bar Mich., Fed. Judges Assn., K.M., K.C. Office: US Ct Appeals US Courthouse 231 W Lafayette Blvd Detroit MI 48226-2700

RYAN, JAMES T., wholesale distribution executive; BS, Miami Univ., Ohio; MBA, DePaul Univ. Mgmt. positions W.W. Grainger Inc., Lake Forest, Ill., 1980—94, pres. parts div., 1994—96, v.p. info. services, 1996—2000, pres. grainger.com, 2000—01, exec. v.p. mktg. & sales, 2001—02, exec. v.p. mktg., sales & svc., 2002—04, group pres., 2004—06, pres., 2006—07, pres., COO, 2007—. Trustee Mus. Sci. & Industry, Chgo. Mem.: Econ. Club Chgo. Office: WW Grainger Inc 100 Grainger Pkwy Lake Forest IL 60045-5201*

RYAN, JOHN, lawyer; BS, Loyola U.; JD, Harvard U., Cambridge, Mass. Former chief admin. officer, corp. devel. leader Hewitt Assoc., CEO, Fin. Svc. Ltd., pres., holding corp., sr. v.p., chief legal officer. Bd. dir. Chgo. Coun. Global Affairs, Legal Club Chgo.; formerly with Ill. Governor's Task Force on Judicial Merit Selection; former dir. Children's Memorial Hosp. (Chgo.) Rsch. Found. Office: Hewitt Assoc 100 Half Day Rd Lincolnshire IL 60069-3342 Office Phone: 847-295-5000.

RYAN, JOHN MICHAEL, landscape architect; b. Chgo., Sept. 27, 1946; s. Terrance Joseph and Norma (Morris) R.; m. Victoria Jean Wheetley, June 26, 1986; children: Micheline Giannasi-Mennecke, Tony Giannasi, Nick Giannasi, Andrew Morris Jennings, Melissa Contance Victoria, Cameron Michael Montgomery. B in Landscape Architecture, U. Ill., 1969. Registered landscape architect, Ill., cert. Mich., registered Ariz., Ind., Wis., Tenn., cert. CLARB. Assoc. landscape architect Carl Garnder & Assocs., Inc., Chgo., 1969-71; sr. landscape architect Collaborative Rsch. & Planning, Chgo., 1971-73; v.p. Michael L. Ives & Assocs., Inc., Downers Grove, Ill., 1973-84; pres. Ives/Ryan Group, Inc., Naperville, 1984—. Prin. works include renovation of Old Orchard Shopping Ctr., Skokie, Ill., Lake Katherine Nature Preserve, Palos Heights, Ill., Crystal Tree Residential Golf Course Cmty., Orland Park, Ill., Corporetum Office Campus, Lisle, Ill., Maravilla Rainforest Atrium, Vernon Hills, Ill. Trustee Wheaton Evangelical Free Ch., 2000—. Recipient Nat. Landscape award Am. Assn. urserymen, 1988, 92, Key award in landscape arch. Home Bldrs. Assn. Greater Chgo., 1981, 84, 90, Best Project Grand award Interiorscape mag., 2001. Mem. Am. Soc. Landscape Archs. (Merit award 1991, 94, 96), Assoc. Landscape Contractors Am. (Environ. Improvement Grand award 1997, 2000, Environ. Improvement honor award 2000), Ill. Landscape Contractors Assn. (Gold award 1991, 96, 2001, Silver award 1986, 90, 93, 2001, Merit award 1988, 91), Chgo. Hort. Soc., Perennial Plant Assn. (Nat. Honor award 1993), Morton Arboretum. Avocations: gardening, travel.

RYAN, JOHN WILLIAM, academic administrator; b. Chgo., Aug. 12, 1929; s. Leonard John and Maxine (Mitchell) R.; m. D. Patricia Goodday, June 20, 1949; children: Kathleen Elynne Ryan Acker, Kevin Dennis Mitchell, Kerrick Charles Casey. BA, U. Utah, 1951; MA, Ind. U., 1958, PhD, 1959; D Pub. Adminstrn., Nat. Inst. Devel. Adminstrn., Thailand, 1991; DLitt (hon.), U. St. Thomas, 1977; LLD (hon.), Ind. U., 1988, U. Notre Dame, 1978, Oakland City Coll., 1981, St. Joseph Coll., 1981, Hanover Coll., 1982, DePauw U., 1983, Manchester Coll., 1983, U. Evansville, 1985, Wabash Coll., 1986, U. Md., 1994, SD State U., 2005, S.Dakota State U., 2004. Rsch. analyst Ky. Dept. Revenue, Frankfort, 1954-55; vis. rsch. prof. U. Thammasat, Bangkok, 1955-57; asst. dir. Inst. Tng. for Pub. Svc. Ind. U., 1957-58; successively asst. prof., assoc. prof. polit. sci., assoc. dir., Bur. Govt. U. Wis., 1958-62; exec. asst. to pres., sec. of univ. U. Mass., Amherst, 1962-63, chancellor Boston, 1965-68; v.p. acad. affairs Ariz. State U., 1963-65; v.p., chancellor regional campuses Ind. U., Bloomington, 1968-71, pres., 1971-87, pres. emeritus, 1987—, prof. polit. sci., 1968-95, prof. pub. and environ. affairs, 1981-95, prof. emeritus, 1995—; cons. AID, 1991-92; chancellor SUNY, Albany, 1996—2000, chancellor emeritus, 2000—; hon. prof. Moscow State U., 1999. Interim pres. Fla. Atlantic U., 1989, U. Md., Balt., 1994; bd. dirs. Ind. U. Found., chmn. 1972-87; chmn. Nat. Adv. Bd. on Internat. Edn. Programs, 1985-89. Contbr. articles to profl. jours. Bd. govs. Pub. Broadcasting Svc., 1973-82; bd. visitors Air U., 1974-81; chmn. Air Force Inst. Tech Subcom., 1976-81; mem. univ. adv. com. Am. Coun. Life Ins.; bd. dirs. Corp. Community Coun., 1976; mem. nat. adv. coun. Pan Am. Games, 1985; mem. adv. bd. Assocs. for Religious and Intellectual Life, 1984—; active United Way Ind. Centennial Commn. Mem. Am. Soc. Pub. Adminstrn. (pres. Ind. chpt. 1969-70, nat. chpt. 1972-73, nat. coun. from 1970, Ind. Soc. Chgo. (non-resident v.p. from 1976, Am. Polit. Sci. Assn., Assn. Asian Studies, Am. Coun. Edn., Assn. Am. Univs. (chmn. 1981-82), Nat. Acad. Public Adminstrn., Ind. Acad., Explorers Club, Adelphia (hon.), Columbia Club (Indpls.), Skyline Club, Cosmos Club (Washington), Athenaeum (London), KC, Equestrian Order of Holy Sepulchre, Elks, Phi Kappa Phi, Phi Alpha Theta, Pi Sigma Alpha, Beta Gamma Sigma, Kappa Sigma (worthy grand master 1985-87). Office: Ind U SPEA 415 1315 E 10th St Bloomington IN 47405-1701 Home Phone: 812-824-9071; Office Phone: 812-855-5780. Personal E-mail: chancem123@aol.com. Business E-Mail: ryan@indiana.edu.

RYAN, JOSEPH W., JR., lawyer; b. Phila., June 24, 1948; s. Joseph W. Sr. and Marie R. (Hillgrube) R.; m. Mary Pat Law, Sept. 11, 1971; children: Caitlin, Joseph W. III. BA, St. Joseph's U., 1970; MA, Villanova U., 1971; JD, U. Va., 1978. Bar: Ohio 1978, U.S. Supreme Ct. 1982. Ptnr. Porter Wright Morris & Arthur LLP, Columbus, Ohio, 1978—. Lectr. Sch. Dentistry Ohio State U., Columbus, 1982-89, CLE Inst., 1984—; trial acad. faculty Internat. Assn. Def. Counsel, Boulder, Colo., 1994, dir.-elect, 2005-06, dir. 2006—. Author: Use of Demonstrative Evidence, 1985; assoc. editor Litigation News, 1986—, editor in chief, 2000-02. Trustee Columbus Zool. Assn., 1980-90; bd. dirs. Columbus Speech and Hearing Ctr., 1988-99, pres., 1995-96. Mem. ABA (sec. litig., co-chair pubs. divsn.), Ohio State Bar Assn., Columbus Bar Assn., Internat. Assn. Def. Counsel, Am. Arbitration Assn. (panel of arbitrators). Republican. Roman Catholic. Office: Porter Wright Morris & Arthur 41 S High St Ste 30 Columbus OH 43215-6101 Office Phone: 614-227-2000. Business E-Mail: jryan@porterwright.com.

RYAN, MARK ANTHONY, architect, lawyer; b. Council Bluffs, Iowa, Sept. 6, 1964; s. Paul Elmer and Darreline Kay (Wyland) Ryan; m. Shelli Ann Hagerbaumer, Sept. 26, 1992. BA in Architecture with distinction, Iowa State U., Ames, 1987; JD summa cum laude, Creighton U., Omaha, 2003. Registered profl. arch., Wis.; bar: Iowa, 2003, Nebr. 2004, U.S Patent and Trademark Office 2005. Project arch. U.S. Army C.E., Omaha, 1987-90, arch., security engr., 1990-91, environ. project mgr., 1991-96; owner, arch. Ryan Designs, Omaha, 1987—2004; project mgr. Bovis Constrn. Corp. and Bovis Lend Lease, Omaha, 1997-2000; CEO Ad Hoc Comm. Resources, LLC, Omaha, 1999—2004, gen. counsel, 2004—; pvt. law practice Ryan Patent Law, 2004—. Bd. advisors Fitness Plus, Council Bluffs, Iowa, 1990—92; expert witness, Iowa, Nebr.,

1991—; law clk. West Corp., 2002; intern law clk. U.S. Dist. Ct., Nebr., 2003. Chmn. City Devel. Commn., Council Bluffs, Iowa, 1992; trustee San. and Improvement Dist. No. 142, Douglas County, Nebr., 1995—96. Scholar, State of Iowa, 1982; Valentino scholar, 2001, Lane Found. scholar, 2002, Abrahams scholar, 2002. Mem.: ABA, AIA (sec. S.W. Iowa sect. 1991, treas. 1992, v.p. 1993, pres. 1994—96), Omaha Bar Assn., ebr. State Bar Assn., Iowa Bar Assn., Golden Key, Phi Delta Phi, Tau Sigma Delta, Phi Kappa Phi. Avocations: bicycling, tennis. Office: Ryan Patent Law 4014 N 154th Ave Omaha NE 68116 Business E-Mail: mark@adhoccr.com.

RYAN, SISTER MARY JEAN, health facility executive; LHD, Webster U., 1994, U. Mo., St. Louis, 2003, Lindenwood U., 2003. Pres., CEO SSM Health Care, 1986—. Presenter in field. Co-author: CQI and the Renovation of an American Health Care System: A Culture Under Construction, 1997. Mem. Excellence in Mo. Found.; chair Taking Care/A Health Forum for Women Religious, Madison, Wis.; bd. dirs. Inst. for Healthcare Improvement, United Way of Greater St. Louis; sec. Hawthorn Found. of Mo.; mem., treas., bd. dirs. St. Louis Regional Chamber and Growth Assn.; bd. dirs. SSM Health Care of Okla., SSM Health Care of Wis., SSM Health Care-St. Louis. Named one of 20 Disting. Women/St. Louis Area, 25 Most Influential Women in Bus. in St. Louis; recipient Brotherhood/Sisterhood award, Nat. Conf. Cmty. and Justice, Gov.'s Quality Leadership award, State of Mo., Corp. that Makes a Difference award, Internat. Women's Forum. Office: SSM Health Care Sys Inc 477 N Lindbergh Blvd Saint Louis MO 63141

RYAN, PATRICK G., insurance company executive; b. Milw., May 15, 1937; m. Shirley Welsh, Apr. 16, 1966; children: Patrick Jr., Robert J., Corbett M. BS, orthwestern U., 1959. Sales agt. Penn Mut., 1959-64, Pat Ryan & Assocs. Chgo., 1964-71; chmn., pres. Ryan Ins. Group Inc., Chgo., 1971-82; pres., CEO Combined Internat. Corp, 1982—87, Aon Corp. (formerly Combined Internat. Corp.), Chgo., 1987—2005, exec. chmn., 1990—. Bd. dirs. Aon Corp. (formerly Combined Internat. Corp.), 1982-, Sears Roebuck and Co., Chgo., Tribune Co., Chgo. Life trustee, past chmn., Rush Univ. Med. Ctr., Chgo.; chmn., trustee orthwestern U.; past trustee Field Mus. Natural History, Chgo. Recipient Lifetime Achievement award, The Review-Worldwide Reinsurance, 2005, Internat. Exec. of the Yr., Brigham Young Univ., 2002, Golden Plate award, Acad. of Achievement, 2002; named to Chgo. Bus. Hall of Fame. Mem., past pres., Econ. Club Chgo. Office: Aon Corp Aon Ctr 200 E Randolph St Chicago IL 60601

RYAN, PAUL, congressman; b. Janesville, Wis., Jan. 29, 1970; s. Paul and Betty Ryan; m. Janna Ryan; 3 children. BS in Econs. and Polit. Sci., Miami U., Ohio, 1992. Aide Staff of US Senator Bob Kasten of Wis., Washington; econ. adv., speechwriter Empower Am., Jack Kemp, Bill Bennett, Washington; legis. dir. US Senate, Washington; mktg. cons. Ryan Inc., Ctrl., Janesville; mem. US Congress from 1st Wis. dist., 1999—, mem. ways and means com., mem. joint econ. com., mem. budget com. Defeated former Kenosha City Coun. Pres. Lydia Spottswood in 1998 to succeed two-term Rep. Mark Neumann, who ran unsuccessfully for the Senate. Mem. Janesville YMCA, Janesville Bowmen Inc. and Ducks Unlimited. Republican. Roman Catholic. Office: US Ho Reps 1113 Longworth Ho Office Bldg Washington DC 20515 Office Phone: 202-225-3031.

RYAN, PRISCILLA E., lawyer; AB, Marquette U., 1969; JD, Loyola U., Chgo., 1982. Bar: Ill. 1982. With IRS, 1986-87; atty.-advisor Office Tax Policy, U.S. Treasury Dept., Washington, 1988-89; ptnr. Sidley & Austin, Chgo. Frequent spkr. on employee benefits. Contbr. articles to profl. jours. Mem. ABA. Office: Sidley & Austin 1 S First National Plz Chicago IL 60603-2000 Fax: 312-853-7036.

RYAN, RAY DARL, JR., academic administrator; b. Joliet, Ill., Dec. 2, 1945; s. Ray D. and Oral Ada (Smiley) R.; m. Marianne Rossetto, Aug. 28, 1965; children: Kimberley, Kristin, Matthew. BS, U. Wis., Menomonie, 1970; MEd, U. Mo., 1973, EdD, 1975; Doctorate (hon.), Tomsk Poly. Inst., Russia, 1992. Cert. vocat./tech. tchr., adminstr., chief sch. officer. Dep. supt. pub. instrn. Nev. Dept. Edn., Carson City; dep. supt. spl. programs Ariz. Dept. Edn., Phoenix, state dir., vocat. educator; exec. dir. Ctr. Edn. and Tng. for Employment Ohio State U., Columbus, assoc. dean rsch., internat. affairs. Bd. dirs., vice-chair Coun. Edn. Devel. and Rsch.; pres., CEO Nat. Occup. Testing Inst., 1999. Mem. OTT, ASTD, Phi Delta Kappa, Epsilon Pi Tau, Omicron Tau Theta. Office: NOCTI 500 N Bronson Ave Big Rapids MI 49307 Home: 1114 Manhattan Ave Apt 2 Brooklyn NY 11222-1086

RYAN, TERRY, professional sports team executive; b. Janesville, Wis., Oct. 26, 1953; m. Karilyn Ryan; children: Tim, Kathleen. Diploma in Phys. Edn., U. Wis., 1979. Profl. baseball player Minn. Twins, 1972-76, scouting dir., 1986-91, v.p. player pers., asst. gen. mgr., 1991-94, v.p., baseball pers., asst. gen. mgr., 1994, v.p., gen. mgr., 1994—2007, sr. adv. to gen. mgr., 2007—; profl. scout NY Mets, 1980-86. Named MLB Exec. of Yr., The Sporting News, 2002, 2006. Office: Minnesota Twins 34 Kirby Puckett Pl Minneapolis MN 55415-1596 Office Phone: 612-375-1366.

RYAN, THOMAS, food service executive; b. Grand Rapids, Mich., Jan. 15, 1957; m. Jody Ryan; three children. B in Food Sci., Mich. State U., M in Lipid Toxicology, D in Flavor Sci. Consumer product rschr. Procter & Gamble, Pillsbury; sr. dir. new product devel. Pizza Hut, 1988-96; v.p. bus. devel. Long John Silvers, Lexington, Ky., 1996-97; v.p. meal mgmt. McDonalds Corp., Oak Brook, Ill. Recipient Silver and Gold awards Am. Mktg. Assn. Avocations: dining, golf, wine collecting.

RYAN, THOMAS F., lawyer; b. Detroit, Nov. 4, 1943; BS, Ferris State U., 1965; JD magna cum laude, Wayne State U., 1971. Bar: Ill. 1972, US Ct. of Appeals (7th cir.) 1972, US Dist. Ct. (no. dist.) Ill. 1972, U.S. Supreme Ct. 1978. Joined Sidley & Austin (now Sidley Austin, LLP), Chgo., 1972—; ptnr. antitrust and bus. counseling Sidley Austin, LLP, Chgo., 1978—. Exec. com. Sidley Austin, LLP; adv. com. on cir. rules 7th Fed. Ct. Appeals. 1st lt. U.S. Army, 1966-68. Decorated Bronze star. Fellow Am. Coll. Trial Lawyers; mem. Chgo. Bar Assn. (mem. jud. evaluation com.), 7th Cir. Bar Assn. (bd. govs. 1986-89, 2nd v.p. 1990-91, pres. 1991-92). Office: Sidley Austin LLP 1 S Dearborn St Chicago IL 60603 Office Phone: 312-853-7497. Office Fax: 312-853-7036. Business E-Mail: tryan@sidley.com.

RYAN, TIMOTHY J., congressman; b. Niles, Ohio, July 16, 1973; s. Rochelle Ryan. Student, Youngstown State U., 1991—92; BA in Polit. Sci., Bowling Green State U., 1995; JD, Franklin Pierce Law Ctr., Concord, NH, 2000. Congl. aide Staff of US Rep. James A. Traficant of Ohio, 1995—97; intern Trumbull County Prosecutor's Office; mem. Ohio State Senate from 32nd dist., Columbus, 2001—02, US Congress from 17th Ohio dist., 2003—, mem. appropriations com., 2006—, co-chair Mfg. Caucus, mem. Dem. steering and policy com., 2006—. Trustee Found. Extended. Recipient Legis. Leadership award on Domestic Mfg., US Bus. and Industry Coun., 2004, Friend of Nat. Pks. award, Nat. Pks. Conservation Assn., 2005. Mem. KC, Sons Italy, Internat. Narcotic Enforcement Officers Assn., Ancient Order Hibernians, Elks. Democrat. Office: 197 W Market St Warren OH 44481 Office Phone: 202-225-5261, 330-373-0074. Office Fax: 330-373-0098.

RYBA, JOHN J., state legislator; b. Aug. 10, 1929; m. Gertrude Ryba, 1954; children: Sue, Sandy, Steve. Former city councilman, Green Bay; former mem. Green Bay Planning Commn. Met. Sewerage Commn. and Transit Authority; Wis. state assemblyman Dist. 90, 1992—. Co-author: Informent Bill, Legalizing Pepper Protection Spray; author: Responsible Beverage Survey. Recipient Spl. Olympics Achievement award, 1991-92. Mem. VFW (life), Elks (life mem. lodge 259, Elk of Yr. 1988-91), Am. Legion (life mem.). Address: 714 Wilson Ave Green Bay WI 54303-4106 Office: Wis Assembly PO Box 8952 Madison WI 53708-8952

RYBAK, R. T., mayor; m. Megan O'Hara; 2 children. BA in Polit. Sci. and Comm., Boston Coll., 1978. Gen. mgr. WCCO TV & WCCO Radio; v.p. Internet Broadcast Sys.; pub., mgr., bus. ops. Twin Cities Reader; mayor City of Minneapolis, Minn., 2001—. Founder, mem. bd. Save the Water in Mpls.; served Minn. Soc. Architects, Night of the Penguin, Hennepin Ave. Adv. Com., Adv. Fedn. Minn., Eiji Oue Inaugural Com.; coach Little League Baseball, Youth Soccer; vol. reader Minn. Pub. Sch.; co-coord. Bill Bradley for Pres., 2000; co-chair Tony Bouza for Gov., 1994; bd. dir. Residents Opposed to Airport Racket. Democrat. Office: City Hall Rm 331 350 S Fifth S Minneapolis MN 55415 Office Phone: 612-673-2700. Office Fax: 612-673-2305.

RYCHLAK, JOSEPH FRANK, psychologist, educator; b. Cudahy, Wis., Dec. 17, 1928; s. Joseph Walter and Helen Mary (Bieniek) R.; m. Lenora Pearl Smith, June 16, 1956; children: Ronald, Stephanie. BS, U. Wis., 1953; MA, Ohio State U., 1954, PhD, 1957. Diplomate Am. Bd. Examiners in Profl. Psychology. Asst. prof. psychology Fla. State U., Tallahassee, 1957-58, Washington State U., Pullman, 1958-61; assoc. prof., then prof. psychology St. Louis U., 1961-69; prof. psychology Purdue U., West Lafayette, Ind., 1969-83, interim dept. head, 1979-80; prof. Loyola U. Chgo., 1983-99, Maude C. Clarke prof. humanistic psychology, 1983—, prof. emeritus, 1999—. Dir. Human Relations Ctr., Pullman, Wash., 1958-61; research cons. AT&T, 1957-82. Author: The Psychology of Rigorous Humanism, 1977, 2d edit., 1988, Discovering Free Will and Personal Responsibility, 1979, A Philosophy of Science for Personality Theory, 2d edit., 1981, Personality and Life Style of Young Male Managers, 1982, (with N. Cameron) Personality Development and Psychopathology, 2d edit., 1985, Artificial Intelligence and Human Reason: A Teleological Critique, 1991, Logical Learning Theory: A Human Teleology and Its Empirical Support, 1994, In Defense of Human Consciousness, 1997, The Human Image in Postmodern America, 2003; assoc. editor Psychotherapy: Theory, Rsch. and Practice, 1965-76, Jour. Mind and Behavior, 1985-94. With USAF, 1946-49. Named Outstanding Contbr. to Human Understanding, Internat. Assn. Social Psychiatry, 1971. Fellow Am. Psychol. Assn. (div. 24 pres. 1977-78, 86-87), Am. Psychol. Soc.; mem. Soc. Personality Assessment, Phi Beta Kappa. Roman Catholic. Home: 12974 Abraham Run Carmel IN 46033 Office Phone: 317-816-0073. E-mail: jrychlak@sbcglobal.net.

RYCUS, MITCHELL JULIAN, urban security and energy planning educator, consultant; b. Detroit, June 20, 1932; s. Samuel Israel and Esther (Mitnick) R.; m. Carole Ann Lepofsky, Aug. 31, 1958; children: Lisa Karen Rycus Mikalonis, Peter Todd. BS in Math., U. Mich., 1958, MS in Math., 1961, MS in Physics, 1965, PhD in Urban and Regional Planning, 1976. Asst. rsch. scientist radiation lab. U. Mich., Ann Arbor, 1958-61, pvt. cons. extension gaming svc., 1972-77, rsch. assoc. Mental Health Rsch. Inst., 1977-80; asst. prof. Coll. Architecture and Urban Planning, Ann Arbor, 1980-83; assoc. prof. U. Mich., Ann Arbor, 1983-86; chmn. Coll. Architecture and Urban Planning, Ann Arbor, 1986-92, prof., 1989—; co-dir. Studies in Urban Security Group U. Mich., Ann Arbor, 1985—; mathematician Bendix Corp. & Rocketdyne, Ann Arbor, 1961-62; group scientist Conductron Corp., Ann Arbor, 1962-70; project assoc. Mich. State C. of C., Lansing, 1970-72. Cons. Community Systems Found., Ann Arbor, 1985— Contbr. rsch. reports, articles. Advisor assessment com. United Way of Washtenaw County, Ann Arbor, 1988-89. With USN, 1950-54. Recipient Faculty Recognition award U. Mich., 1982-83. Mem. AAAS, Am. Planning Assn. Democrat. Jewish. Avocation: computer applications to planning. Office: U Mich Coll Architecture & Urban Planning Ann Arbor MI 48109-2069

RYDELL, CATHERINE M., medical association administrator, former state legislator; b. Grand Forks, ND, May 8, 1950; d. Hilary Harold and Catherine F. (Ireland) Wilson; m. Charles D. Rydell, 1971; children: Kimberly, Jennifer, Michael. BS, U. N.D., 1971. Mem. N.D. Ho. of Reps., 1985—, mem. supreme ct. judicial planning, govt., vet. affairs com., past rep. caucus leader; now exec. dir. Am. Acad. Neurology, St. Paul. Coord. cmty. svc. Bismarck Jr. Coll.; bus. mgr. surg. svc. St. Alexius Med. Ctr. Bd. dirs. Mission Valley Family, YMCA, N.D. Early Childhood Tng. Ctr., Ronald McDonald Found., CHAND; mem. state adv. bd. Casey Family Program, Juvenile Justice; mem. lay adv. bd. St. Alexius; mem. regional adv. bd. Luth. Social Svcs.; mem. N.D. State Centennial Com., N.D. State Mus. Art. Recipient Outstanding Svc. award Tobacco Free N.D., Legislator of Yr. award Children's Caucus, Guardian of Bus. award Nat. Fedn. Ind. Bus. Mem. Philanthropic and Edn. Orgn. Sisterhood, N.D. Med. Assn. (v.p.), Gamma Phi Beta. Office: Am Acad Neurology 1080 Montreal Ave Saint Paul MN 55116-2386

RYDER, ANNE, newscaster; m. Kevin O'Keefe. Grad., U. Mo.; LHD (hon.), Marian Coll., U. Indpls. Creator, prodr. Hope to Tell series WTHR-TV, Indpls., reporter, anchor, 1984—. Columnist: Indpls. Women mag. Named Best Female News Anchor, The Indpls. Star and Indpls. Monthly Mag.; recipient Gabriel award, Wilbur award, Edward R. Murros award, Emmy awards. Office: WTHR-TV 1000 N Meridian St Indianapolis IN 46204

RYDER, HENRY CLAY, lawyer; b. Lafayette, Ind., Feb. 18, 1928; s. Raymond Robert and Mina Elizabeth (Arnold) R.; m. Ann Sater Clay, Nov. 29, 1952 (dec.); children: David C., Sarah Paige Hugon, Anne Ryder O'Keefe; m. Velma Iris Dean, Aug. 27, 1976 (dec.). BS, Purdue U., 1948; LLB, U. Mich., 1951; LLD, Hanover Coll., 1998. Bar: Mich. 1951, Ind. 1952, U.S. Dist. Ct. (so. dist.) Ind. 1953, U.S. Ct. Appeals (7th cir.) 1957, U.S. Supreme Ct. 1981. Assoc. Buschmann, Krieg, DeVault & Alexander, Indpls., 1953-57, ptnr., 1957-60, Roberts & Ryder and successor firms, Indpls., 1960-86, Barnes & Thornburg (merger), Indpls., 1987-95, of counsel, 1996—. Pres. Ind. State Symphony Soc. Inc., 1979-82, bd. dirs., 1972-91, trustee, 1991—; chmn. United Way of Greater Indpls., 1984; vice chmn. Greater Indpls. Progress Com., 1979-86, chmn., 1987-89, mem. exec. com., 1979-2000; trustee Purdue U., 1983-89; trustee Hanover Coll., 1979-2003, chmn., 1988-98; bd. dirs. Hist. Landmarks Found. of Ind., 1985-96, chmn., 1992-95; bd. dirs. Purdue Rsch. Found., 1990-2006; hon. v.p. Ind. Soc. Chgo.; mem. cmty. bd. IUPUI U. Libr., 1998—, chmn. 2003-04; bd. govs. Heartland Film Festival, 2000—04. Lt. U.S. Army, 1951-53. Recipient Jefferson award Indpls. Star, 1983, Whistler award Greater Indpls. Progress Com., 1989; Sagamore of the Wabash, 1984; named Man of Yr., B'nai B'rith Soc., 1984, Ind. Acad., 1992, Lifetime Achievement award Nat. Soc. Fund Raising Execs., 1999, Spirit of Philanthropy award Ind. U. Purdue U. Indpls., 2005. Fellow: Ind. Bar Found., Am. Bar Found.; mem.: ABA, Indpls. Bar Assn., Ind. Bar Assn., Ind. C. of C. (bd. dirs. 1991—94), Purdue U. Alumni Assn. (pres. 1975—77, Alumni Svc. award 1982, Citizenship award 1989), Columbia Club Found. (trustee 1990—), Indpls. Lit. Club (pres. 2004—05), Kiwanis (Downtown Indpls. pres. 1983, Civic award 1981), Columbia Club (bd. dirs. 1987—90, sec. 1988, Benjamin Harrison award 1983, Columbian of Yr. award 2002), USAC Benevolent Found. (bd. dirs., pres. 1999—), USAC Properties (sec., bd. dirs. 1986—), U.S. Auto Club (bd. dirs. 1982—, Pres.'s award 1989, Eddie Edenburn award 2000), Lawyers Club of Indpls. (pres. 1966). Republican. Presbyterian. Office: Barnes & Thornburg 11 S Meridian St Indianapolis IN 46204-3535 Office Phone: 317-231-7521.

RYDER, TOM, state legislator; b. Medora, Ill., May 17, 1949; m. Peggy Ryder; 2 children. BA, No. Ill. U.; JD, Washington and Lee U. Ill. state rep. Dist. 97, 1983—; mem. appropriations II, human svcs. Ill. Ho. Reps., state govt. adminstrn. transp. and motor vehicles coms., chmn. house rep. policy com., mem. health care, labor and commerce com., pub. safety, infrastructure appropriations coms., joint com. adminstrn. rules, minority dep. leader; minority dept. leader; atty. Mem. Ill. Nat. Guard. Mem. Lions, Elks, Moose, Am. Legion. Republican. Home: 309 N Liberty St Jerseyville IL 62052-1516 Office: Ill Ho of Reps Rm 314 State Capitol Springfield IL 62706-0001

RYDZEL, JAMES A., lawyer; b. Worcester, Mass., Nov. 13, 1946; s. Joseph S. and Shirley F. Rydzel; m. Mary C. Chandler; 1 child, Molly. BA, St. Louis U., 1968; JD, Duke U., 1971. Bar: Ohio, 1972, Fla. 1975, U.S. Dist. Ct. (no. dist.) Ohio, U.S. Dist. Ct. (ea. dist.) Mich., U.S. Ct. Appeals (2d, 3d, 4th and 6th cirs.). Ptnr. Jones, Day, Reavis & Pogue, Cleve., 1972—. Adj. prof. law Case Western Res. U. Bd. dirs. New Orgn. Visual Arts, 1990, Greater Cleve. Growth Assn., Citizens League. Mem. ABA (litigation labor and employment law com.), Ohio State Bar Assn., Fla. Bar Assn., Def. Rsch. Inst. Office: Jones Day Reavis & Pogue North Point 901 Lakeside Ave E Cleveland OH 44114-1190

RYERSON, DENNIS, editor; b. Ames, Iowa, Apr. 20, 1948; children: Carey, Kirsten. Student, Iowa State U., U. No. Iowa. Announcer, news dir. Sta. KWBG, Boone, Iowa; reporter, then city editor Cedar Falls Record, 1969—73; news editor Scottsbluff Star-Herald, Nebr., 1973—74; editl. page editor Vancouver Columbian, Wash., 1974—83; chief editl. writer, then editl. dir. Cleve. Plain Dealer, 1983—88; mng. editor news Denver Post, 1988—89; editor editl. pages Des Moines Register, 1989-94; exec. editor Great Falls Tribune, Mont., 1994-95; v.p., editor Des Moines Register, 1995—2001; editl. page editor San Jose Mercury ews, 2001—03; v.p., editor The Indianapolis Star, 2003—. Appeared on TV shows including Good Morning America, MacNeil/Lehrer News Hour, CBS Morning News, PR's All Things Considered. Mem. Nat. Conf. Editl. Writers (past pres.), Am. Soc. Newspaper Editors. Office: Indianapolis Star PO Box 145 Indianapolis IN 46206-0145 Office Phone: 317-444-6169. E-mail: dennis.ryerson@indystar.com.*

RYG, KATHLEEN SCHULTZ, municipal government official; b. Evanston, Ill., Aug. 6, 1952; d. Robert Coyne and Sheila (Hogan) Schultz; m. Martin Lee Ryg, Sept. 21, 1974 (div. Apr. 1986). BS, No. Ill. U., 1974; MA, Roosevelt U., 1979. Tng. counselor Clearbrook Ctr., Elk Grove Village, Ill., 1974-77, dir. residential services Arlington Heights, Ill., 1977-79; employment supr. Condell Hosp., Libertyville, Ill., 1979-80; dir. residential program NW Mental Health Ctr., Arlington Heights, Ill., 1985-89, asst. dir., 1985-89; village clk. Village of Vernon Hills (Ill.), 1989—. V.p. Career Guidance Ctr., Grayslake, Ill., 1980-82, v.p. summer celebration com., Vernon Hills, 1986-89, bd. dirs., 1986; co-chmn. Programs for Alternative Living, Chgo. area, 1984-86. Mem. Lake County Mcpl. Clks., Ill. Mcpl. Clks., Internat. Inst. Mcpl. Clks., Community Alliance Project, Nawthorn Sch. Drug and Alcohol Awareness Com., Jaycees. Roman Catholic. Avocations: tennis, horseback riding. Home: 307 Onwentsia Rd Vernon Hills IL 60061-2120 Office: Village of Vernon Hills 290 Evergreen Dr Vernon Hills IL 60061-2904

RYMER, WILLIAM ZEV, research scientist, administrator; b. Melbourne, Victoria, Australia, June 3, 1939; came to U.S., 1971; s. Jacob and Luba Rymer; m. Helena Bardas, Apr. 10, 1961 (div. 1975); children: Michael Morris, Melissa Anne; m. Linda Marie Faller, Sept. 5, 1977; 1 child, Daniel Jacob. MBBS, Melbourne U., 1962; PhD, Monash U., Victoria, 1971. Resident med. officer dept. medicine Monash U., Victoria, 1964-66; Fogarty internat. fellow NIH, Bethesda, Md., 1971-74; rsch. assoc. Johns Hopkins U. Med. Sch., Balt., 1975-76; asst. prof. SUNY, Syracuse, 1976-78, Northwestern U., Chgo., 1978-81, assoc. prof., 1981-87, prof., 1987—; rsch. dir. Rehab. Inst. Chgo., 1989—. Contbr. articles to profl. jours. Grantee NIH, VA, Dept. of Def., Nat. Inst. Disability Rehab. Rsch., pvt. founds. Fellow Royal Australian Coll. Physicians; mem. Soc. Neurosci., Am. Soc. Biomechanics. Democrat. Avocations: tennis, racquetball. Office: Rehab Inst Chgo 345 E Superior St Chicago IL 60611-4805

RYNKIEWICZ, STEPHEN MICHAEL, journalist; b. Sheboygan, Wis., Oct. 20, 1955; s. Walter Paul and Ruth Catherine (Van Hercke) R.; m. Brenda Gail Russell, Sept. 27, 1986. BA, U. Wis., 1976. Various staff assignments Chgo. Sun-Times, 1979-97, real estate editor, 1990-97; Internet prodr. Chgo. Tribune, 1997—. Pres. Ill. Freedom of Info. Coun., 1991-93; mem. profl. faculty Columbia Coll., Chgo., 1998. Pres. Chgo. Headline Club, 1991-92, treas., 2001-02; chmn. Peter Lisagor Awards for Exemplary Journalism, 2002-06; sec. Headline Club Found., 2004—. Recipient Web Site award, Nat. Assn. Real Estate Editors, 1997—2000, Editor and Pub. Best ewspaper Classified Site award, 2000, award for pub. svc., Online Journalism Assn., 2002, Pub. award, Chgo. Tribune, 2006. Mem. Soc. Profl. Journalists (regional dir. 1992-95, sec.-treas. 1995-96, membership chair 1997-98, diversity chair 1996-97, Peter Lisagor award 2003), Nat. Soc. Real Estate Editors (bd. dirs. 1999-2000), Toastmasters Internat. (asst. div. gov. 2007—), Sigma Delta Chi Found. (bd. dirs. 1995-96), East Village Assn. (bd. mem. 2007-). Office: Ste 400 435 N Michigan Ave Chicago IL 60611-4001

RYPSTRA, ANN, zoology educator; PhD, Pa. State U., 1982. Prof. zoology Miami U., Oxford, Ohio; also dir. Ecology Rsch. Ctr., Oxford, Ohio. Reviewer NSF. Contbr. articles to sci. jours., including Animal Behaviour, Jour. Arachnology, Oikos. Rsch. grantee NSF. Office: Miami U Dept Zoology Oxford OH 45056

RYUN, JIM (JAMES RONALD RYUN), former congressman; b. Wichita, Kans., Apr. 29, 1947; m. Anne Carol Snider, 1969; children: Ned, Drew, Catharine, Heather. BA, U. Kans., 1970. Founder, pres. Jim Ryun Sports, Inc.; mem. US Congressman from 2nd Kans. dist., 1996—2007; mem. armed svcs. com., budget com., fin. svcs. com. US Congress from 2nd Kans. dist. Participant Olympic Games, 1964, 68, 72; Founder Jim Ryun Running Camps. Recipient James E. Sullivan award, 1966, Silver medal 1500 meter run Olympic Games, 1968; Named Sportsman of Yr., SI mag., 1966, Athlete of Yr., ABC Wide World of Soprts, 1966; Named to the US Track & Field Hall of Fame, 2003, Nat. Distance Running Hall of Fame. Republican. Office: PO Box 826 Topeka Lawrence KS 66047 Office Phone: 785-273-8901. E-mail: info@jimryun.com.

SAAD, MICHAEL D., lawyer; b. Zanesville, Ohio, 1941; BS, Ohio State U., 1963, JD summa cum laude, 1966. Bar: Ohio 1966. Law clk. to Chief Justice Ohio State Supreme Ct., 1966—67; ptnr. Squire, Sanders & Dempsey LLP, Columbus, Ohio. Chmn. real estate & hospitality practice group Squire, Sanders & Dempsey LLP. Bd. dir. Ohio Housing Coun. Recipient Founder's Award, Ohio Capital Corp., 2002. Mem.: Order of Coif, Columbus Bar Assn. (fin. institutes com., real estate com., bankruptcy com.), Ohio State Bar Assn., Devel. Com. Ctrl. Ohio, ABA. Office: Squire Sanders & Dempsey LLP 1300 Huntington Ctr 41 South High St Columbus OH 43215-6197 Office Phone: 614-365-2735. Office Fax: 614-365-2499. Business E-Mail: msaad@ssd.com.

SAADA, ADEL SELIM, civil engineer, educator; b. Heliopolis, Egypt, Oct. 24, 1934; came to U.S., 1959, naturalized, 1965; s. Selim N. and Marie (Chahyne) S.; m. ancy Helen Hernan, June 5, 1960; children: Christiane Mona, Richard Adel. Ingénieur des Arts et Manufactures, École Centrale, Paris, 1958; MS, U. Grenoble, France, 1959; PhD in Civil Engring, Princeton U., 1961. Registered profl. engr., Ohio. Engr. Société Dumez, Paris, 1959; research assoc. dept. civil engring. Princeton (N.J.) U., 1961-62; asst. prof. civil engring. Case Western Reserve U., Cleve., 1962-67, asso. prof., 1967-72, prof., 1973—, chmn. dept. civil engring., 1978-98, Frank H. Neff prof. civil engring., 1987. R.J. Carroll Meml. lectr. Johns Hopkins U., 1990; cons., lectr. soil testing and properties Waterways Expt. Sta. (C.E.), Vicksburg, Miss., 1974-79; cons. to various firms, 1962—. Author: Elasticity Theory and Applications, 1974, 2d edit., 1993; contbr. numerous articles on soil mechanics and foundation engring. to profl. jours. Recipient Telford Prize Instn. of Civil Engrs., U.K., 1995, Disting. Leadership award Cleve. Tech. Socs., 2001. Fellow ASCE (named Outstanding Civil Engr. of Yr. Cleve. sect. 1992); mem. Internat. Soc. Soil Mechanics, ASTM, One Two One Athletic Club. Achievements include invention of pneumatic analog computer and loading frame. Home: 3342 Braemar Rd Shaker Heights OH 44120-3332 Office: Case Western Res U Dept Civil Engring Case Sch Engring Cleveland OH 44106 Office Phone: 216-368-2427. Business E-Mail: axs31@case.edu.

SAAL, HOWARD MAX, clinical geneticist, pediatrician, educator; b. NYC, Aug. 20, 1951; s. Josef and Ester S.; m. Cara Tina Schweitzer, May 3, 1987; 1 child, Rebecca. BS, U. Mass., Amherst, 1973, MS, 1975; MD, Wayne State U., 1979. Intern pediatrics U. Conn. Med. Ctr., 1979-80; resident pediatrics U. Conn. Health Ctr., 1980-82; fellow med. genetics U. Wash. Sch. Medicine, 1982-84; dir. cytogenetics U. Conn. Health Ctr., Farmington, 1984-87; vice chmn. med. genetics Children's Nat. Med. Ctr., Washington, 1987-93, head clin. genetics Cin., 1993—. Asst. prof. pediats. George Washington U., Washington, 1987-93, assoc. prof. pediats., 1993; assoc. prof. clin. pediats. U. Cin. Sch. Medicine, 1993—, prof. pediats., 2000—. Contbr. articles to profl. jours. Mem. med. adv. com. Nat. Neurofibromatosis Found., N.Y.C., 1987-93; mem. health profl. adv. com. March of Dimes, Arlington, Va., 1991-93; bd. dirs. Capital Area March of Dimes, 1993. Tng. grantee NIH, 1979-82. Fellow Am. Acad. Pediats. (chmn. exec. com. for sect. on genetics and birth defects 1999-2003, com. genetics 2003—, chmn. com. on genetics 2007—), Am. Coll. Med. Genetics; mem. Am. Soc. Human Genetics, Soc. Craniofacial Genetics (sec.-treas. 1990-96), Accredidation Coun. for Grad. Med. Edn. (med. genetics residency com). Avocation: photography. Home: 3715 Monets Ln Cincinnati OH 45241-3847 Office: Cin Childrens Hosp Med Ctr 3333 Burnet Ave Cincinnati OH 45229-3026 Home Phone: 513-563-0916; Office Phone: 513-636-4760. Business E-Mail: saalhm@cchmc.org.

SABATH, LEON DAVID, internist, educator; b. Savannah, Ga., July 24, 1930; s. Sholom and Sarah (Cherkas) S.; children— Natasha, Joanna, Rachel. AB magna cum laude, Harvard U., 1952, MD, 1956. Diplomat Am. Bd. Internal Medicine, Am. Bd. Infectious Disease. Intern Peter Bent Brigham Hosp., Boston, 1956-57, sr. resident in medicine, 1962-63; jr. resident in medicine Bellevue Hosp., NYC, 1959-60; fellow in infectious disease Harvard U. and Thorndike Meml. Lab., Boston City Hosp., 1960-62; fellow in antibiotic resistance Sir William Dunn Sch. Pathology, Oxford U., Eng., 1963-65; mem.

faculty dept. medicine Harvard U., also; staff physician Boston City Hosp., 1965-74; asst. Harvard Med. Sch., 1965-67, asst. prof., 1967-70, asso. prof., 1970-74; head sect. infectious diseases U. Minn., Mpls., 1974-83, prof. medicine, 1974—. Chmn. coms. U. Minn. Hosps.; adj. faculty Rockefeller U., 1990-91. Editor: Pseudomonas aeruginosa, 1980, Antibiotic Action in Patients, 1982; editl. bd. Clin. Pharmacology and Therapeutics, 1978-80; contbr. articles on antibiotics and their use, bacterial resistance to antibiotics, chlamydia and death associated wiht exercise to profl. jours. Trustee E.P.A. Cephalosporin Fund, Oxford U., 1970—. Capt. M.C. AUS, 1957-59. NIH spl. fellow, 1963-65; recipient Career Devel. award NIH, 1968-72 Fellow ACP, Infectious Disease Soc. Am.; mem. Am. Soc. Clin. Investigation, Am. Soc. Microbiology (vice chmn. div. antimicrobial chemotherapy 1976-77, chmn. 1977-78), Am. Soc. Clin. Pharmacology and Theapeutics, Central Soc. Clin. Research, Am. Fedn. Clin. Research, Soc. Gen. Microbiology, Mass. Med. Soc., Soc. Exptl. Biology and Medicine, Brit. Soc. Antimicrobial Chemotherapy, Sigma Xi. Achievements include research in vancomycin resistance of staphylococcal aureus, and on sudden cardiac death associated with exertion. Home: 2504 Washburn Ave S Minneapolis MN 55416-4351 Office: U Minn Hosps Mayo Meml Blvd D416 Minneapolis MN 55455 Home Phone: 612-377-3773; Office Phone: 612-624-6661. Personal E-mail: leonsabath@yahoo.com.

SABATHIA, C.C. (CARSTEN CHARLES SABATHIA), professional baseball player; b. Vallejo, Calif., July 21, 1980; m. Amber Sabathia; children: Carsten Charles III, Jaeden Arie. Pitcher Cleve. Indians, 2001—. Named to Am. League All-Star Team, 2003—04, 2007; recipient Am. League Cy Young award, 2007, Bullet Rogan Legacy award, Negro Leagues Baseball Mus., 2008. Achievements include leading the American League in fewest hits allowed per 9 innings pitched (7.44), 2001; leading the American League in complete games (6) and shutouts (2), 2006; becoming the youngest pitcher (27 years, 69 days old) to record 100 career wins on September 28, 2007. Mailing: c/o Cleve Indians Jacobs Field 2401 Ontario St Cleveland OH 44115-4003*

SABATINO, THOMAS JOSEPH, JR., lawyer, pharmaceutical executive; b. Norwich, Conn., Dec. 3, 1958; s. Thomas J. and Germaine (Clement) S.; m. Joan Kathryn Turnbull, June 4, 1983. BS cum laude, Wesleyan U., Middletown, Conn., 1980; JD, U. Pa., 1983. Bar: Mass. 1983, Ill. 1985, Calif. 1989. Assoc. Testa, Hurwitz & Thibeault, Boston, 1983-85, Coffield Ungaretti Harris & Slavin, Chgo., 1985-86; corp. counsel Baxter Healthcare Corp., Deerfield, Ill., 1986-90; pres., CEO Secure Med. Inc., Mundelein, Ill., 1990-92; assoc. gen. counsel Am. Med. Internat., Dallas, 1992-93, v.p., gen. counsel, 1993-95; v.p., assoc. gen. counsel Tenet Healthcare Corp., Dallas, 1995—97; v.p., assoc. gen. counsel, asst. sec. Baxter Healthcare Corp., Deerfield, Ill., 1997—2004, sr. v.p., 1997—2004; exec. v.p., gen. counsel Schering-Plough Corp., Kenilworth, NJ, 2004—. Home: 1 Hildebrandt Rd Lebanon NJ 08833-4444

SABBAGHA, RUDY ELIAS, obstetrician, gynecologist, educator; b. Oct. 29, 1931; arrived in U.S., 1965, naturalized; s. Elias C. and Sonia B.S.; m. Asma E. Sahyouny, Oct. 5, 1957; children: Elias, Randa. BA, Am. U., Beirut, 1952, MD, 1958. Diplomate Am. Bd. Ob-Gyn. Sr. physician Tapline, Saudi Arabia, 1958-64, ob-gyn specialist, 1969-70; tchg. fellow U. Pitts./Magee Women's Hosp., 1965-68; fellow diagnostic ultrasound U. Glasgow, Scotland, 1970; asst. prof. ob-gyn U. Pitts., 1970-75; prof. Northwestern U., Chgo., 1975-94; med. dir. Obstet. and Gynecol. Ultrasound S.C., 1994—; clin. prof. U. Chgo. Pritzker Sch. Medicine, 1995-2000; prof. emeritus Northwestern U., Ill., 1995—. Obstetrician, gynecologist Prentice Women's Hosp., Chgo., 1975—. Editor: Ultrasound Applied to Obstetrics and Gynecology, 1980, 3d edit., 1994; co-editor: Fetal Anomalies: Ultrasound Diagnosis and Postnatal Management, 2001; contbr. articles to profl.jours. Fellow Am. Coll. Obstetricians and Gynecologists, Am. Inst. Ultrasound in Medicine; mem. Soc. Gynecol. Investigation, Am. Gynecol. and Obstet. Soc., Ctrl. Assn. Obstetricians and Gynecologists. Research on diagnostic ultrasound, obstetrics and gynecology. Office: 680 N Lake Shore Dr Ste 1430 Chicago IL 60611-8702 E-mail: rsabbagha@comcast.net.

SABERS, RICHARD WAYNE, state supreme court justice; b. Salem, SD, Feb. 12, 1938; s. Emil William and Elrena Veronica (Godfrey) S.; m. Colleen D. Kelley, Aug. 28, 1965 (dec. Feb., 1998); children: Steven Richard, Susan Michelle, Michael Kelley; m. Ellie Schmitz, June 9, 2000. BA in English, St. John's U., Collegeville, Minn., 1960; JD, U. S.D., 1966. Bar: S.D. 1966, U.S. Dist. Ct. S.D. 1966, U.S. Ct. Appeals (8th cir.) 1983. From assoc. to ptnr. Moore, Rasmussen, Sabers & Kading, Sioux Falls, SD, 1966-86; justice SD Supreme Ct., Pierre and Sioux Falls, 1986—. Mem. editorial bd. U. S.D. Law Rev., 1965-66. State rep. March of Dimes, Bismarck, N.D., 1963; bd. dirs. St. Joseph Cathedral, Sioux Falls, 1971-86; trustee, bd. dirs. O'Gorman Found., Sioux Falls, 1978-86; active sch. bd. O'Gorman High Sch., Sioux Falls, 1985-86. Lt. US Army, 1960—63. Named Outstanding Young Religious Leader, Jaycees, Sioux Falls, 1971. Mem. ABA, S.D. Bar Assn., Inst. Jud. Adminstrn., St. John's Alumni Assn. (pres. Sioux Falls chpt. 1975-91). Republican. Roman Catholic. Avocations: tennis, skiing, sailing, sports, wood carving. Office: SD Supreme Ct 500 E Capitol Ave Pierre SD 57501-5070 Home: 5218 S Sweetbriar Ct Sioux Falls SD 57108-2855 Office Phone: 605-367-5926.

SABIN, NEAL F., broadcast executive; b. Chgo., Ill., Sept. 27, 1956; BA, Northwestern U., 1978. Exec. v.p. Weigel broadcasting/WCIU TV, Chgo., 1994—; corp. program mgr. WPWR-TV, Chgo., 1983-94. Home: 180 N Jefferson St Unit 2410 Chicago IL 60661-1450 Fax: (312) 705-2656. E-mail: nsabin@wciu.com.

SABL, JOHN J., lawyer; b. LA, June 16, 1951; AB with distinction, Stanford U., 1973, JD, 1976. Bar: Calif. 1976, Ill. 1977. Assoc. Sidley & Austin, Chgo., 1977-83; ptnr. Sidley Austin Brown & Wood, Chgo., 1983-97, 2000—; exec. v.p., gen. counsel, sec. Conseco, Inc., Carmel, Ind., 1997-2000. Editorial bd. Stanford U. Law Review, 1974-75, assoc. mng. editor, 1975-76. Mem. ABA, Calif. Bar Assn., Ill. Bar Assn., Chgo. Bar Assn. (chmn. securities law commn. 1985-86), Phi Beta Kappa. Office: Sidley & Austin Bank One Plz 10 S Dearborn St Chicago IL 60603 E-mail: jsabl@sidley.com.

SABO, MARTIN OLAV, former congressman; b. Crosby, ND, Feb. 28, 1938; s. Bjorn O. and Klara (Haga) S.; m. Sylvia Ann Lee, June 30, 1963; children: Karin, Julie. BA cum laude, Augsburg Coll., Mpls., 1959; postgrad., U. Minn., 1961-62. Mem. Minn. Ho. Reps. from 57B Dist., 1960-78, minority leader Dem.-Farmer-Labor party, 1969—73, speaker, 1973-78; mem. US Congress from 5th Minn. Dist., 1979—2006; chmn. Dem. Study Group; dep. majority whip 96th to 103rd Congresses; mem. permanent select com. on intelligence 102d Congress; chmn. Ho. Budget Com. 103d Congress; ranking minority mem. house budget com. 104th-106th Congress, mem. standards of official conduct com., appropriations com., ranking minority mem. subcom. on homeland security. Former mem. Nat. Adv. Commn. on Intergovtl. Rels.; past pres. Nat. Legis. Conf.; bd. regents Augsburg Coll. Mgr., player Dem. Congl. Baseball Team, 1987—. Recipient Disting. Alumni citation Augsburg Coll., Arms Control Leadership award Employees Union, Local 113, SEIU, AFL-CIO; named One of 200 Rising Young Leaders in Am. Time mag., 1974; Man of Yr. Mpls. Jr. C.of C., 1973-74, One of Ten Outstanding Young Men of Yr. Minn. Jr. C. of C., 1974; inducted Scandinavian Am. Hall of Fame, 1994. Mem. Nat. Conf. State Legis. Leaders (past pres.). Democrat. Office Phone: 202-225-4755.

SABO, RICHARD STEVEN, retired electronics executive; b. Walkertown, Pa., Jan. 1, 1934; s. Alex S. and Elizabeth (Haluska) Sabo; m. Gail P. Digon, Feb. 15, 1954; children: Gailyn J., Richard A., Kerry S., Dale A. BS in Edn., Calif State U., Pa., 1955; MS in Edn., Edinboro U., Pa., 1965. Tchr. Northwestern Sch. Dist., Albion, Pa., 1955-65; prodn. technician The Lincoln Electric Co., Cleve., 1965-66, staff asst. mktg., 1966-70, mgr. pub. rels., 1971-86, asst. to chmn., 1986-96, dir. cop. comms. and investor rels.; also exec. dir. James F. Lincoln Arc Welding Found.; ret., 1999. Editor: The Procedure Handbook of Arc Welding, 1994, 10 other books on arc welding; contbr. numerous articles to profl. jours. Chmn. Area Recreation Bd., Chesterland, Ohio, 1970, West Geauga Boosters, Chesterland, 1973-77; mem. adv. bd. Breckenridge Village, 2003—. Recipient Svc. award Future Farmers Am., 1970—, Svc. award U.S. Skill Olympics, 1980, Lakeland Community Coll. award, 1990, Ohio State U. Hon. Welding Engring. Alumni award, 1990, Calif. U. (Pa.) medallion of Distinction, 1990, Internat. Bus. Exec. of Yr. Internat. Acad. of Bus. Disciplines, 1997. Mem. Am. Welding Soc. (vice chmn. edn. and fin. com., mem. fin. com. 1988-94, speaker, various awards, Plummer lectr. 1992), Am. Soc. for Engring. Edn., Am. Inst. Steel Cons. (mem. edn. com. 1986—), Steel Plate Fabricators Assn. (past chmn. promotions com., mem. bd. dirs. profit sharing coun. 1991-99—), California U. Alumni Assn. (trustee 1983-99—). Lodges: Masons. Republican. Presbyterian. Avocations: golf, hunting, fishing, classical music.

SACHA, ROBERT FRANK, osteopath, educator; b. East Chicago, Ind., Dec. 29, 1946; s. S. Frank John and Ann Theresa S.; m. Linda T. LePage, 1988; children: Joshua Jude, Josiah Gerard, Anastasia Levon, Jonah Bradley. BS, Purdue U., 1969; DO, Chgo. Coll. Osteo. Medicine, 1975; PharmD, Creighton U., 2004. Diplomate Am. Bd. Pediatrics, Am. Bd. Allery and Immunology. Pharmacist, asst. mgr. Walgreens Drug Store, East Chicago, Ind., 1969-75; intern David Grant Med. Ctr., San Francisco, 1975-76, resident in pediatrics, 1976-78; fellow in allergy and immunology Wilford Hall Med. Ctr., 1978-80; staff pediatrician, allergist Scott AFB (Ill.), 1980-83; practice medicine specializing in allergy and immunology Cape Girardeau, Mo., 1983—. Assoc. clin. instr. St. Louis U., 1980—; clin. instr. Purdue U., 1971-72, Pepperdine U., 1975-76, U. Tex.-San Antonio, 1978-80, assoc. clin. instr. So. Ill. U. Pres., Parent Tchrs. League; bd. gov. Chgo. Coll. Osteopathic Medicine. Maj. M.C. USAF, 1975-83, comdr. USNR. Named one of Top Pediatricians 2002-2003, Pediatric Allergy, Immunology. Fellow Am. Coll. Allergy, Am. Coll. Chest Physicians, Am. Acad. Pediatrics, Am. Acad. Allergy-Immunology, Am. Assn. Cert. Allergists; mem. ACP, AMA, Am. Acad. Allergy, Assn. Mil. Allergists, Am. Coll. Emergency Physicians, Mil. Surgeons and Physicians. Republican. Lutheran. Office: 351 Kelley Ct Cape Girardeau MO 63701 Office Phone: 573-651-4155. E-mail: bsacha@charter.net.

SACHS, ALAN ARTHUR, lawyer; b. Bklyn., Feb. 7, 1947; s. Herman and Clara Sachs; m. Marilyn Mushlin, May 19, 1974; children: David Henry, Stephen Edward. BA, Columbia U., 1967; JD, Harvard U., 1970. Bar: NY 1971, Wis. 1983, Mo. 1989. Law clk. to judge U.S. Dist. Ct. (ea. dist.) N.Y., 1970-71; assoc. Cleary, Gottlieb, Steen & Hamilton, NYC, 1971-79, Paskus, Gordon & Hyman, NYC, 1979-81; sec., gen. counsel The Trane Co., LaCrosse, Wis., 1981-85; sr. v.p., gen. counsel, sec. Edison Bros. Stores Inc., St. Louis, 1985—2001; ptnr. Haar & Woods, LLP, St. Louis, 2001—. Mem.: ABA, Bar Assn. Met. St. Louis. Office: Haar & Woods LLP 1010 Market St Saint Louis MO 63101 Office Phone: 314-241-2224. Business E-Mail: alansachs@haar-woods.com.

SACHS, GREG ALAN, preventive medicine physician; BA in Biology, U. Chgo., 1977—81; MD, Yale U., 1981—85. Diplomate Am. Bd. Internal Medicine, 1988, cert. in Geriatrics Am. Bd. Internal Medicine, 1990. Resident, internal medicine U. Chgo. Hosps. & Clinics, 1985—87; fellow, geriatric medicine U. Chgo., 1987—90, fellow, clin. med. ethics, 1988—90, asst. prof., medicine, 1990—97, dir., ethics consultation svc., 1992—95, asst. dir., MacLean Ctr. for Clin. Med. Ethics, 1993—99, dir., required ambulatory geriatrics rotation for medicine residents, 1993—97, assoc. prof., medicine, 1997—, found co-dir., The Memory Ctr., 1999—, dir., Hartford Found. Ctr. of Excellence in Geriatrics, 2000—, founding sect. chief, geriatrics, 2000—. Mem. editl. bd. Alzheimer's Disease and Assoc. Disorders, An Internat. Jour., 1995—, Second Opinion, 1999—2002, Jour. of Am. Geriatrics Soc., 2000—, reviewer for various jours. Mem. Cook County State's Atty.'s Task Force on Removal of Life-Sustaining Treatment, 1989—90; mem., cmty. ethics com. Chgo. Coun. for Jewish Elderly, 1990—94; reviewer, grant proposals on end-of-life care Retirement Rsch. Found., 1995—; mem., social sci., humanities, and policy adv. bd. The Brookdale Found., 1998—2000. Mem.: ACP, Nat. Alzheimer's Assn. (mem., ethics adv. panel 1995—, bd. dirs., Chgo. chpt. 1998—2000, chair, ethics adv. panel 2000—), Gerontological Soc. Am., Am. Geriatrics Soc. (mem., ethics com. 1992—, rep., coalition for quality end-of-life care 1996—99, chair, ethics com. 1998—2001, mem., pub. policy adv. group 2001—, New Investigator award 1994), Phi Beta Kappa, Alpha Omega Alpha. Office: Univ Chgo Dept Medicine MC6098 5841 S Maryland Ave Chicago IL 60637-1470

SACHS, HOWARD F(REDERIC), federal judge; b. Kansas City, Mo., Sept. 13, 1925; s. Alex F. and Rose (Lyon) S.; m. Susanne Wilson, 1960; children: Alex Wilson, Adam Phinney. BA summa cum laude, Williams Coll., 1947; JD, Harvard U., 1950. Bar: Mo. 1950. Law clk. U.S. Dist. Ct., Kansas City, Mo., 1950-51; pvt. practice law Phineas Rosenberg, Kansas City, 1951-56; with Spencer, Fane, Britt & Browne, 1956-79; U.S. dist. judge Western Dist. Mo., Kansas City, 1979—, chief dist. judge, 1990-92, now sr. judge. Contbr. articles to various publs.; contbr. chpt. to Mid-America's Promise, 1982. Mem. Kansas City Commn. Human Rels., 1967-73; chmn. Jewish Community Rels. Bur., 1968-71, Kansas City chpt. Am. Jewish Com., 1963-65; mem. exec. com. Nat. Jewish Community Rels. Adv. Coun., 1968-71; pres. Urban League Kansas City, 1957-58, Kansas City chpt. Am. Jewish Congress, 1974-77; co-chmn. Kansas City chpt. NCCJ, 1958-60; mem. Kansas City Sch. Dist. Desegregation Task Force, 1976-77; pres. Jackson County Young Democrats, 1959-60; treas. Kennedy-Johnson Club, Jackson County, 1960. Served with USNR, 1944-46. Mem. ABA, Mo. Bar, Kansas City Bar Assn., Am. Judicature Soc., Lawyers Assn. Kansas City, Dist. Judges Assn. (8th cir., pres. 1992-94), Phi Beta Kappa. Office: US Dist Ct US Courthouse 400 E 9th St Kansas City MO 64106-2607

SACHTLER, WOLFGANG MAX HUGO, chemistry professor; b. Delitzsch, Germany, Nov. 8, 1924; arrived in US, 1983; s. Gottfried Hugo and Johanna Elisabeth (Bollmann) S.; m. Anne-Lore Luise Adrian, Dec. 9, 1953; children: Johann Wolfgang Adriaan, Heike Kathleen Julia, Yvonne Rhea Valeska. Diplomchemiker, Tech. U., Braunschweig, Ger., 1949; Dr.rer.nat. (Ph.D), 1952. Rsch. chemist Kon/Shell Lab., Amsterdam, Netherlands, 1952-71; dept. head Kon-Shell Lab., Amsterdam, 1972—83; extraordinary prof. chemistry U. Leiden, Netherlands, 1963-83; V.N. Ipatieff prof. Northwestern U., Evanston, Ill., 1983-96; chmn. Gordon Research Conf. Catalysis, NH, 1985. Rideal lectr. Faraday div. Royal Soc. Chemistry, 1981; F. Gault lectr., 1991. Mem. editl. bd. Jour. Catalysis, 1976-88, Applied Catalysis, 1983-87, Catalysis Letters, 1987—, Advances in Catalysis, 1987—, Catalysis Today, 1996—, Catalysis Reviews, 1997—; contbr. articles to sci. jours. Recipient Deutsche Gesellschaft Mineraloel und Kohle Kolleg award, 1991. Fellow AAAS; mem. Royal Netherlands Acad. Scis., Internat. Congress Catalysis (pres. coun. 1992-96), Am. Chem. Soc. (E.V. Murphee award 1987, Petroleum Chemistry award 1992), Catalysis Soc. N.Am. (Robert L. Burwell award 1985, E. Houdry award 1993). Home: 2141 Ridge Ave Apt 2D Evanston IL 60201-2788 Office: Northwestern Univ 2137 Campus Dr Evanston IL 60208 Business E-Mail: wmhs@northwestern.edu.

SACK, JAMES MCDONALD, JR., radio and television producer, marketing executive; b. London, Ky., Oct. 11, 1948; s. James McDonald and Ruth Elmore (Bryant) S.; m. Cheryl S. Gremaux, July 13, 1969 (div. June 1974); 1 child, Graehm McDonald; m. Svetlana Antsulevich, Oct. 14, 1999. BA in History, Ind. U., 1975, MS in Telecomm., 1976. Coord. Latin Am. Ednl. Ctr., Ft. Wayne, Ind., 1979-81, Mayor's Office, Ft. Wayne, Ind., 1981-83; producer WMEE-WQHK Radio, Ft. Wayne, Ind., 1983-85; owner, operator Festival Mgmt. and Devel., Ft. Wayne, Ind., 1984—; owner Lily Co., Ft. Wayne, Ind., 1991—2001; region sales mgr. Plan Mgmt., Ft. Wayne, Ind., 1995-96; v.p. comm., mktg. United Way of Allen County, Ft. Wayne, Ind., 1989-96; owner The Sack Co., 1996—. Pub. affairs prodr. WBYR/WFWA, Ft. Wayne; co-founder, treas. Vurpar Project (aid to Romania), 1999—. Producer radio documentary, 1985 (First Pl. award Ind. Broadcasters Assn., 1985), WFWA-PBS Eye on the Arts, 1987-89. Founder, pres. Germanfest of Ft. Wayne, 1981-92; pres. cable TV program adv. coun. City of Ft. Wayne; founder Ft. Wayne-Gera (Germany) Sister City Affilation; commr. Ind. Hoosier Celebration, 1988; dir. Ind. Highland Games, 1992, cons., 1993-99; mktg. dir. Germanfest of Ft. Wayne, 1996-98; pres. cmn. adv. bd. Ft. Wayne Cable Fund, 2000-2006; bd. dirs. Ft. Wayne Sister Cities Com., 2000-04; v.p. Ft. Wayne Sister Cities, 2004. Named Ky. Col., 1991. Mem. German Heritage Soc. (founder, bd. dirs. 1986-99), Ind. German Heritage Soc. (founder, bd. dirs. 1986-92, Gov.'s Commendation award 1983), N.Am. Sängerbund (sec. 1985-86), Männerchor Club (Ft. Wayne), Ft. Wayne Sport Club (sec. 1985-86, trustee 1987-89). Lutheran. Avocations: flying, politics, linguistics, travel. Home and Office: 902 West Rudisill Fort Wayne IN 46807 Office Phone: 260-744-1285. Personal E-mail: jimsack@yahoo.com.

SADLER, DAVID G(ARY), manufacturing executive; b. Iowa City, Mar. 14, 1939; s. Edward Anthony and Elsie June (Sherman) S.; m. Karen Sadler; children: Michael Robert, Katherine Louise. Student, St. Ambrose Coll., 1957—59; BS in Indsl. Adminstrn. and Prodn., Kent State U., 1961. Various mgmt. positions Ford Motor Co., Lorain, Ohio, 1962—67, Sperry-New Holland, Lebanon, Ohio, 1967—71; mgr. mfg. Allis Chalmer, Springfield, Ill., 1971—72; dir. mfg. Purolator, Inc., Fayetteville, NC, 1972—73; v.p. mfg. farm equipment and ops. truck divsn. White Motor Co., Eastlake, Ohio and Chgo., 1973—78; corp. v.p. mfg. Massey Ferguson Ltd., Toronto, Ont., Canada, 1978—80, Internat. Harvester, Chgo., 1980—81, sr. v.p. ops. staff, 1981—82, v.p. bus. devel., 1982, pres. diversified group, 1982—83, pres. internat. group, 1983—85; pres. AMI, Inc., Chgo., 1985—86; vice chmn., CEO Savin Corp., Stamford, Conn., 1986, chmn., CEO, 1986—89, also bd. dirs.; pres. Asset Mgmt. Internat., Westport, Conn., 1989—95; chmn., CEO Rowe Internat., Grand Rapids, Mich., 1995—2000, also bd. dirs., 2000—01; CEO Merisel, Inc., El Segundo, Calif., also bd. dirs.; chmn., CEO, bd. dirs. Global Motorsport Group, Inc., Morgan Hill, Calif., 2002—04. Bd. dirs. greater Chgo. Safety Coun., 1981-84,Hellmold Assocs. Opportunity Fund II. Roman Catholic. Home: 751 Bradford Farms Ln NE Grand Rapids MI 49525-3348 Personal E-mail: davidsadler@comcast.net.

SADOWSKI, PETER T., lawyer; b. Warsaw, Oct. 30, 1954; came to U.S., 1968; s. Fryderyk and Maria (Jaklinska) S.; m. Denise A. Decker, Oct. 13, 1979; children: Katherine, Rachel. BA, St. Louis U., 1976; JD, St. Louis U. Law Sch., 1979. Asst. atty. gen. Mo. Atty. Gen.'s Office, Jefferson City, 1979-81; ptnr. The Stolar Partnership, St. Louis, 1981-96; shareholder Goldberg, Katz, Sadowski & Croft, St. Louis, 1996—99; exec. v.p., gen. counsel Fidelity Nat. Fin. Inc., Jacksonville, Fla., 1999—. Chmn. bd. dirs., greater needs com. YMCA, St. Louis, 1995—. Office: Fidelity National Financial 601 Riverside Ave Jacksonville FL 32204 Office Phone: 888-934-3354.

SADOWSKI, RICHARD J., former publishing executive; b. Mar. 26, 1947; Publ. Press-Telegram, Long Beach, Calif., 1992—97; pres., publ. St. Paul Pioneer Press, 1997—2001. Office: St Paul Pioneer Press 345 Cedar St Saint Paul MN 55101-1057

SADOWSKY, MICHAEL J., microbiologist, educator; married; 2 children. BS, U. Wis., Madison, 1977; MS in Biology/Microbiology, U. Wis., Oshkosh; PhD in Microbiology, U. Hawaii, 1983. Rschr. McGill U., 1983—85; molecular biologist Allied Corp.; biologist Nitrogen Fixation and Soybean Genetics Lab. USDA-ARS, Beltsville, Md.; asst. prof. Dept. Soil Sci. and Microbiology U. Minn., St. Paul, 1989, prof. Dept. Soil, Water, and Climate and Biotechnology Inst., dir. grad. studies Microbial Engring. Program, U. McKnight Disting. prof., 2005—. Co-creator Agricultural Microbe Genomes Confs. Editor: (jour.) Applied and Environ. Microbiology; assoc. editor Symbiosis and Microbes and the Environment; contbr. articles to profl. jours. NSF Grant, 2003. Fellow: Am. Acad. Microbiology; mem.: Am. Soc. Microbiology (Region V Coord. and Branch Archivist). Avocations: woodworking, amateur radio electronics. Office: U Minn 439 Borlaug Hall 1991 Upper Buford Cir Saint Paul MN 55108 Office Phone: 612-625-1244. Office Fax: 612-625-2208. E-mail: sadowsky@soils.umn.edu.

SAFFERMAN, ROBERT SAMUEL, microbiologist, researcher; b. Bronx, NY, Dec. 19, 1932; s. Irving and Rose (Schuler) S.; m. Jewel S. Reisman, June 7, 1958; children— Karen M., Sharon L., Steven I. BS, Bklyn. Coll., 1955; PhD, Rutgers U., 1960. With USPHS, Cin., 1959-64; with Dept. Interior, Cin., 1964-70, U.S. EPA, Cin., 1970—; chief virology sect. Environ. Monitoring and Support Lab. EPA, Cin., 1974-88, chief virology br. Environ. Monitoring Systems Lab., 1988-94; chief virology and parasitology br. Environ. Monitoring Sys. Lab., Cin., 1994-95; chief biohazard assessment rsch. br. Nat. Exposure Rsch. Lab., 1995—. Mem. Internat. Com. on Taxonomy of Viruses. Recipient Spl. Service award San. Engring. Ctr., USPHS, 1963; Gans medal Soc. Water Treatment and Examination, Eng., 1970; named Fed. Employee of Yr., Cin., 1974 Fellow Am. Acad. Microbiology; mem. Am. Soc. Microbiology, Sigma Xi. Office: 26 Martin Luther King Dr W Cincinnati OH 45268-0001 Home: 263 Branch Creek Ct Dayton OH 45458-3287

SAFLEY, JAMES ROBERT, lawyer; b. Cedar Rapids, Iowa, Sept. 19, 1943; s. Robert Starr and Jean (Engelman) S.; m. Dianne Lee McInnis; children: Anne Michele, Jamie Leigh. BA, U. Iowa, 1965; JD, Duke U., 1968. Bar: Minn. 1968, U.S. Ct. Appeals (4th, 5th, 6th, 7th, 8th, 9th and 11th cirs.), U.S. Supreme Ct. Law clk. U.S. Dist. Ct. Minn., Mpls., 1968-69; assoc. Robins, Kaplan, Miller & Ciresi, Mpls., 1969-74, ptnr., 1974—. Mem. adv. coun. Women's Intercollegiate Athletics, U. Minn., 1988-94; mem bd. visitors Duke Law Sch, 2004—. Mem. ABA, Minn. State Bar Assn. (antitrust sect. chmn. 1985-87), Hennepin County Bar Assn., Duke Law Alumni Assn. (bd. dirs. 2001-03), Phi Beta Kappa. Office: Robins Kaplan Miller & Ciresi 2800 LaSalle Pla 800 Lasalle Ave Ste 2800 Minneapolis MN 55402-2015 Office Phone: 612-349-8274.

SAGER, DONALD JACK, librarian, consultant, retired publishing executive; b. Milw., Mar. 3, 1938; s. Alfred Herman and Sophia (Sagan) Sager; m. Sarah Ann Long, May 23, 1987; children: Geoffrey, Andrew. BS, U. Wis., Milw., 1963; MSLS, U. Wis., 1964. Sr. documentalist AC Electronics divsn. GM, Milw., 1958-63; teaching asst. U. Wis., Madison, 1963-64; dir. Kingston (N.Y.) Pub. Libr., 1964-66, Elyria (Ohio) Pub. Libr., 1966-71, Mobile Pub. Libr., 1971-75, Pub. Libr. Columbus and Franklin County, Ohio, 1975-78; commr. Chgo. Pub. Libr., 1978-81; dir. Elmhurst Pub. Libr., Ill., 1982-83, Milw. Pub. Libr., 1983-91; pub. Highsmith Press, Ft. Atkinson, Wis., 1991-2000; pres., CEO Gossage Sager Assocs. LLC, NYC, 2000—. Secy Online Computer Library Ctr, 1977—78, disting vis scholar, 1982; chmn investment comt PLA Pub Library, 1985—89, chmn mus comt, 1989—91, mem hist comt, 1993—95, chmn PLA nat conf comt, 1986—88; bd dirs Coun Wis Libraries, 1982—91, Urban Libraries Coun, 1985—93, secy, 1991—93; adj faculty Univ Wis, Milwaukee, 1984—91; consult in field. Author: Reference: A Programmed Instruction, 1970, Binders, Books and Budgets, 1971, Participatory Management, 1981, The American Public Library, 1982, Public Library Administrators Planning Guide to Automation, 1983, Managing the Public Library, 1984, Small Libraries, 1992, 3d rev. edit., 2000; co-editor: Urban Library Management Trends, 1989; contbg. editor: Public Libraries, 1990—2000; contbr. articles to profl. jours. Pres Milwaukee Civic Alliance, 1990—91; chmn Milwaukee United Way Campaign, 1984; pres Milwaukee Westown Asn, 1987—90; treas. Congl. Ch. Deerfield, Ill., 2002—05, bd. dirs., 2005—; bd dirs Goethe House, 1985—91. With AUS, 1956—58. Mem.: ALA (councilor-at-large 1995—2003, policy monitoring comt, awards comt, chmn core values task force, Joseph Lippincott award 2005), Library Admin Asn Wis (chmn 1987—88), Wis Library Asn Found (chmn 1986—88), Wis Library Asn, Chicago Book Clin, Ill Library Asn, Pub Library Asn (pres 1982—83, bd dirs, vpres, pres-elect), Exchange Club Milwaukee (pres 1988—89). Office Phone: 312-961-5536. Business E-Mail: sagerdon@gmail.com.

SAHR, BOB, former state agency administrator; s. Bob and Carla Sahr; m. Christine Sahr. Grad. with honors, U. Colo., 1989, JD. Sales and mktg. exec. Michelin Tire Corp.; gen. counsel Bur. of Pers., State of SD, SD; pub. utilities commr. State of SD, Pierre. Past pres. Oahe Habitat for Humanity; vol. Easter Seals; bd. dirs. Countryside Hospice, Pierre Mcpl. Libr. Mem.: State Bar SD (mem. commn.). Avocations: reading, movies, music, sports.

SAIN, MICHAEL KENT, electrical engineering educator; b. St. Louis, Mar. 22, 1937; s. Charles George and Marie Estelle (Ritch) S.; m. Frances Elizabeth Bettin, Aug. 24, 1963; children: Patrick, Mary, John, Barbara, Elizabeth. BSEE, St. Louis U., 1959, MSEE, 1962; PhD, U. Ill., 1965. Engr. Sandia Corp., Albuquerque, 1958-61, Vickers Electric Corp., St. Louis, 1962; instr. U. Ill., Urbana, 1962-63; asst. prof. U. Notre Dame (Ind.), 1965-68, assoc. prof., 1968-72, prof., 1972-82, Frank M. Freimann prof. elec. engring., 1982—. Vis. scientist U. Toronto, Ont., Can., 1972-73; disting. vis. prof. Ohio State U., Columbus, 1987; cons. Allied-Bendix Aerospace, South Bend, Ind., 1976—, Deere & Co., Moline, Ill., 1981, 82, Garrett Corp., Phoenix, 1984, GM, Warren, Mich., 1984-94; plenary spkr. IEEE Conf. on Decision and Control, 1990. Author: Introduction to Algebraic System Theory, 1981; editor: Alternatives for Linear Multivariable Control, 1978; hon. editor: Ency. of Systems and Control, 1987; editor jour. IEEE Trans. on Automatic Control, 1979-83; contbr. 350 articles to profl. jours., books and refereed proc; founding editor-in-chief, IEEE Circuits and Systems Mag., 2001—. Grantee Army Rsch. Office, NSF, Ames Rsch. Ctr., Lewis Rsch. Ctr. NASA, Office Naval Rsch., Air Force Office Sci. Rsch., Law Enforcement Assistance Adminstrn., Clark-Hurth Components, Visteon. Fellow IEEE (prize papers com. 1992-96, chair 1994-96, awards bd. 1994-96, Alfred Noble prize com. 1995—); mem. Control Sys. Soc. IEEE (bd. govs. 1978-84, Disting. Mem. award 1983, Centennial medal 1984, Axelby prize chair 1991-97, awards com. chair 1993-97), Circuits and Sys. Soc. IEEE (co-chair internat. symposium on circuits and sys. 1990, newsletter editor 1990-2000, v.p. adminstrn. 1992-93, v.p. tech. activities 1994-95, Golden Jubilee medal 1999), Soc. Indsl. and Applied Math. Republican. Roman Catholic. Avocations: photography, swimming, jogging. Office: U Notre Dame Dept Elec Engring 275 Fitzpatrick Hall Notre Dame IN 46556-5637 E-mail: sain.1@nd.edu.

ST. ANTOINE, THEODORE JOSEPH, retired law educator, arbitrator; b. St. Albans, Vt., May 29, 1929; s. Arthur Joseph and Mary Beatrice (Callery) S.; m. Elizabeth Lloyd Frier, Jan. 2, 1960; children: Arthur, Claire, Paul, Sara. AB, Fordham Coll., 1951; JD, U. Mich., 1954; postgrad., U. London, 1957—58. Bar: Mich. 1954, Ohio 1954, DC 1959. Assoc. Squire, Sanders & Dempsey, Cleve., 1954; assoc., ptnr. Woll, Mayer & St. Antoine, Washington, 1958-65; assoc. prof. law U. Mich. Law Sch., Ann Arbor, 1965-69, prof., 1969—81, Degan prof., 1981-98, Degan prof. emeritus, 1998—, dean, 1971-78. Pres. Nat. Resource Ctr. for Consumers of Legal Svcs., 1974—78; mem. pub. rev. bd. UAW, 1973—, chmn., 2000—; spl. counselor on workers' compensation Gov. of Mich., 1983—85; chmn. UAW-GM legal svcs. plan, 1983—95; reporter Uniform Law Commrs., 1987—92; mem. discipline bd. Mich. Atty., 1999—2005, vice chmn. discipline bd., 2000—02, chmn. discipline bd., 2002—05; life mem. Clare Hall, Cambridge (Eng.) U. Co-author: (with R. Smith, L. Merrifield, C. Craver and M. Crain) Labor Relations Law: Cases and Materials, 4th edit., 1968, 11th edit., 2005; editor: The Common Law of the Workplace: The Views of Arbitrators, 2d. edit., 2005; contbr. articles to profl. jours. Bd. dirs. Nat. Workrights Inst., 2005—. 1st lt. JAGC US Army, 1955—57. Fulbright grantee, U. London, 1957—58. Mem. ABA (past sec. labor law sect., coun. 1984-92), Am. Bar Found., State Bar Mich. (chmn. labor rels. law sect. 1979-80), Nat. Acad. Arbitrators (bd. govs. 1985-88, v.p. 1994-96, pres. 1999-2000), Internat. Soc. Labor and Social Security Law (U.S. br. exec. bd. 1983—, vice chmn. 1989-95), Am. Arbitration Assn. (bd. dirs. 2000—), Nat. Workrights Inst. (bd. dirs. 2005-), Labor and Employment Rels. Assn., Coll. Labor and Employment Lawyers, Order of Coif (life). Democrat. Roman Catholic. Home: 1421 Roxbury Rd Ann Arbor MI 48104-4047 Office: U Mich Law Sch 625 S State St Ann Arbor MI 48109-1215 Office Phone: 734-764-9348. Business E-Mail: tstanton@umich.edu.

ST. CYR, JOHN ALBERT, II, cardiovascular surgeon, thoracic surgeon; b. Mpls., Nov. 26, 1949; s. John Albert and Myrtle Lavira (Jensen) St. C.; m. Mary Helen Malinoski, Oct. 29, 1977. BA summa cum laude, U. Minn., 1973, BS, 1975, MS, 1977, MD, 1980, PhD, 1988. Teaching asst. dept. biochemistry U. Minn., Mpls., 1973, rsch. asst. dept. surgery, 1977-78, intern surgery dept. surgery, 1980-81, resident surgery, 1981-88, cardiovascular rsch. fellow dept. surgery, 1983-86, with dept. surgery, 1991-92; rsch. assoc. fellow Cardiovasular Pathology, United Hosp., St. Paul, 1987-88; cardiovascular surg. resident U. Colo., Dept. Cardiovascular Surgery, Denver, 1988-91; med. advisor Organetics, Ltd., Mpls., 1992, med. dir., 1992. Med. advisor Aor Tech., Inc., St. Paul, 1992; bd. dirs. Minn. Acad. Sci.; pres. Virotech, Inc., 1993-94; med./surg. cons. Medtronic, Inc., 1993—; ind. rsch., 1992—; dir. R&D Medcorp Internat., 1996, Jacqmar, Inc., 1996—; med. dir. IHI, 1996, First Circle Med., Inc., 1997-99; med. dir. Bioenergy Inc., 1998—. Contbr. more than 100 articles/abstracts to profl. jours. Rsch. fellow NIH, 1983-86, Grant in Aid Rsch. award Minn. Heart Assn., 1983-85, Med. Student Rsch. award Minn. Med. Found., 1980, Acad. Excellence award Merck Found., 1980. Mem. AAAS, AMA, Assn. Acad. Surgeons, Minn. Acad. for Scis., Am. Physiol. Soc., N.Y. Acad. Scis., Am. Heart Assn., Internat. Soc. Heart Rsch., Phi Kappa Phi. Republican. Achievements include patents in field of subsequent clinical studies. Office Phone: 612-998-9823. Personal E-mail: congenital@aol.com.

ST. EVE, AMY J., federal judge; b. Belleville, Ill., 1965; BA, Cornell U., 1987, JD, 1990. Pvt. practice, NYC, 1990—94; assoc. ind. counsel Whitewater Independent Counsel's Office, Little Rock, 1994—96; asst. U.S. atty. No. Dist. Ill., 1996—2001; sr. counsel Abbott Labs., Abbott Park, Ill., 2001—02; judge U.S. Dist. Ct. (no. dist.) Ill., 2002—. Office: US Dist Ct No Dist Ill Everett McKinley Dirksen Bldg 219 S Dearborn St Chicago IL 60604

ST. PIERRE, GEORGE ROLAND, JR., materials scientist, engineering executive, educator; b. Cambridge, Mass., June 2, 1930; s. George Rol and Rose Ann (Levesque) St. P.; m. Roberta Ann Hansen, July 20, 1956; children: Anne Renee, Jeanne Louise, John David, Thomas George; m. Mary Elizabeth Adams, Dec. 11, 1976; m. Gretchen Ann Butrick, June 29, 2001; 1 dau., Victoria Harris. BS, MIT, 1951, ScD, 1954; DSc (hon.), Ohio State U., 1998. Rsch. metallurgist Inland Steel Co., 1954-56; faculty Ohio State U., 1956—, prof. metall. engring., 1957-88, assoc. dean Grad. Sch., 1964-66, chmn. metall. engring., 1983-88, chmn. mining engring., 1985-92; dir. Ohio Mineral Rsch. Inst., 1984-92, prof., chmn. material sci. and engring., 1988-92, Presdl. prof., 1988-92, chmn., disting. u. prof. emeritus, 1992—; chief scientist Materials Directorate, Wright-Patterson AFB, 1995-96. Cons. in field; vis. prof. U. Newcastle, NSW, Australia, 1975; adv. com. materials sci. MIT, 1990-97; adv. bd. Argonne Nat. Lab., 1994-99. Editor: Physical Chemistry of Process Metallurgy, Vols. 7 and 8, 1961, Advances in Transport Processes in Metallurgical Systems, 1992, Transactions Iron and Steel Soc., 1994-2003; contbr. articles to profl. jours. Bd. dirs. Edward Orton Jr. Ceramic Found., 1989-92. With USAF, 1956-57. Recipient Milton (Mass.) Clarence Boylston Sci. prize, 1947; MacQuigg award, 1971; Alumni Disting. Tchr. award, 1978; named Disting. scholar Ohio State U., 1988, Presdl. prof. Ohio State U., 1988. Fellow Minerals, Metals & Materials Soc., AIME (bd. dirs. 1988-91, 93-96, Educator award 1996), Am. Soc. Materials Internat. (Bradley Stoughton Outstanding Tchr. award 1961, Gold medal 1987, Albert E. White award 1997); mem. Am. Inst. Mining Metall. and Petroleum Engrs. (Mineral Industry Edn. award 1987), Legion of honor 2003, Iron and Steel Soc. (Elliott lectr. 1994), Am. Contract Bridge League (diamond life master), Faculty Club (pres. 1990-92), Sigma Xi. Home: 4906 Stonehaven Dr Columbus OH 43220 Office: Ohio State U Dept Materials Sci/Engring 2041 N College Rd Columbus OH 43210-1124 Home Phone: 614-893-5287; Office Phone: 614-893-5287. Personal E-mail: gstpierr@columbus.rr.com.

ST. PIERRE, RONALD LESLIE, public health and medical educator, academic administrator; b. Dayton, Ohio, Feb. 2, 1938; s. Leslie Frank and Ruth Eleanor (Rhoten) St.P.; m. Joyce A. Guilford, Apr. 1, 1961; children: Michele Christine, David Bryan. BS, Ohio U., 1961; M.Sc., Ohio State U., 1962, PhD, 1965. Instr. anatomy Ohio State U., Columbus, 1965-67, asst. prof., 1967-69, assoc. prof., 1969-72, prof., 1972—2002, chmn. dept. anatomy, 1972-81, assoc. v.p. health scis., 1981-83, sr. assoc. v.p. health scis. and acad. affairs, 1983—2002, assoc. dean Coll. Medicine and Pub. Health, 1987-96, vice dean Coll. of Medicine and Pub. Health, 1996-2000, exec. vice dean, 2000—02, interim dean pub. health, 1999—2002, assoc. v.p., prof. emeritus, 2002—, spl. asst. to sr. v.p. health scis., 2002—06; assoc. dir. Cancer Rsch. Ctr., 1974-78; interim provost, v.p. for acad. affairs Capital U., Columbus, 2006—. Vis. research asso. Duke U., 1966-67; cons. Battelle Meml. Inst., Columbus. Contbr. articles to profl. jours. Chmn. Ohio Gov.'s Com. on Employment of Handicapped, 1970-78; mem. state exec. com. Presdl. Commn. Employment of Handicapped, 1970-78, chmn., 1971-72; mem. planning and adv. council White House Conf. on Handicapped Individuals, 1975-78; mem. Columbus Mayor's Com. on Internat. Yr. of Disabled. Recipient Lederle Med. Faculty award, 1968-71, prize for basic research South Atlantic Assn. Obstetricians and Gynecologists, 1968, Outstanding Individual award Ohio Rehab. Assn., 1969, Gov.'s award for community service, 1973, Coll. Medicine and Mental Health Alumni Faculty Tchg. award, Ohio State U. Coll. Medicine, 2002, Univ. Disting. Svc. award, 2005. Mem. Am. Assn. Anatomists, Am. Assn. Immunologists, Soc. Exptl. Biology and Medicine, Sigma Xi (pres. Ohio State chpt. 1979-80) Republican. Presbyterian. Home: 8586 Button Bush Ln Westerville OH 43082-8675 Office Phone: 614-236-6108. Business E-Mail: rstpierr@capital.edu. E-mail: rstpierre@insight.rr.com.

SAKSENA, MARIAN E., lawyer; BA in Polit. Sci., Grinnell Coll., Iowa, 1993; cert. with high distinction, U. Minn. Grad. Sch. Social Work, 1998; JD, U. Minn. Law Sch., Mpls., 1998. Bar: Minn. 1999, White Earth Band of Chippewa Tribal Ct. 2001. Crisis care provider Mpls. Crisis Nursery, 1993—94; child adv. Cornerstone, Bloomington, Minn., 1993—95; summer law clk. Children's Law Ctr. Minn., 1996; Mansfield fellow, summer law clk. Legal Aid Soc. Mpls., 1997; vol. guardian ad litem Ramsey County Guardian ad Litem Prog., 1997—99; law clk. Office of the Hennepin County Atty., 1998—99; atty. Children's Law Ctr. Minn., 1999—2002, Fredrikson & Byron, P.A., 2002—04; assoc. Walling, Berg & Debele, P.A., Mpls., 2004—. Mem. transitioning from adolescence task force Casey Found./VOA, 2000; mem. juvenile rules com. Minn. Supreme Ct., 2001—, mem. guardian ad litem rules com., mem. adoption rules com.; mem. Uniform Parentage Act Task Force, 2001—02, Statewide Adv. Com. on Long-Term Foster Care, 2002. Youth Support Grp. Facilitator Cornerstone, Bloomington, Minn., 1995—96; bd. dirs. Legal Advocacy for West Bank Women, Mpls., 1995—97. Named Rising Star, Minn. Super Lawyers mag., 2006. Mem.: Nat. Assn. Counsel for Children, Children's Justice Initiative (mem. Hennepin County, state wards subcommittee 2002), Minn. State Bar Assn. (chair children & the law sect. 2001—). Office: Walling Berg & Debele PA 121 S 8th St Ste 1100 Minneapolis MN 55402 Office Phone: 612-335-3233. E-mail: Marian.Saksena@wbdlaw.com.

SALAMME, MATT, reporter; married; 2 children. Airborne reporter WBBM-AM 780, Chgo.; weekend news anchor WLS-AM 890, Chgo.; fill-in airborne reporter Fox 32, Chgo.; reporter News Chopper 12 WISN 12, Milw., 1998—. Office: WISN PO Box 402 Milwaukee WI 53201-0402

SALAMON, MYRON BEN, physicist, educator, dean; b. Pitts., June 4, 1939; s. Victor William and Helen (Sanders) S.; m. Sonya Maxine Blank, June 12, 1960; children: David, Aaron. BS, Carnegie-Mellon U., 1961; PhD, U. Calif., Berkeley, 1966. Asst. prof. physics U. Ill., Urbana, 1966-72, assoc. prof., 1972-74, prof., 1974—, program dir. Materials Research Lab., 1984-91, assoc. dean. Coll. Engring., 2000—06; dean natural sci. and math. U. Tex., Dallas, 2006—. Vis. scientist U. Tokyo, 1966, 71, Tech. U. Munich, Fed. Republic Germany, 1974-75; cons. NSF; Disting. Vis. Prof. Tsukuba (Japan) U., 1995-96. Editor: Physics of Superionic Conductors, 1979; co-editor: Modulated Structures, 1979; divisional assoc. editor: Phys. Rev. Letters, 1992-96; contbr. sci. papers to profl. jours. Recipient Alexander von Humboldt Sr. US Scientist award, 1974-75; NSF coop. fellow, 1964-66; postdoctoral fellow, 1966; A.P. Sloan fellow, 1972-73; Berndt Matthias scholar Los Alamos Nat. Lab., 1995-96; visiting scientist CNRS and Inst. Laue-Langevin Grenoble, France, 1981-82. Fellow Am. Phys. Soc. Office: Univ Tex Dallas Sch Nat Sci and Math POB 830688 FN32 Richardson TX 75083 Office Phone: 972-883-2416. Business E-Mail: salamon@utdallas.edu.

SALE, LLEWELLYN, III, lawyer; b. St. Louis, May 19, 1942; s. Llewellyn Jr. and Kathleen (Rice) S.; m. Cynthia Jean Bricker, Aug. 17, 1968 (div. Apr. 1995); children: Allyson J., Eryn E. AB cum laude, Yale U., 1964; LLB cum laude, Harvard U., 1967. Bar: Mo. 1967, U.S. Dist. Ct. (ea. dist.) Mo. 1967, U.S. Tax Ct. 1982, U.S. Ct. Claims 1985. From assoc. to ptnr. to mng. ptnr. Husch & Eppenberger, St. Louis, 1967-88; ptnr. Bryan Cave LLP, St. Louis, 1988—2004, of counsel, 2005—. Bd. dirs. Washington U. Child Guidance Clinic, St. Louis, 1978-80, Mental Health Assn. St. Louis, 1988-89. Mem. ABA, Bar Assn. Met. St. Louis (chmn. law econs. subcom. 1982), Noonday Club. Avocations: spectator sports, jogging. Office: Bryan Cave 211 N Broadway Ste 3600 Saint Louis MO 63102-2733 Office Phone: 314-259-2649. Business E-Mail: lsale@bryancave.com.

SALENTINE, THOMAS JAMES, pharmaceutical executive; b. Milw., Aug. 8, 1939; s. James Edward and Loretta Marie S.; m. Susan Anne Sisk, Apr. 16, 1966; children: Anne Elizabeth, Thomas James Jr. BS in Acctg., Marquette U., Milw., 1961. CPA, Ind., Wis. Sr. audit mgr. Price Waterhouse, Milw., 1961-74; dir. corp. acctg. Ward Foods Inc., Wilmette, Ill., 1974-78; corp. contr. Johnson Controls Inc., Milw., 1984-85; v.p., contr. Stokely Van Camp Inc., Indpls., 1978-87; exec. v.p., CFO Bindley Western Industries Inc., Indpls., 1987—2001, also bd. dirs.; ptnr. Bindley Capital Ptnrs., LLC, 2001—. Bd. dirs. Priority Healthcare Corp., Nat. Refrigeration Svcs. Inc. Chmn. com. United Way, Indpls., 1989-90. Lt. USN, 1962-65. Mem. AICPA, Fin. Execs. Inst. Republican. Roman Catholic. Home: 3991 Gulf Shore Blvd Naples FL 34103 Office Phone: 317-704-4154.

SALERNO, AMY, state legislator; m. Joe Armeni. BA, Youngstown State U., 1979; JD, Ohio State U., 1982. Bar: Ohio. Lawyer, small bus. owner, Columbus, Ohio; mem. Ohio Ho. of Reps., Columbus. Past chmn. Italian Village Commn; former mem. bd. dirs. St. Mark's Comty. HealthCtr.; former mem. Victorian Village Commn., Downtown Housing Task Force, Columbus. Recipient Appreciation cert. Italian Village Commn, Victorian Village Commn., Columbus City Coun., Outstanding Orgn. award Short North Bus. Assn.

SALIGMAN, HARVEY, retired consumer products and services company executive; b. Phila., July 18, 1938; s. Martin and Lillian (Zitin) S.; m. Linda Powell, Nov. 25, 1979; children: Martin, Lilli Ann, Todd Michael, Adam Andrew, Brian Matthew BS, Phila. Coll. Textiles and Sci., 1960. With Queen Casuals, Inc., Phila., 1960-88, v.p., 1966-68, pres., chief exec. officer, 1968-81, chmn., 1981-88; pres., chief operating officer Interco Inc., St. Louis, 1981-83, chief exec. officer, 1983-85, 1985-89, chmn., 1989-90; ret. Bd. dirs. Ameren Corp. (formerly Union Electric). Trustee Washington U., St. Louis, Nantucket Hist. Assn. Mem. St. Louis Club, Masons.

SALISBURY, ALICIA LAING, state senator; b. NYC, Sept. 20, 1939; d. Herbert Farnsworth and Augusta Belle (Marshall) Laing; m. John Eagan Salisbury, June 23, 1962; children: John Eagan Jr., Margaret Salisbury La Rue. Student, Sweet Briar Coll., 1957-60; BA, Kans. U., 1961. Mem. Kans. Senate, 1985—, v.p., chmn. commerce com., telecomm. stragegic planning, 1995, vice chmn. ways and means com., mem. utilities com., jt. com. on econ. devel., mem. orgn. and calendar rules com., mem. jt. com. corrections and juvenile justice, mem. confirmations oversight com. Elected mem. State Bd. Edn., Topeka, 1981-85, Kans.; past pres. Jr. League of Topeka; trustee Leadership Kans., 1982-89; bd. dirs. Topeka Cmty. Found., 1983—, Topeka Pub. Sch. Found., 1985-89, Capitol Area Pla. Authority, 1989—, Kans. Inc., 1996—, Mid-Am. Mfg. Tech. Ctr., 1994-96, mem. workers' compensation fund oversight com., 1993— Stormont-Vail Hosp. Aux.; mem. adv. commn. Juvenile Offenders Program, Kans., 1985-95; mem. adv. bd. Topeka State Hosp., Kans. Action for Children, 1982—, Kans. Ins. Edn. Found., 1984-95, Youth Ctr. at Topeka, 1987—; steering com. One Stop Career Ctr., 1996, Interstate Cooperation Com. Coun. State Govts.; mem. Nat. Fedn. Rep. Women; past bd. mem. United Way Greater Topeka, ARC, Family Svc. and Guidance, Topeka, Shawnee County Mental Health Assn., Florence Crittenton Svcs., Topeka, Topeka City Commn. Govtl. Adv. Com.; chmn. Topeka State Hosp. Grounds Adv. Com.; mem. Kans. Workforce Investment Partnership Coun. Recipient Woman of Yr. award Topeka Panhellenic Coun., 1997. Mem. Nat. Conf. State Legislators (exec. com.), Nat. Rep. Legislators' Assn. (Nat. Rep. Legislator of Yr. 1993, Gold Rose award 1992, Bus. Guardian award 1990, 99, Outstanding Individual Legis. Achievement award 1989), Shawnee County Rep. Women, Kans. State Hist. Soc. (exec. com.), Kappa Kappa Gamma. Episcopalian. Avocations: tennis, downhill skiing, water sports, horseback ridng, gardening. Office: Kans State Senate State Capital Topeka KS 66612

SALISBURY, ROBERT HOLT, political science professor; b. Elmhurst, Ill., Apr. 29, 1930; s. Robert Holt and Beulah (Hammer) S.; m. Rose Marie Cipriani, June 19, 1953; children: Susan Marie (dec.), Robert Holt, Matthew Gary. AB, Washington and Lee U., 1951; MA, U. Ill., 1952, PhD, 1955. Mem. faculty Washington U., St. Louis, 1955-65, prof., 1965-97, prof. emeritus, 1997—, chmn. dept. polit. sci., 1966-73, 86-92, dir. Center for Study Pub. Affairs, 1974-77, Sidney W. Souers prof. govt., 1982-97. Vis. prof. SUNY, Buffalo, 1965, So. Ill. U., Edwardsville, 1975; affiliated scholar Am. Bar Found., 1981-95; cons. U.S. Conf. Mayors, 1965, Hartford (Conn.) C. of C., 1964, NSF, 1973. Author: Interest Groups Politics in America, 1970, Governing America, 1973, Citizen Participation in the Public Schools, 1980, Interests and Institutions, 1992, The Hollow Core, 1993; contbr. articles to profl. jours. Mem. St. Louis County Charter Commn., 1967, Gov.'s Commn. on Local Govt., 1968-69. Guggenheim fellow, 1990; Rockefeller Ctr. scholar, 1990. Mem. Mo. Polit. Sci. Assn. (pres. 1964-65), Am. Polit. Sci. Assn. (exec. council 1969-71, v.p. 1980-81), Midwest Polit. Sci. Assn. (pres. 1977-78), Pi Sigma Alpha. Democrat. Methodist. Home: 709 S Skinker Blvd Saint Louis MO 63105-3225 Office: Washington U Dept Polit Sci Saint Louis MO 63130

SALITERMAN, RICHARD ARLEN, lawyer; b. Aug. 3, 1946; s. Leonard Slitz and Dorothy (Sloan) S.; m. Laura Shrager, June 15, 1975; 1 child, Robert Warren. BA summa cum laude, U. Minn., 1968; JD, Columbia U., 1971; LLM, NYU, 1974; grad., FBI Citizens Acad., Mpls. and Washington, 2006. Bar: Minn. 1972, DC 1974. Legal staff subcom. on antitrust and monopoly U.S. Senate, Washington, 1971-72; acting dir., dep. dir. compliance and enforcement divsn. Fed. Energy Office, NYC, 1974; mil. atty. Presdl. Clemency Bd., White House, Washington, 1975; pres. Saliterman & Siefferman, PC, Mpls., 1975—. Adj. prof. law Hamline U., 1976-81. Author: Advising Minnesota Corporations and Other Business Organizations, 4 vols., 1975; chmn. Hennepin County Bar Jour., 1985-87. Trustee, sec. Hopkins Edn. Found.; trustee W. Harry Davis Found., 1990-96; pres. Twin Cities Coun.; nat. bd. dirs. Navy League U.S., Washington, 1997—, nat. judge adv., 2001-02; bd. dirs., sec. The Pavek Mus., 1992—; bd. dirs. Mpls. Urban League, 1983-87. Lt. USN, 1972-75, res., 1975—. Office Phone: 612-339-1400. Business E-Mail: rsaliterman@saliterman-law.com.

SALIZZONI, FRANK L., finance company executive; b. 1938; m. Sarah Salizzoni; 3 children. BS, Pa. State U.; MBA, George Washington U. V.p., CFO TWA, 1984-87; exec. v.p., CFO USAir, Inc., 1990-94, pres., COO, 1994-96; pres. H&R Block, Kansas City, Mo., 1996-99, CEO, 1999—. Office: H&R Block 4400 Main St Kansas City MO 64111-1812

SALKIND, MICHAEL JAY, science administrator, metallurgical engineer; s. Milton and Esther (Jaffe) S.; m. Miriam E. Schwartz, Aug. 16, 1959 (div. 1979); children: Michael Jay, Elizabeth Jane, Jonathan Hillson, Joshua Isaac; m. Carol T. Gill, Dec. 23, 1990. B in Metall. Engring., Rensselaer Polytech. Inst., Troy, NY, 1959, PhD, 1962. Chief advanced metallurgy United Techs. Rsch. Labs., East Hartford, 1964-68; chief structures and materials Sikorsky Aircraft div. United Techs. Corp., 1968-75; dir. product devel. Avco Systems div., 1975-76; mgr. structures NASA, 1976-80; dir. aerospace scis. Air Force Office of Sci. Rsch., 1980-89; pres. Ohio Aerospace Inst., 1990—2003, Business Tech Network, 2003—; prin. Indus Internat., 2003—. Adj. faculty metallurgy Trinity Coll., Hartford; adj. faculty aerospace U. Md., College Park, 1982-85; adj. faculty materials Johns Hopkins U., Balt., 1985-89; chair Ohio Math. and Sci. Coalition; adj. faculty Kent State U., Ohio, 2007-Cons. editor Internat. Jour. Fibre Sci. and Tech.; editor Applications Composite Materials, 1973; contbr. to profl. jours. and textbooks. Evaluator Accreditation Bd. Engring. and Tech., 1989—1995; mem. Daniel Guggenheim Medal Bd. Awards, 1984-90; mem. Spirit of St. Louis Medal Bd., 1984-89; bd. dirs. Citizens' Acad. Charter Sch., Cleve. Internat. Program, NCCJ, Cleve. Coun. World Affairs, Sustainable Cleve.; co-chair Buckeye F.I.R.S.T. Robotics Competition; chair industry adv. bd. Kent State U., Coll. Tech. Capt. ord. US Army, 1962-64. Recipient Disting. Leadership award, Cleve. Tech. Socs. Coun., 2002. Fellow AAAS, AIAA (assoc.), ASM Internat.; mem. ASME (Disting. lectr. 1989-93), ASTM (chmn. com. D-30 on high modulous fibers and their composites 1968-74), Am. Helicopter Soc., AIME, Brit. Inst. Metals, Rsch. Soc. Am., Plansee Soc., India Ohio C. of C., Cosmos Club, Union Club, 50 Club, Leadership Cleve., Sigma Xi, Alpha Sigma Mu. Personal E-mail: michaelsalkind@adelphia.net.

SALLEE, MARY LOU, state legislator; Mem. Mo. State Ho. of Reps. Dist. 144. Home: PO Box 128 Ava MO 65608-0128 Office: Mo Ho of Reps State Capitol Building Jefferson City MO 65101-1556

SALLEN, MARVIN SEYMOUR, investment company executive; b. Detroit, Oct. 15, 1930; s. Jack Samuel and Sara S.; m. Nancy Susan Berke; 1 child, Jack Samuel II. AB in Econs., U. Mich., 1952. V.p. Sonnenblick-Goldman Corp., Detroit, 1967-83; sr. v.p. Comerica Bank, Detroit, 1983-87; pres. Comerica Mortgage Corp., Detroit, 1983-87; mng. ptnr. Brick Ltd., Birmingham, Mich., 1988-90; mng. dir. Redcliffe Corp., Birmingham, 1990—; mng. ptnr. Condor Acquisition Ptnr., LLP, 2000—. E-mail: ms865@comcast.net.

SALLER, RICHARD PAUL, classics educator; b. Ft. Bragg, NC, Oct. 18, 1952; s. George E. and Arthea E. (North) S.; m. Carol Joann Fisher, Jan. 12, 1974 (div. Apr. 18, 2002; children: John E., Benjamin T.; m. Tanya M. Luhrmann, Jan. 4, 2003. BA in Greek and History, U. Ill., 1974; PhD in Classics, U. Cambridge, Eng., 1978. Asst. prof. Swarthmore (Pa.) Coll., 1979-84; assoc. prof. U. Chgo., 1984-89, prof., 1990—, dean of social scis., 1994—2001, provost, 2002—06; dean Sch. Humanities and Sci. Stanford U., 2007—. Author: Personal Patronage, 1982, Patriarchy, Property and Death in the Roman Family, 1994; co-editor: Economy and Society in Ancient Greece, 1981; co-author: Roman Empire, 1987; editor Classical Philology, 1991-93. Rsch. fellow Jesus Coll., U. Cambridge, 1978-79; Ctr. for Adv. Study fellow, Stanford U., 1986-87; Trinity Coll., U. Cambridge fellow commoner, 1991. Mem. Am. Philol. Assn., Am. Hist. Assn., Am. Acad. Arts and Scis. Office: Sch Humanities and Scis Stanford Univ Stanford CA 94305 Home: 441 Gerona Rd Stanford CA 94305-8448 Office Phone: 650-723-9784.

SALMANS, LARRY D., state legislator; b. Shamrock, Tex., Nov. 17, 1937; m. Marilyn Salmans. A in Bus. Law, U. Colo; BS in Psychology and Biology, Baylor U.; MD in Guidance Counseling, Phillips U. Cert. alcohol drug counselor. Enlisted USAF, 1960, command pilot, 1960-69, ret., 1969; psychologist Larned State Hosp., 1986-96; farmer, rancher Rock Creek Ranch, 1969-86; ret. dir. drug and alcohol svcs. Kans. State Hosp., Topeka; mem. Kans. Senate, Topeka, 1996—, vice chmn. pub. health and welfare com., mem. transp. and tourism com., mem. ways and means com. Mem. VFW, Kans. Assn. Masters Psychologists, Kans. Alcohol and Drug Assn., Kans. Livestock Assn., Res. Officers Assn., Irrigation Assn. Republican.

SALMELA, DAVID DANIEL, architect; b. Wadena, Minn., Mar. 28, 1945; s. Laurie Fredrick and Lempi Christine (Matti) S.; m. Gladys Elaine Hanka, June 23, 1967; children: Cory, Chad, Tia, Kai, Brit. Grad. high sch., Sebeka, Minn.; LHD (hon.), U. Minn., 2007. Registered profl. architect, Minn., Wis. Draftsman McKenzie Hague & Gilles, Mpls., 1965-66, A.G. McKee, Hibbing, Minn., 1966, ABI Contracting, Virginia, Minn., 1966-69, Archtl. Resources, Hibbing, 1969-70; designer, arch. Damberg Scott Peck & Booker, Virginia, 1970-89; arch. Mulfinger Susanka, Duluth, Minn., 1989-90; prin. Salmela Fospick Ltd., Duluth, 1990-94, Salmela, Arch., Duluth, 1994—. Author: Salmela Architect. Recipient Design award, N.Am. Wood, 1994, 1998, 2 Design awards, 2002, Design award, 2003. Fellow: AIA (18 Minn. Honor awards 1985—2005, WRCL/AIA award 1994, Red Cedar Lumber Hon. award 1994, Record Houses award 1998, Nat. Honor award 1998, AIA/PIA award 2000, Louise Bethune award 2000, ASLA award 2001, 2 Nat. Honor awards 2005); mem.: Nat. Soc. Landscape Artists (Jackson Meadow award 2001, Mayo Woodlands award 2004). Home and Office: Salmelaarchitect 630 W 4th St Duluth MN 55806 Office Phone: 218-724-7517. E-mail: ddsalmela@charter.net.

SALMON, STUART CLIVE, manufacturing engineer; b. London, 1952; BTech in Prodn. Engring. and Engring. Mgmt. with honors, Loughborough U., 1975; PhD, Bristol U., 1979. Apprentice Rolls-Royce Ltd., Derby, Eng., 1969-79; with Gen. Electric Aircraft Engine Group, Cin., 1979-83, engr. Evendale, Ohio, 1980-83; prin. Advanced Mfg. Sci. and Tech., Cin., 1983—. Adj. prof. mfg. engring. U. Cin., 1996—; presenter seminars; founding mem. Internat. Com. Abrasive Tech.; chmn. Internat. Symposium Advances Abrasive Tech. Author: Abrasive Machining Handbook, 1983, Modern Grinding Process Technology, 1992; contbr. articles to profl. jours., to McGraw-Hill Ency., 1982-83; patentee in field. Recipient Jim Bottorf award Abrasive Engring. Soc., 1986, Sir Walter Puckey prize, Inst. Prodn. Engrs., U.K., 1975; Rolls-Royce/Brit. Sci. Rsch. Coun. grantee, 1976. Fellow Soc. Mfg. Engrs. Office: Advanced Mfg Sci and Tech PO Box 60227 Rossford OH 43460-0227 Office Phone: 419-297-9549. Business E-Mail: drsalmon@moderngrindingtechnology.com.

SALOMON, ROGER BLAINE, retired language educator; b. Providence, Feb. 26, 1928; s. Henry and Lucia Angell (Capwell) S.; m. Elizabeth Helen Lowenstein, June 14, 1950; children: Pamela, Wendy. BA, Harvard, 1950; MA, U. Calif., Berkeley, 1951, PhD, 1957. Instr. Mills Coll., Oakland, Calif., 1955-57; instr., then asst. prof. Yale U., New Haven, 1957-66; mem. faculty Case Western Res. U., Cleve., 1966—, prof. English, 1969—, Oviatt prof. English, 1990, chmn. dept., 1974-80, part-time prof. English, 1994-99; Oviatt prof. English emeritus, 1999—. Mem. adv. screening com. Am. lit. Sr. Fulbright-Hayes Program, 1973-76, chmn., 1975; mem. grants-in-aid selection com. Am. Council Learned Socs., 1976-78 Author: Twain and the Image of History, 1961, Desperate Storytelling: Post-Romantic Elaborations of the Mock-Heroic Mode, 1987, Mazes of the Serpent: An Anatomy of Horror Narrative, 2002. Served to 1st lt. USAF, 1952-53. Morse fellow, 1960-61; Guggenheim fellow, 1972-73 Mem. AAUP, MLA. Home: 2830 Coventry Rd Cleveland OH 44120-2231 Office Phone: 216-368-2340.

SALOMONE, JOSEPH ANTHONY, III, emergency medicine physician; b. Reno, June 5, 1958; s. Joseph Anthony and Peggy Ruth (Crompton) S.; m. Cynthia Amelia Douglas, Aug. 10, 1980; children: Joseph Kenneth, Christopher Anthony. BS, U. Nev., 1979, MD, 1983. Diplomate Am. Bd. Emergency Medicine. Intern in gen. surgery Truman Med. Ctr., Kansas City, 1983-84, resident in emergency medicine, 1984-86, fellow in emergency medicine,

1986-87, rsch. dir. emergency medicine, 1987-88, assoc. residency dir., 1990-97, residency dir., 1997—, assoc. prof. emergency medicine, 1994—; med. dir. Met. Ambulance Svcs., Kansas City, 1988-89; staff physician St. Joseph's Med. Ctr., Asheville, N.C., 1989-90. Chmn. Emergency Physicians Adv. Bd., Kansas City, 1992-94; mem. edn. com. SAEM, 1997—. Author: Toxicology Guide for Emergency Medicine, 1988, Emergency Medicine, 1995; editor: Critical Decision in Emergency Medicine, 1995. Cubmaster Pack 397 Boy Scouts Am., Kearney, Mo., 1994-96, webelos leader, 1993-95, den leader, asst. adminstr., 1991-93. Fellow Am. Coll. Emergency Medicine, Am. Acad. Emergency Medicine; mem. Am. Coll. Emergency Physicians (mem. emergency med. svcs. com. Mo. chpt. 1990-94), Soc. for Acad. Emergency Medicine, Coun. Residency Dirs., Nat. Assn. Emergency Med. Svc. Physicians (state liaison 1988-90). Baptist. Avocations: computers, sailing. Office: Truman Med Ctr Dept Emergency Medicine 2301 Holmes St Kansas City MO 64108-2640

SALPETER, ALAN N., lawyer; b. Phila., Oct. 7, 1947; BA with honors, Am. U., 1969; JD, Villanova U., 1972. Bar: Ill. 1972, US Dist. Ct. (no. dist. Ill.) 1972, US Ct. Appeals (5th cir.) 1977, US Ct. Appeals (7th cir.) 1974, US Ct. Appeals (8th cir.) 1981, US Ct. Appeals (11th cir.) 1985, US Ct. Appeals (DC cir.) 1991, US Ct. Appeals (10th cir.) 1998. Assoc. Mayer, Brown & Platt, Chgo., 1972—79; ptnr. Mayer, Brown, Rowe & Maw, Chgo., 1979—2007, LeBoeuf, Lamb, Greene and MacRae LLP, Chgo., 2007—. Adj. prof. Northwestern Law Sch.; lectr. in field. Mng. editor Law Rev., Villanova U.; author in field. Mem. ABA, Chgo. Bar Assn., Chgo. Coun. Lawyers, 7th Cir. Bar Assn. (bd. gov.). Office: LeBoeuf Lamb Greene & MacRae LLP Two Prudential Plaza 180 N Stetson Ave Ste 3700 Chicago IL 60601 Office Phone: 312-794-8088. Business E-Mail: asalpeter@llgm.com.

SALTER, CHRISTOPHER LORD, geography educator; BA, Oberlin Coll., 1961; MA, U. Calif. Berkeley, 1968, PhD, 1970. Tchr. Tunghai U., Taiwan, 1961; prof. Dept. Geography UCLA, 1968—87; coord. Alliance Network Nat. Geog. Alliance, 1987—89; prof. geography U. Mo., Columbia, Mo., 1989—2002, chmn. Dept. Geography, 1989—2002, prof. emeritus, 2002—. Founder Calif. Geog. Alliance, 1983—87. Editor: The China Geographer, 1975—78; author: Social Studies for the 21st Century; editor; author (and editor): over 20 books. Recipient George J. Miller award Nat. Coun. for Geog. Edn., 1992, Disting. Geography Educator award Nat. Geog. Soc., 1990, Disting. Tchg. Achievement award Nat. Coun. for Geog. Edn., 1999, Disting. Faculty award U. Mo. Alumni Assn., 1999. Mem.: Mo. Geog. Alliance, Geography Edn. Proram, Nat. Geog. Soc., Nat. Coun. Geog. Edn. (pres. Calif. chpt. 1975—76, Outstanding Educator award Calif. chpt. 1981), Am. Geog. Soc., Assn. Am. Geographers. Office: Univ Mo Dept Geography Dept Geography 3 Stewart Hall Columbia MO 65211-6170

SALVENDY, GAVRIEL, industrial engineer, educator; b. Budapest, Hungary, Sept. 30, 1938; came to US, 1968; s. Paul and Katarina (Brown) S.; m. Catherine Vivien Dees, Apr. 1, 1966; children: Laura Dorit, Kevin David. MSc in Indsl. Psychology, U. Birmingham, Eng., 1966, PhD in Indsl. Psychology, 1968; D (hon.), Academia Sinica, 1995, Chinese Acad. Scis., 1995. Asst. prof. indsl. engring. SUNY, Buffalo, 1968-71; assoc. prof. indsl. engring. Purdue U., 1971—77, prof., 1977—84, 1999—, NEC prof. indsl. engring., 1984-99; chair prof., head dept. indsl. engring. Tsinghua U., Beijing, 2001—. Fulbright disting. prof. mech. engring. U. Belgrade, Yugoslavia, 1979-81; chmn. Internat. Commn. Human Aspects in Computing, Switzerland, 1986-91. Co-author: Prediction and Development of Industrial Work Performance, 1973, Human Aspects of Computer Aided Design, 1987; sr. editor: Machine-Pacing and Occupational Stress, 1981, Social, Ergonomic and Stress Aspects of Work with Computers, 1987, Designing and Using Human-Computer Interfaces and Knowledge Based Systems, 1989; editor: Handbook of Industrial Engineering, 1982, 3d edit., 2001, Human Computer Interaction, 1984, Handbook of Human Factors, 1987, 3d edit., 2006, Cognitive Engineering in the Design of Human Computer Interaction and Expert Systems, 1987; founding editor: Internat. Jour. on Human-Computer Interaction, Internat. Jour. Human Factors in Mfg., Human-Computer Interaction, 1st and 2d edits., 2002, 07; co-editor: Work with Computers: Organizational Management, Stress and Health Aspects, 1989, Human Computer Interaction: Software and Hardware Interfaces, 1993, Human-Computer Interaction: Applications and Case Studies, 1993, Design of Work and Development of Personnel in Advanced Manufacturing, 1994, Organization and Management of Advanced Manufacturing, 1994, Advanceds in Applied Ergonomics, 1996, Handbook of Human Factors and Ergonomics, 3rd edit. 2006, Design of Computing Systems (2 vols.), 1997, Ergonomics in Manufacturing, 1998, Handbook of Industrial Engineering, 3d edit., 2001; contbr. articles to profl. jours., chpts. to books. Pres. Lafayette Jewish Sunday Sch., 1980-81. Recipient Friendship award Sci. and Engring., Govt. China, 2006, John Fritz medal, Am. Assn. Engring. Socs., 2007. Fellow APA, Inst. Indsl. Engrs. (sr., Phil Carroll award 1973), Human Factors and Ergonomics Soc. (past officer), Ergonomics Soc. (hon., life mem.), Internat. Ergonomics Assn.; mem. NAE. Office: Sch Indsl Engring Purdue U 315 N Grant St West Lafayette IN 47907-2023 Office Phone: 765-463-2628, 765-494-5426. Office Fax: 765-494-0874. E-mail: salvendy@purdue.edu.

SALVO, J. C., lawyer; b. Council Bluffs, Iowa, Dec. 10, 1947; JD, Creighton U. Sch. of Law, Omaha, Neb., 1972. Bar: Iowa 1972, Nebr. 1972, US Dist. Ct. (Dist. ebr.) 1972, US Dist. Ct. (So. Dist. Iowa) 1972, US Supreme Ct. 1980, US Dist. Ct. (No. Dist. Iowa) 1983, US Ct. Appeals (8th Cir.) 1984. County atty., Shelby County, Iowa, 1977—82; ptnr. Salvo, Deren, Schenck & Lauterbach, PC, Harlan, Iowa, 1972—. Shelby County atty., 1977—82. Fellow: Iowa Acad. of Trial Lawyers (pres. 1998); mem.: Iowa Supreme Ct. Nominating Commn., Iowa Supreme Ct. Grievance Commn., Assn. of Trial Lawyers of Am., Am. Bar Assn., Neb. State Bar Assn., Iowa State Bar Assn. (bd. gov. 1999—2003, v.p. 2003, pres.-elect 2004, pres. 2005), Phi Alpha Delta. Office: Salvo Deren Schenck & Lauterbach PC 711 Court St Harlan IA 51537-0509 Office Phone: 712-755-3141. Office Fax: 712-755-3144. Business E-Mail: jasalvo@sdsllaw.com.

SALZMAN, ARTHUR GEORGE, retired architect; b. Chgo., June 20, 1929; s. Russell Harvey Salzman and Mildred Olive (Olsen) Erickson; m. Joan Marie Larson, Aug. 16, 1952; children: Lisa Jo Salzman Braucher, David Ralph. BS in Archtl. Engring., U. Ill., 1952; MArch, Ill. Inst. Tech., 1960. Nat. Coun. Archtl. Registration Bds. Architect Skidmore, Owings & Merrill, Chgo., 1960, Mies van der Rohe, Arch., Chgo., 1960-69; assoc. The Office of Mies Van Der Rohe, Chgo., 1969-81; v.p. FCL Assocs., Chgo., 1981-86; exec. v.p. Lohan Assocs., Chgo., 1986-91; pvt. practice Evanston, Ill., 1992—2007; cons., 2007. Bldg. code restructuring com. City of Chgo., 1994-96, bldg. code electronic version com., 1997, bldg. code rev. com., 1998-2004; adj. prof. arch. Ill. Inst. Tech., Chgo., 2005-06. V.p. Chgo. area Unitarian-Universalist Coun., Chgo., 1974—76; bd. dirs. Savoy-aires, Evanston, Ill., 1985—88, 1990—93, pres., 1992—93; active Chgo. Com. on High Rise Bldgs. Emeritus cpl. US Army, 1952—54. Mem. AIA (bd. dirs. Chgo. chpt. 1992-96, sec. 1994-96, Ill. region bd., alt. del. 1997-98, del. 1999-2000, emeritis 2007—, Disting. Svc. award for profl. excellence 2003), Am. Soc. Testing and Materials Internat., Constrn. Specifications Inst. (emeritus 2007—), Internat. Code Coun. (profl.), Precast-Prestressed Concrete Inst., North Shore Musicians Club. Avocations: acting, singing.

SALZMAN, JERROLD E., lawyer; b. Chgo., Oct. 11, 1940; AB with high distinction, Univ. Mich., 1962; LLB cum laude, Harvard Univ., 1965. Bar: Ill. 1965, US Dist. Ct. no. dist. Ill., US Ct. Appeals 7th cir. Ptnr., commodities & futures litig. & regulation Freeman Freeman & Salzman PC, Chgo.; prin. outside counsel Chgo. Merc. Exch. Editor: Harvard Law Rev.; contbr. articles to profl. jours. Mem.: ABA (mem. exec. council, com. futures regulation), Chgo. Bar Assn., Chgo. Council Lawyers, Phi Beta Kappa. Office: Skadden Arps Slate Meagher & Flom LLP 333 W Wacker Dr Chicago IL 60606 Office Phone: 312-407-0718. Office Fax: 312-827-9406. Business E-Mail: jesalzma@skadden.com.

SAMBOLIN, ZORAIDA, newscaster; b. Chgo. married; 2 children. At, Loyola U. Dir. of broadcasting Chgo. City Colls., Chgo.; host Small Talk for Parents WYCC-TV, Chgo.; host Nuestros Niños WSNS-TV, Chgo., 1999—2002; co-anchor 11am news WMAQ-TV, Chgo., 2002—. Recipient Emmy award. Office: WMAQ-TV NBC Tower 454 N Columbus Dr Chicago IL 60611-5555

SAMEROFF, ARNOLD JOSHUA, developmental psychologist, educator, research scientist; b. NYC, Apr. 20, 1937; s. Stanley and Zeena (Shapiro) S.; m. Susan C. McDonough, Jan. 2, 1982; children: Shira, Rebecca, Crista. BS, U. Mich., 1961; PhD, Yale U., 1965; MA (hon.), Brown U., 1987. Asst. prof. psychology, pediat. and psychiatry U. Rochester, 1967—70, assoc. prof., 1970—73, prof., 1973—78, dir. developmental psychology tng. program, 1975—78; prof. psychology U. Ill., Chgo., 1978—86, assoc. dir. Inst. for Study Devel. Disabilities, 1978—86; assoc. dir., dir. rsch. Ill. Inst. for Devel. Disabilities, Ill. Dept. Mental Health and Deve. Disabilities, 1978—86; prof. psychiatry and human behavior Brown U., Providence, 1986—92; dir. Bradley Hosp., Devel. Psychopathology Rsch. Ctr., East Providence, 1986—92; prof. psychology, rsch. prof. U. Mich., Ctr. for Human Growth and Devel., Ann Arbor, 1992—; dir. devel. and mental health Rsch. Ctr. U. Mich., Ann Arbor, 2000—05. Vis. prof. psychology Birkbeck Coll., U. London, 1974-75; vis. scientist Ctr. for Interdisciplinary Rsch., U. Bielefeld, Fed. Republic Germany, 1977-78; dir. Summer Inst. on Human Devel. and Psychopathology, Ctr. for Advanced Study in Behavioral Scis., Stanford, Calif., 1989; mem. small grants adv. com. NIH, 1977-81, behavioral scis. assessment panel, 1987-88; mem. orgnl. planning com. Internat. Conf. for Infant Studies, 1980-84 Editor: (with R.N. Emde) Relationship Disturbances in Early Childhood: A Developmental Approach, 1989, (with F. Kessel and M. Bornstein) Contemporary Constructions of the Child: Essays in Honor of William Kessen, 1991, (with M. Haith) The Five to Seven Year Shift, 1996 (with F.F. Furstenberg et. al.) Managing to Make It: Urban Families and Adolescent Success, 1999, (with M. Lewis and S. Miller) Handbook of Developmental Psychopathology, 2000, (with S.C. McDonough and K.L. Rosenblum) Treating Early Relationship Problems: Infant, Parent, and Interaction Therapies, 2004; also monographs; mem. editl. bds. Devel. and Psychopathology, 1988-94, Jour. Devel. and Behavioral Pediatrics, 1989-93, Jour. Family Psychology, 1990-91, Parenting: Science and Practice, 2001, others. Mem. social and behavioral scis. rsch. adv. com. March of Dimes Birth Defects Found., 1977-94, rsch. adv. com. Little City Found., 1986-88; bd. dirs. Zero to Three: Nat. Ctr. for Infants Toddlers and Families, exec. com., 1998-2002; mem. program on successful adolescent devel. among youth in high-risk settings John D. and Catherine T. MacArthur Found., 1986-95, network on early childhood transitions, 1989-92; mem. gov. coun. Soc. Rsch. in Child Devel., 1998-. Recipient rsch. scientist award NIMH, 1994-99; GE fellow Yale U., 1961; NIMH predoctoral rsch. fellow Yale U., 1962, NIMH postdoctoral rsch. fellow, 1965-67, Ctr. for Advanced Study in Behavioral Scis. fellow Stanford U., 1984-85. Fellow AAAS, Am. Acad. Mental Retardation, Am. Psychol. Soc., APA (program com. devel. psychology divsn. 1978-90, chair 1979, coun. 1980-83, mem.-at-large exec. com. 1985-88, pres. devel. psychology divsn. 1995-96, G. Stanley Hall rsch. award, Sci. award 2005); mem. AAUP, Soc. for Rsch. in Child Devel. (governing coun. 1999-2005, pre.-elect 2005—, Dist. Scientist award, 2005), World Assn. Infant Mental Health, Internat. Soc. for Infant Studies (pres. 2002-2004), Soc. for Rsch. on Adolescence E-mail: sameroff@umich.edu.

SAMIC, DENNIS R., retired career officer; BSBA, Ohio State U., 1970; M in Systems Mgmt, U. Southern Calif., LA, 1973. Commd. 2d lt. USAF, 1970, advanced through grades to brig. gen., 1994; base cost analysis officer, later base budget officer 306th Combat Support Group, McCoy AFB, Fla., 1970-73; budget analyst to exec. officer to dep. chief staff, comptr. Hdqs. USAF Europe, Ramstein AB, West Germany, 1973-77; comdr.'s aide, to asst. to comptr., asst. chief of staff Hdqs. Army and AF Exch. Svc., Dallas, 1977-80; fin. analyst, to chief Comptr. Plans divsn. Air Force Acctg. and Fin. Ctr., Lowry AFB, Colo., 1981-85, chief Ret. Pay Entitlements divsn., 1981-85; chief, comptr. info. architecture, exec. officer to comptr. Hdqs. USAF, the Pentagon, Washington, 1985-88; dep. chief of staff, contr., comptr. Hdqs. Alaskan Air Command, Elmendorf AFB, Alaska, 1989-90; asst. dep. chief of staff, fin. mgmt., comptr. Hdqs. Mil. Airlift Command, Scott AFB, Ill., 1990-92; comptr. Hdqs. Air Edn. and Tng. Command, Randolph AFB, 1992-95, Hdqs. Air Force Material Command, Wright-Patterson AFB, Ohio, 1995-99; ret., 1999. Decorated Legion of Merit. Office: HQ AFMC/FM 4375 Chidlaw Rd Ste 6 Wright Patterson AFB OH 45433-5066

SAMPANTHAVIVAT, ARUN, chef; b. Thailand; Student, U. Chgo. Owner, chef Arun's, Chgo. Named to Fine Dining Hall of Fame, Nation's Restaurant News; recipient Ivy award, Restaurants & Instns. mag., 1994, DiRoNA award, 1998, 1999. Office: Arun's 4156 N Kedzie Ave Chicago IL 60618

SAMPSON, JOHN EUGENE, food products executive, consultant; b. Feb. 25, 1941; s. Delbert John and Mary Etta (Dodrill) S.; m. Mary Margaret Treanor, Aug. 14, 1965; children: J. Mark, Sharon. AB with distinction, Nebr. Wesleyan U., 1963; MBA, Ind. U., 1964. Mgmt. asst., exec. trainee Office Sec. Def., Washington, 1963—64; mem. staff Com. Econ. Devel., Washington, 1964—69; coord. environ. planning Gen. Mills Inc., Mpls., 1969—72, mgr. devel. planning, 1972—74; dir. corp. planning Cen. Soya Co. Inc., Ft. Wayne, Ind., 1974—76, v.p. corp. planning, 1976—80, v.p. corp. planning and devel., 1980—82, v.p. corp. devel., corp. sec., 1982—84; v.p. corp. planning and devel. Internat. Multifoods, Inc., 1984—96; pres. Sampson Assocs., Edina, Minn., 1996—. Author: How to Sell Your Business and Get the Best Price For It, 2003. Mem. bd. govs. Nebr. Wesleyan U., 1974-80; chmn. bd. trustees St. Joseph United Meth. Ch., Ft. Wayne, 1984; bd. dirs., treas. North Ind. United Meth. Found., 1981-84; lay mem. North Ind. Ann. Conf. United Meth. Ch., 1980-84; bd. dirs. Anthony Wayne coun. Boy Scouts Am., 1984; lay mem. Minn. Ann. Conf. United Meth. Ch., 1985-91, 97-00; chmn. conf. bd. devel. Minn. United Meth. Conf., 1986-91; chmn. bd. trustees Hennepin Ave. United Meth. Ch., Mpls., 1990-92, chair adminstrv. coun., 1993-95, lay leader, 1995-98; chair exec. com. North Naples (Fla.) United Meth. Ch., 2002-05, co-chmn. bldg. com., 2002-05, chair bd. trustees, 2005-. Mem. Ind. U. Sch. Bus. Alumni Assn. (pres. 1984-85), Interlachen Country Club, Country Club of Naples (bd. dirs. 2004—). Home: Unit 1701 4451 Gulf Shore Blvd N Naples FL 34103 Office Phone: 952-928-0800.

SAMPSON, KELVIN DALE, former college basketball coach; b. Laurinburg, NC, Oct. 5, 1955; s. John W. and Eva (Brewington) S.; m. Karen Sue Lowry, June 16, 1979; children: Lauren Elizabeth, Kellen Matthew. BS, Pembroke State U., 1978; MS, Mich. State U., 1980. Asst. coach Mont. Tech. U., 1979—80, head coach, 1981—85; asst. coach Wash. State U., 1985—87, head coach, 1987—94, U. Okla., Norman, Okla., 1994—2006, Ind. U., Bloomington, 2006—08. Contbr. articles to profl. jours. Named Big Eight Coach of Yr., 1995, Nat. Coach of Yr., AP, 1995. Mem. Nat. Assn. Basketball Coaches (Dist. Coach of Yr. 1991, PAC 10 Coach of Yr. 1991, Nat. Coach of Yr., 2002) Avocations: golf, reading, exercise.*

SAMPSON, RONALD ALVIN, advertising executive; b. Charlottesville, Va., Nov. 13, 1933; s. Percy Thomas Sampson and Lucile (Mills) Martin; m. Norvelle Ann Johnson, Aug. 8, 1959; children: David Alan, Cheryl Ann. BS in Commerce, DePaul U., 1956. Advt. sales rep. Ebony Mag., Chgo., 1959-63; merchandising rep. Foote, Cone & Belding Advt., Chgo., 1963-66; account mgr. Tatham, Laird & Kudner Advt., Chgo., 1966-78; account mgr., exec. v.p. Burrell, Advt., Chgo., 1978-81; advt. agy. account mgr., sr. v.p. Darcy McManus Masius, Chgo., 1981-88; advt. agy. account mgr., exec. v.p., dir. corp. devel. Burrell Comm. Group, Chgo., 1990—. Mem. diversity com. Am. Advt. Fedn., 1996—. Bd. dirs. Cmty. Renewal Soc., Chgo., 1969-94; deacon Chgo. United, 1992-94; co-chair Protestants for Common Good, 1996—. With U.S. Army, 1956-58. Office: Burrell Communications 233 N Michigan Ave #29 Chicago IL 60601-5519

SAMPSON, WILLIAM ROTH, lawyer; b. Teaneck, NJ, Dec. 11, 1946; s. James and Amelia (Roth) S.; 1 child, Lara; m. Drucilla Jean Mort, Apr. 23, 1988; stepchildren: Andy, Seth. BA in History with honors, U. Kans., 1968, JD, 1971. Bar: Kans. 1971, Mo. 2004, U.S. Dist. Ct. Kans. 1971, U.S. Dist. Ct. (we. dist.) Mo. 2004, U.S. Ct. Appeals (10th cir.) 1982, U.S. Ct. Claims 1985, U.S. Ct. Appeals (8th cir.) 1992. Assoc. Turner & Balloun, Great Bend, Kans., 1971; ptnr. Foulston & Siefkin, Wichita, Kans., 1975-86, Shook, Hardy & Bacon LLP, Kans. City, 1987. Adj. prof. advanced litig. U. Kans., 1994; mem. faculty trial tactics inst. Emory U. Sch. Law, 1994-97; mem. merit selection panel US Dist. Ct. Kans., 1999; lectr., presenter in field. Author: Kansas Trial Handbook, 1997, 2d edit., 2006; mem. Kans. Law Rev., 1969—71, editor, 1970—71; contbr. articles to profl. jours. Chmn. stewardship com. Univ. Friends Ch., Wichita, 1984-86; bd. dir. Friends U. Retirement Corp., Wichita, 1985-87, Lied Ctr. Kans., 1994-97, Nat. Found. Jud. Excellence, 2004—, program chmn., 2005, 06, pres. elect, 2007; chmn. capital fund drives Trinity Luth. Ch., Lawrence, Kans., 1990-93, mem. ch. coun., 1990-92, stewardship com. Trinity Episcopal Ch., 2002—. Lt., Judge Advocate General's Corps, USNR, 1971-75. Named one of Best Lawyers in Am., 1995—, Kans. Super Lawyers, 2005—, 2006. Fellow: Kans. Bar Found., Am. Bar Found.; mem.: ABA, Lawyers for Civil Justice (bd. dirs. 2003—05), Am. Inn Ct. (Judge Hugh Means chpt. Master of Bench), Kans. U. Law Soc. (bd. govs. 1993—96), Kans. Assn. Def. Counsel (pres. 1989—90, legis. coun. 1991, 1993, William H. Kahrs Disting. Achievement award 1994), Def. Rsch. Inst. (Kans. state rep. 1990—98, nat. bd. dirs. 1998—2000, nat. pres. 2003—04, chmn. strategic planning com. 2006—08, chair commercial litigation program 2007), Internat. Assn. Def. Coun. (faculty mem. trial acad. 1994), Am. Bd. Trial Advs. (pres. Kans. chpt. 1990—91, nat. bd. dir. 1990—91), Wichita Bar Assn. (bd. dirs. 1985—86), Johnson County Bar Assn. (bench-bar com. 1989—, Boss of Yr. award 1990), Douglas County Bar Assn., Kans. Bar Assn. (chmn. Kans. coll. advocacy 1986, CLE com. 1987—88, long-range planning), Assn. Def. Trial Attys., Club at Porto Cima, Order of the Coif, Omicron Delta Kappa, Phi Alpha Theta, Delta Sigma Rho. Republican. Episcopalian. Avocations: jogging, golf, travel, reading. Office: Shook Hardy & Bacon LLP 2555 Grand Ave Kansas City MO 64108-2613 Home Phone: 785-749-5358; Office Phone: 816-474-6550. Office Fax: 816-421-5547. Business E-Mail: wsampson@shb.com.

SAMRA, NICHOLAS JAMES, bishop emeritus; b. Paterson, NJ, Aug. 15, 1944; s. George H. and Elizabeth L. (Balady) S. BA, St. Anselm Coll., 1966; BD, St. John Sem., Brighton, Mass., 1970. Ordained priest Eparchy of Newton, Mass., 1970; assoc. pastor St. Anne Ch., North Hollywood, Calif., 1970—78; pastor Holy Cross Ch., Anaheim, Calif., 1973—78, St. John The Bapt. Ch., Northlake, Ill., 1978—81, St. Michael Ch., Hammond, Ind., 1978—81, St. Anne Ch., West Paterson, NJ, 1981—89; ordained bishop, 1989; aux. bishop Eparchy of Newton, Mass., 1989—2005, aux. bishop emeritus Mass., 2005—. Chaplain Police Athletic League Supporters, North Hollywood, 1970; vicar gen., corp. v.p., and regional bishop of Midwest region Diocese of Newton; transl. articles on Melkite subjects; mem. Ecumenical Commn., LA, 1974—78. Mem.: US Conf. Catholic Bishops, Christian Churches Together in the USA, Cath. Archives Assn. Roman Catholic. Office: 32406 Barclay Sq Warren MI 48093-6101 Office Phone: 586-756-1971. Office Fax: 586-756-1976. E-mail: nsamra@prodigy.net.*

SAMSON, ALLEN LAWRENCE, investor, bank executive; b. Milw., Nov. 16, 1939; s. Harry E. and Rose (Landau) S.; m. Vicki Faye Boxer, July 3, 1977; children: Daniel, Rachel; children from previous marriage: Nancy, David. BS, U. Wis., 1962, LLB, 1965. Bar: Wis. 1965. Asst. dist. atty. Milw. County Dist. Attys. Office, 1965-67, dep. dist. atty., 1968-70; assoc. Samson & Nash, Milw., 1967-68; ptnr. Samson, Friebert, Sutton and Finerty, Milw., 1970-73; v.p., sec. Am. Med. Svcs., Inc., Milw., 1973-83, exec. v.p., chief exec. officer, 1983-86, chmn., chief exec. officer, 1986-90; cons. nursing homes Samson Med. Mgmt. Co., Milw., 1990-93; pres. Liberty Bank, Milw., 1994—2001; vice chmn. State Fin. Bank, 2001—03; trustee State of Wis. Investment Bd., 2003—. Pub. mem. State of Wis. Investment Bd., 2003—; pub. mem. nursing home study Wis. Legis. Bur., 1988-89; mem. bd. visitors U. Wis. Law Sch., 1992—; mem. health policy adv. coun. Med. Coll. Wis., 1992-96. Bd. dirs. Nat. Found. Jewish Culture, 1996—98; trustee Milw. Ballet, 1982—89, Milw. Art Mus., 2001—, pres. bd. trustees, 1992—95; bd. dirs. Milw. Symphony Orch., 1995—2002, treas., 1996—2000; bd. dirs. Wis. Womens Bus. Initiative, War Meml. Corp., 1993—95, Jewish Fedn., 1985—, pres., 2000—02; bd. dirs. Milw. Jewish Home, 1992—96, Jewish Cmty. Ctr., 1985—96; pres. Milw. Parks Found., 1998—; gen. chmn. Wis. Israel Bond Campaign, 1993—94, chmn., 1996—98, bd. dirs., exec. com., 1986—; gen. chmn. ann. camp Milw. Jewish Fedn., 1990—91; pres. Jewish Vocat. Svc., 1976—78; Alexis de Tocqueville's leadership chmn. United Way campaign, 1995. Recipient Kaplan prize for econ. devel. Govt. of Israel, 1986, United Way Fleur de Lys award, 1996, Israel Bonds Star of David award, 1999. Avocations: tennis, skiing, golf. Office: State Fin Bank 815 N Water St Milwaukee WI 53202-3529 Home: 42108 N 101st Way Scottsdale AZ 85262

SAMSON, LINDA FORREST, nursing educator, dean; b. Miami, Dec. 7, 1949; d. Alvin S. and Grace (Kanner) Forrest; m. Mark I. Samson, Jan. 29, 1972; children: Amy, Josh. BSN, Emory U., 1972, MN, 1973; PhD, U. Pa., 1989. RN, Fla., Ga., N.J., Pa., Ill. Nursing instr. Ga. State U., Atlanta, 1974-78; neonatal intensive care nurse Northside Hosp., Atlanta, 1976-78; perinatal clin. specialist Our Lady of Lourdes Med. Ctr., Camden, N.J., 1978-82, per diem staff nurse, ICU nursery, labor and delivery, 1982-88; asst. prof., nursing Kennesaw Coll., Marietta, Ga., 1988-89; asst. prof. Clayton Coll. and State U., Morrow, Ga., 1989-92, assoc. prof., 1992-98, prof., 1998—, head baccalaureate nursing dept. Morrow, Ga., 1991-94, acting dean Sch. Health Scis., 1992-94, dean Sch. Health Scis., 1994—2002; dean Coll. Health Professions, Govs. State U., University Park, Ill., 2002—. Adj. faculty Gloucester County Coll., 1981-83; adj. clin. preceptor U. Pa. Sch. Nursing, 1981-83, lectr. in perinatal nursing, 1983-88; nursing dir. So. N.J. Perinatal Coop., 1982-84; researcher and lectr. in field. Mem. editorial rev. bds.; contbr. chpts. to textbooks, articles to profl. jours. Bd. dirs., chmn. profl. adv. com. South Jersey chpt. March of Dimes, 1980-85. Named Nurse of Yr. N.J. State Nurses Assn., 1985; recipient Network Edn. grant N.J. State Dept. Health, 1982-84, numerous grants for rsch., 1983-89, Outstanding Svc. award March of Dimes, 1983, Disting. Leadership award March of Dimes, 1984; grantee Fuld Inst. Post Secondary Edn., 1997—, Nursing Workforce Diversity Grant, 2000-03, NCMHD, 2003—, Samhsa CSAP, 2002—. Mem. ANA (cert. advanced nursing adminstrn., RNC high risk perinatal nursing), AACN (program com. 1987-88, rsch. com. 1988-89, project devel. task force 1989, strategic planning com. 1989, bd. dirs. 1987-90, bd. dirs. certification corp. 1987-90, chair neonatal and pediatric appeal panels 1992), Am. Orgn. Nurse Execs. (planning com. 1994-95), Nat. Assn. Neonatal Nurses (pub. policy and legis. com. 1994-96), Assn. Women's Health, Obstetrics and Neonatal Nurses, Nat. Perinatal Assn. (program planning com. 1983-85, resolutions com. 1984-88, stds. devel. com. spl. interest group task force 1985-88, bd. dirs. 1985-89, chmn. resolutions com. 1988, fin. com. 1989, pub. health policy com.), Ill. Nurses Assn., Ga. Perinatal Assn. N.J. (pres. 1982-86), Sigma Theta Tau (bylaws com.). Home: 20676 Francisca Way Frankfort IL 60423 Office: Govs State U Coll Health Professions 1 University Pkwy University Park IL 60466-0975 Office Phone: 708-534-4389.

SAMSON, RICHARD MAX, theater director, investment company executive; b. Milw., June 13, 1946; s. Harry E. and Rose (Landau) Samson; m. Nancy K. Pinter; children: Gina Shoshana, Alayna Tamar 1 stepchild, Christopher P. BA, U. Wis., 1968. Dir., owner Puppet Co., Jerusalem, 1972-73; pres. Century Hall, Inc., Milw., 1974-75; dir. purchasing Am. Med. Svcs., Inc., Milw., 1973-74, v.p., 1974-82, exec. v.p., 1982-86, pres., 1986-90, Samson Investments, Milw., 1990—2002. Bd. dirs. Liberty Bank, Milw., 1999—2004; sec. Super Sitters, Mequon, Wis., 1987—2004. Dir.(co-prodr.): (plays) Loss of Breath: The Unfinished Life and Death of Edgar Allan Poe, 1999, (co-creator) Einstein: Hero of the Mind, 2002, Stones of Wisdom, 2003, The Apollo of Bellac, 2004, The Trial -Adapted from Franz Kafka, 2005, Smoldering Fires, 2006; designer: (mask and puppet design), 2006; The Ballad of Josef K., 2008. Pres. bd. dirs. Theatre X, Milw., 1982, Holton Youth Ctr., Milw., 1994, Children's Outing Assn., 1996, Jewish Found. Econ. Opportunity, 1996—2004; v.p. bd. dirs. ArtReach, Milw., 1987; mem. funding bd. Wis. Cmty. Fund, 1989—93; dir. Mask and Puppet Co. Milw., 1992—; treas. nat. bd. dirs. Am. for Peace Now, 2002—04; bd. dirs. Bnai Or Religious Fellowship, 1988—93, Milw. Jewish Coun., 1992—94, The Shalom Ctr., 2006—. Recipient Humanitarian Peace award, Ecumenical Refugee Coun., 1989, Social Justice award, Wis. Cmty. Fund, 1997, Human Rels. award, Wis. region NCCJ, 1998, Cmty. Svc. Human Rels. award, Wis. chpt. Am. Jewish Com., 2000. Avocations: chess, comic book collecting, puppetry. Office: Milwaukee Mask & Puppet Theatre 100A E Pleasant St Milwaukee WI 53212-3975

SAMUEL, ROGER D., newspaper publishing executive; Dir. advt. The Flint (Mich.) Jour., 1991—96, pub., 1996—. Office: The Flint Jour 200 E 1st St Flint MI 48502-1911

SAMUELSON, DONALD B., former state legislator; b. Brainerd, Minn., Aug. 23, 1932; s. Walter H. and Ellen (Gallagher) S.; m. Nancy O'Brien, 1952; children: Stephen, Laura, Paula, Christine. Chmn. 6th Dist. Com. on Polit. Edn. State of Minn., 1960-66; mem. Minn. Ho. of Reps., St. Paul, 1969-76, 1981-82, Minn. Senate from 12th dist., St. Paul, 1982—; pres. Minn. Senate, St. Paul, 2000—02. Chmn. Health & Human Svc. Fin. Div. Com., mem. Commerce and Consumer Protection, mem. Family Svc. Com., mem. Fin. and Health Care Com.; former foreman Bor-Son Construct Co.; union bus. mgr. Chmn. 6th Dist.

Com. on Polit. Edn., Minn., 1960-66; mem. State Ctrl. Com. Dem-Farmer-Labor Party, 1964-66, former chmn. Crow Wing County. Mem. Housing and Redevel. Authority, Minn. AFL-CIO, Bricklayers Union, Am. Legion, Eagles. Democrat. Home: 1018 Portland Ave Brainerd MN 56401-4133

SANCHEZ, MANUEL (MANNY SANCHEZ), lawyer; b. Chgo., Dec. 1, 1947; s. Salomon and Margaret (Flores) S.; children: Annette, Manny, Brian. BA, No. Ill. U., 1970; JD, U. Pa., 1974. Bar: Ill. 1974, US Dist. Ct. (no. dist. Ill.), US Supreme Ct. Assoc. Hinshaw, Culbertson, Moelmann, Hoban & Fuller, Chgo., 1974-80, ptnr., 1980-86; founding ptnr. Sanchez & Daniels, Chgo., 1987—. Mem. gov. bd. Holy Trinity H.S., 1988-94; trustee Holy Cross H.S., 1988-92, Ill. Benedictine Coll., 1993-99, No. Ill. Univ., 1995-; bd. overseers Law Sch. U. Pa., 1991-98; corp. adv. bd. Univ. Ill., Chgo., 1994-; police commr. Village of Lisle; bd. dirs. Wheelabrator Tech., 1992-98, Met. Bank & Trust, 1994-, Alford Group Inc., 1995-, DGA Inc., 1998-, New Am. Alliance, Children's Meml. Hosp., Constl. Rights Found. Chgo., 1992-96, Steppenwolf Theater, Uniter Way, 1990-98, Acion Chgo., Boy's and Girls Clubs of Chgo., St. Ignatius Coll. Prep., 1995-; co-chmn. Chgo. United, 1995-; mem. City Chgo. Mayor's Fellows Bd. Named One of Nation's 100 Most Influential Hispanics, Hispanic Bus. Mag., 1993-95; recipient Vida award, NBC/Hispanic Mag., 1995; Raoul Wallenberg Internat. Humanitarian award, 1998; Guiding Light award, Salute to Chgo., 1997; El Puente award, St. Augustine Coll., 1999; VALE award, No. Ill. Univ., 2000. Mem. ABA (minority counsel demonstration program, co-chmn. litigation individual and small firm com.), Def. Rsch. Inst., Soc. Trial Lawyers, Hispanic Nat. Bar Assn. (sec. 1989-92), Ill. Bar Assn., Chgo. Bar Assn., Trial Lawyers Club Chgo. (pres. 1989, bd. dirs.), Execs. Club of Chgo. (bd. dir.), Soc. Trial Lawyers, L.Am. Bar Assn. (founding mem., bd. dir.), Coalition for Justice, Mex.-Am. Lawyers Def. Edn. Fund (nat. bd. dirs. 1989-93), Neighborhood Justice Chgo. (bd. dirs. 1990-93), Econ. Club, Comml. Club of Chgo. Office: Sanchez & Daniels 333 W Wacker Dr Ste 500 Chicago IL 60606-1225 Office Phone: 312-641-1555. Office Fax: 312-641-3004. Business E-Mail: msanchez@sanchezdaniels.com.

SANCHEZ, VINCENT A., lawyer; b. Bronx, NY, Dec. 12, 1968; BA, Univ. Notre Dame, 1991, JD, 1994; MBA, Northwestern Univ., 2003. Bar: Ill. 1994. Ptnr., co-chmn. Tech. & Sourcing Group DLA Piper US LLP, Chgo. Adj. prof. Loyola Univ. Sch. Law, 2002—; mem. adv. bd. West Suburban Tech. Enterprise Ctr. Editor (in chief): otre Dame Jour. of Legislation. Bd. dir. i.c. stars. 1st Lt. USMC Reserve, 1991—95. Named one of 40 Ill. Attorneys under 40 to Watch, Chgo. Lawyer mag., 2004, Leading Lawyers in Ill. for Tech. & IT Outsourcing, Chambers USA, 2005, 2006. Mem.: ABA. Office: DLA Piper US LLP Ste 1900 203 N LaSalle St Chicago IL 60601-1293 Office Phone: 312-368-3420. Business E-Mail: vincent.sanchez@dlapiper.com.

SAND, DAVID BYRON, lawyer; b. Mpls., Jan. 28, 1946; s. William John and Lois E. (Crane) S.; m. June Ann Striffler, Sept. 14, 1969; children— Kristin, Maren, Brandon. BA cum laude, St. Olaf Coll., 1968; JD, Duke U., 1975. Bar: Minn. 1975, U.S. Dist. Ct. Minn. 1976, U.S. Ct. Appeals (8th cir.) 1978. Assoc. Briggs and Morgan, St. Paul, 1975-80, ptnr., Mpls., 1980—, mem. bd. dirs., 1997-99; mem. panel of constrn. industry arbitrators Am. Arbitration Assn., Mpls., 1981—; commr. North Suburban Cable Commn., 1992—, comm.'s chmn. 2000-2002; mem. panel of mediators for Lex Mundi, Chmn. Arden Hills Park & Recreation (Minn.), 1983—, planning commn., 1999-; chmn. Fiscal and Property Ctrl. Lutheran Ch., Minn., 2002-; bd. trustees Hamline Methodist Ch., St. Paul, 1984-92. Lt. (j.g.) USNR, 1969-72. Recipient Svc. award Minn. Bd. Archtl. Engring. and Land Surveying, 1983. Mem. ABA (litigation sect. and forum com. constrn. industry). Office: 80 S 8th St #2200 Minneapolis MN 55402-2157 E-mail: sandav@briggs.com.

SAND, HARVEY, state legislator; m. Eleanor; 5 children. Mem. N.D. Senate, 1993—, vice chmn. govt. affairs com., mem. bus., labor coms. Mem. Masonic Orders, Am. Legion. Home: HC 2 Box 28 Langdon ND 58249-9501 Office: ND Senate Mems State Capitol Bismarck ND 58505

SANDALOW, TERRANCE, law educator; b. Chgo., Sept. 8, 1934; s. Nathan and Evelyn (Hoffing) Sandalow; m. Ina Davis, Sept. 4, 1955; children: David Blake, Marc Alan, Judith Ann. AB, U. Chgo., 1954, JD, 1957. Bar: Ill. 1958, Mich. 1978. Law clk. to judge Sterry R. Waterman U.S. Ct. Appeals (2d cir.), 1957-58; law clk. to justice Potter Stewart U.S. Supreme Ct., Washington, 1958-59; assoc. Ross, McGowan & O'Keefe, Chgo., 1959-61; assoc. prof. law U. Minn., Mpls., 1961-64, prof., 1964-66; prof. law U. Mich., Ann Arbor, 1966-2000, dean Law Sch., 1978-87, Edson R. Sunderland prof. law, 1987-2000, dean emeritus and Edson R. Sunderland prof. law emeritus, 2000—. Author (with F. I. Michelman): (book) Government in Urban Areas, 1970; author: (with E. Stein) Courts and Free Markets, 1982; contbr. articles to legal jours. and periodicals. Mem. Mpls. Commn. Human Rels., 1965—66. Recipient Profl. Achievement award, U. Chgo. Alumni; fellow, Ctr. Advanced Study in Behavioral Scis., 1972—73. Fellow: Am. Acad. Arts Scis.; mem.: Order of Coif (nat. pres. 2001—04), Phi Beta Kappa (hon.). Office: U Mich Law Sch Hutchins Hall Ann Arbor MI 48109-1215 Home Phone: 734-994-4289. Personal E-mail: terrysan@comcast.net. Business E-Mail: sandalow@umich.edu.

SANDBERG, JOHN STEVEN, lawyer; b. Mpls., Sept. 1, 1948; s. Donald and Margery Susan (Knudsen) S.; m. Cynthia A. Tucker, July 17, 1982; children: Jennifer, Adam, Luke, Abigail. AB with honors, U. Mo., Columbia, 1970, JD cum laude, 1972. Bar: Mo., Ill., U.S. Ct. Appeals (7th and 8th cirs.), U.S. Dist. Ct. (ea. and we. dists.) Mo., U.S. Dist. Ct. (so. and ctrl. dists.) Ill., U.S. Dist. Ct. (we. dist.) Ky. Ptnr. Coburn, Croft & Putzell, St. Louis, 1972-79, Sandberg, Phoenix & von Gontard, St. Louis, 1979—. Author (books) Damages Deskbook, 1988, Missouri Product Liability Law, 1988. Pres. SAFE KIDS, St. Louis, 1989-96. Mem. Am. Bd. Trial Advocates. Office: Sandberg Phoenix & von Gontard One City Ctr Fl 15 Saint Louis MO 63101-1883

SANDER, DONALD HENRY, retired soil scientist; b. Creston, Nebr., Apr. 21, 1933; s. Paul L. and Mable O. (Wendt) S.; m. Harriet Ora Palmateer, Dec. 27, 1953; children: Ben, Joan. BS, U. Nebr., 1954, MS in Agronomy, 1958, PhD in Agronomy, 1967. Soil scientist, researcher USDA Forest Svc., Lincoln, Nebr., 1958-64; asst. prof. agronomy, soil fertility specialist Kans. State U., Manhattan, 1964-67; prof. agronomy U. Nebr., Lincoln, 1967-98; ret., 1998. Contbr. numerous rsch. articles to jours. including Soil Sci. Soc. Am. Jour. 1st lt. U.S. Army, 1954-56, Korea. Recipient Agronomic Achievement award, 1985, USDA Superior Svc. award, 1987, Soil Sci. Applied Rsch. award, 1989, Great Plains Leadership award, Denver, 1990. Fellow Am. Soc. Agronomy, Soil Sci. Soc. Am.; mem. Gama Sigma Delta, Sigma Xi. Republican. Presbyterian. Avocation: woodworking. Office: Univ Nebr Dept Agronomy Lincoln NE 68583

SANDERS, BARRY, retired professional football player; b. Wichita, July 16, 1968; s. William and Shirley Sanders. Student, Okla. State U., 1986—89. Running back Detroit Lions, 1989—99. Co-author (with Mark E. McCormick): Now You See Him: The Barry Sanders Story, 2003. Named NFL Rookie of Yr., 1990, NFL Offensive Player of the Yr., 1997, 1994, NFL Player of the Yr., 1991, 1997; named to Sporting News Coll. All-Am. team, 1987, 1988, Pro Bowl, 1989—98; recipient Heisman Trophy award, 1988. Achievements include holds NCAA single season record in rushing yards (2,628); led NFL in rushing, 1990, 94, 96, 97; #3 all-time on NFL rushing list (15,269); inducted into the pro and college NFL Hall of Fame, 2004. Office Phone: 305-674-7221. Business E-Mail: jb@barry.sanders.com.

SANDERS, DAVID, university press administrator; BFA in Creative Writing, Bowling Green State U., 1977; MFA, U. Ark., 1983, postgrad., 1986-88. Owner, propr. Hays & Sanders Bookshop, Fayetteville, Ark., 1983-86; vis. asst. prof. dept. English U. Ark., Fayetteville, 1984-88; asst. dir. U. Ark. Press, Fayetteville, 1988-89, assoc. dir., 1989-90, assoc. dir., editor-in-chief, 1991-92; dir. Purdue U. Press, West Lafayette, Ind., 1992-95, Ohio U. Press/Swallow Press, Athens, 1996—. Author: Time in Transit, 1995, Nearer to Town, 1998; contbr. translations: Poetry Miscellany; Sparrow. Literature of the Western World, Vol. One, 1988; contbr. poetry to New Orleans Rev., Poetry East, Christian Sci. Monitor, S.I. Rev., Mankato Rev., Kans. Quar., Stand Mag., Yarrow, Caesura, Epigrammatist, Zone 3, Hiram Poetry Rev., others. Recipient Christopher McKean award for poetry, 1982, Kenneth Patchen Poetry award, 1982, Dudley Fitts Translation award, 1986, 87, Lily Peter Found. award, 1987. Office: Ohio Univ Press 19 Circle Dr The Ridges Athens OH 45701

SANDERS, DAVID P., lawyer; b. Chgo., Sept. 24, 1949; BA with distinction, U. Wis., 1971; JD, Georgetown U., 1974. Bar: Ill. 1974, U.S. Ct. Appeals (7th and 4th cirs.) 1974, U.S. Dist. Ct. (no. dist. trial bar) Ill. 1974. Ptnr. Jenner & Block, Chgo. Adj. prof. trial advocacy Northwestern U., Chgo., 1981-91. Editor Am. Criminal Law Rev., 1974. Mem. ABA, Chgo. Coun. Lawyers (chmn. fed. jud. evaluation com. 1989—, mem. def. counsel sect. libel def. resource ctr.). Office: Jenner & Block One IBM Plz Chicago IL 60611

SANDERS, JACQUELYN SEEVAK, psychologist, educator; b. Boston, Apr. 26, 1931; d. Edward Ezral and Dora (Zoken) Seevak; 1 child, Seth. BA, Radcliffe Coll., 1952; MA, U. Chgo., 1964; PhD, UCLA, 1972. Counselor, asst. prin. Orthogenic Sch., Chgo., 1952—65; rsch. assoc. UCLA, 1965—68; asst. prof. Ctr. for Early Edn., LA, 1969—72; assoc. dir. Sonia Shankman Orthogenic Sch., U. Chgo., 1972—73, dir., 1973—93, dir. emeritus, 1993—; curriculum cons. day care ctrs. LA Dept. Social Welfare, 1970—72; instr. Calif. State Coll., LA, 1972; lectr. dept. edn. U. Chgo., 1972—80, sr. lectr., 1980—93, clin. assoc. prof. dept. psychiatry, 1990—93, emeritus, 1993—; instr. edn. program Inst. Psychoanalysis, Chgo., 1979—82. Cons. Osawatomie State Hosp., Kans., 1965—68; reading cons. Foreman HS, Chgo.; treas. Chgo. Inst. Psychoanalysis, 2003—. Author: Greenhouse for the Mind, 1989; editor (with Barry L. Childress): Psychoanalytic Approaches to the Very Troubled Child: Therapeutic Practice Innovations in Residential & Educational Settings, 1989; editor: Severely Disturbed Children and the Parental Alliance, 1992; editor: (with Jerome M. Goldsmith) Milieu Therapy: Significant Issues and Innovative Applications, 1993; editor: The Seevak Family, The Zoken Family; contbr. articles to profl. jours. Mem. vis. com. univ. sch. rels. U. Chgo.; bd. dirs. KAM Isaiah Israel Congregation, 1997—2001; bd. dirs., treas. Chgo. Inst. for Psychoanalysis. Recipient Alumna award, Girls' Latin Sch., Boston, Bettelheim award, Am. Assn. Children's Residential Ctrs., Disting. Svc. award, Radcliffe Assn., 2002; scholar Radcliffe Coll. scholar, 1948—52; Univ. fellow, UCLA, 1966—68. Mem.: Chgo. Inst. for Psychoanalysis, Assn. Children's Residential Ctrs. (past pres.), Harvard Club (bd. dirs. 1986—2001, Chgo.), Radcliffe Club (sec.-treas. 1986—87, pres. 1987—89, Chgo.). Home: 5842 S Stony Island Ave Apt 2G Chicago IL 60637-2033

SANDERS, JOE MAXWELL, JR., pediatrician; b. Hartsville, SC, July 5, 1940; m. Dorothy Garvin, June 6, 1963; children Joe M. III, Eric T. BS, The Citadel, 1962; MD, Med. U. S.C., 1967. Diplomate Am. Bd. Pediatrics. Rotating intern, resident in pediatrics Letterman Army Med. Ctr., San Francisco, 1967-70; fellow in adolescent medicine San Francisco Children's Hosp., 1970-71; chief adolescent medicine svc. Fitzsimmons Army Med. Ctr., 1971-86; dir. adolescent medicine svc. Med. Coll. Ga., 1986-88; assoc. exec. dir. Am. Acad. Pediatrics, Elk Grove Village, Ill., 1988-93, exec. dir., 1993—2004; ret., 2004. Asst. clin. prof. pediatrics U. Colo. Health Scis. Ctr., 1971-76, assoc. clin. prof., 1976-83, clin. prof. 1983-86; assoc. prof. pediatrics Med. Coll. Ga., 1986-88; clin. prof. pediatrics, U. Chgo., 1991—; cons. for adolescent medicine Surgeon Gen. Army, 1976-86; mem. med. com. Rocky Mt. Planned Parenthood, 1981-86; vis. prof. dept. pediatrics U. Kansas (Wichita), 1984, 87, dept. pediatrics and family practice, E. Tenn. State U., Johnson City, 1985, U. Fla., Gainesville, 1987, Fitzsimmons Army Med. Ctr., Denver, 1989, U. Chgo., 1991, Baylor Coll., Houston, 1994, others. Contbr. numerous articles and abstracts to profl. jours., chpts. to books; mem. editl. bd. Jour. Current Adolescent Medicine, 1979-81, Substance Abuse: A Guide for Profls., 1985-88; reviewer Pediatrics, 1984—, Jour. Pediatrics, 1986—, Jour. Adolescent Health, 1986—, Am. Jour. Diseases of Children, 1987—, Jour. Am. Med. Assn., 1987—; guest lectr., speaker at many sci. confs. and med. soc. meetings. Mem. teenage coord. coun. Richmond County Health Dept., 1986-88, head start health adv. com. CSRA Econ. Opportunity Authority, Inc., 1986-88; med. cons. Alexian Bros. Med. Rels. Com. Decorated Legion of Merit, U.S. Army, 1987; recipient Adele Hoffman award, Sect. on Adolescent Health, 1988. Fellow Am. Acad. Pediatrics (com. on adolescence 1980-87, chmn. 1983-87, chmn. uniformed svcs chpt. 1981, 84, mem. exec. com. mil. pediatrics sect. 1976-79, sec.-treas. 1976-77, chmn. 1977-79, mem. steering com. to establish non-geographic mil. dist. chpt., mem sect. on adolescent health 1979—, program com. 1981-83, task force on substance abuse, chmn. 1984-85, cons. 85-87, task force on sch. based clinics, 1987—), Soc. Adolescent Medicine (edn. com., ambulatory care com., 1975-80, chmn. nominating com. 1978, exec. coun. 1980-83, chmn. awards com. 1990-93, pres. 1987-88, past pres's. coun. 1988—, Outstanding Achievement award 1994); mem. AMA (mem. planning com. nat. coalition on adolescent health, rep. Am. Acad. Pediatrics, Soc. Adolescent Medicine to Coalition 1987—, chmn. working group on rsch. agenda 1987-88, adv. com. on unintentional injuries 1987), Ambulatory Pediatric Assn., So. Soc. for Pediatric Rsch., Soc. Med. Cons. to Armed Forces, Order Mil. Med. Merit, Sigma Xi.

SANDERS, KEITH PAGE, journalism educator; b. Ashland, Ohio, Sept. 25, 1938; s. Merwin Morse and Phyllis Pearl (Snyder) S.; m. Jane Carmel Adams, June 11, 1966; children: Paige Ann, Kevin Scott. BS in Journalism, Bowling Green State U., 1960; MS in Journalism, Ohio U., 1964; PhD in Mass. Comm., U. Iowa, 1967. Sports editor Ashland (Ohio) Times Gazette, 1960-61, Dover (Ohio) Daily Reporter, 1961-62; instr. journalism Bowling Green (Ohio) State U., 1963-64, U. Iowa, Iowa City, 1965-67; prof. journalism U. Mo., Columbia, 1967—2001, assoc. dean grad. studies Sch. Journalism, 1986-87, 90-91, O.O. McIntyre disting. prof., 1993, prof. emeritus, 2002—. Cons. in field. Contbr. articles to profl. jours. including Journalism Quar., Mass Media Rev., Jour. Broadcasting, Electronic Jour. of Comm.; assoc. editor Mass Comm. Rev., 1981-92, mem. editl. bd., 1972-98; mem. editl. bd. Journalism Monographs, 1973-80, Mass Comm. and Soc., 1998-2006. Recipient Award for Outstanding Achievement U. Mo. Alumni Assn., 1986; Joyce Swan Disting. Faculty award U. Mo., 1973; inducted into Columbia Bowling Hall of Fame, 1999. Mem.: Soc. Profl. Journalists, Assn. for Edn. in Journalism/Mass Comm. (Trayes Prof. of Yr. 1987), Internat. Soc. for Sci. Study of Subjectivity (treas. 1990—95), Mo. State-US Bowling Congress (2d v.p. 2006—), Mo. State Bowling Assn. (bd. dirs. 2000—06, Dir. of Yr. 2005), Omicron Delta Kappa, Kappa Tau Alpha (exec. dir. 1991—). Avocations: bowling, golf, fishing. Home: 6551 N Creasy Springs Rd Columbia MO 65202-8093 Office: Univ of Missouri Sch Journalism Columbia MO 65211-1200

SANDERS, RICHARD HENRY, lawyer; b. Chgo., Apr. 10, 1944; s. Walter J. and Marian (Snyder) Sikorski; m. Sharon A. Marciniak, July 8, 1967 (dec.); child, Douglas Bennett; m. Susan Gerhardt Nalepa, Feb. 19, 2005. BS, Loyola U., Chgo., 1967; JD, Northwestern U., 1969. Bar: Ill. 1969, Ind. 1990, DC 1990, US Dist. Ct. (no. dist.) Ill. 1970, US Dist. Ct. (no. and so. dists.) Ind. 1990, US Ct. Appeals (7th cir.) 1990, US Supreme Ct. 1990. Assoc. Vedder, Price, Kaufman & Kammholz, Chgo., 1969-76, ptnr., 1976—2003, mem. exec. com., 1991-93, health law area leader, 1989—95, 2001—04, 2006—, shareholder, 2003—, chmn. tech. com., 2003—. Adj. prof. Sch. of Law Northwestern U., 1994—; mem. svc. dispute resolver panel Am. Health Lawyers Assn. Alt. Dispute Resolution, 2000—. Bd. trustees Chgo. Acad. for the Arts, 2006—; bd. dirs. Smart Love Parenting Ctr., 2004—, Breath of Life Found., 2007—. Fellow Am. Bar Found.; mem. ABA, Ill. Bar Assn. (chmn. health sect. 1989-90), Chgo. Bar Assn., Ind. Bar Assn., DC Bar Assn., Am. Health Lawyers Assn., Ill. Assn. Health Attys., Univ. Club, Evanston Golf Club (Skokie). Avocations: skiing, diving, photography, golf. Office: Vedder Price Kaufman & Kammholz 222 N La Salle St Ste 2600 Chicago IL 60601-1100 Office Phone: 312-609-7644. Business E-Mail: rsanders@vedderprice.com.

SANDERS, WALLACE WOLFRED, JR., civil engineer; b. Louisville, June 24, 1933; s. Wallace Wolfred and Mary Jane (Brownfield) S.; m. Julia B. Howard, June 9, 1956; children— Linda, David. B.C.E., U. Louisville, 1955; MS, U. Ill., Urbana, 1957, PhD, 1960; M.Engring., U. Louisville, 1973. Research asst., then research assoc. U. Ill., 1955-60, asst. prof., 1960-64; mem. faculty Iowa State U., Ames, 1964-98, prof. civil engring., 1970-98, assoc. dir. engring. research, 1980-91, assoc. dean research, 1988-91, interim asst. vice provost for research and advanced studies, 1991-92. Cons. to govt. and industry. Contbr. numerous papers to profl. jours. Bd. dirs. Northcrest Cmty., Ames, 1976-82, 92-98, pres., 1987-91, 96-2003; bd. dirs. Am. Bapt. Homes of the Midwest, Mpls., 1998—. Mem. ASCE (R.C. Reese research prize 1978), Am. Welding Soc. (Adams Meml. membership award 1971), Am. Ry. Engring. Assn., Am. Soc. Engring. Edn. Baptist. Home and Office: 1924 Northcrest Cir Ames IA 50010-5113 Home Phone: 515-232-7184. Business E-Mail: wsanders@iastate.edu.

SANDERSON, GEOFF, professional hockey player; b. Hay River, N.W.T., Can., Feb. 1, 1972; m. Ellen Sanderson; children: Benjamin, Jake. Left wing Hartford Whalers, Hartford, 1990—97, Carolina Hurricanes, 1997—98, Vancouver Canucks, 1998, 2004, Buffalo Sabres, 1998—2000, Columbus Blue Jackets, 2000—04, 2005, Phoenix Coyotes, 2005—06, Phila. Flyers, 2006—. Player NHL All-Star Game, 1994, 97. Office: Phila Flyers 3601 S Broad St Philadelphia PA 19148

SANDERSON, GLEN CHARLES, science director; b. Wayne County, Mo., Jan. 21, 1923; married; 2 children. BS, U. Mo., 1947, MA, 1949; PhD, U. Ill., 1961. Game biologist Iowa State Conservation Commn., 1949-55, Ill. Dept. Conservation, 1955-60; from game biologist to prin. scientist emeritus, dir. Ill. Nat. History Survey, Champaign, 1955—90, prin. scientist emeritus, dir., 1990—; prof. U. Ill., 1965—92. Adj. rsch. prof. So. Ill. U., 1964, adj. prof. 1964-84. Editor Jour. Wildlife Mgmt., 1971-72. Recipient Oak Leaf award Nature Conservancy, 1975. Mem. AAAS, Am. Soc. Mammal, Am. Inst. Biol. Sci., Wildlife Soc. (Aldo Leopold Meml. award 1992). Achievements include research in population dynamics of wild animals, especially furbearers, physiological factors of reproductive and survival rates, and lead poisoning in waterfowl. Office: Ill Natural History Survey Ctr Wildlife Ecology 711 S State St Champaign IL 61820-5114 Office Phone: 217-244-2146.

SANDLER, RICHARD H., pediatric gastroenterologist; MD, Mich. State U. Coll. Human Medicine. Resident, pediatrics Mich. State U., Lansing; fellow, pediatric gastroenterology, hepatology, and nutrition Harvard Med. Sch., Boston Children's Hosp.; fellow, human metabolism and nutrition Mass. Gen. Hosp., Boston; asst. in medicine, instr., divsn. of gastroenterology and nutrition The Children's Hosp., Harvard Med. Sch., Boston, 1989—90; dir. Biomed. Acoustics Rsch. Group, Evanston, Ill., 1990—, pres., CEO, 1997—; assoc. prof., pediatrics Rush Med. Coll., Chgo., 1990—; adj. assoc. prof., biomed. engring. U. Ill., Chgo., 2002—. Office: Rush Univ Med Ctr 1725 W Harrison St Chicago IL 60612 Address: 1725 W Harrison St Ste 946 Chicago IL 60612 Office Phone: 312-942-2889.

SANDLIN, STEPHANIE HERSETH, congresswoman, lawyer; b. Aberdeen, SD, Dec. 3, 1970; d. Ralph Lars and Joyce Herseth. BA summa cum laude in Polit. Sci. and Govt., Georgetown U., 1993, MA in Polit. Sci., 1996; JD, Georgetown U. Law Ctr., 1996. Bar: SD. Law clerk Staff of US Dist. Ct. Judge Charles Kornmann, Pierre, 1998—99, Staff of US 4th Cir. Ct. Appeals Judge Diana Gribbon Motz, Balt., 1999—2000; atty. Skadden, Arps, Slate, Meagher & Flom LLP, Washington, 2001; exec. dir. SD Farmers Union Found., 2003—04; mem. US Congress from SD at-large, 2004—, mem. Blue Dog Coalition, mem. agr. com., mem. resources com., mem. vets. affairs com., ranking minority mem. econ. opportunity subcommittee. Prof. Georgetown U. Law Ctr., 1997, Augustana Coll., 2003, SD State U., 2003; tchr. Fund for Am. Studies; counsel on energy and telecom. issues SD Pub. Utilities Commn., Pierre; bd. dir. First Nat. Bank, Brookings, SD. Sr. editor Georgetown U. Law Rev. Mem. Rotary Internat., Brookings, SD; co-chair Rural Working Grp.; legal counsel for the elderly. Recipient Small Bus. Adv., Small Bus. Survival Com., 2004. Mem.: SD Bar Assn., Phi Beta Kappa. Democrat. Lutheran. Office: US Ho Reps 331 Cannon Ho Office Bldg Washington DC 20515-4101 Office Phone: 202-225-2801.

SANDLOW, LESLIE JORDAN, gastroenterologist, educator; b. Chgo., Jan. 7, 1934; s. Harry H. and Rose (Ehrlich) S.; m. Joanne J. Fleischer, June 16, 1957; children: Jay, Bruce, Lisa. BS, U. Ill., 1956; MD, Chgo. Med. Sch., 1960. Intern Michael Reese Hosp. and Med. Ctr., Chgo., 1961, med. resident, rsch. fellow gastrointestinal rsch., 1961-64, physician-in-charge clin. gastroenterology lab., 1963-74, asst. attending physician, 1964-67, assoc. attending physician, 1967-72, vice chmn. divsn. gastroenterology, dir. ambulatory medicine, 1968, dir. ambulatory care, 1969-76, attending physician, 1972—, assoc. med. dir., 1972-73; clin. asst. Chgo. Med. Sch., 1963-68, clin. instr., 1966; asst. prof. dept. medicine Pritzker Sch. Medicine, U. Chgo., 1973-76, assoc. prof., 1976-85, prof., 1985-90; prof. clin. medicine and med. edn. U. Ill. Coll. Medicine, Chgo., 1990-91, prof. medicine and med. edn., 1992—, sr. assoc. dean for grad. and continuing med. edn., 1993—, head dept. med. edn., 1993—, sr. assoc. dean for med. edn. affairs, 1994—. Dep. v.p. profl. affairs Michael Reese Hosp. and Med. Ctr., 1973-78, dir. Office Ednl. Affairs, 1976-81, assoc. v.p. acad. affairs, 1978-82, dir. quality assurance program, 1981-91, v.p. planning, 1982-83, v.p. profl. affairs and planning, 1983-88, dir. divsn. internal medicine, 1986-93, v.p. profl. and acad. affairs, 1988-91, med. dirs. acad. and med. affairs, 1992-94; med. dir. Michael Reese Health Plan, Inc., 1972-74, interim exec. dir., 1976-77; cons. gastroenterologist Ill. Ctrl. Hosp., 1978-80; vis. prof. Pontifica U. Catolica Rio Grande do Sul, Brazil, 1978, U. Fed. Espirito Santo, Brazil, 1978, Nordic Fedn. for Med. Understanding, Akureyri, Iceland, 1978, Seoul Nat. U. Sch. Medicine, 1981, Coll. Physicians and Surgsons, Kharachi, Pakistan, 1994, U. Tex., Ft. Worth, 1977, U. Ariz., Tucson, 1977, Loyola U. Med. Sch., Maywood, Ill., 1979; cons. in field; coord. Health Scis. Librs. in Ill.; mem. Midwest Med. Libr. etwork; mem. subcom. on delivery of ambulatory med. care Inst. Medicine Chgo.; mem. cmty. resources task force Interinstnl. Cardiovascular Ctr.; chmn. steering group Ill. Regional Med. Program; past co-chmn. curriculum com. U. Chgo. Reviewer Rsch. in Med. Edn./Assn. Am. Med. Colls., 1985—, Acad. Medicine/Assn. Am. Med. Colls., 1989; contbr. numerous articles to profl. publs. Mem. Skokie (Ill.) Bd. Health, 1973-85, chmn., 1976-85; bd. dirs. Group Health Assn. Am., 1976-78, Portes Ctr., 1980—; bd. dirs. Good Health Program Skokie Valley Hosp., 1978-80; bd. dirs., exec. com. Rsch. and Edn. Found. of Michael Reese Hosp. Med. Staff, 1992—; pres.-elect Inst. Medicine Chgo., 2003-04, pres., 2004-06. Recipient numerous grants, including NIH 1988, Michael Reese Hosp. Found. 1994-95, Chgo. Cmty. Trust 1994-95, AOA faculty award 2007. Fellow Am. Coll. Gastroenterology; mem. N.Y. Acad. Scis., Inst. Medicine, Assn. Am. Med. Colls., Am. Coll. Physician Execs. (co-chair resource mgmt. com. of quality assurance forum), Soc. Dirs. Med. Coll. Continuing Med. Edn., Soc. Dir. Rsch. in Med. Edn. Home: 2314 N Lincoln Park W Chicago IL 60614-3455 Office: U Ill Coll Medicine Med Edn MC 784 1819 W Polk St Chicago IL 60612-7331

SANDOR, RICHARD LAURENCE, financial company executive; b. NYC, Sept. 7, 1941; s. Randolph Henry and Luba (Mirner) S.; m. Ellen Ruth Simon, June 27, 1963; children: Julie, Penya. BA, CCNY, 1962; PhD, U. Minn., 1967. Asst. prof. applied econs. U. Calif, Berkeley, 1966-72; v.p., chief economist Chgo. Bd. Trade, 1972-75; v.p. ContiCommodity Services, Chgo., 1975-82; dir. ContiFin div. ContiCommodity Services, Chgo., 1975-82; sr. v.p. instl. fin. futures Drexel Burnham Lambert, Inc., Chgo., 1982-90; pres., CEO Indosuez Internat. Capital Markets, Chgo., 1990-93; chmn. Indosuez Carr Futures, 1990-91, Hedge Fin. subs. CNA, 1997—; chmn., CEO Environ., Fin. Products, 1998—. Mem. Chgo. Bd. Trade, 1975—, bd. dirs., vice chmn., 2d vice chmn., 1996-98; exec. mng. dir. Kidder, Peabody Inc., N.Y.C., 1991-94, Non-resident Dir., CBOT; pres., CEO Centre Fin. Products Ltd., 1993-98; chmn., CEO, Environ. Fin. Products LLC, 1998—, mem. Index and Option Market, 1983—; sr. advisor PriceWaterhouseCoopers LLP, 1999—; bd. dirs. Chgo. Mercantile Exch., chmn., Hedge Fin. Products, Inc., 1997-99; dir., Sustainable Asset Mgmt./Sustainable Performance grp.; Internatl. Adv. Bd. of Maché à Terme Internatl. de France (MATIF); bd. dirs., Fin. Products Adv. Com. of The Commodity Futures Trading Comm., Benfield and Rea Investment Trust, Bear Stearns Fin. Products, Inc., Ben Stearns Trading Risk Mgmt., Inc., Altra Energy Bd., Altra Electronic Adv. Bd., Ctr. for Sustainable Devel. in Ams., Nextera Enterprises, Inc.; vis. scholar, Northwestern U., 1999—, bd. visitors of Internatl. Prog. Ctr., U. Oklahoma, Internat. Ctr. Photography, N.Y.C., First Fed. Savs. & Loan Assn. of Chgo., Sch. Art Inst. Chgo., Patsyss. plc, 2000—; vis. scholar Northwestern U., 1972-74; Martin C. Remer vis. Disting. prof. fin. Grad. Sch. Mgmt., 1974-75; cons. agribus. orgns., securities firms, banks, fgn. exchs., govts., 1969—; mem. faculty NYU, 1964; mem. faculty U. Minn., 1963-67; mem. faculty Stanford U., 1969; disting. adj. prof. Grad. Sch. Bus. Columbia U., 1993; expert advisor UNCTAD; guest lectr. various univs., coms. and bds., Banking and Rsch. Ctr., Northwestern U., Columbia U. Futures Ctr.; bd. dirs. Ctrl. and S.W. Corp. Dow Jones Sustainability Group Index GmbH.; life mem. London Internat. Fin. Future and Options Exch., London Clearing House. Contbr. articles to profl. journs., chpts. of books and handbooks. Vice chmn. bd. govs. Sch. of Art Inst. of Chgo.; bd. dirs. Lincoln Park Zool. Soc., 1985—. Summer faculty fellow U. Calif.; NSF grantee Mem. Am. Econ. Assn., Econometric Soc., Am. Fin. Assn., Am. Agrl. Econs. Assn. Clubs: Union League of Chgo.

SANDROK, RICHARD WILLIAM, lawyer; b. Evergreen Park, Ill., July 8, 1943; s. Edward George and Gertrude Jeanette (Van Stright) Sandrok; m. Rebecca Fitz, June 19, 1973; children: Richard William, Jr., Alexander Edward, Philip Robert, Erika Joy. BA, Wheaton Coll., Ill., 1965; JD, U. Ill., 1968. Bar: Ill. 1968, U.S. Dist. Ct. (no. dist.) Ill. 1971, ct. apptd. arbitrator: Cook, DuPage, Kane and Will counties. Assoc. Hinshaw Culbertson Moelmann Hoban & Fuller, Chgo. and Wheaton, 1971-75, ptnr. Wheaton, 1976-89, Lisle, Ill., 1989—2001; sole practice Glen Ellyn, Ill., 2001—. Arbitrator Ill. State Mandatory Arbitration. Reviewer: Legal Checklists. Capt. US Army, 1969—71. Mem.: Ill. Ct. Sys. Arbitrator, Assn. Def. Trial Attys., DuPage County Bar Assn. (chmn. med./legal com. 1978—79), Am. Arbitration Assn. (arbitrator). Home: 818 Revere Rd Glen Ellyn IL 60137-5537 Office: Richard W Sandrok Atty at Law 818 Revere Rd Glen Ellyn IL 60137 Office Phone: 630-790-1583. E-mail: RWS283@yahoo.com.

SANDS, DEANNA, editor; BA in Journalism, U. Nebr., Lincoln, 1972; grad., Ioaw State U., 1974. Intern Nebr. City News Press, 1974; night copy desk editor Omaha World Herald, 1974, night mng. editor, 1990—93, mng. editor, 1993—, 1995—. Office: Omaha World-Herald 1334 Dodge St Omaha NE 68102-1138 Office Phone: 402-444-1000. E-mail: deanna.sands@owh.com.

SANDS, THOMAS, state representative, banker; b. Louisa County, Iowa, Sept. 1954; 3 children. Cert. lay spkr.; real property appraiser. Comml. loan officer Columbus Junction State Bank, Iowa; state rep. dist. 87 Iowa Ho. of Reps., 2003—; mem. pub. safety com.; mem. ways and means com.; mem. econ. devel. appropriations subcom.; vice chair commerce, regulation and labor com. Twp. trustee Concord Twp.; active Young Reps. Columbus Cmty., Columbus Junction United Meth. Ch.; past bd. dirs. Louisa County Farm Bur.; chair fin. com. Columbus Junction City Coun. Mem.: Am. Legion (charter mem., first comdr.). Methodist. Office: State Capitol East 12th and Grand Des Moines IA 50319

SANDSTROM, DALE VERNON, state supreme court justice; b. Grand Forks, ND, Mar. 9, 1950; s. Ellis Vernon and Hilde Geneva (Williams) S.; m. Gail Hagerty, Mar. 27, 1993; children: Jack, Carrie, Anne. BA, N.D. State U., 1972; JD, U. N.D., 1975. Bar: ND 1975, US. Dist. Ct. ND 1975, US Ct. Appeals (8th cir.) 1976. Asst. atty. gen., chief consumer fraud and antitrust div. State of ND, Bismarck, 1975-81, securities commr., 1981-83, pub. svc. commr., 1983-92, pres. public svc. commn., 1987-91; justice ND Supreme Ct., Bismarck, 1992—. Chair ND Commn. on Cameras in the Courtroom, 1993—, Joint Procedure Com., 1996—, mem. adminstrv. coun., 2005-; mem. exec. com. ND Jud. Conf., 1995—, chair-elect, 1997-99, chair, 1999-2001; mem. Gov.'s Com. on Security and Privacy, Bismarck, 1975-76, Gov.'s Com. on Refugees, Bismarck, 1976; chmn. Gov's Com. on Comml. Air Transp., Bismarck, 1983-84. Mem. platform com. ND Reps., 1972, 76, exec. com., 1972-73, 85-88, dist. chmn., 1981-82; former chmn. bd. deacons Luth. Ch.; mem. ch. coun., exec. com., chmn. legal and constl. rev. com. Evang. Luth Ch. Am., 1993—; mem. exec. bd. dirs., No. Lights Coun., dist. chair Boy Scouts Am., 1998-2000. Named Disting. Eagle Scout, Boy Scouts Am., 1997, Master of the Coll. Arts, Humanities, and Social Scis., N.D. State U., 2002; recipient Cmty. Svc. award, N.D. State Bar Assn., 2002. Mem. ABA, ND Bar Assn., Big Muddy Bar Assn., Nat. Assn. Regulatory Utility Commrs. (electricity com.), N.A. Assn. Securities Adminstrs., Order of De Molay (grand master 1994-95, mem. Internat. Supreme coun., Legion of Honor award), Nat. Eagle Scouts Assn. (regent for life), Shriners, Elks, Eagles, Masons (33d degree, chmn. grand youth com. 1979-87, Youth Leadership award 1986), Bruce M. VanSickle Am. Inn of Court (pres. 1999-2001), ND Judges Assn. (v.p. 2005-). Office: State ND Supreme Ct Judicial Wing 1st Fl 600 E Boulevard Ave Bismarck ND 58505 Office Phone: 701-328-2221.

SANDVIG, SALLY, state legislator; m. Henry David Sandvig; 3 children. Student, N.D. State U. Sales rep. Avon; rep. Dist. 21 N.D. Ho. of Reps., mem. human svc. and govt. and vet. affairs coms. Precinct chmn., dist. sec. Dist. 21, Cass, N.D.; 4-H leader; client coun. mem. LAND; mem. Dem. Women. Soroptimist Internat. Tng. Awards scholar, 1988. Mem. Avon Pres.'s Club. Office: ND Ho of Reps State Capitol Bismarck ND 58505 Address: 201 11th St N Fargo ND 58102-4652

SANFILIPPO, ALFRED PAUL, dean, medical educator, pathologist; b. Racine, Wis., Aug. 30, 1949; s. Paul Joseph and Therese (Rhode) Sanfilippo; m. Janet Lee Thompson, 1973; children: Lisa, Joseph. Student, Max Planck Inst. Exptl. Medicine, Gottingen, Germany, 1966—68; BA in Physics, MS in Physics, U. Pa., 1970; PhD in immunology, Duke U., 1975, MD, 1976. Diplomate Am. Bd. Pathology, lic. physician NC, Md. Intern in anatomic pathology Duke U. Hosp., 1976—77, resident in anatomic and clin. pathology, 1977—79, postdoctoral rschr. divsn. tumor virology dept. surgery, 1976—79; asst. prof. pathology and exptl. surgery, lectr. immunology Duke U., 1979—84, from assoc. prof. to prof. pathology, 1984—93, from assoc. prof. to prof. exptl. surgery, 1985—93, prof. immunology, 1990—93; attending pathologist Duke U. and Durham VA Hosps., 1979—93; staff mem. Duke Surg. Pvt. Diagnostic Clinic, 1979—93; dir. Transplantation Lab Durham VA Hosp., 1979—93; dir. immunopathology Duke U. Med. Ctr., 1982—93, exec. com. dept. pathology, 1989—91; Baxley Prof. and chair pathology dept. John's Hopkins U., Balt., 1993—2000; pathologist-in-chief Johns Hopkins Hosp., Balt., 1993—2000; sr. v.p. health scis. Ohio State U., Columbus, 2000—, exec. dean health scis., 2004—, dean. coll. medicine; CEO Ohio State U. Med. Ctr. Mem. Duke Comprehensive Cancer Ctr., 1979—93; dir. rsch. Johns Hopkins Comprehensive Transplant Ctr.; mem. Third Frontier Commn. Adv. Bd., Ohio, 2004—; cons. Battelle Human Affairs Rsch. Ctrs., Seattle, 1985—93, NSF of Switzerland, 1992—93, numerous US govt. adv. coms.; mem. editl. bd. Transplantation, 1985—, Pathobiology, 1989—, Transplantation Now, Japan, 1989—, Pathology, Rsch. and Practice, 1990—, Human Immunology, 1992—, Lab. Investigation, 1993—, Xeno, 1994—, Virchows Archiv, 1998—, Transplant Immunology; reviewer Am. Jour. Kidney Diseases, Am. Jour. Ophthalmology, Am. Jour. Pathology, New Eng. Jour. Medicine, Jour. of AMA, Jour. Am. Soc. Nephrology, Jour. Clin. Investigation, Jour. Leukocyte Biology, Kidney Internat., others; contbr. numerous articles to prof. jours.; speaker and presenter in field. Bd. trustees Omeris, Columbus, Ohio, 2004—. Recipient Kermit G. Osserman Award, Myasthenia Gravis Found., 1976, Wiley D. Forbus Award, NC Soc. Pathologists, 1979, Reach for Sight Physician Investigator Award, 1990; grantee numerous, NIH. Fellow: Am. Soc. Clin. Pathologists (coun. on edn. and rsch. 1994—96); mem.: Southeastern Organ Procurement Found. (exec. com 1992—97, sec. 1992—93, treas. 1993—94, v.p. 1994—95, pres. 1995—96), Assn. for Rsch. in Vision and Ophthalmology, Am. Soc. Nephrology, Am. Soc. Transplant Physicians (pres. 1985—86), Am. Soc. Histocompatibility and Immunogenetics, Transplantation Soc., US-Can. Acad. Pathology, Am. Assn. Med. Colls., Am. Assn. Immunologists, AMA, Am. Soc. Investigative Pathology (pres. 2002—03), Intersociety Pathology Coun., Assn. Pathology Chairs (sr. fellow), Am. Soc. Transplantation (past pres.), Alpha Omega Alpha. Office: Office Dean Ohio State U Coll Medicine 370 W 9th Ave 200 A Meiling Columbus OH 43210

SANFORD, BILL R., medical products executive; BS, Kans. State U. Pres., CEO Steris Corp., Mentor, Ohio, 1987—, also chmn. bd. dirs. Bd. dirs. Key Corp., Cleve. Clinic Found., Edison Biotechnology Ctr., Primus Ventur Ptnrs., neuroControl Corp., BIOMEC, Inc., Cleve. Tomorrow, Case Western Res. U., Health Industries Mfrs. Assn. Office: 5960 Heisley Rd Mentor OH 44060-1834 Fax: 440-639-4457.

SANFORD, SARAH J., healthcare executive; b. Seattle, July 20, 1949; d. Jerome G. and Mary L. (Laughlin) S. BS in Nursing, U. Wash., 1972, MA in Nursing, 1977. Cert. in advanced nursing adminstrn. Critical care staff nurse Valley Gen. Hosp., Renton, Wash., 1972-75, Evergreen Gen. Hosp., Kirkland, Wash., 1975-76; instr. nursing Seattle Pacific U., 1977-79; with Overlake Hosp. Med. Ctr., Bellevue, Wash., 1979-88, critical care coord., 1979-80, dir. acute care nursing, 1980-82, assoc. adminstr., 1982-83, sr. v.p. patient care, 1983-88; exec. dir. AACN, Aliso Viejo, Calif., 1988-90, CEO, 1990-99; exec. dir. Actuarial Found., Schaumburg, Ill. Bd. dirs. Partnership for Organ Donation, Boston, Am. Soc. of Assn. Execs. Found., Washington. Co-editor: Standards for ursing Care of the Critically Ill, 1989; contbr. articles to books and jours. Fellow Am. Acad. Nursing; mem. AACN (pres. 1984-85, bd. dirs. 1981-83), ANA, Am. Coll. Healthcare Execs., Soc. for Critical Care Medicine, Am. Orgn. Nurse Execs., Sigma Theta Tau.

SANFORD, T(HOMAS) DENNY, bank executive; b. Dec. 23, 1935; s. William B. and Edith C. Sanford; m. Colleen Anderson Sanford, 1995 (div. 2003); children: Scott, William. BA in Psychology, U. Minn., 1958. CEO First Premier Bank, 1986—, Premier Bankcard; CEO, chmn. United Nat. Corp. Named one of 50 Most Generous Philanthropists, Business Week, 2006. Donated several million dollars to Sioux Valley Hospitals & Health Systems to transform the facility into a major research institution for children's health. The hospital has promised to rename the institution in his honor Sanford Health. Other recent donations include several millions to convert an abandoned mine into a science laboratory, for the children's hospital, and to the health system to expand projects involving the University of South Dakota's School of Medicine. Office: United National Corp 601 South Minnesota Ave Sioux Falls SD 57104

SANGER, LAWRENCE MARK, editor-in-chief; b. Bellevue, Washington, July 16, 1968; BA in Philosophy, Reed Coll., 1991; MA in Philosophy, Ohio State Univ., 1995, PhD in Philosophy, 2000. Ran website Sanger's Review of Y2K News Reports, 1998—2000; editor-in-chief Nupedia; editor Wikipedia, 2001—02; lectr. Ohio State Univ., 2002—05; dir. distributed content prog. Digital Universe Found. (leave of absence in 2006), 2005—06; founder, editor-in-chief Citizendium.org, Citzendium Found., 2006—. Presenter in field. Controversy as to whether co-founder "chief organizer" of Wikipedia and its name.

SANGER, STEPHEN W., consumer products company executive; b. 1946; BA in History, DePauw U., 1986; MBA, U. Mich., 1970. Marketing and sales positions Procter & Gamble, 1970—73; with Gen. Mills, Inc., Mpls., 1974—, v.p., gen. mgr. Northstar Divsn., 1983—86, v.p., gen. mgr. new bus. devel., 1986, pres. Yoplait USA, 1986—88, pres. Big G Divsn., 1988, sr. v.p., 1989—92, vice chmn., 1992-96, pres., 1993-95, chmn., CEO, 1995—2007, chmn., 2007—. Bd. dirs. Donaldson Co., Inc., Mpls., Target Corp., Wells Fargo & Co., Grocery Manufacturers of Am.; mem. Bus. Council, Bus. Roundtable; bd. adv. Retail Food Industry Ctr. Treas. Guthrie Theatre Found., Mpls.; bd. mem. Catalyst, Minnesota Bus. Partnership. Office: General Mills Inc 1 General Mills Blvd Minneapolis MN 55426

SANNER, JOHN HARPER, retired pharmacologist; b. Anamosa, Iowa, Apr. 29, 1931; s. Lee Michael and Helen (Grace) S.; m. Marilyn Joan Eichorst, Dec. 28, 1958; children: Linda Leigh, Steven Bradley. BS, U. Iowa, 1954, MS, 1961, PhD, 1964. Rsch. investigator G.D. Searle & Co., Skokie, Ill., 1963-69, sr. rsch. investigator, 1969-75, rsch. fellow, 1975-86, ret., 1986—. Contbr. articles to profl. jours. Mem. Deerfield (Ill.) Cable and Telecomm. Commn. 1st lt. USAFR, 1955-57. Mem.: Ill. Videographers Assn. Democrat. Achievements include pioneering research in prostaglandin antagonists. Avocation: video photography and production. Office: Sanner Video Svc PO Box 199 Deerfield IL 60015-0199 Personal E-mail: johnsanner@comcast.net.

SANNER, ROYCE NORMAN, lawyer; b. Lancaster, Minn., Mar. 9, 1931; s. Oscar N. and Clara Sanner; m. Janice L. Sterne, Dec. 27, 1972; children—Michelle Joy, Craig Allen. BS, Minn. State U., Moorhead, 1953; LLB cum laude, U. Minn., 1961. Bar: Minn. 1961, U.S. Dist. Ct. Minn. 1961, U.S. Supreme Ct. 1981. Tchr. English Karlstad (Minn.) High Sch., 1955-57; counsel IDS Life Ins. Co., Mpls., 1961-68, v.p., gen. counsel, 1969-72, exec. v.p., gen. counsel, 1972-77; dir. corp. devel. Am. Express Fin. Advisors, Mpls., 1968-69, v.p., gen. counsel, 1975-78, v.p., 1978-80, sr. v.p., gen. counsel, 1980-82; v.p. law Northwestern Nat. Life Ins. Co., Mpls., 1982-83, sr. v.p., gen. counsel, sec., 1983-96, ReliaStar Fin. Corp. (formerly known as NWNL Cos., Inc.), Mpls., 1988-96; of counsel Maslon Edelman Borman & Brand, Mpls., 1996—. Bd. dirs. Friendship Found., Inc., Fraser Cmty. Svcs. Served with U.S. Army, 1953-55. Mem. ABA, Minn. Bar Assn., Hennepin County Bar Assn., Fed. Bar Assn., Assn. of Life Ins. Counsel, Minn. Corp. Counsel Assn., Rotary. Office: Maslon Edelman Borman & Brand 3300 Wells Fargo Ctr 90 S 7th St Ste 3300 Minneapolis MN 55402-4140 E-mail: royce.sanner@maslon.com.

SANSTEAD, WAYNE GODFREY, school system administrator; b. Hot Springs, Ark., Apr. 16, 1935; s. Godfrey A. and Clara (Buen) S.; m. Mary Jane Bober, June 16, 1957; children: Timothy, Jonathan. BA in Speech and Polit. Sci, St. Olaf Coll., 1957; MA in Pub. Address and Group Comm., Northwestern U., 1966; EdD in Secondary Edn., U. ND, 1974. Tchr., Luverne, Minn., 1959-60; dir. forensics Minot High Sch., ND, 1960-71, tchr. social sci. ND, 1960-78; mem. ND Ho. of Reps., 1965-70, 83-85, ND Senate, 1971-73; lt. gov. State of ND, Bismarck, 1973-81, supt. pub. instrn., 1985—. Served with AUS, 1957-59. Recipient Disting. Alumnus award St. Olaf Coll., 1991, Literacy award, Internat. Reading Assn., 1993, Nat. Fedn. Outstanding Speech Educator award, 1995; named Outstanding Freshman Senator A.P., 1971, Outstanding Young Educator, N.D. Jr. C. of C., 1967, Outstanding Young Man, Minot Jr. C. of C., 1964, Communicator of the Yr., Nat. Forensic League, 1992, Advocate of Yr., Am. Sch. Counselor Assn., 1994; James J. Hill Found. scholar, Coe Family Found. scholar, 1963, Eagleton scholar Rutgers U., 1969. Mem. ND Edn. Assn., NEA (legis. com. 1969—), Central States Speech Assn., Am. Forensic Assn., Jr. C. of C., Sons of Norway, Elks, Toastmasters. Democrat. Lutheran. Home: 1120 Columbia Dr Bismarck ND 58504-6514 Office: State Supt ND Dept Pub Instrn 600 E Boulevard Ave Dept 201 Fl 9-10-11 Bismarck ND 58505-0440 Office Phone: 701-328-4570. Business E-Mail: wsanstead@nd.gov.

SANT, JOHN TALBOT, lawyer; b. Oct. 7, 1932; s. John Francis and Josephine (Williams) S.; m. Almira Steedman Baldwin, Jan. 31, 1959; children: John Talbot Jr., Richard Baldwin, Frank Williams. AB, Princeton U., 1954; LLB, Harvard U., 1957. Bar: Mo. 1957. Assoc. Thompson, Mitchell, Douglas & Neill, St. Louis, 1958-60; atty. McDonnell Aircraft Co., St. Louis, 1960-61; asst. sec., 1961-62; sec., 1962-67, McDonnell Douglas Corp., St. Louis, 1967-76; asst. gen. counsel, 1969-74; corp. v.p. legal, 1974-75; corp. v.p., gen. counsel, 1975-88; bd. dirs., 1978-82; sr. v.p., gen. counsel, 1988-91; ptnr. Bryan Cave, 1991-96; of counsel, 1997. Vestry of St. Michael and St. George, St. Louis, 1979-82, 87-90, 93-95; bd. dirs. Grace Hill Neighborhood Svcs., Inc., St. Louis, 1987-93; pres. Grace Hill Settlement House, 1996-97; mem. transition task force Supt. Elect. of St. Louis Pub. Schs., 1996, found. dir. St. Louis Pub. Schs. Found., chair Partnership For Youth, Inc., 2001—. Mem. ABA (pub. contracts sec., coun. 1987-91), Mo. Bar Assn., St. Louis Bar Assn. Home: 9 Ridgewood St Saint Louis MO 63124-1849 Office: Bryan Cave 1 Metropolitan Sq Ste 3600 Saint Louis MO 63102-2750

SANTANA, JOHAN (JOHAN ALEXANDER SANTANA ARAQUE), professional baseball player; b. Tovar, Merida, Venezuela, Mar. 13, 1979; m. Yasmile Santana; children: Jasmily, Jasmine. Pitcher Minn. Twins, 2000—07, NY Mets, 2008—. Named Am. League Pitcher of Yr., Sporting News, 2004, 2006, Player of Yr., Baseball Am., 2006; named to Am. League All-Star Team, 2005—07; recipient Am. League Cy Young award, 2004, 2006, Player's Choice award for Am. League's most outstanding pitcher, 2004, 2006, Am. League Triple Crown, 2006, Gold Glove award, 2007. Achievements include becoming the first pitcher since 1961 to give up four or fewer hits in ten straight starts; setting a new Twins team season record for strikeouts with 265 in 2004. Mailing: c/o NY Mets Shea Stadium 123-01 Roosevelt Ave Flushing NY 11368

SANTANA, LYMARI JEANETTE, lawyer; b. Augusta, Ga., 1968; married. BA with honors in Polit. Sci., U. PR, Rio Piedras, 1991; JD with honors, Mich. State U. Detroit Coll. Law, 1994. Bar: Mich. 1994, Minn. 2000. With James M. Hacker, P.C., Mt. Clemens, Mich.; asst. prosecutor Village of New Haven, Mich.; asst. US atty. No. Dist. Ala.; founding shareholder Mack & Santana Law Offices, P.C.; of counsel Mansfield, Tanick & Cohen, P.A., Mpls. With Judge Adv. Gen. Corps US Army, 1995—2000, criminal trial def. counselor 82nd Airborne Divsn. US Army, 1998. Decorated Meritorious Svc. medal; named a Rising Star, Minn. Super Lawyers Mag., 2005, 2006, 2007. Mem.: Nat. Hispanic Bar Assn., Minn. Hispanic Bar Assn. (pres. 2004—05, sec. 2001—03), Hennepin County Bar Assn. Avocations: reading, sports, movies. Office: Mack & Santana Law Offices PC 1700 US Bank Plz South 220 S 6th St Minneapolis MN 55402 Office Phone: 612-605-0967. Business E-Mail: lymari@macksantanalaw.com.

SANTE, WILLIAM ARTHUR, II, electronics manufacturing executive; b. NYC, July 16, 1943; s. William Arthur and Grace Elizabeth (Burnat) S.; m. Kathleen Margaret Rourke, July 2, 1966; children: Jennifer, William, Timothy. BS, U. Detroit, 1965; MBA, U. Pitts., 1981. CPA, Mich. Mgr. Deloitte & Touche, Detroit, 1965-78; gen. auditor Rockwell Internat., Pitts., 1978—. Mem. AICPA, Mich. Assn. CPA's, Inst. Internal Auditors, Shannopin Club (Pitts.), Ozaukee Club. Republican. Roman Catholic. E-mail: wasante@ra.rockwell.com.

SANTELLE, JAMES LEWIS, prosecutor; b. Milw., Sept. 10, 1958; s. James Nathaniel and Carol Jean (Hasley) S. BA, Marquette Univ., 1980; JD, Univ. Chgo., 1983. Bar: Wis. 1983, U.S. Dist. Ct. (ea. and we. dist.) 1983, U.S. Ct. Appeals (7th cir.) 1983. Clerk Hon. Judge Robert W. Warren, Milw., 1983-85; asst. U.S. atty. Ea. Dist. Wis., Milw., 1985—, civil divsn. chief, 1993—99, interim U.S. atty., 2001—02; prin. dep. dir. Exec. Office U.S. Attys., U.S. Dept. Justice, Washington, 1999—2001, exec. asst. U.S. atty., 2002—03; civil divsn. chief We. Dist. Mich., Grand Rapids, 2003—04. Mem. profl. responsibility com., investigator Wis. Bd. of Attys., 1993-99. Editor: The Milw. Lawyer, 1986-92. Bd. dirs. Waukesha County Coun. Alcoholism and Other Drug Abuse, 1993-99; citizen counselor Badger Boys State, 1986—; coach Wis. Bar Found. High Sch. Mock Trial Tournament, 1986-99. Mem.: Milw. Bar Assn., 7th Cir. Bar Assn. (liaison 2001—), Ea. Dist. Wis. Bar Assn. (sec. 2001—02). Avocations: running, swimming. Office: US Atty Office 517 E Wisconsin Ave Rm 530 Milwaukee WI 53202-4580 Office Phone: 414-297-1700. Business E-Mail: james.santelle@usdoj.gov.

SANTIAGO, BENITO RIVERA, professional baseball player; b. Ponce, P.R., Mar. 9, 1965; m. Bianca Santiago; 1 child, Benny Beth. Baseball player San Diego Padres, 1986-92, Florida Marlins, 1993-94, Cin. Reds, 1995, 2000—, Philadelphia Phillies, 1996, Toronto Blue Jays, 1997-98; catcher Chgo. Cubs, 1999. Named Nat. League Rookie of Yr. Baseball Writers' Assn. Am., 1987, Sporting News All-Star Team, 1987, 89, 91, 92; recipient Gold Glove award, 1988-90, Silver Slugger award, 1987-88, 90-91; holder maj. league rookie record for most consecutive games batted safely. Office: Cin Reds 100 Cinergy Fld Cincinnati OH 45202-3543

SANTIAGO, MIGUEL A., state legislator; b. PR, May 24, 1953; 2 children. BA, Northwestern Ill. U.; MA, Gov.'s State U. Ill. state rep. Dist. 3, 1989—; mem. exec. fin. inst., vice chmn. human svcs. appropriations Ill. Ho. Reps., mem. reapportionment, regist and regulation, transp. and motor vehicles coms.; tchr. Democrat. Home: 7414 N Octavia Ave Chicago IL 60631-4435 Office: Ill Ho of Reps Rm 618 State Capitol Springfield IL 62706-0001

SANTINI, GINO, pharmaceutical executive; b. Cesena, Italy; Grad. in Mech. Engrng., U. Bologna, Italy, 1981; MBA, U. Rochester, NY, 1983. Pres. SERM and skeletal products; fin. planning assoc. Eli Lilly and Co., Italy, 1983, pharm. dir. Belgium, 1990—91, gen.mgr. Eli Lilly Compania de Mex. Mexico City, 1991, area dir. L.Am., 1994—95, v.p. corp. strategy and bus. devel., 1996—97, pres. women's health bus. unit, 1997—99, pres. US ops., 1999—2004, sr. v.p. corp. strategy and policy, 2004—, mem. policy and strategy com., 2004—, mem. sr. mgmt. coun., 2004—. Bd. trustees Healthcare Leadership Coun.; assoc. mem. bd. Nat. Assn. Chain Drug Stores. Chmn. Nobel of Ind.; mem. exec. com. Indpls. C. of C. Office: Eli Lilly and Co Lilly Corp Ctr Indianapolis IN 46285 Office Phone: 317-276-2000.

SANTISI, TERRI M. (THERESA M. SANTISI), multi-media company executive; b. Mar. 5, 1954; BS magna cum laude, Boston Coll., 1976. With Ernst & Young; CFO EMI Music Publishing Worldwide; exec. v.p., gen. mgr. EMI Music N.Am.; mng. ptnr. KPMG; CFO Interpublic Group of Cos.; exec. v.p., chief fin. & adminstrv. officer IMG, 2006—. Mem. adv. bd. She Made It program Mus. TV and Radio; bd. dirs., mem. exec. com. NYC Outward Bound. Office: IMG 1360 E 9th St Ste 100 Cleveland OH 44114

SANTNER, THOMAS, statistician, educator; b. St. Louis, Aug. 29, 1947; s. Joseph Frank and Margaret Ann (Dolak) S.; m. Gail DeFord, Aug. 29, 1970; children: Emily, Matthew, Abigail, Dominick. BS, U. Dayton, 1969; MS, Purdue U., 1971, PhD, 1973. Asst. prof. Cornell U., Ithaca, N.Y., 1973-80, assoc. prof., 1980-86, prof., 1986-89, dir. stats. ctr., 1982-86; prof. Ohio State U., 1990—, chair dept. stats., 1992—2000. Cons. Hosp. for Spl. Surgery, N.Y.C., 1983—. Co-author: The Statistical Analysis of Discrete Data, 1989, Design and Analysis of Experiments for Statistical Selection, Screening and Multiple Comparasons, 1995, Design and Analysis of Computer Experiments, 2003; co-editor: Design of Experiments: Ranking and Selection, 1984; contbr. articles to profl. jours. ASA and IMS fellow, Fulbright fellow; numerous grants. Mem. Inst. Math. Stats., Biometric Soc., Am. Statis. Assn. Home: 1042 Putney Dr Columbus OH 43085-2903 Office: Ohio State U Dept Stats Columbus OH 43210 Office Phone: 614-292-2866. Business E-Mail: santner.1@osu.edu.

SANTONA, GLORIA, lawyer, food products executive; b. Gary, Ind., June 10, 1950; d. Ray and Elvira (Cambeses) S.; m. Douglas Lee Frazier, Apr. 12, 1980; 1 child, Daniel BS in Biochemistry, Mich. State U., 1971; JD cum laude, U. Mich., 1977. Bar: Ill. 1977. Atty. McDonald's Corp., Oak Brook, Ill., 1977-82, dir., 1982-86, assoc. gen. counsel, 1986-92, asst. v.p., 1989-93, v.p., sec., dep. gen. counsel, 1996-99, v.p., gen. counsel, sec., 1999-2001, sr. v.p., gen. counsel, sec., 2001—03, exec. v.p., gen. counsel, sec., 2003—. Bd. dirs. Aon Corp. Bd. trustees Rush U. Med. Ctr. Named a Women of Achievement, The Anti-Defamation League, 2008. Mem. ABA, Chgo. Bar Assn., Am. Corp. Counsel Assn., Am. Soc. Corp. Secs., Constl. Rights Found. Chgo. Office: McDonalds Corp 1 McDonalds Plz Oak Brook IL 60523-1911

SANTOS, RICHARD J., association administrator; m. Linda Lee Perry; children: Betsy Lee, Lee, Steffen. Ins. claim rep.; nat. comdr. Am. Legion, Indpls., 2001—. Commr. Md. Vets. Commn., Md. Mil. Monuments Commn. With USNR. Mem.: Am. Legion (life; mem. vets. affairs and rehab. commn., citizens flag alliance, policy coordination and action group, vets. planning and coord. com., legis. commn., NEC liaison to V&AR commn., chmn. pub. rels. commn.). Office: American Legion PO Box 1055 700 N Pennsylvania St Indianapolis IN 46206

SAPERSTEIN, LEE WALDO, mining engineering educator; b. NYC, July 14, 1943; s. Charles Levy and Freda Phyllis (Dornbush) S.; m. Priscilla Frances Hickson, Sept. 16, 1967; children: Adam Geoffrey, Clare Freda. BS in Mining Engrng., Mont. Sch. Mines, 1964; DPhil in Engrng. Sci., Oxford U., 1967. Registered profl. engr., Ky., Mo., Pa. Laborer, miner, engr. The Anaconda Co., Butte, Mont., and N.Y.C., 1963-64; asst. prof. mining engrng. Pa. State U., University Park, 1967-71, assoc. prof., 1971-78, prof., 1978-87, sect. chmn., 1974-87; prof., chmn. dept. mine engrng. U. Ky., Lexington, 1987-93; dean Sch. Mines and Metallurgy U. Mo., Rolla, 1993—2004, prof. mining engrng., 1993—2006, prof. emeritus, 2007—, cons., dean emeritus Sch. Mines and Metallurgy, 2004—. Chmn. engrng. accreditation commn., 1989-90, bd. dirs. Accreditation Bd. for Engrng. and Tech., 1992-2001, sec. of bd., 1995-98, pres.-elect, 1998-99, pres. 1999-2000, ABET fellow. Contbr. articles to refereed jours. Rhodes scholar Oxford U., 1964-67; recipient Linton E. Grinter Disting. Svc. award, 2004. Mem. SPE, ASEE, Soc. Mining, metallurgy and Exploration, Inc. (disting. mem. AIME-Soc. Mining Engrs.), Am. Assn. Rhodes Scholars. Home: PO Box 1408 Nantucket MA 02554-1408 Office: 20 New St Nantucket MA 02554 Office Phone: 573-578-7750. Personal E-mail: leesaperstein@comcast.net.

SAPP, JOHN RAYMOND, lawyer; b. Lawrence, Kans., June 18, 1944; s. Raymond Olen and Amy (Kerr) S.; m. Linda Lee Tebbe, July 3, 1965; children: Jeffrey, Jennifer, John. BA, U. Kans., 1966; JD, Duke U., 1969. Bar: Wis. 1969, U.S. Dist. Ct. (ea. dist.) Wis. 1969, U.S. Ct. Appeals (7th cir.) 1974, U.S. Ct. Appeals (4th cir.) 1984, U.S. Supreme Ct. 1974. Assoc. Michael, Best & Friedrich, Milw., 1969-76, ptnr., 1976-90, mng. ptnr., 1990—2004, sr. ptnr., 2004—. Dir. Roadrunner Freight Sys., Milw., 1992-2004, J.J. Keller Co., 2003-. Author: (book) Making Partner, A Guide for Law Firm Associates, 2005. Bd. dirs. Milw. Symphony, 1981-95, mem. exec. com., 1993-95; bd. dirs. Boy Scouts Am., Milw., 1986—, pres. 1990-92; mem. Milw. Arts Bd., 1990, Greater Milw. Com.; bd. dirs. Zool. Soc., 1995-, v.p., 2000-05, chmn., 2005-; bd. dirs. Lex Mundi, 1997-2000, mem. exec. com., 1997-2001; bd. dirs. Jr. Achievement Greater Milw., 2001—04. Avocations: golf, curling, print collecting. Office Phone: 414-271-6563, 414-271-6560. Business E-Mail: jrsapp@michaelbest.com.

SAREMBOCK, IAN JOSEPH, internist, cardiologist; b. Cape Town, South Africa, June 9, 1951; arrived in US, 1982, naturalized, 1986; m. Ghita Marueen Sarembock; children: Craig Murray, Kerri Lauren. MD, U. Cape Town, 1975, PhD, 1988. Diplomate Am. Bd. Internal Medicine, Am. Bd. Cardiovasc. Medicine, Am. Bd. Interventional Cardiology. Sr. house officer dept. internal medicine U. Cape Town and Groote Schuur Hosp., Cape Town, 1979-80, resident in internal medicine, 1980-83, sr. registrar Cardiac Clinic, 1985-86;

Velva Schrire meml. rsch. fellow Cardiac Clinic Groote Schur Hosp., 1983-85; postdoctoral rsch. assoc. divsn. cardiology Yale U., New Haven, 1986-88; attending cardiologist divsn. cardiology VA Ctr., West Haven, Conn., 1987-88; asst. prof. internal medicine cardiovasc. divsn. U. Va. Health Scis. Ctr., Charlottesville, 1988-93, assoc. prof. internal medicine cardiovasc. divsn., 1993-99, dir. coronary care unit, 1988—2007, prof. internal medicine cardiovasc. divsn., 1999—2007; interventional cardiologist, 1988—2007; cardiology cons. Salem VA Med. Ctr., Va., 1988—2000; dir. Ctr. Interventional Cardiology, U. Va. Health System, 2005—07, Ohio Heart & Vascular Ctr., Cin., 2007—. Lectr., presenter in field; invited prof. Heart-Lung Inst., Utrecht, Netherlands, 1992; mem. faculty restenosis summits, Cleve. Clinic, 1992, 93, 97. Contbr. articles to profl. publs. Mem. policy working com., house staff supervision Commonwealth of Va., 1990-2007. With South African Def. Force, Med. Corps, 1977—78. Grantee U. Va. Sch. Medicine, 1989, Beecham Labs., 1989-90, Am. Heart Assn., 1989-91, 91-92, 95-98, NIH, 1991-94, 2000-05; named Harrison DFisting. Tchg. Prof. Internal Medicine, 2006-07. Fellow ACP, Coll. Physicians South Africa, Am. Coll. Cardiology (allied health profls. com. 1993—), Coun. Thrombosis Atherosclerosis and Vascular Biology; mem. AAAS, Am. Heart Assn. (bd. dirs. Charlottesville/Albermarle divsn. 1991—, mem. Va. affiliate rsch. peer rev. subcom. 1992—, thrombosis coun. 1987, fellow coun. on clin. cardiology 1989), South African Med. and Dental Coun. Jewish. Office: Ohio Heart Vascular Ctr 2123 Auburn Ave Ste 136 Cincinnati OH 45219 E-mail: ijs4s@virginia.edu.

SARGUS, EDMUND A., JR., judge; b. Wheeling, W.Va., July 2, 1953; s. Edmund A. Sr. and Ann Elizabeth (Kearney) S.; m. Jennifer L. Smart, Jan. 7, 1978; 2 children. AB with honors, Brown U., 1975; JD, Case Western Res. U., 1978. Bar: Ohio 1978, U.S. Dist. Ct. (so. dist.) Ohio 1979, U.S. Dist. Ct. (no. dist.) Ohio 1981, U.S. Ct. Appeals (6th cir.) 1985, U.S. Dist. Ct. (no. dist.) W.Va. 1988, U.S. Ct. Appeals (4th cir.) 1988. Assoc. Cinque, Banker, Linch & White, Bellaire, Ohio, 1978-79, Stanley C. Burech, St. Clairsville, Ohio, 1980-82; ptnr. Burech & Sargus, St. Clairsville, 1983-93; U.S. Atty. Dept. of Justice, Columbus, Ohio, 1993-96; dist. judge U.S. Dist. Ct. (so. dist.) Ohio, Columbus, 1996—. Spl. counsel Ohio Atty. Gen., Columbus, 1979-93. Solicitor Village of Powhattan Point, Ohio, 1979-93; councilman City of St. Clairsville, 1987-91. Mem. ABA, Ohio Bar Assn. Office: US Dist Ct 85 Marconi Blvd Columbus OH 43215-2823

SARICKS, JOYCE GOERING, librarian; b. Nov. 8, 1948; d. Joe W. and Lovella Goering; m. Christopher L. Saricks, Aug. 21, 1971; children: Brendan James, Margaret Katherine. BA with highest distinction in English and German, U. Kans., 1970; MA in Comparative Lit., U. Wis., 1971; MA/MAT in LS, U. Chgo., 1977. Reference librarian Downers Grove Pub. Library, Ill., 1977-80, head tech. svcs., 1980-83, coord. lit. and audio svcs., 1983—2004; ret., 2004. Columnist Booklist Mag.; adj. prof. Dominican U., River Forest, Ill; lectr., presenter workshops in field. Author: (with Nancy Brown) Readers' Advisory Service in the Public Library, 1989, revised edit., 1997, 3d edit., 2005, The Readers' Advisory Guide to Genre Fiction, 2001. Mem. Read Ill. adv. com., 1990-91. Woodrow Wilson fellow, 1970; recipient Allie Beth Martin award Pub. Library Assn., 1989, No. Ill. Libr. of Yr. award Windy City Romance Writers, 1995, Libr. of the Yr. award Romance Writers of Am., 2000. Mem. ALA, Ill. Library Assn., Adult Reading Round Table (founder), Phi Beta Kappa, Delta Phi Alpha, Pi Lambda Theta, Beta Phi Mu. Home: 1116 61st St Downers Grove IL 60516-1819 E-mail: saricksj@juno.com.

SASS, DAWN MARIE, state official; b. Milw. d. Richard and Patricia S. BA in Hist., Polit. Sci., Univ. Wis., 1994. Probation officer to custody placement specialist Milw. Juvenile Detention Ctr.; child welfare worker Milw. County; office asst. III Wis. Parks Dept.; sales assoc. Boston Store, 2001—07; pharmacy tech. St. Luke's Hosp., 2004—07; former treas. Wis. Electrical Contractors' Corp.; state treas. State of Wis., 2007—. Mem.: Am. Fedn. State, County, Mcpl. Employees, The Nature Conservancy, World Wildlife Fund, Milw. County Zoological Soc. Democrat. Cath. Office: State Treas One S Pinckney St Ste 550 PO Box 7871 Madison WI 53707-7871 Office Phone: 608-266-1714. Office Fax: 608-266-2647. Business E-Mail: treasury@ost.state.wi.us.

SATERFIEL, THOMAS HORNE, education researcher, administrator; b. Hattiesburg, Miss., Dec. 14, 1950; s. Thomas Walton and Maybell (Horne) S.; m. Susan McKinley, June 1, 1974; children: Wayne Thomas, John Michael. BS, Miss. State U., 1972, MEd, 1973; PhD, Fla. State U., 1977; postgrad., Harvard U., 1985. Asst. prin. Tupelo (Miss.) Pub. Schs., 1972-73; tchr. math. Amory (Miss.) Pub. Schs., 1973-74; dir. devel. Blue Mountain (Miss.) Coll., 1974-75; asst. prof. ednl. psychology Miss. State U., Mississippi State, 1976-81, assoc. prof., 1981-85, dir. program. rsch. and evaluation for pub. schs., 1976-85; dep. state supt. Miss. Dept. Edn., Jackson, 1985-90; v.p. for rsch. Am. Coll. Testing (now ACT, Inc.), Iowa City, 1990-98, sr. v.p., 1998—. Mem. outcomes accreditation panel Office Gov. of Miss., Jackson, 1981-83, study commn. Coun. of Chief State Sch. Officers, Washington, 1985-90; chair planning and evaluation Southeastern Ednl. Rsch. Lab., Raleigh, N.C., 1987-90; exec. com. Nat. Forum on Ednl. Stats., Washington, 1989-90. Contbr. articles to profl. jours. Sec.-treas. Optimist Club, Starkville, Miss., 1977-85, bd. dirs., Jackson, 1985-90; deacon 1st Bapt. Ch., Starkville, 1982-85. Recipient Outstanding Young Adminstr. award Phil Hardin Found., 1975; named one of Outstanding Young Men in Am., U.S. Jaycees, 1977; Kellogg Nat. fellow W.K. Kellogg Found., 1983-86. Mem. Nat. Coun. on Measurement in Edn., Am. Ednl. Rsch. Assn., Am. Mgmt. Assn., Phi Kappa Phi, Phi Delta Kappa (pres. Mississippi State chpt. 1983-84, Peer award, 1982, Outstanding Educator award 1984). Avocations: music, running. Home: 49 Samuel Dr Iowa City IA 52245-5652 Office: ACT Inc 2201 N Dodge St Iowa City IA 52243-0001

SATHE, SHARAD SOMNATH, chemical company executive; b. Bombay, Oct. 10, 1940; came to U.S., 1967; s. Somnath Waman and Kamala S. (Bhave) S. m. Usha Moreshwar Tamhankar, Feb. 6, 1966; children: Vandana, Swapna. BS, U. Bombay, 1960; B in Pharmacy, Banaras Hindu U., 1963; PhD, Ind. U., 1971. Rsch. asst. CIBA Rsch. Ctr., Bombay, 1964-67; postdoctoral fellow Rsch. Triangle Inst., Raleigh, N.C., 1971-73; rsch. chemist Mallinckrodt, Inc., St. Louis, 1973-79, tech. supr., 1979-81, group leader, 1981-87, mgr. R & D, 1989-94; assoc. dir. rsch., 1995-98; dir. process rsch. Mallinckrodt Inc., St. Louis, 1998—. Patentee in field; contbr. articles to profl. jours. Pres. India Student Assn., Bloomington, Ind., 1969-70; mem. bd. of trustees India Assn. of St. Louis, 1980-85; pres. Sangeetha, St. Louis, 1986-87. Fellow Am. Inst. Chemistry, N.Y. Acad. Scis.; mem. Am. Chem. Soc. Avocations: music, tennis, reading. Office: Mallinckrodt Inc 2nd & Mallinckrodt St Saint Louis MO 63147

SATHY, ANUP, lawyer; BS with highest honors, U. Ill., 1992; JD cum laude, Northwestern U., 1995. Bar: Ill. 1995, US Dist. Ct. (no. dist. Ill.), US Bankruptcy Ct. (no. Ill., Del., so. NY, ea. La., Md., so. Ohio, so. Tex.). Ptnr. Kirkland & Ellis, Chgo. Contbg. editor: ABI Jour.; asst. editor: Norton Bankruptcy Law & Practice; contbr. articles in law jours. Office: Kirkland & Ellis 200 E Randolph Dr Chicago IL 60601 Office Phone: 312-861-2046. Office Fax: 312-861-2200. E-mail: asathy@kirkland.com.

SATO, PAUL HISASHI, pharmacologist; b. Mt. Vernon, NY, Mar. 22, 1949; s. Yoshio and Lury (Shiogi) S.; m. Jeanne Ellen Courville, June 29, 1996. BS, Jamestown Coll., 1971; MS, NYU, 1972, PhD, 1975. Rsch. assoc. Roche Inst. Molecular Biology, Nutley, N.J., 1975-77; assoc. prof. Mich. State U., East Lansing, 1977—. E-mail: sato@msu.edu.

SATTERLEE, TERRY JEAN, lawyer; b. Kansas City, Mo., Aug. 28, 1948; d. Charles Woodbury and Francis Jean (Shriver) Satterlee; m. William W. Rice, Jan. 9, 1982; children: Cassandra Jean Rice, Mary Shannon Rice. BA, Kans. U., 1970; JD, U. Mo., 1974. Bar: Mo. 1974. Lawyer Arthur Benson Assocs., Kansas City, 1974—77, Freilich & Leitner, Kansas City, 1977—78, U.S. EPA, Kansas City, 1978—83; of counsel Lathrop & Norquist, Kansas City, 1985—87, ptnr., 1987—, Shook Hardy & Bacon LLP, Kansas City, 2006—. Exec. com. Lathrop & Norquist, Kans. City, 1997—2002. Contbr. articles to profl. jours. Chmn. Bd. Zoning Adjustment, Kansas City, 1983—87, Mo. State Pks. Adv. Bd., 1997—2002; mem. hazardous materials com. Kansas City; mem. steering com. COMPASS Met. Planning, Kansas City, 1990—93. Mem.: Kansas City Bar Assn. (environ. com. chmn. 1986—90, chair 2001), Mo. Bar Assn. (chair environ. com. 1990—93), Nat. Assn. Clean Water Agys. (legal affairs com. 1992—, vice chair 2005—06), Women's Pub. Svc. Network (named Top 25 U.W. Women in Bus. 2000), Kansas City C. of C. (environ. com. chmn. 1992), Mo. C. of C. (mem. natural resource coun. 1990—2002, chair 1998—2002, bd. dirs. 1999—2002). Democrat. Episcopalian. Office: Shook Hardy & Bacon LLP 2555 Grand Blvd Kansas City MO 64108 Office Phone: 816-474-6550. Business E-Mail: tsalterlee@shb.com.

SATTERTHWAITE, MARK A., economics professor; BS, Calif. Inst. Tech., 1967; MS, Univ. Wis., Madison, 1969, PhD, 1973. Asst. prof. Kellogg Sch. Mgmt., Northwestern Univ., 1972—78, prof., 1978—83, Earl Dean Howard prof., 1983—2003, IBM rsch. prof., 1979—81, Herman Smith rsch. prof., 1981—83, prof. mgmt. strategy, 1985—, dir. Gen. Motors Rsch. Ctr. for Strategy in Mgmt., 1987—, chmn., dept. Mgmt. & Strategy, 1990—92, assoc. dean, 1992—96, A.C. Buehler prof. hosp. & health svc. mgmt., 2003—. Vis. prof. Calif. Inst. Tech., 1989. Editor (assoc.): Journal of Economic Theory, 1987—; contbr. articles to profl. jour. Fellow: Econometric Soc., Am. Acad. Arts & Sci.; mem.: Game Theory Soc. Office: Kellogg School of Management Northwestern University Evanston IL 60208 Business E-Mail: m-satterthwaite@northwestern.edu.

SAUBERT, WALTER E. (WALLY SAUBERT), trucking and transportation company executive; b. Seattle; m. Alicejo Saubert. BS in Econs., U. Wash. Joined Am. Red Ball Internat., 1972, various mgmt. and exec.-level positions, v.p., gen. mgr., 1983; co-founder Red Ball Corp., 1985, CEO, 1989; chmn., CEO Atlas World Group, 1996—. With USMC, 1965-68, Vietnam.

SAUER, BRAD T., manufacturing executive, mechanical engineer; BS in Mech. Engring., U. Minn.; MBA, St. Thomas U. Joined 3M Co., 1981, gen. mgr., med. solutions bus., Imation Corp., 1997—99, new bus. devel. dir., commercial graphics divsn., 1999, mng. dir., 3M Korea Ltd., 1999—2001, exec. dir., Six Sigma, 2001—02, exec. v.p., electro and comm. bus., 2002—. Office: 3M Co 3M Ctr Saint Paul MN 55144

SAUER, JEFF, university hockey coach; b. St. Paul; m. Jamie Sauer Adler; children: Chip, Beth. BA in Sociology, Colo. Coll., 1965. Asst. hockey, baseball coach Colo. Coll., Colo. Springs, 1966-68, head coach hockey, 1971-82; asst.coach hockey U. Wis., Madison, 1968-71, head coach hockey, 1980—. Mem. U.S. Olympic Hockey Com., 1984; coach Olympic Festival, 1987, USA Select Team, Pravda Cup, Leningrad, Russia, 1989, Team USA, Goodwill Games, 1990, U.S. Nat. Team World Championships, 1995, U.S. Select Team, Tampere Cup, Finland, 1997, coach, organizer youth hockey camps in summer; asst. coach USA World Jr. Team, 2003—; head coach USA Team TUI Cup, Manheim, Germany, Gold medal-winning hockey team Deaf Olympics, Salt Lake City, 2007. Counselor Stan Mikita's Hockey Camp for Hearing Impaired, Chgo. Named We. Coll. Hockey Assn. Coach of Yr. 1972-73, 74-75 (Colo. Coll.); NCAA championship (Wis.) 1983, 90, WCHA championship 1987-88, 97-98, WCHA Playoff Championship, 1982-83, 87-88, 94-95. Office: Western Collegiate Hockey Assn 559 D'onofrio Dr Ste 103 Madison WI 53719 Personal E-mail: coachjsauer@juno.com.

SAUER, MARK, professional sports team executive; b. Bklyn., Nov. 17, 1946; m. Georgia Sauer; children: Peter, Alex. B, U. Ill., 1968; MBA, Columbia U., 1971. V.p. Seven-Up Internat., 1976-80, Busch Entertainment Corp. subs. Anheuser-Busch, 1980-84; pres., CEO Civic Ctr. Corp. subs. Anheuser-Busch; dep. COO St. Louis Cardinals, exec. v.p., COO, 1989-91; pres. Kiel Ctr. Arena Project, St. Louis; pres., CEO Pitts. Pirates subs. Pitts. Assocs., 1991—96, St. Louis Blues, 1996—. Vice chmn. St. Louis Blues Hockey Club, bd. dirs. Co-chmn. Pitts. Minority Bus. Opportunity Com. Mem. Greater Pitts. C. of C. (bd. dirs.). Office: c/o St Louis Blues 1401 Clark Ave Saint Louis MO 63103

SAUL, NORMAN EUGENE, historian, educator; b. LaFontaine, Ind., Nov. 26, 1932; s. Ralph Odis and Jessie (Neff) S.; m. Mary Ann Culwell, June 27, 1959; children: Alyssa, Kevin, Julia. BA, Ind. U.-Bloomington, 1954; MA, Columbia U., 1959, PhD, 1965; postgrad., Leningrad State U., 1960-61. Asst. prof. Brown U., 1965-68; vis. assoc. prof. Northwestern U., 1969-70; assoc. prof. U. Kans., Lawrence, 1970-75, prof. history, 1975—, chmn. dept. history, 1981-89. Inst. Advanced Study, Princeton, 2000. Author: Russia and the Mediterranean 1797-1807, 1970, Sailors in Revolt, 1917, 1978, Distant Friends: The United States and Russia, 1763-1867, 1991, Concord and Conflict: The United States and Russia, 1867-1914, 1996, War and Revolution: The United States and Russia, 1914-1921, 2001, Friends or Foes?: The United States and Soviet Russia, 1921-1941, 2006; editor: Russian-American Dialogue on Cultural Relations, 1776-1914, 1997. Fulbright scholar, London, 1954-55, Helsinki, 1968-69, Soviet Am. Exch. scholar Internat. Rsch. and Exch. Bd., Moscow, 1973-74, 91-92; fellow Ford Found., 1957-59, Hall Ctr. for Humanities, 1989, 95; recipient Byron Caldwell Smith Book award for Distant Friends, 1993, Robert H. Ferrell book award for Concert and Conflict, Soc. Historians Am. Fgn. Rels., 1997, Pub. Scholar award Kans. Humanities Coun., 1997, Higuchi Rsch. award U. Kans., 1997, Steeples award for Svc. to Kans., 2000, Herbert Hoover Libr. Assn. award, 2001, Franklin and Eleanor Roosevelt Inst. award, 2002. Mem. Am. Assn. Advancement of Slavic Studies, Kans. State Hist. Soc., Kans. Assn. Historians, Phi Alpha Theta. Home: 1002 Crestline Dr Lawrence KS 66049-2607 Business E-Mail: nsaul@ku.edu.

SAUL, WILLIAM EDWARD, engineering educator; b. NYC, May 15, 1934; s. George James and Fanny Ruth (Murokh) S.; m. J. Muriel Held Eagleburger, May 11, 1976. BSCE, Mich. Tech. U., 1955, MSCE, 1961; PhD in Civil Engring., Northwestern U., 1964. Registerd profl. engr., Wis., Idaho, Mich., profl. structural engr., Idaho. Mech. engr. Shell Oil Co., New Orleans, 1955-59; instr. engring. mechanics Mich. Tech. U., Houghton, 1960-62; asst. prof. civil engring. U. Wis., Madison, 1964-67, assoc. prof., 1967-72, prof., 1972-84; dean, prof. civil engring. U. Idaho Coll. Engring., Moscow, 1984-90; prof. civil engring. Mich. State U., East Lansing, 1990—2000, chmn. dept. civil and environ. engring., 1990-95, chmn. emeritus, prof. emeritus, 2000. Cons. engr., 1961—; vis. prof. U. Stuttgart, Germany, 1970-71. Co-editor Conf. of Methods of Structural Analysis, 1976. Bd. dirs. Idaho Rsch. Found., 1984-90. Fulbright fellow 1970-71; von Humboldt scholar, 1970-71. Fellow ASCE (pres. Wis. sect. 1983-84), NSPE (bd. dirs.), Mich. Soc. Profl. Engrs. (Steinman award 2003); mem. Internat. Assn. Bridge and Structural Engrs., Am. Concrete Inst., Am. Soc. Engring. Edn., Sigma Xi, Phi Kappa Phi, Tau Beta Pi, Chi Epsilon Avocations: hiking, reading, travel, gadgets. Home: 1971 Cimarron Dr Okemos MI 48864-3905 Office: Mich State U 3546 Engring Bldg E East Lansing MI 48824 Business E-Mail: saul@egr.msu.edu.

SAUNDERS, FLIP (PHILIP D. SAUNDERS), professional basketball coach; b. Cleve., Feb. 23, 1955; m. Debbie Saunders; children: Ryan, Mindy, Rachel and Kimberly (twins). Attended, U. Minn. Asst. coach U. Minn., 1981—86, U. Tulsa, 1986-88; head coach Continental Basketball Assn. Rapid City Thrillers, SD, 1988-89, Continental Basketball Assn. La Crosse Catbirds, Wis., 1989-94, gen. mgr., 1991-93, team pres., 1991-94; head coach Continental Basketball Assn. Sioux Falls Skyforce, SD; gen. mgr., head coach NBA Minn. Timberwolves, 1995—2005; head coach NBA Detroit Pistons, 2005—. Head coach US Men's Basketball Team Goodwill Games (gold medal), Brisbane, Australia, 2001. Named Continental Basketball Assn. Coach of Yr., 1990, 92. Achievements include leading the La Crosse Catbirds to the Continental Basketball Association Championship as head coach, 1990, 92. Office: The Detroit Pistons Four Championship Dr Auburn Hills MI 48326

SAUNDERS, GEORGE LAWTON, JR., lawyer; b. Mulga, Ala., Nov. 8, 1931; s. George Lawton and Ethel Estell (York) S.; children: Kenneth, Ralph, Victoria; m. Terry M. Rose. BA, U. Ala., 1956; JD, U. Chgo., 1959. Bar: Ill. 1960. Law clk. to chief judge U.S. Ct. Appeals (5th cir.), Montgomery, Ala., 1959-60; law clk to Justice Hugo L. Black U.S. Supreme Ct., Washington, 1960-62; assoc. Sidley & Austin, Chgo., 1962-67, ptnr., 1967-90; founding ptnr. Saunders & Monroe, Chgo., 1990—. With USAF, 1951-54. Fellow: Am. Coll. Trial Lawyers; mem.: Law Club, Quadrangle Club, Point-O-Woods Club, Chgo. Club, Order of the Coif, Phi Beta Kappa. Democrat. Baptist. Home: 179 E Lake Shore Dr Chicago IL 60611-1306 Office: Saunders Monroe Law Offices 20 S Clark St Ste 1720 Chicago IL 60603-1847 Personal E-mail: glsaunders@sbcglobal.net.

SAUNDERS, HOSEA, newscaster; BA in Comm. and Journalism, Henderson State U., Ark. With KARK-TV, Little Rock, 1980—81; weekend anchor and reporter KDFW-TV, Dallas, 1981—86, KCBS-TV, LA, 1986—94, weekly talk show host, 1986—94; co-anchor News This Morning WLS-TV, Chgo., 1994—, reporter, host spl. programs. Motivational spkr. Active mentoring programs Alpha Phi Alpha Big Brothers, Chgo. Pub. Sch., NAACP; bd. mem. Open Book Literacy Program, Chgo. Named Man of Yr., Alpha Kappa Alpha, Best Image in Chgo. TV, Internat. Assn. of Image Cons., 2001; recipient six Emmys, Monarch award Outstanding Communicator, Alpha Kappa Alpha, 2001, Illuminati award, Inst. Positive Living, 2003, spl. awards, Chgo. Urban League. Mem.: NATAS, Chgo. Assn. of Black Journalists, Nat. Assn. of Black Journalists. Office: WLS-TV 190 N State St Chicago IL 60601

SAUNDERS, JOHN L., state agency administrator; Dir. Agr. Dept., Jefferson City, Mo. Office: Agr Dept PO Box 630 Jefferson City MO 65102-0630

SAUNDERS, MARTHA DUNAGIN, academic administrator; m. Joseph Bailey; 7 children. BA, U. So. Miss., 1969; MA, U. Ga.; PhD in Comm. Theory, Fla. State U. Asst. prof. comm. U. West Fla., dir. Univ. Honors Prog., dean Coll. Arts and Scis., 1999; v.p. Academic Affairs Columbus State U.; chancellor U. Wis., Whitewater, 2005—07; pres. U. So. Miss., Hattiesburg, 2007—. Author: Eastern's Armageddon: Labor Conflict and the Destruction of Eastern Airlines, 1992. Mem.: Pub. Relations Soc. Am. (Silver Anvil award). Avocations: fishing, gardening. Office: U So Miss Office of Pres 118 College Dr Hattiesburg MS 39406-0001

SAUNDERS, MARY L., career officer; BS in Social Work, Tex. Woman's U., 1970; grad., Squadron Officer Sch., 1973; MA in Guidance and Counseling, Rider Coll., 1978; grad., Air War Coll., 1993; nat. security leadership course, Johns Hopkins U., 1997. Commd. 2d lt. USAF, 1971, advanced through grades to brigadier gen., 1997; air terminal ops. officer 610th Mil. Airlift Support Squadron, Yokota Air Base, Japan, 1973-75; dep. comdr., comdr. Mil. Air Traffic Coordinating Office Mil. Traffic Mgmt. Command, McGuire AFB, N.J., 1976-79; chief of transp. 6168th Combat Support Squadron, Taegu Air Base, South Korea, 1982-83; comdr. 475th Transp. Squadron, Yokota Air Base, Japan, 1983-84; transp. staff officer Joint Deployment Agy., MacDill AFB, Fla., 1986-88, J-5, U.S. Transp. Command, Scott AFB, Ill., 1988-90; chief contingency plans divsn. J-5, U.S. So. Command, Quarry Heights, Panam, 1990-92; chief logistic plans Hdqs. Air Force Res., Robins AFB, GA., 1993-96; dir. transp. Office Dep. Chief Staff Installations/Logistics Hdqs. USAF, The Pentagon, Washington, 1996-98; comdr. Def. Supply Ctr. Columbus Def. Logistics Agy., Columbus, Ohio, 1998—. Decorated Legion of Merit, Def. Meritorious Svc. medal with oak leaf cluster, Meritorious Svc. medal with 2 oak leaf clusters. Mem. AAUS, NAFE, Air Force Assn., Nat. Def. Transp. Assn. Office: Def Supply Ctr Columbus PO Box 3990 Columbus OH 43216-5000

SAUNDERS, TERRY ROSE, lawyer; b. Phila., July 13, 1942; d. Morton M. and Esther (Hauptman) Rose; m. George Lawton Saunders Jr., Sept. 21, 1975. BA, Barnard Coll., 1964; JD, NYU, 1973. Bar: D.C. 1973, Ill. 1976, U.S. Dist. Ct. (no. dist.) Ill. 1976, U.S. Ct. Appeals (7th cir.) 1976, U.S. Supreme Ct. 1983. Assoc. Williams & Connolly, Washington, 1973-75, Jenner & Block, Chgo., 1975-80, ptnr., 1981-86, Susman, Saunders & Buehler, Chgo., 1987-94; pvt. practice Law Offices of Terry Rose Saunders, Chgo., 1995—2002; ptnr. Saunders & Doyle, Chgo., 2002—. Author: (with others) Securities Fraud: Litigating Under Rule 10b-5, 1989. Recipient Robert B. McKay award NYU Sch. Law. Mem. ABA (co-chair class actions and derivative suits com. sect. litig. 1992-95, task force on merit selection of judges, co-chair consumer and personal rights litig. com. sect. litigation 2000-02), Chgo. Bar Assn., Order of Coif, Union League Club. Office Phone: 312-551-0051. Business E-Mail: trsaunders@saundersdoyle.com.

SAUNDERS, THOMAS E., state representative; Former sales and pub. rels.; former assessor Henry County, Ind.; state rep. dist. 54 Ind. Ho. of Reps., Indpls., 1996—, mem. local govt., rds. and transp., and human affairs coms., asst. caucus chmn. Past vice chmn. Henry County Rep. Party. Mem.: County Assessor Assn. (pasts pres.), Heritage in Progress. Republican. Office: Ind Ho of Reps 200 W Washington St Indianapolis IN 46204-2786

SAUNDERS, WARNER, newscaster; b. Chgo. m. Sadako Saunders. BA, Xavier U.; MA, Northwestern U. Instr. sociology Nat. Coll. Edn. Ind. U. Northwest, Gary, Ind., ortheastern Ill. U.; dir. cmty. affairs, host Common Ground Sta. WBBM-TV; with Sta. WMAQ-TV, Chgo., 1980—, sports anchor, reporter, 1982—89, host Warner pub. affairs talk show, 1983—90, co-anchor 6 pm and 10 pm newscasts. Recipient 16 Chgo. Emmy awards in news and programming. Mem.: Chgo. Assn. Black Journalists (past pres., Hull House Jane Addams award 1999). Office: NBC 454 N Columbus Dr Chicago IL 60611

SAUNDERS, W(ARREN) PHILLIP, JR., economics professor, consultant, writer; b. Morgantown, W.Va., Sept. 3, 1934; s. Warren Phillip and Thelma Marie (Dotson) S.; m. Nancy Lee Trainor, June 16, 1956; children: Kathleen M., Kevin W., Keith A., Kent T., Kristine A. BA, Pa. State U., 1956; MA, U. Ill., 1957; PhD, MIT, 1964. Instr. econs. Bowdoin Coll., Brunswick, Maine, 1961-62; rsch. assoc., from asst. to assoc. prof. econs. Carnegie-Mellon U., Pitts., 1962-70; prof. to prof. emeritus in Econ. Ind. U., Bloomington, 1970—; assoc. dean Coll. of Arts and Scis. Ind. U., Bloomington, 1974-78, chmn. dept. econs., 1988-92. Cons. Agy. for Instructional Tech., Bloomington, 1976-78, 81-84, 92-93. Author: (books) Political Dimension of Labor-Management Relations, 1986; author, editor: Framework for Teaching Basic Economic Concepts, 1995; (Workbooks) Introduction to Macroeconomics (18th edit.), 1998, Introduction to Microeconomics (18th edit.), 1998; contbr. articles to Am. Econ. Rev., 1964—. Chmn. staff-parish rels. com. First United Meth. Ch., Bloomington, 1982-94. Recipient Vilard award for disting. rsch., Nat. Assn. Econ. Educators, N.Y.C., 1986, Leavey award for edn. Freedoms Found., Valley Forge, Pa., 1986, Disting. Svc. award. at. Coun. Econ. Edn., 1995. Mem. Am. Econ. Assn., Midwest Econ. Assn. (1st v.p. 1988-89), Soc. Econs. Educators (pres. 1992-93). Home: 3725 E Brownridge Rd Bloomington IN 47401-4209 Office: Ind Univ Dept Econs Bloomington IN 47405 E-mail: saunders@indiana.edu.

SAVAGE, BLAIR DEWILLIS, astronomer, educator; b. Mt. Vernon, NY, June 7, 1941; s. Rufus Llewellyn and Christine (Burney) S.; m. Linda Jean Wilber, June 25, 1966; children: Reid Hamilton, Keith Wesley. B Physics, Cornell U., 1964; MS, Princeton U., 1966, PhD, 1967. Rsch. assoc. Princeton U., 1967-68; asst. prof. U. Wis., Madison, 1968-73, assoc. prof., 1973-78, prof. astronomy, 1978—, chmn. dept., 1982-85, Karl Kansky prof. astronomy, 1999—2006, prof. astronomy emeritus, 2006—. Vis. fellow Joint Inst. Lab. Astrophysics, Boulder, Colo., 1974-75; investigator space astronomy projects NASA, 1968—; bd. pres. Wis., Ind., Yale Nat. Optical Astronomy Obs. Telescope Consortium, 1990-96. Contbr. articles to profl. jours. Peyton fellow Princeton U., 1964-66; NASA fellow Princeton U., 1966-67; research grantee NASA, NSF, 1968—. Mem. Am. Astron. Soc. (councilor 1994-97), Internat. Astron. Union, Nat. Rsch. Coun. (space sci. bd. mem. 1985-88, chmn. com. for space astronomy and astrophysics 1985-88, astronomy and astrophysics survey com. 1989-90, com. for astronomy and astrophysics 1998-2001), Assn. for Univ. Rsch. in Astronomy (bd. dirs. 1989-92, space telescope Sci. Inst. coun. 1999-2002), Tau Beta Pi. Home: 4015 Hiawatha Dr Madison WI 53711-3037 Office: Dept Astronomy U Wis 475 N Charter St Madison WI 53706-1507

SAVAGE, MURRAY, engineering executive; Various fin., mgmt., and strategic planning roles, including CFO Profl. Svc. Industries Inc., Lombard, Ill., pres., 1998—2000, CEO, 2000—. Office: PSI Corp Hdqs Ste 400 1901 S Meyers Rd Oakbrook Terrace IL 60181

SAVAGE, TERRY, television personality, journalist, stockbroker; Grad., U. Mich. Registered investment advisor stocks and commodity futures. Founding mem., 1st woman trader Chgo. Bd. Options Exch.; mem. Internat. Monetary Market; columnist Chgo. Sun Times, Chgo.; personal fin. columnist Barron's Online; featured columnist MSN Money website; owner, columnist pvt. website www.TerrySavage.com. Bd. dirs. Devon Energy, Broadway Stores, Chicago Mercantile Exchange; former bd. mem. McDonald's Corp., Pennzoil-Quaker State Corp.; former co-editor Options Trading Strategies newsletter; spkr. in field. Host Money Talks; author: Terry Savage's New Money Strategies for the 90s, 1993, Terry Savage Talks Money: The Common-Sense Guide to Money Matters, 1999, The Savage Truth on Money, 1999; columnist Chgo. Sun-Times. Dir. Chgo. Mus. Sci. and Industry, Northwestern Meml. Hosp. Found., Econ. Club Chgo., Execs. Club Chgo., Jr. Achievement Ill., Ill. Coun. on Econ. Edn., Women's Bus. Devel. Ctr. Recipient Outstanding Consumer Journalism award Nat. Press Club, 1987, Dir.'s Choice award, 1994, 2 Emmy awards, Outstanding

Personal Finance Columnist award, Northwestern U.; Woodrow Wilson fellow in Am. history and econs. Mem. Phi Beta Kappa. Office: Terry Savage Productions 676 N Michigan Ave Ste 3610 Chicago IL 60611 also: Chicago Sun Times 350 N Orleans St Ste 1270 Chicago IL 60654-2148 E-mail: savage@suntimes.com.

SAVAGE, THOMAS RYAN, lawyer; b. Milw., Dec. 1, 1947; s. John F. and Dorothy R. (Ryan) S.; m. Patricia C. Savage; children: Ryan, Patrick, Molly. BA, Quincy Coll., 1969; JD, Marquette U., 1973. Bar: Wis. 1973, U.S. Dist. Ct. (ea. and we. dists.) Wis. Sr. atty. Clark Oil & Refining Corp., Milw., 1973-82; assoc. Mulcahy & Wherry, Milw., 1982-84; v.p., sec., gen. counsel Sta-Rite Industries, Milw., 1984-92; v.p. adminstrn., gen. counsel Briggs & Stratton Corp., Wauwatosa, Wis., 1992—97, sr. v.p. adminstrn., 1992—. Mem. Dist. Export Coun., Milw., 1983-88, Gov.'s Adv. Coun. on Internat. Trade, Madison, Wis., 1982-85; solicitor United Way, Milw., 1990; bd. dirs. Goodwill Industries Wis., 1995—. Mem. Am. Counsel Assn. (bd. govs. Wis. chpt. 1988-94, pres. 1993-94), Engine Mfrs. Assn. (pres. 2001-02). Office: Briggs & Stratton Corp 12301 W Wirth St Wauwatosa WI 53222-2110 Office Phone: 414-259-5333.

SAVARD, DENIS JOSEPH, professional hockey coach, former professional hockey player; b. Pointe Gatineau, Que., Can., Feb. 4, 1961; m. Mona Savard; 1 child, Tanya. Center Chgo. Blackhawks, 1980—90, 1995—97, Montreal Canadiens, 1990—93, Tampa Bay Lightning, 1993—95; devel. coach Chgo. Blackhawks, 1997, asst. coach, 1997—2006, head coach, 2006—. Player NHL All-Star Game, 1982—84, 1986, 88, 91. Recipient Michel Briere trophy, 1979—80. Achievements include being a member of Stanley Cup Champion Montreal Canadiens, 1993; being inducted into the Hockey Hall of Fame, 2000. Office: Chgo Blackhawks 1901 W Madison St Chicago IL 60612-2459

SAVIA, ALFRED, conductor; b. Livingston, NJ; Asst. condr. Omaha Symphony, 1976-78, Fla. Symphony Orch., 1978-78, assoc. condr., 1979-86, prin. guest condr., 1986-87; asst. condr. Colo. Philharm., 1979-81; resident condr. New Orleans Symphony, 1986-88, assoc. condr., 1988-89; resident condr. Philharm. Orch. Fla. (now Fla. Philharm. Orch.), 1987-89; music dir. Evansville (Ind.) Philharm., 1989—; assoc. condr. Indpls. Symphony Orch., 1990-96, artistic dir., prin. condr. summer season, 1991-96. Guest condr. Indpls. Symphony, New Orleans Symphony, Kitchener-Waterloo Symphony, Can., Presdl. Symphony Ankara, Turkey, Aalborg Symphony, Denmark, Korea Philharm., San Antonio Symphony, Alabama Symphony, Hudson Valley Philharm., Fla. Symphony Orch., Colo. Philharm., Denver Chamber Orch., Lubbock Symphony, Nebr. Chamber Orch., Miami Ballet, Orlando Opera Co., St. Louis Symphony, R.I. Philharm., Nat. Repertory Orch., Ill. Symphony, Grant Park Symphony, Osnabruck Symphony Orch., others. Recipient High Fidelity Musical Am. Young Artist award, 1985. Office: Evansville Philharm Orch PO Box 84 Evansville IN 47701-0084 also: Parker Artists 382 Central Park W Apt 9G New York NY 10025-6032

SAVIANO, ANGELO, state legislator; b. May 20, 1958; m. Julia Thalji, 1987; 1 child, Bianca. BA, DePaul U., 1980. Supr. Leyden Twp., Franklin Park, Ill., 1989-93; Ill. state rep. Dist. 77, 1993—. Office: Ill Ho of Reps State Capitol 2112 N Stratton Bldg Springfield IL 62706-0001

SAVILLE, PAT, state senate official; b. Marysville, Kans., Sept. 10, 1943; Sec. Kans. Senate, Topeka, 1991—. Mem.: Am. Soc. Legis. Clks. and Secs. (past pres.). Office: Kans Senate State House 374 E Topeka KS 66612 Office Phone: 785-296-2456. E-mail: pats@senate.state.ks.us.

SAVINELL, ROBERT FRANCIS, engineering educator; b. Cleve., May 26, 1950; s. Robert D. and Lotte R. Savinell; m. Coletta A. Savinell, Aug. 23, 1974; children: Teresa, Robert, Mark. BSChemE, Cleve. State U., 1973; MS, U. Pitts., 1974, PhD, 1977. Registered profl. engr., Ohio. Rsch. engr. Diamond Shamrock Corp., Painesville, Ohio, 1977-79; assoc. prof. U. Akron, Ohio, 1979-86; prof. Case Western Reserve U., Cleve., 1986—, dir. Ernest B. Yeager Ctr. for Electrochem. Scis., 1991—, assoc. dean engring., 1998—, interim dean of engring., 2000, dean engring., 2001—06. Divsn. editor Jour. Electrochem. Soc., 1988-91; N.Am. editor Jour. Applied Electrochemistry, 1991-97; contbr. articles to profl. jours. Named Presdl. Young Investigator, NSF, Washington, 1984-89, Outstanding Engring. Alumnus, Cleve. State U., 1984. Fellow Electrochem. Soc., AIChE (program chmn. 1986-92), Am. Inst. Chem. Engrs.; mem. Electrochem. Soc. (divsn. officer 1992—), Internat. Soc. Electrochemistry (v.p. 1995-98). Avocations: sailing, skiing. Office: Case Sch Engring CRWU-500 ord Hall Cleveland OH 44106-7220 Office Phone: 216-368-4436. Business E-Mail: rfs2@case.edu.

SAVINI, DAVE, reporter; BA Broadcast Journalism, U. Dayton, 1989. Intern in investigative journalism NBC 5, Chgo., 1988—90; Raleigh bur. chief, investigative reporter Sta. WNCT-TV, Greenville, NC, 1990—92; investigative reporter, weekend anchor Sta. WROC-TV, Rochester, NY; investigative reporter NBC 5, Chgo., 1993—. Named Best Reporter, AP, 1995; recipient 2 Chgo. Emmy awards, 1998, Emmy for Outstanding Achievement award, 1999, 2 Peter Lisagor awards, 2000, award, Chgo. City Coun., Chgo. Emmy award, 1997, RTNDA award, Peter Lisagor award, 15 awards, AP, 5 Regional Radio & TV News Dirs. Assn. awards, 1999. Office: NBC 454 N Columbus Dr Chicago IL 60611

SAVIT, ROBERT STEVEN, physics professor, consultant; b. Chgo., Aug. 21, 1947; BA with honors, U. Chgo., 1969; MS in Physics, Stanford U., 1970, PhD in Physics, 1973. Vis. scientist CERN, Geneva, 1974-75; physicist Fermi Nat. Accelerator Lab., Batavia, Ill., 1975-78; asst. rsch. scientist U. Mich., Ann Arbor, 1978-83, assoc. prof. physics, 1983-90, prof., 1990—, dir. program for study complex sys., 1994—2000; dir. Alaska Summer Inst. in Complex Sys., 2003—. Vis. rsch. scientist Inst. Theoretical Physics, Santa Barbara, Calif., 1981-82; vis. prof. Racah Inst. Physics, Hebrew U., Jerusalem, 1986; rsch. fellow Columbia Futures Ctr., Columbia U., N.Y.C., 1988; cons. Powers Rsch., Jersey City, 1987-88, various fin. instns., non-profit instns., govt. agys., 1988—; mem. fin. strategies group Merrill-Lynch, N.Y.C., 1988. NDEA grad. fellow Stanford U., 1969-71, postdoctoral fellow NATO, Geneva, 1974-75, fellow Am. Swiss Found., 1974-75, rsch. fellow A.P. Sloan Found., 1981-85. Office: U Mich Physics Dept Ann Arbor MI 48109 Office Phone: 734-764-3426. Business E-Mail: savit@umich.edu.

SAWATSKY, BEN, church administrator; Exec. dir. Evangelical Free Church Mission, Bloomington, Minn., 1992. Office: The Evang Free Ch Am 901 E 78th St Bloomington MN 55420-1334

SAWHNEY, MOHANBIR S., finance educator; BSEE, Indian Inst. of Tech., Delhi, India, 1985; MS in Mktg., Indian Inst. Mgmt., Calcutta, India, 1987; MA in Mktg., PhD in Mktg., U. Penn., Wharton Sch., 1993. Asst. prof., mktg. Kellogg Sch. of Mgmt., Northwestern U., 1993—99, McCormick Tribune prof. of tech., 1999—, dir., ctr. for rsch. in tech. and innovation. Former adv. Govt. of Oman, U.S. Jordan Bus. Alliance; bd. dirs. Edmunds.com, IntelliSeek, MarketRx, Confluent Surgical, Autodaq, ConvergeLabs, Instill Corp.; fellow World Economic Forum. Co-author: (books) The Seven Steps to Nirvana: Strategic Insights into eBusiness Transformation, Techventure: New Rules for Value and Profit from Silicon Valley, Kellogg on Technology & Innovation, author numerous jour. articles. Named one of 25 most influential people in e-business, Bus. Week, 40 under 40 bus. leaders, Crain's Chicago Bus. Office: Northwestern U Kellogg Sch of Mgmt Jacobs Ctr Rm 5245B 2001 Sheridan Rd Evanston IL 60208

SAWYER, CHARLES F., lawyer; b. 1956; Student, Northwestern U. Sch. Music, 1974—76; AB in Econ. with honors and high distinction, U. Mich., 1978; JD, U. Chgo., 1981. Bar: Minn. 1982. Law clerk, Hon. Charles L. Levin, 1981—82; assoc. Dorsey & Whitney LLP, Mpls., 1982—88, ptnr., corp. dept., 1989—, and co-chair, securitization group. Exec. editor Univ. Chgo. Law Rev., 1980—81. Office: Dorsey & Whitney LLP Ste 1500 50 S Sixth St Minneapolis MN 55402-1498 Office Phone: 612-343-7986. Office Fax: 612-340-8738. Business E-Mail: sawyer.charles@dorsey.com.

SAWYER, HOWARD JEROME, physician; s. Howard C. and Dorothy M. (Risley) S.; m. Janet Carol Hausen, July 24, 1954; children: Daniel William, Teresa Louise BA in Philosophy, Wayne State U., Detroit, 1952, MD, 1962, postdoctoral, 1969-72. Diplomate Am. Bd. Preventive Medicine in Occupational and Environ. Medicine. Intern William Beaumont Hosp., Royal Oak, Mich., 1962-63, resident in surgery, 1963-64; chief physician gen. parts div. Ford Motor Co., 1964-66; med. dir. metall. products dept. Gen. Electric Co., Detroit, 1966-73, chem. and metal div., 1972-73; staff physician Detroit Indsl. Clinic, Inc., 1973-74; pres., med. dir. OccuMed Assocs., Inc., Farmington Hills, Mich., 1974-84; dir. OccuMed div. Med. Service Corp. Am., Southfield, Mich., 1984-86; dir. occupational, environ. and preventive medicine Henry Ford Hosp., 1987-91; pres. Sawyer Med. Cons., P.C., 1991—. Adj. asst. prof. occupational and environ. health scis. Wayne State U., 1974—, lectr. occpl. and environ. medicine Sch. of Medicine, 1998—; lectr. Sch. Pub. Health, U. Mich., Ann Arbor, 1977-88; cons. med. dir. St. Joe Minerals Corp., 1976-87, Chesbrough Pond's Inc., 1979-83; cons. Anaconda, Bendix, Borg Warner Chems., Fed. Mogul, Gen. Electric, Gt. Lakes Chems., other corps. Contbr. articles to profl. jours., chpts. to textbooks. Fellow Am. Coll. Preventive Medicine, Am. Occupational and Environ. Med. Assn., Mich. Occupational and Environ. Med. Assn. (pres. 1986), Am. Acad. Occupational Medicine; mem. AMA, Detroit Occupational Physicians Assn. (pres. 1984), Mich. State Med. Soc., Oakland County Med. Soc., Am. Indsl. Hygiene Assn., Mich. Indsl. Hygiene Soc. Office: Sawyer Med Cons PC 7072 Edinborough Dr West Bloomfield MI 48322-4025 Home Phone: 248-626-1693; Office Phone: 248-626-8061. Personal E-mail: buzsaw@comcast.net.

SAWYER, JOHN, professional football team executive; s. Charles S.; m. Ruth Sawyer; children: Anne, Elizabeth, Catherine, Mary. Pres., part owner Cin. Bengals, at. Football League; pres. J. Sawyer Co., Ohio, Miss., Mont., Wyo.; vice pres Cin. Bengals. Office: J Sawyer Co Provident Towers Cincinnati OH 45202-3717 also: Cin Bengals One Bengals Dr Cincinnati OH 45204

SAWYER, RAYMOND TERRY, lawyer, consultant, theater producer; b. Cleve., Oct. 1, 1943; s. R. Terry and Fanny Katherine (Young) S.; m. Katherine Margaret Schneider, Aug. 5, 1972; children: Margaret Young, John Terry. BA, Yale U., 1965; LLB, Harvard U., 1968. Bar: Ohio 1969, U.S. Dist. Ct. (no. dist.) Ohio 1970, prin., Sawyer LLC, 2002-. Assoc. Thompson Hine LLP, Cleve., 1968-76, ptnr., 1976—83, 1986—2001, chmn. bus. transactions and org. dept., 1998—2001; exec. dir. Ohio Housing Fin. Agy., Columbus, 1983-84; counsel to gov. State of Ohio, Columbus, 1984, chief of staff, 1985-86, chmn. Gov.'s commn. on housing, 1989-90; prin. Sawyer LLC, Cleve., 2002—. Bd. dirs. Premix, Inc., North Kingsville, Ohio. Assoc. prodr.: Frankie and Johnny in the Clair de Lune, 2002—03 (Tony award nomination for best revival of a play); Match, 2004. Vol. VISTA, East Palo Alto, Calif., 1968—69; mem. Tech. Leadership Coun., 1987—95, Leadership Cleve., 1986—87, Cleve. Found. Study Commn. on Med. Rsch. Edn., 1991—92, George W. Codrington Charitable Found., 1989—, chmn., 1989—2003; mem. Ohio Bd. Regents, Columbus, 1987—96, chmn., 1992—93; trustee Cleve. Ballet, 1987—2000, Cleve. Orch., 1993—, sec., exec. com., 1997—; mem. exec. com. MetroHealth Sys., 1998—; mem. Juilliard Coun. Juilliard Sch.; mem. pres.'s adv. coun. Case Western Res. U. Named Man of Yr. Womanspace, 1982. Mem. Ohio State Bar Assn. (chair corp. law com. 1993-95), Yale U. Alumni Assn. (pres. Cleve. chpt. 1980-81), Assn. Yale Alumni (del. 1996-99). Democrat. Presbyterian. Office: Sawyer LLC 3900 Key Ctr Cleveland OH 44114-1291 Home: 2425 N Park Blvd Apt 3A Cleveland Heights OH 44106-3154 Office Phone: 216-566-5837.

SAWYER, ROBERT MCLARAN, historian, educator; b. St. Louis, Nov. 12, 1929; s. Lee McLaran and Harrie (Alcock) S.; m. Patricia Ann Covert, Nov. 23, 1955; children— Ann Marie, Lee McLaran, Gail Louise. BS, S.E. Mo. State Coll., 1952; MA, U. Ill., 1953; PhD, U. Mo., 1966. Tchr. Rolla Public Schs., Mo., 1955; asst. prof., then asso. prof. history U. Mo., Rolla, 1956-67; mem. faculty U. Nebr., Lincoln, 1967—, prof. history of edn., 1969—2006, chmn. dept. history and philosophy of edn., 1975-81, coun. mem. Coll. Arts and Scis., 1979—2006, emeritus prof., 2007—. Vis. prof. Ark. State U., Jonesboro, 1966; proposal reviewer Nat. Endowment Humanities, 1979 Author: The History of the University of Nebraska, 1929-1969, 1973, The Many Faces of Teaching, 1987, The Art and Politics of College Teaching, 1992, The Black Student's Guide to College Success, 1993, The Handbook of College Teaching, 1994; contbr. articles to profl. jours. With AUS, 1953—55. Mem. Orgn. Am. Historians, History Edn. Soc., Am. Ednl. Studies Assn., Soc. Profs. Edn., Phi Alpha Theta, Phi Delta Kappa. Home: 2640 S 35th St Lincoln NE 68506-6623 Office: Univ Nebr 29 Henzlik Hall Lincoln NE 68588

SAWYER, THOMAS C., former congressman; b. Akron, Ohio, Aug. 15, 1945; m. Joyce Handler, 1968; 1 child, Amanda. BA, U. Akron, 1968, MA, 1970. Pub. sch. tchr., Ohio; adminstr. state sch. for delinquent boys; legis. agt. Ohio Pub. Utilities Commn.; mem. Ohio House Reps., Columbus, 1977-83; mayor City of Akron, 1984-86; mem. U.S. Congress from 14th Ohio dist., Washington, 1987—2003; mem. energy and commerce com. Democrat.

SAWYERS, ELIZABETH JOAN, retired librarian, director; b. San Diego, Dec. 2, 1936; d. William Henry and Elizabeth Georgiana (Price) S. AA, Glendale Jr. Coll., 1957; BA in Bacteriology, UCLA, 1959, M.L.S., 1961. Asst. head acquisition sect. Nat. Library Medicine, Bethesda, Md., 1962-63, head acquisition sect., 1963-66, spl. asst. to chief tech. services div., 1966-69, spl. asst. to assoc. dir. for library ops., 1969-73; asst. dir. libraries for tech. services SUNY-Stony Brook, 1973-75; dir. Health Scis. Library Ohio State U., Columbus, 1975-90, spl. asst. to dir. Univ. librs., 1990—2007. Mem. Assn. Acad. Health Scis. Library Dirs. (sec./treas. 1981-83, pres. 1983-84), Med. Library Assn., Am. Soc. for Info. Sci., Spl. Libraries Assn., ALA

SAWYIER, DAVID R., lawyer; b. Chgo., Feb. 2, 1951; BA, Harvard U., 1972, JD, 1977; MA, Oxford U., 1974; diploma law, Cambridge U., 1979. Bar: Ill. 1977, D.C. 1978. Law clerk U.S. Ct. Appeals D.C. cir., 1977-78; ptnr. commodities & fin. litig. Sidley Austin Brown & Wood LLP, Chgo. Mem. ABA (bus. law sect.), Chgo. Bar Assn. (futures sect.). Office: Sidley Austin Brown & Wood LLP Bank One Plz 10 S Dearborn St Chicago IL 60603 Office Phone: 312-853-7261. Office Fax: 312-853-7036. Business E-Mail: dsawyier@sidley.com.

SAXBE, WILLIAM BART, former United States attorney general, senator, lawyer; b. Mechanicsburg, Ohio, June 24, 1916; s. Bart Rockwell and Faye Henry (Carey) S.; m. Ardath Louise Kleinhans, Sept. 14, 1940; children: William Bart, Juliet Louise Saxbe Blackburn, Charles Rockwell. AB, Ohio State U., 1940; LLB, 1948; degree (hon.), Central State U., Findlay Coll., Ohio Wesleyan U., Walsh Coll., Capital U., Wilmington Coll., Ohio State U., Bowling Green State U. Bar: Ohio 1948, DC. Practiced in, Mechanicsburg, Ohio, 1948-55; ptnr. Saxbe, Boyd & Prine, 1955-58; mem. Ohio Ho. Reps., 1947—54, majority leader, 1951-52, speaker, 1953-54; atty. gen. State of Ohio, 1957-58, 63-68; ptnr. Dargusch, Saxbe & Dargusch, 1960-63; mem. US Senate from Ohio, 1969-74; atty. gen. US, 1974—75; US amb. to India, 1975-77; ptnr. Chester, Saxbe, Hoffman & Wilcox, Columbus, Ohio, 1977-81; of counsel Jones, Day, Reavis & Pogue, Cleve., 1981-84, Pearson, Ball & Dowd (merger Pearson, Ball & Dowd and Reed, Smith & McClay), Washington, 1984-93, Chester Willcox & Saxbe, Columbus, Ohio, 1994—; ind. spl. counsel Central States Teamsters Pension Fund, 1982—. Served with 107th Cav. AUS, 1940-42, 107th Cav. USAAF, 1942-45; col. Res. Mem. ABA, Ohio Bar Assn., Am. Judicature Soc., Chi Phi, Phi Delta Phi. Clubs: Mason (Rufus Putnam Disting. Svc. Award), University, Columbus Athletic, Scioto Country, Urbana Country, Burning Tree Country, Bethesda, Md., Country of Fla., Boynton Beach. Republican. Episcopalian. Office: Chester Wilcox & Saxbe LLP 65 E State St Ste 1000 Columbus OH 43215

SAXENMEYER, MARK HAROLD, television news reporter; b. Neptune, NJ, June 19, 1966; BA in Broadcast Journalism, U. Wis., Madison, 1989. Reporter KOVR-TV (formerly ABC, now CBS), Sacramento, Calif., 1989-93; spl. projects reporter WFLD-TV (Fox), Chgo., 1993—. Recipient Emmy awards, 1993-94, 96, Associated Press award, 1991, 93, 94, 95, 97, United Press Internat. award, 1995, 96, 97, alumni achievement award Minn. Pub. Schs., 1997. Office: WFLD-TV 205 N Michigan Ave Chicago IL 60601-5927

SAXTON, WILLIAM MARVIN, lawyer; b. Joplin, Mo., Feb. 14, 1927; s. Clyde Marvin and Lea Ann (Farnan) S.; m. Helen Grace Klinefelter, June 1, 1974; children: Sherry Lynn, Patricia Ann Painter, William Daniel, Michael Lawrence. AB, U. Mich., 1949, JD, 1952. Bar: Mich. Mem. firm Love, Snyder & Lewis, Detroit, 1952-53, Butzel, Long, Detroit, 1953—, dir., chmn., CEO, 1989-96, dir. emeritus, 1997—. Lectr. Inst. Continuing Legal Edn.; sec., bd. dirs. Fritz Broadcasting, Inc., 1983-97; mem. mediation tribunal hearing panel for 3d Jud. Dist. Mich., 1989—, 6th Jud. Dist., 1994—. Trustee Detroit Music Hall Ctr. Soc. for the Performing Arts, 1984-99; trustee Hist. Soc. US Dist. Ct. (ea. dist.) Mich., 1992-95, pres., 1993-95. Recipient Disting. award Mich. Road Builders Assn., 1987. Master of Bench Emeritus Am. Inn of Court; fellow Am. Coll. Trial Lawyers, Am. Bar Found., Am. Coll. Labor and Employment Lawyers, Mich. Bar Found.; mem. ABA, FBA, Detroit Bar Assn. (dir. 1974-79, Goodnow Pres.'s award 1996), Mich. Bar Assn. (atty. discipline panel, Disting. Svc. award 1998, Champion of Justice award, 2003), Detroit Indsl. Rels. Rsch. Assn. (treas. 1980—, v.p. 1982, pres. 1984-85), Mich. Young Lawyers (pres. 1954-55), Am. Law Inst., Indsl. Rels. Rsch. Assn. Am. Arbitration Assn., U.S. 6th Cir. Ct. Appeals (life, mem. jud. conf., mem. bicentennial com.), Am. Inn Ct., Cooley Club, Renaissance Club, Detroit Golf Club (dir. 1983-89), Detroit Athletic Club. Office: Butzel Long 150 W Jefferson Ave Ste 100 Detroit MI 48226-4416 Office Phone: 313-225-7001. Personal E-mail: saxton214@aol.com.

SAYATOVIC, WAYNE PETER, manufacturing executive; b. Cleve., Feb. 8, 1946; m. Janice Elaine Zajac; children: Jason Scott, Jamie Elizabeth. BA in Econs., Syracuse U., 1967, MBA in Fin., 1969; student in Fin. Mgmt., Gen. Electric Co., 1969—72. Fin. and cost acctg. mgr. Lubriquip divsn. Houdaille Industries Inc., Solon, Ohio, 1972—75, contr. Hydraulics divsn. Buffalo, 1975-77, contr. Strippit divsn. Akron, NY, 1977-79, treas. Ft. Lauderdale, Fla., 1979-86, v.p., treas., sec. Northbrook, Ill., 1986-88, IDEX Corp., Northbrook, 1988—91, v.p. fin., CFO, sec., 1992—94, sr. v.p. fin., CFO, sec., 1994-98, sr. v.p. fin., CFO, 1998—. Mem. Mfrs.' Alliance for Productivity & Innovation (fin. coun.). Office: IDEX Corp 630 Dundee Rd Ste 400 Northbrook IL 60062-2745

SAYERS, GALE, computer company executive, retired professional football player; b. Wichita, Kans., May 30, 1943; s. Roger Earl and Bernice (Ross) S.; m. Ardythe Elaine Bullard, Dec. 1, 1973; children: Gale Lynne, Scott Aaron, Timothy Gale, Gaylon, Guy, Gary. Student phys. edn., Kans. U., N.Y. Inst. Finance. Running back Chgo. Bears Profl. Football Team, 1965—72; then asst. to athletic dir. Kans. U.; athletic dir. So. Ill. U., to 1981; v.p. mktg. Computer Suppy by Sayers, Northfield, Ill., 1984—86; pres. Crest Computer Supply Co., Skokie, Ill., 1986—; pres., CEO Sayers Computer Source, Mt. Prospect, Ill., 1983—2006, chmn.; pres., CEO Sayers40, Inc., Mt. Prospect, Ill., 2006—. Columnist Chgo. Daily News; bd. dir. Global Healthcare Exchange, 2003. Author: (with Al Silverman) I Am Third, 1970, (with Fred Mitchell) Sayers: My Life and Times, 2007 Co-chmn. legal def. fund sports com. NAACP; co-ordinator Reach-Out program, Chgo.; hon. chmn. Am. Cancer Soc.; commr. Chgo. Park Dist. Named NFL Rookie of Yr., 1965; NFL Pro Bowl MVP, 1966, 1967, 1969; named to Pro Football Hall of Fame, 1977 Mem. Kappa Alpha Psi. Office: Sayers Computer Source 1150 Feehanville Dr Mount Prospect IL 60056-6007

SAYERS, MARTIN PETER, pediatric neurosurgeon; b. Big Stone Gap, Va., Jan. 2, 1922; s. Delbert Bancroft and Loula (Thompson) S.; m. Marjorie W. Garvin, May 8, 1943; children: Daniel Garvin Sayers, Stephen Putnam Sayers, Julia Hathaway Sayers Bolton, Elaine King Sayers Buck. BA, Ohio State U., 1943, MD, 1945; postgrad., U. Pa., 1948-51. Intern Phila. Gen. Hosp., 1945-46; resident in neurosurgery U. Pa. Hosps., Phila., 1948-51; practice medicine specializing in neurosurgery Columbus, Ohio, 1951—; mem. faculty Ohio State U., Columbus, 1951-87, clin. prof. neurosurgery, 1968-87, emeritus, chief dept. pediatric neurosurgery, 1960-87. Cons. Bur. Crippled Children Services Ohio.; Neurosurgeon Project Hope, Ecuador, 1964, Ceylon, 1968, Cracow, Poland, 1979. Served as lt. jr. grade M.C. USN, 1946—48. Mem. Am. Assn. Neurol. Surgeons (chmn. pediatric sect.), Congress Neurol. Surgeons (pres.), Neurosurg. Soc. Am. (pres.), Am. Soc. Pediatric Neurosurgery, Soc. Neurol. Surgeons. Office: 931 Chatham Ln Columbus OH 43221-2417

SAYLES BELTON, SHARON, former mayor; b. St. Paul, May 13, 1951; m. Steve Belton, Aug. 29, 1981; 3 children. Student, Macalester Coll., 1969-1973; Doctorate (hon.), Walden U. Asst. dir. Minn. Program for Victims of Sexual Assault; parole officer Minn. Dept. Corrections; city coun. mem., 1983-93; coun. pres., 1989-93; mayor City of Mpls., 1994—2001; sr. fellow Roy Wilkins Ctr. Human Rels. and Social Justice U. Minn., 2001—. Pres., co-founder Nat. Coalition Against Sexual Assault; co-founder, pres. Harriet Tubman Shelter for Battered Women; trustee U.S. Conf. of Mayors, chair Youth Violence Task Forum; bd. dirs. Bush Found., Search Inst., Youth Coordinating Bd., Neighborhood Revitalization Program, Clean Water Partnership, Children's Healthcare and Hosp., Bush Found., U.S. Conf. Mayors, Nat. League Cities. Recipient Gertrude E. Rush Disting. Svc. award, Nat. Bar Assn., Rosa Parks award, Am. Assn. Affirmative Action.

SAYRE, KENNETH MALCOLM, philosophy educator; b. Scottsbluff, Nebr., Aug. 13, 1928; s. Harry Malcolm and Mildred Florence (Potts) S.; m. Lucille Margaret Shea, Aug. 19, 1958 (dec. Apr. 1980); children: Gregory, Christopher, Jeffrey; m. Patricia Ann White, Apr. 4, 1983; 1 child, Michael. AB, Grinnell Coll., Iowa, 1952; MA, Harvard U., 1954, PhD, 1958. Asst. dean Grad. Sch. Arts and Letters Harvard U., Cambridge, Mass., 1953-56; systems analyst MIT, Cambridge, Mass., 1956-58; from instr. to prof. philosophy U. Notre Dame, Ind., 1958—, dir. Philosophic Inst. Ind., 1966—. Author: Recognition, 1965, Consciousness, 1969, Plato's Analytic Method, 1969, Cybernetics and the Philosophy of Mind, 1976, Moonflight, 1977, Starburst, 1977, Plato's Late Ontology, 1983, Plato's Literary Garden, 1995, Parmenides' Lesson, 1996, Belief and Knowledge, 1997, Metaphysics and Method in Plato's Statesmen, 2006. Served with USN, 1946-48 NSF grantee, 1962-79; NEH fellow, 1995-96. Mem. Am. Philos. Assn., Phi Beta Kappa Home: 910 Weber Sq South Bend IN 46617-1850 Office: Univ Notre Dame Dept Philosophy 100 Malloy Hall Notre Dame IN 46556

SCALES, FREDA S., dean, nursing educator; BSN, Okla. Bapt. U., 1965; MSN, Ind. U., 1970; PhD, Purdue U., 1977. Mem. staff faculty Sch. Nursing Ind. U., Inpls., 1970-82; dean Coll. Nursing Valparaiso (Ind.) U., 1982—. Mem. ANA, Am. Assn. Coll. Nursing, Nat. League Nursing. Office: Valparaiso U Coll Nursing Valparaiso IN 46383 Fax: 219-464-5425.

SCALETTA, PHILLIP RALPH, III, lawyer; b. Iowa City, Dec. 18, 1949; s. Phillip Jasper and Helen M. (Beedle) S.; m. Karen Lynn Scaletta, May 13, 1973; children: Phillip, Anthony, Alexander. BSIM, MS, Purdue U., 1972; JD, Ind. U., 1975. Bar: Ind. 1975, U.S. Dist. Ct. Ind. 1975, Ill. 1993. Assoc. Ice Miller, Indpls., 1975-81, ptnr., 1981—, mng. ptnr., 2007—. Contbr. articles to profl. jours. Chmn. Ind. Continuing Legal Edn. Found., Indpls., 1989; mem. Environ. Quality Control Water Com., 1988-98. Mem. Ind. Bar Assn., Indpls. Bar Assn., Def. Rsch. Inst., Internat. Assn. Def. Counsel, Gyro Club Indpls. (v.p. 1992-93, pres. 1993-94, bd. dirs. 1990—). Avocations: golf, skiing, tennis. Home: 7256 Tuliptree Trl Indianapolis IN 46256-2136 Office: Ice Miller 1 American Sq Indianapolis IN 46282-0020 Office Phone: 317-236-2330. Business E-Mail: scaletta@icemiller.com.

SCALLEN, THOMAS KAINE, broadcast executive; b. Mpls., Aug. 14, 1925; s. Raymond A. and Lenore (Kaine) S.; m. Bille Jo Brice; children by previous marriage: Thomas, Sheila, Patrick, Eileen, Timothy and Maureen (twins). BA, St. Thomas Coll., 1949; JD, U. Denver, 1950. Bar: Minn. Asst. atty. gen. State of Minn., Mpls., 1950-55; sole practice Mpls., 1955-57; pres. Med. Investment Corp., Mpls., 1957—, Internat. Broadcasting Corp., Mpls., 1977—; owner Harlem Globetrotters. Pres., exec. producer Ice Capades; chmn. bd. dirs. Century Park Pictures Corp., Los Angeles, chmn. bd. dirs. Blaine-Thompson Co., Inc., N.Y.C; chmn. Apache Plastics, Inc., Stockton, Calif. Served with AUS. Mem. World Pres. Orgn., Minn. Club, Calhoun Beach Club, L.A. Athletic Club. Clubs: University (St. Paul, Mpls.), Rochester (Minn.) Golf and Country, Edina (Minn.) Country, Athletic (Mpls.). Home: Heron Cove Windham NH 03087 Office: Internat Broadcasting Corp 80 S 8th St Ste 4701 Minneapolis MN 55402-2207 Office Phone: 612-333-5100.

SCAMINACE, JOSEPH M., paint store executive; Grad., U. Dayton; MBA, Case Western Res. U. Dir. mfg. Sherwin-Williams Co., Morrow, Ga., 1983, pres., gen. mgr. consumer group/predecessor coatings divsn. Cleve., 1997-99, pres., COO, 1999—. Office: Sherwin-Williams Co 101 Prospect Ave NW Cleveland OH 44115-1075

SCANLAN, JAMES PATRICK, philosophy and Slavic studies educator; b. Chgo., Feb. 22, 1927; s. Gilbert Francis and Helen (Meyers) S.; m. Marilyn A. Morrison, June 12, 1948. BA, U. Chgo., 1948, MA, 1950, PhD, 1956. Research fellow Inst. Philos. Research, San Francisco, 1953-55; instr. Case Inst. Tech., Cleve., 1955-56; from instr. to assoc. prof. Goucher Coll., Balt., 1956-68; prof., dir. Slavic Ctr. U. Kans., Lawrence, 1968-70; prof. Ohio State U., Columbus, 1971-91, dir. Slavic Ctr., 1988-91, prof. emeritus, 1992—. Vis. rsch. scholar Moscow State U., 1964-65, 69, 98, Acad. Scis. USSR, Moscow, 1978, 93, Russian State U. for the Humanities, 1995; fgn. vis. fellow Slavic Rsch. Ctr., Hokkaido U., Sapporo, Japan, 1987-88. Author: Marxism in the USSR, 1985, Dostoevsky the Thinker, 2002, Russian trans., 2006; editor: Historical Letters by Peter Lavrov, 1967, Soviet Studies in Philosophy, 1987—92, Russian Studies in Philosophy, 1992—97, Technology, Culture and Development: The Experience of the Soviet Model, 1992, Russian Thought After Communism, 1994; co-editor: Russian Philosophy, 1965, Marxism and Religion in Eastern Europe, 1976. Served with USMC, 1945-46. Woodrow Wilson Internat. Ctr. fellow, 1982; recipient Translation award Nat. Translation Ctr., 1967, Faculty Rsch. award Fulbright-Hays, 1982-83. Mem. Am. Philos. Assn., Am. Assn. Advancement Slavic Studies, Phi Beta Kappa. Home: 1000 Urlin Ave Apt 206 Columbus OH 43212-3324 Personal E-mail: scanlan.1@osu.edu.

SCANLAN, MICHAEL, priest, academic administrator; b. Far Rockaway, NY, Dec. 1, 1931; s. Vincent Michael and Marjorie (O'Keefe) Scanlan. BA, Williams Coll., 1953; JD, Harvard U., 1956; MDiv, St. Francis Sem., Loretto, Pa., 1975; LittD (hon.), Coll. Steubenville, 1972; LLD (hon.), Williams Coll., Williamstown, Mass., 1978; PdD (hon.), St. Francis Coll., Loretto, Pa., 1987; STM, 3d Order Regular of St Francis, 1996. Ordained priest Roman Catholic Ch., 1964; Cross Pro Ecclesia et Pontifice, 1990. Acting dean Coll. Steubenville, Ohio, 1964-66, dean Ohio, 1966-69; rector pres. St. Francis Major Sem., Loretto, Pa., 1969-74; pres. Franciscan U. Steubenville, 1974-2000, chancellor, 2000—. Pres. (FIRE) Cath. Alliance for Faith, Intercession, Repentence and Evangelism, 1984—. Author: The Power in Penance, 1972, Inner Healing, 1974, A Portion of My Spirit, 1979, The San Damiano Cross, 1983, 2007, Turn to the Lord-A Call to Repentance, 1989, The Truth About Trouble, 1989, rev. edit. 2005, What Does God Want: A Practical Guide to Making Decisions, 1996, (with James Manney) Let the Fire Fall, 1997, The Holy Spirit: Holy Desire, 1998, Rosary Companion with Luminous Mysteries, 2002; chmn. editl. bd. New Covenant mag., 1985-92. Mem. Diocese of Steubenville Ecumenical Commn., 1964-69; bd. dirs. Rumor Control Ctr., Steubenville, 1968-69, C. of C., Steubenville, 1976-79; bd. trustees St. Francis Prep. Sch., Spring Grove, Pa., 1969-74; vice-chmn., bd. trustees St. Francis Coll., Loretto, Pa., 1969-74; trustee United Way, Steubenville, 1975-80; chmn. nat. svc. com. Cath. Charismatic Renewal, 1975-78. Staff judge adv. USAF, 1956-57. Named Sacrae Theologiae Magister Third Order Regular St Francis, 1996. Roman Catholic. Avocations: tennis, golf, skiing. Office: Franciscan U Office of Chancellor 1235 University Blvd Steubenville OH 43952-1796 Office Phone: 740-283-6466.

SCANLAN, RICHARD THOMAS, classics educator; b. St. Paul, May 30, 1928; s. Robert Lawrence and Catherine (Rockstroh) S.; m. Donna Mary Campion, Dec. 29, 1951; children: John, Susan, Catherine, Anne, Margaret. BS, U. Minn., 1951, MA, 1952. Tchr. Hastings High Sch., Minn., 1953-55, Edina High Sch., Minn., 1955-67; prof. classics U. Ill., Urbana, 1967—. Ednl. cons., 1960-75 Author: Power in Words, 1983; computer courses, 1975, 77; Myths of Greece and Rome, 1986 Pres. bd. trustees Champaign Libr., 1980-92. With U.S. Army, 1946-48, Italy. Named Excellent Tchr. Am. Classical League, 1966; recipient Silver medal Nat. Coun. for Advancement of Edn., 1985. Mem. Am. Philol. Assn., Am. Classical League, Archaeol. Assn., Classical Assn. (Excellent Tchr.award 1974) Roman Catholic. Home: 2103 Noel Dr Champaign IL 61821-6552 Office: Univ of Ill Dept of Classics Urbana IL 61801

SCANLAN, THOMAS CLEARY, publishing executive, editor; b. Birmingham, Mich., May 18, 1957; s. Thomas Matthew and Emily (Cleary) S.; m. Sally Sachs, June 20, 1981; children: Bridget C., Thomas M., Patrick J. BS, St. Louis U., 1979. Salesman Walter Heller Co., Chgo., 1979-82; pub., editor Surplus Record, Inc., Chgo., 1982—. Office: Surplus Record Inc 20 N Wacker Dr Chicago IL 60606-2806

SCARFONE, ANTHONY C., lawyer; BA summa cum laude, U. Rochester, 1983; JD magna cum laude, Syracuse U., 1986. Sr. counsel Harris Beach & Wilcox, Rochester, NY, 1986—89, Bausch & Lomb Inc., Rochester, NY, 1989—93; v.p., gen. counsel, sec. Dahlberg, Inc., 1993—99; sr. v.p., gen. counsel, sec. Deluxe Corp., 2000—. Office: Deluxe Corp 3680 Victoria St N Shoreview MN 55126-2966

SCARSE, OLIVIA MARIE, cardiologist, consultant; b. Chgo., Nov. 10, 1950; d. Oliver Marcus and Marjorie Ardis (Olsen) S. BS, North Park Coll., 1970; MD, Loyola U., Maywood, Ill., 1973. Diplomate Am. Bd. Internal Medicine, Am. Bd. Cardiovascular Diseases. Surg. intern Resurrection Hosp., Chgo., 1974; resident in internal medicine Northwestern U., Chgo., 1974-77; cardiovascular disease fellow U. Ill., Chgo., 1977-80; dir. cardiac catherization lab. Cook County Hosp., Chgo., 1981; dir. heart sta. MacNeal Hosp., Berwyn, Ill., 1983; dir. electrophysiology Hines VA Hosp., Maywood, Ill., 1984-85; dir. progressive care Columbus Hosp., Chgo., 1985-88, pvt. practice, 1984—, Ill. Masonic Hosp., Chgo., 1989-96. Founder Physician Cons. for Evaluation of Clin. Pathways, Practice Parameters and Patient Care Outcomes, 1991—. Dir. continuous quality improvement Improvement Columbus, 1990-95; mem. presdl. ad hoc com. on prevention and treatment of domestic violence Chgo. Med. Soc., 1997—. Pillsbury fellow Pillsbury Fund, 1980. Fellow Am. Coll. Cardiology; mem. AMA, ACP, Chgo. Med. Assn., Ill. State Med. Assn., Am. Heart Assn. (coun. on clin. cardiology), Crescent Countries Found. for Med. Care, Physicians Health Network, Cen. Ill. Med. Rev. Orgn. Avocations: dance, acting, modeling, singing. Home and Office: 2650 N Lakeview Ave Apt 4109 Chicago IL 60614-1833

SCHACHT, JOCHEN HEINRICH, biochemistry educator; b. Königsberg, Fed. Republic Germany, July 2, 1939; arrived in U.S., 1969; s. Heinz and Else (Sprenger) S.; m. Helga Hildegard Seidel, Jan.27, 1967; children: Miriam Helga, Daniel Jochen. BS, U. Bonn, Fed. Republic Germany, 1962; MS in Chemistry, U. Heidelberg, Fed. Republic Germany, 1965, PhD in Biochemistry, 1968. Asst. research chemist, Mental Health Research Inst. U. Mich., Ann Arbor, 1969-72, from asst. prof. to assoc. prof. biochemistry, Dept. Biol. Chemistry & Otolaryngology, 1973-84, prof., 1984—, chmn. grad. program in physiol. acoustics, 1981—; hon. prof. Med. Acad. of the Chinese PLA, Beijing, 1998. Vis. prof. Karolinska Inst., Stockholm, 1979-80; acting dir. Kresge Hearing Rsch. Inst., U. Mich., 1983-84, assoc. dir., 1989-99, dir., 2000—; mem. hearing rsch. study sect. USPHS, NIH, Nat. Inst. Neurol. and Communicative Disorders and Stroke, 1986-89, Task Force Nat. Strategic Rsch. Plan, Nat. Insts. Deafness and Communication Disorders, USPHS, NIH; hon. prof. Hunan Med. U., Changsha, China, 1999—, Tonghi Med. U., Wuhan, China, 1999—; guest prof. Fourth Mil. Med. U., Xian, China, 1999—. Mem. editl. bd. Hearing Rsch., 1990—; assoc. editor Audiology & euro-Otol., 1995—; contbr. more than 200 articles to profl. jours., book chpts., revs.; co-editor Neurochemistry of Cholinergic Receptors, 1974. Fogarty Sr. Internat. fellow NIH, 1979, Sen. J. Javitz Neurosci. investigator, 1984; recipient Chercheur Etranger rsch. award INSERM, Paris, 1986, 94, Animal Welfare award Erna-Graff Found., Berlin, 1987, Disting. Faculty Achievement award U. Mich., 1989, Employer of Yr. award Nat. Capital Assoc. Coop. Edn. and Gallaudet U., Washington. Mem. Am. Soc. Neurochemistry, Internat. Soc. Neurochemistry, Soc. for Neurosci., Assn. for Rsch. in Otolaryngology, Am. Soc. Biol. Chemists, Assn. Espanola de Audiologia Exptl. Avocations: photography, travel, birding. Office: U Mich Kresge Hearing Rsch Inst Ann Arbor MI 48109-0506 Home Phone: 734-665-7101; Office Phone: 734-763-3572. Business E-Mail: schacht@umich.edu.

SCHACHT, RICHARD LAWRENCE, philosopher, educator; b. Racine, Wis., Dec. 19, 1941; s. Robert Hugo and Alice (Munger) S.; m. Judith Rowan; children: Eric Lawrence, Marshall Robert. BA, Harvard U., 1963; MA, Princeton U., 1965, PhD, 1967; postgrad, Tübingen U., Fed. Republic Germany, 1966-67. Asst. prof. U. Ill., Urbana-Champaign, 1967-71, assoc. prof., 1971-80, prof. philosophy, 1980—, Jubilee prof. of Liberal Arts and Scis., 1990—, chmn. dept., 1980-91, 2001—, interim dean Coll. Liberal Arts and Scis., 1994. Vis. prof. U. Oreg., 1969, U. Pitts., 1973, U. Mich., 1979; vis. scholar Tübingen U., 1975 Author: Alienation, 1970, Hegel and After, 1975, Nietzsche, 1983, Classical Modern Philosophers, 1984, The Future of Alienation, 1994, Making Sense of Nietzsche, 1995, (with Philip Kitcher) Finding An Ending, 2004; editor: Nietzsche Selections, 1993, Nietzsche, Genealogy, Morality, 1994, Internat. Nietzsche Studies. Mem. Am. Philos. Assn., N.Am. Nietzsche Soc. (exec. dir.), AAUP. Office: U Ill Dept Philosophy 105 Gregory 810 S Wright St Urbana IL 61801-3645 Office Phone: 217-333-2889. Business E-Mail: rschacht@uinc.edu.

SCHADE, STANLEY GREINERT, JR., hematologist, educator; b. Pitts., Dec. 21, 1933; s. Stanley G. and Charlotte (Marks) S.; m. Sylvia Zottu, Mar. 24, 1966; children: David Stanley, Robert Edward. BA in English, Hamilton Coll., 1955; MD, Yale U., 1961. Diplomate Am. Bd. Internal Medicine, Am. Bd. Hematology, Am. Bd. Oncology. Intern, resident, hematology fellow U. Wis., Madison, 1962-66; chief hematology Westside VA Hosp., Chgo., 1971-77; prof. medicine, chief hematology U. Ill., Chgo., 1978—97. Contbr. articles to profl. jour. Served to maj. US Army, 1967-69. Fulbright fellow Tubingen, Fed. Republic of Germany, 1956. Fellow Am. Coll. Physicians; mem. Am. Soc. Hematology. Presbyterian. Avocation: medical ethics. Home: 189 N Delaplaine Rd Riverside IL 60546-2060 Office: Westside VA Med Ctr Dept Medicine MP111 820 S Damen Ave Chicago IL 60612-3728

SCHAEFER, DAVID ARNOLD, lawyer; b. Cleve., May 3, 1948; s. Leonard and Maxine V. (Bassett) S.; m. Riki C. Freeman, Aug. 8, 1971; children: Kevin, Lindsey, Traci. BS, Miami U., Oxford, Ohio, 1970; MA, Northwestern U., 1971; JD, Case Western Res. U., 1974. Bar: Ohio 1974, U.S. Dist. Ct. (no. dist.) Ohio 1974, U.S. Ct. Appeals (6th cir.) 1978, U.S. Supreme Ct. 1978. Ptnr. Guren, Merritt et al, 1980-84, Menexch. Friedlander et al, Cleve., 1984-93, McCarthy, Lebit, Crystal & Haiman, Cleve., 1993—. Author: Deposition Strategy, 1981, 2d edit., 1984; contbr. articles to profl. publs. Mem. ABA, Internat. Assn. Def. Counsel, Fed. Bar Assn. (pres. 1992-93), Nat. Inst. Trail Advocacy (faculty), 8th Cir. Jud. Conf. (life). Office: McCarthy Lebit Crystal & Haiman 1800 Midland Bldg 101 W Prospect Ave Ste 1800 Cleveland OH 44115-1027

SCHAEFER, FRANK WILLIAM, III, microbiologist, researcher; b. Dayton, Ohio, Sept. 1, 1942; s. Frank William Jr. and Irene Josephine (Krouse) S. BA, Miami U., Oxford, Ohio, 1964; MS, U. Cin., 1970, PhD, 1973. Rsch. assoc. parasitologist U. Notre Dame, South Bend, Ind., 1973-78; U.S. EPA EPA, Cin., 1978—. Mem. ASTM, AAAS, Am. Soc. Parasitology, Am. Soc. Microbiology, Am. Water Works Assn., Soc. Protozoologists, Sigma Xi. Home: 9948 McCauley Woods Dr Sharonville OH 45241-1489 Office: US EPA 26 Martin Luther King Dr Cincinnati OH 45268 Office Phone: 513-569-7222. Personal E-mail: f.schaeferiii@att.net. Business E-Mail: schaefer.frank@epa.gov.

SCHAEFER, GEORGE A., JR., bank executive; b. Cincinnati, Ohio, 1945; BS Engineering, U.S. Mil. Acad., West Point, 1967; MBA, Xavier U., 1974. Joined as mgmt. trainee Fifth Third Bancorp, Cin., 1971, pres., 1990—2006, CEO, 1990—2007, chmn., 2006—. Bd. dirs. Fifth Third Bancorp, Fifth Third Bank, Anthem, Inc, Ashland, Inc, Greater Cin./N. Ky. Internat. Airport, Cin. Bus. Com. Chmn., bd. trustees U. Cin.; bd. dirs. Children's Hosp. Med. Ctr., Greater Cin. C. of C., Health Alliance Greater Cin. Served US Army, 1967—70, Europe and Vietnam. Recipient Bronze Star. Office: Fifth Third Bancorp Fifth Third Center 38 Fountain Square Plz Cincinnati OH 45263-0001

SCHAEFER, JOHN FREDERICK, lawyer; b. Detroit, Apr. 10, 1943; s. Gilbert Frederick and Mary Cathryn (Henderson) S.; m. Sharon Kathleen Chalmers, May 22, 1976; children: Kimberly Megan, Kelly Leigh, John Frederick, Charles Frederick. Student, U. Notre Dame, 1961-63; BA, Mich. State U., 1965, LLD, 1996; JD, Detroit Coll. Law, 1968. Bar: Mich. 1969. Ptnr. Buesser, Buesser, Snyder & Blank, Detroit, 1968-73, Williams, Schaefer, Ruby & Williams, Birmingham, Mich., 1973-89; propr. Law Firm of John F. Schaefer, Birmingham, 1989—. Adj. prof. domestic rels. Detroit Coll. Law, 1971—; instr. domestic rels. Mich. Jud. Inst., 1980-81; lectr. in field. Contbr. articles to legal jours. Trustee Detroit Coll. Law, Mich. State U., 1985—, William Beaumont Hosp., 2000; chair Detroit Coll. Law at Mich. State U. Found., 1995—; mem. ICLE Legal Edn. Inst. Fellow: Oakland Bar Found., Mich. State Bar Found. (jud. rev. com. 1997—), Am. Acad. Matrimonial Lawyers (pres. Mich. chpt. 1986—87), State Bar Mich. (family law com. 1972—73, com. on character and fitness 1972—75, coun. family law sect. 1974—, mem. fee arbitration grievance bd. 1976—, chmn. 1978—79); mem.: Oakland County Bar Assn. (mem. character and fitness com. 1973, family law com. 1973—, chmn. com. 1974—77, cir. ct. com. 1985—88, bd. dirs. 1995—, pres.), Detroit Bar Assn. (friend of ct. and domestic rels. com. 1972—, chmn. com. 1975—76, mem. pub. adv. com. 1976—), ABA (family law sect. 1969—, jud. rev. com. 1997—). Roman Catholic. Office: Law Firm of John F Schaefer Ste 320 380 N Old Woodward Ave Birmingham MI 48009-5347 Office Phone: 248-642-6655.

SCHAEFFER, ANDREW, lawyer; b. Cin., July 31, 1974; BA in Economics, Thomas More Coll., 1996, BA in Hist., 1996, AA in Pre-legal Studies, 1996; JD, U. Ky. Coll. of Law, 1999. Bar: Western Dist. Ky. 1999, Ky. 1999, US Dist. Ct. Eastern Dist. Ky. 2000. Atty. Geenebaum Doll & McDonald PLLC, Cin. Vol. firefighter Burlington Fire Protection Dist., 1990—2000, vice chair, 2002—; trustee Thomas More Coll., 1994—96, mem., Found. Bd. Exec. Com., 1999—; fundraiser United Way Ann. Campaign, 2001; mem., Adv. Com. Conrad and Gunpower Creek Park, 2001—02; fundraiser Muscular Dystrophy Assn., 2002; pres. LEGACY, 2003; co-chair Vision 2015. Named one of 40 Under 40, Cin. Bus. Courier, 2005, Ohio's Rising Stars, Super Lawyers, 2005, 2006. Mem.: Cin. Bar Assn., Northern Ky. Bar Assn., Ky. Bar Assn. (mem., Exec. Com. 2000—, chair, Young Lawyers Sect., mem., Ann. Conv. Planning and CLE Com. 2001—02), ABA (mem., The Young Lawyer Editl. Bd. 2001, vice-chair, Ethics & Professionalism Com. 2001, mem., Del. Credentials Com. 2002—, mem., Resolutions Com. 2002—, chair, Young Lawyers Divsn. Nat. Conf. Team 2004, mem., Leadership Adv. Bd. 2004—, prog. dir., Young Lawyers Divsn. Affiliate Outreach 2005—06). Office: Greenebaum Doll & McDonald PLLC RiverCenter I 50 E RiverCenter Blvd Ste 1800 Covington KY 41012-2673 Office Phone: 859-655-4200. Office Fax: 859-655-4239.

SCHAFER, MICHAEL FREDERICK, orthopedic surgeon; b. Peoria, Ill., Aug. 17, 1942; s. Harold Martin and Frances May (Ward) S.; m. Eileen M. Briggs, Jan. 8, 1966; children: Steven, Brian, Kathy, David, Daniel. BA, U. Iowa, 1964, MD, 1967. Diplomate Am. Bd. Orthopedic Surgery. Intern Chgo. Wesley Meml. Hosp., 1967-68; resident in orthop. surgery Cook County Program, Northwestern U., Chgo., 1968-72; asst. prof. orthop. surgery Northwestern U., 1977—; Reyerson prof. and chmn. dept. orthopedic surgery; asso. attending orthopedic surgeon Northwestern Meml. Hosp., 1974—. Adj. staff Children's Meml. Hosp., Chgo., 1974—; cons. VA Lakeside Hosp., 1974—; panelist Bur. Health Manpower, HEW, 1976; sec.-treas. Orthop. Rsch. and Edn. Found.; attending orthop. surgeon Northwestern Meml. Hosp., 1980—, exec. dir. Back and Neck Inst. Contbr. articles to profl. jours. Maj. U.S. Army, 1973-74. Fellow Am. Orthopaedic Assn., Am. Acad. Orthopaedic Surgeons; mem. AMA, Am. Orthopedic Soc. Sports Medicine, Ill. Med. Soc., Chgo. Med. Soc., Scoliosis Rsch. Soc. Roman Catholic. Home: 1815 Ridgewood Ln W Glenview IL 60025-2205 Office: Northwestern U Med School Ste 910 645 N Michigan Ave Chicago IL 60611-2876 Home Phone: 847-724-4228. Business E-Mail: m-schafer@northwestern.edu.

SCHAFER, SHARON MARIE, anesthesiologist; b. Detroit, Mar. 23, 1948; d. Charles Anthony and Dorothy Emma (Schweitzer) Pokriefka; m. Timothy John Schafer, Nov. 12, 1977; children: Patrick Christopher, Steven Michael. BS in Biology, Wayne State U., 1971, MD, 1975; MBA in Practice Mgmt., Madonna U., 2000. Diplomate Am. Bd. Anesthesiology. Intern, resident Sinai Hosp. Detroit, 1975-78; pvt. practice anesthesiology Troy, Mich., 1988—. Mem. AMA, Am. Soc. Anesthesiologists. Roman Catholic. Home and Office: 5741 Folkstone Dr Troy MI 48085-3154 Office Phone: 248-879-6246.

SCHAFFER, HENRY M., lawyer; b. Bklyn., Aug. 22, 1943; AB, Columbia U., 1964; MA, Wash. U., St. Louis, 1964; JD, U. Calif., Berkeley, 1973. Bar: Ill. 1973, Ohio (inactive) 1980, US Dist. Ct. No. Dist. Ill. 1974, US Dist. Ct. No. Dist. Ohio 1980, US Supreme Ct. 1980, US Ct. Appeals 8th Cir. 1985. Atty. Jenner & Block LLP, Chgo., 1973—77, Rothschild, Barry & Myers, Chgo., 1977—78, Cooper, Straub, Walinski & Cramer, Toledo, 1983—87; co-dir. civil law clinic U. Toledo, Ohio, 1979—83, Ohio, 1987—89; ptnr. Howe & Hutton, Ltd., Chgo., 1989—2003; of counsel Jenner & Block LLP, Chgo., 2003—. Office: Jenner & Block LLP 1 IBM Plz Chicago IL 60611-7603 Office Phone: 312-840-7673. Office Fax: 312-840-7773. Business E-Mail: hschaffer@jenner.com.

SCHAFFER, TIM, state representative; b. Columbus, Ohio, Jan. 25, 1963; married. BA in Polit. Sci. and Comm., Mount Union Coll. Exec. dir. Ohio Soc. Profl. Engrs., Columbus; state rep. dist. 5 Ohio Ho. of Reps., Columbus, 2000—, chair, homeland security engring. and archtl. design com., mem. commerce and labor, econ. devel. and tech., and ways and means coms. Pres. Fairfield Ctr. for Disabilities and Cerebral Palsy, 1996—98; chair Fairfield County Rep. Party Exec. Com., Fairfield County Rep. Party, 1996—. Named Advocate of Yr., Trustee of Yr., Nat. Multiple Sclerosis Soc., Advocate of Yr., Nat. Vol. Health Agys. of Ohio, Lewis Urling Party; named one of 40 under 40, Bus. First-Columbus; recipient Lifetime Svc. award, Fairfield Ctr. Disabilities and Cerebral Palsy. Mem.: Ohio Soc. Assn. Execs. (Outstanding Membership Campaign award), Ohio Rural Devel. Partnership (steering com.), Lancaster-Fairfield County C. of C., Ohio C. of C., Ohio League Young Rep. Clubs (vice chair 1991), Fairfield County Young Rep. Club (pres. 1990—92), Fairfield County Lincoln Rep. Club (pres. 1993—95). Republican. Office: 77 S High St 11th fl Columbus OH 43215-6111

SCHAIBLEY, ANN M., lawyer; b. St. Cloud, Minn. BA in Politics, Cornell Coll., Mt. Vernon, Iowa, 1994; JD, Hamline U. Sch. Law, St. Paul, 1997. Bar: Minn. 1997. Law clk. to Hon. Mary L. Davidson Hennepin County Dist. Ct., Family Ct. Divsn., 1997—99; assoc. pvt. practice, 1999—2002; ptnr. Schaibley & Vicchiollo, L.L.C., Edina, Minn., 2001—. Named a Rising Star, Minn. Super Lawyers mag., 2006. Mem.: Internat. Acad. Collaborative Profls., Collaborative Law Inst. Minn. (bd. dirs. 2004—), ABA, Minn. State Bar Assn., Ramsey County Bar Assn. (mem. family law sect.). Office: Schaibley & Vicchiollo LLC Edinborough Corp Ctr 3300 Edinborough Way Ste 550 Edina MN 55435 Office Phone: 612-333-0803. E-mail: ann@mnlaw.us.

SCHAKOWSKY, JANICE, congresswoman; b. Chgo., May 26, 1944; d. Irwin and Tillie (Cosnow) Danoff; m. Harvey E. Schakowsky, Feb. 17, 1965 (div. 1980); children: Ian, Mary; m. Robert B. Creamer, Dec. 6, 1980; 1 stepchild, Lauren. BS, U. Ill., 1965. Cert. elem. tchr., Ill. Tchr. Chgo. Bd. Edn., 1965-67; organizer Ill. Pub. Action Coun., Chgo., 1976-85; exec. dir. Ill. State Coun. Sr. Citizens, Chgo., 1985-90; mem. Ill. Ho. Reps., 1990-98, US Congress from 9th Ill. dist., 1999—; mem. banking and fin. svcs. com., 1999—2000; mem. govt. reform com., 1999—2000; Ho. Dem. leadership team-deputy whip; mem. energy and commerce Com. Bd. dirs. Ill. Pub. Action, 4 C's Day Care Coun., Evanston, Ill.; steering com. mem. Cook County Dem. Women, 1986-90; del. Nat. Dem. Conv., 1988; governing coun. Am. Jewish Congress, 1990—. Named Outstanding Legislator Interfaith Coun. for Homeless, 1993, Legislator of Yr. Ill. Nurses Assn., 1992, Ill. Assn. Cmty. Mental Health Agys., 1994, Coalition of Citizens with Disabilities and Ill. Coun. Sr. Citizens, 1993, Cmty. Action Assn., 1991, Champaign County Health Care Assn., 1992, Rookie of Yr. Ill. Environ. Coun., 1991. Mem. ACLU, NOW, Nat. Coun. Jewish Women, Ill. Pro-Choice Alliance, Evanston Mental Health Assn., Evanston Hist. Soc., Evanston Friends of Libr., Rogers Park Hist. Soc. Democrat. Jewish. Avocations: travel, horsebackriding, reading. Office: US Ho Reps 1027 Longworth Ho Office Bldg Washington DC 20515-1309 also: Dist Office 5533 Broadway St Chicago IL 60640 Office Phone: 202-225-2111.

SCHALLENKAMP, KAY, academic administrator; b. Salem, SD, Dec. 9, 1949; d. Arnold B. and Jennie M. (Koch) Krier; m. Ken Schallenkamp, Sept. 7, 1970; children: Heather, Jenni. BS, No. State Coll., 1972; MA, U. S.D., 1973; PhD, U. Colo., 1982. Prof. No. State Coll., Aberdeen, S.D., 1973-88, dept. chair, 1982-84, dean, 1984-88; provost Chadron (Nebr.) State Coll., 1988-92, U. Wis., Whitewater, 1992-97; pres. Emporia (Kans.) State U., 1997—. Cons. North Ctrl. Assn., nursing homes, hosps. and ednl. instns. Contbr. articles to profl. jours. Commr. North Ctrl. Assn., 1995-99. Bush fellow, 1980; named Outstanding Young Career Woman, Bus. and Profl. Women's Club, 1976. Mem. NCAA (pres.'s coun. 2000—), Kans. C. of C. (bd. dirs. 2000—), Am. Speech and Hearing Assn. (cert.), Rotary. Avocation: martial arts. Office: Emporia State U 1200 Commercial St Emporia KS 66801-5087 E-mail: schallka@emporia.edu.

SCHANFARBER, RICHARD CARL, real estate broker; b. Cleve., June 11, 1937; s. Edwin David and Helen (Newman) S.; m. Barbara A. Berger, Dec. 21, 1958 (div. Sept. 1981); children: Edwin Jeffrey, Lori Jo, Tammy Joy. Grad., NYU, 1959. Lic. FCC broadcast engr. Pres. Erieview Realty, Gates Mills, 1961—, Miller Warehouse, Gates Mills, 1968—2001, ERI Travel Co., Gates Mills, 1974—2001, ERI Sales Co., Gates Mills, 1979—, Eastgate Travel Svcs., Gates Mills, Ohio, 1987—2001. Pres. Shaker Hts. (Ohio) Alumni Assn., 1986-97, chmn. bd., 1997-; pres. Cleve. Area Bd. Realtors, 1981, Cleve. Warehouseman Assn., 1977-79; chmn. City of Cleve. Landmarks Commn., 1983-2002. Mem. NRA (life), Nat. Assn. Realtors, Ohio Assn. Realtors, Cleve. Area Bd. Realtors. Avocation: real estate. Home: 6719 Sandalwood Dr Gates Mills OH 44040-9619 Office Phone: 440-442-3222. Personal E-mail: singhon@yahoo.com. Business E-Mail: richard@eri-group.com.

SCHANWALD, STEVE, professional sports team executive; Grad., U. Md., 1977. Dir. sports mktg. USAF Acad., 1978; dir. promotions Pitts. Pirates, 1979—80; asst. v.p. mktg. Chgo. White Sox, 1981—86; exec. v.p. bus. ops. Chgo. Bulls, 1987—; sr. v.p. mktg. United Ctr., Chgo. Guest lectr. U. Chgo. Bus. Sch., Northwestern Kellogg Grad. Sch. Bus., U. Notre Dame Bus. Sch., Am. Mktg. Assn. Founder, pres. CharitaBulls; bd. mem. James Jordan Boys and Girls Club. Recipient local Emmy award. Mem.: Chgo. Econ. Club. Office: Chgo Bulls United Ctr 1901 W Madison St Chicago IL 60612-2459

SCHAR, STEPHEN L., lawyer; b. Chgo., Oct. 19, 1945; s. Sidney and Lillian (Lieberman) Schar; m. Jessica S. Feit, Aug. 17, 1980; children: Scott Andrew, Elizabeth Loren. BA, U. Chgo., 1967; JD, DePaul U., 1970. Bar: Ill. 1970, U.S. Dist. Ct. (no. dist.) Ill. 1970. Assoc. Aaron, Aaron, Schimberg & Hess, Chgo., 1970-77, ptnr., 1977-80, Aaron, Schimberg, Hess, Rusnak, Deutsch & Gilbert, Chgo., 1980-84, Aaron, Schimberg, Hess & Gilbert, Chgo., 1984, Aaron, Schimberg & Hess, Chgo., 1984, D'Ancona & Pflaum, Chgo., 1985-98; mem. D'Ancona & Pflaum LLC, Chgo., 1999—2003; ptnr. Seyfarth Shaw LLP, Chgo., 2003—. Instr. estate planning Loyola U., Chgo., 1978—79. Bd. dirs. Jewish Children's Bur. Chgo., 1982—2001, pres., 1996—98, hon. dir., 2001—; pres. Faulkner Condominium Assn., Chgo., 1980—82, Carl Sandburg Village Homeowners Assn., Chgo., 1981—82. Mem.: Chgo. Estate Planning Coun., Chgo. Bar Assn. (pres. probate practice divsn. III 1979), Ill. Bar Assn. Home: 2155 Tanglewood Ct Highland Park IL 60035-4231 Office Phone: 312-781-8649. Personal E-mail: sschar@seyfarth.com.

SCHARF, CHARLES W., bank executive; married; two children. B, Johns Hopkins U., 1987; MBA, N.Y. U. With Comml. Credit Corp., 1987-95; various sr. positions to CFO Smith Barney, 1995-98; CFO global corp. & investment bank Citibank, 1998-2000; exec. v.p., CFO Bank One Corp., Chgo., 2000—02, head retail banking, 2002—04; CEO retail fin. services JPMorgan Chase, NYC, 2004—. Office: JPMorgan Chase 270 Park Ave New York NY 10017

SCHARF, STEPHANIE A., lawyer; m. Jeffry Mandell; children: Meredith, Jonathan. BA, Rutgers U.; MA, Stanford U.; PhD, U. Chgo., 1978, JD, 1985. Bar: Ill. 1985, US Dist. Ct. (no., ctrl. and so. dists.) Ill., US Dist. Ct. (no. dist.) Ind., US Dist. Ct. (we. dist.) Mich., US Ct. Appeals (first cir.). Sr. study dir. at. Opinion Rsch. Ctr., Chgo.; ptnr. Schoeman Updike Kaufman & Scharf, Chgo. Author: Consumer Fraud Litigation: Law and Defenses in Illinois, 2004, The Business of Drug Development, 2004, Direct-to-Consumer Advertising of Prescription Pharmaceuticals and Medical Devices, 2004, Through the Glass Ceiling: Best Practices for Women Lawyers and Their Firms, 2004, Benchmarking for Success: Introducing NAWL Assessment Questionnaire, 2004, A Business Approach to Minimizing Product Liability Litigation, 2005, New Rulings In Drug Cases Highlight Debate Over Pre-emption, 2006, Punitive Damages in Supreme Court: How Much is Too Much?, 2007, Foreign Plaintiff's Battle to Keep Class Claims in U.S. Courts, 2007; co-author: The Media and Products Litigation, 1996, Communications Specialists Help With Damage Control, 1997, Marketing Pharmaceutical Products on the Internet: Managing Risks and Limiting Liabilities in the World of E-Commerce, 2001, Post-Sale Duties to Warn, Recall, and Retrofit Defective Products in Illinois, 2003, The Evidentiary Impact of Regulatory Action on Product Litigation in the United States, 2004, Immigration Reform and the Federal Law of Employment Discrimination;: FDA's Comments Herald New Strength for Preemption Defense in Drug Product Litigation, 2006, Foreign Plaintiffs Battle to Keep Class Claims in U.S. Courts, 2007; editor: The Use of Epidemiology in Tort Litigation: A Survey of Federal and State Jurisdictions, 2003; co-editor: The Use of Toxicology in Tort Litigation, 2005; contbr. articles to profl. jours. Bd. mem. The

Youth Campus, Chgo.; chair, Best Interest of the Child Subcommittee Cir. Ct. Cook County, mem. Chief judge's Pub. Guardian Com. Harper Fellow, Univ. Chgo. Mem.: ABA (co-editor Product Liability newsletter 1997—2000, editor Mass Torts newsletter 2001, co-chair sect. litig. products liability com. 2005—, mem. mass torts com., bd. dirs., mem. spl. com. bioethics), Internat. Assn. Def. Counsel, Spl. Com. Bioethics, Pub. Guardian Com., Best Interest of Child Subcom. of Child Protection Adv. Com. (chair 1995—96), Circuit Ct. Cook County, Def. Rsch. Inst., Ill. Bar Found. (bd. mem. 2005—), Univ. Chgo. Women's Bus. Group, Products Liability Adv. Coun. (mem. case selection com.), Nat. Assn. Women Lawyers (pres. 2004—05, chair, Survey of Retention and Promotion of Women in Law Firms 2006—07, chair, com. for evaluation of Supreme Ct. nominees, bd. dirs. 2000—), U. Chgo. Women's Bus. Group. Office: Schoeman Updike Kaufman Scharf 333 W Wacker Dr Ste 300 Chicago IL 60606 Office Phone: 312-726-6000. Business E-Mail: sscharf@schoeman.com.

SCHARFFE, WILLIAM GRANVILLE, academic administrator, educator; b. Saginaw, Mich., Mar. 12, 1942; s. William Edward and Marion Kittie (Granville) S.; m. Mary Jo Whitfield, Sept. 4, 1965; children: Sue L., William W. BA, Mich. State U., 1965, MA, 1969, PhD, 1977. Tchr. English Webber Jr. High Sch., Saginaw, 1965-66; tchr. speech Arthur Hill High Sch., Saginaw, 1966-68; staff asst. for pers. Saginaw City Schs., 1968-73, dir. pers., 1977-94, dir. employee devel. and media ops., 1994-99; prin. Zilwaukee Jr. High Sch., Saginaw, 1973-74; asst. prin. North Intermediate Sch., Saginaw, 1974-75, 1975-77; dir. policy svcs. Mich. Assn. Sch. Bds., Lansing, 1999—. Adj. asst. prof. Mich. State U., East Lansing, 1977; adj. lectr. Ctrl. Mich. U., Mt. Pleasant, 1987, Mich. State U., 1977, Saginaw Valley State U., 1991; cons. in field. Author: Elfred Alanzo & Santa's Surprise, 1987. Bd. dirs. Japanese Cultural Ctr. and Tea House, Saginaw, 1986-97, pres., 1993-95. Recipient Key Man award United Way Saginaw County, 1978, Outstanding Svc. award, 1978. Mem.: Am. Assn. State Policy Svcs. (pres. 2004—05), Soc. For Human Resource Mgmt., Mich. Mid. Cities Pers. and Labor Rels. Task Force (pres. 1980—82), Mich. Assn. Sch. Pers. Assn. (sec., bd. dirs. 1988—90, pres., bd. dirs. 1992—93), Mich. State U. Alumni Club (pres. Saginaw County chpt. 2002—04), Saginaw Club (pres. 1996—97), Exch. Club (Saginaw chpt. pres. 1981), Phi Delta Kappa. Republican. Episcopalian. Avocations: writing, golf, photography, public speaking. Home: 2812 Adams Blvd Saginaw MI 48602-3103 Office Phone: 517-327-5928. Personal E-mail: drbills@charter.net. Business E-Mail: bscharffe@masb.org.

SCHARP-RADOVIC, CAROL ANN, choreographer, classical ballet educator; b. Ypsilanti, Mich., Aug. 9, 1940; d. John Lewis and Mary Vivien (Alther) Keeney; m. Jack Laurel Scharp, July 28, 1958 (div. July 1970); children: Kathryn E., Mark A.; m. Srecko Radovic, Nov. 15, 1989. Studied with Pereslavic, Danilova; student, Harkness Ballet, NYC, Joffrey Ballet, Eglevsky Ballet, Briansky Ballet, Darvesh Ballet, NYC; studied with Jurgen Schneider, Am. Ballet Theatre, 1983-93; studied with Janina Cunova, Luba Gulyeava, Australian & Kirov ballet cos., 1983-93; studied with Ninel Kurgapkina, Ludmila Synelnikova, Genhrich Mayorov, Kirov Ballet, 1987-89; studied with Ludmila Sakharova, Perm Ballet, 1993; studied with Ludmila Synelnikova, Bolshoi Ballet Sch., Moscow, 1989; studied with Inna Zubkhovskaya, Alex. Stiopin, Lydia Goncharova, Valentina Chistova and Mararita Zagurskaya, Vaganova Ballet Acad., St. Petersburg, Russia, 1993, studied with Mdm. Trafimova, Nina Sakhrouskaya and Valentina Rumyantsema, 1993. Ballet mistress Adrian (Mich.) Coll., 1982-84; founder, artistic dir. Ann Arbor (Mich.) Ballet Theatre, 1980—. Former regional field judge Nat. Ballet Achievement Fund; dir. seminars Marygrove Coll., Detroit. Choreographer Cinderella, 1980, Nightingale, 1980, Nutcracker, 1984, Carnival of the Animals, 1981, Carmen, 1983, Midsummer Nights Dream, 1982, Vivaldi's Spring, 1990, Opulence, 1984, La Boutique Fantasque, 1995, Handel's Alcina, 1985, Gymnopedie, 1985, Gershwin's Preludes, 1996, Ravel's Bolero, 1997, Dracula, 1997, others. Ruth Mott grantee for choreography, 1982. Mem. Mich. Dance Assn. Avocations: gardening, reading, writing. Home: 6476 Huron River Dr Dexter MI 48130-9796 Office: CAS Ballet Theatre Sch Ann Arbor Ballet Theatre 548 Church St Ann Arbor MI 48104-2563

SCHATZ, BRETT A., lawyer; b. Cin., Aug. 9, 1972; BSME, U. Cin., 1995; JD, Salmon P. Chase Coll. Law, 2000. Bar: Ohio 2000, Ky. 2000, Ind. 2000, US Dist. Ct. Southern Dist. Ohio, US Dist. Ct. Eastern Dist. Ky., US Dist. Ct. Western Dist. Ky. Adj. prof. Salmon P. Chase Coll. Law, 2000—; assoc. Wood, Herron & Evans, L.L.P., Cin. Named one of Ohio's Rising Stars, Super Lawyers, 2006. Mem.: Am. Intellectual Property Law Assn., Ohio State Bar Assn., Cin. Bar Assn. Office: Wood Herron & Evans LLP 2700 Carew Tower Cincinnati OH 45202 Office Phone: 513-241-2324. Office Fax: 513-241-6234.

SCHAUB, PAUL B., lawyer; b. Waseca, Minn., Jan. 11, 1965; s. Frank Joseph and Marjory Ann (Kean) S. BA, Creighton U., Omaha, 1987, JD, 1991. Bar: Nebr. 1992, U.S. Dist. Ct. Nebr. 1992. Assoc. Peetz, Sonntag & Goodwin, P.C., Sidney, Nebr., 1992-95; county atty. Cheyenne County, Nebr., 1995—. Mem. ABA, Cheyenne County Lawyers Assn., Nebr. State Bar Assn., Assn. Trial Attys. Republican. Office: Office Cheyenne County Atty PO Box 217 Sidney NE 69162-0217 Home: 1932 Maple St Sidney NE 69162-1836 Office Phone: 308-254-6060.

SCHEETZ, SISTER MARY JOELLEN, English language educator; b. Lafayette, Ind., May 20, 1926; d. Joseph Albert and Ellen Isabelle (Fitzgerald) S. AB, St. Francis Coll., 1956; MA, U. Notre Dame, 1964; PhD, U. Mich., 1970. Tchr. English, Bishop Luers High Sch., Fort Wayne, Ind., 1965-67; acad. dean St. Francis Coll. (now U. St. Francis), Fort Wayne, 1967-68, pres. Ft. Wayne, Ind., 1970-93, pres. emeritus, English lang. prof. Ft. Wayne, Ind., 1993—. Mem.: Delta Epsilon Sigma. Office: U St Francis 2701 Spring St Fort Wayne IN 46808-3939 Office Phone: 260-434-3229. Business E-Mail: jscheetz@sf.edu.

SCHEEVEL, KENRIC JAMES, state legislator; b. July 7, 1956; m. Karen Dornink. BA, Northwestern Coll., 1978; BSME, S.D. State U., 1981. Mem. Minn. Senate from 31st dist., St. Paul, 1994—. Address: RR 2 Box 227 Preston MN 55965-9570

SCHEFDORE, RONALD L., dentist; BS in Biology with honors, Southern Ill. U., 1979, DMD, 1983; Implant Cert., Northwestern U., 1985. Pvt. practice, Westmont, Ill. Author & lectr. Dentist Worldwide, 2001—. Author: Better Service Better Dentistry, 2003. Mem.: ADA, Am. Acad. Cosmetic Dentistry, Ill. Dental Assn., Chgo. Dental Soc. Office: 345 West Ogden Ave Westmont IL 60559 Office Phone: 630-971-0682. Office Fax: 630-971-0072. Business E-Mail: celebritysmiles@aol.com.

SCHEIBER, STEPHEN CARL, psychiatrist; b. NYC, May 2, 1938; s. Irving Martin and Frieda Olga (Schor) S.; m. Mary Ann McDonnell, Sept. 14, 1965; children: Lisa Susan, Martin Irving, Laura Ann. BA, Columbia Coll., 1960; MD, SUNY, Buffalo, 1964. Diplomate Am. Bd. Psychiatry and Neurology. Intern Mary Fletcher Hosp., Burlington, Vt., 1964-65; resident in psychiatry Strong Meml. Hosp., Rochester, NY, 1967-70; asst. prof. U. Ariz., Tucson, 1970-76, assoc. prof., 1976-81, prof., 1981-86; exec. sec. Am. Bd. Psychiatry and Neurology, Inc., Deerfield, Ill., 1986-89, exec. v.p., 1989—2006. Adj. prof. psychiatry Northwestern U., Chgo., 1986—, Med. Coll. Wis., Milw., 1986-2006, clin. prof. psychiatry, 2006—. Co-editor: The Impaired Physician, 1983, Certification, Recertification and Lifetime Learning in Psychiatry, 1994, Core Competencies for Psychiatric Practice, 2003, Core Competencies for Neurologists, 2003; contbr. articles to profl. jours. Mem. med. adv. com. Casas de los Ninos, Tucson, 1974-86; mem. mental health adv. com. Tucson Health Planning Coun., 1974-75; med. student interviewer Office of Med. Edn., 1975; mem. Glenbrook (Ill.) North H.S. Boosters Club, 1988-91; treas. Robert E. Jones Found., 1988-96. Surgeon USPHS, 1965-67. Recipient Outstanding Tchr. award, U. Ariz., 1986, Disting. Life and Career Achievement award, SUNY, Buffalo Med. Alumni Assn., 1998; grantee Group Therapy Outcome Studies on Inpatient Svc., 1980, Dialysis and Schizophrenia Pilot Project, NIH, 1978. Fellow: Am. Assn. Dirs. Psychiat. Residency Tng. (pres. 1981—82), Am. Coll. Psychiatrists (bd. regents 1992—2001, treas. 1995—2001, Disting. Svc. award 2007), Group for Advancement of Psychiatry (life; invited mem., chmn. mem. edn. com. 1987—91, bd. dirs., sec. 1993—97, pres.-elect 1997—99, pres. 1999—2001), Am. Psychiat. Assn. (life; chmn. impaired physician com. 1985—88, cons. 1988—92, Disting. Life Fellow 2002, Vestermark award 2007), Assn. Acad. Psychiatry (life; parliamentary sec. 1979—84, treas. 1984—88, pres.-elect 1988—89, pres. 1989—90, Lifetime Educator award 2002, Disting. Life Fellow 2006); mem.: Am. Bd. Med. Specialties (Disting. Svc. award 2007), Benjamin Rush Soc. (sec. treas. 2004—06, v.p. 2006—08, pres. 2008—), Oracle Heights Club (pres. 1983—84). Democrat. Jewish.

SCHEID, LINDA J., state legislator; b. June 16, 1942; 2 children. BA, Coe Coll.; JD, William Mitchell Coll. Law. Bar: Minn. Mem. Minn. Ho. of Reps., 1976, 82-90; mem. 47th dist. Minn. Senate, St. Paul, 1996—. Home: 6625 81st Ave N Brooklyn Park MN 55445-2513 Office: 317 Capitol 75 Constitution Ave Saint Paul MN 55155-1601

SCHEIDT, W. ROBERT, chemistry educator, researcher; b. Richmond Heights, Mo., Nov. 13, 1942; s. Walter Martin and Martha (Videtich) S.; m. Kathryn Sue Barnes, Aug. 9, 1964; children: Karl Andrew, David Martin. BS, U. Mo., 1964; MS, U. Mich., 1965, PhD, 1968; postdoctoral studies, Cornell U., 1970. Asst. prof. U. otre Dame, Ind., 1970-76, assoc. prof., 1976-80, prof., 1980—, William K. Warren prof., 1999—. Vis. prof. U. Wash., Seattle, 1980, U. Paris (Orsay), Paris, 1991, U. René Descartes, 2005, 06, U. Strasbourg, France, 1998; mem. rev. sec. Metallobiochemistry NIH, Bethesda, 1991—96. Contbr. articles to profl. jours. Fellow AAAS; mem. Am. Chem. Soc. (assoc. editor Chem. Revs. jour. 1980-85), Am. Crystallographic Assn., Biophys. Soc., Sigma X. Democrat. Office: U Notre Dame Dept Chemistry Notre Dame IN 46556 Business E-Mail: scheidt.1@nd.edu.

SCHEINFELD, JAMES DAVID, retired travel company executive; b. Milw., Nov. 11, 1926; s. Aaron and Sylvia (Rosenberg) S.; children from previous marriage: John Stephen, Shaina, Robert Alan; m. Elna Magnusson, 1994. BA in Econs. magna cum laude, U. Wis., 1949. With Manpower, Inc., 1948-78, salesman, Chgo., 1949-51, br. mgr., 1951-53, nat. sales mgr., Milw., 1953-56, dir. sales, corp. sec., 1956-59, v.p. sales, 1959-62, exec. v.p. mktg., 1962-65, exec. v.p. (sr.), chief ops. officer, 1965-76, v.p. spl. projects, 1976-78, mem. exec. com., bd. dirs., 1959-76, cons., 1978-84; exec. v.p., chief exec. officer, bd. dirs. Transpersonal, Inc., Any Task Inc., Manpower Argentina, Manpower Europe, Manpower Ltd. (U.K.), Manpower Australia, Manpower Japan, Manpower Germany GmbH, Manpower Norway, Manpower Denmark, Manpower Venezuela, 1966-76; pres. Travway Internat. Inc. -Funway Holidays, Funjet, 1976-81, Aide Svcs., Inc., Tampa, Fla., 1976-81; pres., chief exec. officer Travelpower Inc., 1976-84; sr. v.p. Carlson Travel Network, 1984—2004. Mem. Hickory Travel Systems Inc., 1977-85, bd. dirs., 1978-85, pres., 1980-82, pres. emeritus, 1982—. Contbr. articles to profl. jours. Chmn. Cancer Crusade Milwaukee County, 1970; bd. dirs. Sinai-Samaritan Med. Ctr., Better Bus. Bur. Milw., 1979-90, Found. for Santa Barbara City Coll., 1989—, pres., 1996-2000; trustee U. Wis. Milw. Found., 1981-91, emeritus trustee, 1991—; mem. bus. adv. bd. U. Wis.-Milw., 1987—; chmn. bus. adv. bd. Santa Barbara City Coll., 1988-92; dir. Santa Barbara Trust for Hist. Preservation, 1995—, v.p., 1998-2004, pres. 2004-06; mem. Greater Milw. Com., 1984-97; bd. dirs. Sansum Clinic, 1989—, chmn., 2005-07. With USNR, 1944—46. Pacific Theatre. Decorated Pacific Theatre Ribbon with 1 Star. Mem. Nat. Assn. Temporary Svcs. (bd. dirs. 1969-77, pres. 1975-76), La Cumbre Country Club (Santa Barbara), Rotary Club of Montecito Calif. Home and Office: 129 Rametto Rd Santa Barbara CA 93108-2317 Office Phone: 805-969-5671. Personal E-mail: jimscheinfeld1@cox.net.

SCHELLEN, NANDO, opera director; b. The Hague, The Netherlands, Oct. 11, 1934; came to U.S., 1993; m. Deborah Raymond, June 19, 1991; 4 children. Mng. dir. etherlands Opera, 1969-79, assoc. gen. dir., 1979-87; gen. artistic dir. Sweelinck Conservatory of Music, Amsterdam, 1990-93; gen. dir. Indpls. Opera, 1993-96; dir. opera theatre No. Ariz. U., Flagstaff, 2000—. Freelance stage dir., 1982—. Home: 3841 Woodride E Way Flagstaff AZ 86004

SCHENDEL, DAN ELDON, management consultant, finance educator; b. Norwalk, Wis., Mar. 29, 1934; s. Leonard A. and Marian T. (Koch) S.; m. Mary Lou Sigler, Sept. 1, 1956; children: Suzanne, Pamela, Sharon. BS in Metall. Engring., U. Wis., 1956; MBA, Ohio State U., 1959; PhD (Ford Found. fellow), Stanford U., 1963. With ALCOA, 1956, U.S. Civil Svc., 1959-60, SRI, 1963-65; prof. mgmt., dir. exec. edn. programs Purdue U., Lafayette, Ind., 1965-85, Blake Family endowed chair emeritus in strategic mgmt.; vis. prof. U. Mich., 1988-89, U. Chgo., 1990-91, 1999—2004. Former dean German Grad. Internat. Sch. Mgmt. and Adminstrn., Hannover, Germany, 1999-2005; pres. Strategic Mgmt. Assocs., Inc. Author: (with others) Strategy Formulation: Analytical Concepts, 1978, Divided Loyalties, 1980, Fundamental Issues in Strategy, 1994; editor: (with others) Strategic Management: A New View of Business Policy and Planning, 1979; founding and cons. editor Strategic Mgmt. Jour., 1980-2007; founding editor Strategic Entrepreneurship Jour., 2006—. With USAF, 1956—59. Fellow Acad. Mgmt., Strategic Mgmt. Soc. (founding pres., treas.); mem. Univ. Club Chgo. Home: 1327 N Grant St West Lafayette IN 47906-2463 Office: Krannert Grad Sch Mgmt Purdue U West Lafayette IN 47907 Office Phone: 765-494-4386. Business E-Mail: schendel@purdue.edu.

SCHENKENBERG, MARY MARTIN, principal; b. Oakland, Calif., Nov. 29, 1944; d. Leo Patrick and Florence Kathryn (Brinkoetter) Martin; m. Philip Rawson Schenkenberg III, Aug. 20, 1966; children: Philip Rawson IV, Amy Lynn, Stephen Patrick. BA in English, Fontbonne Coll., 1966; MA Teaching in English, St. Louis U., 1975, PhD in English, 1991. Cert. tchr., Mo. Asst. prof. Fontbonne Coll., St. Louis, 1978-85; English dept. chair Nerinx Hall High Sch., St. Louis, 1979-89; asst. prof. Webster U., St. Louis, 1986-89; co-prin. Nerinx Hall High Sch., St. Louis, 1989-92, prin., 1992—. Adj. prof. St. Louis U., 1985-89; advanced placement reader Ednl. Testing Svc., Princeton, N.J., 1986-89. Author: (with others) The English Classroom in the Computer Age, 1991. Bd. pres. Mary, Queen of Peace Sch., St. Louis, 1977. Mem. ASCD, Nat. Coun. Tchrs. English, Greater St. Louis Tchrs. English (bd. dirs. 1989—). Roman Catholic. Avocations: tennis, theater, travel. Office: Nerinx Hall High Sch 530 E Lockwood Ave Webster Groves MO 63119-3278

SCHEPMAN, STEVEN F., bank executive; BS in Bus. Admin., U. Va. CPA Calif., 1998. Cons. Price Waterhouse LLP, 1996—97; various positions fin. services audit practice KPMG LLP, San Francisco, 1997—99; sr. mgmt. positions First Banks, Inc., St. Louis, 1999—2000, sr. v.p. private banking, wealth mgmt., trust services First Bank, 2000—05, also dir. sub. First Bank, 2001—04, dir., 2004—, sr. v.p., CFO, 2005—. Office: First Banks Inc 135 N Meramec Ave Clayton MO 63105

SCHEPP, RICHARD D., lawyer, retail executive; b. July 1960; m. Beth Schepp. BBA, U. Wis., Eau Claire; JD, U. Wis. Atty. Quarles & Brady, Milw.; dir. legal affairs, asst. corp. sec. Shopko Stores, Inc., 1992—96, v.p. legal affairs, corp. sec., 1996—98, sr. v.p., gen. counsel, 1998—2000; sr. v.p. Kohl's Corp., 2000—01, gen. counsel, sec., 2000—, exec. v.p., 2001—. Office: Kohls Corp N56 W17000 Ridgewood Dr Menomonee Falls WI 53051-5660 Office Phone: 262-703-7000.

SCHERB, JEFF R., publishing executive; BA in Bus. Adminstrn., Computer Sci., Rutgers U. Mgmt. positions Commodore Internat. Ltd, Cullinet Software Inc.; v.p. systems devel. Turner Broadcasting; chief tech. officer, sr. v.p. R & D Dun & Bradstreet Software; sr. v.p., chief tech. officer Tribune Co., Chgo., 1999—. Office: Tribune Co 435 N Michigan Ave Chicago IL 60611-4066

SCHERER, ANITA (ANITA STOCK), gerontologist, marketing consultant; b. Sept. 20, 1938; d. William John Stock and Gertrud Clara (Kaufmann) Bacher; m. Richard Phillip Scherer, ov. 25, 1961; children: William Richard, Christopher Howard. Student, U. Cin., 1956-57; AB, Jones Bus. Coll., 1958; BA, Coll. Mount St. Joseph, 1999. Acct. sec. Northlich, Stolley Inc., Cin., 1978-79, acct. asst., 1979-80, asst. acct. mgr., 1980-81, acct. mgr., 1981-84, mktg. svc. assoc., 1984-89, mgr., 1989-97. Lectr. local schs. and us., Cin. 1980-93; adv. bd. mem. performing arts Coll. Mount St. Joseph, Ohio, 1974-80; mktg. cons. for the over 50 market; trustee Arts and Humanities Resource Ctr. for Older Adults, 1990-2004, chmn. bd., 1991-93. Co-editor: monthly newsletter Badge, 1967-72; designer assorted notepads, 1986. Corr. sec. Delhi Police Assn. Inc., Ohio, 1967—72; pres. Delhi Hills Cmty. Coun., Ohio, 1974—75; v.p. adminstr. Stagecrafters, Cin., 1983—85, publicity chmn., 1984—89; mktg. bd. mem. Contemp. Arts Ctr., 1985—97; chmn. Advt./Graphic Arts div. Fine Arts Fund Campaign, 1988; docent Cin. Art Mus., 2002—; Lector Our Lady of Victory Roman Cath. Ch., Cin., 1972—. Winner nat. competition Am. Assn. Advt. Agys., 1980; recipient Outstanding Performance award Assn. Cmty. Theatres, Cin., 1983, Excellence in Acting award Ohio Cmty. Theatres Assn., 1984, Outstanding Achievement Gerontological Studies, Coll. Mount St. Joseph, 1999; first American to participate in Kalkriese dig, Germany, 1993, 95. Mem.: Acad. Health Svcs. Mktg. (adv. bd. dirs. 1989—91), Am. Mktg. Assn., Cin. C. of C. (lectr. 1984—86), Sigma Phi Omega. Avocations: travel, reading, medieval/renaissance history, community theater, archaeology. Home: 5511 Palomino Dr Cincinnati OH 45238-4143

SCHERER, GEORGE F., construction executive; Exec. v.p., treas., CFO, McCarthy Bldg. Cos., St. Louis. Office: McCarthy Bldg Cos 1341 N Rock Hill Rd Saint Louis MO 63124-1441

SCHERER, NORBERT FRANZ, chemistry professor; b. Milw., July 9, 1960; s. Franz and Ilse Scherer; m. Seung-Eun Choi, June 2, 1990; children: Matthew S., Amanda, Andrew. BS, U. Chgo., 1982; PhD, Caltech., 1989. NSF postdoctoral fellow U. Chgo., 1989-91, postdoctoral assoc., 1991-92; asst. prof. chemistry U. Pa., Phila., 1992-97; prof. chemistry U. Chgo., 1997—. Contbr. articles to sci. publs. Recipient Nat. Young Investigator award NSF, 1993-98; David and Lucile Packard fellow, 1993-98, Arnold and Mabel Beckman fellow, 1994-96, Alfred P. Sloan fellow, 1997; Camille Dreyfus tchr.-scholar, 1996. Mem. Am. Chem. Soc., Am. Phys. Soc., Optical Soc. Am.

SCHERER, RONALD CALLAWAY, voice scientist, educator; b. Akron, Ohio, Sept. 11, 1945; s. Belden Davis and Lois Ramona (Callaway) S.; children: Christopher, Maria. BS, Kent State U., 1968; MA, Ind. U., 1972; PhD, U. Iowa, 1981. Research asst. U. Iowa, Iowa City, 1979-81, asst. research scientist, 1981-83, adj. asst. prof., 1983-88, adj. assoc. prof., 1988—; adj. asst. prof. U. Denver, 1984-86; asst. adj. prof. U. Colo., Boulder, 1984-93, adj. assoc. prof., 1993-96; rsch. scientist Denver Ctr. Performing Arts, 1983—88, sr. scientist, 1988—96; lectr. voice and speech sci. Nat. Theatre Conservatory, Denver, 1990-94; asst. clin. prof. Sch. Medicine U. Colo., Denver, 1988—96; assoc. prof. Bowling Green State U., Ohio, 1996—2001, prof., 2001—05, 2006—. Adj. assoc. prof. U. Okla., 1992-96; affiliate clin. prof. U. No. Colo., 1993-96; Oberlin Coll. affiliate scholar, 1996—; mem. exec. and legis. bd. Nat. Ctr. Voice and Speech, 1990-96; adj. prof. Drexel U., Phila., 2006-; G. Paul Moore lectr., The Voice Found., 2002; rsch. prof. U. Cin., 2005-06. Author: (with Dr. I. Titze) Vocal Fold Physiology: Biomechanics, Acoustics and Phonatory Control, 1983; contbr. articles to profl. jours. Nat. Inst. Dental Research fellow, 1972-76. Fellow: Internat. Soc. Phonetic Scis. (auditor 1988—91); mem.: Am. Assn. Phonetic Scis. (nominating com. 1985—87, counselor 2000—03, councelor 2000—03), Internat. Assn. Logopedics and Phoniatrics, Acoustical Soc. Am., Am. Speech-Lang.-Hearing Assn., Internat. Arts Medicine Assn., Collegium Medicorum Theatri, Sigma Xi, Pi Mu Epsilon (G. Paul Moore lectr.). Office Phone: 419-372-2515.

SCHERER, VICTOR RICHARD, physicist, computer scientist, musician, consultant; b. Poland, Feb. 7, 1940; came to U.S., 1941; s. Emanuel and Florence B. Scherer; m. Gail R. Dobrofsky, Aug. 11, 1963; children: Helena Cecile, Markus David. BS magna cum laude, CCNY, 1960; MA, Columbia U., 1962; PhD, U. Wis., 1974. Health physics asst. Columbia U., NYC, 1961-63; rsch asst. physics. dep. U. Wis., Madison, 1967-74; project assoc., project mgr. Inst. for Environ. Studies, World Climate-Food Rsch. Group, 1974-78; specialist computer systems U. Wis. Acad. Computing Ctr., 1978—; coord., sr. cons. Divsn. Info. Tech. U. Wis., Madison; concert pianist; tchr.; promoter contemporary composers. Researcher in particle physics, agroclimatology, soil-yield relationships and computer graphics; cons. on computer sys., electronic mail, geographic analysis, help desk and supercomputing applications. Fellow AEC, 1960-61. Mem. AAAS, Am. Phys. Soc., Am. Meteorol. Soc., Am. Soc. Agronomy, Assn. Computing Machinery, Nat. Computer Graphics Assn., Phi Beta Kappa, Sigma Xi. Office: U Wis-Madison Divsn Info Tech 1210 W Dayton St Madison WI 53706-1613 Office Phone: 608-262-3570. Business E-Mail: scherer@doit.wisc.edu.

SCHERMER, LLOYD G., publishing and broadcasting company executive; b. St. Louis, 1927; married. Student Amherst U., 1950, Harvard U. Grad. Sch. Bus. Adminstrn., 1952. With Lee Enterprises, Inc., Davenport, Iowa, 1955—, pres., chief exec. officer, from 1974, now pres., also dir.; chmn. Newspaper Advt. Bur.; dir. Davenport Bank & Trust Co., NAPP Systems (USA), Inc. Bd. dirs. U. Mont. Found. Mem. Am. Soc. Newspaper Editors, Am. Newspaper Pubs. Assn. (dir.; dir. Found.). Office: Lee Enterprises Inc 400 Putnam Bldg 215 N Main St Ste 400 Davenport IA 52801-1924

SCHEVE, MAY E., state legislator, political organization worker; b. St. Louis, June 27, 1964; d. Robert Anthony and May Ellen (Braun) S. BA, St. Louis U., 1987; postgrad., Webster U. Rep. Mo. State Ho. Reps. Dist. 98, 1991—2002; adminstr. Dem. Party, Jefferson City, Mo., 2002—. Committeewoman Gravois Twp. Dem. Club; chair, Mo. Dem. Party, 2002-. Mem. Women Legislators, Third Congl. Women's Club (sec.), Women's Dem. Forum, Alpha Gamma Delta, Kappa Beta Phi. Democrat. Office: Mo Democratic Party 419 E High St PO Box 719 Jefferson City MO 65102

SCHICKEL, BILL, state senator, broadcast executive; b. Loveland, Ohio, Mar. 24, 1951; BA, U. Cin. Newspaper editor and reporter; TV news anchor and prodr.; gen. mgr. radio sta.; state rep. dist. 13 Iowa Ho. of Reps., 2003—; mem. edn. com.; mem. judiciary com.; mem. econ. devel. appropriations subcom.; vice chair local govt. com. Vol. YMCA; mayor Mason City, Iowa. Recipient Gov.'s Outstanding Vol. award. Mem.: Jaycees, Toastmasters. Republican. Address: 1443 E State Mason City IA 50401 Office: State Capitol East 12th and Grand Des Moines IA 50319

SCHIELE, MICHELE M., not-for-profit fundraiser, medical association administrator; b. 1967; Grad., Boston U. Coll. Communication, 1989, Northwestern U. Sch. Communication, 1995. V.p. & assoc. dean devel. U. Chgo. Biol. Sciences Divsn./U. Chgo. Hospitals, 2003—. Active in YWCA, Chgo. Named one of 40 Under 40, Crain's Chgo. Bus., 2006. Office: U Chgo Hospitals 5841 S Maryland Ave Chicago IL 60637-1470 also: U Chgo Divsn Biol Sciences 5812 S Ellis St Chicago IL 60637 Office Phone: 773-702-4767. Office Fax: 773-702-1670. E-mail: mschiele@medmail.uchicago.edu.

SCHIESER, HANS ALOIS, education educator; b. Ulm, Germany, July 15, 1931; arrived in U.S., 1965; s. Alois and Anna (Stegmann) S.; m. Margret H. Schröer, June 6, 1962; children: Peter, Elisabeth. BA, Kepler Gymnasium, Ulm, 1952; MA in Philosophy, U. Passau, Fed. Republic Germany, 1959; EdM, Pedagogic Acad., Weingarten, Fed. Republic Germany, 1962; PhD, Loyola U., Chgo., 1970. Head tchr. Pestalozzischule, Ulm, 1964-65; learning disabilities tchr. Jeanine Schultz Meml. Sch., Skokie, Ill., 1966-67; co-dir. Oak Therapeutic Sch., Evanston, Ill., 1967-70; from assoc. prof. to prof. edn. DePaul U., Chgo., 1969-91, prof. emeritus, 1991—. Cons. in field; program cons. Delphian Soc., L.A., 1977-90; rschr., tchr. in Germany, 1991—; active in tchrs. edn. Midwest Montessori Tchr. Tng. Ctr., Evanston, Ill.; guest prof. State U. Chelyabinsk, State Linguistic U., Irkutsk, Russia, 1998-2005; ord. prof., dean of studies Gustav-Siewerth-Akademie, Germany, 1995-2003. Author chpts. in books; contbr. articles to profl. jours.; adv. bd. Am. Edits. Sociology, Dushkin Pub. Group, 1985-91. Pres. N.Am. Family Svc. Found., Oak Lawn, Ill., 1974-91; bd. dirs. S.O.S. Children's Villages USA, Washington, 1986-94; pres. emeritus S.O.S. Children's Village Ill., Inc., Chgo.; bd. govs. Invest-in-Am. Nat. Found., Phila., 1988-90. Rsch. grant DePaul U., 1985-86, Rsch. sabbatical, 1989. Mem. Am. Ednl. Studies Assn., Nat. Soc. for Study of Edn., Philosophy of Edn. Soc. U.S.A., Soc. Educators and Scholars (bd. dirs. 1984-90), Am. Montessori Soc., Thomas More Gesellschaft/Amici Mori Europe, Phi Delta Kappa (pres. Zeta chpt., Chgo. 1973-75). Home: Veilchenweg 9 D-89134 Bermaringen Germany also: 400 E Main/6B/DJURI Evanston IL 60202 Office: DePaul U 2320 N Kenmore Ave Chicago IL 60614-3210 Personal E-mail: profschieser@aol.com, prof_schieser@hotmail.com.

SCHIFF, GILBERT MARTIN, virologist, microbiologist, educator; b. Cin., Oct. 21, 1931; married, 1955; 2 children. BS, U. Cin., 1953, MD, 1957. Intern U. Hosp., Iowa City, 1957-58, resident internal medicine, 1958-59; med. officer lab br. Communicable Diseases Ctr., Ga., 1959-61; head tissue culture investigation unit, perinatal rsch. br. Nat. Inst. Neurol. Diseases and Blindness, 1961-64; dir. clin. virology lab. U. Cin., 1964-78, asst. prof. medicine and microbiology, 1964-67, asst. prof. microbiology, 1967-71, prof. medicine Coll. Medicine, 1971—; pres. James N. Gamble Inst. Medical Rsch., 1984—. Attending physician dept. medicine Emory U., Atlanta, 1959-61; cons. com.

maternal health Ohio State Med. Assn., 1964-70, Hamilton County Neuromuscular Diagnostic Clinic, 1966, 75, Contract Immunization Status in U.S., 1975-77; mem. com. viral hepatitis among dental pers. VA; mem. immunization practice adv. com. Surgeon Gen., 1971-75; dir. Christ Hosp Inst. Med. Rsch., Cin., 1974-83, chairperson libr. com., 1974—, mem. com. cancer programs, 1979—, mem. com. human rsch., 1980—, chairperson search com., dir. radiotherapy, 1980-82; mem. com. infection control, 1981—, mem. com. univ. liaisons, 1982—; mem. subcom. antimicrobial agents U.S. Pharmacopeia, 1977-80; mem. study sect., adv. com., review com. NIH; mem. com. Rubella immunization Ohio Dept. Health; com. Rubella control Cin. Dept. Health. Trustee Children's Hosp. Med. Ctr., rsch. com., 1985—; community adv. com. Hoxworth Blood Ctr., 1991—. Recipient career rsch. devel. award Nat. Inst. Child Health and Human Devel., 1970-74; grantee USPHS, 1964-67, Nat. found., 1965-67. Fellow ACP; mem. AAAS, Am. Soc. Microbiology, Am. Fedn. Clin. Rsch. (sec.-treas. 1967-70), Am. Pub. Health Assn., Sci. Rsch. Soc. Am., Ctrl. Soc. Clin. Rsch. (sec.-treas. 1977-81, v.p. 1983, pres. 1984), Infectious Disease Soc. Am. Am. Soc. Clin. Investigation, Sigma Xi. Office: Dept Pediatrics U Cincinnati Coll Med 3333 Burnet Ave Cincinnati OH 45229-3026 E-mail: gilbert.schiff@cchmc.org.

SCHIFF, JOHN JEFFERSON, JR., finance company executive; BS, Ohio State U., 1965. Chmn., CEO John J. & Thomas R. Schiff & Co., Inc., 1983-96; COO Cin. Fin. Corp., 1998—99, pres., CEO, 1999—2006, CEO, 2006—, also chmn. bd. dirs. Trustee Am. Inst. Chartered Property Casualty Underwriters; dir. Cinergy Corp., Fifth Third Bancorp, Cin. Bengals Inc., John J. & Thomas R. Schiff & Co. Inc., Std. Register Co. Office: Cin Fin Group PO Box 145496 Cincinnati OH 45250-5496

SCHIFFER, JOHN PAUL, physicist, educator; b. Budapest, Hungary, Nov. 22, 1930; came to U.S., 1947, naturalized, 1953; s. Ernest and Elisabeth (Tornai) S.; m. Marianne Tsuk, June 28, 1960; children: Celia Anne, Peter Ernest. AB, Oberlin Coll., 1951; MS, Yale U., 1952, PhD, 1954; DSc (hon.), Notre Dame U., 1999. Research asso. Rice Inst., Houston, 1954-56; asst. physicist Argonne (Ill.) Nat. Lab., 1956-59, asso. physicist, 1960-63, sr. physicist, 1964—, assoc. dir. physics div., 1964-79, 83-99, dir. physics div., 1979-82, 99. Prof. physics U. Chgo., 1968-99, prof. emeritus, 1999; vis. asso. prof. Princeton, 1964; vis. prof. U. Rochester, N.Y., 1967-68; mem. adv. coms. nuclear physics Nat. Acad. Scis.; mem. program adv. or rev. coms. Los Alamos Meson Physics Facility, 1971-73, Ind. U. Cylotron Facility, 1974-77, Lab. for Nuclear Sci., M.I.T., 1975-79, Lawrence Berkeley Lab, Bevalac, 1978-80, Swiss Inst. uclear Research, 1981-85, Max Planck Inst. Nuclear Physics, 1982-85; mem. physics adv. panel NSF, 1971-73; mem. Nuclear Sci. Adv. Com. Dept. Energy/NSF, 1981-85, chmn., 1983-85; chmn. program adv. com. CEBAF, 1986-91; chmn. subcom. Implementation of 1989 Long Range Plan for Nuclear Sci.; chair Com. on uclear Physics, NRC, 1996—; Riken (Japan) Adv. Coun., 1996—. Editor: Comments on Nuclear and Particle Physics, 1971-75; assoc. editor Revs. Modern Physics, 1972-77; mem. editorial bd. Phys. Rev. C, 1983-85; editor: Physics Letters, 1978—; mem. editorial com. ann. revs. of nuclear and particle sci., 1987-91; contbr. articles on nuclear structure physics and nuclear reactions to phys. jours. and books. Mem. cold fusion panel Dept. Energy, 1989. Recipient Alexander V. Humboldt Found. sr. U.S. scientist award, 1973-74; Wilbur Cross medal Yale U., 1985; Guggenheim fellow, 1959-60 Fellow AAAS (mem. coun., chair physics sect. 1992-93), Am. Acad. Arts and Scis., Am. Phys. Soc. (chmn. div. nuclear physics 1975-76, Tom W. Bonner prize 1976); mem. NAS, Royal Danish Acad. Scis. and Letters. Achievements include research on nuclear structure, Mössbauer effect, heavy-ion reactions, pion interactions in nuclei, quark searches, crystalline order in confined cold plasmas. Office: Physics Division Argonne Nat Lab Argonne IL 60439

SCHILKEN, MICHAEL C., lawyer; BS, U. Colo., Boulder, 1987; JD, Creighton U., 1990. Bar: Nebr. 1990, US Tax Ct. Atty. Gross & Welch, P.C., 1990—2004; ptnr. Blackwell, Sanders, Peper & Martin, LLP, Omaha, 2004—. Bd. dirs. Cantorium Found. Named one of Top 100 Attys., Worth mag., 2006. Mem.: Omaha Estate Planning Coun., ebr. State Bar Assn., ABA. Office: Blackwell Sanders Peper & Martin 1620 Dodge St Ste 2100 Omaha NE 68102 Office Phone: 402-964-5018. Office Fax: 402-964-5050. E-mail: mschilken@blackwellsanders.com.

SCHILLER, DONALD CHARLES, lawyer; b. Chgo., Dec. 8, 1942; s. Sidney S. and Edith (Lastick) S.; m. Eileen Fagin, June 14, 1964; children— Eric, Jonathan Student, Lake Forest Coll., 1960-63; JD, DePaul U., 1966. Bar: Ill. 1966, US Dist. Ct. (no. dist.) Ill. 1966, US Supreme Ct. 1972. Ptnr. Schiller, DuCanto & Fleck LLP, Chgo., 1966—; lectr. in law U. Chgo. Law Sch., 2001—. Chair domestic rels. adv. com. Cir. Ct. Cook County, 1993—2001, co-chmn. rules revision com., 2003—; spkr. profl. confs. Contbr. chpts. and articles to profl. publs. Mem. steering com. on juvenile ct. watching, LWV, 1980-81. Named one of Am.'s Best Divorce Lawyers, Town and Country, 1986, 1998, Nat. Law Jour., 1987, Best Lawyers in Am., 1987—, Chgo.'s Best Divorce Lawyers, Crain's Chgo. Bus., 1981, Today Chgo. Woman, 1985, Inside Chgo. Mag., 1988, Chgo. Sun Times, 2000, Worth Mag., 2002, Nat. Top 500 Lawyers, Law Dragon Mag., 2005, 2006, 2007, 10 Top Ill. Lawyers, Super Lawyers Mag., 2006, 2007, Leading Laws Mag., 2006, 2007; recipient Maurice Weigle award, Chgo. Bar Found., 1978, Disting. Alumni award, DePaul U., 1988, various certs. of appreciation from numerous profl. groups. Fellow Am. Bar Found., Am. Acad. Matrimonial Lawyers (nat. chair continuing legal edn. 1993-94); mem. ABA (bd. govs. 1994-97, chmn. family law sect. 1985-86, Ill. State del. 1980-84, mem. Ho. of Dels. 1984-2003, editor-in-chief Family Law Newsletter 1977-79; mem. editorial bd., assoc. editor Family Adv. Mag. 1979-84, speaker at confs. and meetings), Am. Bar Retirement Funds (pres. 2005-06, adv. bd. mem. 2007—), Ill. Bar Assn. (pres. 1987-88, chmn. family law sect. 1976-77, editor Family Law Bull. 1976-77, bd. govs. 1977-83, treas. 1981-84, v.p. 1984-86, chmn. various coms., lectr., incorporator and pres. Ill. State Bar Assn. Mutual Ins. Co., Inc. 1988-89), Chgo. Bar Assn., Am. Coll. Family Law Trial Lawyers (diplomate). Office: Schiller DuCanto & Fleck LLP 200 N La Salle St 30th Fl Chicago IL 60601-1098 Office Phone: 312-609-5560. Business E-Mail: dschiller@sdflaw.com.

SCHILLER, ROBERT E., former school system administrator; PhD, U. Pa. Supt. local sch. districts, NJ, 1984—87; state dep. supt. edn. La., 1988—89; state dep. supt. pub. instrn. Del., 1989—91; supt. pub. instrn. Mich. State Dept. Edn., Lansing, 1992—95; interim CEO Balt. Pub. Schs., 1997—98; supt. Caddo Parish Pub. Sch. Dist., Shreveport, La., 1999—2002; state supt. edn. Ill. Dept. Edn., 2002—04.

SCHILLER, WILLIAM RICHARD, surgeon; b. Bennett, Colo., Jan. 14, 1937; s. Francis T. and Frances M. (Finks) S.; m. Beverlee Schiller; children from previous marriage: Julie, Lisa. BS, Drury Coll., Springfield, Mo., 1958; MD, Northwestern U., 1962; MA in Liberal Arts, St. John's Coll., 2005. Diplomate Am. Bd. Surgery; cert. of added qualifications in surg. critical care, 1987, recertified in surg. critical care, 1994. Intern Passavant Meml. Hosp., Chgo., 1962-63; resident Northwestern U. Clin. Tng. Program, Chgo., 1963-68; assoc. prof. surgery Med. Coll Ohio, Toledo, 1970-78; prof. surgery U. N.Mex, Albuquerque, 1978-83; dir. Trauma Ctr. St. Joseph's Hosp., Phoenix, 1983-89; dir. burn and trauma ctr. Maricopa Med. Ctr., Phoenix, 1989-98; prof. surgery So. Ill. U., Springfield, 1998—2002; ret., 2002. Clin. prof. surgery U. Ariz. Health Sci. Ctr.; prof. surgery Mayo Grad. Sch. Medicine, Rochester, Minn. Contbr. chpts. to books, articles to profl. jours. Served as maj. M.C. U.S. Army, 1968-70, Vietnam. Recipient Disting. Alumnus award for career achievement, Drury Coll., 2004. Fellow ACS; mem. Am. Assn. Surgery of Trauma, Cen. Surg. Assn., Western Surg. Assn., Soc. Surgery of Alimentary Tract, Am. Burn Assn., Internat. Soc. of Surgery. Republican. Home: 784 Aspen Compound Santa Fe NM 87501 Personal E-mail: wrschiller@hughes.net.

SCHILLING, EMILY BORN, editor, professional society administrator; b. Lawton, Okla., Oct. 2, 1959; d. George Arthur and Sumiko (Nagamine) Born; m. Mark David Schilling, June 26, 1995. BS, Ball State U., 1981. Cert. coop. communicator Nat. Rural Electric Coop. Assn. Feature writer The News-Sentinel, Fort Wayne, Ind., 1981-83; wire editor The Noblesville (Ind.) Daily Ledger, 1983; staff writer Ind. Statewide Assn. Rural Electric Coops., Indpls., 1983-84, mng. editor, 1984-85, editor, 1985—. Author: Power to the People, 1985. Mem. Coop. Communicators Assn. (Michael Graznak award 1990), Internat. Assn. Bus. Communicators (award of excellence dist. 7 1985), Women's Internat. Network of Utility Profls. (pres. 1999, Mem. of Yr. 1999, Power award 1994), Nat. Electric Coops. Statewide Editors Assn. Office: Ind Statewide Assn RECs 720 N High School Rd Indianapolis IN 46214-3756

SCHILLING, MIKE, state legislator; Rep. Mo. State Ho. Reps. Dist. 136. Home: 1027 S New Ave Springfield MO 65807-1346 Office: Mo Ho of Reps State Capitol Jefferson City MO 65101

SCHILLING, W. A. HAYDEN, history professor; BA, So. Meth. U., 1959; MA, Vanderbilt U., 1961, PhD, 1970. Faculty mem. Coll. Wooster, Ohio, 1964—, Robert Critchfield prof. English history Ohio, 1982—, dir. Advanced Placement Inst. Ohio. Recipient US Professors of Yr. Award for Outstanding Baccalaureate Coll. Prof., Carnegie Found. for Advancement of Tchg. and Coun. for Advancement and Support of Edn., 2005. Office: Coll Wooster 1189 Beall Ave Wooster OH 44691 Office Phone: 330-263-2452. E-mail: hschilling@wooster.edu.

SCHILLINGS, DENNY LYNN, retired history professor, educational and grants consultant; b. Mt. Carmel, Ill., June 28, 1947; s. Grady Lynn and Mary Lucille (Walters) S.; m. Karen Krek; children: Denise, Corinne. AA, Wabash Valley Coll., 1967; BEd, Ea. Ill. U., 1969, MA in History, 1972; MA in Adminstrn., Govs. State U., 1996; postgrad., Ill. State U., No. Ill. U. Grad. asst. dept. history Ea. Ill. U., Charleston, 1969; tchr. Edwards County High Sch., Albion, Ill., 1969-70, Sheldon (Ill.) High Sch., 1971-73, Homewood-Flossmoor (Ill.) High Sch., 1973—2003, tchr. history, grants and devel. mgr., 1994—2003; supr. history dept. Coll. Liberal Arts and Scis, No. Ill. U., Dekalb, 2003—; ret., 2003; adj. prof. Trinity Christian Coll., 2003—. Participant, con. Atlantic Coun. U.S. and NATO, Washington, 1986, Internat. Soviet-U.S. Textbook Project Conf., Racine, Wis., 1987; moderator Soviet-U.S. Textbook Study: Final Report, Dallas, 1987; chair history content adv. com. Ill. Tchr. Certification Requirements Com. 1986; mem. Ill. State Bd. Edn., Com. to Establish Learner Outcomes, 1984, Joint Task Force on Admission Requirements Ill. State Bd. on Higher Edn., 1986—; mem. adv. com. for Jefferson Found. Sch. Programs, 1987-90, Ill. State Bd. Edn.'s Goals Assessment Adv. Com., 1987-90; chair Ill. Learning Standards Project, 1996-97; pres. Corinne Jeannine Schillings Found., 2004—. Author: (with others) Economics, 1986, The Examination in Social Studies, 1989, Links Across Time and Place: A World History, 1990, Illinois Government Text, 1990, 99, 2003, Challenge of Freedom, 1990; author: The Living Constitution, 1991, 3d edit., 2002; co-editor: Teaching the Constition, 1987; reviewer, cons. for ednl. instns. and organizations; chair editorial bd. Social Edn., 1983; contbg. editor Social Studies Tchr., 1987-88. Mem. steering com. Homewood-Flossmoor High Sch. Found., 1983-84; elected bd. edn. Homewood Elem. Dist. 153, 1999—, found. pres., 2005—. Mem. NEA, Am. Hist. Assn. (James Harvey Robinson prize com. 1990-91), Ill. Coun. Social Studies (v.p. 1981, editor newsletter 1979-84, pres. 1983), Ill. Edn. Assn. (Gt. Lakes coord. com. 1982-83), Nat. Coun. Social Studies (publs. bd. 1983-86, bd. dirs. 1987-90, 94-96, exec. com. 1989-90, chair conf. com. 1989-90, pres. 1993-94, program planning com. 1989, 91), Phi Alpha Theta. Avocations: computers, reading. Home and Office: 18447 Aberdeen St Homewood IL 60430-3525 Home Phone: 708-957-3684; Office Phone: 630-886-0507. Personal E-mail: dschillings1@comcast.net.

SCHILSKY, RICHARD LEWIS, oncologist, researcher; b. NYC, June 6, 1950; s. Murray and Shirley (Cohen) S.; m. Cynthia Schum, Sept. 24, 1977; children: Allison, Meredith. BA cum laude, U. Pa., Phila., 1971; MD with honors, U. Chgo., 1975. Diplomate Nat. Bd. Med. Examiners, Am. Bd. Internal Medicine (subspecialty med. oncology); lic. physician, Mo., Ill. Intern, resident medicine Parkland Meml. Hosp., Southwestern Med. Sch., Dallas, 1975-77; clin. assoc. medicine br. and clin. pharmacology br. Divsn. Cancer Treatment, Nat. Cancer Inst., Bethesda, Md., 1977-80, cancer expert clin. pharmacology br., 1980-81; asst. prof. dept. internal medicine U. Mo. Sch. Medicine, Columbia, 1981-84; asst. prof. dept. medicine U. Chgo. Pritzker Sch. Medicine and Michael Reese Med. Ctrs., 1984-86, assoc. prof. dept. medicine, 1986-89; assoc. dir. joint sect. hematology and med. oncology U. Chgo. and Michael Reese Med. Ctrs., 1986-89; assoc. prof. dept. medicine, assoc. dir. sect. U. Chgo. Pritzker Sch. Medicine, 1989-91, prof. dept. medicine sect. hematology-oncology, 1991—; dir. U. Chgo. Cancer Rsch. Ctr., 1991-99; chmn. Cancer and Leukemia Group B, Chgo., 1995—; assoc. dean clin. rsch. biol. scis. divsn. U. Chgo., 1999—2007. Vivian Saykaly vis. prof. oncology McGill U., 1992; sci. com. Internat. Congress on Anti-Cancer Chemotherapy, 2002; adv. panel on hematologic and neoplastic disease U.S. Pharmacopeial Conv., 1991-95; cancer ctr. support grant rev. com. Nat. Cancer Inst., NIH, 1992-95; expert panel on advances in cancer treatment, 1992-93; mem. Cancer Ctrs. Working Group, 1996-97; oncologic drugs adv. com. FDA, 1996-2000, chmn., 1999-2000; mem. clin. trials implementation com. Nat. Cancer Inst., 1997-98, mem. bd. sci. advisors, 1999—, mem. clin. trials working group, 2004-05, mem. translational rsch. working group, 2005-07, mem. clin. trials adv. com., 2007—. Mem. editl. bd. Investigational New Drugs, 1988-95, Jour. Clin. Oncology, 1990-93, Contemporary Oncology, 1991-95, Jour. Cancer Rsch. and Clin. Oncology, 1991—, Seminars in Oncology, 1997—; assoc. editor Clin. Cancer Rsch., 1994—, Cancer Therapeutics, 1997-99, Cancer, 2000—; contbr. articles to profl. jours., chpts. to books. With USPHS, 1977-80. Recipient Spl. Advancement for Performance award VA, 1983, Fletcher Scholar award Cancer Rsch. Found., 1989; grantee VA, 1981-87, Am. Cancer Soc., 1983-86, 92-95, Ill. Cancer Coun., 1985-86, Michael Reese Inst. Coun., 1985-86, Nat. Cancer Inst., 1987, 88-90, Burroughs-Wellcome Co., 1987-88, NIH/Nat. Cancer Inst., 1988— Fellow ACP; mem. AAAS, Am. Soc. Clin. Oncology (bd. dirs. 2002-05, pres.-elect 2007), Am. Assn. Cancer Rsch. (chmn. Ill. state legis. com. 1992—), Am. Fedn. Clin. Rsch. (senator Midwest sect. 1983-84, councilor 1983-86, chmn. 1988-89), Am. Cancer Soc. (bd. dirs. Ill. divsn. 1997—), Am. Assn. Cancer Edn., Am. Soc. Clin. Pharmacology and Therapeutics, Ctrl. Soc. Clin. Rsch., N.Y. Acad. Scis., Assn. Am. Cancer Insts. (bd. dirs. 1995-99), Chgo. Soc. Internal Medicine, Sigma Xi, Alpha Epsilon Delta, Alpha Omega Alpha. Office: U Chgo Biol Scis Divsn 5841 S Maryland Ave Chicago IL 60637-1463 Office Phone: 773-834-3914. Business E-Mail: rschilsk@medicine.bsd.uchicago.edu.

SCHILTZ, PATRICK JOSEPH, federal judge; b. Duluth, Minn., 1960; BA summa cum laude, Coll. St. Scholastica, 1981; JD magna cum laude, Harvard Law Sch., 1985. Bar: Minn. 1985. Summer assoc. Faegre & Benson LLP, 1985, assoc., 1987—92, ptnr., 1993—95; law clk. to Hon. Antonin Scalia, US Ct. Appeals, DC Cir., 1985—86, US Supreme Ct, 1986—87; assoc. prof. law U. Notre Dame Law Sch., 1995—2000; assoc. dean U. St. Thomas Sch. Law, 2000—03, law prof. & St. Thomas More chair in law, 2003—06; judge US Dist Ct. Minn., 2006—. Office: US Dist Ct 778 Fed Bldg 316 N Robert St Saint Paul MN 55101 Office Phone: 651-848-1900. Office Fax: 651-848-1902.

SCHIMBERG, A(RMAND) BRUCE, retired lawyer; b. Chgo., Aug. 26, 1927; s. Archie and Helen (Isay) S.; m. Barbara Zisook; children: Geoffrey, Kate. PhB, U. Chgo., 1949, JD, 1952. Bar: Ohio 1952, Ill. 1955, U.S. Supreme Ct. 1987. Assoc. Paxton & Seasongood, Cin., 1952-55; ptnr. Schimberg, Greenberger, Kraus & Jacobs, Chgo., 1955-65, Leibman, Williams, Bennett, Baird & Minow, Chgo., 1965-72, Sidley & Austin, Chgo., 1972-92, counsel, 1993-94; ret., 1994. Lectr. U. Chgo., 1953-54; gen. counsel Comml. Fin. Assn., 1978-94; past mem. editl. bd. Lender Liability News. Mng. and assoc. editor U. Chgo. Law Rev., 1951-52; contbr. articles to legal jours. Bd. dirs. U. Chgo. Law Sch. Alumni Assn., 1969-72; dir. vis. com. U. Chgo. Law Sch., 1980-83. Recipient Homer Kripke Lifetime Achievement award for contbns. to comml. fin. law, 1998. Mem. ABA (chmn. subcom. and charter mem. comml. fin. svcs. com.), Am. Coll. Comml. Fin. Lawyers (pres. 1994-95, bd. regents), Ill. Bar Assn. (chair comml. banking, bankruptcy sect. 1972-73), Chgo. Bar Assn. (chair ucc com., 1966, bd. mgrs. 1968-70, chair judiciary com. 1971-72), Law Club Chgo., Mid-Day Club, Lake Shore Country Club. Home: 132 E Delaware Pl Apt 5002 Chicago IL 60611-4944 Office: Sidley & Austin 55 W Monroe St Ste 2000 Chicago IL 60603-5008

SCHIMEK, DIANNA RUTH REBMAN, state legislator; b. Holdrege, Nebr., Mar. 21, 1940; d. Ralph William and Elizabeth Julia (Wilmot) Rebman; m. Herbert Henry Schimek, 1963; children: Samuel Wolfgang, Saul William. AA, Colo. Women's Coll., 1960; student, U. Nebr., Lincoln, 1960-61; BA magna cum laude, U. Nebr., Kearney, 1963. Former tchr. and realtor; mem. Nebr. Legislature from 27th dist., Lincoln, 1989—; chmn. govt., mil. and vets. affairs com. Nebr. Legislature, Lincoln, 1993—94, 1999—2002, vice chair urban affairs com., 1995-98; chmn. Performance audit Com., 2007—. Dem. Nat. committeewoman, 1984-88; chmn. Nebr. Dem. Com., 1980-84; mem. exec. com. Dem. Nat. Com., 1987-88; past pres., sec. bd. dirs. Downtown Sr. Ctr. Found., 1990-96; mem. exec. bd. Midwestern Legis. Conf., 1995—, co-chair health and human svcs. com., 1995-96; exec. dir. Nebr. Civil Liberties Union, 1985; former bd. dirs. Nebr. Repertory Theater, Exon Found., 1997-2000; mem. adv. bd. Martin Luther Home, 1997-2003; chair Midwestern Legis. Conf. Coun. of State Govts., 2000-01, co-chair com. intergovtl. affairs; mem. Midwest Interstate passenger Rail Commn., 2001-05; mem. exec. bd. Coun. State Govts., 2000-05; chair NCSL Task Force on Initiative and Referendum, 2001-02; bd. dirs. Habitat Humanity, 2006—. Recipient Outstanding Alumni award, U. Nebr., 1989, Tribute award, YWCA, 1992, Friend of Psychology award, NE Psychol. Assn., 1998, Woman of Yr. award, Nova Chpt. Bus. & Profl. Women, 1999, Disting. Svc. award, Nat. Guard Assn., 2000, Woman of Distinction award, Soroptomists, 1999, Legis. of Yr. award, NE Dental Hygienists Assn., 2001, Disting. Svc. award, NE League of Municipalities, 2002, Lincoln Interfaith Leadership award, 2003, Harold Steck award, ARC of NE, 2004, Alice Paul award, Lancaster Status of Women Commn., 2006, Civil Libertarian of Yr. award, ACLU Nebr., 2006, Patty Steele Meml. award, Am. Cancer Soc., Ethics in Govt. award, Common Cause, 0207, others, Friend Edn. award, NSEA, 2007, Friend Medicine award, NMA, 2007; Toll fellow, 1999. Mem. Nat. Conf. State Legislators Women's Network (bd. dirs. 1993-96, 1st vice chmn.), PEO, Mayflower Soc., Delta Kappa Gamma (hon.), Mortar Bd. (cmty. advisor 1998, hon.), Rotary Internat. Democrat. Unitarian Universalist. Home: 6437 Lone Tree Dr Lincoln NE 68512 Office: Dist # 27 State Capitol Lincoln NE 68509 Home Phone: 402-423-0262; Office Phone: 402-471-2632. Business E-Mail: dschimek@leg.ne.gov.

SCHIMKE, DENNIS J., former state legislator; m. Olive Young, Dec. 1964 (dec. 1998); 3 children. BS, U. N.D., 1968, MS, 1972. Bison rancher, Coteau Hills, ND, 1987—; tchr. h.s. math. and physics LaMoure, N.D., 1975-2000; lectr. math. N.D. State U., 2001—; rep. Dist. 28 N.D. Ho. of Reps., 1991-93, rep. dist. 26, 1995-97, mem. edn. and agr. com., 1991—93, 1995—97. Founding bd. dirs. N.D. Buffalo Assn., 1991—95. Home: PO Box 525 Edgeley ND 58433-0525

SCHINDEL, DONALD MARVIN, retired lawyer; b. Chgo., Jan. 5, 1932; s. Harry L. and Ann (Schiff) S.; m. Alice Martha Andrews, Apr. 24, 1960; children: Susan Yost, Judith Harris, Andrea Glickman. BS in Acctg., U. Ill., 1953; JD, U. Chgo., 1956. Ptnr. Sonnenschein, Nath & Rosenthal, Chgo., 1956-2000, ret., 2000. Author: Estate Administration and Tax Planning for Survivors, 1987, supplements, 1988-1996. Pres. United Way Highland Park-Highwood, Ill., 2000—03; v.p. campaign United Way of the North Shore, 2004—05; pres. Congregation Beth Or, Deerfield, Ill., 1983—85. Fellow Am. Coll. Trust and Estate Counsel; mem. Chgo. Estate Planning Coun. (Austin Fleming Disting. Svc. award 1999), ABA, Ill. Bar Assn., Chgo. Bar Assn. (chmn. probate practice com. 1981-82). Clubs: East Bank (Chgo.). Avocations: tennis, travel, bridge, golf, running. Home: 636 Rice St Highland Park IL 60035-5012

SCHINK, JAMES HARVEY, lawyer; b. Oak Park, Ill., Oct. 2, 1943; s. Norbert F. and Gwendolyn H. (Hummel) S.; m. Lisa Wilder Haskell, Jan. 1, 1972 (div. 1980); children— David, Caroline, Elizabeth; m. April Townley, Aug. 14, 1982. BA, Yale U., 1965, JD, 1968. Bar: Ill. 1968, Colo. 1982. Assoc. Sidley & Austin, Chgo., 1968; law clk. to judge U.S. Ct. Appeals, Chgo., 1968-69; assoc. Kirkland & Ellis LLP, Chgo., 1969—72, ptnr., 1972—. Sustaining fellow Art Inst. Chgo. Mem. ABA, Ill. Bar Assn., Chgo. Bar Assn., Chgo. Club, Saddle and Cycle Club, Mid-Am. Club, Econ. Club Chgo., Sonnenalp Golf Club, Vail Racquet Club, Vail Mountain Club, Yale Club Chgo., Racquet Club Chgo., Game Creek Club. Republican. Presbyterian. Home: 1530 N State Pkwy Chicago IL 60610-1614 Office: Kirkland & Ellis LLP 200 E Randolph St Ste 6100 Chicago IL 60601-6436 Home Phone: 312-951-0036; Office Phone: 312-861-2258. Business E-Mail: jschink@kirkland.com.

SCHIRN, JANET SUGERMAN, interior designer; b. Jersey City; d. Oscar H. and Mary (Lustig) S.; 1 child, Martha. BFA, Pratt Inst.; MFA, Columbia U.; postgrad. in Architecture, U. Ill. Tchr. N.Y.C. Bd. Edn.; dir. N.Y.C. Bd. Adult Edn.; pres. Janet Schirn Design Group, Chgo., NYC, 1950—; prin. The J S Collection, YC, 1978—. Adj. prof. So. Ill. U., 1991-92; mem. adv. bd. Du Pont Co., Monsanto, 1981-89, Masland, So. Ill. U., 1990-95; mem. adv. bd. interior arch. dept. Columbia Coll., Iowa State U., Mundelein Coll., 1978; program advisor NEOCON World Trade Fair, 1995-. Contbr. articles to interior design mag. Bd. dirs. Washington Archtl. Forum, 1992-96, Chgo. Archtl. Assistance Ctr., 1975, pres., 1982; mem. Met. Planning Coun., Chgo., 1980—, Art Resources Tchg., 1984-95—; mem. aux. bd. Sch. of Art Inst., Ill. Arts Alliance, 1992—. Recipient award Chgo. Lighting Inst., 1989, 92, 93, 95, 97, 98, 2001, Villeroy and Boch gold award, 1990, Designer mag. residential award, 1990, Edward Fields 1st prize Rug Design, 1981, 91, 1st prize project awards ASID, 1993, 95, 96, 98, 99, 2000, 01, 03; named Designer of Distinction, 1998. Mem. UNESCO (steering com. tall bldgs. and urban habitat coun.), Am. Soc. Interior Designers (nat. pres. 1986, nat. treas. 1984, regional v.p. 1981, pres. Ill. chpt. 1977-78, nat. dir. 1979-83, chmn. pub. affairs 1989, rep. to Pres. Commn., 1993-95, rep. to Ctr. for Quality Assurance in Internat. Edn., 1989-92, liaison to NAFTA & U.S. Trade Commn., 1990-93), Illuminating Engring. Soc., Am. Inst. Architects (nat. urban planning and design com. 1981-85), Chgo. Network, Internat. Fedn. Interior Designers (exec. bd. dirs. 1992-96). Home: 220 E Walton St Chicago IL 60611-1507 Office: Janet Schirn Design Group 401 N Franklin St Chicago IL 60610-4400 also: 521 5th Ave New York NY 10175-0003

SCHIZAS, JENNIFER ANNE, law association administrator; b. Grand Island, Nebr., Aug. 18, 1959; d. John Delano and Jacqueline May (Pieper) S. BJ, U. Nebr., 1982. Rschr. U.S. Senator Carl T. Curtis, Washington, 1978; pub. rels. dir. Nebr. Solar Office, Lincoln, 1979; reporter Sta. WOWT-TV, Omaha, 1980-83; bur. chief Sta. KHAS-TV, Hastings, Nebr., 1983-84; divsn. dir. March of Dimes, Lincoln, 1986-90; exec. dir. Lincoln Arts Coun., 1990-92, Nebr. Food Industry Assn., Lincoln, 1992-93; dir. comm. Nebr. Bar Assn., Lincoln, 1993—. Mem. editor's exch. adv. bd. West Pub. CO., Eagan, Minn., 1995. Mem. Am. Soc. Assn. Execs., at. Assn. Bar Execs. (pub. rels. cons. 1995), Nebr. Soc. Assn. Execs. Sertoma Club (v.p.). Democrat. Greek Orthodox. Avocations: running, painting, antique refinishing. Office: Nebr Bar Assn 635 S 14th St Lincoln NE 68508-2700 Home: 1648 N Greenbrier St Arlington VA 22205-3635 E-mail: jschizas@nebar.com.

SCHLAFLY, PHYLLIS STEWART, writer; b. St. Louis, Aug. 15, 1924; d. John Bruce and Odile (Dodge) Stewart; m. Fred Schlafly, Oct. 20, 1949; children: John F., Bruce S., Roger S., Phyllis Liza Forshaw, Andrew L., Anne V. BA, Washington U., St. Louis, 1944, JD, 1978; MA, Harvard U., 1945; LLD, Niagara U., 1976. Bar: Ill. 1979, DC 1984, Mo. 1985, U.S. Supreme Ct. 1987. Syndicated columnist Copley News Svc., 1976—. Broadcaster Spectrum, CBS Radio Network, 1973—78; commentator Matters of Opinion sta. WBBM-AM, Chgo., 1973—75, Cable TV News Network, 1980—83; pres. Eagle Forum, 1975—. Author, pub.: Phyllis Schlafly Report, 1967—; author: A Choice Not an Echo, 1964, The Gravediggers, 1964, Strike From Space, 1965, Safe Not Sorry, 1967, The Betrayers, 1968, Mindszenty The Man, 1972, Kissinger on the Couch, 1975, Ambush at Vladivostok, 1976, The Power of the Positive Woman, 1977, First Reader, 1994, Turbo Reader, 2001, Feminist Fantasies, 2003, The Supremacists: The Tyranny of Judges and How to Stop It, 2004; editor: (book) Child Abuse in the Classroom, 1984, Pornography's Victims, 1987, Equal Pay for Unequal Work, 1984, Who Will Rock the Cradle, 1989, Stronger Families or Bigger Government, 1990, Meddlesome Mandate: Rethinking Family Leave, 1991. Del. Rep. Nat. Conv., 1956, 1964, 1968, 1984, 1988, 1992, 1996, 2004, alt., 1960, 1980, 2000; 1st v.p. Nat. Fedn. Rep. Women, 1964—67; nat. chmn. Stop ERA, 1972—; mem. Ronald Reagan's Def. Policy Adv. Group, 1980, Commn. on Bicentennial of U.S. Constn., 1985—91, Adminstrv. Conf. U.S., 1983—86; pres. Ill. Fedn. Rep. Women, 1960—64; mem. Ill. Commn. on Status of Women, 1975—85. Named Woman of Achievement in Pub. Affairs, St. Louis Globe-Democrat, 1963; named one of 10 Most Admired Women in World, Good Housekeeping poll, 1977—90, 100 Most Important Women of 20th Century, Ladies Home Jour., 1998; recipient 10 Honor awards, Freedom Found., Brotherhood award, NCCJ, 1975. Mem.: DAR (nat. chmn. Am. history 1965—68, nat. chmn. bicentennial com. 1967—70, nat. chmn. nat. def. 1977—80, 1983—95), ABA, Ill. Bar Assn., Phi Beta Kappa, Pi Sigma Alpha. Office: Eagle Forum 7800 Bonhomme Ave Saint Louis MO 63105-1906 Office Phone: 314-721-1213. E-mail: phyllis@eagleforum.org.

SCHLARMAN, STANLEY GIRARD, bishop emeritus; b. Belleville, Ill., July 27, 1933; Student, St. Henry Prep. Sem., Belleville, Gregorian U., Rome, St. Louis U. Ordained priest Diocese of Belleville, Ill., 1958, aux. bishop Ill., 1979—83; ordained bishop, 1979; bishop Diocese of Dodge City, Kans.,

1983—98, bishop emeritus Kans., 1998—. Roman Catholic. Office: Hincke-Sense Residence 2620 Lebanon Ave Belleville IL 62221 Office Phone: 618-235-9601. Office Fax: 618-277-0387. E-mail: sschlarman@diobelle.org.*

SCHLEGEL, FRED EUGENE, lawyer; b. Indpls., July 24, 1941; s. Fred George and Dorothy (Bruce) S.; m. Jane Wessels, Aug. 14, 1965; children: Julia, Charles, Alexandra. BA, Northwestern U., 1963; JD with distinction, U. Mich., 1966. Bar: Ind. 1966. Assoc. lawyer Baker & Daniels, Indpls., 1966-72, ptnr., 1972—; vice chmn. Meridian St. Preservation Commn., Indpls., 1975-90. Contbr. articles to profl. jours. Chmn. Pub. Schs. Edn. Found., Indpls., 1988—90; pres. Festival Music Soc., 1974—75, 1979, 1986—87; bd. dirs. Indpls. Symphony Orch., chmn., 2002—04; bd. dir. Arts Coun., Indpls, 1996—2002. Mem. ABA, Ind. Bar Assn., Energy Bar Assn., Northwestern U. Alumni Club Indpls. (pres. 1992-94). Episcopalian. Office: Baker and Daniels 300 N Meridian St Ste 2700 Indianapolis IN 46204-1782 Office Phone: 317-237-1410. Business E-Mail: fred.schlegel@bakerd.com.

SCHLEGEL, JOHN P., academic administrator; b. Dubuque, Iowa, July 31, 1943; s. Aaron Joseph and Irma Joan (Hingtgen) S. BA, St. Louis U., 1969, MA, 1970; BDiv, U. London, 1973; DPhil, Oxford U., 1977. Joined Soc. of Jesus, 1963, ordained priest Roman Cath. Ch., 1973. From asst. prof. to assoc. prof. Creighton U., Omaha, 1976—79, asst. acad. v.p., 1979—82; dean Coll. Arts and Scis. Rockhurst Coll., Kansas City, Mo., 1982—84, Marquette U., Milw., 1984—88; exec. and acad. v.p. John Carroll U., Cleve., 1988—91; pres. U. San Francisco, 1991—2000, Creighton U., Omaha, 2000—. Cons. Orgn. for Econ. Devel. and Cooperation, Paris, 1975-76. Author: Bilingualism and Canadian Policy in Africa, 1979; editor: Towards a Redefinition of Development, 1976; contbr. articles to profl. jours. Mem. Milwaukee County Arts Coun., 1986—88, Mo. Coun. on Humanities, Kansas City, 1984; trustee St. Louis U., 1985—91, Loyola U., Chgo., 1988—2004, Loyola U. New Orleans, 1995—98, St. Ignatius H.S., Cleve., 1990—91, Loyola Coll. in Md., 1992—98, Xavier U., 1998—2003. Oxford U. grantee, 1974-76; Govt. of Can. grantee, 1977-78. Mem.: Am. Coun. Edn., Omaha Country Club, Bohemian Club. Avocations: racquet sports, classical music, cooking, hiking.

SCHLEICHER, DONALD, music director; Degree, U. Wis., Northwestern U.; studied with Gustav Meier, Simon Rattle, Seiji Ozawa, Maurice Abravanel, Roger Norrington, Joel Smirnoff, Leon Fleisher. Band dir. Williamsville (N.Y.) South High Sch., 1977-84; past mem. music faculty U. Wis., Stevens Point; past mem. conducting faculty U. Mich.; dir. orch. studies, condr. Univ. Symphony Orch., head grad. program in orch. conducting U. Ill.; music dir. Quad City Symphony Orch. Assn., Davenport, Iowa. Conducting fellow Tanglewood Music Ctr., 1993; music dir., prin. condr. Pine Mountain Music Festival, Mich., 1994—; condr. orchs. N.Y., Ala., Wis., Hawaii, R.I., Ill.; guest condr., resident Fla. State U., Ark. State U., U. Minn., U. Akron, Ohio U., U. Buffalo, Ithaca Coll., Ohio State U.; guest condr. orchs. Bridgeport, Conn., Tallahassee, Fla., Lansing, Mich., Ann Arbor, Mich., Southfield, Mich.past dir. Detroit Chamber Winds; guest condr. Chautauqua Festival, 1996, Taiwan Symphony Orch. Wind Ensemble; presenter conducting clinic at nat. convention Music Educators at. Conf., Kansas City, 1996. Condr. operas including La Boheme, Suor Angelica, Il Pagliacci, Susannah, The Barber of Seville, La Traviata, The Marriage of Figaro, Madama Butterfly, Carmen. Office: Quad City Symphony Assn 327 Brady St Davenport IA 52801-1508

SCHLENDER, WILLIAM ELMER, management sciences educator; b. Sawyer, Mich., Oct. 28, 1920; s. Gustav A. and Marie (Zindler) S.; m. Lela R. Pullen, June 9, 1956 (dec. June 1983); m. Margaret C. Krahn, Mar. 3, 1987. AB, Valparaiso U., 1941; MBA, U. Denver, 1947; PhD, Ohio State U., 1955. With U.S. Rubber Co., 1941-43, 46; asst. prof., assoc. prof. bus. adminstrn. Bowling Green State U., 1947-53; asst. prof. bus. orgn., prof. Ohio State U., 1954-65, asst. dean, 1959-62; assoc. dean Ohio State U. (Coll. Commerce and Adminstrn.), 1962-63; prof. mgmt. U. Tex., 1965-68, chmn. dept., 1966-68; dean Cleve. State U. Coll. Bus. Adminstrn., 1968-75, prof. mgmt., 1975-76; Internat. Luth. Laymen's League prof. bus. ethics Valparaiso (Ind.) U., 1976-79, Richard E. Meier prof. mgmt., 1983-86, Richard E. Meier prof. emeritus, 1986—. Vis. assoc. prof. mgmt. Columbia U., 1957-58; vis. prof. mgmt. U. Tex., Arlington, 1981-82; cons. in field; bd. govs. Internat. Ins. Soc., 1972-90. Author: (with M.J. Jucius) Elements of Managerial Action, 3d edit., 1973, (with others) Management in Perspective: Selected Readings, 1965; editor: (with others) Management in a Dynamic Society, 1965; mem. editl. bd. Jour. Acad. Mgmt., 1966-72; contbr. articles to profl. jours. Mem. Assn. Ohio Commodores. Served with AUS, 1943-45. Decorated Bronze Star; Exec. Order of Ohio Commodore in recognition of contbn. to econ. devel., Gov. Ohio, 1972. Fellow Acad. Mgmt.; mem. Indsl. Rels. Rsch. Assn. (pres. N.E. Ohio chpt. 1971-72), Am. Legion, Tau Kappa Epsilon, Rotary, Beta Gamma Sigma, Sigma Iota Epsilon, Pi Sigma Epsilon, Alpha Kappa Psi, Phi Kappa Phi. Home (Summer): PO Box 446 Sawyer MI 49125-0446 Office: Coll Bus Adminstrn Valparaiso U Valparaiso IN 46383 Personal E-mail: bschlend@aol.com.

SCHLENSKER, GARY CHRIS, landscape company executive; b. Indpls., Nov. 12, 1950; s. Christian Frederick and Doris Jean (Shannon) S.; m. Ann Marie Tobin, Oct. 27, 1979; children: Laura Patricia, Christian Frederick II. Student, Purdue U., 1969-71, 73; A Bus. Adminstrn., Clark Coll., 1979; cert. emergency med. technician, Ind. Vocat. Tech. Inst., Lafayette, 1974. Salesman Modern Reference, Indpls., 1971; orthopaedic technician St. Elizabeth Hosp., Lafayette, 1973-75, asst. mgr. ambulance service, 1975; sales asst. Merck, Sharpe & Dohme, Oakbrook, Ill., 1975-77; v.p. Turfco, Inc., Zionsville, Ind., 1977-84; pres. Turfscape, Inc., Zionsville, 1984—. Speaker Midwest Turf Conf., 1991; del. erosion and sediment control econ. summit Internat. Erosion Control Assn., New Orleans, 2000. With U.S. Army, 1971-73. Mem. ASTM (erosion control subcom.), BBB, Nat. Fedn. Ind. Bus., Midwest Turf Found., Ohio Turf Found., Internat. Erosion Control Assn. (bd. dirs. Gt. Lakes chpt. 1998-2002), U.S. C. of C., Zionsville C. of C., Phi Kappa Psi. Presbyterian. Avocations: woodworking, golf. Business E-Mail: gary@turfscapeinc.com.

SCHLESINGER, JOSEPH ABRAHAM, political scientist; b. Boston, Jan. 4, 1922; s. Monroe Jacob and Millie (Romansky) S.; m. Mildred Saks, Sept. 9, 1951; children: Elizabeth Hannah, Jacob Monroe. Student, Hobart Coll., 1938-40; AB, U. Chgo., 1942; A.M., Harvard U., 1947; PhD, Yale U., 1955. Instr. Boston U., 1947-49; teaching fellow Wesleyan U., Middletown, Conn., 1952-53; mem. faculty Mich. State U., East Lansing, 1953—, prof. polit. sci., 1963—. Vis. prof. U. Calif., Berkeley, 1964-65 Author: How They Became Governor, 1957, Ambition and Politics: Political Careers in the United States, 1966, Political Parties and the Winning of Office, 1991, also articles. Del. Ingham County (Mich.) Democratic Conv., 1966-68. Served with AUS, 1943-45. Cowles fellow, 1950-51; Block fellow, 1951-52; grantee Social Sci. Research Council, 1955-57, 68-69; recipient Distinguished Faculty award Mich. State U., 1976, Sr. Fulbright award for Rsch. Western Europe, 1990—. Mem. Am. Polit. Sci. Assn. (coun. 1981-83, 1st ann. award for outstanding pub. paper 1986, Samuel Eldersveld award for lifetime achievement 1993), Midwest Polit. Sci. Assn. (v.p. 1969-70), So. Polit. Sci. Assn., Mich. Conf. Polit. Scientists, Acad. Polit. Sci. Democrat. Jewish. Home: 930 Roxburgh Ave East Lansing MI 48823-3131 Office: Dept Polit Sci Mich State Univ East Lansing MI 48824

SCHLESINGER, LEONARD ARTHUR, academic administrator; b. NYC, July 31, 1952; s. Joe and Edith (Smukler) S.; m. Phyllis Barbara Fineman, Dec. 23, 1972; children: Rebecca, Emily, Katharine. BA, Brown U., 1972; MBA, Columbia U., 1973; DBA, Harvard U., 1979. Mgr. Procter & Gamble, Green Bay, Wis., 1973-75; asst. prof., assoc. prof. bus. sch. Harvard U., Boston, 1978-85; exec. v.p., COO Au Bon Pain, Inc., Boston, 1985-88; prof. bus. adminstrn. Harvard U., Boston, 1988-98; sr. v.p. Brown U., 1998-99; exec. v.p., COO Limited Brands, Columbus, Ohio, 1999—2003, vice chmn., COO, 2003—07; pres. Babson Coll., Wellesly, Mass., 2008—. Past bd. dir. Limited Brands, Columbus, Ohio Editor: Human Resources Mgmt. Jour., Jour. Mgmt. Inquiry; contbr. articles to profl. jours. Jewish. Avocations: travel, music, hiking. Home: 396 Washington St 324 Wellesley MA 02481 Office Phone: 781-239-4624. Business E-Mail: lschlesinger@babson.edu.

SCHLESINGER, MILTON J., virology educator, researcher; b. Wheeling, W.Va., Nov. 26, 1927; s. Milton J. and Caroline (Oppenheimer) S.; m. Sondra Orenstein, Jan. 30, 1955. BS, Yale U., 1951; MS, U. Rochester, 1953; PhD, U. Mich., 1959. Rsch. assoc. U. Mich., Ann Arbor, 1953-56, 59-60; guest rsch. investigator Inst. Superiore di Sanita, Rome, 1960-61; rsch. assoc. MIT, Cambridge, 1961-64; asst. prof. virology Washington U. Sch. Medicine, St. Louis, 1964-67, assoc. prof., 1967-72, prof., 1972-99, chmn. exec. coun. divsn. biol. and biomed. scis., 1992-94, emeritus prof., 1999—. Vis. scientist Imperial Cancer Rsch. Fund, London, 1974-75; vis. scholar Harvard U., Cambridge, 1989-90, 95-96; mem. adv. panels Am. Heart Assn., Dallas, 1975-78, NSF, Washington, 1978-82; mem. sci. adv. bd. Friedrich Miescher Inst., Basel, Switzerland, 1988—, chmn., 1992-98; nat. lectr. Sigma Xi, 1991-93. Editor: Heat Shock, 1982, Togaviridae and Flaviviridae, 1986, Lipid Modification of Proteins, 1992, (monographs) The Ubiquitin System, 1988, Stress Proteins, 1990; mem. editl. bd. virology, 1975-92, Jour. Biol. Chemistry, 1982-87, Molecular and Cellular Biology, 1983-92. Bd. dirs. ACLU, St. Louis, 1966-72, Coalition for Environ., St. Louis, 1989-92. Fellow AAAS; mem. Am. Biol. Chemistry and Molecular Biology, Am. Soc. Microbiology, Am. Soc. Virologists, Am. Chem. Soc. Office: Dept Molecular Micro 8230 Washington U Med Sch 660 S Euclid Ave Saint Louis MO 63110-1010

SCHLICHTER, JOHN M., state representative; b. June 20, 1958; Farmer; state rep. dist. 85 Ohio Ho. of Reps., 2002—, mem. agr. and natural resources com., vice chair, civil and comml. law subcom., transp. and pub. safety subcom., natural resources parks and recreation subcom. Commr. Fayette County, Ohio. Republican. Office: 77 High St 11th fl Columbus OH 43215-6111

SCHLICHTING, CATHERINE FLETCHER NICHOLSON, librarian, educator; b. Huntsville, Ala., Nov. 18, 1923; d. William Parsons and Ethel Loise (Breitling) Nicholson; m. Harry Fredrick Schlichting, July 1, 1950 (dec. Aug. 1964); children: James Dean, Richard Dale, Barbara Lynn. BS, U. Ala., 1944; MLS, U. Chgo., 1950. Asst. libr. U. Ala. Edn. Libr., Tuscaloosa, summers 1944-45; libr. Sylacauga (Ala.) H.S., 1944-45, Hinsdale (Ill.) H.S., 1945-49; asst. libr. Centre for Children's Books, U. Chgo., 1950-52; instr. reference dept. libr. Ohio Wesleyan U., Delaware, 1965-69, asst. prof., 1969-79, assoc. prof., 1979-85, prof., 1985—, curator Ohio Wesleyan Hist. Collection, 1986—, student pers. libr., 1966-72. Author: Introduction to Bibliographic Research: Basic Sources, 4th edit., 1983, Checklist of Biographical Reference Sources, 1977, Audio-Visual Aids in Bibliographic Instruction, 1976, Introduction to Bibliographic Research: Slide Catalog and Script, 1980; info. cons. (documentary) Noble Achievements: The History of Ohio Wesleyan 1942-1992, 1992, 150 Years of Excellence: A Pictorial View of Ohio Wesleyan University, 1992. Mem. adminstrv. bd. Meth. Ch., 1973-81, chmn. adminstrv. bd., 1985—, mem. coun. on ministries, 1975-81, chmn., 1975-77, trustee, 1999—2003. Recipient Algernon Sidney Sullivan award U. Ala., 1944, Hon. Alumna award Ohio Wesleyan U., 1997; Ohio Wesleyan U.-Mellon Found. grantee, 1972-73, 84-85; GLCA Tchg. fellow, 1976-77. Mem. ALA, Ohio Libr. Assn., Midwest Acad. Libr. Conf., Acad. Librs. Assn. Ohio (dir. 1984-86), AAUP (chpt. sec. 1967-68), United Meth. Women (pres. Mt. Vernon dist. 1994-97, newsletter editor 1998-2002), Ohio Wesleyan Woman's Club (exec. bd. 1969-72, 77-79, 81-84, pres. 1969-70, sec. 1977-78), History Club (pres. 1971-72, v.p. 1978-79, 2003-04) Fortnightly Club (pres. 1975-76, 87-88, 2003-04), Am. Field Svc. (pres. Delaware chpt. 1975-76), Kappa Delta Pi, Alpha Lambda Delta. Democrat. Home: 57 Willow Brook Way S Delaware OH 43015 Office: Ohio Wesleyan U La Beeghly Library Delaware OH 43015

SCHLICHTING, NANCY MARGARET, hospital administrator; b. NYC, Nov. 21, 1954; BA, Duke U., 1976; MBA, Cornell U., 1979. Adminstrv. resident Meml. Hosp. Cancer, NYC, 1978; fellow Blue Cross-Blue Shield Assn., Chgo., 1979-80; asst. dirs. ops. Akron (Ohio) City Hosp., 1980-81, assoc. dir. planning, 1981-83, exec. v.p., 1983-88, Riverside Meth. Hosps., Columbus, Ohio, 1988-92, pres., COO, 1992-93, pres., CEO, 1993-96; pres. Ea. region Cath. Health Initiatives, Aston, Pa., 1996-97; exec. v.p., COO Summa Health Sys., Akron, Ohio, 1997—98; sr. v.p., chief adminstrv. officer Henry Ford Healthcare Sys., Detroit, 1998—99, exec. v.p., COO, 1999—2003, pres., CEO, 2003—, Henry Ford Hosp., 2001—03. Bd. dirs. Fifth Third Bank Corp., First Nat. Bank of Ohio, Mich. Health and Hosp. Assn., Greater Detroit Area Health Council, Walgreen Co., 2006—. Trustee Kresge Found. Office: Henry Ford Health Sys 1 Ford Pl Detroit MI 48202

SCHLIEVE, HY C. J., school administrator; b. Mandan, ND, Apr. 4, 1952; s. Calvin L. and Loretta L. (Johnson) S.; m. Terri Ann Hansen, Dec. 30, 1977; children: Derek, Aaron, Jessica. BA, N.D. State U., 1974, MS, 1984; EdD, Calif. Coast U., 1994. Tchr., coach Halliday Pub. Sch., ND, 1974-75, Drake Pub. Sch., ND, 1975-76, Montpelier Pub. Sch., ND, 1976-81; prin. Unity Pub. Sch., Petersburg, ND, 1981-83, Page Pub. Sch., ND, 1983-85; supt. Wolford Pub. Sch., ND, 1985-87, Garrison Pub. Schs., ND, 1987-93; prin. Buhl Joint Sch. Dist. 412, Idaho, 1993-95, Oconto Falls Area Sch. Dist., Wis., 1995-99; supt. Ellendale Pub. Schs. #40, ND, 1999—. Com. mem. NDASA Rsch. and Evaluation, Garrison, 1988-93; fiscal agt. Mo. Hills Consortium, McLean County, N.D., 1989-93; cons. asbestos Garrison Pub. Sch. Dist., 1987-93. Sec. Govtl. Affairs Com., Garrison, 1987-93; mem. Tourism Com., Garrison, 1988-92, Econ. Devel. Com., 1988-89. Recipient Nat. Superintendent of the Yr. awd., North Dakota, Am. Assn. of School Administrators, 1992. Mem. Nat. Assn. Secondary Sch. Prins. (prin. assessor tng. 1990), NSBA Fed. Policy Coords. Network. Avocations: golf, hunting, fishing, bowling, outdoor activities. Office: Ellendale Pub Schs PO Box 400 321 N 1st St Ellendale ND 58436 Home: 1330 12th St N Apt 18 Wahpeton ND 58075-5028

SCHLITTER, STANLEY ALLEN, lawyer; b. Decorah, Iowa, Jan. 27, 1950; s. Joseph Everett and Lillian Helena (Helgerson) S.; m. Sheila Lynn Edwards, Sept. 24, 1977; children: Stephanie Anne, Joseph Allen, John Edward. BS, Iowa State U., 1972; JD, U. Iowa, 1977. Bar: Ill. 1977, U.S. Dist. Ct. (no. dist.) Ill. 1977, U.S. Ct. Appeals (7th cir.) 1981, U.S. Ct. Appeals (Fed. cir.) 1982, D.C. 1989. Assoc. Kirkland & Ellis, Chgo., 1977-84, ptnr., 1984-88, Washington, 1988-91, Jenner & Block, Chgo., 1991—. Mem. ABA, IEEE, Am. Intellectual Property Law Assn. Office: Jenner & Block One IBM Plaza Chicago IL 60611-3608 Office Phone: 312-923-2712. E-mail: sschlitter@jenner.com.

SCHLODER, JOHN E., museum director; BS, Duquesne U., 1969; diplôme d'Ancien Elève, L'Ecole du Louvre, Paris, 1973; licence L'Institut d'Art et d'Archéologie, U. Paris-Sorbonne, 1973, doctorat L'Institut d'Art et d'Archéologie, 1988; MPhil, Columbia U., 1980. Chargé de Mission Musée du Louvre, Paris, 1979-82; asst. curator Cleve. Mus. Art Edn Dept., 1982-85, assoc. curator, 1985-86, adminstr. pub. programs, 1986-88, asst. dir. edn. and pub. programs, 1988-92; dir. Birmingham Mus. Art, Ala., 1992-96, Joslyn Mus. Art, Omaha, 1997—2000, Mus. Fine Arts, St. Petersburg, Fla., 2001—. Vis. prof. Colégio Andrews, Rio de Janeiro, Brazil, 1980-81, Vaculdade Candido Mendes, Rio de Janeiro, 1981-82; adj. prof. dept. art history Case Western Res. U., Cleve., 1984-92; lectr. in field. Mus. rep. Northeastern Ohio Inter-Mus. Coun., 1984-92; trustee Cleve. Sch. Arts, 1991-92; active Southeast Mus. Conf., 1992—; mem. Leadership Birmingham, 1994-95; bd. dirs. Op. New Birmingham, 1993—; mem. Birmingham Olympic programming com., mem. outreach com., 1994—. Lurcy Trust fellowship, 1975, Columbia U. Traveling fellowship, 1975, 76, U. Cambridge, Eng. Leverhulme fellowship, 1977, Kellogg Project fellowship Smithsonian Instn., 1987; scholarship J. Paul Getty Trust, 1989; vis. Scholar grantee The Japan Found., 1995; recipient French Govt. award, 1975, award of achievement for best cmty. event Northern Ohio Live Mag., 1991. Mem. Am. Assn. Mus., Assn. Art Mus. Dirs., Internat. Lab. for Visitor Studies, Visitor Studies Assn., Ala. Mus. Assn., Birmingham Area Mus. Assn., Soc. de l'Histoire de l'Art Français, Rotary Club Birmingham. Office: Museum Fine Arts 255 Beach Drive NE Saint Petersburg FL 33701 Business E-Mail: jschloder@fine-arts.org.

SCHLOERB, PAUL RICHARD, surgeon, educator; b. Buffalo, Oct. 22, 1919; s. Herman George and Vera (Gross) S.; m. Louise M. Grimmer, Feb. 25, 1950; children: Ronald G., Patricia S. Johnson, Marilyn A. Hock, Dorothy S. Hoban, P. Richard. AB, Harvard U., 1941; MD, U. Rochester, 1944. Intern U. Rochester Med. Sch., 1944—45, asst. resident, 1947—48, instr. surgery, 1952; rsch. fellow, resident Peter Bent Brigham Hosp., Boston, 1948—52; faculty U. Kans. Med. Ctr., Kansas City, 1952—79, prof. surgery, 1964—79, 1988—2006, prof. surgery emeritus, 2006—, dean for rsch., 1972—79, dir. nutritional support svc., 1993—2002; prof. surgery U. Rochester (NY) Med Ctr., 1979—88, adj. prof. surgery, 1988—90; surgeon Strong Meml. Hosp., 1979—88, dir. Surg. ICU, 1979—85, dir. surg. nutritional support service. Contbr. over 100 articles to profl. jours. Lt. (j.g.), M.C. USNR, 1944-45; to lt. 1953-55. Mem. AMA, ACS, AAAS, Am. Surg. Assn., Soc. U. Surgeons, Am. Physiol. Soc., Internat. Soc. Surgery, Ctrl. Surg. Assn., Am. Assn. for Surgery of Trauma, Am. Assn. Cancer Rsch., Biomed. Engring. Soc., Am. Inst. Nutrition, Am. Soc. Clin. Nutrition, Sigma Xi. Achievements include first to measure total body water in humans. Office: Dept Surgery U Kansas Med Ctr Kansas City KS 66160-0001 Home Phone: 913-451-8998; Office Phone: 913-588-7565. Business E-Mail: pschloer@kumc.edu.

SCHLOSSMAN, JOHN ISAAC, architect; b. Chgo., Aug. 21, 1931; s. Norman Joseph and Carol (Rosenfeld) S.; m. Shirley Goulding Rhodes, Feb. 8, 1959; children: Marc N., Gail S. Mewhort, Peter C. Student, Grinnell Coll., 1949-50; BA, U. Minn., 1953, BArch, 1955; MArch, MIT, 1956. Registered architect, Ill. Archtl. designer The Architects Collaborative, Cambridge, Mass., 1956-57; architect Loebl Schlossman & Hackl and predecessors, Chgo., 1959-65, assoc., 1965-70, prin., 1970-98, cons. prin., 1998—. Bd. overseers Coll. Arch. Ill. Inst. Tech., Chgo.; adv. bd. Coll. of Arch. and Landscape Arch. U. Minn., 2003-06; founding bd. dirs. Chgo. Archtl. Assistance Ctr., 1974-79 Chmn. Glencoe Plan Commn., Ill., 1977-82; mem. Village of Glencoe Contextual Design Rev. Commn., 2005-0; trustee Com. for Green Bay Trail, Glencoe, 1970-77, Chgo. Arch. Found., 1971-75, Graham Found. for Advanced Studies in Fine Arts, 1995-99, pres. 1999-2001; adv. bd. dirs. Merit Sch. of Music, Chgo., 1983-93, pres., 1988-90, hon. trustee, 1996; governing mem. Chgo. Symphony Orch.; mem. founders coun. Field Mus., Chgo.; mem. zoning and planning com. Greater North Michigan Ave. Assn., Chgo., 2000-01; mem. Nat. Trust Coun., Nat. Trust for Hist. Preservation, Washington. Named dir. for life Young Men's Jewish Coun., Chgo., 1971; Rotch travelling scholar, 1957; sustaining fellow Art Inst. Chgo. Fellow AIA (trustee ins. trust 1971-76, chmn. ins. com. 1974-75, v.p. Chgo. chpt. 1975, chmn. architects liability com. 1976, 80-82, hon. found. trustee 1995—), Tavern Club (gov. 1986-88, v.p. 1990), The Club at Symphony Ctr., The Arts Club, Alpha Rho Chi. Office: Loebl Schlossman & Hackl 232 Mary St Winnetka IL 60093-1522 E-mail: jschloss@worldnet.att.net.

SCHLOTMAN, J. MICHAEL, food products executive; Grad., U. Ky., Lexington. CPA. With The Kroger Co., Cin., 1985—, v.p. fin. svcs. & control, 1995—2000, CFO, 2000—, sr. v.p., 2003—. Office: Kroger 1014 Vine St Cincinnati OH 45202

SCHLOZMAN, BRADLEY J., former prosecutor; b. Overland Park, Kans., Feb. 6, 1971; BA in Hist., U. Pa., 1993; JD, George Washington U. Law Sch., 1996. Clk. Chief US Dist. Judge G. Thomas VanBebber, Dist. Kans., US Ct. Appeals, 10th Cir.; atty. Howrey, Simon, & White, LLP, Washington, 1999—2001; counsel to dep. atty. gen. US Dept. Justice, 2001—03, dep. asst. atty. gen., 2003, acting asst. atty. gen., Civil Rights divsn., prin. dep. asst. atty. gen., Civil Rights divsn., interim US atty. (we. dist.) Mo., 2006—07.

SCHMALTZ, DAVID G., lawyer; b. St. Paul, Aug. 2, 1968; BS cum laude in Civil Engring., Marquette U., 1991; JD cum laude, U. Wis., Madison, 1994. Bar: Wis. 1994, Minn. 1994, US Patent and Trademark Office. Ptnr. Merchant & Gould, P.C., Mpls. Named a Rising Star, Minn. Super Lawyers mag., 2006. Mem.: Wis. State Bar Assn., Minn. State Bar Assn., Minn. Intellectual Property Law Assn., Hennepin County Bar Assn., ABA (tech. and patent sects.). Office: Merchant & Gould PC 3200 IDS Ctr 80 S 8th St Minneapolis MN 55402 Office Phone: 612-332-5300. E-mail: dschmaltz@merchantgould.com.

SCHMALZ, DOUGLAS J., retired agricultural company executive; b. Oct. 28, 1945; BS, U. Minn. CPA. Public acct. Ernst & Young, 1975—85; fin. mgmt. positions Archer Daniels Midland Co., Decatur, Ill., 1985—86, contr., 1985—94, CFO, 1985—2002, sr. v.p., CFO, 2002—08. Bd. mem. Cmty. Found. of Decatur Macon County, Ill., Decatur Mem. Hosp., Boys & Girls Clubs of Decatur, Decatur Area Arts Council.*

SCHMELZER, WILHELM A., manufacturing executive; Degree in Acctg. and Fin., Fachhochschule, Cologne, Germany; student, Albion Coll. Various positions Federal-Mogul Corp., Southfield, Mich., 1969-95, v.p., group exec., 1995-98, exec. v.p. sealing systems, 1998, exec. v.p. Europe, 1998—. Bd. dirs. Federal-Mogul Corp. Fellow Carl Duisberg Found. Office: Federal-Mogul Corp 26555 Northwestern Hwy Southfield MI 48034-2146

SCHMETTERER, JACK BAER, federal judge; b. Chgo., Apr. 11, 1931; s. Samuel and Gertrude (Schiff) Schmetterer; m. Joan L. Ruther, Mar. 18, 1956 (dec.); children: Laura, Mark, Kenneth; m. Barbara Friedman, Sept. 2, 2001. BA, Yale U., 1952, JD, 1955. Bar: Ill. 1956. Instr. polit. sci. Yale U., New Haven, 1954-55, U. Ga., Ga., 1957-58; ptnr. Schmetterer & Schmetterer, Chgo., 1958-63; asst. U.S. atty. U.S. Dist. Ct. (no. dist.) Ill., Chgo., 1963-68, 1st asst. U.S. atty., 1968-70; ptnr. Freeman, Schmetterer, Freeman & Salzman, Chgo., 1970-71; 1st asst. states atty. State's Atty. of Cook County, Chgo., 1971-73; assoc., ptnr., head of litigation Gottlieb & Schwartz, Chgo., 1973—85; US bankruptcy judge US Bankruptcy Ct. (no. dist.) Ill., Chgo., 1985—. Vis. prof. dept. criminal justice U. Ill., Chgo., 1974-76. Bd. dir. Cook County Ct. Watchers, Inc., until 1985, Better Govt. Assn., until 1985; former mem. Northbrook Village Bd., North Shore Mass Transit Dist. Bd. With US Army, 1956-58. Mem.: ABA, John Howard Assn. (chairperson 1997—99, adv. bd.), Fed. Bar Assn. (pres. Chgo. chpt. 1993—94), Fed. Trial Judges Conf., Just the Beginning Found. (v.p.), Decalogue Soc., Law Club Chgo. Office: US Bankruptcy Ct # 600 219 S Dearborn St Rm 600 Chicago IL 60604-1702

SCHMID, HARALD HEINRICH OTTO, biochemistry educator, academic administrator; b. Graz, Styria, Austria, Dec. 10, 1935; Came to U.S., 1962; s. Engelbert and Annemarie (Kletetschka) S.; m. Patricia Caroline Igou, May 21, 1977. MS, U. Graz, 1957, LLD, 1962, PhD, 1964. Rsch. fellow Hormel inst. U. Minn., Austin, 1962-65, rsch. assoc., 1965-66, asst. prof., 1966-70, assoc. prof., 1970-74, prof., 1974—2003, prof. emeritus, 2003—. Cons. NIH, Bethesda, Md., 1977-04; acting dir. Hormel inst. U. Minn., 1985-87, exec. dir., 1987-01; faculty mem. Mayo Med. Sch., Rochester, Minn., 1990-03. Mng. editor Chemistry and Physics of Lipids, Elsevier Sci. Pubs., Amsterdam, The Netherlands, 1984-01; contbr. numerous articles to profl. jours. Rsch. grantee NIH, 1967-01. Mem. AAAS, Am. Soc. Biochemistry and Molecular Biology, Am. Chem. Soc., The Oxygen Soc. Avocations: yacht racing, downhill skiing, classical music. Office: U Minn Hormel Inst 801 16th Ave NE Austin MN 55912-3679 Business E-Mail: hoschmid@hi.umn.edu.

SCHMIDT, ARLO E., state legislator; m. Marion Schmidt; 6 children. Grad., Am. Sch. Auctioneering. Auctioneer; rep. Dist. 12 N.D. Ho. of Reps., mem. indsl. bus. and labor and govt. and vet. affairs coms. Named to N.D. Auctioneers Hall of Fame. Mem. N.D. Auctioneers Assn. (past pres.), Legionnaires. Office: ND Ho of Reps State Capitol Bismarck ND 58505

SCHMIDT, CHUCK, professional football team executive; b. Detroit, Jan. 22, 1947; m. Sharon Schmidt; children: Scott, Krista, Matthew. Degree in bus., U. Mich.; grad. degree in fin., Wayne State U. Formerly with Ernst and Whinney; CPA Detroit Lions, from 1976, also contr., then v.p. fin., until 1987, exec. v.p., chief oper. officer, 1989—. Bd. dirs., sec., treas. Detroit Lions Charities; bd. dirs. CATCH, Pontiac (Mich.) Devel. Found. Office: Detroit Lions Inc 222 Republic Dr Allen Park MI 48101-3650

SCHMIDT, DEREK, state legislator; b. Independence, Kans., Jan. 23, 1968; m. Jennifer Shaw, May 23, 1998. Student, Independence C.C.; B, Kans. U., 1990; M in Internat. Politics, U. Leicester, Eng., 1992; JD, Georgetown U., 1996. Bar: Kans. 1996, DC 1996, US Supreme Ct. 2003. Mem. legis. staff Senator Nancy Kassebaum, 1992—96; gen. counsel, legis. dir. Senator Chuck Hagel, 1996—98; asst. atty. gen. State of Kans., 1999; legis. liaison, spl. counsel to Kans. Gov. Bill Graves, 2000; pvt. practice Scovel, Emert, Heasty & Chubb, Independence, 2000—; mem. Kans. Senate from 15th dist., Topeka, 2001—, majority leader, 2005—, chmn. agr. com., 2001—05, chmn., post audit com., 2004—05, chmn. confirmation oversight com., 2005—, chmn. spl. com on Medicaid reform, 2005. Bd. dirs. Independence Industries, Inc. Grad. Leadership Kans., 1999; trustee, ea. Kans. br. Nat. Multiple Sclerosis Soc.; active Am. Coun. Young Polit. Leaders. Ralph Kirchner scholar U. Leicester; fellow Bowhay Inst. for Legis. Leadership Devel.; Henry Toll fellow, 2002, Simons Pub. Humanities fellow U. Kans., 2006, Aspen Inst. Rodel fellow, 2007-. Mem.: Kans. State Hist. Soc., Inc. (bd. dirs. 2000—07), Rotary. Republican. Office: State Capitol Rm 392E Topeka KS 66612 Office Phone: 785-296-2497.

SCHMIDT, GARY DAVID, language educator; b. Massapequa, NY, Apr. 14, 1957; s. Robert H. and Jeanne A. (Smith) S.; m. Anne E. Stickney, Dec. 22, 1979; six children. BA, Gordon Coll., 1979; MA in Lit., U. Ill., 1981, PhD in

Lit., 1985. Teaching asst. U. Ill., Urbana, 1979-85; prof. English Calvin Coll., Grand Rapids, Mich., 1985—. Book reviewer, 1987—. Author: Robert McCloskey, 1990, Hugh Lofting, 1992, Anson's Way, 1999, Straw into Gold, 2001, A Passionate Usefulness: The Life and Literary Labors of Hannah Adams, 2004, Lizzie Bright and the Buckminster Boy, 2005, Mara's Stories, 2005, First Boy, 2005; co-editor: Voice of the Narrator, 1989, Sitting at the Feet of the Past, 1992, Communities of Discourse, 1992. Mem. Early English Text Soc. Avocation: farming. Office: Calvin Coll English Dept Grand Rapids MI 49546 Home Phone: 616-868-0067; Office Phone: 616-526-6540. E-mail: sdg@calvin.edu.

SCHMIDT, GARY P., lawyer, personal care industry executive; b. Youngstown, Ohio, Mar. 25, 1951; BA, Miami U., 1973; JD, U. Akron, 1976. Gen. counsel Lyphomed, Inc., 1988—90; v.p., sec., gen. counsel Fujisawa USA, Inc., 1990—97; v.p., asst. sec., gen. counsel Alberto-Culver Co., Melrose Park, Ill., 1997—2000, sr. v.p., asst. sec., gen. counsel, 2000—. Mem.: ABA, Patent Law Assn., Ill. State Bar Assn., Chicago Bar Assn. Office: Alberto-Culver Co 2525 Armitage Ave Melrose Park IL 60160

SCHMIDT, GORDON PEIRCE, artistic director; Former dancer; resident choreographer Ballet Chgo., 1990-95; artistic dir. Grand Rapids (Mich.) Ballet, 1999—. Office: Grand Rapids Ballet Co 341 Ellsworth Ave Grand Rapids MI 49503-4045

SCHMIDT, JEAN, congresswoman; b. Cin., Nov. 29, 1951; m. Peter W. Schmidt; 1 child, Emilie. BS in Polit. Sci., U. Cin., 1974. Tchg. cert. in secondary edn. U. Cin., 1986. Trustee, Miami Ohio, 1989—2000; mem. Ohio State Ho. Reps. from Dist. 66, 2001—04, US Congress from 2nd Ohio dist., 2005—. Chmn. Clermont County Rep. Party, 1996—98, Taft for Gov., 1998; mem. agr. com. US Congress, mem. transp. and infrastructure com. Mem. Milford Miami Twp. C. of C., 1989—, Ohio Twp. Assn., 1990—, Clermont County Twp. Assn., 1990—, Clermont County 20/20 Com., 1990—, Clermont County League of Women Voters, 1990—, Clermont County Agrl. Soc., 1990—, Clermont County C. of C., 1990—, mem. econ. devel. com., 1995—2005; mem. Leukemia Soc. Team in Tng., 1994—, mentor, 1996—; bd. trustees Clermont County Libr., 1980—92, 1994—2000, 2005—; bd. mem. Clermont County Mercy Hosp. Found., 1997—, Phoenix Pl., 2005—; founder, chmn. Sauls Found. 5K Race, 1995—. Named Marriage & Family Therapy Legislator of Yr., 2003, Empowerment Coalition Legislator of Yr., 2004, Am. Liver Found. Legislator of Yr., 2004, Bioscience Legislator of Yr., 2004; recipient Clermont County Cmty. Devel. of the Greater Cin. Found. Appreciation award, 2003, Clermont County Mental Health Svc. Recognition Award, 2003, Children's Hosp. Award of Distinction, 2003, So. Ohio Agrl. and Cmty. Devel. Found. Disting. Svc. Award, 2004. Republican. Roman Catholic. Avocations: long distance running, auto racing. Office: US House Reps 238 Cannon House Office Bldg Washington DC 20515 Office Phone: 202-225-3164. Office Fax: 202-225-1992.

SCHMIDT, JOHN R., lawyer; b. Chgo., Nov. 24, 1943; s. Edward F. and Josephine (Roggen) S.; m. Janet Gilroy, Apr. 24, 1982; 1 child, Laura. BA, Harvard U., 1964, JD, 1967. Bar: Ill. 1967, U.S. Dist. Ct. (no. dist.) Ill. 1972, U.S. Supreme Ct. 1972. Assoc. Mayer, Brown & Platt, Chgo., 1967-73, ptnr., 1973-84, Skadden, Arps, Slate, Meagher & Flom, Chgo., 1984-93; Amb., chief US negotiator Uruguay Round, 1993—94; assoc. atty. gen. U.S. Dept. Justice, Washington, 1994—97; ptnr. Mayer, Brown, Rowe & Maw, LLP, Chgo., 1998—. Vis. scholar Northwestern U. Sch. Law, 1997—98. Contbr. articles to profl. jours. Chmn. Ill. Guardianship and Advocacy Commn., 1979-82, Met. Pier and Exposition Authority, Chgo., 1989-94; chief of staff City of Chgo., 1989; co-chmn. Citizens for Ct. Reform, Chgo., 1986-92; trustee Ill. Inst. Tech., 1991-93, 1998-, Chgo. Symphony Orch., 1978-93, 1998-. Recipient Judge Learned Hand Human Rels. award Am Jewish Com., 1992. Fellow Am. Bar Found.; mem. ABA, Chgo. Coun. Lawyers (pres. 1974-76). Office: Mayer Brown Rowe Maw LLP 71 S Wacker Dr Chicago IL 60606-4637 Office Phone: 312-701-8597. Office Fax: 312-706-8397. Business E-Mail: jschmidt@mayerbrownrowe.com.

SCHMIDT, KELLY, state official; b. Elmhurst, Ill. married; 4 children. State treas. State of ND, 2004—. Pres. ND Jump$tart Coalition for Personal Fin. Literacy; trustee ND State Hist. Bd. Found. Mem.: Nat. Assn. State Treas. (pres., Midwest State Treas.), Bus. Profl. Women, AmVets Auxiliary, Am. Legion Auxiliary. Republican. Office: State Treas 600 E Blvd Ave 3d fl Bismarck ND 58505-0130 Office Phone: 701-328-2643. Office Fax: 701-328-3002. Business E-Mail: klschmidt@nd.gov.

SCHMIDT, MARK JAMES, state public health official; b. Milw., July 16, 1955; s. Warren J. and Carolyn Juel (Gissing) S.; m. Janet M. Schmidt, Oct. 5, 1991; children: Andrew T., Rachel M., Malia D.; stepchildren: Nathan A. and Aaron M. Stotts. BA, U. Wis., Eau Claire, 1977; MSc., Ill. State U., 1978. Dir. debate U. No. Iowa, Cedar Falls, 1978-79; dir. comm. Ill. Rep. Party, Springfield, 1979-83; asst. adminstr. driver svc. dept. Office of the Sec. State, Springfield, Ill., 1983-87, asst. to dir., driver svc. dept., 1987-91; dir. pub. affairs Ill. Dept. Ctrl. Mgmt. Svcs., 1991-95; asst. dir. Ill. Dept. Pub. Health, Springfield, 1995-2000, acting dep. dir. Office of Health and Wellness, 1999-2000, dep. dir. Office of Health Promotion, 2000—03, chief divsn. children's health and safety, 2003—. Guest lectr. cert. program in health policy Am. Osteo. Assn., 1997; guest lectr. Ill. Pub. Health Leadership Inst., 1999—2000, Leadership Springfield Conf., 1999, 2000; guest lectr. polit. comm. Ill. State U., Normal, 1980; guest lectr. social mktg. U. Ill., Springfield, 2001—02; cons. 6th Congl. Dist. Rep. Com., Lombard, Ill., 1985—90; rep. Ill. Drivers Lic. Compact Com., Falls Church, Va., 1987—91; mem. Ill. Rural Health Assn.; bd. dirs. Ill. Rural Ptnrs., Inc., 1995—2000, co-chmn. pub. sector, 1997—99; chmn. Rural Transp. Task Force, 1997—2001; mem. Ill. Rural Ptnrs. Telecomm. Commn., 1999—2000; keynote spkr. conf. on managed care Coop. Extension Svc., 1996; keynote spkr. Ill. Rural Poverty Conf., 1998, SIU Cancer Prevention and Control Conf., 2002; leader, mentor Mid-Am. Regional Pub. Health Leadership Inst., 1999—; chair Springfield Pub. Health and Safety Strategy Group, 1999—2003; mem. panel advisors Mayor Karen Hasarn, Springfield; chair Ill. Adoption Registry Adv. Coun., 1999—2001; staff Gov.'s Domestic Preparedness Conf., 2001; lectr. tobacco prevention and control Ill. Sch. Health Days, 2001; guest lectr. cert. program in health policy cancer control conf. So. Ill. U., 2002; spkr. in field. Editor: Driver's Handbook (annual) Rules of the Road, 1984-91; editor Driver Svcs. Dept. newsletter, 1988-91, Rural Health News, 1999-2000; contbg. editor: Lyme Disease Handbook for Physicians, 1997, Management and Treatment of Lyme Disease, 1998; co-editor tng. manual for local bds. of health; contbr. articles to profl. jours. Debate strategist Fahner for Atty. Gen. Ill., 1982, Bertini for Congress, Chgo., 1982; advisor Richard Austin for Congress, Springfield, 1984; designer local advt. Al Salvi for Sec. of State of Ill., 1998; health care developer George Ryan for Gov. of Ill., 1998; coord. Citizens for Jim Edgar, Springfield, 1985-91; sr. staff, Ill. gubernatorial transition team, 1990-91; stage mgr. 1999 Ill. Gubernatorial Inauguration; chmn. pub. info. subcom. Ill. Comml. Drivers License Program, 1989-91; media coord. Lincoln Land C.C. Trustee Campaign, 1997; mem. local advance staff George W. Bush for Pres., 1999-2000; mem. long range planning com. 1st United Meth. Ch., Springfield; mem. Food and Nutrition Work Group, Ill. Farm Bill Task Force, 2001. Recipient Gov. Adminstrs. Recognition award Ill. Primary Health Care Assn., 1997, Presdl. award for Outstanding Contbn. Ill. Rural Health Assn., 1999. Fellow: Ill. Pub. Health Leadership Inst.; mem.: Ill. Pub. Health Assn., Order Ea. Star (chmn. Grand chpt. info. com. 2001—02, co-chmn. home rev. com. 2002—03), Masons. Republican. Methodist. Home: 37 Meander Pike Chatham IL 62629-1569 Office: Ill Dept Pub Health 500 E MonroeSt Springfield IL 62701 E-mail: mschmidt@idph.state.il.us.

SCHMIDT, STEPHEN CHRISTOPHER, agricultural economist, educator; b. Isztimer, Hungary, Dec. 20, 1920; came to U.S., 1949, naturalized, 1965; s. Francis Michael and Anne Marie (Angeli) S.; m. Susan M. Varszegi, Dec. 20, 1945; children— Stephen Peter, David William. Dr.Sc., U. Budapest, Hungary, 1945; PhD, McGill U., Montreal, Que., Can., 1958. Asst. head dept. Hungary Ministry Commerce, Budapest, 1947-48; asst. prof. U. Ky., Lexington, 1955-57, Mont. State U., Bozeman, 1957-59, U. Ill., Urbana-Champaign, 1959-63, assoc. prof., 1963-70, prof. agrl. mktg. and policy, 1970-91, prof. emeritus, 1991—. Fulbright grantee Bulgaria, 1992-93; Ford Found. fellow, 1959; Agrl. Devel. Coun. grantee, 1966, U. Man. Rsch. fellow, 1968-69, Ford Found. rsch. grantee, 1973, 74, Whitehall found. grantee, 1979, Internat. Inst. Applied Systems Analyses (Laxenburg, Austria) rsch. scholar, 1976-77, USDA Intergovtl. Personnel Act grantee, 1983-84. Mem. Am. Agrl. Econs. Assn. (award 1979), Internat. Assn. Agrl. Economists, Am. Assn. Advancement Slavic Studies, Ea. Econ. Assn., Sigma Xi, Gamma Sigma Delta. Office: 1301 W Gregory Dr Urbana IL 61801-9015

SCHMIDT, THOMAS JOSEPH, JR., lawyer; b. New Haven, Jan. 16, 1945; s. Thomas Joseph and Rosemary (O'Shaughnessy) S.; m. Linda Diane Crider, Nov. 16, 1974; children: Elizabeth Anne, Thomas Joseph III, Karen Diana. AB, Xavier U., 1967; JD, U. Cin., 1970. Bar: Ohio 1970, U.S. Ct. Mil. Appeals 1970. Commd. 2d lt. U.S. Army, 1967, advanced through grades to capt., 1969-75; legal officer U.S. Army Corps Engrs., Ft. Hayes, Ohio, 1967-68, Ft. Knox, Ky., 1969-70; atty. U.S. Army JAGC, Ft. Benning, Ga., 1971-75; asst. counsel Midland Enterprises Inc., Cin., 1975-77, assoc. gen. counsel, 1977-83, gen. counsel, 1983-87, gen. counsel, sec., 1987-95, v.p., gen. counsel and sec., 1995—. Republican. Roman Catholic. Office: Midland Enterprises Inc 2500 Chamber Center Dr Ste 200 Lakeside Park KY 41017-1604

SCHMIDT, THOMAS WALTER, airport executive; b. St. Paul, Nov. 16, 1938; s. Elmer John and Margaret Elizabeth (Cunnien) S.; m. Roxanne B. Therrien, Mar. 1, 1980; children: Susan, Johnette, Holly. BA, U. Minn., 1961. Accredited airport exec. Dir. aviation Burlington (Vt.) Internat. Airport, 1970-83; asst. dir. aviation McCarran Internat. Airport, Las Vegas, Nev., 1983-89; exec. dir. Capital Region Airport Authority, Lansing, Mich., 1989—. Dir., mem. exec. com. Greater Lansing Conv. and Visitors Bur., Lansing, 1993—; dir. Capital Choice program C. of C., Lansing, 1995—. Mem. Mich. Athletic Club. Office: Capital Region Airport Authority 4100 Capitol City Blvd Lansing MI 48906-2170

SCHMIT, DAVID E., lawyer; b. Charleston, W.Va., Feb. 18, 1947; BSEE, U. Cin., 1969, MSEE, 1976; JD, No. Ky. U., 1975. Bar: Ohio 1975, U.S. Patent and Trademark Office. Mem. Frost Brown Todd LLC, Cin. Office: Frost Brown Todd LLC 2200 PNC Center 201 E 5th St Cincinnati OH 45202-4182 Office Phone: 513-651-6985. Business E-Mail: dschmit@fbtlaw.com.

SCHMITT, ANDREW B., manufacturing executive; Pres. NL Acme Tool, 1985-88; v.p., gen. mgr. Tri-State Oil Tools, Inc., Bossier City, La., 1988-90, pres., 1990; pres., CEO Layne Christensen Co., Mission Woods. Office: Layne Christensen Co Ste 100 1900 Shawnee Mission Pkwy Mission KS 66205-3600

SCHMITT, GEORGE FREDERICK, JR., materials engineer; b. Louisville, Nov. 3, 1939; s. George Frederick and Jane Limbird (Hurst) S.; m. Ann Cheatham, July 31, 1965; 2 children. BS, U. Louisville, 1962, MS, 1963; MBA, Ohio State U., 1966. Advanced engring devel. mgr. USAF Materials Lab., Wright Patterson AFB, Ohio, 1986-90, chief plans and programs br. Wright AFB, Ohio, 1989-90, asst. chief nonmetallic materials divsn., 1990-96, chief integration and ops. divsn., 1997—2005; dir. internat. programs Air Force Rsch. Lab. USAF Materials Directorate, Wright Patterson AFB, Ohio, 1966—. Guest lectr. U. Dayton, 1970, 95, Cath. U., 1973, U. Mich., 1975. Contbr. articles to profl. jours. Mem. Kettering (Ohio) Civic Band, 1965—, Affiliate Socs. Coun. Dayton, 1972-81; mem. Dayton Philharm Chorus, 1999—, Dayton Letter Carriers Band, 2000—, Windjammers Circus Music Preservation Soc., 2001—. 1st lt. USAF, 1963-66. Named Fed. Profl. Employee of Yr., Dayton, 1972; named one of Ten Outstanding Engrs., Engrs. Week, 1975; recipient Meritorious Civilian Svc. award, USAF, 1994, Burton award, Playhouse South Cmty. Theater, 1998, Tech. Transfer award, Fed. Lab. Consortium, 2001, Internat. Program Supr. award, USAF, 2002, Internat. Program Non-Supr. award, 2007, Internat. award, USAF Materiel Command, 2006. Fellow Soc. for Advancement Materials and Process Engrs. (Best Paper award 1973, nat. sec. 1975-76, nat. membership chmn. 1977-79, nat. v.p. 1979-81, nat pres. 1981-82, chmn. long-range planning com. 1983-87, trustee 1991—, chmn. Internat. SAMPE Symposium 1996, chmn. SAMPE Trophy com. 1998-2004, chmn. internat. conf., 2003, adminstr. Fellows program 1997-2007), AIAA (assoc., materials tech. com.); mem. ASTM (rec. sec. 72-75, chmn. com. on erosion and wear 1976-79, chmn. liaison subcom. 1979-83, award of merit 1981), Am. Chem. Soc., Affiliate Socs. Coun. Dayton (chmn. 1978-79). Republican. Lutheran. Home: 1500 Wardmier Dr Dayton OH 45459-3354 Office: AFRL Materials and Mfg Directorate RXO Wright-Patterson AFB 2977 Hobson Way Bldg 653 Dayton OH 45433-7733 Office Phone: 937-656-9209. Business E-Mail: george.schmitt@wpafb.af.mil.

SCHMITT, HOWARD STANLEY, minister; b. Waterloo, Ont., Can., Oct. 19, 1933; came to U.S., 1971; s. Delton Howard and Beulah (Weber) S.; m. Dorothy Jean West, May 20, 1960; children: Valerie Jean Schmitt Jones, Jeffrey Howard. B Theology, Toronto Bible Coll., Ont., Can., 1963. Ordained to ministry Mennonite Ch., 1963. Pastor Wanner Mennonite Ch., Cambridge, Ont., 1960-71, Calvary Mennonite Ch., Ayr, Ont., 1964-69, S. Union Mennonite Ch., West Liberty, Ohio, 1971-83; hosp. chaplain Mary Rutan Hosp., Bellefontaine, Ohio, 1983-85; dir. devel. Adriel Sch., West Liberty, Ohio, 1985-86; pastor Bay Shore Mennonite Ch., Sarasota, Fla., 1986-95, Sharon Mennonite Ch., Plain City, Ohio, 1995—2004; transitional pastor Oak Grove Mennonite Ch., West Liberty, Ohio, 2004—. Sec. Mennonite Conf. Ont., Cambridge, 1970-71; overseer Ohio Conf. Mennonites, West Liberty, 1972-78, 84-86; moderator Southeast Mennonite Conf., Sarasota, 1989-92; mem. Mennonite Ch. Gen. Bd., 1991-95. Vice chair Mary Rutan Hosp. Bd., 1978-83; sec. Plain City Ch. Fellowship, 1997—2002. Recipient 13 Yrs. Svc. award Vol. Chaplains Group, Mary Rutan Hosp., 1985. Mem. Sarasota Mennonite Mins. Fellowship (past sec., chmn.), Plain City Pastors' Fellowship, Ctrl. Ohio Mennonite Pastor Peer Group, Ohio Conf. Mennonites Coun. Mennonite. E-mail: howjean@prodigy.net.

SCHMITT, MARK FRANCIS, bishop emeritus; b. Algoma, Wis., Feb. 14, 1923; Student, Salvatorian Sem., St. Nazianz, Wis., St. John's Sem., Collegeville, Minn. Ordained priest Diocese of Green Bay, Wis., 1948, aux. bishop, 1070—1978; ordained bishop, 1970; bishop Diocese of Marquette, Mich., 1978—92, bishop emeritus, 1992—. Roman Catholic. Office: Chancery Office 444 S 4th St PO Box 550 Marquette MI 49855-0550 Office Phone: 906-225-1141.*

SCHMITT, WOLF RUDOLF, consumer products executive; b. Koblenz, Germany, Mar. 12, 1944; s. Josef H. and M.H. (Baldus) S.; m. Toni A. Yoder, June 30, 1974. BA, Otterbein Coll., 1966; AMP, Harvard U. Bus. Sch., 1986. With Rubbermaid Inc., Wooster, Ohio, 1966—, pres., gen. mgr. housewares products div., 1984-91, exec. v.p., bd. dirs., 1987-91, pres., chief operating officer, 1991-92; chmn., CEO, 1993-99; ret., 1999. Bd. dirs. Parker Hannifin Corp. Bd. dirs. Otterbein Coll., 1992—, Secrest Arboretum, 2002—. Avocations: horticulture, tennis, sailing. Office: Trends 2 Innovation 105 E Liberty St Wooster OH 44691-4345

SCHMITZ, JOHN, energy and food products executive; BS in Acctg., St. Cloud State U., Minn. CPA, Minn. With Harvest States (merged with Cenex, now CHS Inc.), Inver Grove Heights, Minn., 1974—, v.p., contr., 1986—98, sr. v.p., CFO, 1999, exec. v.p., CFO. Bd. dirs. Nat. Coop. Refinery Assn., Cofina Fin., LLC. Mem. AICPA, Nat. Soc. Accts. for Coops., Minn. Soc. CPAs. Office: CHS Inc PO Box 64089 Saint Paul MN 55164-0089 Office Phone: 651-355-3778. E-mail: john.schmitz@chsinc.com.

SCHMITZ, ROGER ANTHONY, chemical engineer, educator, academic administrator; b. Carlyle, Ill., Oct. 22, 1934; s. Alfred Bernard and Wilma Afra (Aarns) Schmitz; m. Ruth Mary Kuhl, Aug. 31, 1957; children: Jan, Joy, Joni. BSChemE, U. Ill., 1959; PhD in Chem. Engring., U. Minn., 1962. Prof. chem. engring. U. Ill., Urbana, 1962-79; Keating-Crawford prof. chem. engring. U. Notre Dame, Ind., 1979—2005, prof. emeritus, 2005—, chmn. dept. chem. engring. Ind., 1979-81, dean engring. Ind., 1981-87, v.p., assoc. provost Ind., 1987-95. Cons. Amoco Chems., Naperville, Ill., 1966—77; vis. prof. Calif. Inst. Tech., LA, 1968—69. Contbr. articles to profl. jours. With US Army, 1953—55. Fellow, Guggenheim Found., 1968. Mem.: AIChE (A.P. Colburn award 1970, R.H. Wilhelm award 1981), Am. Soc. Engring. Edn. (George Westinghouse award 1977), Nat. Acad. Engring. Roman Catholic. Home: 16865 Londonberry Ln South Bend IN 46635-1444 Office: U otre Dame 305 Cushing Hall Notre Dame IN 46556 Office Phone: 574-631-7798. Business E-Mail: rschmitz@nd.edu.

SCHNABEL, ROBERT VICTOR, retired academic administrator; b. Scarsdale, NY, Sept. 28, 1922; s. Frederick Victor and Louise Elizabeth (Frick) S.; m. Ellen Edyth Foelber, June 7, 1946; children: Mark F., Philip P. Student, Concordia Sem., St. Louis, 1943-45; AB, Bowdoin Coll., 1944; MS, Fordham U., 1951, PhD, 1955; LLD (hon.), Concordia Coll., 1988. Tchr. St. Paul's Sch., Ft. Wayne, Ind., 1945-49; prin. St. Matthew's Sch., NYC, 1949-52; asso. supt. edn. Central Dist., Luth. Ch.-Mo. Synod, 1952-56; asst. prof. philosophy Concordia Sr. Coll., Ft. Wayne, 1956-60, assoc. prof., 1960-65, prof., acad. dean, 1966-71; pres. Concordia Coll., Bronxville, NY, 1971-76; acad. v.p., dean Wartburg Coll., Waverly, Iowa, 1976-78; pres. Valparaiso (Ind.) U., 1978-88. Cons. Luth. Edn. Conf. N.Am., 1977-88. Contbr. articles to profl. jours. Mem. AAUP, Luth. Acad. Scholarship, Assoc. Colls. Ind., Nat. Assn. Ind. Colls. and Univs., Rotary, Phi Delta Kappa. Office: Valparaiso Univ 23 Huegli Hall Valparaiso IN 46383

SCHNEIDER, ARTHUR SANFORD, medical educator; b. LA, Mar. 24, 1929; s. Max and Fannie (Ragin) S.; m. Edith Kadison, Aug. 20, 1950; children: Jo Ann Schneider Farris, William Scott, Lynnellen. BS, UCLA, 1951; MD, Chgo. Med. Sch., 1955. Diplomate Am. Bd. Internal Medicine, Am. Bd. Pathology. Intern, Wadsworth VA Hosp., Los Angeles, 1955-56, resident, 1956-59, chief clin. pathology sect., 1962-68; mem. faculty UCLA, 1961-75, clin. assoc. prof., 1971-75; chair dept. clin. pathology City of Hope Med. Ctr., Duarte, Calif., 1968-75; prof., chair dept. clin. pathology Whittier Coll., 1974-75; prof., chair dept. pathology Chgo. Med. Sch., 1975—; chief lab. service VA Med. Ctr., North Chicago, Ill., 1975-86, chief lab. hematology, 1986-94. Sr. author: BRS Pathology, 1993; sr. author 3d edit., 2006; contbr. chapters to books, articles to profl. jours. Served to capt. M.C., USAF, 1959-61. Fellow: ACP, Am. Soc. Clin. Pathologists, Coll. Am. Pathologists; mem.: AMA, AAUP, Group Rsch. in Pathology Edn., Lake County Med. Soc., Ill. Med. Soc., Am. Soc. Clin. Rsch., Am. Assn. Blood Banks, Am. Soc. Hematology, Acad. Clin. Lab. Physicians and Scientists, Assn. Pathology Chairs, Am. Assn. Investigative Pathology, Internat. Acad. Pathology, Alpha Omega Alpha, Sigma Xi, Phi Delta Epsilon. Office: Chgo Med Sch Rosalind Franklin U Medicine and Sci 3333 Green Bay Rd North Chicago IL 60064-3037 Home Phone: 847-234-5693; Office Phone: 847-578-3260. E-mail: arthur.schneider@rosalindfranklin.edu.

SCHNEIDER, CARL EDWARD, law educator; b. Exeter, NH, Feb. 23, 1948; s. Carl Jacob and Dorothy (Jones) S.; m. Joan L. Wagner, Jan. 6, 1976. BA, Harvard Coll., 1972; JD, U. Mich., 1979. Curriculum specialist Mass. Tchrs. Assn., Boston, 1972-75; law clk. to judge U.S. Ct. Appeals (D.C. cir.), Washington, 1979-80; law clk. Potter Stewart U.S. Supreme Ct., Washington, 1980-81; asst. prof. law U. Mich., Ann Arbor, 1981-84, assoc. prof. law, 1984-86, prof. law, 1986—, prof. internal medicine, 1998—, Chauncey Stillman prof. ethics, morality and practice of law; vis. prof. U. Tokyo, 1998. Disting. vis. prof. US Air Force Acad., 2007. Author: The Practice of Autonomy: Patients, Doctors and Medical Decisions, 1998, (with Margaret F. Brinig) An Invitation to Family Law, 1996, (with Marsha Garrison) The Law of Bioethics, 2003; editor: (book) The Law and Politics of Abortion, 1980, Family Law in Action: A Reader, 1999 (with Margaret F. Brinig and Lee E. Teitelbaum), Law at the End of Life: The Supreme Court and Assisted Suicide, 2000; contbr. articles to profl. jours. Mem. Pres. Coun. Bioethics, 2006—, 2006—. Fellow Am. Council of Learned Socs., Ford Found., 1985, Hastings Ctr.; life fellow Clare Coll., Cambridge. Fellow Am. Coll. Legal Medicine (hon.); mem. Order of Coif. Office Phone: 734-647-4170.

SCHNEIDER, CAROL ANN, staffing services company executive; d. Glenn William and Beatrice Helen Kluth; m. Leon A. Schneider, Feb. 4, 1961; children: Paul, Joel, Neil. BEd in Bus. Edn., U. Wis., Whitewater, 1958; postgrad., U. Wis., 1971-74. Lic. secondary bus. educator, Wis., vocat. bus. educator, Wis.; cert. pers. cons.; sr. prof. in human resources. Bus. divsn. chair Milw. Area Tech. Coll.-North, Mequon, Wis., 1969-80, Port Washington (Wis.) Vocat., Tech. and Adult Sch., 1969-80; founder, CEO, chair of the bd. SEEK, Inc., Grafton, Wis., 1971—. Founder, mgr. The Schneider Co., LLC, Grafton, 1996—, ITech Profls., LLC, Grafton, 1998—, Guardian HealthStaff, LLC, 2002; past pres. Wis. Assn. Staffing Svcs.; presenter in field. Fund raising chair St. Joseph's Ch.; founder, past co-chair Workforce 2010; founder, co-chair Ozaukee County Transp. Mgmt. Assn.; former bd. mem. Ozaukee County Econ. Devel. Corp.; bd. mem., capitol campaign mem. B.A.B.E.S. Recipient Celebrate Success award Wis. Women Entrepreneurs, 1993, named Outstanding Citizen, Grafton C. of C., Nat. Employer of Yr., Coun. for Exceptional Children Divsn. on Career Devel. and Transition, 1998, Outstanding Bus. of Yr., Grafton Area C. of C., 1998, Wis. Welfare-to-Work Small Bus. Person of Yr., U.S. Small Bus. Adminstrn., 1999; named Woman of Yr. Wis. Women Entrepreneurs, 2000. Mem. FOCUS (founder, past pres., past v.p.), Am. Staffing Assn. (nat. temporary help week regional chair), Exec. Women's Orgn. (v.p. Envision program), Wis. Assn. Pers. Svcs. (past pres.), Washington/Ozaukee County Pers. Mgmt. Assn. (past pres.), Ind. Bus. Assn. Wis. (past bd. dirs., past pres., past v.p. state programs, past welfare reform chair, Mem. of Yr. award 1999). Republican. Roman Catholic. Avocations: community service, playing piano, reading, politics. Office: SEEK Inc PO Box 148 Grafton WI 53024-0148

SCHNEIDER, DAN W., lawyer, consultant; b. Salem, Oreg., Apr. 28, 1947; s. Harold Otto and Frances Louise (Warner) S.; m. Nancy Merle Schmalzbauer, Mar. 29, 1945; children: Mark Warner, Edward Michael. BA cum laude, St. Olaf Coll., 1969; JD, Willamette U., 1974; LLM, Columbia U., 1975. Bar: Oreg. 1974, D.C. 1978, Ill. 1987. Trial atty. U.S. Dept. Justice Antitrust, Washington, 1975-79; dep. assoc. dir. U.S. SEC, Washington, 1979-86; gen. ptnr. Schiff Hardin & Waite, Chgo., 1986-95; name ptnr. Smith Lodge & Schneider, Chgo., 1995-98; ptnr. Hopkins & Sutter, Chgo., 1998-2000; internat. ptnr. Baker & McKenzie, Chgo., 2000—. Bd. dirs. NygaarArt, Northfield, Minn. Contbr. articles to profl. jours. Trustee, sec. Ill. Acad. Fine Arts, Chgo., 1990-98; mem. adv. bd. Flaten Art Mus., Northfield, 1990—; mem. adv. bd. Hallie Ford Mus. Art, Salem, Oreg., 1999—; pres. adv. group arts in edn. Willamette U., 2004—. Recipient 1st prize Nathan Burkan Law Essay Competition ASCAP, N.Y., 1974, Christie award Securities Transfer Assn., 1987. Mem. Met. Club. Chgo., Monroe Club, Plaza Club. Avocations: art collecting, art writing, music composition. Office: Baker & McKenzie 1 Prudential Plz 130 E Randolph St Ste 3700 Chicago IL 60601-6342 Business E-Mail: dan.w.schneider@bakernet.com.

SCHNEIDER, DAVID MILLER, lawyer; b. Cleve., July 27, 1937; s. Earl Philip and Margaret (Miller) S.; children: Philip M., Elizabeth Dale. BA, Yale U., 1959; LL.B., Harvard U., 1962. Assoc. Baker & Hostetler, Cleve., 1962-72, ptnr., 1972-89; cons. Progressive Casualty Ins. Co., Cleve., 1989-99; sec. The Progressive Corp., Cleve., 1989-99. Trustee Alcoholism Svcs. of Cleve., 1977—, pres., 1980-82, chmn., 1982-84; v.p. Ctr. for Human Svcs., Cleve., 1980-83; trustee Cleve. chpt. NCCJ, 1986—. Mem. Ohio Bar Assn., Bar Assn. Cleve., Union Club, Tavern Club, Hunt Club, Town Club (Jamestown, N.Y.), Ojibway Club (Pointe au Baril, Ont., Can.). Republican. Episcopalian. Office: The Progressive Corp 300 N Commons Blvd Cleveland OH 44143 Home: 7100 South Ln Willoughby OH 44094-9389

SCHNEIDER, DONALD J., trucking company executive; b. Green Bay, Wis., 1935; married; 5 children. BA, St. Norbert Coll., 1957; MBA, U. Pa. Pres. Schneider Transport Inc., Green Bay, Wis., 1957—; CEO, pres. Schneider National, Inc., 1971—2002, chmn. Office: Schneider National Inc PO Box 2545 Green Bay WI 54306-2545

SCHNEIDER, JAMES JOSEPH, military theory educator, consultant; b. Oshkosh, Wis., June 18, 1947; s. Joseph Edward and Virginia Gertrude Schneider; m. Peggy L. Spees, July 28, 1973 (dec. May 1976); m. Claretta Virginia Burton, Nov. 11, 1984; children: Kevin, Jason, Jenifer, Julie. BA, U. Wis., Oshkosh, 1973, MA, 1974; PhD, U. Kans., 1992. Planning evaluator Winnegago County, Oshkosh, 1978-80; ops. rsch. analyst Tng. and Doctrine Command Analysis Ctr., Ft. Leavenworth, Kans., 1980-84; prof. mil. theory Sch. Advanced Mil. Studies U.S. Army Command and Gen. Staff Coll., Ft. Leavenworth, 1984—. Adj. assoc. prof. history Russian and East European Studies Ctr., U. Kans., 1994—; vis. assoc. prof. philosophy St. Mary Coll., Leavenworth, Kans., 2000. Author: (monograph) Exponential Decay of Armies in Battle, 1985, The Structure of Strategic Revolution, 1994; also numerous articles. With U.S. Army, 1965-68, Vietnam. Recipient medal for civilian achievement Dept. Army, 1989, superior civilian svc. award, 2001, Bronze Order of St. George, U.S. Cav. Assn., 1990 Mem. Am. Hist. Assn., Mil. Ops. Rsch. Soc., Soc. Mil. History, Phi Beta Delta. Office: U S Army Command/Gen Staff Coll Sch Advanced Mil Studies Fort Leavenworth KS 66027

SCHNEIDER, JOHN DURBIN, state legislator; b. St. Louis, Mar. 1, 1937; s. F. John and Kathleen (Durbin) S.; m. Mary Jo Steppan; children: Anne Marie, John Steppan, Robert Durbin. BS, JD, St. Louis U., 1960. Atty. Transit Casualty Co., 1960-65, chief trial atty., 1965-70; rep. Mo. Ho. Reps. Dist. 26, Jefferson City, 1969-70; mem. Mo. Senate Dist. 14, Jefferson City, 1970—. Mem. St. Louis Bar Assn., Phi Delta Phi. Address: 3520 Tremont Dr Florissant MO 63033-3057 also: State Senate State Capitol Bldg Rm 422 Jefferson City MO 65101-1556

SCHNEIDER, MAHLON C., lawyer; b. 1939; BA, U. Minn., 1962, LLB, 1964. Bar: Minn. 1965. Atty. Green Giant Co., 1968—80, Pillsbury, 1980-84, v.p., gen. counsel foods divsn., 1984-89; corp. atty. Hormel Foods Corp., Austin, Minn., 1989-90, v.p., gen. counsel, 1990-99, sr. v.p. external affairs, gen. counsel, 1999—2005. Bd. dirs. HMN Fin. Inc., 2000—. Office: HMN Fin 1016 Civic Center Dr NW Rochester MN 55901 Office Phone: 507-437-5611.

SCHNEIDER, MARLIN DALE, state legislator; b. La Crosse, Wis., Nov. 16, 1942; s. Donald M. and Elva M. (Peterson) S.; m. Georgia Jean Johansen, 1973; children: Jeanine Marie, Molly Anne. BS, U. Wis., La Crosse, 1965; MST, U. Wis., Stevens Point, 1976; MS, U. Wis., 1979; cert. Police Acad., Madison Area Tech. Coll., 1982. Wis. state rep. Dist. 72, 1970—; Wis. state assemblyman Dist. 59, 1971-72. Asst. majority leader, 1989-90; asst. minority leader, 1995—; tchr. Lomira H.S., Wis., 1965-66, Lincoln H.S., Wisconsin Rapids, 1966-71. Mem. Nat. Conf. State Legis. NSF grantee in sociology La. State U., 1970; named one of Outstanding Young Men of Am., 1973, Wis. Men of Achievement, 1976. Mem. Moose (local 819), Sigma Tau Gamma. Democrat. Address: 3820 Southbrook Ln Wisconsin Rapids WI 54494-7548

SCHNEIDER, MARY LEA, college administrator; Student, Cardinal Stritch Univ., 1960-63; BA in Theology and Philosophy, Marquette U., 1966, MA in Theology, 1969, PhD in Religious Studies, 1971. Asst. prof. dept. religious studies Mich. State U., 1971-79, assoc. prof., 1979-84, prof., 1984-90, acting chair dept. religious studies, 1988-90; pres. Cardinal Stritch Coll., Milw., 1990—. Vis. instr. theology dept. U. San Francisco, summer 1969, Creighton U., summers 1974-77; spkr., presenter papers, mem. seminars in field; cons. Lilly Endowment, 1988; various TV and radio interviews, 1985— Contbr. articles, revs. to profl. publs. Trustee Pub. Policy Forum, Mt. St. Clare Coll., Clinton, Iowa, 1995—; mem. program Peter Favre Forum; mem. Greater Milw. Com. NEH travel grantee, 1986-87, 1990, rsch. grantee Coll. Arts and Letters Mich. State U., 1987-88. Mem. Am. Acad. Religion (chair Thomas Merton consultation 1979-81), Coll. Theology Soc. (chair Detroit-Cleve. region 1975-77, mem. com. on membership and objectives 1977-79, program dir., chair ann. conv. 1981-84, 88, convenor ecclesiology sect. ann. conv. 1984-87, pres. 1988-90, bd. dirs. 1990-92), Cath. Theol. Soc. Am., Am. Cath. Hist. Soc., History of Women in Religious etwork, Tempo (Greater Milw. com.), Wis. Assn. Ind. Colls. and Univs. (exec. com. 1995—, chair, 1997—). Home: 225 W Bradley Rd Milwaukee WI 53217-3154 Office: Cardinal Stritch Univ 6801 N Yates Rd Milwaukee WI 53217-3945

SCHNEIDER, MATHIEU, professional hockey player; b. NYC, June 12, 1969; married. Defenseman Montreal Canadiens, 1990-95, NY Islanders, 1995-96, Toronto Maple Leafs, 1996-98, NY Rangers, 1998—2000, LA Kings, 2000—03, Detroit Red Wings, 2003—07, Anaheim Ducks, 2007—. Player NHL All-Star Game, 1996, 2003. Achievements include being a member of Stanely Cup Champion Montreal Canadiens, 1993. Office: Anaheim Ducks 2695 E Katella Ave Anaheim CA 92806

SCHNEIDER, MICHAEL JOSEPH, biologist; b. Saginaw, Mich., Apr. 21, 1938; s. Michael Elias and Jane (Moffitt) S.; m. Janet Marie Potter, Nov. 24, 1967. BS, U. Mich., 1960; MS, U. Tenn., 1962; PhD (Hutchinson Meml. fellow 1963-64, John M. Coulter research fellow 1964-65), U. Chgo., 1965. Resident research asso. Nat. Acad. Scis., Beltsville, Md., 1965-67; USPHS fellow U. Wis., Madison, 1967-68; asst. prof. biology Columbia U., 1968-73; mem. faculty U. Mich., Dearborn, 1973—, prof. biology, 1975—, chmn. dept. natural scis., 1975-80, 83-89, assoc. provost for acad. affairs, 1990, interim provost, vice chancellor for acad. affairs, 1991, prof. emeritus, 2003. Vis. prof. Plant Research Lab., Mich. State U., East Lansing, 1980-81 Contbr. articles profl. jours. Mem. AAAS, Am. Soc. Plant Physiologists, Am. Soc. Photobiology, Sigma Xi. Home: 4654 Mulberry Woods Cir Ann Arbor MI 48105-9767 Office: U Mich-Dearborn Dept Nat Scis Dearborn MI 48128-1491

SCHNEIDER, MICHELLE G., state representative; b. 1954; 2 children. Student, Ohio State U., U. Cin. Small bus. owner; mayor Madeira, Ohio, 1997—99; state rep. dist. 35 Ohio Ho. of Reps., Columbus, 2000—, chair, human svcs. and aging com., mem. banking pensions and securities, health, and pub. utilities coms. Councilwoman Madeira City Coun., 1993—. Mem.: Am. Coll. Health Care Adminstrn. (Disting. Health Care Adminstr. Yr. 1989), Madeira Alumni Assn., Madeira Sch. Found. Office: 77 S High St 11th fl Columbus OH 43215-6111

SCHNEIDER, ROBERT F., treasurer; b. 1961; With Kimball Internat., Inc., Jasper, Ind., corp. contr., 1990—, v.p., dir. acctg., 1992—, exec. v.p., CFO, asst. treas., 1997—. Office: Kimball Internat Inc 1600 Royal St Jasper IN 47549-1001

SCHNEIDER, ROBERT JEROME, lawyer; b. Cin., June 22, 1947; s. Jerome William and Agnes (Moehringer) S.; m. Janice Loraine Eckhoff, Dec. 13, 1968; children: Aaron Haisley, Jared Alan, Margot Laraine. BSME, U. Cin., 1970, JD, 1973. Bar: Ill. 1973, U.S. Dist. Ct. (no. dist.) Ill. 1973, U.S. Ct. Appeals (7th cir.) 1973, U.S. Ct. Appeals (fed. cir.) 1973. Ptnr. Mason, Kolehmainen, Rathburn & Wyss, Chgo., 1973-82; ptnr., asst. chmn. patents, chmn. intellect. property dept. McDermott, Will & Emery, Chgo., 1982-94; chmn. intellectual property dept. Chapman & Cutler, Chgo., 1995—. Mem. ABA, ASME, Ill. Bar Assn., Chgo. Bar Assn., Licensing Execs. Soc., Intellectual Property Law Assn. Chgo. (sec. 1981-83), Fedn. Internat. des Conseils en Proriete Industrielle, Assn. Internationale pour la Protection de la Propertiètè Industrielle, Internat. Pat-Got Assn. (treas. 2001-05, pres. 2005-), Internat. Trademark Assn., Internat. Trade Commn. Trial Lawyers Assn., Am. Intellectual Property Law Assn., Tower Club (bd. govs. 1988—, v.p. 1994-95, pres. 1995—), Univ. Club Chgo. (bd. dirs. 2001-). Republican. Roman Catholic. Home: 1609 Asbury Ave Winnetka IL 60093-1303 Office: Chapman & Cutler Chicago IL 60601 Office Fax: 312-803-3529. E-mail: iplaw@chapman.com.

SCHNEIDER, STEVEN PHILIP, aeronautical engineer, educator; b. Chgo., Aug. 4, 1960; s. Philip Walter and Barbara Jean (Brilla) S.; m. Lynette Diane Brown, Aug. 24, 1985; children: Ariel, Kaitlyn. BS with honor, Calif. Inst. Tech., 1981, MS in Aeronautics, 1984, PhD in Aeronautics, 1989. Engr., scientist Naval Ocean Systems Ctr., San Diego, 1981-83; rsch. fellow Calif. Inst. Tech., Pasadena, 1989; asst. prof. Sch. Aero. and Astronautical Engring., West Lafayette, Ind., 1989-95, assoc. prof., 1995—. Presenter in field. Contbr. articles and abstracts to profl. jours. Achievement Rewards for Coll. Scientists scholar, 1986-87. Fellow AIAA (assoc.); mem. Am. Phys. Soc. (fluid dynamics div. 1983—). Avocations: backpacking, bicycling. Office: Purdue U Airport Aerospace Scis Lab West Lafayette IN 47906

SCHNEIDER, THOMAS PAUL, non-profit agency administrator; b. June 5, 1947; s. Milton and Gloria (Bocaner) S.; m. Susan G. Stein, May 31, 1987; children: Rachel Jenny, Daniel Joshua. BA with honors, U. Wis., 1972, JD, 1972. U.S. atty. U.S. Dist. Dist. Ct. (ea. dist.) Wis., Milw., 1993-2001; exec. dir. youth svcs. COA Youth & Family Ctrs., Milw., 2001—. Mem. Wis. Bar Assn. Democrat. Jewish. Office: COA Youth & Family Ctrs 909 E North Ave Milwaukee WI 53212 Office Phone: 414-263-8383. Business E-Mail: tomschneider@coa-yfc.org.

SCHNEIDER-CRIEZIS, SUSAN MARIE, architect; b. St. Louis, Aug. 1, 1953; d. William Alfred and Rosemary Elizabeth (Fischer) Schneider; m. Demetrios Anthony Criezis, Nov. 24, 1978; children: Anthony, John and Andrew. BArch, U. Notre Dame, 1976; MArch, MIT, 1978. Registered architect, Wis. Project designer Eichstaedt Architects, Roselle, Ill., 1978-80, Solomon, Cordwell, Buenz & Assocs., Chgo., 1980-82; project architect Gelick, Foran Assocs., Chgo., 1982-83; asst. prof. Sch. Architecture U. Ill., Chgo., 1980-86; exec. v.p. Criezis Architects, Inc., Northfield, Ill., 1986—2005; dir. cmty. devel. Village of Kenilworth, 2005—. Graham Found. grantee MIT, 1977, MIT scholar, 1976-78; Prestressed Concrete Inst. rsch. grantee, 1981. Mem. AIA, Chgo. Archtl. Club, Chgo. Women in Architecture, Am. Solar Energy Soc., NAFE, Jr. League Evanston, Evanston C. of C. Roman Catholic. Avocations: tennis, swimming. Office: 419 Richmond Rd Kenilworth IL 60043 Office Phone: 847-251-1666. E-mail: scriezis@villageofkenilworth.org.

SCHNELL, CARLTON BRYCE, lawyer; b. Youngstown, Ohio, Jan. 1, 1932; s. Carlton Wilhelm and Helen Jean (Alexander) S.; m. Dorothy Stewart Apple, Aug. 15, 1953; children: Laura, Margaret, Heidi BA, Yale U., 1953, LL.B., 1956. Bar: Ohio 1956. Assoc. Arter & Hadden, Cleve., 1956-65, ptnr., 1966-96, mng. ptnr., 1977-82, Washington, 1982-84. Exec. comm. mem. Greater Cleve. Growth Assn., Cleve., 1983-97; chmn. Build Up Cleve., 1981-89; profl. chmn. United Way, Cleve., 1983; co-chmn. Charter Rev. Commn., Cleve., 1983-84; pres. Citizen's League Rsch. Inst., 1992-95. Named Vol. of Yr., Leadership Cleve., 1985. Mem. Tex. Club Cleve. (pres. 1972-73), Cleve. Tax Inst. (chmn. 1978), Ohio C. of C. (trustee 1977-80) Clubs: Tavern, Pepper Pike. Republican. Presbyterian. Avocations: golf, tennis. Home: 31450 Shaker Blvd Pepper Pike OH 44124-5153

SCHNELL, ROBERT LEE, JR., lawyer; b. Mpls., Sept. 20, 1948; s. Robert Lee and Dorothy Mae (Buran) S.; m. Jacqueline Irene Husak, Dec. 19, 1969 (div. Aug. 1988); children: Robert Lee III, Elizabeth Anne, Jennifer Irene; m. Julie Ann Bemlott, Sept. 29, 1989; children: Helen Bridget, Michael Henry. BA cum laude, Princeton U., 1970; JD magna cum laude, Harvard U., 1974. Bar: Minn. 1974, U.S. Dist. Ct. Minn. 1974, U.S. Ct. Appeals (8th cir.) 1975, U.S. Supreme Ct. 1990. Assoc. Faegre & Benson, Mpls., 1974-81, ptnr., 1982—. Bd. dirs. United Way of Mpls., 1992-93. Office: Faegre & Benson 2200 Wells Fargo Ctr 90 S St Ste 2200 Minneapolis MN 55402-1109 Office Phone: 612-766-7225. E-mail: rschnell@faegre.com.

SCHNOBRICH, ROGER WILLIAM, lawyer; b. New Ulm, Minn., Dec. 21, 1929; s. Arthur George and Amanda (Reinhart) Schnobrich; m. Angeline Ann Schmitz, Jan. 21, 1961; children: Julie A. Johnson, Jennifer L. Holmers, Kathryn M. Kubinski, Karen L. Holetz. BBA, U. Minn., 1952, JD, 1954. Bar: Minn. 1954. Assoc. Fredrikson and Byron, Mpls., 1956-58; pvt. practice Mpls., 1958-60; ptnr. Popham Haik, Schnobrich & Kaufman, Mpls., 1960-97, Hinshaw & Culbertson, Mpls., 1997—2004; officer Wayworth, Inc., Wayzada, Minn., 2004—. Bd. dirs. numerous corps. With US Army, 1954—56. Mem.: ABA, Order of Coif. Roman Catholic. Avocations: jogging, reading, golf. Home and Office: Wayworth Inc 530 Waycliff Dr N Wayzata MN 55391-1385 Personal E-mail: rnapana@aol.com.

SCHNOLL, HOWARD MANUEL, financial consultant, investment company executive; b. Milw., June 6, 1935; s. Nathan P. and Della (Fisher) Schnoll; m. Barbara Ostach, Dec. 3, 1988; children: Jordan, Terry, Jeffrey, Robert, Tammy, Daniel. BBA, U. Wis., 1958. CPA Wis.; cert. mgmt. cons., registered investment advisor. Mng. ptnr. ankin, Schnoll & Co., S.C., Milw., 1966-86; mng. ptnr., bd. dirs. BDO Seidman, 1986-90; pres., COO Universal Med. Bldgs., L.P., Milw., 1990, also bd. dirs.; pres. Howard Schnoll & Assocs., Milw., 1991; mng. dir. Grande, Schnoll & Assocs., Milw., 1992-93; exec. mng. dir., COO Glaisner, Schilffarth, Grande & Schnoll, Ltd., Milw., 1993-98; exec. v.p., treas., bd. dirs. GS2 Securities, Inc., Milw., 1998—2004; sr. v.p. B. C. Ziegler and Co., Milw., 1999—, mng. dir., 2005—06; sr. v.p. Shilffarth-Schnoll Group, RBC Dain Rauscher, Milw., 2006—. Bd. dirs. Milw. World Festival, Inc., 1968—, pres., 2003—05, chmn. bd., 2005—; bd. dirs. City of Festivals Parade, Milw., 1983—89, Aurora Health Care Ventures, Milw. Heart Rsch. Found., Milw., Milw. Heart Inst., Arthritis Found.; pres. Impact, 1993—, bd. dirs.; pres., treas. Am. Heart Assn., Milw., 1978—82; capt. United Way, Milw., 1985; mem. greater Milw. com. Nat. Found. Ileitis and Colitis. Served to sgt. US Army, 1956—63. Mem.: AICPA, Acct. Computer Users Tech. Exchange, Wis. Inst. CPAs, B'nai Brith (pres. 1960—62), Boca Grove Golf and Tennis (bd. dirs. 2003—, treas. 2006—, v.p. 2005—), Brynwood Country Club (pres. 1988—2000, bd. dirs., treas.). Jewish. Avocations: golf, tennis. Office: RBC Dain Rauscher 1000 N Water St Milwaukee WI 53202-4298 Office Phone: 414-347-7106. Business E-Mail: howard.schnoll@rbcdain.com.

SCHNOOR, JEFFREY ARNOLD, lawyer; b. Winnipeg, Man., Can., June 22, 1953; s. Toby and Ray. BA, U. Man., 1974, LLB, 1977. Bar: Man. 1978. Assoc. McJannet Weinberg Rich, Winnipeg, 1977-84, ptnr., 1984-86; exec. dir. Man. Law Reform Commn., Winnipeg, 1986-97; dir. criminal justice policy Man. Dept. Justice, Winnipeg, 1998—2002, exec. dir. policy devel. and analysis, 2002—05, asst. dep. min. cts. divsn., 2005—. Pres. Fedn. Law Reform Agys. Can., 1995-98; del. Uniform Law Conf. Can., 1986-2003, exec. com. 1996-2001, chair civil sect., 1996-97, v.p., 1998-99, pres., 1999-2000. Trustee United Way of Winnipeg, 1990-97, 99-2005, exec. com., 1990-97, 2001-05, treas., 1991-92, pres., 1994-95, cmty. rels. com. 1995-98, chmn. 1996-97, chair United Way 2005 com., 1997-98, hon. solicitor, 2001-05, chmn. 211 implementation com., 2001—; mem. R&D 2000 steering com., United Way of Can., 1995-98; bd. dirs. Winnipeg Libr. Found., 1997-2001, St. Boniface Gen. Hosp., 2005—; Man. Voluntary Sector Coun., 2001-04, U. Man. Winnipeg area study adv. group, 2001-04. Named Queen's Counsel Govt. of Man., 1992; recipient Chair's award of distinction United Way of Can., 1997. Mem. Law Soc. Man. (lectr. bar admission course 1981-96), Man. Bar Assn. (life, governing coun. 1988-96, recipient Cmty. Svc. award 1999), Can. Bar Assn. (legis. and law reform com. 1994-2000, 01—03, vice-chair 1997-2000, chair 2001-03, nat mag. editl. bd. 2002—). Avocations: travel, languages, performing arts. Office: 235-405 Broadway Winnipeg MB Canada R3C 3L6 Home Phone: 204-475-9069; Office Phone: 204-945-3027. Business E-Mail: jeffrey.schnoor@gov.mb.ca.

SCHNUCK, CRAIG D., grocery store company executive; b. Apr. 20, 1948; s. Donald Schnuck. BS, Cornell U., 1967, MBA, 1971. With Schnuck Markets, Inc., Hazelwood, Mo., 1971—, v.p., 1975-76, exec. v.p., sec., 1976-83, pres., chief exec. officer, 1983-91, also bd. dirs., 1991, chmn., CEO, 1991—. Office: Schnuck Markets Inc 11420 Lackland Rd Saint Louis MO 63146-3559

SCHNUCK, SCOTT C., grocery store executive; b. 1950; Pres., COO Schnuck Markets, Inc., St. Louis, 1992—. Office: Schnuck Markets Inc 11420 Lackland Rd Saint Louis MO 63146-3559

SCHNUCK, TERRY EDWARD, lawyer; b. St. Louis, Oct. 10, 1952; s. Donald Otto and Doris Irene (Letson) S.; m. Sally Barrows Braxton, May 24, 1980; children: Hadley Braxton, Terry Edward Jr. BA in Econs., Tulane U., 1975; MBA, Washington U., St. Louis, 1980; JD, St. Louis U., 1980. Bar: Mo. 1980. Assoc. Greensfelder, Hemker, Wiese, Gale & Chappelow, St. Louis, 1980-84; with Schnuck Markets Inc., Bridgeton, Mo., 1980—, chief legal counsel, sec. Bd. dirs. Arts and Edn. Coun. of Greater St. Louis, 1991—. Bd. dirs. Urban League of Met. St. Louis, 1987—. Mem. ABA, Mo. Bar Assn., Bar Assn. of Met. St. Louis, Better Bus. Bur. (bd. dirs. 1990—), Mo. Retailers Assn. (exec. bd. 1984—), Beta Theta Pi. Clubs: Bellerive Country (St. Louis). Republican. Presbyterian. Office: Schnuck Markets Inc 11420 Lackland Rd Saint Louis MO 63146-3559

SCHNUCKER, ROBERT VICTOR, historian, educator; b. Waterloo, Iowa, Sept. 30, 1932; s. Felix Victor and Josephine (Maasdam) S.; m. Anna Mae Engelkes, Sept. 18, 1955; children: Sarai Ann, Sar Victor, Christjahn Dietrich. AB, NE Mo. State U., 1953; BD, U. Dubuque, 1956; MA, U. Iowa, 1960, PhD, 1969. Ordained to ministry Presbyn. Ch., 1956. Pastor United Presbyn. Ch. USA, Springville, Iowa, 1956-63, Meth.-Presbyn. Ch., Labelle, Mo., 1976-97; asst. prof. N.E. Mo. State U., Kirksville, 1963-65, assoc. prof., 1963-65, prof., 1969—99; interim pastor Bethany Presbyn. Ch., Grundy Center, Iowa, 1999—2001, First Presbyn. Ch., Aplington, 2002—04, Immanuel Presbyn. Ch., Waterloo, Iowa, 2004—05. Dir. Thomas Jefferson U. Press; supr. Bible exam. Presbyn. Ch. USA, Louisville, 1977-89; bd. dir. Ctr. for Reformation Rsch., St. Louis, 1984-99; pres. Conf. of Hist. Jours., 1993; adj. prof. religion U. No. Iowa, 1999—; vis. prof. religion and humanities, 2001-02. Author: A Glossary of Terms for Western Civilization, 1975, Helping Humanities Journal Survive, 1985, History Assessment Test, 1990; editor: Calviniana, 1989, Historians of Early Modern Europe, 1976-93, 97, Network News Exch., 1978-88; pres. 1st and 2d Editing History, Conf. for Hist. Jour., 1985-97; book rev. editor, mng. editor 16th Century Jour., 1972-97; pub. 16th Century Essays and Studies, 1980-97; contbr. articles to profl. jours. Recipient 16th Studies Conf. medal for Significant Achievement in Early Modern Studies, 1997, Presdl. Citation for Contbns. to the Univ., Truman State U., 1997; fellow Soc. Sci. Study of Religion, 1988, Sixteenth Century Studies conf., 1998; NEH grantee for jour. pubs., 1980. Mem. AAUP, Am. Acad. Religion, Renaissance Soc. Am., Am. History Assn. (chmn. Robinson prize com. 1987), Am. Soc. Ch. History, Soc. History of Edn., Soc. Bibl. Lit., Soc. for Reformation Rsch., Soc. Scholarly Pubs., Soc. for Values in Higher Edn., Conf. for Hist. Jour., Am. Coun. Learned Soc. (exec. bd. conf. adminstr. officers 1993-96, sec. 1994, chmn. 1995-96), Conf. Faith and History, 16th Century Studies Cons. (exec. sec. 1972-97), Humanities Iowa (bd. dirs. 1999-2003, pres. 2002-03). Office: Dept Philosophy and Religion U No Iowa Cedar Falls IA 50614-0501 E-mail: rvs@cedarnet.org.

SCHNUR, ROBERT ARNOLD, lawyer, educator; b. White Plains, NY, Oct. 25, 1938; s. Conrad Edward and Ruth (Mehr) S.; children: Daniel, Jonathan. BA, Cornell U., 1960; JD, Harvard U., 1963. Bar: Wis. 1965, Ill. 1966. Assoc. Michael, Best & Friedrich, Milw., 1966-73, ptnr., 1973—. Chmn. Wis. Tax News, 1983-90; adj. prof. tax law U. Wis. Law Sch., 1988—; vis. prof. tax law Cornell U. Law Sch., 2006-. Capt. U.S. Army, 1963-65. Fellow Am. Coll. Tax Counsel; mem. ABA, Wis. Bar Assn. (chmn. tax sect. 1986-88), Milw. Bar Assn. Home: 3093 Timber Ln Verona WI 53593 Office: Michael Best Friedrich 100 E Wisconsin Ave Ste 3300 Milwaukee WI 53202-4108 Business E-Mail: raschnur@michaelbest.com.

SCHOBINGER, RANDY ARTHUR, state legislator; b. Minot, ND, Dec. 15, 1969; Student, Minot State U., 1991-96. Warehouseman, Minot; mem. N.D. Senate from 3rd dist., Bismarck, 1994—; with Movers, Inc. Vice chmn. transp. com. State Senate of N.D., mem. edn. com.; endorsed candidate of the N.D. Repub. Party for State Treasurer, 1996. Office: ND State Capitol 600 Easy St Bismarck ND 58504-6239

SCHOCH, ALEXANDER C., lawyer, energy executive; BA, Kenyon Coll.; JD, Case Western Reserve U. Bar: Ill., Tex., Ohio. Internat. atty. Marathon Oil Co.; v.p., assoc. gen. counsel, sec. Goodrich Corp.; v.p., gen. counsel Emerson Process Mgmt.; exec. v.p., chief legal officer Peabody Energy, St. Louis, 2006—. Mem.: ABA, Am. Soc. Corp. Sec., State Bar Assn., Internat. Bar Assn. Office: Peabody Energy 701 Market St Saint Louis MO 63101

SCHODORF, JEAN, state legislator; b. Cherry Point, NC, June 11, 1950; m. Richard Schodorf; children: Brian, Kelly, Kristin. BA, U. N.Mex., 1972, MS, 1973; PhD, Wichita State U., 1981. Mem. Kans. State Senate, 2000—. Active USD 259 Bd. Edn., 1989—. Republican. Methodist. Home: 3039 Benjamin Ct Wichita KS 67204 Office: State Capitol Rm 143-N Topeka KS 66612 E-mail: jschodor@swbell.net.

SCHOELLER, DALE ALAN, nutrition research educator; b. Milw., June 8, 1948; s. Arthur B. and Anne Clare S.; m. Madeline Mary Juresh, Aug. 22, 1970; children: Nicholas Paul, Gregory Scott, Erica Lee. BS with honors, U. Wis., Milw., 1970; PhD, Ind. U., 1974. Postdoctoral fellow Argonne (Ill.) Nat. Lab., 1974-76; from asst. prof. to prof., also rsch. assoc. U. Chgo., 1976-91, assoc. prof., 1991—, prof., 1996; assoc. prof. U. Wis., Madison, 1997-98, prof., 1998—. Chmn. com. on human nutrition and nutritional biology U. Chgo., 1991-97. Author: (book chpt.) Obesity, 1992; co-author: (book chpt.) Annual Review of Nutrition, 1991. Mem. Am. Soc. Nutritional Scis. (v.p. elect 2001, Mead Johnson award 1987), Am. Soc. for Clin. Nutrition (Herman award 2000), Am. Soc. for Mass Spectrometry, N.Am. Soc. for Study of Obesity. Achievements include development of stable isotope methods for the study of human energy metabolism including first human use of doubly labeled water for measurement of free-living total energy expenditure. Office: U Wis Dept Nutrition 1415 Linden Dr Madison WI 53706-1527 E-mail: dschoell@nutrisci.wisc.edu.

SCHOENBERG, JEFFREY M., state legislator; b. Chgo., July 28, 1959; BA, Columbia U., 1983, Rugers U. Ill. state rep. Dist. 58, 1991—; mem. aging com. appropriations, edn. fin. Ill. Ho. Reps., environ. and energy, health care, human svcs. com.; dir. Roosevelt Ctr. for Am. Policy Studies. Democrat. Office: Ill Ho of Reps Rm M-2 State Capitol Springfield IL 62706-0001 Home: 2744 Lincolnwood Dr Evanston IL 60201-1229

SCHOENDIENST, ALBERT FRED (RED SCHOENDIENST), professional baseball coach, former baseball player; b. Germantown, Ill., Feb. 2, 1923; m. Mary Eileen O'Reilly; children: Colleen, Cathleen, Eileen, Kevin. Infielder St. Louis Cardinals, 1945-56, 61-63, N.Y. Giants, 1956-57, Milw. Braves, 1957-61; coach St. Louis Cardinals, 1961-64, 1979-95, Hitting Coach, mgr., 1964-77; coach Oakland Athletics, Calif., 1977-78. Mem. Nat. League All-Star team, 10 times, player in 9 games; mem. World Series Championship team, 1946, 57, 64; managed team to World Series Championship, 1967; inducted into Major League Baseball Hall of Fame, 1989. Office: Saint Louis Cardinals 250 Stadium Plz Saint Louis MO 63102-1722

SCHOENFELD, HANNS-MARTIN WALTER, finance educator; b. Leipzig, Germany, July 12, 1928; came to U.S., 1962, naturalized, 1968; s. Alwin and Lisbeth (Kirbach) Schoenfeld; m. Margit Frese, Aug. 10, 1956 (dec. Jan. 21, 2005); 1 child, Gabriele. MBA, U. Hamburg, Fed. Republic Germany, 1952, DBA, 1954; PhD, U. Braunschweig, Fed. Republic Germany, 1966. Pvt. practice acctg., Hamburg, 1948-54; bus. cons. Europe, 1958-62; faculty accountancy U. Ill., Champaign/Urbana, 1962—, prof. acctg., bus. adminstrn. Urbana, 1967—, Weldon Powell prof. acctg., 1976, 80-81, H. T. Scovill prof. acctg., 1985-94; prof. emeritus, 1994—; dir. Office of West European Studies, 1982-84. Lectr., cons. in bus. and acctg., Eng., Belgium, Austria, Denmark, Brazil, Mex., Germany, Poland, Indonesia, Korea, Japan, Switzerland, Hungary, Czechoslovakia, 1962—; vis. prof. Econs. U. Vienna, Austria, 1984-2002, Handelshochschule, Leipzig, Germany, 1996-2002. Author: Management Dictionary 2 vols., 4th edit, 1971, Cost Accounting, 8th edit, 1974-95, Management Development, 1967, Cost Terminology and Cost Theory, 1974, (with J. Sheth) Export Marketing: Lessons from Europe, 1981, (with H.P. Holzer) Managerial Accounting and Analysis in Multinational Enterprises, 1986, (with L. Noerreklit) Resources of the Firm, 1996. With German Army, 1944-45. Recipient Dr. Kausch prize for internat. integration of acctg. U. St. Gall, Switzerland, 1996. Mem. Am. Acctg. Assn. (chmn. internat. sect. 1976-77), Acad. Acctg. Historians (v.p. 1976-77, pres. 1978-79, Hour Glass award for best book publs. 1975), Acad. Internat. Bus., German Profs. Bus. Adminstrn., German Assn. Indsl. Engring., European Acctg. Assn., Coun. of European Studies, Internat. Assn. for Acctg. Edn. and Rsch., Beta Gamma Sigma, Beta Alpha Psi. Home: 1014 Devonshire Dr Champaign IL 61821-6620 Office: U Ill Dept Acctg 360 Wohlers Hall 1206 S 6th St Champaign IL 61820-6915 Office Phone: 217-333-0857. Business E-Mail: hschoenf@uiuc.edu.

SCHOENFELD, HOWARD ALLEN, management consultant, lawyer; b. NYC, Apr. 17, 1948; s. Irving and Muriel (Levy) S.; m. Paula Simon; 1 child, Haley Rebecca. BA, U. Pa., 1970; JD, Georgetown U., 1973. Bar: Md. 1973, U.S. Dist. Ct. Md. 1973, Wis. 1976, U.S. Dist. Ct. (ea. dist.) Wis. 1976, U.S. Dist. Ct. (we. dist.) Wis. 1987. Law clk. Md. Ct. Appeals, 1973-74; assoc. Gordon, Feinblatt, Rothman, Hoffberger & Hollander, Balt., 1974-76; ptnr. Trebon & Schoenfeld, Milw., 1976-85, Godfrey & Kahn, Milw., 1985—2002; prs. DSC Advisors, Milw., 2002—. Chmn. John Anderson Campiagn for Pres., Wis., 1980; pres. Milw. Jewish Coun., 1987-89, mem., 1983—. Recipient Young Leadership award Milw. Jewish Fedn., 1983. Mem. ABA, Wis. Bar Assn., Milw. Bar Assn. Office: DSC Advisors 3805 N Oakland Ave Milwaukee WI 53211 Home Phone: 414-351-1919; Office Phone: 414-967-0579. E-mail: hasreorg@aol.com.

SCHOENHARD, WILLIAM CHARLES, JR., health system executive; b. Kansas City, Mo., Sept. 26, 1949; s. William Charles S. and Joyce Evans (Thornsberry) Bell; m. Kathleen Ann Klosterman, June 3, 1972; children: Sarah Elizabeth, Thomas William. BS in Pub. Adminstrn., U. Mo., 1971; M of Health Adminstrn. with honors, Washington U., St. Louis, 1975. V.p., dir. gen. svcs. Deaconess Hosp., St. Louis, 1975-78; assoc. exec. dir. St. Mary's Health Ctr., St. Louis, 1978-81; exec. dir. Arcadia Valley Hosp., Pilot Knob, Mo., 1981-82, St. Joseph Health Ctr., St. Charles, Mo., St. Joseph Hosp. West, Lake St. Louis, 1982—86; exec. v.p., COO SSM Health Care, St. Louis, 1986—. Adv. bd. dirs. Firstar Bank, 1998-01, Midwest Bank Ctr., 2004, Coll. Bus. Mgmt. U. Mo., Columbia, Mo., 2005-. Contbr. articles to profl. jours. Mem. Mo. Commn. on Patient Safety, 2003—04; mem. adv. bd. St. Louis chpt. Lifeseekers, St. Louis, 1985—94; mem. bd. mgrs. Kirkwood-Webster (Mo.) YMCA, 1990—96, sec., 1996; mem. healthcare adv. bd. Sanford Brown Colls., 1992—94; bd. dirs. St. Andrews Mgmt. Svcs., Inc., 1994—2002, Mid Am. Transplant Svcs., 1995—, sec., 2005—; bd. dirs. Lindenwood U., 1997—, Civic Entrepreneurs Orgn.,

1997—2000, Greater St. Louis Boy Scouts Am., 1997—, Benedictine Health Sys., 2002. With USN, 1971—72, Vietnam. Fellow Am. Coll. Health Care Execs. (regent Mo.-Gateway area 1997-01, bd. govs. 2002—, chmn. 2006-07); mem. VFW, Am. Hosp. Assn. (del. regional policy bd. 1999-2005, bd. trustees, 2007—, exec. com., 2008-, ops. com. 2007—), Mo. Hosp. Assn. (bd. trustees 1999-2005, chmn. 2000), Am. Heart Assn. (mem. bd. Greater St. Louis chpt. 2001-03), Cath. Health Assn. U.S. (mem. fin. com. 1999-01), Am. Legion, US Navy League, Westborough Country Club, Phi Eta Sigma, Pi Omicron Sigma, Delta Upsilon, Delta Sigma Pi. Roman Catholic. Avocations: reading, walking. Home: 420 Fairwood Ln Saint Louis MO 63122-4429 Office: SSM Health Care 477 N Lindbergh Blvd Saint Louis MO 63141-7832 Office Phone: 314-994-7810.

SCHOENROCK, TRACY ALLEN, airline pilot, aviation consultant; b. Oshkosh, Wis., Jan. 11, 1960; s. Elder Roy and Shirley Mae (Rutz) S.; m. Kathleen Mary Neumann, Oct. 8, 1983; children: Amanda Beth, Veronica Grace, Shannon Traci. BS in Geography summa cum laude, U. Wis., Oshkosh, 1982. Charter pilot Basler Airlines, Oshkosh, 1977-82; pilot Simmons Airlines, Marquette, Mich., 1982-84, Northwest Airlines, St. Paul, 1984—; owner Cargo Airline, Oshkosh. Lutheran. Avocations: golf, travel, flying, electronics. Home and Office: 1345 Maricopa Dr Oshkosh WI 54904-8150 Office Phone: 920-410-1472.

SCHOLER, SUE WYANT, retired state legislator; b. Topeka, Oct. 20, 1936; d. Zint Elwin and Virginia Louise (Achenbach) Wyant; m. Charles Frey Scholer, Jan. 27, 1957; children: Elizabeth Scholer Truelove, Charles W., Virginia M. Scholer McCal. Student, Kans. State U., 1954-56. Draftsman The Farm Clinic, West Lafayette, Ind., 1978—79; assessor Wabash Twp., West Lafayette, 1979-84; commr. Tippecanoe County, Lafayette, Ind., 1984-90; state rep. Dist. 26 Ind. Statehouse, Indpls., 1990—2004, ret., 2004; legis. cons. Gov.'s Office, 2007. Asst. minority whip, 1992-94, Rep. whip, 1994-2000, asst. Rep. leader, 2001—04; mem. Tippecanoe County Area Plan Commn., 1984-90; chmn. Midwestern legis. conf. CSG, 1998. Bd. dirs. Crisis Ctr., Lafayette, 1984-89, Tippecanoe Arts Fedn., 1990-99, United Way, Lafayette, 1990-93; mem. Lafayette Conv. and Visitors Bur., 1988-90. Recipient Salute to Women Govt. and Politics award, 1986, United Sr. Action award, Outstanding Legislator award, 1993, Small Bus. Champion award, 1995, Ind. Libr. Fedn. Legislator award, 1995, Disting. Legislator award at Alliance for Mentally Ill, 1997,, 2003, West Ctrl. Ind. Advocate award, 2003, Friend of Cmty. Action award, 1999, Disting. Pub. Svc. award Am. Legion, 2004, Family Svcs. Advocacy award Family Svcs., 2004, Sagamore of the Wabash, 2004, Order of the Griffin, Purdue U., 2004. Mem. Ind. Assn. County Commrs. (treas. 1990), Assn. Ind. Counties (legis. com. 1988-90), Greater Lafayette C. of C. (ex-officio bd. 1984-90), LWV, P.E.O., Purdue Women's Club (past treas.), Kappa Kappa Kappa (past pres. Epsilon chpt.)., Delta Delta Delta (past pres. alumnae, house corp. treas.). Republican. Presbyterian. Avocations: golf, needlecrafts, reading. Home: 807 Essex St West Lafayette IN 47906-1534

SCHOLTEN, ROGER KEITH, lawyer; b. Jan. 25, 1955; BA, Northwestern U.; JD, U. Iowa. Atty. Maytag Corp., 1981—87, assoc. gen. counsel, 1987—94, asst. gen. counsel, 1994—2001, v.p. strategic planning & corp. devel., 2000—01, sr. v.p. & gen. counsel, 2001—. Office: Maytag Corp Legal Dept 403 W 4th St N Newton IA 50208 Home: 4106 John Lynde Rd Des Moines IA 50312-3040 Office Phone: 641-791-8309. Office Fax: 641-791-8102. Business E-Mail: rschol@maytag.com.

SCHONBERG, ALAN ROBERT, personnel director; b. NYC, Oct. 23, 1928; s. Julius and Evelyn (Guzik) S.; m. Carole May Kreisman, Dec. 27, 1975; children: William, Evelyn, David, Jeffrey. Nat. sales mgr. Majestic Specialties, Inc., Cleve., 1953-63; pres. Internat. Personnel, Inc., Cleve., 1963-65; chmn. Mgmt. Recruiters Internat., Inc., Cleve., 1965-98, 1998—2000, chmn. emeritus, 2001—. Pres., bd. dirs. Jewish Vocat. Service, Cleve., 1983—; trustees Mt. Sinai Hosp. (now Mt. Sinai Found.), Cleve., bd. dirs. Cleve. Jewish News; gen. chmn. Welfare Fund Campaign; trustee Am. Jewish Commn., Mt. Sinai Med. Ctr., Hebrew Immigrant Aid Soc. Named one of Cleve.'s 86 Most Interesting People, Cleve. Mag., 1986, Man of Yr. local chpt. Orgn. through Rehab. and Tng., 1996, Entrepreneur of Yr. Inc. Mag., Merrill Lynch Ernst & Young, 1995; recipient Human Rels. award Cleve. chpt. Am. Jewish Com., 1998. Mem. Internat. Franchise Assn., Internat. Confederation Pvt. Employment Agys. Assns., Am. Mgmt. Assn., Assn. Human Resource Cons. (chmn. 1980—), Org. for Rehab. and Training (ORT), Assn. Am.-Israel C. of C. (pres.), Ohio Israel C. of C. (co-chmn.), Jewish Family Svcs. Assn. (v.p., pres. 1998-2002). Avocation: travel.

SCHONBERG, WILLIAM PETER, engineering educator, department chairman; b. NYC, Mar. 25, 1960; s. Christian and Tamara (Kalnev) S.; m. Jane Heminover, Sept. 7, 1986; children: Christina Carol, Richard William, Peter James. BSCE cum laude, Princeton U., 1981; MS in Engring., Northwestern U., 1983, PhD, 1986. Asst. prof. civil engring. U. Ala., Huntsville, 1986-91, assoc. prof., 1991-94, prof., 1994-99, chair civil and environ. engring. dept., 1995-99; prof., chair U. Mo., Rolla, 1999—. Mem. working group NASA Boeing Space Sta., 1987-90. Contbr. articles to profl. pubs. Recipient rsch. and creative works award U. Ala.-Huntsville Found., 1992; Walter P. Murphy fellow, 1981-82, summer faculty fellow NASA, 1987, 88, 94, 95, Air Force Office Sci. Rsch., 1992, 93; grantee U. Ala.-Huntsville Rsch. Inst., 1987-92. Fellow AIAA (assoc., Young Engr. of Yr. award 1990, Lawrence Sperry award 1995); mem. ASME, ASCE, Am. Acad. Mechanics, Tau Beta Pi. Avocations: astronomy, stamp collecting/philately, reading, music, travel. Office: U Mo Civil Engring Dept Rolla MO 65401 E-mail: wschon@umr.edu.

SCHÖNEMANN, PETER HANS, psychologist, educator; b. Pethau, Germany, July 15, 1929; arrived in U.S., 1960, naturalized, 2003; s. Max Paul Franz and Hertha Anna (Kahle) S.; m. Roberta Dianne Federbush, Jan. 29, 1962; children: Raoul Dieter, Nicole Deborah. Vordiplom in Psychologie, U. Munich, 1956; Hauptdiplom in Psychologie, U. Goettingen, 1959; PhD, U. Ill., 1964. Thurstone postdoctoral fellow U. N.C., 1965-66; asst. prof., then assoc. prof. Ohio State U., 1966-69; postdoctoral fellow Ednl. Testing Service, Princeton, NJ, 1967-68; vis. prof. Technische Hochschule, Aachen, Fed. Republic Germany, 1981; mem. faculty Purdue U., 1969—, prof. psychology, 1971-2001, emeritus, 2001—. Vis. prof. Univs. Munich, Bielefeld and Braunschweig, 1984-85, Nat. Taiwan U., 1992, 96, 97. Author papers in field. Recipient Found. for the Advancement of Outstanding Scholarship award, Taiwan, 1996. Office: Dept Psychol Scis Purdue U Lafayette IN 47907 Home Phone: 765-583-4807. Personal E-mail: phs@psych.purdue.edu.

SCHONFELD, GUSTAV, medical educator, researcher, administrator; b. Mukacevo, Ukraine, May 8, 1934; arrived in US, 1946, naturalized, 1951; s. Alexander Schonfeld and Helena Gottesmann; m. Miriam Steinberg, May 28, 1961; children: Joshua Lawrence, Julia Elizabeth, Jeremy David. BA, Washington U., St. Louis, 1956, MD, 1960. Diplomate Am. Bd. Internal Medicine. Intern. Bellevue Med. Ctr. NYU, 1960—61, resident in internal medicine, 1961—63; chief resident in internal medicine Jewish Hosp., St. Louis, 1963—64; from NIH trainee in endocrinology & metabolism to Kountz prof. medicine Washington U., St. Louis, 1964—96, Busch prof., chair medicine, 1996—99, Samuel E. Schechter prof. medicine, 2002—; rsch. assoc. Cochran VA Hosp., St. Louis, 1965—66, clin. investigator, 1968—70, cons. in internal medicine, 1972—; rsch. flight med. officer USAF Sch. Aerospace Medicine, Brooks AFB, Tex., 1966—68; from asst. physician to physician Barnes Hosp., St. Louis, 1972—96; physician-in-chief Barnes Jewish Hosp., St. Louis, 1996—99; clin. instr. medicine Harvard U. Med. Sch., Boston, 1970—72; assoc. prof. metabolism and human nutrition, asst. dir. Clin. Rsch. Ctr. MIT, Cambridge, 1970—72. Mem. rsch. com. Mo. Heart Assn., 1978-80; expert witness working group on atherosclerosis Nat. Heart, Lung and Blood Inst., 1979, Nat. Diabetes Adv. Bd., 1979; mem. endocrinologic and metabolic drugs adv. com. USPHS, FDA, 1982-86; mem. nutrition study sect. NIH, 1984-88, spl. reviewer metabolism study sect.; mem. adult treatment guidelines panel Nat. Cholesterol Edn. Program, 1986; mem. Consensus Devel. Conf. on Triglyceride, High Density Lipoprotein and Coronary Heart Disease, 1992; cons. Am. Egg Bd., Am. Dairy Bd., Inst. Shortening and Edible Oils, Ciba-Geigy, Sandoz, Fournier, Parke-Davis, Bristol-Meyers Squibb, Monsanto/Searle; adj. prof. medicine Columbia U. Coll. Physicians & Surgeons, 2006. Past editor: Atherosclerosis, past mem. editl. bd.: Jour. Clin. Endocrinology and Metabolism, Jour. Clin. Investigation, Jour. Lipid Rsch., past assoc. editor: Circulation. Recipient Berg Prize in Microbiology, 1957, 58, Faculty/Alumni award Washington U., 1995; named Physician honoree Am. Heart Assn. Mo. Affiliate, 1995; grantee MERIT status NIH, Vascular Biology Spl. Merit award, Am. Heart Assn. Fellow ACP, AAAS; mem. Assn. Am. Physicians, Am. Soc. for Clin. Investigation, Am. Physiol. Soc., Am. Soc. Biol. Chemists, Am. Inst. Nutrition, Am. Diabetes Assn., Am. Heart Assn. (program com. coun. on atherosclerosis 1977-80, 86-88, nutrition com. 1980-84, pathology rsch. com. 1980-83, budget com. 1991, awards com. 1992, exec. com. 2001—, Spl. Vascular Biology award 2005, G.L. Duff lecture award, 2006), Endocrine Soc., Alpha Omega Alpha. Democrat. Jewish. Office: Washington U Sch Medicine Box 8046 660 S Euclid Ave Saint Louis MO 63110-1010 Office Phone: 314-362-8060. Business E-Mail: gschonfe@wustl.edu.

SCHOOFF, DAN, state legislator; b. Dec. 10, 1971; 1 child. BA, U. Wis., 1994. Mem. Wis. State Assembly, Madison, 1998—, mem. com. on energy and utilities, mem. health com., mem. transp. com., mem. state and local fin. com. Mem. Near East Side Neighborhood Assn.; dir. Neighborhood Housing Svc., Beloit Snappers Baseball Club. Democrat. Home: 1955 Pebble Dr Beloit WI 53511-6721

SCHOONHOVEN, RAY JAMES, retired lawyer; b. Elgin, Ill., May 24, 1921; s. Ray Covey and Rosina Madeline (Schram White) S.; m. Marie Theresa Dunn, Dec. 11, 1943; children: Marie Kathleen (Kamie), Ray James, Jr., Pamela Suzanne, John Philip, Rose Lynn. BSc, U. Notre Dame, 1943; JD, Northwestern U., 1948. Bar: Ill. 1949, U.S. Supreme Ct. 1954, D.C. 1973, U.S. Ct. Mil. Appeals 1954. Assoc. Seyfarth, Shaw Fairweather & Geraldson, Chgo., 1949-57; ptnr. Seyfarth, Shaw Fairweather & Geraldson now Seyfarth Shaw, Chgo., 1957-92; ret. Chief rulings and ops. br. Wage Stabilization Bd. Region VII, Chgo., 1951-52. Book rev. editor: Ill. Law Rev., 1948. Served to lt.comdr. USNR, 1942-62. Mem. ABA, Ill. State Bar Assn., Chgo. Bar Assn., D.C. Bar Assn., Chgo. Athletic Assn., Univ. Club. Chgo., Fed. Bar Assn., Order of Coif. Republican. Roman Catholic. Home: 1182 Lynette Dr Lake Forest IL 60045-4601 Office: Seyfarth Shaw 131 S Dearborn St Ste 2400 Chicago IL 60603-5577 Office Phone: 312-460-5000.

SCHOPF, WILLIAM GRANT, lawyer; b. Muskegon, Mich., Sept. 7, 1948; s. William G. and June Marie (Bodine) Schopf; children: Brody A., Alexandra J., Anais M.E. AB, Princeton U., 1970; JD, Cornell U., 1973. Bar: Ill. 1973, US Dist. Ct. (no. dist. Ill.) 1973, US Supreme Ct. 1977, Tex. 1989, US Dist. Ct. (so. dist. Tex.) 1995, US Dist Ct. (ea. dist. Tex.) 1998, US Dist. Ct. (so. dist. Ill.) 2001, US Dist. Ct. (we. dist. Mich.) 2005, US Ct. Appeals (3rd, 5th, 7th, 8th, 10th and 11th cirs.). Assoc. Keck, Mahin & Cate, Chgo., 1973-79; ptnr. Reuben & Proctor, Chgo., 1979-86, Isham, Lincoln & Beale, Chgo., 1986-87, Schopf & Weiss, Chgo., 1987—. Adj. prof. John Marshall Law Sch., Chgo., 1977-78; owner Music Box Theatre & Schopf Gallery on Lake, Chgo. Author: Money in the Bank, 1988; contbr. articles, chpts. to legal publs. Named an Top 10 Trial Lawyers in Am., Nat. Law Jour., 2004. Mem. ABA, Chgo. Bar Assn., Union Internationale des Avocats, Union League Club (Chgo.), Princeton Club (NYC). Office: Schopf & Weiss 1 S Wacker Dr 28th Fl Chicago IL 60606-4617 Office Phone: 312-701-9308. E-mail: schopf@sw.com.

SCHORER, JOSEPH U., lawyer; b. Baraboo, Wis., June 15, 1953; BA with highest distinction, Northwestern U., 1975; JD cum laude, Harvard U., 1978. Bar: Calif. 1978, US Dist. Ct. (so. dist. Calif.) 1978, Ill. 1981, US Dist. Ct. (no. dist. Ill.) 1981, US Ct. Appeals (7th cir.) 1987, US Ct. Appeals (5th cir.) 1985, US Ct. Appeals (10th cir.) 1984. Law clk. to Hon. Gordon Thompson, Jr. So. Dist. Calif., 1978—80; ptnr. Mayer, Brown & Platt, Chgo., 1985—97; gen. counsel Diamond Homes Svcs., 1997—2000, Globe Bldg. Materials, 1997—2000, Mid-West Spring Mfg. Co., 1997—2000; of counsel Kirkland & Ellis, Chgo., 2000—. Contbr. articles to law jours. Mem.: Chgo. Coun. Lawyers, Chgo. Bar Assn., Phi Beta Kappa. Office: Kirkland & Ellis 200 E Randolph Dr Chicago IL 60601-6636 Office Phone: 312-861-2345. Office Fax: 312-861-2200. E-mail: jschorer@kirkland.com.

SCHORNACK, JOHN JAMES, accountant; b. Chgo., Nov. 22, 1930; s. John Joseph and Helen Patricia (Patrickus) S.; m. Barbara Anne Lelli, June 5, 1965; children: Mark Boyd, Anne Marguerite Schornack Trueman, Erin Keeley Schornack Dickes, Tracy Bevan Schornack Power. BS, Loyola U., 1951; MBA, Northwestern U., 1956; grad., Advanced Mgmt. Program, Harvard Bus. Sch., 1969. With Ernst & Young (formerly Arthur Young & Co.), 1955-91, partner, 1964-91; firm dir. personnel Ernst & Young LLP (formerly Arthur Young & Co.), NYC, 1966-71, asst. mng. ptnr. N.Y.C. office, 1971-72, mng. ptnr., 1972-74, mng. ptnr. Chgo. office, 1976-85, mng. ptnr. Midwest region, vice chmn., 1985-91; mem. mgmt. com. Arthur Young & Co. Mgmt. com. Arthur Young & Co.; vice chmn., mng. ptnr. Midwest region Ernst & Young, 1989-91; bd. dirs., chmn. Ernst & Young Found., 1981-91; chmn., bd. dirs. North Shore Bancorp, Inc., 1992-, Wintrust Fin. Corp., 1996-. Pres. Chgo. Youth Ctrs., 1979-95; bd. govs. Chgo. Symphony, 1979-85, trustee, 1985-2003, life trustee; vol. United Way, 1975-92, dir., 1989-92; vis. adv. com. sch. accountancy DePaul U., 1980-83; mem. Loyola U. Citizens Bd., 1977-94, chmn., 1993-94; mem. adv. com. Northwestern U. Grad. Sch. Mgmt., 1967-91; coun. U. Chgo. Grad. Sch. Bus., 1982-91; bd. dirs. Met. Planning Coun., 1992-95; trustee Kohl Children's Mus., 1994-2005, life trustee, 2005—; trustee Lyric Opera, 1984-92, Cath. Charities Chgo., 2004—, Cath. Theol. Union, 1992-97, Graham Found., 1992-98; trustee Barat Coll., 1983-98, life trustee, 1999-2001, vice chmn., 1985-90, chmn., 1990-97; trustee St. Francis Hosp., 1986-97, vice chmn., 1991-94; trustee Night Ministry, 1998-004 Recipient Order of the Sacred Treas., Emperor of Japan, 1999. Mem. AICPA, Am. Acctg. Assn., Ill. Soc. CPAs, Midwest-Japan Assn. (chmn. 1983-99), Japan Am. Soc., Chgo. Club, Glen View Club, The Little Club. Home: 314 Regent Wood Rd Northfield IL 60093-2762 Office: Ernst & Young LLP Great Lakes Reg Office 233 S Wacker Dr Chicago IL 60606-6306

SCHORR, ROGER J., employee and customer care company executive; Gen. mgr. Convergys Corp., Cin., 1993—. Office: Convergys Corp 4600 Montgomery Rd Cincinnati OH 45212-2697

SCHOTTENFELD, DAVID, retired epidemiologist, educator; b. NYC, Mar. 25, 1931; m. Rosalie C. Schaeffer; children: Jacqueline, Stephen. AB, Hamilton Coll., 1952; MD, Cornell U., 1956; MS in Pub. Health, Harvard U., 1963. Diplomate Am. Bd. Internal Medicine, Am. Bd. Preventive Medicine. Intern in internal medicine Duke U., Durham, NC, 1956-57; resident in internal medicine Meml. Sloan-Kettering Cancer Ctr., Cornell U. Med. Coll., NYC, 1957-59; Craver fellow med. oncology Meml. Sloan-Kettering Cancer Ctr., 1961-62; clin. instr. dept. pub. health Cornell U., NYC, 1963—65, asst. prof. dept. pub. health, 1965-70, assoc. prof. dept. pub. health, 1970-73, prof. dept. pub. health, 1973-86; John G. Searle prof., chmn. epidemiology sch. pub. health U. Mich., Ann Arbor, 1986—2004, prof. internal medicine, 1986—2004, prof. emeritus internal medicine and epidemiology Sch. Pub. Health, 2004—; adj. prof. dept. family medicine and cmty. health U. Mass. Med. Sch., Worcester, 2006—. Vis. prof. epidemiology U. Minn., Mpls., 1968, 71, 74, 82, 86; W.G. Cosbie lectr. Can. Oncology Soc., 1987. Editor: Cancer Epidemiology and Prevention, 1982, 2d. edit., 1996, 3d edit., 2006; author 10 books; contbr. more than 250 articles to profl. jours. Served with USPHS, 1959-61. Recipient Acad. Career award in Preventive Oncology, Nat. Cancer Inst., 1980-85, Disting. Achievement award Am. Soc. Preventive Oncology, 1992; vis. scholar Nat. Cancer Inst., 2007. Fellow AAAS, ACP, APHA (John Snow award 2007), Am. Coll. Preventive Medicine, Am. Coll. Epidemiology (Abraham Lilienfeld award 2002), Armed Forces Epidemiology Bd.; mem. Soc. Epidemiologic Rsch. (pres. 1998-99), Phi Beta Kappa. Office: U Mich Sch Pub Health Dept Epidemiology 109 Observatory St Ann Arbor MI 48109-2029 Home: 25 River Birch Ln Dalton MA 01226-2104 Business E-Mail: daschott@umich.edu.

SCHOTTENSTEIN, JAY L., retail executive; b. 1954; Grad., Ind. U. With Schottenstein Stores, Columbus, Ohio, vice chmn., exec. v.p., CEO, 1992—; chmn. Value City Department Stores, Columbus, Ohio, 1992; CEO Am. Eagle Outfitters, Warrendale, Pa., 1992—2002, chmn., 2002—, Retail Ventures Inc., 2002—. Office: Schottenstein Stores 1800 Moler Rd Columbus OH 43207-1680 Address: Retail Ventures Inc 3241 Westerville Rd Columbus OH 43224 also: American Eagle Outfitters 150 Thorn Hill Dr Warrendale PA 15086-7528

SCHOTTENSTEIN, ROBERT H., construction executive; Pres., vice chair M/I Schottenstein Homes, Columbus, Ohio, 1997—. Office: M/I Schottenstein Homes 3 Eastern Columbus OH 43219

SCHOUMACHER, BRUCE HERBERT, lawyer; b. Chgo., May 23, 1940; s. Herbert Edward and Mildred Helen (Wagner) S.; m. Alicia Wesley (Sanchez), Nov. 4, 1967; children: Liana Cristina, Janina Maria. BS, Northwestern U., 1961; MBA, U. Chgo., 1963, JD, 1966. Bar: Nebr. 1966, U.S. Dist. Ct. Nebr. 1966, Ill. 1971, U.S. Dist. Ct. (no. dist.) Ill. 1971, U.S. Ct. Appeals (7th cir.) 1979, U.S. Supreme Ct. 1982, U.S. Ct. Fed. Claims 1986. Assoc. Luebs, Tracy, and Huebner, Grand Island, ebr., 1966-67, McDermott, Will, and Emery, Chgo., 1971-76; ptnr. McDermott, Will,and Emery, Chgo., 1976-89, Querrey and Harrow, Ltd., Chgo., 1989—. Instr. bus. adminstrn., Bellevue Coll., Nebr., 1967-70; lectr., U. Md. Overseas Program, 1970. Author: Engineers and the Law: An Overview, 1986; contbg. author: Construction Law, 1986, Construction Law Handbook, 1999, Construction Business Handbook, 2004; co-author: Successful Business Plans for Architects, 1992; contbr. articles to profl. jour. Capt., USAF, 1967-71, Vietnam. Decorated, Bronze Star, 1971. Fellow Am. Coll. Constrn. Lawyers; mem. ABA, AIA (profl. affiliate), Nebr. Bar Assn., Ill. State Bar Assn. (ad hoc com. large law firms 1992-98), chmn. membership and bar activities com. 1988-89, coun. ins. law sect., 1986-91, mem. spl. com. on computerized legal rsch. 1986-87, Chgo. Bar Assn. (chmn. fed. civil procedure com. 1982-83), Def. Rsch. Inst., Ill. Assn. Def. Trial Counsel, Chgo. Bldg. Congress (bd. dirs. 1985—, sec. 1987-89, 95—, v.p. 1989-91), Soc. Ill. Constrn. Attys. (steering com. 2004-2005, sec. 2005-07, treas. 2007—), Western Soc. Engr. (assoc.), The Lawyers Club of Chgo., Tower Club, Chgo., Univ. Club Chgo., Rolling Green Country Club, Pi Kappa Alpha, Phi Delta Phi. Republican. Methodist. Office: Querrey & Harrow Ltd 175 W Jackson Blvd Ste 1600 Chicago IL 60604-2827 Office Phone: 312-540-7046. Business E-Mail: bschoumacher@querrey.com.

SCHRADER, DAVID FLOYD, state legislator; b. Oct. 23, 1952; s. Hubert F. and Violet L. (Marshall) S.; m. Roberta J. Sterling, July 15, 1974; children: Todd, JoAnna, Heather, Melissa. Grad. high sch., Monroe, Iowa, 1970. Owner, operator automotive fabrication bus., Monroe, 1970-93; owner, operator amusement and vending bus., 1980-88; mem. Iowa Ho. of Reps., Des Moines, 1987-90, asst. majority leader, 1991-92, asst. minority leader, 1993—, minority leader. Named Legis. Conservationist of 1993, Iowa Wildlife Fedn. Mem. Internat. Motor Contest Assn., NASCAR, Kiwanis. Democrat. Methodist. Office: Iowa Ho of Reps State Capitol Des Moines IA 50319-0001

SCHRADER, KEITH WILLIAM, mathematician; b. Neligh, Nebr., Apr. 22, 1938; s. William Charles and Gail (Hughes) S.; m. Carol Jean Taylor, Dec. 26, 1960; children: Jeffrey, Melinda. BS, U. Nebr., 1959, MS, 1961, PhD, 1966; postgrad., Stanford U., 1961-63. Engr. Sylvania Co., Mountain View, Calif., 1962-63; asst. prof. dept. math U. Mo.-Columbia, 1966-69, assoc. prof., 1969-78, prof., 1978-79, chmn. dept. math. prof., 1979-82, 85-88, prof. dept. math., 1988—. Bd. dirs. Schrader Inst. Early Learning, Columbia, 1970-83; mem. Planning And Zoning Commn., 1980-90. NASA grantee, 1967-68; NSF grantee, 1969-70 Mem. Am. Math. Soc., Sigma Xi, Sigma Phi Epsilon Office: Dept Math U Mo Columbia MO 65211-0001 E-mail: keiths99k@netscape.net.

SCHRAG, EDWARD A., JR., lawyer; b. Milw., Mar. 27, 1932; s. Edward A. and Mabel Lena (Baumbach) Schrag; m. Leslie Jean Israel, June 19, 1954; children: Amelia Marie Schrag Prack, Katherine Allison Schrag Roberts, Edward A. III(dec.). BS in Econs, U. Pa., 1954; JD, Harvard, 1960. Bar: Ohio 1961. From assoc. to ptnr. Vorys, Sater, Seymour & Pease, Columbus, Ohio, of counsel, 1960—. Sec. Ranco Inc., 1972—87; trustee Lake of Woods Water Co., 1972—91; mem. Ohio divsn. Securities Adv. Com. Mem. Downtown Area Com., 1970—74. Served to lt. (j.g.) USNR, 1954—57. Mem.: ABA, Columbus Bar Assn., Ohio Bar Assn., Navy League, Columbus Area C. of C., Ohio State U. Pres.'s Club, Capital Club, Crichton Club, Pi Gamma Mu, Phi Sigma Alpha, Beta Gamma Sigma, Alpha Tau Omega. Episcopalian. Home: 9400 White Oak Ln Westerville OH 43082-9606 Office: Vorys Sater Seymour and Pease PO Box 1008 52 E Gay St Columbus OH 43216-1008 Office Phone: 614-464-6400. Business E-Mail: easchrag@vssp.com.

SCHRECK, ROBERT, commodities trader; b. 1944; With Pillsbury Co., Mpls., 1968-93, v.p.; exec. v.p. Commodity Specialists Co., Mpls., 1993—. Office: Commodity Specialists Co 301 4th Ave S Minneapolis MN 55415-1015

SCHRECK, ROBERT A., JR., lawyer; b. Buffalo; BS in Bus. Adminstrn., Georgetown U., 1974; MBA, Northwestern U., 1975, JD, 1978. Bar: Ill. 1978. Ptnr. McDermott, Will & Emery, Chgo., 1978—. Mem. ABA. Office: McDermott Will & Emery 227 W Monroe St Ste 4400 Chicago IL 60606-5096 E-mail: rschreck@mwe.com.

SCHREIBER, BERTRAM MANUEL, mathematics professor; b. Seattle, Nov. 4, 1940; s. Isador and Amy (Hurwitz) S.; m. Rita Ruth Stusser, June 30, 1963; children: Susannah M. Schreiber Bechhofer, Deborah H. Schreiber Shapiro, Abraham D., Elisabeth T. Schreiber Seigel. BA, Yeshiva U., 1962; MS, U. Wash., 1966, PhD, 1968. Asst. prof. Wayne State U., Detroit, 1968-71, assoc. prof., 1971-78, prof., 1978—, chair dept. math., 1987-90. Vis. prof. Hebrew U., Jerusalem, 1975, 2000, 07, Mich. State U., East Lansing, 1982-83, Nat. U. Singapore, 1992, U. NSW, Sydney, 1992, Indian Statis. Inst., New Delhi and Bangalore, 1993, Tata Inst. Fund Res., Bombay, 1993, Bar Ilan U., Ramat Gan, Isreal, 1993, 2007, Tel Aviv U., 1993, U. Utrecht, The Netherlands, 1993, U. Wroclaw, Poland, 1993, 2006, U. Paris VII, 1999, U. Granada, Spain, 1999-2000, U. Wash., Seattle, 2000, Ecole Poly. Féd. Lausanne, Switzerland, 2006, U. Vienna, 2007, U. Munich, 2007. Contbr. articles to profl. jours. NSF grantee, 1968-87; Sci. and Engring. Rsch. Coun. Gt. Britain fellow U. Edinburgh, Scotland, 1976. Mem. Am. Math. Soc., Math. Assn. Am., Israel Math. Union, Edinburgh Math. Soc. Achievements include research in the fields of harmonic analysis, topological groups, and probability theory. Office: Wayne State U Dept Math Detroit MI 48202 Home Phone: 248-827-1199; Office Phone: 313-577-8838. Business E-Mail: bschreiber@wayne.edu.

SCHREIBER, JAMES RALPH, obstetrician, researcher; b. Rosebud, Tex., May 29, 1946; s. Lester B. and Jane Elinore (Hodges) Schreiber; m. Mary Celia Schmitt, Aug. 16, 1968; children: Lisa, Joseph, Laura, Cynthia. BA, Rice U., 1968; MD, Johns Hopkins U., 1972. Diplomate Am. Coll. Ob-gyn., Am. Bd. Reproductive Endocrinology. Intern. ob-gyn. U. So. Calif. Los Angeles County Hosp., 1972-73, resident ob-gyn., 1973-74, 76-78; fellow reproductive endocrinology NIH, Bethesda, Md., 1974-76; asst. prof. ob-gyn U. Calif., San Diego, 1978-82; assoc. prof. U. Chgo., 1982-87, prof., 1988-91; prof., chmn. dept. Washington U., St. Louis, 1991—. Contbr. articles to profl. jours. Grantee, NIH, 1978—. Mem.: Soc. Gynecologic Investigation. Home: 22 Frontenac Estates Saint Louis MO 63131-2600 Office: Washington U Sch Medicine Dept Ob-Gyn 4911 Barnes Hospital Plz Saint Louis MO 63110-1003 E-mail: schreiberj@msnotes.wustl.edu.

SCHREIBER, LOLA F., former state legislator; m. Marion Schreiber; 2 children. Student, S.D. State U. Mem. S. D. Ho. Reps., to 1997, vice-chmn. edn. com., mem. state affairs com. Chmn. edn. com., mem. judiciary com., mem. tax com., chmn. legislators exec. bd., 1995, 96, chmn. edn. com. Nat. Conf. State Legislators; commr. Edn. Commn. States; mem. policy and priorities com.; mem. adv. bd. Policymakers Inst., Danforth Found.; mem. Fin. Project. Home: 30045 173rd St Gettysburg SD 57442-5301

SCHREIER, BRADLEY, management executive; b. Aug. 19, 1951; m. Marge St. Pierre; children: Ryan, Kyle. BS in Social Studies and Econs., Minn. State U., Mankato, 1973. Letterpress supr. Carlson Craft, Mankato, Minn., 1973-74, custom svc. supr., 1974-76, office mgr., 1976-79; v.p. sales and mktg. Taylor Corp., Mankato, 1980-85, pres., COO, 1985—2001, CEO, 2001—. Bd. dir. Malto Meal Corp., Mpls. Bd. dirs. Mankato Area United Way, 1975-81, v.p., 1979, 80, pres. bd. dirs., 1981; bd. dirs. YMCA, 1983-92, chmn. fin. com., co-chair spl. gifts divsn. 1 million dollar bldg. expansion capital campaign; bd. dirs. Immanuel-St. Joseph's Hosp., 1984-94, treas., 1988, vice chmn., treas, 1989, chmn. med. office bldg. task force, 1990, vice chmn., 1990, chmn. bd. dirs., 1991, 92, mem. exec. com., 1993-94; bd. dirs. Mankato Area Cath. Sch. Found., 1988—; pres. parish coun., mem. coun. Holy Rosary Ch., 1988—, chmn. fin. com., mem. com., 1989—; mem. pers. com. Loyola Cath. High Sch., 1989-90, mem. sch. bd., 1989-90; chmn. Mankato Area Cath. Sch. Bd., 1990—; coach Mankato Area Youth Baseball Assn., 1986—, bd. dirs., 1991—; pres. Mankato Royals Baseball, 1989, 90, bd. dirs., 1989-93; Fitzgerald 7th and 8th grade basketball coach, 1988, mem. Loyola Booster Club; bd. dirs. Mankato Basketball Assn., 1989—, traveling team coach, 1989—; basketball team coach Holy Rosary. Recipient Book of Golden Deeds award for Outstanding Cmty.

Svc., Mankato Exch. Club, 1994, Disting. Alumni award Minn. State U., Mankato, 1994. Mem. KC. Office: Taylor Corp 1725 Roe Crest Dr Mankato MN 56003-1807 Office Phone: 507-625-2828.

SCHREIER, KAREN ELIZABETH, judge; b. Sioux Falls, SD, 1956; AB, St. Louis U., 1978; JD, St. Louis U. Law Sch., 1981. Law clk. to Hon. Francis Dunn, SD Supreme Ct., 1981—82; pvt. practice Sioux Falls, SD, 1982—93; US atty. US Dept. Justice, Sioux Falls, SD, 1993-99; judge US Dist. Ct., Rapid City, SD, 1999—. Office: US Dist Ct 515 9th St Rm 318 Rapid City SD 57701-2626 Office Phone: 605-343-3744.

SCHREINER, ALBERT WILLIAM, internist, educator; b. Cin., Feb. 15, 1926; s. Albert William and Ruth Mary (Neuer) S.; m. Jean Tellstrom, Dec. 12, 1953; 1 child, David William. BS, U. Cin., 1947, MD, 1949. Diplomate Am. Bd. Internal Medicine, 1958. Clin. investigator VA Hosp., Cin., 1957-59, chief med. svc., 1959-68, dir. dept. internal medicine, 1968-93; dir. resident program internal medicine Christ Hosp., Cin., 1978-87; mem. faculty U. Cin. Coll. Medicine, 1955—, assoc. prof. medicine, 1962-67, prof. internal medicine, 1967-98, emeritus prof. internal medicine, 1998—; attending physician Cin. Gen. Hosp., 1957—95. Cons. to med. dir. Gen. Electric, 1987-96; med. dirs. United Home Care Hospice, 1993-99, United Home Care Agy.; chair instnl. rev. bd. The Christ Hosp., 1988—; subinvestigator Sterling Rsch. Group, 2003—. Contbr. articles to profl. jours. Bd. dirs., chmn. health com. Cmty. Action Commn., 1968-71; trustee Drake Meml. Hosp., 1975-78, Leukemia Found. Southwest Ohio, Cancer Control, Am. Cancer Soc., bd. dirs. Hamilton County unit, 1990; bd. dirs., chair profl. affairs com. United Home Care Agy., 1998; bd. dirs. Gamble Inst. Med. Rsch., Cin., 1991-96; chmn. IRB Hilltop Rsch., 2007-. Fellow: ACP; mem.: Am. Soc. Clin. Rsch. Program Dirs. Internal Medicine, Assn. Program Dirs. Internal Medicine, Clin. Soc. Internal Medicine (pres. 1979—80), Ohio Soc. Internal Medicine (trustee 1978, sec.-treas. 1981—85, v.p. 1982—83, pres. 1984—85), Ohio Med. Assn., Am. Fedn. Clin. Rsch., N.Y. Acad. Scis., Am. Cancer Soc. (bd. dirs. Hamilton County unit 1990—92), Am. Leukemia Soc. (med. adv. exec. bd.), Phi Beta Kappa, Sigma Xi. Roman Catholic. Home: 8040 S Clippinger Dr Cincinnati OH 45243-3248 Office: 2139 Auburn Ave Cincinnati OH 45219-2906 Office Phone: 513-585-2742. Business E-Mail: schreia@healthall.com.

SCHRIER, ARNOLD, historian, educator; b. NYC, May 30, 1925; s. Samuel and Yetta (Levine) S.; m. Sondra Weinshelbaum, June 12, 1949; children: Susan Lynn, Jay Alan, Linda Lee, Paula Kay. Student, Bethany Coll., W.Va., 1943-44, Ohio Wesleyan U., 1944-45; BS, Northwestern U., 1949, MA, 1950, PhD (Social Sci. Research Council fellow, Univ. fellow), 1956. Asst. prof. history U. Cin., 1956-61, assoc. prof., 1961-66, prof., 1966-95, dir. grad. studies history, 1969-78, Walter C. Langsam prof. modern European history, 1972-95; Walter C. Langsam prof. history emeritus, 1995—. Vis. asst. prof. history Northwestern U., Evanston, Ill., 1960; vis. assoc. prof. history Ind. U., Bloomington, 1965-66; vis. lectr. Russian history Duke U., 1966; disting. vis. prof. US Air Force Acad., 1983-84; dir. NDEA Inst. World History for Secondary Sch. Tchrs., U. Cin., 1965; Am. del. Joint U.S.-USSR Textbook Study Commn., 1989. Author: Ireland and the American Emigration, 1958, reissued, 1970, paperback edit., 1997, The Development of Civilization, 1961-62, Modern European Civilization, 1963, Living World History, 1964, rev., 1993, Twentieth Century World, 1974, History and Life: the World and Its People, 1977, rev., 1993, A Russian Looks at America, 1979, Irish Immigrants in the Land of Canaan, 2003. Pres. Ohio Acad. History, 1973-74, Midwest Slavic Conf., 1980. Served with USNR, 1943-46, 52-54. Recipient Disting. Svc. award Ohio Acad. History, 1992; Am. Coun. Learned Socs. fgn. area fellow, 1963-64 Mem. World History Assn. (v.p. 1986-88, pres. 1988-90). Home: 10 Diplomat Dr Cincinnati OH 45215-2073 Personal E-mail: arnsond@aol.com.

SCHRIESHEIM, ALAN, science administrator; b. NYC, Mar. 8, 1930; s. Morton and Frances (Greenberg) Schriesheim; m. Beatrice D. Brand, June 28, 1953; children: Laura Lynn, Robert Alan. BS in Chemistry, Poly. Inst. Bklyn., 1951; PhD in Phys. Organic Chemistry, Pa. State U., 1954; DSc (hon.), No. Ill. U., 1991; Laureate, Lincoln Acad., 1996; PhD (hon.), Ill. Inst. Tech., Chgo., 1992, Pa. State U., 2001. Chemist Nat. Bur. Standards, 1954—56; with Exxon Rsch. & Engring. Co., 1956—83, dir. corp. rsch., 1975—79; gen. mgr. Exxon Engring., 1979—83; sr. dep. lab. dir., COO Argonne Nat. Lab., 1983—84, lab. dir., CEO, 1984—96, dir. emeritus, 1996—; prof. chemistry dept. U. Chgo., 1984—96, lectr. Bus. Sch., 1996—99; prin. Washington Adv. Group, 1996—2006; pres. Chgo. Coun. Sci. and Technol., 2007—. Karcher lectr. U. Okla., 1977; Hurd lectr. Northwestern U., 1980; Rosensteil lectr. Brandeis U., 1982; Welsh Found. lectr., 87; com. svc. RC, 1980—; vis. com. chemistry dept. MIT, 1977—82; mem. vis. com. mech. engring. and aerospace dept. Princeton (N.J.) U., 1983—87, mem. vis. com. chemistry dept., 1983—87; mem. Pure and Applied Chemistry Com.; del. to People's Republic of China, 1978; mem. Presdl. Nat. Commn. on Superconductivity, 1989—91, U.S.-USSR Joint Commn. on Basic Sci. Rsch., 1990—93; mem. U.S. nat. com. Internat. Union Pure and Applied Chemistry, 1982—85; mem. magnetic fusion adv. com. Divsn. Phys. Scis. U. Chgo. Magnetic Fusion adv. com. to U.S. DOE, 1983—86; mem. Dept. Energy Rsch. Adv. Bd., 1983—85, Congl. Adv. Com. on Sci. and Tech., 1985—96; mem. vis. com. Stanford (Calif.) U., U. Utah, Tex. A&M U., Lehigh U.; bd. govs. Argonne Nat. Lab., 1984—96; mem. adv. com. on space sys. and tech. NASA, 1987—93; mem. nuc. engring. and engring. physics vis. com. U. Wis., Madison; mem. Coun. Gt. Lakes Govs. Regional Econ. Devel. Commn., 1987—, rev. bd. Compact Ignition Tomamak Princeton U., 1988—91; advisor Sears Investment Mgmt. Co., 1988—89; bd. dirs. HEICO, Smart Signal Corp.; adv. bd. Batterson Venture Ptnrs., Influx, UHV Aluminum, Valley Indsl. Assn., Coun. on Superconductivity for Am. Competitiveness; mem. State of Ill. Commn. on the Future of Pub. Svc., 1990—92; co-chair Indsl. Rsch. Inst. Nat. Labs./Industry Panel, 1984—87; mem. Nat. Acad. Engring. Adv. Commn. on Tech. and Soc., 1991—92, Sun Electric Corp. Bd., 1991—92, U.S. House of Reps. subcom. on Sci.-Adv. Group on Renewing U.S. Sci. Policy, 1992—96, Chgo. Acad. Scis. acad. coun., 1994—; mem. adv. bd. Chemtech; mem. sr. action group on R&D investment strategies Ctr. for strategic and Internat. Studies, 1995; bd. vis. Astronomy and Astrophysics Pa. State U., 1995—; bd. overseers Fermi Nat. Lab., 2003—. Adv. bd.: Chemtech, 1970—85, editl. bd.: Rsch. & Devel., 1988—92, Superconductor Industry, 1988—95; patentee in field. Mem. spl. vis. com. Field Mus. of Natural History, Chgo., 1987—88; trustee The Latin Sch. of Chgo., 1990—92; adv. bd. WBEZ Chicagoland Pub. Radio Cmty., 1990—96; mem. Conservation Found. DuPage County, 1983—96, Econ. Devel. Adv. Commn. of DuPage County, 1984—88, Ill. Gov.'s Commn. on Sci. and Tech., 1986—90, Inst. for Ill. Coun. Advisors, 1988—, Ill. Coalition Bd. Dirs., 1989—, Inst. for Ill. Adv. Rev. Panel, 1986—88, NASA Sci. Tech. Adv. Com. Manpower Requirements Ad Hoc Rev. Team, 1988—91, Ill. Sci. and Tech. Adv. Com., 1989—, chmn., 1997; mem. U. Ill. Engring. Vis. com., Urbana-Champaign, 1986—95; trustee Tchrs. Acad. for Math. and Sci. Tchrs. in Chgo., 1990—96; bd. visitors astronomy and astrophysics Pa. State U., 1995—; bd. dirs. LaRabida Children's Hosp. and Rsch. Ctr., 1987—95, Children's Meml. Hosp., Children's Meml. Inst. for Edn. and Rsch. Recipient Outstanding Alumni Fellow award, Pa. State U., 1985, laureate, Lincoln Acad. Ill., 1996, Disting. fellow, Poly. U., 1989, Disting. Alumni award, Pa. State U., 2005. Fellow: AAAS (coun. del. chem. sect. 1986—92, sci. engring. and pub. policy com. 1992, standing com. audit 1992, bd. dirs. 1992—96, selection com. to bring FSU scientists to ann. mtg. 1995—2000), N.Y. Acad. Scis.; mem.: AIChE (award com. 1992—2000), NAE (adv. com. tech. and soc. 1991—92, mem. program adv. com. 1992—94, chair study fgn. participation in U.S. R&D 1993—96, NRC com. on dual use tech. 1996—97, com. to assess policies and practices of Dept. of Energy to design, ma 1998—99), Chgo. Coun. on Sci. and Tech. (pres. 2007—), NASA Com. on Aeronautics Innovation Models (chmn. 2005—07), Ctr. Strategic and Internat. Studies (sr. action group 1995—96), Indsl. Rsch. Inst. (co-chmn. Nat. Labs. Indsl. Panel 1984—87, fed. adv. com. to Fed. Sci. and Tech. Com. 1992—96, sr. action group on R&D Investment Strategies), Am. Nuc. Soc., Am. Petroleum Inst. (rsch. coord. coun.), Nat. Conf. Advancement Rsch. (conf. com. 1985—, site selection com. 1994, conf. com. 50th ann. 1996), Am. Mgmt. Assn. (R&D coun. 1988—96), Am. Chem. Soc. (joint bd. coun. on sci. 1983—87, chmn. petroleum divsn. 1983—91, councilor, com. on chemistry and pub. affairs 1983—91, petroleum chemistry award 1969, 1995—96), Econ. Club, Comml. Club, Carleton Club (bd. govs. 1992—), Cosmos Club, Phi Lambda Upsilon, Sigma Xi. Home: 1440 N Lake Shore Dr Apt 31ac Chicago IL 60610-5927 Office: Argonne Nat Lab 9700 S Cass Ave Argonne IL 60439-4803 Home Phone: 312-440-9408; Office Phone: 312-630-3872. Personal E-mail: aschries@aol.com. Business E-Mail: schriesheim@anl.gov.

SCHRIVER, JOHN T., III, lawyer; b. Evanston, Ill., May 18, 1945; AB, Coll. of Holy Cross, 1967; JD, Georgetown U., 1970. Bar: Ill. 1971, Fla. 1972. Ptnr. Duane Morris LLC, Chgo. Mem. ABA, Chgo. Bar Assn., Fla. Bar. Office: Duane Morris LLC 227 W Monroe St Ste 3400 Chicago IL 60606-5096

SCHROCK, EDWARD J., state legislator; b. Holdrege, Nebr., Aug. 20, 1943; m. Judith M. Grove, 1965; children: Ted, Tom. BA, Nebr. Wesleyan U., 1965. Farmer, Phelps County, Nebr.; mem. Nebraska Legislature, Lincoln, 1991, 92, 95—. Mem. Phelps County Sch. Bd. Dist. R-4. Mem. Holdrege Area C. of C., Natural Resources Commn., Nebr. Corn Growers Assn., Nebr. Corn Developers (utilization and mkt. coms. bds.), Ctrl. Irrigators Assn., Nebr. Cattlemens Assn.

SCHROCK, HAROLD ARTHUR, manufacturing executive; b. Goshen, Ind., Apr. 10, 1915; s. Arthur E. and Anna (Shaner) S.; m. Thelma A. Hostetler, Sept. 3, 1938; children— Sara (Mrs. William Barrett), Susan (Mrs. John Graff), Cinda (Mrs. Stephen McKinney), Douglas. B.A, Goshen Coll., 1937. Chmn. bd. dirs. Starcraft Co., Goshen, 1967-71. Pres. Goshen Sash & Door Co., Smoker-Craft, Inc., New Paris, Earthway Products, Bristol, Inc., Goshen Iron & Metal Co.; chmn. 1st Nat. Bank of Goshen; v.p. Ind. Capital Co., Ft. Wayne; pres. Ivy Terrace, Inc., Goshen, Marque, Inc., Goshen. Past pres. Greater Goshen Assn., Jr. Achievement, Goshen Gen. Hosp., Goshen Pub. Library; pres. Goshen Hosp. Found. Mem. Goshen C. of C. (pres. 1952) Republican. Lutheran (v.p. vestry). Clubs: Elcona Country (Goshen), Maplecrest Country (Goshen); Vineyards Country, Naples, Fla.; Rotary (past pres.). Home: 506 N Front St Syracuse IN 46567-1257 Office: US 33 E Goshen IN 46526 Also: Goshen Sash & Door Co Inc 603 E Purl St Goshen IN 46526-4044

SCHROEDER, HORST WILHELM, food products executive; b. Schwerin, Germany, May 5, 1941; m. Gisela I. Kammin; 1 child, Bernd; stepchildren: Ralph, Isabel Lange. MBA, U. Gottingen, Hamburg, Fed. Republic Germany, 1965. Sr. auditor Price Waterhouse, Hamburg, 1966-70; fin. contr. Kellogg Co. of West Germany, Bremen, 1970-71, dir. fin., 1971-76, mng. dir., 1976-81; pres., chief exec. officer Kellogg Salada Can., Toronto, 1981-83; pres. Kellogg Internat., Battle Creek, Mich., 1983-86, Kellogg N.A., Battle Creek, 1986-88; exec. v.p. Kellogg Co., Battle Creek, 1988, pres., chief oper. officer, 1988—. Mem. adv. bd. J.L. Kellog Grad. Sch.; Bd. of govs. St. Joseph Acad. of Food Mktg., Phila., 1986-88; mem. com. external affairs U. Ill., Chgo., 1987-88. Mem. Am. Health Found. (bd. dirs. 1987—), KC (pres. 1988—, bd. dirs. 1989—). Avocations: golf, tennis. Office: Am Italian Pasta Co 1000 Italian Way Excelsior Springs MO 64024

SCHROEDER, JOHN H., university chancellor; b. Twin Falls, Idaho, Sept. 13, 1943; s. Herman John and Azalia (Kimes) S.; m. Sandra Barrow; children: John Kimes, Andrew Barrow. BA, Lewis and Clark Coll., Portland, Oreg., 1965; MA, U. Va., 1967, PhD, 1971. Instr. history U. Wis., Milw., 1970-71, asst. prof., 1971-76, assoc. prof., 1976-86, prof., 1986—, Am. Coun. on Edn. fellow, 1982-83, assoc. dean, 1976-82, asst. to vice chancellor, 1982-85, acting vice chancellor, 1985-87, vice chancellor, 1987-90, chancellor, 1990-98, U. Wis. sys. prof., 1998—. Louis M. Sears Meml. lectr. Purdue U., 1978. Author: Mr. Polk's War: American Opposition and Dissent, 1973, The Commercial and Diplomatic Role of the American Navy 1829-1861, 1985, Matthew C. Perry: Antebellum Sailor and Diplomat, 2001 (Theodore and Franklin Roosevelt Naval History prize 2002, John Lyman Naval History award 2002), Commodore John Rodgers: Paragon of the Early American Navy, 2006. V.p. bd. dir. John Michael Kohler Arts Ctr.; bd. dir. Wis. Hist. Soc., We. Golf Assn. Recipient Edward and Rosa Uhrig award U. Wis.-Milw., 1974, Disting. Teaching award AMOCO/U. Wis.-Milw., 1975. Mem. Orgn. Am. Historians, Soc. for History of Early Republic, Soc. for History Am. Fgn. Rels. Office: U Wis Dept History PO Box 413 2310 E Hartford Ave Milwaukee WI 53211-3165 Business E-Mail: jhs@uwm.edu.

SCHROEDER, KENNETH LOUIS, reinsurance company executive; b. Altamont, Ill., Sept. 10, 1921; s. Edwin Samuel and Clara (Bauer) S.; m. Cleo K. Buzzard, May 30, 1943; children: Margery, Gerry, Mark. BS in Banking and Fin., U. Ill., 1947. Supr. investments State Farm Ins. Cos., Bloomington, Ill., 1947-50, mgr. tax dept., 1950-52, asst. comptroller, 1952-62, v.p., treas., 1962-74, v.p. reins., treas., 1974—. Bd. dirs. Bloomington-Normal YMCA, 1966-70; mem. Normal Town Council, 1968-76; trustee Bloomington-Normal San. Dist., 1982—; vice chmn. McLean County Republican Central Com., 1962-68. Mem. Fin. Execs. Inst. Clubs: Bloomington Country (dir. 1966-70, dir. 1979-83).

SCHROEDER, KENT A., lawyer; b. Genoa, Nebr., Apr. 7, 1943; m. Linda J. Sotherspoon, June 24, 1972; 3 children. BS, Iowa State U., 1965; JD, U. Nebr., 1968. Bar: ebr. 68. Ptnr. Ross, Schroeder & Romatzke, Kearney, Nebr. Bd. dirs. Ctrl. C.C.; bd. regents U. Nebr., 1998—; trustee Good Samaritan Hosp., 1988—2001. Mem.: ABA, Nebr. Assn. Trial Attys. (bd. dirs.), Nebr. Bar Assn., Kearney C. of C. (bd. dirs.), Kearney Cosmo. Club, Kearney Country Club (bd. dirs.), Phi Delta Phi, Pi Kappa Alpha. Mailing: 3003 Country Club Ln Kearney NE 68845-4047 Office: Ross Schroeder & Romatzke 220 W 5th St PO Box 1685 Kearney NE 68848-1685

SCHROEDER, STEPHEN ROBERT, psychology researcher; b. Leipsic, Ohio, Oct. 28, 1936; BA, Josephinum Coll., 1958; MA, U. Toledo, 1964; PhD, U. Pitts., 1967. Lic. psychologist, Ohio, N.C. Postdoctoral rsch. assoc. Learning Rsch. and Devel. Ctr., U. Pitts., 1967-68; clin. asst. prof. dept. psychology U. N.C., Chapel Hill, 1968-73, clin. assoc. prof. depts. psychology and psychiatry, 1973-77, rsch. assoc. prof. dept. psychology, 1977-87, rsch. sci. Biol. Scis. Rsch. Ctr., 1973-87, assoc. prof. dept. psychiatry, 1977-86, prof. dept. psychiatry, 1986-87; dir. psychology Murdoch Ctr., Butner, N.C., 1973-75, dir. rsch. and devel., 1975-77; prof. dept. psychology and psychiatry Ohio State U., Columbus, 1987-90, dir. The Nisonger Ctr., 1987-90; prof. dept. human devel. and family life U. Kans., Lawrence, 1990—, prof. dept. pharmacology and toxicology, 1990—, dir. Bur. Child Rsch., 1990—, dir. Schiefelbusch Inst. for Life Span Studies, 1990—. Mem. program com. Gatlinburg Conf. on Mental Retardation and Devel. Disabilities, 1977-92, program chmn., 1992—; mem. N.C. divsn. Mental Health and Mental Retardation Rsch. Grants Rev. Bd., 1977-86; mem. statewide lead screening com. N.C. Dept. Meternal and Child Health, 1979-86; founding chmn. Annie Sullivan Enterprises, Inc., 1982-89, active, 1989-92, chmn., 1992—; mem. rsch. grant rev. bd. Ont. Mental Health Found., 1984—; mem. internat. rsch. exch. subcom. for Rsch. in Ednl. Rehab. in U.S. and German Dem. Republic, 1984-90; gen. ad hoc mem. grant rev. bd. NIMH, 1984; mem. mental retardation study com. NICHD, 1989-90; rsch. cons. Am. Occupational Therapy Found., Inc.; cons. pediats. ward N.C. Meml. Hosp., 1977-86; cons. civil rights divsn. U.S. Dept. Justice, 1987—; cons. No. Va. Tng. Ctr., 1983-85, 91, Murdoch Ctr., Western Carolina Ctr., Caswell Ctr., 1977-89; bd. dirs. Corp. of Guardianship; active Ohio Devel. Disabilities Planning Coun., 1987-90, Kans. Planning Coun. on Devel. Disabilities Svcs., 1990—, Kans. Prevention Task Force, 1991—, Gov. Task Force on Respite Care, 1991—. Author, editor chpts. to books; editor Am. Jour. Mental Retardation, 1987—; co-editor Jour. Applied Rsch. in Mental Retardation, 1980-86, Rsch. in Devel. Disabilities, 1987—; mem. editl. bd. Jour. Applied Behaviour Analysis, 1973-74, Mental Retardation, 1977-93, Analysis and Intervention in Devel. Disabilities, 1981-82; guest reviewer Jour. Applied Behaviour Analysis, Pediat. Psychology, Am. Jour. Psychiatry, Jour. Autism and Childhood Scizophrenia, Child Devel., Sci., Perceptual and Motor Skills, Pediatrics, Neurotoxicology; contbr. articles, papers to profl. jours. Mem. adv. bd. Ohio United Cerebral Palsy, 1988-90; active Ohio Prevention Coalition, 1987-90. Recipient Karl Heinz Renker medallion for interdisciplinary sci. collaboration German Dem. Republic, 1989. Fellow APA (pres. divsn. 33 mental retardation 1986-87, Nicholas Hobbs award 1989); mem. AAAS, Am. Assn. Mental Retardation, Am. Acad. Mental Retardation, Assn. Advancement Behavior Therapy (task force on self-injurious behavior 1981-82), Assn. Behavior Analysis, N.Y. Acad. Scis., Sertoma Club. Office: U Kansas KS Ctr Rsch Mental Retardation 1052 Dole Human Devel Ctr Lawrence KS 66045-0001

SCHROPP, TOBIN, lawyer; b. 1962; BS in Fgn. Svc., Georgetown U., 1984, JD, 1987, LLM in Taxation, 1991. Bar: 1987. Sr. v.p., gen. counsel Peter Kiewit Sons' Inc., Omaha. Office: Peter Kiewit Sons Inc 1000 Kiewit Plaza Omaha NE 68131

SCHTEINGART, DAVID EDUARDO, internist; b. Buenos Aires, Oct. 17, 1930; came to U.S., 1957; s. Mario and Flora (Garfunkel) S.; m. Monica Naomi Starkman, July 3, 1960; children: Miriam, Judith, M. Daniel. MD, U. Buenos Aires, 1955. Diplomate Am. Bd. Internal Medicine. Fellow Mt. Sinai Hosp., NYC, 1957-58, Maimonides Hosp., Bklyn., 1958-59, U. Mich., Ann Arbor, 1959-62, instr., 1962-63, asst. prof., 1963-68, assoc. prof., 1968-72, prof., 1972—. Contbr. articles to profl. jours., books. Pres. Beth Israel Congregation, Ann Arbor, 1974-79, Hebrew Day Sch., Ann Arbor, 1984-86, Jewish Fedn. Washtenaw County, Ann Arbor. Recipient rsch. grants NIH, Bethesda, Md., 1985—. Fellow Am. Coll. Physicians; mem. Endocrine Soc., N.Y. Acad. Scis., Am. Soc. Clin. Nutrition, Cen. Soc. Clin. Rsch., Am. Fedn. Clin. Rsch. Jewish. Avocations: tennis, running, community activities. Office: U Mich Med Sch 1150 W Medical Center Dr Ann Arbor MI 48109-0726

SCHUBERT, HELEN CELIA, public relations executive; b. Washington City, Wis. d. Paul H. and Edna (Schmidt) S. BS, U. Wis., Madison. Dir. pub. rels. United Cerebral Palsy, Chgo., 1961; adminstrv. dir. Nat. Design Ctr., Chgo., 1962-67; owner Schubert Pub. Rels., Chgo., 1967—. Bd. dirs. Fashion Group, Chgo., 1988—95; adj. prof. comm. Roosevelt U., 1992—. Mem. women's bd. Am. Cancer Soc., Chgo., 1988—, Art Resources in Tchg., Chgo., 1988-92. Recipient Comm. award Am. Soc. Interior Designers, Chgo., 1979, 83, 88, 94; named to Chgo. Women's Hall of Fame City of Chgo., 1990. Fellow Nat. Home Fashion League; mem. Women's Ad Club Chgo. (pres. 1981-83, Woman of Yr. award 1987), Women in Comm. (pres. 1969-70, Matrix award Lifetime Achievement 1996), Am. Advt. Fedn. (lt. gov. 1983-85). Lutheran. Personal E-mail: schube@mail.com.

SCHUBERT, WILLIAM HENRY, curriculum studies educator; b. Garrett, Ind., July 6, 1944; s. Walter William and Mary Madeline (Grube) S.; children by previous marriage: Ellen Elaine, Karen Margaret; m. Ann Lynn Lopez, Dec. 3, 1977; children: Heidi Ann, Henry William. BS, Manchester Coll., 1966; MS, Ind. U., 1967; PhD, U. Ill., 1975. Tchr. Fairmount, El Sierra and Herrick Schs., Downers Grove, Ill., 1967—75; clin. instr. U. Wis., Madison, 1969—73; tchg. asst., fellow U. Ill., Urbana, 1973—75, asst. prof. Chgo., 1975—80, assoc. prof., 1981—85, prof., 1985—, coord. secondary edn., 1979—82, coord. instrnl. leadership, 1979—85, dir. grad. studies Coll. Edn., 1983—85, coord. grad. curriculum studies, 1985—2005, coord. edn. studies, 1990—94, 1996—, chair area curriculum and instrn., 1990—94, 2002—05, Univ. scholar, 2005—, coord. PhD program in curriculum and MEd program in edn. studies, 2006—. Vis. assoc. prof. U. Victoria (B.C., Can.), 1981; disting. vis. prof. U. S.C., 1986; presenter in field. Author (with Ann Lopez Schubert): Curriculum Books: The First Eighty Years, 1980; author: Curriculum: Perspective, Paradigm and Possibility, 1986, with Edmund C. Short and George Willis, 1985; author: (with J. Dan Marshall and James T. Sears) Turning Points in Curriculum: A Contemporary American Memoir, 2000; author: (with others) 2d edit., 2007; author: (with Ann Lopez Schubert, Thomas P. Thomas, Wayne M. Carroll) Curriculum Books: The First Hundred Years, 2002; editor (with Ann Lopez): Conceptions of Curriculum Knowledge: Focus on Students and Teachers, 1982; editor: (with George Willis) Reflections from the Heart of Educational Inquiry: Understanding Curriculum Teaching Through the Arts, 1991; editor: (with William Ayers) Teacher Lore: Learning From Our Own Experience, 1992, 2001; editor: (with George Willis, R. Bullugh, C. Kridel, J. Holton) The American Curriculum: A Documentary History, 1993; assoc. editor, mem. editl. bd. Ednl. Theory, mem. editl. bd. Catalyst: Voices of Chicago School Reform, Taboo: The Jour. of Culture and Edn., former mem. editl. bd. Ednl. Studies, former cons. editor Phenomenology and Pedagogy, adv. bd. Tchg. Edn., Pi Lamda Pubs., 1995—, Jour. Curriculum and Supervision, mem. editl. bd. Curriculum and Teaching, Jour. Curriculum and Pedagogy, emeritus editl. bd. Jour. Curriculum Theorizing, 1999—; editor: (book series) Student Lore, 1990—; cons. editor Jour. Curriculum Discourse and Dialogue, mem. adv. bd. Jour. Critical Issues in Curriculum and Instrn., 2000—, contbr. over 200 articles to profl. jours., chpt. to books. Mem.: ASCD (steering com. curriculum com. 1980—83, publs. com. 1987—90, internat. polling panel 1990—), Internat. Acad. Edn., Am. Assn. for Advancement of Curriculum Studies, Internat. Assn. for Advancement of Curriculum Studies, Soc. Profs. of Edn. (exec. bd. 1988—97, pres.-elect 2000—01, pres. 2001—02, Mary Ann Raywid award 2007), John Dewey Soc. (bd. dirs. 1986—95, chair awards com. 1988—90, co-chair lectures commn. 1989—91, 1989—91, pres.-elect 1990—91, pres. 1992—93), Inst. Dem. in Edn., Nat. Soc. Study Edn., World Coun. Curriculum and Instrn., Am. Ednl. Rsch. Assn. (chmn. creation and utilization of curriculum knowledge 1980—82, program chmn. curriculum studies divsn. 1982—83, sec. divsn. B 1989—91, v.p. 2000—01, Lifetime Achievement award in Curriculum Studies 2004), Am. Assn. Colls. Tchr. Edn., Soc. Study Curriculum History (sec.-treas. 1981—82, pres. 1982—83, founder), Profs. of Curriculum (factotum 1984—85), Internat. Acad. Edn., Scottish Rite, Masons, Phi Kappa Phi (pres. U. Ill. Chgo. chpt. 1981—82), Phi Delta Kappa. Office: U Ill Coll Edn M/C 147 1040 W Harrison St Chicago IL 60607-7129 Business E-Mail: schubert@uic.edu.

SCHUBERT, WILLIAM KUENNETH, hospital medical center executive; b. Cin., July 12, 1926; s. Wilfred Schubert and Amanda Kuenneth; m. Mary Jane Pamperin, June 5, 1948; children: Carol, Joanne, Barbara, Nancy. BS, U. Cin., 1949, MD, 1952; LHD (hon.), Coll. Mt. St. Joseph, Cin., 1997. Diplomate Am. Bd. Pediat. Pvt. practice specializing in pediat., Cin., 1956-63; dir. clin. rsch. ctr. Children's Hosp. Med. Ctr., Cin., 1963-76; dir. divsn. gastroenterology Children's Hosp., Cin., 1968-79; prof. pediat. U. Cin., 1969-96, prof. emeritus, 1997—, assoc. sr. v.p. for children's hosp. affairs Coll. Medicine, 1993-96; chief of staff Children's Hosp. Med. Ctr., Cin., 1972-88; chmn. dept. pediat. U. Cin., 1979-93; dir. Children's Hosp. Rsch. Found., Cin., 1979-93; pres., CEO Children's Hosp. Med. Ctr., Cin., 1983-96, trustee, 1983—. V.p. Ohio Solid Organ Transplant Consortium, Columbus, 1986-87, pres., 1987-88, alt. trustee, 1988-96; trustee med. rsch. James N. Gamble Inst., Cin., 1989-95; bd. dirs. Choice Care Found., Health Found. of Greater Cin.; mem. fetal oversight com. Fetal Care Ctr. Cin., 2005—. Contbr. over 100 articles to profl. jours. Trustee Greater Cin. Hosp. Coun., 1986-96, Assn. of Ohio Children's Hosps., Columbus, 1986-96, The Children's Hosp. Found., 1990—, Springer Sch., Cin., 1994-2003, Children's Convalescent Hosp., 1997—, The Children's Hosp., 2001—; chmn. Greater Cin. Hosp. Coun., 1989; co-chmn. Citizen's Com. for Med. Ctr., Cin., 1980-81; chmn. Hosp. Divsn. 1988 Fine Arts Fund, Cin., 1987; hon. trustee Babies' Milk Fund, Children's and Prenatal Clinics, Cin., 1994-2002. Recipient Disting. Alumni award U. Cin., 1992, Donald Newkirk award Ohio Hosp. Assn., 1997, Health Care Heros Lifetime Achievement award Bus. Courier, Cin., 2003, Great Living Cincinnatian award, 2004. Fellow Am. Acad. Pediat. (Murray Davidson award sect. on gastroenterology/nutrition 2003); mem. Am. Pediatric Soc. (councillor 1986-93), Soc. Pediatric Rsch., Assn. Med. Sch. Pediatric Dept. Chmn., Cin. Acad. Medicine, AMA, Midwestern Soc. for Pediatric Rsch., Am. Assn. for Study of Liver Diseases, Ctrl. Soc. Clin. Rsch., Am. Gastroenterological Assn., N.Am. Soc. Pediatric Gastroenterology, Nat. Reye's Syndrome Found. (med. dir. 1976-87), Internat. Assn. Study Liver Diseases. Clubs: Queen City (Cin.). Office: Children's Hosp Med Ctr Cin ML 5005 3333 Burnet Ave Cincinnati OH 45229-3026 Home Phone: 513-751-6007. Business E-Mail: william.schubert@cchmc.org.

SCHUCK, THOMAS ROBERT, lawyer, farmer; b. Findlay, Ohio, Feb. 7, 1950; s. Robert Damon and Katherine Margaretta (Beynon) S. BA, DePauw U., 1972; MA, U. Kent, UK, 1974; JD, Harvard U., 1976. Bar: Ohio 1976, U.S. Dist. Ct. (no. dist.) Ohio 1977, U.S. Dist. Ct. (so. dist.) Ohio 1979, Ariz. 1990, U.S. Ct. Appeals (6th cir.) 1978, U.S. Ct. Appeals (9th cir.) 1991, U.S. Ct. Appeals Armed Forces, 2000, U.S. Supreme Ct. 2001. Law clk. U.S. Dist. Ct., Cleve., 1976-79; assoc. Taft, Stettinius & Hollister, Cin., 1979-87, ptnr., 1987—; owner, operator Rural Hill Farm. Participant Ohio Bench Bar Conf., Columbus, 1990-91, Glenmoor Justice Inst., 2000; barrister Am. Inn of Ct., 1986-87, LEAD Clermont, 1997-98; bar exam com. US Dist. Ct. (so. dist.) Ohio, nen, panel criminal justice act, mem. criminal justice act atty. panel, 2006—; merit panel for bankruptcy judge selection US Ct. Appeals Sixth Cir., 1998, chair, 2002; life mem. Jud. Conf. of 6th Cir., mem. standing com. Author: Federal Employment Litigation Practice Guide, 2006; contbg. author: Aids and the Law, 2d edit. 1992; contbr. articles to profl. jours. Trustee Mental Health Svcs. East, Inc., Cin., 1985-91; sec. bd. trustees Joy Outdoor Edn. Ctr., Inc., 1999-2005; active May Festival Assocs., Cin., 1984-86, WGUC Radio Cmty. Bd., 1984-86, Clermont County Mental Health Bd., Batavia, Ohio, 1992-2000, vice-chmn., 1997-2000; steering com. Clermont County Mental Retardation Developmental Disabilities Levy, 1996, trustee, 2000-02, vice-chmn., 2002; spl. gifts com. Cin. Art Acad., 1987, Ohio Found. Ind. Colls., 1995-, bd. dir., 2003—; pres. Fed. Bar Assn. Found. Cin. Grad. fellow Rotary Internat. Found., 1972-73. Mem. Fed. Bar Assn. (pres. Cin. chpt. 1994-95, v.p. 6th cir. 1996-99, nat. membership chair 1997-99, nat. sec. 2001-2002, nat. treas., nat. v.p. 2002-03, nat. pres.-elect 2003-04, nat. pres. 2004-05, govt. rels. com., pres. Foun. of Cin.), Potter Stewart Am. Inn of Ct. (barrister 1986-87), U.S. Rowing Assn. (asst. referee), Harvard

Club Cin. (pres. 1995-96), Soc. Bacchus Am., Masons (33rd degree, trustee Valley of Cin. 2003-05), Phi Beta Kappa, Delta Chi, Phi Eta Sigma, Sigma Delta Chi. Republican. Methodist. Avocations: reading, photography. Home: PO Box 615 189 State Route 133 Felicity OH 45120 Office: Taft Stettinius & Hollister LLP Ste 1800 425 Walnut St Cincinnati OH 45202-3957 Home Phone: 513-633-1841; Office Phone: 513-381-2838.

SCHUCK, WILLIAM, state legislator; b. Findlay, Ohio, Dec. 12, 1951; s. Robert and Margaretta (Beynon) S. BA, Harvard Univ., 1974; MBA, JD, Cornell Univ., 1982. Mem. Columbus Devel. Com., Ohio, 1985-86; State Rep. Ohio Dist. 29, 1987—; lawyer Porter, Wright, Morris & Arthur, 1984—. Named Outstanding Citizen of Columbus, Jaycees, 1986. Mem. Columbus Athletic Club, Aladdin Shrine, Delta Epsilon. Address: Ohio Ho of Reps 13th Fl State House Columbus OH 43215

SCHUELE, DONALD EDWARD, retired physics professor, dean; b. Cleve., June 16, 1934; s. Edward and Mildred (Matousek) S.; m. Clare Ann Kirchner, Sept. 5, 1956; children: Donna, Karen, Melanie, Judy, Rachel, Ruth. BS, John Carroll U., Cleve., 1956, MS, 1957; PhD, Case Inst. Tech., 1962. Instr. physics and math. John Carroll U., 1956-59; part-time instr. physics Case Inst. Tech., 1959-62, instr., asst. prof., assoc. prof., 1962-70; mem. tech. staff Bell Telephone Labs., 1970-72; assoc. prof. physics Case Western Res. U., 1972-74, prof., 1974—, dean undergrad. coll., 1973-76, chmn. dept. physics, 1976-78; vice dean Case Inst. Tech., 1978-83, v.p. for undergrad. and grad. studies, 1983-84, dean, 1984-86, prof. physics, 1986-88, dean math. and natural sci., 1988-89, Albert A. Michelson prof. physics, 1989—2006, Albert A. Michelson emeritus prof. physics, 2006, acting chmn. elec. engring. and applied physics, 1992-93. Cons. in field. Co-editor: Critical Revs. in Solid State Scis, 1969-84; contbr. articles to profl. jours.; patentee in field. Mem. adv. bd. St. Charles Borromeo Sch., 1970-72; pres. Seed Found., 1986-89; trustee St. Mary's Sem., 1980-93; mem. Olympic Sports Equipment and Tech. Com., 1982-93; trustee Newman Found., 1983—, Northeastern Ohio Sci. Fair, 1983—; mem. Diocesan Pastoral Coun., 1992-94; active Rep. Presdl. task force. Recipient Disting. Physics Alumnus award John Carroll U., 1983; NSF Faculty fellow, 1961-63; Sam Givelber fellow Case Alumni Assn., 2001. Mem.: North Coast Thermal Analysis Soc., Am. Assn. Physics Tchrs., Am. Phys. Soc. (vice chair Ohio sect. 1995—96, chair 1996—97), Newman Apostolate, Case Alumni Coun. (life; 3d v.p. 2001—02, 1st v.p. 2002—03, pres. 2003—04, treas. 1992, chair Case Fund Bd. 2004—), Tau Beta Pi, Sigma Xi, Alpha Sigma Nu. Republican. Roman Catholic. Achievements include patents fluid pressure device, impact wrench torque calibrator, detection of wear particles and other impurities in industrial fluids, electrical oil analysis instrument. Home: 4892 Countryside Rd Cleveland OH 44124-2513 Office: Case Western Res U 10900 Euclid Ave Cleveland OH 44106-1712 Home Phone: 216-382-0561; Office Phone: 216-368-4013. Business E-Mail: des3@case.edu.

SCHUEPPERT, GEORGE LOUIS, financial executive; b. Merrill, Wis., July 1, 1938; s. George Henry and Eleanor Natalie (Pautz) S.; m. Kathleen Kay Carpenter, May 6, 1967; children: Steven Andrew, Stephanie Roanne, Stenning Karl BBA, U. Wis., Madison, 1961; MBA, U. Chgo., 1969. Treas., controller Steiger-Rathke Devel. Co., Phoenix, 1964-65; various positions Continental Ill. Nat., Chgo., 1965-76, 1981-86; mng. dir. Continental Ill. Ltd., London, 1977-81; sr. v.p. Continental Ill. Nat. Bank, Chgo., 1982-86; ptnr. Coopers & Lybrand, Chgo., 1986-87; exec. v.p. fin. CBI Industries Inc, Oak Brook, Ill., 1987-95, also bd. dirs., 1987-95; exec. v.p., CFO Outboard Marine Corp., Waukegan, Ill., 1996-97. Bd. dirs. Wells Mfg. Co., Barrington Bank & Trust Co. Pres. Gt. Books Found., Atlas Rsch. found., West Am. Mortgage Co.; chmn., bd. dirs. De Paul U. Gov. Asst. Program. Lt. (j.g.) USN, 1961-64, trustee Village Barringham. Recipient Herfurth award U. Wis., 1960 Mem. Econ. Club Chgo. (bd. dirs., chmn. membership com.). Republican. Avocations: history, architecture, travel, golf. Home: 97 Otis Rd Barrington IL 60010-5129 Office: Great Books Found 35 E Wacker Dr Ste 400 Chicago IL 60601-2298

SCHUERER, NEAL, state legislator; b. Cedar Rapids, Iowa, Nov. 6, 1954; BA, Ctrl. Coll. Restauranteur, Amana, Iowa; mem. Iowa Senate from 30th dist., Des Moines, 1996—; mem. appropriations com., mem. bus. and labor rels. com.; mem. commerce com., mem. human resources com.; mem. state govt. com. Bd. dirs. Amana Ch. Soc., Sunday sch. supt.; mem. Amana Heritage Soc., Amana Colonies Land Use Dist., Amana Colonies Challenge 2000. Mem. Nat. Restaurant Assn., Iowa Hospitality Assn. Republican. E-mail: neal_schuerer@legis.state.ia.us.

SCHUESSLER, JOHN T. (JACK SCHUESSLER), retired food service executive; b. Dec. 21, 1950; m. Patty A. Schuessler. BS, Spring Hill Coll. Mgr. trainee Wendy's franchise, Atlanta, 1974-76; joined Wendy's Internat., 1976, dist. mgr., dir. area ops., regional dir. various zones US, 1976-83, regional v.p. ea. divsn., 1983-84, zone pres., 1984-86, divsn. v.p., 1986-87, sr. v.p. N.E. region, 1987-95, exec. v.p. US ops., 1995-97, pres., COO US ops., 1997-2000, pres., COO Can., 1999-2000, pres., CEO, 2000—06, chmn., 2001—06. Trustee Wendy's Nat. Advtsg. Program.

SCHUETTE, BILL, state legislator; b. Midland, Mich., Oct. 13, 1953; m. Cynthia; children: Heidi, Billy. Student, U. Aberdeen, 1974-75; BS in Fgn. Svc., Georgetown U., 1976; JD, U. San Francisco, 1979. Bar: U.S. Supreme Ct. 1985. Atty., Midland, Mich., 1981—; Mich. field coordinator George Bush for Pres., 1979; Mich. polit. dir. Reagan/Bush for Pres., 1980; mem. 99th-101st Congresses from 10th Mich. dist., Washington, 1985-91, Mich. Senate from 35th dist., Lansing, 1994—. Dir. Mich. Dept. Agr., 1991-93; chair State Econ. Devel., Internat. Trade and Regulatory Affairs Com., 1995—. Office: PO Box 30036 Lansing MI 48909-7536

SCHUG, KENNETH ROBERT, chemistry professor; b. Easton, Pa., Aug. 27, 1924; s. Howard Lester and Marion Henry (Hulbert) S.; m. Miyoko Ishiyama, June 13, 1948; children: Carey Tyler, Carson Blake, Reed Porter. Student, Johns Hopkins U., 1942-43; BA, Stanford U., 1945; PhD, U. So. Calif., 1955. Instr. Seton Hall Coll., South Orange, N.J., 1948-50; research assoc. U. Wis.-Madison, 1954-56; instr. Ill. Inst. Tech., Chgo., 1956-59, asst. prof., 1959-65, assoc. prof., 1965-75, prof. chemistry, 1975—, chmn. dept. chemistry, 1976-82, 85-87, 89-90, assoc. chair dept. biol. chem. phys. sci., 1999-01. Project dir. Chgo. Area Health and Med. Careers Program, 1979—; project co-dir. Sci. and Math. Initiative for Learning Enhancement, 1985—; project dir. Howard Hughes Med. Inst. Undergrad. Biol. Scis. Program, 1992-97; cons. Argonne (Ill.) Nat. Lab., 1960-62. Co-author: Eigo Kagoku Ronbun no Kakikata, 1979; contbr. articles to profl. jours. Trustee Michael Reese Health Plan, Chgo., 1976-91, Michael Reese Trust, 1991-2003; bd. dirs. Hyde Park Consumers Coop. Soc., 1982-94. Fulbright scholar, 1964-65; grantee in field Mem. Am. Chem. Soc. (dir., officer Chgo. sect. 1978-84). Home: 1466 E Park Pl Chicago IL 60637-1836 Office: Ill Inst Tech Div Chemistry IIT Ctr Chicago IL 60616 Office Phone: 312-567-3438. Business E-Mail: schug@iit.edu.

SCHUH, DALE R., insurance company executive; Joined Sentry Ins. Group, Stevens Point, Wis., 1972, v.p. planning, 1988, pres., COO, 1996, CEO, pres., chmn., 1997—. Office: Sentry Ins Group 1800 North Point Dr Stevens Point WI 54481

SCHUH, G(EORGE) EDWARD, dean, agricultural economist; b. Indpls., Sept. 13, 1930; s. George Edward and Viola (Lentz) S.; m. Maria Ignez, May 23, 1965; children: Audrey, Susan, Tanya. BS in Agrl. Edn, Purdue U., 1952, DAgr, PhD, Purdue U., 1992; MS in Agrl. Econs., Mich. State U., 1954; MA in Econs, U. Chgo., 1958, PhD, 1961; prof. (hon.), Fed. U. Vicosa, Brazil, 1965. From instr. to prof. agrl. econs. Purdue U., 1959-79; dir. Center for Public Policy and Public Affairs, 1977-78; dep. undersec. for internat. affairs and commodity programs Dept. Agr., Washington, 1978-79, chair bd. for internat. food and agrl. devel., 1995—2002; prof. agrl. and applied econs., head dept. U. Minn., Mpls., 1979-84; dir. agr. and rural devel. World Bank, Washington, 1984-87; dean Humphrey Inst. for Pub. Affairs U. Minn., 1987—96; Orville and Jane Freeman Endowed chair Humphrey Inst. for Pub. Affairs, U. Minn., 1996—; regents prof. U. Minn., 1998—. Program advisor Ford Found., 1966-72; sr. staff economist Pres.'s Coun. Econ. Advisors, 1974-75; mem. bd. on agr. and natural resources NRC, 1998—2004; trustee Internat. Food Policy Rsch. Inst., 1997-2003, Internat. Potato Ctr., 2004—. Contbr. articles to profl. jours. Trustee Sasakawa Africa Assn., 1998—. Served with U.S. Army, 1954-56. Recipient 60 at 60 award, Internat. Insts. Cooperation in Agr., Order Sci. Merit, Grand Cruz. Fellow: AAAS, Brazilian Acad. Sci., Brazilian Soc. Rural Econs., Am. Acad. Arts and Scis., Am. Agrl. Econs. Assn. (bd. dirs. 1977—80, pres.-elect 1980—81, pres. 1981—82, Thesis award 1962, Pub. Rsch. award 1971, Article award 1975, Policy award 1979, Publ. of Lasting Value award 1988); mem.: Brazilian Soc. Agrl. Economists, Am. Econ. Assn., Internat. Assn. Agrl. Econs. Office: Humphrey Ctr U Minn 301 19th Ave S Minneapolis MN 55455-0429 Office Phone: 612-625-8388. Business E-Mail: geschuh@hhh.umn.edu.

SCHUL, BILL DEAN, psychological administrator, author; b. Winfield, Kans., Mar. 16, 1928; s. Fred M. and Martha Mildred (Miles) S.; m. Virginia Louise Duboise, Aug. 3, 1952; children: Robert Dean, Deva Elizabeth. BA, Southwestern Coll., 1952; MA, U. Denver, 1954; PhD, Am. Internat. U., 1977. Reporter, columnist Augusta (Kans.) Daily Gazette, 1954-58, Wichita (Kans.) Eagle-Beacon, 1958-61; youth dir. under auspices Kans. Atty. Gen., 1961-65; state dir. 7th Step Found., Topeka, 1965-66; mem. staff Dept. Preventive Psychiatry, Menninger Found., Topeka, 1966-71; dir. cons. Ctr. Improvement Human Functining, Wichita, 1975—. Psychologist Ctr. Human Devel., Wichita; assoc. prof. Holos U. Grad. Seminary, 2002-. Mng. editor The Register, Oxford, Kans., 1988—; author: (with Edward Greenwood) Mental Health in Kansas Schools, 1965, Let Me Do This Thing, 1969, (with Bill Larson) Hear Me, Barabbas, 1969, How to Be An Effective Group Leader, 1975, The Secret Power of Pyramids, 1975, (with Ed Pettit) The Psychic Powre of Pyramids, 1976, Pyramids: The Second Reality, 1979, The Psychic Power of Animals, 1977, Psychic Frontiers of Medicine, 1977, Animal Immortality, 1990, Life Song, 1995, Synchronize Your Brain, 1997, Wayward Angel, 1988. Bd. dirs. Recreation Commn., Topeka, United Funds, Topeka, Acadic Inst., Trees for Life; v.p. Pegasus Way; pres. Intraface Corp., 1989—; mem. adv. bd. Clayton U. With USN, 1945-46. Recipient John H. McGinnis Meml. award Nonfiction, 1972, Am. Freedom Found. award, 1966, Spl. Appreciation award Kans. State Penitentiary, 1967. Mem. Acad. Parapsychology and Medicine, Kans. Coun. Children and Youth (pres. 1965-66), Assn. Strenghtening higher Realities and Aspirations of Man (pres. 1970-71), Smithsonian Instn., Lions (pores. 1957). Address: 1624 E 8th Ave Winfield KS 67156 E-mail: schul@iwinfield.net.

SCHULER, JAMES JOSEPH, vascular surgeon; b. Aurora, Ill., Feb. 12, 1946; s. Ella Schuler; m. Catherine Weller, 1969; children: James Jr., Matthew. BS, St. John's U., 1968; MD with hons., U. Ill., 1972, MS in Biochemistry, 1975. Diplomate Am. Bd. Surgery, Am. Bd. Vascular Surgery. Intern U. Ill., Chgo., 1972-73, resident, 1973-78, chief resident, 1978-79, instr., 1975-79, asst. prof., 1980-85, assoc. prof., 1985-92, prof. surgery, 1992—, chief divsn. vascular surgery, 1988—. Lectr. Cook County Grad. Sch., Chgo., 1991—; attending surgeon Cook County Hosp., Chgo., 1992—, West Side Vets. Hosp., Chgo., 1979—. Assoc. editor: Civilian Vascular Trauma, 1992; co-author numerous book chpts.; contbr. articles to profl. jours. Vascular Surgery fellow U. Ill., 1979-80; rsch. grantee numerous granting bodies, 1980—. Fellow ACS; mem. Am. Venous Forum, Soc. for Vascular Surgery, Western Surg. Assn., Internat. Soc. for Cardiovascular Surgery, Midwestern Vascular Surg. Soc., Alpha Omega Alpha. Republican. Roman Catholic. Avocations: hunting, fishing. Office: U Ill Hosp 1740 W Taylor St Ste 2200 Chicago IL 60612-7232

SCHULER, ROBERT HUGO, chemist, educator; b. Buffalo, Jan. 4, 1926; s. Robert H. and Mary J. (Mayer) S.; m. Florence J. Forrest, June 18, 1952; children: Mary A., Margaret A., Carol A., Robert E., Thomas C. BS, Canisius Coll., Buffalo, 1946; PhD, U. Notre Dame, 1949. Asst. prof. chemistry Canisius Coll., 1949-53; asso. chemist, then chemist Brookhaven Nat. Lab., 1953-56; staff fellow, dir. radiation research lab. Mellon Inst., 1956-76, mem. adv. bd., 1962-76; prof. chemistry, dir. radiation research lab. Carnegie-Mellon U., 1967-76; prof. chemistry U. Notre Dame, Ind., 1976—, dir. radiation lab. Ind., 1976-95, dir. emeritus, 1995—, John A. Zahm prof. radiation chemistry, 1986—; Raman prof. U. Madras, India, 1985-86. Vis. prof. Hebrew U., Israel, 1980. Author articles in field. Recipient Curie medal Poland, 1992. Fellow AAAS; mem. Am. Chem. Soc., Am. Phys. Soc., Chem. Soc., Radiation Research Soc. (pres. 1975-76), Sigma Xi. Clubs: Cosmos. Office: U Notre Dame Radiation Lab Notre Dame IN 46556 Home Phone: 574-272-7323. Business E-Mail: schuler.1@nd.edu.

SCHULER, ROBERT LEO, appraiser, consultant; b. Cin., June 15, 1943; s. Del D. and Virginia D. (Heyl) S.; m. Shelagh J. Moritz, Aug. 11, 1962; children: Robert C., Sherry L. V.p. Comprehensive Appraisal Service, Cin., 1977—. Bd. dirs. Hamilton County Regional Planning Commn., Cin., 1987-88; mem. exec. com., past pres. OKI Regional Coun. Govts., Cin., 1981-92. Councilman City of Deer Park, Ohio, 1979-86; trustee Sycamore Twp., 1988-92; Ohio state rep. 36th dist., 1993—2000; senator, 7th Dist., Ohio, 2003-; active Scarlet Oaks Bus. Adv. Coun. Recipient United Conservatives of Ohio Watchdog of the Treasury award, 1994, 1996, 1998, 2005; Coun. of State Govts. Toll fellow, 2004. Mem. Cin. Bd. Realtors, Ohio Assn. Realtors, Jaycees (v.p.). Republican. Roman Catholic. Home: 3648 Jeffrey Ct Cincinnati OH 45236-1544 Office: State House of Ohio Columbus OH 43215 Office Phone: 614-466-9737.

SCHULFER, ROCHE EDWARD, theater executive director; b. Chgo., Sept. 26, 1951; s. Thomas Florian and Tess (Ronk) S.; m. Arlene Lencioni, June 2, 1973 (div. 1979); m. Linda Kimbrough, Aug. 2, 1986 (div. 1996). BA in Econs., U. Notre Dame. Box office asst. Goodman Theatre, Chgo., 1973-74, asst. to mng. dir., 1974-77, gen. mgr., 1977-80, mng. dir., prodr., producing dir., exec. dir., 1980—. Mem. exec. com. League of Resident Theatres, Chgo., 1981, 83; pres. League of Chgo. Theatres, 1983-85, pres. Chgo. Theatre Found.; bd. dirs. Goodman Theatre, Chgo. Theatre Group, Lifeline Theatre; adj. prof. DePaul U. Mem. Am. Arts Alliance, Ill. Art Alliance. Office: Goodman Theatre 170 N Dearborn St Chicago IL 60601-3205

SCHULKERS, JOAN M., lawyer; Grad., William Mitchell Coll. Law, 1999. Bar: Minn. Ptnr. Borman & Schulkers, P.L.L.P., Mpls. Named a Rising Star, Minn. Super Lawyers mag., 2006. Mem.: Minn. Women Lawyers, Minn. State Bar Assn. (bd. govs. 2001—, chair new lawyers sect. 2003—04, vice chair new lawyers sect. 2002—03, sec. new lawyers sect. 2001—02), Hennepin County Bar Assn. (sec. 2001—02, bd. govs. 2001—04, mem. exec. com. 2002—03, chair new lawyers sect. 2002—03, co-chair litig. sect. 2004—06). Office: Borman & Schulkers PLLP 250 3rd Ave North Ste 530 Minneapolis MN 55401 Office Phone: 612-332-3096. E-mail: joan@bormanschulkers.com.

SCHULLER, DAVID EDWARD, cancer center administrator, otolaryngologist; b. Cleve., Oct. 20, 1944; m. Carole Ann Hauss, June 24, 1967; children: Rebecca, Michael. BA, Rutgers U., 1966; MD cum laude, Ohio State U., 1970. Diplomate Am. Bd. Otolaryngology 1975. Intern dept. surgery U. Hosps. Cleve., 1970-71; resident dept. otolaryngology Ohio State U., Columbus, 1971-72; resident dept. surgery U. Hosps. Cleve., 1972-73; fellow head and neck surgery Pack Med. Found. with John Conley, NYC, 1973; resident dept. otolaryngology Ohio State U. Hosps., Columbus, 1973-75; fellow head and neck oncology and facial plastic and reconstructive surgery U. Iowa, Iowa City, 1975-76; trustee Ohio Cancer Found, 1988—; from clin. instr. to prof. and chmn. dept. otolaryngology The Ohio State U., Columbus, 1971—; dir. Am. Bd. Otolaryngology, 1988—2000, Comprehensive Cancer Ctr., Columbus, 1997—; prof. sect. oral biology, Coll. Dentistry The Ohio State U., 1990—; dir. Arthur G. James Cancer Hosp. & Richard J. Solove Rsch. Inst., Columbus, 1988—; chair dept. otolaryngology Ohio State U., Columbus, 1990—; past pres. American Board of Otolaryngology. Mem., chmn. various coms. Ohio State U. Hosps. and Coll. Medicine, 1976—; dir. CCC head and neck oncology program Ohio State U., 1977—, hosps. physician flr. coord. 10th flr., 1977-82, dir. laser-microsurgery teaching and rsch. lab., 1987-88; mem. various coms. Grant Hosp., 1980-84; mem. Accreditation Coun. for the Grad. Med. Edn. Residency Review Com. for Otolaryngology, 1985—, chmn., 1988—; vis. prof., lectr., ACS prof. clin. Oncology, 1989-94. numerous instns. Author: (books) (with others) Otolaryngology-Head and Neck Surgery-4 Vols., 1986, Textbook of Otolaryngology-7th Edit., 1988, Otolaryngology-Head and Neck Surgery-Update I, 1988, Musculocutaneous Flaps in Head and Neck Reconstructive Surgery, 1989, Otolaryngology-Head and Neck Surgery Update II, 1990, Otorinolaringologia-Cirugia de Cabeza y Culleo, 1991, Otolaryngology-Head and Neck Surgery-4 Vols., 1992; contbr. chpts. to books and articles to profl. jours.; mem. editorial bd. New Horizons in Otolaryngology/Head and Neck Surgery, 1982-87, The Laryngoscope, 1986—, Am. Jour. Otolaryngology, 1988—, Facial Plastic Surgery Internat. Quar. Monographs, 1992—; mem. rev. bd. Jour. Head and eck Surgery, 1985—; mem. editorial rev. bd. Otolaryngology-Head and Neck Surgery, 1990—; reviewer New Eng. Jour Medicine, 1992—. Recipient Cert. of Appreciation, Scioto Meml. Hosp., 1982, Edmund Prince Fowler award Triological Soc., 1984; Henry Rutgers scholar Rutgers U., 1965-66; grantee Nat. Cancer Inst., 1980-88, 90-97, Bremer Found., 1982-83, 87-88, Photomedica Inc., 1986-89, Upjohn Co., 1986-90, others. Mem. AMA (mem. rev. panel Archives of Otolaryngology-Head and Neck Surgery 1984—), Am. Cancer Soc. (mem. instl. grant rev. com. 1980—, chmn. rehab. com. Franklin County unit 1981-82, mem. profl. edn. com. 1981—, chmn. 1982-85, v.p. 1982-83, pres. 1986, 87, trustee Ohio divsn. 1988—), Am. Assn. Cosmetic Surgeons, Am. Acad. Facial Plastic and Reconstructive Surgery (mem. rsch. com. 1977-82, chmn. residency rels. com. 1982-85, mem. program com. 1982-85, v.p. mid. sect. 1983-87, chmn. by-laws com. 1988-90, treas. 1988-90, Honor award 1989), Am. Coll. Surgeons, Am. Cleft Palate Assn., Assn. Am. Cancer Insts., Am. Soc. Head and Neck Injury, Am. Acad. Otolaryngology Head and Neck Surgery (mem. editorial bd. self-instructional package program 1982—, del. bd. govs. 1982-87, Honor award 1983), Am. Soc. Laser Medicine and Surgery, Am. Laryngological, Rhinological, Otological Soc., Inc., Am. Laryngological Assn., Am. Soc. Clin. Oncology (mem. program com. 1989—), Am. Assn. Cancer Researchers, Am. Soc. Head and Neck Surgery (mem. coun. 1983-86, chmn. scholastic and fellowship award com. 1984-86, mem. profl. rels. and pub. edn. com. 1989—), Southwest Oncology Group (chmn. head and neck com. 1983—), Collegium ORLAS, Ohio State Med. Assn. (pres. sect. otolaryngology 1987—), Ohio Soc. Otolaryngology (pres. 1985, 86, 87), Acad. Medicine of Columbus and Franklin County, Columbus E.E.N.T. Soc., Franklin County Acad. Medicine (mem. profl. rels. com. 1982—), Head and Neck Intergroup (vice-chmn. 1984-86, chmn. 1986-89), Assn. Rsch. Otolaryngology, Ohio State U. Med. Alumni Soc. (class rep. 1980—, v.p. 1987-88, pres. 1989-90), Med. Forum, Med. Review Club, Order of Hippocrates (charter), Alpha Omega Alpha. Office: 456 W 10th Ave Columbus OH 43210-1240 also: Ohio State Univ Comp Cancer Ctr 300 W 10th Ave Columbus OH 43210-1240

SCHULMAN, SIDNEY, neurologist, educator; b. Chgo., Mar. 1, 1923; s. Samuel E. and Ethel (Miller) S.; m. Mary Jean Diamond, June 17, 1945; children— Samuel E., Patricia, Daniel. BS, U. Chgo., 1944, MD, 1946. Asst. prof. neurology U. Chgo., 1952-57, assoc. prof., 1957-65, prof., 1965-75, Ellen C. Manning prof., divsn. biol. scis., 1975-93, Ellen C. Manning prof. emeritus, 1993—. Served with M.C. AUS, 1947-49. Mem. Am. Neurol. Assn., U. Chgo. Med. Alumni Assn. (pres. 1968-69, Norman Maclean award 1997), Chgo. Neurol. Soc. (pres. 1964-65)

SCHULT, THOMAS P., lawyer; b. Great Falls, Mont., Sept. 12, 1954; s. Peter Henry and Louise (de Russy) S.; m. Margo C. Soulé, Sept. 18, 1982. BS in Russian History, U. Va., 1976, JD, 1979. Bar: U.S. Dist. Ct. (we. dist.) Mo. 1979, U.S. Ct. Appeals (10th cir.) 1983, U.S. Ct. Appeals (7th, 8th and llth cirs.) 1984, U.S. Ct. Appeals (5th cir.) 1985, U.S. Supreme Ct. 1987, U.S. Ct. Appeals (9th cir.) 1988. Ptnr. Lathrop Koontz & Norquist, Kansas City, Mo., 1979-89, Bryan Cave, Kansas City, 1989-94; Stinson, Mag & Fizzell, Kansas City, 1994-2001; ptnr. Berkowitz Feldmiller, 2001—. Committeeman Jackson County Reps., Kansas City, 1984—. Mem. ABA (products liability com.), Products Liability Adv. Coun., Mo. Bar Assn. (lectr. continuing legal edn.), Fedn. of Ins. and Corporate Counsel, Def. Rsch. Inst. Episcopalian. Office: Stinson Mag & Fizzell 1201 Walnut St Ste 2800 Kansas City MO 64106-2117

SCHULTE, DAVID MICHAEL, investment banker; b. NYC, Nov. 12, 1946; s. Irving and Ruth (Stein) S.; m. Patricia Gordon, Sept. 5, 1999; children: Michael B., Katherine F. BA, Williams Coll., 1968; postgrad., Exeter Coll., Oxford U., Eng., 1968-69; JD, Yale U., 1972. Bar: DC 1973. Law clk. to Mr. Justice Stewart, US Supreme Ct., 1972-73; spl. asst. to pres. NW Industries, Inc., Chgo., 1973-75, v.p. corp. devel., 1975-79, exec. v.p., 1979-80; sr. v.p. Salomon Bros., Chgo., 1980-84; mng. ptnr. Chilmark Ptnrs., Chgo., 1984—. Editor-in-chief: Yale Law Jour, 1971-72. John E. Moody scholar Exeter Coll., Oxford U., 1968-69. Mem. Washington Bar Assn., Chgo. Club, Racquet Club, Farm Neck Golf Club, Vineyard Golf Club. Office: Chilmark Ptnrs 875 N Michigan Ave Ste 3460 Chicago IL 60611-1957 Office Phone: 312-984-9711.

SCHULTE, STEPHEN CHARLES, lawyer; b. Evanston, Ill., June 26, 1952; s. George John and Mary Ruth (Lamping) S.; m. Kathleen Ann O'Donnell, Sept. 4, 1982; children: Kate, Maureen, John. BA magna cum laude, St. Louis U., 1973, JD, 1976. Bar: Ill. 1976, U.S. Dist. Ct. (no. dist.) Ill. 1976, U.S. Ct. Appeals (7th cir.) 1991. Atty. Perz & McGuire, Chgo., 1976-83; ptnr. Winston & Strawn, Chgo., 1983—. Founder, bd. dirs. Greater Orgn. for Less Fortunate (GOLF), Chgo., 1982—; fundraiser for Maryville Acad.; mem. Glenview Park Dist. Commn., 1989—, v.p., 1991-92, 98-99, pres., 1992-93, 99-2000. Mem. ABA, Ill. State Bar Assn., Chgo. Bar Assn., Ill. Trial Lawyers Assn., Ill. Assn. Def. Trial Counsel, Chgo. Vol. Legal Svcs., Nat. Legal Aid Defender Assn., Phi Beta Kappa. Avocations: basketball, baseball, golf, music, travel. Home: 941 Club Cir Glenview IL 60025-3101 Office: Winston & Strawn 35 W Wacker Dr Ste 4200 Chicago IL 60601-1695 E-mail: sschulte@winston.com.

SCHULTS-BERNDT, ELFIE, music educator; Grad. in Piano Performance, SUNY, Buffalo; PhD in Piano Performance, Music Theory and Lit., Mich. State U. Dir. music Lake Mich. Coll., Benton Harbor. Recipient US Prof. of Yr. award, Carnegie Found. for Advancement of Tchg. and Coun. for Advancement and Support of Edn., 2006. Office: Music Prog Lake Mich Coll 2755 E Napier Ave Benton Harbor MI 49022 Office Phone: 269-927-8192. E-mail: berndt@lakemichigancollege.edu.

SCHULTZ, CARL HERBERT, real estate developer; b. Chgo., Jan. 9, 1925; s. Herbert V. and Olga (Swanson) S.; m. Helen Ann Stevesson, June 6, 1948; children: Mark Carl, Julia Ann BS Gen. Engring., Iowa State U., 1948. With Schultz Bros. Co., 1948—, mdse. mgr. and store planner Chgo., 1962—70, v.p. Lake Zurich, Ill., 1968—72, pres., 1972—2000, Ill. Schultz Bros. Co., Ind. Schultz Bros. Co., Iowa Schultz Bros. Co., Wis. Schultz Bros. Co.; chmn. Schultz Bros. Co., 2000—. Mem. Lake Bluff Zoning Bd. Appeals, Ill., 1976-85, chmn., 1978-85. Served with U.S. Army, 1944-46 Mem. Lake Zurich Indsl. Coun. (sec. 1976), Assn. Gen. Mdse. Chains (dir. 1975-86, exec. com. 1983-86, chmn. nat. conv. 1982), Ill. Retail Mchts. Assn. (dir. 1984-89), Wis. Retail Fedn. (dir. 1981-89). Presbyn. Office: 815 Oakwood Rd Unit I Lake Zurich IL 60047 Home: 1100 Pembridge Dr Apt 242 Lake Forest IL 60045-4219 Office Phone: 847-438-3900. Personal E-mail: chs701@sbcglobal.net.

SCHULTZ, CLARENCE JOHN, minister; b. Morris Twp., Wis., Aug. 4, 1937; s. Clarence John Sr. and Ella Mae (Feavel) S.; m. Doroland Kay King, Aug. 24, 1957 (dec. Jan. 1974); children: Sharon Kay Braun, Susan May Schultz Rogers; m. Martha Ann Aylor, Apr. 5, 1975. BS, Bryan Coll., 1960. Ordained to ministry Conservative Congl. Ch., 1961. Min. 1st Congl. Ch., Herreid, SD, 1961-66, Immanuel Evang. Congl. Ch., Sheboygan, Wis., 1966-77, Hope Congl. Ch., Superior, Wis., 1977-83, Zion Evang. Ch., Scottsbluff, Nebr., 1983-89, 1st Congl. Ch., Buffalo Center, Iowa, 1989-92, Kenosha, Wis., 1992-98, St. Lucas Cmty. Ch., Lake Elmo, Minn., 1998—2007; pastor emeritus St, Lucas Cmty. Ch. Mem. Conservative Congl. Christian Conf. (rec. sec. 1973-82, v.p. 1994-96, pres. 1996-99, Rocky Mountain area rep. 1987-89, endorser of chaplains 1988-2000, mem. credentials com. 1988-2006), Rotary (ch. chaplain com. 1993-95). Congregationalist. Avocations: amateur radio, golf. Personal E-mail: cjsmas@sbcglobal.net.

SCHULTZ, DALE WALTER, state legislator; b. Madison, Wis., June 12, 1953; s. Walter Albert and Lillian (Fortman) S.; m. Rachel Weiss, June 20, 1981; children: Katherine Ann, Amanda. BBA, U. Wis., 1975. Farm mgr., Hillpoint, Wis., 1975—; adminstrv. and legis. asst. Wis. State Senate, Madison, 1976-79; planning analyst State of Wis., Madison, 1979-82; mem. Wis. Assembly, Madison, 1982-91, Wis. Senate from 17th dist., Madison, 1991—; chair ins. com. Wis. Senate, Madison, 1995—, mem. audit com. joint com. rev. adminstrv. rules. Mem. citizens adv. bd. Sauk County (Wis.) Health Care Ctr.; mem. Sauk County Farm Bur. Recipient Disting. Svc. award FFA, 1994; named Legislator of Yr., Wis. Tech. Coll. Assn., 1994-95, Guardian of Small Bus., Nat. Fedn. Ind. Bus., 1994, Legislator of Yr., Vietnam Vets. Assn., 1994. Mem.: Rod & Gun (Hillpoint, Wis.), Lions, Masons. Republican. Home: 515 N Central Ave Richland Center WI 53581-1702 Office: PO Box 7882 Madison WI 53707-7882

SCHULTZ, DENNIS BERNARD, lawyer; b. Detroit, Oct. 15, 1946; s. Bernard George and Madeline Laverne (Riffenberg) Schultz; m. Andi Lynn Leslie, Apr. 18, 1967; 1 child, Karanne Anne. BS, Wayne State U., 1970; JD, Mich. State U., 1977. Bar: Mich. 1977, U.S. Dist. Ct. (ea. and we. dists.) Mich., U.S. Ct. Appeals (6th cir.), U.S. Dist. Ct. (we. dist.) Pa. V.p. Barkay Bldg. Co., Ferndale, Mich., to 1976; law clk. Hon. George N. Bashara, Mich. Ct. Appeals, Detroit, 1977; shareholder Butzel Long, Detroit, 1978—. Editor: Detroit Coll. Law Rev., 1977.

Scholar Detroit Coll. Law Alumni Assn., 1976, Mich. Consol. Gas Co., 1977. Mem.: Mich. Bar Assn., Detroit Bar Assn. Republican. Roman Catholic. Avocations: boating, bicycling, golf. Personal E-mail: dbs77@comcast.net.

SCHULTZ, ED (EDWARD ANDREW SCHULTZ), radio personality; b. Norfolk, Va., Jan. 27, 1954; s. George and Mary Schultz; m. Wendy Schultz; 6 children. Student, Moorhead State. Sportscaster WDAY, Fargo, ND; radio host News and Views weekdays Sta. KFGO-AM, Fargo, ND, 1992—2003; host The Ed Schultz Show, 2003—. Author: Straight Talk from the Heartland: Tough Talk, Common Sense, and Hope from a Former Conservative, 2004. Democrat. Avocations: fishing, hunting, flying. Office: The Ed Schultz Show 1020 25th St S Fargo ND 58103-2312

SCHULTZ, KURT LEE, lawyer; b. Chgo., Feb. 13, 1946; s. William Ernst Schultz and Patricia Marie (Chelminski) Facchine; m. Jane Marmet Lerro, Sept. 9, 1972; children: Jane, Melissa, Katherine, Laura. BA, U. Pa., 1967; JD, Ohio State U., 1972. Bar: Ill. 1972, U.S. Dist. Ct. Ill. (no. dist.), U.S. Dist Ct. Mich. (ea. dist.). Law clk. to Judge Richard B. Austin U.S. Dist. Ct. (no. dist.) Ill., Chgo., 1972-73; assoc. Winston & Strawn, Chgo., 1972-78, ptnr., 1978—. Arbitration panelist Nat. Assn. Securities Dealers. Trustee Ravinia Festival, Highland Park, Ill., 1989-97; bd. dirs., past pres. Youth Guidance, Chgo. 1st lt. U.S. Army, 1967-69. Mem. Order of Coif. Office: Winston & Strawn LLP 35 W Wacker Dr Ste 4200 Chicago IL 60601-9703 Office Phone: 312-558-5700. E-mail: kschultz@winston.com.

SCHULTZ, LOUIS EDWIN, management consultant; b. Foster, Nebr., Aug. 8, 1931; s. Louis Albert and Lula Pusey (Cox) S.; m. Mary Kathleen Peck, Mar. 3, 1962; children: Kurt Michael, Kristen Leigh. BSEE, U. Nebr., 1959; MBA, Pepperdine U., 1974. Mktg. mgr. Bell & Howell, Pasadena, Calif., 1962-70; dir. mktg. Cogar Corp., Utica, N.Y., 1970-71; product mgr. Pertec Corp., LA, 1971-73; gen. mgr. Control Data Corp., Mpls., 1973-84; founder Process Mgmt. Internat., Inc., Mpls., Minn., 1984, pres., 1984-99; ptnr., mng. dir. Bluefire Ptnrs., Mpls., 1999—. Bd. dirs. CorCom Cos., Inc., Mpls., PMI Ltd, 1995-98; adv. bd. Inst. for Productivity Through Quality, U. Tenn., Knoxville, 1982-84; ptnr. CorCom Cos., Inc., 1997-99, ptnr.-mng. dir., Bulefire Ptnrs. Author: Managing in the Worldwide Competitive Society, 1984, Quality Management Philosophies, 1985, Profiles in Quality, 1994; co-author: Quality Handbook for Small Business, 1994, Deming, The Way We Knew Him, 1995. Mem. Gov.'s Commn. on Productivity, St. Paul, 1986; chmn. Wirth Park Tree Restoration Com., Mpls., 1983; mem. Productivity Planning Com., St. Paul, 1985—. Staff sgt. USMC, 1952-54; advisor to Deming Forum, 1985—; judge Minn. Quality award, 1992. Recipient Profl. Partnership award U. Minn., 1987. Mem. Am. Soc. Performance Improvement (bd. dirs. 1984-89, outstanding svc. award), Minn. Coun. for Quality (bd. dirs. 1987-97), Human Sys. Mgmt. (editl. bd.), Asia-Pacific Orgn. Quality Control (life), Toastmasters Internat. Republican. Methodist.

SCHULTZ, LOUIS MICHAEL, advertising agency executive; b. Detroit, Aug. 24, 1944; s. Henry Richard and Genevieve (Jankowski) S.; children: Christian David, Kimberly Ann; m. Diane Lee; stepchildren: Vince, Andrea, Frank. BA, Mich. State U., 1967; MBA, Wayne State U., 1970. Staff Campbell-Ewald, Warren, Mich., 1967-74, v.p. group dir., 1975-77, sr. v.p., assoc. dir., 1977-82, group sr. v.p., 1982-83, exec. v.p., 1984-87, Lintas: USA, 1987-94; chmn. Lintas: WW Media Coun., 1991; mem. devel. council IPG, NYC, 1984—; pres., CEO CE Comm., 1994—; vice chmn. Campbell-Ewald, 1998-99; chmn., CEO Initiative Media N.Am., LA, 2000—; chmn. Initiative Media WW, 2000. Advisor, Detroit Renaissance Com., 1981-84. With USAR, 1967-73. Mem. NATAS, Am. Women in Radio and TV, Am. Mktg. Assn., Detroit Advt. Assn., Promotion Mktg. Assn. (bd. dirs. 1999), Ad Club N.Y. (bd. dirs.), Adcraft Club, Old Club, Hidden Valley Club, Longboat Key Club, Detroit Athletic Club, Am. Advt. Fedn. (bd. dirs.), Forest Lake Country Club, Renaissance Club, Detroit Athletic Club. Episcopalian. Avocations: golf, tennis, travel. Office: Initiative Media 5700 Wilshire Blvd Ste 400 Los Angeles CA 90036-3639 Home: 250 Bird Key Dr Sarasota FL 34236-1614

SCHULTZ, LOUIS WILLIAM, retired judge; b. Deep River, Iowa, Mar. 24, 1927; s. M. Louis and Esther Louise (Behrens) S.; m. D. Jean Stephen, Nov. 6, 1949; children: Marcia, Mark, Paul. Student, Central Coll., Pella, Iowa, 1944-45, 46-47; LLB, Drake U., Des Moines, 1949. Bar: Iowa. Claims supr. Iowa Farm Mut. Ins. Co., Des Moines, 1949-55; partner firm Harned, Schultz & McMeen, Marengo, Iowa, 1955-71; judge Iowa Dist. Ct. (6th dist.), 1971-80; justice Iowa Supreme Ct., 1980-93; county atty. Iowa County, 1960-68; ret., 1993. Served with USNR, 1945-46. Mem. Iowa Bar Assn. (bd. govs.), Iowa Judges Assn. (pres.)

SCHULTZ, RICHARD CARLTON, plastic surgeon; b. Grosse Pointe, Mich., Nov. 19, 1927; s. Herbert H. and Carmen (Huebner) S.; m. Pauline Zimmermann, Oct. 8, 1955; children: Richard, Lisa, Alexandra, Jennifer. MD, Wayne State U., 1953. Diplomate Am. Bd. Plastic Surgery. Intern Harper Hosp., Detroit, 1953-54, resident in gen. surgery, 1954-55, U.S. Army Hosp., Ft. Carson, Colo., 1955-57; resident in plastic surgery St. Luke's Hosp., Chgo., 1957-58, U. Ill. Hosp., Chgo., 1958-59, VA Hosp., Hines, Ill., 1959-60; practice medicine specializing in plastic surgery Park Ridge, Ill., 1961-96; ret., 1996; clin. asst. prof. surgery U. Ill. Coll. Medicine, 1966-70, assoc. prof. surgery, 1970-76, prof., 1976-96, head divsn. plastic surgery, 1970-87; pres. med. staff Luth. Gen. Hosp., Park Ridge, 1977-79. Vis. prof. U. Pitts., 1972, U. Miss., 1973, U. Pisa, Italy, 1974, Jikei U. Coll. Medicine, Tokyo, 1976, Ind. U., 1977, U. Helsinki, 1977, U. N.Mex., 1978, U. Milan, 1981, So. Ill. Sch. Medicine, 1982, Tulane U. Med. Sch., 1983, Shanghai 2d Med. Coll., 1984, U. Guadalajara (Mex.), 1986, Gazi U., Turkey, 1988, U. Coll. Medicine Tsuksba, Japan, 1996, Taegu (Korea) U., 1996; sr. Fulbright lectr. U. Uppsala, Sweden, 2003; participant, guest surgeon Physicians for Peace, Turkey and Greece, 1988, Israel and Occupied Ters., 1990, Egypt, 1991, Lithuania, Estonia, 1993 (team leader); leader citizen amb. People to People Internat. Del. Plastic Surgeons to Albania & Russia, 1994, del. leader, Tibet and China, 1998. Author: Facial Injuries, 1970, 3d edit., 1988, Maxillo-Facial Injuries from Vehicle Accidents, 1975, Outpatient Surgery, 1979. Mem. sch. bd., Lake Zurich, Ill., 1966-72, pres., 1968-72; pres. Chgo. Found. for Plastic Surgery, 1966-. Served to capt. M.C., AUS, 1955-57. Fulbright Found. scholar, Sweden, 1960-61; recipient Auto Safety award Med. Tribune, 1967, Robert H. Ivy award 1969, Disting. Sci. Achievement award Wayne U. Coll. Medicine Alumni, 1975, Sanvenero-Rosselli award, 1981; McGregor scholar, U. Mich., 1946-49; grantee Ednl. Found. Am. Soc. Plastic and Reconstructive Surgery, 1964-65. Fellow ACS (pres. local commn. on trauma 1985-87); mem. Am. Assn. Plastic Surgeons (trustee 1990-91), Am. Soc. Plastic and Reconstructive Surgeons, Midwestern Assn. Plastic Surgeons (pres. 1978-79), Chgo. Soc. Plastic Surgeons (pres. 1970-72), Midwestern Assn. Plastic Surgeons (pres. 1978-79), Am. Soc. Maxillofacial Surgeons (pres. 1988-89, award of honor 1986), Am. Assn. Automotive Medicine (pres. 1970-71, A. Merkin award 1982), Am. Cleft Palate Assn., Am. Soc. Aesthetic Plastic Surgery, Tord Skoog Soc. Plastic Surgeons (pres. 1971-75), Can. Soc. Plastic Surgery, Chilean Soc. Plastic Surgery (corr.), Japanese Soc. Plastic Surgery (corr.), Cuban Soc. Maxillofacial Surgery (corr.), Korean Soc. Plastic Surgery (corr.). Office: PO Box 357 Northport MI 49670-0357 Office Phone: 231-386-5950. Business E-Mail: schultz5@coslink.net.

SCHULTZ, RICHARD DALE, national athletic organization executive; b. Grinnell, Iowa, Sept. 5, 1929; s. August Henry and Marjorie Ruth (Turner) S.; m. Jacquilyn Lu Duistermars, June 26, 1949; children: Robert Dale, William Joel, Kim Marie. BS, Ctrl. Coll., Pella, Iowa, 1950; EdD (hon.), Ctrl. Coll., 1987; LLD (hon.), Wartburg Coll., 1988, Alma Coll., 1989, Luther Coll., 1991; PhD (hon.), U.S. Sports Acad., 1993; LLD (hon.), Daniel Webster Coll., 1997, Gettysburg Coll., 1998. Head basketball coach, athletic dir. Humboldt (Iowa) High Sch., 1950-60; freshman basketball coach U. Iowa, Iowa City, 1960-62, head baseball coach, assoc. basketball coach, 1962-70, head basketball coach, 1970-74, asst. v.p., 1974-76; dir. athletics and phys. edn. Cornell U., Ithaca, NY, 1976-81; dir. athletics U. Va., Charlottesville, 1981-87; exec. dir. NCAA, Mission, Kans., 1987-94; pres. Global Sports Enterprises, 1994-95; exec. dir. U.S. Olympic Com., Colorado Springs, Colo., 1995—2000; chmn. Mktg. Assocs. Internat., 2000—04; chmn., CEO, Internat. Partnerships, 2002—. Mem. honors ct. Nat. Football Found. and Hall of Fame, Nat. Basketball Hall of Fame, 1992; chmn. bd. NCAA Found., 1989; organizer Iowa Steel Mill, Inc.; trustee Gettysburg Coll., 1996—99; bd. dirs. Hanspree Corp., Tacipe, Twaian. Author: A Course of Study for the Coaching of Baseball, 1964, The Theory and Techniques of Coaching Basketball, 1970; Contbr. articles to mags. Bd. dirs. Fellowship of Christian Athletes, 1986, chmn., 1990; chmn. Multiple Sclerosis, 1974-75; mem. Knight Found. Commn. on Intercollegiate Athletics, 1990—; mem. adv. com. on svc. acad. athletic programs Def. Dept. Recipient Disting. Alumni award Ctrl. Coll., Pella, 1970, 98, Lifetime Svc. award U. Iowa, 1994, Corbett award Nat. Assn. Collegiate Dirs. Athletics, 1994, medal of honor Ellis Island, 1997, Disting. Alumni award Ctrl. Coll., 1998, Casey award, 1999, Pres. and Mrs. Bush Cmty. Impact award 1999; mem. Basketball Hall of Fame Honor Ct., 1992, Sportsman of Yr. award Marine Corp., 1997; inducted into Iowa Baseball Hall of Fame, 1993, Ctrl. Coll. Hall of Honors, 2002, Des Moines Register Hall of Fame, 2003. Mem. Nat. Assn. Coll. Basketball Coaches, Ea. Coll. Athletic Assn. (mem. exec. com. 1980-81), Am. Basketball Coaches Assn. (Award of Honor 1994), Am. Football Coaches Assn. (internat. dir. CEO forum 2005-, lifetime membership award 1995). Home: 3670 Twisted Oak Cir Colorado Springs CO 80904-4720 Home Phone: 719-685-3238; Office Phone: 719-685-3245. Personal E-mail: dschultzprint2@earthlink.net.

SCHULTZ, RICHARD MICHAEL, biochemistry educator, researcher; b. Phila., Oct. 28, 1942; s. William and Beatrice (Levine) S.; m. Rima M. Lunin, Mar. 7, 1965; children: Carl M., Eli J. BA, SUNY, Binghamton, 1964; PhD, Brandeis U., 1969. Rsch. fellow Harvard U. Med. Sch., Boston, 1969-71; asst. prof. Loyola U. Stritch Sch. of Medicine, Maywood, Ill., 1971-78, assoc. prof., 1978-84, prof., 1984—, chmn. dept. molecular and cellular biochemistry, 1984-2000. Mem. adv. med. bd. Leukemia Rsch. Found., Chgo., 1987-91. Co-author: Textbook of Biochemistry; contbr. articles to profl. jours., chapters to books. Recipient Rsch. grants IH. Achievements include in vivo evidence for the role of protease enzymes and their inhibitors in regulating tumor cell metastasis, ras oncogene pathways in cancer, role of JNK and c-Jun in cancer cell protease expression, obtaining evidence on the nature of the transition-state in serine protease enzyme catalysis, regulation of gene expression by historic modification. Office: Divsn Molecular & Cellular Biochemistry Loyola U Sch Medicine Maywood IL 60153 Home Phone: 708-383-7026; Office Phone: 708-216-9378. E-mail: rschult@lumc.edu.

SCHULTZ, RICHARD OTTO, ophthalmologist, educator; b. Racine, Wis., Mar. 19, 1930; s. Henry Arthur and Josephine (Wagoner) S.; m. Diane Haldane, Sept. 29, 1990; children: Henry Reid, Richard Paul, Karen Jo. BA, U. Wis., 1950, MS, 1954; MD, Albany Med. Coll., 1956; MSc, U. Iowa, 1960. Diplomate Am. Bd. Ophthalmology. Intern, Univ. Hosps., Iowa City, 1956-57, resident in opthalmology, 1957-60; chief ophthalmology sect. div. Indian health USPHS, Phoenix, 1960-63; practice medicine specializing in ophthalmology Phoenix, 1963; NIH spl. fellow in ophthalmic microbiology U. Calif., San Francisco, 1963-64, clin. assoc., 1963-64, research assoc., 1963-64; assoc. prof., chmn. dept. ophthalmology Marquette U. Sch. Medicine (now Med. Coll. Wis.), Milw., 1964-68, prof., chmn., 1968-97, prof. ophthalmology, 1997—2000, prof. emeritus, 2000—. Mem. nat. adv. eye coun. NIH, 1984-88; cons. Froedert Hosp., Milw. Contbr. articles to profl. jours. Served with USPHS, 1960-63. Fellow: ACS (life), Am. Ophthalmol. Soc. (emeritus), Am. Acad. Ophthalmology (life); mem.: Milw. Acad. Medicine, Oxford Ophthalmol. Congress (Eng.), N.Y. Acad. Scis. (emeritus), Pan Am. Assn. Ophthalmology (life), Assn. Rsch. Vision and Ophthalmology (emeritus), Milw. Ophthal. Soc., Assn. Univ. Profs. Ophthalmology (past pres., trustee). Home: 7505 S Kangaroo Lake Rd Baileys Harbor WI 54202 Office Phone: 414-456-7915. Personal E-mail: eyeotto@aol.com.

SCHULZ, KEITH DONALD, corporate lawyer, writer; b. Burlington, Iowa, Dec. 20, 1938; s. Henry Carl and Laura Iral (Bowlin) S.; m. Emily Brook Roane, Apr. 19, 1985; children: Keith Jr., Sarah, Christine, Stefan. BA, U. Iowa, 1960, JD, 1963. Bar: Iowa 1963, Ill. 1966, Wis. 1990. Dep. Sec. of State, State of Iowa, Des Moines, 1965-66; atty. AT&T, Chgo., 1966-67; sec., gen. counsel Borg-Warner Acceptance Corp., Chgo., 1967-74; asst. gen. counsel Borg-Warner Corp., Chgo., 1974-84, v.p., gen. counsel, 1984-88; of counsel Bell, Boyd & Lloyd, Chgo., 1988—. Chmn., CEO Downtown Ptnrs., Inc., 1995-96. Author: (novel) Keepers of the River, 2001; contbr. articles to Harvard Bus. Rev., Jour. for Corp. Growth. Mem. Theatre Bldg. Chgo., 1975-85, chair, 1977-82, bd. dirs., 1977-82; chmn. bd. dirs. Vol. Legal Svcs. Found., Chgo., 1984-91, pres.; bd. dirs. S.E. Iowa Symphony Orch., pres., 1998-2000, 03-07, Heritage Trust Found.; mem. Capitol Theater Found., 2006-, bd. dirs., 2006-. Mem.: Des Moines County Cmty. Found. (bd. drs. 2007—), Assn. Gen. Counsel, Econ. Club, Univ. Club. Avocations: tennis, bicycling, skiing. Office: Bell Boyd & Lloyd 70 W Madison St Ste 3300 Chicago IL 60602-4284 Home Phone: 312-654-0387; Office Phone: 312-372-1121. Personal E-mail: KDons@aol.com.

SCHULZ, MICHAEL JOHN, fire and explosion analyst, consultant; b. Milw., Oct. 7, 1958; s. John F. and JoAnn E. (Carlson) S.; children: Kari L., Brian M. BS in Fire and Safety Engring. Tech., U. Cin., 1996; grad., US Fire Adminstrn. Acad. Cert. fire and explosion investigator; cert. fire protection specialist; cert. fire investigation instr.; cert. fire svc. instr. II; cert. Can. fire investigator. Fire investigator Cedarburg Police Dept., Wis., 1979—90; capt., fire investigator Cedarburg Fire Dept., 1981-90; sr. staff expert John A. Kennedy & Assoc., Hoffman Estates, Ill., 1990-2000; pres. M.J. Schulz Assocs., Inc., 2000—. Cons. US Fire Adminstrn.; instr. fire tech. and police sci. depts. Milw. Area Tech. Coll.; instr. fire sci. tech. dept. William Rainey Harper CC; lectr. in field. Author: Manual for the Determination of Electrical Fire Causes, 1988, Guide for Fire and Explosion Investigations, 1992, 95, 98. Recipient Common Coun. Commendation, City of Cedarburg, Wis., 1986; named Firefighter of Yr., Ozaukee County Assn. Fire Depts., 1985. Mem. ASTM, Nat. Assn. Fire Investigators (bd. dirs. 1987—, nat. cert. bd. 1987—, chmn. edn. com., editor The Nat. Fire Investigator, Man of Yr. 1991), Nat. Fire Protection Assn. (tech. com. on fire investigations 1985—, fire svc. sect., sect. rep. tech. com. on fire investigations 1985-92, sec. rep. nat. conf. on fire investigation instrn., mem. bd. dirs. fire sci. and tech. educators sect.), Fire Marshal's Assn. N.Am. (assoc.), Nat. Inst. Bldg. Scis. (reviewing mem. fire rsch. sub-com.), Bldg. Ofcls. and Code Adminstrs. Internat., Soc. Automotive Enmgrs., Human Factors and Ergonomics Soc., So. Bldg. Code Congress Internat., Internat. Bldg. Code Ofcls., Internat. Assn. Arson Investigators (John Charles Wilson scholarship award 1982), Ill. Chpt. Internat. Assn. Arson Investigators, Internat. Soc. Fire Svc. Instrs., Am. Soc. Safety Engrs., Nat. Conf. Fire Investigation Instrn. (bd. dirs.), Wis. Soc. Fire Svc. Instrs., Ky. Cols. Republican. Lutheran. Avocation: amateur radio. Office Phone: 630-736-0747. Personal E-mail: mjschulz@mjschulz.com.

SCHULZE, CHAD WILLIAM, lawyer; m. Kelly Schulze. BS in Speech Comm. and Polit. Sci., U. SD, Vermillion; JD, Hamline U. Sch. Law, St. Paul, 2002. Bar: Minn. 2002, US Dist. Ct. (dist. Minn.) 2003. Law clk. Rondoni, MacMillan & Schneider, Ltd., 2000—02; atty. Milavetz, Gallop & Milavetz, P.A., Edina, Minn., 2003—. Named a Rising Star, Minn. Super Lawyers mag., 2006, 2007. Mem.: Minn. Trial Lawyers Assn., Am. Trial Lawyers Assn. (mem. Vioxx litig. grp. 2004—, mem. Hurricane Katrina relief grp. 2005—), Ramsey County Bar Assn., Hennepin County Bar Assn., Minn. State Bar Assn., Am. Civil Liberty Union. Avocations: hunting, fishing. Office: Milavetz Gallop & Milavetz PA 6500 France Ave South Edina MN 55435 Office Phone: 952-920-7777. E-mail: attorneyschulze@netscape.net.

SCHULZE, FRANZ, JR., critic, educator; b. Uniontown, Pa., Jan. 30, 1927; s. Franz and Anna E. (Krimmel) Schulze; m. Marianne Gaw, June 24, 1961 (div. 1975); children: F. C. Matthew, Lukas A.; m. Stephanie Mora, 1992 (div. 1996). Student, Northwestern U., Evanston, Ill., 1943; PhB, U. Chgo., 1945; BFA, Sch. Art Inst. Chgo., 1949, MFA, 1950; postgrad., Acad. Fine Arts, Munich, 1956-57. Instr. art Purdue U., 1950-52; chmn. dept. art Lake Forest (Ill.) Coll., 1952-58, artist-in-residence, 1958-61, prof. art, 1961—, Hollender prof. art, 1974-91, Hollender prof. art emeritus, 1991—; art critic Chgo. Daily News, 1962-78, Chgo. Sun-Times, 1978-85. Chgo. corr. art Christian Sci. Monitor, 1958—62; art. and arch. critic Chicagoan, 1973—74; mem. vis. com. dept. art U. Chgo., 1974—87; adj. prof. U. Ill., Chgo., 1996. Co-author: Art, Architecture and Civilization, 1969; co-author: (with Rosemary Cowler and Arthur Miller) Thirty Miles North, 2000, Philip Johnson: Life and Work, 1994; co-author: (with Kevin Harrington) Chicago's Famous Buildings, 2003; co-author: Mariotti II, 2004; author: Fantastic Images: Chicago Art Since 1945, 1972, 100 Years of Chicago Architecture, 1976, Stealing is My Game, 1976, Mies van der Rohe: A Critical Biography, 1985, The University Club of Chicago: A Heritage, 1987, Mariotti, 1988, Illinois Institute of Technology. Campus Guide, 2005, 2007; editor: Mies van der Rohe: Critical Essays, 1989, Mies van der Rohe Archive, 1993; editor: (with Kevin Harrington) Chicago's Famous Buildings, 1993; co-editor: A. James Speyer, Architect, Curator, Exhibition Designer, 1997, The Farnsworth House, 1997, Illinois Institute of Technology, Campus Guide, 2005; contbg. editor: Art News, 1973—, Inland Arch., 1975—94, corr. editor: Art in Am., 1975—. Trustee Ragdale Found., Lake Forest, 1981—. Recipient Harbison award for tchg., Danforth Found. St. Louis, 1971, Disting. Svc. award, Chgo. Phi Beta Kappa soc., 1972, Hon. Mention Hitchcock Book award, Soc. Archtl. Historians, 1987, Excellence in Architecture award, Ill. Inst. Tech., 1999; Adenauer fellow, 1956—57, Ford Found. fellow, 1964—65, Graham Found. for Advanced Studies in the Fine Arts fellow, 1971, 1981, 1993, NEH fellow, 1982, 1988, Skidmore Owings & Merrill Found. fellow, 1983. Mem.: AAUP, Soc. Archtl. Historians (Hon. Mention Hitchcock Book award), Archives Am. Art (mem. adv. com.), Coll. Art Assn. (bd. dirs. 1983—86). Office: Lake Forest Coll Dept Art Lake Forest IL 60045 Office Phone: 847-735-5084. Business E-Mail: schulze@lakeforest.edu.

SCHULZE, JOHN B., manufacturing executive; BBA, So. Meth. U., 1959; Advanced Mgmt. Program, Harvard U., 1984. Group v.p., sr. group v.p., sr. exec. v.p., CEO indsl. products group White Consol. Industries, 1962-87; pres., chief oper. officer Lamson & Sessions Co., Cleve., 1988, pres., chief exec. officer, 1989, chmn., pres., chief exec. officer, 1990—, also bd. dirs. Capt. USMC, 1959-62. Office: Lamson & Sessions 25701 Science Park Dr Cleveland OH 44122-7393

SCHULZE, RICHARD M., retail executive; b. St. Paul, Minn., 1941; married; 9 children. D (hon.), Univ. of St. Thomas, St. Paul, 1998. With No. States Sales Co., 1962-66; founder, chmn. Sound of Music (now Best Buy Co., Inc.), Eden Prairie, Minn., 1966—; CEO Best Buy Co., Inc., Eden Prairie, Minn., 1983—2002, chmn., 2002—. Mem. Minn. Bus. Partnership; bd. dir. Pentair Inc., Nat. Entrepreneur of Yr. Inst., 1992—; bd. of overseers Carlson Sch. of Mgmt.; bd. trustees Univ. of St. Thomas. With Minnesota Air National Guard. Named Corp. Leader of Yr., Juvenile Diabetes Assn., 1999; named one of Top CEOs, Worth Mag., 1999, Am.'s Richest People, Forbes mag., 1999—, Exec. Pay, 1999—, World's Richest People, 2001—; recipient Nat. Entrepreneur of Yr., Ernst & Young, 1999, America's Promise Red Wagon for Cmty. Svc., Gen. Colin Powell, 1999, Outstanding Mktg. Exec of Yr., Minnesota DECA, 2000, Robert C. McDermond Medal for Excellence in Entrepreneurship, Robert C. McDermond Ctr. for Mgmt. and Entrepreneurship, 2000. Office: Best Buy 7601 Penn Ave S Minneapolis MN 55423-3645*

SCHUMACHER, JULIE ALISON, literature and language professor; b. Wilmington, Del., Dec. 2, 1958; d. Frederick George and Winifred Jean (Temple) Schumacher; m. Lawrence Rubin Jacobs, July 9, 1983; children: Emma Lillian Jacobs, Isabella Nan Jacobs. BA, Oberlin Coll., 1981; MFA, Cornell U., 1986. Assoc. prof. U. Minn., Mpls. Author: (book) The Body is Water, 1995, An Explanation for Chaos, 1997, Grass Angel, 2004, The Chain Letter, 2005. Recipient Best Am. Short Stories award, 1983, Prize Stories: the O. Henry awards, 1990, 1996.

SCHUMAN, ALLAN L., chemicals executive; b. 1937; BS, NYU, 1955. With Ecolab Inc., St. Paul, 1957—, v.p. mktg. and nat. acctg., 1972-78, v.p. mktg. devel., 1978-79, pres. svc. group, 1988—92, pres., COO, 1992—95, pres., CEO, 1995—2004, chmn., 2000—06, chmn. emeritus, 2006—. Bd. dir. Tanger Factory Outlet Ctr. Inc., Soap & Detergent Assn. Bd. dir. Ordway Ctr. Performing Arts, Guthrie Theater; bd. overseers Carlson Sch. Mgmt. at U. Minn.; trustee Hamline U., Minn., Culinary Inst. Am., Nat. Restaurant Assn. Office: Ecolab Inc Ecolab Ctr 370 N Wabasha St Saint Paul MN 55102

SCHUMAN, WILLIAM PAUL, lawyer; b. Chgo., May 6, 1954; s. Alvin W. and Gloria (Kayner) S.; m. Caryn Gutmann, Dec. 20, 1980; children: Lindsey J., Lisa A., Jamie L. BBA, U. Mich., 1975; JD, Harvard U., 1979. Bar: U.S. Dist. Ct. (no. dist.) Ill. 1979. Assoc. McDermott, Will & Emery, LLP, Chgo., 1979—84, ptnr., 1985—. Mem. ABA, Ill. Bar Assn., Chgo. Bar Assn. Avocations: softball, golf, basketball. Home: 1863 Clavey Rd Highland Park IL 60035-4373 Office: McDermott Will & Emery LLP Ste 3100 227 W Monroe St Chicago IL 60606-5096 E-mail: wschuman@mwe.com.

SCHUMANN, WILLIAM HENRY, III, corporate financial executive; b. Iowa City, Aug. 28, 1950; s. William Henry Jr. and Eunice Vere (Doak) S. BS, UCLA, 1972; MS, U. So. Calif., 1973. Program mgmt. analyst Hughes Helicopters, Culver City, Calif., 1973-75; mgr. fin. planning Sunkist Growers, Sherman Oaks, Calif., 1975-81; dir. .Am. Ops. Agrl. Products Group, FMC Corp., Chgo., 1981—; treas. FMC Corp., 1987—, exec. dir. corp. development, 1990-93, v.p., 1995—, sr. v.p., CFO, 1999—2001, FMC Techs., 2001—. Bd. dirs. Gt. Lakes Advisors and UAP Holdings. Republican. Office: FMC Technologies 200 E Randolph Dr Chicago IL 60601

SCHUNK, MAE GASPARAC, former state official; b. Chgo., May 21, 1934; m. William Schunk; 1 child. BS in Elem. Edn., U. Wis., Eau Claire, 1958; MA in Curriculum and Instrn., Gifted Edn., U. St. Thomas, St. Paul, 1989, lic. in adminstrv. leadership, 1992. Curriculum specialist, asst. prin., elem. tchr. various pub. schs. in Wis. and St. Paul; lt. gov. State of Minn., St. Paul, 1999—2003; instr. dept. edn. Inver Hills C.C., 2003—. Mem. Minn. Exec. Coun.; chair Capitol Area Archtl. Planning Bd.; co-chair The Minn. Alliance with Youth, the NetDay Minn. Program, Minn. Office of Citizenship and Vol. Svcs. Recipient 1st pl. state award, U. Minn. Coun. on Econ. Edn., 1984, award of commendation, Gov. Perpich, 1986, 1990, award, United Def., 1999, Hmong Am. New Yr., Inc., 1999, St. Paul Fedn. Tchrs., 1999, Mpls. Police Dept., 1999, Minn. Sch. Counselors Assn., 1999, United Vietnamese Mut. Assistance Assn., 1999, Dept. Corrections, 2000, 82d Airborne Divsn. Assn. Am.'s Guard of Honor, 2000, Forward Support Bn., 2000, Outstanding Citizen award, 2000, award, Jobs for Am. Grads., Washington, 2000, Recognition award, Gov. Jesse Ventura, 2002, Minn. State Founders award, Jobs for Minn. Grads. Bd., 2002, proclamation from Gov. Ventura, 2002. Independent. Avocations: flower and vegetable gardening, creative cooking and baking, stained glass, watercolor painting, fishing.

SCHURZ, FRANKLIN DUNN, JR., media executive; b. South Bend, Ind., May 22, 1931; s. Franklin Dunn and Martha (Montgomery) S.; m. Robin Rowan Tullis, Nov. 22, 1975 (div. 1985). AB, Harvard U., 1952, MBA, 1956, A.M.P., 1984. Exec. asst. South Bend Tribune, 1956-60, dir., 1971-76, sec., 1970-75, assoc. pub., 1971-72, editor, pub., 1972-82, exec. v.p., 1975-76, pres., 1976-82; asst. pub. Morning Herald and Daily Mail, Hagerstown, Md., 1960-62, pub., 1962-70, editor, 1966-70; pres. Schurz Communications, Inc., 1982—, treas., 1983-89. Bd. dirs. Atlantic Salmon Fedn., MSTV, CSPAN. Chmn. Ind. Arts Commn., 1979-81; bd. regents St. Marys Coll., Notre Dame, Ind., 1977-83; chmn. adv. coun. Coll. Arts and Letters Notre Dame U., 1980-82; bd. dirs. Ind. Endowment Ednl. Excellence Inc., Indpls., 1987-90; mem. pres.'s coun. Ind. U., Bloomington, 1988-94; bd. dirs. C-Span, 1997—, MSTV, 2001—. 2d lt. U.S. Army, 1952-54. Recipient Presdl. Award of Merit Nat. Newspaper Assn., 1965, Frank Rogers award Rotary, South Bend, 1980 Mem. Am. Press Inst. (bd. dirs. 1985-94), AP (chmn. audit com. 1979-84), Chesapeake AP Assn. (past pres.), Md.-Del.-D.C. Press Assn. (past pres.), Hoosier State Press Assn. (past pres.), Newspaper Advt. Bur. (past bd. dirs.), South Bend Mishawaka Area C. of C. (pres. 1980-82), Am. Soc. Newspaper Editors, Am. women in Radio and TV (Found. hon. trustee 1996—), past bd. mem., Inland Press Assn., Inst. Newspaper Fin. Execs. (past pres.), South Bend Country Club, Nat. Press Club, Soc. Profl. Journalists, MSTV (bd. dir. 2001-), C-SPAN (bd. dir. 1997-). Presbyterian. Home: 1329 Erskine Manor Hl South Bend IN 46614-2186 Office: Schurz Communications Inc 225 W Colfax Ave South Bend IN 46626-1000 Home Phone: 574-291-6470; Office Phone: 574-287-1001. E-mail: fschurz@schurz.com.

SCHURZ, SCOTT CLARK, journalist; b. South Bend, Ind., Feb. 23, 1936; s. Franklin Dunn and Martha (Montgomery) S.; m. Kathryn Joan Foley, Aug. 5, 1967; children: Scott Clark, Alexandra Carol, John Danforth. BA, Denison U., 1957; LHD (hon.), Ind. U., 2000. Asst. instr. U. Md., 1957-58; adminstrv. asst. South Bend Tribune, 1960-66; circulation cons. Imperial Valley Press, El Centro, Calif., 1966; pres. Hoosier Times, Inc.; dir., vice chmn. Schurz Comms., Inc., pub. Pres. Bloomington Boys' Club, 1970-71, Jr. Achievement Monroe County, 1971-73; bd. dirs. United Way Monroe County, 1979-81, Cmty. Found. Area Arts Coun. Served with U.S. Army, 1958-60. Mem.: Ind. U. Found. (bd. dirs. 1986—), Newspaper Advt. Bur. (bd. dirs. 1987—92), Internat. Press Inst. (mem. bd. US), World Press Freedom Com. (adv. bd.), Hoosier State Press Assn. (pres. 1989, 1997), Inter-Am. Press Assn. (bd. dirs. 1995—, hon. pres.), Newspaper Assn. Am. (bd. dirs. 1992—95, 2002—, found. bd. trustees), Inland Daily Press Assn. (pres. 1989), Internat. Newspaper Mktg. Assn. (pres. 1986, treas. 1997—2004), World Assn. Newspapers (bd. dirs., exec. com., v.p.). Republican.

Presbyterian. Office: Hoosier Times Inc 1900 S Walnut St Bloomington IN 47401-7720 Office Phone: 812-332-4401.

SCHUSTER, ELAINE, retired civil rights professional; b. Detroit, Sept. 26, 1947; d. William Alfred and Aimee Isabelle (Cote) LeBlanc; m. James William Schuster, Sept. 6, 1969; 1 child, Cambrian James. BA, Wayne State U., 1972, postgrad., 1974-75, paralegal cert., 1991; student, Bay Mills Com. Coll., 2003—. Asst. payments Mich. Dept. Social Svcs., Detroit, 1972-73; rights rep. Mich. Dept. Civil Rights, Detroit, 1973-80, 82-87, 90, asst. dir. div., 1987-90, supr., 1993-97, dir. Svc. Ctr., 1997-99, contract coord., 1999—2002, ret., 2003; ct. adminstr. Chippewa-Ottawa Conservation Ct., Bay Mills, Mich., 1980-82; quality assurance coord. State Mental Health Facility, Southgate, Mich., 1991-93; acting interim dir. Mich. Indian Commn., Detroit, 1995; proprietor Good Things to Share, 2003—; trainer HIV/AIDS health support profls., 2004—. Author: Walking in Two Worlds, Delivering Culturally Competent Care in the American Indian Community, 2004, Critique, An Indian Tours Michilimackinac, 1981, In the Track of the Bear, Discussion, Coordination of Resources to Fight HIV, 2005; contbr. articles and poems to mags. and profl. jours. Bd. dirs. Tri-County Native Ams., Warren, Mich., 1982-89, sec. Native Am. Sesquicentennial subcom., Mich., 1987; mem. Linking Lifetimes, mentor program for Native Am. youth, 1992-93; sec., newsletter editor various civic orgns.; also other polit. and civic activities. Native Am. fellow Mich. State U., 1989. Mem. NAACP (housing com. S. Oakland br. 2000), ACLU (bd. dirs. Union-Oakland county 1987-88, 2002-04). Democrat. Avocations: exploring local historical and natural places of interest, historical re-enactment, research, exercise. E-mail: ikwewe@comcast.net.

SCHUTTA, HENRY SZCZESNY, neurologist, educator; b. Gdansk, Poland, Sept. 15, 1928; came to U.S., 1962, naturalized, 1967; s. Jakub and Janina (Zerbst) S.; m. Henryka Kosmal, Apr. 29, 1950; children— Katharine, Mark, Caroline. M.B., BS, U. Sydney, Australia, 1955, MD, 1968. Jr. resident, then sr. resident St. Vincent's Hosp., Sydney, 1956-58; acad. registrar, house physician Nat. Hosp. Nervous Diseases, London, 1958-62; neurologist Pa. Hosp., Phila., 1962-73; asso. prof. neurology U. Pa. Med. Sch., 1963-73; prof. neurology, chmn. dept. SUNY Downstate Med. Center, Bklyn., 1973-80; prof. U. Wis. Med. Sch., 1980-98, chmn. dept. neurology, 1980-95, prof. emeritus, 1999; prof. neurology U. Ariz., Tucson, 2001—. Achievements include research on bilirubin encephalopathy, cerebral edema, degeneration and regeneration of muscle, history of medicine. Office: U Hosp 600 Highland Ave Madison WI 53792-0001 Home: 506 Addison Street Philadelphia PA 19147-1404 E-mail: hsschutta@comcast.net.

SCHUTTER, DAVID JOHN, banker; b. Erie, Pa., Apr. 21, 1945; s. Donald John and Ruth Margaret (Hilbert) S. m. Ellen Carol Hoffman, June 18, 1967; children: David, Erica. BS with honors and distinction, Pa. State U., 1967; postgrad., Mich. State U., 1967-68, Ohio State U., 1973-75; cert., Stonier Grad. Sch. Banking, 1981. Asst. v.p. Huntington Nat. Bank, Columbus, Ohio, 1973-80; v.p. Ameritrust Co., Cleve., 1980-81, v.p., mgr. asset based lending dept., 1981-86, sr. v.p. secured lending div., 1986-89, dep. sr. loan adminstr., 1989-90, sr. cred. pol. off., 1990-92; sr. v.p., regional credit exec. Soc. Nat. Bank, Cleve., 1992-94; exec. v.p., chief credit officer, 1994-97; exec. v.p., sr. lending officer Key Bank NA, Cleve., 1997—; exec. v.p., chief credit officer Key Corp., 2000—. Pres. AT Comml. Corp., 1986-96; panelist Robert Morris Assocs., Cleve., 1981, 93, mem., 1986—, Cleve. Bar Assn., 1986. Served to capt. U.S. Army, 1968-72. Mem. Nat. Comml. Fin. Assn. (bd. dirs. 1986—), Key Bank (dir., mem. exec. com., 2000—), Beta Gamma Sigma, Omicron Delta Epsilon. E-mail: david_schutter@keybank.com.

SCHUTZIUS, LUCY JEAN, retired librarian; b. Cin., Dec. 27, 1938; d. Gregory Girard and Harriet Elsa (Wiggers) Wright; m. Paul Robert Wilson, Aug. 25, 1962 (div. 1968); 1 child, Ellen Field; m. William Carl Schutzius, Dec. 12, 1976; stepchildren: Christopher Matthew, Catharine Alexander, John Benedict, Margaret Elizabeth. BA in French, Middlebury Coll., 1960; MLS, U. Ill., 1963. Tech. libr. Chanute AFB, Rantoul, Ill., 1963-65; libr. Coll. Prep. Sch., Cin., 1969-74; pub. svcs. libr. Raymond Walters Coll., Cin., 1974-79, dir. libr., 1979-92, sr. libr., 1988—2001, sr. libr. emerita, 2001—. Access svcs. libr. U. Cin. Coll. Engring., 1992—2001. Mem.: Friends of Univ. Librarians. Home: 3444 Stettinius Ave Cincinnati OH 45208-1204 E-mail: lucy.wilson@uc.edu.

SCHWAB, DAVID, state legislator; b. 1944; m. Phyllis Schwab, 1966; three children. Owner Schwab's Pines; farmer and businessman; rep. Mo. State Ho. Reps. Dist. 157. Former chmn. Farmers for Emerson Com.; former mem. Farmers for Ashcroft Com., Farmers to Elect Sen. Bon State Com.; mem. Mo. State Agr. Stabilization Conservation Com., Gov. Ashcroft's Adv. Coun. on Agr.; former committeeman Ward 6, Byrd; former pres. congregation St. Paul Luth. Ch., Jackson, Mo., Sunday sch. tchr., chmn. bd. elders, chmn. men's club; former mem. St. Paul Sch. Bd. Edn. Mem. Nat. Fedn. Ind. Businessmen, Am. Tree Farm Sys., Mo. State Christmas Tree Growers Assn., Cape County Far Bur. (past pres.), Jackson C. of C., NRA. Office: Mo Ho of Reps State Capitol 201 W Capitol Ave Rm 203B Jefferson City MO 65101-1556

SCHWAB, GRACE S., state legislator; m. Steven Schwab; 3 children. BS, postgrad., Mankato State U. Mem. Minn. State Senate, 2000—, mem. crime prevention com., edn. com., transp. com., E-12 edn. budget divsn. com., taxes com., income and sales tax budget divsn. com. Home: 1858 Greenwood Dr Albert Lea MN 56007

SCHWAB, STEPHEN WAYNE, lawyer; b. Washington, Jan. 25, 1956; s. A. Wayne and Elizabeth (Parsons) S.; m. Debora Zellner, May 26, 1979; children: Benjamin Earl, Jason Edward. BA, Northwestern U., 1979; JD, Pa. State U., 1982. Bar: Ill. 1982, NY 2007, U.S. Dist. Ct. (no. dist.) Ill. 1983, U.S. Ct. Appeals (7th cir.) 1985, U.S. Ct. Claims 1986, U.S. Supreme Ct. 1989, U.S. Ct. Appeals (9th cir.) 1991, D.C. 1994. Assoc. Pretzel & Stouffer, Chgo., 1982-85; ptnr. Piper Rudnick LLP, Chgo., 1985—2004; ptnr., chmn. Insurance & Reinsurance practice group DLA Piper US LLP, Chgo., 2005—. Contbr. chapters to books, articles to profl. jours. Scoutmaster Troop 5 Boy Scouts Am., Wilmette, Ill., 1999—2003; chmn.NE Ill. coun. Jamboree Com., 2003—; lay reader Luth. Ch. of the Ascension, Northfield, Ill., 1998—, endowment com., 2002—. Recipient Nat. Scoutmaster award, Nat. Eagle Scout Assn., 2002, Potawatomi Dist. Merit award, 2003, Wood Badge award, 2003. Mem. ABA, Internat. Bar Assn., Chgo. Bar Assn., ARIAS U.S., Internat. Assn. Insurance receivers, Def. Rsch. Inst., Nat. Conf. Insurance Legislators, Nat. Assn. Insurance Commissioners, Order of Barristers, Phi Eta Sigma. Lutheran. Office: DLA Piper US LLP Fl 19 203 N LaSalle St Chicago IL 60601-1293 Home Phone: 847-251-4056; Office Phone: 312-368-2150. Office Fax: 312-630-7343. Business E-Mail: stephen.schwab@dlapiper.com.

SCHWANDA, TOM, religious studies educator; b. East Stroudsburg, Pa., Oct. 23, 1950; s. Theodore Frank and Madlyn Betty (Backensto) S.; m. Grace Elaine Dunning, July 30, 1977; children: Rebecca Joy, Stephen Andrew. Student, Worcester Polytechnic Inst., 1968-69; BA in Econ., Moravian Coll., 1969-72; student, Gordon-Conwell Sem., 1972-74; MDiv, New Brunswick Sem., 1975; DMin, Fuller Theol. Sem., 1992. Ordained to ministry Reformed Ch. in Am., 1975. Pastor Wanaque (N.J.) Reformed Ch., 1975-87; pastor congl. care Immanuel Reformed Ch., Grand Rapids, Mich., 1987-92; interim sr. pastor Remembrance Reformed Ch., Grand Rapids, 1992-93; rsch. fellow H. Henry Meeter Ctr. for Calvin Studies Calvin Coll., Grand Rapids, 1993-95; instr. spirituality and worship Bethlehem Ctr. for Spirituality, Grand Rapids, 1993—; dir. Reformed Spirituality Network, Grand Rapids, 1992—; assoc. for spiritual formation Reformed Ch. in Am., 1995-99; prof. spiritual formation Reformed Bible Coll., Grand Rapids, Mich., 1999—2006; assoc. prof. Christian formation and ministry Wheaton Coll., Ill., 2006—. Organizer, convener Gathering Reformed Spirituality, 1993, 94, 95, 97, 99, 2001, 2004; chair spirituality com. Synod of Great Lakes, 1989-2000, mem. Christian discipleship com., 1988-94; mem. ch. life, evangelism, missions com. South Grand Rapids Classics, chair, 1992; mem. commn. on worship Reformed Ch. in Am., 1978-94; mem. care of students com. Passaic Classis, 1975, 87, chair, 1978, 83-86, pres., 1979; adj. prof. spirituality and spiritual direction and worship Fuller Theol. Sem., San Francisco Theol. Sem., No. Bapt. Theol. Sem., Western Theol. Sem., Columbia Theol. Sem., Charlotte, Orlando, Reformed Theol. Sem., Charlotte. Author: Celebrating God's Presence: The Transforming Power of Public Worship, 1995; contbr. articles to religious jours.; author poetry; manuscript reader, evaluator religious pub. co. Established, managed Wanaque Cmty. Food Pantry, 1977-87; vol. Domestic Crisis Ctr., Grand Rapids, 1988—; bd. dirs. Nat. Inst. Rehabilitation Engring., Hewitt, N.J., 1984—, pres. bd. dirs., 1986—. Recipient Barnabas award Iglesia Cristiana Ebenezer, 1987. Mem. Czechoslovak Soc. Arts and Sci., Czechoslovak Hist. Conf., Soc. for Study of Christian Spirituality, Evangelical Theol. Soc., Calvin Studies Soc. Mem. Reformed Ch. Am. Avocations: running, landscaping, genealogy, amateur radio. Home: 1999 Nottingham Ln Wheaton IL 60187 Office: Wheaton College 501 College Ave Wheaton IL 60187 Office Phone: 616-988-3680.

SCHWANK, JOHANNES WALTER, chemical engineering educator; b. Zams, Tyrol, Austria, July 6, 1950; came to U.S., 1978; s. Friedrich Karl and Johanna (Ruepp) S.; m. Lynne Violet Duguay; children: Alexander Johann, Leonard Friedrich, Hanna Violet, Rosa Joy. Diploma in chemistry, U. Innsbruck, Austria, 1975, PhD, 1978. Mem. faculty U. Mich., Ann Arbor, 1978—, assoc. prof. chem. engring., 1984-90, acting dir. Ctr. for Catalysis and Surface Sci., 1985-90, prof., interim chmn. dept. chem. engring., 1990-91, assoc. dir. Electron Microbeam Analysis Lab., 1990—2000; chmn. dept. chem. engring., 1991-95; prof. chem. engring. U. Mich., Ann Arbor, 1995—. Vis. prof. U. Innsbruck, 1987-88, Tech. U. Vienna, 1988; cons. in field. Contbr. over 125 articles to profl. jours. Fulbright-Hays scholar, 1978. Mem. Am. Chem. Soc., Am. Inst. Chem. Engrs., Mich. Catalysis Soc. (sec.-treas. 1982-83, v.p. 1983-84, pres. 1984-85). Achievements include patents for bimetallic cluster catalysts, hydrodesulfurization catalysts and microelectronic gas sensors. Home: 5633 Meadow Dr Ann Arbor MI 48105-9368 Office: U Mich Dept Chem Engring 2300 Hayward St Ann Arbor MI 48109-2136 E-mail: schwank@umich.edu.

SCHWARTZ, ALAN EARL, lawyer, director; b. Detroit, Dec. 21, 1925; s. Maurice H. and Sophia (Welkowitz) S.; m. Marianne Shapero, Aug. 24, 1950; children: Marc Alan, Kurt Nathan, Ruth Anne. Student, Western Mich. Coll., 1944-45; BA with distinction, U. Mich., 1947; LLB magna cum laude, Harvard U., Cambridge, Mass., 1950; LLD, Wayne State U., Detroit, 1983, U. Detroit, 1985. Bar: NY 1951, Mich. 1952. Assoc. Kelley, Drye & Warren, NYC, 1950-52; mem. Honigman, Miller, Schwartz & Cohn, Detroit, 1952—. Spl. asst. counsel NY State Crime Commn., 1951; bd. dirs. Pulte Corp. Editor: Harvard Law Rev., 1950. Dir. Detroit Symphony Orch.; v.p., bd. dirs. United Way; bd. dirs. Detroit Renaissance, New Detroit, Jewish Welfare Fedn. Detroit, Wayne State U. Found.; trustee Cmty. Found. for Southeastern Mich.; adv. mem. Arts Commn., City of Detroit; bd. dirs., mem. investment com. Skillman Found., Wayne State U. Found. Served as ensign Supply Corps, USNR, 1945-46. Recipient Mich. Heritage Hall of Fame award, 1984, George W. Romney award for lifetime achievement in volunteerism, 1994, Max M. Fisher Cmty. Svc. award, 1997; named one of Top 200 Collectors, ARTnews, 2004-07. Mem. Mich. Bar Assn., Franklin Hills Country Club, Econ. Club (dir.). Avocation: collecting Old Masters and modern prints. Office: Honigman Miller Schwartz & Cohn 2290 1st National Bldg Detroit MI 48226

SCHWARTZ, ALAN GIFFORD, sport company executive; b. NYC, Nov. 7, 1931; s. Kevie Waldemar and Vera (Isaacs) S.; m. Roslyn Smulian, Sept. 6, 1958; children: Steven, Andrew, Sally, Elizabeth. BS, Yale U., 1952; MBA, Harvard U., 1954. Ptnr. Gifford Investment Co., Chgo., 1954—; CEO Tennis Corp. of Am., Chgo., 1969—, chmn. bd., 1974—. Dir. Firstar Bank Ill., Comtrex Systems, Inc., Mt. Laurel, N.J.; trustee Roosevelt U., 1994—, Inst. European & Asian Studies, 1993—; v.p. U.S. Tennis Assn., 1994—. Contbr. articles to profl. jours.; editorial cons. Club Industry mag., 1985—. Bd. dirs. Grad. Sch. of Bus., Duke U., Durham, N.C., 1977—, McCormick Boys and Girls Club, 1989—. Elected to Club Industry Hall of Fame, 1987. Mem. Standard Club of Chgo., Exec. Club. Chgo. Jewish. Avocations: travel, tennis. Office: Tennis Corp of Am 3611 N Kedzie Ave Chicago IL 60618-4513

SCHWARTZ, ALAN LEIGH, pediatrician, educator; b. NYC, Apr. 25, 1948; s. Robert and Joyce (Goldner) S.; m. Judith Child, June 22, 1974; 1 child, Timothy Child. BA, Case Western Res. U., 1974, PhD in Pharmacology, 1974, MD, 1976. Diplomate Am. Bd. Pediatrics. Intern Children's Hosp., Boston, 1976-77, resident, 1976-78, fellow Dana Farber Cancer Inst., 1978-80; instr. Harvard Med. Sch., Boston, 1980-81, asst. prof., 1981-83, assoc. prof., 1983-86; prof. pediatrics, molecular biology and pharmacology Washington U. Sch. Medicine, St. Louis, 1986—, chmn. dept. pediatrics, 1995—; chmn. faculty practice plan Washington U., 1999—2001. Vis. scientist MIT, Boston, 1979-82; mem. sci. adv. bd. Nat. Inst. Child Health and Human Devel., NIH, Bethesda, Md., 1988-94; investigator Am. Heart Assn. Alumni Endowed Prof. Pediats. Wash. U. Sch. Medicine, 1987-97, Harriet B. Spoehrer Prof. Pediats., 1997—. Mem. Inst. Medicine of NAS. Office: Washington U Sch Medicine Dept Pediatrics Box 8116 One Children's Pl Saint Louis MO 63110-1093 E-mail: schwartz@kids.wustl.edu.

SCHWARTZ, ARTHUR, lawyer; BA, U. Albany; JD cum laude, Benjamin N. Cardozo Sch. Law. With Thacher, Proffit & Wood; founder, bus. devel. leader Greedy Assocs. FindLaw, Inc. Named one of 100 Most Influential Lawyers, Nat. Law Jour., 2000. Office: FindLaw Inc 610 Opperman Dr Eagan MN 55123

SCHWARTZ, DONALD LEE, lawyer; b. Milw., Dec. 8, 1948; s. Bernard L. and Ruth M. (Marshall) S.; m. Susan J. Dunst, June 5, 1971; children: Stephanie Jane, Cheryl Ruth. BA, Macalester Coll., 1971; JD, U. Chgo., 1974. Bar: Ill. 1974. Assoc. Sidley & Austin, Chgo., 1974-80, ptnr., 1980-88, Latham & Watkins, Chgo., 1988—. Chmn. Ill. Conservative Union, 1979-81, bd. dirs. 1977-85. Served with U.S. Army, 1971-77. Mem. ABA (uniform comml. code com., comml. fin. svcs. commn.), Ill. Bar Assn. (sec. coun. banking and bankuprtcy sect. 1982-83), Chgo. Bar Assn. (chmn. comml. law com. 1980-81, fin. insts. com. 1982-83), Ivanhoe Country Club, Sea Pines Country Club, Colleton River Country Club, Met. Club. Republican. Episcopalian. Avocation: golf. Home: 191 Park Ave Glencoe IL 60022-1351 Office: Latham & Watkins Ste 5800 Sears Tower Chicago IL 60606 Office Phone: 312-876-7631. Business E-Mail: donald.schwartz@lw.com.

SCHWARTZ, ELEANOR BRANTLEY, academic administrator; b. Kite, Ga., Jan. 1, 1937; d. Jesse Melvin and Hazel (Hill) Brantley; children: John, Cynthia. Student, U. Va., 1955, Ga. Southern Coll., 1956-57; BBA, Ga. State U., 1962, MBA, 1963, DBA, 1969. Adminstrv. asst. Fin. Agy., 1954, Fed. Govt., Va., Pa., Ga., 1956-59; asst. dean admissions Ga. State U., Atlanta, 1961-66, asst. prof., 1966-70; assoc. prof. Cleve. State U., 1970-75, prof. and assoc. dean, 1975-80; dean, Harzfeld prof. U. Mo., Kansas City, 1980-87, vice chancellor acad. affairs, 1987-91, interim chancellor, 1991-92, chancellor, 1992-99; prof. mgmt. U. Mo. Block Sch., Kansas City, 1999—2003, prof. emeritus, 2003—. Disting. vis. prof. Berry Coll., Rome, N.Y. State U. Coll., Fredonia, Mons U., Belgium; cons. pvt. industry U.S., Europe, Can.; bd. dirs. Rsch. Med. Ctr., Waddell & Reed Funds, Inc., Toy and Miniature Mus., Menorah Med. Ctr. Found., NCAA, NCCJ, Econ. Devel. Corp. of Kansas City, Silicon Prairie Tech. Assn. Author: Sex Barriers in Business, 1971, Contemporary Readings in Marketing, 1974; (with Muczyk and Smith) Principles of Supervision, 1984. Chmn., Mayor's Task Force in Govt. Efficiency, Kansas City, Mo., 1984; mem. comm. unity planning and rsch. coun. United Way Kansas City, 1983-85; bd. dirs. Jr. Achievement, 1982-86. Named Jones Store Career Woman of Yr., Kansas City, Mo., 1989, Ctrl. Exch. Woman of Yr., 1995; named one of 60 Women of Achievement, Girl Scouts Coun. Mid Continent, 1983; recipient Disting. Faculty award, Cleve. State U., 1974, Disting. Svc. award, Kans. State U., 1992, YWCA Hearts of Gold award, 2002. Mem.: Alpha Iota Delta, Golden Key, Phi Kappa Phi. Office Phone: 816-942-1840.

SCHWARTZ, JOHN NORMAN, human services administrator; b. Watertown, Minn., Dec. 13, 1945; s. Norman O. and Marion G. (Tesch) Schwartz. BA, Augsburg Coll., Mpls., 1967; MHA, U. Minn., 1969. Adminstrv. resident Luth. Hosp. and Med. Ctr., Wheat Ridge, Colo., 1968-69; asst. adminstr. St. Luke's Hosp., Milw., 1969-73, med. adminstr., 1973-75, v.p., 1975-84; sr. v.p., COO Good Samaritan Med. Ctr., Milw., 1984-85, pres., CEO, 1985-88; exec. v.p. Aurora Health Care Inc., Milw., 1988-89; gen. mgr. SmithKline Beecham Clin. Labs., Schaumburg, Ill., 1989-90; chief exec. adv. Trinity Hosp. Adv. Health Care, Chgo., 1991—. Bd. dirs. E. Side Bank. Gov.'s appointee Coun. Hemophilia and Related Blood Disorders, Madison, 1978; mem. Sullivan Chamber Ensemble, Milw., 1975—84; bd. dirs. Gt. Lakes Hemophilia Found., Milw., 1975—89, S.E. Chgo. Devel. Commn., 1996—; mem. S. Chgo. YMCA, 1993—. Named Exec. of the Yr., Health and Human Svcs. Ministry, 1999; recipient Bd. Mem. of the Yr. award, Gt. Lake's Hemophilia Found., 1986, Outstanding Cmty. Leadership award, Stony Island C. of C., 1996, Cir. of Distinction award, Am. Hosp. Assn., 1999. Fellow: Am. Coll. Healthcare Execs. (regent 1993—99, Regent's award for sr. exec. leadership 1999). Lutheran. Avocations: jogging, photography, music, choral singing. Office: Adv Trinity Hosp 2320 E 93rd St Chicago IL 60617 E-mail: john.schwartz@advocatehealth.com.

SCHWARTZ, JUDY ELLEN, thoracic surgeon; b. Mason City, Iowa, Oct. 5, 1946; d. Walter Carl and Alice Nevada (Moore) Schwartz. BS, U. Iowa, Iowa City, 1968, MD, 1971; MPH, Johns Hopkins U., Balt., 1996. Diplomate Am. Bd. Surgery, Am. Bd. Thoracic Surgery, Am. Bd. Med. Mgmt., cert. physician exec. Cert. Commn. Med. Mgt. Intern Nat. Naval Med. Ctr., Bethesda, Md., 1971-72, gen. surgery resident, 1972-76, thoracic surgery resident, 1976-78, staff cardiothoracic surgeon, 1979-82, chief cardiothoracic surgeon, 1982-83; chmn. cardiothoracic surg. dept. Naval Hosp., San Diego, 1983-85, quality assurance program dir., 1985-88. Exec. office Rapidly Deployable Med. Facility Four, 1986—88; asst. prof. surgery Uniformed Svcs. U. Health Sci., Bethesda, 1983—99; sr. policy analyst quality assurance Profl. Affairs and Quality Assurance, 1988—90, dep. dir. quality assurance, 1990; dir. clin. policy Health Svcs. Ops., Washington, 1990—94; head performance evaluation and improvement Nat. Naval Med. Ctr., 1994—99; cardiothoracic splty. cons. to naval med. command USN, Washington, 1983—84; Dept. Def. rep. to task force info. mgmt. Joint Commn. Accreditation Health Care Orgn., 1990—93, chmn., 1991—93, mem. task force IMS Tech., 1993—94; chmn. info. mgmt. workshop Fed. Health Care Study Commn.'s Coord. Fed. Health Care, 1993; corp. med. dir. Medcenter One Health Sys., 1999—2002, trustee, 1999—2003; corp. med. dir. ND Dept. Corrections & Rehab., 1990—2002; v.p. med. affairs Medcenter One, 2002; v.p. Surg. Svc. and Electronic Med. Records Informatics, 2003—05, Surg. Svc., 2005—06; bd. dirs. SCCI; mem. adv. com. Blue Cross Blue Shield Care Mgmt., 1999—2002, v.p. med. affairs, 2002; chmn. rsch. and bioethics com. Instnl. Rev. Bd., 2000—06; mem. exec. adv. bd. Surg. Info. Sys., 2005—; examiner Nat. Baldridge award, 2006—07; v.p. med. affairs Knox Cmty. Hosp., 2007—. Contbr. articles to various publs. Mem. nat. physician's leadership coun. VHA, 2000—02; trustee St. Vincent's Nursing Home, 2001—05. Capt. USN, 1969—99, ret. USN, 1999. Decorated Legion of Merit, Commendation Medal Navy and Marine Corps, Meritorious Unit Commendation. Fellow: ACS (mem. com. allied health pers. 1985—91, mem. exec. com. 1987—91, mem. accreditation rev. com. edn. physician asst. 1988—94, treas. accreditation rev. com. 1991—93, sr. mem. com. allied health pers. 1991—94), Am. Coll. Cardiology; mem.: AMA, Am. Coll. Physician Execs., Am. Mgmt. Assn., Am. Med. Women's Assn., Am. Thoracic Soc.

SCHWARTZ, MICHAEL, academic administrator, sociology educator; b. Chgo., July 29, 1937; s. Norman and Lillian (Ruthenberg) S.; m. Ettabelle Slutsky, Aug. 23, 1959 (div. Jan. 1998); children: Monica, Kenneth, Rachel; m. Joanne Rand (Whitmore)Schwartz, Nov. 10, 1998. BS in Psychology, U. Ill., 1958, MA in Indsl. Rels., 1959, PhD in Sociology, 1962; LLD (hon.), Youngstown State U., 1990. Asst. prof. sociology and psychology Wayne State U., Detroit, 1962-64; asst. prof. sociology Ind. U., Bloomington, 1964, assoc. prof. sociology, 1966-70; prof., chmn. dept. sociology Fla. Atlantic U., Boca Raton, 1970-72, dean Coll. Social Sci., 1972-76; v.p. grad. studies and rsch. Kent State U., Ohio, 1976-78, interim pres. Ohio, 1977, acting v.p. acad. affairs Ohio, 1977-78, v.p. acad. and student affairs Ohio, 1978-80, provost, v.p. acad. and student affairs Ohio, 1980-82, pres. Ohio, 1982-91, pres. emeritus and trustee's prof., 1991; interim pres. Cleve. State U., 2001, pres., 2001—. Trustee Ctrl. State U., 1996-97; acting dir. Inst. for Social Rsch., Ind. U., 1966-67; tng. cons. Operation Head Start in Ind., 1964-70; cons. Office of Manpower, Automation and Tng., U.S. Dept. Labor, 1964-65. Cons. editor, Sociometry, 1966-70, assoc. editor, 1970; reader Am. Sociol. Rev. papers; author: (with Elton F. Jackson) Study Guide to the Study of Sociology, 1968; contbr. articles to profl. jours., chpts. to books. Chmn. Mid-Am. Conf. Coun. Pres.; rep. Nat. Coll. Athletic Assn. Pres.'s Commn.; chmn. divsn. I, 1988; corps evaluators North Ctrl. Assn. Colls. and Schs.; mem. bd. visitors Air U., USAF; mem. Akron (Ohio) Regional Devel. Bd., N.E. Ednl. TV of Ohio, Inc., N.E. Ohio Univs. Coll. Medicine; trustee Akron Symphony Orch. Assn.; mem. State of Ohio Post-Secondary Rev. Entity, 1995; mem. Assn. of Governing Bds. Commn. on Strengthening the Presidency. Recipient Disting. Tchr. award Fla. Atlantic U., 1970-71, Meritorious Svc. award Am. Assn. State Colls. and Univs., 1990; Michael Schwartz Ctr., Kent State U., named in his honor, 1991. Mem. Ohio Tchr. Edn. and Cert. Adv. Commn., Pine Lake Trout Club. Office: Office of the President Cleveland State Univ 2121 Euclid Ave Cleveland OH 44115 E-mail: mschwartz@educ.kent.edu.

SCHWARTZ, MICHAEL ROBINSON, management consultant; b. St. Louis, Mar. 18, 1940; s. Henry G. and Edith C. (Robinson) Schwartz; m. Kathleen Nowicki, Dec. 9, 1989; children from previous marriage: Christine, Richard. AB, Dartmouth Coll., 1962; MHA, U. Minn., 1964. Asst. in adminstrn. Shands Tchg. Hosp., Gainesville, Fla., 1966-67, asst. dir., 1967-68, assoc. dir., 1968-73; assoc. adminstr. St. Joseph Mercy Hosp., Pontiac, Mich., 1973-76, pres., 1976-85; exec. v.p. Mercy Health Svcs., Farmington Hills, Mich., 1985-96, COO, 1988-96; exec. v.p. Ea. Mich. region Sisters of Mercy Health Corp., 1991-92; pvt. practice Birmingham, Mich., 1996—2004, 2007—; dir. provider rels. Blue Cross Blue Shield of Mich., 2003—04, v.p. contracting, 2004—05, sr. v.p. network rels. contracting, pharmacy Mich., 2005—07. Non-resident lectr. U. Mich., 1982—93; cons. prof. Oakland U., 1980—88; asst. prof. hosp. adminstrn. U. Fla., 1967—73; pres. Eastern Mich. Regional Bd. Sisters of Mercy Health Corp., 1976—79; v.p. Lourdes Nursing Home, 1981—84, United Way-Pontiac/North Oakland, 1982—84; treas. Oakland Health Edn. Program, 1978—79; bd. dirs. Blue Cross/Blue Shield of Mich., 1982—86, coms., 1978—86, chair hosp. contingent to participating hosp. agreement adv. com., 1989—96; bd. dirs. Vis. Nurse Assn., Inc., 1997—2005, treas., 1998—2004, vice chair, 1999—2000, chair, 2000—02; chmn. bd. dirs., pres. Accord Ins. Co. Ltd., 1983—88; chmn. bd. dirs. Mercy Health Plans, 1986—96, Venzke Svc. Co., 1983—88, pres., 1983—84; chmn. bd. dirs., pres. Venzke Ins. Co. Ltd., 1988—96; mem. audit and fin. com. Am. Healthcare Sys., 1988—92; mem. S.E. Mich. Hosp. Coun., chmn. pub. rels. com., 1983—85; mem. Commonfund Healthcare Coun., 1999—2005, U. Detroit Mercy Health Professions Adv. Bd., 2002—07; trustee Sisters of Mercy Health Corp., 1991—93, sec. bd. trustees, 1993; bd. dirs. Hosp. Fund, 1986—96, Visiting Nurse Svc. Corp., 2007—, DenteMax, 2007—. Mem. charitable trust Sisters of Mercy, Regional Cmty. Detroit, 1999—2004. With US Army, 1964—66. Fellow: Am. Coll. Healthcare Execs. (life; mem. exec. com. higher edn. 1990—93, Mich. Regent's award 1992); mem.: Comprehensive Health Planning Coun. (com. mem. 1976—81), Am. Healthcare Sys. Risk Retention Group (bd. dirs. 1990—91), Mich. Hosp. Assn. (at-large rep. corp. bd. 1990—96, exec. com. 1992—96), Pontiac Urban League (pers. com. 1979). Office Phone: 313-378-8400. Business E-Mail: mschwartzbham@aol.com.

SCHWARTZ, RICHARD BRENTON, English language educator, dean, writer; b. Cin., Oct. 5, 1941; s. Jack Jay and Marie Mildred (Schnelle) S.; m. Judith Mary Alexis Lang, Sept. 7, 1963; 1 son, Jonathan Francis. AB cum laude, U. Notre Dame, 1963; AM, U. Ill., 1964, PhD, 1967. Instr. English, U.S. Mil. Acad., 1967-69; asst. prof. U. Wis.-Madison, 1969-72, assoc. prof., 1972-78, prof., 1978-81, assoc. dean Grad. Sch., 1977, 79-81; prof. English, dean Grad. Sch., Georgetown U., Washington, 1981-98, interim exec. v.p. for main campus academic affairs, 1991-92; interim exec. v.p. for the main campus Georgetown U., Washington, 1995-96; dean Coll. Arts and Sci. U. Mo., Columbia, 1998—2006, prof. English, 1998—. Mem. exec. bd. Ctr. Strategic and Internat. Studies, 1981-87. Author: Samuel Johnson and the New Science, 1971 (runner-up Gustave O. Arlt prize), Samuel Johnson and the Problem of Evil, 1975, Boswell's Johnson: A Preface to the Life, 1978, Daily Life in Johnson's London, 1983, Japanese edit., 1990, After the Death of Literature, 1997, Nice and Noir: Contemporary American Crime Fiction, 2002, (novels) Frozen Stare, 1989, The Last Voice You Hear, 2001, After the Fall, 2002, reissued as Proof of Purchase, 2007, Into the Dark, 2002 (hon. mention genre fiction Writer's Digest), (short stories) The Biggest City in America, 1999 (Choice Mag. citation); editor: The Plays of Arthur Murphy, 4 vols., 1979, Theory and Tradition in Eighteenth-Century Studies, 1990; contbr. articles to profl. jours. Served to capt. U.S. Army, 1967-69. Decorated Army Commendation medal; recipient Presdl. medal Georgetown U., 1998; Disting. Svc. award, U. Mo. Columbia, Coll. Arts and Sci., 2007; Nat. Endowment Humanities grantee, 1970, 87; Inst. for Research in Humanities fellow, 1976; Am. Council Learned Socs. fellow, 1978-79; H.I. Romnes fellow, 1978-81. Mem. Mystery Writers Am., Johnson Soc. So. Calif., Johnson Soc. of London, Am. Soc. Eighteenth-Century Studies, Coun. Grad. Schs., N.E. Assn. Grad. Schs. (exec. com. 1986-88), Assn. Grad. Schs. in Cath. Univs. (exec. com. 1984-87), Assn. Literary Scholars and Critics, Nat. Assn. Scholars, N.Am. Conf. Brit. Studies, Jefferson Club, Mosaic Soc., Eliot Soc., Alpha Sigma Nu, Alpha Sigma Lambda. Roman Catholic.

Home: 5800 Highlands Pkwy Columbia MO 65203-5125 Office: U Mo Dept English 236 Tate Hall Columbia MO 65211-6080 Home Phone: 573-442-2242; Office Phone: 573-884-7038. Business E-Mail: schwartzrb@missouri.edu.

SCHWARTZ, RICHARD JOHN, electrical engineering educator, researcher; b. Waukesha, Wis., Aug. 12, 1935; s. Sylvester John and LaVerne Mary (Lepien) S.; m. Mary Jo Collins, June 29, 1957; children: Richard, Stephen, Susan, Elizabeth, Barbara, Peter, Christopher, Margaret. BSEE, U. Wis., 1957; SM, MIT, 1959, ScD, 1962. Mem. tech. staff Sarnoff Rsch. Labs. RCA, Princeton, NJ, 1957-58; instr. MIT, Cambridge, 1961-62; v.p. Energy Conversions, Inc., Cambridge, 1962-64; assoc. prof. Purdue U., West Lafayette, Ind., 1964-71, prof., 1972—, head dept., 1985-95, dean engring., 1995—2001, dir. Optoelectronic Ctr., 1986-89. Co-dir. Nano Tech. Ctr. Purdue U., W. Lafayette, Ind., 2001—06; cons. solar cells, 1965—. Contbr. chpts. to books, articles to profl. jours. Served to 2nd lt. U.S. Army, 1957-58. Recipient Disting. Svc. medal U. Wis., 1989, Centennial medal, 1991. Fellow: IEEE (William R. Cherry award 1998), Internat. Electronics Con.; mem.: Nat. Elec. Engring. Dept. Heads Assn. (bd. dirs.). Achievements include development of high intensity solar cells, of surface charge transfer device, and of numerical models for solar cells. Office: Purdue U 1285 Electrical Engring West Lafayette IN 47907 Office Phone: 765-494-0619.

SCHWARTZ, ROBERT TERRY, industrial designer, director; b. Irvington, NJ, Sept. 29, 1950; s. Edward Herman and Harriet Selma (Rosenstein) S.; m. Carol Fawn Mullenix, July 27, 1975; children: Zachary Jacob, Allison Lizabeth. BFA, Kansas City Art Inst., 1973; M of Indsl. Design, R.I. Sch. Design, 1975. Red Cross project dir. R.I. Sch. Design, Providence, 1975-76; head indsl. design/architecture Red Cross Nat. Hdqrs., Washington, 1976-88; dir. sci. and tech. Health Industry Mfrs. Assn., Washington, 1988-90; exec. dir., COO Worldesign Found., Great Falls, Va., 1990-96, Indsl. Designers Soc. Am., Great Falls, 1990-99; dir. indsl. design Motorola, Inc., Ft. Lauderdale, Fla., 1999—2003; v.p. new product devel. Levolor Kirsch, High Point, NC, 2003; assoc. dir. global design orgn. Procter and Gamble, 2003—07; gen. mgr. Global Design GE HealthCare. Provider expert testimony before Congress, 1994, commencement address, Kansas City Art Inst., 1995; official delegate to Nat. Medal of Arts Ceremonies, 1997-98; official state delegate for Md. and Va., Nat. Arts Advocacy Days, 1997-99; sr. tech. advisor to Peoples Republic of China, UN, 1998; appointed to curriculum adv. bd., Coll. Arts, Carnegie Mellon U., 1999-; vis. assoc. prof. design, U. Cin. Contbr. chpts. to books, articles to profl. jours.; presenter in field; holder 5 patents, 1 trademark. Recipient Project of Merit award Indsl. Design Mag., 1985, Cert. of Achievement, ARC, 1988, Louis C. Tiffany award ARC, 1987, Personal Recognition award, Industrial Designers Soc. Am., 2000, numerous others; Nat. Endowment for the Arts grantee, 1984, 92, 94; EPA grantee, 1992. Mem. Indsl. Designers Soc. Am. (Personal Recognition award 2000). Avocations: edison antiquities collecting, sailing. Office: GE Healtcare 3000 N Grandview Blvd Waukesha WI 53188*

SCHWARTZ, SHIRLEY E., retired chemist, researcher; b. Detroit, Aug. 26, 1935; d. Emil Victor and Jessie Grace (Galbraith) Eckwall; m. Ronald Elmer Schwartz, Aug. 25, 1957; children: Steven Dennis, Bradley Allen, George Byron. BS, U. Mich., 1957, Detroit Inst. Tech., 1978; MS, Wayne State U., 1962, PhD, 1970. Asst. prof. Detroit Inst. Tech., 1973—78, head divsn. math. sci., 1976—78; mem. rsch. staff BASF Wyandotte Corp., Mich., 1978—81, head sect. functional fluids, 1981; sr. staff rsch. scientist GM Rsch., Warren, Mich., 1981—99; part time contract GM Powertrain, 1999—2003. Part-time contractor GM Powertrain, 2003—. Contbr. articles to profl. jours. Recipient Gold award Engring. Soc. Detroit, 1989 Fellow Soc. Automotive Engrs. (Excellence in Oral Presentation award 1986, 91, 94, Arch T. Colwell Merit award 1991, Lloyd L. Withrow Disting. Spkr. award 1995), Soc. Tribologists and Lubrication Engrs. (treas. Detroit sect. 1981, vice chmn. 1982, chmn. 1982-83, chmn. wear tech. com. 1987-88, bd. dirs. 1985-91, assoc. editor 1989-90, contbg. editor 1989—2003, Wilbur Deutsch award 1987, P.M. Ku award 1994); mem. Am. Chem. Soc., Soc. In Vitro Biology, Soc. Women Engrs. Life Achievement award 1989), Mich. Women's Hall of Fame (lifetime achievement award 1996), Women of Wayne (headliners award 2000), U.S. Nat. Acad. Engring., Mensa, Classic Guitar Soc. Mich., U.S. Power Squadrons, Detroit Navigators, Sigma Xi. Lutheran. Achievements include development of General Motors system that indicates when the engine oil should be changed; patents in field.

SCHWARTZHOFF, JAMES PAUL, foundation executive; b. Waukon, Iowa, June 24, 1937; s. Harold J. and Mary (Regan) Schwartzhoff; m. Mary Lou Hess, Apr. 23, 1960; children: Tammara, Eric, Stephanie, Mark, Laurie, Michelle, Steven. B, U. Iowa, 1962. Asst. chief auditor Wis. Dept. Tax, Madison, 1962-67; mgr. treas. dept. Mead Johnson and Co., Evansville, Ind., 1967-69; v.p., treas., investment officer Kettering Found., Dayton, Ohio, 1969—. Chmn., treas. bd. Pastoral Counseling Ctr., Dayton, 1975-81; treas. Ohio River Rd. Runners, Dayton, 1986-87; spkr. nat. investment confs. Past treas. Nat. Issues Forums Inst., Coun. Pub. Policy Edn., Ctr. for Cmty. and Ednl. Devel.; mem. Donor's Forum Ohio Fin. Com., 1990-92; mem. investment com. U. Dayton; adv. com. JMB Endowment and Found. Realty Funds, 1991-94; advisor to investment com. Fetzer Inst. Cpl. U.S. Army, 1957-59. Mem. AICPA, Found. Fin. Officers Group, Southern Ohio Pension Fund Group. Avocations: bicycling, running, photography, woodworking, skiing. Office: Kettering Found 200 Commons Rd Dayton OH 45459-2799

SCHWARZ, EGON, language educator, writer, critic; b. Vienna, Aug. 8, 1922; arrived in U.S., 1949, naturalized, 1956; s. Oscar and Erna S.; m. Dorothea K. Klockenbusch, June 8, 1950; children: Rudolf Joachim, Caroline Elisabeth, Gabriela Barbara. PhD, U. Wash., 1954; PhD (hon.), U. Vienna, 1997, U. Örebro, Sweden, 2002. Mem. faculty Harvard U., 1954-61; mem. faculty dept. Germanic langs. and lit. Washington U., St. Louis, 1961—, prof. German, 1963—, Rosa May Disting. Univ. prof. in the Humanities, 1975-93, prof. emeritus, 1993—. Vis. prof. U. Hamburg, Fed. Republic Germany, 1962-63, U. Calif., Berkeley, 1963-65, Middlebury Coll., 1969, U. Calif., Irvine, 1977, U. Tübingen, 1986; William Evans prof. U. Otago, Dunedin, N.Z., 1984; Disting. scholar Ohio State U., Columbus, 1987, U. Graz, Austria, 1989, 93, U. Siegen, 1993-94. Author: Hofmannsthal und Calderon, 1962, Joseph von Eichendorff, 1972, Das verschluckte Schluchzen-Poesie und Politik bei Rainer Maria Rilke, 1972, Keine Zeit für Eichendorff: Chronik unfreiwilliger Wanderjahre; an autobiography, 1979, rev., 1992, Dichtung, Kritik, Geschichte: Essays zur Literatur 1900-1930, 1983, Literatur aus vier Kulturen: Essays und Besprechungen, 1987, Ich bin Kein Freund allgemeiner Urteile über ganze Volker: Essays über österreichische, deutsche und jüdische Literatur, 2000, Die japanische Mauer: Ungewöhnliche Reisegeschichten, 2002, Refuge-Chronicle of a Flight from Hitler, 2002, Unfreiwillige Wanderjahre, 2005, Schwarz auf Weiss, others. Recipient Joseph von Eichendorff medal, 1986, Austrian Medal of Honor for Arts and Scis., 1991, Alexander von Humboldt prize for fgn. scholars, 1995; Guggenheim fellow, 1957-58, Fulbright fellow, 1962-63, sr. fellow NEH, 1970-71, fellow Ctr. for Interdisciplinary Studies, Bielefeld, Germany, 1980-81, Grosses Ehrenseichen fur Verdienste un die Republik Osterreich, 2007; grantee Am. Coun. Learned Socs., 1962-63. Mem.: MLA, German Acad. Lang. and Letters, Am. Assn. Tchrs. German, German Acad. Lang. and Lit. (hon.). Home: 1036 Oakland Ave Saint Louis MO 63122-6565 Office: Washington U German Dept Saint Louis MO 63130 Personal E-mail: gabrielas@aol.com. Business E-Mail: eschwarz@artsci.wusl.edu.

SCHWARZ, JOE (JOHN J.H. SCHWARZ), former congressman, physician; b. Battle Creek, Mich., Nov. 15, 1937; s. Frank William and Helen Veronica (Brennan) S.; m. Anne Louise Ennis, Jan. 16, 1971 (dec. Feb. 1990); 1 child, Brennan Louise. BA in History, U. Mich., 1959; MD, Wayne State U., 1964. Operative CIA, 1968—70; physician, surgeon Battle Creek, Mich., 1974—; commr. City of Battle Creek, 1979—85, mayor, 1985-87; mem. Mich. State Senate from 24th dist., Lansing, 1987—2002, pres. pro tempore, 1993—2002; mem. US Congress from 7th Mich. dist., 2005—07, mem. com. agr., com. armed services, com. sci.; chmn., bd. dir. Alumni Assc., U. Mich., 2005—07. Trustee Leila Y. Post Montgomery Hosp. (now Battle Creek Health Sys.), Mich., 1980-82, Olivet Coll., 1991—, Wayland Acad., 1992-96, Libr. Mich., 1994-2003; trustee, treas. Am. Legacy Found; bd. directors Artrain, Ann Arbor, Detroit Receiving Hosp., Kellogg Cmty. Coll. Found., Univ. Musical Soc., Ann Arbor, Wayne State U. Found. Lt. Comdr. USN, 1965—67, Vietnam. Fellow ACS; mem. AMA, Am. Soc. for Head and Neck Surgery, Calhoun County Mich. Med. Soc. (pres. 1971), Mich Otolaryngological Soc., Mich State Med. Soc., Soc. Med. Consultants to Armed Forces, U. Mich. Club of Battle Creek. Republican. Roman Catholic.

SCHWARZ, NORBERT, psychology professor; b. Annweiler, Germany, Mar. 28, 1953; Dipl. Sociol., Universität Mannheim, Germany, 1977, D. Phil., Sociol. & Psychol. summa cum laude, 1980; D. Phil. Habil., Universität Heidelberg, Germany, 1986. Lectr. Universität Mannheim, 1978—80; postdoctoral fellow Univ. Ill., 1980—81; fellow Decision Rsch., Universität Mannheim, 1981—83; asst. prof. Universität Heidelberg, 1981—86, privatdozent, 1986—92; sci. dir. Zentrum für Umfragen Methoden & Analysen, Mannheim, 1987—92; prof. psychol. & rsch prof. Univ. Mich., Ann Arbor, 1993—, prof. mktg., 2002—; rsch. prof. Joint Univ. Md. & Univ. Mich. prog. in survey methodology, 1995—. Contbr. articles to profl. jour.; author: Stimmung als Information, 1987, Cognition and Communication, 1996; co-author: Thinking About Answers, 1996. Recipient Heinz Maier-Leibnitz prize, Fed. Republic of Germany, 1986. Fellow: Soc. Personality & Social Psychol., Am. Psychol. Soc., Am. Acad. Arts & Sci.; mem.: World Assn. Public Opinion Rsch., Assn. Consumer Rsch. (France Nicosia award 2004), Am. Assn. Public Opinion Rsch., Soc. Personality & Social Psychol., Soc. Judgement & Decision Making, German Psychol. Soc. (hon. Wilhelm Wundt medal 2004), Soc. Experimental Social Psychol., Soc. Applied Rsch. Memory & Cognition, Midwestern Psychol. Assn., Internat. Soc. Rsch. on Emotion, European Assn. Experimental Social Psychol., Am. Psychol. Assn. Office: Institute for Social Research 426 Thompson St PO Box 1248 Ann Arbor MI 48106-1248 Office Phone: 734-647-3616. Business E-Mail: nschwarz@umich.edu.

SCHWARZ, STEVEN R., stationary company executive; Exec. v.p. supply divsn. United Stationers, Inc., Des Plaines, Ill., 1997—. Office: United Stationers Inc 2200 E Golf Rd Des Plaines IL 60016-1257

SCHWEICKART, JIM, advertising executive, broadcast executive, consultant; b. Toledo, June 25, 1950; s. Norman Marvin and Anne Belle S.; m. Deborah J., Aug. 14, 1971; children: Jennifer, Kimberly, Stephen. BA in Polit. Sci, Taylor U., Upland, Ind., 1972. News anchor, announcer Sta. WCMR, Elkhart, Ind., 1967-71; news anchor, disc jockey Sta. WWHC, Hartford City, Ind., 1971-72; gen. mgr. Sta. WTUC, Taylor U., 1971; news dir. Sta. WCMR, Elkhart, 1972-74; news anchor Sta. WOWO, Fort Wayne, Ind., 1974-78, Sta. KDKA, Pitts., 1978-79; gen. mgr. Sta. WBCL-FM, Fort Wayne, 1979-85; owner advt. agy., broadcast cons. Schweickart & Assocs. Inc., Fort Wayne, 1984—. Mem. adv. bd. Taylor U., Fort Wayne campus. Republican. Baptist. Office: 3452 Stellhorn Rd Fort Wayne IN 46815-4630 Home Phone: 260-627-0611; Office Phone: 260-486-5428.

SCHWEITZER, PETER, advertising agency executive; b. Chgo., Aug. 31, 1939; children: Mark, Cynthia, Jenifer, Samantha; m. Elaine Elkin, 1986; children: Dana, Taylor. BA, U. of Mich., 1961; MBA, W. Mich. U., 1967. With Post div. Gen. Foods, 1961-69; v.p. Grey Advt., 1969-76; sr. v.p. J. Walter Thompson, 1976-79; sr. v.p. mktg. Burger King Corp., 1990; sr. v.p., gen. mgr., then exec. v.p., gen. mgr. J. Walter Thompson USA, Inc.-Detroit, 1995; v. chmn. of agency ops. J. Walter Thompson Co., Detroit, 1988-95, pres., 1995—, CEO, 2001—. Pres. Internat. Fedn. Multiple Sclerosis. Office: J Walter Thompson Co 500 Woodward Ave 14th Fl Detroit MI 48226-3416 also: 466 Lexington Ave New York NY 10017-3140

SCHWEIZER, KENNETH STEVEN, physics professor; b. Phila., Jan. 20, 1953; s. Kenneth Paul and Grace Norma (Fischer) S.; m. Janis Eve Pelletier, Oct. 18, 1986; children: Gregory Michael, Daniel Patrick. BS, Drexel U., 1975; MS, U. Ill., 1976, PhD, 1981. Postdoctoral rsch. assoc. AT&T Bell Labs., Murray Hill, NJ, 1981-83; sr. mem. tech. staff Sandia Nat. Labs., Albuquerque, 1983-91; prof. materials sci. engring. and chemistry U. Ill., Urbana, 1991—, prof. chem. engring., 1998—, G. Ronald and Margeret H. Morris prof. materials sci., 2001—. Contbr. articles to profl. jours. Recipient Sandia award for Excellence, 1990, R&D 100 award, 1992, Award for Scientific Achievement in Materials Chemistry DOE, 1996, Burnett Tchg. award, 1997, Everitt Tchg. award, 2002. Fellow Am. Phys. Soc. (John H. Dillon medal 1991); mem. Am. Chem. Soc., Soc. Rheology, Sigma Xi, Pi Mu Epsilon. Office: U Ill Dept Materials Sci Engring 1304 W Green St Urbana IL 61801-2920 E-mail: kschweiz@uiuc.edu.

SCHWEMM, JOHN BUTLER, printing company executive, lawyer; b. Barrington, Ill., May 18, 1934; s. Earl M. and Eunice (Butler) S.; m. Nancy Lea Prickett, Sept. 7, 1956; children: Catherine Ann, Karen Elizabeth. AB, Amherst Coll., 1956; JD, U. Mich., 1959. Bar: Ill. 1959. With Sidley & Austin, Chgo., 1959-65; with legal dept. R.R. Donnelley & Sons Co., Chgo., 1965-69, gen. counsel, 1969-75, v.p., 1971-75, pres., 1981-87, chmn., 1983-89, dir., 1980-92. Bd. dirs. William Blair Mut. Funds, Inc., Walgreen Co., USG Corp. Life trustee Northwestern U., Chgo. Mem. Law Club Chgo., Order of Coif, Phi Beta Kappa. Clubs: Chgo., Univ., Hinsdale (Ill.) Golf, Old Elm. Home (Summer): 2 Turvey Ln Downers Grove IL 60515-4530 Home and Office: 565 Sanctuary Dr Ste A401 Longboat Key FL 34228

SCHWEND, MICHAEL T., hospital administrator; m. Mary Jo Fitzpatrick. BS in Psychology, Truman State U., 1983, MA in Counseling and Guidance, 1990; MBA, William Woods U., 1997. Pres., CEO Preferred Family Healthcare, Kirksville, Mo. Mem. White House Commn. on Alcohol and Drug Abuse; sec. bd. govs. Truman State U., Kirksville, 2001—; former mem. Mo. Adv. Coun. on Alcohol and Drug Abuse; peer rev. specialist Tex. Commn. on Alcohol and Drug Abuse; active Kirksville R-III Athletic Booster Club; pres. bd. dirs. K-Life outreach program; active Immaculate Cath. Ch. Office: Preferred Family Healthcare 900 E LaHarpe Kirksville MO 63501

SCHWERTFEGER, TIMOTHY R., investment company executive; b. Mar. 28, 1949; BA in Econs. and Fin., Northwestern U.; JD, Georgetown U.; student, Harvard Bus. Sch., Stanford U. Nat. dir. health care investment banking svcs. Nuveen Investments, Inc. (div. St. Paul Co., Inc.), 1977—86, head corp. mktg., 1987—89, exec. v.p., 1989—96, chmn. Nuveen Mutual Funds & Exch.-traded Funds, 1996—, chmn., CEO, 1996—2007, non-exec. chmn., 2007—. Pres. Hubbard St. Dance Chgo.; bd. dirs. Better Boys Found., Lyric Opera Chgo., Mus. Contemporary Art, Providence St. Mel Sch. Office: Nuveen Investments Inc 333 W Wacker Dr Chicago IL 60606

SCHWOY, LAURIE ANNETTE, professional soccer player; b. Balt., Feb. 14, 1978; Mem. U.S. Nat. Women's Soccer Team, 1997—99, including U.S. Women's Cup, 1997; mem. Under-20 Women's Nat. Team, 1996; including bronze medal team at Nordic Cup Sweden, 1996; championship team Nordic Cup, Denmark, 1997; founder, trainer Laurie Schwoy Summer Soccer Camp, Balt. County, 2005—. Named Soccer Am. Freshman of Yr., 1996, ACC Rookie of Yr., 1996. Avocation: dance. Office: US Soccer Fedn 1801-1811 S Prairie Ave Chicago IL 60616

SCHYVINCK, CHRISTINE, electronics executive; b. Minn., 1967; BS in mech. engring., U. Wis.; MS in engring. mgmt., Northwestern U. Engr., corp. quality divsn. Shure Inc., Niles, Ill., 1989—97, mgr., process engring. dept., 1997—98, v.p. corp. quality, 1998—2000, v.p. ops., 2000—04, exec. v.p. ops., 2004—06, exec. v.p. global mktg. & sales, 2006—. Named one of 40 Under 40, Crain's Chgo. Bus., 2006. Office: Shure Inc 5800 W Touhy Ave Niles IL 60714-4608 Office Phone: 847-600-2000. Office Fax: 847-600-1212. E-mail: info@shure.com.

SCIARRA, JOHN J., obstetrician, gynecologist, educator; b. West Haven, Conn., Mar. 4, 1932; s. John and Mary Grace (Sanzone) S.; m. Barbara Crafts Patton, Jan. 9, 1960; chidren: Vanessa Patton, John Crafts, Leonard Chapman. BS, Yale U., 1953; MD, Columbia U., NYC, 1957, PhD, 1963. Asst. prof. Columbia U., NYC, 1964-68; prof., dept. head U. Minn. Med. Sch., Mpls., 1968-74; prof. Northwestern U. Med. Sch., Chgo., 1974—; chmn. ob-gyn Northwestern Meml. Hosp. and orthwestern U. Med. Sch., Chgo., 1974—2003. Guest prof. Peking U., China, 2005. Editor Gyn-Ob Reference Series, 1973-2005, Internat. Jour. Gyn-Ob, 1985-2006. V.p. med. affairs Chgo. Maternity Ctr., Chgo., 1974—2003; treas. Soc. Family Planning, 2005-. Fellow ACS, Am. Coll. Ob-Gyn. (chmn. internal affairs com. 1985-89), Royal Coll. Ob-Gyn. (ad eundem); Internat. Fedn. Gyn-Ob. (pres. 1991-94, pres. Supporters Assn. 1994-2000); mem. Assn. Profs. Gyn-Ob. (sec. 1976-79, pres. 1980-81, Achievement award 1998, Tchg. award 2003), Am. Assn. Maternal and Neonatal Health (pres. 1980-89), Coun. Resident Edn. in Ob-Gyn., Am. Fertility Soc. (Hartman award 1965, bd. dirs. 1971-73), Assn. Profs. Gyn-Ob. Med. Edn. Found. (sec.-treas. 1987-91, pres. 1991-93), Ctrl. Assn. Ob-Gyn. (trustees 1986-90, pres. 1990-91), Chgo. Gynecol. Soc. (pres. 1990-91), Internat. Soc. Gynecol. Endoscopy (hon. 2005, v.p. 1997-99, pres. 1999-01), Am. Gynecol. Club (pres. 2007-08), Internat. Acad. Human Reprodn., Yale Club N.Y.C., Carleton Club (Chgo.). Avocations: photography, travel. Office: Northwestern U Med Sch Dept Ob-Gyn 680 N Lake Shore Dr Ste 1015 Chicago IL 60611-8702 Office Phone: 312-695-5107. Business E-Mail: jsciarra@northwestern.edu.

SCILLIAN, DEVIN, announcer; m. Corey Scillian; children: Griffin, Quinn, Madison, Christian. BS in Journalism, U. Kans., 1985. Anchor KFOR-TV, Oklahoma City, 1989—95; with WDIV-TV, Detroit, 1995—. Author: Fibblestax, 2000, A Is For America: An American Alphabet, 2001, S is for Sooner, An Oklahoma Alphabet, 2003; singer: (albums) Tulsa, 1999, A is For America, 2001. Recipient Detroit Music award for Best Country Performer, 2001. Office: WDIV-TV 550 W Lafayette Blvd Detroit MI 48226

SCISM, DANIEL REED, lawyer; b. Evansville, Ind., Aug. 27, 1936; s. Daniel William and Ardath Josephine (Gibbs) S.; m. Paula Anne Sedgwick, June 21, 1958; children: Darby Claire, Joshua Reed. BA, DePauw U., 1958; JD, Ind. U., 1965. Bar: Ind. 1965, U.S. Dist. Ct. (so. dist.) Ind. 1965, U.S. Ct. Appeals (7th cir.) 1967, U.S. Supreme Ct. 1976. Reporter Dayton (Ohio) Jour.-Herald, 1958-59; editor Mead Johnson & Co., Evansville, 1961; first assoc., then ptnr. Roberts, Ryder, Rogers & Scism and predecessor firms, Indpls., 1965—86; ptnr. Barnes & Thornburg, Indpls., 1987—2002, of counsel, 2003—. Cons. Ind. Pers. Assn., 1984-2002. Treas. Marion County chpt. Myasthenia Gravis Found., Indpls., 1970; v.p. Marion County Mental Health Assn., Indpls., 1970-71; pres. The Suemma Coleman Agy., Indpls., 1973-74; bd. dirs. Ind. Humanities Coun., 1995-00, chmn. bd., 1997-98; trustee Indpls. Mus. Art, 2001—07; bd. dirs. Westminster Village North, Inc., 2003-06; pres. Persimmon Woods Homeowners Assn., 2001-03, sec. 2003-. With US Army, 1959—62. Edwards fellow Ind. U., 1964. Mem. ABA, Ind. Bar Assn., Woodland Country Club (bd. dirs. 1984-88, sec. 1998-99). Methodist. Home: 10909 300 Yard Dr Fishers IN 46037-9306 Office: Barnes & Thornburg 11 S Meridian St Indianapolis IN 46204-3535

SCOBIE, TIMOTHY FRANKLIN, lawyer; b. Chippewa Falls, Wis., July 8, 1964; s. William Mason and Nancy Anne (Clark) S.; m. Michelle Mae Michael, Aug. 10, 1991; 1 child, Lauren Michael. BA, Boston U., 1987; JD, Hamline U., 1990. Bar: Wis. 1991, Minn. 1991, U.S. Ct. Appeals (7th cir.) 1991. Staff atty. Wiley, Wahl et al, Chippewa Falls, 1990-92; dist. atty. County of Chippewa, Chippewa Falls, 1992—. Mem. bd. alumni Breck Sch., Mpls., 1992—; mem bd. advisors U. Wis., Eau Claire, 1992—. Mem. Jaycees (v.p. 1994). Office: 711 N Bridge St Chippewa Falls WI 54729-1845

SCODEL, RUTH, humanities educator; b. Columbus, Ohio, Feb. 29, 1952; d. Alvin and Barbara (Keith) S.; 1 child, Anna Gabrielle. AB, U. Calif., Berkeley, 1973; PhD, Harvard U., 1978. Asst. prof. Harvard Coll., Cambridge, Mass., 1978-83; assoc. prof. classics of Greek and Latin U. Mich., Ann Arbor, 1983-87, prof., 1987—, dir. LSA Honors program, 1991—97. Author: Trojan Trilogy of Euripides, 1980, Sophocles, 1984, Credible Impossibilities, 1999, Listening to Homer, 2002; editor Transactions of Am. Philol. Assn., 1986-91. Office: Univ Mich Dept Classical Studies 2123 Angell 1003 Ann Arbor MI 48109 E-mail: rscodel@umich.edu.

SCOGLAND, WILLIAM LEE, lawyer; b. Moline, Ill., 1949; s. Maurice William and Harriet Rebecca S.; m. Victoria Lynn, 1976; 1 child, Thomas. BA magna cum laude, Augustana Coll., 1971; JD cum laude, Harvard U., 1975. Bar: Ill. 1975, U.S. Dist. Ct. (no. dist.) Ill. 1975. From assoc. to ptnr. Jenner & Block, Chgo., 1981—. Lectr. in law U. Chgo. Law Sch., 2000—; bd. dirs. Am. Benefits Coun., 2004—; adv. coun. employee welfare and pension benefit plans US Dept. Labor, 2006—. Author: Fiduciary Duty: What Does It Mean?, 1989; co-author Employee Benefits Law, 1987; contr. Tort and Ins. Law Jour., 1989, and others. Fellow: Am. Coll. Employee Benefits Counsel; mem.: Omicron Delta Kappa, Phi Beta Kappa. Republican. Office: Jenner & Block LLP 330 N Wabash Chicago IL 60611 Office Phone: 312-923-2878. Business E-Mail: wscogland@jenner.com.

SCOLES, CLYDE SHELDON, library director; b. Columbus, Ohio, Apr. 14, 1949; s. Edward L. and Edna M. (Ruddock) S.; m. Diane Francis, July 14, 1976; children: David, Kevin, Karen, Stephen. BS, Ohio State U., 1971; MLS, U. Mich., 1972. Libr. Columbus Pub. Libr., 1972-74; libr. dir. Zanesville Pub. Libr., Ohio, 1974-78; asst. dir. Toledo-Lucas County Pub. Libr., 1978-85, dir., 1985—. Adj. lectr., libr. bldg. cons. U. Mich.; v.p. bd. dirs. Read for Literacy. Mem. ALA, Ohio Libr. Assn., Ohio Libr. Coun., Toledo C. of C., Com. of 100, Maumee Hist. Soc. Clubs: Torch (Toledo). Lodges: Rotary. Office: Toledo-Lucas County Pub Libr 325 N Michigan St Toledo OH 43604 Office Phone: 419-259-5256. Business E-Mail: clyde.scoles@toledolibrary.org.

SCOMMEGNA, ANTONIO, obstetrician, gynecologist, educator; b. Barletta, Italy, 1931; came to U.S., 1954, naturalized, 1960; s. Francesco Paola and Antonietta S.; m. Lillian F. Sinkiewicz, May 3, 1958; children: Paola, Frank, Roger. BA, State Lyceum A. Casardi, Barletta, 1947; MD, U. Bari, Italy, 1953. Diplomate: Am. Bd. Obstetrics and Gynecology, also sub-bd. endocrinology and reprodn. Rotating intern New Eng. Hosp., Boston, 1954-55; resident obstetrics and gynecology Michael Reese Hosp. and Med. Center, Chgo., 1956-59, fellow dept. research human reprodn., 1960-61, research asso., 1961; fellow steroid tng. program Worcester Found. Exptl. Biology, also Clark U., Shrewsbury, Mass., 1964-65; asso. prof. obstetrics and gynecology Chgo. Med. Sch., 1965-69; mem. staff Michael Reese Hosp. and Med. Center, 1961—, attending physician obstetrics and gynecology, 1961—, dir. sect. gynecologic endocrinology, 1965-81; dir. ambulatory care obstetrics and gynecology Mandel Clinic, 1968-69, chmn. dept., 1969-89; attending, chief svc. U. Ill. Chgo. Hosp. and Med. Ctr., 1989-98; trustee Mandel Clinic, 1977-80; prof. dept. ob-gyn. Pritzker Sch. Medicine, U. Chgo., 1969-89; prof., head dept. ob-gyn. Coll. Medicine, U. Ill. Chgo., 1989-98, prof. emeritus, 1999—. Contbr. articles to profl. jours. Fulbright fellow, 1954-55 Fellow Am. Coll. Obstetricians and Gynecologists, Endocrine Soc., Chgo. Inst. Medicine, Am. Gynecol. and Obstet. Soc.; mem. AMA, Ill., Chgo. med. socs., Am. Fertility Soc., Chgo. Gynecol. Soc. (sec. 1976-79, pres. 1981-82), Soc. Study Reprodn., AAAS, Soc. for Gynecologic Investigation. Home: 2645 N Dayton Chicago IL 60614 Office Phone: 312-996-0222. Business E-Mail: anmis@uic.edu.

SCORZA, SYLVIO JOSEPH, religion educator; b. Zürich, Switzerland, Mar. 21, 1923; came to U.S., 1929; s. Joseph Peter and Helena Christina (Kopp) S.; m. Phyllis Joan VanSetters, June 6, 1952; children: Christine Marie, Philip Joseph, John Forrest. AA, Woodrow Wilson Jr. Coll., 1942; AB, Hope Coll., 1945; BD, Western Theol. Sem., Holland, Mich., 1953; ThD, Princeton Theol. Sem., 1956; PhD, U. Ill., 1972. Ordained to ministry Ref. Ch. in Am., 1955. Stated supply pastor Hickory Bottom Charge, Loysburg, Pa., 1957-58; prof. religion Northwestern Coll., Orange City, Iowa, 1959-90, prof. emeritus, 1990—. Vis. prof. Lancaster (Pa.) Theol. Sem., 1956-57, Western Theol. Sem., Holland, Mich., 1958-59; v.p. Ref. Ch. in Am., N.Y.C., 1988-89, pres., 1989-90, moderator, exec. com., 1990-91; mem. Iowa Bd. Law Examiners, 1997—2004. Co-editor: Concordance to the Greek and Hebrew Text of Ruth, The Computer Bible, Septuagint series, Vols. XXX, XXX-B, 1988-89; contbr. articles to profl. jours. County del. Iowa Dems., Ft. Dodge, 1984. Recipient Disting. Alumnus award Hope Coll., 1989, Homecoming Honors award Northwestern Coll. N Club, 1990, Handicapped Person of Siouxland award Siouxland Com. for the Handicapped, 1990, Gov.'s award Iowa Commn. of Persons with Disabilities, 1990, Victory award Nat. Rehab. Hosp., 1991, Disting. Alumnus award Western Theol. Sem., 2002. Mem. Internat. Orgn. for Septuagint and Cognate Studies, Smithsonian Instsn., Nat. Geog. Soc., U.S. Chess Fedn., Iowa State Chess Assn. (v.p. 1984-85, dir. postal tournament 1987-97). Mem. Ref. Ch. In Am. Avocations: chess, bridge. Home and Office: 520 2nd St SW Orange City IA 51041-1728 E-mail: scorza@nwciowa.edu.

SCOTT, BRUCE A., otolaryngologist; b. Louisville, Ky., Sept. 30, 1961; m. Christy Scott; 3 children. MD, U. Tex., 1987. Diplomate Am. Bd. Otolaryngology. Intern Sealy Hosp.-U. Galveston, 1987-88; resident in otolaryngology and head and neck surgery U. Tex. Med. Br., Galveston, 1988-92; fellow in facial plastic and reconstructive surgery U. Tex. Health Sci. Ctr., Houston, 1992-93; pvt. practice Lousiville. Tee-ball, baseball coach, basketball coach. Mem. AMA (bd. trustees, com. on membership, nominating com., AMA Found., mem. resident physician sect. governing coun., chairperson, young physician sect. governing coun., del. to ho. of dels. 1997, 98, mem. surg. caucus exec. com., reference com., mem. women in medicine adv. panel, Outreach Awards). Avocations: golf, flying radio control planes.

SCOTT, DEBORAH EMONT, curator; b. Passaic, NJ; d. Harold and Rhoda (Baumgarten) Emont; m. George Andrew Scott, June 4, 1983; children: Meredith Suzanne, Diana Faith. BA, Rutgers U., 1973, Livingston Coll.; MA, Oberlin Coll., 1979. Asst. curator Allen Meml. Art Mus., Oberlin, Ohio, 1977-79; curator collections Memphis Brooks Mus. Art, 1979-83; curator The Nelson-Atkins Mus. Art, Kansas City, 1983—, chief curator, 1998—. Project dir. Kansas City Sculpture Pk., 1986-01. Author: (catalogue) Alan Shields, 1983, (essay) Jonathan Borofsky, 1988, (essay) Judith Shea, 1989, (interview) John Ahearn, 1990, (essay) Gerhard Richter, 1990, (essay) Kathy Muehlemann, 1991, (essay) Nate Fors, 1991, (essay) Julian Schnabel, 1991, (essay) Louise Bourgeois, 1994, (essay) Joel Shapiro, 1995, (essay) Lewis deSoto, 1996, (catalogue) Ursula von Rydingsvard, 1997; contbr.: Celebrating Moore: Works from the Collection of the Henry Moore Foundation, Selected by David Mitchinson, 1998, Modern Sculpture at The Nelson-Atkins Museum of Art: An Anniversary Celebration, 1999, (CD ROM) Masterworks for Learning: A College Collection Catalogue, Allen Memorial Art Museum, Oberlin College, 1998. Office: Nelson-Atkins Mus Art 4525 Oak St Kansas City MO 64111-1873

SCOTT, DELBERT LEE, state legislator; Rep. Mo. State House Reps. Dist. 119. Home: PO Box 147 700 W 7th St Lowry City MO 64763-9550 Office: Mo House of Reps State Capitol Jefferson City MO 65101

SCOTT, JIM, radio personality; b. Bridgeport, Conn. m. Donna Scott. With WSAI, Cin., 1968—84; radio host 700 WLW, Cin., 1984—. Active United Way, The Wellness Cmty. Recipient Marconi Radio award for Large Market Personality of Yr., Nat. Assn. Broadcasters, 2002. Avocation: running. Office: WLW 700 AM The Big One 8044 Montgomery Rd Cincinnati OH 45236-2919 Office Phone: 513-241-9597.

SCOTT, JOHN BELDON, art history educator, writer; BA in history, Ind. U., 1968; MA in art history, Rutgers U., 1975, PhD in art history, 1982. Lectr. U. Pa., 1981—82; asst. prof. to prof. art history U. Iowa, Iowa City, 1982—, Elizabeth M. Stanley Prof. of the Arts, 2004—, head art history divsn. Sch. Art and Art History. Vis. mem. Inst. Advanced Study, Princeton, NJ, 1991—92; mem. US Nat. Com. for the History of Art Internat. Congress of the History of Art, 2001—02. Author: Images of Nepotism: The Painted Ceilings of Palazzo Barberini, 1991, Architecture for the Shroud: Relic and Ritual in Turin, 2003 (Charles Rufus Morey Book Award, Coll. Art Assn., 2004), (articles have appeared in) Art Bulletin, Burlington Mag., Memoirs of Am. Acad. Rome, Storia dell'Arte, Jour. of the Warburg and Courtauld Institutes, Jour. of Soc. Archtl. Historians. Served USAF, 1969—73. Samuel H. Kress Found. Rome Prize Fellowship, Am. Acad. Rome, 1979—81, Gladys Krieble Delmas Found. for Venetian Studies Grant, 1979, Andrew W. Mellon Postdoctoral Rsch. Fellow, U. Pa., 1984—85, Rsch. Fellowship for Recent PhD Recipients, Am. Coun. Learned Societies, 1984, Am. Philos. Soc. Rsch. Grant, 1984, 1989, NEH Travel to Collections Grant, 1986, Gladys Krieble Delmas Found. for Venetian Studies Grant, 1986, Nat. Humanities Ctr. Fellow, 1993—94, Trinity Coll. Barbieri Grant in Italian History, Barbieri Endowment for Italian Culture, 1994, Marta Sutton Weeks Fellow, Stanford Humanities Ctr., Stanford U., 1999—2000, Graham Found. for Advanced Studies in the Visual Arts Rsch. Grant, 1999, Am. Philos. Soc. Sabbatical Fellowship, 2000. Mem.: Midwest Art History Soc. (bd. dirs. 1986—89), Coll. Art Assn. (bd. dirs. nominating com. 1998), Soc. Archtl. Historians (bd. dirs. 1997—2000). Office: U Iowa Sch Art and Art History 120 N Riverside Dr #100 Art Bldg Iowa City IA 52242-1706

SCOTT, JOHN E., state legislator; b. Charleston, Mo., July 24, 1939; Mem. Mo. Ho. Reps., Jefferson City, 1971-76, Mo. Senate from 3rd dist., Jefferson City, 1977—. Office: Mo Senate State Capitol Rm 416 Jefferson City MO 65101

SCOTT, JOHN JOSEPH, lawyer; b. Chgo., Dec. 30, 1950; s. John Joseph and Alice (Pierzhala) S.; m. Maria Crawford, Aug. 17, 1974. BA, Yale U., 1972; JD, U. Chgo., 1975. Bar: Ill. 1975, U.S. Dist. Ct. (no. dist.) Ill. 1976. Assoc. Kirkland & Ellis, Chgo., 1975-82, ptnr., 1982-91; asst. gen. counsel CF Industries Holdings, Inc., Deerfield, Ill., 1991—2006, sr. litig. counsel, 2006—. Mem. ABA, Chgo. Bar Assn., Order of Coif. Roman Catholic. Avocations: reading, swimming, bike riding, playing tennis. Office: CF Industries Holdings Inc 4 Parkway North Ste 400 Deerfield IL 60015-2590

SCOTT, KAREN BONDURANT, consumer catalog company executive; b. East Orange, NJ, June 4, 1946; d. Walter James and Wanda (French) Schmidt; m. Ian James Anderson, May 12, 1982; children: Steven, Michael. BS, U. Mass., 1968; MBA, Northwestern U., 1977. Bus. analyst Dun & Bradstreet, NYC, 1968-69; asst. mgr. Shay Med. Employment, Chgo., 1970-72; mgr. recruitment Michael Reese Med. Ctr., Chgo., 1972-76; brand mgmt., new bus. devel., dir. mergers & acquisitions Kraft Foods, Inc., Glenview, Ill., 1977-95; pres. Chelsea & Scott dba One Step Ahead, Lake Bluff, Ill., 1987—. Sec.-treas. adv. bd. Lincolnshire (Ill.) Nursery Sch., 1987-89; co-leader Boy Scouts Am., Lincolnshire, 1991. Mem. Juvenile Product Mfrs. Assn. (new product judge 1992-99, speaker nat. catalog conf.), at. Assn. Women Bus. Owners (mem. Lake Forest cmty. task force). Office: Chelsea & Scott Ltd 75 Albrecht Dr Lake Bluff IL 60044-2226

SCOTT, MARTHA G., state legislator; b. Ware Shoals, SC, Nov. 10, 1935; d. Harold and Pearl (Wardlaw) Smith; children: Marion Jr., Deborah Ann Gilmore. Student, Highland Park Jr. Coll., 1952-54; DHH, Tenn. Sch. Religion, 1990; DHL, Urban Bible Inst., Detroit, 1994. With Mich. Bell Telephone Co., 1960-86; rep. Mich. Ho. of Reps. Mem. Mich. State Dem. Ctrl. Com., 1974-82; commr. Wayne County Bd. Commrs., 1977-80, chairwoman Human Resources Com., 1978-80; vice chairwoman Wayne County Civil Svc. Commn., 1980-82; pres. Highland Park City Coun., 1984-87; mayor City of Highland Park, 1988; Dem. precinct del. 1st Congl. Dist.; bd. dirs. Nat. Coun. Alcoholism and Other Dependencies, 1979, Detroit Osteopathic Hosp., 1990; vice chairwoman Mich. Women in Mcpl. Govt.; founding mem. Nat. Polit. Congress Black Women; adv. bd. Met. Region Bus. Alliance; vol. Residential Care Alternatives. Recipient Plaque Highland Park Sch. Bd., 1977, Nat. Polit. Congress of Black Women award, 1981, Resolution, Wayne County Bd. Commrs., 1981, Wayne County Auditors, 1981, Dollars and Sense Mag. award, 1989, Spl. Achievement award Amvets, Golden Heritage award for excellence in svc., 1988, Cmty. Svc. award Knoxville Coll. Alumni, 1988. Mem. Gamma Phi Delta. Office: Michigan House of Reps State Capitol Lansing MI 48909

SCOTT, NORMAN LAURENCE, engineering consultant; b. Meadow Grove, Nebr., Oct. 17, 1931; s. Laurence Ray Scott and Ruth Louise Braun; m. Joan Culbertson, Jan. 21, 1956; 1 child, Douglas Jay. BS in Civil Engring., U. Nebr., 1954. Registered profl. engr., Ill., Fla., Md., Minn., Va., Tex.; registered structural engr., Ill. Sales engr. R.H. Wright & Son, Ft. Lauderdale, Fla., 1956-58; mgr. Wright of Palm Beach, West Palm Beach, Fla., 1958-59; exec. sec. Prestressed Concrete Inst., Chgo., 1959-63; gen. mgr. Wiss, Janney, Elstner & Assoc., Northbrook, Ill., 1963-66; pres., chmn. The Consulting Engrs. Group Inc., Mt. Prospect, Ill., 1966—. 1st lt. USAF, 1954-56. Mem. ASCE (life), Am. Concrete Inst. (hon., pres. 1983-84, Henry C. Turner medal 1993), Ill. Soc. Profl. Engrs. (pres. orth Shore chpt. 1962). Republican. Office: The Consulting Engrs Group 55 E Euclid Ave Mount Prospect IL 60056-1283

SCOTT, NORMAN ROSS, electrical engineering educator; b. NYC, May 15, 1918; s. George Norman and Lillias B.H. (Ogg) S.; m. Marjorie M. Fear, Apr. 6, 1950; children: Mari, George, Ian, Charles. BS, MS, MIT, 1941; PhD, U. Ill., 1950. Asst. prof. elec. engring. U. Ill., Urbana, 1946-50; asst. prof. to prof. elec. engring. U. Mich., Ann Arbor, 1951-87, assoc dean Coll. Engring., 1965-68, dean Dearborn Campus, 1968-71, prof. emeritus of elec. engring. and computer sci., 1987—. Cons. Nat. Cash Register Co., Dayton, 1956-65; mem. math. and computer sci. rsch. adv. com. AEC, Washington, 1961-63. Editor-in-chief IEEE Trans. on Computers, N.Y.C., 1961-65; author: Analog and Digital Computer Technology, 1959, Electronic Computer Technology, 1970, Computer Number Systems and Arithmetic, 1985. Maj. U.S. Army, 1941-46. Fellow IEEE. Home: 2260 Gale Rd Ann Arbor MI 48105-9512 Office: U Mich EECS Dept Ann Arbor MI 48109

SCOTT, ROBERT LEE, speech educator; b. Fairbury, Nebr., Apr. 19, 1928; s. Walter Everett and Ann Maria (Jensen) S.; m. Betty Rose Foust, Sept. 13, 1947; children— Mark Allen, Janet Lee, Paul Matthew. BA, U. No. Colo., 1950; MA, U. Nebr., 1951; PhD, U. Ill., 1955. Asst. prof. speech U. Houston, 1953-57; asst. prof. U. Minn., 1957-59, assoc. prof., 1959-63, prof., 1963-2000, prof. emeritus, 2000—, chair dept. speech communication, 1971-89, chair dept. Spanish and Portuguese, 1992-94, dir. Sch. Journalism and Mass Comm., 1995-97. Author: Rhetoric of Black Power, 1969, Moments in the Rhetoric of the Cold War, 1970; contbr. articles to profl. jours. Recipient Teaching award Coll. of Liberal Arts, U. Minn., 1981. Mem. Nat. Comm. Assn. (editor Quar. Jour. Speech 1971-74, Winans-Wichelns Rsch. award 1970, Charles H. Woolbert Rsch. award, 1981, Douglas-Ehninger Disting. Scholar award 1989, Disting. Scholar of Assn. 1992), Ctrl. States Speech Assn., Internat. Soc. for Study of Rhetoric. Office: U Minn Dept Comm Studies 268 Ford Hall 224 Church St S3 Minneapolis MN 55455 E-mail: scott033@umn.edu.

SCOTT, SAMUEL C., food products executive; B in Engring., Fairleigh Dickinson U., 1966, MBA. V.p. CPC Internat. Inc., 1991; pres. N. Am. corn refining Bestfoods, 1989—97, pres. worldwide corn refining, 1995-97; pres., COO Corn Products Internat., Westchester, Ill., 1997—2001, chmn., pres., CEO, 2001—. Bd. dir. Motorola Inc. Dir. ACCION USA; trustee Chgo. Symphony. Office: Corn Products International 5 Westbrook Corporate Ctr Westchester IL 60154

SCOTT, SHIRLEY CLAY, dean; PhD, Kent State U., 1973. Dean Grad. Coll. Western Mich. U.; dean Coll. Liberal Arts Southern Ill. U., 1999—, prof. Office: Office of the Dean Coll Liberal Arts So Illinios U Mailcode 4522 Carbondale IL 62901 Office Phone: 618-453-2466. E-mail: scotts@siu.edu.

SCOTT, STUART L., real estate company executive; b. Montreal; s. David George and Jean (Lothian) S.; m. Anne O'Laughlin, Nov. 26, 1982; children: Alexis L., Sarah Scott Tornes, Charity A., Christina A., Fiona L., Christopher G., Phoebe B. BA in Enlish Lit., Hamilton Coll., 1961; JD, Northwestern U., 1964. Atty. SEC, 1964-66; sr. v.p., asst. to chmn., bd. dirs. Arthur Rubloff & Co., 1966-73; pres. Equity Assocs., Inc. div. LaSalle Ptnrs., Inc., Chgo., 1973-75; from pres. to chmn., CEO LaSalle Ptnrs., Inc., Chgo., 1975—99; chmn. Jones Lang LaSalle Inc., Chgo., 2002—, interim CEO, pres., 2004. Bd. dirs. Hartmarx Corp., LaSalle Hotel Properties. Bd. dirs. Rehab. Inst. Chgo., chmn. 8 yrs.; charter trustee Hamilton Coll., Clinton, N.Y.; trustee Lyric Opera Chgo. Named Real Estate Exec. of Yr. 1998, Comml. Property World. Mem. Chgo. Club, Econ. Club Chgo., Comml. Club Chgo., Old Elm Club. Office: Jones Lang LaSalle Inc 200 E Randolph Dr Chicago IL 60601

SCOTT, TILLIAN PETER, corporate financial executive; b. Topeka, Dec. 11, 1963; s. Donald and Betty Scott; m. Joyce James, Sept. 5, 1995; 1 child, Ronald. BA in Acctg., Wichita State U., Kans., 1990, MBA, 1992. CPA 1992. Accountant Meriks Holdings LLC, Wichita, 1992—94, acct. exec., 1994—96, sr. acct. exec., 1996—2004, v.p. acctg., 2004—. EMT Wichita Vol. EMS, 1990—92; scout master Boy Scouts Am., Wichita, 2002—. Sgt. US Army, 1982—86, Ft. Campbell, Ky. Decorated Disting. Svc. medal US Army. Mem.: AICPA, BBB, Amvets. Republican. Roman Catholic. Avocations: hunting, hiking, fishing, poker. Office: Meriks Holdings LLC 2250 N Rock Rd #118-269 Wichita KS 67226-2304

SCOTT, WALTER, JR., telecommunications industry executive; b. May 21, 1931; m. Suzanne Scott. BS, Colo. State U., 1953; LittD, U. Nebr., 1983; LHD, Coll. St. Mary, 1988; D of Commerce, Bellevue U., 1996. With Peter Kiewit Sons, Inc., Omaha, 1953—, engr., project engr., dist. engr., Cleve. dist., 1959—61, asst. dist. mgr., Cleve. dist., 1961—62, dist. mgr. Cleve. dist. Omaha, 1962-64, v.p., 1964, exec. v.p., 1965-79, chmn. bd., 1964, pres., 1979, chmn. bd. dirs., pres., CEO, 1979-97, chmn. emeritus, 1997—; chmn. Level 3 Communications Inc. (former subs. PKS), Broomfield, Colo., 1997—. Bd. trustee Open World Leadership Ctr.; dir. Berkshire Hathaway, Burlington Resources, Commonwealth Telephone Enterprises, MidAmerican Energy Holdings, RCN Corp., Valmont Industries. Served with USAF, 1954-56. Named Philanthropist of Yr., Nat. Soc. Fund-Raising Execs., 1987, Man of Yr., Mid-Am. Coun. Boy Scouts Am., 1988, King Ak-Sar-Ben XCII, Knights of Ak-Sar-Ben, 1988, Disting. Eagle Scout, Boy Scouts Am., 1991, Citizen of Yr., United Way of the Midlands, 1993, Air Force Assn., 1993, Person of Yr., Pmaha Club, 1996; named one of Forbes Richest Americans, 2006; named to Nebr. Bus. Hall Fame, Nebr. C. of C. and Industry, 1995, Omaha Bus. Hall Fame, Greater Omaha C. of C., 1995; recipient Nebr. Builder award, U. Nebr., 1983, Outstanding Achievement in Construction award, The Moles, 1986, Brotherhood award, Nat. Conf. Christians and Jews, 1986, Horatio Alger award, Horatio Alger Assn., 1997, Spirit Youth award, Uta Halee Girls Village, 1988, Perry W. Branch Disting. Svc. award, U. Nebr. Found., 1989, Golden Beaver for Mgmt., The Beavers, 1990, Order of Tower, U. Nebr., Omaha, 1991, Golden Plate award, Am. Acad. Achievement, 1991, Golden Apple award, Met. Cmty. Coll. Found., 1993, Headliner award, Greater Omaha C. of C., 1996, Nebraskalander award, Nebraskaland Found., 1998, Manresa award, Creighton U., 1998, Cmty. Builder award, Greater Omaha C. of C., 1999, Bus. Vol. of Yr., Nat. Alliance Bus., 1999, Midlander of Yr., Omaha World-Herald, 2000. Mem.: Chi Epsilon Soc. (hon.). Office: Peter Kiewit Sons Inc 1000 Kiewit Plz Omaha NE 68131-3302 also: Joslyn Art Mus 2200 Dodge St Omaha NE 68102-1208 Office: Level 3 Communications Inc 1025 Eldorado Blvd Broomfield CO 80021

SCOTT, WALTER DILL, management educator; b. Chgo., Oct. 27, 1931; s. John Marcy and Mary Louise (Gent) S.; m. Barbara Ann Stein, Sept. 9, 1961; children: Timothy Walter, David Frederick, Gordon Charles. Student, Williams Coll., Williamstown, Mass., 1949-51; BS, Northwestern U., Evanston, Ill., 1953; MS, Columbia U., NYC, 1958. Cons. Booz, Allen & Hamilton, NYC, 1956—58; assoc. Glore, Forgan & Co., NYC, 1958—63, ptnr. Chgo., 1963-65; pntr. Lehman Bros, Chgo., 1965-72, sr. ptnr., 1972-73, also bd. dirs.; assoc. dir. econs. and govt. Office Mgmt. and Budget, Washington, 1973-75; sr. v.p. internat. and fin. Pillsbury Co., Mpls., 1975-78, exec. v.p., 1978-80, also bd. dirs.; pres., CEO, Investors Diversified Svcs., Inc., Mpls., 1980-84; group mng. dir. Grand Met. PLC, Mpls., 1984-86, also bd. dirs.; chmn. Grand Met USA, Mpls., 1984-86; prof., sr. Austin fellow Kellogg Sch. Mgmt., Northwestern U., Evanston, Ill., 1988—. Bd. dirs. Intermatic, Inc.; chmn. Good News Ptnrs. Mem. adv. bd. dirs. Chgo. Cmtys. in Schs.; bd. dirs. Ctr. Exec. Women. Lt. (j.g.) USN, 1953—56. Office: Northwestern U Kellogg Sch Mgmt 2001 Sheridan Rd Evanston IL 60208-0814 Business E-Mail: wds@kellogg.northwestern.edu.

SCOUTON, DAVID EARL, lawyer; b. Jan. 17, 1970; BS in Biochemistry, St. Cloud State U., 1994; JD with honors, U. Minn., 2000. Bar: Minn. 2000. Sr. assoc. Foley & Mansfield, P.L.L.P., Mpls. Named Rising Star, Minn. Super Lawyers mag., 2006. Mem.: Def. Rsch. Inst., Hennepin County Bar Assn., Minn. State Bar Assn. Office: Foley & Mansfield PLLP 250 Marquette Ave Ste 1200 Minneapolis MN 55401 Office Phone: 612-349-9846. E-mail: dscouton@foleymansfield.com.

SCOVANNER, DOUGLAS A., retail executive; BS, Washington and Lee U., 1977; MBA, U. Va., 1979. With Coca-Cola Enterprises and affiliates, Atlanta, 1980-92, v.p., treas., 1989-92; sr. v.p. fin. Fleming Cos., Oklahoma City, 1992-94; sr. v.p. fin., CFO Target Corp., Mpls., 1994—2000, exec. v.p., CFO, 2000—. Trustee Darden Sch. Found. U. Va. Darden Grad. Sch. Bus. Adminstrn.; vice chmn. exec. com. Minn. Orchestral Assn.; bd. mem. Greater Met. Housing Corp. Office: Target Corp 1000 Nicollett Mall Minneapolis MN 55403-2467

SCOVILLE, JAMES GRIFFIN, industrial relations professor; b. Amarillo, Tex., Mar. 19, 1940; s. Orlin James and Carol Howe (Griffin) S.; m. Judith Ann Nelson, June 11, 1962; 1 child, Nathan James. BA, Oberlin Coll., 1961; MA, Harvard U., 1963, PhD, 1965. Economist ILO, Geneva, 1965-66; instr. econs. Harvard U., Cambridge, Mass., 1964-65, asst. prof., 1966-69; assoc. prof. econs. and labor and indsl. relations U. Ill.-Urbana, 1969-75, prof., 1975-80; prof. indsl. rels. Indsl. Rels. Ctr., U. Minn., Mpls., 1979—, dir., 1979-82, dir. grad. studies, 1990-97. Cons. ILO, World Bank, U.S. Dept. Labor, Orgn. for Econ. Cooperation and Devel., USAID; labor-mgmt. arbitrator. Author: The Job Content of the US Economy, 1940-70, 1969, Perspectives on Poverty and Income Distribution, 1971, Manpower and Occupational Analysis: Concepts and Measurements, 1972, (with A. Sturmthal) The International Labor Movement in Transition, 1973, Status Influences in 3rd World Labor Markets, 1991, (with H. Buds) The Ethics of Human Resources and Industrial Relations, 2005. Mem. Am. Econ. Assn., Indsl. Rels. Rsch. Assn. (v.p. internat. sect. 1998, pres. 1999), Internat. Indsl. Rels. Assn. Office: U Minn Ind Rels Ctr 3-289 CSOM Minneapolis MN 55455 Office Phone: 612-624-1579. Business E-Mail: jscoville@csom.umn.edu.

SCOVILLE, JOSEPH GIACOMO, federal magistrate, judge; b. 1949; BA with high honors, Mich. State U., 1971; JD magna cum laude, U. Mich., 1974. Bar: Ill. 1974, U.S. Dist. Ct. (no. dist.) Ill. 1974, Mich. 1976, U.S. Dist. Ct. (we. dist.) Mich. 1976, U.S. Supreme Ct. 1981. Assoc. McDermott, Will & Emery, Chgo., 1974-76; ptnr. Warner, Norcross & Judd, Grand Rapids, Mich., 1976-88; magistrate judge U.S. Dist. Ct. (we. dist.) Mich., Grand Rapids, 1988—. Mem. Fed. Bar Assn., Mich. State Bar, Grand Rapids Bar Assn. Office: US Dist Ct We Dist Mich 685 Fed Bldg 110 Michigan St NW Grand Rapids MI 49503-2313 Fax: (616) 456-2074. E-mail: scoville@miwd.uscourts.gov.

SCOZZIE, JAMES ANTHONY, chemist; b. Erie, Pa., Nov. 3, 1943; AB, Gannon Coll., 1965; MS, Case Western Res. U., 1968, PhD in Chemistry, 1970. Jr. rsch. chemist ctrl. rsch. dept. Lord Corp., 1965; rsch. chemist Diamond Shamrock Corp., 1970-72, sr. rsch. chemist, 1972-76, rsch. supr. pharmaceutics, 1976-78, group leader agrl. chemistry, 1978-81, assoc. dir. agrl. chemistry rsch., 1981-83; dir. agrl. chemistry rsch. SDS Biotech Corp., 1983-85, dir. corp. rsch., 1985—; pres. Ricerca, Inc., Painesville, Ohio, 1986-2000, Ricerca LLC, Painesville, Ohio, 2000—. Chmn. bd. trustees State of Ohio Edison Biotechnology Ctr.; bd. governance Edison Biotechnology Inst. Mem. Am. Chem. Soc. Achievements include research in structure and chemistry of peptide antibiotics, synthesis of biologically active compounds, pesticides, process studies of organic compounds, commercial evaluation, nutrition and animal health, herbicides, plant growth regulants, cardiovascular agents and anti-inflammatory agents. Office: Ricerca LLC PO Box 1000 7528 Auburn Rd Painesville OH 44077-9603

SCRIMSHAW, SUSAN CROSBY, academic administrator; b. Nov. 12, 1945; m. Allan Stern; 1 child from previous marriage, Mary Corey March. AB, Barnard Coll., 1967; MA, Columbia U., 1969, PhD in Anthropology, 1974. Rsch. assoc. Internat. Inst. for Study of Human Reporduction, 1969—75; asst. prof. health adminstrn. Columbia U., 1975; asst. prof. pub. health Div. Population, Family and Internat. Health, Sch. Pub. Health UCLA, 1975—80, assoc. prof. Div. Population and Family Health, 1980—85, assoc. dir. Latin Am. Ctr., 1984—88, prof. pub. health and anthropology, 1985—96, acting chair Dept. Pub. Health, 1988—89, assoc. dean Academic Programs, 1988—94, acting dean, 1991—92, 1992—93; dean, prof. cmty. heath scis. and anthropology U. Ill. Sch. Pub. Health, Chgo., 1995—2006; pres. Simmons Coll., Boston, 2006—. Co-editor: The Handbook of Social Studies in Health & Med. Recipient Margaret Mead award, 1985. Fellow: AAAS; mem.: at. Soc. Med. Anthropology (pres. 1985), Soc. Applied Anthropology, Am. Anthropology Assn., Inst. Medicine NAS (coun. mem. 2006—). Office: Simmons Coll Office of Pres 300 The Fenway Boston MA 02115

SCRIVEN, JOHN G., retired lawyer, retired chemical company executive; Bar: Mich. 1993. Sr. staff counsel Dow Europe S.A., 1981-83; gen. counsel Dow Chem. Co., Midland, Mich., 1983-86, v.p., gen. counsel, 1986-2000, v.p., gen. counsel, sec., 1986-2000; ret., 2000. Office: Dow Chem Co 2030 Dow Ctr Midland MI 48674-0001

SCRIVNER, THOMAS WILLIAM, lawyer; b. Madison, Wis., Sept. 10, 1948; s. William H. and Jane (Gehrz) S.; m. Meredith Burke, Aug. 16, 1980; children: Allison, David. AB, Duke U., 1970, MAT, 1972; JD, U. Wis., 1977. Assoc. Michael, Best & Friedrich LLP, Milw., 1978-85, ptnr., 1985—. Mem. ABA, Wis. Bar Assn., Milw. Bar Assn. (labor sect.), Corp. Practice Inst. (pres. 1989-92). Episcopalian. Home: 4626 N Cramer St Milwaukee WI 53211-1203 Office: Michael Best & Friedrich LLP 100 E Wisconsin Ave Ste 3300 Milwaukee WI 53202-4108 Home Phone: 414-332-1377; Office Phone: 414-271-6560. Business E-Mail: twscrivner@michaelbest.com.

SCULFIELD, TONY, radio personality, comedian; Weekday morning show radio host, weekend afternoon radio host Sta. WGCI-FM, Chgo. Comedian (comedy shows) HBO Russell Simmons' Def Comedy All Star Jam, BET Comic View, (numerous other comedy acts).

SCULLION, ROSEMARIE, literature educator; PhD, Univ. Wis., Madison. Assoc. prof. women's studies & French Univ. Iowa. Co-editor: Celine and the Politics of Difference, 1995, Studies in Twentieth Century Literature, South Central Rev. Substance; contbr. articles to profl. jours. Mem.: Modern Lang. Assn. Am. (exec. coun. 2000—). Office: Univ Iowa 716 Jefferson Bldg 467 Phillips Hall Iowa City IA 52242 E-mail: rosemarie-scullion@uiowa.edu.

SCURRY, BRIANA COLLETTE, professional soccer player; b. Mpls., Sept. 7, 1971; BS in Polit. Sci., U. Mass., 1995. Goalkeeper U.S. Women's Nat. Soccer Team, Chgo., 1994—99, 2002—; profl. soccer player Atlanta Beat (WUSA), 2001—03. Mem. U.S. Olympic Soccer Team, Athens, 2004. Named Goalkeeper of Yr., Mo. Athletic Club Sports Found., 1993; recipient Gold medal, Atlanta Olympics, 1996, Athens Olympic games, 2004, World Cup champion, 1999, Silver medal, Sydney Olympic Games, 2000. Office: US Soccer Fedn US Soccer House 1801 S Prairie Ave Chicago IL 60616-1319

SEABAUGH, WILLIAM F., lawyer; BS magna cum laude, U. Mo., 1978; JD magna cum laude, U. Mich., 1981. Bar: Mo. 1981. Ptnr., group co-leader Transactions Bryan Cave LLP, St. Louis. Office: Bryan Cave LLP One Metropolitan Sq 211 N Broadway, Ste 3600 Saint Louis MO 63102 Office Phone: 314-259-2450. E-mail: wfseabaugh@bryancave.com.

SEAGREN, ALICE, school system administrator, former state legislator; b. 1947; m. Fred Seagren; 2 children, Christina and Greg. BS in Mktg., SE Mo. State U. Mem. Bloomingdale Sch. Bd., 1989—92; Minn. state repr., Dist. 41A Minn. Ho. of Reps., 1992—2002, chmn. K-12 edn. fin. com., 1999—2004, former mem., Edu. Policy, Local Govt & Met. Affairs & Ways & Means, Transportation Policy Committees; former chair Edu. Com., Nat. Coun. of State Legislatures, Assembly of State Issues; commr. of edn. State of Minn., 2004—. Active Bloomington (Minn.) Sch. Bd., 1989-92; bd. dir. Normandale Cmty. Coll. Found., Fraser Cmty. Services Mem. Bloomington C. of C. (bd. dirs. 1990-92), Phi Gamma Nu, Alpha Chi Omega. Republican. Home: 9730 Palmer Cir Bloomington MN 55437-2017 Office: Minn Dept Children, Famlies, Learning 1500 Highway 36 W Roseville MN 55113-4035 Office Phone: 651-582-8204. E-mail: mde.commissioner@state.mn.us.

SEALL, STEPHEN ALBERT, lawyer; b. South Bend, Ind., Oct. 24, 1940; s. Stephen Henry and Mildred Rita (MacDonald) S.; m. Barbara Ann Halloran, June 25, 1966; children: John Paul, Edward Andrew, Ann Marie. BA, Purdue U., 1963; postgrad., Cornell U. Grad. Sch. Bus. Adminstrn., 1963; LLB, U. Notre Dame, 1966. Bar: Ind. 1966, U.S. Claims Ct. 1973, U.S. Tax Ct. 1968, U.S. Ct. Appeals (6th cir.) 1980, U.S. Ct. Appeals (7th cir.) 1969, U.S. Supreme Ct. 1973. Assoc. Thornburg, McGill, Deahl, Harman, Carey & Murray, South Bend, 1966-71; ptnr. Barnes & Thornburg LLP and predecessor firm Thornburg, McGill, Deahl, Harman, Carey & Murray, 1972—2005, vice chmn. and mgmt. com., mng. ptnr. South Bend office, 1985—2001. Spkr. in field. (Mem. editl. bd.) Notre Dame Law Rev., 1964—66. Mem. Mayor's Com. on Downtown Devel., South Bend, 1975-77, Mayor's Com. on Utilization of Downtown Bldgs., South Bend, 1988-96; trustee Project Future, South Bend, 1986-2002; exec. com. Meml. Hosp. South Bend, Inc., 1999-2003; dir. Meml. Health Found., 1992-98, Meml. Health Sys., 1997-2003, United Way of St. Joseph County, Inc., 1992-98, Conv. and Tourism Industry Coun., 1994-2000, CASIE Ctr., Inc., 1998-2006, Home Mgmt. Resources, Inc. 2003-06. Fellow Am. Coll. Tax Counsel, Am. Bar Found., Ind. Bar Found.; mem. ABA (taxation sect.), Ind. State Bar Assn. (chmn. taxation sect. 1977-78), Summit Club (chmn. 1976-77), Morris Park Country Club (bd. dirs., sec. 1998-2001). Democrat. Roman Catholic. Avocations: golf, softball, weightlifting. Office: Barnes & Thornburg LLP 600 1st Source Bank Ctr 100 N Michigan St Ste 600 South Bend IN 46601-1632 Home: 245 Martellago Dr North Venice FL 34275-6710 Office Phone: 574-233-1171.

SEAMAN, IRVING, JR., banker; b. Milw., July 14, 1923; s. Irving and Anne (Douglas) S.; m. June Carry, June 24, 1950, (dec. 2001); children: Peter Stewart, Marion Carry, Terry Osborne, Anne Douglas; m. Barbara P. Gardner, May 22, 2002. BA, Yale U., 1944. With Continental Ill. Nat. Bank & Trust Co., Chgo., 1947-61, v.p., 1959-61; pres., chief exec. officer, dir. Nat. Boulevard Bank, Chgo., 1961-65, chmn. exec. com., chief exec. officer, dir., 1966-76; vice chmn. bd., dir. Sears Bank and Trust Co., Chgo., 1976-77, pres., chief operating officer, dir., 1977-82; sr. cons. Burson-Marsteller, Chgo., 1982-94. Chmn. bd. Associated Bank Chgo., 1985-05. Mem. Northwestern U. Assn.; life mem. bd. dirs.

Lake Forest Hosp.; bd. dirs. United Way of Chgo., 1975-89, pres., 1979; bd. dirs. United Way/Crusade of Mercy, 1980-89, 94-95, vice chmn., 1980-81; trustee Chgo. Symphony Orch., 1987—. Lt. (j.g.) USNR, WWII. Mem. Commonwealth Club, Econ. Club, Chgo. Club, Comml. Club, Racquet Club, Onwentsia Club, Old Elm Club, Shoreacres Club, Augusta Nat. Golf Club, Sawgrass Country Club. Home: 666 N Sheridan Rd Lake Forest IL 60045-1410

SEAMAN, WILLIAM CASPER, retired news photographer; b. Grand Island, Nebr., Jan. 19, 1925; s. William H. and Minnie (Cords) S.; m. Ruth Witwer, Feb. 14, 1945; 1 son, Lawrence William. Grad. high sch. Photographer Leschinsky Studio, Grand Island; news photographer Mpls. Star & Tribune, 1945-82; ret., 1982. Recipient Pulitzer prize, 1959; also awards Nat. Headliners Club; also awards Nat. Press Photographers Assn.; also awards Inland Daily Press Assn.; also awards Kent State U.; also awards Mo. U.; also awards Local Page One; State A.P. contest; Silver Anniversary award Honeywell Photog. Products, 1975 Mem. Nat. Press Photographers Assn., Sigma Delta Chi.

SEARLES, LYNN MARIE, community health nurse; b. Cherryvale, Kans., Oct. 29, 1949; d. Darrell Eugene and Beva Caroline (Waller) Stringer; m. Martin Dale Searles, Aug. 23, 1970; children: Jeremy Dale, Michelle Le Anne. A in Fine Arts, Labette Cmty. Jr. Coll., Parsons, Kans., 1969, ADN, 1970. RN Kans., Calif. Evening med.-surg. charge nurse Coffeyville (Kans.) Meml. Hosp., 1970-72, med.-surg. head nurse, 1972-73, relief evening house supr. and emergency rm. nurse, 1974, head nurse recovery rm., 1974-81; head nurse recovery rm., ambulatory care unit Coffeyville Meml. Med. Ctr., 1981-83, head nurse recovery rm., ambulatory care unit and surgery, 1983-84; dir. family planning, rural home health aide and multi phasic screening clinics, AIDS edn. and counseling Jefferson County Health Dept., Oskaloosa, Kansas, 1984-87; health facility surveyor Kans. Dept. Health and Environ., Topeka, 1988—2004, edn. coord., risk mgmt. specialist, 2004—. Mem.: Am. Soc. Post Anesthesia Nurses (charter), Kans. Pub. Health Assn., Nazarene Healthcare Fellowship. Republican. Nazarene Ch. Avocations: needlecrafts, gardening, interior decorating.

SEARLS, EILEEN HAUGHEY, retired lawyer, law librarian, educator; b. Madison, Wis., Apr. 27, 1925; d. Edward M. and Anna Mary (Haughey) S. BA, U. Wis., 1948, JD, 1950, MS in LS, 1951. Bar: Wis. 1950. Cataloger Yale U., 1951-52; instr. law St. Louis U., 1952-53, asst. prof., 1953-56, assoc. prof., 1956-64, prof., 1964-2000, law libr., 1952-2000. Chmn. Coun. Law Libr. Consortia, 1984-90; sec. Bd. of Conciliaton and Arbitration, Archdiocese of St. Louis, 1986-98. amed Woman of Yr. Women's Commn., St. Louis U., 1986. Mem. ABA, ALA, Wis. Bar Assn., Bar Assn. Met. St. Louis, Am. Assn. Law Librs. (Marian Gould Gallagher Disting. Svc. award 1999), Mid Am. Assn. Law Librs. (pres. 1984-86), Mid Am. Law Sch. Libr. Consortium (chmn. 1980-84), Southwestern Assn. Law Librs., Altrusa Club. Office: 3700 Lindell Blvd Saint Louis MO 63108-3412 Business E-Mail: searlseh@slu.edu.

SEASE, GENE ELWOOD, communications executive; b. Portage, Pa., June 28, 1931; s. Grover Chauncey and Clara Mae (Over) S.; m. Joanne D. Cherry, July 20, 1952; children: David Gene, Daniel Elwood, Cheryl Joanne. AB, Juniata Coll., 1952; BD, Pitts. Theol. Sem., 1956, ThM, 1959; PhD, U. Pitts., 1965, MEd, 1958; LLD, U. Evansville, 1972, Butler U., 1972; LittD, Ind. State U., 1974; DD, U. Indpls., 1989. Ordained to ministry United Methodist Ch., 1956; pastor Grace United Meth. Ch., Wilkinsburg, Pitts., 1952-63; conf. dir., supt. Western Pa. Conf. United Meth. Ch., Pitts., 1963-68; lectr. grad. faculty U. Pitts., 1965-68; mem. staff U. Indpls., 1968-89, asst. to pres., 1968-69, pres., 1970-88, chancellor, 1988-89, pres. emeritus, 1989—; chmn. Sease, Gerig & Assocs., Indpls., 1989—. Bd. dirs. Bankers Life Ins. Co. of NY Author: Christian Word Book, 1968; also numerous articles. Pres. Greater Indpls. Progress Com., 1972-75, Marion County Sheriff's Merit Bd.; mem. Ind. Scholarship Commn.; cons. Time Warner; bd. dirs. Indpls. Conv. Bur., Ind. Law Enforcement Tng. Acad., 500 Festival, Crossroads coun. Boy Scouts Am., Community Hosp. Indpls., St. Francis Hosp.; chmn. Ind. State Fair Commn. Mem. Internat. Platform Assn., English Speaking Union, Japan-Am. Soc. Ind., Ind. C. of C. (bd. dirs.), Indpls. C. of C. (bd. dirs.), Ind. Schoolmen's Club, Ind. State Fair Commn. (chmn.), Econ. Club of Indpls. (bd. dirs.), Skyline Club (bd. dirs.), Phi Delta Kappa, Alpha Phi Omega, Alpha Psi Omega. Clubs: Mason (33 deg., Shriner), Kiwanian, Columbia. Office Phone: 317-634-1171.

SEATON, EDWARD LEE, editor, publishing executive; b. Manhattan, Kans., Feb. 5, 1943; s. Richard Melvin and Mary (Holton) Seaton; m. Karen Mathisen, Sept. 4, 1965; children: Edward Merrill, John David. AB cum laude, Harvard U., 1965; postgrad., U. Ctr., Quito, Ecuador, 1965-66, U. Mo., 1966—67. Staff writer Courier-Jour., Louisville, 1968—69; editor-in-chief, pub. Manhattan Mercury, 1969—. Bd. dirs., officer 8 newspaper and broadcasting affiliates; mem. Pulitzer Prize Bd., 1992—2001, chmn., 2001; mem. adv. com. Knight Internat. Press Fellowship Program, 1994—2006; mem. Cabot Awards bd. Columbia U., 1995—2003. Contbr. articles to profl. jours. Chmn. Alfred M. Landon lecture patrons Kans. State U.; chmn. Latin Am. Scholarship Program Am. Univs., Cambridge, Mass., 1986—87. Decorated comendador Order Christopher Columbus (Dominican Republic); recipient Cabot prize, Columbia U., 1993; Fulbright scholar, 1965. Mem.: Internat. Press Inst., Internat. Ctr. Journalists (bd. dirs. 1990—2001), Inter-Am. Press Assn. (pres. 1989—90, exec. com. 1976—), Am. Soc. Newspaper Editors (Found. pres. 1994—, pres. 1998—99), Kans. C. of C. and Industry (pres. 1987), Fly Club (Harvard U.). Avocations: tennis, cooking. Office: 318 N 5th St Manhattan KS 66505-0787

SEATON, VAUGHN ALLEN, retired veterinary pathology educator; b. Abilene, Kans., Oct. 11, 1928; m. Clara I. Bertelrud; children: Gregory S., Jeffrey T. BS, DVM, Kans. State U., 1954; MS, Iowa State U., 1957. Pvt. practice, Janesville, Wis., 1954; instr. pathology Vet. Diagnostic Lab. Iowa State U., Ames, 1954-57, from asst. to assoc. prof. pathology Vet. Disgnostic Lab., 1957-64, prof., head Vet. Diagnostic Lab., 1964-94. Lab. coord. regional emergency animal disease eradication orgn. Animal and Plant Health Inspection Svc. USDA, 1974—; mem. rsch. com. Iowa Beef Industry Coun., 1972-85; mem. adv. bd. Iowa State Water Resources Rsch. Inst., 1973-80; cons. several orgns. Co-author: (monographs) Feasibility Study of College of Veterinary Medicine, 1972, Veterinary Diagnostic Laboratory Facilities-State of New York, 1970; bd. dirs. Iowa State U. Press, 1985-88, mem. manuscript com., 1982-85; contbr. articles to profl. jours. Trustee Ames Pub. Libr., 1979-85; mem. Iowa State Bd. Health, 1971-77, v.p., 1976-77; bd. dirs. Masonic Edn. Found., 1985-88; v.p. Iowa Scottish Rite Masonic Found. Recipient Disting. Alumnus award, Coll. Vet. Medicine, Kans. State U., 2005. Mem. AVMA, Am. Assn. Vet. Lab. Diagnosticians (bd. govs. 1973-88, pres. 1968, E.P. Pope award 1980), Am. Coll. Vet. Toxicologists, U.S. Animal Health Assn., Iowa Vet. Med. Assn. (pres. 1971), North Ctrl. Assn. Vet. Lab. Diagnosticians, Western Vet. Conf. (exec. bd. 1986-90, v.p. 1994, pres.-elect 1995, pres. 1996), World Assn. Vet. Lab. Diagnosticians (pres. 1980-86), Ames C. of C. (bd. dirs. 1970-73), Phi Kappa Phi, Phi Zeta (pres. 1964), Alpha Zeta, Gamma Sigma Delta. Office: Iowa State U Coll Vet Medicine Vet Diagnostic Lab Ames IA 50011-0001

SEAVER, DERRICK, state representative; b. Oxford, Ohio, Feb. 6, 1982; Student, Wright State U., 2001—. State rep. dist. 78 Ohio Ho. of Reps., Columbus, 2000—, ranking minority mem., agr. and natural resources com., mem. edn. and ins. coms. Mem.: Auglaize County Dem. Exec. Com., Minster Civics Assn., Minster/New Bremen Area Right to Life, NAACP, NRA, Ohio Young Dems., Auglaize County Young Dems., Young Politicians of Am. Democrat. Office: 77 S High St Columbus OH 43215-6111

SEBELIUS, KATHLEEN GILLIGAN, governor; b. Cin., May 15, 1948; d. John J. and Mary K. (Dixon) Gilligan; m. Keith Gary Sebelius, 1974; children: Edward Keith, John McCall. BA, Trinity Coll., 1970; MA in Pub. Adminstrn., U. Kans., 1977. Dir. planning Ctr for Cmty. Justice, Washington, 1971—74; spl. asst. Kans. Dept. of Corrections, Topeka, 1975—78; exec. dir. Kans. Trial Lawyers Assn., 1978—86; mem. Kans. Ho. of Reps., 1987-95; ins. commr. State of Kans., 1995—2002, gov., 2003—. Founder Women's Polit. Caucus; precinct committeewoman, 1980-86; mayor, Potwin, 1985-87; appointed Presdl. adv. commn. consumer protection and quality in Health Care, 1997. Recipient Outstanding Elected Officer, Nat. Fedn. of Dem. Women, 1996, Breaking the Glass Ceiling, Women in Govt., 1997, Svc. Award, Kansas City YMCA. Mem.: Kans. Women's Political Caucus (founder), Nat. Assn. Ins. Commrs. (chair), Common Cause (state bd., nat. gov. bd. 1975—81), Kans. Kids Count (bd. mem.), Friends of Cedar Crest (bd. mem.). Democrat. Roman Catholic. Office: Office of the Gov State Capitol 2nd Fl Topeka KS 66612-1590 Office Fax: 785-296-7973.

SEBO, STEPHEN ANDREW, electrical engineer, educator, researcher, consultant; b. Budapest, Hungary, June 10, 1934; s. Emery Sebo and Elizabeth Thieben; m. Eva Agnes Vambery, May 25, 1968. MSEE, Budapest Poly-tech. U., 1957; PhD, Hungarian Acad. Sci., 1966. Engr. Budapest Elec. Co., 1957-61; asst. prof. Budapest Poly. U., 1961-66, assoc. prof., 1966-68, Ohio State U., Columbus, 1968-74, prof., 1974—82, Am. Electric Power prof. in power sys. engring., 1982—2003, Neal A. Smith prof., 1995—2003, prof. emeritus, 2003—. Recipient Power Educator award Edison Elec. Inst., 1981, Tech. Person of Yr. award Columbus Tech. Coun., 1994. Fellow IEEE (Prize Paper award 1981). Office: Ohio State U Elec Engring 2015 Neil Ave Columbus OH 43210-1272 Office Phone: 614-292-7410. Business E-Mail: sebo.1@osu.edu.

SECCHIA, PETER F., forest products executive, former United States ambassador to Italy; b. Englewood, NJ, Apr. 15, 1937; s. Charles P. and Valerie Margaret (Smith) Secchia; m. Joan Peterson, 1964; children: Mark, Charles, Sandra, Stephanie. BS in Econ., Mich. State U., 1963, HHD (hon.), 1997; AA (hon.), Grand Rapids Cmty. Coll., 1993; LLD (hon.), Grand Valley State U., 1990, Davenport Coll., 1993, Cooley Law Sch., 1993. Positions through v.p. sales Universal Forest Products, Grand Rapids, Mich., 1962—71, dir., 1967—, chmn., pres., CEO, 1971—89, chmn., 1993—2006, chmn. emeritus, 2006; U.S. Amb. to Italy, 1989—93. Chmn. River City Food Co.; mng. ptnr. SIBSCO LLC. Mem. exec. com. Gerald R. Ford Found., past chmn. endowment com.; trustee Bush Presdl. Libr. Found., James A. Baker III Inst. Pub. Policy, Rice Univ, John Cabot Univ., Rome; Mich. del. Rep. Nat. Convention, 1976, 1980, 1984; mem. Rep. Nat. Com., 1980—89, vice chmn. Midwest region, 1984—89; co-chmn. Dole for Pres. Nat. Campaign, 1995—96. Served to sgt. USMC, 1956—59. Named Master Entrepeneur of the Year for Mich., 1994, Businessman of the Year, Econ. Club We. Mich., 1995; recipient Cavaliere di Gran Croce, Govt. of Italy, Disting. Honor award, U.S. Dept. State, 1993, Louis A. Smith Disting. Jurist award, Cooley Law Sch., 1993, Michelangelo D'Oro Children of the World award, 1993, Peace award, Internat. Commn. for Peace. Mem.: Council of Am. Ambassadors. Republican. Methodist. Office: Universal Forest Products 2801 East Beltline NE Grand Rapids MI 49525

SECREST, PATRICIA K., state legislator; Rep. Mo. State House Reps. Dist. 93. Home: 723 Country Heights Ct Ballwin MO 63021-5623

SEDELMAIER, JOHN JOSEF, filmmaker; b. Orrville, Ohio, May 31, 1933; s. Josef Heinrich and Anne Isabel (Baughman) S.; m. Barbara Jean Frank, June 6, 1965; children: John Josef, Nancy Rachel, Adam Frederich. BFA, Art Inst. Chgo. at U. Chgo., 1955. Dir. art Young and Rubicam, Chgo., 1955-61; dir. art, assoc. creative dir. Clinton E. Frank, Chgo., 1961-64; dir. art, producer J. Walter Thompson, Chgo., 1964-67; pres. Sedelmaier Film Prodns., Chgo., 1967—. Spkr. Brit. design and art direction Lectr. Series, London, 1998; spkr. Harvard Bus. Sch., 2003. Exhibitions include Mus. Broadcast Comms., Chgo., 1988, Mus. Broadcasting, LA, 1991, Mus. TV and Radio, NYC, 1992, Represented in permanent collections Acad. TV Arts and Scis. Archive; dir.: (films) OpenMinds, 2003 (Sundance Film Festival Official Selection, 2003). Recipient Golden Ducat award for short film MROFNOC Mannheim Film Festival, 1968, Golden Gate award for short film Because That's Why, San Francisco Film Festival, 1969, 82 Clio awards, 1968-92, numerous Gold, Silver and Bronze Lion awards Cannes Film Festival, 1972-90, Gold Hugo award Chgo. Film Festival, 1976, 91, 2d Ann. IDC Creative award, Chgo., 1980, Internat. Broadcasting award for world's best TV comml., 1980, 86, Clio award for dir. of yr., 1981, London Internat. Advt. awards, 1986-88, numerous awards Internat. Festival of NY, 1984-93, Ann. Achievement award Assn. Ind. Comml. Producers, 1988; named Advt. Person of Yr., Chgo. Advt. Club, 1984, Jewish Communicator of Yr., 1985; named one of 50 Pioneers & Visionaries Who Made TV America's Medium, Advt. Age Mag., 1995; profiled in Communication Arts mag., Mar. 1976, Print mag., Jan. 1982, Fortune mag., June 1983, Newsweek mag., Nov. 1986, numerous others; featured on 60 Minutes, 48 Hours; subject of cover story Esquire mag., Aug. 1983; included in Arts & Entertainment's Top 10 Greatest Commls. of All Time, 1999; inducted The Art Dirs. Hall Fame, 2000; body of work and interview made part of permanent collections Acad. TV Arts and Scis. Archive, 2006. Office Phone: 312-822-0110. Personal E-mail: sedelmaierfilms@gmail.com.

SEDERBURG, WILLIAM ALBERT, academic administrator, former state senator; b. Chadron, Nebr., Aug. 1, 1947; s. Marion E. and Viola A. (Shalender) S.; m. Joyce I. Witte, July 29, 1972; children: Matthew E., Karl A. BA in Edn. and Polit. Sci., Mankato State Coll., 1969; MA in Polit. Sci., Mich. State U., 1972, PhD in Polit. and Pub. Adminstrn., 1974; LLD (hon.), Kalamazoo Coll. Postdoctoral fellow dept. polit. sci. Mich. State U., East Lansing, 1973-75; dir. rsch. and programs, edn. specialist Mich. Ho. Rep. Caucus, Lansing, 1975—77, exec. dir., 1977—78; pres. Survey Rsch. Co., 1974—91; senator, 24th dist. Mich. Senate, Lansing, 1978—91; v.p. pub. policy, dir. Pub. Opinion Rsch. Inst., 1991—94; pres. Ferris State U., Big Rapids, Mich., 1994—2003, Utah Valley State Coll., Orem, Utah, 2003—. Mem. appropriations com., 1983-95, chmn. higher edn. and tech. com., health policy com., 1987-95, Mich. Capitol com., 1989-95. Contbr. articles to profl. jours. Bd. dirs. Luth. Social Svcs. Mich. Recipient Phil Sirotkin award for Higher Edn. Leadership, Pub. Svc. award, Am. Cancer Soc., Am. Lung Assn., award for Contributions to Ind. Higher Edn., Assn. Ind. Colleges and Universities, William P. Faust award, Am. Cancer award, Dir.'s Conf. award, Mich. Dept. Pub. Health, Pub. Svc. award, Mich. Coll. and U. Placement Coun., Outstanding Alumni award, Mich. State U.; NSF fellow, 1970—73. Mem. Phi Beta Kappa, Kappa Delta Pi, Omicron Delta Kappa, Golden Key Soc., Am. Polit. Sci. Assn. Republican. Office: Utah Valley State Coll 800 W Univ Pkwy Orem UT 84058 Business E-Mail: William.Sederburg@uvsc.edu.

SEDGWICK, SALLY BELLE, publishing company executive; b. Chgo., July 6, 1947; d. William Morton and Dorothy Hyde (Dunlap) Price; m. Roger Stephen Sedgwick, Sept. 7, 1968 (div.); children: Peter, Andrew. BA, Lawrence U., 1968; MFA, U. Alaska, 1974; MA, Gen. Theol. Sem., NYC, 1986; DMin, Grad. Theol. Found., Donaldson, Ind., 1996. Instr. Lake Region Jr. Coll., Devils Lake, N.D., 1974-77; dir. Carousel Creative Arts Program, Oakes, N.D., 1978-80; pricing analyst Orgn. Resources Counselors, NYC, 1981-85; exec. dir. Ch. Periodical Club, NYC, 1985-90; assoc. dir. Forward Movement Publs., Cin., 1990—. Bd. mem. Fountain Sq. Fools, Cin., 1992-95; cons. Episcopal Diocese N.D., 1974-80. Mem. Episcopal Communicators, Nat. Network Lay Profls. Episcopalian.

SEDLAK, ROBERT, academic administrator; BS, Calif. State Coll., Pa., 1968; M Ed, Pa. State Univ., 1970, PhD, 1973. Prof. spl. edn., dir. Office Rsch. U. Wis.-Stout, Menomonie, asst. to dean Sch. Ed. and Human Svcs., 1983—85, asst. dean rsch., 1985—88, assoc. vice chancellor, provost, vice chancellor, 1999—. Office: U Wis-Stout Office of Provost 303 Adminstrn Bldg 712 Broadway Menomonie WI 54751-0790

SEDMAK, DANIEL D., academic administrator; b. Columbus, Ohio, Apr. 18, 1952; m. Peggy Sedmak; 5 children. BS in biology, U. Cin.; MD, Ohio State U., 1980. Resident in pathology Cleve. Clinic Found., 1980—84, fellow in immunopathology, 1984—85; joined faculty Ohio State U., 1985; dir. nephropathology and transplant pathology programs Ohio State U. Hosp.; prof. and chair pathology Coll. Medicine and Pub. Health, Ohio State U., 1997, interim dean, sr. assoc. v.p. health sci. and exec. vice dean; exec. dean Georgetown U. Sch. Medicine, 2003—04, exec. v.p. health sci., 2003—04; exec. vice dean, assoc. v.p. health sciences Ohio State Med. Ctr., Columbus, 2003—. Office: Ohio State Univ Med Ctr 200 Meiling Hall 370 West 9th St Columbus OH 43210 Office Phone: 202-687-4600. Business E-Mail: sedmak@georgetown.edu.

SEEBERT, KATHLEEN ANNE, international sales and marketing executive; d. Harold Earl and Marie Anne (Lowery) S. MM, MA, Northwestern U., 1983. Dir. mktg. MidAm. Commodity Exch., 1982—85; internat. trade cons. to Govt. of Ont. Canada, 1985—90; dir. mktg. and program devel. Internat. Orientation Resources, 1990—94; v.p. Am. Internat. Group, 1995—97; dir. KPMG Peat Marwick LLP, 1997—98; cons. Watson Wyatt & Co., 1999—2005, Katzenbach Ptnrs. LLC, 2006—; with Aon Cons., Inc., 2007—. Guest lectr. U. Dayton, U. Notre Dame, Northwestern U., Kellogg Alumni Chgo., French-Am. C. of C., Internat. Employee Relocation Coun., Soc. Intercultural Educators, Trainers and Rschrs., ASTD, Ill. CPA Soc., SBA, KPMG Peat Marwick, Pricewaterhouse-coopers, Ernst & Young, Nat. Fgn. Trade Coun., William M. Mercer, Inc. Nat. bd. dirs. U. Dayton. Mem. Futures Industry Assn. Am. (treas.), Notre Dame Club Chgo., Kellogg Mgmt. Club Chgo. Republican. Roman Catholic. Office: 200 E Randolph St Ste 900 Chicago IL 60611

SEEDER, RICHARD OWEN, infosystems specialist; b. Chgo., May 4, 1947; s. Edward Otto and Betty Jane (Reamer) S. BA, Trinity U., 1969; M in Mgmt., Northwestern U., 1979; MS, DePaul U., 1993. Programmer, analyst R.R. Donnelley & Sons Co., Chgo., 1972-76, project mgr., 1977-80; mgr. systems devel. Joint Commn. Accreditation of Healthcare Orgns., Chgo., 1980-84, dir. mgmt. info. systems, 1985-89; dir. info. svcs., 1989-92; v.p. AApex Info. Systems., Skokie, Ill., 1992—. Cons. Internat. Printworks, Newton, Mass., 1981-82. Served to 1st lt. U.S. Army, 1969-71, Korea. Mem. Assn. MBA Execs., Healthcare Info. and Mgmt. Systems Soc., Am. Mgmt. Assn., Mensa. Clubs: Northwestern U. Mgmt. Avocations: sports, gardening. Home: 2224 Maple Ave Northbrook IL 60062-5208 Office: AApex Info Systems 9230 Lotus Ave Skokie IL 60077-1150 Home Phone: 847-564-0242; Office Phone: 312-421-0777. Personal E-mail: richseeder@att.net.

SEEGER, RONALD L., lawyer; b. Prairie Farm, Wis., June 10, 1930; s. John M. and Mildred G. (Moen) S.; m. Theresa A. Seeger, Sept. 3, 1955; children: Mark, Scott, John, Lynn, Eric. BA, U. Wis., 1951; JD, U. Minn., 1956. Bar: Minn. 1956, U.S. Dist. Ct. 1957, U.S. Supreme Ct. 1983. Pres. Dunlap & Seeger (was Michaels, Seeger, Rosenblad & Arnold), Rochester, Minn., 1956—. Counsel, City of Rochester Charter Commn., 1962-74, chmn., 1971-72; pres. Legal Assistance of Olmsted County, 1973-76; bd. dirs., v.p. Legal Assistace Minn., 1972-74; trustee, chmn. Gamehaven area Boy Scout Found., 1974-76; trustee Rochester Area Found.; dir. Minn. Lawyers Mutual. With U.S. Army, 1951-53, Korea. Fellow Am. Bar Found.; mem. ABA (ho. of dels. 1974-80, 92-96, bd. govs. 1991-95), Minn. State Bar Assn. (bd. govs. 1974-85, pres. 1983-84, Lifetime Svc. award 1997), Minn. Bar Found. (dir.), Minn. Legal Cert. Bd. (chmn. 1985-90). Home: 2924 Salem Point Dr SW Rochester MN 55902-1305 Office: PO Box 549 Rochester MN 55903-0549

SEEGERS, LORI C., lawyer; b. Miami Beach, Fla., June 17, 1955; BA cum laude, U. Pa., 1977; JD, Fordham U., 1982. Bar: N.Y. 1983, Ill. 2002, U.S. Dist. Ct. (so. dist.) N.Y. 1983. Ptnr. Anderson, Kill & Olick, P.C., NYC; gen. counsel PPM Am., Inc. Contbr. articles to profl. jours. Mem. ABA, N.Y. State Bar Assn. (sect. banking, corp. and bus. law), Assn. of Bar of City of N.Y. Office: PPM Am Inc Ste 1200 225 W Wacker Dr Chicago IL 60606-1276 E-mail: lori.seegers@ppmamerica.com.

SEELER, RUTH ANDREA, pediatrician, educator; b. NYC, June 13, 1936; d. Thomas and Olivia Seeler. BA cum laude, U. Vt., 1959, MD, 1962. Diplomate Am. Bd. Pediat., Am. Bd. Pediatric Hematology/Oncology. Intern Bronx (N.Y.) Mcpl. Hosp., 1962—65; pediats. hematology/oncology fellow U. Ill., 1965—67; dir. pediatric hematology/oncology Cook County Hosp., 1967—84; prof. pediatrics and pediatric edn. Coll. Medicine U. Ill., Chgo., 1984—; assoc. chief pediatrics Michael Reese Hosp., Chgo., 1990—97, acting chief pediatrics, 1997—99; pediatrician St. Anthony's Hosp./U. Ill. Coll. Medicine, 1999—2001. Course coord. pediatrics Nat. Coll. Advanced Med. Edn., Chgo., 1987-96; mem. subboard Pediatric Hematology/Oncology, Chapel Hill, 1990-95; chief Midwest Am. Bd. Pediat., 1990-, Mem. editl. bd. Am. Jour. Pediat. Hematology/Oncology, 1985-95. Founder med. dir. camp for hemophiliacs Ill. Hemophilia Found., 1973—2000, pres. Ill., 1981—85; sec. exec. com. U. Vt. Med. Sch. Alumna Assn.; jr. and sr. warden, treas. Ch. Our Saviour, Chgo., 1970—92. Mem.: U. Vt. Med. Sch. Alumna Assn. (pres.-elect), Phi Beta Kappa, Gamma Phi Beta Found. (trustee 1994—2000, 2002—). Avocations: triathalons, biking, swimming. Office: U Ill Coll Medicine Pediats M/C 856 840 S Wood St Chicago IL 60612-7317 Office Phone: 312-355-1021. Business E-Mail: seeler@uic.edu.

SEGAL, MINDY, chef; Grad., Kendall Coll. Pastry asst. Ambria, Chgo.; pastry chef Metropolis 1800, Chgo., Charlie Trotter's, Chgo., Gordon, Chgo., Spago, Chgo., Marche, Chgo., MK the Restaurant, Chgo.; owner, exec. pastry chef Hotchocolate, Chgo., 2005—. Developed dessert menus Mia Francesca, Harvest on Huron, Thyme. Named Best Pastry Chef in Chgo., Chgo. Mag., 2005, Rising Star Pastry Chef, StarChefs.com, 2005. Office: Hotchocolate 1747 N Damen Ave Chicago IL 60647 Office Phone: 773-489-1747. Office Fax: 773-489-1777.

SEGERLIND, LARRY J., agricultural engineering educator; BS in Agrl. Engring., Mich. State U., 1959, MS in Agrl. Engring., 1962; PhD in Agrl. Engring., Purdue U., 1966; BS in Math., Mich. State U., 1981, MS in Math., 1986. Prof. emeritus dept. agrl. engring. Mich. State U. Mem. Am. Soc. Agrl. Engrs. (A.W. Farrall Young Educator award 1976, Paper award, Massey-Ferguson medal 1996) Office: Mich State U Rm 102 AW Farrall Hall East Lansing MI 48824-1323 E-mail: segerlin@egr.msu.edu.

SEGUI, DAVID, professional baseball player; b. Kansas City, Kans., July 19, 1966; Baseball player Balt. Orioles, 1990-93, N.Y. Mets, 1994-95, Mont. Expos, 1995-97, Seattle Mariners, 1998-99, Toronto Blue Jays, 1999, Tex. Rangers, 2000, Cleve. Indians, 2000—01, Balt. Orioles, 2001—04.

SEIBERLICH, JUNE SCHAUT, chaplain; b. Green Bay, Wis., Sept. 30, 1925; d. Clifford Charles and Eleanor Josephine (Arts) Schaut; m. Marshall E. Gillette, Jan. 23, 1946 (div. 1974); children: Ronald Leigh Gillette, Patrick Allen Gillette, Vicki Jeanne Baumann; m. Hubert L. Hirsch, Nov. 7, 1975 (dec. Mar. 2002); m. Richard R. Seiberlich, Dec. 10, 2004. Student, St. Mary's Sch. Nursing, Rochester, Minn., 1943—45, U. Wis., Sheboygan, 1973—75. Cert. med. asst. Med. asst. James W. Faulkner, M.D., Phoenix, 1953-56; med. office mgr. Edward E. Houfek, M.D., Sheboygan, 1956-75; med. office cons. Profl. Mgmt. Inc., Milw., 1975-77; office mgr., adminstrv. asst. Schroeder & Holt Archs. Ltd., Milw., 1977-90; vol. chaplain St. Camillus Health Ctr., Milw., 1991—, Children's Hosp. and Froedert Meml. Hosp., Milw., 1991-95; staff chaplain Froedert Meml. Hosp., 1995—2006; ret., 2005. Instr. med. asst. program Lake Shore Tech., 1975—76. Mem.: Lake Shore Med. Assts. (exec. bd. 1959—75), Am. Assn. Med. Assts. (nat. trustee 1963—66), Wis. Soc. Med. Assts. (life; exec. bd. 1975—89), Lay Camillian Family (pres. Milw. chpt. 2004—07), Nat. Assn. Cath. Chaplains (cert.). Republican. Roman Catholic. Home: 10200 W Bluemound Rd Apt 1032 Milwaukee WI 53226-4372 Office: Froedtert Meml Luth Hosp 9200 W Wisconsin Ave Milwaukee WI 53226-3522

SEIBERT, TROY J., lawyer; b. Mankato, Minn., June 11, 1972; m. Cara Seibert; 2 children. BA, U. Minn., Duluth, 1994; JD magna cum laude, William Mitchell Coll. Law, 1998. Bar: Minn. 1998. Ptnr. Zelle, Hofmann, Voelbel, Mason & Gette, L.L.P., Mpls. Named a Rising Star, Minn. Super Lawyers mag., 2006. Mem.: Minn. State Bar Assn., Hennepin County Bar Assn., ABA. Office: Zelle Hofmann Voelbel Mason & Gette LLP 500 Washington Ave South Ste 4000 Minneapolis MN 55415 Office Phone: 612-339-2020. E-mail: tseibert@zelle.com.

SEIDMAN, DAVID N(ATHANIEL), materials scientist, engineer, educator; s. Charles and Jeanette (Cohen) S.; m. Shoshanah Cohen-Sabban, Oct. 21, 1973; children: Elie, Ariel, Eytan. BS, NYU, 1960, MS, 1962; PhD, U. Ill., Urbana, 1965. Postdoc. assoc. Cornell U., Ithaca, NY, 1964-66, asst. prof. materials sci. and engring., 1966-70, assoc. prof. materials sci. and engring., 1970-76, prof. materials sci. and engring., 1976-85, Northwestern U., Evanston, Ill., 1985-96, Walter P. Murphy prof. materials sci. and engring., 1996—; founding dir. Northwestern U. Ctr. for Atom-Probe Tomography, Evanston, Ill., 2004—. Vis. prof. Technion, Haifa, 1969-70, Tel-Aviv U., Ramat-Aviv, 1972; Lady Davis vis. prof. Hebrew U., Jerusalem, 1978, 80-81, prof. materials sci., 1983-85; vis. scientist C.E. de Grenoble, 1981, C.N.E.T.-Meylan, 1981, C.E. de Scalay, 1989, U. Goettingen, 1989, 92; sci. cons. Argonne Nat. labs., Ill., 1985-94. Editor: Jour. Materials Sci., 2004—06, Materials Rsch. Soc. Bulletin, 2007—; editor-in-chief (jour.) Interface Sci., 2002—04, mem. editl. bd., editor spl. issues, 1993—2001, mem. editl. bd. Materials Sci. Forum, 1996—; contbr. numerous articles to profl. jours. Recipient Max Planck Rsch. prize Max-Planck-Gesellschaft and the A. von Humboldt-Stiftung, 1993; Guggenheim fellow, 1972-73, 80-81, Humboldt fellow, 1989, 92; named chair for phys. metallurgy Gordon Conf., 1982. Fellow Am. Phys. Soc., TMS (mem. fellows award com. 2002-2005, chair, 2006, Hardy Gold medal 1966), Am. Soc. Materials Internat. (Grossman and Howe awards com. 2005-07, Albert Sauveur Achievement award, 2006), AAAS; mem. Materials Rsch. Soc. (editl. bd. Materials Rsch. Bulletin, 2007—), Microscopy Soc. Am., A. von Humboldt Soc. Am., Internat.

Field-Emission Soc. (mem. steering com. 1997-2002, pres. 2000-2002), Böhmische Phys. Soc. Democrat. Jewish. Achievements include research in nanostructural temporal evolution of microstructures in metallic alloys, metal semiconductor reactions, internal interfaces, atomic-scale imperfections in metals and semiconductors, three-dimensional atom-probe tomography and electron microscopy. Avocations: reading, history, travel. Office: Northwestern U MS&E Dept Cook Hall Evanston IL 60208-3108 Office Phone: 847-491-4391. Business E-Mail: d-seidman@northwestern.edu.

SEIFERT, JAMES J., lawyer; b. New Ulm, Minn., Nov. 24, 1956; BA, U. Notre Dame, 1979; MS in Manufacturing Systems, U. St. Thomas, 1994; JD, Creighton U. Sch. of Law, 1982. Bar: Minn. 1983, U.S. Dist. Ct., Dist. of Minn. 1983, Wis. 1992. Law clerk Judge Donald J. Porter U.S. Dist. Judge S.D., Pierre, 1982—83; atty. Carlsen, Greiner and Law, Minneapolis, Minn., 1983—85, Am. Hoist and Derrick Co., 1985—90, The Toro Co., 1990—94, asst. gen. counsel, 1994—99; v.p., gen. counsel, sec. Tennant Co., 1999—2002, Bemis Co., Inc., 2002—. Mem. Minn. House of Reps., 1999—2001. Mem.: ABA. Office: Bemis Co Inc 2300 Piper Jaffray Tower 222 S 9th St Minneapolis MN 55402-4099

SEIFERT, KATHI P., manufacturing executive; b. Appleton, Wis., 1949; m. Steve Seifert; children: Erin, Andrew. BA Valparaiso U., 1971. Various mgmt. positions P&G, Beatrice Foods, Fort Howard Paper Co., 1972—78; from product mgr. to mktg. dir. feminine care products Kimberly-Clark, Inc., Neenah, Wis., 1978—92, pres. feminine care sectory, 1992—94, group pres. N. Am. consumer products, 1994—95, group pres. N. Am. personal care products, 1995—98, group pres. personal care products, 1998—99, exec. v.p., group pres. global personal care products, 1999—, ret.; with Pinnacle Perspectives, LLC. Bd. dirs. Eli Lilly and Co. Bd. dirs. U.S. Fund for UNICEF; bd., dirs. Fox Cities Performing Art Ctr., 1999—, chmn. of bd., 2003—; bd, dirs. Theda Health Care Group, Wis. Commn. in Arts Edn. Office: Pinnacle Perspectives LLC Ste 303 330 W College Ave Appleton WI 54911

SEIFERT, SHELLEY JANE, bank executive; b. Aug. 12, 1954; BS in Consumer Econs. and Journalism, U. Mo., 1976; MBA with honors in Fin., U. Louisville, 1980. Fin. analyst at. City Bank, Ky., 1979-81, compensation analyst, 1981-85, mgr. compensation, 1985-86, mgr. compensation, recruiting and tng., 1986-91; mgr. compensation and devel. Nat. City Corp., Cleve., 1988-91, human resource dir., 1991-94, sr. v.p., 1994—2000, corp. human resource dir., 1994—2004, exec. v.p. corp. svcs., 2000—. Spkr. in field.; bd. dirs., Blair Corp., 2006-. Grad. Leadership Cleve.; vice chair bd. dirs. Bus. Vols. Unlimited, Vis. Nurse Assn. Greater Cleve.; bd. dirs. Arthritis Found.; mem. Cleve. Commn. on Econ. Partnership and Inclusion. Recipient Woman of Distinction award YMCA. Mem. Urban League (bd. dirs., chair employment com., Ohio labor adv. com.). Office: Nat City Corp Nat City Ctr 1900 E 9th St Cleveland OH 44114-3401 Office Phone: 216-222-2000.

SEIGLER, DAVID STANLEY, botanist, educator, chemist; b. Wichita Falls, Tex., Sept. 11, 1940; s. Kenneth R. and Floy M. (Wilkinson) S.; m. Janice Kay Cline, Jan. 20, 1961; children: Dava, Rebecca. BS in Chemistry, Southwestern State Coll., Okla., 1961; PhD in Organic Chemistry, U. Okla., 1967. Postdoctoral assoc. USDA o. Regional Lab., Peoria, Ill., 1967-68; postdoctoral fellow dept. botany U. Tex., Austin, 1968-70; asst. prof. botany U. Ill., Urbana, 1970-76, assoc. prof., 1976-79, prof. botany, 1979—, head dept. plant biology, 1988-93. Curator U. Ill. Herbarium, 1993—. Author: Plant Secondary Metabolism, 1999; editor: Crop Resources, 1977, Phytochemistry and Angiosperm Phylogeny, 1981; contbr. numerous articles to profl. jours. Recipient Fulbright Hays Lecturer award Fulbright Commn., Argentina, 1976, (alternate) Germany, 1995-96, study award Deutsche Akademischer Austauschdienst, Germany, 1995, Rupert Barneby award NY Bot. Garden, 1997. Mem. Phytochem. Soc. N.Am. (pres. 1988-89), Bot. Soc. Am., Am. Chem. Soc., Am. Soc. Plant Taxonomists, Internat. Soc. Chem. Ecology (pres. 1990-91). Mem. Assembly of God Ch. Avocation: genealogy. Home: 510 W Vermont Ave Urbana IL 61801-4931 Office: U Ill Dept Plant Biology 265 Morrill Hall 505 S Goodwin Ave Urbana IL 61801-3707 Home Phone: 217-384-1192; Office Phone: 217-333-7577. Business E-Mail: seigler@life.uiuc.edu.

SEILS, WILLIAM GEORGE, lawyer; b. Chgo., Aug. 9, 1935; s. Harry H. and Hazel C. (Sullivan) S.; m. Evelyn E. Oliver, Sept. 8, 1956; children: Elizabeth Ann, Ellen Carol, Eileen Alison. AB, JD, U. Mich., 1959. Bar: Ill. bar 1959. Since practiced in, Chgo.; ptnr. Arvey, Hodes & Costello & Burman, 1968-87; gen. counsel, sec., sr. v.p. Richardson Electronics, Ltd., LaFox, Ill., 1986—2006, of counsel, 2006. Contbr. articles to profl. jours.; asst. editor: Mich. Law Rev, 1958-59. Mem. Ill. Bar Assn., Order of Coif. Office: Richardson Electronics Ltd PO Box 393 40w267 Keslinger Rd Lafox IL 60147-0393 Office Phone: 630-208-2370. Business E-Mail: wgs@rell.com.

SEITZ, BILL, state representative; b. Cin., Oct. 29, 1954; married; 2 children. BA, JD, U. Cin. State rep. State of Ohio, Youngstown, Ohio, 2000—. Mem. banking, pensions and securities com. Ohio State Ho. Reps., chmn. civil and comml. law com., mem. criminal justice com., mem. mcpl. govt. and urban revitalization com.; mem. Western Econ. Coun. Trustee Green Township, 1994—2000; mem. Ohio Small Govt. Capital Improvement Commn.; Hamilton County Integrating Com., 1995—2000; mem. St. Antoninus Parish Edn. Commn., 1992—95, Cin. Sch. Bd., 1990—93. Named One of 200 Greater Cincinnatians, Cin. Bicentennial Commn., 1987, One of Cin.'s Future Movers and Shakers, Cin. Post, 1986. Mem.: Ohio State Bar Assn., S.W. Ohio Township Assn. (sec.), Hamilton County Township Assn. (pres.), Green Township Civic Assn., Bridgetown Civic Assn. (sec.), Westwood Civic Assn. (pres.), Kiwanis. Office: Ohio House Reps 77 South High St 11th Fl Columbus OH 43215-6111

SELBY, DIANE RAY MILLER, retired fraternal organization administrator; b. Lorain, Ohio, Oct. 11, 1940; d. Dale Edward and Mildred (Ray) Miller; m. David Baxter Selby, Apr. 14, 1962; children: Elizabeth, Susan, Sarah. BS in Edn., Ohio State U., 1962. Sec. Kappa Kappa Gamma Frat., Columbus, Ohio, 1962-63, editor, 1972-86; tchr. Hilliard (Ohio) High Sch., 1963-65; exec. dir. Mortar Bd., Inc. Nat. Office, Columbus, Ohio, 1986—2007; ret., 2007. Editor The Key of Kappa Kappa Gamma Frat, 1972-86 (Student Life award, 1983, 84, 85). Founding officer Cmty. Coordinating Bd., Worthington, Ohio, 1983; pres. PTA Coun., Worthington, 1984, Worthington Band Boosters, 1985; sec., treas. Sports and Recreation Facilities Bd., Worthington, 1986-90; mem. sustaining com. Jr. League Columbus, 1991-93, docent Kelton House, 1979—; libr. fundraising com. Ohio State U. Mortar Bd. Alumni Coun., 2006-. Mem.: Assn. Coll. Honor Soc. (exec. com. 1999—2001, 2003—04, 2004—07, chmn. bylaws com., trustee 2004—07, v.p. 2005—06, pres. 2006—07), Mortar Bd., Inc. (hist. com., grad. fellowship 2007—08), Docent Kelton House, Jr. League Columbus, Mortar Bd. Alumni Columbus Chpt. (pres. 2007—08), Twig 53 Children's Hosp., Ladybugs and Buckeyes, Ohio State U. Retiree's Assn. (conf. co-chair 2007—08, benefit's com. 2007—), Worthington Women's Club, Kappa Kappa Gamma (house bd. v.p. 1997—2000, v.p. heritage museum guild 2007—08). Republican. Lutheran. Home: 6750 Merwin Pl Columbus OH 43235-2838 Business E-Mail: selby.1@osu.edu.

SELF, BILL, men's college basketball coach; b. Okmulgee, Okla., Dec. 27, 1962; m. Cindy Self; children: Lauren, Tyler. BSBA, Okla. State U., 1985, M in Athletic Adminstrn., 1989. Asst. coach U. Kans., 1985-86, head coach, 2003—; asst. coach Okla. State U., 1986-93; head coach Oral Roberts U., 1993-97, U. Tulsa, 1997—2000, U. Ill. Champaign-Urbana, 2000—03. Mem. competition com. USA Men's Basketball, 2005—; bd. mem. Nat. Assn. Basketball Coaches. Finalist aismith Coach of Yr. award 2000, 01, 02, 03; named Don Haskins Coach of Yr., Western Athletic Conf., 2000, John and Nellie Wooden Coach of Yr., Utah Tipoff Club, 2000, Nat. Coach of Yr., The Sporting News, 2000, Big 12 Coach of Yr., 2006. Coached U. Tulsa to Western Athletic Conference titles, 1999, 2000; coached U. Illinois to Big Ten championships, 2001, 02; coached U. Kansas to Big 12 championships, 2005, 06, 07, 08; NCAA tournament championship, 2008. Office: U Kans Men's Basketball Allen Fieldhouse 1651 Naismith Dr Lawrence KS 66045 Office Phone: 785-864-7929.

SELIG-PRIEB, WENDY, sports team executive; JD, Marquette U., 1988. With broadcasting dept. Milw. Brewers, from 1982; exec. trainee Office of Baseball Commr.; corp. atty. Foley & Lardner, to 1990; gen. counsel Milw. Brewers, 1990-95, v.p., gen. counsel, 1995-98, now pres., CEO, 1998—. Office: Milw Brewers Baseball % Miller Park 1 Brewers Way Milwaukee WI 53214-3651

SELIGSON, THEODORE H., architect, interior designer, urban planner; b. Kansas City, Mo., Nov. 10, 1930; s. Harry and Rose (Haith) S.; m. Jacqueline Rose, Dec. 27, 1964 (div. 1976). BArch, Washington U., St. Louis, 1953. Registered architect, Mo., Kans. Intern Marshall & Brown, Kansas City, Mo., 1949-54; designer, head design Kivett & Myers, Kansas City, Mo., 1954-62; prin. Design Assocs., 1955—, Atelier Seligson, Kansas City, Mo., 1962-64; pres. Seligson, Eggen, Inc., Kansas City, 1964-73, Seligson Assocs., Inc., Architects Planners, Kansas City, 1973-97; prin. Foss, Seligson, Lafferty, 1997—. Vis. lectr. adult edn. U. Mo.-Kansas City, 1958-61, vis. prof. arch., 1989—, vis. prof. urban design, 2002-; tchr., critic Kansas City Art Inst., Mo., 1961-64, 71-72, adj. prof., 1986, 89, 91, 92; adj. prof. Kans. State U., 1991-92, 97; vis. prof. Washington U., St. Louis, 1975, 77, 78, 81, 86, 91, U. Kans., Lawrence, 1978, 79, 80, 91, 92; art cons. Design Assocs., Kansas City, Mo., 1955—. Projects pub. in archtl. jours. V.p. Friends of Art Nelson-Atkins Mus. Art, Kansas City, bd. dirs. 1963-67, chmn. selections com., 1981, vis. curator, 1972, 87; chmn. Capitol Fine Arts Commn. Mo., 1983-90, Kansas City Worlds Fair goals and themes subcom., 1985-90; bd. dirs. Westport Tomorrow, Kansas City, 1980-87, Hist. Kansas City Found., 1984-90; pres. Native Sons of Kansas City, 1989, bd. dirs. 1978-94, Westport Cmty. Coun., 1973-75; bd. govs. Truman Med. Ctr., Kansas City, 1998-2002, mem. bd. advisors, 2002--; mem. Kansas City Key to City Commn., 2001-02; bd. dirs. Sacred Structures, 2003—. Recipient Urban Design award Kansas City Mcpl. Art Commn., 1968, 74, 78; Nat. Archtl. award Am. Inst. Steel Constrn., 1970; Nat. award ASID/DuPont Corian, 1989. Fellow AIA (Kansas City chpt. pres. 1983, bd. dirs. 1979-84, Design Excellence award 1966, 68, 70, 74, Ctrl. States Regional award 1974, 78, Honor award for outstanding svc. to chpt. and profession 1982-83); mem. Mo. Coun. Archs., Am. Soc. Interior Designers, Nat. Coun. Archtl. Registration Bds. (task analysis adv. com. 1988-90), Soc. Archtl. Historians (pres. 1973-75, bd. dirs. 1994-97). Jewish. Office: Foss Seligson Lafferty 450 E 4th St Kansas City MO 64106

SELLERS, BARBARA JACKSON, federal judge; b. Richmond, Va., Oct. 3, 1940; m. Richard F. Sellers; children: Elizabeth M., Anne W., Catherine A. Attended, Baldwin-Wallace Coll., 1958-60; BA cum laude, Ohio State U., 1962; JD magna cum laude, Capital U. Law Sch., Columbus, Ohio, 1979. Bar: Ohio 1979, U.S. Dist. Ct. (so. dist.) Ohio 1981, U.S. Ct. Appeals (6th cir.), 1986. Jud. law clk. Hon. Robert J. Sidman, U.S. Bankruptcy Judge, Columbus, Ohio, 1979-81; assoc. Lasky & Semons, Columbus, 1981-82; jud. law clk. to Hon. Thomas M. Herbert, U.S. Bankrupcty Ct., Columbus, 1982-84; assoc. Baker & Hostetler, Columbus, 1984-86; U.S. bankruptcy judge So. Dist. Ohio, Columbus, 1986—. Lectr. on bankruptcy univs., insts., assns. Recipient Am. Jurisprudence prize contracts and criminal law, 1975-76, evidence and property, 1976-77, Corpus Juris Secundum awards, 1975-76, 76-77. Mem. Columbus Bar Assn., Am. Bankruptcy Inst., Nat. Conf. Bankruptcy Judges, Order of Curia, Phi Beta Kappa. Office: US Bankruptcy Ct 170 N High St Columbus OH 43215-2403 Office Phone: 614-469-6638 ext. 250. Business E-Mail: barbara_sellers@ohsb.uscourts.gov.

SELMAN, RUSSELL BERTRAM, lawyer, department chairman; b. Oceanside, NY, May 31, 1954; s. Leon Daniel and Lorraine Thelma (Leichter) S.; m. Elizabeth Friedgut. BA, New Coll., 1975; MPA, Syracuse U., 1978; JD, Washington U., 1980. Bar: Ill. 1987, D.C. 1981, Mo. 1980. Asst. enforcement counsel U.S. Environ. Protection Agy., Washington, 1980-82, atty., advisor, 1983; atty. McKenna, Conner & Cuneo, Washington, 1983-86, Schiff, Hardin & Waite, Chgo., 1986-88, Bell, Boyd & Lloyd, Chgo., 1988-93; ptnr., chmn. environ. law dept. Katten Muchin Rosenman, Chgo., 1993—. Contbr. Chicago Lawyer mag. Office: Katten Muchin Rosenman 525 W Monroe St Ste 1600 Chicago IL 60661-3693 Office Phone: 312-902-5390. Business E-Mail: russell.selman@kattenlaw.com.

SELOLWANE, DIPHETOGO (DIPSY SELOLWANE), professional soccer player; b. Jan. 27, 1978; s. Gertrude Selolwane and Leslie Ramasodi. Attended, Harris Stowe State Coll. Played one season Harris Stowe State Coll., St. Louis; forward Chgo. Fire, Major League Soccer, 2002—. Mem. Botswana Nat. Team, 1998—. Achievements include top goal-scorer, 23-and-under nat. team, Four Nation's Cup, South Africa, 1998. Office: Soldier Stadium 425 E McFetridge Dr Chicago IL 60605-279

SEMONIN, RICHARD GERARD, retired state official; b. Akron, Ohio, June 25, 1930; s. Charles Julius and Catherine Cecelia (Schooley) S.; m. Lennie Stuker, Feb. 3, 1951; children: Cecelia C., Richard G. Jr. (dec.), James R., Patricia R. BS, U. Wash., 1955. With Ill. State Water Survey, Champaign, 1955-91, chief, 1986-91, chief emeritus, 1991—; co-chmn. Ill. Water Rsch. & Land Use Planning Task Force, 1992-94. Adj. prof. U. Ill., 1975-91; chmn. Ill. Low-Level Radioactive Waste Task Group, 1994-96. Contbr. chpts. to books and articles to profl. jours.; co-editor: Atmospheric Deposition, 1983. Staff sgt. USAF, 1948-52. Grantee, NSF, 1957—76, US Dept. Energy, 1965—90. Fellow: AAAS, Am. Meteorol. Soc. (councilor 1983—86); mem.: Ill. Acad. Scis., Weather Modification Assn., at. Weather Assn. (councilor 1978—81), Sigma Xi. Roman Catholic. Avocations: civil war, golf, fishing, genealogy. Home: 1002 Devonshire Dr Champaign IL 61821-6620 Office: Ill State Water Survey 2204 Griffith Dr Champaign IL 61820-7495 E-mail: semonin@uiuc.edu.

SEMPLE, LLOYD ASHBY, lawyer; b. St. Louis, June 7, 1939; s. Robert B. and Isabelle A. S.; m. Cynthia T. Semple, Aug. 26, 1961; children: Whitney, Sarah, Lloyd Jr., Terrell. BA, Yale U., 1961; JD, U. Mich, 1964. Bar: Mich. 1964. Assoc. Dykema Gossett, Detroit, 1964-70, ptnr., 1971—2004, chmn., 1994—2002; chmn. emeritus UD Mercy Sch. of Law, 2004—, vis. prof., 2004—. Bd. dirs. Argon St. Councilman, mayor pro tem City of Grosse Pointe Farms, Mich., 1975—83; chmn. exec. com. Detroit Zool. Soc.; dir., trustee Karmanos Cancer Inst., 1994—2004; chmn. bd. trustees Detroit Med. Ctr. Corp., 1996—2001. Mem. ABA, Mich. Bar Assn., Detroit Bar Assn., Country Club Detroit, Yondotega Club, Detroit Athletic Club, Yale Club (N.Y.C.), Bohemian Club (San Francisco), Audobon Soc. (dir. 2003—) Episcopalian. Home: 57 Cambridge Rd Grosse Pointe Farms MI 48236-3004 Office: Dykema Gossett 400 Renaissance Ctr Ste 3500 Detroit MI 48243-1602 Business E-Mail: lsemple@dykema.com.

SENECHAL, ALICE R., federal magistrate judge, lawyer; b. Rugby, ND, June 25, 1955; d. Marvin William and Dora Emma (Erdman) S. BS, N.D. State U., 1977; JD, U. Minn., 1984. Bar: Minn. 1984, U.S. Dist. Ct. Minn. 1984, N.D. 1986, U.S. Ct. Appeals (8th cir.) 1987. Law clk. U.S. Dist. Judge Bruce M. Van Sickle, Bismarck, ND, 1984-86; with Robert Vogel Law Office, Grand Forks, ND, 1986—. U.S. magistrate judge, 1990—.

SENG, COLEEN JOY, director; b. Council Bluffs, Iowa, Feb. 8, 1936; d. Otis A. and Helen V. (Anderson) McElwain; m. Darrel E. Seng, Oct. 22, 1960 (dec. 1993); children: Marcee Lee, Christopher Charles, Phillip Scott. BA, Nebr. Wesleyan U., 1958. Dist. dir. Girl Scouts U.S.A., Saginaw, Mich., 1958-60, Lincoln, ebr., 1960-62; cmty. ministry 1st United Meth. Ch., Lincoln, 1977-97; mem. Lincoln City Coun., 1987—2003; mayor City of Lincoln, 2003—07; dir. Comty. Ministries First United Methodist Ch., 2007. Mem. Mayor's first multi-cultural task force, co-chair of Gov. Nelson's urban adv. team, chmn. railroad transp. safety dist. Lincoln/Lancaster county joint budget com., mem. Lincoln/Lancaster county homeless coalition; active U. Place Cmty. Orgn. N.E. Family Resource Ctr.; past chair Lincoln/Lancaster county family resource ctr. bd.; past pres. Lincoln Fellowship of Chs.; mem. Lincoln Interfaith Coun.; mem Lincoln Urban Ministries com.; past pres. Homestead Girl Scouts Coun. Democrat. United Methodist. Avocations: reading, movies, gardening. Home: 6101 Walker Ave Lincoln NE 68507-2467 Office: First United Methodist Church 2723 North 50th St Lincoln NE 68504

SENG, JOE, state senator, veterinarian; b. Sept. 1946; 1 child, Heidi Anne. BS in Vet. Medicine, Iowa State U. Veterinarian, Davenport, Iowa; state rep. Iowa Ho. of Reps., 2000—02; state senator dist. 43 Iowa Senate, 2003—; mem. agr. com.; mem. appropriations com.; mem. ways and means com.; mem. agr. and natural resources subcom.; ranking mem. natural resources and environment com. Active NAACP, Ter. Hill Bd.; pres. Marquette Acad. Recipient Past Pres. award, Iowa Vet. Med. Assn., Golden Apple award, Marquette Acad. Mem.: KC. Democrat. Office: State Capitol East 12th and Grand Des Moines IA 50319

SENGUPTA, DIPAK LAL, engineering educator; b. Bengal, India, Mar. 1, 1931; came to U.S., 1959; s. Jayanta Kumar and Pankajini Sengupta; m. Sujata Basu, Aug. 31, 1962; children: Sumit, Mita. BSc in Physics with honors, Calcutta U., India, 1950, MSc in Radio Physics, 1952; PhD, U. Toronto, Ont., Can., 1958. Assoc. rsch. physicist dept. elec. engring. U. Mich., Ann Arbor, 1959-63, rsch. physicist, 1965-75, rsch. scientist, prof. dept. elec. engring., 1975-86; asst. prof. dept. elec. engring. U. Toronto, 1963-64; asst. dir. Cen. Electronics Engring. Rsch. Inst., Pilani, India, 1964-65; prof. elec. engring. U. Detroit Mercy, 1996—2001, chmn. dept. elec. engring. and physics, 1986-95, prof. emeritus, rsch. scientist, 2001—. Fulbright vis. lectr. in India, 1992-93; cons. Ford Motor Co., Dearborn, Mich., 1976-77, Battelle Pacific N.W. Labs., Richland, Wash., 1978. Author: Radar Cross Section Analysis and Control, 1991; contbr. articles to profl. jours. Fellow IEEE (life, Contbn. award 1969, recognition awards 1978-79); mem. Internat. Radio Scientists Union (sec. commn. B 1976-78), Sigma Xi, Eta Kappa Nu. Office: Radiation Lab Dept Elec Engring and Computer Sci U Mich Ann Arbor MI 48109-2122 Home Phone: 734-761-1374. E-mail: sengupdl@eecs.umich.edu.

SENHAUSER, JOHN CRATER, architect; b. New Philadelphia, Ohio, Apr. 7, 1947; s. Edwin Crater and Margaret Jean (Huffman) S.; m. Teri A. Schleyer, June 25, 1988. BS in Architecture, U. Cin., 1971. Registered architect, Ohio, Ky., Fla. Designer Jones, Peacock, Garn & Ptnrs., Cin., 1971-72; project architect Smith Stevens Architects, Cin., 1972-76; project mgr. Herrlinger Enterprises, Cin., 1976-79; prin., owner John C. Senhauser, Architect, Cin., 1979—. Adj. assoc. prof. Sch. Architecture and Interior Design, U. Cin., 1992-98 Exhibited in group shows at Toni Birckhead Gallery, 1990, Contemporary Arts Ctr., Cin., 1993, 98, Canton (Ohio) Art Inst., 1993; prin. works include residences. Mem. historic conservation bd. City of Cin., 1986-98, chmn. 1998—; mem. urban design rev. bd., 1998—; mem. dean's adv. coun. Coll. Design Architecture Art and Planning U. Cin., 1990; mem. design rev. com. U. Cin., 1997—. Recipient Merit award Builder mag., 1985, 88, 94, 96, 99, Grand award, 1990, Grand Best in Region award Profl. Builder, 1988, 90, Grand award for Best Overall Design, Custom Home Mag., 1996, 97, Merit award, 1990, 94, other awards. Fellow AIA (pres. 1991, Honor award Cin. chpt. 1983, 85, 90-96, 2000, 04, Merit award 1990, 93-94); mem. AIA Ohio (bd. dirs., sec. 1997-98, v.p. 1999, pres. 2000, regional dir. nat. bd. dirs. 2001—03, Inst. sec. 2005-06, Honor award 1985, 90-91, 93-94, 99, 2003-04) Office: John Senhauser Architects 1118 Saint Gregory St Cincinnati OH 45202-1724

SENIOR, THOMAS BRYAN A., electrical engineering educator, researcher, consultant; b. Menston, Yorkshire, Eng., June 26, 1928; arrived in U.S., 1957; s. Thomas Harold and Emily Dorothy (Matthews) Senior; m. Heather Margaret Golby, May 4, 1957; children: Margaret, David, Hazel, Peter. B.Sc., Manchester U., 1949, M.Sc., 1950; PhD, Cambridge U., 1954. Sr. sci. officer Royal Radar Establishment, Malvern, Eng., 1952-57; rsch. scientist U. Mich., Ann Arbor, 1957-69, prof. elec. engring., 1969-84, prof. elec. and computer sci., 1984-98, Arthur F. Thurnau prof., 1990-98, prof. emeritus, 1998—, dir. radiation lab., 1975-87, assoc. chmn. elect. engring. & computer sci. dept., 1984-90, acting chmn., 1987-88, assoc. chmn. acad. affairs, 1991-98. Cons. in field. Author: (with Bowman and Uslenghi) Electromagnetic and Acoustical Scattering by Simple Shapes, 1969; Mathematical Methods in Electrical Engineering, 1986; (with Volakis) Approximate Boundary Conditions in Electromagnetics, 1995; contbr. articles to profl. jours. Fellow IEEE (3d Millennium medal, AP-S Disting. Achievement award 2000); mem. Internat. Sci. Radio Union (chmn. U.S. nat. com. 1982-84, vice chmn. Com. B. 1985-87, chmn. 1988-90, pres. 1996-99, Van der Pol Gold medal 1993). Home: 1919 Ivywood Dr Ann Arbor MI 48103-4527 Office: U Mich Dept Elec Engring Comp S Ann Arbor MI 48109 E-mail: senior@eecs.umich.edu.

SENKLER, ROBERT L., insurance company executive; BA in Math. and Stats., Minn. Duluth Coll., 1974. Began Minn. Life Ins. Co., 1974—, v.p. Individual Ins. Divsn., 1987-94; pres. Securian Fin. Group (Minn. Life Ins. Co.), 1994—2007, CEO, 1994—, chmn., 1995—. Past chmn. Ins. Fed. Minn.; pres. Minn. Bus. Prtnrshp., 2003; chmn. Cap. City Partnership. Recipient Univ. Minn.-Duluth Acad. Sci. Engring., 2003. Fellow Soc. Actuaries. Office: Securian Fin Group 400 Robert St Saint Paul MN 55101-2015

SENNET, CHARLES JOSEPH, lawyer; b. Buffalo, Aug. 7, 1952; s. Saunders M. and Muriel S. (Rotenberg) S. AB magna cum laude, Cornell U., 1974; JD with high honors, George Washington U., 1979. Bar: Ill. 1979, U.S. Dist. Ct. (no. dist.) Ill. 1979, U.S. Ct. Appeals (7th cir.) 1982, U.S. Ct. Appeals (D.C. cir.) 1993. Assoc. Reuben & Proctor, Chgo., 1979-83; assoc. counsel Tribune Co., Chgo., 1984-91, sr. counsel, 1991—. Adj. faculty Medill Sch. Journalism, Northwestern U., 1991-94, 2004—; chmn. Television Music Lic. Com., 1995—. Contbr. articles to profl. jours. Chmn. cable royalty distbn. com. Nat. Assn. Broadcasters, 2005—. Mem. ABA (spkr. 1984-88, 91-97, 2000—, mem. gov. bd. Forum on Comms. Law 1995-98), NATAS, Ill. Bar Assn. (chmn. media law com. 1989-91), Chgo. Bar Assn., Fed. Comms. Bar Assn. Office: Tribune Co 435 N Michigan Ave Chicago IL 60611-4066 E-mail: csennet@tribune.com.

SENNETT, JOHN O., lawyer; b. Broken Bow, Nebr., Apr. 10, 1948; BS, Univ. Nebr., 1970, JD, 1972. Bar: Nebr. 1972, US Dist. Ct. (Dist. Nebr.) 1972, US Supreme Ct. 1975, US Ct. Appeals (8th Cir.) 1976. Ptnr. Sennett Duncan Borders & Jenkins PC, LLO, Broken Bow, Nebr. Mem.: ABA, Assn. of Trial Lawyers of Am., Nebr. Trial Lawyers Assn., Custer County Bar Assn., Nebr. State Bar Assn. (Ho. of Del. 1986—92, chmn. 1991—92, bd. trustees 1992—98, pres. 2004—05). Office: Sennett Duncan Borders & Jenkins PC LLO 425 S 7th St Broken Bow NE 68822 Office Phone: 308-872-6868. Office Fax: 308-872-2191. Business E-Mail: jsennett@adb-law.com.

SENNETT, NANCY J., lawyer; b. Milw., Nov. 26, 1951; BS in English & comm. arts with honors, U. Wis., 1973; JD cum laude, Northwestern U., 1979. Bar: Wis. 1979. With Foley & Lardner LLP, Milw., 1979—, chair securities litig. practice group, mng. ptnr. Milw. office. Chair merit selection com. reappointment magistrate judges Ea. Dist. Wis. Notes and comments editor Northwestern U. Law Rev., 1978-79. Active Jr. Achievement. Mem.: ABA (securities litig. com.), Securities Industry Assn. (compliance & legal divsn.), State Wis. Bar Assn., Milw. Bar Assn. (Lawyer Year 2003), ABCD, Inc. (bd. dirs.), Betty Brinn Children's Mus. (founding bd. dirs.), Greater Milw. Com., Tempo & Rotary, U. Wis. Alumni Assn. (bd. dirs., Distinguished Alumni Award 2003). Office: Foley & Lardner LLP US Bank Ctr 777 E Wisconsin Ave Milwaukee WI 53202-5367 Office Phone: 414-297-5522. Business E-Mail: nsennett@foley.com.

SENSENBRENNER, F(RANK) JAMES, JR., congressman; b. Chgo., June 14, 1943; s. F. James and Margaret Sensenbrenner; m. Cheryl Warren, Mar. 26, 1977; children: F. James III, Robert Alan. AB in Polit. Sci., Stanford U., 1965; JD, U. Wis., Madison, 1968. Bar: Wis. 1968, US Supreme Ct. 1972. State rep. Wis. State Assembly, Madison, 1969-75; mem. Wis. State Senate, Madison, 1975-79, asst. minority leader, 1976-79; mem. US Congress from 5th Wis. dist., 1979—, chmn. sci. com., 1997—2001, chmn. judiciary com., 2001—07. Mem. Friends of Milw. Mus., Riveredge Nature Ctr. Mem. Am. Philatelic Soc., Chenequa Country Club, Capitol Hill Club, Energy Independence and Global Warming. Republican. Office: US Ho Reps 2449 Rayburn Ho Office Bldg Washington DC 20515-4905 Office Phone: 202-225-5101.

SERAFYN, ALEXANDER JAROSLAV, retired automotive executive; b. Stare Selo, Ukraine, Mar. 27, 1930; came to U.S., 1949; s. Leon and Ahaphia (Peretiatko) S.; m. Zenia Maria Sylvestruk, July 5, 1958; children: Lesia, Lidia, Myron, Roman. BA, Wayne State U., 1954, MBA, 1960; PhD, Kensington U., 1983. Mgr. fin. analysis Ford (France) S.A., Paris, 1964-66; budget analysis mgr. Ford Motor/Indsl. and Chem. Div., Southfield, Mich., 1967; asst. ops. controller Ford Motor/Paint and Vinyl Ops., Mt. Clemens, Mich., 1968, ops. controller, 1969-71; controller Ford South Africa, Port Elizabeth, 1972-73; asst. div. controller Ford Motor/Metal Stamping Div., Dearborn, Mich., 1974-80, Ford Motor/Body and Assembly Ops., Dearborn, 1981-82; bus. plans and adminstrv. mgr. Ford Motor/Mfg. Ops., Dearborn, 1983-84; program mgr. Mazda Ford Motor/Body and Assembly Ops., Dearborn, 1985-90. Bd. dirs. Selfreliance Fed. Credit Union, Warren, Mich. Contbr. articles to profl. jours. Adviser Ukrainian Nat. Assn., 1994-98, auditor 1998-2006, pres. Detroit dist., 1989—, exec. v.p., 1987-89; treas. Shevchenko Sci. Soc., Detroit, 1989—, v.p., 1997-2003. Named Ukrainian of Yr., Ukrainian Grads. of Detroit and Windsor, 1980, Disting. Alumnus, Wayne State U. Sch. Bus., 1995. Mem. Acad. Engring. Scis. Ukraine, Ukrainian Engrs. Soc. Am. (sr. mem., bd. dirs. 1991-97), Ukrainian Engring. Soc. (pres. Detroit br. 1978-79), Ukrainian Nat. Assn. (Fraternalist of Yr. award 1991, Merit award 2005), World Found. Ukrainian Med. Assns. (bd. dirs. 1996-2002), Am. Ukranian Med. Found. (fin. sec. 2002—), also others. Republican. Ukrainian Catholic. Avocations: golf, skiing, travel, writing, reading. Home: 2565 Timberwyck Trail Dr Troy MI 48098-4103

SERATTI, LORRAINE M., state legislator; b. Oct. 30, 1949; V.p. Wis. Fedn. Taxpayers Orgn.; pres. Florence County Taxpayers Alliance; Wis. state assemblywoman dist. 36, 1992—. Small bus. owner. Mem. Florence Hist. Soc. Mem. NRA. Republican. Address: HC 2 Box 588 Florence WI 54121-9620 Office: Wis Assembly PO Box 8952 Madison WI 53708-8952

SERGI, VINCENT A.F., lawyer; Grad., Beloit Coll.; JD with honors, Northwestern U. With fin. and reorganization dept. Katten Muchin Zavis Rosenman, 1974, dept. head, nat. mng. ptnr., 1996—, mem. bd. dirs., mem. exec. and operating com., chmn. compensation com. Bd. dirs. Goodman Theatre, Joffrey Ballet, Providence-St. Mel Sch. Office: 525 W Monroe St Chicago IL 60661-3693 Office Phone: 312-902-5255. Business E-Mail: vincent.sergi@kmzr.com.

SERLIN, MARSHA, waste management service administrator; CEO/pres. Ill. United Scrap Metal, Cicero, 1978—. Recipient Nat. Small Bus. Subcontractor Yr. award, U.S. Small Bus. Adminstrn., 1996, Mass. Mut.-Nat. Family Bus. of Yr. award, Ernst and Young's Entrepreneur of Yr. award, Outstanding Recycling Bus. award Ill. Recycling Assn.; named Grant Thorton Exec. Woman of Yr.; inductee Jr. Achievement Chgo. Bus. Hall of Fame. Office: United Scrap Metal Inc 1545 S Cicero Ave Chicago IL 60804-1529

SEROTA, SCOTT, medical association administrator; BA, Purdue U.; MA in Health Admin. and Planning, Wash. U. Sch. of Med., St. Louis. Creator, leader Physicians Preferred Health Inc., Mo.; v.p. health care mgmt. PruCare, St. Louis, 1980; v.p. group ops., v.p. health care mgmt. Prudential Ins. Co., Chgo.; pres., CEO Rush Prudential Health Plans, Chgo., 1993—96; exec. v.p. system devel. Blue Cross and Blue Shield Assn., COO, 1994—96, exec. v.p. sys. devel., 1996—2000, pres., CEO, 2000—. Founding mem. Inst. on Healthcare Costs and Solutions Wash. Bus. Group on Health; bd. mem. Council for Affordable Quality Healthcare, Nat. Ctr. for Healthcare Leadership, Partnership for Prevention, Nat. Alliance for Health Info. Tech., Accrediting Commn. on Edn. for Health Services Admin.; mem. Am. Coll. of Healthcare Executives. Office: Blue Cross Blue Shield Assn 225 N Michigan Ave Chicago IL 60601

SERRA, JOE, investment company executive; Pres. Team Mgmt., Dearborn, Mich.; pres., CEO Al Serra Chevrolet, Grand Blanc; pres., COO Saturn Enterprises, Inc., Charlotte, N.C., 1998-99; CEO, chmn. Serra Investments, Grand Blanc, Mich., 1999—. Office: Serra Investments 3118 E Hill Rd Grand Blanc MI 48439-8106

SERRANO, JUSTIN FORBES, education executive; b. 1973; BA, Cornell U.; MBA, Harvard Bus. Sch., 2001. Tchr., student adv. Kaplan, Inc., 1995, mgr., dir., tchr. recruitment and devel.; v.p., graduate programs Kaplan Test Prep and Admissions; pres. SCORE! Ednl. Ctrs., Chgo., 2006—. Office: SCORE! Educational Centers 10 S Wacker Dr Ste 3425 Chicago IL 60606

SERRIN, JAMES BURTON, mathematics professor; b. Chgo., Nov. 1, 1926; s. James B. and Helen Elizabeth (Wingate) S.; m. Barbara West, Sept. 6, 1952; children: Martha Helen Stack, Elizabeth Ruth, Janet Louise Sucha. Student, Northwestern U., 1944-46; BA, Western Mich. U., 1947; MA, Ind. U., PhD, 1951; DSc, U. Sussex, 1972; DSc in Engring., U. Ferrara, Italy, 1992; DSc in Math., U. Padova, Italy, 1992; DSc, U. Tours, France, 2004. With MIT, Cambridge, 1952-54; mem. faculty U. Minn., Mpls., 1955—, prof. math., 1959-95, Regents prof., 1968—, head Sch. Math., 1964-65; emeritus, 1995. Vis. prof. U. Chgo., 1964, 75, Johns Hopkins U., 1966, U. Sussex, 1967-68, 72, 76, U. Naples, 1979, U. Modena, 1988, Ga. Inst. Tech., 1990. Author: Mathematical Principles of Classical Fluid Mechanics, 1957. Mem. Met. Airport Sound Abatement Council, Mpls., 1969—. Recipient Disting. Alumni award Ind. U., 1979 Fellow AAAS; mem. NAS, Am. Math. Soc. (G.D. Birkhoff prize 1973), Math. Assn. Am., Soc. for Natural Philosophy (pres. 1969-70), Finnish Acad. Sci. and Letters. Home: 4422 Dupont Ave S Minneapolis MN 55419-4739

SERRITELLA, JAMES ANTHONY, lawyer; b. Chgo., July 8, 1942; s. Anthony and Angela (Deleonardis) S.; m. Ruby Ann Amoroso, Oct. 3, 1981. LLD, North Park U., 1996; BA, SUNY-S.I., 1965, Pontifical Gregorian U., Rome, 1966; postgrad., DePaul U., 1966-67; MA, U. Chgo., 1968, JD, 1971. Bar: Ill. 1971, U.S. Dist. Ct. (no. and ea. dist.) Ill. 1971, U.S. Supreme Ct. 1976, U.S. Tax Ct. 1985, U.S. Ct. Appeals (fifth cir.) 1995, U.S. Ct. Appeals (sixth cir.) 1992, U.S. Ct. Appeals (seventh cir.) 1993, U.S. Ct. Appeals (ninth cir.) 1996. Ptnr. Kirkland & Ellis, Chgo., 1978; ptnr. Reuben & Proctor, Chgo., 1978-86, Mayer, Brown & Platt, Chgo., 1986-97, Burke, Warren, MacKay & Serritella, PC, Chgo., 1997—. Lectr. in field. Contbr. articles to profl. jours. Exec. bd. govt. rels. com. United Way of Chgo., 1979-84; bd. dirs. Child Care Assn. Ill., 1975-79, Lyric Opera Guild, 1979-84; v.p. Comprehensive Community Svcs. of Met. Chgo., 1976-81; chmn. adv. bd. DePaul U. Coll. Law Ctr. Ch./State Studies, 1982—, dean's vis. com., 1982—; trustee Mundelein Coll., 1982-86, St. Xavier Coll., St. Mary of the Lake Sem., 1982-83, Sta. WTTW Chgo. Pub. TV, 1978-81, Loretto Hosp., 1989-91; mem. geriatrics/gerontology steering com. McGaw Med. Ctr. orthwestern U., 1981-82; adv. bd. N.Am. Coll., 1990-92; mem. Bus. Execs. for Econ. Justice, 1988-94, State wide citizens com. on Child Abuse and Neglect, 1988-94; bd. advisors Alzheimer's Ctr. Rush-Presbyn.-St. Luke's Med. Ctr., 1990—; cons. Union of Bulgarian Founds., 1992, Internat. Acad. for Freedom of Religion and Belief, Budapest, Hungary, 1992. Recipient St. Joseph Sem. Rerum Novarum award, 1999. Fellow Am. Bar Found.; mem. ABA, FBA, NCCJ (adv. com. on ch., state and taxation), Am. Assn. homes for Aging, Nat. Health Lawyers Assn., Ill. State Bar Assn. (bd. govs., spl. com. on jud. redistricting), Ill. Bar Found. (charter), Chgo. Bar Assn. (com. on evaluation of jud. candidates), Cath. Lawyers Guild (bd. govs.), Canon Law Soc. Am. (active mem.), Diocesan Attys. Assn. (exec. com.), Nat. Cath. Cemetery Conf., Cath. Health Assn., The Chgo. Club, Econ. Club, Tavern Club. Office: Burke Warren MacKay & Serritella PC IBM Plaza 22nd Fl 330 N Wabash Ave Chicago IL 60611-3603 E-mail: jserritella@burkelaw.com.

SERRITELLA, WILLIAM DAVID, lawyer; b. Chgo., May 16, 1946; s. William V. and Josephine Dolores (Scalise) S. JD, U. Ill., Champaign, 1971. Bar: Ill. 1971, US Dist. Ct. (no. and cen. dists.) Ill. 1972, US Dist. Ct. (ea. and we. dists.) Wis. 1995, US Ct. Appeals (7th cir.) 1974, US Supreme Ct. 1979, US Dist. Ct. (so. dist.) Ind. 1997. Law clk. U.S. Dist. Ct., Danville, Ill., 1971-72; ptnr. Ross & Hardies, Chgo., 1972—2003, McGuire Woods, Chgo., 2003—07, Johnson & Bell, Ltd., Chgo., 2007—. Arbitrator Am. Arbitration Assn. Named to Leading Lawyers Network, Ill. Super Lawyers, Top Best Lawyers Network. Fellow Am. Bar Found.; mem. ABA, Ill. Bar Assn., Chgo. Bar Assn., Internat. Assn. Def. Counsel, Soc. Trial Lawyers, Defense Rsch. Inst., Trial Lawyers Club (Chgo.), Lawyers Club Chgo. Office: Johnson & Bell Ltd Ste 2700 33 W Monroe St Chicago IL 60603-5404 Business E-Mail: serritellaw@jbltd.com.

SERVAAS, BEURT RICHARD, manufacturing executive; b. Indpls., May 7, 1919; s. Beurt Hans and Lela Etta (Neff) S.; m. Cory Jane Synhorst, Jan. 7, 1950; children: Eric, Kristin, Joan, Paul, Amy. Student, U. Mex., Mexico City, 1938-39; AB, Ind. U., 1940, MD, 1970; postgrad., Purdue U., 1941; D Bus. Mgmt., Ind. Inst. Tech.; LHD (hon.), Butler U. Agt. CIA, China, 1946; v.p. constrn. Vestar Corp., NYC, 1948; founder, chief exec. officer, chmn. bd. No. Vernon Forge, Inc. Rev. Pub. Co., SerVaas Labs., Indpls., 1949—. Chmn. bd. SerVaas, Inc., Indpls. and affiliated cos. Curtis Pub. Co., Forge Mexicana, Edgerton Tool, Dependable Engring., SerVaas Mgmt., SerVaas Rubber, Premier, Indpls. Rubber Co., Bridgeport Brass Co.; bd. dirs. Bank One Ind. Pres. City-County Coun., Indpls.; chmn. Ind. State Commn. Higher Edn., Kirksville Coll. Osteo. Medicine; bd. dirs. Coll. Univ. Corp., Ind. Pub. Health Found., Robert Schuller Ministries; past chmn. bd. dirs. Ind. State Bd. Health, Nat. Fgn. Rels. Commn. With USNR, 1941—45. Decorated Bronze Star, Army Commendation medal; recipient Horatio Alger award, 1980. Mem. NAM, Am. Acad. Achievement (Golden Plate award 1973), Assn. Am. Med. Colls., Ind. C. of C., Indpls. C. of C., Marion County Hist. Soc., Ind. Hist. Soc., Newcomen Soc. N.Am., U.S. Naval Res. Assn., World Future Soc., Am. Legion, Columbia Club, Econ. Club, Indpls. Athletic Club, Indpls. Press Club, Meridian Hills Country Club, Phi Delta Kappa. Presbyterian. Home: 2525 W 44th St Indianapolis IN 46228-3249 Office: Office of the City County Coun 241 City-County Bldg 200 E Washington St Indianapolis IN 46204-3307 also: SerVaas Inc 1000 Waterway Blvd Indianapolis IN 46202-2155

SERVAAS, CORY, editor-in-chief; AB in Journalism, Univ. Iowa; MD, Ind. Univ.; PhD (hon.), Vincennes Univ. Chmn., pres., CEO Curtis Pub. Co., 1975—82; former chmn. Country Gentleman Pub. Co.; founder, pres., CEO Benjamin Franklin Literary and Med. Soc., 1976—; also editorial dir. Children's Better Health Inst., Indpls.; and editor Saturday Evening Post, Indpls., editor-in-chief, 2004—. Mem. Pres. Coun. on Phys. Fitness and Sports, 1990—94. Named to Univ. Iowa Journalism Hall of Fame; recipient Ind. Woman of Achievement award, Nat. Fedn. of Press Women, Kappa Tau Alpha award for outstanding svc., Nat. Journalism Scholarship Soc., Outstanding Bus. Leader award, Northwood Inst. Mem.: Nat. Women's Coalition, Women in Comm. Inc., Indianapolis Arthritis Guild, Am. Med. Women's Assn., Ind. State Med. Assn., AMA, Education CHOICE Charitable Trust, Epsilon Sigma Alpha. Office: Saturday Evening Post 1100 Waterway Blvd Indianapolis IN 46202-2174

SERVER, GREGORY DALE, state legislator, counseling administrator; b. Mpls., Jan. 27, 1939; 3 children. BA, U. Evansville, Ind., 1962; MS, Ind. State U., 1968, MS, 1970, EdS, 1981. Guidance counselor Cen. High Sch., Evansville, 1976; mem. Ind. Senate from 50th dist., 1973—. Bd. dirs. Sta. WNIN-TV. Mem. New Harmony (Ind.) Commn. Served with USN. Mem. Edn. Commn. of States, Evansville Tchrs. Assn., VFW, Phi Delta Kappa. Republican. Methodist. Office: Ind Senate Mems State Capitol Indianapolis IN 46204 Home: 311 W Walnut St Indianapolis IN 46202-3163

SERWER, ALAN MICHAEL, lawyer; b. Detroit, Aug. 31, 1944; s. Bernard Jacob and Marian (Borin) S.; m. Laurel Kathryn Robbert, June 6, 1968; children: David Matthew, Karen Anne. BA in Econs., U. Mich., 1966; JD, Northwestern U., 1969. Bar: Ill. 1969, D.C. 1980, U.S. Dist. Ct. (no. dist.) Ill. 1970, U.S. Ct. Appeals (7th cir.) 1979, U.S. Supreme Ct. 1979, U.S. Ct. Appeals (6th cir.) 1982, U.S. Ct. Appeals (5th cir.) 1983, U.S. Ct. Appeals (9th cir.) 1986. Trial atty. U.S. Dept. Labor, Chgo., 1969-78, counsel safety and health, 1978-79; assoc. Haley, Bader & Potts, Chgo., 1979-82, ptnr., 1983-87; mem. Bell, Boyd & Lloyd, Chgo., 1987—. Ill. Bar Assn., Chgo. Bar Assn. Home: 233 Woodland Rd Highland Park IL 60035-5052 Office: Bell Boyd & Lloyd 70 W Madison St Ste 3200 Chicago IL 60602-4244 Home Phone: 847-432-7338; Office Phone: 312-372-1121. Business E-Mail: aserwer@bellboyd.com.

SERWY, ROBERT ANTHONY, accountant; b. Chgo., Mar. 26, 1950; s. Anthony J. and Bernice (Zubek) S.; m. Margaret A. Smejkal, Aug. 12, 1972; children: Karen, Steven. BS in Engring., U. Ill., 1972; MBA, Northwestern U., 1974. Mgr. cons. Arthur Andersen & Co., Chgo., 1974-83; dir. fin. planning Teepak, Inc., Oak Brook, Ill., 1983-85; sr. mgr. cons. Peat Marwick & Mitchell, Chgo., 1985-86; dir. cons. Warady & Davis, Deerfield, Ill., 1986—. F.C. Austin scholar, 1972. Mem. AICPA, Ill. CPA Soc. Roman Catholic. Avocations: amateur radio, microcomputers, football. Home: 203 Buckingham Ct Grayslake IL 60030-3479 Office: Warady & Davis 1717 Deerfield Rd Ste 3005 Deerfield IL 60015

SESSIONS, BARBARA C., lawyer; b. St. Johns, Mich., Jan. 23, 1961; d. John C. and Patricia H. (Hyland) Cary; m. Rex. L. Sessions, Oct. 10, 1989; 1 child, Isabel P. BA in English, U. Mich., 1983; JD, DePaul U., 1986. Bar: Ill. Comml. litigator Hinshaw & Culbertson, Chgo., 1986-90; sr. acct. exec. Edelman Pub. Rels. Worldwide, NYC, 1990-91; mgr. mktg. and comms. Skadden, Arps, Slate, Meagher & Flom, NYC, 1991-94; ptnr., dir. bus. devel. mktg. and planning Winston & Strawn LLP, Chgo., 1994—. Mem. Jr. League, N.Y.C, 1990-94, Chgo., 1989-99. Mem. Law Mktg. Assn. (pres., pres-elect 1998, bd. dirs. 1996—), Info. Innovators (editl. bd.). Office: Winston & Strawn LLP 35 W Wacker Dr Chicago IL 60601-9703 Office Phone: 312-558-5834. Fax: 312-558-5700. E-mail: bsessions@winston.com.

SESSIONS, JUDITH ANN, dean, university librarian; b. Lubbock, Tex., Dec. 16, 1947; d. Earl Alva and Anna (Mayer) S. BA cum laude, Cen. Fla. U., 1970; MLS, Fla. State U., 1971; postgrad., Am. U., 1980, George Washington U., 1983. Head libr. U. S.C., Salkehatchie, 1974-77; dir. Libr. and Learning Resources Ctr. Mt. Vernon Coll., Washington, 1977-82; planning and systems libr. George Washington U., Washington, 1981-82, asst. univ. libr. for adminstrn. svcs., acting head tech. svcs., 1982-84; univ. libr. Calif. State U., Chico, 1984-88; univ. libr., dean of libr. Miami U., Oxford, Ohio, 1988—. Cons. Space Planning, SC, 1976, DataPhase Implementation, Bowling Green U., 1982, TV News Study Ctr., George Washington U., 1981; asst. prof. dept. child devel. Mt. Vernon Coll., 1978—81; mem., lectr. U.S.-China Libr. Exch. Del., 1986, 91; lectr., presenter in field; mem. coord. com. OhioLink Adv. Coun., 1995—2003, v.p., 1996—97, chair, 1998—2000; mem. gov. bd. OhioLink, exec. com., 1998—2001; mem. OCLC Users Coun., 1998—2001; convenor Pub. Acad. Libr. Group, 1999—2000; mem. OCLC Preservation Resources Interest Group, 1999—2001, chmn., 2001. Contbr. articles, book revs. to profl. jours. Trustee Christ Hosp., Cin., 1990-94, Deaconness Gamble Rsch. Ctr., Cin., 1990-94, OhioNet, 1990-94, treas. 1993; bd. dirs. Hamilton (Ohio) YWCA, 1994-98, pres., 1995-96, v.p., 1996-97, 97-98; mem. OCLC user's coun., 1998—; mem. steering com. Tri City Reading Initiative, 2002-03. Recipient award for outstanding contbn. D.C. Libr. Assn., 1979; rsch. grantee Mt. Vernon Coll., 1980; recipient Fulbright-Hayes Summer Travel fellowship to Czechoslovakia, 1991. Mem. ALA (Olofson award 1978, councillor-at-large policy making group 1981-94, coun. com. on coms. 1983-84, intellectual freedom com. 1984-88, directions and program rev. com. 1989-91, fin. and audit subcom. 1989-90, mem. exec. bd. 1989-94, mem. del. to Zimbabwe Internat. Book Fair 1997), Assn. Coll. and Rsch. Librs. (editorial bd. Coll. and Rsch. Librs. jour. 1979-84, nominations and appointments com. 1983-85, faculty status com. 1984-86), Libr. and Info. Tech. Assn. (chair legis. and regulation com. 1980-81), Libr. Adminstrn. and Mgmt. Assn. (bd. dirs. libr. orgn. and mgmt. sect. 1985-87), Calif. Inst. Librs. (v.p., pres. elect 1987-88), Mid-Atlantic Regional Libr. Fedn. (mem. exec. bd. 1982-84), Jr. Mems. Round Table (pres. 1981-82), Intellectual Freedom Round Table (sec. 1984-85), Freedom to Read Found. (trustee 1984-88, v.p. 1985-86, treas. 1986-87, pres. 1987-88), Rotary, Beta Phi Mu. Office: Miami U Edgar W King Oxford OH 45056 Office Phone: 513-529-2800. E-mail: judith@lib.muohio.edu.

SETSER, CAROLE SUE, food scientist, educator; b. Warrenton, Mo., Aug. 26, 1940; d. Wesley August and Mary Elizabeth (Meine) Schulze; m. Donald Wayne Setser, June 2, 1969; children: Bradley Wayne, Kirk Wesley, Brett Donald. BS, U. Mo., 1962; MS, Cornell U., 1964; PhD, Kans. State U., 1971. Grad. asst. Cornell U., Ithaca, NY, 1962-64; instr. Kans. State U., Manhattan, 1964-72, asst. prof., 1974-81, assoc. prof., 1981-86, prof., 1986-2001, prof. emeritus, 2001—. Vis. prof. Bogazici U., Istanbul, Turkey, 2000—01. Recipient Rsch. Excellence award, Coll. of Human Ecology, Manhattan, 1990. Mem.: Inst. Food Techs. (chmn. sensory evaluation divsn. edn. com. 1989—92, continuing edn. com. 1992—95, sec. product devel. divsn. 1997—99, also other offices), Am. Assn. Cereal Chemists (assoc. editor 1989—93), Kappa Omicron Nu (Excellence for Rsch. award 1987), Sigma Xi, Phi Tau Sigma (Outstanding Food Scientist 1998), Gamma Sigma Delta, Phi Upsilon Omicron, Phi Kappa Phi (Scholar award 1998). Home Phone: 785-537-9449. Business E-Mail: setser@ksu.edu.

SETSER, DONALD WAYNE, chemistry professor; b. Great Bend, Kans., Jan. 2, 1935; s. Leo Wayne and Velma Irene (Hewitt) S.; m. Carole Sue Schulze, June 2, 1969; children: Bradley Wayne, Kirk Wesley, Brett Donald. BS, Kans. State U., 1956, MS, 1958; PhD, U. Wash., 1961. Asst. prof. Kans. State U., Manhattan, 1963-66, assoc. prof., 1966-68, prof. chemistry, 1968-2000, Alumni Disting. prof. chemistry, 1984-2000, prof. emeritus, 2000—. Vis. prof. U. Grenoble, France, 1981, 84, 87, 91, Bogazici U., Turkey, 2000. Editor Reactive Intermediates, 1976; contbr. more than 300 articles to profl. jours. Recipient Rank prize electro-optics divsn., 1992. Fellow Am. Phys. Soc.; mem. Am. Chem. Soc. (Midwest award St. Louis sect. 1984). Home: 414 Wickham Rd Manhattan KS 66502-3751 Office: Kans State U Dept Of Chemistry Manhattan KS 66506 Home Phone: 785-537-9449; Office Phone: 785-532-6665. Business E-Mail: setserdw@ksu.edu.

SETZER, ARLENE J., state representative, retired secondary school educator; b. Dayton, Ohio, Mar. 2, 1944; BS in Bus. Adminstrn., U. Dayton, 1966; MEd, Wright State U., 1973, postgrad. Tchr. bus. and computer applications Vandalia-Butler HS, 1967—2000; rep. Ohio State Ho. Reps., Columbus, 2000—. Mem. agr. and natural resources com. Ohio State Ho. Reps., chmn. edn. com., mem. ins. com. Mem. ins. rev. com. and state govt. com. City of Vandalia, 1998—2000; chair Vandalia-Butler Food Pantry Bldg. Fund; pres. Pres.'s Club of Vandalia, 1997—99; mem. Ednl. Trust Project, Advocates for People with Devel. Disabilities, Montgomery County Ednl. Advancement Dialogue; precinct capt. Montgomery County Rep. Party, mem. ctrl. com., exec. com.; mem. Vandalia City Coun., 1982—2000, vice-mayor, 1986—88, 1995—2000. Named Rep. Woman of Yr., 1997, 2001, 2003; recipient Clara Weisenborn award, 1999, Horace M. Huffman Jr. Svc. to Bicyclists award, Ohio Bicycle Fedn., 2001, Appreciation award, S.W. Ohio Hemophilia Found. and W. Ctrl. Ohio Hemophilia Ctr., 2002, Rep. of Yr. award, Ohio Coll. Rep. Fedn., 2003; Martha Holden Jennings scholar, 1983—84. Mem.: Sister Cities of Vandalia, Montgomery County Farm Bur., Inc., Montgomery County Cattlemen's Assn., Montgomery Agrl. Soc., Sr. Citizens of Vandalia-Butler, Miami Valley Mil. Affairs Assn., Vandalia-Butler (Ohio) Hist. Soc. (v.p. 2000), Rotary (hon.; Dist. 6670 dir. 1992—96, pres. 1994—95, Dist. 6670 scholarship com. 1997, Dist. 6670 bd. dirs., asst. dist. gov. 1998—2000, named to Hall of Fame). Republican. Office: Ohio State Ho of Reps 77 S High St 13th Fl Columbus OH 43215-6111

SEVART, DANIEL JOSEPH, lawyer; b. Oswego, Kans., June 25, 1944; s. Vernon Joseph and Alma Bridget (Carland) S.; m. Shoko Kato, Apr. 17, 1968; 1 child, Eric J. AA, Parsons Jr. Coll., 1964; BA, Washburn U., 1973, JD with honors, 1975. Bar: Kans. 1976, U.S. Dist. Ct. Kans. 1976, U.S. Ct. Appeals (10th cir.) 1976. Assoc. Render & Kamas, Wichita, Kans., 1976-78, ptnr., 1978-82, Schartz & Sevart, Wichita, 1982-83, Sevart & Sevart, Wichita, 1983—. Bd. dirs. Wichita Symphony Soc., Inc., 1989—. Served to staff sgt. USAF, 1965-72. Mem. Assn. Trial Lawyers Am., Kans. Bar Assn. (bd. govs. 1995-98, 2000-01, sec.-treas. 1998-99, v.p. 2001-02, pres.-elect 2002-03, pres. 2003-04, Kans. Trial Lawyers Assn. (bd. govs. 1989—), Wichita Bar Assn. (bd. govs. 1988-90, sec.-treas. 1990-91, v.p. 1991-92, pres.-elect 1992-93, pres. 1993-94), Wichita C. of C. Democrat. Roman Catholic. Avocations: classical music, gardening, fishing, camping, travel. also: 1900 L St NW Ste 500 Washington DC 20036-5031

SEVERINSEN, DOC (CARL H. SEVERINSEN), conductor, musician; b. Arlington, Oreg., July 7, 1927; m. Emily Marshall; children: Nancy, Judy, Cindy, Robin, Allen. Ptnr. Severinsen-Akwright Co.; pops condr. The Phoenix (Ariz.) Symphony Orchestra; prin. pops condr. Minn. Orch., Milw. Symphony Orch., Phoenix Symphony Orch. Mem. Ted Fio Rito Band, 1945, Charlie Barnet Band, 1947—49, Tommy Dorsey Band, Benny Goodman Band, Vaughn Monroe Band, soloist network band Steve Allen Show NBC-TV, 1954—55, mem. orch. Tonight Show, 1962—67, music dir. Tonight Show, 1967—92, host Midnight Spl., rec. artist Brass Roots album RCA Records, 1971, rec. artist Facets album, 1988, rec. artist The Tonight Show Band, Night Journey album. Address: Minn Orch 1111 Nicollet Mall Minneapolis MN 55403-2406 also: c/o William Morris Agency 151 S El Camino Dr Beverly Hills CA 90212-2704 also: c/o The Phoenix Symphony Orch 455 N 3rd St Ste 390 Phoenix AZ 85004-3942

SEVERSON, SALLY, meteorologist; married; 2 children. Student, No. Ill. U., U. Wis., Milw.; BS in Meteorology, Miss. State U. Meteorologist WISN, Milw., 1986—. Vol. Children's Hosp. of Wis. Avocations: hiking, bicycling, astronomy, boating. Office: WISN PO Box 402 Milwaukee WI 53201

SEWELL, ANDREW, music director; m. Mary Anne Sewell; children: Anna, Lydia, Alistair. MMus, U. Mich.; studied with Gustav Meier. Past asst. condr. Memphis Symphony; past resident condr. Toledo Symphony Orch.; music dir. Mansfield (Ohio) Symphony, Wis. Chamber Orch., Madison; music dir., condr. Wichita (Kans.) Symphony Orch., 2000—. Guest condr. orchs. Detroit, Japan, Mex., Can., New Zealand. Recipient Young Achiever's award Australian Guarantee Corp., Star award New Zealand Aotea Performing Arts Trust, 1997. Office: Wichita Symphony Orch 225 W Douglas Ave Ste 207 Wichita KS 67202-3181

SEWELL, JAMES, artistic director; b. Mpls. Student, Sch. Am. Ballet, NYC; studied with David Howard. Dancer Am. Ballet Theatre II, N.Y., Eliot Feld Co.; guest artist N.Y.C. Ballet, Zvi Gottheiner and Dancers, Denishawn, Martine van Hamel's New Amsterdam Ballet. Choreographer over 45 ballets in U.S. and Taiwan including Musical Toys, Minn. Orch., Amahl and the Night Visitors, St. Paul Chamber Orch., Aida, Minn. Opera, 1998, (video) Nutcracker: The Untold Story, cmty.-portrait ballets Swans Island, Maine, Akron, Ohio, Chadron, Nebr. Office: James Sewell Ballet 528 Hennepin Ave Minneapolis MN 55403-1810

SEWELL, RICHARD HERBERT, retired historian, educator; b. Ann Arbor, Mich., Apr. 11, 1931; s. Herbert Mathieu and Anna Louise (Broene) Sewell; m. Natalie Paperno, Jan. 13, 1971; 1 child, Rebecca Elizabeth. AB, U. Mich., 1953; MA, Harvard U., 1954, PhD, 1962. Asst. prof. No. Ill. U., DeKalb, 1962-64, U. Wis., Madison, 1965-67, assoc. prof., 1967-74, prof., 1974-95, chmn., 1982—85, prof. emeritus, 1995—; ret., 1995. Vis. lectr. U. Mich., Ann Arbor, 1964—65; adv. bd. Lincoln and Soldiers Inst. Gettysburg Coll., Pa., 1990—. Author: (book) John P. Hale and the Politics of Abolition, 1965, Ballots for Freedom, 1976, A House Divided, 1988; contbr. articles to profl. jours. Lt. (j.g.) USNR, 1954—57. Fellow: Wis. Hist. Soc. (hon.); mem.: Orgn. of Am. Historians, So. Hist. Assn., Soc. Civil War Historians, Phi Beta Kappa, Phi Kappa Phi. Home: 2206 Van Hise Ave Madison WI 53726 Business E-Mail: rhsewell@wisc.edu.

SEWELL, WILLIAM HAMILTON, JR., historian; b. Stillwater, Okla., May 15, 1940; s. William Hamilton and Elizabeth Lucille (Shogren) S.; m. Ellen Martha Wheeler, June 16, 1962 (dec. July 2001); children: Jessica Ellen, Adrienne Felicity; m. Jan Goldstein, Dec. 2004. BA, U. Wis., 1962; MA, U. Calif., 1963, PhD, 1971. Instr. history U. Chgo., 1968-71, asst. prof. history, 1971-75; assoc. prof. history U. Ariz., Tucson, 1980-83, prof. history, 1983-85; dir. d'etudes associe Ecole de Hautes Etudes en Scis. Sociales, Paris, 1984, 88; prof. history and sociology U. Mich., Ann Arbor, 1985-90; prof. polit. sci. and history U. Chgo., 1990—, Max Palevsky prof., 1996—2004, Frank P. Hixon disting. svc. prof., 2004—07, emeritus prof., 2007; fellow Ctr. for Advanced Study in Behavioral Scis., 1990-91, Nat. Humanities Ctr., 2006—07. Mem. bd. editors Jour. Modern History, 1984-86, French Hist. Studies, 1985-88, Sociol. Theory, 2004—07; mem., bd. dirs. Social Sci. Rsch. Coun., N.Y.C., 1986-92; dir. Program in Comparative Study of Social Transformations, U. Mich., Ann Arbor, 1987-90, Ctr. for Rsch. Social Orgn., 1988-90; dir. Wilder House Ctr. for Politics, History and Culture, U. Chgo., 1999-2004; mem. Sch. Social Sci. Inst. Advanced Study, Princeton, NJ, 1971-72, 75-80, 2002-03. Author: Work and Revolution in France, 1980, Structure and Mobility, 1985, A Rhetoric of Bourgeois Revolution, 1994, Logics of History, 2005. Recipient Herbert Baxter Adams prize Am. Hist. Assn., 1981, William Koren Jr. prize Soc. French hist. studies, 1982; grantee Nat. Sci. Found., 1972-75; Guggenheim fellow, 1990-91, Nat. Humanities Ctr., 2006-. Fellow Am. Acad. Arts and Sci.; mem. Am. Hist. Assn., Soc. French Hist. Studies, Am. Sociol. Assn. (Best Article prize comparitive hist. sociology sect. 1991, culture sect. 1993, theory sect. 1997), Social Sci. History Assn., Coun. European Studies, Am. Polit. Sci. Assn. Office: U Chgo Dept Polit Sci 5828 S University Ave Chicago IL 60637-1515 E-mail: wsewell@uchicago.edu.

SEWRIGHT, CHARLES WILLIAM, JR., mortgage banking advisory services company executive; b. Great Lakes, Ill., Feb. 22, 1946; s. Charles William Sewright Sr. and Selma Joy Kester; m. Bonnie Joyce Knight, July 2, 1967; children: Kimberly Ann, Traci Lynn, Megan Paige. BS in Acctg., Calif. State U., Long Beach, 1969, MBA, 1974. Fin. analyst aeronautic div. Philco-Ford Corp., Newport Beach, Calif., 1969-73; sr. acctg. analyst Calif. Computer Products, Anaheim, 1973-74; product line controller McGaw Labs. div. Am. Hosp. Supply Corp., Irvine, Calif., 1974-75, div. acctg. mgr., 1975-76, fin. planning dir., 1976-80; v.p., controller critical care div. McGaw Park, Ill., 1980-85; v.p., controller EZ Painter Corp., Milw., 1985-86; v.p. dept. mgr. automotive fin. services secondary mkts. Marine Midland Bank, Buffalo, N.Y., 1986-87; pres., chief exec. officer Marine Midland Mortgage Corp., Buffalo, 1987-91, Anchor Mortgage Svcs., Inc., Wayne, NJ, 1991-95; exec. v.p., COO Avondale Fed. Savs. Bank, Chgo., 1997—2000; founder, chmn., CEO Quest Advisors, Inc., Northbrook, Ill., 1995—. Chair credit com. Am. Employees Fed. Credit Union, McGaw Park, Ill., 1980-85; vice chmn. Bd. Am. Employees Fed. Credit Union, 1981-85; mem. Fannie Mae Adv. Bd., 1990-92; speaker in field; mem. bd. trustees Medaille Coll., 1989-92; dir. Avondale Fed. Savs. Bank. Mem. Nat. Assn. Accts., Inst. of Cert. Mgmt. Accts. (cert.), Mortgage Bankers Assn. Am. (legis. com. 1990—), Mortgage Bankers Assn. Am. (bd. govs. 1990-98), Beta Gamma Sigma, Phi Kappa Phi. Avocation: golf. Office: Quest Advisors Inc 3710 Commercial Ave Ste 5 Northbrook IL 60062 Business E-Mail: csewright@questadvisors.com.

SEXTON, CAROL BURKE, finance company executive, consultant; b. Chgo., Apr. 20, 1939; d. William Patrick and Katharine Marie (Nolan) Burke; m. Thomas W. Sexton Jr., June 30, 1962 (div. June 1976); children: Thomas W., J. Patrick, M. Elizabeth. BA, Barat Coll., 1961; cert. legal, Mallinckrodt Coll.,

1974. Tchr. Roosevelt High Sch., Chgo., 1961-63, St. Joseph's Sch., Wilmette, Ill., 1975-80; dir. Jane Byrne Polit. Com., Chgo., 1980-81; mgr. Chgo. Merc. Exch., 1981-84, sr. dir. govt. and civic affairs, 1984-87, v.p. pub. affairs, 1987-94, exec. v.p. corp. rels., 1995-2001. Mem. internat. trade an investment subcom. Chgo. Econ. Devel. Commn., 1989, 90. Bd. dirs. Chgo. Sister Cities, 1992—2000, Ill. Ambs., 1991—98, pres., 1994—98; bd. dirs., sec. Internat. Press Ctr., 1992—97, chmn. bd., 1994. Mem. Chgo. Conv. and Tourism Bur. (sec. 1989-90, exec. com. 1987-2000, chmn.-elect 1990, chmn. 1991-92). Roman Catholic. Avocations: books, gardening, travel.

SEXTON, J. STAN, lawyer; b. Hays, Kans., 1948; BA, Univ. Kans., 1970, JD, 1977. Bar: Kans. 1977, Mo. 2001. Ptnr. complex litigation, toxic tort, insurance practices Shook Hardy & Bacon LLP, Kans. City, Mo. Editor (assoc., note & comment): Kans. Law Rev. Served to Lt. USN, 1970—74. Mem.: Am. Coll. Trial Lawyers, ABA, Def. Rsch. Inst., Kans. Inst. Trial Advocacy, Kans. Assn. Def. Counsel, Kans. Bar Assn., Mo. Bar. Office: Shook Hardy & Bacon LLP 2555 Grand Blvd Kansas City MO 64108 Home Phone: 816-531-7472; Office Phone: 816-474-6550. Office Fax: 816-421-5547. Business E-Mail: jsexton@shb.com.

SEXTON, MIKE W., state legislator; b. Ft. Dodge, Iowa, Aug. 22, 1961; m. Carolyn Sexton; 4 children. AAS in Agrl. Mgmt., Iowa Lakes C.C. Farmer; mem. Iowa Senate from 7th dist., Des Moines, 1998—; vice chair transp. com., mem. state govt. com.; mem. agr. com., mem. edn. com.; mem. small bus., econ. devel., and tourism com. Republican. Presbyterian. E-mail: mike_sexton@legis.state.ia.us.

SEXTON, OWEN JAMES, vertebrate ecology educator, conservationist; b. Phila., July 11, 1926; s. Gordon and Elizabeth May (Evans) S.; m. Mildred Lewis Bloomsburg, Apr. 5, 1952; children: Kenneth, Jean, Ann, Carolyn. Student, Sampson Coll., 1947-48; BA, Oberlin Coll., 1951; MA, U. Mich., 1953, PhD, 1956. Sr. teaching fellow Washington U., St. Louis, 1955-56, instr., 1956-57, asst. prof., 1957-62, assoc. prof., 1962-68, prof. vertebrate ecology, 1968-97, dir. Tyson Rsch. Ctr., 1996-99, prof. emeritus, 1998—, dir. emeritus, 2001—. Vis. prof. U. Mich. Biol. Sta., Pellston, 1975-83; cons. UNESCO, 1974-75; adj. curator St. Louis Sci. Ctr., 1986-88. Pres., bd. dirs. Mo. Prairie Found., Columbia, 1968-99; pres. Wild Canid Survival and Research Ctr., St. Louis, 1971-73; sec. Contemporary Art Soc., 1972-73; bd. dirs. Creve Coeur Figure Skating Club, 1982-89; mem. membership com. U.S. Figure Skating Assn., 1987-90. NSF fellow, 1966-67; vis. research fellow U. New Eng., 1984. Fellow Herpetologists League; mem. Am. Soc. Icthyologists and Herpetologists, Ecol. Soc. Am., Soc. Study of Amphibians and Reptiles, Orgn. Tropical Studies (bd. dir. 1976-85). Democrat. Home: 13154 Greenbough Dr Saint Louis MO 63146-3622 Office: Tyson Rsch Ctr PO Box 258 Eureka MO 63025 E-mail: sexton@biology.wustl.edu.

SEYFERTH, VIRGINIA M., public relations executive; b. Detroit; BA, Grand Valley State U., Allendale, Mich. With pub. rels. dept. St. Jude Children's Rsch. Hosp., 1977-79, AMOCO Oil Co., 1979-81, Amway Corp., 1981-84; pres. Seyferth & Assocs., Inc., Grand Rapids, Mich., 1984—. Office: Seyferth & Assocs Inc Ste 202 40 Monroe Ctr NW Grand Rapids MI 49503

SEYHUN, HASAN NEJAT, finance educator, department chairman; b. Ankara, Turkey, May 19, 1954; came to U.S., 1972; s. Niyazi and Serife (Sayilgan) S.; m. Tamara Z. Cleland, Aug. 10, 1992; children: Kent E., Jon C. and Evan G. BEE, Northwestern U., 1976; MA in Econs., U. Rochester, 1981, PhD in Fin., 1984. Elec. engr. Sungurlar, Istanbul, 1976-77; asst. prof. fin. U. Mich., Ann Arbor, 1983-91, assoc. prof., 1991-93, prof., 1993—, Jerome B. and Eilene M. York prof. bus. adminstrn., 1998—, chmn. fin. dept., 1994-95, 97-00. Vis. prof. Koc U., Istanbul, 2000-01, vis. assoc. prof. U. Chgo., 1988-89, 92, Wissenschaftliche Hochschule für Unternehmens führung, Koblenz, Germany, 1994; co-dir. banking and fin. svcs. program, cons. Citibank, Zurich, Switzerland, 1991; cons. Tweedy Brown, N.Y.C., 1993—, Towneley Capital, N.Y.C., 1994—. Mem. Am. Fin. Assn., Western Fin. Assn., European Fin. Assn., Beta Gamma Sigma. Avocations: volleyball, running. Office: U Mich 701 Tappan Ave Ann Arbor MI 48109-1217 E-mail: nseyhun@umiu.edu.

SEYMOUR, JAMES, state senator, retired health facility administrator; b. Rockford, Ill., Apr. 8, 1939; Student, No. Ill. U., Creighton U. Former healthcare exec.; state senator dist. 28 Iowa Senate, 2003—; mem. appropriations com.; mem. bus. and labor rels. com.; mem. econ. growth com.; mem. local govt. com.; mem. agr. and natural resources subcom.; vice chair human resources com. Vol. Am. Cancer Soc. With USMC Res. Republican. Office: State Capitol East 12th and Grand Des Moines IA 50319

SEYMOUR, MCNEIL VERNAM, lawyer; b. St. Paul, Dec. 21, 1934; s. McNeil Vernam and Katherine Grace (Klein) S.; children: Margaret, McNeil Vernam, James, Benjamin; m. Mary Katherine Velner, May 15, 1993. AB, Princeton U., 1957; JD, U. Chgo., 1960. Bar: Minn. 1960, U.S. Dist. Ct. Minn. 1960. Mem. Seymour & Seymour, St. Paul, 1960-71; mem. firm Briggs & Morgan, St. Paul, 1971—, ptnr., 1976—2005, of counsel, 2005—. Pres. Thomas Irvine Dodge Nature Ctr.; sec., bd. dirs. Ramsey County Law Libr., 1972—76; pres. White Bear Unitarian Ch., treas.; trustee Oakland Cemetery Assn., 2006—. With US Army, 1960—62. Mem. Minn. Bar Assn., Ramsey County Bar Assn., Somerset Country Club. Republican. Unitarian Universalist. Home: 886 S Highview Cir Mendota Heights MN 55118-3686 Office: Briggs & Morgan W-2200 1st Nat Bank Bldg Saint Paul MN 55101 Office Phone: 651-808-6601. E-mail: MSeymour@Briggs.com.

SFERRA, DANIEL J., state legislator, state representative; b. 1949; married; 2 children. Student, Youngstown State U., Ohio. Mem. city coun. Town of Warren, Ohio, 1972—79, mayor, 1980—95; rep. Ohio State Ho. Reps., Columbus, 2000—. Mem. county and township govt. com. Ohio State Ho. Reps., mem. ins. com., mem. mcpl. govt. and urban com., mem. reviatlization com., mem. trans. and publ safety com. Democrat.

SFIKAS, PETER MICHAEL, lawyer, educator; s. Michael E. and Helen (Thureanos) S.; m. Freida Platon, Apr. 24, 1966; children: Ellen M., Pamela C., Sandra N. BS, Ind. U., 1959; JD, Northwestern U., 1962. Bar: Ill. 1962, U.S. Dist. Ct. (no. dist.) Ill. 1963, U.S. Ct. Appeals (7th cir.) 1963, U.S. Supreme Ct. 1970, U.S. Ct. Appeals (9th cir.) 1976, U.S. Ct. Appeals (3d cir.) 1981, U.S. Ct. Appeals (D.C. cir.) 1984, U.S. Ct. Appeals (8th cir.) 1995, U.S. Dist. Ct. (cen. dist.) Ill. 1988. Atty. Legal Aid Bur., United Charities Chgo., 1962-63; sr. ptnr. Peterson & Ross, Chgo., 1970-95; chief counsel, assoc. exec. dir. divsn. legal affairs ADA, Chgo., 1995—2006; ptnr. Bell, Boyd & Lloyd, Chgo., 1996—. Prosecutor Village of LaGrange Park, Ill., 1969-74; mem. rules com. Ill. Supreme Ct., 1975-95, mem. spl. joint com. on discovery rules, 1995; arbitrator Nat. Panel Arbitrators, 1972—; adj. prof. Loyola U. Sch. Law, 1978—; guest lectr. U. Ill. Coll. Dentistry, 1988-95; lectr. corp. counsel inst. Northwestern U. Sch. Law, 1984, lectr. Ray Garret Jr. Corp. and Securities Law Inst., 1996. Co-author: Antitrust and Unfair Competition Practice Handbook, 1996; contbr. articles to profl. jours. Mem. Ill. steering com. Ct. Watching Project, LWV, 1975-77; pres. Holy Apostles Greek Orthodox Ch. Parish Coun., 1987-89; co-pres. Oak Sch. PTO, 1989-90; mem. com. to select sch. supr., dist. 86, DuPage County, Ill., 1993-94. Named Super Lawyer, Chgo. Mag., 2005, 2006, 2007, Leading Lawyer, 2005, 2006, 2007; recipient Maurice Weigle award, Chgo. Bar Found., 1973, Fones award, Conn. Dental Assn., 1998. Fellow Am. Bar Found., Am. Coll. Trial Lawyers, Chgo. Bar Found. (life); mem. ABA (editor in chief Forum Law Jour. sect. ins., negligence and compensation law 1972-76), Ill. Bar Found. (bd. dirs. 1975-77), Northwestern U. Law Alumni Assn. (1st v.p. 1985-86, pres. 1986-87, Svc. award 1990), Ill. State Bar Assn. (bd. govs. 1970-76, chmn. antitrust law sect. coun. 1986-87), Chgo. Bar Assn. (editl. bd. Chgo. Bar Record 1973-84), Bar Assn. 7th Fed. Cir. (chmn. com. on meetings 1973-75), Ill. Inst. Continuing Legal Edn. (chmn. profl. antitrust problems program 1976, author program on counseling corps., antitrust and trade regulation), Am. Nat. Standards Inst. (mem. copyright ad hoc group 2004-06), Legal Club Chgo. (sec.-treas, 1984-86, v.p. 1989-90, pres. 1990-91). Office: Bell Boyd & Lloyd 70 W Madison St Ste 3300 Chicago IL 60602-4284 Home Phone: 630-323-6848; Office Phone: 312-807-4348. Personal E-mail: petersfi@comcast.net. Business E-Mail: psfikas@bellboyd.com.

SHAAR, H. ERIK, academic administrator; V.p. acad. affairs Shippensburg U. of Pa., until 1986; pres. Lake Superior State U., Sault Sainte Marie, Mich., 1986-92, Minot (N.D.) State U., 1992—. Office: Minot State U Office of Pres 500 University Ave W Minot ND 58707-0002

SHABAZ, JOHN C., judge; b. West Allis, Wis., June 25, 1931; s. Cyrus D. and Harriet T. Shabaz; children: Scott J., Jeffrey J., Emily D., John D. LLB, Marquette U., 1957; BS in Polit. Sci., U. Wis., 1999. Comd. 2d. lt. US Army, 1953, assigned to inactive reserves as capt., 1964; pvt. practice law West Allis, Wis., 1957—82; mem. Wis. Assembly, 1965—81; judge US Dist. Ct. (we. dist.) Wis., 1982—96, chief judge, 1996—2001. Office: US Dist Ct PO Box 591 Madison WI 53701-0591

SHABICA, CHARLES WRIGHT, retired geologist, earth science educator; b. Elizabeth, NJ, Jan. 2, 1943; s. Anthony Charles and Eleanor (Wright) S.; m. Susan Ewing, Dec. 30, 1967; children: Jonathan, Andrew, Dana. BA in Geology, Brown U., 1965; PhD, U. Chgo., 1971. Prof. earth sci. Northeastern Ill. U., Chgo., 1971—; disting. prof., 1991; pres. Shabica & Assocs. Coastal Cons., Inc., Northfield, Ill., 1985—. Chmn. bd. dirs. Aesti Corp., 1991-96; rsch. collaborator Nat. Park Svc., 1978-82, 89—; adj. prof. Coll. V.I., St. Thomas, 1980, adj. prof. environ. sci. Northwestern U., Evanston, 1999-2003; Kellogg fellow Northeastern Ill. U., 1979—; chmn. Task Force on Lake Michigan, Chgo., 1986-89; mem. Chgo. Shoreline Protection Commn., 1987-88; cons. Shedd Aquarium, Chgo., 1991; mem. Ft. Sheridan Commn., 1989-90; bd. dirs. Winnetka (Ill.) Hist. Soc. Editor: (with Andrew A. Hay) Richardson's Guide to the Fossil Fauna of Mazon Creek, 1997. Commr., packmaster Boy Scouts Am., Winnetka, Ill., 1984-88. Coop. Inst. for Limnology and Ecosystems Rsch. Lab. fellow. Mem. ASCE, Internat. Assn. for Great Lakes Rsch., Am. Shore and Beach Preservation Assn. (bd. dirs., pres. Great Lakes chpt.), Sigma Xi. Home: 326 Ridge Ave Winnetka IL 60093-3842 Office: 550 W Frontage Rd Ste 3735 Northfield IL 60093-1246 Office Phone: 847-446-1436. Personal E-mail: charles@shabica.com.

SHADID, GEORGE P., state legislator; b. Clinton, Iowa, May 15, 1929; m. Lorraine; two children. Sheriff, Peoria County, Ill., 1976-93; mem. Ill. State Senate Dist. 46, 1993—, mem. judiciary, higher edn. and exec. appts. coms. Office: Ill Senate Mems Rm 309H State Capitol Springfield IL 62706-0001

SHADUR, MILTON IRVING, judge; b. St. Paul, June 25, 1924; s. Harris and Mary Shadur; m. Eleanor Pilka, Mar. 30, 1946; children: Robert, Karen, Beth. BS, U. Chgo., 1943, JD cum laude, 1949. Bar: Ill. 1949, U.S. Supreme Ct. 1957. Pvt. practice, Chgo., 1949-80; assoc. Goldberg, Devoe & Brussell, 1949-51; ptnr. Shadur, Krupp & Miller and predecessor firms, 1951-80; judge U.S. Dist. Ct. (no. dist.) Ill., Chgo., 1980-92, sr. judge, 1992—. Commr. Ill. Supreme Ct. Character and Fitness, 1961-72, chmn., 1971; gen. counsel Ill. Jud. Inquiry Bd., 1975-80; chmn. adv. com. on evidence rules to Jud. Conf. of U.S., 1999-2002, mem. adv. com., 1992-99. Editor-in-chief: U. Chgo. Law Rev., 1948-49. Chmn. visiting com. U. Chgo. Law Sch., 1971-76, mem. vis. com., 1989-92, 99-2002; bd. dirs. Legal Assistance Found. Chgo., 1972-78; trustee Village of Glencoe, 1969-74, Ravinia Festival Assn., 1976-93, exec. com. 1983-93, vice chmn. 1989-93, life trustee, 1994—. Lt. (j.g.) USNR, 1943-46. Fellow Am. Bar Found.; mem. ABA (spl. com. on youth edn. for citizenship 1975-79), Ill. State Bar Assn. (joint com. on rules of jud. conduct 1974), Chgo. Bar Assn. (chmn. legis. com. 1963-65, jud. com. 1970-71, profl. ethics com. 1975-76, sec. 1967-69), Chgo. Council Lawyers, Order of Coif Office: US Dist Ct 219 S Dearborn St Ste 2388 Chicago IL 60604-1800 Office Phone: 312-435-5766.

SHADUR, ROBERT H., lawyer; b. Chgo., June 17, 1947; Upper 2d degree, U. Birmingham, Eng., 1968; BA magna cum laude, UCLA, 1969; JD, U. Chgo., 1972. Bar: Ill. 1973. Former ptnr. Winston & Strawn, Chgo.; ptnr. Barnes & Thornburg, Chgo., 1998—. Mem. ABA, Ill. State Bar Assn., Chgo. Bar Assn., Phi Beta Kappa. Office: 1 N Wacker DR #4400 Chicago IL 60606-2833

SHAEVSKY, MARK, lawyer; b. Harbin, Manchuria, China, Dec. 2, 1935; came to U.S., 1938, naturalized, 1944; s. Tolio and Rae (Weinstein) S.; m. Lois Ann Levi, Aug. 2, 1964; children: Thomas Lyle, Lawrence Keith. Student, Wayne State U., Detroit, 1952—53; BA with highest distinction, U. Mich., Ann Arbor, 1956; JD with highest distinction, U. Mich., 1959. Bar: Mich. 1959. Law clerk to presiding judge US Dist. Ct., Detroit, 1960-61; assoc. Honigman, Miller, Schwartz & Cohn, Detroit, 1961-64, ptnr., 1965-69, sr. ptnr., 1969—2001, of counsel, 2001—05; prin., owner Mark Shaevsky & Assocs., LLC, Farmington Hills, 2006—. Instr. law Wayne State U. Law Sch., Detroit, 1961-64; comml. arbitrator Am. Arbitration Assn., Detroit; bd. dir. Charter One Fin. Inc., Charter One Bank, H.W. Kaufman Fin. Group, Inc., Freya Fanning Mgmt., LLC, USF Ins. Co. Contbr. Wayne State U. Law Rev., U. Mich. Law Rev., 1957-59, asst. editor, 1958-59. Dir. Detroit Mens Orgn. of Rehab. through Tng., 1969—79; trustee William Beaumont Hosp., 1997—, Beaumont Found., 1997—2005, Jewish Vocat. Svcs., 1973—76; mem. exec. bd. Am. Jewish Com., 1965—74; sec., dir. Am. Friends Hebrew U., 1976—84; mem. capital needs com. Jewish Welfare Fedn., 1986—97; bd. dir. William Beaumont Hosp., 2002—, Shaevsky Family Found., 2000—. With US Army, 1959—60. Burton Abstract fellow, 1959. Mem. ABA, Mich. Bar Assn., Franklin Hills Country Club, Detroit Athletic Club, Order of the Coif, Phi Beta Kappa. Home: The Hills of Lone Pine 4750 N Chipping Gln Bloomfield Hills MI 48302-2390 Office: 30883 Northwestern Hwy Ste 200 Farmington MI 48334 Office Phone: 248-737-0808. Business E-Mail: advisors@mshaevsky.com.

SHAFER, ERIC CHRISTOPHER, minister; b. Hanover, Pa., Apr. 10, 1950; s. B. Henry and Doris M. (Von Bergen) S.; m. Kristi L. Owens, Nov. 24, 1973. BA, Muhlenberg Coll., 1972; MDiv, Hamma Sch. Theology, 1976. Ordained to ministry Luth. Ch. Am., 1976. Pastor Holy Trinity Meml. Luth. Ch., Catasauqua, Pa., 1976-83; asst. to Bishop Northeastern Pa. Synod, Wescosville, Pa., 1983-92; staff commn. for fin. support Evang. Luth. Ch. in Am., Chgo., 1988-92, asst. dir. dept. for comm., 1992-93, dir. dept. for comm., 1993—. Contbg. editor The Lutheran mag., 1989-92. Trustee Muhlenberg Coll., Allentown, Pa., 1972-83; bd. dirs. Luth. Film Assn., 1993—; chmn. comm. commn. Nat. Coun. Chs. in USA, 1996—2003, mem. exec. bd., 1996—2003. Democrat. Lutheran. Avocations: running, computers, photography, travel. Office: Evang Luth Ch in Am 8765 W Higgins Rd Chicago IL 60631-4178 Office Phone: 773-380-2960. Business E-Mail: eric.shafer@elca.org.

SHAFF, KAREN E., lawyer, insurance company executive; BA, Northwestern U., Evanston, Ill.; JD, Drake U., Des Moines. Atty. Austin and Gaudineer, Des Moines, 1979—82, Principal Fin. Group, 1982—83, asst. counsel, 1983—86, assoc. counsel, 1986—90, sr. v.p., gen. counsel, 1999—2004, exec. v.p., 2004—, gen. counsel, 2004—. Bd. dir. Sargasso Mut. Ins. Co., GuideOne Mut. Ins. Co., GuideOne Specialty Mut. Ins. Co. Bd. mem. Hospice of Ctrl. Iowa Found., Sci. Ctr. of Iowa; trustee Grinnell Coll.; mem. Greater Des Moines Partnership. Mem.: ABA, Assn. Life Ins. Counsel (bd. mem., pres. elect), Am. Corp. Counsel Assn., Polk County Bar Assn., Iowa State Bar Assn. (mem. bd. gov. 1989—95). Office: Principal Fin Group 711 High St Des Moines IA 50392

SHAFFER, ALAN LEE, manufacturing systems company executive; b. Cin., Aug. 10, 1950; s. Stanley Edward and Stella Pauline (Lilly) S.; Sharon Elizabeth Schleicher, Dec. 7, 1973; children: Alex, Kelly, Adam, Molly. ASMechE, U. of Cin., 1971; BS in Applied Sci., Miami U., Oxford, Ohio, 1973. Sales project engr. Cin. Milacron, 1973-77, product mgr., 1977-80, div. mgr., 1980-82, gen. mgr. products, 1982-84, gen. sales mgr., 1984-85, group mgr., 1985-86, group v.p., 1986—. Bd. dirs. Grinding Wheel Inst., Cleve., 1984. Mem. Oak Hills Bd. Edn., Cin., 1986—; chmn. Sch. Tax Levy Campaign, Cin., 1986-87.

SHAFFER, HARRY GEORGE, economics professor; b. Vienna, Aug. 28, 1919; arrived in U.S., 1940; s. Max Schaffer and Teofilia (Infeld) Schaffer Weissman; m. Betty Rosenzweig, June 7, 1987; children by previous marriages: Bernard Charles, Ronald Eric, Len Joseph, Tanya Elaine; stepchildren: Rene Carlis, Jamie Paul. BS, NYU, 1947, MA, 1948, PhD, 1958. Instr. Concord Coll., Athens, W.Va., 1948-50, U. Ala., Tuscaloosa, 1950-56; from asst. prof. to prof. U. Kans., Lawrence, 1956-69, prof. econs. and Soviet and East European studies, 1969—90, prof. emeritus, 1990—. Vis. prof. Portland State Coll., Oreg., summer 1963, U. Calif.-Davis, 1973-74. Author: English-Language Periodic Publications on Communism, 1971, Periodicals on the Socialist Countries and on Marxism, 1977, Women in the Two Germanies, 1981, American Capitalism and the Changing Role of Government, 1999; author booklet: The U.S. Conquers the West, 1974; editor: The Soviet Economy, 1963, rev. edit., 1969, The Soviet System in Theory and Practice, 1965, 2d edit., 1984, The Communist World: Marxist and Non-Marxist Views, 1967; (with Jan Prybyla) From Under-Development to Affluence: Western, Soviet and Chinese Views, 1968; editor, contbg. author: The Soviet Treatment of Jews, 1974, Soviet Agriculture, 1977, American Capitalism and the Changing Role of Government, 1999; contbr. articles to profl. jours. Served with M.I., US Army, 1943-44 Mem. Am. Econ. Assn., Assn. Comparative Econ. Studies, AAUP, Ams. for Dem. Action, Common Cause, NAACP, Unity Ch., Beta Gamma Sigma Democrat. Jewish. Home: 2510 Jasu Dr Lawrence KS 66046-4537 Office: U Kans Dept Econs 355 Snow Hall Lawrence KS 66045-7522 Office Phone: 785-864-3501.

SHAFFER, MICHAEL L., transportation company executive; b. Eldorado, Ill., Dec. 28, 1945; s. L.E. Jim Shaffer and Berniece (Belva) Andrews; m. Mary Elaine Charboneau, Jan. 30, 1970; children: Michelle, James. Dispatcher Atlas Van Lines, Inc., Long Beach, Calif., 1969-73, ops. mgr. Hyattsville, Md., 1973-75, Evansville, Ind., 1975-80, asst. v.p., 1980-84; v.p., gen mgr. Atlas Van Lines Texas, Austin, 1983-84; v.p. ops. Atlas Van Lines, Inc., Evansville, 1984-88, sr. v.p., 1988-90; pres. U.S. Transp. Group, 1991-98; chmn., CEO Atlas Van Lines, Inc., 1998—. With U.S. Army, 1963-65, Vietnam. Roman Catholic. Home: 3599 Crossgate Ct Newburgh IN 47630-9661 Office: Atlas Van Lines Inc 1212 Saint George Rd Evansville IN 47711-2364

SHAFFER, ROBERT M.M., lawyer; b. Cin., June 6, 1968; BA, Yale U., 1990; JD, U. Cin., 1996. Bar: Ohio 1996. Atty. Warren County Prosecutor's Office, Ohio; assoc. Vorys, Sater, Seymour and Pease LLP, Cin. Named one of Ohio's Rising Stars, Super Lawyers, 2006. Mem.: Ohio State Bar Assn., Cin. Bar Assn. Office: Vorys, Sater, Seymour and Pease LLP Atrium Two Ste 2000 221 E Fourth St PO Box 0236 Cincinnati OH 45202-0236 Office Phone: 513-723-4085. Office Fax: 513-852-7815.

SHAFFER, THOMAS LINDSAY, lawyer, educator; b. Billings, Mont., Apr. 4, 1934; s. Cecil Burdette and Margaret Jeanne (Parker) S.; m. Nancy Jane Lehr, Mar. 19, 1954; children: Thomas, Francis, Joseph, Daniel, Brian, Mary, Andrew, Edward. BA, U. Albuquerque, 1958; JD, U. Notre Dame, 1961; LLD, St. Mary's U., 1983. Bar: Ind. 1961. Assoc. Barnes, Hickam, Pantzer, & Boyd, Indpls., 1961-63; prof. law U. Notre Dame, Ind., 1963-80, assoc. dean, 1969-71, dean, 1971-75, Robert and Marion Short prof., 1988-97; Robert and Marion Short prof. emeritus, 1997—; supervising atty. Notre Dame Legal Aid Clinic, 1991—; prof. law Washington and Lee U., 1980-87, Robert E.R. Huntley prof. law, 1987-88. Vis. prof. UCLA, 1970-71, U. Va., 1975-76, U. Maine, 1982, 87, 98, Boston Coll., 1992; mem. Ind. Constl. Revision Commn., 1969-70, Ind. Trust Code Study Commn., 1968-71; reporter Ind. Jud. Conf., 1963, 67. Author: Death, Property, and Lawyers, 1970, The Planning and Drafting of Wills and Trusts, 1972, 5th edit., 2007, On Being a Christian and a Lawyer, 1981, American Legal Ethics, 1985, Faith and the Professions, 1987, Moral Memoranda From John Howard Yoder, 2002; co-author: Lawyers, Law Students, and People, 1977, Cases in Legal Interviewing and Counseling, 1980, American Lawyers and Their Communities, 1991, Property Cases, Materials and Problems, 1992, 3rd edit., 2006, Lawyers, Clients, and Moral Responsibility, 1994, Legal Interviewing and Counseling, 1976, 4th edit., 2004; co-editor: The Mentally Retarded Citizen and the Law, 1976; contbr. articles to profl. jours. Served with USAF, 1953-57. Frances Lewis scholar Washington and Lee U., 1979; recipient Emil Brown Found. Preventive Law prize, 1966, Presdl. citation U. Notre Dame, 1975, St. Thomas More award St. Mary's U., 1983, Law medal Gonzaga U., 1991, Reinhold Niebuhr award U. Notre Dame, 1991, Jour. Law and Religion award, 1993. Mem. Ind. State Bar Assn., Jewish Law Assn. Roman Catholic. Home: 1865 Champlain Dr Niles MI 49120-8935 Office: otre Dame Legal Aid Clinic 725 Howard St South Bend IN 46617-1529 Office Phone: 574-631-7250. Personal E-mail: shaffer@nd.edu.

SHAH, RAJESH K., auto parts manufacturing executive; B, U. Bombay; MBA, Bowling Green U. CPA. Various sr. level positions including v.p., COO Dayton Walther divsn. Varity Corp.; v.p. fin. and planning Kelsey Hayes; dir. fin. Perkins Engine Peterborough, Eng.; v.p., CFO United Techs. Automotives divsn. United Techs. Corp.; exec. v.p., CFO Collins & Aikman Corp.; leader MIS.

SHAH, SURENDRA POONAMCHAND, engineering educator; b. Bombay, Aug. 30, 1936; s. Poonamchand C. and Maniben (Modi) S.; m. Dorothie Crispell, June 9, 1962; children: Daniel S., Byron C. BE, B.V.M. Coll. Engring., India, 1959; MS, Lehigh U., 1960; PhD, Cornell U., 1965. Asst. prof. U. Ill., Chgo., 1966-69, assoc. prof., 1969-73, prof., 1973-81; prof. civil engring Northwestern U., Evanston, Ill., 1981—, dir. Ctr. for Advanced Cement Based Materials, 1989—, prof. civil engring., 1989—, Walter P. Murphy prof. of engring., 1992—. Cons. govt. agys. and industry, U.S.A., UN, France, Switzerland, People's Republic China, Denmark, The Netherlands; vis. prof. MIT, 1969, Delft U., The Netherlands, 1976, Denmark Tech. U., 1984, LCPC, Paris, 1986, U. Sidney, Australia, 1987; ATO vis. sci. Turkey, 1992; disting. vis. prof. Nat. Singapore U., 1999, vis. chair prof. Denmark Tech. U., 2002; hon. prof. Hongkong Poly. U, 2003-. Co-author: Fiber Reinforced Cement Composites, 1992, High Performance Concrete and Applications, 1994, Fracture Mechanics of Concrete, 1995; contbr. more than 400 articles to profl. jours.; editor 20 books; mem. editorial bds. 2 internat. jours.; editor-in-chief Jour. Materials and Structures, 2001-05. Recipient Thompson award ASTM, Phila., 1983, Disting. US Vis. Scientist award Alexander von Humboldt Found., 1989, Swedish Concrete award, Stockholm, 1993, Engring. News Record award of Newsmaker, 1995, Charles Perkow award, 1997, Fulbright Lectureship award, India, 2007, Della Roy Lecture, Am. Ceramic Soc., Detroit, 2007; named one of 10 Most Influential Persons, Concrete Constrn., 2006. Fellow Am. Concrete Inst. (chmn. tech. com., Anderson award 1989, 99, Henry Crown award 2000, Symposium in his honor 2002, Robert Philbo award 2006), Internat. Union Testing and Rsch. Labs. Materials and Structures (chmn. tech. com. 1989—, mgmt. adv. bd. 1996—, Gold medal 1980, symposium in his honor 2004); mem. NAE, ASCE (past chmn. tech. com., mem. exec. com., mem. adv. bd., Richard J. Caroll Meml. Lectr. 2001). Achievements include dedicated in his honor RILEM 7th international conference on fiber reinforced concrete and was given a special award, Italy, 2004; symposium in his honor during the 13th European fracture conference in Greece, 2006. Home: 921 Isabella St Evanston IL 60201-1773 Office: Northwestern U Tech Inst Rm A130 2145 Sheridan Rd Evanston IL 60208-0834 Home Phone: 847-475-6858; Office Phone: 847-491-3858. Business E-Mail: s-shah@northwestern.edu.

SHAH, Y. T., academic administrator; BSChemE, U. Mich.; MS, ChE, DSc, MIT. Prof. chem. engring. U. Pitts., 1969—87; dean engring. and sci. U. Tulsa, 1987—91; disting. prof., dean Coll. Engring. Drexel U., Phila., 1991—97; sr. vice provost for rsch. and grad. studies, chief rsch. scientist Clemon U., 1997; provost U. Mo., Rolla, 2002—. Mem.: AIChE, Am. Chem. Soc., Am. Soc. Elec. Engring.

SHAHEEN, CHRISTOPHER T., lawyer; b. 1962; BA in Internat. Rels. magna cum laude, Bucknell Univ., 1984; JD cum laude, Harvard Univ., 1987. Bar: Pa. 1989, Minn. 1994. Assoc. Bustamante & Crespo, Ecuador, 1987; law clerk, Hon. Samuel Conti US Dist Ct, No. Dist., Calif., 1988—89; trial atty. US Dept. Justice, civil rights divsn., 1989—94; assoc., litig. dept. Dorsey & Whitney LLP, Mpls., 1994—97, ptnr., trial dept., 1998—, and co-chair, tax, trust, estate litig. group. Bd. dir. Project for Pride in Living, Inc.; chmn. Kenwood Isles Area Assn. Grantee Humphrey Inst. Policy Fellow, Univ. Minn., 1999—2000. Mem.: ABA, Hennepin County Bar Assn., Minn. State Bar Assn. Office: Dorsey & Whitney LLP Ste 1500 50 S Sixth St Minneapolis MN 55402-1498 Office Phone: 612-340-2886. Office Fax: 612-340-2807. Business E-Mail: shaheen.christopher@dorsey.com.

SHAHEEN, GERALD L., manufacturing executive; B in Mktg., Bradley U., 1966, M, 1968. With Caterpillar Inc., Peoria, Ill., 1967—, mng. dir. Geneva, Switzerland, 1995, v.p. engring. products divsn. Peoria, 1995, group pres., 1998—. Chmn. bd. dirs. US C. of C.; bd. dir. UtiliCorp United, National City Corp. Office: Caterpillar Inc 100 NE Adams St Peoria IL 61629-0002 Office Phone: 309-692-0822.

SHAIN, IRVING, retired chemicals executive, academic administrator; b. Seattle, Jan. 2, 1926; s. Samuel and Selma (Blockoff) S.; m. Mildred Ruth Udell, Aug. 31, 1947; children: Kathryn A., Steven T., John R., Paul S. BS in Chemistry, U. Wash., 1949, PhD in Chemistry, 1952. From instr. to prof. U. Wis., Madison, 1952-75, vice chancellor, 1970-75, chancellor, 1977-86; provost, v.p. acad. affairs U. Wash., Seattle, 1975-77; v.p. Olin Corp., Stamford, Conn.,

1987-92, ret., 1992, also bd. dirs. Mem. tech. adv. bd. Johnson Controls, Inc., Milw., 1980-2003; trustee Univ. Rsch. Park, Inc., Madison, pres., 1984-86, v.p., 1987—; mem. Nat. Commn. on Superconductivity, 1989-90. Contbr. articles on electroanalytical chemistry to profl. jours. Bd. dirs. Madison Gen. Hosp., 1972-75; v.p. Madison Cmty. Found., 1984-86; mem. CEO adv. bd. Kamehameha Schs./Bishop Estates, 2002-04; mem. bd. dirs. Madison Symphony Orch., 2006-. With U.S. Army, 1943-46, PTO. Fellow AAAS, Wis. Acad. Scis., Arts and Letters; mem. Am. Chem. Soc., Electrochem. Soc., Conn. Acad. Sci. and Engring., Phi Beta Kappa, Sigma Xi, Phi Kappa Phi, Alpha Chi Sigma (Chemistry Hall of Fame 2006-). Home: 2820 Marshall Ct # 8 Madison WI 53705-2270 Office Phone: 608-441-8000. E-mail: i.shain@att.net.

SHAKNO, ROBERT JULIAN, hospital and social services administrator; b. Amsterdam, Holland, Aug. 15, 1937; came to U.S., 1939, naturalized, 1944; s. Rudy C. and Gertrude S.; m. Linda, June 10, 1962; children: Steven Lee, Deborah Sue. BBA (scholar 1955), So. Methodist U., 1959; M.H.A., Washington U., St. Louis, 1961. Adminstrv. asst. Mt. Sinai Hosp., Chgo., 1961—63; asso. adminstr. Tex. Inst. Rehab. and Research, Houston, 1963—65; asst. adminstr. Michael Reese Hosp., Chgo., 1965—70, v.p., hosp. dir., 1970—73; asso. exec. dir. Cook County Hosp., Chgo., 1973—75; pres. Hackensack Med. Center, NJ, 1975—85, Mt. Sinai Med. Ctr., Cleve., 1985—96; dir. nat. strategy practice KPMG Peat Marwick, 1996-98; v.p. med. affairs, vice dean sch. of medicine Case Western Res. U., 1998—2002; pres., CEO Jewish Family Svc., Cleve., 2002—05; ptnr. Tatum Ptnrs., LLC, Deerfield, Ill., 2005—, exec. svc. corp., Chgo., 2007—. Bd. dirs. Ohio Hosp. Inc. Co. Mem. editorial bd. Mgmt. Series, Am. Coll. Healthcare Execs. Mem. Leadership Cleve.; bd. dirs. Premier Hosp. Alliance, chmn., 1994-96; bd. dirs. The New Cleve. Inc., Univ. Circle Inc., Cleve., Cleve. Sight Ctr.; trustee Hope Lodge, Cleve. chpt. Am. Cancer Soc.; chmn. elect, bd. dirs. Jewish Family Svcs.; chmn. social svcs. divsn. United Jewish Appeal, Cleve., 1987-88, chmn. health cabinet, 1990, gen. co-chmn., 1990—; chmn. Hosp. Pacesetter campaign United Way, chmn. health svcs. portfolio, 1988-89, oversight commn., 1992-93; bd. trustees Mount Sinai Health Sys., Chgo., 2006-. Served to 1st lt. USAR, 1960-66. Named Young Adminstr. of Yr., Washington U., 1968 Fellow Am. Coll. Hosp. Adminstrs.; mem. Am. Hosp. Assn. (coun. urban hosps., del. coun. on met. hosps., rep. regional policy bd.), Washington U. Alumni Assn. (past pres.), Greater Cleve. Hosp. Assn. (bd. dirs.), Ohio Hosp. Assn. (bd. dirs.), Cleve. Sight Ctr. (trustee, bd. dirs.), Sigma Alpha Mu (past pres.). Home: 908 Island Ct Deerfield IL 60015 Office Phone: 312-909-2022. Personal E-mail: lbs1shak@sbcglobal.net.

SHALLENBURGER, TIM, state official; m. Linda N. Shallenburger. Rep. dist. 1 Kans. Ho. of Reps., speaker; state treas. Topeka, Kans., 1999—. Republican. Office: Office Kans State Treas 900 SW Jackson St Rm 201N Topeka KS 66612-1221 Home: 1538 Garfield Ave Baxter Spgs KS 66713-1768

SHANAHAN, BETTY, professional society administrator; BSEE, Mich. State. U.; M of Software Engring., Wang Inst. of Grad. Studies; MBA in Strategic Mgmt., U. Chgo. Grad. Sch. of Bus. Cert. assn. exec. Various positions in devel., engring. mgmt. and mktg. Data Gen., Alliant Computer Sys., 1978—90; mktg. mgmt., including v.p., prod. mgmt. and mktg., software components divsn. Stellent, Inc., 1990—2002; exec. dir. Soc. of Women Engr., Chgo., 2002—. Bd. dir. Women in Engring. Programs and Adv. Network; bd. dirs. JETS; champions bd. Nat. Girls Collaborative Project. Fellow: Soc. Women Engr. (life); mem.: IEEE, Am. Soc. of Assn. Execs., Assn. for Computing Machinery. Office: Exec Dir Soc of Women Engr 230 E Ohio St Chicago IL 60611

SHANAHAN, BRENDAN FREDERICK, professional hockey player; b. Mimico, Ont., Can., Jan. 23, 1969; Left wing NJ Devils, 1987—91, St. Louis Blues, 1991—95, Hartford Whalers, 1995—97, Detroit Red Wings, 1997—2006, NY Rangers, 2006—. Named one of NHL All-Star Game, 1994, 1996—2000, 2002, 2007; named to First All-Star Team, NHL, 1994, 2000, Second All-Star Team, 2002; recipient King Clancy Meml. Trophy, 2003, Mark Messier Leadership Award, 2006. Achievements include being a member of Stanley Cup Champion Detroit Red Wings, 1997, 1998, 2002; being a member of gold medal Canadian Hockey team, Salt Lake City Olympic Games, 2002. Office: NY Rangers Hockey Club 2 Pennsylvania Plaza New York NY 10121

SHANAHAN, MICHAEL FRANCIS, retired manufacturing executive, former hockey team executive; b. St. Louis, Oct. 29, 1939; m. Mary Ann Barrett; children: Megan Elizabeth, Michael Francis Jr., Maureen Patricia. BS in Commerce, St. Louis U.; postgrad., Washington U., St. Louis; LHD (hon.), St. Louis Rabbinical Coll., 1987; PhD (hon.), St. Louis U., 2002. With McDonnell Douglas Automation Co., St. Louis, 1962-73, sales mgr., 1969-71, br. mgr., 1971-72, mktg. dir. cen. region, 1972-73; mktg. v.p. Numerical Control Inc., St. Louis, 1973-74, pres., 1974-79; v.p. Cleve. Pneumatic Co. (formerly Numerical Control Inc.), St. Louis, 1979-82; chmn., chief exec. officer Engineered Air Systems Inc., St. Louis, 1982—; former chmn., ceo St. Louis Blues Hockey Team. Bd. dirs. Engineered Air Systems Inc. (chmn.), St. Louis Blues Hockey Inc. (chmn.); adv. com. Nat. Hockey League; mem. U.S. Senatorial Bus. Adv. Bd.; bd. dirs. Capital Bank and Trust of Clayton, The Graphic Arts Ctr. Inc., Kilo Rsch. Found. (vice chmn.). Bd. dirs. Am. Heart Assn., St. Louis Ambassadors, Catholic Charities of St. Louis, Galway Sister City Com., The Backstoppers, Christmas in St. Louis Found.; nat. bd. dirs. Boys Hope; bd. trustees, pres. coun. St. Louis U.; adv. bd. Safe Kids; hon. bd. Paraquad; hon. chmn. Small Bus. Week in St. Louis, 1989; hon. co-chmn. Veteran's Day Observance and Parade, 1989; co-chairperson AMC Cancer Rsch. Ctr. Community Svc. award. Named St. Louis Ambassador of Yr., 1986, Olivette Businessman of Yr., 1987, St. Louis Bus. Leader of Yr. Coll. Bus. Adminstrn., So. Ill. U. at Carbondale, 1987,Outstanding Philanthropist St. Louis chpt., Nat. Soc. Fund Raising Execs., 1987; recipient Spirit of Life award City of Hope Labor Mgmt., 1987, St. Louis U. Alumni Merit award, 1987, Meritorious Svc. to Sports award MS Soc., 1987, Presdl. Sports award Maryville Coll., 1987, Sales Exec. of Yr. award Sales and Mktg. Execs. of Met. St. Louis, 1988, St. Louis Port Coun.'s Mgmt. Man of the Yr. award Greater St. Louis Area and Vicinity Port Council, Maritime Trades Dept., AFL-CIO., 1989. Mem. Alzeimer's Disease and Related Disorders Assn. (hon.), St. Louis Counts, Hawthorn Found., St. Louis Club, Mo. Athletic Club, Old Warson Country Club, Boone Valley Country Club. Home: 10 Trent Dr Saint Louis MO 63124-1033 Office: Engineered Air Systems Inc 201 Evans Ln Saint Louis MO 63121-1126

SHANAHAN, THOMAS M., judge; b. Omaha, May 5, 1934; m. Jane Estelle Lodge, Aug. 4, 1956; children: Catherine, Thomas M. II, Mary Elizabeth, Timothy F. AB magna cum laude, U. Notre Dame, 1956; JD, Georgetown U., 1959. Bar: Nebr., Wyo. Mem. McGinley, Lane, Mueller, Shanahan, O'Donnell & Merritt, Ogallala, Nebr.; assoc. justice Nebr. Supreme Ct., Lincoln, 1983-93; judge U.S. Dist. Ct. Nebr., Omaha, 1993—. Office: US Dist Ct 111 S 18th Plz Ste 3141 Omaha NE 68102

SHANDS, COURTNEY, JR., lawyer; b. St. Louis, Mar. 17, 1929; s. Courtney and Elizabeth W. (Jones) S.; m. Frances Jean Schellfeffer, Aug. 9, 1952 (div. 1976); children: Courtney III, E.F. Berkley, Elizabeth V.; m. Nancy Bliss Lewis, Oct. 25, 1980. AB, Washington U., St. Louis, 1951; LLB, Harvard U., 1954. Assoc. Thompson and Mitchell, St. Louis, 1954-62, ptnr., 1962-63, Thompson, Walther and Shewmaker, St. Louis, 1963-69, Kohn, Shands, Elbert, Gianoulakis & Giljum, St. Louis, 1970—. Trustee Frank G. and Florence V. Bohle Scholarship Found., Edward Chase Garvey Meml. Found., L.F. Jones Charitable Trust, 1958-60; bd. dirs. St. Louis Fund, 1972—, Law Libr. St. Louis, 1988—, pres. 1995—; bd. dirs. Hope Ednl. & Rsch. Found., 1989—, pres. 1995—, Citizenship Edn. Clearing House, St. Louis, 1985-87, pres. 1986-87, Mark Twain Summer Inst., St. Louis, 1968-89, pres., 1974-79; Andrews Acad., 1989—, v.p., 1989—; pres. com. Goldwater for Pres., Met. St. Louis, 1964, Ea. Mo. chpt. ACLU, 1966-69, nat. bd. dirs. 1969-72. Mem. ABA, Mo. Bar Integrated, Bar Assn. of Met. St. Louis, Selden Soc., Law Libr. Assn. (Mo. sect.), Noonday Club, Racquet Club, St. Louis Club. Republican. Episcopalian. Office: Kohn Shands Elbert 1 Mercantile Ctr Fl 24 Saint Louis MO 63101-1643

SHANE, SANDRA KULI, postal service administrator; b. Akron, Ohio, Dec. 12, 1939; d. Amiel M. and Margaret E. (Brady) Kuli; m. Fred Shane, May 30, 1962 (div. 1972); 1 child, Mark Richard; m. Byrl William Campbell, Apr. 26, 1981 (dec. 1984). BA, U. Akron, 1987, postgrad., 1988-90. Scheduler motor vehicle bur. Akron Police Dept., 1959-62; flight and ops. control staff Escort Air, Inc., Akron and Cleve., 1972-78; asst. traffic mgr. Keen Transport, Inc., Hudson, Ohio, 1978-83; mem. ops. and mktg. staff Shawnee Airways and Essco, Akron, 1983-86; in distbn. U.S. Postal Svc., Akron, 1986—. Rec. sec. Affirmative Action Coun., Akron, 1988-90. Asst. art tchr. Akron Art Mus., 1979; counselor Support, Inc., Akron, 1983-84; com. chmn. Explorer post Boy Scouts Am., Akron, 1984-85. Mem. Bus. and Profl. Women's Assn. (pres.), Delta Nu Alpha. Democrat. Roman Catholic. Avocations: painting, sculpting, fabric design. Home: 745 Hampton Ridge Dr Akron OH 44313

SHANINE, GEORGE, sales executive, information technology executive; b. Peoria, Ill., 1974; Grad., U. Ill., Chgo. With IBM Corp., 1995—, head of Midwest brand sales divsn. Named one of 40 Under 40, Crain's Chgo. Bus. Home: 3803 Looking Post Ct Naperville IL 60564-5928

SHANK, WILLIAM O., lawyer; b. Hamilton, Ohio, Jan. 11, 1924; s. Horace Cooper and Bonnie (Winn) S.; m. Shirleen Allison, June 25, 1949; children—Allison Kay, Kristin Elizabeth. BA, Miami U., Oxford, Ohio, 1947; JD, Yale, 1950. Bar: (Ohio), (Ill.), (US Supreme Ct.). Pvt. practice, Hamilton, Ohio, 1951-55, Chgo., 1955—; mem. firm Shank, Briede & Spoerl, Hamilton, Ohio, 1951-55; assoc. Lord, Bissell & Brook, Chgo., 1955-58; atty. Chemetron Corp., 1958-60, sr. atty., 1960-61, gen. atty., asst. sec., 1961-71, sec., gen. counsel, 1971-78; v.p., gen. counsel, sec. Walgreen Co., Deerfield, Ill., 1978-89; ptnr. Burditt & Radzius, Chartered, Chgo., 1989-98; exec. v.p. Internat. Bus. Resources, Inc., Chgo., 1993—2000; ptnr. Williams Montgomery & John Ltd., Chgo., 1998—2003; of counsel Hinshaw & Culbertson, Crystal Lake, Ill., 2003—. Mem. bus. adv. coun. Miami U., Oxford, Ohio, 1975—; arbitrator 19th and 22d Jud. Cir., Ill., 1995—; adv. bd. eLawForum, Washington, 1999—. Bd. dirs. Coun. for Cmty. Svcs. Met. Chgo., 1973-77; trustee Libr. Internat. Rels., 1971-78; bd. dirs. Chgo. Civic Fedn., 1984-89, Walgreen Drug Stores Hist. Found., 1990—; mem. Chgo. Crime Commn., 1985-89. 1st lt., pilot 8th Air Force, USAAF, World War II, ETO. Fellow Am. Bar Found. (life); mem. ABA (com. corp. gen. counsel), Soc. Corp. Secs. and Governance Profls. (pres. Chgo. regional group 1983-84, nat. bd. dirs. 1984-87), Ill. State Bar Assn., Chgo. Bar Assn. (chmn. com. on corp. law depts. 1971-72, 89-90), Yale U. Law Sch. Assn. (past pres. Ill. Alumni, exec. com. New Haven), Walgreen Alumni Assn. (pres. 1992-94), Legal Club (pres. 1979-80), Law Club, Lawyers Club (Chgo.), Univ. Club, Econ. Club, Yale Club of Chgo., Am. Air Mus. in Britain (sustaining mem. 2004-), Omicron Delta Kappa, Phi Delta Phi, Sigma Chi. Home: 755 S Shore Dr Crystal Lake IL 60014-5530 Office: Hinshaw & Culbertson 500 Coventry Ln Crystal Lake IL 60014 Office Phone: 815-459-5123. E-mail: wshank@hinshawlaw.com.

SHANKEL, DELBERT MERRILL, microbiologist, biologist, educator; b. Plainview, Nebr., Aug. 4, 1927; s. Cecil Wilfred and Gladys Dalton (Dodd) Shankel; m. Carol Jo Mulford, Sept. 10, 1962; children: Merrill, Jill, Kelley. BA, Walla Walla Coll., 1950; PhD, U. Tex., 1959. Tchr. Walla Walla Coll. Acad., College Place, Wash., 1950-51; instr. San Antonio Coll., 1954-55; asst. prof., assoc. prof. microbiology and biology U. Kans., Lawrence, 1959-68, prof., 1968—, asst. dean, assoc. dean arts and sci., 1966-72, acting dean, 1973, exec. vice chancellor, 1974-80, 86, 90-92, acting chancellor, 1980-81, chancellor, 1994-95, chancellor emeritus, 1996. Commr. N. Ctrl. Assn. Colls. and Schs., Chgo., 1991—95, cons., evaluator, 1969—96, NW Comm. Coll., 1997—. Editor: Artimutagenesis and Anticarcinogenesis: Mechanisms vols. I-III, 1986, 1988, 1993; assoc. editor: Mutation Rsch., 1992—95. Active numerous civic orgns. With US Army, 1952—54. Named Disting. Alumnus of the Yr., Walla Walla Coll., 1989; recipient Outstanding Educator award, Mortar Bd., U. Kans., 1982, 1985, 1990; numerous rsch. grantee. Fellow: Am. Acad. Microbiology; mem.: Radiation Rsch. Soc., Soc. Gen. Microbiology (Eng.), Genetics Soc. Am., Environ. Mutagen Soc. (chmn. pub. policy com. 1991—93, mem. nat. coun. 1994—97), Am. Soc. Microbiology (past chmn. edn. com., chmn. numerous coms.), U. Kans. Alumni Assn. (interim pres., CEO 2004), Sigma Xi (pres. U. Kans. chpt. 1967). Republican. Unitarian Universalist. Avocations: sports, music, theater, reading. Office: U Kans 1002 Haworth Hl Lawrence KS 66045-0001 Office Phone: 785-864-3150. Business E-Mail: shankel@ku.edu.

SHANKLIN, CAROL W., dietician, educator; BS in Home Econs. Edn., U. Tenn., Martin, 1973; MS in Food Sys. Adminstrn., U. Tenn., Knoxville, 1974, PhD in Food Sys. Adminstrn., 1976. Asst. prof. foods and nutrition Tex. Tech. U., 1977—78; asst. food svc. dir. Highland Hosp., Lubbock, Tex., 1978; asst. prof. food sys. mgmt. Tex. Women's U., 1978—82, assoc. prof. food sys. mgmt., 1982—88, assoc. prof., chair dept. nutrition and food scis., 1985—87, prof., chair dept. nutrition and food scis., 1987—90; tech. advisor, cons. Miss. Inst. Higher Learning, 1988—89; grad. program dir., prof. dept. hotel, restaurant, instn. mgmt. and dietetics Kans. State U., Manhattan, 1990—2001, asst. dean. Grad. Sch., prof. dept. hotel, restaurant, instn. mgmt. and dietetics, 2001—04, assoc. dean. Grad. Sch., prof. dept. hotel, restaurant, instn. mgmt. and dietetics, 2004—07, prof. Grad. Sch., prof. dept. hotel, restaurant, instn. mgmt. and dietetics, 2007—. Contbr. articles to profl. jours. Recipient Michael Olsen Rsch. Achievement award, U. Del. Mem.: Am. Dietetic Assn. (Medallion award 2001). Achievements include research on environmental issues in the food service and hospitality industry; dietetics and hospitality education; quality service in food service operations; research in food service management, food safety and security in food service operations. Office: Kansas State U Graduate Sch 103 Fairchild Manhattan KS 66502-1404 Office Phone: 785-532-7927. Business E-Mail: shanklin@k-state.edu.

SHANNON, MARGARET ANNE, lawyer; b. Detroit, July 6, 1945; d. Johannes Jacob and Vera Marie (Spade) Van De Graaf; m. Robert Selby Shannon, Feb. 4, 1967. Student, Brown U., 1963-65; BA in History, Wayne State U., 1966, JD, 1973. Bar: Mich. 1973. Housing aide City of Detroit, 1967-68; employment supr. Sinai Hosp., Detroit, 1968-69; assoc. gen. counsel regulatory affairs Blue Cross Blue Shield Mich., Detroit, 1969-80; ptnr. Honigman Miller Schwartz and Cohn, Detroit, 1980-95, of counsel, 1996—. Nat. Merit scholar, 1963-66. Mem. Mich. State Bar (chmn. health care com. 1991, 92, co-chmn. payor subcom. health law sect.). Home: 1111 Orinoco Way Palm Beach Gardens FL 33410 Office: Honigman Miller Schwartz and Cohn 2290 First National Bldg Detroit MI 48226-3583 Office Phone: 313-465-7552. E-mail: mshannon@honigman.com.

SHANNON, WILLIAM NORMAN, III, finance educator, food service executive; b. Chgo., Nov. 20, 1937; s. William Norman Jr. and Lee (Lewis) S.; m. Bernice Urbanowicz, July 14, 1962; children: Kathleen Kelly, Colleen Patricia, Kerrie Ann. BS in Indsl. Mgmt., Carnegie Inst. Tech., 1959; MBA in Mktg. Mgmt., U. Toledo, 1963. Sales engr. Westinghouse Electric Co., Detroit, 1959-64; regional mgr. Toledo Scale, Chgo., 1964-70; v.p. J. Lloyd Johnson Assoc., Northbrook, Ill., 1970-72; mgr. spl. projects Hobart Mfg., Troy, Ohio, 1972-74; corp. v.p. mktg. Berkel, Inc., La Porte, Ind., 1974-79; gen. mgr. Berkel Products, Ltd., Toronto, Canada, 1975-78; chmn. Avant Industries, Inc., Wheeling, Ill., 1979-81; chmn., pres. Hacienda Mexican Restaurants, South Bend, Ind., 1978—95; chmn. Ziker Shannon Corp., South Bend, 1982-88, Hacienda Franchising Group, Inc., South Bend, Ind., 1987—92. Assoc. prof. mktg. and internat. bus. St. Mary's Coll., otre Dame, Ind., 1982—; chmn. Hacienda Franchise Group, Inc., 1987-96, Hacienda Mex. Restaurants Mgmt., Inc., 1994-96; sr. chmn. Hacienda Mex. Restaurants, 1996-2004; mem. London program faculty, 1986, 89, 92, 94, coord. internat. bus. curriculum, 1989—, mktg. curriculum, 1983; advisor Coun. Internat. Bus. Devel., Notre Dame, 1991-2005; mng. dir. Alden & Torch Lake Railway, 1995—. Co-author: Laboratory Computers, 1971; columnist Bus. Digest mag., 1988-1994; mem. editl. bd. Jour. Bus. and Indsl. Mktg., 1986-1992, South Bend Tribune Business Weekly, 1990-1994; contbr. articles to profl. jours. V.p. mktg. Jr. Achievement, South Bend, Ind., 1987-90; pres. Small Bus. Devel. Coun., South Bend., 1987-90; bd. dirs. Ind. Small Bus. Coun., Indpls., 1986—, Mental Health Assn., South Bend, 1987-90, Michiana World Trade Orgn., Internat. Bus. Edn., 1989-91; Entrepreneurs Alliance Ind., 1988-92, Nat. Small Bus. United, Washington, 1989-92, Women's Bus. Initiative, 1986-90, dir. ednl. confs., 1986-90; chmn. bd. trustees, Holy Cross Coll., Notre Dame, Ind., 1987-1993, chmn. edn. com., 1993-1993; chmn. St. Joseph County Higher Edn. Coun., 1988-91, Nat. Coun. Small Bus., Washington, 1988-1994; Midwest region adv. coun. U.S. SBA, 1988-91; at-large mem. U.S. Govt. Adv. Coun. on Small Bus., Washington, 1988-90, 1994-1996, chmn. Bus. and Econ. Devel. Com., 1988-90, 1994-1996; vice chmn. Internat. Trade Com., 1994-1996; nat. adv. coun. Women's Network for Entrepreneur Tng., 1991-1994; vice chmn. State of Ind. Enterprise Zone Bd., 1991-1994; elected del. White House Conf. Small Bus., Washington, 1986; bd. dirs. Ind. Small Bus. Devel. Ctrs. Adv. Bd.; co-pres. Helena Twp. Downtown Devel. Authority, 2002—. Named Small Bus. Person of the Yr., City of South Bend, 1987, Small Bus. Advocate of the Yr., State of Ind., 1987, Ind. Entrepreneur Advocate of the Yr., 1988. Mem. Am. Mktg. Assn. (chmn. Mich./Ind. chpt., pres. 1985-86), U.S. Assn. Small Bus. and Entrepreneurship (nat. v.p. for entrepreneurship edn. 1991-92, nat. v.p. entrepreneurship devel. 1992-1996), Ind. Inst. New Bus. Ventures (mktg. faculty 1987-91), Michiana Investment Network (vice chmn. 1988-91), SBA (adminstrn. adv. coun. 1988-1992, contbg. editor Our Town Michiana mag. 1988-91), U.S. C. of C., Nat. Coun. Small Bus. (Washington), South Bend C. of C. (bd. dirs. 1987-1996, vice chmn. membership 1993-1996), Assn. for Bus. Communications (co-chmn. Internat. Conf. 1986), Univ. Club Notre Dame (vice chmn.), Shamrock Club Notre Dame (exec. dir., trustee 1993-1996), Rotary. Roman Catholic. Office: Saint Mary's Coll Dept Bus Adminstrn Eco Notre Dame IN 46556 Office Phone: 574-284-4508.

SHANTZ, DEBRA MALLONEE, lawyer; b. Springfield, Mo., Aug. 12, 1963; d. Arnold Wayne and Jean Marie (Pyle) Mallonee; m. Joseph Benjamin Shantz, Dec. 26, 1987; children: Benjamin, Riley. BS, S.W. Mo. State U., 1984; JD, U. Mo., 1988. Ptnr. Farrington & Curtis, P.C., Springfield, Mo., 1988-95; corp. counsel John Q. Hammons Hotels, Springfield, Mo., 1995—2003, sr. v.p., gen. counsel, 2003—. Bd. mem. Springfield City Utilities; Discovery Ctr.; Jordan Valley Park Cmty. Improvement Dist. Mem.: ABA, State Bar Mo., Springfield Met. Bar Assn. Home: 1635 E Delmar St Springfield MO 65804-0207 Office: John Q Hammons Hotels Ste 900 300 John Q Hammons Pkwy Springfield MO 65806 E-mail: debbie.shantz@jqh.com.

SHAPIRA, DAVID S., food products and retail grocery executive; b. 1942; married. BA, Oberlin Coll., 1964; MA, Stanford U., 1966. V.p. Giant Eagle, Inc. (formerly Giant Eagle Markets, Inc.), Pitts., 1974—81, pres., 1981—94, CEO, also bd. dirs.; chmn. & CEO Giant Eagle, Youngstown; now chmn. bd. Phar-Mor Inc., Youngstown. Mem. bd. Allegheny Conf. Community Devel.

SHAPIRO, BURTON LEONARD, dentist, geneticist, educator; b. NYC, Mar. 29, 1934; s. Nat Lazarus and Fay Rebecca (Gartenhouse) S.; m. Eileen Roman, Aug. 11, 1958; children: orah Leah, Anne Rachael, Carla Faye. Student, Tufts U., Medford, Mass., 1951-54; DDS, NYU, 1958; MS, U. Minn., 1962, PhD, 1966. Faculty U. Minn. Sch. Dentistry, Mpls., 1962—, assoc. prof. div. oral pathology, 1966-70, prof., chmn. div. oral biology, 1970-79, prof., chmn. dept. oral biology, 1979-88, prof. dept. oral pathology and genetics, 1979-88, dir. grad. studies, mem. grad. faculty genetics, 1966—, prof. dept. oral sci., 1988—2006, mem. grad. faculty pathobiology, 1979; prof. dept. lab. medicine and pathology U. Minn. Sch. Medicine, 1985—; prof. emeritus U. Minn. Sch. Dentistry, 2006; mem. Human Genetics Inst. U. Minn. Sch. Medicine, 1988—, univ. senator, 1968-72, 88-93; also mem. med. staff U. Minn. Health Scis. Center; exec. com. Grad. Sch. U. Minn., chmn. health scis. policy rev. council, chmn. univ. faculty consultative com., 1988-92; chmn. univ. fin. and planning com. Grad. Sch. U. Minn., 1988. Hon. research fellow Galton Lab. dept. human genetics Univ. Coll., London, 1974; spl. vis. prof. Japanese Ministry Edn., Sci. and Culture, 1983 Mem. adv. editorial bd.: Jour. Dental Research, 1971—; Contbr. articles to profl. jours. Served to lt. USNR, 1958-60. Am. Cancer Soc. postdoctoral fellow, 1960-62; advanced fellow, 1965-68; named Century Club Prof. of Yr., 1988. Fellow Am. Acad. Oral Pathology, AAAS; mem. Internat. Assn. Dental Research (councilor 1969), Am. Soc. Human Genetics, Craniofacial Biology Soc. (pres. 1972), Sigma Xi, Omicron Kappa Upsilon. Home: 148 Nina St # 2 Saint Paul MN 55102-2160 Office: U Minn Sch Dentistry Dept Oral Sci Minneapolis MN 55455 Office Phone: 612-624-3991. Business E-Mail: burt@umn.edu.

SHAPIRO, JAMES EDWARD, judge; b. Chgo., May 28, 1930; BS, U. Wis., 1951; JD, Harvard U., 1954. Bar: Wis. 1956, U.S. Dist. Ct. (ea. dist.) Wis. 1956, U.S. Ct. Appeals (7th cir.) 1962, U.S. Supreme Ct. 1971. Sole practice, Milw., 1956-57; resident house counsel Nat. Presto Industries, Eau Claire, Wis., 1957-60; ptnr. Bratt & Shapiro, Milw., 1960-64; sole practice Milw., 1964-74; ptnr. Frank, Hiller & Shapiro, Milw., 1974-82; judge U.S. Bankruptcy Ct., Milw., 1982—, chief judge, 1996-2000. Mem. Bayside Bd. Appeals, Wis., 1969-77; Milwaukee County Ct. commr., 1969-78; dir. Milw. Legal Aid Soc., 1969-77. Served to 1st lt. U.S. Army, 1954-56. Jewish. Office: US Courthouse 140 Fed Bldg 517 E Wisconsin Ave Milwaukee WI 53202-4500 Office Phone: 414-297-3291 ext. 3201. Business E-Mail: james_e_shapiro@wieb.uscourts.gov.

SHAPIRO, KEITH J., lawyer; b. Chgo., Nov. 14, 1958; BS, Univ. Ill., 1980; JD, Emory Univ., 1983. Bar: Ill. 1983. Former chmn., pres. Am. Bankruptcy Inst.; co-mng. shareholder, co-chair nat. bus. reorganization and bankruptcy practice Greenberg Traurig LLP, Chgo. Fellow: Am. Coll. Bankruptcy; mem.: Am. Bankruptcy Bd. of Certification (founder, first chmn. 1992—95), R3, London, Chgo. Bar Assn. (chair, bankruptcy and reorganization com. 1999—2000), Am. Bankruptcy Inst. (pres. 2000—01, chmn.bd. 2002—03). Office: Greenberg Traurig Ste 2500 77 W Wacker Dr Chicago IL 60601 Office Phone: 312-456-8405. Office Fax: 312-456-8435. Business E-Mail: shapirok@gtlaw.com.

SHAPIRO, LARRY J., pediatrician, scientist, dean, educator; b. July 6, 1946; s. Philip and Phyllis Shapiro; m. Carol-Ann Uetake; children: Jennifer, Jessica, Brian. AB, Washington U., St. Louis, 1968, MD, 1971. Diplomate Am. Bd. Pediat., Am. Bd. Med. Examiners, Am. Bd. Med. Genetics. Intern St. Louis Children's Hosp., 1971—72, resident, 1971—73; rsch. assoc. NIH, Bethesda, Md., 1973—75; asst. prof. Sch. Medicine UCLA, 1975—79, assoc. prof., 1979—83, prof. pediat. and biol. chemistry, 1983—91; investigator Howard Hughes Med. Inst., 1987—91, investigator, W.H. and Marie Wattis Disting. prof.; prof., chmn. dept. pediat. U. Calif.-San Francisco Sch. Medicine, 1991—2003; chief pediat. svcs. U. Calif.-San Francisco Med. Ctr., 1991—2003; Spencer T. and Ann W. Olin Disting. prof., exec. vice chancellor for med. affairs, dean Washington U. Sch. Medicine, St. Louis, 2003—. Contbr. numerous articles to profl. publs. Served to lt. comdr. USPHS, 1973—75. Fellow: AAAS, Am. Acad. Pediat. (E. Mead Johnson award in rsch. 1982); mem.: Am. Acad. Arts and Scis., Am. Pediatric Soc. (coun. mem. 1999—2001, pres. 2003—04), Am. Soc. Clin. Investigation, Am. Soc. Human Genetics (coun. 1985—88, pres.-elect 1995, pres. 1997), Assn. Am. Physicians, Soc. for Inherited Metabolic Disease (coun. 1983—88, pres. 1986—87), Western Soc. for Pediatric Rsch. (coun. 1983—87, pres. 1989—90, Ross award in rsch. 1981), Soc. Pediatric Rsch. (coun. 1984—87, pres. 1991—92), Inst. Medicine of NAS. Office: Wash U 660 S Euclid campus box 8106 Saint Louis MO 63110

SHAPIRO, LEO J., social researcher; b. NYC, July 8, 1921; m. Virginia L. Johnson, Feb. 9, 1952; children: David, Erik, Owen, Amy. BA, U. Chgo., 1942, PhD, 1952. Survey specialist Fed. Govt. Agy., Washington, 1941-45, Sci. Rsch. Assn., Chgo., 1948-52; prin., founder Leo J. Shapiro and Assocs., Chgo., 1952-91; pres. SAGE LLC Survival & Growth Enterprise, Chgo., 2002—. Bd. dirs. Field of Flowers. Fellow U. Chgo., 1949. Fellow Social Sci. Rsch. Coun.; mem. Am. Sociol. Assn., Phi Beta Kappa.

SHAPIRO, MARK D., retail executive; With Ernst and Young, Blackman Co., Chemlawn Svcs. Corp.; dir., asst. contr. Consolidated Stores Corp., Columbus, 1992-94, v.p., contr., 1994-2000, sr. v.p., CFO, 2000—. Office: Consolidated Stores Corp 300 Phillipi Rd Columbus OH 43228-0512

SHAPIRO, MATTHEW DAVID, economist, educator; b. Mpls., Apr. 11, 1958; s. Irving and Janet (Reinstein) S.; m. Susan L. Garetz, Oct. 21, 1989; children: Benjamin Avigdor, Molly Kendall. BA summa cum laude, Yale U., 1979, MA, 1979; PhD, MIT, 1984. Jr. staff economist Coun. Econ. Advisers, Washington, 1979-80, sr. economist, 1993-94; asst. prof. Yale U., New Haven, 1984-89; assoc. prof. U. Mich., Ann Arbor, 1989-95, prof., 1995—, L.R. Klein Collegiate prof., 2004—, sr. rsch. scientist, 2000—, chair, 2003—07. Rschr. Nat. Bur. Econ. Rsch., Cambridge, Mass., 1986—; mem. acad. adv. coun. Fed. Res. Bank Chgo., 1995-; mem. com. on nat. stats. NAS, 1999-2002; mem. Fed. Econ. Stats. Adv. Com., 2000—, chmn., 2006—. Bd. editors Am. Econ. Rev., 1993-96, 2000-02, co-editor, 1997-2002; contbr. articles to profl. jours. Recipient Paul A. Samuelson Cert. of Excellence, TIAA-CREF, 1997; Olin fellow Nat. Bur. Econ. Rsch., Cambridge, 1986-87, Alfred P. Sloan fellow Sloan Found., 1991-93. Mem. Am. Econ. Assn., Econometric Soc., Phi Beta Kappa. Office: U Mich Dept Econs 611 Tappan Ave Ann Arbor MI 48109-1220

SHAPIRO, MICHAEL BRUCE, lawyer; b. Akron, Ohio, 1947; BBA summa cum laude, Kent State U., 1969; JD magna cum laude, U. Mich., 1972. Bar: Mich. 1972. Ptnr. Honigman Miller Schwartz & Cohn, LLP, Detroit. Mem. Nat. Assn. of Real Estate Investment Trusts subcom. on state and local taxes, citizens property tax commn. Mich. Senate, 1986-87. Mem. ABA, Am. Property Tax Counsel, State Bar of Mich., Inst. Property Taxation, Order of the Coif, Beta Alpha Psi, Pi Sigma Alpha, Beta Gamma Sigma. Office: Honigman Miller Schwartz & Cohn LLP 2290 1st Nat Bldg Detroit MI 48226 Office Phone: 313-465-7622. Business E-Mail: mbs@honigman.com.

SHAPIRO, RICHARD CHARLES, publishing executive, sales executive, marketing professional; b. Bklyn., May 28, 1936; s. Isidore and Sylvia (Rappaport) Shapiro; m. Marilyn Joyce Baily, Feb. 17, 1957 (div. 1974); children: Joseph, Scott; m. Francine L. Shaw, Sept. 19, 1975. BS in Edn., Golden State U., 1978, MBA, 1981; PhD in Bus. Adminstrn. and Mktg., Honolulu U., 1987. Lic. real estate broker Ill. Sales mgr. Coca Cola Bottling Co. of N.Y., 1955-62; affiliate Effective Motivation Assocs./Success Motivation inst., Bethpage, N.Y., 1965-68; v.p. sales, dir. Field Enterprises, Chgo., 1962-78; pres., CEO Snack-In, Inc., Detroit, 1978-82; sr. ptnr. Directions Growth and Strategy Cons., Chgo., 1982-95; v.p. domestic & internat. mktg. & sales, oper. officer Ency. Brit.-Compton's Learning Co., 1991-93, specialist network mktg. & relationship mktg., CEO, pres., bd. dirs.; CEO Am.'s Home Detailing Corp., 1995—, CEO, chmn. bd., 2001—; pres., COO Am.'s Deep Clean Divsn., Deerfield, Ill., 1995—2000; CEO, chmn. emeritus Am.'s Home Detailing Corp., Deerfield, Ill.; instr. grad. studies mktg. mgmt., instr. human resources mgmt. Robert Morris Coll., Chgo., 2001—; owner, operator PennyPincherDepot.com, 2005—. Instr. planning Life Underwriter Tng. Coun., LI, 1965—66; assoc. editor Media Technics Pub. Assn., Lake Forest, 1988; bd. dirs. Master Deep Clean Co., Nat. Video Libr.; spkr. on mktg., sales and leadership; cons. in field; liaison Chgo. Daily News, Chgo. Sun Times, Sta. WFLD-TV; founder Discovery Toy Divsn.; tennis pro, instr. Frank Sacks Tennis Camps, Chgo., 2001—; profl. tennis registry tennis instr., 2002—; asst. e-bay Auction Svcs., Deerfield, Ill., 2001—; continuing edn. instr. Gen. Contracting, Highland Pk., Ill., 2005—; founder Pennyincberdepot.com, 2005—. Pub.: Real Estate Property Marketing News; author: self-improvement cassettes; contbr. articles to profl. jours. Active Explorers, high schs., youth clubs, 1965—74; founder, pres. Abundance and Goodwill Soc., 1968—. With USAF, 1957—60. Named Sales/Mktg. Execs. Leadership Recruiter/Trainder of Decade award, Profl. Tennis Assocs. Singles champion, 1957, 1958, 1960; recipient Leadership award, Am. Sales Masters, 1968, 1999—2000, POPAI-OMA Best Industry Point of Purchase Display and Mktg. award, 1992. Mem.: Chgo. Computer Soc., Effective Motivation Assocs., Salesman with a Purpose, Deercreek Tennis Club (tchr., mem. rels. 2000—). Avocations: white-water rafting, canoeing, camping, tennis, writing. Home Phone: 847-459-0122; Office Phone: 847-459-3435. Personal E-mail: ahd10@yahoo.com, leadership_01@yahoo.com. E-mail: richard@tennis2win.com, guitarstabb-richard@yahoo.com.

SHAPIRO, ROBYN SUE, lawyer, educator; b. Mpls., July 19, 1952; d. Walter David and Judith Rae (Sweet) S.; m. Charles Howard Barr, June 27, 1976; children: Tania Shapiro-Barr, Jeremy Shapiro-Barr, Michael Shapiro-Barr. BA summa cum laude, U. Mich., 1974; JD, Harvard U., 1977. Bar: D.C. 1977, Wis. 1979, U.S. Supreme Ct. 1990. Assoc. Foley & Lardner, Washington, 1977-79; ptnr. Barr & Shapiro, Menomonee Falls, Wis., 1980-87; assoc. Quarles & Brady, Milw., 1987-92; ptnr. Michael Best & Friedrich, Milw., 1992—2005, chair health law practice, 2003—05; ptnr. Gardner Carton & Douglas LLP, Milw., 2005—06, Drinker Biddle Gardner Carton, Milw., 2006—. Adj. asst. prof. law Marquette U., Milw., 1979-83; assoc. dir. bioethics ctr. Med. Coll. Wis., Milw., 1982-85, dir., 1985—; asst. prof. bioethics Med. Coll. Wis., 1984-89, assoc. prof. bioethics, 1989-97, prof. bioethics, 1997—, Ursula Von der Ruhr prof. bioethics, 2000—; dir. Wis. Ethics Com. Network, 1987-98, Midwest Ethics Com. Network, 1998-2004, Med. Ethics Com. Network, 2004—; bd. dirs. Wis. Health Decisions, 1990-93; drug safety and risk mgmt. adv. com. FDA, 2003-2007; mem. data and safety monitoring bd. Med. Coll. Wis., 2003-; mem. recombinant DNA adv. com. NIH, 2005—, mem. Biosafety Working Group NIH Recombihant DNA adv. com. 2007-, mem. Clinical Trails Working Group NIH Recombihant DNA adv. com. 2007-. Mem. editl. bd. Cambridge Quar., 1991—, HEC Forum, 1988—91, Human Rights, 1998—2007; contbr. articles to profl. jours. Mem. ethics com. St. Luke's Med. Ctr., Milw., 1983—, Elmbrook Meml. Hosp., Milw., 1983-86, Cmty. Meml. Hosp., Menomonee Falls, 1984—, Aurora Sinai Med.Ctr., Milw., 1986—, Milw. County Mental Health Complex, 1984—, Froedtert Meml. Luth. Hosp., 1985—; mem. subcom. organ transplantation Wis. Health Policy Coun., Madison, 1984, bioethics com., 1986-89; mem. com. study on bioethics Wis. Legis. Coun., Madison, 1984-85; bd. dirs. Jewish Home and Care Ctr., 1994-2005, chair ethics com., 1994—; chair Bayside Ethics Bd., 1994—; bd. dirs. Milw. area chpt. Girl Scouts U.S., Am. Bioethics Assn., 1995-97, Wis. Perinatal Found., 1996-99, Am. Soc. Bioethics and Humanities, 1997-00, Manor Park Found., 2002—; mem. sec.'s adv. com. on xenotransplantation U.S. Dept. Health and Human Svcs., 2001-05; mem. sci. adv. com. Alzheimer's Assn. Southeastern Wis., 1997—; mem. data and safety monitoring bd. GlaxoWellcome, 1995-03; mem. med. and cmty. adv. bd. After Breast Cancer Diagnosis, 1999—. James B. Angell scholar, 1971—72. Fellow: Am. Bar Found.; mem.: ACLU, ABA (coordinating com. on bioethics and law 1993—, individual rights and responsibilities sect., health rights com. chair 1994—99, vice chair clin. ethics group 1998—2001, coun. 1999—, working group on health info. privacy 2000—02, misuse of genetic info. study group 2002—, AIDS coordinating com. 2003—, sec. individual rights and responsibilites vice chair 2005—06, chair-elect individual rights and responsibilities sect. 2006—, adv. nat. conf. of commrs. on uniform state laws, health law sec. 2004—, chair 2007—), Profl. Dimensions (Golden Compass award 1994), Internat. Bioethics Assn. (chair task force on ethics coms.), Am. Soc. Transplant Surgeons (ethics com. 1999—), Milw. AIDS Coalition (steering com. 1988—91), Milw. Acad. Medicine (coun. 1992—98, chair bioethics com. 1992—98), Am. Soc. Law, Medicine and Ethics, Assn. Post-Doctoral Programs in Clin. Neurophysiology (bd. dirs.), Wis. Found. (Atty. of Yr. 1988), Assn. Women Lawyers, Wis. Bar Assn. (individual rights sect. coun. 1987—90, chair Wis. health law sect. 1988—89), Am. Hosp. Assn. (spl. com. HIV practitioners 1991—93, bioethics tech. panel 1991—94), Am. Health Lawyers Assn., Susan G. Komen Breast Cancer Found., Phi Beta Kappa (Wis. chpt. scholarship com. chair 1990—93). Home: 9474 N Broadmoor Rd Milwaukee WI 53217-1309 Office: Med Coll Wis Bioethics Ctr 8701 Watertown Plank Rd Milwaukee WI 53226-3548 Office Phone: 414-221-6040. Business E-Mail: rshapiro@mcw.edu, robyn.shapiro@dbr.com.

SHAPIRO, STEPHEN MICHAEL, lawyer; b. Chgo., May 3, 1946; s. Samuel H. and Dorothy A. (D'Andrea) S.; m. Joan H. Gately, Oct. 30, 1982; children: Dorothy Henderson, Michael Clifford. BA magna cum laude, Yale U., 1968, JD, 1971. Bar: Ill. 1971, Calif. 1972, DC 1991, US Dist. Ct. (no. dist. trial bar Ill.) 1992, US Ct. Appeals (all cirs.), US Supreme Ct. 1975. Law clk. US Ct. Appeals (9th cir.), San Francisco, 1971—72; with Mayer, Brown & Platt, Chgo., 1972—78; asst. to solicitor gen. US Dept. Justice, Washington, 1978-80, dep. solicitor gen., 1981—83; sr. mem. Supreme Ct. and Appellate Ct. practice Mayer, Brown LLP, Chgo., 1983—, ptnr., 1983—. Former trustee Product Liability Adv. Found. Co-author: Supreme Ct. Practice, 2007; contbr. articles to profl. jours. Mem. Am. Law Inst. (life), Am. Acad. Appellate Lawyers, 7th Cir. Bar Assn., Inst. Jud. Adminstrn. (bd. dirs.), Phi Beta Kappa. Republican. Jewish. Office: Mayer Brown LLP 71 S Wacker Dr Ste 4430 Chicago IL 60606 Office Phone: 312-701-7327. Office Fax: 312-706-8684. E-mail: sshapiro@mayerbrown.com.

SHAPIRO, STEVEN A., lawyer; b. Chgo., Oct. 22, 1950; BS, U. Ill., 1971; JD, Ill. Inst. Tech., 1975. Bar: Ill. 1975, Fla. 1983. Ptnr. Katten Muchin Zavis Rosenman, Chgo. Mem.: ABA. Office: Katten Muchin Zavis Rosenman 525 W Monroe St Chicago IL 60661 Office Phone: 312-902-5545. Office Fax: 312-577-8881. E-mail: steven.shapiro@kmzr.com.

SHAPO, MARSHALL SCHAMBELAN, lawyer, educator; b. Phila., Oct. 1, 1936; s. Mitchell and Norma (Schambelan) S.; m. Helene Shirley Seidner, June 21, 1959; children: Benjamin, athaniel. AB summa cum laude, U. Miami, 1958, JD magna cum laude, 1964; AM, Harvard U., Cambridge, Mass., 1961, SJD, 1974. Bar: Fla. 1964, Va. 1977, Ill. 1993. Copy editor, writer Miami News, Fla., 1958-59; instr. history U. Miami, 1960-61; asst. prof. law U. Tex., 1965-67, asso. prof., 1967-69, prof., 1969-70; prof. law U. Va., 1970-78, Joseph M. Hartfield prof., 1976-78; Frederic P. Vose prof. Northwestern U. Sch. Law, Chgo., 1978—; of counsel Sonnenschein, Nath & Rosenthal, Chgo., 1991-2001. Vis. prof. Juristisches Seminar U. Gottingen (Fed. Republic Germany), 1976; cons. on med. malpractice and tort law reform U.S. Dept. Justice, 1978-79; mem. panel on food safety Inst. Medicine, NAS, 1978-79; vis. fellow Centre for Socio-legal Studies, Wolfson Coll., Oxford, vis. fellow Wolfson Coll., 1975, Wolfson Coll., Cambridge, 1992, 2001; mem. Ctr. for Advanced Studies, U. Va., 1976-77; cons. Pres.'s Commn. for Study of Ethical Problems in Medicine and Biomed. and Behavioral Rsch., 1980-81; reporter Spl. Com. on Tort Liability System Am. Bar Assn., 1980-84; del. leader People to People Citizen Amb. program delegation to East Asia Tort and Ins. Law, 1986; lectr. appellate judges' seminars ABA, 1977, 83, 90; reporter symposium on legal and sci. perspectives on causation, 1990; advisor Restatement of the Law, Third, Torts: Products Liability, 1992-97. Author: Towards a Jurisprudence of Injury, 1984, Tort and Compensation Law, 1976, The Duty to Act: Tort Law, Power and Public Policy, 1978, A Nation of Guinea Pigs, 1979, Products Liability, 1980, Public Regulation of Dangerous Products, 1980, The Law of Products Liability, 1987, Tort and Injury Law, 1990, (with Richard Peltz) 3d edit., 2006, The Law of Products Liability, 2 vols., 2d edit., 1990, 4th edit., 2001, supplements, 1991, 92, 93, 95, 96, 97, 98, 99, 2002, 03, 04, 05, 06, 07, Products Liability and the Search for Justice, 1993, (with Helene Shapo) Law School Without Fear, 1996, 2d edit., 2002, Basic Principles of Tort Law, 1999, 2d edit., 2003, Tort Law and Culture, 2003, Compensation for Victims or Terror, 2005; (with Page Keeton) Products and the Consumer: Deceptive Practices, 1972, Products and the Consumer: Defective and Dangerous Products, 1970, (with D. Jacobson & A.N. Weber) International e-Commerce: Business & Legal Issues, 2001, (with G. Hernandez & others) eBusiness & Insurance, 2001, Concise Hornbook on Tort Law, 2003; mem. editl. bd. Jour. Consumer Policy, 1980-88, Products Liability Law Jour.; author: A Representational Theory of Consumer Protection: Doctrine, Function and Legal Liability for Product Disappointment, 1975; mem. adv. bd. Loyola Consumer Law Reporter; contbr. articles to legal and med. jours. Recipient Andrew J. Hecker award Fedn. Ins. and Corp. Counsel, 2001, Robert B. McKay Prof. award Am. Bar Assn., 2005, Disting. Alumnus award U. Miami Sch. Law, 2005; NEH sr. fellow, 1974-75 Mem. Am. Law Inst., Am. Assn. Law Schs. (chmn. torts compensation systems sect. 1983-84, torts round table coun. 1970). Home: 1910 Orrington Ave Evanston IL 60201-2910 Office: Northwestern U Sch Law 357 E Chicago Ave Chicago IL 60611-3059 E-mail: m-shapo@law.northwestern.edu.

SHAPPIRIO, DAVID GORDON, biologist, educator; b. Washington, June 18, 1930; s. Sol and Rebecca (Porton) S.; m. Elvera M. Bamber, July 8, 1953; children: Susan, Mark. BS with distinction in Chemistry, U. Mich., 1951; A.M., Harvard U., 1953, PhD in Biology, 1955. NSF postdoctoral fellow in biochemistry Cambridge U., Eng., 1955-56; rsch. fellow in physiology Am. Cancer Soc.-NRC, U. Louvain, Belgium, 1956-57; mem. faculty U. Mich., Ann Arbor, 1957—, prof. zool. and biology, 1967-99, Arthur F. Thurnau prof., 1989-94, prof. emeritus, 1999—, assoc. chair div. biol. scis., 1976-83, acting chair, 1978, 79, 80, 82, coord. NSF undergrad. sci. edn. program, 1962-67, dir. honors program Coll. Lit. Sci. and Arts, 1983-91. Vis. lectr. Am. Inst. Biol. Scis., 1966-68; reviewer, cons. to pubs. on textbook devel.; reviewer rsch. and ednl. tng. grant proposals NSF, NIH, mem. program site visit teams. Author rsch. on biochemistry and physiology growth, devel., dormancy; invited spkr., rsch. symposia of nat. and internat. orgns. in field. Recipient Disting. Teaching award U. Mich., 1967, Excellence in Edn. award, 1991, Bausch & Lomb Sci. award, 1974; Lalor Found fellow, 1953-55; Danforth Found. assoc. Fellow AAAS; mem. Am. Inst. Biol. Scis. (vis. lectr. 1966-68), Am. Soc. Cell Biology, Biochem. Soc., Soc. Exptl. Biology, Assn. Biol. Lab. Edn., Xerces Soc., Phi Beta Kappa (v.p. U. Mich. chpt. 1995-97, pres. 1997—). Office: U Mich Dept Biology 1123 Natural Sci Bldg Ann Arbor MI 48109-1048

SHARF, STEPHAN, automotive executive; b. Berlin, Dec. 30, 1920; arrived in USA, 1947, naturalized, 1952; s. Wilhelm and Martha (Schwartz) S.; m. Rita Schantzer, 1951, (dec. 2001). Degree in Mech. Engring., Tech. U., Berlin, Fed. Republic Germany, 1947; PhD, Oakland U., Rochester, Mich., 2007. Tool and die maker Buerk Tool & Die Co., Buffalo, 1947-50; foreman Ford Motor Co., 1950-53, gen. foreman Chgo., 1953-58; with Chrysler Corp., Detroit, 1958-86, master mechanic Twinsburg stamping plant, 1958-63, mfg. engring. mgr., 1963-66, mrg. prodn. Twinsburg stamping plant, 1966-68, plant mgr. Warren stamping plant, 1968-70, plant mgr. Sterling stamping plant, 1970-72, gen. plants mgr. stamping, 1972-78, v.p. Engine and Casting div., 1978-80, v.p. Power Train div., 1980-81, exec. v.p., mfg., dir., 1981-85, exec. v.p. internat., 1985-86, also bd. dirs.; pres. SICA Corp., Bloomfield Hills, Mich., 1986—. Columnist Ward's Auto World Common Sense mag., 1987—. Bd. dirs. Jr. Achievement, Detroit council Boy Scouts Am.; trustee, v.p. Oakland U. Mem. Soc. Auto Engrs., Detroit Engring. Soc. Clubs: Wabeek Country. Avocations: golf, travel, charity. Home: 966 Adams Castle Dr Bloomfield Hills MI 48304-3713 Office: SICA Corp President 725 Adams Rd Ste 230 Birmingham MI 48009 Personal E-mail: sharfsteve@yahoo.com.

SHARKEY, LEONARD ARTHUR, automobile company executive; b. Detroit, May 21, 1946; s. Percy and Lillian (Peros) S.; m. Irene Johnson, Aug. 9, 1969 (div. Nov. 1991); children: Michelle, Wesley Tucker (step-son). Cert. pvt. pilot. Tool and diemaker Ford Motor Co., Dearborn, Mich., 1965-85, indsl. hazardous substance educator, 1985-86, indsl. health, safety and energy control educator, 1987-88, tool and diemaker leader, 1989—2006; non-fiction author Individual Initiative, Brighton, Mich., 1989—. Author: Journey Into Fear (reprinted title Split Decision, 1997), 1995, Hidden Shadows -An Opening to the Windows of the Mind, 1996. Mem. Nat. Geog. Soc., Nat. Rifle Assn., Boat U.S., Drummond Island Sportsman's Club, Mich. United Conservation Clubs. Avocations: boating, shooting sports, political awareness studies, biblical prophetic studies, theater.

SHARKEY, THOMAS DAVID, botanist, educator; b. Detroit, Jan. 28, 1953; s. Robert Hugh and Patricia June (Elliott) S.; m. Paulette Marie Bochnig June 21, 1974; 1 child, Jessa Sung. BS in Biology with honors, Mich. State U., 1974, PhD in Botany and Plant Pathology, 1980. Postdoctoral fellow Australian Nat. U., Canberra, 1980-82; assoc. rsch. prof. Desert Rsch. Inst., Reno, 1982-87; asst. prof. U. Wis., Madison, 1987-88, assoc. prof., 1988-91, prof., 1991—2008, Dept. Biochemistry and molecular Biology, Mich. State U., 2008—, chair, 2008—. Assoc. dir. Biolog. Scis. Ctr., Reno, Nev., 1983-87; chmn. dept. botany U. Wis., Madison, 1992-94; dir. Inst. Cross-Coll. Biology Edn. Editor: Trace Gas Emissions from Plants, 1991, Photosynthesis: Physiology and Metabolism, 2000; contbr. more than 160 articles to profl. peer-reviewed jours. Mem.: AAAS, Internat. Soc. Photosynthesis Rsch., Am. Soc. Plant Biologists. Office: MI State Univ Dept Biochemistry Mol Biology 210 Biochemistry Bldg East Lansing MI 48824 Home: 1210 Prescott Drive East Lansing MI 48823 Office Phone: 608-262-6802, 517-353-3257. Business E-Mail: tsharkey@msu.edu.

SHARP, ALLEN, federal judge; b. Washington, Feb. 11, 1932; s. Robert Lee and Frances Louise (Williams) S.; children: Crystal Catholyn Sharp Bauer, Scarlet Frances Thomas. Student, Ind. State U., 1950-53; AB, George Washington U., 1954; JD, Ind. U., 1957; MA, Butler U., 1986. Bar: Ind. 1957. Practiced in, Williamsport, 1957-68; judge Ct. of Appeals Ind., 1969-73, U.S. Dist. Ct. (no. dist.) Ind., South Bend, 1973—. Served to JAG USAF, Res. Mem.: Ind. Judges Assn., Phi Delta Kappa, Tau Kappa Alpha, Pi Gamma Mu, Blue Key. Republican. Mem. Christian Ch. Club: Mason. Office: US Dist Ct 124 Fed Bldg 204 S Main St South Bend IN 46601-2122

SHARPE, ROBERT FRANCIS, JR., lawyer, food products executive; b. Long Branch, NJ, Mar. 9, 1952; s. Robert Francis and Audrey Carolyn (Rembe) Sharpe; m. Maria Renna, Sept. 9, 2000; 1 child, Robert Francis III. BA, DePauw U., Greencastle, Ind., 1974; JD, Wake Forest U., Winston-Salem, NC. Bar: NC 1978. V.p. Tyco Internat. Ltd.; with RJR Nabisco Holdings Corp., sr. v.p., gen. counsel; sr. v.p. pub. affairs, gen. counsel, sec. Pepsico Inc., Purchase, NY, 1998—2002; ptnr. Brunswick Group, LLP, 2002—05; exec. v.p. legal & external affairs ConAgra Foods, Inc., Omaha, 2005—. Bd. dirs. Ameriprise Fin. Mem.: ABA, Am. Corp. Counsel Assn., C Bar Assn. Republican. Episcopalian. Avocations: golf, fishing. Office: ConAgra Foods Inc 1 ConAgra Dr Omaha NE 68102 Office Phone: 402-595-4000.

SHAUGHNESSY, EDWARD LOUIS, language educator; b. Sewickley, Pa., July 29, 1952; s. James Francis and Marie Rosalia (Kraus) S.; m. Gina Lynn Look, May 15, 1976 (div. Sept. 1992); m. Elena Valussi, Sept. 6, 1997; children Guilia, Maria. BA, U. Notre Dame, 1974; MA, Stanford U., 1980, PhD, 1983. Asst. prof. U. Chgo., 1985-90, assoc. prof., 1990-96, prof., 1996—, Lorraine J. and Herrlee G. Creel prof. of early China, disting svc. prof., 2006—. Assoc. editor: Early China, 1985-88, editor, 1988-96; editor: New Sources of Early Chinese History: An Introduction to the Reading of Inscriptions and Manuscripts, 1997, (with Michael Loewe) The Cambridge History of Ancient China: From the Origins of Civilization to 221 R.C., 1999, China Empire and Civilization, 2000; author: Sources of Western Zhou History: Inscribed Bronze Vessels, 1991, I Ching, The Classic of Changes: The First English Translation of the Newly Discovered Second-Century B.C. Mawangdui Manuscripts, 1996, Before Confucius: Studies in the Creation of the Chinese Classics, 1997, Ancient China: Life, Myth and Art, 2005, Rewriting Early Chinese Texts, 2006, (with Robert Poor and Harrie A. Vanderstappen) Ritual and Reverence: Chinese Art at the University of Chicago, 1989, (with Cai Fangpei and James F. Shaughnessy) A Concordance of the Xiaotun Nandi Oracle-Bone Inscriptions, 1988; contbr. essays to books. Andrew W. Mellon fellow for Chinese studies, 1984-85; Divsn. of Humanities jr. faculty fellow U. Chgo., 1986; J. William Fulbright fellow in China, 2003-04, Nat. Endowment for Humanities, 2007-. Office: U Chgo East Asian Langs/Civilizat 1050 E 59th St Chicago IL 60637-1559 Home: 1050 E 59th St Chicago IL 60637-1559 Business E-Mail: e-shaughnessy@uchicago.edu.

SHAUGHNESSY, THOMAS WILLIAM, retired librarian; b. Pitts., May 3, 1938; s. Martin T. and LaVerne (O'Brien) Shaughnessy; m. Marlene D. Reuben, Aug. 11, 1968; 1 child, Mark Andrew. AB, St. Vincent Coll., 1961; MLS, U. Pitts., 1964; PhD, Rutgers U., 1970. Asst. dean Rutgers U., New Brunswick, NJ, 1969-71, libr. dir. Newark, 1971-74; assoc. dean U. So. Calif., LA, 1974-78; asst. libr. dir. U. Houston, 1978-82; libr. dir. U. Mo., Columbia, 1982-89; univ. libr., dir. U. Minn., Mpls.-St. Paul, 1989—2002; dir. Metronet, St. Paul, 2005—. Rsch. dir. Chgo. Pub. Libr. Survey, 1968—69; cons. U. Tulsa Libr., 1982—83; mem. faculty exch. USIA, Poland, 1998; trustee OCLC, Inc., 1997—2004. Author (with Lowell A. Martin): (book) Library Response to Urban Change, 1969, Developing Leadership Skills: A Source Book for Librarians, 1990. Recipient Hugh C. Atkinson Meml. award, 1996; fellow, Coun. Libr. Resources, 1973; U.S. Office Edn. grantee, Rutgers U., 1971, Sr. fellow, Coun. Libr. Resources, 1985. Mem.: ALA, Minn. Libr. Assn. (Disting. Achievement award 2002), Assn. Rsch. Librs. (cons. tng. fellow 1981, bd. dirs. 1989—92), Assn. Coll. and Rsch. Librs. Home: 5705 Wycliffe Rd Minneapolis MN 55436-2264 E-mail: tws@umn.edu.

SHAVER, JOAN LOUISE FOWLER, dean, women's health nurse; BS in Nursing, U. Alberta, Can., 1966; M in Nursing, U. Wash., 1968-70, PhD in Physiology and Biophysics, 1976. ursing instr. chair med. surgical prog. Holy Cross Hosp. Sch. Nursing, Calgary, Canada, 1966-68; staff nurse Virginia Mason Hosp., Seattle, 1970-71; asst. prof. Sch. Nursing U. Ariz., Tucson, 1976-77; assoc. prof. U. Calgary, Canada, 1977-80; asst. prof. Dept. Physiological Nursing U. Wash., Seattle, 1980-85, rsch. affil. Regl. Primate Rsch. Ctr., 1983-86, assoc. prof., 1985-89, chair Dept. Physiological Nusring, 1988-95, prof., 1989-95, prof., chair Dept. Biobehavioral Nursing & Health Systems, 1995-96, co-dir. Ctr. Women's Health Rsch., 1989-96; prof., dean Coll. Nursing U. Ill., Chgo., 1996—, co-dir. Rsch. Core Nat. Ctr. Excellence in Women's Health, 1997—. Mem. editl. bd. Health Care for Women Internat., 1984—, Heart and Lung: The Jour. of Critical Care, 1988-90, Jour. of Applied Nursing Rsch., 1988-91, IMAGE: Jour. Nursing Scholarship, editl. adv. bd. Nursing Rsch., 1997—, Biol. Rsch. for ursing, 1999—, Jour. Nursing Scholarship, 2000—; contbr. artilces to profl. jours. Abe Miller Meml. scholar Alberta Assn. Registered Nurses, 1968-69; Kathryn McLaggen Meml. fellow Can. Nurses Found., fellow Am. Acad. Nursing Am. Nurses Assn., 1988—. Office: U Ill Coll Nursing 845 S Damen Ave Mc802 Chicago IL 60612-7350

SHAW, CHARLES ALEXANDER, judge; b. Jackson, Tenn., Dec. 31, 1944; s. Alvis and Sarah S.; m. Kathleen Ingram, Aug. 17, 1969; 1 child, Bryan Ingram. BA, Harris Stowe State U., 1966; MBA, U. Mo., 1971; JD, Cath. U. Am., 1974. Bar: D.C. 1975, Mo. 1975, U.S. Ct. Appeals (8th and D.C. cirs.) 1975, U.S. Dist. Ct. (ea. dist.) Mo. 1976, U.S. Ct. Appeals (6th and 7th cirs.) 1976. Tchr. St. Louis Pub. Schs., 1966-69, D.C. Pub. Schs., Washington, 1969-71; law clk. U.S. Dept. Justice, Washington, 1972-73, NLRB, Washington, 1973-74, atty., 1974-76; assoc. Lashly, Caruthers, Theis, Rava & Hamel, St. Louis, 1976-80, asst. U.S. atty., 1980-87; judge Mo. Cir. Ct., St. Louis, 1987-94, asst. presiding judge, 1993-94; judge U.S. Dist. Ct., St. Louis, 1994—. Hearing officer Office of the Mayor, Washington, 1973-74; instr. U. Mo., St. Louis, 1980-81. State bd. dirs. United Negro Coll. Fund, St. Louis, 1979-83; trustee St. Louis Art Mus., 1979-82, 89-96; bd. dirs. Arts and Edn. Coun., 1992-96, Metro Golf Assn., 1993-2000, Landmarks Assn., St. Louis, 1980-82. Recipient Silver Gavel award Fed. Def. Bar, 2005; named Disting. Alumnus, Cath. U., 2001; fellow Danforth Found., 1978-79; scholar Cath. U. Am., 1971-74. Mem. D.C. Bar Assn., Mo. Bar Assn., Mound City Bar Assn., Bar Assn. Met. St. Louis, Harris-Stowe State Coll. Alumni Assn. (Disting. Alumni 1988), Nat. Assn. Guardsmen (sec. St. Louis chpt. 1999-2001), Phi Alpha Delta (svc. award 1973-74), Sigma Pi Phi (pres. St. Louis chpt. 1999-2001). Avocation: golf. Office: 111 S 10th St Saint Louis MO 63102 Office Phone: 314-244-7480.

SHAW, JOHN, sports association administrator; b. NY; 1 dau., Alexandra. BS in Acctg., U. San Diego; JD, NYU. Lawyer, Calif.; acct. Arthur Andersen & Co.; pres. St. Louis Rams, 1980—. Primary advisor to chmn. and owner St. Louis Rams; mem. NFL Mgmt. Coun. Exec. Com. Bd. dirs. Greater St. Louis United Way; mem. Coun. Trustees LEARN, St. Louis. Office: St Louis Rams 1 Rams Way Earth City MO 63045-1525

SHAW, JOHN W., lawyer; b. Mo., 1951; m. Cynthia Shaw; children: Sarah Ann, Katherine Kennan, Amy Elizabeth. BA, MA, U. Mo., 1973, JD, 1977. Bar: Mo. 1977. Ptnr. Lathrop & Norquist, 1983-92, Bryan Cave LLP, 1992-98, Berkowitz Oliver Williams Shaw & Eisenbrandt LLP (formerly Berkowitz Stanton Brandt Williams and Shaw LLP), Kansas City, 1998—. Bd. advisors, dept. personal fin. planning U. Mo.-Columbia, bd. advisors, Coll. Arts and Sci., Mo. 100 adv. group of bus. leaders to pres. Named Commencement Keynote Spkr., Coll. Arts and Sci., U. Mo.-Columbia, 2003, Best of the Bar, Kansas City Bus. Jour., 2003; named one of Mo. Super Lawyers, Law and Politics, 2006—07, Best Lawyers in Am., 2007—08; recipient Disting. Alumni award, Coll. Arts and Sci., U. Mo.-Columbia, 2005. Mem. ABA, Securities Industry Assn. (legal and compliance group), Mo. Bar, Def. Rsch. Inst. (chmn. firearms litigation subcom.), Order of Coif. Office: Berkowitz Oliver Williams Shaw & Eisenbrandt LLP 2600 Grand Blvd Ste 1200 Kansas City MO 64108 Home Phone: 913-491-9332; Office Phone: 816-561-7007. Business E-Mail: jshaw@bowse-law.com.

SHAW, MELVIN PHILLIP, physicist, engineering educator, psychologist; b. Bklyn., Aug. 16, 1936; s. Harry and Yetta (Stutsky) S.; m. Carol Joan Phillips, Sept. 5, 1959 (div. Feb. 1987); children: Adam, Evan; m. Bernetta Berger, May 16, 1987. BS, Bklyn. Coll., 1959; MS, Case Western Res. U., 1963, PhD, 1965; MA, Ctr. for Humanistic Studies, 1988. Research scientist United Techs. Research Labs., E. Hartford, Conn., 1964-68, scientist-in-charge, 1966-70; prof. Wayne State U., Detroit, 1970-96, prof. emeritus, 1997—; adminstrv. dir. Assocs. of Birmingham/Kingswood Hosp., 1991-93. Cons. Energy Conversion Devices, Troy, Mich., 1970-92. Co-author: The Gunn-Hilsum Effect, 1979, The Physics and Applications of Amorphous Semiconductors, 1988, The Physics of Instabilities in Solid State Electron Devices, 1992, Creativity and Affect, 1994. Fellow Am. Phys. Soc.; mem. IEEE (sr.), Am. Psychol. Assn. (assoc.). Avocations: cooking, walking, exercise, travel. Office Phone: 248-644-8330. E-mail: bunny3336@talkamerica.net.

SHAW, MICHAEL ALLAN, lawyer; b. Evanston, Ill., July 14, 1940; s. Frank C. and Mabel I. (Peacock) S.; m. Genevieve Schrodt, Aug. 16, 1964; children: M. Ian, Trevor A. BA, Colo. State U., 1962; JD, U. Denver, 1965; MBA, DePaul U., 1969; postgrad., Columbia U., 1970. Bar: Ill. bar 1965. Practiced in, Chgo., 1965-83; asst. counsel, staff asst. to v.p. traffic Jewel Cos., Inc., Melrose Park, Ill., 1965-71; corp. sec., asst. treas., house counsel Wieboldt Stores, Inc., Chgo., 1972-83; pvt. practice law Naperville, Ill., 1983-89; pres. Kingston Korner, Inc., Naperville, Ill., 1983—, Aztec Corp., Naperville, Ill., 1989—. Pres. Folk Era Prodns., producers folk music concert series, records, 1985—; editor Folk Music Editor, 1984; contbr. articles to legal jours. Mem. Village Planning Commn., Itasca, Ill., 1973-77; bd. dirs. Crimestoppers, Naperville, 1984—, chmn., 1988-94; session mem. Naperville Lumen Christi United Presbyn. Ch., 1984-85; chmn. bldg. fin. com. Naperville Presbyn. Ch., 1989-93. Mem. Fox Valley Folklore Soc. (bd. dirs. 1991—). Home: 6 S 230 Cohasset Rd aperville IL 60540 Office: Aztec Corp 705 S Washington St Naperville IL 60540-6696 E-mail: allan@folkera.com.

SHAW, SCOTT ALAN, photojournalist; b. Danville, Ill., 1963; BS in Journalism, So. Ill. U., 1985. Formerly with The Comml. News, Danville; with The Paragould (Ark.) Daily Press, 1985-86; staff photographer The Odessa (Tex.)

Am., 1986-89; with St. Louis Sun, 1989-90; now staff photographer The Plain Dealer, Cleve., 1990—. Recipient Pulitzer Prize for spot news photgraphy, 1988. Office: The Plain Dealer 1801 Superior Ave E Cleveland OH 44114-2198

SHAW, STANLEY MINER, pharmacist, educator; b. Parkston, SD, July 4, 1935; s. George Henry and Jensina (Thompson) S.; m. Excellda J. Watke, Aug. 13, 1961; children: Kimberly Kay, Renee Denise, Elena Aimee. BS, S.D. State U., 1957, MS, 1959; PhD, Purdue U., 1962. Instr. S.D. State U., 1960-62; asst. prof. bionucleonics Purdue U., West Lafayette, Ind., 1962-66, assoc. prof., 1966-71, prof. nuclear pharmacy, 1971—2005, prof. emeritus nuclear pharmacy, 2005—, head. divsn. nuclear pharmacy, 1990—2004, acting head Sch. Health Scis., 1990-93. Bd. pharm. spltys. Splty. Council Nuclear Pharmacy, 1978-82. Contbr. articles to profl. jours. Recipient Lederle Pharmacy faculty award, 1962, 1965, Parenteral Drug Assn. Rsch. award, 1970, Henry Heine Outstanding Tchr. award, Sch. Pharmacy Purdue U., 1989, 1993, 1999, Disting. Alumnus award, S.D. State U., 1991, Coll. Pharmacy Disting. Alumnus award, 2006, Disting. Pharmacy Educator award, Am. Assn. Colls. Pharmacy, 1994. Fellow Acad. Pharmacy Practice (chmn. sect. nuclear pharmacy 1979-80, historian 1981-85, mem.-at-large 1993-95, chmn.-elect 1995-96, chmn. 1996-97, Disting. Achievement award 1998), Am. Soc. Hosp. Pharmacy, Am. Pharm. Assn. (ho. of dels. 1977, 79, 86, 92, Founder's award, Daniel B. Smith Practice Excellence award 2000); mem. Health Physics Soc., Sigma Xi, Phi Lambda Upsilon, Phi Lambda Sigma, Rho Chi. Home: 7208 W Greenview Dr Battle Ground IN 47920-9732 Office: Purdue U Sch Pharmacy West Lafayette IN 47907-1336 Business E-Mail: sshaw@pharmacy.purdue.edu.

SHAW, WILLIAM, state legislator; b. Fulton, Ark., July 31, 1937; s. McKinley and Gertrude (Henderson) S.; m. Shirley Shaw, 1957; children: Gina, Victor, Shawn, 3 stepchildren. Grad. high sch. Adminstrv. asst. to Alderman Wilson Frost 34th Ward; precinct capt. 24th ward and inspector City of Chgo.; pres. 9th ward Regional Dem. Orgn.; Ill. state rep. Dist. 34, 1983—; mem. appropriations I com. labor and commerce com. Ill. Ho. Reps., exec. and vet. affairs com., registration com., vice chmn. fin. insts. com., chmn. ins. com.; mem. Ill. State Senate Dist. 15, 1993—; asst. dir. Supportive Svcs., Chgo. Mem. Masons, C. of C. Home: 12126 S Perry Ave Chicago IL 60628-6627

SHAW, WILLIAM, broadcast executive; V.p., gen. mgr. WGN Superstation Tribune Co., Chgo., 2002—; pres., CEO Fox TV Sales (subs. Rupert Murdoch's News Corp. Ltd.), NY; v.p. sales Tribune TV. Office: Tribune Co 435 N Michigan Ave Chicago IL 60611

SHAYMAN, JAMES ALAN, nephrologist, educator; b. Chgo., June 14, 1954; s. Benjamin and Chernie (Abrams) S.; children: Rebecca Lynn, David Aaron. AB, Cornell U., 1976; MD, Washington U., St. Louis, 1980. Intern and resident Barnes Hosp., St. Louis, 1980-83; instr. Washington U., St. Louis, 1985-86; asst. prof. U. Mich., Ann Arbor, 1986-92, assoc. prof., 1992-97; prof. internal medicine and pharmacology, 1997—; assoc. chair rsch. programs dept. internal medicine U. Mich., Ann Arbor, 1997—. Mem. Am. Soc. Nephrology, Internat. Soc. Nephrology, Am. Diabetes Assn., Am. Soc. Clin. Investigation, Am. Physiol. Soc., Phi Beta Kappa, Phi Kappa Phi, Alpha Omega Alpha. Achievements include research in renal inositol phosphate metabolism and renal glycolipid metabolism.

SHEA, DANIEL BARTHOLOMEW, JR., literature and language professor, educator; b. Mpls., Oct. 29, 1936; s. Daniel Bartholomew and Dorothea (Lonergan) S.; m. Kathleen Anne Williams, June 3, 1978; children: Timothy, Matthew, Catherine, Daniel, Emily. BA summa cum laude, Coll. St. Thomas, 1958; MA, Stanford U., 1962, PhD, 1966. Teaching asst. Stanford U., 1959-61; instr. to prof. English Washington U., St. Louis, 1962—, chmn. dept., 1978-84, 95-98; acting chair performing arts, prof. drama, 1995. Fulbright-Hays lectr. Univs. of Caen and Nice, France, 1968-69; vis. fellow Clare Hall, U. Cambridge, Eng., 1984-85 Author: Spiritual Autobiography in Early America, 1968, 2d edit., 1988; editorial bd.: Early Am. Lit, 1972-74; sect. editor: Columbia Literary History of the United States; contbr. chpts. to books. Woodrow Wilson fellow, 1958; NEH summer grantee, 1971 Mem. MLA (del. gen. assembly 1977-78), AFTRA, Equity, Phi Beta Kappa. Office: Washington Univ Dept of English Saint Louis MO 63130 E-mail: dbshea@artsci.wustl.edu.

SHEA, JAMES F., manufacturing executive; CEO Fairmont Homes, Nappanee, Ind. Office: Fairmont Homes 502 S Oakland Ave Nappanee IN 46550-2332

SHEARER, DAVID A., JR., lawyer; b. Lexington, Ky., Apr. 20, 1968; married; 2 children. BA, Vanderbilt U., 1990; JD, U. Ky., 1993. Bar: Ky. 1993, US Dist. Ct. Eastern Dist. Ky. 1993, US Ct. of Appeals Sixth Cir. 1993, Ohio 1999. Ptnr. Freund, Freeze & Arnold, Cin. Named one of Ohio's Rising Stars, Super Lawyers, 2006. Mem.: Ohio Assn. Civil Trial Attorneys, ABA, Ohio State Bar Assn., Ky. Bar Assn., Northern Ky. Bar Assn., Cin. Bar Assn. Avocations: skiing, hunting, fishing, golf. Office: Freund Freeze & Arnold Fourth and Walnut Ctr 105 E Fourth St Ste 1400 Cincinnati OH 45202-4035 Office Phone: 513-665-3500. Office Fax: 513-665-3503.

SHEARER, LINDA, museum director; b. LI, NY, Feb. 13, 1946; BA, Sarah Lawrence Coll., Bronxville, NY, 1968. Assoc. curator Solomon R. Guggenheim Mus., NYC, 1969—80; exec. dir. Artists Space, NYC, 1980—85; curator painting and sculpture Mus. Modern Art, NYC, 1985—89; dir. Williams Coll. Mus. Art, Williamstown, Mass., 1989—2004; Alice & Harris Weston dir. Contemporary Arts Ctr., Cin., 2004—06; interim dir. Contemporary Arts Mus Houston, 2007—. Tchr. contemporary art Williams Coll., Sch. Visual Arts, NYC. Bd. trustees Am. Fedn. of Arts; adv. com. Skowhegan Sch. of Painting and Sculpture; chair Phila. Exhibition Initiative, 2003. Mem.: Am. Fedn. of Arts (former trustee), Assn. Art Mus. Dirs. (former trustee). Office: Contemporary Arts Mus Houston 5216 Montrose Blvd Houston TX 77006-6598 Office Phone: 713-284-8250. Office Fax: 713-284-8275.

SHEARER, MARK SMITH, state legislator; b. Burlington, Iowa, Aug. 11, 1952; Student, U. Iowa. Broadcast journalist Stas. KCII, KICR, KCRG, 1968-79; mem., chair Iowa Arts Coun., 1981-88; mem. Iowa House, Des Moines, 1989-92; salesperson U.S. Cellular, 1995-98; comms. cons.; mem. Iowa Senate from 49th dist., Des Moines, 1998—; mem. agr. com., mem. edn. com., mem. human resources com.; ranking com. small bus., econ. devel., and tourism; mem. appropriations com. Editor: Columbus Gazette, 1979-95. Democrat. E-mail: mark.shearer@legis.state.ia.us.

SHEA-STONUM, MARILYN, federal bankruptcy judge; b. 1947; AB, U. Calif., Santa Cruz, 1969; JD, Case Western Res. U., 1975. Law clk. to Hon. Frank J. Battisti, Cleve., 1975-76; ptnr. Jones, Day, Reavis & Pogue, Cleve., 1984—94; bankruptcy judge U.S. Dist. Ct. (no. dist.) Ohio, Akron, 1994—. Editor-in-chief Am. Bankruptcy Law Jour., Nat. Conf. Bankruptcy Judges. Mem. Order of Coif. Office: US Bankruptcy Ct No Dist Ohio 240 Fed Bldg 2 S Main St Akron OH 44308-1813 Office Phone: 330-252-6130.

SHEDLOCK, JAMES, library director, consultant; b. Detroit, Nov. 25, 1950; BA in English, U. Notre Dame, 1974; AM in LS, U. Mich., 1977. Reference and serials libr. St. Joseph Mercy Hosp., Pontiac, Mich., 1977-79; document delivery libr. Wayne State U. Med. Libr., Detroit, 1979-81; coord. online search svc. U. .C. Health Scis. Libr., Chapel Hill, 1982-84; head pub. svcs. Med. Libr., Northwestern U., Chgo., 1985-88, assoc. dir., 1988-91, dir. Galter Health Scis. Libr., 1991—. Cons. U.N. High Commr. for Refugees, Cyprus, 1993-94, Med. Coll. Wis. Libr., 1996-97, La Porte (Ind.) Hosp., 1998. Mem. ALA, Med. Libr. Assn. (bd. dirs. 1997-99), Am. Med. Informatics Assn., Assn. Acad. Health Scis. Libr. Dirs. (rep.), Acad. Health Info. Profls. (disting.). Office Phone: 312-503-8133. E-mail: j-shedlock@northwestern.edu.

SHEEDY, PATRICK THOMAS, judge; b. Green Bay, Wis., Oct. 31, 1921; s. Earl P. and Elsie L. (Brauel) S.; m. Margaret P. Mulvaney, Sept. 6, 1952; children: Michael, Mary, Kathleen, Patrick Thomas, Ann, Maureen. BS in Bus. Adminstrn., Marquette U., 1943, JD, 1948; LLM in Taxation, John Marshall Law Sch., 1972. Bar: Wis. 1948. Pvt. practice, Milw., 1948-80; judge Wis. Cir. Ct., Milw., 1980-90; chief judge 1st Jud. Dist., Milw., 1990-98. Past vice chmn. Archdiocesan Sch. Bd., Milw., chairperson, 1986—. Served to col. USAR, 1942-73. Decorated Legion of Merit. Mem.: ABA (state del. 1983—85, 1989—92, bd. govs. 1985—88), Wis. Bar Assn. (pres. 1974—75, bd. govs., exec. com.), Exchange (pres.). Roman Catholic.

SHEEHAN, CAROL SAMA, magazine editor; Editor-in-chief Country Home Mag., Des Moines, 1997—. Office: Country Home Magazine 1716 Locust St Des Moines IA 50309-3038

SHEEHAN, JAMES PATRICK, printing company executive, former media company executive; b. Jersey City, June 6, 1942; s. John Patrick and Helen Teresa (Woods) S.; m. Mary Ellen Finnell, July 1, 1967; children: James, Christopher. BS, Seton Hall U., 1965; MBA, Wayne State U., 1973. Contr. Otis Elevator Co. N.Am., Farmington, Conn., 1976-78, dir. mfg. Yonkers, N.Y., 1978-80; v.p., contr,. Pratt & Whitney Aircraft, East Hartford, Conn., 1980-82; sr. v.p. A. H. Belo Corp., Dallas, 1982-84; CFO, A.H. Belo Corp., Dallas, 1984-86, pres., COO, 1987-93, CEO, 1993-99; pres., CEO, chmn. Goss Graphic Systems, Westmont, Ill., 1999—. Mem. devel. bd. U. Tex.-Dallas, 1985—; bd. dirs. United Way, The Dallas Partnership, The Dallas Morning News Charities; trustee St. Paul Med. Ctr. Found. Served to Lt. (j.g.) USN, 1967-69, Vietnam. Mem. Am. Newspaper Pubs. Assn., So. Newspaper Pubs. Assn. Roman Catholic. Avocations: tennis, racquetball, golf, running. Office: Goss International 3 Territorial Ct Bolingbrook IL 60440-3557

SHEEHAN, KEVIN EDWARD, venture capitalist; b. Deerfield, Mass., June 17, 1945; s. Walter Francis and Lillian (Fontaine) S.; m. Barbara Ann Frank, July 6, 1974; children: Timothy John, James Frank. BA, Williams Coll., 1966; MBA, Harvard U., 1971. Traffic mgr. New England Tel., Boston, 1966-69; foreman H Block Line Cummins Engine Co., Columbus, Ind., 1971, employee rels. mgr., 1972-75, dir. employee rels., 1975-77, mgr. engine plant, 1977-80, v.p. mgmt. systems, 1980-83, v.p. parts, 1984, v.p. parts and distbn., 1984-86, v.p. components group, 1986; gen. ptnr. CID Equity Partners, 1994—. Bd. dirs. One Call Comm., Hetsco, Inc., SPS Commerce; bd. observer SmartSignal, Emerald BioAgr.; non-exec. chmn. Flowserve Corp. Pres., bd. dirs. Quinco Mental Health Ctr., Columbus, 1976-80, St. Agnes Parish, Nashville, Ind., 1980-84. Mem. Country of Brown County Club (Nashville, Ind., pres., bd. dirs. 1984-88). Avocations: golf, reading, nature study. Office: CID Capital 1 American Sq Ste 2850 Indianapolis IN 46282 Office Phone: 317-269-2350. Business E-Mail: kevins@cidcap.com.

SHEEHAN, SAMANTHA, gymnast; b. Cin., May 20, 1986; d. Kevin and Cindy Sheehan. Gymnast Cincinnati Gymnastics/U.S. Natl. Team, 2002—. Achievements include Level 10 ational Bar Champion; Level 10 State Champion; Qualified to 2001, 02 U.S. Gymnastics Championships, World Championships, 2002; Bronze Medal Floor Exercise, World Championships, 2002; 1st place All Around, USA-Belgium dual competition, 2003. Office: 3635 Woodbridge Blvd Fairfield OH 45014

SHEEHY, RICK, lieutenant governor, former mayor; b. Hastings, Nebr., Oct. 3, 1959; m. Connie Sheehy; children: Maggie, Joel. Attended, Ctrl. CC, U. ebr.-Lincoln. City coun. mem. City of Hastings, Nebr., 1994—2005, mayor, 2000—05; lt. gov. State of Nebr., Lincoln, 2005—. Market gen. mgr., paramedic Rural/Metro Ambulance, 1982—. Exec. com. mem. Cottonwood Festival; mem. Nebr. State Trauma Adv. Bd., Mary Lanning Hosp. Found. Bd., Crane Meadows Bd. Dirs., Nebr. Rural Health Assn. Mem.: Hastings C. of C. (former chair), Hastings Noon Rotary, Hastings Sertoma Club (past pres.). Republican. Office: Lt Gov State Capitol, Rm 2315 PO Box 94863 Lincoln NE 68509-4863 Office Phone: 402-471-2256. Office Fax: 402-471-6031.

SHEFFEL, IRVING EUGENE, health facility administrator; b. Chgo., July 5, 1916; s. Joseph and Jennie (Leibson) S.; m. Beth Silver, Aug. 2, 1942 (dec.); 1 child, Anita (dec.); m. Peggy Shelton, Apr. 6, 1996. AB, U. Chgo., 1939; M.P.A., Harvard U., 1946; LHD (hon.), Washburn U., 1987. Insp., wage and hour div. Dept. Labor, Chgo., 1940-41; mgmt. and budget analyst VA, Washington, 1946-48; budget analyst U.S. Bur. of Budget, Washington, 1948-49; controller, treas. Menninger Found., Topeka, 1949-73, v.p., 1973-93, v.p. emeritus, 1993—. Instr. Menninger Sch. Psychiatry. Bd. dirs. Washburn U. Art Center, 1969—, pres., 1971-73; treas. Karl Menninger lect. series, 1983—. Served to maj. U.S. Army, 1942-45. Fellow Assn. Mental Health Adminstrs. (charter); mem. Am. Soc. Public Adminstrn. (charter), Topeka Opera Soc. (treas. 1985—). Jewish. Home: 1215 SW 29th Ter Topeka KS 66611-2192

SHEFFIELD, GARY ANTONIAN, professional baseball player; b. Tampa, Fla., Nov. 18, 1968; s. Betty and Harold Jones (Stepfather); m. DeLeon Sheffield, Feb. 5, 1999; children: Ebony, Carissa, Gary Jr. Outfielder Milw. Brewers, 1986-92, Fla. Marlins, 1993-98, LA Dodgers, 1999—2001, Atlanta Braves, 2002—03; third baseman San Diego Padres, 1992-93; outfielder, designated hitter NY Yankees, 2004—06, Detroit Tigers, 2006—. Co-author (with David Ritz): Inside Power, 2007. Founder Gary Sheffield Found., 1995—. Recipient Silver Slugger award, 1992, 1996, 2003-05; named Player of Yr. Sporting News, 1992, Nat. League Comeback Player of Yr., 1992; named to Nat. League All-Star Team, 1992-93, 96, 98-2000, 2003, Am. League All-Star Team, 2004-05. Achievements include becoming the youngest batting champion (1992) since Tommy David. Office: Detroit Tigers Comerica Park 2100 Woodward Ave Detroit MI 48201*

SHEFFIELD, JEFFREY T., lawyer; b. Oct. 1954; BA phi beta kappa, U. Chgo., 1976; JD, Harvard Law Sch., 1979. Bar: Ill. 1980. Law clk. Mass. Supreme Jud. Ct., Mass., 1979—80; ptnr., mem. firm mgmt. com. Kirkland & Ellis LLP, Chgo. Former adj. prof. IIT/ Chgo. Kent Coll. Law; former lecturer U. Chgo. Sch. Law. Contbr. articles to profl. jours. Office: Kirkland & Ellis LLP 200 E Randolph Dr Chicago IL 60601 Home: 125 Laurel Ave Wilmette IL 60091-2830 Home Phone: 847-251-1270; Office Phone: 312-861-2454. Office Fax: 312-861-2200. Business E-Mail: jsheffield@kirkland.com.

SHEFFIELD, JOHN WILLIAM, mechanical engineering educator; b. Ft. Worth, May 3, 1950; s. James G. and Sarah E. (Laney) S.; m. Mary White, May 21, 1977; children: Jennifer Marie, Katherine Elaine, Christopher William robert. B of Engring. Sci., U. Tex., 1971; M of Engring. Mechanics, N.C. State U., 1973, PhD in Engring. Sci. and Mechanics, 1975. Sr. analytical engr. Pratt & Whitney Aircraft, United Tech. Corp., East Hartford, Conn., 1975-76, sr. exptl. engr. West Palm Beach, Fla., 1976-78; rsch. asst. prof. of mech. engring. U. Miami, Coral Gables, Fla., 1978-80; asst. prof. U. Mo., Rolla, 1980-84, assoc. prof., 1984-89, prof. of mech. and aerospace engring., 1989—. Asst. dir. Indsl. Assessment Ctr., 1994—; asst. editor Internat. Assn. for Hydrogen Energy, 1978-82; assoc. editor Internat. Assn. Hydrogen Energy, 1983—; dir. Office of U. Outreach and Extension, 1997—. Contbr. numerous articles to profl. jours. Mem. ASHRAE (Dist. Svc. award 1991, mem. various coms.), ASME, AIAA, Am. Soc. Engring. Edn., Sigma Xi, Phi Kappa Phi, Tau Beta Pi, Pi Tau Sigma. Home: 11870 Forest Lake Dr Rolla MO 65401-7382 Office: Univ Mo Rolla Dept Mech & Aerospace Engrg 108 USBN Bldg 1 1300 Bishop Rolla MO 65409-0001

SHEFFIELD, LEWIS GLOSSON, physiologist; b. Adel, Ga., Oct. 30, 1957; s. Eugene Davis and Martha Sue (Sinclair) S.; m. Mary Frances Tanner, July 18, 1980. MS, Clemson U., 1980; PhD, U. Mo., 1983. Rsch. asst. Clemson (S.C.) U., 1978-80, U. Mo., Columbia, 1980-83; postdoctoral assoc. Mich. State U., East Lansing, 1983-86; asst. prof. dairy sci. dept. U. Wis., Madison, 1986-91, assoc. prof. dairy sci., 1991—, dir. endocrinology-reproductive physiology program, 1990—. Contbr. articles to profl. jours. Recipient First award NIH, 1988. Mem. Am. Dairy Sci. Assn. (milk synthesis chair 1991-92), Com. on Mammary Gland Biology, Endocrine Soc., Sigma Xi. Achievements include demonstration that epidermal growth factor interacts with estrogen and progesterone to regulate mammary devel. and are working to understand the cellular and molecular basis of that interaction; that prolactin causes a decrease in epidermal growth factor-induced growth responses, which appears to be related to mammary gland differentiation. The molecular regulation of this response is also under investigation. Office: U Wis 864 Animal Scis Bldg 1675 Observatory Dr Madison WI 53706-1205

SHEFSKY, LLOYD EDWARD, lawyer; b. Lake Village, Ark., Feb. 18, 1941; s. Samuel Martin and Esther Louise (Bender) S.; m. Natalie E. Shefsky, June 19, 1977; children: Dawn, Julie, Douglas. BS in Commerce, DePaul U., 1962; JD, U. Chgo., 1965. Bar: Ill. 1965, Fla. 1973; CPA, Ill. From assoc. to ptnr. Grossman, Kasakoff, Magid & Silverman, Chgo., 1965-70; ptnr. Shefsky & Froelich, Ltd., Chgo., 1970—95; of counsel Shefsky & Froelich Ltd.; clin. prof. Kellogg Grad. Sch. Mgmt., Northwestern U., 1995—. Lectr. various schs. and seminars; legal counsel Govt. Isreal, Mid-west Region; founder, chmn. The Inst. for Entrepreneurship. Author: Entrepreneurs Are Made Not Born, 1996; contbg. editor The Entertainment Law and Finance Jour. Former bd. dirs. Ill. Inst. for Entrepreneurial Edn.; past pres., dir. Am.-Israel C. of C.; bd. govs. Econs. Am., Ill. Coun. on Econ. Edn.; mem. adv. bd. Kellogg-Recanati Internat. Exec. MBA Prog.; mem. nat. coun. and regional bd. Anti Defamation League. Recipient Disting. Alumnus Award, DePaul U., 1980. Mem. Sports Lawyers Assn. (past pres., Award of Excellence, 1993), Am. Jewish Congress, Am-Israel Cultural Found., Office: Kellogg Sch Mgmt Ctr Family Enterprises 2001 Sheridan Rd Evanston IL 60208 E-mail: l-shefsky@kellogg.northwestern.edu.

SHEI, H. RAY, food products executive; b. Ind., Nov. 26, 1950; m. Janet Shei; 1 child. A in Computer Sci., Purdue U. Sr. mgr. transp. and logistics Keebler Co., 1991—97, v.p. info. sys., 1997—2001; v.p. Kellogg Co., 2001, sr. v.p., 2003—, chief info. officer, 2002—. Office: Kellogg PO Box 3599 1 Kellogg Sq Battle Creek MI 49016-3599

SHELBY, DON, radio personality; Anchor news at 6 pm and 10 pm Sta. WCCO-TV, Mpls., 1978—; radio host, news anchor Sta. WCCO, Mpls. Recipient 3 nat. Emmy awards, Columbia-duPont citation, Scripps-Howard award for Excellence, 2 George Foster Peabody awards, Disting. Svc. award, Soc. Profl. Journalist. Office: WCCO Radio 625 2nd Ave S Minneapolis MN 55402

SHELDON, GILBERT IGNATIUS, bishop emeritus; b. Cleve., Sept. 20, 1926; s. Ignatius Peter and Stephanie Josephine (Olszewski) Sheldon. Student, John Carroll U.; M.Div., St. Theol. Sem., 1970; D.Min., St. Mary Sem. and Ohio Consortium of Sems., 1974; HHD, Jesuit U. of Wheeling, 1993; STD, Franciscan U., Steubenville, 1994. Ordained priest Diocese of Cleve., 1953, assoc. pastor, 1953-64, diocesan dir. propagation of faith, 1964-74; pastor, Episcopal vicar Lorain County, Ohio, 1974-76; aux. bishop Diocese of Cleve., 1976—92; ordained bishop, 1976; vicar for Summit County, 1979-80, So. Region, 1980-92; bishop Diocese of Steubenville, Ohio, 1992—2002, bishop emeritus Ohio, 2002—. Bd. dirs. Soc. Propagation of Faith, 1968-74, Diocesan Presbyteral Coun.; instr. theology St. John Coll.; clergy adv. bd. econ. edn. Akron U.; mem. Bishop's Com. Latin Am.; adv. bd., Franciscan U.; bd. trustees St. Mary Seminary, Diocesan Health Ins. Adv. Bd., Cath. Charities Corp.; former mem. bd. trustees Borromeo Coll.; mem. acad. bd. St, Mary Seminary; bd. dirs. Bishops' Com. Latin Am., adminstrv. com. Nat. Conf. Cath. Bishops/USCC, Nat. Adv. Coun., Bishops' Com. for Missions, Nat. Bd. Soc. for Propagation of Faith; bd. trustees Pontifical Coll. Josephinum, Bishop Emeritus of Steubenville, 2002, Adj. Faculty, Franciscan U. of Steubenville, 2003. Goals for Greater Akron. With USAF, 1944—45. Mem. Nat. Conf. Cath. Bishops (adminstrv. bd. 1985—), Am. Legion, Cath. War Vets., Knights of Columbus, Order of Alhambra., Rotary Club Akron and Steubenville. Clubs: K.C. Lodges: Rotary (Akron). Roman Catholic. Avocations: golf, astronomy, photography, history, travel. Home: 609 N 7th St Steubenville OH 43952-1748 Home Phone: 740-283-9608. Business E-Mail: lnichols@diosteub.org.

SHELDON, INGRID KRISTINA, retired mayor, controller; b. Ann Arbor, Mich., Jan. 30, 1945; d. Henry Ragnvald and Virginia Schmidt Blom; m. Clifford George Sheldon, June 18, 1966; children: Amy Elizabeth, William David. BS, Eastern Mich. U., 1966; MA, U. Mich., 1970; doctorate (hon.), Cleary U., 2001. Cert. tchr., Mich. Tchr. Livonia (Mich.) Pub. Schs., 1966-67, Ann Arbor Pub. Schs., 1967-68; bookkeeper Huron Valley Tennis Club, Ann Arbor, 1978—; acct. F.A. Black Co., Ann Arbor, 1984-88; coun. mem. Ward II City of Ann Arbor, 1988-92, mayor, 1993-2000. Commr. Housing Bd. Appeals, Ann Arbor, 1988—91; vice chmn. fin. and budget com. S.E. Mich. Coun.Govts.; treas. Huron Valley Child Guidance Clinic, Ann Arbor, 1984—, Ann Arbor Hist. Found., 1985—, Parks Adv. Commn., 1987—92, Ann Arbor Planning Commn., 1988—89; excellence com. Ann Arbor Pub. Schs. reorgn., 1985; treas. SOS Cmty. Crisis Ctr., Ypsilanti, Mich., 1987—93; chair United Meth. Retirement Cmty., Ann Arbor, 2003—06; trustee Cmty. Found., 2001—05; chair Ann Arbor Summer Festival, 2005; treas. Dixboro United Meth. Ch., 2006—. Recipient Cmty. Svc. award Ann Arbor Jaycees, 1980, DAR Cmty. Svc. award, 1997; AAUW fellow, 1982. Mem.: Mich. Mcpl. League (life; del. 1989—97, hon. life mem. 1994, trustee 1997—2000, pres. 1999—2000), Ann Arbor Rotary (pres.-elect 2006—, pres. 2006—07), Ann Arbor Women's City Club (fin. com. 1987—90, chair endowment com. 1989—90, treas. 2003), Alpha Omicron Pi, Kappa Delta Pi. Republican. Methodist. Avocation: musical theatre. Home: 1416 Folkstone Ct Ann Arbor MI 48105-2848 Personal E-mail: aasheldon@aol.com.

SHELDON, TED PRESTON, library dean; b. Oak Park, Ill., July 5, 1942; s. Preston and Marjorie Sheldon; m. Beverly Stebel; children: Kathy, Mark. BA, Elmhurst Coll., Ill., 1964; MA, Ind. U., 1965, PhD, 1976; MLS, U. Ill., 1977. Asst. archivist U. Ill., Urbana, 1976-77; reference librarian U. Kans., Lawrence, 1977-79, head collection devel., 1979-81; assoc. dir. libraries SUNY, Binghamton, 1981-83, U. Mo., Kansas City, 1983-85, dean libraries, 1985—2005. Pres. Mo. Libr. etwork Corp., 1991-95. Author: Population Trends, 1976, Kans. Coll. Devel. Policy, 1978, History, Sources Social Science, 1985; co-author: ANSI/ISO/AES audio/video data preservation stds., 1997—. Mem. ALA, Am. Nat. Stds. Inst./Audio Engring. Soc. (joint tech. commn. 1994—), Internat. Assn. Sound Archives, Assn. Recorded Sound Collection (mng. editor jour 1988-95, pub. jour. 1995—, pres. 1996-98, pub. 1996—). Office: U Mo Libraries 5100 Rockhill Rd Kansas City MO 64110-2499 Office Phone: 816-235-1531. Business E-Mail: sheldont@umkc.edu.

SHELL, OWEN GLADSTONE, JR., retired bank executive; b. Greenville, SC, June 19, 1936; s. Owen and Katherine S.; m. Mary Ruth Trammell, Aug. 9, 1980; children: Katherine Sloan, Mary Carroll, Robert Owen, James Walker. BS, U. S.C., 1960; postgrad., Stonier Grad. Sch. Banking, 1971; grad., Advanced Mgmt. Program, Harvard U., 1979. V.p. Citizens & So. Nat. Bank S.C., Columbia, 1968-71, sr. v.p., 1971-74, exec. v.p., 1974-79; pres., dir., chief exec. officer First Am. Nat. Bank, ashville, 1979-86; vice chmn. bd., dir. First Am. Corp., 1979-86; chmn., pres., chief exec. officer Sovran Bank/Tenn., Nashville, 1986-91; pres. Nations Bank of Tenn. (formerly Sovran Bank), Nashville, 1992-96; pres. asset mgmt. group NationsBank Corp., St. Louis, 1997-99; pres. Asset Mgmt. Bank of Am., Charlotte, 1997—2002; ret., 2002. Bd. dirs. Nashville br. Fed. Res. Bank, Atlanta, Ctrl. Parkine, Inc., chmn. bd., Lifepoint Hosp. Inc. Chmn. Leadership ashville, Tenn. Performing Arts Found., Mid. Tenn. coun. Boy Scouts Am., Vanderbilt U. Owen Grad. Sch. Mgmt.; trustee Met. Nashville Pub. Edn. Found.; chmn. bd. INROADS/Nashville; bd. dirs. Tenn. Bus. Roundtable, Tenn. Tomorrow. Mem.: Assn. Res. City Bankers, Old Warson Country Club (St. Louis), Harvard Club N.Y.C., Belle Meade Country Club (Nashville), Kappa Alpha. Presbyterian. Home: 4412 Chickering Ln Nashville TN 37215-4915 also: 114 Tern Dr Anna Maria FL 34216

SHELLEY, WALTER BROWN, dermatologist, educator; b. St. Paul, Feb. 6, 1917; s. Patrick K. and Alfaretta (Brown) S.; m. Marguerite H. Weber, 1942 (dec.); children: Peter B., Anne E. Kiselewich, Barbara A. (dec.); m. E. Dorinda Loeffel, 1980; children: Thomas R., Katharine D., William L. BS, U. Minn., 1940, PhD, 1941, MD, 1943; MA honoris causa, U. Pa., 1971; MD honoris causa, U. Uppsala, Sweden, 1977; DSc (hon.), Med. U. Ohio, 2006. Diplomate: Am. Bd. Dermatology (pres. 1968-69, dir. 1960-69). Instr. physiology U. Pa., Phila., 1946-47, asst. instr. dermatology and syphilology, 1947-49, asst. prof. dermatology, 1950-53, assoc. prof., 1953-57, prof., 1957-80, chmn. dept., 1965-80; prof. dermatology U. Ill. Peoria Sch. Medicine, 1980-83; prof. medicine (dermatology) Med. Coll. Ohio, 1983-97, emeritus prof. medicine, 1997—. Instr. dermatology Dartmouth Coll., 1949-50; Regional cons. dermatology VA, 1955-59; mem. com. on cutaneous system NRC, 1955-59, Commn. Cutaneous Diseases, Armed Forces Epidemiological Bd., 1958-61, dep. dir., 1959-61; cons. dermatology Surgeon Gen. USAF, 1958-61, U.S. Army, 1958-61; mem. NRC, 1961-64 Author (with Crissey): Classics in Clinical Dermatology, 1953, 2003; author: (with Pillsbury, Kligman) Dermatology, 1956; author: Cutaneous Medicine, 1961; author: (with Hurley) The Human Apocrine Sweat Gland in Health and Disease, 1960; author: (with Botelho and Brooks) The Endocrine Glands, 1969; author: Consultations in Dermatology with Walter B. Shelley, 1972, 2006, Consultations II, 1974; author: (with Shelley) Advanced Dermatologic Therapy, 1987; author: Advanced Dermatologic Diagnosis, 1992, A Century of International Dermatological Congresses, 1992, Advanced Dermatogical Therapy II, 2001, Shelley's 77 Skins, 2001, Consultations in Dermatology, 2006, The Skin Around Me: Adventure in Dermatology, 2007; mem. editl. bd. Jour. Investigative Dermatology, 1961—64, Archives of Dermatology, 1961—62, Skin and Allergy News, 1970—93, Excerpta Medica Dermatologica, 1960—, Cutis, 1972—, Jour. Geriatric Dermatol, 1993; assoc. editor: Jour.

Cutaneous Pathology, 1972—81; editl. cons. Medcom, 1972—. Served as capt. M.C. AUS, 1944-46. Recipient Spl. award Soc. Cosmetic Chemists, 1955, Hellerstrom medal, 1971, Am. Med. Writers Assn. Best Med. Book award, 1973, Dohi medal, 1981, Rothman medal Soc. for Investigative Dermatology, 1987, Rose Hirschler award, 1990, Humane Dermatologist award, 2005. Master ACP; fellow Assn. Am. Physicians, St. John's Dermatol. Soc. London (hon.); mem. AMA (chmn. residency rev. com. for dermatology 1963-67, chmn. sect. dermatology 1969-71), Assn. Profs. Dermatology (pres. 1972-73), Pacific Dermatol. Assn. (hon.), Am. Dermatol. Assn. (hon., dir., pres. 1975-76), Soc. Investigative Dermatology (hon. pres. 1961-62), Am. Physiol. Soc., Phila. Physiol. Soc., Brit. Dermatol. Soc. (hon.), Phila. Dermatol. Soc. (pres. 1960-61), Mich. Dermatol. Soc., Ohio Dermatol. Soc. (hon.), Am. Acad. Dermatology (Gold medal 1992, hon. pres. 1971-72), Pa. Acad. Dermatology (pres. 1972-73), Am. Soc. Dermatologic Surgery, N.Am. Clin. Dermatol. Soc. (hon.), Noah Worcester Dermatol. Soc., Royal Soc. Medicine; corr. mem. Nederlandse Vereniging Van Dermatologen, Israeli Dermatol. Assn., Finnish Soc. Dermatology, Swedish Dermatol. Soc., French Dermatologic Soc.; fgn. hon. mem. Danish Dermatol. Assn., Japanese Dermatol. Assn., Dermatol. Soc. S.Africa, Austrian Dermatol. Soc. Home: 21171 W River Rd Grand Rapids OH 43522-9703 Office: U Toledo Coll Medicine 3000 Arlington Ave Toledo OH 43614 Home Phone: 419-832-0648; Office Phone: 419-383-3720. Business E-Mail: walter.shelley@utoledo.edu.

SHELTON, KEVIN L., geology educator; Prof. geology U. Mo., Columbia. Recipient Lindgren award Soc. Economic Geologists, 1991. Office: Univ of Missouri Columbia Dept of Geol Scis 303 Geol Scis Bldg Columbia MO 65211-0001

SHELTON, O. L., state legislator; b. Greenwood, Miss., Feb. 6, 1946; s. Obie and Idell (McClung) S.; m. Linda Kay, July 21, 1980; children: Eric, Jaimal, Schron, Kiana. AB, Lincoln U., 1970. Youth specialist Mo. Ext. Svc., St. Louis, 1972-82. Committeeman 4th ward Dem. party, St. Louis, 1988—; vice-chmn. Dem. Party; advisor Ville Area Neighborhood Housing Assn.; active Black Leadership Roundtable, Mary Rydar Homes, Williams Community Sch. Mem. Early Childcare Devel. Corp. Home: 1803A Cora Ave Saint Louis MO 63113-2221

SHEN, SIN-YAN, physicist, acoustical engineer, musicologist; b. Singapore, Nov. 12, 1949; came to the U.S., 1969, naturalized, 1984; s. Shao-Quan and Tien-Siu (Chen) S.; m. Yuan-Yuan Lee, Aug. 4, 1973; children: Jia, Jian. BSc, U. Singapore, 1969; MS, Ohio State U., 1970, PhD, 1973. Concert recitalist on Erhu Chinese fiddle, 1963—; instr. math. U. Singapore, 1969; asst. prof. physics Northwestern U., Evanston, Ill., 1974-77, assoc. prof., 1977-81; faculty assoc. Argonne (Ill.) Nat. Lab., 1974-77, scientist, 1977-83, sr. rsch. leader, 1983—. Dir. rsch. divsn. natural resource mgmt. SUPCON Internat., 1988—; prof. Harvard U., 1989—; meeting series reviewer NSF, Washington, 1981—; coord. Tech. Rev., Argonne, Atlanta, Phoenix, Portland, Oreg., 1983—; dir. Global Warming Internat. Ctr., 1991—, chmn. Internat. Conf. Chgo., 1990-93, San Francisco, 1994-95, Vienna, 1996, Columbia U., N.Y.C., 1997, Hong Kong U. Sci. and Tech., 1998, Yamanashi Inst. Environ. Scis., 1999, Harvard U., 2000, Cambridge U., 2001, Max Planck Inst., 2002, Mass. Inst. Tech., 2003; Chinese Music Internat. Conf., 1991, 94, 2002; advisor Internat. Energy Agy., 1986—, Gas Rsch. Inst., 1984—, SUPCON Internat., 1986—, Nat. Geog., 1986—, Internat. Boreal Forest Rsch. Assn., 1991—, Electric Power Rsch. Inst., 1992—, World Climate Rsch. Programme WMO, 1993—, UN Devel. Program, 1993—, World Bank, 1994—, US Dept. Energy and US EPA, 1995—; prof. Chinese Acad. Forestry, 1986—; panel on biol. diversity Nat. Acad. Scis., Smithsonian Instn., 1986; chmn. internat. program com. Austrian Acad. Scis., 1995-96, Columbia U., 1996-97, Japan Environ. Agy., 1998-99, Intergovt. Panel on Climate Change, 1999—; music dir. Orch. Chinese Music Soc. N.Am., 1976—, Silk & Bamboo Ensemble, 1981—; adv. Ctrl. Traditional Orch., 1984—; del. leader, UN Conf. Environ. and Devel., Rio, 1992; del. chmn. Third All China Arts Festival, Kunmin, 1992; panelist Nat. Endowment for Arts, 1981—, New Eng. Found. for Arts, 1987—, Arts Midwest, 1985—, Ill. Arts Coun., 1982—, Chgo. City Arts, 1990—, Ill. Art's Alliance Found., adv. coun., 1992—, adv. coun. Mid-Am. Arts Alliance, 1992—, bd. dirs.; tech. adv. Shanghai Nat. Musical Instrument Co., 1985—; adv. West Lake Qin Soc., Hangzhou, China, 1991—. Author: Superfluidity, 1982, Acoustics of Ancient Chinese Bells, 1987, Chinese Music and Orchestration: A Primer om Principles and Practice, 1991, Global Warming Science and Policy, 1992, The Boreal Forests and Global Change, 1993, Global Warming Eludidated, 1994, Chinese Musical Instruments, 1999, Global Warming and Public Health, 1999, China: A Journey through Its Musical Art, 1999, Chinese Music in the 20th Century, 2001; editor-in-chief Chinese Music Internat. Jour., 1978—; mem. internat. editl. bd. World Resource Rev., 1989—, Internat. Boreal Forest Rsch., 1992—, Ency. of Life Support Sys., 1994—; adv. Ency. Brit., 1983—; contbr. over 300 articles to profl. jours.; patentee molten liquids, 1974, 80. Recipient Mich. Heritage award, 1992; Fulbright scholar U.S. State Dept., 1969; merit scholar Govt. Singapore, 1967; named Artistic Treasure Gov. Jim Edgar of Ill., 1998. Mem. AAAS, Am. Phys. Soc., Ops. Rsch. Soc. Am., Acoustical Soc. Am., Chinese Music Soc. N.Am. Achievements include rsch. in renewable energy and materials techs.; global change and global warming; extreme event index; indsl. sonic techs.; energy policy, planning and economics; acoustics; cultural acoustics. also: SUPCON Internat PO Box 5275 Woodridge IL 60517-0275 Office Phone: 630-910-1551.

SHEPARD, IVAN ALBERT, securities and insurance broker; b. Springfield, Mass., Sept. 28, 1925; s. Albert Joseph and Mary (Harrigan) S.; m. Miriam Murray, May 20, 1950; children: Kirk, Robin, Mark. BS in Edn., Ohio State U., Columbus, 1949. Registered rep. Divisional mgr. Confedn. Life, Columbus, Ohio, 1953-62; regional v.p. Western Res. Life, Cleve., 1962-69; v.p. Computer Life-Pan Western, Columbus, 1969-74; ins. broker Shepard and Assocs., Rocky River, Ohio, 1974—. Bd. dirs., v.p., sec. Computer Life Ohio, 1969-72. With U.S. Navy, 1943-45. Home: 29318 Lake Rd Bay Village OH 44140-1321 Office: Shepard and Assocs 20525 Center Ridge Rd Cleveland OH 44116-3424

SHEPARD, MICHAEL J., prosecutor; Atty. U.S. Dept. Justice, Chgo., 1993—, asst. atty.

SHEPARD, RANDALL TERRY, state supreme court chief justice; b. Lafayette, Ind., Dec. 24, 1946; s. Richard Schilling and Dorothy Ione (Donlen) S.; m. Amy Wynne MacDonell, May 7, 1988; one child, Martha MacDonell. AB cum laude, Princeton U., 1969; JD, Yale U., 1972; LLM, U. Va., 1995; LLD (hon.), U. So. Ind., 1995, U. S.C., 1996. Bar: Ind. 1972, U.S. Dist. Ct. (so. dist.) Ind. 1972. Spl. asst. to under sec. U.S. Dept. Transp., Washington, 1972-74; exec. asst. to mayor City of Evansville, Ind., 1974-79; judge Vanderburgh Superior Ct., Evansville, 1980-85; assoc. justice Ind. Supreme Ct., Indpls., 1985-87, chief justice, 1987—. Instr. U. Evansville, 1975-78, Indiana U., 1995, 99; pres. Nat. Conference of Chief Justices, 2005—. Author: Preservation Rules and Regulations, 1980, Indiana Legal History, 2005; contbr. articles to profl. publs. Bd. advisors Nat. Trust for Hist. Preservation, 1980-87, chmn. bd. advisors, 1983-85, trustee, 1987-96; dir. Hist. Landmarks Found. Ind., 1983—, chmn., 1989-92, hon. chmn., 1992—; chmn. State Student Assistance Commn. Ind., 1981-85; chmn. Ind. Commn. on Bicentennial of U.S. Constn., 1986-91; vice chmn. Vanderburgh County Rep. Ctrl. Com., 1977-80. Recipient Disting. Svc. award Evansville Jaycees, 1982, Herbert Harley award Am. Judicature Soc., 1992, Wickler award Nat. Assn. Women Judges, 2004. Mem. ABA (coun. mem. sect. on legal edn. 1991—, chair sect. on legal edn. 1997-98, chair appellate judges conf. 1996-97), Ind. Bar Assn., Ind. Judges Assn., Princeton Club (N.Y.), Capitol Hill Club (Washington), Columbia Club (Indpls.), Woodstock Club (Indpls.). Republican. Methodist. Home: 3644 Totem Ln Indianapolis IN 46208-4171 Office: Ind Supreme Ct 315 State House Indianapolis IN 46204-2213 Office Phone: 317-232-2550.

SHEPARD, W. BRUCE, academic administrator; m. Cyndie Shepard. BA in Polit. Sci., U. Calif., Riverside, 1969, MS in Polit. Sci., 1970, PhD in Polit. Sci., 1972. Prof. polit. sci., provost, v.p. acad. affairs Ea. Oreg. U., LaGrande, 1995—2002; mem. faculty dept. polit. sci. Oreg. State U., Oreg.; chancellor U. Wis., Green Bay, Wis., 2002—. Vis. scientist Population Study Ctr., Seattle; vis. fellow Sch. Comm. and Liberal Studies MItchell Coll. Advanced Edn., Bathurst, Australia. Office: U Wis Office Chancellor 2420 Nicolet Dr Green Bay WI 54311-7001

SHEPHERD, DANIEL MARSTON, executive recruiter; b. Madison, Ind., Apr. 8, 1939; s. Marston Vincent and Edith America (Brunson) S.; m. Bonnie Lynn Brawley, June 27, 1970 (div. Nov. 1987); children: Vincent, David, Christopher, Megan; m. Gail Lenore Sanborn, Oct. 3, 1989; children: Heather, Shannon. BS in Civil Engring., U. Ky., 1962; MBA, Harvard Bus. Sch., 1964. Mfg. and distbn. mgr. Procter & Gamble Co., Staten Island, N.Y., 1966-70; distbn. and ops. mgr. Mattel, Inc., Gardenia, Calif., 1970-73; gen. mgr., dir. ops. Fuqua Industries, Inc., Atlanta, 1973-76; v.p. product/market mgmt. Masonite Corp., Chgo., 1976-78; v.p. Heidrick & Struggles, Chgo., 1978-82, Lamalie Assocs., Chgo., 1982-86; prin. Sweeney Shepherd Bueschel Provus Harbert & Mummert, Chgo., 1986-91, Shepherd Bueschel & Provus, Inc., Chgo., 1991—. Capt. U.S. Army, 1964-66. Decorated Army Commendation medal, 1966; recipient Am.'s Top 150 Recruiters award Harper Bus., N.Y.C., 1992. Mem. Assn. Exec. Search Cons., Inc., Harvard Bus. Sch. Club. Republican. Episcopalian. Avocations: coin and art collecting, skiing, baseball, food, wine. Home: 100 Buckboard Pl Pagosa Springs CO 81147 Office: 401 N Michigan Ave Ste 3020 Chicago IL 60611-4257 E-mail: sbp401@aol.com.

SHEPHERD, JOHN THOMPSON, physiologist; b. No. Ireland, May 21, 1919; s. William Frederick and Matilda (Thompson) S.; m. Helen Mary Johnston, July 28, 1945; children: Gillian Mary, Roger Frederick John; m. Marion G. Etzwiler, Apr. 22, 1989. Student, Campbell Coll., Belfast, No. Ireland, 1932-37; MB, BCh, Queen's U., Belfast, 1945, MChir, 1948, MD, 1951, DSc, 1956, DSc (hon.), 1979; MD (hon.), U. Bologna, 1984, U. Gent, 1985. Lectr. physiology Queen's U., 1948-53, reader physiology, 1954-57; assoc. prof. physiology Mayo Found., 1957-62, prof. physiology, 1962—, chmn. dept. physiology and biophysics, 1966-74; bd. govs. Mayo Clinic, 1966-80; trustee Mayo Found., 1969-81, dir. rsch., 1969-77, dir. for edn., 1977-83, chmn. bd. devel., 1983-88; dean Mayo Med. Sch., 1977-83; assoc. dir. Gen. Rsch. Ctr. Mayo Clinic, Rochester, 1992-94. Chmn. U.S. Nat. Com. for the Internat. Union of Physiol. Scis., 1991-95; vis. prof. U. Auckland, New Zealand, 1997; vis. prof. cardiovasc. divsn. U. Minn., 1995; Soma Weiss meml. lectr. Third Internat. Congress WHMA, Pecs, Hungary, 1996. Author, editor: Physiology of the Circulation in Human Limbs in Health and Disease, 1963, Cardiac Function in Health and Disease, 1968, Veins and Their Control, 1975, Human Cardiovascular System, 1979, Handbook of Physiology, The Cardiovascular System Peripheral Circulation and Organ Blood Flow, 1983, Vascular Diseases in the Limbs, 1993, Nervous Control of the Heart, 1996; co-editor: Exercise: Regulation and Integration of Multiple Systems. Handbook of Physiology, 1996; mem. editl. bd. Hypertension, 1973—, Am. Jour. Physiology, Am. Heart Jour., Microvascular Rsch.; cons. editor Circulation Rsch., 1981—; editor-in-chief News in Physiol. Sci., 1988-94; mem. editl. adv. bd. Clin. Autonomic Rsch., 1990—, Jour. Autonomic Nervous Sys., 1994—, Exptl. Physiology, 1994—, Vascular Medicine, 1995—, Internat. Angiology Adv. Com., 1994—, Cardiovasc. Rsch., 1997—; contbr. more than 590 sci. articles to profl. jours. Recipient NASA Skylab Achievement award, 1974, A. Ross McIntyre medal for achievement, 1991; Brit. Med. Assn. scholar, 1949-50, Fulbright scholar, 1953-54; Anglo-French Med. exch. bursar, 1957; Internat. Francqui chair, 1978; Einthoven lectr. 1981, Volhard lectr., 1990. Fellow Am. Coll. Cardiology (hon.), Royal Coll. Physicians (London, hon.), Royal Coll. Physicians Ireland (hon.), Royal Acad. Medicine (Belgium); mem. NAS (space sci. bd. 1973-74, chmn. com. space biology and medicine 1973), Am. Physiol. Soc. (Disting. Svc. award 1990, Ray G. Daggs award 1997), Louis Rapkine Assn., Am. Heart Assn. (dir. 1968—, pres. 1975-76, chmn. vascular medicine and biology task force 1990, hon. fellow coun. clin. cardiology), Physiol. Soc. Gt. Brit., Med. Rsch. Soc. London, Assn. Am. Physicians, Internat. Union of Angiology (hon.), Worldwide Hungarian Med. Acad. (hon.), Rappaport Inst. Israel (sci. adv. bd.), Sigma Xi. Office: Mayo Clinic Plummer Bldg N-10 Rochester MN 55905 Home Phone: 507-282-9161; Office Phone: 507-284-2691.

SHEPHERD, STEWART ROBERT, lawyer; b. Chgo., Sept. 9, 1948; s. Stewart and LaVina Beatrice (Nereim) S.; m. Margaret Brownell Shoop, Aug. 14, 1970; children: Elisabeth Ashby, Megan Brownell, Blair Stewart. BA, Rockford Coll., 1970; JD, U. Chgo., 1973. Bar: Calif. 1973, U.S. Dist. Ct. (no. dist.) Calif. 1973, Ill. 1976, U.S. Dist. Ct. (no. dist.) Ill. 1976. Assoc. Heller, Ehrman, White & McAuliffe, San Francisco, 1973-75, Hopkins & Sutter, Chgo., 1975-79, ptnr., 1979-96, Sidley Austin LLP, Chgo., 1996. Mem. ABA, Order of Coif, Phi Beta Kappa. Office Phone: 312-853-2654. E-mail: sshepherd@sidley.com.

SHEPHERD, TERRY L., health facility administrator; BS, Purdue U.; MBA, Ind. U. V.p., CFO Cardiac Pacemakers, Inc.; dir. bus. devel. med. devices and diagnostics divsn., CFO Lilly Industries, Ltd., U.K.; pres. Hybritech Eli Lilly and Co.; pres. heart valve divsn. St. Jude Med. Inc., St. Paul, 1994, mgr. internat. ops., 1996, pres., CEO, 1999—, chmn., 2002—. Office: St Jude Med Inc 1 Lillehei Plz Saint Paul MN 55117-9983

SHEPHERD, WAYNE, radio personality; b. Lapeer, Mich., Jan. 14; m. Becky Shepherd, 1973; children: Levi, Jennifer. Grad., Cedarville Coll. Radio host of Open Line and Proclaim Sta. WMBI Radio, Chgo. Avocations: snowmobiling, riding ATVs. Office: WMBI 820 N LaSalle Blvd Chicago IL 60610

SHER, SUSAN, lawyer; b. 1948; children: Graham, Evan. BA, George Wash. U.; JD, Loyola U. Bar: Ill. 1974. With Mayer, Brown & Platt; former dir. labor and litigation U. Chgo.; asst. corp. counsel City of Chgo., 1989—93, corp. counsel, 1993—97; v.p., gen. counsel U. Chgo. Hosps., 1997—, v.p. legal and govt. affairs, 2001—. Mem. steering com. Ill. Hosp. Assn., 2004; spkr. in field. Office: Univ Chgo Hosps 5841 S Maryland Ave MC 1114 Chicago IL 60637 Office Phone: 773-702-1000.

SHERBIN, DAVID M., lawyer; b. Detroit, Sept. 6, 1959; m. Abbe H. Sherbin. BA with honors, Oberlin College, 1981; JD, Cornell Law Sch., 1987. Assoc. Katten Muchin & Zavis, Chgo., 1987—91; sr. counsel Heller Fin. Inc., 1992—97; assoc. gen. counsel Fed. Mogul Corp., Southfield, Mich., 1997—2001, sec., 1999—, v.p., dep. gen. counsel, sec., 2001—04, sr. v.p., gen. counsel, sec., 2004—05; v.p., gen. counsel, sec. Pulte Homes, Inc., Bloomfield Hills, Mich., 2005; v.p., gen. counsel, chief compliance officer Delphi Corp., Troy, Mich., 2005—. Mem.: Chgo. Bar Assn., ABA. Office: Delphi Corp 5725 Delphi Dr Troy MI 48098-2815 Office Phone: 248-813-3009. Office Fax: 248-813-2491.

SHERE, DENNIS, lawyer, writer, retired publishing executive; b. Cleve., Nov. 29, 1940; s. William and Susan (Luskay) S.; m. Maureen Jones, Sept. 4, 1965 (div. Aug. 23, 2005); children: Rebecca Lynn, David Matthew, Stephen Andrew. BS in Journalism, Ohio U., 1963, MS in Journalism, 1964; JD, DePaul U., 2003. Staff writer Dayton (Ohio) Daily News, 1966-69; asst. prof. Sch. Journalism Bowling Green (Ohio) State U., 1969-70; fin. editor Detroit News, 1970-72, city editor, 1973-75; editor Dayton Jour. Herald, 1975-80; pub. Springfield (Ohio) Newspapers Inc., 1980-83, Dayton Newspapers, Inc., 1983-88; gen. mgr. Media Group Moody Bible Inst., 1989—2001; with death penalty trial assistance divsn. Il. State Appellate Defender's Office, 2004—05; asst. pub. defender Kane County Pub. Defender's Office, Ill., 2005—07. Author: Cain's Redemption -A Story of Hope & Transformation in America's Bloodiest Prison, 2005. Served with AUS, 1964-66. Mem. Sigma Alpha Epsilon, Omicron Delta Kappa. Business E-Mail: Dennis.Shere@moody.edu.

SHERIDAN, JAMES EDWARD, history professor; b. Wilmington, Del., July 15, 1922; s. Phillip Lambert and Ida Alverna (Green) S.; m. Sonia Landy, Sept. 27, 1947; 1 son, Jamy. BS, U. Ill., 1949, MA, 1950; PhD, U. Calif., Berkeley, 1961. Lectr. Chinese history Stanford U., 1960; mem. faculty Northwestern U., 1961—, prof. history, 1968—, chmn. dept., 1969-74, assoc. dean Coll. Arts and Scis., 1985-89, prof. emeritus, 1992—. Author: Chinese Warlord: The Career of Feng Yu-hsiang, 1966, China: A Culture Area in Perspective, 1970, China in Disintegration: The Republican Era in Chinese History, 1912-1949, 1975, A Community of Caring: An Introduction to Kendal at Hanover, 1998; editor: The Transformation of Modern China series, 1975—. Served to ensign USN, 1941-46. Fulbright fellow, France, 1950-51; Ford Found. fellow, 1958-60; grantee Am. Coun. Learned Socs.-Social Sci. Rsch. Coun., 1966-67, 71-72 Home: 80 Lyme Rd Apt 438 Hanover NH 03755-1236 Office: Northwestern Univ Dept History Evanston IL 60201 E-mail: james.e.sheridan@valley.net.

SHERIDAN, PATRICK MICHAEL, retired finance company executive; b. Grosse Pointe, Mich., Apr. 13, 1940; s. Paul Phillip and Frances Mary (Rohan) S.; m. Diane Lorraine Tressler, Nov. 14, 1986; children: Mary, Patrick, Kelly, Kevin, James. BBA, U. Notre Dame, 1962; MBA, U. Detroit, 1975. Acct. Peat, Marwick, Mitchell & Co., Detroit, 1962-72, audit mgr., 1969-72; exec. v.p. fin. Alexander Hamilton Life Ins. Co., Farmington, Mich., 1973-76; sr. v.p. ops. Sun Life Ins. Co. Am., Balt., 1976-78, exec. v.p., 1978-79; pres. Sun Ins. Services, Inc., 1979-81; pres., chief exec. officer Am. Health & Life Ins. Co., Balt., 1981-85; chief exec. officer Gulf Ins. Co., 1985-86; sr. v.p., chief fin. officer Comml. Credit Co., 1985-86, sr. v.p. audit, 1987; exec. v.p., chief fin. officer Anthem, Inc., Indpls., 1987-99, ret., 1999. Author: (book) Bottle-Cap Sundaes, Beneath The Radar, The Doer, God Lets a Dog. Rep. candidate for U.S. Congress, 1972; past pres. Charlesbrooke Cmty. Assn.; past. v.p. Jr. Achievement of Met. Balt., 1984-85; bd. dirs. Goodwill Industries of Balt., 1986, bd. govs. 1994; bd. dirs. Family Svcs. Assn., 1994, Goodwill Industries of Indpls., 1994; mem. adv. coun. Clowes Meml. Hall. Capt. AUS, 1963-65. Recipient various Jaycee awards. Fellow Life Mgmt. Inst.; mem. Am. Mgmt. Assn. (pres.'s assn.), AICPAs, Mich. Assn. CPAs, Md. Assn. CPAs, Am. Soc. CLUs, U.S. Jaycees (treas. 1973-74), Mich. Jaycees (pres. 1971-72), Detroit Jaycees (pres. 1968-69), Balt. C. of C. (bd. dirs.), Mensa, Notre Dame Club.

SHERMAN, JENNIFER L., lawyer; BBA, U. Mich., 1986, JD, 1989. Bar: Ill. 1989. Assoc. Barack Ferrazzano Kirschbaum Perlman & Nagelberg LLC, 1989—93; corp. counsel Hook-SupeRx, Inc./Revco Drug Stores, 1993—94; dep. gen. counsel, asst. sec. Fed. Signal Corp., Oak Brook, Ill., 1994—2004, v.p., gen. counsel, sec., 2004—. Office: Fed Signal Corp 1415 W 22nd St Oak Brook IL 60521 Office Phone: 630-954-2000.

SHERMAN, JEREMY P., lawyer; b. Chgo., Mar. 8, 1951; BA magna cum laude, Am. U., 1973; JD with honors, George Washington U., 1976. Bar: Ill. 1976. Mem. Seyfarth Shaw LLP, Chgo., 1976, ptnr. Nat. chairperson Labor and Employment Practice Group, Ill. Office: Seyfarth Shaw LLP Ste 2400 131 S Dearborn St Chicago IL 60603 Office Phone: 312-460-5901. Business E-Mail: jsherman@seyfarth.com.

SHERMAN, LOUIS ALLEN, biology professor, department chairman; b. Chgo., Dec. 16, 1943; s. Stanley E. and Sarah R. Sherman; m. Debra Meddoff, June 15, 1969; children: Daniel, Jeff. BS in Physics, U. Chgo., 1965, PhD in Biophysics, 1970. Postdoctoral fellow Cornell U., Ithaca, NY, 1970-72; asst. prof. U. Mo., Columbia, 1972-78, assoc. prof., 1978-83, prof., 1983-88, dir. biol. scis., 1985-88; prof., head dept. biol. scis. Purdue U., West Lafayette, Ind., 1989-2000, prof. biol. scis., 1989—. Vis. scholar Hebrew U., Jerusalem, 2004—05. Contbr. articles to profl. jours. NIH fellow, 1965-72; Fulbright Hayes scholar, The etherlands, 1979-80; NSF travel grantee, Fed. Republic Germany, Japan; grantee NIH, USDA, Dept. Energy. Fellow: AAAS, Am. Acad. Microbiology; mem.: AAUP, Plant Molecular Biology Soc., Biophys. Soc., Am. Soc. Plant Biologists, Am. Soc. Microbiology. Office: Purdue U Dept Biol Scis Lilly Hall West Lafayette IN 47907

SHERMAN, STUART, internist, gastroenterologist; b. NYC, Feb. 21, 1955; s. Sol and Rhoda (Kaplan) S.; m. Leslie Jane Derus, Oct. 5, 1991; children: Matthew, Benjamin. BA, SUNY, Binghampton, 1977; MD, Washington U., St. Louis, 1982. Diplomate Am. Bd. Internal Medicine. Resident in internal medicine U. Pitts., 1982-85, rsch. fellow, 1985-86; gastroenterology fellow Sch. of Medicine UCLA, 1986-89; therapeutic endoscopy fellow Sch. Medicine Ind. U., 1989-90; asst. prof. medicine and pancreaticobiliary endoscopy UCLA, 1990-92; asst. prof. medicine Ind. U., 1992-95, assoc. prof., 1995—, assoc. prof. radiology, 1996—. Cons. Bard Interventional Products Adv. Panel, Tewksbury, Mass., 1994—. Contbr. articles to profl. jours. Recipient Glaxo Award for excellence in gastroenterology Midwest Am. Fedn. Clin. Rsch., 1993, Young Scholars Rsch. award World Congress of Gastroenterology, L.A., 1994. Fellow Am. Coll. Gastroenterology (mem. editl. bd. Gastrointestinal Endoscopy); mem. ACP, Am. Soc. for Gastrointestinal Endoscopy, Am. Gastroent. Assn. Avocations: travel, skiing, tennis, golf. Office: Ind U Med Ctr 550 University Blvd Ste 2300 Indianapolis IN 46202-5149 E-mail: ssherman@induni.edu.

SHERREN, ANNE TERRY, chemistry professor; b. Atlanta, July 1, 1936; d. Edward Allison and Annie Ayres (Lewis) Terry; m. William Samuel Sherren, Aug. 13, 1966. BA, Agnes Scott Coll., 1957; PhD, U. Fla., Gainesville, 1961. Grad. tchg. asst. U. Fla., Gainesville, 1957-61; from instr. to asst. prof. Tex. Womans U., Denton, 1961-66; rsch. participant Argonne Nat. Lab., 1973-80, 93-94; assoc. prof. chemistry North Cen. Coll., Naperville, Ill., 1966-76, prof., 1976-2001, prof. emeritus, 2001—. Contbr. articles to profl. jours. Ruling elder Knox Presbyn. Ch., 1971—, clk. of session, 1976-94. Mem. Am. Chem. Soc., Am. Inst. Chemists, Sigma Xi, Delta Kappa Gamma (chpt. pres. 2002-2004), Iota Sigma Pi (nat. pres. 1978-81, nat. dir. 1972-78, nat. historian 1989—). Presbyterian. Office: North Ctrl Coll Dept Chemistry Naperville IL 60566 Business E-Mail: atsherren@noctrl.edu.

SHERRER, GARY, former state lieutenant governor, bank executive; m. Judy (Waller), 1965; children: Stuart and Nancy. Grad., Emporia State U. Sec. Kans. Dept. Commerce and Housing, 1995—2002; lt. gov. State of Kans., 1996—2003; exec. v.p. Gold Banc, Leawood, Kans., 2002—. Vice chmn. Governor's Cabinet. Recipient Disting. Alumni Award Emporia State U., 1994, Award of Excellence, 1995; Carl Perkins Humanitarian Award, 2000; Toll fellow, 1999. Mem. Nat. Conf. Lt. Govs. (chmn.). Republican.

SHERRICK, DANIEL WILLIAM, lawyer; b. Rochester, Minn., Jan. 24, 1958; s. Donald William and Jean Karol (Loudon) S.; m. Ellen Moss, Mar. 6, 1989. BA, Yale U., 1980; JD, U. Mich., 1984. Bar: Mich. 1984, US Ct. Appeals (6th cir.) 1985, US Ct. Appeals (11th cir.) 1985, US Supreme Ct. 1991. Assoc. gen. counsel Internat. Union UAW, Detroit, 1984—98, gen. counsel, 1998—. Office: UAW Legal Dept 8000 E Jefferson Ave Detroit MI 48214-3963 Office Phone: 313-926-5216.

SHERRILL, GREGG M., automotive executive; BSME, Tex. A&M; MBA, Ind. U. Plant mgr. Ford Motor Com., Dearborn, Mich., dir., supplier tech. assistance; with Johnson Controls, Inc., 1998—2007, v.p., gen. mgr., North Am. automotive ops., 2000—01, grp. v.p., mng. dir., Europe, South Africa, South Am., automotive systems grp., 2001—03, grp. v.p., mng. dir., Japan and Asia Pacific, grp. v.p., gen. mgr., battery ops., automotive systems grp., 2003—07, v.p., pres., power solutions; chmn., CEO Tenneco Inc., Lake Forest, Ill., 2007—. Office: Tenneco Inc 500 N Field Drive Lake Forest IL 60045 Office Phone: 847-482-5000. Office Fax: 847-482-5940.

SHERRILL, THOMAS BOYKIN, III, retired newspaper publishing executive; b. Tampa, Fla., Nov. 19, 1930; s. Thomas Boykin Jr. and Mary Emma (Addison) S.; m. Sandra Louise Evans, Dec. 27, 1969; children: Thomas Glenn, Stephen Addison. Circulation dir. Tampa (Fla.) Tribune, 1962—67, Sarasota (Fla.) Herald-Tribune, 1967—75; v.p. circulation The Dispatch Printing Co., Columbus, Ohio, 1975—78, v.p. mktg., 1978—97, bd. dirs., 1977—97; v.p., bd. dirs. Ohio Mag., Inc., Columbus, 1979—97; ret., 1997. Bd. dirs., past chmn. bd. dirs. Salvation Army; trustee, past chmn. bd. dirs. Better Bus. Bur. Ctrl. Ohio, Inc.; bd. dirs. Ctrl. Ohio Ctr. Econ. Edn.; v.p., trustee Columbus Dispatch Charities; past pres. Wesley Glen United Meth. Retirement Ctr.; pres.'s adv. bd. Meth. Theol. Sch. With USN, 1951-56. Recipient Disting. Svc. award Editor and Pub. Mag., 1978; named hon. pres. Troy State U., 1979, hon. Ky. Col., 1980, hon. lt. col. aide-to-camp to Gov. State of Ala., 1984. Mem. Internat. Newspaper Mktg. Assn., Ohio Newspaper Assn. (bd. dirs. 1984-97, pres. 1986-88, Pres.'s award 1990), So. Circulation Mgrs. Assn. (life; pres. 1967-68, sec. and treas., 1968-75, C.W. Bevinger Meml. award 1972), Audit Bur. Circulations (bd. dirs. 1980-90), Am. Advt. Fedn., Navy League, Ohio Newspapers Found., Ohio Circulation Mgrs. Assn (life; Pres.' award 1989), Columbus Area C. of C., SAR, Internat. Platform Assn., Athletic Club of Columbus, Muirfield Village Country Club, Kiwanis Club of Columbus (life, pres. 1982, George F. Hixon fellow). Republican. Home: 5215 Hampton Ln Columbus OH 43220-2270

SHERRY, PAUL HENRY, minister, religious organization administrator; b. Tamaqua, Pa., Dec. 25, 1933; s. Paul Edward and Mary Elizabeth (Stein) Sherry; m. Mary Louise Thornburg, June 4, 1957; children: Mary Elizabeth, Paul David. BA, Franklin and Marshall Coll., 1955; ThM, Union Theol. Sem., NYC, 1958, PhD, 1969; D (hon.), Ursinus Coll., 1981, Elmhurst Coll., 1990, Defiance Coll., 1991, Lakeland Coll., Sheboygan, Wis., 1991, Reformed Theological Acad., Debrecen, Hungary, 1994, United Theol. Sem. Twin Cities, 1995, Eden Theol. Sem., St. Louis, 2000, Chgo. Theol. Sem., 2000. Ordained to ministry United Ch. Christ, 1958. Pastor St. Matthew United Ch. of Christ, Kenhorst, Pa.,

1958—61, Community United Ch. of Christ, Hasbrouck Heights, NJ, 1961—65; mem. staff United Ch. Bd. Homeland Ministry, NYC, 1965—82; exec. dir. Community Renewal Soc., Chgo., 1983—89; pres. United Ch. of Christ, Cleve., 1989—99, pub. policy cons., 2000—02. Mem. gen. bd. Nat. Coun. Chs., NYC, 1989—99, coord. anti-poverty program; cons. Ctr. for Cmty. Change, 2001—05; mem. ctrl. com. World Coun. Chs., 1990—99; del. 8th Assembly, Harare, Zimbabwe, 1998, 7th Assembly, Canberra, Australia, 1991; Coord. NCC Anti Property Program, 2003—07. Co-author: A Just Minimum Wage, 2005; editor: The Riverside Preachers, Jour. Current Social Issues, 1968—80; contbr. articles to religious jours.; host (weekly programs local sta.), 1974—78, 1984—85, 1993—97, lect. (Union Theo. Seminar) NYC, 2008. Bd. dirs. Nat. Interfaith Com. Worker Justice, 2000—. Democrat. Mem. United Ch. Of Christ. Avocations: reading, hiking, cultural events. Home: 12700 Lake Ave # 1612 Lakewood OH 44107 Office Phone: 216-221-9722. Personal E-mail: psher973@aol.com.

SHERTZER, BRUCE ELDON, education educator; b. Bloomfield, Ind., Jan. 11, 1928; s. Edwin Franklin and Lois Belle S.; m. Carol Mae Rice, Nov. 24, 1948; children: Sarah Ann, Mark Eldon. BS, Ind. U., Bloomington, 1952, MS, 1953, EdD, 1958. Tchr., counselor Martinsville H.S., Ind., 1952-56; dir. div. guidance Ind. Dept. Pub. Instrn., 1956-58; assoc. dir. project guidance of superior students North Ctrl. Assn. Coll. and Secondary Sch., 1958-60; asst. prof. Purdue U., 1960—, assoc. prof., 1962-65, prof., 1965-95, head dept. ednl. studies, 1989-95, prof. emeritus of counseling, 1995—. Vis. prof. ednl. psychology U. Hawaii, 1967; Fulbright sr. lectr., Reading, Eng., 1967-68; vis. prof. U. So. Calif. Overseas Grad. Program, 1975, 82; chmn. Nat. Adv. Council for Career Edn., 1976 Author: Career Exploration and Planning 1973, 2d edit., 1976, Fundamentals of Counseling, 3d edit., 1980, Fundamentals of Guidance, 4th edit., 1981, Individual Appraisal, 1979, Career Planning, 3d edit., 1985, also articles. Chmn. bd. trustees Found. Am. Assn. of Counseling and Devel., 1986-87. With AUS, 1946-47. Mem. Am. Counseling Assn. (pres. 1973-74, Disting. Profl. Svc. award 1986). Home: 1620 Western Dr West Lafayette IN 47906-2236 Office: Beering Hall Purdue University West Lafayette IN 47907

SHERWIN, BYRON LEE, religion educator, college official; b. NYC, Feb. 18, 1946; s. Sidney and Jean Sylvia (Rabinowitz) S.; m. Judith Rita Schwartz, Dec. 24, 1972; 1 child, Jason Samuel. BS, Columbia U., NYC, 1966; B of Hebrew Lit., Jewish Theol. Sem. of Am., 1966, M of Hebrew Lit., 1968; MA, NYU, 1969; PhD, U. Chgo., 1978; DHL (hon.), Jewish Theol. Sem. Am., 1996. Ordained rabbi, 1970. Prof. Jewish philosophy and mysticism Spertus Coll. Judaica, Chgo., 1970—, v.p. acad. affairs, 1984-2001. Author: Judaism, 1978, Encountering the Holocaust, 1979, Abraham Joshua Heschel, 1979, Garden of the Generations, 1981, Jerzy Kosinski: Literary Alarm Clock, 1981, Mystical Theology and Social Dissent, 1982, The Golem Legend, 1985, Contents and Contexts, 1987, Thank God, 1989, In Partnership with God: Contemporary Jewish Law and Ethics, 1990, No Religion Is an Island, 1991, Toward a Jewish Theology, 1991, How To Be a Jew: Ethical Teachings of Judaism, 1992, The Theological Heritage of Polish Jews, 1995, Sparks Amongst the Ashes: The Spiritual Legacy of Polish Jewry, 1997, Crafting the Soul: Creating Your Life as a Work of Art, 1998, Why Be Good?, 1998, John Paul II and Interreligious Dialogue, 1999, Perché Essere Buonil?, 1999, Por Que Ser Bueno?, 1999, Jewish Ethics for the Twenty-First Century, 2000, Creating an Ethical Jewish Life, 2001 Golems Among Us, 2004, Works of Wonders, 2005, The Cubs and the Kabbalist, 2006, Kubbulah: Introduction to Jewish Mysticism, 2006; contbr. articles to profl. jours. Recipient Man of Reconciliation award Polish Coun. Christians and Jews, 1992, Presdl. medal, Officer of Order of Merit, Republic of Poland, 1995. Mem. Midwest Jewish Studies Assn. (founding pres.), Am. Philos. Assn., Rabbinical Assembly, Authors Guild. Republican. Avocations: cooking, book collecting. Office: Spertus Coll Judaica 618 S Michigan Ave Chicago IL 60605-1901 Office Phone: 312-922-9012. Business E-Mail: bsherwin@spertus.edu.

SHETLAR, JAMES FRANCIS, physician; b. Wichita, Dec. 26, 1944; MD, U. Kans., 1970. Resident in family practice Saginaw Cooperative Hosp., 1970-72; staff Covenant Hosp.; asst. clin. prof. Mich. State U. Mem. AMA, Am. Acad. Family Physicians, Mich. Acad. Family Physicians. Office: 163 Churchgrove Rd Frankenmuth MI 48734-1025 Home Phone: 989-652-0098; Office Phone: 989-652-9969.

SHEVITZ, MARK H., sales promotion and marketing executive; b. Dioles, France, July 10, 1955; came to U.S., 1956; s. Arthur E. and Marilyn (Sigoloff) S. Student, U. Mo., 1973-75, Rockhurst Coll., 1983-84; MBA, Washington U., St. Louis, 1988. Program dir. KFMZ-FM, Columbia, Mo., 1974-81; mgmt. supr. Bernstein-Rein Advt., Kansas City, Mo., 1981-84; account supr. The Hermann Group, St. Louis, 1984-86; dir. promotions, food svc. products divsn. Seven-Up Co., St. Louis, 1986-87; pres. Landing Assocs., St. Louis, 1987-88, SJI, Inc., St. Louis, 1988-98, SJI Fulfillment, Inc., St. Louis, 1991—; CEO SJI Inc., St. Louis. Lectr. Washington U., St. Louis, 1988—, Bowling Green (Ohio) State U., 1977-89, Stephens Coll., Columbia, Mo., 1976-89, U. Mo., Columbia, 1975-81. Contbr. articles to profl. jours. Chpt. chmn. March of Dimes, mid.-Mo., 1978-81; mem. devel. bd. Cardinal Glennon Children's Hosp., St. Louis, 1984-88; event chmn. March of Dimes, St. Louis, 1990. Named Entrepreneur of Yr. St. Louis region, 1993. Mem. Assn. Promotion Mktg. Agys. Worldwide (sec./treas. 1998-2000), Porsche Club Am. (pres. St. Louis region 1986).

SHEWARD, RICHARD S., judge; b. Jackson, Ohio, May 21, 1944; s. D.J. and M.A. (Rapp) S.; children: Carrin E., Alison M. BBA, Ohio U., 1967; JD, Capital U., 1974. Bar: Ohio 1974, U.S. Dist. Ct. (so. dist.) Ohio 1975, U.S. Supreme Ct. 1978. Asst. pros. atty. Franklin County (Ohio), 1974-76; ptnr. Sheward & Weiner, Columbus, Ohio, 1976-87; judge Franklin County Mcpl. Ct., 1987-91, Franklin County Ct. Common Pleas, 1991—, presiding judge, 1993—; instr. real estate law Columbus Tech. Inst., 1977-80. Mem. Upper Arlington (Ohio) Civic Assn.; mem. Franklin County Republican Central Com., 1978-87; bd. dirs. Easter Seal Soc. Columbus, 1990-93. Served with U.S. Army, 1968-71. Decorated Bronze Star, Air medal. Mem. ABA, Ohio Bar Assn., Columbus Bar Assn. (common pleas ct., chmn. criminal law com. 1985-86, 86-87), Franklin County Trial Lawyers Assn. (pres. 1984-85), Am. Arbitration Assn. (labor panel), Franklin County Pros. Atty. Alumni Assn. (chmn. 1979-87), Buckeye Rep. Club (pres. 1981), Touchdown Club, Agonis Club, Charity Newsies, Am. Inns Ct. (pres. Robert Duncan chpt. 1994-95), Masons (32 deg.). Office: Franklin County Common Pleas Ct 369 S High St Fl 9-c Columbus OH 43215-4516 Home: 7540 James River Close New Albany OH 43054-9026 Office Phone: 614-462-3770. E-mail: richard_sheward@fccents.org.

SHIBA, WENDY C., lawyer; BA, Mich. State U., 1973; JD cum laude, Temple U. Sch. of Law, 1979. Atty. corp. and securities law O'Melveny & Myers, Los Angeles & YC; corp. chair Phila. Law Dept., Phila.; v.p., sec., asst. gen. counsel Bowater, Inc., Greenville, SC, 1993—2000; gen. counsel PolyOne Corp., Avon Lake, Ohio, 2000—01, v.p., chief legal officer, sec., 2001—07; exec. v.p., gen. counsel, corp. sec. KB Home, LA, 2007—. Former bd. mem. Legal Services Agency of Western Carolina, S.C. Bd. of Accountancy, Greenville Little Theater, Palmetto Soc. of United Way of Greenville County; former mem. United Way of Greenville County Campaign Cabinet, Palmetto Soc. Women's Leadership Council, Greenville Professional Women's Forum. Office: KB Home 10990 Wilshire Blvd Los Angeles CA 90024

SHIBILSKI, KEVIN W., state legislator; b. June 28, 1961; married. BS, U. Wis., Stevens Point, 1972. With Portage County Bd. Suprs., 1982-87, Portage County Register Deeds, 1987-95; mem. Wis. Senate from 24th dist, Madison, 1995—. Bd. dirs. Portwage County Red Cross. Mem. Izaak Walton League, Whitetails Unlimited, Ducks Unlimited, Wis. Bowhunters Assn., Lions.

SHIELDS, CHARLES W., state legislator; b. Kansas City, Mo., July 25, 1959; m. Brenda Brandt; children: Brandt, Bryce. BA, BS, MA, U. Mo. Project coord. Heartland Health Systems; mem. Mo. State Ho. of Reps., 1990—, minority whip, 1996—. Mem. appropriations/health and mental health com., budget com., elem. and secondary end. com., higher edn. com., automation com. Mo. Ho. of Reps., mem. joint com. on health care rules, joint rules and bills, interim desegregation com. Mem. applications com. United Way; mem. Pony Express coun. Boy Scouts Am.; bd. dirs. Children's Healthcare Clinic; mem. adv. bd. Project Discovery, Mo. Rural Health Assn., Mo. Job Corps Coalition, United Way, Mid-Buchanan Sch. Bd.; co-chair arts fund drive Allied Arts Coun., 1997. Mem. Lions Club (v.p.), Buchanan County Rep. Club. Home: 47 SE Erin Ct Saint Joseph MO 64507-7984

SHIELDS, ROBERT EMMET, merchant banker, lawyer; b. Ridley Park, Pa., May 18, 1942; s. Joseph Leonard and Kathryn J. (Walsh) S.; m. Mary Katherine Reid, July 22, 1967; children: Christopher D., David R., Kevin M., Kathleen. AB, Coll. Holy Cross, 1964; LLB cum laude, NYU, 1967. Bar: Pa. 1968. Mem. faculty Boalt Hall Sch. Law U. Calif., Berkeley, 1967-68; assoc. Drinker Biddle & Reath, Phila., 1968-74, ptnr., 1974-94, mng. ptnr., 1979-83, 85-94, head corp. and securities group, 1983-93, CFO, 1993-94; mng. dir., prin., ptnr., COO Questor Gen. Ptnr., L.P., 1995—2003, Questor Ptnrs. Funds, L.P. and Questor Mgmt. Co., 1995—2003; vice chmn. AlixPartners Holdings, Inc., Southfield, Mich., 2003—07, Questor Ptnrs. Holdings, Inc., Southfield, 2003—, TK Aluminum, Ltd., Hamilton, Bermuda, 2003—08; pres., CEO Lakeview Capital, Inc., Southfield, 2007—. Sec. Wallquest Inc.; bd. dirs. Plainfield Direct, Inc.; mem. bd. trustees Archmere Acad. Author: (with Eliot B. Thomas) Federal Securities Act Handbook, 4th edit, 1977; (with Robert H. Strouse) Securities Practice Handbook, 1987. Mem.: ABA, Turnaround Mgmt. Assn., Phila. Bar Assn., Pa. Bar Assn., Am. Law Inst. (life), Skyline Club (Southfield, Mich.). Office: Lakeview Capital Inc 2000 Town Ctr Ste 2400 Southfield MI 48075-1406 Office Phone: 248-213-2200. E-mail: rshields@alixpartners.com.

SHIELDS, THOMAS CHARLES, lawyer; b. Evergreen Park, Ill., Apr. 26, 1941; s. Thomas James and Adelaide (McElligott) Shields; m. Nicoline M. Murphy, Sept. 14, 1974; children: Thomas James II, Nicoline M. E., Suzanne Adelaide, Kerry Anne. AB, Georgetown U., 1963; JD cum laude, Northwestern U., 1966. Bar: Ill. 1966, U.S. Dist. Ct. (no. dist.) Ill. 1966, U.S. Ct. Appeals (7th cir.) 1966, U.S. Tax Ct. 1968, U.S. Supreme Ct. 1977. Assoc. Hopkins & Sutter, Chgo., 1966-73, ptnr., 1973-93; mem., chair health law dept. Bell, Boyd & Lloyd, Chgo., 1994—; chief counsel Cath. Health Assn. U.S., St. Louis, 1994—2005. Lectr. Ill. Inst. Continuing Legal Edn., 1973; mem. adv. bd. Health Law Inst. Loyola U. Sch. Law, Chgo., 1984—89, Health Law Inst. DePaul U. Sch. Law, Chgo., 1985—96. Contbr. articles to profl. jours. Trustee Village of Riverside, Ill., 2001—; mem. Ill. Health Facilities Authority, 2000—03; governing mem. Chgo. Zool. Soc., Chgo., Cath. Charities Chgo.; bd. dirs. Cancer Rsch. Found., Chgo., 1987—, Brother Louie and Fannie Roncoli Found., 1994—2006. Mem.: Chgo. Bar Assn., Ill. Assn. Healthcare Attys. (bd. dir. 1983—89, pres. 1987—88), Ill. Bar Assn., Am. Hosp. Assn. (tax adv. group 1987—90), Am. Health Lawyers Assn. (bd. dir. 1983—91, pres. 1989—90), Chgo. Power Squadron, U.S. Power Squadron (legal officer 2005—06), Mid-Am. Club Chgo. (bd. govs. 2001—, sec. 2004—), Order of Coif. Avocations: skiing, bicycling, golf, boating. Office: Bell Boyd & Lloyd 3 First Nat Plz 70 W Madison St Ste 3100 Chicago IL 60602 Office Phone: 312-807-4232. Business E-Mail: tshields@bellboyd.com.

SHIELDS, THOMAS WILLIAM, surgeon, educator; b. Ambridge, Pa., Aug. 17, 1922; s. John Jr. and Elizabeth (Flanagan) S.; m. Dorothea Ann Thomas, June 12, 1948; children: Thomas William, John Leland, Carol Ann. BA, Kenyon Coll., Gambier, Ohio, 1943, DSc (hon.), 1978; MD, Temple U., Phila., 1947. Resident surgery orthwestern U. Med. Sch., Chgo., 1949-55, prof. surgery, 1968-92, prof. Emeritus of surgery, 1992—; practice medicine specializing in surgery Chgo., 1956—; chief of surgery VA Lakeside Hosp., Chgo., 1968-87; chief thoracic surgery VA Lakeside Med. Ctr., Chgo., 1987-90. Editor: General Thoracic Surgery, 1972, 5th edit., 2000, 6th edit 2004, Bronchial Carcinoma, 1974, Mediastinal Surgery, 1991; assoc. editor Surgery, Gynecology and Obstetrics, Annals of Thoracic Surgery, 1993-2002; mem. editl. bd. Annals of Thoracic Surgery, Lung Cancer; contbr. articles to profl. jours. Served with U.S. Army, 1951-53. Mem. ACS, AMA, Am. Assn. for Thoracic Surgery, Soc. Thoracic Surgery, Central, Western Surg. Assns., Société Internationale de Chirurgie, Soc. for Surgery of Alimentary Tract, Internat. Assn. for Study Lung Cancer, Japanese Assn. Thoracic Surgery (hon.), Pa. Assn. Thoracic Surgery (hon.), Pan Pacific Surg. Assn., Phi Beta Kappa, Sigma Xi, Alpha Omega Alpha. Home: 10513 E Cinnabar Ave Scottsdale AZ 85258-4908 Office: Northwestern U Feinberg Sch Medicine Galter 3-150 201 E Huron St Chicago IL 60611 Office Phone: 480-451-8296. Personal E-mail: twshields@comcast.net.

SHIELDS, V. SUE, federal magistrate judge; b. 1939; AB, Ball State U., 1959; LLB, Ind. U., 1961. Atty. Office of the Regional Counsel, IRS, 1961; dept. atty. gen. Office of the Atty. Gen. of Ind., 1962-64; judge Hamilton Superior Ct., 1965-78, Ind. Ct. Appeals, 1978-94; magistrate judge U.S. Dist. Ct. for So. Dist. Ind., Indpls., 1994—. Office: 256 US Courthouse 46 E Ohio St Indianapolis IN 46204-1903 Office Phone: 317-229-3670.

SHIELY, JOHN STEPHEN, manufacturing executive, lawyer; b. June 19, 1952; s. Vincent Robert and Mary Elizabeth (Hope) Shiely; m. Helen Jane Pauly, Aug. 29, 1981; children: Michael, Erin, Megan. BBA, U. Notre Dame, 1974; JD, Marquette U., 1977; M in Mgmt., Northwestern U., 1990. With Arthur Andersen & Co., Milw., 1977-79, Hughes Hubbard & Reed, Milw., 1979-83, Allen-Bradley Co., Milw., 1983-86, Rockwell Internat. Corp., Milw., 1985-86, Briggs & Stratton Corp., Milw., 1986—, gen. counsel, 1986-90, v.p., gen. counsel, 1990-91, pres., COO, 1994-2001, pres., CEO, 2001—03, chmn., pres., CEO, 2003—. Bd. dirs. Briggs & Stratton Corp., Quad/Graphics, Inc., Pewaukee, Wis., 1996—, Marshall & Ilsley Corp., Milw., 1999—, Scotts Miracle-Gro Co., 2007—. Mem. Greater Milw. Com., 2000—; chmn. bd. Children's Hosp. and Health Sys., 2005—; mem. bd. regents Milw. Sch. Engring., 1995—; trustee Med. Coll. Wis., 2003—; mem. corp. bd. dirs. Rock and Roll Hall of Fame and Mus.; bd. dirs. Outdoor Power Equipment Inst. Mem.: Assn. Corp. Growth (past pres. Wis. chpt. 1988—). Office: Briggs & Stratton Corp PO Box 702 Milwaukee WI 53201-0702

SHIFMAN, MIKHAIL, physicist; b. Riga, Latvia, Apr. 4, 1949; came to U.S., 1990; s. Arkady and Raisa (Yakovich) S.; m. Margarita Pusynya, Apr. 21, 1971; children: Julia, Anya. MA in Theoretical Physics, Moscow Inst. Physics & Tech., Dolgoprudny, Russia, 1972; PhD, Inst. Theoretical Exptl. Phys., Moscow, 1976. From jr. rsch. fellow to sr. rschr. Inst. Theoretical & Exptl. Physics, Moscow, 1976-89; prof. theoretical physics U. Minn., Mpls., 1990—. Lectr. on particle physics and field theory. Author: Vacuum Structure and QCD Sum Rules, 1992, Instantons in Gauge Theories, 1994, ITEP Lectures on Particle Physics and Field Theory, 2 vols., 1999, The Many Faces of the Superworld, 2000, The Supersymmetric World, 2000; At the Frontiers of Particle Physics, 4 Vol., 2001 Recipient Humboldt Rsch. award Alexander-von-Humboldt Stiftung, Bonn, Germany, 1993, Rsch. award Japan Soc. for Promotion Sci., 1993, 96. Fellow Am. Phys. Soc. (Sakurai prize 1999, Lilienfeld prize, 2006). Achievements include invention (with others) invisible axion; rsch. in hadronic physics/quantum chromodynamics, SVZ sum rules, heavy-flavor hadrons based on the heavy quark expansions, supersymmetric guage theories in the strong coupling regime. Office: Theoretical Phys Inst Univ Minn 116 Church St SE Minneapolis MN 55455-0149 E-mail: shifman@umn.edu.

SHILLING, JENNIFER, state official; b. Oshkosh, Wis., July 4, 1969; married. BA, U. Wis., 1992. State assemblywoman, Wis., 2000—. Mem. fin. instns. com.; mem. health com.; mem. ins. com.; mem. Minn.-Wis. Boundary Area Commn.; mem. personal privacy com. Congl. aide to U.S. Rep. Ron Kind; mem. La Crosse County Dem. Party, La Crosse County LWV. Democrat. Office: State Capitol PO Box 8953 Madison WI 53708-8953

SHILLINGSBURG, MIRIAM JONES, literature educator, academic administrator; b. Balt., Oct. 5, 1943; d. W. Elvin and Miriam R. Jones; m. Peter L. Shillingsburg, Nov. 21, 1967; children: Robert, George, John, Alice, Anne Carol. BA, Mars Hill Coll., 1964; MA, U. S.C., 1966, PhD, 1969; BGS, Miss. State U., 1994. Asst. prof. Limestone Coll., Gaffney, SC, 1969, Miss. State U., 1970—75, assoc. prof., 1975—80, prof. English, 1980—96, assoc. v.p. for acad. affairs, 1988—96, dir. summer sch., 1990—96, dir. undergrad. studies, 1994—96; dean arts and scis. Lamar U., Tex., 1996—99; dean liberal arts and scis. Ind. U., South Bend, 2000—04, dean sch. edn., 2005—06. Disting. acad. visitor Mark Twain Ctr., 1993, 2001; Simms rsch. prof. U. S.C., 1998; vis. fellow Australian Def. Force Acad., 1989; Fulbright lectr. U. New South Wales, Duntroon, Australia, 1984-85. NEH fellow in residence, Columbia U., 1976-77. Author: Mark Twain in Australasia, 1988; editor: Conquest of Granada, 1988, The Cub of the Panther, 1997, Confession, 2005; mem. editl. bd. Works of W.M. Thackeray, Miss. Quar., So. Quar.; contbr. articles to profl. jours. and mags. Mem. South Ctrl. 18th Century Soc., Am. Lit. Assn., Pop Culture Assn., Sigma Tau Delta, Phi Kappa Phi, Simms Soc. (pres. 1996-97). Business E-Mail: mshillin@iusb.edu.

SHILTS, NANCY S., automotive executive, lawyer; b. Clinton, Mass., Feb. 10, 1942; BA, Smith Coll., 1963; JD, U. Mich., 1980. Bar: Mich. 1980. Assoc. gen. counsel Fed.-Mogul Corp., Southfield, Mich. Mem. ABA, State Bar Mich. Office: Fed Mogul Corp 26555 Northwestern Hwy Southfield MI 48034-2199

SHIMKUS, JOHN MONDY, congressman; b. Collinsville, Ill., Feb. 21, 1958; s. Gene Louis and Kathleen (Mondy) S.; m. Karen Kay Muth; children: David, Joshua, Daniel. BS, U.S. Mil. Acad., 1980; MBA, So. Ill. U., Edwardsville, 1997. Advanced through grades to capt. U.S. Army, 1980-86; stationed at U.S. Army Base, Columbus, Ga., 1980-81, 85, served at Bamberg, Germany, 1981-84, stationed at Monterey, Calif, 1985-86; tchr. Metro East Luth. H.S., Edwardsville, Ill., 1986-90; treas. Madison County, Edwardsville, 1990-96; mem. U.S. Congress from 19th Ill. dist., 1997—, mem. energy and commerce com. Liaison officer U.S. Mil. Acad., 1987-96; treas. So. Ill. Law Enforcement Commn., 1990-96. Bd. dirs. Sr. Citizen Companion Program, Belleville, Ill., 1991; trustee Collinsville Twp., Ill., 1989-93; Rep. precinct committeeman, Collinsville, 1988—. Lt. col. USAR, 1985—. Mem. Nat. Assn. County Treas. and Fin. Officers (bd. dirs.), Ill. County Treas. Assn., Am. Legion Post 365. Republican. Lutheran. Home: 504 Sumner Blvd Collinsville IL 62234-1934 Office: US Ho Reps 513 Cannon Ho Office Bldg Washington DC 20515-1319 also: Springfield Dist Office Ste C 3130 Chatham Rd Springfield IL 62704

SHIN, HYOUN-WOO, aircraft engineer; Sr. engr. GE Aircraft Engines, Cin. Mem. ASME (Meville Medal 1998). Office: GE Aircraft Engines 1 Neumann Way MD/A411 Cincinnati OH 45215-1915 E-mail: jamie.jewell@ae.ge.com.

SHINDELL, SIDNEY, preventive medicine physician, educator, department chairman; b. New Haven, May 31, 1923; s. Benjamin Abraham and Freda (Mann) S.; m. Gloria Emhoff, June 17, 1945; children: Barbara, Roger, Lawrence, Judith. BS, Yale U., 1944; MD, L.I. Coll. Medicine, 1946; postgrad., Emory U., 1948-49; LLB, George Washington U., 1951. Diplomate Am. Bd. Preventive Medicine in Occupl. Medicine, Am. Bd. General Preventive Medicine. With USPHS, 1947-52; med. dir. Conn. Commn. on Chronically Ill and Aged, 1952-57, Am. Joint Distbn. Com., 1957-59; asst. prof. preventive medicine U. Pitts., 1960-65; dir. Hosp. Utilization Project Western Pa., 1965-66; prof. dept. preventive medicine Med. Coll. Wis., Milw., 1966-93, chmn. dept., 1966-89, dir. Office Internat. Affairs, 1989-93, prof. emeritus, 1993—; exec. dir. Health Svc. Data of Wis., 1967-73. Mem. bd. sci. advisors Am. Coun. Sci. and Health, 1978—87, 1992—, chmn., 1988—92; mem. Nat. Adv. Com. on Occupl. Safety and Health U.S. Dept. Labor, 1982—84; cons. Caribbean Epidemiology Ctr. Pan Am. Health Orgn./WHO, 1988; field edpiemiology tng. program Ctr. Disease Control, Thailand, 1989; field epidemiology tng. program Nat. Office Occupl. and Environ. Medicine Royal Thai Ministry of Pub Health, 1990; mem. gov.'s white paper com. on health care reform, Wis., 93; acad. cons. Facilities of Medicine Padjadjaran U., Airlangga U., Indonesia, 1993, 94; cons. Project C.U.R.E., 2002—. Author: Statistics, Science and Sense, 1964, A Method of Hospital Utilization Review, 1966, The Law in Medical Practice, 1966, A Coursebook on Health Care Delivery, 1976; contbr. 120 articles to profl. jours. Trustee Med. Coll. Wis., 1996-2002; mem. sch. bd. Fox Point-Bayside (Wis.), Sch. Dist., 1970-71; vice chmn. Citizens' Adv. Com. Met. Problems, 1971-72; bd. dirs. Med. Care Evaluation S.E. Wis., 1973-76; trustee Interfaith Caregivers Aliance, 2001-2002. With AUS, 1943-46. Recipient Frank L. Babbott Meml. award SUNY Health Sci. Ctr., Bklyn., 1996. Fellow Am. Coll. Preventive Medicine (mem. bd. regents 1982-85), APHA, Am. Coll. Occupl. and Environ. Medicine (Pres.'s award 1999), Am. Coll. Legal Medicine; mem. Am. Assn. Health Data Sys. (sec. 1972-73), Assn. Tchrs. Preventive Medicine (dir. 1973-74, pres. 1976-77, spl. recognition award 1992, Duncan Clark award 2002), Assn. Occupl. Health Profls. (pres. 1980-90), Wis. Med. Soc. (mem. coun. on health care financing and delivery, mem. coun. on govt. affairs, mem. ho. of dels., 50 Yr. recognition award 1996, svc. award 2000), Am. Coll. Physician Execs., Internat. Commn. on Occupl. Health, Aircraft Owners and Pilots Assn., Masons, CAP. Home and Office: One Polo Creek Unit 201 2400 Cherry Creek South Drive Denver CO 80209-3251 Office Phone: 303-778-0141.

SHINDLER, DONALD A., lawyer; b. New Orleans, Oct. 15, 1946; s. Alan and Isolene (Levy) S.; m. Laura Epstein, 1969; children: Jay, Susan. BSBA, Washington U., St. Louis, 1968; JD, Tulane U., 1971. Bar: La. 1971, U.S. Dist. Ct. (ea. dist.) La. 1971, U.S. Tax Ct. 1974, Ill. 1975, U.S. Dist. Ct. (no. dist.) Ill. 1975; CPA, La.; lic. real estate broker, Ill. Assoc. Pope, Ballard, Shepard & Fowle, Chgo., 1975-78, Rudnick & Wolfe, Chgo., 1978-81, ptnr., 1981-99; gen. counsel America's Second Harvest Nat. Food Bank Network, 1998-2000; ptnr. Piper Marbury Rudnick & Wolfe, Chgo., 1999—2002, Piper Rudnick LLP, Chgo., 2002—05, DLA Piper Rudnick Gray Cary US LLP, Chgo., 2005—. Lectr. in field. Contbr. articles on real estate to legal jours. Trustee Glencoe (Ill.) Pub. Libr., 1981-87, pres., 1986-87; alumni bd. govs. Washington U., 1992-93; mem. Glencoe Zoning Commn./Bd. Appeals, 1994-2000; Glencoe Plan Commn, 1986-87. Lt. JAGC, USNR, 1971-75. Fellow Am. Coll. Mortgage Attys.; mem. ABA, Ill. Leading Lawyers, La. State Bar Assn., Chgo. Bar Assn. (com. chmn. 1979-80, 83-84, 90-94, 96-99, editor land trust seminars 1984-96), Ill. Super Lawyers, Urban Land Inst. (mem. steering com. Chgo. dist. coun.), Ill. Super Lawyers (R/E), CoreNet Global (pres. Chgo. chpt. 1997-98, dir. 1991-2003), Internat. Assn. Attys. and Execs. in Corp. Real Estate (fall forum co-chair 2002, spring conf. co-chair, 2003, bd. dirs. 2003—), Union League Club (chair real estate group 1993-96), Order of Coif, Beta Gamma Sigma, Omicron Delta Kappa. Office: DLA Piper Rudnick Gray Cary US LLP Ste 1900 203 N La Salle St Chicago IL 60601-1210 Office Phone: 312-368-2175. Business E-Mail: donald.shindler@dlapiper.com.

SHIPLEY, TONY L(EE), software company executive; b. Elizabethton, Tenn., July 19, 1946; s. James A. and Edith J. (Crowder) S.; m. Lynda Anne Jenkins, Nov. 19, 1971; children: Blake Alan, Sarah Robyn. BS in Indsl. Engring., U. Tenn., 1969; MBA, U. Cin., 1975. Indsl. engr. Monsanto Co., Pensacola, Fla., 1969—72; mktg. mgr. SDRC, Cin., 1972—76; v.p. sales and mktg. Anatrol Corp., Cin., 1977—81; pres. Entek Sci. Corp., Cin., 1981—96; pres., CEO Entek IRD Internat. Corp., 1996—2000; founding mem. Queen City Angels, chmn. Bd. dirs. Ohio IT Alliance, chmn., CHMack; bd. dirs. The Circuit, U. Cin. E-Ctr., RhinoCyte, Forte Industries, U. Cin. Named Small Bus. Person of Yr., Greater Cin. C. of C., 1994, Entrepreneur of Yr. in Cin., No. Ky. Region, 1996; recipient Entrepreneurial Excellence award U. Cin., 2001, C.H. Lindner Outstanding Bus. Achievement award U. Cin., 2004; Hamilton County Bus. Ctr., Larry Albice Entrpreneurship award, 2006. Mem. ASME, Soc. Automotive Engrs., Greater Cin. Software Assn. (pres. 1996-97, chmn. 1997-99, bd. dirs.), Greater Cin. C. of C., Leadership Class XVIII, Terrace Park (Ohio) Country Club (past pres.). Republican. Avocations: golf, boating. Home: 7825 Calderwood Ln Cincinnati OH 45243-1319 Personal E-mail: tshipley@fuse.net.

SHIRBROUN, RICHARD ELMER, veterinarian, cattleman; b. Coon Rapids, Iowa, Oct. 22, 1929; s. Francis Clyde and Clara Mable (Bell) S.; m. Treva Margaret Teter (div.), Sept. 9, 1951; children: Randal Mark, Camille Leean, James Bradley; m. Wava Lynne Frank, Nov. 11, 1989. DVM, Iowa State U., 1952. Owner, vet. Shirbroun Vet. Med. Ctr., Coon Rapids, 1955-2001; trust rep. Am. Vet. Med. Assn., Chgo., 2001—. Lt. USAF, 1952-55. Mem. AVMA (trustee 1982-2000), Am. Assn. Bovine Practitioners (bd. dirs. 1982-1990, Excellence Preventive Medicine award 1987), Am. Assn. Swine Practitioners, Iowa Vet. Med. Assn. (pres. 1981, Pres.' award 1985), Soc. for Theriogenology, N.Am. Limousin Found. (founding mem. 1968), Nat. Cattlemen Assn., Iowa Cattlemen Assn., Am. Legion, Rotary (pres. Coon Rapids 1965). Republican. Methodist. Home: 32104 Millard Circle Warrenville IL 60555-3988 Office: Am Vet Med Assn 55 E Jackson PO Box 1629 Chicago IL 60690-1629 Office Phone: 312-279-4669. Business E-Mail: richard.shirbroun@avmaplit.com.

SHIRLEY, BRYAN DOUGLAS, lawyer; b. Sacramento, Sept. 12, 1972; BA, U. Wis., Madison; JD cum laude, Hamline U., 2001. Bar: Minn. 2001. Assoc. Kennedy & Graven, Chartered, Mpls. Bd. dirs. Rakhma Homes, Inc. Named a Rising Star, Minn. Super Lawyers mag., 2006. Mem.: Minn. State Bar Assn.

SHIRLEY, VIRGINIA LEE, advertising executive; b. Kankakee, Ill., Mar. 24, 1936; d. Glenn Lee and Virginia Helen (Ritter) S. Student, Northwestern U., 1960-61. With prodn. control dept. Armour Pharm., Kankakee, 1954-58; exec. sec. Adolph Richman, Chgo., 1958-61; mgr. media dept. Don Kemper Co., Chgo., 1961-63, 65-69; exec. sec. Playboy mag., Chgo., 1964-65; exec. v.p. SMY Media inc., Chgo., 1969-96, CEO, chmn. bd., 1996-2000, CEO, 2000—. Mem. Tavern Club. Home: 1502-J S Prairie Ave Chicago IL 60605-2856

SHIVELY, DANIEL JEROME, retired transportation executive; b. Akron, Ohio, Sept. 2, 1924; s. Richard Miles and Josephine (Pellicer) S.; m. Pamela Marion Kurfess, July 31, 1954; children: Jennifer, Laurie, Thomas. Grad., U.S. Mcht. Marine Acad., King's Point, NY, 1945. Chief officer (tanker) Trinidad Corp., NYC, 1946-51; co-owner, mgr. Shively Bros. Jersey Farm, Quaker City, Ohio, 1952-54; staff asst. Gulf Oil Corp., Phila., 1955-57; distbn. coord. Standard Oil Co., Cleve., 1957-73; budget coord. BP Oil Co., Wilmington, Del., 1973-79; mgr. mktg. budget and planning Standard Oil Co., Cleve., 1979-85; owner, mgr. Shively & Assocs., Cleve., 1985-88. Served to lt. (j.g.) USNR, 1945-61. Mem. Transp. Practitioners Assn. (exec. com. 1984-90, pres. local chpt. 1984-85), Kings's Point Club (treas. N.E. Ohio chpt. 1989-94, sec. 1999-2003), KC (chancellor 1986, dep. grand knight 1987-91). Republican. Roman Catholic. Avocations: farming, sailing. Home: 21347 Erie Rd Rocky River OH 44116-2133

SHIVELY, WILLIAM PHILLIPS, political scientist, educator; b. Altoona, Pa., Mar. 31, 1942; s. Arthur and Ruth Shively; m. Barbara Louise Shank, Aug. 29, 1964; children: Helen, David. BA, Franklin and Marshall Coll., 1963; PhD, U. NC, 1968. Mem. faculty U. Oreg., Eugene, 1967-68, Yale U., 1968-71; mem. faculty U. Minn., Mpls., 1971—, prof. polit. sci., 1979—, provost arts, scis. & engring., 1995-97. Author: Craft of Political Research, 1974, 7th edit., 2008, Research Process in Political Science, 1985, Power and Choice, 1986, rev. edit., 1989, 11th edit., 2008, Comparative Governance, 1995, (with Christopher Achen) Cross-Level Inference, 1995; editor Am. Jour. Polit. Sci., 1977-79; contbr. articles on elections and voting to profl. jours. Home: 1572 Northrop St Saint Paul MN 55108-1322 Office: U Minn Dept Polit Sci 1414 Social Scis Tower Minneapolis MN 55455 Business E-Mail: shively@umn.edu.

SHNIDER, BRUCE JAY, lawyer; b. Lansing, Mich., Oct. 16, 1950; s. Harold A. and Raynor (Seidner) Shnider; m. Patricia Lynn Strandness, Dec. 28, 1973; 1 child, Ruth Strandness. AB magna cum laude, Dartmouth Coll., 1972; MPP, JD magna cum laude, Harvard U., 1977. Bar: Minn. 1977, US Dist. Ct. Minn. 1977, US Tax Ct. 1978, US Ct. Appeals (8th cir.) 1980, US Supreme Ct. 1981. Asst. to dir. Mich. Dept. Commerce, Lansing, 1972-73; law clk. United Mineworkers Am. Health/Retirement Funds, 1975; summer assoc. Robins, Davis & Lyon, Mpls., 1976; assoc. Dorsey & Whitney, Mpls., 1977-82, ptnr., 1983—2006, chmn. diversity com., 1990-93, chmn. tax practice group, 1994-98, of counsel, 2007—. Vis. disting. prof. Law. Sch., U. Minn., 2006—. Bd. dirs. Minn. Justice Found., Mpls., 1989—91; v.p. Emergency Food Shelf Network, 2003—05, pres., 2005—07. Mem.: ABA, Hennepin County Bar Assn., Minn. State Bar Assn. Home: 1908 James Ave S Minneapolis MN 55403-2831 Office: Dorsey & Whitney 50 S 6th St Ste 1500 Minneapolis MN 55402-1498 Office Phone: 612-340-2862. Business E-Mail: shnider.bruce@dorsey.com.

SHOAFF, THOMAS MITCHELL, lawyer; b. Ft. Wayne, Ind., Aug. 21, 1941; s. John D. and Agnes H. (Hanna) S.; m. Eunice Swedberg, Feb. 7, 1970; children: Andrew, Nathaniel, Matthew-John. BA, Williams Coll., 1964; JD, Vanderbilt U., 1967. Bar: Ind. 1968. Assoc. Isham, Lincoln & Beale, Chgo., 1967-68; ptnr. Baker & Daniels, Ft. Wayne, Ind., 1968—. Bd. dirs. Weaver Popcorn Co., Inc., Ft. Wayne, Dreibelbiss Title Co., Inc., Ft. Wayne, Am. Steel Investment Corp., Ft. Wayne. Bd. dirs. McMillen Found., Ft. Wayne, Wilson Found., Ft. Wayne. Mem. ABA, Allen County Bar Assn., Ind. State Bar Assn. Presbyterian. Avocations: golf, sailing. Office: Baker & Daniels 111 E Wayne St Ste 800 Fort Wayne IN 46802-2603 Office Phone: 260-460-1618. Business E-Mail: thomas.shoaff@bakerd.com.

SHOEMAKER, JOHN CALVIN, aeronautical engineer, engineering company executive; b. Portland, Ind., Dec. 21, 1937; s. Homer Vaughn and Thelora Maxine (Avey) S.; m. Ruby ell Johnson, Aug. 3, 1957; children: Gena Rebecca, Lora Rachele, John Calvin II; foster child, Jeanine Louise Patterson. BS in Aero. Engring., Ind. Inst. Tech., Ft. Wayne, 1960. Project engr. Wayne Pump Co., Ft. Wayne, 1960-63, Daybrook Ottawa Co., Bowling Green, Ohio, 1963-65; engring. mgr. Globe Wayne div. Dresser Industries, Ft. Wayne, 1965-67; sales engr. Taylor-Newcomb Engring., Ft. Wayne, 1967-74; prin. Shoemaker, Inc., Ft. Wayne, 1974—. Patentee in field. Rep. precinct committeeman, 1984—. Served with USAR, 1960-67. Mem. Am. Inst. Plant Engrs. Lodges: Lions (pres. local chpt. 1972). Avocations: gospel music, ch. choristering, directing choir. Home and Office: 12120 Yellow River Rd Fort Wayne IN 46818-9702

SHOEMAKER, MICHAEL C., state legislator; b. Nippen, Ohio, July 2, 1945; m. Vicki Shoemaker; children: Michale Todd, Angela Lynn. BS, Capital U., 1967; MEd, Xavier U., Cin., 1973. Tchr. Paint Valley H.S., 1967-70, Waverly H.S., 1970-72, Smith Jr. H.S., 1972-73, Unioto H.S., 1973-77; carpenter, 1977; mem. Ohio Ho. of Reps., Columbus, 1983-97; mem. 17th dist. Ohio Senate, Columbus, 1997—. Vice chmn. Health & Retirement Com., mem. Edn. Pub. Utilities & Fin. & Appropriations com., mem. Coll. & Univ. com. Named Athletic of Yr. Capital Univ.; recipient Svc. to Edn. award Ohio Univ. 1989, Friend of Edn. award, COTA, 1989. Mem. Bainbridge Hist. Soc., Paint Valley Athletic Boosters, Ross County Farm Bureau, Twp. Trustee and Clerks Assn., Scioto Valley Habitat for Humanity. Home: PO Box 577 Bourneville OH 45617-0577

SHOENER, JERRY JAMES, state legislator; BBA, Nat. Am. U., Rapid City, SD. Mem. S.D. State Senate, mem. transp. com., chmn., commerce vice chmn., local govt. mem., mem. transp. com., chmn. rules com., mem. legis. exec. bd.; v.p., circulation dir. Rapid City Newspaper. Office: SD Senate Mems State Capitol Pierre SD 57501 Home: 4022 Oakmont Ct Rapid City SD 57702-5300

SHOHET, JUDA LEON, electrical and computer engineering educator, researcher, information technology executive; b. Chgo., June 26, 1937; s. Allan Sollman and Frannye Ina (Turner) S.; m. Amy Lenore Scherz, Sept. 5, 1969; children: Aaron, Lena, William. BS, Purdue U., 1958; MS, Carnegie Mellon U., 1960, PhD, 1961. Registered profl. engr., Wis. Asst. prof. Johns Hopkins U., Balt., 1961-66; assoc. prof. U. Wis., Madison, 1966-71, prof., 1971—, chmn. dept. elec. and computer engring., 1986-90, dir. Torsatron/Stellarator Lab., 1974—99, dir. Engring. Rsch. Ctr. for Plasma-Aided Mfg., 1986—97; dir. Plasma Processing and Tech. Lab., 1999—. Pres. Omicron Tech., Inc., Madison, 1985—; cons., presenter in field. Author: The Plasma State, 1979, Flux Coordinates and Magnetic Field Structure, 1991; contbr. over 150 articles to profl. jours. Recipient Frederick Emmons Terman award Am. Soc. for Engring. Edn., 1978, John Yarborough Meml. medal British Vacuum Coun., 1993. Fellow IEEE (Centennial medal 1984, Richard F. Shea Disting. Mem. award 1992), Am. Phys. Soc.; mem. IEEE Nuclear and Plasma Scis. Soc. (pres. 1980-82, Merit award 1978, Plasma Sci. and Applications prize 1990). Achievements include patents in field. Avocations: skiing, sailing, hiking. Home: 1937 Arlington Pl Madison WI 53726-4001 Office: U Wis Dept Elec & Computer Engring 1445 Engring Hall Madison WI 53706 Office Phone: 608-262-1191. Business E-Mail: shohet@engr.wisc.edu.

SHORE, SHELDON G., chemist, educator; With Ohio State Univ., 1957—, prof. chemistry, Charles H. Kimberly Chair Chemistry. Recipient award in inorganic chemistry, Am. Chem. Soc., 2007. Achievements include patents in field. Office: Ohio State U 2042 Evans Laboratory 88 W 18th Ave Columbus OH 43210 Office Phone: 614-292-6000. Business E-Mail: shore.1@osu.edu.

SHORE, THOMAS SPENCER, JR., retired lawyer; b. Akron, Ohio, Jan. 1, 1939; s. T. Spencer and Harriet G. (Delicate) S.; m. Margaret F. Kudzma, Aug. 12, 1961; children— Thomas Spencer III, John Christopher, Daniel Andrew, Mary Margaret. BA, Brown U., 1961; JD, Northwestern U., 1964. Bar: Ohio 1964. Assoc. Taft, Stettinius and Hollister, Cin., 1964-69, Rendigs, Fry, Kiely & Dennis, Cin., 1969-71, ptnr., 1972—2003; ret., 2003. Adj. asst. prof. Chase Law Sch., U. No. Ky. Bd. dirs. United Cerebral Palsy of Cin., 1978—; bd. dirs., sec. Boys Club Am., Cin.; trustee emeritus Family Svc. of Cin. Area; past pres. Vis. Nurse Assn. of Cin., hon. trustee; mem. Kennebunkport Zoning Bd. Appeals. Mem. Ohio Bar Assn., Cin. Country Club, Queen City Club, Webhanet Club, Edgcomb Tennis Club. Office: 900 4th and Vine Tower 1 W 4th St Cincinnati OH 45202 Home: PO Box 629 Kennebunkport ME 04046 E-mail: t.shore@rendigs.com.

SHORS, JOHN DENNIS, lawyer; b. Ft. Dodge, Iowa, July 21, 1937; s. George A. and Catherine (Shaw) S.; m. Patricia Ann Percival, Oct. 7, 1967; children: John, Tom, Matt, Luke. BSEE, Iowa State U., 1959; JD, U. Iowa, 1964. Bar: Iowa, U.S. Supreme Ct. Assoc. then shareholder Davis, Brown, Koehn, Shors & Roberts, P.C., Des Moines, 1964—. Co-author: Closely Held Corporations in Business and Estate Planning, 1982. Pres. Mercy Hosp. Found., Des Moines, 1981-84; chair Iowa State U. Found., Ames, 1989-92; bd. dirs. Mercy Housing, Denver, 1992—. Cpl. U.S. Army, 1960-61. Recipient Iowa State U. Alumni medal, YLS Merit award Iowa State Bar Assn. Mem. Iowa State Bar Assn. (pres. 1992) Iowa Women Profl. Corp. (Good Guy award 1987), Iowa Rsch. Coun. (bd. dirs. 1994—), Am. Judicature Soc. (bd. dirs. 1974-79), Polk County Bar Assn. (pres. 1986), Rotary (Des Moines chpt.), DM Club. Republican. Roman Catholic. Office: Davis Brown Koehn Shors & Roberts PC 666 Walnut St Ste 2500 Des Moines IA 50309-3904 Business E-Mail: johnshors@lawiowa.com.

SHORT, MARIANNE DOLORES, lawyer; b. Mpls., Mar. 12, 1951; d. Robert Earl and Marion (McCann) S.; m. Raymond Louis Skowyra Jr., Nov. 1, 1980; 2 children, R. Louis Skowyra III & Nicholas Skowyra. BA in Philos. and Polit. Sci., Newton Coll. of Sacred Heart, 1973; JD, Boston Coll. Law Sch., 1976. Bar: Minn. 1976, Mass. 1977, US Dist. Ct. Minn. 1976, US Dist. Ct. Mass. 1980, US Dist. Ct. ND 2000, US Ct. Appeals (8th cir.) 1980, US Supreme Ct. 1988; civil trial specialist, Minn. State Bar Assn. Spl. asst. atty. gen., St. Paul, 1976-77; assoc. Dorsey & Whitney LLP, Mpls., 1977-82, ptnr., litig. practice, 1983—88, mem. policy com., 1987—88, 2000—, mem. profl. pers. com., 2000—02, mem. capital contbn. com., 2001—03, mem. ptnr. compensation com., 2002—03, mng. ptnr, 2007—; judge Minn. Ct. Appeals, 1988—2000. Chmn. recruiting com. Dorsey & Whitney, Mpls., 1985-87. Trustee Boston Coll., 1985—, Visitation Convent, St. Paul, 1985-91, St. Thomas Acad., 2000—; bd. overseers Boston Coll. Law Sch., 1998—, U. Minn. Law Sch., 2001—. Named Minn. Super Lawyer, Minn. Law & Politics Mag., 2000—07, Women to Watch, Bus. Jour., 2005, Atty. of Yr., Minn. Lawyer, 2005; named one of 15 Top Attys. in Minn., Minn. Lawyers, 2005; recipient Corp. Woman of Achievement award, Nat. Assn. Women Bus. Owners, 2004. Mem. ABA, Mass. Bar Assn., Minn. Bar Assn., Hennepin County Bar Assn. (ethics com.), Ramsey County Bar Assn., Am. Arbitration Assn. (arbitrator), Acad. Cert. Trial Lawyers Minn. Clubs: Town and Country (St. Paul), Mpls. Club (bd. govs.), Am. Acad. Appellate Lawyers, Am. Coll. Trial Lawyers. Avocations: running, skiing. Office: Dorsey & Whitney LLP Ste 1500 50 S Sixth St Minneapolis MN 55402-1498 Home Phone: 651-645-9015; Office Phone: 612-340-2833. Office Fax: 612-340-2807. Business E-Mail: short.marianne@dorsey.com.

SHORT, MARION PRISCILLA, neurogenetics educator; b. Milford, Del., June 12, 1951; d. Raymond Calistus and Barbara Anne (Ferguson) S.; m. Michael Peter Klein; 1 child, Asher Calistus Klein. BA, Bryn Mawr Coll., 1973; diploma, U. Edinburgh, Scotland, 1975; MD, Med. Coll. Pa., 1978. Diplomate Am. Bd. Psychiatry and eurology, Am. Bd. Internal Medicine. Intern in internal medicine Hahnemann Med. Coll. Hosp., Phila., 1978-79; med. resident in internal medicine St. Lukes-Roosevelt Hosp., NYC, 1979-81; neurology resident U. Pitts. Health Ctr., 1981-84; fellow in med. genetics Mt. Sinai Med. Ctr., NYC, 1984-86; fellow in neurology Mass. Gen. Hosp., Boston, 1986-90, asst. neurologist, 1990-95; asst. prof. dept. neurology Harvard Med. Sch., Boston, 1990-95; asst. prof. dept. neurology, pediat. and pathology U. Chgo., 1995—2000, clin. assoc. pediat. neurosurgery, 2000—, fellow McLean Ctr. for Clin. Med. Ethics, 2002—03, sr. fellow McLean Ctr. for Clin. Med. Ethics, 2003—04; program dir. genetics, transplantation and clin. rsch. AMA, Chgo., 1997—2002. Recipient Clin. Investigator Devel. award, NIH, 1988—93; fellow, Inst. Medicine, Chgo., 1999. Mem. AMA, Am. Acad. Neurology, Am. Soc. for Human Genetics, Am. Coll. Med. Genetics. Office: Pediat Neurosurgery U Chgo MC 4066 5481 S Maryland Ave Chicago IL 60637-4325 Office Phone: 773-702-2475. Business E-Mail: mpshort@surgery.bsd.uchicago.edu.

SHOSS, DEANNA, theatre executive; m. Eugenio Shoss; children: Andre, Lucca. BA in Comparative Lit., Indiana U., 1985; MA, DePaul U., 2003. Exec. dir. Newbury Street League, Boston, 1986—93; account exec. Arnold Pub. Relations, Boston, 1994; marketing and communications mgr. Lakefront Region, Chgo. Pk. Dist.; dir. promotions Chgo. Dept. Aviation, 1997—2005; pres. & CEO League of Chgo. Theatres, 2005—. Office: Chgo League Theatres 228 S Wabash Ave Ste 900 Chicago IL 60604

SHOSTAK, BURTON H., lawyer; b. St. Louis, Mar. 20, 1936; AB, Wash. U., 1958, JD, 1960. Bar: Mo. 1960, U.S. Tax Ct. 1973, U.S. Supreme Ct. 1982. Spl. asst. atty. gen., Mo., 1963—68; ptnr. Moline, Shostak & Mehan LLC, St. Louis. Mem. moot ct. Wash. U.; faculty mem. Nat. Criminal Def. Coll., 1988—; counsel com. to investigate dept. revenue Mo. Ho. of Reps., 1982; mem., chmn. Mo. Pub. Defender Commn., 1976—82, 1994—. Recipient Trial Lawyer award, Mo. Bar Found., 1971. Mem.: NACDL (bd. dirs.), Am. Arbitration Assn., Mo. Assn. Trial Lawyers, Assn. Trial Lawyers Am., Lawyers Assn. St. Louis (treas. 1968, mem. exec. com. 1970—71, v.p. 1971—73, pres.-elect 1973—74, pres. 1974—75), Fla. Bar Assn. (mem. bd. govs. 1976—86, Pres. award 1984), St. Louis County Bar Assn., Bar Assn. Met. St. Louis, Phi Delta Phi. Office: Moline Shostak & Mehan LLC The Berkley Bldg 8015 Forsyth Blvd Saint Louis MO 63105 Office Phone: 314-725-3200 307. Office Fax: 314-725-3275. E-mail: bshostak@msmattorneys.com.

SHOTWELL, MALCOLM GREEN, minister; b. Brookneal, Va., Aug. 14, 1932; s. John Henry and Ada Mildred (Puckett) S.; m. LaVerne Brown, June 19, 1954; children: Donna (dec.), Paula. BA in Sociology, U. Richmond, 1954; MDiv, Colgate Rochester Div. Sch., 1957; D Ministry, Ea. Bapt. Theol. Sem., 1990; DD (hon.), Judson Coll., 1990. Ordained to ministry Am. Bapt. Ch. in U.S.A., 1957. Student asst. Greece Bapt. Ch., Rochester, NY, 1954-57; pastor 1st Bapt. Ch., Cuba, NY, 1957-62, sr. pastor Galesburg, Ill., 1962-71, Olean, NY, 1971-81; area minister Am. Bapt. Chs. of Pa. and Del., 1981-90; regional exec. minister Am. Bapt. Chs. of Great Rivers Region, Ill. and Mo., 1990-96; interim pastor First Bapt. Ch., Jacksonville, Ill., 2002, Galesburg, Ill., 2003, Decatur, Ill., 2005—06. Mem. Midwest Commn. on Ministry Am. Bapt. Chs. U.S.A., 1990—96, mem. task force for So. Bapt. Am. Bapt. Chs. Relationships, 1990—96; cons. for ch. growth and planning. Author: Creative Programs for the Church Year, 1986, Renewing the Baptist Principle of Associations, 1990; contbg. writer Baptists in the Balance, 1997; rschr., writer, performer: (dramatic monologue) Our Neighbors, the Lincolns: A Clergyman Remembers, 1999—. Trustee No. Bapt. Theol. Sem., Lombard, Ill., 1993-96; mem. gen. exec. coun., 1990-96, regional exec. ministers coun., 1990-96; trustee Judson Coll., 1990-2003, trustee emeritus, 2003-, chmn., 1997-00, chmn. presdl. search com., 1997-98; bd. dirs. Ctrl. Bapt. Theol. Sem., Kansas City, Kans., 1990-96, Old State Capitol Found., 2004-; sec. bd. dirs. Shurtleff Fund, Springfield, Ill., 1990-96; tchr., libr. Ctrl. Bapt. Ch., Springfield, 1997-05; mem. Hist. Commn. Am. Bapts. Ill. and Mo., 1998-02; retreat leader in stress mgmt., 1985—; conf., spkr., pulpit supply preacher Bapt. Ch.; mentor ILCS Elem. Sch., Old State Capital Reenactment of Lincoln-Douglas Debates, 1999-01, 03-08; tour guide Old State Capital, Springfield, 2003—, Abraham Lincoln Presdl. Libr. and Mus., 2005-. Recipient George Younge Biennal award The Am. Bapt. Hist. Soc., 2006; Walter Pope Binns fellow William Jewell Coll., 1995. Mem. Ministers Coun. Ill. and Mo., Coun. Ret. Execs., Abraham Lincoln Assn., Am. Bapt. Men of Ill. and Mo. (v.p., coord. disaster relief ministries).

SHOULTZ, DONALD L., state representative; b. Muscatine, Iowa, Aug. 2, 1936; AA, Muscatine Jr. Coll., Iowa, 1959; BS, U. No. Iowa, 1962; MEd, U. Ga., 1971. Educator Waterloo (Iowa) Ind. Schs., 1962—90; econ. devel. coord. Hawkeye C.C., 1989—94; mem. Iowa Ho. Reps., DesMoines, 1983—, ranking mem. ways and means com., mem. environ. protection com., mem. health and human rights com., mem. appropriations com., mem. judiciary com. Active Izaak Walton League; mem. adv. bd. Iowa Waste Reducation Ctr. With USMC, 1954—57. Mem.: NEA, Waterloo Edn. Assn. (former pres.), United Tchg. Profession, Sierra Club, Nat. Wildlife Fedn., Kiwanis Internat. Democrat. Office: State Capitol East 12th and Grand Des Moines IA 50319 also: 259 Kenilworth Rd Waterloo IA 50701

SHOWALTER, SHIRLEY H., former academic administrator; b. July 30, 1948; BA cum laude in English, Ea. Mennonite U., Harrisonburg, Va., 1970; MA in Am. civilization, U. Tex., Austin, 1974, PhD in Am. civilization, 1981. Tchr. English Harrisonburg HS, Va., 1970—72; tchg. asst. English and Am. Studies depts. U. Tex., Austin, 1973—75, asst. instr. Am. Studies dept., 1976; dir. continuing edn. Goshen Coll., Ind., 1979—82, project dir. Title II tech. and liberal arts devel. grant, 1982—85, project dir. Consortium Advancemet of Pvt. Higher Edn. grant, 1985—86, asst. to prof. English, 1967—, pres., 1997—2004. Coord. Humanities program Harrisonburg (Va.) H.S., 1970—72; co-dir. Study-Svc. Term in Haiti Goshen Coll., 1981—82; rsch. asst. Consortium Advancement of Pvt. Higher Edn., Washington, 1986—87, interim v.p., 1987; chair English dept. Goshen Coll., 1990—93; sr. fellow Lilly Fellows program in Humanities and Arts Valparaiso U., Ind., 1993—94; co-dir. Study-Svc. Term in Ivory Coast Goshen Coll., 1993; lectr. and spkr. in humanities. Contbr. chapters to books, articles to profl. jours. Bd. mem. South Bend Symphony Assn.; mem. blue ribbon adv. group Boys and Girls Club; vice chair and mem. Hist. Com. of Mennonite Ch., 1984—88; co-sponsor Kid's Club No. Va. Mennonite Ch., 1987—88; chair curriculum com. Sojourner's Sunday Sch. class Coll. Mennonite Ch., 1987—88, mem. constn. revision com., 1988—92, tchr. H.S. age class, 1988—91, mem. worship commn., 1994—96; bd. mem. Coun. Christian Coll. and U., 2000—, Ind. Colls. of Ind., 1999—, Lantz Ctr. Christian Vocations, Indpls., 1998—; dir. Coun. Ind. Colls., 1999—; bd. dir. Mennonite Mutual Aid Trust; dir. Elkhart County Cmty. Found. Recipient Tchg. Excellence and Campus Leadership award, Sears Roebuck Found., 1990, Faculty Rsch., Goshen Coll., 1990, Knight Presdl. Leadership award, John S. and James L. Knight Found., 1999, 1999; fellow, George H. Gallup Rsch. Inst., 1999—2000, Coolidge Fellow, Yale U., Assn. Religion in Intellectual Life, 1996; grantee Faculty Rsch., Goshen Coll., 1977, 1982, Summer Stipend, Lilly Endowment, 1991. Mem.: AAUW, Am. Studies Assn., Am. Assn. Higher Edn. (Goshen Coll. rep. Forum on Exemplary Tchg. 1992, bd. dir. 1992—96), No. Ind. Partnership for the Arts, Willa Cather Pioneer Mem., Ind. Hist. Soc., Ellen Glasgow Soc., Blue Sky Assoc. Office: VP Programs Fetzer Inst 9292 West KL Ave Kalamazoo MI 49009-9398

SHRACK, CHRISTOPHER GEORGE, curator; b. Wichita, Kans., June 17, 1949; s. George William and Phyllis Star Shrack; m. Marsha Carol Gates, Mar. 20, 1986; children: Samuel Cody, Chelsea Christine, Emma Leigh, Gates Kipp. BFA in Graphic Design, Wichita State U., Kans., 1973; AS in Biology, Pratt CC, Kans., 1987. Cert. arborist Kans., 1978, housing inspector Kans., 1995, sci. and art tchr. Kans. Bd. Edn., 2006. Graphic artist Chikaskia, Golden Belt and Indian Hills Assns., Pratt, 1976—81; instr. art and sci. Pratt CC and Pratt and Stafford Counties Pub. Schs., 1981—2002; gen. maintenance repair tech. Kans. Dept. Wildlife and Pks., 2002—05, wildlife mus. curator, edn. ctr. coord., 2005—. Freelance graphic artist, photographer, pub., 1971—; presenter in field; spkr. in field. Photo exhibition, Kans. Dept. Wildlife and Pks., 2006; contbr. Vol. Pratt Regional Med. Ctr., 2006—; mem. transition team First United Meth. Ch., 2004—, mem. worship com., 2004—, jr. high Sunday sch. tchr., 2005—, mem. hist. com., 2005—; leader Stephen Ministry, St. Louis, 2006—; bd. dirs. Pratt Teen Ctr., 2003—. Sgt. nat. guard USAF, 1967—72. Named Tchr. of Yr., Stafford County Soil Conservation, 1991—92, 1993—94; recipient Outstanding Svc. award, Pratt CC, 1990. Mem.: Kans. Dept. Wildlife and Parks Employees Group. Meth. Avocations: hunting, fishing, beekeeping, gardening, photography. Office: Kansas Department of Wildlife and Parks 512 SE 25th Ave Pratt KS 67124-8174 Office Phone: 620-672-0776. Office Fax: 620-672-6020. Business E-Mail: chriss@wp.state.ks.us.*

SHRADER-FRECHETTE, KRISTIN, science educator; m. Maurice Frechette; children: Danielle, Eric. B in Math. summa cum laude, Edgecliff Coll., Xavier U., 1967; PhD in Philosophy, U. Notre Dame, 1972. Asst. prof., philosophy Edgecliff Coll., 1971—73; prof., philosophy, natural sciences U. Louisville, 1973—82; prof., philosophy of sci., environ. studies U. Calif., Santa Barbara, 1982—84; prof., philosophy, natural sciences U. Fla., 1984—87; disting. rsch. prof., philosophy, environ. scis. U. So. Fla., 1987—98; O'Neill Family prof., dept. biol. sci. and dept. philosophy U. Notre Dame. Vis. philosopher Coun. on Philosophical Studies, 1980, 87; US NAS/NRC coun. del. Internat. Union Hist. & Phil. Sci., 1987; chair, internat. geosphere/biosphere program. Internat. Union Hist. & Phil. Sci. & Internat. Conf. Scientific Unions, 1988—91; chair, sci. and ethics com. Internat. Conf. Scientific Unions, 1990—96; mem. adv. bd. Tech., Risk, and Soc.: An Internat. Series in Risk Analysis, 1983—, Earth Ethics Rsch. Group, 1990—, Integration, Environ. Assessment and Environ. Indicators, EPA, 1992—, Planet Ctrl. TV Cable Network (environ. issues), 1993—, Vision for 2010, PBS TV series on the environment, 1993—, Ont. Soc. for Environ. Ethics, 1994—; panelist referee Nat. Endowment for the Humanities, 1979—, NSF, 1980—, EPA, Atmospheric Rsch. and Exposure Assessment, 1992—; mem. Blue Ribbon Panel US Dept. Energy Performance Evaluation of US Nuclear Facilities, 1994—96, US Dept. Energy Performance Evaluation of Sites for Mixed ulcear Wastes, 1994—97; mem. adv. bd. Inst. Hydrology and Water Quality, 1995—; chair, sci. ethics com. 10th Congress of Logic, Methodology, Philosophy Sci., 1995; chair World Congress Philosophy Sect. on Philosophy and Tech., 1998; chair com. bioethics EPA, mem. sci. adv. bd., 2003—; prin. investigator grants NSF, Nat. Endowment for the Humanities, Coun. Philosophical Studies, U.S. Dept. Energy; dir., Ctr. for Environmental Justice and Children's Health U. Notre Dame; invited lectr. in field. Author: (books) Nuclear Power and Public Policy, 1983, Environmental Ethics, 1991, Four Methodological Assumptions in Cost Benefit Analysis, 1983, Science, Policy, Ethics, and Economic Methodology, 1984, Risk Analysis and Scientific Method, 1985, Nuclear Energy and Ethics, 1991, Risk and Rationality, 1991, Burying Uncertainty: Risk and the Case Against Geological Disposal of Nuclear Waste, 1993, Method in Ecology, 1993, The Ethics of Scientific Research, 1994, Environmental Justice: Creating Equality, Reclaiming Democracy, 2002, Taking Action, Saving Lives: Our Duties to Protect Environmental and Pub. Health, 2007; co-editor: Technology and Human Values, 1996; co-author: Policy for Land: Law and Ethics, 1992; assoc. editor: Bioscience, 1994—2002, editor-in-chief: Oxford U. Press monograph series Environ. Ethics and Sci. Policy, 1988—; mem. editl. bd. Humanities and Tech., 1980—, Environmental Ethics, 1981—, Philosophy and Tech., 1986—, Jour. Agr. and Environ. Ethics, 1986—, Pub. Affairs Quarterly, 1987—, Jour. Law and Pub. Policy, 1987—, Studies in Religion and the Social Order, 1991—, Risk: Issues in Health and Safety, 1991—, Syntheis: An Internat. Jour. in Logic, Epistemology and Philosophy of Sci., 1993—, Eco Spheres, 1993—, Organization and Environ., 1995—, Ethics and the Environment, 1995—, Environmental Values, 1995—, Encyclopedia of Philosophy Sci., 1996—, Poiesis and Praxis, 1999—, Europaische Akademie, 1999—, Bus. Ethics Quarterly, 2002—, Biological Theory, 2004—, Accountability in Rsch., 2004—; Article Referee Behavioral Science, 1975-, Philosophy Sci., 1977-, Sci., Tech., and Human Values, 1980-, Sci., 1982-, Jour. Bus. Ethics, 1983-, Energy Policy Studies, 1984-, Synthese, 1984-, Environment International, 1985-, Risk Analysis, 1985-,Environmental Management, 1985-, Ethics, 1987-, Hypatia, 1988-, Soc. and Natural Resources, 1989-, Biology and Philosophy, 1993, Economics and Philosophy, 1992-, Conservation Biology, 1993-, Bulletin Ecological Soc. Am., 1995-, Environmental Professional, 1995-, Newsletter on Philosophy and Tech., 1995-, Environ. Sci. and Tech., 1996-, Environ. Health Perspectives, 2005-present; Book Referee MIT Press, 1981-, Reidel Press, 1981-, Macmillan Publishers, 1984-, Prentice-Hall, 1984-, Univ. Calif. Press, 1984-, Oxford Univ. Press, 1987-, Kluwer Academic Publishers, 1988-, Cambridge Univ. Press, 1991-, Rowman and Littlefield, 1991-, Univ. Ariz. Press, 1991-, Temple Univ. Press, 1992-, Univ. Press Kans., 1992-, Univ. Georgia Press, 1994-, Yale Univ. Press, 1994-; contbr. several articles to profl jours. including Ethics, Jour. Philosophy, Philosophy of Sci., Synthese, Trends in Ecology Revolution, others Named Kentucky's Outstanding Young Women, 1977; recipient NEH/NSF Interdisciplinary Incentive award, 1982, NSF Scholar's award in Philosophy of Sci., 1982, World Tech. award in Ethics, 2004; Woodrow Wilson Nat. Fellowship, 1967—68, NSF Fellow, 1968—71, Carnegie Found. Fellowship in Philosophy Sci., 1971. Mem.: NAS ((with NRC) bd. dirs. environ. studies and toxicology 1993—96, (with NRC) oversight com. environ. monitoring and assessment program 1993—96, (with NRC) com. risk characterization 1994—96, (with NRC) com. to evaluate zinc-cadmium-sulfide 1995—96, (with NRC) mem. com. on ecosystems svcs. 2002—03), Humanities and Tech. Assn. (bd. mem. 1980—90), Assn. Internat. de Cyberétique (mem. Am. bd. 1976—78), Internat. Soc. Environ. Ethics (mem. nominating com. 1992—, mem. adv. bd. 1995—, pres. 2000—03), Risk Assessment and Policy Assn. (pres. 1995—98, chair, mtg. program com. 1997), Soc. Philosophy and Tech. (v.p./pres.-elect 1983—85, pres. 1985—87, past pres.), Philosophy Sci. Assn. (mem. nominating com. 1981—82, mem. program com. 1986, mem. mtg. program com. 1986, 1996, mem. program com. 1998, mem. mtg. program com. 1998, mem. program com. 2006), Am. Philosophical Assn. (mem. program com. 1981, mem. adv. com. on ethics 1989—92, mam. adv. bd. Newsletter on Feminism and Philosophy 1992—), DAR. Avocations: scuba diving, canoeing, hiking, volunteer work. Office: Dept Philosophy and Dept Biol Scis 100 Malloy Hall Univ Notre Dame Notre Dame IN 46556-5639 Office Phone: 574-631-2647. Office Fax: 574-631-8209. Business E-Mail: kristin.shrader-frechette.1@nd.edu.

SHRAUNER, BARBARA WAYNE ABRAHAM, electrical engineer, educator; b. Morristown, NJ, June 21, 1934; d. Leonard Gladstone and Ruth Elizabeth (Thrasher) Abraham; m. James Ely Shrauner, 1965; children: Elizabeth Ann, Jay Arthur. BA cum laude, U. Colo., 1956; AM, Harvard U., 1957, PhD, 1962.

Postdoc. mrschr. Free U. Brussels, 1962-64, NASA-Ames Rsch. Ctr., Moffett Field, Calif., 1964-65; asst. prof. Washington U., St. Louis, 1966-69, assoc. prof., 1969-77, prof., 1977—2003, sr. prof., 2003—. Sabbatical Los Alamos (N.Mex.) Sci. Lab., 1975-76, Lawrence Berkeley Lab., Berkeley, Calif., 1985-86; cons. Los Alamos Nat. Lab., 1979, 84, ASA, Washington, 1980, Naval Surface Weapons Lab., Silver Spring, Md., 1984. Contbr. articles on transport in semiconductors, hidden symmetries of differential equations, plasma physics to profl. jours. Fellow Am. Phys. Soc. (sr. divsn. plasma physics, exec. com. 1980-82, 96-98); mem. IEEE (sr.; sr. exec. com. of standing tech. com. on plasma sci. and applications 1996-98), AAUP (local sec.-treas. 1980-82), Am. Geophys. Union, Phi Beta Kappa, Sigma Xi, Eta Kappa Nu, Sigma Pi Sigma. Home: 7452 Stratford Ave Saint Louis MO 63130-4044 Office: Washington U Dept Elec and Systems Engring 1 Brookings Dr Saint Louis MO 63130-4899 Home Phone: 314-727-1012; Office Phone: 314-935-6134. Business E-Mail: bas@wustl.edu.

SHRINER, THOMAS L., JR., lawyer; b. Lafayette, Ind., Dec. 15, 1947; s. Thomas L. Sr. and Margaret (Kamstra); m. Donna L. Galchick, June 5, 1971; children: Thomas L. III, John H., Joseph P., James A. AB, Ind. U., 1969, JD, 1972. Bar: Wis. 1972, U.S. Dist. Ct. (ea. dist.) Wis. 1973, U.S. Dist. Ct. (we. dist.) Wis. 1977, U.S. Dist. Ct. Colo. 2005, U.S. Ct. Appeals (7th cir.) 1972, U.S. Ct. Appeals (8th cir.) 1989, U.S. Ct. Appeals (fed. cir.) 1990, U.S. Supreme Ct. 1978. Law clk to Hon. John S. Hastings U.S. Ct. Appeals (7th cir.), Chgo., 1972-73; assoc. Foley & Lardner, Milw., 1973-79, ptnr., 1979—. Adj. prof. Law Sch. Marquette U., Milw., 2005—. Chmn. bd. trustees Cath. Charities of Archdiocese of Milw., 2001—02. Fellow Am. Coll. Trial Lawyers; mem. 7th Cir. Bar Assn. (pres. 1993-94), Phi Beta Kappa. Republican. Roman Catholic. Office: Foley & Lardner LLP 777 E Wisconsin Ave Ste 3800 Milwaukee WI 53202-5306 Home Phone: 414-964-6315; Office Phone: 414-297-5601. Business E-Mail: tshriner@foley.com.

SHRIVER, DUWARD FELIX, chemistry professor, researcher, consultant; b. Glendale, Calif., Nov. 20, 1934; s. Duward Laurence and Josephine (Williamson) S.; m. Shirley Ann Clark; children: Justin Scott, Daniel Nathan. BS, U. Calif., Berkeley, 1958; PhD, U. Mich., 1961. From instr. to assoc. prof. chemistry Northwestern U., Evanston, Ill., 1961-70, prof., 1970-87, Morrison prof. of chemistry, 1987—, chmn. dept. chem., 1992-95; mem. Inorganic Syntheses Inc., 1974—, pres., 1982-85. Vis. staff mem. Los Alamos (N.Mex.) Nat. Lab., 1976-85, cons., 1985-92; vis. prof. U. Tokyo, 1977, U. Wyo., 1978, U. Western Ont., Can., 1979. Author: The Manipulation of Air-Sensitive Compounds, 1969, edit., 1987; co-author: Inorganic Chemistry, 1990, 2d edit., 1994, 3d edit., 1998; editor-in-chief Inorganic Syntheses, vol. 19, 1979; co-editor: The Chemistry of Metal Cluster Complexes, 1990; editl. bd. Inorganic Synthesis, 1979—, Advances in Inorganic Chemistry, 1986—, Jour. Coordination Chemistry, Inorganic Chimca Acta, 1988—, Chemistry of Materials, 1988-90, 92—, Jour. Cluster Sci., 1990-97, Organometallics, 1993-95; contbr. articles to profl. jours. Alfred P. Sloan fellow, 1967-69; Japan Soc. Promotion of Sci. fellow, 1977; Guggenheim Found. fellow, 1983-84. Fellow AAAS; mem. Am. Chem. Soc. (Disting. Svc. in Inorganic Chemistry award 1987), Royal Soc. Chemistry London (Ludwig Mond lectr. 1989), Electrochem. Soc., Materials Rsch. Soc. (medal 1990). Home: 1100 Colfax St Evanston IL 60201-2611 Office: Northwestern U Dept Chemistry Evanston IL 60208-0001 E-mail: shriver@chem.nwu.edu.

SHRIVER, JOSEPH DUANE, state legislator; b. Arkansas City, Kans., Oct. 13, 1959; s. John Francis and Carolyn Joan (Thornhill) S.; m. Mindi Sue Peterson, 1982; 1 child, Jayme Dawn. AA, Cowley County C.C., 1981. Mem. from dist. 79 Kans. State Ho. of Reps., 1994—, mem. tax and judiciary coms. Mem. Kans. Joint Commn. on Adminstv. Rules and Regulations and Spl. Com. on Motor Fuel Tax, U.s. Dept. Revenue. Recipient Outstanding Svc. award Kans. Dem. Party, 1990. Mem. Arkansas City C. of C. (legis. chmn. 1990-91), Firefighter Relief Assn. (pres. 1991-94), Firefighters Local 2101.

SHRIVER, PHILLIP RAYMOND, academic administrator; b. Cleve., Aug. 16, 1922; s. Raymond Scott and Corinna Ruth (Smith) S.; m. Martha Damaris Nye, Apr. 15, 1944; children: Carolyn (Mrs. William Shaul), Susan (Mrs. Lester LaVine), Melinda (Mrs. David Williams), Darcy, Raymond Scott II. BA, Yale U., New Haven, Conn., 1943; MA, Harvard U., Cambridge, Mass., 1946; PhD, Columbia U., NYC, 1954; LittD, U. Cin., 1966; LLD, Heidelberg Coll., Tiffin, Ohio, 1966, Ea. Mich. U., Ypsilanti, 1972, Ohio State U., 1973; DH, McKendree Coll., Lebanon, Ill., 1973; DPS, Albion Coll., Mich., 1974; LHD, Ctrl. State U., Wilberforce, Ohio, 1976, No. Ky. State U., 1980, Miami U., 1984, U. Akron, Ohio, 1988. Mem. faculty Kent (Ohio) State U., 1947-65, prof. Am. history, 1960-65; dean Coll. Arts and Scis., 1963-65; pres. Miami U., Oxford, Ohio, 1965-81, pres. emeritus, prof. Am. history, 1981-99. Pres. Ohio Coll. Assn., 1974-75; chmn. coun. pres.'s Mid-Am. Conf., 1971-77; chmn. Ohio Bicentennial Commn. for NW Ordinance and U.S. Constn., 1985-89, Ohio Tuition Trust Authority, 1989-92; chmn. coun. pres.'s Nat. Assn. State Univs. and Land Grant Colls., 1975-76, mem. exec. coun., 1976-78. Author: The Years of Youth, 1960, George A. Bowman: The Biography of an Educator, 1963, (with D.J. Breen) Ohio's Military Prisons of the Civil War, 1964, A Tour to New Connecticut in 1811: The Narrative of Henry Leavitt Ellsworth, 1985, Miami University: A Personal History, 1998, (with C.E. Wunderlin Jr.) The Documentary Heritage of Ohio, 2000, (with E.F. Puff) The History of Presbyterianism in Oxford, Ohio, 2000. Bd. dirs. Cin. Ctr. Sci. and Industry, 1965-70, Fed. Reserve Bank Cincinnati, 1968-72, chmn. bd. 1971-72; trustee Ohio Coll. Library Center, 1968-74; chmn. bd. Univ. Regional Broadcasting, 1975-76, 78-79. Served to lt. (j.g.) USNR, 1943-46, PTO. Decorated Order of Merit (Grand Duchy of Luxembourg); recipient Disting. Acad. Svc. award AAUP, 1965, Gov.'s award 1969, A.K. Morris award, 1974, Ohioana Career medal, 1987, Converse award, 1990, award of merit Am. Assn. for State and Local History, 1993, Bjornson award Ohio Humanities Coun., 2001, John E. Dolibois History prize, 2003, Statesman award Cin. Soc. Assn. Execs., 2004. Mem. Orgn. Am. Historians, Ohio Acad. History (pres. 1983-84, Disting. Svc. award 1991), Archaeol. Inst. Am., Ohio Hist. Soc. (trustee 1982-91, v.p. 1983-84, pres. 1984-86), Ohio Humanities Coun. (Bjornson award 2001), Am. Studies Assn., Mortar Board, Phi Beta Kappa, Omicron Delta Kappa, Phi Alpha Theta, Alpha Kappa Psi, Kappa Delta Pi, Phi Eta Sigma, Phi Kappa Phi, Kappa Kappa Psi, Alpha Lambda Delta, Beta Gamma Sigma, Sigma Delta Pi, Alpha Phi Omega, Delta Upsilon (Disting. Alumni Achievement award 1985) Clubs: Rotary. Presbyterian. Home: 5115 Bonham Rd Oxford OH 45056-1428 Business E-Mail: shrivepr@muohio.edu.

SHTOHRYN, DMYTRO MICHAEL, librarian, educator; b. Zvyniach, Ukraine, Nov. 9, 1923; came to U.S., 1950; s. Mykhailo and Kateryna (Figol) S.; m. Eustachia Barwinska, Sept. 3, 1955; children: Bohdar O., Liudoslava V. Student, Ukrainian Free U., Munich, 1947-48, U. Minn., 1954; MA in Slavic Studies, U. Ottawa, Can., 1958, B.L.S., 1959, PhD in Slavic Studies, 1970. Slavic cataloger U. Ottawa, 1959; cataloger NRC Can., Ottawa, 1959-60; Slavic cataloger, instr. library adminstrn. U. Ill., Urbana, 1960-64, head Slavic cataloging, asst. prof. library adminstrn., 1964-68, head Slavic cataloging, assoc. prof., 1968-75, head Slavic cataloging, prof., 1975-85, lectr. Ukrainian lit., 1975-91, assoc. Slavic librarian, prof., 1985-95, prof. Ukrainian lit., 1991-95, prof. emeritus, 1995—. Vis. prof. Ukrainian lit. U. Ottawa, 1974; assoc. prof. Ukrainian lit. Ukrainian Cath. U., Rome, 1978—; prof. Ukrainian lit. Ukrainian Free U., Munich, 1983—, Ukrainian lang. and lit., U. Ill., 1991-95, Ukrainian culture, 1996—; chmn. Ukrainian Research Program U. Ill., 1984—. Editor: Catalog of Publications of Ukrainian Academy of Sciences, 1966, Ukrainians in North America: A Bibliographical Directory, 1975; author: Ukrainian Literature in the U.S.A.: Trends, Influences, Achievements, 1975, The Rise and Fall of Book Studies in Ukraine, 1986, Oleh Kandyba-Olzhych: Bibliography, 1992; editor: Bull. Ukrainian Libr. Assn. Am., 1982-88; mem. editl. bd. Ukrainian Historian, 1985-98, Ethnic Forum, 1985-95, Crossroads, 1986-97, Ukrainian Quar., 1993—, Ukrainian Problems, 1997—, Ukrainian Rev., 1997-99. Counselor Boy Scouts Am., Champaign, Ill., 1967-85; bd. dirs. Ukrainian-Am. Found., Chgo., 1978-87. Recipient Grant Future Credit Union Toronto, 1956, Grant U. Ill., 1977, 1982, Silver medal, Parliament of Can. Librarian, Ottawa, 1959, award, Glorier Soc. Can., 1959, citation plaque, Ukrainian Congress Com. Am., Chgo., 2000, Medal, V. Stefanyk Subcarpathian State U., 2001. Fellow Shevchenko Sci. Soc. (exec. com., M. Hrushevsky medal 1998); mem. ALA (chmn. Slavic and East European sect. 1968-69), Ukrainian Libr. Assn. Am. (pres. 1970-74, 82-87), Ukrainian Acad. and Profl. Assn. (charter, sec. 1985-89, pres. 1989—), I. Franko Internat. Soc. (founding mem., pres. 1978-79, 81-82), Ukrainian-Am. Assn. Univ. Profs. (exec. com. 1981-96), Ukrainian Hist. Assn. (exec. com. 1983-97), Ukrainian Acad. Arts and Scis. in U.S. (exec. com. 1993-98), Ukrainian Congress Com. of Am. Scholarly Coun., Ukrainian Writers' Assn. Slovo, Am. Assn. Ukrainian Studies, Libr. Congress Assocs. (charter mem.). Ukrainian Catholic. Home: 403 Park Lane Dr Champaign IL 61820-7729 Office: Dept Slavic Langs & Lits 3092 Fgn Langs Bldg U ill 707 S Mathews Ave Urbana IL 61801-3625 E-mail: shtohryn@uiuc.edu.

SHUCK, JERRY MARK, surgeon, educator; b. Bucyrus, Ohio, Apr. 23, 1934; s. James Edwin and Pearl (Mark) S.; m. Linda Wayne, May 28, 1974; children: Jay Steven, Gail Ellen, Kimberly Ann, Lynn Meredith, Steven James. BS in Pharmacy, U. Cin., 1955, MD, 1959, DSc, 1966. Intern Colo. Gen. Hosp., Denver, 1959-60; resident in surgery U. Cin. Integrated Program, 1960-66; mem. faculty dept. surgery U. N.Mex., Albuquerque, 1968-80, prof., 1974-80; prof. surgery Case-Western Res. U., Cleve., 1980—, Oliver H. Payne prof. dept. surgery, 1980—2005, chmn. dept., 1980-2000, prof. anatomy, 1999—, interim v.p. for med. affairs, 1993-95, dir., assoc. dean grad. med. edn., 2002—. Cons. FDA, 1972-77 Contbr. articles to profl. jours. Served to capt. U.S. Army, 1966-68. Mem. ACS, Am. Surg. Assn., Am. Bd. Surgery (bd. dirs., chmn. 1993-94, residency rev. com. for surgery 1994-2000, vice chmn. 1997-2000), Soc. Univ. Surgeons, Am. Ass n. S urgery Trauma, Am. Trauma Soc. (founding mem.), Univ. Assn. Emergency Medicine (founding mem.), Am. Burn Assn. (founding mem.), We. Surg. Assn., Ctrl. Surg. Assn. (pres. 1996-97), Assn. Acad. Surgery, S.W. Surg. Assn., Cleve. Surg. Soc. (pres. 1988-89), Ohio Med. Assn., Acad. Medicine Cleve., Halsted Soc., Surg. Infection Soc. (founding mem.), B'nai B'rith, Jewish Cmty. Ctr. Club, The Temple Club. Democrat. Jewish. Office: Case Western Reserve U Dept Surgery 11100 Euclid Ave Cleveland OH 44106-2602

SHUEY, JOHN HENRY, manufacturing executive; b. Monroe, Mich., Mar. 14, 1946; s. John Henry and Bertha (Thomas) S.; children: Katherine, John Henry, John Joseph Satory. BS in Indsl. Engring., U. Mich., 1968, MBA, 1970. With Tex. Instruments Co., Dallas, 1970-74; asst. treas. The Trane Co., La Crosse, Wis., 1974-78, treas., 1978-81, v.p., treas., 1981-83, v.p. fin., chief fin. officer, 1983-86; also v.p., group exec. Am. Standard; sr. v.p. and chief fin. officer AM Internat. Inc., Chgo., 1986-91; exec. v.p. Amcast Indsl. Corp., Dayton, Ohio, 1991-93, pres., COO, 1993-95, pres., CEO, 1995—, also chmn. bd. dirs., chmn. bd., pres., CEO, 1997—. Bd. dirs. Cooper Tire and Rubber Co., Findlay, Ohio, EMTEC. Bd. dirs. Wright State Univ. Found., 1996—; bd. trustees Dayton Ballet, 1996—, Ohio Found. of Ind. Colleges, 1994—. Mem. Fin. Execs. Inst. Congregationalist. also: Elkhart Products Corp 1255 Oak St Elkhart IN 46514-2277

SHUGARS, DALE L., state legislator; b. May 6, 1953; m. Debra; 1 child, Meaghan. BSBA, Western Mich. U. CPA. Mem. Mich. Ho. of Reps. from 47th dist., Lansing, 1991-92, Mich. Ho. of Reps. from 61st dist., Lansing, 1993-94, Mich. Senate from 21st dist., Lansing, 1994—. Chmn. health policy & sr. citizens com. Mich. State Senate, vice chmn. econ. delvel. com., vice chmn. internat. rels. com., vice chmn. regulatory affairs com., mem. fin. com. Vol. Big Brothers and Big Sisters of Kalamazoo. Mem. Lions Club, Rotary, Kalamazoo C. of C. Address: PO Box 30036 Lansing MI 48909-7536 Office: Mich Senate Mems State Capitol PO Box 30036 Lansing MI 48909-7536 Home: 1722 N 10th St Kalamazoo MI 49009-9157

SHUGHART, DONALD LOUIS, retired lawyer; b. Kansas City, Mo., Aug. 12, 1926; s. Henry M. and Dora M. (O'Leary) Shughart; m. Mary I. Shughart, July 25, 1953; children: Susan C. Hogsett, Nancy J. Goede. AB, U. Mo., Columbia, 1949, JD, 1951. Bar: Mo. 1951, U.S. Dist. Ct. (we. dist.) Mo. 1951, U.S. Tax Ct. 1979. With Shughart, Thompson & Kilroy, PC, Kansas City, Mo., 1951—2002, ret., 2002. With AC, U.S. Army, 1944-47. Mem. Kansas City Bar Assn. (chmn. bus. orgns. com. 1990-91), Mo. Bar Assn. (chmn. corp. com. 1980-81, 82-83), Lawyers Assn. Kansas City, Am. Judicature Soc., Mo. Orgn. Def. Lawyers (pres. 1971-72), U. Mo. Law Soc., Phi Delta Phi, Sigma Chi. Republican. Roman Catholic. Home: 1242 W 67th Ter Kansas City MO 64113-1941 Office Phone: 816-333-3819.

SHULA, ROBERT JOSEPH, lawyer; b. South Bend, Ind., Dec. 10, 1936; s. Joseph Edward and Bertha Mona (Buckner) S.; m. Gaye Ann Martin, Oct. 8, 1978; children: Deirdre Regina, Robert Joseph II, Elizabeth Martin. BS in Mktg., Ind. U., 1958, JD, 1961. Bar: Ind. 1961. Ptnr. Bingham Summers Welsh & Spilman, Indpls., 1965-82, sr. ptnr., 1982-89; ptnr. Price & Shula, Indpls., 1989-91, Lowe Gray Steele & Darko, Indpls., 1991—2003; of counsel Norris Choplin and Schroeder, Indpls., 2003—05; pvt. practice Indpls., 2005—. Mem. faculty Nat. Inst. Trial Advocacy; guest lectr. Brit. Medicine and Law Soc., 1979, Ind. U. Sch. Law; medico-legal lectr. Ind. U. Schs. Medicine, Dentistry, and Nursing. Bd. dirs. Arts Ind., Indpls., 1995-99; founding pres. Oriental Arts Soc., Indpls., 1975-79, Meridian Women's Clinic, Inc., Indpls.; trustee Indpls. Mus. Art, 1975-78, life trustee, 1984—; bd. dirs. Ind. Repertory Theatre, Indpls., 1982-92, chmn. bd. dirs., pres., 1985-89; pres. Repertory Soc., 1993-96; v.p., bd. dirs. Flanner House of Indpls., Inc., 1977-88, chmn., 1988-99; pres. Internat. Ctr. of Indpls., Inc., 1993-96; commr. Indpls. Met. Devel. Commn., 2005. Maj. JAGC, USAFR, 1961—65. Recipient Gov.'s award of Sagamore of the Wabash, 1998. Master Am. Inns of Ct.; fellow 20th Fighter Wing Assn. (v.p. 2005—); mem. ABA, FBA, Am. Assn. for Justice, Am. Law Inst. (diplomate), Am. Bd. Trial Advs. (pres. 2000), Am. Coll. Legal Medicine, Ind. Bar Assn., Indpls. Bar Assn., Ind. Trial Lawyers Assn., Ind. Trial Lawyers Assn., Am. Assn. for Justice. Democrat. Episcopalian. Avocations: flying, art. Home: 7924 Beaumont Green Pl Indianapolis IN 46250-1663 Office: 3891 Eagle Creek Pkwy Ste C Indianapolis IN 46254 Home Phone: 317-845-1857; Office Phone: 317-299-0400. Business E-Mail: shulalaw@sprynet.com.

SHULL, DOUG, state senator; b. Sac City, Iowa, Jan. 14, 1943; m. Carol Shull; children: Lynne, Greg. BS, U. S.D. Mem. Iowa State Senate, DesMoines, 2003—, vice chair econ. growth com., vice chair ways and means com., mem. appropriations com., mem. state govt. com., mem. transp. com. Acct., adj. prof. acctg., sr. v.p. Simpson Coll. Bd. mem. Keep Iowa Beautiful; treas. First United Meth. Ch., Indianola, Iowa; trustee Simpson Coll. Mem.: AICPA, Iowa Soc. CPA. Office: State Capitol Bldg East 12th and Grand Des Moines IA 50319 Home: 901 Scott Felton Rd Indianola IA 50125

SHULMAN, CAROLE KAREN, professional society administrator; b. Mpls., Nov. 25, 1940; d. Allen Eldon and Beulah Ovidia (Blomsness) Banbury; m. David Arthur Shulman, Mar. 26, 1962; children: Michael, Krista, Tracy, Robbyn. Student, Colo. Coll., 1958-61, California Coast U., 1983-84. Profl. instr. Rochester (Minn.) Figure Skating Club, 1962-84, dir. skating, 1964-79, cons., 1979—; exec. dir. Profl. Skaters Assn., Rochester, 1984—, master rating examiner, 1971—, world profl. judge, 1976, 79, 87-88. Editor Professional Skater mag., 1984—; prodr. U.S. Open Profl. Figure Skating Championships, 1987, 89—. Pres. Rochester Arts Council, 1983. Recipient Achievement award Rochester Arts Coun., 1983, Mayor's Medal of Honor, 1997; named triple gold medalist U.S. Figure Skating Assn., Colorado Springs, Colo., 1959, 63, Master Rated Coach Profl. Skaters Assn., 1970, Sr. Rated Coach in Dance Profl. Skaters Assn., 1970. Mem. Am. Harp Soc., Profl. Skaters Assn. (hon., Lifetime Achievement award 1989). Mem. Covenant ch. Avocations: harp, skiing. Office: Profl Skaters Assn Internat 3006 Allegro Park SW Rochester MN 55902-0886

SHULMAN, YECHIEL, engineering educator; b. Tel Aviv, Jan. 28, 1930; came to the U.S., 1950; s. David and Rachel (Chonowski) S.; m. Ruth Danzig, June 29, 1950; children: Elinor D., Ron E., Orna L. BS in Aero. Engring., MIT, 1954, BS in Bus. and Engring. Adminstrn., 1954, MS in Aero. Engring., 1954, DSc Aero. and Astro., 1959; MBA, U. Chgo., 1973. Assoc. prof. mech. engring. Northwestern U., Evanston, Ill., 1959-67; v.p. adv. engring. Anocut, Inc., Elk Grove Vill., Ill., 1967-72; v.p. corp. devel. Alden Press, Elk Grove Vill., Ill., 1973-84; pres. MMT Environ., Inc., Shoreview, Minn., 1984-87; cons. Shulman Assocs., Mpls., 1987-89; prof. mech. engring. dept. U. Minn., Mpls., 1989-2000, H. W. Sweatt chair in technol. leadership and dir. ctr. for devel. technol. leadership, 1989-2000, dir. grad. studies mgmt. of tech. program, 1990-2000, prof. emeritus mech. engring. dept., 2000—. Mem. ASME, Internat. Assn. for Mgmt. of Tech. Business E-Mail: shulman@umn.edu.

SHULRUFF, STUART P., lawyer; b. Chgo., Apr. 28, 1959; BS, U. Ill., 1981; JD cum laude, Loyola U., 1984. CPA Ill., 1981; bar: Ill. 1984. Ptnr. Katten Muchin Zavis Rosenman, Chgo. Mem.: Ill. Bar Assn., Chgo. Bar Assn. Office: Katten Muchin Zavis Rosenman 525 W Monroe St Chicago IL 60661 Office Phone: 312-902-5694, 312-577-8680. E-mail: stuart.shulruff@kmzr.com.

SHULTS, ANNA, elementary school educator; BA in Elem. Edn., Anderson Univ., 1996; MA in Elem. Edn., Ind. Wesleyan Univ. Nominee Disney's Am. Tchr. award, 2000; named Fall Creek Elem. Tchr. of Yr., 2006, Hamilton Southeastern Tchr. of Yr., 2006, Ind. Tchr. of Yr., 2007; recipient Hamilton Southeastern Thank An Educator award (five). Office: Fall Creek Elem Sch 12130 Olio Rd Fishers IN 46037 Office Phone: 317-594-4180. Business E-Mail: ashults@hse.k12.in.us.

SHUMAKER, ROGER LEE, lawyer; b. Sept. 6, 1950; s. Donald E. and Helen Jeannette (Gary) Shumaker; m. Cheralyn Jean Fee, Aug. 28, 1971; children: Donald Lawrence, William Lee, Cristin Leigh. BA, Manchester Coll., 1972; JD, Case Western Res. U., 1976. Bar: Ind. 1976, Ohio 1976, cert.: (specialist in estate planning, trust and probate law). Assoc. Kiefer, Knecht, Rees, Meyer & Miller, Cleve., 1976—79; ptnr. Knecht, Rees, Meyer, Mekedis & Shumaker, Cleve., 1979—86; shareholder McDonald, Hopkins Co LPA, Cleve., 1986—. Trustee Manchester Coll., Ind., 1983—87, Ohio Presbyn. Retirement Svcs. Found., 1992—97, 1997sec., 1995—97. Active Breckenridge Village Coun., Ohio Presbyn. Cmtys., Willoughby, Ohio, 1981—97; adv. com. Salvation Army Adv. Bd., Cleve., 1986—, sec., 1998—2000, chmn., 2002—04; faculty Notre Dame Estate Planning Inst., 1986, 1990, Heckerling Inst. on Estate Planning. Fellow: Am. Coll. Trust & Estate Counsel (tech. in the practice com. 1989—, charitable planning and exempt orgn. com. 2003—); mem.: ABA (chmn. software evaluation com. 1983—85, chmn. com. on tech. and econs. in probate and planning 1985—89, software editor Planning and Probate 1991—97, mem. coun. sect. real property, probate and trust law 1991—97, software coord. commn. legal tech. 1992—96), Estate Planning Coun. (chmn. program com. 1987, treas. 1988, sec. 1989, v.p. 1990, pres. 1991), Bar Assn. Greater Cleve. (chmn. estate planning inst. 1983), Ohio State Bar Assn. Democrat. Methodist. Office: McDonald Hopkins Co LPA 600 Superior Ave E Ste 2100 Cleveland OH 44114-2653 Home Phone: 216-382-5848; Office Phone: 216-348-5801. Business E-Mail: rshumaker@mcdonaldhopkins.com.

SHUMAN, ANN, investment company executive; b. 1968; BA in Eng., Trinity Univ., San Antonio, Tex.; JD, Univ. Chgo. Atty., derivatives, investments products group Sidley & Austin, Chgo.; with Chgo. Merc. Exch. Holdings, Inc., Chgo., 2000—, dir., co-head copr. devel., 2005—. Named one of 40 Under Forty, Crain's Bus. Chgo., 2005.

SHUMAN, R. BAIRD, academic administrator, consultant, language educator, writer; b. Paterson, NJ, June 20, 1929; s. George William and Elizabeth (Evans) Shuman. AB (Trustees scholar), Lehigh U., 1951; M.Ed., Temple U., 1953; PhD (Univ. scholar), U. Pa., 1961; cert. in philology, U. Vienna, Austria, 1954. Tchr. Phila. Pub. Schs., 1953-55; asst. instr. English U. Pa., 1955-57; instr. humanities Drexel U., Phila., 1957-59; asst. prof. English San José (Calif.) State U., 1959-62; asst. prof. English, edn. Duke U., 1962-63, assoc. prof., 1963-66, prof. edn., 1966-77; prof. English, 1977-93, dir. English edn. U. Ill., Urbana-Champaign, 1977-85, dir. freshman rhetoric, 1979-84, coord. Univ. Associates in Rhetoric Program, 1978-84, dir. devel., 1988-93, acting dir. Ctr. for Study of Writing, 1989-90, prof. emeritus, 1993—. Vis. prof. Moore Inst. Art, 1958, Phila. Conservatory Music, 1958—59, Lynchburg Coll., 1965, King Faisal U., Saudi Arabia, 1978, Saudi Arabia, 81, Bread Loaf Sch. English, Middlebury Coll., 1980, E. Tenn. State U., Johnson City, 1980, Olivet azarene Coll., 1984, 86, 88, U. Tenn., Knoxville, 1987; com. mem. William Inge Nat. Festival, 1989—95; contbg. cons. Lit. Rsch. Ctr.; cons. in field. Author: Clifford Odets, 1962, Robert E. Sherwood, 1964, William Inge, 1965, Strategies in Teaching Reading: Secondary, 1978, Elements of Early Reading Instruction, 1979, The First R: Strategies in Early Reading Instruction, 1987;: rev. edit., 1989, Classroom Encounters: Problems, Case Studies, Solutions, 1989, Resources for Writers, 1992, American Drama 1918-1960, 1992, Georgia O'Keeffe, 1993; author: (with Robert J. Krajewski) The Beginning Teacher: A Guide to Problem Solving, 1979; author: (with Eric Hobson) Reading and Writing in High School; author: (with Denny T. Wolfe Jr.) Teaching English Through the Arts, 1990; editor: Nine Black Poets, 1968, An Eye for an Eye, 1969, A Galaxy of Black Writing, 1970, Creative Approaches to the Teaching of English: Secondary, 1974, Questions English Teachers Ask, 1977, Educational Drama for Today's Schools, 1978, Education in the 80's-English, 1980, The Clearing House: A Closer Look, 1984, 70th anniversary issue Clearing House, 1995, Great American Writers: 20th Century, 13 vols., 2002, Cyclopedia of Literary Places, 3 vols., 2003, The Clearing House: A Retrospective, 2004, Ednl. Leadership, 1989—96; exec. editor: Clearing House Jour., 1976—2006, cons. editor: Poet Lore, 1977—90, Cygnus, 1978—2001, Jour. Aesthetic Edn., 1978—82, contbg. editor: Reading Horizons, 1975—85. Active Nat. Trust Hist. Preservation. NEH grantee, Trinity Coll., Dublin, Ireland, 1985. Mem.: MLA, Union Profl. Employees (editor newsletter, mem. exec. com. 1988—92, mem. editl. bd. Poeteka 2005—), Am. Fedn. Tchrs., Nat. Soc. Study Edn., Internat. Assn. Univ. Profs. English, Internat. Reading Assn. (coord. symposium cultural literacy Queensland, Australia 1988), Conf. English Edn. (mem. exec. com. 1976—79), Internat. Fedn. Tchrs. English, Nat. Coun. Tchrs. English (evaluator ERIC Clearing House, mem. com. alt. careers English profs.). Democrat. Home: PO Box 27647 Las Vegas NV 89126-1647 Personal E-mail: rbaird@intermind.net.

SHUMATE, ALEX, lawyer; b. DeKalb, Miss., June 14, 1950; m. Sharon Louise Holley, Aug. 3, 1974; children: John Alexander, Aaron Michael. BA in Polit. Sci., Ohio Wesleyan U., 1972; JD, U. Akron, 1975. Bar: Ohio 1975, U.S. Dist. Ct. (no. and so. dists.) Ohio 1976, U.S. Supreme Ct. 1980. Asst. atty. gen. State of Ohio, Columbus, 1975-83; atty. Brownfield, Bally & Goodman, Columbus, 1983-85; chief counsel, dep. chief of staff Gov., State of Ohio, Columbus, 1985-88; mng. ptnr.-Columbus, Ohio Office Squire, Sanders & Dempsey L.L.P., Columbus, 1988—. Bd. dirs. Bank One Corp., Chgo, Bank One, N.A., Columbus, Intimate Brands, Inc., Columbus, William Wrigley Jr. Co., Chgo. Bd. trustees Ohio State U., Ohio Wesleyan U., Columbus Mus. of Art; governing com. The Columbus Found.; 1st vice chmn. Columbus Urban League; bd. trustees, exec. com. BalletMet; bd. govs. Pub. Policy Com., United Way of Franklin County; exec. com. 29th Dist. Citizens Caucus, 1992 Commn., Christopher Columbus Quincentennial Jubilee Commn.; founding trustee Participation 2000, Berwick Civic Assn. Recipient Jewish Nat. Fund Tree of Life award 1996, Robert S. Crane Trusteeship award Leadership Columbus, 1995, Spl. Achievement award NAACP, 1989, Disting. cmty. Svc. award Columbus Urban League, 1987, Cert. of Outstanding Achievement 116th Ohio Gen. Assembly 1985, Polit. Leadership award 29th Dist. Citizens Caucus, 1984, Outstanding Legal Cmty. Svc. award Captial U. Sch. of Law, 1982, Superior Achievement award United Negro Coll. Fund, 1982; named Outstanding Alumni U. Akron Law Sch., 1994, Disting. Alumnus Ohio Wesleyan U., 1992. Fellow Columbus Bar Assn. (governing bd., Cmty. Svc. award 1986), Ohio State Bar Assn. (coun. of dels.); mem. Lambda Boule, John Mercer Langston Bar Assn., Greater Columbus C. of C. (1st vice chair), The Capital Club (bd. govs.). Office: Squire Sanders & Dempsey LLP 41 S High St Ste 1300 Columbus OH 43215-6197 Office Phone: 614-365-2739. Office Fax: 614-365-2499. Business E-Mail: ashumate@ssd.com.

SHUTZ, BYRON CHRISTOPHER, real estate company officer; b. Kansas City, Mo., Feb. 16, 1928; s. Byron Theodore and Maxine (Christopher) S.; m. Marilyn Ann Tweedie, Mar. 30, 1957; children: Eleanor S. Gaines, Byron Christopher, Collin Reid, Allison S. Moskow, Lindley Anne Baile. AB in Econs, U. Kans., 1949. Ptnr. Herbert V. Jones & Co., Kansas City, Mo., 1953-72; pres. Herbert V. Jones Mortgage Corp., Kansas City, 1967-72, The Byron Shutz Co., Kansas City, 1973—. Dir. 1st Am. Financial Corp., Rothschild's, Inc., Bus. Men's Assurance Co., Faultless Starch, Bon Ami Co. Chmn. bd. trustees U. Kansas City, 1979-81; trustee Pembroke-Country Day Sch., 1974-77, Midwest Rsch. Inst., 1980-89; chmn., bd. govs. Kansas City Art Inst., 1960-62; chmn. bd. dirs. Ctr. for Bus. Innovation, Inc., 1985-87; bd. dirs. Kansas City Crime Commn. 1st lt. USAF, 1951-53. Mem. Mortgage Bankers Assn. Am. (bd. govs. 1966-74), Am. Inst. Real Estate Appraisers. Clubs: Kansas City Country, University, Mercury (pres. 1978-79); Fla. Yacht (Jacksonville), Ocean Reef (Key Largo, Fla.). Home: 1001 W 58th Ter Kansas City MO 64113-1159 Office: 800 W 47th St Kansas City MO 64112-1251 E-mail: arrowrock3@sbcglobal.net.

SIBBALD, JOHN RISTOW, management consultant; b. Lincoln, Nebr., June 20, 1936; s. Garth E.W. and Rachel (Wright) S.; div.; children: Allison, John, Wright. BA, U. ev., 1958; MA, U. Ill., 1964. Office mgr. Hewitt Assocs., Libertyville, Ill., 1964-66; coll. rels. mgr. Pfizer Inc., NYC, 1966-69; pres., CEO Re-Con Systems, NYC, 1969-70; v.p. Booz, Allen & Hamilton, NYC, 1970-73, Chgo., 1973-75; pres., founder John Sibbald Assocs., Inc., Chgo., 1975. Mem. Nat. Advisory Coun., Nat. Club Assn. Author: The Career Makers, 1990, 92, The

New Career Makers, 1995; pub. Club Leaders Forum; contbr. articles to profl. jours. Capt. AUS, 1958-64. Mem. St. Louis Club. Episcopalian. Office: 7733 Forsyth Blvd Saint Louis MO 63105-1817 Home: 3220 Oleander Way Lauderdale By The Sea FL 33062 Office Phone: 314-727-0227. Business E-Mail: jsibbald@sibbaldassociates.com.

SIBLEY, WILLIS ELBRIDGE, anthropology educator, consultant; b. Nashville, Feb. 22, 1930; s. Elbridge and Elizabeth Reynolds (LaBarre) S.; m. Barbara Jean Grant, June 9, 1956 (dec.); m. Marjorie Arielle Hegge, July 6, 2002; children: Sheila Katherine, Anthony Grant, Michael David. BA, Reed Coll., 1951; MA, U. Chgo., 1953, PhD, 1958. Instr. sociology and anthropology Miami (Ohio) U., 1956-58; asst. prof. anthropology U. Utah, 1958-60; from asst. prof. to prof. anthropology Wash. State U., 1960-71; prof. anthropology Cleve. State U., 1971—, chmn. dept., 1971-77, Cleve. (City) faculty fellow, 1987, interim chmn., 1989-90, prof. emeritus, 1990—; sr. program analyst EPA, Washington, 1977-78; Govtl. fellow Am. Coun. on Edn., 1978; Rockefeller Found. vis. prof. anthropology U. Philippines, Quezon City, 1968-69; postdoctoral fellow in society and tech. Carnegie-Mellon U., 1981-82. Fulbright grantee, 1954-55, 64; NIMH grantee, 1959-61; NSF grantee, 1964-71; Nat. Acad. Scis.-NRC travel grantee, 1966; Office Edn., HEW research grantee, 1967 Fellow AAAS, Assn. Profl. Anthropologists (pres. Washington chpt. 1999—), Am. Anthropol. Assn. (treas. 1989-91, com. on pub. policy 2000-2002), Soc. Applied Anthropology (sec. 1977-80, pres. 1981-82, Sol Tax Disting. Svc. award 2006); mem. AAUP (treas. Wash. State U. chpt. 1962-63, v.p. 1963-64, pres. 1965-66, pres. Cleve. State U. chpt. 1979-80, treas. 1980-81, interim pres. 1989-90), ACLU (pres. Pullman chpt. 1963, 66), Ctrl. States Anthropol. Soc. (past mem. exec. bd., treas. 1986-89), Wash. Assn. Profl. Anthropologists, Edgewater Yacht Club (Cleve., commodore 1991), Chesapeake Yacht Club (Shady Side, Md.) (gov. 1999, 2000). Democrat. Unitarian Universalist. Avocation: sailing. Home: 1190 Cedar Ave Shady Side MD 20764 Office: Cleve State U Dept Anthropology Cleveland OH 44115 Home Phone: 301-261-9404; Office Phone: 301-261-9404. Personal E-mail: shadyside1190@comcast.net.

SICHERMAN, MARVIN ALLEN, lawyer; b. Cleve., Dec. 27, 1934; s. Harry and Malvina (Friedman) S.; m. Sue Kovacs, Aug. 18, 1957; children: Heidi Joyce, Steven Eric. BA, Case Western Res. U., 1957, LLB, 1960, JD, 1968. Bar: Ohio 1960, US Dist. Ct. (no. dist.) Ohio 1961, Ct. Appeals (6th cir.) 1969, US Supreme Ct. 1975. Mng. prin. Dettelbach, Sicherman & Baumgart, Cleve., 1971—. Mem. editl. bd.: Case-Western Res. Law Rev, 1958-60; contbr. articles to legal jours. Mem. Beachwood Civic League, Ohio, 1972-92; mem. Beachwood Bd. Edn., 1978-86, pres., 1981, 85, v.p., 1984; trustee Beachwood Arts Coun., 1977-84. Mem. Ohio Bar Assn. (lectr. truth in lending 1969, lectr. bankruptcy 1972, 81, 84, 99, 2000-06, Meritorious Service awards 1971, 77, 78, 79, 83, 84, 85, 86, 87), Cleve. Bar Assn. (lectr. practice and procedure clinic 1960-80, 82-87, chmn. bankruptcy ct. com. 1971-73; award established in his honor by Bankruptcy & Commercial Law Sect., 2007), Jewish Chautauqua Soc., Tau Epsilon Rho, Zeta Beta Tau. Jewish (trustee Temple brotherhood 1968-76, sec. 1971-73). Jewish. Home: 24500 Albert Ln Cleveland OH 44122-2302 Office: Dettelbach Sicherman & Baumgart 1100 Ohio Savings Plz Cleveland OH 44114 Office Phone: 216-696-6000. Business E-Mail: msicherman@dsb-law.com.

SICILIANI, ALESSANDRO DOMENICO, conductor; b. Florence, Italy; s. Francesco and Ambra Siciliani; 1 child, Giacomo Francesco. Student, Giuseppe Verdi Milano Cons., Rome, Santa Cecilia; studied with, Franco Ferrara. Music advisor Columbus Symphony Orch., 1991—2006, music dir., 1992—2006. Condr. Nat. Radio Orchs. of Rome and aples, Symphony of Abruzzi, Palermo Symphony Orch., Cagliari Symphony Orch., Bari Symphony Orch., N.Y. City Opera, Opera Co. of Phila., New Orleans Opera, Ky. Opera, Teatro San Carlo, Naples, Italy, Teatro dell'Opera, Rome, Teatro Massimo, Palermo, Italy, Verdi, Pisa, Italy, also Barcelona, Spain, Marseille, France, Avignon, and Liege; condr. revivals Cavalleria Rusticana, Pagliacci, N.Y. City Opera's revival La Rondine, Am. premiere Schubert's Fierrabras; appeared with Pitts. Symphony, Nat. Symphony, Washington, D.C., Munich Symphony Orch., Cologne Symphony Orch., Dresden Symphony Orch., Stockholm Symphony Orch., Goteborg Symphony Orch., Hong Kong Symphony Orch., Nat. Arts Ctr. Orch. of Ottawa, English Chamber Orch., Symphonia Varsovia, Perugia Chamber Orch., Padova Chamber Orch.; participant festivals including Schleswig-Holstein, Panatenee Pompeiane, Printemps Festival of Praha, Spring Festival in Saratoga Springs, Sagra Musicale Umbra; prin. guest condr. Orch. Teatro Colon, Buenos Aires, Teatro Mcpl. Sao Paulo. Recipient Amerigo Vespucci award, 1992.

SIDLIK, THOMAS W., automotive executive; b. New Britain, Conn., Nov. 14, 1949; BS with hon. in Econ. & Fin., N.Y.U., 1971; MBA in Fin., U. Chgo., 1973. With controller's office car product devel. Ford Motor Co., 1973—80; mgr., car product fin. analysis Chrysler Corp., 1980, mgr., advanced product analysis, 1981, mgr., engring. and product devel. fin. control, 1982, controller, svc. and parts org., 1984, mgr., corp. fin. analysis, 1984, dir., engring. ops., 1987, gen. mgr. special projects engring., 1989, controller, product devel. group, 1989, group controller, product devel. & procurement, 1990, gen. mgr., sales & mktg. ops. planning, 1991, exec. dir., sales & mktg, planning and warranty programs, 1992, v.p., customer satisfaction and vehicle quality, 1992, v.p., chmn., Chrysler Fin. Corp., 1994, 1996, gen. mgr., small car ops., 1996; mem., bd. of mgmt. procurement & supply Chrysler Group DaimlerChrysler AG, 1998—, gen. mgr. Jeep Ops., 1998—. Mgmt. bd. Daimler Chrysler, 1998—; exec. sponsor Automotive Industry Action Group (AIAG). Vice-chmn. Nat. Minority Supplier Devel. Coun. (NMSDC); chmn. Coun. Exec. Com.; bd. overseers Leonard N. Stern Sch. of Bus., NYU. Office: Daimler Chrysler Corp 1000 Chrysler Drive Auburn Hills MI 48326-2766

SIDMAN, ROBERT JOHN, lawyer; b. Cleve., Aug. 4, 1943; s. Charles Frances and Louise (Eckert) S.; m. Mary Mato, July 29, 1967; children: Christa Mary, Alicia Mary. BA, Benedictine Coll., 1965; JD, U. Notre Dame, 1968. Bar: Ohio 1968, U.S. Dist. Ct. (so. dist.) Ohio 1970, U.S. Ct. Appeals (6th cir.) 1971, U.S. Supreme Ct. 1971. Law clk. U.S. Dist. Ct. (so. dist.) Ohio, Columbus, 1968-70; assoc. Mayer, Tingley & Hurd, Columbus, 1970-75; judge Bankruptcy Ct. U.S. Dist. Ct. (so. dits.) Ohio, Columbus, 1975-82; ptnr. Vorys, Sater, Seymour & Pease, Columbus, 1982—. Prof. Ohio State U. Law Sch., Columbus, 1984, 85, 86. Mem. at. Conf. Bankruptcy Judges (bd. dirs. 1981-82), Assn. Former Bankruptcy Judges (bd. dirs. 1983-89, treas. 1986-87, pres. 1988-89). Office: Vorys Sater Seymour & Pease PO Box 1008 52 E Gay St Columbus OH 43215-3161 E-mail: rjsidman@vssp.com, rsidman843@aol.com.

SIEBEN, JEFFREY SCOTT, lawyer; b. Hastings, Minn., 1975; BA, St. John's U., Collegeville, Minn., 1997; JD, William Mitchell Coll. Law, St. Paul, 2001. Bar: Minn. 2001. Assoc. Sieben, Grose, Von Holtum & Carey, Ltd., Mpls. Named a Rising Star, Minn. Super Lawyers mag., 2006. Mem.: Minn. Trial Lawyers Assn., ABA, Minn. State Bar Assn., Dakota County Bar Assn., Hennepin County Bar Assn. Office: Sieben Grose Von Holtum & Carey Ltd 900 Midwest Plz East Bldg 800 Marquette Ave Minneapolis MN 55402 Office Phone: 612-333-9713. E-mail: jeffrey.sieben@knowyourrights.com.

SIEBEN, TODD, state legislator; b. Geneso, Ill., July 11, 1945; m. Kay Sieben; children: Rachel, Brandon, Meredith. BS, Western Ill. U., 1967. Commnr. Geneso Park Dist., 1977-87; mem. Henry County Planning Commn., 1978-80, 85-86; Ill. state rep. Dist. 73, 1987-92; vice chmn. fin. inst. com., mem. pub. utilities com. Ill. Ho. Reps., state govt. adminstrn. com., energy, environ. com., natural resources com., aging com., children com., small bus. com.; mem. Ill. State Senate Dist. 37, 1993—. Co-owner, v.p. Sieben Hybrids, Inc. Mem. Am. Legion, Geneso Rotary, VFW, Farm Bur., Masons. Office: Ill Senate Mems State Capitol Rm 307 Springfield IL 62706-0001 Home: 13467 N 2150th Ave Geneseo IL 61254-9002

SIEBENBURGEN, DAVID A., airline company executive; b. Cin., Sept. 18, 1947; s. Joseph and Elsie (Diersing) S.; m. Marcia Altieri, Sept. 27, 1974; 1 child, Brian. BBA, Xavier U., 1972. CPA, Ohio. Acct. Arthur Andersen & Co., Ohio, Ohio, 1974—; pres., COO Comair, Inc., Cin., 1984—. Mem. St. James Ch., Cin., 1980—, Community Chest, Cin. Republican. Roman Catholic. Office: Comair Inc 77 Comair Blvd Erlanger KY 41018

SIEBERT, CALVIN D., economist, educator; b. Hillsboro, Kans., Feb. 11, 1934; s. Ira and Margaret (Everett) S.; m. Valerie Dawn Nanninga, Feb. 18, 1960; children— Douglas Erik, Derek Christopher. BA, U. Kans., 1958, MA, 1960; PhD in Econs., U. Calif., Berkeley, 1966. Asst. prof. econs. U. Iowa, 1965-68, assoc. prof., 1968-75, prof., 1975—, chmn. dept., 1969-71, 75-79. Rockefeller Found. vis. asso. prof. U. Philippines, 1971-72 Contbr. articles to profl. jours. With U.S. Army, 1954-56. Ford Found. grantee, 1964-65 Mem. Am. Econ. Assn., Phi Beta Kappa. Home: 341 N 7th Ave Iowa City IA 52245-6003 Office: U Iowa Dept Econs S318 Pbb Iowa City IA 52242 Business E-Mail: calvin_siebert@uiowa.edu.

SIEDLECKI, NANCY THERESE, lawyer, funeral director; b. Chgo., May 30, 1954; d. LeRoy John and Dorothy Josephine (Wilczynski) Schielka; m. Jonathan Francis Siedlecki, June 18, 1977; children: Samantha Ann, Abigail Marie. Grad. funeral dir., Worsham Coll., 1974; student, Loyola U., Chgo., 1974—76, U. Ill., 1976—77; JD with honors, Chgo.-Kent Coll. Law, 1980. Bar: Ill. 1980. Paralegal in real estate Rosenberg, Savner & Unikel, Chgo., 1974—77; pvt. practice law Burr Ridge, Ill., 1980—; cons. wills, trusts, probate and small bus. corps., Chgo., 1980—. Mem.: ABA, DuPage Bar Assn., DuPage County Bar Assn., Chgo. Bar Assn., Ill. State Bar Assn., NFDA, Ill. Funeral Dirs. Assn., Union League Club of Chgo., Lyric Opera Chgo. Roman Catholic. Office: Village Law Bldg 5300 Main St Downers Grove IL 60515-4846 Office Phone: 630-969-1009. Business E-Mail: nsvillagelaw@aol.com.

SIEDLER, ARTHUR JAMES, nutrition and food science educator; b. Milw., Mar. 17, 1927; s. Arthur William and Margaret (Stadler) Siedler; m. Doris Jean Northrop, Feb. 23, 1976; children: William, Nancy Siedler Wilhite, Sandra Siedler Goodner, Roxanne Rose Butler, Randy Rose. BS, U. Wis., 1951; MS, U. Chgo., 1956, PhD, 1959. Chief divsn. biochemistry and nutrition Am. Meat Inst. Found., Chgo., 1959-64; group leader Norwich (N.Y.) Pharmacal Co., 1964-65, chief physiology sect., 1965-69, chief biochemistry sect., 1969-72; acting dir. divsn. nutritional scis. U. Ill., Urbana, 1978-81, head dept. food sci., 1972-89, prof. food sci., internal medicine and nutritional scis., 1972-94, prof. emeritus, 1994—. With USCG, 1945—46, PTO. Grantee, Nat. Livestock and Meat Bd., 1959—64; NIH Rsch. grantee, 1960—63. Mem.: Coun. Agrl. Sci. and Tech., Am. Soc. Nutritional Scis., Am. Chem. Soc., Inst. Food Technologists, VFW, Elks, Eagles. Achievements include patents in field. Home: 8 Stanford Pl Champaign IL 61820-7620 Office: 382M Ag Eng Sci 1304 W Pennsylvania Ave Urbana IL 61801-4713 E-mail: asiedler@uiuc.edu.

SIEFERS, ROBERT GEORGE, banker; b. Pitts., Aug. 28, 1945; s. George Francis and Idella Alice (Eiler) S.; m. Janice Lynn Kirkpatrick, Mar. 25, 1970; children: Robert Scott, Jillian Stewart BA, Mt. Union Coll., 1967; MBA, Kent State U., 1971; JD, Cleveland Marshall Law Sch., 1976. Security analyst Nat. City Bank, Cleve., 1971-76, v.p., investment rsch. dir., 1976-80, v.p. adminstrn. and rsch., 1980-82; sr. v.p. corp. planning Nat. City Corp., Cleve., 1982-85; sr. v.p. corp. banking Nat. City Bank, Cleve., 1985-86; pres., chief exec. officer Ohio Citizens Bank (affiliate Nat. City Corp.), Toledo, 1986-90; vice chmn., CFO Nat. City Corp., Cleve., 1997—. Bd. dirs. HCR Corp. Bd. trustees Mt. Union Coll. Republican. Presbyterian Club: Chagrin Valley Country.

SIEG, STANLEY A., military official; B in Bus. Adminstrn., U. N.Mex., 1970; M in Bus. Adminstrn., U. Okla., 1971; grad., Squadron Officer Sch., 1974, Armed Forces Staff Coll., 1981, Air War Coll., 1987. Commd. 2d lt. USAF, 1970, advanced through grades to brigadier gen., 1998; chief Comdr.'s Mgmt. Rsch. Office, exec. officer to comdr. Hdqs. Air Force Contract Mgmt. Divsn., Kirtland AFB, N.Mex., 1977-81; comdr., DOD plant rep. Def. Contract Adminstrn. Svcs. Plant Rep. Office, ITT, Nutley, N.J., 1981-84; comdr. Air Force Contract Maintenance Ctr., Kimhae Internat. Airport, South Korea, 1984-86; chief item mgmt. divsn. Oklahoma City Air Logistics Ctr., Tinker AFB, Okla., 1987-89; chief sys. and logistics contracting divsn. Office of Asst. Sec. of Air Force for Acquisition, USAF, Washington, 1989-91; inspector gen. Hdqs. Air Force Materiel Command, Wright-Patterson AFB, Ohio, 1993-95; dir. propulsion Oklahoma City Air Logistics Ctr., Tinker AFB, 1995-97; dir. logistics Hdqs. Air Force Materiel Command, Wright-Patterson AFB, 1997—, dir. contracting, 2000—. Decorated Legion of Merit with oak leaf cluster, Def. Meritorious Svc. medal, Meritorious Svc. medal with 2 oak leaf clusters. Office: 4375 HQ AFMC/PK Chidlaw Rd S208 Wright Patterson AFB OH 45433-5006

SIEGAL, BURTON LEE, product designer, consultant, inventor; b. Chgo., Sept. 27, 1931; s. Norman A. and Sylvia (Vitz) S.; m. Rita Goran, Apr. 11, 1954; children: orman, Laurence Scott BS in Mech. Engring., U. Ill., 1953. Torpedo designer U.S. Naval Ordnance, Forest Park, Ill., 1953-54; chief engr. Gen. Aluminum Corp., Chgo., 1954-55; product designer Chgo. Aerial Industries, Melrose Park, Ill., 1955-58; chief designer Emil J. Paidar Co., Chgo., 1958-59; founder, pres. Budd Engring. Corp., Chgo., 1959—. Dir. Dur-A-Case Corp., Chgo.; design cons. to numerous corps. Holder more than 127 patents in more than 40 fields including multimemory for power seats and electrified office panel sys., Piezo ink jet valves; contbr. articles to tech. publs. Mem. math., sci. and English adv. bds. Niles Twp. High Schs., Skokie, Ill., 1975-79; electronic cons. Chgo. Police Dept., 1964. Nominee Presdl. medal Tech., Sen. Paul Simon and Rep. Dan Rostenkowski, 1986; named Winner, Internat. Extrusion Design Competition, 1975, Inventor of Yr., Patent Law Assn. Chgo., 1986, Disting. Alumni, Coll. Engring., U. Ill., 2005. Mem. ASME, Soc. Plastics Engrs., Soc. Mfg. Engrs., Inventors Coun., Soc. Automotive Engrs., Pres.'s Assn. Ill. Office: Skokie IL 60076

SIEGAL, RITA GORAN, engineering company executive; b. Chgo., July 16, 1934; d. Leonard and Anabelle (Soloway) Goran; m. Burton L. Siegal, Apr. 11, 1954; children: orman, Laurence Scott. Student, U. Ill., 1951-53; BA, DePaul U., 1956. Cert. elem. tchr. Ill. Tchr. Chgo. Public Schs., 1956-58; founder, chief exec. officer Budd Engring. Corp., Skokie, Ill., 1959—; founder, pres. Easy Living Products Co., Skokie, 1960—; pvt. practice in interior design, Chgo., 1968-73; dist. sales mgr. Super Girls, Skokie, 1976. Guest spkr. nat. radio and TV, 1979—; lectr. Northwestern U., 1983. Contbr. articles to profl. jours. Mem. adv. bd. Skokie HS, 1975—79; advisor Cub Scouts Skokie coun. Boy Scouts Am., 1975; leader Great Books Found., 1972; founder Profit Plus Investment, 1970; bus. mgr. Nutrition Optimal Health Assn., Winnetka, Ill., 1980—82, pres., 1982—84, v.p. med./profl., 1985—93; bd. dirs. Noha, Internat. Named Prominent Alumni, Sullivan HS, 2001; recipient Cub Scout awards, Boy Scouts Am., 1971—72, Nat. Charlotte Danstrom award, Nat. Women of Achievement, 1988, Corp. Achievement award, 1988, Frannie Award, U. Ill., 1998. Mem.: Inventors Coun., Pres. Assn. Ill. (bd. dirs. 1990—94, membership chair 1991—93), North Shore Women Mgmt. (pres. 1987—88), Oriental Art Soc. Chgo. (publicity chair).

SIEGEL, BARRY ALAN, radiologist; b. Nashville, Dec. 30, 1944; s. Walter G. Siegel and Lillian B. Ivener; m. Pamela M. Mandel, Aug. 18, 1968 (div. Mar. 1981); children: Peter A., William A.; m. Marilyn J. Siegel, Jan. 29, 1983. AB, Washington U., St. Louis, 1966, MD, 1969. Diplomate Am. Bd. Nuc. Medicine, Am. Bd. Radiology. Intern Barnes Hosp., St. Louis, 1969-70; from resident in radiology to prof. Mallinckrodt Inst. Radiology Washington U., 1970—79, prof. radiology Mallinckrodt Inst. Radiology, 1979—, dir. divsn. nuc. medicine Mallinckrodt Inst. Radiology, 1973—, mem. Siteman Cancer Ctr., 1996—. Dir. Am. Bd. Nuc. Medicine, LA, 1985—90, sec., 1990; chmn. adv. com. on med. uses of isotopes NRC, Washington, 1990—96; chmn. radiopharm. drugs adv. com. FDA, Rockville, Md., 1982—85, radiol. devices panel, 1992—95; mem. U.S. Pharmacopeia Adv. Panel on Radiopharms., 1975—2000, Armed Forces Radiobiol. Rsch. Inst., Bethesda; cons. experts, chair radiopharm. expert com. U.S. Pharmacopoeial Conv., 2000—05; co-chair working group Nat. Oncologic PET Registry, 2005—; cons. in field. Author, editor 33 books; contbr. articles to profl. jours., chpts. in books. Maj. USAF, 1974—76. Recipient Commr.'s Spl. citation U.S. FDA, 1988, Honor citation U.S. Pharmacopeial Conv., 1995, 2000. Fellow: ACP, Am. Coll. Nuc. Physicians, Am. Coll. Radiology (vice chmn. commn. nuc. medicine 1981—93, editor-in-chief profl. self evaluation program 1988—2002, chmn. nuc. medicine com. imaging network 1998—2006, med. dir. PET core lab. imaging network 2006—, Gr. Deputy Co-Chair Imaging Network 2008—); mem.: ACS (chmn. diagnostic imaging com. oncology group 1998—2007, mem. exec. com. 2000—07), AMA, Acad. Molecular Imaging (chair inst. Clin. PET coun. 2001—02, bd. dirs. 2004—), Soc. Nuc. Medicine (trustee 1981—85, 1987—91, Georg Charles de Hevesy Nuclear Pioneer award 2003), Radiol. Soc. N.Am., Assn. Univ. Radiologists, Am. Roentgen Ray Soc. Office: Washington U Mallinckrodt Inst Radiology 510 S Kingshighway Blvd Saint Louis MO 63110-1016 Home Phone: 314-367-3650; Office Phone: 314-362-2809. Business E-Mail: siegelb@mir.wustl.edu.

SIEGEL, HOWARD JEROME, lawyer; b. Chgo., July 29, 1942; s. Leonard and Idele (Lehrner) S.; m. Diane L. Gerber; children: Sari D., Allison J., James G. BS, U. Ill., 1963; JD, Northwestern U., 1966. Bar: Ill. 1966, U.S. Dist. Ct. (no. dist.) Ill. 1967. Assoc. Ancel, Stonesifer & Glink, Chgo., 1966-70; ptnr. Goldstine & Siegel, Summit, Ill., 1970-75; sole practice Chgo., 1975-77; pres. Wexler, Siegel & Shaw, Ltd., Chgo., 1978-82; ptnr. Keck, Mahin & Cate, Chgo., 1982-95, eal Gerber & Eisenberg, Chgo., 1995-99; counsel Fagel & Haber, Chgo., 1999—. Bd. dirs. various corps. Mem.: ABA, Chgo. Bar Assn., Ill. Bar Assn., Twin Orchard Country Club (Long Grove, Ill.). Office: FabelHaberLLC 55 E Monroe 40th Fl Chicago IL 60603 Office Phone: 312-580-2248. Business E-Mail: hsiegel@fagelhaber.com.

SIEGEL, ROBERT, heat transfer engineer; b. Cleve., July 10, 1927; s. Morris and Mollie (Binder) S.; m. Elaine Jane Jaffe, July 19, 1951; children: Stephen, Lawrence. BS, Case Inst. Tech., 1950, MS, 1951; ScD, MIT, 1953. Heat transfer engr. GE, Schenectady, NY, 1953-54; heat transfer analyst Knolls Atomic Power Lab., Schenectady, 1954-55; rsch. scientist NASA Lewis Rsch. Ctr., Cleve., 1955-99; tech. cons., 1999—. Adj. prof. U. Toledo, 1981, 85, 95, adj. prof. mech. engring. U. Akron (Ohio), 1987, adj. prof. mech. engring. Cleve. State U., 1989, 91; mem. adv. coun. U. Akron, 1989-96. Author: Thermal Radiation Heat Transfer, 1972, 4th edit., 2002; tech. editor ASME, 1973-83, AIAA, 1986-98; author numerous sci. papers. With U.S. Army, 1945-47. Recipient Exceptional Sci. Achievement medal NASA, 1986, Space Act award, 1993, ASME-AIChE Max Jakob Meml. award, 1996. Fellow ASME (Heat Transfer Meml. award 1970, Max Jakob Bd. of award 1999-2002), AIAA (Thermophysics award 1993); mem. Sigma Xi, Tau Beta Pi. Jewish. Avocations: ballroom dancing, piano. Home and Office: 3052 Warrington Rd Shaker Heights OH 44120-2425

SIEGEL, ROBERT HAROLD, English literature educator, writer; b. Aug. 18, 1939; married; 3 children. Student, Denison U., 1957-59; BA in English, Wheaton Coll., 1961; MA, Johns Hopkins U., 1962; PhD in English, Harvard U., 1968. Instr. Dartmouth Coll., 1967-68, asst. prof., 1968-75; vis. lectr. Princeton (N.J.) U., 1975-76; poet-in-residence, McManes vis. prof. Wheaton (Ill.) Coll., 1976; asst. prof. U. Wis., Milw., 1976-79, assoc. prof. English, 1979-83, prof., 1983—99, prof. emeritus, 1999—. Poet on faculty Summer Writers' Inst., Wheaton Coll., 1980, Wesleyan U., 1982, 83, New Eng. Young Writers Conf., 2002-2006; vis. prof. J. W. v. Goethe U., Frankfurt, Fed. Republic Germany, 1985; lectr., reader various univs. Author: (fiction) Alpha Centauri, 1980, Whalesong, 1981, The Kingdom of Wundle, 1982, White Whale, 1991, The Ice at the End of the World, 1994; (poetry) The Beasts and the Elders, 1973, In A Pig's Eye, 1980, The Waters Under the Earth, 2005, A Pentecost of Finches: New and Selected Poems, 2006; contbr. poems to Atlantic Monthly, Sewanee Rev., other jours. Recipient Margaret O'Loughlin Foley award Am. mag., 1970, award Cliff Dwellers' Arts Found., 1974, Chgo. Poetry prize Soc. Midland Authors, 1974, Poetry prize Prairie Schooner, 1977, Jacob Glatstein Meml. prize Poetry mag., 1977, award Ingram Merrill Found., 1979, Gold medallion ECPA, 1981, Book of Yr. award Campus Life mag., 1981, 1st Pl. prize for juvenile fiction Coun. for Wis. Writers, 1981, 1st Pl. prize poetry Soc. Midland Authors, 1981, Matson award Friends of Lit., 1982, Golden Archer award Sch. Libr. Sci., U. Wis., Oshkosh, 1986, 1st prize Milton Ctr. Poetry Contest, 1994, EPA 1st place in poetry, 2003; Dartmouth Coll. faculty fellow, 1971; Gilman fellow Johns Hopkins U., 1961-62; tchg. fellow Harvard U., 1965-67, Yaddo Artists' Colony, 1974, 75, Transatlantic Rev. fellow Bread Loaf Writers Conf., 1974, Nat. Endowment for Arts, 1980; grantee U. Wis., 1978, 84, 88-89, 96-97. Office: U Wis English Dept Milwaukee WI 53201 Business E-Mail: grindel@msn.com, siegelrh@uwm.edu.

SIEGLER, MARK, internist, educator; b. NYC, June 20, 1941; s. Abraham J. and Florence (Sternlieb) S.; m. Anna Elizabeth Hollinger, June 4, 1967; children: Dillan, Alison, Richard, Jessica. AB with honors, Princeton U., 1963; MD, U. Chgo., 1967. Diplomate Am. Bd. Internal Medicine. Resident, chief resident internal medicine U. Chgo., 1967-71; hon. sr. registrar in medicine Royal Postgrad. Med. Sch., London, 1971-72; asst. prof. medicine U. Chgo., 1972-78, assoc. prof. medicine, 1979-85, acting dir. div. gen. internal medicine, 1983-85, dir. MacLean Ctr. Clin. Med. Ethics, 1984—, prof. medicine, 1985—, Lindy Bergman prof., 1997-2000, Lindy Bergman Disting. Svc. prof., 2000—, dir. fellowship tng. program in clin. med. ethics, 1986—. Vis. asst. prof. medicine U. Wis., Madison, 1977; vis. assoc. prof. medicine U. Va., Charlottesville, 1981-82. Co-author: Clinical Ethics, 1981, 6th edit., 2006, An Annotated Bibliography of Medical Ethics, 1988, Institutional Protocols for Decisions About Life-Sustaining Treatment, 1988; co-editor: Changing Values in Medicine, 1985, Medical Innovations and Bad Outcomes, 1987; editl. bd.: Am. Jour. Medicine, 1979—94, 1997—, Archives Internal Medicine, 1979—90, Bibliography of Bioethics, Jour. Med. Philosophy, 1978—89, Jour. Med. Philosophy, 1978—89, Jour. Clin. Ethics, 1989—; contbr. articles to profl. jours. Mem. adv. bd. Bioethics Inst., Madrid, Notre Dame Ctr. for Ethics and Culture; trustee Princeton U., 2006—. Grantee Andrew W. Mellon Found., Henry J. Kaiser Family Found., Pew Charitable Trusts, Field Found. Ill., Ira De Camp Found., Gaylord & Dorothy Donnelley Found., Irving Harris Found.; Phi Beta Kappa vis. scholar, 1991-92, Chirone prize Italian Nat. Acad. Medicine, 1996; mem. NAS Cloning Panel, 2001-02, others. Fellow ACP (human rights com., ethics com. 1985-90), Hastings Ctr.; mem. ACS (ethics com. 1992—), Assn. Am. Physicians, Chgo. Clin. Ethics Program (pres. 1989-90). Office: Univ Chgo MC 6098 MacLean Ctr Clin Med Ethics 5841 S Maryland Ave Chicago IL 60637-1463 Office Phone: 773-702-1453. E-mail: msiegler@medicine.bad.uchicago.edu.

SIEKERT, ROBERT GEORGE, retired neurologist, educator; b. Milw., July 23, 1924; s. Hugo Paul and Elisa (Kraus) S.; m. Mary Jane Evans, Feb. 17, 1951; children: Robert G. Jr., John E., Friedrich A.P. BS, Northwestern U., 1945, MS, 1947, MD, 1948. Diplomate Am. Bd. Psychiatry and Neurology. Instr. anatomy U. Pa., Phila., 1948-49; fellow neurology Mayo Found., Rochester, Minn., 1950-54; cons. Mayo Clinic, Rochester, 1954-91, head neurology sect., 1966-76, bd. govs., 1973-80, prof. neurology med. sch., 1969-91, prof. emeritus neurology, 1991—. Chmn. Internat. Stroke Conf. Am. Heart Assn., 1976-93. Editor Mayo Clinic Procs., 1982-86; cons. editor Jour. Stroke, 1992-2001; contbr. articles to profl. jours.; described transient cerebral ischemic attacks. Trustee Mayo Found., Rochester, 1973-81, chmn. emeritus com., 1997-98. Served to lt. j.g. M.C., USNR, 1950-52. Recipient Disting. Achievement award, Am. Heart Assn., 1984, Merit award, 1989, Robert G. Siekert Young Investigator award Am. Heart Assn., 1986. Fellow Am. Coll. Physicians; mem. Am. Neurol. Assn., orthwestern U. Med. Sch. Alumni Assn. (Service award 1983), Swiss Neurol. Soc. (corr.), Alpha Omega Alpha. Avocation: stamp collecting/philately. Office: Mayo Clinic 200 1st St SW N-10 Rochester MN 55905-0002

SIEKMANN, DONALD CHARLES, accountant; b. St. Louis, July 2, 1938; s. Elmer Charles and Mabel Louise (Blue) S.; m. Linda Lee Knowles, Sept. 10, 1966; 1 child, Brian Charles. BS, Washington U., St. Louis, 1960. CPA, Ohio, Ga. Regional mng. ptnr. Arthur Andersen & Co., Cin., 1960-98. Trustee Touchstone Group Mut. Funds, Riverfront Group Mut. Funds, Constellation Group Mutual Funds; exec. Duro Bag Mfg. Co. Columnist Cin. Enquirer, 1983-86, Gannett News Services, 1983-86; editor "Tax Clinic" column Tax Advisor mag., 1974-75. Mem. bd. Cin. Zool. Soc., 1985-88; officer, bd. dirs. Cin. Found. for Pub. TV, 1984-88, Cin. Symphony Orch., 1973-85, Cin. Ballet Co., 1973-88, Atlanta Symphony Orch., 1988-91, The Atlanta Opera, 1988-91, Cin. Theatrical Assn., Jewish Hosp., 1993—, Cin. Assn. for Performing Arts, 1992—, Cin. United Way, 1992-99, Cin. Pk. Bd. Found., 1995-98; pres. Greater Cin. Arts and Edn. Ctr., 1996-99; mem. Friends of Sch. for Creative and Performing Arts, 1996-99, Cin. Arts Festival, 1992-96, Ronald McDonald House, 1998—. Mem. AICPA, Ohio Soc. CPAs, Cin. Country Club (trustee 1983-88), Optimists Club (pres. Queen City chpt. 1986). Clubs: Cin. Country (trustee 1983-88). Lutheran. Home: 5495 Waring Dr Cincinnati OH 45243-3933 Office Phone: 859-581-8200. E-mail: dsiekmann@aol.com.

SIEMER, PAUL JENNINGS, public relations executive; b. St. Louis, Jan. 24, 1946; s. Robert Vincent and Pauline Mary (Nece) S.; m. Susan MacDonald Arnott, Aug. 26, 1967 Student, U. Notre Dame, 1964-67. Reporter South Bend Tribune, Ind., 1967-69; reporter St. Louis Globe-Democrat, 1969-76; account exec. Fleishman-Hillard Inc., St. Louis, 1976-79, v.p., sr. ptnr., 1979-84, exec. v.p., sr. ptnr., 1984-95; ptnr. Stolberg & Siemer Inc., St. Louis, 1995—. Mem. Pub. Relations Soc. Am. Roman Catholic. Home: 2961 Hatherly Dr Saint Louis MO 63121-4551 Office: Stolberg & Siemer Inc 818 Lafayette Ave Saint Louis MO 63104-3702 Office Phone: 314-436-6577.

SIEPMANN, JOERN ILJA, chemistry professor; b. Cologne, Germany, June 28, 1964; came to U.S., 1993; m. Silke Schmid, Mar. 22, 1990; children: Tim Christoph, Ines Vivian. PhD, Cambridge U., Eng., 1992. Postdoctoral fellow IBM Zurich Rsch. Lab., Rüschlikon, Switzerland, 1991-92, Koninklijke/Shell Lab., Amsterdam, The etherlands, 1992-93; rsch. assoc. U. Pa., Phila., 1993-94; asst. prof. chemistry U. Minn., Mpls., 1994-2000, assoc. prof. chemistry, 2000—. Recipient Dreyfus New Faculty award Dreyfus Found., 1994; Alfred P. Sloan Rsch. fellow, 1998. Mem. AIChE, Am. Chem. Soc. Achievements include research on configurational bias Monte Carlo of complex fluids. Office: U Minn Dept Chemistry 207 Pleasant St SE Minneapolis MN 55455-0431

SIERLES, FREDERICK STEPHEN, psychiatrist, educator; b. Bklyn., Nov. 9, 1942; s. Samuel and Elizabeth (Meiselman) S.; m. Laurene Harriet Cohn, Oct. 25, 1970 (div. Aug. 1990); children: Hannah Beth Alterson, Joshua Caleb. AB, Columbia U., 1963; MD, Rosalind Franklin U., 1967. Diplomate Am. Bd. Psychiatry and Neurology. Intern Cook County Hosp., Chgo., 1967-68; resident in psychiatry Mt. Sinai Hosp., NYC, 1968-69, assoc. attending psychiatrist Chgo., 1973-74; resident in psychiatry Rosalind Franklin U., North Chgo., Ill., 1969-71, chief resident, 1970-71, instr. psychiatry, 1973—74, asst. prof., 1974-78, assoc. prof., 1978-88, dir. med. student edn., 1974—94; staff psychiatrist U.S. Reynolds Army Hosp., Ft. Sill, Okla., 1971-73. Cons. psychiatry Cook County Hosp., 1974-79, St. Mary of Nazareth Hosp., 1979-82, Gt. Lakes Naval Hosp., 1987-90, Jackson Park Hosp., 1987-89, Mt. Sinai Hosp., 1988—, Elgin Mental Health Ctr., 1997—; chief mental health clinic, North Chicago VA Hosp., 1982-85, chief psychiatry svc., 1983-85. Author: (wth others) General Hospital Psychiatry, 1985, Behavioral Science for the Boreds, 1987, rev. 2d edit., 1989, rev. 3d edit., 1993, USMLE Behavioral Science Made Ridiculously Simple, 1998; editor: Clinical Behavioral Science, 1982, Behavioral Science for Medical Students, 1993; mem. editl. bd. Acad. Psychiatry, 2000—; contbr. articles to profl. jours. Coach Glenview (Ill.) Youth Baseball, 1987-89, mgr. 1990 (age 10-12 Glenview World Series winner 1990), Glenview Tennis Club, 1986-90 (3.5 Men's Doubles League winner 1989-90). Maj. M.C., U.S. Army, 1971-73. N.Y.State Regents scholar, 1959-63; NIMH grantee, 1974-83, Chgo. Med. Sch. grantee, 1974-83; recipient Seymour Vestermark award NIMH/Am. Psychiat. Assn., 2003. Fellow Am. Psychiat. Assn. (disting. life fellow, 2006-, coun. edn and career devel. 1993-95); mem. Ill. Psychiat. Soc. (fellowship com. 1985-99), Columbia Coll. Alumni Secondary Schs. Com., Assn. Dirs. Med. Student Edn. in Psychiatry (exec. coun. 1985-99, chmn. program com. 1987-88, treas. 1989-91, pres-elect 1991-93, pres. 1993-95, immediate past pres. 1995-99), Alliance for Clin. Edn., Am. Assn. Dirs. Psychiat. Residency Tng. (exec. coun. 2000-03, chair workforce coalition 2000-03), Sigma Xi, Alpha Omega Alpha, Phi Epsilon Pi. Office: Rosalind Franklin Univ Chgo Med Sch 3333 Green Bay Rd North Chicago IL 60064-3037 Business E-Mail: frederick.sierles@rosalindfranklin.edu.

SIERRA-AMOR, ROSA ISABEL, health facility administrator; b. Tampico, Mex., Apr. 28, 1954; Licensure Degree in Clin. Biochemistry, Nat. Autonomous U. Mexico, 1979, MS, 1992, PhD, 1995; postgrad., U. Reading, Eng., 1986. Fellow dept. endocrinology and metabolism Jewish Hosp. and Washington U. Sch. Medicine, St. Louis, 1982; mem. staff dept. nephrology and mineral metabolism, assoc. investigator Nat. Inst. Nutrition Salvador Zubiran, Mexico City, 1978-90; dir. Mineral Metabolism Rsch. Lab., divsn. neonatology Children's Hosp.-U. Cin. Med. Ctr., 1990-96; lab. mgr. Pediat. Bone Rsch. Ctr. Children's Hosp. Med. Ctr., 1996—. Lectr. in field. Contbr. articles to profl. jours. Recipient Ames/Bayer L.Am. award, 1993, award Mexican Coll. Profls. in Chemistry, 1994. Mem.: Spanish Soc. Clin. Chemistry and Molecular Pathology, Iberoamerican Soc. for Rsch. on Bone Metabolism, Nat. Acad. Pharm. Scis. (Mexico), Mexican Assn. Clin. Biochemistry, Am. Assn. for Bone and Mineral Rsch., Am. Assn. for Clin. Chemistry (mem. internat. rels. com. 1992—94, chair OVS membership com. 1994, mem. internat. adv. panel 1994—96, chair exch. program in clin. chemistry OVS 1994—, chair Ohio Valley sect. awards com. 1997—, treas. pediat. materno-fetal divsn. 2002—, Internat. Fellowship award 1996, Bernard Katchman ann. award 2001), Mex. Assn. Clin. Biochemistry (chair continuing edn. com., chmn. sci. proc. 8th internat. congress on lab. automation, mem. sci. program), Internat. Fedn. Clin. Chemistry (alt. rep. to Mexican Assn. Clin. Biochemistry 1992—96, newsletter corr. and reviewer jour. 1992—, mem. sci. program XVII Internat. Congress in Clin. Chemistry 1996—, assoc. mem. com. in metabolic bone disease and bone markers sci. divsn 1996—, mem. at large 1997—99, mem. EB 2000—02, co-chmn. sci. com. XIX ICCC 2005).

SIEVERS, BRYAN, state senator, farmer; b. Iowa; m. Lisa Sievers; 2 children. Grad., Iowa State U. Farmer; state rep. Iowa Ho. of Reps., 2000—02; state senator Iowa Senate, 2003—. Vol. Scott County Farm Bur., Iowa Farm Bur.; former mem. Bennett Cmty. Sch. Bd.; pres. Durant Cmty. Schs. Athletic Boosters. Republican. Address: 27135 1st Ave New Liberty IA 52765

SIFFERLEN, NED, academic administrator; m. Joyce Sifferlen; 2 children (twins). BS, U. Dayton, 1963, MS, 1967; EdD, U. Cin., 1974. Instr. bus. techs. Miami Jacobs Jr. Coll., 1963-65; from instr. to asst. prof. to assoc. prof. bus. techs. Sinclair C.C., Dayton, Ohio, 1965-69, dean bus. techs., 1969-79, v.p. for adminstrn., 1979-81, v.p. for instrn., 1981-91, pres., 1997—. Cons. on ednl. programs Am. Coun. on Edn., Washington; workshop presenter on experience-based edn. Am. Tech. Assn., Cin.; chair examining teams for propietary cosmetology schs. Cosmetology Accrediting Commn., Washington; reviewer coll. and univ. ednl. programs Mil. Installation Vol. Edn. Rev., Rota, Spain and Redstone Arsenal, Ala.; presenter experiential edn. concepts Union Coll., Barbourville, Ky; editor Nat. Coun. for Occupl. Edn. Quar. Co-author: (manual) Participative Management Manual; contbr. articles to profl. publs. Sec. Dayton Area Progress Coun.; bd. dirs. Goodwill Industries, Downtown Dayton Assn.; mem. supt.'s adv. com. for vocat. edn. Dayton City Schs.; pres. Nat. Coun. Occupl. Edn., Washington; past pres. coun. chief instrnl. officers Ohio Tech. and C.C. Assn., Columbus; chair various divsn. United Way. Office: Sinclair CC 444 W 3rd St Dayton OH 45402-1421

SIGERSON, CHARLES WILLARD, JR., insurance agency executive; b. Biloxi, Miss., Mar. 6, 1945; s. Charles Willard S.; m. Elizabeth Ann Moss, Dec. 9, 1967; children: Anthea Louise, Andrew Charles. B in Gen. Studies, U. Nebr., Omaha, 1971. Pres., owner Sigerson Ins. Agy., Inc., Omaha, 1973—. Pres. Floyd Rogers Diabetic Found., Lincoln, Nebr., 1981—; mem. state bd. dirs. Nebraska Stroke Found., 2002—; chmn. Douglas County Rep. Com., Omaha, 1982-83, 90-93; mem. exec. com. Nebr. Rep. Com., Lincoln, 1982-83, 86-88, 90-2001, elected pres. Omaha City Coun., 2001; chmn. Nebr. Rep. Party, 1995-2001. Staff sgt. USAF, 1964-71. Recipient Cosmopolitan of Yr.award I-80 Cosmopolitan Club, 1982, Patrick hodgins award I-80 Cosmopolitan Club, 1983, Legion of Honor ward State Farm Ins. Co., 1984. Mem. Nat. Assn. Health Underwriters, Nat. Assn. Ins. and Fin. Advisors, Soc. Fin. Svc. Profls., Nat. Assn. Life Underwriters, Rotary Internat., Masons, Christian Missionary Alliance. Avocations: genealogy, antique book and newspaper collecting, coin collecting/numismatics. Office: Sigerson Ins Agy Inc 10766 Fort St Omaha NE 68134-1230 Home: 15835 California St Omaha NE 68118-2231

SIGMON, JOYCE ELIZABETH, professional society administrator; b. Stanley, NC, Oct. 4, 1935; d. Rome Alfred and Pearl Elizabeth (Beal) S. BS, U. N.C., 1971; MA, Loyola U., 1980. Cert. assn. exec. Dental asst. Dr. Paul A. Stroup, Jr., Charlotte, N.C., 1953-63; instr. Wayne Tech. Inst., Goldsboro, N.C., 1963-65, Ctrl. Piedmont CC, Charlotte, 1965—69; dir. Dental Assisting Edn. ADA, Chgo., 1971-85, asst. sec. Coun. Prosthetics Svcs., 1985-87, mgr. Office Quality Assurance, 1987—90, exec. dir. Aux., 1990-92; dir. adminstrv. activities Am. Acad. of Implant Dentistry, Chgo., 1993—; exec. sec. Am. Bd. of Oral Implantology/Implant Dentistry, 1993-99. Deacon 4th Presbyn. Ch., 1973-75, elder 1975-77, 88-91, 2002-05, trustee, 1991-94; moderator Presbyn. Women in 4th Ch., 1987-91, Stephen min., 1997-99 Mem. Am. Soc. Assn. Execs., Chgo. Soc. Assn. Execs. (chair CAE com. 1991-92), Am. Dental Assts. Assn., N.C. Dental Assn. (pres. 1968-69), Charlotte Dental Assts. Soc. Presbyterian. Home: 260 E Chestnut St Chicago IL 60611-2401 Office: Am Acad Implant Dentistry 211 E Chicago Ave Chicago IL 60611-2637 Home Phone: 312-642-8242. Personal E-mail: jesigmon@aol.com.

SIH, CHARLES JOHN, pharmaceutical chemistry professor; b. Shanghai, Sept. 11, 1933; s. Paul Kwang-Tsien and Teresa (Dong) S.; m. Catherine Elizabeth Hsu, July 11, 1959; children: Shirley, Gilbert, Ronald. AB in Biology, Caroll Coll., 1953; MS in Bacteriology, Mont. State Coll., 1955; PhD in Bacteriology, U. Wis., 1958. Sr. research microbial biochemist Squibb Inst. for Med. Research, New Brunswick, N.J., 1958-60; mem. faculty U. Wis.-Madison, 1960—, Frederick B. Power prof. pharm. chemistry, 1978, Hilldare prof., 1987—. Recipient 1st Ernest Volwiler award, 1977; Roussel prize, 1980, Am. Pharm. Assoc. award 1987. Mem. Am. Chem. Soc., Soc. Am. Biol. Chemists, Acad. Pharm. Scis., Soc. Am. Microbiologists. Home: 10 Coyote Ct Madison WI 53717-2736

SIKKEMA, KENNETH R., state legislator; b. Cadillac, Mich., Feb. 10, 1951; s. Peter John and Kathryn Mae (Laarman) S.; m. Carla Chase, Oct. 12, 1985; 1 child, Zachary Chase. BA in History cum laude, Harvard U., 1974; MBA with distinction, U. Mich., 1984. Legis. asst. Mich. Ho. of Reps., Lansing, 1974-75; adminstrv. asst. Mich. State Senate, Lansing, 1975-79; mktg. mgr. Herman Miller, Inc., Zeeland, Mich., 1984-86; exec. dir. West Mich. Environ. Action, Grand Rapids, 1979-82; mem. Mich. Ho. of Reps., Lansing, 1987-98, Mich. Senate from 31st dist., Lansing, 1999—. Republican. Mem. Reformed Ch. in Am. Home: 4309 Del Mar Ct Grandville MI 49418 Office: State Senate Capitol Bldg Lansing MI 48913-0001 E-mail: senksikkema@senate.michigan.gov.

SIKORA, SUZANNE MARIE, dentist; b. Kenosha, Wis., Dec. 4, 1952; d. Leo F. and Ida A. (Dupuis) S. BS, U. Wis., Parkside, 1975; DDS, Marquette U., 1981. Assoc. Paul G. Hagemann, DDS, Racine, Wis., 1981-84; pvt. practice dentistry Racine, 1984—. Cons. Westview Health Care Ctr., Racine, 1981—89, Lincoln Luth. Home, Racine, 1981—2001, Becker-Shoop Ctr., Racine, 1981—2000, Lincoln Village Convalescent Ctr., Racine, 1986—2000, Lincoln Luth Cmty. Care Ctr., 1989—2000. Mem. ad hoc study com. County Health Dept., Racine, 1982—83. Mem.: ADA, Racine County Dental Soc. (pres.-elect 2001, v.p. 2002, pres. 2003, membership chairperson 2003—), Wis. Dental Assn. (coun. on access prevention and wellness com. 1984—86, impaired provider program intervenor 1990—2001, del. 1993—2006, Dental Care for Older Persons award 2000). Office: 1900 Lathrop Ave Racine WI 53405-3707 Home Phone: 262-598-9860; Office Phone: 262-632-0719.

SIKORSKI, JAMES ALAN, research chemist; b. Stevens Point, Wis., Nov. 9, 1948; s. John Paul and Florence Lucille (Wierzba) S.; m. Jeanne Delaney, Apr. 15, 1968 (div. 1975); 1 child, Christine René; m. Georgina Weber, Nov. 19, 1977. BS, Northeast La. State Coll., 1970; MS, Purdue U., 1976, PhD, 1981. With Monsanto Agrl. Co., St. Louis, 1976-91, sci. fellow, 1987-91, Monsanto Corp. Rsch., St. Louis, 1991-93; sci. fellow med. chem. G.D. Searle R&D, St. Louis, 1994-2000; sci. fellow med. chemistry Pharmacia Discovery Rsch., St. Louis, 2000—. Instr. organic chemistry St. Louis C.C., 1977-78; adj. prof. biochemistry Ctrl. Meth. Coll., 1995-97; invited spkr. tech. presentations and seminars. Contbr. chpts. to books, rev. articles, symposia-in-print and articles to profl. jours.; patentee and co-patentee in field. Mem. AAAS, Am. Chem. Soc. (St. Louis ACS award St. Louis Mo. sect. 1994, Kenneth A. Spencer award Kansas City Mo. sect. 1999, Internat. Soc. Heterocyclic Chemistry. Avocations: hiking, canoeing, skiing, photography, snorkeling. E-mail: james.a.sikorski@pharmacia.com.

SILBERMAN, ALAN HARVEY, lawyer; b. Chgo., Oct. 22, 1940; s. Milton J. and Mollie E. (Hymanson) S.; m. Margaret Judith Auslander, Nov. 17, 1968; children: Elena, Mark. BA with distinction, Northwestern U., 1961; LLB, Yale U., 1964. Bar: Ill. 1964, U.S. Dist. Ct. (no. dist.) Ill. 1966, U.S. Ct. Appeals (7th cir.) 1970, (5th and 9th cir.) 1977, (D.C. cir.) 1979, (4th cir.) 1980, (11th cir.) 1981, (3rd cir.) 1982, (8th and 10th cirs.) 1993, U.S. Supreme Ct. 1978. Law clk. U.S. Dist. Ct., Chgo., 1964-66; assoc. Sonnenschein Nath & Rosenthal, Chgo., 1964-71, ptnr., 1972—. Mem. antitrust adv. bd. Bur. Nat. Affairs, Washington, 1985—; mem. Ill. Atty. Gen. Franchise Adv. Bd., 1996—; bd. dirs., mem. exec. com. Mercaz, USA. Contbr. articles to profl. jours. Bd. dirs., v.p., sec. Camp Ramah in Wis., Inc., Chgo., 1966-86, pres., 1986-94; bd. govs. Northwestern U. Libr., 2004-; bd. dirs. Nat. Ramah Commn., Inc. of Jewish Theol. Sem. Am., N.Y.C., 1970—, v.p., 1986-94, pres., 1994-99, sr. v.p., 1999-2003; mem. U.S. del. 33d World Zionist Congress, Jerusalem, 1997, 34th World Zionist Congress, Jerusalem, 2002, 35th World Zionist Congress, Jerusalem, 2006; bd. dirs., mem. exec. com. Masorti Olami/World Coun. of Conservative Synagogues, 2002—, v.p. 2005, pres., 2005—; bd. govs. Jewish Agy. Israel, 2006-; mem. presidium World Zionist Orgn. Gen. Cou., 2006-. Mem. ABA (chmn. antitrust sect. FTC com. 1981-83, chmn. nat. insts. 1983-85, mem. coun. antitrust sect. 1985-88, fin. officer 1988-90, sect. del. ho. of dels. 1990-92, chmn.-elect 1992-93, chmn. 1993-94), Ill. Bar Assn. (chmn. antitrust sect. 1975-76), Northwestern U. 1851 Soc. (chair 1994-97), Lex Mundi Assn. Ind. Law Firms (bd. dirs. 2005—, vice chmn. com. antitrust competition and trade 1999-2003, internat. chair elect 2003-05, chair 2005—). Home: 430 Oakdale Ave Glencoe IL 60022-2113 Office: Sonnenschein Nath Ste 7800 233 S Wacker Dr Chicago IL 60606-6491 Office Phone: 312-876-8103. Business E-Mail: ASilberman@sonnenschein.com.

SILBERSACK, MARK LOUIS, lawyer; b. Cin., Dec. 27, 1946; s. Joseph Leo and Rhoda Marie (Hinkler) S.; m. Ruth Ann Schwallie, Sept. 7, 1985. AB, Boston Coll., 1968; JD, U. Chgo., 1971. Bar: Ohio 1971, U.S. Dist. Ct. (so. dist.) Ohio 1973, U.S. Ct. Appeals (6th cir.) 1974, U.S. Supreme Ct. 1975. Atty. Dinsmore & Shohl LLP, Cin., 1971—. Lectr. Ohio CLE Inst., Columbus, 1981-91. Co-author: Managed Care: The PPO Experience, 1990, Information Sharing Among Health Care Providers, 1994. Bd. dirs. United Way, Cmty. Chest, 1985-89, 2001—, chmn. pub. policy com., 1998—; vice-chmn. Ohio United Way, Columbus, 1989-94, chmn. bd. dir., 1994-96; pres. Hyde Park Neighborhood Coun., Cin., 1989-91, Hyde Park Ctr. for Older Adults, 1989-91; active Cin. Bd. Health, 1991-97, chmn., 1995-97; bd. dirs. Cath. Social Svc. of S.W. Ohio, 1998-2003, Children, Inc., 2003-; mem. Cincinnatus Assn., 2000—. Mem. ABA, FBA, Ohio State Bar Assn. (chmn. antitrust sect. 2005-07), Cin. Bar Assn., Cin. Assn., Cincinnatus Assn., Hyde Park Golf and Country Club. Republican. Roman Catholic. Avocations: reading, travel, theater. Home: 3465 Forestoak Ct Cincinnati OH 45208-1842 Office: Dinsmore & Shohl LLP 1900 Chemed Ctr 255 E 5th St Cincinnati OH 45202-4700 Home Phone: 513-321-1806; Office Phone: 513-977-8243. Business E-Mail: mark.silbersack@dinslaw.com.

SILBERSTEIN, EDWARD BERNARD, nuclear medicine educator, oncologist, researcher; b. Cin., Sept. 3, 1936; s. Bernard Gumpert and Harriet Louise (Kahn) S.; m. Jacqueline Rose Mervis, Oct. 2, 1988; children: Scott, Lisa. BS magna cum laude, Yale U., 1958; MD, Harvard U., 1962; postgrad. in art history, U. Cin. Bd. cert. in Internal Medicine, Hematology, Nuclear Medicine, Med. Oncology Am. Bd. Internal Medicine. Intern Cin. Gen. Hosp., 1962—63, resident in internal medicine, 1963—64; resident Univ. Hosps. Cleve., 1966—67; NIH fellow in hematology New Eng. Med. Ctr., Boston, 1967—68; asst. prof. radiol. medicine U. Cin. Med. Ctr., 1968—72, assoc. prof. radiol. medicine, 1972—76, prof. radiol. medicine, 1976—, Eugene L. and Sue R. Saenger prof. radiol. scis., 1998—2000, prof. emeritus of radiology and medicine, 2000—. Assoc. dir. E.L. Saenger Radioisotope Lab., 1980—; chmn. Environ. Safety Health Com. Dept. Energy Fernald Facility, 1986-91; mem. U.S. Pharmacopeia Com. of Revision, 1990—; mem. Nat. Coun. on Radiation Protection and Measurement, 1997—; cons. Nuc. Regulatory Commn., 1988—; dir. divsn. nuc. medicine Jewish Hosp., 1976-95; cancer pain panel Agy. for Health Care Planning and Rsch., 1992-93; mem. Am. Nuclear Soc. Com. on Isotope Assurance, 2003-05; vis. prof. various lecturerships; reviewer in field. Author: Differential Diagnosis in Nuclear Medicine, 1984, Bone Scintigraphy, 1984, Diagnostic Patterns in Nuclear Medicine, 1998; contbr. articles to profl. jours., chpts. to books. Active Race Rels. Commn. Greater Cin., 1995—2000; trustee Cin. Opera Assn., 1993—, v.p., 2003—; active Jewish Cmty. Rels. Coun., 1992—; trustee Isaac M. Wise Temple, 1992—2000, treas., 1997—2000; bd. dirs. Talbert House, 1969—, Air Pollution Control League, Cin., 1980—95. Capt. US Army Med. Corps, 1964—66. Recipient Pearl S. Gantz award for Cmty. Svc., United Way of Cin., 2002, VIP Volunteerism award, Hamilton County Mental Health Bd., 2005; fellow, Am. Col. Nuc. Physicians. Mem.: Am. Bd. uclear Medicine (chmn. 1999), Soc. Nuc. Medicine (sec. 1989—92, 1989—92, bd. dirs. 1989—99, pres. S.E. chpt. 1990—91, chair sci. program 1992—94, spkr. Ho. of Dels. 2002—04, Speaker's award 2004, Marshall Brucer award 2002), Literary Club, Sigma Xi, Phi Beta Kappa. Jewish. Avocations: tennis, history of art, archaeology, travel. Office: U Cin Med Ctr Mont Reid Pavilion G026 234 Goodman St Cincinnati OH 45219-2364 Office Phone: 513-584-9032. Business E-Mail: silbereb@healthall.com.

SILVER, ALAN IRVING, lawyer; b. St. Paul, Sept. 17, 1949; s. Sherman J. Silver and Muriel (Bernstein) Brawerman; m. Janice Lynn Gleekel, July 8, 1973; children: Stephen, Amy. BA cum laude, U. Minn., 1971, JD cum laude, 1975. Bar: Minn. 1975, U.S. Dist. Ct. Minn. 1975, U.S. Dist. Ct. (ea. dist.) Wis. 1975, U.S. Ct. Appeals 8th and 10th cirs.) 1975. Assoc. Doherty, Rumble & Butler, P.A., St. Paul, 1975-80, ptnr. Mpls., 1980-99, Bassford, Remele (formerly called Bassford, Lockhart, Truesdell & Briggs, P.A.), Mpls., 1999—. Mem. 2d Jud. Dist. Ethics Com., St. Paul, 1985-88, 4th Jud. Dist. Ethics Com., Mpls., 1990-97. Author: Building a New Foundation: Torts, Contracts and the Economic Class Doctrine, 2000, other numerous continuing edn. seminar material. Vol. atty. Legal Assistance Ramsey County, St. Paul, 1975-82; mem. St. Louis Park (Minn.) Sch. Bd., 1993-99, chair, 1995-97; mem. St. Louis Park Human Rights Commn., 1987-91; chmn. site mgmt. coun. Susan Lindgren Sch., St. Louis Park, 1986-93; bd. dirs. Jewish Cmty. Rels. Coun., Anti-Defamation League Minn. and Dakotas, 1987-93, 97—, treas., 1992-93, v.p., 2003-06, pres., 2006-. Mem. ABA, Minn. Bar Assn. (exec. bd. antitrust sect. 1984, litigation chair probate and trust sect.), Hennepin County Bar Assn. Avocations: running, guitar, reading. Home: 4320 W 25th St Minneapolis MN 55416-3841 Office: Bassford Remele Ste 3800 33 S 6th St Minneapolis MN 55402-1501 Office Phone: 612-376-1634. Business E-Mail: alans@bassford.com.

SILVER, DONALD, surgeon, educator; b. NYC, Oct. 19, 1929; s. Herman and Cecilia (Meyer) S.; m. Helen Elizabeth Harnden, Aug. 9, 1958; children: Elizabeth Tyler, Donald Meyer, Stephanie Davies, William Paige. AB, Duke U., 1950, BS in Medicine, MD, 1955. Diplomate Am. Bd. Surgery, Am. Bd. Gen. Vascular Surgery, Am. Bd. Thoracic Surgery. Intern Duke Med. Ctr., 1955-56, asst. resident, 1958-63, resident, 1963-64; mem. faculty Duke Med. Sch., 1964-75, prof. surgery, 1972-75; cons. Watts Hosp., Durham, 1965-75, VA Hosp., Durham, 1970-75, chief surgery, 1968-70; prof. surgery, chmn. dept. U. Mo. VA Med. Ctr., Columbia, 1975-98, chmn. univ. physicians, 2002—. Cons. Harry S. Truman Hosp., Columbia, 1975—2000; mem. bd. sci. advisers Cancer Research Center, Columbia, 1975—; mem. surg. study sect. A NIH; dir surg. svcs. U. Mo. Health System, 2001-2003. Contbr. articles to med. jours., chpts. to books; editorial bds.; Jour. Vascular Surgery, Postgrad. Gen. Surgery, Vascular Surgery. Served with USAF, 1956-58. James IV Surg. traveler, 1977 Fellow ACS (gov. 1995-99), Deryl Hart Soc.; mem. AMA, AAAS, Mo. Med. Assn., Boone County Med. Soc., Internat. Cardiovascular Soc., Soc. Univ. Surgeons, Am. Heart Assn. (Mo. affiliate rsch. com.), Soc. Surgery Alimenatry Tract, Assn. Acad. Surgery, So. Thoracic Surg. Assn., Internat. Soc. Surgery, Soc. Vascular Surgery, Am. Assn. Thoracic Surgery, Am. Surg. Assn., Ctrl. Surg. Assn. (pres.-elect 1990-91, pres. 1991-92), Western Surg. Assn., Midwestern Vascular Surg. Soc. (pres. 1984-85), Ctrl. Surg. Assn. Found. (treas. 1992-93, 2d v.p. 1993-94, 1st v.p. 1994-95, pres. 1995-96). Home: 3 Silver Maple Ct Durham NC 27705-5642 Office Phone: 573-882-1612. Business E-Mail: Silverd@health.missouri.edu.

SILVERMAN, GARY R., lawyer; b. 1961; BA, Brandeis U., 1983; JD, Northwestern U., 1986; MBA, U. Chgo., 1990, MLA, 2006. Bar: Ill. 1986, Colo. 1987, DC 1988, NY 1994. Ptnr. Corp. & Fin. Dept. Kaye Scholer LLP, Chgo., NYC. Mem.: ABA. Office: Kaye Scholer LLP Ste 4100 3 First Nat Plaza Chicago IL 60602 also: 425 Park Avenue New York NY 10022 Office Phone: 312-583-2330. Business E-Mail: gsilverman@kayescholer.com.

SILVERMAN, HENRY JACOB, history professor; b. New Haven, Feb. 22, 1934; s. Morris Samuel and Ethel (Ullman) S.; m. Ann Beryl Snyder, Apr. 12, 1957; children— Edwin Stodel, Emily Davies. BA (Univ. scholar), Yale U., 1955, MA, 1956; MA (Ford Found. fellow); postgrad., Stanford U., 1959-60; PhD, U. Pa., 1963. Fgn. service officer Dept. States, 1961-63; bibliographer Am. history Library of Congress, Washington, 1963-64; asst. prof. Am. thought and lang. Mich. State U., East Lansing, 1964-68, assoc. prof., 1968-71, prof., 1971-89, prof. history, 1988—, chmn. dept. Am. thought and lang., 1977-87, sec. for acad. governance, 1989-95, chmn. dept. history, 1995-99. Author: American Radical Thought, 1970. Fulbright scholar, Munich, 1956-57; Danforth Found. Assoc., 1969-73; Nat. Endowment for Humanities/U. Iowa grantee, 1979 Mem. AAUP (mem. exec. bd. Mich. State U. chpt. 1975-77), ACLU (mem. Laxing exec. bd., 1975-78, v.p. 1991-96, pres. 1996—, Mich. exec. bd. 1993—), Am. Hist. Assn., Am. Studies Assn., Orgn. Am. Historians. Home: 1099 Woodwind Trl Haslett MI 48840-8978 Office: Mich State U Dept History East Lansing MI 48823

SILVERMAN, NORMAN ALAN, cardiac surgeon; b. Boston, Dec. 19, 1946; BA, Dartmouth Coll., 1968; MD, Boston U., 1971. Prof. surgery U. Ill., Chgo., 1980-89; divsn. head Henry Ford Hosp., Detroit, 1989—; prof. surgery Case-Western Res. U., Cleve., 1992—. Contbr. 200 scientific articles to profl. jours. Lt. comdr. USPHS, 1973-75. Fellow Am. Coll. Surgeons, Am. coll. Cardiology, Am. Coll. Chest Physicians. Avocation: sailing. Office: Henry Ford Hosp 2799 W Grand Blvd Detroit MI 48202-2689 Home Phone: 313-881-0302; Office Phone: 313-916-2695. Business E-Mail: nsilver1@hfhs.org.

SILVERMAN, RICHARD BRUCE, chemist, biochemist, educator; b. Phila., May 12, 1946; s. Philip and S. Ruth (Simon) Silverman; m. Barbara Jean Kesner, Jan. 9, 1983; children: Matthew, Margaret, Philip. BS, Pa. State U., 1968; MA, Harvard U., Cambridge, Mass., 1972, PhD, 1974. From asst. prof. to prof. Northwestern U., Evanston, Ill., 1976—86, prof., 1986—, mem. Inst. Neurosci., 1990—. Mem. adv. panel NIH, Bethesda, Md., 1981, 83, 85, 87-91, 2001; expert analyst CHEMTRACTS; scientific adv. bd. Influx, Inc., 1998-2003, Protez Pharml., 2004—, Synchem, 2003—. NIGMS adv. coun., 2002, 2005; mem. Faculty of 1900; cons. in field. Mem. editl. bd.: Jour. Enzyme Inhibition, 1988—2002, Archives Biochem. & Biophys., 1993—, Jour. Medicinal Chemistry, 1995—2000, Enzyme Inhibition and Medicinal Chemistry, 2002—, Letters in Drug Design & Discovery, 2003—, Bioorganic & Medicinal Chemistry, 2003—, Bioorganic & Medicinal Chemistry Letters, 2003—, Current Enzyme Inhibition, 2004—. Mem. adv. bd. Ill. Math. & Scis. Acad., 1988. With U.S. Army, 1969-71. Recipient Career Devel. award USPHS, 1982-87, E. LeRoy Hall award for tchg. excellence, 1999, Northwestern Alumni Tchg. award, 2000; postdoctoral fellow Brandeis U., Waltham, Mass., 1974-76, DuPont Young Faculty fellow, 1976, Alfred P. Sloan Found. fellow, 1981-85; grantee various govt. and pvt. insts., 1976—. Arthur C. Cope. Sr. scholar ACS, 2003. Fellow: AAAS; mem.: Am. Chem. Soc. (nat. elected nominating com. divns. biol. chemistry 1993—96, long-range planning com. divsn. med. chem. 1999—2002), Am. Soc. Biochem. Molecular Biology, Am. Inst. Chemists. Avocations: golf, tennis. Office: Northwestern U Dept Chemistry 2145 Sheridan Rd Evanston IL 60208-3113 Office Phone: 847-491-5653. Business E-Mail: Agman@chem.northwestern.edu.

SILVERMAN, ROBERT JOSEPH, lawyer; b. Mpls., Apr. 4, 1942; s. Maurice and Toby (Goldstein) S.; 1 child, Adam Graham-Silverman; m. Suzanne M. Brown; 1 child, Thomas B. BA, U. Minn., 1964, JD, 1967. Bar: Minn. 1967. Assoc. Dorsey & Whitney, Mpls., 1967-72, of counsel, 1972—2001. Lectr. William Mitchell Coll. Law, St. Paul, 1977-78, Hamline Law Sch., St. Paul, 1990-96, Minn. Continuing Legal Edn., Mpls, 1985-01. Bd. dirs. Courage Ctr., Golden Valley, Minn., 1978-84, 85-95, v.p., 1983-86, pres., 1988-89. With USAR, 1967-73. Mem. ABA, Minn. Bar Assn., Hennepin County Bar Assn., Am. Coll. Real Estate Lawyers. Jewish. Office: Dorsey & Whitney 50 S 6th St Ste 1500 Minneapolis MN 55402-1498 E-mail: silverman.robert@dorseylaw.com.

SILVERMAN, ROSS O., lawyer; b. Toledo, Aug. 3, 1960; BA, Ohio State U., 1982; JD cum laude, U. Toledo, 1985. Bar: Ga. 1986, DC 1989, Ill. 1995, NY 2003, US Dist. Ct., So. and Ea. Dist. NY, No. Dist. Ill., US Ct. Appeals, 7th Cir. Trial atty. Criminal Sect. Tax Div., US Dept. Justice, 1988—90; asst. US atty. No. Dist. Ill., 1990—94; ptnr. Katten Muchin Zavis Rosenman, Chgo. Mem.: DC Bar, State Bar Ga., Ill. State Bar Assn., Chgo. Bar Assn. Office: Katten Muchin Zavis Rosenman 525 W Monroe St Chicago IL 60661 Office Phone: 312-902-5240. Office Fax: 312-577-8989. E-mail: ross.silverman@kmzr.com.

SILVERS, GERALD THOMAS, retired publishing executive; b. Cin., Aug. 26, 1937; s. Steve Allen and Tina Mae (Roberts) S.; m. Ann Gregory Woodward, July 25, 1964. BA, U. Ky., Lexington, 1960. Asst. rsch. svcs. mgr. Cin. Enquirer, 1963-72, rsch. svcs. dir., 1972-74, rsch. dir., 1974-90, v.p. mktg. svcs., 1990-94, v.p. market devel., 1994—2003; ret., 2003. Active U. Ky. Devel. Coun., Lexington, 1986—; trustee Neediest Kids of All, 1991—; region 5 exec. com. Ohio Sch. to Work, 1997-2000; corps. com. St. Elizabeth Med. Ctr. Found., 1998-2007; bd. overseers Taft Mus. Art, 1999—, treas., bd. govs., 2002—, vice chmn., 2007. 1st lt. U.S. Army, 1960-62. Recipient Thomas H. Copeland award of merit, 1991. Mem. U. Ky. Alumni Assn. Cin. Chpt. (pres. 1985), Newspaper Rsch. Coun. (pres. 1985-86), Internat. Newspaper Market Assn., Am. Mktg. Assn., Am. Art Soc. Cin. (pres. 1999-2001). Presbyterian. Home: 229 Watch Hill Rd Fort Mitchell KY 41011-1822

SILVERSTEIN, IRA I., state legislator; m. Debra; 4 children. Grad., Loyola U., 1982, John Marshall Law Sch., 1985. Mem. from 8th dist. Ill. Senate, Springfield, 1999—, chmn. exec. com. Past pres. Northtown Cmty. Coun.; past bd. dirs. Korean Sr. Ctr.; mem. Greek Pan-Hellenic Laconian Orgn.; bd. dirs. Bernard Horwitz Jewish. Cmty. Ctr., Arie Crown Hebrew Day Sch., Akiba Schechter Jewish Day Sch. Democrat. Office: State Capitol Capitol Bldg 121B Springfield IL 62706-0001 also: Ira Silverstein 2951 W Devon Ave Chicago IL 60659-1555

SIM, RICHARD GUILD, utilities executive; b. Glasgow, Scotland, Sept. 9, 1944; came to U.S., 1970; BSc, Glasgow U., 1965; PhD, Cambridge U., Eng., 1968. Engr. Westinghouse Electric, 1970-71; gen. mgr. Gen. Electric, 1972-85; CEO, chmn. Applied Power, Milw., 1985—; chmn., pres. & CEO APW Ltd., Waukesha, Wis. Bd. dirs. Gehl Co., Wis., IPSCO, Inc., Sask., Can.

SIMECKA, BETTY JEAN, marketing executive; b. Topeka, Apr. 15, 1935; d. William Bryan and Regina Marie (Rezac) S.; m. Alex Pappas, Jan. 15, 1956 (div. Apr. 1983); 1 child, Alex William. Student, Butler County C.C., 1983—85. Freelance writer and photographer, L.A., also St. Marys, Kans., 1969-77; co-owner Creative Enterprises, El Dorado, Kans., 1977-83; coord. excursions into history Butler County C.C., El Dorado, 1983-84; dir. Hutchinson Conv. & Visitors Bur., Kans., 1984-85; dir. mktg. divsn. Exec. Mgmt., Inc., Wichita, 1985-87; exec. dir. Topeka Conv. and Visitors Bur., 1987-91, pres., CEO, 1991-96; pres. Internat. Connections, Inc., 1996-97, Simecka and Assoc., 1996-99, Pinnacle Prodns., L.L.C., 1997-99; pres., CEO Cultural Exhbns. and Events, L.L.C., 1999—2003; organizer Czars: 400 Years of Imperial Grandeur exhbn., 2002—04; v.p. mktg. Sunflower Exhbns., LLC, 2003—04; mktg. cons., 2003—06; employment cons. Joblink, Cottonwood, Inc., Lawrence, Kans., 2006—. Dir. promotion El Dorado Thunderboat Races, 1977-78. Contbr. articles to jours. and mags.; columnist St. Marys Star, 1973-79. Pres. El Dorado Art Assn., 1984; chair Santa Fe Trail Bike Assn., Kans., 1988-90; co-dir. St. Marys Summer Track Festival, 1973-81; chair spl. events Mulvane Art Mus., 1990, sec., 1991-92; membership chair, 1993-94, bd. dirs., 1995-96; bd. dirs. Topeka Civic Theater, 1991-96, co-chair spl. events, 1992; Kans. chair Russian Festival Com., 1992-93; vice-chair Kans. Film Commn., 1993-94, chair, 1994; bd. dirs. Kans. Expoctr. Adv. Bd., 1990-96, Brain Injury Assn. Greater Kansas City, Concerned Citizens Topeka, 1998-2000; pres. Kans. Internat. Mus., 1994-96. Recipient Kans. Gov.'s Outstanding Tourism award Kans. Broadcaster's Assn., 1993, Disting. Svc award City of Topeka, 1995, Hist. Ward Meade Disting. award Topeka Parks and Recreation Dept., 1995; named Kansan of Yr., Topeka Capitol-Jour., 1995, Sales and Mktg. Exec. of Yr., 1995, Internat. Soroptomists, Topeka chpt., Woman of Distinction, 1996. Mem. Nat. Tour Assn., Sales and Mktg. execs. (bd. dirs. 1991-92), Internat. Assn. Conv. and Visitors Burs. (co-chair rural tourism com. 1994), Am. Soc. Assn. Execs., Travel Industry Assn. Kans. (membership chair 1988-89, sec. 1990, pres. 1991-92, Outstanding Merit award 1994), St. Marys C. of C. (pres. 1975), I-70 Assn. (v.p. 1989, pres. 1990), Optimists (social sec. Topeka chpt. 1988-89). Independent. Methodist. Holder at. AAU record for 100-yard dash, 1974.

SIMMONS, ADELE SMITH, foundation executive, former educator; b. Lake Forest, Ill., June 21, 1941; d. Hermon Dunlap and Ellen T. (Thorne) Smith; m. John L. Simmons; children: Ian, Erica, Kevin BA in Social Studies with honors, Radcliffe Coll., 1963; PhD, Oxford U., Eng., 1969; LHD (hon.), Lake Forest Coll., 1976, Amherst Coll., 1977, Franklin Pierce Coll., 1978, U. Mass., 1978, Alverno Coll., 1982, Marlboro Coll., 1987, Smith Coll., 1988, Mt. Holyoke Coll., 1989, Am. U., 1992, Tufts U., 1994. Asst. prof. Tufts U., Boston, 1969-72; dean Jackson Coll., Medford, Mass., 1970-72; asst. prof. history, dean student affairs Princeton U., NJ, 1972-77; pres. Hampshire Coll., Amherst, Mass., 1977-89, John D. and Catherine T. MacArthur Found., Chgo., 1989—99; vice chair, sr. exec. Chgo. Metropolis 2020, 1999—; sr. assoc. Ctr. for Internat. Studies U. Chgo., 1999—2005. Bd. dirs. Marsh & McLennan Cos., N.Y.C., Shorebank Corp., Chgo., Union Concerned Scientists, Synergos Inst., Environ. Def., bd. mem., Am. Prospect; bd. dirs. Field Mus., Chgo., Mexican Fine Arts Ctr. Mus., Chgo. Coun. on Fgn. Rels., Winning Worlplaces; emeritus mem. bd. dirs. Rocky Mountain Inst.; former corr. in Mauritius and Tunisia for N.Y. Times, The Economist; high level adv. bd. UN, 1993—; mem. adv. com. World Bank Inst.; mem. bd. overseers Harvard U., 1972-78; chair Fair Labor Assn.; sr. advisor World Econ. Forum. Co-author: (with Freeman, Dunkle, Blau) Exploitation from 9 to 5: Twentieth Century Fund Task Force Report on Working Women, 1975; author: Modern Mauritius, 1982; contbr. articles on edn. and pub. policy in The N.Y. Times, Christian Sci. Monitor, The Bulletin of Atomic Scientist, Harper's, The Atlantic Monthly and others. Commr. Pres.'s Commn. on World Hunger, Washington, 1978-80, Pres.'s Commn. on Environ. Quality, 1991-92; mem. Commn. Global Governance; trustee Carnegie Found. for Advancement Teaching, 1978-86; chair Mayor Richard Daley's Youth Devel. Task Force, 1993-95. Named one of Chgos. 100 Most Influential Women, Crain's Chgo. Bus., 2004. Fellow Am. Acad. Arts and Scis.; mem. Phi Beta Kappa. Office: Chgo Metropolis 2020 30 W Monroe St Chicago IL 60603 Home Phone: 773-404-5566; Office Phone: 312-332-8161. Business E-Mail: adele.simmons@cm2020.org.

SIMMONS, CHARLES E., state official; Sec. Dept. Corrections, Topeka, Kans. Office: Dept Corrections 900 SW Jackson St 400 Topeka KS 66612-1220

SIMMONS, EMORY G., mycologist, microbiologist, botanist, educator; b. Ind., Apr. 12, 1920; AB, Wabash Coll., 1941; AM, DePauw U., 1946; PhD in Botany, U. Mich., 1950; DSc in Microbiology (hon.), Kasetsart U., Thailand, 1988. Instr. bacteriology & botany DePauw U., Greencastle, Ind., 1946-47; asst. prof. botany Dartmouth Coll., Hanover, N.H., 1950-53; mycologist U.S. Army Natick Labs., 1953-58, head mycology lab., 1958-74; prin. investor Devel. Ctr. Cult Collection of Fungi, 1974-77; prof. botany U. Mass., Amherst, 1974-77, prof. microbiology, 1977-87, ret., 1987; rsch. assoc. Wabash Coll., Crawfordsville, Ind., 1987—. Chmn. adv. com. fungi Am. Type Cult Collection; U.S. rep. Expert Group on Fungus Taxonomy, Orgn. Econ. Coop. & Devel.; rsch. fellow Sec. Army, Thailand Indonesia, 1968-69; adj. prof. U. R.I., 1972-74; mem. exec. bd. U.S. Fedn. Cult Collections, 1974-76, pres., 1976-78; pres., chmn. bd. dirs. Second Internat. Mycology Congress Inc., 1975-78; mem. adv. com. cult collections UN Environ. Program/UNESCO/Internat. Cell Rsch. Orgn., 1977—. Mem AAAS, Mycological Soc. Am. (sec.-treas. 1963-65, v.p. 1966, pres. 1968, Disting. Mycologist award 1990), Brit. Mycological Soc., Internat. Assn. Plant Taxonomists. Achievements include research in taxonomic mycology, taxonomy of Fungi imperfecti, taxonomy and cultural characteristics of Ascomycetes. Office: 717 Thornwood Rd Crawfordsville IN 47933-2760

SIMMONS, LEE GUYTON, JR., zoological park director; b. Tucson, Feb. 20, 1938; s. Lee Guyton and Dorothy Esther (Taylor) S.; m. Marie Annette Geim, Sept. 6, 1959; children: Lee Guyton, Heather, Heidi. Student, Cen. State Coll.; DVM, Okla. State U. Resident veterinarian Columbus Zoo, Powell, Ohio, 1963-66, Henry Doorly Zoo, Omaha, 1966-70, dir., 1970—. Research cons. VA Hosp.; assoc. instr. U. Nebr. Med. Ctr., Omaha; assoc. clin. prof. Creighton U. Sch. Dentistry. Contbr. articles to profl. jours. Bd. dirs. Nebr. State Mus., Lincoln. Served with USAR. Recipient Nat. Idealism award City of Hope, 1979; named Man of Yr., Lions Club, 1978. Fellow AVMA, Am. Assn. Zool. Veterinarians (pres.), Am. Assn. Zool. Parks, Nebr. Vet. Med. Assn. (Veterinarian of Yr. 1979). Lodges: Rotary. Office: Henry Doorly Zoo Office of the Director 3701 S 10th St Omaha NE 68107-2200

SIMMONS, ROBERTA JOHNSON, public relations firm executive; b. St. Louis, June 28, 1947; d. Robert Andrew and Thelma Josephine (Bunch) J.; m. Clifford Michael Simmons, Aug. 10, 1968; children: Andrew Park, Matthew Clay, Jordan Michael. BA, Ind. U., South Bend, 1972. Lic. real estate broker, Ind.; accredited pub. rels. practitioner; mem. Inst. Residential Mktg. Account exec., supr. Juhl Advt., Inc., Mishawaka, Ind., 1971-74, pub. rels. dir., 1974-79, v.p., 1979, v.p., pub. rels. dir. Mishawaka and Indpls., 1984-89; v.p. E.L. Yoder & Assocs., Inc., Granger, Ind., 1979-80; pres. Simmons Communications, Inc., Mishawaka, 1981-82; v.p., gen. mgr. Juhl Bldg. Communications, Inc., South Bend, 1983-84; sr. v.p. Wyse Advt., Inc., Indpls., 1989-90; v.p., pub. rels. dir. Caldwell VanRiper, Inc., Indpls., 1990-94; v.p. Pub. Rels. Network, Indpls., 1995—. Contbr. articles to profl. publs. Mem. pub. rels. com. Ind. Adult Literacy Coalition, Indpls., 1989; chairperson pub. rels. com. Crossroads of Am. coun. Boy Scouts Am., Indpls., 1990-91; dep. community info. com. Indpls. C. of C. Infrastructure Study, 1990-91. Mem. PRSA (accredited, mem. counsellors acad., Hoosier chpt. job bank com. 1993—, Nat. Assembly Del., 1996—, v.p. programs, 1997), Nat. Sales Mktg. Coun. (trustee 1991-92), Inst. Residential Mktg. Elder Christian Ch. (Disciples of Christ). Avocations: travel, reading. Office: Pub Rels Network 111 Monument Cir Ste 882 Indianapolis IN 46204-5173

SIMMS, LOWELLE, synod executive; b. Sterling, Colo., June 16, 1931; s. Griffin L. and Irene O. (Geer) S.; m. Lois A. Streeter, Aug. 8, 1959. BA, Park Coll., 1953; MDiv, Union Theol. Sem., 1956. Ordained min. Presbyn. Ch., 1956. Pastor East Trenton Presbyn. Ch., Trenton, N.J., 1957-61, Calvary Presbyn. Ch., Phila., 1961-66; min. of mission First, North, Westminster Chs., Kalamazoo, Mich., 1966-69; assoc. exec. Presbytery of Sccoto Valley, Columbus, Ohio, 1969-80; administr. interims Presbytery and Synods Presbyterian Ch., 1980-83; synod exec. Synod of the Covenant, Columbus, 1993. Avocation: photography.

SIMON, ARTHUR JOSEPH, lawyer; b. Berwyn, Ill., June 4, 1954; s. Frank and Bessie (Bauer) S.; m. Donna Casey, July 30, 1977; children: James Casey, John Arthur, Jane Mayer. BS, Vanderbilt U., 1975; JD, Northwestern U., 1979. Bar: U.S. Dist. Ct. (no. dist.) Ill. 1979. Assoc., then ptnr. Gardner, Carton & Douglas, Chgo.; ptnr. Sonnenschein, Nath & Rosenthal, Chgo.; gen. counsel William Blair & Co., Chgo. Mem. ABA, Union League (Chgo.). Avocations: sports, woodworking. Office: William Blair & Co LLC 222 W Adams St Chicago IL 60606 Office Phone: 312-236-1600.

SIMON, BARRY PHILIP, lawyer, retired air transportation executive; b. Paterson, NJ, Nov. 22, 1942; s. Alfred Louis and Rhoda (Tapper) S.; m. Hinda Bookstaber, Feb. 9, 1964; children: Alan, John, Eric. BA, Princeton U., NJ, 1964; LLB, Yale U., New Haven, 1967. Bar: NY 1965, Tex. 1986. Assoc. atty. Hughes, Hubbard & Reed, NYC, 1967-69, Sullivan & Cromwell, NYC, 1969-72, Shea & Gould, NYC, 1972-73; v.p., gen. counsel Teleprompter Corp., NYC, 1973-82; v.p., sec., gen. counsel Continental Airlines, LA and Houston, 1982-86, v.p. in-charge internat. divsn. Houston, 1987-90, sr. v.p. legal affairs, gen. counsel, sec., 1990-92, sr. v.p. internat. ops. Houston, 1996—2004; sr. v.p. Tex. Air Corp., 1986-87; sr. v.p. legal affairs, gen. counsel, sec. Ea. Airlines, Miami, Fla., 1987-90; exec. v.p., gen. counsel GAF Corp., Wayne, NJ, 1993-95, N.W. Airlines Corp., Eagan, Minn., 2004—06. Bd. dirs. Amadeus Reservations Sys., at. Energy and Gas Transmission. Mem. copyright com. Nat. Cable TV Assn., Washington, 1974-76, mem. utilities com., 1973-82; bd. dirs. Houston Grand Opera, Inprint, Alley Theatre. Recipient Class of 1888 Lit. prize Princeton U., 1961

SIMON, BERNECE KERN, retired social worker; b. Denver, Nov. 27, 1914; d. Maurice Meyer and Jennie (Bloch) Kern; m. Marvin L. Simon, Feb. 26, 1939 (dec.); 1 child, Anne Elizabeth. BA, U. Chgo., 1936, MA, 1942. Social worker Jewish Children's Bur. Chgo., 1938-40, U. Chgo. Hosps. and Clinics, 1940-44; mem. faculty U. Chgo., 1944-81, instr., 1944-48, asst. prof., 1948-60, prof. social casework, 1960—81, prof. emeritus, 1981—, Samuel Deutsch prof. Sch. Social Service Adminstrn., 1960—. Mem. bd. editors 17th Edit. Ency. Social Work, 1975—77, Social Svc. Rev., 1975—99, Social Work, 1978—82; book rev. editor: Social Work, 1982—87, cons. editor: Jour. Social Work Edn.; contbr. articles to profl. jours., chapters to books. Mem.: NASW, Nat. Acads. Practice Social Work, Acad. Cert. Social Workers, Coun. Social Work Edn. (mem. nat. bd. dirs., sec. 1972—74).

SIMON, EVELYN, lawyer; b. NYC, May 13, 1943; d. Joseph and Adele (Holzschlag) Berkman; m. Fredrick Simon, Aug. 18, 1963; children: Amy Jocelyn, Marcie Ann. AB in Physics, Barnard Coll., 1963; MS in Physics, U. Pitts., 1964; JD, Wayne State U., 1978; LLB, Monash U., Melbourne, Australia, 1980. Bar: Mich. 1980, Victoria (Australia) 1981. Supr. engring. Chrysler Corp., Detroit, 1964-72; edn. and profl. mgr. Engring. Soc. Detroit, 1972-78; solicitor Arthur Robinson & Co., Melbourne, 1980-81; sr. atty. Ford Motor Co., Detroit, 1981-89; assoc. gen. counsel Sheller-Globe Corp., Detroit, 1989-90; v.p. planning, gen. counsel United Techs. Automotive Inc., Dearborn, Mich., 1991-94, v.p. bus. devel. and legal affairs, 1995-96, v.p. Asian bus. devel., 1997-98; pvt. practice, 1999—. Cons. internat. bus. devel., 1998—. Mem.: Mich. Bar Assn. Office: 1787 Alexander Dr Bloomfield Hills MI 48302-1204 Home Phone: 248-855-5664; Office Phone: 248-539-0969. E-mail: evelynsimon@prodigy.net.

SIMON, GEORGE T., lawyer; BA, Trinity Coll., 1969; JD, Harvard U. Law Sch., 1972. Bar: N.Y. 1973, Ill. 1982. Staff atty. SEC, Washington, 1976—81; ptnr. Foley & Lardner LLP, Chgo., 1991—, mem. mgmt. com. Mem.: SEC Hist. Soc. (chmn., market regulation com.), Trinity Coll. (bd. fellows 1998—2002), Securities Industry Assn., ABA, Northwestern U. Law Sch. Garrett Inst. (exec. com.). Office: Foley & Lardner LLP 321 N Clark St Ste 2800 Chicago IL 60610-4764 Office Phone: 312-832-4554. Business E-Mail: gsimon@foley.com.

SIMON, HERBERT, real estate developer, professional sports team owner; b. Bklyn., Oct. 23, 1934; s. Max and Mae Simon; m. Bui Simon; children: Jennifer, Stephen, Sarah, Rachel, Asher, Sean. Grad., CCNY. With Albert Frankel Co., Indpls., 1959; co-founder Melvin Simon and Assocs., Inc., Indpls., 1959—; co-owner NBA Ind. Pacers, Indpls., 1983—, chmn., CEO, 2008—; went pub. and became Simon Property Group, 1993; CEO Simon Property Group, Inc., 1993—95; merged with DeBartolo Realty Corp. and became Simon DeBartolo Group, 1996; name changed back to Simon Property Group, 1998; co-chmn. bd. Simon Property Group, Inc., 1995—. Named one of Forbes' Richest Ams., 2006. Office: Ind Pacers 125 S Pennsylvania St Indianapolis IN 46204 also: Simon Property Group Inc 225 W Washington St Indianapolis IN 46204*

SIMON, JANOS, computer science educator; b. Budapest, Hungary, June 11, 1946; came to U.S., 1976; s. Sandor and Ilona (Neufeld) S.; married; children: Sandor, Kyle, Trevor. BS in Physics, U. São Paulo, Brazil, 1968, diploma in engring., 1969; PhD, Cornell U., 1975. Instr. State U. São Paulo, 1969-75; asst. prof. U. at Campinas, Brazil, 1975-76, assoc. prof. computer sci. dept., 1976-79, head dept., 1975-79; asst. prof. computer sci. dept. Pa. State U., State College, 1979-83, assoc. prof., 1983-85, prof., 1985, U. Chgo., 1985—. Editor-in-chief Chgo. Jour. Theoretical Computer Sci.; mem. editl. bd. SIAM Jour. Computing, CALCOLO; contbr. articles to profl. jours. Recipient Jabuti prize Brazilian Pubs. Assn. Mem. Assn. for Computing Machinery, IEEE (com. on theory of computing).

SIMON, JOHN BERN, lawyer; b. Cleve., Aug. 8, 1942; s. Seymour Frank and Roslyn (Schultz) S.; children: Lindsey Helaine, Douglas Banning. BS, U. Wis., 1964; JD, DePaul U., 1967. Bar: Ill. 1967. Asst. U.S. atty. U.S. Justice Dept., Chgo., 1967-70, dep. chief civil div., 1970-71, chief civil div., 1971-74; spl. counsel to dir. Ill. Dept. Pub. Aid, Chgo., 1974-75; legal cons. to Commn. on Rev. of Nat. Policy Toward Gambling, Chgo., 1975-76; ptnr. firm Friedman & Koven, 1975-85, mem. exec. com., 1983-85; ptnr. firm Jenner & Block, 1986—. Spl. cons. to adminstr. DEA Dept. Justice, 1976-77; counsel to Gov.'s Revenue Study Commn. on Legalized Gambling, 1977-78; spl. counsel Ill. Racing Bd., 1979-80; lectr. tng. seminars and confs.; instr. U.S. Atty. Gen.'s Advocacy Inst., Washington, 1974; lectr. Nat. Conf. Organized Crime, Washington, 1975, Dade County Inst. Organized Crime, Ft. Lauderdale, Fla., 1976; faculty Cornell Inst. Organized Crime, Ithaca, N.Y., 1976, judge Miner Moot Ct. competition Northwestern U., 1971-73; mem. law coun. DePaul U., 1974-83, mem. alumni assn., 1984-85, chmn., 1975-79; adj. prof. DePaul U. Coll. Law, 1977, 81; faculty Practising Law Inst., Chgo., 1984. Contbr. articles to profl. jours. Bd. dirs. Lawyer's Trust Fund of Ill., 1998-2004, treas., 2000-01, v.p., 2002-03, pres., 2003-04, Cmty. Film Workshop of Chgo., 1977-90, Friends of Glencoe Parks, 1977-78, sec., 1978-79; mem. nominating com. Glencoe Sch. Bd., 1978-81, chmn. rules com., 1980-81; pres. Glencoe Hist. Soc., 1979-82; mem. Glencoe Zoning Bd. Appeals, Zoning Commn., Sign Bd. Appeals, 1981-86, chmn., 1984-86; mem. Ill. Inaugural Com., 1979, 83, 87, 95; bd. dirs., mem. exec. com. Chgo. World's Fair 1992 Authority, 1983-85; mem. Chancery divsn. task force Spl. Commn. on Adminstrn. of Justice in Cook County, 1985-87; trustee De Paul U., 1990, chair phys. plant and property com., 1992-94, vice chair, 1995-2004, chair, 2004—; commr. Ill. Racing Bd., 1990—2006; gen. trustee Lincoln Acad. Ill., 1993—, regent, 1999—, chancellor, 2001—; mem. Ill. Supreme Ct. Planning and Oversight Com. for Jud. Performance Evaluation Program, 1997-98, 2000-05, Ill. Supreme Ct. Rules Com., 2004—. Recipient Bancroft-Whitney Am. Jurisprudence award, 1965, 66, Judge Learned Hand Human Rels. award Am. Jewish Com., 1994, award for outstanding svc. to legal profession DePaul U. Coll. Law, 1996, Am. ORT Jurisprudence award, 1999. Mem. ABA (com. on liaison with the judiciary 1983-95), Fed. Bar Assn., Chgo. Bar Assn. (fed. civil procedure com. 1979-85, chmn. 1985-86, bd. mgrs. 1987-89, chmn. house com. 1989-90, treas. 1990-91, 2d v.p. 1991-92, 1st v.p. 1992-93, pres. 1993-94), Ill. State Bar Assn., Women's Bar Assn., Ill. Police Assn., Ill. Sheriffs Assn., U.S. Treasury Agts. Assn., Chgo. Bar Assn., DePaul U. Alumni Assn. (pres. 1985-87, chmn. spl. gifts com. campaign, chmn. Simon Commn. 1989-91, nat. chair for ann. giving 1991-94), Std. Club. Office: Jenner & Block One IBM Plz 42nd Fl Chicago IL 60611

SIMON, LOU ANNA KIMSEY, academic administrator; BA in Math., Ind. State U., 1969, MS in Student Personnel and Counseling, 1970; PhD in Higher Edn., Mich. State U., 1974. Faculty mem. Mich. State U., asst. dir. Office Instl. Rsch., 1974—78, asst. provost gen. academic adminstrn., 1981—87, assoc. provost, 1987—92, v.p. acad. affairs, 1993—2004, interim pres., 2003, pres., 2005—. Office: Mich State U 450 Administration Bldg East Lansing MI 48824-1046 Office Phone: 517-355-6560. Business E-Mail: presmail@msu.edu.

SIMON, MELVIN, real estate developer, professional sports team owner; b. Oct. 21, 1926; s. Max and Mae Simon; m. Bren Burns, Sept. 14, 1972; children: Deborah, Cynthia, Tamme, David, Max. BS in Acctg., CCNY, 1949, MBA in Real Estate, 1983; PhD (hon.), Butler U., 1986, Ind. U., 1991. Leasing agt. Albert Frankel Co., Indpls., 1955-60; co-founder Melvin Simon & Assocs., Indpls., 1959—, pres., 1960-73, co-chmn. bd., 1973; co-owner NBA Ind. Pacers, Indpls., 1983—; went pub. becoming Simon Property Group, 1993; chmn. bd. Simon Property Group, Inc., Indpls., 1993—95, co-chmn. bd. dirs., 1995—; merged with DeBartolo Realty Corp. to become Simon DeBartolo Group, 1996; reverted to Simon Property Group, 1998. Adv. bd. Wharton's Real Estate, Phila., 1986—. Prodr.: (films) Porky's. Adv. bd. dean's coun. Ind. U., Bloomington; bd. dirs. United Cerebral Palsy, Indpls., Muscular Dystrophy Assn., Indpls., Jewish Welfare Found., Indpls.; trustee Urban Land Inst., Internat. Coun. Shopping Ctrs. Served in US Army. Recipient Horatio Alger award Boy's Club Indpls., 1986; named Man of Yr., Jewish Welfare Found., 1980; named one of Forbes' Richest Ams., 1999—, World's Richest People, 2005—. Democrat. Jewish. Office: Simon Property Group Inc 225 W Washington St Indianapolis IN 46204 also: Indiana Pacers 125 S Pennsylvania St Indianapolis IN 46204

SIMON, PAUL H., newspaper editor; Bur. chief AP, Omaha, 1978—. Office: 909 N 96th St Ste 104 Omaha NE 68114-2508

SIMONS, DOLPH COLLINS, JR., publishing executive, editor; b. Lawrence, Kans., Mar. 11, 1930; s. Dolph Collins and Marie (Nelson) S.; m. Pamela Counseller, Feb. 7, 1952; children: Pamela, Linda, Dolph Collins, Dan. AB, U. Kans., 1951; LLD (hon.), Colby Coll., 1972. Reporter Lawrence Jour.-World, 1953, asso. pub., 1957, pub., 1962—2004, editor, 1978—, pres., 1969—2004; reporter The Times, London, 1956, Johannesburg (South Africa) Star, 1958; chmn. World Co. Mem. Pulitzer Awards Jury, 1977, 78, 80, 81. Trustee, past pres. William Allen White Found.; trustee Midwest Rsch. Inst.; former trustee Menninger Found., Nat. Parks Conservation Assn.; former mem. governing bd. Children's Mercy Hosp., Kansas City, Mo.; former trustee, former chmn. U. Kans. Endowment Assn.; past bd. dirs. Greater Kansas City Cmty. Found., Commerce Bancshares, Kansas City, Mo.; former trustee The Freedom Forum, Kans. Nature Conservancy; former mem. Kans. Biosci. Authority Bd. Served to capt. USMRC, 1951—53. Recipient Elijah Parish Lovejoy award, 1972; Fred Ellsworth award for significant service to U. Kans., 1976; Disting. Service citation, 1980 Mem. Newspaper Advt. Bur. (past dir.), Am. Soc. Newspaper Editors, Inland Daily Press Assn. (past dir.), Kans. Press Assn. (past pres., dir.), AP (past dir.), Am. Newspaper Pubs. Assn. (past dir., past nat. sec.), Lawrence C. of C. (past pres., dir.), U. Kans. Alumni Assn. (past pres., dir.), Lawrence Country Club, Kansas City Country Club, Kansas City River Club, Masons, Rotary, Sigma Delta Chi, Phi Delta Theta. Republican. Episcopalian. Home: 2425 Vermont St Lawrence KS 66046-4761 Office: 609 New Hampshire St Lawrence KS 66044-2243 Personal E-mail: dsimonsjr@ljworld.com.

SIMONS, GALE GENE, nuclear and electrical engineer, educator; b. Kingman, Kans., Sept. 25, 1939; s. Robert Earl and Laura V. (Swartz) S.; m. Barbara Irene Rinkel, July 2, 1966; 1 child, Curtis Dean. BS, Kans. State U., 1962, MS, 1964, PhD, 1968. Engr. Argonne Nat. Lab., Idaho Falls, Idaho, 1968-77, mgr. fast source reactor, head exptl. support group, 1972-77; prof. nuc. engring. Kans. State U., Manhattan, 1977—2001, assoc. dean for rsch., dir. rsch. coun. Coll. Engring., 1983-97, emeritus prof., 2001—, bd. dirs. Rsch. Found., 1988-97, Presdl. lectr., 1983-96, career counselor, 1984-96. Bd. dirs. Kans. Tech. Enterprise Corp., Topeka; com. mem. Kans. Gov.'s Energy Policy Com., Topeka, 1992-97; presenter, cons. in field Contbr. over 100 articles to sci. jours.; patentee radiation dosimeter. Expert witness State of Kans., Topeka, 1986. Fellow AEC, 1964-67; recipient numerous rsch. grants Mem. AAAS, IEEE, Am. uclear Soc., Health Physics Soc., Am. Soc. for Engring. Edn., Masons, Rotary, Phi Kappa Phi, Tau Beta Pi, Pi Mu Epsilon. Home: 2395 Grandview Ter Manhattan KS 66502-3729

SIMONSON, BRUCE MILLER, geologist, educator; b. Washington, May 13, 1950; s. Roy Walter and Susan (Miller) S.; m. Sue Mareske, June 28, 1974; children: Joseph Walter, Sonja Anne, Maya Beth. BA with high honors, Wesleyan U., Middletown, Conn., 1972; PhD, Johns Hopkins U., 1982. Field mapper Nat. Geog. Inst., Honduras, 1973-74; instr. dept. geology Oberlin Coll., 1979—81, asst. prof., 1982—85, assoc. prof., 1986—88, prof., 1989—, Biggs prof. natural scis., 2001—06, chmn. dept. geology, 1986—89, 1993—97, 2000—05. Adj. faculty Case Western Res. U., Cleve., 1983—2000; vis. scientist Geol. Survey Western Australia, summers, 1985—87, 1989, 93; tchr. U.S. Geol. Survey, Reston, Va., 1985, vis. prof., Denver, 1992—93. Contbr. articles to profl. jours. Recipient Bradley award Geol. Soc. Washington, 2000; grantee Nat. Geog. Soc., 1986-89, 93-94, 96-97, 99-2000, NSF, 1977-79, 84, 91-94, Rsch. Corp., 1983, Petroleum Rsch. Fund, 1982-84. Fellow: Geol. Soc. Am.; mem.: Meteoritical Soc., SEPM (Gt. Lakes sect. 1986—90), No. Ohio Geol. Soc., Geol. Soc. Australia, Sigma Xi. Office: Oberlin Coll Dept Geology Oberlin OH 44074-1052 Office Phone: 440-775-8347. Business E-Mail: bsimonso@oberlin.edu.

SIMOVIC, LASZLO, architect; b. O Becej, Yugoslavia, May 11, 1957; s. Mihaly and Eva (Daku) S. BArch, Ill. Inst. Tech., 1982; postgrad., Mass. Inst. Tech., 1984. Architect Marton Sass & Assoc., Chgo., 1974-82, Imre & Anthony Halasz Inc., Boston, 1984-85, Skidmore, Owings & Merrill, NYC, 1985-86, Chgo., 1986-87, Loebl, Schlossman & Hackl, Chgo., 1987-89; pvt. practice Chgo., 1989—. Home: 6512 N Artesian Ave Chicago IL 60645-5328 Office Phone: 773-338-2225. Office Fax: 773-338-2226. Personal E-mail: LaszloArch@aol.com.

SIMPKIN, LAWRENCE JAMES, engineering company executive; b. Sault Ste Marie, Mich., Jan. 1, 1933; s. Fred Bernard and Helen Clara (Goetz) S.; m. Agnes Diane L'Huillier, Sept. 3, 1960; children: Lawrence J., Lynn Marie, Dawn Catherine. BS in Elec. Engring, Mich. Technol. Inst., 1954; MS, Wayne State U., 1965. Registered profl. engr., Mich. Engr. Detroit Edison Co., 1957-67, supr. engring. instrumentation, 1967-69, dir. elec. div., 1969-72, dir. engring. research, 1972-75, dir. tech. systems planning, 1975-76, gen. dir. div. services, 1976-82, dir. outage mgmt., 1982-84, dir. nuclear engring., 1985-87, gen. dir. generation engring., 1987-95, engring. cons., 1995—; pres. Sunrise Solutions Inc., 1996—. Lectr. Lawrence Inst. Tech., 1965-72; adj. prof. U. Mich., 1974 Contbr. articles to profl. jours. Served to capt. USAF, 1954-57. Mem. IEEE, Engring. Soc. Detroit, Sigma Xi. Home: 4615 S US 23 Greenbush MI 48738 also: 4615 Us Highway 23 Greenbush MI 48738-9753

SIMPSON, A.W. BRIAN, law educator; b. 1931; Degree (hon.), Dalhousie Law Sch., Can., 2003, U. Kent at Canterbury, Eng., 2003. Fellow Oxford U., Eng., 1955-72; prof. U. Kent, Canterbury, Eng., 1972-84, U. Chgo., 1984-87, U. Mich. Law Sch., Ann Arbor, 1987—, Charles F. and Edith J. Clyne Prof. of Law. Lectr. Centre for Human Rights, London Sch. Econs., 2003. Author: Human Rights and the End of Empire: Britain and the Genesis of the European Convention, History of the Common Law of Contract, Biographical Dictionary of the Common Law, Cannibalism and the Common Law, A History of the Land, Law, Legal Theory and Legal History, In the Highest Degree Odious: Detention Without Trial in Wartime Britain, Leading Cases in the Common Law; contbr. articles to law jours. Named Hon. Queen's Coun., 2001. Fellow: Am. Acad. Arts and Scis.,

Lincoln Coll., Oxford (hon.); mem.: British Acad. Office: U Mich Law Sch 409 Hutchins Hall 625 S State St Ann Arbor MI 48109-1215 Office Phone: 734-763-0413. Business E-Mail: bsimpson@umich.edu.

SIMPSON, JACK BENJAMIN, medical technologist, business executive; b. Tompkinsville, Ky., Oct. 30, 1937; s. Benjamin Harrison and Verda Mae (Woods) S.; m. Winona Clara Walden, Mar. 21, 1957; children: Janet Lazann, Richard Benjamin, Randall Walden, Angela Elizabeth. Student, Western Ky. U., 1954-57; grad., Norton Infirmary Sch. Med. Tech., 1958. Asst. chief med. technologist Jackson County Hosp., Seymour, Ind., 1958-61; chief med. technologist, bus. mgr. Mershon Med. Labs., Indpls., 1962-66; founder, dir., officer Am. Monitor Corp., Indpls., 1966-77; founder, pres., dir. Global Data, Inc., Ft. Lauderdale, Fla., 1986—. Mng. ptnr. Astroland Enterprises, Indpls., 1968—, 106th St. Assocs., Indpls., 1969-72, Keystones Ltd., Indpls., 1970-82, Delray Rd. Assoc. Ltd., Indpls., 1970-71, Allisonville Assocs. Ltd., Indpls., 1970-82, Grandview Assocs. Ltd., 1977—, Rucker Assocs. Ltd., Indpls., 1974—; mng. ptnr. Raintree Assocs. Ltd., Indpls., 1978—, Westgate Assocs. Ltd., Indpls., 1978—; pres., dir. Topps Constrn. Co., Inc., Bradenton, Fla., 1973-91, Acrovest Corp., Asheville, N.C., 1980—; dir. Indpls. Broadcasting, Inc.; founder, bd. dirs. Bank of Bradenton, 1986-92; founder, CFO Biomass Processing Tech., Inc., West Palm Beach, Fla., 1996—; also bd. dirs. Mem. Am. Soc. Med. Technologists (cert.), Indpls. Soc. Med. Technologists, Fla. Soc. Med. Technologists, Am. Soc. Clin. Pathologists, Am. Assn. Clin. Chemistry, Royal Soc. Health (London), Internat. Platform Assn., Am. Mus. Natural History, Columbia of Indpls. Club, Harbor Beach Surf Club, Fishing of Am. Club, Marina Bay Club (Ft. Lauderdale), Elks. Republican. E-mail: jack_simpson@msn.com.

SIMPSON, JOHN W., lawyer; b. Wichita, Kans., 1960; BA with highest distinction, U. Kans., 1982, JD, 1985. Bar: Mo. 1985, US Dist. Ct., We. Dist. of Mo., US Ct. of Appeals, Tenth Cir. 1986, US Tax Ct. 1989, US Dist. Ct., Dist. of Kans. Ptnr., chmn Tax Practice Group Shook, Hardy & Bacon LLP, Kansas City, Mo. Mem. bd. dirs. Higher M-Pact. Mem.: Kansas City Met. Bar Assn., Phi Kappa Phi, Phi Beta Kappa. Office: Shook, Hardy & Bacon LLP 2555 Grand Blvd Kansas City MO 64108 Office Phone: 816-559-2453. Office Fax: 816-421-5547. E-mail: jsimpson@shb.com.

SIMPSON, MICHAEL, retired metals service center executive; b. Albany, NY, Dec. 10, 1938; s. John McLaren Simpson and Constance (Hasler) Ames; m. Barbara Ann Bodtke, Jan. 5, 1963; children: Leslie Ann, Elizabeth S. Wessel. BA, U. Mich., 1965, MBA, 1966. Product mgr. Armour & Co., Chgo., 1966-68; with A.M. Castle & Co., Franklin Park, Ill., 1968—, pres. Hy-Alloy Steels Co. divsn., 1974-79, v.p. Midwestern region, 1977-79, chmn. bd., 1979—2004, also bd. dirs.; chmn. emeritus, 2004—. Trustee Rush U. Med. Ctr., Chgo., 1978—, mem. exec. com., 1980—, vice chmn., 1991—; trustee Oldfields Sch., Glencoe, Md., 1982-87, 95-2003, chmn. bd., 1998-2000; bd. dirs. Lake Forest Hosp. Found. and Lake Forest Hosp., Ill., 1998-2008; chmn. bd. overseers Rush U., Chgo., 1996-. Office: AM Castle & Co 3400 N Wolf Rd Franklin Park IL 60131-1319 Office Phone: 847-349-2500.

SIMPSON, VI, state senator; b. LA, Mar. 18, 1946; d. Lloyd M. and Helen (Chacon) Sentman; m. William D. McCarty; children: Jason, Kristina. Student, Ind. U., Indpls. Asst. to chmn. Com. on Status of Women, Calif., 1974-75; dir. pub. affairs Calif. Parks and Recreation Soc., Sacramento, 1975-77; county auditor Monroe County, Ind., 1980-84; mem. Ind. Senate, Indpls., 1984—; exec. dir. Heritage Edn. Found., Indpls., 1989—. Editor Equal Rights Monitor mag., 1974-76; syndicated newspaper columnist Know You Rights, 1975-76. Named Fresman Dem. Senator of Yr., Ind. Broadcasters Assn., 1985, Legislator of Yr., Ind. State Employees Assn., 1985, various legis. awards Sierra Club, Ind. Wildlife Fedn., Isaac Walton League, Ind. Parks and Recreation Assn. Mem. NAACP, AAUW. Methodist. Office: Heritage Edn Found 7821 W Morris St Indianapolis IN 46231-1364 also: Ind Senate Dist 40 200 W Washington St Indianapolis IN 46204-2728

SIMPSON, VINSON RALEIGH, manufacturing executive, director; b. Chgo., Aug. 9, 1928; s. Vinson Raleigh and Elsie (Passeger) S.; m. Elizabeth Caroline Matte, Sept. 9, 1950; children: Kathleen Simpson Zier, Nancy Simpson Ignacio, James Morgan. SB in Chem. Engring, MIT, 1950; MBA, Ind. U., 1955. With Trane Co., LaCrosse, Wis., 1950-75, mgr. mktg. services, 1957-64, mgr. dealer devel., 1964-66; mng. dir. Trane Ltd., Edinburgh, Scotland, 1966-67; v.p. internat. Trane Co., LaCrosse, Wis., 1967-68, exec. v.p., 1968-70; exec. v.p., gen. mgr. comml. air conditioning div., 1970-73; pres., dir., 1973-75, Simpson and Co., La Crosse, 1975-76; pres., chief operating officer, dir. Marathon Electric Mfg. Corp., Wausau, Wis., 1976-80; chmn., pres., chief exec. officer Marion Body Works, Inc., Wis., 1980-93, chmn., 1993—. Bd. dirs. Clintonville Area Found. Past trustee, treas. Fox Valley Tech. Coll.; bd. dirs., past pres. Fox Valley Tech. Coll. Found.; past pres., bd. dir. Wausau Area Jr. Achievement; mem. Marion Minutemen; past 20 yr. trustee, chair endowment com., trustee emeritus orthland Coll.; past dir. Wis. Mfrs. and Commerce; mem. investments com. Comty. Found. for Fox Valley Region, Inc. Decorated Korean War Commendation ribbon. Mem. Am. Legion, Kappa Kappa Sigma, Alpha Tau Omega, Beta Gamma Sigma (dirs. table). Lodges: Masons, Shriners, Rotary (past. pres. Marion club, Paul Harris fellow). Congregationalist. Avocations: running, snorkeling, cross country skiing, playing the trombone. Home: 171 Fairway Dr Clintonville WI 54929-1071

SIMPSON, WILLIAM ARTHUR, insurance company executive; b. Oakland, Calif., Feb. 2, 1939; s. Arthur Earl and Pauline (Mikalasic) S.; m. Nancy Dougery Simpson, Mar. 31, 1962; children: Sharon Elizabeth, Shelley Pauline BS, U. Calif.-Berkeley, 1961; postgrad. Exec. Mgmt. Program, Columbia U. CLU. V.p. mktg. Countrywide Life, LA, 1973-76; v.p. agy. Occidental Life of Calif., LA, 1976-79; pres., CEO Vol. State Life, Chattanooga, 1979-83; exec. v.p. Transam. Occidental Life Ins. Co., LA, 1983-86, pres., 1986-88, pres., CEO, COO, 1988-90, also bd. dirs.; dir. USLIFE Corp., NYC, 1990—; pres., CEO All Am. Life Ins. Co., Pasadena, Calif., 1990-94, USLIFE Life Ins. div. USLIFE Corp., 1994, USLIFE Corp., 1995-97. Chmn. Franklin Life Ins. Co. Pres. Chattanooga coun. Boy Scouts Am., 1982, bd. dirs., LA, 1983, v.p., 1983-85, vice-chmn LA area, 1989, chmn., 1989; pres. bd. councillors LA County Am. Cancer Soc.; trustee Verdugo Hills Hosp. Found., Ill. Symphony Orch.; bd. dirs. Abraham Lincoln coun. Boy Scouts Am., Meml. Medical Ctr., Springfield, Ill. 1st lt. US Army, 1961—64. Mem. Am. Soc. CLUs, Life Ins. Mktg. and Rsch. Assn. (bd. dirs. 1986-89), Ctl. Ill. Ins. Co. (bd. dirs.), Rotary. Republican. Presbyterian. Avocations: golf, skiing. Office: Franklin Life Ins Co 1 Franklin Sq Springfield IL 62713-0002 E-mail: neswas@aol.com.

SIMPSON, WILLIAM MARSHALL, academic administrator; b. Chgo., Aug. 26, 1943; s. Marshall Wayne and Edith Berniece (Smith) S.; m. Joyce Ann Heald, Dec. 23, 1966; children: Katherine, Diane. BA, Monmouth Coll., 1965; MA, Ill. State U., 1968, EdD, 1979. Faculty mem. Carl Sandburg Coll., Galesburg, Ill., 1968-79; dir. community svc. Black Hawk Coll., Kewanee, Ill., 1979-82; dir. continuing edn. Olympic Coll., Bremerton, Wash., 1982-85, dir. bus. and engring., 1985-86, assoc. dean instrn., 1986-90; dean of the coll. Marshalltown (Iowa) C.C., 1990-97; v.p. acad. affairs Iowa Valley C.C. Dist., 1992-97; pres. John Wood C.C., Quincy, Ill., 1997—. Pres. Adult Edn. Dirs. of Wash., 1984-85; dir. Nat. Coun. Instrnl. Adminstrs., 1986-88; cons. evaluator North Cen. Assn. Colls. and Schs., 1992—; mem. adv. coun. Iowa Youth Apprenticeship, 1993-95. Contbr. articles to profl. jours. Elder First Presbyn. Ch., Galesburg, 1976-79, pres. trustees, 1980-82; elder Cen. Kisap Presbyn. Ch., Bremerton, 1983-86, Marshalltown First Presbyn. Ch., 1993-96; campaign cabinet mem. Marshalltown United Way, 1990, 92, bd. dirs., 1991-97, allocation chair, 1992-93, v.p., 1994-95, pres. 1995-96; mem. adv. com. dept. ednl. adminstrn., Ill. State U., 1991-94; mem. Gov.'s adv. bd. on Literacy, 2000-02; bd. dirs. Quincy YMCA, 2001-05; profl. divsn. leader campaign United Way, 2003, bd. dirs., 2004—, v.p. allocations, 2006; bd. trustees Monmouth Coll. Alumni, 2006—. Named one of Outstanding Young Men in Am., 1971, Regional Person of Yr. Nat. Coun. on Community Svcs. and Continuing Edn., 1985; NEH grantee, 1975; League for Innovation in the C.C. Exec. Leadership Inst., Class of 1993, Iowa Assn. for Bus. and Industry Leadership Iowa Class of 1994-95; named to Ill. State. U. Coll. Edn. Hall of Fame. Mem.: Nat. Jr. Coll. Athletic Assn. (presdl. rep. 2001—07, Svc. award 2007), Quincy Rotary Club (pres. 2002—03), Blue Key, Sigma Phi Epsilon, Phi Delta Kappa, Phi Theta Kappa (Shirley B. Gordon Distinction award 2006), Pi Gamma Mu. Office: 1301 S 48th St Quincy IL 62305-8736 E-mail: simpson@jwcc.edu.

SIMS, BETTY, state legislator; b. St. Louis, Mo., Dec. 15, 1935; Mem. Mo. Senate from 24th dist., Jefferson City, 1994—. Active United Way, Girl Scout Coun., Jr. League Girls, Inc., 1972—. Office: Mo State Mems Rm 226 State Capitol Bldg Jefferson City MO 65101

SIMS, HOWARD F., architectural firm executive; BA in Architecture, MA in Architecture, U. Mich.; Doctorate of Public Service (hon.), Eastern Mich. U. Chmn., CEO Sims Design Group, 1964—. Architectural projects include Museum of African Am. History, various projects at Detroit Metropolitan Airport, Stroh River Place, Cleveland Hopkins Internat. Airport, George Bush Intercontinental Airport Houston, Willow Run Airport. Trustee Community Found. for Southeastern Mich., W. K. Kellogg Found.

SIMS-CURRY, KRISTY, women's college basketball coach; b. Olla, La., 1967; m. Kelly Curry, 2 dau. BS in Health and Phys. Edn., N.E. La. U., 1988; MS in Kinesiology, Stephen F. Austin U., Nacogdoches, Tex., 1992. Coach Weston H.S., Mansfield H.S., La.; women's asst. basketball coach Tulane U., 1991-93, Stephen F. Austin U., 1993-94, Tex. A&M U., 1994-96; asst. coach La. Tech. U., 1996-99; head coach Purdue U., West Lafayette, 1999—. Office: care Women's Basketball 1790 Mackey Arena Rm 44 West Lafayette IN 47907-1790

SINCLAIR, VIRGIL LEE, JR., judge, writer; b. Canton, Ohio, Nov. 10, 1951; s. Virgil Lee and Thelma Irene S.; children: Kelly, Shannon; m. Janet Brahler Sinclair. BA, Kent State U., 1973; JD, U. Akron, 1976; postgrad., Case Western Res. U., 1939. Adminstr. Stark County Prosecutor's Office, Canton, 1974-76; mem. faculty Walsh Coll., Canton, 1976-78; asst. pros. atty. Stark County, Canton, 1976-77; ptnr. Amerman Burt Jones Co. LPA, Canton, 1976-91, Buckingham, Doolittle and Burroughs Co., L.P.A., Canton, 1991-95; judge Stark County Common Pleas Ct., 1995—, adminstrv. judge, 1996, presiding judge, 1999. Mem. faculty Ohio Jud. Coll., 1991—, lead faculty, 1998—; mem. legal adviser Mayor's Office, City of North Canton, Ohio, 1978-79; referee Stark County Family Ct., Canton, 1981, Canton Mcpl. Ct., 1991—; spl. referee Canton Mcpl. Ct., 1985-86. Author: Law Enforcement Officers' Guide to Juvenile Law, 1975, Lawy Manual of Juvenile Law, 1976, Handling Capital Punishment Cases, 1998, Ohio Jury Institutions, Capital Punishment Approved, Jury Instructions, 2000; editor: U. Akron Law Rev.; contbr. to Ohio Family Law, 1983, also articles to profl. jours. Mem. North Canton Planning Comm., 1979-82; bd. mgrs. North Canton YMCA, 1976—, Camp Tippecanoe, Ohio, 1981—; profl. adviser Parents Without Partners, 1980—; spl. sep. Stark County Sheriff Dept., 1983—; trustee Palace Theatre Assn., Canton, 1983—. Recipient Disting. Service award U.S. Jaycees, 1984; named to Hall of Distinction, Plain Local Schs., 1999, Jud. Hall of Fame, U. Akron Sch. Law, 2000. Mem. ABA, Ohio Bar Assn., Stark County Bar Assn. (lects. 1984), Ohio Trial Lawyers Assn., Assn. Trial Lawyers Am., Nat. Dist. Attys. Assn., Akron Law Sch. Alumni Assn. (trustee), Jaycees, Elks, Eagles, Masons, Delta Theta Phi (bailiff 1976, nat. key winner 1975-76). Republican. Methodist. Office Phone: 330-451-7789.

SINCOFF, MICHAEL Z., human resources and marketing executive, educator; b. Washington, June 28, 1943; s. Murray P. and Anna F. (Jaffe) S. m. Kathleen M. Dunham, Oct. 9, 1983. BA, U. Md., 1964, MA, 1966; PhD, Purdue U., 1969. Instr. U. Tenn., Knoxville, 1968; asst. prof. Ohio U., Athens, 1969-74, dir. Ctr. for Comm. Studies, 1969-76, assoc. prof., 1974-76; vis. prof. U. Minn., St. Paul, 1974; dir. personnel devel. Celanese Corp., NYC, 1976-79; dir. employee comm. The Mead Corp., Dayton, Ohio, 1979-81, dir. edn. and tng., 1981-83; assoc. dean Sch. of Bus. Adminstrn., Georgetown U., Washington, 1983-84; v.p. human resources ADVO-Sys., Hartford, Conn., 1984—87; v.p. human resources, corp. officer DIMAC Direct Inc., St. Louis, 1987-88; sr. v.p. human resources and adminstrn., sr. corp. officer DIMAC Mktg. Corp. (parent of DIMAC Direct Inc.), St. Louis, 1988-97, also sec., asst. treas., exec. com., 1988-97; sr. v.p. human resources, exec. corp. officer Brooks Fiber Properties, Inc., St. Louis, 1997-98; pres., CEO Michaelson Group Ptnrs., Dayton, Ohio, 1969—. Vis. prof. Wright State U., Dayton, Ohio, 1999-2001, assoc. prof., 2001-07, prof., 2007-; assoc. grad. faculty mem. Ctrl. Mich. U., Mt. Pleasant, 1999—. Author, editor human resources sect. Am. Mgmt. Assn. Mgmt. Handbook, 3d edit.; author approximately 50 books and articles; mem. edtl. adv. bd. Jour. Applied Comm. Rsch., 1991-97; sr. adv. dir., sr. editor Franklin Pub. Co., 2007-. Life mem. Internat. Comm. Assn. (bus. mgr.-exec. sec. 1969-73, fin. com. 1982-85); mem. Am. Mgmt. Assn. (human resources coun. 1990-2000), Printing Industries of Am. (employer resources group 1989-97), mem. Franklin Publ. Co. (sr. editor, sr. advisor, dir. 2007-).

SINDLINGER, VERNE E., bishop; Bishop Lincoln Trails Synod, Indpls.; exec. SYNOD, 1994. Office: Presbyterian Church USA 1100 W 42d St Ste 220 Indianapolis IN 46208-3345

SINES, RAYMOND E., former state legislator; m. Suanne Sines; children: Stephanie, Amanda, Victoria. Student, Lakeland Coll., Aldenson-Broadus Coll. Mem. Ohio Ho. of Reps., Columbus, 1993-97; state rep. Ohio Dist. 69, 1993; owner Sines & Sons, Inc., Painesville, Ohio. Bd. dirs. Humane Soc. Mem. Am Legion, United Way, C. of C., Farm Bureau, Ahtletic Assocs. Home: 4287 Harper St Perry OH 44081-9744 Office: 2481 N Oak Ridge Rd Painesville OH 44077

SINGER, ELEANOR, sociologist, editor; b. Vienna, Mar. 4, 1930; arrived in U.S., 1938; d. Alfons and Anna (Troedl) Schwarzbart; m. Alan Gerard Singer, Sept. 8, 1949; children: Emily Ann, Lawrence Alexander. BA, Queens Coll., 1951; PhD, Columbia U., 1966. Asst. editor Am. Scholar, Williamsburg, Va., 1951-52; editor Tchrs. Coll. Press, NYC, 1952-56, Dryden-Holt, NYC, 1956-57; rsch. assoc., sr. rsch. assoc., sr. rsch. scholar Columbia U., NYC, 1966-94; sr. rsch. scientist Inst. for Social Rsch. U. Mich., Ann Arbor, 1994—2003, acting assoc. dir., 1998-99, assoc. dir., 1999—2002, rsch. prof., 2004—06, prof. emeritus, 2006—; editor Pub. Opinion Quar., NYC, 1975-86. Author (with Carol Weiss): The Reporting of Social Science in the Mass Media, 1988; author: (with Phyllis Endreny) Reporting On Risk, 1993; author: (with Robert M. Groves et. al.) Survey Methodology, 2004; editor (with Herbert H. Hyman): Readings in Reference Group Theory and Research, 1968; editor: (with Stanley Presser) Survey Research Methods: A Reader, 1989; editor: (with Stanley Presser, others) Methods for Testing and Evaluating Survey Questionnaires, 2004; editor: (with James S. House, others) A Telescope on Society, 2004; contbr. articles to profl. jours. Mem. Am. Assn. Pub. Opinion Rsch. (pres. N.Y.C. chpt. 1983-84, pres. 1987-88, Exceptionally Disting. Achievement award 1996), Am. Sociol. Assn., Am. Statis. Assn. Office: U Mich Inst Social Rsch PO Box 1248 Ann Arbor MI 48106-1248 Home Phone: 734-747-7441; Office Phone: 734-647-4599.

SINGER, J. DAVID, political science professor; b. Bklyn., Dec. 7, 1925; s. Morris L. and Anne (Newman) S.; m. C. Diane Macaulay, Apr., 1990; children: Kathryn Louise, Eleanor Anne. BA, Duke U., 1946; LLD (hon.), Northwestern U., 1983; PhD, NYU, 1956. Instr. NYU, 1954-55, Vassar Coll., 1955-57; vis. fellow social relations Harvard U., 1957-58; vis. asst. prof. U. Mich., Ann Arbor, 1958-60, sr. scientist Mental Health Research Inst., 1960-82, assoc. prof., 1964-65, prof. polit. sci., 1965—, coordinator World Politics Program, 1969-75, 81-90; vis. prof. U. Oslo and Inst. Social Research, 1963-64, 90, Carnegie Endowment Internat. Peace and Grd. Inst. Internat. Studies, Geneva, 1967-68, Zuma and U. Mannheim (W. Ger.), 1976, Grad. Inst. Internat. Studies, Geneva, 1983-84; U. Groningen, The Netherlands, 1991; Nat. Chengchi U., Taiwan, 1998. Author: Financing International Organization: The United Nations Budget Process, 1961, Deterrence, Arms Control and Disarmament: Toward a Synthesis in National Security Policy, 1962, rev. 1984, (with Melvin Small) The Wages of War, 1816-1965: A Statistical Handbook, 1972, (with Susan Jones) Beyond Conjecture in International Politics: Abstracts of Data Based Research, 1972, (with Dorothy La Barr) The Study of International Politics: A Guide to Sources for the Student, Teacher and Researcher, 1976, Correlates of War I and II, 1979, 80, (with Melvin Small) Resort to Arms: International and Civil War, 1816-1980, 1982, Models, Methods, and Progress: A Peace Research Odyssey, 1990, (with Paul Diehl) Measuring the Correlates of War, 1998, (with D. Geller) Nations at War, 1998; monographs; contbr. articles to profl. jours.; mem. editorial bd. ABC: Polit. Sci. and Govt., 1968-84, Polit. Sci. Reviewer, 1971—, Conflict Mgmt. and Peace Sci., 1978—, Etudes Polemologiques, 1978—, Internat. Studies Quar., 1989—, Jour. Conflict Resolution, 1989—, Internat. Interactions, 1989—. With USNR, 1943-66. Ford fellow, 1956; Ford grantee, 1957-58; Phoenix Meml. Fund grantee, 1959, 1981-82; Fulbright scholar, 1963-64; Carnegie Corp. research grantee, 1963-67; NSF grantee, 1967-76, 1986-89, 1992-94; Guggenheim grantee, 1978-79 Mem. Am. Polit. Sci. Assn. (Helen Dwight Reid award com. 1967, 95, chmn. Woodrow Wilson award com., chmn. nominating com. 1970), Internat. Polit. Sci. Assn. (chmn. conflict and peace rsch. com. 1974—), World Assn. Internat. Rels., Internat. Soc. Polit. Psychology, Internat. Soc. Rsch. on Aggression, Social Sci. History Assn., Peace Sci. Soc., Internat. Peace Rsch. Assn. (pres. 1972-73), Consortium on Peace Rsch., Fedn. Am. Scientists (nat. coun. 1991-95), Union Concerned Scientists, Arms Control Assn., Internat. Studies Assn. (pres. 1985-86), Com. Nat. Security, Am. Com. on East-West Accord, World Federalist Assn. Office: U Mich Dept Polit Sci 505 S State St Ann Arbor MI 48109-1045 E-mail: jdsinger@umich.edu.

SINGER, WILLIAM S., lawyer; BA, Brandeis U., 1962; LLB, Columbia U. Law Sch., 1965. Bar: Ill. 1965. Law clk. to US Dist. Judge Hubert L. Will Ill. Supreme Ct., Chgo., 1965—67; of counsel atty. Kirkland & Ellis LLP, Chgo., 1967—. Office: Kirkland & Ellis LLP 200 E Randolph Dr Chicago IL 60601 Business E-Mail: wsinger@kirkland.com.

SINGH, RAJENDRA, mechanical engineering educator, director; b. Dhampur, India, Feb. 13, 1950; came to U.S., 1973; s. Raghubir and Ishwar (Kali) S.; m. Veena Ghungesh, June 24, 1979; children: Rohit, Arun. BS with honors, Birla Inst., 1971; MS, Indian Inst. Tech., 1973; PhD, Purdue U., 1975. Grad. instr. Purdue U., West Layfayette, Ind., 1973-75; sr. engr. Carrier Corp., Syracuse, NY, 1975-79; asst. prof. Ohio State U., Columbus, 1979-83, assoc. prof., 1983-87, prof., 1987—, Donald D. Glower chair in engring., 2001—, dir. Smart Vehicle Concepts Ctr., 2006—, sr. fellow Ctr. Automotive Rsch., 2006—. Adj. lectr. Syracuse (N.Y.) U., 1977-79; bd. dirs. Inst. of Noise Control Engring., 1994-96, 99—, v.p. tech. activities, 2000-02, pres., 2003; gen. chmn. Nat. Noise Conf., Columbus, 1985; leader U.S. delegation to India-U.S.A. Symposium on Vibration and Noise Engring., 1996; vis. prof. U. Calif., Berkeley, 1987-88; pres. Inter-Noise 2002 Congress; chmn. India-USA Symposium on Vibration and Noise, 2001; cons., lectr. in field. Author: Emerging Trends in Vibration and oise Engineering, 1996; contbr. more than 350 articles to profl. jours.; guest editor jours. Recipient Gold medal U. Roorkee, 1973, R. H. Kohr Rsch. award Purdue U., 1975, Excellence in Tchg. award Inst. Noise Control Engring., 1989, Rsch. award Ohio State U., 1983, 87, 91, 96, 01, 06, Educator of Yr. award GM Tech. Edn. Program, 1998. Fellow ASME, Acoustical Soc. Am., Soc. Auto Engring.; mem. Inst. Noise Control Engring.(cert.), Am. Soc. Engring. Edn. (George Westinghouse award 1993). Achievements include patent for rolling door; development of new analytical and experimental techniques in machine dynamics, acoustics, vibration and fluid control. Home: 4772 Belfield Ct Dublin OH 43017-2592 Office: Ohio State U Mech Engring Dept 201 W 19th Ave Columbus OH 43210 Home Phone: 614-761-8855; Office Phone: 614-292-9044.

SINGHVI, SURENDRA SINGH, financial consultant; b. Jodhpur, Rajasthan, India, Jan. 16, 1942; arrived in US, 1962, naturalized, 1986; s. Rang Raj and Ugam Kanwar (Surana) Singhvi; m. Sushila Bhandari, July 7, 1965; children: Seema, Sandeep. B in Commerce, Rajasthan U., 1961; MBA, Atlanta U., 1963; PhD, Columbia U., NYC, 1967. CPA, cert. mgmt. acct. Asst. prof. fin. Miami U., Oxford, Ohio, 1967-69, assoc. prof. fin., 1969-70; adj. prof. fin., 1970-95; fin. mgr. ARMCO Inc., Middletown, Ohio, 1970-79, asst. treas., 1979-83, gen. fin. mgr., 1983-86; v.p. and treas. Edison Bros. Stores, Inc., St. Louis, 1986-90; pres. Singhvi & Assocs., Inc., Dayton, Ohio, 1990—. Bd. dirs. Columbia Indsl. Sales Corp., Hauer Music Co., Oasis Property Inc., Om Hospitality, Inc. Author: Planning for Capital Investment, 1980; co-editor: Frontiers fo Financial Management, 4th edit., 1984, Global Finance 2000 -A Handbook of Strategy and Organization (The Conference Board), 1996; contbr. articles to profl. jours. Trustee South Ctrl. Ohio Minority Bus. Coun., 2000—. Recipient Chancellor's Gold medal, Rajasthan U., Ahimsa (Non-Violence) award, Fedn. Jaina Assns. N.Am., 1999. Mem.: Dayton Minority Supplier Devel. Coun. (dir. 1997—, chmn. 2000), Fin. Mgmt. Assn., Fin. Execs. Inst., Inst. Mgmt. Accts. (Bayer Silver medal 1978), India Club (pres. Dayton chpt. 1980), Rotary (dir. internat. program Middletown chpt. 1973—86, Dayton chpt. 1995—, treas., dir. 2001—02). Avocations: swimming, kanasta, travel, writing. Home and Office: Singhvi and Assocs Inc 439 Ridge Line Ct Dayton OH 45458-9546 Office Phone: 937-885-7414. Personal E-mail: s.singhvi@yahoo.com.

SINGLETON, MARVIN AYERS, state legislator, otolaryngologist; b. Baytown, Tex., Oct. 7, 1939; s. Henry Marvin and Mary Ruth Singleton. BA, U. of the South, 1962; MD, U. Tenn., 1966. Diplomate Am. Bd. Otolaryngology. Intern City of Memphis Hosps., 1966-67; resident in surgery Highland Alameda City Hosp., Oakland, Calif., 1967-68; resident in otolaryngology U. Tenn. Hosp., Memphis, 1968-71; fellow in otolaryngic pathology Armed Forces Inst. Pathology, Washington, 1971; fellow in otologic surgery U. Colo. at Gallup (N.Mex.) Indian Med. Ctr., 1972; practice medicine specializing in otolaryngology/allergies Joplin, Mo., 1972—. Founder, operator Home and Farm Investments, Joplin, 1975—, staff mem. Freeman Hosp., Dameron Hosp. Stockton, St. John's Hosp., Joplin; cons. in otolaryngology Mo. Crippled Children's Service; pres. Ozark Mfg. Co., Inc., Joplin; mem. St. Joaquin Commn. on Aging, 2005—; dir. St. Mary's Interfaith Svcs., Stockton, 2007—; med. dir. Health Choice NW Mo. Mem. Internat. Arabian Racing Bd., 1983-88; mem. Mo. State Senate, 1990-2003; del. Rep. Nat. Conv., 1988, 92. Served with USNG, 1966-72. Fellow Am. Coll. Surgeons, Am. Acad. Otolaryngologic Allergy (past pres.), Am. Assn. Acad. Asthma, Allergy and Immunology; mem. AMA (Mo. del.), Mo. State Med. Assn., So. Med. Assn., Mo. State Allergy Assn., Ear Nose & Throat Soc. Mo. (past. pres.), Calif. Med. Assn. (trustee 2005—), San Joaquin Med. Soc. (pres. 2006-07), Masons (32d degree), Sigma Alpha Epsilon, Phi Theta Kappa, Phi Chi. Republican. Episcopalian. Home: 1637 W Swain Rd Stockton CA 95207-4172 Office: 7373 W Ln Stockton CA 95210 Home Phone: 209-951-7273; Office Phone: 209-476-5623. Personal E-mail: senatorsingleton@hotmail.com.

SINHA, KUMARES CHANDRA, engineering educator, consultant; b. Calcutta, India, July 12, 1939; s. Amares Chandra and Asha Rani (Mitra) S.; m. Anne Elizabeth Kallina; children: Shohini Sarah, Rahul Norman, Nabina Justine, Arjun Daniel, Ishan Edmund. BSCE, Jadavpur U., 1961; diploma in town and regional planning, Calcutta U., 1964; MSCE, U. Conn., 1966, PhD, 1968. Registered profl. engr., Ind. Asst. engr. Pub. Works Dept., West Bengal, Calcutta, 1961-64; asst. prof. civil engring. Marquette U., Milw., 1968-72, assoc. prof., dir. urban transp. program, 1972-74; assoc. prof. civil engring. Purdue U., West Lafayette, Ind., 1974-78, prof., 1978—, assoc. dir. Ctr. Pub. Policy, 1978-79, head transp. and urban engring., 1981—. Vis. prof. MIT, Cambridge, 1980, U. Roorkee, India, 1981; systems engring. cons. Southeastern Wis. Regional Planning Commn., Waukesha, 1969-76; cons. Ind. Transp. Assn. Inc., Indpls., 1985, UN Devel. Program, India, 1985, Chinese Ministry of Communications, Beijing, 1986, World Bank, 1988—. Author or co-author over 200 tech. publs. on transp. engring. and mgmt. Recipient Fred Burggraff award Transp. Research Bd., Washington, 1972; 50 research grants and contracts NSF, U.S. Dept. Transp., Ind. Dept. Transp., 1968—. Fellow ASCE (chmn. urban transp. div. 1982-83, Frank M. Masters award 1986), Inst. Transp. Engrs. (chmn. tech. coms. 1978-84); mem. Am. Inst. Cert. Planners, Am. Pub. Works Assn., Am. Soc. Engring. Edn. Hindu. Avocation: reading. Home: 2224 Miami Trl West Lafayette IN 47906-1924 Office: Purdue Univ Sch Civil Engring West Lafayette IN 47907

SINICKI, CHRISTINE, state official; b. Mar. 28, 1960; married; 2 children. Mgr. small bus.; state assemblywoman Wis., 1998—; del. U.S. Presdl. Electoral Coll., 2000. Mem. children and families com.; mem. edn. com.; mem. edn. reform com.; mem. personal privacy com.; mem. Wis. Housing and Econ. Devel. Authority. Mem. Milw. Sch. Bd., 1991—98. Democrat. Office: State Capitol Rm 321F W PO Box 8953 Madison WI 53708-8953

SINOR, DENIS, history professor, linguist; b. Kolozsvar, Hungary, Apr. 17, 1916; s. Miklos and Marguerite (Weitzenfeld) S.; m. Eugenia Trinajstic (dec.); children: Christophe (dec.), Sophie. BA, U. Budapest, 1938; MA, Cambridge U., Eng., 1948; Doctorate (hon.), U. Szeged, Hungary, 1971, U. Humanities, Kazan, Russia, 2007. Attache Centre National de la Recherche Scientifique, Paris, 1939-48; univ. lectr. Altaic studies Cambridge U., 1948-62; prof. Uralic and Altaic studies and history Ind. U., Bloomington, 1962-81, disting. prof. Uralic and Altaic studies and history, 1975-86, disting. prof. emeritus Uralic and Altaic studies and history, 1986—, chmn. dept. Uralic and Altaic studies, 1963-1981, dir. Lang. and Area Ctr., 1963-88, dir. Asian studies program, 1965-67, dir. Asian Studies Rsch. Inst., 1967-79, dir. Rsch. Inst. for Inner Asian Studies (renamed Denis Sinor Inst. for Inner Asian Studies), 1979-1981, 85-86. Sec. gen. Permanent Internat. Altaistic Conf., 1961-2007; rsch. project dir. U.S. Office Edn., 1969-70; sec. Internat. Union Orientalists, 1954-64; vis. prof. Inst. Nat. des Langues et Civilisations Orientales, Paris, spring 1974; scholar-in-residence

Rockefeller Found. Study Ctr., Bellagio, 1975; vice chmn. UNESCO Commn. for History Civilization Cen. Asia, 1981-2005, consultative com. UNESCO Silk Rd. Project, 1990-97; summer seminar dir. NEH, 1988, 2005; hon. prof. Inst. Oriental Studies, Russian Acad. Scis. Author: Orientalism and History, 1954, History of Hungary, 1959, Introduction à lètude de l'Eurasie Centrale, 1963, Aspects of Altaic Civilization, 1963, Inner Asia, 1968, Inner Asia and Its Contacts with Medieval Europe, 1977, Tanulmányok, 1982, Essays in Comparative Altaic Linguistics, 1990, Studies in Medieval Inner Asia, 1997; editor, contbr.: Modern Hungary, 1977, Studies in Finno-Ugric Linguistics, 1977, Uralic Languages, 1988, Essays on Uzbek History, Culture and Languages, 1993, Cambridge History of Early Inner Asia, Handbook of Uralic Studies, Jour. Asian History, Ind. U. Uralic and Altaic Series; mem. editl. bd. Britannica-Hungarica. Served with Forces Françaises de l'Intérieur, 1943-44. With Free French Army, 1944—45. Rsch. grantee Am. Coun. Learned Soc., 1962, Am. Philos. Soc., 1963, NEH grant, 1981, 87-88; Guggenheim fellow, 1968-69, 1981-82; recipient Jubilee prize U. Budapest, 1938, Barczi Geza Meml. medal, 1981, Gold medal Permanent Internat. Altaistic Conf., 1982, 1996, Arminius Vambery Meml. medal, 1983, Thomas Hart Benton Mural medal Hungarian Order of Star, 1986, UNESCO Avicenna medal, 1998, medal for outstanding svcs. U. Szeged, 2002, UNESCO 60th Anniversary medal, 2005, Middle Cross Hungarian Order of Merit, 2006, John W. Ryan award, Ind. U., 2006; named Denis Sinor Inst. for Inner Asian Studies in his honor, 2006. Fellow Körösi Csoma Soc. (hon.); mem. Royal Asiatic Soc. (hon. sec. 1954-64, Denis Sinor medal for Inner Asian Studies named in his honor 1992), Am. Oriental Soc. (pres. Midwest br. 1968-70, nat. pres. 1975-76, medal of honor 1999), Assn. Asian Studies, Am. Hist. Soc., Soc. Asiatique (hon.), Tibet Soc. (pres. 1969-74), Mongolia Soc. (pres. 1987-94), Correspondant de l'Académie des inscriptions et belles lettres (Paris), Hungarian Acad. Scis. (hon.), Acad. Europaea (fgn.), Deutsche Morgenlandische Gesellschaft, Suomalais-Ugrilaisen Seura (hon.), Soc. Uralo-Altaica (v.p. 1964-94, hon.), Internat. Union Oriental and Asian Studies (v.p. 1993—), Cosmos Club Washington, Explorers Club NYC, United Oxford and Cambridge Club London. Achievements include reached the North Pole on a Russian icebreaker, 2004. Home: 5581 E Lampkins Ridge Rd Bloomington IN 47401-8674 Office: Indiana U Dept Ctrl Eurasian Studies Goodbody Hall Bloomington IN 47405 E-mail: sinord@indiana.edu.

SIPES, CONNIE W., state legislator, educator; b. New Albany, Ind., Aug. 6, 1949; m. Stephen Sipes; children: Cassie, Zachary. BS, Ind. U.-S.E., 1971, MS in Edn., 1975, MS in Adminstrn., 1991. Prin. Fairmont Elem. Sch., New Albany, Ind., 1991—; mem. Ind. Senate from 46th dist., Indpls., 1997—; mem. edn. com., mem. pension and labor com.; ranking minority elections com.; mem. transp. and interstate coop. com. Mem. Dem. Women's Club. Recipient Woman of Achievement award BPW, 1986. Mem. LWV, Ind. State Prins. Assn., Nat. Assn. Elem. Prins. Avocation: running. Office: 200 W Washington St Indianapolis IN 46204-2728

SIPES, KAREN KAY, communications executive; b. Higginsville, Mo., Jan. 8, 1947; d. Walter John and Katherine Marie (McLelland) Heins; m. Joel Rodney Sipes, Sept. 24, 1971; 1 child, Lesley Katherine. BS in Edn., Ctrl. Mo. State U., 1970. Reporter/news editor Newton Kansan, 1973—76; sports writer Capital-Jour., Topeka, 1976—83, spl. sects. editor, 1983—85, editl. page editor, 1985—92, mng. editor/features, 1992—2002, asst. editl. page editor, 2002—03; dir. commn. Kans. Dept. Aging, Topeka, 2003—. Co-chair Mayor's Commn. on Literacy, Topeka, 1995-96; mem. Act Against Violence Com., Topeka, 1995-96, Mayor's Task Force on Race Rels., 1998; planning com. Leadership Greater Topeka, 1997; Great Am. Cleanup, 1999-2001, ERC/Resource and Referral, 2001-07; com. mem. Martin Luther King Living the Dream Bus. Ptnrs., 2001-2004; Centennial planning com. Family Svc. and Guidance Ctr., 2003-04; mem. Project Topeka Com., 2004—, Arthritis Walk Com., 2004-05, Faith in Action-No Place Like Home Coalition, 2003—; bd. dirs. Western Swing Music Soc. Kans., 2003—. Mem. Ctrl. Mo. State U. Alumni Assn. (bd. dirs. 1996-2002, v.p. 1999, pres. 2000). Avocations: music, gardening, art. Office: Kans Dept Aging New England Bldg 503 S Kans Ave Topeka KS 66603-3404 Home Phone: 785-862-4119; Office Phone: 785-368-7196. Personal E-mail: critterkaren@aol.com. Business E-Mail: karen.sipes@aging.state.ks.us.

SIPKINS, PETER W., lawyer; b. Mpls., 1944; BA, U. Minn., 1966, JD, 1969. Bar: Minn. 1969, Wis. 1982. Spl. asst. atty. gen. State Minn., 1971-73, solicitor gen., 1974-76; mem. Dorsey & Whitney, Mpls., ptnr., trial practice group; co-chmn., products & tech. liability litig. group. Adj. prof. law, legal writing, appellate advocacy William Mitchell Coll. Law, 1974-77. Mem. Phi Delta Phi. Office: Dorsey & Whitney Ste 1500 50 S 6th St Minneapolis MN 55402-1498 Office Phone: 612-343-7903. Office Fax: 612-340-2807. Business E-Mail: sipkins.peter@dorsey.com.

SIROTKA, MIKE, professional baseball player; b. Chgo., May 13, 1971; Baseball player Chgo. White Sox, 1995—. Office: Chgo White Sox 333 W 35th St Chicago IL 60616

SIVE, REBECCA ANNE, public relations executive; b. Jan. 29, 1950; d. David and Mary (Robinson) S.; m. Clark Steven Tomashefsky. BA, Carleton Coll., 1972; MA in Am. History, U. Ill., Chgo., 1975. Asst. to chmn. of pres.' task force on vocations Carleton Coll., Northfield, Minn., 1972; rsch. asst. Jane Addams Hull House, Chgo., 1974; instr. Loop Coll., Chgo., 1975, Columbia Coll., Chgo., 1975-76; dir. Ill. Women's History Project, 1975-76; founder, exec. dir. Midwest Women's Ctr., Chgo., 1977-81; exec. dir. Playboy Found., 1981-84; v.p. pub. affairs/pub. rels. Playboy Video Corp., 1985—85; v.p. pub. affairs Playboy Enterprises, Inc., Chgo., 1985-86; pres. The Sive Group, Inc., Chgo., 1986—. Instr. Roosevelt U., Chgo., 1977-78; dir. spl. projects Inst. on Pluralism and Group Identity, Am. Jewish Com.; trainer Midwest Acad. Contbr. articles to profl. jours. Commr. Chgo. Park Dist., 1986-88; del.-at-large at. Women's conf., 1977; mem. Ill. Human Rights Commn., 1980-87, Ill. coordinating com., Internat Womens Yr.; coord. Ill. Bicentennial Photog. Exhbn., 1977; mem. Ill. Employment and Tng. Coun.; bd dirs. Nat. Abortion Rights Action League and NARAL Found., Ill. div. ACLU, Midwest Women's Ctr. Recipient award for outstanding cmty. leadership YWCA Met. Chgo., 1979, award for outstanding cmty. leadership Chgo. Jaycees, 1988. Office: The Sive Group Inc 1235 Astor St Chicago IL 60610-5213 Office Phone: 312-397-9857. Business E-Mail: rsive@sivegroup.com.

SIX, FRED N., retired state supreme court justice; b. Independence, Mo., Apr. 20, 1929; AB, U. Kans., 1951, JD with honors, 1956; LLM in Judicial Process, U. Va., 1990. Bar: Kans. 1956. Asst. atty. gen. State of Kans., 1957-58; pvt. practice Lawrence, Kans., 1958-87; judge Kans. Ct. Appeals, 1987-88; justice Kans. Supreme Ct., Topeka, 1988—2003. Editor-in-chief U. Kans. Law Review, 1955-56; lectr. on law Washburn U. Sch. Law, 1957-58, U. Kans., 1975-76. Served with USMC, 1951-53; USMCR, 1957-62. Recipient Disting. Alumnus award, U. Kans. Sch. Law, 1994, Disting. Alumni Achievement award, U. Kans. Coll. Liberal Arts and Sci., 2000—01. Fellow Am. Bar Found. (chmn. Kans. chpt. 1983-87); mem. ABA (jud. adminstrn. divsn.), Am. Judicature Soc., Kans. Bar Assn., Kans. Bar Found., Kans. Law Soc. (pres. 1970-72), Kans. Inn of Ct. (pres. 1993-94), Order of Coif, Phi Delta Phi. Address: 1180 E 1400 Rd Lawrence KS 66046

SIX, STEPHEN N., state attorney general, former judge; b. Dec. 11, 1965; s. Frederick N. Six; m. Betsy Six; children: Emily, Sam, Henry, Will. B, Carleton Coll., orthfield, Minn., 1988; JD, U. Kans. Sch. Law, Lawrence, 1993. Law clk. to Hon. Deanell R. Tacha US Ct. Appeals (10th Cir.), 1993—94; ptnr. Shamberg, Johnson & Bergman, Kansas City, Mo., 1994—2005; dist. judge Kans. Jud. Dist., Douglas County, 2005—08; atty. gen. State of Kans., Topeka, 2008—. Contbg. editor: Kans. Law Rev., 1993. Bench-bar com. US Dist. Ct. Kansas; bd. trustees Kans. Bar Found. Mem.: Kans. Bar Assn. (bd. govs., bench-bar com., chmn. mandatory malpractice disclosure com.), Order of the Coif. Democrat. Office: Office Atty Gen Memorial Hall Fl 2 120 SW 10th St Topeka KS 66612*

SIZEMORE, WILLIAM CHRISTIAN, retired academic administrator, county official; b. South Boston, Va., June 19, 1938; s. Herman Mason and Hazel (Johnson) S.; m. Anne Catherine Mills, June 24, 1961; children: Robert C., Richard M., Edward S. BA, U. Richmond, 1960; BD, Southeastern Bapt. Theol. Sem., Wake Forest, NC, 1963; MLS, U. .C., 1964; MLS (advanced), Fla. State U., 1971, PhD, 1973; postgrad., Harvard U., 1989. Library asst. U. N.C., Chapel Hill, 1963-64; assoc. librarian, instr. grad. research Southeastern Bapt. Theol. Sem., 1964-66; librarian, assoc. prof. South Ga. Coll., Douglas, 1966-71, acad. dean, prof., 1971-80, dean coll., prof., 1980-83, acting pres., 1982-83; pres. Alderson-Broaddus Coll., Philippi, W.Va., 1983-94, William Jewell Coll., Liberty, Mo., 1994-2000, chancellor, 2000—02; dir. bus. expansion Clay County Econ. Devel. Coun., Kansas City, Mo., 2003—. Cons. Continental R&D, Shawnee Mission, Kans., 1987-92, So. Assn. Colls. and Schs., Atlanta, 1977, S.C. Commn. on Higher Edn., Columbia, 1975-76, State Coun. Higher Edn. for Va., Richmond, 1969-70, Software Valley Corp., 1989-94; adv. bd. Software Valley Found., 1991-94. Contbr. articles to profl. jours. Active Barbour County Devel. Authority, Philippi, 1984-94, Barbour County Emergency Food and Shelter Bd., 1985-94, Barbour County Extension Com., 1990-94; mem. exec. coun. Yellow Pine area Boy Scouts Am., Valdosta, 1974-76; pres. Satilla Librarians Ednl. Coun., Douglas, 1969-71; lectr., workshop leader on Bible studies various orgns., 1966—; bd. advisors Swatow Kakwang Profl. Acad., Peoples Republic China; pres. bd. dirs. W.Va. Intercollegiate Athletic Conf., 1985-86, coun. of pres. Nat. Assn. Intercollegiate Athletics; bd. dirs., mem. exec. com. Broaddus Hosp., Philippi, 1983-94; chmn. W.Va. Productive Industry Efforts Found., 1989-92; mktg. com. W.Va. Life Scis. Park Found., 1989-94, Gov.'s Partnership for Progress, 1989-94; mem. adv. panel W.Va. Rural Health Initiative, 1991-94; gov. bd., bd. dirs. W.Va. Alliance of Hosps., 1991-94; bd. dirs. Clay-Platte Econ. Devel. Coun., 1996—; bd. dirs. ARC, Kansas City, 1996-02, exec.com. 2000-02; adv. com. Mo. Conservation Heritage Found. Discovery Ctr. Campaign, 1998-2002; mem. Clay County Millennium Hist. Bd., 2002-; mem. Liberty HIstory Book Steering Com., 2001-04; bd. dirs., v.p. Immaculata Manor, 2003-; adv. bd. North Kansas City Schs., 2003-; mem. steering com., co-chair Freedom House, 2004-. Joseph Ruzicka scholar N.C. Library Assn., 1963; recipient Douglas Pilot Club Edn. award, 1981, Good Citizenship medal Nat. Soc. Sons of Am. Revolution, 1999. Mem. ALA, Am. Assn. for Higher Edn., Am. Assn. Univ. Adminstrs., Nat. Coun. Instrnl. Adminstrs., W.Va. Assn. Coll. and Univ. Pres. (exec. com., v.p., pres. 1992), Mountain State Assn. Colls., W.Va. Found. for Ind. Colls. (dir. 1983-84, v.p. 1988-92), Mo. Colls. Fund (exec. com. 1997-98), Barbour County C. of C. (bd. dirs. 1988-94, v.p. 1988-90, pres. 1990-92, chmn. bd. 1992-94), Liberty Area C. of C. (bd. dirs. 1995-97), Clay County Hist. Soc. (life), SAR, Pi Kappa Alpha. Democrat. Baptist. Avocations: woodworking, gardening. Home: 1417 Woodbury Dr Liberty MO 64068-1266 Office: Clay County Econ Devel Coun Office 110 NW Barry Rd Kansas City MO 64155

SKAGGS, BILL, state legislator; b. Sylacanga, Ala., Jan. 24, 1942; Student, Ctrl. Mo. State U. Rep. Mo. State Ho. Reps. Dist. 34, 1983-93, Mo. State Ho. Reps. Dist. 31, 1993—. Office: Mo Ho of Reps State Capitol Jefferson City MO 65101 Home: 3509 North Park Kansas City MO 64116

SKAGGS, ROBERT C., JR., utilities executive, lawyer; BA, Davidson Coll.; JD, W. Va. Univ.; MBA, Tulane Univ. With Columbia Energy Group, 1981—2000, law dept., 1981—96, pres., Columbia Gas Ohio & Ky., 1996—2000; pres. Bay State Gas, No. Utilities, other Columbia cos. NiSource Inc., 2000—03, exec. v.p., 2003—04, pres., 2004—, CEO, 2005—. Bd. dir. Southeastern Gas Assn.; mem. Midwest Energy Assn.; mem. leadership council Am. Gas Assn. Mem.: ABA, Energy Bar Assn., W. Va. Bar Assn. Office: NiSource Inc 801 E 86th Ave Merrillville IN 46410

SKELTON, IKE (ISAAC NEWTON SKELTON IV), congressman; b. Lexington, Mo., Dec. 20, 1931; s. Isaac Newton and Carolyn (Boone) S.; m. Susan B. Anding, July 22, 1961 (dec. Aug. 23, 2005); children: Ike, Jim, Page. AA, Wentworth Mil. Acad., 1951; student, U. Edinburgh, Scotland, 1953; AB in Hist., U. Mo., Columbia, 1953, LLB, 1956. Bar: Mo. 1956. Atty. pvt. practice, Lexington, Mo.; pros. atty. Lafayette County, Mo., 1957-60; spl. asst. atty. gen. Mo., 1961-63; mem. Mo. State Senate from 28th dist., 1971—76, US Congress from 4th Mo. dist., 1977—, chmn. armed svcs. com. Vice chmn. bd. trustees Harry S. Truman Scholarship Found. Named Minuteman of Yr., Res. Officers Assn. of US, 1995; recipient W. Stuart Symington award, Air Force Assn., 1994, Henry M. Jackson Disting. Svc. award, Jewish Inst. at. Security Affairs, 1999, Hon. commandant award, Indsl. Coll. Armed Forces, 2005, Mil. Order of Iron Mike award, Marine Corps League. Mem. Phi Beta Kappa, Sigma Chi, Masons, Shriners, Elks, Boy Scouts Am., Mo. Bar Assn. Democrat. Mem. Christian Ch. Office: US House Reps 2206 Rayburn House Office Bldg Washington DC 20515-2504 Office Phone: 202-225-2876.

SKIBNIEWSKI, MIROSLAW JAN, engineering educator; MEng, Warsaw Tech. U., 1981; MS, Carnegie-Mellon U., 1983, PhD, 1986; cert. in advanced studies, Harvard U. Grad. Sch. Edn., 2000. Staff engr. engring. dept. Pitts. Testing Lab., 1981-82; rsch. and tchg. asst. dept. civil engring. Carnegie-Mellon U., Pitts., 1982-86; asst. prof. Sch. Civil Engring. Purdue U., West Lafayette, Ind., 1986-90, assoc. prof. Sch. Civil Engring., 1990-95, prof. Sch. Civil Engring., 1995—, asst. exec. v.p. acad. affairs, 1997-2001, assoc. provost, 2001—02, dean internat. programs, dir. internat. rsch., 2002—04; A. James Clark endowed chair prof. U. Md., College Park, 2005—. Vis. sr. rsch. scientist divsn. bldg., constrn. and engring. Commonwealth Scientific and Indsl. Rsch. Orgn., Melbourne, Australia, 1992; vis. rsch. prof. Inst. Mechanized Constrn. and Rock Mining, Warsaw, 1993; hon. prof. civil engring. Warsaw Tech. U., 2004—; rsch. engr. Robotics Ctr. Constrn. Engring. Rsch. Lab. U.S. Army C.E., Champaign, Ill., 1993; presenter workshops. Editor-in-chief constrn. techs. and engring. Automation in Constrn.; guest editor Microcomputers in Civil Engring.; mem. editl. bd. Internat. Jour. Cont. Engirng. Edn. and Lifelong Learning, Real Estate Valuation and Investment, Constrn. Mgmt. and Econs., Constrn. Rsch. jours.; contbr. articlest to over 100 profl. jours., chpts. to books. Recipient Best Paper award Am. Soc. Engring. Edn., 1991; named Presdl. Young Investigator NSF, 1987-92. Mem. ASCE Ind. gel. dist. 9 coun. 1986-91) mem. control group aerospace divsn. tsk force on constrn. robotics 1987-89, constrn. rsch. coun. 1987—, expert sys. and artificial intelligence com. 1987—, data base and info. ech. com. 1988—, com. on field sensing and robotics in civil engring. 1990— (Walter L. Huber Civil Engring. Rsch. prize 1998), Internat. Assn. Automation and Robotics in Constrn. (founding mem., co-dir. 1991—, chmn. newsletter com. 1993-95 chmn. Comms. Com. 1997, v.p. 1990-2000, pres. 2000—), Internat. Coun. Bldg. Rsch. Studies and Documentation (Mem. W-75 working commn. on conrstrn. equipment and mechanization 1989-96, task group on computer-aided learning in constrn. and property, W-89 commn. on bldg. rsch. and edn. 1993— TG27 Task Group on Human Machine Technologies in Constrn.), Internat. Coun. on Tall Bldgs. and Urban Habitat (co-chmn. com. 65 robots and tall bldgs. 1991—, mem. com. on applications of emerging techs 1994-95) Internat. Stds Orgn. (U.S. rep. on behalf of Am. Nat. Stds. Inst. to tech. com. on constrn., machinery and equipment 1994—) Constrn. Industry Inst., Sigma Xi. Achievements include development of a decision support system for managing a fleet of construciton robotics, a computerized constructabilty review system for advanced construction technologies applications. Office: U Md 1188 Glenn L Martin Hall College Park MD 20742-3021 Office Phone: 301-405-9364. Fax: (765) 494-0644; Office Fax: 301-405-2585. E-mail: mirek@umd.edu.

SKILES, JAMES JEAN, electrical and computer engineer, educator; b. St. Louis, Oct. 16, 1928; s. Coy Emerson and Vernetta Beatrice Skiles; m. Deloris Audrey McKenney, Sept. 4, 1948; children: Steven, Randall, Jeffrey. BSEE, Washington U., St. Louis, 1948; MS, Mo. Sch. Mines and Metallurgy (now U. Mo.-Rolla), 1951; PhD, U. Wis., Madison, 1954. Engr. Union Electric Co., St. Louis, 1948-49; instr. U. Mo., Rolla, 1949-51; instr. elec. engring. U. Wis., Madison, 1951—54, prof., 1954-89, prof. emeritus, 1989—, chmn. dept. elec. engring., 1967-72, dir. univ. industry rsch. program, 1972-75, dir. Energy Rsch. Ctr., 1975-95. Cons. in field. Contbr. articles to profl. jours. Mem. Monona Grove Dist. Schs. Bd., Wis., 1961—69; mem. adv. com. Wis. Energy Office, Madison, 1979—80, Wis. Pub. Svc. Commn., 1980—81. Recipient Kiekhofer Tchg. award, 1955, Wis. Electric Utilities Professorship in Energy Engring., U. Wis., 1975—89, Benjamin Smith Reynolds Tchg. award, 1980, Acad. Elec. Engring. award, U. Mo. -Rolla, 1982. Mem.: IEEE (sr.), Am. Soc. Engring. Edn. Home: 8099 Coray Ln Verona WI 53593-9073 Office: Univ of Wisconsin Dept Elec & Computer Engring 1415 Engineering Dr Madison WI 53706-1607 Business E-Mail: skiles@engr.wisc.edu.

SKILES, SCOTT ALLEN, professional basketball coach; b. LaPorte, Ind., Mar. 5, 1964; m. Kim Skiles; children: Scott Jr., Sean, Shelby. Grad., Mich. State U. Profl. basketball player Milw. Bucks, 1986—87, Ind. Pacers, 1987—89, Orlando Magic, 1989—94, Washington Bullets, 1994—95, Phila. 76ers, 1995—96; head coach PAOK Thessaloniki BC, Greece, 1996—97; asst. coach Phoenix Suns, 1997-99, head coach, 1999—2002, Chgo. Bulls, 2003—07, Milw. Bucks, 2008—. Named NBA Most Improved Player, 1991. Achievements include holding the NBA record for most assists in a game with 30, Dec. 30, 1990. Office: Milw Bucks 1001 N Fourth St Milwaukee WI 53203*

SKILLING, RAYMOND INWOOD, lawyer; b. Enniskillen, Eng., July 14, 1939; s. Dane and Elizabeth (Burleigh) Skilling; m. Alice Mae Welsh, Aug. 14, 1982; 1 child from previous marriage, Keith A. LLB, Queen's U., Belfast, UK, 1961; JD, U. Chgo., 1962. Solicitor: English Supreme Ct. 1966, bar: Ill. 1974. Assoc. Clifford-Turner (name now Clifford Chance), London, 1963-69, ptnr., 1969-76; exec. v.p., chief counsel Aon Corp. (and predecessor cos.), Chgo., 1976—2003, sr. advisor, 2004—. Recipient McKane medal, Queen's U., Belfast, 1961; Commonwealth fellow, U. Chgo., 1961—62, Bigelow Tchg. fellow, U. Chgo. Law Sch., 1962—63, Fulbright scholar, U.S. Ednl. Commn., London, 1961—63. Mem.: Bucks Club London, Racquet Club Chgo. Office: Aon Corp 200 E Randolph Chicago IL 60601

SKILLING, THOMAS ETHELBERT, III, meteorologist, educator; b. Pitts., Feb. 20, 1952; s. Elizabeth Clarke. Student, U. Wis., 1970-74; Dr. Humanities (hon.), Lewis U., Romeoville, Ill., 1995. Meteorologist Sta. WKKD-AM-FM, Aurora, Ill., 1967-70, Sta. WLXT-TV, Aurora, 1969-70, Sta. WKOW-TV, Madison, Wis., 1970-74, Sta. WTSO, Madison, 1970-74, Sta. WTLV-TV, Jacksonville, Fla., 1974-75, Sta. WITI-TV, Milw., 1975-78, Sta. WAUK, Waukesha, Wis., 1976-77, Sta. WGN-TV, Chgo., 1978—. Weather forecaster Wis. Farm Broadcast Network, Madison, 1970-74; weather cons. Piper, Jaffray & Hopwood, Madison, 1972-74; instr. meteorology Columbia Coll., Chgo., 1982-92, Adler Planetarium, Chgo., 1985-86. Prodr. weather page Chgo. Tribune. Vol. Chgo. chpt. Muscular Dystrophy Assn. Recipient Emmy award for "It Sounded Like a Freight Train," 1991, "The Cosmic Challenge," 1994, Peter Lisagor awards for weather spls. aired on WGN, 1991, 93, Pub. Svc. award OAA-Nat. Weather Svc., 1998. Fellow Am. Meteorol. Soc. (v.p. Chgo. chpt. 1985-86, TV Seal of Approval, Outstanding Svc. award 1997), Nat. Weather Assn., Soc. Profl. Journalists, Chgo. Acad. TV Arts and Scis. Avocations: hiking, cross country skiing. Home: 6033 N Sheridan Rd Apt 31C Chicago IL 60660-3048 Office: Sta WGN-TV 2501 W Bradley Pl Chicago IL 60618-4701

SKILLMAN, BECKY SUE, lieutenant governor, former state legislator; b. Bedford, Ind., Sept. 26, 1950; d. Jack Delmar and Catherine Louise (Flinn) Foddrill; m. Stephen E. Skillman, 1969; 1 child, Aaron. Dep. recorder Lawrence County, 1971-76, county recorder, 1977-84; clk. Lawrence County Cir. Ct., 1985—92; mem. Ind. State Senate from 44th dist., 1992—2005; lt. gov. State of Ind., Indpls., 2005—. Co-dir. Lawrence County Young Reps., 1973-78; co-chmn. State Young Reps. Conv., 1975, 77; vice chmn. Lawrence County Rep. Ctrl. Com. Named The Outstanding Elected Official of 2000, Ind. Assn. Area Agencies, "Legislator of the Year", Ind. Library Found., 2002; recipient "Champion of Small Bus." award, Small Bus. Coun, 1995, Disting. Pub. Policy award, Ind. Rural Health Policy award, 2003. Republican. Office: Office Lt Governor State Capitol Rm 333 Indianapolis IN 46204 Office Phone: 317-232-4545. Office Fax: 317-232-4788.

SKILLMAN, THOMAS GRANT, endocrinology consultant, former educator; b. Cin., Jan. 7, 1925; s. Harold Grant and Faustina (Jobes) S.; m. Elizabeth Louise McClellan, Sept. 6, 1947; children: Linda, Barbara. BS, Baldwin-Wallace Coll., 1946; MD, U. Cin., 1949. Intern Cin. Gen. Hosp., 1949-50, resident, 1952-54; instr. medicine U. Cin., 1952-57; asst. prof. medicine Ohio State U., Columbus, 1957-61, dir. endocrinology and metabolism Coll. Medicine, 1967-74, Ralph Kurtz prof. endocrinology, 1974-81, prof. emeritus, 1981—, cons. to v.p. med. affairs, 1981—. Asso. prof. medicine Creighton U., Omaha, 1961-67 Editor: Case Studies in Endocrinology, 1971; Contbr. numerous articles to med. jours. Served with USNR, 1943-45; 1950-52, Korea. Recipient Golden Apple award Student Am. Med. Assn., 1966 Mem. Am. Diabetes Assn., Central Soc. Clin. Investigation, Am. Fedn. for Clin. Research, Alpha Omega Alpha. Clubs: Ohio State Golf (Columbus). Home: 4179 Stoneroot Dr Hilliard OH 43026-3023

SKILLRUD, HAROLD CLAYTON, minister, retired bishop; b. St. Cloud, Minn., June 29, 1928; s. Harold and Amanda Skillrud; m. Lois Dickhart, June 8, 1951; children: David, Janet, John. BA magna cum laude, Gustavus Adolphus Coll., 1950; MDiv magna cum laude, Augustana Theol. Sem., Rock Island, Ill., 1954; STM, Luth. Sch. Theology, Chgo., 1969; DD (hon.), Augustana Coll., 1978, Newberry Coll., 1988. Ordained to ministry Evang. Luth. Ch. in Am., 1954. Supply pastor Saron Luth. Ch., Big Lake, Minn., 1950-51; mem. staff 1st Luth. Ch., Rock Island, Ill., 1951-52; intern, organizer new mission Faith Luth. Ch., Syosset, NY, 1952-53; sr. pastor St. John's Luth. Ch., Bloomington, Ill., 1954-79, Luth. Ch. of the Redeemer, Atlanta, 1979-87; bishop Southeastern Synod Evang. Luth. Ch. in Am., Atlanta, 1987-95, regional rep. bd. pensions, 1995—2007. Del. to various convs. Luth. Ch. in Am., Luth. World Fedn. in Helsinki, 1963, mem. bd. publ., 1976-84, pastor-evangelist Evang. Outreach Emphasis program, 1977-79, mem. exec. bd. Ill. synod, 1977-79, pres. bd. publ., 1980-84, leader stewardship cluster Southeastern synod, 1983, mem. exec. bd. Southeastern synod, 1984-87; mem. exec. coun., Luth. Ch. in Am., 1984-87; mem. task force on new ch. design Commn. on New Luth. Ch., task force on ch. pub. house, 1985; del. constituting conv. Evang. Luth. Ch. in Am., 1987, del. assemblies Evang. Luth. Ch. in Am., 1989, 91, 93, 95; mem. commn. on clergy confidentiality Luth. Coun. in USA, 1987; co-chair USA Luth.-Roman Cath. Dialogue, 1990-97; mem. Task Force on Theol. Edn. Author: LSTC: Decade of Decision, 1969; co-editor Scripture and Tradition, Lutherans and Catholics in Dialogue, 1995; mem. edtl. bd. Partners mag., 1978-80; contbr. articles and sermons to religious jours. Former bd. dirs. Augustana Theol. Sem.; bd. dirs. Augustana Coll., 1969-77, chmn. bd., 1976-77; bd. dirs. Kessler Reformation Collection, Newberry Coll., Luth. World Relief, Augsburg Fortress; chmn. bd. dirs. Luth. Sch. Theology, Chgo., 1962-69; mem. Leadership Atlanta, 1980-81, United Way, Atlanta, 1980-81; mem. Bishop's Commn. on Econ. Justice, 1985-86; pres. bd. dirs. Atlanta Samaritan House, 1986-87. Recipient Alumni award Luth. Sch. Theology, Chgo., 1976, award Leadership Atlanta, 1981, The Rev. John Bachman award, Luth. Theol. Sem., Columbia, S.C., 1996. Mem. Luth. Sch. Theology Alumni Assn. (pres. 1975-77), Conf. of Bishops, Kiwanis (pres. Midtown chpt. 1984-85). Lutheran. Avocations: travel, photography. Home: 104 Hawthorne Lake Dr Bloomington IL 61704 Personal E-mail: hcskillrud@aol.com.

SKILTON, JOHN SINGLETON, lawyer; b. Washington, Apr. 13, 1944; s. Robert Henry and Margaret (Neisser) S.; m. Carmen Fisher, Jan. 28, 1967; children: Laura Anne, Susan Elizabeth, Robert John. BA, U. Wis., 1966, JD, 1969. Bar: Wis. Supreme Ct. 1969, U.S. Dist. Ct. (ea. and we. dists.) Wis. 1969, U.S. Ct. Appeals (7th cir.) 1969, U.S. Supreme Ct. 1989, U.S. Ct. Appeals (Fed. cir.) 1991. Law clk. 7th Cir. Ct. Appeals, Milw., 1969-70; assoc. Foley & Lardner, Milw., 1970-77, ptnr. Madison, Wis., 1977-2000; shareholder Heller, Ehrman, White & McAuliffer, Washington, 2000—. Bd. visitors U. Wis. Law Sch., Madison, 1982-90, chmn., 1988-89; chair Wis. Fed. Nominating Commn., 1994; mem. Gov.'s Task Force on Bus. Ct., 1994-95, Govs. Internat. Trade Coun., 2004-; pres. Wis. Law Found., 2000-02, Wis. Internat. Trade Co. 2004-. Recipient Eisenberg Lifetime Achievement award, Equal Justice Fund, 2003. Fellow Am. Bar Found., Am. Coll. Trial Lawyers, Internat. Acad. Trial Lawyers; mem. ABA (chmn. standing com. on delivery of legal svcs. 1996-2000, chmn. consortium legal svcs. and pub. 2000-02), Am. Law Inst., Am. Acad. Appellate Lawyers, 7th Cir. Bar Assn. (pres. 1985-86, chmn. 7th cir. adv. com. on rules 1994-2000), State Bar Wis. (pres. 1995-96, Pres.'s award of excellence 1989, 2004, 2006, Sinykin award for publ svc. 1996), Western Dist. Wis. Bar Assn. (pres. 1992-93), Western Dist. Adv. Group (chmn. 1991), Wis. Law Found. (pres. 2000-02), James E. Doyle Am. Inn of Ct. (coun. 1992-94), Am. Inns of Ct. Found. (trustee 1995-98), U. Wis. Law Alumni Assn. (bd. dirs. 1991-97, pres. 1993-95), Lawyers Com. Civil Rights (co-chair, 2003-2005), recipient Lawyers Com. Lifetime Achievement award, 2007 Home: 917 Woodward Dr Madison WI 53704 Office: 1 E Main St Madison WI 53703-5118 Office Phone: 608-663-7474.

SKINDELL, MICHAEL J., lawyer; b. Medina, Ohio, Aug. 31, 1962; s. Vincent M. and Carol A. (Kaska) S. BA, Walsh U., 1983; JD, Cleve.-Marshall Coll. of Law, 1987. Asst. atty. gen. Ohio Atty. Gen., Columbus, Ohio, 1987-89; assoc. atty. Scaman & Assoc. Co. L.P.A., Cleve., 1989—. Hearing officer Ohio Dept. of Health, Cleve., 1989—. Chmn. Citizens Adv. Com., Lakewood, Ohio, 1996; candidate for state rep. Ohio Gen. Assembly, 1996; v.p. Lakewood Dem. Club, 1993—. Mem. Ohio Acad. of Trial Lawyers, Lakewood Jaycees. Roman Catholic. Home: 16800 Delaware Ave Lakewood OH 44107-5517

SKINDRUD, RICK, state legislator; b. Sept. 15, 1944; Bd. dirs. Dane County, Wis.; planning commn. Town of Primrose, Wis.; assemblyman Wis. State Dist. 79, 1993—. Former dairy farmer; chmn. State Affairs Com., Consumer Affairs

Com., Colo. Land Conservation Com., Colo. Extension Com. Past pres. Mt. Vernon Park Assn. Mem. Govs. Coun. on Tourism. Office: Wis Assembly PO Box 8952 Madison WI 53708-8952 Home: 1303 La Follette Rd Mount Horeb WI 53572-2932

SKINNER, CALVIN L., JR., state legislator; b. Easton, Md., June 11, 1942; s. Calvin L. Sr. and Eleanor (Stevens) S.; m. Robin Meredith Geist, 1977 (div.); m. Michele M. Giangrasso, 1990; children: Alexandra, Steven. BA, Oberlin Coll., 1964; MPA, U. Mich., 1971. Treas. McHenry County, 1966-70; mem. Ill. Ho. of Reps., Springfield, 1973—81, 1993—2001. Rep. candidate for comptr. State of Ill., 1982; precinct committeeman Algonquin Twp. Rep. Com., 1986-2000; Libertarian Party candidate for Ill. Gov., 2002; mem. Ill. AIDS Adv. Coun., 1988-92, 93-97. Mem. McHenry County Defenders. Home: 275 Meridian St Crystal Lake IL 60014-5411

SKINNER, JAMES A., food products executive; b. Davenport, IA; m. Kathleen Skinner; 1 child. Grad, Roosevelt U. Restaurant mgr. trainee to numerous positions within the US Co. McDonald's Corp., 1971—, US zone v.p., 1987—92; sr. v.p., relationship ptnr., 1992—95; exec. v.p., internat. relationship ptnr. McDonald's Ctrl. Europe, Middle East, Africa, India, 1995—97; pres. McDonald's Europe, 1997—2001; pres., COO McDonald's Europe/Asia/Pacific and Middle East, 2001—02, McDonald's Restaurant Group, 2002—03; vice chmn. McDonald's Corp., 2003—04, vice-chmn., CEO, 2004—. Adv. dir. bd. dirs. (twice) McDonald's Corp.; bd. dirs. Walgreen Co., 2005—. Bd. mem. Ronald McDonald House Charities. Office: McDonald's Corp McDonald's Plz 2111 McDonalds Dr Oak Brook IL 60523

SKINNER, JAMES LAURISTON, chemist, educator; b. Ithaca, NY, Aug. 17, 1953; s. G. William and Carol (Bagger) S.; m. Wendy Moore, May 31, 1986; children: Colin Andrew, Duncan Geoffrey. AB in Chemistry and Physics with highest honors, U. Calif., Santa Cruz, 1975; AM in Physics, Harvard U., 1977, PhD in Chem. Physics, 1979. Postdoctoral rsch. assoc. Stanford U., Calif., 1980-81; from asst. prof. to prof. chemistry Columbia U., NYC, 1981-90; Joseph O. Hirschfelder prof. chemistry U. Wis., Madison, 1990—, dir. Theoretical Chemistry Inst., 1990—, chair dept. chemistry, 2004—07. Vis. scientist Inst. Theol. Physics U. Calif., Santa Barbara, 1987; vis. prof. physics U. Jos. Fourier, Grenoble, France, 1987, U. Bordeaux, France, 1995. Mem. editl. bd.: Jour. Chem. Physics, 1999—2001, Single Molecules, 2000—03, Jour. Phys. Chemistry, 2004—06, Chem. Physics, 2005—; mem. editl. bd. mol. Physics, 2008—; contbr. articles to profl. jours. Recipient Fresenius award Phi Lambda Upsilon, 1989, Camille and Henry Dreyfus Tchr.-Scholar award, 1984, Presdl. Young Investigator award SF, 1984-89, Kellett Mid-Career award U. Wis., 1995, Pharmacia Tchg. award, 2000, Chancellor's Disting. Tchg. award, 2003; named Sr. Scientist Humboldt Found., 1993-97; NSF grad fellow, 1975, NSF postdoctoral fellow, 1980, Alfred P. Sloan Found. fellow, 1984, Guggenheim fellow, 1993-94. Fellow: AAAS, Am. Acad. Arts & Sciences, Am. Phys. Soc. Achievements include fundamental research in condensed phase theoretical chemistry. Office: U Wis Dept Chemistry Theoretical Chem Inst 1101 University Ave Madison WI 53706-1322

SKINNER, MARY JACOBS, lawyer; b. 1957; m. Sam Skinner, Aug. 17, 1989; stepchildren: Thomas, Steven, Jane. BA cum laude, Harvard U., 1978; JD, Northwestern U., 1981. Bar: Ill. 1981, D.C. 1990, U.S. Supreme Ct. 1990. With Sidley Austin Brown & Wood, Chgo., 1981—, ptnr., 1989—; counsel to spkr. Ill. Ho. of Reps., Springfield, Ill., 1983—85. Intern White House, 1979. Former trustee RAdcliffe Coll.; participant leadership coun. Greater Chgo. Fellowship Program, 1984. amed One of Forty under 40 Most Outstanding Leaders in Chco., Crain's Chgo. Bus. Mem. Harvard Alumni Assn. (bd. dirs.), Radcliffe Coll. Alumni Assn. (past pres.). Office: Sidley Austin Brown and Wood Bank One Plz 10 S Dearborn St Chicago IL 60603

SKINNER, THOMAS, broadcast executive; b. Poughkeepsie, NY, Aug. 17, 1934; s. Clarence F. and Frances D. S.; m. Elizabeth Burroughs, June 22, 1957; children: Kristin Jon, Karin Anne, Erik Lloyd. BS, SUNY, Fredonia, 1956; MA, U. Mich., Ann Arbor, 1957, PhD, 1962. Instr. speech U. Mich., 1960; assoc. prof., exec. producer dept. broadcasting San Diego State U., 1961-66; asst. mgr. Sta. WITF-TV, Hershey, Pa., 1966-70; v.p. Sta. WQED-TV, Pitts., 1970-72; exec. v.p., COO QED Communications Inc. (WQED-TV, WQED-FM, Pittsburgh mag., WQEX-TV), 1972-93; founder, pres., exec. prodr. Windrush Assocs., 1993—; v.p. Programming Resolution Prodns., Burlington, Vt., 1996—; mng. dir. Inland Seas Edn. Assn., 2000—; exec. prodr. Free to Choose Media, 2004—. Exec. prodr.: spls. and series including (for PBS) Nat. Geog. spls. Planet Earth, The Infinite Voyage, Conserving America, (for TBS) Pirate Tales, (for A&E) Floating Palaces, California and the Dream Seekers, The Story of Money, (for Discovery) Battleship, The Secret World of Air Freight, (for PBS) The Power of Choice: The Life and Ideas of Milton Friedman, (for HDNET) The Ultimate Resource. Recipient award as exec. prodr. DuPont Columbia, 1979, Oscar award as dir. Acad. Motion Picture Arts and Scis., 1967, Emmy award as exec. prodr. Nat. Acad. TV Arts and Scis., 1979, 83-84, 86-87, Peabody award as exec. prodr., 1980, 86. Office Phone: 231-883-1659. Personal E-mail: ski361@aol.com.

SKINNER, TIMOTHY D., state senator; m. Mary Lou Skinner; 4 children. B in Secondary Edn., M in Secondary Edn., Ind. State U. Tchr. Vigo County Sch. Corp., Ind.; state sen. dist. 38 Ind. State Senate, Indpls., 2002—. Elected Vigo County Coun., Ind.; Otter Creek precinct committeeman. Democrat. Office: Ind State Senate 200 W Washington St Indianapolis IN 46204-2787

SKLARSKY, CHARLES B., lawyer; b. Chgo., June 13, 1946; s. Morris and Sadie (Brenner) S.; m. Elizabeth Ann Hardzinski, Dec. 28, 1973; children: Jacob Daniel, Katherine Gabrielle, Jessica Leah. AB, Harvard U., 1968; JD, U. Wis., 1973. Bar: Wis. 1973, Ill. 1973, U.S. Dist. Ct. (no. dist.) Ill. 1973, U.S. Ct. Appeals (7th cir.) 1978, U.S. Ct. Appeals (2d cir.) 1986. Asst. states atty. Cook County, Chgo., 1973-78; asst. U.S. atty. (no. dist.) Ill. US Dept. Justice, Chgo., 1978-86; ptnr. Jenner & Block LLP, Chgo., 1986—. Mem. ABA, Am. Coll. Trial Lawyers, Chgo. Bar Assn. Office: Jenner & Block One IBM Plz Chicago IL 60611-3586 Office Phone: 312-923-2904. E-mail: csklarsky@jenner.com.

SKLBA, RICHARD JOHN, bishop; b. Racine, Wis., Sept. 11, 1935; Student, Old St. Francis Minor Sem., Milw., Pontifica. Bibl. Inst., Rome. Ordained priest Archdiocese of Milw., Wis., 1959; ordained bishop, 1979; aux. bishop Archdiocese of Milw., 1979—. Roman Catholic. Office: Archdiocese of Milwaukee PO Box 07912 3501 S Lake Dr Milwaukee WI 53207-0912 Office Phone: 414-769-3300. Office Fax: 414-769-3300.*

SKOCHELAK, SUSAN E., dean; BS, Mich. Tech. U., 1975, MS in Biol. Sci., 1977; MD, U. Mich., 1981; MPH, U. N.C., 1986. Diplomae Am. Bd. Family Medicine. Intern, resident family medicine U. N.C.-N.C. Meml. Hosp., Chapel Hill, 1977-81; assoc. dean Academic Affairs U. Wis., Madison, 1993—. Cons. in field; assoc. prof. U. Wis. Author: (with others) Preceptor Education Project, Handbook for Clerkship Directors. Mem. Wis. Rural Health Dev. Council, Consortium Primary Care in Wis.; co-dir. Wis. Area Health Edn. Sys. Recipient National award Patient Care mag., 1997. Mem. AMA, Soc. Tchrs. Family Medicine, Assn. Am. Med. Colls., Am. Med. Women's ssn., ACPHE. Office: Univ Wisconsin Med School 1300 University Ave Madison WI 53706-1510

SKOGSBERGH, JAMES H., health facility administrator; BS, Iowa State U.; M in health admin., U. Iowa. Exec. v.p. Iowa Health Sys., Des Moines; pres. CEO Iowa Meth. Med. Ctr., Iowa Luth. Hosp., Blank Children's Hosp.; admin. resident to exec. v.p., chief oper. officer Mem. Health Sys., South Bend, Ind., 1982—91; exec. v.p. Iowa Meth. Med. Ctr., 1991; chief operating officer Advocate Health Care, Oak Brook, Ill., 2001—02, pres., CEO, 2002—. Fellow: Am. Coll. Healthcare Exec.; mem.: Ill. Hosp. Assoc. Advocacy Coun., Metro. Chgo. Healthcare Coun., Young Pres. Organ., Chgo. Econ. Club. Office: Advocate health Care 2025 Windsor Dr Oak Brook IL 60523-1586

SKOIEN, GARY, real estate company executive; BS cum laude, Colgate U., 1976; M Pub. Policy with honors, U. Mich., 1978. Asst. to James R. Thompson Gov. of Ill., Springfield, 1980-83; exec. dir. Ill. Capital Devel. Bd., 1983-90; sr. v.p., COO retail divsn. PGI (name now Prime Retail Inc.), 1991-92; exec. v.p., COO Prime Group, Inc., 1991—; chmn. bd., pres., CEO Horizon Group, Inc., Chgo., 1998—. Vice-chmn. bd. dirs. Civic Fedn.; chmn. bd. trustees No. Ill. U.; chmn. Cook County Rep. Party. Mem. Chicagoland C. of C. (bd. dirs.). Office: 6250 N River Rd Ste 10-400 Rosemont IL 60018

SKOLNIK, DAVID ERWIN, financial analyst; b. Cleve., Oct. 31, 1949; s. Marvin and Ruth (Kovit) S.; m. Linda Susan Pollack, Mar. 31, 1973; children: Carla Denise, Robyn Laurel. BS in Acctg., Ohio State U., 1971. CPA, Ohio. Chief acct. Gray Drug Fair, Cleve., 1976-82, mgr. acctg. systems, 1982-84; fin. systems analyst Soc. Corp., Cleve., 1984, fin. systems officer, 1984-86, fin. systems rsch. officer, 1986-90, sr. fin. systems officer, 1990-91, strategic rsch. officer, 1991-92; mgmt. acctg. officer Keycorp, Cleve., 1992-96, asst. v.p., 1996—. Scoutmaster Boy Scouts Am., Cleve., 1971-77; coach Girls Softball League, South Euclid, Ohio, 1989-97. Mem. AICPAs, Ohio Soc. CPAs, Am. Inst. Banking, Am. Mgmt. Assn., Tau Epsilon Phi. Jewish. Avocations: golf, bowling, home repairs. Home: 33892 Hanover Woods Trl Solon OH 44139-4473 Office: Keycorp 127 Public Sq Cleveland OH 44114-1306 Home Phone: 440-498-2163; Office Phone: 216-689-7176. Business E-Mail: dave_skolnik@keybank.com.

SKRAINKA, ALAN FREDERICK, securities analyst; b. St. Louis, May 8, 1961; s. Frederick Ralph and Yvonne M. (Oelawder) S.; m. Julie Lynn Wussler, Jan. 24, 1987. BBA in Acctg. and Fin., U. Mo., 1983; MBA, Washington U., 1990. Chartered fin. analyst. Utility analyst Edward D. Jones & Co., St. Louis, 1983—, ltd. ptnr. Maryland Heights, Mo., 1986-88, gen. ptnr., 1988—, chief market strategist, Investment Policy Adv. Com., 1996—. Mem. Fin. Analysts Fedn. Office: Edward D Jones & Co PO Box 190489 Saint Louis MO 63119-6489

SKROWACZEWSKI, STANISLAW, conductor, composer; b. Lwow, Poland, Oct. 3, 1923; came to U.S., 1960; s. Pawel and Zofia (Karszniewicz) S.; m. Krystyna Jarosz, Sept. 6, 1956; children: Anna, Paul, Nicholas. Diploma faculty philosophy, U. Lwow, 1945; diploma faculties composition and conducting, Acad. Music Lwow, 1945, Conservatory at Krakow, Poland, 1946; L.H.D., Hamline U., 1963, Macalester Coll., 1972; L.H.D. hon. doctorate, U. Minn.; Doctorate (hon.), U. Wroclaw, Poland, 2003. Guest condr. in, Europe, S.A., U.S., 1947—; Composer, 1931—; pianist, 1928—; violinist, 1934—; condr., 1939—; permanent condr., music dir. Wroclaw (Poland) Philharmonic, 1946-47, Katowice (Poland) Nat. Philharmonic, 1949-54, Krakow Philharmonic, 1955-56, Warsaw Nat. Philharmonic Orch., 1957-59, Minnesota Orch., 1960-79; prin. condr., mus. adviser Halle Orch., Manchester, Eng., 1984-91; musical advisor St. Paul Chamber Orchestra, 1986—87, Milw. Symphony, 1995—97; prin. condr. Yominri Nippon Symphony Orch., Tokyo, 2007—; prin. conductor Nippon Symphony Orch., Tokyo, 2007—. First symphony and overture for orch. written at age 8, played by Lwow Philharm. Orch., 1931; adv. music Milw. Symphony, 1994-97. Composer: 4 symphonies Prelude and Fugue for Orchestra (conducted first performance Paris), 1948, Overture, 1947 (2d prize Szymanowski Concours, Warsaw 1947); Cantiques des Cantiques, 1951, String Quartet, 1953 (2d Prize Internat. Concours Composers, Belgium 1953), Suite Symphonique, 1954 (first prize, gold medal Composers Competition Moscow 1957), Music at Night, 1954, Ricercari Notturni, 1978 (3d prize Kennedy Center Friedheim Competition, Washington), Concerti for Clarinet and Orch., 1980, Violin Concerto, 1985, Concerto for Orch., 1985, Fanfare for Orch., 1987, Sextett for Oboe, Violin, Viola, Orchestra, 1980, String Trio for Violin, Viola, 1990, Triple Concerto for Violin, Clarinet, Piano, Orchestra, 1992, Fantasie per Tre (Flute, Oboe, Cello), 1993, Chamber Concerto, 1993, Passacaglia Immaginaria for Orch., 1995, Musica a Quattro for Clarinet, Violin, Viola, Cello, 1998, Concerto for Orch., 1998, Symphony, 2003; also music for theatre, motion pictures, songs and piano sonatas, English horn concerto; rec. by Mercury, Columbia, RCA, Albany, Victor, Vox, EMI, Angel. Decorated comdrs. cross Polonia Restituta, Highest Polish award Gold medal, Gloria Artist, 2007; recipient nat. prize for artistic activity Poland, 1953, 1st prize Santa Cecilia Internat. Concours for Condrs., Rome, 1956, Cannes Festival award for best rec. of 19th century symphonic music, 2002, Disting. Artist award McKnight Found., 2004. Mem. Union Polish Composers, Internat. Soc. Modern hon. doctorate at New England Consenatory Boston 2008 Music, Nat. Assn. Am. Composers-Condrs., Am. Music Center. Office: PO Box 700 Wayzata MN 55391

SKULINA, THOMAS RAYMOND, lawyer; b. Cleve., Sept. 14, 1933; s. John J. and Mary B. (Vesely) S. AB, John Carroll U., 1955; JD, Case Western Res. U., 1959, LLM, 1962. Bar: Ohio 1959, U.S. Supreme Ct. 1964, ICC 1965. Ptnr. Skulina & Stringer, Cleve., 1967-72, Riemer Oberdank & Skulina, Cleve., 1978-81, Skulina, Fillo, Walters & Negrelli, 1981-86, Skulina & McKeon, Cleve., 1986-90, Skulina & Hill, Cleve., 1990-97; atty. Penn Ctrl. Transp. Co., Cleve., 1960-65, asst. gen. atty., 1965-78, trial counsel, 1965-76; with Consol. Rail Corp., 1976-78; pvt. practice Cleve., 1997—. Tchr. comml. law Practicing Law Inst., N.Y.C., 1970; practicing labor arbitrator Fed. Mediation and Conciliation Svc., 1990—; arbitrator Mcpl. Securities Rulemaking Bd., 1994-98, N.Y. Stock Exch., 1995—, ASD, 1996—; mediator NASD, 1997—, AAA Comml., 1997—; mediator vol. panel EEOC, 1997-99, contract panel, 1999-2000; arbitrator Better Bus. Bur., 2000—. Contbr. articles to legal jours. Income tax and fed. fund coord. City of Warrensville Heights, Ohio, 1970—77; spl. counsel City of North Olmstead, Ohio, 1971—75; spl. counsel to Ohio Atty. Gen., 1983—93, Cleve. Charter Rev. Commn., 1988, referee, 1986—; fact-finder State Employees Rels. Bd., Ohio, 1986—; hearing officer Human Resource Commn., Summit County, Ohio, 2000—03. With US Army, 1959. Mem. ABA (R.R. and motor carrier com. 1988-96, jr. chmn. 1989-96, alt. dispute resolution com. 1998—), FBA, Assn. Conflict Resolution, Cleve. Bar Assn. (grievance com. 1987-93, chmn. 1997-98, trustee 1993-96, ADR com. 1997—), Ohio Bar Assn. (bd. govs. litigation sect. 1986-98, negligence law com. 1989-96, ethics and profl. responsibility com. 1990-91, alt. dispute resolution com. 1996—), Am. Arbitration Assn. (practicing labor arbitrator 1987—), Nat. Acad. Arbitrators, Nat. Assn. R.R. Trial Counsel (emeritus), Internat. Assn. Law and Sci., Pub. Sector Labor Rels. Assn., Internat. Indsl. Rels. Rsch. Assn., Soc. Fed. Labor and Employee Rels. Profls. Democrat. Roman Catholic. Home: 3162 W 165th St Cleveland OH 44111-1016 Office: 24803 Detroit Rd Westlake OH 44145 Home Phone: 216-221-4910; Office Phone: 440-899-1911. E-mail: tskulina@sbcglobal.net.

SKYES, GREGORY, food products executive; New products mktg. mgr. Hillshire Farm & Kahn's, 1984; pres., CEO Ball Park Brands, 1995; mgr. State Fair Foods, Best Kosher; v.p. Sara Lee Foods, Chgo.; pres., CEO Sara Lee Foods Retail, Chgo. Office: Sara Lee Corp 3 First National Plz Chicago IL 60602-4260

SLADE, ROY, artist, college president, museum director; b. Cardiff, U.K., July 14, 1933; came to U.S., 1967, naturalized, 1975; s. David Trevor and Millicent (Stone) S. N.D.D., Cardiff Coll. Art, 1954; A.T.D., U. Wales, 1954; D of Arts, Art Inst. So. Calif., 1994. Tchr. art and crafts Heolgam High Sch., Wales, 1956-60; lectr. art Clarendon Coll., Nottingham, Eng., 1960-64; sr. lectr. fine art Leeds Coll. Art, Eng., 1964-67; prof. painting Corcoran Sch. Art, Washington, 1967-68, assoc. dean, 1969-70, dean, 1970-77; dir. Corcoran Gallery of Art, Washington, 1972-77; pres., dir. Cranbrook Acad. Art, Bloomfield Hills, Mich., 1977-94, now dir. emeritus. Sr. lectr. Leeds Coll. Art, England, 1968—69; vis. Boston Mus. Fine Arts, 1970; dir. emeritus Cranbrook Art Mus., 2000—. Exhibited one-man shows Howard Roberts Gallery, Cardiff, Wales, 1958, New Art Ctr., London, 1960, U. Birmingham, 1964, 69, Herbert Art Gallery and Mus., Coventry, 1964, Va. State Art League, 1967, Mus. of Arts and Crafts, Columbus, Ga., 1968, Jefferson Place Gallery, Washington, 1968, 70, 72, 73, Park Sq. Gallery, Leeds, 1969, St. Mary's Coll., Md., 1971, Guelph U., Ont., Can., 1971, Hood Coll., 1974, Pyramid Gallery, Washington, 1976, Robert Kidd Gallery, 1981, 92, Herman Miller, Inc., Mich., 1985; group shows in U.K., Washington, Can.; represented in permanent collections Arts Council Gt. Brit., Contemporary Art Soc., Nuffield Found., Ministry of Works, Eng., Brit. Embassy, Washington, Brit. Overseas Airways Corp., U. Birmingham, Wakefield City Art Gallery, Clarendon Coll., Cadbury Bros., Ltd., Eng., Lord Ogmore, Local Edn. Authorities. Mem. D.C. Commn. on Arts.; bd. dirs. Artists for Environment Found., Nat. Assn. Schs. Art; chmn. Nat. Council Art Adminstrs., 1981. Served with Brit. Army, 1954-56. Decorated knight 1st class Order of White Rose (Finland), Royal Order of Polar Star (Sweden); recipient award Welsh Soc., Phila., 1974, Gov.'s Arts Orgn. award, 1988; Fulbright scholar, 1967-68. Mem. Nat. Soc. Lit. and Arts, AIA (hon. Detroit chpt.), Assn. Art Mus. Dirs. (hon.). Home: 31 Island Way Apt 801 Clearwater FL 33767-2206 Personal E-mail: royslade@verizon.net.

SLANSKY, JERRY WILLIAM, investment company executive; b. Chgo., Mar. 8, 1947; s. Elmer Edward and Florence Anna (Kosobud) S.; m. Marlene Jean Cannella, Jan. 29, 1950; children: Brett Matthew, Blake Adam. BA, Elmhurst Coll., 1969; MA, No. Ill. U., 1971. Mktg. rep. Bantam Book Co., Chgo., 1972-73, Charles Levy Circulating Co., Chgo., 1973-76; account exec. Merrill Lynch, Chgo., 1976-77, Oppenheimer & Co., Inc., Chgo., 1977—, asst. v.p., 1978, v.p., 1979, sr. v.p., 1981, mng. dir., 1986, ptnr., 1986—. Bd. dirs. Lake Geneva (Wis.) Beach Assn., 1987-02, Glen Ellyn Youth Ctr., Glenbard West H.S., pres., 1998-99; bd. dirs. Buttonwood Cove, Longboat Key, Fla., 2006-; mem. bus. affairs com. Presbytery of Chgo., 1999-04. Mem. Nat. Assn. Securities Dealers (arbitrator 1988—), .Y. Stock Exch., Chgo. Bd. Options, Am. Arbitration. Assn, Omaha C. of C. Presbyterian. Avocations: swimming, water-skiing, golf, skiing, kayaking. Office: Oppenheimer & Co Ste 4000 500 W Madison St Chicago IL 60661 Office Phone: 312-360-5553. Personal E-mail: jerry.slansky@opco.com.

SLATON, DANIELLE VICTORIA, professional soccer player; b. San Jose, Calif., June 10, 1980; Majored in psychology, Santa Clara U., Calif., 1998—2001. Capt. U.S. Under-16 at. Team, 1996—97; mem. U.S. Under-21 Nat. Team, 1999, starter, Nordic Cup championship team, 1999; soccer player, defender U.S. Women's Nat. Team, 1999—; mem. U.S. soccer team Summer Olympics, Sydney, Australia, 2000; team mem. Carolina Courage, WUSA. Finalist Mo. Athletic Club award, 2000, 2001, Hermann trophy, 2001; named third team All-Am., NSCAA, 1998, first team All-Am., 1999, 2001, 2002. Office: US Soccer Fedn 1801 S Prairie Ave Chicago IL 60616

SLATOPOLSKY, EDUARDO, nephrologist, educator; b. Buenos Aires, Dec. 12, 1934; married, 1959; 3 children. BS, Nat. Coll. Nicolas Avellaneda, 1952; MD, U. Buenos Aires, 1959. Postdoctoral rschr. renal USPHS, renal divsn., Dept. Internal Medicine Washington U. Sch. Medicine, 1963—65, instr. med. nephrology, 1965—67, asst. prof. to assoc. prof. medicine dept. nephrology, 1967—75, dir. Chromalloy Am. Kidney Ctr. St. Louis, 1967—97, co-dir. renal divsn. Chromalloy Am. Kidney Ctr., 1972—97, prof. medicine, nephrology dept. Chromalloy Am. Kidney Ctr., 1975—, Joseph Friedman Prof. renal disease medicine Chromalloy Am. Kidney Ctr., 1991—. Adv. mem. regional med. prog., renal prog. sch. medicine Washington U., 1970-75; chmn. transplantation com. Barne Hosp., 1975—; fellow com. Kidney Found. Ea. Mo. and Metro.-East, 1978; mem. adv. com. artificial kidney-chronic uremia prog. NIH, 1978-90, rep. Latin-Am. nephrology, 1983-88; mem. study sect. Gen. Med., NIH, 1984-88. Recipient Frederick C. Bartter award, 1991. Mem. AAAS, Am. Fedn. Clin. Rsch., Internat. Soc. Nephrology (Amgen Internat. prize for Therpeutic Advancement in Nephrology), Am. Soc. Nephrology, Endocrine Soc., Sigma Xi. Achievements include research in pathogenesis and treatment of secondary hyparathyroidism and bone disease in renal failure; studies conducted at both levels: clinical, on patients maintained on chronic dialysis and on animals with experimentally induced renal feilure; detailed studies of the effects of calcitriol on PTH MRNA and the extra-renal production of calcitriol by macrophages; vitro studies in primary culture of bovine parathyroid cells used to understand the mechanisms that control the secretion of PTH. Office: Washington U Chromalloy Am Kidney Ctr PO Box 8126 Saint Louis MO 63156-8126 Office Phone: 314-362-7208. Office Fax: 314-362-7875. E-mail: eslatopo@wustl.edu.

SLAUGHTER ANDREW, ANNE, lawyer; b. Evansville, Ind., Sept. 23, 1955; d. Owen L. and Marjorie (Specht) Slaughter; m. Joseph J. Andrew, Sept. 9, 1989. BA, Georgetown U., 1977; JD cum laude, Ind. U., 1983. Bar: Ind. 1983, U.S. Dist. Ct. (so. dist.) Ind. Ptnr. Baker & Daniels, Indpls. Adj. prof. environ. law Ind. U. Sch. Law, Indpls. Editor-in-chief Ind. U. Law Rev., 1982-83; contbr. articles to profl. jours. Bd. dirs. Nature Conservancy, 1997—, Ind. Natural Resources Found., 1994—; mem. Indpls. Pub. Sch. Found. Com., 1997—; mem. Brownfield Remediation Adv. Com., 1997—. Mem. ABA (chair state and regional environ. coop. com. 1996-98), Ind. Bar Assn. (chair environ. law sect. 1992-93), Ind. C. of C. (govt. affairs commn.). Office: Baker & Daniels 300 N Meridian St Ste 2700 Indianapolis IN 46204-1782

SLAVENS, THOMAS PAUL, library science educator; b. Cincinnati, Iowa, Nov. 12, 1928; s. William Blaine and Rhoda (Bowen) S.; m. Cora Hart, July 9, 1950; 1 son, Mark Thomas. BA, Phillips U., 1951; MDiv, Union Theol. Sem., 1954; MA, U. Minn., 1962; PhD, U. Mich., 1965. Ordained to ministry Christian Ch., 1953. Pastor First Christian Ch., Sac City, Iowa, 1953-56, Sioux Falls, SD, 1956-60; librarian Divinity Sch., Drake U., Des Moines, 1960-64; teaching fellow Sch. Info., U. Mich., Ann Arbor, 1964-65; instr. U. Mich., Ann Arbor, 1965-66, asst. prof., 1966-69, assoc. prof., 1969-77, prof., 1977—2003, prof. emeritus, 2003—. Vis. prof. U. Minn., 1967, U. Coll. of Wales, 1978, 80, 93; vis. scholar U. Oxford, Eng., 1980; cons. Nutrition Planning Abstracts-UN, N.Y.C., 1977-79. Author-editor: Library Problems in the Humanities, 1981, (with John F. Wilson) Research Guide to Religious Studies, 1982, (with W. Eugene Kleinbaur) Research Guide to the History of Western Art, 1982, (with Terrence Tice) Research Guide to Philosophy, 1983, Theological Libraries at Oxford, 1984, (with James Pruett) Research Guide to Musicology, 1985, The Literary Adviser, 1985, A Great Library through Gifts, 1986, The Retrieval of Information, 1989, Number One in the U.S.A.: Records and Wins in Sports, Entertainment, Business, and Science, 1988, Doors to God, 1990, Sources of Information for Historical Research, 1994, Introduction to Systematic Theology, 1992, Reference Interviews Questions and Materials, 3d edit., 1994, Using the Financial and Business Literature, 2004. Served with U.S. Army, 1946-48. Recipient Warner Rice Faculty award U. Mich., 1975; H.W. Wilson fellow, 1960; Lilly Endowment fellow Am. Theol. Libr. Assn., 1963. Mem. Assn. Libr. and Info. Sci. Edn. (pres. 1972), Beta Phi Mu.

SLAVIN, CRAIG STEVEN, management and franchising consultant; b. Tucson, Sept. 7, 1951; s. Sidney and Eileen (Gilbert) S.; m. Carol Lynn Haft, Aug. 30, 1982; children: Carly Blair, Samantha Illyna. Student, U. Ariz., 1969—73, U. Balt., 1978. Dir. franchising and sales Evelyn Wood Reading Dynamics, Walnut Creek, Calif., 1974-75; dir. franchising Pasquale Food Co., Birmingham, Ala., 1975-77; exec. v.p. Franchise Concepts, Flossmoor, Ill., 1977-80; pres. Franchise Architects, Chgo., 1980-88; mng. dir. franchise practice Arthur Andersen & Co., Chgo., 1988-91; chmn. Franchise Architects, Bannockburn, Ill., 1991—. Founder, bd. dirs. Franchise Broadcast Network, Riverwoods, 1991—; founder Franchise Success System, 1991, The Original Franchise Match, 1992. Author: Complete Guide to Self-Employment in Franchising, 1991, Franchising for the Growing Company, 1993, AMACON, The Franchising Handbook. Mem. ABA (faculty), Am. Arbitration Assn., Internat. Franchise Assn., Nat. Assn. Info. Suppliers, Water Quality Assn., Inst. Mgmt. Cons., Coun. Franchise Suppliers (adv. bd. dirs.), Nat. Restaurant Assn. Avocations: golf, chess. Office: Franchise Architects 2275 Half Day Rd Ste 350 Bannockburn IL 60015-1277

SLAVIN, RAYMOND GRANAM, allergist, immunologist; b. Cleve., June 29, 1930; s. Philip and Dinah (Baskind) S.; m. Alberta Cohrt, June 10, 1953; children: Philip, Stuart, David, Linda. AB, U. Mich., 1952; MD, St. Louis U., 1956; MS, Northwestern U., 1963. Diplomate Am. Bd. Internal Medicine, Am. Bd. Allergy and Immunology (treas.). Intern U. Mich. Hosp., Ann Arbor, 1956-57; resident St. Louis U. Hosp., 1959-61; fellow in allergy and immunology Northwestern U. Med. Sch., 1961-64; asst. prof. internal medicine and microbiology St. Louis U., 1965-70, assoc. prof., 1970-73, prof., 1973—, dir. divsn. allergy and immunology, 1965—. Mem. NIH study sect., 1985-89; cons. U.S. Army M.C. Contbr. numerous articles to med. pubs.; editl. bd.: Jour. Allergy and Clin. Immunology, 1975-81. Chmn. bd. Asthma and Allergy Found. Am., 1985-88. With M.C., U.S. Army, 1957-59. Grantee NIH, 1967-70, 84—, Nat. Inst. Occupl. Safety and Health, 1974-80. Master: ACP; fellow: Am. Acad. Allergy and Immunology (exec. bd., historian, pres. 1983—84, Disting. Svc. award 1995, Disting. Clinician award 2005); mem.: AAAS, Ctrl. Soc. Clin. Rsch., Am. Assn. Immunologists. Democrat. Jewish. Home: 631 E Polo Dr Saint Louis MO 63105-2629 Office: 1402 S Grand Blvd Saint Louis MO 63104-1004 Office Phone: 314-977-8829. Business E-Mail: slavinrg@slu.edu.

SLAY, FRANCIS G., mayor; b. St. Louis, Missouri; s. Francis R. and Anna Slay; m. Kim Slay; children: Francis Jr., Katherine. Law degree, Saint Louis U. Sch. Law, 1980; postgrad in political sci., Quincy Coll., Ill., 1977. Mayor City of St. Louis, 2001—; pvt. lawyer 20 yrs.; law clerk Judge Paul J. Simon, Mo. Court Appeals, 1981; ptnr. Guilfoil, Petzall & Shoemake. Mem. St. Louis Bd. Alderman, 1995, elected pres. Office: City Hall Rm 200 1200 Mrk St Saint Louis MO 63103*

SLAYMAKER, GENE ARTHUR, public relations executive; b. Kenton, Ohio, Sept. 15, 1928; s. Edwin Paul and Anna Elizabeth (Grable) S.; divorced; children: Jill Brook, Scott Wood, Leslie Beth; m. Julie Ann Graff, Feb. 3, 1979; 1 adopted child, Peter Fredric Bannon II; stepchildren: Jennifer Elizabeth Nash, David Frank Nash. BA in Radio Journalism, Ohio State U. Announcer, reporter WLWC-TV, Columbus, Ohio, 1951-52; anchor, reporter WKBN-AM-FM-TV, Youngstown, Ohio, 1952-56, KYW-TV, Cleve., 1956-60; editor news Sta. WFBM-AM-FM-TV, Indpls., 1960-68; pres., founder Slaymaker & Assocs. Pub. Rels., 1969—; dir. news, sports, pub. affairs WTLC-FM and WTUX-AM, Indpls., 1976-92; community rels. liaison Marion County Pros. Atty. Office, Indpls., 1993. Pres., founder Slaymaker and Assocs., Indpls., 1969—. Mambo dancer (movie) Going All the Way, 1996. Past bd. dirs. Park-Tudor Father's Assn.; mem. Meridian Kessler Neighborhood Assn., pres., 1968-69. Recipient Disting. Service award (2). Mem. Ind. AP Broadcasters Assn. (awards), UPI (awards), Nat. Fedn. Press Women, Soc. Profl. Journalists (awards Ind. chpt., bd. dirs., chpt. pres. 1991-92, Radio-TV News Dirs. Assn. (region bd. dirs. 1987-91), Indpls. Press Club, Woman's Press Club Ind., Players Club, Lambs Club (pres. 2000—). Clubs: Nat. Headliners, Unity. Democrat. Avocations: writing, painting, singing, gardening, tennis. Home: 5161 N Washington Blvd Indianapolis IN 46205-1071 Office: Slaymaker Assoc 5161 N Washington Blvd Indianapolis IN 46205-1071

SLEDGE, CARLA ELISSA, county official; b. Detroit, July 20, 1952; d. Thomas Biggs Sr. and Zephrie (Heard) Griffin; m. Willie Frank Sledge, July 20, 1974; children: Arian Darkell, Ryan Marcel. B in Acctg., Wayne State U., 1973; MA, Eastern Mich. U., 1982. Tchr. Taylor (Mich.) Bd. Edn., 1974-81, Met. Detroit Youth Found., 1981-86; auditor Deloitte & Touche, Detroit, 1982—95; chief dep. fin. officer Wayne County, Mich., 1995—2002; CFO, 2002, 2005—; pres. Govt. Fin. Officers Assn. bd. dirs. Mich. Assn. Cert. Pub. Accountants. Coordinator Tiger Cub Boy Scouts Am., Detroit, 1985—. Mem. Nat. Assn. Black Accountants. Democrat. Avocations: reading, music, travel. Office: Govt Fin Officers Assn 203 N LaSalle St Suite 2700 Chicago IL 60601

SLEIK, THOMAS SCOTT, lawyer; b. La Crosse, Wis., Feb. 24, 1947; s. John Thomas and Marion Gladys (Johnson) S.; m. Judith Mattson, Aug. 24, 1968; children: Jennifer, Julia, Joanna. BS, Marquette U., 1969, JD, 1971. Bar: Wis. 1971, U.S. Dist. Ct. (we. dist.) Wis. 1971. Assoc. Hale Skemp Hanson Skemp & Sleik, La Crosse, 1971-74, ptnr., 1975—. Bd. mem. Wis. Lawyer Mut. Ins. Co., 1999—. State pres. Boy Scouts Am., 1981—83, bd. dirs. Gateway Area Con., 1973—99, pres., 1980—81; trustee La Crosse Pub. Libr., 1981—, chair, bd. trustees, 2006—; bd. dirs. Children's Mus. of La Crosse, 1997—2002, Greater La Crosse Area United Way, 1985—92, campaign chmn., 1986, pres., 1987; mem. Sch. Dist. La Crosse Bd. Edn., 1973—77, v.p., 1977; festmaster Oktoberfest (LaCross Festivals Inc.), 2001, trustee, 2001—; bd. mem. Franciscan Skemp Healthcare, 2003—. Fellow Am. Acad. Matrimonial Lawyers (pres. Wis. chpt. 1999-2000); mem. ABA, State Bar Wis. (bd. govs. 1987-94, pres. 1992-93). Roman Catholic. Home: 4082 Glenhaven Dr La Crosse WI 54601-7503 Office: Hale Skemp Hanson Skemp & Sleik 505 King St Ste 300 La Crosse WI 54602-1927 Business E-Mail: tss@haleskemp.com.

SLEMMONS, ROD, museum director, art educator, curator; BA, U. Iowa, MA in English; MFA, Rochester Inst. Tech., 1976—78. Curator prints and photog. Seattle Art Mus., 1982—96; dir. Mus. of Contemporary Photog., Columbia Coll., Chgo., 2002—. Tchr. hist. photog. and grad. mus. studies U. Wash., Seattle. Curator Eye of the Mind/Mind of the Eye, 1988, Water: The Renewable Metaphor, 1997, Beyond Novelty: New Digital Art, 2000. Office: Mus Contemporary Photog Columbia Coll Chgo 600 S Michigan Ave Chicago IL 60605

SLICHTER, CHARLES PENCE, physicist, researcher; b. Ithaca, NY, Jan. 21, 1924; s. Sumner Huber and Ada (Pence) S.; m. Gertrude Thayer Almy, Aug. 23, 1952 (div. Sept. 1977); children: Sumner Pence, William Almy, Jacob Huber, Ann Thayer; m. Anne FitzGerald, June 7, 1980; children: Daniel Huber, David Pence AB, Harvard U., 1946, MA, 1947, PhD, 1949; DSc (hon.), U. Waterloo, 1993; LLD (hon.), Harvard U., 1996. Rsch. asst. Underwater Explosives Rsch. Lab., Woods Hole, Mass., 1943-46; faculty U. Ill., Urbana, 1949—, prof. physics, 1955-97, prof. Ctr. for Advanced Study, 1968-97, prof. chemistry, 1986-97, rsch. prof. physics, 1997—, prof. emeritus, 1997—. Morris Loeb lectr. Harvard U., 1961; mem. Pres.'s Sci. Adv. Com., 1964-69, Com. on Nat. Medal Sci., 1969-74, Nat. Sci. Bd., 1975-84, Pres.'s Com. Sci. and Tech., 1976 Author: Principles of Magnetic Resonance, 1963, 3d edit., 1989; Contbr. articles to profl. jours. Former trustee, mem. corp. Woods Hole Oceanog. Instn.; mem. Harvard Corp., 1970-95. Recipient Langmuir award Am. Phys. Soc., 1969, Buckley prize, 1996; Alfred P. Sloan fellow, 1955-61. Fellow AAAS, Am. Phys. Soc., Internat. Electron Paramagnetic Resonance Soc.; mem. NAS (Comstock prize 1993), Am. Acad. Arts and Scis., Am. Philos. Soc., Internat. Soc. Magnetic Resonance (pres. 1987-90, Triennial prize 1986). Home: 61 Chestnut Ct Champaign IL 61822-7121

SLINGER, MICHAEL JEFFERY, law librarian, director; b. Pitts., Apr. 12, 1956; s. Maurice and Mary Helen (Kengerski) S.; m. Cheryl Blaney, Apr. 19, 1980; children: Rebecca, Sarah. BA, U. Pitts., 1978; M Librianship, U. S.C., 1979; JD, Duquesne U., 1984. Reference libr. Duquesne U. Sch. Law, Pitts., 1983-84; rsch. libr. U. otre Dame Sch. Law, Ind., 1984-85, head rsch. svcs., 1985-86, assoc. dir. pub. svcs., 1986-90; law libr. dir., assoc. prof. law Suffolk U. Sch. Law, Boston, 1990-93, law libr. dir., prof. law, 1994-95; law libr. dir., prof. law, assoc. dean Cleve. State U., 1995—. Contbr. articles to profl. jours., chpt. to book. Mem.: ALA, ABA, Ohio Regional Assn. Law Librs. (v.p. 1987—88, pres. 1988—89, Pres. award 1989), New Eng. Law Libr. Consortium (treas. 1992—95), Am. Assn. Law Schs. (exec. bd. sect. on law librs. 1993—94), Am. Assn. Law Librs. (chair acad. law libr. spl. interest sect. 2005—). Avocations: reading, sports. Office: Cleve-Marshall Coll Law Libr 1801 Euclid Ave Cleveland OH 44115-2223 Office Phone: 216-687-3547. Business E-Mail: michael.slinger@law.csuohio.edu.

SLOAN, DAVID W., lawyer; b. Rahway, NJ, June 23, 1941; s. Harper Allen and Margaret (Walker) S.; m. Margaret J. Neville, Oct. 23, 1965; children: Matthew A., John S. AB, Princeton U., 1963; MS, Stanford U., 1965; JD, Harvard U., 1970. Bar: Calif. 1971, Ohio 1974. Assoc. Brobeck, Phleger & Harrison, San Francisco, 1970-73; assoc. and ptnr. Burke, Haber & Berick, Cleve., 1973-83; ptnr. Jones, Day, Reavis & Pogue, Cleve., 1983—. Adj. prof. law Case Western Reserve U., 1975. Vol. Peace Corps., Turkey, 1965-67; sr. warden St. Paul's Episcopal Ch., Cleveland Heights, 1993-96. Mem. ABA (former council mem. sect. on science and technology, bus. law sect., intellectual property law sect.), Ohio Bar Assn., Cleve. Bar Assn., Computer Law Assn., Princeton Assn. No. Ohio (pres. 1990-94), Sigma Xi, Alzheimer's Assn. (former trustee and v.p.). Office: Jones Day Reavis & Pogue North Point 901 Lakeside Ave E Cleveland OH 44114-1190

SLOAN, HUGH WALTER, JR., automotive executive; b. Princeton, NJ, Nov. 1, 1940; s. Hugh Walter and Elizabeth (Johnson) Sloan; m. Deborah Louise Murray, Feb. 20, 1971; children: Melissa, Peter, Jennifer, William. AB in History with honors, Princeton U., 1963. Staff asst. to Pres. U.S. White House, Washington, 1969-71; treas. Pres. Nixon's Re-election Campaign, Washington, 1971; spl. asst. to pres. Budd Co., Troy, Mich., 1973-74, exec. asst. internat., 1974-77, mgr. corp. mktg., 1977-79; pres., gen. mgr. Budd Can. Inc., Kitchener, Ont., Canada, 1979-85; pres. automotive Woodbridge Group, Troy, 1985-98, dep. chmn., 1998—. Bd. dirs. Woodbridge Foam Corp., Mfrs. Life Ins. Co., Wescast Industries. Trustee Spartan Motors, Inc., Beaumont Hosp.; gov. Cranbrook Schs. Lt. USNR, 1963—65. Recipient Outstanding Bus. Leader award, Wilfrid Laurier U., 1987. Mem.: Bloomfield Hills (Mich.) Country Club. Republican. Office: Woodbridge Group 1515 Equity Dr Troy MI 48084-7146 Office Phone: 248-280-6571. Business E-Mail: hugh_sloan@woodbridgegroup.com.

SLOAN, JUDI C., former physical education educator; b. Kansas City, Mo., July 17, 1944; d. Oscar H. Wilde and Florance (Janes) Wilde Graupner; m. Richard J. Sloan; children: Blake, Tracy. BS in Phys. Edn., No. Ill. U., 1966, postgrad.; MS in Phys. Edn., Ind. U., 1970; postgrad., U. Ill., DePaul U., Loyola U., at. Louis U. Tchr. phys. edn., coach Niles West High Sch., Skokie, Ill., 1966-99. Former coach gymnastics, tennis; coach cross-country; coop. tchr.; creator, dir. Galibo Gymnastics Show, 1968-75; founder, co-chair staff wellness com., Niles Township Sch. Dist., 1988—, curriculum coun., 1988-91; creator phys. mgmt. course, sophomore health and fitness program, evening children's, summer girls' gymnastics programs; co-dir. Indian Cross Country Invitational, Niles West Gymnastics Invitational; adv. com. cross country Ill. High Sch. Assn. Recipient All-Am. High Sch. Gymnastics Coach award U.S. Gymnastics Fedn., 1981, award of Honor Nat. Sch. Pub. Rels. Assn., 1990, Ill. Disting. Educator award, 1992; Named Ill. Tchr. Yr., 1992-93. Mem. AAHPERD, Am. Fedn. Tchrs., Nat. Assn. Secondary Physical Edn., Nat. Coaches Fedn., Ill. Fedn. Tchrs., Ill. Assn. Heatlh, Phys. Edn., Recreation, Dance (Outstanding Phys. Edn. award 1986), Nat. Assn. Girls' and Women's Sports, Ill. Track and Cross Country Coaches Assn., Ill. Girls' Coaches Assn. Office: Niles West High Sch 5701 Oakton St Skokie IL 60077-2681

SLOAN, SCOTT, radio personality; Grad., Bowling Green State U. Radio host WSPD, Toledo; radio personality 700 WLW, Cin.

SLOGOFF, STEPHEN, dean, anesthesiologist, educator; b. Phila., July 7, 1942; s. Israel and Lillian (Rittenberg) S.; m. Barbara Anita Gershman, June 2, 1963; children: Michele, Deborah. AB in Biology, Franklin and Marshall Coll., 1964; MD, Jefferson Med. Coll., 1967. Diplomate Am. Bd. Med. Examiners, Am. Bd. Anesthesiology (jr. assoc. examiner 1977-80, sr. assoc. examiner 1980-81, bd. dirs. 1981-93, pres. 1989-90, joint coun. on in-tng. exams, vice chmn. 1983-86, chmn. 1986-92). Intern Harrisburg (Pa.) Hosp., 1967-68; resident in anesthesiology Jefferson Med. Coll. Hosp., 1968-71; chief anesthesia sect. U.S. Army, Brooke Army Med. Ctr., Fort Sam Houston, Tex., 1971-74; staff anesthesiologist Baylor Coll. Medicine, Houston, 1974-75; attending cardiovascular anesthesiologist U. Tex. Health Sci. Ctr., Houston, 1974-93, clin. asst. prof., 1977-81, clin. assoc. prof., 1981-85, clin. prof., 1985-93; prof., chmn. dept. anesthesiology Loyola U., Chgo., 1993—; sr. v.p. for clin. affairs Loyola U. Health Sys., 1999—; dean, Strich Sch. Medicine Loyola U., Chgo., 1999—. Chmn. rsch com., co-dir. rsch. labs Tex. Heart Inst., Houston, 1990-93. Contbr. articles to profl. jours. Trustee Loyola U. Health Sys., Chgo., 1996—; chmn. Loyola U. Physicians Found., 1995-99. Mem. Am. Soc. Anesthesiologists, Alpha Omega Alpha. Avocations: tennis, jogging. Office: Loyola U Med Ctr Office of Dean 2160 S 1st Ave Maywood IL 60153-3304 Office Phone: 708-216-3223. Office Fax: 708-216-6227. E-mail: sslogof@luc.edu.

SLORP, JOHN S., retired academic administrator; b. Hartford, Conn., Dec. 5, 1936; Student, Ocean Coll., Calif., 1956, Taft Coll., 1961; BFA Painting, Calif. Coll. Arts and Crafts, 1963, MFA Painting, 1965. Grad. tchr. U. N.D., Grand Forks, 1964; in house designer Nat. Canner's Assn., Berkeley, Calif., 1965; faculty Md. Inst. Coll. Art, Balt., 1965-82, chmn. Found. Studies, 1972-78; faculty Emma Lake program U. Sask., Can., 1967-68, 70; selection, planning group for Polish Posters Smithsonian Instn., Md. Inst. Coll. Art, Warsaw, 1977; planner, initiator visual arts facility, curriculum Balt. High Sch. Arts, 1979-81; adjudicator Arts Recognition and Talent Search, Princeton, N.J., 1980-82; mem. Commn. Accredation Nat. Assn. Schs. Art and Design, 1985-88; pres. Memphis Coll. Art, 1982-90, Mpls. Coll Art and Design, 1990—2002, prof. emeritus, 2002—. Com. Advanced Placement Studio Art Ednl. Testing Svc., Princeton, J., 1975-82; chair Assn. Memphis Area Colls. and Univs., 1986-88. Prodr. film A Romance of Calligraphy; calligrapher various brochures, manuscripts, album covers, children's books. Mem. Hotel adv. com. City of Memphis and Shelby County Convention Hotel, 1982; adv. bd. Memphis Design Ctr.; bd. trustees Opera Memphis, 1985—, ART Today Memphis Brooks Mus., 1988—. Avocations: painting, calligraphy, computer graphics.

SLOVUT, GORDON, reporter; Health and science reporter The Mpls. Star Tribune, Minn. Home: 17545 46th Ave N Minneapolis MN 55446-2375

SLY, WILLIAM S., biochemist, educator; b. East St. Louis, Ill., Oct. 19, 1932; MD, St. Louis U., 1957. Intern, asst. resident ward medicine Barnes Hosp., St. Louis, 1957-59; clin. assoc. nat. heart inst. NIH, Bethesda, Md., 1959-63, rsch. biochemist, 1959-63; dir. divsn. med. genetics, dept. medicine and pediatrics, sch. medicine Washington U., St. Louis, 1964-84, from asst. prof. to prof. medicine, 1964-78, from asst. prof. to prof. pediatrics, 1967-78, prof. pediatrics, medicine and genetics, 1978-84; prof. biochemistry and pediat. St. Louis U., 1984—, chmn. Edward A. Doisy dept. biochemistry-molecular biology, 1984—. Vis. physician Nat. Heart Inst., 1961-63, pediatric genetics clinic U. Wis., Madison, 1963-64; Am. Cancer Soc. fellow lab. enzymol Nat. Ctr. Sci. Rsch., Gif-sur-Yvette, France, 1963, dept. biochemistry and genetics U. Wis., 1963-64; attending physician St. Louis County Hosp., Mo., 1964-84; asst. physician Barnes Hosp., St. Louis, 1964-84, St. Louis Children's Hosp., 1967-84; genetics cons. Homer G. Philips Hosp., St. Louis, 1969-81; mem. genetics study sect. divsn. rsch. grants NIH, 1971-75; mem. active staff Cardinal Glennon Children's Hosp., St. Louis, 1984—; mem. med. adv. bd. Howard Hughes Med. Inst., 1989-92. Recipient Merit award NIH, 1988; elected to Nat. Acad. Sci., 1989; named Passano Found. laureate, 1991. Mem. NAS, AMA, AAAS, Am. Soc. Human Genetics (mem. steering com. human cell biology program 1971-73, com. genetic counseling 1972-76), Am. Soc. Clin. Investigation, Am. Chem. Soc., Genetics Soc. Am., Am. Soc. Microbiology, Soc. Pediatric Rsch., Sigma Xi. Achievements include research on lysosomal enzyme replacement in storage diseases, inherited carbonic anhydrase deficiencies, and hereditary hemochromatosis. Office: St Louis U Med Sch Dept Biochemistry 1402 S Grand Blvd Saint Louis MO 63104-1004 Business E-Mail: slyws@slu.edu.

SMALE, JOHN GRAY, diversified industry executive; b. Listowel, Ont., Can., Aug. 1, 1927; s. Peter John and Vera Gladys (Gray) S.; m. Phyllis Anne Weaver, Sept. 2, 1950; children: John Gray, Jr., Catherine Anne, Lisa Beth, Peter McKee. BS, Miami U., Oxford, Ohio, 1949; LLD (hon.), Kenyon Coll., Gambier, Ohio, 1974, Miami U., Oxford, Ohio, 1979; DSc (hon.), DePauw U., 1983; DCL (hon.), St. Augustine's Coll., 1985; LLD (hon.), Xavier U., 1986. With Vick Chem. Co., NYC, 1949-50, Bio-Rsch., Inc., NYC, 1950-52; asst. brand mgr. Procter & Gamble Co., 1952-54, brand mgr., 1954-58, assoc. advt. mgr., 1958-63, mgr. advt. dept. toilet goods divsn., 1963-66, mgr. toilet goods divsn., 1966-67, v.p. toilet goods divsn., 1967-68, v.p. bar soap and household cleaning products divsn., 1968-69, v.p. packaged soap and detergent divsn., 1969-70, v.p. group exec., 1970-72, mem. bd. dirs., 1972, exec. v.p., 1973-74, pres., 1974-81, pres., chief exec., 1981-86, chmn. of bd., chief exec., 1986-90, chmn. exec. com. of bd. of dirs., 1990-95; chmn. GM, 1992-95, chmn. exec. com., 1995-2000, chmn. bd. dirs. Detroit, 1996-2000, chmn. exec. com., 1996-2000, also bd. dirs.; ret., 2000. Emeritus trustee Kenyon Coll. With USNR, 1945-46. Mem. Comml. Club, Queen City Club, Cin. Country Club. Office: Procter & Gamble PO Box 599 Cincinnati OH 45201-0599

SMALL, JOYCE GRAHAM, psychiatrist, educator; b. Edmonton, Alta., Can., June 12, 1931; came to U.S., 1956; d. John Earl and Rachel C. (Redmond) Graham; m. Iver Francis Small, May 26, 1954; children: Michael, Jeffrey. BA, U. Sask., Saskatoon, Can., 1951; MD, U. Man., Alta., Can., 1956; MS, U. Mich., 1959. Diplomat Am. Bd. Psychiatry and Neurology, Am. Bd. Electroencephalography. Instr. in psychiatry Neuropsychiat. Inst. U. Mich., Ann Arbor, 1959-60; instr. in psychiatry med. sch. U. Oreg., Portland, 1960-61, asst. prof. in psychiatry med. sch., 1961-62; asst. prof. in psychiatry sch. of medicine Washington U., St. Louis, 1962-65; assoc. prof. in psychiatry sch. of medicine Ind. U., Indpls., 1965—69, prof. psychiatry sch. of medicine, 1969—2004, prof. emerita, 2004—. Mem. initial rev. groups NIMH, Washington, 1972-76, 79-82, 87-91; assoc. mem. Inst. Psychiat. Rsch., Indpls., 1974—. Mem. editl. bd. Quar. Jour. Convulsive Therapy, 1984-2000, Clin. EEG, 1990—; contbr. articles to profl. jours. Rsch. grantee NIMH, Portland, Oreg., 1961-62, St. Louis, 1962-64, Indpls., 1967-95, Epilepsy Found., Dreyfus Found., Indpls., 1965; recipient Merit award NIMH, Indpls., 1990, Career award EEG and Clin. Neurosci. Soc., 2003. Fellow Am. Psychiat. Assn., Am. EEG Soc. (councillor 1972-75, 1982); mem. Soc. Biol. Psychiatry, Cen. Assn. Electroencephalographers (sec., treas. 1967-68, pres. 1970, councillor 1971-72). Business E-Mail: jgsmall@iupui.edu.

SMALL, MELVIN, historian, educator; b. NYC, Mar. 14, 1939; s. Herman Z. and Ann (Ashkinazy) S.; m. Sarajane Miller, Oct. 23, 1958; children: Michael, Mark. BA, Dartmouth Coll., 1960; MA, U. Mich., 1961, PhD, 1965. Asst. prof. history Wayne State U., Detroit, 1965-68, assoc. prof., 1968-76, prof., 1976—, chmn. dept. history, 1979-86, disting. prof., 2004—. Vis. prof. U. Mich., Ann Arbor, 1968, Marygrove Coll., Detroit, 1971, Aarhus (Denmark) U., 1972—74, 1983, Windsor (Ont., Can.) U., 1977—78; Fulbright sr. specialist CIES, 2007—. Author: Was War Necessary, 1980, Johnson, Nixon and the Doves, 1988, Covering Dissent, 1994, Democracy and Diplomacy, 1996, The Presidency of Richard Nixon, 1999, Antiwarriors, 2002, At The Water's Edge, 2005; co-author: Wages of War, 1972, Resort to Arms, 1982; editor: Public Opinion and Historians, 1970; co-editor: International War, 1986, Appeasing Fascism, 1991, Give Peace a Chance, 1992, The Good Fight Continues, 2006; mem. editl. bd. Internat. Interactions, 1987-91, Peace and Change, 1989—; restaurant critic Detroit Metro Times, 1982-95, 2006—; reviewer Detroit Free Press, 1988-95. Hon. bd. Swords into Plowshares Mus., 1992—; bd. dirs. Abraham Lincoln Brigade Archives, 1998—, Ctr. on Peace and Liberty, 2003—, David S. Wyman Inst. for Holocaust Studies, 2003-. Recipient Disting. Faculty award Mich. Assn. Governing Bds., 1993; Am. Coun. Learned Socs. fellow, 1969; Stanford Ctr. for Advanced Study fellow, 1969-70, Rsch. fellow NATO, 1996; grantee Am. Coun. Learned Socs., 1983, Johnson Libr., 1982, 88, Can. Govt., 1987; named to Hewlett-Woodmere Alumni Hall of Fame, 2005. Mem. Coun. on Peace Rsch. in History (nat. coun. 1986-90, pres. 1990-92), Am. Hist. Assn., Atlantic Coun. (acad. assoc.), Orgn. Am. Historians, Soc. Historians of Am. Fgn. Rels. (Warren Kuehl prize 1989). Home: 1815 Northwood Blvd Royal Oak MI 48073-3919 Office: Wayne State U Dept History 3119 Fab Detroit MI 48202 Office Phone: 313-577-6138. Business E-Mail: M.Small@Wayne.edu.

SMALLEY, WILLIAM EDWARD, bishop; b. New Brunswick, NJ, Apr. 8, 1940; s. August Harold and Emma May (Gleason) S.; m. Carole A. Kuhns, Sept. 12, 1964; children: Michelle Lynn, Jennifer Ann. BA in Sociology, Lehigh U., 1962; MDiv, Episcopal Theol. Sch., 1965; MEd, Temple U., 1970; D of Ministry, Wesley Theol. Sem., 1987. Ordained to ministry Episcopal Ch., 1965, bishop, 1989; oblate Order of St. Benedict. Vicar St. Peter's Episcopal Ch., Plymouth, Pa., 1965-67, St. Martin-in-the-Fields Ch., Nuangola, Pa., 1965-67; rector All Saints' Episcopal Ch., Lehighton, Pa., 1967-75; fed. program adminstr. Lehighton Area Schs., 1970-72; rector Episcopal Ministry of Unity, Palmerton, Pa., 1975-80, Ch. of Ascension, Gaithersburg, Md., 1980-89; bishop Episcopal Diocese Kans., Topeka, 1989—. Pres. Gaithersburg (Md.) Pastoral Counseling Inc., 1986-89; bd. dirs. Washington Pastoral Counseling, 1988-89; chmn. Turner House Inc., Kansas City, Kans., 1989—, Episcopal Social Svcs., Wichita, Kans., 1989—; bd. dirs. Christ Ch. Hosp., Topeka, 1989—, St. Francis Acad., Atchison, Kans., 1989—; v.p. Province VII, The Episcopal Ch., 1993-95, pres. Province VII, 1995—; pres. Province VII House of Bishops; mem. Ch. Deployment Bd., vice chair, 1997-2000; chair Presiding Bishop's Coun. Advice; mem. joint nominating com. for Presiding Bishop; pres. Friends of Topeka and Shawnee County Pub. Libr., 1998-2000. Mem. Omicron Delta Kappa. Democrat. Avocations: gardening, swimming, cross-stitching, reading. Address: 833 SW Polk St Topeka KS 66612-1620

SMARR, LARRY LEE, science administrator, astrophysicist, educator; b. Columbia, Mo., Oct. 16, 1948; s. Robert L. Jr. and Jane (Crampton) S.; m. Janet Levarie, June 3, 1973; children: Joseph Robert, Benjamin Lee. BA, MS, U. Mo., 1970; MS, Stanford U., 1972; PhD, U. Tex., 1975. Rsch. asst. in physics U. Tex., Austin, 1972-74; lectr. dept. astrophys. sci. Princeton U., 1974-75; rsch. assoc. Princeton U. Obs., 1975-76; rsch. affiliate dept. physics Yale U., New Haven, Conn., 1978-79; asst. prof. astronomy dept. U. Ill., Urbana, 1979-81, asst. prof. physics dept., 1980-81, assoc. prof. astronomy and physics dept., 1981-85, prof. astronomy and physics dept., 1985—; dir. Nat. Ctr. for Supercomputing Applications, Champaign, Ill., 1985—, Nat. Computational Sci. Alliance, 1997—. Cons. Lawrence Livermore Nat. Lab., Calif., 1976—, Los Alamos (New Nex.) Nat. Lab., 1983—; mem. Commn. on Phys. Sci., Math. and Resources, NRC, Washington, 1987-90, commn. on Geoscience, Environ. and Resources, 1990—, adv. panel on Basic Rsch. in the 90's Office Tech. Assesment, 1990—. Editor: Sources of Gravitational Radiation, 1979; mem. editoral bd. Science mag., 1986-90; contbr. over 50 sci. articles to jours. in field. Co-founder, co-dir. Ill. Alliance to Prevent Nuclear War, Champaign, 1981-84. Recipient Fahrney medal Franklin Inst., Phila., 1990; NSF fellow Stanford U., 1970-73, Woodrow Wilson fellow, 1970-71, Lane Scholar U. Tex., Austin, 1972-73, jr. fellow Harvard U., 1976-79, Alfred P. Sloan fellow, 1980-84. Fellow Am. Phys. Soc.; mem. NAE, AAAS, Am. Astron. Soc., Govt. Rsch. Roundtable U. Ind. Avocations: marine aquarium, gardening.

SMART, GEORGE M., energy executive, former packaging company executive; BS, Defiance Coll.; MBA, Wharton Sch., U. Penn. With Central States Can Co. (div. of Van Dorn Co.), 1970—78, pres., CEO, 1978—93; chmn., pres. Phoenix Packaging Corp., 1993—2001; pres. Sonoco-Phoenix, Inc., 2001—03; bd. dirs. FirstEnergy Corp., Akron, Ohio, 1997—, chmn., 2004—. Bd. dirs. Ohio Edison Co., 1988—, Ball Corp., 2005—. Office: FirstEnergy Corp 76 S Main St Akron OH 44308

SMART, JILL BELLAVIA, financial consultant; b. Chgo., Oct. 16, 1959; d. Salvatore and patricia (Foran) B.; m. Stephen D. Smart; two children. BS, U. Ill., 1981; MBA, U. Chgo., 1991. Assoc. ptnr. Accenture Ltd., Chgo., 1981—89, mng. ptnr. human resource delivery/Chgo. office, lead ptnr., 1989—. Bd. trustee Accenture Found. Vol. Treehouse Animal Found., Chgo., 1986-90, Chgo. Area Runners Assn., 1986—; bd. dirs. Goodman Theater, Chgo.; dir. United Way Met. Chgo.; mem. pres. adv. com. U. Ill. Named one of Chgos. 100 Most Influential Women, Crain's Chgo. Bus., 2004. Republican. Roman Catholic. Avocations: jogging, aerobics, travel, reading, skiing. Office Phone: 312-693-0161.

SMEDINGHOFF, THOMAS J., lawyer; b. Chgo., July 15, 1951; s. John A. and Dorothy M. Smedinghoff; m. Mary Beth Smedinghoff. BA in Math., cum laude, Knox Coll., 1973; JD cum laude, U. Mich., 1978. Bar: Ill. 1978, U.S. Dist. Ct. (no. dist.) Ill. 1978. Assoc. McBride, Baker & Coles and predecessor McBride & Baker, Chgo., 1978—84, ptnr., 1985—99, Baker & McKenzie, Chgo., 1999—2006, Wildman, Harrold, Allen & Dixon LLP, Chgo., 2006—. Adj. prof. info. tech. & privacy law John Marshall Law Sch., Chgo., 1985-; adj. prof. bus. law Brennan Grad. Sch. Bus. Dominican U., Chgo., 2004—; chair Ill. Commn. on Electronic Commerce and Crime, 1996—; mem. US Del. to UN Commn. on Internat. Trade Law; mem. legal working group, UN Ctr. For Trade Facilitation and Elec. Bus., 2004-. Author: The Legal Guide to Developing, Protecting & Marketing Software, 1986, Multimedia Law Handbook, 1995, Online Law, 1996. Fellow: Am. Bar Found.; mem.: ABA (chair electronic commerce divsn. 1995—2003, chair sect. Sci. and Tech. Law 1999—2000, chair Internat. Policy Coord. Com. 2003—). Office: Wildman Harrold Allen & Dixon LLP 225 W Wacker Dr Ste 3000 Chicago IL 60606 Home Phone: 708-366-2329; Office Phone: 312-201-2021. Business E-Mail: smedinghoff@wildman.com.

SMERZ, NANCY, entrepreneur; Chair Air Comfort Corp., Broadview, Ill. Office: Air Comfort Corp 2550 Braga Dr Broadview IL 60155-3987

SMETANA, MARK, food products executive; CFO Eby-Brown Co., Naperville, Ill. Office: 280 Shuman Blvd Ste 280 Naperville IL 60563-2578

SMETANKA, MARY JANE, reporter; Grad., U. Minn.-Twin Cities. Reporter, Minn., ND, Conn.; higher edn. reporter Mpls. Star Tribune, Mpls. Mem.: Edn. Writers Assn. (pres.). Achievements include being a Minn. Master Gardener. Office: Mpls Star Tribune 425 Portland Ave Minneapolis MN 55488-1511

SMILEY, WYNN RAY, nonprofit corporation executive; b. Danville, Ill., May 18, 1961; s. Arthur Glen and Lois Jean (Lawrence) S. BS in Agriculture Comms., U. Ill., 1983. Asst. prodr. Sta. WCIA-TV, Champaign, Ill., 1982-83, news prodr., 1983-87, gen. assignments reporter, 1987-91, host, anchor news show, 1988-99; founder, owner, pres. Advisory Inc., Indpls., 1989—; dir. communications Alpha Tau Omega Nat. Hqrs., 1991-98; CEO Alpha Tau Omega, 1997—. Facilitator Leadershape Inc., Champaign, 1990—. Editor: The Positive Experience, 1992, 96, 2000; pub. Live Life Intentionally!, 1996; prodr. (CD-ROM) Live Life Intentionally!, 1996. Chmn. bd. Am. Cancer Soc., Champaign, 1991-93; bd. dirs., sec. Meadowbrook Cmty. Ch., 1994-98; bd. fraternity affairs, U. Ill., 1993-2001. Avocations: running, outdoor ropes course, weightlifting. Office: ATO 12th Fl One N Pennsylvania St Indianapolis IN 46204

SMIT, NEIL, telecommunications industry executive; BS, Duke U.; M in internat. bus., Tufts U. Mgmt. positions Pillsbury Co.; regional v.p. Nabisco; with Am. Online, Inc., 2000—05, COO Mapquest.com, COO AOL Local, sr. v.p. product and programming team, exec. v.p. mem. services, 2002—03, exec. v.p. mem. devel., 2003—04, pres. access bus., 2004—05; pres., CEO Charter Comm., Inc., St. Louis, 2005—, also dir., 2005—. Served to lt. comdr. Navy SEALS USN. Office: Charter Comm Inc Ste 1000 12405 Powerscourt Dr Saint Louis MO 63131-3660

SMITH, ADRIAN DEVAUN, architect; b. Chgo., Ill., Aug. 19, 1944; s. Alfred D. and Hazel (Davis) S.; m. Nancy L. Smith, Aug. 17, 1968; children: Katherine, Jason. Student, Tex. A&M U., 1962-66; BArch, U. Ill., Chgo., 1969. Registered architect, Ill., Mass., Fla. Design ptnr. Skidmore, Owings, & Merrill, Chgo.,

1980—2003, cons. ptnr., 2003—06; founding ptnr. CEO Adrian Smith & Gordon Gill Arch., 2006—. Vis. faculty Sch. Architecture, U. Ill., Chgo., 1984; chmn. U. Ill. Sch. Archtl. Alumni Assn., AIA Jury on Inst. Honors; adv. jury AIA gold metal and architecture firm award, 2000; chmn. nat. AIA awards jury for architecture and 25 yr. award, 2004; chmn. Skidmore Owings Merrill Found., 1989-95; pres. Chgo. Ctrl. Area, 1997-99; bd. dirs. Greater State Street Coun. trustee; bd. govs. Sch. Art Inst. Chgo., 1999—; repr., RIBA British Archtl. Libr. Trust, British Schs. and Univ. Found.; dir., U. Ill. Alumni Found., 88-89. Designer numerous projects including 919 North Michigan Ave, Chgo., 1982, Chgo. Ctrl. Area Plan, 1984, 1992 Chgo. World's Fair, 1980-85, Olympia Ctr., Chgo., 1986, 222 N. LaSalle, Chgo., 1986, Art Inst. Chgo. 2nd Fl. Galleries, 1987, Arthur Anderson Tng. Ctr., St. Charles, Ill., 1987, Rowes Wharf, Boston, 1988, AT&T Corp. Ctr., Chgo., 1989, NBC Tower at Cityfront Ctr., Chgo., 1989, 75 State St., Boston, 1989, Continental Bank First Fl. Renovation, Chgo., 1990, Dearborn Tower, Chgo., 1991, USG Hdqs., Chgo., 1991, Washington Univ. Psychology Bldg., Lab., & Animal Facility, St. Louis, 1996, Chgo. Transit Authority, Green Line Rehabilitation, Chgo., 1995, Heller Internat. Tower, Chgo., 1992, State St. Renovation, 1997 (AIA honor award urban design, 1998), Washington Univ. Arts & Scis. Bldg., St. Louis, Mo., 2000, Campus Crusade for Christ Internat., Orlando, Fla., 2000, Millennium Park, Chgo., 2002, 7 South Dearborn Tower, Chgo., 2002, Manulife Fin., Boston, 2003, GM Global Hdqrs. at Resaissance Ctr., Detroit, 2003, Lakeshore East, Chgo., 2004, Trump Internat. Hotel & Tower, Chgo., 2006, Monterey Cultural Ctr., Mex., 1978, Bally of Switzerland, 1982, Hdqs. Canary Wharf Fin. Ctr., London, Eng., 1988, United Gulf Bank, Manama, Bahrain, 1986, 10 Fleet Place, Ludgate Office Bldg., London, 1992, 100 Ludgate Hill, Ludgate Office Bldg., London, 1992, Aramco Hdqrs., Dhahran, Saudi Arabia, 1993, Xiamen Posts & Telecommunications Bldg., China, 1994, Frankfurter Allee, 1991, Tower Palace III, Seoul, Korea, 1996, Kowloon MTR Tower, Hong Kong, 1997, Pidemco GSCP MSCP Towers, Singapore, 1997, McGraw Hill European Headquarters, Canary Wharf (FC-2), London, 1990, Canary Wharf, London, 1991, Canary Wharf (DS4), 2002, CSFB European Headquarters, Canary Wharf (DSI), 2002, Morgan Stanley Headquarters for Europe (HQI), Canary Wharf, 2002, Burj Dubai Tower (World's Tallest Bldg., 2009), United Arab Emirates, Jin Mao Tower (World's Tallest Mixed-Use Project), Shanghai, China (Nat. AIA award for interior architecture 2000), 1998, BankBoston Hdqrs., Sao Paulo, Brazil, 2000, 201 Broadgate, London, Eng., 2008, Nanjing Guozi Greenland Fin. Ctr., Nanjing, China, Chemsunny Office Bldg., Beijing, 2008, Shanghai Grand Office Tower, 2008, Shanghai, Pearl River Zero Energy Tower, Guanghou, China; author: Monograph of Adrian P. Smith, 2002, The Architecture of Adrian Smith 1980-2006: Toward a Sustainable Future, contbr. articles to profl. jours.; subject numerous pubs. in architecture. Mem. com. Task Force for New City Plan, Chgo., Light Up Chgo., Ctrl. Area Com. Task Force Chgo.; chmn. Senator Richard A. Newhouse Bldg. Competition Jury, 1982, Progressive Architecture Design Jury, 1985; bd. dirs. State St. Coun.; lifetime gov., Urban Land Inst. Found.; trustee, Chgo. Architecture Found., 93-99, Bldg. Experiences Trust, 91-95. Recipient silver award, Ill. Ctr. Masonry Coun., 1981, Gold award, 1982, Urban Design and Planning First award, 32nd Annual Progressive Architecture Mag., 1986, Energy award program, Am. Refrigerating & Air Conditioning Engrs., NBC 1988, AT&T 1988, Build Am. award, Assoc. General Contractors of Am. and Motorola, 1989, Excellence on the Waterfront Honor award, 1990, Civic Trust award, Ludgate Office Complex, 1994, Alumni Achievement award, U. Ill., 1995, First Prize, European Commercial Property Development Awards, 1995, Excellence in Engrng., ASHRAE, 1995, spl. achievement award, Internat. Downtown Assn., 1997, Best Structure award, Structural Engineers Assn. Ill. 1998, Architect Creation award, World Architect Conf., 2001, Merit award, Illuminating Engrng. Soc. N. Am., 2001, award of excellence, ULI, 2004, Pres. award, Korea Inst. Architects, 2005, Am. Architecture award, Chgo. Athenaeum; named Best of Competition, Inst. Bus. Designers, Interior Design Mag., Bally Switzerland, Chgo., 1982. Fellow AIA, chmn. nat. jury arch. and 25 yr. award 2004, Banco de Occidente, 1980, 81, Interior Architecture Award, Citation of Merit, 1984, Interior Architecture award, 1989, Disting. Bldg. award 1981, 87, 90, 91, 92, 94, 97, 98, 2003, 04, 06, Nat. Honor award, 1988, 94, 98), Royal Inst. Brit. Architects, Archtl. Registration Coun., U.K., Nat. Coun. Archtl. Registration Bds., Architecture Soc. of Art Inst. Chgo., Chgo. Arch. Found., Chgo. Archtl. Club, Urban Found. (bd. trustees) University Club, Arts Club; Am. Acad. Rome (Midwest dir., 85-86); mem. Economic Club Chgo. Office: Adrian Smith & Gordon Gill Architecture 111 W Monroe St #2300 Chicago IL 60603 Office Phone: 312-920-1888. Office Fax: 312-920-1775.

SMITH, ADRIAN M., congressman, real estate agent; b. Scottsbluff, Nebr., Dec. 19, 1970; BS in Mktg. Edn., U. Nebr., 1993, postgrad., Portland State U. Legis. page ebr. Legislature, 1992; mem. Nebr. Legislature from 48th dist., Lincoln, 1998—; staff internat., mktg. specialist Nebrs. Gov.'s Office, 1992; rsch. asst. U. Nebr. Found., 1992-93; educator, staff devel. project mgr. Ednl. Svc. Unit 13, 1994-97; real estate agt., mktg. specialist Buyers Realty, 1997—; mem. US Congress from 3rd Nebr. dist., 2007—, asst. whip, 2007—. Mem. Scotts Bluff County Bd. Realtors. Mem. Gering City Coun., 1994-98, We. Nebr. Regional Airport Ops. Bd., Scotts Bluff County Visitors Adv. Com., 1995-96, N. Platte Valley Hist. Soc., Riverside Zool. Soc., Wyo-Braska Mus. Natural History, Calvary Meml. Evang. Free Ch., Farm and Ranch Mus. Assn.; chmn. land use task force Vision 2020; bd. dirs. Twin Cities Devel. Mem. Scottsbluff Kiwanis Club (bd. dirs. Camp Kiwanis). Republican. Office: US House Reps 503 Cannon House Office Bldg Washington DC 20515 Office Phone: 202-225-6435. Office Fax: 202-225-0207.

SMITH, AKILI, professional football player; b. Aug. 21, 1975; Student, U. Oreg. Football player Cin. Bengals, 1999—2003. Avocations: weightlifting, Bible reading. Office: 14654 Lyons Valley Jamul CA 91935

SMITH, ALMA WHEELER, state legislator; b. Aug. 6, 1941; BA, U. Mich. Legis. coord. Senator Lane Pollack; mem. Mich. Senate from 18th dist., Lansing, 1995—; mem. appropriations com. Mem. South Lyon (Mich.) Bd. Edn.

SMITH, ARTHUR B., JR., lawyer; b. Abilene, Tex., Sept. 11, 1944; s. Arthur B. and Florence B. (Baker) S.; m. Marya Argetsinger, 1968 (div. 1996); children: Arthur C., Sarah R.; m. Tracey L. Truesdale, 1999; children: Thomas A. BS, Cornell U., 1966; JD, U. Chgo., 1969. Bar: Ill. 1969, N.Y. 1976. Assoc. Vedder, Price, Kaufman & Kammholz, Chgo., 1969-74; asst. prof. labor law N.Y. State Sch. Indls. and Labor Rels., Cornell U., 1975-77; ptnr. Vedder, Price, Kaufman & Kammholz, Chgo., 1977-86; founding mem. Murphy, Smith & Polk, Chgo., 1986-98; shareholder Ogletree, Deakins, Chgo., 1999—. Guest. lectr. Northwestern U. Grad. Sch. Mgmt., 1979, Sch. Law, spring 1980; chmn. hearing bd. Ill. Atty. Registration and Disciplinary Commn. Author: Employment Discrimination Law Cases and Materials, 6th edit., 2006, Construction Labor Relations, 1984, supplement, 1993; co-editor-in-chief: 1976 Annual Supplement to Morris, The Developing Labor Law, 1977; chpt. editor: The Developing Labor Law, 5th edit., 2006; contbr. articles to profl. jours. Recipient award for highest degree of dedication and excellence in tchg. N.Y. State Sch. Indsl. and Labor Rels., Cornell U., 1977; listed in The Best Lawyers in Am., 2003—. Fellow Coll. Labor and Employment Lawyers; mem. ABA (co-chmn. com. on devel. law under Nat. Labor Rels. Act, Sect. Labor Rels. Law 1976-77), N.Y. State Bar Assn., Phi Eta Sigma, Phi Kappa Phi, Union Leauge Club Chgo. Presbyterian. Office: Ogletree Deakins et al 2 First National Plz Fl 25 Chicago IL 60603 Office Phone: 312-558-1230. Business E-Mail: Arthur.Smith@odnss.com.

SMITH, ARTHUR EDWARD, JR., lawyer; b. Oct. 8, 1949; s. Arthur and Audre Smith; m. Janis O'Hara: children: Gregory, Jeffrey. BA in Biology, Columbia U., 1971, MA in Environ. Sci., 1972, MS in Environ. Sci., 1973; JD with distinction, U. Puget Sound, 1976. Bar: Wash. 1976. Assoc. regional counsel Region V, EPA, Chgo., 1976-91; spl. asst. US Atty. (no. dist.) Ill., 1989; environ. officer, counsel NIPSCO Industries (now NiSource), Merrillville, Ind., 1991—2000; sr. v.p., environ. counsel NiSource Inc., Merrillville, Ind., 2000—. Recipient bronze medal EPA, 1985, 91, Silver medal Am. Gas Assn., 2007; environ. fellow Columbia U. 1972; scholar U. Puget Sound. Home: 300 S Ashland Ave La Grange IL 60525-6308 Office: 801 E 86th Ave Merrillville IN 46410

SMITH, ARTHUR LEE, lawyer; b. Davenport, Iowa, Dec. 19, 1941; s. Harry Arthur Smith and Ethel (Hoffman) Duerre; m. Georgia Mills, June 12, 1965 (dec. Jan. 1984); m. Jean Bowler, Aug. 4, 1984; children: Juliana, Christopher, Andrew, Wendy. BA, Augustana Coll., Rock Island, Ill., 1964; MA, Am. U., 1968; JD, Washington U., St. Louis, 1971. Bar: Mo 1971, DC 1983. Telegraph editor Davenport Morning Democrat, 1962-64; ptnr. Peper Martin Jensen Maichel & Hetlage, 1971-95, Husch & Eppenberger, St. Louis, 1995—. Arbitrator Nat Asn Security Dealers, 1980—, Am Arbitration Assn, 1980—2004; dir. St. Louis Bar Found., 2005—, v.p., 2005—. Columnist: St Louis Lawyer, syndicated columnist: Technolawyer.com and other publications. Dir. P. Buckley Moss Found. for Children's Edn., 2001—03; mem. Sedona Conf. Working Group on Electronic Document Prodn.; mem. electronic discovery and ethics com. DRI, Inc., 2007—. Lt USN, 1964—68. amed Mo.-Kans. Superlawyer, 2006, 2007; named one of Best Lawyers in Am., 2005, 2006, 2007, Best Lawyers in Info.-Tech. in Am., 2006. Mem.: ABA (co-chair electronic discovery subcom.), Bar Assn. Met. St. Louis (chmn law mgt comt 1993—96, chair technology comt 1996—99, Pres.'s award Exceptional Service 1995, 1997), P. Buckley Moss Soc. (dir 1994—2006, v.p. 1998—2000, exec vpres 2001—02, pres. 2002—06), Mo. Bar Assn. (vice-chair ins programs comt 1981—83, vice-chair antitrust comt 1981—83, chair admin law comt 1995—97), D.C. Bar Assn. (chmn law practice mgt 1990—91), Order of Coif. Office: Husch & Eppenberger Ste 600 190 Carondelet Plz Saint Louis MO 63105-3441 Home Phone: 636-532-0354; Office Phone: 314-480-1500. Business E-Mail: arthur.smith@husch.com.

SMITH, BARBARA JEAN, lawyer; b. Washington, Jan. 9, 1947; d. Harry Wallace and Jean (Fraser) S.; m. Philip R. Chall, July 13, 1991; children: Brian C.S. Brown, Craig F.S. Brown, Amy E. Spiers, Carrie A. Chall. BA, Old Dominion Coll., 1968; MBA, Pepperdine U., 1974; JD, Case Western Res. U., 1977. Bar: Ohio 1977. Assoc. Squire, Sanders & Dempsey, Cleve., 1977—88, ptnr., 1988—93; shareholder McDonald, Hopkins, Burke & Haber Co., L.P.A., Cleve., 1993—2003; ptnr. Shottenstein, Zox & Dunn Co., LPA, Cleve., 2003—05; founding mem. Smith & Hultin LLC, Chagrin Falls, Ohio, 2005—. Bd. editors Health Law Jour. of Ohio, 1989-95; contbr. articles to health jours. and periodicals. Trustee Urban Community Sch., Cleve., 1984-86, Alzheimer's Assn. Greater Cleve., 2000-2005. Mem. Ohio Women's Bar Assn. (pres. 1994-95), Cleve. Bar Assn. (pres. 1998-99, trustee 1992-95, chair health law sect. 1991-92), Am. Health Lawyers Assn., Ohio State Bar Assn. (health law com. 1991—), Soc. Ohio Hosp. Attys., Sci. Edn. Coun. Ohio. Democrat. Mem. United Ch. of Christ. Avocations: reading, hiking. Home: 416 Fairway Vw Chagrin Falls OH 44023-6718 Office: Smith & Hultin LLC 100 N Main St Ste 350 Chagrin Falls OH 44022 Office Phone: 440-247-2620. Business E-Mail: smith@smithhultin.com.

SMITH, BILL, advertising and marketing executive; V.p. advt. and mktg. Meijer, Inc., Grand Rapids, Mich., 1987—. Office: Meijer Inc 2929 Walker Ave NW Grand Rapids MI 49544-9428

SMITH, BRIAN J., lawyer; b. 1951; BA in Polit. Sci., Bradley U., 1973; JD, U. Mich., 1976. Bar: Mich. 1976. Mem. legal dept., specialty prods. div., Hospital Prods. Div., Specialty Prods. Div. Hospira, Inc., Chgo., 1979—84, div. counsel Abbott Diagnostics Division and the Pharmaceutical Products Division, 1984—91, intl. legal dept., 1991—95, v.p., domestic legal ops., 1995—2001, now sr. v.p., gen. counsel, sec. Sec. Clara Abbot Found. Office: Hospira Inc 275 North Field Dr Lake Forest IL 60045

SMITH, C. LEMOYNE, retired publishing executive; b. Atkins, Ark., Sept. 15, 1934; s. Cecil Garland and Salena Bell (Wilson) S.; m. Selma Jean Tucker, May 23, 1964; 1 child, Jennifer Lee BS, Ark. Tech. U., 1956; M.Ed., U. Ark., 1958. Tchr. pub. schs., Little Rock, 1956-58; instr. bus. adminstrn. Ark. Tech. U., Russellville, 1958-60; sales rep. South-Western Pub. Co., Cin., 1960-67, editorial staff, 1967-82, pres., chief exec. officer, 1982-90, chmn., 1990-91, ret., 1991. Bd. dirs. Cin. Council on World Affairs, 1983-95. Mem.: Nat. Bus. Edn. Assn., Delta Pi Epsilon. Republican. Presbyterian. Avocations: bridge, travel, golf. Office: South-Western Pub Co 5191 Natorp Blvd Mason OH 45040-7980

SMITH, CARL BERNARD, education educator; b. Feb. 29, 1932; s. Carl R. and Elizabeth Ann (Lefeld) S.; m. Virginia Lee Cope, Aug. 30, 1958; children: Madonna, Anthony, Regina, Marla. BA, U. Dayton, 1954; MA, Miami U., Oxford, Ohio, 1961; PhD, Case Western Res. U., 1967. Tchr. Cathedral Latin H.S., Cleve., 1954-57; customer corr. E.F. MacDonald Co., Dayton, 1958-59; tchr. Kettering (Ohio) H.S., 1959-61; editor Reardon Baer Pub. Co., Cleve., 1961-62; tchr., rschr. Case Western Res. U., Cleve., 1962-65, Cleve. Pub. Schs., 1966-67; asst. prof. edn. Ind. U., Bloomington, 1967-69, assoc. prof., 1970-72, prof., 1973—99, prof. emeritus, 1999—. Dir. ERIC Ctr., 1988-2004, Family Literacy Ctr., 1990—; pres. Grayson Bernard Pub. Co., 1988—, Am. Family Learning Corp., 1996—. Author: Reading Instruction through Diagnostic Teaching (Pi Lambda Theta Best Book in Edn. award 1972), Getting People to Read, 1978; sr. author: Series r, 1983, New View, 1993, Teaching Reading and Writing Together, 1984, Connect! Getting Your Kids to Talk to You, 1994, Word History A Resource Book, 1995, Self-Directed Learner Curriculum, 1998, (videotape) Make a Difference, 1996, Improving Your Child's Writing Skills, 1999, Gotcha Grandpa, 2000, Talk to Your Children About Books, 2001, Teaching Children to Learn, 2002, Reading to Learn, 2003, Parents Guide to Character Development, 2003, The Spriritual Family, 2005, Teaching Parents How To Listen and Learn, 2007. Pres. Bd. Edn., St. Charles Sch., Bloomington, 1976-80. Recipient Sch. Bell award NEA, 1967, Literacy award Ind. State Reading Assn., 1997. Mem. ASCD, Internat. Reading Assn., Nat. Coun. Tchrs. of English, Am. Ednl. Rsch. Assn., Phi Delta Kappa. Republican. Roman Catholic. Home: 4915 E Cedarcrest Dr Bloomington IN 47401 Office: Reading and English Clearinghouse Smith Rsch Ctr Bloomington IN 47405 Home Phone: 812-336-1800; Office Phone: 812-345-0985. Business E-Mail: smith2@indiana.edu.

SMITH, CAROLE DIANNE, retired lawyer, editor, writer, product developer; b. Seattle, June 12, 1945; d. Glaude Francis and Elaine Claire (Finkenstein) S.; m. Stephen Bruce Presser, June 18, 1968 (div. June 1987); children: David Carter, Elisabeth Catherine. AB cum laude, Harvard U., Radcliffe Coll., 1968; JD, Georgetown U., 1974. Bar: Pa. 1974. Law clk. Hon. Judith Jamison, Phila., 1974—75; assoc. Gratz, Tate, Spiegel, Ervin & Ruthrouff, Phila., 1975—76; freelance editor, writer Evanston, Ill., 1983—87; editor Ill. Inst. Tech., Chgo., 1987—88; mng. editor LawLetters, Inc., Chgo., 1988—89; editor ABA, Chgo., 1989—95; product devel. dir. Gt. Lakes divsn. Lawyers Coop. Pub., Deerfield, Ill., 1995—96; product devel. mgr. Midwest Market Ctr. West Group, Deerfield, Ill., 1996—97; mgr acquisitions, bus. and fin. group CCH, Inc., Riverwoods, Ill., 1997—2002; ret. Author Jour. of Legal Medicine, 1975, Selling and the Law: Advertising and Promotion, 1987; (under pseudonym Sarah Toast) 79 children's books and stories, 1994-2002; editor The Brief, 1990-95, Criminal Justice, 1989-90, 92-95 (Gen. Excellence award Soc. Nat. Assn. Pubs. 1990, Feature Article award-bronze Soc. Nat. Assn. Pubs. 1994), Franchise Law Jour., 1995; mem. editl. bd. The Brief, 1995-2000, editor-in-chief, 1998-2000. Dir. Radcliffe Club of Chgo., 1990-93; mem. parents coun. Latin Sch. Chgo., 1995-96; trustee Winnetka-Northfield Libr. Dist., 2003—, pres. trustees, 2005-; mem. Winnetka Plan Commn. 2003-05, Winnetka Forestry Commn., 2004-05 Mem. ABA (editor-in-chief The Brief 1998-2000, mem. publs. editl. bd. tort trial and ins. practice sect. 2003-05, chair 2005—).

SMITH, DANIEL C., dean, finance educator; BBA, U. Toledo, 1980, MBA, 1982; PhD in bus. adminstrn., U. Pitts., 1988. Asst. prof. U. Wis. Sch. Bus., Madison; asst. to assoc. prof. U. Pitts. Joesph M. Katz Grad. Sch. Bus.; joined faculty Kelley Sch. Bus., Ind. U., 1996, MBA program chair, 1998—2001, chair mktg. dept., 2002—03, Clare W. Barker chair mktg., 2002—, assoc. dean academics, 2003—04, interim dean, 2004—05, dean, 2005—. Mem. editl. rev. bd. Jour. Mktg., Jour. Acad. Mktg. Sci., Jour. Competitive Intelligence, Jour. Personal Selling and Sales Mgmt., Jour. Market Focused Mgmt. Avocations: fly fishing, food and wine. Office: Indiana Univ Kelley Sch Business 1575 E 10 St Ste 2010 Bloomington IN 47405 Office Phone: 812-855-8489. Business E-Mail: dansmith@indiana.edu.

SMITH, DAVID BRUCE, lawyer; b. Moline, Ill., May 9, 1948; s. Neal Schriever and Barbara Jean (Harris) S.; children: Neal, Stephanie. BSME, U. Iowa, 1970; JD, U. Tex., 1973. Bar: Tex. 1973, Wis. 1975. Patent examiner U.S. Patent and Trademark Office, Washington, 1973—74; atty., intellectual property practice coord. Michael Best & Friedrich, Milw., 1978—. Co-chair Intellectual Property Com. of Lex Mundi. Pres. Milw. County coun. Boy Scouts Am., Milw., 1994-95. Mem. ABA, Am. Intellectual Property Law Assn., State Bar Wis., Wis. Intellectual Property Law Assn., Ozaukee Country Club, Milw. Club. Office: Michael Best & Friedrich 100 E Wisconsin Ave Ste 3300 Milwaukee WI 53202-4108 E-mail: dbsmith@mbf-law.com.

SMITH, DAVID JAMES, lawyer; b. 1955; BS, Western Ill. U.; JD, John Marshall Law Sch. Asst. sec. Archer Daniels Midland, Decatur, Ill., 1988-97, asst. gen. counsel, 1995-97, v.p., sec., gen. counsel, 1997—2001, sr. v.p., sec., gen. counsel, 2002—03, exec. v.p., sec. and gen. counsel, 2003—. Office: Archer Daniels Midland Co 4666 E Faries Pkwy Decatur IL 62526-5666 Office Phone: 217-424-5200.

SMITH, DAVID JOHN, JR., plastic surgeon; b. Indpls., Feb. 20, 1947; s. David John and Carolyn (Culp) S.; m. Nancy Loonsten, June 7, 1975; children: Matthew, Peter, Hadley. BA, Wesleyan U., 1969; MD, Ind. U., 1973. Diplomate Am. Bd. Plastic Surgery. Resident Emory U.-Grady Hosp., Atlanta, 1973-78; resident Ind. U. Med. Ctr., Indpls., 1978-80; Christine Kleinert fellow in hand surgery, 1979; asst. prof. surgery Ind. U. Sch. Medicine, 1980-84; assoc. prof. of surgery Wayne State U. Sch. Medicine, 1984-87; assoc. prof. plastic surgery, surgery sect. head U. Mich. Med. Ctr., Ann Arbor, 1987-92, prof. surgery sect. head, 1992—2001; prof. surgery Coll. Medicine U. South Fla., 2004—, Juan Bolivar chair in surg. oncology, dir. divsn. plastic and reconstructive surgery, 2004—. Mem. Residency Rev. Com. for Plastic Surgery, 1992-2000, vice chmn., 1994, chmn. 1996-99; vis. prof. Ctr. Cutaneous Rsch. Queen Mary U., London, Eng., 2004—, Anglia Polytech. U., Cambrige, Eng., 2004—. Mem. editl. bd. Jour. of Surg. Rsch., 1989-95, Annals of Plastic Surgery, 1992-2002, assoc. editor, 1994-2002, Yearbook of Hand Surgery, 1989—; guest reviewer Surgery, 1988—, Plastic and Reconstructive Surgery, 1988—; contbr. articles to profl. jours. Recipient numerous grants. Fellow ACS (com. mem.), Am. Assn. Plastic Surgeons, Am. Surg. Assn., Am. Bd. Plastic Surgeons (vice chmn. 1997-98, chair-elect 1998-99, chmn. oral exam 1995-97, chmn. 1999-2000), Ctrl. Surg. Assn., Am. Soc. for Surgery of the Hand, Am. Soc. Plastic Surgeons, Plastic Surgery Ednl. Found. (bd. dirs. 1988-99, treas. 1994, v.p., pres.-elec., pres., chair nominating com. 1997-98), Plastic Surgery Rsch. Coun., Am. Burn Assn. (chmn. com. on organization and delivery of burn care 1995-98), Am. Burn Life Support Nat. Faculty, Am. Assn. for Hand Surgeons (pres. 1994), Assn. Acad. Chmn. Plastic Surgery (pres.-elect 1997, pres. 1998-99, chmn. nominating com. 1999-2000). Home: 3107 Prospect Rd Tampa FL 33629 Office: Divsn Plastic Surgery 4 Columbia Dr Ste 650 Tampa FL 33606 Home Phone: 813-250-9160. Business E-Mail: dsmith3@health.usf.edu.

SMITH, DAVID WALDO EDWARD, pathology and gerontology educator, physician; b. Fargo, ND, Apr. 3, 1934; s. Waldo Edward and Martha (Althaus) S.; m. Diane Leigh Walker, June 18, 1960. BA, Swarthmore Coll., 1956; MD, Yale U., 1960. Intern, asst. resident, research fellow pathology Yale U. Med. Sch., 1960-62; research assoc. lab. molecular biology Nat. Inst. Arthritis and Metabolic Diseases, 1962-64, investigator lab. exptl. pathology, 1964-67; assoc. prof. pathology and microbiology Ind. U. Med. Sch., 1967-69; prof. pathology Northwestern U. Med. Sch., 1969—, dir. Ctr. on Aging, 1988—, prof. emeritus, 2000—. Guest investigator Internat. Lab. Genetics and Biophysics, Naples, Italy, 1969; mem. ad hoc biochemistry study sect. NIH, 1974-75, mem. pathobiol. chemistry study sect., 1975-79, cons., 1982; sabbatical leave NIH, 1986-87; chmn. NIH Conf. on Gender and Longevity: Why Do Women Live Longer Than Men?, 1987. Author: Human Longevity, 1993, also research papers, chpts. in books.; editorial bd. Yale Jour. Biology and Medicine, 1957-60. Sr. surgeon USPHS, 1958-67. Recipient Career Devel. award NIH, 1968-69 Mem. AAAS, Sigma Xi, Alpha Omega Alpha. Home: 1212 N Lake Shore Dr Apt 33 Chicago IL 60610-2371

SMITH, DONALD E., banker, director; b. Terre Haute, Ind., Nov. 4, 1926; s. Henry P. and Ruth I. (Bius) S.; m. Mary F. Ryan, June 25, 1947; children: Virginia Lee, Sarah Jane. Student, Ind. U., 1945-47, Ind. State U., 1947-48. Chmn. Deep Vein Coal Co., Terre Haute, Ind., 1947—, R.J. Oil Co., Inc., 1948—, Princeton Mining Co., Terre Haute, 1947—; pres. Terre Haute Oil Corp., 1947—; chmn. bd. Terre Haute 1st Nat. Bank, 1969—; pres. 1st Fin. Corp., Terre Haute, 1969—. Trustee Ind. State U.; bd. mgrs. Rose-Hulman Inst. Tech., 1978—; treas. Terre Haute Econ. Devel. Commn., 1981—; mem. Ind. Econ. Devel. Coun. Mem. Terre Haute C. of C. (bd. dirs. 1982—), Elks, Country Club of Terre Haute. Home: 94 Allendale Terre Haute IN 47802-4751 Office: First Fin Bank One First Financial Pla PO Box 540 Terre Haute IN 47808-0540

SMITH, DONALD NICKERSON, food service executive; b. Can., Sept. 12, 1940; came to U.S., 1946, naturalized, 1956; s. Fred Raymond and Hazel (Nickerson) S.; m. Beverley Thorell, Dec. 1961 (div.); children: Jeffrey, Stacy, Darby; m. Angela Dangerfield, Mar. 8, 1984. BA, U. Mont., 1962; D in Bus. Adminstrn. (hon.), Upper Iowa U., 1980. Sr. exec. v.p., sr. ops. officer McDonald's Corp., Oak Brook, Ill., 1964-77; pres., chief exec. officer Burger King Corp., Miami, 1977-80; sr. v.p., pres. food svc. div. PepsiCo, Inc., Purchase, N.Y., 1980-83; pres., chief exec. officer Chart House, Inc. (name changed to Diversifoods, Inc.), Itasca, Ill., 1983-85; chmn., chief exec. officer Tenn. Restaurant Co., Itasca, 1985—; chmn., pres., CEO Friendly Holding Corp., Wilbraham, Mass. With USMCR, 1957-65. Named Adman of the Yr., Advt. Age mag., 1979.

SMITH, EDWARD BYRON, JR., bank executive; b. Washington, Oct. 1, 1944; s. Edward Byron and Louise de Marigny (Dewey) S.; B.A. in History, Yale, 1966; M.B.A. in Fin., Columbia, 1969, M.Internat. Affairs, 1970; M.B.A. in Econs., N.Y. U., 1974; m. Maureen Dwyer, June 22, 1974; children— Edward Byron III, Peter Byron. With No. Trust Co., Chgo., 1970-87, v.p., 1976-81, sr. v.p., 1981-87; sr. v.p. Bear, Stearns & Co., 1987—. Trustee Art Inst. Chgo., Chgo. Hist. Soc.; bd. dirs. Lincoln Park Zoo, Chgo.; governing mem. Brookfield (Ill.) Zoo, Field Mus., Chgo.; mem. fine arts com. U. Cjhgo.; mem. Mus. Contemporary Art Circle; mem. assocs. bd. Presbyterian-St. Lukes Hosp., Chgo. Mem. Econ. Club Chgo., Onwentsia Club, Racquet Club (Chgo.)., The Chgo. Club, Casino Club, Kinckerbocker Club (N.Y.C.).

SMITH, ELIZABETH ANGELE TAFT, curator; Degree in Art History, Columbia U. Curator Mus. Contemporary Art, LA, 1983—99, James W. Alsdorf Chief Curator Chgo., 1999—. Adj. prof. pub. art studies program U. So. Calif., 1992—98; bd. advisors Independent Curators Internat., NYC; bd. overseers, Sch. Architecture, Ill. Inst. Tech., Chgo. Curator (exhibitions) Blueprints for Modern Living: History and Legacy of the Case Study Houses, Mus. Contemporary Art, LA, 1989, Urban Revisions: Current Projects for the Public Realm, 1994, Cindy Sherman: Retrospective, 1997, At the End of the Century: One Hundred Years of Architecture, 1998, The Architecture of R.M. Schindler, 2001 (Named Best Architecture or Design Exhibition of Yr., Internat. Assn. Art Critics/USA, 2001), Matta in America: Painting and Drawings of the 1940s, Mus. Contemporary Art, Chgo., 2001, Donald Moffett: What Barbara Jordan Wore, 2002, Lee Bontecou: A Retrospective, 2003 (Named Best Monographic Mus. Show Nationally, Internat. Assn. Art Critics/USA, 2004); author: (books) Techno Architecture, 2000, Case Study Houses: The Complete CSH Program 1945-66, 2002; co-editor: Lee Bontecou: A Retrospective of Sculpture and Drawing, 1958-2000, 2003. Named Woman of Yr., Chgo. Soc. Artists, 2004. Office: Mus Contemporary Art 220 E Chgo Ave Chicago IL 60611

SMITH, ERIK, announcer; m. Sharon Smith; children: Kristian. Sarah. Bachelor (hon.), Wayne State Coll., 1998. Soundman WXYZ-TV, Detroit, 1962—63, part-time report, 1963—65; with WKNR-AM Radio, 1965—68, WXYZ-TV, Detroit, 1968—72, KPIX-TV, San Francisco, WXYZ-TV, Detroit, 1976—, host (series) From the Heart, 1997—, co-anchor Action News This Morning. Recipient 7 Emmy awards, 2001. Office: WXYZ-TV 20777 W Ten Mile Rd Southfield MI 48037

SMITH, F. ALAN, automobile manufacturing company executive; b. 1931; BBA, Dartmouth Coll., 1952, MBA, 1953. Statistician, analyst GM Corp., 1957—63, staff asst. Office of Chmn., 1963—65, sect. dir. treas.'s staff, 1965—68, dir. fin. analysis, 1968—70, asst. treas., 1970—73, gen. asst. treas., then corp. treas., 1973—75, corp. v.p. fin. staff, 1975—81; pres., gen. mgr. GM Can. Ltd., 1978—81, exec. v.p. fin., 1981—, also bd. dirs. With USN, 1953—56.

SMITH, FRANK EARL, retired trade association administrator; b. Fremont Ctr., NY, Feb. 4, 1931; s. Earl A. and Hazel (Knack) S.; m. Caroline R. Gillin, Aug. 14, 1954; children: Stephen F., David S., Daniel E. BS, Syracuse U., 1952. With Mellor Advt. Agy., Elmira, NY, 1954-55; asst. mgr. Elmira Assn. of Commerce, 1955-56; retail dept. mgr. C. of C., Binghamton, NY; mgr. Better Bus. Bur., Broome County, NY, 1956-60; exec. v.p. C. of C., Chemung County, Elmira, 1960-65, Schenectady County (N.Y.) C. of C., 1965-69, Greater Cin. C. of C., 1969-78; pres. Greater Detroit C. of C., 1978-95; ret., 1995. Bd. dirs., sec. Presbyn. Devel. Corp. of Detroit, Inc., 1995-2006. 1st lt. USAF, 1952-54.

Named Young Man of Yr. Jr. C. of C. Elmira, 1964. Mem. C. of C. Execs. Mich., Am. C. of C. Execs. (past chmn.), NY State C. of C. Execs. (past pres.), Ohio C. of C. Execs. (past pres.), C. of C. of US (past bd. dirs. Ctr. Internatl Pvt. Enterprise, past chmn. nat. bd. regents, Inst. for Orgn. Mgmt.). Presbyterian. Home: 1626 Shallow Shores Dr Gaylord MI 49735

SMITH, FREDERICK COE, retired manufacturing executive; b. Ridgewood, NJ, June 3, 1916; s. Frederick Coe and Mary (Steffee) S.; m. Ruth Pfeiffer, Oct. 5, 1940; children: Frederick Coe, Geoffrey, Roger, William, Bart. BS, Cornell U., 1938; MBA, Harvard U., 1940. With Armstrong Cork Co., Lancaster, Pa., 1940-41; with Huffy Corp., Dayton, Ohio, 1946-86, pres., chief exec. officer, 1961-72, chmn., chief exec. officer, 1972-76, chmn., 1976-78, chmn. exec. com., 1979-86. Past chmn. Sinclair C.C. Found.; past chmn. nat. bd. dirs. Planned Parenthoo Fedn.; past dir. Internat. Parenthood Fedn.; past chmn. Dayton Found.; trustee emeritus Alan Gutmacher Inst., Ohio United Way; past chmn. employment and tng. com. Gov.'s Human Investment Coun. Lt. col. USAAF, 1941-46. Decorated Legion of Merit. Home Phone: 937-434-1654. Office Fax: 937-223-1441. Personal E-mail: dotti8@aol.com.

SMITH, FREDERICK ROBERT, JR., social studies educator, educator; b. Lynn, Mass., Sept. 19, 1929; s. Frederick Robert and Margaret Theresa (Donovan) S. m. Mary Patricia Barry, Aug. 28, 1954; children: Brian Patrick, Barry Frederick, Brendan Edmund. AB, Duke U., 1951; M.Ed., Boston U., 1954; PhD, U. Mich., 1960. Tchr. social studies public, Jackson, Mich., 1954-58; instr. Eastern Mich. U., 1959, U. Mich., 1959-60; mem. faculty Sch. Edn., Ind. U., Bloomington, 1960-94, prof., 1969-94, chmn. social studies edn., 1965-69, chmn. secondary edn. dept., 1969-72, chmn. dept. curriculum and instrn., 1983-84, assoc. dean adminstrn. and devel., 1975-78, dir. external rels., 1991-94; dir. devel. Bloomington campus and annual giving Ind. U. Found., 1984-90; prof. emeritus retired, 1994. Vis. prof. U. Wis., summer 1967, U. Hawaii, 1968. Co-author: New Strategies and Curriculum in Social Studies, 1969, Secondary Schools in a Changing Society, 1976; co-editor 2 books. Bd. overseers St. Meinrad Coll. and Sem., 1991-98, trustee, 1995-97; treas. Bloomington Pk. and Recreation Found., 1996-98; bd. dirs. Monroe County YMCA, 1995-2002. With USAF, 1951-53. Recipient Booklist award Phi Lambda Theta, 1965, 69 Mem. Ind. Coun. Social Studies (pres. 1968-69), Phi Delta Kappa, Kappa Sigma, Phi Kappa Phi. Roman Catholic. Home: 3165 E Wyndam Bloomington IN 47401-6839 Office: Indiana Univ Sch of Edu Rm 3032 Bloomington IN 47405

SMITH, GARY LEE, lawyer; b. Seymour, Ind., June 24, 1961; s. Adam Donald and Noretta Joyce (Johnston) S.; m. Carol Stith, May 19, 1990. BA, Ind. U., 1984, JD, 1988. Bar: Ind. 1988, U.S. Dist. Ct. (no. and so. dists.) Ind. 1988. Assoc. Beck and Harrison, P.C., Columbus, Ind., 1988-90; pros. atty. Jennings County, orth Vernon, Ind., 1991—. State of Ind. scholar, 1980. Mem. Ind. Bar Assn., Jennings County Bar Assn. (pres. 1990—), Am. Trial Lawyers Assn., Ind. Trial Lawyers Assn., NRA, Moose, Optimists (charter). Democrat. Baptist. Avocations: fishing, firearms, softball, coin collector. Office: Jennings County Office of Prosecutor Courthouse Annex Vernon IN 47282

SMITH, GEOFFREY C., state legislator, state representative; b. 1968; BA in Polit. Sci., Ohio State U. Rep. Ohio State Ho. Reps., Columbus, 2000—. Mem. banking, pensions and securities com. Ohio State Ho. Reps., mem. health com., chmn. ins. com., mem. pub. utilities com. Vol. Big Brothers/Big Sisters; bd. dir. Prevent Blindness Ohio. Mem.: Charity Newsies, Columbus (Ohio) Blues Alliance, Columbus (Ohio) Mus. Art. Republican. Office: Ohio State House Reps 77 South High Street 13th Floor Columbus OH 43215-6111

SMITH, GEORGE CURTIS, judge; b. Columbus, Ohio, Aug. 8, 1935; s. George B. and Dorothy R. Smith; m. Barbara Jean Wood, July 10, 1963; children: Curtis, Geoffrey, Elizabeth Ann. BA, Ohio State U., 1957, JD, 1959. Bar: Ohio 1959, U.S. Dist. Ct. (so. dist.) Ohio 1987. Asst. city atty. City of Columbus, 1959-62; exec. asst. to Mayor of Columbus, 1962-63; asst. atty. gen. State of Ohio, 1964; chief counsel to pros. atty. Franklin County, Ohio, 1965-70; pros. atty., 1971-80; judge Franklin County Mcpl. Ct., Columbus, 1980-85, Franklin County Common Pleas Ct., 1985-87; sr. judge U.S. Dist. Ct., 2002—. Mem. 2003 Ohio Bicentennial Com.; mem. Historical Marker com., 2003; mem. Ohio Supreme Ct. Coun. on Victims Rights; judge in residence Law Sch. U. Cin.; chair Fed. Ct. Case Settlement Seminar; faculty Ohio Jud. Coll., Litig. Practice Inst.; chmn., Fed. Bench-Bar Conf.; lectr. ABA Anti-Trust Sec.; alumni spkr. law graduation Moritz Coll. Law, Ohio State U.; pres. Young Rep. Club; chmn. Perry Group, 2005; exec. com. Franklin County Rep. Party, 1971-80 Elder Presbyn. Ch. Recipient Superior Jud. Svc. award Supreme Ct. Ohio, Outstanding Pub. Svc. award Fr. Co. Rep. Orgn., 2001, Judge W.K. Thomas award Ohio State U. Law Alumni, Disting. Jurist, 2006, Ohio Pros. of Yr. award Ohio Pros. Attys. Assn., 1976, Hon. Leadership award, 1977. Mem. Columbus Bar Assn., Columbus Bar Found., Columbus Athletic Club (pres. 1980, dir.), Lawyers Club of Columbus (pres. 1975), Masons (pres. 33rd assn.), Shriners, Gyro Club (pres. 2003), Putin Bay Yacht Club (commodore 2007). Office: 85 Marconi Blvd Columbus OH 43215-2823 Office Phone: 614-719-3220.

SMITH, GLEE SIDNEY, JR., lawyer; b. Rozel, Kans., Apr. 29, 1921; s. Glee S. and Bernice M. (Augustine) S.; m. Geraldine B. Buhler, Dec. 14, 1943; children: Glee S., Stephen B., Susan K. AB, U. Kans., 1943, JD, 1947. Bar: Kans. 1947, U.S. Dist. Ct. 1951, U.S. Supreme Ct. 1973, U.S. Ct. Mil. Appeals 1988. Ptnr. Smith Burnett & Larson, Lanred, Kans., 1947—. Of counsel Barber, Emerson et. al., Lawrence, Kans., 1992—. Kans. state senator, 1957-73, pres. Senate, 1965-73; mem. Kans. Bd. Regents, 1975-83, pres., 1976; bd. govs. Kans. U. Law Soc., 1967—; mem. Kans. Jud. Coun., 1963-65; county atty. Pawnee County, 1949-53; mem. bd. edn. Larned, 1951-63; Kans. commr. Nat. Conf. Commn. on Uniform State Laws, 1963—; bd. dirs. Nat. Legal Svcs. Corp., 1975-79. Served to 1st lt. U.S. Army Air Corps, 1943-45. Recipient disting. svc. award U. Kans. Law Sch., 1976; disting. svc. citation U. Kans., 1984. Fellow Am. Coll. Probate Counsel, Am. Bar Found.; mem. ABA (bd. of govs. 1987-90, chmn. ops. com. 1989-90, exec. com. 1989-90, chmn. task force on solo and small firm practitioners 1990-91, chmn. com. on solo and small firm practitioners 1992-94, chmn. task force on applying fed. legis. to congress 1994-96), Kans. Bar Assn. (del. to ABA ho. of dels. 1982-92, bd. govs. 1982-92, leadership award 1973, medal of distinction 1993), Southwest Kans. Bar Assn., Am. Jud. Soc., Kiwanis, Masons, Rotary. Republican. Presbyterian. Home: 4313 Quail Pointe Rd Lawrence KS 66047-1966 Business E-Mail: glees@ku.edu.

SMITH, GLORIA RICHARDSON, nursing educator; b. Chgo., Sept. 29, 1934; BSN, Wayne State U., 1955; MPH, U. Mich., 1959; cert., UCLA, 1971; MA in Anthropology, U. Okla., 1977; PhD, Union for Experimenting Colls. and Univs., 1979; D Honoris Causa (hon.), U. Cin., 1992. Pub. health nurse Detroit Vis. Nurse Assn., 1955-56, sr. pub. health nurse, 1957-58, asst. dist. office supr., 1959-63; asst. prof. nursing Tuskegee Inst. Sch. Nursing, Ala., 1963-66, Albany (Ga.) State Coll., 1966-68; cons. nurse home health care Okla. State Health Dept., 1968-70, medicare nurse cons., 1970-71; asst. prof. U. Okla. Coll. Nursing, Oklahoma City, 1971-73, assoc. prof. and interim dean, 1973-75; state health dir. Mich. Dept. Pub. Health, 1983-88; prof., dean Coll. Nursing Wayne State U., 1988-91; coord., program dir. in health WK Kellogg Found., 1991-95, v.p. programs in health, 1995—. Chair Mich. Task Force on Nursing Issues, 1989-90, at. Commn. on Nursing Shortage, 1990-91; cons. on nursing Colo. Commn. Higher Edn., 1990, U. N.C., 1990; mem. adv. com. nursing Okla. State Regents for Higher Edn., 1973-83; cons. VA Hosp., 1975-77, HEW, 1977-78, U. Mich. External Rev. Sch. Nursing, 1980. Contbr. articles on health care and nursing edn. to profl. publs. Mem. Mayor's Com. to Study In-Migrants, Detroit, 1963; bd. dirs. St. Peter Claver Cmty. Credit Union, 1961-63, YMCA, Oklahoma City, 1972-76, Better Homes Found. for Homeless, 1986—; mem. steering com. Kellogg Fellowship Internat. Program in Health, 1985-89; mem. study com. health care for homeless Inst. Medicine, 1987-88. Recipient Outstanding Svc. award Franklin Settlement, 1963, Disting. Alumni award Wayne State U., 1984, Disting. Scholar award Am. Nurses Found., 1987—. Mem. Nat. League Nursing (dir. from 1979), Am. Nurses Assn. (mem. commn. on nursing edn. 1978-82), Okla. League ursing, Midwest Alliance in Nursing (dir. 1977-80), Black Pers. (exec. com. 1974-76), Am. Assn. Colls. Nursing (exec. com. from 1976), Nat. Black Nurses Assn. (dir. 1972-78), Okla. State Nurses Assn. (Nurse of Yr. 1972), Am. Assn. for Higher Edn., Okla. State Assn. for Black Pers. in Higher Edn. (rec. sec. 1976-78), Am. Acad. Nursing (governing coun. 1983-85), Assn. State and Territorial Health Officers, Am. Pub. Health Assn., Okla. Pub. Health Assn., Sigma Gamma Rho (Outstanding Sigma of Yr. 1963), Sigma Theta Tau.

SMITH, GORDON HOWELL, lawyer; b. Syracuse, NY, Oct. 26, 1915; s. Lewis P. and Maud (Mixer) S.; m. Eunice Hale, June 28,1947; children: Lewis Peter, Susan S. Rizk, Catherine S. Maxson, Maud S. Daudon. BA, Princeton U., 1932-36; LL.B., Yale U., 1939. Bar: N.Y. 1939, Ill. 1946. Asso. Lord, Day & Lord, NYC, 1939-41, Gardner, Carton & Douglas, Chgo., 1946-51; partner Mackenzie, Smith & Michell, Syracuse, 1951-53, Gardner, Carton & Douglas, 1954-57, 60-85, of counsel, 1986-96, retired ptnr., 1996—. Sec., dir. Smith-Corona, Inc., 1951-54, v.p., Syracuse, 1957-60 Bd. dirs. Rehab. Inst. Chgo., chmn., 1974-78, 83-86; bd. dirs. United Way Met. Chgo., 1962-85. Served to lt. comdr. USNR, 1941-46. Mem. Am. Soc. Corporate Secs., Am., Ill., Chgo. bar assns. Clubs: Comml., Law, Econ., Legal, Chgo., Old Elm (Chgo.).

SMITH, GREGORY ALLGIRE, academic administrator; b. Washington, Mar. 31, 1951; s. Donald Eugene and Mary Elizabeth Smith; m. Susan Elizabeth Watts, Oct. 31, 1980; 1 child, David Joseph Smith-Watts. BA, Johns Hopkins U., 1972; MA, Williams Coll., 1974. Adminstrv. asst. Washington Project for Arts, 1975; intern Walker Art Ctr., Mpls., 1975—76; asst. devel. officer Sci. Mus. Minn., St. Paul, 1977; asst. dir. Akron Art Inst., Ohio, 1977—80; asst. to dir. Toledo Mus. Art, 1980—82, asst. dir. adminstrn., 1982—86; exec. v.p. Internat. Exhbns. Found., Washington, 1986—87; dir. Telfair Mus. Art, Savannah, Ga., 1987—94, Art Acad. Cin., 1994—98, pres., 1998—. Trustee Greater Cin. Consortium of Colls. and Univs., vice chmn., 2001—03, chmn., 2003—05; trustee Assn. Ind. Colls. of Art and Design; grad. Leadership Savanah, 1990—92, Leadership Cin., 2003—04. Mem.: Coll. Art Assn., Ohio Found. on the Arts (v.p. 1981—83, trustee 1981—84), Assn. Art Mus. Adminstrs. (founder 1984—85), Am. Assn. Mus., Rotary (dir. Cin. club 2000—01, sec.-treas. 2001—02, pres. 2002—03), Univ. Club. Avocation: collecting arts and crafts movement objects, landscape design, gardening. Home: 8380 Springvalley Dr Cincinnati OH 45236-1356 Office: Art Academy Of Cincinnati 1212 Jackson St Cincinnati OH 45202-7106 Office Phone: 513-562-8743. E-mail: gasmith@artacademy.edu.

SMITH, HAROLD B., manufacturing executive; b. Chgo., Apr. 7, 1933; s. Harold Byron and Pauline (Hart) S. Grad., Choate Sch., 1951; BS, Princeton U., 1955; MBA, orthwestern U., 1957. With Ill. Tool Works, Inc., Chgo., 1954—, exec. v.p., 1968-72, pres., 1972-81, vice chmn., 1981, chmn. exec. com., 1982—, also bd. dirs. Bd. dirs. W.W. Grainger, Inc., No. Trust Corp Mem. Rep. Nat. Com., 1976-99; chmn. Ill. Rep. Com., 1993-99; del. Rep. Nat. Conv., 1964, 76, 88, 92, 96, 2000, 04; bd. dirs. Adler Planetarium, Boys and Girls Clubs Am., Northwestern U., Rush U. Med. Ctr., Newberry Libr. Mem.: Chicago, Commercial, Commonwealth, Economic, Northwestern, Princeton (Chgo.). Office: Ill Tool Works Inc 3600 W Lake Ave Glenview IL 60026-1215

SMITH, HARTMAN WILLIAM, supermarket executive; b. Corpus Christi, Tex., June 18, 1944; s. Laban Conrad and Margaret (Hayes) S.; m. Nancy Marie Foster, June 6, 1964; children: Kelly Lynn, Christopher Brock, Megan Marie. BS, Ind. U., 1966. CPA Ind. R&D adminstr., then tax auditor Ind. Dept. Revenue, 1964—66; audit mgr. Arthur Andersen & Co., Indpls., 1966—74; v.p. fin., sec.-treas. Marsh Supermarkets, Inc., Yorktown, Ind., 1974—. Assoc. mem. faculty acctg. dept. Ind. U.-Purdue U., Indpls., 1972—73. Named Sagamore of Wabash, 1967. Mem.: AICPA, Fin. Execs. Inst., Soc. Corp. Secs., Ind. Assn. CPAs. Office: Marsh Supermarkets Inc Depot St Yorktown IN 47396-1510

SMITH, HARVEY, social science research administrator; Dir. Social Sci. Rsch. Inst. No. Ill. U., De Kalb, Ill., 1993—. Office: No Ill U Social Sci Rsch Inst Dekalb IL 60115 E-mail: hsmith@niu.edu.

SMITH, HENRY CHARLES, III, symphony orchestra conductor; b. Phila., Jan. 31, 1931; s. Henry Charles Jr. and Gertrude Ruth (Downs) S.; m. Mary Jane Dressner, Sept. 3, 1955; children: Katherine Anne, Pamela Jane, Henry Charles IV. BA, U. Pa., 1952; artist diploma, Curtis Inst. Music, Phila., 1955. Solo trombonist Phila. Orch., 1955-67; condr. Rochester (Minn.) Symphony Orch., 1967-68; assoc. prof. music Ind. U., Bloomington, 1968-71; resident condr., ednl. dir. Minn. Orch., Mpls., 1971-88; prof. music U. Tex., Austin, 1988-89, Frank C. Erwin Centennial Prof. of Opera, 1988-89; music dir. S.D. Symphony, Sioux Falls, 1989-2001; prof. Ariz. State U., Tempe, 1989-93, prof. emeritus, 1993—. Vis. prof. U. Tex., Austin, 1987-88; founding mem. Phila. Brass Ensemble, 1956—; music dir. World Youth Symphony Orch., Interlochen, Mich., 1981-96; artistic advisor, prin. guest conductor Cedar Rapids Symphony, Iowa, 2004-. Composer 5 books of solos for trombone including Solos for the Trombone Player, 1963, Hear Us As We Pray, 1963, First Solos for the Trombone Player, 1972, Easy Duets for Winds, 1972; editor 14 books 20th century symphonies lit. Served to 1st lt. AUS, 1952-54. Recipient 3 Grammy nominations, 1967, 76, 1 Grammy award for best chamber music rec. with Phila. Brass Ensemble, 1969. Mem. Internat. Trombone Assn. (dir.), Am. Symphony Orch. League, Music Educators Nat. Conf., Am. Guild Organists, Am. Fedn. Musicians, Tubist Universal Brotherhood Assn., Acacia Fraternity. Republican. Congregationalist. Home: 8032 Pennsylvania Rd S Bloomington MN 55438-1135

SMITH, HERALD ALVIN, JR., transportation executive; b. Beaconsfield, Iowa, Dec. 23, 1923; s. Herald Alvin and Iva Viola (Briggeman) S.; m. Miriam Gayle Armstrong, Oct. 5, 1946; children: Sharon Konchar, John, Susan Johnson, Jim. Student, U. Iowa, 1942-43, Coe Coll., Cedar Rapids, Iowa, 1944-45. Pres., chmn. bd. CRST, Inc., Cedar Rapids, 1955-77, chmn. bd., chief exec. officer, 1977-83; chmn. bd. CRST Internat., Inc., Cedar Rapids, 1983—. Chmn. bd., pres. Crest Microfilm, Inc., Cedar Rapids, 1980—. Mem. Gov.'s Blue Ribbon Task Force on Transp., Iowa, 1982; trustee Regional Transit Authority, Cedar Rapids, 1967-78; campaign mgr. United Way, 1973-74; bd. dirs. CMC Colls. Associated, 1979, Cornell Coll., Mt. Vernon, Iowa, 1979-87, Four Oaks Treatment Ctr., 1986—. Mem. Am. Trucking Assn., Inc. (interstate carriers conf. 1st v.p. 1980-81, pres. 1981-82, chmn. 1982-83), Iowa Motor Truck Assn. (pres., chmn. bd. 1978-79, exec. bd. 1979—). Avocations: tennis, sailing, running a resort. Office: CRST Internat Inc 3930 16th Ave SW Cedar Rapids IA 52404-2332

SMITH, IAN CORMACK PALMER, biophysicist; b. Winnipeg, Man., Can., Sept. 23, 1939; s. Cormack and Grace Mary Smith; m. Eva Gunilla Landvik, Mar. 27, 1965; children: Brittmarie, Cormack, Duncan, Roderick. BS, U. Man., 1961, MS, 1962; PhD, Cambridge U., Eng., 1965; PhD (hon.), U. Stockholm, 1986; DSc (hon.), U. Winnipeg, 1990, Brandon U., 2001, Cracow Polish Acad. Sci., 2006; diploma in tech. (hon.), Red River Coll., 1996. Fellow Stanford U., 1965-66; mem. rsch. staff Bell Tel. Labs., Murray Hill, NJ, 1966-67; rsch. officer divsn. biol. scis. NRC, Ottawa, Canada, 1967-87, dir. gen., 1987-91, Inst. Biodiagnostics, Winnipeg, Canada, 1992—. Adj. prof. chemistry and biochemistry Carleton U., 1973—90, U. Ottawa, 1976—92; adj. prof. biophysics U. Ill., Chgo., 1974—80; adj. prof. chemistry, radiology, physics and anatomy U. Man., 1992—; allied scientist Ottawa Civic Hosp., 1985—98, Ottawa Gen. Hosp., 1989—98, Ont. Cancer Found., 1989—91, St. Boniface Hosp., 1992—, Health Scis. Ctr., 1993—, Econ. Tech. Innovation Coun., Man., 1994—98; exec. com. Man. Health Rsch. Coun., 1996—98, 2007—, Econ. Tech. Innovation Coun., Man., 1996—98; chmn. Man. Health Rsch. Coun., 1998—2002, 2007; mem. adv. bd. Loeb Inst., Ottawa, 1999—2001, Keystone Ventures, 1999—2002, Western LIfe Scis. Fund, 2002—, Novadaq, 2004—, St. Boniface Hosp. Rsch. Enterprise, 2006—, Cancer Care Man.; bd. govs. U. Manitoba, Canada, 2000—06; bd. dirs. ENSIS Growth Fund, DIASPEC Holdings, IMRIS Inc., Magnetic Resonance Vets., Photonics Rsch. Ont., Spectex Pty., Biomed. Commercialization Can., Ontario Centres of Excellence, Genome Prairie, Cancer Care Man. Contbr. chapters to books, articles to profl. jours. Mem. adv. bd. Smart Winnipeg, 2000—03; mem. Premier's Econ. Adv. Bd., Man., 2001—, exec. com. Man., 2004—; bd. govs. U. Man., 2000—06. Decorated Order of the Star of Romania; recipient Barringer award, Can. Spectroscopy Soc., 1979, Herzberg award, 1986, Organon Teknika award, Can. Soc. Clin. Chemists, 1987, Sr. Scientist award, Sigma Xi, 1995, Queen's Jubilee medal, 2003, Star of Romania, 2004, Paul Harris award, Rotary Club, 2006. Fellow: Soc. Magnetic Resonance Medicine (mem. exec. com. 1989—94), Royal Soc. Can. (Flavelle medal 1996), Chem. Inst. Can. (Merck award 1978, Labatt award 1984); mem.: U. Manitoba (bd. gov. 1991—97), Ont. Ctr. Photonics (chmn. bd. mgmt. 2002—), Ont. Ctrs. Excellence (bd. dirs. 2002—), Internat. Union Pure and Applied Biophysics (mem. coun. 1993—, v.p. 1996—99, 2002—05, pres. 2005—08), Biophys. Soc. Can. (pres. 1992—94), Can. Biochem. Soc., Biophysical Soc., Internat. Coun. Sci. Unions (mem. gen. com. 1989—94), U. Man. Alumni Assn. (bd. dirs. 1994—2000, v.p. 1997—98, pres. 1998—99). Office: Inst Biodiagnostics Winnipeg MB Canada R3B 1Y6 Home Phone: 204-897-0650; Office Phone: 204-983-7526. Business E-Mail: ian.smith@nrc-cnrc.gc.ca.

SMITH, JAMES ALBERT, lawyer; b. Jackson, Mich., May 12, 1942; s. J. William and Mary Barbara (Browning) S.; m. Lucia S. Santini, Aug. 14, 1965; children: Matthew Browning, Aaron Michael, Rachel Elizabeth. BA, U. Mich., 1964, JD, 1967. Bar: Mich. 1968, U.S. Dist. Ct. (ea. dist.) Mich., U.S. Ct. Appeals (6th and D.C. cirs.), U.S. Supreme Ct. Assoc. Bodman, Longley & Dahling, Detroit, 1967-75, ptnr., 1975—. Mem. panel Atty. Discipline Bd., Wayne County, Mich., 1987—; arbitrator Am. Arbitration Assn., 1975—; mem. Banking Commrs. com. on Contested Case Adminstrn., 1978. Mem. pro bono referral group Call For Action, Detroit, 1982—. Mem. ABA, State Bar Mich., Detroit Bar Assn. Roman Catholic. Avocations: sailing, travel. Office: Bodman LLP 1901 Antoine St 6th Fl Detroit MI 48226

SMITH, JAMES C., entrepreneur; B, Northeastern U., 1963. Sales exec. Tex. Instruments; founder ARC Mgmt.; pres., CEO First Health; chmn. Concentra, 2000—. Mem.: ortheastern U. Gov. Bd., Internat. Found. Employee Benefit Plans (chmn. strat. planning and devel. com., adv. dir., mem. edn. com.), Health Ins. Assn. Am. (mem. bd. dirs.), Healthcare Leadership Coun. (treas., mem. exec. com.). Office: 3200 Highland Grove Downers Grove IL 60515-1282

SMITH, JAMES WARREN, pathologist, educator, microbiologist, parasitologist; b. Logan, Utah, July 5, 1934; s. Kenneth Warren and Nina Lou (Sykes) S.; m. Nancy Chesterman, July 19, 1958; children: Warren, Scott. BS, U. Iowa, 1956, MD, 1959. Diplomate Am. Bd. Pathology. Intern Colo. Gen. Hosp., Denver, 1959—60; resident U. Iowa Hosps., Iowa City, 1960—65; asst. prof. pathology U. Vt., Burlington, 1967—70; prof. pathology Ind. U., Indpls., 1970—98, chmn. dept. pathology and lab. medicine, 1992—98, Nordshow prof. of lab. medicine, 1997—98, prof. emeritus, 1998—. Contbr. articles to profl. jours. Served to lt. comdr. USN, 1965-67. Recipient Outstanding Contbn. to Clin. Microbiology award South Ctrl. Assn. Clin. Microbiology, 1977. Fellow Coll. Am. Pathologists (chmn. microbiology resource com. 1981-85); mem. AMA, Infectious Disease Soc. Am., Am. Soc. Investigative Pathology, Royal Soc. Tropical Medicine and Hygiene, Am. Soc. Clin. Pathology, Am. Soc. Microbiology, Am. Soc. Tropical Medicine and Hygiene, U.S.-Can. Acad. Pathology, Assn. Pathology Chairs, Binford Dammin Soc. Infectious Disease Pathologists, Soc. Protozoologists. Home: 4375 Cold Spring Rd Indianapolis IN 46228-3327 Office: Ind U Med Ctr 635 Barnhill Dr Rm A128 Indianapolis IN 46202-5126

SMITH, JAY LAWRENCE, financial planning company executive; b. Detroit, June 10, 1954; s. Paul Edward Smith and Gloria D. Lawrence; m. Janice Irene Acheson, May 21, 1978; children: Kevin Hamilton, Travis Jay. Student, Oakland U., 1972-75. CFP. Asst. tng. dir. Equitable Cos., Troy, Mich., 1978-81; pres. JLS Fin. Planning Corp., Oxford, Mich., 1978—. Adj. faculty Oakland U., Rochester, Mich., 1986-87; commentator TV show Your Money and You, 1987. Cons. Practicing Fin. Planning, 1990; contbr. articles to profl. jours. Mem. Internat. Assn. Fin. Planning (v.p. 1985-87, bd. dirs. 1987-89), Inst. Cert. Fin. Planners (bd. dirs. 1988-90), Inst. Cert. Fin. Planners-Mich. (pres. 1992-93), Fin. Profl. Adv. Panel, Internat. Bd. Cert. Fin. Planners, Rotary (bd. dirs. 1984-86, treas. 1985-87, pres. Oxford 1992-93). Republican. Methodist. Avocations: skiing, music, raquetball. Office: Investment Mgmt & Rsch Inc PO Box 4 28 S Washington St Oxford MI 48371-4985

SMITH, JOHN FRANCIS, JR., (JACK SMITH), retired automotive executive; b. Worcester, Mass., Apr. 6, 1938; s. John Francis and Eleanor C. (Sullivan) S.; children: Brian, Kevin; m. Lydia G. Sigrist, Aug. 27, 1988; 1 stepchild, Nicola. BBA, U. Mass., 1960; MBA, Boston U., 1965. Fisher Body divsn. mgr. GM, Framingham, Mass., 1961-73, asst. treas. NYC, 1973-80, comptr. Detroit, 1980-81, dir. worldwide product planning, 1981-84, pres., gen. mgr. Oshawa, Ont., Canada, 1984-85, exec. v.p. internat. ops. Detroit, 1988-90, vice chmn. internat. ops., 1990, bd. dirs., mem. fin. com., 1990-98, COO, 1992, CEO, 1992—2000, pres., 1992—98, chmn. bd., 1996—2003; exec. v.p. GM Europe, Glattbrugg, Switzerland, 1986-87, pres., 1987-88. Mem. US Japan Bus. Coun.; bus. coun. Meml. Sloan-Kettering Cancer Ctr.; bd. dirs. Procter & Gamble Co., 1995-2008, Delta Air Lines Inc., 2000-2007, non-exec. chmn., 2004-2007; chmn. adv. bd. Alix Ptnrs. LLC/Questor Ptnrs. Funds. Mem. chancellor's exec. com. U. Mass., dir.; trustee United Way SE Mich., New Am. Revolution, Boston U.; bd. dirs. The Nature Conservancy. Mem. Am. Soc. Corp. Execs., Am. Auto Mfrs. Assn. (bd. dirs.), Econ. Club Detroit (bd. dirs.), The Bus. Coun., Beta Gamma Sigma (pres.), Dirs. Table. Roman Catholic.

SMITH, JOHN M., trucking executive; b. 1948; Degree in econs., Cornell Coll., 1971; MBA, Cornell U., 1974. With CRST Internat. Inc., Cedar Rapids, Iowa, 1971—, pres., CEO, 1987—. Named Regional Entrepreneur of the Yr., 1992. Mem. Am. Trucking Assn. (exec. com.), ITCC. Office: CRST Internat Inc 3930 16th Ave SW Cedar Rapids IA 52404-2332

SMITH, JOHN ROBERT, physicist, department chairman; b. Salt Lake City, Oct. 1, 1940; married; 2 children. BS, Toledo U., 1962; PhD in Physics, Ohio State U., 1968. Aerospace engr. surface physics Lewis Rsch. Ctr. NASA, 1965-68; sr. rsch. physicist, head surface and interface physics group Gen. Motors, Warren, Mich., 1972-80, sr. staff scientist, head solid state physics group, 1980-86, prin. rsch. scientist rsch. lab., 1986-99, head engineered surfaces program, 1995-99; group mgr. mfg. process Delphi Rsch. Labs, Shelby, Mich., 1999—. Adj. prof. dept. physics U. Mich., 1983—. Air Force Office Sci. Rsch., Nat. Rsch. Coun. fellow U. Calif., 1970-72. Fellow Am. Phys. Soc. (David Adler Lectureship award in field of materials sci. 1991); mem. Am. Vacuum Soc., Sigma Xi. Achievements include research in the theory and experiment of solid surfaces, electronic properties, magnetic properties and chemisorption, adhesion, metal contact electronic structure, defects and universal features of bonding in solids, as well as manufacturing processes including machining and coatings. Office: M/C 483-478-107 51786 Shelby Pkwy Shelby Township MI 48315-1786

SMITH, KATIE (KATHERINE MAY SMITH), professional basketball player; b. Logan, Ohio, June 4, 1974; d. Don Smith. Degree in zoology, Ohio State U., 1996. Profl. basketball player Columbus Quest, ABL, 1997—98, Minn. Lynx, WNBA, 1999—, Lotos VBW Clima, EuroLeague, Gdynia, Poland, 2001—02. Named Ohio State Female Athlete of the Century, Columbus Touchdown Club, 2002; named to ABL All-Star Team, 1997, 1998, All-ABL First Team, 1998, WNBA All-Star Team, 2000, 2001, 2002, 2003, All-WNBA First Team, 2001, 2003. Achievements include mem., Columbus Quest ABL Championship Team, 1997, 98; mem., US Women's Basketball Gold Medal Team, FIBA World Championships, 1998, 2002; mem., US Women's Basketball Gold Medal Team, Sydney Olympics, 2000; mem., US Women's Basketball Team, Athens Olympics, 2004; first female in history of Ohio State U. to have number retired, Jan. 21, 2001. Office: Minn Lynx 600 First Ave North Minneapolis MN 55403

SMITH, K(ERMIT) WAYNE, computer company executive; b. Newton, NC, Sept. 15, 1938; s. Harold Robert and Hazel K. (Smith) S.; m. Audrey M. Kennedy, Dec. 19, 1958; 1 son, Stuart W. BA, Wake Forest U., 1960; MA, Princeton U., 1962, PhD, 1964; postgrad., U. So. Calif., 1965; LLD (hon.), Ohio U., 1992; LHD (hon.), Ohio State U., 1998. Instr. Princeton U., 1963; asst. prof. econs. and polit. sci. U.S. Mil. Acad., 1963-66; spl. asst. to asst. sec. def. for sys. analysis Washington, 1966-69; program mgr. def. studies RAND Corp., Santa Monica, Calif., 1969-70; dir. program analysis NSC, Washington, 1970-72; group v.p. planning Dart Industries, LA, 1972-73, group pres. resort devel. group, 1973-76; exec. v.p. Washington Group, Inc., 1976-77; mng. ptnr. Coopers & Lybrand, Washington, 1977-80, group mng. ptnr., 1980-83; chmn., CEO World Book, Inc., 1983-86; prof. Wake Forest U., 1986—88, 2001—; CEO OCLC Online Computer Libr. Ctr., Inc., Dublin, Ohio, 1989-98, pres. emeritus, 1998—. Sr. cons. Dept. Def., Dept. State, NSC, NASA, Dept. Energy, OMB, GAO; bd. dirs. Nat. City Bank, K. Wayne Smith and Assocs.; con. prof. (hon.) Tsinghua U., Beijing, 1996; chmn. Rainbow Care For Kids Found., 1999-2000. Author: How Much is Enough? Shaping the Defense Program, 1961-69, 1971, reprinted as RAND classic, 2005; editor: OCLC 1967-97: Thirty Years of Furthering Access to the World's Information, 1998; contbr. articles to profl. jours. Mem. vis. com. Brookings Instn., Washington, 1971-79; mem. bd. visitors Wake Forest U., 1974-78, 82-90, chmn. bd. visitors, 1976-78, trustee, 1991-95, 96-00, 01-05, 06-, vice chmn., 2006-07, chmn., 2007—; mem. bd. visitors Def.

Sys. Mgmt. Coll., 1982-85, Lenoir Rhyne Coll., 1988-94, Mershon Ctr. Ohio State U., 1990-92, Columbus Assn. for Performing Arts, 1991-95, U. Pitts. Sch. Libr. and Info. Sci., 1992-95; mem. bd. visitors Bowman Gray Bapt. Hosp. Med. Ctr., 1992-95, chmn. bd. visitors, 1993-95; bd. dirs. Wake Forest U. Bapt. Med. Ctr., 2007—. Danforth fellow, Woodrow Wilson fellow Princeton U., 1962-64. Mem. ALA (hon., life), Coun. Fgn. Rels., Internat. Inst. Strategic Studies, Inst. Internat. Edn., Coun. Higher Edn., Am. Assn. Higher Edn., Chgo. Club, Lakes Golf and Country Club, Capital Club, Phi Beta Kappa, Omicron Delta Kappa, Kappa Sigma. Methodist. Home: 2606 Sigmon Dairy Rd Newton NC 28658-7609 Office: Online Computer Libr Ctr Inc 6565 Frantz Rd Dublin OH 43017-5308

SMITH, LEROY HARRINGTON, JR., mechanical engineer, consultant; b. Balt., Nov. 3, 1928; s. Leroy Harrington and Edna (Marsh) S.; m. Barbara Ann Williams, July 7, 1951; children: Glenn Harrington, Bruce Lyttleton, Cynthia Ann. BS in Engring., Johns Hopkins U., 1949, MS, 1951, Dr. Engring., 1954. Compressor aerodynamacist Gen. Electric Co., Cin., 1954-61, mgr. turbomachinery devel., 1961-68, mgr. compressor & fan design tech., 1968-75, mgr. turbomachinery aerodynamics tech., 1975-92, cons. technologist Turbomachinery Aerodynamics, 1992-94, cons., 1994—. Contbr. articles to ASME Trans. Recipient Perry T. Egbert Jr. awards, 1969, 83, Charles P. Steinmetz award, 1987 Gen. Electric Co. Fellow ASME (Gas Turbine award 1981, 87, R. Tom Sawyer award 1987, Aircraft Engine Tech. award 1993); mem. NAE, Internat. Soc. Air Breathing Engines (award 2001), Ohio River Launch Club. Achievements include patents in field. Office: GE Aviation 30 Merchant St Princeton Hill P20 Cincinnati OH 45246 Office Phone: 513-552-5702. E-mail: leroy.smith@ae.ge.com.

SMITH, LINDA JEANE, allied health educator; b. Alton, Ill., Mar. 22, 1952; d. LeRoy Homer and Jeane (Garrett) Campbell; m. Gary L. Smith, Mar. 14, 1998; children: Mary Jeane, Barbara Jo. BSN, St. Louis U., 1974, MS in Nursing of Children, 1976; EdD, So. Ill. U., 1993. RN, Ill., Mo. Staff nurse St. Louis Children's Hosp., 1973-75; faculty allied health Lewis and Clark C.C., Godfrey, Ill., 1976-87, coord. assoc. deg. nursing program, 1987—2000. Pres. Am. Lung Assn. of Ill., Springfield, 1994-95. Mem. Coun. of Deans and Dirs. of Assoc. Deg. Nursing Programs (chair 1990-92), Nat. League for Nursing, Order Ea. Star, Sigma Theta Tau, Kappa Delta Pi. Presbyterian. Home: 226 Forest Ct Edwardsville IL 62025-5389 Office: Lewis & Clark C C 5800 Godfrey Rd Godfrey IL 62035-2426

SMITH, LOUIS, sports association administrator; m. Sharon Smith; 4 children. BSEE, U. Mo., Rolla; MBA, Rockhurst Coll.; postgrad., U. Kans. Assoc. engr. to asst. gen. mgr. AlliedSignal Inc., Kansas City, Mo., 1966-86, v.p. prodn. ops. Bendix Aerospace Sector Arlington, Va., 1986-88; v.p. mfg. AlliedSignal Aerospace Co., Torrance, Calif., 1988-89; asst. gen. mgr., adminstrn. AlliedSignal Inc., Kansas City, 1989-90, pres., 1990-95; pres., COO, bd. dirs. Ewing Marion Kauffman Found., Kansas City, 1995—. Bd. dirs. Western Resources, Commerce Bank Kansas City. Bd. dirs. Kansas City Royals, Greater Kansas City C. of C., Midwest Rsch. Inst., Civic Coun. Greater Kansas City, The Learning Exch.; mem. exec. com. Kansas City Area Devel. Coun., Rockhurst Coll. Bd. Trustees; mem. numerous coms. U. Mo.-Rolla, U. Kans.;;past chmn. corp. devel. coun., mem. Acad. Elec. Engring. U. Mo.-Rolla; adv. bd. U. Kans. Sch. Engring. On Board of Directors of KC Royals since 1992. Office: Kansas City Royals Kauffman Stadium PO Box 419969 Kansas City MO 64141-6969

SMITH, LOVIE, professional football coach; b. Gladewater, Tex., May 8, 1958; m. MaryAnne Smith; children: Mikal, Matthew, Miles. BA, U. Tulsa, 1979. Head coach Big Sandy HS Football Team, 1980, Cascia Hall Prep, Tulsa, 1981, U. Tulsa, 1983—86, U. Wis., 1987, Ariz. State U., 1988—91, U. Ky, 1992, U. Tenn., 1993—94, Ohio State U., 1995, Chgo. Bears, 2004—; linebacker coach Tampa Bay Buccaneers, 1996—2001; defensive coord. St. Louis Rams, 2001—03. Named two-time All-American, three-time All-Mo. Conf., Coach of Yr., AP, 2005. Achievements include becoming one of two first African-Am. Coaches in Super Bowl, 2007. Office: Chgo Bears 1000 Football Dr Lake Forest IL 60045

SMITH, MARGARET TAYLOR, volunteer; b. Roanoke Rapids, NC, May 31, 1925; d. George Napoleon and Sarah Luella (Waller) T.; m. Sidney William Smith Jr., Aug. 15, 1947; children: Sarah Smith, Sidney William Smith III, Susan Smith, Amy Smith. BA in Sociology, Duke U., 1947. Chair emeritus bd. trustees Kresge Found., Troy, Mich., 1985—; chmn. Nat. Coun. for Women's Studies Duke U., NC, 1986—, chmn. Trinity Bd. Visitors NC, 1988-98; chair emeritus. Chmn. bd. visitors Wayne State U. Med. Sch., 1993; bd. dirs., mem. exec. com. Detroit Med. Ctr.; mem. bd. govs. Detroit Med. Ctr. Recipient the Merrill-Palmer award Wayne State U., Detroit, 1987, Zimmerman award Gtr. Detroit Health Coun., Athena award C. of C., 1998, Women of Achievement award Mich. Women's Fedn., 1999, disting. svc. award Wayne State U., 1999; named disting. alumna award Duke U. Mem. The Village Club, Internat. Women's Forum, Pi Beta Phi, Phi Beta Kappa. Methodist. E-mail: sidmyth@aol.com.

SMITH, MARK D., state representative; b. Jan. 1952; State rep. dist. 43 Iowa Ho. of Reps., 2001—; mem. appropriations com.; mem. human resources com.; mem. human svcs. appropriations com.; mem. labor and indsl. rels. com. Democrat. Office: State Capitol East 12th and Grand Des Moines IA 50319 Address: 816 Roberts Ter Marshalltown IA 50158

SMITH, MARSCHALL IMBODEN, lawyer; b. San Antonio, Oct. 3, 1944; s. Lowell B. and Jacqueline I. Smith; m. Elizabeth Braswell (div. 1973); m. Ann McNamara, June 3, 1976; children: Catherine, Elizabeth, Margaret, Austin, Lillian. AB in Hist. cum laude, Princeton U., NJ, 1966; JD, U. Va., 1973; MBA, U. Chgo., 1987. Bar: NY 1974, US Ct. Appeals (2nd cir.) 1974, US Dist. Ct. (so. dist. NY) 1974, Ill. 1980. Assoc. Debevoise & Plimpton, NYC, 1973-75, Paul, Weiss, Rifkind, Wharton & Garrison, NYC, 1975-81; atty. Baxter Travenol Labs., Deerfield, Ill., 1980-82, Baxter Internat. Inc., Deerfield, Ill., 1982-83, 1983-85, asst. gen. counsel, 1985-87, assoc. gen. counsel, 1987—92; v.p., gen. counsel Am. Med. Holdings Inc., 1992—93; sr. v.p., gen. counsel, sec. IMC Global Inc. (formerly IMC Fertilizer Group Inc.), Northbrook, Ill., 1993—99; exec. v.p., gen. counsel Digitas Inc., Boston, 1999—2001; v.p., gen. counsel, corp. sec. Brunswick Corp., Lake Forest, Ill., 2001—07; sr. v.p. legal affairs, gen. counsel 3M Co., St. Paul, 2007—. Adj. faculty Lake Forest Grad. Sch. Mgmt., 1985—88. Maj. USMC, 1966—73, Vietnam. Mem.: Assn. Corp. Counsel, Christian Legal Soc., Chgo. Bar Assn. Office: 3M Co 3M Corp HQ 3m Ctr Saint Paul MN 55144-1000 Office Phone: 847-735-4430.

SMITH, MICHAEL JAMES, industrial engineering educator; b. Madison, Wis., May 12, 1945; s. James William and Ruth Gladys (Murphy) S.; m. Patricia Ann Bentley, June 22, 1968; children: Megan Colleen, Melissa Maureen. BA, U. Wis., 1968, MA, 1970, PhD, 1973. Rsch. analyst Wis. Dept. Industry Labor, Madison, 1971-74; rsch. psychologist Nat. Inst. for Occupational Safety and Health, USPHS, Cin., 1974-84; prof. U. Wis., Madison, 1984—. Owner, prin. M.J. Smith Assocs. Inc., Madison, 1991—. Contbr. articles to profl. jours. Mem. APA, Inst. Indsl. Engrs. (sr.), Human Factors Soc., Assn. Computer Machinery, Am. Soc. Testing and Measurement. Avocation: tennis. Home: 6719 Shamrock Glen Cir Middleton WI 53562-1144 Office: U Wis Dept Indsl Engring Human Factors Rsch Lab 1513 University Ave Madison WI 53706-1539 Office Phone: 608-263-6329. Business E-Mail: mjsmith@engr.wisc.edu.

SMITH, MICHAEL KENT, state legislator; b. Canton, Ill., May 23, 1966; m. Donna Shaw. BA, Bradley U., 1988. Legis. asst. to Rep. Thomas J. Homer Ill. State House of Reps., Springfield, 1986-92, mem. from dist. 91, 1994—, mem. agr., mem. consumer protection, mem. elem. and secondary sch. com., mem. judiciary criminal law com. Trustee Graham Hosp.; field coord. Dukakis/Bentsen Presdl. Campaign, 1988; precinct committeeman Dem. Com., 1984—; chmn. Fulton County Dem. Ctrl. Com., 1990—; trustee Canton Twp., 1991-94; citizen's advocate Ill. Atty. Gen., Peoria, 1992-95. Mem. Canton Area C. of C. (past pres.), Am. Heart Assn., Dem. County Chmn.'s Assn. (v.p. 1992—). Office: Ill House of Reps Rm 2068L State Capitol Springfield IL 62706-0001 Address: 301 45 E Side Sq Canton IL 61520-2603

SMITH, MORTON EDWARD, ophthalmology educator, dean; b. Balt., Oct. 17, 1934; BS, U. Md., 1956, MD, 1960. Bd. cert. Ophthalmology Bd.; lic. physician Mo., Md., Wis. Rotating intern Denver Gen. Hosp., 1960-61; resident, nat. inst. of neorol. diseases and blindness fellow in opthalmology Washington U. Sch. Medicine-Barnes Hosp., 1961-63; NIH spl. fellow in ophthalmic pathology Armed Forces Inst. of Pathology, Washington, 1964; chief resident, instr. ophthalmology Washington U. Sch. Medicine, St. Louis, 1965-66, instr. ophthalmology, 1966-67, asst. prof. ophthalmology and pathology, 1967-69, assoc. prof. ophthalmology and pathology, 1969-75, prof. ophthalmology and pathology, 1975—, asst. dean, 1978-91, assoc. dean, 1991-96, prof. emeritus, assoc. dean emeritus, 1996—; prof. ophthalmology U. Wis., Madison, 1995-2001. Vis. scholar Eye Inst., Columbia Presbyn. Med. Ctr., N.Y.C., 1966; prof./lectr. Montefiore Hosp., Pitts., 1969, U. Ark., 1970, 77, 80, 82, 84, 86, 88, U. Fla., 1972, 81, U. Tex. and Lackland AFB, San Antonio, 1973, U. Colo., 1974, 82, U. Mo., 1974, 79, 80, 88, So. Ill. U., Springfield, 1974, U. Md., 1975, Montreal (Can.) Gen. Hosp., 1975, U. Wis., 1976, 87, 93, U. Pitts., 1977, 83, 87, U. Iowa, 1977, 87, Cleve. Clinic, 1978, Colo. Ophthalmol. Soc., 1978, Brooke Army Hosp., San Antonio, 1979, Wills Eye Hosp., Phila., 1980, USPHS Hosp., San Francisco, 1981, U. Calif., Davis, 1981, Sinai Hosp., Balt., 1985, 89, 94, U. Calif., San Diego, 1985, Tufts U., Boston, 1985, Cornell U., N.Y.C., 1988, U. Wash., Seattle, 1990, Brown U., Providence, 1990, Vanderbilt U., Nashville, 1991, Duke U., Durham, N.C., 1992; Chandler lectr. Harvard U., 1988; The Lois A. Young-Thomas Meml. lectr. U. Md., 1991; Braley lectr. U. Iowa, 1993; Havener Meml. lectr. Ohio State, 1994. Editor pathology sect.: Perspectives in Ophthalmology, 1977; mem. editl. bd. Ophthalmic Plastic & Reconstructive Surgery, 1986-90; contbr. articles to profl. jours. With USAR M.C., 1958-66. Scholar U. Md., 1958, 59. Fellow Am. Acad. Ophthalmology (ophthalmic pathology com. 1977-83, chmn. ophthalmic com. 1979-83, Honor award for svc. 1981, Sr. Honor award 1992); mem. AMA, Am. Bd. Ophthalmology (diplomate, bd. dirs. 1992—), Assn. for Rsch. in Vision and Ophthalmology (chmn. sect. pathology ann. meeting 1971), Am. Assn. Ophthalmic Pathologists (pres. 1977-80), Assn. Am. Med. Colls. (group med. edn. 1985—), Mo. Med. Assn., Mo. Ophthalmol. Soc., Verhoeff Soc., Theobald Soc., St. Louis Med. Soc., St. Louis Ophthalmol. Soc., Soc. Med. Coll. Dirs. for Continuing Med. Edn., Alpha Omega Alpha (sec.-treas. chpt. 1993-95, councillor 2003—). Home: 1275 Castle Gate Dr Saint Louis MO 63132 Office: Campus Box 8096 660 S Euclid Ave Saint Louis MO 63110-1093 Office Phone: 314-747-5559. Business E-Mail: smithm@vision.wustl.edu.

SMITH, MURRAY THOMAS, transportation company executive; b. Hudson, SD, 1939; s. Rex D. and Frances M. Smith; m. Diane R. Cramer, Dec. 4, 1959 (div. June 1994); children: Lisa B., Thomas M., Amy R.; m. Donna Thomas Kjonaas, Jan. 1995. V.p. Overland Express Inc., Indpls., 1978-82; v.p. ops. R.T.C. Transp. Inc., Forest Pk., Ga., 1982-83; with Midwest Coast Transport L.P., Sioux Falls, S.D., 1983—, sr. v.p., 1983-84; pres. Midwest Coast Transport L.P., Sioux Falls, S.D., 1984-89, prin., pres., chief exec. officer, 1989—, also bd. dirs.; pres. Willis Shaw Express, Elm Springs, Ark., 1999—. Bd. dirs. Interstate Carrier Conf., Nat. Perishable Logistics Assn. Bd. dirs. Sioux Valley Hosp., 1991-2000, United Way, Sioux Falls, 1991-2000. Office: Midwest Coast Transport LP 1600 E Benson Rd Sioux Falls SD 57104-0822 E-mail: smithm@mct-comcar.com.

SMITH, N. LINDSEY, lawyer; m. Christine Smith; children: Alex, Emily, Max. BSBA, Bowling Green State U., Ohio; JD, U. Toledo Coll. Law. With legal dept. Nat. City Bank; founder Smith & Condeni, LLP, Cleve., 1980, head estate and bus. planning group. Author: Wealth Management Through Estate Planning. Named one of Top 100 Attys., Worth mag., 2005. Mem.: Soc. Fin. Svcs. Profls. (past pres. Cleve. chpt.). Office: Smith & Condeni LLP 600 Granger Rd 2d Fl Cleveland OH 44131 Office Phone: 216-771-1760. Office Fax: 216-771-3387. E-mail: lindsey@smith-condeni.com.

SMITH, NANCY HOHENDORF, sales executive, marketing professional; b. Detroit, Jan. 30, 1943; d. Donald Gerald and Lucille Marie (Kopp) Hohendorf; m. Richard Harold Smith, Aug. 21, 1978 (div. Jan. 1984). BA, U. Detroit, 1965; MA, Wayne State U., 1969. Customer rep. Xerox Corp., Detroit, 1965-67, mktg. rep. Univ. Microfilms subs. Ann Arbor, Mich., 1967-73, mktg. coord., 1973-74, mgr. dir. mktg., 1975-76, mgr. mktg. Can., 1976-77, major account mktg. exec. Hartford, Conn., 1978-79, New Haven, 1979-80, account exec. State of N.Y. NYC, 1981, N.Y. region mgr. customer support Greenwich, Conn., 1982, N.Y. region sales ops. mgr., 1982, State of Ohio account exec. Columbus, 1983, new bus. sales mgr. Dayton, Ohio, 1983, major accounts sales mgr., 1984, info. systems sales and support mgr., quality specialist Detroit, 1985-87, new product launch mgr., ops. quality mgr., 1988, dist. mktg. mgr., 1989-92, major accounts sales mgr., 1992—; graphics arts industry sales mgr., 1998—; sales mgr. corp. accounts Sprint-Nextel Comms., Farmington Hills, Mich., 2005—. Reg. graphic arts industry cons. mgr., 1999. Mem. exec. leadership team Am. Heart Assn. Named to Outstanding Young Women of Am., 1968, Outstanding Bus. Woman, Dayton C. of C., 1984, Women's Inner Circle of Achievement, 1990. Mem. NAFE, Am. Mgmt. Assn., Am. Heart Assn. (mem. exec. leadership team 2005-06), Women's Econ. Club Detroit, Detroit Inst. Arts Founders' Soc., Detroit Hist. Soc., Detroit Hist. Soc., Greater Detroit C. of C. Republican. Roman Catholic. Avocations: interior decorating, reading, music, art. Home: 6462 West Oaks Dr West Bloomfield MI 48324-3269 Home Phone: 248-363-5898; Office Phone: 248-866-0601. Personal E-mail: nancyhsmith@sbcglobal.net.

SMITH, NEAL EDWARD, congressman; b. Hedrick, Iowa, Mar. 23, 1920; s. James N. and Margaret M. (Walling) S.; m. Beatrix Havens, Mar. 23, 1946; children— Douglas, Sharon. Student, U. Mo., 1945-46, Syracuse U., 1946-47; JD, Drake U., 1950. Bar: Iowa 1950. Farmer, Iowa, 1937—; sole practice Des Moines, 1950-58; atty. 50 sch. bds. in Iowa, 1951-58; asst. county atty. Polk County, Iowa, 1951; mem. from 4th Dist. Iowa US Ho. of Reps, 1959—94; ptnr. Davis, Hockenberg, Wine, Brown, Koehn & Shors, 1994, of counsel, 1995—. Chmn. Polk County Bd. Social Welfare, 1954-56; pres. Young Democratic Clubs Am., 1953-55. Served with AUS, World War II. Decorated Air medal with 4 oak leaf clusters, Purple Heart, nine battle stars. Mem. Am. Bar Assn., Farm Bur., Farmers Union, DAV. Clubs: Masons. Home: Plaza Box 90 300 Walnut Des Moines IA 50309 Office: Davis Brown Koehn Shors The Financial Ctr 666 Walnut St Ste 2500 Des Moines IA 50309-3904 Office Fax: 515-243-0654.

SMITH, NICK H., former congressman, archivist, farmer; b. Addison, Mich., Nov. 5, 1934; s. LeGrand John and Blanche (Nichols) S.; m. Bonnalyn Belle Atwood, Jan. 1, 1960; children: Julianna, Bradley, Elizabeth, Stacia. BA, Mich. State U., 1957; MS, U. Del., 1959. Radio & TV farm editor Sta. WDEL, Wilmington, Del., 1957-59; radio editor Sta. KSWD, Wichita Falls, Tex., 1959-60; capt. intelligence USAF, 1959-61; mem. twp. bd. Somerset Twp., Addison, 1962-68; asst. dep. adminstr. USDA, Washington, 1971—74; state rep. Mich. Ho. of Reps., Lansing, 1978-82; state senator, pres. pro-tem Mich. State Senate, Lansing, 1982-92; mem. U.S. Congress from 7th Mich. dist, 1993—2005, mem. agr., sci., and internat. rels. coms. Mem. budget com. Mich. State Senate, 1993—99, chmn. sci. rsch. com., 1999—2005. Del. Am. Assembly on World Population & Hunger, Washington, 1973; nat. del. on U.S.-Soviet Cooperation and Trade, 1991; deacon Somerset Congl. Ch. Capt. USAF, 1959-61. Fellow Kellogg Found., 1965; named Hon. FFA State Star Farmer, 1987, SCF Conservator of Yr. Hillsdale County, 1988. Mem. Mich. Farm Bur. (bd. dirs.), Jackson C. of C., Mich. State U. Varsity Club, Masons. Republican.

SMITH, ORTRIE D., judge; b. Jonesboro, Ark., Apr. 30, 1946; m. Christine Wendel, 1968; married; 4 children. BA, U. Mo., 1968, JD with distinction, 1971. Bar: Mo., 1971. Ptnr. Ewing, Smith & Hoberock, Nevada, Mo., 1971-95; judge western dist. U.S. Dist. Ct., Kansas City, Mo., 1995—. Adj. prof. Sch. Law, U. Mo.-Kansas City, 1999; spkr. in field. Bd. trustees U. Mo.-Kansas City Law Sch. Found., 1997-2004; treas. Vernon County (Mo.) Dems., 1982-95; pres. bd. dirs. region 9 coun. Mo. Sch. Bds. Assn., 1990; pres. Nevada Cmty. Betterment, 1981, Cmty. Coun. Perfomring Arts, 1980, Vernon County chpt. Am. Red Cross, 1976; trustee Mo. Bar Ctr., 1991-92. Recipient Appreciation award Mo. Jud. Conf.; named to Raytown Schs. Alumni Hall Fame, 2005. Fellow Am. Bar. Found., Mo. Bar Found. (trustee, Spurgeon Smithson award 2005); mem. ABA (vice chmn. trial evidence com. litig. sect., Ho. Dels. 1993-97), Mo. Bar Assn. (pres. 1991-92, chmn. fin. com., bd. govs. 1978-93, mem. Young Lawyers Counsel 1975-82, exec. com. young Lawyers Counsel 1978-82, exec. com. Mo. Bd. Govs., Tom Cochran Cmty. Svc. award Young Lawyers Sect.), Vernon County Bar Assn. (sec.-treas. 1972-75), Am. Law Inst., Bench and Robe Honor Soc. (pres. 1983), Nevada Rotary Club (Citizen of Yr. award), Vernon County C. of C. (pres. 1975), Nevada Jaycees (Key Man of Yr.). Baptist. Avocations: skiing, squash, golf, horseback riding, fishing. Office: US Dist Ct 400 E 9th St Ste 7652 Kansas City MO 64106-2675 Office Phone: 816-512-5645.

SMITH, OZZIE (OSBORNE EARL SMITH), retired professional baseball player; b. Mobile, Ala., Dec. 26, 1954; m. Denise Jackson, Nov. 1, 1980; children: Osborne Earl Jr., Dustin Cameron. Grad., Calif. State Poly. U., San Luis Obispo. Shortstop San Diego Padres Baseball Club, Nat. League, 1977—82, St. Louis Cardinals Baseball Club, at. League, 1982—96; baseball analyst St. Louis Cardinals Sta. KPLR, St. Louis, 1997—. Named Member of World Series Championship Team, 1982; named to All-Star Team, Nat. League, 1981—92, 1994, Sporting News, 1982, 1984—87, Baseball Hall of Fame, 2002; recipient Most Valuable Player award, Nat. League Championship Series, 1985, Golden Glove award, 1980—92, Silver Slugger award, 1987. Avocations: jazz, word puzzles, backgammon.

SMITH, PAUL LETTON, JR., geophysicist; b. Columbia, Mo., Dec. 16, 1932; s. Paul Letton and Helen Marie (Doersam) S.; m. Mary Barbara Noel; children: Patrick, Melody, Timothy, Christopher, Anne. BS in Physics, Carnegie Inst. Tech., 1955, MSEE, 1957, PhD in Elec. Engring., 1960. From instr. to asst. prof. Carnegie Inst. Tech., Pitts., 1955-63; sr. engr. Midwest Rsch. Inst., Kansas City, Mo., 1963-66; from rsch. engr. to sr. scientist and group head Inst. Atmospheric Scis., S.D. Sch. Mines and Tech., Rapid City, 1966-81; vis. prof. McGill U., Montreal, Que., Canada, 1969-70; chief scientist Air Weather Svc. USAF, Scott AFB, Ill., 1974-75; dir. Inst. Atmospheric Scis., S.D. Sch. Mines and Tech., Rapid City, 1981-96, prof. emeritus, 1996—. Lectr. Tech. Svc. Corp., Silver Spring, Md., 1972-91; vis. scientist Alberta Rsch. Coun., Edmonton, Can., 1984-85; dir. S.D. Space Grant Consortium, Rapid City, 1991-96; Fulbright lectr. U. Helsinki, 1986; nat. assoc. Nat. Acads., 2004—. Contbr. over 60 articles to profl. jours. Fellow Am. Meteorol. Soc. (Editor's award 1992, Remote Sensing lectr. 2006); mem. IEEE (life, sr.), NRC (assoc.), Weather Modification Assn. (Thunderbird award 1995), Sigma Xi. Home: 2107 9th St Rapid City SD 57701-5315 Office Phone: 605-394-2291. Business E-Mail: paul.smith@sdsmt.edu.

SMITH, PETE A., lawyer; b. St. Marys, Ohio, Mar. 29, 1969; BA, U. Cin., 1991; JD, U. Notre Dame, 1994. Bar: Ohio 1994, Ky. 1995. Ptnr. Strauss & Troy, Cin. Pro-bono legal adv. Covington Cmty. Ctr.; mem., Bd. Dirs. Southland Hall Assn. Named one of Ohio's Rising Stars, Super Lawyers, 2006. Mem.: ABA, Ky. Bar Assn., Ohio State Bar Assn., Cin. Bar Assn., Omicron Delta Kappa, Pi Kappa Alpha, Phi Beta Kappa. Office: Strauss & Troy 50 E RiverCenter Blvd Covington KY 41011 Office Phone: 513-621-8900. Office Fax: 513-629-9444.

SMITH, PHILIP G., lawyer; b. Louisiana, Mo., Oct. 4, 1946; m. Andrea K. Smith; children: Andrew Gentry, James Lyndon. BS, N.E. Mo. State U., 1968; JD, U. Mo., 1972. Atty. Mem. Rotary Club, Elks, Masons, Mo. Alumni Assn., Mo. State U. Alumnus Assn. Home: PO Box 486 Louisiana MO 63353-0486

SMITH, RALPH ALEXANDER, cultural and educational policy educator; b. Ellwood City, Pa., June 12, 1929; s. J. V. and B. V. Smith; m. Christiana M. Kolbe, Nov. 16, 1955. AB, Columbia Coll., 1954; MA, Columbia Tchrs. Coll., 1959, EdD, 1962. Faculty art history and arts edn. Kent (Ohio) State U., 1959-61, Wis. State U., Oshkosh, 1961-63, SUNY, New Paltz, 1963-64; faculty edn. and art edn. U. Ill., Urbana-Champaign, 1964—, prof. cultural and ednl. policy & aesthetic edn., prof. emeritus, 1996—. First Italo DeFrancesca Meml. lectr. Kutztown State U., 1974; Leon Jackman Meml. lectr., Perth, Australia, 85; Dean's lectr. Coll. Fine Arts and Comm., Brigham Young U., 1985; disting. vis. prof. Ohio State U., 1987; sr. scholar Coll. Edn., U. Ill., 1991; Dunbar lectr. Millsaps Coll., 1993; John Landrum Bryant lectr. Harvard U., 1999. Founder, editor: Jour. Aesthetic Edn., 1966—2000; editor: (book) Aesthetics and Criticism in Art Education, 1966, Aesthetic Concepts and Education, 1970, Aesthetics and Problems in Education, 1971, Regaining Educational Leadership, 1975, Cultural Literacy and Arts Education, 1991, Discipline-Based Art Education, 1989; editor: (with Alan Simpson) Aesthetics and Arts Education, 1991; editor: (with Bennett Reimer) The Arts, Education and Aesthetic Knowing, 1992; editor: (with Ronald Berman) Public Policy and the Aesthetic Interest, 1992; editor: General Knowledge and Arts Education, 1994, Excellence II: The Continuing Quest Art Education, 1995, Online Bibliography: Discipline Based Art Education, 1997, Readings in Discipline-Based Art Education: A Literature of Educational Reform, 2000; co-author: Research in the Arts and Aesthetic Education: A Directory of Investigators and Their Fields of Inquiry, 1978, Excellence in Art Education: Ideas and Initiatives, 1987, The Sense of Art: A Study in Aesthetic Education, 1989, Culture and the Arts in Education, 2006; author (with Albert William Levi): (book) Art Education: A Critical Necessity, 1991; contbg. editor: Arts Edn. Policy Rev., 2001—. With Med. Svc. US Army, 1954—57. Recipient spl. merit recognition, Coll. Edn., U. Ill., 1975, Disting. Lectr. Studies in Art Edn. award, 1991. Fellow: Nat. Art Edn. Assn. (Disting., Manuel Barkan Meml. award 1973, Nat. Educator award 2000); mem.: Ill. Art Edn. Assn. (Disting.), Coun. Policy Studies Art Edn. (1st exec. sec. 1978—82). Home: 2909 Heathwood Ct Champaign IL 61822-7659 Office: 360 Education 1310 S 6th St Champaign IL 61820-6925 Business E-Mail: ras@uiuc.edu.

SMITH, RALPH EDWARD, psychology assistant; b. Bellfountaine, Ohio, May 19, 1953; s. Ralph Raymond and Virginia (Picklesimer) S.; m. Melody Lee Welbaum Smith, Sept. 3, 1988. B of Gen. Studies, Ohio U., 1980; MS in Edn., U. Dayton, 1987. Houseparent Roweton Boys Ranch, Chillicothe, Ohio, 1974-86, social worker, 1981-82; employment counselor Ross County Community Action, Chillicothe, 1980-81, 83; social worker Roweton Residential Ctr., Chillicothe, 1986-87; psychology asst. Ross Correctional Inst., Chillicothe, 1988-89, 97—, Chillicothe Correctional Inst., State of Ohio, 1989-97. Pres. H.Y.S. Fed. Credit Union, Chillicothe, 1981-86. Vol. Ross County Community Action, Inc., Chillicothe, 1983-87, commodity distbn. vol. Mem. Sons of Union Veterans, Sons and Daughters of Pioneer Rivermen. Avocations: music, films, books. Office: Ross Correctional Institution PO Box 7010 Chillicothe OH 45601-7010 E-mail: msrs@horizonview.net.

SMITH, RAYMOND THOMAS, anthropology educator; b. Oldham, Lancashire, Eng., Jan. 12, 1925; s. Harry and Margaret (Mulchrone) S.; m. Flora Alexandrina Tong, June 30, 1954; children: Fenela, Colin, Anthony. BA, Cambridge U., Eng., 1950, MA, 1951, PhD, 1954. Sociol. research officer govt., Brit. Guiana, 1951-54; research fellow U. West Indies, 1954-59, sr. lectr. sociology, prof. anthropology, 1962-66; prof. sociology U. Ghana, 1959-62; prof. anthropology U. Chgo., 1966-95, prof. emeritus, 1995—, chmn. dept. anthropology, 1975-81, 84-85, 94-95. Vis. prof. U. Calif.-Berkeley, 1957-58, McGill U., Montreal, 1964-65; mem. com. on child devel. rsch. and pub. policy NRC, 1977-80; dir. Caribbean Consortium Grad. Sch., 1985-86. Author: The Negro Family in British Guiana, 1956, British Guiana, 1962, 2d edit., 1980, Kinship and Class In The West Indies, 1988, The Matrifocal Family, 1996; co-author: Class Differences in American Kinship, 1978; editor: Kinship Ideology and Practice in Latin America, 1984; contbr. articles to profl. jours. Co-investigator urban family life project U. Chgo., 1986-90. Served with RAF, 1943-48. Guggenheim fellow, 1983-84 Fellow Am. Anthrop. Assn.; mem. Assn. Social Anthropologists. Office: Univ Chicago Dept Anthropology 1126 E 59th St Chicago IL 60637-1580 Office Phone: 831-471-0471. Business E-Mail: r-smith@uchicago.edu.

SMITH, RICHARD NORTON, library director; b. Leominster, Mass., Oct. 2, 1953; s. Frank Chandler and Ruth Adeline (Richards) S. BA in Govt. magna cum laude, Harvard Coll., 1975. Intern The White House, Washington, 1975; freelance writer Washington Post, The Real Paper, and other publs., various cities, 1975-77; speechwriter Sen. Edward Brooke, Boston, 1977-78, Sen. Robert Dole, Washington, 1979-85; biographer, rschr. book on Thomas E. Dewey Rochester, N.Y., 1980-81; speechwriter, cons. various fed. officials, Washington, 1981-87; staff speechwriter Sen. Pete Wilson, Washington, 1984-87; dir. various presdl. libraries and foundations, including Herbert Hoover Libr., Dwight D. Eisenhower Ctr., Ronald Reagan Libr., Gerald R. Ford Mus. and Libr., 1987—2001; speechwriter Pres. Ronald Reagan, V.P. and Mrs. Dan Quayle, and others, Washington, 1989; dir. Robert J. Dole Inst. of Politics, Lawrence, Kans., 2001—03; exec. dir. Abraham Lincoln Presdl. Libr. and Mus., Springfield, Ill., 2003—. Cons. Nixon and Reagan Librs., 1989-91. Author: Thomas E. Dewey and His Times, 1982, An Uncommon Man: The Triumph of Herbert Hoover, 1984, The Harvard Century, 1986, Patriarch: George Washington and the New American Nation, 1992; co-author: (with Robert and Elizabeth Dole) Unlimited Partners, 1988. Mem. White House bicentennial planning com., Washington, 1990—; mem. World War II 50th anniversary planning com. Nat. Archives, Washington, 1991—. Republican. Christian Scientist. Avocations: reading, travel. Office: Abraham Lincoln Presdl Library & Museum 112 North Sixth St Springfield IL 62701 Office Phone: 217-558-8882.

SMITH, RICHEY, manufacturing executive; b. Akron, Ohio, Nov. 11, 1933; s. Thomas William and Martha (Richey) S.; m. Sandra Cosgrave Roe, Nov. 25, 1961; children: Mason Roe, Parker Richey. Grad., Hotchkiss Sch.; BS, U. Va., Charlottesville, 1956. Asst. to pres. Sun Products Corp., Barberton, Ohio, 1960-64, v.p., 1964-67, gen. mgr., dir., 1967-69, chmn., CEO, 1969-76; prin. A.T. Kearney Co., Cleve., 1977-87; chmn., CEO Richey Industries, Inc., Medina, Ohio, 1987—. Bd. dirs. Jaite Packaging, Inc. Exec. com. Gt. Trail coun. Boy Scouts Am.; chmn. capital funds dr. Summit County Planned Parenthood; trustee, found. pres. Old Trail Sch., Barberton Citizens Hosp., Medina County Arts Coun., Akron Regional Devel. Bd.; treas. Friends of Metro Park; found. trustee, vestryman St. Paul's Episcopal Ch.; corp. bd. Cleve. Mus. of Art; bd. govs. The Hotchkiss Sch. Lt. USN, 1957—60, lt. comdr. USNR, 1961—69. Mem. Ohio Commodores, Bluecoats (trustee), Navy League (pres. Akron coun. 1972-73), Young Pres. Orgn., Portage Country Club (bd. dirs.), Mayflower Club, Sawgrass Country Club (Fla.) Farmington Country Club (Charlottesville, Va.), Rotary (trustee Akron 1974-75), Yale Club (N.Y.C.), Rockwell Springs Trout Club, Chi Psi (pres.). Office: 910 Lake Rd Medina OH 44256-2453 Home: 333 N Portage Path Akron OH 44303 Office Phone: 330-725-4997 x 304. Personal E-mail: rsmith@richeyind.com.

SMITH, ROBERT FREEMAN, history professor; b. Little Rock, May 13, 1930; s. Robert Freeman and Emma Martha Gottlieb (Buerkle) S.; m. Alberta Vester, Feb. 1, 1951 (dec. 1985); children: Robin Ann, Robert Freeman III; m. Charlotte Ann Coleman, Sept. 9, 1985. BA, U. Ark., 1951, MA, 1952; PhD, U. Wis., Madison, 1958. Instr. U. Ark., Fayetteville, 1953; asst. prof. Tex. Luth. Coll., Seguin, 1958-62; assoc. prof. U. R.I., Kingston, 1962-66, U. Conn., Storrs, 1966-69; prof. history U. Toledo, 1969-86, disting. univ. prof., 1986—. Vis. prof. U. Wis., Madison, 1966-67. Author: The United States and Cuba: Business and Diplomacy 1917-1960, 1961 (Tex. Writers' Roundup award 1961), What Happened in Cuba: A Documentary History of U.S.-Cuban Relations, 1963, The United States and Revolutionary Nationalism in Mexico, 1916-1932, 1973 (Ohio Acad. History award 1973), The Era of Caribbean Intervention, 1890-1930, 1981, The Era of Good eighbors, Cold Warriors, and Hairshirts, 1930-82, 1983, The Caribbean World and the United States: Mixing Rum & Coca-Cola, 1994; contbr. to numerous publs. Retired Col. 7th Hist. Detachment, Ohio Mil. Res. 1st lt. U.S. Army, 1953-55. Knapp fellow in history U. Wis., 1957; Tom L. Evans rsch. fellow Harry S. Truman Libr., Independence, Mo., 1976-77, Mexican Ministry Fgn. Rels. fellow, 1991-92. Mem. Soc. Historians of Am. Fgn. Rels., Soc. Mil. History, U.S. Naval Inst., Ohio Acad. History, So. Hist. Assn., Orgn. Am. Historians, Assn. U.S. Army, State Guard Assn. of U.S., Am. Legion, Masons, Scottish Rite, Shriners, Army Hist. Found., Inst. Land Warfare, Sons of Confederate Vets., Phi Beta Kappa, Phi Alpha Theta. Episcopalian. Avocation: photography. Home: 4110 Dunkirk Rd Toledo OH 43606-2217 Office: U Toledo Dept History Toledo OH 43606

SMITH, ROBERT HUGH, retired engineering construction company executive; b. Wichita, Kans., Dec. 29, 1936; s. Richard Lyon and E. Eileen (O'Neal) S.; m. Melinda Louise Fitch, Sept. 26, 1959 (div. Dec. 1969); children: Robert Blake, Thomas Hugh; m. Margaret Anne Moseley, Dec. 11, 1971; 1 child, Steven Richard. BS, Kans. State U., 1959; MS, U. Kans., 1964, PhD, 1970. Sr. process engr. FMC Corp., Lawrence, Kans., 1959-64; rsch. engr. Phillips Petroleum Co., Bartlesville, Okla., 1964-66; group leader Standard Oil of Ohio, Warrenville Heights, Ohio, 1966-67; sr. rsch. assoc., group leader Atlantic Richfield, Plano, Tex., 1970-80; regional mgr., sr. mgr., sales mgr. Fluor Daniel, Houston and Marlton, NJ, 1980-90; v.p., gen. mgr. Badger Design & Construction, Tampa, Fla., 1990-93; exec. v.p., COO Process divsn. Black & Veatch, Overland Park, 1993-2000; ret., 2000. Patentee in the field; contbr. to profl. jours. Adv. bd. dept. chem. engring, coll. of engring. U. Kans., Lawrence, 1993—; mem. adv. bd. coll. engring. Kans. State U., 1998-2005. Recipient Disting. Svc. award Kans. State U., 1998; named to Engring. Hall of Fame Kans. State U., Chem. and Petroleum Engring. Hall of Fame, U. Kans., 2000. Fellow AIChE (chmn., vice chmn., sec. Dallas chpt. 1962—, exec. bd. Engr. and Cons. Contracting divsn., 1995-97, bd. dirs. 2002-04, career and edn. ops. coun. 2002-03, bd. trustees 2007—, Engr. of Yr. award Dallas chpt. 1980), Phi Lambda Upsilon, Sigma Xi. Avocations: tennis, sailing, skiing, reading. Personal E-mail: bobsmith29@everstkc.net.

SMITH, ROY ALLEN, United States marshal; b. Columbus, Ohio, Sept. 29, 1946; s. Chester Allen and Frances (Goff) S.; m. Janet Lee Coldicott, Aug. 13, 1967 (dec. Apr. 13, 1999); 2 children. BS in Secondary Edn., Ohio U., 1971, PhD in Ednl. Leadership, 1993; MS, Ea. Ky. U., 1980. Dep. sheriff Pike County, Ohio, 1969-71, chief probation officer, 1973-77; state probation parole officer Ohio Parole Authority, 1972-73; U.S. marshal so. dist. Ohio U.S. Marshal's Office, 1977-81, 94—; chief dep. sheriff Richland County, Ohio, 1981; dir. Pike County Dept. Human Svcs., 1981-94. Tech. advisor ct. security com. Ohio Supreme Ct., security advisor. With USMC, 1964-68. Recipient Nat. Def. medal, Vietnam Def. Ribbon, Vietnamese Campaign medal with 2 stars, Vietnam unit Cross of Gallantry, Presdl. Navy unit Citation, 1966, Good Conduct medal. Mem. U.S. Marshals Svc. (dir.'s adv. com., past chair), Fin./Human Resources Allocation Com., Chillicothe, York Rite Bodies (Aladdin Shrine Temple), Orient Lodge, Order of Ea. Star (Waverly chpt.), Am. Legion (life). Methodist. Avocations: tom clancy novels, pistol shooting, helping young people into college.

SMITH, S. KINNIE, JR., lawyer; BA in Econs., Yale U., New Haven, Conn., 1953; JD, U. Wisc. Law Sch., 1956. Ptnr. Sidley & Austin, Chgo., 1964—75; gen. counsel through vice chmn., Am. Natural Resources Company; sr. v.p. and dir. Coastal Corp., 1975—87; pres., vice chair, gen. counsel CMS Energy, Jackson, Mich., 1988—96; counsel Skadden, Arps, Slate, Meagher & Flom, 1996—2002; vice chmn., gen. counsel CMS Energy, Jackson, Mich., 2002—06; sr. counsel Miller, Canfield, Paddock & Stone, P.L.C., Detroit, 2006—. Mem. bd. vis. Univ. Wis. Law Sch. Mem.: ABA, Mich. Bar Assn., Chgo. Bar Assn. Office: Miller Canfield Paddock & Stone Ste 2500 150 W Jefferson Detroit MI 48226-4415 Office Phone: 313-496-8477. Office Fax: 313-496-8452. E-mail: smithsk@millercanfield.com.

SMITH, SAM, columnist, writer; b. Bklyn., Jan. 24, 1948; s. Leon and Betty (Pritzker) S.; m. Kathleen Ellen Rood, Jan. 24, 1976; children: Connor, Hannah-Li. BBA in Acctg., Pace U., NYC, 1970; MA in Journalism, Ball State U., Muncie, Ind., 1974. Acct. Arthur Young & Co., NYC, 1970-72; reporter Ft. Wayne (Ind.) News Sentinal, Ft. Wayne, 1973-76, States News Svc., Washington, 1976-79; press sec. U.S. Senator Lowell Weicker Jr., 1979; writer/reporter Chgo. Tribune, 1979-90, columnist, 1991—. Commentator ESPN Radio. Author: The Jordan Rules, 1991, Second Coming, 1995; co-author: Total Basketball Encyclopedia, 2004, The Perfect Team, 2006; columnist: Hoop Japan msnbc-.com; contbr. to publs. With USAR, 1970-76. Named Ball State U. Journalism Alumnus of Yr.; named to Ball State U. Journalism Hall of Fame, 2002; recipient Journalism awards, AP, UPI, Sigma Delta Chi, Sports Local Emmy award, WGN-TV. Mem.: Basketball Writers Assn. (pres. 1998—2005). Office: Chicago Tribune 435 N Michigan Ave Chicago IL 60611-4066 Office Phone: 312-222-5445. Business E-Mail: sasmith@tribune.com.

SMITH, SAMUEL, JR., state legislator; m. Diane Taylor; children: Emerald, Danielle. Grad., Worsham Coll. Mortuary Sci. Pres. Div. Funeral Home, Inc.; mem. Ind. Senate from 2nd dist., Indpls., 1998—. Mem. Magic City Consistory, Gary, Ind., Mahomet Temple, E. Chgo., Mt. Herman Bapt. Ch., E. Chgo. Mem. Nat. Funeral Dirs. Assn., Nat. Funeral Dirs. and Morticians Assn., Lakeside Lodge, Gary Shriners. Avocation: reading. Office: State House Dist 2 200 W Washington St Indianapolis IN 46204-2728 also: PO Box 3812 East Chicago IN 46312-1312 E-mail: s2@ai.org.

SMITH, SCOTT CLYBOURN, publishing executive; b. Evanston, Ill., Sept. 13, 1950; s. E. Sawyer and Jerolanne (Jones) S.; m. Martha Reilly, June 22, 1974; children: Carolyn Baldwin, Thomas Clybourn. BA, Yale U., 1973; M.Mgmt., Northwestern U., 1976. With Northern Trust Co., Chgo., 1973-77, Tribune Co., Chgo., 1977—93, sr. v.p., chief fin. officer, 1989-91, sr. v.p. for devel., 1991-93; pres., pub., CEO Sun Sentinel Co., Ft. Lauderdale, Fla., 1993-97, Chgo. Tribune Co., 1997—2004, interim pres., pub., CEO, 2006—; pres. Tribune Publishing, 2005—. Bd. dirs. McCormick Tribune Found., Chgo. Pub. Edn. Fund, Northwestern Meml. Healthcare, Chgo. Symphony Orch., Nat.-Louis U. Mem.: Newspaper Assn. Am. (chmn. pub. policy com.). Episcopalian. Office: Tribune Co 435 N Michigan Ave Chicago IL 60611-4066*

SMITH, SHIRLEY A., state legislator, state representative; b. 1950; 2 children. AA, Cuyahoga CC; BA, Cleve. State U. Rep. Ohio State Ho. Reps., Columbus, 1998—. Mem. banking, pensions and securities com. Ohio State Ho. Reps., mem. juvenile and family law com., mem. fin. instns., real estate and securities com., ranking minority mem. health com., mem. joint legis. com. on health care oversight. Vice chair Ohio Women's Dem. Caucus; chair region IX exec. com. Nat. Black Caucus of State Legislators; sec. Ohio Legis. Black Caucus; active Cuyahoga County Dem. Del. Mem.: NOW, Ohio Legis. Women's Caucus, Nat. Black Caucus of State Legis., Women in Govt., Emily's List. Democrat. Office: Ohio State House Reps 77 South High Street 10th Floor Columbus OH 43215-6111

SMITH, SIDONIE, literature educator; Student, U. Sheffield, Eng., 1965; BA, MA, U. Mich., 1966; PhD, Case Western Res. U., 1971. Tchg. asst. Case Western Res. U., 1968—70; instr. Cuyahoga C.C., 1969—71; asst. dean Coll. Continuing Edn. Roosevelt U., 1971—72; asst. prof. U. Ariz., 1973—78, assoc. prof., 1978—83; assoc. prof. Eng. and women's studies Binghamton U., 1983—89, prof. Eng., comparative lit., and women's studies, 1989—96; Martha Guernsey Colby Collegiate prof. of English & Women's Studies, chair English dept. U. Mich., Ann Arbor, 1996—. Program officer instl. grants edn. divsn. NEA, Washington, 1981—82; assoc. dean acad. affairs, arts and sci. and Harpur Coll. SUNY, Binghamton, assoc. dean adminstrn., arts and sci., and Harpur Coll., acting dean arts and sci. and Harpur Coll., interim dean arts and sci. and Harpur Coll.; dir. grad. studies dept. Eng. Binghamton U., NY, 1991—93; dir. women's studies U. Mich., Ann Arbor, 1996—. Author: Where I'm Bound: Patterns of Slavery and Freedom in Black American Autobiography., 1974, A Poetics of Women's Autobiography: Marginality and the Fictions of Self-Representation, 1987, Subjectivity, Identity, and the Body: Women's Autobiographical Practices in the Twentieth Century., 1993, Moving Lives: Women's Twentieth Century Travel Narratives, 2001; co-author: Reading Autobiography: A Guide for Interpreting Life arratives, 2001, Human Rights and Narrated Lives: The Ethics of Recognition, 2004; co-editor: De/Colonizing the Subject: Gender and the Politics of Women's Autobiography, 1992, Getting a Life: Everyday Uses of Autobiography, 1996, Writing New Identities: Gender, Nation, and Immigration in Contemporary Europe, 1997, Indigenous Australian Voices: A Reader, 1998, Women, Autobiography, Theory: A Reader, 1998, Interfaces: Women's Visual and Performance Autobiography, 2002; contbr. articles to profl. jours. Fellow Canterbury fellow, 1993; grantee Ford grant, 1971, Travel grant, U. Ariz. Found., 1978; scholar Sr. Fulbight scholar, 1994. Mem.: Comparative Lit. Assn., Soc. Study of Narrative Lit., Midwest Modern Lang. Assn., Modern Lang. Assn. Am. (exec. coun. 2000—, exec. bd. divsn. life writing 1989—94, exec. bd. divsn. women's studies lit. 1994—99). Office: Univ Mich 234 West Hall Ann Arbor MI 48109-1092 E-mail: sidsmith@umich.edu.

SMITH, STAN VLADIMIR, economist, finance company executive; b. Rhinelander, Wis., Nov. 16, 1946; s. Valy Zdenek and Sylvia Smith; children: Cara, David. BS in Ops. Research, Cornell U., 1968; MBA, U. Chgo., 1972, PhD in Econs., 1997. Diplomate Am. Bd. Disability Analysts. Lectr. U. Chgo., 1973; economist bd. govs. Fed. Res. System, Washington, 1973-74; staff economist First Nat. Bank of Chgo., 1974; assoc. December Group, Chgo., 1974-77; founding pres. Seaquest Internat., Chgo., 1977-85; mgr., ptnr. Ibbotson Assocs., Chgo., 1981-85; pres. Smith Econ. Group Ltd. divsn. Corp. Fin. Group, Chgo., 1985—. Expert econ. witness in field; adj. prof. DePaul U. Coll. Law, Chgo., 1990. Author: Economic/Hedonic Damages, 1990; founding editor Stocks, Bonds, Bills and Inflation yearbook, 1983-01; editor Jour. Forensic Econs., 1990-01; contbr. articles in field. Founder, exec. dir. Inst. for Value of Life, 1996. Fellow Allied Chem., 1967, John McMullen Trust, 1969; grantee Ford Found., 1972, U.S. Fed. Res., 1973. Fellow: Am. Coll. Forensic Examiners (bd. cert. 1996—); mem.: Soc. Litig. Economists (bd. govs. 1999—), Acad. Econ. and Fin. Experts, Am. Bd. Forensic Examiners, Nat. Future Assn. (arbitrator), Am. Arbitration Assn. (arbitrator 1994—96), Nat. Acad. Econ. Arbitrators (founder 1989—), Nat. Assn. Forensic Econs. (v.p. 2000—03), Am. Fin. Assn., Am. Econ. Assn., Alpha Delta Phi. Office: Smith Econ Group Ltd Ste 600 1165 N Clark St Chicago IL 60610-7861 Office Phone: 312-943-1551. Business E-Mail: stan@smitheconomics.com.

SMITH, STANTON KINNIE, JR., lawyer; b. Rockford, Ill., Feb. 14, 1931; s. Stanton Kinnie Smith and Elizabeth (Brown) Stanton; m. Mary Beth Sanders, July 11, 1953; children: Stanton E., Kathryn A., Dana. BA, Yale U., 1953; JD, U. Wis., 1956. Bar: Ill. 1956, Mich. 1976. Ptnr. Sidley & Austin Law, Chgo., 1964—84; vice chmn., gen. counsel Am. Natural Resources Co., Detroit, 1975—87; sr. v.p. The Coastal Corp., Houston, 1985—87; vice chmn., gen. counsel CMS Energy Corp., Jackson, Mich., 1987—88, pres., 1988—92, vice chmn., 1992—96, vice chmn., bd. dirs., 2002—05; sr. spl. counsel Skadden, Arps, Slate, Meagher & Flom, NYC, 1996—2002; vice chmn. Trans-Elect, Inc., 2002. Bd. dirs. Clarcor Corp., Mich. Natural Corp., Mich. Nat. Bank. Trustee Founders Soc., Detroit Inst. Arts, Rockford Coll.; devel. bd. mem. Yale U.; trustee Mich. Opera Theatre; bd. advisors U. Wis. Law Sch., Mich. State U., Pub. Utility Inst. Mem.: ABA, Chgo. Bar Assn., Mich. Bar Assn. Office: CMS Energy Corp One Energy Plaza Jackson MI 49201 Business E-Mail: sksmith@cmsenergy.com.

SMITH, STEVE C., lawyer, state legislator; b. Hutchinson, Minn., Nov. 29, 1949; s. Charles H. and Laura G. Smith; married; 1 child, Ryan. BA, U. Minn., 1972; JD, Oklahoma City U., 1975. City coun. mem. City of Mound, Minn., 1984-86, mayor Minn., 1986-90; state rep. Minn. Ho. of Reps., St. Paul, 1990—. Served with U.S. Army, 1971-75. Republican. Home: 2710 Clare Ln Mound MN 55364-1812 Office: 353 State Office Bldg Saint Paul MN 55155-0001

SMITH, STEVEN J., communications company executive; b. Milw., Apr. 10, 1950; married; 2 children. BA in Communication Arts, U. Wis., 1972; Cert. Advanced Mgmt. Program, Harvard U., 1995. Advt. salesperson Sta. WTMJ-AM, subs. Jour. Comm., Milw., 1976; gen. mgr. Sta. WKTI-FM, Milw., 1980-83; v.p., gen. mgr. WTMJ-AM and WKTI-FM, subs. Jour. Comm., Milw., 1983-85, KTNV-TV, ABC-TV affiliate, Las Vegas, 1985; pres. Jour. Broadcast Group Inc. subs. Jour. Comm., 1987-92, Jour. Comm., 1992—, COO, 1996—, CEO, chmn., 1998—. Trustee Faye McBeath Found., Med. Coll. of Wis., Boys and Girls Club of Greater Milw.; bd. dirs. YMCA of Greater Milw., United Performing ArtsFund, Milw. Met. Assn. of Commerce; co-chair Safe & Sound, Milw.; past chmn. bd. dirs. Am. Heart Assn. of Wis. Mem. Wis. Broadcasters Assn. (past bd. dirs.), Milw. Area Radio Stas. (past pres.).

SMITH, TEFFT WELDON, lawyer; b. Evanston, Ill., Nov. 18, 1946; s. Edward W. and Margery T. (Weldon) S.; m. Nancy Jo Smith, Feb. 25, 1967; children: Lara Andrea, Tefft Weldon II. BA, Brown U., 1968; JD, U. Chgo., 1971. Bar: Ill. 1971, D.C. 2000, U.S. Supreme Ct. 1977. Sr. litigation ptnr. Kirkland & Ellis LLP, Chgo., 1971—, chair, competition and antitrust practice group. Mem. adv. bd. Bur. Nat. Affairs Antitrust and Trade Regulation Reporter; instr. trial advocacy. Contbr. numerous articles on trial practice and antitrust issues to law jours. Mem. ABA (litigation sect., antitrust law sect.), Econ. Club., Univ. Club, Mid-Am. Club, Sea Pines Country Club (Hilton Head, S.C.). Avocations: squash, ferraris, sculpture. Office: 655 15th St NW Washington DC 20005-5701 also: Kirkland & Ellis 200 E Randolph St Fl 54 Chicago IL 60601-6636 Home: 700 New Hampshire Ave NW Washington DC 20037 Office Phone: 202-879-5212. Business E-Mail: tsmith@kirkland.com.

SMITH, THOMAS GORDON, architect; b. Oakland, Calif., Apr. 23, 1948; s. Sheldon Wagers and Margaret (Prendergast) S.; m. Marika Wilson, Dec. 19, 1970; children— Alan, Stuart, Demetra, Andrew, Philip, Duncan. A.B., U. Calif.-Berkeley, 1970, M.Arch., 1975. Lic. architect, Calif. Prin. Thomas Gordon Smith, Architect, Chgo., 1980—; instr. archtl. history Coll. of Marin, Kentfield, Calif., 1976-77; guest instr. archtl. design So. Calif. Inst. Architecture, Santa Monica, 1983; guest lectr., seminar leader Kunstegeschichtlieches Institut der Philipps Universitat, Marburg, W.Ger., 1983; guest tchr. U. Ill., Chgo., UCLA, 1984; assoc. prof. U. Ill., Chgo.; chmn. Sch. Architecture U. Notre Dame, Ind., 1989-98. Exhibited art in shows at Santa Barbara Mus. Art, 1977, Cooper-Hewitt Mus., Chgo. Art Inst., 1980, Louisiana Mus. Modern Art, Copenhagen, 1981, Venice Biennale, 1980, Smith Coll. Mus. Art, 1981, La Jolla Mus. Modern Art, Calif., 1982, Deutsches Architekturmuseum, Frankfurt, W.Ger., 1984; revision of Modern IBM Gallery, N.Y., 1987; author: Classical Architecture: Rule and Invention, 1987, Vitruvias on Architecture, 2003. Bd. dirs. Soc. Cath. Liturgy. U. Calif. grad. fellow, 1974, John K. Branner fellow, 1975, Rome Prize fellow, Am. Acad., 1979; grantee Graham Found. Advanced Study in Fine Arts, 1984, 87, Am. Philos. Soc., 1987. Mem. AIA (Grad. fellow 1973), Soc. Archtl. Historians. Home: 1903 Dorwood Dr South Bend IN 46617-1818 Office: 2025 Edison Rd South Bend IN 46637 E-mail: archtgs@aol.com.

SMITH, TODD A., lawyer; b. Chgo., Aug. 27, 1949; married; 2 children. BSB, U. Kans., 1971; MBA, Northwestern U., 1973; JD, Loyola U., 1976. Bar: Ill. 1976, U.S. Dist. Ct. (no. dist.) Ill. 1980, U.S. Ct. Appeals (7th cir.) 1991, U.S. Supreme Ct. 1980. Asst. Cook County Public Defender, Chgo.; atty. Corboy & Demetrio P.C., Chgo., ptnr., Powers, Rogers, & Smith P.C., Chgo. Adj. prof. law De Paul Coll., 1985—88; mock trial judge, 1978—83; bd. dir. Trial Lawyers Club of Chicago, 1987—; lectr. John Marshall Law Sch., 1985, Loyola U. Sch. Law, 1981—85, 1988; bd. gov Assoc. Trial Lawyers of Am. (ATLA), 1989—, mem. exec. comm., 1998—, treas., 2000—01, sec., 2001—02, v.p., 2002—03, pres. elect, 2003—04, pres., 2004—05; bd. dir. ATLA Endowment, 1999—, ISBA Mutual Insurance Co., 1995—, Ill. Bar Found., 2000—. Assoc. editor: Ill. Trial Lawyers Jour.; contbr. articles to profl. jours. Named Person of the Yr., Chicago Lawyer Mag., 1998; named one of The Best Lawyers in Am., 1997—2004; fellow Internat. Soc. of Barristers, 1996, Am. College of Trial Lawyers, 1996, Am. Bar Found., 1996, Internat. Acad. of Trial Lawyers, 1998, Am. Bd. of Trial Advocates, 1999. Fellow: Am. Coll. Trial Lawyers, Internat. Soc. Barristers, Internat. Acad. Trial Lawyers; mem.: Ill. State Bar Assn. (past pres.). Office: Powers, Rogers, Smith 70 W Madison St 55th Fl Chicago IL 60602

SMITH, TODD P., marketing executive; b. 1968; MBA, U. Iowa, 1996. Worked for Saturn, Daimler Chrysler Corp.; founder, CEO Clear!Blue, Birmingham, Mich., 2000—. amed one of 40 Under 40, Crain's Detroit Bus., 2006. Avocations: music, travel. Office: Clear!Blue 135 North Old Woodward Birmingham MI 48009 Office Phone: 248-644-0800. Office Fax: 248-644-0818.

SMITH, TUBBY, men's college basketball coach; b. Scotland, Md., June 30, 1951; s. Guffrie & Parthenia Smith; m. Donna Smith; children: Orlando, Shannon, Saul, Brian. BS in Health & Phys. Edn., High Point Coll., 1973. Head basketball coach Gt. Mills (Md.) H.S., 1973-77; head coach Hoke County H.S., Raeford, 1977-79; asst. coach Va. Commonwealth U., 1979-86, U. S.C., 1986-89, Ky. U., 1989-91; head coach U. Tulsa, 1991-95, U. Ga., Athens, 1995-97, U. Ky., Lexington, 1997—2007, U. Minn., Mpls., 2007—. Asst. basketball coach US Men's Nat. Basketball Team, 1999; head coach US Olympic Basketball Team, Sydney, 2000; bd. dirs. Nat. Assn. Basketball Coaches. Founder The Tubby Smith Found., 1987—. Named Jim Phelan Coach of Yr., 2005, Naismith Coll. Coach of Yr., 2003; recipient Henry Iba award, 2003. Coached the U. Ky. to five Southeastern Conf. Titles, 1998-2001, 2003-2004 & 1 NCAA Men's Divsn. I Basketball Championship, 1998. Office: U Minn 205 BFAB 516 15th Ave SE Minneapolis MN 55455

SMITH, VERNON G., education educator, state legislator; b. Gary, Ind. BS, Ind. U., 1966, MS, 1969, EdD, 1978; postgrad., Ind.U.-Purdue U., 1986-90. Tchr. Gary Pub. Schs. Systems, 1966-71, resource tchr., 1971-72; asst. prin. Ivanhoe Sch., Gary, 1972-78; prin. Nobel Sch., Gary, 1978-85, Williams Sch., Gary, 1985-92; part-time counselor edn. div. Ind. U. N.W., Gary, 1967-69, adj. lectr., 1987-92, assoc. prof., 1992—; mem. Ind. Ho. of Reps., Indpls., 1990—. Columnist Gary Crusader, 1969-71; speaker Devel. Tng. Inst., 1986—. Author: (with D. McClam) Building Bridges Instead of Walls—History of I.U. Dons, Inc., 1979; also articles. Mem. Gary City Coun., 1972-90; precinct committeeman Gary Dem. Com., 1972-92; founder, chmn. Gary City-wide Festival Com.; bd. dirs. .W. Ind. Urban League; founder, pres. I.U. Dons, Inc.; past pres. Gary Cmty. Mental Health Bd.; v.p. Gary Common Coun., 1982, 85-87, pres., 1976, 83-84, 88; past mem. bd. dirs. Little League World series; founder, past sponsor Youth Ensuring Solidarity, Young Citizens' League; chmn. Ind. Commn. on Status of Black Males, 1992—; mem. Gov.'s Commn. for Drug-Free Ind., 1990—. Recipient citation in edn. Gary NAACP, 1970, Good Govt. award Gary Jaycees, 1977, Outstanding Svc. award Gary Young Dems., 1979, Businessman of Yr. award Gary Downtown Mchts., 1979, Bd. Dirs. Svcs. award Gary Cmty. Health Ctr., 1982, G.O.I.C. Dr. Leon H. Sullivan award, 1982, Gary Jaycees Youth award, 1983, Info Newspaper Outstanding Citizen of N.W. Ind. and Info. Newspaper's Outstanding Educator award, 1984, Post Tribune Blaine Marz Tap award, 1984, Gary Cmty. Sch. Corp. Speech Dept. Recognition award, 1984, Gary Cmty. Mental Health Ctr.'s 10th Yr. Svc. award, 1985, Roosevelt H.S. Exemplary Svc. award, 1985, Gary Crusader 25th Anniversary award, 1986, Purdue U. Ednl. Opportunity Programs Black History Svc. award, 1986, Educator Par Excellence award Williams Sch., 1987, Black Woman Hall of Fame Found. Success award, 1987, Black Women Hall of Fame Bethune-Tubman-Truth award, 1987, Our Lady of Perpetual Help Ch. Hon. Mem. award, 1987, Gary Educator of Christ Adminstr. Leadership award, 1988, NBC-LEO Appreciation award, 1988, Gary Cmty. Schs. Presenters award, 1991, Mr. G.'s Svc. award, 1991, Appreciation award Ind. Assn. Chiefs Police, 1992, Meth. Hosp., 1992, Bros. Keeper, 1992, Svc. award Ind. Assn. Elem. and Mid. Sch. Prins., 1992, N.W. Ind. Black Expo's Sen. Carolyn Mosby Above and Beyond award, 1995, In the Bethune Tradition award Nat. Coun. Negro Women, 1996, Citizen Yr. award NASW (Ind. chpt.), 1997, 98, Appreciation award Ind. chpt., 1997, Presenters award, Gary Cmty. Sch. Corp. Parent Involvement Program, 1996, Appreciation award, Pitman Square Sch., 1997, 98, 99, Alumni Appreciation award, Froebel High Sch., 1997, 98, 2002, Svc. award, Ind. League Municipal Clerks and Treas., 1998, Facet Excellence in Tchg. award, 1998, Brothers Keeper Appreciation award, 1999, Appreciation award, Lake County Assn. for the Retarded, 1999, New Hope award, 1999, New Hope Men's Day award, 2000; featured cover story Big Brothers Big Sisters Am. Newsletter for Diversity, 2000, Appreciation award, Hoosier Boys Town, 2000, Appreciation award, Gary Reading Coun., 2000, Outstanding Commitment award, Nat. Assn. Social Workers Region I, 2000, Svc. award, Ivanhoe Sch., 2002, Drum Major award, Gary Frontiers, 2002, Majestic Star award, 2002, Appreciation award, City of Lake Station, 2002, New Hope African Am.-Frederic Douglas award, 2003. Mem.: NAACP (life Ovington award 1999), No. Ind. Assn. Black Sch. Educators (founder), Ind. Assn. Sch. Prins., Ind. U. N.W. Alumni Assn. (life Disting. Educator award 1992), Phi Delta Kappa (25 Yr. award (N.W. Ind. chpt.) 1996), Omega Psi Phi (life Omega Man Yr. award 1974, Citizen Yr. award 10th dist. 1989, appreciation award Omicron Rho chpt. 1991, Citizen Yr. award (Alpha Kappa Kappa chpt.) 2003, Man Yr. award (Alpha Kappa Kappa chpt.) 2003). Baptist. Home: PO Box M622 Gary IN 46401-0622 Office: Ind U NW 3400 Broadway # 339 Gary IN 46408-1101 Office Phone: 219-980-7120. Business E-Mail: vesmith@iun.edu.

SMITH, VERONICA LATTA, real estate company officer; b. Wyandotte, Mich., Jan. 13, 1925; d. Jan August and Helena (Hulak) Latta; m. Stewart Gene Smith, Apr. 12, 1952; children: Stewart Gregory, Patrick Allen, Paul Donald, Alison Veronica Hurley, Alisa Margaret Lyons, Glenn Laurence. BA in Sociology, U. Mich., 1948. Tchr. Coral Gables (Fla.) Pub. Sch. Sys., 1949—50; COO Latta Ins. Agy, Wyandotte, 1950—62; treas. L & S Devel. Co., Grosse Ile, Mich., 1963—84; v.p. Regency Devel., Riverview, Mich., 1984—. Active U. Mich. Bd. Regents, 1985-92, regent emeritus, 1993—; mem. Martha Cook Bd. Govs., U. Mich., pres., 1976-78; del. Rep. County Conv., Grand Rapids, Mich., 1985, 87, 89, 91, 92, 94, 96, Lansing, Mich., 1996, Detroit, 1986, 88, 90, 92, 97; mem. pres. adv. com. Campaign for Mich., 1992-97, mem. campaign steering com., 1992-97. Mem. Mich. Lawyers Aux. (treas. 1975, chmn. 1976, 77, 78, 79), Nat. Assn. Ins. Women (cert.), Faculty Women's Club U. Mich. (hon.), Radrick Farms Golf Club (Ann Arbor), Pres.'s Club U. Mich., Investment Club (pres. 1976, sec. 1974-75, treas. 1975-76), Alpha Kappa Delta. Home: 22225 Balmoral Dr Grosse Ile MI 48138-1403

SMITH, VIRGIL CLARK, state legislator; b. Detroit, July 4, 1947; s. Virgil Columbus and Eliza (Boyer) S.; m. Evelyn Owens (div.); children: Virgil Kai, Adam Smith; m. Elizabeth Ann Little. BA in polit. sci., Mich. State U., 1969; JD, Wayne State U., 1972. Legal advisor various community groups, Detroit, 1972-73; supervising atty. Wayne County Legal Svcs., Detroit, 1973-74; sr. asst.corp. counsel law dept. City of Detroit, 1974-75; mem. Mich. State Ho. Reps., 1976-88, Mich. State Senate, 1988—. Mem. Appropriations Comm. Mem. Nat. Caucus Black State Legislators, Nat. Caucus of State Legistlators, Mich. Legis. Black Caucus (2d chair 1991-92). Democrat. Avocations: golf, swimming, bowling, skiing. Office: State Senate PO Box 30036 Lansing MI 48909-7536 Address: 475 Keelson Dr Detroit MI 48215-3076

SMITH, WAYNE ARTHUR, export company executive; b. Detroit, Jan. 28, 1945; s. Edson Alvin Smith and Helen Margaret (Hofer) McKnight. PhB, Wayne State U., 1966, JD, 1969. Bar: Mich. 1969, U.S. Dist. Ct. (ea. dist.) Mich. 1969, U.S. Ct. Appeals (6th cir.) 1970. V.p. R.G. Corace, P.C., Detroit, 1970-76; pvt. practice, Detroit, 1976-80; pres. Tech. Pers. Svcs. of Mich., Ltd., Royal Oak, Mich., 1980-81; v.p. McRae Energy Resources, Inc., Harper Woods, Mich., 1981-82; pres. Diversified Energy Corp. and subs., Deckerville, Mich., 1982—. Mem. ABA, State Bar of Mich., World Trade Club, Can. Legion, Elks (P.E.R. 1990-91, Elk of Yr. Royal Oak chpt. 1992-93). Republican. Avocation: charitable activities. Office: Diversified Energy Corp PO Box 580 Deckerville MI 48427-0580

SMITH, WILBUR LAZAR, radiologist, educator; b. Warwick, NY, Oct. 11, 1943; s. Wilbur and Betty (Norris) S.; m. Rebecca Rowlands, June 19, 1965; children: Jason, Daniel, Joanna, Noah, Ethan, Jacob. BA, SUNY, Buffalo, 1965, MD, 1969. Diplomate Am. Bd. Radiology, Am. Bd. Pediat., Am. Bd. Pediatric Radiology. Intern, then resident Buffalo Children's Hosp., 1969-71; resident in pediatric radiology Cin. Gen. and Children's Hosp., 1971-74; asst. prof. pediatrics and radiology Ind. U., Indpls., 1975-78, assoc. prof., 1978-80, acting dir. pediatric radiology, 1979-80; assoc. prof. U. Iowa, Iowa City, 1980-82, prof., 1982—, dir. med. edn. in radiology, 1980-86, vice chmn. dept. radiology, 1986-94, interim head, 1994-96, dir. pediatric radiology, 1980-92; chmn. dept. radiology Henry Ford Health Sys., Detroit, 1998-99; prof. radiology Wayne State U., Detroit, 2000—, chmn. dept. radiology, 2002—; staff radiologist Mich. Children's Hosp., Detroit, 2000—. Vice chmn. radiology for academics Wayne State U., 2001, radiology residency dir., 01, prof., chmn. dept. radiology, 2002—. Assoc. editor Gastrointestinal Imaging in Pediatrics, Acad. Radiology, 1992—, Quar. Rev. Child Abuse, 1998, Radiology 101, co-author, 2d edit. 2004; exec. assoc. editor Acad. Radiology, 1997-2000, assoc. editor, 2000—02; contbr. articles to profl. jours. Vol. soccer coach, 1980-99; physician cons. in child abuse, 1980-; mem. equity adv. com. Iowa City Sch. Bd., 1983-87. With USAR, 1969—77, hon. discharge USAR. Fellow Am. Acad. Pediatrics, Am. Coll. Radiology; mem. AMA, Radiol. Soc. N.Am.(second v.p. 2004-05), Iowa Radiol. Soc. (pres. 1987-88), Assn. Univ. Radiologists (pres. 1995-96, sr. adv. 2001—, Gold medal 2006), Soc. Pediat. Radiology (treas. 1995-98, rep. coun. Acad. Socs. of AAMC 1996-02), Mich. Radiol. Soc. (bd. dirs. 2004—). Mem. Soc. Of Friends. Avocation: photography. Home: 10124 Lasalle Blvd Huntington Woods MI 48070-1162 Office: Detroit Receiving Hosp Dept Radiology (3L8) 4201 St Antoine Detroit MI 48201 Home Phone: 248-582-1521; Office Phone: 313-745-4443, 313-745-3433. Business E-Mail: wlsmith@med.wayne.edu.

SMITH, WILLIAM G., transportation executive; Chmn., pres., CEO Smithway Motor Xpress Corp., Ft. Dodge, Iowa, 1993—. Office: Smithway Motor Xpress Corp 2031 Quail Ave Fort Dodge IA 50501-8511 Fax: 515-576-8794.

SMITHEY, DONALD LEON, airport authority director; b. St. Louis, Aug. 31, 1940; children: Kelly, Jill. Student, St. Ambrose Coll., 1962; BS in Bus. Mgmt., So. Ill. U., 1966; postgrad., U. Mo., St. Louis, 1973-74. Asst. ops. dispatcher Ozark Airlines, 1971-72; transp. analyst Olin Corp., 1972-78, cost acct., 1978-80; commr. St. Louis Regional Airport Authority, 1971-80, chmn., 1974-80, airport dir., 1980-83; asst. dir. Cedar Rapids Mcpl. Airport, 1983-85; dir. adminstrn. Omaha Airport Authority, 1985-87, dep. exec. dir., 1987-89, exec. dir., 1989—. With USN Air Res. 1963-66, USN, 1966-68. Mem. Am. Assn. Airport Execs. (Great Lakes chpt.), Airports Coun. Internat., Iowa Airport Exec. Assn. (past pres.), Ill. Pub. Airports Assn. (past v.p.), Exptl. Aircraft Assn., Omaha Rotary Club, Masonic Lodge (Bethalto, Ill.), Tangier Shrine (Omaha), Quiet Birdmen Assn., Silver Wings Fraternity. Office: Omaha Airport Authority 4501 Abbott Dr Omaha NE 68110-2698

SMOKVINA, GLORIA JACQUELINE, nursing educator; b. East Chgo., Ind., July 29, 1937; Diploma in nursing, St. Margaret Hosp. Sch. Nursing, 1959; BSN, DePaul U., 1964; MSN, Ind. U., 1966; PhD in Nursing, Wayne State U., 1977. RN, Ind. Staff and charge nurse surgical units St. Catherine Hosp., East Chgo., Ind., 1959-61, charge nurse surgical units, 1962-64; asst. head nurse ICU El Camino Hosp., Mountain View, Calif., 1961-62; instr. nursing South Chgo. Community Hosp., Chgo., 1964-65; asst. prof. med.-surgical nursing U. Evansville, Ind., 1966-70; assoc. prof. nursing Purdue U. Calumet, Hammond, Ind., 1970-80, prof. nursing, 1980—, acting head dept. nursing, 1986-87, head dept. nursing, 1987—, head sch. nursing, 1996—, dean schs. of profl. programs, 1996—2002, dean Sch. of ursing, 2002—. Bd. dir. Health East Chgo. Cmty. Bd., St. Catherine Hosp.; cons. ICU St. Catherine Hosp., 1971, 74, 77, 79, 81, staff nurse, 71, 74, 77, 79, 81; cons. Vis. Nurses Assn., 1979, 80, Klapper, Issac & Parish Law Firm, Indpls., 1995; mem. adv. com. Vis. Nurse Assn. of NW Ind., 1977—; mem. Statewide Task Force on Nursing in Ind., 1987—; mem. Health E. Chgo. Task Force, 1996—; peer reviewer Coll. Nursing Valparaiso U., Ind., 1989; mem. gov. bd. St. Margaret Mercy Healthcare Ctrs. Inc., 1992—, chair quality svcs. com., 1992—, v.p., 1998—2001; mem. gov. bd. Sisters of St. Francis Regional Bd.; expert witness in several cases. Contbr. chpt. to Normal Aging: Dimensions of Wellness, 1986, Medical-Surgical Nursing, 1981; contbr. articles to profl. jours.; numerous rsch. projects. Mem. planning com. Lake County Health Fair, 1975, 77, nursing chair, 1978-80; chmn. nominations com. Ind. League for ursing, 1995—; mem. adv. bd. Horizon Career Coll., Merriville, Ind., 1994—; mem. adv. com. Community Ctr. Devel. Corp., Hammond, 1993—, Three City Empowerment Zone E. Chgo., Gary and Hammond, 1994-95, grad. edn. Ind. U. Purdue U., 1981-85, Westhaysen Med. Edn. Trust Com. Calument Nat. Bank, Hammond, 1987—; mem. panel Healthy E. Chgo., 1994-96; mem. Community Health Assn., 1979-84; v.p. Am. Heart Assn. N.W. Ind. affiliate, 1984-87, mem. edn. com. 1982-87; bd. dirs. Our Lady of Mercy Hosp., Dyer, Ind., 1989-92, Health Adv., 1979-82; bd. dirs. Am. Heart Assn. Ind. affiliate, 1981-87, chair community programs, 1982-87; bd. dirs. Lakeshore Health Care System, 1988-89, quality assurance com. Grantee HHS, 1983-85, 84, 85-88, 90—, Helene Fuld Health Trust, 1989, 92, 93-94, Pub. Health Svc., 1989-90, 1990-91, Meth. Hosp., 1993-98; recipient Meritorious Svc. award Am. Cancer Soc. of N.W. Ind., 1979, Lake Area United Way, 1979, Cert. of Recognition Am. Heart Assn., 1983-84, Med. and Sci. Disting. Program award, 1985, Franciscan Award, Svc. Recogn. St. Margaret Mercy Healthcare Ctr., 2002. Mem. AACN, N.W. Ind. Orgn. Nurse Execs., Nurse Exec. Resource Group (U. Chgo.), Nat. League for Nursing, Ind. Deans and Dirs. of AD, BS and Higher Degree Programs, Nurse Exec. Forum, Wayne State Alumni Assn., St. Margaret Alumni Assn. (v.p. program com., chmn. scholarship com.), Ind. U. Alumni Assn., Mu Omega (chpt. commitment award 1994, chair fin. com. 1991—), Sigma Theta Tau (hon.). Office: Purdue U Calumet 2200 169th St Hammond IN 46323-2068 E-mail: smokvina@calumet.purdue.edu.

SMOLEN, LEE M., lawyer; b. 1960; BS with highest honors, U. Ill., 1982; JD, U. Chgo., 1985. CPA; bar: Ill. 1985. Assoc. real estate group Sidley Austin LLP, 1985—93, ptnr. real estate group, 1993—. Chair Chgo. real estate group Sidley Austin LLP, 2004—, co-chair practice devel. com. Mem.: ABA. Office: One S Dearborn St Chicago IL 60603 Office Phone: 312-853-7823. Office Fax: 312-853-7036. Business E-Mail: lsmolen@sidley.com.

SMOLYANSKY, JULIE, consumer products company executive; b. Russia; arrived in US, 1976; d. Michael and Ludmila Smolyansky. BA, U. Ill., 1996. Dir. sales and mktg. Lifeway Foods Inc., Morton Grove, Ill., 1997—2002, pres., 2002—, CEO, 2002—, CFO, 2002—, treas., 2002—, dir. Avocation: running. Office: Lifeway Foods Inc 6431 West Oakton Ave Morton Grove IL 60053

SMOTHERS, ANN ELIZABETH, museum director; b. Chgo., Dec. 20, 1946; With adminstn. Mercy Hosp., Iowa City, 1982-85; asst. dir. Old Capital Mus., Iowa City, 1985-95, dir., 1995—. Recipient Hon. Achievement for Women award YWCA, 1996. Mem. Altrusa. Office: Old Capitol Mus Univ Iowa 24 Old Capitol Iowa City IA 52242 E-mail: ann.smothers@niowa.edu.

SMUCKER, RICHARD K., food products executive; m. Emily Delp; 1 child. Grad., Miami U., Ohio; MBA, Wharton Sch. Bus., U. Penn. Pres. The J.M. Smucker Co., 1987—, co-CEO, 2001—. Bd. dirs. The J.M. Smucker Co., Wm. Wrigley Jr., Co., Internat. Multifoods, The Sherwin-Williams Co., Internat. Foodservice Mfr. Assoc.; bd. trustees Cleveland Orchestra, Culinary Inst. Am. Office: 1 Strawberry Ln Orrville OH 44667-1241

SMUCKER, TIMOTHY P., food products executive; m. Jennifer Coddington; 3 children. BS Economics, Coll. of Wooster, 1967; MBA Mktg., Wharton Sch. Bus., U Penn, 1969. Chmn. The J.M. Smucker Co., 1984—, co-CEO, 2001—. Bd. dirs. The J.M. Smucker Co., Huntington BancShares, Inc., Dreyer's Grand Ice Cream, Inc., Grocery Mfr. Am., Inc.; bd. trustees Coll. of Wooster; mem. steering com. Heartland Edn. Community. Office: 1 Strawberry Ln Orrville OH 44667-1241

SMYNTEK, JOHN EUGENE, JR., editor; b. Buffalo, Aug. 24, 1950; BA, U. Detroit, 1972. Asst. instr. Mich. State U., East Lansing, 1981; features editor Free Press, Detroit, 1985-92; dir. online svcs. and dir. libr. Free Press Plus, Detroit, 1992-95, spl. features and syndicate editor, 1995—; asst. instr. U. Detroit Mercy, 2000—01. Vis. fellow in journalism Duke U., 1988; profl. student publs. advisor U. Detroit Mercy, 1992—94; bd. visitors Wayne State U. Coll. Fine, Performing and Comm. Arts, 2001—05. Recipient Fine Arts Reporting award, Detroit Press Club, 1985. Roman Catholic. Office: Detroit Free Press 600 W Fort St Detroit MI 48226-2706 Office Phone: 313-222-5169. Business E-Mail: jsmyntek@freepress.com.

SMYTH, ROBERY M., lawyer; b. Pitts., Apr. 2, 1969; married; 3 children. BA, Miami U., 1991; JD, U. Cin., 1994. Bar: Ohio 1994, US Dist. Ct. Southern Dist. Ohio 1995. Clerk 1st Dist. Ohio, Ct. of Appeals; ptnr. Drew & Ward, Cin. Named one of Ohio's Rising Stars, Super Lawyers, 2005, 2006. Fellow: Cin. Acad. Leadership for Lawyers; mem.: Ohio State Bar Assn., ABA, Cin. Bar Assn. (sec., Ct. of Appeals Com. 2004—, former co-chair, Young Lawyers Membership Com.). Avocation: genealogy. Office: Drew & Ward Co LPA 1 W Fourth St Ste 2400 Cincinnati OH 45202 Office Phone: 513-621-8210. Office Fax: 513-621-5444.

SNADER, JACK ROSS, retired publishing company executive; b. Athens, Ohio, Feb. 25, 1938; s. Daniel Webster and Mae Estella (Miller) S.; m. Sharon Perschnick, Apr. 4, 1959; children: Susan Mae, Brian Ross. BS, U. Ill., 1959. Cert. mgmt. cons. With mktg. Richardson-Merrell, Cin., 1959-65, Xerox Corp., NYC, 1965-67, Sieber & McIntyre, Chgo., 1967-69; pres. Systema Corp., Northbrook, Ill., 2008—; ret., 2008. Mem. exec. adv. bd. bus. program Trinity Internat. U. Author Systematic Selling, 1987, The Sales Relationship, 1988. Mem. ASTD, Inst. Mgmt. Cons. Home Phone: 866-271-1734.

SNEED, MICHAEL (MICHELE SNEED), columnist; b. Mandan, ND, Nov. 16, 1943; d. Richard Edward and June Marie (Ritchey) S.; m. William J. Griffin, Sept. 16, 1978; 1 child, Patrick BS, Wayne State U., 1965. Tchr. Barrington High Sch., Ill., 1965-66; legis. asst. Congressman Ray Clevenger, 1966-67; reporter City News Bur., Chgo., 1967-69, Chgo. Tribune, 1969-86, columnist, 1981-86; pres. sec. Mayor Jane Byrne, Chgo., 1979; gossip columnist Chgo. Sun-Times, 1986—. Co-editor Chgo. Journalism Rev., 1971-72 Vice pres. No. Mich. U. chpt. Young Democrats, 1962 Mem.: Women's Athletic. Roman Catholic. Avocation: gardening. Office: Chicago Sun Times 350 N Orleans St Ste 1270 Chicago IL 60654-2148

SNELL, BRUCE M., JR., judge; b. Ida Grove, Iowa, Aug. 18, 1929; s. Bruce M. and Donna (Potter) Snell; m. Anne Snell, Feb. 4, 1956; children: Rebecca, Brad. AB, Grinnell Coll., 1951; JD, U. Iowa, 1956. Bar: Iowa 1956, N.Y. 1958. Law clk. to presiding judge U.S. Dist. Ct. (no. dist.) Iowa, 1956-57; asst. atty. gen., 1961-65; judge Iowa Ct. Appeals, 1976-87; justice Iowa Supreme Ct., Des Moines, 1987—2001, sr. justice, 2001—. Comments editor: Iowa Law Rev. Mem.: ABA, Am. Judicature Soc., Iowa State Bar Assn., Order Coif. Methodist. Home: PO Box 192 Ida Grove IA 51445-0192

SNELL, RICHARD A., equipment manufacturing company executive; b. 1942; BA, Union Coll., Albany, NY; MBA, U. Pa. Brand mgmt. position Procter & Gamble, Cin.; various sr. positions, including v.p. maktg. SmithKline Beecham; exev. v.p. Quaker State Corp., until 1986; various positions Tenneco, Inc., 1987-96, in charge automotive retail bus., sr. v.p., head Walker Mfg. divsn., until 1993, pres., CEO Tenneco Automotive, 1993-96; chmn., CEO, pres. Fed.-Mogul Corp., Southfield, Mich., 1996—. Bd. dirs. Schneider Nat. Nat. bd. dirs. Big Bros. Am.; bd. dirs. United Way Cmty. Svcs. Mem. Equipment Mfrs. Assn. (past chmn.). Office: Fed-Mogul Corp 26555 Northwestern Hwy Southfield MI 48034-2199

SNIDER, LAWRENCE K., lawyer; b. Detroit, Dec. 28, 1938; s. Ben and Ida (Hertz) S.; m. Maxine Bobman, Aug. 12, 1962; children: Stephanie, Suzanne. BA, U. Mich., 1960, JD, 1963. Bar: Mich. 1964, Ill. 1991. Ptnr. Jaffe, Snider, Raitt & Heuer, Detroit, 1968-91, Mayer, Brown & Platt, Chgo., 1991—. Mem. Nat. Bankruptcy Conf., Am. Coll. Bankruptcy, 1991—. Contbr. articles to profl. jours. Mem. Mich. Coun. for the Arts, 1990-91. Avocations: photography, collections.

SNIVELY, DAVID FREDERICK, agricultural products company executive, lawyer; b. Logansport, Ind., Apr. 26, 1954; s. Howard Woodrow Snively and Rebecca S. (Merrell) Hoover; m. Diane Marie Hepper, Aug. 7, 1976; children: Matthew David, Christine Marie, Evan David. BS magna cum laude, Ball State U., 1976; JD magna cum laude, Ind. U., 1979. Bar: Ind. 1979, Mo. 1987, US Dist. Ct. (so. dist. Ind.) 1979, US Ct. Appeals (7th cir.) 1979, US Supreme Ct. 1984. Assoc. Barnes & Thornburg, Indpls., 1979-84; litig. atty. Monsanto Co., St. Louis, 1984-87, asst. litig. counsel, 1987-89, assoc. litig. counsel, 1989-97, asst. gen. counsel litig., dep. gen. counsel, sr. v.p., sec., gen. counsel, 2006—. Note and devel. editor, contbr. Ind. Law Rev., 1978-79. Mem. ABA (co-chair subcommittee on product liability and toxic torts, com. on corp. counsel 1995—), Ind. Bar Assn., Mo. Bar Assn., Lawyers for Civil Justice (bd. dirs. 1990—), Def. Rsch. Inst. (co-chmn. corp. counsel sect.), Phi Delta Phi. Democrat. Roman Catholic. Avocations: marathon running, backpacking, skiing, rollerblading, bicycling. Office: Monsanto Co 800 N Lindbergh Blvd Saint Louis MO 63167-0001

SNODDY, ANTHONY L., manufacturing executive; Degree in indsl. tech., Ea. Mich. U., 1973. Mem. staff materials and purchasing mgmt. GE Corp., 1973-91; pres. Exemplar Mfg. Co., 1991—. Office: 506 S Huron St Ypsilanti MI 48197-5455

SNODDY, JAMES ERNEST, education educator; b. Perrysville, Ind., Oct. 6, 1932; s. James Elmer and Edna May (Hayworth) S.; m. Alice Joanne Crowder, Aug. 15, 1954; children: Ryan Anthony, Elise Suzanne. BS, Ind. State U., 1954; MEd, U. Ill., 1961, EdD, 1967. Tchr. Danville (Ill.) Pub. Schs., 1954-57, prin., 1961-64; instr. U. Ill., Champaign, 1965-67; prof. edn. Mich. State U., East Lansing, 1967-72, 78-96, chmn. dept. elem. and spl. edn., 1972-78, ret., 1996, prof. emeritus, 1997—; dir. Program CORK, 1978-82. With U.S. Army, 1955-57. Mem. Am. Assn. for Adult and Continuing Edn., Commn. of Profs. of Adult and Continuing Edn. Methodist. Home: 1926 Creek Lndg Haslett MI 48840-8704 Office: Mich State U 419 Erickson Hall East Lansing MI 48824-1034 Office Phone: 517-339-6548. Business E-Mail: jsnoddy@msu.edu.

SNOEYINK, VERNON L., civil engineer, educator; BS in Civil Engring., U. Mich., 1984, MS in Sanitary Engring., 1966, PhD in Water Resource Engring., 1968. Asst. prof. sanitary engring. U. Ill., Urbana, 1969-73, from assoc. prof. to prof. environ. engring., 1973—, Ivan Racheff prof. environ. engring., 1989—2004, prof. emeritus, 2005—. Mem.: NAE. Office: U Ill Dept Civil Engring Newmark Civil Engring Lab 205 N Mathews Ave Urbana IL 61801 Home Phone: 217-352-0698. Business E-Mail: snoeyink@uiuc.edu.

SNYDER, ARTHUR E., academic administrator; m. Camille Snyder; children: Melanie, Chris. BA, MBA, Barry U.; EdD, Wilmington Coll. Gen. mgr. AT&T, Fort Lauderdale, Fla.; exec. v.p., chief oper. officer Ensec, Inc., Miami, Fla., Sao Paulo, Brazil; chmn. Dept. Mktg., dean profl./grad. studies Lynn U., Boca Raton, Fla., 1992—2001; dean Tabor Sch. Bus., Dwayne O. Andreas chair exec. mgmt. Millikin U., Decatur, Ill., 2001—03; pres. Indiana Tech., Fort Wayne, 2003—. Chmn. Sister's of Providence Mission Adv. Bd., Downtown Ednl. Partnership. Mem.: Fort Wayne Bus. Forum. Office: Indiana Tech 1600 E Washington Blvd Fort Wayne IN 46803 Office Phone: 260-422-5561.

SNYDER, BARBARA ROOK, academic administrator; b. July 23, 1955; BA, Ohio State U., 1976; JD, U. Chgo., 1980. Bar: Ill. 1980. Law clk. for Judge Luther M. Swygert U.S. Ct. Appeals for the Seventh Cir.; with Sidley & Austin, Chgo.; joined law faculty Case Western Res. U., 1983, Ohio State U., Columbus, 1988, assoc. dean for acad. affairs, 2000—01, vice provost for acad. policy and human resources, 2001—03, interim provost, 2003—04, exec. v.p., provost, 2004—07, Joanne W. Murphy/Class of 1965 professorship Moritz Coll. Law; pres. Case Western Reserve U., Cleve., 2007—. Office: Case Western Reserve U Office of Pres 10900 Euclid Ave Cleveland OH 44106-7001 E-mail: barbara.snyder@case.edu.

SNYDER, BILL, football coach; b. St. Joseph, Mo., Oct. 7, 1939; m. Sharon Snyder; children: Sean, Ross, Shannon, Meredith, Whitney. BA, William Jewell Coll., 1963; MA, Ea. N.Mex. U., 1965. Asst. coach Indio (Calif.) H.S., 1964—66, head coach, 1969—73; grad. asst. U. So. Calif., 1966—67; offensive coord. football, head swimming coach Austin Coll., Sherman, Tex., 1979; coach U. Iowa, 1979—89; head football coach Kans. State U., Manhattan, 1989—. Coached in numerous bowl games, including Copper, Aloha, Holiday, Cotton, Fiesta, Alamo. Named Nat. Coach of Yr., Walter Camp Found., Bobby Dodd Coach of Yr. Found., Paul "Bear" Bryant Award, Schutt Sports Group, ESPN, 1991, CNN, 1994, AP, 1990, 1991, 1993. Mem.: Am. Football Coaches Assn. (mem. rules com., mem. ethics com.). Office: Vanier Football Complex 2201 Kimball Ave Manhattan KS 66502

SNYDER, CAROLYN ANN, education educator, librarian, director; b. Elgin, Nebr., Nov. 5, 1942; d. Ralph and Florence Wagner. Student, Nebr. Wesleyan U., 1960—61; BS cum laude, Kearney State Coll., 1964; MS in Librarianship, U. Denver, 1965. Asst. libr. sci. and tech. U. Nebr., Lincoln, 1965—67, asst. pub. svc. libr., 1967—68, 1970—73; from pers. libr. to interim devel. officer Ind. U. Librs., Bloomington, 1973—89, interim dean, 1989—91; adminstrv. army libr. Spl. Svcs. Agy., Europe, 1968—70; dean libr. affairs So. Ill. U., Carbondale, 1991—2000, prof. libr. affairs, 2000—06, dir. found. rels., 2000—06. Team leader Midwest Univs. Consortium for Internat. Activities-World Bank IX project to develop libr. sys. and implement automation U. Indonesia, Jakarta, 1984-86; libr. devel. cons. Inst. Tech. MARA/Midwest Univs. Consortium for Internat. Activities Program in Malaysia, 1985; ofcl. rep. EDUCAUSE, 1996-2000; mem. working group on scholarly comm. Nat. Commn. on Librs. and Info. Sci., 1998-2000. Editor: Library and Other Academic Support Services for Distance Learning, 1997; contbr. chpt. to book and articles to profl. jours. Active Carbondale Pub. Libr. Friends, 1991-, Morris Libr. Friends, 1991—; br. pres. AAUW, Carbondale, 2004-05; bd. dirs. Carbondale Cmty. Arts Bd., 2006-, Carbondale Info. and Telecomm. Commn., 2006-. Cooperative Rsch. grant Coun. on Libr. Resources, Washington, 1984. Mem. ALA (councilor 1985-89, Bogle Internat. Travel award 1988, H.W. Wilson Libr. Staff devel. grant 1981), Libr. Adminstrn./Mgmt. Assn. (pres. 1981-82, numerous others), Com. on Instnl. Coop./Resource Sharing (chair 1987-91), Coalition for Networked Info. (So. Ill. U. at Carbondale rep. 1991-00), Coun. Dirs. State Univ. Librs. in Ill. (chair 1992-93, 99-00), Coun. on Libr. and Info. Resources Digital Leadership Inst. Steering Com. (Assn. Rsch. Librs. rep. 1998-00), Ill. Assn. Coll. and Rsch. Librs. (chair Ill. Bd. Higher Edn. liaison com. 1993-94), Ill. Network (bd. dirs.), Ind. Libr. Assn. (chair coll./univ. divsn. 1982-83), U.S. Grant Assn. (bd. dirs. 1992—), Ill. Libr. Computer Sys. Orgn. (policy coun. 1992-95, 96-00), Nat. Assn. State Univs. and Land-Grant Colls. (commn. on info. tech. and its distance learning and libr. bds. 1994-96), NetIllinois (bd. dirs. 1994-96), OCLC Users Coun. (elected rep. 1995-98), Big 12 Plus Libr. Consortium (chair 1997-98), Nat. Commn. on Librs. and Info. Sci. Working Group on Scholarly Comm., Assn. Rsch. Libr. (vis. program officer 2000-01). Avocations: antiques, theater, movies, reading. Office: So Ill U Ctrl Devel Carbondale IL 62901-6632 Home Phone: 618-457-3689; Office Phone: 618-453-1447.

SNYDER, EDWARD ADAMS, dean, economics professor; b. Danville, Pa., July 3, 1953; s. Harry Coolidge and Fay (Adams) S.; m. Kimberly Marie Snyder; children: Alison Marie, Jeffrey Adams, Kevin James. Ba in Econs. and Govt., Colby Coll., 1975; M of Pub. Policy, U. Chgo., 1978, PhD in Econs., 1984. Staff economist Antitrust div. U.S. Dept. Justice, Washington, 1978—82; asst. prof. bus. econs. and pub. policy Sch. Bus. Adminstrn. U. Mich., Ann Arbor, 1982—90, assoc. prof. Sch. Bus. Adminstrn., 1990-94, prof. Sch. Bus. Adminstrn., 1994-98, chair bus. econ. and pub. policy, Sch. Bus. Adminstrn., 1992—95; dean Darden Bus. Sch. U. Va., Charlottesville, 1998—2001; dean U. Chgo. Grad. Sch. Bus., 2001—, prof., 2001—02, George Pratt Shultz prof. economics, 2002—. Rsch. fellow Office for Study of Pub. and Pvt. Instns., U. Mich.; cons. Antitrust div. U.S. Dept. Justice, Chgo., 1982-85, Fed. Home Loan Bank Bd., Washington, 1989; antitrust expert, 1985—; John M. Olin vis. assoc. prof. U. Chgo., 1991-92; dir. William Davidson Inst. Mich. Bus. Sch., 1992-95. Author: Crisis Resolution in the Thrift Industry, 1989; contbr. articles to econ. jours. and law revs., 1985-98. Avocations: foreign policy, sports, sailing. Office: U Chgo Grad Sch of Bus 5807 S Woodlawn Ave Chicago IL 60637 Office Phone: 773-702-1680. E-mail: tsnyder@chicagogsb.edu.

SNYDER, GEORGE EDWARD, lawyer; b. Battle Creek, Mich., Feb. 7, 1934; s. Leon R. and Edith (Dullabahn) S.; m. Mary Jane Belt, July 27, 1957 (div. Sept. 23, 1982); children: Sara Lynn, Elizabeth Jane; m. Claudia Gage Brooks, Feb. 25, 1984 BS, Mich. State U., 1957; JD, U. Mich., 1960. Bar: Mich. 1961, U.S. Dist. Ct. (we. and ea. dists.) Mich. 1961. With Gen. Electric Co., 1957-58; assoc. firm Miller, Johnson, Snell & Commisky, Grand Rapids, 1960-62, Goodenough & Buesser, Detroit, 1962-66; partner firm Buesser, Buesser, Snyder & Blank, Detroit and Bloomfield Hills, 1966-85, Meyer, Kirk, Snyder & Lynch PLLC, Bloomfield Hills, 1985—2007; of counsel Meyer & Kirk, PLLC, 2007. Chmn. bd. dirs. Bill Knapps Mich., Inc., 1998-2000. Chmn. E. Mich. Environ. Action Council, 1974-78; pub. mem. inland lakes and streams rev. com. Mich. Dept. Natural Resources, 1975-76. Served as 2d lt. AUS, 1957. Named one of Best Lawyers in Am., Woodward White, 1992—2007, Mich. Super Lawyers, Law and Politics, 2006—07. Fellow Am. Acad. Matrimonial Lawyers (pres. Mich. chpt. 1991-92), Am. Coll. Family Trial Lawyers, Am. Bar Found., Internat. Acad. Matrimonial Lawyers, Mich. Bar Found; mem. ABA, Am. Judicature Soc., Am. Arbitration Assn. (panel arbitrators), State Bar Mich. (chmn. family law com. 1968-72, mem. rep. assembly 1972-78, chmn. rules and calendar com. 1977-78, mem. family law sect. coun. 1973-76, environ. law sect. coun. 1980-85, prepaid legal svcs. com. 1973-82, com. on judicial selection 1974, com. on specialization 1976-82), Detroit Bar Assn. (chmn. family law com. 1966-68), Oakland County Bar Assn., Delta Upsilon (chmn. trustees, alumni chpt. dep. 1965-70), Tau Beta Pi, Pi Tau Sigma, Phi Eta Sigma. Detroit Athletic Club, Birmingham (Mich.) Athletic Club, Bloomfield Hills Country Club. Episcopalian. Home: 32965 Outland Trl Bingham Farms MI 48025-2555 Office: Meyer & Kirk PLLC Ste 100 100 W Long Lake Rd Bloomfield Hills MI 48304-2773 Home Phone: 248-540-1698; Office Phone: 248-647-5111. Business E-Mail: gsnyder@meyerkirk.com.

SNYDER, HARRY COOPER, retired state legislator; b. July 10, 1928; Student, Wilmington Coll., Ohio U. Mem. Ohio State Senate, Columbus, 1979-96; ret., 1996; chmn. edn. and retirement com. Ohio State Senate, Columbus. Former mem. exec. com. Ohio Sch. Bds. Assn.; commr. Ohio High Speed Rail Devel. Authority; mem. Edn. Commn. of the States; chmn. Ohio Retirement Study Commn.; chmn. Legis. Office on Edn. Oversight; ad hoc mem. State Bd. Edn., Ohio Bd. Regents; mem. Jobs for Ohio Grads.; founder Clinton County Family Y; mem. Clinton County Bd. Edn. Recipient Outstanding Legis. Svc. award Citizens United for Responsible Edn., Ohio Ret. Tchrs. Assn., Ohio Coalition for Edn. of Handicapped Children, Ohio Assn. Civil Trial Attys., Guardian of Small Bus. award Nat. Fedn. Ind. Bus., Outstanding Contbr. to Edn. in Ohio award Ohio Confedn. Tchr. Edn. Orgn., Disting. Govtl. Svc. award Ohio Coun. Pvt. Colls. and Schs., Legis. of Yr. Ohio Sch. and Transit Assn. Mem. Am. Legis. Exch. Coun. (edn. com., Outstanding State Legis.-Jefferson award), Nat. Conf. State Legislatures (state/fed. assembly, edn. and job tng. com., assembly of legislature, edn. com.), Rotary Club (pres.), Great Oaks Task Force. Republican. Methodist. Avocations: reading, gardening, sailing. Home: 6508 Spring Hill Dr Hillsboro OH 45133-9209

SNYDER, JEAN MACLEAN, lawyer; b. Chgo., Jan. 26, 1942; d. Norman Fitzroy and Jessie (Burns) Maclean; m. Joel Martin Snyder, Sept. 4, 1964; children: Jacob Samuel, oah Scot. BA, U. Chgo., 1963, JD, 1979. Bar: Ill. 1979, U.S. Dist. Ct. (no. dist.) Ill. 1979, U.S. Ct. Appeals (7th cir.) 1981. Ptnr. D'Ancona & Pflaum, Chgo., 1979-92; prin. Law Office of Jean Maclean Snyder, Chgo., 1993-97, 2004—; trial counsel The MacArthur Justice Ctr. U. Chgo. Law Sch., 1997—2004, of counsel, 2004—05. Contbr. articles to profl. jours. Bd. dirs. Citizens Alert, 2005—07. Mem.: Lawyers for the Creative Arts (bd. dirs. 1995—97), ACLU of Ill. (bd. dirs. 1996—99), ABA (mem. coun. on litigation sect. 1989—92, editor-in-chief Litigation mag. 1987—88, co-chair First Amendment and media litigation com. 1995—96, co-chair sect. litigation task force on gender, racial and ethnic bias 1998—2001, standing com. on strategic comms. 1996—2001). Home Phone: 773-285-2245; Office Phone: 773-285-5100. Business E-Mail: jeansnyder@sbcglobal.net.

SNYDER, JILL, museum director; b. Trenton, NJ, June 28, 1957; d. Barry and Arline (Gellar) S. BA, Wesleyan U., Middletown, Conn., 1979. Exec. assoc. Guggenheim Mus., NYC, 1983-88, edn. assoc., 1989-91; dir./curator Freedman Gallery, Albright Coll., Reading, Pa., 1993-95; dir. The Aldrich Mus. of Contemporary Art, Ridgefield, Conn., 1995—96; exec. dir. Mus. Contemporary Art Cleve., 1996—. Mem. curatorial rev. panel Abington Art Ctr., Jenkintown, Pa., 1995; staff lectr. Mus. of Modern Art, N.Y.C., 1989-94, Guggenheim Mus., 1988-92; adj. faculty N.Y. Sch. Interior Design, 1988-92, Mary Schiller Myers Sch. Art, U. Akron. Author: Caring for Your Art, 1991, In the Flesh (catalogue), 1996, Impossible Evidence: Contemporary Artists View the Holocaust (catalogue), 1994, Against the Stream: Milton Avery, Adolph Gottlieb and Mark Rothko in the 1930s (catalogue), 1994. Bd. dirs. Forum for U.S.-Soviet Dialogue, Washington, 1990-91. Milton and Sally Avery Found. fellow, 1990, Shelby and Leon Levy fellow, 1988. Mem. Art Table, Am. Assn. Mus., Coll. Art Assn. Office: Mus Contemporary Art Cleve 8501 Carnegie Ave Cleveland OH 44106 E-mail: jsnyder@MOCAcleveland.org.

SNYDER, LEWIS EMIL, astrophysicist, educator; b. Ft. Wayne, Ind., Nov. 26, 1939; s. Herman Lewis and Bernice (McKee) S.; m. Doris Jean Selma Lautner, June 16, 1962; children: Herman Emil, Catherine Jean. BS, Ind. State U., 1961; MA, So. Ill. U., 1964; PhD, Mich. State U., 1967. Research assoc. Nat. Radio Astronomy Obs., Charlottesville., Va., 1967-69; prof. astronomy dept. U. Va., Charlottesville, 1969-73, 74-75; vis. fellow Joint Inst. for Lab. Astrophysics, U. Colo., Boulder, 1973-74; prof. astronomy dept. U. Ill., Urbana, 1975—2005, prof. emeritus, 2005—, chair astronomy dept., 2002—05. Co-editor: Molecules in the Galactic Environment, 1973; contbr. articles to sci. jours. NASA-Am. Soc. Engring. Edn. summer fellow, 1972, 73; Alexander von Humboldt Found. sr. U.S. scientist award, 1983-84. Mem. AAAS, Am. Phys. Soc., Am. Astron. Soc., Internat. Astron. Union, Union Radio Scientifique Internationale, Alexander von Humboldt Assn. Am. Lutheran. Office: U Ill 1002 W Green St Urbana IL 61801-3074

SNYDER, PETER M., medical educator, medical researcher; BA in Biology summa cum laude, Luther Coll., 1984; MD, U. Iowa, 1989. Diplomate Am. Bd. Internal Medicine, Am. Bd. Cardiovasc. Disease. Resident in internal medicine U. Tex., Dallas, 1989—92; fellow in cardiovasc. diseases Dept. Internal Medicine U. Iowa Hosp. & Clinics, Iowa City, 1992—96, asst. prof. Dept. Internal Medicine, 1996—2000, assoc. prof. internal medicine and physiology and biophysics, 2000—. Contbr. articles to profl. jours. Recipient Clinician Scientist award, 1996, Katz Basic Sci. award, 1998; fellow, U. Iowa, 1985, Am. Heart Assn., 1987—88. Mem.: ACP, Alpha Omega Alpha. Achievements include research in sodium channel structure and function. Office: U Iowa Coll of Medicine Dept Internal Medicine 200 Hawkins Dr Iowa City IA 52242-1009

SNYDER, THOMAS J., automotive company executive; With Delco Remy divsn. of GM Corp., 1962-94, product mgr. heavy duty systems; pres., CEO, dir. Delco Remy Internat., Inc., Anderson, Ind., 1994—. Bd. dirs. St. John's Health Systems. Office: Delco Remy Internat Inc 2902 Enterprise Dr Anderson IN 46013

SNYDER, WILLIAM W., corporate financial executive; m. Valerie Snyder; 2 children. BSBA, U. Mo., M in Accountancy. CPA. With pub. acctg. Deloitte & Touche; corp. contr. Enterprise Rent-A-Car, 1984—89, asst. v.p. to v.p. corp. acctg., 1989—94, v.p. fleet adminstrn., 1994—95, v.p. info. sys., 1995—98, sr. v.p., chief info. officer, 1998—2002, sr. v.p., CFO, 2002—03, exec. v.p., CFO, 2003—. Office: Enterprise Rent-A-Car 600 Corporate Park Dr Saint Louis MO 63105

SO, FRANK S., educational association administrator; b. Youngstown, Ohio, Apr. 25, 1937; BA cum laude, Youngstown U., 1959; MA, Ohio State U., 1961. Dir. planning and cmty. devel. City of Harvey, Ill., 1964-67; cons. advisor to village mgr. Village of Flossmoor, Ill., 1980-96; exec. dir. Am. Planning Assn., Chgo., 1996—. Adj. prof. Govs. State U., University Park, Ill.; spkr. in field. Editor-in-chief: The Practice of Local Government Planning, 3 edits., The Practice of State and Regional Planning; contbr. articles to profl. jours. Vol. planning career advisor to Peace Corps. Mem. Am. Planning assn., Am. Inst. Cert. Planners, Lambda Alpha Internat. Office: Am Planning Assn 122 S Michigan Ave Ste 1600 Chicago IL 60603-6190

SOAVE, ANTHONY, manufacturing executive; Pres., CEO, founder City Mgmt. Corp., Detroit, 1974—98, Soave Enterprises LLC, Detroit. Dir. Titan Internat., Inc., 1994—. Office: Soave Enterprises LLC 3400 E Lafayette St Detroit MI 48207-4962

SOBEL, ALAN, electrical engineer, physicist; b. NYC, Feb. 23, 1928; s. Edward P. and Rose (Naftalison) S.; m. Marjorie Loebel, June 15, 1952; children: Leslie Ann, Edward Robert. BSEE, Columbia U., 1947, MSEE, 1949; PhD in Physics, Poly. Inst. Bklyn., 1964. Lic. Profl. Engr., N.Y. and Ill. Asst. chief engr. The Electronic Workshop, NYC, 1950-51; head, functional engr. Fairchild Controls Corp., 1951-56; project engr. Skiatron Electronics and TV Corp., 1956-57; sr. rsch. engr. Zenith Radio Corp., Glenview, Ill., 1964-78; v.p. Lucitron inc., Northbrook, Ill., 1978-87, pres., 1987; pvt. practice cons. Evanston, Ill., 1988—; v.p. Machine Vision and Control Internat. Inc., 1994—2003, LightWave Technologies Corp., 2000—. Asst., instr. Poly. Inst. Bklyn.,1957-64; mem. program coms. SID Internat. Symposium, Internat. Display Rsch. Conf., 1970—. Inventor: 14 patents on various display and electron devices; editor Jour. Soc. Info. Display, 1991-99, assoc. editor, 2000—; adv. editor Info. Display Mag., 1991-2003; assoc. editor: IEEE Trans. on Electron Devices, 1970-77; contbr. articles to profl. jours. NSF fellow, 1959, 60. Fellow Soc. Info. Display (Lewis and Beatrice Winner award 2002); mem. IEEE (sr., life), SPIE, Am. Phys. Soc., Sigma Xi. Democrat. Home and Office: 1307 Beechwood Dr Ann Arbor MI 48103 Office Phone: 734-995-8414. Personal E-mail: as1285@columbia.edu.

SOBEL, HOWARD BERNARD, osteopath, educator; b. NYC, May 15, 1929; s. Martin and Ella (Sternberg) S.; m. Ann Louise Silverbush, June 16, 1957 (dec. May 1978); children: ancy Sobel Michel, Janet Sobel Medow, Robert; m. Irene S. Miller, June 8, 1980; stepchildren: Avner Saferstein, Daniel Saferstein, Naomi Saferstein AB, Syracuse U., 1951; D.O., Kansas City Coll. Osteopathy and Surgery, 1955. Intern Zieger Osteo. Hosp., Detroit, 1955-56; gen. practice osteo. medicine Redford Twp., Mich., 1956-74, Livonia, Mich., 1974—2005; ret., 2005. Chief of staff Botsford Gen. Hosp., Farmington, Mich., 1978; mem. faculty Mich. State U. Coll. Osteo. Medicine, 1969—, clin. assoc. prof. family practice, 1973—; mem. exec. and med. adv. coms. United Health Orgn. Mich.; mem. Venereal Disease Action Com., Mich.; apptd. to asst. impaired osteo. physicians Mich., 1983 Mem. Am. Osteo. Assn. (ho. of dels. 1981—), Mich. Assn. Osteo. Physicians and Surgeons (ho. of dels.), Am. Coll. Osteo. Rheumatologists, Coll. Am. Osteo. Gen. Practitioners, Osteo. Gen. Practice Mich., Wayne County Osteo. Assn. (pres.) Jewish. Home: 6222 Northfield Rd West Bloomfield MI 48322-2431

SOBKOWICZ, HANNA MARIA, retired neurologist; b. Warsaw, Jan. 1, 1931; arrived in U.S., 1963; d. Stanislaw and Jadwiga (Ignaczak) S.; m. Jerzy E. Rose, Mar. 12, 1972. BA, Girls State Lyceum, Gilwice, Poland, 1949; M.D, Med. Acad., Warsaw, 1954, PhD, 1962. Intern. 1st Internal Med. Clinic Med. Acad., Warsaw, 1954-55; resident 1st Internal Med. Clinic, Med. Acad., Warsaw, 1955-59, Neurol. Clinic, Med. Acad., 1959, jr. asst., 1959-61, sr. asst., 1961-63; research fellow neurology Mt. Sinai Hosp., NYC, 1963-65; Nat. Multiple Sclerosis Soc. fellow Columbia U., NYC, 1965-66; asst. prof. neurology U. Wis., Madison, 1966-72, assoc. prof., 1972-79, prof., 1979—2006, prof. emerita, 2006—. Contbr. articles to profl. jours. NIH rsch. grantee, 1968—2002. Mem. Internat. Brain Rsch. Orgn., Soc. Neurosci., Internat. Soc. Devel. Neurosci. (editl. bd. 1984—). Business E-Mail: hmsobkow@wisc.edu.

SOBOL, LAWRENCE RAYMOND, lawyer; b. Kansas City, Mo., May 8, 1950; s. Haskell and Mary (Press) S.; m. Maureen Patricia O'Connell, May 29, 1976; children: David, Kevin. BBA, U. Tex., 1972; JD, U. Mo., 1975. Bar: Mo. 1975, U.S. Dist. Ct. (ea. dist.) Mo. 1975. Gen. counsel, gen. ptnr. Edward D. Jones & Co., Maryland Heights, Mo., 1975—. Allied mem. N.Y.C. Stock Exchange, 1977—; sec. Lake Communications Corp., Conroe, Tex., 1984-86, LHC Inc., EDJ Holding Co. Inc., Unison Capital Corp., 1990—, Cornerstone Mortgage Investment Group, 1987-92; sec., bd. dirs. Cornerstone Mortgage Inc., St. Louis, 1986; v.p., bd. dirs. Tempus Corp., St. Louis, 1984—. Omar Robinson Meml. scholar U. Mo., 1974-75. Mem. ABA (securities law com. 1982—), Met. St. Louis Bar Assn. (securities law sect.), Nat. Assn. Securities Dealers (dist. bus. com., registered prin. officer, nat. arbitration com. 1991—), Securities Industry Assn. (fed. regulation securities com. 1987-88), Persimmon Woods Country Club, Lake Las Vegas South Shore Country Club, Phi Eta Sigma. Avocations: tennis, golf. Office: Edward D Jones & Co 12555 Manchester Rd Saint Louis MO 63131-3729

SOBRERO, KATE (KATHRYN MICHELE SOBRERO), professional soccer player; b. Pontiac, Mich., Aug. 23, 1976; BA in Bus., U. Notre Dame, 1997. Mem. U.S. Nat. Women's Soccer Team, 1995—2001; profl. soccer player Boston Breakers (WUSA), 2001—03. Mem. U.S. Under-20 Nat. Team, 1993—. Named Defensive Most Valuable Player, NCAA Final Four, 1995. Achievements include on cover of Soccer Am. mag., 1995; member Notre Dame NCAA National Championship Team, 1995; member U.S. World Cup Championship Team, 1999; member U.S. Olympic Silver Medal Team, 2000. Office: US Soccer Fedn 1801-1811 S Prairie Ave Chicago IL 60616

SOBUS, KERSTIN MARYLOUISE, physician, physical therapist; b. Washington, June 16, 1960; d. Earl Francis and Dolores Jane (Gill) G.; m. Paul John Jr., March 10, 1990; children: Darlene Marie, Julieann Marie, Gwendolyn Rose Marie. BS in Phys. Therapy summa cum laude, U. ND, 1981, MD, 1987. Clinic instr. pediatric physical therapy U. ND Sch. Medicine, Grand Forks, 1981-83; pediat. phys. therapist child evaluation-treatment program Med. Rehab. Ctr., Grand Forks, 1981-83, med. dir. program, 1997—; asst. prof. dept. pediatrics, asst. prof. dept. physical medicine and rehab. U. Ark. for Med. Scis., Little Rock, 1992-96; resident in internal medicine Sinai Hosp. Balt., 1987-88; resident in phys. medicine and rehab. Johns Hopkins program Sinai Hosp., Balt., 1988-91; pediatric rehab. clin. and rsch. fellow Alfred I. DuPont Inst., Wilmington, Del., 1991-92; pediatric pysiatrist Altru Health System, Grand Forks, 1997—. Contbr. articles to med. jours. Mem. Am. Acad. Cerebral Palsy and Devel. Medicine, Alpha Omega Alpha Honor Soc. Office: Altru Health Sys PO Box 6002 1300 S Columbia Rd Grand Forks ND 58201-4012 Home: 7451 S 25th St Grand Forks ND 58201 Office Phone: 701-780-2482.

SOCHEN, JUNE, history professor; b. Chgo., Nov. 26, 1937; d. Sam and Ruth (Finkelstein) S. BA, U. Chgo., 1958; MA, Northwestern U., 1960, PhD, 1967. Project editor Chgo. Superior and Talented Student Project, 1959-60; high sch. tchr. English and history North Shore Country Day Sch., Winnetka, Ill., 1961-64; instr. history Northeastern Ill. U., 1964-67, asst. prof., 1967-69, assoc. prof., 1969-72, prof., 1972—. Author: The New Woman, 1971, Movers and Shakers, 1973, Herstory: A Woman's View of American History, 1975, 2d edit., 1981, Consecrate Every Day: The Public Lives of Jewish American Women, 1981, Enduring Values: Women in Popular Culture, 1987, Cafeteria America: New Identities in Contemporary Life, 1988, Mae West: She Who Laughs Lasts, 1992, From Mae to Madonna: Women Entertainers in 20th Century America, 1999; editor: The New Feminism in 20th Century America, 1972, Women's Comic Visions, 1991; contbr. articles to profl. jours. Nat. Endowment for Humanities grantee, 1971-72 Office: Northeastern Ill U 5500 N Saint Louis Ave Chicago IL 60625-4679 Office Phone: 773-442-5607. Business E-Mail: j-sochen@neiu.edu.

SOCOL, MICHAEL LEE, obstetrician, gynecologist, educator; b. Chgo., Oct. 3, 1949; s. Joseph and Bernice (Bofman) S.; m. Donna Kaner, Dec. 17, 1972. BS, U. Ill., 1970; MD, U. Ill., Chgo., 1974. Diplomate Am. Bd. Ob-Gyn., Am. Bd. Maternal-Fetal Medicine. Resident obstetrics and gynecology U. Ill. Hosp., Chgo., 1974-77; clin. rsch. fellow dept. obstetrics and gynecology L.A. County-U. So. Calif. Med. Ctr., 1977-79; assoc. attending physician Northwestern Meml. Hosp., Chgo., 1980-86, attending physician dept. ob-gyn., 1986—; co-dir. Northwestern Perinatal Ctr., Chgo., 1987—; chief obstetrics Northwestern Meml. Hosp., Chgo., 1987—, dir. maternal-fetal medicine fellowship program, 1987-99, asst. prof. obstetrics and gynecology, 1979-84, assoc. prof., 1984-92, prof., 1992—. Vice chmn. dept. ob-gyn Northwestern Meml. Hosp., Chgo., 1992—. Author: (with others) Clinical Obstetrics and Gynecology, 1982, 1984, Diagnostic Ultrasound Applied to Obstetrics and Gynecology, 1987, Principles and Practice of Medical Therapy in Pregnancy, 1992; peer reviewer Am. Jour. Obstetrics and Gynecology, 1980—, Obstetrics and Gynecology, 1984—; contbr. numerous articles to profl. jours. Fellow Am. Coll. Ob-Gyn., Soc. Maternal-Fetal Medicine, Soc. for Gynecol. Investigation, Am. Gynecol. and Obstet. Soc.; mem. Assn. Profs. Gynecology and Obstetrics. Avocation: marathon running. Office: 333 E Superior St Ste 410 Chicago IL 60611-3015 Home: 30 W Oak St Apt 208 Chicago IL 60610 Office: 250E Superior St Ste 3-2303 Chicago IL 60611

SOCOLOFSKY, JON EDWARD, banker; b. Chgo., Mar. 27, 1946; s. E. E. and Jane C. (Ward) S.; married; 1 child, Brian Edward. BA, DePauw U., 1968; MBA, Ind. U., 1970. Auditor No. Trust Co., Chgo., 1970-79, v.p., 1979-86, sr. v.p., 1986—. Pres. Cass Sch. Dist. # 63, Darien, Ill., 1987-93. Mem. Internat. Ops. Assn. Republican. Congregationalist. Avocations: water-skiing, volleyball, motorcycling. Office: The Northern Trust Co 50 S La Salle St Chicago IL 60603-1003 Home: 3600 S Ocean Blvd Apt 502 Palm Beach FL 33480-6302

SODERBERG, LEIF G., electronics company executive; BA, Harvard Coll.; MS in Mgmt., MIT. Various positions ending with ptnr. McKinsey & Co., Cleveland and Scandinavia, 1978-93; head bus. strategy Land Mobile Products Sector, Network Svcs. Bus. Motorola Inc., 1993-94, v.p., gen. mgr. Network Svcs. and Bus. Strategies Group Ill., 1994—98, sr. v.p. Systems Solutions Group Ill., 1998—2000, sr. v.p., gen. mgr., strategy, business development and industry relations, 2000—02, sr. v.p., dir., Motorola's global strategy and corporate development organization, 2002—. Mem. Clearnet's Nominating Com.

SODREL, MICHAEL EUGENE, former congressman, small business owner; b. Louisville, Dec. 17, 1945; s. Robert Eugene Sodrel and Nora Baily (Vermillion) Keller, m. Marquita Dean, Nov. 24, 1967; children: Michael Noah, Keesha. Student, Ind. U., Jeffersonville, 1963. Dir. maintenance Sodrel Truck Lines, Inc., Jeffersonville, 1969-72, dir. ops., 1972-74, v.p., 1974-76, exec. v.p., 1976-81, pres., CEO, 1981—2004; mem. US Congress from 9th Ind. dist., 2005—07; mem. sci. com., small bus. com., transp. and infrastructure com. Pres., chief exec. officer, Salem Stage, Inc., Jeffersonville, 1974-2004, The Free Enterprise System, Inc., 1976-2004. Bd. dirs. George Rogers Clark council Boy Scouts Am., New Albany, Ind., 1988—. Served to staff sgt. Nat. Guard US Army, 1966—73. Recipient Spl. Tourism award State of Ind., 1987; named to Hon. Order Ky. Col, 1983. Mem. Nat. Star Route Mail Contractor's Assn. (pres., chmn. bd. 1978-88), Am. Bus. Assn. (bd. dirs. 1987—), So. Ind. C. of C. Clubs: Skal (pres. 1986-87). Lodges: Rotary (pres. 1988—, Paul Harris fellow 1976). Republican. Presbyterian.

SOENEN, MICHAEL J., consumer products company executive; b. 1970; BA, Kalamazoo Coll., 1992. Investment banker Salomon Brothers Inc., 1993—96; assoc. Perry Corp., 1996; pres., CEO FTD.com, 1999—2002; v.p. mktg. FTD Grp. Inc., Downers Grove, Ill., 1997—99, dir. sales and promotions, 1997—99, dir., 2002—04, pres., COO, 2002—04, pres., CEO, 2004—. Mem. Chgo. Gateway Green. Mem.: Young Presidents' Orgn., Econ. Club, Chgo. Club. Office: FTD Group Inc 3113 Woodcreek Dr Downers Grove IL 60515 Office Phone: 630-719-7800. Office Fax: 630-719-6170.

SOENS, LAWRENCE DONALD, bishop emeritus; b. Iowa City, Aug. 26, 1926; Student, Loras Coll., Dubuque, Iowa, St. Ambrose Coll., Davenport, Iowa, Kenrick Sem., St. Louis, U. Iowa. Ordained priest Diocese of Davenport, Iowa, 1950; ordained bishop, 1983; bishop Diocese of Sioux City, 1983—98, bishop emeritus, 1998—. Roman Catholic. Office: Chancery Office PO Box 3379 1821 Jackson St Sioux City IA 51102-3379 Office Phone: 712-233-7512. Office Fax: 712-233-7598.*

SOERGEL, KONRAD HERMANN, physician; b. Coburg, Germany, July 27, 1929; came to U.S., 1954, naturalized, 1962; s. Konrad Daniel and Erna Henrietta (Schilling) S.; m. Rosina Klara Rudin, June 24, 1955; children: Elizabeth Ann, Karen Theresa, Marilyn Virginia, Kenneth Thomas. MD, U. Erlangen, Germany, 1954, Dr. med., 1958. Intern Bergen Pines County Hosp., Paramus, NJ, 1954-55; resident in pathology West Pa. Hosp., Pitts., 1955-56; rsch. asst. U. Erlangen, Germany, 1956-57; resident in medicine Mass. Meml. Hosp., Boston, 1957-58; fellow in gastroenterology Boston U. Med. Sch., 1958-60, instr., 1960-61; mem. faculty Med. Coll. Wis., Milw., 1961—, prof. medicine, 1969—2002, prof. medicine emeritus, 2003—, prof. physiology, 1993—2002, chief sect. gastroenterology, 1961-93. Chmn. gastroenterology and clin. nutrition study sect. NIH, 1979-80 Contbr. articles to profl. jours., chpts. to books. Recipient Rsch. Career Devel. award USPHS, 1963-72; Alexander von Humboldt Found. sr. fellow, 1973-74 Mem. Am. Gastroenterol. Assn., Am. Soc. Clin. Investigation, Am. Assn. Physicians, German Soc. for Digestive and Metabolic Disorders (hon.), Ger. Soc. Internal Medicine (hon.). Home: 14245 Hillside Rd Elm Grove WI 53122-1677 Office: Med Coll Wis 9200 W Wisconsin Ave Milwaukee WI 53226-3522 Personal E-mail: k.soergel@comcast.net.

SOETEBER, ELLEN, journalist, editor; b. East St. Louis, Ill., June 14, 1950; d. Lyle Potter and Norma Elizabeth (Osborn) S.; m. Richard M. Martins, Mar. 16, 1974. BJ, Northwestern U., 1972. Edn. writer, copy editor Chgo. Today, 1972-74; reporter Chgo. Tribune, 1974-76, asst. met. editor, 1976-84, assoc. met. editor, 1984-86, TV and media editor, 1986, met. editor, 1987-89, assoc. mng. editor for met. news, 1989-91, dep. editor editorial page, 1991-94; mng. editor South Fla. Sun-Sentinel, Ft. Lauderdale, 1994-2001; editor St. Louis Post-Dispatch, 2001—05. Vis. faculty Poynter Inst. Journalism Studies, 2006-; presenter in field; Gaylord vis. prof. journalism and ethics, Ariz. State U., 2008. Named to Hall of Achievement, Medill Sch. Journalism, 2003; Journalism fellow, U. Mich., Ann Arbor, 1986—87. Office Phone: 480-965-7873. Personal E-mail: ellsoeteber@aol.com.

SOGG, WILTON SHERMAN, lawyer; b. Cleve., May 28, 1935; s. Paul P. and Julia (Cahn) S.; m. Saralee Frances Krow, Aug. 12, 1962 (div. July 1975); 1 child, Stephanie; m. Linda Rocker Lehman, Dec. 22, 1979 (div. Dec. 1990); m. Nancy Rosenfield Walsh, June 2, 1991. AB, Dartmouth Coll., 1956; JD, Harvard U., 1959; postgrad., London Grad. Sch. Bus. Studies, 1974-76. Bar: (Ohio) 1960, (Fla) 1970, (U.S. Tax Ct.) 1961, (U.S. Supreme Ct.) 1969. Assoc. Gottfried, Ginsberg, Guren & Merritt, 1960-63, ptnr., 1963-70, Guren, Merritt, Feibel, Sogg & Cohen, Cleve., 1970-84; of counsel Hahn, Loeser, Freedheim, Dean and Wellman, Cleve., 1984-85; ptnr. Hahn Loeser & Parks LLP, Cleve., 1986-2000; of counsel McCarthy, Lebit, Crystal & Liffman Co., Cleve., 2001—. Trustee, pres. Cleve. Jewish ews; adj. prof. Cleve. State U. Law Sch., 1960—; lectr. Harvard U. Law Sch., 1978-80. Author: (with Howard M. Rossen) new and rev. vols. of Smith's Review Legal Gems series, 1969—; editor: Harvard Law Rev.; contbr. articles to profl. jours. Trustee Jewish Cmty. Fedn. of Cleve., 1966-72; bd. overseers Cleveland Marshall Coll. Law, Cleve. State U., 1969—, vis. com. Coll. Bus. Adminstrn., 1996-2001, 2003-; mem. U.S. and State of Ohio Holocaust commns.; pres. bd. trustees Ohio Audubon Adv. Bd., 2005-07. Fulbright fellow U. London, 1959-60. Mem. Ohio Bar Assn., Fla. Bar Assn., Germany Philatelic Soc., Chagrin Valley Hunt, Rowfant Club, Phi Beta Kappa. Home: PO Box 278 Gates Mills OH 44040-0278 Office: McCarthy Lebit Crystal & Liffman 101 W Prospect Ave Ste 1800 Cleveland OH 44115-1088 Business E-Mail: wss@mccarthylebit.com.

SOKOL, DAVID LEE, utilities company executive; b. Omaha, Nebr., 1956; m. Peggy Sokol; children: D.J.(dec.), Kelly. BSCE, U. Nebr., Omaha, 1978; Ph.D (hon.), Bellevue U., Nebr., 1997. With Henningson, Durham and Richardson, Inc. (HDR, Inc.), 1978—82, Citicorp, 1982—83; pres., CEO Ogden Projects, Inc., 1983—91, Peter Kiewit Energy Company, 1991; chmn., pres., CEO MidAmerican Energy Holdings Co. (formerly CalEnergy Co., Inc.), Des Moines, 1991—2008, chmn., 2008—. Co-chmn. for Campaign Nebr., U. Nebr. Found., chmn. Omaha Met. Entertainment & Convention Authority; bd. dirs. Creighton U., Coll. World Series Omaha, Inc., Omaha Airport Authority, Strategic Command Consultation Co., Joslyn Art Mus., River City Roundup and Rodeo, Nebr. Easter Seal Soc., Mt. Michael Abbey H.S., Archdiocese of Omaha, Girls, Inc., Mid-Am. Coun. Boy Scouts Am., Muscular Sclerosis Soc.-Midlands Chpt., United Way Midlands, Edison Electric Inst.; mem. bd. dirs. NCAA Leadership Advisory Named Exec. of Yr., Alternative Sources Energy mag., 1988, Maverick Man of Yr., U. Nebr., 1996, CEO of Yr., Financial Times Energy, 2000, Volunteer of Yr., Greater Omaha C. of C., 2001; named one of 40 Under 40, Crain's NY Bus., 1990; recipient Alumnus Achievement award, U. Nebr. Alumni Assn., 1992, Whitney M. Young, Jr. award, Boy Scouts America-Mid. America Coun., 1993, Heritage Patron award, 1993, Silver Beaver award, 1996, Viking of Distinction award, Omaha North H.S., 1996, Industrial Entrepreneur of Yr., Iowa/Nebr. Region, 1997, Disting. Grad. award, Nat. Catholic Edn. Assn., 1998, Order of the Tower award, U. Nebr., 1998, Community Svc. award, Chancellor's Commn. on Status of Women, U. Nebr., 1999, Mancuso award, Omaha Sportscasters Assn., 2000, Individual Achievement award, The Energy Daily, 2001, Omaha Bus. Hall of Fame award, Greater Omaha Found., 2004, Waite Medal for Leadership award, Creighton U., 2004. Mem. Del. Assn. Profl. Engrs., Neb. Soc. Profl. Engrs.; life mem., Omicron Delta Kappa U. Nebr., 1994-, Horatio Alger Assn., 2004-; bd. govs. Knights of Ak-Sar-Ben Avocations: hockey, hunting, fishing, horseback riding. Office: MidAm Energy Holdings Co 666 Grand Ave PO Box 657 Des Moines IA 50303-0657

SOKOL, ROBERT JAMES, obstetrician, gynecologist, educator; b. Rochester, NY, Nov. 18, 1941; s. Eli and Mildred (Levine) S.; m. Roberta Sue Kahn, July 26, 1964; children: Melissa Anne, Eric Russell, Andrew Ian. BA in Philosophy with highest distinction, U. Rochester, 1963, MD with honors, 1966. Diplomate Am. Bd. Ob-gyn. (assoc. examiner 1984-86), Sub-Bd. Maternal-Fetal Medicine. Intern Barnes Hosp., Washington U., St. Louis, 1966—67, resident in ob-gyn., 1967—70, asst. in ob-gyn., 1966—70, rsch. asst., 1967—68, instr. clin. ob-gyn., 1970; Buswell fellow in maternal fetal medicine Strong Meml. Hosp.-U. Rochester, 1972—73; fellow in maternal-fetal medicine Cleve. Met. Gen. Hosp.-Case Western Res. U., 1974—75, assoc. obstetrician and gynecologist, 1973—83, asst. prof. ob-gyn., 1973—77; asst. program dir. Perinatal Clin. Rsch. Ctr., 1973—78, co-program dir., 1978—82, program dir., 1982—83, acting dir. obstetrics, 1974—75, co-dir., 1977—83, assoc. prof., 1977—81, prof., 1981—83, assoc. dir. dept. ob-gyn., 1981—83; prof. ob-gyn. Wayne State U., Detroit, 1983—2000, dist. prof. ob-gyn., 2000—, chmn. dept. ob-gyn., 1983—89, mem. grad. faculty dept. physiology, 1984—, interim dean Med. Sch., 1988—89, dean, 1989—99, pres. Fund for Med. Rsch. and Edn., 1988—99, interim dir. Applied Genomics Ctr., 2004—; chief ob-gyn. Hutzel Hosp., Detroit, 1983—89; interim chmn. med. bd. Detroit Med. Ctr., 1988—89, chmn. med. bd., 1989—99, sr. v.p. med. affairs, 1992—99, trustee, 1990—99; past pres. med. staff Cuyahoga County Hosps.; mem. profl. adv. bd. Educated Childbirth Inc., 1976—80; dir. C.S. Mott Ctr. for Human Growth and Devel., 1983—89, 1999—. Sr. obstet. cons. Symposia Medicus; cons. Grant Planning Task Force Robert Wood Johnson Found., Nat. Inst. Child Health and Human Devel., Nat. Inst. Alcohol Abuse and Alcoholism, Ctr. for Disease Control, NIH, Health Resources and Svcs. Adminstrn., Nat. Clearinghouse for Alcohol Info., APA; mem. alcohol psychosocial rsch. rev. com. at. Inst. Alcohol Abuse and Alcoholism, 1982-86; mem. ob-gyn. adv. panel U.S. Pharmacopial Conv., 1985-90, adv. com. on policy Am. Jour. Ob-gyn., 1999-2001, internat. adv. bd. Karmanos Cancer Inst., Detroit, Mich., 2002-04; mem. clin. rsch. task force Assn. Am. Med. Colls., 1998-2000; mem. WSU Faculty Devel. Coun., 2003—. Mem. internat. editl. bd. Israel Jour. Obstetrics and Gynecology; reviewer med. jours.; mem. editl. bd. Jour. Perinatal Medicine; editor-in-chief Interactions: Programs in Clinical Decision-Making, 1987-90; rschr. computer applications in perinatal medicine, alcohol-related birth defects, perinatal risk and neurobehavioral devel.; contbr. chpts. to books and articles to profl. jours. Mem. Pres.'s leadership coun. U. Rochester, 1976—80, permanent trustee, 1986—; mem. exec. com. bd. trustees Southeast Mich. Ctr. Med. Edn., 1987—2000; chmn. Friends of the Grand Theatre, 2005—; mem. rsch. adv. com. Wayne State U., 2005—; mem. fetal alcohol spectrum disorders prevention adv. com. CDC and Prevention, 2005—07, mem. sci. review group, 2007; bd. dirs. Am. U. Caribbean, 2001—, vice chair, 2007—, 2004; trustee Stratford Am., 2004—, pres., 2007—, Grand Theatre, London, Ont., Canada, 2007, bd. dirs., 2002—. Maj. M.C. USAF, 1970—72. Recipient 15 sci. rsch. awards, 1986—, Disting. Svc. award, Wayne State U. Mem.: APHA, ACOG (chmn. steering com. drug and alcohol abuse contract 1986—87, rep. ctr. for disease control & prevention task force 2000—07, editor-in-chief ACOG Update 2001—, Outstanding Dist. Svc. Excellence award 2006), NAS (Inst. of Medicine, com. to study fetal alcohol syndrome 1994—96), AMA, Am. Bd. Addiction Medicine, Soc. Maternal-Fetal Medicine Found. (found. bd. chmn. 2003—06, award for dedication and leadership 2007), Soc. Physicians Reproductive Choice and Health, World Assn. Perinatal Medicine, Internat. Soc. Computers in Obstetrics, Neonatology, Gynecology (v.p. 1987—89, pres. 1989—92), Soc. for euroscis. (Mich. chpt.), Am. Med. Soc. on Alcoholism and Other Drug Dependencies, Am.

Gynecol. and Obstet. Soc., Neurobehavioral Teratology Soc., Soc. Perinatal Obstetricians (pres.-elect 1987—88, pres. 1988—89, v.p., Achievement award 1995), Rsch. Soc. Alcoholism, Ctrl. Assn. Obstetricians-Gynecologists (pres.-elect 1997—99, pres. 1999—2000), Detroit Acad. Medicine (pres.-elect 1999—2001, pres. 2001—02), Wayne County Med. Soc., Mich. Med. Soc., Royal Soc. Medicine, Assn. Profs. Ob-gyn., Perinatal Rsch. Soc., Soc. Gynecologic Investigation, Am. Med. Informatics Assn., Chgo. Gynecol. Soc. (hon.), Detroit Physiol. Soc. (hon.), Wayne State U. Acad. Scholars (pres. 2006—07), Alpha Omega Alpha, Sigma Xi, Phi Beta Kappa. Republican. Jewish. Home: 7921 Danbury Dr West Bloomfield MI 48322-3581 Office: Wayne State U CS Mott Ctr for Human Growth and Devel Detroit MI 48201 Home Phone: 248-851-5048; Office Phone: 313-577-1337. Business E-Mail: rsokol@moose.med.wayne.edu.

SOKOLOFF, STEPHEN PAUL, lawyer; b. Mt. Kisco, NY, July 27, 1953; s. Martin A. and Vivienne A. (Albam) S.; m. Amy H. Newberry, May 28, 1976 (div. 1980); m. Freddi Diann Killebrew, Sept. 3, 1981. BA, Pace U., 1978; JD, U. Mo., 1979. Bar: Mo. 1979, U.S. Tax Ct. 1981, U.S. Dist. Ct. (ea. dist.) Mo. 1985. Asst. pros. atty. Dunklin County, Kennett, Mo., 1979-84; assoc. Law Office of Stephen R. Sharp, Kennett, 1979-84; ptnr. Hilfiker & Sokoloff, Malden, Mo., 1984-87, Sharp & Sokoloff, Kennett, Mo., 1987-90, Sokoloff & Tinsley, Kennett, 1991—. City atty. City of Kennett, 1987-91, City of Clarkton (Mo.), 1986—, City of Holcomb (Mo.), 1989—; pros. atty. Dunkin County, 1990—; treas. Delmo Housing Corp., Lilbourn, Mo., 1986—; instr. bus. law S.E. Mo. State U., Cape Girardeau, 1980-82; mem. U. Mo. Bd. Advocates; spl. asst. U.S. atty. Ea. Dist. Mo., 1991—. Contbg. author: Missouri Criminal Law Enforcement Handbook, 1978. Trustee, Dunklin County Youth Devel. Project, Kennett, 1985-88; pres. Dunklin County Probation Community Adv. Bd., Kennett, 1985-86. Mem. ABA, Assn. Trial Lawyers Am., Mo. Assn. Trial Attys., Dunklin County Bar Assn. (sec.-treas. 1988—), Nat. Dist. Attys. Assn., Mo. Assn. Pros. Attys. (chair edn. com. 1990), Semo Little Theater Inc. (pres., bd. dirs. 1988—), Kennett Country Club, Kennett Optimist Club (pres. 1988-90), Eagles, Phi Delta Phi. Avocations: painting, bonsai, cooking, golf, art collecting. Home: 301 N Everett St Kennett MO 63857-1872 Office: Sokoloff & Tinsley Donklin County Courtho Kennett MO 63857

SOKOLOV, RICHARD SAUL, real estate company executive; b. Phila., Dec. 7, 1949; s. Morris and Estelle Rita S.; m. Susan Barbara Saltzman, Aug. 13, 1972; children: Lisa, Anne, Kate. BA, Pa. State U., 1971; JD, Georgetown U., 1974. Assoc. Weinberg & Green, Balt., 1974-80, ptnr., 1980-82; v.p., gen. counsel The Edward J. DeBartolo Corp., Youngstown, Ohio, 1982-86, sr. v.p. devel., gen. coun., 1986-94; pres., CEO DeBartolo Realty Corp., Youngstown, Ohio, 1994-96; pres., COO Simon DeBartolo Group, Indpls., 1996-98; pres, COO Simon Property Group, Indpls., 1998—. Mem. investment com. Jewish Fedn., Youngstown, 1992—; trustee U. Wis.-Madison Ctr. for Urban Land Econs. Rsch., Youngstown/Mahoning Valley United Way. Alumni fellow Pa. State U., 2000. Mem. Internat. Coun. Shopping Ctrs. (trustee 1994—, chmn. 1998-99), Urban Land Inst. (assoc.). Office: Simon Property Group 115 W Washington St Ste 1465 Indianapolis IN 46204-3464

SOLAND, NORMAN R., corporate lawyer; b. Duluth, Minn., Oct. 17, 1940; m. Carol A. Isaacson, Aug. 29, 1964; children: Kirk, Lisa, Kari, Chad. BA, U. Minn., 1963; JD, Am. Univ., 1972. Bar: Minn. 1973. Analyst CIA, 1963-73; assoc. Thompson, Hessian, Fletcher, McKay & Soderberg, Thompson, Fletcher, Stone & Morse, 1973-79; corp. counsel Nash-Finch Co., Mpls., 1979-84, asst. sec., counsel, 1984-86, sec., gen counsel, 1986-88, v.p., sec. & gen. counsel, 1988-98, sr. v.p., sec., gen. counsel, 1998—. Mem. ABA, Minn. State Bar Assn., Hennepin County Bar Assn., Am. Corp. Counsel Assn. Office: Nash Finch Co PO Box 355 Minneapolis MN 55440-0355

SOLARO, ROSS JOHN, physiologist, biophysicist; b. Wadsworth, Ohio, Jan. 9, 1942; s. Ross and Lena (Chuppa) S.; m. Kathleen Marie Cole, Sept. 18, 1965; children: Christopher, Elizabeth. BS, U. Cin., 1965; PhD, U. Pitts., 1971. Asst. prof. Med. Coll. Va., Richmond, 1973-77; assoc. prof. pharmacology and physiology U. Cin., 1977-81, prof. pharmacology and cell biophysics, 1981-85, prof. physiology, 1981-88; prof. physiology, head U. Ill., Chgo., 1988—, disting. univ. prof., 1998—. Sec. gen. Internat. Soc. Heart Rsch., 1989-93, sec./treas., 1995-98, pres., 1999, assoc. chair dept. physiology; chmn. exptl. cardiovasc. study sect. NIH, 1990-92; vice-chmn. physiology U. Cin., 1987-88. Editor: Protein Phosphorylation in Heart Muscle, 1986, Handbook of Physiology: The Heart, 2001; co-editor Handbook of Physiology: The Heart, 2001; contbr. articles to profl. jours. including Nature, Jour. Biol. Chemistry, Circulation Rsch. Chmn. rsch. coun. Am. Heart Assn., Met. Chgo., 1990-92. Grantee NIH, 1977—, Fogarty fellow, 1986; Brit. Am. Heart fellow Am. Heart Assn., 1974-75; Sr. Internat. fellow U. Coll. London, 1987. Mem. Am. Physiol. Soc. (chmn. subgroup), Am. Soc. Pharm. Exptl. Therapeutics, Biophys. Soc. (chmn. subgroup 1983-84). Office: U Ill at Chgo MC901 Physiology & Biophysics 835 S Wolcott Ave Chicago IL 60612-7340 Business E-Mail: solarorj@uic.edu.

SOLBERG, ELIZABETH TRANSOU, public relations executive; b. Dallas, Aug. 10, 1939; d. Ross W. and Josephine V. (Perkins) Transou; m. Frederick M. Solberg Jr., Mar. 8, 1969; 1 son, Frederick W. BJ, U. Mo., 1961. Reporter Kansas City (Mo.) Star, 1963-70, asst. city editor, 1970-73; reporter spl. events, documentaries Sta. WDAF-TV, Kansas City, Mo., 1973-74; prof. dept. journalism Park Coll., Kansas City, Mo., 1975-76, advisor, 1976-79; mng. ptnr. Fleishman-Hillard Inc., Kansas City, Mo., then exec. v.p., sr. ptnr., gen. mgr. Kansas City br., now regional pres., sr. ptnr.; pres. Fleishman-Hillard/Can., 1994—99. Mem. Kansas City Commn. Planned Indsl. Expansion Authority, 1974-91; bd. dirs. Ferrellgas, Midwest Airlines. Mem. long range planning com. Heart of Am. coun. Boy Scouts Am., 1980-82, bd. dirs., 1986-89; mem. Clay County (Mo.) Devel. Commn., 1979-88; bd. govs. Citizens Assn., 1975—; mem. exec. com. bd. Kansas City Area Devel. Coun., 1989-96, co-chair, 1991-93; trustee Pembroke Hill Sch., 1987-93, U. Kansas City, 1990-2002, exec. com., 1992-2002, Midwest Rsch. Inst., 1995-2002; bd. dirs. Greater Kansas City Cmty. Found. and Affiliated Trusts, 1996-2005, Starlight Theatre, 1996-2002, Union Sta. Bd., 1998-2002, Mo. Devel. Fin. Bd., 2000—, chair, 2003—; regent Rockhurst Coll., 1984-96; active Bus. Coun., Nelson Gallery Found., Nelson-Atkins Mus. Art, 1990—; bd. dirs. Civic Coun. Greater Kansas City, 1992—, chair civic coun., 2003-2005; mem. Jr. League Kansas City. Recipient award for contbn. to mental health Mo. Psychiat. Assn., 1973, Arthur E. Lowell award for excellence in orgn. comm. Kansas City/IABC, 1985, Kansas City Spirit award Gillis Ctr., 1994. Mem. Pub. Rels. Soc. Am. (nat. honors and awards com., co-chmn. SilverAnvil com. 1983, Silver Anvil award 1979-82, chair nat. membership com. 1989-91, assembly del.-at-large 1995-96), Counselor's Acad. (exec. com. 1991-92), Mo. C. of C. Pub. Rels. Coun., Greater Kans. City C. of C. (chair 1994-95, bd. exec. com.), River Club, Carriage Club. Office: Fleishman Hillard Inc 2405 Grand Blvd Ste 700 Kansas City MO 64108-2522

SOLBERG, JAMES JOSEPH, industrial engineering educator; b. Toledo, May 27, 1942; s. Archie Norman and Margaret Jean (Olsen) S.; m. Elizabeth Alice Snow, May 28, 1966; children: Kirsten Kari, Margaret Elizabeth. BA, Harvard U., 1964; MA, MS, U. Mich., 1967, PhD, 1969. Asst. prof. U. Toledo, 1969-71; assoc. prof. Purdue U., West Lafayette, Ind., 1971-81, prof., 1981—, dir. engring. rsch. ctr., 1986—. Author: Operations Research, 1976 (Book of the Yr. 1977); contbr. over 100 articles to profl. jours. Mem. NAE, Inst. Indsl. Engrs. (Disting. Rsch. award 1982), Soc. Mfg. Engrs., AAAS. Achievements include invention of CAN-Q which is a method for predicting performance of manufacturing systems used by hundreds of companies. Office: Purdue U Sch Industrial Engineering West Lafayette IN 47907-1287

SOLBERG, KENNETH R., state legislator; b. Minot, ND, Jan. 10, 1940; m. Chris; children: Tom, Brad, Stacy. Mem. N.D. Senate from 7th dist., Bismark, 1991—; mem. judiciary, agr., transp., joint constn. rev. coms. N.D. Senate, mem. appropriations com. Owner, mgr. Rugby Livestock Sales, 1965—. Mem. Rugby City Coun., 1966-72; bd. dirs. Regional Selective Svc., 1980, Good Samaritan Hosp., 1981-87, pres., 1985-86, chmn. health found., 1988; alt. del. Nat. Rep. Conv., 1988. Recipient DSA award N.D. Jaycees, 1965. Mem. Eagles Club, Am. Legion, Stockmens Assn. (bd. dirs. 1985), Cattlemen's Assn., Rugby C. of C. Home: 207 Sunset Ln Rugby ND 58368-2510 Office: ND Senate State Capitol Bismarck ND 58505

SOLBERG, LOREN ALBIN, state legislator, secondary education educator; b. Blackduck, Minn., Nov. 3, 1941; s. Albin Andy and Mabel Ethel (Bergen) S.; m. Joan Maxine Olsen, Aug. 9, 1969; children: Sean, John, Previn, Kjirstin. BS, Bemidji State U., Minn., 1965, MS, 1974; MPA, Harvard U., 1990. Tchr. math. Ind. Sch. Dist. 316, Coleraine, Minn., 1965—; mem. Minn. Ho. of Reps., St. Paul, 1983—. Instr. math. Itasca C.C., Grand Rapids, Minn., 1981-83; instr. computer sci. Harvard U., Cambridge, Mass., 1988. Mayor City of Bovey, Minn., 1970-82. Democrat. Lutheran. Office: Minn Ho of Reps State Office Bldg Saint Paul MN 55155-0001

SOLBERG, WINTON UDELL, historian, educator; b. Aberdeen, SD, Jan. 11, 1922; s. Ole Alexander and Bertha Georgia (Tschappat) S.; m. Ruth Constance Walton, Nov. 8, 1952; children: Gail Elizabeth, Andrew Walton, Kristin Ruth. AB magna cum laude, U. S.D., 1943, LHD (hon.), 1987; student, Biarritz Am. U., France, 1946; A.M., Harvard, 1947, PhD, 1954. Instr., then asst. prof. social scis. U.S. Mil. Acad., 1951-54; instr., then asst. prof. history Yale U., 1954-58; fellow Pierson Coll., 1955-58, Morse fellow, 1958; James Wallace prof. history Macalester Coll., 1958-62; vis. prof. U. Ill., 1961-62, assoc. prof. history, 1962, prof., 1967—, chmn. dept. history, 1970-72. Rsch. fellow Ctr. Study History of Liberty in Am., Harvard U., 1962-63; rsch. scholar Henry E. Huntington Library, San Marino, Calif., 1959; dir. Coe Found. Am. Studies Inst., summers 1960-62; lectr., cons. Army War Coll., 1959-62; lectr. U.S. Command and Gen. Staff Sch., 1963-64; Fulbright lectr. Johns Hopkins U. Bologna, 1967-68, Moscow (USSR) State U., 1978, U. Calcutta India, 1993; vis. prof. Konan U., Kobe, Japan, 1981; USIA Lectr., Korea and Malaysia, 1985, Korea, 1992. Author: The Federal Convention and the Formation of the Union of the American States, 1958, The Constitutional Convention and the Formation of the Union, 1990, The University of Illinois, 1867-1894, An Intellectual and Cultural History, 1968, Redeem the Time: The Puritan Sabbath in Early America, 1977, History of American Thought and Culture, 1983, Cotton Mather, The Christian Philosopher, 1994, The University of Illinois, 1894-1904: The Shaping of the University, 2000, Reforming Medical Education:The University of Illinois, Coll. Medicine 1880-1920, 2008; also articles. Mem. Ill. Humanities Council, 1973-75; sec. Council on Study of Religion, 1981-85. Maj. inf. AUS, 1943-46, 51-54; lt. col. U.S. Army Res. Recipient Faculty Achievement award Burlington No. Found., 1986, Disting. Teaching award U. Ill. Coll. Liberal Arts and Scis., 1988; NEH sr. fellow, 1974-75; Rsch. grantee NSF, 1981-82 Mem. Am. Hist. Assn., So. Hist. Assn., Orgn. Am. Historians, Am. Studies Assn. (pres. Mid-Am. 1985-86), Am. Soc. Ch. History (pres. 1985-86), AAUP (chpt. pres. 1965-66, mem. council 1969-72, 1st v.p. 1974-76), Phi Beta Kappa. Episcopalian. Home: 8 Lake Park Rd Champaign IL 61822-7101 Office: U Ill History Dept Urbana IL 61801 Office Phone: 217-333-4193. Business E-Mail: wsolberg@uiuc.edu.

SOLGANIK, MARVIN, real estate executive; b. Chgo., Nov. 7, 1930; s. Harry and Dora (Fastoff) S.; m. Judith Rosenberg, Sept. 11, 1960; children: Randall, Janet, Robert. BBA, Case Western Res. U., 1952. Real estate broker, Cleve., 1950-65, Herbert Laronge Inc., Cleve., 1965-68; sr. v.p. real estate Revco D.S., Inc., Twinsburgh, Ohio, 1968—, corp. dir., 1974—. Adj. prof. Ohio No. U.; guest lectr. Cleve. State U., Case Western Res. U. Sch. Law, Cuyahoga C.C., Ohio o. U., Cleve. Real Estate Bd., CASE Sch. Law. Vol. jewish Welfare Fund, Shaker heights, Ohio; chmn. capital and budget coms. Jewish Fedn.; chmn. Agnon Sch. Bdlg. Com.; bd. dirs. Bellfair-J.C.B.-Home for Emotionally Disturbed Children, Visconsi Cos, Cleve. Inst. Music. Recipient Appreciation award Am. Soc. Real Estate Appraisers, Akron-Cleve. chpt., 1971 Mem. Nat. Assn. Corp. Real Estate Officers, Internat. Council Shopping Ctrs. Office: D S Revco 22925 Holmwood Rd Shaker Heights OH 44122-3005

SOLICH, FRANK, coach; b. Cleve., Sept. 8, 1944; s. Frank Solich Sr.; m. Pamela Solich; children: Cindy, Jeff. BS, U. Nebr., 1966, MEd, 1972. Coach football, runningbacks U. Nebr., Lincoln, head coach football, freshman, head coach football. Office: U Nebr 221 S Stadium Lincoln NE 68588

SOLL, BRUCE A., retail executive; Degree in Econs. and Polit. Sci., Claremont McKenna Coll., 1979; degree in Law, So. Calif. Law Sch., 1982. Bar: Calif. Former counsel US Sec. Commerce; sr. v.p., counsel Ltd. Brands, Columbus, Ohio, 1991—. Mem. Ohio Bicentennial Commn.; bd. dirs. Columbus Symphony Orch., Ohio State U. Wexner Ctr. Found. Office: Ltd Brands Three Ltd Pkwy Columbus OH 43230

SOLLARS, FRANK B., automobile insurance company executive; Chmn., dir. Nationwide Mut. Ins. Co., Columbus, Ohio.

SOLOMON, DAVID EUGENE, engineering company executive; b. Milton, Pa., June 22, 1931; s. Oren Benjamin and Bernardine Claire Solomon; m. Joyce Marie Hoffman, June 24, 1950; children: Timothy, Melissa, Daniel. AB, Susquehanna U., 1958; MS, Bucknell U., 1960; MBA, Ea. Mich. U., 1974. Sr. engr. Westinghouse Electric Corp., Balt., 1959-65; rsch. engr. U. Mich., 1965-67; chief engr. Electro-Optics divsn. Bendix Corp., 1967-72; v.p. ops. KMS Fusion, Inc., Ann Arbor, Mich., 1972-85; pres., CEO Solohill Engring. Inc., 1985—. Bd. dirs. Ann Arbor Engring. Inc., SoloHill Labs. Inc. Patentee in field. With USN, 1950-55. Fellow IEEE. Office: 4220 Varsity Dr Ann Arbor MI 48108-2241 E-mail: solomon@ic.net.

SOLOMON, RANDALL LEE, lawyer; b. Dayton, Ohio, June 8, 1948; BA summa cum laude, Wright State U., 1970; JD, Case Western Res. U., 1973. Bar: Ohio 1973, U.S. Dist. Ct. (no. dist.) Ohio 1973, U.S. Ct. Appeals (6th cir.) 1973, U.S. Ct. Appeals (fed. cir.) 1988, U.S. Supreme Ct. 2002. Ptnr. Baker & Hostetler, Cleve. Life mem. Sixth Circuit Jud. Conf., Eighth Dist. Jud. Conf., Ohio; speaker in field. Fellow Am. Coll. Trial Lawyers; mem. ABA (mem. litigation, tort and ins. practice sects.), Ohio State Bar Assn., Cleve. Bar Assn. (chair litig. sect. 1991-92), Nat. Inst. Trial Advocacy (mem. nat. session 1978), Def. Rsch. Inst., Anthony J. Celebrezze Inn. of Ct. (master). Office: Baker & Hostetler LLP 3200 Nat City Ctr 1900 E 9th St Ste 3200 Cleveland OH 44114-3475 Office Phone: 216-861-7327. Business E-Mail: rsolomon@bakerlaw.com.

SOLOMON, RAYMAN LOUIS, dean, law educator; b. Helena, Ark., June 5, 1947; s. David and Miriam (Rayman) S.; m. Carol Avins, Aug. 10, 1975. BA, Wesleyan U., 1968; MA in History, U. Chgo., 1972, JD, 1976, PhD in History, 1986. Bar: Ill. 1976, U.S. Ct. Appeals (7th cir.) 1978, U.S. Ct. Appeals (6th cir.) 1979. Dir. court history project U.S. Ct. Appeals (7th cir.), Chgo., 1976-78; law clk. to presiding judge U.S. Ct. Appeals (6th cir.), Cin., 1978-79; Bigelow fellow instr. U. Chgo. Law Sch., 1979-80; research fellow Am. Bar Found., Chgo., 1980-89, assoc. dir., 1986-89; assoc. dean Northwestern U. Sch. Law, Chgo., 1989—98; prof. law Rutgers U. Sch. Law, Camden, NJ, 1998—, dean, 1998—. Instr. Kent-Ill. Inst. Tech. Coll. Law, Chgo. 1982, Northwestern U., Evanston, Ill. 1986. Author: History of the Seventh Circuit, 1981; editor Am. Bar Found. Research Jour., 1985-87. Bd. dirs. Family Counseling Svc. of Evanston, 1985—, BPI, 1990—. Served with USN, 1969-70. Mem. ABA, Law and Soc. Assn., Selden Soc., Am. Soc. Legal Hist. (bd. dirs. 1985-88). Democrat. Jewish. Office: Rutgers State U Sch Law 217 North Fifth St Camden NJ 08102 Office Phone: 856-225-6191. Office Fax: 856-225-6487. E-mail: raysol@camlaw.rutgers.edu.

SOLOMON, WAYNE C., aerospace engineer, educator; BS in Chemistry, U. Idaho, 1956; PhD in Chemistry, U. Oreg., 1963. Staff scientist Air Force Rocket Propulsion, Edwards, Calif., 1963—67; vis. prof. U. Goettingen Inst. Phys. Chemistry, Germany, 1967—69; chief kinetics and thermodynamics Air Force Astronautics Lab., Edwards, 1969—73; dir. high energy laser tech. Bell Aerospace Textron, Wheatfield, NY, 1973—80, dir. advanced tech., 1980—82, progs. dir. prototype laser systems, 1982—86, dir. engring. for advanced systems, 1987—88; prof. aero. and astronautical engring. U. Ill. Urbana-Champaign, 1988—, head aero. and astronautical engring. dept., 1988—99, dir. Ill. Space Grant Consortium, 1991—; pres. CU Aerospace, 1998—. Contbr. articles to sci. jours. Fellow: AIAA. Office: U Ill Dept Aerospace Engring 306 Talbot Lab 104 S Wright St Urbana IL 61801 Office Phone: 217-244-7646. E-mail: wsolomon@uiuc.edu.

SOLOSKI, JOHN, journalism and communications educator; AB cum laude, Boston Coll., 1974; MA in Journalism, U. Iowa, 1976, PhD, 1978. Copy editor, reporter Iowa City Press Citizen, 1977-78; instr. Univ. Iowa, 1977-78, asst. prof. sch. journalism and mass communication, 1978-84, assoc. prof. sch. journalism and mass communication, 1984-85, assoc. prof., head of grad. studies, 1985-92, prof., head of grad. studies, 1992-94, prof., acting dir., 1994-95, prof. sch. of journalism and mass communication, 1995-96, prof., dir. sch. of journalism and mass communication, 1996—, prof. law, 1996—2001; dean Grady Coll. Journalism and Mass Comm. U. Ga., 2001—04, prof. Grady Coll. Journalism and Mass Comm., 2004—. Con. Ottumwa Courier, 1976-77, Iowa City Press-Citizen, 1976-77; speaker in field; vis. prof. Univ. Tech., Sydney, Australia, 1995. Co-author: Reforming Libel Law, 1992, Libel and the Press: Myth and Reality, 1987, Taking Stock: Journalism nad the Publicly Traded Newspaper Company, 2001; contbr. numerous articles to profl. jours.; editor: Journalism and Communication Monographs, 1994—. Recipient Soc. of Profl. Journalists Disting. Svc. award, 1988; numerous rsch. grants. Mem.: Assn. Schs. Journalism and Mass Comm. (pres. 2003—04). Office: Henry W Grady College of Journalism and Mass Communication The University of Georgia Athens GA 30602-3018 Office Phone: 706-542-1704. Business E-Mail: jsoloski@uga.edu.

SOLOVY, JEROLD SHERWIN, lawyer; b. Chgo., Apr. 10, 1930; s. David and Ida (Wilensky) S.; m. Kathleen Hart; children: Stephen, Jonathan. BA with honors, U. Mich., 1952; LLB cum laude, Harvard U., 1955. Bar: Ill. 1955, DC 1955. Mem. bd. of editors Harvard Law Review, 1953—55; mem. visiting com. Harvard Law Sch., 1986—92; mem. Harvard Com. U. Resources, 1993—98; assoc. Jenner & Block LLP, Chgo., 1955-63, ptnr., 1963—, chmn., 1991—2997, chmn. emeritus, 2007—. Chmn. Spl. Commn. on Adminstrn. Justice in Cook County, 1984-91, Ill. Supreme Ct. Spl. Commn. on Adminstrn. of Justice, 1992-93, Criminal Justice Project of Cook County, 1987-91. Mem. Cook County Jud. Adv. Council, Chgo., 1975-77, 82-89, chmn., 1989-91; trustee U.S. Supreme Ct. Hist. Soc., 1993—. Named one of 100 Most Influential Lawyers, Nat. Law Jour., 1991, 1994, 1997, 2000, 2006, 500 Leading Leading Lawyers in Am., Lawdragon Mag., 2005, 2006, 500 Leading Litigators in Am., 2006; recipient Pro Bono Award, Seventh Cir. Bar Assn., 1993, Professionalism Award, Am. Inns of Ct., 2004, Lifetime Achievement Award, Decalogue Soc. of Lawyers, 2004, John Minor Wisdom Pub. Svc. and Professionalism Award, Am. Bar Assn., 2005, Lifetime Achievement award, The Am. Lawyer mag., 2007. Fellow Am. Coll. Trial Lawyers; mem. ABA, Chgo. Bar Assn., Ill. State Bar. Assn., Am. Law Inst. Clubs: Standard; Lake Shore Country (Chgo.), Phi Eta Sigma, Phi Kappa Phi, Phi Beta Kappa, Pi Sigma Alpha. Office: Jenner & Block 330 N Wabash Avenue Chicago IL 60611-7603 E-mail: jsolovy@jenner.com.

SOLOW, MICHAEL BARRY, lawyer; b. Chgo., Jan. 6, 1959; s. Gilbert and Eunice (Eres) S.; m. Dale Susan Weinbaum, Aug. 21, 1983; children: Corey Francis, Andrew Wenbaum. AB summa cum laude, U. Ill., 1981; JD, Harvard U., 1984. Bar: Ill. 1984, NY 2003, U.S. Dist. Ct. (no. dist.) Ill. 1984, U.S. Dist. Ct. (no. dist.) Tex. 1987, U.S. Dist. Ct. Ariz. 1991, U.S. Dist. Ct. (we. dist.) Mich. 2003, U.S. Dist. Ct. (so. dist.) NY 2004, U.S. Ct. Appeals (7th cir.) 1984, U.S. Ct. Appeals (8th cir.) 1992, U.S. Ct. Appeals (4th cir.) 1993, U.S. Ct. Appeals (6th cir.) 1997, U.S. Supreme Ct. 1993. Law clk. to presiding justice Ill. Supreme Ct., 1984-85; assoc. Hopkins and Sutter, Chgo., 1985-90, ptnr., 1990—2001; ptnr., co-chair Bus. Reorganization and Creditors' Rights Dept., mem. Exec. Com. Kaye Scholer LLP, Chgo., NYC, 2001—. Mem. ABA, Chgo. Bar Assn., Phi Beta Kappa. Office: Kaye Scholer LLP 3 First Nat Plaza, Ste 4100 70 West Madison St Chicago IL 60602 also: 425 Park Ave New York NY 10022 Home Phone: 847-940-7691; Office Phone: 312-583-2310, 212-836-7240. Business E-Mail: msolow@kayescholer.com.

SOLOWAY, ALBERT HERMAN, medicinal chemist; b. Worcester, Mass., May 29, 1925; s. Bernard and Mollie (Raphaelson) S.; m. Barbara Berkowicz, Nov. 29, 1953; children: Madeleine Rae, Paul Daniel, Renee Ellen. Student, U.S. Naval Acad., 1945-46; BS, Worcester Poly. Inst., 1948; PhD, U. Rochester, 1951. Postdoctoral fellow at. Cancer Inst. at Sloan-Kettering Inst., NYC, 1951-53; research chemist Eastman Kodak Co., Rochester, NY, 1953-56; asst. chemist Mass. Gen. Hosp., Boston, 1956-61, asso. chemist, 1961-73; asso. prof. med. chemistry Northeastern U., Boston, 1966-68, prof. medicinal chemistry, chmn. dept., 1968-71, prof. medicinal chemistry and chemistry, chmn. dept. medicinal chemistry and pharmacology, 1971-74; dean Coll. Pharmacy and Allied Health Professions, 1975-77; dean Coll. Pharmacy Ohio State U., Columbus, 1977-88, prof. medicinal chemistry, 1977-98, Kimberly prof. pharmacy, 1997-2000, dean, prof. emeritus, 1998—. Author rsch. in medicinal chemistry, boron neutron capture therapy of cancer. Recipient Disting. Achievements in Boron Sci. award, Boron USA, 1994. Fellow AAAS, Acad. Pharm. Soc.; mem. AHS (50 Yr. mem.), Am. Chem. Soc., Am. Assn. Coll. Pharmacy, Am. Assn. Cancer Rsch., Torch Club Columbus (pres. 2004-05) Office: Ohio State U 500 W 12th Ave Columbus OH 43210-1214 Business E-Mail: soloway.1@osu.edu.

SOLSO, THEODORE M., manufacturing executive; m. Denny; 3 children. BA, DePauw U., 1969; MBA, Harvard U., 1971. Asst. to v.p. personnel Cummins Engine Co., Inc., Columbus, Ind., 1971—72; employment dir. Holset Engring. Co., Ltd. (Cummins' U.K. subs.), Columbus, 1972—74, dir. devel. & tng., 1974—77; exec. dir. personnel Cummins Engine Co., Inc., Columbus, 1977-80; v.p., mng. dir. Holset Engring. Co., Ltd. (Cummins' U.K. subs.), 1980-84; v.p. spl. engine markets Cummins Engine Co., Inc., Columbus, 1984-86, v.p. mktg., 1986-88, v.p., gen. mgr. engine bus., 1988-92, exec. v.p. opers., 1992—94, exec. v.p. & COO, 1994—95, pres. & COO, 1995-00, chmn., CEO, 2000—. Bd. dirs. Ashland, Inc., Cyprus Amax Minerals, Inc. Bd. trustees DePauw U.; bd. advisors U. Mich. Sch. Bus.; past bd. dirs. Heritage Fund Bartholomew County, Ind.; chmn. campaign Bartholomew County United Way; bd. dirs. Otter Creek Golf Course, Columbus, Ind. Mem. Mfrs. Alliance (bd. trustees). Office: Cummins Inc 500 Jackson St Columbus IN 47201*

SOMER, THOMAS JOSEPH (T.J. SOMER), lawyer; b. Chicago Heights, Oct. 13, 1953; m. Cynthia Flamini; 2 children. BA, Nat. Louis U., 1987; JD, John Marshall Law Sch., 1991. Republican candidate for U.S. House, 2d dist., Ill., 1996. Roman Catholic.

SOMMER, ANNEMARIE, pediatrician; b. Königsberg, Prussia, Federal Republic Germany, Jan. 1, 1932; came to U.S., 1955; d. Heinrich Otto and Maria Magdalena (Kruppa) S. BA, Wittenberg U., Springfield, Ohio, 1960; MD, Ohio State U., 1964. Diplomate Am. Bd. Pediat., Am. Bd. Med. Genetics. Intern Grant Hosp., Columbus, Ohio, 1964-65; resident in pediat. Children's Hosp., Columbus, 1965-67; NIH fellow in med. genetics, 1968-70; from asst. prof. pediatrics to assoc. prof. Coll. Medicine Ohio State U., Columbus, 1975-97, prof., 1997-99, chief genetics div., 1984-98. Mem. adv. bd. Heinzerling Found., Columbus, 1980—; bd. dirs. Regional Genetics Ctr., Columbus. Contbr. articles to profl. jours. Com. mem. Ohio Prevention MR/DD Coalition, Columbus, 1987; bd. dirs. Franklin County Bd. Health, Columbus, 1985—. Fellow Am. Acad. Pediatrics, Am. Bd. Med. Genetics, Am. Coll. Med. Genetics (founder); mem. Ctrl. Ohio Pediatric Soc., Midwest Soc. for Pediatric Research, Dublin (Ohio) Hist. Soc. Lutheran. Home: 4700 Brand Rd Dublin OH 43017-9530 Office: Ohio State Coll Medicine Sect Human and Molecular Genetics 700 Childrens Dr Columbus OH 43205-2664

SOMMERS, DAVID LYNN, architect; b. Salem, Ohio, June 17, 1949; s. Carl Ervin and Jean (Mohr) S. BArch, Kent State U., 1974. Registered architect, Ohio. Designer, draftsman Rice & Stewart, Architects, Painesville, Ohio, 1974-76; assoc. architect Prentiss Brown Assoc., Kent, Ohio, 1977-81; project architect Edward W. Prusak, Assoc., Ravenna, Ohio, 1982-83; pvt. practice Kent, 1983—. Mem. archtl. adv. com. Kent Planning Commn., 1985—; mem. Franklin Twp. Bd. Zoning Appeals; bd. bldg. appeals, City of Kent Bldg. Dept.; bd. dirs. Townhall II Drug and Crisis Intervention Ctr., Kent, 1986-92, 2001—. Named one of Outstanding Young Men of Am., 1979-81. Mem. AIA (pres. Akron chpt. 1991—), Archs. Soc. Ohio, Jaycees (pres. Kent chpt. 1981-82, Jaycee of Yr. 1980, Keyman of Yr. 1981), Rotary (bd. dirs. 1994-96). Office: 136 N Water St # 208 Kent OH 44240-2450

SOMMESE, ANDREW JOHN, mathematics professor; b. NYC, May 1948; s. Joseph and Frances S.; m. Rebecca Rooze DeBoer, June 7, 1971; children: Rachel, Ruth. BA in Math., Fordham U., 1969; PhD in Math., Princeton U., 1973. Gibbs instr. Yale U., New Haven, 1973-75; asst. prof. Cornell U., Ithaca, NY, 1975-79; assoc. prof. U. otre Dame, Ind., 1979-83, prof. of math. Ind., 1983—, chair dept. math. Ind., 1988-92, Vincent J. Duncan and Annamarie Micus Duncan chair math. Ind., 1994—, dir. Ctr. Applied Math. Ind., 2005—. Mem. Inst. for Advanced Study, Princeton, N.J., 1975-76; guest prof. U. Bonn, Germany, 1978-79; guest rschr. Max Planck Inst. for Math., Bonn, 1992-93; cons. GM Rsch., Warren, Mich., 1986-97. Editor: Manuscripta Mathematica jour., 1986-93, Advances in Geometry, 2000;mem. editl. bd. Milan Jour. Math., 2002; contbr. articles to profl. publs. Recipient Rsch. award for Sr. U.S. Scientists, Alexander Von Humboldt Found., 1993; A.P. Sloan Found. rsch. fellow, 1979. Mem. Am. Math. Soc., Soc. for Indsl. and Applied Math., Phi Beta Kappa. Office: U Notre Dame Dept Math otre Dame IN 46556

SONDEL, PAUL MARK, pediatric oncologist, educator; b. Milw., Aug. 14, 1950; s. Robert F. and Audrey J. (Dworkus) S.; m. Sherie Ann Katz, Jan. 1, 1973; children: Jesse Adam, Beth Leah, Elana Rose, Jodi Zipporah. BS with honors, U. Wis., Madison, 1971, PhD in Genetics, 1975; MD magna cum laude, Harvard Med. Sch., Boston, 1977. Diplomate Nat. Bd. Med. Examiners, Am. Bd. Pediatrics; lic. physician, Wis. Postdoctoral rsch. fellow Harvard Med. Sch., Boston, 1975-77; intern in pediatrics U. Minn. Hosp., Mpls., 1977-78; resident in pediatris U. Wis. Hosp. and Clinics, Madison, 1978-80; asst. prof. pediatrics, human oncology and genetics U. Wis., Madison, 1980-84, assoc. prof., 1984-86, prof. pediatrics, human oncology and genetics, 1987—, head divsn. pediatric hematology/oncology, program leader, 1990—; assoc. dir. U Wisc. Cancer Ctr., 1996-99, U. Wis. Cancer Ctr., 2006—; vice chair rsch. dept. pediatrics U. Wis., Madison, 2006—. Sub-fellow pediat. oncology; Midwest Children's Cancer Ctr., Milw., 1980; vis. scientist dept. cell biology Weizmann Inst. Sci., Rehovot, Israel, 1987, 2000; chmn. immunology com. Children's Cancer Group 1990-2001; cancer ctr. rev. com. Nat. Cancer Inst., 1997-2000, bd. sci. counselors, 2005— Sr. editor Clin. Cancer Rsch., 1996-99; mem. editl. bd. Jour. Immunology, 1985-87, Jour. Nat. Cancer Inst., 1987—, Jour. Biol. Response Modifiers, 1990—, BLOOD, 1992—, Natural Immunity, 1992—; contbr. articles to Jour. Exptl. Medicine, Jour. Immunology, Cellular Immunology, Immunol. Revs., Med. Pediatric Oncology, Wis. State Med. Jour., Jour. Biol. Response Modifiers, Jour. Pediatrics, Jour. Clin. Oncology, Jour. Clin. Investigation, others State of Wis. Regents scholar, 1968; J.A. and G.L. Hartford Found. fellow, 1981-84. Mem. Am. Assn. Immunologists, Am. Assn. Clin. Histocompatibility Typing, Am. Fedn. Clin. Rsch., Am. Soc. Pediatric Hematology/Oncology, Am. Assn. Cancer Rsch., Am. Soc. Transplant Physicians, Am. Soc. Clin. Oncology, Am. Acad. Pediatrics, Leukemia Soc. Am. (bd. dirs. Wis. chpt. 1987-90 Achievements include patent for Typing Leukocyte Antigens; research on clinical and immunological effects of human recombinant Interleukin-2 and monoclonal antibodies. Home: 1114 Winston Dr Madison WI 53711-3161 Office: U Wis K4/448 Clin Sci Ctr 600 Highland Ave Madison WI 53792-3284 Business E-Mail: pmsondel@humonc.wisc.edu.

SONDERBY, SUSAN PIERSON, federal bankruptcy judge; b. Chgo., May 15, 1947; d. George W. and Shirley L. (Eckstrom) Pierson; m. James A. De Witt, June 14, 1975 (dec. 1978); m. Peter R. Sonderby, Apr. 7, 1990. AA, Joliet Jr. Coll., Joliet, Ill., 1967; BA, U. Ill., 1969; JD, John Marshall Law Sch., 1973. Bar: Ill., 1973; U.S. Dist. Ct. (cen. and so. dists.) Ill., 1978,; U.S. Dist. Ct. (no. dist.) Ill., 1984; U.S. Ct. Appeals (7th Cir.), 1984. Assoc. O'Brien, Garrison, Berard, Kusta, and De Witt, Joliet, Ill., 1973-75, ptnr., 1975-77; asst. atty. gen. consumer protection div., litig. sect. Office of the Atty. Gen., Chgo., 1977-78, asst. atty. gen., chief consumer protection divsn. Springfield, Ill., 1978-83; U.S. trustee (no. dist.) Ill. Chgo., 1983-86; judge U.S. Bankruptcy Ct. (no. dist.) Ill., Chgo., 1986—, chief fed. bankruptcy judge, 1998—2002. Mem. law faculty Fed. Jud. Tng. Ctr., Ill., Practicing Law Inst., Ill., U.S. Dept. Justice, Ill., Nat. Bankruptcy Inst., Ill., Ill. Continuing Edn.; spl. asst. atty. gen., Ill., 1972—78; adj. faculty De Paul U. Coll. Law, Chgo., 1986; past mem. U.S. Trustee adv. com., Ill.; consumer adv. coun. Fed. Res. Bd., Ill.; past sec. of State Fraudulent I.D. com. Dept. of Ins. Task Force on Improper Claims Practices, Ill.; former chair pers. rev. bd., mem. task force race and gender bias, U.S. Dist. Ct.; jud. conf. planning com. 7th Cir. Jud. Conf.; former mem. Civil Justice Reform Act Adv. Com., Adminstrv. Office of the U.S. Cts. Bankruptcy Judges Adv. Group, Ct. Security com., Adminstrv. Office of the U.S. Cts. Budget and Fin. Coun. Contbr. articles to profl. jour. Mem. Fourth Presbyn. Ch., Art Inst. Chgo.; past mem. Westminster Presbyn. Ch., Chgo. Coun. of Fgn. Rels.; past bd. dirs. Land of Lincoln Coun. Girl Scouts U.S.; past mem. individual guarantors com. Goodman Theatre, Chgo.; past chair clubs and orgns. Sangamon County United Way Capital campaign; past bd. dirs., chair house rules com. and legal subcom. Lake Point Tower; past mem. Family Svc. Ctr., Aid to Retarded Citizens, Henson Robinson Zoo. Named Young Career Woman, Bus. and Profl. Women, One of Ten Outstanding Bankruptcy Judges, Turnarounds and Workouts, 2002; named one of 500 Leading Judges in Am., Law Dragon mag., 2006; recipient Spl. Achievement Award, Dept. Justice, 1984, Disting. Svc. Alumni Award, Joliet Jr. Coll., 1987, Disting. Alumni Award, John Marshall Law Sch., 1988, Dir. Award, Exec. Office U.S. Trustee, Leadership Award, Internat. Orgn. Women Exec., Outstanding Svc. to Bench, Am. Bankruptcy Inst., 1990. Master: Abraham Lincoln Marovitz Inn of Ct. (former pres., membership com.); fellow: Am. Coll. Bankruptcy (circuit admissions com.); mem.: ATLA, Comml. Law League Am. (former exec. coun. mem., bankruptcy and insolvency sect., coord. with nat. conf. bankruptcy judges com.), Nat. Conf. Bankruptcy Judges (co-chair edn. program com. conf. 2001, liaison with bankruptcy rev. commn. com.), Bar Assn. (7th cir.) (former treas., judicial conf. planning com.), Am. Bankruptcy Inst. (bd. dirs. Chgo. chpt.), Fed. Bar Assn., Chgo. Archtl. Found., John Marshall Law Sch. Alumni Assn. (bd. dirs.), Nordic Law Club (past legis. com.), Lawyers Club Chgo. (hon.). Avocations: travel, flying, interior decorating. Office: US Bankruptcy Ct 219 S Dearborn St Ste 638 Chicago IL 60604-1702

SONG, DAVID, plastic surgeon, medical educator; b. 1970; MD, UCLA. Cert. Plastic Surgery. Surg. resident Univ. Chgo. Hospitals, plastic surgeon, chief plastic surgeon, 2004—. Spkr. in field; bd. mem. Med. Aid for Children of Latin Am. Contbr. articles to numerous profl. jours. Med. Aid for Children Latin Am. Named one of 40 Under Forty, Crain's Bus. Chgo., 2005. Mem.: Am. Coll. Plastic Surgeons, Am. Coll. Surgeons. Office: Univ Chgo Hosps MC 6035 5841 S Maryland Ave Chicago IL 60637 Office Phone: 773-702-6302. Office Fax: 773-702-1634. E-mail: dsong@surgery.bsd.uchicago.edu.

SONNEDECKER, GLENN ALLEN, pharmaceutical historian, educator; b. Creston, Ohio, Dec. 11, 1917; s. Ira Elmer and Leta (Linter) S.; m. Cleo Bell, Apr. 3, 1943; 1 child, Stuart Bruce. BS, Ohio State U., 1942, DSc honoris causa, 1964; MS, U Wis., 1950, PhD, 1952; DSc honoris causa, Phila. Coll. Pharmacy and Sci., 1989; PharmD honoris causa, Mass. Coll. Pharmacy, 1974. Lic. pharmacist. Mem. editorial staff Sci. Service, Washington, 1942-43; editor Jour. Am. Pharm. Assn. (practical pharmacy edit.), Washington, 1943-48; asst. prof. U. Wis., 1952-56, asso. prof., 1956-60, prof., 1960-81, Edward Kremers prof., 1981-86; sec. Am. Inst. History of Pharmacy, 1949-57, dir., 1957-73, 81-85, hon. dir. life, chmn. bd., 1988-89; editor-in-chief RPh, 1978-80. Sec., bd. dirs. Friends of Hist. Pharmacy, 1945-49; chmn. Joint Com. on Pharmacy Coll. Librs., 1960-61; US del. Internat. Pharm. Fedn., 1953, 55, 62; US rep. to Mid. East Pharm. Congress, Beirut, 1956; sec. sect. history of pharmacy and biochemistry Pan-Am. Congress Pharmacy and Biochemistry, 1957. Co-author books; contbr. to pharm. and hist. publs. Recipient Edward Kremers award (for writings), 1964, Nat. award Rho Chi, 1967, Schelenz plaquette Internat. Soc. for History of Pharmacy, 1971, Remington honor medal Am. Pharm. Assn., 1972, Urdang medal, 1976, Folch Andreu prize, Spain, 1985, Profile award Am. Found. Pharm. Edn., 1994; Am. Found. fellow, 1948-52, Guggenheim fellow, 1955, Fulbright Rsch. scholar, Germany, 1955-56. Mem. Am. Pharm. Assn. (life; sec. sect. history of pharmacy 1949-50, vice chmn. 1950-51, chmn. 1951-52, rsch. assoc. 1964-65, chmn. joint task force with Acad. Pharm Scis. 1985, hon. chmn. bd. trustees 1985), Internat. Acad. History Pharmacy (1st v.p. 1970-81, pres. 1983-91, hon. pres. 1991—), Am. Assn. History of Medicine (exec. coun. 1966-69), Internat. Gesellschaft fur Geschichte der Pharmazie (exec. bd. 1965-89), hon. mem. socs. for history of pharmacy of Italy, Benelux, pan-Arab, Spain; mem. Sigma Xi, Rho Chi (mem. nat. exec. coun. 1957-59), Phi Delta Chi. Unitarian. Home: 2030 Chadbourne Ave Madison WI 53726-4047

SONNENSCHEIN, HUGO FREUND, academic administrator, writer, economist, educator; b. NYC, Nov. 14, 1940; s. Leo William and Lillian Silver Sonnenschein; m. Elizabeth Gunn, Aug. 26, 1962; children: Leah, Amy, Rachel. AB, U. Rochester, 1961; MS, Purdue U., 1963, PhD, 1964, PhD (hon.), 1996; PhD (hon.), Tel Aviv U., 1993; D (hon.), U. Autonoma Barcelona, Spain, 1994; PhD (hon.), Lake Forest Coll., 1995, North Ctrl. Coll., 2001, U. Chgo., 2002. Faculty dept. econs. U. Minn., 1964—70, prof., 1968—70; prof. econs. U. Mass., Amherst, 1970—73, Northwestern U., 1973—76, Princeton (N.J.) U., 1976—87, Class of 1926 prof., 1987—88, provost, 1991—93; dean, Thomas S. Gates prof. U. Pa. Sch. Arts & Scis., Phila., 1988—91; pres. U. Chgo., 1993—2000, Hutchinson disting. prof., pres. emeritus, 2000—. Vis. prof. U. Andes, Columbia, 1965, Tel Aviv U., 1972, Hebrew U., 1973, U. Paris, 1978, U. Aix-en-Provence, France, 1978, Stanford U., 1984—85; bd. dirs. Van Kampen Mutual Funds. Editor: Econometrica, 1977—84; mem. editl. bd.: Jour. Econ. Theory, 1972—75, Jour. Math. Econs., 1974—, SIAM Jour., 1976—80; contbr. articles to profl. jours. Trustee U. Rochester, 1992—, U. Chgo., 1993—. Fellow, Social Sci. Rsch. Coun., 1967—68, NSF, 1970—, Ford Found., 1970—71, Guggenheim Found., 1976—77. Fellow: Econometric Soc. (pres. 1988—89), Am. Acad. Arts and Scis.; mem.: NAS, Am. Philos. Soc. Business E-Mail: h-sonnenschein@uchicago.edu.

SONS, LINDA RUTH, mathematician, educator; b. Chicago Heights, Ill., Oct. 31, 1939; d. Robert and Ruth (Diekelman) Sons. AB in Math., Ind. U., 1961; MS in Math., Cornell U., 1963, PhD in Math., 1966. Tchg. asst. Cornell U., Ithaca, NY, 1961-63, instr. math., summer 1963, rsch. asst., 1963-65; from asst. prof. to assoc. prof. math. No. Ill. U., De Kalb, 1965—78, prof., 1978—, presdl. tchg. prof., 1994-98, disting. tchg. prof., 1998—, dir. undergrad. studies math. dept., 1971—77, exec. sec. univ. coun., 1978—79, chair faculty fund, 1982—. Author (with others): A Study Guide for Introduction to Mathematics, 1976, Mathematical Thinking in a Quantitative World, 1990, 2003; contbr. articles to profl. jours. Bd. dirs., treas. DeKalb County Migrant Ministry, 1967—78; pres. Luth. Women's Missionary League, 1974—87; mem. campus ministry com. No. Ill. Dist. Luth. Ch./Mo. Synod, Hillside, 1977—2001; mem. ch. coun. Immanuel Luth. Ch., DeKalb, 1978—85, 1987—89, 2005—. Recipient Excellence in Coll. Tchg. award, Ill. Coun. Tchrs. Math., 1991; NSF Rsch. grantee, 1970—72, 1974—75. Mem.: London Math. Soc., Ill. Sect. Math. Assn. Am. (past pres. 1982—87, bd. dirs. 1989—92, v.p. sect., pres., pres.-elect, Disting. Svc. award 1988), Math. Assn. Am. (mem. nat. bd. govs. 1989—92, mem. com. undergrad. program math. 1990—96, chmn. subcom. on quantitative literacy 1990—96, chmn. coun. awards 1997—2003, chmn. Adler award com. 2004—, Disting. Coll. or Univ. Tchg. Math. Sect. award 1995, Cert. Meritorious Svc. Nat. award 1998), Assn. Women in Math., Am. Math. Soc., Sigma Xi (past chpt. pres.), Phi Beta Kappa (pres. No. Ill. assn. 1981—85). Achievements include research in mathematics education and classical complex analysis, especially value distribution for meromorphic functions with unbounded characteristic in the unit disc. Office: o Ill U Dept Math Scis Dekalb IL 60115 Office Phone: 815-753-6760.

SOPER, LAVERN G., appliance and houseware manufacturer; b. 1917; married. With Nat. Presto Industries, Inc., Eau Claire, Wis., 1946—, v.p., 1954—70, exec. v.p., 1970—75, pres., dir., 1975—. With USAF, 1942—46. Office: Nat Presto Industries Inc 3925 N Hastings Way Eau Claire WI 54703-0485

SOPRANOS, ORPHEUS JAVARAS, manufacturing executive; b. Evanston, Ill., Oct. 4, 1935; s. James Javaras and Marigoula (Papalexatou) S.; m. Angeline Buches, Dec. 31, 1959; children: Andrew, Katherine. AB, MBA, U. Chgo., 1957. Mgmt. trainee Ford Motor Co., Chgo., 1958-59; with Amsted Industries, Chgo., 1959—, dir. bus. research, 1966-70, treas., 1970-80, v.p., 1980—; pres. Amsted Internat., 1991-93, corp. v.p., 1993-2000, ret. Served with U.S. Army, 1958, 61-62. Mem. Univ. Club (Chgo.), Skokie Country Club.

SORENSEN, CHARLES W., academic administrator; V.p. acad. affairs Winona (Minn.) State U., until 1988; chancellor U. Wis., Stout, 1988—. Office: U Wis-Stout Office of Chancellor Menomonie WI 54751

SORENSON, CHRISTOPHER J., lawyer; b. Laramie, Wyo., May 1, 1970; 4 children. BA, Macalester Coll., 1993; JD cum laude, William Mitchell Coll. Law, 1996. Bar: Minn. 1996, US Dist. Ct. (dist. Minn.) 1996, US Dist. Ct. (dist. Colo.) 1996, US Ct. Appeals (1st, 7th, 8th and Fed. cirs.) 1996. Ptnr. Merchant & Gould, P.C., Mpls. amed a Rising Star, Minn. Super Lawyers mag., 2006. Avocation: fishing. Office: Merchant & Gould PC 3200 IDS Ctr 80 S 8th St Minneapolis MN 55402 Office Phone: 612-336-4645. E-mail: csorenson@merchant-gould.com.

SORIANO, ALFONSO GUILLEARD, professional baseball player; b. San Pedro De Macoris, Dominican Republic, Jan. 7, 1976; Player NY Yankees, 1999—2004, Tex. Rangers, 2004—05, Wash. Nationals, 2005—06, Chgo. Cubs, 2007—. Named All-Star Game MVP, 2004; named to Am. League All-Star Team, Maj. League Baseball, 2002—05, Nat. League All-Star Team, 2006—07; recipient Silver Slugger award, 2002, 2004—06. Achievements include leading the Am. League in hits (209), runs scored (128), and stolen bases (41), 2002. Mailing: c/o Chgo Cubs Wrigley Field 1060 W Addison St Chicago IL 60613-4397*

SOSVILLE, DICK, sales and marketing executive; V.p. sales and mktg. The Dow Chem. Co., Midland, Mich., v.p. engring. plastics, 1997—. Office: The Dow Chem Co 2030 Dow Ctr Midland MI 48674-0001

SOTELINO, GABINO, chef; b. Vigo, Spain; Mem. staff Hotel Ritz, Madrid, Plaza Athanee, Paris, Koons Hotel, Switzerland, Hilton Internat. Hotels, Montreal Expo., Madison Hotel, Washington; exec. chef Capitol Hill Restaurants, Washington, Le Perroquet, Chgo.; head chef The Pump Room, Chgo., 1980; owner, chef Ambria, Chgo., 1980—, Un Grande Cafe, Chgo., 1981—, Cafe Ba-Ba-Reeba!, Chgo., 1985—, Mon Ami, Chgo., 1998—. Named Chef of Yr., Chefs of Am., 1990; recipient Perrier-Jouet Chef of Midwest award, James Beard Found., 1997, Medalla Merito Nacional os Fpain, 1990, Academie Culinaire de France. Mem.: Euro-Toque Inc. (pres. U.S. chpt.), Grand Master Chefs Assn. (nat. chmn.), Commanderie des Corden Bleus de France. Office: Ambria 2300 N Lincoln Park W Chicago IL 60614

SOTIR, MARK, automotive rental executive; B in Econs., Amherst Coll.; MBA, Harvard U. Group mktg. mgr. Coca-Cola Co.; sr. v.p. worldwide mktg. Budget Rent-A-Car Corp., 1997-98, pres., 1999-2000; v.p. ops. and reservations Budget Group, Inc., Daytona Beach, Fla., 1998-99, pres. worldwide reservation svcs., 1999-2000, pres. N.Am. vehicle rental ops., pres., COO, 2000—.

SOUDER, MARK EDWARD, congressman; b. Ft. Wayne, Ind., July 18, 1950; s. Edward Getz and Irma (Fahling) S.; m. Diane Kay Zimmer, July 28; children: Brooke Diane, athan Elias, Zachary. BS, Ind. U., Ft. Wayne, 1972; MBA, U. Notre Dame, 1974. Mgmt. trainee Crossroads Furniture Co., Houston, 1974; mktg. mgr. Gabberts Furniture & Studio, Mpls., 1974-76; mktg. mgr., exec. v.p. Souder's Furniture & Studio, Grabill, Ind., 1976-80, pres., 1981-84; econ. devel. liaison for U.S. Rep. Dan Coats, from 1983; mem. U.S. Congress from Ind. 3rd Dist. (formerly 4th), 1995—, Ho. Select Com. on Homeland Security. Mem. edn. and workforce com., govt. reform and oversight com., small bus. com., natural resources com. Publicity chmn. Grabill County Fair, 1977—; advisor Dan Coats for Congress Com., 1980-81; mem. Ind. Area Devel. Coun.; mem. bus. alumni adv. com. Ind. U.-Ft. Wayne. Mem. Midwest Home Furnishings Assn. (dir. 1976-84, past treas., exec. v.p.), Ft. Wayne, Grabill C. of C., Allen County Hist. Soc., Alumni Assn. Ind. U. at Ft. Wayne (dir., past pres.), Alumni Assn. U. Notre Dame. Republican. Mem. Apostolic Christian Ch. Home: 13733 Ridgeview Ct Grabill IN 46741 Office: US Ho Reps 2231 Rayburn Ho Office Bldg Washington DC 20515-1403 Office Phone: 202-225-4436. Office Fax: 202-225-3479. E-mail: souder@mail.house.gov.

SOUKUP, BETTY A., state legislator; b. Clarksburg, W.Va. m. Robert Soukup; 3 children. AS in Bus. Mgmt., BA in Comms. Arts. Mem. Iowa Senate from 15th dist., Des Moines, 1998—; mem. agr. com., mem. appropriations com.; mem. small bus., econs. devel. and tourism com. Iowa Senate, Des Moines, mem. ways and means com. Democrat. E-mail: betty_soukup@legis.state.ia.us.

SOULE, GEORGE ALAN, literature educator; b. Fargo, ND, Mar. 3, 1930; s. George Alan and Ruth Georgia (Knudsen) S.; m. Carolyn Richards, Nov. 24, 1961; 1 child, Katherine. BA, Carleton Coll., 1951; postgrad., Corpus Christi Coll., Cambridge U., Eng., 1952-53; MA, Yale U., 1956, PhD, 1960. Instr. English lit. Oberlin (Ohio) Coll., 1958-60; asst. prof. U. Wis., Madison, 1960-62; from asst. prof. to prof. Carleton Coll., Northfield, Minn., 1962-95, prof. emeritus, 1995—, chair English dept., 1980—83; tchr. Cannon Valley Elder Collegium, 1998—, vice chair, 2003—05, chair, 2005—07, also bd. dirs. Cons. Ednl. Testing Svc., Princeton, NJ, 1967-84, 94-97; lectr. Wordsworth Winter Sch., Grasmere, UK, 2003-07. Author: Four British Women Novelists: An Annotated and Critical Secondary Biblioigraphy, 1998; editor: Theatre of the Mind, 1974; contbr. articles to profl. jours. Libr. bd. City Northfield, 1997-00; bd. dirs. orthfield Area Found., 2001-02. With US Army, 1954-55. Internat. fellow Rotary, 1952-53, Sterling pre-doctoral fellow Yale U., 1957-58. Mem.: Anthony Powell Soc., The Iris Murdoch Soc., Friends of Dove Cottge, Boswell Soc. of Auchinleck, Johnson Soc. of Lichfield, Mayflower Soc., Oxford and Cambridge Club, Rotary, Phi Beta Kappa. Episcopalian. Avocations: cooking, travel, Jeopardy (Champion Sr. Tournament 1990). Home: 313 Nevada St Northfield MN 55057-2346 Office Phone: 507-646-4322. Fax: 507-645-5099. E-mail: gsoule@charter.net.

SOUSANIS, NICK, art web site designer; b. 1973; Tchr., pub. speaking Wayne State U.; co-founder, pub., editor-in-chief Thedetroiter.com, 2002—. Trustee Contemporary Art Inst. Detroit. Named one of 40 Under 40, Crain's Detroit Bus., 2006. Office: Museum of Contemporary Art Detroit 4454 Woodward Ave Detroit MI 48201

SOUTAS-LITTLE, ROBERT WILLIAM, mechanical engineer, educator; b. Oklahoma City, Feb. 25, 1933; s. Harry Glenn and Mary Evelyn (Miller) Little; m. Patricia Soutas, Sept. 3, 1982; children: Deborah, Catherine, Colleen, Jennifer, Karen. BS in Mech. Engring, Duke U., 1955; MS, U. Wis., 1959, PhD, 1962. Design engr. Allis Chalmers Mfg. Co., Milw., 1955-57; instr. mech. engring. Marquette U., 1957-59; instr. U. Wis., Madison, 1959-62, asst. prof., 1962-63, Okla. State U., 1963-65; prof. Mich. State U., 1965—2001, chmn. dept. mech. engring., 1972-77, chmn. dept. biomechanics, 1977-90; dir. biomechanics evaluation lab., 1989—; prof. emeritus Mich. State U., Lansing, 2001—. Cons. A. C. Electronics Co., Ford Motor Co., CBS Research Lab., B. F. Goodrich Co.; lectr. AID, India, 1965 Author: Elasticity, 1973, Engineering Mechanics: Statics, 1999, Engineering Mechanics: Dynamics, 1999; contbr. articles to profl. jours. Vice pres. Okemos (Mich.) Sch. Bd., 1967-72; mem. Meridian Twp. (Mich.) Charter Commn., 1969-70, Meridian Twp. Zoning Bd. Appeals, 1969-71. Recipient award for excellence in instrn. engring. students Western Electric Co., 1970-71, Disting. Faculty award, 1996; NSF grantee, 1964-69, 79, NIH grantee, 1973-75, 79—. Fellow ASME; mem. Soc. Engring. Sci., Am. Soc. Biomechanics, Internat. Soc. Biomechanics, N.Am. Soc. Clin. Gait and Movement Analysis, Sigma Xi, Pi Tau Sigma, Ta Beta Pi. Home: 187 S Highland Dr Leland MI 49654-1143 Office: PO Box 1143 Leland MI 49654-1143 Home Phone: 231-256-7646; Office Phone: 231-256-7646. Business E-Mail: soutas@egr.msu.edu.

SOUTHGATE, MARIE THERESE, physician, editor; b. Detroit, Apr. 27, 1928; d. Clair and Josephine Marie (Hoefeyzers) S. BS, Coll. St. Francis, 1948, LLD (hon.), 1974; MD, Marquette U., 1960. Duplomate Nat. Bd. Med. Examiners. Rsch. editor Ill. Inst. Tech. Rsch. Inst., Chgo., 1951-55; intern St. Mary's Hosp., San Francisco, 1960-61; sr. editor Jour. of AMA, Chgo., 1962-75, dep. editor, 1975-88, sr. contbg. editor, 1988—. Mem. editorial bd. Forum, from 1978; mem. ad hoc com. on biol. scis. Ill. Bd. Huigher Edn., 1969-70; mem. ad hoc com. on lay deacons Archdiocese Chgo., 1973; trustee Coll. St. Francis, from 1978. Editor-in-chief Marquette Med. Rev., 1959-60. Mem. AMA, AAAS, Am. Med. Women's Assn. (v.p Chgo. chpt. 1967-68, mem. continuing med. edn. com. from 1978), Coun. Biology Editors. Office: JAMA 515 N State St Chicago IL 60610-4325

SOWALD, HEATHER GAY, lawyer; b. Columbus, Ohio, Dec. 26, 1954; d. Martin M. and Beatrice (Kronick) S.; m. Robert Marc Kaplan, June 12, 1977; children: Andrew Scott, Alexis Beth. BA, Case Western Res. U., 1976; JD, Capital U., 1979. Bar: Ohio 1979, U.S. Dist. Ct. (so. dist.) Ohio 1980, U.S. Ct. Appeals (6th cir.) 1981, U.S. Supreme Ct., 1987. Ptnr. Sowald & Sowald, Columbus, 1979-85, Sowald & Daneman, Columbus, 1985-1987, Sowald, Sowald & Mas, Columbus, 1988, Sowald, Sowald & Clouse, Columbus. Hearing officer Cert. Need Rev. Bd. State of Ohio, 1982—, Dept. Adminstrv. Services, 1982—, Dept. Mental Health, 1986—, Dept. Mental Retardation, 1986-88, Dept. Health, 1986-89, Ohio Dept. Liquor Control, 1989—. Bd. dirs. Wilderness Bond, Inc., Franklin County, Ohio, 1982-86, Youth Svcs. Adv. Bd., Franklin County, 1984—, chmn. 1987—, Ohio Bd. of Nursing, 1988—; legal advisor United Way League Against Child Abuse, Franklin County, 1986-87. Mem. Ohio State Bar Assn. (council of dels. 1986, pres. 2004, mem. family law com.), Columbus Bar Assn. (chmn. juvenile law com. 1982-84, chmn. admissions to bar 1984-86, 2005-07, chmn. publications com., 1987-88, chmn. family law com. 1988—, ethics com. 1988—, pres. 1998-99), Franklin County Trial Lawyers Assn. (trustee 1985-88, treas. 1988-89. pres.-elect 1989—, pres. 1989-90), Women Lawyers of Franklin County (pres. 1984-85), Capital U. Law Sch. Alumni Assn. (pres. 1984-86), Ohio Bar Found. (head trustee 2003—), Columbus Bar Found. (head trustee 1999—, mem. grants com. 2007—), Legal Aid Soc. Ctrl. Ohio (head trustee 2006—). Democrat. Jewish. Office: Sowald Sowald & Clouse One Americana 400 S 5th St Ste 101 Columbus OH 43215

SOZEN, METE AVNI, engineering educator; b. Turkey, May 22, 1930; m. Joan Bates; children: Timothy, Adria, Ayshe. BCE, Roberts Coll., Turkey, 1951; MCE, U. Ill., 1952, PhD in Civil Engring., 1957; doctorate (hon.), Bogazici U., Istanbul, Turkey, 1988, Janus Pannonius U., Pecs, Hungary, 1998, Georgian Tech. U., Tblisi, 2005. Registered structural engr., Ill. Jr. engr. Kaiser Engrs., Oakland, Calif., 1952; structural engr. Hardesty and Hanover, NYC, 1953; research asst. civil engring. U. Ill., Urbana, 1953-55, research assoc., 1955-57, asst. prof. civil engring., 1957-59, assoc. prof., 1959-63, prof., 1963-94, Purdue U., 1994—. Cons. problems related to earthquake-resistant constrn. VA, various firms Europe, S.Am., U.S., UNESCO, UN Devel. Programs; cons. criteria for mass housing projects P.R.; adv. com. structural safety VA, rsch. project NSF, Applied Tech. Coun., Los Alamos and Sandia Nat. Labs.; chief investigator various NSF contracts and grants. Contbr. over 125 tech. papers, monographs, procs., reports to profl. jours.; presenter numerous papers to profl. meetings U.S.A, Japan, Italy, India, Turkey, Mexico. Recipient Drucker award U. Ill., 1986, Howard award, 1987, Boase award, 1988, Parlar Sci. and Tech. prize Mid. East Tech. U., Ankara, Turkey, 1995, ASEE Gen. Electric Sr. Rsch. award, 1997, Ill. Sect. Structural Group Lifetime Achievement award, 1998. Mem. NAE, ASCE (hon., Rsch. prize 1963, Raymond C. Reese award 1971, 94, Moiseiff award 1972, Howard award 1987, Raymond C. Reese Rsch. award 1994), Am. Concrete Inst. (Kelly award 1975, Bloem award 1985, Lindau award 1993), Am. Arbitration Assn. (nat. panel) Seismological Soc. Am., Swedish Royal Acad. Engring. Office: Purdue Univ Sch Civil Engring 1284 Civil Engineering West Lafayette IN 47907-1284 E-mail: sozen@ecn.purdue.edu.

SPACE, ZACK (ZACHARY T. SPACE), congressman; b. Dover, Ohio, Jan. 27, 1961; s. Socrates and Sandra (Gallion) Space; m. Mary Wade, 1988; children: Gina, Nicholas. BA in Polit. Sci., Kenyon Coll., Gambier, Ohio, 1983; JD, Ohio State U., Columbus, 1986. Atty. Space & Space Co., LPA, 1986—, Pub. Defender's Office; spl. counsel to Ohio Attys. Gen. Anthony Celebrezze and Lee Fisher State of Ohio; law dir. City of Dover, Ohio, 2000—06, city atty. Ohio, 2000—06; mem. US Congress from 18th Ohio dist., 2007—, mem. agr. com., transp. & infrastructure com., vets.' affairs com. Mem. St. George Greek Orthodox Ch., Massillon, Ohio. Democrat. Greek Orthodox. Office: 315 Cannon Ho Office Bldg Washington DC 20515 also: 137 E Iron Ave Dover OH 44622 Office Phone: 330-343-2430, 202-225-6265, 330-364-4300. Office Fax: 330-364-2599, 330-364-4330.

SPADA, ROBERT F., state legislator; b. Cleve. BS, Cleveland State Coll.; MBA, Baldwin Wallace Coll. Business owner, accountant; mem. Ohio Senate from 24th dist., Columbus, 1999—. Mem. Parma Heights City Coun., Parma Area C. of C. Republican. Office: Senate Bldg 24 Dist 1st Fl Rm 143 Columbus OH 43215

SPAETH, NICHOLAS JOHN, lawyer, former state attorney general; b. Mahnomen, Minn., Jan. 27, 1950; m. Cindy Spaeth; children: Gawain Kevin, Carl Wilson, William James, Elizabeth Bedont. AB, Stanford U., 1972, JD, 1977; BA, Oxford U., Eng., 1974. Bar: Minn. 1979, US Dist. Ct. Dist. Minn. 1979, US Ct. Appeals 8th cir. 1979, ND 1980, US Dist. Ct. Dist. ND 1980, US Supreme Ct. 1984, Calif. 1999, US Dist. Ct. Calif. 1999, Mo. 2005. Law clk. US Ct. Appeals 8th cir., Fargo, D, 1977-78; law clk. to Justice Byron White US Supreme Ct., Washington, 1978-79; atty. pvt. practice, 1979-84; atty. gen. State of ND, Bismarck, 1985—93; ptnr. Dorsey & Whitney, Fargo, ND, 1993-99, Oppenheimer Wolff & Donnelly, Mpls., 1999, Cooley Godward, Palo Alto, Calif., 1999—2000; sr v.p., gen. counsel, sec. GE Employers Reinsurance Corp., Overland Park, Kans., 2000—03, Intuit Inc., Mountain View, Calif., 2003—04; sr. v.p., chief legal officer H&R Block Inc., Kansas City, Mo., 2004—. Adj. prof. law U. Minn., 1980-83. Rhodes scholar, 1972-74. Democrat. Roman Catholic. Office: H&R Block Inc 4400 Main St Kansas City MO 64111 Business E-Mail: nspaeth@hrblock.com.

SPAID, GREGORY P., academic administrator, art educator; b. Mishawaka, Ind. m. Susan R. Spaid. BA in Art, Kenyon Coll., 1969; MFA, Ind. U., 1976. Mem. faculty Berea (Ky.) Coll., 1976—79; prof. art Kenyon Coll., Gambier, Ohio, 1979—, chair art dept., 1984—88, assoc. provost, 1999—2002, acting provost, 2002—03, provost, 2003—. Tchr. summer programs Kenyon Coll., Gambier, Ohio, Santa Fe, Bozeman, Mont., Nantucket Island Sch. Design Art. Photography published in books, The Man Who Created Paradise, 2001, On

Nantucket, 2002, Represented in permanent collections Mus. Modern Art, N.Y.C., J. Paul Getty Mus., L.A., Santa Barbara (Calif.) Mus. Art, Smithsonian Instn., Nat. Mus. Am. Art, Washington, Dayton (Ohio) Art Inst., Chase Manhattan Bank, N.Y.C. Fellow Photo Educators fellow, Eastman Kodak, 1993; Individual Artist's fellow, Ohio Arts Coun., 1984, 1986, 1995, 2000, Fulbright Rsch. fellow, Italy, 1987, Profl. Devel. Assistance grantee, Ohio Arts Coun., 1990, Artist Project grantee, 1995. Office: Ransom Hall 21 Kenyon College Gambier OH 43022-9623

SPAINHOUR, J. PATRICK (JAMES PATRICK SPAINHOUR), outsourcing company executive, former apparel executive; b. 1950; married. B, Miss. State Univ., 1972. Positions through v.p. fin. & adminstrn. Kellwood Co., 1972—83; exec. v.p. fin. & ops. Seminole Mfg. Co., 1983; sr. v.p. sourcing Gap Inc., 1988—93; exec. v.p. fin. & ops. Stride Rite Corp., 1993—94; exec. v.p., CFO Donna Karen Co., 1994—96; pres., COO Ann Taylor Stores Corp., 1996, chmn., CEO, 1996—2005; interim chmn., CEO Servicemaster Co., Downers Grove, Ill., 2006, chmn., CEO, 2006—07; CEO Servicemaster Co., Servicemaster lLobal Holdings, Downers Grove, Ill., 2007—. Bd. dir. Tupperware Corp., Circuit City Stores Inc., 2004—, Servicemaster Co., 2005—. Office: Servicemaster Co Ste 600 3250 Lacey Rd Downers Grove IL 60515

SPAINHOWER, JAMES IVAN, retired college president; b. Stanberry, Mo., Aug. 3, 1928; s. Elmer Enoch and Stella Irene (Cox) S.; m. Joanne Steanson, June 10, 1950; children: Janet Dovell, James Jeffrey. BA, Phillips U., Enid, Okla., 1950, LLD (hon.), 1967; BD, Lexington Theol. Sem., Ky., 1953; MA in Polit. Sci., U. Mo., Columbia, 1967, PhD, 1971, U. Ark., 1954; diploma, U. Pacific Sch. Religion, Berkeley, Calif., 1958; DPA (hon.), Culver-Stockton Coll., 1973; LL.D. (hon.), Maryville Coll., St. Louis, 1976; Litt.D. (hon.), Kirksville Coll. Osteo. Medicine, Mo., 1977; D.H.L. (hon.), Mo. Valley Coll., 1984; LLD (hon.), Eureka Coll., 1989, Lynchburg Coll., 1993. Ordained to ministry Christian Ch. (Disciples of Christ), 1950; pastor chs. in Ark. and Mo., 1953-70; mem. Mo. Ho. of Reps. from, Saline County, 1963-70; pres. Assn. Med. Schs. Mo., Jefferson City, 1970-72; part-time prof. polit. sci. Lincoln U., Jefferson City, 1970-72; treas. State of Mo., 1973-80; pres. Sch. of Ozarks, Point Lookout, Mo., 1981-82, Lindenwood Coll., St. Charles, Mo., 1983-89; pres. divsn. higher edn. Christian Ch. (Disciples of Christ), 1989-93. Author: Pulpit, Pew and Politics, 1979. Chmn. Mo. del. Dem. Nat. Conv., 1976; elected mem. Acad. Squires, 1981; 1st chmn. Mo. Children's Trust Fund, 1984-86. Recipient Mental Health award Mo. Mental Health Assn., 1967, Meritorious Service award St. Louis Globe Dem., 1968, Harry S. Truman award Saline County Young Democrats, 1970, citation of merit Alumni Assn. U. Mo., 1975; named Mo. Lay Educator of Year Mo. chpt. Phi Delta Kappa, 1968 Home and Office: 1616 W Long Blvd Raymore MO 64083 Personal E-mail: jspriny@comcast.net.

SPALTY, EDWARD ROBERT, lawyer; b. New Haven, Oct. 1, 1946; s. Kermit and Elinor Turgeon; m. Suzy Clune; children: Thomas John, Kathleen Tess. BA, Emory U., 1968; JD, Columbia U., 1973. Bar: Mo. 1975, Nebr. 1997, Kans. 1998, Colo. 2003, U.S. Dist. Ct. (we. dist.) Mo. 1975, U.S. Ct. Claims 1977, U.S. Ct. Appeals (8th cir.) 1984, U.S. Ct. Appeals (10th cir.) 1999, U.S. Supreme Ct. 1994, U.S. Dist. Ct. (ea. dist.) Wis. 2004. Assoc. Webster & Sheffield, NYC, 1973-74; mng. ptnr. Armstrong Teasdale LLP, Kansas City, Mo., 1991-2001, ptnr., 1980—. Contbr. articles to profl jours. Chmn. bd. dirs. Mo. Easter Seals, 1990—92; founding mem. Heartland Franchise Assn.; bd. dirs., mem. exec. com. Nat. Easter Seal Soc.; bd. dirs. Mo. Easter Seals, 1984—. With US Army, 1968—70. Named a Superlawyer, Mo., 2006, Kans., 2006; named Best of the Bar, Kans. City Bus. Jour., 2006; named one of Best Lawyers in Am., Chambers USA, 2007—, Woodward White, 1995—; recipient BTI Client Svc. award, Chambers USA, 2007. Mem.: ABA (litigation sect, franchising forum comt), Intern. Rels. Coun. Kansas City, Def. Rsch. Inst., Mo. Orgn. Def. Attys., Lawyers Assn. Kansas City, Kansas City Met. Bar Assn. (chmn antitrust and franchise law comt, co-chair 14th and 16h ann Nat Franchise Law Inst), Mo. Bar Assn. (civil rules and procedures comt), Lex Mundi (regional vice chair N.Am. dispute resolution, antitrust practice group), German-Am C. of C. (v.p. Kansas City chpt), Nat. Golf Club Kansas City (founder), Phi Delta, Pi Sigma Alpha, Sigma Nu. Home: 13703 NW 73rd St Parkville MO 64152-1120 Office: Armstrong Teasdale LLP 2345 Grand Blvd Ste 2000 Kansas City MO 64108-2617 Office Phone: 816-221-3420. Business E-Mail: espalty@armstrongteasdale.com.

SPANGLER, DOUGLAS FRANK, state legislator; m. Mary Clare Spangler. BS, Kans. State U., 1985; MPA, U. Kans., 1993. Small bus. owner; mem. from dist. 36 Kans. State Ho. of Reps., Topeka. Dem. precinct committeeman, Wyco Dem. Ctrl. Com., 1986-88. Office: Kans Ho of Reps State House Topeka KS 66612 Address: 212 N 4th St Edwardsville KS 66111-1303

SPANOGLE, ROBERT WILLIAM, marketing and advertising company executive, association administrator; b. Lansing, Mich., Nov. 13, 1942; s. William P. and Mary A. (Lenneman) S.; m. Ruth Ann Long, Jan. 14, 1967; children: John Paul Stephen Donald, Amy Lynn. AA, Lansing C.C., 1969; BA, Mich. State U., 1971; postgrad., U. Pa., 1985. Cons. Nat. League Cities, Washington, 1971-72, Am. Legion, Indpls., 1972-75, dir. membership, 1975-79, exec. dir. Washington, 1975-81, nat. adjutant, 1981—; chmn. HP Direct, Inc., Indpls., 1985—, chmn. exec. com. Washington, 1989—. Mem. individual investors adv. com. N.Y. Stock Exch., N.Y.C., 1989-92. Bd. govs. USO, Washington, 1986-92, Childrens Miracle Network, 2001—; trustee St. Mary of the Woods Coll., Terre Haute, Ind., 1991-2001; treas. Civil War Battle Flags Commn. State of Ind., Indpls., 1994—; sec. 500 Festival Assocs., Indpls., 1985-91; mem. Vet.'s Day Coun., Indpls., 1989; bd. dirs. Indpls. Athletic Club, 1989-93, Crossroads Coun. Boy Scouts Am., 1985-92; civilian aide Sec. Army India, 2003-. With U.S. Army, 1962-65. Recipient Silver Buffalo award, Nat. Council Boy Scouts Am., 2004. Mem. Am. Legion of Mich. (Hon. Comdr. 1985), Kiwanis (exec. com. 1989-92). Roman Catholic. Avocations: golf, hunting, reading. Home: 7420 Killarney Dr Indianapolis IN 46217-5472 Office: Am Legion 700 N Pennsylvania St Indianapolis IN 46204-1129 Office Phone: 317-630-1236.

SPARBERG, MARSHALL STUART, gastroenterologist, educator; b. Chgo., May 20, 1936; s. Max Shane and Mildred Rose (Haffron) S.; m. Eve Gaymont Enda, Mar. 15, 1987. BA, orthwestern U., 1957, MD, 1960. Intern Evanston Hosp., Ill., 1960-61; resident in internal medicine Barnes Hosp., St. Louis, 1961-63; fellow U. Chgo., 1963-65; practice medicine specializing in gastroenterolgy Chgo., 1967—; asst. prof. medicine Northwestern U., 1967-72, assoc. prof., 1972-80, prof. medicine, 1980—; instr. Wash. U., St. Louis, 1961-63, U. Chgo., 1963-65. Author: Ileostomy Care, 1969, Primer of Clinical Diagnosis, 1972, Ulcerative Colitis, 1978, Inflammatory Bowel Disease, 1982; contbr. numerous articles to profl. jours. Pres. Fine Arts Music Found., 1974-76, Crohn's Disease and Colitis Found. of Am., pres. Ill. chpt., 1994-97; bd. dirs. Lyric Opera Guild, 1974-94, Chamber Music Soc. North Shore Chgo., 1984—; physician to Chgo. Symphony Orch., 1981-97. With USAF, 1965-67. Named Outstanding Tchr. Northwestern U. Med. Sch., 1972 Mem. AMA, ACP, Am. Gastroent. Assn., Am. Coll. Gastroent. (bd. govs.), Chgo. Med. Soc., Chgo. Soc. Internal Medicine, Chgo. Soc. Gastroenterology (pres.), Chgo. Soc. Gastrointestinal Endoscopy (pres.) Office: 676 N Saint Clair St Ste 1525 Chicago IL 60611-2862

SPARKS, DONALD EUGENE, interscholastic activities association executive; b. St. Louis, May 26, 1933; s. Lloyd Garland and Elsie Wilma (Finn) S.; m. Gloria Helle, Sept. 22, 1951; children: Robert, Michael, Donna Lyn. BS in Edn., Truman State Univ., 1956, MA, 1959, postgrad., 1962-63. Cert. tchr. and principal, Mo. High sch. coach, athletic dir. The Parkway Sch. Dist., Chesterfield, Mo., 1959-77; assoc. dir. Mo. High Sch. Activity Assn., Columbia, 1977-81; asst. dir. Nat. Fedn. State High Sch. Assns., Kansas City, Mo., 1981-98, retired, 1998. Recipient spl. Nat. Athletic Dir.'s and Nat. Coach and Nat. Ofcl. citations Nat. Fedn. State High Sch. Assns., 1972; named to Truman State U. Athletics Hall of Fame, 1996, Greater St. Louis Athletics Hall of Fame, 1978. Mem. Nat. Interathletic Adminstrs. Assn. (Disting. Service award 1979). Home: 20 Whispering Sands Dr Sarasota FL 34242-1665 Office: Nat High Sch Athletic Hall of Fame 2000 PO Box 690 Indianapolis IN 46206-0690

SPARKS, RICHARD EDWARD, aquatic ecologist; b. Kingston, Pa., Apr. 19, 1942; s. Raymond Earl and Marjory Bernice (Coffey) S.; m. Ruth Marie Cole, Dec. 30, 1966; children: Amelia Mary, Carolyn Denise. BA, Amherst Coll., 1964; MS, U. Kans., 1968; PhD, Va. Poly. Inst., 1971. Instr. Meth. Tchr. Tng. Coll., Uzuakoli, igeria, 1964-66; rsch. assoc. Va. Poly. Inst. and State U., Blacksburg, 1971-72; asst. aquatic biologist Ill. Natural History Survey, Champaign, 1972-77, assoc. aquatic biologist, 1977-80, aquatic biologist, 1980—. Contbr. articles to profl. jours.; author and co-author 11 spl. publs. and refereed symposia. Mem. Ill. Chpt. Am. Fisheries Soc. (pres. 1980, north cen. div. exec. com. 1980), Sigma Xi. Achievements include research in how the flood regulates and enhances biological productivity in large floodplain rivers. Home: RR 1 Ipava IL 61441-9801 Office: Ill Natural History Survey River Rsch Lab PO Box 590 Havana IL 62644-0590

SPARKS, WILLIAM B., JR., consumer products company executive; BA, U of Notre Dame; MBA, Cornell U. Pres. Down River Internat., Greif Bros. Corp, 1978—80, chmn., CEO, 1980—95; mem. bd. dir. Greif Bros. Corp., 1995—, Pres., COO, 1995—. Office: 425 Winter Rd Delaware OH 43015

SPARKS, WILLIAM SHERAL, retired librarian; b. Alden Bridge, La., Oct. 30, 1924; s. Fred DeWitt and Truda (Bradford) S.; m. Joy Eleanor Young, Aug. 8, 1947; 1 child, David Frederick. AB, Phillips U., 1946; MDiv, Christian Theol. Sem., 1949; ThM, Iliff Sch. of Theology, 1955, ThD, 1957; MA, U. Denver, 1962. Pastor chs., 1950-60; asst. libr. Kans. Wesleyan U., Salina, 1962-66; dir. libr. and info. svcs. St. Paul Sch. of Theology, Kansas City, Mo., 1966-93, ret., 1993. Horowitz Found. fellow Hebrew Union Coll.-Jewish Inst. of Religion, Cin., 1949-52. Mem. Am. Theol. Libr. Assn.

SPARLING, PETER DAVID, dancer, educator; b. Detroit, June 4, 1951; s. Robert Daniel and Emily Louise (Matthews) S. BFA, Juilliard Sch., NYC, 1973. Dancer José Limón Co., NYC, 1971-73; co. instr. London (Eng.) Contemporary Dance Theatre, 1983-84; prin. dancer Martha Graham Dance Co., NYC, 1973-87; asst. prof. dance U. Mich., Ann Arbor, 1984-87, chmn. dance dept., assoc. prof., 1987-94, prof. of dance, 1994—. Artistic dir. Peter Sparling Presents Solo Flight, N.Y.C., 1977-82, Peter Sparling Dance Co., N.Y.C., 1980-84; co-dir. Ann Arbor Dance Works, 1984-94; artistic dir. Dance Gallery/Peter Sparling & Co., 1993—; guest choreographer Victorian Coll. Arts, 1981, 84, Dance Uptown, Am. Ballet Theatre II, Cloud Dance Theatre, Taiwan, Ballet Gulbenkian, Lisbon, Utah Repertory Dance Theatre, Joseph Holmes Dance Theatre, Corning Dances, Fla. State U., Danza Una, Costa Rica. Choreographer Divining Rod, 1973, Little Incarnations, 1974, Three Farewells, 1977, Suite to Sleep, 1978, A Thief's Progress or The Lantern Night, 1979, Excursions of Chung Kuei, 1978, Nocturnes for Eurydice, 1978, Once in a Blue Moon, 1978, Herald's Round, 1979, Hard Rock, 1979, What She Forgot He Remembered, 1979, Sitting Harlequin, 1979, In Stride, 1979, Elegy, 1979, The Tempest, 1980, Orion, 1980, Landscape with Bridge, 1980, Nocturnes, Modern Life, Bright Bowed River, A Fearful Symmetry, Alibi, Rounding the Square, De Profundis, Rondo, Wings, Witness, The Boy Who Played With Dolls, Jealousy, Bride of Grand Prairie, Travelogue, The Four Seasons, New Bach, Popular Songs, Johnny Angel, Unfinished, The Pursuit of Happiness, Sonata, Philistines, Seven Enigmas, Berliner Mass, Ask/Tell; contbr. poetry to Mich. Quarterly Rev. Louis Horst Meml. scholar Juilliard Sch., 1973; Nat. Endowment for the Arts fellow 1971, 79, 83; grantee U. Mich., 1985-86, 89, 96-97, Mich. Coun. for the Arts, 1986, 93-98; faculty fellow U. Mich. Inst. for Humanities, 1996-97; recipient Choreographer's award Mich. Dance Assn., 1988, Artist's award Arts Found. Mich., 1989, 1997. Office: Univ of Michigan Dept of Dance 1310 N University Ct Ann Arbor MI 48109-1037

SPARROW, EPHRAIM MAURICE, mechanical engineering scientist, educator; b. Hartford, Conn., May 27, 1928; s. Charles and Frieda (Gottlieb) S.; m. Ruth May Saltman, Nov. 2, 1952; 1 child, Rachel Bernarr. BS, MIT, 1948, MS, 1949; MA, Harvard Coll., 1950, PhD, 1956; PhD (hon.), U. Brazil, 1967. Heat transfer specialist Raytheon Mfg. Co., 1952-53; rsch. specialist Lewis Rsch. Ctr., NASA, Cleve., 1953-59; prof. mech. engring. U. Minn., 1959—, Inst. prof., 1994—, chmn. fluid dynamics program, 1968-80, Morse alumni disting. tchg. prof., 1980—. Program dir. NSF, 1986-87, dir. chem., biochem. and thermal engring. divsn., 1986-88; vis. prof., chief AID mission U. Brazil, 1966-67; adv. prof. Xi'an Jiaotong U., 1984—; cons. in field, 1960—; pres. 1st Brazilian Symposium on Heat Transfer and Fluid Mechanics, 1966; mem. solar energy panel Fed. Coun. on Sci. and Tech., 1972; U.S. sci. committeeman 5th Internat. Heat Transfer Conf., 1973-74. Author: (with R.D. Cess) Radiation Heat Transfer, 1966, 2nd edit., 1978; editor: Handbook of Numerical Heat Transfer, 1988, Advances in Numerical Heat Transfer, vol. 1, 1997, vol. 2, 2000; hon. mem. editl. bd. Internat. Jour. Heat Mass Transfer, 1964—, Internat. Comm. in Heat Mass Transfer, 1975—; sr. editor Jour. Heat Transfer, 1972-80; editor Series in Computational and Phys. Processes in Mechanics and Thermal Scis., 1980—; chmn. editl. adv. bd. umerical Heat Transfer, 1978—; contbr. over 560 tech. articles to profl. jours. Recipient Ralph Coates Roe award Am. Soc. Engring. Edn., 1978, Outstanding Teaching award U. Minn., 1985, Fed. Engr. of Yr. award NSF, 1988, Sr. Rsch. award Am. Soc. Engring. Edn., 1989, Horace T. Morse award for outstanding contbns. to undergraduate teaching, 1993, Disting. Tchg. award Acad. Disting. Tchrs., U. Minn., 1997, 99, Donald Q. Kern award, Am. Inst. Chemical Engrs., 1999; named George Hawkins Disting. lectr. Purdue U., 1985. Fellow ASME (Meml. award for outstanding contbn. to sci. heat transfer 1962, Max Jakob award for eminent contbn. 1976, Centennial medal 1980, Disting. Svc. award heat transfer divsn. 1982, Charles Russ Richards Meml. award 1985, Worcester Reed Warner medal 1986, 50th Anniversary award heat transfer divsn. 1988, Disting. lectr. 1986-91, 93-94); mem. NAE, Biomed. Engring. Soc. (faculty advisor 1994—), Sigma Xi (Monie A. Ferst medal for contbn. to rsch. through edn. 1993), Pi Tau Sigma. Home: 2105 West Hoyt Ave Saint Paul MN 55108-1314 Office: U Minn Dept Mech Engring Minneapolis MN 55455-0111 Home Phone: 651-647-0787; Office Phone: 612-625-5502. Business E-Mail: esparrow@umn.edu.

SPARROW, HERBERT GEORGE, III, lawyer, educator; b. Ft. Bragg, NC, May 26, 1936; s. Herbert George and Virginia (Monroe) S.; m. Nancy Woodruff, Mar. 4, 1962; children: Amy Winslow, Edward Harrison, Herbert G. IV, Alison Kidder. AB cum laude, Princeton U., 1958; JD, U. Mich., 1961. Bar: Mich. 1961, Calif. 1964, D.C. 1979, U.S. Ct. Claims 1982, U.S. Tax Ct. 1983, U.S. Ct. Mil. Appeals 1962, U.S. Supreme Ct. 1976. Assoc. Dickinson Wright PLLC, Detroit, 1965-70, ptnr., 1970—. Adj. prof. Detroit Coll. Law, Mich. State U., 1977-99. Author numerous articles environ. law.; speaker in field. Bd. dirs. Family Life Edn. Coun., Grosse Pointe, Mich., 1982-88, Adult Well-Being Svcs., Inc., Detroit, 1995-2001; cons. Adult Well-Being Svcs. Inc., 2001—. Capt. JAGC, U.S. Army, 1962-65. Mem. Mich. Bar Assn. (rep. assembly 1979-85, environ. law sect. coun. 1985-91), Calif. Bar Assn., Detroit Bar Assn., Am. Arbitration Assn. (panel arbitrators 1975—), Mich. State Bar Found. (fellow 1989-93), Environment Law Inst. (former assoc.), Phi Delta Phi (pres. Kent Inn Assn., Ann Arbor 1985-97). Office: Dickinson Wright PLLC 500 Woodward Ave Ste 4000 Detroit MI 48226-3416

SPAULDING, DAN, public relations executive; BA, MA, U. Mich. Lt. USN; aide, pub. affairs officer to comdr. Tng. Command U.S. Pacific Fleet, San Diego, 1969-72; news anchor/prodr./reporter Staf. WFRV-TV, Green Bay, Wis., Sta. WEYI-TV, Flint-Saginaw, Mich.; mem. faculty U. Wis., Green Bay; news dir. Sta. KOMU-TV, Columbia, Mo., Sta. WOTV-TV 8; with Seyferth & Assocs., Inc., Grand Rapids, Mich., 1989-94, exec. v.p., 1994—. Active West Mich. Environ. Action Coun. Mem. Pub. Rels. Soc. Am. (accredited). Office: Seyferth Spaulding Tennyson 40 Monroe Center NW, Suite 202 Grand Rapids MI 49503-3003 Business E-Mail: info@seyferthpr.com.

SPEAR, ALLAN HENRY, state legislator, historian, educator; b. Michigan City, Ind., June 24, 1937; s. Irving S. and Esther (Lieber) S. BA, Oberlin Coll., 1958, LLD (hon.), 1997; MA, Yale U., 1960, PhD, 1965. Lectr. history U. Minn., Mpls., 1964-65, asst. prof., 1965-67, assoc. prof., 1967-2000; mem. Minn. State Senate, St. Paul, 1973-2000, chmn. jud. com., 1983-93; chmn. crime prevention com., 1993-2000; pres. Minn. State Senate, 1993—2000; vice-chair Minn. Campaign Fin. and Pub. Disclosure Bd., 2001—03. Vis. prof. Carleton Coll., Northfield, Minn., 1970, Stanford U., Palo Alto, Calif., 1970. Author: Black Chicago, 1967. Mem. Internat. Network Gay and Lesbian Ofcls. Avocations: cooking, travel, reading, classical music. Home: 2429 Colfax Ave S Minneapolis MN 55405-2942

SPEAR, PETER D., retired academic administrator; BA, Rutgers U., 1966; PhD in Physiol. Psychology, Yale U., 1970. Postdoctoral fellow dept. neurology Stanford U. Sch. Medicine, Calif., 1970—72; asst. prof. psychology Kans. State U., 1972, U. Wis., Madison, 1976—78, assoc. prof., 1978—81, prof., 1981, chair dept. psychology, 1990—94, assoc. dean social sci. Coll. Letters and Sci., 1994—96, provost, vice chancellor for acad. affairs, 2001—05; dean Coll. Arts and Scis. U. Colo., Boulder, 1996—2001; ret., 2005. Co-author: Psychology: Perspectives on Behavior. Business E-Mail: pspear@wisc.edu.

SPEAR, THOMAS TURNER, history educator; b. Coral Gables, Fla., Dec. 23, 1940; BA, Williams Coll., 1962; MA, U. Wis., 1970, PhD, 1974; postgrad., Sch. Oriental and African Studies, 1976-77. Sr. lectr. La Trobe U., Melbourne, Australia, 1973-80; Charles R. Keller prof. Williams Coll., Williamstown, Mass., 1981-92; prof. U. Wis., Madison, 1993—, dir. African studies program, 1995-98, chair dept. history, 2001—. Reviewer NEH, Social Sci. Rsch. Coun./Am. Coun. Learned Socs., Am. Philos. Soc. Author: The Kaya Complex: A History of the Mijikenda Peoples of the Kenya Coast to 1900, 1978, Kenya's Past: An Introduction to Historical Method in Africa, 1981, (with Derek Nurse) The Swahili: Reconstructing the History and Language of and African Soc., 800-1500, 1985, Mountain Farmers: Moral Economics of Land and Agricultural Development in Arusha and Meru, 1997; editor: (with Richard Waller) Being Maasai: Ethnicity and Identity in East Africa, 1993, (with Isaria N. Kimambo) East African Expressions of Christianity, 1999; editor Jour. of African History, 1997-2001; contbr. articles to profl. jours. Grantee Williams Coll., 1984, 87-89, 91-92, NEH, 1984, Am. Coun. Learned Socs., 1982, La Trobe U., 1976-77; recipient A.C. Jordan prize U. Wis., 1972, Fgn. Area fellowship Social Sci. Rsch. Coun./Am. Coun. Learned Socs., 1970-72, Coll. Tchrs. fellowship NEH, 1987-88, Guggenheim fellowship, 1995-96, U. Wis., 1995—. Mem. Am. Hist. Soc. (contbr. Guide to Hist. Lit.), African Studies Assn., African Studies Assn. Australia (founder, exec. sec. 1978-80), Internat. African Inst. Office: U Wis Dept History 3211 Humanities 455 N Park St Madison WI 53706-1405

SPEARS, KENNETH GEORGE, chemistry professor; b. Erie, Pa., Oct. 23, 1943; BS, Bowling Green State U., 1966; MS, PhD in Phys. Chemistry, U. Chgo., 1970. NIH predoctoral fellow U. Chgo., 1968-70; NRC-NOAA postdoctoral fellow NOAA, Boulder, Colo., 1970-72; prof. dept. chemistry Northwestern U., 1972—, mem. biomedical engring. dept., 1987—. Bd. editors The Rev. Scientific Instruments, 1980-83; conbtr. articles to profl.jours. Alfred P. Sloan Found. fellow, 1974-76. Fellow AAAS; mem. Am. Phys. Soc., Am. Chem. Soc. Office: Northwestern U Dept Chemistry 2145 Sheridan Rd Evanston IL 60208-3113 Office Phone: 847-491-3095, 847-491-3424. E-mail: k-spears@northwestern.edu.

SPECHT, JAMES E., agronomist, educator; b. Scottsbluff, Nebr., Sept. 12, 1945; s. Henry W. and Lydia (Marsh) S.; m. Pamela S. Hammers, May 31, 1969. BS, U. Nebr., 1967; MS, U. Ill., 1971; PhD, U. Nebr., 1974. Rsch. assoc. dept. agronomy U. Nebr., Lincoln, 1974, asst. prof., 1974-80, assoc. prof., 1980-85, prof., 1985—. Mem. editorial bd. Crops Sci., 1983-86, Field Crops Rsch. Jour., 1987-90. Contbr. numerous articles to profl. jours; presenter many rsch. lectures, 1975-85. Sgt. US Army, 1969-71, Vietnam. Recipient, Agronomic Acheivement award American Society of Agronomy, 1994. Fellow AAAS, Crop Sci. Soc. Am., Am. Soc. Agronomy. Democrat. Avocations: travel, investments, reading, computers. Office: Univ Nebr Plant Sci Rm 279 PO Box 830915 Lincoln NE 68583-0915

SPECK, SAMUEL WALLACE, JR., state official; b. Canton, Ohio, Jan. 31, 1937; s. Samuel Wallace Sr. and Lois Ione (Schneider) S.; m. Sharon Jane Anderson, Jan. 20, 1962; children: Samuel Wallace III, Derek Charles. BA, Muskingum Coll., 1959; postgrad., U. Zimbabwe, 1961; MA, Harvard U., 1963, PhD, 1968. Prof. polit. sci. Muskingum Coll., New Concord, Ohio, 1964-83, asst. to pres., 1986-87, exec. v.p., 1987, acting pres., 1987-88, pres., 1988-99; assoc. dir. Fed. Emergency Mgmt. Agy., 1983-86; mem. Ohio Ho. of Reps., 1971-76; state senator from Ohio 20th Dist., 1977-83; dir. Dept. Natural Resources, mem. Gov's. cabinet State of Ohio, 1999—2007. Bd. dirs. Camco Fin. Corp., Cambridge, Ohio, 1990-2007; pres. Eastern Ohio Devel. Alliance, 1990-92; Fund for Improvement of Postsecondary Edn., 1990-92, chmn. 1991. Contbr. numerous articles on African and Am. govt. and pub. policy. Bd. dirs. Ohio Tuition Trust Authority, 1991-93, Internat. Ctr. for Preservation Wild Animals, 1988-99, Lake Erie Commn., 1999-2007; bd. dirs., chmn. Ohio Water Resources Coun. 1999-2005; mem. Great Lakes Commn., 1999-2007, chmn., 2002-04; mem. Ohio Power Siting Bd., 1999-2007; mem. Ohio Pub. Works Commn., 2003-07; chmn. coun. Great Lakes water mgmt. working group, 2002-05; mem. Ohio Higher Edn. Financing Commn., 2007—. Recipient Outstanding Legislator award VFW/DAV/Am. Legion, Conservation Achievement award State of Ohio, Disting. Svc. award, Nat. Gov. Conf., 2004, Conservation Leadership award, Ohio Nature Conservancy. Republican. Home: 240 Greenbriar Ct Worthington OH 43085-3055

SPECTOR, DAVID M., lawyer; b. Rock Island, Ill., Dec. 20, 1946; s. Louis and Ruth (Vinikour) S.; m. Laraine Fingold, Jan. 15, 1972; children: Rachel, Laurence. BA, orthwestern U., 1968; JD magna cum laude, U. Mich., 1971. Bar: Ill. 1971, U.S. Dist. Ct. (no. dist.) Ill. 1971, U.S. Ct. Appeals (7th cir.) 1977, U.S. Ct. Appeals (4th cir.) 1984, U.S. Dist. Ct. (cen. dist.) Ill. 1984, U.S. Supreme Ct. 1999, N.Y. 2002, U.S. Ct. Appeals (2d cir.) 2002. Clk. Ill. Supreme Ct., Chgo., 1971-72; ptnr., assoc. Isham, Lincoln & Beale, Chgo., 1972-87; ptnr. Mayer, Brown & Platt, Chgo., 1987-97, Hopkins & Sutter, Chgo., 1997-2001, Schiff, Hardin LLP, Chgo., 2001—. Chmn. ABA Nat. Inst. on Ins. Co. Insolvency, Boston, 1986; co-chmn. ABA Nat. Inst. on Internat. Reins.: Collections and Insolvency, NY, 1988; chmn. ABA Nat. Inst. on Life Ins. Co. Insolvency, Chgo., 1993; spkr. in field. Editor: Law and Practice of Insurance Company Insolvency, 1986, Law and Practice of Life Insurer Insolvency, 1993; co-editor: Law and Practice of International Reinsurance Collections and Insolvency, 1988; contbr. articles to profl. jour. Mem. ABA (chair Nat. Inst. on Life Insurer Insolvency 1993), Chgo. Bar Assn., Lawyer's Club of Chgo. Office: Schiff Hardin LLP 6600 Sears Tower Chicago IL 60606 Home: 1418 N Lake Shore Dr Chicago IL 60610-1642 Office Phone: 312-258-5552. Business E-Mail: dspector@schiffhardin.com.

SPECTOR, GERSHON JERRY, otolaryngologist, educator, researcher; b. Rovno, Poland, Oct. 20, 1937; came to U.S., 1949; naturalized, 1956; m. Patsy Carol Tanenbaum, Aug. 28, 1965. BA, Johns Hopkins U., 1960; MD cum laude, U. Md., 1964. Intern Beth Israel Hosp., Boston, 1964-65; resident in surgery Sinai Hosp., Balt., 1965-66; resident in otolaryngology Mass. Eye and Ear Infirmary, Boston, 1966-69, Peter Bent Brigham Hosp., Boston, 1968-69; teaching fellow in otolaryngology Harvard U. Med. Sch., Boston, 1968-69; assoc. physician Ill. Crippled Children's Svc., Carbondale, 1971; mem. faculty Washington U. Med. Sch., St. Louis, 1971—, assoc. prof. otolaryngology, 1974-76, prof., 1976—; chief dept. otolaryngology St. Louis County Hosp., 1971-77. Mem. staff Washington U. Med. Ctr., Barnes Hosp.; dir. temporal bone bank, 1971-81; guest examiner Am. Bd. Otolaryngology, 1975-77; rsch. cons. neurosci. group, G.D. Searle Pharm. Corp. Mem. editl. bd. Laryngoscope, 1978, editor-in-chief, 1984-94; contbr. articles to med. jours. With U.S. Army, 1969-71. Hancock scholar, 1962. Fellow ACS; mem. AAAS, AMA, Am. Acad. Ophthalmology and Otolaryngology (Honor award 1979), St. Louis Med. Soc., St. Louis County Med. Soc., Am. Coun. Otolaryngology, St. Louis Ear, Nose and Throat Club (pres. 1986), So. Med. Assn., Deafness Rsch. Found., Pan. Am. Assn. Otorhinolaryngology and Broncho Esophagology, Am. Soc. Head and Neck Surgery, Soc. Univ. Otolaryngologists, Am. Laryngol., Rhinol. and Otol. Soc. (Edmund Prince Fowler award 1974), Am. Soc. Cell Biology, Electron Microscopy Soc., N.Y. Acad. Scis., Am. Assn. Anatomists, Am. Acad. Facial Plastic and Reconstructive Surgery, Am. euro-Otology Soc., Gesellschaft fur Neurootologie und Aequilibrimoetrie A.V., Barany Soc., Am. Radium Soc., Assn. Acad. Surgery, Am. Fedn. Clin. Oncologic Socs., Am Otol. Soc., Acoustical Soc. Am., Soc. for Neurosci., Internat. Skull Base Soc. (founding), Brazilian Skull Base Soc. (hon.), Centurion Club, Alpha Omega Alpha, Psi Chi. Home: 7365 Westmoreland Dr Saint Louis MO 63130-4241 Office: Washington U Med Sch Saint Louis MO 63110 Office Phone: 314-362-7252. Business E-Mail: spectorg@wustl.edu.

SPEER, DAVID BLAKENEY, chemicals executive; b. Sault Ste. Marie, Ont., Apr. 6, 1951; s. Richard Norwood and Mary (Davis) S.; m. Barbara Ann Brugenhemre, June 22, 1974; children: Blake, Sarah. BS in Indsl. Engring., Iowa State U., 1973; MBA, Northwestern U., 1977. Sales engr. Precision Paper, Wheeling, Ind., 1976-78, sales mgr., 1976-78; regional sales mgr. ITW Buildex, Itasca, Ill., 1978-81, nat. sales mktg. mgr., 1981-84, v.p., gen. mgr., 1984-92, ITW Paslode, Lincolnshire, Ill., 1992; group v.p., constrn. products Ill. Tool Works Inc. (ITW), 1994—95, exec. v.p. global constrn. products bus. Glenview, Ill., 1995—2004, exec. v.p. finishing systems bus., 1997—2004, exec. v.p. global Wilsonart laminate bus. unit, 2003—04, pres., 2004—, CEO, 2005—, chmn., 2006—. Bd. dirs. Rockwell Automation, Inc. Mem. adv. bd. Northwestern U. Master of Mgmt. and Mfg. program. Mem. Am. Mgmt. Assn., Am. Mktg. Assn., Am. Soc. Indsl. Engrs., Midwest Indsl. Mfg. Assn. Achievements include brokering historic number of acquisitions within company, 2006. Office: Ill Tool Works Inc 3600 W Lake Ave Glenview IL 60026-1215 Office Phone: 847-724-7500. Office Fax: 847-657-4572.

SPEHR, STEVEN, real estate company executive; Sr. v.p. Coldwell Banker Ira E. Berry, St. Louis.

SPEICHER, CARL EUGENE, pathologist; b. Carbondale, Pa., Mar. 21, 1933; s. William Joseph and Elizabeth Marcella (Connolly) S.; m. Mary Louise Walsh, June 21, 1958; children: Carl E. Jr., Gregory, Erik. BS in Biology, King's Coll., 1954; MD, U. Pa., 1958; student, Sch. of Aerospace Medicine, Brooks AFB, Tex., 1969. Diplomate Am. Bd. Pathology. Intern U. Pa. Hosp., Phila., 1958-59, resident, 1959-63; chief lab. svcs. USAF Hosp., London, Eng., 1963-66, USAF Med. Ctr. Wright Patterson, Dayton, Ohio, 1966-70; dir. clin. labs. and chmn. dept. pathology Wilford Hall USAF Med. Ctr., San Antonio, 1971-77; prof. dept. pathology Ohio State U., Columbus, 1977—2000, vice chair dept. pathology, 1992—2000, prof. emeritus dept. pathology, 2000—; dir. clin. svcs. Ohio State U. Med. Ctr., Columbus, 1977—2000; dir. clin. lab. Stoneridge Med. Ctr., Ohio State U., 2000—. Co-author: Choosing Effective Laboratory Tests, 1983; author: The Right Test, 1990, 3d edit., 1998. Col. USAF, 1956-77. Decorated Legion of Merit; fellow in med. chemistry SUNY, Syracuse, 1970-71. Mem. AMA, Ohio Soc. Pathologists, Ctrl. Ohio Soc. Pathologists, Am. Assn. for Clin. Chemistry, Assn. Clin. Scientists, Coll. Am. Pathologists, Am. Soc. Clin. Pathologists, Alpha Omega Alpha.

SPELLMIRE, GEORGE W., lawyer; b. Oak Park, Ill., June 10, 1948; Student, Brown U.; BA, Ohio State U., 1970; JD, De Paul U., 1974. Bar: Ill. 1974, US Dist. Ct. (no. dist.) Ill. 1974, US Tax Ct. 1984, US Ct. Appeals (7th cir.) 1984, US Supreme Ct. 1994. Ptnr. Hinshaw & Culbertson, Chgo., 1982-98, D'Ancona & Pflaum, Chgo., 1998—2003, Spellmire & Sommer, Chgo., 2003—. Author: Attorney Malpractice: Prevention and Defense, 1988, supplemental edit., 1990; co-author: Accounting, Auditing and Financial Malpractice, 1998, supplemental edit., 2000, Accountants' Legal Liability Guide, 1990, Illinois Handbook on Legal Malpractice, 1982, Associates Primer for the Prevention of Malpractice, 1987. Mem. ABA, Am. Coll. Trial Lawyers, Soc. Trial Lawyers, Fed. Trial Bar, Internat. Assn. Def. Counsel (legal malpractice com., def. counsel practice mgmt. com.), Ill. State Bar Assn. Office: 77 W Wacker Dr Ste 4800 Chicago IL 60601-1664 Office Phone: 312-606-8722. Business E-Mail: gws@spellmireSommer.com.

SPENCE, KENNETH F., III, lawyer, insurance company executive; b. Balt., Apr. 18, 1955; BA summa cum laude, Dickinson Coll., 1977; JD with honors, U. Md., 1982. Bar: Md. 1982, US Fed. Ct. 1982. Mem. litig. dept. Miles & Stockbridge, Balt., 1983—96, ptnr., 1990—96; with USF&G (merged with St. Paul Cos. Inc.), 1996—98; v.p. corp. litig. St. Paul Cos. Inc. (merged with Travelers Property Casualty Corp.), 1998—2004; v.p. legal services divsn., dep. gen. counsel St. Paul Travelers Cos. Inc., 2004, exec. v.p., gen. counsel, 2004—. Mem.: Md. State Bar, Minn. State Bar. Office: St Paul Travelers Companies Inc 385 Washington St Saint Paul MN 55102

SPENCE, MARY LEE, historian, educator; b. Kyle, Tex., Aug. 4, 1927; d. Jeremiah Milton and Mary Louise (Hutchison) Nance; m. Clark Christian Spence, Sept. 12, 1953; children: Thomas Christian, Ann Leslie. BA, U. Tex., 1947, MA, 1948; PhD, U. Minn., 1957. Instr., asst. prof. S.W. Tex. State U., San Marcos, 1948-53; lectr. Pa. State U., State College, 1955-58; mem. faculty U. Ill., Urbana-Champaign, 1973—, asst. prof., assoc. prof., 1973-81, 81-89, prof. history, 1989-90, prof. emerita, 1990—. Editor (with Donald Jackson) The Expeditions of John Charles Fremont, 3 vols., 1970-84, (with Clark Spence) Fanny Kelly's Narrative of Her Captivity Among the Sioux Indians, 1990, (with Pamela Herr) The Letters of Jessie Benton Fremont, 1993, The Arizona Diary of Lily Fremont, 1878-1881, 1997; contbr. articles to profl. jours. Mem. Children's Theater Bd., Urbana-Champaign, 1965-73. Grantee Nat. Hist. Pub. and Records Commn., Washington, 1977-78, 87-90, Huntington Libr., 1992; recipient Excellent Advisor award Liberal Arts and Sci. Coll./U. Ill., 1986. Mem. Western History Assn. (pres. 1981-82), Phi Beta Kappa (exec. sect. Gamma chpt. 1985-89, pres. 1991-92), Phi Alpha Theta. Episcopalian. Home: 101 W Windsor Rd #1211 Urbana IL 61802-6663 Office: U Ill Dept History 810 S Wright St Urbana IL 61801-3644

SPENCER, C. STANLEY, insurance company executive; b. Canton, Pa., Sept. 24, 1940; s. Clarence N. and Maude E. (Phipps) S.; m. Carol M. Vest, Aug. 23, 1962; children: Greg, Mike. BS in Agrl. Engring., Pa. State U., 1961. Regional sales mgr. W.T. Grant Co., NYC, 1966-76; engr. Hoover Well Service, Zion, Ill., 1976-80, ielson Iron Works, Racine, Wis., 1980-82; spl. agent Prudential Ins. Co., Racine, 1982-84, div. mgr., from 1984; v.p. legal dept. Am. Family Mut. Ins. Co., Madison, Wis. Recipient 1st Place Barbershop Chorus award, Racine, 1984, Kenosha, 1985, Manitowoc, 1986, 1st Place Barbershop Quartet award, Kenosha, Wis., 1986. Mem. Life Underwriters Assn. (v.p. 1985-86), Soc. for the Preservation and Encouragement of Barber Shop Quartet Singing in Am. (pres. Racine 1984-85). Clubs: Toastmasters (1st Place 1985). Republican. Home: 6234 Larchmont Dr Racine WI 53406-5120 Office: American Family Mutual Insurance Company 6000 American Pkwy Madison WI 53783-0001

SPENCER, DAVID JAMES, lawyer; b. Altadena, Calif., June 23, 1943; s. Dorcy James and Dorothy Estelle (Pingry) S.; m. Donna Rae Blair, Aug. 22, 1965; children: Daniel, Matthew. BA, Rocky Mountain Coll., 1965; JD, Yale U., 1968. Bar: Minn. 1968, U.S. Dist. Ct. Minn. 1968, U.S. Ct. Appeals (8th cir.) 1970. Mem. firm Briggs and Morgan, P.A., Mpls. and St. Paul, 1968—2003. Bd. dirs. RS Eden, Inc. Contbg. author 10 William Mitchell Law Rev., 1984; contbr. articles to profl. jours. Trustee Rocky Mountain Coll., Billings, Mont., 1980-01; bd. dirs. River Valley Arts Coun., 1996-01, Stillwater Area Arts Ctr. Alliance, 1998-01, Homeward Bound, Inc., 1999—; pres., bd. dirs. St. Croix Friends of Arts, Stillwater, Minn., 1981-84; bd. dirs. Valley Chamber Chorale, Stillwater, 1989-92; v.p. Minn. Jaycees, St. Paul, 1974; elder Presbyn. Ch. Recipient Silver Key St. Paul Jaycees, 1974; Disting. Svc. award Rocky Mountain Coll., 1981, Outstanding Svc. award, 1988, Disting. Achievement award, 1992. Fellow Am. Coll. Real Estate Lawyers; mem. ABA, Minn. Bar Assn., Ramsey County Bar Assn., Stillwater Country Club, Stillwater Sunrise Rotary Club (bd. dirs. 1997-99). Presbyterian. Avocations: trout fishing, golf, singing. Home: 10135 Waterfront Dr Woodbury MN 55129 E-mail: dspencer36@earthlink.net.

SPENCER, DONALD SPURGEON, historian, academic administrator; b. Anderson, Ind., Jan. 29, 1945; s. Thomas E. and Josephine (Litz) S.; m. Pamela Sue Roberts, June 19, 1965; 1 child, Jennifer Wynne. BA, Ill. Coll., 1967; PhD, U. Va., 1973. Asst. prof. history Westminster Coll., Fulton, Mo., 1973-76, Ohio U., Athens, 1976-77; from asst., assoc. to full prof., assoc. dean, asst. provost U. Mont., Missoula, 1977-90; provost SUNY, Geneseo, 1990-93; pres. Western Ill. U., Macomb, 1994—. Author: Louis Kossuth and Young America, 1978, The Carter Implosion: Jimmy Carter and the Amateur Style of Diplomacy,1989; contbr. articles to jours. in field. With U.S. Army, 1968-71, Korea. Woodrow Wilson Found. fellow, 1968; Danforth Found. univ. teaching fellow, 1971. Mem. Phi Beta Kappa. Congregationalist. Home: 124 Links Of Leith Williamsburg VA 23188-7461

SPENCER, GARY L., state government lawyer; b. Amboy, Ill., Sept. 4, 1949; s. W. Leslie and Mabel E. (Smith) S.; m. Julie A. Swanson, Mar. 14, 1987; children: Erin, Elizabeth, Nichole, Nathan. BS, Ill. State U., Normal, 1971; JD, Drake U., 1979. Bar: Ill. 1979, U.S. Dist. Ct. (no. dist.) Ill. 1981. Asst. state's atty. Whiteside County, Morrison, Ill., 1979-81, state's atty., 1981—. Mem. Ill. State Bar Assn., Whiteside County Bar Assn., Kiwanis Club Moarrison (2d v.p. 1993—). Methodist. Avocation: boating. Office: Whiteside County Courthouse 200 E Knox St Morrison IL 61270-2819

SPENCER, RICHARD HENRY, lawyer; b. Kansas City, Mo., Nov. 29, 1926; s. Byron Spencer and Helen Elizabeth (McCune) Hockaday; m. Barbara G. Rau, Aug. 2, 1952 (div. 1955); 1 chlid, Christina G. Cuevas; m. Katherine Graham, Dec. 28, 1957; children: Elisabeth M., Katherine S. Rivard. BS in Engring., Princeton U., 1949; LLB, U. Mo., 1952. Bar: Mo. 1952, U.S. Dist. Ct (we. dist.) Mo. 1955. Assoc. Spencer, Fane, Britt & Browne, Kansas City, 1952-59, ptnr., 1959-94; ret. ptnr., 1995—. Sec., bd. dirs. Met. Performing Arts Fund, Kansas City, 1984—; trustee Barstow Sch., Kansas City, 2002—; dir. Kansas City Symphony, 2004—. Mem. ABA, Mo. Bar Assn., Kansas City Club (pres. 1974), Kansas City Country Club (pres. 1986). Episcopalian. Avocations: hunting, golf, travel. Home: 77 Le Mans Ct Shawnee Mission KS 66208-5230 Office: Spencer Fane Britt & Browne 1400 Commerce Bank Bldg 1000 Walnut St Kansas City MO 64106-2140 Home Phone: 913-341-5205; Office Phone: 816-474-8100. E-mail: rhs@spencertone.com.

SPENCER, RUTH, announcer; b. San Diego; m. Jerry Aaron Spencer, 1992; 1 child, Amy. BS in Broadcast Journalism, San Francisco State U. With KSTP-TV, Mpls., 1985—89, WDIV-TV, Detroit, 1990—. Office: WDIV-TV 550 W Lafayette Blvd Detroit MI 48226

SPENDLOVE, STEVE DALE, broadcast executive; b. LA, Calif., July 20, 1955; V.p. and gen. mgr. KSAS, Wichita, Kans., 1992-96, WFTC-TV, Mpls., 1996—. Mem. Minn. Broadcasters Assn. (bd. dirs.), TV Music License Fee Com. (bd. dirs.). Office: 11358 Viking Dr Eden Prairie MN 55344-7238

SPERELAKIS, NICHOLAS, SR., retired physiology and biophysics educator, researcher; b. Joliet, Ill., Mar. 3, 1930; s. James and Aristea (Kayaidakis) S.; m. Dolores Martinis, Jan. 28, 1960; children: Nicholas Jr., Mark (dec.), Christine, Sophia, Thomas, Anthony. BS in Chemistry, U. Ill., 1951, MS in Physiology, 1955, PhD in Physiology, 1957. Cert. in electronics, radio and radar US Navy & Marine Corps Electronics Sch., 1952. Tchg. asst. U. Ill., Urbana, 1954-57; instr. Case Western Res. U., Cleve., 1957-59, asst. prof., 1959-66, assoc. prof., 1966; prof. U. Va., Charlottesville, 1966-83; Joseph Eichberg prof. physiology Coll. Medicine U. Cin., 1983-96, chmn. dept., 1983-93, Eichberg prof. emeritus, 1996—. Cons. NPS Pharm., Inc., Salt Lake City, 1988-95, Carter Wallace, Inc. Cranbury, N.J., 1988-91; vis. prof. U. St. Andrews, Scotland, 1972-73, U. San Luis Potosi, Mex., 1986, U. Athens, Greece, 1994; Rosenblueth prof. Centro de Investigacion y Avanzades, Mex., 1972; mem. sci. adv. com. several internat. meetings, editl. bds. numerous sci. jours. Co-editor: Handbook of Physiology: Heart, 1979; editor: Physiology and Pathophysiology of the Heart, 1984, 2d edit., 1988, 3rd edit., 1994, 4th edit., 2000, Calcium Antagonists: Mechanisms of Action on Cardiac Muscle and Vascular Smooth Muscle, 1984, Cell Interactions and Gap Junctions, vols. I and II, 1989, Frontiers in Smooth Muscle Research, 1990, Ion Channels in Vascular Smooth Muscle and Endothelial Cells, 1991, Essentials of Physiology, 1993, 2d edit., 1996, Cell Physiology Source Book, 1995 (Outstanding Acad. Book, Choice Am. Libr. Assn. 1996, 98), 3d edit., 2001, Electrogenesis of Biopotentials, 1995; assoc. editor Circulation Rsch., 1970-75, 75-80, Molecular Cellular Cardiology; regional editor Current Drug Targets, 2000-02; contbr. more than 500 articles to profl. jours. Lectr. Project Hope, Peru, 1962. Sgt. USMC, 1951—53, Korean War, with USMCR, 1953—59. Recipient Disting. Alumnus award Rockdale (Ill.) Pub. Schs., 1958, Rsch. Excellence award Am. Heart Assn. Ohio, 1995, Visionary award Am. Heart Assn., S.W. Ohio, 1996; U. Cin. Grad. fellow, 1989; NIH grantee, 1959-99. Mem. IEEE, Engring. in Medicine and Biology, Am. Physiol. Soc. (chair steering com. sect. 1981-82), Biophys. Soc. (coun. 1990-93), Am. Soc. Pharmacology and Exptl. Therapeutics, Internat. Soc. Heart Rsch. (coun. 1980-89, 92-98), Am. Hellenic Ednl. Progressive Assn. (pres. Charlottesville chpt. 1980-82), Ohio Physiol. Soc. (pres. 1990-91), Phi Kappa Phi. Independent. Greek Orthodox. Avocations: ancient Greek coins, stamp collecting/philately. Personal E-mail: nicksperel@aol.com.

SPERLING, JAC, professional sports team executive; CEO Minn. Wild Minn. Hockey Ventures Group, St. Paul, 1997—; ptnr. Hogan & Hartson, Washington. Office: 317 Washington St Saint Paul MN 55102

SPERTUS, EUGENE, frame manufacturing company executive; b. 1940; BS, U. Mich., 1962; MSE, Columbia U., 1963. With Hypertech Co., 1969—74, Intercraft Industries Corp., Chgo., 1963—69, 1974—, v.p., 1977—79, pres., COO, 1979—, also dir.

SPERZEL, GEORGE E., JR., former personal care industry executive; b. 1951; BS in Bus. Adminstrn./Mgmt., U. Louisville, 1977. With General Electric Co., 1977-93; v.p., CFO Andrew Jergens Co., Cin., 1993-2000, Kao Am. Inc., Wilmington, Del., 1995-2000; svp and CFO Alliant Exchange, Inc., 2000—. Office: Alliant Food Service 9933 Woods Dr Skokie IL 60077-1057

SPICER, HOLT VANDERCOOK, retired theater educator; b. Pasadena, Calif., Feb. 1, 1928; s. John Lovely and Dorothy Eleanor (Clause) S.; m. Marion Arel Gibson, Aug. 16, 1952; children: Mary Ellen, Susan Leah, Laura Alice, John Millard. BA, U. Redlands, 1952, MA, 1957; PhD, U. Okla., 1964. From instr. speech and theatre to prof. S.W. Mo. State Coll., 1952-93, emeritus prof., 1993—, head dept. speech and theatre, 1967-71, dean Sch. Arts and Humanities, 1971-85. Chmn. Dist. 4 at. Debate Tournament Com., 1955, 58, 64, 68 Vestryman Episcopalian Ch., 1981—85, 1998—2001; bd. dirs. Springfield (Mo.) Cmty. Ctr., 1981—. Named Debate Coach of Decade U.S. Air Force Acad., 1965, Holt V. Spicer Debate Forum, 1988; recipient Alumni Achievement award in Speech and Debate U. Redlands, 1991, Alumni award of appreciation S.W. Mo. State U., 1996; team won CEDA Nat. Debate championship, 1992. Mem.: AAUP, Am. Forensic Assn., Speech Communication Assn. Episcopalian. Home: 2232 E Langston St Springfield MO 65804-2646 E-mail: holtspicer9@mchsi.com.

SPICER, S(AMUEL) GARY, lawyer, writer, educator; b. Dickson, Tenn., Jan. 8, 1942; s. Clark and E. Maybelle (Hogin) S.; children: Victoria, S. Gary Jr., Matthew, Katy, Mark, David. BA, Adrian Coll., 1964; MBA, Wayne State U., 1965; JD, Detroit Coll. Law, 1969; LLD (hon.), Adrian Coll., 2002. Bar: Mich. 1969, Tenn. 1969. With pers. dept. GM Truck & Coach, Detroit, 1964-66; with trust dept. Nat. Bank Detroit, 1966-69; acct. Price Waterhouse & Co., Detroit, 1969-71; propr. Law Firm of S. Gary Spicer, Detroit, 1971—. Adj. prof. law, sports and entertainment Mich. State U., Lansing, 2002—; adj. prof. law, sports U. Detroit, 2006—. Author: Surviving Success, 1990. Co-chmn. endowment com. Adrian (Mich.) Coll., 1982-94, Don and Dolly Smith Found., Detroit, 1981—; trustee Grosse Pointe Acad., 1983-95, Joseph Sloan Bonsall and Mary Ann Bonsall Found., 1988—, Don Baylor Found., 1995—, JoAnne Nicolay Found., 1996—, Richard A. and Donna L. Sterban Found., 1997—, Pam Lewis Found, 1997—, Detroit Sch. Arts, 2004—; Detroit Tigers Players Home Clubhouse Scholarship Fund, Doris and Don Duchene, Sr. Found., Mary I. McLeod Found.; former elder, treas., Fort St. Presbyn. Ch.; memorabilia cons. Ernie Harwell Libr. Sports. With USAR, 1965-71 Recipient Young Alumni Achievement award Adrian Coll. Alumni Assn., 1987; named to Athletic Hall of Fame, Adrian Coll., 1996. Mem. Detroit Athletic Club Avocations: Russian literature, squash. Office Phone: 313-884-9700. Personal E-mail: sgspicer@aol.com.

SPIEGEL, GABE, newscaster; b. Akron, Ohio; married. BA in Mass Comm./Broadcasting, Anderson U. Anchor, reporter Sta. WUPW-TV, Toledo; anchor KPTM-TV, Omaha, Sta. SWYX/WTTE-TV, Columbus, Ohio, 2000—. Office: WSYX/WTTE-TV 1261 Dublin Rd Columbus OH 43215

SPIEGEL, S. ARTHUR, federal judge; b. Cin., Oct. 24, 1920; s. Arthur Major and Hazel (Wise) S.; m. Louise Wachman, Oct. 31, 1945; children: Thomas, Arthur Major II, Andrew, Roger Daniel. BA, U. Cin., 1942, postgrad., 1949; LLB, Harvard U., 1948. Assoc. Kasfir & Chalfie, Cin., 1948-52; assoc. Benedict, Bartlett & Shepard, Cin., 1952-53, Gould & Gould, Cin., 1953-54; ptnr. Gould & Spiegel, Cin., 1954-59; assoc. Cohen, Baron, Druffel & Hogan, Cin., 1960; ptnr. Cohen, Todd, Kite & Spiegel, Cin., 1961-80; judge U.S. Dist Ct. Ohio, Cin., 1980—; sr. status, 1995—. Served to capt. USMC, 1942-46. Mem. ABA, FBA, Ohio Bar Assn., Cin. Bar Assn., Cin. Lawyers Club. Democrat. Jewish. Office: US Dist Ct 838 US Courthouse 5th Walnut St Cincinnati OH 45202

SPIEGLER, JOSEPH ANDREW, lawyer; b. LI, NY, Apr. 4, 1968; BA magna cum laude, NYU, 1990; JD, U. Notre Dame, 1994. Bar: Ill. 1994, US Dist. Ct. (no. dist. Ill.). Ptnr. Winston & Strawn, Chgo., 1994—2007, Much Shelist, Chgo., 2007—. Office: Much Shelist 191 N Wacker Dr Chicago IL 60606-1615 Office Phone: 312-521-2765. Business E-Mail: jspiegler@muchshelist.com.

SPIGARELLI, JAMES L., science administrator; BA in Chemistry, MS in Chemistry, PhD in Chemistry, Kans. State Coll. Various positions Midwest Rsch. Inst., Kansas City, Mo., 1961—78, v.p., 1978—91, sr. v.p., 1991—97, exec. v.p., 1997—98, COO, 1998—99, pres., CEO, 1999—. Bd. dirs. Sci. City at Union Sta., Kansas City Mus., KCCatalyst, Brush Creek Cmty. Ptnrs., Sci. Pioneers; founding bd. mem. Kansas City Area Life Sci. Inst., Inc., 2000; trustee Univ. Mo.-KC, Avila Coll., Rockhurst Univ. R&D task force Kansas City Area Life Scis. Inst., 1999; trustee U. Mo., Kansas city, Avila Coll., Rockhurst U.; bd. dirs. Kansas City Area Life Scis. Inst., 2000. Lt. Chemical Corps US Army, Rocky Mt. Arsenal. Named Tech. Leader of Yr., Silicon Prairie Tech. Assn., 2000; recipient Meritorious Achievement award, Pitts. State U., 1993. Fellow: Coll. Arts and Scis. Alumni, Kans. State U. Office: Midwest Rsch Inst 425 Volker Blvd Kansas City MO 64110

SPINDLER, GEORGE S., lawyer, retired oil industry executive; BCE, Ga. Inst. Tech., 1961; JD, DePaul U., 1966. Bar: Ill. 1966. Asst. gen. counsel, patents and licensing Amoco Corp., Chgo., 1979-81, gen. mgr. info. svcs., 1981-85, v.p. planning and adminstrn., 1985-87, assoc. gen. counsel, 1987-88, dep. gen. counsel, 1988-89, v.p., gen. counsel, 1989-92, sr. v.p., gen. counsel, 1992-95, sr. v.p. law and corporate affairs, 1995-99; ret., 1999. Dir. Methode Electronics Inc, 2004—. Office: Methodde Electronics 7401 W Wilson Ave Chicago IL 60706

SPINELL, RICHARD E., financial services company executive; Ptnr. Mid-Am. Asset Mgmt., Inc., Oakbrook Terrace, Ill., 1993—. Office: Mid-Am Asset Mgmt Inc 2 Mid-Am Plz Ste 330 Oakbrook Terrace IL 60181

SPIOTTO, JAMES ERNEST, lawyer; b. Chgo., Nov. 25, 1946; s. Michael Angelo and Vinnetta Catherine (Henninger) S.; m. Ann Elizabeth Humphreys, Dec. 23, 1972; children: Michael Thomas, Mary Catherine, Joan Elizabeth, Kathryn Ann. AB, St. Mary's of the Lake, 1968; JD, U. Chgo., 1972. Bar: Ill. 1972, U.S. Dist. Ct. (no. dist.) Ill. 1973, U.S. Ct. Appeals (7th cir.)1974, US Ct.Appeal(3d cir.), 1992, U.S. Supreme Ct. 1978, U.S. Ct. Appeals (9th cir.) 1984, U.S. Dist. Ct. (so. dist.) Calif. 1984. Exclusionary rule study-project dir. Law Enforcement Assistance Agy. Grant, Chgo., 1972; law clk. to presiding justice U.S. Dist. Ct., Chgo., 1972-74; assoc. Chapman and Cutler, Chgo., 1974-80, ptnr., 1980—. Chmn. program on defaulted bonds and bankruptcy Practising Law Inst., 1982—, chmn program on troubled debt financing, 1987—. Author: Troubled Debt Financing: Litig. Bankruptcy, 1987, Defaulted Bonds and Bankruptcy, 1988, Defaults, Litig., Bankruptcy, and Workouts, 1988, Troubled Debt Securities, 1988, The Problems of Indenture Trustees and Bondholders, 1988, Bonds and Bankruptcy, 1989, Defaulted Securities, 1990; co-author with Joseph C. Daley Current Disclosure of Obligations for Mcpl. Securities, 1988, Mcpl. Bond Disclosure, 1987, The Law of State and Local Govt. Debt Financing, 2001; contbr. numerous articles to profl. jours. With USAR, 1969-75. Recipient Mcpl. Industry Contbn. award, Nat. Fedn. of Mcpl. Analysts, Carlson Prize, 1995. Mem. ABA, Chgo. Bar Assn., Econ. Club of Chgo., Nat. Assn. Bond Lawyers, Soc. Mcpl. Analysts, Law Club of City of Chgo., Union League, Econs. Club Chgo. Roman Catholic. Office: Chapman and Cutler 111 W Monroe St Ste 1700 Chicago IL 60603-4006 Office Phone: 312-845-3000. Office Fax: 312-701-2361.

SPIRES, ROBERT CECIL, foreign language educator; b. Mo. Valley, Iowa, Dec. 1, 1936; s. Roy C. and Ellen M. (Epperson) S.; m. Roberta A. Hyde, Feb. 2, 1963; children: Jeffrey R., Leslie Ann. BA, U. Iowa, 1959, MA, 1963, PhD, 1968. Asst. prof. Ohio U., Athens, 1967-69; asst. prof. Dept. Spanish and Portuguese U. Kans., Lawrence, 1969-72, assoc. prof., 1972-78, prof., 1978—, prof. emeritus, chmn. dept., 1983-92. Author: La novela española de posguerra, 1978, Beyond the Metafictional Mode, 1984, Transparent Simulacra, 1988, Post-Totalitarian Spanish Fiction, 1996; contbg. editor SigloXX/20th Century; editl. bd. Jour. of Interdisciplinary Literary Studies, 1993—, Ind. Jour. of Hispanic Lit., 1992—. Served with U.S. Army, 1959-61. NEH fellow, 1981-82, U.S.-Spain Joint Com. fellow, 1985-86, Hall Ctr. for Humanities fellow, 1992, Program Cultural Coop. fellow, 1993. Mem. Revista de Estudios Hispánicos (editorial bd. 1985—), Anales de Literatura Contemporánea (editorial bd. 1981—), Letras Peninsulares (editorial bd. 1987—), MLA (del. assembly 1989-91), MLA 20th Century Spain (exec. com. 1983-89), 20th Century Spanish Assn. Am. (v.p. 1989-92). Office: U Kans Dept Spanish & Portuguese 1445 Jayhawk Blvd Lawrence KS 66045-0001 Home Phone: 785-842-6820; Office Phone: 785-864-3851. E-mail: rspires@ku.edu.

SPITZE, ROBERT GEORGE FREDERICK, agricultural studies educator; b. Berryville, Ark., Oct. 12, 1922; s. Wesley Henry and Nora Catherine (Stullken) Spitze; m. Hazel Cleo Taylor, Mar. 4, 1944; children: Glenna Dean, Ken Rollin. Student, Columbia U., 1944; BS (Sears Roebuck nat. fellow), U. Ark., 1947; PhD (Knapp research fellow), U. Wis., 1954. Instr. U. Wis., Madison, 1950; asst. prof. to prof. U. Tenn., Knoxville, 1951-60; prof. agrl. econs. U. Ill., Urbana, 1960-93. Vis. prof. Wye Coll., U. London, 1967-68; vis. research prof. policy U.S. Dept. Agr., Washington, 1975; vis. lectr. various univs., U.S. and Eng.; cons. Fed. Intermediate Credit Bank, 1958-59, Ill. Gen. Assembly Commn. on Revenue, 1963, Tex. A&M U., 1970, Am. Farm Bur. Fedn., Chgo., 1971, Ill. Gov.'s Commn. on Farm Income, 1972, Nat. Agrl. Research Policy Adv. Com., 1975, U.S. Dept. Agr. Econs. Research Service, 1976, Wharton Econometric Forecasting Inc., 1977, at. Rural Center, Washington, 1979-80, Nat. Public Policy Com., 1980, Okla. State U., 1986; mem. Ill. Gov.'s Council Econ. Advisers, 1974-76 Co-author: Food and Agricultural Policy, Economics and Politics, 1994; co-editor Policy Rsch. Notes, 1975-92, Food, Agriculture, and Rural Policy into the Twenty-first Century, 1994; editor Agricultural and Food Policy: Issues and Alternatives for the 1990s, 1990; contbr. articles to profl. jours., chpts. to books Lt. USNR, 1943—47. Recipient Funk recognition award, 1973, Excellence in Teaching award U. Ill., 1977, Outstanding Agr. Coll. Alumni award U. Ark., 1994; co-recipient Outstanding Philanthropist Award Nat. Agrl. Alumni Devel. Assn., 2004 Mem. AAAS, Am. Econ. Assn., Am. Agrl. Econs. Assn. (Disting. Policy award 1981, Disting. Teaching award 1972, travel study grantee to France 1964), Internat. Assn. Agrl. Econs., Agrl. Econs. Soc. (U.K.), AAUP, Blue Key, Sigma Xi, Omicron Delta Kappa, Gamma Sigma Delta, Phi Eta Sigma, Alpha Zeta, Phi Sigma Office: U Ill Dept Agr Econ 1301 W Gregory Dr Dept Agr Urbana IL 61801-9015

SPITZER, ALAN, automotive executive; Student, Baldwin Wallce Coll. Gen. mgr. Dodge dealership Spitzer Mgmt. Inc., Ohio, dealer, operator Akron, Ohio, CEO Elyria, Ohio, 1990—, also chmn. bd. dirs. Mem. nat. dealer coun. Ford Motor Co., Chrysler Corp.; mem. Key Bank USA Dealer Adv. Bd. Office: Spitzer Mgmt Inc 150 E Bridge St Elyria OH 44035-5219

SPITZER, JOHN BRUMBACK, lawyer; b. Toledo, Mar. 6, 1918; s. Lyman and Blanche (Brumback) S.; m. Lucy Ohlinger, May 10, 1941 (dec. Oct. 13, 1971); children: John B., Molly (Mrs. Edmund Frost), Lyman, Adelbert L.; m. Vondah D. Thornbury, July 3, 1972 (dec. Nov. 2001); stepchildren: Vondah, Barbara, James R. Thornbury. Grad., Phillips Andover Acad., 1935; BA, Yale U., 1939, LLB, 1947. Bar: Ohio 1947. Law clk. to U.S. Supreme Ct. Justice Stanley Reed, 1947-48; ptnr. Marshall, Melhorn, Cole, Hummer & Spitzer, Toledo, 1955-86, Hummer & Spitzer, Toledo, 1986-89; with Hummer Legal Svcs. Corp., 1990—2002; ptnr. Spitzer and Hummer, 1990—. Pres. Spitzer Paper Box Co., 1955-63; v.p. Spitzer Bldg. Co., 1960-91, pres. 1992—. Pres. Toledo Symphony Orch., 1956-58, v.p., sec., 1958-86, trustee, 1986—. Maj. AUS, World War II. Mem.: Belmont Country Club. Congregationalist. Home: 29620 Gleneagles Rd Perrysburg OH 43551-3530 Office: Spitzer Bldg Co Rm 430 Spitzer Bldg 520 Madison Ave Toledo OH 43604 Office Phone: 419-255-1440. Personal E-mail: info@winelandlegal.com.

SPLINTER, WILLIAM ELDON, agricultural engineering educator; b. North Platte, Nebr., Nov. 24, 1925; s. William John and Minnie (Calhoun) Splinter; m. Eleanor Love Peterson, Jan. 10, 1952 (dec. Jan. 6, 1999); children: Kathryn Love, William John, Karen Ann, Robert Marvin; m. Elizabeth Butters Calhoun, Feb. 9, 2002. BS in Agrl. Engring., U. Nebr., 1950; MS in Agrl. Engring., Mich. State U., 1951, PhD in Agrl. Engring., 1955. Instr. agrl. engring. Mich. State U., East Lansing, 1953-54; assoc. prof. biology and agrl. engring. N.C. State U., Raleigh, 1954-60, prof. biology and agrl. engring., 1960-68; head agrl. engring. dept. U. Nebr., Lincoln, 1968—88, vice chancellor rsch., 1988—93; interim dean Coll. Engring. & Tech. U. Nebr., 1994—95, 2001—02; interim dir. Nebr. State Mus., 2002—. Cons. engr.; exec. bd. Am. Assn. Engring. Socs.; hon. prof. Shengyang (People's Republic of China) Agrl. U. Contbr. articles to tech. jours.; patentee in field. Vol. dir. L.F. Larsen Tractor Mus. Served with USNR, 1946-51. Recipient Massey Ferguson Gold medal, 1978, John Deere Gold medal, 1995, Disting. Svc. award Kiwanis, 1994, George Howard-Loiuse Pound award, 2001; named to Nebr. Hall of Agrl. Achievement; named Disting. Alumni, U. Nebr., Lincoln, 2000, Mich. State U., 2005; named U. Nebr. Splinter Rsch. Lab. in his honor, 2004. Fellow AAAS, NSPE, Am. Soc. Agrl. Engrs. (pres., adminstrv.

council, found. pres., Presdl. citation 1999); mem. Nat. Acad. Engring., Soc. Automotive Engrs., Am. Soc. Engring. Edn., Sigma Xi, Sigma Tau, Sigma Pi Sigma, Pi Mu Epsilon, Gamma Sigma Delta, Phi Kappa Phi, Beta Sigma Psi. Home: 4801 Bridle Ln Lincoln NE 68516-3436 Office: U Nebr Lincoln PO Box 830833 Lincoln NE 68583-0833 Office Phone: 402-472-8389. Business E-Mail: wsplinter1@unl.edu.

SPODEK, BERNARD, early childhood educator; b. Bklyn., Sept. 17, 1931; s. David and Esther (Lebenbaum) S.; m. Prudence Debb, June 21, 1957; children: Esther Yin-ling, Jonathan Chou. BA, Bklyn. Coll., 1952; MA, Columbia U., 1955, EdD, 1962. Cert. early childhood edn. tchr., N.Y. Tchr. Beth Hayeled Sch., NYC, 1952-56, N.Y. City Pub. Schs., Bklyn., 1956-57, Early Childhood Ctr., Bklyn. Coll., 1957-60; asst. prof. elem. edn. U. Wis.-Milw., 1961-65; assoc. prof. early childhood edn. U. Ill., Champaign, 1965-68, prof. dept. curriculum and instrn., 1968-97, dir. dept. grad. programs, 1986-87, chair dept., 1987-89, dir. hons. program, Coll. Edn., 1984-86, mem. faculty Bur. Ednl. Rsch., 1981-85, prof. emeritus, 1997—; adv. prof. Hong Kong Inst. of Edn., 1999-2001. Dir. insts. Nat. Def. Edn. Act, 1965-67, dir. experienced tchr. fellowship program, 1967-69, co-dir. program for tchr. trainers in early childhood edn., 1969-74; vis. prof. Western Wash. State U., 1974, U. Wis., Madison, 1980, Kobe Shinwa Women's U., Japan, 2004, 07; vis. scholar Sch. Early Childhood Studies, Brisbane (Australia) Coll. Advanced Edn., Delissa Inst. Early Childhood Studies, S. Australia Coll. Advanced Edn., 1985, Beijing Normal U., anjing Normal U., East China Normal U., Shangai, People's Republic China, 1986; rsch. fellow Kobe U., Japan, 1996; adj. prof. Queensland (Australia) U. Tech., 2000. Author or co-author: (with others) A Black Studies Curriculum for Early Childhood Education, 1972, 2d edit., 1976, Teaching in the Early Years, 1972, 3d edit., 1985, Early Childhood Education, 1973, Studies in Open Education, 1975 (Japanese trans.), Early Childhood Education: Issues and Perspectives, 1977, (with Nir-Janiv and Steg) International Perspectives on Early Childhood Education, 1982 (Hebrew trans.), with Saracho and Lee (Mainstreaming Young Children, 1984, (with Saracho and Davis) Foundations of Early Childhood Education, 1987, 2d edit. (Japanese trans.), 1991, Right from the Start, 1994 (Chinese, Portuguese and Korean translations), Dealing with Individual Differences in the Early Childhood Classroom, 1994; editor: Handbook of Research in Early Childhood Education, 1982, rev. edit., 2005, Today's Kindergarten, 1986; (with Saracho and Peters) Professionalism and the Early Childhood Practitioner, 1988; (with Saracho) Early Childhood Teacher Education, 1990, Issues in Early Childhood Curriculum, 1991, Educationally Appropriate Kindergarten Practices, 1991, Issues in Childcare, 1992, Handbook of Research on the Education of Young Children (Portuguese tranls.), 1993, Language and Literacy in Early Childhood Education, 1993, Issues in Early Childhood Educational Evaluation and Assessment, 1996, Multiple Perspectives on Play in Early Childhood Education, 1998, Contemporary Perspectives in Early Childhood Curriculum, 2002, Contemporary Perspectives on Literacy in Early Childhood Education, 2002, Contemporary Perspectives on Play in Early Childhood Education, 2003, Studying Teachers in Early Childhood Settings, 2003, Contemporary Perspectives on Language Policy and Literacy Instruction, 2004, Contemporary Perspectives on Families, Communities, and Schools for Young Children, 2005, International Perspectives on Research in Early Childhood Education, 2005, Handbook of Research on the Education of Young Children, 2d edit., 2006, Contemporary Perspectives on Socialization and Social Development in Early Childhood Education, 2007, Contemporary Perspectives on Social Learning in Early Childhood Education, 2007; (with Safford and Saracho) Early Childhood Special Education, 1994; (with Garcia, McLaughlin & Saracho) Meeting the Challenge of Cultural and Linguistic Diversity, 1995; (with Saracho and Pellegrini) Issues in Early Childhood Educational Research, 1998, others; series editor Yearbook in Early Childhood Education, early childhood edn. publs., 1990-00; series co-editor: Contemporary Perspectives in Early Childhood Education, 2002—; guest editor Studies in Ednl. Evaluation, 1982, Early Education and Child Development, 1995; also contbr. chpts to books, articles to profl. jours. Mem. Am. Ednl. Rsch. Assn. (chair early childhood and child devel. spl. interest group 1983-84, publs. com. 1984-86), Nat. Assn. Edn. Young Children (sec. 1965-68, bd. govs. 1968-72, pres. 1976-78, editl. adv. bd. 1972-76, book rev. editor, 1972-74, cons. editor, 1985-87 Young Children jour., tchr. edn. commn. 1981-88, chair commn. on appropriate edn. 4-5 yr. old children, 1984-85, cons. editor Early Childhood Rsch. Quar. 1987-90), Nat. Soc. for Study of Edn. (1972 yearbook com., Asia-Pacific edn. rev.), Pacific Early Childhood Edn. Rsch. Assn. (pres. 2000—). Office: Univ Ill Dept Curriculum & Instrn 1310 S 6th St Champaign IL 61820-6925 Home Phone: 217-352-1482. Business E-Mail: b-spodek@uiuc.edu.

SPOERRY, ROBERT F., manufacturing executive; b. 1955; B Mech. Engring., Fed. Inst. Tech., Zurich Switzerland; MBA, U. Chgo. Mgmt. positions with Mettler-Toledo Internat., 1983—87, head. indsl. & retail (Europe), 1987—93, pres., CEO, 1993—98, chmn., pres., CEO, 1998—2007, exec. chmn., 2008—. Bd. dirs. Mettler-Toledo Internat., 1996—, Phonak Group, Sonova Holding AG. Bd. dir. Swiss-Am. C. of C. Office: Mettler-Toledo Internat 1900 Polaris Pkwy Columbus OH 43240 Office Phone: 614-438-4511.

SPOHN, HERBERT EMIL, psychologist; b. Berlin, June 10, 1923; s. Herbert F. and Bertha S.; m. Billie M. Powell, July 28, 1973; children: Jessica, Madeleine. BSS., CCNY, 1949; PhD, Columbia U., 1955. Research psychologist VA Hosp., Montrose, NY, 1955-60, chief research sect., 1960-64; sr. research psychologist Menninger Found., Topeka, 1965-80, dir. hosp. research, 1979-94, dir. research dept., 1981-94; ret., prof. emeritus for rsch., 1994—. Mem. mental health small grant com. NIMH, 1972-76, mem. treatment assessment rev. com., 1983-86, chmn. 1986-87. Author: (with Gardner Murphy) Encounter with Reality, 1968; assoc. editor: Schizophrenia Bull, 1970-87, 91—; contbr. articles to profl. jours. Served with AUS, World War II. USPHS grantee, 1964— Fellow Am. Psychopath. Assn.; mem. AAAS, N.Y. Acad. Sci., Soc. Psychopath. Research, Phi Beta Kappa, Sigma Xi. Office: 1906 SW Village Dr Topeka KS 66604-3714 E-mail: hspohn@prodigy.net.

SPOKANE, ROBERT BRUCE, biophysical chemist; b. Cleve., Aug. 5, 1952; s. Herbert Norman and Marjorie Ellen (Firsten) S.; m. Linda Carol Wright, June 20, 1976; children: Lea, Hannah, Tara. BS in Chemistry, Ohio U., 1975; MS in Biophys. Chemistry, U. Colo., 1978, PhD in Biophys. Chemistry, 1981. Cert. full cave diver. Tchg. asst. dept. chemistry U. Colo., Boulder, 1975-77, rsch. asst. dept. chemistry, 1977-81; staff scientist Procter & Gamble Co., Cin., 1981-84; rsch. scientist dept. neurophysiology Children's Hosp., Cin., 1984-90; sr. scientist, product mgr. YSI Co., Yellow Springs, Ohio, 1990—2005; sr. rsch. scientist U. Dayton, Ohio, 2006—. Cons. Synthetic Blood Internat., Yellow Springs, 1992. Contbr. articles to profl. jours. Rescuer, treas. Boulder Emergency Squad, 1980; rescue diver Kitty Hawk Scuba, Dayton, Ohio, 1992. Recipient Merck Index award Ohio U., 1975. Mem. Am. Chem. Soc., N.Y. Acad. Sci., Am. Physiol. Soc., Nat. Speleological Soc. (cave diving sect.), Sigma Xi. Achievements include research in implantable glucose sensors; oxygen tonometer for peritoneal oxygen measurements; interferant removal system for biosensors for methanol, ethanol, glutamate, and glutamine, optical carbon dioxide sensor, water chemistry in submerged caves. Home: 1715 Garry Dr Bellbrook OH 45305-1362 Office: UDRI 300 Collose Pk Dayton OH 45469-0181 Office Phone: 937-767-7241. Business E-Mail: rspokane@ysi.com.

SPONG, DOUGLAS K., public relations executive; B in English, Iowa State U. With Colle & McVoy, sr. v.p., mng. dir., also bd. dirs.; mng. ptnr. Carmichael Lynch Spong, 1990—. Office: Carmichael Lynch Spong Pub Rels 800 Hennepin Ave Minneapolis MN 55403-1817

SPOOR, WILLIAM HOWARD, food products executive; b. Pueblo, Colo., Jan. 16, 1923; s. Charles Hinchman and Doris Field (Slaughter) S.; m. Janet Spain, Sept. 23, 1950; children: Melanie G., Cynthia F., William Lincoln. BA, Dartmouth Coll., 1949; postgrad., Denver U., 1949, Stanford U., 1965. Asst. sales mgr. N.Y. Export divsn. Pillsbury Co., 1949-53; mgr. N.Y. office Pillsbury Co., 1953-62, v.p. export divsn. Mpls., 1962-68, v.p., gen. mgr. internat. ops., 1968-73, CEO, 1973-85, also bd. dirs., chmn. exec. com., 1987, pres., CEO, 1988, past chmn. bd. dirs. Bd. dirs. Coleman Co. Mem. regional export expansion coun. Dept. Commerce, 1966-74; bd. dirs. exec. Coun. Fgn. Diplomats, 1976-78; mem. bd. visitors Nelson A. Rockefeller Ctr., Dartmouth Coll., 1992-95; Minn. Orchestral Assn., United Negro Coll. Fund, 1973-75; chmn. Capitol City Renaissance Task Force, 1985; trustee Mpls. Found., 1985-92; mem. sr. campaign cabinet Carlson Com. U. Minn., 1985; mem. corps. rels. com. Nature Conservancy, 1985; mem. Nat. Cambodia Crisis Com., pres. pvt. sector Dept. Transp, task force, 1982, pres. pvt. sector survey on cost control, 1983; chmn. YWCA Tribute to Womwn in Internat. Industry. 2d lt. inf. U.S. Army, 1943-46. Recipient Golden Plate award, Am. Acad. Achievement, Disting. Bus. Leadership award, St. Cloud State U., Miss. Valley World Trade award, Outstanding Achievement award, Dartmouth Coll., Horatio Alger award, 1986, Medal of Merit, U.S. Savs. Bond Program; honored with William H. Spoor Dialogues on Leadership, Dartmouth Coll., honored Fair Player Minn. Women's Polit. Caucus, 1989. Mem.: Nat. Fgn. Trade Coun., Grocery Mfrs. Am. (treas. 1973—84), Minn. Bus. Partnership, Minn. Hist. Soc. (mem. exec. com. 1983, bd. dirs.), Mpls. Club (bd. govs. 1985, pres. 1986), Old Baldy Club, Woodhill Country Club, River Club NYC, The Country Club Salt Lake City, Alta Club, Phi Beta Kappa. Home: 1173 Oak Forest Rd Salt Lake City UT 84103 Office: 4900 IDS Ctr Minneapolis MN 55402 Office Phone: 612-330-4621.

SPORE, KEITH KENT, newspaper executive; b. Milw., May 29, 1942; s. G. Keith and Evelyn A. (Morgan) S.; divorced; children: Bradley, Julie, Justine; m. Kathy Stokebrand. BS in Journalism, U. Wis., Milw., 1967. City editor Milw. Sentinel, 1977-81; asst. mng. editor/news, 1981-89; mng. editor Milw. Jour. Sentinel, 1989-91, editor, 1991-95, editl. page editor, 1995, pres., 1995—, pub., 1996—2004. Author: (novels) The Hell Masters, 1977, Death of a Scavenger, 1980. With U.S. Army, 1961-64. Recipient Freedom of Info. award Soc. Profl. Journalists, 1995; named Mass Comms. Alumnus of Yr., U. Wis.-Milw., 1994. Mem. Greater Milw. Com. Office: Milw Jour Sentinel PO Box 661 Milwaukee WI 53201-0661 E-mail: kspore@onwis.com.

SPRAGUE, CHARLES W., lawyer, finance company executive; b. Orange, NJ, Nov. 14, 1949; BA cum laude, Yale U., 1971; MBA, JD, NYU, 1975. Bar: NY 1976, DC 1993, Wis. Atty. Sullivan & Cromwell, 1975—83, Reboul MacMurray, 1983—92, Sprague & Coultas, 1992—94; exec. v.p., gen. counsel, sec. Fiserv, Inc., Brookfield, Wis., 1994—, chief admin. officer, 1999—. Mem.: ABA, Wis. State Bar Assn., DC Bar Assn., Internat. Bar Assn. Office: Fiserv Inc PO Box 979 255 Fiserv Dr Brookfield WI 53045 Office Phone: 262-879-5000.

SPRANG, MILTON LEROY, obstetrician, gynecologist, educator; b. Chgo., Jan. 15, 1944; s. Eugene and Carmella (Bruno) S.; m. Sandra Lee Karabelas, July 16, 1966; children: David, Christina, Michael. Student, St. Mary's Coll., 1962-65; MD, Loyola U., 1969. Diplomate Am. Bd. Ob-gyn; Nat. Bd. Med. Examiners; CME accreditation. Intern St. Francis Hosp., Evanston, Ill., 1969-70, resident, 1972-75, sr. attending physician, 1985—; assoc. attending phsycian Evanston Hosp., 1975-79, attending physician, 1980-84, sr. attending physician, 1985—, v.p. med. staff, 1990-91, pres.-elect, 1991-92, pres., 1992-93; also bd. dirs., 1991-94; sec. exec. com. Evanston Hosp., 1993-94; chmn. ob-gyn Cook County Grad. Sch. Medicine, Chgo., 1983-91. Instr. Northwestern U. Med. Sch., Chgo., 1975-78, asst. prof., 1984-95, assoc. prof., 1995-04, prof., 2004—; pres. Northwestern Healthcare Network Physician Leadership, 1994; lectr. acad. and civic groups Ob-Gyn. Nat. Ctr. Advanced Med. Edn., 1991—; bd. dirs. Ill. Found. Med. Rev.; bd. trustees Ill. State Ins. Svcs., 1992—, chair, 1998-00, chair rates and res., 2002—; bd. govs. Ill. State Med. Inter-Inst. Exch., 1987-92; adv. bd. practicing physicians Sec. Health and Human Svc. and Ctr. for Medicare Svcs., 2005—, Ctrs. Medicare and Medicaid. Editor: Profl. Staff News, 1992-93; chmn. editorial bd. Jour. Chgo. Medicine, 1986-91; contbr. articles to profl. jours. Bd. dirs. Am. Cancer Soc., chmn. profl. edn. com. North Shore unit, 1982-85; bd. dirs. Chgo. Community Info. Network, 1994-95; mem. Nat. Rep. Congrl. Com., 1981—, Ill. Med. Polit. Action Com.; bd. advisors Nat. Youth Leadership Forum on Medicine, Chgo., 1998—; trustee Midwest Ctr. Women's Healthcare, 2002—, pres., 2002—; adv. patients and med. profession. With USN, 1970-72. Fellow: ACOG (chmn. Ill. sect. 1975—76), ACS, Inst. Medicine Chgo.; mem.: AMA (com. to select pub. mem. 2003—, Physician Recognition award 1977, 1980, 1983), Gt. Lakes States Coalition of Dels. to AMA (chmn. 2003—), Orgn. State Med. Assn. Presidents (steering com. 2003—06, sec. 2006—, v.p. 2007), Chgo. Found. Med. Care (med. care evaluation and edn. com. 1980—83, nominating com. 1980—84, practice guidelines com. 1984), Ednl. and Scientific Found. (bd. dirs. 1994—98), Chgo. Med. Soc. (adv. com. advt. stds. 1978—84, physician's rev. com. 1980—85, trustee ins. bd. 1982—, nominating com. 1985—, treas. 1986—89, chmn. fin. com. 1986—89, trustee 1986—92, sec. 1989—90, pres.-elect 1990—91, chmn. bd. trustees 1990—91, pres. 1991—92, chmn. ethical rels. com. 1994—), Ill. Med. Soc. (del. to AMA 1987—, govt. affairs com. 1988—, chmn. reference com. 1989, chmn. fin. com. 1992—94, sec.-treas. 1994—96, chmn. bd. trustees 1996—98, chmn. bylaws com. 1998—99, pres. 2000—01), Physician Benefit Trust (chmn. fin. com. 1993—2004, chmn. 2004—, adv. coun. 2005—). Roman Catholic. Avocations: reading, swimming. Home: 4442 Concord Ln Skokie IL 60076-2606 Office: AGSO 1000 Central St Evanston IL 60201-1777 Home Phone: 847-677-5890; Office Phone: 847-869-3300. E-mail: sprangml@aol.com.

SPRECHER, CHRISTINA M., lawyer; b. Wabash, Ind., Apr. 1, 1970; BA, Ind. U., Bloomington, 1992; JD, Valparaiso U. Sch. Law, 1995. Bar: Ohio 1996. Ptnr. Frost Brown Todd LLC, Cin. Mem., Bd. Trustees, Exec. Com. Cin. Ballet; pres. BRAVO!. Named one of Ohio's Rising Stars, Super Lawyers, 2006; recipient Inspiring Fine Arts Vol. award, Inspire Mag., 2006. Mem.: Internat. Coun. Shopping Centers, Moot Ct. Soc., ABA (mem., Probate and Trust Law Sect.), Ohio State Bar Assn., Cin. Bar Assn. Office: Frost Brown Todd LLC 2200 PNC Ctr 201 E Fifth St Cincinnati OH 45202-4182 Office Phone: 513-651-6800. Office Fax: 513-651-6981.

SPRECHER, KEVIN S., lawyer; b. Willingboro, NJ, Feb. 24, 1968; BS Indsl. Engring., Purdue U., 1992; JD, Valparaiso U., 1995. Bar: Ohio 1995, US Ct. of Appeals Fed. Cir. 1995, registered: US Patent and Trademark Office. Ptnr. Frost Brown Todd LLC, Cin. Mem. Purdue U. President's Coun. Named one of Ohio's Rising Stars, Super Lawyers, 2006. Mem.: Ohio State Bar Assn., Cin. Bar Assn., Cin. Intellectual Property Law Assn., Am. Intellectual Property Law Assn., Inst. Indsl. Engineers, ABA, Purdue Club of Cin. Office: Frost Brown Todd LLC 2200 PNC Ctr 201 E Fifth St Cincinnati OH 45202-4182 Office Phone: 513-651-6121. Office Fax: 513-651-6981.

SPRENGER, GORDON M., hospital administrator; b. Albert Lea, Minn., Apr. 30, 1937; Bachelors degree, St. Olaf Coll., 1959; masters degree, U. Minn., 1961. Registrar USAF Hosp., Hamilton AFB, Calif., 1961-64; with St. Luke's Hosp., Milw., 1964-67, Northwestern Hosp., Mpls., 1967-71; exec. v.p. Abbott-Northwestern Hosp., Mpls., 1971-75, pres. ceo., 1975-88, LifeSpan, 1982-92; exec. ofcr HealthSpan, 1992-94; chief exec. ofcr Allina Health, 1994—. Prof. U. Minn., 1976—; acad. lectureship; preceptor. Mem. ACHE and AHA; Affiliated Hosp. Srvs: Past Sec. Bd mem., 1971-74; Council of Community Hosp., chair. 1980-81; Governor's Task Force on Nursing, 1981; Health Political Action Comm. of Minn., chair. 1981; Minn. Hosp. Assoc. Governmntl Relations Comm., chair. 1979, bd mem, 1978-81, exec. comm. treas., 1981; chair. elect, Minn. Hosp. Assoc., 1982; MMI Cos bd mem, currently vice chair., preceptor and faculty mem., U of Minn. Hosp. and Health Care Admin., 1982 bd of Minnehaha Acad.; disting. alumnus, St. Olaf Coll., mem. bd of regents; Voluntary Hosp. of Amer., past chair., mem. Medtronics, Inc., bd of dirs., 1991-; mem. St. Paul Cos., bd of dirs. Office: Allina Health System 5601 Smetana Dr PO Box 9310 Minneapolis MN 55440-9310 Home: 6244 Ridge Rd Chanhassen MN 55317-9438

SPREWELL, LATRELL FONTAINE, professional basketball player; b. Milw., Sept. 8, 1970; s. Latoska Fields and Pamela Sprewell; children: Aquilla, Page, Latrell II. Student, Three Rivers C.C., Poplar Bluff, Mo., 1988—90, Ala. U., 1990—92. Profl. basketball player Golden State Warriors, Oakland, Calif., 1992—98; profl. Basketball Player New York Knicks, NYC, 1998—2003, Minnesota Timberwolves, 2003—. Named an NBA All-star, 1994, 1995, 1997, 2001. Avocations: music, repairing stereo equipment. Office: c/o Minn Timberwolves 600 First Ave N Minneapolis MN 55403

SPRIESER, JUDITH A., former software company executive; BA in Linguistics, Northwestern U., MBA in Fin. CPA, Ill., 1982. Comml. banker Harris Bank, Chgo., 1974-81; dir. treasury ops. Esmark, 1981-84; asst. treas. internat. Nalco Chem. Co., 1984-87; asst. treas. corp. fin. Sara Lee Corp., 1987-90; sr. v.p., CFO Sara Lee Bakery N.Am., 1990-93, pres., CEO, 1993-94; sr. v.p., CFO Sara Lee Corp., 1994-99, CEO, Foods and Food Svc., 2000-2001; CEO Transora, Chgo., 2001—05. Bd. dirs. USG Corp., Reckitt Benckiser, Allstate Corp., 1999-, Kohl's Corp., 2003-, CBS Corp., 2005-Bd. dirs. Hinsdale Hosp. Found.; trustee Northwestern U. Mem. AICPA, Chgo. Network, Young Pres. Orgn., Chgo. coun. Fgn. Rels., Econ. Club, Conf. Bd. Coun. Fin. Execs. Mailing: Bd Dir Allstate Corp 2775 Sanders Rd Northbrook IL 60062-6127

SPRIESTERSBACH, DUANE CARYL, academic administrator, speech pathology/audiology services professional, educator; b. Pine Island, Minn., Sept. 5, 1916; s. Merle Lee and Esther Lucille (Stucky) Spriestersbach; m. Bette Rae Bartell, Aug. 31, 1946; children: Michael Lee, Ann. BEd, Winona State Tchrs. Coll., 1939; MA, U. Iowa, 1940, PhD, 1948. Asst. dir. pers. rels. Pacific Portland Cement Co., San Francisco, 1946-47; prof. speech pathology U. Iowa, Iowa City, 1948-89, prof. emeritus, 1989—, dean. Grad. Coll., v.p. ednl. devel. and rsch., 1965-89, v. pres. and dean emeritus, 1989—, acting pres., 1981-82; v.p. ops. Breakthrough, Inc., Oakdale, Iowa, 1993-94; freelance cons., 1994—2006. Com. mem. Nat. Inst. Neurol. Disease and Blindess; chmn. dental tng. com. Nat. Inst. Dental Rsch., 1967—72, chmn. spl. grants rev., 1978—82; chmn. bd. dirs. Midwest Univs. Cons. Internat. Activities, Columbus, 1978—87. Author: (book) Psychosocial Aspects of Cleft Palate, 1973; author: (with others) Diagnostic Methods in Speech Pathology, 1978; co-editor: Cleft Palate and Communication, 1968, Diagnosis in Speech Language Pathology, rev. edit., 1999, The Way It Was: The University of Iowa 1964-1989, 1999. Pres. Iowa City Cmty. Theater, 1964, 1977, 1983. Served to lt. col. US Army, 1941—46, ETO. Decorated Bronze Star; fellow Nat. Inst. Dental Rsch., 1971. Fellow: AAAS; mem.: Midwestern Assn. Grad. Schs. (chmn. 1979—80), Am. Cleft Palate Assn. (pres. 1961—62, disting. svc. award), Am. Speech and Hearing Assn. (pres. 1965, honor award), Assn. Grad. Schs. (pres. 1979—80), Cosmos Clug (Washington), Mortar Bd., Sigma Xi. Home: 2 Longview Knoll NE Iowa City IA 52240-9148 Office: Univ Iowa M212 Oakdale Hall Iowa City IA 52242-5000 Home Phone: 319-351-8756; Office Phone: 319-335-4012. Business E-Mail: duane-spriestersbach@uiowa.edu.

SPRING, TERRI, political organization executive; BA, U. Wis., 1975. 2d vice chair Dem. Party—Wis., Madison, 1994-97, state chair, 1997; legis. asst. State Senate, Madison, 1996-00; state chair Dem. Party-Wis., Madison, 2000—. Mem. Assn. State Dem. Chairs.

SPRINGER, JERRY (GERALD NORMAN SPRINGER), television talk show host, radio personality; b. London, Feb. 13, 1944; BA in Polit. Sci., Tulane U.; JD, Northwestern U., 1968. Presdl. campaign aide Sen. Robert F. Kennedy; elected mem. at large Cin. Coun., 1971-77; elected mayor Cin., 1977; polit. reporter, commentator WLWT-TV, Cin., 1982-84, anchor, mng. editor, 1984-93; host The Jerry Springer Show, 1991—, Springer on the Radio, Air Am. Radio, 2005—06. Author Ringmaster, 1998; video collection Jerry Springer: Too Hot for TV; actor: (films) A Fair to Remember, 1998, Citizen Verdict, 2003, The Defender, 2004, (TV films) Since You've Been Gone, 1998, Talking to Americans, 2001; actor, prodr.: (films) Ringmaster, 1998; performer, Dancing With the Stars, 2006; host America's Got Talent, 2007-. On-site reporter Cin. Reaches Out; mem. adv. bd. Audrey Hepburn Hollywood for Children Fund; co-host Stars Across America Muscular Dystrophy Labor Day Telethon; v.p. bd. Nat. Muscular Dystrophy Assn.; founder scholarship fund Kellman Sch., Chgo. Recipient 7 Emmy awards for nightly news commentaries; named Best Anchor Cin. Mag. 5 times. Achievements include top rated daytime talk show series in the U.S. Office: Jerry Springer Show 454 N Columbus Dr Fl 2 Chicago IL 60611-5514 also: Air America Radio 641 Avenue Of The Americas Fl 4 New York NY 10011-2038

SPRINGER, NEIL ALLEN, manufacturing executive; b. Fort Wayne, Ind, May 2, 1938; s. Roy V. and Lucille H. (Gerke) S.; m. Janet M. Grotrian, Sept. 3, 1960; children: Sheri Lynn, Kelly Jean, Mark Allen. BS, U. Ind, 1960; MBA, U. Dayton, 1966. CPA, Ill. Staff asst. acctg. Internat. Harvester Co. (now Navistar Internat. Corp.), Bridgeport, Conn., 1966-68, asst. comptroller Fort Wayne, Ind., 1968-70, staff asst. Chgo., 1970-75, asst. corp. compt., 1975-77, v.p. fin., 1977-79, v.p. gen. mgr. trucks, 1979-81, pres. truck group, 1981-84, pres., chief operating officer, 1984-87; chmn., pres., chief exec. officer Navistar Internat. Transp. Corp., Chgo., 1987-90; pres., chief oper. officer Navistar Internat. Corp./Navistar Internat. Transp. Corp., Chgo., 1990; pres. cen. region Alexander Proudfoot, Deerfield, Ill., 1991—. Bd. dirs. Century Cos. Am., Waverly, Iowa, IDEX Corp., Northbrook, Ill., TNT Freightsways, Rosemont, Ill. Active bus. dean's adv. coun. Ind. U., 1988—. Mem. Ill. Soc. CPAs.

SPROGER, CHARLES EDMUND, retired lawyer; b. Chgo., Feb. 18, 1933; s. William and Minnette (Weiss) Sproger. BA (David Himmelblau scholar), Northwestern U., 1954, JD, 1957. Bar: Ill. 1957. Assoc. Ehrlich & Cohn, 1958-63, Ehrlich, Bundesen, Friedman & Ross, 1963-72; partner Ehrlich, Bundesen, Broecker & Sproger, 1972-77; pvt. practice, 1977—2000; ret., 2000. Mem. adv. com. curriculum Ill. Inst. Continuing Legal Edn., Chgo., 1976—90; v.p. Mediation Coun. of Ill., 1986-87; arbitration panelist for Cir. Ct. Cook County, 1990—. Editor: Family Lawyer, 1962-63; contbr. articles to legal publs. Mediator Pastoral Psychotherapy Inst., 1982-86, vol. Coun. for Jewish Elderly, Chgo., 2002-. Recipient Vol. of Yr. award, Coun. for Jewish Elderly, 2004. Fellow Am. Acad. Matrimonial Lawyers (bd. examiners 1972-86, chmn. Law Day U.S.A. 1975); mem. ABA, Ill. Bar Assn. (chmn. coun. family law 1970-71), Chgo. Bar Assn. (matrimonial law com. 1958-2000), Am. Arbitration Assn. (divorce mediation com. 1983-92), Decalogue Soc., U. Mich. Club Chgo. (pres. 1988-89, bd. dirs. 1987-2004), Phi Alpha Delta. Address: 2800 W Birchwood Ave Chicago IL 60645-1218

SPRUNGER, KEITH L., historian, educator; b. Berne, Ind., Mar. 16, 1935; s. Arley and Lillian (Mettler) S.; m. Aldine Mary Slagell, June 13, 1959; children: David, Mary, Philip. BA, Wheaton Coll., 1957; MA, U. Ill., 1958, PhD, 1963. Tchr. Berne (Ind.) High Sch., 1958-60; Oswald H. Wedel prof. history Bethel Coll., N. ewton, Kans., 1963—2001. Author: Dutch Puritanism, 1982, The Learned Doctor William Ames, 1972, Voices Against War, 1973, Auction Catalogue of The Library of William Ames, 1988, Trumpets From The Tower, 1994, Campus, Congregation, and Community, 1997. Mem. Newton Historic Preservation Commn.; bd. dirs. Germantown Mennonite Historic Trust. Recipient Harbison award Danforth Found., 1972; fellow Social Sci. Rsch. Coun., 1969, Am. Coun. Learned Soc. fellow, 1976, Huntington Libr. fellow, 1982, 90; grantee Am. Philos. Soc., 1967, 1969, 83, The Netherlands Orgn. for Advancement of Pure Rsch., 1983. Fellow Pilgrim Soc.; mem. AAUP, Am. Hist. Assn., Am. Soc. Ch. History (coun. 1974-76), Conf. on Faith and History, Dutch Mennonite Hist. Cir. Mennonite. Avocation: book and postcard collecting. Home: 2412 Clg Ave North Newton KS 67117 Office: Bethel Coll 300 E 27th St North Newton KS 67117 Office Phone: 316-283-2500. Business E-Mail: sprunger@bethelks.edu.

SPURRIER-BRIGHT, PATRICIA ANN, professional society administrator; b. El Paso, Tex., Feb. 27, 1943; d. James Ray and Lucile Gray (Lafferty) Spurrier; m. Martin Oliver Bright, Sept. 18, 1964 (div. 1967); 1 child, James R. Student, Frederick Coll., 1962-64. Planning technician Reston Va, Inc./Gulf Reston, Inc., 1966-75; adminstrv. asst. Gulf Oil, Tulsa, 1975-79; planner Conde Engring., El Paso, Tex., 1979-82; adjutant U.S. Horse Cavalry Assn., Ft. Bliss, Tex., 1983-91; exec. dir. U.S. Cavalry Assn., Ft. Riley, Kans., 1991—, sec., 1991—. Sec. U.S. Cavalry Meml. Found., Fort Riley, 1994—; trustee Spurrier Trust, El Paso, 1990—; mem. Bigheart Cemetery Found., Barnsdale, Okla., 1989—; bd. dirs. 1st Kans. Territorial Capital. Editor The Cavalry Jour., 1990—. Mem. U.S. Army Daus. Republican. Avocations: painting, genealogy. Home: 1517 Leavenworth St Manhattan KS 66502-4154 Office: US Cavalry Assn PO Box 2325 Fort Riley KS 66442-0325 E-mail: cavalry@flinthills.com.

SPYERS-DURAN, PETER, librarian, educator; b. Budapest, Hungary, Jan. 26, 1932; came to U.S., 1956, naturalized, 1964; s. Alfred and Maria (Almasi-Balogh) S-D; m. Jane F. Cumber, Mar. 21, 1964; children: Kimberly, Hilary, Peter. Certificate, Free U. Budapest, 1955; MA in L.S, U. Chgo., 1960; Ed.D., Nova S Ea. U., 1975. Profl. asst. libr. adminstrn. div. ALA, Chgo., 1961-62; assoc. dir. librs., assoc. prof. U. Wis., 1962-67; dir. librs., prof. Western Mich. U., 1967-70; dir. librs., prof. libr. sci. Fla. Atlantic U., 1970-76; dir. libr. Calif. State U., Long Beach, 1976-83; prof. libr. and info. sci., dir. libr. Wayne State U., Detroit, 1983-86, dean, prof. libr. and info. sci. program, 1986-95, dean and prof. emeritus, 1995—; cons. Spyers-Duran Assocs., 1995—; acting univ. libr. Nova Southeastern U., Ft. Lauderdale, Fla., 1996-97. Vis. prof. State U. N.Y. at Geneseo, summers 1969-70; cons. publs., libr. and info. scis.-related enterprises; chmn. bd. internat. confs., 1970—. Author: Moving Library Materials, 1965, Public Libraries -A Comparative Survey of Basic Fringe Benefits, 1967; editor: Approval and Gathering Plans in Academic Libraries, 1969, Advances in Understanding Approval Plans in Academic Libraries, 1970, Economics of Approval Plans in Research Libraries, 1972, Management Problems in Serials Work, 1973, Prediction of Resource Needs, 1975, Requiem for the Card Catalog: Management Issues in Automated Cataloging, 1979, Shaping Library Collections for the 1980's, 1981, Austerity Management in Academic Libraries, 1984, Financing Information Systems, 1985, Issues in Academic Libraries, 1985; mem. editorial bd. Jour. of Library Adminstration, 1989-95. Mem. Kalamazoo County Library Bd., 1969-70; Bd. dirs. United Fund. Reciient G. Flint Purdy award for outstanding contbns. Wayne State U., 1999. Mem. ALA, Mich. Libr. Assn., Internat. Fed. Libr. Assns., Assn. Info. Sci., Fla. Libr. Assn., Calif. Libr. Assn., Fla. Assn. Community Colls., Boca Raton C. of C., U. Chgo. Grad. Libr. Sch. Alumni Club (pres. 1973-75), Solinet Mich. Libr. Consortium (founder charter bd. mem. 1973—, bd. dirs. 1973-76), Detroit Area Libr. Network (pres. bd. dirs. 1985-95), Mich. Ctr. for Book (pres. 1988-89), Am. Soc. Info. Sci., Assn. Libr. and Info. Sci. Edn., Sago Point Homeowners Assn. (pres., bd. dirs. 2001-05), Bayou Club Cmty. Assn. (pres., bd. dirs. 2005—). Home: 7295 Maidencane Ct Largo FL 33777-4900 Office: Wayne State Univ Librs Detroit MI 48202 Business E-Mail: spyers-duran@wayne.edu, ae8249@wayne.edu.

SQUIRES, JOHN HENRY, judge; b. Oct. 21, 1946; married; five children. AB cum laude, U. Ill., 1968, JD, 1971. Bar: Ill. 1971, U.S. Dist. Ct. (cen. dist.) Ill. 1972, U.S. Tax Ct. 1978. Assoc. Brown, Hay & Stephens, Springfield, Ill., 1971-76, ptnr., 1977-87; judge U.S. Bankruptcy Ct. No. Dist. Ill. ea. divsn., 1988—2001, reappointed, 2002—. Trustee in bankruptcy, 1984-87; adj. prof. law John Marshall Law Sch., Chgo., 1994, DePaul U., Chgo., 1995-96; lectr. Am. Bankruptcy Inst., Sangamon County Bar Assn., Winnebago County Bar Assn., Chgo. Bar Assn., Ill. Inst. CLE, Comml. Law League Am., DuPage County (Ill.) Bar Assn. Mem. Nat. Conf. Bankruptcy Judges, Am. Bankruptcy Inst., Fed. Bar Assn., Am. Bus. Club, Union League Club Chgo.

SQUIRES, VERNON T., lawyer; b. 1935; BA, Williams Coll.; LLB, Harvard U. Bar: Ill., 1960. V.p., sec. and gen. counsel The Service Master Co., Downers Grove, Ill. Mem. ABA.

SRIVASTAVA, ANURAG K., research scientist; b. Azamgarh, Uttar Pradesh, India, June 30, 1976; s. Suresh C. Sinha and Kamla Srivastava. B Tech., Harcourt Butler Tech. Inst., Kanpur, India, 1997; M Tech., BHU, Varanasi, India, 1999; PhD, Ill. Inst. Tech., 2005. Sr. rsch. assoc. Indian Inst. Tech., Kanpur, 1999—2000; tchg. asst. Ill. Inst. Tech., Chgo., 2001—05, rsch. assoc., 2001—. Rsch. fellow Asian Inst. Tech., Bangkok, 2000—01. Coord. Nat. Svc. Scheme, Kanpur, Uttar Pradesh, 1996—97. Named Dean's scholar, Ill. Inst. Tech., 2001; scholar, Univ. Grant Commn., 1998—99. Mem.: IEEE (mem. editl. bd. Transactions on Power Sys. 2002), Student Employee Assn. IIT (pres. 2005), IEEE Power Engring. Soc., IEEE Computer Soc., Eta Kappa Nu, Sigma Xi. Office: Ill Inst Tech 3301 S Dearborn St Ste 136 Chicago IL 60616 Home: 60 E 32d St Apt 902 Chicago IL 60616 Personal E-mail: anurags@ieee.org. Business E-Mail: srivanu@iit.edu.

STABENOW, DEBORAH ANN, senator, former congresswoman; b. Gladwin, Mich., Apr. 29, 1950; d. Robert Lee and Anna Merle (Hallmark) Greer; m. Dennis Stabenow (div. 1990); children: Todd Dennis, Michelle Deborah. m. Tom Athans, Feb. 16, 2003; 1 stepdaughter, Gina BS magna cum laude, Mich. State U., 1972, MSW magna cum laude, 1975. With spl. svcs. Lansing (Mich.) Sch. Dist., 1972-73; county commr. Ingham County, Mason, Mich., 1975-78; state rep. State of Mich., Lansing, 1979—91, state senator, 1991—94; mem. 103rd-106th Congress from Mich. 8th dist. U.S. Ho. Reps., 1997—2001; US Senator from Mich., 2001—. Founder Ingham County Women's Commn.; co-founder Council Against Domestic Assault. Recipient Service to Children award Council for Prevention of Child Abuse and eglect, 1983, Disting. Service to Mich. Families award Mich. Council Family Relations, 1983, Outstanding Leadership award Nat. Council Community Mental Health Ctrs., 1983, Snyder-Kok award Mental Health Assn. Mich., Awareness Leader of Yr. award Awareness Communications Team Developmentally Disabled, 1984, Communicator of Yr. award Woman in Communications, 1984, Lawmaker of Yr. award Nat. Child Support Enforcement Assn., 1985, Disting. Service award Lansing Jaycees, 1985, Disting. Service in Govt. award Retarded Citizens of Mich., 1986, Cmty. award Mich. Mental Health, 1988, Boxing Glove award Nat. Com. to Preserve Social Security and Medicare, 1999, Home Health Hero Nat. Assn. for Home Care, 1999, Friend of Farm Bur. Mich. Farm Bur., 1999, Leadership award Nat. Coun. of Space Grant Dirs., 1998, Outstanding Achievement Nat. Farmers Union, 1998, Legislator of Yr. award Nat. Multiple Sclerosis Soc., 1992, Assn. for Children's Mental Health, 1991, Mich. Assn. of Vol. Adminstrs., 1989, Citizens Alliance to Uphold Spl. Edn., 1989, Recognition award State 4-H Alumni, 1991, Public. Elected Ofcl. award Nat. Assn. Social Workers, 2004, Congressional Support for Sci. award Inst. Food Technologists, 2004, Cmty. Health Defender award Nat. Assn. Cmty. Health Centers, 2005; named One of Ten Outstanding Young Ams. Jaycees, 1986. Mem. NAACP, Nat. Assn. Social Workers, Lansing Regional C. of C., Delta Kappa Gamma. Democrat. Meth. Office: US Senate 702 Hart Senate Office Bldg Washington DC 20510 also: District Office Ste 100 221 W Lake Lansing Rd East Lansing MI 48823-8661 Office Phone: 202-224-4822, 517-203-1760. Office Fax: 202-228-0325, 517-203-1778. E-mail: senator@stabenow.senate.gov.*

STACK, JIM, professional sports team executive; Grad., Northwestern U., 1983. Draft pick Houston Rockets, 1983; profl. basketball player Belgium, Israel and France, 1983—88; scout Chgo. Bulls, 1988—89, spl. asst. to v.p. basketball ops., 1989—96, asst. v.p. basketball ops., 1996—2000; asst. coach Ind. Pacers, 2000—03; advanced scout NY Knicks, 2003—04; gen. mgr. Minn. Timberwolves, 2004—. Office: Minn Timberwolves 600 First Ave N Minneapolis MN 55403

STACK, JOHN WALLACE, lawyer; b. Chgo., May 30, 1937; s. Wallace and Irma Evelyn (Anderson) S.; divorced; children: James Randolph, Linnea Claire, Theodore. BBA, U. Wis., 1960; JD, U. Calif., Berkeley, 1963. Bar: Ill. 1963, D.C. 1972, U.S. Ct. Appeals (7th cir.) 1963, U.S. Supreme Ct. 1972. Assoc. Pattishall, McAuliffe & Hofstetter, Chgo., 1963-64, Winston & Strawn, Chgo., 1964-70, ptnr., 1970-99; ret., 1999; adminstrv. law judge City of Evanston, Ill. Contbg. editor U. Calif. Law Rev., 1963. Mem. ABA (antitrust sect.), Am. Arbitration Assn., W Club of U. Wis. (Madison), Order of Coif, Phi Delta Phi, Beta Gamma Sigma. Republican. Lutheran. Avocations: sports, gardening, reading. Home: 2906 Lincoln St Evanston IL 60201-2047 Office: Winston & Strawn 40th Fl 35 W Wacker Dr Fl 40 Chicago IL 60601-1614

STACK, STEPHEN S., manufacturing executive; b. DuPont, Pa., Apr. 25, 1934; s. Steve and Sophie (Baranowski) Stasenko; m. Lois Sims Agnew, May 25, 1996. BSME, Case Western Res. U., 1956; postgrad., Syracuse Univ. registered profl engr., Ill. Mech. engr. Kaiser Aluminum, Erie, Pa., 1956-58; instr. Gannon Univ., Erie, Pa., 1958-60, Syracuse U., NY, 1960-61; engrg. supr. A.O. Smith Corp., Erie and Los Angeles, 1961-66; gen. mgr. Am. Elec. Fusion, Chgo., 1966-67; mgr.new products Maremont Corp., Chgo., 1967-69; dir. market planning Gulf and Western Ind., Bellwood, Ill., 1969-71; mgmt. and fin. cons. Stack & Assocs., Chgo., 1971-76; founder, pres. Seamcraft, Inc., Chgo., 1976—. Mem. Ill. Legis. Small Bus. Conf., 1980, Gov.'s Small Bus. Adv. Commn., 1984-94, Ill. State House Conf. on Small Bus., 1984, 86, 99; chmn. West Cell Svcs., 1988-2000; chmn., founder Bridge Pers. Svcs. Corp., 1989—; vice pres., founder Ind. Bus. Assn. Ill., 1993-94; small bus. adv. coun. Fed. Res. Bank Chgo., 1989-91, Nat. Fedn. Ind. Bus., 1980—, mem. Ill. State. Leadership Coun. 1999-, del. White House Conf. on Small Bus., 1986, Nat. Small Bus. Attitudes Rsch. Panel, 1987-, pres. Chgo. Marine Heritage Soc., 1999—, mem. Navy League of US, 1991—, del. Congl. Small Bus. Summit, 1998, 2000, 02, 04, 06; with Ill. Small Bus. Leadership Coun., 2000—. Treas. Sem. Townhouse Assn., 1993-94; active Lincoln Park Conservation Assn., Sheffield Neighbors Assn.; mem. adv. coun., DePaul U. Coll. Commerce, 2000—, mem. planning com. Cathedral Prep HS, Erie, Pa, 2007. Recipient Am. Legion award, 1948, Case Western Res. U. Honor key, 1956, Eagle Scout award, 1949. Mem. Ill. Mfrs. Assn. (bd. dirs. 1986-98, vice chmn. 1995-98), Small Mfrs. Action Couns. (vice chmn. 1986-87, chmn. 1988-89), Mfrs. Polit. Action Com. (exec. com. 1987-98, vice chmn. 1993-95, chmn. 1995-98), Am. Mgmt. Assn., Pres. Assn., Blue Key, Beta Theta Pi, Theta Thau, Pi Delta Epsilon. Chgo. Yacht Club, East Bank Club, Fullerton Tennis Club (pres. 1971-79, treas. 1979-83, bd. dirs. 1983-86), Lake Shore Ski Club (v.p. 1982, 91), Lincoln Park Tennis Assn. Patentee in liquid control and metering fields. Office: 932 W Dakin St Chicago IL 60613-2922

STACKHOUSE, DAVID WILLIAM, JR., retired furniture systems installation contractor; b. Cumberland, Ind., Aug. 29, 1926; s. David William and Dorothy Frances (Snider) S.; BS, Lawrence Coll., Appleton, Wis., 1950; m. Shirley Pat Smith, Dec. 23, 1950; 1 child, Stefan Brent. Indsl. designer Globe Am. Co., Kokomo, Ind., 1951-53; product designer, chief engr. Midwest Foundry & Workwall divsn. LA Darling Co., Bronson, Mich., 1954-66; contract mgr. Brass Office Products, Indpls., 1966-73; mfrs. rep., Nashville, Ind., 1973-78; mktg. exec. Brass Office Products, Inc., Indpls., 1978-80; office furniture systems installation contractor, 1980-92; creator This Great House, The Story of This Home, 1995; founder Half-High Hill Prodns., Inc., 1996. Served with USNR, 1944-46; Beta Theta Pi. Anglican. Clubs: Lions, American Legion, VFW. Patentee interior structural systems. Home: 410 Pocono Ct Arden NC 28704-8475 E-mail: davenshirleypat@bellsouth.net.

STADLER, GERALD P., transportation executive; b. 1937; married. Student, Loyola U. Chmn. S&M Moving Sys., Santa Fe, Calif.; sec. United Van Lines, Fenton, Mo., 1982—84, vice chmn., 1984—2001, also bd. dirs., 1978—, chmn., 2001—; chmn., CEO UniGroup Inc., 2001—. Mem.: American Moving Storage Assn. (bd. dirs.). Office: United Van Lines Inc 1 United Dr Fenton MO 63026-2578

STADTHERR, MARK A., chemical engineer, educator; b. Austin, Minn. BChE in Chem. Engring., U. Minn., Mpls., 1972; PhD in Chem. Engring., U. Wis., Madison, 1976. Faculty U. Ill., Urbana-Champaign, 1976-95; chem. engring. faculty U. Notre Dame, Ind., 1996—. Lectr. in field. Contbr. articles to profl. jours. Recipient Xerox award for engring. rsch., 1982, Computing in Chem. Engring. award AIChE, 1998; named GTE Emerging scholar lectr. U. Notre Dame, 1986. Mem.: ASEE, SIAM, ACS, AICHE (chair Computing and Sys. Tech. Divsn. 2002—03). Achievements include research on advanced computational strategies for process engineering, application of interval analysis to chemical engineering problems, environmentally conscious process design, ecological modeling. Office: Dept Chem Engring Univ Notre Dame Notre Dame IN 46556 Business E-Mail: markst@nd.edu.

STADTMUELLER, JOSEPH PETER, federal judge; b. Oshkosh, Wis., Jan. 28, 1942; s. Joseph Francis and Irene Mary (Kilp) S.; m. Mary Ellen Brady, Sept. 5, 1970; children: Jeremy, Sarah. BS in Bus. Adminstrn., Marquette U., 1964, JD, 1967. Bar: Wis. 1967, U.S. Supreme Ct. 1980. With Kluwin, Dunphy, Hankin and McNulty, 1968-69; asst. U.S. atty. Dept. Justice, Milw., 1969-74, 1st. asst. U.S. atty., 1974-75; with Stepke, Kossow, Trebon and Stadtmueller, Milw., 1975-76; asst. U.S. atty. Dept. Justice, 1977-78, dep. U.S. atty., 1978-81, U.S. atty., 1981-87; judge U.S. Dist. Ct. (ea. dist.) Wis., Milw., 1987—, chief judge, 1995—2002. Mem. 7th Cir. Jud. Coun., 1995—2002. Recipient Spl. Commendation award Atty. Gen. U.S., 1974, 80. Mem. ABA, State Bar Wis. (bd. govs. 1979-83, exec. com. 1982-83), Am. Law Inst., Fed. Judges Assn. (bd. dirs. 1995—, sec. 2001--). Clubs: University (Milw.). Republican. Roman Catholic. Office: 471 US Courthouse 517 E Wisconsin Ave Milwaukee WI 53202-4500

STAFFORD, ARTHUR CHARLES, medical association administrator; b. Cleve., May 10, 1947; s. Charles Arthur and Florence Mildred (Hovey) S.; m. Patricia Anne Cz, Dec. 20, 1991. BS, Kent State U., 1977; MBA, Lake Erie Coll., 1984. Med. tech. VA, Cleve., 1977-81, supr. med. tech., 1981-97; lab. mgr. Univ. Hosps. Health System Meml. Hosp. of Geneva, Ohio, 1998-99; instr. Lake Erie Coll., Painesville, Ohio, 1980-82; mgr. customer svc. Giant Eagle Supermarket, Madison, Ohio, 2001—02; instr. Cuyahoga C.C., Cleve., 1988-91, 2003—05; preferred team Progressive Ins. Co., Highland Heights, 2004—. Pres. Kent State U. Veterans Assn., 1974, mem. Kent State U Budget Review Com., 1975. Contbr. articles to profl. jour. Mem. Am. Legion, 1974, VFW, 1973. With USN, 1968-72. Mem.: Rock and Roll Hall of Fame, Founders Club. Republican. Avocations: genealogy, computers, antiques, chess, cooking. Home: 2193 Chimney Ridge Dr Madison OH 44057-2588 E-mail: czstafford@ncweb.com.

STAFFORD, FRANK PETER, JR., economics professor, consultant; b. Chgo., Sept. 17, 1940; s. Frank Peter and Ida Gustava (Tormala) S.; m. Lilian Elisabeth Lundin, Aug. 8, 1964; children: Craig Peter, Jennifer Elisabeth, Christine Anna BA, Northwestern U., 1962; MBA, U. Chgo., 1964, PhD, 1968. Asst. prof. econs. U. Mich., 1966-71, assoc. prof., 1971-73, 74-75, prof., 1976—, chmn. dept. econs., 1980—, rsch. scientist Inst. Social Rsch., 1995—, chair budget study com., 1995—, assoc. dir. Inst. for Social Rsch., 2000—. Vis. assoc. prof. Grad. Sch. Bus.-Stanford U., 1973-74; spl. asst. for econ. affairs U.S. Dept. Labor, Washington, 1975-76; vis. prof. dept. econs. U. Saarlandes, Fed. Republic Germany, 1986; faculty rsch. assoc. Inst. Social Rsch., Ann Arbor, 1979—; vis. scholar Indsl. Inst. for Econs. and Social Rsch., Stockholm, 1979, 83, 90, Worklife Study Ctr., Stockholm, 1988, 90; Tinbergen Found. prof. U. Amsterdam, 1992, 94; panel mem. Social Sci. Rsch. Coun., N.Y.C., 1979—; rsch. assoc. Nat. Bur. Econ. Rsch., Cambridge, Mass., 1983—; prof. econs. Tinbsrgne Found. U. Amsterdam, 1992; vis. scholar U. Stockholm, 1994. Author, editor: Time Use Goods and Well Being, 1986, Studies in Labor Market Behavior: Sweden and the United States, 1981; mem. editorial bd.: Am. Econ. Rev., 1976-78; contbr. articles to profl. jours. Dir. Panel Study of Income Dynamics, 1995—. Grantee SF, 1973, 80, 95—, 2002—, NICHD, 1995—, Nat. Ins. on Aging, 1999—. Mem. Am. Econs. Assn. Home: 3535 Daleview Dr Ann Arbor MI 48105-9686 Office: U Mich Dept Econs Lorch Hall Rm 312 Ann Arbor MI 48105 Business E-Mail: fstaffor@umich.edu.

STAFFORD, LORI, reporter; b. Birmingham, Ala. m. Jeff Stafford. Student, Auburn U., U. Ala.; MA, Northwestern U. Mem. staff TV sta., Reno, Cin., Chattanooga, Evansville, Ind.; reporter WISN, Milw. Office: WISN PO Box 402 Milwaukee WI 53201-0402

STAGE, BRIAN, hotel executive; BSBA, Coll. William and Mary, 1974; grad. mgmt. exec. program, U. Minn., 1995. Mgr. Sheraton Boston Hotel and Towers, 1981; ops. mgr. Inn Am., area dir. ops. and corp. dir. sales and mktg.; v.p. sales and mktg. Inn Am. Corp.; regional v.p. ops. Radisson Hotels Worldwide, 1990-95, exec. v.p. sales and mktg., 1995-97, pres., COO Mpls., 1997-99; exec. v.p. sales, reservations and distbn. Carlson Hotels Worldwide, Mpls., 2000. E-mail: bstage@carlson.com.

STAGEBERG, ROGER V., lawyer; B in Math. with distinction, U. Minn., 1963, JD cum laude, 1966; MA in History and Theology, Luther Seminary, 2006. Assoc. Mackall, Crounse & Moore, Mpls., 1966-70, ptnr., 1970-86; shareholder and officer Lommen, Abdo, Cole, King & Stageberg, P.A., Mpls., 1986—. Co-chmn. joint legal svcs. funding com. Minn. Supreme Ct., 1995-96. Mem. U. Minn. Law Rev. Bd. dirs. Mpls. Legal Aid Soc., 1970-2003, treas., 1973, pres., 1977, dir. of fund, 1980—, chmn. of fund, 1998-2000; chmn. bd. trustees Colonial Ch. of Edina, 1975, chmn. congregation, 1976, pres. found., 1978; officer, trustee Mpls. Found, 1983-88. Mem. Minn. State Bar Assn. (numerous offices and coms., pres. 1994), Hennepin County Bar Assn. (chmn. securities law sect. 1979, chmn. attys. referral svc. com. 1980, sec. 1980, treas. 1981, pres. 1983), Order of Coif. Office: Lommen Abdo Cole King & Stageberg PA 80 S 8th St Ste 2000 Minneapolis MN 55402-2119 Home Phone: 612-378-3001; Office Phone: 612-336-9335. Business E-Mail: roger@lommen.com.

STAGGERS, KERMIT LEMOYNE, II, history and political science professor, state legislator, municipal official; b. Washington, Pa., Nov. 2, 1947; s. Kermit LeMoyne and Christine Ruby (Scherich) S.; m. June Ann Wenda, Aug. 22, 1970; children: Ayn Kristen Staggers Bird, Kyle Lee Staggers. BS, U. Idaho, 1969, MA, 1975; PhD, Claremont Grad. U., 1986. Instr. history Troy (Ala.) State U., 1975-76, U. Idaho, Moscow, 1977, Northwestern Coll., Orange City, Iowa, 1979-80, Coll. Lake County, Grayslake, Ill., 1981-82; lectr. history Chapman Univ., Orange, Calif., 1979, U. Md.-Europe, Heidelberg, Germany, 1988-89; vis. instr. history Trinity Internat. U., Deerfield, Ill., 1980; adj. instr. history U. St. Francis, Joliet, Ill., 1982; prof. history and polit. sci. U. Sioux Falls (S.D.), 1982—; mem. S.D. Senate, Pierre, 1995—2002, Sioux Falls City Coun., 2002—. Lectr. Diplomatic Acad. Ukrainian Fgn. Ministry and Nat. U. Kiev-Mohyla Acad., 2001; expert analyst on polit. and social issues for local radio and TV. Contbr. articles to profl. jours. Chair Senate Transp. Com., 1997-99; bd. dirs. Siouxland Heritage Museums, Sioux Falls, 2006—. Capt. USAF, 1970-76. Recipient Guardian Small Bus. award Nat. Fedn. Ind. Bus., 1996; Malone Faculty fellow, 1993. Mem. Orgn. Am. Historians, Great Plains Polit. Sci Assn. (pres. 2000-01), Federalist Soc., Fulbright Assn., Hist. Soc., Kiwanis, Phi Alpha Theta, Phi Kappa Phi. Republican. Avocations: book collecting, travel. Home: 616 E Wiswall Pl Sioux Falls SD 57105-2030 Office: U Sioux Falls Dept History/Polit Sci 1101 W 22nd St Sioux Falls SD 57105-1699 Office Phone: 605-331-6754. Business E-Mail: kermit.staggers@usiouxfalls.edu.

STAGLIN, GAREN KENT, computer company executive, venture capitalist; b. Lincoln, Nebr., Dec. 22, 1944; s. Ramon and Darlene (Guilliams) S.; m. Sharalyn King, June 8, 1968; children: Brandon Kent, Shannon King. BS in Engring. with honors, UCLA, 1966; MBA, Stanford U., 1968. Assoc. Carr Mgmt. Co., NYC, 1971-75; v.p. Crocker Nat. Bank, San Francisco, 1975-76; dir. fin. Itel Corp., San Francisco, 1976-77, pres. ins. services divsn., 1977-79; corp. v.p., gen. mgr. ADP Automotive Svcs. Group, San Ramon, Calif., 1978-91; chmn., CEO Safelite Glass Corp., Columbus, Ohio, 1991-97, chmn., 1998-2000; owner Staglin Family Vineyard, Rutherford, Calif., 1985—; pres., CEO eOne Global L.L.C., Napa, Calif., 2000—05; sr. advisor FT Ventures, San Francisco, 2005—. Bd. dir. Certive Corp., Specialized Bicycle Corp., Global Document Solutions, Inc., Solera, Inc., ExL Svcs., Inc., Kestrel Wireless, Free Run Techs., Bottomline techs. Bd. dir. Peralta Hosp. Cancer Inst., 1977-78, Berkeley Reportory Theatre, 1979-85, Nat. Alliance for Rsch. Schizophrenia & Depression, 2000-; trustee Justin Sienna HS, Napa, Calif., 1995-20; chmn. major gifts program East Bay region Stanford U., Calif., 1989-92; mem. adv. bd. Stanford Bus. Sch., 1995-2000; judge Cambridge Bus. Sch., 2004-; chmn. 75th anniversary campaign Stanford Grad. Sch. Bus., 1998-00; capital campaign UCLA Coll. Letters Sci., 2004-; pres. bd. trustees Am. Ctr. Wine, Food and Arts, Napa, Calif., 1998-03; pres. Rutherford Charitable Orgn., 1994-. Lt. USN, 1968—71. Recipient Gold Spike award, Stanford U., 2000, Honors Fellow award, UCLA, 2006. Mem. Stanford Assocs. (bd. govs. 1985-92), World Pres. Orgn., Internat. Inst. Soc. (bd. govs. 1985-92), Nappa Valley Vintners Assn. Democrat. Lutheran. Home: PO Box 680 1570 Bella Oaks Ln Rutherford CA 94573 Office Phone: 707-280-5374. Business E-Mail: garen.stagline@staglinfamily.com.

STAHELI, KORY D., law librarian; BA, Brigham Young U., 1984, JD, 1987, MLIS, 1991. Atty. Snow, Nuffer, Engstrom & Drake, St. George, Utah, 1987—90; reference libr. Brigham Young U. Law Library, Provo, Utah, 1990—91, head of reference svcs., 1991—95, assoc. dir. pub. svc. Howard W. Hunter Law Libr., 1995—98, assoc. dir. collection devel. and faculty outreach, 2004—05, dir., 2005—; assoc. dir., head pub. svcs. Wiener-Rogers Law Libr., U. Nev., Las Vegas, 1998—2004, interim dir., 2002. Spkr. in field. Contbr. articles to profl. jours. Mem.: Am. Assn. Law Libs. Office: Howard W Hunter Law Lib 256 JRCB PO Box 28000 Provo UT 84602-8000 Office Phone: 801-422-9223. E-mail: stahelik@lawgate.byu.edu.

STAIR, CHARLES WILLIAM, former service company executive; b. Ida Grove, Iowa, Oct. 21, 1940; s. Frderic Cleveland and Eunice (Carlson) S.; m. Patricia Ellen Gramley, June 15, 1963; children: Kerry John, Andrew Charles, Melissa Kathrine. BA, Wheaton Coll., 1963. Coordinating mgr. The ServiceMaster Co., Downers Grove, Ill., 1963-65, regional ops. mgr., 1966-68, area ops. mgr., 1969-70, div. v.p., 1971, exec. v.p., 1972-73, div. pres., 1974-75, group v.p. east group, 1976-77, group pres. east group, 1978-79, group pres. west group, 1980-82, group pres. cen. group, 1983-85, exec. v.p. healthcare/edn., 1986, exec. v.p. mgmt. svcs., 1987-88, also bd. dirs., exec. v.p., chief oper. officer mgmt. svcs., 1989-90, pres., chief ops. officer mgmt. svcs., 1990-2000; ret., 2000. Exec. chmn. bd. dirs. Tyndale House Pubs. Inc., Wheaton. Republican. Avocations: tennis, golf, fishing, hunting. Office: ServiceMaster Co 1 ServiceMaster Way Downers Grove IL 60515-1700 Home: 1516 E Prairie Ave Wheaton IL 60187-3756

STAKE, JAMES B., manufacturing executive; Mng. dir., 3M Mfg. Venezuela 3M Co., mng. dir., 3M Italy and regional mng. dir., so. European region, 1996—98, mng. dir., 3M Italy, 1998—99, v.p., packaging sys. divsn., 1999—2000, v.p., indsl. tape and specialties divsn., 2000—02, v.p., indsl. tape and specialties divsn. and v.p., mktg., indsl. markets, 2002, exec. v.p., display and graphics bus., 2002—. Office: 3M Co 3M Ctr Saint Paul MN 55144

STALEY, HENRY MUELLER, manufacturing executive; b. Decatur, Ill., June 3, 1932; s. Augustus Eugene, Jr. and Lenore (Mueller) S.; m. Violet Lucas, Feb. 4, 1955; children— Mark Eugene, Grant Spencer. Grad., Governor Dummer Acad., 1950; BS in Psychology, Northwestern U., 1954, MBA in Finance, 1956. Salesman Field Enterprises, Chgo., 1953; salesman A.E. Staley Mfg. Co., 1951, mgmt. trainee, 1956-57, ins. mgr., 1957-59, asst. treas., 1959-65, treas., asst. sec., 1965-73, v.p., treas., asst. sec., 1973-77, v.p. bus. and econ. analysis, 1977-87, also dir., 1969-85; pvt. investor Decatur, 1987—. Dir. Staley Continental, Inc., 1985-88. Crusade chmn. Macon County unit Am. Cancer Soc., 1964-65, mem. bd. dirs., 1965-71, vice chmn. bd., 1965-66, chmn. bd., 1966-69; bd. dirs. United Way Decatur and Macon County, 1972-74; mem. adv. council Millikin U., 1968-91, chmn. adv. coun., 1970-71; mem. Decatur Meml. Hosp. Devel. Council, 1969-71, mem. finan. com., bd. dirs., 1970-79, mem. long-range planning com., 1976-77, mem. devel. and community relations com., 1977-78. Mem. Decatur C. of C. (dir. 1967-72), Sigma Nu, Decatur Country.Club. Home and Office: 276 N Park Pl Decatur IL 62522-1952

STALEY, ROBERT W., mechanical engineer, utilities executive; b. 1935; BSME, Cornell U., 1958, MBA, 1959. Dir. corp. devel. Trane Co., 1960-75; v.p. corp. tech. Emerson Electric Co., St. Louis, 1975-77, internat. v.p., 1977-78, chief fin. officer, sr. v.p. fin., 1978-81, sr. v.p., group v.p., 1981-83, exec. v.p., 1983-88, vice chmn., 1988—, also bd. dirs. Capt. U.S. Army, 1959-66. Office: Emerson Electric Co 8100 W Florissant Ave Saint Louis MO 63136-1494

STALEY, WARREN R., agricultural products and diversified services company executive; b. Springfield, Ill., May 14, 1942; BS in Elec. Engring., Kans. State U., 1965; MS in Bus. Adminstrn., Cornell U., 1967. With Cargill, Inc., Mpls., 1969—, gen. mgr., European corn milling bus., 1978—82, gen. mgr., Argentine ops., 1983—87, pres. for N.Am. and Latin Am., to 1998, pres., COO, 1998—2000, CEO, 1999—2007, chmn., 2000—07. Bd. dirs., Cargill, Inc., 1995-, U.S. Bancorp, 1999-, Target Corp., 2001-; apptd. mem. President's Export Coun. (PEC), 2003, chmn. Cargill Found. Bd. dirs. Greater Twin Cities United Way, Minn. Pvt. Coll. Coun.

STALLMEYER, JAMES EDWARD, engineering educator; b. Covington, Ky., Aug. 11, 1926; s. Joseph Julius and Anna Catherine (Scheper) S.; m. Mary Katherine Davenport, Apr. 11, 1953; children: Cynthia Marie, James Duncan, Michael John, Catherine Ann, John Charles, Gregory Edward. BS, U. Ill., 1947, MS, 1949, PhD, 1953. Jr. engr. So. Ry. System, 1947; research asst. U. Ill., Urbana, 1947-49, research asso., 1951-52, asst. prof. civil engring, 1952-57, assoc. prof., 1957-60, prof., 1960-91, prof. emeritus, 1991—. Cons. on structural problems various indsl. and govt. agys. Author: (with E.H. Gaylord Jr.), Design of Steel Structures; editor: (with E.H. Gaylord Jr.) Structural Engineering Handbook; contbr. to Shock and Vibration Handbook. Served with USN, 1944-46. Standard Oil fellow, 1949-51; recipient Adams meml. award, 1964, Everitt award for teaching excellence, 1981 Mem. ASCE, Am. Concrete Inst., Am. Ry. Engring. Assn., ASTM, Am. Welding Soc., Am. Soc. Metals, Soc. Exptl. Stress Analysis, Scabbard and Blade, Sigma Xi, Chi Epsilon, Sigma Tau, Tau Beta Pi, Phi Kappa Phi. Clubs: KC. Republican. Roman Catholic. Office: Newmark Civil Engring 205 N Mathews Ave Urbana IL 61801-2350 Business E-Mail: jestall26@gmail.com.

STALLWORTH, ALMA GRACE, former state legislator; Grad., Highland Park Community Coll., 1956; student, Wayne State U., 1956. Mem. Mich. Ho. of Reps., Lansing, 1970-74, 81-96; dep. dir. Hist. Dept. City of Detroit, 1975-78, job developer, 1978-79. Mem. exec. com. Nat. Conf. State Legislatures, 1986-89. Commr. Wayne County Charter, Detroit, 1978-79, Martin Luther King Commn., Detroit, 1987; chair bd. dirs. Task Force on Infant Mortality, Mich. Legislature, 1987; pres. Nat. Black Child Devel. Inst., Detroit; vol. United Negro Coll. Fund, 1987—; founder, adminstr. Black Caucus Found. of Mich., 1987—. Recipient cert. of appreciation Mich. Dept. Edn., 1986, Advs. award Mich. Health Mothers, Health Babies Coalition, 1987; named Woman Leader in Pub. Health, Mi ch. Assn. Local Pub. Health, 1987, Woman of Yr., Minority Women's Network, 1988. Mem. NAACP, Nat. Conf. State Legislators (exec. commr. 1986), Nat. Black Caucus State Legislators, (sec. women's caucus), Mich. Legis. Black Causus (chair 1987), Alpha Kappa Alpha. Clubs: Cameo, Top Ladies of Distinction. Democrat. Home: 19793 Sorrento St Detroit MI 48235-1149

STALLWORTH, SAM, broadcast executive; b. Washington, Sept. 4, 1946; BS in Mktg., U. Ala., 1968. V.p. sales CBS on TV, NYC, 1975-95; v.p., gen. mgr. WSYX-TV, Columbus, Ohio, 1995—. Mem. RTNDA, NAD, United Way. Office: WSYX TV 1261 Dublin Rd Columbus OH 43215-7000

STALLWORTH, STANLEY B., lawyer; b. 1963; BS summa cum laude, Ala. Agrl. and Mech. U., 1985; JD, U. Wis., 1990. Bar: Ala. 1990, Ill. 1990, Wis. 1990. Joined Sidley Austin Brown & Wood, Chgo., 1990—, now ptnr. real estate practice, and co-chmn. com. on racial and ethnic diversity. Articles editor Univ. Wis. Multi-Cultural Law Jour., 1989—90. Bd. trustees Univ. Wis. Law Alumni Assn.; chmn. bd. trustees Chgo. Acad. for Arts. Mem.: Chgo. Coun. of Lawyers (bd. dir.), Nat. Bar Assn., ABA, Cook County Bar Assn. (past mem. exec. bd. dir.). Office: Sidley Austin Brown & Wood LLP Bank One Plz 10 S Dearborn St Chicago IL 60603 Office Phone: 312-853-4715. Office Fax: 312-853-7036. Business E-Mail: sstallworth@sidley.com.

STAMM, KEITH G., energy executive; BS in Mech. Engring., U. Mo., Columbia; MBA in Fin., Rockhurst Coll. Lic. Staff Aquila's Mo. Pub. Svc.; CEO Aquila Merchant Svcs.; chmn., CEO United Energy Ltd.; pres., COO Aquila Global Networks Group; sr. v.p., COO Aquila, Kans. City, Mo., 2002—. Former bd. mem. Alinta Ltd., Uecomm. Office: Aquila 20 W 9th St Kansas City MO 64105-1711

STAMOS, JOHN JAMES, judge; b. Chgo., Jan. 30, 1924; s. James S. and Katherine (Manolopoulos) S.; m. Helen Voutiritsas, Sept. 3, 1955 (dec. 1981); children— James, Theo, Colleen, Jana; m. Mary Sotter, March 21, 1986. LL.B., DePaul U., 1948. Bar: Ill. 1949. Since practiced in, Chgo.; asst. corp. counsel City Chgo., 1951-54; asst. states atty. Cook County, 1954-61; chief criminal div. States Attys. Office, 1961-64, 1st asst. states atty., 1964-66, states atty., 1966-68; judge Appellate Ct. of State of Ill., 1968-88; Judge Ill. Supreme Ct., Springfield, 1988-90; ret., 1990; of counsel Stamos and Trucco, Chgo., 1991—. Served with AUS, 1943-45. Office: Stamos & Trucco 30 W Monroe St #1600 Chicago IL 60603-2418

STANALAJCZO, GREG CHARLES, computer company executive; b. 1959; Degree, Oakland U. With CDI Computer Svc., Inc., Troy, Mich., 1986-95, pres., 1993-95; exec. v.p., COO, co-owner Trillium Teamologies, Inc., Royal Oak, Mich., 1996—; pres., owner Stano Enterprises, LLC, Stano Transp. Svcs., LLC, Stano Electronics & Tech., LLC; owner, ptnr. Sullivan Investment Group, 3rd St. Properties; ptnr. Heritage Pewter LLC; founder, pres. Trillium Charities, Inc.; owner, pres. Stano Electronics and Tech., LLC; co-owner, sec. and v.p. i-mdo.USA, Inc.; COO, co-owner, co-founder i-mob USA, Inc. Office: Trillium Teamologies Inc 219 S Main St Ste 300 Royal Oak MI 48067-2611 Office Phone: 248-584-2080. E-mail: greg_stano@compuserve.com.

STANDEN, CRAIG CLAYTON, newspaper executive; b. Camden, NJ, Oct. 3, 1942; s. Charles Raymond and Maxine Jeanette (Lundgren) S.; m. Marcia Claire Peterson, Feb. 10, 1968; children: Kimberly Ruth, Charles Arthur. BA, Denison U., 1964; MBA, Northwestern U., 1966. Assoc. product mgr. Gen. Foods Corp., White Plains, N.Y., 1969-73; dir. mktg. services R.J. Reynolds Tobacco Co., Winston-Salem, N.C., 1973-80; pres. Newspaper Advt. Bur., NYC, 1980-90; v.p. mktg. and advt. Scripps Howard, Cin., 1990—. Mem. Leadership Cin., 1992-93; bd. dirs. ARC, Cin. Chpt., 1993—, Jr. Achievement, 1993—. Mem. Pres. Assn. Advt. Coun. N.Y.C. (dir. 1981—), Media Advt. Partnership for Drug Free Am. (bd. dirs. 1986-89), Country Club of Darien (Conn., bd. dirs. 1989-90), Kenwood Country Club (Cin.), Ivy Hills Country Club (Cin.). Home: 6280 Shawnee Pines Dr Cincinnati OH 45243-3150 Office: Scripps Howard 312 Walnut St Ste 2800 Cincinnati OH 45202-4040

STANFIELD, REBECCA, radio personality; b. Newport Beach, Calif. Grad. Broadcast Journalism and History, U. Southern Calif. Assignment editor, sr. reporter Sta. KRCR-TV, Redding, Calif.; gen. assignment reporter Cable 12 News, Brooklyn Park; freelance writer Fox TV, Mpls.; news anchor Sta. WCCO Radio. Navigator Great Am. Race. Office: WCCO 625 2nd Ave S Minneapolis MN 55402

STANGE, JAMES HENRY, architect; b. Davenport, Iowa, May 25, 1930; s. Henry Claus and Norma (Ballhorn) S.; m. Mary Suanne Peterson, Dec. 12, 1954; children: Wade Weston, Drew Dayton, Grant Owen. BArch, Iowa State U., 1954. Registered architect, Iowa, Nebr., Kans., Mo., Okla. Designer Davis & Wilson, Lincoln, Nebr., 1954-62, v.p., 1962-68; v.p., sec. Davis, Fenton, Stange, Darling, Lincoln, Nebr., 1977-92, pres., 1976—93, chmn., 1978—94. Mem. State Bd. Examiners for Engrs. and Architects, 1989-92, chmn. region V NCARB, 1991. Prin. works include Dorsey Labs., 1960, East H.S., Lincoln, 1966, Lincoln Gen. Hosp., 1967, Lincoln Airport Terminal, Sq. D Mfg. Plant, Lincoln, Bryan Meml. Hosp. (masterplans and additions), 1970, 80, 90, Bryan Ambulatory Care Ctr. Med. Office Bldg., Same Day Surgery Conf. Ctr., Parking Garage, 1993-95, Nebr. Wesleyan Theatre, Lincoln, Hasting (Nebr.) YMCA, various structures U. Nebr., Lincoln, ctr. and br. offices Am. Charter Fed. Savs. & Loan, Lincoln South East HS (addition), 1984, U. Nebr. Animal Sci. Bldg., 1987, Beadle Ctr., UNL, 1991, Carriage Park Parking Garage, 1995. V.p. Nebr. Jazz Orch., 1995, 2000—, pres., 1997, Nebr. Art Assn. Bd., 1996—99; deacon 1st Presbyn. Ch., 1960, chmn. bd. trustees, 1968—90, elder, 1972—, 1997—99, chmn. property com., 1998—2000, found. bd. trustees, 2005—; bd. dirs. Capitol Assn. Retarded Citizens, 1968—72, 1994—, pres., 1970; chmn. United Way Campaign, 1986, chmn. bd., 1988; chmn. endowment com. Bryan Hosp. Found., 1988—90; bd. dirs. Delta Dental, 1987—92, Downtown Lincoln Assn., 1975—94, mem. steering com., 1989, pres., 1979; mem. mayor's com. Study Downtown Redevel., 1989, pub. bldg. commn., masterplan rev. com., 1994; bd. dirs. Bryan Lincoln Gen. Hosp. Found.; pres. Lincoln Ctr. Assn., 1979. Recipient Honor award Conf. on Religious Architecture-First Plymouth Ch. Addition, 1969, also numerous state and nat. awards from archtl. orgns.; inducted into Hall of Fame, Iowa H.S. Athletic Assn., 2001. Mem. AIA (Nebr. bd. dirs. 1964-65, treas. 1965, sec. 1966, v.p. 1967, pres. Nebr. 1968, mem. com. on architecture for health 1980-94, Regional Design award 1976, 88, 96), Am. Assn. Health Planners, Interfaith Forum on Religion, Art, Architecture, Lincoln C. of C. (bd. dirs. 1982), Exec. Club (pres. 1972), Crucible Club, 12 Club, Hillcrest Country Club (pres. 1977), Lincoln U. Club (sec. 1992, bd. dirs. 1991-97, pres. 1995, 96, teammates mentor 2000—). Avocations: travel, photography, golf. Home: 3545 Calvert St Lincoln NE 68506-5744 Office: Davis Design 211 N 14th St Lincoln NE 68508-1616 Personal E-mail: jh3545@aol.com.

STANGE, KURT C., medical educator; MD, Albany Med. Coll., 1983; PhD, U. N.C., 1989. Diplomate Am. Bd. Family Practice, Am. Bd. Preventive Medicine. Prof. family medicine, epidemiology, biostatistics, oncology and sociology Case Western Reserve U., Cleve.; physician, tchr., rschr. dept. family medicine U. Hosps. Cleve.; assoc. dir. prevention, control and population rsch. Ireland Cancer Ctr. at U. Hosps. Cleve. and Case Western Reserve U.; dir., Family Medicine Res. Div. Case Western Reserve U., Cleve. Mem. Inst. Medicine, Rsch. Assn. Practicing Physicians. Office: Case Western Reserve U Sch Medicine Dept Family Medicine 10900 Euclid Ave Cleveland OH 44106-1712 also: Dept Family Medicine U Circle Rsch Ctr 11001 Cedar Ave Ste 306 Cleveland OH 44106-3043 Fax: 216-368-4348. E-mail: kcs@po.cwru.edu.

STANGL, PETER E., transportation executive; BA, MA, Univ. Conn. With Met. Transp. Authority, NY, 1980—95; pres. Metro North Railroad, NY, 1983—91; chmn., CEO Met. Transp. Authority, NY, 1991—95; pres. Bombardier Transit Corp., 1995—2000, Bombardier Transp. US, 2000—03; non-exec. chmn. Laidlaw Internat., Naperville, Ill., 2003—. Past vice chmn. Am. Public Transit Assn. Office: Laidlaw International Ste 400 55 Shuman Blvd Naperville IL 60563

STANHAUS, JAMES STEVEN, lawyer; b. Evergreen Park, Ill., Oct. 22, 1945; s. Wilfrid Xavier and Mary (Komanecky) S.; m. Naomi Evelyn Miller, June 27, 1971; 1 child, Heather. AB magna cum laude, Georgetown U., 1966; JD magna cum laude, Harvard U., 1970. Bar: Ill. 1970, U.S. Dist. Ct. (no. dist.) Ill. 1970. Assoc. Mayer, Brown, Rowe & Maw LLP, Chgo., 1971-76, ptnr., 1977—2005, sr. counsel, 2005—. Mem. ABA, Ill. Bar Assn., Chgo. Bar Assn., Chgo. Coun. Lawyers, Chgo. Estate Planning Coun., Met. Club, Riverpark Club (Chgo.), Phi Beta Kappa. Avocations: computers, tennis, racquetball. Office: Mayer Brown Rowe & Maw LLP 71 S Wacker Dr Ste 3300 Chicago IL 60606-4637 Office Phone: 312-701-7135. Business E-Mail: jstanhaus@mayerbrownrowe.com.

STANLEY, ELLEN MAY, historian, consultant; b. Dighton, Kans., Feb. 3, 1921; d. Delmar Orange and Lena May (Bobb) Durr; m. Max Neal Stanley, Nov. 5, 1939; children: Ann Y. Stanley Epps, Janet M. Stanley Horsky, Gail L. Stanley Peck, Kenneth D., Neal M., Mary E. Stanley McEniry. BA in English and Journalism, Ft. Hays State U., Kans., 1972, MA in History, 1984. Pvt. practice local/state historian, cons., writer local history, Dighton, 1973—; cons. genealogy, 1980—. Vice chmn. State Preservation Bd. Rev., Kans., 1980-87; area rep. Kans. State Mus. Assn., 1978-84. Author: Early Lane County History: 12,000 B.C.--A.D. 1884, 1993 (Cert. of Commendation, Am. Assn. for State and Local History, 1994), Cowboy Josh: Adventures of a Real Cowboy, 1996, Early Lane County Development, 1993, Golden Age, Great Depression and Dust Bowl, 2001 (Ferguson Kans. History Book award Kans. Author Club, 2002); contbr. articles to profl. jours. Precinct woman com. Alamota Township, Kans., 1962-86; mem. Dem. State Affirmative Action Com., 1975. Recipient hon. mention for photography Ann. Christian Arts Festival, 1974, Artist of Month award Dane G. Hansen Mus., 1975. Mem. Kans. State Hist. Soc. (pres. 1990-91), Lane County Hist. Soc. (sec. 1970-78). Methodist. Avocations: fossil hunting, walking, photography, antiques. Home: 100 N 4th Dighton KS 67839 Office: 110 E Pearl St Dighton KS 67839

STANLEY, HUGH MONROE, JR., lawyer; b. Ft. Lewis, Wash., Oct. 25, 1944; s. Hugh Monroe Sr. and Rita (McHugh) S.; m. Patricia Page, Aug. 17, 1968; children: Allison Michelle, Matthew Monroe, Trevor Marshall. BA magna cum laude, U. Dayton, 1966; JD, Georgetown U., 1969. Bar: Ohio 1969, U.S. Ct. Appeals (6th cir.) 1983, U.S. Supreme Ct. 1979. Assoc. Arter & Hadden, Cleve., 1969-76, ptnr., 1976—2003, chmn. litigation dept., 1983-96; ptnr. Tucker Ellis & West LLP, 2003—. Fellow Am. Bar Found., Bar Assn. Greater Cleve., Am. Coll. Trial Lawyers, Internat. Acad. Trial Lawyers, Internat. Soc. Barristers, Nat. Assn. R.R. Trial Counsel; mem. ABA, Fed. Bar Assn., Def. Rsch. Inst., Cleve. Assn. Civil Trial Attys., Ohio Assn. Civil Trial Attys. Republican. Roman Catholic. Avocation: reading. Office: Tucker Ellis & West 1150 Huntington Bldg 925 Euclid Ave Ste 1100 Cleveland OH 44115-1475 Home Phone: 440-338-6920; Office Phone: 216-696-3934. Business E-Mail: hstanley@tucherellis.com.

STANLEY, KELLY N., foundation administrator; m. Donna K.; children: Laura Keppler, Casey Stanley, Marci Robinson. Grad., Miami U.; JD, Ind. Sch. Law. Past pres., CEO Ontario Corp., Muncie, Ind.; pres. BMH Found., Muncie, Ind., 2003—. Past vice-chmn. Cardinal Health Sys., past chmn. Ball Meml. Hosp.; dir. Old Nat. Bancorp, Ind. State C. of C., U.S. C. of C. (chmn. 2000-2001). Office: BMH Foundation 120 W Charles St Muncie IN 47305

STANLEY, RICHARD HOLT, consulting engineer; b. Muscatine, Iowa, Oct. 20, 1932; s. Claude Maxwell and Elizabeth Mabel (Holthues) S.; m. Mary Jo Kennedy, Dec. 20, 1953; children: Lynne Elizabeth, Sarah Catherine, Joseph Holt. BSEE, BSME, Iowa State U., 1955; MS in Sanitary Engring., U. Iowa, 1963. Registered profl. engr., Iowa. With Stanley Cons. Inc., Muscatine, Iowa, 1955—, pres., 1971-87, chmn., 1984—. Vice chmn. HNI Corp., 1979-05; chmn Nat. Constrn. Industry Coun., 1978, Com. Fed. Procurement Archtl.-Engring. Svcs., 1979; pres. Ea. Iowa CC, Bettendorf, 1966-68; mem. indsl. adv. coun. Iowa State U. Coll. Engring., Ames, 1969-97, chmn., 1979-81; bd. dirs. Stanley Cons. Inc., Muscatine, Iowa. Contbr. articles to profl. jours. Bd. dirs. N.E.-Midwest Inst., 1989-95, treas., 1991-93, chmn., 1993-95; bd. dirs. Stanley Found., 1956—, pres., 1984—, chmn., 1995—; bd. dirs. Muscatine Health Support Found., pres., 1984—; bd. dirs. Muscatine United Way, 1969-75, Iowa State U. Meml. Union, 1968-83, U. Dubuque, Iowa, 1977-93, Inst. Social and Econ. Devel., 1992-2001, Unity Healthcare, 1999-2005, chmn. 1999-2002; bd. govs. Iowa State U. Found., 1982-96. Recipient Young Alumnus award Iowa State U. Alumni Assn., 1966, Disting. Svc. award Muscatine Jaycees, 1967, Profl. Achievement citation Coll. Engring., Iowa State U., 1977, Anson Marston medal Iowa State U., 1991, Harry S. Truman disting. svc. award Am. Assn. C.C., 1998; Disting. Alumni Achievement award U. Iowa Alumni Assn., 1999, award for Citizen Diplomacy, Nat. Coun. for Internat. Visitors, 2000, Hoover medal, 2001, Order of Knoll Cardinal and Gold award Iowa State U., 2004; named Sr. Engr. of Yr., Joint Engring. Com. Quint Cities, 1973; named to Disting. Engring. Alumni Acad., U. Iowa, 1998; named to Muscatine H.S. Hall of Honor, 2000. Fellow ASCE, Am. Cons. Engrs. Cos. (chmn. 1976-77, Cmty. Svc. award 1997, Disting. Award of Merit 1998), Iowa Acad. Sci.; mem. IEEE (sr.), ASME, Am. Soc. Engring. Edn., Nat. Soc. Profl. Engrs., Cons. Engrs. Coun. Iowa (pres. 1967), Iowa Engring. Soc. (pres. 1973-74, John Dunlap-Sherman Woodward award 1967, Disting. Svc. award 1980, Voice of Engr. award 1987, Herbert Hoover Centennial award 1989), Muscatine C. of C. (pres. 1972-73), C. of C. of U.S. (constrn. action coun. 1976-91), Rotary, Tau Beta Pi, Phi Kappa Phi, Pi Tau Sigma, Eta Kappa Nu. Presbyterian (elder). Home: 516 Hogan Ct Muscatine IA 52761-2740 Office: Stanley Cons Inc Stanley Bldg Muscatine IA 52761

STANO, SISTER DIANA, academic administrator; AB, Ursuline Coll.; PhD, Ohio State U. Prof. edn. Ursuline Coll., Pepper Pike, Ohio, chair edn. dept., dir. grad. program in non-pub. sch. adminstrn., dir. master's degree program, dean of grad. studies, dir. of instl. rsch., pres., 1996—. Bd. trustees Coll. of New Rochelle; sec. bd. trustees Ohio Found. Ind. Coll.; cons. in field. Recipient YWCA Women of Profl. Excellence award, No. Ohio Live Rainmaker in Edn. award. Mem.: In Counsel With Women, Exec. Women's Leadership Forum. Office: Ursuline Coll 2550 Lander Rd Pepper Pike OH 44124-4398

STANTON, KATHRYN, retail executive; b. Nov. 29, 1954; BS in Acctg., U. Ill., 1976; MBA, U. Chgo., 1996. CPA, Ill. From auditor to mgr. Arthur Anderson, Chgo., 1976-81, mgr., 1981-86; from controller to v.p. finance, CFO Follett Corp., Chgo., River Grove, Ill., 1986-97, v.p. finance, CFO River Grove, Ill., 1997—. Bd. dirs. Mus. Sci. and Industry, Chgo. Mem. Am. Inst. CPAs, Financial Exec. Inst., Ill. CPA Soc., Chgo. Council Foreign Rels. Office: Follett Corp 2233 N West St River Grove IL 60171-1895 Fax: 708-452-9347.

STANTON, R. THOMAS, lawyer; b. Moline, Ill., 1943; BA, Knox Coll., 1965; postgrad., Harvard U., 1966—67; JD, Northwestern U., 1969. Bar: Ohio 1969, N.Y. 1982. Mng. ptnr. Squire Sanders & Dempsey LLP, chmn. Cleve., 1990—, chmn., mgmt. com. Bd. editors Northwestern U. Law Review, 1969. Bd. chair Leadership Cleve., Univ. Circle, Inc.; trustee The Musical Arts Assn./The Cleve. Orchestra, Ohio Bus. Roundtable; mem. law bd. Northwestern Univ.; mem. Dean's Adv. Coun. Case Western Reserve Law Sch. Mem. Order of Coif. (chmn. mgmt. com.). Office: Squire Sanders & Dempsey LLP 4900 Key Tower 127 Public Sq Cleveland OH 44114-1304 Office Phone: 216-479-8728. Fax: 216-479-8780. Business E-Mail: rstanton@ssd.com.

STANTON, ROGER D., lawyer; b. Oct. 4, 1938; s. George W. and Helen V. (Peterson) S.; m. Judith L. Duncan, Jan. 27, 1962; children: Jeffrey B., Brady D. (dec.), Todd A. AB, U. Kans., 1960, JD, 1963. Bar: Kans. 1963, U.S. Dist. Ct. Kans. 1963, U.S. Ct. Appeals (10th cir.) 1972, U.S. Supreme Ct. 1973. Assoc. Stanley, Schroeder, Weeks, Thomas & Lysaught, Kansas City, 1963—68; ptnr. Weeks, Thomas & Lysaught, Kansas City, 1969—81, also bd. dirs., chmn. exec. com., 1981-82; ptnr. Stinson, Mag & Fizzell, Kansas City, 1983-96, chmn. products practice group, also bd. dirs., 1993-95; ptnr. litig. practice Berkowitz Stanton Brandt Williams & Shaw LLP, Prairie Village, Kans., 1997—2005; pvt. practice Overland Pk., Kans., 2005—. Chmn. bd. editors Jour. Kans. Bar Assn., 1975-83; contbr. articles to profl. jours. Active Boy Scouts Am., 1973-79; pres. YMCA Youth Football Club, 1980-82; co-chmn. Civil Justice Reform Act com. Dist. of Kans., 1991-95; bd. dirs. Kans. Appleseed Found., 2000—. Fellow: Am. Coll. Trial Lawyers (state SRSC Com. 1983—88, state chmn. 1984—86, state SRSC Com. 2001—02); mem.: Hist. Soc. Tenth Cir. (bd.dirs. 2005—), Earl O'Conner Inn of Ct. (founding mem. 1991—), Kans. Assn. Def. Counsel (pres. 1977—78), Johnson County Bar Assn. (chmn. bench, bd. dirs. bar com., bd. dirs.), Johnson County Bar Found. (pres., trustee), Kans. Bar Assn. (Pres.'s award 1982), Def. Rsch. Inst. (state co-chmn. 1979—90, Exceptional Performance award 1979), Internat. Assn. Def. Counsel, U. Kans. Kansas City Alumni (bd. dirs. 2001—), U. Kans. Sch. Law Alumni Assn. (bd. dirs. 1975—76, 1985—86), Phi Delta Phi. Office: Ste 500 Bldg 51 9393 W 110th St Overland Park KS 66210 Office Phone: 913-451-6958. Business E-Mail: rstanton@stanton-law.com.

STAPLES, DAVID M., corporate financial executive; B in Acctg., Mich. State U. Audit and bus. adv. practice Arthur Andersen LLP, 1985—96; divisional v.p., strategic planning and reporting Kmart Corp., 1996—2000; v.p. fin. Spartan Stores, Grand Rapids, Mich., 2000, exec. v.p., CRO, 2000—. Office: Spartan Stores PO Box 8700 Grand Rapids MI 49518-8700

STAPLES, THORI YVETTE, former soccer player; b. Balt., Apr. 17, 1974; Student in sports mgmt., N.C. State U. Asst. women's soccer coach Va. Poly. Inst. and State U. Mem. silver medal U.S. squad1993 World Univ. Games, Buffalo; mem. 3d-place U.S. team FIFA Women's World Cup, Sweden, 1995; alt. U.S. Olympic Team, 1996; 1994 NSCAA All-Am.; 3-time All-Atlantic Coast Conf. and All-South Region selection for N.C. State U. Wolfpack. Nominee Mo. Athletic Club Nat. Player of Yr., 1994, 1995; named winner N.C. state championships in long jump, 400-meter dash, 800-meter run, ACC Rookie of Yr., 1994, 5-yr. player, Columbia (Md.) Crusaders; recipient Gold medal heptathlon, Nat. Amateur Athletic Union Jr. Olympics, 1991, 1992. Office: US Soccer Fedn 1801-1811 S Prairie Ave Chicago IL 60616

STAPLETON, JAMES HALL, retired statistician, educator; b. Royal Oak, Mich., Feb. 8, 1931; s. James Leo and Dorothy May (Hall) S.; m. Alicia M. Brown, Apr. 3, 1963; children: James, Lara, Sara. BA, Eastern Mich. U., 1952; MS, Purdue U., 1954, PhD, 1957. Statistician Gen. Electric Co., 1957-58; asst. prof. stats. and probability Mich. State U., East Lansing, 1958-63, assoc. prof., 1963-72, prof., 1972—2007, chmn. dept., 1968-75, grad. dir., 1987—2006. Cons. Gen. Telephone Co. of Ind.; vis. prof. U. Philippines, 1978-79 Mem. USS-Mich. Swim Com., AAU, 1976-84, chmn., 1976-78; mem. Mich. AAU Exec. Bd., 1976-81. NSF fellow, 1966-67 Mem. Inst. Math. Stats., Am. Statis. Assn. Office: Mich State U Dept Statistics East Lansing MI 48823 Office Phone: 517-355-9678. E-mail: stapleton@stt.msu.edu, staplet5@aol.com.

STARK, GEORGE ROBERT, health science association administrator; b. NYC, July 4, 1933; s. Jack and Florence (Israel) S.; m. Mary Susan Beck, Aug. 19, 1956; children: Robert Braden, Janna Elizabeth. BA in Chemistry, Columbia Coll., NYC, 1955; PhD in Chemistry, Columbia Coll., 1959. Rsch. assoc., asst. prof. Rockefeller U., NYC, 1959-63; asst. prof. dept. biochemistry Stanford (Calif.) U., 1963-66, assoc. prof., 1966-71, prof., 1971-83; sr. scientist Imperial Cancer Rsch. Fund, London, 1983-85, asst. dir. rsch., 1985-89, assoc. dir. rsch., 1989-92; chair Lerner Rsch. Inst. Cleve. Clinic Found., 1992—. Reilly lectr. Notre Dame U., 1972; mem. physiol. chemistry study sect. NIH, 1974-77, study sect. Am. Cancer Soc., 1981-83; mem. European Molecular Biology Orgn. Coun., 1990; mem. sci. com. Cancer Rsch. Campaign, 1990-92 Mem. editl. bd. Jour. Biol. Chemistry, 1970-75, Cell, 1983-88, European Molecular Biology Orgn. Jour., 1990-93; contbr. over 180 articles to profl. jours. including European Molecular Biology Orgn. Jour., Jour. Biol. Chemistry, Molecular Cellular Biology, ature, Oncogene, Proceedings of the Nat. Acad. Scis., among others. Trustee Cleve. Playhouse, 1993—. Guggenheim fellow, 1970-71, Josiah Macy, Jr. fellow, 1977-78; Yamagiwa-Yoshida Study grantee Internat. Union Against Cancer, 1981; named H.A. Sober Meml. lectr. Am. Soc. Biol. Chemists. Fellow Royal Soc.; mem. NAS, Am. Soc. Biochemistry Molecular Biology (rep. U.S. nat. com. biochemistry 1995—), European Molecular Biology Orgn. Achievements include discoveries in enzyme chemistry, interferon signaling and mammalian genetics; contributions to methodology in protein chemistry and molecular biology. Home: 2900 W Park Blvd Shaker Heights OH 44120-1812 Office: Cleve Clinic Found 9500 Euclid Ave Cleveland OH 44195-0001

STARK, HENRY, technology educator; BSEE, CCNY, 1961; MSEE, Columbia U., 1964, D in Engring. Sci., 1968. Project engr. Bendix Corp., 1961—62; rsch. engr. Columbia U., NYC, 1962—69; assoc. prof. Yale U., New Haven, 1970—77; prof. Rensselaer Poly. Inst., Troy, NY, 1977—87; prof., chmn. dept. Ill. Inst. Technology, Chgo., 1988—97; Bodine disting. prof. elec. and computer engring., 1988—. Co-author: Modern Electrical Communications: Theory and Systems, 1979, Probability, Random Processes and Estimation Theory for Engineers, 1986, Modern Electrical Communications: Analog, Digital and Optical Systems, 1988, Probability and Random Processes with Applications to Signal Processes, 2002, Vector Space Projections: A Numerical Approach to Signal and Image Processing, Neural Nets and Optics, 1998; editor: Applications of Optical Fourier Transforms, 1981, Image Recovery: Theory and Practice, 1987; co-editor: Signal Processing Methods for Audio, Images and Telecommunications, 1995; contbr. articles to profl. jours., chapters to books. Grantee, NSF. Fellow: IEEE, Optical Soc. Am. (Ester Hoffman Beller prize 2000). Office: Ill Inst Technology Dept Elec/Computer Engring 3301 S Dearborn Chicago IL 60616 E-mail: eestark@ece.iit.edu.

STARK, JOAN SCISM, education educator; b. Hudson, NY, Jan. 6, 1937; d. Ormonde F. and Myrtle Margaret (Kirkey) S.; m. William L. Stark, June 28, 1958 (dec.); children: Eugene William, Susan Elizabeth, Linda Anne, Ellen Scism; m. Malcolm A. Lowther, Jan. 31, 1981. BS, Syracuse U., 1957; MA (Hoadly fellow), Columbia U., 1960; Ed.D., SUNY, Albany, 1971. Tchr. Ossining (N.Y.) High Sch., 1957-59; free-lance editor Holt, Rinehart & Winston, Harcourt, Brace & World, 1960-70; lectr. Ulster County Community Coll., Stone Ridge, NY, 1968-70; asst. dean Goucher Coll., Balt., 1970-73, asso. dean, 1973-74; assoc. prof., chmn. dept. higher postsecondary edn. Syracuse (N.Y.) U., 1974-78; dean Sch. Edn. U. Mich., Ann Arbor, 1978-83, prof., 1983-2001, prof. and dean emeritus, 2001—; dir. Nat. Ctr. for Improving Postsecondary Teaching and Learning, 1986—91. Editor: Rev. of Higher Edn., 1991-96; contbr. articles to various publs. Leader Girl Scouts U.S.A., Cub Scouts Am.; coach girls Little League; dist. officer PTA, intermittently, 1968-80; mem. adv. com. Gerald R. Ford Library, U. Mich., 1980-83; trustee Kalamazoo Coll., 1979-85; mem. exec. com. Inst. Social Research, U. Mich., 1979-81; bd. dirs. Mich. Assn. Colls. Tchr. Edn., 1979-81. Mem. Am. Assn. for Higher Edn., Am. Ednl. Rsch. Assn. (Div. J. Rsch. award 1998), Assn. Study Higher Edn. (dir. 1977-79, v.p. 1983, pres. 1984, Rsch. Achievement award 1992, svc. award 1998, Disting. Career award 1999), Assn. Innovation Higher Edn. (nat. chmn. 1974-75), Assn. Instl. Rsch. (disting. mem., Sidney Suslow award 1999), Assn. Colls. and Schs. Edn. State Univs. and Land Grant Colls. (dir. 1981-83), Acctg. Edn. Change Commn., Phi Beta Kappa, Phi Kappa Phi, Sigma Pi Sigma, Eta Pi Upsilon, Lambda Sigma Sigma, Phi Delta Kappa, Pi Lambda Theta.

STARK, PATRICIA ANN, psychologist; b. Ames, Iowa, Apr. 21, 1937; d. Keith C. and Mary L. (Johnston) Moore. BS, So. Ill. U., Edwardsville, 1970, MS, 1972; PhD, St. Louis U., 1976. Counselor to alcoholics Bapt. Rescue Mission, East St. Louis, Ill., 1969; rschr. alcoholics Gateway Rehab. Ctr., East St. Louis, 1972; psychologist intern Henry-Stark Counties Spl. Edn. Dist. and Galesburg State Rsch. Hosp., Ill., 1972—73; instr. Lewis and Clark C.C., Godfrey, Ill., 1973—76, asst. prof., 1976—84, assoc. prof., 1994, coord. child care svcs., 1974—84; mem. staff dept. psychiatry Meml. Hosp., St. Elizabeth's Hosp., 1979—2001; supr. students interns, 1974—94. Dir. child and family svc. Collinsville Counseling Ctr., 1977-82; clin. dir., owner Empas-Complete Family Psychol. and Hypnosis Svcs., Collinsville, 1982—; cons. cmty. agys., 1974—; mem. adv. bd. Madison County Coun. on Alcoholism and Drug Dependency, 1977-80. Mem. APA, Ill. Psychol. Assn., Midwestern Psychol. Assn., Am. Soc. Clin. Hypnosis, Internat. Soc. Hypnosis. Office: 2802 Maryville Rd Maryville IL 62062 Office Phone: 618-345-6632.

STARK, SUSAN R., film critic; b. NYC, July 9, 1940; d. Albert A. and Lillian H. (Landau) Rothenberg; m. Allan F. Stark, June 26, 1968 (div. 1983); children: Allana Fredericka, Paula-Rose. BA, Smith Coll., 1962; MAT., Harvard U., 1963. Film critic Detroit Free Press, 1968-79, Detroit News, 1979—. Mem. Phi Beta Kappa Office: Detroit News 615 W Lafayette Blvd Detroit MI 48226-3197

STARKMAN, GARY LEE, lawyer; b. Chgo., Sept. 2, 1946; s. Oscar and Sara (Ordman) Starkman. AB, U. Ill., 1968; JD cum laude, Northwestern U., 1971. Bar: Ill. 1971, U.S. Dist. Ct. (no. dist.) Ill. 1972, U.S. Ct. Appeals (7th cir.) 1972, U.S. Supreme Ct. 1974, Trial Bar U.S. Dist. Ct. (no. dist.) Ill. 1982, U.S. Ct. Appeals (3d cir.) 1984, U.S. Ct. Appeals (D.C. cir.) 1984. Asst. U.S. Atty. No. Dist. Ill., 1971-75; gen. counsel, dir. rsch. Citizens for Thompson Campaign Com., 1975-77; counsel to Gov. of Ill., 1977-81; admissions com. U.S. Dist. Ct. (no. dist.) Ill., 1982-90; ptnr. Ross & Hardies, Chgo., 1990—2003, McGuire Woods LLP, Chgo., 2003—. Co-author: (textbook) Cases and Comments on Criminal Procedure, 1974, 6th edit., 2003; contbr. articles to profl. jours.; reviewer in field. Chmn. state agys. divsn. Jewish United Fund Met. Chgo., 1978-81; chmn. Ill. Racing Bd., 1991-96; bd. dirs. Internat. Assn. Racing Commn., 1992-94; cmty. adv. bd. Jr. League Chgo., 1979-83. Named one of Ten Outstanding Young Citizens, Chgo. Jr. C. of C., 1978; recipient John Marshall award for appellate litigation, Atty. Gen. U.S., 1974, Nat. Svc. award, Tau Epsilon Pi, 1968. Mem.: ABA (litigation sect.), Chgo. Bar Assn. (constl. law com.), Decalogue Soc., Northwestern U. Law Alumni Assn. Office: McGuire Woods LLP 77 W Walker Dr Ste 4100 Chicago IL 60601-1681 Home Phone: 773-929-4422; Office Phone: 312-750-2788. Business E-Mail: gstarkman@mcguirewoods.com.

STARKS, DANIEL J., medical technology and services executive; BA, Shimer Coll., Waukegan, Ill.; JD magna cum laude, U. Minn. Law Sch., 1979. Comml. litigation atty. Nichols, Starks, Carruthers and Kaster, 1979—85; gen. counsel to pres., CEO Daig Corp. (bought by St. Jude Medical Inc.), 1985—96; pres., CEO,

Daig Corp. St. Jude Medical Inc., St. Paul, 1996—98, dir., 1996—, pres., CEO Cardiac Rhythm Mgmt. div., 1998—2001, pres., COO, 2001—04, chmn., pres., CEO, 2004—. Bd. dir. Urologix Inc. Office: St Jude Medical Inc 1 Lillehei Plz Saint Paul MN 55117-9913

STARRETT, FREDERICK KENT, lawyer; b. Lincoln, Nebr., May 23, 1947; s. Clyde Frederick and Helen Virginia (Meyers) Starrett; m. Linda Lee Jensen, Jan. 19, 1969; children: Courtney, Kathryn, Scott. BA, U. Nebr., 1969; JD, Creighton U., 1976. Bar: Nebr 1976, Kans 1977, US Dist Ct Nebr 1976, US Dist Ct Kans 1977, US Ct Appeals (8th and 10th cirs) 1983, Mo 1987, US Dist Ct (we dit) Mo 1987, US Supreme Ct 1993. Pvt. practice law, Gt. Bend, Kans., 1976-77, Topeka, 1977-86; with Miller, Bash & Starrett, P.C., Kans. City, Mo., 1986-90; ptnr. Lathrop Norquist & Miller, 1990-91, Lathrop and Norquist, Overland Pk., Kans., 1991-95, Lathrop & Gage L.C., Overland Pk., Kans., 1996—. Judicial nominating commr 10th Judicial Dist, 2000—04. Lt (jg) USNR, 1969—72. Named one of, Mo./Kans. Super Lawyers, 2006. Mem.: ABA, Litigation Counsel Am., Kans. Assn. of Defense Counsel, Mo. Orgn. Def. Lawyers, Def. Rsch. Inst. (state rep. Kans. 1998—2001, bd. dirs. 2002—05), Am. Bd. Trial Advs. (pres. Kans. chpt. 1997), Kans. Bar Assn. (pres. litig. sect. 1985—86), Civitan Club (pres. 1985—86, Disting. Pres. award 1985—86). Democrat. Presbyterian. Avocations: aviation, scuba diving, sailing. Office: Lathrop & Gage LC 10851 Mastin Blvd Bldg 82 Ste 1000 Shawnee Mission KS 66210-1669 Home Phone: 913-469-8271; Office Phone: 913-451-5140. Business E-Mail: fstarrett@lathropgage.com.

STARZEL, ROBERT F., rail transportation executive; BS, Ariz. State U.; JD, Harvard U. Sr. v.p. corp. rels. Union Pacific Corp., Omaha, 1997—. Office: Union Pacific Railroad 1400 Douglas St Omaha NE 68179-1001

STASHOWER, DAVID L., advertising executive; Chmn., CEO Liggett-Stashower Inc., Cleve. Active Cleve. Play House, Cleve. Opera. Inducted into Cleve. Advt. Club Hall of Fame, 1986. Mem. Am. Assn. Advt. Agys. (nat. sec./treas., trustee pension & profit sharing plans), Advt. & Mktg. Internat. Network, Ohio Motorists Assn., Cleve. Advt. Club, Neighborhood Ctrs. Assn. Office: Liggett-Stashower Inc 1228 Euclid Ave Cleveland OH 44115-1831

STASSEN, JOHN HENRY, lawyer; b. Joliet, Ill., Mar. 22, 1943; s. John H. and Florence C. (McCarthy) S.; m. Sara A. Gaw, July 6, 1968; children: John C., David A. BS, Northwestern U., 1965, JD, Harvard U., 1968. Bar: Ill. 1968. Assoc. Kirkland & Ellis, LLP, Chgo., 1968, 73-76, ptnr. 1977—. Contbr. articles to legal jours. Mem. bd. govs. Northwestern U. Libr., chmn., 2003-07; bd. dirs. Landmarks Preservation Coun. Ill., chmn., 2001-03. Lt. comdr., JAGC, USNR, 1969-79. Mem. ABA (past chmn. com. on futures regulation), Ill. Bar Assn., Chgo. Bar Assn., Phila. Soc., Mid America Club. Office: Kirkland & Ellis 200 E Randolph St Ste 5900 Chicago IL 60601-6436 Home: 16346 Timber Ln New Buffalo MI 49117 Office Phone: 312-861-2238. Business E-Mail: jstassen@kirkland.com.

STATES, DAVID JOHNSON, biomedical scientist, physician; b. Boston, July 12, 1953; m. Angel W. Lee, Sept. 1, 1979. BA, Harvard Coll., 1975; MD, PhD, Harvard U., 1983. Diplomate Am. Bd. Internal Medicine. Staff scientist Nat. Magnel Lab. MIT, Cambridge, 1983-84; resident and intern in internal medicine U. Calif., San Diego, 1984-86; staff fellow NIH, Bethesda, Md., 1986-89; sr. staff fellow Nat. Ctr. Biotechnology Info. Nat. Libr. Medicine, Bethesda, 1989-92; dir., assoc. prof. inst. biomedical computing Washington U., St. Louis, 1992—. Lt. Comdr. USPHS, 1990—. Mem. AAAS, Am. Fedn. Clin. Rsch., Intenrat. Soc. Computational Biology. Office: Washington Univ Inst Biomedical Computing Campus Boc 8036 Saint Louis MO 63110

STAUDER, ALFRED MAX, wire products company executive; b. Mexico City, May 25, 1940; s. Hans and Charlotte (Mueller) S.; m. Deanna J. Woods, June 12, 1962; children— Carl, Monique. B.A., Principia Coll., 1962. Chief exec. officer Woods Wire Products, Inc., Carmel, Ind., 1965—. Served to 1st lt. U.S. Army, 1962-65. Mem. Young Pres. Orgn. Republican. Christian Scientist. Club: Palm Beach Polo and Country (Fla.). Office: Woods Wire Products Inc 510 3rd Ave SW Carmel IN 46032-2063 Home: 348A Abbedale Ct Carmel IN 46032-7009

STAVITSKY, ABRAM BENJAMIN, immunologist, educator; b. Newark, May 14, 1919; s. Nathan and Ida (Novak) S.; m. Ruth Bernice Okney, Dec. 6, 1942; children: Ellen Barbara, Gail Beth. AB, U. Mich., 1939, MS, 1940; PhD, U. Minn., 1943; VMD, U. Pa., 1946. Research fellow Calif. Inst. Tech., 1946-47; faculty Case Western Res. U., 1947—, prof. microbiology, 1962—, prof. molecular biology and microbiology, 1983-89, emeritus, 1989; mem. expert com. immunochemistry WHO, 1963-83; mem. microbiology fellowship com. NIH, 1963-66; mem. microbiology test com. Nat. Bd. Med. Examiners, 1970-73; chmn. microbiology test com. Nat. Bd. Podiatry Examiners, 1978-82; adj. staff in pathobiology Lerner Rsch. Inst., Cleve. Clinic Found., 2006—. Mem. editl. bd. Jour. Immunological Methods, 1979-88, Immunopharmacology, 1983-96. Vice pres. Ludlow Community Assn., 1964-66. Fellow AAAS; mem. Am. Assn. Immunologists, Am. Soc. Microbiology, Sigma Xi. Home: 14604 Onaway Rd Shaker Heights OH 44120-2845 Office: 2119 Abington Rd Cleveland OH 44106-2333 Home Phone: 216-752-8631. Business E-Mail: abs7@case.edu.

STAY, BARBARA, zoologist, educator; b. Cleve., Aug. 31, 1926; d. Theron David and Florence (Finley) S. AB, Vassar Coll., 1947; MA, Radcliffe Coll., 1949, PhD, 1953. Entomologist Army Research Center, Natick, Mass., 1954-60; vis. asst. prof. Pomona Coll., 1960; asst. prof. biology U. Pa., 1961-67; asso. prof. zoology U. Iowa, Iowa City, 1967-77, prof., 1977—. Fulbright fellow to Australia, 1953; Lalor fellow Harvard U., 1960 Fellow AAAS, Entomol. Soc. Am.; mem. Soc. Comparative and Integrative Biology, Am. Inst. Biol. Scis., Am. Soc. Cell Biology, Iowa Acad. Scis., Sigma Xi. Office: Univ Iowa Dept Biology Iowa City IA 52242 Home Phone: 319-351-5036. E-mail: barbara-stay@uiowa.edu.

STAYTON, THOMAS GEORGE, lawyer; b. Rochester, Minn., May 1, 1948; m. Barbara Joan Feck, Aug. 8, 1970; children: Ryan, Megan. BS, Miami U., Oxford, Ohio, 1970; JD, U. Mich., 1973. Bar: Ind. 1973, U.S. Dist. Ct. (so. dist.) Ind. 1973, U.S. Ct. Appeals (7th cir.) 1977. Ptnr. Baker & Daniels, Indpls., 1973—. Sustaining mem. Product Liability Adv. Coun. Recipient Sagamore of the Wabash Gov. of Ind., 1988. Mem. ABA, Ind. State Bar Assn., Indpls. Bar Assn. Office: Baker & Daniels 300 N Meridian St Ste 2700 Indianapolis IN 46204-1782 Home Phone: 317-733-0516; Office Phone: 317-237-1260. E-mail: tstayton@bakerd.com.

STEAD, JAMES JOSEPH, JR., securities company executive; b. Chgo., Sept. 13, 1930; s. James Joseph and Irene (Jennings) S.; m. Edith Pearson, Feb. 13, 1954; children: James, Diane, Robert, Caroline. BS, DePaul U., 1957, MBA, 1959. Asst. sec. C. F. Childs & Co., Chgo., 1957-62; exec. v.p., sec. Koenig, Keating & Stead, Inc., Chgo., 1962-66; 2d v.p., mgr. midwest mcpl. bond dept. Hayden, Stone Inc., Chgo., 1966-69; sr. v.p., nat. sales mgr. Ill. Co. Inc., 1969-70; mgr. instl. sales dept. Reynolds and Co., Chgo., 1970-72; partner Edwards & Hanly, 1972-74; v.p., instnl. sales mgr. Paine, Webber, Jackson & Curtis, 1974-76; v.p., regional instl. sales mgr. Reynolds Securities, Inc., 1976-78; sr. v.p., regional mgr. Oppenheimer & Co., Inc., 1978-88; sr. v.p., regional mgr. fixed income Tucker Anthony, 1988—; instr. Mcpl. Bond Sch., Chgo., 1967—. With AUS, 1951-53. Mem. Security Traders Assn. Chgo., Nat. Security Traders Assn., Am. Mgmt. Assn., Mcpl. Fin. Forum Washington. Clubs: Execs., Union League, Mcpl. Bond, Bond (Chgo.); Olympia Fields Country (Ill.); Wall Street (N.Y.C.). Home: 1005 Hickory Ridge Ct Frankfort IL 60423-2114 Office: 1 S Wacker Dr Chicago IL 60606-4614 Office Phone: 312-853-2820 ext. 118.

STEADMAN, DAVID WILTON, retired museum director, deacon; b. Honolulu, Oct. 24, 1936; s. Alva Edgar and Martha (Cooke) S.; m. Kathleen Carroll Reilly, Aug. 1, 1964; children: Alexander Carroll, Kate Montague. BA, Harvard U., Cambridge, Mass., 1960, MAT., 1961; MA, U. Calif.-Berkeley, 1966; PhD, Princeton U., NJ, 1974; M Theol. Studies, Ch. Divinity Sch. of Pacific, 2002. Ordained deacon Episcopal Ch., 2004. Lectr. Frick Collection, NYC, 1970-71; asst. dir., acting dir., assoc. dir. Princeton U. Art Mus., 1971-73; dir. galleries Claremont Colls., Calif., 1974-80; art cons. Archtl. Digest, LA, 1974-77; rsch. curator Norton Simon Mus., Pasadena, Calif., 1977-80; dir. Chrysler Mus., Norfolk, Va., 1980-89, Toledo Mus. Art, Ohio, 1989-99; ret., 2000. Author: Graphic Art of Francisco Goya, 1975, Works on Paper 1900-1960, 1977, Abraham van Diepenbeeck, 1982. Trustee Phillips Collection, Washington, Norton Simon Mus., Pasadena. Chester Dale fellow Nat. Gallery Art, Washington, 1969-70 Episcopalian. Personal E-mail: punto31157@aol.com.

STEADMAN, JACK W., professional football team executive; b. Warrenville, Ill., Sept. 14, 1928; s. Walter Angus and Vera Ruth (Burkholder) S.; m. Judy Tewksbury, Oct. 17, 1998; children: Thomas Edward, Barbara Ann, Donald Wayne. BBA, So. Methodist U., 1950. Accountant Hunt Oil Co., Dallas, 1950-54; chief accountant W.H. Hunt, Dallas, 1954-58, Penrod Drilling Co., Dallas, 1958-60; gen. mgr. Dallas Texans Football Club, 1960-63, Kansas City Chiefs Football Club, 1963-76, exec. v.p., 1966-76, pres., 1976-88; also chmn. bd., 1988—. Chmn. benefit com. NFL; chmn. Hunt Midwest Enterprises, Inc., Kansas City; former dir. Commerce Bank of Kansas City, Pvt. Industry Coun.; former chmn. Full Employment Coun. Former bd. dirs. Children's Mercy Hosp., bd. dirs. Civic Council, Starlight Theatre Assn., Kansas City, Am. Royal Assn.; pres. Heart of Am. United Way, 1981; adv. trustee Research Med. Ctr., Kansas City; trustee Midwest Research Inst.; mem. First Bapt. Ch. of Raytown; past chmn. C. of C. of Greater Kansas City. Recipient Kans. Citian of Yr. award, 1988. Mem. Indian Hills Country Club, Kansas City Club (pres. 1988), 711 Inner, River, Carriage, Man-of-the-Month Fraternity. Home: 6436 Wenonga Ter Shawnee Mission KS 66208-1732 Office: Kansas City Chiefs Football Club, Inc 1 Arrowhead Drive Kansas City MO 64129 Home: 6436 Wenonga Ter Mission Hills KS 66208-1732

STEARNS, NEELE EDWARD, JR., investment company executive; b. Chgo., Apr. 2, 1936; s. Neele Edward Sr. and Grace (Kessler) S.; m. Bonnie Ann Evans; children: Katherine Stearns Sprenger, Kendra Stearns Drozd. BA magna cum laude, Carleton Coll., 1958; MBA with distinction, Harvard U., 1960. Audit staff Arthur Andersen Co., 1962-66, audit mgr., 1966-67; asst. gen. mgr. internat. divsn. Imperial-Eastman Corp., 1967-68; asst. treas. Allied Products Corp., 1968-69, treas., 1969-72; v.p. Henry Crown (Ill.) and Co., 1972-75, v.p., controller, 1975-79; exec. v.p., COO Henry Crown and Co., 1979—86; pres., CEO, CC Industries, Inc., Chgo., 1986-95; chmn. exec. com. Barnes Internat., Inc., Northbrook, Ill., 1996-99; chmn. Wallace Computer Svcs., Inc., 2000, Fin. Investments Corp., Chgo., 2001—. Bd. dir. Schwarz Supply Source Inc. Trustee Evanston Northwestern Healthcare; bd. dir. Presbyn. Homes. Mem. Comml. Club Chgo., Econ. Club Chgo., Country Club Fla., Chgo. Club, Old Elm Club, Skokie Country Club, Phi Beta Kappa. Office: Fin Investments Corp 405 N Wabash River Plz 2E Chicago IL 60611 Office Phone: 312-494-4513. Business E-Mail: nstearns@fic-cep.com.

STEARNS, ROBERT LELAND, curator; b. LA, Aug. 28, 1947; s. Edward Van Buren and Harriett Ann (Hauck) S.; m. Sheri Roseanne Lucas, Oct. 2, 1982 (div. 1994); children: Marissa Hauck, Caroline Lucas. Student, U. Calif., San Diego, 1965-68, BFA, 1970; student, Calif. Poly. State U., San Luis Obispo, 1968. Asst. dir. Paula Cooper Gallery, NYC, 1970-72; prodn. asst. Avalanche Mag., NYC, 1972; dir. Kitchen Ctr. for Video/Music, NYC, 1972-77, Contemporary Arts Ctr., Cin., 1977-82; dir. performing arts Walker Art Ctr., Mpls., 1982-88; dir. Wexner Ctr. for Arts, Columbus, Ohio, 1988-92; mem. Wexner Ctr. Found., Columbus, 1990-92; dir. Stearns & Assocs./Contemporary Exhbn. Svcs., Columbus, Ohio, 1992—2000; sr. prgm. dir. Arts Midwest, Mpls., 1998—2005; cons. curator Franklin Park Conservatory, Columbus, Ohio, 2005—, Bellevue Arts Mus., Wash., 2008—. Adj. prof. dept. art, assoc. dean Coll. Art, Ohio State U., Columbus, 1988-92; lectr. Sch. of the Art Inst. Chgo., 2002; cons. McKnight Found., St. Paul, 1978, Jerome Found., 1978-79; chmn. Artists TV Workshop, N.Y.C., 1976-77; bd. dirs., chmn. Minn. Dance Alliance, Mpls., 1983-88; bd. dirs. Haleakala, Inc., N.Y.C.; mem. various panels Nat. Endowment for Arts, Washington, 1977-91; mem. pub. arts policy Greater Columbus Arts Coun., 1988-90; adv. coun. Bklyn. Acad. Music, 1982-84, Houston Grand Opera, 1991-93; fundraising cons. Art for Life Columbus AIDS Task Force, 2000-; mem. Advocacy Com. Ballet Met, Columbus, 2003-. Author, editor: Robert Wilson: Theater of Images, 1980, Photography and Beyond in Japan, 1995; author: Mexico Now: Point of Departure, 1997, Robert Wilson: Scenografie e Installazioni, 1997, Illusions of Eden: Visions of the American Heartland, 2000, Aspirations: Toward a Future in the Middle East, 2001, The View from Here: Recent Pictures from Central Europe and the American Midwest, 2002, Russel Wright: Living with Good Design, 2006, Bending Nature, 2008; editor: Dimensions of Black, 1970; exec. editor: Breakthroughs: Avant Garde Art in Europe and America 1950-1990, 1991; author and editor numerous catalogues. Mem. gov.'s residence com. State of Ohio, 2004—. Decorated chevalier Order of Arts and Letters (France); Travel grantee Jerome Found., 1986, Japan Found., 1991, Can. Cultural Ministry, 2004. Office: 2218 N Sunshine cir Palm Springs CA 92264 Office Phone: 614-288-7150. E-mail: arts2020@aol.com.

STEBBINS, DONALD J., car parts manufacturing company executive; BS in Fin., Miami U., Ohio; MBA, U. Mich. With Citibank, Bankers Trust Co.; v.p., treas., asst. sec. Lear Corp., Southfield, Mich., 1992, sr. v.p., CFO, treas., 1997, pres., COO Americas, pres., COO Europe, Asia and Africa; pres., COO Visteon Corp., 2005—. Office: Visteon Corp One Village Center Dr Belleville MI 48111

STEC, JOHN ZYGMUNT, retired real estate company officer; b. Stalowawola, Poland, Jan. 21, 1925; Came to U.S.A. 1947. s. Valenty and Maria (Madej) S. m. Wanda G. Baca, Oct. 13, 1956; children: David, Maria, Monica. Student, Poland, 1941-44, Kent State U., Ohio, 1965-66, student, 1966-67. Cert. Master of Corporate Real Estate. With The Singer Co., Cleve., 1952-54, dis. mgr., 1954-60, sales supr., 1960-67, dir. real estate Detroit and Chgo., 1967-73; v.p. Fabri Center of Am., Beachwood, Ohio, 1973—; sr. v.p. real estate Fabri-Centers of Am., Inc., Beachwood, Ohio, 1987—2005, spl. counsel to pres., 2005—; ret., 2005. Cons. in field. With U.S. Army, 1950-52. Mem. Nat. Assoc. of Corporate Real Estate (speaker, organizer 1974-77, audit Com. 1977-79, bd. dirs. 1970-82, Outstanding Achievement award 1982). Chagrin Valley Club. Repulican. Roman Catholic. Avocations: swimming, hiking, reading. Home: 725 Sagewood Dr Chagrin Falls OH 44023-6733 Office: Coventry Investment Real Estate Advisors 8401 Chagrin Rd Ste 1 Chagrin Falls OH 44023 Office Phone: 216-789-2278. Business E-Mail: jstec@coventryadvisors.com.

STECHER, KENNETH W., financial corporation executive; With Inter-Ocean Life Ins. Co. (acquired by Cin. Fin. Corp.); joined Cin. Fin. Corp., 1973—, sr. v.p., treas., co. sec., 1997—, CFO, 2001—. Office: 6200 S Gilmore Rd Fairfield OH 45014-5141

STECK, THEODORE LYLE, biochemistry and molecular biology educator, physician; b. Chgo., May 3, 1939; s. Irving E. and Mary L. S.; children: David B., Oliver M. BS in Chemistry, Lawrence Coll., 1960; MD, Harvard U., 1964. Intern Beth Israel Hosp., Boston, 1964-65, fellow, 1965-66; research assoc. Nat. Cancer Inst., NIH, Bethesda, Md., 1966-68, Harvard U. Med. Sch., Boston, 1968-70; asst. prof. medicine U. Chgo., 1970-74, asst. prof. biochemistry and medicine, 1973-74, assoc. prof., 1974-77, prof., 1977-84, chmn. dept. biochemistry, 1979-84, prof. biochemistry and molecular biology, 1984—, chair environ. studies program, 1993—. Office: 920 E 58th St Chicago IL 60637-5415

STECKO, PAUL T., packaging company executive; With Internat. Paper Co.; pres., CEO Tenneco Packing, 1993-96, COO, 1997-98, pres., COO, 1998-99; CEO, chmn. bd. Packaging Corp. of Am., Lake Forest, Ill., 1999—. Bd. dirs. Tenneco, Am. Forest and Paper Assn., State Farm Mut. Ins. Co. Office: Packaging Corp of Am 1900 W Field Ct Lake Forest IL 60045-4828

STEEL, DUNCAN GREGORY, engineering educator; b. Cleve., Jan. 11, 1951; s. Robert John and Mildred (Graham) S.; children: Adam, Benjamin. BA, U. N.C., 1972; MS, U. Mich., 1973-75, PhD, 1976. Physicist Exxon Rsch. and Engring., Linden, NJ, 1977-78, Hughes Rsch. Labs., Malibu, Calif., 1975-85; prof. U. Mich., Ann Arbor, 1985—; sr. rsch. scientist Inst. Gerontology Sch. Medicine, U. Mich., Ann Arbor, 1986—, sr. rsch. scientist biophys. rsch. divsn., 1992—2007, area chair optical scis., dir. optical scis. lab., 1989—2007, chair biophysics, 2007—, Robert J. Hiller prof., 2005—, Peter S. Fuss prof., 2001—05. Topical editor Jour. Optical Soc., Washington, 1986—92. Contbr. articles to profl. jours. Guggenheim fellow, 1999. Fellow IEEE, Optical Soc. Am., Am. Phys. Soc. Achievements include development of first phase conjugate laser; first high resolution nonlinear laser spectroscopy of semiconductor heterostructures; research in of collision induced resonances in atoms; low noise (below the standard quantum limit) room temperature semiconductor lasers; of first demonstration of coherence optical control and wave function engineering in quantum dots; of first demonstration of wave function engineering; first deimonstration quantum entanglement in a single quantum dot; demonstration of in vitro tryptophan phosphorescence for studies of protein structure in solution; discovery of of structural annealing in proteins during protein folding. Office: U Mich Physics Dept 500 E University Ave Ann Arbor MI 48109-1120 Home: 11516 Waters Rd Chelsea MI 48118-9615 Home Phone: 734-433-9034. Business E-Mail: dst@umich.edu.

STEELE, BRENT E., state legislator; m. Sally Steele. BS, JD, Ind. U. Atty. Steele, Steele, McSoley & McSoley; mem. Ind. State Ho. of Reps. Dist. 65, mem. agr. and rural devel. com., mem. cts. and criminal code com., mem. judiciary com., vice-chmn. fin. inst. com. Vice precinct committeeman, Ind.; former pres. Bedford City Planning Bd.; mem. Rep. Ctr. Fin. Com. Mem. Lions Club. Office: Ind Ho of Reps State Capitol Indianapolis IN 46204

STEELE, JAMES L., researcher; Rschr. USDA-ARS, Manhattan, Kans. Fellow Am. Soc. Agrl. Engrs. Office: US Grain Mktg Rsch Lab USDA-ARS CMPRC 1515 College Ave Manhattan KS 66502-2736

STEELE, WILLIAM M., career military officer; b. July 24, 1945; Commd. 2d lt. U.S. Army, advanced through grades to lt. gen., 1996—, comdg. gen. Office: Combined Arms Center 415 Sherman Ave Fort Leavenworth KS 66027-2300

STEELMAN, SARAH, state official; m. David Steelman; children: Sam, Joe, Michael; 1 stepchild, Amanda. Economist Mo. Dept. Revenue; dep. dir. Mo. Dept. Natural Resources-Divsn. Geology and Land Survey, 1988—93; mem. Mo. State Senate, 1998—2004, mem. civil and criminal jurisprudence com., chair commerce and environment com., mem. edn. com., vice chair judiciary com., vice chair pub. health and welfare com.; state treas. State of Mo., 2005—. Chair Mo. Higher Edn. Savings Bd., Mo. Housing Develop. Commn.; mem. governing bd. Mo. State Employee Retirement Sys.; mem. Bd. Fund Commr.; bd. trustee Mo. Consolidated Health Plan; served on Joint Task Force on Terrorism, Bio-Terrorism and Homeland Security; adj. prof. economics Lincoln U. Investment broker, exec. dir. Big Brothers and Big Sisters Program, Rolla. Recipient Mo. Watch-Defender of Patient Safety award, James Kirkpatrick award, Associated Industries Voice of Mo. Bus. award, Pathway Partnership award, Sheriff's Assn. Senator of Yr. award, Mo. Osteopathic Disting. Health Legis. award, Outstanding Legislator award, Speech, Lang. Hearing Assn. Republican. Achievements include being the first Republican woman in Missouri history to be elected to the office of State Treasurer. Office: PO Box 210 Jefferson City MO 65102 Fax: 573-751-2745.

STEEN, LYNN ARTHUR, mathematician, educator; b. Chgo., Jan. 1, 1941; s. Sigvart J. and Margery (Mayer) S.; m. Mary Elizabeth Frost, July 7, 1940; children: Margaret, Catherine. BA, Luther Coll., 1961; PhD, MIT, 1965; DSc (hon.), Luther Coll., 1986, Wittenberg U., 1991, Concordia Coll., Minn., 1996. Prof. math. St. Olaf Coll., Northfield, Minn., 1965—. Vis. scholar Inst. Mittag-Leffler, Djursholm, Sweden, 1970-71; writing fellow Conf. Bd. Math. Sci., Washington, 1974-75; exec. dir. Math. Sci. Edn. Bd., Washington, 1992-95; spl. asst. to provost St. Olaf Coll. Author: Counterexamples in Topology, 1970, Everybody Counts, 1989; editor: Mathematics Today, 1978, On the Shoulders of Giants, 1990, Math. Mag., 1976-80, Why Numbers Count, 1997, Mathematics and Democracy, 2001, Achieving Quantitative Literacy, 2004, Math and Biology 2010, 2005; contbg. editor: Sci. News, 1976-82. NSF Sci. faculty fellow, 1970-71, Danforth Found. grad. fellow, 1961-65. Fellow AAAS (sec. math. sect. 1982-88); mem. Am. Math. Soc., Math. Assn. Am. (pres. 1985-86, Disting. Svc. award 1992), Coun. Sci. Soc. Pres. (chmn. 1989), Sigma Xi (Bd. Dirs. Spl. award 1989). Home: 716 Saint Olaf Ave Northfield MN 55057-1523 Office: St Olaf Coll Dept of Math Northfield MN 55057 E-mail: steen@stolaf.edu.

STEENLAND, DOUGLAS M., air transportation executive; married; 2 children. BA in History, Calvin Coll.; JD, George Washington U., 1976. Sr. ptnr. Verner, Liipfert, Bernhard, McPherson and Hand, Washington; v.p., dep. gen. counsel Northwest Airlines Corp., Eagan, Minn., 1991—94, sr. v.p., gen. counsel Minn., 1994—98, exec. v.p., gen. counsel and alliances Minn., 1998—99, exec. v.p., chief corp. officer Minn., 1999—2001, pres. Minn., 2001—, CEO, 2004—, also bd. dirs. Minn., 2001—. Mem. bd. dirs. MAIR Holdings, Inc., The Guthrie Theater, The Minn. Symphony Orch.; mem. Super Bowl XL-Detroit 2006 Host Com. Office: orthwest Airlines Corp 2700 Lone Oak Pkwy Eagan MN 55121 Office Phone: 612-726-2111.

STEER, ROBERT L., food products executive; V.p., CFO Seaboard Corp., Shawnee Mission, Kans. Office: Seaboard Corp 9000 W 67th St Shawnee Mission KS 66202

STEFFAN, MARK THIEL, lawyer; b. Algona, Iowa, Nov. 27, 1956; s. Willard Henry and Dorothy (Thiel) S.; m. Becky Sue Veld, Feb. 14, 1984; children: Camorah, John, Michael. BA, Mankato State U., 1979; JD, U. Minn., 1987. Bar: Minn. 1988, U.S. Dist. Ct. Minn. 1989. Pvt. practice, Windom, Minn., 1989-90; atty. County of Jackson, Minn., 1990—. Instr. Southwestern Tech. Coll., Jackson, 1990-94, mem. adv. bd., 1990-94; instr. Jackson County Law Enforcement, 1990-94. Graduation speaker DARE Program, Jackson, 1991-94; advisor Mock Trial Program, Jackson, 1991-94; presenter Wellness Day, Jackson, 1994. Mem. ABA, Nat. Dist. Attys. Assn., Minn. State Bar Assn., Ptnrs. in Prevention. Office: Jackson County Atty PO Box 374 Jackson MN 56143-0374

STEFFEN, ALAN LESLIE, entomologist; b. Ansonia, Ohio, Feb. 27, 1927; s. Henry William and Maude Moiselle (DuBois) S.; m. Genevieve Carlyle, Dec. 27, 1950 (dec. Jan. 6, 1989); m. Doris Mae Rable, Jan. 20, 1990. AB, Miami U., 1948; MSc in Entomology, Ohio State U., 1949; diploma, Malaria Tng. Ctr., 1959; postgrad., WHO, Sri Lanka and The Philippines, 1967-68. Registered profl. entomologist. Malaria specialist Agy. for Internat. Devel., Jakarta, Indonesia, 1959-65, chief malaria advisor Kathmandu, Nepal, 1966-72, Addis Ababa, Ethiopia, 1972-76, Kathmandu, 1976-78, Islamabad, Pakistan, 1978-80; malaria specialist Ctr. Disease Control, Songkhla, Thailand, 1965-66; tropical disease cons. Ill., 1981—. Cons. U.S. AID, Port Au Prince, Haiti, 1981, WHO, Geneva, 1981—, Tifa, Ltd., Millington, N.J., 1982, John Snow, Inc., Boston, 1984, Vector Biology and Control Project, Arlington, Va., 1986. Mem. Nature Conservancy, Washington, 1986-88. With U.S. Army, 1945-46, ETO. Recipient Meritorious Honor award U.S. Dept. State, 1972. Fellow Royal Soc. Tropical Medicine; mem. Entomol. Soc. Am., Am. Registry Profl. Entomologists, Nat. Assn. Ret. Fed. Employees (life), Am. Fgn. Svc. Assn., Ohio State Alumni Assn. (life), VFW. Avocations: stamp collecting/philately, study of asian art. Home and Office: 3666 E Cromwell Ln Springfield MO 65802-2487

STEFFY, MARION NANCY, state agency administrator; b. Fairport Harbor, Ohio, Sept. 23, 1937; d. Felix and Anna (Kosaber) Jackopin; 1 child, Christopher C. BA, Ohio State U., 1959; postgrad., Butler U., 1962-65, Ind. U., 1983. Exec. sec. Franklin County Mental Health Assn., Columbus, Ohio, 1959-61; caseworker Marion County Dept. Pub. Welfare, Indpls., 1961-63, supr., 1963-66, asst. chief supr., 1966-73; dir. divsn. pub. assistance Ind. Dept. Pub. Welfare, Indpls., 1973-77, asst. adminstr., 1977-85; regional adminstr. Adminstrn. Children and Families Ill. Dept. Health and Human Svcs., Chgo., 1985-98; nat. dir. Performance Initiative, 1998—. Lectr. Ball State U., Lockyear Coll., Ind. U. Grad. Sch. Social Work; mem. Ind. Devel. Disabilities Coun., 1979-81, Ind. Cmty. Svcs. Adv. Coun., 1978-81; Ind. Child Support Adv. Coun., 1976-82, Welfare Svc. League, 1968—; chmn. rules com. Ind. Health Facilities Coun., 1974-81; chmn. Lawrence Twp. Roundtable, 1983—; dir. Palette and Chisel Acad. Fine Arts, 2003. Mem. Nat. Assn. State Pub. Welfare Adminstrs., Am. Pub. Welfare Assn., Network of Women in Bus. Roman Catholic.

STEGALL, MARK D., surgeon, medical educator; b. Lubbock, Tex., June 24, 1957; BA, Harvard Coll., 1979; postgrad., Trinity Coll., Oxford (Eng.), 1979; MD, Columbia U., 1984. Diplomate Am. Bd. Surgery. Resident in surgery Presbyn. Hosp., NYC, 1984-91; post-doctoral rsch. scientist Columbia U., NYC, 1987-89; fellow in transplantation U. Wis., Madison, 1991-93; asst. prof. surgery, dir. pancreas and islet transplantation U. Colo., Denver, 1993-98; dir. kidney and pancreas transplantation surgery Mayo Clinic, Rochester, Minn., 1998—, chmn. divsn. transplantation surgery, 2002—; assoc. prof. surgery Mayo Med. Sch., Rochester, 1998—. Post-Doctoral Rsch. fellow N.Y. State Diabetes Fund, 1987-88; recipient NIH-NIAID Individual Nat. Rsch. Svc. award, 1988-89, Upjohn prize N.Y. State Transplantation Soc., 1988. Mem. Am. Soc.

Transplant Surgeons (Upjohn award 1989, Ortho Faculty Devel. award 1995), Soc. Univ. Surgeons, Assn. Acad. Surgery. Office: Mayo Clinic Campus Box C-318 200 1st St SW Rochester MN 55905-0002

STEGER, EVAN EVANS, III, retired lawyer; b. Indpls., Oct. 24, 1937; s. Charles Franklin and Alice (Hill) S.; m. Suzy Gillespie, July 18, 1964; children: Cynthia Anne, Emily McKee. AB, Wabash Coll., 1959; JD, Ind. U., 1962. Bar: Ind. 1962, U.S. Dist. Ct. (so. dist.) Ind. 1962, U.S. Ct. Appeals (7th cir.) 1972, U.S. Tax Ct. 1982, U.S. Supreme Ct. 1982. Assoc. Ice, Miller, Donadio and Ryan and predecessor firm Ross, McCord, Ice and Miller, Indpls., 1962-69, ptnr., 1970-96, mng. ptnr., 1996-99, ret., 2000. Fellow Am. Coll. Trial Lawyers. Democrat. Presbyterian. Office: Ice Miller Box 82001 1 American Sq Indianapolis IN 46282-0020 E-mail: essteger@comcast.net.

STEGLICH, DAVID M., museum administrator, lawyer; b. Wis. BA in Math. and Philosophy, St. Olaf Coll., Minn., 1989; studied econs. and polit. theory, Trinity Coll., Dublin, Ireland, 1990; JD, Yale U., 1995. Law clk. for Chief Judge Paul A. Magnuson US Dist. Ct., St. Paul, 1995—97; atty. Corp. Law Dept. Dorsey & Whitney, Minn., 1997—2000; with McKinsey & Co., Mpls., 2000, assoc. prin.; COO Walker Art Ctr., Mpls., 2006—. Office: Walker Art Ctr 1750 Hennepin Minneapolis MN 55403

STEHMAN, FREDERICK BATES, gynecologic oncologist, educator; b. Washington, July 20, 1946; s. Vernon Andrew and Elizabeth Coats (Bates) S.; m. Helen Sellinger, July 17, 1971; children: Christine Renee, Eileen Patricia, Andrea Kathleen, Lara Michelle. AB, U. Mich., 1968, MD, 1972. Diplomate Am. Bd. Ob-gyn. Resident in ob-gyn. U. Kans. Med. Ctr., Kansas City, 1972-75, resident in surgery, 1975-77; fellow in gynecol. oncology UCLA, 1977-79; asst. prof., attending staff Ind. U. Med. Ctr., Indpls., 1979-83, assoc. prof., 1983-87, prof., 1987—, chief gynecol. oncology, 1984-88, interim chmn., 1992-94, chair 1994—; chief ob-gyn service Wishard Meml. Hosp., Indpls., 1987-95. Author: (with B.J. Masterson and R.P. Carter) Gynecologic Oncology for Medical Students, 1975; also articles. Nat. Cancer Inst. grantee, 1981-89. Fellow Am. Coll. Obstetricians and Gynecologists, ACS (chpt. dir. 1984-92); mem. AMA, Am. Soc. Clin. Oncology, Am. Cancer Soc., Am. Gynecology and Obstetrics Soc., Ind. Med. Assn., Assn. Profs. Gynecology and Obstetrics, Central Assn. Obstetricians and Gynecologists, Gynecol. Oncology Group, K.E. Krantz Soc., Marion County Med. Soc., Soc. Gynecol. Oncologists, Western Assn. Gynecol. Oncologists, Phi Chi. Office: Ind U Med Ctr 550 University Blvd # 2440 Indianapolis IN 46202-5149

STEHR, JOHN, newscaster; b. Pitts. m. Amy Stehr; children: Jared, Morgan, Connor, Riley, Jeanie. Grad., Gannon U. Anchor, reporter Sta. WOTV-TV, Grand Rapids, Mich., Sta. WSEE-TV, Erie, Pa.; anchor, prodr., chief reporter Nightbeat Sta. WISH-TV, Indpls.; anchor, reporter Sta. KUTV-TV, Salt Lake City; anchor CNBC, NYC; reporter, anchor Sta. WCBS-TV, 1991—95; anchor Sta. WTHR-TV, Indpls., 1995—. Office: WTHR-TV 1000 N Meridian St Indianapolis IN 46204

STEIL, GEORGE KENNETH, SR., lawyer; b. Darlington, Wis., Dec. 16, 1924; s. George John and Laura (Donahoe) S.; m. Mavis Elaine Andrews, May 24, 1947; children: George Kenneth, John R., MIchelle Steil Bryski, Marcelaine Steil-Zimmermann. Student, Platteville State Tchrs. Coll., 1942-43; JD, U. Wis., Madison, 1950. Bar: Wis. 1950, U.S. Tax Ct. 1971, U.S. Dist. Ct. (western dist.) Wis. 1950. Assoc. J. G. McWilliams, Janesville, 1950-53; ptnr. McWilliams and Steil, Janesville, 1954-60, Brennan, Steil, Basting & MacDougall, Janesville, 1960-72; pres. Brennan, Steil & Basting (S.C., and predecessor), Janesville, 1972—. Lectr. law U. Wis., 1974; bd. dirs. Acuity Ins. Co., Sheboygan, Wis.; mem. fin. coun. Roman Cath. Diocese of Madison; mem. Wis. Supreme Ct. Bd. Atty. Profl. Responsibility, 1982-87, chmn., 1984-87; chmn. gov.'s adv. coun. jud. selection State of Wis., 1987-92; chmn. Wis. Lottery Bd., 1987-90. Bd. dirs. St. Coletta Sch. for Exceptional Children, Jefferson, Wis., 1972-76, 78-84, 86-89, chmn., 1982-83; bd. regents U. Wis., 1990-97, pres., 1992-94; bd. dirs. U. Wis. Hosp. Authority, 1996—2004, chmn., 2002-04; bd. dirs., chair U. Wis. Med. Found., 1996-99. Recipient Disting. Svc. award U. Wis. Law Alumni, 1991, Cath. Leadership awrd Diocese of Madison, 1998; named Knight of St. Gregory, Pope John Paul II, 1997. Fellow Am. Bar Found. (life), Am. Coll. Trust and Estate Counsel; mem. ABA, Jamesville Area C. of C. (pres. 1970-71), State Bar Wis. (pres. 1977-78), Wis. Bar Found. (bd. dirs. 1976-2003, Charles L. Goldberg Disting. Svc. award 1990). Roman Catholic. Home: 2818 Cambridge Ct Janesville WI 53548-2797 Office: PO Box 1148 1 E Milwaukee St Janesville WI 53545 Home Phone: 608-754-7119; Office Phone: 608-756-4141. Business E-Mail: gsteilsr@brennansteil.com.

STEIL, GLENN, state legislator; b. Aug. 29, 1940; AAS, Davenport Coll.; BSBA, Aquinas Coll. Bus. owner; mem. Mich. Senate from 30th dist., Lansing, 1995—; mem. appropriations and legis. coun. coms.; vice chmn. govt. ops. com. Office: Mich State Senate State Capitol PO Box 30036 Lansing MI 48909-7536

STEIMAN, H. ROBERT, dean, dental educator; BS, ND State U., 1964; MS, Wayne State U., 1967, PhD in physiology, 1969; DDS, U. Detroit, 1973; MS in endodontics, Ind. U., 1979. Diplomate Am. Bd. Endodontics. Chmn. dept. physiology, dept. basic scis. U. Detroit-Mercy Sch. Dentistry, named chmn. dept. endodontics, 1980, interim dean, 2000—01, dean, 2001—. Office: 8200 W Outer Dr Box 98 Detroit MI 48219 Office Phone: 313-494-6621. Office Fax: 313-484-6627. Business E-Mail: steimanr@udmercy.edu.

STEIN, ERIC, retired law educator; b. Holice, Czechoslovakia, July 8, 1913; arrived in US, 1940, naturalized, 1943; s. Zikmund and Hermina (Zalud) Stein; m. Virginia Elizabeth Rhine, July 30, 1955. JUD, Charles U., Prague, Czechoslovakia, 1937; JD, U. Mich., 1942; Dr. honoris causa, Vrije U., Brussels, 1978, U. Libre, 1979, West-Bohemian U., Pilsen, Czech Republic, 1997. Bar: Ill. 1946, DC 1953. Practiced law, Prague, 1937; with State Dept. Bureau United ations Justice Orgn., 1946-55; acting dep. dir. Office UN Polit. Affairs, 1955; mem. faculty U. Mich. Law Sch., Ann Arbor, 1956, prof. internat. law and orgn., 1958-76, Hessel E. Yntema prof. law, 1976-83, emeritus prof., 1983—; co-dir. internat. legal studies, 1958-76; dir., 1976-81. Vis. prof. Stanford Law Sch., 1956, 77, Law Faculties, Stockholm, Uppsala, Lund, Sweden, 1969, Inst. Advanced Legal Studies U. London, London, 1975, U. Ariz., 1991, 92; lectr. Hague Acad. Internat. Law, 1971; vis. lectr. European U. Inst., Florence, Italy, 1983, Jean Monnet prof., 91; vis. lectr. Acad. European Law, Beijing, 1986, Wahen, Shanghai, 90, U. Tokyo, Kyoto, 1986, Coll. Europe, Madrid, 1988, Bruges, Paris, Heidelberg, Germany, Hamburg, Germany, 82; Henry Morris lectr. Kent Coll. Law, Chgo., 1992; Jeanne Kiewit Taylor disting. vis. lectr. U. Ariz., 1993; adviser US del. UN Gen. Assembly, 1947—55; mem. adv. panel, cons. Bur. European Affairs, State Dept., 1966—73; cons. US rep. for trade negotiations, 1979; vice chmn. com. Atlantic studies Atlantic Inst., 1966—68; mem. adv. coun. Inst. European Studies Free U., Brussels, 1965—70; mem. US Com. Legal Edn. Exch. with China, 1983—91; lectr. Acad. European Law, Florence, 1990. Author (with others): American Enterprise in the European Common Market-A Legal Profile, vols I, II, 1960; author: (with H. K. Jacobson) Diplomats, Scientists and Politicians: The United States and the Nuclear Test Ban Negotiations, 1966 (U. Mich. Press Best Book of Yr. award); author: Harmonization of European Company Law: National Reform and Transnational Coordination, 1971, Impact of New Weapons Technology on International Law-Selected Aspects, 1971, Un Nuovo Diritto per l'Europa, 1991, Czecho/Slovakia: Ethnic Conflict, Constitutional Fissure, Negotiated Breakup, 1997, Czech translation, 2000, Thoughts from a Bridge: A Retrospective of Writings on New Europe and American Federalism, 2000 (U. Mich. Press Best Book of Yr. award); editor (with Peter Hay): Law and Institutions in the Atlantic Area, Readings, Cases and Problems, 1987; editor: (with Peter Hay and Michel Waelbrock) European Community Law and Institutions in Perspective, 1976; co-author, co-editor: Courts and Free Markets-Perspectives from the United States and Europe, 1982; bd. editors Am. Jour. Internat. Law, 1965—, mem. adv. bd. Common Market Law Rev., 1964—, Legal Issues of European Integration, 1974—, Rivista di Diritto Europeo, 1978—, Columbia Jour. E. European Law, 1994—, Columbia Jour. European Law, 1994—; contbr. articles to profl. jours. Mem. Internat. Com. Revision Czechoslovak Constn., 1990—92. With US Army, 1943—46. Decorated Bronze Star, Order Italian Crown, Italian Mil. Cross; named Hon. Citizen of Hometown Holice, Czech. Republic, 2001, Establised Collegiate Chair, U. Mich. Law Sch., 2007; recipient Lifetime Achievement medal, Am. Soc. Comparative Law, 2004, Lifetime Contbn. prize, European Union Studies Assn., 2005, First Degree Outstanding Scholarly Achievement medal, Pres. Czech. Republic, 2001, Gold medal, Charles U., Prague, 2005; fellow, Inst. Advanced Study, Berlin, 1984—85; Gugenheim fellow, 1962—63, Social Sci. Rsch. Coun. grantee, Rockefeller Found. scholar-in-residence, Bellagio, Italy, 1965, 1973, Alexander von Humboldt Stiftung grantee, 1982, Rsch. grantee, IREX, 1995. Mem.: ABA (co-chmn. European law com. 1982, mem. coun. sect. internat. law and practice 1983—84), Internat. Acad. Comparative Law, Brit. Inst. Internat. and Comparative Law, Am. Soc. Internat. Law (exec. coun. 1954—57, bd. rev. and devel. 1965—67, 1970—75, hon. v.p. 1982—2000), European Studies Assn., Coun. Fgn. Rels., Internat. Law Assn. Home: 2649 Heather Way Ann Arbor MI 48104-2850 Office Phone: 734-764-0541. E-mail: steine@umich.edu.

STEIN, GERALD, real estate and diversified holding company executive; b. Milw., Dec. 4, 1937; s. Rudolph and Mary (Uberstine) S.; m. Louise Sharon Mendelson, Sept. 6, 1959; children— Debra, Leslie, Leigh. B.B.A., U. Wis.-Milw., 1959; J.D., Marquette U., Milw., 1962. Bar: Wis. 1962; C.P.A., Wis. Exec. v.p. Towne Realty Inc., Milw., 1957-80; vice chmn. Unicare Services Inc., Milw., 1968-83; pres. Zilber Ltd., Milw., 1980—; dir. Universal Mortgage, Milw. Pres. Jewish Vocat. Service, Milw., 1982; pres. Milw. Pub. Mus., 1984, v.p. Milw. Jewish Fedn., 1984. Served as 1st lt. U.S. Army, 1962-64. Mem. Wis. Bar Assn. Club: Milw. Athletic. Office: Zilber Ltd 710 N Plankinton Ave Fl 11 Milwaukee WI 53203-2411

STEIN, RICHARD PAUL, lawyer; b. New Albany, Ind., Sept. 2, 1925; s. William P. and Lillian M. (Russell) S.; m. Mary Charlotte Key, June 22, 1959; children: Richard Paul, William, Patricia. Student, Milligan Coll., Tenn., 1943-44, Duke, 1944-45; JD, U. Louisville, 1950. Bar: Ind., 1950. With labor relations Goodyear Engring. Co., Charlestown, Ind., 1952-54; ptnr. Naville & Stein, New Albany, 1954-61; pros. atty. 52d Jud. Circuit Ind., 1956-61; U.S. atty. So. Dist. Ind., 1961-67; chmn. Pub. Service Commn. of Ind., 1967-70; legis. counsel Eli Lilly Co., Indpls., 1970-74; v.p. pub. affairs Pub. Service Co. Ind., 1974-90; atty., pub. affairs cons., 1990-98; of counsel Stewart, Irwin, 1999—. Dir. Indpls. Indians; Co-counsel New Albany-Floyd County Bldg. Authority, 1960-62; mem. State Bd. Tax Commrs. Adv. Bd., Jud. Study Commn. Sec. New Albany Dist. Dem. Com., 1956-61; chmn. New Albany United Way, 1957. Served to lt. USNR, 1943-46, 50-51; lt. Res. Named Floyd County Young Man of Yr. Floyd County Jr. C. of C., 1955, Outstanding Young Man of Yr. New ALbany Jaycees, 1958. Mem. Ind. Bar Assn., Marion County Bar Assn., Ind. Prosecutors Assn. (pres. 1960-61), Ind. Electric Assn. (dir.), Am. Legion, Plum Creek Country Club, K.C. Roman Catholic. Avocations: tennis, golf, reading. Home: 12414 Medalist Pkwy Carmel IN 46033-8933 Home Phone: 317-844-5816; Office Phone: 317-846-4799.

STEIN, ROBERT ALLEN, lawyer, educator, former legal association administrator; b. Mpls., Sept. 16, 1938; s. Lawrence E. and Agnes T. (Brynildson) S.; m. Sandra H. Stein; children: Linda Stein Routh, Laura Stein Conrad, Karin Stein O'Boyle. BS in Law, U. Minn., 1960, JD summa cum laude, 1961; LLD (hon.), Uppsala U., Sweden, 1993. Bar: Wis. 1961, Minn. 1967. Assoc. Foley, Sammond & Lardner, Milw., 1961-64; prof. U. Minn. Law Sch., Mpls., 1964-77, dean, 1979-94, Everett Fraser prof. law, 2006—; assoc. dean U. Minn., 1976-77, v.p. adminstrn. and planning, 1978-80, faculty rep. men's intercollegiate athletics, 1981-94; of counsel Mullin, Weinberg & Daly, PA, Mpls., 1970-80, Gray, Plant, Mooty, Mooty & Bennett, Mpls., 1980-94, 2006—. Vis. prof. UCLA, 1969-70, U. Chgo., 1975-76; commr. Uniform State Laws Commn. Minn., 1973—; v.p. Nat. Uniform Laws Com., 1991-93, exec. comm., 1991—, sec., 1997—; acad. fellow Am. Coll. Trusts and Estates Counsel, 1975—; vis. scholar Am. Bar Found., Chgo., 1975-76; trustee Gt. No. Iron Ore Properties, 1982—, Uniform Laws Found., 1992—; advisor Restatement of Law Second, Property, 1977—, Restatement of Law Trusts (Prudent Investor Rule), 1989-90, Restatement of Law Third, Trusts, 1993—; chmn. bd. dirs. Ednl. Credit Mgmt. Corp., 1993—; bd. dirs. Fiduciary Counselling Inc. Author: Stein on Probate, 1976, 3d edit., 1995, How to Study Law and Take Law Exams, 1996, Estate Planning Under the Tax Reform Act of 1976, 2d edit, 1978, In Pursuit of Excellence: A History of the University of Minnesota Law School, 1980, contbr. articles to profl. jours. Founding bd. dirs. Park Ridge Ctr., 1985-95; co-chair Gov.'s Task Force on Ctr. for Treatment of Torture Victims, 1985, bd. dirs., 1985-87. Fellow Am. Bar Found (bd. dirs. 1987-94), Am. Coll. Tax Counsel; mem. ABA (coun. sect. of legal edn. and admission to bar 1986-91, vice chairperson 1991-92, chair-elect 1992-93, chair 1993-94, exec. dir. 1994-2006), Internat. Acad. Estate and Trust Law (academician), Internat. Bar Assn. (profl. and pub. interest divsn. sec. 2004-06, vice chair 2006—), Am. Judicature Soc. (bd. dirs. 1984-88), Am. Law Inst. (coun. mem. 1987—, exec. com. 1993—), Minn. Bar Assn. (bd. govs. 1979-94, exec. coun., probate and trust law sect. 1973-77), Hennepin County Bar Assn., U. Minn. Alumni Assn. (nat. pres. 2005-06). Office: U Minn Law Sch 229 19th Ave S Minneapolis MN 55455 Home Phone: 763-545-1701; Office Phone: 612-625-3047. Business E-Mail: stein@umn.edu.

STEIN, TRISHA, advocate; b. 1971; Commn. analyst Mich. House, House of Commons, London; dir., millage campaign Suburban Mobility Authority for Regional Transp., 1996; exec. asst. Wayne County executive's office, 1998; campaign mgr. Mike Duggan, Wayne County prosecutor, 2000; exec. dir. One United Mich., 2004—. Named one of 40 Under 40, Crain's Detroit Bus., 2006. Office: One United Michigan PO Box 81156 Lansing MI 48908 Office Phone: 877-482-1438.

STEINBERG, GREGG MARTIN, financial and management consultant, investment banker; b. Columbus, Ind., Mar. 26, 1962; s. Jerry H. and Sharla C. (Waitzman) S.; m. Stacy A. Schneider, Nov. 6, 1988; 2 children. BSBA, U. Ariz., 1982; M in Mgmt., Am. Grad. Sch. Internat. Mgmt., Glendale, Ariz., 1984. V.p. fin. Bera Hotels Ltd., Phoenix, 1984-85; gen. mgr. Les Jardains Hotel, Phoenix, 1985-87; asst. dir., sr. negotiator GVA Mergers & Acquisitions, Phoenix, 1987-88; pres. Gregg M. Steinberg Ltd., Phoenix and Chgo., 1987—89; prin. Berger, Goldstein Capital Group, Inc., Chgo., 1989-91; joined Internat. Profit Assocs. and Integrated Bus. Analysis (IPA-IBA), Buffalo Grove, Ill., 1992, CFO, 1995—97, pres., 1997—. Chmn., Midwestern region Am. Com. for Weizmann Inst. Sci., 2005—. Bd. dirs., chmn. N.W. com. Jewish Coun. for Youth Svcs., Chgo., 1989-92; bd. dirs. J.C.C., 1997—. Avocations: golf, squash.

STEINBERG, MORTON M., lawyer; b. Chgo., Feb. 13, 1945; m. Miriam C. Bernstein, Aug. 25, 1974; children: Adam Michael, Shira Judith. AB with honors, U. Ill., 1967; JD, orthwestern U., 1971. Bar: Ill. 1971, DC 1994, Colo. 1995, NY, 2003, US Dist. Ct. (no. dist.) Ill. 1971, US Dist. Ct. Colo. 1998, US Ct. Appeals (7th cir.) 1971, US Supreme Ct. 1974. Assoc. Caffarelli & Wiczer, Chgo., 1971-73, Arnstein, Gluck, Lehr, Barron & Milligan, Chgo., 1974-76, ptnr., 1977-86, DLA Piper US LLP (and predecessor firms), 1986—. Spkr. in field. Sr. editor Jour. Criminal Law and Criminology, Northwestern U., 1969-71. Chmn. Chgo. region Leaders Tng. Fellowship, 1962-63; bd. dirs. Camp Ramah Wis., Inc., Chgo., 1974—, sr. v.p., 1992-94, pres. 1994-2003, chmn. bd. trustees, 2003-; bd. dirs., pres. Ramah Day Camp, Inc., Chgo., 2001-03; bd. dirs., v.p. Camp Ramah Wis. Endowment Corp., 1993-2003, pres. 2003-; bd. dirs. North Suburban Synagogue Beth-El, Highland Park, Ill., 1978—, corp. sec., 1983-87, pres., 1989-91, chmn. bd. trustees, 1991-93, trustee, 1991—; mem. Nat. Ramah Commn., Jewish Theol. Sem., 1987—, v.p., 1994-2003, pres., 2003-2007, chariman bd. trustees, 2007-; mem. bd. overseers Albert A. List Coll., 2004—; mem. leadership coun. Conservative Judaism, 2004-2007; bd. dirs. MERCAZ USA 2006-, Found. Conservative Judaism in Israel, 1985-90; Midwest region bd. dirs. United Synagogue of Conservative Judaism, 1989-91, 94-2003; mem. editor's cir. Jewish Forward Newspaper, 1997-2000; trustee Am. Jewish Hist. Soc., 1998—; charter mem. US Holocaust Meml. Mus., 1992; pro bono counsel Frank Lloyd Wright Preservation Trust, Oak Park, Ill., 1996—; elected del. from US to 35th World Zionist Congress, Jerusalem, 2006; bd. govs. State Israel Bonds, 2007-. With 801st Gen. Hosp. USAR, 1969—75. Recipient Youth Leadership award Nat. Fedn. Jewish Men's Clubs, NYC, 1963; Merit cert. US Dist. Ct. Fed. Defender Program, Chgo., 1969, Pras Ramah, The Ramah award Nat. Ramah Commn., 2007; named Ill. Super Lawyer, Chgo. Mag., 2005-08. Mem. ABA, DC Bar, NY State Bar Assn., Ill. State Bar Assn., Chgo. Bar Assn., Profl. Assn. Diving Instrs. (cert. scuba open water diver 2005), Standard Club. Jewish. Home: 1320 Lincoln Ave S Highland Park IL 60035-3459 Office: DLA Piper US LLP Ste 1900 203 N La Salle St Chicago IL 60601-1225

STEINBERG, SALME ELIZABETH HARJU, academic administrator, historian; b. NYC; d. Johan Edward and Jenny Lydia (Peltonen) Harju; m. Michael Stephen Steinberg, Sept. 15, 1963; children: William, Katharine Lovisa. BA, Hunter Coll., 1960; MA, CCNY, 1962; PhD, Johns Hopkins U., 1971. Lectr. history Goucher Coll., Towson, Md., 1971—72; asst. prof. history Northwestern U., Evanston, Ill., 1972—75; prof. Northeastern Ill. U., Chgo., 1975—83, chmn. dept., 1983—87, assoc. provost then acting provost, 1987—92, provost, v.p. for acad. affairs, 1992—95, pres., 1995—. Author: Reformer in the Marketplace: Edward W. Bok and The Ladies' Home Journal, 1979; contbr. articles to profl. jours. Named to, Hunter Coll. Hall of Fame, 1997; recipient 14th Ann. award Appreciation, Asian Am. Coalition Chgo., 1997; grantee, Danforth Found., 1967—68. Episcopalian. Avocations: opera, theater. Office: Northeastern Ill U Office of President 5500 N Saint Louis Ave Chicago IL 60625-4679

STEINBRINK, JOHN P., state official; b. Kenosha, Wis., Apr. 17, 1949; married; 3 children. Student, Carthage Coll., U. Wis. Grain farmer; town supr. Pleasant Prairie, 1985—89; village trustee, 1989—95; state assemblyman Wis., 1996—. Mem. agr. com.; mem. govt. ops. com.; mem. natural resources com.; mem. tourism and recreation com. Mem. Sr. Action Coun., Pleasant Prairie Police Aux., Pleasant Prairie Planning Commn.; treas. Conservative F.S.; mem. Wis. Electric Cmty. Round Table, Danish Brotherhood; former pres., v.p. Kenosha County Farm Bur.; mem. Wis. League Municipalities. Mem.: Wis. Towns Assn. Democrat. Office: State Capitol Rm 307 W PO Box 8952 Madison WI 53708-8952

STEINDLER, HOWARD ALLEN, lawyer; b. Cleve., June 12, 1942; s. Sidney and Lois Jean (Rosenberg) S.; m. Terri Cowan Steindler; c. Rebecca, Allison, Daniel. BS, Miami U., Oxford, Ohio, 1964; JD, Ohio State U., 1967. Bar: Ohio 1967. Mem. firm Benesch, Friedlander, Coplan & Aronoff, Cleve., 1967—. Pres. bd. trustees Cleve. Scholarship Program, 1987-97, trustee, 1997—; trustee Downtown Cleve. Partnership, Inc., The Ratner Sch. Office: Benesch Friedlander Coplan & Aronoff 2300 BP Tower 200 Public Sq Cleveland OH 44114-2378 E-mail: hsteindler@bfca.com.

STEINDLER, MARTIN JOSEPH, chemist; b. Vienna, Jan. 3, 1928; came to U.S., 1938; s. J.P. and M.G. S.; m. Joan Long, Aug. 16, 1952; children: M.H., T.P. PhB, U. Chgo., 1947, BS, 1948, MS, 1949, PhD, 1952. Chemist Argonne (Ill.) Nat. Lab., 1953-74, sr. chemist, 1974—, assoc. dir. div. chem. engring., 1978-84, dir. chem. tech. div., 1984-93, sr. tech. advisor, 1993—. Mem. adv. com. on nuclear waste NRC, Washington, 1988-96, chmn. 1995; adminstrv. judge ASLBP, 1973-90. Conibr. articles to profl. publs.; patentee in field. Pres. Matteson-Park Forest (Ill.) Sch. Bd., 1959-78. Recipient Disting. Performance medal U. Chgo., 1992, Meritorious Svc. award for Scientific Excellence, U.S. NRC, 1996, Lawroski award, ANL Chem. Tech. Divsn., 2002. Mem. AAAS, Am. Nuclear Soc., Am. Inst. Chem. Engrs. (Robert E. Wilson award 1990). Office: Argonne Nat Lab 9700 Cass Ave Argonne IL 60439-4803

STEINER, CHARLES K., museum director, painter; b. Champaign, Ill., Apr. 27, 1951; s. Gilbert Y. and Louise (King) S.; m. Mary B. Shepard; children: Frances Shepard, Hope Bradley. BFA, Cornell U., 1973; MFA, George Washington U., 1976. Aide, educator Perceva, St. Prex, Switzerland, 1973-74; Rockefeller Found. fellow Met. Mus. Art, NYC, 1976-77, asst. and assoc. mus. educator, 1977-86; asst. dir. The Art Mus., Princeton U., NJ, 1986—90, assoc. dir. NJ, 1990—2000; dir. Wichita Art Mus., Kans., 2000—. Bd. dirs. Save Outdoor Sculpture, N.J., 1994-95, Arts Coun. Princeton, 1972-76; mem. art bd. Bellevue Hosp., N.Y.C., 1983-86; vis. painter Edward Albee Found., Montauk, N.Y., 1977-78. Exhibited in solo shows in N.Y.C. and Princeton; group shows at George Washington U., Washington, 1982, Delphine Gallery, Santa Barbara, Calif., 1987, Braithwaite Fine Arts Gallery/So. Utah U., Cedar City, 1993, Lexington Gallery, Lawrenceville, N.J., 1993, others; represented in collections at 3M, Mpls., N.Y. Health and Hosp. Corp., Montgomery County (Md.) Collection; author publs. in field. Spears travel grantee Princeton U., 1995; Met. Mus. Art travel grantee, Europe, 1981. Office: Wichita Art Mus 1400 West Museum Blvd Wichita KS 67203-3296

STEINGASS, SUSAN R., lawyer; b. Cambridge, Mass., Dec. 18, 1941; BA in English Lit., Denison U., 1963; MA in English Lit. with honors, Northwestern U., 1965; JD with honors, U. Wis., 1976. Bar: Wis. 1976, US Dist. Ct. Wis. 1976. Instr. dept. English La. State U., 1965—66, Calif. State Coll., LA, 1966—68, U. Wis., Stevens Point, 1968—72; law clk. Hon. Nathan S. Heffernan Wis. Supreme Ct., 1976—77; ptnr. Stafford, Rosenbaum, Reiser and Hansen, 1977—85; judge Dane County Cir. Ct., Wis., 1985—93; ptnr. Habush, Habush & Rottier, S.C., Madison, Wis., 1993—. Lectr. civil procedure, environ. law, evidence, trial advocacy Law Sch., U. Wis., 1981—, dir. comm. and advocacy programs, 2003—; instr. Nat. Inst. for Trial Advocacy, 1987—, trustee, 2002—; instr. Nat. Jud. Coll., 1993—. Note and comment editor Wis. Law Rev., 1974-76; co-editor: Wisconsin Civil Procedure Before Trial, 1994, The Wisconsin Rules of Evidence: A Courtroom Handbook, 1998—. Chair Wis. Equal Justice Task Force, 1989—91, Wis. Sentencing Commn., 2003—; mem., chair Wis. Jud. Selection Com., 2003—. Recipient Disting. Svc. award Am. Assn. Mediators, 1991, Presdl. award of excellence State Bar Wis., 2000; named Wis. Trial Judge of Yr. Am. Bd. Trial Advocates, 1992. Fellow Wis. Bar Found.; mem. ATLA, ABA (ho. dels. 2000—06), Am. Bar Found., Am. Law Inst., Wis. Bar Assn. (pres. 1998-99), Wis. Law Alumni Assn. (bd. dirs., pres. 2001-05), Wis. Acad. Trial Lawyers, Wis. Equal Justice Fund (pres. 2000-05), Wis. Trust Account Found. (bd. dirs. 1999), Order of the Coif (Marygold Melli Achievement award 2001). Office: Habush Habush Davis & Rottier SC 150 E Gilman St Ste 2000 Madison WI 53703-1481 also: Univ Wis Law School 975 Bascom Mall Madison WI 53706 Business E-Mail: ssteingass@habush.com.

STEINGER, CHRIS, state legislator; b. Kansas City, Jan. 8, 1962; m. Shari Steinger. BS, Kans. State U., 1986; MS, U. Kans., 1992. Stock broker, 1988-90; tax auditor Kans. Dept. Rev., 1993-95; devel. dir. Cross-Lines Coop. Coun., 1995—; mem. Kans. Senate, Topeka, 1996—, mem. assessment and tax, commerce com., mem. elections and local govt. com., mem. pub. health and welfare com., ranking minority mem., mem. joint com. on legis. post audit com., mem. joint com. on health care reform com. Staff asst. U.S. Rep. Jim Slattery, 1987-88; v.p. Mid-County Dem. Club; bd. pres. Grinter Pl. Friends; bd. dirs. Kaw Valleys Arts and Humanties, Wyandotte County Hist. Soc.; bd. sec. Kans. Dem. Leadership Coun.; treas. Southside Dem. Club. Office: 300 SW 10th Ave Topeka KS 66612-1504

STEINGRABER, FREDERICK GEORGE, management consultant; b. Mpls., July 7, 1938; s. Frederick F. and Evelyn (Luger) S.; m. Veronika Agnes Wagner, Aug. 9, 1974; children: Karla, Frederick. BS, Ind. U., 1960; MBA, U. Chgo., 1964. Cert. mgmt. cons. Internat. banker Harris Trust, Chgo., 1960-61; with comml. loan and credit No. Trust Co., Chgo., 1963—68; assoc. A.T. Kearney, Chgo., 1969—72, prin., 1972—, officer/ptnr., 1972—, pres., COO, 1981—82, CEO, chmn. bd., 1983—2000, chmn. emeritus, 2002, chmn., bd. advs., 2002, also bd. dirs.; mem. adv. bd. L.L.C., 1999—. Bd. dirs. Continental AG, 1989—, John Hancock Fin. Trend Funds3, PLC, 2001—, Maytag Corp., 2004—, Elkay Mfg., 2004—, Chgo. Stock Exch.; chmn. Talent Intelligence Adv. Bd., Global Bus. Coun. Adv. Bd. Chief crusader United Way Crusade of Mercy, Chgo., 1983—90; divsn.chmn., bd. dirs.l Ill. Coalition, 1989; fin. rsch. aand adv. com. City of Chgo., 1989—; mem., past chmn. dean's adv. coun. Ind. U. Bus. Sch., Bloomington, 1985—; bd. dirs. Ind. U. Found.; mem. bd. dirs. Grad. Sch. Bus. U. Chgo.; mem. Northwestern U. Assocs., Evanston, Ill.; exec. com. Mid. Am. Com., 1985—; mem. Chgo. Com., 1994—; bd. dirs. Northwestern Healtcare Network, 1989—96, Children's Meml. Hosp., Chgo., 1985—. Recipient Disting. Alumnus award U. Chgo., 1996, Disting. Corp. Exec. award U. Chgo., 1996, Disting. Corp. and Comm. Leadership award Am. Jewish Com., 1998, Disting. Alumnus award Ind. U., 2000. Mem. NAM (bd. dirs.), Chgo. Coun. Fgn. Rels. (bd. dirs., exec. com.), Ill. State C. of C. (bd. dirs. 1982-88, exec. com. 1984-88, chmn. Ill. Alliance for Econ. Initiatives), Coun. Grad. Sch. Bus. (life), Pres.'s Cir., Exec. Club Chgo., Acad. Alumni Fellows Ind. U. (award), Chgo. Club, Econ. Club (bd. dirs.), Comml. Club, Met. Club, Glenview Club, Beta Gamma Sigma, others. Office: Bd Advisors LLC 615 Warwick Rd Kenilworth IL 60043 Office Phone: 847-251-5386. Business E-Mail: fgs@bradadvisors.com.

STEINHAFEL, GREGG W., retail executive; b. Wis., 1955; m. Denise Steinhafel. BBA, Carroll Coll., 1977; MBA, Northwestern U., 1979. With Target Corp., Mpls., 1979—, sr. v.p., gen. mdse. mgr., 1987—94, exec. v.p. merchandising, 1994—99, pres. Target Stores, 1999—. Bd. dirs. The Toro Co., 1999—, Target Corp., 2007—. Dir. Walker Art Ctr. Mem.: Retail Industry Leaders Assn., Tree House. Office: Target Corp 1000 Nicollet Mall Minneapolis MN 55403-2467*

STEINHORN, ROBIN H., neonatologist, educator; b. Akron, Ohio, June 12, 1956; d. Paul Henry and Marion Robinson Heise; m. David Marc Steinhorn; children: Rachel, Benjamin. BS, U. Akron, 1976; MD, Washington U., 1980. Bd. cert. pediat. Am. Bd. Pediat., bd. cert. neonatal-perinatal medicine. Neonatologist Children's Hosp. Buffalo, 1991—99; chief neonatology Children's Meml. Hosp., Chgo., 1999—; intern Wash. U., St. Louis, 1980—81; resident, fellow U. Minn., 1982—88. Assoc. prof. pediat. SUNY, Buffalo, 1991—99; prof. pediat. Northwestern U., Chgo., 1999—2002, Raymond and Hazel Speck Berry chair neonatology, 2002—. Editor: (book) Extracorporeal Cardiopulmonary Support in Critical Care, 2000; contbr. articles to profl. jours. Grantee, NIH, 1995—. Fellow: Am. Heart Assn. (leadership coun. 2004—, Established Investigator award 1998); mem.: Am. Pediat. Sco., Soc. for Pediat. Rsch., Am. Thoracic Soc., Am. Acad. Pediat. Achievements include innovations in treatment of newborn pulmonary hypertension. Office: Childrens Meml Hosp Neonatology #45 2300 Childrens Plaza Chicago IL 60614 Office Phone: 773-880-4142. Business E-Mail: r-steinhorn@northwestern.edu.

STEINMETZ, JON DAVID, health facility administrator, psychologist; b. NYC, June 4, 1940; s. Lewis I. and Rose (Josefsberg) S.; m. Jane Audrey Hilton, Dec. 24, 1964; children: Jonna Lynn, Jay Daniel. BA, NYU, 1962; MA, Bradley U., 1963. Lic. psychologist, Ill. Intern in psychology Galesburg (Ill.) State Rsch. Hosp., 1963-64; staff psychologist Manteno (Ill.) State Hosp., 1964-68, program dir., 1968-70, asst. dir., 1970-72; dep. dir. Manteno Mental Health Ctr., 1972-80, Tinley Park (Ill.) Mental Health Ctr., 1980-88; dir. Chgo. Read Mental Health Ctr., 1988-91; ret., 1991. Clin. dir. Jane Addams Hull House Assn., 1992-98. Trustee Village of Park Forest, Cook, Will Counties, Ill.; officer, bd. dirs. various civic orgns., Park Forest; dir. SOS Children's Village Ill., Lockport, 2004—05. Home: 200 Hickory St Park Forest IL 60466-1016

STEINMETZ, JOSEPH EDWARD, neuroscience and psychology educator; b. Marine City, Mich., Jan. 6, 1955; s. James Robert and Catherine Elizabeth (Gould) S.; m. Sandra Sue Bieth, Aug. 8, 1975; children: Jacob Joseph, Adam Benjamin. BS, Cen. Mich. U., 1977, MA, 1979; PhD, Ohio U., 1983. NIMH postdoctoral fellow Stanford (Calif.) U., 1983-85, rsch. assoc., 1985-87; from asst. prof. to prof. neurosci. Ind. U., Bloomington, 1987-95, prof., chair psychology, 1995—. Cons. editor: Behavior Research Methods, Instruments and Computer Jour., 1989—, Behavior Neuroscience, 1993—; contbr. numerous articles to profl. jours. NIMH grantee, 1988; recipient Troland Rsch. award NAS, 1996. Fellow Am. Psychol. Soc. (charter, bd. dirs. 1997—); mem. Internat. Brain Rsch. Orgn., Soc. for eurosci., Sigma Xi. Democrat. Roman Catholic. Office: Program in Neural Sci Ind U Dept Psychology Bloomington IN 47405-6801 Home: 3606 Jordans Way Bloomington IN 47401-2410

STEINMILLER, JOHN F., professional sports team executive; b. Mt. Prospect, Ill. m. Corinne Steinmiller; children: John Henry, Mary Kate. V.p. bus. ops. Milw. Bucks, 1977—. Bd. dirs. Midwest Athletes Against Childhood Cancer Fund, Metro Milw. YMCA; chmn. Milw. Conv. and Visitors Bur. VISIT Milw.; mem. Greater Milw. Com. Recipient Contardi Commitment award Midwest Athletes Against Childhood Cancer Fund, 1991, Vol. of Yr. award YMCA, 1996. Office: Milw Bucks 1001 N Fourth St Milwaukee WI 53203-1314 Office Phone: 414-227-0500. E-mail: jsteinmiller@milwaukeebucks.com.

STELLA, VALENTINO JOHN, chemistry professor; b. Melbourne, Victoria, Australia, Oct. 27, 1946; came to U.S., 1968; s. Giobatta and Mary Katherine (Sartori) S.; m. Mary Elizabeth Roeder, Aug. 16, 1969; children: Catherine Marie, Anne Elizabeth, Elise Valentina. B of Pharmacy, Victorian Coll. Pharmacy, Melbourne, 1967; PhD, U. Kans., 1971. Lic. pharmacist, Victoria. Pharmacist Bendigo (Victoria) Base Hosp., 1967-68; asst. prof. Coll. Pharmacy U. Ill., Chgo., 1971-73; from asst. prof. to assoc. prof. to prof. Sch. Pharmacy U. Kans., Lawrence, 1973-90, Univ. disting. prof., 1990—. Dir. Ctr. for Drug Delivery Rsch.; cons. to 15 pharm. cos., U.S, Japan, Europe. Co-author: Chemical Stability of Pharmaceuticals, 2d edit., 1986; co-editor: Prodrugs as Novel Drug Delivery Systems, 1976, Directed Drug Delivery, 1985, Lymphatic Transport of Drugs, 1992; author numerous papers, revs., abstracts. Fellow AAAS, Am. Assn. Pharm. Scientists, Am. Acad. Pharm. Scientists. Roman Catholic. Achievements include 16 U.S. patents; rsch. in application of phys./organic chemistry to the solution of pharm. problems. Office: U Kans West Campus Dept Pharm Chemistry 2095 Constant Ave Lawrence KS 66047-3729 Home: 1135 W Campus Rd Lawrence KS 66044-3115

STELLAR, ARTHUR WAYNE, school system administrator; b. Columbus, Ohio, Apr. 12, 1947; s. Fredrick and Bonnie Jean (Clark) S. BS, Ohio U., 1969, MA, 1970, PhD, 1973. Tchr. Athens City Schs., Ohio, 1969-71; curriculum coord., tchr. Belpre City Schs., Ohio, 1971-72; prin. elem. schs., head tchr. learning disabilities South-Western City Schs., Grove City, Ohio, 1972-76; dir. elem. edn. Beverly Pub. Schs., Mass., 1976-78; coord. spl. projects and systemwide planning Montgomery County Pub. Schs., Rockville, Md., 1978-80; asst. supt. Shaker Heights, Ohio, 1980-83; supt. schs. Mercer County Pub. Schs., Princeton, W.Va., 1983-85, Oklahoma City Pub. Schs., 1985-92, Cobb County, Ga., 1992-93, Kingston Sch. Dist., NY, 1996—2001; dep. supt. Boston Pub. Schs., 1993-95, acting supt., 1995-96; pres., CEO High/Scope Ednl. Rsch. Found., Ypsilanti, Mich., 2001—03; v.p., chief edn. officer Renaissance Learning, Madison, Wis., 2003—04; sr. assoc. Proact Search, Inc., Milw., 2004—; rep. Docufide, Inc., LA, 2004—05, also adv. bd. dirs., 2004—05; supt. Taunton Pub. Schs., Mass., 2005—. Mem. ednl. adv. bd. Tchrs. Support Network, 2004—; adj. prof. Lesley Coll., Cambridge, Mass., 1976-78; adj. faculty Harvard U., 1992-93; assoc. Sch. Match, Ohio, 2004—. Author: Educational Planning for Educational Success, Effective Schools Research: Practice and Promise; editor: Effective Instructional Management; cons. editor, book rev. editor Jour. Ednl. Pub. Rels.; mem. editl. bd. Jour. Curriculum & Supervision, Reading Today's Youth; contbr. articles to profl. jours. Mem. Urban Ctr. Ednl. Adv. Bd., US Dept. Edn. Urban Supt. Network, Coun. Great City Schs. Bd., Urban Edn. Clearing House Adv. com., U. Okla. Adminstrn. cert. program com., Cmty. Literacy Coun. Bd.; chmn. bd. dirs. Langston U.; bd. dirs. Oklahoma County chpt. ARC, Jr. Achievement Greater Oklahoma City Bd., Okla. State Fair Bd., Horace Mann League, 1993—, v.p. 2000-01, pres.-elect, 2001-02, pres. 2002-03, past pres. 2003-04, mem. found. com., 2003-05; v.p. Last Frontier Coun. Bd., v.p. NY State PTA, 1996-2000, Kingston chpt. Rip Van Winkle Coun.; v.p. Boy Scouts Am., 1996-2001, membership chmn., 1996-97; exec. bd. Nat. Dropout Prevention Ctr. Network, 1998-2008, chmn., 2003-07; curriculum com. NY State Coun. Sch. Supts., 1996-2001; bd. dirs. Friends Historic Kingston, 1996-2001, Friends Senate House, Kingston, 1996-2001, Project Contemporary Competitiveness Inc., 2005—. Named a Friend, Horace Mann League, 2006; named to Linden McKinley H.S. Acad. Hall of Fame, 2003; recipient Silver Beaver award, Boy Scouts Am., 1990, Amb. award, Horace Mann League, 1995—2007, Crystal Star Leadership award, NDPC/N, 2007; fellow, Charles Kettering Found. IDEA, 1976, 1978, 1980, EH, Danforth Found., 1987—88. Mem. ASCD (life, exec. coun., pres. 1994-95, rev. coun. 1997-2002), Mich. ASCD, Mass. ASCD, Ohio ASCD, Okla. ASCD (Publ. award 1989), NY ASCD, Wis. ASCD, Internat. Soc. Ednl. Planning, Internat. Reading Assn. (govt. rels. com. 2003-04), Nat. Soc. Study Edn., Nat. Planning Assn., Nat. Assn. Gifted Children (life), Nat. Assn. Edn. Young Children (life), Nat. Coun. Tchrs. English (life), Music Educators Nat. Conf. (life), Nat. Orgn. Legal Problems Edn., Nat. Policy Bd. Ednl. Adminstrn., Am. Assn. Sch. Adminstrs. (life, Leadership for Learning award 1991, Dr. Effie Jones Humanitarian award 2007), Coll. Bd. Advanced Placement Spl. Recognition award 1991, Nat. Assn. Elem. Sch. Prins. (life), Am. Edn. Fin. Assn., Nat. Assn. Edn. Young Children (life), Nat. Sch. Pub. Rels. Assn. (Honor award 1991), Am. Mus. Natural Hist. (assoc.), Mass. Assn. for Sch. Supts., Mass. Assn. for Edn. of Young Children, Harvard U. Roundtable of Supts., Mass. Urban Supts., Nat. Sch. Pub. Rels. Assn., Taunton Area C. of C., World Coun. Curriculum and Instrn. (life, bd. dirs. N.Am. chpt. 1996-2000, pres. 2000-02), Coun. Basic Edn., Ohio Assn. Elem. Sch. Adminstrs., Buckeye Assn. Sch. Adminstrs., Ohio U. Coll. Edn. (disting. alumnus award 1991), Okla. Assn. Sch. Adminstrs., Mass. Assn. Sch. Adminstrs., Okla. Coalition Pub. Edn., Okla. Commn. Ednl. Leadership, Urban Area Supts. (Okla. br.), Ohio U. Alumni Assn. (nat. dir. 1975-78, pres. Ctrl. Ohio chpt. 1975-76, pres. Mass. chpt. 1976-78, life mem. trustees acad.), World Future Soc. (life) Greater Oklahoma City C. of C. (bd. dirs.), Okla. Heritage Assn., Heritage Hills Assn. (bd. dirs.), Victorian Soc. (New England chpt.), Nat. Eagle Scout Assn. (life), Aerospace Found. (hon. bd. dirs.), PLATO, Learning, Inc. (bd. dirs. 2000-03), Tchrs. Support etwork (adv. bd. dirs. 2004—), Am. Bus. Card Club, Coca Cola Collectors Club, Internat. Club, Mgmt. Consortium (bd. advisors),Fulbright Alumni Assn. (life), Tau Kappa Epsilon Alumni Assn. (regional officer Mass. 1976-78, named Alumni Nat. Hall of Fame 1986, Nat. Alumnus of Yr. 1993, Excellence in Edn. award 1993), Kappa Delta Pi (life; advisor Ctrl. Okla. chpt., nat. publs. com.), Phi Delta Kappa (life). Methodist. Office Phone: 508-821-1201. Business E-Mail: astellar@tauntonschools.org.

STELLATO, LOUIS EUGENE, lawyer; b. Bethlehem, Pa., 1950; BBA, U. Tex., 1972; JD, U. Pitts., 1977; LLM, Temple U., 1979. Bar: PA. 1977. With Touche Ross & Co., 1979-81; with tax dept. Sherwin-Williams Co., 1981-87, sr. corp. counsel, 1987-90, asst. secy., corp. dir. taxes, 1990-91, v.p., gen. counsel, sec., 1991—. Office: Sherwin Williams Co 101 Prospect Ave NW Cleveland OH 44115-1075 Office Phone: 216-566-2000.

STELLMACHER, JON MICHAEL, corporate financial executive; b. Green Bay, Wis., Feb. 25, 1956; s. Leroy Frederick and Helen Mae (Koss) S.; m. Rebecca Jean Hein, Aug. 20, 1976; children: James Michael, Paul Frederick, Abigail Joy. BBA with distinction, U. Wis., 1978. Underwriting clk. State Life Insur. Fund, Madison, Wis., 1977-78; actuarial student Aid Assn. for Luths., Appleton, Wis., 1978-79, actuarial asst., 1979-83, asst. actuary, 1983-85, assoc. actuary, 1985-87, 2nd v.p., actuary, 1987—97, v.p., 1997—99, sr. v.p., 1999—2002; exec. v.p. Thrivent Fin. for Luths., Appleton, 2002—05, exec. v.p., chief adminstrv. officer, 2005—. Chpt. reviewer Health Ins. Textbook, Soc. Actuaries, 1984-85; chmn. actuaries sect. Health Workshop Nat. Fraternal Congress Am., 1986, 88; mem. actuarial adv. com. Wis. Health Ins. Risk Sharing Pool, 1987—92; co-chmn. workshop, spring meeting Soc. Actuaries, 1989, 91, Loma Ins. Comm., 1999-2000. Acting pres., v.p. coun. 1st English Luth. Ch., Appleton, 1984; mission interpreter Am. Luth. Ch., Appleton area, 1985-87, Sunday Sch. tchr., 1984-2006, stewardship com., 1981-90, social concerns com. 1991-94, Elderly Housing Task Force, 1990-91, Benevolence Task Force, 1994; co-chair Capital Appeal, 2000; asst. den leader Cub Scouts, Boy Scouts Am., Appleton, 1989-91; asst. coach Appleton Soccer Club, 1990-93, Odyssey of the Mind, 1990-93; coach Appleton Park and Recreation Dept., 1990-98; vice chmn. Arthur Krempin Sch. Music and Art, 2003-04; bd. dirs. Appleton Boychoir, 1994—, pres., 1999—; bd. dirs. Appleton Med. Ctr. Found., 2000—, sec., 2001—; bd. dirs. United Way Fox Cities, 2001—, co-chmn. campaign com., 2002, vice-chair, 2006, chair, 2007; mem. sr. adv. bd. Jr. Achievement, 2001—; bd. dirs. YMCA of the Fox Cities, 2002—, vice-chair, 2006-07, co-chair capital campaign, 2006-07; bd. dirs. Fox Cities Performing Arts Ctr., 2003—, ThedaCare, 2006—, Wis. Mfrs. and Commerce, 2006—; mem. Theda Care Quality Coun., 2003—, Cmty. Health Action Team, 2005—; co-chair Emergency Shelter Endowment Campaign, 2005-06; bd. regents Luther Coll., 2007—, ptnr. Nisconsins Econ. Success, 2007-. Fellow Soc. Actuaries; mem. Am. Acad. Actuaries. Office: Thrivent Fin for Luths 4321 N Ballard Rd Appleton WI 54919 Home: 3124 E Sandpiper Ln Appleton WI 54913-7771 Office Phone: 920-628-2002. Business E-Mail: jon.stellmacher@thrivent.com.

STELZNER, PAUL BURKE, textile company executive; b. Iowa City, Iowa, Jan. 1, 1935; s. Glenn W. and Ruth (Schroder) S.; m. Martha Jane Schneeberger, Aug. 23, 1958; children: Martha Elizabeth Beuke and Barrie Jane Lubbering. BS, Muskingum Coll., 1960; postgrad., Akron U., 1961-65. Tech. dir. Buckeye Fabric Finishing Co., Coshocton, Ohio, 1963-74; sec., sales mgr. Excello Fabric Finishers Inc., Coshocton, 1966-74; gen. mgr. Mineral Fiber Mfg. Corp., Coshocton, 1974-76, dir., 1998—2007; v.p., gen. mgr. Kellwood Co. Recreation Group, 1976-85; v.p. Am. Recreation Products, Inc., New Haven, Mo., 1985-88; v.p., gen. mgr. John Boyle & Co., Statesville, NC, 1989-93, pres., CEO, 1993—2005, dir., 1999—2007. Bd. dirs. Indsl. Fabrics Found., 1998-2002. Served with USN, 1953-57. Mem. Indsl. Fabrics Assn. Internat. (dir. 1973-74, 82-88, 94-99). Presbyterian. Home: 843 Scenic Ridge Dr Washington MO 63090

STEM, CARL HERBERT, business educator; b. Eagleville, Tenn., Jan. 30, 1935; s. Marion Ogilvie and Sara Elizabeth (Jones) Stem; m. Linda Marlene Wheeler, Dec. 28, 1963; children: Anna Elizabeth, Susan Kathleen, John Carl, David Leslie. BA, Vanderbilt U., Nashville, 1957; AM (Woodrow Wilson fellow, Harvard scholar), Harvard U., Cambridge, Mass., 1960, PhD, 1969. Internat. fin. economist, bd. govs. Fed. Res. System, Washington, 1963—70; from assoc. prof. to prof. econs. Tex. Tech. U., Lubbock, 1970—75; from assoc. prof. to prof. internat. fin. Tex. Tech U., Lubbock, 1970—2001; prof. emeritus Tex. Tech. U., Lubbock, 2001—; from chmn. fin., adminstr. grad. programs, exec. assoc. dean to dean Tex. Tech U. Rawls Coll. Bus. Adminstrn., Lubbock, 1971—97; dean emeritus Tex. Tech U. Coll. Bus. Adminstrn., Lubbock, 1997—. Sr. econ. adviser Office Fgn. Direct Investments, U.S. Dept. Commerce, Washington, 1973-74; cons. US Dept. Treasury, 1974-75; mem. faculty Grad. Sch. Credit and Fin. Mgmt., Lake Success, NY, 1974-87; adj. scholar Am. Enterprise Inst. Pub. Policy Rsch., Washington, 1974-88; treas. Mission Jour., Inc., 1969-88. Editor (with Makin and Logue): Eurocurrencies and The International Monetary System; contbr. articles to profl. jours. Trustee St. Mary Plains Hosp., Lubbock, Tex., 1987-92, chmn., 1992; v.p. Tex. Coun. Collegiate Edn. Bus., 1977-78, pres., 1978-79; mem. acad. adv. bd. United Arab Emirates U., Al Ain, 1996-03; mem. Coun. on Podiat. Med. Edn., Washington, 1998—; bd. visitors Abilene Christian U., 1998-2007; elder Broadway Ch. of Christ, Lubbock, 2001-04; elder Overland Pk. Ch. of Christ, Kans., 2007—. Capt. Security Agy. AUS, 1961-62. Fulbright scholar, U. Reading, Eng., 1957—58. Fellow Phi Beta Kappa; mem. Southwestern Bus. Adminstrn. Assn. (pres. 1982-83), Nat. Assn. for Bus. Econs., So. Bus. Adminstrn. Assn. (v.p. 1985-86, pres. 1986-87), Lubbock Econ. Coun. (pres. 1973), Am. Assembly Collegiate Schs. Bus. (stds. com. 1981-84, bd. dirs. 1993-96), Lubbock Club (bd. of dirs. 1983-1987, pres. 1986-87), Omicron Delta Kappa, Phi Kappa Phi, Beta Gamma Sigma, Tau Kappa Alpha, Phi Beta Kappa. Avocations: genealogy, history. Home: 12508 W 123rd St Overland Park KS 66213 Personal E-mail: cstem@sbcglobal.net.

STEMBRIDGE, JOHN REESE, mathematics professor; PhD in combinatorics and algebra, MIT, 1985. Prof. math. Univ. Mich., Ann Arbor. Grantee Guggenheim Fellowship, 2000. Achievements include being one of 18 top mathematicians and computer scientists (Atlas of Lie Groups Project) from the US to successfully map E8, one of the largest and most complicated structures in mathematics. Office: 4854 East Hall Math Dept Univ Mich 525 E Univ Ave Ann Arbor MI 48103-1043 Office Phone: 734-936-1790. Office Fax: 734-936-0937. Business E-Mail: jrs@umich.edu.

STEMMONS, RANDEE SMITH, lawyer; b. Springfield, Mo., July 15, 1958; d. Robert Lee and Connie (Smith) S. BA, William Woods Coll., 1980; JD, U. Mo., 1983. Bar: Mo. 1983, U.S. Dist. Ct. (we. dist.) Mo., 1983. Ptnr. Stemmons & Stemmons, Mt. Vernon, Mo., 1983—. V.p. Democratic Alliance, Springfield, 1984—; mem. adv. bd. Hospice. Recipient Profl. Responsibility award Am. Jurisprudence, 1983. Mem. ABA, Assn. Trial Lawyers Am., Mo. Assn. Trial Lawyers, 39th Judicial Cir. Bar Assn. (pres. 1984—), Student Bar Assn. (v.p. 1982-83), Mt. Vernon C. of C. (bd. dirs., v.p. 1984-87, pres. 1987), Order of the Coif, Phi Delta Phi. Democrat. Presbyterian. Home: 520 E Center St Mount Vernon MO 65712-1208 Office: 101 E Dallas St Mount Vernon MO 65712-1401

STEMPEL, GUIDO HERMANN, III, journalism educator; b. Bloomington, Ind., Aug. 13, 1928; s. Guido Hermann Jr. and Alice Margaret (Menninger) S.; m. Anne Elliott, Aug. 30, 1952; children: Ralph Warren, Carl William, Jane Louise. Student, Carnegie Tech., 1945-46; AB in Journalism, Ind. U., 1949, AM in Journalism, 1951; PhD in Mass Communication, U. Wis., 1954. Sports editor Frankfort (Ind.) Times, 1949-50; instr., asst. prof. Sch. Journalism, Pa. State U., University Park, 1955-57; from assoc. prof. to prof. Dept. Journalism, Cen. Mich. U., Mt. Pleasant, 1957-65; assoc. prof. Sch. Journalism, Ohio U., Athens, 1965-68, prof., 1968-82, Disting. prof., 1982—96, Disting. prof. emeritus, 1996—, dir., 1972-79, dir. Scripps Survey Rsch. Ctr., 2002—07. Rsch. cons. Ohio Newspaper Assn., Columbus, 1985—; chmn. rsch. com. Coll. Media Advisors, 1963-69, 79-84; adv. bd. dept. comm. arts U. West Fla., 1987-00; survey coord. Scripps Howard News Svc., 1992—. Co-author: The Media in the 1984 and 1988 Presidential Campaigns, 1991; assoc. editor, Newspaper Rsch. Jour., 1992-2001; co-editor Web Jour. of Mass Comm. Rsch., 1997—; editor, co-author: The Practice of Political Communication, 1994; co-editor, co-author: Research Methods in Mass Communications, 1981, 2d edit., 1989, The Media in the 1984 and 1988 Presidential Campaigns, 1991, Historical Dictionary of Political Communication in the United States, 1999, Mass Communication Research and Theory, 2003; author: Media and Politics in America, 2003; editor: Journalism Quar., 1972-89; sr. rsch. editor Newspaper Research Jour., 2000—; contbr. articles to profl. jours. Mem. bd. visitors Def. Info. Sch., Ft. Meade, 1985-96. amed to Ctrl. Mich. Journalism Hall of Fame, 2004; recipient Chancellor's award, U. Wis., 1977, Francis Asbury award, West Ohio Meth. Conf., 2004, Harold C. Nelson award, U. Wis., 2004. Mem. Assn. for Edn. in Journalism and Mass Comm. (chmn. rsch. com. 1968-71; Eleanor Blum award 1989, Trayes Tchr. of Yr. 1997, Disting. Svc. award 1999, award for excellence in contbns. to journalism 2005, Paul Deutschmann award for excellence in rsch. 2007), Soc. Profl. Journalists, Rotary (pres. Athens unit 1984-85). Democrat. Methodist. Home: 7 Lamar Dr Athens OH 45701-3730 Office: Ohio Univ Sch of Journalism Athens OH 45701 Business E-Mail: stempel@ohio.edu.

STEMPEL, ROBERT C., automobile manufacturing company executive; b. 1933; BSME, Worcester Polytech Inst., 1955, PhD, 1977; MBA, Mich. State U., 1970. Sr. detailer chassis design dept. Oldsmobile div. GM, Detroit, 1958-62, sr. designer, 1962—64, transmission design engr., 1964—69, motor engr., 1969—72, asst. chief engr., 1972—73, spl. asst. to pres., 1973—74; chief engines and components engr. Chevrolet div., GM, 1974—75, dir. engring., 1975—78, corp. v.p. and gen. mgr. Pontiac div., 1978—80, corp. v.p. European passenger car ops., Fed. Republic Germany, 1980—82, corp. v.p., gen. mgr. Chevrolet divsn., 1982—84, corp. v.p., group exec. Buick-Oldsmobile-Cadillac Group, 1984—86, corp. exec. v.p. Worldwide Truck & Bus Group, Overseas Group, 1986—87, corp. pres., COO, 1987—90, chmn., CEO, 1990—92; bd. dirs. Energy Conversion Devices, Inc., Troy, Mich., 1995—, chmn. Served with US Army, 1956—58. Mem.: Electric Drive Transportation Assn. (bd. dirs.), NAE. Office: ECD Energy Conversion Devices 2956 Waterview Dr Rochester Hills MI 48309-3484

STEMPL, ROBERT C., energy company executive; b. 1932; Pres. GM Corp., 1987-90, chmn., CEO, 1990-92; mem. bd. mgrs. GM Ovonic; chmn. Ovonic Battery; sr. bus. and tech. advisor to chmn. Energy Conversion Devices, Inc., Troy, Mich., chmn. bd. dirs., exec. dir., 1999—. Bd. dirs. United Solar and Ovonyx, Alliance Bd. of Ovonic Media, Southwall Technologies, Inc.; mem. mgmt. com. Texaco Ovonic Fuel Cell Co., Bekaert ECD Solar Systems; others. Office: Energy Conversion Devices Inc 2956 Waterview Dr Rochester MI 48309

STENBERG, DONALD B., lawyer; b. David City, Nebr., Sept. 30, 1948; s. Eugene A. and Alice (Kasal) Stenberg; m. Susan K. Hoegemeyer, June 9, 1971; children: Julie A., Donald B. Jr., Joseph L., Abby E. BA, U. Nebr., 1970; MBA, Harvard U., 1974, JD cum laude, 1974. Bar: Nebr. 1974, U.S. Dist. Ct. Nebr. 1974, U.S. Ct. Appeals (fed. cir.) 1984, U.S. Ct. Claims 1989, U.S. Ct. Appeals (8th cir.) 1989, U.S. Supreme Ct. 1991. Assoc. Barlow, Watson & Johnson, Lincoln, Nebr., 1974—75; ptnr. Stenberg and Stenberg, Lincoln, 1976—78; legal counsel Gov. of Nebr., Lincoln, 1979—82; sr. prin. Erickson & Sederstrom, Lincoln, 1983—85, of counsel, 2003—; pvt. practice Lincoln, 1985—90; atty. gen. State of Nebr., Lincoln, 1991—2002. Mem.: Phi Beta Kappa. Republican. Office: Erickson & Sederstrom Regency Westpointe 10330 Regency Pkwy Dr Ste 100 Omaha NE 68114-3761 Office Phone: 402-397-7120. Business E-Mail: donstenberg@eslaw.com.

STENEHJEM, BOB, state legislator; m. Kathy; 4 children. Degree, Bismarck State Coll. Mem. N.D. Senate from 30th dist., Bismark, 1992—; mem. human svc. com. N.D. Senate, chmn. transp. com. Mem. NRA, Elks, Ducks Unlimited, N.Am. Boone and Crockett Club. Home: 7475 41st St SE Bismarck ND 58504-3200 Office: ND State Senate State Capitol Bismarck ND 58505

STENEHJEM, WAYNE KEVIN, state attorney general, lawyer; b. Mohall, ND, Feb. 5, 1953; s. Martin Edward and Marguerite Mae (Peg) (McMaster) Stenehjem; m. Tama Lou Smith, June 16, 1978 (div. Apr. 1984); 1 child, Andrew; m. Beth D. Bakke, June 30, 1995. AA, Bismarck Jr. Coll., ND, 1972; BA, U. ND, 1974, JD, 1977. Bar: N.D. 1977. Ptnr. Kuchera & Stenehjem, Grand Forks, ND, 1977—2000; spl. asst. atty. gen. State of ND, 1983—87, atty. gen., 2000—; mem. ND Indsl. Commn., 2001—; chair RAGA, 2001—02; mem. ND Ho. Reps., 1976—80, ND State Senate, 1980—2000, pres. pro tempore, 1998—99; bd. Univ. and Sch. Lands, 2001—. Chmn. Senate Com. on Social Svcs., 1985—86, Senate Com. on Judiciary, 1995—2000, Interim Legis. Judiciary Com., 1995—2000, Legis. Coun., 1995—2000; mem. Nat. Conf. Commrs. on Uniform State Laws, 1995—2000, Gov.'s Com. on Juvenile Justice. Exec. bd. dirs. No. Lights coun. Boy Scouts Am., 2005—; chmn. Dist. 42 Reps., Grand Forks, 1986—88; bd. dirs. Christus Rex Luth. Ch., pres., 1985—86; bd. dirs. no. lights coun. Boy Scouts Am., 2005—; bd. dirs. ND Spl. Olympics, 1985—89, Bismarck Mandan Big Bros. Big Sisters, 2001—. Named Champion of People's Right to Know, Sigma Delta Chi, 1979, ND Friend of Psych., ND Psychol. Assn., 1990, Outstanding Young Man of ND, Jaycees, 1985, Scandinavian-Am. Hall of Fame, Norsk Høstfest, 2007; recipient Excellence in County Govt. award, D Assn. Counties, 1991, Love Without Fear award, Bismarck Abused Adult Resource Ctr., 2003, Lone Eagle award, ND Peace Officers Assn., 2005, Public Svc. award, Lignite Energy Coun., 2005. Mem.: Grand Forks County Bar Assn., N.D. State Bar Assn. (Legis. Svc. award 1995). Republican. Home: 1216 Crestview Ln Bismarck ND 58501 Office: Office of the Atty Gen State Capitol Bldg 600 E Boulevard Ave Bismarck ND 58505-0040

STENGEL, JAMES R., marketing executive; b. Lancaster, Pa., May 5, 1955; BA, Fraklin & Marshall Coll., 1977; MA, Pa. State U., 1983. With Time, Inc., 1977—81; brand asst. Duncan Hines RTS Cookies Procter & Gamble, 1983, asst. brand mgr. Jif, 1984—86, brand mgr. Jif, 1986—89, assoc. advt. mgr., Jif, Duncan Hines, 1989—91, advt. mgr. Olestra, 1991—93, mktg. dir. US Cosmetics Products, 1993—95, gen. mgr. Europe, Middle East, Africa, 1995—99, v.p. Europe baby care, 1999—2000, v.p. global baby care strategic planning, mktg., new bus. devel., 2000—01, v.p., global mktg. officer, 2001—. Trustee Chatfield Coll., St. Martin, Ohio, 1989—93, Bryn Mawr Sch., Balt., 1993—95, Seven Hills Sch., 2003—; chmn. Assn. Nat. Advts. Inc., 2004—06; trustee Cin. Ballet, 2001—; bd. mem, dir. Motorola Inc., 2005—. Mem.: Heart Am. Found. (exec. adv. bd.). Mailing: Procter & Gamble Co Corp Hdqs One P & G Plaze Cincinnati OH 45202*

STEP, EUGENE LEE, retired pharmaceutical executive; b. Sioux City, Iowa, Feb. 19, 1929; s. Harry and Ann (Keiser) S.; m. Hannah Scheuermann, Dec. 27, 1953; children: Steven Harry, Michael David, Jonathan Allen. BA in Econs., U. Nebr., 1951; MS in Acctg. and Fin., U. Ill., 1952. With Eli Lilly Internat. Corp., London and Paris, 1964-69, dir. Elanco Internat. Indpls., 1969-70, v.p. marketing, 1970-72, v.p. Europe, 1972; v.p. mktg. Eli Lilly and Co., Indpls., 1972-73, pres. pharm. div., 1973-86, exec. v.p., 1986—. Bd. dirs. Cell-Genesys. 1st lt. U.S. Army, 1953-56. Mem. Pharm. Mfrs. Assn. (bd. dirs. 1980-92, chmn. 1989-90), Internat. Pharm. Mfrs. Assn. (pres. 1991-92). Home: PO Box 8997 Rancho Santa Fe CA 92067-8997 Office Phone: 858-759-8958.

STEPAN, FRANK QUINN, JR., (F. QUINN STEPAN JR.), chemical company executive; b. 1960; married; 3 children. BA, U. Notre Dame, 1982; MBA, U. Chgo., 1988. With Monsanto Co., 1983—87, Stepan Co., orthfield, Ill., 1987—, v.p., gen. mgr. Surfactant dept., pres., 1999—2005, CEO, 2005—. Dir. Follett Corp.; bd. dirs. Am. Chem Coun. Office: Stepan Co 22 W Frontage Rd Northfield IL 60093 Office Phone: 847-446-7500, 847-501-2100.

STEPHAN, ALEXANDER FRIEDRICH, German language and literature educator; b. Lüdenscheid, Fed. Republic Germany, Aug. 16, 1946; arrived in US, 1968; s. Eberhard and Ingeborg (Hörnig) S.; m. Halina Konopacka, Dec. 15, 1969; 1 child, Michael. MA, U. Mich., 1969; PhD, Princeton U., 1973. Instr. German Princeton (NJ) U., 1972-73; from asst. prof. to prof. German UCLA, 1973-85; prof. German U. Fla., Gainesville, 1985-2000, chmn., 1985-93; prof. German, Ohio Eminent scholar, sr. fellow Mershon Ctr., Ohio State U., 2000—. Author: Christa Wolf, 1976, Die deutsche Exilliteratur, 1979, Christa Wolf (Forschungsbericht), 1981, Max Frisch, 1983, Anna Seghers im Exil, 1993, Im Visier des FBI, 1995, paperback edit. 1998, English transl. Communazis, 2000, Anna Seghers: Das siebte Kreuz. Welt und Wirkung eines Romans, 1997; editor: Peter Weiss: Die Ästhetik des Widerstands, 1983, 3d edit., 1990, Exil. Literatur und die Künste, 1990, Exil-Studien, 1993—, Christa Wolf: The Author's Dimension, 1993, 2d edit., 1995, Themes and Structures, 1997, Uwe Johnson: Speculations about Jakob and Other Writings, 2000, Early 20th Century German Fiction, 2003, Anna Seghers, Die Entscheidung, 2003, Americanism and Anti-Americanism. The German Encounter with American Culture after 1945, 2004, Exile and Otherness: New Approaches to the Experience of the Nazi Refugees, 2005, The Americanization of Europe: Culture, Diplomacy, and Anti-Americanism After 1945, 2006; co-editor: Studies in GDR Culture and Society, 1981—90, Schreiben im Exil, 1985, The ew Sufferings of Young Werther and Other Stories from the GDR, 1997, Rot=Braun? Brecht Dialog, 2000, Nationalsozialismus und Stalinismus bei Brecht und Zeitgenossen, 2000, Jeans, Rock und Vietnam. Amerikanische Kultur in der DDR, 2002, Refuge and Reality: Feuchtwanger and the European Emigres in California, 2005, Das

Amerika der Autoren von Kafka bis, 2006, America On My Mind, 2006; co-prodr.: (TV films) Im Visier des FBI, 1995, Das FBI und Marlene Dietrich, 2000, Das FBI und Brechts Telephon, 2002, Exilanten und das OSS, 2002, Thomas Mann und der CIA, 2002. Grantee, NEH, 1974, 1984, 1997, Am. Coun. Learned Socs., 1976, 1977, 1984, Am. Philos. Soc., 1979, 1981, 1992, Humboldt Found., 1988, 1994, 1998—99, 2002—03, Guggenheim Found., 1989, German Acad. Exch. Svcs., 1993, 1997, Feuchtwanger Meml. Libr., 1998, Weichmann Stiftung, 1998, Transcoop/AvH, 2002—04; Fulbright Sr. Specialist, 2005—. Mem.: German PEN, German Assn. for Am. Studies, German Studies Assn., Internat. Anna Seghers Soc., Soc. Exile Studies. Office: Ohio State U Dept Germanic Lang Lit 498 Hagerty Columbus OH 43210-1340 Office Phone: 614-247-6068. Business E-Mail: stephan.30@osu.edu.

STEPHAN, KENNETH C., state supreme court justice; b. Omaha, Oct. 8, 1946; m. Sharon Ross, Apr. 19, 1969; 3 children. BA, U. Nebr., 1968, JD with high distinction, 1972. Bar: Nebr. Atty. pvt. practice, 1973-97; judge Nebr. Supreme Ct., Lincoln, 1997—. With US Army, 1969—71. Mem.: Am. Coll. Trial Lawyers (jud. fellow). Office: Nebr Supreme Ct State Capitol Bldg Rm 2211 PO Box 98910 Lincoln NE 68509-8910 Office Phone: 402-471-3737. Business E-Mail: kstephan@nsc.state.ne.us.

STEPHENS, D. RICHARD, manufacturing executive; married; 2 children. BS in chem. engring., U. Akron, 1972; MBA, Bowling Green U., 1990; grad. advanced mgmt. program, Harvard Bus. Sch., 1997. Pres. Cooper Tire & Rubber Co., Findlay, Ohio, 2001—, truck devel. chemist, 1978—79, compound devel. mgr., 1979—85, product devel. mgr., 1985—90, dir. tech., 1990—94, v.p. tech., 1994—2000, v.p. tech. and comm. tire oper., 2000; pres. Cooper Tire & Rubber Co., Internat. Tire Dvsn., 2000—01. Mem. bd. trustees U. Findlay, 2000—; mem. Findlay-Hancock County C. of C., 1992; mem. bd. trustees Vennard Coll. Fin. Com., 1994—96. Office: Cooper Tire Rubber Co 701 Lima Ave Findlay OH 45840

STEPHENS, LEE-ANN WILLIAMS, elementary school educator, educator; b. Cleve., July 9, 1962; d. Joseph Ernest Williams and Joan Lee (Campbell) Warren; m. Terry Brian Stephens, Sept. 21, 1985. BA in Internat. Studies, Miami U., 1984; postgrad., U. Mex., 1984; BS in Elem. Edn., U. Minn., 1989. Cert. elem. tchr., Minn. Asst. adult probation officer Alliance (Ohio) Mcpl. Courthouse, 1982-83; assoc. buyer Dayton Hudson Dept. Store Co., Mpls., 1985-88; elem. tchr. Dowling Pub. Sch., Mpls., 1989; now tchr. Park Spanish Immersion Sch., Minn. Math tutor African Am. Acad. for Accelerated Learning, Mpls., 1989—; coord. Mpls. Council Chs. Tutoring Program, 1988-89. Named Minn. Tchr. of Yr., 2007. Mem. ASCD, Nat. Coun. Tchrs. Math. Avocations: aerobics, bowling, reading. Office: Park Spanish Immersion Sch 6300 Walker St Minneapolis MN 55416

STEPHENS, NORMAN L., former academic administrator; b. Hinsdale, Ill. m. Laurie Stephens; 4 children. Doctorate, U. Fla., 1971. Various positions including faculty mem., dean coll. sys. St. Petersburg Jr. Coll., Pinellas County, Fla.; founding provost Brandon (Fla.) campus Hillsborough C.C.; v.p. acad. svcs. Lincoln Land C.C., Springfield, Ill., 1990-92, pres., 1992-99. Active cmty. svc. orgns. and programs. Fellow U. Fla., 1971. Office: Lincoln Land C C 5250 Shepherd Rd Springfield IL 62703-5402

STEPHENS, RICHARD, aerospace transportation executive; BS in Math., U. So. Calif., 1974; MS in Computer Sci., Calif. State U., Fullerton, 1984. V.p., gen. mgr. Integrated Def. Sys. Homeland Security and Svcs. Boeing Co., Chgo., sr. v.p. Internal Svcs., pres. Shared Svcs. Grp., sr. v.p. Human Resources and Adminstrn., 2005—; mem. Boeing Exec. Coun. Vice chmn. Orange County Bus. Coun.; mem. Pvt. Sector Sr. Adv. Com. Dept. Homeland Security, 2003—; mem. Sec. of Edn.'s Commn. on Future of Edn., 2005. Officer USMC. Recipient Profl. of Yr. Award, Am. Indian Sci. & Engring. Soc., 2004, Gold. Silver Knight and Excellence in Leadership awards, Nat. Mgmt. Assn. Fellow: AIAA; mem.: Pala Band of Mission Indians (chmn. 1988—89). Office: Boeing Co 100 N Riverside Chicago IL 60606-1596 Office Phone: 312-544-2000.

STEPHENS, RONALD EARL, state legislator; b. East St. Louis, Ill., Feb. 19, 1948; s. Earl Evered and Velma Juanita (Wills) S.; m. Karen Kay Angleton, 1975; children: Wendi, Chad, Kent, Tod, Molly. BS, St. Louis Coll. of Pharmacy. Pres., CEO Stephens Pharmacy, Inc., 1975, Freedom Pharmacy, Inc., 1982; pres. Caseyville Township Rep., Ill., 1980-82, trustee, 1981-82; Ill. state rep. Dist. 110, 1985-89, 93—. Rep. candidate Ill. House, 1982. Decorated Purple Heart, Bronze Star. Mem. Nat. Pharmacists Assn., Lions, Jaycees (state dir. 1982), Shriners, Kiwanis, Kappa Psi (Man of Yr. 1980). Office: Ill House of Reps Rm 2003-G State Capitol Springfield IL 62706-0001 Address: 535 Edwardsville Rd Ste 110 Troy IL 62294-1399

STEPHENS, THOMAS G., automotive executive; BS in Mech. Engring., U. Mich., 1971. With GM, Mich., 1969—; exptl. engr., staff project engr. GM Cadillac Motor Car Divsn., Detroit, 1971—80, supr. product engring., 1980—82, staff engr. emission, transmissions, 1982—85; sr. staff engr. transmission, powertrain controls GM Buick-Oldsmobile-Cadillac Powertrain Divsn., 1985—88; plant mgr. GM Buick-Oldsmobile-Cadillac Powertrain Livonia Engine Plant, 1988—90; dir. engring. GM Engine Divsn., 1990—91; dir. engine engring. GM Powertrain, 1991—93, engring. ops. gen. mgr. Pontiac, 1993—94; v.p. GM, Detroit, 1994; v.p., group dir. engring. ops. GM Truck Group., 1996—2000; v.p. vehicle integration GM, 2001; group. v.p. GM Powertrain, 2001—. Mem.: NAE, U. Mich. Nat. Adv. Coun., Detroit Sci. Ctr. (bd. trustees).

STEPHENS, THOMAS M(ARON), education educator; b. Youngstown, Ohio, June 15, 1931; s. Thomas and Mary (Hanna) S.; m. Evelyn Kleshock, July 1, 1955. BS, Youngstown Coll., 1955; MEd, Kent State U., 1957; EdD, U. Pitts., 1966. Lic. psychologist, Ohio. Tchr. Warren (Ohio) public schs., 1955-57, Niles (Ohio) public schs., 1957-58; psychologist Montgomery County, Ohio, 1958-60; dir. gifted edn. Ohio Dept. Edn., Columbus, 1960-66; assoc. prof. edn. U. Pitts., 1966-70; prof. edn. Ohio State U., 1970—, chmn. dept. exceptional children., 1972-82, chmn. dept. human services edn., 1982-87, assoc. dean Coll. Edn., 1987-92, prof., 1987-92, prof. emeritus, 1992—; clin. prof. edn. U. Dayton, Ohio, 1993—; exec. dir. Sch. Study Coun. Ohio, Columbus, 1987—2007, exec. dir. emeritus, 2007—; pvt. practice, 2007—. Mem. Higher Edn. Consortium for Spl. Edn., chmn., 1976-77; pub., pres. Cedars Press, Inc. Author: Directive Teaching of Children with Learning and Behavioral Handicaps, 2d edit, 1976, Implementing Behavioral Approaches in Elementary and Secondary Schools, 1975, Teaching Skills to Children with Learning and Behavioral Disorders, 1977, Teaching Children Basic Skills: A Curriculum Handbook, 1978, 2d edit., 1983, Social Skills In The Classroom, 1978, 2d edit., 1991, Teaching Mainstreamed Students, 1982, 2d edit., 1988, Social Behavior Assessment Scale, 1991; dir.: Jour. Sch. Psychology, 1965-75, 80—; exec. editor: The Directive Tchr.; assoc. editor: Spl. Edn. and Tchr. Edn., Techniques, Behavioral Disorders, Spl. Edn. and Remedial Edn.; contbr. articles to profl. jours. Named to Ohio State U. Coll. of Edn. Hall of Fame, 1999; U.S. Office of Edn. fellow, 1964-65. Mem. APA, ASP (charter), State Dirs. for Gifted (pres. 1962-63), Coun. for Exceptional Children (gov., Tchr. Educator of Yr. tchr. edn. divsn. 1985), Coun. Children with Behavioral Disorders (pres. 1972-73). Home: 551 E Cooke Rd Columbus OH 43214-2813 Office: Sch Study Coun of Ohio 2080 Citygate Dr Columbus OH 43219 Office Phone: 614-785-0481. Business E-Mail: tstephens@ssco.org.

STEPHENSON, HUGH EDWARD, JR., retired surgeon; b. Columbia, Mo., June 1, 1922; s. Hugh Edward and Doris (Pryor) S.; m. Sarah Norfleet Dickinson, Aug. 15, 1964; children— Hugh Edward III, Ann Dunlop. AB, BS, U. Mo., Columbia, 1943; MD, Washington U., St. Louis, 1945. Diplomate Am. Bd. Surgery, Am. Bd. Thoracic Surgery. Mem. faculty U. Mo. Sch. Medicine, Columbia, 1953—; prof. surgery U. Mo. Hugh E. Stephenson Jr. Dept. Surgery, Columbia, 1956—, chmn. dept. surgery, 1956—60, chief div. gen. surgery, 1976—87, chief staff, 1982—94; John Growdon Disting. prof. surgery emeritus U. Mo. Sch. Medicine, Columbia, 1987—, interim dean, 1988—89, assoc. dean, 1989—92, dist. prof. surgery emeritus, 1993; curator U. Mo. System, 1996—. Pres. bd. curators U. Mo., 2000; Markle scholar acad. medicine, 1954-60. Author: Immediate Care of the Acutely Ill and Injured, 2d edit, 1974, Cardiac Arrest and Resuscitation, 4th edit., 1975, The Kicks That Count; Contbr. articles to profl. jours. Named one of Outstanding Young Men of Nation, Nat. Jr. C. of C., 1956, James IV Surg. Traveler Gt. Britain, 1962, Dist. Faculty award, 1989. Mem. ACS, AMA (del., chmn. coun. on med. edn. 1994-95, co-chmn. liaison com. on med. edn. 1995, pres. surgical caucus 1996, Stephenson Endowed chair of Surgery), Vascular Surgery Soc., Soc. Thoracic Surgeons, So. Thoracic Surgery Assn., So. Med. Assn. (coun., pres. 2001), Mo. Med. Assn. (chmn. jud. coun. 1986-, v.p. 1986-), Beta Theta Pi (trustees, pres. gen. frat. 1978-81), Delta Sigma Theta (master bd.). Baptist. Home: 5 Danforth Cir Columbia MO 65201-3509 Office: University of Missouri Hugh E Stephenson Jr Dept Surgery 1 Hospital Dr Columbia MO 65201-5276 Home Phone: 573-442-3834; Office Phone: 573-882-5645.

STEPHENSON, VIVIAN M., former retail executive; B Math., NYU; MBA, U. Havana: PhD (hon.), Mills Coll., Oakland. Mgmt. positions Rand Info. Sys., Occidental Petroleum Corp., Assoc. Credit Burs. Svcs., Inc.; dir. info. sys. devel. Mervyn's, 1989-90, v.p. MIS, 1990-94, sr. v.p., 1994-95; sr. v.p., chief info. officer Dayton Hudson Corp., Mpls., 1995-2000; exec. v.p., chief info. officer Target Corp., Mpls., —2000; ret., 2000. Bd. dirs. MobiNetrix Sys. Inc.; mem. info. sys. customer adv. coun. IBM; mem. Tandem Americas Customer Coun; chmn. bd. dir. Mills Coll. Chair bd. dirs. San Francisco AIDS Found.; mem. Nat. Retail Fedn. Info. Sys. Bd. Mem. Calif. C. of C. Office: Target Corp 1000 Nicollet Mall Minneapolis MN 55403-2467

STEPP, CATHY, state senator; b. Aug. 17, 1963; married. Supr., New Home Consultants First Stepp Builders, Inc., Racine, Wis.; state sen. Wis. State Senate, Madison, 2002—. 3-time judge Met. Milw. Area Parade of Homes; chair Parade of Homes, 1998—99; apptd. dept. natural resources bd. former Gov. Tommy Thompson, 2000—; bd. dirs. Girl Scouts of Racine County. Mem.: Wis. Builders Assn. (bd. dirs. 1996—), Racine-Kenosha Builders Assn. (pres. 1998—99, past sec.), Nat. Assn. Home Builders (bd. dirs. 1999—). Office: State Capitol Rm 7 S PO Box 7882 Madison WI 53707-7882

STERN, CARL WILLIAM, JR., management consultant; b. San Francisco, Mar. 31, 1946; s. Carl William and Marjorie Aline (Gunst) S.; m. Karen Jaffe, Sept. 7, 1966 (div. Mar. 1972); 1 child, David; m. Holly Drick Hayes, Mar. 21, 1985; children: Kenneth, Matthew. BA, Harvard U., 1968; MBA, Stanford U., 1974. Cons. Boston Cons. Group, Inc., Menlo Park, Calif., 1974-77, mgr., 1977-78, London, 1978-80, v.p. Chgo., 1980-87, sr. v.p., 1987-97, pres., CEO, 1998—2003, co-chmn. bd., 2004—07, chmn. bd., 2007—. Lt. USNR, 1968-71. Office: Boston Consulting Group Inc 200 S Wacker Dr Ste 2700 Chicago IL 60606-5846

STERN, DAVID MARK, dean, educator; b. Great Neck, NY; s. Robert and Florence Stern; m. Kathleen Shirley Stern; children: Eric David, Alan Robert. BS, Yale U., 1973; MD, Harvard U., 1978. Mem. faculty Coll. Physicians and Surgeons, Columbia U., NYC, 1983—2002, named Gerald & Janet Carrus Prof. of Surg. Sci., 1998, dir. Ctr. Vascular and Lung Pathobiology, dir. Juvenile Diabetes Rsch. Ctr.; dean sch. medicine, sr. v.p. clin. activities Med. Coll. Ga., Augusta, 2002—05, prof. medicine, physiology and grad. studies, 2002—05; Christian R. Holmes prof. medicine U. Cincinnati, 2005—, dean Coll. Medicine, 2005—. Mem.: Am. Assn. Physicians, Am. Soc. Clin. Investigation. Office: Univ Cincinnati Coll Medicine 231 Albert Sabin Way PO Box 670552 Cincinnati OH 45267-0552 Office Phone: 513-558-7334. Business E-Mail: dstern@mail.mcg.edu. E-mail: david.stern@uc.edu.

STERN, EDWARD, performing company executive; Producing artistic dir. Cin. Playhouse in the Park. Office: Cincinnati Playhouse in the Park PO Box 6537 Cincinnati OH 45206-0537

STERN, GARY B., lawyer; b. 1957; BA, Univ. Mich., 1979; JD cum laude, Northwestern Univ., 1982. Bar: Ill. 1982. Ptnr., head banking & securitization group Sidley Austin Brown & Wood LLP, Chgo. Mem.: ABA, Chgo. Bar Assn., Order of the Coif. Office: Sidley Austin Brown & Wood LLP Bank One Plz 10 S Dearborn St Chicago IL 60603 Office Phone: 312-853-7267. Office Fax: 312-853-7036. Business E-Mail: gstern@sidley.com.

STERN, GARY HILTON, bank executive; b. San Luis Obispo, Calif., Nov. 3, 1944; s. Robert Earl and Joy Merdis (Shimon) S.; m. Mary Katherine Nelson, Aug. 17, 1969; children: Matthew Stuart, Meredith Faulkner. AB, Washington U., St. Louis, 1967; MA, Rice U., 1970, PhD, 1972. Economist Fed. Res. Bank of N.Y., NYC, 1970-73, mgr. domestic research, 1973-77; mgr. fixed income research Loeb Rhoades, Hornblower, NYC, 1977-78; sr. economist A.G. Shilling & Co., NYC, 1978-81; sr. v.p. Fed. Res. Bank Mpls., 1982-85, CFO, 1983, pres., CEO, 1985—. Adj. assoc. prof. NYU, 1980-82; adj. asst. prof. Columbia U., 1976-79 Author: In the Name of Money, 1980. Trustee West Side Montessori Sch., N.Y.C., 1978-79; bd. dirs. Nat. Coun. Econ. Edn., N.W. Area Found., Carlson Sch. Mgmt. U. Minn.; bd. trustees Hamline U., Mpls. Coll. Art and Design. NDEA scholar, 1969-70; Bache & Co. scholar, 1963-67; univ. scholar Washington U.-St. Louis, 1964-67, Rice U.-Houston, 1967-70 Mem.: Mpls. Club (treas.). Office: Fed Res Bank Mpls 90 Hennepin Ave Minneapolis MN 55401 Office Phone: 612-204-5000.

STERN, GEOFFREY, lawyer; b. Columbus, Ohio, Nov. 29, 1942; s. Leonard J. and Anastasia (Percin) S.; m. Barbara Feuer; children: Emily Staheli, Elizabeth Leskowyak; 3 stepchildren. Student, Williams Coll., 1960-63; BA cum laude, Ohio State U., 1965, JD summa cum laude, 1968. Bar: Ohio 1968. Assoc. Alexander, Ebinger, Holschuh & Fisher, Columbus, Ohio, 1968-72; ptnr. Folkerth, Calhoun, Webster & O'Brien, Columbus, Ohio, 1972-80, Arter & Hadden, Columbus, Ohio, 1980-93; disciplinary counsel Supreme Ct. of Ohio, 1993-97; counsel Kegler, Brown, Hill & Ritter, Columbus, 1997-2000, dir., 2000—. Nat. coordinating counsel for asbestos litigation Combustion Engring. Inc. and Basic, Inc., 1985-93; lectr. on legal ethics and profl. responsibility; mem. Spl. Commn. to Review Ohio Ethics Rules, 1995-98, Spl. Commn. on Legal Edn., 1995-98; mem. symposium on ethics and Chinese legal sys., Shanghai, 1998; keynote spkr. Faith and Law Symposium, 1999; spl. investigator Bd. Commrs. Character and Fitness Ohio Supreme Ct., 1998. Sr. editor Ohio State Law Jour., 1967-68. Pres. Bexley (Ohio) City Coun., 1977-80, mem., 1973-80, mem. Bexley Civil Svc. Commn., 1983-85; v.p., trustee Creative Living, Columbus, 1981-89, Ohio Citizens Com. for Arts, Columbus, 1982-88; mem. Nat. Def. Com. on Asbestos in Bldgs. Litigation, 1986-92; pub. mem. Ohio Optical Dispensers Bd., Columbus, 1978-82. Recipient Am. Jurisprudence Evidence award Ohio State U. Coll. Law, 1967, Verdict Top Attorneys, Best Lawyers in Am., Ohio Superlawyer. Fellow Am. Bar Found., Columbus Bar Found., Ohio State Bar Found.; mem. Ohio State Bar Assn. (com. on legal ethics and profl. conduct, sec. 1981-90, vice chmn. 1990-92, chmn. 1992-93), Columbus Bar Assn. (profl. ethics com. 1975-86, 90-93, Liberty Bell award for Cmty. and Profl. Svc. 1998), Order of Coif, Phi Beta Kappa, Pi Sigma Alpha. Home: 278 Crossing Crk N Columbus OH 43230-6108 Office: Kegler Brown Hill & Ritter 65 E State St Ste 1800 Columbus OH 43215-4294 Office Phone: 614-462-5400. Business E-Mail: gstern@keglerbrown.com.

STERN, GERALD DANIEL, poet; b. Pitts., Feb. 22, 1925; s. Harry and Ida (Barach) S.; m. Patricia Miller, Sept. 12, 1952 (div.); children: Rachel, David. BA, U. Pitts., 1947; MA, Columbia U., 1949. English tchr., prin. Lake Grove (N.Y.) Sch., 1951-53; English tchr. Victoria Dr. Secondary Sch., Glasgow, Scotland, 1953-54; English instr. Temple U., Phila., 1956-63; assoc. prof. English Indiana (Pa.) U. of Pa., 1963-67; prof. English Somerset (N.J.) County Coll., 1968-82; prof. English, Writers' Workshop, U. Iowa, Iowa City, 1982-96. Lectr. Douglas Coll., New Brunswick, N.J., 1968; vis. poet Sarah Lawrence Coll., Bronxville, N.Y., 1978, U. Pitts., 1978; vis. prof. Columbia U., N.Y.C., 1980, Bucknell U., Lewisburg, Pa., 1988, NYU, 1989, 91, Princeton U., 1989; Fanny Hurst prof. Washington U., St. Louis, 1985; Coal chair creative writing U. Ala., Tuscaloosa, 1984. Author: (poetry) Pineys, 1971, The Naming of Beasts, 1972, Rejoicings: selected Poems 1966-72, 1973, Lucky Life, 1977 (Lamont Poetry selection 1977, Nat. Book Critics Cir. award for poetry nominee 1978), The Red Coal, 1981 (Melville Caine award Poetry Soc. Am. 1982), Paradise Poems, 1984, Lovesick, 1987, Two Long Poems, 1990, Leaving Another Kingdom: Selected Poems, 1990, Bread Without Sugar, 1992, Odd Mercy, 1995, This Time: New and Seleced Poems, 1998 (Nat. Book award), Last Blue, 2000, American Sonnets, 2002; (essays) Selected Essays, 1988, What I Can't Bear Losing: Notes from a Life, 2003. Guggenheim fellow, 1980, Am. Acad. Poets fellow, 1993; NEA grantee to be master poet for Pa. 1973-75, Creative Writing grantee, 1976, 81, 87, State of Pa. Creative Writing grantee, 1979; recipient Gov. award for excellence in arts State of Pa., 1980, Bess Hokin award Poetry, 1980, Bernard F. Connor's award Paris Rev., 1981, Am. Poetry Rev. award, 1982, Jerome J. Shestack Poetry prize Am. Poetry Rev., 1984, Ruth Lilly prize, 1996. Fellow Acad. Am. Poets. Office: U Iowa 436 EPB Iowa City IA 52242

STERN, LEO G., lawyer; b. Mpls., Apr. 10, 1945; s. Philip J. and June I. (Monasch) S.; m. Christine E. Lamb, June 29, 1968; children: Alison M., Zachary A. BA, U. Calif., Davis, 1967; JD cum laude, U. Minn., 1970. Bar: Minn. 1970, U.S. Dist. Ct. Minn. 1971, Calif. 1971, U.S. Ct. Appeals (6th, 7th and 8th cirs.) 1985, U.S. Supreme Ct. 1993, Wis. 1999; cert. mediator and arbitrator, Minn. Ptnr. Cox, King & Stern, Mpls., 1970-77, Wright, West & Diessner, Mpls., 1977-84, Fredrikson & Byron, P.A., Mpls., 1984—. Mem. Minn. Bar Assn. (governing coun. environ. and natural resources law sect. 1989-95, governing coun. litig. sect. 1995-99), Am. Arbitration Assn. (arbitrator, mediator), Nat. Arbitration Forum, Nat. Assn. Securities Dealers, Internat. Inst. Conflict Prevention and Resolution. Avocations: sailing, jogging. Home: 206 Central Ave S Wayzata MN 55391-1818 Office: Fredrikson & Byron PA 4000 US Bank Plz 200 S 6th St Minneapolis MN 55402 Home Phone: 952-476-2461; Office Phone: 612-492-7061. Business E-Mail: lstern@fredlaw.com.

STERN, LOUIS WILLIAM, marketing educator, consultant; b. Boston, Sept. 19, 1935; s. Berthold Summerfield Stern and Gladys (Koch) Cohen; m. Rhona L. Grant; children: Beth Ida, Deborah Lynn. AB, Harvard U., 1957; MBA in Mktg, U. Pa., 1959; PhD in Mktg, Northwestern U., 1962. Mem. staff bus. research and consumer mktg. sects. Arthur D. Little, Inc., Cambridge, Mass., 1961-63; from asst. prof. bus. orgn. to prof. Ohio State U., Columbus, Ohio, 1963—70, prof. mktg., 1970—73; from prof. mktg. to A. Montgomery Ward prof. mktg. Northwestern U., 1973—83, John D. Gray disting. prof. mktg., 1983—2001, John D. Gray disting. prof. emeritus mktg., 2001—; on leave as exec. dir. Mktg. Sci. Inst., Cambridge, Mass., 1983-85; Thomas Henry Carroll Ford Found. vis. prof. Harvard U. Grad. Sch. Bus. Adminstrn., 1984-85; Dorinda and Mark Winkelman Disting. Scholar sr. fellow, co-dir. Jay H. Baker Retailing Initiative, The Wharton Sch., U. Pa., 2004—06; mem. bd. trustees Williston Northhampton Sch., Easthampton, Mass. Mem. staff Nat. Commn. on Food Mktg., Washington, 1965-66; vis. assoc. prof. bus. adminstrn. U. Calif., Berkeley, 1969-70; guest lectr. York U., U. Minn., U. Ky., UCLA, Ohio State U., U. N.C., Duke U., U. Wis., U. Pitts., U. Chgo., MIT, U. Mich., U. Pa., Cornell U., U. Mo., Norwegian Sch. Econs. and Bus. Adminstrn.; faculty assoc. Hernstein Inst., Vienna, Austria, 1976-77, Mgmt. Centre Europe, 1988-96; faculty assoc. Gemini Cons. Inc., Montvale, N.J., 1977-96, mem. midwest adv. bd., 1989-94; Xerox rsch. prof. Northwestern U., 1981-82; cons. to FTC, 1973, 80; vis. scholar U. Calif., Berkeley, 1997-2001; mem. faculty adv. bd. CSC Index, 1997-98; co-dir. Jay H. Baker Retailing Initiative Wharton Sch., U. Pa., 2004; bd. dirs., Acad. Urban Sch. Leadership, Chgo. Author: Distribution Channels: Behavioral Dimensions, 1969, (with Frederick D. Sturdivant and others) Managerial Analysis in Marketing, 1970, Perspectives in Marketing Management, 1971, (with John R. Grabner, Jr.) Competition in the Marketplace, 1970, (with Anne T. Coughlan, Erin Anderson and Adel I. El-Ansary) Marketing Channels, 6th edit., 2001, (with Thomas L. Eovaldi) Legal Aspects of Marketing Strategy: Antitrust and Consumer Protection Issues, 1984; (with Adel I. El-Ansary and James R. Brown) Management in Marketing Channels, 1989; mem. editl. bd. Jour. Mktg. Rsch., 1976-82, Jour. Mktg., 1979-83, Mktg. Letters, 1988-94; contbr. articles to profl. jours. Mem. exec. com. Northwest Area Coun. on Human Rels., Columbus, 1971—72. Rsch. grantee Ohio State U., 1964-73, Mktg. Sci. Inst., 1976-77, 88-90, 92-94; recipient Harold H. Maynard award best article Jour. Mktg., 1980, Kellogg's Spl. Lifetime Achievement Award for Tchg. Excellence, 1999; named Mktg. Educator of Yr. Sales and Mktg. Execs. Internat., 1989, also Chgo. chpt. 1990, Outstanding Profl. of Yr. award, 1992, and named One of Top 6 Profs. in Kellogg Sch., Northwestern U., Grad. Mgmt. Assocs., 1984-94, (named 6 times Outstanding Prof. Exec. Masters Program), One of Top 12 Tchrs. in U.S., U.S. Bus. Schs., Bus. Week; named Dorinda and Mark Winkelman Disting. scholar, Sr. fellow Wharton Sch., U. Pa., 2004. Mem. AAUP, Am. Mktg. Assn. (mem. program com. educators conf. 1971, chmn. com. 1978, Paul D. Converse award 1986, Richard D. Irwin Disting. Mktg. Educator of Yr. 1994), Hellenic Inst. Mktg. (hon.), Beta Gamma Sigma. Home: Apt 1401 800 Elgin Rd Evanston IL 60201-5629 Office: Northwestern U Kellogg Sch Mgmt Dept Mktg Evanston IL 60208-2001 Home Phone: 847-866-8952; Office Phone: 847-491-2718. Business E-Mail: lwstern@kellogg.northwestern.edu.

STERN, NOAH J., lawyer; b. Albany, NY, Apr. 26, 1971; BA, U. Calif. Berkeley, 1993; MA, Ind. U. Bloomington, 1996; JD, NY U. Sch. Law, 1999. Bar: Ohio 1999, US Tax Ct. Assoc. Dinsmore & Shohl LLP, Cin. Mem., Bd. Trustee Adath Israel Synagogue. Named one of Ohio's Rising Stars, Super Lawyers, 2006, 2007. Mem.: Ohio State Bar Assn., Cin. Bar Assn. Office: Dinsmore & Shohl LLP 255 E Fifth St Ste 1900 Cincinnati OH 45202-4700 Office Phone: 513-977-8460. Office Fax: 513-977-8141.

STERN, RICHARD GUSTAVE, writer; b. NYC, Feb. 25, 1928; s. Henry George and Marion (Veit) S.; m. Gay Clark, Mar. 14, 1950 (div. Feb. 1972); children: Christopher Holmes, Kate Macomber, Andrew Henry, Nicholas Clark; m. Alane Rollings, Aug. 9, 1985. BA, U. N.C., 1947; MA, Harvard U., 1950; PhD, State U. Iowa, 1954. Mem. faculty U. Chgo., 1955—, prof. English, 1965—, Helen Regenstein prof. English, 1990—2002, prof. emeritus, 2002. Author: Golk, 1960, Europe and Up and Down with Baggish and Schreiber, 1961, In Any Case, 1962, Teeth, Dying and Other Matters, 1964, Stitch, 1965, 1968: A Short Novel, An Urban Idyll, Five Stories and Two Trade Notes, 1970, The Books in Fred Hampton's Apartment, 1973, Other Men's Daughters, 1973, Natural Shocks, 1978, Packages, 1980, The Invention of the Real, 1982, A Father's Words, 1986, The Position of the Body, 1986, Noble Rot: Stories, 1949-88, 1989 (book of yr. award Chgo. Sun-Times 1990), Shares and Other Fictions, 1992, One Person and Another, 1993, A Sistermony, 1995 (Heartland award, nonfiction book of year), Pacific Tremors, 2001, What Is What Was, 2002, Almonds to the Zhoof: The Collected Stories of Richard Stern, 2005; editor: Honey and Wax, 1966. Recipient Longwood Found. award, 1960, Friends of Lit. award, 1963, fiction award Nat. Inst. Arts and Letters, 1968; Nat. Coun. Arts and Humanities fellow, 1967-68, Carl Sandburg award for fiction, 1979, Arts Coun. awards, 1979, 81, Am. Acad. and Inst. of Arts and Letters medal of Merit for Novel, 1985; Rockefeller fellow, 1965, Guggenheim fellow, 1973-74. Fellow Ctr. Advanced Studies in the Behavioral Scis.; mem. Am. Acad. Arts and Scis. Business E-Mail: rstern@uchicago.edu.

STERN, TODD, restaurant manager; b. 1967; Founder, mng. ptnr. Small Plates, Detroit, 2002—. Named one of 40 Under 40, Crain's Detroit Bus., 2006; recipient Best of Yr. award for Small Plates, Bon Appetit mag., 2004, Wine Enthusiast, 2004. Office: Small Plates 1521 Broadway Detroit MI 48226 Office Phone: 313-963-0497.

STERNER, FRANK MAURICE, manufacturing executive; b. Lafayette, Ind., Nov. 26, 1935; s. Raymond E. and Maudelene M. (Scipio) S.; m. Elsa Y. Rasmusson, June 29, 1958; children: Mark, Lisa. BS, Purdue U., 1958, MS, 1959, PhD, 1962. Sr. staff specialist Gen. Motors Inst., Flint, Mich., 1962-63; dir. personnel and orgnl. research Delco Electronics, Milw., 1963-66, dir. personnel devel. and research, 1966-68; partner Nourse & Sterner, Inc., Milw., 1968-69; pres., 1969-73; assoc. dean, prof. Krannert Grad. Sch. of Mgmt., Purdue U., West Lafayette, Ind., 1973-79; v.p. strategic mgmt. Johnson Controls, Inc., Milw., 1979-89; pres., chief exec. officer E.R. Wagner Mfg. Co., 1989—; pres., owner Ridgeway Devel. Inc., Milw., 1993—. Bd. dirs. Wausau Homes, Inc., E.R. Wagner Mfg. Co., Ridgeway Devel. Inc., Greenheck Fan Corp. Home: 1440 E Standish Pl Milwaukee WI 53217-1958 Office: ER Wagner Mfg Co 4611 N 32nd St Milwaukee WI 53209-6000 Office Phone: 414-449-8204. Business E-Mail: frank.sterner@erwagner.com.

STERNLIEB, LAWRENCE JAY, marketing professional, writer; b. Akron, Ohio, Aug. 19, 1951; s. Max and Mollie (Atleson) S. BA in English, Kent State U., 1974, BA in Sociology, 1974, MA in Sociology, 1977. Lic. social worker, Ohio. Social program specialist State of Ohio, Cleve., 1976—79; sr. mktg. exec. Xerox Corp., Cleve., 1979—82; sr. acct. mgr. McDonnell Douglas Corp., Independence, Ohio, 1983—87; sr. mktg. rep. Prime Computer Inc., Independence, 1987—90; acct. exec. GE Cons. Svcs., Independence, 1990—94; mgr. major acct. Gen. Data Comm., Inc., Cleve., 1995—2000; pres. LSS, LLC, Cleve., 2000—. Instr. Cuyahoga C.C., Cleve., 1980-81, 92. Author: Barry Storm, 1995. Mem. Cleve. Playhouse. Avocations: acting, modeling, writing, sports, physical fitness. Office Phone: 440-230-0826.

STERNSTEIN, ALLAN J., lawyer; b. Chgo., June 7, 1948; s. Milton and Celia (Kaganove) Sternstein; m. Miriam A. Dolgin, July 12, 1970 (div. July 1981); children: Jeffery A., Amy R.; m. Beverly A. Cook, Feb. 8, 1986 (div. 2004); 1 child, Julia S. BS, U. Ill., 1970; MS, U. Mich., 1972; JD, Loyola U. Sch. Law, Chgo., 1977. Bar: US Patent and Trademark Office 1974, Ill. 1977, US Dist. Ct.

(no. dist.) Ill. 1977, US Dist. Ct. (no. dist.) Ohio 1977, US Dist. Ct. (ea. dist) Mich. 1986, US Dist. Ct. (we. dist.) Mich. 1990, US Ct. Customs and Patent Appeals 1978, US Ct. Appeals (7th cir.) 1979, US Ct. Appeals (Fed. cir.) 1982, US Dist. Ct. (ea. dist.) Wis. 2003, US Ct. Appeals (5th cir.) 2003, US Dist. Ct. (ea. dist.) Tex. 2007. Patent agt. Sunbeam Corp., Oak Brook, Ill., 1972—76; ptnr. Neuman, Williams, Anderson & Olson, Chgo., 1976—84; divsn. patent counsel Abbott Labs., North Chgo., Ill., 1984—87; ptnr. Brinks Hofer Gilson & Lione, Chgo., 1987—2005, mng. ptnr., 1996—99; ptnr., dir. IP and IP litigation Dykema Gossett, Chgo., 2005—. Adj. prof. law John Marshall Sch. Law, 1989—90, DePaul U. Sch. Law, 1990—92, U. Ill., 1992—; lectr. U. Victoria, Canada, 2002, 04, Oxford U., England, 2003. Co-author: Designing an Effective Intellectual Property Compliance Program; contbr. articles to profl. jours. Legal advisor Legal Aid Soc., Chgo., 1974—76, Pub. Defender's Office, Chgo., 1974. Mem.: ABA, Intellectual Property Owners Assn., Am. Intellectual Property Law Assn., Intellectual Property Law Assn. Chgo. (com. chmn. 1982), Chgo. Bar Assn., Phi Eta Sigma, Sigma Gamma Tau, Sigma Tau, Tau Beta Pi. Jewish. Office: Dykema Gossett 10 S Wacker Dr Ste 2300 Chicago IL 60606 Office Phone: 312-627-2143.

STETLER, DAVID J., lawyer; b. Washington, Sept. 6, 1949; s. C. Joseph and Norine (Delaney) S.; m. Mary Ann Ferguson, Aug. 14, 1971; children: Brian, Christopher, Jennifer. BA, Villanova U., 1971, JD, 1974. Bar: U.S. Supreme Ct. 1978, Ill. 1988, U.S. Ct. Appeals (7th cir.) 1988, U.S. Ct. Appeals (3d cir.) 1992, U.S. Dist. Ct. (ctrl. dist.) 1994, U.S. Ct. Appeals (8th cir.) 1994. Atty. IRS, Washington, 1974-79; spl. atty. tax divsn. Dept. Justice, Washington, 1975-79; asst. atty. U.S. Atty.'s Office, Chgo., 1979-88, dep. chief spl. prosecutions div., 1985-86, chief criminal receiving and appellate divsns., 1986-88; ptnr. McDermott, Will & Emery, Chgo., 1988-98; prin. Stetler & Duffy, Ltd., Chgo., 1998—. Lectr. Atty. Gen. Trial Advocacy Inst., Washington, 1977—. Fellow Internat. Soc. Barristers, Am. Coll. Trial Lawyers; mem. ABA (chmn. midwest subcom. White Collar Crime com. 1991-93), Wong Sun Soc. San Francisco. Office: 11 S LaSalle St Ste 1200 Chicago IL 60603 Office Phone: 312-338-0202. E-mail: dstetler@stetlerandduffy.com.

STEVENS, BRAD K., men's college basketball coach; m. Tracy Stevens; 1 child, Brady. BA in Econs., DePauw U., Greencastle, Ind., 1999. Mktg. assoc. Eli Lilly and Co., Indpls.; coord. basketball ops. Butler U., Indpls., 2000—01, asst. coach, 2001—07, head coach, 2007—. Office: Butler Mens Basketball 510 W 49th St Indianapolis IN 46208 Office Phone: 317-940-9897. E-mail: bksteven@butler.edu.

STEVENS, DAN, state legislator; b. Feb. 23, 1950; m. Barbara; four children. Student, U. Minn. Mem. Minn. Senate from 17th dist., St. Paul, 1993—; bus. mgr.; farmer. Office: Minn State Members 100 Constitution Ave Saint Paul MN 55155-1232

STEVENS, GREG, state official; b. Estherville, Iowa, Mar. 23, 1960; m. Laura Stevens; children: Matthew, Daniel. AA, Iowa Lakes C.C., 1980; BA, U. S.D., 1982; MA, Mankato State U., 1994. State rep., 1999—; instr. Freeman Pub. Schs., 1982—84, Terrill Comty. Schs., 1984—87; tchr. HS English Okoboji Cmty. Schs., 1987—. Asst. minority leader, edn. com., agrl. com.; econ. growth com.; mem. Dem. Cen. Com., 1984—98, Dickinson County Dem. Cen. Com., 1993—97; campaign mgr. Aumer for Statehouse, 1995—96. Coach Nat. Forensics League, Two Diamonds Key, 1995—2004; exec. bd. Iowa HS Speech Assn., 1996—2004; pres., coach Okoboji Little League, 1990—2000; active Cath. Daus. Scholarship Com., West Iowa Debate Com., 1994—2004, Iowa Access Adv. Coun., Info. Tech. Coun., Iowa Child Care Adv. Coun. Mem.: Okoboji Edn. Assn. (chief negotiator 1989—99). Democrat. Roman Catholic.

STEVENS, JANE, advertising executive; Exec. v.p., exec. media dir. Bernstein-Rein Advertising Inc, Kansas City, Mo., 1990—. Office: Bernstein-Rein Advertising Inc 4600 Madison Ave Ste 1500 Kansas City MO 64112-3016

STEVENS, JEREMY R., lawyer; b. Spring Valley, Minn., Sept. 5, 1974; m. Christina Stevens; 2 children. BS in Polit. Sci., Luther Coll., 1997; JD, Hamline U. Sch. Law, 2000. Bar: Minn. 2000. Ptnr. Bird, Jacobsen & Stevens, P.C., Rochester, Minn. Articles editor: Hamline Jour. Law and Pub. Policy. Named a Rising Star, Minn. Super Lawyers mag., 2006. Mem.: Am. Trial Lawyers Assn., Minn. Trial Lawyers Assn., Minn. State Bar Assn. Office: Bird Jacobsen & Stevens PC 305 Ironwood Sq 300 3rd Ave SE Rochester MN 55904 Office Phone: 507-282-1503. E-mail: jeremy@birdjacobsen.com.

STEVENS, KENNETH T., retail executive; b. 1952; Grad., DePauw U., 1974; student, U. Redlands; MBA, U. So. Calif. Former ptnr. McKinsey & Co., Inc.; former sr. v.p. and treas. Pepsico; exec. v.p. mktg. Taco Bell divsn. of Pepsico, 1993—94, pres. and COO, 1994—97; chmn. and CEO Banc One Retail Group, 1997—2000; pres. and COO inChord Comm., 2001—02; exec. v.p. and COO Bath & Body Works divsn. of Ltd. Brands, Inc., 2002—03, pres., 2003—04; CEO Express (subs. Limited Brands), 2004—06; exec. v.p., CFO Limited Brands, Inc., 2006; pres., COO,sec., treas. Tween Brands, Inc., 2007—, also bd. dir., 2007—. Bd. mem. Spartan Stores, 2002—. Office: Tween Brand Inc 8323 Walton Pkwy New Albany OH 43054-9522

STEVENS, LINDA K., lawyer; BA cum laude, Kalamazoo Coll., 1984; JD cum laude, U. Mich., 1987. Bar: Ill. 1987, US Dist. Ct. (no. dist. Ill.) 1987, US Dist. Ct. (ctrl. dist. Ill.), US Ct. Appeals (7th cir.) 1993, US Ct. Appeals (4th cir.). Ptnr. Schiff Hardin, Chgo. Adj. faculty Northwestern U. Sch. Law, Nat. Inst. Trial Advocacy. Contbr. articles to law jours. Mem.: ABA. Office: Schiff Hardin 6600 Sears Tower Chicago IL 60606-6473 Office Phone: 312-258-5667. Office Fax: 312-258-5600. E-mail: lstevens@schiffhardin.com.

STEVENS, MARK, banker; b. Chgo., May 24, 1947; s. Joseph K. and Phoebe (Copeland) S.; m. Joyce Sue Skinner, Aug. 22, 1970; children: Mark Benjamin, Katherine Joyce. BA, W.Va. U., 1969, JD, 1972. V.p. Continental Ill. Nat. Bank & Trust Co., Chgo., 1972-79, No. Trust Co., Chgo., 1979-81; pres., CEO, No. Trust Bank Fla., Sarasota, 1981-87, chmn., pres., CEO, 1987-96; exec. v.p. No. Trust Co. & No. Trust Corp., 1996-98, pres. personal fin. svcs., 1998—. Pres. No. Trust Fla. Corp., Miami, 1987-96, chmn., 1996—. Trustee Ctr. Fine Arts, 1988-94, 1988-94, Miami Children's Hosp. Found., 1993-96, South Fla. Performing Arts Ctr. Found., 1993—, U. Miami, 1994, Beacon Coun., 1990—; mem. U. Miami Citizens Bd., 1988-89, Young Pres.'s Orgn., 1988—; bd. dirs. Miami Coalition and Task Force, 1988—, New World Symphony, 1991—; charter mem. Coun. of 100 Fla. Internat. Univ. Found., 1990—; hon. bd. dirs. Audubon House; mem. Orange Bowl Com., 1994. Mem. Young Pres. Orgn., Riviera Country Club, Miami Club. Office: The No Trust Co 50 S Lasalle St Chicago IL 60603-1006

STEVENS, PAUL, newspaper editor; Bur. chief AP, Kansas City, Mo., 1980—. Office: 215 W Pershing Rd Kansas City MO 64108-4317

STEVENS, PAUL G., JR., brokerage house executive; b. 1944; With Saul Lerner Co., NYC, 1968-71, Lombard Street Inc., NYC, 1971-72, Ragner Option Corp., NYC, 1975-89, Am. Stock Exch., NYC, 1989—, pres., COO, treas.; pres. Options Clearing Corp., Chgo., 1989—.

STEVENS, ROBERT JAY, magazine editor; b. Detroit, July 25, 1945; s. Jay Benjamin and Louise Ann (Beyreuther) S.; m. Dahlia Jean Conger, Aug. 15, 1970; children— Sandra Lee, Julie Ann. Student, Huron Coll., SD, 1963-66, Wayne State U., 1968-71. Sr. staff writer Automotive News, Detroit, 1968-71; editor Excavating Contractor mag., Cummins Pub. Co., Oak Park, Mich., 1971-78, Chevrolet's Pro Jour., Sandy Corp., Southfield, Mich., 1978—79, Cars and Parts mag., Cars and Parts Corvette mag. Amos Press, Sidney, Ohio, 1979—; truck editor Automotive Design & Devel. mag., 1971-78. Lectr., speaker in field. Contbr. articles to profl. jours.; author: numerous poems. Served with AUS, 1966-68, Vietnam. Decorated Air medal, Bronze star, Commendation medal; recipient Alphomega Publs. award, 1965—, Robert F. Boger Meml. award for outstanding constrn. journalism, 1975, U.L.C.C. nat. editl. award, Am. Pub. Works Assn., 1978, Moto award for outstanding automotive journalism, Internat. Automotive Media Conf., 1997, 1998, 1999, 2000, 2001, Internal. Automotive Media Conf., 2002, Best of Divsn. award, Internat. Automotive Media Conf., 2001, Folio mag. Editl. Excellence award, 2001. Mem. Detroit Auto Writers (past dir.), Internat. Motor Press Assn., Antique Automobile Club Am. (Lifetime Achievement award 2005. Republican. Presbyterian. Home: 653 Ridgeway Dr Sidney OH 45365-3432 Office: PO Box 482 911 Vandemark Rd Sidney OH 45365 E-mail: bstevens@carsandparts.com.

STEVENS, STANLEY M., lawyer; b. Dec. 21, 1948; m. Kristin Stevens. BA, U. Mo., Columbia, 1970; JD, U. Chgo., 1973. Bar: Ga. 1973, US Dist. Ct. No. Dist. Ga. 1974, Ill. 1976, US. Dist. Ct. No. Dist. Ill. 1977, Fla. 1987, US Dist. Ct. Mid. Dist. Fla. 1987. Exec. v.p., chief legal counsel, sec. Equity Office Properties Trust, Chgo., 1996—2007; ptnr. Sidley Austin LLP, Chgo., 2007—. Office: Sidley Austin LLP One S Dearborn Chicago IL 60603

STEVENS, THOMAS CHARLES, lawyer; b. Auburn, NY, Oct. 17, 1949; s. Alice (Kerlin) S.; m. Christine Eleanor Brown, June 2, 1973; children: Erin, Leigh, Timothy. BA, SUNY, Albany, 1971; JD, Duke U., 1974. Bar: Ohio 1974. Mng. ptnr. Thompson, Hine & Flory, Cleve., 1991-96; vice-chmn. KeyCorp., Cleve., 1996—, chief adminstrv. officer, 1996—. Bd. dirs. KeyCorp. Trustee Greater Cleve. Growth Assn., 1993-96, Greater Cleve. Roundtable, 1993-2003,(chmn. of bd. trustees), Playhouse Sq. Found., 1998—, Greater Cleve. (Ohio) Partnerships, 2003—; active Leadership Cleve., 1992-93, Young Audiences, 1999—, 1999 United Way Campaign; mem. Fin. Svcs. Roundtable, 1997—. Mem. ABA, Cleve. Bar Assn., Am. Soc. Corp. Secs., N.Y. Bankers Assn., Nisi Prius. Office: KeyCorp 127 Public Sq Cleveland OH 44114-1306 E-mail: thomas_stevens@keybank.com.

STEVENS, TONY, broadcast executive, radio personality; b. Jersey City, June 7, 1955; s. Baldassare and Josephine Frances (Costanza) Restivo; m. Maria Ciliberti, July 31, 1976 (div.); children: Anthony Jr., Paul; m. Geri Suzanne Hastert, Oct. 24, 1987; 1 child, Nicholas. BA in Comm., U. Mo., Kansas City, 1985. Profl. musician, Kansas City, Mo., 1974—; owner Wizards Arcade, Independence, Mo., 1982-85; news dir. Sta. KBSM, Blue Springs, Mo., 1984-85; program dir. Sta. KCKM, Kansas City, Kans., 1985-87; on air personality, music dir., asst. program dir. Sta. KFKF, Kansas City, Mo., 1984—. Music cons. Sta. WLLR, Davenport, Iowa, 1990—; feature writer Country Star mag., 1990. Hon. chmn. Multiple Sclerosis Soc., Kansas City, Mo., 1991-92. Roman Catholic. Avocations: collecting records, softball.

STEVENSON, ADLAI EWING, III, lawyer, retired senator; b. Chgo., Oct. 10, 1930; s. Adlai Ewing and Ellen (Borden) S.; m. Nancy L. Anderson, June 25, 1955; children: Adlai Ewing IV, Lucy W., Katherine R., Warwick L. Grad., Milton Acad., 1948; AB, Harvard U., 1952, LL.B., 1957. Bar: Ill. 1957, D.C. 1977. Law clk. Ill. Supreme Ct., 1957-58; assoc. Mayer, Brown & Platt, Chgo., 1958-66, ptnr., 1966-67, 81-83, of counsel, 1983-91; treas. State of Ill., 1967-70; U.S. senator from Ill., 1970-81; chmn. SC&M Internat. Ltd., Chgo., 1991-95, pres., 1995-98, chmn. bd., 1998—; co-chmn. Huamei Capital Co., Inc., 2005—. Mem. Ill. Ho. of Reps., 1965-67; Dem. candidate for gov. of Ill., 1982, 86. Capt. USMCR, 1952-54. Office: Ste 2760 71 S Wacker Dr Chicago IL 60606

STEVENSON, CHERYL D., science educator, researcher; PhD, Tex. A&M Univ., 1969. With Ill. State Univ., 1977—, disting. prof., phys. chemistry. Contbr. several articles to peer-reviewed jours. Recipient award for Rsch. at an Undergraduate Institution, Am. Chem. Soc., 2007. Office: 219 Science Laboratory Bldg 214 Julian Hall 4160 Dept Chemistry Illinois State University Normal IL 61790-4160 Office Phone: 309-438-7300. Business E-Mail: cdsteve@ilstu.edu.

STEVENSON, DAN CHARLES, state legislator; m. Dawn Stevenson. Student, Calumet Coll. Steelworker Inland Steel Co.; mem. Ind. State Ho. of Reps. Dist. 11, mem. labor and employment com., mem. local govt. and pub. safety com. Mem. Jaycees, Ind. Young Dems. (former pres.), Hessville Dem. Club. Office: Ind House of Reps State Capitol Indianapolis IN 46204

STEVENSON, JO ANN C., federal bankruptcy judge; b. 1942; AB, Rutgers U., 1965; JD cum laude, Detroit Coll. Law, 1979. Bar: Mich. 1979. Law clk. to Vincent J. Brennan, Mich. Ct. Appeals, Detroit, 1979; law clk. to Cornelia G. Kenendy, U.S. Ct. Appeals for 6th Cir., Detroit, 1980; assoc. Hertzberg, Jacob & Weingarten, P.C., Detroit, 1980-87; chief judge U.S. Bankruptcy Ct., Grand Rapids, Mich., 1987—. Office: US Bankruptcy Ct NW1 1 Divsn Grand Rapids MI 49503

STEVENSON, JUDY G., instrument manufacturing executive; Bookeeper Magnetrol, Naperville, Ill., 1964-65, accounting supr./mgr., 1965-76, treas./admin. v.p., 1967-75, pres., 1975-78, owner, 1978—. Bd. trustees N. Ctrl. Coll.; established Harold E. Meiley, Judy G. Stevenson, African Scholarship Funds; supports Naperville Heritage Soc., Edward Hosp., the Riverwalk, Millennium Carillon Found., Good Samaritan Hosp., DuPage Intergenerational Village. Recipient YWCA Businesswoman Yr. DuPage Co., 1985, YWCA Outstanding Woman Leader DuPage Co., 1997, Top 500 Woman-Owned Businesses, Working Woman Mag., 1998. Mem. Chief Exec. Officers Club, Nat. Assn. Women Bus. Owners, Nat. Assn. Female Execs., Eastern Star. Avocations: gardening, gourmet cooking, music, ballet, horses. Office: Magnetrol Internat 5300 Belmont Rd Downers Grove IL 60515-4499

STEVENSON, KENNETH LEE, chemist, educator; b. Ft. Wayne, Ind., Aug. 1, 1939; s. Willard Henry and Luella Marie (Meyer) S.; m. Virginia Grace Lowe, Dec. 26, 1959 (dec. Mar. 1991); children: Melinda Anne, Jill Marie; m. Carmen Ramona Kmety, May 9, 1992; 1 child, Sarah Ann. BS, Purdue U., 1961, MS, 1965; PhD, U. Mich., 1968. Tchr. Ladoga High Sch., Ind., 1961-63; tchr. Central High Sch., Pontiac, Mich., 1963-65; prof. chemistry Ind.-Purdue U., Ft. Wayne, 1968—, chmn. dept. chemistry, 1979—86, 1987—2003, acting dean Sch. Sci. and Humanities, 1986-87. Sabbatical visitor Solar Energy Research Inst., Golden, Colo., 1980; vis. faculty N.Mex. State U., Las Cruces, 1975-76 Author: Charge Transfer Photochemistry of Coordination Compounds, 1993, also numerous rsch. papers. Mem. Am. Chem. Soc. (chmn. Northeastern Ind. sect. 1978-79, Chemist of Yr. 1979, 93), Inter-Am. Photochem. Soc., Phi Kappa Phi, Sigma Xi. Office: Ind U-Purdue U Dept Chemistry Fort Wayne IN 46805 E-mail: stevenso@ipfw.edu.

STEVENSON, ROBERT BENJAMIN, III, prosthodontist, writer; b. Topeka, Feb. 13, 1950; s. Robert Benjamin and Martha (McClelland) S.; m. Barbara Jean Sulick, June 6, 1975; children: Jody Ann, Robert Woodrow. BS, U. Miami, Coral Gables, Fla., 1972; DDS, Ohio State U., 1975, MS, MA, 1980, cert. in prosthodontics splty. tng., 1980. Practice dentistry specializing in prosthodontics, Columbus, Ohio, 1981—; clin. asst. prof. Ohio State U., Columbus, 1981-87, 98—. Chmn. oral cancer com. Columbus Dental Soc., 1981-85, Am. Cancer Soc., Columbus, 1985-97; trustee Ohio Divsn, 1997-2000; vol. dentist Provodencialis Ctr., Turks and Chicos Islands, Brit. West Indies, 1982-87. Editor Columbus Dental Soc. Bull., 1981-87, 89-92; assoc. editor Ohio State U. Dental Alumni Quar., 1982—, Am. Med. Writer's Assn. Ohio Newsletter, 1983-86, Ohio State Journalism Alumni Assn. Newsletter, 1986-88, alumni spotlight editor, 1995—; assoc. editor Jour. Prosthetic Dentistry, 1987-92; mem. editl. coun. Jour. Prosthetic Dentistry, 2002—05; inventor intraoral measuring device. Vol. Am. Cancer Soc., Columbus, 1982—. Served to capt. USAF, 1975-78. Fellow Am. Coll. Dentists; mem. ADA, Am. Coll. Prosthodontists, Ohio Dental Assn. (alt. del. 1982-89, del. 1990-92, 97-2003, editor new products newsletter 1988-97), Carl Boucher Prosthodontic Conf. (editor 1987-92, sec. 1992-98, treas. 1998—), Procrastinator's Club Am, Columbus Downtown Quarterback Club, Agonis Club. Avocations: playing electric organ, golf, music, reading. Home: 1300 Southport Cir Columbus OH 43235-7642 Office: Riverview Profl Village 3600 Olentangy River Rd Columbus OH 43214 Office Phone: 614-451-2767. Personal E-mail: lesgobucks@aol.com.

STEWARD, DAVID L., technology company executive; b. Clinton, Mo. m. Thelma Steward; children: David, Kimberly. BS, Ctrl. Mo. State U., 1973. Various sales and mktg. positions Wagner Elec., Mo. Pacific Railroad, Fed. Express; founder, chmn. World Wide Tech., Maryland Heights, Mo., 1990—. Bd. dir. St. Louis Cmty. Coll. Found., Civic Progress of St. Louis, St. Louis Regional Chamber and Growth Assn., Mo. Tech. Corp., Webster U., First Banks, Inc., St. Louis Sci. Ctr., United Way of Greater St. Louis Bd., Greater St. Louis Area Coun. of Boy Scouts of Am., Harris-Stowe State Coll. African-Am. Bus. Leadership Coun., RCGA, Barnes-Jewish Hosp.; chaired (with wife) United Way's 2000 African-American Leadership Giving Initiative. Named 14th Best Am. Entrepreneur, Success Mag., 1998, Minority Small Bus. Person of Yr., Small Bus. Adminstrn., 1997—98, Entrepreneur of Yr. in Tech., Ernst & Young, 1998, #1 African-Am.-Owned Bus. in US, Black Enterprise Mag., 2000; named to Small Bus. Adminstrn. Hall of Fame, 2001. Office: World Wide Technology 60 Weldon Pkwy Maryland Heights MO 63043-3237

STEWARD, JAMES, museum director, art history educator; BA, U. Va., Charlottesville; MA, NYU, NYC; PhD in art hist., Oxford U., England. Prof. hist. art U. Mich., Ann Arbor; dir. U. Mich. Mus. Art, Ann Arbor. Office: U Mich Mus Art 915 E Washington St Ste 0540 Ann Arbor MI 48109 Office Phone: 734-764-0395. E-mail: jsteward@umich.edu.

STEWARD, WELDON CECIL, architecture educator, architect, consultant; b. Pampa, Tex., Apr. 7, 1934; s. Weldon C. and Lois (Maness) S.; m. Mary Jane Nedbalek, June 9, 1956; children: Karen A., W. Craig. Cert. in architecture and planning, Ecole des Beaux Arts, Fontainebleu, France, 1956; B.Arch., Tex. A&M U, 1957; MS in Architecture, Columbia U., 1961; LHD (hon.), Drury Coll., 1991. Registered architect, Tex., Nebr. Designer Perkins & Will, Architects, White Plains, NY, 1961-62; asst. prof. architecture Tex. A&M U., College Station, 1962-67, assoc. chmn. Sch. Architecture, 1966-69, assoc. dean, prof. Coll. Environ. Design, 1969-73; dean, prof. Coll. Architecture U. Nebr., Lincoln, 1973-2000, emeritus dean, prof. arch. and planning, 2000—; founding pres. Joslyn Castle Inst. Sustainable Cmtys., Omaha, 1996—; W. Cecil Steward dist. chair sustainable arch. U. Nebr., Lincoln, 2000—02; founding dir. Nebr. Ctr. for Sustainable Constrn., 2003; editor-in-chief Greensource Report, Atlanta, 2002—04; founding chmn. UN-Habitat North/North Network Urban Sustainability and Leadership, 2004—. Adj. prof. Sch. Arch. U. Hawaii, 1999—; ednl. cons. People's Republic of China, 1979--; project dir. Imo State U. Planning, Nigeria, 1981-88; vis. prof. Tong ji U., Shanghai, 1984; hon. prof. N.W. Inst. Architects Engrs., Xian, 1989; specialist Design USA, USSR, 1990; co-chmn. nat. coordination com. AIA Nat. Coun. Archtl. Registration Bd. Intership, Washington, 1980-81; bd. visitors Drury Coll., 1980-97, Coll. Arch. U. Miami, Fla., 1993-96, Judson Coll., 1998-2000; mem. nat. design rev. bd. GSA, Washington, 1994—; mem. founding bd. dirs. East/West Pacific Arch., U. Hawaii, 1995—; vice chmn. Design Futures Coun., Reston, Va., 1995-2000; sr. fellow Design Futures Coun., 1999. Designer, Quinnipiac Elem. Sch., New Haven, Conn., 1961 (Am Assn. Sch. Adminstrs. Exhibit 1969), J.J. Buser Residence, Bryan, Tex., 1969, Steward Urban Residence, Lincoln, Nebr., 1994. Mem. Lincoln Architects, Engrs. Selection Bd., 1979-88; mem. Nat. Com. for U.S.-China Rels., N.Y.C., 1981—, Nebr. Capitol Environ. Commn., 1989-97; bd. dirs. Downtown Lincoln Assn., 1996-2006, KZUM Pub. Radio, 1997-2001; mem. Lincoln/Lancaster County Planning Commn., 1996-2004, chmn., 2003-04; co-chmn. steering com. City of Lincoln Downtown Master Plan, 2004—; bd. dirs. Lincoln Children's Mus., 1996-2001; profl. adviser nat. design competition Wick Alumni Ctr., Lincoln, 1981; steering com. Internat. Coun. Tall Bldgs., 1992-96. Recipient T.R. Russel award for Newsletters, 2003; named Disting. Alumnus, Tex. A&M U., 1998; Grad. fellow Columbia U., 1960. Mem. AIA (pres. Brazos chpt. 1969, chmn. profl. devel. com. 1979, bd. dirs. 1979-90, dir. Cen. States 1987-90, nat. pres. 1991-92, Coll. of Fellows 1983, Tri-Nat. com. 1991-02, Nebr. Gold medal 1997, nat. AIA/ACSA Topaz award for excellence in architecture 1999, honor award for excellence in urban design 2005, charter award for excellence Congress for New Urbanism 2005); mem. Am. Planning Assn. (chair Dubai Internat. award for sustaining cmty. 2000), Nebr. Soc. Architects (bd. dirs. 1977-2000), Archtl. Found. Nebr. (bd. dirs. 1981-94, treas. 1981-94), Assn. Collegiate Schs. Architecture (bd. dirs. 1975-79), Nat. Archtl. Accrediting Bd. (bd. dirs. 1986-89, pres. 1988-89), Kazakhstan Union Architecture, Assn. Siamese Architects, Royal Inst. Canadian Architects, Fedn. Mexican Achitects, Japan Inst. Architects (hon.), Tau Sigma Delta (medal 1999), Phi Kappa Phi, Phi Beta Delta. Home: 125 N 11th St Lincoln NE 68508-3605 Office: U Nebr Coll Architecture Lincoln NE 68588 Home Phone: 402-475-1275; Office Phone: 402-472-0087. Business E-Mail: csteward1@sustainabledesign.com. E-mail: csteward1@unl.edu.

STEWART, ALBERT ELISHA, safety engineer, engineering executive; b. Urbana, Mo., Dec. 20, 1927; s. Albert E. and Maurine (Lighter) S.; m. Elizabeth O. Tice, May 31, 1958 (div.); children: Sheryl E., Mical A. BA, U. Kans., 1949; MS, U. Mo., 1958, MBA, 1970; PhD, Western States U., 1984. Registered profl. engr., Calif., cert. safety engr., cert. indsl. hygenist. Sales engr. Kaiser Aluminum and Chem. Co., Toledo, 1949-56; tchr. Kansas City (Mo.) Pub. Schs., 1959-65; indsl. hygienist Bendix Corp., Kansas City, 1960-65; safety adminstr. Gulf R&D, Merriam, Kans., 1968-71; sr. indsl. hygienist USDOL-OSHA, Kansas City, 1971-77; pres. Stewart Indsl. Hygiene, Kansas City, 1977—. Adj. prof. Cen. Mo. State U. Mem. Boy Scouts Am. With U.S. Army, 1950-53. Mem. Am. Indsl. Hygiene Assn., Am. Chem. Soc., Am. Acad. Indsl. Hygiene, Am. Soc. Safety Engrs., Am. Welding Soc., Nat. Mgmt. Assn., Nat. Sci. Tchrs. Assn., Adminstrv. Govt. Soc., DAV, ARC, Alpha Chi Sigma. Episcopalian. Avocations: fishing, golf, travel.

STEWART, DAN, state representative; b. Columbus, Ohio; Student in Polit. Sci., Ohio State U. Legis. dir. Hilltop Internat. Union Dist. 1199; state rep. dist. 25 Ohio Ho. of Reps., Columbus, 2002—, ranking minority mem., regulatory reform subcom., mem. commerce and labor, energy and environment, pub. utilities, and state govt. coms., and ethics and elections subcom. Hilltop Area Commr. Office: 77 S High St 11th fl Columbus OH 43215-6111

STEWART, J. DANIEL, air force official; b. Savannah, Ga., June 20, 1941; s. Benjamin F. and Bessie L. (Edenfield) S.; m. Rebecca M. Smith; children: Daniel, Laura. BS in Aero. Engring., Ga. Inst. Tech., 1963, MS in Aero. Engring., 1965, PhD in Aero. Engring., 1967; M. in Mgmt. Sci., Stanford U., 1979. Mem. tech. staff applied mechanics divsn. Aerospace Corp., El Segundo, Calif., 1967-74; br. chief tech. divsn. Air Force Rocket Propulsion Lab., Edwards AFB, Calif., 1974-78, asst. for R&D mgmt., 1979-81; divsn. chief Air Force Armament Divsn., Eglin AFB, Fla., 1981-83; dir. drone control program office 3246 Test Wing, Eglin AFB, Fla., 1983-85, joint dir. US/Allied munitions program office, 1985-86; tech. dir. rsch./devel./acquisitions Air Force Armament Divsn., Eglin AFB, Fla., 1986-88; asst. to comdr. Air Force Munitions Divsn., Eglin AFB, Fla., 1988-90; tech. dir. Air Force Devel. and Test Ctr., Eglin AFB, 1990-93, exec. dir., 1993-98, Air Armament Ctr., Eglin AFB, Fla., 1998-99, Air Force Materiel Command, Wright-Paterson AFB, Ohio, 1999—. Mem. policy coun. Scientist and Engr. Career Program, Randolph AFB, Tex., 1994—, chmn. career devel. panel, 1994-96. Bd. dirs. Internat. Found. for Telemetering, Woodland Hills, Calif., 1991-95; mem. enging. adv. bd. U. Fla., Gainesville, 1988—; mem. citizens adv. com. U. West Fla., Pensacola, 1991—; mem. civilian exec. adv. bd. Air Force Materiel Command, 1990—, also former chmn.; mem. curricular adv. com. Def. Test and Evaluation Profl. Inst., 1991—. Recipient Presdl. Meritorious Rank award Pres. of U.S., 1993. Mem. Air Force Assn. (Lewis H. Brereton award 1994), Sr. Exec. Assn., Am. Def. Preparedness Assn., Internat. Test and Evaluation Assn. (Cross medal 1994), Assn. of Old Crows, Fed. Exec. Inst. Alumni, Gulf Coast Alliance for Tech. Transfer. Avocations: tennis, golf, fishing. Office: Air Force Materiel Command 4375 Chidlaw Rd Wright Patterson AFB OH 45433

STEWART, JAMES BREWER, historian, writer, college administrator; b. Cleve., Aug. 8, 1940; s. Richard Henry and Marion Elizabeth (Brewer) S.; m. Dorothy Ann Carlson; children: Rebecca Ann, Jennifer Lynn. BA, Dartmouth Coll., 1962; PhD, Case Western Res. U., 1968. Asst. prof. history Carrol Coll., Waukesha, Wis., 1968-69, Macalester Coll., St. Paul, 1969-79, prof. history, 1979—, James Wallace prof. history, 2002—, provost St. Paul, 1986—91. Cons. Am. Coun. of Learned Socs., NYC, 1988-92. Author: Joshua R. Giddings & the Tactics of Radical Politics, 1970, Holy Warriors: Abolitionists & Slavery, 1976, rev. editon 1997, Liberty's Hero: Wendell Phillips, 1986 (Best Biography award, Soc. Midland Authors 1986), William Lloyd Garrison and the Challenge of Emmancipation, 1992, To Heal the Scourge of Prejudice: The Life and Writings of Hosea Easton, 1999, Race and the Construction of the Republican State, 2000. Rsch. fellow EH, 1973, Am. Coun. Learned Socs., 1984. Mem. Am. Hist. Assn., Orgn. Am. Historians (nom. com. 1988-92), Soc. Historians of the Early Republic (exec. com. 1987-94, editl. bd. 1999—, pres.-elect 2003—), Phi Beta Kappa. Avocations: camping, gardening, furniture restoration. Home: 1924 Princeton Ave Saint Paul MN 55105-1523 Office: Macalester Coll Dept Of History Saint Paul MN 55105 E-mail: stewart@macalester.edu.

STEWART, JIMMY, state representative; BBA in Econs., Marshall U.; MBA, Xavier U. Salesman Caterpillar Equipment, Athens, Ohio, 1995—98; state rep. dist. 92 Ohio Ho. of Reps., Columbus, 2002—, vice chmn., higher edn. subcom., mem. banking pensions & securities, econ. devel. and tech., homeland security engring. and archtl. design, and fin. and appropriations coms. Councilman, 1st ward Athens (Ohio) City Coun., 1997—98, chmn., sts. and recreation com.; appt. city auditor Athens, 1998—. Office: 77 S High St 11th fl Columbus OH 43215-6111

STEWART, JOHN HARGER, music educator; b. Cleve., Mar. 31, 1940; s. Cecil Tooker and Marian (Harger) S.; m. Julia Wallace, Aug. 14, 1977; children: Barbara, Cecily Bronwen. BA, Yale U., 1962; MA, Brown U., 1972; cert., New Eng. Conservatory, 1965. With various operas including Santa Fe Opera, N.Y.C. Opera, Met. Opera, U.S. and Europe, 1965—; lectr. Mt. Holyoke Coll., South Hadley, Mass., 1988-90; dir. vocal activities Washington U., St. Louis, 1990—, dir. Friends of Music. Office: Dept Music Washington U Campus Box 1030 One Brookings Dr Saint Louis MO 63130-4899 Home Phone: 314-533-0665; Office Phone: 314-935-5597. Business E-Mail: jstewart@wustl.edu.

STEWART, MELBOURNE GEORGE, JR., physicist, researcher; b. Detroit, Sept. 30, 1927; s. Melbourne George and Ottilie (Tuholke) S.; m. Charlotte L. Ford, Jan. 23, 1954; children— Jill K., John H., Kevin G. AB, U. Mich., 1949, MS, 1950, PhD, 1955. Research assoc. dept. physics AEC, Ames Lab., Iowa State U., 1955-56, asst. prof., 1956-62, assoc. prof., 1962-63; prof. Wayne State U., Detroit, 1963-94, prof. emeritus, 1994—, chmn. dept. physics, 1963-73, assoc. provost for faculty relations, 1973-86; hon. research fellow Univ. Coll., London, 1986-87,93. Editorial bd.: Wayne State U. Press, 1969-73. Served with AUS, 1946-47. Mem. Am. Phys. Soc., AAAS, Sigma Xi, Phi Beta Kappa. Office: Dept Physics Wayne State U Detroit MI 48202

STEWART, MIZELL, III, editor; b. Ohio, 1966; m. Valerie Morgan-Stewart. BA, Bowling Green State U., Huron, Ohio, 1991. Reporter Springfield News-Sun, Ohio; reporter & editor Dayton Daily News, Ohio; local news editor Akron Beacon Jour., Ohio, 1994—2000, mng. editor, 2006, editor, 2006—; mng. editor Tallahassee Dem., Fla., 2000—03, editor & v.p., 2003—05. Office: Akron Beacon Journal PO Box 640 Akron OH 44309-0640 Office Phone: 330-996-3700. Office Fax: 330-376-9235.

STEWART, RICHARD DONALD, internist, educator, writer; b. Lakeland, Fla., Dec. 26, 1926; s. LeRoy Hepburn and Zoa Irene (Hachet) S.; m. Mary Leeuw, June 14, 1952; children: R. Scot, Gregory D., Mary E. AB, U. Mich., 1951, MD, 1955, MPH, 1962; MA, U. Wis. Milw., 1979; PhD in English, U. Wis., Milw., 1997. Diplomate Am. Bd. Internal Medicine, Am. Bd. Med. Toxicology, Acad. Toxicol. Scis. Intern Saginaw (Mich.) Gen. Hosp., 1955-56; resident in internal medicine U. Mich. Med. Ctr., Ann Arbor, 1959-62; dir. med. rsch. sect. Dow Chem. Co., Midland, Mich., 1962-66; staff physician Midland Hosp., 1962-66; assoc. prof. preventive medicine Med. Coll. Wis., Milw., 1966-68, prof., chmn. dept. environ. medicine, 1968—78, prof. emergency med., 1989—91, adj. prof. dept. pharmacology and toxicology, 1978—. Cons. Children's Hosp. Wis., 1989-93, Internal Medicine St. Mary's Hosp., Racine, Wis., 1983-93; prof., dir. med. toxicology fellowship Dept. Emergency Medicine Milw. Regional Med. Ctr., 1989-91; sr. attending staff, 1967-90; staff Internal Medicine St. Luke's Hosp., Racine, 1983-93; med. dir. Poison Control Ctr. Southeastern Wis., 1989-93; corp. med. advisor S.C. Johnson & Son, Inc., Racine, 1971-78, corp. med. dir., 1978-89. Author: (med. biography) Leper Priest of Molokai, 2000. Mem. adv. med. staff Milw. Fire Dept., 1975—. Cadet USAF, 1945-46. Fellow ACP, Am. Coll. Occupl. Medicine, Am. Acad. Clin. Toxicology, Acad. Toxicological Scis.; mem. AMA, Soc. Toxicology, Wis. State Med. Soc., Racine Acad. Medicine, Rotary Internat., Phi Theta Kappa, Phi Kappa Phi, Sigma Tau Delta. Achievements include invention of medical devices including the hollow fiber artificial kidney and capillary artificial lung; being leader of team that performed first human dialyses with the Hollow Fiber Artificial Kidney, beginning Aug.4, 1967. This artificial kidney is universally used for long-term dialysis. Avocations: hiking, literature, creative writing. Home and Office: 5337 Wind Point Rd Racine WI 53402-2322 Office Phone: 262-639-6483.

STEWART, ROGER, state senator; b. Oct. 1931; m. Jennie Stewart; 3 children. Student, Cornell Coll. Mem. Iowa State Senate, DesMoines, 2003—, mem. commerce com., econ. growth com., local govt. com., ways and means com. Active Regional Workforce Investment Bd., Maquoketa Contact Team for Econ. Devel., Jackson County Revolving Loan Fund. Recipient Chamber Friends of Agr. award, Nat. Banking award. Home: 3936 317th Ave Preston IA 52069 Office: State Capitol Bldg East 12th and Grand Des Moines IA 50319

STEWART, TODD I., military officer; BSCE, Mich. Technol. U., 1968; MS in Engring. Adminstrn., So. Meth. U., 1971; disting. grad., Squadron Officer Sch., 1974; PhD in Mgmt., U. Nebr., 1980; disting. grad., Air Command and Staff Coll., 1982; grad., Air War Coll., 1989. Commd. 2d lt. USAF, 1968, advanced through grades to brigadier gen., 1995; chief of programs 4683d Air Base Group, Thule Air Base, Greenland, 1971-72; civil engring. staff officer Hdqs. Strategic Air Command, Offutt AFB, Nebr., 1972-77; assoc. prof. mgmt. Grad. Sch. Sys. and Logistics Air Force Inst. Tech., Wright-Patterson AFB, Ohio, 1977-81; chief programs divsn., dep. dir. programs dir. engring./svc. Hdqs. U.S. Air Forces in Europe, Ramstein Air Base, West Germany, 1982-85; comdr. 36th Civil Engring. Squadron, Bitburg Air Base, West Germany, 1985-88; dir. plans and programs Office of Civil Engr. Hdqs. USAF, Washington, 1989-91, dep. civil engr. Office of Civil Engr., 1991-94; command civil engr. Hdqs. Air Edn. and Tng. Command, Randolph AFB, Tex., 1994-95, Hdqs. Air Force Materiel Command, Wright-Patterson AFB, 1995—; maj. gen. USAF. Decorated Legion of Merit, Meritorious Svc. medal with 3 oak leaf clusters; recipient Curtina ward Soc. Mil. Engrs., 1988, Newman medal Soc. Mil. Engrs., 1993. Office: HQ AFMC/XP 4375 Chidlaw Rd Wright Patterson AFB OH 45433-5066

STIEFF, JOHN JOSEPH, lawyer; b. Indpls., Feb. 28, 1952; s. James Frederick and Mary Therese (Bisch) S.; m. Dusty Lee-Ann Warner, Apr. 21, 1989(dec.); stepchildren: Robert Franklin Russell, E.I. Annie Russell. BA with Distinction, Ind. U., 1973, JD, 1977. Bar: Ind. 1977. Sr. atty. Office of Bill Drafting & Rsch., Legislative Svcs. Agy., Indpls., 1977-86; dep. dir. and asst. revisor of statutes Office of Code Revision, Legislative Svcs. Agy., Indpls., 1986-92, dir. and revisor of statutes, 1992—. Adj. prof. law Ind. Univ., Bloomington, 1985-86; instr. continuing legal edn. Ind. Gen. Assembly, Indpls., 1987-96; faculty mem. Nat. Conf. State Legislatures, Denver, Colo., 1988-89; supervising atty. program on law and state govt. Ind. U. Sch. Law, Indpls., 2001—; assoc commr. Nat. Conf. Commrs. on Uniform State Laws, Chgo., 1993—; mem. style com. Nat. Conf. Commrs. on Uniform State Laws, 2005-. Editor in chief: (books) The Acts of Indiana, 1986—, The Indiana Code, 1993—; ast. editor, The Indiana Code, 1986-92. Poetry instr. Gage Inst. for Gifted Children, Indpls., 1982-86. Named Hoosier Scholar, Indiana Commn. for Higher Edn., 1970-73. Mem. Writer's Ctr. of Indpls. (founding mem.), Ind. U. Varsity Club. Avocations: travel, photography, writing poetry, American blues music. Home: 7707 Windy Hill Way Indianapolis IN 46239-8749 Office: Legislative Svcs Agy Office Code Revision 1 N Capitol Ave Ste 420 Indianapolis IN 46204-2097

STIEGEL, MICHAEL ALLEN, lawyer; b. Greenfield, Mass., Sept. 15, 1946; s. Sid James and Ida Eleanor (Solomon) S.; m. Marsha Palmer, Sept. 10, 1983. BA, U. Ariz., Tucson, 1968; JD cum laude, Loyola U., Chgo., 1971. Bar: Ill. 1971, US Dist. Ct. Ill. 1971, US Ct. Appeals (7th cir.) 1971, US Ct. Appeals (1st cir.) 1975, US Ct. Appeals (6th cir.) 1991, US Supreme Ct. 1975, Wis. 1985, Fla. 1987. Law clk. to fed. judge William Lynch U.S. Dist. Ct. Ill., Chgo., 1971—72; mng. ptnr. Arnstein & Lehr, Chgo., 1985—98; ptnr. Michael Best and Friedrich, 1998—, co-chair trial dept., 1998—2003, elected mgmt. com., 2003—. Adj. prof. law orthwestern U.; faculty Nat. Inst. Trial Advocacy, La. State U. Trial Advocacy Program, 1995-2000. Contbr. articles to profl. jours. Mem. fin. com. Lynn Martin for Senate, Ill., 1989-90. Mem. ABA (pres., sects. on litig. and bus. law, vice chmn. trial evidence com. litig. sect. 1990-91, co-chmn. trial evidence com. 1991-95, lawyers conf. stds.andards for admissibility of technologically sophisticated evidence comm., co-chair nat. CLE programs 1995-97, coun. 1997-2000, mem. exec. com. 2000—, budget officer 2000-02, revenue officer, 2002-06, litig. sect. advisor, uniform laws commn., litig. sect. liaison, drafting com. on Model Punitive Damages Act, appointee to Nat. Conf. Attys. & CPA, 2005, atty.-client privilege task force liaison), Ill. Bar Assn., Fla. Bar Assn., Wis. Bar Assn., Chgo. Bar Assn. (chair large firm com. 2002-04), Econ. Club Chgo. (membership com.). Avocations: sports, reading, horse racing syndications. Office: Michael Best Friedrich 70 W Madison St Ste 3500 Chicago IL 60602-4224 Office Phone: 312-836-5073. Business E-Mail: mastiegel@michaelbest.com.

STIEHL, WILLIAM D., federal judge; b. 1925; m. Celeste M. Sullivan; children: William D., Susan M. Student, U. N.C., 1943-45; LLB, St. Louis U., 1949. Pvt. practice, 1952-78; ptnrs. Stiehl & Hess, 1978-81; ptnr. Stiehl & Stiehl, 1982-86; judge, former chief judge U.S. Dist. Court, (so. dist.) Ill., East Saint Louis, 1986—96, sr. judge, 1996—. Spl. asst. atty. gen. State of Ill., 1970-73. Mem. bd. Belleville Twp. High Sch. and Jr. Coll., 1949-50, 54-56, pres., 1956-57, Clair County, Ill., county civil atty., 1956-60. Mem. Ill. State Bar Assn., St. Clair County Bar Assn. Office: US Dist Ct 750 Missouri Ave East Saint Louis IL 62201-2954

STIER, MARY P., publishing executive; b. Memphis, Nov. 9, 1956; m. Jeff Stier; 2 children. BA in comm., broadcasting, U. Iowa, 1978; DHL (hon.), Grand View Coll., Des Moines. With Gannett Co., 1982—2007, v.p. Ctrl. Region Newspaper Divsn., 1990—93, pres. Midwest Newspaper Group, 1993—2000, sr. group pres. Midwest Newspaper Group, 2000—07; retail advt. mgr. Iowa City Press-Citizen, 1982—84, advt. dir., 1984—87, pres., pub., 1987—91, Rockford (Ill.) Register Star, 1991—2000, The Des Moines Register, 2000—07; founder, CEO Brilliance Group, Des Moines, 2007—. Bd. trustees Drake U. Named one of Top 30, Nat. Orgn. Female Execs., Most Powerful Women in Bus., Fortune mag., 2002; recipient Athena award, Council of 100, Star of Hope award, Juvenile Diabetes Rsch. Found., Iowa ch., 2006. Mem.: The Greater Des Moines Partnership, Am. Press Inst., Iowa Newspaper Assn., Newspaper Assn. Am., Phi Beta Kappa. Office: Des Moines Register PO Box 957 Des Moines IA 50304-0957 Office Phone: 515-284-8041. E-mail: mpstier@dmreg.com, mary@thebrilliancegroup.net.

STIFF, PATRICK JOSEPH, internist, hematologist, oncologist, educator; b. Toledo, Nov. 27, 1950; BS, U. Toledo, 1972; MD, Loyola U., 1975. Intern Cleve. Clinic, 1975-76, resident in medicine, 1976-78; fellow in hematology and oncology Meml. Sloan-Kettering Med. Ctr., NYC, 1978-81; asst. prof. medicine Sch. Medicine So. Ill. U., 1981-86; asst. prof. medicine Loyola U. Med. Ctr., Maywood, Ill., 1986-92; assoc. prof. medicine Loyola U. Med. Ctr.-Stritch Sch. Medicine, Maywood, Ill., 1992-96; prof. medicine and pathology Loyola U. Med. Ctr., Maywood, Ill., 1996—, dir. Cardinal Bernardin Cancer Ctr., 2003—, dir. divsn. hematology and oncology, 2003—. Chair transplant subcom. Ill. State Med. Adv. Com., 1999—. Mem. Internat. Soc. Exptl. Hematology, Internat. Soc. Hematotherapy and Graft Engrs., S.W. Oncology Group, Am. Soc. Clin. Oncology, Am. Soc. Hematology. Office: Loyola Univ Med Ctr 2160 S 1st Ave Maywood IL 60153-3304 Office Phone: 708-327-3148. Business E-Mail: pstiff@lumc.edu.

STIFLER, VENETIA CHAKOS, dancer, educator, choreographer; b. Chgo., Feb. 27, 1950; d. Theodore and Ruth (Pastirsky) Chakos; m. John G. Stifler, Jan. 28, 1972 (dec. 1977); m. Michael Hugos, 1994. BA, U. Ill., Chgo., 1983; MFA equivalency, Union Inst., Cin., 1987, PhD, 1992. Tchr. workshops Urban Gateways, Chgo., 1977; tchr. Chgo. Dance Ctr., Chgo., 1971-78, Smith Coll., Northampton, Mass., 1975, Wilson Coll., Chambersburg, Pa., 1984; guest tchr., artistic dir. composition/improvisation U. Wis., Madison, 1980-81, 85, 87; tchr. modern, jazz and ballet Venetia Stifler & Concert Dance, Inc., Chgo., 1978—; tchr. choreography workshop Bell Elem. Sch., Chgo., 1987; tchr./artist in residence Mundelein Coll., Chgo., 1982-90; asst. prof., chair dance program ortheastern Ill. U., Chgo., 1987—; tchr. modern technique So. Ill. U., Carbondale, 1975. Lectr. Mundelein Coll., Chgo., 1983, 84, 85, 86, Mayor's Office of Spl. Events, Chgo., 1980program dir. and choreogrpaher spl. programs Chgo. Symphony Orch., 1985, 87; pres. bd. dirs. Chgo. Dance Arts Coalition, 1983-85; adv. dance panel Ill. Arts Coun., 1983-85, Chgo. Office of Fine Arts, 1983-86; guest speaker Chgo. Office of Fine Arts, 1987; choreographer Sears Fashion Files, BoMay Prodns., 1983, 84, 86; prodn. asst. Audio Visual Prodns., 1970-71; artistic dir. Ruth Page Dance Series, 1992—; centennial dir. Ruth Page Found. Centennial, 1999; exec. dir. Ruth Page Found., 2000-. Choreographer Between Us, 1991, Magic Spaces, 1985, 86, Fugues, 1981, 82, Corporate Cases, 1988, Private places, 1987, Bell School Scrimmage, 1987, Blessings, 1986, Don't Dance with Your Back to the Moon, 1986, Imagery & Concept in the Dances of Venetia Stifler, 1985, Rhymes, 1984, Arriving at Onion, 1984, Pulse, 1983, Haiku, 1982, Mundelein Madness, 1981, Solo Crane, 1981, Tales of a Winter's Night, 1980, Jackson Park-Howard, 1979, La Gaite Parisienne (opera), 1976, Chicago Sketches, 1995, Veils, 1996, Over Weight Over Wrought Over You, 1997, Three German Songs, 1999, Shenandoah. Recipient Ruth Page award; named for Outstanding Artistic Achievement, Chgo. Dance Coalition, 1985. Avocations: films, art. Office: Northeastern Ill U 5500 N Saint Louis Ave Chicago IL 60625-4679 also: Ruth Page Ctr Arts 1016 N Dearborn Parkway Chicago IL 60610 E-mail: Venetia@ruthpage.org, V-Stifler@neiu.edu.

STIFTEN, EDWARD J., corporate financial executive; Corp. contr. Gen. Dynamics Corp.; exec. v.p., chief adminstrv. officer Clark Refining & Mktg., Inc.; v.p., CFO BJC HealthCare, 1998—2004; sr. v.p., CFO Express Scripts, Inc., Md. Heights, Mo., 2004—. Office: Express Scripts Inc 13900 Riverport Dr Maryland Heights MO 63043 Office Phone: 314-702-7667. Office Fax: 314-702-7037.

STIGLER, STEPHEN MACK, statistician, educator; b. Mpls., Aug. 10, 1941; s. George Joseph and Margaret (Mack) S.; m. Virginia Lee, June 27,1964; children: Andrew, Geoffrey, Margaret, Elizabeth. BA, Carleton Coll., 1963, DSc (hon.), 2005; PhD, U. Calif., Berkeley, 1967. Asst. prof. U. Wis., Madison, 1967-71, assoc. prof., 1971-75, prof., 1975-79, U. Chgo., 1979—, chmn. dept., 1986—92, 2005—, Ernest DeWitt Burton Disting. Svc. prof., 1992—. Trustee Ctr. Advanced Study in the Behavioral Scis., Stanford, Calif., 1986-92, 93-2006, chmn., 1995-99, 2002-06; trustee JSTOR, 1998-. Author: The History of Statistics, 1986, Statistics on the Table, 1999; contbr. articles to jours. in field. Recipient Rsch. award Humboldt Found., 2005; Guggenheim Found. fellow, 1976-77; Ctr. for Advanced Study in Behavioral Scis. fellow, 1978-79. Fellow: AAAS, Royal Statis. Soc. (Fisher lectr. 1986), Am. Statis. Assn. (editor Jour. 1979—82), Inst. Math. Stats. (Neyman lectr. 1988, pres. 1993—94, LeCam lectr. 2006), Am. Acad. Arts and Scis. (mem. coun. 1995—99); mem.: Am. Philos. Soc., Brit. Soc. for History Sci., History of Sci. Soc., Bernoulli Soc., Statis. Soc. Can., Internat. Statis. Inst. (mem. coun. 1999—2001, pres. 2003—05), Quadrangle Club, Phi Beta Kappa, Sigma Xi. Office: U Chgo Dept Statistics 5734 S University Ave Chicago IL 60637-1514 Office Phone: 773-702-8328. Business E-Mail: stigler@uchicago.edu.

STILLE, LEON E., state legislator; b. Olive, Mich., Nov. 21, 1939; m. Zinnie; four children. BS, Mich. State U. Market rep., mgr. IBM, 1966-92; mayor Ferrysburg, Mich.; mem. Mich. Ho. of Reps. from 89th dist., Lansing, 1993-94; Rep. asst. whip, 1993-94; mem. Mich. Senate from 32nd dist., Lansing, 1995—. Chair regularity subcom. 1993-94, transportation subcom., 1993-94; mem. higher edn. subcom., 1993-94, gen. govt. subcom., 1993-94. Mem. Rotary. Home: PO Box 511 Spring Lake MI 49456-0511 Office: Mich State Senate State Capitol PO Box 30036 Lansing MI 48909-7536

STILLMAN, NINA GIDDEN, lawyer; b. NYC, Apr. 3, 1948; d. Melvin and Joyce Audrey (Gidden) S. AB with distinction, Smith Coll., 1970; JD cum laude, Northwestern U., 1973. Bar: Ill. 1973, U.S. Dist. Ct. (no. dist.) Ill. 1973, U.S. Dist. Ct. (ea. dist.) Wis. 1979, U.S. Dist. Ct. (no. dist. trial bar) Ill. 1983, U.S. Ct. Appeals (7th cir.) 1974, U.S. Supreme Ct. 1981, U.S. Dist. Ct. (ctrl. dist.) Ill. 1994, U.S. Dist. Ct. (ea. dist.) Tex., 1996, U.S. Dist. Ct. (Colo.), 1999, U.S. Dist. Ct. (ND) 2002. Assoc. Vedder, Price, Kaufman & Kammholz, Chgo., 1973-79, ptnr., 1980—2004, Morgan, Lewis and Bockius, LLP, Chgo., 2004—. Adv. bd. occupational health and safety tng. program U. Mich., Ann Arbor, 1980-83; adj. faculty Inst. Human Resources and Indsl. Rels., Loyola U., Chgo., 1983-86, bd. advisors, 1986—. Author: (with others) Women, Work, and Health: Challenge to Corporate Policy, 1979, Occupational Health Law: A Guide for Industry, 1981, Employment Discrimination, 1981, Personnel Management: Labor Relations, 1981, Occupational Safety and Health Law, 1988; contbg. author: Occupational Medicine: State of the Art Reviews, 1996; contbr. articles to profl. jours. Legal advisor, v.p. Planned Parenthood Assn. Chgo., 1979—81; sec. jr. governing bd. Chgo. Symphony Orch., 1983; trustee Merit Sch. Music, 2000—, vice chmn. bd. trustees, 2001—. Recipient Svc. award Northwestern U., 1994. Mem.: ABA (occupl. safety and health law com. 1978—), Human Resources Mgmt. Assn. Chgo. (bd. dirs. 1986—88, officer), Am. Inns of Ct. (v.p. Wigmore chpt. 1988—89), Chgo. Bar Assn. (chmn. labor and employment law com. 1986—87), Northwestern U. Sch. Law Alumni Assn. (pres. 1991—92), Univ. Club Chgo. (bd. dirs. 1988—2001, sec. 1999—2000, v.p. 2000—01), The Chgo. Com., Econ. Club Chgo., Lawyers Club, Smith Coll. Club Chgo. (pres. 1972). Avocations: travel, reading, the arts, collecting art. Office: Morgan Lewis and Bockius LLP 77 W Wacker Dr Ste 600 Chicago IL 60601 Office Phone: 312-324-1150. Business E-Mail: nstillman@morganlewis.com.

STILWELL, RUSSELL, state representative; b. Oakland City, Ind., Mar. 3, 1948; m. Joanna Stilwell; 2 children. BS in Polit. and Social Sci., U. So. Ind. Coal miner, Warrick County, Ind., 1969—81; polit. field dir. United Mine Workers Am., Warrick County, Ind., 1981—; state rep. dist. 74 Ind. Ho. of Reps., Indpls., 1996—, vice chmn., rules and legis. procedures com., mem. appointments and claims, and labor and employment coms., Dem. fl. leader, asst. majority whip, 1998—. Election observer, South Africa, 1994; del. Dem. Nat. Conv., 1984, 1988, 1996; mem. Ind. Air Pollution Control Bd., 1992—96, Ind. Hazardous Waste Bd., 1990—92, Utility Regulatory Nom. Com., 1988—90. Served to E-4 US Army, 1968—69, Vietnam. Mem.: VFW, United Mine Workers of Am., Moose, Elks, Am. Legion. Democrat. Methodist. Office: Ind Ho of Reps 200 W Washington St Indianapolis IN 46204-2786

STINE, ROBERT HOWARD, retired pediatrician, allergist; b. Nov. 1, 1929; s. Harry Raymond and Mabel Eva (Newhard) S.; m. Lois Elaine Kihlgren, Oct. 22, 1960; children: Robert E., Karen E. Burnham, Jonathan N. BS in Biology, Moravian Coll., 1952. Diplomate in pediatrics and in pediatric allergy Am. Bd. Pediatrics, Am. Bd. Allergy and Immunology. Intern St. Luke's Hosp., Bethlehem, Pa., 1960-61, resident in surgery, 1961-62; physician Jefferson Med. Coll., Phila., 1956-60; resident in pediatrics U. N.Y., Syracuse, 1962-64; resident in allergy Robert A. Cooke Inst. Allergy Roosevelt Hosp., NYC, 1964-65; clin. instr. pediatrics U. Ill., Chgo., 1965-71; mem. courtesy staff Proctor Community Hosp., Peoria, Ill., 1966-77, mem. active staff, 1977—, chmn. dept. medicine, 1988—89; pres. elect. med. staff, 1990-91; pres. med. staff, 1991-92; mem. teaching staff St. Francis Hosp., Peoria, 1969—2002; clin. instr. pediatrics Rush-Presbyn. St. Luke's Hosp., Chgo., 1971—2002; ret. Vol. Heartland Cmty. Health Clinic, Peoria, Ill., 2002—04. Lt. (j.g.) USN, 1953—56. Fellow Am. Acad. Pediatrics (emeritus), Am. Acad. Allergy Asthma and Immunology, Am. Coll. Allergy and Asthma, Am. Assn. Cert. Allergists Am. Coll. Chest Physicians (emeritus); mem. Ill. Soc. Allergy and Clin. Immunology, Peoria Med. Soc. (pres.-elect 1993, pres. 1994), Christian Med. and Dental Soc. Home: 105 Hollands Grove Ln Washington IL 61571-9623

STINEHART, ROGER RAY, lawyer; b. Toledo, Jan. 27, 1945; s. Forrest William and Nettie May (Twyman) S.; m. Martha Jean Goodnight, Sept. 19, 1970; children: Amanda Jean, Brian Scott. BS, Bowling Green State U., Ohio, 1968; JD, Ohio State U., 1972. Bar: Ohio 1972. Fin. analyst Gen. Electric, Detroit, 1968-69; assoc. Gingher & Christensen, Columbus, Ohio, 1972-76, ptnr., 1976-80; sr. v.p., gen. counsel, sec. G.D. Ritzy's, Inc., Columbus, 1983-85; ptnr. Jones, Day, Reavis & Pogue, Columbus, 1980—83, 1985—2000, Jones Day, Columbus, Ohio, 2000—. Adj. prof. law Capital U., Columbus, 1976-79; mem. adv. com. Ohio securities divsn. Dept. Commerce, Columbus, 1979—; fellow Columbus Bar Found., 1992—; adv. bd. The Entrepreneurship Inst., 1992-95. Contbr. Ohio State U. Coll. Law Jour., 1970-72. Gen. counsel, trustee Internat. Assn. Rsch. on Leukemia and Related Diseases, 1975-2000; v.p., trustee Hospice of Columbus, 1978-80; trustee Cen. Ohio chpt. Leukemia Soc. of Am., Columbus, 1983-93, v.p., 1985-87; trustee Ohio Cancer Rsch. Assocs., Columbus, 1983—, v.p., 1990—; dir. Rotary Internat., Columbus Chapter, 2004-, v.p., 2005-; chmn. Social Com., 2001-03, Internat. Com., 2003-04, Adopt-a-School Com., 2003-04, group study exchange com., team leader, Dist. 6690, 2004-05, dist. chmn., 2005-06. With USMCR, 1963-68. Mem. ABA (bus. law com., franchise law com.), Ohio State Bar Assn. (corp. law com., franchise law com.), Columbus Bar Assn. (securities law com., chmn. 1981-83, bus. law com., franchise law com.), Sigma Tau Delta, Beta Gamma Sigma. Home: 2155 Waltham Rd Columbus OH 43221-4149 Office: Jones Day 325 J McConnell Blvd Columbus OH 43215-5017

STINES, FRED, JR., publisher; b. Newton, Iowa, Mar. 16, 1925; s. Fred and Nella (Haun) S.; m. Dorothy G. McClanahan, Sept. 5, 1953 (dec.); children: Steven, Scott, Ann; m. Mary K. Devin, Sept. 12, 1989. B.C.S., U. Iowa, 1949. With Meredith Corp., Des Moines, 1949-90, sales promotion and mdse. mgr., 1955-63, advt. dir., 1963-66, pub., 1966-73, pub. dir. mag. div., 1973-76, v.p., gen. mgr. books and newspapers, 1976-83, sr. v.p., 1983-87, pres. book pub., 1986-90, corp. v.p. spl. projects, 1988-90; pres., prin. Concepts in Mktg., 1990—. Cert. instr. Dale Carnegie courses, 1958-63. Bd. dirs. Des Moines Ballet Assn., orth Am. Outdoor Group, Mpls., 1992-95; bd. dirs., v.p. Jr. Achievement of Ctrl. Iowa. Served with AUS, 1946-49. Named Farm Marketing Man of Year, 1972 Mem. Future Farmers Am. Found. (nat. chmn. 1971), Rotary Internat., Des Moines Golf and Country Club, Phi Gamma Delta (sect. chief 1983, nat. bd. dirs. 1985-89), Alpha Kappa Psi, Alpha Delta Sigma. Clubs: Des Moines Golf and Country (dir., pres. 1981, pres. Ednl. Found.). Home: Concepts in Mktg 680 58th Pl West Des Moines IA 50266-6007

STINGER, FANCHON, newscaster; d. Edward and Zelma Stinger; m. Tony Camilleri. BA in English and Comm., U. Mich., 1993. Reporter WJBK-TV, Detroit, 1997—, editor and co-anchor 5:30pm news, 2000—. Recipient 5 Emmy awards, NATAS, 1998—, Best Reporter award, AP-Mich., 2000, Insp. Gen.'s Integrity award, U.S. Dept. HHS, 2002. Office: WJBK-TV Fox 2 PO Box 2000 Southfield MI 48037-2000

STINNETT, J. DANIEL, lawyer; b. 1945; BA, Vanderbilt U., 1967; JD, U. Mo., 1972. Bar: Mo. 1972. Assoc. counsel Commerce Bank, Kans. City, Mo., 1975—78; v.p., dep. gen. counsel, asst. sec. Commerce Bancshares, Inc., Kans. City, Mo., 1978—95; sec. Commerce Bank, 1978—95; sec., gen. counsel Commerce Bancshares, Inc., 1996; sr. v.p. Commerce Bank, 1996, gen. counsel.

STINSON, KENNETH E., construction and mining company executive; b. Chgo., May 24, 1946; BS in Civil Engring., U. Notre Dame; MS in Civil Engring., Stanford U. Pres. Kiewit Constrn. Grp. Inc., Omaha, 1992—96, chmn., 1993—96; pres. Peter Kiewit Sons' Inc., Omaha, 1997—2000, chmn., 1997—, CEO, 1998—2004. Bd. dirs. ConAgra Foods, Inc., Omaha, 1996—, Valmont Industries, Inc., Omaha, 1996—. Recipient Outstanding Projects and Leaders awards, ASCE, 2003, Star of Courage award, Nebr. Med. Ctr., 2005. Mem.: NAE. Office: Kiewit Corp 3555 Farnam St Omaha NE 68131 Office Phone: 402-342-2052. Office Fax: 402-271-2939.

STIRITZ, WILLIAM P., food products executive; b. Jasper, Ark., July 1, 1934; s. Paul and Dorothy (Bradley) Stiritz; m. Susan Ekberg, Dec. 4, 1972; children: Bradley, Charlotte, Rebecca, Nicholas. BS, Northwestern U., 1959; MA, St. Louis U., 1968. Mem. mktg. mgmt. staff Pillsbury Co., Mpls., 1959—62; staff Gardner Advt. Co., St. Louis, 1963; with Ralston Purina Co., St. Louis, 1963—97, pres., CEO, chmn., 1981—97; chmn., CEO Agribrands Internat., St. Louis, 1997—2001; chmn. Ralcorp Holdings, St. Louis, Energizer Inc. Bd. dirs. Am. Freightways, Angelica Corp., Ball Corp., Boatmen's Bancshares, Inc., Gen. Am. Life Ins. Co., May Dept. Stores, S.C. Johnson & Son, Reins. Group Am., Vail Resorts; bd. dirs., chmn. Ralston Purina, Ralcorp.; chmn. Westgate Equity Group, LLC; bd. dirs. Fedennted Dept. Stores. Served USN, 1954—57. Business E-Mail: william.stiritz@purina.nestle.com.

STIRLING, ELLEN ADAIR, retail executive; b. Chgo., June 21, 1949; d. Volney W. and Ellen Adair (Orr) Foster; m. James P. Stirling, June 6, 1970; children: Elizabeth Ginevra, Diana Leslie, Alexandra Curtiss. Student, U. Chgo., 1970-71; BA, Wheaton Coll., Norton, Mass., 1971; postgrad., U. London, 1974. Pres., CEO, The Lake Forest Shop, 1986—; CEO Zita, 2005—. Bd. dirs. Lake Forest Bank and Trust. Founder, v.p. aux. bd. Art Inst. Chgo., 1972-91; dir. Friends of Ryerson Woods, 1992—; mem. women's bd. Lyric Opera, Chgo., 1992—, Lake Forest Coll., 1989—; mem. adv. bd. Hope C. McCormick Costume Ctr.; mem. costume coun. Chgo. Hist. Soc.; trustee Nat. Louis U., 1999—; bd. dirs. Lake Forest OPen Lands, 1990—. Mem. Onwentsia Club, Racquet Club, Chgo. Club, Econ. Club Chgo. Office: The Lake Forest Shop 165 E Market Sq Lake Forest IL 60045

STIRLING, JAMES PAULMAN, investment banker; b. Chgo., Mar. 30, 1941; s. Louis James and Beverly L. (Paulman) S.; m. Ellen Adair Foster, June 6, 1970; children— Elizabeth Ginevra, Diana Leslie, Alexandra Curtiss. AB, Princeton U., 1963; MBA, Stanford U., 1965. CFA. Vice pres. corp. fin. Kidder, Peabody & Co. (now UBS), NYC and Chgo., 1965-71, 84-86, sr. v.p. corp. fin., 1987—; asst. to sec. U.S. Dept. Commerce, Washington, 1976-77. Chmn. bd. Northwestern Meml. Mgmt. Corp., Chgo., 1989—; trustee Northwestern Meml. Hosp.,

Chgo., 1985—. Pres. jr. bd. Chgo. Symphony, 1968—70; mem. exec. coun. Chgo. Metropolis 2020; trustee Chgo. Symphony, 1970—75, Tchrs. Acad. for Math. Sci., 1991—95. Mem. CFA Soc. Chgo. (bd. dirs.), CFA Leadership Coun. (chmn.), Bond Club Chgo., Nat. Econ. Hon. Soc., Chicago Club, Racquet Club (Chgo.), Onwentsia Club (Lake Forest, Ill.). Office: UBS Tower One N Wacker Dr Ste 2500 Chicago IL 60606-4302

STITH, LAURA DENVIR, state supreme court justice; b. St. Louis, Oct. 30, 1953; m. Donald George Scott; children: Lisa, Rebecca, Cynthia. BA magna cum laude, Tufts U., 1975; JD magna cum laude, Georgetown U., 1978. Law clk. to Hon. Robert E. Seiler, Mo. Supreme Ct., 1978—79; assoc. Shook, Hardy & Bacon, Kansas City, Mo., 1979—84, ptnr., 1984—94; judge. Mo. Ct. Appeals (we. dist.), 1994—2001; judge Mo. Supreme Ct., 2001—. Speaker Mo. New Judges Sch. Author: articles on appellate practice, products liability and civil procedure. Tutor, mentor Operation Breakthrough, St. Vincent's Sch.; founding dir., mem. Lawyers Encouraging Academic Performance. Mem.: Assn. Women Lawyers of Greater Kansas City (speaker, past pres.), Mo. Bar Assn., Kansas City Metropolitan Bar Assn. Office: Supreme Ct Mo PO Box 150 Jefferson City MO 65102

STIVERS, STEVE, state senator; BA, MBA, Ohio State U. State sen. dist. 16 Ohio State Senate, Columbus, 2003—, vice chair judiciary-civil justice com., mem. hwy. and transp., judiciary-criminal justice, and state and local govt. and vets. affairs coms. Bd. dirs. Contemporary Am. Theatre Co., 1997—; bd. dirs., treas. Alvis House, 1997—. Mem.: Ohio Bankers Assn., Ohio NG Officers Assn., Ohio Bankers Assn. BANKPAC, Leadership Columbus, Columbus Athletic Club. Democrat. Office: Senate Bldg Rm # 34 ground fl Columbus OH 43215

STOCK, ANITA See SCHERER, ANITA

STOCK, LEON MILO, chemist, educator; b. Detroit, Oct. 15, 1930; s. J.H. Frederick and Anna (Fischer) S.; m. Mary K. Elmblad, May 6, 1961; children: Katherine L., Ann V. BS in Chemistry, U. Mich., 1952; PhD in Chemistry, Purdue U., 1959. Instr. U. Chgo., 1958-61, asst. prof., 1961-65, assoc. prof., 1965-70, prof. dept. chemistry, 1970-96, master Phys. Scis. Collegiate div., 1970-96, prof. emeritus dept. chemistry, 1997—, assoc. dean div. Phys. Scis., 1976-81, assoc. dean, 1976-81, chmn. dept. chemistry, 1985-88; faculty assoc. Argonne (Ill.) Nat. Lab., 1984-85, joint appointment chemistry div., 1985-96, dir. chemistry div., 1988-95. Exploratory rsch. assoc. Elec. Power Rsch. Inst., 1989; adv. bd. Ctr. for Applied Rsch., U. Ky., 1990-95; Brown lectr. Purdue U., 1992; Given lectr. Pa. State U., 1995; cons. Westinghouse Hanford Co., 1995-96, Phillips Petroleum Co., 1964-95, Amoco Oil Co., 1989-95, Argonne Nat. Lab., 1995—, Pacific N.W. Nat. Lab., 1996—, Fluor Daniel Hanford Co., 1996—; faculty assoc. Wash. State U., 1997—. Recipient L.J. and H.M. Quantrell prize, 1974, H.H. Storch award Am. Chem. Soc., 1987. Mem. NAS (energy engrng. bd.), Am. Chem. Soc. (com. on sci. 1990-92), Coun. of Gordon Rsch. Confs. (chmn. Gordon Conf. on Fuel Sci. 1983), NRC (mem. panel on coop. rsch. in fossil energy 1984, energy engrng. bd. 1984-90, mem. panel on strategic petroleum rsch. 1985, panel on rsch. needs of advanced process tech. 1992-93), Ill. Coal Bd. (program panel 1986-90, panel on prodn. techs. for transp. fuels 1990, editl. bd. Jour. Organic Chemistry 1981-86, Energy and Fuels, 1986-96, mem. panel on new strategy for safety issue resolution at Hanford, 1996, mem. panel rsch. needs radiation chemistry, 1998). Office: Argonne Nat Lab Chem Divsn Argonne IL 60439

STOCKING, GEORGE WARD, JR., anthropology educator; b. Berlin, Dec. 8, 1928; came to U.S., 1929; s. George Ward and Dorothé Amelia (Reichhard) S.; m. Wilhelmina Davis, Aug. 19, 1949 (div. 1965); children: Susan Hallowell, Rebecca, Rachel Louise, Melissa, Thomas Shepard; m. Carol Ann Bowman, Sept. 29, 1968. BA, Harvard U., 1949; PhD, U. Pa., 1960. From instr. to assoc. prof. history U. Calif., Berkeley, 1960-68; assoc. prof. anthropology and history U. Chgo., 1968-74, prof. anthropology, 1974—2000, Stein-Freiler Disting. Svc. prof., 1990—, prof. emeritus, 2000—, dir. Fishbein Ctr. for History Sci. and Medicine, 1981-92. Vis. prof. U. Minn., Mpls., 1974, Harvard U., Cambridge, Mass., 1977, Stanford U., Palo Alto, Calif., 1983, U. Ill., Urbana, 1999. Author: Race, Culture and Evolution, 1968, Victorian Anthropology, 1987, The Ethnographer's Magic, 1992, After Tylor, 1995, Delimiting Anthropology, 2001; author, editor: The Shaping of American Anthropology, 1974; editor History of Anthropology, 1983-97. Active labor union and radical polit. activity, 1949-56. Fellow Ctr. for Advanced Study in Behavioral Scis., 1976—77, John Simon Guggenheim Meml. Found., 1984—85, Inst. for Advanced Study, 1992—93; scholar Getty Ctr. for History of Art and Humanities, 1988—89, Dibner Inst., MIT, 1998; emeritus fellow, Andrew W. Mellon Found., 2005. Fellow Am. Anthropol. Assn. (Franz Boas award 1998), Am. Acad. Arts and Scis.; mem. Royal Anthropol. Inst. (Huxley medal 1993), History Sci. Soc. Avocation: needlepoint. Office: Univ Chicago Dept Anthropology 1126 E 59th St Chicago IL 60637-1580 Office Phone: 773-702-7702. E-mail: g-stocking@uchicago.edu.

STOCKLOSA, GREGORY A., printing company executive; BS, U. Mich.; M in Mgmt., Northwestern U. Fin. staff Kraft Gen. Foods, Inc.; asst. treas. global corp. fin. R.R. Donnelley & Sons Co., Chgo., 1993-94, v.p., treas., 1994-99, v.p., corp. contr., 1999-2000, acting CFO, 2000, exec. v.p., CFO, 2000—. Office: RR Donnelley Sons Co 77 W Wacker Dr Chicago IL 60601-1696

STODDARD, ROBERT H., geography educator; b. Auburn, Nebr., Aug. 29, 1928; s. Hugh P. and Nainie L. (Robertson) S.; m. Sally E. Salisbury, Dec. 10, 1955; children: Martha, Andrew R., Hugh A. BA, Nebr. Wesleyan, Lincoln, 1950; MA, U. Nebr., 1960; PhD, U. Iowa, 1966. Instr. Nebr. Wesleyan, 1961-63, asst. prof., 1963-67, U. Nebr., Lincoln, 1967-71, assoc. prof., 1971-81, prof., 1981—2001. Vis. prof. Tribhuvan U., Kathmandu, Nepal, 1975-76, U. Colombo, Sri Lanka, 1986; inst. instr. Okla. State U., Stillwater, 1966; TV instr. Nebr. Ednl. TV Higher Edn., Lincoln, 1969; instr. Career Opportunity Program, Lincoln, 1973; dir. Geog. Edn. of Nebr., Lincoln, 1989-95. Author: Field Techniques, 1982; 1st author: Human Geography, 1986, 2d edit., 1989; editor and contbr.: Sacred Places, 1997. Mem. subcom. Lincoln-Lancaster Planning Com., 1974-78. Recipient Robert Stoddard award for Svc., Geography of Religion and Belief Systems, 2005. Mem. Assn. Am. Geographers, Nat. Coun. for Geog. Edn. (Disting. Tchg. Achievement award 1992). Democrat. Unitarian Universalist. Office: U ebr Geog Program Lincoln NE 68588-0368 Business E-Mail: rstoddard1@unl.edu.

STODDART, J(AMES) FRASER, chemistry professor, researcher; b. Edinburgh, May 24, 1942; widowed; 2 children. BSc, Edinburgh U., Scotland, 1964; PhD, Edinburgh U., 1966, DSc, 1980; DSc (hon.), Birmingham U., 2005, U. Twente, 2006; DSc, U. Sheffield, 2008. Postgrad. student U. Edinburgh, Scotland, 1964-66; NRC postdoctoral fellow Queen's U., Kingston, Ont., Canada, 1967-70; Imperial Chem. Industries rsch. fellow U. Sheffield, England, 1970, lectr. in Chemistry, 1970—82, reader in Chemistry, 1982—91; sci. rsch. coun. sr. vis. fellow UCLA, 1978; rschr. ICI Corp. Lab., Runcorn, England, 1978-81; prof. Org. Chem. Birmingham U., England, 1990-97, hon. prof. chemistry, 1997—2002, chair organic chemistry, 1990, head Sch. Chem., 1993-97; Saul Winstein chair, organic chemistry UCLA, 1997—2003, Fred Kavil Chair Nanosystems Sciences, 2003—07; acting co-dir. Calif. NanoSystems Inst., 2002—03, bd. dir., 2000, dir., 2003—07; prof. chemistry, dir. Ctr. for Chemistry of Integrated Sys. Northwestern U., Evanston, Ill., 2008—. Vis. prof. Tex. A&M U., 1980, Messina U., Italy, 1985-87, Ecole Nationale Supérieure de Chemie de Mulhouse, 1987; invited lectr. in supramolecular and macromolecular sci.; hon. prof. East China U. Sci. and Tech. in Shanghai, 2005; Carnegie Centenary vis. professorship, U. Scotland, 2005; mem. scientific adv. bd. Ctr. for Nanoscale Sci. and Tech., Rice U. Mem. editl. adv. bd. Crystal Growth and Design, Journal Organic Chemistry, Organic Letters; mem. internat. adv. bd. Collection of Czechoslovak Chem. Communications, Angewandte Chemie; mem. editl. bd. Chemistry-A European Jour., Organic Letters; editor Royal Society of Chemistry Series of Monographs on Supramolecular Chemistry; contbr. a significant number of articles to profl. jours. Recipient Hope prize 1964, RSC Perkin Divsn. Career award 1980, 81, 82, Internat. Izatt-Christensen award in macrocyclic chemistry, 1993, Chaire Bruylants award, U. Louvaine-La-Neuve, Belgium, 1994, Adolf Steinhofer Found. award, 1995, Nagoya Gold Medal award in organic chemistry, 2004, Mack Meml. award, Ohio State U., 2006. Fusion award, U. Nev., 2006, King Faisal Internat. prize Sci. King Faisal Found., Tetrahedron prize for creativity in organic chemistry, 2007, Feynman prize for nanotech., 2007, Albert Einstein award of sci., 2007; Leverhulme rsch. fellow, 1988-89, Humboldt Fellowship, 1998; named Alumnus of Yr., U. Endinburgh, 2005, Knight Bachelor, 2006. Fellow Royal Soc., Royal Soc. Chem., German Acad. Natural Scis., AAAS, Sci. Divsn. Royal Netherlands Acad. Arts and Sciences; mem. Chem. Soc.(Carbohydrate Chemistry award, 1978), Am. Chem. Soc. (Arthur C. Cope Scholar award, 1999, 2008, PSME Divsn. Arthur K. Doolittle award, 2005). Achievements include being co-creator of the world's densest memory circuit in 2007. Office: Northwestern U Dept Chemistry 2145 Sheridan Rd, #K148 Evanston IL 60208-3113 Office Phone: 847-491-3793. Office Fax: 847-491-1009. Business E-Mail: stoddart@northwestern.edu.*

STOECKER, DAVID THOMAS, retired banker; b. St. Louis, June 8, 1939; s. John Garth and Marie (Zahler) S.; m. Ann E. Conrad, Aug. 18, 1962; children—Lisa Ann, Susan Jane. BS, Ind. U., 1963. Sr. v.p. comml. loans Mercantile Trust Co. N.Am., St. Louis, 1965-80; pres. Gravois-Merc. Bank, St. Louis, 1980-87; pres., chief exec. officer Bank of South County, St. Louis, 1987-95; chmn. bd., CEO Ctrl. West End Bank, St. Louis, 1996—2006; ret., 2006. Served to 1st lt. AUS, 1963—65. Mem.: Robert Morris Assocs. (pres. St. Louis 1980), Sunset Country Club. Methodist. Office: 415 Debaliviere Saint Louis MO 63112

STOEFFLER, DAVID BRUCE, publishing executive; b. Boscobel, Wis., Mar. 8, 1959; s. Raymond Elwood and Arlene Mary (Laufenberg) S.; m. Rose Mary Hromadka, June 9, 1978; 1 child, Christine Elizabeth. BA in English, Viterbo Coll., LaCrosse, 1981. Reporter LaCrosse Tribune, LaCrosse, Wis., 1979-81, Wis. State Jour., Madison, Wis., 1981-88, asst. city editor, 1988-93, city editor, 1993-95; editor LaCrosse Tribune (subs. Lee Enterprises), LaCrosse, 1995—97, Lincoln (Nebr.) Journal (subs. Lee Enterprises), 1997—2005; v.p. news Lee Enterprises, Davenport, Iowa, 2001—05; editor & pub. Ariz. Daily Star (subs. Lee Enterprises), Tucson, 2005; gen. mgr. Suburban Jours. of Greater St. Louis, 2007—. Recipient Cmty. Svc. award Inland Daily Press Assn., 1990, 94. Mem. Soc. of Profl. Journalists (pres. Madison Pro chpt.; mem. chmn. Region 6). Roman Catholic. Avocation: boating. Office: Suburban Journals 14522 S Outer Forty Rd Town And Country MO 63017 Office Phone: 314-744-5798. Office Fax: 314-821-0745. E-mail: dstoeffler@yourjournal.com.

STOERI, WILLIAM R., lawyer; b. 1955; BA in History and Phil. summa cum laude, Kalamazoo Coll., 1978; student, U. Erlangen, Nurenberg, Germany, 1978—79; JD, Yale U., 1982. Bar: Minn. 1982. Law clerk, Hon. Diana E. Murphy US Dist. Ct., Minn. Dist., 1982—84; assoc. Dorsey & Whitney LLP, Mpls., 1984—89, ptnr., trial dept., 1990—, and co-chair, profl. malpractice group. Mem.: Phi Beta Kappa. Office: Dorsey & Whitney LLP Ste 1500 50 S Sixth St Minneapolis MN 55402-1498 Office Phone: 612-343-7942. Office Fax: 612-340-8800. Business E-Mail: stoeri.bill@dorsey.com.

STOERMER, EUGENE FILMORE, biologist, educator; b. Webb, Iowa, Mar. 7, 1934; s. Edward Filmore and Agnes Elizabeth (Ekstrand) S.; m. Barbara Purves Ryder, Aug. 13, 1960; children: Eric Filmore, Karla Jean, Peter Emil. BS, Iowa State U., 1959, PhD, 1963. Assoc. rsch. scientist, rsch. scientist U. Mich., Ann Arbor, 1965-79, assoc. prof., 1979-85, prof., 1985—. Editl. advisor Jour. Paeleolimonology. Contbr. over 225 articles to profl. jours. Fellow Acad. Natural Scis., Phila., 1980; recipient Darbaker prize, Bot. Soc. Am., 1993. Mem. Phycological Soc. Am. (pres. 1988-89), Internat. Assn. for Diatom Rsch. (pres. 1992-94). Home: 4392 Dexter Ave Ann Arbor MI 48103-1636 Office: U Mich Sch Nat Resources Ann Arbor MI 48109 E-mail: stoermer@umich.edu.

STOHR, DONALD J., federal judge; b. Sedalia, Mo., Mar. 9, 1934; s. Julius Leo and Margaret Elizabeth (McGaw) Stohr; m. Mary Ann Kuhlman, July 31, 1957; 5 children. BS, St. Louis U., 1956, JD, 1958. Bar: Mo. 1958, U.S. Dist. Ct. (ea. dist.) Mo. 1958, U.S. Ct. Appeals (8th cir.) 1966, U.S. Supreme Ct. 1969. Assoc. Hocker Goodwin & MacGreevy, St. Louis, 1958-63, 66-69; asst. counselor St. Louis County, 1963-65, counselor, 1965-66; U.S. atty. Ea. Dist. Mo., St. Louis, 1973-76; ptnr. Thompson & Mitchell, St. Louis, 1969-73, 76-92; judge U.S. Dist. Ct. (ea. dist.) Mo., St. Louis, 1992—. Mem. ABA, Mo. Bar Assn., Am. Judicature Soc., St. Louis Met. Bar Assn. Office: 111 S 10th St Rm 16 182 Saint Louis MO 63102

STOKAN, LANA J. LADD, state legislator; b. El Dorado, Ark., Sept. 5, 1958; children: Garrett, Adair. BA, So. Ill. U., MA in Secondary Edn. and History. Rep. dist. 76 State of Mo. also: State Capital Rm 305A Jefferson City MO 65101 Home: 2961 E Jennie Lake Rd Ashland MO 65010-9845

STOKES, KATHLEEN SARAH, dermatologist, educator; b. Springfield, Mass., Oct. 18, 1954; d. John Francis and Margaret Cecelia (MacDonnell) Stokes; m. William Walter Greaves; children: Ian R., Spencer W., Malcolm W. BS, U. Utah, 1978, MS, 1980; MD, Med. Coll. Wis., 1987. Diplomate Am. Bd. Dermatology. Intern in internal medicine Med. Coll. Wis., Milw., 1987-88, resident in dermatology, 1988-90, chief resident, 1990-91, asst. clin. prof. dermatology, 1991—; pvt. practice, Milw., 1991—. Contbr. articles to med. jours., including Critical Care Medicine, Jour. Pediatric Dermatology. Named A Top Physician, Milw. mag., 1996, 2000, 04 Fellow Am. Acad. Dermatology, Milw. Acad. Medicine; mem. AMA, Wis. Dermatol. Soc. (sec.-treas. 2003-04, pres. 2005-06), Women's Dermatologic Soc., Tempo, Alpha Omega Alpha. Office: Affiliated Dermatologists 2300 N Mayfair Rd Milwaukee WI 53226-1505

STOKES, PATRICK T., brewery company executive; b. Washington, Aug. 11, 1942; m. Anna-Kristina Stokes. BS, Boston Coll., 1964; MBA, Columbia U., 1966. Fin. analyst Shell Oil Co., 1966-67; v.p. materials acquisitions Anheuser-Busch Cos., Inc., St. Louis, 1979-81, v.p., group exec., 1981—86; COO Campbell Taggart Inc. (subs. Anheuser-Busch Cos. Inc.), Dallas, 1986-90, CEO, 1990—2002; sr. exec. v.p. Anheuser-Busch Cos., Inc., St. Louis, 2000—02, pres., CEO, 2002—06, chmn., 2006—, Anheuser-Busch Internat., Inc, 1999—. Bd. dirs. Anheuser-Busch Cos. Inc., 2000—. Served to 1st lt. U.S. Army, 1967-69. Recipient Award of Excellence in Commerce, Boston Coll. Alumni Assn., 1991. Office: Anheuser-Busch Companies Inc 1 Busch Place Saint Louis MO 63118-1852

STOKES, RODNEY, state agency administrator; Dir. Mich. Pks. and Recreation Divsn., Lansing, 1996—. Office: Mich Pks & Recreation Divsn PO Box 30028 Lansing MI 48909-7528 Fax: 517-335-4242.

STOKEY, NANCY L., economist, educator; BA in Economics, U. Pa., 1972; PhD in Economics, Harvard U., 1978. Asst. prof. Kellogg Grad. Sch. Mgmt., Northwestern U., 1978—82, assoc. prof., 1982—83, prof., 1983—87, dept. chmn., 1987—89, Harold L. Stuart prof. managerial economics, 1988—90; vis. lectr. Harvard U., 1982; vis. prof. economics U. Minn., 1983, U. Chgo., 1983—84, prof. ecnomics, 1990—96, Frederick Henry Prince prof. economics, 1997—. Vis. scholar rsch. dept. Fed. Reserve Bank, Mpls., 2000—01. Author (with Robert E. Lucas, Jr. and Edward C. Prescott): Recursive Methods in Economic Dynamics, 1989. Fellow: Am. Econ. Assn. (v.p. 1996—97, nominating com. 1998, exec. com. 2000—02), Am. Acad. Arts and Scis., Econometric Soc. (coun. mem. 1996—98, 1999—2001); mem.: AS. Home Phone: 773-477-9640; Office Phone: 773-702-0915. Office Fax: 773-702-8490. Business E-Mail: n-stikey@uchicago.edu.

STOKLOSA, GREGORY A., publishing executive; BS, U. Mich.; MA in Mgmt., Northwestern U. Various fin. positions Kraft Gen. Foods, Inc.; from asst. treas. global corp. fin. to exec. v.p., CFO RR Donnelley & Sons, Chgo., 1993—2000, exec. v.p., 2000—05, CFO, 2000—05; v.p., CFO Hollinger Internat. Inc., Chgo., 2005—. Office: Hollinger International Inc 350 N Orleans St Chicago IL 60654 Office Phone: 312-321-2299. Office Fax: 312-321-0629.

STOKSTAD, MARILYN JANE, art history educator, curator; b. Lansing, Mich., Feb. 16, 1929; d. Olaf Lawrence and Edythe Marian (Gardiner) S. BA, Carleton Coll., 1950; MA, Mich. State U., 1953; PhD, U. Mich., 1957; postgrad., U. Oslo, 1951-52; LHD (hon.), Carleton Coll., 1997. Instr. U. Mich., Ann Arbor, 1956-58; mem. faculty U. Kans., Lawrence, 1958—, assoc. prof., 1961-66, prof., 1966-80, Univ. Disting. prof. art history, 1980-94, Judith Harris Murphy disting. prof. art, 1994—, dir. mus. art, 1961-67, research assoc., summers 1965-66, 67, 71, 72; assoc. dean Coll. Liberal Arts and Scis., U. Kans., 1972-76; research curator Nelson-Atkins Mus. Art, Kansas City, Mo., 1969-80, consultative curator medieval art, 1980—. Bd. dirs. Internat. Ctr. Medieval Art, 1972-75, 81-84, 88-96, v.p., 1990-93, pres., 1993-96, sr. advisor, 1996-97; cons., evaluator North Ctrl. Assn. Colls. and Univs., 1972—, commr.-at-large, 1984-89. Author: Santiago de Compostela, 1978, The Scottish World, 1981, Medieval Art, 1986, Art History, 1995, rev. edit., 1999, Art: A Brief History, 2000. Recipient Disting. Service award Alumni Assn. Carleton Coll., 1983, Kans. Gov.'s Arts award, 1997; Fulbright fellow, 1951-52; NEH grantee, 1967-68 Fellow AAUW; mem. AAUP (nat. coun. 1972-75), Archeol. Inst. Am. (pres. Kans. chpt. 1960-61), Midwest Coll. Art Conf. (pres. 1964-65), Coll. Art Assn. (bd. dirs. 1970-80, pres. 1978-80), Soc. Archtl. Historians (chpt. bd. dirs. 1971-73). E-mail: stokstad@ku.edu.

STOLAR, HENRY SAMUEL, lawyer; b. St. Louis, Oct. 29, 1939; s. William Allen and Pearl Minnette (Schukar) S.; m. Mary Goldstein, Aug. 26, 1962 (dec. Nov. 1987); children: Daniel Bruce, Susan Eileen; m. Suzanne Chapman Jones, June 2, 1989. AB, Washington U., 1960; JD, Harvard U., 1963. Bar: Mo. 1963, U.S. Supreme Ct. 1972. Assoc. then ptnr. Hocker, Goodwin & MacGreevy, St. Louis, 1963—69; v.p., sec., gen. counsel LaBarge Inc., St. Louis, 1969—74; from v.p., assoc. gen. counsel then sr. exec. v.p., gen. counsel, sec. Maritz Inc., St. Louis, 1974—. Sec., bd. dirs. New City Sch. Inc., St. Louis, 1968-75, Ctrl. West End. Assn., 1993-2000; mem. St. Louis Bd. Aldermen, 1969-73, Bd. Freeholders City and County St. Louis, 1987-88; bd. dirs. Forest Park Forever, Inc., 1991-2003. Mem. ABA, Mo. Bar, Bar Assn. Met. St. Louis, Triple A Club, Phi Beta Kappa. Office: Maritz Inc 1375 N Highway Dr Fenton MO 63099-0001 Home: 1500 Ocean Dr Apt 803 Miami Beach FL 33139-3132

STOLL, JOHN ROBERT, lawyer, educator; b. Phila., Nov. 29, 1950; s. Wilhelm Friedrich and Marilyn Jane (Kremser) S.; m. Christine Larson, June 24, 1972; children: Andrew Michael, Michael Robert, Meredith Kirstin, Alison Courtney. BA magna cum laude, Haverford Coll., 1972; JD, Columbia U., 1975. Bar: Ind. 1975, U.S. Dist. Ct. (no. and so. dists.) Ind. 1975, U.S. Ct. Appeals (7th cir.) 1978, U.S. Dist. Ct. (no. dist.) Ill. 1980, (so. dist.) N.Y. 1993, Ill. 1981, N.Y. 1989. Atty. Barnes & Thornburg, South Bend, Ind., 1975-80, Mayer, Brown & Platt, Chgo. and N.Y.C., 1980—. Adj. prof. law Northwestern U., Chgo., 1985—94, DePaul U., Chgo., 1987; lectr. in bus. St. Mary's Coll., Notre Dame, Ind., 1977-78. Contbr. articles to profl. jours. Fellow Am. Coll. Bankruptcy; mem. ABA, Ind. State Bar Assn., Am. Bankruptcy Inst., Phi Beta Kappa. Office: Mayer Brown & Platt 71 S Wacker Dr Chicago IL 60606-4637

STOLL, ROBERT W., principal; Prin. Harrison (Ohio) Elem. Sch., 1989—. Recipient Elem. Sch. Recognition award U.S. Dept. Edn., 1989-90. Office: Harrison Elem Sch 600 Broadway Harrison OH 45030-1323

STOLL, STEVE M., state legislator; b. St. Louis, Apr. 3, 1947; m. Kathleen Woods; children: Emily, Laura, Amy, Andrew. Student, S.E. Mo. State U., 1965-67; BA, U. Mo., 1970, postgrad., 1979. Tchr., 1078-93; mem. Mo. Ho. of Reps. from 103d dist., Jefferson City, 1993-98, Mo. Senate from 22nd dist., Jefferson City, 1998—. Mem. Appropriations, Natural and Econ. Resources, Edn., Labor, Profl. Registration, Licensing and Budget Coms. Mo. Ho. of Reps. Councilman Ward II, Crystal City, Mo., 1983, 85, 87, 89, 91, Mayor Pro Tem, 1987-92. Mem. KC, Am. Legion. Democrat. Home: 716 Richard Dr Festus MO 63028-1077 Office Phone: 751 149 2.

STOLL, WILHELM, mathematics professor; b. Freiburg, Germany, Dec. 22, 1923; arrived in U.S., 1960; s. Heinrich and Doris (Eberle) S.; m. Marilyn Jane Kremser, June 11, 1955; children: Robert, Dieter, Elisabeth, Rebecca. PhD in Math, U. Tübingen, Fed. Republic Germany, 1953, habilitation, 1954. Asst. U. Tübingen, 1953-59, dozent, 1954-60, ausserplanmässiger prof., 1960; vis. lectr. U. Pa., 1954-55; temp. mem. Inst. Advanced Study, Princeton, 1957-59; prof. math. U. otre Dame, 1960-88, Vincent J. Duncan and Annamarie Micus Duncan prof. math., 1988-94, prof. emeritus, 1994—, chmn. dept., 1966-68, co-dir. Ctr. for Applied Math., 1992. Vis. prof. Stanford U., 1968-69, Tulane U., 1973, U. Sci. and Tech., Hefei, Anhui, People's Republic of China, summer, 1986; adviser Clark Sch., South Bend, Ind., 1963-68; Japan Soc. Promotion Sci. fellow, vis. prof. Kyoto U., summer 1983. Publs. in field. Fellow: AAAS. Achievements include research in complex analysis several variables. Home: 2601 Covington Commons Dr #44-46 Fort Wayne IN 46804-7333

STOLLER, JOHN R., lawyer; b. NYC, Oct. 16, 1948; BA, Valparaiso U., 1970, JD, 1973. Bar: Minn. 1973, Colo. 1978, Mich. 1993. Editor-in-chief Calparaiso U. Law Rev., 1972—73; law clk. to Justice Walter F. Rogscheske Minn., 1973—74; assoc. HArstad & Rainbow, 1974—78; spl. asst. atty. gen. Minn. Dept. Transp., 1974—78; atty. The Mountain States Telephone and Telegraph Co., 1978—83; v.p., gen. counsel, sec. Beta West Properties, Inc., 1984—90; gen. counsel, sec. Pulte Homes, Inc., Bloomfield Hills, Mich., 1990—2005, sr. v.p., 1999—2005. Mem.: ABA, Am. Soc. Corp. Secs., Am. Corp. Counsel Assn., State Bar Mich., Denver Bar Assn., Colo. Bar Assn., Minn. Bar Assn.

STOLZ, BENJAMIN ARMOND, foreign language educator; b. Lansing, Mich., Mar. 28, 1934; s. Armond John and Mabel May (Smith) S.; m. Mona Eleanor Seelig, June 16, 1962; children: Elizabeth Mona, John Benjamin. AB, U. Mich., Ann Arbor, 1955; certificat, U. Libre de Bruxelles, Belgium, 1956; A.M., Harvard U., 1957, PhD, 1965. Mem. faculty U. Mich., 1964-2001, prof. Slavic langs. and lits., 1972-2001, chmn. dept., 1971-85, 89-91; prof. emeritus, 2001—. Cons. in field. Editor: Papers in Slavic Philology, 1977, Studies in Macedonian Language, Literature, and Culture, 1995; co-editor: Oral Literature and the Formula, 1976, Cross Currents, 1982-85, Language and Literary Theory, 1984, Mich. Slavic Publs., 1990—; co-editor, translator: (Konstantin Mihailovic): Memoirs of a Janissary, 1975; contbr. articles to profl. pubs. Served to lt. (j.g.) USNR, 1957-60. Recipient Orion E. Scott award humanities U. Mich., 1954, Fulbright scholar, 1955-56; Fgn. Area fellow Yugoslavia, 1963-64; Fulbright-Hays rsch. fellow Eng. and Yugoslavia, 1970-71; grantee Am. Coun. Learned Socs., 1968-70, 73, Internat. Rsch. and Exchs. Bd., 1985, 87, Woodrow Wilson Ctr., 1992. Mem. Am. Assn. Advancement Slavic Studies, Am. Assn. Tchrs. Slavic and East European Langs., Phi Beta Kappa, Phi Kappa Phi, Delta Upsilon. Home: 3423 Riverbend Dr Ann Arbor MI 48105

STOLZER, LEO WILLIAM, bank executive; b. Kansas City, Mo., Oct. 14, 1934; s. Leo Joseph and Lennie Lucille (Hopp) S.; m. Eleanor Katherine Griffith, Aug. 17, 1957; children: Joan Ellen Stolzer Bolen, Mary Kevin Stolzer Giller. BS in Acctg., Kans. State U., 1957. Teller Union Nat. Bank & Trust Co., Manhattan, Kans., 1960-62, asst. cashier, 1962-63, asst. v.p., 1963-64, v.p., 1964-69, exec. v.p., 1969-72, pres., 1972-80, chmn., CEO, 1980-95; chmn., 1995—. Bd. dirs. Commerce Bankshares Inc., Commerce Bank-Manhattan; chmn., CEO Griffith Lumber Co., Cmty. Bancorporation of N.Mex., Inc. Trustee, past treas., past vice-chair Kans. State U. Found.; trustee Midwest Rsch. Inst.; chmn. Riley County Savs. Bond. Capt. USAF, 1957-60. Recipient Disting. Service award Manhattan Jr. C. of C., 1968, Kans. State U. Advancement award. Fellow Coll. Bus. Adminstrn. Alumni; mem. Am. Bankers Assn. (past treas., past exec. com., past bd. dirs.), Assn. U.S. Army (bd. dirs. Ft. Riley Ctl. Kans. chpt., past chair), Kans. U. Alumni Assn. (devel. com.), Newcomen Soc. in N.Am. (past Kans. chmn.), KC, Beta Theta Pi. Avocation: skiing. Office: Commerce Bank 727 Poyntz Ave Manhattan KS 66502-0118

STONE, ALAN, container company executive; b. Chgo., Feb. 5, 1928; s. Norman H. and Ida (Finkelstein) S.; m. Joanie B. Stone; children: Christie-Ann Stone Weiss, Joshua. BSE, U. Pa., Phila., 1951; cert. in Advanced Mgmt., U. Chgo., 1960. Trainee, salesman Stone Container Corp., Chgo., 1951-53, dir. mktg. service, 1954-64, gen. mgr., regional mgr., 1964-72, sr. v.p. adminstrn., gen. mgr. energy div., 1972—, also dir., sr. v.p. purchasing and transp.; pres. orth La. and Gulf R.R./Ctrl. La. and Gulf R.R., 1985-92, Atlanta St. Andrews and Bay Line R.R., 1992-94, Abbeville-Grimes R.R., 1992-94, Apache R.R., 1992-94. Bd. dirs., exec. com. Stone Container Corp., 1960—; cons. Chgo. Mfg.; pres. No. La. Gulf Railroad, 1985, Ctrl. La. Gulf Railroad, 1985. Pres. Jewish Vocat. Svc., Chgo., 1975-77, bd. dirs., 2005—; v.p. Sinai Temple, Chgo., 1977-84; bd. dirs. Jewish Fedn. Chgo., 2005; vice-chmn. Roycemore Sch., Evanston, Ill., 1982-87; pres. Emergency Fund for Needy People, 1993-2007, chmn., 2003—; trustee Brewster Acad., Wolfeboro, N.H.; vol. exec. for overseas needs Citizen's Democracy Corps; vol. cons. Exec. Svc. Corps., 1992—, project mgr., 1997, bd. dirs., 2002—; bd. dirs. Gastrointestinal Rsch. Found., Intermodal Transp. Inst., U. Denver, 1997—; cancer adv. bd. Northwestern U. Mem. Standard Club, Tavern Club, Bryn Mawr Country Club, Tamarisk Country Club, Long Boat Key Club, Execs. Club Chgo., Beta Alpha Psi, Phi Eta Sigma, Zeta Beta Tau. Avocations: golf, sports, reading, travel, cultural activities. Office: Stone Container Corp 645 N Michigan Ave Ste 800 Chicago IL 60611-3775 Home Phone: 312-649-5727; Office Phone: 312-981-5016. Personal E-mail: alanstone3@aol.com.

STONE, ALAN JAY, retired academic administrator; b. Ft. Dodge, Iowa, Oct. 15, 1942; s. Hubert H. and Bernice A. (Tilton) S.; m. Jonieta J. Smith; 1 child, Kirsten K. Stone Morlock. BA, Morningside Coll., Sioux City, Iowa, 1964, HD, 2001; MA, U. Iowa, Iowa City, 1966; MTh, U. Chgo., 1968, DMin, 1970; PhD (hon.), Kyonggi U., Korea, 1985; LLD, Stillman Coll., Tuscaloosa, Ala., 1991, Sogong U., Korea, 1992, Alma Coll., Mich., 2001. Admissions counselor Morningside Coll., Sioux City, Iowa, 1964-66; dir. admissions, asso. prof. history George Williams Coll., Downers Grove, Ill., 1969-73; v.p. coll. relations Hood Coll., Frederick, Md., 1973-75; v.p. devel. and fin. affairs W.Va. Wesleyan Coll., Buckhannon, 1975-77; dir. devel. U. Maine, 1977-78; pres. Aurora U., Ill., 1978-88, Alma Coll., 1988-2000; pres., CEO Alzheimer's Assn., Chgo., 2001—02; ret., 2002; lectr. for cruises. Home: 28897 N 94th Pl Scottsdale AZ 85262 Personal E-mail: thestones3@cox.net.

STONE, BERNARD LEONARD, vice mayor, alderman, lawyer; b. Chgo., Nov. 24, 1927; s. Sidney and Rebecca (Spinka) S.; m. Lois D. Falk, Aug. 28, 1949 (dec. 1995); children: Holly (dec.), Robin, Jay, Ilana, Lori. JD, John Marshall Law Sch., 1952. Alderman, 50th Ward City Coun. City of Chgo., 1973—; vice mayor City of Chgo., 1998—. Chmn. com. on bldgs., City of Chgo. Del. North Town Community Coun., 1963—, bd. dirs.; zoning chmn. Hood Ave. Civic Improvement Assn., 1954-58; dist. leader Am. Cancer Soc., 1959; bd. dirs. Congregation Ezras Israel, 1958—, Bernard Horwich Jewish Community Ctr., 1974-78, Assoc. Talmud Torahs, 1983—, Chgo. Assn. Retarded Citizens, 1979—; bd. govs. Bonds for Israel, 1972—; past campaign chmn. govt. agys. div. Jewish United Fund, 1978-79; commr. .E. Ill. Planning Commn., 1977-83; mem. Cook County Commn. on Criminal Justice, 1977-82. Mem. Ill. Bar Assn., Decalogue Soc. of Lawyers, Am. Legion, Westridge C. of C., B'nai B'rith (1st pres. Jacob M Arvey Pub. Svc. Lodge), Jewish War Vets. (past state judge adv., post comdr.). Office: City of Chgo City Hall Rm 203 121 N La Salle St Chicago IL 60602-1204

STONE, GEOFFREY RICHARD, lawyer, educator; b. Nov. 20, 1946; s. Robert R. and Shirley (Weliky) S.; m. Nancy Spector, Oct. 8, 1977; children: Julie, Mollie. BS, U. Pa., 1968; JD, U. Chgo., 1971. Bar: N.Y. 1972. Law clk. to Hon. J.S. Kelly Wright U.S. Ct. Appeals (D.C. cir.), 1971-72; law clk. to Hon. William J. Brennan, Jr. U.S. Supreme Ct., 1972-73; asst. prof. U. Chgo., 1973-77, assoc. prof., 1977-79, prof., 1979-84, Harry Kalven Jr. disting. svc. prof., 1984—, dean Law Sch., 1987-93, provost, 1994—2002, Harry Kalven, Jr. Disting. Svc. Prof. Law, 2003—. Author: Constitutional Law, 1986, 5th edit., 2005, The Bill of Rights in the Modern State, 1992, The First Amendment, 1999, Eternally Vigilant: Free Speech in the Modern Era, 2001, Perilous Times: Free Speech in Wartime, 2004 (25th Annual Robert F. Kennedy Book award, 2005); editor The Supreme Ct. Rev., 1991—; contbr. articles to profl. jours. Recipient Robert F. Kennedy Book award, Los Angeles Times Book prize for Best Book of Yr. in History. Fellow AAAS; mem. Chgo. Coun. Lawyers (bd. govs. 1976-77), Am. Law Inst. Assn. Am. Law Schs. (exec. com. 1990-93), Order of Coif. Office: U Chgo 1111 E 60th St Chicago IL 60637-5418 Business E-Mail: gstone@uchicago.edu.

STONE, HARRY H., retail executive; b. Cleve., May 21, 1917; s. Jacob and Jennie (Kantor) Sapirstein; m. Lucile Tabak, Aug. 10, 1960; children: Phillip, Allan, Laurie (Mrs. Parker), James Rose, Douglas Rose. Student, Cleve. Coll., 1935-36. With Am. Greetings Corp., Cleve., 1936—, v.p., 1944-58, exec. v.p., 1958-69, vice chmn. bd., chmn. finance com., chmn audit com., 1969-78, dir., 1944—2003, dir. emeritus, 2004—. Mem. Ofcl. U.S. Mission to India and Nepal, 1965; cons. U.S. Dept. Commerce, U.S. Dept. State; adviser U.S. del. 24th session UN Econ. Commn. for Asia and Far East, Canberra, Australia, 1968; cons. at. Endowment for Arts, Nat. Council on Arts. Treas. Criminal Justice Co-ordinating Council., 1968-82; trustee emeritus Brandeis U., also univ. fellow. Mem. Rotary (hon. pres.). Office: The Courtland Group Inc 1621 Euclid Ave Ste 1600 Cleveland OH 44115-2195

STONE, HERBERT MARSHALL, architect; b. NYC, July 12, 1936; s. Irving and Rose (Gelb) S.; m. Linda Ann Baskind, May 30, 1960; children: Ian Howard, Matthew Lloyd. BArch, Pratt Inst., NYC, 1958, postgrad., 1958-59. Registered architect, N.Y., Iowa, Kans., Ill., Wis., Minn. Designer Henry Dreyfuss Indsl. Design, NYC, 1960-63; architect Max O. Urbahn Architect, NYC, 1963-66; project architect Brown Healey Bock, P.C., Cedar Rapids, Iowa, 1966-73; ptnr. Brown Healey Stone & Sauer, Cedar Rapids, Iowa, 1973—, pres., 1994—. Guest lectr. U.S. Inst. Theatre Tech., Seattle, 1978; speaker on design of pub. librs. ALA Nat. Conv., Miami, Fla., 1994. Prin. works include Strayer-Wood Theatre, 1978, KUNI radio sta. U. No. Iowa, 1978, Cedar Rapids Pub. Libr., 1984, Greenwood Terr. Sr. Citizen Housing, 1986, Iowa State Hist. Mus., 1988, Nat. Hot Air Balloon Mus., 1988 (Spectrum Ceramic Tile Grand award 1989), Student Ctr. Grinnell Coll., 1992, Hall of Pride, Iowa H.S. Athletic Assn., 1995. Pres. Cedar Rapids Trust for Hist. Preservation, 1981—; bd. dirs. Art in Pub. Places Com., Cedar Rapids, 1988, Cedar Rapids/Marion Arts Coun., 1988, Jane Boyd Community House, Cedar Rapids, 1988; mem. Cedar Rapids Hist. Commn. Mem. AIA, Am. Mus. Assn. Avocations: bicycling, skiing, reading, ceramics. Home: 3411 Riverside Dr NE Cedar Rapids IA 52411-7405 Office: Brown Healey Stone & Sauer PC 800 1st Ave E Cedar Rapids IA 52402-5002

STONE, JACK, religious organization administrator; Sec., hdqs. ops. officer Ch. of the Nazarene, Kansas City, Mo., 1991—. Office: Ch of Nazarene 6401 The Paseo Kansas City MO 64131-1213

STONE, JAMES HOWARD, management consultant; b. Chgo., Mar. 4, 1939; s. Jerome H. and Evelyn Gertrude (Teitelbaum) S.; divorced; children: Margaret Elisa, Emily Anne, Phoebe Jane. AB cum laude, Harvard U., 1960; MBA, Harvard Bus. Sch., 1962. Cert. mgmt. cons., 1977. From staff analyst to exec. com. Stone Container Corp., Chgo., 1962—83, former exec. and audit coms., 1983—96; founder, owner, CEO, pres. Stone Mgmt. Corp., Chgo., 1969—; dir. privately-owned beverage mfr. Sheridan Beverage Co., Chgo., 1989—96; dir. privately-owned distributor and fabricator metals and metal products Fullerton Metals Co., Northbrook, Ill., 1993—98; pres. JEMP, Inc., Chgo., 2002—. Mem. strategic alliance Boston Cons. Group, 1990—; trustee, sec., exec. com. Roosevelt U., Chgo., 1983—, exec. com. edn. alliance, 1994—; co-chmn. commn. fgn. and domestic affairs Northwestern U., Evanston, Ill., 1981-85, bus. plan judge Kellogg Grad. Sch. Mgmt., 1994—; mem. vis. com. libr., lectr. U. Chgo., 1980—, The Chgo. Com., 1986—, Mid-Am. Com., Chgo., 1993-98; bd. overseers, lectr. IIT Stuart Sch. Bus., 1993—; bd. dirs. Cinema Chgo./Chgo. Film. Festival, Pilgrim Chamber Players, pres.; past pres., regional dir. Chgo. chpt. Inst. Mgmt. Cons.; past dir. Chgo. Roundtable Coun. Logistics Mgmt.; past pres., dir. Harvard Bus. Sch. Club Chgo. Contbr. articles in various trade jours. Mem. Chgo. Coun. Fgn. Rels., 1967, bd. dirs., 1974-78; bd. dirs., mem. exec. com. NCCJ, Chgo., 1985, presiding co-chmn., 1990-97; trustee Hadley Sch. Blind, Winnetka, Ill., 1985-96, chmn. planning com., 1989-96, Hadley life trustee, 1996—; vice chmn. fin. com. North Shore Congregation Israel, 1995-98; bd. dirs. Suzuki-Orff Sch., 1997-03; pres. Pilgrim Chamber Players, 2002—; former presiding co-chair Chgo. region Nat. Conf. Christians and Jews; sec., trustee, mem. exec. com. Roosevelt U.; mem. Chgo. Alliance Com.; life trustee Hadley Sch. for the Blind; vis. com. libr., patron U. Chgo.; with orthwestern U. Asher Sch. Psychiatry, Med. Sch.; bd. overseers Ill. Inst. Tech. Stuart Sch. Bus.; pres.'s cir., former dir. Chgo. Coun. Fgn. Rels.; advisor DCFS; mem. JVS Duman Loan Com.; dir. Blue Gargoyle, Little City Found.; past vice chmn. fin. com. North Shore Congregation Israel. Recipient Spirit of Life award, 2003. Mem. Coun. Logistics Mgmt. (dir. Roundtable-Chgo. 1990-94, lectr. Northwestern U. Ill. Inst. Tech.), The Exec. Club Chgo., Econs. Club Chgo., Harvard Club Chgo. (dir. 1995—), Harvard Bus. Sch. Club Chgo. (dir. 1992—, pres. 1997-99), Traffic Club Chgo., Std. Club, Northmoor Country Club, Mid-Day Club, The Casino Club, MidAm. Club, Arts Club, Juvenile Protective Assn. (trustee 1999—, dir.), The East Bank Club, Little City Found. Avocations: reading, golf, travel, writing. Office Phone: 312-236-0800. Business E-Mail: stonem@stonemgmt.com.

STONE, JEFFREY, state official; b. Topeka, Jan. 28, 1961; m. Lynn Stone. BA, Washburn U., 1983. Mgr. printing bus., 1983—87; owner, oper. printing bus., 1987—98; alderman City of Greenfield, 1994—98; pres. city coun., 1997—98; state assemblyman Wis., 1998—. Mem. campaign and elections com.; mem. edn. reform com.; mem. Joint Legis. Coun.; mem. labor and workforce devel. com.; mem. Milw. Child Welfare Partnership Coun.; chair transp. com. Mem. Friends of Greenfield Libr. Mem.: Milw./Racine Printing House Craftsmen (alderperson City of Greenfield 1995—98), Greenfield Bus. Assn. (pres.), S.W. Suburban Chamber Coalition, Greenfield C. of C., Met. Assn. Commerce in Milw., Greenfield C. of C. (past sec.), Greendale Lycus Club. Republican. Lutheran. Office: State Capitol Rm 320 E PO Box 8953 Madison WI 53708-8953

STONE, JOHN TIMOTHY, JR., writer; b. Denver, July 13, 1933; s. John Timothy and Marie Elizabeth (Briggs) S.; m. Judith Bosworth Stone, June 22, 1955; children: John Timothy III, George Williams. Student, Amherst Coll., 1951—52, U. Mex., 1952; BA, postgrad., U. Miami, 1955, U. Colo., 1959—60. Sales mgr. Atlas Tag, Chgo., 1955-57; br. mgr. Household Fin. Corp., Chgo., 1958-62; pres. Janeff Credit Corp., Madison, Wis., 1962-72, Recreation Internat., Mpls., 1972-74, Continental Royal Svcs., NYC, 1973-74; dir. devel. The Heartlands Group/Tryon Mint, Toronto, Ont., Can., 1987-89; spl. cons. Creative Resources Internat., Madison, 1988-90, Pubs. Adv. Group, 1990—; spl. cons. art and antiques Treasure Hunt Assocs., 1994—. Bd. dirs. Madison Credit Bur., Wis. Lenders' Exch. Author: Mark, 1973, Going for Broke, 1976, The Minnesota Connection, 1978, Debby Boone So Far, 1980, (with John Dallas McPherson) He Calls Himself "An Ordinary Man", 1981, Satiacum, The Chief Who's Winning Back the West, 1981, Runaways, 1983, (with Robert E. Gard) Where the Green Bird Flies, 1984, The Insiders Guide to Buying Art, 1993, Anyone's Treasure Hunt, 1995; syndicated columnist The Great American Treasure Hunt, 1983-87. Served with CIC, U.S. Army, 1957-59. Mem. Minarani Club, African First Shotters Club, Sigma Alpha Epsilon. Presbyterian.

STONE, RANDOLPH NOEL, law educator; b. Milw., Nov. 26, 1946; s. Fisher and Lee Della Stone; m. Cheryl M. Bradley; children: Sokoni, Rahman, Marisa, Lee Sukari. BA, U. Wis., Milw., 1972; JD, Madison, 1975. Bar: D.C., 1975, Wis. 1975, Ill. 1977. Staff atty. Criminal Def. Consortium of Cook County, Chgo., 1976-78; clin. fellow U. Chgo. Law Sch., 1977-80; ptnr. Stone & clark, Chgo., 1980-83; staff atty., dep. dir. Pub. Defender Svc. for D.C., Washington, 1983-88; pub. defender Cook County Pub. Defender's Office, Chgo., 1988-91; lectr. U. Chgo. Law Sch., 1990, clin. prof. law, dir. Mandel Legal Aid Clinic, 1991—. Adj. prof. Ill. Inst. Tech. Chgo.-Kent Coll. Law Sch., 1991, bd. overseers, 1990; lectr. law Harvard U., 1991—; mem. Ill. Bd. Admissions to the Bar, 1994—; bd. dirs. The Sentencing Project, 1986—; instr. trial advocacy workshop Harvard Law Sch., 1985-89. Adv. bd. Neighborhood Defender Svc. (Harlem), N.Y.C. Reginald Heber Smith fellow Neighborhood Legal Svcs. Program, Washington, 1975-76. Mem. ABA (sect. criminal justice coun. 1989-95, chair 1993, commn. domestic violence 1994-97), Ill. State Bar Assn. (sect. criminal justice coun. 1989-92), Chgo. Bar Assn. (bd. dirs. 1990-92), Nat. Legal Aid and Defender Assn. (def. com. 1988-96). Office: U Chgo Law Sch Mandel Legal Aid Clinic 6020 S University Ave Chicago IL 60637-2704

STONE, STEVEN MICHAEL, sports announcer, former baseball player; b. Euclid, Ohio, July 14, 1947; BS in Edn., Kent State U., 1969. Pitcher San Francisco Giants, 1971-72, Chgo. White Sox, 1973, Chgo. Cubs, 1974-76, Chgo. White Sox, 1977-78, Balt. Orioles, 1979—81; color commentator, Chgo. Cubs WGN Continental Broadcasting Co., Chgo., 1983—2000, 2003—04; baseball analyst WSCR Radio, Chgo., 2005—, commentator, White Sox, 2008—. Restaurant owner, Scottsdale, Ariz. Co-author (with Barry Rozner): (book) Where's Harry?, 1999. Named Am. League Pitcher of Yr., The Sporting News, 1980; named to Am. League All-Star Team, 1980; recipient Cy Young award, 1980. Achievements include leading the American League in wins (25) during the 1980 season. Office: WSCR Radio 455 N Cityfront Plaza Dr Chicago IL 60611 Office Phone: 312-245-6000.

STONE, SUSAN A., lawyer; b. 1961; BA summa cum laude, Yale U., 1983; JD cum laude, Harvard U., 1987. Bar: Calif. 1987, U.S. Dist. Ct. (no. dist.) Calif. 1987, U.S. Ct. Appeals (9th cir.) 1987, U.S. Dist. Ct. (ctrl. dist.) Calif. 1988, Ill. 1990, U.S. Dist. Ct. (no. dist.) Ill. 1990, U.S. Ct. Appeals (7th cir.) 1990. Asst. U.S. atty. U.S. Dept. Justice, LA; law clk. to Judge William J. Orrick, U.S. Dist. Ct. for No. Dist. Calif.; ptnr. Sidley & Austin (until 2001 merger), Chgo.; ptnr. litig. Sidley Austin Brown & Wood, Chgo., 2001—, and co-chair practice devel. com. Former adj. prof. trial practice DePaul U. Coll. Law, Chgo. Named one of Top Young Litigators Under 40, Ill. Legal Times, One of 40 Attorneys Under 40, Chgo. Lawyer,. Mem. ABA, Ill. Bar Assn., Calif. State Bar, Phi Beta Kappa. Office: Sidley Austin Brown & Wood LLP Bank One Plz 10 S Dearborn St Chicago IL 60603 Office Phone: 312-853-2177. Fax: 312-853-7036. E-mail: sstone@sidley.com.

STONECIPHER, HARRY CURTIS, former aerospace transportation executive; b. Robbins, Tenn., May 16, 1936; s. Harry Sheldon and Jennie Mae Stonecipher; m. Joan Stonecipher; 2 children. BS, Tenn. Poly. Inst., 1960; DSc (hon.), Washington U., 2002. With GE, 1960—61, 1962—79, Martin Aircraft Co., 1961-62; v.p., gen. mgr., comml. & mil. transp. ops. GE, 1979—84, v.p., gen. mgr., aircraft engine ops. Evendale, Ohio, 1984—87; exec. v.p. Sundstrand Corp., 1987, pres., COO, 1987-88, pres., CEO, 1988-94, chmn., 1991-94, also past bd. dirs.; pres., CEO McDonnell-Douglas Corp., St. Louis, 1994-97; pres., COO The Boeing Co., 1997—2001, vice chmn., 2001—02, pres., CEO, 2003—05. Bd. dirs. PACCAR, Inc., The Boeing Co., 1997-2005. Bd. trustees Mus. Contemporary Art; bd. dirs. Lyric Opera Chgo.; bd. mem. US-China Bus. Coun., US-Saudi Arabia Bus. Coun., exec. com. mem. Recipient John R. Allison award, 1996, Rear Adm. John J. Bergen Leadership medal Navy League, 1996, Wings Club Disting. Achievement award, 2001, John W. Dixon award, U.S. Army Assn., 2002. Fellow Royal Aero. Soc., 1998.

STONEMAN, WILLIAM, III, plastic surgeon, educator; b. Kansas City, Mo., Sept. 8, 1927; s. William and Helen Louise (Bloom) S.; m. Elizabeth Johanna Wilson, May 19, 1951; children: William Laurence, Sidney Camdon (dec.), Cecily Anne Erker, Elizabeth Wilson, John Spalding. Student, Rockhurst Coll., 1944-46; BS, St. Louis U., 1948, MD, 1952. Diplomate: Am. Bd. Surgery, Am. Bd. Plastic Surgery. Intern Kansas City Gen. Hosp., 1952-53; resident in surgery St. Louis U., 1953-57, resident in plastic surgery, 1957-59, mem. faculty, 1959—, assoc. prof. surgery, assoc. prof. community medicine, 1975-84, prof. surgery, community medicine, 1984-94, prof. surgery, community medicine emeritus, 1994, assoc. dean Sch. Medicine, 1973-76; exec. assoc. dean St. Louis U. (Sch. Medicine), 1976-82, dean, 1982-95, dean emeritus, 1995—, assoc. v.p. med. ctr., 1983-95. Mem. adj. faculty Washington U. Sch. Medicine, St. Louis, 1968-74; chief exec. officer Bi-State Regional Med. Program, 1968-74; bd. dirs. St. Louis Office Mental Retardation/Developmentally Disabled Resources, 1980-82, Combined Health Appeal of Mo., 1990-94. Editor: Parameters, 1976-94; contbr. articles on plastic surgery, health care delivery planning to profl. jours. Served with AUS, 1946-47. Fellow ACS; mem. AMA (chmn. sect. on med. schs. 1987-88, sect. alt. del. 1989-91, del. 1992-94), Mo. Med. Assn., Mem. St. Louis Met. Med. Soc., St. Louis Surg. Soc., Am. Soc. Plastic and Reconstructive Surgeons, Midwestern Assn. Plastic Surgeons. Roman Catholic. E-mail: stoneman@slu.edu.

STONER, GARY DAVID, cancer researcher; b. Bozeman, Mont., Oct. 25, 1942; married; 2 children. BS, Mont. State U., 1964; MS, U. Mich., 1968, PhD in Microbiol., 1970. Asst. rsch. scientist U. Calif., San Diego, 1970-72, assoc. rsch. scientist, 1972-75; cancer expert Nat. Cancer Inst., 1976-79; assoc. prof. pathology Med. Coll. Ohio, 1979-83; prof. pathology, 1983-92; prof. internal medicine and pathology Ohio State U., Columbus, 1992, assoc. dir. Ctr. for Molecular and Environ. Health, 1993—2003, assoc. dir. basic rsch. Comp Cancer Ctr, 1994—, prof., chmn. divsn. environ. health scis. Sch. Pub. Health, 1995—2003; prof. internal medicine, dir. program Ohio State U. Comprehensive Cancer Ctr., Columbus. Cons. Nat. Heart Lung & Blood Inst., 1974—, EPA, 1979—, Nat. Cancer Inst., 1979—, Nat. Toxicol. Program, 1981—; mem. study sect. NIH, 1980-92, 2003—, Am. Cancer Soc., Ohio, 1982—, Am. Cancer Soc., Nat., 1995-2002. Grantee Nat. Cancer Inst., EPA, U.S. Army R & D Command. Fellow AAAS; mem. Soc. Toxicology, Am. Assn. Cancer Rsch., Am. Assn. Pathologists, Internat. Soc. Cancer Chemoprevention. Achievements include research in carcinogenesis in human and animal model respiratory and esophageal tissues, carcinogenic metabolism, mutagenesis, in vitro transformation of epithelial cells and chemoprevention. Office: Ohio State U Divsn Hematology/Oncology Dept Internal 1148 CHRI 300 W 10th Ave Columbus OH 43210-1240 Home Phone: 614-888-2133; Office Phone: 614-293-3268. Business E-Mail: stoner.21@osu.edu.

STOOKEY, GEORGE KENNETH, retired director, retired dental educator; b. Waterloo, Ind., Nov. 6, 1935; s. Emra Gladison and Mary Catherine (Anglin) Stookey; m. Nola Jean Meek, Jan. 15, 1955; children: Lynda, Lisa, Laura, Kenneth. AB in Chemistry, Ind. U., 1957, MSD, 1962, PhD in Preventive Dentistry, 1971. Asst. dir. Preventive Dentistry Rsch. Inst. Ind. U., Indpls., 1968-70, assoc. prof. preventive dentistry Sch. Dentistry, 1973-78, prof., 1978-98, disting. prof., 1998—, prof. emeritus, 2001, assoc. dir. Oral Health Rsch. Inst., 1974—81, 1999—2001, dir., 1981-99, assoc. dean rsch. Sch. Dentistry, 1987-97, 00-01, acting dean, 1996, assoc. dean acad. affairs, 1997-98, exec. assoc. dean, 1998-2000. Cons. USAF, San Antonio, 1973—, ADA, Chgo., 1972—, Nat. Inst. Dental Rsch., Bethesda, 1978—82, Bethesda, 1991—95. Author (with others): (book) Introduction to Oral Biology and Preventive Dentistry, 1971, Preventive Dentistry in Action, 1972 (Meritorious award, 1973), Preventive Dentistry for the Dental Assistant and Dental Hygienist, 1977; contbr. articles to profl. jours. Mem.: ADA, Am. Assn. Lab. Animal Sci., European Orgn. Caries Rsch., Internat. Assn. Dental Rsch. Republican. Office: Ind U Emerging Techs Ctr 351 W 10th St Ste 222 Indianapolis IN 46202-4119 E-mail: gstookey@iupui.edu.

STOOKSBURY, WALTER ELBERT, insurance company executive; b. Harriman, Tenn., June 19, 1940; s. Maurice Claude and Thelma Marie (Dyer) S.; m. Mary Evelyn Farmer, Dec. 21, 1964; children: Kevin, Andrew. BS, U. Tenn., 1962. Tchr. Anderson County Schs., Clinton, Tenn., 1963-67; agt. Horace Mann Ins. Co., Springfield, Ill., 1967-68, agy. mgr., 1968-70, zone v.p., 1970-77, v.p. casualty div., 1977-92, sr. v.p. casualty div., 1992—, exec. v.p. property & casualty divsn., 1992—, also bd. dirs. Bd. dirs. Allegiance Ins. Co., Allegiance Life Ins. Co., Assn. and Consumer Mktg. Svc. Corp., Educators Life Ins. Co. Am., Horace Mann Svc. Corp., Sr. Mktg. Ins. Svc. Corp., Tchrs. Ins. Co. Mem. Am. Assn. Ins. Svcs. (bd. dirs., exec. dir. 1980—), Sangamo Club. Methodist. Avocations: golf, antique cars. Home: 3210 Victoria Dr Springfield IL 62704-1045 Office: Horace Mann Educators Corp 1 Horace Mann Plz Springfield IL 62715

STORANDT, MARTHA, psychologist; b. Little Rock, June 2, 1938; d. Farris and Floy (Montgomery) Mobbs; m. Duane Storandt, Dec. 15, 1962; 1 child, Eric AB, Washington U., St. Louis, 1960, PhD, 1966. Lic. psychologist, Mo. Staff psychologist VA, Jefferson Barracks, Mo., 1967-68; asst. prof. to prof. Washington U., St. Louis, 1968—. Mem. nat. adv. council on aging Nat. Inst. on Aging, 1984-87; editor-in-chief Jour. Gerontology, 1981-86 Author: Counseling and Therapy with Older Adults, 1983; co-author: Memory, Related Functions and Age, 1974; co-editor: The Clinical Psychology of Aging, 1978, The Adult Years: Continuity and Change, 1989, Neuropsychological Assessment of Dementia and Depression in Older Adults: A Clinician's Guide, 1994. Recipient Disting. Service award Mo. Assn. Homes for the Aging, 1984. Fellow APA (pres. divsn. 20 1979-80, council rep. 1983-84, 86-88, Disting. Sci. Contbn. award divsn. adult devel. and aging 1988, Master Mentor award divsn. adult devel. and aging 2000, Disting. Contbns. to Clin. Geropsychology divsn. clin. psychology 2002), Gerontol. Soc. Am. Office: Washington U Dept Psychology Saint Louis MO 63130

STORB, URSULA BEATE, molecular genetics and cell biology educator; b. Stuttgart, Germany; came to U.S., 1966; d. Walter M. Stemmer and Marianne M. (Kämmerer) Nowara. MD, U. Freiburg, Germany, 1960. Asst. prof. dept. microbiology U. Wash., Seattle, 1971-75, assoc. prof., 1975-81, prof., 1981-86, head. div. immunology, 1980-86; prof. dept. molecular genetics and cell biology U. Chgo., 1986—. Mem. editl. bd. Immunity, Current Opinion in Immunology, Internat. Immunology, Immunol. Revs.; contbr. articles to sci. jours. Grantee NIH, NSF, Am. Cancer Soc., 1973—. Fellow Am. Acad. Arts and Scis.; mem. AAAS, Assn. Women in Sci., Am. Assn. Immunologists. Office: U Chgo 920 E 58th St Chicago IL 60637-5415 E-mail: stor@midway.uchicago.edu.

STORK, DONALD ARTHUR, advertising executive; b. Walsh, Ill., June 17, 1939; s. Arthur William and Katherine Frances (Young) S.; m. Joanna Gentry, June 9, 1962; 1 child, Brian Wesley. BS, So. Ill. U., 1961; postgrad., St. Louis U., 1968—69. With Naegele Outdoor Advt., Mpls. and St. Louis, 1961—63; acct. exec. Richard C. Lynch Advg., 1963—64; media exec. Gardner Advt. Co., 1964—69; v.p. mktg. Advanswers Media/Programming, 1975—79; pres. Advanswers divsn. Wells/BDDP, NYC, 1979—98; pres. Advanswers unit Omnicom, St. Louis, 1998—2002, pres. PHD unit, 2002—04; ret., 2004. Bd. dirs. Trailblazers, Inc.; corp. devel. St. Louis Art Mus., 1999—2005. Capt. Mo. Air N.G., 1961—67. Recipient Journalism Alumnus of Yr. award So. Ill. U., Alumni Achievement award. Mem. St. Louis Advtsg. Club, Mensa, Mo. Athletic Club, St. Clair Country Club (bd. dirs. 2001), Alpha Delta Sigma (Aid to Advtg. Edn. award). Home: 27 Symonds Dr Belleville IL 62223-1905 Office: Media Mgmt Inc 14755 N Outer Forty Dr Chesterfield MO 63017 Office Phone: 314-910-0373. Personal E-mail: dastork@sbcglobal.net.

STORNES, MARK, professional sports team executive; married; children: Matt, Ryan, Scott, Meghan. BBA in Acctg., Cleve. State U., 1983. Sr. auditor Grant Thornton, 1983—87; positions up to exec. v.p., COO TransAmerica Mailings, Inc., 1987—96; sr. v.p. fin. and adminstrn., CFO Cleve. Cavaliers/Quicken Loans Arena, 1996—2001, exec. v.p., COO, 2001—02, CEO, 2003—. Exec. dir. Cavaliers Charities, 1999; treas. Downtown Cleve. Alliance; trustee Berea Ednl. Fund Found. Mem.: Bluccoats, Inc. Office: Cleve Cavaliers One Center Ct Cleveland OH 44115-4001

STORY, KENDRA, wholesale distribution executive; CFO Am. Bldrs. & Contrs. Supply Co., Inc., Beloit, Wis. Office: Am Bldrs & Contrs Supply One ABC Pkwy Beloit WI 53511 Office Fax: (608) 362-6215.

STOUT, GLENN EMANUEL, retired science administrator; b. Fostoria, Ohio, Mar. 23, 1920; AB, Findlay U., 1942, DSc, 1973. Head atmosphere scis. sec. Ill. State Water Survey, 1952—71; sci. coord. NSF, 1969-71; asst. to chief Ill. State Water Survey, Champaign, 1971-74; prof. Inst. Environ. Studies, Urbana, Ill., 1973-94, dir. task force, 1975-79; dir. Water Resources Ctr. U. Ill., Urbana, 1973-94; rsch. coord. Ill.-Ind. Sea Grant Program, 1987-94; emeritus, 1994—. Mem. Ill. Gov.'s Task Force on State Water Plan, 1980-94; bd. dirs. Univ. Coun. Water Resources, 1983-86, chmn. internat. affairs, 1989-92; mem. nomination com. for Stockholm Water Prize, 1994-96. Contbr. articles to profl. jours. Bd. govs. World Water Coun., 1996-98. Mem. Am. Water Resources Assn., Internat. Water Resources Assn. (sec. gen. 1985-91, v.p. 1992-94, exec. dir. 1984-95, pres. 1995-97, hon.), Am. Meteorol. Soc., Am. Geophys. Union, .Am. Lake Mgmt. Soc., Ill. Lake Mgmt. Assn. (bd. dirs. 1985-88), Am. Water Works Assn., Kiwanis (pres. local club 1979-80, lt. gov. 1982-83), Sigma Xi (pres. U. Ill. chpt. 1985-86). Achievements include first to record radar pattern of the hooked echo, depicting a major tornado, 1953. Home: 401 Burwash Ave Apt 216 Savoy IL 61874-9574

STOUT, MICHAEL W., communications executive; BSBA, U. Colo. Various mgmt. pos. United Airlines, Covia Partnership, and Galileo Internat.; v.p., chief tech. and info. officer GE Capital, 1995—2003; exec. v.p., chief info. officer Sprint Corp., Overland Park, Kans., 2003—. Office: Sprint Corp 6200 Sprint Pkwy Overland Park KS 66251

STOVALL, CARLA JO, former state attorney general; b. Hardner, Kans., Mar. 18, 1957; d. Carl E. and Juanita Joe (Ford) Stovall. BA, Pittsburg State U., Kans., 1979; JD, U. Kans., 1982, MPA, 1993. Bar: Kans. 1982, U.S. Dist. Ct. Kans. 1982. Pvt. practice, Pitts., 1982—85; atty. Crawford County, Pitts., 1984—88; gov. Kans. Parole Bd., Topeka, 1988—94; atty. gen. State of Kans., Topeka, 1995—2002. Lectr. law Pittsburg State U., 1982—84. Mem. bd. govs. U. Kans. Sch. Law; at. Ctr. Missing and Exploited Children; Am. Legacy Found.; Nat. Crime Prevention Coun.; Coun. State Govts.; mem. bd. govs. Kans. Children's Cabinet; pres. NAAG, 2001—02, chmn. exec. com. midwest region, sexually violent predator com., 1995—96; Bd. dirs., sec. Pittsburg Family YMCA, 1983—88. Named Outstanding Atty. Gen., Nat. Assn. Attys. Gen., 2001, Topeka Fraternal Order of Police's Amb. to Law Enforcement; recipient Champion award, Campaign Tobacco Free Kids, 2002, Adam Walsh Children's Fund Rainbow award, Nat. Ctr. Missing and Exploited Children, 2001, Kelley-Wyman award, Nat. Assn. Attys. Gen., 2001, Person of the Yr., Kans. Peace Officer Assn.'s Law Enforcement, Morton Baud Allied Profl. award, Nat. Orgn. Victim Assistance, Father Ken Czillinger award, Nat. Parents Murdered Children, Disting. Svc. to Kans. Children award, Kans. Children's Svc. League, Woman of Achievement award, Miss Kans. Pageant. Mem.: NAAG (pres. 2001—02), AAUW (bd. dirs. 1983—87), ABA, Bus. and Profl. Women Assn. (Young Careerist award 1984), Nat. Coll. Dist. Attys., Kans. County and Dist. Attys. Assn., Crawford County Bar Assn. (sec. 1984—85, v.p. 1985—86, pres. 1986—87), Kans. Bar Assn., Kans. Assn. Commerce and Industry (Leadership Kans. award 1983), Pittsburg Area C. of C. (bd. dirs. 1983—85, Leadership

Pitts. award 1984), Pittsburg State U. Alumni Assn. (bd. dirs. 1983—88). Republican. Methodist. Avocations: travel, photography, tennis. Home: 138 S Blue Bells Ct Garden Plain KS 67050-9225

STOWELL, JOSEPH, III, academic administrator; Pres. Moody Bible Inst., Chgo., 1987—. Office: Moody Bible Inst 820 N La Salle Dr Chicago IL 60610-3263 also: Sta WKES-FM PO Box 8888 Saint Petersburg FL 33738-8888

STOWERS, JAMES EVANS, JR., investment company executive; b. Kansas City, Mo., Jan. 10, 1924; s. James Evans Sr. and Laura (Smith) S.; m. Virginia Ann Glasscock, Feb. 4, 1954; children: Pamela, Kathleen, James Evans III, Linda. AB, U. Mo., 1946, BS in Medicine, 1947. Chmn. bd. Am. Century Investment Mgmt. Inc., Am. Century Cos., Inc.; Am. Century Group of Mutual Funds, Kansas City, 1958—. Author: Why Waste Your Money on Life Insurance, 1967, Principles of Financial Consulting, 1971, Yes, You Can.Achieve Financial Independence, 1992; co-author: (with Jack Jonathan) The Best is Yet to Be: A Story of Innovation, Generosity & Success, 2007 Co-founder, chmn. Stowers Inst. for Med. Rsch., Kansas City, 1995—. Capt. USAAF, 1943-45; with USAFR, 1945-57. Mem. Kansas City C. of C., Sigma Chi Republican. Office: Am Century Svcs 4500 Main St Kansas City MO 64111-1816

STOWERS, JAMES W., III, data processing executive; b. 1958; With Twentieth Century Svcs., Kansas City, Mo., 1979—, pres.; CEO Am. Century Cos., Kansas City, Mo. Office: Am Century Investments 4500 Main St Kansas City MO 64111-1816

STOWMAN, DAVID L., lawyer; b. Rothsay, Minn., 1943; m. Judy Stowman; 4 children. BA, Moorehead State Univ.; JD, Univ. N.D. Co-founder NW Minn. Legal Services. Capt. USMC, 1965—69, Vietnam (1968-69). Named one of Minn. Top 25 Lawyers, Law & Politics mag., 2001. Mem.: ABA, Minn. State Bar Assn. (pres.-elect 2003, pres. 2004). Avocations: running, water-skiing. Office: Stowman Law Office PO Box 845 Detroit Lakes MN 56502-0845 also: Stowman Law Office 1100 W Lake Dr Detroit Lakes MN 56501 Office Phone: 218-847-5644.

STRAHORN, FRED, state representative; b. Cin., Mar. 20, 1965; 1 child. BA in Aviation Mgmt., Ohio State U. Rep. Ohio State Ho. Reps., Columbus, 2000—. Mem. banking, pensions and securities com. Ohio State Ho. Reps., mem. econ. devel. and tech. com., mem. fin. and appropriations com., mem. primary and secondary edn. subcom., mem. pub. utilities com. Mem.: Rotary (mem. itnernat. group study exchange team to Sweden 1999). Democrat. Office: Ohio State House Reps 77 South High Street 10th Floor Columbus OH 43215-6111

STRAIGHT, CATHY, editor; Dep. mng. editor Nashville Tennessean; with editor-development program Pioneer Press divsn. Knight Ridder; mng. editor features and sports St. Paul Pioneer Press, 2002—. Recipient Newsroom Supr. Recognition award, Gannett, 1999. Office: St Paul Pioneer Press 345 Cedar St Saint Paul MN 55101

STRAIN, JAMES ARTHUR, lawyer; b. Alexandria, La., Oct. 11, 1944; s. William Joseph and Louise (Moore) S.; m. Cheryl Sue Williamson, Aug. 19, 1967; children: William Joseph, Gordon Richard, Elizabeth Parks. BS in Econs., Ind. U., 1966, JD, 1969. Bar: Ind. 1969, U.S. Dist. Ct. (so. dist.) Ind. 1969, U.S. Ct. Appeals (7th cir.) 1972, U.S. Supreme Ct. 1975, U.S. Ct. Appeals (5th cir.) 1978. Instr. Law Sch. Ind. U., Indpls., 1969-70; law clk. to Hon. John S. Hastings 7th Cir. Ct. Appeals, Chgo., 1970-71; assoc. Cahill, Gordon & Reindel, NYC, 1971-72; law clk. to Hon. William H. Rehnquist U.S. Supreme Ct., Washington, 1972-73; assoc. Barnes, Hickam, Pantzer & Boyd, Indpls., 1973-75; ptnr. Barnes, Hickam, Pantzer & Boyd (name changed to Barnes & Thornburg), 1976-96, Sommer Barnard, PC, Indpls., 1996—. Adj. asst. prof. law Ind. U. Sch. Law, 1986-92, 2003-07. Mem., bd. dirs. The Penrod Soc., Indpls., 1976—, Indpls. Symphonic Choir, 1988-91, Festival Music Soc., Indpls., 1990-96. Mem. 7th Cir. Bar Assn. (meetings chmn. Ind. chpt. 1979-88, portraits 1988-89, bd. govs. 1989—, 1st v.p. 1995, pres. 1996). Avocations: photography, music. Office: Sommer Barnard PC Ste 3500 One Indiana Sq Indianapolis IN 46204 Home Phone: 317-686-1928; Office Phone: 317-713-3500. Business E-Mail: strain@sommerbarnard.com.

STRAMPEL, WILLIAM DERKEY, dean, medical educator; b. Saugatuck, Mich., Feb. 8, 1948; married; 3 children. BA, Hope Coll., 1970; DO, Chgo. Coll. Osteopathic Medicine, 1976. Intern Madigan Army Med. Ctr., Fort Lewis, Wash., 1976—77, resident in medicine, 1977—79; fellow in pulmonary disease Fitzsimons Army Med. Ctr., Aurora, 1980—82; staff internal medicine svc. and dir. intensive care 121 Evacuation Hosp., Seoul; pulmonary staff and dir. intensive care Fitzsimons Army Med. Ctr., Aurora, Colo.; divsn. surgeon First Infantry Divsn. Irwin Army Cmty. Hosp., Fort Riley, Kans., dep. comdr., dir. med. edn., Evans Army Cmty. Hosp., Fort Carson, Colo.; chief Quality Assurance Divsn., Dept. of Army, Office Surgeon Gen., 1991—94; dir. med. edn. Brooke Army Med. Ctr., 1994—96; comdr. Brooke Army Med. Ctr. and Great Plains Med. Command, 1996—97; dir. quality mgmt. Office Sec. Def.; chief med. officer Tricare Mgmt. Activity; spl. asst. for ops. and readiness to U.S. surgeon gen.; leader Mich. State U. Health Team; sr. assoc. dean Mich. State U., Coll. Osteo. Medicine, 1999—2002, prof. internal medicine, 2001—, acting dean, 2001—02, dean, 2002—. Served to col. US Army. Office: A314 E Free Hall East Lansing MI 48824-1316

STRANDJORD, M. JEANNINE, telecommunications industry executive; B in Acctg. and Bus. Adminstrn., U. Kans. CPA. V.p. fin. Macy's Midwest; with Kans. city Power & Light Co., Ernst and Whinney; v.p. fin. and distrbn. AmeriSource, Inc. (subs. Sprint), 1985—90, controller, 1986—90, sr. v.p., treas., 1990—98, sr. v.p. fin. global markets group, 1998—2003; sr. v.p. fin. svcs. Sprint Corp., 2003, sr. v.p., chief integration officer, 2003—. Bd. dirs. Am. Century Mutual Funds, DST Sys., Inc., Euronet Worldwide. Trustee Rockhurst U. Office: 6200 Spring Pkwy Overland Park KS 66251

STRANG, JAMES DENNIS, editor; b. Ashtabula, Ohio, June 23, 1945; s. Delbert Devoe and Mildred Edith (Green) S.; m. Margaret Florence Littell, Aug. 25, 1974; children: Megan Lisbeth, Amy Colleen, Benjamin Jefferson. BS in Journalism, Kent State U., 1969. Cert. firearms instr. Reporter The Star-Beacon, Ashtabula, Ohio, 1966, The Record-Courier, Kent, Ohio, 1966-69, The Cleve. Press, 1969-71; cons. Tom Rall & Assocs., Washington, 1971-72; reporter, editor The Plain Dealer, Cleve., 1973-75, assoc. editor, 1975—. Instr. journalism Lorain County C.C., Elyria, Ohio, 1973-74. Recipient Nat. Comdrs. award DAV, 1980, Best Editorial award AP Soc. Ohio, 1988. Mem. Nat. Conf. Editorial Writers, Soc. Profl. Journalists, Nat. Rifle Assn. (life). Unitarian-Universalist. Avocation: shooting sports. Office: The Plain Dealer 1801 Superior Ave E Cleveland OH 44114-2198

STRANG, RUTH HANCOCK, pediatrician, educator, cardiologist, priest; b. Bridgeport, Conn., Mar. 11, 1923; d. Robert H.W. and Ruth (Hancock) Strang. BA, Wellesley Coll., 1944, postgrad., 1944—45; MD, N.Y. Med. Coll., 1949; MDiv, Seabury We. Theol. Sem., 1993. Diplomate Am. Bd. Pediat.; ordained deacon Episc. Ch., 1993, priest Episc. Ch., 1994. Intern Flower and Fifth Ave. Hosp., NYC, 1949—50, resident in pediat., 1950—52; mem. faculty N.Y. Med. Coll., NYC, 1952—57; fellow cardiology Babies Hosp., NYC, 1956—57, Harriet Lane Cardiac Clinic, Johns Hopkins Hosp., Balt., 1957—59, Children's Hosp., Boston, 1959—62; mem. faculty U. Mich. Hosp., Ann Arbor, 1962—89, prof. pediat., 1970—89, prof. emeritus, 1989—; priest-in-charge St. Johns Episcopal Ch., Howell, Mich., 1994—. Dir. pediat. Wayne County Gen. Hosp., Westland, Mich. 1965-85; mem. staff U. Mich. Hosps., 1962-89; mem. med. adv. com. Wayne County chpt. Nat. Cystic Fibrosis Rsch. Found., 1966-80, chmn. med. adv. com. nat. found., Detroit, 1971-78; cons. cardiology Plymouth (Mich.) State Home and Tng. Sch., 1970-81; diocesan coun. Diocese Mich., 2003-05, mem. com. on nominations and elections Diocesan Conv., 2003, chmn. com., 2004. Author: Clinical Aspects of Operable Heart Disease, 1968; contbr. numerous articles to profl. jours. Mem. citizen's adv. coun. Juvenile Ct., Ann Arbor, 1968—76; mem. med. adv. bd. Ann Arbor Continuing Edn. Dept., 1968—77; v.p. Am. Heart Assn. Mich., 1989, pres., 1991; bd. dirs. Livingston Cmty. Hospice, 1995—99; bd. mgrs. Emrich Episcopal Retreat Ctr., 1998—; mem. Diocesan Com. for World Relief, Detroit, 1970—72; trustee Episcopal Med. Chaplaincy, Ann Arbor, 1971—96; mem. bishop's com. St. Aidan's Episc. Ch., 1966—69, sec., 1966—68, vestry, 1973—76, 1978—80, 1984—86, 1990—91, sr. warden, 1975—76, 1978, 1986, 1990; del. Episc. Diocesan Conv., 1980, 1991; mem. Congl. Life Circle Episcopal Diocese Mich., 1995—2001, mem. loans and grants com., 1995—99, mem. com. on reference ann. diocesan conv., 1995-98, chmn., 1996; mem. Diocese Mich. Clergy Family Project, 1996—98; co-dean Huron Valley area coun. Diocese Mich., 1998—2000; bd. trustees Ecumenical Theol. Sem., 1996—, chair acad. affairs com., 2000—; mem. Congl. Devel. Commn., 2001—03; bd. dirs. Livingston County Cath. Social Svcs., 2004—. Recipient Alumnae Life Achievement award, Baldwin Sch., 2005. Mem. AMA, Am. Acad. Pediat., Am. Coll. Cardiology, Mich. Med. Soc., Washtenaw County Med. Soc., N.Y. Acad. Medicine, Am. Heart Assn., Women's Rsch. Club (membership sec. 1966-67), Ambulatory Pediat. Assn., Am. Assn. Child Care in Hosps., Am. Assn. Med. Colls., Assn. Faculties of Pediat. Nurse Assn./Practitioners Programs (pres. 1978-81, exec. com. 1981-84), Episc. Clergy Assn. Mich., Northside Assn. Ministries (pres. 1975, 76, 79-80), Soc. Companions of Holy Cross. Home: 4500 E Huron River Dr Ann Arbor MI 48105-9335 E-mail: stjohns@saintjohnsepiscopalhowell.org.

STRANO, MICHAEL, chemical engineer; BS, Polytechnic U., Bklyn., 1997; PhD, U. Del., 2002. Asst. prof. dept. chem. & biomolecular engring. U. Ill., Urbana-Champaign. Contbr. articles to profl. jours. Named one of Top 100 Young Innovators, MIT Tech. Review, 2004; recipient DuPont Young Investigator award, 2004.

STRASSMANN, W. PAUL, economics professor; b. Berlin, July 26, 1926; s. Erwin Otto and Ilse (Wens) S.; m. Elizabeth Marsh Fanck, June 27, 1952; children— Joan, Diana, Beverly BA magna cum laude, U. Tex., Austin, 1949; MA, Columbia U., 1950; PhD, U. Md., 1956. Econ. analyst Dept. Commerce, 1950-52; instr. U. Md., 1955; mem. faculty Mich. State U., East Lansing, 1956—, assoc. prof. econs., 1959-63, prof., 1963—. Sr. research dir. ILO, Geneva, 1969-70, 73-74; cons. World Bank, AID Author: Risk and Technological Innovation, 1959, Technological Change and Economic Development, 1968, The Transformation of Housing, 1982, (with Jill Wells) The Global Construction Industry, 1988. Served with USN, 1944-46 Mem. Am. Econ. Assn., Latin Am. Studies Assn., Am. Real Estate and Urban Econs. Assn., Assn. Evolutionary Econs., European Housing Rsch. Network, Phi Beta Kappa. Office: Mich State Univ Dept Econs East Lansing MI 48824 Home Phone: 517-351-7468. E-mail: strassma@msu.edu.

STRASSNER, HOWARD TAFT, JR., obstetrician, educator; b. Tulsa, Okla., Dec. 2, 1948; BA in Biochemistry, U. Chgo., 1970, MD, 1974. Diplomate Am. Bd. Ob-gyn. Intern Columbia Presbyn. Med. Ctr., NYC, 1974, resident ob-gyn., 1974—78; fellow maternal fetal medicine L.A. County-U. So. Calif. Med. Ctr., 1978—80; physician, dir. sect. maternal fetal medicine Rush U. Med. Ctr., Chgo., 1980—, co-dir. Rush Perinatal Ctr. John M. Simpson prof., chmn. Rush U. Med. Ctr., Chgo. Office: Rush Med Ctr 1653 W Congress Pkwy Chicago IL 60612 Office Phone: 312-942-6678. Business E-Mail: howard.t.strassner@rush.edu.

STRATING, SHARON L., elementary school educator, professional staff developer, educational consultant; b. Jamestown, ND, Jan. 20, 1949; d. Walter and Evelyn Darlene (Lang) Remmick; m. Rick Donald Strating, Dec. 24, 1978 (presently divorced); children: Heather Dawn, Amber Nicole, Ashley Renee. BS in Secondary Edn., S.W. Mo. State U., 1971; MEd in Sci. Edn., N.W. Mo. State U., 1992. Cert. elem. tchr., Mo. Tchr. Cassville R-III Sch., 1971-76, Savannah R-III Sch. Sys., Mo., 1976-91; instr. 4th grade Horace Mann Lab. Sch., Maryville, Mo., 1991—2003; prof. staff developer Regional Profl. Devel. Ctr., N.W. Mo. State U., Maryville, 2003—. Facilitator for Environ. Edn. Pilot Project Kans. U., Lawrence; co-chair EPA Pollution Prevention Adv. Task Force; mem. biol. sci. curriculum study Elem. Tchr. Module Project, 1993; instr. for coll. practicum students; Map 2000 Sr. Leader for performance-based assessment sys., Mo., 1994—. Author: Living the Constitution Through the Eyes of the Newspaper, 1987, Tabloid Teaching Tool, 6 edits., 1986-91; tchr. guides in lit. revised editions for Sadako and the Thousand Paper Cranes, The Kid in the Red Jacket, Missing Gator of Gumbo Limbo, Owls in the Family, Where the Waves Break: Life at the Edge of the Sea, 2000-2001; author: Open the Eyes of Children to the World of Literacy Through Comprehensive Literacy, Prof. Develop. Program, 2002. Chairperson March of Dimes, 1972-76, Cystic Fibrosis, 1972-78; scout leader Brownies, 1976-77; exec. bd. dirs. PTA, 1976-82, fund raising chairperson, 1976-83; program chairperson presch. PTA, 1976-80;chairperson community environ. activities, 1976—, Adopt a Hwy. Program, 1976-91; mem. Mo. Stream Team Effort, 1976—. Recipient Nat. Pres. Environ. Youth award, 1988, 89, Presdl. award State of Mo., 1992, 93, Nat. Presdl. award, 1992-93; named Mo. State Tchr. of Yr., 1990-91, Disney Salutes the Am. Tchr. award, 1995. Mem. Nat. Hist. Soc., Internat. Reading Assn., Nat. Bd. for Profl. Tchng. Standards and Mid.-Age Child in Sci., Nat. Sci. Tchrs. Assn., Nat. Assn. Lab. Schs. (sec. 1994-95), Sci. Tchrs. Mo. Lutheran. Avocations: travel, ecology, creative writing, motivational speaking, arts and crafts. Office: Northwest Mo State U McKemy Ctr for Lifelong Learning Maryville MO 64468 Home: 711 Highland Ave Maryville MO 64468 Office Phone: 660-562-1515.

STRATMANN, GAYLE G., lawyer, consumer products company executive; b. Columbia, Mo., Sept. 13, 1956; BS, MEd, U. Mo., 1979; JD cum laude, U. Mo. Sch. of Law, 1987. Bar: Mo. 1987, Ill. 1988. Atty. Greensfelder, Hemker & Gale, St. Louis, Eveready Battery Co., Inc. (div. of Energizer Holdings), 1990—96, asst. gen. counsel, 1996—2002, v.p. legal ops., 2002—03; sr. v.p., gen. counsel Energizer Holdings, 2003—. Author: Church Employment and the First Amendment, 1986; contbr. articles to numerous profl. jours. Mem.: ABA, Mo. Bar Assn., St. Louis Bar Assn. Office: Energizer Holdings 533 Maryville University Dr Saint Louis MO 63141

STRATTON, EVELYN LUNDBERG, state supreme court justice; b. Bangkok, Feb. 25, 1953; came to US, 1971 (parents Am. citizens); d. Elmer John and Corrine Sylvia (Henricksen) Sahlberg; children: Luke Andrew, Tyler John; m. Jack A. Lundberg. Student, LeTourneau Coll., Longview, Tex., 1971-74; AA, U. Fla., 1973; BA, U. Akron, 1976; JD, Ohio State U., 1978. Bar: Ohio 1979, U.S. Dist. Ct. (so. dist.) Ohio 1979, U.S. Ct. Appeals (6th cir.) 1983. Assoc. Hamilton, Kramer, Myers & Cheek, Columbus, 1979-85; ptnr. Wesp, Osterkamp & Stratton, 1985-88; judge Franklin County Ct. Common Pleas, 1989-96; justice Ohio Supreme Ct., 1996—. Vis. prof. Nat. Jud. Coll., 1997—; spkr. legal seminars. Contbr. articles to profl. jours. Trustee Ohio affiliate Nat. Soc. to Prevent Blindness, 1989—, bd. dirs., trustee Columbus Coun. World Affairs, 1990-99, chmn. bd. dirs., 1999—; bd. dirs., trustee Dave Thomas Adoption Found., 1996—, ArChSafe Found., 1997—; mem. women's bd. Zephyrus League Cen. Ohio Lung Assn., 1989—; mem. Alliance Women Cmty. Corrections, 1993—. Recipient Gold Key award LeTourneau Coll., Gainesville, Fla., 1974, Svc. commendation Ohio Ho. of Reps., 1984, Scholar of Life award St. Joseph's Orphanage, 1998. Mem. ABA, ATLA, Columbus Bar Assn. (bd. govs. 1984-88, 90—, lectr.), Ohio Bar Assn. (jud. adminstrv. and legal reform com., coun. dels. 1992-96, Ohio Cmty. Corrections Orgn. (trustee 1995—), Columbus Bar Found. (trustee 1986-91, officer, sec. 1986-87, v.p. 1987-88), Am. Inns of Ct., Women Lawyers Franklin County, Phi Alpha Delta (pres. 1982-83). Office: Ohio Supreme Ct 65 S Front St Columbus OH 43215

STRATTON, STEVEN F., real estate executive; m. Sarah Stratton. Degree in fin., U. Ill. Mng. prin. corp. svcs. Tanguay-Burke-Stratton, Chgo., 1987—. Past. bd. dirs. St. Joseph's Hosp. Celebrity Golf Invitational; mem. bd. dirs. St. Joseph Found., LaSalle St. Coun.; active Anti-Defamation League Chgo. Recipient Tenant Rep. of Yr. award Chgo. Sun Times, 1993. Mem. Chgo. Office Leasing Brokers Assn. (past bd. dirs., COLBY Teamwork award 1996), Chgo. Real Estate Orgn., Chgo. Bd. Realtors. Office: Tanguay Burke Stratton 321 N Clark St Ste 900 Chicago IL 60610-4765

STRATTON-CROOKE, THOMAS EDWARD, financial consultant; b. NYC, June 28, 1933; s. Harold and Jeanne (Stifft); children: Karen, John Ryland; m. Suzanne Williams, Oct. 21, 1989 Student, Hunter Coll., 1951-52; BS in Marine Engring. and Transp., U.S. Maritime Acad., 1952-56; student, Washington U., St. Louis, 1961; MBA in Internat. Mktg., Banking and Fin., NYU, 1967. Commd. ensign USN, 1956, advanced through grades to lt., 1957; with Goodyear Internat. Corp., Akron, Ohio, 1960-63, Esso Internat., NYC, 1963—67; dir. market info. and devel. Hotel Corp. Am., Boston, 1967—71; with Continental Grain Co., NYC, 1971—75; dir. charter contracts Conoco, Stamford, Conn., 1975—77; cons. A. T. Kearney, Cleve., 1977—79; investment banker E. F. Hutton, Cleve., 1979—82, AG Edwards and Sons, Inc., Cleve., 1982—89; sr. fin. advisor, registered investment advisor, asst. v.p., sr. fin. cons. Merrill Lynch, Cleve., 1989—. Chmn. Indsl. Devel. Resch. Coun., Atlanta, 1970, Indsl. Devel. Resch. Coun., Snow Mass, Colo., 1971; lectr. bus. U. R.I., Kingston, 1968-70, tchr. Bus. Coll. Internat., 1986-89 Contbr. articles to profl. jours. Mem. Findley Lake (N.Y.) Hist. Soc.; mem. Nat. Task Force Reps. for Pres. Reagan, Cleve., 1982— Officer (ret.) USN. Mem. Naval Res. Officers Assn., Naval Res. Assn., Great Lakes Hist. Soc., Soc. Naval Architects/Engrs., Findley Lake N.Y. Area C. of C., Navy League, Civil War Roundtable, NYU Alumni Assn., U.S. Coast Guard Club (Cleve.), Univ. Club, Circumnavigators Club (life), Internat. Shipmasters Assn., Propeller Club, Army Club, Navy Club, French Creek Hist. Soc., Town Club (Jamestown, N.Y.), Masons (32d degree), Naval Masonic Lodge, Shriners, Cleve. City Club, Kings Point Alumni Assn., Civil War Round Table, U.S. Mcht. Marine Acad., English Speaking Union (chpt. bd. dirs.), York & Scottish Rites Avocations: sailing, skiing, birdwatching, gardening, sports car and motorcycle enthusiast. Office: Merrill Lynch One Cleveland Ctr 1375 E 9th St Cleveland OH 44114-1798 Office Phone: 216-363-6717, 877-375-6717. Office Fax: 216-539-0941. Personal E-mail: tommyes@aol.com. Business E-Mail: thomas_stratton-crooke@ml.com.

STRAUCH, JOHN L., lawyer; b. Pitts., Apr. 16, 1939; s. Paul L. and Delilah M. (Madison) S.; m. Gail Lorraine Kohn, Dec. 5, 1991; children: Paul L., John M., Lisa E. BA summa cum laude, U. Pitts., 1960; JD magna cum laude, NYU Sch. Law, 1963. Law clk. to Judge Sterry Waterman US Ct. Appeals (2d cir.), St. Johnsbury, Vt., 1963-64; assoc. Jones, Day, Reavis & Pogue, Cleve., 1964-70, ptnr., litig. group, 1970—, chair, litig. group, 1993—2004. Mem. Statutory Com. on Selecting Bankruptcy Judges, Cleve., 1985-88; mem. lawyers com. Nat. Ctr. for State Cts. Editor-in-chief: NYU Law Rev., 1962-63; contbr. chpt. to book. Pres., trustee Cleve. Task Force on Violent Crimes, 1985-88; trustee Legal Aid Soc., Cleve., 1978, Cleve. Greater Growth Assn., 1985-86, Citizens Mental Health Assembly, 1989-90, lawyers com. Nat. Ctr. for State Cts., 1989—. Fellow Am. Coll. Trial Lawyers (life); mem. ABA, Ohio Bar Assn., Cleve. Bar Assn. (trustee 1980-83, pres. 1985-86), Fed. Bar Assn. (trustee Cleve. chpt. 1978-79, v.p. Cleve. chpt. 1979-80), Sixth Fed. Jud. Conf. (life), Ohio Eighth Jud. Conf. (life), Order of Coif, Inns of Ct., Oakmont Country Club, The Country Club, Kiawah Island Club, Phi Beta Kappa. Office: Jones Day North Point 901 Lakeside Ave Cleveland OH 44114-1190

STRAUMANIS, JOAN, academic administrator, consultant; b. NYC, Feb. 10, 1937; d. Herbert S. and Mollie (Brandt) Cole; m. Irwin H. Pomerantz, June 25, 1956 (div. 1969); children: Rebecca, Joel; m. Eric R. Straumanis, June 7, 1969 (dec. 1996); 1 child, Andrei. BA Polit. Sci., Math., Antioch Coll., 1957; MS math., U. Colo.; PhD Philosophy, U. Md., 1974. Prof. Denison U., Granville, Ohio, 1971-82; acad. dean, prof. Kenyon Coll., Gambier, Ohio, 1982-86; dean faculty, prof. Rollins Coll., Winter Park, Fla., 1986-92; program officer Fund for Improvement of Postsecondary Edn. U.S. Dept. Edn., Washington, 1992—95; dean arts and scis. Lehigh U., Bethlehem, Pa., 1995—98; program officer Fund for Improvement of Postsecondary Edn. U.S. Dept. Edn., Washington, 1998—2002; pres. Antioch Coll., Yellow Springs, Ohio, 2002—04. Office Phone: 202-277-1937. E-mail: JoanStraumanis@earthlink.net.

STRAUS, KATHLEEN NAGLER, academic administrator, educator; b. NYC, Dec. 3, 1923; d. Maurice and Mildred (Kohn) Nagler; m. Everet M. Straus, May 29, 1948 (dec. Nov. 1967); children: Peter R., Barbara L. BA in Econs., Hunter Coll., 1944; postgrad., Columbia U., 1944—45, Am. U., 1946—47, Wayne State U., 1976—78. Various positions, 1944—50, 1966; dep. dir. Model Neighborhood Agy., City of Detroit, 1968—70; dir. social svcs. Southeastern Mich. Coun. Govts., Detroit, 1970—74; staff coord. Edn. Task Force, Detroit, 1974—75; exec. dir. People and Responsible Orgns. for Detroit, 1975—76; staff dir. edn. com. Mich. Senate, Lansing, 1976—79; assoc. exec. dir. Mich. Assn. Sch. Bds., Lansing, 1979—86; dir. cmty. rels. and devel. Ctr. for Creative Studies, Detroit, 1986—87, pres., 1987—91; mem. Mich. Bd. Edn., 1992—, pres., 2003. Mem. Mich. Bd. for Pub. Jr. and C.C.s, Lansing, 1980-92, v.p., 1989, pres., 1991; cons. Met. Columbus (Ohio) Schs. Com., 1975-76; mem. steering com. Mich. Edn. Seminars, 1979-86; mem. Adv. Com. on Higher Edn. Needs in S.W. Mich., 1971-72, Ad Hoc Com. on Equal Access to Higher Edn., 1970-71, Citizens Action Com. on Sch. Fin. Contbr. articles to profl. jours. Active numerous civic orgns.; vice chmn. downtown br. Met. Detroit YWCA, 1970-74; bd. dirs. Citizens for Better Care, Inc., 1973-78; mem. edn. com. New Detroit, Inc., 1972—; trustee Detroit Sci. Ctr., Inc., 1975—; founder, pres. Mich. Tax Info. Coun., 1982—; v.p. bd. dirs. Univ. Cultural Ctr. Assn., 1986-91; trustee Comprehensive Health Planning Coun. Southeastern Mich., 1977-78; mem. Wayne County Art and History Commn., 1988; co-chmn. Nat. Arts Program, 1987-88; bd. dirs. North Ctrl. Regional Edn. Libr.; bd. dirs. North Ctrl. Regional Edn. Lab.; bd. mem. Midwest Regional Edn. Lab. Recipient Amity citation, Detroit, 1966, Disting. Cmty. Svc. award Am. Jewish Com., 1988, Common Coun., Detroit, 1976, resolution Mich. Ho. of Reps., 1986, Mich. Senate, 1988, Educator of Yr. Wayne State U., 1999, Disting. Warrior award Detroit Urban League, 2000; named to Mich. Edn. Hall of Fame, 1997; inducted into Mich. Women's Hall of Fame, 2000, Lifetime Achievement award Anti Defamation League, 2004, Multi Cultural Edn. award Nat. Conf. Cmty. and Justice, 2004, Lifetime Achievement award Communities in Schs., 2006. Mem.: LWV (pres. Detroit 1961—63), Alpha Chi Alpha. Democrat. Avocations: travel, theater, concerts. Home: 7431 Deep Run 210 Bloomfield Hills MI 48301 Office: State Bd Edn PO Box 30008 Lansing MI 48909-7508 Office Phone: 517-373-3900. Business E-Mail: strausk@michigan.gov.

STRAUS, LORNA PUTTKAMMER, biology professor; b. Chgo., Feb. 15, 1933; d. Ernst Wilfred and Helen Louise (Monroe) Puttkammer; m. Francis Howe Straus II, June 11, 1955; children: Francis, Helen, Christopher, Michael. BA magna cum laude, Radcliffe Coll., 1955; MS, U. Chgo., 1960, PhD, 1962. Rsch. assoc. dept. anatomy U. Chgo., 1962—64, instr., 1964—67, asst. prof., 1967—73, assoc. prof., 1973—87, prof., 1987—, asst. dean, then dean students, 1967—82, dean admissions, 1975—80, marshal, 1999—. Trustee Radcliffe Coll., Cambridge, Mass., 1973-83; chmn. Cmty. Found., Mackinac Island, Mich., 1994—. Recipient silver medal Coun. for Advancement and Support Edn., 1987. Mem.: North Ctrl. Assn. (commr. 1998—, pres.-elect 2001—02, pres. 2002—04), Harvard U. Alumni Assn. (bd. dirs. 1980—83), Phi Beta Kappa. Avocations: travel, gardening. Home: 5642 S Kimbark Ave Chicago IL 60637-1606 Office: U Chgo 5845 S Ellis Ave Chicago IL 60637-1476 Business E-Mail: hlps@uchicago.edu.

STRAUSBAUGH, JEFFREY ALAN, lawyer; b. Lima, Ohio, Nov. 24, 1956; s. Stanley L. Strausbaugh and Margaret E. (Ebersole) Rutter; m. Sue Ann Webb, Nov. 29, 1975; children: Erin, Erica, Emily, Stanley, Sarah. BA, Defiance Coll., Ohio, 1983; JD, U. Toledo, 1985. Bar: Ohio 1986. Supr., driver Webb Bros. Trucking & Excavating, Defiance, Ohio, 1975_83; ptnr. Ryan, Borland, Snavely & Strausbaugh, Defiance, Ohio, 1986-90; pvt. practice, Defiance, 1990—. Chmn. Defiance County Rep. Cen. and Exec. Coms., 1988—; pres. Defiance County Young Reps., 1987. Mem. ABA, Ohio Bar Assn., NW Ohio Bar Assn., Defiance County Bar Assn., Rotary. Republican. Office: 414 W 3rd St Defiance OH 43512-2137

STRAUSS, DAVID, political organization administrator, former federal official; b. Fargo, ND, Apr. 2, 1950; BA magna cum laude, Moorhead State U., 1973, BS Polit. Sci. and Edn. magna cum laude, 1973; postgrad., Harvard U., 1992. Exec. dir. ND Dem. Party, 1975-76; dir. ND Agrl. Stblzn. and Conservation Svc., 1977-81; adminstrv. asst. Senator Quentin Burdick of ND, 1981-88; staff dir. US Senate Com. on Environment and Pub. Works, Washington, 1988-92; chief of staff US Senator Jocelyn Birch Burdick of ND, Washington, 1992, Senator John Breaux of La., Washington, 1993; dep. chief of staff Office of Vice Pres., Washington, 1993-97; exec. dir. Pension Benefit Guaranty Corp. (PBGC), Washington, 1997; chmn. reelection campaign for Congressman Earl Pomeroy, 2002, 2004; chair ND Dem.-NPL Com., 2005—. Vis. lectr. Ctr. Health Policy Rsch. and Ethics, George Mason U., Fairfax, Va., 2001—; lectr. Ctr. Study of Congress and the Presidency, Am. U., Washington. Grantee Eastman Kodak Congl. Fellow for Sr. Mgrs. in Govt. Program, John F. Kennedy Sch. Govt., Harvard U. Democrat. Office: ND Dem-NPL Com 1902 E Divide Ave Bismarck ND 58501 Office Phone: 701-255-0460. Office Fax: 701-255-7823.*

STRAUSS, JOHN STEINERT, dermatologist, educator; b. New Haven, July 15, 1926; s. Maurice Jacob and Carolyn Mina (Ullman) Strauss; m. Susan Thalheimer, Aug. 19, 1950; children: Joan Sue, Mary Lynn. BS, Yale U., 1946, MD, 1950. Intern U. Chgo., 1950-51; resident dermatology U. Pa., Phila., 1951-52, 54-55, fellow dermatology, 1955-57, instr., 1956-57; mem. faculty Boston U. Med. Sch., 1958-78, prof., 1966-78; head dept. dermatology U. Iowa,

Iowa City, 1978-98, prof. dermatology, 1978-00, prof. emeritus, 2000—. Mem. editl. bd.: Archives of Dermatology, 1970—79, Jour. Am. Acad. Dermatology, 1979—89, Jour. Investigative Dermatology, 1977—82; contbr. articles to profl. jours. With USNR, 1952—54. Fellow James H. Brown Jr., 1947—48, USPHS, 1955—57; grantee. Fellow: Am. Acad. Dermatology (pres.); mem.: Internat. Com. Dermatology (pres. 1992—97), Internat. League Dermatol. Socs. (pres. 1992—97), 18th World Congress Dermatology (pres.), Am. Bd. Med. Spltys. (exec. com. 2001—04), Coun. Med. Splty. Socs. (pres.), Am. Fedn. Clin. Rsch., Ctrl. Soc. Clin. Rsch., Assn. Am. Physicians, Am. Dermatol. Assn. (sec., pres.), Am. Bd. Dermatology (bd. dirs., pres., assoc. exec. dir., exec. cons.), Dermatology Found. (pres.), Soc. Investigative Dermatology (sec.-treas., pres.). Achievements include research in sebaceous glands and pathogenesis of acne. Office: U Iowa Hosp & Clinics Dept Dermatology 200 Hawkins Dr # BT2045-1 Iowa City IA 52242-1009 Office Phone: 319-356-7546.

STRAUSS, WILLIAM VICTOR, lawyer; b. Cin., July 5, 1942; s. William Victor and Elsa (Lovitt) S.; m. Linda Leopold, Nov. 9, 1969; children: Nancy T., Katherine S. AB cum laude, Harvard U., 1964; JD, U. Pa., 1967. Bar: Ohio 1967. Pres. Security Title and Guaranty Agy., Inc., Cin., 1982—, Strauss & Troy, Cin., 1995—. Trustee Cin. Psychoanalytic Inst., 1990—, Downtown Cin., Inc., 2005—, Cin. Contemporary Arts Ctr., 1997-2004; mem. adv. coun. U. Cin. Real Estate. Mem. ABA, Nat. Assn. Office and Indsl. Properties, Ohio State Bar Assn., Cin. Bar Assn., Ohio Land Title Assn Home: 40 Walnut Ave Wyoming OH 45215-4350 Office: Strauss & Troy Fed Res Bldg 150 E 4th St Fl 4 Cincinnati OH 45202-4018 Office Phone: 513-629-9416.

STREETER, STEPHANIE ANNE, former printing company executive; b. Boston, Sept. 19, 1957; d. Andrew Geoffrey Galef and Suzanne Jane (Cohen) Sidy; m. Edward Stanley Streeter, Feb. 22, 1980. BA in Polit. Sci., Stanford U., 1979. Mgr. market analysis Xerox Small Bus. System, Sunnyvale, Calif., 1980-81; regional sales mgr. Xerox Office Products Divsn., Sunnyvale, Calif., 1981-83; product mgr. Decision Data Computer Corp., Horsham, Pa., 1983-85; sr. product mgr. Avery Dennison Corp., Covina, Calif., 1985-88, bus. mgr. indexes, 1988-89, bus. mgr. computer supplies, 1989-90, dir. mktg., computer products, 1990-91, v.p. gen. mgr. label divsn. Diamond Bar, Calif., 1991-93, v.p., gen. mgr., Avery Dennison Brands, 1993—96, worldwide group v.p., 1996—2000; COO idealab!, Pasadena, Calif., 2000; pres., COO Banta Corp., Menasha, Wis., 2001—02, pres., CEO, 2002—04, chmn., pres., CEO, 2004—07. Bd. dirs. Banta Corp., 2001—07, Kohl's Corp., 2007—. Bd. dirs. Wis. Mfrs. and Commerce. Fellow Internat. Women's Forum. Democrat. Avocations: bicycling, skiing.

STREETMAN, JOHN WILLIAM, III, museum director; b. Marion, NC, Jan. 19, 1941; s. John William, Jr. and Emily Elaine (Carver) S.; children: Katherine Drake, Leah Farrior, Burgin Eaves. BA in English and Theatre History, Western Carolina U., 1963; cert. in Shakespeare studies, Lincoln Coll., Oxford (Eng.) U., 1963. Founding dir. Jewett Creative Arts Ctr., Berwick Acad., South Berwick, Maine, 1964-70; exec. dir. Polk Mus. Art, Lakeland, Fla., 1970-75; dir. Mus. Arts and Sci., Evansville, Ind., 1975—; chmn. mus. adv. panel Ind. Arts Commn., 1977-78. Mem. Am. Assn. Museums, Assn. Ind. Museums (bd. dirs.) Episcopalian. Office: Evansville Mus Arts History and Sci 411 SE Riverside Dr Evansville IN 47713-1037

STREFF, WILLIAM ALBERT, JR., lawyer; b. Chgo., Aug. 12, 1949; s. William Albert Streff Sr. and Margaret (McKeough) Streff Fisher; m. Kathleen Myslinski, Sept. 29, 1984; children: Amanda, William III, Kimberly. BS, Northwestern U., 1971, JD cum laude, 1974. Bar: Ill. 1974, U.S. Dist. Ct. (no. dist.) Ill. 1974, U.S. Dist. Ct. (no. dist.) N.Y. 1987, U.S. Dist. Ct. (no. dist.) Calif. 1988, U.S. Ct. Appeals (7th cir.) 1980, U.S. Ct. Appeals (9th cir.) 1988, U.S. Ct. Customs and Patent Appeals, 1978, U.S. Ct. Appeals (3rd cir.), 1992, U.S. Ct. Internat. Trade, 1996, Supreme Ct. State Ill. Legal writing instr. Law Sch. orthwestern U., Chgo., 1973—74; assoc. Kirkland & Ellis LLP, Chgo., 1974—80, ptnr., 1980—. Lectr. Ill. Inst. Continuing Legal Edn., 1984; adj. prof. orthwestern U. Law Sch., 1992-94, 97-2000, Chgo. Kent-IIT Law Sch., 1998, John Marshall Law Sch., 2000-03. Contbr. articles to profl. jours. Mem. adv. bd. Ill. Inst. Tech./Chgo.-Kent, 1983-86; trustee Northwestern U., Evanston, 1984-86, mem. vis. com. Law Sch., Chgo., 1988-94. Mem. ABA. Office: Kirkland & Ellis LLP 200 E Randolph Dr Chicago IL 60601-6636 Office Phone: 312-861-2126. Office Fax: 312-861-2200. Business E-Mail: wstreff@kirkland.com.

STREICHER, JAMES FRANKLIN, retired lawyer; b. Ashtabula, Ohio, Dec. 6, 1940; s. Carl Jacob and Helen Marie (Dugan) S.; m. Sandra JoAnn Jennings, May 22, 1940; children: Cheryl Ann, Gregory Scott, Kerry Marie. BA, Ohio State U., 1962; JD, Case Western Res. U., 1966. Bar: Ohio 1966, U.S. Dist. Ct. (no. dist.) Ohio 1966. Assoc. Calfee, Halter & Griswold, Cleve., 1966—2005; ret., 2005. Bd. dirs. Provider Gateway, Inc., Sensir Technologies, Stamford, Conn., Mid Am. Consulting; mem. Divsn. Securities Adv. Bd., State of Ohio; lectr. Case Western Res. U., Cleve. State U.; mem. pvt. sector com. John Carroll U. Former trustee Achievement Ctr. for Children, Western Res. Hist. Soc., Make-A-Wish Found. Endowment. Mem. ABA, Fed. Bar Assn., Ohio State Bar Assn., Assn. for Corp. Growth, Ohio Venture Assn., No. Ohio Venture Assn. (trustee), Greater Cleve. Bar Assn. (founding chmn. corp., banking, bus. law sect.), Ohio State U. Alumni Assn., Case Western Res. U. Alumni Assn., Newcomen Soc., Bluecoats Club (Cleve.), Mayfield Country (bd. dirs. 1985-89), Union Club, The Pepper Pike Club, The Tavern Club, Beta Theta Pi, Phi Delta Phi. Roman Catholic. Republican. Office Phone: 216-408-3919. Office Fax: 216-241-0816. Business E-Mail: jstreicher@comcast.com.

STREIFFER, JENNY, former soccer player; b. Metairie, La., May 25, 1978; Student, U. Notre Dame. Alt. U.S. Women's Olympic Soccer Team, 1996; mem. U-20 Nat. Team ordic Cup championship, Denmark, 1997. Named Big East Rookie of Yr. and NSCAA 3d Team All-Am., freshman yr., U. Notre Dame. Achievements include scoring winning goal U-20 Nat. Team Nordic Cup championship, Denmark; midfield Notre Dame, NCAA championship freshman yr., undefeated regular season sophomore year. Office: US Soccer Fedn 1801-1811 S Prairie Ave Chicago IL 60616

STREIT, MICHAEL J., state supreme court justice; b. Sheldon, Iowa, Apr. 14, 1950; married; 1 child. BA, U. Iowa, 1972; grad., U. San Diego Sch. Law, 1975. Cert.: (U.S. Ct. Appeals) 1996. Atty. priv. practice, 1975—83; asst. atty. Lucas County, 1975—79, atty., 1979—83; judge Iowa Dist. Ct., Fifth Judicial Dist., 1983—96, Iowa Ct. of Appeals, 1996—2001; justice Iowa Supreme Ct., 2001—. Mem. Iowa Supreme Ct. Education Advisory Com., Iowa Supreme Ct. Judicial Technology Com., Judges Assn. Education Com. Mem.: Iowa State Bar Assn., Blackstone Inn of Ct., Iowa Jud. Inst. Office: Iowa Supreme Ct Jud Branch Bldg 1111 E Ct Ave Des Moines IA 50319

STRETCH, JOHN JOSEPH, social worker, educator, management consultant; b. St. Louis, Feb. 24, 1935; s. John Joseph and Theresa Carmelita (Fleming) S.; children: Paul, Leonmarie, Sylvan, Adrienne, Sharonalice; m. Barbara Ann Stewart, Mar. 16, 1985; children: Margaret, Thomas. AB, Maryknoll Coll., Glen Ellyn, Ill., 1957; MSW, Washington U., St. Louis, 1961; PhD, Tulane U., 1967; MBA, St. Louis U., 1980. LCSW 1985. Instr. Tulane U., 1962—68, asst. prof., 1968; assoc. prof. social work St. Louis U., 1968—71, prof., 1972—, asst. dean Sch. Social Service, 1976-87, dir. doctoral studies, 1976-94, dir. MSW. program, 1985-86, bd. dirs., exec. com. Ctr. for Social Justice, 1987—, instnl. rev. bd. Sch. Social Svc., 1987—92; dir. rsch. Social Welfare Planning Coun. Met. New Orleans, 1962—69. Cons. to United Way Met. St. Louis, Cath. Charities of Archdiocese of St. Louis, Cath. Svcs. for Children and Youth, Full Achievement, Mo. Province of S.J., Cath. Commn. on Housing, Cath. Family Svcs., Youth Emergency Svcs., Mo. State Dept. Social Svcs., U. Mo. Extension Svc., St. Joseph's Home for Boys, Marian Hall Ctr. for Adolescent Girls, Boys Town-Girls Town of Mo., A World of Difference, Anti Defamation League of B'nai Brith, Prog. Youth Ctr., Foster Care Coalition of Greater St. Louis, Rankin-Jordan Children's Rehab. Hosp., 1999-2000, Ill. St. Claire County Sch. Sys.'s Old Man River Project, 2002—05, Prison Performing ARts, 2005-06, Family Resource Ctr., 2004—; expert witness on homeless U.S. House Select Com. on Families, Children and Youth, 1987; resource spl. task force on homeless Office of Sec. U.S. Dept. HUD, 1989; survey design cons. U.S. Office of The Insp. Gen., 1990; methodology expert on homelessness U.S. Census Bur., 1989; expert homeless policy GAO hearings, 1992; chair Mo. Assn. for Social Welfare Low Income Housing, 1982—; chmn. St. Louis Low Income Housing Preservation Com., 1985; mem. Comprehensive Housing Affordabiltiy Strategies (CHAS) Mo. Statewide Planning Group, Mo. Housing Devel. CHAS citizen's com., State of Mo. Affordable House Task Force, Mo. Housing Devel. Corp., 1998-2002, Mo. Inst. Psychiatry, 1995, University City Sch. Dist., 1990; mgmt. cons. People's Issues Task Force Agrl. div. Monsanto Chem. Inc., 1992, regional office NCCJ, 1990-92; vis. prof. Nat. Cath. U. Am. Sch. Social Svcs., 1991, 92, U. Bristol, Eng., 1992, U. Calif. Sch. Pub. Health, Berkeley, 1990; cons. Mo. Speaker of the Ho. statewide legis. task force, 1990-92, Russian Am. Summer U., 2000; statewide grant project reviewer emergency shelter grant program Mo. Dept. Social Svcs., 1989—, chair, 2000—; homeless svcs. grant reviewer City of St. Louis, 1996-97; book award judge Alpha Sigma Nu. Mem editl. bd. Social Work, 1968-74, Health Progress, 1988—01, Social Work Administration, 2003—; manuscript referee Jour. Social Svc. Rsch., 1977-99; mgmt. and evaluation content referee Wadsworth Press, Human Svcs. Press, Thompson Press, Allyn and Bacon Press, Sage Press, Haworth Press; editor, contbr. chpts. to books, articles to profl. jours. Mem. Mo. Assn. Social Welfare, 1980—, Salvation Army Family Haven, 1987, 2000—; mem. leadership coun. Success by Six, 1990—2004; organizer Mo. State Nat. Coalition for the Homeless, 1989; mem. DuBourg Soc. St. Louis U., 1989; evaluation cons. Prison Performing Arts, 2005—06; bd. dirs. Beyond Housing, Inc., 1985—, pres., 1993—95; bd. dirs. Housing Comes First, 1995—99, Adequate Housing for Missorians, 2002—, Neighborhood Housing Svc., 2004—05, at. Coalition for Homeless, 2004—05; mem. adv. bd. Salvation Army Family Haven, 1988—; bd. dirs., mem. exec. com. Cmty. Asset Mgmt. Co.; chmn. venture grant com. United Way of Greater St. Louis, 1988—91, vice chmn. day care allocation com., 1985—95, mem. process and rev. com., 1991—93, mem. inter-orgnl. priorities com., 1991—93; appointee instnl. representation nat. Jesuits social concern group St. Louis U., 1993—2004, mem. exec. and support tng. group, 1987—92, mem. instnl. rev. bd., 1979—2004. NIMH Career Leadership Devel. fellow, 1965-67, Fed. Ednl. grantee Ill. Sch. Sys., 2002; recipient Scholar of Yr. award Sch. Social Svc., St. Louis U., 1987; named Vol. of Yr. Ecumenical Housing Prodn. Corp., 1990; Presdl. scholar Sch. Social Svc., 1992, Fulbright Sr. scholar, 2004—. Mem.: ACLU (chair compensation benefits com. St. Louis faculty senate 2004—05), AAUP (St. Louis U. chpt. exec. com. 1990—2002, pres. 1994—2002), U.S. Census Bur. (subcom. health stats. for minorities and spl. populations of U.S. 1988—2004), Nat. Consumers Union (com. on vital and health stats.), Coun. on Social Work Edn., Mo. Assn. for Social Welfare (bd. dirs., evaluation cons. family resource ctr. 2005—, Outstanding State-Wide Mem. of Yr. 1987, nominee Elaine Aber Humanitarian award 2005), Nat. Assn. Social Workers, Acad. Cert. Social Workers (charter mem.), Amnesty Internat., Common Cause. Democrat. Roman Catholic. Home: 9100 Litzsinger Rd Saint Louis MO 63144-2214 Office: 3550 Lindell Blvd Saint Louis MO 63103-1021 Office Phone: 314-977-2715. Business E-Mail: stretchj@slu.edu.

STREVEY, GUY DONALD, insurance company executive; b. Norcatur, Kans., Mar. 8, 1932; s. Guy Ross Strevey and Maxine Elizabeth (Johnson) Gruse.; m. Irene Franklyn Corey Nov. 7, 1953; children: Richard A., Janet E. Bolte, Philip E., Melinda K. Halvorson. BS, Okla. A&M U., 1953. Cert. CFP, CLU, ChFC. Agt. Penn Mut. Life Ins. Co., Tulsa, 1955-62, regional mgr., 1958-62, gen. agt. Omaha, 1962-69, 2005agt., 1979—2005; ptnr. Strevey and Assocs. Inc., 1979—2005; registered rep. Hornor, Townsend & Kent, Inc., Omaha, 1985—; pres. Guy Strevey & Assocs., Inc., 2005—. Bd. dirs. Citipower LLC, 1997-2004, A Del. Corp., 1996-2004; cons. Appalachian Gas Assocs. I-XII; cons. Fortuna I and II Natural Gas Exploration Co; advisor Brush Mountain I, II, III, IV, V, VI Natural Gas Exploration Co. Deacon Hillcrest Bapt. Ch., Omaha, 1960, Westside Bapt. Ch., Omaha, 1978, chmn., 1979-81. 1st lt. U.S. Army, 1953-55. Mem. NAIFA (Nat. Quality award 1970-94), Soc. Fin. Svc. Profls., Nat. Assn. Ins. & Fin. Advisors, Million Dollar Roundtable (life), F.P.A. Assoc. (pres. 1997—, chmn. bd. 1998-99, named Mem. of Yr. 2002). Republican. Avocations: sports, travel. Home: 3518 S 106th St Omaha NE 68124-3614 Office: Guy Strevey & Assocs Inc 11422 Miracle Hills Dr Ste 305 Omaha NE 68154-4420 Office Phone: 402-493-0253. Business E-Mail: guy@strevey.omhcoxmail.com. E-mail: gstrevey@htk.com.

STREVEY, TRACY ELMER, JR., army officer, surgeon, health facility administrator; b. Shorewood, Wis., Apr. 24, 1933; s. Tracy Elmer and Margaret (Rees) S.; m. Victoria Crowley (div.); children: Virginia Ann, Tracy Elmer III, Andrew Victor; m. Elizabeth Sommers; children: Stephanie Jean, James Sommers. Student, Pomona Coll., 1951-54; MD, U. So. Calif., 1958; student, Armed Forces Staff Coll., 1970-71, U.S. Army War Coll., 1977-78. Diplomate Am. Bd. Surgery, Am. Bd. Thoracic Surgery. Intern Los Angeles County Gen. Hosp., 1958-59; commd. officer U.S. Army, 1959, advanced through grades to maj. gen., 1983; resident in gen. surgery Letterman Gen. Hosp., San Francisco, 1962-66; resident in thoracic and cardiovascular surgery Walter Reed Gen. Hosp., Washington, 1968-70; comdg. officer 757 Med. Detachment OA, Ludwigsburg, Germany, 1959-61; ward officer orthopaedic svc. 75th Sta. Hosp., Stuttgart, Fed. Republic Germany, 1961-62; chief profl. svc., chief surgery 85th Evacuation Hosp., Qui Nhon, Vietnam, 1967; comdg. officer 3d Surg. Hosp., Dong Tam, Vietnam, 1967-68; asst. chief thoracic and cardiovascular surgery service Fitzsimons Army Med Ctr., Denver, 1971-73, chief thoracic and cardiovascular surgery service, 1973-75; asst. dir. med. activities and dir. Profl. Edn. Gorgas Hosp., Panama Canal Zone, 1975-77; chief dept. surgery Walter Reed Army Med. Ctr., Washington, 1978-81; comdr. Brooke Army Med. Ctr., Ft. Sam Houston, Tex., 1981-83, Tripler Army Med. Ctr., Hawaii, 1983-86, U.S. Army Health Svcs. Command, San Antonio, 1986-88; ret. U.S. Army, 1988; CEO Nassau County Med. Ctr., 1988-93; pres., CEO N.Y. Hosp Med. Ctr. Queens, NYC, 1993-94; v.p. N.Y. Hosp. Care etwork, NYC, 1994-95; v.p. for med. affairs Sisters of Mercy Health Sys., St. Louis, 1995-99; prin. Strevey Cons. Assocs., LLC, 1999—2003. Asst. clin. prof. surgery U. Colo. Med. Ctr., Denver, 1973-75; prof. surgery Uniformed Services U. Health Scis., Bethesda, 1978-2003, vice chmn. dept. surgery, 1978-81 Contbr. articles to profl. jours. Mem. reg. bd. Am. Heart Assn. Decorated D.S.M., Legion of Merit with 2 oak leaf clusters, Meritorious Service medal with 2 oak leaf clusters, Purple Heart, Army Commendation Medal for Valor, Vietnam Cross of Gallantry with Palm; recipient Outstanding Service award U. So. Calif. Med. Alumni Assn., 1983 Fellow ACS, Am. Coll. Chest Physicians, Am. Coll. Cardiology, Am. Coll. Physician Execs. (disting.); mem. Assn. Mil. Surgeons U.S., Soc. Thoracic Surgeons, Western Thoracic Surg. Assn., Am. Assn. Thoracic Surgery, Masons. Avocations: ham radio, scuba diving, golf, computers. Home and Office: 1509 Woodgate Dr Saint Louis MO 63131-4724 Personal E-mail: tstrevey@aol.com.

STRICKLAND, ARVARH EUNICE, history professor; b. Hattiesburg, Miss., July 6, 1930; s. Eunice and Clotiel (Marshall) S.; m. Willie Pearl Elmore, June 17, 1951; children: Duane Arvarh, Bruce Elmore. BA, Tougaloo Coll., 1951; MA, U. Ill., 1953, PhD, 1962; LHD (hon.), Tougaloo Coll., 2007. Tchr. Hattiesburg Schs., 1951-52; instr. Tuskegee Inst., 1955-56; prin. supr. Madison County Schs., Canton, Miss., 1956-59; asst. prof. history Chgo. State U., 1962-65, assoc. prof. history, 1965-68, prof., 1968-69, U. Mo., Columbia, 1969-96, prof. emeritus, 1996—, chmn. dept. history, 1980-83, interim dir. black studies program, 1994-96, sr. faculty assoc., Office of V.P. acad. affairs, 1987-88, assoc. v.p. acad. affairs, 1989-91. Author: History of the Chicago Urban League, 1966, reprint, 2001, (with Reich and Biller) Building the United States, 1971, (with Reich) The Black American Experience to 1877, 1974, The Black American Experience since 1877, 1974; editor: Working with Carter G. Woodson, (with Lorenzo J. Greene) The Father of Black History: A Diary, 1928-1930, 1989, Selling Black History for Carter G. Woodson: A Diary, 1930-33, 1996, (with Robert E. Weems) The African American Experience: A Historiographical and Bibliographical Guide, 2000. Commr. Planning and Zoning, Columbia, Mo., 1977-80, Boone County Home Rule Charter, 1982, Mo. Peace Officers Standards and Tng. Commn., 1988-89; co-chmn. Mayors Com. to Commemorate Contbns. of Black Columbians, Columbia, 1981; mem. exec. subcom. Mayor's Ad Hoc Election '82 Com., 1982; bd. dirs. Harry S. Truman Library Inst., 1987-96, U. of Mo.-Columbia Health Sys., 2003—. Recipient Disting. Svc. award Ill. Hist. Soc., 1957, Byler Disting. Prof. award U. Mo., 1994, St. Louis Am.'s Educator of Yr. award, 1994, Disting. Faculty award U. Mo.-Columbia Alumni Assn., 1995, Tougaloo Coll. Alumni Hall of Fame, 1995, Alumni Achievement U. Ill. Coll. Liberal Arts and Scis., 1997, Disting. Svc. award State Hist. Soc. Mo., 1997. Mem. Orgn. Am. Historians, Am. Hist. Assn., Assn. Study Afro-Am. Life and History (Carter Godwin Woodson Scholars medallion 1999), So. Hist. Assn., State Hist. Soc. Mo. (Disting. Svc. award 1997), Boone County Hist. Soc. (bd. dirs. 1998-2002, 2d v.p. 1999, 1st v.p. 2000-02), Kiwanis, Alpha Phi Alpha, Phi Alpha Theta (internat. v.p. 1991-93, pres. 1994-95, chair adv. bd. 1996-97, Disting. Svc. award 1997, Columbia Values Diversity award, 2005). Democrat. Methodist. Home: 4100 Defoe Dr Columbia MO 65203-0252 Office: U Mo Dept History 101 Read Hall Columbia MO 65211-7500 E-mail: stricklanda@missouri.edu.

STRICKLAND, HUGH ALFRED, lawyer; b. Rockford, Ill., May 3, 1931; s. Hugh and Marie (Elmer) S.; m. Donna E. McDonald, Aug. 11, 1956; children: Amy Alice, Karen Ann. AB, Knox Coll., 1953; JD, Chgo. Kent Coll. Law, 1959. Bar: Ill. 1960. Partner firm McDonald, Strickland & Clough, Carrollton, Ill., 1961—; asst. atty. gen. Ill., 1960-67; spl. asst. gen. Ill., 1967-69; pres. McDonald Title Co. Mem. Greene County Welfare Svcs. Com., 1963—, Ill. Heart Assn., 1961-65; trustee Thomas H. Boyd Meml. Hosp., 1972-95; pres. Long Lake Assn. Vilas County, Inc., 2002—. With AUS, 1953-55. Recipient award for meritorious service Am. Heart Assn., 1964 Fellow Ill. Bar Found. (charter); mem. ABA, Ill. Bar Assn., Greene County Bar Assn. (past pres.), Southwestern Bar Assn. (past pres.), Ill. Def. Counsel, Am. Judicature Soc., Def. Rsch. Inst., Elks Club, Westlake Country Club (v.p. 1968-70, dir.), Big Sand Lake Country Club, Phi Delta Theta, Phi Delta Phi. Methodist. Home: 827 7th St Carrollton IL 62016-1421 Office: 524 N Main St PO Box 71 Carrollton IL 62016-1027 Office Phone: 217-942-3115. Personal E-mail: mcdslawyers@aol.com. Business E-Mail: has3@irtc.net.

STRICKLAND, TED, governor, former congressman; b. Lucasville, Ohio, Aug. 4, 1941; s. Orville and Carrie Strickland; m. Frances Smith. BA in Hist., Asbury Coll., Wilmore, Ky., 1963; MDiv, Asbury Theol. Seminary, Wilmore, Ky., 1967; PhD in Counseling Psych., U. Ky., Lexington, 1980. Min.; dir. social svcs. Ky. Meth. Home; consulting psychologist So. Ohio Correctional Facility, 1985—92, 1994—96; asst. prof. psych. Shawnee State U., Portsmouth, Ohio, 1988—92, 1994—96; mem. US Congress from 6th Ohio dist., 1993—95, 1997—2007, mem. energy & commerce com., vets. affairs com., ranking minority mem. oversight and investigations subcommittee; gov. State of Ohio, Columbus, 2007—. Dem. nominee for Gov., Ohio, 2006. Co-recipient Outstanding Psychologist award, Nat. Alliance Mentally Ill, 2004. Mem.: Ohio Psychol. Assn., APA. Democrat. Methodist. Office: Office Gov Vern Riffe Ctr 77 S High St 30th Fl Columbus OH 43215-6117

STRICKLER, CHUCK, newscaster; m. JoJo Strickler; children: Nikolas, Kristofer. With Sta. WVVA-TV, Bluefield, W.Va., STa. WOWK-TV, Charleston, Sat. KIII-TV, Corpus Christi, Tex.; anchor Sta. WBNS-TV, Columbus, Ohio, 1998—. Recipient Best Reporter award, Ohio Soc. Profl. Journalists, 1999, 2000, 2003, Ohio Associated Press, 1998. Office: WBNS-TV 770 Twin Rivers Dr Columbus OH 43215

STRICKLER, IVAN K., dairy farmer; b. Carlyle, Kans., Oct. 23, 1921; s. Elmer E. and Edna Louise (James) S.; m. Madge Lee Marshall, Aug. 7, 1949; children— Steven Mark, Thomas Scott, Douglas Lee. BS, Kans. State U., 1947. Owner, mgr. dairy farm, Iola, Kans., 1947—; tchr. farm tng. to vets. World War II, 1947-54; judge 1st and 2d Nat. Holstein Show, Brazil, 1969-70, Internat. Holstein Show, Buenos Aires, 1972, Nat. Holstein Show, Ecuador, 1978, 10th Nat. Holstein Show, Brazil, 1980, Holstein Show, Australia, Mex. and Argentina, 1981, Lang Lang, 1984, Adelaide (Australia) Royal Show, 1987; pres Mid-America Dairymen, Inc., Springfield, Mo., 1981—. Appointed chmn. Nat. Dairy Bd., 1985-90; dairy leader 4-H Club, 1962-75; dir. Iola State Bank; rep. U.S. Internat. Dairy Symposium, 1994, Belo Horinzote, Brazil. Author: Wholly Cow We Did It, 1996 (Centennia Honor roll 1997). Trustee Allen County Community Jr. Coll.; mem. agr. edn. and rsch. com. Kans. State U. (recipient Medallion-highest honor, 2000), U.S. Agrl. Trade and Devel. Mission, Algeria and Tunisia, 1989. With USN, 1942-46, PTO. Recipient Silver award Holstein Friesian Assn. Brazil, 1969, Top Dairy Farm Efficiency award Ford Found., 1971, Master Farmer award Kans. State U. and Kans. Assn. Commerce and Industry, 1972, Gold award Holstein Friesian Assn. Argentina, 1972, Richard Lynng award Nat. Dairy Bd., 1990, award of merit Gamma Sigma Delta, 1987, Alumni medallion Kans. State U., 1999; named Man of Yr. World Dairy Exposition, 1978; portrait in Dairy Hall of Fame Kans. State U., 1974; Guest of Hon. Nat. Dairy Shrine, 1985; selected First Dairy Leader of Yr., 1996; inductee Kans. Co-op Hall of Fame, 1999. Mem. Mid Am. Dairymen (sec. corporate bd. 1971-81, pres. 1981-95), Holstein Friesian Assn. Am. (nat. dir. 1964-72), Dairy Shrine (nat. dir. 1971-81), United Dairy Industry Assn. (dir. 1971-79), Nat. Holstein Assn. Am. (pres. 1979-80), Alpha Gamma Rho (highest honor 1989, Hall of Fame 1998). Mem. Christian Ch. (elder, bd. dirs.). Club: Nat. Dairy Shrine (pres. 1978). Home: PO Box 365 Iola KS 66749-0365 Office: Mid America Dairymen Inc 1641 N Dakota Rd Iola KS 66749

STRIEFSKY, LINDA A(NN), lawyer; b. Carbondale, Pa., Apr. 27, 1952; d. Leo James and Antoinette Marie (Carachilo) S.; m. James Richard Carlson, Nov. 3, 1984; children: David Carlson, Paul Carlson, Daniel Carlson. BA summa cum laude, Marywood Coll., 1974; JD, Georgetown U., Washington, DC, 1977. Bar: Ohio 1977. Assoc. Thompson Hine LLP (formerly Thompson, Hine & Flory), Cleve., 1977-85, ptnr., 1985—. Loaned exec. United Way N.E. Ohio, Cleve., 1978; trustee ideastream, Mus. Theater Edn. Programming. Mem. ABA (real estate fin. com. 1980-87, vice chmn. leader liability com. 1993-97, mem. non-traditional real estate fin. com. 1987—, chair securitization and spl. financing techniques com. 2006—), Am. Bar Found., Am. Coll. Real Estate Lawyers (bd. govs. 1994-98, 06—, treas. 1999), Internat. Coun. Shopping Ctrs., Nat. Assn. Office and Indsl. Parks, Urban Land Inst. (chmn. Cleve. dist. coun. 1996-2000), Cleve. Real Estate Women (mem. adv. bd. 2007-), Ohio Bar Assn. (bd. govs. real property sect. 1985-97), Greater Cleve. Bar Assn. (chmn. bar applicants com. 1983-84, exec. coun. young lawyers sect. 1982-85, chmn. 1984-85, mem. exec. coun. real property sect. 1980-84, Merit Svc. award 1983, 85), Pi Gamma Mu. Democrat. Roman Catholic. Home: 2222 Delamere Dr Cleveland OH 44106-3204 Office: Thompson Hine LLP 3900 Key Ctr 127 Public Square Cleveland OH 44114-1216 Office Phone: 216-566-5733. Business E-Mail: linda.striefsky@thompsonhine.com.

STRIER, KAREN BARBARA, anthropologist, educator; b. Summit, NJ, May 22, 1959; d. Murray Paul and Arlene Strier. BA, Swarthmore Coll., 1980; MA, Harvard U., 1981, PhD, 1986. Lectr. anthropology Harvard U., Cambridge, Mass., 1986—87; asst. prof. Beloit Coll., Wis., 1987—89, U. Wis., Madison, 1989—92, assoc. prof., 1992—95, prof., 1995—, dept. chair, 1994—96. Panel mem. U.S. Dept. Edn., Washington, 1989—92. Author: (book) Faces in the Forest, 1999, Primate Behavioral Ecology, 2d edit., 2003; co-author: Planning, Purposing, and Presenting Science Effectively; mem. editl. bd.: Internat. Jour. Primatology, 1990—, Primates, 1991—, Yearbook of Phys. Anthropology. Recipient Presdl. Young Investigator award, NSF, 1989—94. Fellow: AAAS, Am. Anthropol. Assn.; mem.: NAS, Animal Behavior Soc., Internat. Primatological Soc., Am. Assn. Phys. Anthropologists. Office: U Wis Dept Anthropology 5403 Social Sci Bldg 1180 Observatory Dr Madison WI 53706-1320 Office Phone: 608-262-0302. E-mail: kbstrier@wisc.edu.

STRIMBU, VICTOR, JR., lawyer; b. New Phila., Ohio, Nov. 25, 1932; s. Victor and Veda (Stancu) S.; m. Kathryn May Schrote, Apr. 9, 1955 (dec. 1995); children: Victor Paul, Michael, Julie, Sue; m. Marjorie Bichsel, Oct. 23, 1999. BA, Heidelberg Coll., 1954; postgrad., Western Res. U., 1956-57; JD, COlumbia U., 1960. Bar: Ohio 1960, U.S. Supreme Ct. 1972. With Baker & Hostetler LLP, Cleve., 1960—, ptnr., 1970—. Bd. dirs. North Coast Health Ministry; mem. Bay Village (Ohio) Bd. Edn., 1976-84, pres., 1978-82; mem. Bay Village Planning Commn., 1967-69; life mem. Ohio PTA; mem. Greater Cleve. Growth Assn.; trustee New Cleve. Campaign, 1987-94—, North Coast Health Ministry, 1989-2001, Heidelberg Coll., 1996—; mem. indsl. rels. adv. com. Cleve. State U., 1979—, chmn., 1982,1999, vice chmn., 1998. With AUS, 1955-56. Mem. ABA, Ohio Bar Assn., Greater Cleve. Bar Assn., Ohio Newspaper Assn. (minority affairs com. 1987-90), Ct. of Nisi Prius Club. Republican. Presbyterian. Office: Baker & Hostetler LLP 3200 National City Ctr 1900 E 9th St Ste 3200 Cleveland OH 44114-3485 Office Phone: 216-621-0200.

STRINGER, EDWARD CHARLES, judge, lawyer; b. St. Paul, Feb. 13, 1935; s. Philip and Anne (Driscoll) S.; m. Mary Lucille Lange, June 19, 1957 (div. Mar. 1991); children: Philip, Lucille, Charles, Carolyn; m. Virginia L. Ward, Sept. 10, 1993. BA, Amherst Coll., 1957; LLD, U. Minn., 1960. Bar: Minn. Ptnr. Stringer, Donnelly & Sharood, St. Paul, 1960-69, Briggs & Morgan, St. Paul, 1969-79; sr. v.p., gen. counsel Pillsbury Co., Mpls., 1980-82, exec. v.p., gen. counsel, 1982-83, exec. v.p., gen. counsel, chief adminstrv. officer, 1983-89; gen. counsel U.S. Dept. Edn., Washington, 1989-91; chief of staff Minn. Gov. Arne H. Carlson, 1992-94; assoc. justice Minn. Supreme Ct., St. Paul, 1994—2002. Mem. ABA, Minn. State Bar Assn., Ramsey County Bar Assn. (sec. 1977-80), Order of Coif, Mpls. Club. Congregationalist. Home: 712 Linwood Ave Saint Paul MN 55105-3513 Office: W-2200 First Nat Bank Bldg Saint Paul MN 55101-

STROBECK, CHARLES LEROY, real estate company executive; b. Chgo., June 27, 1928; s. Roy Alfred and Alice Rebecca (Stenberg) Strobeck; m. Janet Louise Halverson, June 2, 1951; children: Carol Louise, Nancy Faith, Beth Ann, Jane Alison, Jean Marie. BA, Wheaton Coll., Ill., 1949. Mgr. Sudler & Co., Chgo., 1949-50, ptnr., 1951-63; chmn. bd. dirs. Strobeck, Reiss & Co., Chgo., 1964-82; pres. Strobeck Real Estate, Chgo., 1983-94, chmn. bd. dirs., 1994—. Bd. dirs. Am. Slide-Chart Corp., Carol Stream. Bd. dirs. YMCA, Ill. Humane Soc., 1982—2004; pres. Chgo. Youth Ctrs., 1981—83, bd. dirs., 1985—2007; trustee Wheaton Sanitary Dist., 1976—91. Mem.: Am. Arbitration Assn. (former bd. dirs.), Mental Health Assocs. Greater Chgo. (bd. dirs.), Am. Soc. Real Estate Counselors, Inst. Real Estate Mgmt. (pres. 1970—71), Long Boat Key Club, Chgo. Club, Chgo. Golf Club (bd. dirs. 1984—86), Laurel Oak Country Club, Union League Club (pres. 1975—76), Lambda Alpha. Republican. Home: 642 Maplewood Dr Wheaton IL 60187-8067 Office Phone: 630-954-2400.

STROBEL, MARTIN JACK, lawyer, manufacturing and distribution company executive; b. NYC, July 4, 1940; s. Nathan and Clara (Sorgen) S.; m. Hadassah Orenstein, Aug. 15, 1965; children: Gil Michael, Karen Rachel. BA, Columbia U., 1962; JD, Cleve. Marshall Law Sch., 1966; completed advanced bus. mgmt. program, Harvard U., 1977. Bar: Ohio bar 1966. Counsel def. contract adminstrn. services region Def. Supply Agy., Cleve., 1966-68; with Dana Corp., Toledo, 1968—, gen. counsel, 1970—, dir. govt. relations, 1970-71, asst. sec., 1971—, v.p., 1976—, sec., 1982—. Mem. ABA, Fed. Bar Assn., Machinery and Allied Products Inst., Ohio Bar Assn., Toledo Bar Assn. Office: Dana Corp 4500 Dorr St Toledo OH 43615

STROBEL, PAMELA B., former energy executive; b. Chgo., Sept. 9, 1952; BS highest honors, U. Ill., 1974, JD cum laude, U. Ill., 1977. Bar: Ill. 1977, U.S. Dist. (ctrl. and no. dists.) Ill. 1977, U.S. Ct. Appeals (7th cir.) 1981, U.S. Claims Ct. 1983, U.S. Ct. Appeals (fed. cir.) 1985. Ptnr. Sidley & Austin, Chgo., 1988-93; exec. v.p., gen. counsel Commonwealth Edison Co., Chgo., 1993—2000; exec. v.p. Exelon Corp., Chgo., 2000—03, exec. v.p., chief adminstrv. officer, 2003—05; pres. Exelon Energy Delivery Co., Chgo., 2000—05, vice-chair, 2000—01, CEO, vice-chair, 2001—02, chmn., CEO, 2002—03. Bd. dirs. State Farm Mutual Automobile Ins. Co., 2004—, Illinois Tool Works Inc., 2008—. Mem. Kappa Tau Alpha (staff 1975-77).*

STROBEL, RUSS M., gas industry executive, lawyer; b. NYC, May 2, 1952; BA, Northwestern U., 1974; JD magna cum laude, U. Ill., 1977. Bar: Ill. 1977. Ptnr. Jenner & Block, Chgo., Friedman & Koven; sr. v.p., gen. counsel, & sec. Nicor Inc., Naperville, Ill., 2000—02; pres. Nicor Gas, Naperville, Ill., 2002—, CEO, 2003—, chmn., 2005—; exec. v.p. Nicor Inc., Naperville, Ill., 2002, pres., 2002—05, chmn., pres., CEO, 2005—. Dir., mem. exec. com. Am. Gas Assn. Bd. dir. USO Ill.; mem. adv. com. Gene Siskel Film Ctr., Art Inst. Chgo. Mem.: Econ. Club Chgo., Comml. Club Chgo. (mem. civic com.), Order of the Coif. Office: icor Inc 1844 Ferry Rd Naperville IL 60563-9600

STRODE, GEORGE K., sports editor; b. Amesville, Ohio, Nov. 10, 1935; s. Mac and Edith M. (Murphey) S.; m. Jennifer Lanning (div. 1973); m. Ruth E. Wingett, July 15, 1973. BJ, Ohio U., 1958. Sports editor Zanesville (Ohio) Times Reporter, 1958, Athens (Ohio) Messenger, 1958-62; sports reporter Dayton (Ohio) Daily ews, 1962-63, Columbus (Ohio) Citizen Jour., 1963-69; Ohio sports editor AP, Columbus, 1969-85; sports editor Columbus Dispatch, 1985—, exec. sports editor, 1999—. Mem. Ohio AP Sports Writers Assn. (v.p. 1984—), U.S. Golf Writers Assn., U.S. Harness Writers Assn. (pres. Ohio chpt. 1968-69). Republican. Methodist. Avocations: golf, horse racing. Office: Columbus Dispatch 34 S 3rd St Columbus OH 43215-4241

STRODEL, ROBERT CARL, lawyer; b. Evanston, Ill., Aug. 12, 1930; s. Carl Frederick and Imogene (Board) S.; m. Mary Alice Shonkwiler, June 17, 1956; children: Julie Ann, Linda Lee, Sally Payson. BS, Northwestern U., 1952; JD, U. Mich., 1955. Bar: Ill. 1955, U.S. Supreme Ct. 1970; diplomate Am. Bd. Profl. Liability Attys.; cert. civil trial specialist Am. Bd. Trial Advocacy. Mem. firm Davis, Morgan & Witherell, Peoria, Ill., 1957—59; pvt. practice Peoria, 1959—69; prin. Strodel, Kingery & Durree Assoc., Peoria, Ill., 1969—92, Law Offices of Robert C. Strodel, Ltd., Peoria, 1992—; asst. state's atty. Peoria, 1960—61; instr. bus. law Bradley U., Peoria, 1961—62; lectr. Belli seminars, 1969—87. Mem. U.S. Presdl. Commn. German-Am. Tricentennial, 1983; lectr. in trial practice and med.-legal litigation. Author: Securing and Using Medical Evidence in Personal Injury and Health-Care Cases, 1988; contbr. articles to profl. jours. Gov. appointee Ill. Dangerous Drugs Adv. Coun., 1970-71; gen. chmn. Peoria-Tazewell Easter Seals, 1963, Cancer Crusade, 1970; pres. Peoria Civic Ballet, 1969-70; mem. Mayor's Commn. on Human Rels., 1962-64; chmn. City of Peoria Campaign Ethics Bd., 1975; chmn., builder City of Peoria Mil. Svcs. Meml. Plaza Project, 1998; Peoria County Rep. Sec., 1970-74; campaign chmn. Gov. Richard Ogilvie, Peoria County, 1972, Sen. Ralph Smith, 1970; treas. Michel for Congress, 1977-94, campaign coord., 1982; bd. dirs. Crippled Children's Ctr., 1964-65, Peoria Symphony Orch., 1964-68. Served with AUS, 1956-64. Decorated Officer's Cross of Order of Merit (Fed. Republic Germany); named Outstanding Young Man Peoria, Peoria Jr. C. of C., 1963. Mem. ATLA (bd. govs. 1987-96), ABA, Ill. Trial Lawyers Assn. (bd. mgrs. 1985—), Ill. Bar Assn. (Lincoln awards for legal writing 1961, 63, 65), Am. Inns of Ct. (charter master of bench, Lincoln Inn-Peoria, Ill.), Civil Justice Found. (pres., charter founder, trustee 1986-2002, Masons, Scottish Rite. Office: 927 Commerce Bldg Peoria IL 61602 Office Phone: 309-676-4500. Personal E-mail: stro927@aol.com.

STROGER, TODD H., former state legislator; b. Chicago, IL, Jan. 14, 1963; BA, Xavier U., 1988; postgrad., DePaul U., 1991. Adminstrv. asst. Chgo. Park Dist.; jury supr. Cook County Jury Commn.; statistician Office of Chief Judge Cook County Cir. Ct.; 2nd v.p. Young Dems. of Ill.; mem. for dist. 31 Ill. Ho. of Reps., formerly, 1990—; candidate Cook Co. Bd. Dir., Ill., 2006. Home: 8534 S Cottage Grove Chicago IL 60619-6527

STROHM, BRUCE C., lawyer, real estate company executive; b. 1955; BS, U. Ill.; JD, Northwestern U. Ptnr. Rosenberg & Liebentritt, PC, Chgo.; exec. v.p., gen. counsel, sec. Equity Residential, Chgo., 1995—. Office: Equity Residential 2 N Riverside Plaza Chicago IL 60606 Office Phone: 312-474-1300.

STROM, LYLE ELMER, judge; b. Omaha, Jan. 6, 1925; s. Elmer T. and Eda (Hanisch) Strom; m. Regina Ann Kelly, July 31, 1950 (dec.); children: Mary Bess, Susan Frances(dec.), Amy Claire, Cassie A., David Kelly, Margaret Mary, Bryan Thomas. Student, U. Nebr., 1946-47; AB, Creighton U., 1950, JD cum laude, 1953. Bar: Nebr. 1953. Assoc. Fitzgerald, Brown, Leahy, Strom, Schorr & Barmettler and predecessor firm, Omaha, 1953-60, ptnr., 1960-63, gen. trial ptnr., 1963-85; judge U.S. Dist. Ct. Nebr., Omaha, 1985-87, chief judge, 1987-94, sr. judge, 1995—. Adj. prof. law Creighton U., 1959-95, clinical prof., 1996—; mem. com. pattern jury instrns. and practice and proc. Nebr. Supreme Ct., 1965-91; spl. legal counsel Omaha Charter Rev. Commn., 1973; chair gender fairness task force U.S. Ct. Appeals (8th cir.), 1993-97. Exec. com. Covered Wagon Coun. Boy Scouts Am., 1953—57, bd. trustees, exec. com. Mid-Am. Coun., 1988—; chmn. bd. trustees Marian H.S., 1969—71; mem. pres. coun. Creighton U., 1990—95. With U.S. Maritime Svc., 1943—46. Fellow Am. Coll. Trial Lawyers, Internat. Acad. Trial Lawyers; mem. Nebr. Bar Assn. (ho. of dels. 1978-81, exec. coun. 1981-87, pres. 1989-90), Nebr. Bar Found. (bd. trustees 1998—), Omaha Bar Assn. (pres. 1980-81), Am. Judicature Soc., Midwestern Assn. Amateur Athletic Union (pres. 1976-78), Rotary (pres. 1993-94), Alpha Sigma Nu (pres. alumni chpt. 1970-71). Republican. Roman Catholic. Office: US Dist Ct Roman Hruska Courthouse 111 S 18th Plz Ste 3190 Omaha NE 68102 Office Phone: 402-661-7320.

STROM, ROGER, radio personality; m. Mary Strom; 2 children. Farm broadcaster, Waterloo, Iowa, Rochester, Minn., Oshkosh, Wis., Fargo, ND; farm dir. Country Day syndicated TV show, Sta. WCCO Radio, Mpls., 1988—. Spkr. in field. Master of ceremonies Princess Kay Coronation. Recipient Chem Agra award for Farm Broadcasting Excellence, Farm Bur. Communicator award. Avocation: do it yourselfer. Office: WCCO 625 2nd Ave S Minneapolis MN 55402

STROME, STEPHEN, former music distribution company executive; b. Lynn, Mass., June 20, 1945; s. David and Rose (Cantor) S.; m. Phyllis Ruth Fields, Jan. 14, 1967; children: Michael, Rochelle. BA, Hillsdale Coll., Mich., 1967; MBA, Wayne State U., 1968. Trainee KMart Corp., Detroit, 1968-69, mgr. work measurement Troy, Mich., 1970-73; mgr. tng., edn. Fruehauf Corp., Detroit, 1974-76, regional mgr. labor relations, 1976-78; dir. ops. Handleman Co., Clawson, Mich., 1978-80, account exec., 1980-82, v.p. computer software div. Troy, 1983-85, pres. computer software/video div., 1986-87, exec. v.p., 1987-89, exec. v.p., chief oper. officer, 1990, pres., CEO, 1991-2001, chmn., CEO, 2001—07, cons., 2007—. Office: Handleman Co 500 Kirts Blvd Troy MI 48084-4142

STRONG, JOHN DAVID, insurance company executive; b. Cortland, NY, Apr. 12, 1936; s. Harold A. and Helen H. Strong; m. Carolyn Dimmick, Oct. 26, 1957; children: John David, Suzanne. BS, Syracuse U., 1957; postgrad., Columbia U., 1980. With Kemper Group, 1957-90, Kemper Corp., 1990-96, Empire sales divsn. mgr., 1972-74, CEO, 1988-93, chmn. bd., 1989-93; vice chmn. Millikin Assocs., 1993-96, chmn., 1996; exec. v.p., dir. Facilitators, Inc., 1995-98. Mem. adv. coun. Sch. Bus., Millikin U., 1975-79, 84—; bd. dirs. United Way of Decatur and Macon County, Ill., 1976-83, campaign chmn., 1978-79, pres. bd. dirs., 1979-81; pres. United Way of Ill., 1981-83; bd. dirs. DMH Commn. Svcs. Corp., 1985-97, chmn., 1988-90; bd. dirs. Decatur-Macon County Econ. Devel. Found., 1983-88, DMH Health Systems, 1987-94, Richland C.C. Found., 1987-90, Symphony Orch. Guild of Decatur, 1992-96, DMH Found., 1988-97; bd. dirs. Ill. Ednl. Devel. Found., 1983-90, pres., 1986-87; bd. dirs. Decatur Meml. Hosp., 1985-94, vice chmn., 1988, chmn., 1990-92; bd. dirs. Ctrl. Ill. Health Assocs., Inc., 1994, vice chmn., 1994-96; mem. steering com. Decatur Advantage, 1981-93, pres., 1988-93. Capt. USAR, 1958-69. Mem. Metro Decatur C. of C. (bd. dirs. 1977-80, chmn. 1983-84), Decatur Club (bd. dirs. 19080-83, pres. 1983), Country Club of Decatur (bd. dirs. 1993-99, pres. bd. 1995-97), Union League Club Chgo., Bull Valley Golf Club, Anvil Club, Alpha Kappa Psi. Personal E-mail: jack@strongs.net.

STRONG, RICHARD S., investment company executive; married; 1 child. Master's degree, U. Wis. Founder, CEO Strong Capital Mgmt., Menomonee Falls, Wis., 1974—, dir., 1981—, security analyst, portfolio mgr., 1985—, chmn., 1991—, chief investment officer, 1996—; former chmn. Strong Mutual Funds, Menomonee Falls, Wis.

STROPKI, JOHN M., JR., electric power industry executive; BS indsl. engring., Purdue Univ.; MBA, Ind. Univ. Sales trainee Lincoln Electric Holdings, 1972, dist. mgr., nat. sales mgr., 1992—94, exec. vice-pres., 1996, dir., 1998—, COO, 2003—04, CEO, 2003—04, chmn., pres., CEO, 2004—. Mem. Am. Lung Assn.; Juvenile Diabetes Research Found.; mem. bd. Greater Cleveland Growth Assn., Great Lakes Sci. Ctr. Mem.: Nat. Electrical Manufacturers Assn. (mem. bd. gov.), Gas & Welding Distbr. Assn., Manufacturers Alliance/MAPI (pres. coun.), Am. Welding Soc. (hon.). Office: Lincoln Electric Holdings 22801 St Clair Ave Cleveland OH 44117 Office Phone: 216-481-8100. Office Fax: 216-486-1751.

STROSCIO, MICHAEL ANTHONY, physicist, researcher; b. Winston-Salem, NC, June 1, 1949; s. Anthony and Norma Lee (Sidbury) S.; m. Mitra Dutta; children: Elizabeth de Clare, Charles Marshall Sidbury, Gautam Dutta. BS, U. N.C., 1970; MPhil in Physics, Yale U., 1972, PhD in Physics, 1974. Physicist Los Alamos Sci. Lab., N.Mex., 1975-78; sr. staff mem. Johns Hopkins U. Applied Physics Lab., Laurel, Md., 1978-80; prof. mgr. for electromagnetic research Air Force Office of Sci. Research, Washington, 1980-83; spl. asst. to research dir. Office of Under Sec. Def., Washington, 1982-83; policy analyst White House Office of Sci. and Tech. Policy, Washington, 1983-85; prof. dir. for microelectrons, prin. scientist U.S. Army Research Office, Research Triangle Park, NC, 1985—2001; adj. prof. depts. physics and elec. and computer engring. N.C. State U., Raleigh, 1985—; Richard and Loan Hill prof. depts. bioengring., elec. and computer engring., physics U. Ill., Chgo., 2001—, dir. grad. studies, 2002—04. Adj. prof. depts. elec. engring. and physics Duke U., Durham, 1986-2005, dept. physics U. Ill., Chgo., 2002—; vis. prof. dept. elec. engring. U. Va., Charlottesville, 1990-95, U. Md., College Park, 1996-97; mem. congrl. coun. Duke U. Chapel, 1989-91; lectr. UCLA, 1987, U. Mich., 1988; cons. U.S. Dept. Energy, Washington, 1985-90; vice-chmn. White House Panel on Sci. Comm., Washington, 1983-84; chmn. Dept. Def. Rsch. Instrumentation Com., Washington, 1982; assoc. mem. Adv. Group on Electron Devices, 1985-91, liaison Nat. Laser Users Facility, Rochester, N.Y., 1984; liaison Panel on Sci. Comm. and Nat. Security, NAS, 1982, Panel on Materials for High-Density Electron Packaging, 1987-90; U.S. Army liaison to JASON, 1991-2001; mem. U.S. Govt. coord. com. on Semicondr. Rsch. Corp., 1992-2001; reviewer Irish Sci. Found. Author: Positronium: A Review of the Theory, 1975, Onslow Families, 1977, Quantum Heterostructures: Microelectronics and Optoelectronics, 1999, Phonons in anostructures, 2001, Biological Nanostructures and Applications of Nanostructures in Biology, 2004, Introduction to Nanoelectronics, 2007; editor: Quantum-Based Electronic Devices and Systems, 1998, Advanced Semiconductor Lasers and Applications to Optoelectronics, 2000, Advanced Semiconductor Heterostructures, 2003; reviewer: Army Rsch. Office, US Dept. Energy, NSF, Office of Naval Rsch., Dept. Commerce and the Natural Scis., Engring. Rsch. Coun. Can., 1981—, Irish Sci. Found., 2003, referee jours., —; contbr. articles to profl. jours. Capt. USAF, 1974-75. Grantee Los Alamos Sci. Lab., 1977, Air Force Office Sci. Rsch., 2002—, Army Rsch. Office, 2003—, Def. Advanced Rsch. Projects Agy., 2002—, Dept. Homeland Security, Def. Threat Reduction Agy., NSF, SRC, 2004-06. Fellow AAAS, APS, IEEE (exec. com. for plasma sci. 1983—, Harry Diamond Meml. award 1998), Yale Sci. and Engring. Assn. (exec. bd. dirs. 1983—), Editorial Bd. of Proceedings of IEEE, 2008; mem. Nat. Geneal. Soc., Phi Beta Kappa, Nat. Rsch. Coun. Bd., Army Sci. Tech, 2008-. Achievements include patents in field. Home: 2045 Central Ave Wilmette IL 60091-2383 Office: U Ill Dept Elec and Computer Engring MC154 851 S Morgan St Chicago IL 60607 Home Phone: 847-920-1479; Office Phone: 312-413-5968. Business E-Mail: stroscio@uic.edu, m.stroscio@gte.net.

STROSS, JEOFFREY KNIGHT, internist, educator; b. Detroit, May 2, 1941; s. Julius Knight and Molly Ellen S.; m. Ellen Nora Schwartz; children: Wendy, Jonathan. BS in Pharmacy, U. Mich., 1962, MD, 1967. Diplomate Am. Bd. Internal Medicine. Intern Univ. Mich. Hosp., Ann Arbor, 1967-68, resident in internal medicine, 1971-73; instr. internal medicine U. Mich., Ann Arbor, 1973-74, asst. prof., 1974-79, assoc. prof., 1979-87, prof., 1987—. Contbr. numerous articles to med. jours. Served to maj. USAF, 1969-71. Nat. Heart, Lung and Blood Inst. grantee, 1975—. Fellow ACP; mem. Soc. for Gen. Internal Medicine (regional chmn. 1984-86). Jewish. Home: 824 Asa Gray Dr Ann Arbor MI 48105-2853 Office: U Mich Med Sch 3119 Taubman Ann Arbor MI 48109-0376 E-mail: jstross@umich.edu.

STROTHER, JAY D., legal editor; b. Wichita, Kans., May 31, 1967; m. Cynthia L. Mehnert, Sept. 7, 1991; children: Garrett, Claire. BA, U. Tulsa, 1989. Editor U.S. Jr. C. of C., Tulsa, 1990-93, Assn. Legal Adminstrs., Vernon Hills, Ill., 1993—; editor-in-chief Legal Mgmt. Mag. Author: ALA News. Mem. Am. Soc. Assn. Execs., Soc. Nat. Assn. Publs. (bd. dirs. Chgo. chpt.), Internat. Assn. Bus. Communicators (bd. dirs., suburban v.p. 1994-95), Am. Soc. Bus. Press Editors. Office: Legal Adminstrs 75 Tri State Intl Ste 222 Lincolnshire IL 60069-4435 E-mail: jstrother@alanet.org.

STROUCKEN, ALBERT P. L., consumer products company executive, former chemical company executive; b. July 9, 1947; Exec. v.p. industrial chemicals divsn. Bayer Corp., 1992—97; gen. mgr. inorganic chemicals divsn. Bayer AG, 1997—98; pres., CEO H.B. Fuller Co., St. Paul, 1998—2006, chmn., 1999—2006; chmn., CEO Owens-Illinois, Inc., Toledo, 2006—. Bd. dir. Baxter Internat., Owens Illinois. Bd. dir. Twin Cities United Way; chmn. Minn. Bus. for Early Learning. Office: Owens-Illinois Inc One SeaGate Toledo OH 43666

STROUD, RHODA M., elementary school educator; Tchr. Webster Magnet Elem. Sch., St. Paul. Apptd. mem. Minn. Bd. Edn. for State of Minn. Recipient State Tchr. of Yr. Elem. award Minn., 1992. Office: Webster Magnet Elem Sch 707 Holly Ave Saint Paul MN 55104-7126

STROUP, JOHN S., high speed electronic industry executive; BS in Mechanical Engring., Northwestern U., 1988; MBA, U. of Calif. Berkeley, 1994. Field application engr. Compumotor Div., various mktg. mgmt. positions Parker Hannifin, 1988—96; v.p. gen. mgr. gen. motion control bus. Rockwell Automation, 1996—98; v.p. mktg., gen. mgr. Scientific Technologies, Inc., 1998—2000; v.p. bus. develop. motion group Danaher Corp., 2000, pres. Kollmorgen Indsl. and Comml. div., 2001, pres. Gen. Purpose Systems, 2001, group exec. Danaher Motion, 2003—05; pres., CEO Belden CDT Inc., St. Louis, 2005—. Office: Belden CDT 7701 Forsyth Blvd Ste 800 Saint Louis MO 63105

STROUP, KALA MAYS, former education commissioner, educational alliance administrator; BA in Speech and Drama, U. Kans., 1959, MS in Psychology, 1964, PhD in Speech Comm. and Human Rels., 1974; EdD (hon.), Mo. Western State Coll., 1996; LHD (hon.), Harris-Stowe State Coll., 2000. V.p. acad. affairs Emporia (Kans.) State U., 1978-83; pres. Murray State U., Ky., 1983-90, S.E. Mo. State U., Cape Girardeau, 1990-95, Am. Humanics, Kansas City, Mo., 2002—; commr. higher edn., mem. gov.'s cabinet State of Mo., Jefferson City, 1995—2002. Pres. Mo. Coun. on Pub. Higher Edn.; mem. pres.'s commn. NCAA; cons. Edn. Commn. of States Task Force on State Policy and Ind. Higher Edn.; adv. bd. NSF Directorate for Sci. Edn. Evaluation; adv. com. Dept. Health, Edn. and Welfare, chair edn. com.; citizen's adv. coun. on state of Women U. S. Dept. Labor, 1974-76. Mem. nat. exec. bd. Boy Scouts Am., nat. exploring com., former chair profl. devel. com., mem. profl. devel. com., exploring com., Young Am. awards com., 1986-87, north ctrl. region strategic planning com., bd. trustees, nat. mus. chair; mem. Gov.'s Coun. on Workforce Quality, State of Mo.; bd. dirs. Midwestern Higher Edn. Commn.; chair ACE Leadership Commn.; mem. bd. visitors Air U.; v.p. Missourians for Higher Edn.; bd. dirs. St. Francis Med. Ctr. Found., 1990-95, Cape Girardeau C. of C., 1990-95, U. Kans. Alumni Assn.; pres. Forum on Excellence, Carnegie Found.; adv. bd. World Trade Ctr., St. Louis, Svc. Mems. Opty. Colls., 1997—; mem. Mo. Higher Edn. Loan Authority, 1995—, depts. econ. devel. & agrl. Mo. Global Partnership, 1995—, Mo. Tng. & Employment Coun., 1995-2002, Concordia U. Sys. Advancement Cabinet, State Higher Edn. Exec. Officers, 1995—, mem. com. workforce edn. and tng., 1996; bd. govs. Heartland's Alliance Minority Participation, 1995-2002; chair, mem. workforce devel. com. NPEC coun. U.S. Office of Edn., 1997—; bd. dirs. Midwestern Higher Edn. Com. Distributed Learning Workshop, 1998-2002, Dept. Natural Resources Minority Scholarship Adv. Bd.; chair Show Me Results sub-cabinet Educated Missourians; mem. Pub. Policy Initiative Stakeholder Com., 1999—; mem. Coun. Higher Edn. transfer and pub. interest com.; mem. access/diversity com. State Higher Edn. Exec. Officers; trustee, mem. adv. coun. Assn. Governing Bds. of Univs. and Colls. Ctr. for Pub. Edn., 2000—. ACE fellow; recipient Alumni Honor Citation award U. Kans., Award Distinction Profl. Black Men's Club, S.E. Mo., 1990, Dist. Svc. to Edn. award Harris-Stowe State Coll., 1996; named to U. Kans. Womans Hall of Fame, Ohio Valley Conf. Hall of Fame, 1997. Mem. Am. Assn. State Colls. and Univs. (past bd. dirs., mem. Pres.'s Commn. on Tchr. Edn., Task Force on Labor Force Issues and Implications for the Curriculum), Mortar Board, Phi Beta Kappa, Omicron Delta Kappa, Phi Kappa Phi, Rotary (found. Ednl. awards com.). Office Phone: 816-561-6415.

STRUBEL, ELLA DOYLE, advertising executive, public relations executive; b. Chgo., Mar. 14, 1940; d. George Floyd and Myrtle (McKnight) D.; m. Richard Craig G'sell, Apr. 26, 1969 (div. 1973); m. Richard Perry Strubel, Oct. 23, 1976; stepchildren: Douglas Arthur, Craig Tollerton. BA magna cum laude, U. Memphis, 1962; MA, U. Ill., 1963. Staff asst. Corinthian Broadcasting Co., NYC, 1963-65; dir. advt. and pub. rels. WANE-TV, Ft. Wayne, Ind., 1965-66; asst. dir. advt. WBBM-TV, Chgo., 1966-67, mgr. sales promotion, 1967-69, dir. advt. sales promotion and info. svcs., 1969-70; dir. pub. rels. Waltham Watch Co., Chgo., 1973-74; mgr. advt. promotion and pub. rels. WMAQ-TV, Chgo., 1974-76; v.p. corp. rels. Kraft, Inc., Glenview, Ill., 1985-87; sr. v.p. corp. affairs Leo Burnett Co., Inc., Chgo., 1987-92, exec. v.p., 1992-98; mng. dir. EllaQuent Designs, 2002—. Pres. women's bd. Rehab. Inst. Chgo., 1982—84, chair, 1998—2001, Chgo. Network, 1994—95; vice chair Chgo. Pub. Libr. Found., 2005—07; bd. dirs. Econ. Club, Acad. for Urban Sch. Leaership. Named Outstanding Woman in Comms. in Chgo., YWCA, 1995, one of 100 Most Influential Women in Chgo., Crain's Chgo. Bus., 1996, Who's Who in Chgo. Bus., 2002. Mem. Casino Club, Econ. Club. Democrat. Presbyterian. Office: #1254 55 W Goethe St Chicago IL 60610-7406 Office Phone: 312-255-0235. Business E-Mail: estrubel@aol.com.

STRUBEL, RICHARD PERRY, Internet company executive; b. Evanston, Ill., Aug. 10, 1939; s. Arthur Raymond and Martha (Smith) S.; m. Linda Jane Freeman, Aug. 25, 1961 (div. 1974); children: Douglas Arthur, Craig Tollerton; m. Ella Doyle G'sell, Oct. 23, 1976. BA, Williams Coll., 1962; MBA, Harvard U., 1964. Assoc. Fry Cons., Chgo., 1964-66, mng. prin., 1966-68; with N.W. Industries, Inc., Chgo., 1968-83, v.p. corp. devel., 1969-73, group v.p., 1973-79, exec. v.p., 1979-83, pres., 1983; chmn. bd., pres. Buckingham Corp., NYC, 1972-73; pres., chief exec. officer Microdot Inc., Chgo., 1983-94; mng. dir. Tandem Ptnrs. Inc., Chgo., 1990-99; with UNext Inc., Deerfield, Ill., 1999, pres., COO, 1999—2004, vice chmn., dir., 2004—. Chmn. bd. trustee Mut. Funds of The No. Trust Co., Chgo., and various mutual funds of Goldman Sachs Asset Mgmt., N.Y.C.; bd. dirs. Gildan Activewear, Inc., Montreal, Que., Can. Trustee U. Chgo.; mem. visiting com. Divinity Sch., U. Chgo.; mem. adv. bd. Martin Marty Ctr. Mem. Casino Club, Chicago Club, Comml. Club, Racquet Club of Chicago, Commonwealth Club, Econ. Club. Presbyterian. Office: UNext Inc Ste 455 111 N Canal St Chicago IL 60606

STRUNK, ROBERT CHARLES, physician; b. Evanston, Ill., May 29, 1942; s. Norman Wesley and Marion Mildred (Ree) S.; m. Juanita; children: Christopher Robert, Alix Elizabeth. BA in Chemistry, Northwestern U., 1964, MS in Biochemistry, 1968, MD, 1968. Lic. MD, Ariz., Colo., Mass., Mo. Resident in pediatrics Cin. Children's Hosp., 1968-70; pediatrician Newport (R.I.) Naval Hosp., 1970-72; rsch. fellow in pediatrics Harvard Med. Sch., Boston, 1972-74; asst. prof. pediatrics U. Ariz. Health Sci. Ctr., Tucson, 1974-78; dir. clin. svcs. Nat. Jewish Ctr. for Immunology and Respiratory Med., Denver, 1978-87; sabbatical leave Boston Children's Hosp., 1984-85; dir. divsn. allergy and pulmonary medicine Children's Hosp., St. Louis, 1987-98; pediatrician Barnes and Allied Hosp., St. Louis, 1987—; prof. pediatrics Washington U. Sch. Medicine, St. Louis, 1987—, Strominger prof., 2002—. Recipient Allergic Disease Acad. award at Inst. Allergy and Infectious Disease of NIH. Mem. Am. Acad. Allergy and Immunology, Am. Thoracic Soc. Office: Washington U Sch Med Dept Pediatrics 1 Childrens Pl Saint Louis MO 63110-1002

STRUTHERS, MARGO S., lawyer; BA, Carleton Coll., 1972; JD cum laude, U. Minn., 1976. Atty., shareholder Moss & Barnett, P.A. and predecessor firms, Mpls., 1976-93; ptnr. Oppenheimer Wolff & Donnelly, LLP, Mpls., 1993—. Mem. Am. Health Lawyers Assn., Minn. State Bar Assn. (bus. law sect., former chair nonprofit com., former chair and former mem. governing coun. health law sect.). Office: Oppenheimer Wolff & Donnelly LLP Plaza VII 45 S 7th St Ste 3300 Minneapolis MN 55402-1614 Office Phone: 612-607-7427, 612-607-7000. Business E-Mail: mstruthers@oppenheimer.com.

STRUYK, DOUG, state official; b. Omaha, Aug. 1, 1970; BS, Iowa State U.; JD cum laude, Creighton U. Chief agrl. diversification bur. Struyk Turf Maintenance, Inc.; atty.; mem. Iowa Dept. Agr. and Land Stewardship; state rep. Iowa, 2003—. Mem. transp., infrastructure and capitals appropriations subcom.; mem. agr. standing com.; mem. econ. growth standing com.; mem. judiciary standing com. Pres. Council Bluffs Trees Forever; mem. Iowa Dept. Agr. and Land Stewardship, West Pottawattamie County Ext. Coun. Office: State Capitol E 12th and Grand Des Moines IA 50319

STRUYK, ROBERT JOHN, lawyer; b. Sanborn, Iowa, May 17, 1932; s. Arie Peter and Adriana (VerHoef) S.; m. Barbara Damon, Sept. 7, 1963; children: Arie Franklin, Damon icholas, Elizabeth Snow. BA, Hope Coll., 1954; MA, Columbia U., 1957; LLB, U. Minn., 1961. Bar: Minn., U.S. Dist. Ct. Minn. Secondary tchr. Indianola (Iowa) Pub. Schs., 1957-58; assoc., then ptnr. Dorsey & Whitney, Mpls., 1961—. Mem.: Mpls., Minikahda. Episcopalian. Office: Dorsey & Whitney 50 S 6th St Ste 2200 Minneapolis MN 55402-1498

STUART, JAMES, bank executive, advertising executive, announcer; b. Lincoln, Nebr., Apr. 11, 1917; s. Charles and Marie (Talbot) S.; m. Helen Catherine Davis, July 24, 1940; children: Catherine, James, William Scott. BA, BS, U. Nebr., 1940, HHD (hon.), HHD (hon.), DHL (hon.), U. Nebr., 1990. Chmn. bd. Stuart Mgmt. Co.; mng. ptnr. Stuart Enterprises; chmn. exec. com., bd. dirs. Nat. Bank Commerce, Lincoln; pres. Stuart Found. Founder, trustee Nebr. Human Resources Rsch. Found., 1948—; trustee Bryan Meml. Hosp., 1952-58, U. Nebr. Found., 1956—, Nebr. U. Endowment Fund for Disting. Tchrs.; mem. Lincoln Found., 1955—, Lincoln Sch. Bd., 1961-64, pres., 1964; chmn. bd. trustees 1st Plymouth Ch., Lincoln, 1956; pres. Lincoln Community Chest, 1960. With AUS, 1942-45. Named Outstanding Young Man of Lincoln,

1952; recipient Disting. Svc. award U. Nebr., 1961, Svc. to Mankind award Sertoma Club, 1972, Alumni Achievement award, 1980, Kiwanis Disting. Svc. award, 2002, Disting. Alumni Scholarship award Talent Plus, 2003; named Nebraskan of Yr., Lincoln Rotary, 1997; named to Nebr. Skeet Shooting Assn. Hall of Fame, 1989, Nebr. Bus. Hall of Fame, 1999. Mem. U. Nebr. Alumni Assn. (past pres.), Country Club of Lincoln, Gitchigami Club (Duluth, Minn.), Sunrise Country Club (Rancho Mirage, Calif.), Thunderbird Country Club, Phi Delta Theta, Theta Nu Epsilon, Kappa Beta Phi. Home: 3500 Faulkner Dr Apt A209 Lincoln NE 68516 Office: 1248 O St Ste 852 Lincoln NE 68508

STUART, ROBERT, container manufacturing executive; b. Oak Park, Ill., Aug. 3, 1921; s. Robert S. and Marie (Vavra) Solinsky; m. Lillian C. Kondelik, Dec. 5, 1962 (dec. May 1978); m. Lila Winterhoff Peters, May 21, 1968, (dec., Dec. 07). BS, U. Ill., Chgo., 1943, LLD, 1982. Sec.-treas., gen. mgr. Warren Metal Decorating Co., 1947-49; asst. to gen. mgr. Cans, Inc., 1950-52; asst. to v.p., then v.p. Nat. Can Corp., Chgo., 1953-59, exec. v.p., 1959-63, pres., 1963-69, chief exec., 1966-69, chmn. bd., CEO, 1969-73, chmn. bd., 1973-83, chmn. fin. com., 1983, mem. corp. devel. com., until 1986, chmn. emeritus, 1986—. Past pres., bd. dirs. Corp. Responsibility Group of Greater Chgo. Past pres., bd. dirs. Chgo. Crime Commn.; past dir. Nat. Crime Prevention Coun.; founding chmn. Nat. Minority Supplier Devel. Coun., 1972-73, Lloyd Morey Scholarship Fund: Freedoms Found. at Valley Forge, past trustee; past mem. adv. bd. Salvation Army, Broader Urban Involvement and Leadership Devel.; chmn. emeritus World Federalist Assn.; past bd. dirs., past moderator Millard Congl. Ch.; past pres. Ctrl. Ch. Chgo.; chmn. emeritus Assn. to Unite the Democracies. Capt. AUS, 1943-46. Mem.: Rotary (past pres. Chgo. club, past dist. gov.), Little Ship Club (London), Yacht Club, Chgo. Club, Masons (32d degree, Red Cross of Constantine), Alpha Kappa Lambda (past nat. pres.). Lutheran. Home and Office: 233 SW 43d Ter Cape Coral FL 33914

STUART, WILLIAM CORWIN, judge; b. Knoxville, Iowa, Apr. 28, 1920; s. George Corwin and Edith (Abram) S.; m. Mary Elgin Cleaver, Oct. 20, 1946; children: William Corwin II, Robert Cullen, Melanie Rae, Valerie Jo. BA, State U. Iowa, 1941, JD, 1942. Bar: Iowa 1942. Pvt. practice, Chariton, 1946-62; city atty., 1947-49; mem. Iowa Senate from, Lucas-Wayne Counties, 1951-61; justice Supreme Ct. Iowa, 1962-71; judge U.S. Dist. Ct., So. Dist. of Iowa, Des Moines, 1971-86, sr. judge, 1986—. With USNR, 1943-45. Recipient Outstanding Svc. award Iowa Acad. Trial lawyer, 1987, Iowa Trial Lawyers Assn., 1988, Spl. award Iowa State Bar Assn., 1987, Disting. Alumni, U. Iowa Coll. Law, 1987. Mem. ABA, Iowa Bar Assn., Am. Legion, All For Iowa, Order of Coif, Omicron Delta Kappa, Phi Kappa Psi, Phi Delta Phi. Clubs: Mason (Shriner). Presbyterian. Home: PO Box 130 Chariton IA 50049-0130

STUBBLEFIELD, ROBERT F., travel agency executive; married Judy Stubblefield; children: Matt, Rob, Kaarin, Erik. BSBA, U. Nebr. Enlisted U.S. Army, served to inf. capt., ret.; former asst. gen. merchandise mgr. Brandeis & Co.; pres. AAA, Omaha, 1976—. Active Nebr. Spl. Olympics; mem. North Hill Hunt Club; bd. dirs. numerous civic bds.; active Mid-Am. Coun. Boy Scouts. Office: AAA 10703 J St Omaha NE 68127-1023

STUBBS, JERALD D., career military officer; BA, U. Ga., 1967; JD, Harvard Law Sch., 1970. Commd. USAF, advanced through grades to brigadier gen., 1999; asst. staff judge advocate Elec. Sys. Divsn., Hanscom AFB, Mass., 1970-73; dep. staff judge advocate 21st Composite Wing, Elmendorf AFB, Alaska, 1973-76, 314th Mil. Airlift Wing, Little Rock AFB, 1978-80; trial atty. Air Force Contract Trial Team, Wright-Patterson AFB, Ohio, 1980-84; staff judge advocate 51st Tactical Fighter Wing, Osan Air Base, South Korea, 1984-86; chief adminstrn. law HQ USAF, Pentagon, 1986-89; staff judge advocate Warner Robins Air Logistics Ctr, Robins AFB, Ga., 1990-92; dep. staff judge advocate HQ Air Force Materiel Command, Wright-Patterson AFB, 1992-95; staff judge advocate HQ U.S. Space Command Air Force Space Command, Peterson AFB, Colo., 1995-96; comdr. Air Force Legal Svcs. Agy., Bolling AFB, D.C., 1996-99; staff judge advocate HQ Air Force Materiel Command, Wright-Patterson AFB, 1999—. Office: HQ AFMC/JA 4225 Logistics Ave Ste 23 Wright Patterson AFB OH 45433-5769

STUDDERT, ANDREW PAUL, air transportation executive; married; 3 children. BS, San Francisco State U., 1979. Various exec. positions First Interstate Bancorp, LA, exec. v.p.; sr. v.p. info. svcs. divsn., chief info. officer United Airlines, Chgo., sr. v.p. fleet ops., 1997—99, COO, 1999—. Office: UAL Corp and United Airlines World Hqrs PO Box 66100 Chicago IL 60666-0100

STUDER, WILLIAM JOSEPH, library director; b. Whiting, Ind., Oct. 1, 1936; s. Victor E. and Sarah G. (Hammersley) S.; m. Rosemary Lippie, Aug. 31, 1957 (dec.); children: Joshua E., Rachel Marie. BA, Ind. U., 1958, MA, 1960, PhD (Univ. fellow), 1968. Grad. asst. divsn. libr. sci. Ind. U., 1959-60, reference asst., 1960-61; spl. intern Libr. of Congress, 1961-62, reference libr., sr. bibliographer, 1962-65; dir. regional campus librs. Ind. U., Bloomington, 1968-73, assoc. dean univ. librs., 1973-77; dir. librs. Ohio State U., Columbus, 1977-2000, prof. emeritus libr. sci., 2000—, coord. univ. oral history program, 2001—. Mem. Libr. Svcs. and Constrn. Act Adv. Com. of Ind., 1971-76; mem. Adv. Coun. on Fed. Libr. Programs in Ohio, 1977-85, chmn., 1980-81; adv. coun. Libr. Svcs. and Tech. Act, 1997-99; mem. ARL Office Mgmt. Studies Adv. Com., 1977-81, ARL Task Force on Nat. Libr. Network Devel., 1978-83, bd. dirs., 1981-84, chmn., 1981-83, com. on preservation, 1985-88, vice-chmn., 1989-90, chmn., 1991-92, task force on scholarly comm., 1983-87, com. stats. and measurement, 1993-99, chmn., 1997-98; network adv. com. Libr. Congress, 1981-88; libr. study com. Ohio Bd. Regents, 1986-87; mem. steering com. Ohio Libr. and Info. etwork (OhioLINK), 1987-90; vice-chmn. Ctr. Rsch. Librs., 1993-94, chmn., 1994-95, sec., chmn. membership com., 1990-93; adv. coun. OhioLink Libr., 1992-2000, chmn., 1991-92, policy adv. coun., governing bd., 1991-92. Contbr. articles to profl. jours. Trustee Online Computer Libr. Ctr. Inc., 1977-78; del. Online Computer Libr. Ctr. Users Coun., 1983-91; rsch. librs. adv. com. Online Computer Libr. Ctr., 1989-95, vice-chmn., chmn.-elect, 1993-94, chmn., 1994-95; bd. dirs. Ohio Network of Librs. Ohionet, 1977-87, chmn., 1980-82, 86-87, treas., 1983-86; mem. Columbia U. Sch. Libr. Svc. Conservation Programs, vis. com., 1987-90; nat. adv. coun. to commn. on preservation and access, 1989-92; treas. Monroe County (Ind.) Mental Health Assn., 1968-76; budget rev. com. United Way, 1975-77; bd. dirs. Mental Health Assn. Recipient citation for participation MARC Insts., 1968-69, Disting. Alumni award Ind. U., 1978, OhioLINK Founders award, 2002. Mem. ALA, Ohio Libr. Assn. (bd. dirs. 1980-83), Assn. Coll. and Rsch. Librs. (bd. dirs. 1977-81, com. on activities model for 1990, 1981-82, chmn. libr. sch. curriculum task force 1988-89), Ohio State U. Retirees Assn. (pres.-elect 2004-05, pres., 2005-06), Acad. Libr. Assn. Ohio, Torch Club (pres. 1993-94), Phi Kappa Phi (pub. rels. officer 1982-83, sec. 1983-85), Phi Eta Sigma, Alpha Epsilon Delta., Beta Phi Mu. Home: 724 Olde Settler Pl Columbus OH 43214-2924 Office: Ohio State U William Oxley Thompson Meml Libr 1858 Neil Ave Columbus OH 43210-1286 Office Phone: 614-688-0204. Business E-Mail: studer.2@osu.edu.

STUECK, WILLIAM NOBLE, small business owner; b. Elmhurst, Ill., May 20, 1939; s. Otto Theodore and Anna Elizabeth (Noble) S.; m. Martha Lee Hemphill Stueck, June 2, 1963; children: Matthew Noble, Erika Lee. BS, U. Kans., 1963. Owner, pres. Suburban Lawn & Garden, Inc., Overland Park, Kans., 1953—. Chmn. bd. Mark Twain Bank South, Kansas City., Mo., 1984—. Bd. dirs. Ronald McDonald House, Kansas City; ambassador Am. Royal, Kansas City, 1983. Mem. Am. Assn. Nurserymen, Mission Valley Hunt Club (master 1986—), Leavenworth Hunt Club, Saddle & Sirloin Club. Office: PO Box 480200 Kansas City MO 64148-0200 also: Suburban Lawn & Garden Inc 13635 Wyandotte St Kansas City MO 64145-1516

STUELAND, DEAN THEODORE, emergency physician; b. Viroqua, Wis., June 24, 1950; s. Theodore Andrew and Hazel Thelma (Oftedahl) S.; m. Marlene Ann McClurg, Dec. 30, 1972; children: Jeffrey, Michael, Nancy, Kevin. BSEE, U. Wis., 1972, MSEE, 1973, MD, 1977; MPH, Med. Coll. Wis., 1997. Diplomate Am. Bd. Internal Medicine, Am. Bd. Geriatric Medicine, Am. Bd. Emergency Medicine; cert. in addictions medicine, cert. med. rev. officer. Resident Marshfield (Wis.) Clinic, 1977-80, emergency physician, dir. emergency svc., 1981-93; emergency physician Riverview Hosp., Wisconsin Rapids, Wis., 1980-81. Med. dir. Nat. Farm Medicine Ctr., Marshfield, 1986—, alcohol and other drug abuse unit St. Joseph's Hosp., Marshfield, 1988-99; exec. com. Marshfield Clinic, 1989-91, 93-95, treas., 1993-95, v.p., 1997—. ACLS state affiliate faculty Am. Heart Assn., 1984-98, nat. faculty, 1992-97; mem. emergency med. svcs. adv. bd. State of Wis., 1994-97, ECC com., 1998—. Contbr. articles to profl. jours. Charter mem., pres. Hewitt (Wis.) Jaycees, 1984; bd. dirs. Northwood County chpt. ARC, 1988-95, Wood County Partnership Coun., 1993-98. Fellow ACP, Am. Coll. Emergency Physicians (bd. dirs. Wis. chpt. 1984-90, v.p. 1990-91, pres. 1991-92, counselor 1993-98), Am. Coll. Preventive Medicine; mem. Biomed. Engring. Soc. (sr. mem.), Am. Soc. Addictions Medicine. Mem. Missionary Alliance Ch. (bd. govs., treas. 1991-97).

STUFFLEBEAM, DANIEL LEROY, education educator; b. Waverly, Iowa, Sept. 19, 1936; s. LeRoy and Melva Stufflebeam; m. Carolyn T. Joseph; children: Kevin D., Tracy Smith, Joseph. BA, State U. Iowa, 1958; MS, Purdue U., 1962, PhD, 1964; postgrad., U. Wis., 1965. Prof., dir. Ohio State U. Evaluation Ctr., Columbus, 1963-73; prof. edn. Western Mich. U. Evaluation Ctr., Kalamazoo, 1973—, dir., 1973—2002; Beula McKee prof. edn. Western Mich. U., 1997—, disting. univ. prof., 2002—. Author monographs and 15 books; contbr. chpts. to books, articles to profl. jours. With USAR, 1960—68. Recipient Paul Lazersfeld award Evaluation Rsch. Soc., 1985, Jason Millman award Consortium for Rsch. on Ednl. Accountability and Tchr. Evaluation, 1999. Mem.: Am. Evaluation Assn. Baptist. Office: Western Michigan Univ The Evaluation Ctr Kalamazoo MI 49008-5237 Office Fax: 269-387-5923. Personal E-mail: dlstfbm@aol.com.

STUHAN, RICHARD GEORGE, lawyer; b. Braddock, Pa., July 1, 1951; s. George and Pauline Madeline (Pavlocik) S.; m. Mary Ann Cipriano, Aug. 23, 1975; children: Brendan George, Sara Katherine, Brian Christopher, Caitlin Emily. BA summa cum laude, Duquesne U., 1973; JD, U. Va., 1976. Bar: Va. 1976, D.C. 1977, U.S. Ct. Appeals (D.C. cir.) 1977, U.S. Ct. Appeals (4th cir.) 1977, U.S. Claims Ct. 1979, U.S. Supreme Ct. 1980, U.S. Ct. Appeals (3d cir.) 1981, U.S. Ct. Appeals (11th cir.) 1982, U.S. Dist. Ct. (no. dist.) Ohio 1985, Ohio 1986. Assoc. Arnold & Porter, Washington, 1976-84; of counsel Jones Day, Cleve., 1984-86, ptnr., 1987—. Pres. Womankind Maternal and Prenatal Care; chmn. devel. com. Doan Brook Watershed Partnership. Mem. Va. Law Review, 1974-76. Recipient Gold Medal for Gen. Excellence, Duquesne U., 1973; named Ohio Super Lawyer, Law and Politics Media, Inc. Mem. Cleve. Bar Assn. (chmn. jury svc. com.), Internat. Assn. Def. Counsel, Order of Coif. Democrat. Roman Catholic. Avocations: tennis, swimming, basketball, home repair. Home: 2865 Falmouth Rd Shaker Heights OH 44122-2838 Office: Jones Day 901 Lakeside Ave Cleveland OH 44114-1190 Home Phone: 216-561-3595; Office Phone: 216-586-7148. Business E-Mail: rgstuhan@jonesday.com.

STUHR, ELAINE RUTH, state legislator; b. Polk County, Nebr., June 19, 1936; m. Boyd E. Stuhr, 1956; children: Cynthia (Stuhr) Zluticky, Teresa (Stuhr) Robbins, Boyd E., Jr. BS, U. Nebr. Tchr. jr. and sr. vocat. h.s. Nebr. schs.; senator Nebr. Unicameral, Lincoln, 1994—2006; chmn. Nebr. retirement sys. com.; vice chair natural resources com.; commr. edn. com. of states; farmer Bradshaw, Nebr. Former asst. instr. U. Nebr., Lincoln; participant farmer to farmer assignment to Russia with Winrock, Internat., 1993, to Lithuania with Vol. Overseas Coop. Asistance, 1993; former pres. Agrl. Womens Leadership Network; former mem. bd. dirs. Feed Grains Coun., Nebr. Corn Bd. Past pres., bd. dirs. Found. for Agrl. Edn. and Devel.; former mem. exec. com. and bd. dirs. Agrl. Coun. Am.; nat. pres. Women Involved in Farm Econs., state pres.; mem. adv. com. Nebr. Extension Sv.; bd. dirs. Heartland Ctr. for Leadership Devel.; past chmn. ebr. Agrl. Leadership Coun. Republican. Office Phone: 402-471-2756. E-mail: estuhr@unicam.state.ne.us.

STUKEL, JAMES JOSEPH, academic administrator, mechanical engineer, educator; b. Joliet, Ill., Mar. 30, 1937; s. Philip and Julia (Mattivi) S.; m. Mary Joan Helpling, ov. 27, 1958; children: Catherine, James, David, Paul. BS in Mech. Engring, Purdue U., 1959; MS, U. Ill., Urbana-Champaign, 1963, PhD, 1968. Research engr. W.Va. Pulp and Paper Co., Covington, Va., 1959-61; mem. faculty U. Ill., Urbana-Champaign, 1968—, prof. mech. engring., 1975—, dir. Office Coal Research and Utilization, 1974-76, dir. Office Energy Research, 1976-81, dir. pub. policy program Coll. Engring., 1981-84, assoc. dean Coll. Engring. and dir. Expt. Sta., 1984-85; dean Grad. Coll., vice chancellor for research U. Ill. at Chgo., 1985-86, exec. vice chancellor, vice chancellor academic affairs, 1986-91, interim chancellor, 1990-91, chancellor, 1991-95, pres., 1995—. V.p. Chgo. Tech. Park Corp., 1985-88, pres., 1990-91; exec. sec. midwest Consortium Air Pollution, 1972-73, chmn. bd. dirs., 1973-75; mem. adv. bd. regional studies program Argonne (Ill.) Nat. Lab., 1975-76; adv. com. Energy Resources Commn., 1976; chmn. panel on dispersed electric generating techs. Office Tech. Assessment, U.S. Congress, 1980-81; chmn. rev. adv. bd. tech. rev. dist. heating and combined heat and power systems Internat. Energy Agy, OECD, Paris, 1982-83; cons. in field. Contbr. articles to profl. jours. Pres. parish council Holy Cross Roman Cath. Ch., Urbana, 1967-68. Mem. ASCE (State-of-the-Art of Civil Engring. award 1975), ASME, AAAS, Sigma Xi, Phi Kappa Phi, Pi Tau Sigma. Home: 2650 N Lakeview Ave Apt 1610 Chicago IL 60614-1819 Office: 364 Henry Adm Bldg M/C 346 Urbana IL 61801

STUMPF, DAVID ALLEN, pediatric neurologist; b. LA, May 8, 1945; s. Herman A. and Dorothy F. (Davis) S.; children: Jennifer F., Kaitrin E.; m. Elizabeth Dusenbery, Feb. 2, 1989; children: Todd Coleman, Shilo Walker. BA, Lewis and Clark Coll., 1966; MD cum laude, U. Colo., 1972, PhD, 1972. Diplomate Am. Bd. Pediat., Am. Bd. Psychiatry and Neurology, lic. MD State of Ill. Pediatric intern Strong Meml. Hosp., Rochester, NY, 1972-73, resident, 1973-74; resident in neurology Harvard Med. Sch., Boston, 1974-77; dir. pediatric neurology U. Colo. Health Sci. Ctr., Denver, 1977-85; chief neurology Children's Meml. Hosp., Chgo., 1985-89; chmn. neurology, Benjamin and Virginia T. Boshes prof. Northwestern U., 1989-98, prof. neurology and pediatrics, 1999—2001; pres. and CEO Oyxis, LLC, 1999—2001; med. dir. United Healthcare, Chgo., 2005—. Mem. sci. adv. com. Muscular Dystrophy Assn., 1981-87; bd. dirs. Northwestern Meml. Corp., Chgo. Mem. editl. bd. Neurology, 1982-87; contbr. articles to sci. jours. Recipient Lewis and Clark Coll. Disting. Alumni award, 1991; NIH grantee, 1979-84; Muscular Dystrophy Assn. grantee, 1977-89; March of Dimes grantee, 1983-85. Fellow Am. Acad. Neurology (treas. 2005-07); mem. Child Neurology Soc. (counsellor 1982-84, pres. 1985-87), Am. Neurol. Assn., Am. Pediatric Soc., Soc. Pediatric Rsch., Internat. Child Neurology Assn. (sec. 2002-04). Presbyterian. Home: 540 Judson Ave Evanston IL 60202-3084 Office Phone: 312-424-6905. E-mail: david@stumpf.org.

STUPAK, BART (BARTHOLOMEW THOMAS STUPAK), congressman, lawyer; b. Milw., Feb. 29, 1952; m. Laurie Ann Olsen; children: Ken, Bart Jr. (dec. May 14, 2000) AA in Criminal Justice, orthwestern Mich. C.C., Traverse City, 1972; BS in Criminal Justice, Saginaw Valley State Coll., 1977; JD, Thomas M. Cooley Law Sch., 1981. Patrolman Escanaba City Police Dept., 1972-73; state trooper Mich. Dept. State Police, 1973-84; instr. State Police Tng. Acad., 1980-82; atty., 1981-84, Hansley, eiman, Peterson, Beauchamp, Stupak, Bergman P.C., 1984-85; ptnr. Stupak, Bergman, Stupak P.C., 1985-88; mem. Mich. Ho. of Reps., 1989-90; prin. Bart T. Stupak P.C., 1991—; mem. US Congress from 1st Mich. dist., 1993—. Mem. commerce subcom., ranking dem. on oversights and investigation, telecom. and Internet, environment and hazardous materials, commerce trade, consumer protection. Nat. committeeman Boy Scouts Am., coach Menominee Youth Baseball Assn., Little League; active Wildlife Unltd., Menominee Woods and Streams Assn., Menominee County Hist. Soc.; adv. com. Bay Pines Juv. Detection Ctr.; bd. dir. Cmty. Action Agy. Recipient Fed. Legislator of Yr. award, Mich. Credit Union League, Great Lakes legis. of Yr. award, Great Lakes Maritime Task Force, 2003. Mem. Nat. Rifle Assn., Sons of the Am. Legion, Knights of Columbus, Elks Club, State Employees Retirees Assn., fin. com. Holy Spirit Catholic Ch. Democrat. Roman Catholic. Office: US Congress 2352 Rayburn House Office Bldg Washington DC 20515-2201 also: Iron County Courthouse Ste 3 2 S Sixth St Crystal Falls MI 49920-1438 Office Phone: 202-225-4735, 906-875-3751. Office Fax: 202-225-4744, 906-875-3889. E-mail: stupak@mail.house.gov.

STURGESS, GEOFFREY J., aeronautical research engineer; Aero. and mech. rsch. engr. Innovative Scientific Solutions, Inc., Beavercreek, Ohio. Recipient Energy Systems award AIAA, 1994. Office: 2766 Indian Ripple Rd Dayton OH 45440-3638

STURKEN, CRAIG C., retail executive; Sr. v.p. Big Star Food Stores, 1989—90; chmn. Can. ops. Spartan Stores Inc., 1990—93, group v.p. Mich. ops., then pres. A&P Mich., 1993—97, chmn., CEO midwest region, 1997—2000, pres., CEO atlantic region, 2000—03, chmn., pres., CEO, 2003—. Office: Spartan Stores 850 76th St SW Grand Rapids MI 49518

STURTZ, W. DALE, state legislator; m. Fay Sturtz. Grad., Nat. Sheriffs Inst., FBI Acad. Sheriff LaGrange County, Ind., 1980-90; investigator, legal adminstr. Yoder Law Offices, 1990—; mem. from 52d dist. Ind. State Ho. of Reps., 1992—, chmn. judiciary com., mem. agr., natural resources/rural devel. com., mem. cts. and criminal codes com. Mem. Nat. Sheriffs Inst., Fraternal Order of Police, Meridian Sun Lodge, Exch. Club, Scottish Rite. Office: Ind House of Reps State Capitol Indianapolis IN 46204 also: 1080 E 480 N Howe IN 46746-9726

STUTZMAN, MARLIN, state representative; Attended, Glen Oaks C.C. Farmer, owner Stuzman Farms Trucking, Ind.; state rep. dist. 52 Ind. Ho. of Reps., Indpls., 2002—, mem. environ. affairs, human affairs, and rds. and transp. coms. Mem. Leaders of Young Reps. LaGrange County; music dir. LaGrange (Ind.) Bapt. Ch. Republican. Office: Indiana Ho of Reps 200 W Washington St Indianapolis IN 46204-2786

STYLES, BONNIE W., museum director, archaeologist; b. Mesa, Ariz., Nov. 11, 1950; d. Lois M. and James E. Whatley; m. Thomas R. Styles, May 15, 1976; children: Megan A., Todd E. BA in Anthropology, Ariz. State U., 1972; MA in Anthropology, Northwestern U., 1973, PhD in Anthropology, 1978. Chair, assoc. curator anthropology Ill. State Mus., 1977—83, chair, curator anthropology, 1983—88, dir. scis. Springfield, 1988—99, assoc. dir., 1999—2006, dir., 2006—. Mem. nat. accreditation commn. for mus. Am. Assn. Mus., 2007—; presenter in field. Project dir. (natural history exhbn.) Changes (IAM Superior Achievement, 2004); contbr. articles to profl. jours. Sci. adv. com. Ill. River Coordinating Coun.; bd. dirs. Natural Sci. Collections Alliance, 1999—2002, Soc. for Am. Archaeology, 1997—2000; pres. Ill. Archaeol. Survey, Champaign-Urbana, Ill., 1983—85. Named Prin. Investigator Emeritus, NSF, 2007; grantee, Inst. Mus. and Libr. Svcs., 2001—03; Miss. RiverWeb Mus. Consortium grant, NSF, 1998—2001, Mus. Tech. Acad. grant, 2004, Learning Opportunities grant, Inst. Mus. and Libr. Svcs., 2003—05, MuseumLink grant, US Dept. Commerce, 1997—2000. Fellow: Ill. State Acad. Sci. (bd. of directors 1998—2001), AAAS; mem.: Soc. Am. Archaeology, Ill. State Mus. Soc. (exec. sec. 2005—), Am. Assn. Mus. (mem. accreditation com. 2007—), Assn. Sci. Mus. Dirs. (sec.-treas. 2006—), Midwest Archaeol. Conf. (pres. 2006—), Am. Quaternary Assn. (bd. dirs. 1997—2000, sec. 1998—2004), Sigma Xi. Achievements include research in prehistoric subsistence practices. Avocations: travel, hiking. Office: Ill State Mus Sys 502 S Spring St Springfield IL 62706 Office Phone: 217-782-7011. Office Fax: 217-785-2857. Business E-Mail: director@museum.state.il.us.*

STYNES, STANLEY KENNETH, retired chemical engineer, educator; b. Detroit, Jan. 18, 1932; s. Stanley Kenneth and Bessie Myrtle (Casey) S.; m. Marcia Ann Meyers, Aug. 27, 1955; children: Peter Casey, Pamela Kay, Suzanne Elizabeth. BS, Wayne State U., 1955, MS, 1958; PhD, Purdue U., 1963. Lab. asst. U. Chgo., 1951; instr. Purdue U., 1960-63; asst. prof. chem. engring. Wayne State U., Detroit, 1963-64, assoc. prof., 1964-71, prof., 1971-92, dean engring., 1972-85, prof. emeritus, 1992—. Dir. Energy Conversion Devices, Inc., Rochester Hills, Mich., 1978—2005, MacMedia, Holland, Mich.; cons. Schwayder Chem. Metallurgy Co., 1965, chemistry dept. Wayne State U., 1965—66, Claude B. Schneible Co., Holly, Mich., 1968. Contbr. engring. articles to profl. jours. Mem. coun. on environ. strategy S.E. Mich. Coun. Govts., 1976—81; sec.-treas. Mich. Ednl. Rsch. Info. Triad; trustee Sci. Ctr. Met. Detroit, 1980—92; mem. ops. com. MACTV, 2000; sec. Friends of Herrick Dist. Libr., 2003; bd. dirs. Program for Minorities in S.E. Mich., Sci. and Engring. Fair of Met. Detroit, pres., 1983; bd. dirs. Midwest Program for Minorities in Engring., Friends of Herrick Dist. Libr.; treas. bd. dirs. Mac Media, 2002—; bd. dirs. Hope Acad. Sr. Profls., 2004. Ford Found. fellow, 1959-63; DuPont fellow, 1962-63; Wayne State U. faculty research fellow, 1964-65 Fellow: AIChE (past chmn. Detroit sect.), Mich. Soc. Profl. Engrs. (pres. 1987—88), Engring. Soc. Detroit (past bd. dirs.); mem.: Adult Learning Inst. (bd. dirs. 1994—99), Engring. Sci. Devel. Found. (pres. 1992—94), Am. Chem. Soc., Hope Acad. Sr. Profls. (bd. dirs. 2004—), Phi Lambda Upsilon, Omicron Delta Kappa, Tau Beta Pi, Sigma Xi. Presbyterian. Home: 145 Columbia #609 Holland MI 49423-2980 Personal E-mail: stanley.stynes@sbcglobal.net.

SUAREZ, BENJAMIN, consumer products company executive; Pres., CEO Suarez Corp. Office: Suarez Corp 7800 Whipple Ave NW Canton OH 44767-0002

SUAREZ, RAY, city official; b. Yauco, PR, Oct. 26, 1946; m. Marta. Coord. CETA program Dept. Streets & Sanitation, Chgo., 1974, asst. commr., 1974-91; alderman of the 31st ward City of Chgo., 1991—, chmn. com. on housing and real estate. Chair human rels. com. Chgo. City Coun., 1994—, budget and govt. ops. com., bldgs. com., rules & ethics com., fin. com., spl. events and cultural affairs com., zoning, transportation & pub. ways com., 1994. Served in USMC, Vietnam. Mem. Caballeros de San Juan (pres.), Lions. Office: 31st Ward 4502 W Fullerton Ave Chicago IL 60639-1934

SUBLETT, ROGER H., academic administrator; b. Ark. m. Cynthia Sublett; 3 children. BS, MA, U. Ark.; PhD in Am. History, Tulane U. Assoc. v.p. academic affairs U. Evansville, Ind., dean Coll. of Grad. and Continuing Studies Ind., dir. spl. programs Coll. of Alternative Programs Ind.; dir. Kellogg Nat. Fellowship/Leadership Program W. K. Kellogg Found., 1991—2001, program dir. Higher Edn. and Leadership, 1991—2001; faculty mem. Union Inst. & Univ., Cin., 2001—, interim v.p. for nat. undergraduate programs, provost, COO, acting pres., pres., 2003—. Co-author: Leading from the Heart. Bd. trustees Ctr. for Ethical Leadership, Seattle, OmniMed, Boston. Named Leadership Scholar, James MacGregor Burns Acad. of Leadership, U. Md.; recipient Spirit of Leadership Award, Kellogg Fellows Leadership Alliance, 2005. Fellow: James MacGregor Burns Acad. Leadership; mem.: Coalition for Adult Edn. Orgns. (pres. 1989—90), Assn. for Continuing Higher Edn. (life; v.p. 1984—89, Outstanding Svc. Award), Ctr. for Ethical Leadership (sr. scholar). Office: Union Inst & Univ Office of the President 440 E McMillan St Cincinnati OH 45206-1925

SUCH, DOMINGO P., III, lawyer; BA cum laude, Washington U., St. Louis, MBA; JD cum laude, Loyola U. Chgo. Sch. Law. Ptnr. McDermott, Will & Emery LLP, Chgo. Mem. profl. adv. com. Chgo. Cmty. Trust, Loyola U. Med. Ctr.; mem. Body of Knowledge com. of bd. dirs. Family Firm Inst., mem. faculty; lectr. Loyola U. Chgo. Sch. Law and Grad. Sch. Bus. Contbr. articles to profl. publs. Named one of Top 100 Attys., Worth mag., 2006. Mem.: Chgo. Estate Planning Coun., Asian Am. Bar Assn., ABA, Chgo. Bar Assn. (chair, former legis. liaison Trust Law Com., past chmn. probate practice com.). Office: McDermott Will & Emery LLP 227 W Monroe St Chicago IL 60606-5096 Office Phone: 312-984-7683. Office Fax: 312-984-7700. E-mail: dsuch@mwe.com.

SUCHOMEL, MARK, publishing executive; With Contemporary Books, Chgo.; sales mgr. Chgo. Rev. Press (acquired by IPG), Chgo., 1986—87; with Independent Pub. Group, Chgo., 1987—, v.p. sales, mktg., pres., 1998—. Exec. coun. The Quills. Named One of 11 for the Millennium-those who will help shape publ. in 21st century, Publishers Weekly. Office: IPG 814 N Franklin St Chicago IL 60610 Office Phone: 312-337-0747. Office Fax: 312-337-0747.

SUDBRINK, JANE MARIE, sales and marketing executive; b. Sandusky, Ohio, Jan. 14, 1942; niece of Arthur and Lydia Sudbrink. BS, Bowling Green State U., 1964; postgrad., Kinderspital-Zurich, Switzerland, 1965. Field rep. Random House and Alfred A. Knopf Inc., Mpls., 1969-72, Ann Arbor, Mich., 1973, regional mgr. Midwest and Can., 1974-79, Can. rep., mgr., 1980-81; psychology and ednl. psychology adminstrv. editor Charles E. Merrill Pub. Co. div. Bell & Howell Corp., Columbus, Ohio, 1982-84; sales and mktg. mgr. trade products Wilson Learning Corp., Eden Prairie, Minn., 1984-85; fin. cons. Merrill Lynch Pierce Fenner & Smith, Edina, Minn., 1986-88; sr. editor Gorsuch Scarisbrick Pubs., Scottsdale, Ariz., 1988-89; regional mgr. Worth Pubs., Inc. -von Holtzbrinck Pub. Grp., NYC, 1988-97; mktg. assoc. Harcourt Brace Coll. Pubs., Northbrook, Ill., 1997-98, cons. Mid-Atlantic Region, Midwest, Manitoba, Can., 1998—; mktg. assoc. W.W. Norton & Co., Northbrook, Ill., 1998—. Lutheran. Home and Office: 3801 Mission Hills Rd Northbrook IL 60062-5729 Business E-Mail: jsudbrink@wwnorton.com.

SUDER, SCOTT, state official; b. Medford, Wis., Sept. 28, 1968; married. BA, U. Wis., Eau Claire, 1991. State assemblyman, Wis., 1998—; legis. aide; small businessman. Mem. agr. com.; mem. census and redistricting com.; mem. corrections and the cts. com.; chair criminal justice com.; mem. law revision com.; mem. transp. com. Mem.: NRA, Lublin Am. Legion-Sons of Am. Legion, Chippewa Falls C. of C., Abbotsford C. of C., Loyal Sportsman's Club, Neillsville Rod and Gun Club, Abbotsford Sportsman Club, Ducks Unltd. Republican. Office: State Capitol Rm 21 N PO Box 8953 Madison WI 53708-8953

SUDHOLT, TOM, radio personality; 1 child, Kate. Radio host Classic 99, St. Louis. Avocations: history, astronomy, meteorology. Office: Classic 99 85 Founders Ln Saint Louis MO 63105

SUGARBAKER, EVAN R., nuclear science research administrator; b. Mineola, NY, Nov. 17, 1949; married, 1985; 1 child. BA, Kalamazoo Coll., 1971; PhD in Physics, U. Mich., 1976. Rsch. assoc. nuclear structural rsch. lab. U. Rochester (N.Y.), 1976-78; vis. asst. prof. physics U. Colo., 1978-80; asst. prof. physics Ohio State U., Columbus, 1981-86, assoc. prof. physics, 1986-94, prof. physics, 1994—, vice chmn. dept., 2001—. Co-prin. investigator NSF grant, 1981-88, 95—, prin. investigator, 1988-95; bd. dirs. Los Alamos Meson Physics Facility Users Group, Inc., 1990-92; cons. Los Alamos Nat. Lab., 1991-94. Mem. AAAS, Am. Phys. Soc., Am. Assn. Physics Tchrs. Office: Dept Physics Ohio State U 174 W 18th Ave Columbus OH 43210-1106

SUGDEN, RICHARD LEE, pastor; b. Compton, Calif., Apr. 13, 1959; s. L. Fred Sugden and Nancy Jane (Motherwell) Coulter; m. Rebecca Lynn Travis, June 1981; children: Richard Lee II, Ryan Leon, Rachel Lynn, Lawrence Fred, Nicole Irene. BA, Pensacola Christian Coll., Fla., 1981. Ordained pastor, 1985. Assoc. pastor Chippewa Lake Bapt. Ch., Medina, Ohio, 1981-84; dir., evangelist Victory Acres Christian Camp, Warren, Ohio, 1985; asst. pastor Bible Bapt. Temple, Campbell, Ohio, 1985-93; missionary evangelist Sugden Evang. Ministries, Struthers, Ohio, 1993—. Del. pastors' sch. 1st Bapt. Ch., Hammond, Ind., 1982—. Author: Philippians on Your Level, 1990, James on Your Level, 1991, I Timothy On Your Level, 1991. Founder, dir. Penn-Ohio Bapt. Youth Fellowship. Mem. Christian Law Assn., Buckeye Ind. Bapt. Fellowship. Republican. Avocations: gardening, home improvements. Home and Office: Sugden Evang Ministries 71 Harvey St Struthers OH 44471-1538 Personal E-mail: ricsugden@juno.com.

SUGG, REED WALLER, lawyer; b. Morganfield, Ky., Dec. 1, 1952; s. Matt Waller and Iris (Omer) S. BA, Furman U., 1975; JD, Vanderbilt U., 1978. Bar: Mo. 1978, Ill. 1979, U.S. Ct. Appeals (8th, 9th and 7th cirs.), U.S. Dist. Ct. (ea. dist.) Mo., U.S. Dist. Ct. (so. dist.) Ill. Atty. Coburn, Croft, Shepherd & Herzog, St. Louis, 1978-79, Shepherd, Sandberg & Phoenix, St. Louis, 1979-90, Sandberg, Phoenix & von Gontard, St. Louis, 1990—. Mem. ABA, Bar Assn. Met. St. Louis, Christian Legal Soc., Lawyers Assn. St. Louis, Aviation Ins. Assn., Lawyer-Pilots Bar Assn., Phi Beta Kappa. Clubs: Mo. Athletic, Westborough Country (St. Louis). Republican. Presbyterian. Avocations: basketball, golf, reading. Home: 12825 Brighton Woods Dr Saint Louis MO 63131-1413 Office: Sandberg Phoenix & von Gontard 1 City Ctr Ste 1500 Saint Louis MO 63101-1880 Home Phone: 314-984-8272; Office Phone: 314-446-4220. Business E-Mail: rsugg@spvg.com.

SUHRE, RICHARD L., transportation company executive; Pres. Cassens Transport Co., Edwardsville, Ill., 1994—. Office: Cassens Transport Co 145 N Kansas St Edwardsville IL 62025-1770

SUHRHEINRICH, RICHARD FRED, federal judge; b. Lincoln City, Ind., 1936; BS, Wayne State U., 1960; JD cum laude, Detroit Coll. Law, 1963; LLM (hon.), U. Va., 1990, Detroit Coll. Law, 1992. Bar: Mich. Law clerk Stringari, Fritz & Fiott, 1963; assoc. Moll, Desenberg, Purdy, Glover & Bayer, 1963—67; asst. prosecutor Macomb County, 1967; ptnr. Rogensues, Richard & Suhrheinrich, 1967; assoc. Moll, Desenberg, Purdy, Glover & Bayer, 1967—68; ptnr. Kitch, Suhrheinrich, Saurbier & Drutchas, 1968—84; assoc. prof. of law Detroit Coll. of law, 1975—85; judge US Dist. Ct. (ea. dist.) Mich., Detroit, 1984—90, US Ct. Appeals (6th cir.), Lansing, 1990—2001, sr. judge, 2001—. Law prof. Thomas M Cooley Law Sch., 2003—; mem. State of Mich. Atty. Discipline Bd., Atty. Grievance Commn. Bd. trustees Brighton Hosp. Mem.: Ingham County Bar Assn., State Bar Mich., Mich. State Univ.-Detroit (bd. trustees 1985—2003, pres. 1999—2001). Office: US Ct Appeals 6th Cir USPO & Fed Bldg 315 W Allegan St Rm 241 Lansing MI 48933-1514

SULKIN, HOWARD ALLEN, academic administrator; b. Detroit, Aug. 19, 1941; s. Lewis and Vivian P. (Mandel) S.; m. Constance Annette Adler, Aug. 4, 1963; children— Seth R., Randall K. PhB, Wayne State U., 1963; MBA, U. Chgo., 1965, PhD, 1969; LHD (hon.), De Paul U., 1990. Dir. program rsch., indsl. rels. ctr. U. Chgo., 1964-72; dean Sch. for New Learning, De Paul U., Chgo., 1972-77; v.p. De Paul U., Chgo., 1977-84; pres. Spertus Inst. Jewish Studies, Chgo., 1984—, CEO. St. Paul's vis. prof. Rikkyo U., Tokyo, 1970—; cons., evaluator North Ctrl. Assn., Chgo., 1975—. Contbr. articles to profl. jours. Sec.-treas. Grant Park Cultural and Ednl. Cmty., Chgo., 1984—; bd. dirs. Chgo. Sinai Congregation, 1972—, pres., 1980-83; bd. dirs. Grant Park Conservancy, Legacy Charter Sch., Parliament of World's Religions, 1989—, chmn., 1989-; mem. exec. com. Loop Alliance, bd. dirs. Hegeler Carus Found., 2001-. Mem.: Tavern, The Standard. Office: Spertus Inst of Jewish Studies 618 S Michigan Ave Chicago IL 60605-1901

SULLIVAN, ALFRED DEWITT, academic administrator; b. New Orleans, Feb. 2, 1942; s. Dewitt Walter and Natalie (Alford) Sullivan; m. Marilyn Janie Hewitt, Sept. 1, 1962 (div. May 1989); children: Alan, Sean; m. Dorothy Madeleine Hess, Apr. 1993. BS, La. State U., 1964, MS, 1966; PhD, U. Ga., 1969. Asst. prof. Va. Poly. Inst. and State U., Blacksburg, 1969—73; assoc. prof., then prof. Miss. State U., Starkville, 1973—88; dir. Sch. Forest Resources Pa. State U., University Park, 1988—93; dean coll. natural resources U. Minn., St. Paul, 1993—2002, vice provost academic programs & facilities Mpls., 2002—06, spl. asst. to pres., 2006—. Assoc. Danforth Found., 1981. Contbr. articles to profl. jours. Fellow, Am. Coun. Edn., 1987—88, NDEA fellow, U. Ga., 1966—69. Mem.: Soc. Am. Foresters. Office: U Minn 234 MorH 0262 100 Church St SE Minneapolis MN 55455 Office Phone: 612-626-3838. E-mail: sulli031@umn.edu.

SULLIVAN, AUSTIN PADRAIC, JR., retired diversified food company executive; b. Washington, June 26, 1940; s. Austin P. and Janet Lay (Patterson) Sullivan; m. Judith Ann Raab, June 1, 1968 (dec. Oct. 1995); children: Austin P. III, Amanda, Alexander; m. Marie Elise de Golian, Aug. 1, 1997; stepchildren: Lauren Gibbons, Georgia Gibbons, Samuel Gibbons. BA cum laude, Princeton U., 1964. Spl. asst. to dep. dir. N.J. Office Econ. Opportunity, Trenton, NJ, 1956—66; prof. staff mem. Com. on Edn. and Labor, U.S. Ho. of Rep., Washington, 1967—71, legis. dir., 1971—76; dir. govt. relations Gen. Mills, Inc., Mpls., 1976—78, v.p., corp. dir. govt. rels., 1978—79, v.p. pub. affairs, 1979—93, v.p. corp. comm. and pub. affairs, 1993—94, sr. v.p. corp. rels., 1994—2005; ret., 2005. Lectr. fed. labor market policies Harvard U., Mass., 1972—76, Boston U., 1972—76. Mem. Nat. Commn. on Employment and Tng., 1979—81, U.S. Sec. Agr. Adv. Com. on Agrl. Biotech., 2000—03; chmn. Governor's Coun. on Employment and Tng., 1976—82; bd. dir., exec. com. Urban Coalition Mpls., 1978—80, Guthrie Theatre, Mpls., 1978—84, Minn. Citizens for the Arts, 1980—83; co chmn. Governor's Commn. on Dislocated Workers, Minn., 1988—89; chmn. Pub. Affairs Coun., 1993—94; bd. dir. Minn. C. of C., 1993—99; trustee Minn. Pub. Radio, 1999—; bd. advisors Dem. Leadership Coun., 1986—. Served in USMC, 1957—59. Recipient Eleanor Roosevelt Fellow in Interracial Rels., 1964—65. Mem.: Grocery Mfr. Assn. (govt. affairs coun. 1991—2004, chmn. biotech. task force 1999—2004), Coun. of Pub. Affairs Exec. (chmn. 1989—90), Medica (bd. dir. 2001—), Greater Mpls. C. of C. (exec. com. 1980—86, 1990—93, bd. dir.), Mpls. Club (bd. governor's 2001—). Home: 17830 County Rd 6 Minneapolis MN 55447-2905 Office: Ste 252 700 Twelve Oaks Center Dr Wayzata MN 55391

SULLIVAN, BARRY, lawyer; b. Newburyport, Mass., Jan. 11, 1949; s. George Arnold and Dorothy Bennett (Furbush) S.; m. Winnifred Mary Fallers, June 14, 1975; children: George Arnold, Lloyd Ashton. AB cum laude, Middlebury Coll., 1970; JD, U. Chgo., 1974. Bar: Mass. 1975, Ill. 1975, Va. 1995, US Dist. Ct. (no. dist.) Ill. 1976, US Ct. Appeals (7th cir.) 1976, US Ct. Appeals (10th cir.) 1977, US Supreme Ct. 1978, US Ct. Appeals (11th cir.) 1986, US Ct. Appeals (5th and 9th cirs.) 1987, US Ct. Appeals (fed. cir.) 1993, US Ct. Appeals (DC cir.) 1994, US Ct. Appeals (4th cir.) 1997, US Ct. Appeals (2d and 3d cirs.) 2002, US Ct. Appeals (6th and 8th cirs.) 2004, US Dist. Ct. (ctrl. dist.) Ill. 2006. Law clk. to judge John Minor Wisdom U.S. Ct. Appeals (5th cir.), New Orleans, 1974-75; assoc. Jenner & Block, Chgo., 1975-80; asst. to solicitor gen. of U.S. U.S. Dept. of Justice, Washington, 1980-81; ptnr. Jenner & Block, Chgo., 1981-94, 2001—; prof. law Washington and Lee U., Lexington, Va., 1994-2001, dean, 1994-99, v.p., 1998-99; Fulbright prof. U. Warsaw, Poland, 2000—01; lectr. in law U. Chgo., 2001—02; spl. asst. state's atty. Cook County, Ill., 2002—03. Vis. fellow Queen Mary and Westfield Coll., U. London, 2001; spl. asst. atty. gen. State of Ill., 1989—90; lectr. in law Loyola U., Chgo., 1978—79; adj. prof. law Northwestern U., Chgo., 1990—92, 1993—94, vis. prof., 1992—93; vis. prof. Ctr. for Am. law studies U. Warsaw, 2002—03, 2005; sr. lectr. Irving B. Harris Grad. Sch. Pub. Policy, U. Chgo., 2005—; Jessica Swift Meml. lectr. constl. law Middlebury Coll., 1991; Rufus Monroe and Sophie Payne lectr. U. Mo., Columbia, 2003; Charles L. Ihlenfeld lectr. pub. policy and ethics W.Va. U., 2005. Assoc. editor U. Chgo. Law Rev., 1973-74; mem. editl. bd. Dublin U. Law Jour., 2004-; contbr. articles to profl. jours. Mem. nat. adv. bd. Ctr. for Religion, The Professions, and The Pub., U. Mo., Columbia, 2003—; trustee Cath. Theol. Union at Chgo., 1993—2003, trustee emeritus, 2003—; mem. vis. com. Irving B. Harris Grad. Sch. Public Policy Studies U. Chgo., 2001—, U. Chgo. Divinity Sch., 1987—2001; mem. adv. panel Fulbright Sr. Specialist Program, 2001—04; mem. adv. bd. Internat. Human Rights Law Inst. DePaul U., 2003—; trustee U. Chgo. Court Theatre, 2003—05; mem. bd. visitors So. Ill. U. Sch. Law, 2006—; mem. adv. bd. Project DV-Leap, George Washington U. Law. Sch., 2006—, Cmty. Renewal Soc. Chgo., 2006—. Fellow, Woodrow Wilson Found., 1970; scholar, Yeats Soc., 1968; Nat. Honor scholar, Univ. Chgo., 1970—74. Fellow Am. Bar Found., Phi Beta Kappa; mem. ABA (chmn. coord. com. on AIDS 1988—94, standing com. on amicus curiae briefs 1990—97, coun. sect. individual rights and responsibilities 1993—98, sect. legal edn. com. on law sch. adminstrn. 1994—98, chair sect. legal edn. com. on professionalism 1999—2000, co-chair sect. individual rights/responsibilities com. amicus briefs 2002—04, mem. sect. legal edn. stds. rev. com. 2002—05, co-chair sect. individual rights/responsibilities com. bill rights 2002—07, mem. standing com. amicus curiae briefs 2004-07, mem. standing com. profl. discipline, 2007—), Lawyers Club Chgo., Supreme Ct. Hist Soc. (Ill. membership chair 2002—03), Ill. State Bar Assn., Appellate Lawyers Assn., Am. Law Inst., Bar Assn. 7th Fed. Cir. (vice chmn. adminstrn. justice com. 1985—86), Va. State Bar (chair sec. on edn. lawyers 1998—99) Democrat. Roman Catholic. Home: 5555 S Everett Apt A1-2 Chicago IL 60637 Office: Jenner & Block LLP 330 N Wabash Ave Chicago IL 60611 Office Phone: 312-923-2652. Business E-Mail: bsullivan@jenner.com.

SULLIVAN, BERNARD JAMES, accountant; b. Chgo., June 25, 1927; s. Bernard Hugh and Therese Sarah (Condon) S.; m. Joan Lois Costello, June 9, 1951; children: Therese Lynn Scanlan, Bernard J., Geralyn M. Snyder. BSc, Loyola U., Chgo., 1950. CPA, Ill. Staff Bansley and Kiener, Chgo., 1950-66, ptnr., 1966-82, mng. ptnr., 1982—2007. Bd. dirs. Associated Acctg. Firms, Internat.; exec. com. Moore Stephens and Co., 1984—2006, Arbitrator Nat. Assn. Security Dealers. Served with USN, 1945-46. Mem. Am. Inst. CPA's, Ill. Soc. CPA's, Govt. Fin. Officer Assn., Internat. Found. Employee Benefit Plans, Delta Sigma Pi. Clubs: Beverly Country (Chgo.), Metropolitan (Chgo.). Lodges: Elks, K.C. Avocations: golf, sports, travel. Home: 9636 S Kolmar Ave Oak Lawn IL 60453-3214 Office: Bansley & Kiener 8745 W Higgins Rd Ste 200 Chicago IL 60631-2704 Home Phone: 708-423-1990; Office Phone: 312-263-2700. Business E-Mail: bsullivan@bk-cpa.com.

SULLIVAN, BILL M., church administrator; USA/Can. Mission/Evangelism dept. dir. Church of the Nazarene, Kansas City, Mo., 1980. Office: Church of Nazarene 6401 The Paseo Kansas City MO 64131-1213

SULLIVAN, DAVE, state legislator; b. Chgo., Dec. 29, 1964; m. Dru; 4 children. BA in Polit. Sci., Marquette U. Mem. Ill. Senate, Springfield, 1999—, mem. lic. activities com., environ. & energy com.; Rep. spokesman Environ. & Energy com. V.p., precinct capt. Maine Twp. Regular Rep. Orgn.; exec. asst. intergovtl. affairs Sec. of State George H. Ryan, 1992-98; cons. several Ill. campaigns. Republican. Address: 1699 Wall St Ste 123 Mount Prospect IL 60056-3457

SULLIVAN, DENNIS W., power systems company executive; b. Chgo., 1938; Grad., Purdue U., 1960, Case Western Res. U., 1969. Exec. v.p. Parker Hannifin Corp., Cleve., 1981—, bd. dirs., 1983—. Bd. dirs. Soc. Bat. Bank. Office: Parker Hannifin Corp 6035 Parkland Blvd Cleveland OH 44124-4141

SULLIVAN, E. THOMAS, law educator; b. Amboy, Ill., Dec. 4, 1948; s. Edward McDonald and Mary Lorraine (Murphy) S.; m. Susan A. Sullivan, Oct. 2, 1971. BA, Drake U., 1970; JD, Ind. U., Indpls., 1973. Bar: Ind. 1973, Fla. 1974, D.C. 1975, Mo. 1980. Law clk. to Judge Joe Eaton, U.S. Dist. Ct. for So. Dist. Fla., Miami, 1973-75; trial atty. U.S. Dept. Justice, Washington, 1975-77; sr. assoc. Donovan, Leisure, Newton & Irvine, Washington, 1977-79; prof. law U. Mo., Columbia, 1979-84; assoc. dean, prof. Washington U., St. Louis, 1984-89; dean U. Ariz. Coll. Law, Tucson, 1989-95; William S. Pattee prof. law, dean U. Minn. Law Sch., Mpls., 1995—2002, Irving Younger prof. law, 2002—, sr. vice-pres., provost, 2004—. Fellow Am. Bar Found.; mem. Am. Law Inst., Am. Econ. Assn. Office: U Minn Law Sch Walter F Mondale Hall Office 381 229 19th Ave S Minneapolis MN 55455 Home: 182 Bank St Se Minneapolis MN 55414-1042

SULLIVAN, EDWARD, periodical editor; b. Sharon, Pa., 1956; BA in Journalism, Johns Hopkins U., 1979. From news editor to mgr. publs. Am. Soc. Quality Control, 1979-87; acquisitions editor Panel Publishers, 1987-89; editor Trade Press Pub., Milw., 1989—. Office: Trade Press Pub Bldg Operating Mgmt Mag 2100 W Florist Ave Milwaukee WI 53209-3721

SULLIVAN, FRANK, JR., state supreme court justice; b. Mar. 21, 1950; s. Frank E. and Colette (Cleary) S.; m. Cheryl Gibson, June 14, 1972; children: Denis M., Douglas S., Thomas R. AB cum laude, Dartmouth Coll., 1972; JD magna cum laude, Ind. U., 1982; LLM, U. Va., 2001. Bar: Ind. 1982. Mem. staff Office of U.S. Rep. John Brademas, 1974-79, dir. staff, 1975-78; with Barnes & Thornburg, Indpls., 1982-89; budget dir. State of Ind., 1989-92; exec. asst. Office of Gov. Evan Bayh, 1993; assoc. justice Ind. Supreme Ct., 1993—. Chair Ind. Supreme Ct. Judicial Technology & Automation Com. Mem. ABA (vice chair appellate judges conf.), Ind. State Bar Assn., Indpls. Bar Assn. Home: 5854 Lawton Loop West Dr Indianapolis IN 46216-2009 Office: Ind Supreme Ct State House Rm 321 Indianapolis IN 46204-2728 Home Phone: 317-549-3926; Office Phone: 317-232-2548.

SULLIVAN, FRANK C., manufacturing executive; BA, U. N.C., 1983. Various comml. lending corp. fin. 1st Union Nat. Bank and Harris Bank, 1983-87; regional sales mgr. AGR Co. RPM Group, Inc., 1987-89, dir. corp. devel., 1989-91, v.p., 1991-93, CFO, 1993-98, exec. v.p., 1998-99, pres., 1999—2002, pres., CEO, 2002—. Bd. dir. Timken Co. Bd. mem. Greater Cleveland Chpt., Am. Red Cross, Cleveland Rock & Roll Hall of Fame & Mus. Morehead scholar, 1983. Mem.: Cuyahoga County Bluecoats. Office: RPM International PO Box 777 2628 Pearl Rd Medina OH 44256 Office Phone: 330-273-5090.

SULLIVAN, JAMES GERALD, small business owner; b. Bad Axe, Mich., Sept. 13, 1935; s. John Thomas and Frances Eugena (O'Henley) Sullivan; m. Florence Marie Tack, Sept. 12, 1959; children: Kevin Michael, Kathleen Marie. Student, U. Detroit, 1957—58, Highland Park Coll., 1959—60. Owner Jerry's Barber Shop, Kinde, Bad Axe, Mich., 1963-66, 79—; purchasing agt. Thumb Elec. Coop., Ubly, Mich., 1966-79, Walbro Corp., Cass City, Mich., 1979-80; sales rep. Thumb Blanket, Bad Axe, Mich., 1980-81, Sta. WLEW, Bad Axe, 1981-82; regional mgr. Pri Am. Fin. Svcs., Bad Axe, 1985—; treas. Colfax Twp., Bad Axe, 1979-90; rural letter carrier U.S. Postal Svc., Bad Axe, 1982-98, ret., 1998. Loss clk., Toplis & Harding Wagner & Gliddon, Detroit, 1959-61; inventory control clk., Carrick Products Co., Royal Oak, Mich., 1957-59. Pres. Huron County Twp. Assn., Mich., 1988—90; leader Boy Scouts Am., Bad Axe, 1975—77; lector Ushers Club, Sacred Heart Ch., Eucharistic min. With US Army, 1954—56. Mem. Huron County Rural Letter Carriers Assn. (pres. 1988-2003), Armed Forces Vets. Club of the Nat. Rural Letter Carriers Assn. (Mich. divsn., state sec. 1999—), Am. Legion, 4-H Club (pres. 1948-50), Lions (pres. 1979-80, 2006-07), Cmty. Club (pres. 1976-77), KC (mem. coun. #1546), Tip of the Thumb Dance Club (pres. 2005). Republican. Roman Catholic. Avocations: gardening, golf, swimming, fishing. Home: 122 W Richardson Rd Bad Axe MI 48413-9108

SULLIVAN, JOHN E., III, lawyer; b. Boston, Nov. 11, 1958; BA magna cum laude in Hist. and Econs., Boston Coll., 1980; JD, U. Tex. Sch. Law, 1984. Bar: Mass. 1985, Ill. 1985, Ohio 1986, US Dist. Ct. (no. dist. Ohio) 1987, US Dist. Ct. (no. dist. Tex.) 1987, US Ct. Appeals (5th cir.) 1988, US Ct. Appeals (6th cir.) 1991, US Supreme Ct. 1995, US Tax Ct. 1997. Founding mem. Sullivan & Sullivan, Ltd. Contbr. articles to profl. jours. Named one of Top 100 Attys., Worth mag., 2005. Mem.: Ohio State Bar Assn., Cleve. Estate Planning Coun., Internat. Tax Planning Assn. Office: Sullivan & Sullivan Ltd Ste 350 25201 Chagrin Blvd Beachwood OH 44122 Office Phone: 216-896-0001. Office Fax: 216-896-0002. E-mail: jesullivan3@sullivanandsullivan.com.

SULLIVAN, KATHRYN D., geologist, former astronaut, former science association executive; b. Paterson, NJ, Oct. 3, 1951; d. Donald P. and Barbara K. Sullivan (dec.). BS in Earth Scis., U. Calif., Santa Cruz, 1973; PhD in Geology, Dalhousie U., Halifax, NS, Can., 1978; Dr. (hon.), Halhousie, Halifax, NS, Can., 1985, SUNY, Utica, 1990, Stevens Inst., 1992, Ohio Dominican U., 1998, Kent State U., 2002; Doctorate (hon.), St. Bonaventure U., 2005. Astronaut NASA, 1979—93, mission specialist flight STS-41G, 1984, mission specialist flight STS-31, 1990, payload comdr. flight STS-45, 1992; chief scientist NOAA, Washington, 1993—96; pres., CEO Ctr. Sci. and Industry, Columbus, Ohio, 1996—2005, sci. advisor; dir. Battelle Ctr. for Math. and Sci. Edn. Policy John Glenn Sch. Pub. Affairs, Ohio State U., Columbus, Ohio, 2006—. Adj. prof. Rice U., Houston, 1985-92, geology, Ohio State U., Columbus, Ohio; mem. Nat. Commn. on Space, 1985-86; mem. exec. panel Chief of Naval Ops., 1988-96; chair, Ohio Aerospace and Defense Adv. Coun., 2003; mem. Nat. Sci. Bd., 2004—, vice chmn., 2006—; served on Pews Oceans Commn.; advisor, Nat. Geographic, Smithsonian Inst., Pub. TV; bd. dirs. Am. Electric Power. Oceanography officer, Capt. USNR; private pilot. Recipient Space Flight medal NASA, 1984, 90, 92, Exceptional Svc. medal, 1988, 91, Nat. Air and Space Mus. trophy Smithsonian Instn., 1985, Outstanding Leadership medal, 1992, AAS Space Flight Achievement award, 1991, AAS Prather Eva award, 1992, Lone Sailor award, US Navy Meml. Found., 1997, Juliette award for Nat. Women of Distinction, Girl Scouts U.S.A., 2002, Aviation Week & Space Tech. Aerospace Legend award, 2005; named one of Ten Outstanding Young People of the World award, Jaycees Internat., 1987, Ten Outstanding Young Americans award, US Jaycees, 1987; inductee Ohio Veteran's Hall of Fame, 2001, Ohio Women's Hall of Fame, 2002, Astronaut Hall of Fame, 2004. Fellow AAAS; mem. AIAA (Haley Space Flight award, 1991, Legends Aerospace Laureate 2005), Geol. Soc. Am., Am. Geophys. Union, Soc. Women Geographers, Nat. Sci. Bd. (Public Svc. award, 2003), Explorers Club, Woods Hole Oceanographic Institution, Assn. Space Explorers. First Am. woman to walk in space.

SULLIVAN, LAURA PATRICIA, lawyer, insurance company executive; b. Des Moines, Oct. 16, 1947; d. William and Patricia S. BA, Cornell Coll., Iowa, 1971; JD, Drake U., 1972. Bar: Iowa 1972. Various positions Ins. Dept. Iowa, Des Moines, 1972-75; various legal positions State Farm Mut. Auto Ins. Co., Bloomington, Ill., 1975-81, sec. and counsel, 1981-88, v.p., counsel and sec., 1988—; v.p., sec., dir. State Farm Cos. Found., 1985—; sec. State Farm Lloyd's, Inc., 1987—; v.p., counsel and sec. State Farm Fire and Casualty Co., 1988—, State Farm Gen. Ins. Co., 1988—, also bd. dirs.; v.p. counsel, sec., dir. State Farm Life and Accident Assurance Co.; v.p. counsel, sec. State Farm Annuity and Life Assurance Co., State Farm Life Ins. Co.; dir. State Farm Indemnity Co., Bloomington, Ill., 1995—; sec., dir. State Farm Fla. Ins. Co., 1998—. Bd. dirs. Ins. Inst. for Hwy. Safety, Nat. Conf. Ins. Guaranty Funds, chmn., 1995-97. Trustee John M. Scott Indsl. Sch. Trust, Bloomington, 1983-86, Cornell Coll., 1999—; bd. dirs. Scott Ctr., 1983-86, Bloomington-Normal Symphony, 1980-85, YWCA of McLean County, 1993-95; chmn. Ins. Inst. for Hwy. Safety, 1987-88. Mem. ABA, Iowa State Bar Assn., Am. Corp. Counsel Assn., Am. Soc. Corp. Secs. Office: State Farm Mut Automobile Ins Co 1 State Farm Plz Bloomington IL 61710-0001

SULLIVAN, MARCIA WAITE, lawyer; b. Chgo, Nov. 30, 1950; d. Robert Macke and Jacqueline (Northrop) S.; m. Steven Donald Jansen, Dec. 20, 1975; children: Eric Spurlock, Laura Macke, Brian Northrop. BA, DePauw U., 1972; JD, Ind. U., 1975. Assoc. Arnstein, Gluck, Weitzenfeld & Minow, Chgo., 1975-76; ptnr. Greenberger and Kaufmann, Chgo., 1976-86, Katten Muchin Rosenman LLP, Chgo., 1986—. Adj. prof. Kent Coll. Law, Ill. Inst. Tech., Chgo., 1991—94; pres. Chgo. Real Estate Exec. Women, 2000—01. Mem. editl. adv. bd.: Real Estate Chgo., 2001—02. Mem. NNCREW Found. Grant Making Com, 2003—04. Mem.: ABA, Chgo. Bar Assn. Avocations: bicycling, cross country skiing, gardening, camping. Office: Katten Muchin Rosenman LLP 525 W Monroe St Chicago IL 60661-3693 Home Phone: 847-256-2496; Office Phone: 312-902-5535. Business E-Mail: marcia.sullivan@kattenlaw.com.

SULLIVAN, MICHAEL FRANCIS, III, educational consultant; b. DuBois, Pa., Mar. 11, 1948; s. Michael F. and Mary Jane (Borger) S.; m. Janice Marie Calame, May 30, 1969 (dec.); children: Courtney, Shannon, Michael IV; m. Rosa Leigh Gillespie, Aug. 16, 1997. BS in English & Speech, Bowling Green State U., 1969; MEd in Curriculum Devel., Wright State U., 1971; EdD in Instructional Technology, Va. Polytech Inst. & State U., 1976. Specialist in instructional design Md. State Dept. Edn., Balt., 1974-80, asst. state supt. in instructional technology, 1980-86; sr. edn. cons. UNISYS Corp., Bluebell, Pa., 1986-87, product mktg. mgr., 1987-88, dir. strategic planning and devel., 1988-90; exec. dir. Agy. for Instructional Technology, Bloomington, Ind., 1990—. Contbr. articles to profl. jours. Office: Agency for Instructional Tech Box A Bloomington IN 47402

SULLIVAN, MICHAEL PATRICK, food service executive; b. Dec. 5, 1934; s. Michael Francis and Susan Ellen (Doran) S.; m. Marilyn Emmer, June 27, 1964; children: Katherine, Michael, Maureen, Bridget, Daniel, Thomas. BS, Marquette U., 1956; JD, U. Minn., 1962. Bar: Minn. 1962, U.S. Dist. Ct. Minn. 1962, U.S. Supreme Ct. 1975, U.S. Ct. Appeals (8th cir.) 1978. Assoc. Gray, Plant, Mooty, Mooty & Bennett, Mpls., 1962-67, ptnr., 1968-87, mng. ptnr., 1976-87; pres., CEO Internat. Dairy Queen, Inc., Mpls., 1987-2001, chmn. bd., 2001—. Bd. dirs. The Valspar Corp., Allianz Life Ins. Co. N.Am., Opus Corp.; instr. U. Minn. Law Sch., 1962-67; lectr. continuing legal edn.; spl. counsel to atty. gen. Minn., 1971-79, 82-84; bd. dirs. Met. Mpls.YMCA, chmn. bd. dirs., 1997-99; pres. Uniform Law Commn., 1987-89. Contbr. articles to profl. jours. Bd. regents St. John's U., 2000; bd. dirs. YMCA Met. Mpls.; bd. trustees St. Paul Sem. Served with USN, 1956-59. Mem. ABA (ho. of dels., 1984-89), Minn. Bar Assn. (gov. 1974-86), Hennepin County Bar Assn. (pres. 1978-89), Am. Bar Found., Am. Law Inst., Am. Arbitration Assn. (bd. dirs.), Order of Coif. Roman Catholic. Office: Internat Dairy Queen 7505 Metro Blvd Minneapolis MN 55439-3020

SULLIVAN, PAUL F., career officer; b. Wellesley, Mass. m. Ann Sullivan; children: Shane, Morgan. BS with distinction, U.S. Naval Acad., 1970; MS in Ocean Engring., MIT, 1975; postgrad., Nuclear Power Sch. Commd. ensign USN, 1970, advanced through grades to rear adm.; supply officer USS Caiman; various engring. assignments USS Dace; engr. officer USS George C. Marshall; exec. officer USS Richard B. Russell; commdr. USS Birmingham, Pearl Harbor, Hawaii, USS Fla., Bangor, Wash.; mem. tactical analysis group COMSUBDEVRON 12; dep. commdr. tng. & ops. COMSUBDERVON 17; dep. dir. current ops. Ops. Directorate Joint Staff, Washington; commdr. Submarine Group 9, Silverdale, Wash., now rear admiral. Decorated Def. Superior Svc. Medal, Legion Merit award, 2 Meritorious Svc. Medals, 3 Navy Commendation Medals, 3 Navy Achievement Medals.

SULLIVAN, PEGGY, librarian, consultant; b. Kansas City, Mo., Aug. 12, 1929; d. Michael C. and Ella (O'Donnell) Sullivan. AB, Clarke Coll., 1950; MS in Libr. Sci., Cath. U. Am., 1953; PhD, U. Chgo., 1972. Children's pub. libr., Mo., Md., Va., 1952-61; sch. libr. specialist Montgomery County (Md.) Pub. Schs., 1961-63; dir. Knapp Sch. Librs. Project, 1963—68, Jr. Coll. Libr. Info. Ctr., 1968-69; asst. prof. U. Pitts., 1971-73; dir. Office for Libr. Pers. Resources, ALA, Chgo., 1973-74; dean of students, assoc. prof. Grad. Libr. Sch., U. Chgo., 1974-77; asst. commr. for ext. svcs. Chgo. Pub. Libr., 1977-81; dean Coll. Profl. Studies, No. Ill. U., DeKalb, 1981-90; dir. univ. librs. No. Ill. U., 1990-92; exec. dir. ALA, 1992-94; assoc. Tuft & Assocs., 1995-98; dean Grad. Sch. Libr. and Info. Sci. Rosary Coll., 1995-97. Instr. grad. libr. edn. programs, 1958-73, UNESCO cons. on sch. librs., Australia, 1970; trustee Clarke Coll., 1969-72; sr. ptnr. Able Cons., 1987-92; cons. in field. Author: The O'Donnells, 1956, Many Names for Eileen, 1969, Problems in School Media Management, 1971, Carl H. Milam and the American Library Association, 1976, Opportunities in Library and Information Science, 1977; co-author: Public Libraries: Smart Practices in

Personnel, 1982; editor: Realization: The Final Report of the Knapp School Libraries Project, 1968. Mem.: ALA, Ill. Libr. Assn., Cath. Libr. Assn., Caxton Club, Chgo. Lit. Club. Roman Catholic. Home and Office: 2800 N Lake Shore Dr Apt 816 Chicago IL 60657-6266 Office Phone: 773-549-5361. Business E-Mail: pslibcon@alumni.uchicago.edu.

SULLIVAN, STEVEN R., lawyer; b. St. Louis, Aug. 1960; BBA summa cum laude, U. Mo., St. Louis, 1981; JD with distinction, U. Mo., Kans. City, 1994. CPA 1982. Atty. Arthur Andersen & Co., Kohn, Shands, Elbert, Gianoulakis & Giljum, 1985—87, Union Electric Co. (now Ameren EU), 1987—95; assoc. gen. counsel Anheuser-Busch Co., 1995—98; v.p. regulatory policy, gen. counsel, sec. Ameren EU, 1998—2003; sr. v.p. govtl./regulatory policy, gen. counsel, sec. Ameren Corp., St. Louis, 2003—. Mem.: Mo. Bar Assn., Bar Assn. Met. St. Louis, Mo. Soc. CPA., Am. Soc. Corp. Sec., Edison Electric Inst. Office: Ameren Corp 1 Ameren Plz 1901 Chouteau Ave Saint Louis MO 63103 Office Phone: 314-621-3222. Office Fax: 314-554-3801.

SULLIVAN, TERESA ANN, law and sociology educator, academic administrator; d. Gordon Hager and Mary Elizabeth (Finnegan) S.; m. H. Douglas Laycock, June 14, 1971; children: Joseph Peter, John Patrick. BA, Mich. State U., 1970; MA, U. Chgo., 1972, PhD, 1975. Asst. prof. sociology U. Tex., Austin, 1975-76, assoc. prof. sociology, 1981-87, dir. women's studies, 1985-87, prof. sociology, 1987—, prof. law, 1988—, assoc. dean grad. sch., 1989-90, 1992-95, chair dept. sociology, 1990-92, vice provost, 1994-95, v.p., grad. dean, 1995—2002; asst. prof. sociology U. Chgo., 1977-81; exec. vice-chancellor acad. affairs U. Tex. Sys., 2002—06; provost, exec. v.p. academic affairs U. Mich., Ann Arbor, 2006—. Pres. Southwestern Sociol. Assn., 1988-89; mem. faculty adv. bd. Hogg Found. Mental Health, 1989-92; mem. sociology panel NSF, 1983-85. Author: Marginal Workers Marginal Jobs, 1978; co-author: As We Forgive Our Debtors, 1989 (Silver Gavel 1990), Social Organization of Work, 1990, 4th edit., 2007; co-author: The Fragile Middle Class, 2000; contbr. articles and chpts. to profl. jours. Bd. dirs. Calvert Found., Chgo., 1978, CARA, Inc., Washington, 1985; mem. U.S. Census Bur. Adv. Com., 1989-95, chmn., 1991-92; mem. sociology panel SF, 1983-85; trustee St. Michael's Acad., 1996-2001. Leadership Tex. 1994. Fellow AAAS (liaison to Population Assn. Am. 1989-91, chair sect. K 1996), Sociol. Rsch. Assn., Am. Sociol. Assn. (sec. 1995—, editor Rose Monograph Series 1988-92), Philos. Soc. Tex., Soc. Study of Social Problems (chair fin. com. 1986-87), Population Assn. Am. (bd. dirs. 1989-91, chair fin. com. 1990-91), Assn. Grad. Schs. (pres. 2001-2002). Roman Catholic. Avocation: reading. Office: 503 Thompson St Ann Arbor MI 48109-1340 Home: 2197 Gray Fox Ct Ann Arbor MI 48103 Office Phone: 734-764-9292. Business E-Mail: tsull@umich.edu.

SULLIVAN, TERRI, newscaster, reporter; married. BS in Broadcast Journalism, Boston U. With Sta. WBNS-TV, Columbus, Ohio, WNBC-TV, NYC; anchor, reporter Sta. WRKL, Sta. WSYX-WTTE-TV, Columbus, 1993—; anchor Sta. QJZA-FM, 1997—. Office: WSYX/WTTE-TV 1261 Dublin Rd Columbus OH 43215

SULLIVAN, THOMAS CHRISTOPHER, coatings company executive; b. Cleve., July 8, 1937; s. Frank Charles and Margaret Mary (Wilhelmy) S.; m. Sandra Simmons, Mar. 12, 1960; children: Frank, Sean, Tommy, Danny, Kathleen, Julie. BS, Miami U., Oxford, Ohio, 1959. Div. sales mgr. Republic Powdered Metals, Cleve., 1961-65, exec. v.p., 1965-70; chmn. bd., CEO RPM, Internat., Medina, Ohio, 1971—2002, chmn. bd., 2003—. Bd. dirs. Cleve. Clinic Found., Kaydon Corp., Ann Arbor, Mich. Trustee emeritus Culver (Ind.) Ednl. Found.; former trustee Cleve. Tomorrow; bd. advisors Urban Cmty. Sch., Cleve., Malachi House, Cleve.; trustee City Year Cleve.; trustee Cath. Diocese of Cleve. Found. Lt. (j.g.) USNR, 1959-60. Mem.: Nat. Assn. Securities Dealers (bd. govs. 1986—88, long-range strategic planning com.), Nat. Paint and Coatings Assn. (past chmn. bd., CEO, mem. exec. com.). Roman Catholic. Office: RPM Internat 2628 Pearl Rd Medina OH 44256-7623 Office Phone: 330-273-8800. Business E-Mail: tsullivan@rpminc.com.

SULLIVAN, THOMAS PATRICK, lawyer; b. Evanston, Ill., Mar. 23, 1930; s. Clarence M. and Pauline (DeHaye) Sullivan; m. Anne Landau; children from previous marriage: Margaret Mary, Timothy Joseph, Elizabeth Ann. Student, Loras Coll., 1947—49; LLB cum laude, Loyola U., Chgo., 1952; LLD (hon.), U. Notre Dame, 2006. Bar: Ill. 1952, Calif. 1982, N.Mex 1997. Assoc. Jenner & Block, Chgo., 1954—62, ptnr., 1963—77, 1981—; US atty. (no. dist.) Ill. US Dept. Justice, Chgo., 1977—81. Co-chair Ill. Gov.'s Commn. Capital Punishment, 2000—02; chair Capital Punishment Reform Study Com., 2005—. Contbr. articles to profl. jours. With US Army, 1952—54. Decorated Bronze Star; named Llaureate, Acad. Ill. Lawyers, Person of Yr., Chgo. Lawyer Mag., 2004; recipient Medal of Excellence, Loyola U. Law Sch., 1965, Ill. Pub. Defender Assn. award, 1972, Justice John Paul Stevens award, 2000, Ctr. on Wrongful Convictions award, Northwestern U., 2003, Albert E. Jenner, Jr. Pro Bono award, 2003, Damen award, Loyola U. Law Sch., 2004, Lifetime Achievement award, Legal Assistance Found. Chgo., 2005, The Am. Lawyer mag., 2007. Fellow: Am. Coll. Trial Lawyers; mem.: ABA (John Minor Wisdom Pub. Svc. and Professionalism award 2003), Chgo. Coun. Lawyers, Am. Judicature Soc. (Justice award 2004), Am. Law Inst., Fed. Bar Assn., Chgo. Bar Assn., Fed. 7th Cir. Bar Assn., Ill. Bar Assn. Office: Jenner & Block 330 N Wabash Ave Ste 4100 Chicago IL 60611-5697 Office Phone: 312-923-2928. Business E-Mail: tsullivan@jenner.com.

SULLIVAN, THOMAS PATRICK, academic administrator; b. Detroit, July 8, 1947; s. Walter James and Helen Rose (Polosky) S.; m. Barbara Jean Fournier, Aug. 9, 1968; children: Colleen, Brendan. BA in English, U. Dayton, 1969; M. Edn. and Adminstrn., Kent State U., 1971; postgrad., U. Mich., 1988. Tchr. Resurrection Elem. Sch., Dayton, Ohio, 1968-69; adminstr. residence hall Kent (Ohio) State U., 1969-71; program mgr. residence hall Ea. Mich. U., Ypsilanti, 1971-73, adminstrv. assoc., 1973-76, dir. housing, 1976-83; assoc. provost Wayne County Community Coll., Belleville, Mich., 1983-84, dir. budget and mgmt. devel. Detroit, 1984-85, sr. v.p. acad. affairs, acting provost, 1985-86, acting exec. dean Belleville, 1986-88, dir. budget and mgmt. devel. Detroit, 1988-89; pres. Cleary Univ., Ypsilanti, 1989—. Part-time instr. English and math. Schoolcraft Coll., Livonia, Mich., 1980-90. Home: 9835 Whisperwood Ln Brighton MI 48116-8859 Office: Cleary Univ 3601 Plymouth Rd Ann Arbor MI 48105-2659

SUMICHRAST, JOZEF, illustrator, designer; b. Hobart, Ind., July 26, 1958; s. Joseph Steven and Stella Sumichrast; m. Susan Ann Snyder, June 22, 1972; children— Kristin Ann, Lindsey Ann Student, Am. Acad. Art, Chgo. Illustrator Stevens Gross, Chgo., 1971-72; illustrator Eaton & Iwen, Chgo., 1972-73, Graphique, Chgo., 1973-74; pres. Jozef Sumichrast, Deerfield, Ill., 1975—. Author, illustrator: Onomatopoeia, Q is For Crazy; exhbns. include: 200 Years of Am. Illustration, N.Y. Hist. Soc. Mus., Chgo. Hist. Soc., Finland Lath Mus., Library of Congress, Los Angeles County Mus. Art, Md. Inst. Graphic Art, State Colo. Community Coll., Tokyo Designers Gakiun Coll.; represented in permanent collections: Soc. Illustrators, Chgo. Hist. Soc., Milw. Art Dirs. Club, Phoenix Art Dirs. Club, Columbia Coll., U. Tex., contbr. numerous articles to profl. periodicals. Recipient award for children's book Chgo. Book Clinic, 1978; Gold medal Internat. Exhibition of Graphic Arts, Brazil, 1981; Gold medal Chgo. Artist Guild, 1980, 81; Silver medal N.Y. Art Dirs. Club, 1983; numerous others Mem. Soc. Illustrators

SUMMERS, DAVID ARCHIBALD, research mining engineer, educator, director; b. Newcastle-on-Tyne, Eng., Feb. 2, 1944; married, 1972; 2 children. BSc, U. Leeds, 1965, PhD in Mining, 1968. Asst. prof. mining U. Mo., Rolla, 1968-74, assoc. prof. mining, 1974-77, prof. mining, 1977-80, prof., 1980—, sr. investor Rock Mech. and Explosives Rsch. Ctr., 1970-76, dir. Rock Mech. and Explosives Rsch. Ctr., 1976-84, dir. High Pressure Water Jet Lab., 1984—, dir. High Pressure Waterjet Lab. Rock Mech. Facility and Explosives Rsch. Ctr. Recipient Rock Mechanics award Soc. Mining, Metallurgy & Exploration, 1993. Fellow Brit. Inst. Mining Engrs., Brit. Inst. Mining and Metallurgy, Brit. Tunneling Soc., Cleaning Equipment Mfr. Assn., Water Jet Technol. Assn. (pres. 1986-87); mem. ASME, Am. Inst. Mining, Metall. and Petroleum Engrs., Brit. Hydromech. Rsch. Assn. (hon.). Achievements include research in water jet cutting, surface energy of rock and minerals, novel methods of excavation, cavitation at high pressure, coal mining, geothermal development, strata control. Home: 808 Cypress Dr Rolla MO 65401-3804 Office: U Mo High Pressure Waterjet Lab Rock Mech Facility 116 1006 Kingshighway St 116 Rolla MO 65409-0001

SUMMERS, DON, state legislator; Rep. dist. 2 State of Mo. Office: Rte 4 Box 209 Unionville MO 63565-9273 also: Mo Ho of Reps State Capitol Jefferson City MO 65101

SUMMERS, VANESSA, state legislator; m. Nicholas T. Barnes. Grad., Mid-Am. Coll. Funeral Svcs. State rep., mem. aged & aging, pub. policy, ethics, vet. affairs & urban affairs coms., chmn. interstate coop. com. Ind. Ho. of Reps., Indpls., 1991—; funeral dir. Summers Funeral Chapel. Named one of Top Ladies of Distinction. Mem. Alpha Kappa Alpha, Alpha Mu Omega. Democrat. Office: 1140 Brook Ln Indianapolis IN 46202-2255

SUMMERS, WILLIAM B., JR., brokerage house executive; b. 1950; With McDonald & Co. Investments Inc., Cleve., 1971—; pres., CEO and chmn. McDonald & Co. Securities, Cleve., 1983—; chmn. McDonald Investments Inc., Cleve., 1995—; exec. v.p. KeyCorp, 1998—2000; chmn. Key Capital Partners, 1998—2000. Office: McDonald Investment Inc 800 Superior Ave E Cleveland OH 44114-2601

SUMNER, DAVID SPURGEON, surgeon, educator; b. Asheboro, NC, Feb. 20, 1933; s. George Herbert and Velna Elizabeth (Welborn) S.; m. Martha Eileen Sypher, July 25, 1959; children: David Vance, Mary Elizabeth, John Franklin. BA, U. N.C., 1954; MD, Johns Hopkins U., 1958. Diplomate Am. Bd. Surgery; cert. spl. qualification gen. vascular surgery. Intern Johns Hopkins Hosp., Balt., 1958-59, resident in gen. surgery, 1960-61, U. Wash. Sch. Medicine, Seattle, 1961-66; clin. investigator in vascular surgery VA Hosp., Seattle, 1967, 70-73; asst. prof. surgery U. Wash. Sch. Medicine, Seattle, 1970-72, assoc. prof. surgery, 1972-75; prof. surgery, chief sect. peripheral vascular surgery So. Ill. U. Sch. Medicine., Springfield, 1975-84, Disting. prof. surgery, chief sect. peripheral vascular surgery, 1984-98, disting. prof. emeritus, 1998. Staff surgeon Seattle VA Hosp., 1973-75, Univ. Hosp., Seattle, 1973-75, St. John's Hosp., Springfield, 1975-98, Meml. Med. Ctr., Springfield, 1975-98; mem. VA Merit Review Bd. Surgery, 1975-78; mem. vascular surgery rsch. award com. The Liebig Found., 1990-95, chmn., 1994; bd. dirs. Am. Venous Forum Found., 1993-95; vis. prof. Cook County Hosp., Chgo., 1971, Washington U., St. Louis, 1976, U. Tex., San Antonio, 1978, Wayne State U., Detroit, 1978, U. Ind., Indpls., 1979, Ea. Va. Med. Sch., Norfolk, 1979, Case-Western Res. U., Cleve., 1980, U. Chgo., 1981, U. Manitoba, Winnipeg, Can., 1983, others; dist. lectr. Yale U., 1982; guest examiner Am. Bd. Surgery, St. Louis, 1982, assoc. examiner, 1989; lectr. in field. Author: (with D.E. Strandness Jr.) Ultrasonic Techniques in Angiology, 1975, Hemodynamics for Surgeons, 1975; (with R.B. Rutherford, V. Bernhard, F. Maddison, W.S. Moore, M.O. Perry) Vascular Surgery, 1977; (with F.B. Hershey, R.W. Barnes) Noninvasive Diagnosis of Vascular Disease, 1984; (with R.B. Rutherford, G. Johnson Jr., R.F. Kempczinski, W.S. Moore, M.O. Perry, G.W. Smith) Vascular Surgery, 3d edit., 1989; (with A.N. icolaides) Investigation of Patients With Deep Vein Thrombosis and Chronic Venous Insufficiency, 1991; (with R.B. Rutherford, G. Johnson, K.W. Johnston, R.F. Kempczinski, W.C. Krupski, W.S. Moore, M.O. Perry, A.J. Comerota, R.H. Dean, P. Gloviczki, K.H. Johansen, T.S. Riles, L.M. Taylor Jr.) Vascular Surgery, 4th edit., 1995; (with K.A. Myers, A.N. Nicolaides Lower Limb Ischaemia, 1997; author 150 chpts. to books; mem. editl. bd. Vascular Diagnosis and Therapy, 1980-84, Jour. Soc. Non-Invasive Vascular Tech., 1987—, Jour. Vascular Surgery, 1987-97; series editor Introduction to Vascular Tech., 1990—; mem. exec. editl. com. Phlebology, 1987-91, mem. internat. editl. adv. bd., 1991-2000; mem. editl. com. Internat. Angiology, 1992—; contbr. over 150 articles to profl. jours. Lt. col. U.S. Army, 1967-70. Fellow in surg. rsch. Johns Hopkins U. Sch. Medicine, 1959-60, Am. Cancer Soc., Inc. fellow, 1965-66; Appleton-Century Crofts scholar, 1956, Mosby scholar, 1958. Fellow Am. Coll. Surgeons (Wash. chpt. 1971-75, Ill. chpt. counselor 1981-83), Cyprus Vascular Soc. (hon.); mem. AMA, Soc. Univ. Surgeons, Soc. Vascular Surgery (constn. and by-laws com. 1983, Wiley Fellowship com. 1990), Internat. Soc. Cardiovascular Surgery (N.Am. chpt. program com. 1985-88), Am. Surg. Assn., Am. Heart Assn. (stroke coun., cardiovascular surgery coun. 1978), Soc. oninvasive Vascular Tech. (hon.), Vascular Surgery Biology Club, Am. Venous Forum (organizing com. 1987, founding mem. 1988, chmn. membership com. 1988-91, treas. 1992-95, pres. elect 1998, pres. 1999-2000), Cardiovascular Sys. Dynamics Soc., Internat. Soc. Surgery, Vascular Soc. So. Africa (hon.), orth Pacific Surg. Assn., Ctrl. Surg. Assn., Midwestern Vascular Surg. Soc. (counselor 1977-79, pres.-elect 1980-81, pres. 1981-82), So. Assn. for Vascular Surgery, Ill. Heart Assn., Ill. Med. Soc., Ill. Surg. Soc., Chgo. Surg. Soc., Seattle Surg. Soc., Sangamon County Med. Soc., Henry N. Harkins Surg. Soc., Harbinger Soc., Phi Eta Sigma, Phi Beta Kappa, Sigma Xi, Alpha Omega Alpha. Presbyterian. Achievements include research in surgical hemodynamics and noninvasive methods for diagnosing peripheral vascular disease. Home: 2324 W Lake Shore Dr Springfield IL 62712-9521 E-mail: dsumner1@aol.com.

SUMNER, WILLIAM MARVIN, anthropology and archaeology educator; b. Detroit, Sept. 8, 1928; s. William Pulford Jr. and Virginia Friel (Umberger) S.; m. Frances Wilson Morton, June 21, 1952 (div. 1975): children: Jane Cassell, William Morton; m. Kathleen A. MacLean, Apr. 7, 1989. Student, Va. Mil. Inst., 1947-48; BS, U.S. Naval Acad., 1952; PhD, U. Pa., 1972. Dir. Am. Inst. Iranian Studies, Tehran, Iran, 1969-71; asst. prof. Ohio State U., Columbus, 1971-73, assoc. prof., 1974-80, prof. anthropology, 1981-89, prof. emeritus, 1989—; dir. Oriental Inst., prof. Near Eastern langs. and civilizations U. Chgo., 1989-98. Dir. excavations at Tal-e Malyan (site of Elamite Anshan) sponsored by Univ. Mus., U. Pa., 1971—; v.p. Am. Inst. Iranian Studies, 1983-86. Contbr. chpts. to books, articles and essays to profl. jours. Served to lt. comdr. USN, 1952-64. Grantee NSF, 1975, 76, 79, NEH, 1988. E-mail: sumner.1@osu.edu.

SUND, JEFFREY OWEN, retired publishing company executive; b. Bklyn., June 19, 1940; children: Catherine, Meredith. BA, Dartmouth Coll., 1962. Sales rep. Prentice-Hall, Englewood Cliffs, N.J., 1967-73, Houghton Mifflin, Boston, 1973-74, coll. div. editor, 1974-77, editor-in-chief, 1977-86, v.p., editorial dir., 1986-89; pres., chief exec. officer Richard D. Irwin, Burr Ridge, Ill., 1989-96; pres. McGraw-Hill Higher Edn., Burr Ridge, 1996-2000; ret. Lt. USN, 1962-66.

SUNDAY, JACK, radio personality; Midday weekday radio host Sta. KFGO-AM, Fargo, ND. Office: KFGO 1020 25th St S Fargo ND 58103

SUNDBERG, MARSHALL DAVID, biology professor; b. Apr. 18, 1949; m. Sara Jane Brooks, Aug. 1, 1977; children: Marshall Isaac, Adam, Emma. BA in Biology, Carleton Coll., 1971; MA in Botany, U. Minn., 1973, PhD in Botany, 1978. Lab. technician Carleton Coll., Minn., 1973-74; teaching asst. U. Minn., Mpls., 1974-76, rsch. asst., 1976-77; adj. asst. prof. Biology U. Wis., Eau Claire, 1978-85, mem. faculty summer sci. inst., 1982-85; instr. La. State U., Baton Rouge, 1985-88, asst. prof. Biology, 1988-91, coord. dept. Biology, 1988-93, assoc. prof. Biology, 1991-97; prof., chair dept. biol. scis. Emporia State U., 1997—. Author: General Botany Laboratory Workbook, 5th revision, 1984, General Botany 1001 Laboratory Manual, 1986, General Botany 1002 Laboratory Manual, 1987, Biology 1002 Correspondence Study Guide, 1987, Boty 1202: General Botany Laboratory Manual, 1988, Biol 1208: Biology for Science Majors Laboratory Manual, 1988, 2d edit., 1989, Instructor's Manual for J. Mauseth, Introductory Botany, 1991; contbr. articles to profl. jours. Brand fellow U. Minn., 1976-77, Faculty Grants scholar U. Wis., 1984-85. Fellow Linnaean Soc. London; mem. NSTA, AAAS, Am. Inst. Biol. Scis. (coun. mem. at large 1992-95, edn. com. 1994-95, 98-2002), Nat. Sci. Tchrs. Assn., Assn. Biology Lab. Edn., Bot. Soc. Am. (chmn. tchg. sect. 1985-86, workshop com. tchg. sect. 1983-84, slide exch./lab. exch. tchg. sect. 1980-89, edn. com. 1991, 92, editor Plant Sci. Bull. 2000—, Charles H. Bessey award 1992, Centennial award 2006), Internat. Soc. Plant Morphologists, Nat. Assn. Biology Tchrs. (Outstanding 4-Yr. Coll. Tchr. award 1997, 2003), Soc. Econ. Botany, The Nature Conservancy, Sigma Xi (chpt. sec. 1982-84, 93-95, 2000-02, v.p. 1984-85, 96-97, pres. 1996, 99, 2005). Home: 1912 Briarcliff Ln Emporia KS 66801-5404 Office: Emporia State U Dept Biol Scis 1200 Commercial St Emporia KS 66801-5087

SUNDERLAND, HENRY D., retail company executive; Sr. v.p. Sears Roebuck & Co.

SUNDERMAN, DUANE NEUMAN, chemist, research and development company executive; b. Wadsworth, Ohio, July 14, 1928; s. Richard Benjamin and Carolyn (Neuman) S.; m. Joan Catherine Hoffman, Jan. 31, 1953; children: David, Christine, Richard. BA, U. Mich., 1949, MS, 1954, PhD in Chemistry, 1956. Researcher Battelle Meml. Inst., Columbus, Ohio, 1956-59, mgr., 1959-69, assoc. dir., 1969-79, dir. internat. programs, 1979-84; sr. v.p. Midwest Rsch. Inst., Kansas City, Mo., 1984-90, exec. v.p., 1990-94, Golden, Colo., 1990-94. Dir. Nat. Renewable Energy Lab., Golden, Colo., 1990-94, dir. emeritus, 1994—. Contbr. numerous articles to profl. jours. Bd. dirs. Mid-Ohio chpt. ARC, 1982-83, U. Kansas City, 1985-90, Mo. Corp. for Sci. and Tech., Jefferson City, 1986-90, Colo. Energy Sci. Ctr., 2000-04. With USNR, 1949—59. Mem. Am. Chem. Soc. Presbyterian. Avocation: paleontology.

SUNDQUIST, ERIC JOHN, American studies educator; b. McPherson, Kans., Aug. 21, 1952; s. Laurence A. and Frances J. (Halene) S.; m. Tatiana Kreinine, Aug. 14, 1982; children: Alexandra, Joanna, Ariane. BA, U. Kans., 1974; MA, Johns Hopkins U., 1976, PhD, 1978. Asst. prof. English Johns Hopkins U., Balt., 1978-80, U. Calif., Berkeley, 1980-82, assoc. prof., 1982-86, prof. English, 1986-89, UCLA, 1989-97, chair dept. English, 1994-97; dean Judd A. and Marjorie Weinberg Coll. Arts and Scis. Northwestern U., Evanston, Ill., 1997—. Vis. scholar U. Kans., 1985, dir. Holmes grad. seminar, 1993; dir. NEH Summer Seminar for Coll. Tchrs., U. Calif., Berkeley, 1986, 90, UCLA, 1994; cons. Calif. Coun. for Humanities, 1986-87; prof. Bread Loaf Sch. English, Middlebury (Vt.) Coll., 1987, 89, Sante Fe, 95; mem. fellowship com. Newberry Libr., 1987, 88, 92; dir. NEH Summer Seminar for Secondary Sch. Tchrs., Berkeley, 1988; vis. prof. UCLA, 1988; Andrew Hilen vis. prof. U. Wash., 1990; Lamar Meml. lectr. in so. states Mercer U., 1991; Gertrude Conaway Vanderbilt prof. English Vanderbilt U., Nashville, 1992-93; mem. fellowship cons. Nat. Humanities Ctr., 1992, 93; acad. specialist in Am. studies Tel Aviv U., 1994; mem. adv. bd. Colloquium for the Study of Am. Culture, Claremont (Calif.) Grad. Sch. & Huntington Libr., 1994—. Author: Home as Found: Authority and Genealogy in ineteenth-Century American Literature, 1979 (Gustave Arlt award Coun. Grad. Schs. in U.S. 1980), Faulkner: The House Divided, 1983, The Hammers of Creation: Folk Culture in Modern African-American Fiction, 1992, To Take the Nations: Race in the Making of American Literature, 1993 (Christian Gauss award Phi Beta Kappa 1993, James Russell Lowell award MLA 1993, Choice Outstanding Acad. Book 1994); co-author: Cambridge History of American Literature, Vol. II, 1995; editor: American Realism: New Essays, 1982, New Essays on Uncle Tom's Cabin, 1986, Frederick Douglass: New Literary and Historical Essays, 1990, Mark Twain: A Collection of Critical Essays, 1994, Cultural Contexts for Ralph Ellison's Invisible Man, 1995, Oxford W.E.B. DuBois Reader, 1996; mem. adv. bd. Studies in Am. Lit. and Culture, 1987-90, gen. editor, 1991-97; mem. editl. bd. Am. Lit. History, 1987—, Ariz. Quar., 1987—; assoc. editor Am. Nat. Biography, 1990—; cons. The Libr. of Am., 1992—; consulting reader African-Am. Rev., 1992—; contbr. articles to profl. jours. Am. Coun. Learned Socs. fellow, 1981, NEH fellow, 1989-90, Guggenheim fellow, 1993-94. Mem. MLA (chair adv. coun. Am. lit. sect. 1994, mem. exec. com. divsn. 19th Century Am. lit. 1994-97), Am. Studies Assn. (chair John Hope Franklin Prize com. 1993, mem. nat. coun. 1994-97, mem. fin. com. 1995-97, and other coms.), Am. Lit. Assn., Orgn. Am. Historians, So. Hist. Assn., So. Am. Studies Assn. (mem. exec. com. 1993-97), Phi Beta Kappa. Office: Northwestern U Coll Arts and Scis 1918 Sheridan Rd Evanston IL 60208-0847

SUNI, ELLEN Y., dean, law educator; BA magna cum laude, CCNY; JD magna cum laude, Boston U. Law clerk to Chief Justice Mass. Supreme Judicial Ct., dep. legal asst. to Justices; dir. legal writing prog. Boston U. Sch. Law, asst. dean, lectr.; faculty mem. U. Mo.-Kansas City Sch. Law, 1980—, interim assoc. dean, interim dean, prof. law, 2004—, Marvin Lewis Rich Faculty Scholar. Fed. prosecutor U.S. Atty. Office, 1987—88; mem. Eighth Cir. Criminal Jury Instrns. Sub-com.; bd. mem. Pub. Interest Litigation Clinic, Police Law Inst. Contbr. articles to law jours. Legal dir. Kansas City Youth Ct.; pres. Midwestern Innocence Project. Recipient Legal Leader of Yr. Award, 2004. Office: U Mo-Kansas City Sch Law 5100 Rockhill Rd Kansas City MO 64110 Office Phone: 816-235-2372. E-mail: sunie@umkc.edu.

SUNSTEIN, CASS ROBERT, law educator; b. Salem, Mass., Sept. 21, 1954; AB, Harvard U., 1975, JD, 1978. Law clk. to Hon. Benjamin Kaplan Supreme Jud. Ct. of Mass., 1978—79; law clk. to Hon. Thurgood Marshall US Supreme Ct., Washington, 1979-80; atty.-advisor, Office of Legal Counsel US Dept. Justice, Washington, 1980-81; asst. prof. U. Chgo. Law Sch., 1981—83, U. Chgo. Law Sch. & U. Chgo. dept. polit. sci., 1983—85, prof. law, 1985—88, Karl N. Llewellyn Prof. Jurisprudence, 1988—93, Karl N. Llewellyn Disting. Svc. Prof. Jurisprudence, 1993—. Assoc. editor Ethics, 1986—88; bd. editors Studies Am. Polit. Devel., 1989—, Constitutional Polit. Econ., 1991, Jour. Polit. Philosophy, 1991—; contbg. editor The Am. Prospect, 1989, The New Republic, 1999—; vis. prof. Columbia Law Sch., NYC, 1986, Harvard Law Sch., Cambridge, Mass., 1987, 2005; co-dir. Ctr. Constitutionalism Ea. Europe U. Chgo., 1990—97; mem. Presdl. Adv. Com. Pub. Svc. Obligations of Digital TV, 1997—98; cons. project on social norms IRS, 1999—. Author: (book) After the Rights Revolution: Reconceiving the Regulatory State, 1990, Democracy and the Problem of Free Speech, 1993 (Goldsmith Book Award, 1994), The Partial Constitution, 1993, Legal Reasoning and Political Conflict, 1996, Free Markets and Social Justice, 1997, One Case At A Time: Judicial Minimalism on the Supreme Court, 1999, Designing Democracy: What Constitutions Do, 2001, Republic.com, 2001, Free Markets and Social Justice, 2002, Risk and Reason, 2002, The Cost-Benefit State, 2002, Why Societies Need Dissent, 2003, The Second Bill of Rights: Franklin Delano Roosevelt's Constitutional Vision and Why We Need It More Than Ever, 2004, The Laws of Fear: Beyond the Precautionary Principle, 2005, Radicals in Robes: Why Extreme Right-Wing Courts Are Wrong for America, 2005; co-author: Administrative Law and Regulatory Policy, 1999, The Cost of Rights, 1999, Constitutional Law, 2001, Punitive Damages: How Juries Decide, 2002; editor: Feminism and Political Theory, 1990, Behavioral Law and Economics, 2000; co-editor: The Bill of Rights and the Modern State, 1992, Clones and Clones: Facts and Fantasies About Human Cloning, 1998, The Vote: Bush, Gore & the Supreme Court, 2001, Animal Rights: Current Controversies and New Directions, 2004. Mem.: ABA (vice chmn. Sect. Govtl. Orgn. & Separation Powers 1986—87, coun. Sect. Adminstr. Law 1987—88, vice-chmn. Jud. Rev. Com. 1991—, co-chair Com. Regulatory Policy 2001—, Cert. Merit Award 1991), Am. Acad. Arts and Sci., Am. Law Inst., Inst. Medicine Com., World Wildlife Fund. Office: Sch Law U Chgo 1111 E 60th St Chicago IL 60637-2776 E-mail: csunstei@midway.uchicago.edu.

SUPPELSA, MARK, newscaster, reporter; b. Milw. B Broadcast Comms., Marquette U., 1984. Weekend anchor, reporter Sta. WFRV-TV, Green Bay, Wis., 1984—87; anchor, reporter Sta. KSTP-TV, 1987—90, co-anchor 10 pm newscast, 1990—93; with NBC 5, Chgo., 1993—, weekend anchor, reporter, co-anchor early afternoon newscasts, now anchor 4:30 pm and 5 pm newscast. Recipient Regional award, AP, award, Soc. Profl. Journalists, Chgo. Emmy, 1995—96. Office: NBC 454 N Columbus Dr Chicago IL 60611

SURFACE, CHUCK L., state legislator; b. Webb City, Mo., Feb. 5, 1944; s. Hubert Basil and Hazel (Ulmer) S.; m. Sherry Louzader, 1978; children: Jason, Christi, Kimberly. BS, So. State Coll., 1969. Agt. Shelter Ins., 1970—; mem. Mo. Ho. of Reps. from 129th dist., 1985—. Mem. Joplin (Mo.) Zoning and Planning Commn., 1977-82, chmn., 1981-82; mem. Joplin City Coun., 1982-85. Mem. Am. Legion, Sertoma, Mo. So. State Coll. Alumni Assn. (past bd. dirs.), Jaycees (past pres. Joplin chpt.), Elks. Republican. Home: 2401 W 29th St Joplin MO 64804-1425 Office: Mo House of Reps State Capitol Jefferson City MO 65101

SURI, JASJIT S., research scientist; BS in Computer Engrng., Regional Engrng. Coll., Bhopal, India, 1988; MS, U. Ill., Chgo., 1991; PhD in Elec. Engrng., U. Wash., 1997. Lectr. dept. electronic and computer engrng. Regional Engrng. Coll., Bhopal, 1988-89; rsch. asst. biomed. visualization dept. U. Ill., Chgo., 1989-90; rsch. programmer image sci. group IBM Palo Alto (Calif.) Sci. Ctr., summer 1990-91; rsch. assoc. U. Wash., Seattle, 1992-97; rsch. software engr. radiation treatment planning group Siemens Med. Sys., Calif., 1991-92; rsch. scientist Gammex Inc., Middleton, Wis., 1997, Sch. Medicine, U. Wis., Madison, 1997; rsch. scientist software devel. TSI, N.Y., 1997; rsch. staff scientist image guided surgery dept. Image Processing and Computer Graphics Picker Internat., Cleve., 1999—. With Bharat Heavy Elec. Ltd., Bhopal, 1986, Larsen & Tubro Ltd., Bombay, India, 1987, Nat. Info. Tech. Ltd., Bhopal, 1987; presenter in field; mem. Mayo Clinic Procs., Rochester, Minn.; rev. com. Internat. Conf. in Pattern Analysis and Applications, Plymouth, Eng., 1998. Author: (with others) Model Based Segmentation, 2d. rev. edit., 2000; mem. editl. bd. Radiology, Jour. Computer Assisted Tomography, Internat. Jour. Pattern Analysis and Applications, Internat. Conf. Pattern Analysis and Applications; contbr. over 150 articles. to profl. jours.; patentee in field. Scholar Regional Engrng. Coll., 1985-88 Mem. IEEE, Assn. Computing Machinery,

Artificial Intelligence, Optical Engring. Soc. Am., Engring. in Medicine and Biology Soc. (mem. editl. bd.), Am. Assn. Artificial Int., USENIX-Tcl/Tk. Office: Case Western Res U Biomed Engring Dept Cleveland OH Office Phone: 720-936-6362. Personal E-mail: suri0256@msn.com.

SURLES, CAROL D., academic administrator; b. Pensacola, Fla., Oct. 7, 1946; d. Elza Allen and Versy Lee Smith; divorced; children: Lisa Surles, Philip Surles. BA, Fisk U., 1968; MA, Chapman Coll., 1971; PhD, U. Mich., 1978. Personnel rep. U. Mich., Ann Arbor, 1973-78, vice-chancellor-adminstrn. Flint, 1987-89; exec. asst. to pres., assoc. v.p. for human resources U. Ctrl. Fla., Orlando, 1978-87; v.p. acad. affairs Jackson State U., Miss., 1989-92; v.p. adminstrn. and bus. Calif. State U., Hayward, 1992-94; pres. Tex. Woman's U., Denton, 1994-99, Ea. Ill. U., Charleston, 1999—2001. Trustee Pub. Broadcasting Ch. 24, Orlando, 1985-87; bd. dirs. First State Bank, Denton, Tex., Tex.-N.Mex. Power Co., TNP-Enterprise. Recipient Outstanding Scholar's award Delta Tau Kappa, 1983. Mem. AAUW, Am. Assn. Colls. and Univs., Golden Key Honor Soc., Mortar Bd. Soc., Dallas Citizens' Coun., Dallas Women's Found., Coun. of Pres. (Austin, Tex.), Phi Kappa Phi, Alpha Kappa Alpha. Episcopal. Avocation: piano. Home: 1227 Parasol Pl Pensacola FL 32507

SURSA, CHARLES DAVID, banker; b. Muncie, Ind., Nov. 5, 1925; s. Charles Vaught and Ethel Fay (Schukraft) S; m. Mary Jane Palmer, Feb. 2, 1947; children: Ann Elizabeth, Janet Lynne, Charles Vaught, Laura Jane. BSChemE, Purdue U., 1946; MBA, Harvard, 1948. Executive NBD Bank N.A. (formerly Summit Bank, Indsl. Trust & Savings), Muncie, Ind., 1946-51, pres., 1951-80, chmn. bd., pres., 1980-88, chmn. bd., CEO, 1988-90, chmn. bd., 1990-94, chmn. emeritus, 1994—. Bd. dirs. Old Rep. Life Ins. Co., Chgo., Home Owners Life Ins. Co., Chgo., Old Rep. Internat. Corp., Chgo., Ball Meml. Hosp., Inc., Old Rep. Ins. Co., Greensburg, Pa., Internat. Bus. & Merc. Ins. Group, Chgo., Am. Bus. & Merc. Reassurance Co., Chgo., bd. dirs., pres. Com. Svcs. Coun. of Del. County, 1973-74. Treas. Muncie Symphony Assn., 1949-62, pres., 1962-72, 2d v.p., 1978-80, dir., 1991-97; bd. dirs., pres. The Cmty. Found. of Muncie and Del. County, Inc., 1985-97. Recipient Outstanding Young Man award Ind. Jr. C. of C., 1956, Hon. Jaycees award, 1974. Mem. Ind. Banker's Assn., Ind. Pres.'s Orgn. (treas. 1980-86), Delaware County C. of C., Ind. State C. of C., Muncie C. of C. (pres. 1959-60), Rotary (pres. 1964-65), Delaware Country Club (pres., bd. dirs. 1964), Elks, Phi Gamma Delta. Republican. Presbyterian. Home: 3410 W University Ave Muncie IN 47304-3970

SURYANARAYANAN, RAJ GOPALAN, pharmacist, researcher, consultant, educator; b. Cuddalore, Tamil Nadu, India, Apr. 19, 1955; came to U.S., 1985; s. Natesan and Pushpa (Subramanian) Rajagopalan; m. Shanti Venkateswaran, Nov. 24, 1985; children: Priya Mallika Sury, Meera Sindu Sury. B in Pharmacy, Banaras Hindu U., Varanasi, India, 1976, M in Pharmacy, 1978; MS, U. BC, Vancouver, Can., 1981, PhD, 1985. Mgmt. trainee Indian Drugs and Pharms. Ltd., Rishikesh, India, 1978; supr. Roche Products, Bombay, 1979; tchg. asst. U. B.C., Vancouver, Can., 1979, 82-83; asst. prof. pharmaceutics U. Minn., Mpls., 1985-92, assoc. prof., 1992-99, prof., 1999—, dir. grad. studies, 1994-98, William and Mildred Peters endowed chair, 2006—. Cons. numerous pharm. cos. in U.S., 1987—. Contbr. articles to profl. jours.; patentee quantitative analysis of intact tablets. Recipient numerous grants for rsch., U.S., 1985—. Mem. Am. Assn. Pharm. Scientists, Am. Assn. Colls. Pharmacy. Hindu. Avocation: sports. Office: U Minn Coll Pharmacy 308 Harvard St SE Minneapolis MN 55455-0353 Home: 2025 Autumn Pl Saint Paul MN 55113-5417 E-mail: surya001@umn.edu.

SUSLICK, KENNETH SANDERS, chemistry professor; b. Chgo., Sept. 16, 1952; s. Alvin and Edith Suslick. BS with honors, Calif. Inst. Tech., 1974; PhD, Stanford U., 1978. Rsch. and tchg. asst. Stanford (Calif.) U., 1974-78; chemist Lawrence Livermore (Calif.) Lab., 1974-75; asst. prof. U. Ill., Urbana, 1978-84, assoc. prof., 1984-88, prof. chemistry, 1988—; prof. Beckman Inst. for Advanced Sci. and Tech., Urbana, 1989-92; prof. materials sci. and engring. U. Ill., Urbana, 1993—, William H. and Janet Lycan prof. chemistry, 1997—2004, Marvin T. Schmidt prof. chemistry, 2004—; founder ChemSensing, Inc., 2001—. Vis. fellow Balliol Coll., Inorganic Chemistry Lab., Oxford (Eng.) U., 1986; cons. in field. Editor: High Energy Processes in Organometallic Chemistry, 1987, Ultrasound: Its Chemical, Physical and Biological Effects, 1988, Comprehensive Supramolecular Chemistry, vol. 5, 1996; co-editor: Sonochemistry and Sonoluminescence, 1999; editl. bd. Ultrasonics, 1992-96, Ultrasonic Sonochemistry, 1996—, Accounts of Chemical Research, 2005—, Jour. Am. Chem. Soc., 2006-; patentee isotope separation by photochromatography, sonochemistry, protein microspheres, drug delivery, blood substitutes, sensors, smell-seeing, artificial olfaction; contbr. articles to profl. jours. Recipient Rsch. Career Devel. award NIH, 1985-90, NSF Spl. Creativity award 1992-94, Material Rsch. Soc. medal, 1994, R.S.C. Sir George Stokes medal 2007; fellow DuPont Found., 1979-80, Sloan Found., 1985-87; A.C.S. Sr. Cope scholar, 2004. Fellow AAAS, Am. Acoustical Soc. Royal Soc. Arts, Mfrs. and Commerce (Silver medal 1974); mem. Am. Chem. Soc. (chmn. sect. 1987-89, Nobel Laureate Signature award 1994, Sr. Cope Scholar award 2004). Avocations: sculpting, music. Office: U Ill Dept Chemistry 600 S Mathews Ave Urbana IL 61801-3602 Business E-Mail: ksuslick@uiuc.edu.

SUSMAN, MILLARD, geneticist, educator; b. St. Louis, Sept. 1, 1934; s. Albert and Patsy Ruth S.; m. Barbara Beth Fretwell, Aug. 18, 1957; children: Michael K., David L. AB, Washington U., St. Louis, 1956; PhD, Calif. Inst. Tech., 1962. With microbial genetics research unit Hammersmith Hosp., London, 1961-62; asst. prof. genetics U. Wis., Madison, 1962-66, assoc. prof., 1966-72, prof., 1972—2002, prof. emeritus, 2002—, chmn. lab. genetics, 1971-75, 77-86, assoc. dean med. sch., 1986-95, acting dean Sch. Allied Health Professions, 1988-90, vice dean med. sch., 1994-95, spl. advisor to the dean med. sch., 1995; dir. Ctr. for Biology Edn., Madison, 1996—2002. Phage course instr., Cold Spring Harbor, N.Y., 1965; v.p. scis., Wis. Acad. Scis., Arts and Letters, 2000—. Co-author: Life on Earth, 2d edit., 1978, Human Chromosomes: Structure, Behavior, Effects, 3d edit., 1992; contbr. articles to sci. jours. Mem Genetics Soc. Am., AAAS, Sigma Xi, Phi Beta Kappa, Phi Eta Sigma, Omicron Delta Kapp. Home: 2707 Colgate Rd Madison WI 53705-2234 Office: 2432 Genetics/Biotech Ctr Bldg Madison WI 53706 Office Phone: 608-263-5075. Business E-Mail: msusman@wisc.edu.

SUSSMAN, ARTHUR MELVIN, law educator, foundation administrator; b. Bklyn., Nov. 17, 1942; m. Rita Padnick; children: Eric, Johanna. BS, Cornell U., 1963; JD magna cum laude, Harvard U., 1966. Bar: NY 1967, Ill. 1970. Assoc. atty. Cahill, Gordon, Reindel & Ohl, NYC, 1966-67; from assoc. atty. to ptnr. Jenner & Block, Chgo., 1970-77; legal counsel So. Ill. U., Carbondale, 1977-79; gen. counsel, v.p. U. Chgo., 1979-84, gen. counsel, v.p. adminstrn., Arsonne Nat. Lab., 1984-2001, lectr. law Grad. Sch. Bus., 1986-94, bd. dirs. Lab. Schs., 1985-01, lectr. law sch., 1998—; v.p. & sec. John D. and Catherine T. MacArthur Found., 2001—. Presenter in field. Contbr. articles to profl. jour. Mem. Ill. Sec. of State's Com. on Not-for-Profit Corp. Act, 1984—85; chmn. regional selection panel Harry S. Truman Scholarship Found.; bd. dir. Chapin Hill for Children, 1986—; chmn., bd. dir. Ency. Brit., Inc., 1995—96. Capt. JAGC US Army, 1967—70. Fulbright fellow, London, 0197. Mem.: Am. Coun. Edn., Nat. Assn. Coll. and Univ. Attys. Office: The MacArthur Foundation 140 S Dearborn St Chicago IL 60603 also: Law Sch U Chicago 1111 East 60th St Chicago IL 60637 Home Phone: 773-935-9315; Office Phone: 312-516-1529, 773-703-7241. E-mail: asussman@macfound.org.

SUSTER, RONALD, judge, former state legislator; b. Cleve., Oct. 31, 1942; s. Joseph and Frances (Pryatel) S.; m. Patricia Hocevart, 1974; children: Jennifer, Joseph, Michael. BA, Western Res. Univ., 1964, JD, 1967. Lawyer, 1967; asst. law dir. City of Cleveland, 1967; asst. county prosecutor Cuyahoga, Ohio, 1968-71; law dir. City of Highland Heights, 1976-80; asst. atty. gen. Ohio, 1971-80; legal adv. Euclid Dem. Exec. Com., Ohio, 1975-76; state rep. Ohio Dist. 19, 1981-92, Ohio Dist. 14, 1993; judge Common Pleas Ct. of Cuyahoga County, 1995—. Mem. Labor-Mgmt. Rels. subcom., chmn. ethics com. 1983-84, chmn. Civil & Comml. Law com., 1985-87; chmn. Fin. Inst. Com., 1987; exec. com. mem. Cuyahoga County Dem., 1974-78. Mem. Am. Fedn. of State, County & Mcpl. Employees, Fraternal Order of Police Auxiliary, Northern Ohio Patrolmen Benevolent Assn., Internat. Assn. Firefighters, Am. Arbit Assn. Home: 18519 Underwood Ave Cleveland OH 44119-2927 Office: 1200 Ontario St Cleveland OH 44113-1678

SUTER, ALBERT EDWARD, manufacturing executive; b. East Orange, NJ, Sept. 18, 1935; s. Joseph Vincent and Catherine (Clay) S.; m. Michaela Sams Suter, May 28, 1966; children: Christian C., Bradley J., Allison A. BME, Cornell U., 1957, MBA, 1959. Pres., chief exec. officer L.B. Knight & Assocs., Chgo., 1959-79; v.p. internat. Emerson Electric Co., St. Louis, 1979-80, pres. motor div., 1980-87, group v.p., 1981-83, exec. v.p., 1983-87, vice chmn., 1987; pres., chief operating officer, dir. Firestone Tire & Rubber Co., Akron, Ohio, 1987-88; pres., chief operating officer Whirlpool Corp., Benton Harbor, Mich., from 1988; exec. v.p. Emerson Electric Co., St. Louis, until 1990, pres., COO, 1990-92, sr. vice chmn., COO, 1992-97; CAO, 1999—2001; ret. sr. advisor, COO Emerson Electric Co., St. Louis, 2001. Bd. dirs. Furniture Brands Internat. Bd. dirs. Jr. Achievement Nat. Bd., Colorado Springs, Colo., Jr. Achievement Miss. Valley, St. Louis Sci. Ctr. Bd.; chmn. Torch div. St. Louis chpt. United Way, 1982-86. Mem. Glenview (Ill.) Country Club, St. Louis Club, Old Warson Country Club, Log Cabin Club. Republican. Episcopalian. Office: Emerson Electric Co PO Box 4100 Saint Louis MO 63136-8506

SUTERA, SALVATORE PHILIP, mechanical engineer, educator; b. Balt., Jan. 12, 1933; s. Philip and Ann (D'Amico) S.; m. Celia Ann Fielden, June 21, 1958; children: Marie-Anne, Annette Nicole, Michelle Cecile. BS in Mech. Engring, Johns Hopkins, 1954; postgrad., U. Paris, 1955-56; MS, Calif. Inst. Tech., 1955; PhD, Cal. Inst. Tech., 1960; MA (hon.), Brown U., 1965. Asst. prof. mech. engring. Brown U., Providence, 1960-65, asso. prof., 1965-68, exec. officer div. engring., 1966-68; prof. dept. mech. engring. Washington U., St. Louis, 1968-97, chmn. dept., 1968-82, 86-97, Spencer T. Olin prof. engring. and applied sci., 1997—2003, prof. biomed. engring., 1997—2003, sr. prof., 2003—07. Vis. prof. U. Paris VI, 1973. Assoc. editor: Jour. Biomech. Engring., 1993-97; mem. editorial bd. Circulation Rsch., 1975-82. Pres. St. Louis-Lyon Sister Cities, Inc., 2000—. Fulbright fellow Paris, 1955; recipient Nat. Marconi Sci. award UNICO, 1999. Fellow ASME, Am. Inst. of Med and Biol. Engring. (founding); mem. Biomed. Engring. Soc. (bd. dirs. 1997-2000), Internat. Soc. Biorheology, N.Am. Soc. Biorheology (pres.-elect 1986-89, pres. 1989-90), Am. Soc. Artificial Internal Organs, Am. Soc. Engring. Edn., AAAS (Lindbergh award St. Louis sect. 1988), AIAA, European Acad. Sci., Tau Beta Pi, Pi Tau Sigma. Republican. Roman Catholic. Achievements include research in fluid mechanics, heat transfer, blood flow, rheology of suspensions. Home: 830 S Meramec Ave Saint Louis MO 63105-2539 Business E-Mail: sps@wustl.edu.

SUTHERLAND, DONALD GRAY, retired lawyer; b. Houston, Jan. 19, 1929; s. Robert Gray and Elizabeth (Cunningham) S.; m. Mary Reynolds Moodey, July 23, 1955; children: Stuart Gray, Elizabeth Dana. BS, Purdue U., 1954; LLB, Ind. U., Bloomington, 1954. Bar: Ind. 1954, U.S. Dist. Ct. (so. dist.) Ind. 1954, U.S. Tax Ct. 1956, U.S. Ct. Claims 1957, U.S. Ct. Appeals (7th cir.) 1981, U.S. Ct. Appeals (3d cir.) 1984, U.S. Ct. Internat. Trade 1987, U.S. Supreme Ct. 1987. Assoc. IceMiller, Indpls., 1954-64, ptnr., 1965-98, ret., 1998. Practitioner in residence Ind. U. Sch. of Law, Bloomington, 1987; trustee, pres. Pegasus Funds, Detroit, 1992-99; trustee, chmn. bd. dirs., pres. Bison Money Market Fund., Indpls., 1982-92. Contbr. articles to numerous profl. jours. Bd. dirs., v.p. Japan-Am. Soc. of Ind., Inc., Indpls., 1988-97; bd. dirs. Conner Prairie Inc., Fishers, Ind., 1988-97, v.p., 1989-90, chmn. bd., 1990-93; tennis ceremonies 10th Pan-Am. Games, Indpls., 1987; bd. dirs. The Children's Bur. Indpls., 1962-73, v.p., 1968-70, pres., 1970-72; bd. dirs. Orchard Country Day Sch., Indpls., 1970-73, Episc. Cmty. Svcs., Indpls., 1965-73, v.p., 1968, pres., 1969; trustee United Episc. Charities, Indpls., 1970-71, pres., 1971. With USMC, 1946-48. Mem.: Nat. Jr. Tennis League of Indpls. (bd. dirs. 2003—), Econ. Club (bd. dirs. Ind. chpt. 1988—94), Contemporary Club of Indpls. (pres. 2003—04), Woodstock Club. Republican. Avocations: golf, tennis, opera. Office: Ice Miller 1 American Sq Indianapolis IN 46282-0020

SUTHERLAND, JOHN STEPHEN, lawyer; b. Ft. Scott, Kans., July 24, 1950; s. Carl Mason and Mary Jane (Harryman) S.; m. Maureen Elaine Boyle, Nov. 30, 1985; children: Ian, Ryan, Patrick. BA in History, Baker U., 1972; JD, Washburn U., 1975; AA in Data Processing, Johnson County C.C., Overland Park, Kans., 1982. Bar: Kans., Mo.; U.S. Dist. Ct. (fed. dist.) Kans., U.S. Dist. Ct. (we. dist.) Mo. Pvt. practice, Kansas City, Kans., 1975—. Office: Bank Midwest 5th & Minnesota Kansas City KS 66117-1094

SUTTER, WILLIAM PAUL, lawyer; b. Chgo., Jan. 15, 1924; s. Harry Blair and Elsie (Paul) S.; m. Helen Yvonne Stebbins, Nov. 13, 1954; children: William Paul, Helen Blair Sutter. AB, Yale U., 1947; JD, U. Mich., 1950. Bar: Ill. 1950, Fla. 1977, U.S. Supreme Ct. 1981. Assoc. Hopkins & Sutter (and predecessors), Chgo., 1950-57, ptnr., 1957-89, of counsel, 1989—2001. Mem. Ill. Supreme Ct. Atty. Registration Commn., 1975-81 Contbr. articles on estate planning and taxation to profl. jours. Chmn. Winnetka Caucus Com., 1966-67; pres., trustee Lucille P. Markey Charitable Trust, 1983-98; precinct capt. New Trier Twp. (Ill.) Rep. party, 1960-68; asst. area chmn. New Trier Rep. Orgn., 1968-72; trustee Gads Hill Center, pres., 1962-70, chmn., 1971-80; trustee Northwestern Meml. Hosp., 1983-98, life trustee, 1998—; bd. dirs. Chgo. Hort. Soc., 1982-2005, life dir., 2005—; mem. dean's coun. Sch. Medicine, Yale U., 1991-97; bd. visitors Waisman Ctr., U. Wis., 1996-2002; corr. sec. Yale U. Class of 1945, 1990—. Served to 1st lt. AUS, 1943-46 Fellow Am. Bar Found., Am. Coll. Trust and Estate Counsel (bd. regents 1977-83, exec. com. 1981-83); mem. ABA (ho. dels. 1972-81, chmn. com. on income estates and trusts, taxation sect. 1973-75), Ill. Bar Assn. (bd. govs. 1964-75, pres. 1973-74), Chgo. Bar Assn. (chmn. probate practice com. 1963-64), Am. Law Inst., Internat. Acad. Estate and Trust Law, Am. Judicature Soc., Ill. LAWPAC (pres. 1977-83), Order of Coif, Phi Beta Kappa, Phi Delta Phi, Chi Psi, Mid-Day Club, Indian Hill Club, Gulf Stream Golf Club, Country Club Fla., Ocean Club (Fla.) (bd. govs. 1993-99, sec. 1993-97, pres. 1997-99), Lawyers Club Chgo. Episcopalian. Home: 2 Par Club Cir Village Of Golf FL 33436 Personal E-mail: WPSutter@aol.com.

SUTTIE, JOHN WESTON, biochemist; b. La Crosse, Wis., Aug. 25, 1934; married; 2 children. BS, U. Wis., 1957, MS, 1958, PhD, 1960. Fellow biochemist Nat. Inst. Med. Rsch, England, 1960-61; asst. prof. to assoc. prof. biochemistry U. Wis., Madison, 1961-69, prof., 1969—2001, chair nutrition sci., 1988-97, Katherine Berns Van Donk Steenbock prof. nutrition, 2000, prof. emeritus, 2002—. Mem. Bd. on Agriculture & Natural Resources, 1996—2001, Food and Nutrition Bd., 2004—07. Assoc. editor Jour Nutrition, 1991-97; editor Jour. Nutrition, 1997-2003; asst. editor Ann. Rev. Nutrition, 2005—. Recipient Disting. Achievement in Nutrition Rsch., Bristol-Myers Squibb/Mead Johnson, 2002. Fellow Am. Heart Assn. Coun. Nutrition, Physical Activity and Metabolism, Am. Soc. for utrition (Osborne and Mendel award 1980, Mead Johns award 1974, Conrad Elvehjem award, 2004); mem. NAS, Am. Soc. Expl. Biology and Medicine, Am. Soc. Biochemistry and Molecular Biology, Internat. Soc. Thrombosis and Hemostasis (Hemostasis Career award 1989). Business E-Mail: suttie@biochem.wisc.edu.

SUTTLE, DEBORAH S., state legislator; b. Charleston, W.Va., Dec. 28, 1945; m. James H. Suttle, June 4, 1966; children: Virginia Adele, Amber Karolyn. BS, W.Va. U., 1967; postgrad., U. Nebr., Omaha, 1989-91. Former RN; mem. Nebr. Legislature from 10th dist., Lincoln, 1997—. Vol. Douglas County election commr.; mem. United Meth. Ch., Omaha, League Women Voters, 1980—, Voices for Children; former mem. Omaha 2000 Task Force, Pulling Ams. Communities Together, Omaha Pub. Sch. Supt. Adv. Com., Nebr. Partnership Com., Douglas County Corrections Adv. Com.; mem. various PTA's, Omaha, 1976-93; former pres. LWV for Greater Omaha, 1991-93, Laura Dodge Elem. Parent-Tchr. Assn., 1978-79; vol. lobbyist Omaha PTA/PTSA Coun., 1980-91, Nebr. PTA, 1986-89; v.p. Optimist Internat., 1995-96; vol. lobbyist Nebr. LWV, 1994-96; vol. lobbyist, bd. dirs. PRIDE-Omaha, 1984-96. Mem. Nebr. Nurses' Assn. Home: 6054 Country Club Oaks Pl Omaha E 68152-2009 Office: State Capitol Dist 10 PO Box 94604 Rm 1000 Lincoln NE 68509 Fax: 402-571-6901.

SUTTON, BETTY, congresswoman, lawyer; b. Barberton, Ohio, July 31, 1963; m. Doug Sutton; 2 children. BA in Polit. Sci., Kent State U., 1985; JD, U. Akron, 1990. Coun.-at-large Barberton City Coun., 1990-91; v.p. Summit County Coun., 1991-92; mem. Ohio Ho. Reps. from dist. 47, 1993—2000; atty. Faulkner, Muskovitz & Phillips LLP, 2001—06; mem. US Congress from 13th Ohio dist., 2007—, mem. rules com., budget com., 2007—. Vice chmn. Judiciary & Criminal Justice Com., mem. Civil & Comml. Law, Ways & Means, Ins. Pub. Utilities & Elec. Twp. Com. Recipient Outstanding Performance in Const. Law Fed. Bar Assn., 1989, Am. Jurisprudence award, 1989. Mem. ABA, Akron Child Guidance Adv. Coun., Assn. Trial Lawyers Am., Ohio Acad. Trial Lawyers, Summit County Trial Lawyers, Fed. Dem. Women. Democrat. Office: 1721 Longworth House Office Bldg Washington DC 20515 also: 1655 W Market St Rm 435 Akron OH 44313 Office Phone: 330-865-8450. Office Fax: 330-865-8470.

SUTTON, GREGORY PAUL, obstetrician, gynecologist; b. Tokyo, Dec. 12, 1948; (parents Am. citizens); s. Vernon S. And Vonna Lou (Streeter) S.; m. Judith Craigie Holt, June 26, 1977; children: Anne Craigie, James Streeter. BS in Chemistry with honors, Ind. U., 1970; MD, U. Mich., 1976. Diplomate Am. Bd. of Ob/Gyn. Prof. gynecol. oncology Ind. U. Sch. Medicine, Indpls., 1986-97; Mary Fendrich Hulman prof. Gynecologic Oncology Ind. U. Sch. Med., Indpls., 1997-2000; mem. staff St. Vincent Hosp. and Health Svcs., 2000—01. Cancer Clin. fellow Am. Cancer Soc., Phila., 1981-83; recipient Career Devel. award Am. Cancer Soc., 1986-89. Fellow: Am. Coll. Obstetrics and Gynecology (chair Ind. sect. 2000—03); mem.: ACS (com. on cancer, Ind. state liaison), Hoosier Oncology Group, Soc. of Gynecologic Oncologists, Bayard Carter Soc., Ind. State Med. Soc., Marion County Med. Soc., Gynecologic Oncology Group (cert. Spl. Competence in Gynecologic Oncology 1985). Avocations: swimming, bicycling, woodworking, sailing, crossword puzzles. Office: 8301 Harcourt Rd Ste 202 Indianapolis IN 46260-1453 E-mail: gsutton@stvincent.org.

SUTTON, JEFFREY S., federal judge; b. Dhahran, Saudi Arabia, 1960; BA, Williams Coll., 1983; LLB, Ohio State Univ., 1990. Clk. Second Circuit Ct. for Judge Thomas Meskill, 1990—91, Supreme Ct. for Justice Scalia and ret. Justice Powell, 1991—92; assoc. Jones, Day, Reavis & Pogue, Columbus, Ohio, 1992—95; adj. law prof. Ohio State Univ., Ohio, 1994—; Solicitor Ohio State, Ohio, 1995—98; ptnr. Jones, Day, Reavis & Pogue, Columbus, Ohio, 1998—2003; judge US Ct. Appeals, (6th cir.), Cin., 2003—. Office: Office Clerk US Ct Appeals 6th Cir 532 Potter Stewart US Cthse 100 E 5th St Cincinnati OH 45202-3988

SUTTON, LYNN SORENSEN, librarian; b. Detroit, July 31, 1953; d. Leonard Arthur Edward and Dorothy Ann (Steele) Sorensen. AB, U. Mich., 1975, MLS, 1976. Dir. Med. Libr. South Chgo. Cmty. Hosp., 1976-77; corp. dirs. librs. Detroit-Macomb Hosp. Corp., Detroit, 1977-86; dir. librs. Harper Hosp., Detroit, 1987-88; dir. Sci. and Engring. Libr. Wayne State U., Detroit, 1989-95, dir. undergrad. libr., 1996—2004; dir. Z. Smith Reynolds Libr. Wake Forest U., Winston-Salem, NC, 2004—. Cons. Catherine McAuley Health Sys., Ann Arbor, Mich., 1993. Contbr. articles to profl. jours. Mem. ALA, Assn. Coll. and Rsch. Librs. (budget and fin. com. 1995—), Mich. Health Scis. Librs. Assn. (pres. 1987-88), Met. Detroit Med. Libr. Group (pres. 1983-84), Phi Beta Kappa, Beta Phi Mu. Office: Z Smith Reynolds Libr Wake Forest U Box 7777 Reynolda Station Winston Salem NC 27109 Office Phone: 336-758-5090. Business E-Mail: suttonls@wfu.edu.

SUTTON, RAY SANDY, lawyer, food products executive; b. Springfield, Mo., Sept. 4, 1937; AB, S.W. Mo. State U., 1959; postgrad., U. Mo., 1959-60; JD, Washburn U., 1966; grad., U.S. Command/Gen. Staff Coll., 1975. With Ross, Wells & Barnett, Kansas City, Brenner, Lockwood & O'Neal, Kansas City, J.F. Pritchard Co., Kansas City; legal asst. Interstate Brands, 1971-76, legal dir., 1976-77, v.p., gen. counsel, 1977-85; v.p. parent co. Interstate Bakeries Corp., Kansas City, Mo., 1979—, corp. sec., 1985—. Col. AUSR, 1960-62; ret. Mem. ABA, Am. Corp. Counsel Assn., Am. Soc. Corp. Secs., Kans. City Met. Bar Assn., Mo. Bar Assn., Lawyers Assn. Kansas City-Mo., Res. Officers Assn., Masons, Phi Alpha Delta. Office: 12 E Armour Blvd Kansas City MO 64111-1202

SUZUKI, HIDETARO, violinist; b. Tokyo, June 1, 1937; arrived in U.S., 1956; s. Hidezo and Humi (Sakai) S.; m. Zeyda Ruga, May 16, 1962; children: Kenneth Hideo, antel Hiroshi, Elina Humi. Diploma, Toho Sch. Music, Tokyo, 1956, Curtis Inst. Music, 1963. Prof. violin Conservatory Province Que., Canada, 1963-79, Laval U., Quebec, Canada, 1971-77, Butler U., Indpls., 1979—. Concertmaster Que. Symphony Orch., 1963-78, Indpls. Symphony Orch., 1978-2005; performed as concert violinist Can., U.S., Ea. and Western Europe, Cuba, Japan, S.E. Asia, India, USSR 1951-; guest condr. orchs. in numerous concerts, broadcasts, 1968—; mem. jury Mont. Internat. Competition, 1979, Internat. Violin Competition, 1979, jury for Internat. Violin Competition of Indpls., 1982, 86, 90, 94; artistic dir. Suzuki and Friends chamber music series, 1980-, founder Pro Musica Washington, 2007-; rec. artist (CDs, violin and piano) Dialogue, Dialogue II, Pas de deux.

SUZUKI, TSUNEO, molecular immunologist; b. Nagoya, Aichi, Japan, Nov. 23, 1931; s. Morichika and Toshiko (Kita) S.; widowed; children: Riichiro, Aijiro, Yozo. BS, U. Tokyo, 1953, MD, 1957; PhD, U. Hokkaido, 1967. Asst. prof. U. Kans. Med. Ctr., Kansas City, 1970-79, assoc. prof., 1979-83, prof., 1983—2003, prof. emeritus, 2003—, interim chair, 1994-98. Mem. NIH Study Sect., Washington, 1983-87. Contbr. articles to profl. jours. Fellow U. Wis., 1963-66, 69-70, U. Lausanne, Switzerland, 1966-67, U Toronto, 1967-69; recipient Travel award Fulbright Found., 1962, Sr. Investigator award U. Kans. Med. Ctr., 1990. Mem. Am. Assn. Immunologists, Am. Soc. Biological Chemists (Travel award 1988). Home: 3620 W 73rd St Prairie Village KS 66208-2903 Office: U Kans Med Ctr/Dept Microbiology 3901 Rainbow Blvd Rm 3001 Orr Major Kansas City KS 66160-0001 E-mail: tsuzuki@kumc.edu.

SVÄRD, N. TRYGVE, electrical engineer; b. Gothenburg, Sweden; came to U.S., 1973; s. Owe V. and Berit S. (Heden) S.; children: Michael, Stefan. BEE, Gothenburg U., Sweden, 1966. Registered profl. engr. Engr. Volvo Car Div., Gothenburg, 1969-73; from project engr., sr. sect. engr. to program mgr. Honeywell Inc., Mpls., 1973-90; sr. program mgr., internat. programs Alliant Techsystems, Inc., Mpls., 1990-99; ret., 1999. Pres. Nord Mark Inc., Mpls., 1986—; pres., mktg. dir. Ekelund Textiles, 2002—. Sgt. Swedish Coast Arty., 1967-68. Mem. Am. Swedish Inst. Republican. Home and Office: 12075 48th Ave N Minneapolis MN 55442-2129 Personal E-mail: trygves@aol.com.

SVEDJAN, KEN, state legislator; m. Lorretta; 1 child. BS, MS, U. N.D. Mem. from dist. 17 N.D. Ho. of Reps., 1991—; pres. Altru Health Found. Pres. United Health Found.; chmn. bd. Third St. Clinic. With U.S. Army, 1968-70. Recipient Disting. Svc. award Am. Diabetes Assn. Mem. Rotary Internat. (bd. dirs.), Grand Forks C. of C., Elks. Republican. Home: 4697 Harvest Cir Grand Forks ND 58201-3502 Office: ND House of Reps State Capitol Bismarck ND 58505

SVEEN, GERALD O., state legislator; m. Ruth Ellen; 3 children. Student, U. N.D., Temple U. Retired dentist; mayor Bottineau, 12 yrs.; mem. N.D. Ho. of Reps., 1993—, mem. edn., transp. coms. Pres. Internat. Peace Garden. With USAF, WWII and Korea. Recipient Cmty. Svc. award. Mem. Am. Legion, Lions, Oak Creek Cemetery Assn. (pres.). Republican. Presbyterian. Office: ND House of Reps State Capitol Bismarck ND 58505 Home: 6624 Viking Ct NE Bemidji MN 56601-7092 E-mail: gsveen@state.nd.us.

SVETLOVA, MARINA, ballerina, retired choreographer; b. Paris, May 3, 1922; arrived in U.S., 1940; d. Max and Tamara (Andreieff) Hartman. Studied with Vera Trefilova, Paris, 1930-36, studied with L. Egorova and M. Kschessinska, 1936-39; studied with A. Vilzak, NYC, 1940-57; D (hon.), Fedn. Francaise de Danse, 1988. Ballet dir. So. Vt. Art Ctr., 1959-64; dir. Svetlova Dance Ctr., Dorset, Vt., 1965-95; prof. ballet dept. Ind. U., Bloomington, 1969-92, prof. emeritus, 1992—, chmn. dept., 1969-78. Choreographer Dallas Civic Opera, 1964—67, (ballets) Ft. Worth Opera, 1967—83, San Antonio Opera, 1983, Seattle Opera, Houston Opera, Kansas City Performing Arts Found., The Fairy Queen, 1966, L'Histoire du Soidat, 1968, ballerina Ballet Russe de Monte Carlo, 1939—41, guest ballerina Ballet Theatre, 1942, London's Festival Ballet, Teatro dell Opera, Rome, Nat. Opera Stockholm, Suomi Opera, Helsinki, Finland, Het Nederland Ballet, Holland, Cork Irish Ballet, Paris Opera Comique, London Palladium, Teatro Colon, Buenos Aires, others, prima ballerina Met. Opera, 1943—50, N.Y.C. Opera, 1950—52; performer: (ballets) Graduation Ball; contbr. articles to profl. jours. Mem.: Nat. Soc. Arts and Letters (nat. dance chmn.), Conf. Ballet in Higher Edn., Am. Guild Mus. Artists (bd. dirs.). Office: 2100 E Maxwell Ln Bloomington IN 47401-6119 Office Phone: 812-330-0567.

SVIGGUM, STEVEN ARTHUR, farmer, state representative; b. Minn., Sept. 15, 1951; m. Debra Beegh; children: Hans, Erik, Marit. BA in Math., St. Olaf Coll., 1973. Tchr. math., coach Belgrade (Minn.) High Sch., 1973-77, West Concord (Minn.) High Sch., 1977-78; farmer, 1973—; state rep. State of Minn., 1992—, speaker of the ho., 1999—. Bd. dirs. Riverview Manor, Inc., Wanamingo, Minn.; Rep. caucus leader Minn. Ho. of Reps., St. Paul, 1992—. Recipient Hutchinson award Am. Assn. for Mentally Retarded, 1991, Recognition of Disting. Svc. award Minn. Assn. Rehab. Facilities and Minn. Devel. Achievement Ctr. Assn., 1991, Champion of Small Bus. award Nat. Fedn. Ind. Bus. Minn., 1991; named Legislator of Yr., Assn. Retarded Citizens, 1986. Mem. Kenyon (Minn.) Lions, Kenyon Sportsmen's Club. Lutheran. Avocations: baseball, basketball, coaching. Home: 42490 60th Ave Kenyon MN 55946-3224 Office: 463 State Office Bldg Saint Paul MN 55155-0001 E-mail: rep.steve.sviggum@house.leg.state.mn.us.

SWAIMAN, KENNETH FRED, pediatric neurologist, educator; b. St. Paul, Nov. 19, 1931; s. Lester J. and Shirley (Ryan) S.; m. Phyllis Kammerman Sher, Oct. 1985; children: Lisa, Jerrold, Barbara, Dana. BA magna cum laude, U. Minn., 1952, BS, 1953, MD, 1955; postgrad., 1956-58. Diplomate Am. Bd. Psychiatry and Neurology, Am. Bd. Pediatrics, Am. Bd. Psychiatry and Neurology with Spl. Competence in Child Neurology. Intern Mpls. Gen. Hosp., 1955-56; resident in pediatrics, fellow in pediatrics to chief resident U. Minn. Hosp., 1956-58, spl. fellow in pediatric neurology, 1960-63, dir. pediatric neurology tng. program, 1968-94, various to interim head dept. neurology, 1994-96; chief pediatrics U.S. Army Hosp., Ft. McPherson, Ga., 1958-60; asst. prof. pediatrics, neurology U. Minn. Med. Sch., Mpls., 1963-66, prof., dir. pediatric neurology, 1969-96, mem. internship adv. coun. exec. faculty, 1966-70, interim head dept. neurology, 1994-96; postgrad. fellow pediatric neurology Nat. Inst. Neurologic Diseases and Blindness, 1960-63, assoc. prof., 1966-69. Cons. pediatric neurology Hennepin County Gen. Hosp., 1963—, Mpls., St. Paul-Ramsey Hosp., St. Paul Children's Hosp., Mpls. Children's Hosp.; vis. prof. numerous univs. including Loyola U., 1982, U. N.Mex., 1982, U. Ind. Med. Sch., 1983, U. Kyushu, Shiga, Nagoya, Tokyo, 1985, Driscoll Children's Hosp., Corpus Christi, Tex., 1986, Inst. Nacional de Pediatria, Mexico City, 1986, U. de Concepion, Chile, 1989, Beijing U. Med. Sch., 1989, Xian Med. U., China, 1989, Children's Hosp. of Mich., Detroit, 1990, Hong Kong Child Neurology Soc., 1995, Tartu, Estonia, 1997, Krem, Austria, 1997, Santiago, Chile, 1997, Kaunas, Lithuania, 1998, ICNA Ednl. Seminar, Tartu, 1998, Montevideo, Uruguay, 1999, others; lectr. in field; guest worker NIH, NICHD, Bethesda, Md., 1978-79, 79-81. Author: (with Francis S. Wright) Neuromuscular Diseases in Infancy and Childhood, 1969, Pediatric Neuromuscular Diseases, 1979, (with Stephen Ashwal) Pediatric Neurology Case Studies, 1978, 2d edit., 1984, Pediatric Neurology: Principles and Practice, 1989, 4th edit., 2006; editor: (with John A. Anderson) Phenylketonuria and Allied Metabolic Diseases, 1966, (with Francis S. Wright) Practice Pediatric Neurology, 1975, 2d edit., 1982, Pediatric eurology: Principles and Practice, 4th edit., 2006; mem. editl. bd. Annals of Neurology, 1977-83, Neurology Update, 1977-82, Pediatric Update, 1977-85, Brain and Devel. (Jour. Japanese Soc. Child Neurology), 1980—, Neuropediatrics (Stuttgart), 1982-92; editor-in-chief: Pediatric Neurology, 1984—; contbr. articles to sci. jours. Chmn. Minn. Gov.'s Bd. for Handicapped, Exceptional and Gifted Children, 1972-76; mem. human devel. study sect. NIH, 1976-79, guest worker, 1978-81. Served to capt. M.C. U.S. Army, 1958-60. Fellow Am. Acad. Pediatrics, Am. Acad. Neurology (rep. to nat. coun. Nat. Soc. Med. Rsch., A.B. Baker Neurol. Edn. Lifetime Achievement award 2005); mem. Soc. Pediatric Rsch., Ctrl. Soc. Clin. Rsch., Ctrl. Soc. Neurol. Rsch., Internat. Soc. eurochemistry, Am. Neurol. Assn., Minn. Neurol. Soc., AAAS, Midwest Pediatric Soc., Am. Soc. Neurochemistry, Child Neurology Soc. (1st pres. 1972-73, Hower award 1981, Founder's award 1996, chmn. internat. affairs com., 1991-96, mem. long range planning com. 1991-97, chmn. fin. com. 1995—), Internat. Assn. Child Neurologists (exec. com. 1975-79, chmn. global edn. com. 1996-99), Profs. of Child Neurology (1st pres. 1978-80, mem. nominating com. 1986-92), Japanese Child Neurology Soc. (Segawa award 1986, mem. nominating com. 1986-92, chair internat. affairs com. 1991—, mem. long range planning com. 1991-98), Soc. de Psiquiatria y Neurologia de la Infancia y Adolescencia, Internat. Child Neurology Assn. (chair internat. edn. com. 1996-99), Lithuanian Child Neurology Soc. (hon., mem. 2000—), Child Neurology Found. (pres. 2000-03), Phi Beta Kappa, Sigma Xi. Office: U Minn Med Sch Dept Pediatric Neurology 1821 University Ave W Saint Paul MN 55104-2801 also: UMHC Box 486 420 Delaware St SE Minneapolis MN 55455-0374 E-mail: pncomm@uswet.net.

SWAIN, DENNIS MICHAEL, lawyer; b. Jackson, Mich., June 15, 1948; s. Donald Elliot and Rose Therese (Flynn) S.; m. Jacque Lee Wallace, Mar. 20, 1971; 1 child, Jason Patrick. BA, Mich. State U., 1974; JD, Thomas M. Cooley Law Sch., 1978. Bar: Mich. 1979, U.S. Dist. Ct. (we. dist.) Mich. 1983. Assoc. Law Office of Zerafa P.C., Elk Rapids, Mich., 1978-81; ptnr. Gockerman & Swain, Manistee, Mich., 1981-85; pros. atty. Manistee County, 1985—. Instr. West Shore Community Coll., Scottville, Mich., 1985—, bd. dirs. law enforcement adv. bd.; bd. chmn. Region 10 Detectives, Manistee, 1985—. Fellow Mich. Bar Found.; mem. ABA, Mich. Bar Assn. (rep. state assembly 1983—), Manistee County Bar Assn. (pres. 1985-86), Assn. Trial Lawyers Am., Pros. Attys. Assn. of Mich., at. Dist. Attys. Assn. Lodges: Elks. Republican. Episcopalian. Avocations: hunting, fishing, skiing, shooting. Office: Manistee County Prosecutor 402 Maple St Manistee MI 49660-1617 Home: 71 Oak St Manistee MI 49660-1516

SWAIN, PAUL JOSEPH, bishop; b. Newark, NY, Sept. 12, 1943; s. William and Gertrude (Mohr) Swain. BA, Ohio Northern U., 1965; MA in Polit. Sci., U. Wis., 1967, JD, 1974; MDiv, Blessed John XXIII Nat. Sem., Weston, Mass., 1988. Ordained priest Diocese of Madison, Wis., 1988; ordained bishop, 2006; bishop Diocese of Sioux Falls, SD, 2006—. Pvt. practice, Madison, Wis., 1974—79; legal counsel, dir. policy Gov. Lee Sherman Dreyfus, Wis., 1979—83. Intelligence officer USAF, 1967—72, Vietnam. Decorated Bronze star. Mem.: Knights of Columbus (chaplain U. Wis. coun.), Equestrian Order of the Holy Sepulchre of Jerusalem. Roman Catholic. Office: Cath Diocese of Sioux Falls 523 N Duluth Ave Sioux Falls SD 57104 Office Phone: 605-334-9861. Office Fax: 605-334-2092.*

SWAN, BARBARA J., lawyer, utilities executive; BA in History, Macalester Coll., St. Paul, 1973; JD, William Mitchell Coll. of Law, St. Paul, 1979. Atty. Axley Brynelson Law Firm, 1981—87; assoc. gen. counsel Wis. Power and Light (subs. Alliant Energy), 1987—93, gen. counsel, 1993—94, v.p., gen. counsel, 1994—98, pres., 2004—; exec. v.p., gen. counsel Alliant Energy, 1998—. Mem. Edison Electric Inst. Gen. Counsel Com. Bd. mem. Nat. Assn. Mfrs., 2001—07; pres. Alliant Energy Found., 2004—; bd. mem. Forward Wisconsin, Madison Symphony Orch., 2004—, Greater Madison C. of C., 2005—, Am. Players Theater, 2007—, Arcadian networks Advisory Bd., 2008—. Office: Alliant Energy PO Box 77007 4902 N Biltmore Ln Madison WI 53707-1007 Office Phone: 608-458-3431. E-mail: barbaraswan@alliantenergy.com.

SWAN, SCOTT, newscaster; m. Janae Swan; 3 children. Degree in Broadcast Journalism, Pepperdine U., 1985. With Sta. KITV-TV, Honolulu, Sta. KESQ-TV, Palm Springs, Calif., Sta. KHJ-TV, LA, Disneyland Broadcast Svcs.; anchor, reporter Sta. WISH-TV, Indpls., 1996—2000, Sta. KTVX-TV, Salt Lake City, 2000—02; anchor Sta. WTHR-TV, Indpls., 2002—. Office: WTHR-TV 1000 N Meridian St Indianapolis IN 46204

SWANEY, THOMAS EDWARD, lawyer; b. Detroit, Apr. 25, 1942; s. Robert Ernest and Mary Alice (Slinger) S.; m. Patricia Louise Nash, Sept. 9, 1967; children: Julia Bay, Mary Elizabeth, David Paul. AB, U. Mich., 1963, JD, 1967; postdoctoral, London Sch. Econs., 1967-68. Bar: Ill. 1968. From assoc. to ptnr. Sidley & Austin, Chgo., 1968—. Bd. dirs. Corey Steel Co., Cicero, Ill., Gertrude B. Nielsen Child Care & Learning Ctr., Northbrook, Ill., Ward C. Rogers Found., Chgo., Working in Schs., Chgo., Ill. Trustee H. Earl Hoover Found., Glencoe, Ill., 1986—, RF Found., Chgo., 1992—; trustee, bd. pres. 1st Presbyn. Ch., Evanston, Ill., 1984-87, 96-98; bd. dirs. Lakeland Conservancy, Minocqua, Wis., 1987—; vol. sch. dists., Chgo., 2000—. Mem. ABA, Chgo. Bar Assn., Legal Club Chgo.

SWANSON, ALFRED BERTIL, orthopaedic and hand surgeon, educator; b. Kenosha, Wis, Apr. 16, 1923; s. O.P. and Esther (Person) S.; children: Karin Louise, Miles Raymond; m. Genevieve de Groot, MD, Dec. 27, 1969; 1 son, Eric Alfred. BS, U. Ill., 1944, MD, 1947. Diplomate: Am. Bd. Orthop. Surgery. Intern St. Luke's Hosp., Chgo., 1947; spl. tng. orthop. surgery Ill. Crippled Children's Hosp. Sch., Chgo., 1948, St. Luke's Hosp., 1949, Northwestern U. Med. Sch., 1950, Ind. U. Med. Ctr., 1951; practice medicine specializing in orthopaedic/hand surgery Grand Rapids, Mich., 1954—2001; chief hand surgery fellowship, orthopaedic research dir. Blodgett Meml. Hosp.-Spectrum Health East, 1962—; dir. emeritus Grand Rapids Orthopaedic Surgery Residency Tng. Program. Chief of staff Mary Free Bed Children's Hosp. and Orthop. Ctr., Juvenile Amputee Clin., 1963-65, 67-68, 73-78; prof. surgery Mich. State U., Lansing; chmn. Grand Rapids Internat. Symposium on Implant Arthrophasty, 1970-92; nat. and internat. lectr. in field. Author: Implant Resection Arthroplasty in the Hand and Extremities, 1973; Contbr. numerous sci. articles and exhibits in field; producer teaching films. Served with USNR, 1944-45; served to capt. M.C. AUS, 1952-54. Decorated medal of Honor So. Vietnam, 1967; recipient Profl. Medicine award Mich. Internat. Council, 1977; recipient Resolution of Tribute State of Mich., 1986, Order of Merit Orthop. Rsch. Soc., 1982, 89, 91, Disting. Svc. in Health Care award Hosp. Council West Mich., 1984, Nat. Vol. Svc. Citation Arthritis Found., 1984, U. Ill. Alumni Achievement award, 1985, Orthop. Overseas Spl. award for personal svc. and recruitment of orthop. and hand surgery vols. for So. Vietnam and Peru, Disting. Svc. award Arthritis Found., 1990, Cert. of Appreciation, Lifetime Sci. Achievement Award, Nat. Arthritis Found., 2003; Op. Desert Storm, US Dept. VA, 1991; named prof. h.c. Orthop. Alumni of Shriners Hosp. Crippled Children Mexico City; named to Grand Rapids Hall of Fame, 2001. Fellow ACS; mem. Am. Med. Writers Assn., AMA (Disting. Svc. award 1966, 69, Sci. Achievement award 1996), Am. Acad. Orthop. Surgeons (Kappa Delta award 1982), Pan Am. Med. Assn., Pan Pacific Surg. Assn., Assn. Mil. Surgeons, Am. Acad. Cerebral Palsy, Brit. Club Surgery of Hand, Italian Soc. Surgery of Hand, Brazilian, Colombian, South African, Japanese, Argentinian, So. Am., Caribbean Hand soc., Internat. Fedn. Soc. Surgery Hand (sec.-gen. 1978-83, pres. 1983-89, hist. 1989—, Pioneer in Hand Surgery award 1995), Groupe d'Etude de la Main, Am. Assn. Hand Surgeons, Am. Soc. Surgery Hand (pres. 1979-80), Am., Clin., Mich., Lamplighter's orthop. soc., Am. Orthop. Assn., Am. Orthop. Foot Soc., Am. Soc. Plastic and Reconstructive Surgeons, Peruvian Soc. Plastic and Reconstructive Surgeons, Mich. Med. Soc. (Disting. Service award 1966, Nat. Pres. award 1979, 84, Cmty. Svc. award 1993), Assn. Orthop. Chmn., European Rheumatoid Arthritis Surg. Soc., Norwegian Soc. Rheumatoid Surgery, Ga. Orthop. Soc., Fla. Orthop. Soc., Ark. Orthopaedic Soc., Orthop. Letters Club, Brazilian, Latin Am., Chilean, Columbian, Internat., Argentinian, Peruvian, Belgian, Turkish soc. Orthop. Surgery and Traumatology, Internat. Soc. Rehab. Disabled, Rheumatoid Arthritis Surg. Soc., Soc. Am. Inventors, Soc. Biomaterials, Internat. coll. Surgeons, Internat. Soc. Orthop. and Traumatology Rsch., Internat. Soc. Prosthetics and Orthotics Alternative Methods Internat. Stability (founder, chmn. 1983—), Internat. Trees Corps (founder, chmn. 1983—), Airplane Owners and Pilots Assn., World Affairs Coun. Western Mich. (chmn. numerous coms.), Cascade Hills Country Club (Grand Rapids), Rotary Internat. (Paul Harris award), many others. Congregationalist. Achievements include inventing implants for replacement arthritic joints. Office: Spectrum Health Blodgett Campus 1840 Wealthy St SE MC-504 Grand Rapids MI 49506-2969

SWANSON, DAVID P., lawyer; b. 1955; BA, St. Cloud State U., 1978; JD, Vanderbilt U., 1981. Bar: Ill. 1981, Minn. 1983. Ptnr., co-chair, project devel., fin. group Dorsey & Whitney LLP, Mpls., and chair, agribus., coop. law. Dir. North Country Devel. Fund, Ralph K. Morris Found. Recipient Honored Cooperator award, at. Coop. Bus. Assn. Mem.: Nat. Soc. of Accountants for Cooperatives, Nat. Coop. Bus. Assn. Office: Dorsey & Whitney LLP Ste 1500 50 S Sixth St Minneapolis MN 55402-1498 Office Phone: 612-343-8275. Office Fax: 612-340-7800. Business E-Mail: swanson.dave@dorsey.com.

SWANSON, DON RICHARD, university dean; b. LA, Oct. 10, 1924; s. Harry Windfield and Grace Clara (Sandstrom) S.; m. Patricia Elizabeth Klick, Aug. 22, 1976; children— Douglas Alan, Richard Brian, Judith Ann. BS, Calif. Inst. Tech., 1945; MA, Rice U., 1947; PhD, U. Calif., Berkeley, 1952. Physicist U. Calif. Radiation Lab., Berkeley, 1947-52, Hughes Research and devel. Labs., Culver City, Calif., 1952-55; research scientist TRW, Inc., Canoga Park, Calif., 1955-63; prof. Grad. Library Sch., U. Chgo., 1963-92, dean, 1963-72, 77-79, 86-90, prof. bio-sci. coll. divsn. and divsn. humanities, 1992-96, prof. emeritus, 1996—. Mem. Sci. Info. Council, NSF, 1960-65; mem. toxicology info. panel Pres.'s Sci. Advisory Com., 1964-66; mem. library vis. com. Mass. Inst. Tech., 1966-71; mem. com. on sci. and tech. communication Nat. Acad. Scis., 1966-69 Editor: The Intellectual Founds. of Library Education, 1965, The Role of Libraries in the Growth of Knowledge, 1980; co-editor: Operations Research: Implications for Libraries, 1972, Management Education: Implications for Libraries and Library Schools, 1974; mem. editorial bd.: Library Quarterly, 1963-93; contbr.: chpt. to Ency. Brit, 1968—; sci. articles to profl. jours. Trustee Nat. Opinion Research Center, 1964-73; Research fellow Chgo. Inst. for Psychoanalysis, 1972-76. Served with USNR, 1943-46. Recipient Award of Merit Am. Soc. for Info. Sci. and Tech., 2000. Mem.: Am. Soc. for Info. Sci. Home: 5468 S Ingleside Ave Chicago IL 60615-5062 Office: U Chgo Divsn Humanities 1010 E 59th St Chicago IL 60637-1512 Business E-Mail: d-swanson@uchicago.edu.

SWANSON, DONALD FREDERICK, retired food company executive; b. Mpls., Aug. 6, 1927; s. Clayton A. and Irma (Baiocchi) S.; m. Virginia Clare Hannah, Dec. 17, 1948; children— Donald Frederick, Cynthia Hannah, Janet Clare Webster. BA, U. Minn., 1948. With Gen. Mills, Inc., 1949-85, div. v.p., dir. marketing flour, dessert and baking mixes, 1964-65, v.p., gen. mgr. grocery products div., 1965-68, v.p., corporate adminstrn. officer consumer foods group, fashion div., transp. and purchasing depts., advt. and marketing services, 1969, exec. v.p. craft, game and toy group, fashion group, direct marketing group, travel group, dir., 1968-76, sr. exec. v.p. consumer non-foods, 1976-85, chief financial officer, 1977-79, sr. exec. v.p. restaurants and consumer non-foods, 1980-81, vice chmn. restaurants and consumer non-foods, 1981-85. Ret. chmn. bd. Soo Line Corp. Served with AUS, 1946-47. Mem. Mpls. Club, Wayzata Country Club, Royal Poinciana Golf Club, Phi Kappa Psi. Home: 2171 Gulf Shore Blvd N Apt 504 Naples FL 34102-4685

SWANSON, LORI A., state attorney general, lawyer; b. Dec. 16, 1966; m. Gary Swanson. BA in Journalism and Polit. Sci. with distinction, U. Wis., Madison, 1989; JD magna cum laude, William Mitchell Coll. Law, St. Paul, 1995. Atty. Hatch, Eiden & Pihlstrom, Mpls., 1995—99; dep. atty. gen. State of Minn., St. Paul, 1999—2002, solicitor gen., 2003—06, atty. gen., 2007—. Chair consumer adv. coun. Fed. Res. Bd. Govs., Washington, 2004—. Democrat. Office: Office of Atty Gen 1400 Bremer Tower 445 Minnesota St Saint Paul MN 55101 Office Phone: 651-296-3353.

SWANSON, PATRICIA KLICK, retired academic administrator, retired foundation administrator; b. St. Louis, May 8, 1940; d. Emil Louis and Patricia (McNair) Klick; 1 child, Ivan Clatanoff. BS in Edn., U. Mo., 1962; postgrad., Cornell U., 1963; MLS, Simmons Coll., 1967. Reference librarian Simmons Coll., Boston, 1967-68, U. Chgo., 1970-79, sr. lectr. Grad. Library Sch., 1974-83, 86-88, head reference service, 1979-83, asst. dir. for sci. libraries, 1983-93, acting asst. dir. for tech. svcs., 1987-88, assoc. provost, 1993-98; program officer MacArthur Found., 1999—2005; ret., 2005. Project dir. Office Mgmt. Svcs., Assn. Rsch. Librs., 1982-83; speaker in field; cons. on libr. mgmt., planning and space. Author: Great is the Gift that Bringeth Knowledge: Highlights from the History of the John Crerar Library, 1989; contbr. articles to profl. jours. Program officer MacArthur Found., 1999—2001.

SWANSON, WAYNE HAROLD, lawyer; b. Aitkin, Minn., May 6, 1943; s. Edwin and Alma (Sundholm) Swanson; m. Joanne Maxine Case, June 22, 1968; children: Tamara K., Scott E. BA, U. Minn., 1967; JD, William Mitchell Coll. Law, St. Paul, 1974. Bar: Minn. 1974, U.S. Dist. Ct. Minn. 1983. County atty. Polk County, Crookston, Minn., 1979—2002; pvt. practice Crookston, 1976—. Mem.: ABA, Riverview Hosp. Assn., 14th Dist. Bar Assn., Minn. State Bar Assn., Crookston C. of C., Crookston Gun Club (officer), Lions, Eagles. Lutheran. Home: 23544 265th St SW Crookston MN 56716-9127 Office: 213R N Broadway Crookston MN 56716-0555 Home Phone: 218-281-5922; Office Phone: 218-281-4343. Business E-Mail: lawfirm@wayneswanson.com.

SWANSTROM, THOMAS EVAN, economist; b. Green Bay, Wis., May 17, 1939; s. Alfred Enoch and Elizabeth Nan (Thomas) S.; m. Nancy Anne Roche; children: Amy, Scott. Student, U. Notre Dame, 1957-59; BA, U. Wis., 1962, MA, 1963; postgrad., Am. U., 1963-66. Economist, U.S. Bur. Labor Statistics, Washington, 1963-66. Dir. rsch/ Population Ref. Bur., Washington, 1966-68; economist Sears, Roebuck & Co., Chgo., 1968-70, market analyst, 1970-72, mgr. catalog rsch., 1972-75, asst. mgr. econ. rsch., 1974-80, chief economist, 1980-90; pres. Consumer Econs., Chgo., 1991—; mem. bus. rsch. adv. coun. Bur. Labor Stats. Contbr. articles to industry publs. Mem. Conf. Bus. Economists, The Caxton Club, The Literary Club. Home Phone: 312-315-7829. Personal E-mail: tevanswan@aol.com.

SWANTON, VIRGINIA LEE, writer, publisher; b. Oak Park, Ill., Feb. 6, 1933; d. Milton Wesley and Eleanor Louise (Linnell) Swanton. BA, Lake Forest Coll., Ill., 1954; MA in English Lit., Northwestern U., 1955; cert. in acctg., Coll. of Lake County, Ill., 1984. Editorial asst. Publs. Office, Northwestern U., Evanston, Ill., 1955-58; reporter Lake Forester, Lake Forest, 1959; editor Scott, Foresman & Co., Glenview, Ill., 1959-84; copy editor, travel coord. McDougal Littell/Houghton Mifflin, Evanston, 1985-94; sr. bookseller B. Dalton Bookseller, Lake Forest, Ill., 1985—2004; author, pub. poetry books, reference works Gold Star Publ. Svcs., Lake Forest, 1994—. Contbr. articles to profl. jours. Former sec. bd. dirs., newsletter editor Career Resource Ctr., Inc., Lake Forest; vol. Lake Forest/Lake Bluff Sr. Ctr.; mem. bd. deacons First Presbyn. Ch. Lake Forest. Mem.: Lake Forest/Lake Bluff Hist. Soc. (vol.), Chgo. Women in Pub. Presbyterian. Avocation: gardening. Office: Gold Star Publ Svcs PO Box 125 Lake Forest IL 60045-1333

SWARTZ, B. K., JR., (BENJAMIN KINSELL SWARTZ JR.), archaeologist, educator; b. LA, June 23, 1931; s. Benjamin Kinsell and Maxine Marietta (Pearce) S.; m. Cyrilla Casillas, Oct. 23, 1966; children: Benjamin Kinsell III, Frank Casillas. AA summa cum laude, L.A. City Coll., 1952; BA, UCLA, 1954, MA, 1958; PhD, U. Ariz., Tucson, 1964. Curator Klamath County Mus., Oreg., 1959-61, rsch. assoc., 1961-62; asst. prof. anthropology Ball State U., Muncie, Ind., 1964-68, assoc. prof., 1968-72, prof., 1972-2001, prof. emeritus, 2001—. Vis. sr. lectr. U. Ghana, 1970-71; exch. prof. U. Yaoundé, Cameroon, 1984-85; field rschr. N.Am. and West Africa; mem. exec. bd., pres. Am. Com. to Advance the Study of Petroglyphs and Pictographs and its rep. to Internat. Fedn. Rock Art Orgns.; mem. overseas ed. bd. Rock Art Rsch.; mem. adv. bd. Am. Com. for Preservation of Archaeol. Collections. Contbr. revs. and articles to profl. jours.; author books, monographs in field, including: West African Culture Dynamics, 1980, Indiana's Prehistoric Past, 1981, Rock Art and Posterity, 1991, Procs. of 1st Internat. South African Rock Art Assn. Conf., 1991. Klamath County chmn. Oreg. Statehood Centennial, 1959. With USN, 1954-56. Fellow AAAS, Ind. Acad. Sci.; mem. Current Anthropology (assoc.), Soc. Am. Archaeology, Internat. Com. Rock Art, Sigma Xi, Lambda Alpha (nat. coun., exec. sec.). Home: 805 W Charles St Muncie IN 47305-2235 Personal E-mail: 01bkswartz@bsu.edu.

SWARTZ, DONALD EVERETT, broadcast executive; b. Mpls., Mar. 7, 1916; s. Albert L. and Sara (Shore) S.; m. Helen Gordon, Mar. 24, 1940; children: Stuart, Lawrence, Gary. Grad. high sch. Owner Ind. Film Distbrs., 1940-53, Tele-Film Assocs., 1953-57; pres., gen. mgr. KMSP-TV, Mpls., 1957-79; pres. United TV, Inc. (subs. 20th Century Fox Film Corp. until 1981); operating KMSP-TV, KTV4, Salt Lake City, KBHK-TV, San Francisco KMOL-TV, San Antonio; CEO United Television, Inc., Mpls., 1979-85; cons. KMOL-TV, 1985—; founder Tele-Video Assocs., 1985—, Tele-Video Entertainment, 1985—; owner/mgr. Donald Investment Co., 1989—. Vice pres. Twin City Broadcast Skills Bank (scholarship program), St. Paul Arts and Sci. Inst.; pres. U. Minn. Heart Hosp.; mem. Gov.'s Commn. Bicentennial; bd. dirs. Mpls. United Jewish Fund and Council; Mem. Mpls. Inst. Arts, Mpls., St. Paul chambers commerce, Minn. Orch. Assn., Citizens League. Named Minn. Pioneer Broadcaster of Yr., 1992, charter mem. Hall of Fame, Panck Mus. of Broadcasting, 2001; recipient Silver Circle award, St. Paul chpt. NATAS., 2000. Mem. Press Club (Mpls.), Advt. Standard Club (Mpls.), Hillcrest Country Club (St. Paul), Variety Club, Mission Hills Country Club (Rancho Mirage, Calif.), Oak Ridge Country Club (Mpls.), B'nai B'rith. Jewish (pres. temple). Office: Ste 224 10505 Wayzata Blvd Minnetonka MN 55305

SWARTZ, JACK, retired chamber of commerce executive; b. Nov. 24, 1932; s. John Ralph and Fern (Cave) S.; m. Nadine Ann Langlois, Aug. 4, 1956; children: Dana, Shawn, Tim, Jay. AA, Dodge City C.C., 1953; student, St. Mary of Plains Coll., 1953-55, 58; BBA, Washburn U., 1973, BA in Econs., 1974. V.p. D.C. Terminal Elevator Co., Dodge City, Kans., 1957-65; exec. v.p. Kans. Jaycees, Hutchinson, 1965-68, Kans. C. of C. and Industry, Topeka, 1968-82; pres. Nebr. C. of C. and Industry, Lincoln, 1982—2000, ret., 2000. Past chmn., bd. regents U.S. C. of C. Inst. U. Colo. With U.S. Army, 1955-57, USAR, 1961. Named Outstanding Local Pres. in State, Kans. Jaycees, 1961, Outstanding Young Man of Yr., Dodge City Jaycees, 1961, Outstanding State V.P., U.S. Jaycees, 1962, Outstanding Nat. Dir., 1963; named to Nebr. Bus. Hall of Fame, 2000, Sublette H.S. Wall of Honor, 2002. Mem. Am. Soc. Assn. Execs. (cert.), Am. C. of C. Execs. (bd. dirs., cert.), Nebr. C.of C. Execs. (sec.-treas.), Nebr. Soc. Assn. Execs. (past pres.), Nebr. Fedn. Bus. Assns. (pres. 1986-88), Nebr. Thoroughbred Breeders Assn. (past bd. dirs.), Washburn U. Alum. (past bd. dirs.), Am. Legion, Rotary. Republican. Roman Catholic. Home: 625 W Gibraltar Ln Phoenix AZ 85023-5243

SWARTZ, JAMES EDWARD, chemistry professor, educator, dean; b. Washington, June 12, 1951; s. Donald M. and Geneva R. (Henderson) S.; m. Louanne L. Curtis, June 6, 1980 (dec. 1986); m. Cynthea Mosier, Apr. 1, 1988. BS in Chemistry, Stanislaus State Coll., Turlock, Calif., 1973; PhD in Chemistry, U. Calif., Santa Cruz, 1978. Instr. U. Calif., Santa Cruz, 1978; rsch. fellow Calif. Inst. Tech., Pasadena, 1978-80; asst. prof. Grinnell (Iowa) Coll., 1980-86, assoc. prof. chemistry, 1986-93, prof., 1993—, v.p. acad. affairs, dean, 1998—. Vis. prof. U. Minn., Mpls., 1986—87; mem. adv. coun. Iowa Energy Ctr., chair, 2006—; cons.-evaluator Commn. Higher Edn., N. Cent. Assn., 1995—; bd. dirs. Am. Conf. Acad. Deans, 2000—03; mem. exec. com. Associated Colls. of the Midwest, 2003—06. Contbr. articles to profl. jours. Grantee Petroleum Rsch. Fund, 1981-83, Rsch. Corp., 1981-83, 84-86, 86-88, NSF, 1982-84, 90-93, 91-94. Mem. AAAS, Am. Chem. Soc., Iowa Acad. Scis., Am. Wind Energy Assn. Home: 1233 Summer St Grinnell IA 50112-1547 Office: Grinnell Coll Office of Dean Grinnell IA 50112-1690 Home Phone: 641-236-5204; Office Phone: 641-269-3100. Business E-Mail: swartz@grinnell.edu.

SWARTZ, THOMAS R., economist, educator; b. Phila., Aug. 31, 1937; s. Henry Jr. and Elizabeth (Thomas) S.; m. Jeanne Marie Jourdan, Aug. 12, 1961; children: Mary Butler, Karen Miller, Jennifer, Anne, Rebecca. BA, LaSalle U., 1960; MA, Ohio U., 1962; PhD, Ind. U., 1965. Asst. prof. U. Notre Dame, Ind., 1965-70, assoc. dept. chair Ind., 1968-70, assoc. prof. Ind., 1970-78, acting dir. grad. studies Ind., 1977-78, prof. econs. Ind., 1978—85, dir. program econ. policy Ind., 1982-85; resident dir. U. Notre Dame London Program, 1990-91, U. Notre Dame Austraulia Program, Fremantle, 1996. Vis. prof. U. Notre Dame London Program 1982, 85, 90-91, 2001—; fellow Inst. for Ednl. Initiatives, 1997-2005; dir. London Summer Program, 2001—; found. bd. Mich. Coll., 2004—; fiscal cons. Ind. Commn. State Tax, Indpls., 1965-68, spl. tax cons., 1971-81, City of South Bend, Ind., 1972-75; cons. in field. Co-editor: The Supply Side, 1983, Changing Face of Fiscal Federalism, 1990, Urban Finance Under Siege, 1993, Taking Sides, 11th edit., 2004, America's Working Poor, 1995; contbr. articles to profl. jours. Bd. dirs. Forever Learning Inst., South Bend, Ind., 1988-93; mem. steering com. Mayor's Housing Forum, South Bend, 1989-95; chair Com. Svcs. Block Grant, South Bend, 1985-90, Econ. Devel. Task Force, South Bend, 1985; Rsch. fellow Nat. Ctr. Urban Ethnic Affairs, 1979-85, Found. Bd. S.W. Mich. Coll. Bd., 2004-, v.p., 2005-. Rsch. fellow Nat. Ctr. Urban Ethnic Affairs, 1979-85, Found. Bd. S.W. Mich. Coll. Bd., 2004-, v.p., 2005-; recipient Danforth Assoc. award Danforth Found., 1972-86, Tchg. award Kanzajian Found., 1974, Tchg. awards Notre Dame; Rsch. grantee Mellon Found., 1998-2003. Fellow Inst. Ednl. Initiatives. Democrat. Roman Catholic. Avocations: racquetball, golf. Office: U Notre Dame Dept Econs and Policy Studies 414 Decio Hall Notre Dame IN 46556-5644 Office Phone: 574-631-7737. Business E-Mail: swartz1@nd.edu.

SWARTZBAUGH, MARC L., lawyer; b. Urbana, Ohio, Jan. 3, 1937; s. Merrill L. and Lillian K. (Hill) S.; m. Marjory Anne Emhardt, Aug. 16, 1958 (deceased May 20, 2000); children: Marc Charles, Kathleen Marie, Laura Kay. BA magna cum laude, Wittenberg Coll., 1958; LLB magna cum laude, U. Pa., 1961. Bar: Ohio 1961, U.S. Dist. Ct. (no. dist.) Ohio 1962, U.S. Claims Ct. 1991, U.S. Ct. Appeals (6th cir.) 1970, U.S. Ct. Appeals (3d cir.) 1985, U.S. Ct. Appeals (Fed. cir.) 1995, U.S. Supreme Ct. 1973. Law clk. to judge U.S. Ct. Appeals (3d cir.), Phila., 1961-62; assoc. Jones, Day, Reavis & Pogue, Cleve., 1962-69, ptnr., 1970-98; ret., 1998; cons., 1998—. Note editor U. Pa. Law Rev., 1960-61; co-author: Ohio Legal Ethics, 2001, Ohio Legal Ethics Law under the New Rules, 2006; contr. articles to profl. jours. Co-chmn. Suburban Citizens for Open

Housing, Shaker Heights, Ohio, 1966; v.p. Lomond Assn., Shaker Heights, 1965-68; trustee The Dance Ctr., Cleve., 1980-83; amb. People to People Internat., 1986; chmn. legal divsn. Cleve. campaign United Negro Coll. Fund, 1989-96; tutor Cleve. Reads, 2003; endower of keyboard instruments chair, Cleve. Orch., 2004. Mem. ABA (litigation sect., sr. lawyers divsn.), Fed. Bar Assn., Ohio Bar Assn., Cleve. Bar Assn., Rowfant Club, Order of Coif, Beta Theta Pi. Democrat. Avocations: poetry, painting, music, photography, book collecting. Office: Jones Day N Point 901 Lakeside Ave E Cleveland OH 44114-1190

SWATOS, WILLIAM HENRY, JR., priest, sociologist; b. Paterson, NJ, Sept. 25, 1946; s. William H. Sr. and Lucille (MacNab) S.; children (by previous marriage): Giles S., Eric B.; m. Joanne Longstreet, Oct. 29, 2002. AB, Transylvania U., 1966; MDiv summa cum laude, Episc. Theol. Sem., Lexington, Ky., 1969; MA, U. Ky., 1969, PhD, 1973. Ordained to ministry Episcopal Ch., 1969. Mem. sociology faculty King Coll., Bristol, Tenn., 1973-80; vicar St. Mark's Episc. Ch., Silvis, Ill., 1980-94; mem. sociology faculty No. Ill. U., 1984-88; chair dept. edn. Diocese of Quincy, 1988-90, 93-96. Mem. faculty Black Hawk and Scott CC, Moline, Ill., Bettendorf, Iowa, 1988-96; adj. prof. Augustana Coll., Rock Island, Ill., 2005—; priest-in-charge Christ Ch. Limestone Twp., Ill., 2006—. Editor: Sociol. Analysis/Sociology of Religion, 1989-94, The Power of Religious Publics, 1999, The Protestant Ethic Turns 100, 2005, On the Road to Being There, 2006; editor-in-chief Encyclopedia of Religion and Society, 1998; mng. editor Interdisciplinery Jour. Rsch. on Religion, 2004—; co-author Sociology of Religion, 2nd edit., 2008; contbr. articles to profl. jours. Recipient Templeton prize in humility theology, 1996; full grantee World Soc. Found., Zurich, Switzerland, 1987, grantee NEH, 1974, 79, 85, 89, rsch. grantee Soc. for the Sci. Study of Religion, 1984-85, 91-92; Inst. Studies Religion sr. fellow Baylor U, 2004—; named Disting. Alumnus Dept. Sociology, U. Ky., Lexington, 1990. Fellow Soc. Sci. Study of Religion (program chair 2004); mem. Assn. for the Sociology of Religion (editor 1989-94, book rev. editor 1986-88, exec. coun. 1984-86, exec. officer 1996—, gen. editor Religion and the Social Order Series 2004—), Religious Rsch. Assn. (sec. 1990-91, bd. dirs. 1986-89, exec. officer 1994—). Home and Office: 618 SW 2nd Ave Galva IL 61434-1912 E-mail: bill4329@hotmail.com.

SWEARER, WILLIAM BROOKS, lawyer; b. Hays, Kans. Grad., Princeton U., 1951; law degree, U. Kans., 1955. Bar: Kans. 1955. Pvt. practice, Hutchinson, Kans., 1955—; ptnr., now counsel Martindell, Swearer & Shaffer, LLP, Hutchinson, 1955—. Mem. Kans. Bd. Discipline for Attys., 1979-92, chmn., 1987-92; mem. Kans. Commn. on Jud. Qualifications, 2003-. With U.S. Army, 1952-53, Korea. Mem. ABA (ho. of dels. 1995-2000), Am. Bar Found. (state chair 1998-2002), Kans. Bar Assn. (pres. 1992-93, various offices, mem. coms.), Kans. Assn. Sch. Attys. (pres. 1989-90), Reno County Bar Assn. Office: PO Box 1907 Hutchinson KS 67504-1907 Office Phone: 620-662-3331. Business E-Mail: wbs@martindell-law.com.

SWEENEY, JAMES RAYMOND, retired lawyer; b. Chgo., Feb. 19, 1928; s. John Francis and Mae J. (McDonald) S.; m. Rhoda W. Davis, May 15, 1987; children from previous marriage: Margaret Elizabeth, John Francis, Thomas Edward. BS, U. Notre Dame, 1950; JD, Northwestern U., 1956. Bar: Ill. 1956. With firm Schroeder, Hofgren, Brady & Wegner, Chgo., 1956-61; ptnr. Hofgren, Wegner, Allen, Stellman & McCord, Chgo., 1962-71, Coffee, Wetzel, Sweeney, Chgo., 1971-72, Coffee & Sweeney, 1972-76, Mason, Kolehmainen, Rathburn & Wyss, Chgo., 1976-82, Mann, McWilliams, 1983-86, Mann McWilliams Zummer and Sweeney, 1986—89, Lee, Mann, Smith, McWilliams & Sweeney, 1989-91, Lee, Mann, Smith, McWilliams, Sweeney & Ohlson, 1991—2002; dir. ctr. intellectual property law John Marshall Law Sch., 1998—2003; ptnr. Barnes & Thornburg, 2003—04, ret., 2004. Commr. for disbarment matters Ill. Supreme Ct., 1963-73; mem. hearing div. Atty. Registration and Discipline Commn., 1974-77, chmn. commn. 1983-90; chmn. Ctr. for Intellectual Property Law adv. bd. John Marshall Law Sch., 1997-2002. Bd. dirs., sec. Highland Park (Ill.) Hosp., 1972-79. Served as lt. (j.g.) USN, 1950-53; lt. comdr. Res. ret. Mem. ABA (coun. patent, trademark and copyright sect., sec. 1978-82), Ill. State Bar (assembly 1990-96), Chgo. Bar Assn. (sec. 1977-79), Bar Assn. 7th Cir., Intellectual Property Law Assn. Chgo., Patent Law Assn. Chgo. (pres. 1974), The Law Club, Skokie (Ill.) Country Club, Union League Club. Home Phone: 312-644-7303. Business E-Mail: jrsweeney@btlaw.com.

SWEENEY, MIKE (MICHAEL JOHN SWEENEY), professional baseball player; b. Orange, Calif., July 22, 1973; m. Shara Nettles, Nov. 9, 2002; children: Michael, McKara. Designated hitter/first baseman Kansas City Royals, 1995—. Co-founder Mike & Shara Sweeney Family Found., 1996—; spokesman Enjoy the Game; vol. Children's Mercy Hosp., Boys and Girls Club of Greater Kansas City; active Fellowship of Christian Athletes, Kansas City, Youth Front, Kansas City. Named a Good Guy in Sports, The Sporting News, 2003, 2004; named to Am. League All-Star Team, 2000—03, 2005; recipient Hutch award, 2007. Roman Catholic. Mailing: c/o Kansas City Royals Kauffman Stadium One Royal Way Kansas City MO 64129

SWEENEY, THOMAS BELL, III, retail company executive; b. Washington, 1936; Grad., Yale U., 1959. V.p. mdse. group Sears Roebuck & Co., Chgo.

SWEENEY, THOMAS LEONARD, chemical engineering educator, researcher; b. Cleve., Dec. 12, 1936; s. Patrick and Anne (Morrin) S.; m. Beverly Marie Starks, Dec. 30, 1961; children: Patrick E., Thomas J., Michael S., Kevin E. BS, Case Inst. Tech., 1958, MS, 1960, PhD, 1962; JD, Capital U., Columbus, Ohio, 1974. Bar: Ohio 1974, U.S. Supreme Ct. 1978. Registered profl. engr., Ohio. Asst. prof. then assoc. prof. chem. engring. The Ohio State U., Columbus, 1963-73, prof., 1973-94, assoc. v.p. rsch., 1982-94, acting v.p. rsch. and grad., 1989-91, emeritus prof., assoc. v.p., 1995—; pres. The Ohio State U. Research Found., Columbus, 1989-91, exec. dir., 1988-94. Mem. Ohio Hazardous Waste Facility Bd., Columbus, 1984-93; asst. v.p., dir. office rsch., prof. chem. engring. U. otre Dame, 1994—; mem. bd. dirs. Children's Hosp. Rsch. Found., Columbus, 1990-94; cons. numerous orgns. Editor: Hazardous Waste Management, 1982, Management of Hazardous and Toxic Waste, 1985; contbr. articles to profl. jours. Mem. Am. Inst. Chem. Engrs. (exec. com., cen. Ohio sect., 1970-72), Am. Chem. Soc., Am. Soc. for Engring. Edn. (chmn. environ. engring. div., 1973-74, mem. coun. govtl. rels. bd. dirs., 1993—). Roman Catholic. Office: U Notre Dame Rsch Office 511 Main Building Notre Dame IN 46556-5602

SWEET, CHARLES WHEELER, retired executive recruiter; b. Chgo., June 11, 1943; s. Charles Wheeler and Alice Naomi (Grush) Sweet; m. Joy Ann Weidernmiller, Mar. 23, 1968; children: Charles III, Kimberly Ann, Rebecca Townsend. AB, Hamilton Coll., Clinton, NY, 1965; MBA, U. Chgo., 1968. Salesman Procter & Gamble, Chgo., 1965-67; with pers. Ford, Dearborn, Mich., 1968-69, R.R. Donnelley, Chgo., 1969-72; exec. recruiter A.T. Kearney Inc. Exec. Search, Chgo., 1972—87, pres., 1987-99, chmn., 2000—01; ret., 2001. Bd. dirs. Gt. Bank Algonquin. Chmn. bd. dirs., exec. advisor No. Ill. U., 1979—88; bd. dirs. Rehab. Inst. Chgo., 1987—. Mem.: Assn. Exec. Search Cons., Barrington Hills Country Club (bd. dirs. 1993—96). Avocations: tennis, bridge. Home: 92 Meadow Hill Rd Barrington IL 60010-9601

SWEET, CYNTHIA R., historian, genealogist, historic museum director; b. Iowa, 1958; d. Garth Wayne and Shirley Jean Huffman; m. Stanton L. Sweet, 1981; children: Ashley A., Devin L., Tyler B. BA with honors, U. No. Iowa, 1979, MA in History, 2007. Office mgr. Midway Devel. Corp., Cedar Falls, Iowa, 1979-84; adminstrv. asst. D.T.S., Inc., Cedar Falls, 1984—2006, Montessori Sys. Sch., Cedar Falls, 1995—2002; owner Sweet Press, 2002—; writer, spl. projects facilitator Cedar Falls Tourism and Visitors Bur., 2004—07; exec. dir. Iowa Mus. Assn., 2007—. Author: Nuts and Bolts -How to Build a Bell Program, 1986, The Rottink Family of the Netherlands, 1986, Silver Celebration: A History of the Sturgis Falls Celebration, 2000; co-author: The Descendants of John Bond, 1992, David Elliott, Loyalist, and his Descendants, 1995, The Life and Family of Rev. Joshua Sweet, 2001, Since I Started For The War: The Letters and Diary of Solomon B. Humbert, Co. B, 31st Iowa Volunteer Infantry, 2007; editor: Sturgis Falls Celebration Program Book, 1996-2006; editor, compiler, Letters to Emma, 2001, Places To Go, People To See, 2004, 2d edit., 2006; contbr. articles to profl. jours. Adminstrv. asst. Sturgis Falls Celebration, Inc., Cedar Falls, 1987-2006; music dir. handbell program First United Meth. Ch., Cedar Falls, 1979-95. Home and Office: 1116 Washington St Cedar Falls IA 50613-3070

SWEET, DAVID CHARLES, academic administrator; b. Rochester, NY, May 16, 1939; s. Charles J. and Esther W. Sweet; m. Patricia Mayer; children: Britton, Melissa, Marc, Kathryn. BA, U. Rochester, 1961; MA, U. N.C., 1963; PhD, Ohio State U., 1970. Program dir. social/system scis. sect., dir. econs. div. Battelle Inst., Columbus, Ohio, 1963-70; mem. gov.'s cabinet, dir. dept. econ./community devel. State of Ohio, Columbus, 1971-75; commr. Pub. Utilities Commn. of Ohio, Columbus, 1975-78; chair Ohio bd. regents Urban Univ. Program, 1980—2000; dean Levin Coll. Urban Affairs, prof. urban studies Cleve. State Univ., 1978—2000; pres. Youngstown State Univ., Ohio, 2000—. Bd. dirs. Indsl. Info. Inst. Edn. Inc., 2000-, Northeast Ohio Coun. Higher Edn., 2000-, Northeastern Ohio Universities Coll. Medicine, 2000-, Northeastern Ednl. TV Ohio, Inc., 2000-, United Cmty. Fin. Corp., 2004-, Ohio Transp. Rsch. Ctr., 1971-75, mem. exec. com., 1974-75; bd. dirs. N.E.-Midwest Inst., 1983-90, 94-2000, chair devel. com., 1986-90; chmn. bd. dirs. Nat. Regulatory Rsch. Inst., Ohio State U., 1977-78, CityScape, 2004-. Contbr. articles to profl. jours. Bd. trustees Butler Inst. Am. Art, 2000-; bd. dirs. Youngstown Cent. Area Cmty. Improvement Corp., 2000-, Youngstown/Warren Reg. Chamber, 2000-, Wick Neighbors, Inc., 2003-. Fellow Nat. Acad. of Public Admin., 1998. Mem. Am. Econ. Devel. Coun. (hon. life, bd. dirs., 1979-85, vice chmn. fin., 1980, chmn., 1983-84), Am. Soc. for Pub. Adminstrn. (Pub. Adminstr. of Yr. in N.E. Ohio 1987). Office: Office of Pres Youngstown State Univ One Univ Plz Youngstown OH 44555

SWEET, STUART C., pediatrician; BS in Chemistry with highest distinction, U. Mich., 1981, MD with distinction, 1989, PhD, 1989. Resident in pediatrics St. Louis Children's Hosp., 1990-93, fellow in pediatric pulmonology, 1993-96; fellow pediatric pulmonology dept. pediatrics Wash. U. Med. Sch. Mem. physicians adv. com. St. Louis Children's Hosp. Contbr. articles to profl. publs. Burton L. Baker Cancer Rsch. fellowship Mich. Cancer Inst., 1986-87. Mem. Phi Beta Kappa. Office: Wash U Sch Medicine Dept Pediatrics One Children's Pl Saint Louis MO 63110-1093

SWEETS, HENRY HAYES, III, curator; b. Lexington, Ky., May 8, 1949; s. Henry Hayes Jr. and Elizabeth (Keith) S.; m. Nancy Riley, Jan. 28, 1984; children: Amy Louisa, Henry Hayes IV. BS in Chemistry, U. Ill., 1971, MEd., 1973; MA in History, U. Del., 1978. Tchr. Scotch Plains (N.J.)-Fanwood High Sch., 1972-74, Byron (Ill.) High Sch., 1974-76; mus. dir. Mark Twain Mus., Hannibal, Mo., 1978—. Author: A Sesquicentennial History of the Hannibal, Missouri Presbyterian Church; editor The Fence Painter. Mem. bd. edn. Hannibal, Mo. Pub. Schs., 1991—. Mem. Nat. Trust for Hist. Preservation. Methodist. Office: Mark Twain Home Foundation 120 N Main St Hannibal MO 63401-3537

SWENSEN, COLE, poet, educator; BA, MA, San Francisco State U.; PhD in Comparative Lit., U. Calif., Santa Cruz. Dir. creative writing prog. U. Denver; assoc. prof. U. Iowa Writers' Workshop. Author: It's Alive, She Says, New Math, 1988 (Nat. Poetry Series winner), Park, 1991, Numen, 1995, Noon, 1997 (New Am. Poetry Series Award), Try, 1999, Oh, 2000 (Iowa Poetry Prize), Such Rich Hour, 2001, Goest, 2004 (Nat. Book Award finalist, 2004); contbg. editor American Letters and Commentary, Shiny, translation editor How2. Office: Grad Prog Creative Writing U Iowa 102 Dey House Iowa City IA 52242-1408 Office Phone: 319-335-0416.

SWENSON, DALE, state legislator; b. Wichita, K.S., Mar. 2, 1957; m. Roberta Swenson. Mem. from dist. 97 Kans. State Ho. of Reps., Topeka, 1994—. Address: 3351 S McComas St Wichita KS 67217-1158 Office: Kans House of Reps State House Topeka KS 66612

SWENSON, DOUGLAS, state legislator; b. Aug. 1945; m. Sandie; two children, three grandchildren. BS, Gustavus Adolphus Coll.; JD, William Mitchell Coll. Minn. State Rep. Dist. 51B, 1987—2000; judge Chicago County Dist. Ct., Center City, Minn., 1998; atty. Home: 9429 Jewel Lane Ct N Forest Lake MN 55025-9169 Office: Chicago County Courthouse 313 N Main St Center City MN 55063-1620

SWENSON, GEORGE WARNER, JR., engineering educator; b. Mpls., Sept. 22, 1922; s. George Warner and Vernie (Larson) Swenson; m. Virginia Laura Savard, June 26, 1943 (div. 1970); children: George Warner III, Vernie Laura, Julie Loretta, Donna Joan; m. Joy Janice Locke, July 2, 1971. BS, Mich. Coll. Mining and Tech., Houghton, 1944, E.E., 1950; MS, MIT, Cambridge, 1948; PhD, U. Wis., Madison, 1951. Asso. prof. elec. engring. Washington U., St. Louis, 1952-53; prof. U. Alaska, 1953-54; asso. prof. Mich. State U., 1954-56; faculty U. Ill., Urbana, 1956—, prof. elec. engring. and astronomy, 1958-88, prof. emeritus, 1988—, acting head dept. astronomy, 1970-72, head dept. elec. and computer engring., 1979-85. Dir. Vermilion River Obs., 1968-81; vis. scientist Nat. Radio Astronomy Obs., 1964-68; cons. to govt. agys. and other sci. bodies; resident cons. US Army Constrn. Engring. Rsch. Lab., 1988--; adj. prof. elec. engring. Mich. Technol. U., 1996—. Author: Principles of Modern Acoustics, 1953, An Amateur Radio Telescope, 1980; co-author: Interferometry and Synthesis in Radio Astronomy, 1986, 2d edit., 2001, also Russian edits.; contbr. articles to profl. jours. 1st lt. signal corps US Army, WWII. Recipient citation for disting. service to engring. U. Wis., 1984; Guggenheim fellow, 1984-85 Fellow IEEE, AAAS; mem. NAE, Am. Astron. Soc., Internat. Sci. Radio Union (U.S. nat. com. 1965-67, 80-82), Internat. Astron. Union, Inst. Noise Control Engring. (cert.), Sigma Xi, Eta Kappa Nu, Tau Beta Pi, Phi Kappa Phi. Achievements include chairing conceptual design group which produced the concept/proposal for the Very Large Array of National Radio Astronomy Observatory; designed and built two large innovative radio telescopes for the University of Illinois. Home: 1107 Kenwood Rd Champaign IL 61821-4718 Office: U Ill 328 CSL 1308 W Main St Urbana IL 61801-2307

SWENSON, HOWARD, state legislator, farmer; b. Dec. 20, 1930; m. Jane Swenson; 5 children. Farmer, Nicollet, Minn.; mem. Minn. Ho. of Reps., St. Paul, 1994—. Independent-Republican.

SWENSON, LYLE W., protective services official; U.S. marshal U.S. Marshal's Svc., Sioux Falls, S.D., 1997—. Mem. Nat. Sheriffs' Assn. (sec.), S.D. Peace Officers Assn. (past pres.), S.D. Sheriffs's Assn. (past pres.). Office: US Marshal Svc Fed Bldg 400 S Phillips Ave Rm 216 Sioux Falls SD 57104-6851

SWERDLOW, MARTIN ABRAHAM, pathologist, educator; b. Chgo., July 7, 1923; s. Sol Hyman and Rose (Lasky) Swerdlow; m. Marion Levin, May 19, 1945; children: Steven Howard, Gary Bruce. Student, Herzl Jr. Coll., 1941—42; BS, U. Ill., 1945; MD, U. Ill., Chgo., 1947. Diplomate Am Bd Pathology. Intern Michael Reese Hosp. and Med. Center, Chgo., 1947-48, resident, 1948-50, 51-52, mem. staff, 1974—, chmn. dept. pathology, v.p. acad. affairs, 1974-90; pathologist Menorah Med Ctr, Kansas City, Mo., 1954—57. Asst prof, pathologist Univ Ill Col Med, Chicago, 1957—59, assoc prof, 1959—60, clin prof, 1960—64, prof, pathologist, 1966—72, assoc dean, prof pathology, 1970—72; prof pathology, chmn Univ Mo, Kansas City, 1972—74; prof pathology Univ Chicago, 1975—89, Geever prof, head pathology emeritus, 1993—; mem comt standards Chicago Health Sys Agency, 1976—. With MC US Army, 1944—45. Recipient Alumnus of the Yr Award, Univ Ill Col Med, 1973, Instructorship Award, Univ Ill, 1960, 1965, 1968, 1971, 1972. Mem.: Inst. of Medicine, Am. Soc. Dermatopathology, Internat. Acad. Pathology, Coll. Am. Pathologists, Am. Soc. Clin. Pathologists, Chgo. Pathology Soc. (pres 1980—). Jewish. Office Phone: 847-831-2983. Business E-Mail: maswerdl@uic.edu.

SWIBEL, HOWARD JAY, lawyer; b. Chgo., July 9, 1950; s. Charles Robert and Seena (Minkus) S.; m. Sheryl Siegel, June 19, 1973; children: Matthew, Brian, Justin, Alison. BA cum laude, Harvard U., 1972, JD cum laude, 1975. Bar: Ill. 1975, US Dist. Ct. (no. dist. Ill.) 1975, US Ct. Appeals (7th cir.) 1978. Ptnr. Kirkland & Ellis, Chgo., 1975-83, Arnstein & Lehr, Chgo., 1983—, mem. exec. comm., 1983—2005. Mem. Nat. Conf. Commrs. on Uniform State Laws, Chgo., 1976— (pres.); vice chair Midwest Regional Bd. Anti-Defamation League; v.p. Holocaust Meml. Found. Ill., 2002—; arbitrator, NASD Contbr. articles to law jours. Mem. instl. rev. bd. Ill. Cancer Coun., Chgo., 1986-90; pres. Cmty. Found. Jewish Edn. Met. Chgo., 2000-02. Mem. ABA, Ill. Bar Assn., Chgo. Bar Assn., Harvard Club (bd. dirs. Chgo. 1975-85). Jewish. Avocations: investments, tennis, skiing, travel. Office: Arnstein & Lehr LLP 120 S Riverside Plz Ste 1200 Chicago IL 60606-3910 Office Phone: 312-876-7164. E-mail: hjswibel@arnstein.com.

SWIBEL, STEVEN WARREN, lawyer; b. Chgo., July 18, 1946; s. Morris Howard and Gloria Swibel; m. Leslie Swibel; children: Deborah, Laura. BS, MIT, 1968; JD, Harvard U., 1971. Bar: Ill. 1971, U.S. Dist. Ct. (no. dist.) Ill. 1971, U.S. Tax Ct. 1973, U.S. Ct. Appeals (7th cir.) 1981. Assoc. Sonnenschein Carlin Nath & Rosenthal, Chgo., 1971-78, ptnr., 1978-84, Rudnick & Wolfe, 1984-93, Schwartz, Cooper, Chartered, Chgo., 1993—. Adj. prof. taxation Ill. Inst. Tech. Kent Coll. Law, Chgo., 1989—2001; lectr. in field. Contbr. articles to profl. jours. Ednl. counselor MIT, 1979—; bd. dirs. MIT Alumni Fund, 1992—95, MIT Enterprise Forum, Chgo., 2002—, Kids in Danger, 1998—, Ragdale Found., 1987—2000, treas., 1987—92. Recipient Lobdell Disting. Svc. award, MIT Alumni Assn., 1989. Mem.: ABA (com. partnerships sect. taxation), Chgo. Bar Assn. (mem. exec. subcom. 1984—2004, chmn. subcom. real estate and partnerships 1986—87, vice-chmn. 1988—89, chmn. 1990, mem. fed. taxation com.), Ill. Bar Assn., MIT Club (sec. 1980—87, dir. Chgo. chpt. 1980—91, pres. 1987—89, dir. Chgo. chpt. 1996—), Met. Club, Sigma Xi, Eta Kappa Nu, Tau Beta Pi. Office: Schwartz Cooper Chartered 180 N La Salle St Ste 2700 Chicago IL 60601-2757 Office Phone: 312-346-1300. Business E-Mail: sswibel@schwartzcooper.com.

SWIFT, CHRISTOPHER J., lawyer; b. Piqua, Ohio, Mar. 6, 1955; BA summa cum laude, Ohio Wesleyan U., 1977; JD summa cum laude, Ohio State U., Michael E. Moritz Coll. of Law, 1980. Bar: Ohio 1980, US Dist. Ct., No. Dist. of Ohio 1980, US Tax Ct. 1983, US Ct. of Appeals, Sixth Circuit 1987. Ptnr. Baker & Hostetler, Cleveland, Ohio, mem. policy com. coord., tax, personal planning and employee benefits group. Lecturer Cleveland Tax Inst., 1986—2004, Cleveland Health Care Law Inst., 1987—98, Cleveland Bar Assn., Columbus Bar Assn., Com. on State Taxation. Co-author: (articles) Will An F Reorganization Receive A Passing Grade As An Ohio Franchise Tax Planning Technique, The Ohio Tax Aspects To Consider When Transferring A Business. Named Ohio Super Lawyer, 2003. Mem.: ABA (mem. taxation and health sections), Ohio State Bar Assn. (mem. taxation and health sections), Cleveland Bar Assn. (chair, State and Local Tax Inst. 1988, chair, General Tax Com. 1990—91, mem. taxation and health sections). Office: Baker & Hostetler 3200 Nat City Ctr 1900 E 9th St Cleveland OH 44114-3485 Home Phone: 216-283-4093; Office Phone: 216-861-7461. Office Fax: 216-696-0740. Business E-Mail: cswift@bakerlaw.com.

SWIFT, EDWARD FOSTER, III, investment banker; b. Chgo., Nov. 1, 1923; s. Theodore Philip I and Elizabeth (Hoyt) S.; m. Joan McKelvy, July 2, 1947; children: Theodore Philip II, Edward McKelvy, Lockhart McKelvy, Elizabeth Hoyt; m. Carol Coffey Whipple, June 21, 1968. Grad., Hotchkiss Sch., 1941; BA, Yale U., 1945. With Esmark, Inc. (formerly Swift & Co.), 1947-75, asst. to v.p. charge meat packing plants, 1958, asst. v.p., 1958-59, v.p. for provisions, fgn., casings and storage, 1959-64, exec. v.p., 1964-75; vice-chmn. Chgo. Corp., 1975-79; vice chmn. Bacon, Whipple & Co., Chgo., 1980-84; mng. dir. A.G. Becker Paribas Inc., Chgo., 1984-85; with E.F. Hutton and Co., Chgo., 1985-87; mng. dir. Shearson Lehman Hutton Inc, Chgo., 1987-92. Bd. dirs. Santa Fe Pacific Pipelines, Inc. Chmn. So. Ind. chpt. United Negro Coll. Fund, 1956; trustee Northwestern U., Evanston, Ill.; bd. dirs. Northwestern Meml. Hosp., Chgo. Served to capt. U.S. Army, 1942-46. Mem. Chgo. Assn. Commerce and Industry (bd. dirs.), Scroll and Key, Chgo. Club, Racquet Club, Econ. Club, Valley Club, Comml. Club, Onwentsia Club, Old Elm ClubBirnam Wood Golf Club, Aurelian Honor Soc. Home: 1100 Pembridge Dr Apt 129 Lake Forest IL 60045

SWIGER, ELINOR PORTER, lawyer; b. Cleve., Aug. 1, 1927; d. Louie Charles and Mary Isabelle (Shank) Porter; m. Quentin Gilbert Swiger, Feb. 5, 1955; children: Andrew Porter, Calvin Gilbert, Charles Robinson. BA, Ohio State U., 1949, JD, 1951. Bar: Ohio 1951, Ill. 1979. Sr. assoc., now of counsel Robbins, Schwartz, icholas, Lifton & Taylor, Ltd., Chgo., 1979—. Author: (book) Mexico for Kids, 1971, Europe for Young Travelers, 1972, The Law and You, 1973 (Literary Guild award), Law in Everyday Life, 1977, Careers in the Legal Professions, 1978, Women Lawyers at Work, 1978. Mem. Glenview (Ill.) Fire and Police Commn., 1976—86; chmn. Glenview Zoning Bd. Appeals, 1987—97. Mem.: Chgo. Bar Assn. (chmn. legis. exec. com. 1990—92), Women Bar Assn. Ill., Ill. Coun. Sch. Attys. (past chmn.), Ohio State U. Coll. Law Alumni Coun., Soc. Midland Authors. Republican. Home: 1933 Burr Oak Dr Glenview IL 60025 Office: Robbins Schwartz Nicholas Lifton & Taylor 20 N Clark St Ste 900 Chicago IL 60602-4115

SWIGERT, JAMES MACK, lawyer; b. Carthage, Ill., Sept. 25, 1907; s. James Ross and Pearl (Mack) S.; m. Alice Francis Titcomb Harrower, July 7, 1931 (dec. 1990); children: Oliver, David Ladd, Sally Harper (Mrs. Hamilton). Student, Grinnell Coll., 1925-27; SB, Harvard U., 1930, LLB, 1935. Bar: Ill. 1935, Ohio 1937. With Campbell, Clithero & Fischer, Chgo., 1935-36, Taft, Stettinius & Hollister, Cin., 1936—, ptnr., 1948-79, sr. ptnr. and chmn. exec. com., 1963-79; dir., chmn. audit com. Philips Industries, 1975-82. Author articles on labor rels. and labor law. Bd. dirs. Cin. Symphony Orch., 1976-78; trustee, chmn. exec. com. Am. Music Scholarship Assn., 1987-92. Recipient Lifetime Achievement in Law award, Cin. Bar Fund, 2002, Great Living Cincinnatian award, 2004. Mem.: Harvard Law Club (past pres.), Recess Club (past pres.), Tennis Club (past pres.), Queen City Club, Queen City Optimists Club (past pres., psat bd. dirs.), Cin. Country Club (past v.p., dir.). Republican. Presbyterian. Home: 2121 Alpine Pl Cincinnati OH 45206-2690 Office: 425 Walnut St Ste 1800 Cincinnati OH 45202 Home Phone: 513-221-4983; Office Phone: 513-357-9360. Business E-Mail: swigert@taftlaw.com.

SWINAND, ANDREW, advertising executive; b. 1968; m. Laura Swinand; children: Tanner, Georgia. BS economics, U. of Pa., 1990. Account supervisor BBDO, Los Angeles; brand mgr. Procter & Gamble Co., Cincinnati; gen. mgr. Starcom USA, San Francisco, 2000—02, Chicago, 2002—05, exec. v.p., 2005—. Reserve 3rd infantry div USAR, 1990—94. Named one of the best 40 under 40 in business, Crain's Chicago Business, 2005; scholar Reserve Officers' Training Corps, U.S. Army. Office: c/o Starcom 35 W Wacker Dr Chicago IL 60601

SWINGLE, HARRY MORLEY, JR., prosecutor; b. Cape Girardeau, Mo., Apr. 21, 1955; s. Harry Morley and Alberta (Pointer) S.; m. Candace Ann Ely, Aug. 1, 1980; children: Olivia Ann, Veronica Candace. AB in English, U. Mo., 1977, JD, 1980. Bar: Mo., U.S. Dist. Ct. (ea. and we. dists.) Mo. 1980. Intern to presiding justice Mo. Supreme Ct., Jefferson City, spring 1980; assoc. Spradling & Spradling, Cape Girardeau, 1980-82; asst. pros. atty. Cape Girardeau County, Cape Girardeau, 1982-86, pros. atty., 1987—. Guest instr. Mo. Hwy. Patrol Tng. Acad., Jefferson City, 1980, 90, Mo. Judicial Coll., 1994—, Mo. Prosecuting Atty.'s Assn., 1992—, Kansas Dist. Atty.'s Assn., 1994, Iowa Dist. Atty.'s Assn., 1995; guest lectr. criminal justice dept. S.E. Mo. State U., Cape Girardeau, 1986—. Contbr. chpt. to Criminal Practice in Missouri, 1989, 96; contbr. articles to profl. publs. Bd. dirs. Cape River Heritage Mus., Cape Girardeau, 1982-84; pres. Firends of Pub. Libr., Cape Girardeau, 1984. Mem. Nat. Assn. Trial Lawyers, Nat. Dist. Attys. Assn., Mo. Pros. Attys. Assn., Cape Girardeau County Bar Assn. Republican. Methodist. Avocations: reading, running, bridge, writing. Home: 226 N Sunset Blvd Cape Girardeau MO 63701-5216 Office: Office of Prosecuting Atty Courthouse 100 Court St Jackson MO 63755-1875 Office Phone: 573-243-2430.

SWINNEY, CAROL JOYCE, secondary school educator; Langs. tchr. Hugoton (Kans.) High Sch., 1972-98; dir. distance learning S.W. Plains Regional Svcs. Ctr., Kans., 1998—. Named Kans. Tchr. of Yr., Disney for Lang. Tchr. of Yr., 1993, Milken Nat. Educator, 1992. Office: PO Drawer 1010 Sublette KS 67877-1010

SWITZ, ROBERT E., telecommunications executive; BS in Mktg. and Econs., Quinnipiac Coll., 1969; MBA in Fin., U. Bridgeport, 1973. Sr. fin. mgmt. staff PepsiCo., AMF, Olin Corp.; v.p. European ops., ventures and fin. Burr-Brown Corp., Tucson, 1988-94; CFO ADC Telecom., 1994—2003, sr. v.p. to exec. v.p., 1997—2003, pres. broadband access & transport group, 2000—01, pres., CEO, 2003—. Bd. dirs. Hickory Tech. Corp., Mpls. Youth Trust. Office: ADC Telecommunications 13625 Technology Dr Eden Prairie MN 55344 E-mail: bob_switz@adc.com.

SWITZER, JO YOUNG, college president; b. Huntington, Ind., Mar. 4, 1948; d. John Frederick and Miriam Lucile (Kindy) Young; children: Sarah Kate Keller, John Christian Keller. BA, Manchester Coll., 1969; MA, U. Kans., 1977,

PhD, 1980; postdoctoral, Ind. U., 1983, Harvard U., 1995. Asst. instr. U. Kans., Lawrence, 1977-79; asst. prof. Ind. U.-Purdue, Ft. Wayne, Ind., 1979-82; assoc. prof. Manchester Coll., North Manchester, Ind., 1982-87, Ind. U.-Purdue, Ft. Wayne, Ind., 1987-93; v.p., dean for acad. affairs and prof. comm. studies Manchester (Ind.) Coll., 1993—2004, pres., 2004—. Bd. dirs. BCA Study Abroad Consortium, Indpls. Peace Inst. Recipient E. C. Buehler award U. Kans., 1978; grantee NEH, 1983. Mem. Central States Comm. Assn. (Outstanding Young Educator award 1982), Coun. of Ind. Colls., Am. Coun. on Edn., Am. Assn. Colls. and Univs. Office: Manchester Coll Office of Pres 604 E College Ave North Manchester IN 46962-1276 Home: Tall Oaks 1408 East St North Manchester IN 46962 Office Phone: 260-982-5050. Office Fax: 260-982-5042. Business E-Mail: jyswitzer@manchester.edu.

SWITZER, JON REX, architect; b. Shelbyville, Ill., Aug. 22, 1937; s. John Woodrow and Ida Marie (Vadalabene) S.; m. Judith Ann Heinlein, July 7, 1962; 1 child, Jeffrey Eric. Student, U. Ill., 1955-58; BS, Millikin U., 1972; MA, U. Ill., Springfield, 1981. Registered architect Ill., Mo., Ohio, Colo.; registered interior designer, Ill. Arch. Warren & Van Praag, Inc., Decatur, Ill., 1970-72; prin. Decatur, 1972-81, Bloomington, Ill., 1981-83; arch. Hilfinger, Asbury, Cufaude, Abels, Bloomington, 1983-84; ptnr. Riddle/Switzer, Ltd., Bloomington, 1984-86; with bldg., design and constrn. divsn. State Farm Ins. Cos., Bloomington, 1986-89; arch. The Riddle Group, Bloomington, 1989-91; prin. J. Rex Switzer, Arch., Bloomington, 1991—. Elder Presbyn. Ch., 1996. With U.S. Army, 1958-61. Mem. AIA (emeritus, pres. Bloomington chpt. 1983, Decatur chpt. 1976, v.p. Ill. chpt. 1986-87, sec. 1985, treas. 1984), Am. Archtl. Found., Chgo. Architecture Found., Nat. Trust Hist. Preservation, Frank Lloyd Found., Decatur C. of C. (merit citation 1974, merit award 1979), Am. Legion, Masons (32d degree). Republican. Presbyterian. Avocations: swimming, hunting, fishing, reading, drawing. Home: 9 Mary Ellen Way Bloomington IL 61701-2014 Office: 2412 E Washington St Ste 6A Bloomington IL 61704-1613

SWITZER, ROBERT LEE, biochemistry professor; b. Clinton, Iowa, Aug. 26, 1940; s. Stephen and Elva Delila (Allison) S.; m. Bonnie George, June 13, 1965; children: Brian, Stephanie. BS, U. Ill., 1961; PhD, U. Calif., Berkeley, 1966. Research fellow Lab. Biochemistry, Nat. Heart Inst., Bethesda, Md., 1966-68; asst. prof. biochemistry U. Ill., Urbana, 1968—73, assoc. prof., 1973—78, prof. biochemistry and basic med. scis., 1978—2002, prof. emeritus, 2002—, dept. head, 1988—93. Mem. biochemistry study sect. NIH, 1985-89, chmn., 1987-89; guest prof. U. Copenhagen, 1995; mem. microbial physiology and genetics study sect., IH, 1998-2000. Author: (with Liam F. Garrity) Experimental Biochemistry, 3rd rev. edit., 1999; mem. bd. editors Jour. Bacteriology, 1977-82, 1985—2002, Archives Biochemistry and Biophysics, 1977-98, Jour. Biol. Chemistry, 1980-85; contbr. articles to profl. jours. NSF predoctoral fellow, 1961-66; NIH postdoctoral fellow, 1966-68; Guggenheim fellow, 1975. Fellow Am. Acad. Microbiology; mem. Am. Soc. for Biochemistry and Molecular Biology, Am. Soc. Microbiology, Am. Chem. Soc., AAAS, Sigma Xi. Home: 404 W Michigan Ave Urbana IL 61801-4948 Office: U Ill Dept Biochemistry 600 S Mathews Ave Urbana IL 61801-3602 Office Phone: 217-333-3940. Business E-Mail: rswitzer@uiuc.edu.

SWOBODA, LARY JOSEPH, state legislator; b. Luxemburg, Wis., May 28, 1939; s. Joseph Francis and Catherine Magdalene (Daul) S.; m. Janice Marie Hendricks, Nov. 16, 1968. BS in Speech and Edn., U. Wis., Milw., 1963, MS in Polit. Sci., 1965, EdS, 1988; PhD in Ednl. Adminstrn., U. Wis., Madison, 1999. Cert. ednl. specialist. Tchr. speech and English, So. H.S., Brussels, Wis., 1963-67; tchr. civics and govt. Luxemburg Schs., 1967-70; mem. Wis. State Assembly, Madison, 1970—, chmn. adminstrv. rules com., 1993—; exec. dir. Wis. Nat. and Cmty. Svc. Bd., Madison; prin. Oneida Nation Elem. Sch. Active Dem. County Unit; Kewnauci County Hist. Soc. Mem. Luxemburg C. of C., KC, Lions, Phi Eta Sigma, Kappa Delta Pi, Phi Kappa Phi, Phi Delta Kappa. Roman Catholic. Avocations: reading, music, drama. Home: 1505 Meadows Ln Luxemburg WI 54217-1363

SYKES, ALAN O'NEIL, lawyer, educator; b. Bethesda, Md., Oct. 10, 1954; s. Alan O'Neil and Emily (Adams) S.; m. Maureen J. Gorman, June 29, 1980; children: Madeleine, Sophie. BA, Coll. William and Mary, 1976; JD, Yale U., 1982, PhD in Econs., 1987. Bar: Mass., D.C. Atty. Office of Arnold & Porter, Washington, 1982-86; asst. prof. law U. Chgo., 1986-90, prof. law, 1990—, Frank and Bernice Greenberg prof., 1996—. Vis. prof. law Harvard U., Cambridge, Mass., 1991, YU, 1996. Author: (book) Product Standards for Internationally Integrated Goods Markets, 1995; co-author: Legal Problems of International Economic Relations, 2002; co-editor: Implementing the Uruguay Round, 1997. NSF fellow, 1976-79. Mem. ABA, Am. Econ. Assn., Am. Law and Econs. Assn. (bd. dirs. 1999—). Office: U Chgo Sch of Law 1111 E 60th St Chicago IL 60637 Business E-Mail: alan_sykes@law.uchicago.edu.

SYKES, BARBARA, state legislator, state representative; b. Holly Grove, Ark., Apr. 12, 1955; married; 2 children. BA in Social Work, U. Akron, MPA. Rep. Ohio State Ho. Reps., Columbus, 2000—. Mem. econ. devel. and tech. com. Ohio State Ho. Reps., mem. pub. utilities com., mem. ways and means com. Mem.: NAACP, Friends of Maple Libr., PTA Firestone HS. Democrat. Office: Ohio State House Reps 77 South High Street 10th Floor Columbus OH 43215-6111

SYKES, CHARLIE, radio personality; 3 children. Reporter The Jour., Milw.; editor-in-chief Milw. Mag.; radio host 620 AM WTMJ, Milw. Author: Dumbing Down Our Children: Why American Children Feel Good About Themsleves but Can't Read, Write or Add, Profscam? Professors and the Demise of Higher Education, The End of Privacy, A Nation of Victims: The Decay of the American Character, The Hollow Men: Politics and Corruption in Higher Education. Nominee Pulitzer prize. Office: WTMJ 720 E Capital Dr Milwaukee WI 53212

SYKES, DIANE S., federal judge, former state supreme court justice; b. Milw., Dec. 23, 1957; 2 children. BA, Northwestern U., 1980; JD, Marquette U., 1984. Reporter Milw. Jour.; law clk. to Hon. Terence T. Evans US Dist. Ct. (ea. dist.) WI, 1984—85; assoc. Whyte & Hirschboeck S.C., 1985—92; judge Milw. County Ct., 1992—99, Wis. Supreme Ct., Madison, 1999—2004, US Ct. Appeals (7th cir.), 2004—. Mem.: St. Thomas More Soc., Milw. Lawyers Chpt., Federalist Soc., Fairchild Inn, Am. Inns of Ct., Assn. for Women Lawyers, Seventh Cir. Bar Assn., Milw. Bar Assn., Wis. Bar Assn. Office: US Ct Appeals 7th Cir 716 US Court House 517 E Wisconsin Ave Milwaukee WI 53202 also: Dirksen Fed Bldg Rm 2742 219 S Dearborn St Chicago IL 60604 Office Phone: 414-727-6988.

SYKES, GREGORY, food products executive; New products mktg. mgr. Hillshire Farms & Kahn's, 1984; pres., CEO Ball Park Brands, 1995, State Fair Foods, Best Kosher, Ball Park and Hillshiar Farm & Kahn's groups; v.p. Sara Lee Corp., Chgo.; pres., CEO Sara Lee Foods Retail, Chgo. Office: Sara Lee Corp 3 First ational Plz Chicago IL 60602-4260

SYKES, VERNON L., state legislator; b. Oct. 2, 1951; m. Barbara Sykes; children: Stancy, Emilia. BS, Ohio Univ., 1974; MS, Wright State Univ., 1980; MPA, Harvard Univ., 1986. Planner, rsch. & eval., asst. Fiscal Officer Summit Coun. Criminal Justice Com., Akron, Ohio, 1976-79; city councilman Akron, 1980-83; Ohio State Rep. Dist. 42, 1983-92, Dist. 44, 1993—; chmn. Interstate Coop Com.; real estate agt. Clarence K. Allen Realty, Akron, 1982. Mem. Ohio Housing Fin. Agy., Econ. Devel. & Small Bus, Financial Inst., Econ. Affairs & Fed. Rels., Transp. & Urban Affairs Com., mem. jt. Com. on Agy. Rule Rev; tchr. Akron Bd. Edn., Ohio, 1974-75, sr. mgmt. specialist United Neighborhood Coun. Inc., Akron, 1975-76; instr. Univ. Akron & Southern Ohio Coll., 1980; pres. Harvard Group, 1987, mem. BancOne Cmty. adv. bd., 1996—. Named Legis. of Yr. Nat. Assn. Social Workers, 1986. Mem. Akron Pvt. Indsl. Coun., Akron Cmty. Action Agy., Western Econ. Assn. Internat. Cuyahoga Valley Assn. Office: Ohio House of Reps State House Columbus OH 43215 Home: 133 Furnace Run Dr Akron OH 44307-2259

SYKORA, BARBARA ZWACH, state legislator; b. Tracy, Minn., Mar. 5, 1941; d. John M. and Agnes (Schueller) Zwach; m. Robert G. Sykora, 1965; children: Mona, John, Kara, Mary. BA, St. Catherine Coll., 1963. Tchr. Springfield (Mass.) Sch., 1963-64, Roseville (Minn.) Sch., 1964-66; mem. Minn. Ho. of Reps., St. Paul, 1994—. Bd. dirs. Beacon Bank. Vice chmn. 2d Congl. Dist. Rep. Com., Minn., 1978-82; chmn. 6th Congl. Dist. Rep. Com., 1982-86, 2d congl. dist. Senator Durenberger Campaign, 1980-82, Senator Pillsbury Campaign, Wayzata, Minn., 1980; chair Ind. Rep. State Com., Minn., 1987-93; dist. dir. Office Congressman Rod Grams, 1993-94; bd. dirs. Animal Humane Soc. Hennepin County, Minn. Acad. Excellence Found.; chair Family and Early Childhood Edn. Com., 1999-2002, Edn. Policy, 2003—; chair Legis. Commn. on IEcon. Status of Women, 2001—; asst. majority leader Rep. State Com., Minn. 2003—. Mem. Excelsior C. of C., Minnetonka Rotary. Republican. E-mail: bsykora@uswestmail.net.

SYLVESTER, RONALD CHARLES, newspaper writer; b. Springfield, Mo., Feb. 10, 1959; s. Edgar Donald and Barbara Jean (Hedgecock) S.; m. Angela Sylvester; children: Christian Alexander, Lauryn Ayiana. Sports writer Springfield (Mo.) News-Leader, 1976-88, entertainment writer, 1988-96, gen. assignment news reporter, 1996—. Mem. media panel Leadership Music, Nashville, 1993. Author: Branson: On Stage in the Ozarks, 1994; contbr. articles to New Country Music, Gannett News Svc., Colliers Ency. Bd. dirs. Entertainers Guild of Branson, Mo., 1993-94. Recipient Media award Mo. Pub. Health Assn., 1998, 99. Mem. Soc. of Profl. Journalists. Mem. Christian Ch. (Disciples Of Christ). Avocations: music, reading, outdoor recreation. Office: Springfield News-Leader 651 N Boonville Ave Springfield MO 65806-1039

SYMENS, PAUL N., state legislator, farmer; b. Marshall County, SD, July 15, 1943; m. Faye Bovendam; 5 children. AA, Northwestern Coll., Iowa, 1993. Mem. S.D. Senate from 1st dist., Pierre, 1987-94, 97—. Mem. S.D. Farmers Union, Marshall County Farmers Union. Democrat. Presbyterian. Office: State Capitol Bldg 500 E Capitol Ave Pierre SD 57501-5070 also: 41547 105th St Amherst SD 57421

SYMMONDS, RICHARD EARL, gynecologist; b. Greensburg, Mo., Mar. 19, 1922; s. Emmett E. S. AB, Central Coll., Fayette, Mo., 1943; MD, Duke U., 1946; MS in Ob-Gyn, U. Minn., 1953. Intern Los Angeles County Hosp., 1946, resident in Ob-Gyn, 1950-53, resident in gen. surgery, 1954-56; practice medicine specializing in gen. surgery Rochester, Minn., 1958—; mem. faculty Mayo Clinic, Rochester, 1953—, prof. gynecologic surgery, 1960—, chmn. dept., 1970-84, chmn. emeritus, 1984—. Contbr. articles to profl. jours. Served with USN, 1947-49. Fellow A.C.S.; mem. Am. Gynecol. Soc., Am. Assn. Obstetricians and Gynecologists, Soc. Pelvic Surgeons, Soc. Gynecologic Oncologists, Am. Coll. Obstetricians and Gynecologists. Office: 200 1st St SW Rochester MN 55905-0001

SYTSMA, FREDRIC A., lawyer; b. Grand Rapids, Mich., Jan. 12, 1944; BA, Mich. State U., 1964; JD, U. Mich., 1968. Bar: Mich. 1968. Mem. Varnum, Riddering, Schmidt & Howlett, Grand Rapids. Fellow Am. Coll. Trust and Estate Counsel; mem. ABA, State Bar Mich. (mem. coun. probate and estate planning sect. 1977—, chmn. 1986-87), Grand Rapids Bar Assn. Office: Varnum Riddering Schmidt & Howlett PO Box 352 333 Bridge St NW Grand Rapids MI 49501-0352 Office Phone: 616-336-6000. Business E-Mail: fasytsma@varnumlaw.com.

SYVERSON, DAVE, state legislator; b. Chgo., June 29, 1957; m. Shirley Syverson. Student, Rock Valley Coll. Mem. Ill. State Senate, Dist. 34; ptnr. Market Ins. Group. Mem. Rockford Boys and Girls Club; bd. govs. Luth. Social Svc. Recipient Humanitarian award Office Internat. Conf., 1994, Activator award Famr Bur., Voice of Employer award; named Freshman Legislator of Yr. Hosp. Assn. Home: 6757 Flower Hill Rd Rockford IL 61114-6636 Office: Ill Senate State Capitol Springfield IL 62706-0001

SZABO, BARNA ALADAR, engineering educator; b. Martonvasar, Hungary, Sept. 21, 1935; arrived in US, 1967, naturalized, 1974; s. Jozsef and Gizella (Ivanyi) S.; m. Magdalin Gerstmayer, July 23, 1960; children: Mark, Nicholas. BASc., U. Toronto, Ont., Can., 1962; MS, SUNY, Buffalo, 1966, PhD, 1968; D honoris causa, U. of Miskolc, Hungary, 1998. Registered profl. engr., Mo. Mining engr. Internat. Nickel Co. Can., 1960-62; engr. Acres Cons. Services Ltd., Niagara Falls, Can., 1962-66; instr. SUNY, Buffalo, 1966-68; from mem. faculty to sr. prof. Washington U., St. Louis, 1968—2006, sr. prof. mech. engring., 2006—; chmn. Engring. Software R&D, Inc., St. Louis, 1989—. Author: (with Ivo Babuska) Finite Element Analysis, 1991; contbr. articles to profl. jours. Fellow, St. Louis Acad. Sci. Fellow: Hungarian Acad. Sci., US Assn. Computational Mechanics (founding mem.). Office: PO Box 1129 Saint Louis MO 63188-1129 Office Phone: 314-935-6352. Business E-Mail: szabo@wustl.edu.

SZAREK, STANISLAW JERZY, mathematics professor; b. Ladek Zdroj, Poland, Nov. 13, 1953; arrived in US, 1980, naturalized, 1994; s. Mieczyslaw and Bronislawa (Brzezinska) S.; m. Malgorzata Chwascinska, June 22, 1980 (separated 1996, div. 2002); children: Martina, Natalia; 1 stepchild, Olga; m. Margaretmary Daley, May 15, 2004; 1 child, Emily; stepchildren: Blake, Devin. M in Math., Warsaw U., Poland, 1976; PhD in Math. Scis., Polish Acad. Scis., Warsaw, 1979. Rsch. asst. Math. Inst. Polish Acad. Scis., Warsaw, 1976-79, rsch. fellow, 1979-83; asst. prof. Case Western Res. U., Cleve., 1983-87, prof., 1987—, chair math. dept., 1994-96; prof. U. Paris, 1996—. Vis. positions U. Ill., Urbana, 1980, Ohio State U., Columbus, 1981, U. Tex., Austin, 1981-83, Inst. des Hautes Etudes Scientifiques, Bures-Sur-Yvette, France, 1986-89, U. Paris, 1990, 92, 95, Math. Scis. Rsch. Inst., Berkeley, Calif., 1996; invited spkr. Internat. Congress Math., Madrid, 2006 Contbr. articles to profl. jours. Recipient Prize of Sci. Sec., Polish Acad. Scis., 1979, Langevin prize Acad. Scis., France, 2007; Rsch. grantee NSF, 1983—, U.S.-Israel Binat. Sci. Found., 1993-97, 2003—; Sloan fellow Alfred P. Sloan Found., 1986-88. Mem.: Am. Math. Soc. Avocations: skiing, sailing, diving, bridge, travel. Office: Case Western Res U Dept of Math Cleveland OH 44106 Home Phone: 216-283-0303; Office Phone: 216-368-2880. Business E-Mail: szarek@cwru.edu.

SZEWCZYK, ALBIN ANTHONY, engineering educator; b. Chgo., Feb. 26, 1935; s. Andrew Aloysius and Jean Cecelia (Wojcik) S.; m. Barbara Valerie Gale, June 16, 1956; children: Karen Marie Knop, Lisa Anne, Andrea Jean Simpson, Terese Helen Sinka. BS, U. Notre Dame, 1956, MS, 1958; PhD, U. Md., 1961. Staff engr. Northrop Aircraft Corp., Hawthorne, Calif., 1956-57; grad. asst. U. Notre Dame, Ind., 1957-58, asst. prof. engring. Ind., 1962-65, assoc. prof. Ind., 1965-67, prof. Ind., 1967—, chmn. dept. Ind., 1978-88; research asst. U. Md., College Park, 1958-61, postdoctoral researcher, 1961-62; mem. tech. staff Aerospace Corp., El Segundo, Calif., 1962. Cons. Argonne (Ill.) Nat. Lab., 1968-80, Miles Lab., Elkhart, Ind., 1983-88, Chung Shan Inst. Sci. and Tech., Taiwan, 1987-89; vis. prof. Imperial Coll., London, 1989, 99, Kernforschungzentrum, Karlsruhe, Germany, 1990. Editor: Development in Mechanics, 1971. Fellow ASME, AIAA (assoc.); mem. AAAS, Am. Phys. Soc., Am. Soc. Engring. Edn., N.Y. Acad. Sci., Sigma Xi, Pi Tau Sigma, Sigma Gamma Tau. Clubs: South Bend Country (bd. dirs. 1982-89, pres. 1986-88). Roman Catholic. Avocations: golf, model railroading. Office: U Notre Dame Dept Aero & Mech Engring Notre Dame IN 46556 Home: 5815 Vanderbilt Ct Granger IN 46530-4484

SZEWS, CHARLES, transportation executive; BBA, U. Wis., Eau Claire. CPA. With Ernst & Young; v.p., contr. Fort Howard Corp., Green Bay, Wis.; v.p., CFO Oshkosh (Wis.) Truck Corp., 1996-97, exec. v.p., CFO, 1997—. Office: Oshkosh Truck Corp 2307 Oregon St Oshkosh WI 54902

SZYBALSKI, WACLAW, geneticist, educator; b. Lwów, Poland, Sept. 9, 1921; arrived in U.S., 1950, naturalized, 1957; s. Stefan and Michalina (Rakowska) Szybalski; m. Elizabeth Hunter, Feb. 5, 1955; children: Barbara A. Szybalski Sandor, Stefan H. BSChemE, Politechnika Lwów, 1944; MSChemE, Politechnika Slaska, Gliwice, Poland, 1945; DSc, Inst. Tech., Gdansk, Poland, 1949, PhD (hon.), 2001, U. Marie Curie, Lublin, Poland, 1980, U. Gdansk, 1989, Med. Acad. Gdansk, 2000. Asst. prof. Inst. Tech., Gdansk, 1945—50; staff Cold Spring Harbor (N.Y.) Biol. Labs., 1951—55; asst. prof. Inst. Microbiology, Rutgers U., New Brunswick, J, 1955-60; prof. oncology McArdle Lab., U. Wis., Madison, 1960—. Mem. recombinant DNA adv. com. NIH, 1974—78; Wendel H. Griffith meml. lectr. St. Louis U., 1975; Raine vis. prof. U. Western Australia, Perth, 1997. Author: numerous papers, revs., abstracts and books in field; editor-in-chief: Gene, 1976—96, hon., founding editor-in-chief:, 1996—; mem. editl. bd. other jours. Decorated Order of Merit Republic of Poland; recipient Karl A. Forster lectr. award, U. Mainz, 1970, A. Jurzykowski Found. award in biology, 1988, Hilldale award in biology, U. Wis., 1994, G. J. Mendel Gold medal for merit in biol. scis., Acad. Scis. Czech Republic, 1995, Cogene lectr. Internat. Union Biochemistry, Nairobi, 1987, Cairo, 1988, Harare, Zimbabwe, 1989;, chemistry bldg. at Inst. Tech. Gdansk named in his honor, 2004. Mem.: AAAS, Polish Inst. Arts and Scis. Am. (C. Funk Natural Sci. award 2003), Polish Acad. Scis., European Molecular Biology Orgns. (lectr. 1971, 1976), Am. Soc. Microbiologists (chmn. virology divsn. 1972—74, chmn. divsn. IV 1974—75), Genetic Soc. Am., Am. Soc. Biochemists, Polish Med. Alliance (hon.), Italian Soc. Exptl. Biology (hon.), Polish Soc. Microbiologists (hon.). Home: 1124 Merrill Springs Rd Madison WI 53705-1317 Office: U Wis McArdle Lab Madison WI 53706 Home Phone: 608-238-3015. E-mail: szybalski@oncology.wisc.edu.

SZYGENDA, RALPH J., automotive executive; b. McKeesport, Pa., Sept. 6, 1948; BS in Computer Sci., U. Mo., 1970; MEE, U. Tex., 1975; ED (hon.), U. Mo. With Tex. Instruments Inc., 1972—93; v.p., chief info. officer Bell Atlantic Corp., Arlington, Va., 1993—96, GM Corp., 1996—2000, group v.p., chief info. officer, 2000—. Bd. dir. Handleman Co. Mem.: GM Automotive Stratey Bd., U. Mo. Sch. Mgmt. Info. Sys. (chmn. advisory bd.), InformationWeek Mag. (editl. bd.), Rsch. Bd. Office: GM Corp 300 Renaissance Ctr PO Box 300 Detroit MI 48265-3000

SZYMONIAK, ELAINE EISFELDER, retired state senator; b. Boscobel, Wis., May 24, 1920; d. Hugo Adolph and Pauline (Vig) Eisfelder; Casimir Donald Szymoniak, Dec. 7, 1943; children: Kathryn, Peter, John, Mary, Thomas. BS, U. Wis., 1941; MS, Iowa State U., 1977. Speech clinician Waukesha (Wis.) Pub. Sch., 1941-43, Rochester (N.Y.) Pub. Sch., 1943-44; rehab. aide U.S. Army, Chickasha, Okla., 1944-46; audiologist U. Wis., Madison, 1946-48; speech clinician Buffalo Pub. Sch., 1948-49, Sch. for Handicapped, Salina, Kans., 1951-52; speech pathologist, audiologist, counselor, resource mgr. Vocat. Rehab. State Iowa, Des Moines, 1956-85; mem. Iowa Senate, Des Moines, 1989—2000; ret., 2000. Bd. dir. On With Life, Terrace Hill Found. Adv. bd. Iowa State Inst. for Social and Behavioral Health; mem. Child Care Resource and Referral Cmty. Empowerment Bd., Greater Des Moines Coun. for Internat. Understanding, United Way, 1987—88, Urban Dreams, Iowa Maternal and Child Health com.; pres. Chrysalis Found., 1997; mem. City-County Study Commn.; Mem. Des Moines City coun., 1978—88; bd. dirs. Nat. League Cities, Washington, 1982—84, Civic Ctr., House of Mercy, Westminster House, Iowa Leadership Consortium, Iowa Comprehensive Health Assn. amed Woman of Achievement, YWCA, 1982, Visionary Woman, 1993, Young Women's Resource Ctr., 1989; named to Iowa Women's Hall of Fame, 1999; named Des Moines Woman of Influence, Bus. Record, 2000. Mem. Am. Speech Lang. and Hearing Assn., Iowa Speech Lang. and Hearing Assn. (pres. 1977-78), Nat. Coun. State Legislators (fed. state com. on health, adv. com. on child protection), Women's Polit. Caucus, Nexus (pres. 1981-82, mem. Supreme Ct. Select Com.), Wellmark Found. (adv. bd.), Des Moines (Iowa) Women's Club (bd. dir. 2003—), Prairie Club. Avocations: reading, travel, swimming, whitewater rafting. Home: 2909 Woodland Ave Apt 1011 Des Moines IA 50312-3877 Personal E-mail: ElaineSzy@aol.com.

SZYPULSKI, WAYNE R., controller, food products executive; b. 1951; BS in Acctg., MS in Acctg., No. Ill. U., DeKalb. Acctg mgr. Sara Lee Corp., Chgo., 1983, asst. corp. controller, 1991—93, controller, 1993—, corp. v.p., 1994—2001, sr. v.p., 2001—, chief acctg. officer. Office: Sara Lee Corp 3 First Nat Plaza Chicago IL 60602-4260

TAAM, RONALD EVERETT, physics and astronomy educator; b. NYC, Apr. 24, 1948; s. Lawrence and Julia (Louie) T.; m. Rosa Wen Mei Yang, Oct. 19, 1974; children: Jonathan, Alexander. BS, Poly. Inst., NYC, 1969; MA, Columbia U., 1971, PhD, 1973. Postdoctoral fellow U. Calif., Santa Cruz, 1973-76, vis. faculty Berkeley, 1976-78; asst. prof. Northwestern U., Evanston, Ill., 1978-83, assoc. prof., 1984-86, prof. physics and astronomy, 1986—, chmn. physics and astronomy, 1995-98. Fellow Am. Phys. Soc.; mem. Am. Astron. Soc., Royal Astron. Soc., Internat. Astron. Union. Office: Dept Physics and Astronomy orthwestern U 2145 Sheridan Rd Evanston IL 60208-0834 E-mail: r-taam@northwestern.edu.

TABACZYNSKI, RON, state legislator; m. Mary Tabaczynski. AA, BA, Calumet Coll., St. Joseph. Legis. asst. House Dem. Caucus, 1988-90; mem. from 1st dist. Ind. State Ho. of Reps., 1992-98; govt. cons. SRI, Inc., Indpls. Mem. commerce and econ. devel. com., elections and apportionment com., ins., corps. and small bus. com., environ. affairs com., labor com. Formerly Dem. Precinct Committeeman; del. Dem. State Conv. Mem. N.W. Ind. World Trade Coun., Hammond Mohawks Conservation Club, FDR Club, Elks, KC. Home: 550 141st St Hammond IN 46327-1249 Office: SRI Inc 8082 Dash St Indianapolis IN 46250

TABATABAI, M. ALI, chemist, biochemist; b. Karbala, Iraq, Feb. 25, 1934; BS, U. Baghdad, 1958; MS, Okla. State U., 1960; PhD in Soil Chemistry, Iowa State U., 1965. Rsch. assoc. soil biochemistry Iowa State U., Ames, 1966-72, from asst. prof. to assoc. prof., 1972-78, prof. soil chemistry and biochemistry, 1978—. Cons. Electric Power Rsch. Inst., Palo Alto, 1978-83. Fellow AAAS, Am. Inst. Chemists, Am. Soc. Agronomy (Soil Sci. rsch. award 1992), Soil Sci. Soc. Am., Iowa Acad. Sci. (Disting. scientist, Disting. fellow); mem. Coun. Agrl. Sci. and Tech., Am. Chem. Soc., Am. Soc. Microbiology, Am. Soc. Agronomy, Soil Sci. Soc. Am., Assn. Univ. Profs., Iowa Acad. Sci., Gamma Sigma Delta (Alumni award of merit Iowa Beta chpt. 1993), Sigma Xi, Phi Kappa Phi. Achievements include research in soil enzymology and chemistry of sulfur, nitrogen and phosphorus in soils, nutrient cycling in the environment. Office: Iowa State U Sci & Tech Dept Agronomy Ames IA 50011-0001 E-mail: malit@iastate.edu.

TABER, MARGARET RUTH, retired engineering technology educator; b. St. Louis, Apr. 29, 1935; d. Wynn Orr and Margaret Ruth (Feldman) Gould Stevens; m. William James Taber, Sept. 6, 1958 B of Engring. Sci., Cleve. State U., 1958, BEE, 1958; MS in Engring., U. Akron, 1967; EdD, Nova Southeastern U., 1976; postgrad., Western Res. U., 1959-64. Registered profl. engr., Ohio; cert. engring. technologist. From engring. trainee to tng. dir. TOCCO divsn. Ohio Crankshaft Co., Cleve., 1954-64; from instr. elec.-electronic engring. tech. to prof. Cuyahoga C.C., Cleve., 1964-79, chmn. engring. tech., 1977-79; assoc. prof. elec. engring. tech. Purdue U., West Lafayette, Ind., 1979-83, prof., 1983-2000, prof. emeritus, 2000—. Lectr. Cleve. State U., 1963-64; mem. acad. adv. bd. Cleve. Inst. Electronics, 1981—; cons. in field. Author: (with Frank P. Tedeschi) Solid State Electronics, 1976; (with Eugene M. Silgalis) Electric Circuit Analysis, 1980; (with Jerry L. Casebeer) Registers, 1980; (with Kenneth Rosenow) Arithmetic Logic Units, 1980, Timing and Control, 1980, Memory Units, 1980; 6809 Architecture and Operation, 1984, Programming I: Straight Line, 1984; contbr. articles to profl. jours. Bd. dirs. West Blvd. Christian Ch., deaconess, 1974-77, elder, 1977-79; deacon Federated Ch., 1981-84, 86-89, Stephen Leader, 1988—2002; mem. Cancer Support Group; vol. Lafayette Adult Resource Acad., 1992—; vol. ednl. resource, vol. tchr. Sunburst Farm/Rainbow Acres, Ariz., 1988—. Recipient Helen B. Schleman Gold Medallion award Purdue U., 1991, The Greater Lafayette Cmty. Survivorship award, 1994, Outstanding Alumni award U. Akron Coll. Engring., 1994, Disting. Alumni award, Cleve. State U., 2002; Margaret R. Taber Microcomputer Lab. named in her honor Purdue U., 1991; NSF grant, 1970-73, 78; Rainbow Acres Computer Lab named The Marge Taber Computer Lab., 2002. Fellow Soc. Women Engrs. (counselor Purdue chpt. 1983-94, Disting. Engring. Educator award 1987); mem. IEEE (life sr.), Am. Cancer Soc. (co-chair svc. and rehab com. 1992-94, vol. coord. CanSurmount 1993-98, chair Cmty. Connections, mem. Resource, Info. and Guidance CoreTeam, 1994-98, v.p. Tippecanoe bd. dirs. 1996-98, relay for life hon. chair 1999), Am. Bus. Women's Assn. (ednl. chmn. 1964-66), Am. Soc. Engring. Edn., Am. Tech. Edn. Assn., Tau Beta Pi (hon.), Phi Kappa Phi. Avocations: robotics, computers. Home: 3036 State Rd 26 W West Lafayette IN 47906-4743 Office: Purdue U Elec Engring Tech Dept Knoy Hall Tech West Lafayette IN 47907

TABIN, JULIUS, lawyer, physicist; b. Chgo., Nov. 8, 1919; s. Sol and Lillian (Klingman) T.; m. Johanna Krout, Sept. 7, 1952; children: Clifford James, Geoffrey Craig. BS, U. Chgo., 1940, PhD in Physics, 1946; LLB, Harvard U., 1949. Bar: Calif., D.C. 1949, Ill. 1950. Jr. physicist metall. lab. U. Chgo., 1943-44; physicist Los Alamos Sci. Lab. (U. Calif.), N.Mex., 1944-45, Argonne Nat. Lab., AEC, Chgo., 1946; staff mem., group supr. Inst. Nuc. Studies, MIT, 1946-49; patent examiner U.S. Patent Office, Washington, 1949-50; assoc. firm Fitch, Even, Tabin & Flannery, Chgo., 1950-52; mem. firm Fich, Even, Tabin &

Flannery, Chgo., 1952—. Lectr. U. Chgo., 1959. Mem. Am., D.C., Calif., Ill., Chgo. bar assns., Sigma Xi. Home: 162 Park Ave Glencoe IL 60022-1352 Office: 120 S La Salle St Chicago IL 60603-3403 Office Phone: 312-577-7000. E-mail: jtabin@fitcheven.com.

TABLER, BRYAN G., lawyer; b. Louisville, Jan. 12, 1943; s. Norman Gardner and Sarah Marie (Grant) T.; m. Susan Y. Beidler, Dec. 28, 1968 (div. June 1987); children: Justin Elizabeth, Gillian Gardner; m. Karen Sue Strome, July 24, 1987. AB, Princeton U., 1969; JD, Yale U., 1972. Bar: Ind. 1972, U.S. Dist. Ct. (so. dist.) Ind. 1972, U.S. Dist. Ct. (no. dist.) Ind. 1976, U.S. Ct. Appeals (7th cir.) 1976, U.S. Supreme Ct. 1976. Assoc. Barnes & Thornburg, Indpls., 1972-79, ptnr., chmn. environ. law dept., 1979-94; v.p., gen. counsel, sec. IPALCO Enterprises, Inc., 1994—; sr. v.p., gen. coun., sec. Indpls. Power & Light Co., 1994—. Mem. exec. com. Environ. Quality Control, Inc., Indpls., 1985-97. Mem. Indpls. Mus. of Art, 1972—; bd. dirs. Indpls. Symphony Orch., 1995—. 1st lt. U.S. Army, 1964-68, Vietnam. Mem. ABA, Ind. Bar Assn., Bar Assn. of the 7th Cir., Indpls. Bar Assn. Avocation: golf. Home: 137 Willowgate Dr Indianapolis IN 46260-1471 Office: Indpls Power & Light Co One Monument PO Box 1595 Indianapolis IN 46206-1595

TABLER, NORMAN GARDNER, JR., lawyer; b. Louisville, Oct. 15, 1944; s. Norman Gardner and Marie (Grant) T.; m. Dawn Carla Martin, May 6, 1989; 1 child, Rachel Ann Tabler. BA, Princeton U., 1966; MA, Yale U., 1968; JD, Columbia U., 1971. Bar: Ind. 1971, U.S. Dist. Ct. (so. dist.) Ind. 1971. Assoc. Baker & Daniels, Indpls., 1971-77, ptnr., 1978-96; sr. v.p. corp. affairs, gen. counsel, chief compliance officer, sec. Clarian Health Ptnrs., Inc., Indpls., 1996—. Adj. prof. Ind. U. Law Sch., Indpls., 1984-88; mem. adv. com. Ctr. for Law and Health, Ind. U., Indpls., 1987-91; mem. antitrust task force Ind. Dept. Health, 1993-94; lectr. Ind. U. Law Sch., 1992-96; chmn. bd. dirs. CH Assurance Ltd., 2002-, Clarian Health Risk Retention Group, Inc., 2004—, Emergency Medicine Group, Inc., 2004—. Bd. dirs. Clarina Transplant Inst., 2007-, Methodist Cardiology Physician, 2006-, Clarina West Med. Ctr., 2004-, Ind. Repertory Theatre, Inc., Indpls., 1984-97, 2005-06, Indpls. Art Ctr., 1988-93, 2006-07, chmn., 1989-92; bd. dirs. Indpls. 500 Festival, 1992-98, Brickyard 400 Festival, 1993-98; bd. dirs. Indpls. Pub. Broadcasting, 1992—, chmn., 1997-2001, 05-07; mem. Ind. Sec. of State's Com. on Revision of Ind. Nonprofit Corp. Act, 1989-92, Ind. Ednl. Fin. Authority, 1989-93; mem. Ind. Recreational Devel. Commn., 1993-2004, vice chmn., 2002-04; mem. Medicaid Task Force Ind. Commn. Health Policy, 1990-92, Ind. Commn. on CLE, 1999-2005; mem. nat. bd. lay reps. PBS, 1997-2003. Mem. ABA (health care com. sect. antitrust law, health law sect.), Ind. Bar Assn. (health law sect.), Indpls. Bar Assn. (health law sect.), Am. Health Lawyers Assn., Ind. Health and Hosp. Assn. (com. on hosp. governance 1999-2007), Ind. U. Parents Assn., Ind. U. Parents Ann. Fund (nat. chmn. 1995-98), Princeton Alumni Assn. Ind. (pres. 1988-97), Indpls. Athletic Club (bd. dirs. 1994-2000), Skyline Club (bd. govs. 1992—), Princeton Club N.Y., Lawyers Club (Indpls., pres. 2007—), Highland Golf & Country Club (Indpls.), Carmel Racquet Club (Ind.). Methodist. Avocations: reading biographies, squash, kayaking. Office: General Counsel & Sr VP Legal Dept Clarian Health Ptnrs Inc PO Box 1367 Indianapolis IN 46206-1367

TACHA, DEANELL REECE, federal judge; b. Goodland, Kans., Jan. 26, 1946; m. John Allen Tacha; children: John Reece, David Andrew, Sarah Nell, Leah Beth. BA, U. Kans., 1968; JD, U. Mich., 1971. Spl. asst. to US Sec. of Labor, Washington, 1971—72; assoc. Hogan & Hartson, Washington, 1973, Thomas J. Pitner, Concordia, Kans., 1973—74; dir. Douglas County Legal Aid Clinic, Lawrence, Kans., 1974—77; assoc. prof. law U. Kans., Lawrence, 1974—77, prof., 1977—85, assoc. dean, 1977—79, assoc. vice chancellor, 1979—81, vice chancellor, 1981—85; judge US Ct. Appeals (10th cir.), Denver, 1985—2001, chief judge, 2001—07; mem. US Sentencing Commn., 1994—98; nat. pres. Am. Inns. of Ct., 2004—. Office: US Ct Appeals 643 Massachusetts St Ste 301 Lawrence KS 66044

TACKER, WILLIS ARNOLD, JR., medical educator, researcher; b. Tyler, Tex., May 24, 1942; s. Willis Arnold and Willie Mae (Massey) T.; m. Martha J. McClelland, Mar. 18, 1967; children: Sarah Mae, Betsy Jane, Katherine Ann. BS, Baylor U., 1964, MD, PhD, 1970. Lic. physician, Ind., Alaska, Tex. Intern Mayo Grad. Sch. Medicine Mayo Clinic, Rochester, Minn., 1970-71; pvt. practice Prudhoe Bay, Alaska, 1971; instr. dept. physiology Baylor Coll. Medicine, Houston, 1971-73, asst. prof. dept. physiology, 1973-74; clin. prof. family medicine Ind. U. Sch. Medicine, West Lafayette, Ind., 1981—; vis. asst. prof. Biomed. Engring. Ctr., Purdue U., West Lafayette, 1974-76, assoc. prof. Sch. Vet. Medicine, 1976-79; assoc. dir. William A. Hillenbrand Biomed. Engring. Ctr., Purdue U., West Lafayette, 1980-93, prof. Sch. Vet. Medicine, 1979—, acting dir., 1991-93; exec. dir. Hillenbrand Biomed. Engring. Ctr., 1993-95. Vis. rsch. fellow Sch. Aerospace Medicine, Brooks AFB, San Antonio, 1982; with Corp. Sci. and Tech., State of Ind., 1985-88; presenter, cons. in field. Author: Some Advice on Getting Grants, 1991; co-author: Electrical Defibrillation, 1980; author: (with others) Handbook of Engineering and Medicine and Biology, 1980, Implantable Sensors for Closed-Loop Prosthetic Systems, 1985, Encyclopedia of Medical Devices and Instrumentation, 1988, (with others) Defibrillation of the Heart, 1994; contbr. numerous articles to profl. jours. Chmn. bd. dirs. Assn. Advancemt Med. Instrumentation Found., Arlington, Va., 1987-95. Mem. Am. Heart Assn. (bd. dirs. Ind. affiliate 1975-81, med. edn. com. 1975-81, pub. health edn. com. 1975-81, chmn. ad hoc com. CPR tng. for physicians 1976-77, rsch. review com. 1988-90), Am. Physiol. Soc., Ind. State Med. Assn., Tippecanoe County Med. Soc., Assn. Advancement Med. Instrumentation (chmn. various coms., bd. dirs. 1981-84, pres. 1985-86), Am. Men and Women Sci., Alpha Epsilon Delta, Beta Beta Beta, Soc. Sigma Xi. Achievements include research in biomedical engineering, cardiovascular physiology, medical education, emergency cardiovascular care, motor evoked potentials, skeletal muscle ventricle; patents for an apparatus and method for measurement and control of blood pressure, electrode system and method for implantable defibrillators, pressure mapping system with capacitive measuring pad. Office: Purdue U Basic Med Scis 625 Harrison St West Lafayette IN 47907-2006 E-mail: tacker@vet.purdue.edu.

TADDIKEN, MARK, state legislator; b. Clay Center, Kans., Jan. 27, 1950; m. Debra Taddiken; children: Tawnya, Bria, Shawn. BS, Ft. Hays State U., 1972. Mem. Kans. State Senate, 2000, vice chair natural resources com., mem. agr. com., assessment and taxation com., utilities com. Sec., treas. Riverdale Cemetery Dist., 1993—; mem. Clay County Ext. Coun., 1997—. Mem. Farmers Coop Shipping Assn. (pres. 1980's), Lower Rep. Water Users Assn. (v.p. 1991—), Kans. Soybean Assn. (v.p. 1994—), Bluestem Rural Electric Cooperative (pres. 1994—). Republican. Episcopalian. Office: 2614 Hackberry Rd Clifton KS 66937 Fax: 785-926-3210. E-mail: taddiken@senate.state.ks.us.

TAFF, GERRY, reporter; With WFAA-TV, Dallas, WJRT-TV, Flint, Mich., WTNH-TV, New Haven; news anchor WISN 12, Milw., 1979—. Recipient spl. medallion, S.W. Journalism Forum. Office: WISN PO Box 402 Milwaukee WI 53201-0402

TAFLOVE, ALLEN, electrical engineer, educator, researcher, consultant; s. Harry and Leah T.; m. Sylvia Hinda Friedman, Nov. 6, 1977; children: Michael Lee, athan Brent. BS with highest distinction, Northwestern U., 1971, MS, 1972, PhD Cabell Fellow, 1975. Assoc. engr. IIT Rsch. Inst., Chgo., 1975-78, rsch. engr., 1978-81, sr. engr., 1981-84; assoc. prof. Northwestern U., Evanston, Ill., 1984-88, prof., 1988—, Charles Deering McCormick prof., 2000—03; master Lindgren/Slivka Residential Coll. Sci. & Engring., 2000—05. Author: Computational Electrodynamics: The Finite-Difference Time-Domain Method, 1995, 3rd edit., 2005; co-author: Computational Electromagnetics: Integral Equation Approach, 1993; editor: Advances in Computational Electrodynamics: The Finite-Difference Time-Domain Method, 1998. Fellow: IEEE. Achievements include pioneer of finite-difference time-domain method in computational electrodynamics. Office: Northwestern U Dept Elec Engring and Computer Sci 2145 Sheridan Rd Evanston IL 60208-0834 Home Phone: 847-674-0597; Office Phone: 847-491-4127. Business E-Mail: taflove@ece.northwestern.edu.

TAFT, BOB (ROBERT ALPHONSO TAFT II), former governor, educator; b. Conn., Jan. 8, 1942; great grandson of William Howard Taft, 27th President of US; m. Hope Taft; 1 child, Anna. BA in Govt., Yale U., 1963; MA, Princeton U., 1967; JD, U. Cin., 1976. Budget officer, asst. dir. Ill. Bur. Budget, 1967—73; mem. Ohio Ho. of Reps., Columbus, 1976-80; commr. Hamilton County, Ohio, 1981-90; sec. of state State of Ohio, Columbus, 1991-99, gov., 1999—2007; disting. rsch. assoc. U. Dayton, Ohio, 2007—. Vol. Peace Corps., Tanzania, 1963—65. Republican. Protestant. Office: U Dayton 300 College Park Dayton OH 45469*

TAFT, SHELDON ASHLEY, retired lawyer; b. Cleve., Mar. 2, 1937; s. Kingsley Arter and Louise Parsons (Dakin) T.; m. Rebecca Sue Rinehart, Dec. 26, 1962; children: Mariner R., Ashley A., Curtis N. BA, Amherst Coll., 1959; LLB, Harvard U., 1962. Bar: Ohio 1962. Assoc. Vorys, Sater, Seymour & Pease, Columbus, Ohio, 1965-69, 71-73; chief legal counsel Pub. Utilities Commn. Ohio, 1969-71; ptnr. Vorys, Sater, Seymour & Pease, Columbus, Ohio, 1974—2001, of counsel, 2002—04, ret., 2005. Ohio bd. advisors Chgo. Title Ins. Co., 1967-98. Rep. candidate for justice Ohio Supreme Ct., 1974; trustee Opera Columbus, 1989—, pres., 1991-93, life trustee, 1995—; trustee Columbus Bach Ensemble 2002—, pres. 2002-06; trustee Chamber Music Columbus, 2006—;trustee Columbus Symphony orchestra, 2007—; councilor New England Hist. and Geneal. Soc., 2005—. 1st lt. USAF, 1963-65. Mem. Ohio State Bar Assn. (pres. pub. utilities com. 1984-87), Columbus Bar Assn., Ohio Camera Collectors Soc. (pres. 1985-87), Rocky Fork Hunt and Country Club, Hillsboro Club, 41 Club, Review Club. Congregationalist. Avocation: camera collecting. E-mail: staft@columbus.rr.com.

TAGATZ, GEORGE ELMO, retired obstetrician, gynecologist, educator; b. Milw., Sept. 21, 1935; s. George Herman and Beth Elinore (Blain) T.; m. Susan Trunnell, Oct. 28, 1967; children: Jennifer Lynn, Kirsten Susan, Kathryn Elizabeth. AB, Oberlin Coll., 1957; MD, U. Chgo., 1961. Diplomate Am. Bd. Obstetricians and Gynecologists, Am. Bd. Reproductive Endocrinology (examiner, bd. reproductive endocrinology 1976-79). Rotating intern Univ. Hosps. of Cleve., 1961-62, resident in internal medicine, 1962-63; resident in ob-gyn U. Iowa, 1965-68; sr. research fellow in endocrinology U. Wash. dept. obstetrics and gynecology, 1968-70; from asst. prof. ob-gyn to prof. emeritus Med. Sch. U. Minn., 1970—2000, prof. emeritus Med. Sch., 2000—. Fertility and maternal health adv. com. FDA, USPHS, HHS, 1982-86; cons. in field. Ad hoc editor: Am. Jour. Ob-Gyn, Fertility and Sterility; contbr. articles to profl. publs. Served with M.C. U.S. Army, 1963-65. Mem. AMA, Minn., Hennepin County med. socs., Minn. Obstet. and Gynecol. Soc., Am. Coll. Ob-Gyn (subcom. on reproductive endocrinology 1979-82), Endocrine Soc., Am. Fertility Soc., Central Assn. Obstetricians and Gynecologists, U. Iowa Ob-Gyn Alumni Soc. Home: 5828 Long Brake Trl Edina MN 55439-2622 Home Phone: 952-941-7930. Personal E-mail: getagatz@comcast.net.

TAGGART, DAVID D., trucking executive; Chmn., CEO Crouse Cartage Co., Lenexa, Kans., 1994—. Office: Crouse Cartage Co 8245 Nieman Rd Lenexa KS 66214-1508

TAGGART, THOMAS MICHAEL, lawyer; b. Sioux City, Iowa, Feb. 22, 1937; s. Palmer Robert and Lois Allette (Sedgwick) T.; m. Dolores Cecilia Baroway Renfro, Jan. 4, 1963; children: Thomas Michael Jr., Theodore Christopher; m. Mary Ann Gribben, Feb. 7, 1976. BA, Dartmouth Coll., 1959; JD, Harvard U., 1965. Bar: Ohio 1965, U.S. Dist. Ct. (so. dist.) Ohio 1967, U.S. Dist. Ct. (no. dist.) Ohio 1981, U.S. Supreme Ct. 1997. Ptnr. Vorys, Sater, Seymour & Pease, Columbus, Ohio, 1965—, now of counsel. Lectr. Ohio Legal Ctr. Inst., Ohio Mfrs. Assn., Capitol U. Ctr. for Spl. and Continuing Legal Edn. Capt. USMC, 1959-63. Mem. ABA, Ohio Bar Assn. (bd. govs. 1991-99, liability ins. com. 1996-, pres. 1997-98, trustee Found. 1996-98, 2000—, pres 2005—, chair commn. on jud. evaluations 2000, Ohio Bar medal 1999), Columbus Bar Assn. (bd. govs., pres. 1989-90), Am. Bd. Trial Advocates, Columbus Area C. of C. Methodist. Home: 145 Stanbery Ave Columbus OH 43209-1465 Office: Vorys Sater Seymour & Pease 52 E Gay St Columbus OH 43215-3161 Office Phone: 614-464-6252. E-mail: tmtaggart@vssp.com.

TAGUE, JOHN PATRICK, air transportation executive; married; 2 children. Dir., then sr. v.p. Midway Airlines, 1985—91; with ATA Holdings, 1991—95; co-chmn., CEO The Pointe Group, 1995—97; pres., CEO ATA Holdings, 1993—2002; exec. v.p., customer United Airlines Corp., 2003—04, exec. v.p. mktg., sales and revenue, 2004—06, exec. v.p., chief revenue officer, 2006—.

TAI, CHEN-TO, electrical engineering educator; b. Soochow, China, Dec. 30, 1915; came to U.S., 1943; m. Chia Ming Shen, Apr. 28, 1941; children: Arthur, Bing, Julie, David, James. BSc, Tsing Hua U., Beijing, 1937; DSc, Harvard U., 1947. Rsch. fellow Harvard U., Cambridge, Mass., 1947-49; sr. rsch. scientist Stanford Rsch. Inst., Palo Alto, Calif., 1949-54; assoc. prof. Ohio State U., Columbus, 1954-56, prof., 1960-64, Tech. Inst. Electronics, Brazil, 1956-60, U. Mich., Ann Arbor, 1964-86, prof. emeritus, 1986—. Author: Dyadic Green's Functions, 1971, 2d edit., 1994, Generalized Vector and Dyadic Analysis, 1991, 2d edit., 1997; contbr. numerous articles to profl. jours. Fellow IEEE (life, Centennial award 1985, Heinrich Hertz medal 1998); mem. U.S. Nat. Acad. Engring. Home: 1155 Arlington Blvd Ann Arbor MI 48104-4023 Office: Univ of Mich Dept EECS Ann Arbor MI 48109 E-mail: ctnming@aol.com, tai@eecs.umich.edu.

TAIGANIDES, E. PAUL, agricultural and environmental engineer, consultant; b. Polymylos, Macedonia, Greece, Oct. 6, 1934; s. Pavlos Theodorou and Sophia ((Elezidou) T.; m. Maro Taiganides, Dec. 25, 1961; children: Paul Anthony, Tasos E., Katerina. BS in Agri. Engring., U. Maine, 1957; MS in Soil and Water Engring., Iowa State U., 1961, D of Environ. Engring., 1963. Cert. engr., Iowa, Colo. Rsch. assoc., asst. prof. Iowa State U., Ames, 1957-65; prof. Ohio State U., Columbus, 1965-75; mgr., chief tech. adviser UN, FAO, Singapore, Singapore, 1975-84, mgr., chief engr., 1984-85, mgr., chief tech. adviser Kuala Lumpur, Malaysia, 1985-87; mgr., owner EPT Cons., Columbus, 1987—. Cons. EPD/Hong Kong, 1988-92, WHO, UN, Denmark, Poland, Czechoslovakia, 1972-75, Internat. Devel. Rsch. Ctr., Can., China, Asian, 1984-89, NAE, Thailand, 1990, FAO, Malaysia, Foxley & Co., Nu-Tek Foods; environ. advisor to Bertam Devel. Corp., Kuala Lampur, Malaysia, 1992—; waste cons. to U.S. Feed Grains Coun., Taiwan, Malaysia, 1992, Venezuela, 1993; pres. Fan Engring., (US) Inc., 1991—, Red Hill Farms, Ohio, 1992—. Author: (video) Waste Resources Recycle, 1985, Pig Waste Treatment and Recycle, 1992; editor: Animal Wastes, 1977; co-editor Agricultural Wastes/ Biological Wastes, 1979; contbr. articles to profl. jours. Bd. govs., v.p. Singapore Am. Sch., Singapore, 1978-83; clergy-leity congress Greek Orthodox Ch., Houston, 1974. Recipient rsch. awards EPA, 1971-75, Water Resources Inst., 1968-73; rsch. grantee UNDP, FAO, IDRC, GTZ, Asean, 1975-88. Fellow Am. Soc. Agrl. Engrs. (chmn. dept., A.W. Farral award 1974), Am. Assn. Environ. Engrs. (diplomate); mem. Am. Soc. Engring. Edn. (div. chmn.), Singapore Lawn Tennis Assn. (v.p. 1980-84), Am. Club (mgmt. com. 1980-85), Sigma Xi. Greek Orthodox. Avocations: tennis, classical music, folk dancing.

TAIT, ROBERT E., lawyer; b. Lima, Ohio, Sept. 3, 1946; s. Robert and Helen (Smith) T.; m. Donna G. Dome, June 22, 1968; children: Heather, Jennifer, Robert. BA, Kenyon Coll., Gambier, Ohio, 1968; JD, U. Mich., Ann Arbor, 1973. Bar: Ohio 1973, US Dist. Ct. (so. dist.) Ohio. 1976, US Dist. Ct. (no. dist.) Ohio 1976, US Dist. Ct. Md. 1980, US Ct. Appeals (6th cir.) 1981, US Supreme Ct. 1982. Ptnr. Vorys, Sater, Seymour & Pease, LLP, Columbus, Ohio, 1973—. Staff counsel Govs. Select Com. on Prevention Indsl. Accidents, Columbus, 1977-78. Served with US Army, 1969-70. Fellow Ohio Bar Found., Columbus Bar Found.; mem. ABA (litigation sect., products liability com.), Ohio Bar Assn. (worker's compensation com.), Columbus Bar Assn. (workers compensation and professionalism coms.), Def. Rsch. Inst. (workers compensation com.), Am. Bd. Trial Advocates, Assn. Def. Trial Attys. (exec. com. 1991-94, treas., 2002-07, v.p. 2007-), Dept. Energy and Contractors Attys. Assn., Fedn. Def. and Corp. Counsel (toxic torts com). Home: 2045 Wickford Rd Columbus OH 43221-4223 Office: Vorys Sater Seymour & Pease PO Box 1008 52 E Gay St Columbus OH 43215-3161 Home Phone: 614-488-4003; Office Phone: 614-464-6341. Business E-Mail: retait@vssp.com.

TAKAHASHI, JOSEPH S., neuroscientist, educator; b. Tokyo, Dec. 16, 1951; s. Shigeharu and Hiroko (Hara) T.; m. Barbara Pillsbury Snook, June 28, 1985; children: Erika S., Matthew N. BA, Swathmore Coll., Pa., 1974; PhD, U. Oreg., 1981. Pharmacology rsch. assoc. NIMH, NIGMS, Bethesda, Md., 1981-83; asst. prof. orthwestern U., Evanston, Ill., 1983-87, assoc. chmn. neurobiology and physiology, 1988-96, assoc. prof. neurobiology and physiology, 1987-91, prof. neurobiology and physiology, 1991-96, Walter and Mary Elizabeth Glass prof. life scis., 1996—, acting assoc. dir. Inst. for Neurosci., 1988-95; investigator Northwestern U. Howard Hughes Med. Inst., Evanston, 1997—. Psychobiology and behavior rev. com. NIMH, 1988-92; mem. Nat. Mental Health Adv. Coun., 1997—; neurosci. adv. com. Klingenstein Fund, 1999—. Assoc. editor Neuron; mem. adv. bd. Jour. Biol. Rhythms, 1984—; contbr. over 120 articles to profl. jours. Grantee Bristol-Myers Squibb, 1995—; recipient Alfred P. Sloan award A.P. Sloan Found., 1983-85, Searl Scholars award Chgo. Cmty. Trust, 1985-88, Merit award NIMH, 1987, Honma prize in biol. rhythms Honma Found., 1986, Presdl. Young Investigator award NSF, 1985-90, 6th C.U. Ariens Kappers award Netherlands Soc. for Advancement Nat. Scis., Medicine and Surgery, 1995, W. Alden Spencer award Columbia U., 2001. Fellow Am. Acad. Arts and Sci.; mem. NAS, Am. Soc. Human Genetics, Genetics Soc. Am., Soc. Neurosci., Soc. for Rsch. on Biol. Rhythms (adv. bd. 1986—), Mammalian Genome Soc., German Soc. Biochemistry and Molecular Biology (Eduard Buchner prize 2003), Am. Coll. Neuropsychopharmacology. Achievements include discovery of the expression of circadian oscillations in cells from vertebrates; and identification of first circadian clock gene in mice. Office: Northwestern U Howard Hughes Med Inst 2205 Tech Dr Evanston IL 60208-3520

TALBOT, EMILE JOSEPH, French language educator; b. Brunswick, Maine, Apr. 12, 1941; s. Joseph Emile and Flora Talbot; m. Elizabeth Mullen, Aug. 6, 1966; children: Marc, Paul. BA, St. Francis Coll., Biddeford, Maine, 1963; MA, Brown U., 1965, PhD, 1968. From instr. French to prof. U. Ill., Urbana, 1967—86, prof., 1986—2004, prof. emeritus, 2004—, head dept. French, 1988-94. Editor: (book) La Critique Stendhalienne, 1979; author: Stendhal and Romantic Esthetics, 1985, Stendhal Revisited, 1993, Reading Nelligan, 2002; rev. editor: The French Rev., 1979—82, Quebec Studies, 1988—93, mem. editl. bd.:, 1993—96; mem. editl. bd. Quebec Studies, 2003—05; mem. editl. bd.: Nineteenth-Century French Studies, 1986—2003, La Revue Francophone, 1990—96, Etudes Francophones, 1996—2004, Nouvelles Etudes Francophones, 2004—; editor: Quebec Studies, 2004—. Decorated chevalier Ordre des Palmes Académiques (France); recipient prize, Quebec, 2006; fellow, Ctr. Advanced Study U. Ill., 1973, Assoc., 1988, NEH, 1973—74, Camargo Found., France, 1976. Mem.: MLA, Am. Coun. Que. Studies (v.p. 1995—97, pres. 1997—99), Assn. Can. Studies in U.S., Am. Assn. Tchrs. French. Roman Catholic. Office: U Ill Dept French 707 S Mathews Ave Urbana IL 61801-3625 Home Phone: 217-351-6039; Office Phone: 217-244-2728.

TALBOT, PAMELA, public relations executive; b. Chgo., Aug. 10, 1946; BA in English, Vassar Coll., 1968. Reporter Worcester, Mass. Telegram and Gazette, 1970—72; account exec. Daniel J. Edelman, Inc., Chgo., 1972—74, account supr., 1974—76, v.p., 1976—78, sr. v.p., 1978—84, exec. v.p., gen. mgr., 1984—90; pres. Edelman West, Chgo., 1990—95; pres., CEO Edelman U.S., 1995—. Named a Pub. Rels. All Star, PR Mag.; recipient Silver Anvil award, Publicity Club Chgo., 1985, Golden Trumpet award, 1982, 1985. Mem.: Pub. Relations Soc. Am., Chgo. Network, Execs. Club Chgo. Office: Edelman Pub Rels 200 E Randolph Dr Ste 6300 Chicago IL 60601-6436 Business E-Mail: pam.talbot@edelman.com.

TALENT, JAMES MATTHES, former senator, congressman, lawyer; b. Des Peres, Mo., Oct. 18, 1956; m. Brenda Lyons, 1984; children: Michael, Kathleen Marie, Christine. BA in Polit. Sci., Washington U., 1978; JD, U. Chgo. Law Sch., 1981. Law clk. to Hon. Richard A. Posner US Ct. Appeals (7th Cir.), 1982—83; adj. prof. law Washington U. Sch. Law, 1984—86; mem. Mo. State Ho. Reps., 1985—93, minority leader, 1989-93; mem. US Congress from 2nd Mo. Dist., 1993—2001, mem. edn. and the workforce com., armed svcs. com., chmn. small bus. com., 1993—2001; US Senator from Mo., 2002—07. Legislative Achievement award Mo. Hosp. Assn., 1989, Legis. of Yr. award Dept. Mo. Veterans Fgn. Wars, Spirit Enterprise award, Mo. C. of C., 1990, Nat. Public Policy award Nat. Assn. Women Bus. Owners, Lifetime Achievement award Vietnam Veterans of Am. 2000, Lawmaker of Yr. award Independent Electrical Contractors, Inc., 2004 Mem. Mo. Bar Assn. (Award for significant contbns. to adminstrv. justice 1989), Mo. C. of C. (Spirit of Enterprise award 1990), Order of the Coif. Republican. Presbyterian.

TALLACKSON, HARVEY DEAN, state legislator, real estate and insurance salesman; b. Grafton, ND, May 15, 1925; s. Arthur J. and Mabel R. (McDougald) T.; m. Glenna M. Walstad, Aug. 4, 1946; children: Lynda, Thomas, Debra, Amy, Laura. Grad. h.s., Park River, ND. Grain and potato farmer, Grafton, 1946-68; ins. agt. Tallackson Ins., Grafton, 1968—; mem. N.D. Senate, Bismark, 1976—; real estate salesman Johnson Real Estate, Grafton, 1982—. Chmn. appropriation com. N.D. Senate, 1987-93. Bd. dirs. Nodak Rural Electric Coop., Grand Forks, N.D., 1965—; bd. dirs. Minnkota Power Coop., Grand Forks, 1979—, pres., 1990—. Recipient Pub. Svc. award N.D. Lignite Coun., 1989; named Outstanding Young Farmer by Area Chamber of Walsh & Pembina Counties, 1951-52. Mem. Nat. Coun. Ins. Legislatures (mem. exec. com. 1985—, pres. 1996-97), Lions (pres. 1977-79), Masons. Democrat. Lutheran. Avocations: golf, curling, travel, reading. Office: Tallackson Ins & Real Estate 53 W 5th St Grafton ND 58237-1468

TALLCHIEF, MARIA, former ballerina; b. Fairfax, Okla., Jan. 24, 1925; d. Alexander Joseph and Ruth Mary (Porter) Tallchief; m. Henry Paschen, Jr., June 3, 1956; 1 child, Elise Paschen. DFA (hon.), Lake Forest Coll., Ill., Colby Coll., Waterville, Maine, 1968, Ripon Coll., 1973, Boston Coll., Smith Coll., 1981, orthwestern U., Evanston, Ill., 1982, Yale U., 1984, St. Mary of the Woods Coll., 1984, Dartmouth Coll., 1985, St. Xavier Coll., 1989, U. Ill., 1997. Ballerina Ballet Russe de Monte Carlo, 1942-47; with NYC Ballet Co., 1947-65, prima ballerina, 1947-60; founder Chgo. City Ballet, 1981, artistic dir., 1981—87; now ballet dir. Lyric Opera Chgo., 1979—. Ballerina Ballet Russe de Monte Carlo, 1942—47, N.Y.C. Ballet Co., 1947—65, prima ballerina, 1947—60; founder Chgo. City Ballet, 1979; dir. ballet Lyric Opera Chgo., 1979—. Prima ballerina Am. Ballet Theatre, 1960, founder Sch. Chgo. Ballet, guest star Paris Opera, 1947, Royal Danish Ballet, 1961, created role Danses Concertantes, 1944, Night Shadow, 1946, Four Temperaments, 1946, 1946, Orpheus, 1948, The Firebird, 1949, Bourée Fantastique, 1949, Capriccio Brillante, 1951, A la Françaix, 1951, Swan Lake, 1951, Caracole, 1952, Scotch Symphony, 1952, The utcracker, 1954, Allegro Brillante, 1956, The Gounod Symphony, 1958; performer: (films) Presenting Lily Mais, 1943, Million Dollar Mermaid, 1953. Named Hon. Princess, Osage Indian Tribe, 1953; named to Nat. Women's Hall of Fame, 1996, Internat. Women's Forum Hall of Fame, 1997; recipient Disting. Svc. award, U. Okla., 1972, Dance Mag. award, 1960, Jane Addams Humanitarian award, Rockford Coll., 1973, Order of Lincoln award, 1974, Bravo award, Rosary Coll., 1983, award, Dance Educators Am., 1956, Achievement award, Women's Nat. Press Club, 1953, Capezio award, 1965, Nat. Medal of Arts, Pres. Clinton, 1999. Mem.: Nat. Soc. Arts and Letters. Office: Lyric Opera Ballet 20 N Wacker Dr Ste 860 Chicago IL 60606-2874

TALLEY, MELVIN GARY, academic administrator; b. West Chester, Pa., Feb. 26, 1945; s. Melvin G. and Alberta M. (Faddis) T.; m. Jolene Keller (div.); children: Kristin Jolene, Mark Gary. BS, Pa. State U., 1967; D (hon.), Bristol (Tenn.) Coll., 1988; MBA, U. Mo., 1998. Registered rep. DeHaven & Townsend, Phila., 1967-68; dir. Brown Mackie Coll., Salina and Overland Park, Kans., 1968-72, pres., 1972—94, emeritus, also bd. chmn.; mng. ptnr. ETG Partnership, LP, 2002—. Pres. Realty Mgmt. Investment Co., Salina, 1976—94; advisor region VI HEW, 1976-86, chmn. Region VII Adv. Proprietary Coun., 1989; mem. adv. bd. U.S. Office of Edn., 1988; chmn. region VII Coun. for Pvt. Career Colls. and Schs., 1989. Author: Reassessing Values in Postsecondary Edn., 1977. Bd. dirs. St. Francis Boys Home, Salina, 1975; trustee duPont, Hagley Mus. and Libr., 2004—. Mem. Pvt. Edn. Research Council, Inner Circle, Assn. Ind. Colls. and Schs. (bd. dirs. Washington chpt. 1968-78), Claymont Savings and Loan Assn. (bd. dirs.), Hagley Mus. and Libr. (trustee, 2004—). Home: 4609 W 113th Terr Brittany Ct Leawood KS 66211 Office: ETG Partnership LP 4609 W 113th Terr Leawood KS 66217 Office Phone: 913-491-9348.

TALLEY, ROBERT COCHRAN, academic administrator, cardiologist; b. May 26, 1936; m. Katherine Ann Plocar; children: Andrew, Katherine, David. BS, U. Mich., 1958; MD, U. Chgo., 1962. Diplomate Nat. Bd. Med. Examiners (medicine com. 1984-88, com. chair 1988-93). Asst. prof., dept. physiology and medicine U. Tex. Med. Sch., San Antonio, 1969—71, head, sect. cardiovascular diseases, 1971—75, assoc. prof., dept. medicine, 1971—75; acting chief medicine VA Hosp., San Antonio, 1974, chief cardiology svc., 1973—75; chmn. dept. internal medicine U. SD Sch. Medicine, Sioux Falls, 1975—87, Freeman prof. medicine, 1984—87, interim v.p., dean, 1986—87, v.p., dean, 1987—2004, dir. residency program, 2004—. Mem. liaison com. med. edn., 1998—. Contbr. articles to med. jours. Surgeon USPHS, 1966—68. Tchg. scholar, Am. Heart Assn. U. Chgo., 1972—75. Fellow: ACP, Am. Coll.

Cardiology; mem.: AMA, Liaison Com. on Med. Edn., Assn. Am. Med. Coll. (mem. coun. deans new dean mentoring program, mem. adminstrn. bd. coun. deans 1999—2004), Am. Fedn. Clin. Rsch., Am. Heart Assn. (bd. dirs. Dakota affiliate). Home: 1305 Cedar Ln Sioux Falls SD 57103-4512 Office: U SD Sch Medicine 1400 W 22nd St Sioux Falls SD 57105-1505 Business E-Mail: rtalley@usd.edu.

TALLON, DALE, professional sports team executive; b. Oct. 19, 1950; m. Meg Tallon; 2 children. Player Vancouver Canucks, 1970—73, Chicago Blackhawks, 1973—78, Pittsburgh Penguins, 1978—80; color analyst Chicago Blackhawks, 1981—97, dir. of Player Personnel, 1998—2002, color analyst, 2002—03, asst. gen. mgr., 2003—05, gen. mgr., 2005—. Named to NHL All-Star Team, 1971, 1972. Office: c/o Chicago Blackhawks 1901 W Madison St Chicago IL 60612

TALMAGE, LANCE ALLEN, obstetrician, gynecologist, military officer; b. Vandergrift, Pa., Feb. 23, 1938; s. Guy Wesley and Martha Lois (Bradstock) T.; m. Diana Elizabeth Heywood, June 23, 1962; children: Tamara, Lance Jr., Tenley. BS in Chem. Engring., U. Toledo, Ohio, 1960; MD, U. Mich., 1964. Flight surgeon 24th Infantry Divsn. US Army, 1966-69; resident U. Mich. Med. Ctr., Ann Arbor, 1969-73; clin. prof. Med. Univ. Ohio, Toledo, 1987—; med. dir. Ctr. for Women's Health, Toledo, 1987—2003. Brigadier gen. 112th Med. Brigage Ohio Army Nat. Guard, Columbus, 1995-97; pres. med. staff Toledo Hosp., 1989-91, chair dept. Ob-gyn., 1979-86; pres. Toledo Lucas County Acad. Medicine, 1994-95; mem. Toledo Hosp. Found. Bd., 2000-05, Ohio State Med. Bd., 1999—, supervising sec., 2003—. Cabinet mem. United Way, Toledo, 1994-96; hon. chmn. March of Dimes Mothers-March, Toledo, 1989; pres. Ottawa Hills Athletic Boosters, Ohio, 1986-88, team physician, 1981-2003; trustee U. Toledo Found., 1999—. Decorated Legion of Merit; named to, Ohio Vets. Hall Fame, 2001; recipient Disting. Alumni award, Waite H.S., 1996, Garde Nationale Trophy, N.G. Assn. U.S., 1998, Outstanding Team Physician, Ohio H.S. Athletic Assn., 2002, Blue T award, U. Toledo, 2002, Outstanding Chem. Engr. Grad. award, 2002—03. Fellow ACS, ACOG (dist. chair 1996-99, v.p. 2000-01, Disting. Dist. Svc. award, 2004), Fedn. State Med. Bds. (editl. com.), Fedn. State Medical Bds. Editional Com.; mem. AMA (mem. ho. of dels.), Am. Soc. Reproductive Medicine, Ohio State Med. Assn. (pres. 1998-99), Pi Kappa Phi Alumni Assn. (Beta Iota chpt. Hall of Fame), U. Toledo Alumni Assn. (trustee 1996-2002, pres. 2000-01, athletic com., 2005—), Res. Officers Assn., Soc. Med. Cons. to Armed Forces, Am. Legion Post 335, Mil. Officers Assn. Am. (life), Assn. Mil. Surgeons US (life), Nat. Guard Assn. US (life). Republican. Lutheran. Office: The Toledo Hosp 2150 W Ctrl Ave Toledo OH 43606 Office Phone: 419-291-2193. Personal E-mail: latalmage@bex.net.

TAMBRINO, PAUL AUGUST, college president; m. Faye M. Thompson; children: Paul, Jeffrey, Mark, Lauren. BA, Cen. Coll., Pella, Iowa, 1958; postgrad., Am. Inst. Banking, YC, 1958-59; MS, Hofstra U., 1966; EdD, Temple U., 1973. Cert. quality transformation cons. Group acturial supr. N.Y. Life Ins. Co., NYC, 1960-64; tchr. acctg. and bus. N. Babylon (N.Y.) Sr. High Sch., 1964-68; instr. econs. and acctg. coord. Ursinus Coll., Collegeville, Pa., 1968-70; asst. prof. acctg. and edn. Hofstra U., Hempstead, N.Y., 1970-78; dean bus. and art div. Northampton County C.C., Bethlehem, Pa., 1978-83; coll. dean Warren County C.C., Washington, N.J., 1984-91; pres., CEO Iowa Valley C.C. Dist., Marshalltown, 1991—. Cons. N.J. Dept. Higher Edn., 1989—, Pfizer, Inc., N.Y.C., 1974-78, John Wiley & Sons, 1984, Union Coll., 1982, Verbatim, Inc.,m 1974-78, McGraw-Hill, 1967-74. Contbr. chpt. to Accountants Encyclopedia, 1978; revised Careers and Opportunities in Accounting, 1978; contbr. articles to profl. jours. 1st lt. USAR, 1959-65. Mem. Rotary Internat., C. of C., Beta Alpha Psi, Delta Pi Epsilon. Office: Iowa Valley CC Dist Marshalltown IA 50158 Home: 1511 N Carolwood Blvd Casselberry FL 32730-2453

TAMM, ELEANOR RUTH, retired accountant, writer; b. Hansell, Iowa, July 20, 1921; d. Horace Gerald and Sibyl (Armstrong) Wells; m. Roy C. Tamm, Oct. 18, 1941 (dec. Jan. 1980); children: Larry LeRoy, Marilyn Ruth Tamm-Schmitt. Grad., Am. Soc. Travel Agts., Inc., 1970; student, Iowa Cen. C.C., 1983-85; grad., Inst. Children's Lit., 1994. Tchr. Howard County Rural Sch., Riceville, 1939-41; bookkeeper, cashier Cen. States Power and Light Co., Elma, Iowa, 1941-42; office supr. J.C. Penney Co., Goldsboro, N.C., 1942-44, bookkeeper West Palm Beach, Fla., 1945; head teller Iowa State Bank, Clarksville, Iowa, 1955-69; office and group mgr. Allen Travel Agy., Charles City, Iowa, 1969-81, tour conductor, tour organizer and planner, 1971-81; office mgr. Arora Clinics, P.C., Fonda, Iowa, 1986-90; freelance collaborator on children's books Clarksville, 1989—. Author: Flight to the Everlands, 1993, Firm Foundations, 1996, Adventure Down Under, 2001, Critter Capers, 2004, Squirrel Tales, 2006, Memorial to Howard, 2006, The Case of The Missing Meow, 2007. Leader Girl Scouts U.S.A., Clarksville, 1946-47; tchr. St. John Luth. Ch., Clarksville, 1946-66, ch. sec., 1954-66, sec.-treas. Altar Guild, 1993-94; United Fund sec.-treas. Clarksville Cmty. Fund, 1956-66; sec.-treas. Clarksville Band Boosters, 1964-66. Lutheran. Avocations: reading, music, writing, decorating, designing and sewing fashions. Home: 408 E 3rd St Fonda IA 50540-0425

TAMMEUS, WILLIAM DAVID, journalist, columnist; b. Woodstock, Ill., Jan. 18, 1945; s. W. H. and Bertha H. (Helander) T.; m. Marcia Bibens, Nov. 29, 1996; children: Lisen Tammeus Mann, Kate Tammeus Willaredt; stepchildren: Christopher L. Johnston, Daniel Bednarczyk, Kathryn B. Dandino, David Bednarczyk. BJ, U. Mo., Columbia, 1967; postgrad., U. Rochester, 1967-69. Reporter Rochester (N.Y.) Times-Union, 1967-70; reporter Kansas City (Mo.) Star, 1970-77, columnist, 1977—; syndicated columnist N.Y. Times News Svc., 1989-99, Knight Ridder/Tribune Info. Svcs., 2000—06; ret., 2006. Author: A Gift of Meaning, 2001; editor-at-large Presbyn. Outlook, 1993; contbg. editor Mo. Life mag., 1980-81; commentator Sta. KCPT-TV, 1979-90. Co-recipient Pulitzer prize for gen. local reporting of Hyatt Regency Hotel disaster, 1982; recipient 1st pl. opinion-editl. divsn. Heart of Am. award Kansas City Press Club, 1991, 93, 1st pl. column divsn., 1994, 1st pl. award best column/humor divsn. Mo. Press Assn., 1997, 2002, Best In-Depth Reporting on Religion award Am. Acad. Religion, 2001, David Steele Disting. Writer award Presbyn. Writers Guild, 2003, 1st pl. religion coverage Kans. Press Assn., 2004, Wilbur Column Writing award, Religion Communicators Coun., 2005, 1st pl. best feature column divsn. Mo. Press Assn., 2006. Mem. Nat. Soc. Newspaper Columnists (v.p. 1990-92, pres. 1992-94, 1st pl. items divsn. Writing award 1992, 3d place humor writing, 1999, 2000), Soc. Profl. Journalists. Presbyterian. Personal E-mail: wtammeus@kc.rr.com.

TAN, HUI QIAN, computer science, civil engineering educator; b. Tsingtao, China, June 12, 1948; s. Dumen Tan and Ruifan Rao; m. Ren Zhong, June 16, 1994; children: William W., Danny D, Yulia BA, Oberlin Coll., 1982; MS, Kent State U., 1984, PhD, 1986. Asst. prof. computer sci. and civil engring. U. Akron, Ohio, 1986-89, assoc. Ohio, 1990—; rsch. prof. Kent (Ohio) State U., 1987. Contbr. articles to profl. jours. Grantee NASA, 1987—, 91—, NSF, 1988-92. Mem. IEEE Computer Soc., Assn. for Computing Machinery, SIGSAM Assn. for Computing Machinery, Phi Beta Kappa. Avocations: classical music, history, literature, swimming, bicycling.

TANDON, RAJIV, psychiatrist, educator; b. Kanpur, India, Aug. 3, 1956; arrived in US, 1984, naturalized, 1988; s. Bhagwan Sarup and Usha (Mehrotra) T.; m. Chanchal Nammi Vohra; children: Neeraj, Anisha, Gitanjali. Student, St. Xavier's Coll., Bombay, India, 1974; BS, All India Inst., New Delhi, 1980; MD, at. Inst. of MH, India, 1983. Sr. resident Mental Health and Neuro-Scis., India, 1983-84; resident U. Mich. Hosps., Ann Arbor, 1984-87, attending psychiatrist, 1987-2000. Dir. schizophrenia program, dir. hosp. svcs. divsn. U. Mich., Ann Arbor, 1987—2000, assoc. prof., 1993—99, prof., 1999—2004; cons. Lenawee County Cmty. Mental Health, Adrian, Mich., 1985—99. Author: Biochemical Parameters of Mixed Affective States; Negative Schizophrenic Symptoms: Pathophysiology and Clinical Implications; contbr. over 250 articles to profl. jours. Recipient Young Scientist's award Biennial Winter workshop on Schizophrenia, 1990, 92, Travel award Am. Coll. Neuropsychopharmacology/Mead, 1990, Rsch. Excellence award Am. Assn. Psychiatrists from India, 1993, Sci. award, Best Drs. in Am. award, 1994-98, Gerald Klerman award for outstanding rsch. by a Nat. Alliance for Rsch. in Schizophrenia and Depression young investigator, 1995, FuturPsych award CINP, 1997. Mem. Am. Psychiat. Assn. (Wisniewski Young Psychiatrist Rschr. award 1993), World Fedn. Mental Health, Soc. for Neurosci., N.Y. Acad. Scis., Soc. Biol. Psychiatry, Mich. Psychiat. Soc. Independent. Hindu. Office Phone: 850-488-9998. Business E-Mail: rtandon@umich.edu.

TANDY, KAREN POMERANTZ, communications executive, former federal agency administrator; b. Ft. Worth, 1954; married; 2 children. Grad., Tex. Tech. U., Tex. Tech. Law Sch., 1977. Law clk. No. Dist. Tex.; asst. U.S. atty. (ea. dist.) Va. US Dept. Justice, 1979—90, asst. U.S. atty. (we. dist.) Wash., 1979—90, supr. dept. drug and forfeiture litig. criminal divsn., 1990—99; assoc. dep. atty. gen., dir. Organized Crime Drug Enforcement Task Forces, US Dept. Justice, 1999—2003, mgr., 2001—03; adminstr. Drug Enforcement Adminstrn. (DEA), Alexandria, Va., 2003—07; sr. v.p. global govt. rels. & pub. policy divsn. Motorola, Inc., Schaumburg, Ill., 2007—. Chief asset forfeiture unit U.S. Attys. Office Western Dist., Wash., 1988—90; clk. Chief Judge of No. Dist., Tex.; dep. chief Narcotics and Dangerous Drug Sect.; lectr. in field. Recipient Atty. Gens. award for disting. svc., Award for Extraordinary Achievement, US Dept. Justice, Award for Superior Svc., U.S. Atty. Dir., Disting. Alumni award, Tex. Tech U., 2006. Office: Motorola Inc 1303 E Algonquin Rd Schaumburg IL 60196*

TANG, CYRUS, investment company executive; b. Chiangsu Province, China, 1930; arrived in US, 1950; married; 2 children. Attended, Widener U., Ill. Inst. Tech. CEO, pres., chmn. Tang Industries, Mt. Prospect, Ill. Office: 1650 W Jefferson Ave Trenton MI 48183-2136 Address: Tang Industries 3773 Howard Hughes Pkwy Ste 350N Las Vegas NV 89109

TANGUAY, MARK H., real estate company executive; Mng. prin. Tanguay-Burke-Stratton, Chgo., 1987—. Office: Tanguay-Burke-Stratton 321 N Clark St Ste 900 Chicago IL 60610-4765

TANK, ALAN, trade association administrator; BA in Animal Sci., Iowa State U. Field dir. Iowa Pork Prodrs. Assn., 1980; mem. staff Congressman Jim Leach, Wash.; lobbyist Wash.; v.p. pub. policy Nat. Pork Prodrs. Council, Des Moines, 1991, chief exec. officer. Office: National Pork Producers Council 1776 NW 114th St Clive IA 50325-7000

TANNER, HELEN HORNBECK, historian, consultant; b. Northfield, Minn., July 5, 1916; d. John Wesley and Frances Cornelia (Wolfe) Hornbeck; m. Wilson P. Tanner, Jr., Nov. 22, 1940 (dec. 1977); children: Frances, Margaret Tanner Tewson, Wilson P., Robert (dec. 1983) AB with honors, Swarthmore Coll., 1937; MA, U. Fla., 1949; PhD, U. Mich., 1961. Asst. to dir. pub. rels. Kalamazoo Pub. Schs., 1937-39; with sales dept. Am. Airlines Inc., NYC, 1940-43; tchg. fellow, then tchg. asst. U. Mich., Ann Arbor, 1949-53, 57-60, lectr. ext. svc., 1961-74, asst. dir. Ctr. Continuing Edn. for Women, 1964-68; project dir. Newberry Libr., Chgo., 1976-81, rsch. assoc., 1981-95, sr. rsch. fellow, 1995—. Expert witness in Indian treaty litig., 1963—; dir. D'Arcy McNickle Ctr. for Indian History, 1984-85; mem. Mich. Commn. Indian Affairs, 1966-70; cons. in field Author: Zespedes in East Florida 1784-1790, 1963, 89, General Green Visits St. Augustine, 1964, The Greeneville Treaty, 1974, The Territory of the Caddo Tribe of Oklahoma, 1974, The Ojibwas, 1992; editor: Atlas of Great Lakes Indian History, 1987, The Settling of North America: An Atlas, 1995, Powhatan's Mantle, 2006, Beyond Red Power, 2007. Named to Mich. Women's Hall of Fame, 2006; EH grantee, 1976, fellow, 1989; ACLS grantee, 1990. Mem. Am. Soc. Ethnohistory (pres. 1982-83), St. Augustine Hist. Soc., Conf. L.Am. History, Soc. History Discoveries, Chgo. Map Soc., Hist. Soc. Mich., Ctr. French Colonial Studies. Home: 5178 Crystal Dr Beulah MI 49617-9618 Personal E-mail: hhtanner@charter.net.

TANNER, JIMMIE EUGENE, retired dean; b. Hartford, Ark., Sept. 27, 1933; s. Alford C. and Hazel Ame (Anthony) Tanner; m. Carole Joy Yant, Aug. 28, 1958; children: Leslie Allison, Kevin Don. BA, Okla. Baptist U., 1955; MA, U. Okla., 1957, PhD, 1964. Prof. English Okla. Bapt. U., Shawnee, 1958—64, 1965—72; assoc. prof. Franklin Coll., Ind., 1964—65; v.p. acad. affairs Hardin-Simmons U., Abilene, Tex., 1972—78, La. Coll., Pineville, 1978—80; dean William Jewell Coll., Liberty, Mo., 1980—97, prof., 1997—2003, interm pres., 1993—94; ret., 2003. Contbg. author: The Annotated Bibliography of D. H. Lawrence, Vol. 1, 1982, Vol. 2, 1985. Mem. Shawnee Sch. Bd., 1966—72; edn. commn. So. Bapt. Conv., 1967—72; bd. dirs. Mo. Coun. for Humanities, 2003—. So. Fellowships Fund fellow, 1960—61, Danforth fellow, 1962—63. Mem.: SAR. Democrat. Baptist. Avocations: tennis, photography. Home: 609 Lancelot Dr Liberty MO 64068-1023

TANNER, MARTIN ABBA, statistician, educator; b. Highland Park, Ill., Oct. 19, 1957; s. Meir and Esther Rose (Bauer) T.; m. Anat Talitman, Aug. 14, 1984; 1 child, oam Ben. BA, U. Chgo., 1978, PhD, 1982. Asst. prof. stats. and human oncology U. Wis., Madison, 1982-87, assoc. prof., 1987-90; dir. lab., prof. and dept. chair biostatistics U. Rochester, 1990-94; prof. dept. statistics Northwestern U., 1994—. Cons. Kirkland & Ellis, 1980-82; mem. Nat. Inst. Allergy and Infectious diseases study sect., 1994-98; reviewer NIH, NSF, VA. Assoc. editor Jour. Am. Stat. Assn., 1987-99; editor Jour. Am. Statis. Assn., 1999-03, Chapman & Hall, 2002-; contbr. articles to profl. jours. Recipient New Investigator Rsch. award NIH, 1984, Mortimer Spiegelman award Am. Pub. Health Assn., 1993; NSF grantee, 1983, 95, NIH grantee, 1986—. Fellow Royal Statis. Soc., Am. Statis. Assn. (Continuing Edn. Excellence award); mem. AAAS, Mensa, Sigma Xi. Avocations: classical guitar, medieval poetry. Office: Northwestern U 2006 Sheridan Rd Evanston IL 60208-0852 Home Phone: 847-491-2700; Office Phone: 847-491-2700. Business E-Mail: mat132@northwestern.edu.

TANNER, RALPH M., state legislator; b. Jefferson County, Ala., Dec. 10, 1926; m. Judith Tanner. BA, Birmingham-Southern Coll., 1954, MA, 1967; PhD, U. Ala., 1967. Rep. dist. 10 Kans. Ho. of Reps., 1994—. Republican. Office: Kans Ho of Reps Rm 426 -S Topeka KS 66612

TAPKEN, MICHELLE G., prosecutor; BA in Edn., U. SD, 1967, MA in Ednl. Psychology, 1970, JD, 1989. Bar: South Dakota; lic. Psychologist. Fed. law clerk, Lincoln, ebr., 1989—90; prosecutor US Atty. Office, Sioux Falls, SD, 1990—2001; interim US atty. Dist. SD US Dept. Justice, 2001, 2002, 1st asst. US atty. Dist. SD, 2005—. Recipient Director's award, US Dept. Justice, 1996, 2006. Office: 325 S 1st Ave Sioux Falls SD 57104

TARASZKIEWICZ, WALDEMAR, physician; b. Wilno, Poland, July 6, 1936; arrived in U.S., 1979; s. Michal Taraszkiewicz and Nina (Lutomska) Dylla; m. Teresa Barbara Szwarc, Oct. 15, 1966. MD, Med. Acad., Gdansk, Poland, 1961, internal medicine specialty, 1967; internal medicine specialty II, Med. Acad., 1972. Diplomate Am. Bd. Family Practice. Family physician Out Patient Clinic, Sopot, Poland, 1962—64; resident U. Hosp., Gdansk, 1965—71; allergist Clinic of Allergy, Gdansk, 1965—75; physician Cardiology Dept., Gdansk, 1971—75, Hopital Civil, Telagh, Algeria, 1975—79; surg. asst. Hinsdale (Ill.) Hosp., 1979—82; resident physician St. Mary of Nazareth Hosp., Chgo., 1982—85, emergency room physician, 1984—85; family practice medicine Brookfield, Ill., 1985—88, Westmont, Ill., 1988—89, Chgo., 1987—; med. dir. Winston Manor Nursing Home, Chgo., 1989—90; clin. asst. prof. U. Ill. Med. Coll., 1994—. Sr. asst. dept. cardiology Univ. Hosp., Gdansk, 1971—75; mem. adminstrv. com., pres. med. staff Hopital Civil, Telagh, 1976—79. Contbr. articles to profl. jours. Recipient Bronze medal, Polski Zwiazek Wedkarski, 1970, cert. 3d pl., 1971. Fellow: Am. Acad. Family Practice; mem.: AMA (Continuing Edn. award), N.Y. Acad. Scis., Polish Med. Alliance, Am. Coll. Allergy and Immunology, Am. Acad. Allergy and Immunology, World Med. Assn., Chgo. Med. Soc. (mem. practice mgmt. com.), Ill. Med. Soc. Avocations: art collecting, fishing. Office: 5946 N Milwaukee Ave Chicago IL 60646 E-mail: waldemar_taraszkiewicz@yahoo.com.

TARDY, MEDNEY EUGENE, JR., retired otolaryngologist, facial plastic surgeon; b. Scottsburg, Ind., Dec. 3, 1934; MD, Ind. U., 1960. Diplomate Am. Bd. Otolaryngology (v.p. 1993, pres. 1994). Intern Tampa Gen. Hosp., 1960—61; resident in otolaryngology U. Ill. Hosp., 1963—67, fellow head, neck and plastic surgery, 1967—68; otolaryngologist St. Joseph Hosp., Chgo.; prof. clin. otolaryngology U. Ill.; pvt. practice Chgo.; dir. divsn. facial plastic and reconstructive surgery U. Ill.; prof. clin. otolaryngology Ind. U. Med. Ctr., Indpls.; pvt. practice Chgo.; ret. Bd. govs. Chgo. Symphony Orch., Hubbard St. Dance Co., Chgo. Mem.: Soc. Univ. Otolaryngologists, Am. Rhinol. Soc., Am. Laryngol. Soc., Am. Acad. Otolaryngology-Head and Neck Surgery (past pres.), Am. Acad. Facial Plastic and Reconstructive Surgery (past pres.), ACS.

TARLOV, ALVIN RICHARD, foundation administrator, physician, educator; b. Norwalk, Conn., July 11, 1929; s. Charles and Mae (Shelinsky) T.; m. Joan Hylton, June 12, 1956 (div. 1976); children: Richard, Elizabeth, Jane, Suzanne, David. BA, Dartmouth Coll., 1951; MD, U. Chgo., 1956. Intern Phila. Gen. Hosp., 1956-57; resident in medicine U. Chgo. Hosps., 1957-58, 62-63, research assoc., 1958-61; asst. prof. medicine U. Chgo., 1963-68, assoc. prof., 1968-70, prof., 1970-84, prof. medicine, 2006—, chmn. dept. medicine, 1969-81; chmn. grad. med. edn. nat. adv. com. HHS, Washington, 1980; pres. Henry J. Kaiser Family Found., Menlo Park, Calif., 1984-90; sr. scientist New Eng. Med. Ctr., Boston, 1990-99, exec. dir. The Health Inst., 1995-99; prof. pub. health Harvard U., Boston, 1990-99; prof. of medicine Tufts U., 1990-99. Dir. Tex. Program for Soc. and Health, James Baker III Inst. for Pub. Policy, Rice U., 1999-2005. Pres. Med. Outcomes Trust, Inc., 1993-2000; chmn. bd., pres. Mass. Health Data Consortium, 1994-98. Served to capt. U.S. Army, 1958-61. Recipient Research Career Devel. award NIH, 1962-67; John and Mary Markle Found. scholar, 1966-71. Mem. ACP (master), Inst. Medicine of Nat. Acad. Scis. Home: 540 N State St Apt 3801 Chicago IL 60610-7240 E-mail: atarlov@gmail.com.

TARNOVE, LORRAINE, medical association executive; b. Atlantic City, July 26, 1947; d. Leonard Robert Tarnove and Jeanne Tarnove Yudkin; m. Steven B. Friedman, June 1, 1969; children: K. Brooke, Ari-Benjamin. BA, U. Md., 1969. Pres. Lorraine Tarnove Consulting, Columbia, Md., 1985-93; exec. dir. Am. Med. Dirs. Assn., Columbia. Contbr. chpt. to book. Office: AMDA 10840 Little Patuxent #760 Columbia MD 21044

TARONJI, JAIME, JR., lawyer; b. NYC, Nov. 20, 1944; s. Jaime and Ruth T.; m. Mary Taronji, May 16, 1970; children: Ian A., Mark N., Nicole V. BA, George Washington U., 1972; JD, Georgetown U., 1976. Bar: Va. 1977, DC 1978. Asst. to dep. staff dir. U.S. Commn. on Civil Rights, Washington, 1972-76; antitrust enforcement atty. FTC, Washington, 1976-79; antitrust counsel Westinghouse Electric Corp., Pitts., 1979-81; group legal counsel Dana Corp., Toledo, 1982-88; v.p., gen. counsel Packaging Corp. Am. subs. Tenneco, Evanston, Ill., 1988-95; law v.p. NCR Corp., Dayton, 1996-99; v.p., gen. counsel, sec. Dayton Superior Corp., Dayton, 1999—2003; of counsel antitrust practice group Howrey LLP, Washington, 2004—. Mem. adv. bd. Corp. Counsel Inst., Georgetown U. Law Ctr. Author: The 1970 Census Undercount of Spanish Speaking Persons, 1974; editor: Puerto Ricans in the U.S., 1976. Capt. M.I., U.S. Army, 1965-70, Vietnam. Mem. ABA (antitrust sect.), Hispanic Nat. Bar Assn., Hispanic Bar Assn. DC. Democrat. Roman Catholic. Office: Howrey LLP 1299 Pennsylvania Ave NW Washington DC 20004-2402 Office Phone: 202-383-7406. E-mail: taronjij@howrey.com.

TARPY, THOMAS MICHAEL, lawyer; b. Columbus, Ohio, Jan. 4, 1945; s. Thomas Michael and Catherine G. (Sharshal) T.; m. Mary Patricia Canna, Sept. 9, 1967; children: Joshua Michael, Megan Patricia, Thomas Canna, John Patrick. AB, John Carroll U., 1966; JD, Ohio State U., 1969. Bar: Ohio 1969, U.S. Dist. Ct. (so. dist.) Ohio 1972, U.S. Dist. Ct. (no. dist.) Ohio 1974, U.S. Ct. Appeals (6th cir.) 1982, U.S. Supreme Ct. 1997. Assoc. Vorys, Sater, Seymour & Pease LLP, Columbus, 1969-76, ptnr., 1977—85, 1985—87, 1987—2005; v.p. Liebert Corp., Columbus, 1985-87. Chmn. Columbus Graphics Commn., 1980; mem. Columbus Area Leadership Program, 1975. With U.S. Army, 1969-75. Fellow Coll. Labor and Employment Lawyers, Ohio Mgmt. Lawyers Assn. (founding mem.); mem. ABA, Ohio Bar Assn., Columbus Bar Assn. Office: Vorys Sater Seymour & Pease LLP PO Box 1008 52 E Gay St Columbus OH 43215-3161 E-mail: tmtarpy@vssp.com.

TARUN, ROBERT WALTER, lawyer; b. Lake Forest, Ill., Sept. 1, 1949; s. Donald Walter and Bonnie Jean (Cruickshank) T.; m. Helen J. McSweeney, May 1, 1987; children: Abigail Esch, Tyler Vincent, Parker Donald, Aimée Dakota. AB, Stanford U., 1971; JD, DePaul U., 1974; MBA, U. Chgo., 1982. Bar: Ill. 1974, Calif. 1975, US Dist. Ct. (no. dist. Ill.) 1974, US Dist. Ct. (we. dist. Ark.) 1986, US Dist. Ct. (so. dist. Ind.) 1995, US Dist. Ct. (no. dist. Calif.) 1995, US Dist. Ct. (ea. dist. Mich.) 1996, US Dist. Ct. (ea. dist. Wis.) 2000, US Dist. Ct. (ctrl. dist. Ill.) 2001, US Ct. Appeals (7th cir.) 1975, US Ct. Appeals (5th cir.) 1992, US Ct. Appeals (3rd cir.) 1993, US Ct. Appeals (fed. cir.) 1995, US Ct. Appeals (9th and 11th cirs.) 1996, US Supreme Ct. 1978. Asst. atty. gen. State of Ill., Chgo., 1974-76; asst. US atty. US Dept. Justice, Chgo., 1976-79, dep. chief criminal divsn., 1979-82, exec. asst. U.S. atty. no. dist. Ill., 1982-85; ptnr. Reuben & Proctor, Chgo., 1985-86, Isham, Lincoln & Beale, Chgo., 1986-88, Winston & Strawn, Chgo., 1988—2003, Latham & Watkins, LLP, Chgo., 2003—07, Baker & McKenzie, San Francisco and Chgo., 2007—. Instr. Atty. Gen.'s Advocacy Inst., Washington, 1980—85, Nat. Inst. Trial Advs., 1990; adj. prof. Northwestern U. Sch. Law, 1999—2001; lectr. in law white collar criminal and bus. litig. U. Chgo. Law Sch., 2001—05. Author (with Dan K. Webb): Corporate Internal Investigations, 1993—2005. Bd. dirs. Chgo. Ctrl. Area Com., 1994—2003. Named one of Best Lawyers in Am., Euroguide's Guide to World's Leading Litigators, Chambers USA Leading Bus. Lawyers, Top 100 Lawyers in Ill. Fellow Am. Coll. Trial Lawyers (chair. fed. criminal procedure com. 2003-2004, admission to fellowship com. 1997-2000), bd. regents, 2004-; mem. ABA (white collar crime inst. 1997—, planning com.), Bar Assn. San Francisco, Chgo. Bar Assn., U. Chgo. Grad. Sch. Bus. Alumni Assn. (bd. dirs. 1986), Racquet Club, Wong Sun Soc. (San Francisco), Kenilworth Club, H.O.G. (Black Hills chpt.), Chgo. Stanford Assn. Presbyterian. Avocations: architecture, writing screenplays, motorcycling. Office: Baker & McKenzie 2 Embarcadero Ctr 1100 San Francisco CA 94111 also: Baker & McKenzie 130 E Randolph St Chicago IL 60601 Office Phone: 415-591-3220, 312-861-2533. Business E-Mail: robert.w.tarun@bakernet.com.

TARVESTAD, ANTHONY M., psychiatrist; BA magna cum laude, Winona State U., 1973; JD, William Mitchell Coll. of Law, 1977. Exec. dir. Am. Bd. Physical Medicine and Rehab. Named Super Lawyer Minn. Jour. Law and Politics, 1994. Mem. Am. Coll. Healthcare Execs., Am. Health Laywers Assn., ABA, Am. Arbitration Assn. (arbitrator), Minn. State Bar. Assn. Office: Am Bd Physical Medicine and Rehabilitation 3015 Allegro Park Lane SW Rochester MN 55902-4139 Office Phone: 507-282-1776. Office Fax: 507-282-9242. E-mail: tarvestad@abpmr.org.

TATAR, JEROME F., business products executive; V.p., operating officer Mead Corp., Dayton, Ohio, 1994—96, pres., COO, 1996—97, chmn., CEO, 1997—2002; chmn. MeadWestvaco Corp., 2002. Bd. mem. Robbins & Myers Inc., Nat. City Corp., Bartech Group Inc. Office: Mead Corp Courthouse Plz NE Dayton OH 45463-0001

TATE, PHIL, state legislator; b. Mar. 21, 1946; m. Nancy Cassity; 1 child, Aaron Phillip. BS, U. Mo. Oil jobber; mem. Mo. Ho. of Reps. from 3d dist.; dir. bus. expansion and attractions Dept. Econ. Devel., Jefferson City, Mo. Vice chmn. Misc. Bill and Resolution Com. Mo. Ho. of Reps., mem. Agr., Appropriations, Health and Mental Health, Edn., Legis. Rsch. Coms. Mem. Jaycees, Rotary. Democrat. Home: 901 W Grand St Gallatin MO 64640-1610 Office: Dept Econ Devel PO Box 118 Jefferson City MO 65102-0118

TATHAM, RON, marketing executive; BBA, U. Texas, Austin; MBA, Texas Tech U; PhD, U. Ala. CEO Burke Inc. Mem. Mktg. Rsch. Adv. Bd. U. Ga., U. Tex. at Arlington; adv. bd. U. Wis.; presenter in field. Co-author: Multivariate Data Analysis, 4th edition, 1994; contbr. articles to prof. jours. Office: Burke Inc 805 Central Ave Fl 5 Cincinnati OH 45202-5747

TAUB, RICHARD PAUL, social sciences educator; b. Bklyn., Apr. 16, 1937; s. Martin Glynn and Frances (Israel) T.; m. Doris Susan Leventhal, Aug. 14, 1961 (dec. Feb. 1996); children: Neela Robin, Zachariah Jacob; m. Betty G. Farrell, June 21, 2000. BA, U. Mich., 1959; MA, Harvard U., Cambridge, Mass., 1962, PhD in Social Relations, 1966. Asst. prof. sociology Brown U., Providence, 1965-69; from asst. prof. to Paul Klapper prof. of social scis. U. Chgo., 1969—, assoc. dean coll. of Univ., 1982-86, chmn. dept. comparative human devel., 2000—. Adv. bd. Neighborhood Preservation Initiative, 1993-2000; chair adv. bd. at. Comty. Devel. Initiative, 1991-95; dir. South Ark. Rural Devel. Study, 1988-96; Disting. visitor Mac Arthur Found., 1998. Author: Bureaucrats Under Stress, 1969; (with D. Garth Taylor and Jan Dunham) Paths of Neighborhood Change, 1984, Community Capitalism, 1988; (with Doris L. Taub) Entrepreneurship in India's Small Scale Industries, 1989, Doing Development in Arkansas, 2004; (with William Julius Wilson) There Goes the Neighborhood, 2006; editor: (with Doris L. Taub) American Society in Tocqueville's Time and Today, 1974; contbr. articles to profl. jours. Chmn. bd. St. Thomas the Apostle Sch., Chgo., 1983-86; bd. dirs. Hyde Park Kenwood Cmty. Conf., Chgo., 1972-75; bd. seminary Coop Bookstore, Chgo., 1994—. Angell scholar U. Mich., 1956; Woodrow Wilson fellow Harvard U., 1959-60, W.E.B. DuBois Inst. fellow, 1997-98; grantee Am. Inst. Indian Studies, Ford Found.,

MacArthur Found., NSF, Wieboldt Found., Nat. Inst. Justice; recipient Quanctrell award U. Chgo., 1976, Outstanding Grad. Tchg. award U. Chgo., 2004. Mem. Am. Sociol. Assn., Midwest Sociol. Soc. Avocations: hiking, music. Office: Univ Chgo 5730 S Woodlawn Ave Chicago IL 60637 Office Phone: 773-702-3971. Business E-Mail: rpt2@uchicago.edu.

TAUB, ROBERT ALLAN, lawyer; b. Denver, Nov. 25, 1923; s. Clarence Arthur and Mary Frances (Jones) T.; m. Doris Irene Schroeder, Dec. 22, 1945; children: Amanda, Jonathan, Barbara. BA, U. Chgo., 1944, JD, 1947. Bar: Ill. 1947. Legal staff Marshall Field & Co., Chgo., 1947-50; mgr. exec. compensation Ford Motor Co., Dearborn, Mich., 1950-63, asst. sect., 1963-74, dir. corp. affairs planning, 1974-98. Pres. Dearborn Community Arts Council, 1971-72; trustee Internat. Mus. Photography, George Eastman House, Rochester, N.Y., 1976-2006, chmn., 1979-82; mem. adv. bd. U. Mich. Dearborn, 1980—, Met. Mus. Art, N.Y.C., 1987—; trustee Henry Ford Hosp., Detroit, 1983-2006; chmn. Dearborn Pub. Libr., 1986—; bd. dirs., mem. exec. com., chmn. fin. com., Health Alliance Plan, 1992-2006. Mem. ABA, Ill. Bar Assn, Art Inst. Chicago, 1998—. Presbyterian. Home: 1824 Hawthorne St Dearborn MI 48128-1448 E-mail: robert@rataub.org.

TAUBMAN, A. ALFRED, real estate developer; b. Pontiac, Mich., Jan. 31, 1924; s. Philip and Fannie Ester (Blustin) T.; m. Reva Kolodney, Dec. 1, 1949 (div. July 1977); children: Gayle Kalisman, Robert S., William S.; m. Judith Mazor, June 17, 1982. Student, U. Mich., 1945-48, LLD (hon.), 1991; student, Lawrence Inst. Tech., 1948-49, DArch (hon.), 1985; D in Bus. (hon.), Eastern Mich. U., 1984; D in Edn. (hon.), Mich. State U., 1993; HHD (hon.), No. Mich. U., 1995. Chmn. The Taubman Co., Bloomfield Hills, Mich., 1950—, Taubman Ctrs., Inc., Bloomfield Hills, Mich., 1992—. Prin. shareholder Sotheby's Holdings, Inc., N.Y.C., 1983-2001. Author: Threshold Resistance: The Extraordinary Career of a Luxury Retailing Pioneer, 2007. Trustee Ctr. for Creative Studies, Detroit, Harper-Grace Hosps., Detroit; chmn. emeritus Archives Am. Art Smithsonian Inst., Washington, U. Pa. Wharton Real Estate Ctr., Phila.; pres. Arts Commn. of Detroit; mem. nat. bd. Smithsonian Assocs.; established Taubman Ctr. for State and Local Govt. Harvard U., Cambridge, Mass., chmn. Mich. Partnership for New Edn., Program in Am. Instns., U. Mich., Brown U.'s Pub. Policy and Am. Instns. Program; prin. benefactor A. Alfred Taubman Health Care Ctr. and A. Alfred Taubman Med. Libr., U. Mich.; bd. dirs. Detroit Renaissance, Inc., Friends of Art and Preservation in Embassies, Washington; active State of Mich. Gaming Commn. Recipient Bus. Statesman award Harvard Bus. Sch. Club of Detroit, 1983, Sportsman of Yr. award United Found. Detroit, SE Mich. Chpt. March of Dimes Birth Defects, 1983; named Michiganian of Yr. The Detroit News, 1983; named one of Forbes' Richest Americans, 2006 Mem. Urban Land Inst. (trustee), Nat. Realty Com. (bd. dirs.).

TAUBMAN, ROBERT S., real estate developer; b. Detroit, Dec. 27, 1953; s. A. Alfred and Reva (Kolodney) T.; m. Julie Reyes, Aug. 27, 1999; 1 child, Alexander Alfred. BS in Econs., Boston U., MA. With Taubman Co. Inc., Bloomfield Hills, Mich., 1976—, exec. v.p., 1984—, exec. v.p., chief oper. officer, 1988-90; pres. chief exec. officer, 1990—. Bd. dirs. Taubman Ctrs. Inc., Comerica, Inc., Sotheby's Holdings, Inc., fashionmall.com. Chmn. Mich. campaign drive UNCF; bd. dirs. Beaumont Hosp.; trustee Cranbrook Ednl. Cmty. Mem. Nat. Sssn. Real Estate Investment Trusts (bd. govs.), Real Estate Roundtable (bd. dirs.), Urban Land Inst. (trustee, chmn. Detroit regional dist. coun.). Office: Taubman Co Inc 200 E Long Lake Rd Bloomfield Hills MI 48304-2360

TAUREL, SIDNEY, pharmaceutical executive; b. Casablanca, Morocco, Feb. 9, 1949; came to US, 1986; US citizen, 1995; s. Jose and Marjorie (Afriat) T.; m. Kathryn H. Fleischmann, Mar. 22, 1977; children: Alexis, Patrick, Olivia. BSBA, Ecole des Hautes Etudes Commerciales, Paris, 1969; MBA, Columbia U., NYC, 1971. Mktg. assoc. Eli Lilly Internat. Corp., Indpls., 1971-72, pres., 1986-91, exec. v.p. pharm. divsn., 1991; mktg. planning mgr. Eli Lilly Do Brasil Limitada, Sao Paulo, Brazil, 1972-75, gen. mgr., 1981—83; mgr. pharm. ops. Ea. Europe Eli Lilly und Elanco Gesmbh, Vienna, 1976; sales mgr. pharm. Eli Lilly France SA, Paris, 1977-79, mktg. dir. pharm., 1980-81; v.p. Europe Lilly European ops., London, 1983—85; exec. v.p. Eli Lilly & Co., 1993—98, pres. pharm. divsn., 1993, COO, 1996—98, pres., 1996—2005, CEO, 1998—2008, chmn., 1999—. Bd. dirs. Eli Lilly & Co., 1991-, The McGraw-Hill Companies, Inc., 1996-, IBM Corp., 2001-; bd. overseers Columbia Bus. Sch.; mem. President's Homeland Security Adv. Coun., 2002-03, Pres.'s Export Coun., 2003-06, Adv. Com. for Trade Policy & Negotiation, 2007-. Bd. dirs. RCA Tennis Championships. Recipient Ellis Island Medal of Honor, 2000; named a chevalier (Knight) of the French Legion of Honor, 2001. Mem. Pharm. Rsch. and Mfrs. Assn.(PhRMA), Bus. Coun., Bus. Roundtable; trustee, Indpls. Mus. Art Avocations: tennis, music. Office: Eli Lilly and Co Lilly Corp Ctr Indianapolis IN 46285 Office Phone: 317-276-2000. E-mail: staurel@lilly.com.*

TAVARES, CHARLETA B., former state legislator; Student, Spelman Coll., Ohio State U. Mem. Ohio Ho. of Reps., Columbus, 1993-98; council mem. City of Columbus, OH. Mem. Met. Human Svc. Commn. Vol. Huckleberry House, Literacy Initiative. Recipient award Black Students in Comm. Ohio State U., 1992, Ctrl. Comty House award, 1992, Pub. Children's Svc. Assn. award, 1993; named Franklin County Dem. Women's Club Sweetheart, 1993. Mem. LWV, Far East Dem. Women's Club, Columbus Area Women's Polit. Caucus, Coalition of 100 Black Women.

TAVLIN, MICHAEL JOHN, real estate company and manufacturing executive; b. Lincoln, Nebr., Dec. 16, 1946; BEd, Okla. City U., 1970; JD, U. Nebr., 1973; LLM in Taxation, Washington U., St. Louis, 1977. Bar: Nebr. 1973, Mo. 1974. Ptnr. Nelson & Harding, Lincoln, 1973-77; sr. tax. mgr. Deloitte & Touche, Lincoln and Tulsa, 1979-84, PriceWaterhouseCoopers, Tulsa, 1984-86; v.p., treas., sec. Aliant Comm. Inc. and subs., Lincoln, 1986-99; sr. v.p., CFO, treas., sec. Interactive Intelligence, Inc. and subs., Indpls., 1999—2001; CFO, gen. counsel Speedway Motors, Inc and Speedway Properties, Lincoln, 2001—. Bd. dirs., treas. Cmty. Health Endowment, Lincoln, 1998-2004; bd. dirs. Woods Charitable Fund, Lincoln, 2000-06, pres., 2005-06. Named Disting. Alumnus Oklahoma City U., 1995. Office: Speedway Motors Inc PO Box 81906 Lincoln NE 68501 Office Phone: 402-323-3122.

TAYLOR, ALLEN M., community foundation executive; b. Cedar Rapids, Iowa, Dec. 22, 1923; AB, Princeton U., 1946; LLB, Yale U., 1949. Bar: Wis. Assoc. Foley & Lardner, Milw., 1949-57, ptnr., 1957-88, sr. ptnr., 1988-93, of counsel, 1993; chmn., CFO The Chipstone Found., Milw., 1994—. Vice-chmn., bd. dirs. The Lynde and Harry Bradley Found.; bd. dirs. Stark Hosp. Found., Med. Coll. Wis. Health Policy Inst.; adv. bd. dirs. Med. Coll. Wis. Mem. The Greater Milw. Found.; chmn. capital fund drive Milw. Symphony Orch.; steering com. Pabst Theatre Reconstruction Campaign. With USMC, 1942-45. Mem. ABA, Wisconsin Bar Assn., Assn. Bank Holding Cos. (past chmn. lawyers com.), Milw. Country Club (past pres., sec., bd. dirs.), The Milw. Club, Cap and Gown Princeton, Princeton Club N.Y. Home: 2825 E Newport Ave Milwaukee WI 53211-2922 also: 750 N Lincoln Memorial Dr Rm 405 Milwaukee WI 53202-4020

TAYLOR, ANDREW C., rental and leasing company executive; b. 1947; BSBA, Denver U., 1970. With RLM Leasing Co., San Francisco, 1970—73, Enterprise Rent-A-Car, St. Louis, 1973—, pres., COO, 1980—91, CEO, 1991—, chmn., 2001—. Dir. Anheuser Busch Co., Commerce Bancshares; pres., CEO Crawford Group. Trustee, conference co-chair National Urban League; trustee Washington U., St. Louis Symphony Orch.; bd. dirs. United Way Greater St. Louis; life trustee Mo. Bot. Garden. Office: Enterprise Rent-A-Car 600 Corporate Park Dr Saint Louis MO 63105-4204

TAYLOR, ANNA DIGGS, federal judge; b. Washington, Dec. 9, 1932; d. Virginius Douglass and Hazel (Bramlette) Johnston; m. S. Martin Taylor, May 22, 1976; children: Douglass Johnston Diggs, Carla Cecile Diggs. BA, Barnard Coll., 1954; LLB, Yale U., 1957. Bar: D.C. 1957, Mich. 1961. Atty. Office Solicitor Gen. US Dept. Labor, 1957-60; asst. prosecutor Wayne County, Mich., 1961-62; asst. US atty. (ea. dist.) Mich. US Dept. Justice, 1966; ptnr. Zwerdling, Maurer, Diggs & Papp, Detroit, 1970-75; asst. corp. counsel City of Detroit, 1975-79; judge US Dist. Ct. (ea. dist.) Mich., Detroit, 1979—. Hon. chair United Way, Cmty. Found., S.E. Mich.; trustee emeritus Detroit Inst. Arts; co-chair, vol. Leadership Coun.; vice-chair Henry Ford Health Sys. Mem. Fed. Bar Assn., State Bar Mich., Wolverine Bar Assn. (v.p.), Yale Law Assn. Episcopalian. Office: US Dist Ct 740 US Courthouse 231 W Lafayette Blvd Detroit MI 48226-2700

TAYLOR, BILL, manufacturing engineer; Attended, Clemson U., NC State U., MIT. Dir. R & D, comml. vehicle emissions group Arvin Meritor, Inc., 1996—. Named one of Top 100 Young Innovators, MIT Tech. Review, 2004. Office: Arvin Meritor Inc 2135 W Maple Rd Troy MI 48084

TAYLOR, CLIFFORD WOODWORTH, state supreme court justice; b. Delaware, Ohio, Nov. 9, 1942; s. Alexander E. and Carolyn (Clifford) T.; m. Lucille Taylor; 2 children. BA, U. Mich., 1964; JD, George Washington U., 1967. Asst. prosecuting atty. Ingham County, 1971-72; ptnr. Denfield, Timmer & Taylor, 1972-92; judge Mich. Ct. of Appeals, 1992-97; justice Mich. Supreme Ct., 1997—, chief justice, 2005—. Mem. standing com. on professionalism Mich. State Bar, 1992. Bd. dirs. Mich. Dyslexia Inst., 1991—, Friends of the Gov.'s Residence, 1991—; mem. St. Thomas Aquinas Ch. With USN, 1967-71. Fellow Mich. State Bar Found.; mem. Mich. Supreme Ct. Hist. Soc., Federalist Soc., Cath. Lawyers Guild, State Bar. Home: 9760 Sunny Point Dr Laingsburg MI 48848 Office: Mich Supreme Ct PO Box 300052 Lansing MI 48909

TAYLOR, COLLETTE, public relations executive; Sr. v.p. human resources Golin/Harris Internat., Chgo., 1998, chief adminstrv. officer, 1998—. Office: Golin/Harris Internat 111 E Wacker Dr Chicago IL 60601-3713

TAYLOR, DORIS ANITA, molecular biology educator; b. San Francisco, Feb. 21, 1956; d. Benton and Julia P. (Williams) T. BS in Biology, Miss. U. for Women, 1977; PhD in Pharmacology, Southwestern Med. Sch., Dallas, 1988. Lab.instr. med. pharmacology U. Tex. Southwestern Med. Sch., Dallas, 1981-83, lectr. physician's assts. pharmacology course, 1981-86; molecular biology tng. dept. microbiology and immunology Albert Einstein Coll. Medicine, Bronx, NY, 1988-91; med. rsch. assoc. dept. medicine divsn. cardiology Duke U. Med. Ctr., Durham, NC, 1991-96, asst. rsch. prof. depts. medicine-surgery divsn. cardiology, 1996—, asst. rsch. prof. dept. biomed. engring., 1997; with U. Minn., 2003—, prof. medicine and physiology, Medtronic Bakken Chair in Cardiovascular Repair, dir., Ctr. for Cardiovascular Repair. Dir. molecular biology course immunologist fellowship tng. program Bronx-Lebanon Hosp., 1991; cons. drug utilization rev. program 1st Health Svcs. Corp., Chapel Hill, N.C., 1993-95; cons. Medtronic, Mpls. and Fridley, Minn., 1997-99; ad hoc reviewer surgery and bioengring. study sect. NIH, 1998-99; co-moderator Am. Heart Assn. 63rd Ann. Sci. Sessions, Dallas, 1998; mem. scientific committee and jury, Grand Prix Lefoulon-Delande Found., Inst. France; presenter in field, 1991—. Mem. editl. bd. Jour. MOlecular and Cellular Cardiology, 1997—; Assoc. editor Jour. Cardiac Vascular Regeneration, 1998—; contbr. several articles and abstracts to sci. jours., including Jour. Biol. Chemistry, Am. Jour. Med. Scis., Jour. Molecular Biology, Devel. Biology, Jour. Molecular Cell Cardiology, Egyptian Heart Jour., Molecular Cell Biochemistry, Am. Jour. Physiology, Nature Medicine. Bd. dirs. Our Own Place, cmty. ctr., Durham, 1994-96, N.C. Pride PAC, Raleigh, 1996-97; chpt. pres. People's Alliance, Durham, 1999-00. Profiled in Pitts. Tissue Engring. Initiative, 1997, Blackwell Corp. for Pub. Broadcasting, 1998; grantee Am. Cancer Soc., 1992-93, N.C. Heart Assn., 1995-97, Medtronic Inc., 1996-98, 99-00, Duke Heart Ctr., 1996-97, NIH, 1997-04, N.C. Biotech. Assn., 1998-99. Mem. AAAS, Am. Heart Assn. (coun. on basic sci.), Am. Assn. Engring. Eductors, Heart Failure Assn. Am., Tissue Culture Assn., Internat. Soc. for Heart Rsch., Internat. Soc. for Heart and Lung Transplantation (co-chair cell therapy tissue engring. coun.), Rsch. NC (spkr.'s bur.), N.C. Assn. for Biomed. Rsch. Democrat. Medical firsts with team members include: Repair of function in an injured heart with cell therapy in 1998; prevention and reversal of atherosclerosis with cells in 2003 and 2007; Robot-based cell delivery in heart (in animals) in 2007; found new stem cells in adult heart that can generate blood vessels and both left and right ventricular cardiocytes in 2007; showed male and female stem cells differ in their ability for repair in 2007; measured endogenous repair in heart disease in 2008; perfusion decellularization of whole organs in 2008; created a completely new beating rat heart in the laboratory on January 14, 2008. This breakthrough is expected to pave the way for future research to eventually create entire replacement organs based on the patient's own cells, which would eliminate the need for transplants or drugs to prevent rejection. Mailing: U Minn Biomedical Engring Inst 7-105 BSBE 1191 312 Church St SE Minneapolis MN 55455 Office: U Minn Biomedical Engring Inst 7-112 BSBE Minneapolis MN 55455 Office Phone: 612-626-1416.*

TAYLOR, E. JANE, lawyer; b. Niagra Falls, NY, Dec. 16, 1954; BA cum laude, Kent State U., 1977; JD, U. Akron, 1980. Bar: Ohio 1981, U.S. Dist. Ct. No. Dist. Ohio 1981, U.S. Ct. Appeals (6th cir.) 1985, U.S. Dist. Ct. So. Dist. Ohio 2002. Assoc. atty. Guy Lammert & Towne, Akron, Ohio, 1981—90, ptnr., 1990—. Mem. Akron Law Rev., 1979—80. Mem. bd. trustees United Way Summit County, 1995—2002, past chair svc. rev. team, mem. cmty. investment coun., chair portfolio coun. improving health and wellness, past mem. planning and allocations com., co-chair task force multi-yr. funding. Named one of 100 Women of Distinction, Akron Area YWCA, 2001. Mem.: ABA, Comml. Law League Am., Ohio Women's Bar Assn., Nat. Conf. Bar Presidents, Ohio State Bar Assn. (mem. coun. delegates 1996—2003, mem. bd. govs. 2000—03, pres.-elect 2004—, pres. 2005), Akron Bar Assn. (chair bar applicants and students com. 1988—90, mem. bankruptcy and comml. law sect. 1989—, bd. trustees 1990—93, v.p. 1993—94, pres. 1994—95, outstanding com. chairperson 1997—98). Office: Guy Lammert & Towne 2210 First National Tower Akron OH 44308 Office Phone: 330-535-2151. Office Fax: 330-535-9048. E-mail: guylaw2210@aol.com.

TAYLOR, GLEN A., printing, direct mail and technology executive, professional sports team owner; b. Apr. 20, 1941; m. Becky Taylor; children: Terri, Jean, Taylor Moor, Jeff, Kendahl. BS in Math., Physics and Social Sci., Mankato State U., 1962; student, Harvard Grad. Sch. Bus.; D (hon.), Mankato State U., 1997. Chmn., CEO Taylor Corp., North Mankato, Minn., 1975—2001, chmn., 2001—; mem. Minn. State Senate, 1980—90; owner NBA Minn. Timberwolves and Minn. Lynx, Mpls., 1995—. Named Exec. of Yr., Corp. Report mag., 1987; named one of Forbes' Richest Ams., 2006; named to Minn. Hall of Fame, Twin Cities Monthly mag., 2002; recipient Sales Exec. of Yr. award, Sales and Mktg. Execs. Mpls./St. Paul, 1999. Office: Taylor Corp 1725 Roe Crest Dr North Mankato MN 56003-1807 also: Minn Timberwolves Target Ctr 600 1st Ave N Minneapolis MN 55403-1416

TAYLOR, J. MARY (JOCELYN MARY TAYLOR), museum director, educator, zoologist; b. Portland, Oreg., May 30, 1931; d. Arnold Llewellyn and Kathleen Mary (Yorke) T.; m. Joseph William Kamp, Mar. 18, 1972 (dec.); m. Wesley Kingston Whitten, Mar. 20, 2001. BA, Smith Coll., 1952; MA, U. Calif., Berkeley, 1953, PhD, 1959. Instr. zoology Wellesley Coll., 1959-61, asst. prof. zoology, 1961-65; assoc. prof. zoology U. B.C., 1965-74; dir. Cowan Vertebrate Mus., 1965-82, prof. dept. zoology, 1974-82; collaborative scientist Oreg. Regional Primate Research Ctr., 1983-87; prof. (courtesy) dept. fisheries and wildlife Oreg. State U., 1984-95; dir. Cleve. Mus. Nat. History, 1987-96, dir. emerita, 1996—. Adj. prof. dept. biology Case Western Res. U., 1987-96. Assoc. editor Jour. Mammalogy, 1981-82. Contbr. numerous articles to sci. jours. Trustee Benjamin Rose Inst., 1988-93, Western Res. Acad., 1989-94, U. Circle, Inc., 1987-96, The Cleve. Aquarium, 1990-93, Cleve. Access to the Arts, 1992-96; corp. bd. Holden Arboretum, 1988-98, The Cleve. Mus. Natural History, 1996—, The Catlin Gabel Sch., 1998-2000, The Inst. for the Northwest, 1999—2001. Recipient Lake County Environ. award, Lake county metro parks.; Fulbright scholar, 1954-55; Lalor Found. grantee, 1962-63; NSF grantee, 1963-71; NRC Can. grantee, 1966-84; Killam Sr. Rsch. fellow, 1978-79 Mem.: Rodent Specialist Group of Species Survival Commn. (chmn. 1989—93), Assn. Sci. Mus. Dirs. (v.p. 1990—93), Cooper Ornithol., Australian Mammal Soc. (hon. life), Am. Soc. Mammalogists (1st v.p. 1978—82, pres. 1982—84, hon. life, Hartley T. Jackson award 1993), Soc. Women Geographers, Sigma Xi. Home: 2718 SW Old Orchard Rd Portland OR 97201-1637 E-mail: taylorwhitten@comcast.net.

TAYLOR, JACK CRAWFORD, rental and leasing company executive; b. 1922; With Lindburg Cadillac, St. Louis, 1944-50, Forrest Cadillac, St. Louis, 1951-56; chmn. bd. Enterprise Rent-A-Car, St. Louis, 1980—2001, chmn. emeritus, 2001—. Served with USN. Named one of Forbes Richest Americans, 2006, World's Richest People (with family), Forbes Mag., 2007. Office: Enterprise Rent-A-Car 600 Corporate Park Dr Saint Louis MO 63105-4204

TAYLOR, JEFF, reporter, editor; Reporter Kansas City Star; asst. mng. editor Detroit Free Press. Recipient Pulitzer prize for nat. reporting, 1992, Sigma Delta Chi award, George Polk award. Office: Detroit Free Press 600 W Lafayette Blvd Detroit MI 48226-2703

TAYLOR, JOEL SANFORD, government agency administrator, retired lawyer; b. Hazleton, Pa., Oct. 8, 1942; s. Robert Joseph and Alice Josephine (Sanford) T.; m. Donna Rae Caron, Mar. 26, 1967; children: Jason, Adam, Jeremy. BA in Polit. Sci. and Internat. Rels., Swarthmore Coll., 1965; LLB, Columbia U., 1968. Bar: NY 1969, US Ct. Appeals (2d cir.) 1970, US Dist. Ct. (no. dist.) Ohio 1974, US Supreme Ct. 1974, US Dist. Ct. (so. dist.) Ohio 1975, US Ct. Appeals (6th cir.) 1975, US Dist. Ct. (ea. dist.) Ky. 1979. Law clk. hon. Constance B. Motley US Dist. Ct., NYC, 1968-69; assoc. Paul, Weiss, Rifkind, Wharton & Garrison, YC, 1969-72; exec. asst. Ohio Office Budget and Mgmt., Columbus, 1972-74; asst. atty. gen. Ohio Atty. Gen., Columbus, 1974-83, chief counsel, 1983-91; ptnr. Dinsmore & Shohl, Columbus, 1991-2000; dir. fin. and mgmt. City of Columbus, 2000—. Pres. Ohio Sundry Claims Bd., Columbus, 1972-74, Ohio State Controlling Bd., Columbus, 1973-74; mem., bd. trustees Ohio State Tchrs. Retirement Sys., Columbus, 1986-91, Solid Waste Authority Ctrl. Ohio, 2001—. Mem.: Govt. Fin. Officers Assn., Nature Conservancy, Nat. Wildlife Fedn., Columbia Law Alumni Assn. Office: City Hall 90 W Broad St Columbus OH 43215-9000 Home Phone: 614-237-5854; Office Phone: 614-645-7036. E-mail: jstaylor@columbus.gov.

TAYLOR, KATHLEEN (CHRISTINE TAYLOR), physical chemist, researcher; b. Cambridge, Mass., Mar. 16, 1942; d. John F. and Anna M. T. BA in Chemistry, Douglass Coll., New Brunswick, NJ, 1964; PhD in Phys. Chemistry, Northwestern U., 1968. Postdoctoral fellow U. Edinburgh, Scotland, 1968-70; assoc. sr. rsch. chemist Gen. Motors Rsch. Labs., Warren, Mich., 1970-74, sr. rsch. chemist, 1974-75, asst. phys. chemistry dept. head, 1975-83, environ. sci. dept. head, 1983-85, phys. chemistry dept. head, 1985-96; physics and phys. chemistry dept. head Gen. Motors Global Rsch. & Devel. Operations, Warren, Mich., 1995-98, materials and processes dir., 1998—2002. Recipient Mich. Sci. Trailblazer award Detroit Sci. Ctr., 1986. Fellow AAAS, Soc. Automotive Engrs. Internat., mem. NAE, Am. Chem. Soc. (Garvan medal 1989), Materials Rsch. Soc. (treas. 1984, 2d v.p. 1985, 1st v.p. 1986, pres. 1987), N.Am. Catalysis Soc., Am. Acad. Arts Sci, Sigma Xi.

TAYLOR, KOKO, singer; b. Memphis, Sept. 28, 1935; m. Robert "Pops" Taylor (dec.). Singer: (albums) I Got What It Takes, 1975, The Earthshaker, 1978, From the Heart of a Woman, 1981, Queen of the Blues, 1985, Live from Chgo.: An Audience with the Queen, 1987, Jump for Joy, 1990, Force of Nature, 1993, Royal Blue, 2000, Deluxe Edition, 2002. Named to Blues Hall of Fame, 1997; recipient Legend of Yr., Clearly Canadian, 1993, Howlin' Wolf award, 1996, Outstanding Generosity award, Children's Brittle Bone Found., 1997; Nat. Heritage Fellowship, NEA, 2004. Achievements include 2 Grammy awards, 8 Grammy nominations; March 3, 1993 declared by mayor "Koko Taylor Day" in Chgo. Office: Alligator Records care Nora Kinnally PO Box 60234 Chicago IL 60660-0234

TAYLOR, MARK DOUGLAS, publishing executive; b. Geneva, Ill., Jan. 16, 1951; s. Kenneth Nathaniel and Margaret Louise (West) T.; m. Carol E. Rogers, May 28, 1973; children: Jeremy Peter, Kristen Elizabeth, Margaret Louise, Rebecca Cynthia, Stephen Rogers. BA, Duke U., 1973. Exec. dir. Tyndale House Found., Wheaton, Ill., 1973-78, pres., CEO, 2004—; v.p. Tyndale House Pubs., Wheaton, Ill., 1978-84, pres., chief exec. officer, 1984—. Dir. Living Bibles Internat., aperville, Ill., 1972-92; trustee Taylor U., 1998—. Author The Complete Book of Bible Literacy, 1992. Mem. Wheaton Liquor Control Commn., 1986—, chmn., 1994—; chmn. bd. dirs. Outreach Cmty. Ctr., 1986-93. Mem. Internat. Bible Soc. (bd. dirs. 1992-96). Office: Tyndale House Publishers Inc PO Box 80 Wheaton IL 60189-0080

TAYLOR, MARY, state official; M in Taxation, U. Akron. CPA. Sr. mgr. Bober, Markey, Fedorovich & Co.; state rep. dist. 43 Ohio Ho. of Reps., Columbus, 2002—06, mem. edn., econ. devel. & environ. ways and means; state auditor State of Ohio, 2007—. Councilwoman, fin. com. chair, mem. rules & pers. and intergovtl. and utilities coms. Green (Ohio) City Coun., 2001—. Republican. Mailing: 3431 Parfoure Blvd Uniontown OH 44685 Home Phone: 330-699-3031; Office Phone: 614-466-1790.

TAYLOR, MICHAEL ALAN, psychiatrist; b. NYC, Mar. 6, 1940; s. Edward D. and Clara D. T.; m. Ellen Schoenfield, June 28, 1963; children— Christopher, Andrew. BA, Cornell U., 1961; MD, N.Y. Med. Coll., 1965. Intern Lenox Hill Hosp., NYC, 1965-66; resident N.Y. Med. Coll., 1966-69, asst. prof. psychiatry, 1971-73; asso. prof. SUNY Med. Sch., Stony Brook, 1973-76; prof. psychiatry Univ. Health Scis., Chgo. Med. Sch., 1976—, dept., 1976-94. Author: The europsychiatric Mental Status Examination, 1981; sr. author: General Hospital Psychiatry, 1985, The Neuropsychiatric Guide to Modern Everyday Psychiatry, 1993, The Fundamentals of Neuropsychiatry, 1999; editor-in-chief Neuropsychiat., Neuropsychology and Behavioral Neurology Jour.; also numerous articles. Served to lt. comdr. M.C. USNR, 1969-71. Grantee NIMH, 1971-73; Grantee Ill. Dept. Mental Health, 1976-81; VA grantee, 1985-93. Mem. Am. Psychopath. Assn. Office: FUHS Chgo Med Sch 3333 Green Bay Rd North Chicago IL 60064-3037

TAYLOR, RAY, state senator; b. Steamboat Rock, Iowa, June 4, 1923; s. Leonard Allen and Mary Delilah (Huffman) T.; m. Mary Allen, Aug. 29, 1924; chidlren: Gordon, Laura Rae Taylor Hansmann, Karol Ann Taylor Rogers, Jean Lorraine Taylor Mahl. Student, U. No. Iowa, 1940-41, Baylor U., 1948-49. Farmer, Steamboat Rock, Iowa, 1943—; mem. Iowa Senate, 1973-95. Bd. dirs., sec. Am. Legis. Exch. Coun., 1979-94; sec. Hardin County Farm Bur., 1970-72; mem. Iowa divsn. bds. Am. Cancer Soc.; chmn. Am. Revolution Bicentennial com.; mem. Steamboat Rock Cmty. Sch. Bd., 1955-70; coord. Rep. youth, 1968-72; bd. Faith Bapt. Bible Coll., past chmn. acad. com.; bd. dirs. Eldora Area Chamber and Devel. Coun., 1998—2003; mem. Eldora Indsl. Corp., 1998—; exec. coun. Am. Coun. Christian Chs.; chmn. Iowans for Responsible Govt.; bd. dirs. Iowans for Tax Relief, 1995—; chmn. Steamboat Rock Schoolhouse Com., 2000—. Named Guardian of Small Bus. NFIB/Iowa, 1989-90, for outstanding support for good govt. and accessible, affordable health care in Iowa, Iowa Physician Asst. Soc., 1991; Ind. Bapt. fellow of the Midwest, Christian Patriots, 1994, Hon. alumnus Faith Bapt. Bible Coll. & Theol. Sem., 1995; recipient Contenders award Am. Coun. Christian Chs., 1991, Legislator of Yr. award Iowa Soc. of Friends, 1991-92. Mem. Wildlife Club, Eldora Rotary (pres. 2003—). Baptist. Home: 31363 185th St Steamboat Rock IA 50672

TAYLOR, RICHARD D., state representative; b. Algona, Iowa, Apr. 5, 1931; m. Jan Taylor; 2 children. Attended, Milw. Sch. Engring., State U. Iowa. Electrician, project mgr., 1951—93; cons., hire Occupl. Safety and Health Adminstr. Constrn., 1993—2000; state rep. dist. 33 Iowa Ho. of Reps., Des Moines, 2000—, mem. commerce and regulation, labor and indsl. rels., local govt., and ways and means coms., mem. econ. feasibility study for Linn County caucus. Mem.: VFW (chair co-vets. com.). Democrat. Methodist.

TAYLOR, ROGER LEE, academic administrator, lawyer; b. Canton, Ill., Apr. 6, 1941; s. Ivan and Pauline Helen (Mahr) T.; m. E. Anne Zweifel, June 13, 1964. BA, Knox Coll., 1963; JD cum laude, Northwestern U., 1971. Bar: Ill. 1971, U.S. Dist. Ct. (no. dist.) Ill. 1971, U.S. Dist. Ct. (no. dist.) Tex. 1975, U.S. Ct. Appeals (7th cir.) 1972, U.S. Ct. Appeals (5th and 11th cirs.) 1981, U.S. Supreme Ct. 1975. Assoc. Kirkland & Ellis, Chgo., 1971-78, ptnr., 1978—; pres. Knox Coll., Galesburg, Ill., 2002—. Trustee Knox Coll., pres. 2002; trustee Ill. Hist. Preservation Agy., dir. Assoc. Coll. of Midwest, dir. Assoc. Coll. of Ill. Mem. Order of Coif, Univ. Club, Soangetaha Country Club (Galesburg, Ill.). Office: Knox College Galesburg IL 61401

TAYLOR, RONALD LEE, academic administrator; b. Urbana, Ill., Nov. 11, 1943; s. Lee R. and Katherine L. (Becker) Taylor; m. Patricia D. Fitzimmons, Mar. 10, 1973; children: Jamie, Lara, Meredith, Dana. AB, Harvard U., 1966; MBA, Stanford U., 1971. Asst. contr. Bell & Howell, Chgo., 1971-73; pres., CEO DeVry Inc., Chgo., 1973—2004, CEO, 2004—06, co-founder, sr. advisor, 2006—. Trustee Higher Learning Commn., North Ctrl. Assn. Colls. and Schs., 1985—2006; bd. dirs. La Petite Acad., Inc., 1997—2007. Trustee Rehabilitation Inst. Chgo.; mem. mgmt. bd. Stanford U. Sch. Bus., 2003—06. 1st lt. US Army, 1966—69. Decorated Commendation medal US Army, Oak Leaf Cluster;

recipient Outstanding Pub. Svc. medal, Sec. Def., 1998. Achievements include feature in Crain's Mag. Chgo., 2006. Office: DeVry Inc 1 Tower Ln Ste 2350 Oakbrook Terrace IL 60181-4663 Business E-Mail: rtaylor@devry.com.

TAYLOR, S. MARTIN, utilities executive; BS, Western Mich. U., 1964; JD, Detroit Coll. Law, 1967. Dir. Mich. Employment Security Commn., 1971—84, Mich. Dept. Labor, 1983—84; pres. New Detroit Inc., 1985—89; v.p. corp. and public affairs Detroit Edison (now DTE Energy Co.), 1989—99, current sr. v.p. human resources and corp. affairs. Bd. regents U. Mich., Ann Arbor, 1996—; pres. Detroit Zool. Commn.; chmn. Detroit's Future; mem., former chmn. Citizen's Rsch. Coun.; mem. Detroit Urban League; chmn. mayoral campaign Mayor Dennis Archer, Detroit; former bd. dirs. Marygrove Coll., Detroit Symphony Orch., Karmanos Cancer Inst. Democrat. Office: 2000 2nd Ave Ste 2428 WCB Detroit MI 48226-1279

TAYLOR, SCOTT, radio personality; Radio host KUDL, Westwood, Kans. Office: KUDL 4935 Belinder Shawnee Mission KS 66205

TAYLOR, STEPHEN ANDREW, composer, music educator; b. 1965; m. Hua Nian; 2 children. PhD, Cornell U., 1994. Assoc. prof. U. Ill., Urbana-Champaign; condr. U. Ill. New Music Ensemble. Composer: Unapproachable Light, 1996, Quark Shadows, 2001, Seven Memorials, 2004, Nebulae, 2005. Goddard Lieberson fellowship, AAAL, 2008. Office: U Ill Sch Music 1114 W Nevada St Urbana IL 61801 Office Phone: 217-333-3712. E-mail: staylor7@uiuc.edu.*

TAYLOR, STEPHEN LLOYD, toxicologist, educator, food scientist; b. Portland, Oreg., July 19, 1946; s. Lloyd Emerson and Frances Hattie (Hanson); m. Susan Annette Kerns, June 23, 1973; children: Amanda, Andrew. BS in Food Sci. Tech., Oreg. State U., 1968, MS in Food Sci. Tech., 1969; PhD in Biochemistry, U. Calif., Davis, 1973. Research assoc. U. Calif., Davis, 1973-74, research fellow, 1974-75; chief food toxicology Letterman Army Inst., San Francisco, 1975-78; asst. prof. food toxicology U. Wis., Madison, 1978-83, assoc. prof., 1983-87; head dept. food sci. technology, dir. Food Processing Ctr. U. Nebr., Lincoln, 1987—2004, prof. dept. food sci. tech., 2004—. Cons. in field. Contbr. articles to profl. jours. Fellow: Inst. Food Technologists (divsn. chmn. 1981—82, sect. chmn. 1984—85, exec. com. 1988—91); mem.: Soc. Toxicology, Am. Chem. Soc., Am. Acad. Allergy, Asthma and Immunology. Democrat. Presbyterian. Home: 941 Evergreen Dr Lincoln NE 68510-4131 Office: U Nebr Dept Food Sci Tech Lincoln NE 68583-0919 Home Phone: 402-488-6477; Office Phone: 402-472-2833. Business E-Mail: staylor2@unl.edu.

TAYLOR, STEVE HENRY, zoologist; b. Inglewood, Calif., Mar. 18, 1947; s. Raymond Marten and Ardath (Metz) T.; 1 child, Michael Travis; m. Sarah Margaret Young, May 14, 1993. BA in Biology, U. Calif.-Irvine, 1969. Animal keeper Los Angeles Zoo, 1972-75, assoc. curator, 1975-76; children's zoo mgr. San Francisco Zoo, 1976-81; zoo dir. Sacramento Zoo, 1981-88; dir. Cleve. Met. Zoo, 1989—. Bd. dirs. Sacramento Soc. Prevention Cruelty to Animals, 1983-87, Sacramento Red Cross, 1988-89, Conv. and Visitor Bur. of Greater Cleve., 1995-03, 06-, Leadership Cleve. Class 1997; mem. admissions com. United Way, 1999. Recipient Robert P. Bergman Impact award Convention & Visitors Bur. Greater Cleve., 2000. Fellow Am. Assn. Zool. Parks and Aquariums (infant care diet advisor 1979, 85, bd. dirs. 1987-93, pres. 1991-92, chmn. pub. edn. com. 1987-89, bd. regents, mgmt. sch., chmn. accreditation com. 1998, 99, Outstanding Svc. award 1979, 85, 88, 89, 91, 95, 98, 99, 2001); mem. Conservation Breeding Specialist Group, World Assn. Zoos and Aquariums, Sierra Club, Audubon Soc. Democrat. Home: 1265 Elmwood Rd Rocky River OH 44116-2236 Office: Cleveland Metroparks Zoo 3900 Wildlife Way Cleveland OH 44109-3132 Home Phone: 440-333-7564; Office Phone: 216-635-3331. Business E-Mail: sht@clevelandmetroparks.com.

TAYLOR, SUSAN S., performance consultant; b. Minneapolis, Oct. 17, 1945; d. Lucius O. and Mary Elizabeth (McNaughton) T. BS in Edn., U. Minn., 1967; MS in Ednl. Rsch. & Testing, Fla. State U., Tallahassee, 1971, PhD in Instl. Sys., 1974. Cert. tchr., Minn., Mo. Tchr. Minnetonka (Minn.) Pub. Schs., 1967—68; tchr./author CAI Lab.-Kansas City Pub. Schs., 1968-70; grad. asst. Fla. State U., Tallhassee, 1970-74; cons./mgr. Control Data Corp., 1974-88; tech. dir. WICAT Sys., Orem, Ut., 1989-90; owner/cons. SST Enterprises, Bloomington, Minn., 1990—. Presenter in field. Author: (book chpt.) CREATE: A Computer-Based Authorizing Curriculum, 1979. Sec. Minn. Episcopal Cursillo Coun., Minn., 1998—2001. Mem. Internat. Soc. Performance Improvement (co-chair independent cons., past pres., treas. Minn. chpt.), Am. Soc. Tng. & Devel. Avocations: gardening, genealogy, reading, walking, crafts. Office: SST Enterprises 7430 Autumn Chace Dr Ste 203 Bloomington MN 55438-1115

TAYLOR, TODD, state representative; b. Cedar Rapids, Iowa, May 21, 1966; BA, Graceland Coll., 1988; BS, U. No. Iowa, 1990. Legis. asst., 1992; legis. Iowa State House Dist. 54, 1994—98; mem. Iowa Ho. Reps., DesMoines, 1995—, ranking mem. labor and indsl. rels. com., mem. adminstrn. and regulation com., mem. appropriations com., mem. state govt. com. Active Boy Scouts Am. Democrat. Mem. Lds Ch. Office: State Capitol East 12th and Grand Des Moines IA 50319 also: 5710 Johnson Ave SW #215 Cedar Rapids IA 52404

TAYLOR, WILLIAM, state legislator; Mem. from dist. 63 Ohio State Ho. of Reps., 1995—. Address: 100 Eastwood Dr Norwalk OH 44857-1105 Office: Ohio Ho of Reps State House Columbus OH 43215

TEAGAN, JOHN GERARD, publishing executive; b. Detroit, Sept. 23, 1947; s. Stanley John and Margaret Suzanne (Sullivan) T.; m. Carla Kay Eurich, Sept. 13, 1975; 1 child, Elizabeth Margaret. BBA, U. Notre Dame, 1969. CPA Mich. Audit supr. Ernst & Whinney (C.P.A.s), Detroit, 1969-73; acctg. mgr. Detroit Free Press, 1973-77, treas., controller, 1977-83, v.p. fin., treas., 1983-89, v.p., bus. mgr., 1989—2005; CFO Duluth News Tribune, 2005—. Adv. bd. Providence Hosp., Southfield, Mich., 1984-93, sec., 1989, vice chmn. 1990, chmn., 1991; trustee Grosse Pointe (Mich.) Acad., 1990-96, Children's Home Detroit, Grosse Pointe, 1997-2005; bd. dirs., treas. Free Press Charities, Inc.; bd. dirs. Providence Hosp. and Med. Ctrs., Southfield, 1998-2005; Metro Detroit bd. dirs. Am. Heart Assn., 1999-2005, chair, 2004-05; bd. dirs. Holy Cross Children's Svcs., 2001-05; mem. cmty. adv. bd. Knight Found., 2002-05. Mem. AICPA, Internat. Newspaper Fin. Execs., Mich. Assn. CPAs, Grosse Pointe Yacht Club. Roman Catholic. Business E-Mail: jteagan@duluthnews.com.

TEASDALE, KENNETH FULBRIGHT, lawyer; b. St. Louis, Nov. 8, 1934; s. Kenneth and Ann (Fulbright) T.; m. Elizabeth Driscol Langdon, June 13, 1964; children: Caroline, Doug, Cindy. AB, Amherst Coll., 1956; LLB, Washington U., St. Louis, 1961. Bar: Mo. 1961. Atty. antitrust div. U.S. Dept. Justice, Washington, 1961-62; asst. counsel Dem. Policy Com. U.S. Senate, Washington, 1962—64, gen. counsel Dem. Policy Com., asst. to majority leader, 1963-64; assoc. Armstrong, Teasdale, Kramer & Vaughan, St. Louis, 1964-67, ptnr., 1967-86; mng. ptnr. Armstrong, Teasdale, Schlafly & Davis, St. Louis, 1986-93, chmn. of firm, 1993—. Trustee United Way Greater St. Louis, Sci. Ctr. St. Louis, St. Louis Art Mus.; trustee, St. Louis U.; mem. nat. coun. Washington U. Law Sch., 1988—. Mem. ABA, Bar Assn. Mo., Bar Assn. St. Louis, St. Louis Coalition for Plant and Life Scis., Racquet Club, Noonday Club, Old Warson Country Club. Episcopalian. Office: Armstrong Teasdale LLP Ste 2600 One Metropolitan Sq Saint Louis MO 63102-2733 Office Phone: 314-621-5070. Business E-Mail: kteasdale@armsteasdale.com.

TECHAR, FRANK J., bank executive; b. Minn. BS in engring., Princeton U., 1978; MBA, U. Denver, 1983; exec. program, USC, 1992. Various banking positions First Interstate Bank, Denver; various engring. positions USG Corp., Oakfield, NY; sr. v.p., gen. mgr. BMO Fin. Group, London; acct. officer, corp. banking Bk. of Montreal, Denver, 1984, mgr. dir., corp. banking Houston, 1993—95, exec. v.p., small bus. banking Canada, 1999—2002; pres., CEO Harris Bankcorp, Toronto, Canada, 2002—06; pres., CEO Personal & Comml. Banking Canada BMO Fin. Group, 2006—. Mem.: Northwestern U. Bus. Sch. Adv. Coun., Chicagoland C.of.C. (bd. mem.), Exec. Club Chgo. (bd. mem.), U. Club, Chgo. Club, Econ. Club, Comml. Club of Chgo. Office: BMO Fin Group 1 First Canadian Pl M5X 1H3 Toronto ON Canada

TEETERS, JEFFREY R., lawyer; b. Jackson Ctr., Ohio, July 18, 1968; BA, U. Dayton, 1990; JD, U. Cin., 1993. Bar: Ohio 1993, US Dist. Ct. Southern Dist. Ohio 1993, US Ct. of Appeals Sixth Cir. 1998, US Supreme Ct. 2005, US Dist. Ct. Northern Dist. Ohio 2006. Ptnr. Frost Brown Todd LLC, Cin., chair, Unfair Competition Litig. Practice Grp., mem., Recruiting Com. Mentor U. Cin. Coll. Law, 1997—2003; baseball and basketball coach Mariemont Recreation Assn., 2003—; mentor Sr. High Youth, Lutheran Ch. of Good Shepherd, 1997—2002; ministry, Bd. Trustees U. Cin. Luth. Campus, 2003—. Named one of Ohio's Rising Stars, Super Lawyers, 2005, 2006. Mem.: ABA (co-editor, Bus. Torts Jour. 2004—), Ohio State Bar Assn. (mem., Litig. Sect., Antitrust Sect.), Cin. Bar Assn. Office: Frost Brown Todd LLC 2200 PNC Ctr 201 E Fifth St Cincinnati OH 45202-4182 Office Phone: 513-651-6715. Office Fax: 513-651-6981.

TEETERS, JOSEPH LEE, mathematician, consultant; b. Caney, Kans., Dec. 10, 1934; s. Jesse L. and Marie (Tapper) Teeters; m. Janet L. Hamm, June 18, 1984; children: Jeffrey, Susan, Christopher. Student, Colo. Sch. Mines, 1956, U. Kans., 1957; MA in Math., U. No. Colo., 1960, EdD in Math., 1968. Cert. secondary sch. tchr., Colo., Ill., hazard waste profl., OSHA. Exploration geologist Ohio Oil Co., Rawlings, Wyo., 1956-57; instr. Stout State U., Menomonie, Wis., 1960-62; asst. prof. Baker U., Baldwin City, Kans., 1962-65; temp. instr. U. No. Colo., Greeley, 1965-68; asst. prof. Western State Coll., Gunnison, Colo., 1968-69; prof. U. Wis., Eau Claire, 1969-88; cons. assoc. Delphi Data, Corona, Calif., 1989-98; ind. mathematician and cons., Lake Zurich, Ill., 1998—. Land surveying cons. Donaldson Engring., Menomonie, 1960-62; land boundary cons. ACLU, Eau Claire, 1974; lectr., spkr., cons. in field. Author: Creating Escher-Type Drawings, 1977; designer tessellation art; contbr. cover designs for profl. publs. Active Forest Lake (Ill.) Cmty. Assn., 1990—; sr. citizen trainer Marathon Challenge, St. Louis, 1994; mem. Golden Colo. Civic Orch., 1956; unicyclist Kans. State Sunflower State Games. Grantee NSF, 1965, U. New Orleans, 1987. Mem. Internat. Assn. for Math. Geology, Internat. Platform Assn., Stanton County Kans. Hist. Assn., No Man's Land Hist. Soc., Santa Fe Trail Assn., Kans. Trails Assn., Am. Volkssport Assn. (triathlete), Colo. Sch. Mines Assn., Tiblow Trailblazers (sports cons. 1994—), Sherman County Kans. Hist. Soc., Ill. Running Club, Kappa Kappa Psi, Sigma Gamma Epsilon, Phi Delta Kappa. Achievements include drill site improvisation of a magnetic fishing tool for small sand screen well openings; invention of a multi-function recursive algorithm which yields (with each use) a unique random lottery number ball quick-pick selection result; two successful completions of the Boston Marathon as well as six other 26.2 mile running events; design and development of motion activated vortiginous reflector system(s) for bicycles. Avocations: raising St. Bernards, planning and building full size windmills, designing birdhouses. Home and Office: 8683 Felsview Dr Laurel MD 20723

TEICHNER, BRUCE A., lawyer; b. Chgo. BA, U. Iowa, 1981; JD, De Paul U., 1985; MBA, U. Chgo., 1997. Legal writing tchg. asst. Coll. Law De Paul U., Chgo., 1982-83; assoc. coun. Allstate Ins. Co., Northbrook, Ill. Mem. writing staff De Paul Law Rev., 1983-85; contbr. articles to profl. jours. Mem. ABA, Chgo. Bar Assn. (corp. law coms.), Am. Corp. Counsel Assn. (assoc. counsel), Phi Beta Kappa. Office: Allstate Ins Co 3075 Sanders Rd Ste G5A Northbrook IL 60062-7127 E-mail: bteichner@allstate.com.

TEICHNER, LESTER, general management executive; b. Chgo., Apr. 21, 1944; s. Ben Bernard and Eva Bertha (Weinberg) T.; m. Barbara Rae Bush, Jan. 30, 1966 (div. Aug. 1969); m. Doris Jean Ayres, Jan. 31, 1980; children: Lauren Ayres, Caroline Ayres. BSEE, U. Ill., 1965; MBA in Mktg. and Fin., U. Chgo., 1969. Sales engr. Westinghouse Electric Corp., Chgo., 1965-69; v.p. ops. Intec Inc., Chgo., 1969-74; pres., CEO The Chgo. Group Inc., 1974—2000, Guttermonster, LLC, 2005—; pres., COO Republic Window & Doors, 2000—05. Bd. dirs. Golub & Co., Inc., Strategic Processing Inc., NYC, Dees Comms. Ltd., Vancouver, B.C., Maxcor Mfg. Co., Colorado Springs; CEO, bd. dirs. Axcess Worldwide Ltd., Coal Gasification, Inc., Chgo.; guest lectr. U. Chgo. Grad. Sch. Bus., 1982-95. Co-inventor U.S. patent electronic marketplace; contbr. articles to profl. publs. Mem. The Chgo. Forum, 1976—; bd. dirs. Am. Israeli C. of C. Mem. Am. Mgmt. Assn., Am. Mktg. Assn., Midwest Planning Assn. (bd. dirs. 1981). Republican. Jewish. Avocations: astronomy, skiing. Home: 2230 N Seminary Ave Chicago IL 60614-3507 Office: The Chicago Group Inc 2230 N Seminary Ave Chicago IL 60614-3507 Office Phone: 773-371-0357. Personal E-mail: lteichner@aol.com.

TEITELBAUM, STEVEN LAZARUS, pathology educator; b. Bklyn., June 29, 1938; s. Hyman and Rose Leah (Harnick) T.; m. Marilyn Ruth Schaffner; children: Caren Beth, Aaron Michael, Rebecca Lee. BA, Columbia U., NYC, 1960; MD, Washington U., St. Louis, 1964; DSc (hon.), CUNY SI Coll., 2004. Intern Washington U. Sch. Medicine, St. Louis, 1964-65, 3d. yr. asst. resident, ACS clin. fellow, 1967-68; intern NYU, 1965-66, 2d yr. resident, 1966-67; assoc. pathologist Jewish Hosp. at Washington U. Med. Ctr., St. Louis, 1969-89, pathologist-in-chief, 1987-96; assoc. pathologist Barnes-Jewish Hosp., St. Louis, 1986—; pathologist St. Louis Shriners Hosp. for Crippled Children, 1986—; Wilma and Roswell Messing prof. pathology Washington U. Sch. Medicine, St. Louis, 1987—. Mem. Othopedics and Musculoskeletal Study Sect. NIH, 1983-87; adv. counsel NIH, 2003—. Contbr. numerous sci. articles to med. jours., 1965—, 12 chpts. to med. books and texts, 1976—; mem. editorial bd. Calcified Tissue Internat., 1980-85, 89-91, Human Pathology; mem. bd. assoc. editors Jour. Orthopaedic Rsch., Jour. Cellular Biochemistry. Recipient 2nd Century award, Washington U. Sch. Medicine, 2004, Rouse-Whipple award, Am. Soc. Investigative Pathology, 2006. Mem. Am. Soc. Clin. Investigation, Assn. Am. Physicians, Am. Acad. Orthopaedic Surgeons (Ann Doner Vaughan Kappa Delta award 1988), Paget's Disease Found. (adv. panel), Am. Soc. for Bone and Mineral Rsch. (pres. 1993, William F. Neuman award 1998), Fed. Am. Soc. Expl. Biology (bd. dirs. 1997—, pres. 2002—). Office: Washington U Sch Medicine 216 S Kingshighway Blvd Saint Louis MO 63110-1026 Business E-Mail: teitelbs@wustl.edu.

TEITELMAN, RICHARD B., state supreme court judge; BA in Math., U. Pa., 1969; JD, Washington U., 1973. Bar: Mo. 1974. Pvt. practice, St. Louis, 1974-75; staff atty. Legal Svcs. Ea. Mo., St. Louis, 1975-76, mng. atty., 1976-80, exec. dir., gen. counsel, 1980—; judge Mo. Ct. Appeals (ea. dist.), 1998—2002, Mo. Supreme Ct., 2002—. Bd. dirs. Citizens for Mo.'s Children, St. Louis, 1988—. Recipient Durward K. McDaniel award Am. Coun. of Blind, 1986. Mem. The Mo. Bar, Kansas City Met. Bar Assn., Mound City Bar Assn., Lawyers Assn., St. Louis, Women Lawyers' Assn. Greater St. Louis, St. Louis County Bar Assn., Am. Blind Lawyers Assn., Am. Judicature Soc. (bd. dirs. 1986-2005), St. Louis Bar Found., Leadership St. Louis. Office: Mo Supreme Court PO Box 150 Jefferson City MO 65102 Home Phone: 314-367-5541; Office Phone: 573-751-1004. Business E-Mail: rteitelm@courts.mo.gov.

TELFER, MARGARET CLARE, internist, hematologist, oncologist; b. Manila, Apr. 9, 1939; came to U.S., 1941; d. James Gavin and Margaret Adele (Baldwin) T. BA, Stanford U., 1961; MD, Washington U., St. Louis, 1965. Diplomate Am. Bd. Internal Medicine, Am. Bd. Hematology, Am. Bd. Oncology; lic. Ill., Mo. Resident in medicine Michael Reese Hosp., Chgo., 1968, fellow in hematology and oncology, 1970, assoc. attending physician, 1970-72, dir. Hemophilia Ctr., 1971—, interim dir. div. hematology and oncology, 1971-74, 81-84, 89—, attending physician, 1972—, Rush-Presbyn. St. Luke's Hosp., 1999—, Olympia Fields (Ill.) Hosp., 1999—2006, Cook County Hosp., Chgo., 2000—, dir. hematology/oncology fellowship, 2004—; asst. prof. medicine U. Chgo., 1975-80, assoc. prof. medicine, 1980-85, assoc. prof. clin. medicine, 1985-89; assoc. prof. medicine U. Ill., Chgo., 1990-2001, Rush U., Chgo., 2001—. Mem. med. adv. bd. Hemophilia Found. Ill., 1971, chmn., 1972—83, lectr. annual symposium, 1978—84; mem. med. adv. bd. State of Ill. Hemophilia Program; dir. hematology-oncology fellowship program Michael Reese Hosp., 1971—75, 1981—84, 1989—2000, dir. Cook County Fellowship Program, 2004—, mem. numerous coms.; lectr. in field. Contbr. articles to profl. jours. Fellow ACP; mem. Am. Soc. Clin. Oncology, Am. Assn. Med. Colls., Am. Soc. Hematology, World Fedn. Hemophilia, Blood Club (Chgo.), Thrombosis Club (Chgo.). Office: Stroger Cook County Hosp Rm 750 Adminstrn Bldg 1900 W Polk Chicago IL 60612 Office Phone: 312-864-7250. Business E-Mail: mtelfer@ccbhs.org.

TEMKIN, HARVEY L., lawyer; b. Madison, Wis., Jan. 1, 1952; s. Joe L. and Sylvia Temkin; m. Barbara, June 13, 1976; children: James, Daniel, Eli. BA, U. Wis., 1974; JD, U. Ill., 1978. Bar: Wis. 1978. Assoc. Foley & Lardner, Madison, 1978—83; prof. Tulane Law Sch., New Orleans, 1983-87; ptnr. Foley & Lardner, Madison, 1987—2002; shareholder Reinhart Boerner Van Deuren, s.c., Madison, 2002—. Lectr. U. Wis. Law Sch., 1990-93; mem. U.S. Senator Feingold's Bus. Adv. Group. First v.p. Hillel Found., Madison, 1982-83, bd. dirs., 1987-95; chmn. edn. com. Beth Israel Synagogue, Madison, 1980-82; chmn. Jewish edn. panel Madison Jewish Cmty. Coun., 1993-98, bd. dirs., 1998-03; bd. dirs. Hospice Care, Inc. Fellow Am. Coll. Real Estate Lawyers (chmn. title insurance coverage subcom.); mem. ABA (real property probate and trust sect., reporter significant legis. panel 1983-85, significant lit. panel 1985-87), Downtown Madison, Inc. (chmn. 1989-91), Hospice Care Inc. (bd. dirs. and audit com.). Office: Reinhart Boerner Van Deuren 22 East Mifflin St PO Box 2018 Madison WI 53701-2018 Business E-Mail: htemkin@reinhartlaw.com.

TEMMER, JAMES DONALD, museum director; BA, U. Wis., 1987; MA, Marquette U., 1991; postgrad., Pa. State U., 2002—. Dir. Stonefield, Wis., 1996—99, H.H. Bennett & History Ctr., Wisconsin Dells, Wis., 1999—2002, Charles Allis/Villa Terr. Art Mus., Milw., 2002—. Recipient Nancy Hanks award for Profl. Excellence, Am. Assn. Mus., 2001. Mem.: State Hist. Soc. Wis. Office: Charles Allis Art Museum 1801 N Prospect Ave Milwaukee WI 53202

TEMPLE, WAYNE CALHOUN, historian, writer; b. Richwood, Ohio, Feb. 5, 1924; s. Howard M. and Ruby March (Calhoun) T.; m. Lois Marjorie Bridges, Sept. 22, 1956 (dec. Apr. 1978); m. Sunderine Wilson, Apr. 9, 1979; stepson, James C. Mohn. AB cum laude, U. Ill., 1949, AM, 1951, PhD, 1956. Rsch. asst. history U. Ill., 1949-53, tchg. asst., 1953-54; curator ethnohistory Ill. State Mus., 1954-58; editor-in-chief Lincoln Herald, Lincoln Meml. U., 1958-73, assoc. editor, 1973—, also dir. dept. Lincolniana, dir. univ. press, John Wingate Weeks prof. history, 1958-64; with Ill. State Archives, 1964—, now chief dep. dir. Lectr. U.S. Mil. Acad., 1975; sec.-treas. Nat. Lincoln-Civil War Council, 1958-64; mem. bibliography com. Lincoln Lore, 1958—; hon. mem. Lincoln Sesquicentennial Commn., 1959-60; advisory council U.S. Civil War Centennial Commn., 1960-66; maj. Civil War Press Corps, 1962—; pres. Midwest Conf. Masonic Edn., 1985; mem. adv. com. Abraham Lincoln Bicentennial Commn., 2000—. Author: Indian Villages of the Illinois Country: Historic Tribes, 1958, rev. edits., 1966, 77, 87, Lincoln the Railsplitter, 1961, Abraham Lincoln and Others at the St. Nicholas, 1968, Alexander Williamson-Tutor to the Lincoln Boys, 1971, (with others) First Steps to Victory: Grant's March to Naples, 1977, Lincoln and Grant: Illinois Militiamen, 1981, Stephen A. Douglas: Freemason, 1982, Lincoln as a Lecturer, 1982, By Square and Compasses: The Building of Lincoln's Home and Its Saga, 1984, Lincoln's Connections with the Illinois and Michigan Canal, 1986, Dr. Anson G. Henry: Personal Physician to the Lincolns, 1988, Abraham Lincoln: From Skeptic to Prophet, 1995, Thomas and Abraham Lincoln as Farmers, 1996, Alexander Williamson: Friend of the Lincolns, 1998, By Square and Compass: Saga of the Lincoln Home, 2002, The Taste Is In My Mouth a Little.Lincoln's Victuals and Potables, 2004, Abraham Lincoln and Illinois' Fifth Capitol, 2006, Abraham Lincoln's Travels on the River Queen, 2007; co-author: Illinois's Fifth Capitol: The House that Lincoln Built, 1988; contbg. author: Capitol Centennial Papers, 1988; editor: Campaigning with Grant, 1961, 72, The Civil War Letters of Henry C. Bear, 1961; 71 radio scripts A. Lincoln 1809-1959, Indian Villages of the Illinois Country: Atlas Supplement, 1975; mem. editl. bd. Am. Biog. Inst., 1971—, Ency. Indians of Ams., 1973—; contbr. articles to profl. jours., encys. Sponsor Abraham Lincoln Bay, Washington Nat. Cathedral; mem. Ill. State Flag Commn., 1969—; trustee, regent Lincoln Acad. Ill., 1970-82; bd. govs. St. Louis unit Shriners Hosps. for Crippled Children, 1975-81; commissioning com., hon. crew mem. and plank owner USS Springfield submarine, 1990—; hon. crew mem. USS Abraham Lincoln aircraft carrier, 1989—. With U.S. Army, 1943-46, gen. Res. (ret.). Decorated Bronze Star Medal, Silver Citizenship Medal SAR, 1993, Literary Merit Gold medal Ill. Lodge of Rsch., 1993; recipient Order of Arrow Boy Scouts Am., 1957, Scouters award, 1960, Scouter's Key, also medallion, 1967, Lincoln medallion Lincoln Sesquicentennial Commn., 1960, award of Achievement U.S. Civil War Centennial Commn., 1965, Algernon Sydney Sullivan medallion, 1969, Distinguished Service award Ill. State Hist. Library, 1969, 77, I.H. Duval Distinguished Service award, 1971, legion of honor Internat. Supreme Council, Order of De Molay, 1972, Disting. Service award Civil War Round Table of Chgo., 1983, 91, Cert. Excellence Ill. State Hist. Soc., 1985, Archbishop Richard Chenevix Trench award, 1999; Lincoln Diploma Honor, Lincoln Meml. U., Harrogate, Tenn., 1963, Lifetime Achievement award 2001; named Hon. Ky. Col., Marshal of Okla. Territory. Fellow Royal Soc. Arts (life); mem. NRA, KT (Red Cross Constantine), Lincoln Group D.C. (hon.), U. Ill. Alumni Assn., Ill. State Hist. Soc., Board of Advisors, The Lincoln Forum, Ill. Profl. Land Surveyors Assn., Ill. State Dental Soc. (citation plague 1966), Res. Officers Assn., Lincoln Fellowship of Wis., Iron Brigade Assn. (hon. life), Mil. Order Loyal Legion U.S. (hon. companion), Mil. Order Fgn. Wars U.S., Army and Navy Union, Masons (33 degree, Meritorious Svc. award, grand rep. from Grand Lodge of Colo.), Shriners, Kappa Delta Pi, Phi Alpha, Phi Alpha Theta (Scholarship Key award), Chi Gamma Iota, Phi Beta Kappa, Tau Kappa Alpha, Alpha Psi Omega, Sigma Pi Beta (Headmaster), Sigma Tau Delta (Gold Honor Key award for editorial writing), Zeta Psi. Presbyterian (elder). Home: 1121 S 4th Street Ct Springfield IL 62703-2200 Office: Ill State Archives Springfield IL 62756-0001 Office Phone: 217-782-3501.

TEMPLETON, ALAN ROBERT, biology professor; b. Litchfield, Ill., Feb. 28, 1947; s. John Smith and Lois Arlene (McCormick) T.; m. Bonnie A. Altman, Dec. 20, 1969; children: Jeremy Alan, Jeffrey Alan. BA, Washington U., 1969; MS in Stats., U. Mich., 1972, PhD in Genetics, 1972. Jr. fellow Mich. Soc. Fellows, Ann Arbor, 1972-74; asst. prof. U. Tex., Austin, 1974-77; assoc. prof. Washington U., St. Louis, 1977-81, prof., 1981—, Charles Rebstock prof. biology, 2001—; prof. Inst. Evolution, Haifa, Israel, 2007—. Cons. St. Louis Zool. Park, 1979—; founding mem., dir. Soc. for Conservation Biology, 1985—. Editor: Theoretical Population Biology, 1981-91; mem. editl. bd. Molecular Phylogenetics & Evolution, 1991—, Brazilian Jour. Genetics, 1991-97, Genetics and Molecular Biology, 1998-2001, Animal Conservation, 2004—, Evolutionary Bioinformatics Online, 2005—; assoc. editor Am. Naturalist, 2002-05; contbr. numerous article to profl. jours. Grantee NSF, 1974-80, 90—, NIH, 1980—, Nixon Griffis Fund for Zool. Rsch., 1986-87, Burroughs Welcome Fund for Functional Genomics, 2000—04. Fellow AAAS; mem. Soc. for Study Evolution (v.p. 1982, pres. 1996-97), Soc. Conservation Biology (bd. dirs. 1985-88), Nature Conservancy (trustee Mo. chpt. 1988—, v.p. 1996-2000). Avocations: hiking, caving, ethnomusicology, scuba diving, flying. Office: Washington U Dept Biology Saint Louis MO 63130-4899

TEMPLIN, KENNETH ELWOOD, paper company executive; b. Mason City, Nebr., Jan. 26, 1927; s. Otto Rudolph and Marianna (Graf) T.; m. Harriet Elaine Ressel, Aug. 24, 1951; children: Steven, David, Daniel, Benjamin, Elizabeth. BSBA, U. Nebr., Lincoln, 1950; MBA, Wayne State U., Detroit, 1981. Fin. analyst Ford Motor Co., 1950-54; fin. analyst, corp. staff Chrysler Corp., 1955-60, div. controller marine engine div., 1961-63, gen. sales mgr., 1964-65; v.p. Marsh and Templin, YC, 1966-69; v.p., gen. mgr. operating group Saxon Industries, NYC, 1970-79, group v.p., 1979-82, sr. v.p., c.o.o., 1982-85; v.p.-converting Paper Corp. Am., Wayne, Pa., 1985-86; exec. v.p. Quality Park Products Inc., St. Paul, 1986-88, 1986-88, pres., 1988-96, ret., 1996. Mem. exec. com. Single Service Inst., 1971-79 Regional chmn. Minn. devel. com. Nat. Multiple Sclerosis Soc., 1970-71; co-pres. Home and Sch. Assn., Bernardsville, N.J., 1975-76; bd. dirs. West Hennepin Counseling Svcs., Inc., 1996-2000, Brain Injury Assn. Minn., 1997-2001; mem. Svc. Corps Ret. Execs. (SCORE), 1996—, chmn. Mpls. chpt., 1999-2000; bd. dirs. Hennepin History Mus., 2000-06. With U.S. Army, 1945-47, 50-51. Mem. Envelope Mfrs. Assn. Am. (postal affairs com. 1989-96, fin. com. chmn. 1994-95, bd. dirs. 1990-91, 93-95). Presbyterian. Office Phone: 612-339-5200. E-mail: templink@aol.com.

TEMPORITI, JOHN J., political organization administrator, lawyer; BA, Cardinal Glennon Coll., 1971; JD, St. Louis U., 1975. Chief of staff Mayor of City of St. Louis, 1981—85; ptnr., mem. mgmt. com. Gallop, Johnson & Neuman, LC, St. Louis, 1985—97, now of counsel; exec. v.p. UniGroup, 1997; pres., CEO Mayflower Van Lines, 1998—99, Vanliner Insurance Co., 1999—2004; chief of govtl. affairs St. Louis County, 2004—07; chmn. Mo. Dem. Party, 2007—; mem. Dem. Nat. Com., 2007—. Mem.: ABA, Bar Assn. of Met. St. Louis, Mo. Bar Assn. Democrat. Office: Mo Dem Party 208 Madison St PO Box 719 Jefferson City MO 65102 Office Phone: 573-636-5241. Office Fax: 573-634-8176.*

TENHOLDER, EDWARD J., pharmaceutical executive; Sr. v.p. client svcs. and ops. Right Choice Managed Care, Inc., 1994—97; exec. v.p., COO Blue Cross and Blue Shield Mo., 1997—2000; sr. v.p., chief info. officer Express Scripts, Inc., Maryland Heights, Mo., 2000—, chief adminstrn. officer, 2003—. Office: Express Scripts Inc 13900 Riverport Dr Maryland Heights MO 63043

TENHOUSE, ART, state representative, farmer; b. Dec. 27, 1950; m. Sharon Roberts; children: Kate, Andy, Adam. BS in Agrl. Sci., Econs., U. Ill., 1973, MBA in Fin. Acctg., 1974. CPA, Ill. Cash mgr. DeKalb (Ill.) Inc.; ptnr. Four-Ten Famrs; state rep. 96th dist. State of Ill., 1989—. Chmn. Ho. Rep. Conf.; past chmn. Pub. Sfaety Appropriations Com.; bd. dirs. U. Ill. Coll. Agr. Alumni Assn.; instr. agrl. credit and fin. John Wood C.C. Burton Twp. clk., 1981-89; chmn. Adams County Farm Bur. Polit. Involvement Fund, 1988-89; 4-H leader Burton Flyers 4-H Club; treas. Farm Bur., Adams County, 1983-85, state utility spl. study com., 1986, legis. chmn., 1985-89, past. pres., v.p., 1985-89. Home: PO Box 1161 Quincy IL 62306-1161 Office: Rep Art Tenhouse 640 Maine St Quincy IL 62301-3908

TENNEFOS, JENS JUNIOR, retired state senator; b. Fargo, ND, Feb. 15, 1930; s. Jens Peterson and Iva M. (Gilbraith) T.; m. Jeanne P. Quamme, 1960; children: Daniel J., David A., Judie A., Mary J. Student, N.D. State U., 1947-49. Pres. Tennefos Constrn., 1951-74, Tennefos Enterprises, 1975-96; mem. N.D. Ho. of Reps., 1974-76, N.D. Senate, 1977-96, chmn. fin. and taxation com., mem. transp. com., pres. pro tempore, 1995-97. Past chmn., bd. trustees Constrn. Employees Pension, Trust and Health and Welfare Plan, capitol ground com., 1976-95. Featured in front page picture and article Modern Hwy. Mag., 1960, Local Guide Mag., 1980. Bd. regents Oak Grove Luth. H.S., 1970—, also v.p.; bd. dirs. Friendship, Heritage Hjemkosmst Interpretive Ctr., 1998—. Mem. Assn. Gen. Contractors N.D. (hon., past pres., Disting. Svc. Citation 1969), Elks, Am. Legion, Sons of Norway, Masons, Sigma Alpha Epsilon. Home: 310 8th St S Apt 304 Fargo ND 58103-1867

TENTORI, GIUSEPPE, chef; b. Italy, 1973; Grad., Antica Osteria la Rampina, Milan. Cook Carlos', Highland Park, Ill.; sous chef Metropolitan, Salt Lake City; chef de cuisine Charlie Trotter's, Chgo.; exec. chef Boka, Chgo., 2007—. Named one of America's Best New Chefs, Food & Wine Mag., 2008. Office: Boka 1729 N Halsted ST Chicago IL 60614 Office Phone: 312-337-6070.*

TEPE, THOMAS M., JR., lawyer; b. Cin., June 16, 1972; BA, Ohio State U., 1995; JD, Mich. State U. Detroit Coll. Law, 1999. Bar: Ohio 1999, US Dist. Ct. Southern Dist. Ohio 1999, US Ct. of Appeals Sixth Cir. 2001. Ptnr. Keating Muething & Klekamp PLL, Cin. Trustee Starfire Coun. Greater Cin., Inc.; com. mem. Bus. Devel. and Permit Ctr. Adv., Cin. Named one of Ohio's Rising Stars, Super Lawyers, 2005, 2006. Mem.: Ohio State Bar Assn., Cin. Bar Assn. Office: Keating Muething & Klekamp PLL One E Fourth St Ste 1400 Cincinnati OH 45202 Office Phone: 513-639-3947. Office Fax: 513-579-6457.

TEPHLY, THOMAS ROBERT, pharmacologist, educator, toxicologist; b. Norwich, Conn., Feb. 1, 1936; m. Joan Bernice Clifcorn, Dec. 17, 1960; children: Susan Lynn, Linda Ann, Annette Michele. BS, U. Conn., 1957; PhD, U. Wis., 1962; MD, U. Minn., 1965. Research asst. U. Wis., Madison, 1957-62, instr., 1962; asst. prof. U. Mich., Ann Arbor, 1965-69, assoc. prof., 1969-71; prof. pharmacology U. Iowa, Iowa City, 1971—2003, prof. emeritus, 2003. Contbr. articles to profl. jours. Rsch. scholar Am. Cancer Soc., 1962-65; recipient John Jacob Abel award, 1971, Kenneth P. Dubois award, 1992; Fogarty sr. internat. fellow NIH, 1978; rsch. grantee NIH, 1966—. Mem. Am. Soc. Pharmacology and Exptl. Therapeutics, Soc. Toxicology, AAAS, Am. Soc. Biochem. Molecular Biologists. Home: 6 Lakeview Dr NE Iowa City IA 52240-9142 Office: U Iowa Dept Pharmacology 2-452 BSB Iowa City IA 52242

TERKEL, STUDS (LOUIS TERKEL), writer, journalist; b. NYC, May 16, 1912; s. Samuel and Anna (Finkel) T.; m. Ida Goldberg, July 2, 1939; 1 son, Dan. PhB, U. Chgo., 1932, JD, 1934. Disting. Scholar in Residence, Chgo. Hist. Soc., 1998—. Stage appearances include Detective Story, 1950, A View From the Bridge, 1958, Light Up the Sky, 1959, The Cave Dwellers, 1960; moderator: (TV program) Studs Place, 1950-53, (radio programs) Wax Museum, 1945— (Ohio State Univ. award 1959, UNESCO Prix Italia award 1962), Studs Terkel Almanac, 1952—, Studs Terkel Show, Sta. WFMT-FM, Chgo.; actor (films) Beginning to Date, 1953, Eight Men Out, 1988; (TV movies) The Dollmaker, 1984; master of ceremonies Newport Folk Festival, 1959, 60, Ravinia Music Festival, 1959, U. Chgo. Folk Festival, 1961, others; panel moderator, lectr., narrator films; Author: Giants of Jazz, 1957, Division Street: America, 1967, Hard Times: An Oral History of the Great Depression, 1970, Working: People Talk about What They Do All Day and How They Feel about What They Do, 1974 (Nat. Book award nomination 1975), Talking to Myself: A Memoir of My Times, 1977, American Dreams: Lost and Found, 1980, The Good War: An Oral History of World War II (Pulitzer prize for Non-fiction 1985), Chicago, 1986, The Great Divide: Second Thoughts On The American Dream, 1988, Race: How Blacks and Whites Think and Feel About the American Obsession, 1992, Coming of Age: The Story of Our Century by Those Who've Lived It, 1995, My American Century, 1997, The Spectator: Talk About Movies and Plays With Those Who Make Them, 1999, Will the Circle Be Unbroken: Reflections on Death, Rebirth and Hunger for a Faith, 2001, Hope Dies Last: Keeping the Faith in Difficult Times, 2003, And They All Sang: Adventures of an Electric Disc Jockey, 2005, The Studs Terkel Reader: My American Century, 2007; co-author: (with Sydney Lewis) Touch and Go: A Memoir, 2007; author: (play) Amazing Grace, 1959 Named Communicator of Yr. U. Chgo. Alumni Assn., 1969; recipient Nat. Humanities Medal, 1997, Nat. Book Critics Circle Lifetime Achievement award, 2004, Dayton Lit. Peace prize, 2006. Office: Disting Scholar in Residence Chgo Hist Soc Clark St at North Ave Chicago IL 60614

TERNBERG, JESSIE LAMOIN, pediatric surgeon, educator; b. Corning, Calif., May 28, 1924; d. Eric G. and Alta M. (Jones) T. AB, Grinnell Coll., Iowa, 1946, ScD (hon.), 1970; PhD, U. Tex., Austin, 1950; MD, Washington U., St. Louis, 1953; ScD (hon.), U. Mo., St. Louis, 1981. Diplomate: Am. Bd. Surgery. Intern Boston City Hosp., 1953—54; asst. resident in surgery Barnes Hosp., St. Louis, 1954-57, resident in surgery, 1958-59; rsch. fellow Washington U. Sch. Medicine, 1957-58; practice medicine specializing in pediatric surgery St. Louis, 1966—; instr., DGMS trainee in surgery Washington U., 1959-62, asst. prof. surgery, 1962-65, assoc. prof. surgery, prof., 1965-71, prof. surgery, 1971-96, chief divsn. pediatric surgery, 1972-90, prof. emeritus, 1996—; mem. staff Barnes Hosp., 1959—90; gen. surgeon in chief Children's Hosp. of St. Louis, 1974-90. Mem. staff Children's Hosp., dir. pediatric surgery, 1972-90. Contbr. numerous articles on pediatric surgery to profl. jours. Trustee Grinnell Coll., 1984—. Recipient Alumni award Grinnell Coll., 1966, Faculty/Alumni award Washington U. Sch. Medicine, 1991, 2nd Century award 2006, 1st Aphrodite Jannopaulo Hofsommer award, 1993, Local Legend Changing the Face of Medicine award AMWA. Fellow AAAS; mem. SIOP, Am. Pediatric Surg. Assn., We. Surg. Assn. (2d v.p. 1984-85), St. Louis Med. Soc., Soc. Surgery of the Alimentary Tract, Am. Acad. Pediatrics, Soc. Pelvic Surgeons (v.p. 1991-92), Brit. Assn. Paediatric Surgeons, Assn. Women Surgeons (disting. mem. 1995), Mo. State Surg. Soc., St. Louis Surg. Soc. (pres. 1980-81), St. Louis Pediatric Soc., Soc. Surg. Oncology, Pediatric Oncology Group (chmn. surg. discipline 1983-96), St. Louis Childrens Hosp. Soc. (pres. 1979-80), Acad. Sci. St. Louis (Trustees award 2002), St. Louis Met. Med. Soc. (hon., councilor, trustee), Barnes Hosp. Soc., Phi Beta Kappa, Sigma Xi, Iota Sigma Pi, Alpha Omega Alpha. Office: St Louis Childrens Hosp 1 Childrens Pl Saint Louis MO 63110-1002 Business E-Mail: ternbergj@wudosis.wustl.edu.

TERNUS, MARSHA K., state supreme court chief justice; b. Vinton, Iowa, May 30, 1951; married; 3 children. BA, U. Iowa, 1972; JD, Drake U., 1977. Bar: Iowa 1977, Ariz. 1984. With Bradshaw, Fowler, Proctor & Fairgrave, Des Moines, 1977—93; justice Iowa Supreme Ct., Des Moines, 1993—, chief justice, 2006—. Former mem. Iowa Jury Instructions Com.; former bd. mem. Polk County Legal Aid Soc.; pres. bd. of counselors Drake U. Law Sch.; former mem. Iowa Supreme Ct. Commn. on Planning for the 21st Century, MultiState Perf. Test Policy Com., Nat. Conf. of Bar Examiners. Editor-in-chief: Drake Law Rev., 1976—77. Mem.: Iowa State Bar Assn. (bd. governors), Polk County Bar Assn. (pres. 1984—85), Order of Coif, Phi Beta Kappa. Office: Iowa Supreme Ct Jud Branch Bldg 1111 E Ct Ave Des Moines IA 50319-0001

TERP, DANA GEORGE, architect; b. Chgo., Nov. 5, 1953; s. George and June (Hansen) T.; m. Lynn Meyers, May 17, 1975; children: Sophia, Rachel. BA in Architecture, Washington U., St. Louis, 1974; postgrad., Yale U., 1975-76; MArch, Washington U., 1977. Registered architect, Ill., Calif., Fla. Architect Skidmore Owings & Merrill, Chgo., 1976, 1978-84, Terp Meyers Architects, Chgo., 1984—; prin. Arquitectonica Chgo. Inc., 1986—. Exhibited in group shows at Moming Gallery, Chgo., 1980, Printers Row Exhibit, 1980, Frumkin Struve Gallery, Chgo., 1981, Chgo. Art Inst., 1983; pub. in profl jours. including Progressive Architecture, Los Angeles Architect; work featured in various archtl books; exhibited 150 Yrs. of Chgo. Architecture. Bd. dirs. Architecture Soc. Art Inst. Chgo. Recipient hon. mention Chgo. Townhouse Competition, 1978, award Progressive Architecture mag., 1980, Archtl. Record Houses, 1989, GLOBAL Architecture Ga. Houses/26, 1989, Casa Vogue, 1989, 2d place award Burnham Prize Competition, 1991. Office: Terp Meyers Architects Inc 2314 N Lincoln Park W Apt 13N Chicago IL 60614-3462

TERP, THOMAS THOMSEN, lawyer; b. Fountain Hill, Pa., Aug. 12, 1947; s. Norman T. and Josephine (Uhran) T.; m. Pamela Robinson; children: Stephanie, Brian, Adam; step-children: Taylor Mefford, Grace Mefford. BA, Albion Coll., Mich., 1969; JD, Coll. of William and Mary, 1973. Bar: Ohio 1973, US Dist. Ct. (so. dist.) Ohio 1973, US Ct. Appeals (6th cir.) 1973, US Supreme Ct. 1979. Assoc. Taft, Stettinius & Hollister, Cin., 1973-80, ptnr., 1981—, chmn., mng. ptnr., 2007—. Bd. dirs. Starflo Corp., Orangeburg, SC, Attorneys' Liability Assurance Soc., Ltd., Hamilton, Bermuda, ALAS, Inc., Chgo. Editor-in-chief William & Mary Law Rev., 1972-73; mem. bd. editors Jour. of Environ. Hazards, 1988—, Environ. Law Jour. of Ohio, 1989—. Mem. Cin. Athletic Club, Camargo Club, Epworth Assembly (Ludington, Mich.), Lincoln Hills Golf Club (Ludington), Queen City Club. Avocations: tennis, golf, travel. Office Phone: 513-357-9354. Business E-Mail: terp@taftlaw.com.

TERRASSA, JACQUELINE, museum director; MFA, U. Chgo., 1994. Staff mem. Columbia Coll., Chgo.; edn. dir. Hyde Park Art Ctr., David and Alfred Smart Mus. Art, U. Chgo., 1998—, interim dir., 2004—05, established SmART Explorers sch. program, dep. dir. collections, programs, & interpretation, 2005—.

TERRY, LEE RAYMOND, congressman, lawyer; b. Omaha, Jan. 29, 1962; s. Leland R. Terry; m. Robyn L. Terry, Feb. 14, 1992; children: Nolan E., Ryan, Jack. BA in Polit. Sci., U. Nebr., Lincoln, 1984; JD, Creighton U. Sch. Law, Omaha, 1987. Bar: Nebr. 1987, US Dist. Ct. Nebr. 1987. Staff atty. Schrempp & Salerno, Omaha, 1987-92; ptnr. Schrempp, Salerno & Terry, Omaha, 1992-93, Terry & Kratville, Omaha, 1993-98; mem. City Coun., Omaha, 1991—98, US Congress from 2nd Nebr. dist., 1999—, mem. energy & commerce com. Co-author: Trying the Soft Tissue Case in Nebraska, 1995. V.p. Omaha City Coun., 1993-94, pres., 1995-97; chair elect Am. Diabetes Assn., Great Plains, 1996-97, chair Nebr. area, 1997-99; co-chmn. Impact Aid Coalition. Named One of Ten Outstanding Young Omahans, Omaha Jaycees, 1994, Outstanding Young Nebraskan Nebr. Jaycees, 1997; recipient Spirit of Enterprise award US C. of C., 2002 Mem. Nebr. Assn. Trial Attys. (dir. 1995), Suburban Rotary. Republican. Meth. Avocations: travel, playing, spending time with family. Office: US House Reps 1524 Longworth House Office Bldg Washington DC 20515-2702 Office Phone: 202-225-4155.

TERRY, LEON CASS, neurologist, educator; b. Dec. 22, 1940; s. Leon Herbert and Zella Irene (Boyd) T.; m. Suzanne Martinson, June 27, 1964; children: Kristin, Sean. Pharm. D., U. Mich., 1964; MD, Marquette U., 1969; PhD, McGill U., 1982; MBA, U. So. Fla., 1994. Diplomate Am. Bd. Psychiatry and Neurology, Am. Bd. Med. Mgmt. Intern U. Rochester, NY, 1969-70; staff assoc. NIH, 1970-72; resident in neurology McGill U., Montreal, Que., Canada, 1972-75; MRC fellow, 1975-78; assoc. prof. U. Tenn., Memphis, 1978-81; prof. neurology U. Mich., Ann Arbor, 1981-89; assoc. prof. physiology, 1982-89; asst. chief neurology VA Med. Ctr., Ann Arbor, 1982-89; chmn. dept. neurology Med. Coll. of Wis., Milw., 1989—2000, prof. neurology and physiology, 1989—2003; chief med. officer exostherapeuticals, 2003—; pres., CEO Neurologic Cons., LLP, 2004—, Longevitech, 2004—. Dir. clin neurosci. ctr. and multiple sclerosis clinic, Med. Coll. Wis.; assoc. dean for amb. care, 1996-98; vice chief of staff Froedtert Hosp., 1994-97; chief of staff, 1997-98; chief med. officer cenegenics, 1997-98. Contbr. articles to profl. jours, chpts. to books. Served to lt. comdr. USPHS, 1970-72. NIH grantee, 1981-92; VA grantee, 1980-92; VA Clin. Investigator award, 1980-81. Mem. AMA, Am. Soc. Clin. Investigation, Cen. Soc. Clin. Investigation, Am. Neurol. Assn., Am. Coll. Physician Execs. (vice chmn. academic health ctr. soc. 1994-95, chair, 1995-98, leader forum health care delivery 1995-98), Am. Coll. Healthcare Execs., Endocrine Soc., Am. Acad. Neurology, Internat. Soc. Neuroendocrinilogy, Internat. Soc. Psychoeuroendocrinilogy, Soc. Neurosci., Soc. Rsch. Biol. Rhythms, Milw. Acad. Physicians, Wis. Neurol. Assn., Wis. State Med. Soc. (del.-elect 1995-96), Med. Soc. Milw. County, Milw. Neuropsychiatric Soc. (pres.-elect.). Avocations: pilot, skiing, scuba diving, computers. Office: Neurologic Consultnats LLP Suite 209 1009 W Glen Oaks Lane Mequon WI 53092 Home Phone: 414-234-9207; Office Phone: 262-241-8512. E-mail: cass@cass-terry.com, drcassterry@wi.rr.com.

TERRY, NICHOLAS P., law educator; b. London, Eng., Dec. 5, 1952; BA, Kingston Univ., UK, 1975; LLM, Univ. Cambridge, 1977. Lectr. Univ. Exeter, England; prof. Saint Louis U. Sch. Law, 1980—, co-dir. Ctr. Health Studies, 2000—; prof. Saint Louis U. Sch. Pub. Health, 2003—. Vis. prof. Univ. Mo. Columbia Sch. Law, 1986—87, Washington Univ. Sch. Law, 1986—99; dir. Legal Edn. LEXIS-NEXIS, Dayton, Ohio, 1996—97; sr. fellow Melbourne Law Sch., Australia, 2001—. Co-author: Cases, Materials and Problems in the Law of Torts, 2002, Products Liability, Cases, Material, Problems, 2002; contbr. articles to prof. jour.; co-editor (in-chief): Jour. Health Law, 2000—. Mem. bd. dir. Ctr. for Computer Assisted Legal Instruction, 1998—; mem. editl. bd. Jour. Medical Internet. Rsch., 2000—; mem. internat. bd. adv. Medical Law Rev., Oxford Univ. Press, 1992—; mem. bd. adv. Melbourne Law Sch., Australia, 2001—. Mem.: ABA, Am. Health Lawyers Assn., Am. Soc. Law & Medicine (mem. bd. dir.), Health Law Tchr. Assn. Office: Saint Louis U Sch Law 3700 Lindell Blvd Saint Louis MO 63108 Office Phone: 314-977-3998. Business E-Mail: terry@slu.edu.

TERRY, ROBERT BROOKS, food products executive, lawyer; b. Kansas City, Mo., July 7, 1956; s. Frank R. and Susan S. (Smart) T.; m. Penny Susan Kanterman, July 2, 1987; children: Ryan, Kevin, Erin. Student, Vanderbilt U., 1974-75; BS in Acctg., U. Mo., 1978, JD, 1981. Bar: Mo. 1981, U.S. Dist. ct. (we. dist.) Mo. 1981, U.S. ct. Appeals (8th and 10th cirs.) 1983. Assoc. Spencer, Fane, Britt & Browne, Kansas City, Mo., 1981—89; v.p., gen. counsel Farmland Industries, Inc., Kansas City, 1993—, pres., CEO, 2002—. Mem. ABA, Kansas City Mo. Bar Assn., Lawyers' Assn. Kansas City, Order of Coif. Avocation: baseball. Home: 4952 W 132nd Ter Leawood KS 66209-3460

TERRY, ROBIN, museum director; b. 1969; Degree in Telecom. and Film, Eastern Mich. U., 1992. Dir., Pub. Rels. Motown Hist. Mus., Detroit, 1992—95, dep. dir., 2002—04, exec. dir., 2004—; worked for D'Arcy Masius Benton & Bowles Inc., Troy, Mich., 1995, Gable Grp.; dir., Pub. Rels. Coll. for Creative Studies; devel. officer Focus: HOPE, 1998—2002. Named one of 40 Under 40, Crain's Detroit Bus., 2006. Office: Motown Historical Museum 2648 W Grand Blvd Detroit MI 48208 Office Phone: 313-875-2264.

TERSCHAN, FRANK ROBERT, lawyer; b. Dec. 25, 1949; s. Frank Joseph and Margaret Anna (Heidt) T.; m. Barbara Elizabeth Keily, Dec. 28, 1974; 1 child, Frank Martin. BA, Syracuse U., 1972; JD, U. Wis., 1975. Bar: Wis. 1976, U.S. Dist. Ct. (ea. and we. dists.) Wis. 1976, U.S. Ct. Appeals (7th cir.) 1979, U.S. Ct. Appeals (10th cir.) 1989, U.S. Supreme Ct. 1992. From assoc. to ptnr. Frisch, Dudek & Slattery Ltd., Milw., 1975-88; ptnr. Slattery and Hausman Ltd., Milw., 1988-94, Terschan & Steinle Ltd., Milw., 1994-96, Terschan, Steinle & Ness, Milw., 1996—. Chmn. MBA Fee Adminstrn. Com., 2000—; mem. Wis. Jud. Conduct Adv. Com., 2002—. Treas., sec. Ville du Park Homeowners Assn., Mequon, Wis., 1985-86; cubmaster Boy Scouts Am., 1989-90, asst. scoutmaster, 1991-93. Mem. ABA, Am. Bd. Trial Advocates, Wis. Bar Assn., Milw. Bar Assn., Am. Assn. for Justice, Wis. Assn. for Justice (bd. dirs. 1996—), 7th Cir. Bar Assn., Order of Coif. Republican. Lutheran. Avocations: swimming, coin collecting/numismatics, reading, outdoor activities. Home: 10143 N Lake Shore Dr Mequon WI 53092-6109 Office: 309 N Water St Ste 215 Milwaukee WI 53202 Office Phone: 414-258-1010. Business E-Mail: frt@tsn-law.com.

TERWILLEGER, GEORGE E., state legislator; m. Jackie Johnson; children: DeWayne, DeLanna, DeAnna. AA, Xavier Univ. Trustee Hamilton Twp., 1969-74; state rep. Ohio Dist. 2, 1996—. Mem. Nat. Land Use com., Nat. Assn. Towns & Townships, County Commn. Assn.; vice chair Clinton Warren Counties Solid Waste Policy com., chair County Reg. Planning Com. Corp. dir. spl. svc. Otterbein Homes, Lebanon, Ohio; treas. Watchdog. Named County Clerk of Yr. Mem. Scottish Rite Club (pres.), County Assn. of Trustees (pres.), Warren County Bd. Realtors (dir., pres.). Home: 10609 Rochester Cozaddale Rd Goshen OH 45122-9607 Office: Ohio Ho of Reps State House Columbus OH 43215

TERWILLIGER, ROY W., state legislator; b. June 20, 1937; m. Mary Lou; three children. BS, U. S.D.; MA, U. Iowa. Mem. Minn. Senate from 42nd dist., St. Paul, 1992—; banker. Office: Minn Senate State Capitol Saint Paul MN 55155-0001 Home: 7723 Shaughnessy Rd Minneapolis MN 55439-2639

TESCHER, JENNIFER, bank executive; b. 1971; Grad., Northwestern U.; MA in pub. policy, U. Chgo. With ShoreBank Corp., Chgo., 1996—, ShoreBank Adv. Services, Chgo., 2002—04; dir. Ctr. Fin. Services Innovation, Chgo., 2004—. Pres. bd. Ctr. Econ. Progress, Chgo.; monthly columnist Am. Banker. Named one of 40 Under 40, Crain's Chgo. Bus., 2006. Office: Ctr Fin Services Innovation Ste 200 2230 S Michigan Ave Chicago IL 60616 Office Phone: 312-881-5856. Office Fax: 312-881-5801. E-mail: cfsi@cfsinnovation.com.

TETTLEBAUM, HARVEY M., lawyer; m. Ann Safier; children: Marianne, Benjamin. AB, Dartmouth Coll., 1964; JD, Washington U. Sch. Law, 1968, AM in History, 1968. Asst. dean Washington U. Sch. Law, 1969-77; asst. atty. gen., chief counsel Consumer Protection and Anti-Trust Div., 1970-77; pvt. practice Jefferson City, Mo., 1977-90; mem., chmn. health law practice group Husch & Eppenberger, LLC, Jefferson City, Mo., 1990—. Mem. selection com. US Magistrate, 1988; mem. Fed. Jud. Merit Selection Commn., 1991. Contbr. articles to profl. jours. Treas. Mo. Rep. State Com., 1976—2004; v.p. Moniteau County R-1 Sch. Dist. Bd., 1991-95, pres., 1995-96; mem. Calif. R-1 Sch. Bd., 1990-96, v.p., 1993-95, pres., 1995-96. Named Best Lawyers in Am., 2008; named one of, 2005, 2006, 2007; recipient Legis. award, Legal Svcs. Ea. Mo., 1999. Mem. Am. Health Lawyers Assn. (bd. dirs. 1993-99, co-chair long-term care and the law program 1993-01, chair 2001—07, chair long-term care and law program 2001—07, former chair long term care practice group 1997-01), Mo. Bar Assn. (health and hosp. law com., chmn. adminstrv. law com., vice chair delivery legal svc. com., Mo. statewide legal svc. com., President's award 2000, 03), Am. Health Care Assn. (legal subcom. 1994—, chair 2004-06), Rep. Nat. Lawyers Assn. (bd. dirs. 1988-, 1st v.p. 2002—, pres. 2003-06, Lawyer of Yr. 2006). Republican. Jewish. Home: 56295 Little Moniteau Rd California MO 65018-3069 Office: Husch & Eppenberger LLC Monroe House Ste 300 235 E High St PO Box 1251 Jefferson City MO 65102-1251 Office Phone: 573-761-1107. Business E-Mail: harvey.tettlebaum@husch.com.

TETZLAFF, THEODORE R., lawyer; b. Saukville, Wis., Feb. 27, 1944; AB magna cum laude, Princeton U., 1966; LLB, Yale U., 1969. Bar: Ind. 1969, D.C. 1969, Ill. 1974. Legis. asst. to Congressman John Brademas, 1970; exec. dir. Nat. Conf. Police Community Rels., 1970-71; acting dir. US Office Legal Svcs., Office Econ. Opportunity, Washington, 1972-73; counsel, Com. Judiciary US Ho. of Reps., Washington, 1974; v.p., legal and external affairs Cummins Engine Co., 1980-82; gen. counsel Tenneco, Inc., Greenwich, Conn., 1992-99; ptnr. Jenner & Block, Chgo., 1976—80, 1982—2001, McGuireWoods LLP, Chgo., 2002—05, mng. ptnr. Chgo. office; gen. counsel Peoples Energy, 2003—05; ptnr. Ungaretti & Harris LLP, Chgo., 2005—. Bd. dirs. Continental Materials Corp., Chgo. Pres. Chgo. area Found. Legal Svcs., 1983—; commr. Pub. Bldg. Commn. Chgo., 1990-2005; chmn. Met. Pier and Expo Authority, 2005—. Reginald Heber Smith fellow, 1969-70. Mem. ABA (chair sect. litigation 1991-92), Ill. State Bar Assn., Ind. State Bar Assn., D.C. Bar. Office: Ungaretti & Harris LLP 3500 Three First Nat Plz Chicago IL 60602 Office Phone: 312-977-4150. Business E-Mail: tedt@mycingular.blackberry.net.

THACH, WILLIAM THOMAS, JR., neurologist, educator; b. Okla. City, Jan. 3, 1937; s. William Thomas and Mary Elizabeth T.; m. Emily Ransom Otis, June 30, 1963 (div. 1979); children: Sarah Brill, James Otis, William Thomas III. AB in Biology magna cum laude, Princeton U., 1959; MD cum laude, Harvard U., 1964. Diplomate Am. Bd. Psychiatry and Neurology (in Neurology). Intern Mass. Gen. Hosp., Boston, 1964-65, asst. residency, 1965-66; staff assoc. physiology sect. lab. clin. sci. NIMH, Bethesda, Md., 1966-69; neurology resident, clin. and rsch. fellow Mass. Gen. Hosp., 1969-71; from asst. prof. neurology to assoc. prof. neurology Yale U. Sch. Medicine, New Haven, Conn., 1971-75; assoc. prof. neurobiology and neurology dept. anatomy and neurobiology Washington U. Sch. Medicine, St. Louis, 1975-80, prof. neurobiology and neurology dept. anatomy and neurobiology, 1980—, chief divsn. neurorehab. dept. neurology, 1992—. Acting dir. Irene Walter Johnson Rehab. Inst. Washington U. Sch. Medicine, 1989-91, dir., 1991-92; attending neurologist Barnes Hosp., med. dir. dept. rehab.; attending neurologist Jewish Hosp., St. Louis Regional Hosp.; bd. sci. counselors NINCDS, 1988-92; mem. NIH Study Sect. Neurology A, 1981-85. Assoc. editor Somatosenory and Motor Research; contbr. numerous articles to profl. jours. Fulbright grantee U. Melbourne, Australia, 1959-60; NIH grantee, 1971— Mem. Physiol. Soc., Am. Acad. Neurology, Soc. Neurosci., Am. Neurol. Assn., Am. Soc. Neurorehab., Phi Beta Kappa, Sigma Xi, Alpha Omega Alpha. Achievements include research on brain control of movement and motor learning, roles of the basal ganglia and the cerebellum in health and disease. Home: 7520 Clayton Rd Saint Louis MO 63117-1418 Office: Washington Univ Dept Anatomy & Neurobiol 600 S Euclid Ave Dept Anatomy& Saint Louis MO 63110-1010 E-mail: thachw@peg.wustl.edu.

THADEN, EDWARD CARL, history professor; b. Seattle, Apr. 24, 1922; s. Edward Carl and Astrid (Engvik) T.; m. Marianna Theresia Forster, Aug. 7, 1952. BA, U. Wash., 1944; student, U. Zurich, Switzerland, 1948; PhD, U. Paris, 1950. Instr. Russian history Pa. State U., 1952-55, asst. prof., 1955-58, assoc. prof., 1958-64, prof., 1964-68, U. Ill., Chgo., 1968—92, chmn. dept. history, 1971—73, prof. emeritus, 1992—. Vis. prof. Ind. U., 1957, U. Marburg, 1965, U. Ill., Urbana, 1980, U. Halle, Germany, 1988, U. Helsinki, Finland, 1990; editl. cons. Can. Rev. Studies in Nationalism, 1973—78; vis. rsch. scholar USSR Acad. Scis., 1975, 88, 90; project prin. rschr. Ford Found., 1975—78; U.S. rep. Internat. Congress of Hist. Scis., 1980; project dir. NEH grant, 1980—82. Author: Conservative Nationalism in Nineteenth-Century Russia, 1964, Russia and the Balkan Alliance of 1912, 1965, Russia Since 1801: The Making of a New Society, 1971, Russia's Western Borderlands, 1710-1870, 1984, Interpreting History: collected Essays on Russia's Relations with Europe, 1990, Essays in Russian and East European History: Festschrift in Honor of Edward C. Thaden, 1995, The Rise of Historicism in Russia, 1999; co-author, editor: Russification in the Baltic Provinces and Finland, 1855-1914, 1981; co-author, co-editor: Finland and the Baltic Provinces in the Russian Empire, 1984; mem. editorial bd. Jour Baltic Studies, 1984-93, assoc. editor, 1987-93, East European Quarterly, 1998—. Served to lt. (j.g.) USNR, 1943-46. Carnegie Inter-Univ. Com. travel grantee to USSR, 1956; Fulbright rsch. grantee Finland, 1957-58, Germany, 1965, Poland and Finland, 1968; Soc. Sci. Rsch. Coun. grantee, 1957; Am. Coun. Learned Socs. grantee, 1963, 65-66; fellow Woodrow Wilson Internat. Ctr. for Scholars, 1980 Mem. Am. Hist. Assn. (life), Nat. History Ctr. (founding mem.), Am. Assn. for Advancement Slavic Studies (pres. Midwest br. 1975-76, exec. sec. 1980-82), Chgo. Consortium for Slavic and Ea. European Studies (pres. 1982-84), Baltische Historische Kommission, Göttingen (corr. mem. 1985—), Commn. Internat. des Etudes Historiques Slaves (v.p. 1985-95, pres. 1995-2000, pres.d'honneur 2000—). Office: U Ill Dept History 913 UH (M/C 198) 601 S Morgan St Chicago IL 60607-7100

THAI-TANG, HAU, automotive engineer; b. Saigon, Vietnam, Sept. 12, 1966; m. Jenny Thai-Tang. BS in mech. engring., Carnegie-Mellon U.; MBA, U. Mich. Ford Coll. grad. trainee Ford Motor Co., 1988, vehicle engring. mgr. Mustang line, Ford N. Am. car chief engr. Thunderbird, Mustang, and Windstar lines, vehicle engring. mgr. 2000 Lincoln LS, 1997—99. Race engr. Nigel Mansell's CART team Ford Racing, 1993, race engr. Newman-Haas Racing team, 93, race engr. Mario Andretti Racing team; lead recruiter for Ford Motor Co. Carnegie-Mellon U.; leader/tchr. New Bus. Leader program Ford, 2000. Recipient Young Leadership and Excellence award, Automotive Hall Fame, Dearborn, Mich., 2001. Achievements include Lincoln LS earned Motor Trend Car Yr. award, Autoweek's Ten Best award, Consumer Report's "Promising" rating, and was named best driving domestic sedan, Road and Track mag; led the devel. and launch of 2001 Mustang GT, V-6, Cobra and Bullitt GT models for Ford Motor Co; responsible for devel. of Nigel Ansell's and Mario Andretti's race cars. Office: Ford Motor Co PO Box 6248 Dearborn MI 48126

THALDEN, BARRY, architect; b. Chgo., July 5, 1942; s. Joseph and Sibyl (Goodwin) Hechtenthal; m. Irene L. Mittleman, June 23, 1966 (div. 1989); 1 child, Stacey; m. Kathryn McKnight, Sept. 1996. BArch, U. Ill., 1965; M in Land Architecture, U. Mich., 1969. Landscape arch. Hellmuth, Obata, Kassebaum, St. Louis, 1969-70; dir. landscape architecture PGAV Archs., St. Louis, 1970-71; pres. Thalden Corp. Archs., St. Louis, 1971—; ptnr. Thalden-Boyd-Emery Archs., St. Louis, 1998—. Prin. works include Rock Hill Park, 1975 (AIA award, 1977), Wilson Residence, 1983 (AIA award), Nat. Bowling Hall of Fame, 1983 (St. Louis RCGA award, 1984), Village Bogey Hills (Home Builders award, 1985, St. Louis ASLA award, 1994), St. Louis U. Campus Mall (St. Louis ASLA award, 1989), Horizon Casino Resort, Lake Tahoe, Nev., St. Louis Airport's Radisson Hotel, Lady Luck, Treasure Bay, Palace Casinos, Biloxi, Miss., Boomtown Casino, New Orleans, Pres. Casino on the Admiral, St. Louis, Plaza of Champions, Busch Stadium, Ho Chunk Casino, Wisconsin Dells (ABC award Best Bldg. in Wis., 2000), Potowatomi Casino, Milw., Terrible's Casino, Las Vegas, Chumash Casino Resort, Santa Ynez, Calif., Casino Morongo, Palm Springs, Calif., Paragon Casino Resort, Marksville, La. Bd. dirs. St. Louis Open Space Coun., 1973—83, St. Louis Art., Ednl. Coun.; bd. trustees Las Vegas Art Mus.; apptd. Mo. Lands Architect Coun., 1990—94. Named Architect of Yr. Builder Architect mag., 1986. Fellow Am. Soc. Landscape Architects (nat. v.p. 1979-81, pres. St. Louis chpt. 1975, trustee 1976-79, nat. conv. chair 1991); mem. AIA, World Future Soc. (pres. St. Louis chpt. 1984-94, keynote conf. spkr. 1995). Avocations: painting, gardening, tennis, guitar. Home: 2204 Chatsworth Ct Henderson NV 89074-5307 Office: Thalden-Boyd Emery Archs 8085 Manchester Rd Saint Louis MO 63144

THALL, ROBERT, photographer, educator; b. Chgo., Dec. 6, 1948; BA in Design, U. Ill., 1972, MFA in Photography, 1986. Prof. photography Columbia Coll., Chgo., 1976—, chmn. Photography Dept. Vis. artist U. Ill., Chgo., 1975, adj. asst. prof. art, 80; lectr. in field. One-man shows include Evanston (Ill.) Art Ctr., 1980, Morning Art and Dance Ctr., Chgo., 1980, Edwynn Houk Gallery, 1984, Art Inst. Chgo., 1994, Ehlers Caudill Gallery, Chgo., 1995, City of Chgo. Photography Gallery at Water Tower, 1999, Mus. Contemporary Photography, 1999, exhibited in group shows at Hodges Taylor Gallery, Charlotte, N.C., 1996, Mus. Contemporary Art, Chgo., 1996, Mus. Van Bommel-Van Dam, Venlo, The Netherlands, 1997, Milw. Art Mus., 1999, others; curated exhbns. include Truman Coll., 1980, Chgo. Ctr. Contemporary Photography, Columbia Coll., 1983; commns. include, Historic Bldgs. Iowa, 1976, Ctrl. Mfg. Dist., 1983, Midway Airport Pub. Art Competition, 1999, others, Represented in permanent collections Art Inst. Chgo., Calif. Mus. Photography, Riverside, Calif., Can. Ctr. Arch., Montreal, Chgo. Hist. Soc., Getty Ctr. History Art and Humanities, Santa Monica, Calif., Hallmark Collection, Kansas City, Mo., Milw. Art Mus., Mus. Fine Art, Houston, Mus. Folkwang, Essen, Germany, Mus. Modern Art, N.Y.C., Seagram Collection, Victoria and Albert Mus., London, others; book and exhbn. reviewer Exposure and New Art Examiner, 1980—83; author: The Perfect City, 1994; The New American Village, 1999, City Spaces, 2002. Grantee Project Completion grantee, Ill. Arts Coun., 1980; Graham Found. grantee, 1998, John Simon Guggenheim Meml. Found. fellow, 1998. Office: Columbia Coll Dept Photography 600 S Michigan Ave Chicago IL 60605-1900

THAMAN, MICHAEL H., building material systems executive; b. Mar. 5, 1964; BSEE, Princeton U., 1986, BS in Computer Sci., 1986. V.p. Mercer Mgmt. Cons., NYC, 1986—92; dir. corp. devel. Owens Corning, 1992-94, plant mgr. Toronto insulation facility, 1994-96, gen. mgr. OEM solutions group Louisville, 1996-97, v.p., pres. engineered pipe systems bus. Brussels, 1997-99, v.p., pres. exterior systems bus. Toledo, 1999-2000, sr. v.p., 2000—02, CFO, 2000—07, chmn., 2002—, pres., CEO, 2007—. Bd. dirs. Owens Corning, 2002—, FPL Group, Inc., 2003—. Office: Owens Corning One Owens Corning Pkwy Toledo OH 43659

THANE, RUSSELL T., state legislator; b. Denver, July 14, 1926; s. Joseph and Bernice (Steere) T.; m. Betty Jo Chowning, 1952; children: Ronald, Kathleen. Degree, .D. State Sch. Sci., 1949, N.D. State U., 1955. Dir. Home Mutual Ins. Co., Wahpeton, 1968—; mem. N.D. Senate from 25th dist., Bismark, 1971—; asst. majority floor whip N.D. Senate, Bismark, 1981-82, mem. appropriations com., chmn. human svc., mem. interim adv. com. on intergovt. rels. Farmer; dir. Red River Valley Beet Growers, 1969—. Precinct committeeman 25th dist., N.D., 1964-70; mem. adv. bd. N.D. State Sch. Sci. Drug and Alcohol Prevention, Wahpeton Cmty. Devel. Corp., State Hosp. Mem. N.D. Cattle Feeders Assn. (sec.-treas. 1964-70), Zagal Shrine, Elks, Masons, Eagles, Am. Legion (life), Farm Bur. Office: Rte 1 Box 142 Wahpeton ND 58075-9801 also: ND Senate State Capitol Bismarck ND 58505 Home: 7660 178th Ave SE Wahpeton ND 58075-9615

THARALDSON, GARY DEAN, hotel developer, owner; b. Valley City, ND, Oct. 17, 1945; BA in Phys. Edn., Valley City State U.; postgrad., N.D. State U. Tchr., Leonard, .D.; ins. agt., agy. owner, 1969-89; owner of 350 hotels, Valley City, 1982; pres. Tharaldson Enterprises, Fargo, N.D., 1982—. Office: Tharaldson Enterprises 1202 Westrac Dr Fargo ND 58103-2344

THEEN, ROLF HEINZ-WILHELM, political science educator; b. Stadthagen, Germany, Feb. 20, 1937; came to U.S., 1956, naturalized, 1962; s. Walter and Gertrud (Tysper) T.; m. orma Lee Plunkett, June 14, 1959; children: Tanya Sue, Terrell René. BA magna cum laude, Manchester Coll., 1959; MA, Ind. U., 1962, cert. with high distinction Russian and East European Inst., 1962, PhD, 1964. From asst. prof. to assoc. prof. Iowa State U., 1964-70; assoc. prof. polit. sci. Purdue U., West Lafayette, Ind., 1971-73, prof., 1974—. Dir. Purdue U.-Ind. U. study program U. Hamburg, 1980-81; translator, editor U.S. Joint Publs. Rsch. Svc. Author: Lenin: Genesis and Development of a Revolutionary, 1973, 74, 79; co-author: Comparative Politics: An Introduction to Seven Countries, 1992, 4th edit., 2000; editor, translator: The Early Years of Lenin (N. Valentinov), 1969; editor: The USSR First Congress of People's Deputies: Complete Documents and Records, 4 vols., 1991; contbr. articles to profl. jours., chpts. to books. Recipient Wilton Park award Iowa State U., 1971; Fgn. Area Tng. fellow Russian and East European Inst., 1962-64; grantee Am. Philos. Soc., Inter Univ. Com., Joint Com. Slavic Studies, Fulbright grantee, 1995; NEH sr. fellow, 1974-75, rsch. fellow Kennan Inst. Advanced Russian Studies, Woodrow Wilson Internat. Ctr. for Scholars, 1976, Ctr. Humanistic Studies fellow Purdue U., 1982, 88, 91. Mem. Am. Polit. Sci. Assn., Am. Assn. Advancement Slavic Studies, Am. Acad. Social and Polit. Sci. Mem. Ch. of the Brethren. Office: Purdue U Dept Polit Sci Liberal Arts/Edn Bldg 2221 West Lafayette IN 47907-1363 Home (Winter): 6415 Midnight Pass Rd Unit 611 Sarasota FL 34242 E-mail: theen@polscipurdue.edu.

THEISEN, HENRY J., manufacturing executive; b. 1953; BSChemE, U. Wis. Pres. Curwood Inc., 1998—2003; v.p. ops., pres. high barrier products Bemis Co., Inc., 2002—03, exec. v.p., COO, 2003—07, pres., COO, 2007—08, pres., CEO, 2008—. Bd. dirs. Bemis Co., Inc. Office: Beamis Co Inc One Neenah Ctr 4th Fl Neenah WI 54956 Office Phone: 920-727-4100. Office Fax: 612-376-3150.*

THELEN, BRUCE CYRIL, lawyer; b. St. Johns, Mich., Nov. 24, 1951; BA, Mich. State U., 1973; JD, U. Mich., 1977. Bar: NY 1978, Mich. 1980, Ill. 1992. Assoc. Dewey, Ballantine, Bushby, Palmer & Wood, NYC, 1977-80, Dickinson, Wright, Moon, Van Dusen & Freeman, Detroit, 1981-83; ptnr. Dickinson Wright PLLC, Detroit, 1984—. Mem. US Dept. Commerce-Mich. Dist. Export Coun., 1995—. Contbr. articles to profl. jours. Mem. allocation panel, mem. spkrs. bur., chmn. rsch. and info. svcs. com., mem. strategic planning com. and cmty. leaders coun. United Way Cmty. Svcs., 1987—; mem. Mich. Task Force Internat. Trade, Lansing, 1990, Detroit Com. Fgn. Rels., Greater Detroit-Windsor Japan Am. Soc.; mem. global partnership Mich. Econ. Devel. Corp.; mem. adv. coun. Ctr. Internat. Bus. Edn., U. Mich. Sch. Bus. Decorated Order of Merit Germany. Mem.: German Am. C. of C. Mich. (pres. 1994—2004, chmn. 2004—), Internat. Inst. Detroit (bd. dirs. 1997—99, v.p. 1999—2000, adv. coun. 2001—), Ill. Bar Assn. (internat. law sect.), Am. Soc. Internat. Law, Internat. Bar Assn. (chmn. fin. aspects internat. sales subcom. 2003—05, vice chmn. internat. sales com. 2006—07, sr. vice chmn. internat. sales com. 2007—), State Bar Mich. (chmn. internat. law sect. 1990—91), NY Bar Assn. (internat. law sect.), Wayne State U. (mem. office Internat. programs, mem. Internat. Bridge Coun. and bd. visitors), Detroit Regional Chamber (mem. Leadership Detroit VIII program 1986—87, chmn. European mission com. 1991, 1992, mem. export com. 1992—95, mem. exec. com. world trade club and internat. bus. coun. 1992—, chmn. adv. bd. European mission com. 1995, ptnr. 2007—), Mich. Israel C. of C. (bd. dirs. 1997—2001), German Am. C. of C. Midwest (bd. dirs. 1992—2006), French-Am. C. of C. Detroit, Detroit Athletic Club, Econ. Club Detroit. Office: Dickinson Wright PLLC 500 Woodward Ave Ste 4000 Detroit MI 48226-3416 Office Phone: 313-223-3624. Business E-Mail: bthelen@dickinsonwright.com.

THEOBALD, THOMAS CHARLES, banker; b. Cin., May 5, 1937; m. Gigi Mahon, Jan. 1987 AB in Econs., Coll. Holy Cross, 1958; MBA in Fin. with high distinction, Harvard U., 1960. With Citibank, N.A. div. Citicorp, 1960-87; vice-chmn. Citicorp, NYC, 1982-87; CEO, chmn. Continental Bank Corp., Chgo., 1987-94; chmn. bd. dirs. Continental Bank N.A., Chgo., 1987-94; mng. dir. Blair Capital Ptnrs., Chgo., 1994—. Bd. dir. Jones, Lang LaSalle US Realty Income & Growth Fund, Anixter Internat., Liberty Funds, MONY Group, Ambac Financial Group; bd. chmn. Columbia Mutual Funds. Trustee Northwestern U.; bd. dirs. MacArthur Found.; bd. of adv. Harvard Bus. Sch. Office: William Blair Capital Partners 222 W Adams St Chicago IL 60606-5307

THIBODEAU, GARY A., academic administrator; b. Sioux City, Iowa, Sept. 26, 1938; m. Emogene J. McCarville, Aug. 1, 1964; children: Douglas James (dec.), Beth Ann. BS, Creighton U., 1962; MS, S.D. State U., 1967, MS, 1970, PhD, 1971. Profl. service rep. Baxter Lab., Inc., Deerfield, Ill., 1963-65; tchr., researcher dept. biology S.D. State U., Brookings, 1965-76, asst. to v.p. for acad. affairs, 1976-80, v.p. for adminstrn., 1980-85; chancellor U. Wis., River Falls, 1985-2000; sr. v.p. acad. affairs U. Wis. Sys., 2000—01. Mem. investment com. U. Wis., River Falls Found.; trustee W. Cen. Wis. Consortium U. Wis. System; bd. dirs. U. Wis. at River Falls Found.; mem. Phi Kappa Phi nat. budget rev. and adv. comm., Phi Kappa Phi Found. investment comm., comm. on Agrl. and Rural Devel., steering commn. Coun. of Rural Colls. and Univs., Joint Coun. on Food and Agrl. Scis., USDA. Author: Basic Concepts in Anatomy and Physiology, 1983, Athletic Injury Assessment, 1994, Textbook of Anatomy and Physiology, 2006, Structure and Function of the Body, 2008, The Human Body in Health and Disease, 2005, Anatomy and Physiology, 2006. Mem. AAAS, Am. Assn. Anatomists, Am. Assn. Clin. Anatomists, Human Anatomy and Physiology Soc., Sigma Xi, Phi Kappa Phi, Gamma Sigma Delta, Gamma Alpha. Office: U Wis 116 N Hall River Falls WI 54022

THIEMANN, CHARLES LEE, banker; b. Louisville, Nov. 21, 1937; s. Paul and Helen (Kern) T.; m. Donna Timperman, June 18, 1960; children: Laura Gerette, Charles Lee, Rodney Gerard, Jeffrey Michael, Matthew Joseph. BA in Chemistry, Bellarmine Coll., 1959; MBA, Ind. U., 1961, DBA, 1963. Mem. rsch. dept. Fed. Res. Bank, St. Louis, 1963-64; with Fed. Home Loan Bank, Cin., 1964—, sr. v.p., then exec. v.p., 1974, pres., 1976—. Past chmn. bd. dirs. Office Fin.; trustee Fin. Instns. Retirement Fund; past mem. First Step Home. Bd. dirs. Habitat for Humanity Internat., Bellarmine U. Named Bellarmine Coll. Alumnus of Yr., 1999. Mem. Rotary Club, Queen City Club. Roman Catholic. Office: Fed Home Loan Bank 221 E 4th St Ste 1000 Cincinnati OH 45202-5139

THIEN-STASKO, VICKI LYNN, civil engineer; b. Scott AFB, Ill., Apr. 22, 1953; d. Cordell Albert Knepper and Erna Rose (Studnicka) Knepper; m. Michael Lee Stasko, Nov. 19, 1988; stepchildren: Julie Stasko, Elliott Stasko; m. William Frederick Thien, Mar. 12, 1971 (div.); 1 child, Kyle Thien. Associates of Arch., Belleville Area Coll., 1982, Associates of Applied Sci., 1988; BSc cum laude, Greenville Coll., 1998. Civil engr. tech. St. Clair County Hwy. Dept., Belleville, Ill., 1982—; part-time real estate agent Better Homes & Gardens /Strano, Belleville, Ill., 1993—94. Census enumerator U.S. Dept. Commerce, Belleville, 2000—01; co-chmn. Operation Bag-It, Belleville, 1998—2002; owner, designer Bagapalooza Purse Co., 2004—. Exhibitions include Not a Creature was Stirring, 1996 (Best of Show, 1996), Nuts Anyone?, 1997 (Merchant's award, 1997), Frosty the Gingerbread Snowman, 1998 (Downtown Merchant's award, 1998), Crayola Factory, 2002 (first place profl. divsn.), Mr. G. Shops Downtown Belleville, 2000 (Best of Show, 2000). Precinct committeewoman Dem. Party, Belleville, 1978—91; sec. Belleville Dem. Orgn., Belleville, 1979—91; mayoral appointment/mem. Belleville Re-develop. Com., Belleville, 1982—84; member St. Clair County Hist. Soc., Belleville, 2000—02; ch. sch. bd. mem., tchr. Christ United Ch. of Christ, Belleville, 1987—91. Recipient Ill. Gov.'s Hometown award, State of Ill., 1999. Avocations: gardening, remodeling, travel. Office: St Clair County Hwy Dept 1415 N Belt W Belleville IL 62226

THIES, RICHARD BRIAN, lawyer; b. Chgo., Dec. 14, 1943; s. Fred W. and Loraine C. (Mannix) T.; m. Anita Marie Rees, Aug. 5, 1972; children: Emily Marie, Richard Clarke. BA, Miami U., 1966; JD, Loyola U., 1974. Bar: (Ill. 1974), 1989 (U.S. Tax Ct.). Assoc. Wilson & McIlvaine, Chgo., 1974-78; assoc.-ptnr. Isham, Lincoln & Beale, Chgo., 1978-88; ptnr. Wildman, Harrold, Allen & Dixon, Chgo., 1988—2005, mem. exec. com., 1999—2005; pvt. ptnr. Bd. govs. Chgo. Heart Assn., 1980-87, exec. com., 1982-87; bd. dirs. Juvenile Protective Assn., Chgo., 1984—; v.p. Samaritan Counseling Ctr., Evanston, 1989-94, pres., 1994. Mem. ABA, Chgo. Bar Assn., Chgo. Estate Planning Coun. Avocations: photography, music. Home: 305 Driftwood Ln Wilmette IL 60091-3441 Office: Ste 3800 200 S Wacker Dr Chicago IL 60606 Office Phone: 312-650-8620.

THIES, RICHARD LEON, lawyer, director; b. Nov. 7, 1931; s. Arnold C. Thies and Wilma J. (Pattison) Player; m. Marilyn Lucille Webber, June 15, 1954; children: David, ancy, Susan, John, Anne. BA, U. Ill., 1953; JD, 1955. Bar: Ill. 1955, U.S. Dist. Ct. (ea. dist.) Ill. 1958, U.S. Supreme Ct. 1986. Instr. engring. law U. Ill., Urbana, 1955-56; ptnr. Webber & Thies, P.C., Urbana, 1958—. Past mem. Urbana Park Dist. Bd.; bd. dirs., past mem. Nat. Acad. Arts, Champaign-Urbana Urban League; past bd. dirs., past pres. Salvation Army, Champaign County. Served as 1st lt. USAF, 1956-58. Fellow Am. Bar Found (chair 1993-94), Ill. State Bar Found.; mem. ABA (ho. of dels. 1984-2005, bd. govs. 1988-91, exec. com. 1990-91, state del. 1993-2005), Am. Bar Retirement Assn. (bd. 1992-2000, chair 1997-99), Am. Law Inst. Ill. Bar Assn. (various offices, pres. 1986-87), Bar Assn. Ctrl. and So. Fed. Dists. Ill. (pres., co-founder, bd. dirs. 2001—), Champaign County Bar Assn. (v.p.), Urbana C. of C. (pres.), Urbana Country Club, Kiwanis (pres. Champaign-Urbana). Democrat. Presbyterian. Office: Webber & Thies PC 202 Lincoln Sq PO Box 189 Urbana IL 61803-0189 Office Phone: 217-367-1126. Business E-Mail: rthies@webberthies.com.

THIMESCH, DANIEL J., state legislator; m. Ruth A. Thimesch. Contractor; mem. from dist. 93 Kans. State Ho. of Reps., Topeka. Address: 30121 W 63rd St S Cheney KS 67025-8775 Office: Kans House of Reps State House Topeka KS 66612

THIMMIG, DIANA MARIE, lawyer; b. Germany, May 5, 1959; BA cum laude, John Carroll U., 1980; JD, Cleve. State U., 1982. Bar: Ohio 1983, U.S. Dist. Ct. (no. dist.) Ohio 1983, U.S. Ct. Appeals (6th cir.) 1983, U.S. Supreme Ct. 1983, U.S. Ct. Appeals (3d cir. 1996); cert. Am. Bankruptcy Bd. for Consumer and Bus. Bankruptcy. Ptnr. Roetzel & Andress, Cleve. Contbr. articles to profl. jours. Trustee Geauga United Way Svcs. Coun., 1992-96, Altenheim, 1992-97, Internat. Svcs. Ctr., 1998-04; trustee Cuyahoga County Bar Assn., 1995-05, pres., 2005-06; trustee Legal Aid Soc., 1998-2006, pres., 2003-05. Named Hon. Consul, Germany, 1988—. Mem. Women's City Club Cleve. (pres. 1995-97). Office: Roetzel & Andress 1375 East Ninth St One Cleveland Ctr Ninth Floor Cleveland OH 44114 Office Phone: 216-696-7078. Business E-Mail: dthimmig@ralaw.com.

THISTED, RONALD AARON, statistician, educator, consultant; b. LA, Mar. 2, 1951; s. Dale Owen and Barbara Jean (Walker) T.; m. Linda Jeane Soder, Dec. 30, 1972; 1 child, Walker. BA, Pomona Coll., 1972; PhD, Stanford U., 1977. Asst. prof. statistics U. Chgo., 1976-82, assoc. prof. statistics, 1982-92, assoc. prof. anesthesia and critical care, 1989-92, prof. stats. and anesthesia and critical care, 1992—, prof. health studies, 1996—, chmn. health studies, 1999—. Co-dir. Clin. Rsch. Training Program, 1999—. Author: Elements of Statistical Computing, 1988; contbr. more than 90 articles to profl. jours. Fellow AAAS, Am. Statis. Assn.; mem. Assn. for Computing Machinery, Inst. for Math. Stats. Office: U Chgo MC 2007 5841 S Maryland Ave Chicago IL 60637-1463 Home Phone: 773-947-9243; Office Phone: 773-834-1242.

THISTLETHWAITE, SUSAN BROOKS, religious organization administrator; BA, Smith Coll.; MDiv summa cum laude, Duke Div. Sch.; PhD, Duke Univ. Ordained minister United Ch. Christ, 1974—; former prof. theol. Chgo. Theol. Sem., former dir., PhD ctr., pres., 1999—. Translator two translations of Bible; leadership adv. com. Assn. of Theol. Schools, 2000—; adv. com. Lilly Endowment, 2000—; bd. dir. Medill Ctr. for Religion and the News Media, Northwestern Univ., 2001—. Author: Metaphors for the Contemporary Church, 1983, Sex, Race, and God: Christian Feminism in Black and White, 1989; co-author (with Rita Nakashima Brock): Casting Stones: Prostitution and Liberation in Asia and the US, 1996; co-author: (with Mary Potter Engel) Lift Every Voice: Constructing Christian Theologies from the Underside, 1998; contbg. editor: Adam, Eve and the Genome: The Human Genome Project and Theology, 2003; editorial bd.: Theology Today, 1993—. Named one of Chicago's Most Influential Women, Crain's Chicago Business mag., 2004. Office: Office of President Chgo Theol Seminary 5757 S Univ Ave Chicago IL 60637

THOMAN, HENRY NIXON, lawyer; b. Cin., May 5, 1957; s. Richard B. and Barbara (Lutz) Thoman; m. Anne Davies, May 25, 2002; children: Victoria E., Nicholas B. BA, Duke U., 1979; JD, U. Chgo., 1982. Bar: Ohio 1982, U.S. Dist. Ct. (so. dist.) Ohio, 1982. With Taft, Stettinius & Hollister, Cin., 1982-88; sr. atty. John Morrell & Co., Cin., 1988-90; sr. counsel Chiquita Brands Internat. Inc., Cin., 1990-91, corp. planner, 1991-92; sr. dir. CTP ops. Chiquita Brands, Inc., Cin., 1993-94, chief adminstrv. officer Armuelles divsn., 1994-95; corp. counsel The Loewen Group, Covington, Ky., 1995-97; asst. chief counsel, asst. v.p. The Midland Co., Amelia, Ohio, 1997-99; v.p. orgnl. devel. Kendle Internat. Inc., 1999-2000, v.p. complementary ops., 2000—02; pvt. atty., 2002—05; exec. dir. Madisonville Edn. and Assistance Ctr., 2004—05; dir. acquisitions, corp. counsel Unifund CCR Ptnrs., 2004—. Mem. counselors com. U.S. Swimming, Colo., 1983-89; bd. dirs. Friends of Cin. Parks, 1990-93, 96-98, Starshine Children's Hospice, 1996-99, Cin. Aquatic Club, 1997-2002, Kids Helping Kids, 2000-2001, Summerbridge, Cin., 2006—, Mariemont Aquatic Club, v.p., 1992-93; pres. Club Atletico Y Socialde Chiriqui, 1994-95. Mem. ABA, Ohio State Bar, Cin. Bar Assn. E-mail: thoman.henry@fuse.net.

THOMAN, MARK EDWARD, pediatrician; b. Chgo., Feb. 15, 1936; s. John Charles and Tasula Mark (Petrakis) T.; m. Theresa Thompson, 1984; children: Marlisa Rae, Susan Kay, Edward Kim, Nancy Lynn, Janet Lea, David Mark. AA, Graceland Coll., 1956; BA, U. Mo., 1958, MD, 1962. Diplomate Am. Bd. Pediat., Am. Coll. Toxicology (examiner), 1975-90. Intern U. Mo. at Columbia, 1962—63; resident in pediat. Blank Meml. Children's Hosp., Des Moines, 1963—65; cons. in toxicology USPHS, Washington, 1965—66; chief dept. pediat. Shiprock (N.Mex.) Navajo Indian Hosp., 1966—67; dir. N.D. Poison Info. Ctr.; also practice medicine specializing in pediat. Quain & Ramstad Clinic, Bismarck, ND, 1967—69; dir. Iowa Poison Info. Ctr., Des Moines, 1969—99; mem. pediat. exec. com. Broadlawns Med. Ctr., Des Moines, 1969—2000, pres. med. staff, 2000—01. Accident investigator FAA, 1976—2005, sr. aviation examiner, 1977—2000; lectr. aviation seminars, 1977—; mem. faculty Des Moines U., 1969—2005, dir. cystic fibrosis clin., 1973—82; dir. Mid-Iowa Drug Abuse Program, 1972—76; mem. med. adv. bd. La Leche League Internat., 1965—; chief med. officer Broadlawns Med. Ctr., Des Moines, 2000—02; sci. rev. panel Nat. Libr. Medicine, 2003—; med. cons., expert witness Office Hearings and Appeals Social Security Adminstrn., 2003—; cons. in field. Editor-in-chief AACTION, 1975-90; monthly columnist Aviation Medicine Twin and Turbine Mag., 2005-06. Bd. dirs. Polk County Pub. Health Nurses Assn., 1969-77, Des Moines Speech and Hearing Ctr., 1974-79, Ecumenical Coun. Iowa, 1990-99; bd. govs. Mo. U. Sch. Medicine Alumni, 1988—; pres. parish coun. Greek Orthodox Ch., 2007—. With USMCR, 1954-59; lt. comdr. USPHS, 1965-67; capt. USNR, 1988-96, ret. 1996; dir. Dept. Health Svcs. USNR. Recipient N.D. Gov.'s award of merit, 1969, Cystic Fibrosis Rsch. Found. award, 1975, Am. Psychiat. Assn. Thesis award, 1962. Fellow Am. Coll. Med. Toxicology (diplomate 1996), Acad. Clin. Toxicology; mem. AMA (del. 1970-88), APHA, NRA (life), Assn. Am. Physicians & Surgeons (chief of staff, pres. Broadlawns Polk County Med. Ctr. 2000-02), Polk County Med. Soc., Iowa State Med. Assn., Aerospace Med. Assn., Res. Officers Assn., Civil Aviation Med. Assn., Soc. Adolescent Medicine, Inst. Clin. Toxicology, Internat. Soc. Pediat., Am. Acad. Pediat. (chmn. accident prevention com. Iowa chpt. 1975-2000), Cystic Fibrosis Club, Am. Acad. Clin. Toxicology (trustee 1969-90, pres. 1982-84), Am. Assn. Poison Control Ctrs., Am. Coll. Physician Execs., U.S. Naval Inst., Flying Physicians Club, Aircraft Owners and Pilots Assn, Nat. Pilots Assn. (Safe Pilot award). Republican. Greek Orthodox. Home: 5355 Crane Ave E Port Orchard WA 98366 Office Phone: 360-871-2219. Office Fax: 360-871-4436. Personal E-mail: paro1795@aol.com.

THOMAS, ANDREW P., state representative; JD, Valparaiso U. Atty.; adj. prof. Ind. State U.; rep. dist. r44 Ind. Ho. of Reps., Indpls., 2002—, ranking Rep. mem. local govt. com., mem. tech., R & D, and judiciary coms. Former pres. Clay County Coord. Coun., Gov.'s Task Force for Drug Free Ind.; trustee Brazil (Ind.) Libr. Bd.; chmn. bd. South Ind. Conf. Bd. Pensions, United Meth. Ch. Mem.: Clay County Farm Bur., Clay County Meml. Found., Clay County Cmty. Found., Parke County C. of C., Greater Greencastle C. of C., Clay County C. of C. Republican. Office: Ind Ho of Reps 200 W Washington St Indianapolis IN 56204-2786

THOMAS, CHERRYL T., former federal agency administrator; b. Oct. 31, 1946; BS Biology & Chem., Marquette U.; MS Physiology, U. Illinois, Chicago. Dir., mgmt. services Dept. Aviation, 1983—89; dir., personnel policy & utilization Dept. Water, 1989—92; deputy chief of staff Mayor Richard M. Daley City of Chgo., 1992—94, commr. Dept. Bldgs., 1994-98, chmn. U.S. Railroad Retirement Bd., 1998—2003. Mem., bd. trustees U. Chgo., 2000—. Home: 5020 S Lake Shore Dr Apt 2716N Chicago IL 60615-3220

THOMAS, DANIEL J., health services executive; BS, U. No. Iowa. Cert. public acct. Various positions Med. Care Internat., Inc.; exec. v.p. and COO OccuSystems, 1993—96, dir., pres. and COO, 1997, exec. v.p. and pres. practice mgmt. svcs., 1997—98; pres. and COO Concentra, 1998, CEO and dir., 1998—. Office: Concentra 3200 Highland Ave Downers Grove IL 60515

THOMAS, DUKE WINSTON, lawyer; b. Scuddy, Ky., Jan. 25, 1937; s. William E. and Grace T. Thomas; m. Jill Staples, Oct. 24, 1964; children: Deborah L., William E. II, Judith A. BSBA, Ohio State U., 1959, JD, 1964. Bar: Ohio 1964, U.S. Dist. Ct. Ohio 1966, U.S. Ct. Appeals (3d cir.) 1971, U.S. Ct. Appeals (6th cir.) 1972, U.S. Supreme Ct. 1973, U.S. Ct. Appeals (7th cir.) 1979. Ptnr. Vorys, Sater, Seymour and Pease, LLP, Columbus, Ohio, 1964—2005. Chmn. bd. dirs. Ohio Bar Liability Ins. Co. Fellow: Columbus Bar Found., Ohio Bar Found., Am. Coll. Trial Lawyers (chmn. Ohio joint select com. jud. compensation 1987), Internat. Soc. Barristers, Am. Bar Found. (life); mem.: ABA (ho. of dels. 1985—99, state del. 1989—95, bd. govs. 1995—98), Columbus Bar Assn. (pres. 1978), Ohio Bar Assn. (pres. 1985), The Golf Club, Columbus Athletic Club, Pres.'s Club Ohio State U. Home: 2090 Sheringham Rd Columbus OH 43220-4358 Office: Vorys Sater Seymour & Pease LLP PO Box 1008 52 E Gay St Columbus OH 43215-3161 Office Phone: 614-464-6263. Business E-Mail: dwthomas@vssp.com.

THOMAS, DYNDA A., lawyer; b. Springfield, Ill., 1959; BA magna cum laude, Miami U., 1982; JD, U. Cin., 1986. Bar: Ohio 1986. Ptnr. Squire, Sanders & Dempsey LLP, Cleve., co-chmn., Project Fin. Practice Group. Mem.: ABA (global infrastructure com., Pub. Utility, Comm. & Transp. Law Sect.), Cleve. Bar Assn. (Real Property, Probate & Trust Law Sect.). Office: Squire Sanders & Dempsey LLP 4900 Key Tower 127 Public Sq Cleveland OH 44114-1304 Office Phone: 216-479-8583. Office Fax: 216-479-8780. Business E-Mail: dthomas@ssd.com.

THOMAS, EVELYN B., agricultural products supplier; Sec., treas., bookkeeper Brandt Fertilizer, Pleasant Plains, Ill., 1953—; co-owner Har Brand, 1963-67, Brandt Chem., 1967; sec./treas. Brandt Consol., Pleasant Plains. Office: Brandt Consol PO Box 350 Pleasant Plains IL 62677-0277 Business E-Mail: bcadmin@brandtconsolidated.com.

THOMAS, FRANK EDWARD, professional baseball player; b. Columbus, Ga., May 27, 1968; Student, Auburn U. With Chgo. White Sox, 1990—2006, Oakland Athletics, 2006, Toronto Blue Jays, 2006—. Named Maj. League Player of Yr., Sporting News, 1993, AL Comeback Player Yr., Players Choice Awards, 2006; named to All-Star Coll. All Am. team, Sporting News, 1989, All-Star Team, 1991, 1993—94, Am. League, 1993—95; recipient Silver Slugger award, 1991, 1993, 1994, Most Valuable Player award, Am. League, 1994. Achievements include becoming the 21st player in major league history to hit 500 home runs, June 28, 2007. Office: Toronto Blue Jays Ste 3200 1 Blue Jays Way M5V 1J1 Toronto ON Canada

THOMAS, FREDERICK BRADLEY, lawyer; b. Evanston, Ill., Aug. 13, 1949; s. Frederick Bradley and Katherine Kidder (Bingham) T.; m. Elizabeth Maxwell, Oct. 25, 1975; children: Bradley Bingham, Stephens Maxwell, Rosa Macaulay. AB, Dartmouth Coll., 1971; JD, U. Chgo., 1974. Bar: Ill. 1974. Law clk. to hon. judge John C. Godbold U.S. Ct. Appeals (5th cir.), Montgomery, Ala., 1974-75; assoc. Mayer, Brown, Rowe & Maw, LLP, Chgo., 1975—80, ptnr., 1981—. Bd. trustees La Rabida Children's Hosp., 1990—; bd. mgrs. YMCA Met. Chgo., 2002—. Mem.: ABA, Chgo. Coun. Lawyers. Republican. Episcopalian. Office: Mayer Brown LLP 71 South Wacker Dr Chicago IL 60606-4637

THOMAS, GARY L., retired academic administrator; b. Willows, Calif., May 12, 1937; s. Leonel Richard and Myrtle Blanch (Moncur) T.; m. Margaret Anderson, Aug. 11, 1960 (div. 1975); children: Katelin, Elizabeth Ann, Derek Alan. AA, Modesto Jr. Coll., 1958; BS in Elec. Engring., U. Calif., Berkeley, 1960, MA in Physics, 1962, PhD in Elec. and Computer Engring., 1967. Acting asst. prof. U. Calif., Berkeley, 1967; asst. prof. elec. engring. SUNY, Stony Brook, 1967-70, assoc. prof. elec. engring., 1970-73, assoc. dean grad. sch., 1973-74, chairperson, prof. elec. engring., 1975-79; congl. fellow A.A.A.S., Washington, 1974-75; provost, v.p. acad. affairs N.J. Inst. Tech., Newark, 1980-98, prof. elec. and computer engring., 1980—2000; chancellor U. Missouri-Rolla, Rolla, Mo., 2000—05. Student asst. bd. Dept. Higher Edn., N.J., 1980-97; chairperson rsch. adv. bd. PSE & G, Newark, 1986-90, Regional Transp. Rsch. Bd., N.Y. and N.J., 1987-90; bd. dirs. Kessler Inst. for Rehab., West Orange, N.J., 1988—; chair bd. dirs. Kessler Med. Rehab. Rsch. & Edn. Corp., 1997-2002. Author, editor: Fundamentals of Electrical and Computer Engineering, 1983. State of Calif. scholar, 1960, Schumberger scholar, 1961; NSF grantee, 1973-79. Home: 7 Vosseler Ct West Orange NJ 07052-3911

THOMAS, J. MIKESELL (MIKE THOMAS), former bank executive; b. Grand Rapids, Mich., Jan. 19, 1951; s. Joseph Alexander and Betty Jane (Mikesell) T.; m. Phyllis Scholl, Aug. 3, 1973. AB, Duke U., 1973; MBA, U. Chgo., 1976. Treas. First Chgo. Corp., 1981-86, chief fin. officer, 1986-89; exec. v.p., co-head corp. instl. banking First at. Bank Chgo., 1989—94; mng. dir. Lazard Freres & Co. LLC, 1995—2001; ind. fin. adv., 2001—04; pres., CEO Fed. Home Loan Bank Chgo., 2004—08. Bd. dirs. Jr. Achievement Chgo., 1986, Evanston Hosp., Ill., 1991, Leadership Greater Chgo., 1991.*

THOMAS, JOHN, mechanical engineer, artist; b. Tiruvalla, Kerala, India, Jan. 2, 1946; arrived in U.S., 1974; s. Munnencheril Varghese and Rachel (Mathai) Thomas; m. Mary Parapat Varghese, Apr. 28, 1975; children: Joel George, Sayana Rachel. BSMechE, Birla Inst. Tech., Ranchi, India, 1969; MSMechE, U. Waterloo, Ont., Can., 1974. Registered profl. engr., Wis. Lectr. mech. engring. U. Kerala, 1970-71; design engr. Combustion Engring., Inc., Springfield, Ohio, 1974-76; mech. engr. Ingersoll-Rand Co., Painted Post, NY, 1977-80; engr. Allis-Chalmers Corp., Milw., 1980-82; pvt. practice engring. cons. Milw., 1982-84; sr. technology devel. engr Cross & Trecker divsn. Kearney & Trecker Corp., Milw., 1984-87; prin. John Thomas & Assocs., Brookfield, Wis., 1988-90; sr. product engr. N.W. Water Group, Pub. Ltd. Corp. (now U.S. Filter Corp.), Waukesha, Wis., 1989-94; pres. Thomas Products Co., Brookfield, Wis., 1995—; staff engr. Milsco Mfg. Co. unit of Jason Inc., Milw., 1997—2003. Mem.: ASME, U. Waterloo Alumni Assn. Achievements include patents in field. Avocations: photography, golf. Home: 18330 Benington Brookfield WI 53045-5419 Office: Thomas Products Co The Nature Arts Gallery PO Box 401 Brookfield WI 53008-0401

THOMAS, JOHN ARLEN, pharmacologist, educator, science administrator; b. LaCrosse, Wis., Apr. 6, 1933; s. John M. and Eva Hazel (Nelson) T.; m. Barbara A. Fisler, June 22, 1957; children: Michael J., Jane L. BS in Sci. Edn., U. Wis., 1956; MA in Physiology, U. Iowa, 1958, PhD in Physiology, 1961. Diplomate Am. Acad. Toxicologic Sci. Instr. U. Iowa, Iowa City, 1961; asst. prof. U. Va., Charlottesville, 1961-64; assoc. prof. Creighton U., Omaha, 1964-67, W.Va. U., Morgantown, 1968-69, prof. pharmacology, 1970-80; asst. dean W.Va. Sch. Medicine, Morgantown, 1973-75, assoc. dean, 1973-80; v.p. corp. rsch. Baxter Internat. Travenol Labs., Round Lake, Ill., 1980-87; v.p. acad. svcs. U. Tex. Health Sci. Ctr., San Antonio, 1988-99, prof. emeritus pharmacology dept. toxicology, 1988—; prof. Ind. U. Sch. Medicine. Chmn. expert adv. com. Can. Network Toxicol. Ctr., 1999-02; sci. adv. bd. USAF, 2002-05, FDA, 2003—; adj. prof. pharmacology Ind. U. Sch. Medicine, Indpls., 2005; cons. to NIH, Inst. of Medicine, NRC, NAS. Author (with M.G. Mawhinney): Synopsis of Endocrine Pharmacology, 1978; author: (with E.J. Keenan) Principles of Endocrine Pharmacology, 1986; editor (with others): Basic and Clinical Toxicology of Lead, 1985; editor: Endocrine Toxicology, 1985, 1996, Drugs Athletes & Physical Performance, 1988, Biotechnology and Safety Assessment, 1993; editor: (with Laurie A. Myers) Biotechnology and Safety Assessment 2d edit., 1981; editor: (with Roy L. Fuchs) Biotechnology and Safety Assessment, 3d edit., 2002; editor: Endocrine Methods, 1996, Toxic Substances Mechanism Jour.; contbr. articles to profl. jours. Sgt. U.S. Army, 1951-53. Recipient Cert. Svc. US EPA, 1977, Commn. Spl. citation FDA, 2006, Advis Commn. Svc. award FDA, 2007; named Outstanding Tchr., W.Va. U., 1971, 73, 79, Outstanding alumnus U. Wis., La Crosse, 1978, Disting. Alumni, U. Iowa, 1997, Adv. Com. Svc. award FDA, 2007; named to Hall of Excellence-LaCrosse, 2002. Fellow Acad. Toxicol. Sci. (pres. 2001); mem. Endocrine Soc., Soc. Toxicology (councilor, Merit award 1998), Am. Soc. Pharmacology and Exptl. Therapeutics, Am. Coll. Toxicology (councilor, pres., disting. fellow 2004, Disting. Svc. award), Teratology Soc., Am. Acad. Vet. Pharmacology, Am. Chem. Soc. (pres. chem. toxicology pathology), Tex. Soc. Biomed. Rsch. (bd. sci. advisors 1989-99, Disting. Svc. award 1996), Russian Acad. Med. Sci. (fgn. fellow-elect 1995). Home and Office: 7258 Pymbroke Cir Fishers IN 46038 Office Phone: 317-845-5224. Personal E-mail: jat-tox@sbcglobal.net.

THOMAS, JOHN KERRY, chemistry professor; b. Llanelli, Wales, May 16, 1934; came to U.S., 1960; s. Ronald W. and Rebecca (Johns) T.; m. June M. Critchley, Feb. 28, 1959; children: Delia, Roland, Roger. BS, U. Manchester, Eng., 1954, PhD, 1957, DSc, 1969. Rsch. assoc. Nat. Rsch. Coun. Can., Ottawa, 1957-58; sci. officer Atomic Energy. U.K., Harwell, Eng., 1958-60; rsch. assoc. Argonne (Ill.) Nat. Lab., 1960-70; prof. chemistry U. Notre Dame, Ind., 1970-82, ieuwland prof. chemistry Ind., 1982—. Author: Chemistry of Excitation at Interfaces, 1984; mem. editorial bd. Macromolecules Langmuir, Jour. of Colloid and Interface Soc. Recipient of Rsch. Awd., 1994, Radiation Rsch, Am. Chem. Soc. award in Colloid or Surface Chemistry, 1994. Fellow Royal Soc. Chemistry; mem. Am. Chem. Soc. (award in colloids and surface 1994), Radiation Rsch. Soc. (editorial bd. jours., Rsch. award 1972, 94), Photochem. Soc. Home: 17704 Waxwing Ln South Bend IN 46635-1327 Office: Univ Notre Dame Dept Chemistry Notre Dame IN 46556

THOMAS, JOHN THIEME, management consultant; b. Detroit, Aug. 21, 1935; s. John Shepherd and Florence Leona (Thieme) T.; m. Ellen Linden Taylor, June 27, 1959; children: Johnson Taylor, Evan Thurston. BBA, U. Mich., 1957, MBA, 1958. Mfg. dept. mgr. Procter & Gamble Co., Cin., 1958-60, brand mgr., 1960-63; sr. cons. Glendinning Cos. Inc., Westport, Conn., 1964-66, v.p. London, 1967-69, exec. v.p. Westport, 1970-74, also bd. dirs.; exec. v.p., chief operating officer Ero Industries, Chgo., 1974-76; v.p. Lamalie Assocs. Inc., Chgo., 1977-81; pres. Wilkins & Thomas Inc., Chgo., 1981-87; ptnr. Ward Howell Internat., Chgo., 1987—, mng. dir., cons. practice, 1992-98, chief of staff, 1995-98; also bd. dirs.; cons. ret. LAI Ward Howell, Chgo., 1999—, El Jefe, Thomas Ent. Inc., 1989—. Exec. dir. Procter & Gamble Alumni Assn., Chgo., 1981—. Pub. Procter & Gamble Mktg. Alumni directory, 1981—; author articles in profl. jours. Chmn. bd. dirs. Winnetka (Ill.) Youth Orgn., 1986—2005; chmn. United Way Winnetka, 2001—, United Way North Shore; bd. dirs. No. Ill. Girl Scouts Coun., 2002—; mem. planning commn. City Winnetka, 2003—05; selector Winnetka Town Coun., 1978, 1980, 1984, Winnetka Zoning Bd., 2002—04, 2006—; selector com., chmn. Winnetka Caucus Exec. Com., 1997—2001; commr. Winnetka Pks., 2005—. Mem. Nat. Assn. Corp. & Profl. Recruiters, Assn. Exec. Search Cons., Am. Soc. Pers. Adminstrn. Clubs: Fairfield (Conn.) Hunt (treas. 1971-74). Avocations: gardening, music, tuba. Home and Office: 525 Ash St Winnetka IL 60093-2601 Office Phone: 847-446-5401. Business E-Mail: pngalumni@aol.com.

THOMAS, LLOYD BREWSTER, economics professor; b. Columbia, Mo., Oct. 22, 1941; s. Lloyd B. and Marianne (Moon) T.; m. Sally Leach, Aug. 11, 1963; 1 child, Elizabeth. AB, U. Mo., 1963, AM, 1964; PhD, Northwestern U., 1970. Instr. Northwestern U., Evanston, Ill., 1966-68; asst. prof. econs. Kan. State U., Manhattan, 1968-72, assoc. prof., 1974-81; asst. prof. Fla. State U., Tallahassee, 1973-74; prof. Kans. State U., Manhattan, 1983—, head dept., 2004—. Vis. prof. U. Calif., Berkeley, 1981-82, U. Del., 1993, U. Ind., Bloomington, 1997-98, Adelaide U., 2002; prof., chair dept. econs. U. Idaho, 1989. Author: Money, Banking and Economic Activity, 3d edit., 1986, Principles of Economics, 2d edit, 1993, Principles of Macroeconomics, 2d edit, 1993, Principles of Microeconomics, 2d edit, 1993, Money, Banking and Financial Markets, 2006; contbr. articles to profl. jours. Mem. Am. Econs. Assn., Midwest Econs. Assn., Phi Kappa Phi. Avocations: tennis, classical music. Home: 1501 N 10th St Manhattan KS 66502-4607 Home Phone: 785-539-1108; Office Phone: 785-532-4584. Business E-Mail: lbt@ksu.edu.

THOMAS, MARGARET JEAN, clergywoman, religious research consultant; b. Detroit, Dec. 24, 1943; d. Robert Elcana and Purcella Margaret (Hartness) T. BS, Mich. State U., 1964; MDiv, Union Theol. Sem., Va., 1971; DMin, San Francisco Theol. Sem., 1991. Ordained to ministry United Presbyn. Ch., 1971. Dir. rsch. bd. Christian edn. Presbyn. Ch. U.S., Richmond, Va., 1965-71, dir. rsch. gen. coun. Atlanta, 1972-73; mng. dir. rsch. div. support agy. United Presbyn. Ch. U.S.A., NYC, 1974-76, dep. exec. dir. gen. assembly mission coun., 1977-83; dir. N.Y. coordination Presbyn. Ch. (U.S.A.), 1983-85; exec. dir. Minn. Coun. Chs., Mpls., 1985-95; synod exec. Synod of Lakes and Prairies Presbyn. Ch. (U.S.A.), Bloomington, Minn., 1995—. Mem. Permanent Jud. Commn., Presbyn. Ch. (U.S.A.), 1985-91, moderator, 1989-91, mem. adv. com. on constn., 1992-98, moderator, 1997-98, mem. synod exec. forum, 1995—, mem. coop. com. on partnership funding, 1997-98, chair, 1998, gen. assembly coun., 2000—; sec. com Contbr. articles to profl. jours. Active alumni bd. Union Theol. Seminary Va., 1980-85; mem. adv. panel crime victims svcs. Hennepin County Atty.'s Office, 1985-86, Police and Cmty. Rels. Task Force, St. Paul, 1986; mem. adv. panel Hennepin County Crime Victim Coun., 1990-93, chair 1990-93; bd. dirs. Minn. Foodshare, 1985-95, Minn. Coalition on Health, 1986-92, Minn. Black-on-Black Crime Task Force, 1988, Twin Cities Coalition Affordable Health Care, 1986-87, Presbyn. Homes of Minn., 1995—, Clearwater Forest, Deerwood, Minn., 1995-96; co-chmn. Minn. Interreligious Com., 1988-95; bd. dirs. Abbott Northwestern Pastoral Counseling Ctr., 1988-91, chair 1990-91; chaplains adv. panel, Immortal Chaplains Found., 1999—. Recipient Human Rels. award Jewish Community Rels. Coun./Anti-Defamation League, 1989, Gov.'s Cert. of Commendation for Women's Leadership, 1993. Mem. NOW (Outstanding Woman of Minn. 1986). Mem. Democrat-Farm-Labor Party. Office: Synod Of Lakes And Prairies 2115 Cliff Dr Saint Paul MN 55122-3327

THOMAS, MARLIN ULUESS, industrial engineer, academic administrator, educator; b. Middlesboro, Ky., June 28, 1942; s. Elmer Vernon and Helen Lavada (Banks) T.; m. Susan Kay Stoner, Jan. 18, 1963; children: Pamela Claire Thomas Davis, Martin Phillip. BSE, U. Mich., Dearborn, 1967; MSE, U. Mich., Ann Arbor, 1968, PhD, 1971. Registered profl. engr., Mich. Asst. and assoc. prof. dept. ops. rsch. Naval Postgrad. Sch., Monterey, Calif., 1971-76; assoc. prof. systems design dept. U. Wis., Milw., 1976-78; mgr. tech. planning and analysis vehicle quality-reliability Chrysler Corp., Detroit, 1978-79; prof. dept. indsl. engring. U. Mo., Columbia, 1979-82; prof. indsl. engring., chmn. dept. Cleve State U., 1982-88, acting dir. Advanced Mfg. Ctr., 1984-85; prof., chmn. indsl. engring. Lehigh U., Bethlehem, Pa., 1988-93; prof., head Sch. Indsl. Engring. Purdue U., West Lafayette, Ind., 1993-98; dir. Inst. Interdisciplinary Engring. Studies, West Lafayette, 1998—. Program dir. NSF, Washington, 1987-88. Contbr. numerous articles on indsl. engring. and ops. rsch. to profl. jours. With USN, 1958-62; capt. USNR, 1971—. Named Outstanding Tchr., U. Mo. Coll. Engring., 1980, Coll. Man of Yr., Cleve. State U. Coll. Engring., 1985, Disting. Alumnus of Yr., U. Mich.-Dearborn, 1996, Engr. Excell Engagement Svc. award, Purdue U., 2003, IIE Holzman Disting. Educator award, 2004. Fellow Inst. Indsl. Engrs. (past pres., recipient Frank Groseclose Medallion award, 2005), Am. Soc. for Quality, Inst. for Ops. Rsch. and Mgmt. Scis.; mem. Am. Soc. for Engring. Edn., Am. Indian Sci. and Engr. Soc., VFW, Seabee Vet. Am. Office: Sch Indsl Engring Purdue Univ 315 N Grant St West Lafayette IN 47907-2023 Home Phone: 765-497-4586. Office Fax: 765-494-1299. Business E-Mail: muthomas@ecn.purdue.edu.

THOMAS, PAMELA ADRIENNE, special education educator; b. St. Louis, Oct. 28, 1940; d. Charles Seraphin Fernandez and Adrienne Louise (O'Brien) Fernandez Reeg; divorced, 1977; m. Alvertis T. Thomas, July 22, 1981. BA in Spanish and EdS, Maryville U., 1962; Cert. EdS, U. Ky., 1966-67; MA in Edn., St. Louis U., 1974. Cert. learning disabilities, behavior disorders, educable mentally retarded, Spanish, Mo. Tchr. Pawnee Rock Kans. Sch., 1963-64; diagnostic tchr. Frankfort State Hosp. Sch., Ky., 1964-67; spl. edn. tchr. St. Louis City Pub. Schs., 1968-71, itinerant tchr., 1971-73, ednl. strategist, 1973-74, elem. level resource tchr., 1974-78, secondary resource tchr., dept. head, 1978—, head dept. spl. edn., 1978—, resource tchr., 1998—, dept. head, 1998; ret., 2000. Co-author: Sophomore English Resource for Credit Curriculum Handbook, 1991. Co-author: Teaching Foreign Language to Handicapped Secondary Students, 1990. Pres. Council for Exceptional Children, local chpt. #103, 1982-83, Mo. Division of Mentally Retarded, 1985-87. Mem. Alpha Delta Kappa (St. Louis chpt. pres. 1982-84, 2008-). Avocations: travel, reading, swimming, theater, crafts. Home: 4534 Ohio Ave Saint Louis MO 63111-1324

THOMAS, PHILIP STANLEY, economist, educator; b. Hinsdale, Ill., Oct. 23, 1928; s. Roy Kehl and Pauline (Grafton) Thomas; m. Carol Morris, Dec. 27, 1950; children: Lindsey Carol, Daniel Kyle, Lauren Louise, Gay Richardson. BA, Oberlin Coll., 1950; MA, U. Mich., 1951, PhD, 1961; postgrad., Delhi U., 1953—54. Instr. U. Mich., 1956-57; asst. prof. Grinnell (Iowa) Coll., 1957-63, assoc. prof., 1963-65; assoc. prof. econs. Kalamazoo Coll., 1965-68, prof. econs., 1968-94, prof. emeritus, 1994—. Econ. advisor Pakistan Inst. Devel. Econs., 1963—64, USAID, 1965—68, 1971, Planning Commn., Pakistan, 1969—70, Ctrl. Bank Swaziland, 1974—75, Ministry Planning, Kenya, 1980—81, 1983—85, 1986—88, Ministry Fin., Swaziland, 1990, Kenya, 91, 92, Ministry Indsl. Devel., Sri Lanka, 1997, Res. Bank Malawi, 1998—99, Jordan-U.S. Bus. Partnership, 2000—01. Contbr. articles to profl. jours. Mem. alumni coun. Oberlin Coll., 1961—63, 1974—76, 1983—86, 1995—2001, treas. alumni coun., 2004—06, exec. bd. mem alumni coun., 2007—. With AUS, 1954—56. Fellow Overseas, Ford Found., 1953—54; scholar Fulbright. Mem.: Am. Econs. Assn., Phi Beta Kappa. Home and Office: 313A S Shabwasung St Northport MI 49670-9604 E-mail: pcmthomas@charter.net.

THOMAS, RICHARD LEE, banker; b. Marion, Ohio, Jan. 11, 1931; s. Marvin C. and Irene (Harruff) Thomas; m. Helen Moore, June 17, 1953; children: Richard L., David Paul, Laura Sue. BA, Kenyon Coll., 1953; postgrad. (Fulbright scholar), U. Copenhagen, Denmark, 1954; MBA (George F. Baker scholar), Harvard U., 1958. With First Nat. Bank Chgo., 1958—, asst. v.p., 1962-63, v.p., 1963-65; v.p., gen. mgr. First Nat. Bank Chgo. (London br.), 1965-66; v.p. term loan divsn. First Nat. Bank, Chgo., 1968; sr. v.p., gen. mgr. First Chgo. Corp., 1969-72, exec. v.p., 1972-73, vice chmn. bd., 1973-75, pres., 1975-92, chmn., pres., CEO, 1992-95; chmn. First Chgo. NBD Corp., 1995-96, ret. chmn., 1996. Bd. dirs. Sara Lee Corp., Sabre Holdings Corp, IMC Global Inc., PMI Group Inc., EXELON Corp. Trustee, past chmn. bd. trustees Kenyon Coll., Chgo. Symphony Orch.; life trustee Kenyon Coll., Chgo. Symphony Orch., Northwestern U.; trustee Rush-Presbyn.-St. Luke's Med. Ctr., Northwestern U. With AUS, 1954—56. Mem.: Chgo. Coun. Fgn. Rels., Old Elm Club Highland Park, Ill., Indian Hill Club Winnetka, Ill., Mid-Am. Club, Chgo. Club, Econ. Club (past pres.), Sunningdale Golf Club London, Comml. Club (past chmn.), Casino Club, Beta Theta Pi, Phi Beta Kappa. Office: First Chgo NBD Corp 1 Bank One Plz Ste IL1-0518 Chicago IL 60670-0001 E-mail: richard_l_thomas@bankone.com.

THOMAS, ROBERT LEIGHTON, physicist, researcher; b. Dover-Foxcroft, Maine, Oct. 10, 1938; s. Tillson Davis and Ruth (Leighton) T.; m. Sandra Evenson, June 23, 1962; 1 child, Stephen Leighton. AB, Bowdoin Coll., 1960; PhD, Brown U., 1965. Rsch. assoc. Wayne State U., Detroit, 1965-66, from asst. to assoc. prof. physics, 1966-76, prof. physics, 1976—, dir. Inst. for Mfg. Rsch., 1986—. Chmn. Gordon Rsch. Conf. in Nondestructive Evaluation, 1991-92. Assoc. editor Rsch. in ondestructive Evaluation; contbr. more than 150 articles to sci. jours. Fellow Am. Phys. Soc.; mem. Acad.Scholars, Sigma Xi (chpt. pres. 1990-91). Achievements include patents for Thermal Wave Imaging Apparatus, for Vector Lock-in Imaging System for Single Beam Interferometer, and for Confocal Optical Microscope. Office: Wayne State U Inst for Mfg Rsch Detroit MI 48202

THOMAS, ROBERT R., state supreme court justice; b. Rochester, NY, Aug. 7, 1952; m. Maggie Thomas; 3 children. BA in govt., U. Notre Dame, 1974; JD, Loyola U., 1981. Cir. ct. judge DuPage County, 1988, acting chief judge, 1989—94; judge Appellate Ct. Second Dist., 1994—2000; justice Ill. Supreme Ct., 2000—, chief justice, 2006—. Named to Academic All-Am. Hall of Fame; recipient NCAA Silver Anniversary award, 1999. Mem.: DuPage County Bar Assn., Acad. All-Am. Hall of Fame (life NCAA Silver Ann. Award 1999). Office: Illinois Supreme Ct 160 N LaSalle St Chicago IL 60601

THOMAS, ROGER D., state representative; b. Delwein, Iowa, Dec. 13, 1950; m. Rosemary Thomas; 3 children. BS, Upper Iowa U., 1966. Paramedic Ctrl. Ambulance Svc., 1992—; mechanic, 1996; state rep., dist. 24 Iowa Ho. of Reps., Des Moines, 1996—, mem. agr. and natural resources, econ. devel., edn., and transp. coms., mem. sch. fin. reform and oil overcharge caucuses. Trustee Northeast Iowa C.C., 1996; mem. 4H Ext. Coun., 1986; past pres. Northeast Iowa EMS Coun.; candidate Iowa State Senate, Dist. 16, 2000; adv. bd. Iowa Safety Found. Served USAF, 1969—75. Mem.: Farm Bur. (bd. dirs.), Mountak Hist. Soc., ARC (bd. dirs.), VISTA (bd. dirs.), Am. Legion, Masons (bd. dirs.). Democrat. Lutheran. Office: State Capitol E 12th and Grand Des Moines IA 50319

THOMAS, STEPHEN PAUL, lawyer; b. Bloomington, Ill., July 30, 1938; s. Owen Wilson and Mary Katherine (Paulsen) T.; m. Marieanne Sauer, Dec. 7, 1963 (dec. June 1984); 1 child, Catherine Marie; m. Marcia Aldrich Toomey, May 28, 1988; 1 child, Ellen Antonia. BA, U. Ill., 1959; LLB, Harvard U., 1962; student in MLA Program, U. Chi, 2005—. Bar: Ill. 1962; cert. naturalist Morton Arboretum, 2001, treekeeper Openlands Found., 2004. Vol. Peace Corps, Malawi, Africa, 1963-65; assoc. Sidley Austin LLP, Chgo., 1965-70, ptnr., 1970-2000; mem. Borrister's Big Band and Scales of Justice Asemble; founder Pianist Beverly. Lectr. on law Malawi Inst. Pub. Adminstrn., 1963-65. Pres. Hyde Park-Kenwood Cmty. Conf., Chgo., 1988-90; life trustee Chgo. Acad. for Arts, chmn., 1992-97; life trustee Union League Civic and Arts Found., Chgo., 1999—. Recipient Paul Cornell award Hyde Park Hist. Soc., 1981. Mem. ABA, Chgo. Bar Assn., Chgo. Fedn. Musicians, Ill. State Hist. Soc., Union League Club Chgo., Chgo. Lit. Club (pres. 2007-), Ill. Geog. Soc, Natural Areas Assoc, Ill. Geol. Soc. Democrat. Roman Catholic. Avocations: jazz piano playing, naturalist studies. Home: 9756 S Longwood Dr Chicago IL 60643-1610 Office: Sidley Austin LLP One S Dearborn St Ste 900 Chicago IL 60603 Office Phone: 312-853-7516. Business E-Mail: sthomas@sidley.com.

THOMASON, LARRY, state official; b. Jefferson City, Mo., Oct. 31, 1948; m. Diane Bush, 1978; 1 child, Sarah. BS, Ark. State U. Mem. Mo. Ho. of Reps. from 163d dist., 1988-98; dir. Mo. Hwy. Reciprocity Commn., 1998—. Mem. Agr.-Bus., Appropriations, Comm., Transp. Coms. Mo. Ho. of Reps.; cons. econ. devel.; mem. adv. bd. Internat. Bus. Inst. S.E. Mo. State U., Dyersburg C.C. Assoc. dir. Mo. Indsl. Devel. Commn.; active S.E. Mo. Regional Growth Assn., Hwy. 412 Corridor Assn. Mem. Kennett C. of C. (exec. dir.), Am. Legion, Lions. Democrat. Home: 1009 Falcon Dr Kennett MO 63857-3312

THOME, JAMES J., financial executive; Exec. v.p., COO BHA Group Holdings Inc., 1993—. Office: 8800 E 63d St Kansas City MO 64133

THOME, JIM, professional baseball player; b. Peoria, Ill., Aug. 27, 1970; s. Chuck and Joyce; m. Andrea Pacione, Nov. 7, 1998; children: Lila Grace, Landon. Student Illinois Central College. Designated hitter Cleve. Indians, 1991—2002, Phila. Phillies, 2003—05, Chgo. White Sox, 2006—. Hon. co-chmn. United Way Softball Slam. Named to Am. League All-Star Team, 1997—99, Nat. League All-Star Team, 2004, 2006; recipient Roberto Clemente award, 2002, Lou Gehrig Meml. award, 2004. Achievements include leading the National League in home runs (47), 2003; hitting 400th career home run, June 13, 2004; hitting 500th career home run, September 16, 2007. Avocations: cooking, hunting, fishing. Office: Cellular One Field 333 W 35th St Chicago IL 60616

THOMFORDE, CHRISTOPHER MEREDITH, minister; b. Cleve., Jan. 25, 1947; s. Fredrich Henry and Marie (Meredith) T.; m. Christine Elizabeth Stone Huber, June 10, 1972; children: Christopher, Rebecca, Sarah, Jonathan. BA, Princeton U., 1969; MDiv, Yale U., 1974. Ordained to ministry Luth. Ch. in Am., 1976. Asst. chaplain Colgate U., Hamilton, N.Y., 1974-78; pastor St. Paul's Luth. Ch., Dansville, N.Y., 1978-86; chaplain Susquehanna U., Selinsgrove, Pa., 1986—. Pres. Dansville Ministerim, 1979-81. Sec. ARC, Danville, 1983-86. Named Citizen of Yr., Dansville, 1986. Office: Susquehanna U Chaplain's Office Selinsgrove PA 17870 Home: 1215 Saint Olaf Ave Northfield MN 55057-1534

THOMOPULOS, GREGS G., consulting engineering company executive; b. Benin City, Nigeria, May 16, 1942; s. Aristoteles and Christiana E. (Ogiamien) Thomopulos; m. Patricia Walker, Sept. 4, 1966 (div. 1974); 1 child, Lisa; m. Mettie L. Williams, May 28, 1976; children: Nicole, Euphemia. BSCE with highest distinction, U. Kans., 1965; MS in Structural Engring., U. Calif., Berkeley, 1966; PhD (hon.), Teikyo Marycrest U., 1996. Sr. v.p. internat. div. Stanley Cons., Inc., Muscatine, Iowa, 1978-84, sr. v.p. project divsn., 1984-87; pres., CEO Stanley Consultants, Inc., Muscatine, Iowa, 1987—2007, chmn., CEO, 2007—; exec. v.p. SC Co., Inc., Muscatine, 1992-98; pres., COO, 1998-99; pres., CEO, 2000—; also bd. dirs. SC Co., Inc., Muscatine; chmn., CEO Stanley Environ., Inc., Chgo., 1991—, also bd. dirs.; chmn., CEO SC Power Devel., Inc., 1992—. Chmn., CEO Stanley Design-Build, Inc., 1995—; bd. dirs. Stanley Cons., Inc., Muscatine, Wellmark, Inc., Blue Cross Blue Shield Iowa and S.D., 1999—; mem. adv. bd. U. Kans. Sch. Engring., 2002—; mem. industry adv. panel US Dept. State, 2006—07. Mem. adv. bd. Coll. Engring. U. Iowa, 1992-2000, Hydraulics Inst., 2000-06. Fellow ASCE, Am. Coun. Engring. Cos. (vice chair., mem. exec. com.); mem. NSPE, Internat. Fedn. Cons. Engrs. (v.p., mem. exec. com.), 33 Club (pres. 1987), Rotary. Presbyterian. Avocations: tennis, computers, music. Home: 75 Shagbark Ct Iowa City IA 52246-2786 Office: Stanley Cons Inc 225 Iowa Ave Muscatine IA 52761-3765 Personal E-mail: thomopulos@home.com. Business E-Mail: thomopulosg@stanleygroup.com.

THOMPSON, ADRIENNE, secondary school educator; Tchr. advanced placement art history Sch. for Creative and Performing Arts, Cin. Mem. arts assessment steering com. Ohio Art Coun. Named Music Educator of the Yr., Ohio Art Edn. Assn. Mus. Divsn., 2000; recipient Ohio Govs. award for excellence in tchg., 1998, Outstanding Excellence award, Cin. Pub. Schs., 1999. Mem.: Nat. Bd. for Profl. Tchg. Stds. (bd. mem.). Office: Sch for Creative and Performing Arts 1310 Sycamore St Cincinnati OH 45202

THOMPSON, BARBARA STORCK, state official; b. McFarland, Wis., Oct. 15, 1924; d. John Casper and Marie Ann (Kassabaum) Storck; m. Glenn T. Thompson, July 1, 1944; children—David C., James T. BS, Wis. State U., 1956; MS, U. Wis., 1959, PhD, 1969; L.H.D. (hon.), Carroll Coll., 1974. Tchr. pub. schs., West Dane County, Mt. Horeb, Wis., 1944-56; instr. Green County Tchrs. Coll., Monroe, Wis., 1956-57; coordinator curriculum Monroe Pub. Schs., 1957-60; instr. U. Wis., Platteville, 1960; supr. schs. Waukesha County Schs., Wis., 1960-63, supt. schs., 1963-65; prin. Fairview Elem. Schs., Brookfield, Wis., 1962-64; adminstrv. cons. Wis. Dept. Pub. Instrn., Madison, 1964-72, state coordinator, 1971-72; instr. U. Wis., Madison and Green Bay, 1972; supt. pub. instrn. Madison, Wis., 1973—81. Mem. Wis. State Bd. Vocat. Edn., 1973-81, Wis. Edn. Comm. Bd., 1973-81, Univ. Wis. Sys. Bd. Regents, 1973-1981. Author: A Candid Discussion of Critical Issues, 1975; mem. editorial bd.: The Education Digest, 1975—; contbr. articles to profl. jours. Mem. White House Conf. Children, 1970, Gov.'s Com. State Conf. Children and Youth, 1969-70, Manpower Council, 1973-81; bd. dirs. Vocational, Tech. and Adult Edn., 1973-81, Ednl. Communications, 1973-81, Higher Edn. Aids, 1973-81, Agy. Instructional TV, 1975-81; mem. nat. panel on SAT score decline; bd. regents U. Wis., 1973-81, U.S. office f Edn. Visiting Sch. Team -England, GErmany, Sweden, Poland, Iran, Syria, India, and Japan. Recipient State Conservation award Madison Lions CLub, 1956; Waukesha Freeman award, 1961 Mem. ASCD, NEA, Nat. Coun. Adminstrv. Women in Edn. (named Woman of Year 1974), Nat. Coun. State Cons. in Elem. Edn. (pres. 1974-75), Wis. Assn. Sch. Dist. Adminstrs., Wis. ASCD, Southwestern Wis. ASCD, Southeastern Wis. ASCD (mem. exec. coun. 1972-73), Dept. Elem. Sch. Prins., Wis. Elem. Sch. Prins. Assn., Wis. Edn. Assn. (pres. local chpt. 1970-71); life mem. So. Wis. Edn. Assn., Wis. Ednl. Rsch. Assn., Dept. Elem.-Kindergarten-Nursery Edn., Assn. Childhood Edn. Internat., Assn. Childhood Edn., Coun. Chief State Sch. Officers, Edn. Commn. States, Nat. Coun. State Cons. in Elem. Edn. (pres.

1974-75), Am. Assn. Sch. Dist. Adminstrs. (chmn. policy com. 1963-81), Madison Ctrl. Internat. Lions Club, U. Wis. Alumni Orgn. (Sarasota, Fla. and Madison), U. Wis. League (Madison chpt.), Delta Kappa Gamma, Pi Lambda Theta. Office: Apt 123 325 S Yellowstone Dr Madison WI 53705-4301 also: 1700 3rd Ave W Apt 1015 Bradenton FL 34205-5937

THOMPSON, BERTHA BOYA, retired education educator; b. New Castle, Pa., Jan. 31, 1917; d. Frank L. and Kathryn Belle (Park) Boya; m. John L. Thompson, Mar. 27, 1942; children: Kay Lynn Thompson Koolage, Scott McClain. BS in Elem. and Secondary Edn., Slippery Rock State Coll., Pa., 1940; MA in Geography and History, Miami U., Oxford, Ohio, 1954; EdD, Ind. U., Bloomington, 1961. Cert. elem. and secondary edn. tchr. Elem. tchr., reading specialist New Castle Sch. Sys., Pa., 1940—45; tchr., chmn. social studies Talawanda Sch. Sys., Oxford, Ohio, 1954—63; assoc. prof. psychology and geography, chair edn. dept. Western Coll. for Women, Oxford, 1963-74; assoc. prof. edn., reading clinic Miami U., Oxford, 1974-78, prof. emeritus, 1978—. Contbr. articles to profl. jours. Folk art com. Miami U. Art Mus., Oxford, 1974—76; adv. com. Smith libr., Oxford Pub. Libr., 1978—81. Mem. AAUP, Nat. Coun. Geographic Edn. (exec. bd. dirs. 1966-69), Nat. Soc. for Study Edn., Assn. Am. Geographers, Soc. Women Geographers, Nat. Coun. for the Social Studies, Pi Lambda Theta, Zeta Tau Alpha, Pi Gamma Mu, Gamma Theta Upsilon, Kappa Delta Pi. Avocations: antiques, reading, travel, tennis. Home: 6073 Contreras Rd Oxford OH 45056-9708

THOMPSON, CHARLES MURRAY, lawyer; b. Childress, Tex., Oct. 13, 1942; s. Walter Lee and Lois S. (Sheehan) T.; children: Murray, McLean. BS with honors, Colo. State U., Ft. Collins, 1965; JD cum laude, U. SD, Vermillion, 1969, LLD (hon.), 1995. Bar: SD 1969, US Dist. Ct. SD 1969, US Ct. Claims 1989, US Ct. Appeals (8th cir.) 1972, US Supreme Ct. 1973. Ptnr. May, Adam, Gerdes & Thompson, Pierre, SD, 1969—. Bd. dirs. Bank West, Pierre, SD; past pres., dir. Delta Trust, 1997-2002; spkr. in field. Editor S.D. Law Rev., 1969 Pres. SD Coun. Sch. Attys., 1984-86. Fellow Am. Bar Found. (chmn. 1991-92, bd. dirs. 1989-92), Coll. Law Practice Mgmt., Am. Coll. Trial Lawyers; mem. ABA (ho. of dels. 1978-2002, bd. govs. 1983-86, standing com. on fed. judiciary (2004-06), ATLA, Am. Bd. Trial Advs., Am. Counsel Assn., Am. Judicature Soc. (bd. dirs. 1981-85), Am. Bar Endowment (bd. dirs. 1991-2006, dir. emeritus 2006-, pres. 2000-02), AEFC (Pension Plan Bd., 1987-90, 2005-), Nat. Conf. Bar Pres.'s (exec. coun. 1986-94, pres. 1992-93), State Bar S.D. (pres. young lawyers sect. 1974-75, pres. 1986-87), SD Bar Found. (pres. 1991), SD Trial Lawyers Assn. (pres. 1980-81), Jackrabbit Bar Assn. (chancellor 1981-82, ABA, Am. Bar Endowment, Am. Bar Found., Nat. Jud. Coll. pension bd., 1987-90, adminstrv. com., 2005-), SD Cmty. Found., Kiwanis (pres. local club 1977). Democrat. Avocations: flying, ranching. Home and Office: PO Box 160 Pierre SD 57501-0160 Office Phone: 605-224-8803.

THOMPSON, CLIFTON C., retired chemistry professor, academic administrator; b. Franklin, Tenn., Aug. 16, 1939; s. Clifton C. and Ruby M. Thompson; m. Sarah Ellen Gaunt, Dec. 1, 1978; children: Brenda Kay, Victoria Lea. BS, Middle Tenn. State U., 1961; PhD, U. Miss., 1964. Asst. prof. Rutgers U., New Brunswick, NJ, 1965, Marshall U., Huntington, W.Va., 1965-66; assoc. prof. Middle Tenn. State U., Murfreesboro, 1966-68, U. Memphis, 1968—74; prof. chemistry, dept. head, dean Coll. Sci. and Math., dir. Ctr. for Sci. Rsch., assoc. v.p. for grad. studies and rsch. Mo. State U., Springfield, 1974-96, prof. emeritus, 1996—; prof. chemistry Cen. Mich. U., Mt. Pleasant, 1996-98. Rsch. assoc. U. Tex., Austin, 1964-65; rschr. Oak Ridge Nat. Lab., 1968; cons. Mid-South Research Assocs., Memphis, 1969-71; mem. med. tech. rev. com. Nat. Accrediting Agy. for Clin. Lab. Sci., Chgo., 1974-80; vis. prof. So. Ill. U., Carbondale, 1995. Author: Ultraviolet-Visible Absorption Spectroscopy, 1974; contbr. articles to profl. jours. Mem. health care com. Springfield C. of C., 1978-79, mem. econ. devel. com., 1983-89; bd. dirs. United Hebrew Congregation, Springfield, 1983-86, United Hebrew Found., Inc., 1994-96. NSF fellow, 1961-64; Sigma Xi grantee-in-aide, 1970; NSF sr. fgn. scientist grantee, 1971; NSF coop-coll. sch. sci. grantee, 1972; Higher Edn. Applied Projects grantee, 1987-90. Mem.: Royal Soc. Chemistry, Am. Chem. Soc., Phi Kappa Phi, Sigma Xi. Office: Mo State U Dept Chemistry Springfield MO 65804

THOMPSON, DON, food products executive; m. Elizabeth Thompson; children: Xavier, Maya. BSc in elec. engring., Purdue U. Engr. specialist, def. systems divsn. orthrop Corp., Rolling Meadows, Ill.; restaurant systems engr. McDonald's Corp., 1990—91, project mgr., 1991—93, staff dir., then dir. ops. for Denver region, 1993, regional v.p., San Diego region, 1998, sr. v.p., restaurant support officer, Midwest divsn., 1998—2000; pres., Midwest divsn. McDonald's USA, 2000—01; pres., West divsn. McDonald's Corp., 2001—04, exec. v.p. restaurant Solutions, 2004—05, exec. v.p., COO McDonald's USA, 2005—06, pres. McDonald's USA, 2006—. Office: McDonald's Corp McDonald's Plaza Oak Brook IL 60523

THOMPSON, HERBERT STANLEY, neuro-ophthalmologist; b. Shansi, China, June 12, 1932; arrived in U.S., 1949, naturalized, 1955; s. Robert Ernest and Ellen Thompson; m. Delores Lucille Johnson, June 27, 1953; children: Geoffrey, Peter, Kenneth, Philip, Susan. Student, Methodist Coll., Belfast, No. Ireland, 1947—49; BA, U. Minn., 1953, MD, 1961; MS, U. Iowa, 1966. Diplomate Am. Bd. Ophthalmology (assoc. examiner 1972-88, bd. dirs. 1989-96, chmn. ABO 1996). Intern U. Iowa, Iowa City, 1961—62, resident in ophthalmology, 1962—66; fellow in pupillography Columbia Coll. Physicians and Surgeons, 1962; fellow in clin. neuro-ophthalmology U. Calif., San Francisco, 1966—67; prof. ophthalmology U. Iowa, Iowa City, 1976—97, emeritus prof., 1997—, dir. neuro-ophthalmology unit, 1967—97; practice medicine specializing in neuro-ophthalmology Iowa City, 1967—97. Editor: Topics in Neuro-ophthalmology, 1979; assoc. editor: Am. Jour. Ophthalmology, 1981—84, book rev. editor:, 1984—91, cons.: Stedman's Med. Dictionary, 26th edit. Served with AUS, 1954-55. Recipient rsch. career devel. award, NIH, 1968—72; fellow spl. fellow, 1966—67. Fellow: N.Am. Neuro-ophthalmol. Soc., Am. Acad. Ophthalmology; mem.: Cogan Ophthalmic History Soc. (Charles Snyder lectr. 1995), Am. Ophthalmol. Soc. Office: U Iowa Dept Ophthalmology Iowa City IA 52242

THOMPSON, JAMES ROBERT, JR., lawyer, former governor; b. Chgo., May 8, 1936; s. James Robert and Agnes Josephine (Swanson) Thompson; m. Jayne Carr, 1976; 1 child, Samantha Jayne. Student, U. Ill., Chgo., 1953-55, Washington U., St. Louis, 1955-56; JD, Northwestern U., 1959. Bar: Ill. 1959, US Supreme Ct. 1964. Asst. state's atty., Cook County, Ill., 1959-64; assoc. prof. law Northwestern U. Law Sch., 1964-69; asst. atty. gen. State of Ill., 1969-70; chief criminal divsn., 1969; chief dept. law enforcement and pub. protection, 1969-70; 1st asst. U.S. atty. (No. dist.) Ill. US Dept. Justice, 1970-71, U.S. atty., 1971-75; counsel Winston & Strawn LLP, Chgo., 1975-77, ptnr., 1991—, chmn., CEO, 1993—2006, chmn. exec. com., 1991—2006, head gov. rels. practice; gov. State of Ill., Springfield, Ill., 1977-91. Chmn. Rep. Govs. Assn., 1982, Nat. Govs. Assn., Midwest Govs. Assn., Coun. Gt. Lakes Govs., 1985, Pres.' Intelligence Oversight Bd., 1989—93; adv. bd. Fed. Emergency Mgmt. Agy., 1991—93; bd. govs. Chgo. Bd. Trade; mem. ABA Commn. on Separation of Powers & Jud. Independence, 1996—97; commr. The Nat. Commn. on Terrorist Attacks Upon the U.S. (The 9-11 Commn.), 2002—04; bd. dirs. FMC Tech., Inc., Navigant Cons. Inc., Maximus, Inc. Co-author: Cases and Comments on Criminal Justice, 1974, Criminal Law and Its Administration. Bd. dirs. Civic Com., Comml. Club Chgo. Mem.: ABA, Chgo. Bar Assn., Ill. Bar Assn. Republican. Office: Winston & Strawn LLP 35 W Wacker Dr Ste 4200 Chicago IL 60601-9703 Home Phone: 312-640-0420; Office Phone: 312-558-7400. Office Fax: 312-558-5700. Business E-Mail: jthompson@winston.com.

THOMPSON, JEFF, state representative; BS, Purdue U. Tchr. chemistry and physics Danville Cmty. H.S., Ind.; state rep. dist. 28 Ind. Ho. of Reps., Indpls., 1998—, mem. elections and ways and means coms. Mem. Ind. State Fair Bd.; mem. Ind. State Fair Commn.; mem. Hendricks County 4-H Fair Bd.; mem. Hendricks County Extension Bd.; precinct committeeman Rep. State Conv. Mem.: Hoosier Assn. Sci. Tchrs., Ind. Farm Bur., Purdue Alumni Assn. Republican. Office: Ind Ho of Reps 200 W Washington St Indianapolis IN 46204-2786

THOMPSON, LEE (MORRIS THOMPSON), lawyer; b. Hutchinson, Kans., Nov. 29, 1946; s. Morris J. and Ruth W. (Smith) T.; m. M. Susan Morgan, May 26, 1974; children: Deborah, Erin, Andrew, Christopher. BA, Wichita State U., 1968; MA, Emporia State U., 1970; JD, George Washington U., 1974. Bar: Kans., 1974, U.S. Dist. Ct. Kans., 1974, U.S. Ct. Appeals (10th cir.) 1976, U.S. Supreme Ct., 1978. Instr., lectr. Emporia State U., Kans., 1969-70; lctr. in speech George Washington U., Washington, 1970-71; asst. to Senator James Pearson Washington, 1971-75; assoc. Martin, Pringle, et al., Wichita, Kans., 1976-78, ptnr., 1979-89; U.S. atty. for dist. of Kans., Dept. Justice, Wichita, 1990-93; ptnr. Triplett, Woolf & Garrets, LLC, Wichita, 1993—2001; mng. mem. Thompson Law Firm, LLP (previously Thompson Stout & Goering LLC), Wichita, 2001—. Treas. Kansans for Kassebaum, Wichita, 1978-88; mem. Kans. State Rep. Cen. Com., Topeka, 1978-79, 88-90; candidate U.S. Ho. of Reps., Kans., 1988; chmn. civil issues subcom. Atty. Gen.'s Adv. Com. of U.S. Attys., 1992-93. Mem. Kans. Bar Assn. (pres. criminal law sect. 1994-95). Methodist. Office: Thompson Law Firm 106 E 2nd St Wichita KS 67202 Office Phone: 316-267-3933. Office Fax: 316-267-3901. E-mail: lthompson@tslawfirm.com.

THOMPSON, MARGARET M., physical education educator; b. Merrifield, Va., Aug. 1, 1921; d. Lesley L. and Madeline (Shawen) T. BS, Mary Washington Coll., 1941; MA, George Washington U., 1947; PhD, U. Iowa, 1961. Tchr., supr. phys. edn. Staunton (Va.) City Schs., 1941-44; tchr. jr. high sch. phys. edn. Arlington County, Va., 1944-47; instr. women's phys. edn. Fla. State U., Tallahassee, 1947-51; instr., asst. prof., assoc. prof. phys. edn. Purdue U., Lafayette, Ind., 1951-65, dir. gross motor therapy lab., 1963-65; assoc. prof. phys. edn. U. Mo., Columbia, 1965-68, prof., 1968-71, dir. Cinematography and Motor Learning Lab. Dept. Health and Phys. Edn., 1965-71; prof. phys. edn. U. Ill., Champaign-Urbana, 1971-87, prof. emeritus, 1987—. Vis. prof. Escola de Educacão Fisica, U. de Saõ Paulo, Brazil, 1985; vis. prof. phy. edn. Inst. Bioscis. de Rio Claro, U. Estadual Paulista, Brazil, 1991. Author: (with Barbara B. Godfrey) Movement Pattern Checklists, 1966, (with Chappelle Arnett) Perceptual Motor and Motor Test Battery for Children, 1968, (with Barbara Mann) An Holistic Approach to Physical Education Curriculum: Objectives Classification System for Elementary Schools, 1977, Gross Motor Inventory, 1976, revised edit., 1980, Developing the Curriculum, 1980, Setting the Learning Environment, 1980, Sex Stereotyping and Human Development, 1980; also film strips, articles. Mem.: AAHPER. Home and Office: 1311 Wildwood Ln Mahomet IL 61853-9770

THOMPSON, MARK K., lawyer; b. St. Paul, Aug. 1, 1967; BA in Polit. Sci., U. St. Thomas, St. Paul, 1996; JD, William Mitchell Coll. Law, St. Paul, 1999. Bar: Minn. 1999, US Dist. Ct. (dist. Minn.) 2000, US Ct. Appeals (8th cir.) 2001, US Dist. Ct. (we. dist. Wis.) 2003. Assoc. Dudley & Smith, P.A., St. Paul, 1999—. Co-founder, pres. Computer Legal Internet Com. William Mitchell Law Sch. Contbr. articles to profl. publs. Named a Rising Star, Minn. Super Lawyers mag., 2006. Mem.: Minn. Trial Lawyers Assn., ABA, Minn. State Bar Assn., Ramsey County Bar Assn. Office: Dudley & Smith PA 2602 US Bank Ctr 101 E 5th St Saint Paul MN 55101 Office Phone: 651-291-1717. E-mail: mkt@dudleyandsmith.com.

THOMPSON, MARY EILEEN, chemistry professor; b. Mpls., Dec. 21, 1928; d. Albert C. and Blanche (McAvoy) T. BA, Coll. St. Catherine, 1953; MS, U. Minn., 1958; PhD, U. Calif., Berkeley, 1964. Tchr. math. and sci. Derham Hall H.S., St. Paul, 1953-58; mem. faculty Coll. of St. Catherine, St. Paul, 1964-69, prof. chemistry, 1969-2000, chmn. dept., 1969-90, prof. emerita, 2000—. Project dir. Women in Chemistry, 1984-98. Contbr. articles to profl. jours. Named one of 100 persons honored, Coll. St. Catherine's 100th Anniversary. Mem. AAAS, Am. Chem. Soc. (chmn. women chemists com. 1992-94, award for encouraging women into chem. scis. careers 1997), Coun. Undergrad. Rsch. (councillor 1991-96), N.Y. Acad. Scis., Chem. Soc. London, Sigma Xi, Phi Beta Kappa (senator 1997-2003). Democrat. Roman Catholic. Achievements include research interests in Cr(III) hydrolytic polymers, kinetics of inorganic complexes, Co(III) peroxo/superoxo complexes. E-mail: MTHOM17349@aol.com.

THOMPSON, MORLEY PUNSHON, textile company executive; b. San Francisco, Jan. 2, 1927; s. Morley Punshon and Ruth (Wetmore) T.; m. Patricia Ann Smith, Jan. 31, 1953 (dec.); children: Page Elizabeth Tredennick, Morley Punshon; m. Katharine Shaw Wallace. AB, Stanford U., 1948; MBA, Harvard U., 1950; JD, Chase Law Sch., 1969; LLD, Xavier U., 1981. CPA, Ohio. Chmn. Stearns Tech. Textiles Co., Cin., 1985—, Stearns Can., Inc., Cin., 1985—. Bd. dirs. Cin. Inst. Fine Arts. Lt. Supply Corps USNR, 1952-54. Mem. Beta Theta Pi. Home: 450 Belvedere Ave Belvedere Tiburon CA 94920-2429

THOMPSON, NANCY P., state legislator; b. Sioux Falls, SD, Oct. 26, 1947; m. James Thompson, July 4, 1970; children: Kevin, Matthew, Cynthia, Joseph. BA, Creighton U., 1969, MA, 1982. Dist. staff mem. U.S. Rep. John Cavanaugh; dep. chief of staff Gov. Ben Nelson; former tchr.; mem. Nebr. Legislature from 14th dist., Lincoln, 1997—. Former exec. dir. Omaha Cmty. Partnership; mem. Sarpy County Bd. Commrs. Office: State Capitol Dist 14 PO Box 94604 Rm 1117 Lincoln NE 68509-4604 Home: 9406 Bayberry Ct La Vista NE 68128-3220 E-mail: nthompson@unicam.state.ne.us.

THOMPSON, NORMAN WINSLOW, surgeon, educator; b. Boston, July 12, 1932; s. Herman Chandler and Evelyn Millicent (Palmer) T.; m. Marcia Ann Veldman, June 12, 1956; children: Robert, Karen, Susan, Jennifer. BA, Hope Coll., Holland, Mich., 1953; MD, U. Mich., 1957; MD (hon.), U. Linköping, Sweden, 1995. Diplomate Am. Bd. Surgery. From intern to prof. emeritus surgery U. Mich., Ann Arbor, Mich., 1957—2001, prof. emeritus surgery, 2001—. Contbr. articles to profl. jours. Trustee Hope Coll., 1973-88. Fellow Royal Australasian Coll. Surgeons (hon.), Royal Coll. Physicians and Surgeons of Glasgow; mem. ACS (gov. 1979-85), Ctrl. Surg. Assn., Western Surg. Assn. (1st v.p. 1992-93, pres. 1994-95), F.A. Coller Surg. Soc. (pres. 1986), Am. Surg. Assn., Am. Thyroid Assn., Soc. Surg. Alimentary Tract, Internat. Assn. Endocrine Surgeons (pres. 1989-91), Internat. Soc. Surgeons (v.p. 1995—), Am. Assn. Endocrine Surgeons (pres. 1980-81, 81-82), Royal Soc. Medicine, Brit. Assn. Endocrine Surgeons, Spanish Assn. Surgeons (hon.), Assn. French Endocrine Surgeons, Scandanvian Surg. Soc., Soc. Surg. Oncology, Turkish Assn. Endocrine Surgeons, European Soc. Endocrine Surgeons (hon.), Spanish Soc. Surgeons (hon.), Alpha Omega Alpha. Home: 465 Hillspur Rd Ann Arbor MI 48105-1048 Office: Surgery Emeritus Faculty 1327 Jones Dr Ste 201 Ann Arbor MI 48105 Office Phone: 734-998-0167. Office Fax: 734-998-0173. Business E-Mail: normant@med.umich.edu.

THOMPSON, PAUL C., labor union administrator; m. Roberta Thompson; 2 children. Fireman Atchison, Topeka & Santa Fe Railway, 1959; with Kans. City Southern; pres. Local 298, United Transp. Union, 1968—70, chairperson, 1970—82; internat. v.p. United Transp. Union, 1983—99, gen. sec., treas., 1999—2001, asst. pres., 2001—04, internat. pres., 2004—. Labor rep. to Pres. Clinton's Sch./Work program com., 1993. Office: UTU 14600 Detroit Ave Cleveland OH 44107-4250 Office Phone: 216-228-9400. Business E-Mail: President@utu.org.

THOMPSON, RICHARD L., retired manufacturing executive; B in Engring., Stanford U. With Caterpillar Inc., 1983—2004, v.p. Customer Services, Solar Turbines Inc., pres. Solar Turbines Inc., v.p. engring. divsn., 1990-95, group pres., 1995—2004; ret., 2004. Bd. dir. Gardner Denver, Inc., Lennox Internat., 1993—, vice chmn., 2005—06, chmn., 2006—. Office: Lennox Internat 2140 Lake Park Blvd Richardson TX 75080

THOMPSON, RICHARD LLOYD, retired pastor; b. Lansing, Mich., May 8, 1939; s. Lloyd Walter and Gladys V. (Gates) T.; m. Dianne Lee Tuttle, Nov. 14, 1958; children: Matthew, Beth Anne, Douglas. BA, Azusa Pacific U., 1969; MDiv, Concordia Theol. Sem., 1973; DD, Concordia U., Mequon, Wis., 1997. Aerospace industry test engr. Hycon Mfg. Co., Monrovia, Calif., 1961-69; pastor Trinity Luth. Ch., Cedar Rapids, Iowa, 1973-84, Billings, Mont., 1984-94, Good Shepherd Luth. Ch., Watertown, Wis., 1994—2001; ret., 2001. Chmn. mission com. Iowa E. dist. Luth. Ch. Mo. Synod, 1979-81, 2nd v.p. Iowa dist. E, Cedar Rapids, 1981-84, cir. counselor so. cir. and 2d v.p. Mont. dist., bd. mgr. Concordia plans, St. Louis, 1983-86, bd. dirs., St. Louis, 1986-98, chmn. bd. dirs., 1992-98, mem. commn. on theology and ch. rels., 2001; chmn. bd. dirs. Ambs. and Reconciliation, 2005-; served on various task forces and coms. dealing with structure and vision setting for chs. at local, dist. and nat. level, 1975—. Mem. Nat. Exch. Club, Cedar Rapids, 1982-84, Billings, 1986; pro tem com. structure Commn. Doctrinal Rev., 2001—. With USN, 1957—61. Mem. Kiwanis. Lutheran. Avocations: attending auctions, yard work, travel, exercise activity. Home Phone: 406-656-0006. Personal E-mail: diarich39@msn.com, rlt50@hotmail.com.

THOMPSON, RICHARD THOMAS, academic administrator; b. Buffalo, Oct. 11, 1939; m. Nancy A. Streeter, Aug. 29, 1959; children: Elizabeth Thompson Grapentine, Richard Thomas Jr., David Bryant. BA, Ea. Mich. U., 1961, MA, 1963; LLD (hon.), Walsh Coll., 2000. Cert. tchr. Mich. Tchr. Warren Consol. Sch., Mich., 1961—66; dean, pres. Highland Lake campus Oakland C.C., Union Lake, 1966—75, pres. Orchard Ridge campus Farmington, 1975—84, v.p. Bloomfield, 1984—88, vice chancellor, 1988—91, pres. Auburn Hills campus, 1995—96, chancellor, 1996—2004, chancellor emeritus, 2004. Arbitrator Better Bus. Bur., Detroit, 1987—96; bd. dirs., past chair Providence Hosp., Southfield; cons. examiner North Ctrl. Assn. Commn. Higher Learning, 1988—2004. Contbr. articles to profl. jours. Pres. Oakway Symphony Orch., Livonia, Mich., 1981—85; chair Oakland Literacy Coun., Pontiac, 1988—2002. Recipient Leadership award, Oakland County C. of C., 1987, Tricounty Disting. Svc. award, Detroit Coll. Bus., 1996, Shirley B. Gordon award Distinction, Phi Theta Kappa Internat., 2001. Mem.: watershed center grand traversee boy (chair), Phi Delta Kappa. Home: 6868 W Harbor Dr Elk Rapids MI 49629

THOMPSON, ROBY CALVIN, JR., orthopedic surgeon, educator, department chairman; b. Winchester, Ky., May 1, 1934; s. Roby Calvin and Mary Davis (Guerrant) T.; m. Jane Elizabeth Searcy, May 2, 1959; children: Searcy Lee, Roby Calvin, III, Mary Alexandria. BA, Va. Mil. Inst., 1955; MD, U. Va., 1959. Diplomate Am. Bd. Orthopaedic Surgery (mem. bd. 1983). Intern Columbia Presbyn. Med. Center, NYC, 1959-60, asst. resident, then resident in orthopedic surgery, 1963-67; instr. orthopaedic surgery Coll. Phys. and Surg. Columbia U., 1967-68; mem. faculty Med. Sch. U. Va., 1968-74, prof. orthopaedic surgery, vice chmn. dept. Med. Sch., 1973—94; prof., chmn. dept. Med. Sch. U. Minn., 1974—94; chief med. officer U. Minn. Health Sys., 1995-96, v.p. clin. and acad. affairs, 1996—2001; sr. assoc. dean clin. affairs U. Minn. Sch. Medicine, 1996—. Merit rev. bd. VA, 1977-80; study sect. on applied physiology and orthopedics NIH, 1980-83; adv. coun. NIH, Nat. Inst. Arthritis, Musculoskeletal Disease and Skin, 1987-91; chmn. bd. dirs. U. Minn. Physicians, 2001-05, CEO, 2001—. Trustee Jour. Bone and Joint Surgery, 1988-94, chmn. bd. trustees, 1991-94; contbr. articles to med. jours. Capt. M.C. USAR, 1960-61. Grantee John Hartford Found., NIH Mem. ACS, Orthopaedic Rsch. and Edn. Found. (bd. trustees 1990-96), Am. Acad. Orthopaedic Surgeons (bd. dirs. 1975-76, 83-90, pres. 1986), Orthopaedic Rsch. Soc. (pres. 1978), Am. Orthopaedic Assn., Musculoskeletal Tumor Soc. (pres. 1988-89), U. Va. Med. Alumni Assn. (bd. dirs. 1979-84), Woodhill Club (Wayzata). Republican. Presbyterian. Office: U Minn MMC 293 420 Delaware St SE Minneapolis MN 55455-0374

THOMPSON, RONALD L., manufacturing executive; BBA, U. Mich.; MS, PhD, Mich. State U. Chmn., CEO Evaluation Techs., Inc.; chmn. bd. dirs., pres. GR Group Inc., 1980—; chmn., CEO Midwest Stamping and Mfg. Co. (subs. of GR Group Inc.), Bowling Green, Ohio, 1993—2005; chmn. TIAA-CREF, Charlotte, NC, 2008—. Mem. faculty Old Dominion U., Va. State Coll., U. Mich.; bd. dirs. Mcdonnell Douglas Corp.; trustee TIAA-CREF 1995-Recipient Nat. Minority Entrepreneur of Yr. award U.S. Dept. Commerce, 1989, Disting. Svc. to Edn. award Harris-Stowe State Coll., 1991, disting. Cmty. Svc. award So. Ill. U., Edwardsville, 1990. Mailing: TIAA-CREF PO Box 1259 Charlotte NC 28201*

THOMPSON, RONELLE KAY HILDEBRANDT, library director; d. Earl E. and Maxine R. (Taplin) Hildebrandt; m. Harry Floyd Thompson II, Dec. 24, 1976; children: Clarissa, Harry III. BA in Humanities magna cum laude, Houghton Coll., 1976; MLS, Syracuse U., 1976; postgrad., U. Rochester, 1980-81; cert., Miami U., 1990. Libr. asst. Norwalk (Conn.) Pub. Libr., 1977; elem. libr. Moriah Ctrl. Schs., Port Henry, NY, 1977—78; divsn. coord. pediat. gastroenterology and nutrition U. Rochester (N.Y.) Med. Ctr., 1978—81, cons., pediat. housestaff libr. com., 1980—81; dir. Medford Libr. U. S.C., Lancaster, 1981—83; dir. Mikkelsen Libr., Libr. Assocs., Ctr. for Western Studies, mem. libr. com. Augustana Coll., Sioux Falls, SD, 1983—, adminstrv. pers. coun., 1989—94, 1997—2004. Presenter in field. Contbr. articles to profl. jours. Mem. S.D. Symphony; advisor pers. dept. City of Sioux Falls. Recipient leader award YWCA, 1991; Gaylord Co. scholar Syracuse U., 1976; named S.D. Libr. of Yr., 1998. Mem. ALA, AAUW, Assn. Coll. and Rsch. Librs. (nat. adv. coun. coll. librs. sect. 1987—), Mountain Plains Libr. Assn. (chair acad. sect., nominating com. 1988, pres. 1993-94), S.D. Libr. Assn. (chair interlibr. coop. task force 1986-87, pres. 1987-88, chair recommended minimum salary task force 1988, chair local arrangements com. 1989-90, 2002-03), S.D. Libr. Network (adv. coun. 1986—, exec. com. 1992-96, 1998-2000, 2006-, chair adv. coun. 1994-96, 98-2000, 2006-). Office: Augustana Coll Mikkelsen Libr 29th & Smt Sioux Falls SD 57197-0001 Office Phone: 605-274-4921. Business E-Mail: ronelle.thompson@augie.edu.

THOMPSON, STANLEY B., church administrator; Pres., CEO, dir. The Free Meth. Found., Spring Arbor, Mich.; chmn., CEO, dir. King Trust Co., N.A.; CEO, chmn., dir. King Trust Charitable Gift Fund; ret., 2003. Office: Free Methodist Foundation PO Box 580 Spring Arbor MI 49283-0580 Home: PO Box 284 Spring Arbor MI 49283-0284 E-mail: stanleythompson@comcast.net.

THOMPSON, STEPHEN ARTHUR, sales consultant; b. Englewood, NJ, Jan. 24, 1934; s. Stephen Gerard and Doris Lillian (Evans) T.; m. Joan Frances O'Connor, May 12, 1955 (div. 1978); children: Stephen Andrew, Craig Allen, David John; m. Sandra Rene Fingernut, May 27, 1979. BS, Ohio State U., 1961. Physicist Rocketdyne div. North Am. Aviation, Canoga Park, Calif., 1961-62, Marquardt Corp., Van Nuys, Calif., 1962-63; mem. tech. staff Hughes Rsch. Labs., Malibu, Calif., 1963-69; editor Electronic Engr. mag. Chilton Co., LA, 1969-72, in advt. sales Instruments and Controls Sys., mag., 1972-77; regional advt. sales Design News mag. Cahners Pub. Co., LA, 1977-84, sales mgr. Design News mag. Newton, Mass., 1984-87, pub. Design News mag., 1987-95, group. pub. mfg. group, 1989-93, sr. v.p. integrated mktg., 1993-94, gen. mgr. Boston divsn., 1995-96, gen. mgr. mfg. mktg. divsn., 1995-97, sr. v.p. tng., 1996-97; gen. mgr. OEM/processing group Advanstar Comms., Cleve., 1997-99; sales training cons. Bentleyville, Ohio, 1999-2000. Founder Design News Engring. Edn. Found., Newton, 1991-97; pub. Design News Mag., 1994-95; group pub. Mfg. Group. Author: Basketball for Boys, 1970; contbr. articles to Jour. Spacecraft/Rockets, 1966. Club leader YMCA, Canoga Park, 1963-78; active PTA, Canoga Park, 1961-80; bd. dirs. Chatsworth (Calif.) High Booster Club, 1972-80. 1st lt., jet fighter pilot USAF, 1952-58. Mem. Bus. Profl. Advt. Assn. (Golden Spike award 1980, 81, 82, 83), L.A. Mag. Reps. Assn. (life), Nat. Fluid Power Assn., BPA Internat. (bd. dirs.). Achievements include patents for ion source, system and method for ion implantation of semiconductors. Office: 7500 Old Oak Blvd Cleveland OH 44130-3343

THOMPSON, THEODORE ROBERT, pediatric educator; b. Dayton, Ohio, July 18, 1943; s. Theodore Roosevelt and Helen (Casey) J.; m. Lynette Joanne Shenk; 1 child, S. Beth. BS, Wittenberg U., 1965; MD, U. Pa., 1969. Diplomate Am. Bd. Pediatrics (Neonatal, Perinatal Medicine). Resident in pediat. U. Minn. Hosp., Mpls., 1969—72, chief resident in pediat., 1971—72, fellow neonatal, perinatal, 1974—75, asst. prof., 1975—80, dir. divsn. neonatology and newborn intensive care unit, 1977—91, assoc. prof., 1980—85, prof., 1985—, co-dir. Med. Outreach, 1988—91, med. dir. med. outreach, 1991—2000, assoc. chief pediat. svcs., 1988—2003, assoc. head pediat. edn. and cmty. programs, 2003—04, assoc. head cmty. affairs, 2004—; med. dir. outreach, bd. dirs. U. Minn. Physicians, 1992—2008. Med. exec. com., sec.-treas. U. Minn. Med. Ctr., Fairview, 2002—04, chief of staff elect, 2004—07, chief of staff, 2007—. Editor: Newborn Intensive Care: A Practical Manual, 1983. Bd. dirs. Life Link III, St. Paul, 1987—; cons. Maternal and Child Health, Minn. Bd. Health, 1975-94; bd. dirs. Minn. Med. Found., 1995-99. With USPHS. 1972-74. Recipient Advocacy award, U. Minn. Med. Sch., Pres.'s award for outstanding svc., U. Minn., Alumni Catalogs award, Wittenberg U., 2005. Fellow: Am. Acad. Pediats.; mem.: Acad. Med. Educators, Gt. Plains Orgn. for Perinatal Health Care (Sioux Falls, SD Kunshe award 1989). Lutheran. Office: MMC 39 420 Delaware St SE Minneapolis MN 55455-0374 Office Phone: 612-626-2841. Business E-Mail: thomp005@umn.edu.

THOMPSON, THOMAS ADRIAN, sculptor; b. Sidney, Mont., Aug. 28, 1944; s. Vernon Eugene and Helen Alice (Torstenson) T.; m. M. Aileen Braun, June 7, 1968; children: Blair C., Meghann C. BA, Concordia Coll., 1966; postgrad., Mich. State U., 1968-69, Oakland U., 1970-72. Art tchr. Carman Ainsworth Sch. Dist., Flint, Mich., 1966-98; ret., 1998. Chmn. Flint Art Curriculum Com., 1980. Mem. adv. bd. Equine Art Guild; mem. Gand Blanc Arts Coun. Mem. NEA, Nat.

Art. Edn. Assn., Mich. Art Edn. Assn. (liaison mem.), Internat. Arabian Horse Assn., Arabian Horse Registry. Lutheran. Avocations: painting, sculpture, golf. Home: 1409 Kings Carriage Grand Blanc MI 48439-1622 E-mail: tathomps@sbcglobal.net.

THOMPSON, VERN, political organization executive; b. Maddock, ND, Aug. 23, 1956; m. Cindy; one child, Will. Former city councilman; former twp. supr.; rep. N.D. State, 1989-91, state senator, 1997—2000. Exec. dir. ND Dem. Party, 2001—. Recipient N.D. Weekly N.D. POI. Figure of the Yr., 1995, Minnewaukan Citizen of the Yr., 1996. Democrat. Home: 2214 Victoria Rose Dr S Fargo ND 58104-6813

THOMPSON, WADE FRANCIS BRUCE, manufacturing executive; b. Wellington, New Zealand, July 23, 1940; came to US, 1961, naturalized, 1990. m. Angela Ellen Barry, Jan. 20, 1967; children: Amanda and Charles (twins). B in Commerce, Cert. Acctg., Victoria U., Wellington, 1961; MSc, NYU, 1963; PhD of Commerce (hon.), Victoria U., 2007. Dir. diversification Sperry & Hutchinson, NYC, 1967-72; v.p. Texstar Corp., NYC, 1972-77; chmn. Hi-Lo Trailer Co., Butler, Ohio, 1977—2003; chmn., pres., CEO Thor Industries Inc., Jackson Center, Ohio, 1980—. Trustee Mystic Seaport Mus., Conn., 1984—; trustee Wade F.B. Thompson Charitable Found. Inc., 1985—, Mcpl. Art Soc., NYC, 1993—, Seventh Regiment Armory Conservancy, NYC, 1997—; founder The Drive Against Prostate Cancer. Recipient Oliver R. Grace award for Disting. Svc., Cancer Rsch. Inst., 2007, Jacqueline Kennedy Onassis award for Outstanding Contbn. to NYC, Mcpl. Art Soc., 2007. Mem. Union Club, NY Yacht Club (NYC). Avocations: tennis, collecting contemporary art. Office: Thor Industries Inc PO Box 629 Jackson Center OH 45334-0629

THOMPSON, WILLIAM EDWARD, state official; b. Lima, Ohio, Apr. 17, 1948; s. Richard Edward and Claudine (Burt) T.; m. Kay Swick, 1974; children; Marshall Burt, Kendra Lea, Parker Sherman. BS, Ohio State Univ., 1972. Mem. Ohio Ho. of Reps., 1987-97; chairperson Indsl. Commn. of Ohio, Columbus, 1997—. V.p. Thompson Seed Farm, Inc., 1977; mem. extension adv. com. Mem. Ohio Seed Improvement Assn., Ohio Seed Dealers Assn., Agrl. Genetic Rsch. Assn., Masonic Lodge, Ohio Farm Bureau, Phi Kappa Psi. Office: 30 W Spring St # L-30 Columbus OH 43215-2241 Home: 5616 Hardwell Dr Hilliard OH 43026-8092

THOMPSON, WILLIAM HARKINS, lawyer; b. Indpls., Aug. 6, 1957; s. William Richard and Nancy Pauline (Harkins) T. BS in Pub. Health, Ind. U., 1980; MS in Health Adminstrn., Ind. U., Indpls., 1983, JD, 1987. Bar: Ind. 1987, U.S. Dist. Ct. (no. and so. dists.) Ind. 1987. Adminstrv. asst. nursing dept. Wishard Meml. Hosp., Indpls., 1980-82, adminstr. pulmonary svcs., 1982-83; asst. adminstr. Ind. U. Med. Ctr., Indpls., 1983-87; assoc. to shareholder, health law, antitrust & corp. practices Hall, Render, Killian, Heath & Lyman, Indpls., 1987—. Lectr. Ind. U. Med. Ctr., 1987—; speaker and cons. in field. Contbr. articles to profl. jours. Tchr. Wheeler Rescue Mission, Indpls., 1987—; active YMCA, Indpls. Mem. ABA, Ind. Bar Assn., Indpls. Bar Assn., Am. Coll. Health Care Execs., Am. Health Lawyers Assn., Am. Soc. Law and Medicine, Indpls. Rugby Club. Republican. Lutheran. Office: Hall Render Killian Heath & Lyman Suite 2000 Box 82064 1 American Sq Indianapolis IN 46282 Office Phone: 317-633-4884. Fax: 317-633-4878. Business E-Mail: bthompson@hallrender.com.

THOMSON, JAMES ALEXANDER, molecular biologist, educator; b. Oak Park, Ill., Dec. 20, 1958; married; 2 children. BS in Biophysics, U. Ill., 1981; DVM magna cum laude, U.Pa., 1985, DS in molecular biology, 1988. Cert. Am. Coll. Veterinary Pathologists. Joined U. Wis., Madison, 1991, assoc. veterinarian; chief pathologist Wis. Regional Primate Rsch. Ctr., dir., 1999—; John D. McArthur Prof., dept. anatomy U. Wis.-Madison Med. Sch., 2002—. Adj. prof., molecular, cellular, and develop. biology dept. U. Calif., Santa Barbara, 2007—. Contbr. articles to profl. sci. jours. Named a finalist for World Tech. award in health and medicine, The Economist, London, 1999; named one of The Most Intriguing People, People Mag., 2001; recipient Ill. Gen. Assembly award, 1978, Eastman Kodak award in Biol. Scis., 1979, Golden Plate award, Am. Acad. Achievement, 1999, Man of the Year, Madison Mag., 2001, World Tech. Award, 2002, LIFE Internat. Rsch. Award, 2002, Frank Annunzio award, Christopher Columbus Fellowship Found., 2003, Outstanding Achievement Award, Am. Coll. of Veterinary Pathologists, 2003, Disting. Service Award for Enhancing Edn. through Biol. Rsch., The Nat. Assn. of Biology Teachers, Inc., 2005, Nathan R. Brewer Sci. Achievement Award, Am. Assn. for Lab. Animal Sci. (AALAS), 2006; fellow Undergrad. Rsch. Participation, Princeton U., N.J., 1979, Wis. Acad. of Sciences, Arts, and Letters, 2002; scholar Nat. Merit, 1977. Mem.: Soc. for Devel. Biology, Internat. Soc. for Stem Cell Rsch., Am. Coll. of Veterinary Pathologists, Phi Zeta, Phi Beta Kappa. Achievements include first to isolate and culture nonhuman primate embryonic stem cells in 1995, and human ES cells in 1998. Office: Univ Wisconsin Genome Ctr of WI 425 Henry Mall Rm 4420 Madison WI 53706 E-mail: thomson@primate.wisc.edu.*

THOMSON, STEVE, radio personality; b. St. Paul; m. Michele Thomson, 1989; 2 children. Student, U. Minn., Brown Inst. With radio stas., Montevideo, Minn., Sioux Falls, SD; with WCCO Radio, Mpls., 1997—, weekend afternoon radio host, 1998, announcer. Avocations: golf, reading. Office: WCCO 625 2nd Ave S Minneapolis MN 55402

THORESON, LAUREL, state legislator; m. Betty Thoreson; 3 children. Rep. N.D. Ho. of Reps., Bismarck, 1994—. Mem. human svc. and govt. and vet. affairs com. N.D. Ho. of Reps. Mem. Amvets. Office: ND House of Reps State Capitol Bismarck ND 58505

THORLAND, TIMOTHY, architectural firm executive; b. 1967; Degree in Architecture, Lawrence Technol. U. Joined Lighthouse of Oakland County, 1992—95; real estate profl. Hope Network Southeast Divsn., 1995—99; dir., real estate Southwest Housing Solutions Corp., Detroit, 1999—2004, exec. dir., 2004—. Founder Housing Opportunity Ctr., Southwest Housing Solutions Corp., 2004. Named one of 40 Under 40, Crain's Detroit Bus., 2006. Mem.: NeighborWorks Am.

THORMODSGARD, DIANE L., bank executive; b. 1950; m. Gaylord Thormodsgard. BA in Math., Econ. & Acctg., Luther Coll.; MBA, U. Minn. Controller, asst. treas. First Bank System (now US Bancorp), 1978, sr. v.p. Regional Cmty. Banking, 1985—89, sr. v.p. ops., 1989—93, sr. v.p., treas., chief adminstr. officer, 1993—95, sr. v.p., chief adminstr. officer Corp. Trust, 1995—99, pres. Corp. Trust., Inst. Trust and Custody Svcs., 1999—2007, vice chmn., head wealth mgmt., 2007—. Bd. mem. St. Paul C of C, St. Paul Chamber Orch., Minn. Church Found., Central Corridor Partnership. Named one of The Top 15 Women in Fin., Finance & Commerce, 2005, 25 Most Powerful Women in Banking, US Banker, 2006. Mem.: Am. Inst. of Certified Pub. Accountants, Minn. Soc. of Certified Pub. Accountants, Lutheran Social Services Fin. Com. Office: US Bancorp US Bancorp Ctr 800 Nicollet Mall Minneapolis MN 55402 Office Phone: 612-303-7936. E-mail: diane.thormodsgard@usbank.com.

THORNBURGH, RON E., state official; b. Burlingame, Kans., Dec. 31, 1962; m. Annette Thornburgh; 2 children. BA in Criminal Justice, Washburn U., 1985. Dep. asst. sec. state to asst. sec. state State of Kans., Topeka, 1985-87, asst. sec. state, 1991-95, sec. state, 1995—. Vice chairperson blue ribbon panel on ethical conduct State of Kans., 1989. Mem. Kids Voting Kans. Exec. Com.; mem. adv. com. United Way. Toll fellow Henry Toll Fellowship Prog., 1995, Digital Govt. Agent of Change award, MIT, 2002, Lee Ann Elliott Election Excellence award, Kids Voting USA, 2004. Mem. Washburn U. Alumni Bd., 20/30 Club Internat. Republican. Methodist. Office: Office Sec State Memorial Hall First Floor 120 SW 10th Ave Topeka KS 66612-1504 Office Phone: 785-296-4575. Office Fax: 785-368-8033.

THORNE-THOMSEN, THOMAS, lawyer; b. El Dorado, Kans., Oct. 22, 1949; s. Fletcher and Barbara (Macoubrey) T.-T. BA, Vanderbilt U., 1972; JD, U. Colo., 1976; LLM in Taxation, NYU, 1983. Bar: Colo. 1976, Ga. 1977, Ill. 1983. Law clk. to Chief Judge Alfred A. Arraj U.S. Dist. Ct. Colo., Boulder, 1976-77; assoc. Alston & Bird, Atlanta, 1977-82; assoc., ptnr. Keck, Mahin & Cate, Chgo., 1983-95; ptnr. Schiff, Harden & Waite, Chgo., 1995-98, Applegate & Thorne-Thomsen, Chgo., 1998—. Bd. dirs. Century Place Devel. Corp., Chgo., 1989—, Sutherland Neighborhood Devel. Corp., Chgo., 1989—, South Shore Neighborhood Devel. Crop. Chgo. 1990—, Argyle Neighborhood Devel. Corp., Chgo., 1991—, Heartland Alliance for Human Rights and Human Need, 1995—, Howard Brown Health Ctr., Chgo., 1991-94; com. mem. Chgo.'s Comprehensive Housing Affordability Strategy, Chgo., 1992—; mem. bond leverage trust fund task force Ill. Housing Authority, 1993. Mem. ABA, Colo. State Bar Assn., Ill. State Bar Assn., Ga. State Bar Assn. Avocations: jogging, biking, swimming, boating, horses. Home: 233 E Wacker Dr Apt 606 Chicago IL 60601-5106 Office: Applegate & Thorne-Thomsen 322 S Green St Ste 412 Chicago IL 60607-3544

THORNTON, JERRY SUE, community college president; BA, MA, Murray State U., Ky.; PhD, U. Tex.; DHL, Coll. St. Catherine, St. Paul. Tchr. jr. high sch., Earlington, Ky., Murray H.S., Triton Coll., RiverGrove, Ill., dean arts ans scis.; pres. Lakewood C.C., White Bear Lake, Minn., 1985-92, Cuyahoga C.C., Cleve., 1992—. Bd. dirs. Nat. City Bank, Applied Indsl. Techs. Author books, book chpts. and articles. Bd. dirs. Greater Cleve. Growth Assn., Greater Cleve. Roundtable, Urban League of Greater Cleve., United Way Svcs., Rock and Roll Hall of Fame and Mus., Cleve. Found. Mem. Alpha Kappa Alpha. Office: Cuyahoga CC Office of Pres 700 Carnegie Ave Cleveland OH 44115-2833

THORNTON, JOHN T., corporate financial executive; b. NYC, Oct. 22, 1937; s. John T. and Catherine (Burke) T.; m. Patricia C. Robertson; children: Kevin, Brian, Vincent, Elizabeth, Monica. BBA, St. John's U., 1959, JD, 1972. Bar: N.Y.; CPA. Auditor Peat, Marwick, Mitchell & Co., NYC, 1961-67; asst. controller Texasgulf Inc., Stamford, Conn., 1967-81, v.p., controller, 1981-84; sr. v.p., controller Norwest Corp., Mpls., 1984-87, exec. v.p., chief fin. officer, 1987-97; owner, mgr. JT Investments, Inc., 2005—; dir. XL Capital Ltd. Bd. dirs. Exel., Ltd., Stock Exch. Listed Co., Arcadia Resources. Office: c/o Arcadia Resources Inc Ste 200 26777 Central Pakr Blvd Southfield MI 48076 Office Phone: 248-352-7530. Office Fax: 248-352-7534.

THORNTON, THOMAS NOEL, former publishing executive; b. Marceline, Mo., Apr. 23, 1950; s. Bernard F. and Helen F. (Kelley) T.; m. Cynthia L. Murray, Nov. 26, 1971; children: T. Zachary, Timothy. B.J., U. Mo., 1972. Asst. to editor Universal Press Syndicate, Kansas City, Mo., 1972, v.p., 1974, dir. mktg., 1976; v.p., dir. mktg. Universal Press Syndicate and Andrews McMeel Pub., Kansas City, 1976-87; pres., COO Andrews McMeel Pub., 1987—2002, pres., CEO, 2003—05. Bd. dirs. Andrews McMeel Universal. Office Phone: 816-932-6700. Business E-Mail: tthornton@amuniversal.com.

THORPE, NORMAN RALPH, lawyer, automotive executive, retired military officer; b. Carlinville, Ill., Oct. 17, 1934; s. Edwin Everett and Imogene Midas (Hayes) T.; m. Elaine Frances Pritzman, Nov. 1, 1968; children: Sarah Elizabeth Chisholm, Carrie Rebecca Keough. AB in Econs., U. Ill., 1956, JD, 1958; LLM in Pub. Internat. Law, George Washington U., 1967. Bar: Ill. 1958, Mich. 1988, U.S. Supreme. Ct. 1969. Commd. 2d lt. USAF, 1956, advanced through grades to brig. gen., 1983; legal advisor U.S. Embassy, Manila, 1969-72; chief internat. law hdqrs. USAF, Washington, 1972-77; staff judge adv. 21st Air Force, McGuire AFB, N.J., 1977-80, USAF Europe, Ramstein AB, Fed. Republic Germany, 1980-84; comdr. Air Force Contract Law Ctr., Wright-Patterson AFB, Ohio, 1984-88; mem. legal staff, group counsel GM Def. and Power Products Gen. Motors Corp., Detroit, 1988—98; counsel GMR&D Planning and Fuel Cell Activity, 1998—2003; ret., 2003. Legal advisor Dept. of Def. Blue Ribbon Com. on Code of Conduct, 1975; USAF del. Internat. Aero. and Astronautical Fedn., Budapest, 1983; adj. prof. U. Dayton Sch. Law, 1986-87; partnership counsel U.S. Advanced Battery Consortium, Legal Advisor U.S. Coun. Automotive Rsch., Chrysler Corp., Ford Motor Co., GM, 1990—. Contbr. articles to profl. jours. Mem. staff Commn. on Police Policies and Procedures, Dayton, 1986; trustee Dayton Philharm. Orch., 1987-88; mem. bd. visitors U. Ill. Law Sch., 2002-; bd. dirs. Friends of Ctrl. European and Eurasian Law Inst., 2003—. Recipient Disting. Svc. medal Legion of Merit. Mem. ABA (chmn. com. internat. law sect. 1977-80, coun. mem. pub. contract law sect. 1986-88, chmn. com. pub. contract law sect. 1988-95, sec. pub. contract law sect. 2000-01, vice chair 1999-2000, chair-elect 2000-01, chair 2001-02), Air Force Assn., Dayton Coun. on World Affairs, Army/Navy Club, Detroit Econ. Club, Renaissance Club. Republican. Avocations: music, piano, gardening. Home: 498 Abbey Rd Birmingham MI 48009-5618 Home Phone: 248-644-8105; Office Phone: 248-644-8105. Business E-Mail: nthorpe@ameritech.net.

THORSEN, MARIE KRISTIN, radiologist, educator; b. Milw., Aug. 1, 1947; d. Charles Christian and Margaret Josephine (Little) T.; M. James Lawrence Troy, Jan. 7, 1978; children: Katherine Marie, Megan Elizabeth. BA, U. Wis., Madison, 1969; MBA, George Washington U., Washington, 1971; MD, Columbia Coll. Physicians and Surgeons, 1977. Diplomate Am. Bd. Radiology. Intern. Columbia-Presbyn. Med. Ctr., NYC, 1977-78, resident dept. radiology, 1978-81; asst. prof. radiology Med. Coll. Wis., 1982-84, assoc. prof., 1984-89, prof., 1989-94; dir. computed tomography Waukesha Meml. Hosp., 1994—, Oconomowoc Meml. Hosp., 1994—. Contbr. articles to profl. jours. Fellow, Med. Coll. Wisc., Milw., 1981—82. Fellow Am. Coll. Radiology, Radiol. Soc. N. Am., Wis. Radiologic Assn. (v.p., 2005, pres., 2007). Home Phone: 262-567-4532. Personal E-mail: mkthorsen@aol.com.

THORSON, JOHN MARTIN, JR., electrical engineer, consultant; b. Armstrong, Iowa, Dec. 16, 1929; s. John Martin and Hazel Marguerite (Martin) T.; m. Geraldine Carol Moran, Apr. 21, 1956 (dec. 1975); children— John Robert, James Michael; m. Lee Houk, Sept. 24, 1977 BSE.E., Iowa State U., 1951. Transmission engr. No. States Power Co., Mpls., 1953-58, system operation relay engr., 1962-74, telephone engr. Minot, N.D., 1958-62; utility industry mktg. mgr. Control Data Corp., Mpls., 1974-77, product/program mgr. utilities, 1977-84, sr. cons. energy mgmt. systems, 1984-90; pres. Thorson Engrs., Inc., Chanhassen, Minn., 1991—. Inductive coordination cons. SNC Corp., Oshkosh, Wis., 1985—; tech. cons. Power Technologies, Inc., Schenectady, N.Y., 1991—, Control Corp., Osseo, Minn., 1992-93, Control Data, Plymouth, Minn., 1991-92, Hathaway, Denver, 1992-93, Scottish Hydro-Electric, PLC, Perth, Scotland, 1992—, NRG Energy Inc., Mpls., 1993—, Stanford Rsch. Inst., 1995—, Univ. Online, Inc., 1995—, GE, 1996—, No. States Power Co., 1998-2000, Siemens, 2000—; head U.S. nat. com. Internat. Electrotech. Com., TC57, 1985-2001. Contbr. tech. papers to profl. jours. Dist. commr. Boy Scouts Am., Minn., 1954-58, 64-65, coun. commr. N.D., Mont., 1959-62; mem. coun. St. Philip Luth. Ch., Wayzata, Minn., 1968-69; mem. coun. Family of Christ Luth. Ch., Chanhassan, 2001--; county del. Rep. Com., Chanhassen, 1980-82. 1st lt. USAF, 1951-53. Recipient Alumni Service award Iowa State U., 1972 Fellow IEEE (life mem., bd. dirs. 1981-82, dir. region 4, 1981-82, mem. U.S. activities bd. 1981-82, regional activities bd. 1981-82, Centennial medal 1984, Millenium medal 2000); mem. Internat. Conf. on Large High Voltage Electric Sys. (Atwood assoc. 2000), Iowa State U. Alumni Assn. (v.p., pres. 1963-66). Independent. Avocations: canoeing, backpacking, mountain climbing. Home and Office: 7320 Longview Cir Chanhassen MN 55317-7905

THRASH, PATRICIA ANN, retired educational association administrator; b. Grenada, Miss., May 4, 1929; d. Lewis Edgar and Weaver (Betts) T. BS, Delta State Coll., 1950; LHD, Delta State U., 2007; MA, Northwestern U., Evanston, Ill., 1953, PhD, 1959; cert. Inst. Edn. Mgmt., Harvard U., Cambridge, Mass., 1983; EdD (hon.), Vincennes U., Ind., 1997; LHD, Drake U., Des Moines, 1997, Adrian Coll., Mich., 1998, Delta State U., Cleveland, Miss., 2007. Tchr. high sch. English, Clarksdale, Miss., 1950-52; head resident Northwestern U., 1953-55, asst. to dean women, 1955-58, asst. dean women, 1958-60, lectr. edn., 1959-65, dean women, 1960-69, assoc. prof. edn., 1965-72, assoc. dean students, 1969-71; asst. exec. sec. Commn. on Instns. Higher Edn., North Central Assn. Colls. and Schs., 1972-73, assoc. exec. dir., 1973-76, assoc. dir., 1976-87, exec. dir., 1988-96; exec. dir. emeritus, 1997—. Adv. panel Am. Coun. on Edn., MIVER program evaluation mil. base program, 1991-94; nat. adv. panel Nat. Ctr. Postsecondary Tchg., Learning & Assessment, 1991-95. Author (with others): Handbook of College and University Administration, 1970; editor Jour. Northwestern U. Inst. for Learning in Retirement, 2000-02, course coord., 2000—; contbr. articles to ednl. jours. Bd. dirs. Delta State U. Found., 2000-02. Mem. Nat. Assn. Women Deans and Counselors (v.p. 1967-69, pres. 1972-73), Ill. Assn. Women Deans and Counselors (sec. 1961-63, pres. 1964-66), Am. Coll. Pers. Assn. (editl. bd. jour. 1971-74), Coun. Student Pers. Assns. in Higher Edn. (program nominations com. 1974-75, adv. panel Am. Coll. Testing Coll. Outcome Measures project 1977-78, staff Coun. on Postsecondary Accreditation project for evaluation nontraditional edn. 1977-78, mem. editl. bd. Jour. Higher Edn. 1975-80, guest editor Mar.-Apr. 1979, co-editor NCA Quar. 1988-96, vice-chair regional accrediting dirs. group 1993, exec. com. Nat. Policy Bd. for Higher Edn. Inst. 1993-95), Mortar Bd. (hon.), Phi Delta Theta, Pi Lambda Theta, Alpha Psi Omega, Alpha Lambda Delta. Methodist. Home: 2337 Hartrey Ave Evanston IL 60201-2552 Personal E-mail: patsy1941@comcast.net.

THULIN, INGE G., manufacturing executive; b. Sweden; Mng. dir., Russian markets 3M Co., v.p., skin health divsn., v.p., Europe and Middle East, 2002—03, exec. v.p., internat. opers., 2003—. Office: 3M Co 3M Ctr Saint Paul MN 55144

THULL, TOM (JOHN THOMAS THULL), state agency administrator; m. Shelley Thull. Grad. in Agr. Edn., Kans. State U., 1975. Loan specialist; v.p. Midland Nat. Bank, Ctrl. Bank & Trust; pres. Ctrl. Nat. Bank, Newton, Kans.; mayor Town of North Newton; mem. Kans. House Reps. from Dist. 72, 2003—07; commr. Office of State Bank Commr., Kans., 2007—. Pres. Harvey County Bankers Assn., Harvey County Econ. Devel. Coun.; dir. Newton C. of C.; mem. adv. bd. Bethel Coll. Democrat. Office: Office of State Bank Commr 700 Jackson Ste 300 Topeka KS 66603 Office Phone: 785-296-2266. Office Fax: 785-296-0168. E-mail: tom.thull@osbckansas.org.

THUNE, JOHN RANDOLPH, senator; b. Murdo, SD, Jan. 7, 1961; m. Kimberley Jo Weems, 1984; children: Brittany, Larissa. BBA, Biola U., Calif., 1983; MBA, U. SD, 1984. Legis. asst. to Senator James Abdnor US Senate, 1985-87; dep. staff dir. to the ranking rep. Senate Small Bus. Com., 1987-89; exec. dir. South Dakota Rep. Party, 1989-91; dir. railroad divsn. State of SD, 1991-93; exec. dir. SD Mcpl. League, 1993-96; founder The Thune Group LLC; mem. US Ho. Reps. from SD, 1997—2003; US Senator from SD, 2005—. Mem. com. armed services US Senate, com. environment and public works, com. small bus. and entrepreneurship, com. veterans affairs. Republican. Protestant. Avocations: basketball, pheasant hunting. Office: US Senate 383 Russell Senate Office Bldg Washington DC 20510 also: District Office 320 North Main Ave Sioux Falls SD 57104-6056 Office Phone: 202-224-2321, 605-334-9596. Office Fax: 202-228-5429, 605-334-2591.

THURBER, JOHN ALEXANDER, lawyer; b. Detroit, Nov. 9, 1939; s. John Levington and Mary Anne (D'Agostino) T.; m. Barbara Irene Brown, June 30, 1962; children: John Levington II, Sarah Jeanne. AB in History, U. Mich., 1962, JD, 1965. Bar: Ohio 1965, Mich. 1968. Assoc. Hahn, Loeser and Parks, Cleve., 1965-67, Miller, Canfield, Paddock and Stone, Birmingham, Mich., 1967-73; sr. mem. Miller, Canfield, Paddock and Stone, P.L.C., Troy, Mich., 1974—. Treas. Birmingham Community House, 1971-73; pres. Birmingham Village Players, 1983-84; bd. dirs. Oakland Parks Found., Pontiac, Mich., 1984—, pres., 1989-92; mem. capital com. Lighthouse Found.; trustee Oakland Land Conservancy. Avocations: reading, theater, walking, sports. Office: Miller Canfield Paddock & Stone PLC 840 W Long Lake Rd Ste 200 Troy MI 48098-6358 E-mail: thurberj@millercanfield.com.

THURBER, PETER PALMS, lawyer; b. Detroit, Mar. 23, 1928; s. Cleveland and Marie Louise (Palms) T.; m. Ellen Bodley Stites, Apr. 16, 1955; children: Edith Bodley, Jane Chenoweth, Thomas, Sarah Bartlett. BA, Williams Coll., 1950; JD, Harvard U., 1953. Bar: Mich., 1954. With Miller, Canfield, Paddock and Stone, Detroit, 1953-93, of counsel, 1994—. Trustee McGregor Fund, Detroit, 1979-2003. Bd. dirs. Detroit Symphony Orch., Inc., 1974-93; trustee Community Found. for Southeastern Mich., 1990-2000, Coun. Mich. Founds., 1991-2000. With U.S. Army, 1953-55. Fellow Am. Bar Found.; mem. Clubs: Country of Detroit (Grosse Pointe Farms, Mich.). Roman Catholic. Avocations: reading, travel, sports. Home: 28 Provencal Rd Grosse Pointe Farms MI 48236-3038

THURSFIELD, DAVID W., automotive executive; Plant mgr. Ford Motor Co., 1979—84, gen. mfg. mgr. and gen. ops. mgr. various locations in Europe, 1984—92, dir. body and assembly ops. Ford of Europe, mgr. vehicle ops. Ford automotive ops., 1996—98, v.p. vehicle ops. Ford automotive ops., 1998—2001, group v.p. internat. ops. and global purchasing, 2001, chmn., CEO, and pres. Ford of Europe, 2001—02, exec. v.p. and pres. internat. ops. and global purchasing, 2002—.

THURSTON, JAMES KENDALL, lawyer; b. NYC, July 1, 1962; s. David Wheeler and Frances Davis Thurston; m. Camille Nadia Khodadad, June 16, 1995; children: Taylor Frances, Isabel Jena. BA in Arch., U. Pa., 1984; postgrad., Yale U., 1988-89; JD magna cum laude, Marquette U., 1989. Bar: Ill. 1989, Wis. 1989, US Dist. Ct. (no. dist.) Ill., US Ct. Appeals (4th and 6th cir.). Assoc. Lord, Bissell & Brook, Chgo., 1989-92, Altheimer & Gray, Chgo., 1992-94, Peterson & Ross, Chgo., 1994-95; ptnr. Wilson, Elser, Moskowitz, Edelman & Dicker, Chgo., 1995—. Contbr. articles to legal jours. Mem. ABA. Office: Wilson Elser et al 120 N Lasalle St Chicago IL 60602-2424 Office Phone: 312-704-0550 125. Office Fax: 312-704-1522. E-mail: thurstonj@wemed.com.

THURSTON, STEPHEN JOHN, pastor; b. Chgo., July 20, 1952; s. John Lee and Ruth (Hall) T.; m. Joyce DeVonne Hand, June 18, 1977; children: Stephen John II, Nicole D'Vaugh, Teniece Rael, Christian Avery Elijah. BA in Religion, Bishop Coll., 1975; Hon. degree, Chgo. Baptist Inst., 1986. Co-pastor New Covenant Missionary Bapt. Ch., Chgo., 1975-79, pastor, 1979—; pres. National Baptist Convention, Inc. Third v.p. Nat. Bapt. Conv. Am., mem. exec. com. Christian Edn. Congress; pres. Ill. Nat. Bapt. State Conv.; mem. Christian Fellowship Dist. Assn.; lectr. various orgns.; instr. New Covenant Bapt. Ch., Fellowship Bapt. Ch. Co-chmn. religious affairs div. People United to Save Humanity (PUSH); bd. dirs. nat. alumni assn. Bishop Coll.; active NAACP; trustee, fin. chmn. Chgo. Bapt. Inst. Named one of 100 Most Influential Black Americans, Ebony mag., 2006. Mem. Broadcast Ministers Alliance, Bapt. Ministers Conf. Chgo. (Ministerial Pioneer award). Clubs: Bishop Coll. (Chgo.). Office: New Cov Miss Baptist Church 740 E 77th St Chicago IL 60619-2553

THURSWELL, GERALD ELLIOTT, lawyer; b. Detroit, Feb. 4, 1944; s. Harry and Lilyan (Zeitlin) T.; m. Lynn Satovsky, Sept. 17, 1967 (div. Aug. 1978); children: Jennifer, Lawrence; m. Judith Linda Bendix, Sept. 2, 1978 (div. May 1999); chldren: Jeremy, Lindsey. LLB with distinction, Wayne State U., 1967. Bar: Mich. 1968, .Y. 1984, D.C. 1985, Colo. 1990, Ill. 1992, U.S. Dist. Ct. (ea. dist.) Mich. 1968, U.S. Ct. Appeals (6th cir.) 1968, U.S. Supreme Ct. 1994, U.S. Dist. Ct. (western dist.) Mich. 2004. Student asst. to U.S. Atty. Eas. Dist. Mich., Detroit, 1966; assoc. Zwerdling, Miller, Klimist & Maurer, Detroit, 1967-68; st. prnt. The Thurswell Law Firm, Southfield, Mich. Arbitrator Am. Arbitration Assn., Detroit, 1969—; mediator Wayne County Cir. Ct., Mich., 1983—, Oakland County Cir. Ct. Mich., 1984—, also facilitator, 1991; twp. atty. Royal Oak Twp., Mich., 1982—; lectr. Oakland County Bar Assn. People's Law Sch., 1988. Pres. Powder Horn Estates Subdivsn. Assn., West Bloomfield, Mich., 1975, United Fund, West Bloomfield, 1976. Arthur F. Lederly scholar Wayne State U. Law Sch., 1965; Wayne State U. Law Sch. grad. profl. scholar, 1965, 66. Mem. ATLA (treas. Detroit mt. chpt. 1986-87, v.p. 1989-90, pres. 1991-93), Mich. Bar Assn. (investigator/arbitrator grievance bd., atty. discipline bd., chmn. hearing panel), Mich. Trial Lawyers Assn. (legis. com. on govtl. immunity 1984, exec. bd. 2004-, PAC 2004), Detroit Bar Assn. (past panel pub. adv. com. jud. candidates), Oakland County Bar Assn. Office: The Thurswell Law Firm 1000 Town Ctr Ste 500 Southfield MI 48075-1221 Office Phone: 248-354-2222.

THYEN, JAMES C., furniture company executive; b. Jasper, Ind., 1943; BS, Xavier U., 1965; MBA, Ind. U., 1967. With Kimball Internat. Inc., Jasper, 1967—, sr. exec. v.p., treas., 1982—, also bd. dirs. Home: 1440 W Schuetter Rd Jasper IN 47546-9545 Office: Kimball Internat Inc 1038 E 15th St Jasper IN 47546-2225

TIAHRT, TODD (W. TODD TIAHRT), congressman, former state senator; b. Vermillion, SD, June 15, 1951; s. Wilbur E. and Sara Ella Marcine (Steele) T.; m. Vicki Lyn Holland, Aug. 14, 1976; children: Jessica, John, Luke. Student, SD Sch. Mines & Tech., Rapid City, 1969-72; BA, Evangel Coll., 1975; MBA, S.W. Mo. State U., 1989. Property estimator Crawford & Co., Springfield, Mo., 1975-78; project engr. Zenith Electronics, Springfield, 1978-81; cost engr. Boeing, Wichita, Kans., 1981-94, proposal mgr., 1991-94; state senator State of Kans., Topeka, 1993—95; mem. US Congress from 4th Kans. dist., Washington, 1995—; mem. appropriations com., 1997—. Chmn. 4th dist. Rep. party, 1990-92; exec. com. Kans. Rep. party, 1990-92, nat. security com., sci. com. Mem. Pachyderm (bd. dirs. 1991-92), Delta Sigma Phi. Republican. Office: US Ho Reps 2441 Rayburn Ho Office Bldg Washington DC 20515-1604

TIBBLE, DOUGLAS CLAIR, lawyer; b. Joliet, Ill., May 26, 1952; BA, DePaul U., 1974; JD, Syracuse U., 1977. Bar: Ill., US Dist. Ct. (no. dist.) Ill., US Ct. Appeals (7th cir.), US Supreme Ct. Ptnr. McDermott, Will & Emery, 1977—95, McBride, Baker & Coles, Oakbrook Terrace, Ill., 1996—2003, Brooks, Adams and Tarulis, aperville, Ill., 2003—. Mem. ABA, DuPage County Bar Assn., Illinois State Bar Assn. Office: Brooks Adams and Tarulis 101 N Washington St Naperville IL 60540-4511 Office Phone: 630-355-2101. Business E-Mail: dtibble@naperville.com.

TIBERI, PATRICK JOSEPH, congressman, former state legislator; b. Columbus, Ohio, Oct. 21, 1962; m. Denice Tiberi; 1 child. BA in Journalism, Ohio State U., 1985; HHD (hon.), Capital U., 2005. Realtor ReMax Achievers; asst. dist. mgr. Staff of US Rep. John Kasich; mem. Ohio State Ho. Reps. from Dist. 26, 1993—2001, majority leader; mem. ins. and vets. affairs coms. Ohio Ho. Reps.; mem. US Congress from 12th Ohio dist., 2001—, mem. ways and means com. Mem. adv. bd. Columbus chpt. ARC, Columbus Italian Cultural Ctr.; pres., co-founder Windsor Terrace Learning Ctr. Recipient Pres.'s award Northland Cmty. Coun., Vet. Admin Commendation award, Svc. award ARC, Watchdog of Treas. award United Conservatives of Ohio, Giving from the Heart award Alzheimer's Assn. Ctrl. Ohio Chpt. Mem. Sons of Italy. Republican. Roman Catholic. Office: 3000 Corporate Exchange Dr Ste 310 Columbus OH 43231-7689 Office Phone: 614-523-2555, 202-225-5355. Office Fax: 614-818-0887.

TICE, CAROL HOFF, intergenerational specialist, consultant; b. Ashville, NC, Oct. 6, 1931; d. Amos H. and Fern (Irvin) Hoff; m. (div.); children: Karin E., Jonathan H. BS, Manchester Coll., North Manchester, Ind., 1954; MEd, Cornell U., 1955. Cert. tchr., Mich., N.Y., N.J. Tchr. Princeton (N.J.) Schs., 1955-60, Ann Arbor (Mich.) Schs., 1964—; dir. intergenerational programs Inst. for Study Children and Families Eastern Mich. U., Ypsilanti, 1985-96. Founder, pres. Lifespan Resources, Inc., Ann Arbor, 1979—; presdl. appointee to U.S. Nat. Commn. Internat. Yr. of the Child, Washington, 1979-81; del. to White House Conf. on Aging, Washington, 1995; founder, bd, mem. Tchg.-Learning Community. Innovator; program, Tch. Learning Intergenerational Communities, 1971; author: Guide Books and articles, Community of Caring, 1980; co-producer, Film, What We Have, 1976 (award, Milan, Italy Film Festival 1982). Trustee Blue Lake Fine Arts Camp, Twin Lake, Mich., 1975—; dir. Visual Arts Colony, 1990—. Recipient Program Innovation award, Mich. Dept. Edn., 1974—80, C.S. Mott Found. award, 1982, Nat. Found. Improvement in Edn. award, Washington, 1986, Disting. Alumni award, Manchester Coll., 1979, A+ Break the Mold award, U.S. Sec. of Edn., 1992, Ann Arbor Sch. Supts. Golden Apple award, 1999, Disting. Svc. award, Mich. Art Edn. Assn., 2001; fellow Ford Found. fellow, Ithaca, N.Y., 1955. Mem. AAUW (agt. 1979, Agent of Change award), Generations United (hon. com. for Margaret Mead Centennial 2001, 1998—, Pioneer award 1989), Mich. Edn. Assn. (hon. mention Program Innovation 2000), Optimist Club (Humanitarian award). Democrat. Presbyterian. Office: Scarlett MS 3300 Lorraine St Ann Arbor MI 48108-1970

TICE, MIKE (MICHAEL P. TICE), former professional football coach; b. Bayshore, NY, Feb. 2, 1959; m. Diane Tice; children: Adrienne, Nathan. Student, U. Md., 1977—80. Tight end Seattle Seahawks, 1981—88, 1990—91, Washington Redskins, 1989, Minn. Vikings, Eden Prairie, 1992—93, 1995, coach tight ends, 1996, offensive line coach, 1997—2001, asst. head head coach, 2001, head coach, 2002—05.

TIEDJE, JAMES MICHAEL, microbiologist, ecologist, educator; b. Newton, Iowa, Feb. 9, 1942; married, 1965; 3 children. BS, Iowa State U., 1964; MS, Cornell U., 1966, PhD in Soil Microbiology, 1968. From asst. prof. to prof. Mich. State U., 1968-78, disting. prof., 1991—; dir. sci. and tech. ctr. microbial ecology NSF, 1988—. Vis. assoc. prof. U. Ga., 1974-75; cons. NSF, 1974-77; vis. prof. U. Calif. Berkeley, 1981-82; mem. biotech. sci. adv. com. EPA, 1986-89, chair sci. adv. coun. GPA, 1988-90. Editor: Applied Microbiology, 1974—, editor-in-chief, 1980-86. Recipient Carlos J. Finley prize, UNESCO, 1993. Mem. AAAS, Am. Soc. Agronomy (Soil Sci. award 1990), Internat. Inst. Biotech., Am. Soc. Microbiology (award in applied and environ. microbiology 1992), Soil Sci. Soc. Am., Ecol. Soc. Am., Internat. Soc. Soil Sci. (chair soil biology divsn.). Achievements include research in dentrification, microbial metabolism of organic pollutants, and molecular microbiol. ecology. Office: Michigan State U Microbial Ecology Ctr 540 Plant & Soil Scis Bldg East Lansing MI 48824-1325

TIEFENTHAL, MARGUERITE AURAND, school social worker; b. Battle Creek, Mich., July 23, 1919; d. Charles Henry and Elisabeth Dirk (Hoekstra) Aurand; m. Harlan E. Tiefenthal, ov. 26, 1942; children: Susan Ann, Daniel E., Elisabeth Amber, Carol Aurand. BS, Western Mich. U., 1941; MSW, U. Mich., 1950; postgrad., Coll. of DuPage, Ill., 1988-90. Tchr. No. High Sch., Flint, Mich., 1941-44, Cen. High Sch., Kalamazoo, 1944-45; acct. Upjohn Co., Kalamazoo, 1945-48; social worker Family Svc. Agy., Lansing, Mich., 1948-50, Pitts., 1950-55; sch. social worker Gower Sch. Dist., Hinsdale, Ill., 1962-70, Hinsdale (Ill.) Dist. 181, 1970-89, cons., 1989—; sch. social worker Villa Park (Ill.) Sch. Dist. 45, 1989; addictions counselor Mercy Hosp., 1990-92; asst. prof. sch. social work, liaison to pub. schs. Loyola U., Chgo., 1990-98, ret., 1998. Field instr. social work interns U. Ill., 1979-88; impartial due process hearing officer; mem. adv. com. sch. social work Ill. State Bd. Edn. approved programs U. Ill. and George Williams Coll.; speaker Nat. Conf. Sch. Social Work, Denver, U. Tex. Joint Conf. Sch. Social Work in Ill.; founder Marguerite Tiefenthal Symposium for Ill. Sch. Social Work Interns. Co-editor The School Social Worker and the Handicapped Child: Making P.L. 94-142 Work; sect. editor: Sch. Social Work Quarterly, 1979. Sec. All Village Caucus Village of Western Springs, Ill., mem. village disaster com.; deacon Presbyn. Ch. Western Springs, Sunday sch. tchr., mem. choir; instr. Parent Effectiveness, Teacher Effectiveness, STEP; trainer Widowed Persons Service Tng. Program for Vol. Aides AARP. Recipient Ill. Sch. Social Worker of Yr., 1982. Mem. Nat. Assn. Social Workers (chmn. exec. council on social work in schs.), Ill. Assn. Sch. Social Workers (past pres., past conf. chmn., conf. program chmn.), Ladies Libr. Assn., Sch. Social Workers Supervisors Group (del. to Ill. Commn. on Children), Programs. for Licensure of Social Work Practice in Ill., Ladies Libr. Assn. (Kalamazoo), LWV, DKG, PEO. Avocation: sewing. also: 3151 West B Ave Plainwell MI 49080

TIEKEN, ROBERT W., relocation services company executive, retired tire manufacturing company executive; b. Decatur, Ill., May 6, 1939; married; 2 children. BS, Ill. Wesleyan U., 1961. With GE Co., mem. corp. audit staff; mgr. fin. ops. GE Nuclear Energy, GE Transp. Sys.; with GE Aerospace, v.p. fin. and info. tech.; corp. v.p. GE Co., 1988; v.p. fin. Utah Internat., Inc., Martin Marietta Corp., Bethesda, Md., 1993—94; exec. v.p., CFO Goodyear Tire & Rubber Co., Akron, Ohio, 1994—2004; interim CEO SIRVA, Inc., Westmont, Ill., 2007, pres., CEO, 2007—. Bd. dir. Graphic Packaging Corp. Office: SIRVA Inc 700 Oakmont Ln Westmont IL 60559

TIEMEYER, CHRISTIAN, conductor; m. Pattie Farris; children: Jeanie, Hank, Elisa. Grad., Peabody Conservatory; D of Musical Arts, Cath. U. of Am. Assoc. condr. Dallas Symphony, 1978-83; interim artistic dir., prin. guest condr. Omaha Symphony; music dir. Cedar Rapids Symphony, 1982—; founder Symphony Sch. of Music, 1986. Chmn. string and conducting faculties U. Utah; faculty Brigham Young U.; founding condr. Snowbird Summer Arts Inst.; founder Bear Lake Music Festival, 1992; guest condr. Preucil Orch. Prin. cellist Utah Symphony. Avocations: fly fishing, boating, outdoor activities. Office: Cedar Rapids Symphony 119 3rd Ave Se Cedar Rapids IA 52401-1403

TIEN, H. TI, biophysics and physiology educator, researcher; b. Beijing, Feb. 01; came to U.S., 1947; s. Fang-cheng and Wen-tsun (Chow) T.; children: Stephen, David, Adrienne, Jennifer; m. Angelica Leitmannova, 1992. B.Sc., U. Nebr., 1953; PhD, Temple U., 1963. Chem. engr. Allied Chem. Corp., Phila., 1953-57; med. scientist Eastern Pa. Psychiat. Inst., Phila., 1957-63; assoc. prof. Northwestern U., Boston, 1963-66, Mich. State U., East Lansing, 1966-70, prof. biophysics, 1970—, chmn. dept., 1978-82. Cons. Hungarian Acad. Sci., Szeged, 1975-76; rsch. prof. Acad. Sinica, Beijing, 1978; cons. prof. Sichuan U., 1984—; cons. Tianjin Econ. Tech. Devel. Area, China; external dir. Ctr. Interface Scis., Slovak Tech. U., Slovakia; cons. prof. Jilin U., Peoples Republic China; frequent lectr. many countries. Author: Bilayer Lipid Membranes, 1974; co-author: Membrane Biophysics, 2000; contbr. chpts. to books. Research grantee NIH, 1964—, NSF, 1978, Dept. Energy, 1980-83, U.S. Naval Rsch. Office, 1985— Mem. AAAS, Biophys. Soc. (council 1972-75), Nat. Inst. Peer Reviewer Achievements include research in membrane biophysics, bioelectrochemistry, photobiology, solar energy conversion via semiconductor septum electrochemical photovoltaic cells (SC-SEP); biomolecular electronic devices. Office: Mich State U Physiology Dept Giltner Hall East Lansing MI 48824 E-mail: tien@msu.edu.

TIGERMAN, STANLEY, architect, educator; b. Chgo., Sept. 20, 1930; s. Samuel Bernard and Emma Louise (Stern) T.; m. Margaret I. McCurry; children: Judson Joel, Tracy Leigh. Student, MIT, Cambridge, 1948-49; BArch, Yale U., New Haven, 1960, MArch, 1961. Archtl. draftsman firm George Fred Keck, Chgo., 1949-50, Skidmore, Owings and Merrill, Chgo., 1957-59, Paul Rudolph, New Haven, 1959-61, Harry Weese, Chgo., 1961-62; ptnr. firm Tigerman & Koglin, Chgo., 1962-64; prin. firm Stanley Tigerman & Assos., Chgo., 1964-82; ptnr. Tigerman Fugman McCurry, Chgo., 1982-88, Tigerman McCurry Archs., Chgo., 1988—. Prof. architecture U. Ill.-Chgo., 1967-71, 80-93, dir. Sch. Architecture, 1985-93; vis. lectr. Yale U., 1974, Cornell U., Ithaca, N.Y., 1963, Cooper Union, 1970, U. Calif. at Berkeley, 1968, Cardiff (Wales) Coll., 1965, Engring. U., Bangladesh, 1967; chmn. AIA com. on design, coordinator exhbn. and book Chicago Architects, 1977; Charlotte Shepherd Davenport prof. architecture Yale U., 1979; architect-in-residence Am. Acad. in Rome, 1980; vis. prof. architecture Harvard U., 1982; William Henry Bishop Chair. prof. architecture Yale U., 1984, Sarrinen prof., 1993; dir. post-professional grad. program U. Ill.-Chgo.; co-founder Archeworks, Design Lab., Chgo., 1993; mem. adv. com. Princeton U., 1997. Prin. works include Ounce of Prevention Educare Ctr., Chgo., Fukuoka Apt. Complex, Japan, Power House, Zion, Ill., Chgo. Children's Adv. Ctr., Holocaust Mus. and Edn. Ctr., Skokie, Ill., Pacific Garden Mission, Chgo.; author: Versus, 1982, Architecture of Exile, 1988, Stanley Tigerman: Buildings and Projects, 1966-89, 1989; contbr. Design of the Housing Site, 1966, Chicago on Foot, 1969, Art Today, 1969, New Direction in American Architecture, 1969, Contemporary Jewelry, 1970, Urban Structures for the Future, 1972, Spaces for Living, 1973, Chicago 1930-70, 1974, Interior Spaces Designed by Architects, 1976, 100 Years of Architecture in Chicago, 1976, 100 Years of Architecture in Chicago, 1986, Mies Reconsidered, 1986, Chicago Architecture 1872-1922, 1988, articles; exhibitions include Venice Biennale, 1976, 1980, Calif. Condition, 1982;, author essay; exhibitions include Chicago Architecture, The New Zeitgeist: In Search of Closure, 1989; author: (catalog) Chicago Architecture, The New Zeitgeist: In Search of Closure, 1989. Pres. Yale Arts Assn., 1969-70; bd. dirs. Bangladesh Found.; adv. com. Yale Sch. Architecture, 1976-2006. Served with USN, 1950-54. Recipient Alpha Rho Chi medal, Yale, 1961, Archtl. Record award, 1970, Masonry award, 1974, Masonry gold medal, 1974, Alumni Art award, Yale U., 1985, Design award for Art Inst. Chgo. Schinkel Exhbn., Am. Soc. Interior Designers, 1995, Humanitarian award, Holocaust Meml. Found. Ill., 2001, Grand award of Excellence, NAHB, 2001, 2003, Recognition award, World Trade Ctr. Meml., 2004, Cultures Achievement award, Univ. Club Chgo., 2004, AIA Topaz medallion, 2007; grantee Advanced Studies in Fine Art, Graham Fedn., 1965. Fellow AIA (chmn. com. design 1976-77, adv. com., Disting. Svc. award Chgo. chpt. 1983, Chgo. Honor awards 1977-79, Nat. Honor award 1982, 84, 87, 91, 98, Nat. Modern Income Housing award 1970, Nat. Homes for Better Living award 1974, 75, Ill. award 1976, Nat. award of Merit 1970, 74, 75, named to Hall of Fame 1990, Disting. Bldg. award for pvt. residence Chgo. chpt. 1991, Chgo. Interior Archtl. Award of Excellence 1981, 83, 87, 91, 92, Nat. Interior Archtl. Award of Excellence 1992-93, Chgo. Disting. Bldg. award 1971, 73, 75, 77, 79, 81, 82, 84, 85, 86, 91, 94, Italian Ceramic Tile Design award 1995, Fukuoka Urban Beautification award 1995, 6 citations of merit Chgo. chpt. 1994, Interior Design award for A.I.C. Schinkel Exhibit 1996, Chgo. Interior Architecture award 1997, Chgo. Chpt. Arch. award 1998, Nat. Interior Architecture award 1998, Louis Sullivan award 2000), Ill./Ind. Masonry Coun. (Silver Award for Excellance in Masonry 2003); mem. Arts Club of Chgo., Yale Club of N.Y.C., Phi Kappa Phi. Office: Tigerman McCurry Archs 444 N Wells St Ste 206 Chicago IL 60610-4522 Office Phone: 312-644-5880. E-mail: tma@tigerman-mccurry.com.

TILL, CHARLES EDGAR, nuclear engineer; b. Can., June 14, 1934; BE, U. Sask., Can., 1956, MS, 1958; PhD in Reactor Physics, U. London, 1960. Jr. rsch. officer physics at. Rsch. Coun. Can., 1956-58; reactor physicist Can. Gen. Electric, 1961-63; asst. physicist Argonne (Ill.) Nat. Lab., 1963-65, assoc. physicist, 1965-66, sect. head exp devel. sect., 1966-68, head critical exp anal sect., 1968-72, mgr. zero power reactor program, 1968-72, assoc. dir. applied physics divsn., 1972-73, dir. applied physics, 1973-80, assoc. lab. dir. engring. rsch., 1980-97, sr. counsellor to lab. dir., 1998; ret., 1998; sr. cons., 1998—. Mem. NAE, Am. Nuc. Soc. (Cisler award 1995), Nat. Acad. Rsch. Office: Argonne Nat Lab 9700 Cass Ave Bldg 208 Argonne IL 60439-4842 Office Phone: 208-254-2812.

TILLER, THOMAS C., manufacturing executive; BA, MIT, 1983; MBA, Harvard U., 1991; M in Mech. Engring., U. Vt. Engr. GE, 1983; mgr. GE Appliances; v.p., gen. mgr. GE Silicones; pres., COO Polaris Industries Inc., Mpls., 1998—99, pres., CEO, 1999—2005, CEO, 2005—. Bd. dir. KTM Power Sports AG. Office: Polaris Industries Inc 2100 Highway 55 Medina MN 55340

TILTON, GLENN F., air transportation executive; b. Washington, Apr. 9, 1948; BA in Internat. Rels., U. S.C., 1970. Sales trainee U.S. mktg. ops. Texaco Inc., Washington, 1970, various assignments, 1970—76, div. supr. mktg. East Brunswick, NJ, 1976—78, area mgr. resale N.Y. div. NYC, 1978, asst. to gen. mgr. northeastern region, 1978—79, mktg. mgr. resale Phila. div., 1979—81, staff coord. corp. planning and econs. dept. Harrison, NY, 1981—83; asst. gen. mgr. sales Texaco Europe, 1983—84, gen. mgr. mktg., 1984—87; v.p. mktg. Texaco U.S.A., Houston, 1984—88; pres. Texaco Refining and Mktg. Inc., Houston, 1988—91; v.p. Texaco Inc., 1989; chmn. Texaco Ltd., 1991—92; pres. Texaco Eruope, 1992—94, Texaco USA, Houston, 1994—2002; sr. v.p. Texaco Inc., 1995—2002; pres. Texaco Global Bus. Unit; CEO Texaco, White Plains, NY, 2001; chmn., pres., CEO UAL Corp. and United Airlines, 2002—. Mem.: bd. dirs., Chevron Texaco (chmn., 2002). Office: UAL PO Box 66100 Chicago IL 60666

TIMBERLAKE, CHARLES EDWARD, historian, educator; b. South Shore, Ky., Sept. 9, 1935; s. Howard Ellis and Mabel Viola (Collier) T.; m. Patricia Alice Perkins, Dec. 23, 1958; children: Mark Brewster, Daniel Edward, Eric Collier BA, Berea Coll., 1957; Calif. State Teaching Credential, Claremont Grad. Sch., 1958, MA, 1962; PhD, U. Wash., 1968. Tchr. Barstow H.S., Calif., 1959-60, Claremont City Sch., Calif., 1960-61; tchg., rsch. asst. U. Wash., Seattle, 1961-64; asst. prof. history U. Mo., Columbia, 1967-73, assoc. prof., 1973-81, prof. history, 1981—, Byler disting. prof., 1996, chmn. dept., 1996—2000, asst. dir. Honors Coll., 1988-90. Exch. prof. Moscow State U., 1985, U. Manchester, England, 1987—88; hon. prof. history Lanzou U., China, 1991; dir. edn. svcs. Leisure Voyages, 1992—2000; vis. prof. Joensuu (Finland) U., 1996, 98, 2000, 03, adj. prof., 2005—. Author: The Fate of Russian Orthodox Monasteries and Convents Since 1917, 1995; editor: Essays on Russian Liberalism, 1972, Detente: A Documentary Record, 1978, Religious and Secular Forces in Late Tsarist Russia, 1992, Profiles of Finland series, 1991-94, (microfiche) The St. Petersburg Collection of Zemstvo Publs., 1992-2000; contbr. chpts. to books, articles to profl. jours. Mem. Citizens Alliance for Progress, Columbia, Mo., 1969—75, pres., 1969—70; founding mem. High Edn. Rescue Operation, Mo., 1983—91; mem. Columbians Against Throw-Aways, 1980—83, Friends of Rock Bridge State Park, 2005—, Friends of Mus. Russian Art, 2005—; assoc. Mus. Art and Archaeology, 2006—. Recipient Disting. Alumnus award Berea Coll., 2002; Fgn. Area fellow, 1965-66, fellow Internat. Rsch. and Exchs. Bd., 1971, 95, 2001, Am. Coun. Learned Socs., 1978-79, Fulbright-Hays fellow, 1995; grantee NEH, 1972, 79, 87; Am. Couns. for Internat. Edn. grantee, 2005. Mem. Am. Assn. Advancement Slavic Studies (bd. dirs. 1980-82, 84-86, chmn. council regional affiliates 1981-82, 85-86, chmn. permanent membership com. 1981-84), Western Slavic Conf., Am. Hist. Assn. (exec. council Conf. on Slavic and East European History 1987-89), Central Slavic Conf. (sec.-treas. 1967-68, pres. 1968-69, 76-77, 83-84, 88-89, 2001-02, exec. bd. 1972—, custodian archive 1972—), Mo. Conf. History (pres. 1992, sec.-treas. 1996-2000), State Hist. Soc. Mo., Fulbright Assn. (pres. Mo. chpt. 1997-2000). Avocations: hiking, travel, theater. Home: 9221 S Rt N Columbia MO 65203-9312 Home Phone: 573-442-4580. Business E-Mail: timberlakec@missouri.edu.

TIMM, MIKE, state legislator; m. Sonia Timm; 4 children. Student, Minot State U., ND. Pres., mgr. Timm Moving & Storage Co.; mem. N.D. Ho. of Reps. from 5th dist., 1973-85, 89—. Chmn. Fin. & Taxation Com. N.D. Ho. of Reps., mem. Transp. Com., spkr. of the house, 1997—. Named Outstanding Jaycee, 1965. Mem. Elks, Eagles, Moose, Am. Legion, Lions. Republican. Home: PO Box 29 Minot ND 58702-0029

TIMM, ROGER K., lawyer; b. Bay City, Mich., May 21, 1947; BS, U. Mich., 1969; JD, Harvard U., 1972. Bar: Mich. 1972. Mem. Dykema Gossett, Detroit. Mem.: ABA, State Bar Mich. Office: Dykema Gossett 400 Renaissance Ctr Detroit MI 48243-1668 Office Phone: 313-568-6597. E-mail: rtimm@dykema.com.

TIMMONS, ROBBIE, news anchor; m. Jim Brandstatter. Grad., Ohio State U. Anchor WILX-TV, Lansing, Mich., 1972—76, WJBK-TV, Detroit, 1976—82, WXYZ-TV, Detroit, 1982—. Recipient numerous Emmy awards, Silver Cir. award, Nat. Acad. TV Arts and Scis., 1998, Most Powerful Woman in Mich., 2002. Achievements include being the first woman in the US to anchor TV news at 6 & 11pm. Office: WXYZ-TV 20777 W Ten Mile Rd Southfield MI 48037 Office Phone: 248-827-9413. Business E-Mail: rtimmons@wxyz.com.

TINDER, JOHN DANIEL, federal judge; b. Indpls., Feb. 17, 1950; s. John Glendon and Eileen M. (Foley) T.; m. Jan M. Carroll, Mar. 17, 1984 BS, Ind. U., 1972, JD, 1975. Bar: Ind. 1975, U.S. Dist. Ct. (so. dist.) Ind., U.S. Ct. Appeals (7th cir.), U.S. Supreme Ct. Assoc. Tinder & O'Donnell, 1975; asst. US atty. (so. dist.) Ind. US Dept. Justice, Indpls., 1975-77; ptnr. Tinder & Tinder, Indpls., 1977—82; pub. defender Marion County Criminal Ct., Indpls., 1977-78; chief trial dep. Marion County Pros. Office, Indpls., 1979-82; assoc. Harrison & Moberly, Indpls., 1982-84; US atty. (so. dist.) Ind. US Dept. Justice, Indpls., 1984-87; judge US Dist. Ct. (so. dist.) Ind., 1987—2007, US Ct. Appeals (7th Cir.), 2007—. Adj. prof. Ind. U. Sch. of Law, Indpls., 1980—88; mem. Supreme Ct. Character & Fitness Com., Ind., 1982— Co-founder Turkey Trot Invitational Race, Indpls., 1980 Recipient Cert. of Appreciation award Bur. Alcohol, Tobacco & Firearms, Indpls., 1976; Service award Marion County Prosecutor, Indpls., 1981 Mem. ABA, Ind. State Bar Assn. (dir. criminal justice sect. 1984—), Indpls. Bar Assn., 7th Circuit Ct. Bar Assn., Fed. Bar Assn. Republican. Roman Catholic. Office: US Ct Appeals 301 Fed Bldg 204 S Main St South Bend IN 46601

TINKER, H(AROLD) BURNHAM, chemical company executive; b. St. Louis, May 16, 1939; s. H(arold) Burnham and Emily (Barnicle) T.; m. Barbara Ann Lydon, Feb. 20, 1965; children: Michael B., Mary K., Ann E. BS in Chemistry, St. Louis U., 1961; MS in Chemistry, U. Chgo., 1964, PhD in Chemistry, 1966. Sr. research chemist Monsanto, St. Louis, 1966-69, research specialist, 1969-73, research group leader, 1973-77, research mgr., 1977-81; tech. dir. Mooney Chems., Inc., Cleve., 1981-90, v.p. rsch. and devel., 1991-94; v.p. corp. devel., 1994—. Patentee in field; contbr. article to profl. jours. Mem. scis. adv. coun. U. Akron, 1995—. Mem. Am. Chem. Soc. (chmn. bd. St. Louis sect. 1978-79), Cleve. Assn. Rsch. Dirs. (v.p. 1989, pres. 1990, bd. dirs. 1991—). Roman Catholic. Avocation: computers. E-mail: burn.tinker@omqi.com.

TINKER, JOHN HEATH, anesthesiologist, educator; b. Cin., May 18, 1941; s. Leonard Henry and Georgia (Reeves) T.; m. Martha Iuen (div. Jan., 1989); children: Deborah H. Lynne, Karen Sue, Juliette Kay; m. Bonnie Howard, Mar. 18, 1989. BS magna cum laude, U. Cin., 1964, MS summa cum laude, 1968. Diplomate Am. Bd. Anesthesiology (sr. examiner 1976—). Surg. intern, resident Harvard Med. Sch., Peter Bent Brigham Hosp., Boston, 1969-70, resident in anesthesiology, 1970-72; cons. anesthesiology Mayo Clinic, Rochester, Minn., 1974-83, chief cardiovascular anesthesiology, 1978-83; prof. anesthesiology U. Iowa Coll. Medicine, Iowa City, 1983-97, chmn. dept., 1983-97; prof., chmn. anesthesiology U. Nebr., Med. Ctr., Omaha, 1997—. Mem. pharm. scis. rev. com., NIH, Bethesda, Md., 1986—; dir. Matrix Med. Inc., Orchard Park, N.Y., 1988—; frequent guest lectr. Author: Controversies in Cardiopulmonary Bypass, 1989 (monograph award Soc. Cardiovascular Anesthsiologists); editor: Anesthesia and Analgesia, Jour. Internat. Anesthesiology Rsch. Soc., 1983—; contbr. over 185 articles to profl. jours. Maj. U.S. Army, 1972-74. NIH grantee, 1977-87. Fellow Royal Coll. Surgeons Australia; mem. Am. Soc. Anesthesiologists (active numerous coms. 1972—), Soc. Cardiovascular Anesthesiologists, Assn. Univ. Anesthetists. Avocations: fishing, golf, modeling ships and airplanes. Office: U Nebr 984455 Nebr Med Ctr Omaha NE 68198-0001

TINKHAM, THOMAS W., lawyer; b. Milw., June 29, 1944; s. Richard Perry and Helen (Savage) T.; m. Jackie Hauser; children: Tamara, Liza, Taylor. BS with honors, U. Wis., 1966; JD with honors, Harvard U., 1969. Bar: Minn. 1969. Ptnr. Dorsey & Whitney, Mpls., 1974—, now ptnr.-in-charge Mpls. off, chmn., comml. contract. litig. Mem. Minn. State Bar (pres. 1991), Hennepin County Bar Assn. (pres. 1980). Office: Dorsey & Whitney Ste 1500 50 S 6th St Minneapolis MN 55402-1498 Office Phone: 612-340-2829. Office Fax: 612-340-2868. Business E-Mail: tinkham.tom@dorsey.com.

TINSMAN, MARGARET NEIR, state legislator; b. Moline, Ill., July 14, 1936; d. Francis Earl and Elizabeth (Lourie) Neir; m. Robert Hovey Tinsman Jr., Feb. 21, 1959; children: Robert Hovey III, Heidi Elizabeth, Bruce MacAlister. BA in Sociology, U. Colo., 1958; MSW, U. Iowa, 1974. Health care coord. Community Health Care, Inc., Davenport, Iowa, 1975-77; assoc. dir. Scott County Info., Referal, and Assistance Svc., Davenport, Iowa, 1977-79; county supr. Scott County Bd. Suprs., Davenport, Iowa, 1978-89; mem. Iowa Senate from 21st dist., Des Moines, 1989—, asst. minority leader, 1992—96, chmn. health and human svcs. appropriations subcom. Chair Iowa Adv. Commn. on Inter-govt. Rels., 1982—84; U.S. country rep. to the German-Am. Symposium German Marshall Plan, 1983; commr. Iowa Dept. Elder Affairs, Des Moines, 1983—89. Chair planning com. Quad City United Way, Davenport; bd. dirs. Bi-State Met. Planning Commn., Davenport, 1981-89, Quad City Devel. Group, Davenport, 1988-90, Am. Lung Assn. Ill., Iowa, Goodwill Industries S.E. Iowa; mem. structure commn. Nat. Episcopal Ch. Named Iowa Social Worker of Yr., NASW, 1978. Mem. Am. Lung Assn. of Ill.-Iowa (bd. dirs. 1989—), Davenport C. of C. (local/state govt. com. 1989—), Nat. Assn. Legislators, Nat. Assn. of Counties (bd. dirs. 1984-89, pres. Women Ofcl. 1984-89), Iowa State Assn. of Counties (bd. dirs. 1983-89, chair), Jr. League (sustaining mem. 1989), Vol. Action Ctr. (pres. 1989), Phi Beta Kappa. Republican. Avocations: tennis, golf, sailing, water and snow skiing. Home: 2865 Hickory Hill Ln Bettendorf IA 52722 Office: 3541 E Kimberly Rd Davenport IA 52807-2552 Office Phone: 563-359-3624.

TIPSORD, MICHAEL L., insurance company executive; b. Ill. B in Acctg., Ill. Wesleyan U.; JD, U. Ill., Urbana-Champaign. CPA; CLU 1991, CPCU 1995. Asst. tax counsel, 1988; with State Farm Ins. Cos., 1988—, dir. acctg., 1995—96, asst. contr., 1996—97, exec. asst., 1997—98, v.p., asst. treas., 1998—2001, v.p., treas., 2001—02, sr. v.p., CFO, 2002—04, vice chmn., CFO, 2004—. Bd. dir. State Farm Lloyds, Inc., Ins. Placement Svc., Inc., State Farm Investment Mgmt. Corp., State Farm V.P. Mgmt. Corp., State Farm Bank, FSB; trustee State Farm Mutual Fund Trust, State Farm Variable Product Trust, State Farm Assoc.'s Funds Trust, State Farm Ins. Co. Employee Retirement Trust, State Farm Ins. Co. Savings and Thrift Trust for US Employees; prof., dept. accountancy U. Ill., Urbana-Champaign. Bd. trustees Ill. Wesleyan U. Mem.: Ill. State Bar Assn., ABA. Office: State Farm Ins Cos 1 State Farm Plz Bloomington IL 61710-0001

TIPTON, DANIEL L., religious organization executive; Gen. supt. Chs. of Christ in Christian Union, Circleville, Ohio, 1990—. Office: Chs of Christ in Christian Union Box 30 1426 Lancaster Pike Circleville OH 43113-9487

TIRONE, BARBARA JEAN, retired health insurance administrator; b. Celina, Ohio, Nov. 19, 1943; d. Vincent James and Theresa Barbara (Goettermoeller) G. BA, Miami U., 1965; MBA, U. Chgo., 1977. Asst. dir. for internat. trade State of Ill., Chgo., Brussels, Hongkong and Sao Paulo, Brazil, 1973-76; dir. office of mgmt. and planning Office Human Devel. Svcs., Chgo., 1976-79; dep. regional adminstr. Health Care Financing Adminstrn., Chgo., 1979-82, regional adminstr., 1982-87, dir. bur. of prog. ops. Balt., 1987-92; dir. health stds. and quality bur. Health Care Fin. Adminstrn., Balt., 1992-96; pres., CEO AdminaStar, Inc., Indpls., 1996-2001; ret., 2002. Recipient Presdl. Disting. Rank award 1988, 94,

Presdl. Meritorious Rank award 1987, 92; named Fed. Exec. of Yr., 1987. Home: 11212 Appaloosa Dr Reisterstown MD 21136 Office Phone: 410-833-5570. Personal E-mail: bgageltirone@verizon.net.

TISHLER, WILLIAM HENRY, landscape architect, educator; b. Baileys Harbor, Wis., June 22, 1936; s. William John and Mary Viola (Sarter) T.; m. Betsy Lehner, Sept. 23, 1961; children: William Phillip, Robin Elizabeth. BS in Landscape Architecture, U. Wis., 1960; M in Landscape Architecture, Harvard U., 1964. Urban planner City of Milw., 1961-62; mem. faculty dept. landscape architecture U. Wis., Madison, 1964—; assoc. Hugh A Dega & Assocs. (Landscape Archs.), 1964-66; prin. Land Plans Inc. (Land and Hist. Preservation Planning Cons.), Madison, 1966—. Advisor emeritus Nat. Trust for Hist. Preservation; bd. dirs. The Hubbard Ednl. Trust. Author: American Landscape Architecture: Designers and Places, 1989, Midwestern Landscape Architecture, 2000, Door County's Emerald Treasure: A History of Peninsula State Park, 2005; contbr. articles to profl. jours. With C.E., U.S. Army, 1960. Recipient Design Arts Program award NEA, 1981, Hawthorn award Friends of The Clearing, 1997, Outstanding Educator award Coun. Educators in Landscape Architecture, 1998; Attingham (Eng.) Program fellow Soc. Archtl. Historians, 1980; Dumbarton Oaks sr. fellow, 1990. Fellow Am. Soc. Landscape Archs. (Horace Cleve. vis. prof. U. Minn. 1993, nat. merit award 1971, 97, 99, honor award 1980, 89, Wis. chpt. Lifetime Achievement award 2000), Coun. Educators Landscape Arch.; mem. Wis. Acad. Arts, Letters and Scis., Pioneer Am. Soc. (Henry Douglas award), Hist. Madison (hon.), Vernacular Architecture Forum (past pres.), Madison Trust for Hist. Preservation, Alliance for Hist. Landscape Preservation (founder), The Clearing Landscape Inst. (founder, dir.), Phi Kappa Phi, Sigma Lambda Alpha, Gamma Sigma Delta, Sigma Nu. Meth. Home: 3925 Regent St Madison WI 53705-5222 Office: U Wis Dept Landscape Architecture Madison WI 53706 Business E-Mail: wtishler@wisc.edu.

TITLEY, LARRY J., lawyer; b. Tecumseh, Mich., Dec. 9, 1943; s. Leroy H. and Julia B. (Ruesink) T.; m. Julia Margaret Neukom, May 23, 1970; children: Sarah Catherine, John Neukom. BA, U. Mich., 1965, JD, 1972. Bar: Va. 1973, Mich. 1973. Assoc. Hunton & Williams, Richmond, Va., 1972-73, Varnum, Riddering, Schmidt & Howlett, Grand Rapids, Mich., 1973—. Trustee Friends Pub. Mus., 1985—94; bd. dirs. Pub. Mus. Found., 1988—97, 2004—, pres., 1992—95; bd. dirs. Camp Optimist YMCA, 1993—98, Peninsular Club, 1994—2003, pres., 1997. Mem. ABA, Mich. Bar Assn., Grand Rapids Bar Assn. Home: 520 Roundtree Dr NE Ada MI 49301-9707 Office: Varnum Riddering Schmidt & Howlett Bridgewater Pl PO Box 352 Grand Rapids MI 49501-0352 E-mail: ljtitley@vrsh.com.

TITLEY, ROBERT L., lawyer; b. Tecumseh, Mich., Dec. 15, 1947; AB, U. Mich., 1970; JD, Duke U., 1973. Bar: Wis. 1973, Mich. 1974. Ptnr. Quarles & Brady, Milw. Mem. editorial bd. Duke Law Jour., 1972-73. Mem. State Bar Mich., State Bar Wis., Order of Coif. Office: Quarles & Brady LLP 411 E Wisconsin Ave Milwaukee WI 53202-4497

TITUS, JACK L., pathologist, educator; b. South Bend, Ind., Dec. 7, 1926; s. Loren O. and Rutha B. (Orr) T.; m. Beverly Harden, June 18, 1949; children—Jack, Elizabeth Ann Titus Engelbrecht, Michael, Matthew, Joan, Marie Titus Davis. BS, Notre Dame U., 1948; MD, Washington U., St. Louis, 1952; PhD, U. Minn., 1962. Practice medicine, Rensselaer, Ind., 1953-57; fellow in pathology U. Minn., 1957-61; assoc. prof. pathology Mayo Grad. Sch., Rochester, Minn., 1961-72; prof. pathology Mayo Med. Sch., 1971-72, coordinator pathology tng. programs, 1964-72; W.L. Moody Jr. prof., chmn. dept. pathology Baylor Coll. Medicine, Houston, 1972-87; chief pathology service Meth. Hosp., Houston, 1972-87; pathologist-in-chief Harris County Hosp. Dist., Houston, 1972-87; chmn. dept. pathology Med. Ctr. Hosp., Conroe, Tex., 1982-87, Woodlands Community Hosp., 1984-87; dir. registry for cardiovascular diseases United Hosp., 1987—95, 1997—2005, sr. cons. registry, 1996-97, dir., 1997—2004; prof. pathology U. Minn., 1987—. Adj. prof. pathology Baylor Coll. Medicine, 1987—; sr. cons. in pathology U. Tex. System Cancer Ctr., Houston, 1974—. Mem. editl. bd. Circulation, 1966-72, Am. Heart Jour., 1972-77, Modern Pathology, 1987-95, Human Pathology, 1988—, Am. Jour. of Cardiovascular Pathology, 1987-94, Cardiovascular Pathology, 1991—, Advances in Pathology, 1998--; contbr. articles to med. jours. With US Army, 1945—47. Recipient Billings gold medal AMA, 1968, Hoektoen gold medal, 1969, Disting. Achievement award Soc. Cardiovascular Pathology, 1993, Scholarly Achievement award Houston Soc. Clin. Pathology, 1993. Mem. Internat. Acad. Pathology, Am. Assn. Pathologists, Am. Soc. Clin. Pathologists, AAAS, AMA, Am. Heart Assn., Coll. Am. Pathologists, Minn. Med. Assn., Minn. Heart Assn., Minn. Soc. Clin. Pathologists, Minn. Acad. Medicine (pres. 1998-99), Ramsey County Med. Soc., Soc. for Cardiovascular Pathology (pres. 1995-97), Sigma Xi, Alpha Omega Alpha. Methodist. Office: 333 Smith Ave Ste 4625 Saint Paul MN 55102-2518

TITZE, INGO ROLAND, physics professor; b. Hirschberg, Silesia, Germany, July 8, 1941; came to U.S. 1955; s. Kurt Herrmann and Marta Emma (Bettermann) T.; m. R. Katherine Pittard, July 19, 1969; children: Karin, Michael, Jason, Gregory BSEE, U. Utah, 1963, MS in Elec. Engring. and Physics, 1965; PhD in Physics, Brigham Young U., 1972. Rsch. engr. N. Am. Aviation, Tulsa, 1965-66, Boeing Co., Seattle, 1968-70; lectr. Calif. State Poly. U., Pomona, 1973-74; asst. prof. U. Petroleum and Minerals Dhahran, Saudi Arabia, 1974-76, Gallaudet Coll., Washington, 1976-79; disting. prof. speech sci. and voice U. Iowa, Iowa City, 1979—. Cons. Bell Labs., Murray Hill, N.J., 1977-78; exec. dir. Wilbur James Gould Voice Rsch. Ctr., Denver Ctr. Performing Arts, 1983—; pres. Voice Cons. Inc., 1985—; panelist, site visitor NRC-NAS, 1984—; regular cons. divsn. rsch. grants NIH, 1986—; chmn. task force on voice Nat. Inst. Deafness and Other Comm. Disorders, 1989; adj. prof. Westminster Choir Coll., Princeton, N.J., 1989-94; dir. Nat. Ctr. for Voice and Speech, 1990—. Author: Principles of Voice Production, 1993, The Myoelastic Aerodynamic Theory of Phonation, 2006; editor: Vocal Fold Physiology: Biomechanics, Acoustics and Phonatory Control, 1985, Vocal Fold Physiology: Frontiers in Basic Science, 1992; assoc. editor Jour. of Voice; contbr. articles to profl. jours. Adv. bd. Voice Found., N.Y.C., 1980—; young men's pres. Latter Day Saints Ch. and Boy Scouts Am., Iowa City, 1982— Jacob Javits Neurosci. Investigator grantee NIH, 1984; recipient William and Harriot Gould Found. award, 1983, Claude Pepper award, 1989, Quintant award Voice Found., 1990, U. Iowa Regents award, 1995; ASHA fellow, 1992. Fellow Acoustical Soc. Am. (tech. coun., awards com. 1989, Silver medal 2007), Am. Laryngological Assn. (hon.; award 1996); mem. Am. Speech-Hearing-Lang. Assn., Nat. Assn. Tchrs. Singing (rsch. coun. 1977—, editl. bd. 1986—), Internat. Assn. Rsch. Singing (dir. publs. 1982—), Am. Assn. Phonetic Scis., Internat. Assn. Logopedics and Phoniatrics, Collegium Medicorium Teatri. Republican. Avocations: singing, tennis, home building. Office: at Ctr for Voice & Speech Univ of Iowa 330 Wjshc Iowa City IA 52242-1012 Home: 1551 Larimer St No 2301 Denver CO 80202

TJEPKES, DAVID A., state representative, protective services official; b. Iowa, Apr. 1944; State trooper, Iowa; state rep. Dist. 50 Iowa House of Reps., 2003—. Mayor City of Gowrie, Iowa. Republican. Office: Iowa House of Reps State Capitol East 12th and Grand Des Moines IA 50319

TKACHUK, KEITH, professional hockey player; b. Melrose, Mass., Mar. 28, 1972; m. Chantel Oster; children: Matthew, Braeden, Taryn. Attended, Boston U., 1990—91. Left wing Winnipeg Jets, 1992—96, Phoenix Coyotes (formerly Winnipeg Jets), 1992—2001, St. Louis Blues, 2001—07, 2007—, Atlanta Thrashers, 2007. Mem. Team USA, World Cup of Hockey, 1996, 2004, USA Olympic Hockey Team, Nagano, Japan, 1998, Salt Lake City, 2002, Torino, Italy, 06. Named NHL Second Team All-Star, 1995, 1998; named to NHL All-Star Game, 1997—99, 2004. Achievements include being a member of World Cup Champion Team USA, 1996; being a member of silver medal winning USA Hockey Team, Salt Lake City Olympics, 2002. Office: St Louis Blues Hockey Club Scottrade Ctr 1401 Clark Ave Saint Louis MO 63103

TOALE, THOMAS EDWARD, school system administrator, minister; b. Independence, Iowa, Aug. 30, 1953; s. Francis Mark and Clara R. (DePaepe) T. BS in Biology, Loras Coll., 1975, MA in Ednl. Adminstrn., 1986; MA in Theology, St. Paul Sem., 1980; PhD in Ednl. Adminstrn., U. Iowa, 1988. Ordained priest Roman Cath. Ch., 1981; cert. tchr., prin., supt., Iowa. Tchr. St. Joseph Key West, Dubuque, Iowa, 1975-77, Marquette High Sch., Bellevue, Iowa, 1981-84, prin., 1984-86; assoc. supt. Archdiocese of Dubuque, 1986-87, supt. schs., 1987—2006, vicar for edn., 2002—. Assoc. pastor St. Joseph Ch., Bellevue, 1981-84; pastor Sts. Peter and Paul Ch., Springbrook, Iowa, 1984-86, St. Peter, Temple Hill, Cascade, Iowa, 1986—. Mem. Nat. Cath. Edn. Assn. (past pres., chief adminstrn. Cath. edn.). Office: Archdiocese of Dubuque 1229 Mount Loretta Ave Dubuque IA 52003-7826

TOAN, BARRETT A., former health products executive; s. Winthrop A. and Edith Byrne Toan; m. Polly O'Brien; children: Elliot, Frannie. BA in history, Kenyon Coll., 1969; MBA, U. Pa., 1974. With budget bur. State of Ill., Springfield; positions with State of Pa.; cons. PriceWaterhouse, Washington; commr. divsn. social svcs. State of Ark., 1979—81; dir. dept. social svcs. State of Mo., 1981—85; exec. dir., COO Sanus Health Plan of St. Louis, 1985—91; pres. Express Scripts Inc., Maryland Heights, Mo., 1990—2002, CEO, 1992—2005, chmn., 2000—06. Bd. dirs. Pharm. Care Mgmt. Assn., Sigma-Aldrich Corp. Mem. bd. dirs., treas. Mentor St. Louis. Named Entrepreneur of Yr. Inc. Mag., 1994.

TOBACCOWALA, RISHAD, marketing professional; b. Bombay, 1959; BA in Maths., U. Bombay, 1979; MBA, U. Chgo., 1982. Media buyer Leo Burnett USA, Chgo., 1982-84, account supr., 1984-92, v.p., account dir. direct mkg., 1992-94, dir. interactive mktg., 1994-96; pres. Giant Step, Chgo., 1996; now v.p., acct. dir. interactive mktg. Leo Burnett USA, Chgo., exec. v.p. Starcom IP, 2000—. Office: Leo Burnett USA 35 W Wacker Dr Chicago IL 60601-1614

TOBIAS, CHARLES HARRISON, JR., lawyer; b. Cin., Apr. 16, 1921; s. Charles Harrison and Charlotte (Westheimer) T.; m. Mary J. Kaufman, June 15, 1946 (dec. May 2, 2005); children— Jean M., Thomas Charles, Robert Charles. BA cum laude, Harvard U., 1943, LL.B., 1948. Bar: Ohio 1949. Assoc. firm Steer, Strauss and Adair, Cin., 1949-56; ptnr. firm Steer, Strauss, White and Tobias, Cin., 1956-90; mem. Kepley MacConnell & Eyrich, Cin., 1990-93; mediator U.S. Ct. Appeals (6th crct.), Cin., 1993—. Bd. dirs. Cin. City Charter Com., 1955-75; mem. Wyoming (Ohio) City Council, 1972-77, vice mayor, 1974-77; bd. govs., past chmn. Cin. Overseers, Hebrew Union Coll.-Jewish Inst. Religion; pres. Met. Area Religious Coalition of Cin., 1977-80, Jewish Fedn. Cin., 1972-74; mem. nat. bd. govs. Am. Jewish Com., 1981-87. With USN, 1943-46. Mem. Cin. Bar Assn., Losantiville Country Club. Office: US Ct Appeals Potter Stewart US Courthse 5th and Walnut St Cincinnati OH 45202 Home: 2115 Evergreen Ridge Dr Cincinnati OH 45215-5713 Office Phone: 513-564-7330.

TOBIAS, PAUL HENRY, lawyer; b. Cin., Jan. 5, 1930; s. Charles H. and Charlotte (Westheimer) T.; 1 child, Eliza L. AB magna cum laude, Harvard U., 1951, LLB, 1958. Bar: Mass. 1958, Ohio 1962. Assoc. Stoneman & Chandler, Boston, 1958-61, Goldman & Putnick, Cin., 1962-75; ptnr. Tobias, Kraus and Torchia, Cin., 1976—. Instr. U. Cin. Law Sch., 1975-77. Author: Litigating Wrongful Discharge Claims, 1987; co-author: Job Rights and Survivor Strategies, a Handbook for Terminated Employees, 1997; contbr. articles to profl. jours. Mem. Cin. Bd. of Park Commrs., 1973-81, Cin. Human Rels. Commn., 1980-84, Cin. Hist. Conservation Bd., 1990-91. With U.S. Army, 1952-54. Mem. ABA, Nat. Employment Lawyers Assn. (founder), Nat. Employee Rights Inst. (chmn.; editor-in-chief Employee Rights quar. 2000-02), Ohio State Bar Assn., Cin. Bar Assn. (past chmn. legal aid com.), Phi Beta Kappa. Home: 15 Hill And Hollow Ln Cincinnati OH 45208-3317 Office: Tobias Kraus Torchia 911 Mercantile Libr Bldg Cincinnati OH 45202 Office Phone: 513-241-8137. Business E-Mail: tkt@tktlaw.com.

TOBIN, PATRICK JOHN, dermatologist; b. Bay City, Mich., Sept. 20, 1938; s. John Howard and Dorothy Ida (De Matio) T.; m. Suzanne Lane Bumstead, Apr. 11, 1959; children: Jennifer Lane, Suzannah Lane, Benjamin Lane. AS, Bay City Jr. Coll., 1958; MD, U. Mich., 1964. Diplomate Am. Bd. Dermatology. Intern Munson Med. Ctr., Traverse City, Mich., 1964-65, mem. active staff, 1970—; resident Univ. Hosp., Ann Arbor, Mich., 1965-68. Lt. comdr. USN, 1968-70. Fellow Am. Acad. Dermatology; mem. Mich. State Med. Soc., AMA, Am. Soc. for Dermatologic Surgery, Alpha Omega Alpha, Grand Traverse Yacht Club (commodore 1977), Grand Traverse Ski Club (pres. 1975). Avocations: skiing, bicycling, sailing, travel, reading. Home: 7777 Truesdale Ln Traverse City MI 49686-1667 Office: orthwestern Mich Dermatol 550 Munson Ave Ste 200 Traverse City MI 49686-3580 Home Phone: 231-946-2264; Office Phone: 231-935-8717.

TOCCO, JAMES, pianist; b. Detroit, Sept. 21, 1943; s. Vincenzo and Rose (Tabbita) T.; 1 child, Rhoya. Prof. music Ind. U., Bloomington, 1977-91; prof. Musikhochschule, Lübeck, Germany, 1990—2006, Manhattan Sch. Music, 2002—; eminent scholar, artist-in-residence U. Cin. Coll.-Conservatory Music, 1991—; artistic dir. Great Lakes Chamber Music Festival, 1994—. Debut with orch., Detroit, 1956, since performed with Chgo. Symphony, LA Philharm., Cin. Symphony, Detroit Symphony, Nat. Symphony, Balt. Symphony, Atlanta Symphony, Denver Symphony, Montreal Symphony, Philharm. Orch., London Symphony, London Philharm., BBC Orch., Berlin Philharm., Moscow Radio-TV Orch., Amsterdam Philharm., Munich Philharm., Bavarian Radio Orch., Royal Concertebouw Orch., also recitals, US and abroad, and performances, CBS and NBC networks; guest performer, White House; Recs. include the complete preludes of Chopin, collected piano works of Leonard Bernstein, complete piano works of Charles Tomlinson Griffes, 4 piano sonatas of Edward MacDowell, selected piano works of Aaron Copland, complete Bach-Liszt organ transcriptions, piano works of John Corigliano. concertos of Igor Stravinsky, Leonard Bernstein, and John Corigliano. Recipient Bronze medal Tchaikovsky Competition, Moscow 1970, Queen Elisabeth of Belgium Competition, Brussels 1972, Salzburg Festival, 1st prize Piano Competition of Americas, Rio de Janeiro 1973, Munich Internat. Competition 1973. Office: U Cin Coll Conservatory Musi Cincinnati OH 45221-0001 Business E-Mail: toccojv@ucmail.uc.edu.

TODD, JOHN JOSEPH, lawyer; b. St. Paul, Mar. 16, 1927; s. John Alfred and Martha Agnes (Jagoe) Todd; m. Dolores Jean Shanahan, Sept. 9, 1950; children: Richard M., Jane E., John P. Student, St. Thomas Coll., 1944, 46-47; BSc and Law, U. Minn., 1949, LLB, 1950. Bar: Minn. 1951. Practice in, South St. Paul, Minn., 1951-72; partner Thuet and Todd, 1953-72; asso. justice Minn. Supreme Ct., St. Paul, 1972-85; sole practice West St. Paul, 1985-92; of counsel Brenner & Glassman Ltd., Mpls., 1992—99, Orme & Assoc., Eagan, Minn., 1999—. With USNR, 1945—46. Mem.: VFW. Home: 6689 Argenta Trl W Inver Grove Heights MN 55077-2208 Office: Orme & Assocs 4040 Nicols Rd Saint Paul MN 55121 Home Phone: 651-454-1113; Office Phone: 651-688-7646. Personal E-mail: jjbtodd@comcast.net. Business E-Mail: jtodd@ormelaw.com.

TODD, ROBERT FRANKLIN, III, oncologist, educator; b. Granville, Ohio, Apr. 16, 1948; m. Susan Erhard, 1977; children: Currier Nathaniel, Andrew Joseph. AB, Duke U., 1970, PhD, 1975, MD, 1976. Diplomate Am. Bd. Internal Medicine. Intern Peter Bent Brigham Hosp., Boston, 1976-77, resident, 1977-78; fellow in oncology Sidney Farber Cancer Inst., Boston, 1978-80; clin. fellow in medicine Harvard Med. Sch., Boston, 1978-81; postdoctoral fellow divsn. tumor immunology Sidney Farber Cancer Inst., Boston, 1979-81; asst. prof. medicine Harvard Med. Sch., Boston, 1981-84; assoc. prof. internal medicine U. Mich., Ann Arbor, 1984-88, assoc. prof. cellular and molecular biology, 1985-88, assoc. dir. divsn. hematology-oncology internal medicine, 1987-91, prof. internal medicine, 1988—, assoc. chair for rsch. dept. internal medicine, 1989-91, assoc. chair dept. internal medicine, 1991-93, chief divsn. hematology-oncology dept. internal medicine, 1993—2007, assoc. v.p. rsch., 1999—2005, Frances and Victor Ginsberg prof. hematology/oncology, 1999—, interim chair, dept. internal medicine, 2007—. Attending physician U. Mich. Hosps., 1984—. Contbr. numerous articles to profl. jours.; patentee in field. Mem.: Assn. Am. Physicians, Am. Soc. Clin. Investigation, S.W. Oncology Group, Ctrl. Soc. Clin. Rsch. (councilor 1997—, pres. 2001—02), Am. Fedn. Clin. Rsch. (councilor midwest chpt. 1986—89), Am. Soc. Hematology (councilor 2005—), Soc. Leukocyte Biology (councilor 1996—99), Am. Soc. Clin. Oncology, Am. Assn. Cancer Rsch., Am. Assn. Immunologists, ACP, Alpha Omega Alpha, Phi Beta Kappa. Office: U Mich Med Sch 1500 E Med Ctr Dr 3101 Taubman Ctr Ann Arbor MI 48109-5368 Business E-Mail: robtodd@umich.edu.

TODD, WILLIAM MICHAEL, lawyer; b. Cleve., Dec. 13, 1952; s. William Charles and Jennie Ann (Diana) T. BA with hon., U. Notre Dame, 1973; JD cum laude, Ohio State U., 1976. Bar: Ohio 1976, U.S. Dist. Ct. (so. dist.) Ohio 1977, U.S. Supreme Ct. 1987. Assoc. Porter, Wright, Morris & Arthur, Columbus, Ohio, 1976-82, ptnr., 1983-93, Squire, Sanders & Dempsey, Columbus, 1993—2006; of counsel Benesch Friedlander, Columbus, 2006—. Trustee Callvac Svcs., Columbus, Ohio, 1985—91, pres., 1988; trustee Opera Columbus, 2004—. Mem. ABA (governing com. forum on health law 1988-91), Ohio Bar Assn., Columbus Bar Assn., Am. Soc. Med. Assn. Counsel, Am. Bd. Trial Advocates, Ohio Soc. Healthcare Attys. (pres. 1999-2000), Am. Health Lawyers Assn., Rep. Nat. Lawyers Assn. (chmn. Ohio chpt. 2005—), Columbus Athletic Club. Roman Catholic. Avocations: music, recreational sports. Office: Benesch Friedlander et al 41 S High St Columbus OH 43215-6101 Office Phone: 614-223-9348, 614-885-7136. Business E-Mail: wtodd@bfca.com.

TOELKES, DIXIE E., state legislator; m. Roger Toelkes. Educator; mem. from dist. 53 Kans. State Ho. of Reps., Topeka. Office: Kans House of Reps State House Topeka KS 66612 Home: 1514 SE 43rd Pl Topeka KS 66609-1685

TOFT, RICHARD P(AUL), title insurance executive; b. St. Louis, Sept. 20, 1936; s. Paul C. and Hazel F. T.; m. Marietta Von Etzdorf, Oct. 5, 1963; children: Christopher P., Douglas J. BSBA, U. Mo., 1958. With Lincoln Nat. Life Ins. Co., 1959—69, group and pension sales mgr., 1969—73; 2d v.p. Lincoln Nat. Sales Corp., Ft. Wayne, Ind., 1973—74, v.p., 1974—80, v.p., treas., 1980—81; pres. Chgo. Title Ins. Co., 1981—82; pres., CEO, dir. Chgo. Title Ins. Co. and Chgo. Title and Trust Co., 1982—. Dir. Lincoln Nat. Devel. Corp. Trustee Chgo. Cmty. Trust, 1982. 2d lt. US Army, 1958—59. Mem.: Am. Land Title Assn., Union League Chgo. Congregationalist. Office: Chgo Title & Trust Co 171 N Clark St Chicago IL 60601-3203

TOIRAC, S(ETH) THOMAS, software engineering executive, consultant; b. Ft. Wayne, Ind., May 17, 1951; s. Florent D. and Dorothy M. (Lee) T.; m. Martha J. Rife, Dec. 20, 1969 (div. 1979); 1 child, Kristina M.; m. Linda D. Benecke, Aug. 2, 1987 (div. 1999); children: Danielle Shari, Anthony David; m. Deborah L. Schiller, ov. 16, 2001. Student, Grace Coll., 1970. Computer operator United Telephone Co., Warsaw, Ind., 1968-69; programmer-analyst GTE Data Svcs., Ft. Wayne, 1970-76, systems programmer, 1976-79, systems supr., 1979-82; mgr. software N.Am. Van Lines, 1982-84, dir. computing svcs., 1984-90; founder, exec. dir. Pioneer Missionary, Inc., 1990-94; CFO Pillar Pub., New Carlisle, 1990-94; exec. v.p. Kessington Network, Indpls., 1990-91; info. mgmt. cons., 1991-95; sr. consulting engr. Lexis-Nexis, Inc., Dayton, Ohio, 1995-98, mgr. devel. svcs., 1998—2001, mgr. sys. support, 2001—. Chmn. GTE Tech. Adv. Group, 1978—79; cons. in field. Sec.-treas. bd. dirs. Greater Ft. Wayne Crime Stoppers, 1986-91; lay min. Wesleyan Meth. Ch., Ft. Wayne, 1974-75; mem. Share, Inc., 1976-81. Republican. Avocations: photography, personal computers. E-mail: tom.toirac@lexisnexis.com.

TOLAND, CLYDE WILLIAM, lawyer; b. Iola, Kans., Aug. 18, 1947; s. Stanley E. and June E. (Thompson) T.; m. Nancy Ellen Hummel, July 27, 1974; children: David Clyde, Andrew John, Elizabeth Kay. BA in History, U. Kans., 1969, JD, 1975; MA in 17th Century English History, U. Wis., Madison, 1971. Bar: Kans. 1975, U.S. Dist. Ct. Kans. 1975, U.S. Supreme Ct. 1980. Atty. Toland and Thompson LLC, Iola, 1975—2006; pvt. practice Iola, 2006—. Contbr. articles to profl. publs. Mem. exec. com. Friends of Libr., U. Kans., 1977-92, pres., 1988-91, Allen County Hist. Soc., Inc., 1990-95, v.p. 1998-2006, exec. dir., curator, 2006-; founder Ann. Buster Keaton Celebration, Iola, co-chmn., 1993-97; leader restoration Frederick Funston Boyhood Home, 1991-95; Chief planner, remodeling designer Allen County Mus., 2003—2005. Recipient Appreciation cert. DAR, 1995, First Cmty. Svc. award Current Events Club, Iola, 1998; co-recipient (with US Sen. Nancy Kassebaum) First Alumni Disting. Achievement award Coll. Liberal Arts and Scis. U. Kans., 1996; Paul Harris fellow Rotary Internat., 1986;. Fellow Kans. Bar Found.; mem. ABA, Kans. Bar Assn. (Outstanding Svc. award 1988), Allen County Bar Assn., U. Kans. Alumni Assn. (Strickland award 1969), Iola Rotary Club (pres. 1985-86, Outstanding Cmty. Svc. plaque 1996), Iola Jaycees, Phi Beta Kappa, Order of Coif, Omicron Delta Kappa (presdl. plaque 1969). Republican. Presbyterian. Avocations: speaking on estate planning and history, historical field trips. Office: PO Box 163 Iola KS 66749*

TOLBERT, NATHAN EDWARD, biochemistry educator, plant pathologist; b. Twin Falls, Idaho, May 19, 1919; s. Edward and Helen (Mills) T.; m. Evelynne Cedarlund, June 21, 1952 (dec. Nov. 1963); children— Helen, Carol, James; m. Eleanor Dalgleish, June 22, 1964 BS in Chemistry, U. Calif., Berkeley, 1941; PhD in Biochemistry, U. Wis., 1950. Prof. biochemistry Mich. State U., East Lansing, 1958-89, prof. emeritus, 1989—. Editor: Biochemistry of Plants, Vol. 1, 1980; editor 3 sci. jours.; contbr. numerous papers, revs., abstracts to profl. publs.; patentee in field Served to capt. USAF, 1943-45, PTO Named disting. prof. Mich. State U., 1963, Mich. Scientist of Yr., 1985; Fulbright fellow, 1969; grantee NSF, NIH Mem. Nat. Acad. Sci., Am. Soc. Plant Physiology (pres. 1983-84, Stephen Hale award 1980), Am. Soc. Biol. Chemists, Am. Chem. Soc., Nat. Acad. Sci. Avocation: travel. Office: Mich State U Dept Biochemistry East Lansing MI 48824

TOLCHINSKY, PAUL DEAN, organization design psychologist; b. Cleve., Sept. 30, 1946; s. Sanford Melvin and Frances (Klein) T.; m. Laurie S. Schermer, Nov. 3, 1968 (div. Jan. 1982); m. Kathy L. Dworkin, June 19, 1988; children: Heidi E., Dana M. BA, Bowling Green State U., 1971; PhD, Purdue U., 1978. Asst. br. mgr., tng. instr. Detroit Bank and Trust, 1971-73; mgr. tng. and devel. nuclear divsn. Babcock and Wilcox Co., Barberton, Ohio, 1973-75; internal cons. food products divsn. Gen. Foods Corp., West Lafayette, Ind., 1975-77; grad. tchg. asst. Krannert Grad. Sch. Mgmt. Purdue U., West Lafayette, 1975-78; asst. prof. mgmt. Coll. Bus. Adminstrn. Fla. State U., Tallahassee, 1978-79, U. Akron, Ohio, 1979-81; pres. Performance Devel. Assocs., Cleve., 1975—; ptnr. Dannemiller Tyson Assocs., Cleve., 1994-99; mng. ptnr. Performance Devel. Assocs., 2000—. Sr. lectr. Case Western Res. U., 2002—. Contbr. articles to profl. publs. Bd. dirs. Temple Tiferth Israel, Cleve., 195, Cleve. Jewish News, Jewish Family Svcs. Assn. Cleve. With U.S. Army, 1966-69, Vietnam. Mem. APA, Acad. Mgmt. Democrat. Jewish. Avocations: running, travel. Office: Performance Devel Assocs 50 Fox Glen Rd Moreland Hills OH 44022 Home Phone: 440-349-1441; Office Phone: 440-349-1990. Personal E-mail: kdtpdt@aol.com.

TOLEDO-PEREYRA, LUIS HORACIO, transplant surgeon, researcher, historian educator; b. Nogales, Ariz., Oct. 19, 1943; s. Jose Horacio and Elia (Pereyra) Toledo; m. Marjean May Gilbert, Mar. 21, 1974; children: Alexander Horacio, Suzanne Elizabeth. BS magna cum laude, Regis Coll., 1960; MD, Nat. U. Mex., 1967, MS in Internal Medicine, 1970; PhD in Surgery, U. Minn., 1984. Intern Hosp. Juarez, Nat. U. Mex., 1966; resident in internal medicine Instituto Nacional de la utricions, Nat. U. Mex., 1968, 70; resident in surgery U. Minn., 1970-76; resident in thoracic and cardiovascular surgery U. Chgo., 1976-77; dir. surg. rsch. Henry Ford Hosp., Detroit, 1977-79; co-dir. transplantation, 1977-79; chief transplantation, dir. surg. rsch. Mt. Carmel Mercy Hosp., Detroit, 1979-89; chief transplantation, dir. rsch. Borgess Med. Ctr., Kalamazoo, 1990-99, 90—; clin. prof. surgery Mich. State U., 1993-96, prof. surgery, 1996—. Adj. prof. Sch. Health Sci. Mercy Coll., Detroit, 1983-91, history Western Mich. U., 1990—, biol. sci., 1991-96; prof. surgery Nat. U. Mex., 1990-96. Guest editor various med. and transplant jours.; mem. editl. bd. Dialysis and Transplantation, 1979—, Rsch. in Surgery, 1991—, Cirugia Iberoamericana, 1992—, clin. adv. bd. Transpl. Proc., 1993—, Medico Interamericano, 1993—, Cirugia Espanola, 1994—; assoc. editor Transplantology, 1990—; contbr. over 800 publs. on organ preservation, transplantation, other surg. and med. related areas, and the history of medicine to profl. jours. Recipient Outstanding Achievement award U. Mex., 1961, 64, 67; Resident Rsch. award Assn. Acad. Surgery, 1974; Cecil Lehman Mayer Rsch. award Am. Coll. Chest Physicians, 1975, Surgery Rsch. Nat. award Mex. Assn. Gen. Surgery, 1993. Mem. AMA, Transplantation Soc., Assn. Acad. Surgery, Am. Soc. Transplant Surgery, Soc. Organ Sharing (pres., founder), Am. Assn. History Medicine, Am. Soc. Nephrology, Am. Assn. Immunologists, Am. Physiol. Soc., Soc. Exptl. Biology and Medicine, Am. Soc. Artificial Organs, Am. Diabetes Assn., European Soc. Study of Diabetes, No. Am. Soc. Dialysis Transplantation (pres., founder), Pan Am. Soc. Dialysis Transplantation (pres. elect, founder), Transplantation Soc. Mich. (pres., exec. bd.). Roman Catholic. Home: 3598 Whistling Ln Portage MI 49024-5545 Office: Borgess Med Ctr 1631 Gull Rd Ste 110 Kalamazoo MI 49048-1626

TOLIA, VASUNDHARA K., pediatric gastroenterologist, educator; b. Calcutta, India; came to U.S., 1975; d. Rasiklal and Saroj (Kothari) Doshi; m. Kirit Tolia, May 30, 1975; children: Vinay, Sanjay. MBBS, Calcutta U., 1968-75. Intern, resident Children's Hosp. Mich., Detroit, 1976-79, fellow, 1979-81, dir. pediat. endoscopy unit, 1984-90, dir. pediat. gastroenterology and nutrition, 1990—2005. Instr. Wayne State U., Detroit, 1981—83, asst. prof., 1983—91, assoc. prof., 1991—97, prof., 1997—2005; adjunct prof. pediat. Mich. State U., 2008—. Mem. editl. bd. Inflammatory Bowel Diseases, 1999-2005 Am. Jour. Gastroenterology, 1999-2005, Rev. of World Lit. in Pediatrics, 1999—, AAP Grand Rounds and Therapy, 2006—; contbr. articles to profl. jours. Named Woman of Distinction, Mich. chpt. Crohn's and Colitis Found. Am., 1991. Fellow Am. Coll. Gastroenterology (chair ad-hoc com. pediat. gastroenterology 1998-2000), Am. Acad. Pediats.; mem. Am. Gastroenterology Assn., N.Am. Soc. Pediat. Gastroenterology and Nutrition, Soc. Pediat. Rsch. Office Phone: 248-568-1500.

TOLL, DANIEL ROGER, corporate financial executive, volunteer; b. Denver, Dec. 3, 1927; s. Oliver W. and Merle D'Aubigne (Sampson) T.; m. Sue Andersen, June 15, 1963; children: Daniel Andersen, Matthew Mitchell. AB magna cum laude (Pyne prize), Princeton U., 1949; MBA with distinction, Harvard U., 1955. With Deep Rock Oil Corp., Tulsa, 1949-51, asst. mgr. product supply and distbn.; with Helmerich & Payne, Tulsa, 1955-64, roughneck, landman, exploration mgr., pipeline constrn. mgr., v.p. fin., 1961-64; with Sunray DX Oil Co., Tulsa, 1964-69, treas., v.p. corp. planning and devel.; v.p. Sun Oil Co., 1969; with Walter E. Heller Internat. Corp., Chgo., 1970-85, sr. v.p. fin., dir., 1970-80, pres., dir., 1980-85, corp. and civic dir., 1985—. Bd. dirs. Mallinckrodt, Inc. (formerly IMCERA Group Inc.), Kemper Nat. Ins. Co., Lincoln Nat. Income Fund, Inc., Lincoln Nat. Convertible Securities, Inc. Vice chmn. Tulsa Cmty. Chest, 1964-66; v.p., bd. dirs. Tulsa Opera, 1960-69; bd. dirs. Tulsa Little Theatre, 1963-69, Internat. House, Chgo., 1984-87; bd. dirs. Inroads, Inc., 1973-95, nat. vice chmn., 1982-95; bd. dirs. Chgo. Area coun. Boy Scouts Am., 1976-94, pres., 1981-83; mem. Kenilworth (Ill.) Sch. Bd. Dist. 38, 1975-81, pres., 1978-81; bd. dirs., mem. exec. com., chmn. fin. and hosp. affairs coms. Evanston (Ill.) Northwestern Healthcare, Inc., 1982—; bd. dirs. Chgo. Met. Planning Coun., 1989—, pres., 1991-94; bd. dirs. Northwestern Healthcare Network, Inc., 1995-99; trustee Princeton U., 1990-94. Lt. (j.g.) USNR, 1951-52. Baker scholar Harvard U., 1955. Mem. Chgo. Assn. Commerce and Industry (bd. dirs. 1979-86), Chgo. Club, Comml. Club, Econ. Club, Harvard Bus. Sch. Club (past pres., bd. dirs. 1971-91), Indian Hill Club (bd. govs. 1987-90), Princeton Club (past pres., bd. dirs. 1985—), Phi Beta Kappa. Home: 1005 Mount Pleasant Rd Winnetka IL 60093-3614 Office: Ste 300 560 Green Bay Rd Winnetka IL 60093-2242

TOLL, PERRY MARK, lawyer, educator; b. Kansas City, Mo., Oct. 28, 1945; s. Mark Irving and Ruth (Parker) T.; m. Mary Anne Shottenkirk, Aug. 26, 1967; children: Andrea Lynne, Hillary Anne. BS in Polit. Sci. and Econs., U. Kans., 1967, JD, 1970. Bar: Mo. 1970 1970, U.S. Dist. Ct. (we. dist.) Mo. 1970, U.S. Tax. Ct. 1979, U.S. Supreme Ct. 1979. With Shughart, Thomson & Kilroy P.C., Kansas City, 1970—, pres., 1995—2006, past chmn. bus. dept. Asst. prof. deferred compensation U. Mo., Kansas City, 1979-83; bd. dirs., pres. Heart of Am. Tax Inst., Kansas City, 1975-87. Mem., chmn. Prairie Village (Kans.) Bd. Zoning Appeals, 1977-95. Mem. ABA, Mo. Bar Assn., Am. Health Lawyers Assn., Am. Agr. Law Assn., Mo. Merchants and Mfrs. Assn., Greater Kansas City Med. Mgrs. Assn., Lawyers Assn. Kansas City, East Kans. Estate Planning Coun. (bd. dirs., pres.), Phi Kappa Tau (bd. dirs. Beta Theta chpt.). Office: Shughart Thomson & Kilroy 12 Wyandotte Plz 120 W 12th St Ste 1500 Kansas City MO 64105-1929

TOLL, SHELDON SAMUEL, lawyer; b. Phila., June 6, 1940; s. Herman and Rose (Ornstein) T.; m. Roberta Darlene Pollack, Aug. 11, 1968; children: Candice Moore, John Maitland, Kevin Scott. BA, U. Pa., 1962; MA, Oxford U., Eng., 1964; JD, Harvard U., 1967. Bar: Pa. 1967, Mich. 1972, Ill. 1990, Tex. 1990, U.S. Dist. Ct. (ea. dist.) Pa. 1968, U.S. Ct. Appeals (3d cir.) 1970, U.S. Supreme Ct. 1971, Mich. 1972, U.S. Dist. Ct. (ea. dist.), U.S. Ct. Appeals (6th cir.) 1973, U.S. Ct. Appeals (5th cir.) 1978, U.S. Dist. Ct. (no. dist.) Calif. 1986, U.S. Ct. Appeals (9th cir.) 1987, U.S. Dist. Ct. (ea. dist.) Wis. 1989. Assoc. Montgomery, McCracken et al, Phila., 1967-72; sr. ptnr. Honigman Miller Schwartz and Cohn, Detroit, 1972—2003; prin. Sheldon S. Toll PLLC, Southfield, Mich., 2003—. Panelist Bankruptcy Litigation Inst., N.Y.C., 1984-94. Author: Toll's Pennsylvania Crime Code, 2005, Bankruptcy Litigation Manual, 2004. Bd. dirs. Southeastern Mich. chpt. ARC, Detroit. Mem. Fed. Bar Assn. (past pres. Detroit chpt.), ABA, Pa. Bar Assn., Phila. Bar Assn., Franklin (Mich.) Hills Country Club, Mar-a-Lago Club (Palm Beach, Fla.), Phi Beta Kappa. Democrat. Jewish. Office: Sheldon S Toll PLLC 2000 Town Ctr Ste 2100 Southfield MI 48075 Office Phone: 248-351-5480. Business E-Mail: lawtoll@comcast.net.

TOLLEFSON, BEN C., state legislator, retired utilities executive; b. Minot, ND, June 14, 1927; s. Ben K. and Hannah G. (Espeseth) T.; m. Lila R. Adams, Apr. 11, 1949; children: Robb, LuAnn, David, Richard. Student, Minot State U., 1946-48. Advt. salesman Minot Daily News, 1956-57; utility salesman No. States Power Co., Minot, 1957-72, sales mgr., 1972-89; retired, 1989; advisor Ctrl. Venture Capital, Minot, 1990-95; mem. N.D. Ho. of Reps., Bismark, 1984-99, N.D. Senate from 38th dist., Bismark, 2001—. Pres. Minot Jaycees, 1957. Served with USN, 1945-47. Recipient Clara Barton Svc. award Am. Red Cross, 1969; named one of Outstanding Young Men Am., Minot Jaycees, 1958, State Ofcl. Yr., Nat. Assn. Home Builders, 1992. Mem. Kiwanis (Minot lt. gov. 1973, Outstanding Lt. Gov. 1973). Republican. Lutheran. Avocations: hunting, public speaking. Home: 500 Twenty Fourth St NW Minot ND 58701

TOLLEFSON, LEE, architect; BArch, U. Minn.; MArch, U. Pa. Adj. prof., design studio & N. Am. Indian architecture U. Minn., Mpls., 1970—; ptnr. Rafferty, Rafferty, Tollefson Archs., St. Paul, 1983—. Fellow: AIA. Office: CALA Ralph Rapson Hall 89 Church St SE Minneapolis MN 55455 E-mail: tolle001@umn.edu.

TOLLESTRUP, ALVIN VIRGIL, physicist; b. Los Angeles, Mar. 22, 1924; s. Albert Virgil and Maureen (Petersen) T.; m. Alice Hatch, Feb. 26, 1945 (div. Nov. 1970); children: Kristine, Kurt, Eric, Carl; m. Janine Cukay, Oct. 11, 1986. BS, U. Utah, 1944; PhD, Calif. Inst. Tech., 1950. Mem. faculty Calif. Inst. Tech., Pasadena, 1950-77, prof. physics, 1968-77; scientist Fermi Nat. Lab., Batavia, Ill., 1977-93; co-spokesman CDF Collaboration, 1977-93. Co-developer superconducting magnets for Tevatron, Fermi Lab. Served to lt. (j.g.) USN, 1944-46. NSF fellow; Disting. Alumni award Calif. Inst. Tech., 1993. Fellow AAAS, NAS, Am. Phys. Soc. (R.R. Wilson prize 1989, Nat. medal for tech. 1989). Democrat. Office: Fermi Nat Lab PO Box 500 Batavia IL 60510-0500

TOLVA, JOHN, information technology manager; b. Chgo., 1972; m. Robyn Tolva; 3 children. BA, Vanderbilt U.; MA in Eng. Lit., Washington U.; MS in Info. Design & Tech., Georgia Inst. Tech. Prodr., events webcasting group IBM Corp., Atlanta, 1997—2000; global program. mgr. cultural strategy & programs IBM Corp. Comty. Relations, Chgo., 2000—; creative dir. Ctr. IBM e-Bus. Innovation, Chgo. Named one of 40 Under 40, Crain's Chgo. Bus., 2006. Home Phone: 773-755-2563; Office Phone: 312-529-2840. E-mail: jtolva@us.ibm.com, john@ascentstage.com.

TOMAC, STEVEN WAYNE, state legislator, farmer; b. Hettinger, ND, Nov. 23, 1953; s. Robert and Betty Ann (Schmidt) T. BS, N.D. State U., 1976. Loan officer Bank of .D., Bismarck, 1976-79; v.p. 1st Southwest Bank, Mandan, N.D., 1979-80; dir. mktg. N.D. Dept. Agr., Bismarck, 1980-81; exec. dir. N.D. Grain Growers, Bismarck, 1981-86; rodeo clown PRCA, Colorado Springs, 1971—; farmer/rancher St. Anthony, N.D., 1982—; mem. N.D. Ho. of Reps., Bismarck, 1986-90, N.D. Senate from 31st dist., Bismarck, 1990—. Mem. Accredited Rural Appraisers, Am. Soc. Farm Mgrs. and Rural Appraisers (appraiser 1981—). Democrat. Roman Catholic. Home: 2498 59th St Saint Anthony ND 58566-9640 Office: ND Senate 600 E Boulevard Ave Bismarck ND 58505-0660

TOMAIN, JOSEPH PATRICK, law educator, retired dean; b. Long Branch, NJ, Sept. 3, 1948; s. Joseph Pasquale and Bernice M. (Krzan) T.; m. Kathleen (Corcione), Aug. 1, 1971; children: Joseph Anthony, John Fiore. BA, U. Notre Dame, 1970; JD, George Washington U., 1974. Bar: NJ, Iowa. Assoc. Giordano and Halleran, Middletown, NJ, 1974-76; asst. to prof. law Drake U. Sch. Law, Des Moines, 1976-83; prof. law U. Cin., 1983—, acting dean, 1989—90, dean, 1990—2004, ippert prof. law, 1990—, dean emeritus, 2004. Vis. prof. law U. Tex., Austin, 1986—87. Author: Energy Law in a Nutshell, 1981, Nuclear Power Transformation, 1987; co-author: Energy Decision Making, 1983, Energy Law and Policy, 1989, Energy and Natural Resources Law, 1992, Regulatory Law and Policy, 1993, 2d edit., 1998, 3rd edit., 2003, Energy, The Environment and the Global Economy, 2000. Trustee Ctr. for Chem. Addictions Treatment, Cin., Vol. Lawyers for Poor, Cin.; mem. steering com. BLAC/CBA Round Table, Cin.; chair Knowledge Works Found.; trustee Ohio State Bar Found., Ohio Legal Assitance Found.; gov. Greater Cin. Found. Served in USAR, 1970-76. Mem. ABA, Am. Law Inst., Ohio State Bar Assn. (del.), Mercantile Libr. Assn. (v.p.). Roman Catholic. Home: 3009 Springer Ave Cincinnati OH 45208-2440 Office: U Cin Coll Law Office Dean PO Box 210040 Cincinnati OH 45221-0040 Home Phone: 513-871-3800; Office Phone: 513-556-0067. Business E-Mail: joseph.tomain@uc.edu.

TOMAR, RUSSELL HERMAN, pathologist, educator, researcher; b. Phila., Oct. 19, 1937; s. Julius and Ethel (Weinreb) T.; m. Karen J. Kent, Aug. 29, 1965; children: Elizabeth, David. BA in Journalism, George Washington U., 1959, MD, 1963. Diplomate Am. Bd. Pathology, Am. Bd. Allergy and Immunology, Am. Bd. Pathology, Immunopathology. Intern Barnes Hosp., Washington U. Sch. Medicine, 1963-64, resident in medicine, 1964-65; asst. prof. medicine SUNY, Syracuse, 1971-79, assoc. prof., 1979-88, assoc. prof. microbiology, 1980-84, prof., 1984-88, asst. prof. pathology, 1974-76, assoc. prof., 1976-83, prof., 1983-88, dir. immunopathology, 1974-88, attending physician immunodeficiency clinic, 1982-88, acting dir. microbiology, 1977-78, 82-83, interim dir. clin. pathology, 1986-87; prof. pathology and lab. medicine U. Wis. Ctr. for Health Scis., Madison, 1988—2003; dir. div. lab medicine U. Wis., Madison, 1988-95, dir. immunopathology and diagnostic immunology, 1995-98, prof. population health scis., 1999—2003, vis. prof. population health scis., 2003—07; chair dept. pathology Stroger Hosp. Cook County, Chgo., 1999—; prof. pathology Rush U., 1999—. Past mem. numerous coms. SUNY, Syracuse, U. Wis., Madison; mem. exec. com., chair and med. cons. AIDS Task Force Cen. N.Y., 1983-88. Assoc. editor Jour. Clin. Lab. Analysis; contbr. articles, rev. to profl. jours. Mem. pub. health com. Onondaga County Med. Soc., 1987-88. Lt. comdr. USPHS, 1965-67. Allergy and Immunology Div. fellow U. Pa. Fellow Coll. Am. Pathologists (diagnostics immunology rsch. com. 1993-2003, stds. com. 1995-97, commn. on clin. pathology 1997-2003), Am. Soc. Clin. Pathology (com. on continuing edn. immunopathology 1985-91, pathology data presentation com. 1976-79, pathology rep. coun. med. subspecialty socs. 2004—), Am. Acad. Allergy (penicillin hypersensitivity com. 1973-77); mem. AAAS, Am. Assn. Immunologists, Am. Assn. Pathology (chmn. 2002—), Acad. Clin. Lab. Physicians and Scientists (com. on rsch. 1979-81, chairperson immunology 1979), Clin. Immunology Soc. (clin. lab. immunology com., chair coun. 1991-96, pathology rep. to Coun. Med. Subspecialty Socs. 2003—). Office: Stroger Cook County Dept Pathology 1901 W Harrison St Chicago IL 60612 Personal E-mail: rtomar@comcast.net. Business E-Mail: russell.tomar@hektoen.org.

TOMASKY, SUSAN, electric power industry executive; b. Morgantown, W.Va., Mar. 29, 1953; m. Ron Ungvarsky; 1 child, Victoria. BA cum laude, U. Ky., Lexington, 1974; JD with honors, George Washington U., 1979. Staff mem. House Com. Interstate and Fgn. Commerce, Washington, 1974—76; with Office Gen. Counsel FERC, Washington, 1979—81, gen. counsel, 1993—97; assoc. Van Ness, Feldman & Curtin, Washington, 1981—86; ptnr. Van Ness, Feldman & Curtis, Washington, 1986—93, Hogan & Harts, Washington, 1997-98; sr. v.p., gen. coun., sec. Am. Electric Power Svc. Corp., Columbus, Ohio, 1998—2000, exec. v.p., gen. counsel, sec., 2000—01, exec. v.p., CFO, 2001—06, exec. v.p. Shared Svcs., 2006—. Staff mem. George Washington U. Law Rev., 1979. Trustee Columbus Symphony Orch., Columbus Sch. for Girls; co-chair Keystone Energy Bd. Mem. Greater Columbus C. of C., Phi Beta Kappa. Office: Am Electric Power Svc Corp 1 Riverside Plz Columbus OH 43215-2373 Office Phone: 614-716-1600.

TOMBLINSON, JAMES EDMOND, architect; b. Flint, Mich., Feb. 12, 1927; s. Carl and Edna Ethel (Spears) T.; m. Betsy Kinley, Sept. 26, 1959; children: Amy Lisa, John Timothy (dec.). B.Arch., U. Mich., 1951. Draftsman firms in, Detroit, 1951-53, Flint, 1953-54, 56-57, San Francisco, 1955-56; field engr. Atlas Constructors, Morocco, 1952-53; architect Tomblinson, Harburn, & Assocs., Inc. (and predecessors), Flint, 1958—, pres., 1969-95; chmn. bd. Tomblinson, Harburn & Assocs., Inc. (and predecessors), 1995—2001; chmn. Mich. Bd. Registration Architects, 1975-77; sec. Mundy Twp. Planning Commn., 1974-85, Grand Blanc Planning Commn., City of Mich., 1985—; chmn., 1988—. Pres. Flint Beautification Commn., 1968-69; bd. dirs. Grand Blanc Beautification Commn., 1969-84; founding mem. bd. dirs. Flint YMCA, 1969-75, chmn. camp com., 1971-75; founding mem. bd. dirs. Flint Environ. Action Team, 1971-77, v.p., 1971-73; elder First Presbyn. Ch. Flint, 1983, trustee, 1986-99; exec. com. Tall Pine council Boy Scouts Am., 1975—; bd. dirs. New Paths, 1994-2004, pres., 1985-86, 94—; trustee Grand Blanc Cmty. Found., 1997-2004; mem. vestry St. Christopher's Ch., 2004—. Served with AUS, 1945-46. Recipient various civic service awards. Fellow AIA; mem. Mich. Soc. Architects, Flint Area C. of C. Clubs: Greater Flint Jaycees (dir. 1957-63, v.p. 1963), Flint City, U. Mich. (pres. Flint chpt. 1980—). Lodges: Rotary (pres. 1984-85). Home: 686 Applegate Ln Grand Blanc MI 48439-1669 Office: THA Architects Engrs 817 E Kearsley St Flint MI 48503-2076 Office Phone: 810-767-5600. Personal E-mail: jetomblinson@aol.com. E-mail: jtomblinson@tha-flint.com.

TOMKINS, ANDY, state commissioner education; BA, East Ctrl. State U., 1969; MEd, Emporia State U., 1973; PhD, U. Kans., 1977. Tchr. Kans. High Schs.; prin., supr. Kans. Sch. Dist.; dean sch. edn. Pitts. State U.; commr. edn. Kans. State Dept. Edn., Topeka, 1996—. Recipient Kans. Supr. Yr. award, 1991-92. Office: Kansas State Dept Education 120 SE 10th Ave Topeka KS 66612-1103

TOMKOVICZ, JAMES JOSEPH, law educator; b. LA, Oct. 10, 1951; s. Anthony Edward and Vivian Marion (Coory) T.; m. Nancy Louise Abboud, June 27, 1987; children: Vivian Rose, Michelle Evelene, Henry James. BA, U. So. Calif., 1973; JD, UCLA, 1976. Bar: Calif. 1976, U.S. Dist. Ct. (so. dist.) Calif., U.S. Ct. Appeals (9th and 10th cirs.), U.S. Supreme Ct. Law clk. to Hon. Edward J. Schwartz, San Diego, 1976-77; law clk. to Hon. John M. Ferren Washington, 1977-78; atty. U.S. Dept. Justice, Washington, 1979-80; assoc. prof. law U. Iowa, Iowa City, 1982-86, prof., 1986—. Vis. prof. U. Iowa, Iowa City, 1981, U. Mich., Ann Arbor, 1992, UCLA, 2003, U. San Diego, 2004; adj. prof. UCLA, 1981-82. Author: (casebook) Criminal Procedure, 5th edit. (with W. White), 2004, (book) The Right to the Assistance of Counsel, 2002; (outline) Criminal Procedure, 1997; contbr. articles to profl. jours. Mem. Order of Coif, Phi Beta Kappa. Democrat. Roman Catholic. Avocations: running, softball. Office: U Iowa Coll Law Melrose & Byngton Iowa City IA 52242 E-mail: james-tomkovicz@uiowa.edu.

TOMLINSON, JOSEPH ERNEST, manufacturing executive; b. Sycamore, Ill., Apr. 22, 1939; s. Bernie Gilbert and Elizabeth Lowe (Hoffman) T.; m. Judith Ann Worst, Sept. 20, 1969; children: Mark Joseph, Amy Ann. BS in Acctg., U. Ill., 1962. CPA. Staff acct. Price Waterhouse and Co., Chgo., 1962-65, sr. acct., 1965-69, audit mgr. Indpls., 1969-74; corp. contr. Inland Paperboard and Pkg., Indpls., 1974-82; v.p., treas., contr. Inland Container Corp., Indpls., 1982—. Congl. chmn. Carmel Luth. Ch., Ind., 1983-86, v.p., 1988-91; mem. bd. dirs. Luth. Child and Family Svcs., Indpls., 1994-97. With Ill. N.G. 1963-69. Mem. Fin. Execs. Inst. (treas. Indpls. chpt. 1986-87, sec. 1987-88, 2d v.p. 1988-89, 1st v.p. 1989-90, pres. 1990-91). Clubs: Crooked Stick Golf. Republican. Home: 2204 Mason Point Pl Wilmington NC 28405-5276

TOMLINSON, ROBERT MARK, state legislator; b. Linclon, NE, May 6, 1957; m. Carole Tomlinson. BSE, Kansas U., 1980; MLA, Baker U., 1987. Special svcs. teacher Shawnee Mission AEP, Kans., 1985—; Kans. state rep. Dist. 24, 1993—2003; asst. commr. ins. State of Kans., 2003—. Spl. svc. tchr. Address: 5722 Birch Roeland Park KS 66205 Home Phone: 913-831-1905; Office Phone: 785-296-2676. Business E-Mail: btomlinson@ksinsurance.org.

TOMLJANOVICH, ESTHER M., retired judge; b. Galt, Iowa, Nov. 1, 1931; d. Chester William and Thelma L. (Brooks) Moellering; m. William S. Tomljanovich, Dec. 26, 1957; 1 child, William Brooks Tomljanovich. AA, Itasca C.C., 1951; BSL, St. Paul Coll. Law, 1953, LLB, 1955. Bar: Minn. 1955, U.S. Dist. Ct. Minn. 1958. Asst. revisor of statutes State of Minn., St. Paul, 1957-66, revisor of statutes, 1974-77, dist. ct. judge Stillwater, 1977-90; assoc. justice Minn. Supreme Ct., St. Paul, 1990—98, ret., 1998. Adv. bd. women offenders Minn. Dept. Corrections, 1999—; leadership com. So. Minn. Legal Svcs. Corp., 1999—. Former mem. North St. Paul Bd. Edn., Maplewood Bd. Edn., Lake Elmo Planning Commn.; trustee William Mitchell Coll. Law, 1995—2004, Legal Rights Ctr., 1995—2004, pres., 1999; bd. dirs. Itasca C.C. Found., 1996—, Medica Health Ins. Co., 2001—, vice chair, 2003—. Recipient Centennial 2000 award William Mitchell Coll., Disting. Alumna award, First Ann. Esther Tomljanovich Lifetime Achievement award, 2005, Disting. Junior award Academy Trial Lawyers, 2007; named one of One Hundred Who Made a Difference William Mitchell Coll. Law, One of 100 Most Influential Lawyers of All Time, Law & Politics Mag., 2007. Mem. Minn. State Bar Assn., Bus. and Profl. Women's Assn. St. Paul (former pres.), Minn. Women Lawyers (founding mem.). Home and Office: 8533 Hidden Bay Trail Lake Elmo MN 55042 Home Phone: 612-777-5970; Office Phone: 612-777-5970.

TOMPKINS, CURTIS JOHNSTON, government agency administrator; b. Roanoke, Va., July 14, 1942; s. Joseph Buford and Rebecca (Johnston) T.; m. Mary Katherine Hasle, Sept. 5, 1964; children: Robert, Joseph, Rebecca. BS, Va. Poly. Inst., 1965, MS, 1967; PhD, Ga. Inst. Tech., 1971. Indsl. engr. E.I. DuPont de Nemours, Richmond, Va., 1965-67; instr. Sch. Indsl. and Systems Engring., Ga. Inst. Tech., Atlanta, 1968-71; assoc. prof. Colgate Darden Grad. Sch. Bus. Adminstrn., U. Va., Charlottesville, 1971-77; prof., chmn. dept. indsl. engring. W.Va. U., Morgantown, 1977-80, dean Coll. Engring., 1980-91; pres. Mich. Technol. U., Houghton, 1991—2004, pres. emeritus, univ. prof., 2004—; dir., mem. sr. exec. svc. John A. Volpe Nat. Transp. Sys. Ctr., U.S. Dept. Transp., 2004—. Mem. engring. accreditation commn. Accreditation Bd. for Engring. and Tech., 1981-86; mem. exec. bd. Engring. Deans Coun., 1985-89, vice chmn., 1987-89; mem. engring. adv. com., chmn. of planning com. NSF, 1988-91, chm. Mich. Univs. pres. coun., 1996-98; Pres. Coun. Assn. Governing bds. 1996-2004, Gov's. Workforce Commn., 1996-2002; mem. engring. adv. bd. U. Cin., 1996-99 Author: (with L.E. Grayson) Management of Public Sector and Nonprofit Organizations, 1983, (with others) Maynard's Industrial Engineering Handbook, 1992; contbr. chpt. to Ency. of Profl. Mgmt, 1978, 83. Co-chmn. W.Va. Gov.'s Coun. on Econ. Devel.; bd. dirs. Pub. Land Corp. W.Va., 1980-89, Mich. C. of C., 1997—, vice chmn., 2002—; mem. faculty Nat. Acad. Voluntarism, United Way Am., 1976-91; mem. Morgantown Water Commn., 1981-87, Morgantown Utility Bd., 1987-91, steering com. W.Va. Conf. on Environ., 1985-89, Coun. on Competitiveness, 1998-2004, Mich. Higher Edn. Assistance Authority, The Mich. Higher Edn. Student Loan Authority, 2002-04; chmn. Monogalia County United Way, 1989-90; campaign chmn. Copper Country United Way, 1995-96. Named to Com. of 100 Va. Tech. Coll., Disting. Alumni Acad. dept. indsl. engring, hon. alumnus Mich. Technol. U., 2004; recipient Frank and Lillian Gilbreth Indsl. Engring. award Inst. Indsl. Engrs., 1998. Fellow Inst. Indsl. Engrs. (life mem., trustee 1983-90, pres. 1988-89), Nat. Soc. Profl. Engrs., Am. Soc. Engring. Edn. (pres. 1990-91), Mich. Soc. Profl. Engrs.; mem. Am. Assn. Engring. Soc. (bd. govs. 1987-90, exec. com. 1987-90, sec.-treas. 1989-90), Jr. Engring. Tech. Soc. (bd. dirs. 1988-91), Nat. Soc. for Sci., Tech. and Society (bd. dirs. 1991-94), Internat. Hall of Fame of Sci. and Engring. (hon. trustee), Ga. Tech. Coll. Engring. Disting. Alumni Acad., Ga. Tech. Sch. Indsl. and Sys. Engring. Disting. Alumni Acad., W.Va. U. Dept. Indsl. Engring. Disting. Alumni Acad. (hon.), Mich. C. of C. (bd dirs 1997-2004), Blue Key (hon.), Sigma Xi, Phi Kappa Phi, Tau Beta Pi, Alpha Pi Mu. Methodist. Home: 199 Coolidge Ave #111 Watertown MA 02472 Home Phone: 617-744-0283; Office Phone: 617-494-2222. E-mail: curtisj42@yahoo.com.

TOMPKINS, P. KELLY, lawyer, manufacturing executive; BA, Mercyhurst Coll.; JD, Cleveland-Marshall Law Sch., 1981. Bar: Ohio, Tex., US Supreme Ct. Corp. atty. Reliance Electric Co., 1981—85; litigation atty. Exxon Corp., 1985—87; various positions including sr. corp. counsel, dir. corp. devel., dir. investor relations Reliance Electric Co., 1987—96; asst. gen. counsel RPM Internat., 1996—98, v.p., 1998—2002, gen. counsel, sec., 1998—, sr. v.p., 2001—. Mem.: ABA, Defense Rsch. Inst., Am. Corp. Counsel Assn., Nat. Paint & Coatings Assn. (chair corp. adv. group), Cleveland Bar Found. (trustee), Cleveland Bar Assn. (trustee 2000—03, v.p. 2003, pres.-elect 2004—, mem. fiscal policy, planning, capital & exec. comm.). Office: RPM Internat 2628 Pearl Rd PO Box 777 Medina OH 44258

TOMPSON, MARIAN LEONARD, professional society administrator; b. Chgo., Dec. 5, 1929; d. Charles Clark and Marie Christine (Bernardini) Leonard; m. Clement R. Tompson, May 7, 1949 (dec. 1981); children: Melanie Tompson Kandler, Deborah Tompson Frueh, Allison Tompson Fagerholm, Laurel Tompson Davies, Sheila Tompson Doucet, Brian, Philip. Student public and parochial schs., Chgo. and Franklin Park, Ill. Co-founder La Leche League (Internat.), Franklin Park, 1956, pres., 1956-80, dir., 1956—, pres. emeritus, 1990—; exec. dir. Alternative Birth Crisis Coalition, 1981-85; founder, pres., CEO Another-Look, Inc., 2001—. Cons. WHO; bd. dirs. N.Am. Soc. Psychosomatic Ob-Gyn, Natural Birth and Natural Parenting, 1981-83; mem. adv. bd. Nat. Assn. Parents and Profls. for Safe Alternatives in Childbirth, Am. Acad. Husband-Coached Childbirth; mem. adv. bd. Fellowship of Christian Midwives; mem. profl. adv. bd. Home Oriented Maternity Experience; guest lectr. Harvard U. Med. Sch., UCLA Sch. Pub. Health, U. Antioquia Med. Sch., Medellín, Columbia, U. Ill. Sch. Medicine, Chgo., U. W.I., Jamaica, U. N.C., Nat. Coll. of Chiropractic, Am. Coll. Nurse Midwives, U. Parma, Italy, Inst. Psychology, Rome, Rockford (Ill.) Sch. Medicine, orthwestern U. Sch. Medicine, NGO Forum/4th World Conf. on Women, Beijing; mem. family com. Ill. Commn. on Status of Women, 1976-85; mem. perinatal adv. com. Ill. Dept. Pub. Health, 1980-83; mem. adv. bd. Internat. Nutrition Comm. Svc., 1980—; bd. cons. We Can, 1984—; exec. adv. bd. United Resources for Family Health and Support, 1985-86; mem. internat. adv. coun. World Alliance of Breast Feeding Action, 1996; mem. US Breastfeeding Com., 2006— Author: (with others) Safe Alternatives in Childbirth, 1976, 21st Century Obstetrics Now!, 1977, The Womanly Art of Breastfeeding, 6th edit., 1997, Five Standards for Safe Childbearing, 1981, But Doctor, About That Shot., 1988, The Childbirth Activists Handbook, 1983; author prefaces and forwards in 11 books; columnist La Leche League News, 1958-80; columnist People's Doctor Newsletter, 1977-88, mem. adv. bd., cons., 1988-92; assoc. editor Child and Family Quar., 1967—; mem. med. adv. bd. East West Jour., 1980—; also articles. Mem. adv. bd. Shelters for Healthy Environments, 1998—2002. Recipient Gold medal of honor Centro de Rehabilitacao Nossa Senhora da Gloria, 1975, Night of 100 Stars III Achiever award Actors Fund Am., 1990, N.Y. Soc. Ethical Culture Ethical Humanist award, 1999, 100 Women Making a Difference Today's Chgo. Woman, Health Humanity award Svc. Humanity, 2007. Mem. Nat. Assn. Postpartum Care Svcs. (adv. bd.), Chgo. Cmty. Midwives (adv. bd.), World Alliance for Breast Feeding Action (mem. internat. adv. coun. 1997). Office: 957 N Plum Grove Dr Schaumburg IL 60173 Office Phone: 847-869-1278. Personal E-mail: m.tompson@comcast.net. E-mail: mt@anotherlook.org.

TOMSICH, ROBERT J., heavy machinery manufacturing executive; Chmn. Blaw Knox Corp., Pitts.; pres., chmn., founder Nesco, Inc., Cleve., 1956—. Office: Nesco 6140 Parkland Blvd Cleveland OH 44124-4187

TONACK, DELORIS, elementary school educator; Elem. tchr. math. and sci. Goodrich Jr. High Sch., 1996—. Recipient Nebr. State Tchr. of Yr. award math./sci., 1992. Office: Sci Focus Program 1222 S 27th St Lincoln NE 68502-1832

TONDEUR, PHILIPPE MAURICE, mathematician, educator; b. Zurich, Switzerland, Dec. 7, 1932; came to U.S., 1964, naturalized, 1974; s. Jean and Simone (Lapaire) T.; m. Claire-Lise Ballansat, Dec. 20, 1965. PhD, U. Zurich, 1961. Rsch. fellow U. Paris, 1961-63; lectr. math. U. Zurich, 1963-64, U. Buenos Aires, 1964, Harvard U., Cambridge, Mass., 1964-65, U. Calif., Berkeley, 1965-66; asso. prof. Wesleyan U., Middletown, Conn., 1966-68; assoc. prof. U. Ill., Urbana, 1968-70, prof., 1970—2002, prof. emeritus, 2002—, chair dept. math., 1996-99. Vis. prof. Auckland U., 1968, Eidg. Techn. Hochschule U. Heidelberg, 1973, U. Zurich, 1987, U. Rome, 1984, Ecole Poly., Paris, 1987, U. Santiago de Compostela, Spain, 1987, Max Planck Inst., 1987, U. Leuven (Belgium), 1990, Keio U., Yokohama, Japan, 1993; assoc. mem. Ctr. Advanced Study U. Ill., 1977—78, 1991—92; dir. divsn. math. sci. NSF, 1999—2002. Contbr. articles to profl. jours. Recipient Divsn. Math. Scis. Govtl. Math. award; fellow Swiss Nat. Sci. Found., Harvard U., U. Ill. Mem.: Math. Assn. Am., Soc. Indsl. and Applied Math. (Frederick A. Howes pub. svc. award), Soc. Math. France, Schweiz Math. Gesellschaft, Am. Math. Soc. Office: U Ill Math Dept Urbana IL 61801 Business E-Mail: tondeur@math.uiuc.edu.

TOOHEY, BRIAN FREDERICK, lawyer; b. Niagara Falls, NY, Dec. 14, 1944; s. Matthew and Marilyn (Hoag) T.; m. Mary Elizabeth Monihan; children: Maureen Elizabeth, Matthew Sheridan, Margaret Monihan, Mary Catherine, Elizabeth Warner. BS, Niagara U., 1966; JD, Cornell U., 1969. Bar: N.Y. 1969, N.Mex. 1978, Ohio 1980. Ptnr. Jones Day, Cleve., 1981—. Lt. JAG Corps, USNR, 1970-73. Mem. ABA, N.Y. State Bar Assn., State Bar N.Mex., Ohio

State Bar Assn., Greater Cleve. Bar Assn. Roman Catholic. Home: 25 Pepper Creek Dr Cleveland OH 44124-5279 Office: Jones Day N Point 901 Lakeside Ave E Cleveland OH 44114-1190 Office Phone: 216-586-7246. E-mail: bftoohey@jonesday.com.

TOOHEY, JAMES KEVIN, lawyer; b. Evanston, Ill., July 16, 1944; s. John Joseph and Ruth Regina (Cassidy) T.; m. Julie Marie Crane, Nov. 1, 1969 (div. Aug. 1977); children: Julie Colleen, Jeannne Christine; m. Anne Margaret Boettingheimer, May 28, 1983; children: James Robert, Kevin John, Casey Anne. BBA, U. Notre Dame, 1966; JD, Northwestern U., 1969. BAr: Ill. 1969, U.S. Dist. Ct. (no. dist.) Ill. 1971, U.S. Dist. Ct. (ctrl. dist.) Ill. 1991, U.S. Ct. Appeals (7th cir.) 1973, U.S. Ct. Appeals (8th cir.) 1975, U.S. Supreme Ct. 1988. Assoc. Taylor, Miller, Magner, Sprowl & Hutchings, Chgo., 1970-71; asst. U.S. Atty. Office U.S. Atty., Chgo., 1971-74; assoc. Ross, Hardies, O'Keefe, Babcock & Parsons, Chgo., 1974-77; ptnr. Ross & Hardies, Chgo., 1978—2003, McGuire Woods, LLP, 2003—05, Johnson & Bell, Ltd., 2005—. Mem. St. Mary of the Wood Parish Coun., 1999-2002 Mem. Ill. State Bar Assn., Soc. Trial Lawyers, Assn. Advancement of Automotive Medicine, Ill. Assn. Def. Attys., Trial Lawyers Club Chgo., Edgebrook Sauganash Athletic Assn. (bd. dirs., commr. 1993-96; softball, baseball, and basketball coach), Evanston Golf Club. Office: Johnson & Bell Ltd 33 W Monroe St Chicago IL 60603 Office Phone: 312-984-0280.

TOOMAJIAN, WILLIAM MARTIN, lawyer; b. Troy, NY, Sept. 26, 1943; s. Leo R. Tooomajian and Elizabeth (Gundrum) Toomajian; children: Andrew, Philip. AB, Hamilton Coll., 1965; JD, U. Mich., 1968; LLM, NYU, 1975. Bar: N.Y. 1968, Ohio 1978. Mem. firm Cadwalader, Wickersham & Taft, NYC, 1971—77, Baker Hostetler LLP, Cleve., 1977—. Lt. U.S. Coast Guard, 1968—71. Mem.: ABA, Cleve. Tax Club, Cleve. Bar Assn., Ohio Bar Assn. Home: 3582 Lytle Rd Cleveland OH 44122-4908 Office: Baker Hostetler LLP 3200 National City Ctr 1900 E 9th St Ste 3200 Cleveland OH 44114-3475 Business E-Mail: wtoomajian@bakerlaw.com.

TOPACIO, ANGELA, marketing executive; b. Germany, 1968; m. Matt DiDio. Brand mgr. Saks Inc.; project mgr. Gyro Creative Grp., Detroit, 1999, majority owner. amed one of 40 Under 40, Crain's Detroit Bus., 2006. Office: Gyro Creative Group 400 Grand River Ave Ste 200 Detroit MI 48226 Office Phone: 313-964-0100. Office Fax: 313-964-0101.

TOPEL, DAVID GLEN, agricultural studies educator; b. Lake Mills, Wis., Oct. 24, 1937; BS, U. Wis., 1960; MS, Kans. State U., 1962; PhD, Mich. State U., 1965; DSc (hon.), Szent Istvan U., Godallo, Hungary, 2002. Assoc. prof. animal sci. and food tech. Iowa State U., Ames, 1967-73, prof. animal sci. and food tech., 1973-79, dean Coll. Agr., 1988-2000, dir. agr. and home econs. experiment sta., 1988-2000; prof., head dept. Auburn U., Ala., 1979—88, M.E. Ensminger endowed chair animal sci., 2000—. Cons., presenter, lectr. in field; mem. Gov. of Iowa's Sci. Adv. Coun., 1990-2000, Gov. of Iowa's Livestock Revitalization Task Force, 1993-98; chair Gov.'s Environ. Agr. Com., 1994; mem. Iowa Corn Promotion Bd.; mem. faculty Royal Vet. and Agrl. U., Denmark, 1971-72; vis. prof. Nat. Taiwan U., 1972. Author: The Pork Industry -Problems and Progress, 1968. Secretariat World Food Prize, Iowa State U., Ames, 1991-96. Fulbright-Hays scholar Royal Vet. and Agrl. U., 1971-72; recipient award of merit Knights of Ak-Sar-Ben, 1973, Commr.'s award Agrl. Commr. Republic of China, 1977, disting. Achievement award Block and Bridle Club, 1979, Ala. Cattlemen's Assn.,1 984, Hon. State Farmer Degree, Ala., 1986, Harry L. Rudnick Educator's award Nat. Assn. Meat Purveyors, 1989, USDA Honor award, 1999, Hon. Prof. award Gyöngyös Coll., Hungary, 2000; named hon. prof. Ukrainian State Agrl. U., 1993. Fellow Am. Soc. Animal Sci. (Disting. Rsch. award in meat sci. 1979, Bouffault Internat. Agr. award 2002); mem. Am. Meat Sci. Assn., Inst. Food Tech., Iowa Crop Improvement Assn., Extension and Tchg. (pres. North Ctrl. Region 1992), Nat. Assn. State Univs. and Land-Grant Colls. (chair bd. agr. 1993, mem. commn. on food, environ. and renewable resources 1992-99), Ukrainian Acad. Agrl. Scis., Sigma Xi (Outstanding Achievement award Iowa chpt. 1993), Alpha Zeta, Gamma Sigma Delta (Internat. award). Presbyterian. Avocations: fishing, golf. Office: Iowa State U Coll Agriculture 2374 Kildee Hall Ames IA 50011-0001 Home: 4108 Laura Ct Ames IA 50010 Home Phone: 515-292-7543; Office Phone: 515-294-6304.

TOPILOW, CARL S., symphony conductor; b. Jersey City, Mar. 14, 1947; s. Jacob Topilow and Pearl (Roth) Topilow Josephs; m. Shirley; 1 child, Jenny Michelle. BMus., Manhattan Sch. Mus., 1968, MMus., 1969. Exxon/Arts Endowment Condr. Denver Symphony Orch., 1976-79, asst. condr., 1979-80; mus. dir. Denver Chamber Orch., 1976-81, Denver Youth Orch., 1977-80, Grand Junction Symphony, Colo., 1977-80, Nat. Repertory Orch., Breckenridge, Colo., 1978—; dir. orchs. Cleve. Inst. Mus., 1981—, condr. Summit Brass 1986—, Cleve. Pops Orch., 1995—. Recipient Conducting fellowship Nat. Orch. Assn., NYC, 1972-75, Aspen Mus. Festival, Colo., 1976; winner 1st place Balt. Symphony Conducting Competition, Md., 1976. Office: Cleve Inst Music 11021 East Blvd Cleveland OH 44106-1705

TOPINKA, JUDY BAAR, state official, political organization worker; b. Riverside, Ill., Jan. 16, 1944; d. William Daniel and Lillian Mary (Shuss) Baar; 1 child, Joseph Baar. BS, Northwestern U., 1966. Features editor, reporter, columnist Life Newspapers, Berwyn and LaGrange, Ill., 1966-77; with Forest Park (Ill.) Rev. and Westchester News, 1976-77; coord. spl. events dept. fedn. comm. AMA, 1978-80; rsch. analyst Senator Leonard Becker, 1978-79; mem. Ill. Ho. of Reps., 1981-84, Ill. Senate, 1985-94; treas. State of Ill., Springfield, 1995—; chmn. State Rep. Party, 2002—; candidate Gov. Ill., 2006. Former mem. judiciary com., former chmn. senate health and welfare com.; former mem. fin. instn. com.; former co-chmn. Citizens Coun. on Econ. Devel.; former co-chmn. U.S. Commn. for Preservation of Am.'s Heritage Abroad, serves on legis. ref. bur.; former mem. minority bus. resource ctr. adv. com. U.S. Dept. Transp.; former mem. adv. bd. Nat. Inst. Justice. Founder, pres., bd. dirs. West Suburban Exec. Breakfast Club, from 1976; chmn. Ill. Ethnics for Reagan-Bush, 1984, Bush-Quayle 1988; spokesman Nat. Coun. State Legislatures Health Com.; former mem. nat. adv. coun. health professions edn. HHS; mem., GOP chairwoman Legis. Audit Commn. of Cook County; chmn. Riverside Twp. Regular Republican Orgn., 1994—. Recipient Outstanding Civilian Svc. medal, Molly Pitcher award, Abraham Lincoln award, Silver Eagle award U.S. Army and N.G. Office: Office of Ill State Treasurer 100 W Randolph St Ste 15-600 Chicago IL 60601-3232

TOPLIKAR, JOHN M., state legislator; m. Dianne Lee. Kans. state rep. Dist. 15, 1993—. Bus. owner, carpenter. Home: 507 E Spruce St Olathe KS 66061-3356

TOPOL, ERIC JEFFREY, academic administrator, cardiologist, educator; b. NYC, June 26, 1954; s. Erwin and Susan (Lepp) T.; m. Susan Leah Merriman, May 5, 1979; children: Sarah, Evan. BA with highest distinction, U. Va., 1975; MD with honors, U. Rochester, 1979. Med. resident U. Calif., San Francisco, 1979-82; fellow Johns Hopkins U. Med. Ctr., Balt., 1982-85; asst. prof. U. Mich. Sch. Medicine, Ann Arbor, 1985-87, assoc. prof., 1987-90, prof., 1990; dir. cardiac catheterization labs. and interventional cardiology U. Mich. Med. Ctr., Ann Arbor, 1986-91; chmn. dept. cardiovasc. medicine Cleve. Clinic Found., dir. Ctr. for Thrombosis and Arterial Biology, 1991—; founder, provost, chief acad. officer Cleve. Clinic Lerner Coll. Medicine, Case Western Reserve Univ., 2002—05, prof. medicine, 2004—06; prof. genetics Case Western Reserve Univ. Sch. Medicine, 2006—. Editor: Acute Coronary Intervention, 1988, Textbook of Interventional Cardiology, 1990, 4th edit., 2002, Textbook of Cardiovascular Medicine, 1st and 2d edits.; mem. editl. bd. Circulation, Circulation Rsch., Am. Jour. Cardiology, Coronary Art Disease, Jour. Am. Coll. Cardiology, Brit. Heart Jour.; mem. editl. bd. of several med. publs.; contbr. articles to profl. jours. Recipient Clin. Rsch. Innovator award, Doris Duke Charitable Found., 2003, Andres Gruentzig award, European Soc. Cardiology, 2004. Fellow ACP, Am. Coll. Cardiology (editor jour., Simon Dack award, 2005), Am. Soc. Clin. Investigation, Am. Heart Assn. (mem. coun. on clin. cardiology, coun. on circulation and thrombosis), European Soc. Cardiology; mem. Cen. Soc. Clin. Rsch., Am. Fedn. for Clin. Rsch. (councilor), Assn. Am. Physicians, AMA (Dr. William Beaumont award in Medicine 2002), IOM, NAS, John Hopkins Soc. Scholars. being one of the first scientists to raise doubts about the safety of Vioxx, and was a key witness in lawsuits against Merck & Co. Office: Case Western Reserve Univ Sch Medicine 10900 Euclid Ave Cleveland OH 44106 Office Phone: 216-445-9490.

TORDOFF, HARRISON BRUCE, retired zoologist, educator; b. Mechanicville, NY, Feb. 8, 1923; s. Harry F. and Ethel M. (Dormandy) T.; m. Jean Van Nostrand, July 3, 1946; children: Jeffrey, James. BS, Cornell U., 1946; MA, U. Mich., 1949, PhD, 1952. Curator Inst. of Jamaica, Kingston, 1946-47; instr. U. Kans., 1950-52, asst. prof., 1952-57, assoc. prof., 1957; asst. prof. U. Mich., 1957-59, assoc. prof., 1959-62, prof., 1962-70; former dir. Bell Mus. Natural History; prof. ecology U. Minn., Mpls., 1970-91, dean coll. biol. scis., 1986-87. Contbr. articles in ornithology to profl. jours. Served with USAF, 1942-45. Decorated D.F.C., 17 Air medals. Fellow Am. Ornithologists Union (pres. 1978-80); mem. Nature Conservancy (chmn. bd. Minn. chpt. 1975-77), Wilson Ornithol. Soc. (editor 1952-54), Cooper Ornithol. Soc. Office: 100 Ecology 1987 Upper Buford Cir Saint Paul MN 55108-1051 Home: 189 11th St Lake Placid FL 33852-9460 E-mail: tordoff@ecology.umin.edu.

TORF, PHILIP R., lawyer, pharmacist; b. Chgo., Aug. 4, 1952; m. Donna Torf; 3 children. BS, U. Ill., 1976; JD, John Marshall Law Sch., 1984. Dem. candidate 10th dist. Ill. U.S. House of Reps., 1996. Jewish.

TORGERSEN, TORWALD HAROLD, architect, consultant; b. Chgo., Sept. 2, 1929; s. Peder and Hansine Malene (Hansen) T.; m. Dorothy Darlene Peterson, June 22, 1963. BS in Archtl. Engring. with honors, U. Ill., 1951. Lic. architect Ill., D.C., real estate broker, Ill., interior designer, Ill., pvt. pilots, scuba diver; registered architect Nat. Coun. Archtl. Registration Bds. Ptnr. Coyle & Torgersen Architects-Engrs., Washington, Chgo. and Joliet, Ill., 1955—56; coord. project Skidmore, Owings & Merrill, Chgo., 1956—60; corp. architect, dir. architecture, constrn. and interiors Container Corp. Am., Chgo., 1960—86; prin. in charge of orgn. and adminstrn. Jack Train Assocs. Inc., Chgo., 1987—88; cons. Torwald H. Torgersen, AIA, FASID, Chgo., 1988—. Guest lectr. U. Wis. Capt. USNR, 1951-82. Recipient Top Ten Design award Factory mag., 1964 Fellow Am. Soc. Interior Designers; mem. AIA, Naval Res. Assn., Ill. Naval Militia, Am. Arbitration Assn., Am. Soc. Mil. Engrs., Paper Industry Mgmt. Assn. (hon.), Sports Car Club Am., Nat. Eagle Scout Assn., 20 Fathoms Club. Home and Office: 3750 N Lake Shore Dr Chicago IL 60613-4238

TORGERSON, JAMES PAUL, energy company executive; b. Cleve., Nov. 30, 1952; s. Alfred Paul and Alice Marie (Kola) T.; m. Mary Ann Gadzinski, Sept. 9, 1978; children: Paul David, Beth Ann. BBA in Acctg., Cleve. State U., 1977; postgrad., So. Meth. U., 1980-81. Sr. budget acct. Diamond Shamrock Corp., Cleve., 1977-79, fin. planning supr., 1979, fin. staff analyst Dallas, 1979-80, sr. fin. analyst, 1980-81, planning analyst Lexington, Ky., 1981-83, mgr. planning and devel., 1983-86, gen. mgr. planning systems, 1986—, v.p., Development Dallas; exec. v.p., Chief Adminstrv. Officer and CFO Washington Energy Co., Seattle; v.p. and CFO Puget Sound Energy, Inc., Seattle; CFO and treas. DPL, Inc., Dayton, OH, 1998—. Republican. Roman Catholic. Avocations: golf, aerobics.

TORGERSON, JIM, state legislator; m. Analene Torgerson; 4 children. BS, Minot State U. Operator restaurant and marina, Ray, N.D.; mem. from dist. 2 N.D. State Ho. of Reps., Bismarck, 1993-98, mem. edn. and natural resources coms. Office: HC 1 Box 22 Ray ND 58849-9615

TORGERSON, KATHERINE P., media consultant, corporate communications specialist; Now v.p. human resources and exec. adminstrn. Penton Media, Inc., Cleve., with.

TORGERSON, LARRY KEITH, lawyer; b. Albert Lea, Minn., Aug. 25, 1935; s. Fritz G. and Lu (Hillman) Torgerson. BA, Drake U., 1958, MA, 1960, LLB, 1963, JD, 1968; MA, Iowa U., 1962; cert., The Hague Acad. Internat. Law, The Netherlands, 1965-69; LLM, U. Minn., 1969, Columbia U., 1971, U. Mo., 1976; PMD, Harvard U., 1973; EdM, 1974. Bar: Minn. 1964, U.S. Dist. Ct. Minn. 1964, Wis. 1970, Iowa 1970, U.S. Dist. Ct. (no. dist.) Iowa 1971, U.S. Tax Ct. 1971, U.S. Supreme Ct. 1972, U.S. Dist. Ct. (ea. dist.) Wis. 1981, U.S. Ct. Appeals (8th cir.) 1981. Asst. corp. counsel 1st Bank Stock Corp. (88 Banks), Mpls., 1963-67, 1st Svc. Corp. (27 ins. agys., computer subs.), Mpls., 1965-67; v.p., trust officer Nat. City Bank, Mpls., 1967-69; sr. mem. Torgerson Law Firm, Northwood, Iowa, 1969-87; trustee, gen. counsel Torgerson Farms, Northwood, 1967—, Redbirch Farms, Kensett, Iowa, 1987—2002, Sunburst Farms, Grafton, Iowa, 1987—, Gold Dust Farms, Bolan, Iowa, 1988—, Torgerson Grain Storage, Bolan, 1988—, Indian Summer Farms, Bolan, 1991—, Sunset Farms, Bolan, 1992—, Sunrise Farms, Grafton, 1994—. CEO, gen. counsel Internat. Investments, Mpls., 1983-96, Transoceanic, Mpls., 1987-96, Torgerson Capital, Northwood, 1996—, Torgerson Investments, Northwood, 1984—, Torgerson Properties, Northwood, 1987—, Torgerson Ranches, Sundance, Wyo., 1998—, Hawaiian Investments Unltd., Maui, Hawaii, 1998—. Internat. Investments Unltd., San Pedro, Belize, 1999—. Recipient All-Am. Journalism award Thomas Arkle Clark Outstanding Achievement award, 1958, Dennis E. Brumfield Outstanding Achievement award, 1958, Johnny B. Guy Outstanding Leadership award, 1958; named to Outstanding Young Men of Am., U.S. Jaycees; Hagen scholar, Honor scholar. Mem. ABA, Am. Judicature Soc., Iowa Bar Assn., Minn. Bar Assn., Wis. Bar Assn., Hennepin County Bar Assn., Mensa, Drake Student-Faculty Coun., Drake Student Alumni Coun. (chmn.), Jaycees, Harvard Bus. Sch. Study (pres., exec. com., univ. editor in chief), Psi Chi, Circle K (pres. local chpt.), Phi Alpha Delta, Omicron Delta Kappa (pres. local chpt.), Pi Kappa Delta (pres. local chpt.), Alpha Tau Omega (pres. local chpt., Silver Bullet Outstanding Leadership award, 1965, 66), Pi Delta Epsilon (founder, chpt. pres.), Alpha Kappa Delta, Alpha Scholastic Hon. (U. editor-in-chief), Harvard Bus. Sch. Exec. Com. (U. editor-in-chief). Lutheran.

TORIUMI, DEAN MICHAEL, facial, plastic and reconstructive surgeon, educator; b. Chgo., Ill., 1958; Degree in biology, Knox Coll., 1980; grad., Norwestern U. Med. Ctr.; MD, Rush Med. Coll., 1981. Cert. otolaryngology 1988. Resident, gen. surgery U. Ill., Chgo., 1983—85; resident, otolaryngology Northwestern U. Med. Sch., Chgo., 1985—87; fellowship, facial plastic and reconstruction surgery Tulane Med. Sch., New Orleans, 1988, Va. Mason Med. Ctr., Seattle, 1989; assoc. prof. U. Ill., Dept. Otolaryngology, Chgo. Co-author: Open Structure Rhinoplasty; contbr. articles various profl. papers, chapters to books. Mem.: Am. Acad. Facial Plastic and Reconstructive Surgery (pres.). Office: U Ill Chgo Coll Medicine Dept Otolaryngology 1855 W Taylor St Rm 242 Chicago IL 60612-7242 Address: 60 E Del Pl Chicago IL 60611-1495 also: 900 N Mich Ave Chicago IL 60611-1542

TORR, GERALD R., state representative; b. Greencastle, Ind., Nov. 28, 1957; m. Stephanie Torr. Attended, Hanover Coll., 1976—77; grad., Musicians Inst., Hollywood, Calif., 1978. Claims adjuster Farm Bur. Ins., 1982—85, Quality Claims Inc., 1985—98, Monroe Guaranty Ins. Co. Quality Claims, Inc., 1998—; state rep. dist. 39 Ind. Ho. of Reps., Indpls., 1996—, mem. ins., corps. and small bus., judiciary, and labor and employment coms.; mem. Ind. Lt. Gov.'s Ins. Industry Task Force. Past Rep. precinct committeeman. Mem.: Ctrl. Ind. Claims Assn., Ind. Forum for Fair Liability Laws (past sec.-treas.), State Adjusters Assn. (dir., past pres.), Nat. Soc. Profl. Ins. Investigators, Westfield-Washington C. of C., Fishers C. of C., NRA, Carmel/Clay C. of C., Am. Contract Bridge League. Republican. Office: Ind Ho of Reps 200 W Washington St Indianapolis IN 46204-2786

TOSCANO, JAMES VINCENT, medical foundation president; b. Passaic, NJ, Aug. 8, 1937; s. William V. and Mary A. (DeNigris) T.; m. Sharon Lee Bowers; children: Shawn Truelson, Lauren Bjorklund, David Brendan, Dania Toscano Miwa. AB summa cum laude, Rutgers U., 1959; MA, Yale U., 1960. Lectr. Wharton Sch., U. Pa., 1961-64; chief opinion analyst Pa. Opinion Poll, 1962-64; mng. dir. World Press Inst., St. Paul, 1964-68, exec. dir., 1968-72; dir. devel. Macalester Coll., St. Paul, 1972-74; v.p. resource devel. and pub. affairs Mpls. Soc. Fine Arts, 1974-79; pres. Minn. Mus. Art, 1979-81; exec. v.p. Park Nicollet Inst., 1981—2006; corp. sec. Park Nicollet Clinic, 1983-86; sr. v.p. Am. Med. Ctrs., Inc., 1985-87; pres. Mpls. Heart Inst. Found., 2006—. Adj. prof. sch. of mgmt. U. St. Thomas, 1989-01; co-chair prin. practices nonprofit excellence com. MCN, 1994-98, 2004—05; lectr. Grad. Sch. Mgmt., Hamline U., 2003—. Author: The Chief Elected Official in the Penjerdel Region, 1964; co-author, co-editor: The Integration of Political Communities, 1964. Bd. dirs., exec. com., sec.-treas. World Press Ins., 1972-2007; bd. dirs., chmn. Southside Newspaper Mpls., 1975-79; chmn. com. to improve student behavior St. Paul Pub. Schs., 1977-79; bd. dirs. Planned Parenthood St. Paul, 1965-72, Mpls. Action Agy., 1976-79; emeritus dir. Help Enable Alcoholics Receive Treatment; mem. St. Paul Heritage Preservation Commn., 1979-82, vice chmn., 1981; mem. Citizens Adv. Com. on Cable Comm.; bd. dirs. Minn. Newspaper Found., 1987-92, Minn. Coun. Nonprofits, 1989-95, 1997-2003; bd. mem. Vocal Essence, 1993-96, alt. Minn. Healthcare Commn., 1993-95, mem. Minn. Healthcare Commn., 1995-97, chair task force med edn. rsch. costs, 1994-96. com. med. rsch. edn. costs, 1996-2003; chair, 1996-99; liason health tech adv. com., 1993-97; pres. 2000-03, bd. dirs. Summit Ave Residential Preservation Assn., 2000-06, Skylight Club, Informal Club, bd. dirs. Citizens League, 1980, African-Am. Culture Ctr., 1979-82, Am. Composers Forum, 1981-85, St. Paul Chamber Orch., 1976-80, 83-89, United Theol. Sem., 1985-88; dir. emeritus Minn. Citizens for the Arts; mem. exec. com., chmn. Med. Alley Assn., 1986-96, bd. dirs., 1986-96, task force on tech. assessment Med. Alley, 1992-93; mem. health affairs adv. com. Acad. Health Ctr. U. Minn., 1988-95; bd. dirs. Mother Cabrini House, 1985-92, Minn. Civil Justice Coalition, 1987-91, also chmn.; chmn. Gov.'s Task Force on Health Care Promotion, 1985-86, mem. Gov.'s Com. Promotion Health Care Resources, 1986-87; chmn. bd. Minn. Fin. Counseling Svcs., Inc., 1990-93; mem. task force cost effectiveness Med. Alley, 1994-95; bd. dirs. Meml. Blood Bank, 1995-2001, mem. exec. com., 1996-2001; bd. dirs. Bakken Mus., 1997-2003, Stevens Sq. Cmty. Orgn., 1997-99; bd. dirs. Rainbow Rsch., Inc., 2002—, chmn. bd., 2004-07; bd. dirs. Friends of the St. Paul Libr., 2004-07; bd. dirs., treas. Pub. Arts St. Paul, 2004-2007, Minn. Charities Rev. Coun., 2004-07, chmn., 2007—; mem. West Summit Neighborhood Adv. Coun., 2004-; co-chair, 2004-05. Woodrow Wilson Nat. fellow, 1960. Minn. Charities Rev. Coun. (chair 2007-). Congregationalist. Address: 1982 Summit Ave Saint Paul MN 55105-1460 Office: Mpls Heart Inst Fund 920 E 28th St Ste 100 Minneapolis MN 55407 Home Phone: 651-699-1765; Office Phone: 612-863-3978. Personal E-mail: jvt2@comcast.net. Business E-Mail: jtoscano@mhif.org.

TOSHACH, CLARICE OVERSBY, real estate developer, retired computer company executive; b. Firbank, Westmoreland, Eng., Nov. 21, 1928; came to U.S., 1955; d. Oliver and Nora (Brown) Oversby; m. Daniel Wilkie Toshach, July 30, 1965 (dec. Aug. 1992); 1 child, Duncan Oversby Toshach; 1 child from previous marriage, Paul Anthony Beard. Textile designer Storeys of Lancaster, Eng., 1949-55; owner, operator Broadway Lane, Saginaw, Mich., 1956-70; pres., owner Clarissa Jane Inc., Saginaw, 1962-70, Over-Tosh Computers, Inc. dba Computerland, Saginaw and Flint, Mich., 1983-95; mgr., ptnr. Mich. Comml. Devel. L.L.C., Saginaw, 1995—. Trustee Saginaw Gen. Hosp., 1977-83, Home for the Aged, 1978-80; bd. dirs. Vis. Nurse Assn., pres., 1981-83; bd. dirs. Hospice of Saginaw, Inc., v.p., 1981-83; mem. long range planning com. United Way of Saginaw, 1982-83; cmty. advisor Jr. League of Saginaw, 1982-83; pres. Saginaw Gen. Hosp. Aux., 1972-82, pres., 1976-77.

TOSTE, ANTHONY PAIM, chemistry educator, researcher; b. Mountain View, Calif., June 26, 1948; BS in Chemistry with honors, Santa Clara U., Calif., 1970; PhD in Biochemistry and Chemistry, U. Calif., Berkeley, 1976. Rsch. fellow Cardiovasc. Rsch. Inst., San Francisco, 1977—79; rsch. scientist Battelle Meml. Inst. Pacific N.W. Nat. Lab., Richland, Wash., 1980—88; asst. prof. Mo. State U., Springfield, 1988—94, assoc. prof., 1994—99, prof., 1999—. Cons. Mitsubishi Metal Corp., Tokyo, 1984-87, Dow Chem., Tex., 1994-96; presenter in field. Contbr. articles to jours. in field, cmty. svc. presentations. Bd. dirs. Mid Columbia Arts Coun., Richland, 1987-88, Bot. Soc. S.W. Mo., Springfield, 1997-2002; pres. bd. dirs. Springfield Sister Cities Assn., 1993-96; co-founder, leader Internat. Friendship Dels. to Japan, 1996, 99, 2001, 03, 05, 07. Rsch., equipment grantee NSF, 1990; recipient Diverse Cmty. award Sister Cities Internat., Boston, 1996, STA Rsch. fellow, Japan, 1998 Mem. Am. Chem. Soc. (treas. Ozark sect. 1989-91, chmn.-elect 2000, chmn. 2000-01), Am. Nuc. Soc. (Best Poster award 1987), Assn. Ofcl. Analytical Chemists (program chair 1986, 90), Mo. Acad. Sci. (program chair 1997, 2002). Avocations: picture framing, collecting fine art, woodworking, reading, cinema. Home: 2113 E Woodhaven Pl Springfield MO 65804-6767 Office: Mo State U Dept Chemistry 901 S ational Ave Springfield MO 65804 Home Phone: 417-883-1051; Office Phone: 417-836-5150. Business E-Mail: anthonytoste@missouristate.edu.

TOTH, BRUCE A., lawyer; b. Toledo, Feb. 14, 1953; s. Louis W. and Marianne (Tschann) T.; m. Christina Maria Schwarz, Aug. 28, 1976. BS, Ga. Inst. Tech., 1976; MBA, JD, Stanford U., 1980. Bar: Ill., 1981. V.p. Prescott, Ball & Turben, Cleve., 1980-82; assoc. Winston & Strawn, Chgo., 1982-87, ptnr., 1987—, mem. exec. com. Republican. Office: Winston & Strawn 35 W Wacker Dr 45th Fl Chicago IL 60601-1695 Office Fax: 312-558-5700. E-mail: btoth@winston.com.

TOUHILL, BLANCHE MARIE, retired academic administrator, historian, educator; b. St. Louis, Mo., July 1, 1931; d. Robert and Margaret (Walsh) Van Dillen; m. Joseph M. Touhill, Aug. 29, 1959. BA in History, St. Louis U., 1953, MA in Geography, 1954, PhD in History, 1962. Prof. history and edn. U. Mo., St. Louis, 1965-73, assoc. dean faculties, 1974-76, assoc. vice chancellor for acad. affairs, 1976-87, vice chancellor, 1987-90, chancellor, 1991—2002, chancellor emeritus, 2002—. Bd. dirs. Peabody Energy, Inc. Author: William Smith O'Brien and His Irish Revolutionary Companions in Penal Exile, 1981, The Emerging University UM-St. Louis, 1963-83, 1985; editor: Readings in American History, 1970, Varieties of Ireland, 1976. Named Outstanding Educator St. Louis chpt. Urban League, 1976; recipient Leadership award St. Louis YWCA, 1986. Mem. Nat. Assn. State Univs. and Land Grant Colls. (exec. com. 1988—), Am. Com. on Irish Studies (pres. 1991—), Phi Kappa Phi, Alpha Sigma Lambda. E-mail: j_touhill@hotmail.com.

TOURLENTES, THOMAS THEODORE, retired psychiatrist; b. Chgo., Dec. 7, 1922; s. Theodore A. and Mary (Xenostathy) T.; m. Mona Belle Land, Sept. 9, 1956; children: Theodore W., Stephen C., Elizabeth A. BS, U. Chgo., 1945, MD, 1947. Diplomate Am. Bd. Psychiatry and Neurology (sr. examiner 1964-88, 90). Intern Cook County Hosp., Chgo., 1947-48; resident psychiatry Downey (Ill.) VA Hosp., 1948-51; practice medicine specializing in psychiatry Chgo., 1952, Camp Atterbury, Ind., 1953, Ft. Carson, Colo., 1954, Galesburg, Ill., 1955-71; staff psychiatrist Chgo. VA Clinic, 1952; clin. instr. psychiatry Med. Sch., Northwestern U., 1952; dir. mental hygiene consultation service Camp Atterbury, 1953-54, Ft. Carson, 1953-54; asst. supt. Galesburg State Research Hosp., 1954-58, supt., 1958-71; dir. Comprehensive Community Mental Health Ctr. Rock Island and Mercer Counties; dir. psychiat. services Franciscan Hosp., 1971-85; chief mental health services VA Outpatient Clinic, Peoria, Ill., 1985-88; clin. prof. psychiatry U. Ill., Chgo. and Peoria, 1955—96; preceptor in hosp. adminstrn. State U. Iowa, Iowa City, 1958-64; ret., 1996. Councilor, del. Ill. Psychiat. Soc.; chmn. liaison com. Am. Hosp. and Psychiat. Assns., 1978-79, chmn. Quality Care Bd., Ill. Dept. Mental Health, 1995-97. Contbr. articles profl. jours. Mem. Gov. Ill. Com. Employment Handicapped, 1962-64; zone dir. Ill. Dept. Mental Health, Peoria, 1964-71; mem. Spl. Survey Joint Commn. Accreditation Hosps.; chmn. Commn. Cert. Psychiat. Adminstrs., 1979-81; pres. Knox-Galesburg Symphony Soc., 1966-68; bd. dirs. Galesburg Civic Music Assn., pres., 1968-70; chair Knox county United Way Campaign, 1989; pres. Civic Art Ctr., 1990-92. Capt. M.C. AUS, 1952-54. Fellow AAAS, AMA, Am. Psychiat. Assn. (chair hosp. and cmty. psychiatry award bd. 1989-90, dist. life fellow, 2002), Am. Coll. Psychiatrists, Am. Coll. Mental Health Adminstrs.; mem. Ill. Med. Soc. (chmn. aging com. 1968-71, coun. on mental health and addictions 1987-89), chair mental health substance abuse com. 1987-89), Ill. Psychiat. Soc. (pres. 1969-70), Am. Pub. Health Assn., Soc. Biol. Psychiatry, Ill. Hosp. Assn. (trustee 1968-70), Am. Coll. Hosp. Adminstrs., Assn. for Rsch. Nervous and Mental, Am. Assn. Psychiat. Adminstrs. (pres. 1980), Ctrl. Neuorpsychiat. Assn. (pres. 1988-89). Home and Office: 138 Valley View Rd Galesburg IL 61401-8524 Office Phone: 309-344-1177. E-mail: tourlentes@gallatinriver.net.

TOWEY, ANNE C., lawyer; BA, Coll. St. Catherine, 1996; JD, William Mitchell Coll. Law, 2000. Pvt. practice atty. Anne C. Towey, P.L.L.C., Edina, Minn. Named a Rising Star, Minn. Super Lawyers mag., 2006. Mem.: Minn. Women Lawyers, Hennepin County Bar Assn. (mem. family law sect., mem. juvenile and the law sect.), Minn. State Bar Assn. (mem. professionalism com., mem. family law sect., mem. juvenile and the law sect.), Collaborative Law Inst., Internat. Acad. Collaborative Profls. Office: Anne C Towey PLLC 3300 Edinborough Way Ste 550 Edina MN 55435 Office Phone: 952-405-2030. E-mail: actowey@comcast.net.

TOWNE, JONATHAN BAKER, vascular surgeon; b. Youngstown, Ohio, Jan. 10, 1942; m. Sandra Green Towne, Aug. 24, 1963; children: Timothy, Heidi, Crista. BS, U. Pitts., 1963; MD, U. Rochester, NYC, 1967. Intern in surgery U. Mich., Ann Arbor, 1967-68, resident I, 1968-69; resident II, III, IV U. Nebr., Omaha, 1969-72; chief gen. surgery USAF Hosp., Vandenberg AFB, Calif., 1972-74; asst. prof. surgery Med. Coll. Wis., Milw., 1975-79, assoc. prof., 1979-84, prof., 1984—, chair vascular surgery, 1984—. Editor: (book) Complications Vascular Surgery, 1980, Complications Vascular Surgery, II, 1985, Complications Vascular Surgery, III, 1991. Mem.: Wis. Surg. Soc. (pres. 1991—92), Assn. Program Dirs. Vascular Surgery (pres. 1997—98), Ctrl. Surg. Assn. (recorder 1992—97, pres.-elect 2001), Soc. Vascular Surgery (sec. 1994—98, pres.-elect 1999, pres. 2000). Avocation: photography. Office: Med Coll Wis 9200 W Wisconsin Ave Milwaukee WI 53226-3522 Home Phone: 262-784-0588; Office Phone: 414-805-9160. Business E-Mail: jtowne@mcw.edu.

TOWNS, DEBI, state legislator; b. Feb. 12, 1956; MSE, U. Wis., Whitewater, 1999. Dairy farm owner; former fin. cons. and sch. adminstr.; mem. Wis. State Assembly, Madison, 2002—, vice chair com. on edn., mem. agr. com., mem. coll. and univ. com., mem. edn. reform com., mem. fin. instns. com. Republican. Office: State Capitol Bldg Rm 302 N PO Box 8953 Madison WI 53708 Address: 7930 N Eagle Rd Janesville WI 53545

TOWNSEND, JOHN F., state official; b. May 23, 1938; married; 2 children. BS, Wayne State U., 1960, MBA, 1967. Small bus. ptnr., corp. exec. Mem. colls. and univs. com.; chair econ. devel. com.; mem. edn. com.; mem. vets. and mil. affairs. Mem. adv. bd. Fond du Lac Salvation Army; mem. Fond du Lac Pub. Libr. Bd., 1992—98. With USN, Vietnam. Mem.: Fond du Lac Noon Rotary. Republican. Office: State Capitol Rm 22 W PO Box 8953 Madison WI 53708-8953

TOWNSEND, LEROY B., chemistry professor, researcher, academic administrator; b. Lubbock, Tex., Dec. 20, 1933; s. L.B. and Ocie Mae (McBride) T.; m. Sammy Beames, Sept. 15, 1953; children: Lisa Loree, LeRoy Byron. BA in Chemistry and Math., N.Mex. Highlands U.-Las Vegas, 1955, MS, 1957; PhD, Ariz. State U.-Tempe, 1965; DSc. (hon.), U. Nebr. Assoc. prof. medicinal chemistry U. Utah, Salt Lake City, 1971-75, prof., 1975-78, adj. prof. chemistry, 1975-78; prof. medicinal chemistry U. Mich., Ann Arbor, 1979—, Albert B. Prescott prof. medicinal chemistry, 1985—, prof. chemistry, 1979—, chmn., dir. interdept. grad. program in medicinal chemistry, 1979—99. Chmn. drug discovery and devel. program Comprehensive Cancer Ctr.; mem. cancer rsch. com. Nat. Cancer Inst., 1979—99, mem. com. on devel. treatments for rare genetic disease dept. human genetics; mem. nat. adv. com. on AIDS to NIAID; mem. steering com. on chemotherapy of malaria WHO; mem. study sect. on chemotherapy of cancer Nat. Am. Cancer Soc.; mem. Am. Cancer Soc. study sect. drug devel. hematology and pathology; mem. various ad hoc site visit teams Nat. Cancer Inst.; chmn. purines and pyrimidines Gordon Rsch. Conf.; chmn. Nat. Medicinal Chemistry Symposium; pres. Internat. Congress Heterocyclic Chemistry; participant symposia in field; lectr. various nat. and internat. sci. congresses. Contbr. articles to profl. jours.; assoc. editor Internat. Jour. Heterocyclic Chemistry; mem. editorial bd. Jour. Carbohydrates, Nucleosides, Nucleotides, Jour. ucleosides and Nucleotides, Jour. Chinese Pharm. Soc., Jour. Medicinal Chemistry. Recipient Smissman-Bristol Myers-Squibb award in medicinal chemistry, Taito O. Soine Meml. award; various grants; named Disting. prof. MAGB. Fellow AAAS; mem. Am. Chem. Soc. (chmn., counsilor medicinal chemistry div.), Internat. Soc. Heterocyclic Chemistry (treas., pres. 1973-79), Nat. Am. Chem. Soc. (chmn. divsn. of medicinal chemistry), Sigma Xi, Phi Kappa Phi. Office: U Mich Coll Pharmacy Coll Pharmacy 4569 Pharmacy CC Little Bldg Ann Arbor MI 48109-1065

TOWNSEND, ROBERT J., lawyer; b. Charlotte, Mich., Nov. 11, 1938; s. Robert Wright and Rhea Lucille (Jennings) T.; m. Thea E. Kolb, Aug. 1, 1964; children: Melissa, Bradley. BA, Mich. State U., 1960; LLB, Harvard U., 1963. Bar: Ohio 1964, U.S. Dist. Ct. (so. dist.) Ohio 1964, U.S. Ct. Appeals (6th cir.) 1971, U.S. Supreme Ct. 1992. Assoc. Taft, Stettinus & Hollister, Cin., 1963-72, ptnr., 1972—. With U.S. Army, 1963-64, 68-69. Office: 1800 US Bank Tower 425 Walnut St Cincinnati OH 45202-3923 E-mail: townsend@taftlaw.com.

TRACY, ALLEN WAYNE, management consultant; b. Windsor, Vt., July 25, 1943; s. J. Wayne and Helen (Bernard) T.; m. Karla Noelte, Dec. 14, 1969; children: Tania, Tara. BA, U. Vt., 1965; MBA cum laude, Boston U., 1974. Retail salesman Exxon Corp., Boston, 1965-72; mgr. mfg. Leonard Silver Mfg. Co., Inc., Boston, 1974-78, v.p. ops., 1979-81; pres. OESM Corp., NYC, 1978-81; pres., bd. dirs. Gold Lance Inc., Houston, 1981-91; v.p. ops. Town & Country Corp., 1989-92; sr. v.p. L.G. Balfour Co., 1990-92; asst. to pres. Syratech Corp., Boston, 1993; dir. ops. Goldman-Kolber Co., Inc., Norwood, Mass., 1994; exec. v.p., COO, George H. Fuller & Son Co., Inc., Pawtucket, R.I., 1994-97; COO, BioMatrix Techs., Inc., Lincoln, R.I., 1997-98; mgmt. cons. IPA, Buffalo Grove, Ill., 1998—. Bd. dirs. Verilyte Gold, Inc., L.G. Balfour Co., Inc. Mem. Ashland Bd. Selectmen, 1977-78; chmn. Ashland Study Town Govt. Com., 1976-77; vice chmn. ch. coun. Federated Ch. Ashland, 1979-80, chmn., 1981; bd. dirs. Nottingham Forest Civic Assn., 1886. With U.S. Army, 1965-68. Mem. Nottingham Forest Club (bd. dirs. Houston 1986), Beta Gamma Sigma. Home: 118 Lakeview Dr Nokomis FL 34275 Office: IPA 1250 Barclay Blvd Buffalo Grove IL 60089-4500

TRACY, JAMES DONALD, historian, educator; b. St. Louis, Feb. 14, 1938; s. Leo W. and Marguerite M. (Meehan) T.; m. Nancy Ann McBride, Sept. 6, 1968 (div. 1993); children: Patrick, Samuel, Mary Ann; m. Suzanne K. Swan, May 2, 1997. BA, St. Louis U., 1959; MA, Johns Hopkins U., 1960, Notre Dame U., 1961; PhD, Princeton U., 1967. Instr. U. Mich., 1964-66; instr. to prof. history U. Minn., Mpls., 1966—, dept. chmn., 1988-91, Union Pacific prof. early modern history, 2001—04. Vis. prof. U. Leiden, Netherlands, 1987, U. Paris IV, 2001, U. Amsterdam, 2004. Author: Erasmus: The Growth of a Mind, 1972, The Politics of Erasmus: A Pacifist Intellectual and His Political Milieu, 1979, True Ocean Found.: Paludanus's Letters on Dutch Voyages to the Kara Sea, 1980, A Financial Revolution in the Habsburg Netherlands: Renten and Renteniers in the County of Holland, 1515-1565, 1985, Holland Under Habsburg Rule: The Formation of a Body Politic, 1506-1566, 1990, Erasmus of the Low Countries, 1996, Europe's Reformations, 1450-1650, 1999, 2d edit., 2006, Emperor Charles V, Impresario of War, 2002, The Low Countries in the Sixteenth Century: Erasmus, Religion and Politics, Trade and Finance, 2005; editor: Luther and the Modern State in Germany, 1986, The Rise of Merchant Empires: Long Distance Trade in the Early Modern Era, 1350-1750, 1990, The Political Economy of Merchant Empires: Long Distance Trade and State Power in the Early Modern World, 1991; editor: (with T.A. Brady and H.A. Oberman) Handbook of European History in the Late Middle Ages, Renaissance and Reformation, Vol. 1, 1994, Vol. 2, 1995, City Walls: The Urban Enceinte in Global Perspective, 2000; editor: (with T.A. Brady, K.G. Brady and S. Karant-Nunn) The Work of Heiko A. Oberman, 2003; editor: (with Marguerite Ragnow) Religion and the Early Modern State: Views from China, Russia and the West, 2004; editor: (with K.L. Reyerson and T.G. Stavrov) Pre-Modern Russia and Its World: Essays in Honor of Thomas S. Noonan, 2006; co-editor: Jour. Early Modern History, 1997—2000; editor, 2000—; mem. editl. bd. Sixteenth Century Jour., 1979—2000. Guggenheim fellow, 1972-73; NEH summer grantee, 1977, 85; Fulbright rsch. grantee, Belgium, 1979, Netherlands, 1980; resident fellow Netherlands Inst. for Advanced Studies, 1993-94. Mem. Am. Cath. Hist. Soc. (pres. 1999-00), Soc. Reformation Rsch. (pres. 1995-97), 16th Century Studies Conf. (pres. 1985-86). Republican. Roman Catholic. Home: 757 Osceola Ave # 2 Saint Paul MN 55105-3327 Office: U Minn History 614 Social Sci Bldg Minneapolis MN 55455 Home Phone: 651-227-0466; Office Phone: 612-624-0808. Business E-Mail: tracy001@umn.edu.

TRACY, SAUNDRA J., academic administrator; m. Doug Tracy; children: Steve, Elaine. BA in Spanish, Carroll Coll., Waukesha, Wis., 1968; M Ed in Fgn. Lang. Instrn., U. Pitts., 1971; PhD in Edn. Adminstrn., Purdue U., West Lafayette, Ind., 1981. Dir. Greater Cleve. Adminstr. Assessment Ctr., 1968—88; asst. to assoc. prof. edn. Cleve. State U., 1981—88; exec. dir. sch. study coun. Lehigh U., 1989—91, dir. ednl. programs Lee Iacocca Inst., 1990—92, assoc. prof. to prof. edn., 1988—94; dean of coll. of edn. Butler U., 1994—98; v.p. acad. affairs Mt. Union Coll., 1998—2001; pres. Alma Coll., 2001—. Fellow, Am. Coun. of Edn., 1992—93. Office: Alma Coll 614 West Superior St Alma MI 48801-1599 Office Phone: 989-463-7146.

TRADER, JOSEPH EDGAR, orthopedic surgeon; b. Milw., Nov. 2, 1946; s. Edgar Joseph and Dorothy Elizabeth (Senzig) T.; m. Janet Louise Burzycki, Sept. 23, 1972 (div. ov. 1987); children: James, Jonathan, Ann Elizabeth; m. Rhonda Sue Schultz, May 26, 1990. Student, Marquette U., 1964-67; MD, Med. Coll. Wis., 1971. Diplomate Am. Bd. Orthop. Surgery. Physician emergency rm. Columbia, St. Joseph's Hosps., Milw., 1972—76; orthop. surgeon, pres. Orthop. Assn., Manitowoc, Wis., 1979—. Mem. exec. com. Holy Family Meml. Med. Ctr., Manitowoc, 1985-96, chief-of-staff, 1994-96, ethics com., 1995—, chair instnl. rev. com. Former pres., bd. dirs. Holy Innocents Mens Choir; county del. State Med. Soc. Charitable Sci. and Edn. Found.; mem. bd. dirs. (trustee), mem. cobia com. Wis. Maritime Mus. Fellow ACS, Am. Acad. Orthopaedic Surgeons; mem. AMA, Wis. State Med. Soc., Wis. Orthop. Soc., Midwest Orthop. Soc., Am. Coll. Sports Medicine, Orthop. Assn. Manitonoc (pres.), Crown and Anchor, Wis. Maritime Mus. (cobia com. mem., bd. dirs.), Manitowoc Yacht Club, Phi Delta Epsilon, Psi Chi. Roman Catholic. Avocations: singing, tennis, skiing, sailing, golf. Home: 1021 Memorial Dr Manitowoc WI 54220-2242 Office: Orthopaedic Assocs 501 N 10th St Manitowoc WI 54220-4039 Office Phone: 920-682-6376. Personal E-mail: jetrader@lakefield.net. E-mail: jetrader@comcast.net.

TRAINOR, JIM, animator, filmmaker; b. Phila. BA, Columbia U., 1983. Asst. prof.-film, video & new media Sch. Art Inst. Chgo., 2000—. Dir.: (films, screening), Whitney Biennial; (films) From Microbe to Man, 1974, Antrozous, 1976, Torn Up, 1994, The Bat & the Virgin, 1997, The Fetish, 1997, The Bats, 1998, The Ordovicians, The Magic Kingdom, Sun Shames Headhunting Moon: Story of Nazr, Serene Velocity, The Skulls & the Skulls, the Bones & the Bones, The Moschops, 2000, A Net, 2000, Harmony, 2004, Could Be Tropical Fish, 2005, Leafy, Leafy Jungle, 2005, Blood, 2005, New Diagonal Symphony, 2005. Recipient, San Francisco Film Festival, Black Maria Film Festival, NY Underground Film Festival, Cinematexas Film Festival, Big Muddy Film Festival, Ann Arbor Film Festival.

TRAISMAN, HOWARD SEVIN, retired pediatrician; b. Chgo., Mar. 18, 1923; s. Alfred Stanley and Sara (Sevin) T.; m. Regina Gallagher, Feb. 29, 1956; children: Barry D. Lifschultz, Edward S., Kenneth N. BS in Chemistry, Northwestern U., 1943, MB, 1946, MD, 1947. Intern Cook County Hosp., Chgo., 1946-47; resident in pediat. Children's Meml. Hosp., Chgo., 1949-51, attending physician divsn. endocrinology, 1951—2002; mem. faculty Med. Sch. Northwestern U., Evanston, Ill., 1951—2002, prof. pediat., 1973—2002, pres., 1999—2002; ret., 2002. Author articles in field, chpts. in books. Capt. M.C. AUS, 1943-46, 47-49. Recipient Alumni Merit award, 1995, Northwestern U., Alumni medal, 2005, Ravitch award, 2007. Mem. Am. Diabetes Assn. (Disting. Svc. award 1976), Am. Pediatric Soc., Am. Acad. Pediat., Endocrine Soc., Lawson Wilkins Pediatric Endocrine Soc., AMA, Midwest Soc. Pediatric Rsch., Ill. Med. Soc., Chgo. Pediatric Soc., Chgo. Med. Soc., Inst. Medicine Chgo. Democrat. Jewish. Office: 1325 Howard St Evanston IL 60202-3766

TRAKAS, JAMES PETER, state legislator, state representative; b. Cleve., May 5, 1965; BA in Social Behavioral Sci., Ohio State U., 1987. Rep. Ohio State Ho. Reps., Columbus, 1998—; councilman at large City of Indep. Mem. fin. and appropriations com. Ohio State Ho. Reps., mem. higher edn. subcom., mem. rules and ref. com., mem. state govt. com. Named one of Outstanding Young Men of Am., 1989. Mem.: Western Res. Hist. Soc., Cleve. (Ohio) Mus. Art, City Club of Cleve., Order of the AHEPA. Greek Orthodox. Office: Ohio State House Reps 77 South High Street 14th Floor Columbus OH 43215-6111 Home: 6924 Brettin Ct Independence OH 44131

TRAMBLEY, DONALD BRIAN, lawyer; b. Anna, Ill., Aug. 31, 1967; s. Donald Ralph and Nona June (Brimm) T.; m. Michelle Lynne Pierson, Dec. 26, 1991; children: Kirsten Elizabeth Marie, Brian Andrew. BA, So. Ill. U., 1990; JD, Miss. Coll. Sch. Law, 1993. Bar: U.S. Dist. Ct. (so. dist.) Ill. Pub. defender Union County Cir. Ct., Jonesboro, Ill., 1994-96; state's atty. Johnson County Cir. Ct., Vienna, Ill., 1996—. Pres. Nazarene World Missionary Soc., Anna, 1995—, Rep. Booster Club, Vienna, 1995—. Mam. ABA, ATLA, Ill. State Bar Assn. Avocations: reading, parenting, christian fellowship. Office: Johnson County State's Atty PO Box 1257 Vienna IL 62995-1257

TRAMMELL, ALAN STUART, professional baseball coach, retired professional baseball player; b. Garden Grove, Calif., Feb. 21, 1958; m. Barbara Leverett, Feb. 21, 1978; children: Lance, Kyle, Jade Lynn. Shortstop Detroit Tigers, 1977—96, asst. to baseball ops., 1996—98, mgr., 2003—05; first base coach San Diego Padres, 2000—02; bench coach Chgo. Cubs, 2006—. Named Most Valuable Player, So. League, 1977; winner Gold Glove award, 1980, 81, 83-84; Silver Slugger award, 1987-88, 90; mem. Am. League All-Star Team, 1980, 84, 87, 88, 90, World Series Championship Team, 1984; named Most Valuable Player 1984 World Series. Office: Chgo Cubs Wrigley Field 1060 W Addison St Chicago IL 60613

TRAMMELL, KENNETH R., automotive executive; married; 2 children. BBA in acctg., U. Houston. Cert. CPA Tex. Sr. mgr. Arthur Andersen LLP; asst. contr. Tenneco Automotive, 1996—97, corp. contr., 1997—99, v.p., contr., 1999—2003, sr. v.p., CFO Lake Forest, Ill., 2003—. Office: Tenneco Automotive 500 N Field Dr Lake Forest IL 60045

TRAMONTO, RICK, chef; b. Rochester, NY; m. Gale Gand. Grill/saute cook The Scotch & Sirloin; chef Strathallen; garde-mgr. chef Tavern on the Green; chef Gotham Bar & Grill, Aurora, Avanzare, Chgo., The Pump Room, Chgo., Scoozi!, Chgo., Charlie Trotter's, Chgo., Stapleford Park Hotel, London; owner, chef Tru, Chgo., 1999—, Brasserie T., Chgo. Appeared on Oprah TV program. Named one of Am.'s rising Star Chefs, Robert Mondavi, 1995; named to Ten Best New Chefs, Food & Wine, 1994; recipient Outstanding Svc. award, James Beard Found., 2007.

TRAN, NANG TRI, research scientist, electrical engineer, entrepreneur; b. Binh Dinh, Vietnam, Jan. 2, 1948; came to the U.S., 1979, naturalized, 1986; s. Cam Tran and Cuu Thi Nguyen; m. Thu-Huong Thi Tong, Oct. 14, 1982; children: Helen, Florence, Irene, Kenneth. BSEE, Kyushu Inst. Tech., Kitakyushu, Japan, 1973, MSEE, 1975; PhD in Materials Sci./Solid State Device, U. Osaka Prefecture, Sakai, Japan, 1979. Rsch. assoc. U. Calif. Irvine, 1979; engr., rsch. scientist Sharp Electronics, Irvine, 1979-80; sr. rsch. scientist Arco Solar Industries, Chatsworth, Calif., 1980-84; sr. rsch. specialist, group leader 3M Co., St. Paul, 1985-96; sr. staff scientist Imation Corp., Oakdale, Minn., 1996—2007; exec. Khanti Inc., Am. Thin Films. McKnight disting. vis. prof. Ho Chi Minh Nat. U., U. Minn., Mpls., adj. prof.; cons., lectr. Japan industry mgmt.; reviewer NSF; sr. advisor to Vietnamese univs. Author: (poetry) My Journey; contbr. articles to profl. jours. Mem. tech. com. various internat. confs. Recipient R&D awards, Photonic Cir. Excellence award; fellow, Govt. South Vietnam, Japan, USAID, Rotary Internat., 1968—79. Mem. IEEE (sr.), Japan Soc. Applied Physics, N.Y. Acad. Scis. Achievements include invention of direct digital x-rays for chest and mammography; transparent conducting zinc oxide doped with group III elements which has become the standard material in many thin film solar cells; thin film transistors on flexible substrate; structured phosphors; copper indium diselenide and selenium-based solar cells; patents in field; research in amorphous silicon solar cells; image sensors; solid state memory; photoconductors; CD; high density data storage media; diamond like carbon evaporated lubricant; transparent conducting oxide films. Office: Univ Minn Inst Tech 200 Union St SE 4-174 D EE C Sci Bldg Minneapolis MN 55455 Office Phone: 612-378-2710. Business E-Mail: tranx051@umn.edu.

TRAPP, JAMES MCCREERY, lawyer; b. Macomb, Ill., Aug. 11, 1934; BA, Knox Coll., 1956; JD, U. Mich., 1961. Bar: Ill. 1961. Ptnr. McDermott, Will & Emery, Chgo., 1961-98, sr. counsel, 1998—. Chmn. Ill. Inst. Continuing Legal Edn., 1978-79, bd. dirs., 1980-86, pres., 1984-85. Fellow Am. Coll. Trust and Estate Coun. (Ill. chmn. 1980-83, nat. regent 1983—, treas. 1989-90, sec. 1990-91, v.p. 1991-92, pres.-elect 1992-93, pres. 1993-94, exec. com. 1986-94), Am. Bar Found., Ill. Bar Found.; mem. ABA, Ill. State Bar Assn., Chgo. Bar Assn. (chair trust law com. 1972-73, com. on coms. 1972-74), Internat. Acad. Estate and Trust Law, Am. Law Inst. (pres.), Chgo. Estate Planning Coun. Office: McDermott Will & Emery 227 W Monroe St Chicago IL 60606-5096

TRASK, THOMAS EDWARD, religious organization administrator; b. Brainard, Minn., Mar. 23, 1936; m. Shirley Burkhart; children: Kimberly, Bradley, Todd, Tom. BA, North Ctrl. Bible Coll., 1956, DDiv (hon.), 1994. Ordained min. Assemblies of God, 1958. Pastor First Assembly of God, Hibbing, Minn., 1956-60, pastor Vicksburg, Mich., 1960-64; Mich. dist. youth and Sunday sch. dir. Assembly of God, 1964-68; pastor First Assembly of God, Saginaw, Mich., 1968-73, Brightmoor Tabernacle, Southfield, Mich., 1976-88; supt. Mich. Dist. Coun., Dearborn, 1973-76; gen. treas. The Gen. Coun. Assemblies of God, Springfield, Mo., 1988-93, gen. supt., 1993—2007. Co-author: Back to the Altar: A Call to Spiritual Awakening, 1994, Back to the Word, A Call to Biblical Authority, 1996, The Battle: Defeating the Enemies of Your Soul, 1997, The Blessing: Experiencing the Power of the Holy Spirit Today, 1998, The Choice: Embracing God's Vision in the New Millennium, 1999, The Fruit of the Spirit, 2000, Ministry for a Lifetime, 2001. Mem. Assemblies Of God Ch.

TRAUTH, JOSEPH LOUIS, JR., lawyer; b. Cin., Apr. 22, 1945; s. Joseph L. and Margaret (Walter) Trauth; m. Barbara Widmeyer, July 4, 1970; children: Jennifer, Joseph III, Jonathan, Braden, Maria. BS in Econs., Xavier U., 1967; JD, U. Cin., 1973. Bar: Ohio 1973, U.S. Dist. Ct. (so. dist.) Ohio 1973, U.S. Ct. Appeals (6th cir.) 1973, U.S. Supreme Ct. 1988, Ky. 2000. Ptnr. Keating, Muething & Klekamp, PLL, Cin., 1973-80, Keating, Muething & Klekamp, Cin., 1980—. Spkr. real estate law, 1974—. Contbr. articles to profl. jours. Mem. Parish Coun., Cin., 1990. Mem.: Cin. Bar Assn. (mem. grievance com., mem. real estate com., mem. negligence com.). Roman Catholic. Avocations: tennis, reading. Office: Keating Muething & Klekamp 1400 Provident Tower 1 E 4th St Ste 1400 Cincinnati OH 45202-3717 Office Phone: 513-579-6515. E-mail: jtrauth@kmklaw.com.

TRAUTMANN, THOMAS ROGER, history professor, anthropology educator; b. Madison, Wis., May 27, 1940; s. Milton and Esther Florence (Trachte) T.; m. Marcella Hauolilani Choy, Sept. 25, 1962; children: Theodore William, Robert Arthur. BA, Beloit Coll., 1962; PhD, U. London, 1968. Lectr. in history Sch. Oriental and African Studies, U. London, 1965-68; asst. prof. history U. Mich., Ann Arbor, 1968-71, assoc. prof., 1971-77, prof., 1977—, Richard Hudson rsch. prof., 1979, prof. history and anthropology, 1984—, chmn. dept. history, 1987-90, Steelcase rsch. prof., 1993-94, dir. Inst. Humanities, Mary Fair Croushore prof. humanities, 1997—2002, Marshall D. Sahlins coll. prof. history and anthropology, 1997—. Author: Kautilya and the Arthasastra, 1971, Dravidian Kinship, 1981, Lewis Henry Morgan and the Invention of Kinship, 1987; author: (with K.S. Kabelac) The Library of Lewis Henry Morgan, 1994; author: (edit. with Diane Owen Hughes) Time: Histories and Ethnologies, 1995, Aryans and British India, 1997; author: (edit. with Maurice Godelier and Franklin Tjon Sie Fat) Transformations of Kinship, 1999, Languages and Nations: The Dravidian Proof in Colonial Madras, 2006; editor: Comparative Studies in Society and History, 1997—2006; contbr. articles on India, kinship and history of anthropology;: The Aryan Debate, 2005. Sr. Humanist fellow NEH, 1984. Mem. Am. Anthrop. Assn., Assn. Asian Studies, Am. Inst. Indian Studies (mem. exec. com. trustee, sr. rsch. fellow in India 1985, 97), Phi Beta Kappa. Office: U Mich Dept History Ann Arbor MI 48109-1003

TRAVIS, DAVID M., state legislator; b. Pawtucket, RI, Sept. 21, 1948; s. Gideon and Jessie (Campbell) T.; married. BA, U. Wis., Milw., 1980; MA, U. Wis. Adminstrv. asst. Wis. State Legis., 1971-72; analyst Senate Dem. Caucus, 1972-73, dir., 1973-78; mem. Joint Fin. Com.; Wis. state assemblyman dist. 81, 1978—. Majority leader; chmn. rules com.; mem. orgn. com., Joint Com. on Employ Rels. and Spl. Com. on Reapportionment; del. Dem. Nat. Conv., 1980; instr. polit. sci. Mem. Northside Comty. Coun., Eastmorland and Elvehjem Comty. Assn. Democrat. Home: 5440 Willow Rd Apt 31 Waunakee WI 53597-8429

TRAVIS, DEMPSEY JEROME, real estate company executive; b. Chgo., Feb. 25, 1920; s. Louis and Mittie (Strickland) T.; m. Moselynne Hardwick, Sept. 17, 1949. BA, Roosevelt U., 1949; grad., Sch. Mortgage Banking, Northwestern U., 1969; D.Econs., Olive Harvey Coll., 1974; D.BA (hon.), Daniel Hale Williams U., Chgo., 1976; PhD (hon.), Kennedy-King Coll., 1982; DHL (hon.), Governor State U., 2001. Cert. property mgr.; cert. real estate counselor. Pres. Travis Realty Co., Chgo., 1949—, Urban Rsch. Press, 1969—. Author: Don't Stop Me Now, 1970, An Autobiography of Black Chicago, 1981, An Autobiography of Black Jazz, 1983, An Autobiography of Black Politics, 1987, Real Estate is the Gold in Your Future, 1988, Harold: The People's Mayor, 1989, Racism: American Style a Corporate Gift, 1990, I Refuse to Learn to Fail, 1992, Views From the Back of the Bus During World War II and Beyond, 1995, The Duke Ellington Primer, 1996, The Louis Armstrong Odessey: From Jazz Alley to America's Jazz Ambassador, 1997, Racism: Revolves Like a Merry Go 'Round: 'Round 'n 'Round It Goes, 1998, They Heard a Thousand Thunders, 1999, The Life and Times of Redd Foxx, 1999, The Victory Monument: The Beacon of Chicago's Bronzeville, 1999, J. Edgar Hoover's FBI Wired the Nation, 2000, The FBI Files on the Tainted and the Damned, 2001, An American Story: In Red, White and Blue, 2002, Norman Granz The White Moses of Black Jazz, 2003, Jimmie Lumceford: The King of Jazzmocracy, 2004. Trustee Northwestern Meml. Hosp., Chgo., Chgo. Hist. Soc., Auditorium Theater, Chgo., Roosevelt U.; bd. dirs. Columbia Coll. With AUS, 1942-46. Recipient award Soc. Midland Authors, 1982, Chgo. Art Deco Soc., 1985, The Human Rights award The Gustavus Myers Ctr. for Study of Human Rights in N.Am., 1995, Humanitarian award Kennedy-King Coll., 1997, Art Deco award, 1983, Soc. Midland Authors award for nonfiction, 1981; named to Jr. Achievement Chgo. Bus. Hall of Fame, 1995; named embedded in sidewalk of Bronzeville Walk of Fame, Chgo; inductee Internat. Literary Hall of Fame, Chgo. State U., 2000. Mem. United Mortgage Bankers Assn. Am. (pres. 1961-74), Dearborn Real Estate Bd. (pres. 1957-59, 70-71), Nat. Assn. Real Estate Brokers (1st v.p. 1959-60), Inst. Real Estate Mgmt., Soc. Profl. Journalists, Soc. Midland Authors (pres. 1988-90), NAACP (pres. Chgo. 1959-60), Econs. Club, Forty Club Chgo., Assembly Club, Cliff Dwellers, The Caxtons Club. Office: Travis Realty Co 840 E 87th St Chicago IL 60619-6298 E-mail: travisDT88@aol.com.

TRAVIS, RICHARD L., lawyer; b. Mobridge, SD, 1954; BA, U. SD, 1976, JD, 1980. Bar: SD 1980, US Dist. Ct. (Dist. SD) 1980. Atty. Frieberg Frieberg & Peterson, Beresford, SD, 1980; dep. state atty. Union County, SD; atty. May & Johnson PC, Sioux Falls, SD, 1990—, ptnr. Mem.: SD Def. Lawyers Assn., Def. Rsch. Inst., SD Trial Lawyers Assn. (bd. gov. 1991—93), State Bar SD (pres. young lawyers sect. 1985—86, bar commr. 1989—94, disciplinary bd. mem. 1994—2000, pres.-elect 2006—07), Second Judicial Cir. Bar Assn. Office: May & Johnson PC 4804 S Minnesota Ave Sioux Falls SD 57108 Office Phone: 605-336-2565. Office Fax: 605-336-2604.

TRAVIS, TRACEY THOMAS, retail executive; MBA in Fin. and Ops. Mgmt., Columbia U. With Pepsi, 1987—97; CFO Rexam Beverage Can Ams., 1997—99; v.p. fin., CFO Intimate Brands, Inc., 2001—02; sr. v.p. fin. Ltd. Brands, Inc., Columbus, Ohio, 2003—. Bd. dirs. Jo-Ann Stores, Inc. Office: Ltd Brands Three Ltd Pkwy Columbus OH 43230

TRAYNOR, DANIEL M., state representative; Postgrad in law, U.N.D., 1997. Lic.: N.D. (Law). Elected state chmn. N.D. Rep. party, 2001—; law clerk N.D. Supreme Court. District 15 chmn.; vol. Political Campaigns, 1988; dir. N.D. Rep. Party Election, 1992; mem., delegate rules com. Rep. Nat. Convention, Phila., 2000. Republican. Office: PO Box 1917 Bismarck ND 58502-1917

TRAYNOR, JOHN THOMAS, JR., state legislator, lawyer; b. Devils Lake, ND, June 14, 1955; s. John Thomas and Kathryn Jane (Donovan) T. BA, U. N.D., 1977, JD, 1980. Bar: N.D. 1980, U.S. Dist. Ct. N.D. 1980. Assoc. Traynor & Rutten, Devils Lake, 1980-82; ptnr. Traynor, Rutten & Traynor, Devils Lake, 1982—; mem. N.D. Senate from 15th dist., Bismark, 1990—. Mcpl. judge, Devils Lake, 1983-84; dir. 1st Ins. Agy., Devils Lake, 1984—. Editor Law Rev., U. N.D., 1979-80. Bd. dirs. Cmty. Devel. Corp., Devils Lake, 1983—, treas., 1984; pres. Lake Region Devel. Corp., Devils Lake, 1983-84, bd. dirs., 1983—. Recipient Book award Am. Jurisprudence, 1980. Mem. ABA, N.D. Bar Assn., N.E. Jud. Dist. Bar Assn., Lake Region Bar Assn. (pres. 1980-83), Devils Lake C. of C. (dir. 1982—), Jaycees, Rotary, KC, Elks (officer 1982—). Republican. Roman Catholic. Home: PO Box 838 Devils Lake ND 58301-0838 Office: Traynor Rutten & Traynor 509 5th St Devils Lake ND 58301-2571

TREACY, JOHN C., insurance company executive; b. 1963; With Ernst & Young, 1984—89; with investment reporting dept. St. Paul Co., 1989—96, fin. reporting officer, 1996—99, v.p., contr. fire and marine, 1999—2001, corp. contr., 2001—. Bd. dirs. Cath. Charities. Mem.: Am. Ins. Assn. (mem. fin. mgmt. issues com.). Office: St Paul Cos Inc 385 Washington St Saint Paul MN 55102

TREADWAY, JOSEPH L., state legislator; b. St. Louis, Mar. 23, 1947; m. Marlene Kroeger, 1982; 2 children. Diploma, Forest Pk. C.C. Office mgr.; real estate broker; mem. Mo. Ho. of Reps. from 96th dist., 1983—. Mem. C. of C. Democrat. Home: 2226 Telford Dr Saint Louis MO 63125-3288

TRECKELO, RICHARD M., lawyer; b. Elkhart, Ind., Oct. 22, 1926; s. Frank J. and Mary T.; m. Anne Kosick, June 25, 1955; children: Marla Treckelo Buck, Mary Treckelo Lucchesi. AB, U. Mich., 1951, JD, 1953. Bar: Ind. 1953, U.S. Dist. Ct. (no. and so. dists.) Ind. Pvt. practice, Elkhart, 1953-70; ptnr. Barnes and Thornburg, Elkhart, South Bend, others, 1971-91, of counsel, 1992—. Sec. Skyline Corp., Elkhart, 1959-94, bd. dirs., 1961-91. Bd. dirs. Elkhart Gen. Hosp. Found., Elkhart Park Found.; co-chmn. Elkhart Constl. Bicentennial Commn. Served with USAF, 1945-46. Mem. ABA, Elkhart City Bar Assn. (pres. 1975), Ind. Bar Assn., Elkhart County Bar Assn., Pres.'s Club (U. Mich.), Christiana Country Club, Michiana Club (chmn., U. Mich. Elbel Scholarship award), Rotary. Republican. Office: Barnes & Thornburg 121 W Franklin St Ste 200 Elkhart IN 46516-3200 Office Phone: 574-293-0681.

TREDWAY, THOMAS, college president; b. North Tonawanda, NY, Sept. 4, 1935; s. Harold and Melanya (Scorby) T.; m. Catherine Craft, Jan. 12, 1991; children: Daniel John, Rebecca Elizabeth. BA, Augustana Coll., 1957; MA, U. Ill., 1958; BD, Garrett Theol. Sem., 1961; PhD, Northwestern U., 1964. Instr. history Augustana Coll., Rock Island, Ill., 1964-65, asst. prof., 1965-69, assoc. prof., 1969-71, prof., 1971—, v.p. acad affairs, 1970-75, pres., 1975—. Vis. prof. ch. history Waterloo Lutheran Sem., 1967-68 Mem. Phi Beta Kappa, Omicron Delta Kappa Lutheran. Office: Augustana Coll Office of President 639 38th St Rock Island IL 61201-2210

TREFFERT, DAROLD ALLEN, psychiatrist, writer, hospital administrator; b. Fond du Lac, Wis., Mar. 12, 1933; s. Walter O. and Emma (Leu) T.; m. Dorothy Marie Sorgatz, June 11, 1955; children: Jon, Joni, Jill, Jay. BS, U. Wis., 1955, MD, 1958. Diplomate Am. Bd. Psychiatry and Neurology. Resident in psychiatry U. Wis. Med. Sch., 1959-62, clin. prof. psychiatry, 1965—; chief children's unit Winnebago (Wis.) Mental Health Inst., 1962-64, supt., 1964-79, Ctrl. State Hosp., Waupun, Wis., 1977-78; dir. Dodge County Mental Health Ctr., Juneau, Wis., 1964-74; mem. staff St. Agnes Hosp., Fond du Lac, 1963—; exec. dir. Fond du Lac County Mental Health Ctr., 1979-92. Chmn. Controlled Substances Bd. Wis.; chmn. med. examining bd. State of Wis. Author: Extraordinary People: Understanding Savant Syndrome, 1989, 3d edit., 2006, edits. in U.S., U.K., Italy, Japan, Netherlands, Sweden, Korea, China, Mellowing: Lessons from Listening, 2006; autism cons. (movie) Rainman, 1988. Fellow Am. Coll. Psychiatrists; mem. AMA, Wis. Med. Soc. (pres. 1979-80), Wis. Psychiat. Assn. (pres.), Am. Assn. Psychiat. Adminstrs. (pres.), Alpha Omega Alpha. Home: W 4065 Maplewood Ln Fond Du Lac WI 54935-9562 Office: 430 E Division St Fond Du Lac WI 54935-4560 Office Phone: 920-921-9381. Business E-Mail: daroldt@charter.net.

TREINAVICZ, KATHRYN MARY, application developer; b. Nov. 25, 1957; d. Ralph Clement and Frances Elizabeth (O'Leary) T. BS, Salem State Coll., Mass., 1980. Tchr. Brockton Pub. Schs., 1980-81; instr. Quincy CETA Inc., Mass., 1981-82; programmer Systems Architects Inc., Randolph, Mass., 1982; programmer analyst Dayton, Ohio, 1982-84; sr. programmer analyst System Devel. Corp., Dayton, 1984-86; project mgr. Unisys Inc., Dayton, 1986-87; software engr. Computer Scis. Corp. (formerly Systems & Applied Corp. 1988), 1987-89; project mgr. Computer Sci. Corp. (formerly Atlantic Rsch. Corp. 1994), Fairborn, Ohio, 1989-96; dept. mgr., 1996-98; sr. test analyst, 1998—. Mem.: NAFE. Democrat. Roman Catholic. Avocations: steven king novels, needlepoint, knitting, crocheting. Personal E-mail: kathy_t@msn.com.

TRENBEATH, THOMAS L., state legislator, lawyer; b. Neche, ND, July 23, 1948; m. Rose Trenbeath; children: Ian, Britta. BS, U. N.D., 1970, JD, 1978. Underwriting atty. Chgo. Title Ins. Co., Denver, 1981-84; v.p. Ticor Title Ins. Co., Denver, 1984—86; ptnr. Fleming, DuBois & Trenbeath, Attys., 1986-97; city adminstr., atty., 1997—; mem. N.D. Senate from 10th dist., 2001—. Mem. ct. svcs. adminstrn. com. N.D. Supreme Ct., 1995—; dir. Red River Regional Coun., 1999—. Capt. USAR, 1971-78. Mem. N.D. Assn. Mcpl. Power Sys. (v.p. 1999—), N.D. Bar Assn., N.D. Humanities Coun. Republican. Lutheran. Office: PO Box 361 Cavalier ND 58220-0361 E-mail: rosentom@polarcomm.com, ttrenbea@state.nd.us.

TRENT, DARRELL M., ambassador, academic administrator, transportation executive; b. Neosho, Mo., Aug. 2, 1938; s. Clarence Melvin and Edna Ruth T.; children: Darrell Michael, Derek Montgomery, Mercy Ruth. AB, Stanford U., 1961; postgrad., Internat. Law Sch., The Hague, Netherlands, summer 1961, Wharton Grad. Sch. Bus., U. Pa., summer 1962; MBA, Columbia U., 1964. Owner, mgr. Trent Enterprises, Kans. and Mo., 1963-66; pres., CEO N.Am. Carmen, Ltd., Del., 1965-68, Assoc. Stores, Inc., Okla., 1967-69, Plz. Supermarkets, Inc., Kans., 1966-69, Food Svc., Inc., Kans., 1966-69, Supermarkets, Inc., Kans., 1966-69, Acton Devel. Co., Inc., Kans., 1966-81; rsch. writer Nixon for Pres., 1968; staff dir. for pers. Presdl. Transition, 1968-69; commr. Property Mgmt. and Disposal Svc., GSA, 1969; dep. asst. to Pres. U.S., 1969-70; exec. dir. Property Rev. Bd., Exec. Office of Pres., 1969-73; dep. dir. Office Emergency Preparedness, 1970-72, acting dir., 1973; mem. Cost of Living Coun., 1973, Oil Policy Com., 1973; chmn. Joint Bd. Fuel Supply and Fuel Transp., 1973; mem. NSC, 1973; chmn. Pres.'s Adv. Coun. CD, 1973; U.S. mem. NATO Sr. Civil Emergency Planning Com., 1973; sr. rsch. fellow Hoover Inst., Stanford U., 1974-81, 89-94, sr. advisor, 1998—, assoc. dir., 1974-81, bd. overseers, 1985-89; dep. campaign mgr. Citizens for Reagan, 1976; dep. campaign mgr., cons. Reagan for Pres. Com., 1979-80, sr. policy advisor, 1980; dir. Office Policy Coordination, Presdl. Transition, 1980-81; U.S. alt. rep. Nato Com. Challenges of Modern Soc., 1982-83; dep. sec. U.S. Dept. Transp., 1981-82, acting sec., 1982-83; chmn. U.S. del. European Civil Aviation Com., U.S. Amb., 1983-88; chmn. Action Devel. Corp., Inc., 1988—; chmn., CEO Rollins Environ. Svcs., Inc., 1983-88, TEC Systems, Inc., 1990-91, Clean Earth Tech., Inc., 1992-93; amb., sr. adv. Ministry of Transp., Iraq, 2003—04; sr. adv. Sec. Def., 2001—04, Transition on Trans. and Budget, 2000; chmn. Trans Adv. Com., Bush Cheney, 2000. Chmn. Fed. Home Loan Bank Pitts., 1983-91; cons. ACDA, 1974-81, HUD, 1974, Dept. Commerce, 1974-76; bd. advisors Chronicle Info. Svcs., Inc., 1984-87; bd. mem. Continental Materials Corp., 1998—. Author: The U.S. and Transnational Terrorism, 1980, Transportation: Policy, Goals, Accomplishments, 1984; co-author: Terrorism: Threat, Reality, Response, 1979; contbr. articles to profl. publs. Bd. regents Pepperdine U., 1985-92; bd. dirs. Found. Teach Econs., 1988-90; dep. chmn. Ronald Reagan Presdl. Found., 1985-88. Mem. Bohemian Club. Republican. Methodist. Office: 1610 S Broadway St Pittsburg KS 66762-5845 Personal E-mail: darrell.trent@att.net. Business E-Mail: darrell@trent.org.

TREPPLER, IRENE ESTHER, retired state senator; b. St. Louis County, Mo., Oct. 13, 1926; d. Martin H. and Julia C. (Bender) Hagemann; student Meramec Community Coll., 1972; m. Walter J. Treppler, Aug. 18, 1950; children: John M., Steven A., Diane V. Anderson, Walter W. Payroll chief USAF Aero. Chart Plant, 1943-51; enumerator U.S. Census Bur., St. Louis, 1960, crew leader, 1970; mem. Mo. Ho. of Reps., Jefferson City, 1972-84; mem. Mo. Senate, Jefferson City, 1985-96; chmn. minority caucus, 1991-92. Alt. del. Rep. Nat. Conv., 1976, 84. Recipient Spirit of Enterprise award Mo. C. of C., 1992, appreciation award Mo. Med. Assn., Nat. Otto Nuttli Earthquake Hazard Mitigation award, 1993, Disting. Legislator award Cmty. Colls. Mo., 1995; named Concord Twp. Rep. of Yr., 1992. Mem. Nat. Order Women Legislators (rec. sec. 1981-82, pres. 1985), at. Fedn. Rep. Women, Tesson Ferry Twp. Rep. Club. Mem. Evangelical Ch. Office Phone: 314-487-4959. Personal E-mail: treppler@att.net.

TRESSEL, JIM (JAMES PATRICK TRESSEL), college football coach; b. Mentor, Ohio, Dec. 5, 1952; s. Lee and Eloise Tressel; m. Ellen Watson; children: Zak, Carlee, Eric, Whitney. BS cum laude in Edn., Baldwin-Wallace Coll., Berea, Ohio, 1975; MS in Edn., Akron U., Ohio, 1977. Grad. asst. Akron U., 1975; quarterbacks, receivers & running backs coach U. Akron, 1976—78; quarterbacks & receivers coach Miami U., Ohio, 1979—80; quarterbacks coach Syracuse U., NY, 1981—83; quarterbacks, receivers & running backs coach Ohio St. U., Columbus, 1983—85, head coach, 2001—, Youngstown St., 1986—2000. Named Ohio Valley Conf. Coach of Yr., 1987, Regional Coach of Yr., Am. Football Coaches Assn., 1987, 1993, Nat. Coach of Yr., 1991, 1994, 2002, Chevrolet Nat. Coach of Yr., 1993—94, 1997, Eddie Robinson Nat. Coach of Yr., Football Writers Assn., 1994, 2002; recipient Paul "Bear" Bryant award, Nat. Sportscasters & Sportswriters Assn., 2002. Mem.: Fellowship Christian Athletes, Am. Football Coaches Assn. Achievements include coaching Ohio St. U. to the 2002 BCS Nat. Championship; leading Youngstown U. to Divsn. I-AA Nat. Championship, 1991, 93, 94, 97. Office: Woody Hayes Athletic Ctr 2491 Olentangy River Rd Columbus OH 43210

TRESTMAN, FRANK D., distribution company executive, director; b. Mpls., Sept. 3, 1934; s. Saul and Rose (Hyster) T.; m. Carol Lynn Wasserman, Apr. 3, 1960; children— Lisa Ellen, Jill Susan BBA with high distinction, U. Minn., 1955. Exec. v.p., treas. Napco Industries, Inc., Mpls., 1965-74, pres., dir., 1974-84; chmn, CEO Mass Merchandisers, Inc., Hopkins, Minn., 1984-86; pres. Trestman Enterprises, Golden Valley, Minn., 1987—. Bd. dirs. Best Buy Co., Mpls., Western Container Corp., Mpls.; chmn. Avalon Real Estate Group., Mpls., Camir Investment Co., Mpls. Mem. bd. govs. Mt. Sinai Hosp., Mpls., 1978-91, Abbott Northwestern Hosp., 1993-2002; chmn. bd. trustees Mpls. Fedn. Endowment Fund; bd. dirs. Harry Kay Found. With USN, 1957-58. Mem. Oak Ridge Country Club (Hopkins). Office: Trestman Enterprises 5500 Wayzata Blvd Ste 1045 Minneapolis MN 55416-1241 Business E-Mail: frank@trestmanenterprises.com.

TRESTON, SHERRY S., lawyer; BA, Dominican U., 1972; MS, Purdue U., 1973; MBA, U. Chgo., 1979; JD with honors, DePaul U., 1983. Bar: Ill. 1983. With planning dept. Fed. Res. Bank, Chgo., 1973—77; with sys. dept. Sears Bank & Trust Co., Chgo., 1977—78; with trust dept. 1st Nat. Bank Chgo., 1978—83; assoc. Sidley Austin LLP, Chgo., 1983—91, ptnr., 1991—. Trustee Dominican U. Office: Sidley Austin LLP 1 S Dearborn Chicago IL 60603-2000 Fax: 312-853-7036.

TREUMANN, WILLIAM BORGEN, university dean; b. Grafton, ND, Feb. 26, 1916; s. William King and Dagny Helen (Borgen) T.; m. Mildred Elizabeth Jenkins, Aug. 14, 1948; children— Richard Roy, Robert Evan, Beverly Kay. BS, U. N.D., 1942; MA, U. Ill., 1944, PhD, 1947. Teaching asst. chemistry U. Ill., 1942-45, teaching asst. math., 1945-46, vis. prof., summers 1948-50; from asst. prof. to prof. chemistry N.D. State U., 1946-55; mem. faculty Minn. State U. Moorhead, 1960—, prof. chemistry, 1962—, asso. dean acad. affairs, 1968-70, dean faculty math. and sci., 1970—. Contbr. to profl. jours. Research Corp. Am. grantee, 1954; Minn. U. Bd. grantee, 1967 Fellow Am. Inst. Chemists; mem. Am. Chem. Soc., Am. Assn. U. Profs., Minn. Acad. Sci., Fedn. Am. Scientists, Phi Beta Kappa, Sigma Xi. Home: 1809 11th Ave S Fargo ND 58103 Office: Math Dept Moorhead State U Moorhead MN 56560 Personal E-mail: btreumann@yahoo.com.

TREVES, SAMUEL BLAIN, geologist, educator; b. Detroit, Sept. 11, 1925; s. Samuel and Stella (Stork) T.; m. Jane Patricia Mitoray, Nov. 24, 1960; children: John Samuel, David Samuel. BS, Mich. Tech. U., 1951; postgrad., U. Otago, New Zealand, 1953-54; MS, U. Idaho, 1953; PhD, Ohio State U., 1959. Geologist Ford Motor Co., 1951, Idaho Bur. Mines and Geology, 1952, Otago Catchment Bd., 1953-54; mem. faculty U. Nebr., Lincoln, 1958—2004, prof. geology, 1966—2004, chmn. dept., 1964-70, 74-89, assoc. dean Coll. Arts and Scis., 1989-96, emeritus, 2004. Curator geology Nebr. State Mus., 1964—; participant expdns. to Antarctica and Greenland, 1960, 61, 63, 65, 70, annually 72-76. Rsch. and publs. on geology of igneous and metamorphic rocks of Idaho, New Zealand, Mich., Antarctica, Nebr., Can., Greenland with emphasis on origin of Precambrian granite complexes and basaltic volcanic rocks. Fulbright scholar U. Otago, New Zealand, 1953-54. Fellow Geol. Soc. Am.; mem. Am. Mineral Soc., Am. Geophys. Union, Sigma Xi, Tau Beta Pi, Sigma Gamma Epsilon. Home: 1710 B St Lincoln NE 68502-1524 Office Phone: 402-472-0872. Business E-Mail: streves1@unlnotes.unl.edu.

TREVOR, ALEXANDER BRUEN, information technology consultant; b. NYC, Apr. 12, 1945; s. John B. Jr. and Evelyn (Bruen) T.; m. Ellen Ruth Armstrong, Sept. 21, 1974; children: Anne Wood Roebel, Alexander Jay Bruen. BS, Yale U., 1967; MS, U. Ariz., 1971. Rsch. asst. U. Ariz., Tucson, 1971; systems analyst CompuServe Inc., Columbus, Ohio, 1971-73, dir. systems, 1973-74, v.p., 1974-81, exec. v.p., chief tech. officer, 1981-96, also bd. dirs., 1985-96; pres. Nuvocom, Inc., Columbus, 1996—. Bd. dirs. State Auto Fin. Corp., Columbus. Author (software program) CB Simulator, 1980. Trustee Aviation Safety Inst., Worthington, Ohio. 1st lt. Signal Corps, U.S. Army, 1968-70, Vietnam. Decorated Bronze Star. Mem. IEEE (sr.), SAR (N.Y.), Union Club (N.Y.). Republican. Episcopalian. Home: 1987 My Tern Ct Sanibel FL 33957

TRIANDIS, HARRY CHARALAMBOS, psychologist, educator; b. Patras, Greece, Oct. 16, 1926; s. Christos Charalambos and Louise J. (Nikokavouras) T.; m. Pola Fotitch, Dec. 23, 1966; 1 child, Louisa. B.Engring., McGill U., 1951; M.Commerce, U. Toronto, Ont., Can., 1954; PhD, Cornell U., 1958; Doctorate (hon.), U. Athens, Greece, 1987. Asst. prof. U. Ill., Champaign, 1958-61, assoc. prof., 1961-66, prof. psychology, 1966-97; cons. USIA, 1970-75, NSF, 1968-75; prof. emeritius, 1997—. Author: Attitudes and Attitude Change, 1971, The Analysis of Subjective Culture, 1972, Varieties of Black and White Perception of the Social Environment, 1975, Interpersonal Behavior, 1977, Culture and Social Behavior, 1994, Individualism and Collectivism, 1995; editor: Handbook of Cross-Cultural Psychology, Vol. 1-6, 1980-81, Handbook of Industrial and Organizational Psychology, Vol. 4, 1994; editorial cons.; Jour. Personality and social Psychology, 1963-71, Jour. Applied Psychology, 1970-79, Sociometry, 1971-74, Jour. Cross-Cultural Psychology, 1974—, others. Chmn. fgn. grants com. Am. Psychol. Found., 1968-90. Sr. fellow Ford Found., 1964-65; Guggenheim fellow, 1972-73; grantee USPHS, 1956-60, 62; grantee Office Naval Research, 1960-68, 80-85; grantee Social and Rehab. Service, HEW, 1968-73; grantee Ford Found., 1973-75; recipient award Interam. Soc. Psychology, 1981 Mem. Soc. for Psychol. Study of Social Issues (pres. 1975-76), Internat. Assn. Cross-Cultural Psychology (pres. 1974-76), Interam. Soc. Psychology (pres. 1985-87), Soc. for Exptl. Social Psychology (chmn. 1972-74), Soc. for Personality and Social Psychology (pres. 1976-77), Internat. Assn. Applied Psychology (pres. 1990-94). Office: 603 E Daniel St Champaign IL 61820-6232 Home: 2008 Eagle Ridge Ct Apt A Urbana IL 61802-8695 Business E-Mail: triandis@uiuc.edu.

TRIBBETT, CHARLES, executive recruiter; b. Alexandria, La., Oct. 25, 1955; m. Lisa Tribbett; children: Jillian, Charlie, Jason. BA magna cum laude, Marquette U.; JD, U. Va. Former corp. securities atty. Skadden, Arps, Slate, Meagher & Flom, NYC; ptnr. Abraham & Sons; with Russell Reynolds Assoc., Chgo., 1989—; mng. dir., co-head, CEO/bd. services practice Russel Reynolds Assoc., Chgo., 1994—. Bd. trustees Northwestern J.L. Kellogg Bus. Sch.; bd. dirs. Chgo. Children's Mus., AON Pension and Investment Fund, Chgo. Union League. Office: Russell Reynolds Assoc 200 S Wacker Dr Ste 2900 Chicago IL 60606 Business E-Mail: ctribbett@russellreynolds.com.

TRICASE, ELIZABETH, gymnast; b. Elmhurst, Ill., July 26, 1986; d. Pino and Sheila. Gymnast Ill. Gymnastics Inst./U.S. Natl. Team, 2001—; competed in U.S. Gymnastics Championships, Cleve., 2001, 2002, 2003, Spring Cup, Burlington, Ontario, Canada, 2002, Pacific Alliance Championships, Vancouver, Canada, 2002, U.S. Classic, Pomona, Calif., 2001, Virginia Beach, Va., 2002, San Antonio, 2003, FL Gym Open, Luxembourg City, Luxembourg, 2004, Am. Classic, Ontario, Calif., 2004, Nat. Elite Podium Meet, NYC, 2004. Named U.S. Nat. Vault Champion, 2002; recipient 1st place vault, U.S. Gymnastics Championships, 2002, FL Gym Open, 2004. Avocations: soccer, basketball, running track. Office: 145 Plaza Dr Westmont IL 60559

TRICK, TIMOTHY NOEL, electrical and computer engineering educator, researcher; b. Dayton, Ohio, July 14, 1939; s. Edmund Louis and Roberta Elizabeth (Heckel) T.; m. Dorothe Lee Jacobs, Feb. 18, 1958; children: Patricia, Michael, Thomas, William, Gregory, Andrew. BSEE, U. Dayton, 1961; MSEE, Purdue U., 1962, PhD, 1966. Instr. Purdue U., West Lafayette, Ind., 1963-65; asst. prof. elec. and computer engring. U. Ill., Urbana, 1965-70, assoc. prof., 1970-75, prof., 1975—, dir. Coordinated Sci. Lab., 1984-86, head dept. elec. and computer engring., 1985-95. Author: Introduction to Circuit Analysis, 1978. Fellow AAAS, IEEE (bd. dirs. 1986-89, v.p. publs. 1988-89, Guillemin-Cauer award 1976, Centennial medal 1984, Meritorious Svc. award 1987); mem. Circuits and Sys. Soc. of IEEE (pres. 1979, Van Valkenburg award 1994), Am. Soc. Engring. Edn. Avocations: hiking, camping. Office: U Ill Dept Elec & Computer Engring 1406 W Green St Urbana IL 61801-2918

TRIPLEHORN, CHARLES A., entomologist, educator; b. Bluffton, Ohio, Oct. 27, 1927; s. Murray E. and Alice Irene (Lora) T.; m. Wanda Elaine Neiswander, June 12, 1949 (dec. Nov. 1985); children: Bradley Alyn, Bruce Wayne; m. Linda Sue Parsons, July 11, 1987. B.Sc., Ohio State U., 1949, MS, 1952; PhD, Cornell U., 1957. Asst. prof. entomology U. Del., Newark, 1952-54; teaching asst. entomology Cornell U., Ithaca, NY, 1954-57; asst. prof. entomology Ohio Agrl. Research and Devel. Ctr., Wooster, Ohio, 1957-61, Ohio State U., Columbus, 1961-62, assoc. prof. entomology, 1962-66, prof. entomology, 1966-92, prof. emeritus, 1992—. Econ. entomologist U.S. AID/Brazil, Piracicaba, Sao Paulo, 1964-66; vis. curator Field Mus. Natural History, Chgo., 1974, Can. Nat. Collection, Ottawa, Ont., 1977, Am. Mus. Natural History, N.Y.C., 1982, U. Mich., 1989, U. Ariz., 1989, Nat. Mus. of Natural History, 1998, Cornell U., 1999, Colo. State U., 2000, Brigham Young U., 2000. Co-author: Introduction to the Study of Insects, 7th edit., 2004. Cubmaster Boy Scouts Am., Wooster, Ohio, 1959-60, scoutmaster, Columbus, 1971-72; football coach Upper Arlington Football Assn., Ohio, 1968-71 Grantee Am. Philos. Soc., 1963, NSF, 1979, 85, 92. Mem. Entomol. Soc. Am. (pres. 1985), Coleopterists Soc. (pres. 1976), Royal Entomol. Soc. London, Entomol. Soc. Washington, Sigma Xi, Gamma Sigma Delta Clubs: Wheaton (pres.). Republican. Methodist. Avocations: sports, music, reading, writing. Home: 3943 Medford Sq Hilliard OH 43026-2219 Office: Mus Biol Diversity Div Insects The Ohio State University 1315 Kinnear Rd Columbus OH 43212-1157 Office Phone: 614-292-6839. Personal E-mail: ctriplhrn@aol.com.

TRIPP, APRIL, special education services professional; BS, Calif. State U., Fullerton, Calif., 1981; MA with hons., Calif. State U., Long Beach, Calif., 1985; MS, Johns Hopkins U., 1994; PhD with hons., Tex. Woman's U., 1989. 1st coord. adapted physical edn. Balt. County Pub. Schs.; assoc. prof. U. Ill., Urbana-Champaign, Ill. Chmn. adapted physical edn. section Md. AHPERD; mem. Nat. Cert. for Adapted Physical Edn. Standards Com., Spl. Olympics. Recipient Excellence in Edn. award-Spl. Tchr. of Yr. Balt. County, Mabel Lee award Am. Alliance Health, Phys. Edn., Recreation and Dance, 1994; grantee Nat. Handicapped Sports. Mem. Nat. PTA (hon. life award 1993), ARAPCS (mem. adapted physical activity coun. exec. com.) Office: Dept Kinesiology Univ Ill Louise Freer Hall 906 S Goodwin Ave Urbana IL 61801 E-mail: atripp3@uiuc.edu.

TRIPP, MARIAN BARLOW LOOFE, retired public relations executive; b. Lodgepole, Nebr., July 26; d. Lewis Rockwell and Cora Dee (Davis) Barlow; m. James Edward Tripp, Feb. 9, 1957; children: Brendan Michael, Kevin Mark. BS, Iowa State U., 1944. Writer Dairy Record, St. Paul, 1944-45; head product promotion divsn., pub. rels. dept. Swift & Co., Chgo., 1945-55; mgmt. supr. pub. rels. J. Walter Thompson Co., NYC and Chgo., 1956-76, v.p. consumer affairs Chgo., 1974-76; pres. Marian Tripp Communications Inc., Chgo., 1976-94. Mem. Am. Inst. Wine and Food, Confriere de la Chaine des Rotisseriers (officer Chgo. chpt.), Mayflower Soc., Daughters of the Am. Revolution, Les Dames D'Escoffier. Episcopalian.

TROGANI, MONICA, ballet dancer; b. Newark, Sept. 2, 1963; m. Jay Brooker, July 3, 1993. Grad. high sch., 1980. Ballet dancer N.J. Ballet, West Orange, 1980-83; field asst., coder Reichman Rsch., Inc., NYC, 1984-86; ballet mistress, prin. dancer Dance Theatre of L.I., Port Washington, N.Y., 1984-88; exec. sec. programming dept. The First N.Y. Internat. Festival of the Arts, NYC, 1987-89; guest regisseur Alta. Ballet, Edmonton, Can., 1988-89, ballet mistress, asst. to artistic dir., 1989-93; guest regisseur Ballet du Nord, Roubaix, France, 1991, Dance Theatre of Harlem, NYC, 1993-94; ballet mistress Les Grands Ballets Canadiens, Montreal, 1994—2003; rehearsal dir. Hubbard Street Dance Chicago, 2003—. Avocation: singing. Office: Hubbard St Dance Chicago 1147 W Jackson Blvd Chicago IL 60607

TROLANDER, HARDY WILCOX, engineering executive, consultant; b. Chgo., June 2, 1921; s. Elmer Wilcox and Freda Marie (Zobel) T.; m. Imogen Davenport, July 3, 1946 (dec.); children: Megan, Patricia. BS in Engring., Antioch Coll., 1947. Instr. Antioch Coll., Yellow Springs, Ohio, 1947-48; co-founder, CEO Yellow Springs Instrument Co., Inc., 1948-86. Dir., co-founder Cook Design Ctr., Dartmouth Coll., Hanover, N.H., 1975-88; bd. dirs. Deban Inc., Yellow Springs, Camax Tool co., Arvada, Colo.; mem. evaluation panel Inst. Basic Stds., Nat. Bur. Stds., 1977-79. Contbr. articles to profl. jours.; patentee in field. Co-founder, trustee Yellow Springs Community Found., 1974-83; trustee Autioch Coll., 1968-74, chmn. bd., 1972-74; trustee Engring. and Sci. Found., Dayton, 1982-96, Engrs. Club Dayton Found., 1994-2005, Engring. and Sci. Hall of Fame, 1994-2002; mem. adv. bd. Coll. Engring. and Computer Sci. Wright State U., 1993-2005; bd. dirs. united Way Greater Dayton Area, 1984-92; small bus. innovative rsch. grant panels Nat. Sci. Found., 1988—. 1st lt. USAF, 1943-46. Named Outstanding Engr., Dayton Affiliate Socs., 1967, 89. Fellow Dayton Engrs. Club, Am. Inst. for Med. and Biol. Engring.; mem. ACLU, Nat. Acad. Engring., Am. Inst. Biol. Scis. (bioinstrumentation adv., coun. 1969-75), Internat. Orgn. of Legal Metrology (tech. advisor, sec. 1975-82), Amnesty Internat. Democrat. Achievements include co-development of melting point of gallium which has become recognized as a primary defining point of the International Temperature Scale. Home and Office: 3 Aspen Ct Yellow Springs OH 45387-1326 Office Phone: 937-767-4551.

TROPMAN, JOHN ELMER, social sciences educator; b. Syracuse, NY, Sept. 14, 1939; s. Elmer and Elizabeth (Overfield) T.; m. Penelope Savino, June 20, 1964; children: Sarah, Jessica, Matthew. AB, Oberlin Coll., 1961; AM, U. Chgo., 1963; PhD, U. Mich., 1967. Asst. prof. U. Mich., Ann Arbor, 1965-70, assoc. prof., 1970-76, prof. social work and social sci., 1976—. Author: Policy Management, 1984, American Values and Social Welfare, 1989, Catholic Ethic in American Society, 1996, Making Meetings Work, 1996, 2002, Successful Community Leadership, 1997, Managing Ideas in the Creating Organization, 2001, Catholic Ethic and the Spirit of Community, 2002, The Total Compensation Solution, 2003, Supervision and Management in Nonprofit Organizations, 2006. Recipient Monsignour O'Grady award Catholic U., Washington, 1986. Mem. Mich. Soc. Fellows (chair 1988-89). Avocations: fly and spin fishing, medical mysteries. Home: 3568 River Pines Dr Ann Arbor MI 48103-9516 Office Phone: 734-763-6275. Business E-Mail: tropman@umich.edu.

TROST, EILEEN BANNON, lawyer; b. Teaneck, NJ, Jan. 9, 1951; d. William Eugene and Marie Thelma (Finlayson) Bannon; m. Lawrence Peter Trost Jr., Aug. 27, 1977; children: Lawrence Peter III, William Patrick, Timothy Alexander. BA with great distinction, Shimer Coll., 1972; JD cum laude, U. Minn., 1976. Bar: Ill. 1976, U.S. Dist. Ct. (no. dist.) Ill. 1976, Minn. 1978, U.S. Tax Ct. 1978, U.S. Supreme Ct. 1981. Assoc. McDermott, Will & Emery, Chgo., 1976-82, ptnr., 1982-93; v.p. No. Trust Bank Ariz. N.A., Phoenix, 1993-95; ptnr. Sonnenschein Nath & Rosenthal, Chgo., 1995—2006, Bell, Boyd & Lloyd LLP, Chgo., 2006—. Mem. Am. Coll. Trust and Estate Coun., Minn. Bar Assn., Internat. Acad. Estate and Trust Law, Chgo. Estate Planning Coun. Roman Catholic. Office: Bell Boyd & Lloyd LLP 70 W Madison St #3100 Chicago IL 60602 Home Phone: 630-681-8063; Office Phone: 312-807-4411. Business E-Mail: etrost@bellboyd.com.

TROTTER, CHARLIE, chef; Degree in polit. sci., U. Wis., 1982. Owner, chef Charlie Trotter's, Chgo., Trotter's To Go, Lincoln Park, Ill., 2000—, "C", Los Cabos, Mexico, 2004—. Founder Charlie Trotter Culinary Edn. Found., 1999—. Author: Lessons in Excellence, 1999, Kitchen Sessions with Charlie Trotter, 1999, Gourmet Cooking for Dummies, 1999, Great Restaurants of the World: Charlie Trotter's, 2000, Charlie Trotter Cooks at Home, 2000, Charlie Trotter's, 2001, Charlie Trotter's Vegetables, 2001, Charlie Trotter's Seafood, 2001, Charlie Trotter's Desserts, 2001, Charlie Trotter's Meat and Game, 2001, Lessons in Service, 2001, Raw, 2003, Workin' More Kitchen Sessions with Charlie Trotter, 2004, The Cook's Book, 2005, Spa Cuisine; host: (tv series) Kitchen Sessions with Charlie Trotter. Named Best Chef: Midwest, James Beard Found., 1992; named to Who's Who in Food & Beverage in Am., 1996; recipient Grand award, Wine Spectator, 1993—, Humanitarian of Yr. award, Internat. Assn. Culinary Professionals, 2005, Outstanding Chef award, James Beard Found., 1999. Achievements include being one of 5 heroes to be honored by America's Promise. Office: 816 W Armitage Ave Chicago IL 60614

TROTTER, CORTEZ, city official, former fire commissioner; b. Chgo. First dep. fire commr. Chgo. Fire Dept., fire commr., 2001—06; exec. dir. Office of Emergency Mgmt. and Comm. (formerly Office of Emergency Comm.), 2006—. Apptd. to bd. dirs. Emergency Comm. (911) Bd., 1990—. Recipient Martin Luther King Jr. Excellence in Leadership award, Suburban Human Rels. Com. Office: City Hall 121 N La Salle Chicago IL 60602

TROTTER, DONNE E., state legislator, hospital administrator; b. Cairo, Ill., Jan. 30, 1950; s. James and Carita (Caldwell) T.; m. Rose Zuniga; 4 children. BA, U. Chgo., 1976, Chgo. State U.; MJ, Loyola U. Sch. Law. Sr. hosp. adminstr. Cook County Hosp., Chgo., 1981—; house rep. Ill. Ho. of Reps., Springfield, 1988-93; state senator Ill. Senate, Springfield, 1993—. State rep.

State of Ill., Chgo., 1988—; vice-chmn. Health Care Commn., Ill. Gen. Assembly, 1991, mem. human svcs. com., 1988—, mem. minority caucus. Adv. bd. mem. 8th Ward Region Dem., 1983—; mem. Ill. Black United Front. Mem. APHA, Ill. Pub. Health Assn., Nat. Assn. of Health Care Adminstrs., Nat. Conf. State Legislators, Nat. Conf. Black State Legislators. Office: 417 Capitol Bldg Springfield IL 62706-0001 Address: 8704 S Constance Ave Ste 324 Chicago IL 60617-2756

TROTTER, THOMAS ROBERT, lawyer; b. Akron, Ohio, Apr. 11, 1949; s. Fred and Josephine (Daley) Trotter; m. Martha Kaltenbach, 2003. BA, Ohio U., 1971; JD, Tulane U., 1975. Bar: Ohio 1975, D.C. 2000, U.S. Dist. Ct. (no. dist.) Ohio 1975. Assoc. Squire, Sanders & Dempsey, Cleve., 1975-80; shareholder Buckingham, Doolittle & Burroughs, Akron, 1980—2007; of counsel Vorys, Sater, Seymour and Pease LLP, Akron, Ohio, 2007—. Trustee Cascade Capital Corp., Akron, 1983-2000; chair taxation and legis. com. Greater Akron C. of C., 1988-95; trustee Akron-Summit Solid Waste Mgmt. Authority, 1994-97 Trustee Akron Symphony Orch., 1984-93, trustee Weathervane Cmty. Playhouse, 1996-2003, 06—, pres., 1999-2001. Mem. ABA, Ohio Bar Assn. (chair local govt. law com.), Akron Bar Assn., Nat. Assn. Bond Lawyers, Sigma Alpha Epsilon. Democrat. Home: 180 W Fairlawn Blvd Akron OH 44313 Office: Vorys Sater Seymour and Pease LLP 106 S Main St Ste 1100 Akron OH 44308 also: Vorys Sater Seymour and Pease LLP 2100 One Cleveland Ctr 1375 E Ninth St Cleveland OH 44114-1724 Office Phone: 330-208-1126, 216-479-6107. Business E-Mail: trtrotter@vssp.com, trtrotter@vorys.com.

TROUPE, CHARLES QUINCY, state legislator; b. St. Louis, May 12, 1936; Qiploma, Nat. Inst. Electronics & Tech, Denver. Elec. contrator; mem. Mo. Ho. of Reps. from 63d dist., 1978-82, Mo. Ho. of Reps. from 62d dist., 1982—. Chmn. Appropriations, Social Svc. and Corrections Coms. Mo. Ho. of Reps., mem. Budget, Banks & Fin. Instns., Local Govt. Accounts, Ops. and Fin Coms.; mem. Mo. Legis. Black Caucus. V.p. Local 788 ATU. Democrat. Home: PO Box 150019 Saint Louis MO 63115-8019

TROUT, MICHAEL GERALD, airport administrator; b. Apr. 16, 1959; B in Urban Adminstrn. with honors, U. Mich., 1993, MPA, 1996. Owner, operator Arrow Video, 1985-90; airport planning cons. GTA, 1990-93; prin. aviation planner SEMCOG, 1993-96; dep. dir. Detroit City Airport, 1996-2000; dep. dir. maintenance ops. Flint (Mich.) Bishop Airport, 2000—. Mgr. Whatley Farm Domino's Farms, 1989. Mem. Am. Assn. Airport Execs., Am. Planning Assn., Am. Inst. Cert. Planners, Am. Soc. Pub. Adminstrn., Mich. Assn. Airport Execs. Office: Fliint Bishop Airport G 3425 W Bristol Rd Flint MI 48507

TROY, DANIEL PATRICK, former state legislator, county official; b. Cleveland, Ohio, May 6, 1948; s. John Edward and Marjorie (Farrell) T. BA in Polit. Sci., U. Dayton, 1970. City councilman Ward I, Willowick, Ohio, 1972-77, coun. pres., 1980-82; pres. Lake County Coun. Govt., Ohio, 1975-78; committeeman Lake County Dem. Com., 1976; Ohio State Rep. Dist. 60., 1983-92, Dist. 70, 1993-97; del. Dem. Nat. Conv., 1984; pres., bd. dirs. Lake County (Ohio) Commrs., Painesville. Tech. Kahoe Air Balance Co., 1967-74; prof. Balance Co., 1975-80, proj. engr., 1980. Recipient Legis. Svc. award, 1983-84, Ohio Sea grant Disting. Svc. award, 1988, Legis. Leadership award Ohio Coalition for Edn. Handicapped Children, 1989, 91, Voc. Edn. Person of Yr. award, 1989, Ohio Edn. Broadcasting award, 1983, Friends of Cmty. Coll. Excellence award, 1994. Mem. AFL, East Side Irish-Am. Club. Home: 31600 Lakeshore Blvd Willowick OH 44095-3522

TROYER, LEROY SETH, architect; b. Middlebury, Ind., Nov. 23, 1937; s. Seth and Nancy (Miller) T.; m. Phyllis Eigsti, May 24, 1958; children: Terry, Ronald, Donald. BArch, U. Notre Dame, 1971. Founder, pres. LeRoy Troyer and Assocs., South Bend, Ind., 1971; chmn. Troyer Group, Inc. (formerly LeRoy Troyer and Assocs.), Mishawaka, Ind., 1988—; pres. Southfield, Inc., 1988—. Pres. Lead Devel., Inc.; founder, sec., treas. Am. Countryside, LLC, Midwest Farmers Market, LLC Author numerous documents; contbr. numerous papers and articles to publs. Past pres., chair Environic Found. Internat., Inc.; bd. dirs. Habitat for Humanity Internat. Americus, Ga., 1987-93, global leadership coun., 2003—; chair The Fuller Ctr. for Housing Ams., Ga., 2006—; bd. dirs. Coun. of Christian Colls. and Univs., 1991-96, Habitat for Humanity St. Joseph County, Ind., 1992-99, 2001-, Bethel Coll. 1988-97, 2001-, bd. chair 2005-, Evangelicals for Social Action, Wynnewood, Pa., 1997-2003, Mishawaka, CONNECT, HHS, South Bend, 1999-2003; bd. dirs., exec. com., trustee Fourth Freedom Forum Internat., 1996—, vice-chmn., 2005—; chmn., Miracle of Nazareth Internat. Found., 2000-03, 07-; trustee 2000—; bd. trustee Fuller Ctr. Housing, Americus, Ga., 2005—, chmn. 2006—. Recipient numerous local, state and nat. awards and honors. Fellow AIA (practice mgmt. com., chmn. 1983-84), Ind. Soc. Archs., Mennonite Econ. Devel. Assn. Internat. (chmn. bd., 1987-91). Avocations: photography, travel, reading, art, woodworking. Home: 1442 Deerfield Ct South Bend IN 46614-6429 Office: The Troyer Group Inc 550 Union St Mishawaka IN 46544-2346 Office Phone: 574-259-9976. Business E-Mail: leroy@troyergroup.com.

TROZZOLO, ANTHONY MARION, chemistry professor; b. Chgo., Jan. 11, 1930; s. Pasquale and Francesca (Vercillo) T.; m. Doris C. Stoffregen, Oct. 8, 1955; children: Thomas, Susan, Patricia, Michael, Lisa, Laura. BS, Ill. Inst. Tech., 1950; MS, U. Chgo., 1957, PhD, 1960. Asst. chemist Chgo. Midway Labs., 1952-53; assoc. chemist Armour Rsch. Found., Chgo., 1953-56; tech. staff Bell Labs., Murray Hill, NJ, 1959-75; Charles L. Huisking prof. chemistry U. Notre Dame, 1975-92, Charles L. Huisking prof. emeritus, 1992—; asst. dean U. Notre Dame Coll. Sci., 1993-98; P.C. Reilly lectr. U. Notre Dame, 1972, Hesburgh Alumni lectr., 1986, Disting. lectr. sci., 1986. Vis. prof. Columbia U., N.Y.C., 1971, U. Colo., 1981, Katholieke U. Leuven, Belgium, 1983, Max Planck Inst. für Strahlenchemie, Mülheim/Ruhr, Fed. Republic Germany, 1990; vis. lectr. Academia Sinica, 1984, 85; Phillips lectr. U. Okla., 1971; C.L. Brown lectr. Rutgers U., 1975; Sigma Xi lectr. Bowling Green U., 1976, Abbott Labs., 1978; M. Faraday lectr. No. Ill. U., 1976; F.O. Butler lectr. S.D. State U., 1978; Chevron lectr. U. Nev., Reno, 1983; J. Crano lectr. U. Akron, 2000; plenary lectr. various internat. confs.; founder, chmn. Gordon Conf. on Organic Photochemistry, 1964; trustee Gordon Rsch. Confs., 1988-92; cons. in field. Assoc. editor Jour. Am. Chem. Soc., 1975-76; editor Chem. Revs., 1977-84; editorial adv. bd. Accounts of Chem. Rsch., 1977-85; cons. editor Encyclopedia of Science and Technology, 1982-92; contbr. articles to profl. jours.; patentee in field. Fellow AEC, 1951, NSF, 1957-59; named Hon. Citizen of Castrolibero, Italy, 1997; recipient Pietro Bucci prize U. Calabria/Italian Chem. Soc., 1997. Fellow: AAAS (life), Inter-Am. Photochem. Soc., N.Y. Acad. Scis. (chmn. chem. scis. sect. 1969—70, Halpern award in photochemistry 1980), Am. Inst. Chemists (Student award 1950); mem.: Am. Chem. Soc. (lectr., Tex. lectr. 1975, Disting. Svc. award St. Joseph Valley sect. 1979, Coronado lectr. 1980, Pacific Coast lectr. 1981, Coronado lectr. 1993, N.Y. State lectr. 1993, Hoosier lectr. 1995, Ozark lectr. 1995, Rocky Mountain lectr. 1996, Coronado lectr. 1998, Osage lectr. 1998, Rocky Mountain lectr. 2002, SE Tex. lectr. 1996), Sigma Xi. Roman Catholic. Home: 53419 Hansel Ln South Bend IN 46637-5248 Office: U Notre Dame Dept Chemistry-Biochemistry Notre Dame IN 46556-5670 Home Phone: 574-271-7291; Office Phone: 574-631-5768. Business E-Mail: trozzolo.4@nd.edu.

TRUCANO, MICHAEL, lawyer; b. Washington, May 28, 1945; s. Peter Joseph and Fern Margaret (Bauer) T.; m. Doreen E. Struck, 1969; children: Michael, David. BA, Carleton Coll., 1967; JD, NYU, 1970. Assoc. Dorsey & Whitney, Mpls., 1970-75, ptnr., 1976—2004, head of office, 2000—03, of counsel, 2005—. Office: Dorsey & Whitney LLP Ste 1500 50 S 6th St Minneapolis MN 55402-1498 Office Phone: 612-340-2673. Business E-Mail: trucano.mike@dorsey.com.

TRUCE, WILLIAM EVERETT, chemist, educator; b. Chgo., Sept. 30, 1917; s. Stanley C. and Frances (Novak) T.; m. Eloise Joyce McBroom, June 16, 1940; children: Nancy Jane, Roger William. BS, U. Ill., 1939; PhD, Northwestern U., 1943. Mem. faculty Purdue U., 1946-88, prof. chemistry, 1956-88, prof. chemistry emeritus, 1988—, asst. dean Grad. Sch., 1963-66. Com. mem. numerous univ.; chmn. profl. meetings; exec. officer Nat. Organic Symposium, 1961; chmn. Gordon Rsch. Conf. on Organic Reactions and Processes; cons. in field. Co-author book; contbr. articles to profl. jours., chpts. to books. Guggenheim fellow Oxford U., 1957 Mem. Am. Chem. Soc., Phi Beta Kappa (sec. Purdue chpt.), Sigma Xi (pres. Purdue chpt.). Achievements include research in new methods of synthesis, devel. new kinds of compounds and reactions. Home: 350 Ponca Pl Boulder CO 80303-3802

TRUCKSIS, THERESA A., retired library director; b. Hubbard, Ohio, Sept. 1, 1924; d. Peter and Carmella (DiSilverio) Pagliasotti; m. Robert C. Trucksis, May 29, 1948 (dec. May 1980); children: M. Laura, Anne, Michele, Patricia, David, Robert, Claire, Peter; m. Philip P. Hickey, Oct. 19, 1985 (dec. May 1993). BS in Edn., Youngstown Coll., 1945; postgrad., Youngstown State U., 1968-71; MLS, Kent State U., 1972. Psychometrist Youngstown (Ohio) Coll., 1946-49; instr. ltd. svc. Youngstown State U., 1968-71; libr. Pub. Libr. Youngstown & Mahoning County, Youngstown, 1972-73, asst. dept. head, 1973-74, asst. dir., 1985-89, dir., 1989-97, NOLA Regional Libr. System, Youngstown, 1974-85. Contbr. articles to profl. jours. Mem. bd. Hubbard Sch. Dist., 1980-85. Mem. ALA, Ohio Libr. Assn. (bd. dirs. 1979-81), Pub. Libr. Assn. Address: 133 Viola Ave Hubbard OH 44425-2062

TRUDEAU, GARRETSON BEEKMAN (GARRY TRUDEAU), cartoonist; b. NYC, July 21, 1948; m. Jane Pauley, June 14, 1980; children: Ross and Rachel (twins), Thomas. BA, Yale U., 1970, MFA, 1973, DHL, 1976. Syndicated cartoonist, writer. Creator: comic strip Doonesbury; syndicated nationwide comic strip; author: Still a Few Bugs in the System, 1972, The President is a Lot Smarter Than You Think, 1973, But This War Had Such Promise, 1973, Call Me When You Find America, 1973, Guilty, Guilty, Guilty, 1974, Joanie, 1974, The Doonesbury Chronicles, 1975, What Do We Have for the Witnesses, Johnnie?, 1975, Dare to Be Great, Ms. Caucus, 1975, Wouldn't A Gremlin Have Been More Sensible?, 1975, We'll Take it From Here, Sarge, 1975, Speaking of Inalienable Rights, Amy., 1976, You're Never Too Old for Nuts and Berries, 1976, An Especially Tricky People, 1977, As the Kid Goes For Broke, 1977, Stalking the Perfect Tan, 1978, Any Grooming Hints for Your Fans, Rollie?, 1978, Doonesbury's Greatest Hits, 1978, But The Pension Fund was Just Sitting There, 1979, We're Not Out of the Woods Yet, 1979, A Tad Overweight, but Violet Eyes to Die For, 1980, And That's My Final Offer!, 1980, The People's Doonesbury, 1981, He's Never Heard of You, Either, 1981, In Search of Reagan's Brain, 1981, Ask for May, Settle for June, 1982, Unfortunately, She Was Also Wired for Sound, 1982, Adjectives Will Cost You Extra, 1982, Gotta Run, My Government is Collapsing, 1982, The Wreck of the Rusty Nail, 1983, You Give Great Meeting, Sid, 1983, Guess Who Fish Face, 1983, It's Supposed to be Yellow Pinhead: Selected Cartoons From Ask For May, Settle For June, Vol. I, 1983, Do All Birders Have Bedrooms, 1983, Farewell to Alms, 1984, Doonesbury Dossier: The Reagan Years, 1984, Doonesbury: A Musical Comedy, 1984, Check Your Egos at the Door, 1985, That's Doctor Sinatra, You Little Bimbo, 1986, Death of a Party Animal, 1986, Doonesbury Deluxe: Selected Glances Askance, 1987, Downtown Doonesbury, 1987, Calling Dr. Whoopee, 1987, The Doonesbury Desk Diary 1988, 1987, Talking Bout My G-G-Generation, 1988, We're Eating More Beets, 1988, Read My Lips, Make My Day, Eat Quiche & Die! A Doonesbury Collection, 1989, Small Collection, 1989, The Doonesbury Stamp Album, 1990, 1990, Recycled Doonesbury: Second Thoughts on a Gilded Age, 1990, You're Smokin' Now, Mr. Butts! A Doonesbury Book, 1990, Welcome to Club Scud: A Doonesbury Book, 1991, Action Figure: The Life and Times of Doonesbury's Uncle Duke, 1992, The Portable Doonesbury, 1993, In Search of Cigarette Holder Man: A Doonesbury Book, 1994, Doonesbury Nation, 1995, Flashbacks: Twenty-five Years of Doonesbury, 1995, The Bundled Doonesbury: A Pre-Millennial Anthology, 1998, Peace Out, Dawg! Tales from Ground Zero, 2002, Got War?, 2003, The Long Road Home: One Step at a Time, 2005; co-author: Tales From the Margaret Mead Taproom, 1979; plays include: Doonesbury, 1983, Rapmaster Ronnie, A Partisan Review (with Elizabeth Swados), 1984 Pulitzer Prize for Editorial Cartooning, 1975, Commander's Award for Pub. Svc., US Dept. Army, 2006.

TRUE, STEVE, radio personality; Student, U. Wis. Radio host 1130 WISN, Greenfield, Wis., 1989—. Office: WISN Radio 12100 W Howard Ave Greenfield WI 53228

TRUHLAR, DONALD GENE, chemist, educator; b. Chgo., Feb. 27, 1944; s. John Joseph and Lucille Marie (Vancura) T.; m. Jane Teresa Gust, Aug. 28, 1965; children: Sara Elizabeth, Stephanie Marie. BA in Chemistry summa cum laude, St. Mary's Coll., Winona, Minn., 1965; PhD in Chemistry, Calif. Inst. Tech., 1970. Asst. prof. chemistry and chem. physics U. Minn., Mpls., 1969—72, assoc. prof., 1972—76, prof., 1976—93, Inst. of Tech. prof., 1993—98, Inst. of Tech. disting. prof., 1998—, Lloyd H. Reyerson prof., 2002—. Cons. Los Alamos Sci. Lab.; vis. fellow Joint Inst. for Lab. Astrophysics, 1975-76; sci. dir. Minn. Supercomputer Inst., 1987-88, dir., 1988—. Editor Theoretical Chemistry Accounts (Theoretica Chemica Acta), 1985—2001, Computer Physics Comms., 1986—, Topics Phys. Chemistry, 1992—99, Understanding Chem. Reactivity, 1990—92, mem. editl. bd. Jour. Chem. Physics, 1978—80, Chem. Physics Letters, 1982—, Jour. Phys. Chemistry, 1985—87, Understanding Chem. Reactivity, 1993—, Advances in Chem. Physics, 1993—, Internat. Jour. Modern Physics C., 1994—, IEEE Computational Sci. and Engring., 1994—98, Internat. Jour. Quantum Chemistry, 1996—2000, Computing in Sci. and Engring., 1999—, Jour. Chemical Theory and Computation, 2004—, Chemical Physics, 2005, chief adv. editor Theoretical Chemistry Accounts, 2002—. Recipient Minn. award, 2003, NAS award for Sci. Reviewing, 2004, award for sci. computing, NAS, 2004; fellow, Alfred P. Sloan Found., 1973—77; grantee, NSF, 1971—, NASA, 1987—95, U.S. Dept. Energy, 1979—, NIST, 1995—98, Dept. of Def., 2001—; scholar, Ruhland Walzer Meml. scholar, 1961—62; John Stauffer fellow, 1965—66, NDEA fellow, 1966—68. Fellow AAAS, Am. Phys. Soc.; mem. Am. Chem. Soc. (sec.-treas. theoretical chemistry subdivsn. 1980-89, councilor 1985-87, assoc. editor jour. 1984—, Award for computers in chem. and pharm. rsch. 2000, Peter Debye award in phys. chemistry 2006). Achievements include research, numerous publications in field. Home: 5033 Thomas Ave S Minneapolis MN 55410-2240 Office: U Minn 207 Pleasant St SE Minneapolis MN 55455-0431 Office Phone: 612-624-7555. Business E-Mail: truhlar@umn.edu.

TRUITT, WILLIAM HARVEY, private school educator; b. Alton, Ill., May 27, 1935; s. Howard Earl and Mary Margaret (Haper) T.; m. Janetha Mitchell, Aug. 5, 1961; children: Joy Elizabeth, Janita Ann. BA, Principia Coll., 1957; MA, So. Ill. U., 1964. Headmaster Forman Schs., Litchfield, Conn.; prin. upper and lower sch. The Principia, St. Louis, headmaster; ret., 1998. Musician: The Worlds Greatest Love Songs, Sing Unto the Lord, A New Song. Mem. NASSP, Mo. Assn. Secondary Prins., St. Louis Ind. Sch. Heads, Mo. Ind. Schs. (pres. 1983-84), Am. Coun. for Am. Pvt. Edn. (v.p. 1983-84), North Cen. Accrediting Assn. (exec. bd. dirs. 1988-91). Office: 4002 Radcliffe Place Ct Wildwood MO 63025 Business E-Mail: bill@billtruitt.com.

TRUJILLO, ANGELINA, endocrinologist; b. Long Beach, Calif. BA in Psychology, Chapman Coll., 1974; postgrad., U. Colo., 1974-75, MD, 1979. Resident in internal medicine Kern Med. Ctr., Bakersfield, Calif., 1979-82; fellow in endocrinology UCLA, Sepulveda, Calif., 1982-84, chief resident dept. internal medicine, 1985-86; chief diabetes clinic Sepulveda (Calif.) VA Med. Ctr., 1986-89; physician specialist Olive View Med. Ctr., Sylmar, Calif., 1989; chief divsn. endocrinology U. S.D. Sch. Medicine, Sioux Falls, 1990—2001; ACOS R&D Royal C. Johnson VA Med. Ctr., Sioux Falls, 1998—2001. Adj. instr. UCLA, 1982-84, adj. asst. prof. medicine, 1985-89, clin. asst. prof. family medicine, 1994-2001; asst. prof. U. S.D. Sch. Medicine, 1990-94, assoc. prof., 1994—, assoc. dir. internal medicine residency program, 1992-95; spkr. in field. Pub. spkr. in diabetes, women and heart disease. Grantee NIH, 1986-89, Am. Diabetes Assn., 1985-87, Pfizer, Inc., 1990-91, Nat. Heart, Lung, and Blood Inst., 1994—, Bristol-Myers Squibb, 1994-2001 Mem. ACP, Am. Fedn. Clin. Rsch. (med. sch. rep., endo/metabolism subspecialty coun.), Am. Soc. Hypertension, Am. Diabetes Assn., Assn. Program Dirs. in Internal Medicine, Assn. Clerkship Dirs. in Internal Medicine, S.D. State Med. Assn., Seventh Dist. Med. Soc., Wilderness Med. Soc. (mem. environ. coun.).

TRURAN, JAMES WELLINGTON, JR., astrophysicist, educator; b. Brewster, NY, July 12, 1940; s. James Wellington and Suzanne (Foglesong) T.; m. Carol Kay Dell'Acy, June 26, 1965; children— Elaina Michelle, Diana Lee, Anastasia Elizabeth. BA in Physics, Cornell U., Ithaca, NY, 1961; MS in Physics, Yale U., New Haven, Conn., 1963, PhD in Physics, 1966. Postdoctoral rsch. assoc. NAS-NRC Goddard Inst. Space Studies, NASA, NYC, 1965-67; asst. prof. physics Belfer Grad. Sch. Sci., Yeshiva U., 1967-70; rsch. fellow in physics Calif. Inst. Tech., 1968-69; assoc. prof. Belfer Grad. Sch. Sci., Yeshiva U., 1970-72, prof., 1972-73; prof. astronomy U. Ill., Urbana, 1973-91; sr. vis. fellow, Guggenheim Meml. Found. fellow Inst. Astronomy, U. Cambridge, Eng., 1979-80; trustee Aspen Ctr. Physics, 1979-85, 91-93, 96-99, v.p., 1985-88; assoc. U. Ill. Ctr. for Advanced Study, 1979-80, 86-87; prof. astronomy astrophysics U. Chgo., 1991—; sr. physicist Argonne Nat. Lab., 2003—. Alexander von Humboldt-Stiftung sr. scientist Max-Plank Inst., Munich, Germany, 1986-87, 94; Beatrice Tinsley vis. prof. U. Tex., Austin, 1999; Biermann lectr. in astrophysics, Max-Planck Inst., Munich, 2001. Contbr. articles to profl. jours.; co-editor: ucleosynthesis, 1968, Nucleosynthesis— Challenges and New Developments, 1985, Nuclear Astrophysics, 1987, Type Ia Supernovae: Theory and Cosmology, 2000, Cosmic Chemical Evolution, 2002; editor: Physics Letters B, 1974-80. Co-recipient Yale Sci. and Engring. Assn. annual award for advancement basic or applied sci., 1980 Fellow AAAS, Am. Phys. Soc.; mem. Am. Astron. Soc., Am. Phys. Soc., Internat. Astron. Union. Home: 210 Wysteria Dr Olympia Fields IL 60461-1202 Office: U Chgo Dept Astronomy Astrophysics 5640 S Ellis Ave Chicago IL 60637-1433 Business E-Mail: truran@nova.uchicago.edu.

TRUSKOWSKI, JOHN BUDD, lawyer; b. Chgo., Dec. 3, 1945; s. Casimer T. and Jewell S. (Kirk) T.; m. Karen Lee Sloss, Mar. 21, 1970; children: Philip K., Jennifer B. BS, U. Ill., 1967; JD, U. Chgo., 1970. Bar: Ill. 1970, U.S. Dist. Ct. (no. dist.) Ill. 1970, U.S. Tax Ct. 1977. Assoc. Keck, Mahin & Cate, Chgo., 1970-71, 74-78, ptnr., 1978-97, Lord, Bissell & Brook, Chgo., 1997—. Author, editor Callaghan's Federal Tax Guide, 1987. Lt., USNR, 1971-74. Mem. ABA, Ill. State Bar Assn., Chgo. Bar Assn. Republican. Unitarian. Avocations: model railroading, stamp collecting/philately. Home: 251 Kimberly Ln Lake Forest IL 60045-3862 Office: Lord Bissell & Brook Harris Bank Bldg 115 S Lasalle St Chicago IL 60603-3801 Office Phone: 312-443-0257.

TRUWIT, MITCHELL, private equity; b. 1969; BS in Polit. Sci., Vassar College, Poughkeepsie, NY; MBA, Harvard Univ., 1997. Dir. bus. devel. Oxford Health Plans, Conn., 1997; sr. v.p. corp. devel. Priceline.com, COO, exec. v.p. Conn.; pres, CEO Orbitz Worldwide, Travelport, Chgo.; ptnr. Apax Partners, L.P., NYC, 2006—. Spkr. in field; adv. mem. Travelport bd. dirs., 2006—. Advisory bd. mem. Special Olympics, Conn. Named one of 40 Under Forty, Crain's Bus. Chgo., 2005. Avocation: squash. Office: Apax Partners LP 153 E 53rd St 53rd Fl New York NY 10022 Office Phone: 212-753-6300. Office Fax: 312-894-5001, 646-514-7242.

TRYLOFF, ROBIN S., food products executive; BS, U. Mich.; MS, U. Chgo. Exec. dir., cmty. rels. Sara Lee Corp.; exec. dir. Sara Lee Found., pres., 2002—. Chair, bd. dirs. Donors Forum of Chgo., 2004. Office: Sara Lee Found 3 First Nat Plz Chicago IL 60602-4260

TSALIKIAN, EVA, physician, educator; b. Piraeus, Greece, June 22, 1949; came to U.S., 1974; d. Vartan and Arousiak (Kasparian) T.; m. Arthur Bonfield, Apr. 8, 2000. MD, U. Athens, 1973. Rsch. fellow U. Calif., San Francisco, 1974-76; resident in pediats. Children's Hosp., Pitts., 1976-78, fellow in endocrinology, 1978-80; rsch. fellow Mayo Clinic, Rochester, Minn., 1980-83; from asst. prof. to prof. dept. pediats. U. Iowa, 1983—2004, dir. pediat. endocrinology hosps. and clinics, 1988—, prof. pediats., 2004—, interim chmn. dept. pediatrics, 2004, vice chmn. clin. affairs Dept. Pediats., 2005—; chief staff hosp. U. Iowa Health Ctr., 2006—. Recipient Young Physician award, AMA, 1977; fellow, Juvenile Diabetes Found., 1978—80, Heinz Nutrition Found., 1980—81. Mem. Am. Diabetes Assn. (bd. dirs. Mid-Am. sect.), Endocrine Soc., Soc. Pediat. Rsch., Am. Pediat. Soc., Lawson Wilkins Soc. for Pediat. Endocrinology, Internat. Soc. Pediat. and Adolescent Diabetes, Midwest Pediat. Endocrino Soc. (pres. 1996-99). Home: 206 Mahaska Dr Iowa City IA 52246-1606 Office: U Iowa Dept Pediatrics 2856 JPP Iowa City IA 52242

TSAO, GEORGE T., chemical engineer, educator; b. Nanking, China, Dec. 4, 1931; married; 3 children. BSc, Nat. Taiwan U., 1953; MSc, U. Fla., 1956; PhD in Chem. Engring., U. Mich., 1960. Asst. prof. physics Olivet Coll., 1959-60; chem. engr. Merck & Co., Inc., 1960-61; rsch. chemist TVA, 1961-62; sect. leader hydrolysis and fermentation, rsch. dept. Union Starch & Refining Co. divsn. Miles Labs., Inc., 1962-65, asst. rsch. dir., 1965-66; from assoc. prof. to prof. chem. engring. Iowa State U., 1966-77; prof. chem. engring. Purdue U., West Lafayette, Ind., 1977—, dir. Lab. Renewable Resources Engring., 1978-99. Recipient John Ericsson award Dept. Energy, 1989. Mem. AIChE, Am. Chem. Soc., Am. Soc. Engring. Edn. Office: Purdue U Lab Renewable Resources Engring 1295 Potter Dr West Lafayette IN 47906-1333

TSOULFANIDIS, NICHOLAS, engineering educator, dean; b. Ioannina, Greece, May 6, 1938; arrived in US, 1963; s. Stephen and Aristea (Ganiou) T.; m. Zizeta Koutsombidou, June 21, 1964; children: Stephen, Lena. BS in Physics, U. Athens, Greece, 1960; MS in Nuclear Engring., U. Ill., 1965, PhD in Nuclear Engring., 1968. Registered profl. engr., Mo. Prof. nuclear engring. U. Mo., Rolla, 1968—2002, vice chancellor acad. affairs, 1985-86, assoc. dean for rsch. Sch. Mines and Metallurgy, 1989; prof. chem. and metall. engring. U. Nevada, Reno. Sr. engr. Gen. Atomic Co., San Diego, 1974-75; researcher Cadarache France, 1986-87. Author: Measurement and Detection of Radiation, 1984, 2d edit. 1995; co-author: The Nuclear Fuel Cycle: Analysis and Management, 1990; editor: Nuclear Technology, 1997-. Recipient Glenn Murphy award, outstanding contributions in profession and tchg. of nuclear engring., Am. Soc. for Engring. Edn., 1995. Mem. Am. Nuclear Soc. (chmn. radiation protection shielding div. 1987-88), Health Physics Soc., Nat. Soc. Profl. Engring., Rotary. Office: Chemical & Metallurgical Engring Univ Nevada Mail Stop 388 Reno NV 89557 Office Phone: 775-784-8287. Office Fax: 775-327-5059. E-mail: nikost@unr.edu.

TSUBAKI, ANDREW TAKAHISA, theater director, educator; b. Chiyoda-ku, Tokyo, Japan, Nov. 29, 1931; s. Ken and Yasu (Oyama) T.; m. Lilly Yuri, Aug. 3, 1963; children: Arthur Yuichi, Philip Takeshi. BA in English, Tokyo Gakugei U., Tokyo, Japan, 1954; postgrad. in Drama, U. Saskatchewan, Saskatoon, Canada, 1958-59; MFA in Theatre Arts, Tex. Christian U., 1961; PhD in Speech & Drama, U. Ill., 1967. Tchr. Bunkyo-ku 4th Jr. High Sch., Tokyo, 1954—58; instr., scene designer Bowling Green (Ohio) State U., 1964—68; asst. prof. speech & drama U. Kans., Lawrence, 1968—73, assoc. prof., 1973—79; vis. assoc. prof. Carleton Coll., orthfield, Minn., 1974; lectr. Tsuda U., Tokyo, 1975; vis. assoc. prof. theatre Tel-Aviv (Israel) U., 1975—76; vis. prof. theatre Mo. Repertory Theatre, Kansas City, Mo., 1976, Nat. Sch. Drama, New Delhi, 1983; prof. theatre, film, east Asian Languages and Cultures U. Kans., Lawrence, 1979—2000, prof. emeritus, 2000—. Dir. Internat. Theatre Studies Ctr., U. Kans., Lawrence, 1971-2000, Operation Internat. Classical Theatre, 1988—; Benedict disting. vis. prof. Asian studies Carleton Coll., 1993; area editor Asian Theatre Jour., U. Hawaii, Honolulu, 1982-94; chmn. East Asian Langs. and Cultures, U. Kans., Lawrence, 1983-90; mem. editl. bd. Studies in Am. Drama, Oxford, Miss., 1985-88. Dir. plays Kanjincho, 1973, Rashomon, 1976, 96, King Lear, 1985, Fujito and Shimizu, 1985, Hippolytus, 1990, Busu and the Missing Lamb (Japan) 1992, Suehirogari and Sumidagawa, 1992, 93, Tea, 1995; choreographed Antigone (Greece), 1987, Hamlet (Germany), 1989, The Resistible Rise of Arturo Ui, 1991, Man and the Masses (Germany), 1993, The Children of Fate (Hungary), 1994, The Great Theatre of the World (Germany); editor Theatre Companies of the World, 1986; contbg. author to Indian Theatre: Traditions of Performance, 1990; contbr. 7 entries in Japanese Traditional plays to the Internat. Dictionary of Theatre, vol. 1, 1992, vol. 2, 1994. Named to Order of Sacred Treasure, Govt. of Japan, 2006; recipient citation, Min. Fgn. Affairs Japan, 2003, Statement of Appreciation, Chmn. and Bd. Dirs. Hiratsuka Internat. Exch. Assn., 2004; World Univ. Svc. scholar, U. Saskatchewan, 1958—59, University fellow, U. Ill., 1961—62, Rsch. fellow, The Japan Found., 1974—75, 1990, Rsch. Fulbright grantee, 1983. Fellow Coll. Am. Theatre (elected 2002); mem. Am. Theatre Assn., Asian Theatre Program (chair 1976-79), Assn. for Asian Studies, Assn. Kans. Theatres., Assn. Kans. Theatres U/C Div. (chmn. 1980-82), Assn. for Theatre in Higher Edn., Assn. for Asian Performance. Democrat. Buddhist. Avocations: ki-aikido (5th dan), photography, travel. Home: 924 Holiday Dr Lawrence KS 66049-3005

TUAN, DEBBIE FU-TAI, chemist, educator; b. Kiangsu, China, Feb. 2, 1930; arrived in U.S., 1958; d. Shiau-gien and Chen (Lee) T.; m. John W. Reed, Aug. 15, 1987. BS in Chemistry, Nat. Taiwan U., Taipei, 1954, MS in Chemistry, 1958, Yale U., New Haven, Conn., 1960, PhD in Chemistry, 1961. Rsch. fellow Yale U., New Haven, 1961-64; rsch. assoc. U. Wis., Madison, 1964-65; asst. prof. Kent (Ohio) State U., 1965-70, assoc. prof., 1970-73, prof., 1973—; vis. scientist Yeshiva U., NYC, summer 1966; rsch. fellow Harvard U., Cambridge, 1969-70; vis. scientist SRI Internat., Menlo Park, Calif., 1981; rsch. assoc. Cornell U., Ithica, N.Y., 1983. Vis. prof. Acad. Sinica of China, Nat. Taiwan U. and Nat. Tsing-Hwa U., summer 1967, Ohio State U., 1993, 95. Contbr. articles to profl. jours. Recipient NSF Career Advanced award, 1994—; U. Grad. fellow

Nat. Taiwan U., 1955-58, F.W. Heyl-Anon F fellow Yale U., 1960-61, U. Faculty Rsch. fellow Kent State U., 1966, 68, 71, 85; Pres. Chiang's scholar Chinese Women Assn., 1954, 58, Grad. scholar in humanity and scis. China Found., 1955. Mem.: Am. Chem. Soc., Am. Phys. Soc., Sigma Xi. Office: Kent State U Chemistry Dept Williams Hl Kent OH 44242-0001

TUCKER, DON EUGENE, retired lawyer; b. Rockbridge, Ohio, Feb. 3, 1928; s. Beryl Hollis and Ruth (Primmer) T.; m. Elizabeth Jane Parke, Aug. 2, 1950; children: Janet Elizabeth, Kerry Jane, Richard Parke. BA, Aurora Coll., 1951; LL.B., Yale, 1956. Bar: Ohio 1956. Since practiced in, Youngstown, Ohio; asso. Manchester, Bennett, Powers & Ullman, 1956-62, ptnr., 1962-73, of counsel, 1973-87; gen. counsel Comml. Intertech Corp., Youngstown, 1973-75, v.p., gen. counsel, 1975-83, also dir., sr. v.p., gen. counsel, 1983-87, sr. v.p., 1987-93; ret., 1993. Solicitor Village of Poland, Ohio, 1961-63; former chmn. bd., pres., trustee United Cerebral Palsy Assn., Youngstown and Mahoning County; trustee Mahoning County Tb and Health Assn.; former trustee, pres. Indsl. Info. Inst.; former pres., trustee Ea. Ohio Lung Assn.; trustee, former chmn. Cmty. Corp.; trustee, former pres. Butler Inst. Am. Art. With USMCR, 1946-48, 51-53. Mem. Ohio Bar Assn., Mahoning County Bar Assn. (pres. 1972, trustee 1970-73), Youngstown Area C. of C. (chmn. bd. dirs. 1979). Methodist. Home: 6005 Martins Point Rd Kitty Hawk NC 27949-3819

TUCKER, KEITH A., investment company executive; b. 1945; BBA, U. Tex., 1967, JD, 1970. With KPMG Peat Marwick, Dallas, 1970-85, Stephens, Inc., Little Rock, 1985-87, Trivest Inc., Miami, Fla., 1987-91; dir. Waddell & Reed Inc., Shawnee Mission, Kans., 1989—, vice chmn., 1991—, chmn. Home: 3831 Turtle Creek Blvd Apt 6h Dallas TX 75219-4412

TUCKER, MICHAEL, elementary school principal; Prin. Grace Abbott Elem. Sch., Omaha, 1982—. Recipient Elem. Sch. Recognition award U.S. Dept. Edn., 1989-90. Office: Grace Abbott Elem Sch 1313 N 156th St Omaha NE 68118-2371

TUCKER, RAYMOND A., chemical company executive; Various positions Bayer Corp., Pitts., 1968-99, sr. v.p. inorganics products; CFO, treas. HB Fuller Co., St. Paul, 1999—. Office: HB Fuller Co 1200 Willow Lake Bvld Saint Paul MN 55110

TUCKER, THOMAS RANDALL, public relations executive; b. Indpls., Aug. 6, 1931; s. Ovie Allen and Oris Aleen (Robertson) T.; m. Evelyn Marie Armuth, Aug. 9, 1953; children: Grant, Roger, Richard. AB, Franklin Coll., 1953. Grad. asst. U. Minn., 1953-54; dir. admissions registrar Franklin Coll., 1954-57; with Cummins Engine Co., Inc., Columbus, Ind., 1957, dir. pub. rels., 1968-88; pub. rels. cons. Mem. sch. bd. trustees Bartholomew County, Ind., 1966-72, pres., 1968-69; mem. Ind. State Bd. Edn., 1977-89; treas. Bartholomew County Rep. Ctrl. Com., 1960-80; sec. Columbus Learning Ctr. Mgmt. Corp.; hon. trustee Franklin Coll.; trustee Ind. State Mus. Mem. Pub. Rels. Soc. Am., Columbus (Ind.) C. of C. (Cmty. Svc. award 1986), Rotary, Sagamore of the Wabash, Kappa Tau Alpha, Phi Delta Theta, Sigma Delta Chi. Lutheran. Home: 4380 N Riverside Dr Columbus IN 47203-1123 Office: PO Box 3005 Columbus IN 47202-3005

TUCKER, WATSON BILLOPP, lawyer; b. Dobbs Ferry, NY, Nov. 16, 1940; s. Watson Billopp and Mary (Prema) T.; children: Robin, Craig, Christopher, Alexander, John. BS, orthwestern U., Evanston, Ill., 1962; JD magna cum laude, Northwestern U., 1965. Bar: Ill. 1965, US Dist. Ct. (no. dist.) Ill. 1966, US Supreme Ct. 1971, US Dist. Ct. (no. dist.) NY 1976, US Ct. Appeals (2d, 3d, 5th, 6th, 7th, and 9th cirs.). Ptnr. Mayer, Brown, Rowe & Maw, Chgo., 1972-99, Smith Tucker & Coghlan, Sycamore, Ill., 1999—. Fellow Am. Coll. Trial Lawyers. Office Phone: 815-787-7033. Business E-Mail: wbtucker@smithtucker.com.

TUCKMAN, BRUCE WAYNE, educational psychologist, educator, researcher; b. NYC, Nov. 24, 1938; s. Jack Stanley and Sophie Sylvia (Goldberg) T.; children: Blair Z., Bret A. BS, Rensselaer Poly. Inst., 1960; MA, Princeton U., 1962, PhD, 1963. Rsch. assoc. Princeton (N.J.) U., 1963; rsch. psychologist Naval Med. Rsch. Inst., Bethesda, Md., 1963-65; assoc. prof. edn. Rutgers U., New Brunswick, N.J., 1965-70, prof., 1970-78, dir. Bur. R&D, 1975-78; dean Coll. Edn. Baruch Coll., CUNY, 1978-82; sr. rsch. fellow CUNY, 1982-83; dean Coll. Edn. Fla. State U., Tallahassee, 1983-86, prof., 1983—98; prof., dir. W.E. Dennis Learning Ctr., Ohio State U., Columbus, 1998—. Author: Preparing to Teach the Disadvantaged, 1969 (N.J. Assn. Tchrs. of English Author's award 1969), Conducting Educational Research, 1972, 5th rev. edit., 1999 (Phi Delta Kappa Rsch. award 1973), Evaluating Instructional Programs, 1979, 2d rev. edit., 1985, Analyzing and Designing Educational Research, 1979, Effective College Management, 1987, Testing for Teachers, 1988; (novel) Long Road to Boston, 1988, Educational Psychology: From Theory to Application, 1992, 96, 98, 2002, Learning and Motivation Strategies: Your Guide to Success, 2002. Rsch. dir. Task Force on Competency Stds. Trenton, N.J., 1976. N.Y. State Regents scholar, 1956; Kappa Nu grad. scholar, 1960; NIMH predoctoral fellow, 1961, 62; Rutgers U. faculty study fellow, 1974-75 Fellow: APA; mem.: Am. Ednl. Rsch. Assn. Office: 250B Younkin Success Ctr 1640 Neil Ave Columbus OH 43201-2333 Office Phone: 614-688-8284.

TUCKNER, MICHELLE, newscaster; b. Hudson, Wis. BS in Journalism/Broadcast News, U. Kans. Weekend news reporter KTKA, Topeka; anchor/reporter WEAU-TV Channel 13, 2000—. Recipient award, Kans. Assn. Broadcasters, William Randolph Hearst Journalism awards; scholar, Assn. for Women in Sports Media, 1999. Office: WEAU PO Box 47 Eau Claire WI 54702

TUCKSON, REED V., physician, health insurance company executive; Grad., Howard U.; MD, Georgetown U. Residency & fellowship in internal med. Hosp. Univ. Pa.; commr. pub. health Washington, 1986—90; sr v.p. progs. March of Dimes Birth Defects Found., 1990—91; pres. Charles R. Drew U., LA, 1991—97; sr. v.p. profl. stds. AMA, Chgo., 1998—2000; sr. v.p. consumer health and med. care advancement UnitedHealth Group, Mpls., 2000—06, exec. v.p., head med. affairs, 2006—. Office: UnitedHealth Grp PO Box 1459 Minneapolis MN 55440*

TULLY, ROBERT GERARD, lawyer; b. Dubuque, Iowa, Sept. 7, 1955; s. Thomas Alois and Marjorie May (Fosselman) T. BA, U. Notre Dame, 1977; postgrad., U. Notre Dame, London, summer 1979; JD, Drake U., 1981. Bar: Iowa 1981, U.S. Dist. Ct (no. and so. dists.) Iowa 1981, U.S. Ct. Appeals (8th cir.) 1981, U.S. Supreme Ct. 1986. Assoc. Verne Lawyer & Assocs., Des Moines, 1981-93, Michael J. Galligan Law Firm; ptnr. Galligan, Tully, Doyle & Reid P.C., 1993, Anderson & Tully, Des Moines, 2003—. Bd. dirs. Dubuque Lumber Co., sec., treas., 1984-87; lectr. Nat. Collegiate Mock Trial Drake U., Des Moines, 1984-93, atty., coach, 1985-93; bd. counselors Drake U. Law Sch., 1986-92, 2005—, chmn. alumni rels. com. Contbr. articles to profl. jours. Com. mem. Dubuque County Dem. party, 1976-78, Polk County Dem. party, 1982-83, 87-89, 92—, del. state convs., 1988, chmn. IA Dem. Party, 1999-2007; bd. dirs. nat. Coun. Alcoholism and Other Drug Dependencies for Des Moines Area, pres. 1985-92; mem. nat. commn. on future of Drake U.; Dem. candidate for U.S. Congress 2d Dist., 1998. Fellow Iowa Acad. Trial Lawyers (compiler various profl. publs.); mem. ABA, ATLA (state del. 1991—, bd. govs. 1993-2003, key peron com.), Iowa Bar Assn. (Uniform Jury Instructions rules com., young lawyers sect., com. legal svcs. for elderly chmn. fed. practice com., law related edn. com.), Assn. Trial Lawyers Iowa (pres. 1992-93, pres.-elect 1991-92, v.p. legis. 1988-91, bd. govs. 1985—, Outstanding Key Person 1983-84, 91-92, chmn. key person com. 1985-88), Polk County Bar Assn. (bd. dirs. 1993—, grievance com.), Iowa Citizens Action Network (bd. dirs. 1989-98), Blackstone Inn of Ct., Notre Dame Club of Des Moines (pres. 1981-83), Drake Student Bar Assn. (pres. 1980-81), Phi Alpha Delta. Roman Catholic. Home: 4315 Greenwood Dr Des Moines IA 50312 Office: Anderson and Tully 700 W Towers 1200 Valley West Dr West Des Moines IA 50266-1908 E-mail: tully@andersontullylaw.com.

TULLY, THOMAS ALOIS, building materials executive, consultant, educator; b. Dubuque, Iowa, Nov. 11, 1940; s. Thomas Aloysius and Marjorie Mae (Fosselman) T.; m. Joan Vonnetta Dubay, Nov. 30, 1963; children: Thomas Paul, Maureen Elizabeth. BA, Loras Coll., 1962; postgrad., Georgetown U., 1963-66; MPA, Harvard U., 1968. Mgmt. trainee Office of Sec. Def., Washington, 1962-63, fgn. affairs officer, 1963-70; v.p. Dubuque Lumber Co., 1970-84, pres., 1984-91, Tully's, 1991-92, LBM Mktg. Assocs., Inc., 1992—; gen. mgr. Kane How Appraisor Svcs., 2006—. Adj. instr. Divine Word Coll., 1971, Loras Coll., 1972; adj. instr. Clarke Coll., 1987-89, instr., 1989-91, asst. prof., 1992-97, chmn. dept. acctg. and bus., 1993-97, dir. small bus. inst., 1994-97; dir. MBA program U. Dubuque, 1997-2000; founder, exec. dir. Dubuque Area Com. on Fgn. Rels., 2001—, pres., 2002—; pres. Hills and Dales Child Devel. Ctr., Inc., 1992-96; trustee Alverno Apts., 1995-2001, pres., 1999-2001. Mem. Dubuque Human Rights Commn., 1974—75, chmn., 1975, Iowa State Com. for Employer Support of Guard and Res. Forces, 1988—, area chmn., 2000—05, Iowa state coord., 2004—06, state vice chair, 2006—07; city councilman Dubuque, 1975—79; bd. dirs. League Iowa Municipalities, 1977—79; mayor City of Dubuque, 1978; vice chmn. Iowa Temporary State Land Preservation Policy Com., 1978—79; pres. N.E. Iowa Regional Coordinating Coun., 1985—93, East Ctrl. Intergovtl. Assn. Bus. Growth, Inc., 1987—2002, chmn., 1993—2002; bd. dirs. Pvt. Industry Coun. of Dubuque and Delaware Counties, Inc., 1983—86; trustee Divine Word Coll., 1989—97; pres. Barn Cmty. Theatre, 1988—89; chmn. bd. trustees United Way Svcs. of Dubuque, 1990, campaign chmn., 1991, bd. mem., 1980—94; trustee Carnegie-Stout Pub. Libr., 2001—05, pres., 2003—04; Iowa state chair Nat. Security Network, 2006—. Recipient Meritorious Civilian Svc. award Sec. of Def., 1970, Gov.'s Vol. award, 1989. Mem. Nat. Lumber and Bldg. Material Dealers Assn. (exec. com. 1988-90), Iowa Lumbermen's Assn. (pres. 1984, chmn. legis. com. 1985-90), Northwestern Lumbermen Assn. (bd. dirs. 1984-87, 2d v.p. 1988, 1st v.p. 1989-90, pres. 1990-91). Democrat. Roman Catholic. Home: 838 Stone Ridge Pl Dubuque IA 52001-1362 Office: LBM Mktg Assocs 838 Stone Ridge Pl Dubuque IA 52001 Home Phone: 563-556-1904; Office Phone: 563-590-6565. E-mail: tully.thomas@alumni.ksg.harvard.edu.

TUMA, JOHN, former state legislator, lawyer; b. Sept. 25, 1962; m. Wendy Tuma; 1 child. BA, Mankato State U.; JD, U. Minn. Bar: Minn. Mem. Minn. Ho. of Reps., St. Paul, 1994—. Independent-Republican.

TUNHEIM, JAMES RONALD, state legislator, farmer; b. Drayton, ND, June 6, 1941; s. Olaf and Grace (Doran) T.; m. Diana Lee Rojas, 1964; children: Christopher Alan, Aaron Cory, Nicolle Anne. Student, Thief River Falls Vocat. Sch., 1959-61. Owner, mgr. James Tunheim Farms, Kennedy, Minn., 1964—; mem. Minn. Ho. of Reps., St. Paul, 1982—. Vice chmn. commerce and econ. devel. tourism divsn., mem. regulated industry, edn., ethics, and transp. coms. Treas. Kennedy (Minn.) Sch. Dist., 1975; del. Minn. Dem. Conv., 1978; past chmn. Kittson County (Minn.) Dem.-Farmer-Labor Com.; mem. bd. Maria Luth. Ch., 1975. Mem. Nat. Rural Water Assn., Minn. Rural Water Assn. (bd. dirs. 1978), Lions, Masons, Shriners (sec., treas.).

TUNHEIM, JERALD ARDEN, academic administrator, physicist, educator; b. Claremont, SD, Sept. 3, 1940; s. Johannes and Annie Tunheim; children: Jon, Angie, Alec. BS in Engring. Physics, S.D. State U., 1962, MS in Physics, 1964; PhD in Physics, Okla. State U., 1968. Vis. scientist Sandia Corp., Albuquerque, 1970-71, Ames (Iowa) AEC Labs., 1972; asst. prof. S.D. State U., Brookings, 1968-73, assoc. prof., 1973-78, prof., 1978-80, prof., head physics dept., 1980-85; dean Ea. Wash. U., Cheney, 1985-87; pres. Dakota State U., Madison, S.D., 1987—. Bd. dirs. Nat. Skill Stds. Bd., 1998—. Co-author: Elementary Particles and Unitary Symmetry, 1966, Quantum Field Theory, 1966; contbr. articles to profl.jours. Bd. dirs. Lake Area Improvement Corp. Grantee USDA, 1987-88, S.D. Govt. Office Edn. Devel., 1988-89, U.S. Dept. Edn., Eisenhower Program, 1985-86, 87-90, 92-93, 95-96, U.S. Dept. Edn. Math. and Sci. Program, 1989-92; named Tchr. of Yr. S.D. State U., 1972. Mem. NSPE, Am. Phys. Soc., Am. Assn. Physics Tchrs., Madison C. of C. (bd. dirs. 1990—), Rotary. Republican. Lutheran. E-mail: Jerald.Tunheim@dsu.edu.

TUNHEIM, KATHRYN H., public relations executive; b. Sacred Heart, Minn., 1956; BA in Polit. Sci., U. Minn., 1979. Staff asst. U.S. Senator Wendell Anderson, 1977-79; mgr., bus. planning NCR Comten, 1979-81; corp. pub. rels. mgr. Honeywell, 1981-84, dir. corp. pub. rels., 1985-86; v.p. pub. rels. and internal comm. Honeywell Inc., 1987-90; pres., CEO Tunheim Santrizos, Mpls., 1990—. Office: Tunheim Santrizos 1100 Riverview Tower 8009 34th Ave S Minneapolis MN 55425-1608

TUPPER, LEON F., manufacturing executive; BS in Indsl. Psychology, Wayne State U.; MS in Indsl. Psychology, U. Mich.; postgrad., Dartmouth U. Tng. mgr. Am. Motors Corp., Detroit, 1972-77, buyer/procurement specialist, 1977-83, sr. buyer interior trim group, 1983-86, purchasing mgr. interior trim group, 1986-88; sales mgr. steering divsn. Sheller-Globe Corp., Toledo, Ohio, 1984-88; dir. sales and engring. Gilreath Mfg., Inc., Howell, Mich., 1988-91, pres., CEO, owner, 1991—. Trustee Cleary Coll., Ypsilanti, Mich.; treas., trustee High/Scope Edn. Rsch. Found.; bd. trustees Rehab. Inst. of Mich., Detroit Med. Ctr.; bus. sch. bd. exec. advisors Wayne State U.; mem. friends of the Detroit Area Pre-Coll. Engring. Program, Nat. Conf. for Cmty. Justice, 100 Black Men of Detroit. Address: PO Box 408 Howell MI 48844-0408 Fax: 248-728-1753.

TURANO, DAVID A., lawyer; b. Ashtabula, Ohio, Sept. 9, 1946; s. Egidio A. and Mary Agnes (Bartko) T.; m. Karen J. Emmel, Aug. 29, 1970; children: Aaron, Thad, Bethen, Kyle. BS, Kent State U., 1968; JD, Ohio State U., 1971. Bar: Ohio 1971. Staff atty. The Pub. Utilities Commn. Ohio, Columbus, 1971-72; assoc., then ptnr. George, Greek, King, McMahon and McConnaughey, Columbus, 1972-79; ptnr. Baker & Hostetler, Columbus, 1979-96, Harris, Carter, Mahota, Turano & Mazza, Columbus, 1996-97, Harris, Turano & Mazza, Columbus, 1997—2003; of counsel Shoemaker, Howarth & Taylor, LLP, Columbus, 2003—. Mem. ABA, Ohio State Bar Assn., Columbus Bar Assn., Transp. Lawyers Assn. Roman Catholic. Office: Shoemaker Howarth & Taylor LLP 471 E Broad St Ste 2001 Columbus OH 43215 Home Phone: 614-888-4686; Office Phone: 614-232-0426. Business E-Mail: dturano@midohiolaw.com.

TURILLI, M. LOUISE, lawyer; Grad., Oberlin Coll., Ohio; M, U. Cin.; law degree, U. Conn. Sch. Law. Ptnr. east coast law firm; law v.p., asst. sec. NCR Corp.; v.p., assoc. gen. counsel Bellsouth Corp., Atlanta; v.p., dep. gen. counsel Qwest Comm. Internat. Inc., Denver; v.p., gen. counsel Ryerson Inc., Chgo., 2007—. Office: Ryerson Inc 2621 W 15th Pl Chicago IL 60608-1712

TURLEY, MICHAEL ROY, lawyer; b. St. Louis, Mar. 7, 1945; s. W. Richard and Mary Jeanne (Ogle) T.; m. Patricia Ederle, Aug. 21, 1968; children: James, Alisyn. AB, Princeton U., 1967; JD, Mo. U., 1970. Bar: Mo. 1970, U.S. Dist. Ct. (ea. dist.) Mo. 1975. Assoc. Lewis, Rice & Fingersh (formerly Lewis & Rice), St. Louis, 1970-71, 74-80, ptnr., 1980—. Mem. Jefferson County Planning and Zoning Commn., 1987—2000; chmn., sec.-treas. Ctr. for Emerging Techs. Mem. ABA, Mo. Bar Assn., St. Louis Met. Bar Assn., Princeton Club. Episcopalian. Office: Lewis Rice & Fingersh 500 N Broadway Ste 2000 Saint Louis MO 63102-2147 E-mail: mturley@lewisrice.com.

TURNBULL, ANN PATTERSON, special education educator, consultant, research director; b. Tuscaloosa, Ala., Oct. 19, 1947; d. H. F. and Mary (Boone) Patterson; m. H. Rutherford Turnbull III, Mar. 23, 1974; children: Jay, Amy, Kate. BS in Edn., U. Ga., 1968; MEd, Auburn U., 1971; EdD, U. Ala., 1972. Asst. prof. U. N.C., Chapel Hill, 1972-80; disting. prof., co-dir. Beach Ctr. U. Kans., Lawrence, 1980—. Author: Free Appropriate Public Education, 2000, Exceptional Lives: Special Education in Today's Schools, 2004, Families, Professionals and Exceptionality, 2006. Recipient Rose Kennedy Internat. Leadership award, Kennedy Found., 1990, 20th Century award in Mental Retardation, 1999; Joseph P. Kennedy Jr. Found. fellow, 1987-88. Mem.: The Arc-U.S. (named Educator of Yr. 1982), Am. Assn. on Mental Retardation (bd. dirs. 1986—88, v.p. 2001, pres.-elect 2002, pres. 2003—04, Rsch. award 2004). Democrat. Avocations: travel, exercise. Office: Univ Kans Beach Ctr 3136 1200 Sunnyside Dr Lawrence KS 66045-7534 Home: 730 New Hampshire St Ste 3K Lawrence KS 66044 Home Phone: 785-843-9500; Office Phone: 785-864-7608. E-mail: turnbull@ku.edu.

TURNBULL, CHERYL LANKARD, investment company executive; b. Chicago Heights, Ill., Aug. 21, 1960; d. David Reid and Bettina Anne (Priamvera) L.; m. Michael Lambo Turnbull. BBA, Miami U., 1982; Masters of Mgmt. in Fin. & Internat. Bus., Northwestern U., 1987. Analyst corp. fin. divsn. Continental Ill. Nat. Bank & Trust Co.; assoc., Mergers & Acquisitions dept. Prudential Securities, 1987—90; v.p. Prudential Bache Interfunding, 1990—91; mng. dir. Aston Ltd. Partners, LP, 1992—95; with Bank One Corp., 1996—2003; spl. limited ptnr. Phronesis Partners LP, Columbus, Ohio, 2005—. Bd. dirs. Quick-Med Technologies Inc., 2006—. Mem. Kellogg Alumni Assn. Office: Phronesis Partners LP 180 E Broad St Ste 1704 Columbus OH 43215

TURNBULL, H. RUTHERFORD, III, lawyer, educator; b. NYC, Sept. 22, 1937; s. Henry R. and Ruth (White) T.; m. Mary M. Slingluff, Apr. 4, 1964 (div. 1972); m. Ann Patterson, Mar. 23, 1974; children: Jay, Amy, Katherine. Grad., Kent (Conn.) Sch., 1955; BA, Johns Hopkins U., 1959; LLB with honors, U. Md., 1964; LLM, Harvard U., 1969. Bar: Md., N.C. Law clk. to Hon. Emory H. Niles Supreme Bench Balt. City, 1959-60; law clk. to Hon. Roszel C. Thomsen U.S. Dist. Ct. Md., 1962-63; assoc. Piper & Marbury (now LDA Piper), Balt., 1964-67; prof. Sch. Govt. U. N.C., Chapel Hill, 1969—80, U. Kans., Lawrence, 1980—. Disting. prof. spl. edn., courtesy prof. law U. Kans. Editor-in-chief Md. Law Rev. Cons., author, lectr., co-founder, co-dir. Beach Ctr. on Disability, U. Kans.; pres. Full Citizenship Inc., Lawrence, 1987-93; spl. staff-fellow U.S. Senate subcom. on disability policy, Washington, 1987-88; bd. dirs. Camphill Assn. N.Am., Inc., 1985-87; trustee Judge David L. Bazelon Ctr. Mental Health Law, 1993-2007, chmn., 2000-05. With US Army, 1960-65. Recipient Nat. Leadership award at. Assn. Pvt. Residential Resources, 1988, Internat. Coun. for Exceptional Children, 1996, Am. Assn. on Mental Retardation, 1997, Century award Nat. Trust for Hist. Preservation in Mental Retardation, 1999, Nat. Adv. award Am. Music Therapy Assn., 2002, Leadership award Camphill Assn. N.Am., 2004, Leadership award The Arc of the US, 2004, U. Kans. Gene A. Budig Disting. Tchg. Professorship award, 2005, Nat. award advocacy positive supports Assn. Persons with Severe Handicaps, 2005, Kans.U. Sch. of Edn. Disting. Leadership award, 2005, Burton Blatt award Coun. Exceptional Children, 2006; named Nat. Educator of Yr., The Arc of the U.S., 1982; Pub. Policy fellow Joseph P. Kennedy, Jr. Found., 1987-88. Fellow Am. Assn. on Mental Retardation (pres. 1985-86, bd. dirs. 1980-86); mem. ABA (chmn. disability law commn. 1991-95), U.S.A. Assn. for Retarded Citizens (sec. and dir. 1981-83), Assn. for Persons with Severe Handicaps (treas. 1988, bd. dirs. 1987-90), Nat. Assn. Rehab. Rsch. and Tng. Ctrs. (chair govt. affairs com. 1990-93), Internat. Assn. Sci. Study of Mental Deficiency, Internat. League of Assns. for Persons with Mental Handicaps, Johns Hopkins U. Alumni Assn. (pres. N.C. chpt. 1977-79). Democrat. Episcopalian. Office: U Kans 3111 Haworth Hall 1200 Sunnyside Ave Lawrence KS 66045-7534 Office Phone: 785-864-7600. Business E-Mail: Rud@ku.edu.

TURNER, ARTHUR L., state legislator; b. Chgo., Dec. 2, 1950; m. Rosalyn Turner; 2 children. BS, Ill. State U.; MS, Lewis U. Ill. state rep. Dist. 9, 1981—; vice chmn. consumer protection, higher edn. Ill. Ho. Reps., ins., labor and com. revenue, chmn. housing com., health care, ins. com., dep. majority leader; treas. Ill. Minority Caucus, 1987—. Exec. com. Nat. Conf. of Black State Legislators, 1987-89; mem. housing com. Nat. Conf. of State Legislators, 1987-89; mem. NCSL, Reapportionment Task Force, 1988—; vice chmn. edn. com., 1989—. Mem. Lawndale Cmty. Econ. Devel. Corp.; active Operation Brotherhood, YMCA. Mem. NAACP, Urban League. Home: 2102 S Avers Ave Chicago IL 60623-2467 Office: Ill House of Reps State Capitol Springfield IL 62706-0001

TURNER, EVAN HOPKINS, retired art museum director; b. Orono, Maine, Nov. 8, 1927; s. Albert Morton and Percie Trowbridge (Hopkins) T.; m. Brenda Winthrop Bowman, May 12, 1956; children: John, Jennifer. AB cum laude, Harvard U., 1949, MA, 1950, PhD, 1954; degree (hon.), Swarthmore Coll., Sir George Williams U., Cleve. State U.; Case Western Res. U., 2001. Head docent svc. Fogg Mus., Cambridge, Mass., 1950-51; curator Robbins Art Collection of Prints, Arlington, Mass., 1951; teaching fellow fine arts Harvard U., 1951-52; lectr., research asst. Frick Collection, NYC, 1953-56; gen. curator, asst. dir. Wadsworth Atheneum, Hartford, Conn., 1956-59; dir. Montreal Mus. Fine Arts, Que., Can., 1959-64, Phila. Mus. Art, 1964-77, Ackland Art Mus., 1978-83, Cleve. Mus. Art, 1983-93. Adj. prof. art history U. Pa., U. N.C., Chapel Hill, 1978-83; disting. vis. prof. Oberlin Coll., 1993-95. Author: Ray K. Metzker: Photographs, 2001. Recipient Chevalier L'Ordre Arts Lettres. Mem. Assn. Art Mus. Dirs., Coll. Art Assn. Am., Am. Mus. Assn., Century Assn. Club. Home: 2125 Cypress St Philadelphia PA 19103-6507

TURNER, FRANK, announcer; m. Nicky Turner, 1999; 1 child. BA in Broadcast Comm., Columbia Coll., Chgo., 1982. Gen. assignment reporter, anchor WFLD-TV, Chgo., WWL-TV, New Orleans; co-anchor Action News Weekend, WXYZ-TV, Detroit, 1990—95, co-anchor Action News at 5pm, 1995—98, co-anchor, 2000—. Recipient Emmy award, Broadcasters award, AP, Michele Clark Fellowship award, Radio and TV News Dirs. Assn., TV award, N.Y. Festivals. Office: WXYZ-TV 20777 W Ten Mile Rd Southfield MI 48037

TURNER, FRED L., retired fast food company executive; b. 1933; married. BS, Drake U., 1954. With McDonald's Corp., Oak Brook, Ill., 1956—2004, exec. v.p., 1967—68, pres., chief adminstrv. officer, 1968—73, CEO, 1973—87, chmn., 1977—90, sr. chmn., 1990—2004, hon. chmn. With U.S. Army, 1954-56. Office: McDonald's Corp One Kroc Dr Oak Brook IL 60523

TURNER, HAROLD EDWARD, retired education educator; b. Hamilton, Ill., Nov. 22, 1921; s. Edward Jesse and Beulah May (White) T.; m. Catherine Skeeters, Apr. 5, 1946; children: Michele Turner Nimerick, Thomas, Barbara Turner McMahon, Krista Turner Landgraf. AB, Carthage Coll., 1950; MS, U. Ill. -Urbana, 1951, Ed.D. (George Peabody fellow), 1956. Tchr. Taylorville (Ill.) Jr. H.S., 1951-52, Moline (Ill.) Jr. H.S., 1952-54; dir. elem. edn. Jefferson County, Colo., 1955-57; prin. Jefferson County H.S., 1957-60; asst. prof. edn. North Tex. State U., Denton, 1960-63; asst. supt. curriculum Sacramento City Schs., 1963-66; assoc. prof., chmn. dept. curriculum and instrn. U. Mo., St. Louis, 1966-69, prof., 1971-85, prof. emeritus, 1985—, chmn. dept. adminstrn., founds., secondary edn., 1977-78, dept. chmn., 1983-85. Vis. prof. Adams State Coll., Alamosa, Colo., 1959, U. Ga., Athens, 1981-82; adj. prof. NYU, 1965, U. Ill., 1980; cons. various sch. dists., Tex., Mo.; spl. cons. Mo. State Dept. Edn., 1973. Author: (with Adolph Unruh) Supervision for Change and Innovation, 1970; contbr. articles to profl. jours. Served with USNR, 1942-46. Presbyterian. Home: 685 S La Posada Cir # AL 52 Green Valley AZ 85614 E-mail: gazvk@aol.com.

TURNER, JOHN, manufacturing executive; Exec. v.p. The LTV Corp., Cleve., 1999—. Office: LTV Steel Co 5800 Steel Ctr Ste 255 Seven Hills OH 44131-6913

TURNER, JOHN GOSNEY, insurance company executive, director; b. Springfield, Mass., Oct. 3, 1939; s. John William and Clarence Oma (Gosney) T.; m. Leslie Corrigan, June 23, 1962; children: John Fredric, Mary Leslie, James Gosney, Andrew William. BA, Amherst Coll., 1961; student, Advanced Mgmt. Program, Harvard U., 1980. Assoc. actuary Monarch Life Ins. Co., Springfield, Mass., 1961-67; group actuary Northwestern Nat. Life Ins. Co., Mpls., 1967-75, sr. v.p. group, 1975-79, sr. v.p., chief actuary, 1979-81, exec. v.p., chief actuary, 1981-83, pres., chief operating officer, 1983—; chmn., CEO Northwestern Nat. Life Ins. Co. (now ReliaStar Fin. Corp.), Mpls., 1993—. Dir. NWNL Reins. Co., NWNL Gen. No. Life, North Atlantic Life Ins. Co. N.Y. Trustee Abbott-Northwestern Hosps., Evans Sch. Found.; chmn. Minn. Trustees of the Evans Scholars Found. Fellow Soc. Actuaries; mem. Am. Acad. Actuaries, Western Golf Assn. (dir.), Minn. Golf Assn. Clubs: Minikahda (Mpls.). Home: 301 Kenwood Pkwy Apt 502 Minneapolis MN 55403-1165

TURNER, JOHN W., state legislator; b. Lincoln, Ill., 1956; m. Kimberly Turner; 1 child, Jack. BA, U. Ill., 1978; JD, DePaul U., 1981. Pub. defender Logan County, 1984-87, state atty., 1988-94; mem. Blue Ribbon Com., Firearm Transfer Inquiry Program, 1992—; Ill. state rep. Dist. 90, 1994—; atty. Kavanagh, Scully Sudow, White & Frederick PC, 1981-82, Turner & Rossi, 1982-87. Bd. dirs. Lincoln YMCA, chmn. fin. com.; active Lincoln Jaycees. Mem. Logan County Tri-Police Assn., Elks, Phi Beta Kappa, Phi Kappa Phi. Office: Wallace Computer Svcs Inc 4600 Roosevelt Rd Hillside IL 60162-2034

TURNER, JONATHAN SHIELDS, computer science educator, researcher; b. Boston, Nov. 13, 1953; m. Helen Gaddy; 1 child, Gregory. AB, Oberlin Coll., 1977; BS in Computer Sci., Washington U., St. Louis, 1977, BSEE, 1977; MS in Computer Sci., Northwestern U., 1979, PhD in Computer Sci., 1982. Mem. tech. staff Bell Labs., aperville, Ill., 1977-83; asst. to assoc. prof. computer sci. Washington U., St. Louis, 1983-90, prof., 1990—, chmn. computer sci. dept., 1992-97, Henry Edwin Sever prof. engring., 1994—2006, Barbara J. and Jerome R. Cox Jr. prof. computer sci., 2006—. Adv. NSF, 1990; co-founder Growth

Networks. Editl. bd. IEEE/Assn. Computing Machinery Transactions on Networking, 1993; contbr. numerous articles to profl. jours.; patentee in field. Recipient Tech. Devel. award St. Louis, Econ. Coun., 1995. Fellow IEEE (Koji Kobayashi Computers and Comm. award 1994), Assn. Computing Machinery; mem. NAE. Avocations: music, tennis, reading. Office: Computer Sci and Engring Dept Washington U Campus Box 1045 Saint Louis MO 63130-4899 Office Fax: 314-935-7302.

TURNER, LEE, travel company executive; b. 1952; BS, Worcester Polytechnic Inst., 1974; MBA, Dartmouth, 1976. With Baxter Healthcare, Deerfield, Ill., 1976-79, 82-87, Southeastern Pub. Svc. Co., Miami Beach, Fla., 1979-82; exec. v.p. BTI Ams., Inc., Northbrook, Ill., 1987-98; CFO WorldTravel Ptnrs., orthbrook, 1998—. Office: World Travel Ptnrs 2700 Patriot Blvd Ste 200 Glenview IL 60025-8064

TURNER, MICHAEL R., congressman; b. Dayton, Ohio, Jan. 11, 1960; s. Ray and Vivian Turner; m. Lori Turner; 2 children. BS in Polit. Sci., Ohio No. U., Ada, 1982; JD, Case Western Res. U. Sch. Law, 1985; MBA, U. Dayton, Ohio, 1992. Bar: Ohio 1985. Corp. counsel Modern Technologies Corp., Dayton, Ohio; pres. JMD Devel.; mayor Ohio, 1994—2002; mem. US Congress from 3rd Ohio dist., 2003—. Mem. armed svcs. com. US Congress, 2003—, mem. govt. reform com., 2003—, chmn. federalism and the census subcommittee, 2005—, mem. vets. affairs com., 2005—. Recipient Nat. Legis. Leadership award, US Conf. Mayors, 2005, Restore Am. Hero award, Nat. Trust Hist. Preservation and HGTV, 2005. Mem.: Am. Corp. Counsel Assn., Ohio Bar Assn., Dayton Bar Assn., ABA. Republican. Office: US House Reps 1740 Longworth House Office Bldg Washington DC 20515 Office Phone: 202-225-6465. Office Fax: 202-225-6754.

TURNER, MICHAEL STANLEY, astrophysics professor, researcher, science administrator; b. LA, July 29, 1949; s. Paul Joseph and Janet Mary (Lindholm) Turner; m. Terri Lee Shields, Aug. 1978 (div. Sept. 1980); m. Barbara Lynn Ahlberg, Sept. 10, 1988; children: Rachel Mary, Joseph Lucien. BS in Physics, Calif. Inst. Tech., Pasadena, 1971; MS in Physics, Stanford U., Calif., 1973, PhD in Physics, 1978; DSc (hon.), Mich. State U., East Lansing, 2005. Enrico Fermi fellow U. Chgo., 1978-80, from asst. to assoc. prof. physics and astronomy and astrophysics, 1980-85, prof., 1985—, chmn. dept. astronomy and astrophysics, 1997—2003, Bruce V. and Diana M. Rauner Disting. Svc. prof., 1998—, scientist Fermi Nat. Accelerator Lab., Batavia, Ill., 1983—2003, 2006—; asst. dir. US SF, 2003—06; chief scientist Argonne Nat. Lab., 2007—. Trustee Aspen Ctr. Physics, Colo., 1984—97, pres., 1989—93, hon. trustee, 2002—; Halley lectr. Oxford U., 1994; Klopsteg lectr. Am. Assn. Physics Tchrs., 1999; Neils Bohr lectr. Copenhagen U., 2001; Marker lectr. Pa. State U., 2002; W. Paul fellow Bonn U., 2000; Houston lectr. Rice U., 2003; Herzfield lectr. Cath. U., 2004; Buhl lectr. Carnegie Mellon U., 2004; Heinrich Hertz lectr. DESY-Germany, 2004; Kaczmarczk lectr. Dexel U., 2004; Buhl lectr. Carnegie Mellon, 2004; Fisher lectr. Brandeis U., 2005; Centennial lectr. Purdue U., 2005; Shaw lectr. So. Ill. U., 2005; Mohler Prize lectr. U. Mich., 2007. Author: (with E.W. Kolb) The Early Universe, 1990; contbr. over 200 articles to profl. jours. Trustee Ill. Math. Sci. Acad., 1998-2003, Project Exploration, Ill., 2002-03, Fermi Rsch. Alliance, 2006-. Sloan fellow A.P. Sloan Found., 1983-88; recipient Disting. Alumni award Caltech, 2006. Fellow AAAS (chair physics sect. 2003), Am. Acad. Arts and Scis., Am. Phys. Soc. (mem. exec. bd. 1992-94, chmn. publ. oversight com. 1993-94, chmn. nominating com. 1999-2000, Lilienfeld prize 1997, Primakoff lectr., 2003, chair-elect, dir. astrophysics, 2007), Phi Beta Kappa (nat. lectr. 2002-2003); mem. NAS (NRC astronomy astrophysics survey com. 1998-2000, chair NRC com. Physics of Universe, 2000-02, chair physics sect. 2007-, bd. on physics and astronomy, 2007), Am. Astron. Soc. (Helen B. Warner prize 1984), Internat. Astron. Union, Sigma Xi. Office: U Chgo Astron & Astrophysics Ctr 5640 S Ellis Ave Chicago IL 60637-1433 Office Phone: 630-252-3575. Business E-Mail: mturner@uchicago.edu.

TURNER, MONICA GOIGEL, ecologist; b. NYC, Dec. 9, 1958; d. Peter Joseph and Dorothy Ann (Burger) Goigel; m. Michael G. Turner, Aug. 28, 1982. BS in biology summa cum laude, Fordham U., 1980; PhD in ecology, U. Ga., 1985. Environ. specialist US Nat. Park Svc., Washington, 1981; grad. non-teaching asst. U. Ga., Athens, 1980-83, rsch. asst. Inst. Ecology, 1983-85, postdoctoral rsch. assoc. Inst. Ecology, 1985-87; Hollaender fellow Oak Ridge Nat. Lab., Tenn., 1987-89, rsch. staff scientist environ. scis. divsn., 1989—94; asst. prof. zoology U. Wis., 1994—95, assoc. prof. zoology, 1995—99, prof. zoology, 1999—. Adj. asst. prof. ecology U. Tenn., 1990—94. Editor: Landscape Heterogeneity and Disturbance, 1987; co-editor-in-chief: Ecosystems; mem. editl. bd.: BioScience, Conservation Ecology, Ecological Applications. Mem. Internat. Assn. Ecology, Internat. Assn. Landscape Ecology (program chair U.S. chpt. 1986—), AAAS, Am. Inst. Biol. Scis., Ecol. Soc. Am., NAS, Phi Beta Kappa, Phi Kappa Phi. Roman Catholic. Office: Univ Wis Dept Zoology 432 Birge Hall 430 Lincoln Dr Madison WI 53706 Office Phone: 608-262-2592. E-mail: turnermg@wisc.edu.

TURNER, PAUL ERIC, state legislator; m. Cyndy Rush. BS, Taylor U., 1975. Pres., CEO Family Sales Co. & T-3 Investments, Gas City, Ind.; mem. Ind. State Ho. of Reps. Dist. 32, 1982-86, 1994—, mem. elec. and apportionment com., mem. ways and means com. Former state chmn. Am. Legis. Exch. Coun.; mem. small bus. adv. coun. Fed. Res. Bank. Active State Enterprise Zone. Mem. Am. Pyrotechnics Assn., Taylor U. Trojan Club (bd. mem.), Gas City C. of C. (bd. mem.). Office: Ind House of Reps State Capitol Indianapolis IN 46204

TURNER, REGINALD MAURICE, JR., lawyer; b. Detroit, Feb. 25, 1960; s. Reginald and Anne Laura (Mims) T.; m. Marcia Holland, June 10, 1989. BS in Indsl. Psychology, Wayne State U., 1982; JD, U. Mich., 1987. Bar: Mich. With UPS, Livonia, Mich., 1977-83, Profl. Pers. Svc. div. B.P.A. Enterprises, Detroit, 1983-84; summer assoc. Office of the Gen. Counsel GM Corp., Detroit, 1985, 86; law clk. Sachs, Nunn, Kates, Kadushin, O'Hare, Helveston & Waldman, Detroit, 1987; jud. law clk. to Hon. Dennis W. Archer Mich. Supreme Ct., Detroit, 1987-89; ptnr. Sachs, Waldman PC, Detroit, 1989—2000; atty. Clark Hill PLC, Detroit, 2000—. Vice chair Detroit Police Found.; active Mich. State Bd. Edn., 2003—, Detroit Bd. edn., 2000-2003. White House fellow, 1996-97; recipient Irving Stenn Jr. award U. Mich. Law Sch., 1987; named Barrister of the Yr., Outstanding Young Lawyer State Bar Mich., 1999; named one of the Best Lawyers in Am., 2002-; named to Super Lawyers, 2006-; named one of Most Influential Black Americans, Ebony mag., 2006. Mem. ABA, ACLU, NAACP, Fed. Bar Assn., Nat. Bar Assn. (pres. 2005—), State Bar Mich. (commn., pres. 2002-03), Wolverine Bar Assn. (pres. 1994-95, Damon J. Keith award 2004), Detroit Bar Assn., Alpha Phi Alpha. Office: Clark Hill PLC 500 Woodward Ave Ste 3500 Detroit MI 48226-3435 E-mail: rturner@clarkhill.com.

TURNER, ROBERT LLOYD, state legislator; b. Columbus, Miss., Sept. 14, 1947; s. Roosevelt and Beatrice (Hargrove) T.; m. Gloria Harrell; children: Roosevelt, Robert, Ryan. BS, U. Wis., Racine, 1976. Mgr. French Quarter Restaurant, Racine, 1989; legislator Wis. State Assembly, Madison, 1990—, mem. transp. com. bldg. commn., mem. ways and means com., labor com., fin. institutions com., minority vice chmn. caucus, highway com., chmn. Dem. Caucus. Br. sales mgr. ETG Temporaries, Inc., Racine, 1989—; pub. Communicator News, Racine, 1989—; v.p. Racine Raider Football Team. State chmn. Dem. Black Polit. Caucus, Madison; pres. Bd. Health, Racine; chmn. Wis. State Elections Bd., Madison, 1990; alderman Racine City Coun., 1976—; chair Econ. Devel. Com., Racine; regional dir. Badger State Games, Racine; active Pvt. Industry Coun. Southeastern Wis., 1988-89, bd. dirs. Racine County Youth Sports Assn.; active Racine Juneteenth Day Com., bd. advisors Big Bros./Big Sisters. Sgt. USAF, 1967-71, Vietnam. Decorated Commendation medal; named Man of Yr. 2d Missionary Bapt. Ch., 1983. Mem. Dem. Caucus (chmn. 2003, 05), Urban League (pres. bd. dirs.), NAACP (2d v.p.), VFW, Vietnam Vets. Am. (life mem.), Am. Legion, Masons (supreme coun. 33rd degree), Shriners. Democrat. Home: 36 Mckinley Ave Racine WI 53404-3414 Office: Wis Assembly PO Box 8953 Madison WI 53708-8953

TURNER, RONALD L., information services executive; BS in Aerospace Engring., U. Tenn.; MS in Engring., U. Fla.; MS in Mgmt., MIT. Sys. command USAF, 1968—73; sys. mgr. through v.p. Martin Marietta, 1973—87; pres., CEO GEC Marconi Electronic Sys., 1987—93; pres., CEO computing devices internat. Ceridian Corp., Mpls., 1993—97, exec. v.p. ops., 1997—98, pres., COO, 1998—2000, chmn., pres., CEO, 2000—06, pres., CEO, 2006. Bd. dir. Ceridian Corp., Brink's Co.; mem. bd. gov. Electronic Industries Alliance. Bd. dir. Danny Thompson Meml., Minn. Bus. Partnership; mem. Bus. Roundtable. Office: Ceridian Corp 3311 E Old Shakopee Rd Minneapolis MN 55425-1640

TURNER, WILLIAM V., bank executive; b. Aug. 13, 1932; m. Ann Turner; children: Julie Ann Brown, Joseph William. BS in Bus. and Pub. Adminstrn., U. Mo., 1956. Regional sales and credit mgr. Kraft Foods Co., 1956-60; chief mgmt. assistance sect. Small Bus. Adminstrn., 1961-68; v.p. comml. and consumer lending, exec. v.p., pres., CEO Citizens Bank, 1966-74; pres. Greater So. Bank, Springfield, Mo., 1974-97, chmn., CEO, 1997-99, chmn., 1999—. Dir., vice chmn. Fed. Home Loan Bank Des Moines; dir. Fed. Savs. and Loan Adv. Coun., Washington; com. mem. U.S. Savs. and Loan League, Mo. Savs. and Loan League. Pres. Springfield Area C. of C., Springfield Bapt. Hosp.; pres., mem. Springfield R-12 Sch. Dist.; chmn. Greene County Cancer Crusade, Boy Scouts Am., Campaign Fund Dr. for Mental Retardation; bd. mem. Greene County ARC; dir., pres. Am. Cancer Soc., Greene County; dir., pres. Cox Health Sys. Bd. Dirs.; trustee, chmn. Pres. Club, Drury Coll.; trustee Ozarks Playgrounds Assn., Springfield Boy's Club, S.W. Bapt. Coll.; bd. mem. Springfield Girls Club; dir. Cmty. Found.; treas. exec. com. YMCA; mem. Pub. Safety Com., Mayor's Commn. on Human Rights; chmn. Better Bus. Bur. S.W. Mo. Recipient Civic Contbr. award North Springfield Betterment Assn., Springfieldian award, 1979. Office: Great So Bank PO Box 9009 Springfield MO 65808-9009

TURNEY, SHAREN JESTER, retail executive, cosmetics executive; b. 1956; BA in Bus. Edn., U. Okla., 1974. With Foley's, 1979—88, Byer Calif. Federated Dept. Stores; sr. v.p., gen. merchandise mgr. Neiman Marcus stores, 1997—98; exec. v.p. merchandising, creative prodn., advt., pub. rels. Neiman Marcus, 1998; pres., CEO eiman Marcus Direct, 1999—2000, Victoria's Secret Direct, 2000—06, Victoria's Secret Megabrand and Intimate Apparel, 2006—. Campaign chmn. United Way, Dallas; hon. co-chair Children's Hunger Alliance, Ohio, 2006; bd. dirs. Winston Sch., Addison Theater, Columbus Coalition Against Family Violence, Jay H. Retailing Initiative Adv. bd., Wharton Sch., U. Pa. Named to Hall of Fame Bus. Edn., U. Okla., 2005; recipient Fashion Medal Hon. for Fashion Retailing, 1997, Dr. Catherine White Achievement award, HeartShare Human Services, 2005. Office: Victoria's Secret PO Box 16589 Columbus OH 43216-6589

TUROW, SCOTT F., writer, lawyer; b. Chgo., Apr. 12, 1949; s. David D. and Rita (Pastron) Turow; m. Annette Weisberg, Apr. 4, 1971 (div. 2007); 3 children. BA magna cum laude, Amherst Coll., 1970; MA, Stanford U., 1974; JD cum laude, Harvard U., 1978. Bar: Ill. 1978, U.S. Dist. Ct. (no. dist.) Ill. 1978, U.S. Ct. Appeals (7th cir.) 1979. Asst. U.S. atty. US Dept. Justice (no. dist.) Ill., Chgo., 1978—86; ptnr. Sonnenschein Nath & Rosenthal LLP, Chgo., 1986—. E.H. Jones lectr. Stanford U., 1972—75; pres. Author's Guild, 1997—98. Author: (novels) Presumed Innocent, 1987, The Burden of Proof, 1990, Pleading Guilty, 1993, The Laws of Our Fathers, 1996, Personal Injuries, 1999, Reversible Errors, 2002, Ordinary Heroes, 2005, Limitations, 2006, (non-fiction) One L.: An Inside Account of Life in the First Year at Harvard Law School, 1977, Ultimate Punishment: A Lawyer's Reflections on Dealing With the Death Penalty, 2003 (Robert F. Kennedy Book award, 2004); contbr. articles to profl. jours. Mem.: Chgo. Coun. Lawyers, Chgo. Bar Assn. Office: Sonnenschein Nath Rosenthal 233 S Wacker Dr Ste 8000 Chicago IL 60606-6491 E-mail: sturow@sonnenscheim.com.

TUSHMAN, J. LAWRENCE, wholesale distribution executive; Ptnr., mgr. Sherwood Food Distbrs., Detroit. Office: Sherwood Food Distributors 18615 Sherwood St Detroit MI 48234-2813

TUTTLE, WILLIAM MCCULLOUGH, JR., history professor; b. Detroit, Oct. 7, 1937; s. William McCullough and Geneva (Duvall) T.; m. Linda Lee Stumpp, Dec. 12, 1959 (div.); children: William McCullough III, Catharine T., Andrew S.; m. Kathryn Nemeth, May 6, 1995. BA, Denison U., 1959; MA, U. Wis., 1964, PhD, 1967. From mem. faculty to prof. history U. Kans., Lawrence, 1967—2000, prof. Am. studies, 2000—, John Adams disting. Fulbright chair in Am. history, 2007. Vis. scholar Radcliffe Coll., 1993—94; Charles Warren fellow Harvard U., Cambridge, Mass., 1972—73; sr. fellow Johns Hopkins U., 1969—70; vis. prof. U. S.C., Columbia, 1980; fellow Humanities Ctr. Stanford U., 1983—84; rsch. assoc. U. Calif., Berkeley, Calif., 1986—88. Author: Race Riot: Chicago in the Red Summer of 1919, 1970, 2d edit., 1996, W.E.B. Du Bois, 1973, (with David M. Katzman) Plain Folk, 1982, (with others) A People and A Nation, 1982, 7th edit., 2005, Daddy's Gone to War: The Second World War in the Lives of America's Children, 1993, (with others) World War II and the American Home Front, 2007; contbr. chpts. to books, articles to profl. jours. Dem. precinct committeeman, Lawrence, 1980-90. Lt. USAF, 1959-62. Recipient Merit award Am. Assn. for State and Local History, 1972, Balfour S. Jeffrey Rsch. Achievement award Humanities and Social Scis., 2004, Chancellors Club Career Tchg. award, 2004, Steeples Svc. to Kans. award, 2006; Younger Humanist fellow NEH, 1972-73, Guggenheim fellow, 1975-76, NEH fellow, 1983-84, rsch. fellow Hall Ctr., 1990, Kemper fellow for tchg. excellence, 1998; Evans grantee, 1975-76, Beveridge grantee, 1982; NEH grantee, 1986-89. Mem. Soc. Am. Historians (elected), Am. Hist. Assn., Orgn. Am. Historians, Am. Studies Assn., Assn. for Study of African Am. Life and History, Lawrence Trout Club, Golden Key (hon.), Omicron Delta Kappa, Phi Beta Delta, Phi Gamma Delta. Home: 713 Louisiana St Lawrence KS 66044-2339 Office: U Kans Dept Am Studies Lawrence KS 66045-0001 Office Phone: 785-864-9476. Business E-Mail: tuttle@ku.edu.

TYER, TRAVIS EARL, librarian, consultant; b. Lorenzo, Tex., Oct. 23, 1930; s. Charlie Earl and Juanita (Travis) T.; m. Alma Lois Davis, Nov. 6, 1951; children: Alan Ross, Juanita Linn. BS, Abilene Christian U., 1952; BLS, U. North Tex., 1959; AdM in LS, Fla. State U., 1969, postgrad., 1969-71. Librarian, tchr. pub. schs., Gail, Lubbock, and Seminole, Tex., 1952-61; with Dallas Pub. Library, 1961-66, coordinator young adult services, 1962-66; library dir. Lubbock Pub. Library, 1966, Lubbock City-County Libraries, 1967-68; grad. library sch. faculty-state personnel coordinator Emporia (Kans.) State U., 1971-72; sr. cons. profl. devel. Ill. State Library, Springfield, 1972-80; exec. dir. Great River Libr. Sys., Quincy, Ill., 1980-94; cons. pub. rels. and comm. Alliance Libr. Sys., Quincy, 1994-97; ind. libr. cons., 1997—. Lectr. summer workshops Tex. Woman's U., U. Okla., U. Utah, Fla. State U., U. North Tex.; adj. faculty U. Mo., 1986-89; cons. in field; mem. adv. com. Ill. State Libr., 1984-87, 93-96; pres. Resource Sharing Alliance West Ctrl. Ill., Inc., 1981-94, sec., 1994-97; pres. Ill. Libr. System Dirs. Orgn., 1992-94. Contbr. articles to library jours. Inductee U. North Tex. Libr. and Info. Sci. Hall of Fame, 1990. Mem. ALA, Ill. Libr. Assn., Ill. Ctr. for the Book, Friends of Librs. U.S.A., U. North Tex. Sch. Libr. and Info. Sci. (life), Friends Lubbock City-County Librs. (life), Ill. Sch. Libr. MEdia Assn. Democrat. Mem. Ch. of Christ. Home and Office: 2008 S Arrowood Ct Quincy IL 62305-8961 Office Phone: 217-223-5024.

TYLER, SEAN, radio personality; Radio personality KPRS, Kanss City, Mo. Office: Charter Broadcast Group 11131 Colorado Ave Kansas City MO 64137

TYLER, W(ILLIAM) ED, finance company executive; b. Cleve., Nov. 3, 1952; s. Ralph Tyler and Edith (Green) Kauer; m. Vickie Sue Boggs, Feb. 7, 1976; children: Stacia Leigh, Adam William. BSEE, Ind. Inst. Tech., 1974; MBA, Ind. U., 1977; postgrad., Harvard U., 1981, Baruch U., 1988. From electronic engr. to exec. v.p. R.R. Donnelley & Sons Co., Warsaw, Ind., 1974—95, exec. v.p. & chief tech. officer, 1995—98; CEO, pres. Moore Corp. Ltd., 1998—2001, Willoughby Capitol, Lake Forest, Ill., 2001; CEO Ideapoint Ventures, 2002—. Home: 1000 N Lake Shore Plz Ste 45A Chicago IL 60611 Office Phone: 847-567-7111.

TYLER, WILLIAM HOWARD, JR., advertising executive, educator; b. Elizabethton, Tenn., May 21, 1932; s. William Howard and Ethel Margaret (Schueler) T.; m. Margery Moss, Aug. 31, 1957; children: William James, Daniel Moss. Student, Iowa State U., 1950-52, U. Iowa, 1952; AB in Lit., BJ in Advt., U. Mo., 1958, MA in Journalism, 1966. Advt. mgr. Rolla (Mo.) Daily News, 1958-59; instr. sch. journalism U. Mo., Columbia, 1959-61; copy writer, then v.p. copy dir. D'Arcy Advt. Agy., St. Louis, 1961-67; writer, producer, creative supr. Gardner Advt. Co., St. Louis, 1967-69; sr. v.p., creative dir. D'Arcy, McManus, Masius, St. Louis, 1969-77; exec. v.p., creative dir. Larson Bateman Advt. Agy., Santa Barbara, Calif., 1977-80; v.p. advt. Pizza Hut, Inc., Wichita, Kans., 1980-82; v.p., creative dir. Frye-Sills/Y&R, Denver, 1980; exec. v.p., creative dir. Gardner Advt. Co., St. Louis, 1982-88; exec. v.p., ptnr., creative dir. Parker Group, St. Louis, 1988-91; pres. Tylertoo Prodns., St. Louis, 1991—. Assoc. prof. St. Louis U., 1993-2003, prof., 2003—. Mng. editor St. Louis Advt. Mag., 1992-95. Trustee Blackburn Coll., Carlinville, Ill., 1983—84; bd. advisors U. Mo. Journalism Sch., 1986—91. 1st lt. USMC, 1952—55, Japan, Korea. Named AAF 9th Dist. Educator of Yr., 1998, 2007; recipient Faculty and Excellence Award, 2001, 2002, Outstanding Advisor awards, 1999, 2007. Mem. U. Mo. Alumni Assn. (bd. dirs. 1969-70), Advt. Club Greater St. Louis, Golden Key (hon.), Mensa, Kappa Tau Alpha (hon.). Episcopalian. Office: Saint Louis U Dept Comm Xavier 300 3733 W Pine Blvd Saint Louis MO 63108-3305 Office Phone: 314-977-3190. Business E-Mail: tylerwh@slu.edu.

TYLEVICH, ALEXANDER V., sculptor, architect; b. Minsk, Belarus, Sept. 12, 1947; arrived in U.S., 1989; s. Wulf Tylevich and Asia Klebanova; m. Poline M. Dvorkin, Jan. 22, 1981; children: Alexei, Katherine. BA in Arch., Minsk Archtl. Inst., 1965; MA in Arch., Byelorussian Poly. Inst., Minsk, 1971. Prin., sr. arch. Minskprojekt, 1971-84; artist, arch. Fine Arts Found., Minsk, 1984-89; sculptor-arch. Tylevich Studio Inc., St. Paul, 1989—. Prin. works include Vincentian Letter, DePaul U., Chgo., Letterdance, Minn. State U., Mankato, River of Memory, La. State Mus., Baton Rouge, Four Suspended Mobiles, DCT Coll. Rosemont, Mont., Midtown Exchange Sculpture, Mpls., Inver Hills C.C., Inver Grove Heights, Minn., St. Francis de Sales, Morgantown, W.Va., Thomas More Chapel, U. St. Thomas, Mpls., Suspended Cross, Church of St. Peter, Mendota, Minn., St. Victoria Ch., Victoria, Minn., Processional Cross, Cathedral of Christ the King, Superior, Wis., Blue Springs.Net, Blue Springs, Mo., Letters of Creation, Wayzata, Minn., Montessori's Vision: Through the Eyes of a Child, Lake Country Sch., Mpls., Tree of Life, U. Minn., Mpls., Sculpture Anoka Ramsey C.C., Coon Rapids, Minn., Resurrection, Ch. of St. Stephen, Anoka, Minn., Madonna and Child, The Ch. of St. Mary, Alexandria, Minn., Gateway to Belief/Point of Belief, St. Mary's U., Winona, Minn., Thomas Becket, Cath. Cmty. of Thomas Becket, Eagan, Minn., Tribute to Erich Mendelsohn, FORECAST Pub. Artwork, St. Paul, Zenon Possis, North Meml. Hosp., Mpls., Winona Tech. Coll. Aviation Facility, North Shore Synagogue, Syosset, N.Y., Mt. Zion Temple, St. Paul, St. Paul Sem., St. Joseph Abbey, St. Benedict, La., Mepkin Abbey, S.C., Immaculate Conception Cath. Ch., Durham, N.C., Ctr. of Minsk, Minsk City Govt. Bldg., Subway Sta., pvt. collections, St. Thomas Aquinas Chapel, St. Paul, Minn., exhibited in group shows at Monumental Art of Byelorussia, Minsk, 1989, Nat. Jewish Mus., Washington, 1993, Harvard U. Grad. Sch. Design New Eng., 1993, St. John's U., Collegeville, Minn. Recipient Internat. Design Honor award Interfaith Forum Religion, Art, and Architecture, 2006, Henry Hering Meml. medal, 2007; grantee Minn. Met. Regional Arts Coun., 1991, Howard B. Brin Arts Endowment, 1991, FORECAST Pub. Artworks, 1993. Fellow Archtl. Assn. USSR. Home: 1937 Highland Pkwy Saint Paul MN 55116-1350 Personal E-mail: tyleart@aol.com.

TYLKA, GREGORY L., plant pathologist, educator; BS in Biology, California U. Pa., 1983, MS in Biology, 1985; PhD in Plant Pathology, U. Ga., 1990. Asst. prof. dept. plant pathology Iowa State U., Ames, 1990-95, assoc. prof. dept. plant pathology, 1995—. Recipient Prodn. Rsch. award United Soybean Bd., 1998. Mem. Agronomy Soc. Am., Am. Phytopathol. Soc. (Excellence in Ext. award 1999), Am. Soybean Assn., Iowa Soybean Assn., Helminthological Soc. Washington, Soc. ematologists, Soil Sci. Soc. Am., Sigma Xi, Beta Beta Beta (Outstanding Alumnus award 1992), Gamma Sigma Delta. Achievements include research on the effects of cultural practices and soybean resistance and tolerance on soybean cyst nematode population densities and soybean yields. Office: Iowa State U Dept Plant Pathology 321 Bessey Hall Ames IA 50011 Fax: 515-294-3851. E-mail: gltylka@iastate.edu.

TYMESON, JODI, state official; b. Boone, Iowa, June 27, 1955; BA, U. No. Iowa; MPA, Drake U. Tchr.; state rep. Iowa, 2001—. Mem. edn. com.; mem. human resources com.; mem. oversight and comms. com.; vice chair appropriations com.; mem. ways and means com. Inspector gen. Iowa N.G. Republican. Office: State Capital E 12th and Grand Des Moines IA 50319

TYNER, HOWARD A., retired publishing executive, newspaper editor, journalist; b. Milw., May 30, 1943; s. Howard Arthur and Katharine Elizabeth Tyner; m. Elizabeth Jane Adams, May 3, 1969; children: Sophie Elizabeth, Ian Adams. BA, Carleton Coll., 1965; MSJ, Northwestern U., 1967. Sports editor Chippewa Herald-Telegram, Chippewa Falls, Wis., 1965—66; fgn. corr. UPI, 1967—77; with Chgo. Tribune, Chgo., 1977—2001, fgn. corr. Moscow, 1982—85, fgn. editor Chgo., 1985—88, asst. mng. editor, 1988—90, dep. mng. editor, 1990—92, assoc. editor, 1992—93, v.p., editor, 1993—2001; v.p. editorial Tribune Pub. Co., 2001—03. Mem. adv. bd. Alfred Friendly Press Fellowships, Washington, 1988—; mem. exec. bd. World Press Inst., 1994—2007, bd. dirs., 1997—2007, chmn. Recipient US Editor of Yr. award, Nat. Press Found., 2001. Mem.: Found. for Am. Comms. (adv. bd. 1997—), Am. Press Inst. (bd. dirs. 1997—), Am. Soc. ewspaper Editors (mem. found. bd. 1994—). Home: 2700 Park Pl Evanston IL 60201-1337 Office: World Press Inst 1576 Summit Ave Saint Paul MN 55105 E-mail: HatManGuy@aol.com.

TYNER, WALLACE EDWARD, agricultural economics educator; b. Orange, Tex., Mar. 21, 1945; s. Richard D. and Jeanne (Gullahorn) T.; m. Jean M. Young, May 2, 1970; children: Davis, Jeffrey. BS in Chemistry, Tex. Christian U., 1966; MA in Econs., U. Md., 1972, PhD in Econs., 1977. Vol. Peace Corps., India, 1966-68, math, sci., ednl. skill desk chief Washington, 1968-70; grad. teacher asst. U. Md., Balt., 1971-73; assoc. scientist Earth Satellite Corp., Washington, 1973-74; rsch. assoc. Cornell U., Ithaca, NY, 1974-77; asst. prof., assoc. prof. natural resource econs. and internat. devel. policy Purdue U., West Lafayette, Ind., 1977-84, prof., asst. dept. head, 1983-88, dept. head, 1989—2002. Cons. UN Food and Agrl. Orgn., Rome, Office Tech. Assessment, Washington, U.S. Dept. Interior, Washington, OECD, Paris, World Bank, Washington, USDA, Washington. Author: Energy Resources and Economic Development in India, 1978, A Perspective on U.S. Farm Problems and Agricultural Policy, 1987. Recipient Disting. Policy Contbn. award, Am. Agrl. Economics Assn., 2005. Mem. Am. Assn. Agrl. Economists, Am. Econs. Assn., Internat. Assn. Agrl. Economist, Sigma Xi, Gamma Sigma Delta. Home: 116 Arrowhead Dr West Lafayette IN 47906-2105 Office: Purdue U Krannert Bldg West Lafayette IN 47907-1145 Office Phone: 765-494-0199. Business E-Mail: wtyner@purdue.edu.

TYREE, ALAN DEAN, clergyman; b. Kansas City, Mo., Dec. 14, 1929; s. Clarence Tillman and Avis Ora (Gross) T.; m. Gladys Louise Omohundro, Nov. 23, 1951; children: Lawrence Wayne, Jonathan Tama, Sharon Avis. BA, U. Iowa, 1950; postgrad., U. Mo.-Columbia, 1956-58, U. Mo.-Kansas City, 1961-62. Ordained to ministry Cmty. of Christ, 1947. Appointee min., Lawrence, Kans., 1950-52; mission adminstr. (Mission Sanito), French Polynesia, 1953-64; regional adminstr. Denver, 1964-66; mem. Council Twelve Apostles, Independence, Mo., 1966-82, sec., 1980-82, mem. First Presidency, 1982-92; ret. First Presidency, 1992; pastor East 39th Street Congregation Cmty. of Christ, Independence, 2000—02. Mem. Joint Coun. and Bd. Appropriations, 1966-92; originator music appreciation broadcasts Radio Tahiti, 1962-64, Mission Sanito Radio Ministry, 1960-64; instr. Music/Arts Inst., 1992-2005, Met. C.C.'s, 1994-2005. Editor: Cantiques des Saints French-Tahitian hymnal, 1965, Exploring the Faith: A Study of Basic Christian Beliefs, 1987; mem. editing com.: Hymns of the Saints, 1981; author: The Gospel Graced by a People: A Biography of Persons in Tahiti, 1993, Evan Fry: Proclaimer of Good News, 1995, Priesthood: For Other's Sake, 1996, God: Getting to Know the Unknown, 1998. Bd. dirs. Outreach Internat. Found., 1979-82, mem. corp. body, 1982-92; mem. corp. body Independence Regional Health Ctr., 1982-92, v.p., 1983-92, bd. dirs., 1984-93; mem. bd. publs. Herald House, 1984-92; mem. corp. body Restoration Trail Found., 1982-92; chmn. Temple Art Com., 1988-94; bd. dirs. Independence Symphony Orch., 1992-96, pres., 1995-96; mem. human rels. commn. city of Independence, 1995-97, chmn., 1996-97. Recipient Elbert A. Smith Meml. award for publ. articles, 1968, 72 Mem. Phi Beta Kappa, Phi Eta Sigma. Home and Office: 3408 S Trail Ridge Dr Independence MO 64055 Office Phone: 816-373-8151. E-mail: adtyree@gmail.com.

TYREE, JAMES C., insurance company executive; b. 1957; m. Eve Tyree; 3 children. BS in Finance, Ill. State U., 1978, MBA, 1980. With Mesirow Ins. Svcs. Inc., Chgo., 1980—, chmn., CEO, 1994—. Mem. Juv. Diabetes Rsch. Found. Internat.; bd trustee Roosevelt Univ.; bd. dirs. Illinois State U. Found., Saint Xavier U., Marist High Sch.; chmn. bd. City Colleges of Chgo. Named Person of the Year, Juv. Diabetes Rsch. Found., 2004; recipient E. Burton Mercier Service award, Illinois State U., 2000, Coll. of Business Alumni Hall of Fame, 2003, Disting. Alumni award, 2005. Mem.: Exec. Club, Econ. Club. Office: Mesirow Ins Svcs Inc 350 N Clark St Chicago IL 60610-4712

TYRRELL, THOMAS NEIL, former metal processing executive; b. Valdosta, Ga., Feb. 5, 1945; s. Thomas W. and Marilynn (Bowler) T.; children from previous marriage: Tracey, Torrey, Taryn; m. Diane Montague, 1995. BA in Bus. Adminstra., Elmhurst Coll., 1967; LLD (hon.), Baldwin-Wallace Coll., 1992. Sales loop trainee Bethlehem (Penn.) Steel Corp., 1967; gen. product sales person Bethlehem Steel Sales Office, Greensboro, N.C., 1968-73; product specialist Bethlehem Steel Corp., 1973-78; v.p. mktg. Raritan River Steel, Perth Amboy, N.J., 1978-86; CEO Am. Steel & Wire Corp., Cuyahoga Hgts., Ohio, 1986-94; vice chmn., CAO Birmingham (Ala.) Steel Corp., 1994-96; pres., ceo Bar Technologies, Inc., 1996-98; ceo Republic Engineered Steels, Akron, Ohio, 1998-99; ceo. Republic Technologies Intl.(merger USS/KOBE, Bar Technologies & Republic Engineered Steels), Akron, Ohio, 1999-00. Bd. dirs. Birmingham Steel Corp. Contbr. articles to profl. jours. Vol. Leadership Cleve., 1987, Baldwin Wallace Coll., 1989—, Elmhurst Coll., 1990—, Ohio Valley Corridor Commn. emeritus, 1990—. amed Entrepreneur of Yr. Northeast Ohio, Venture Inc. mag., 1988; recipient Register award for Bus. and Commerce, Esquire mag., 1988. Mem. Wire Assn. Internat., Cold Finished Bar Inst., Am. Wire Producers Assn., Indsl. Fastener Inst., Concrete Reinforced Steel Inst., Am. Inst. Steel Engrs., Summit Club (Birmingham), Old Overton C. of C. Roman Catholic. Avocations: running, fishing, scuba diving, weight training. Office: Republic Technologies Intl 3770 Embassy Pkwy Akron OH 44333-8367

TYSON, EUGENE, state legislator; b. Omaha, July 26, 1931; m. Barbara Tyson, Apr. 7, 1956 (dec.); children: Ann, Claire, Catherine, Elizabeth, Brian, Joseph. Grad., Creighton U., 1958. Collection mgr. loan ctr. First Nat. Bank Omaha, 1960-68; controller Vulcraft div. Nucor Corp., 1968-73; controller Nucor Steel, 1973-77, sales mgr., 1977-95; mem. Nebr. Legislature from 19th dist., Lincoln, 1996—. Former mem. Norfolk City Coun., Norfolk Planning Commn., orfolk Libr. Bd. With USAF, 1950-54. Mem. N.E. Nebr. Shooting Assn. (pres.). Home: 2406 Norfolk Ave Norfolk NE 68701-3522 Office: State Capitol Dist 19 PO Box 94604 Rm 1021 Lincoln NE 68509-4604

TYSON, JOSEPH B., JR., lawyer; b. Roanoke Rapids, NC, Feb. 19, 1949; AB, U. N.C., 1971; JD, U. Va., 1977. Bar: N.Y. 1978, Wis. 1979. Ptnr. Foley & Lardner LLP, Milw., chmn. bus. law dept. Mem. ABA, State Bar Wis., Phi Beta Kappa, U. Club (officer & dir.). Office: Foley & Lardner LLP Firstar Ctr 777 E Wisconsin Ave Ste 3800 Milwaukee WI 53202-5367 Office Phone: 414-297-5631. Office Fax: 414-297-4900. Business E-Mail: jtyson@foley.com.

TYSON, KIRK W. M., management consultant; b. Jackson, Mich., July 2, 1952; s. George Carlton and Wilma Marion (Barnes) Tyson; m. Terri Lynn Long, Mar. 25, 2000; 1 child, Gabriel 1 stepchild, Robert. BBA, Western Mich. U., 1974; MBA, DePaul U., Chgo., 1982. CPA, Ill.; cert. mgmt. cons. Bus. cons. Arthur Andersen & Co., Chgo., 1974-84; v.p. cons. First Chgo. Corp., 1984; chmn. Kirk Tyson Internat., 1984-2000; pres. The Perpetual Strategist, Chgo., 2001—; adj. prof. of mgmt. Wright State U., 2007—. Adj. prof. coll. bus. Write State U., 2007—. Author: Business Planning, 1982, Business Intelligence: Putting It All Together, 1986, Competitor Intelligence: Manual and Guide, 1990, Competition in the 21st Century, 1996, The Complete Guide to Competitive Intelligence, 1998, 4th rev. edit. 2006. Pres., Chgo. Jr. Assn. Commerce and Industry Found., 1977-79; active Easter Seals Soc., 1977, Am. Blind Skiing Found., 1977-78, Jr. Achievement, 1976-77, United Way Met. Chgo., 1979-80, Urban Gateways, 1975; Rep. precinct committeeman Downers Grove Twp., 1985-88; treas. St. Charles H.S. Football Booster club, 1994-95. Fellow Soc. Competitive Intelligence Profls. (Meritorious award, 2005); mem. Rotary Club of Springboro (asst. dist. gov., 2005-), Alpha Kappa Psi (Disting. Alumni Svc. award 1974-86, named Alumnus of Yr. 2003) Centerville-Washington Found. (trustee 2007-). Office: The Perpetual Strategist 30 S Wacker Dr Ste 2200 Chicago IL 60606-7456 Office Phone: 312-466-5733. Business E-Mail: kirk.tyson@perpetualstrategist.com.

TYSON, ROBERT, state legislator; b. Ottawa, Kans., Sept. 29, 1940; m. Linda Tyson; 2 children. Grad., Ottawa U., 1963. Rancher, Linn County; airline pilot TWO, 1966-92; mem. Kans. Senate from 12th dist., Topeka, 1997—. Mem. Young Reps.; mem. com. Ottawa Franklin County; chmn. Bob Dole's 1st U.S. Senate Campaign; mem. Prairie View United Sch. Dist., sch. bd., (8 yrs). Mem. Am. Hereford Assn., Kans. Livestock Assn. (Kans. Environ. Stewardship award 1992), Kans. Farm Bur., Ottawa C. of C. Republican.

TYSOR, RONALD W., retail executive; CFO Federated Dept. Stores, Inc., Cin., federated vice chmn. fin., real estate, 1990—. Mem. Federated Direct; pres., COO Campeau Corp., 1989. Office: Federated Dept Stores 7 W 7th St Cincinnati OH 45202

UBER, LARRY R., transportation executive; BA, Pa. State U. With Ingersoll-Rand, 1967-90, pres. Prodn. Equipment Group, 1990-95, pres. Constrn. and Mining Group, 1995-98; pres., CEO, N.Am. Van Lines, Fort Wayne, Ind., 1998—. Office: NAm Van Lines 5001 Us Highway 30 W Fort Wayne IN 46818-9701

UCHIDA, HIROSHI, diagnostic equipment company executive; BA, Brown U.; MA, PhD, Harvard U. Sr. mgmt. positions Arthur D. Little, Bain Cons.; v.p., gen. mgr. Asia-Pacific region Dade Behring, Deerfield, Ill., 1997-99, pres. Asia divsn., 1999—.

UCKO, DAVID ALAN, science foundation official; b. NYC, July 9, 1948; s. Lawrence L. and Helen H. Ucko; m. Barbara Alice Clark, Aug. 13, 1972; 1 child, Aaron. BA, Columbia Coll., NYC, 1969; PhD, MIT, 1972. Asst. prof. chemistry Hostos C.C., CUNY, Bronx, 1972-76, Antioch Coll., Yellow Springs, Ohio, 1976-79, assoc. prof. chemistry, 1979; rsch. coord. Mus. Sci. and Industry, Chgo., 1979-80, dir. sci., 1981-87, v.p., 1986-87; dep. dir. Calif. Mus. Sci. and Industry, LA, 1987-90; pres. Kansas City (Mo.) Mus., 1990-2000, Sci. City at Union Sta., 1999-2000; exec. dir. Koshland Sci. Mus. and Sci. Outreach, NAS, Washington, 2001—02; pres. Mus. + More LLC, 2002—; program dir. Informal Sci. Edn. NSF, 2003—07, head sci literacy section, 2004—07, dep. dir. divsn. rsch. learning in formal and informal settings, 2007—08; guest faculty mus. mgmt. program U. Colo., Boulder, Colo., 2001. Rsch. assoc. and assoc. prof. dept. edn. U. Chgo., 1982—87; adj. staff scientist C. F. Kettering Rsch. Lab., Yellow Springs, Ohio, 1977—79; mem. pub. engagement working group, nanoscale sci. edn. and tech. subcom. Nat. Sci. and Tech. Coun., 2005—. Author: (book) Basics for Chemistry, 1982, Living Chemistry, 2d edit., 1986; contbr. articles to profl. jours.; host, prodr. (radio program) Science Alive!, 1983—87, developer numerous mus. exhibits. Apptd. Nat. Mus. Svcs. Bd., 1996—2003; trustee Mus. Without Walls, 1996—2000, Sci. Pioneers, 2000. Recipient Up and Comers award, Jr. Achievement Mid.-Am., 1992; fellow Woodrow Wilson, 1969, NIH postdoctoral, 1972; grantee, NSF, NEH, U.S. Dept. Edn., Ill. Humanities Coun., 1976—88. Fellow: AAAS (at large sect. Y 1987—93); mem.: Am. Assn. Museums (mus. assessment program adv. com. 2000—03), Assn. Sci. Tech. Ctrs. (publs. com. 1984—94, chmn. 1988—94, ethics com. 1994—95, legis. com., chmn. 1996—2000), Phi Lambda Upsilon, Sigma Xi, Alpha Sigma Nu (hon.). Home: 2528 Queen Anne's Ln NW Washington DC 20037-2148 Office Phone: 703-292-5126. Personal E-mail: d.ucko@verizon.net.

UECKER, BOB, actor, radio announcer, former baseball player, television personality; b. Milw., Jan. 26, 1935; m. Judy Uecker, 1976 (div. 2001); 4 children. Major league baseball player Milw. Braves, Nat. League, 1962, 63; major league baseball player St. Louis Cardinals, 1964, 65, Phila. Phillies, 1966-67, Atlanta Braves, 1967; commentator ABC Monday Night Baseball, 1976-82; commentator playoff and world series NBC Baseball, 1994-98; radio-TV baseball announcer Milw. Brewers, 1971—. Host War of the Start, Bob Ueckers Wacky World of Sports, Saturday Night Live; guest Tim Conway show, Who's the Boss, Peter Marshall Show; appeared in Fatal Instinct. Co-star TV series Mr. Belvedere, ABC-TV, 1985-1990; guest TV appearances include Late Night with David Letterman, The Tonight Show, Midnight Special, LateLine, 1998; also numerous comms.; author: Catcher in the Wry, 1985; films include: Major League, 1989, Major League 2, 1994, (voice over) Homeward Bound II: Lost in San Francisco, 1996, Major League: Back to the Minors, 1998, Andre the Giant: Larger Than Life, 1999. Recipient Big B.A.T. award Baseball Assistance Team, 1995; inducted Wis. Performing Artists Hall of Fame, 1993, Wis. Broadcasters Assn. Hall of Fame, 1994, Wis. Sports Hall of Fame, 1998. Office: Milw Brewers Baseball Club Milw County Stadium 1 Brewers Way Milwaukee WI 53214-3651

UHI, JUDD R., lawyer; b. Sept. 18, 1973; m. Leslee Uhi. BA in Hist., Miami U., Ohio, 1995, BA in Polit. Sci., 1995; JD, U. Akron, 1999. Bar: Ohio 1999, US Dist. Ct. Northern Dist. Ohio 1999, US Dist. Ct. Southern Dist. Ohio 1999, Ky. 2003. Adj. prof., Trial Advocacy Ohio State U., 2000—01; assoc. Freund, Freeze & Arnold, Cin. Named one of Ohio's Rising Stars, Super Lawyers, 2006. Mem.: Ohio Assn. Civil Trial Attorneys, Ohio State Bar Assn., Ky. Bar Assn., orthern Ky. Bar Assn., Cin. Bar Assn. Avocations: indoor soccer, travel, horseracing, softball. Office: Freund Freeze & Arnold Fourth and Walnut Ctr 105 E Fourth St Ste 1400 Cincinnati OH 45202 Office Phone: 513-665-3500. Office Fax: 513-665-3503.

UHLMANN, FREDERICK GODFREY, securities trader; b. Chgo, Dec. 31, 1929; s. Richard F. and Rosamond G. (Goldman) U.; m. Virginia Lee Strauss, July 24, 1951; children: Richard, Thomas, Virginia, Karen, Elizabeth. BA, Washington and Lee U., 1951. Ptnr. Uhlmann Grain Co., Chgo., 1951-61; v.p. Uhlmann & Co., Inc., Chgo., 1961-65; sr. v.p. H. Hentz & Co., Chgo., 1965-73, Drexel Burnham Lambert Inc., Chgo., 1973-84; exec. v.p., dir. bus. futures Dean Witter Reynolds Inc., Chgo., 1984-85; sr. v.p., mgr. commodity dept. Bear, Stearns & Co., Inc., Chgo., 1985-88; exec. v.p. Rodman & Renshaw, Inc., 1988-95; sr. v.p. LIT-Divsn. of First Options Inc., Chgo., 1995-98; chmn. Chgo Bd. Trade, Ill., 1973-74; sr. v.p., exec. dir. MAN Financial, 1998—. Ptnr. Uhlmann Price Securities LLC. Bd. dir. Dist. 113 H.S. Found., 1990—, Mt. Sanai Hosp. Inst., Chgo., 1999—. Mem. Nat. Futures Assoc. (dir. 1981-2000, vice chair 1998-2000), Futures Industry Assn. (bd. dir., chmn. 1975-76), Futures Industry Inst. (bd. dir.). Home: 783 Whiteoaks Ln Highland Park IL 60035-3656 Office Phone: 847-444-1104. E-mail: fgu73@aol.com.

UJVAGI, PETER, state representative, manufacturing executive; b. Budapest, Hungary, Mar. 31, 1949; m. Betty Ujvagi; children: Andrew, Krisztina, Elizabeth, Szuszi. Student, U. Toledo, 1967—72. Field coord. Nat. Ctr. Urban Ethnic Affairs, 1972—75; v.p. E&C Mfg., 1975—; rep. Ohio State Ho. Reps., Columbus, Ohio, 2002—. Councilman City of Toledo; White Ho. Commr. Commn. on Neighborhoods, 1977—81; chmn. Lucas County Dem. Party, 1982—92; pres. Toledo (Ohio) City Coun., 1981—. Democrat. Roman Catholic. Office: Ohio State House Reps 77 South High Street 11th Fl Columbus OH 43215-6111

ULABY, FAWWAZ TAYSSIR, academic administrator, engineering educator; b. Damascus, Syria, Feb. 4, 1943; came to US, 1964; s. Tayssir Kamel and Makram (Ard) Ulaby; children: Neda, Aziza, Laith. BS in Physics, Am. U. Beirut, 1964; MSEE, U. Tex., Austin, 1966, PhD in Elec. Engring., 1968. With Boeing Co., 1966; asst. prof. elec. and computer engring. U. Kans., Lawrence, 1968-71, assoc. prof., 1971-76, prof., 1976-84; prof. elec. engring. and computer sci. U. Mich., Ann Arbor, 1984—. dir. NASA Ctr. for Space Terahertz Tech., 1988, R. Jamison and Betty Williams Disting. prof. elec. engring. and computer sci., 1993—, v.p. for rsch., 1999—2005; founding provost, exec. v.p. King Abdullah U. Sci. and Tech., 2008—. Author: Microwave Remote Sensing, Vol. 1, 1981, Vol. 2, 1982, Vol. 3, 1986, Radar Polarimetry, 1990. Recipient Kuwait prize in applied scis. Govt. of Kuwait, 1987, NASA Grp. Achievement award, 1990. Fellow IEEE (gen. chmn. internat. symposium 1981, Disting. Achievement award 1983, Centennial medal 1984, Edison medal 2006, Geoscience and Remote Sensing Soc. Edn. award 2006); mem. IEEE Geoscience and Remote Sensing Soc. (exec. editor jour., pres. 1979-81), Internat. Union Radio Sci., NAE. Avocations: flying kites, racketball. Office: U Mich 3228 Elec Engring and Computer Sci 1301 Beal Ave Ann Arbor MI 48109-2122 E-mail: ulaby@eecs.umich.edu.*

ULETT, GEORGE ANDREW, psychiatrist; b. Needham, Mass., Jan. 10, 1918; s. George Andrew and Mabel Elizabeth (Caswell) U.; m. Pearl Carolyn Lawrence; children: Richard Carlton, Judith Anne, Carol Lynn. BA in Psychology, Stanford U., 1940; MS in Anatomy, U. Oreg., 1943, PhD in Anatomy, 1944, MD, 1944. Diplomate Am. Bd. Psychiatry and Neurology. Asst. psychiatrist Barnes Hosp., St. Louis, 1950-64; med. dir. Malcolm Bliss Hosp., St. Louis, 1951-61; dir. Mo. Dept. Mental Health, Jefferson City, Mo., 1962-72; prof., chair Mo. Inst. Psychiatry, St. Louis, 1964-73; dir. psychiatry Deaconess Hosp., St. Louis, 1973-94; interim dir. Mo. Inst. of Mental Health, St. Louis, 1990-91, assoc. dir. for policy and ethics, 1991-94; clin. prof. dept. family and cmty. medicine St. Louis U. Sch. Medicine, 1995-98. Mem. adv. coun. Mental Health Assn. St. Louis, 1965-66, 69-70, mem. profl. adv. com., 1965; chair health and hosp. com. Health & Welfare Coun. St. Louis, 1960; mem. alcohol rev. com., psychopharmacology study sect., alcoholism study sect., 1993, grants rev. com. for alternative medicine NIMH, Rockville, Md.; prof. psychiatry Washington U. Sch. Medicine, St. Louis, 1956-61; clin. prof. psychiatry St. Louis U. Sch. Medicine, 1981-89, U. Mo. Sch. Medicine, 1990—. Author 12 books, including The Biology of Acupuncture, 2001, Sleight of Mind, 2006; contbr. over 270 articles to profl jours. Capt. U.S. Air Force, 1946-47. Recipient Ann. award Mo. Assn. for Mental Health, 1966, Recognition award, 1970, AMA Honorable Mention award Foster Com. Exhibit, 1974, Pax Mundi Fellowship award for profl. excellence, 1989, Silver Key award Mental Health Assn. Greater St. Louis, 2005; named hon. mem. Turkish Coll. Neuropharmacology, 1969. Fellow Am. Psychiat. Assn.; mem. Am. Soc. Acupuncture (past pres.), Am. Soc. of Med. Psychiatry (past pres.), Mo. Acad. Psychiatry (past pres.). Office: Mo Inst Mental Health 5400 Arsenal St Saint Louis MO 63139-1400 Office Phone: 314-877-6480. E-mail: george.ulett@mien.edu.

ULLIAN, JOSEPH SILBERT, philosophy educator; b. Ann Arbor, Mich., Nov. 9, 1930; s. Hyman Benjamin and Frieda G. (Silbert) U. AB, Harvard U., 1952, AM, 1953, PhD, 1957. Instr. philosophy Stanford U., Calif., 1957-58; asst. prof. philosophy Johns Hopkins U., Balt., 1958-60; vis. asst. prof. philosophy U. Pa., Phila., 1959-60, rsch. assoc. in linguistics, 1961-62; vis. asst. prof. philosophy U. Chgo., 1962-63; asst. prof. U. Calif., Santa Barbara, 1964-66; assoc. prof. Washington U., St. Louis, 1965-70, prof., 1970—. Lectr. U. Calif., Berkeley, 1961; cons. Rsch. Directorate System Devel. Corp., Santa Monica, Calif., 1962-70. Co-author: The Web of Belief, 1970, 2d edit., 1978; contbr. articles to profl. jours. Mem. Am. Philos. Assn., Assn. for Symbolic Logic (exec. com. 1974-77), Am. Soc. for Aesthetics, Phi Beta Kappa. Democrat. Avocations: sports, theater, music. Home: 984 Tornoe Rd Santa Barbara CA 93105-2229 Office: 1 Brookings Dr Saint Louis MO 63130-4899

ULLMAN, NELLY SZABO, statistician, educator; b. Vienna, Aug. 11, 1925; came to U.S., 1939; d. Viktor and Elizabeth (Rosenberg) Szabo; m. Robert Ullman, Mar. 20, 1947 (dec.); children: Buddy, William John, Martha Ann, Daniel Howard. BA, Hunter Coll., 1945; MA, Columbia U., 1948; PhD, U. Mich., 1969. Rsch. assoc. MIT Radiation Lab, Cambridge, Mass., 1945; instr. Polytechnic Inst. of Bklyn., 1945-63; from asst. prof. to prof. Ea. Mich. U., Ypsilanti, 1963—2002, prof., 2002; ret., 2002. Author: Study Guide To Actuarial Exam, 1978; contbr. articles to profl. jours. Mem. Am. Math. Assn., Am. Assn. Univ. Profs. E-mail: nullman@emich.edu.

ULMER, EVONNE GAIL, health science association administrator; b. Bagley, Minn., Sept. 12, 1947; d. John Ferdinand and Elsie Mabel (McCollum) Lundmark; m. G. Bryan Ulmer, Jan. 11, 1969; 1 child, G. Bryan. Diploma, St. Luke's Hosp., Duluth, Minn., 1968; BS, St. Joseph's Coll., N. Windam, Maine, 1981; MHA, U. Minn., 1984; JD, T.M. Cooley Law Sch., Lansing, Mich., 1997. Bar: Mich. 1997. Staff nurse Baton Rouge Gen., 1969—70, St. Luke's Hosp., Duluth, Minn., 1968—69, 1971—72; asst. adminstr. Hickory Heights Care Ctr., Metarie, La., 1972—73; asst. head nurse Eisenhower Hosp., Colorado Springs, Colo., 1973—74; dir. patient care svcs. St. Vincent's Gen. Hosp., Leadville, Colo., 1974—78; dir. insvc., quality assurance Watsatch Hosp., Heber City, Utah, 1979; adminstr. Prospect Park Living Ctr., Estes Park, Colo., 1982—84; asst. adminstr. Estes Park Med. Ctr., 1979—84; CEO Weston County Hosp. and Manor, Newcastle, Wyo., 1984—92, Ionia County Meml. Hosp., Mich., 1992—; pres. Ionia County Health Sys., 1995—, Ulmer Law Firm Evonne G. Ulmer, PLC, 2006—. Mem. Am. Hosp. Assn. Chgo. (trustee 1998-01, past tech. small and rural governing coun., past del. region and policy bd., past chair small and rural governing com., leadership com.), Am. Soc. Healthcare Risk Mgmt. (edtl. adv. bd.), Medicare Geog. Reclassification Rev. Bd., Mich. Health and Hosp. Assn. (past bd. dirs., vice-chair smaller hops. coun.). Republican. Lutheran. Home: 536 Skyview Dr Ionia MI 48846-9776 Home Phone: 616-527-6627; Office Phone: 616-523-1000. Personal E-mail: evonneulmer@hotmail.com. Business E-Mail: eulmer@ioniahospital.org.

ULMER, JAMES HOWARD, potter; b. Carrington, ND, Oct. 12, 1945; s. James Francis and Lois Adelle (Wolf) U.; m. Ann Cecile Gerlach, May 28, 1977; children: Jesse Gerlach, Matthew James. BSBA, N.D. State U., 1969; MS, U. N.D., 1973. Geologist UND Engring. Sta., Grand Forks, N.D., 1974-76; potter Stoneware by Jim Ulmer, Frazee, Minn., 1972—. Dir. Lake Region Arts Coun., Fergus Falls, Minn., 1990-92; dir. intern program U.N.D., Grand Forks, 1976-93, Moorhead (Minn.) State U., 1976-93. Author of poems. Mem. Mich. Guild Artists, Minn. Craft Coun. Home and Office: 15158 330th Ave Frazee MN 56544-8810 E-mail: ulmerstoneware@yahoo.com.

ULMER, JOHN D., state representative; BA, Mich. State U.; JD, Ind. U. Lawyer, sr. ptnr. Yoder, Ainlay, Ulmer & Buckingham, Ind.; state rep. dist. 49 Ind. Ho. of Reps., Indpls., 1998—, mem. agr., natural resources and rural devel., cts. and criminal code, and judiciary coms. Past chmn. March of Dimes; past bd. trustees Goshen (Ind.) Cmty. Schs.; past bd. dirs. Camp Fire Girls. Fellow: Am. Coll. Trial Lawyers; mem.: Ind. State Bar Assn. (past bd. mgrs., chair civil rights com.), Goshen C. of C. Republican. Office: Ind Ho of Reps 200 W Washington St Indianapolis IN 46204-2786

ULMER, MELVILLE PAUL, physics and astronomy educator; b. Washington, Mar. 12, 1943; s. Melville Jack and Naomi Louise (Zinkin) U.; m. Patricia Elifson, Dec. 28, 1968; children: Andrew Todd, Jeremy John, Rachel Ann. BA, Johns Hopkins U., 1965; PhD, U. Wis., 1970. Asst. research U. Calif., San Diego, 1970-74; astrophysicist Harvard Smithsonian Ctr. for Astrophysics, Cambridge, Mass., 1974-76; dir. Lindheimer and Dearborn Obs. Northwestern U., 1982—; asst. prof. Dept. Physics and Astoronomy, Northwestern U., Evanston, Ill., 1976-82, assoc. prof., 1982-87, dir. astrophysics program, 1982—, prof., 1987—, former chmn. Co-investigator on Gamma Ray Ob. experiment and Orbiting Solar Ob. 7. Contbr. articles to profl. jours. Fellow Am. Phys. Soc.; mem. Am. Astron. Soc., Soc. Photo-optical Instrumentation Engrs., Internat. Astron. Union. Office: Northwestern U Dearborn Obs 2131 Tech Dr Evanston IL 60208-2900 Office Fax: 847-491-3135. E-mail: m-ulmer2@northwestern.edu.

ULRICH, ROBERT GENE, judge; b. St. Louis, Nov. 23, 1941; s. Henry George Ulrich and Wanda Ruth (Engram) Webb; m. JoAnn Demark, July 3, 1965; children— Jill Elizabeth, Jane Ashley BA, William Jewell Coll., 1963; JD, U. Mo., Kansas City, 1969, LLM, 1972, U. Va., 2001. Bar: Mo. 1969. Assoc. Von Erdmannsdorff, Voigts & Kuhlman, North Kansas City, Mo., 1969—72; pvt. practice Raytown, Mo., 1972; asst. U.S. atty. Dept. Justice, Kansas City and Springfield, Mo., 1973-76, 78-81; ptnr. Pine & Ulrich, Warrensburg, Mo., 1976-77; litigation atty. Shifran, Treiman, et al., Clayton, Mo., 1977-78; U.S. atty. We. Dist. Mo., Kansas City, 1981-89; judge Mo. Ct. Appeals (we. dist.), Kansas City, 1989—, chief judge, 1996-98. Mem. U.S. Atty. Gen.'s Econ. Crime Council, 1983-89, Atty. Gen.'s Adv. Com. of U.S. Attys., 1983-89, chmn. 1986-89, adv. com. U.S. Ct. Appeals (8th cir.), 1983-86; bd. trustees U. Mo., Kansas City, 2002—, William Jewell Coll., 2004—. Appointed mem. steering com. Protect our Children Campaign, Gov. of Mo., chmn. legis. subcom., 1985; mem. resource bd., personnel mgmt. bd. Dept. Justice, 1985-89; trustee Liberty Meml. Assn., 1989—; vice chmn. Orgn. Crime Drug Enforcement Task Force Nat. Program, Dept. Justice, 1987-89. Col. USMCR, 1963-66. Mem.: U. Mo.-Kansas City Alumni Assn. (v.p. 1997—98, pres. 1998—2000), U. Mo.-Kansas City Law Found. (emeritus), U. Mo.-Kansas City Law Sch. Alumni Assn. (v.p. 1994—95, pres. 1995—96), Marine Corps Res. Officers' Assn. (exec. councillor 1986—87), Kansas City Met. Bar Assn., Mo. Bar Assn., Inst. Jud. Adminstrn., Am. Judicature Soc., U. Mo. Alliance. Office: Missouri Ct Appeals 1300 Oak St Kansas City MO 64106-2904 Office Phone: 816-889-3602.

ULRICH, ROBERT J., retail executive; b. Mpls., Minn., 1944; 2 children. BA, U. Minn., 1967. With Dayton Hudson Corp., Mpls., 1967—2000, exec. v.p. Target Stores divsn., 1981-84, pres. Target Stores divsn., 1984-87, chmn., CEO Target Stores divsn., 1987-93; chmn, CEO Target Corp. (formerly Dayton Hudson Corp.), Mpls., 2000—, Dayton Hudson Corp., Mpls., 1994—2000. Bd. dirs. Dayton Hudson Corp., 1993—2000, Target Corp., 2000—, Yum Brands!, Inc., 1997—2007. Named CEO of Yr., Chief Exec. mag., 2007; recipient Gold Medal award, Nat. Retail Fedn., 2001. Office: Target Corp 1000 Nicollet Mall Minneapolis MN 55403-2467

ULRICH, WERNER, b. Munich, Mar. 12, 1931; came to U.S., 1940, naturalized, 1945; s. Karl Justus and Grete (Rosenthal) U.; m. Ursula Wolff, June 28, 1959; children: Greta, Kenneth. BS, Columbia U., 1952, MS (NSF fellow 1952-53), 1953, Dr.Engring. Sci., 1957; MBA, U. Chgo., 1975; JD, Loyola U., Chgo, 1985. Bar: Ill. 1985. With AT&T Bell Labs, Naperville, Ill., 1953-95; head electronic switching dept. AT&T Bell Labs., Naperville, Ill., 1964-68; dir. Advanced Switching Tech., Naperville, 1968-77, head maintenance architecture dept., 1977-81; sr. atty. Intellectual Property Law Orgn., Naperville, 1981-95; pvt. practice Glen Ellyn, Ill., 1995—2007; ret., 2007. Vis. lectr. U. Calif., Berkeley, 1966-67 Inventor of over 20 telecommunications inventions; patentee electronic switching systems. Fellow IEEE; mem. ABA, Ill. State Bar Assn., Tau Beta Pi, Beta Gamma Sigma.

UMANS, ALVIN ROBERT, manufacturing executive; b. NYC, Mar. 11, 1927; s. Louis and Ethel (Banner) U.; m. Nancy Jo Zadek, June 28, 1953 (div.); children: Kathi Lee Umans Lind, Craig Joseph; m. Madeleine Sayer, Sept. 21, 1985; 1 child, Valentine Brett. Student, U. Rochester, NY, 1944—45. Sales mgr. Textile Mills Co., Chgo., 1954-56; regional sales mgr. Reflector Hardware Corp., Melrose Park, Ill., 1956-58, nat. sales mgr., 1959-62, v.p., 1962-65, pres., treas., dir., 1965-92; pres., CEO RHC/Spacemaster Corp., Melrose Park, 1992-97, chmn., CEO, 1997—2003, Commerce Nat. Group, Chgo., 2004—. Past chmn., bd. dirs. Goer Mfg. Co., Inc., Charleston, SC, Morgan Marshall Industries, Inc., Ill., Capitol Hardware, Inc., Ill., Spartan Showcase Inc., Mo.; v.p., dir. Adams Comm., Chgo.; bd. dirs. Monroe Comm., Chgo.; trustee Driehaus Mut. Funds, 1996—, chmn. bd., 2005—; mem. adv. bd. Capsonic Group, Elgin, Ill. Trustee Mt. Sinai Hosp. Med. Ctr., Chgo., 1970—, chmn. bd., 1987-89; trustee Schwab Rehab. Hosp., Chgo., 1987—, chmn. bd., 1987-89; trustee Sinai Health Sys., Chgo., 1993—, chmn., 1995-97; mem. Cook County Bur. Adv. Com., 1994—; bd. dirs. Milton & Rose Zadek Fund, 1965-78; governing bd. mem. Cinema/Chgo., 1988-89. Served with US Army, 1945-46. Mem. Nat. Assn. Store Fixture Mfrs. (dir. 1969-70), World Pres.'s Orgn., Chgo. Pres.'s Orgn. Clubs: Standard (Chgo.). Home: 132 E Delaware Pl Chicago IL 60611-1445 Office: Commerce Nat Group 194 E Delaware Pl Ste 501 Chicago IL 60611 Office Phone: 312-654-9150. Office Fax: 312-654-9180. Business E-Mail: arumans@gmail.com.

UMBARGER, DWAYNE, state legislator; b. Chanute, Kans., Aug. 2, 1952; m. Toni Umbarger. AA, Neosho C.C., 1972; student, Pittsburg State U. Rural mail carrier U.S. Postal Svc., 1984-86; mem. Kans. Senate from 14th dist., Topeka, 1996—; mem. agr. com., mem. commerce com., mem. edn. com.; mem. joint com. on children and families com. Mem. site coun. Thayer Pub. Schs.; bd. dirs. Thayer Christian Ch.; mem. Neosho County Farm Bur.; mem. Hidden Haven Christian Camp Bd. Republican. Office: 300 SW 10th Ave Topeka KS 66612-1504

UMBDENSTOCK, RICHARD J., medical association administrator; b. 1950; BA in Politics, Fairfield U., Conn., 1972; MSc in Health Services Adminstrn., SUNY, Stony Brook, 1974; LLD (hon.), Gonzaga U., Spokane, Washington, 2003. Diplomate Am. Coll. Healthcare Executives. Independent cons. for voluntary hosp. governing boards in the US and Can.; pres., CEO Providence Services, Spokane, Wash., 1993—2006; chmn. Premier, Inc., Charlotte, NC, 2006; exec. v.p. Providence Health & Services (merger of Providence Services and Providence Health System), 2006; spl. asst. to pres. Am. Hosp. Assn., Inc., Chgo., trustee, 2000—04, chmn.-elect, 2005, chmn., 2006, COO, 2006, pres.-elect, 2006, pres., 2006—. Mem. nat. bd. advisors Ctr. for Healthcare Governance. Author: of several books and articles for the hosp. bd. audiences, nat. survey reports for Am. Hosp. Assn., Health Rsch. Ednl. Trust, and Am. Coll. Healthcare Executives. Office: Am Hosp Assn One North Franklin St Chicago IL 60606-3421 Office Phone: 312-422-3000. Office Fax: 312-422-4796.

UNAKAR, NALIN JAYANTILAL, biological sciences educator; b. Karachi, Sindh, Pakistan, Mar. 26, 1935; came to U.S., 1961; s. Jayantilal Virshankar and Malati Jaswantrai (Buch) U.; m. Nita Shantilal Mankad; children: Rita, Rupa. BS, Gujerat U., Bhavnagar, India, 1955; MSc, Bombay U., 1961; PhD, Brown U., 1965. Research asst. Indian Cancer Research Ctr., Bombay, 1955-61; USPHS trainee in biology Brown U., Providence, 1961-65; research assoc. in pathology

U. Toronto, Ont., Canada, 1965-66; asst. prof. biology Oakland U., Rochester, Mich., 1966-69, assoc. prof., 1969-74, prof., chmn. biology dept., 1974-87, prof., 1974-2000, prof. emeritus, 2000—, adj. prof. biomed. scis., 1984—. Mem. coop. cataract research group Nat. Eye Inst., Bethesda, Md., 1977—; mem. visual scis. study sect. NIH, Bethesda, 1982-86, mem. cataract panel, 1980—. Mem. vis. bd. Lehigh U., Bethlehem, Pa., 1986-89. Grantee Nat. Cancer Inst., NIH, 1967-70, Nat. Eye Inst., NIH, 1976-97. Mem. AAAS, Am. Soc. Cell Biology, Assn. Rsch. in Vision and Ophthalmology, Sigma Xi. Home: 2822 Rhineberry Rd Rochester Hills MI 48309-1912

UNANUE, EMIL RAPHAEL, immunopathologist; b. Havana, Cuba, Sept. 13, 1934; married, 1965; 3 children. B.Sc., Inst. Secondary Edn., 1952; MD, U. Havana Sch. Medicine, Cuba, 1960; MA, Harvard U., 1974. Assoc. exptl. pathology Scripps Clin. and Research Found., 1960-70; intern in pathology Presbyn. Univ. Hosp., Pitts., 1961-62; research fellow in exptl. pathology Scripps Clin. and Research Found., 1962-65; research fellow immunology Nat. Inst. Med. Research, London, 1966-68; from asst. prof. to assoc. prof. pathology Harvard U. Med. Sch., Boston, 1971-74, prof., 1974-77, Mallinckrodt prof. immunopathology, 1977—; prof., chmn. dept. pathology Washington U. Sch. Medicine, St. Louis, 1988—. Recipient T. Duckett Jones award, Helen Hay Whitney Found., 1968, Park-Davis award, Am. Soc. Exptl. Pathology, 1973, Albert Lasker award for Basic Med. Rsch., Lasker Found., 1995, Gairdner Found. award, 2000. Office: Washington U Sch Medicine Dept Pathology and Immunology Box 8118 Saint Louis MO 63110-1093 Office Phone: 314-362-7440. Office Fax: 314-362-4096. E-mail: unanue@pathbox.wustl.edu.

UNDERHEIM, GREGG, state legislator; b. Aug. 22, 1950; BS, U. Wis., La Crosse, 1972. Former mem. Winnebago County Bd.; former congl. aide; Wis. state assemblyman dist. 54, 1987—. Former h.s. tchr. Republican. Home: 1652 Beech St Oshkosh WI 54901-2808 Office: Wis Assembly PO Box 8952 Madison WI 53708-8952

UNDERWOOD, JULIE K., dean, former law educator; b. 1954; d. Kenneth and Shirley Underwood; m. William Young, July 4, 1991; children: David, Chris, Kate, Maggie. BA in Polit. Sci. and Sociology, DePauw U., 1976; JD, Ind. U., 1979; PhD, U. Fla., 1984. Clk. Ind. Ct. Appeals, 1979-81; instr. sch. law U. Fla., Gainesville, 1981-82, rsch. assoc. Inst. Edn1. Fin., 1981-82; asst. prof. edn1. adminstrn. U. N.D., 1982-85, assoc. prof., 1982-86, asst. dean Ctr. Teaching and Learning, 1986; asst. prof. dept. edn1. adminstrn. U. Wis., Madison, 1986-89, prof., edn. adminstrn., 1990-93, chair, dept. edn. adminstrn., 1993—94, assoc. prof. sch. law, 1992—95, dean, Sch. Edn., 2005—; interim counsel Wis. Dept. Pub. Instrn., Madison, 1990; dean, Sch. Edn. & Allied Professions Miami Univ., Ohio, 1995—98; assoc. exec. dir, gen. counsel Coun. Sch. Attys, Nat. Sch. Bds. Assn., Alexandria, Va., 1998—2005. 2d level spl. edn. reviewing officer State Wis., 1988; hearing officer Wis. Tchr. Cert., 1993. Author: Legal Aspects of Special Education and Pupil Services, 1994; editor: (with D. Monk) Microlevel School Finance: Issues and Implications for Policy, 1988, (with W. Camp and M. Connelly) Principals' Handbook: Current Issues in School law, 1989, (with D. Verstegen) The Impact of Litigation and Legislation on Public School Finance, 1989, (with W. Camp, M. Connelly and K. Lane) The Principal's Legal Handbook, 1993; asst. editor Jour. Edn. Fin., 1981-83, legis. editor, 1985-88, legal editor, 1988—; mem. author's com. Edn. Law Reporter, 1982—; editor The Sch. and the Cts.; contbr. articles to profl. jours., chpts. to books. Grantee U. Wis., 1988, 89, 90-93. Mem. Am. Edn. Fin. Assn. (bd. dirs. 1984-88, chair Outstanding Svc. award 1987-88), Nat. Orgn. Legal Problems of Edn. (chair membership com. 1987-88, bd. dirs. 1987-91, chair ann. conf. program com. 1988-89, chair publs. com. 1989-91, constl. review com. 1990-92). Office: Dean Sch Edn 123 Edn Bld Univ Wisconsin 1000 Bascom Mall Madison WI 53706-1398 Office Phone: 608-262-6137.

UNDERWOOD, ROBERT LEIGH, venture capitalist; b. Paducah, Ky., Dec. 31, 1944; s. Robert Humphreys and Nancy Wells (Jessup) Underwood; m. Susan Lynn Doscher, May 22, 1976; children: Elizabeth Leigh, Dana Whitney, George Gregory. BS with great distinction, Stanford U., 1965, MS, 1966, PhD, 1968; MBA, Santa Clara U., 1970. Rsch. scientist, project leader Lockheed Missiles & Space Co., Sunnyvale, Calif., 1967—71; spl. asst. for engring. scis. Office Sec., Dept. Transp., Washington, 1971—73; sr. mgmt. assoc. Office Mgmt. and Budget, Exec. Office Pres., 1973; with TRW Inc., LA, 1973—79, dir. retail nat. accts., 1977—78, dir. product planning and devel., 1978—79; pres., CEO OMEX, Santa Clara, Calif., 1980—82; v.p. Heizer Corp., Chgo., 1979—85; pres. No. Capital Corp., Chgo., 1985—86; mng. ptnr. ISSS Ventures, 1986—88; founding ptnr. N.Am. Bus. Devel. Co., Chgo., 1988—; pres., CEO Polymer Corp., Rockland, Mass., 2003—. Trustee Burridge Mut. Funds, 1996—98. Contbr. articles to profl. jours. Sch. bd. Avoca Dist. 37, 1990—99, v.p., 1996—99; adv. bd. Leavy Sch. Bus. and Adminstrn. Santa Clara U., 1995—; adv. com. on indsl. innovation NSF, 1982—96; trustee Kenilworth Union Ch., 2003—; elder Presbyn. Ch., 1978—79. Fellow, ASA, NSF; scholar, Alcoa. Mem.: IEEE, Farmington Country Club (Charlottesville, Va.), Indian Hill Club (Winnetka, Ill.), Union League Chgo., Chgo. Club, Beta Gamma Sigma, Tau Beta Pi, Phi Beta Kappa, Sigma Xi. Home: 59 Woodley Rd Winnetka IL 60093-3748 Office: 135 S La Salle St Chicago IL 60603-4159

UNGAR, IRWIN ALLAN, botany educator; b. NYC, Jan. 21, 1934; s. Isidore and Gertrude (Fageles) U.; m. Ana Celia Del Cid, Aug. 10, 1959; children: Steven, Sandra, Sharon. BS, CCNY, 1955; MA, U. Kans., Lawrence, 1957, PhD, 1961. Instr. U. R.I., Kingston, 1961-62; asst. prof. Quincy Coll., Ill., 1961-66, Ohio U., Athens, 1966-69, assoc. prof., 1969-74, prof. botany, 1974—, chmn. dept. botany, 1984-89. Dir. Dysart Woods Lab., 1985—99, Environ. Studies Program, 1991—95; vis. prof. dept. plant scis. and vis. fellow Wolfson Coll., Oxford (Eng.) U., 1990—91; panelist Nat. Sea Grant Program, 1984; grant proposal reviewer NSF, 1980—2002. Contbr. articles to profl. jours.; manuscript reviewer Am. Jour. Botany, Internat. Jour. Plant Scis. NSF grantee, 1974-76, 76-78, 80-83, 94-95, 98-2001; rsch. grantee Petroleum Environ. Rsch. Forum, 1992-96. Fellow Ohio Acad. Sci.; mem. AAAS, Am. Inst. Biol. Scis., Bot. Soc. Am., Ecol. Soc. Am., Sigma Xi. Home: 44 Walker St Athens OH 45701-2252 Office: Ohio Univ Dept Of Botany Athens OH 45701 E-mail: ungar@ohio.edu.

UNGARETTI, RICHARD ANTHONY, lawyer; b. Chgo., May 25, 1942; s. Dino Carl and Antoinette (Calvetti) U.; children: Joy A., Paul R. BS, DePaul U., 1964, JD, 1970. Bar: Ill. 1970, U.S. Dist. Ct. (no. dist.) Ill. 1970, U.S. Supreme Ct. 1980. Assoc. Kirkland & Ellis, Chgo., 1970-74; ptnr. Ungaretti & Harris, Chgo., 1974—. Mem. adv. coun. DePaul Coll. Law, Chgo., 1988. Mem. ABA, Chgo. Bar Assn., Ill. State Bar Assn., Internat. Coun. Shopping Ctrs., Am. Coll. Real Estate Lawyers, Justinian Soc., Urban Land Inst. (assoc.), Lamda Alpha Avocations: golf, fishing, hunting. Office: Ungaretti & Harris 3500 Three First Nat Plz Chicago IL 60602 Office Phone: 312-977-4430. Business E-Mail: raungaretti@uhlaw.com.

UNGER, SUSAN J., automotive executive; b. Detroit, Apr. 8, 1950; BA in Economics, Mich. State U., 1972; MBA in Fin., Wayne State U., 1976. Fin. analyst, sales and mktg. DaimlerChrysler AG, 1972, various financial positions, fin. dir. product devel. and Jeep/Truck Ops., exec. dir. mgmt. info. sys., 1993, sr. v.p., 1998—, chief info. officer, 1998—. Mem., past pres., Eli Broad Bd., Coll. Bus. Mich. State U.; bd. dir. Cyberstate.org; nat. adv. com. Coll. of Engring. U. Mich.; adv. tech. bd. Oakland U. Named 100 Leading Women in N.Am. Auto Industry, Automotive News, 2002, CIO of Yr., Automation Alley, 2002, Salomon Smith Barney, 2002, Disting. Alumnus of Yr., Wayne State U. Sch. Bus. Adminstrn., 2002; named one of Detroit's Most Influential Women, Crain's Detroit Bus., 2002; recipient Top Am. Woman award, Assn. Woman in Computing, 2003, Pioneer award, Phoenix Hill Women's Mus., 2004, Disting. Svc. Citation, Automotive Hall of Fame, 2006. Mem.: Automotive Womens Alliance, Kleiner Perkins CIO Strategy Exch. Forum. Office: Daimler-Chrysler Corp 1000 Chrysler Dr Auburn Hills MI 48326-2766

UNHJEM, MICHAEL BRUCE, lawyer; b. Fargo, ND, Aug. 22, 1953; s. Kalmer Joseph and Lorelei Mae (Myhra) U.; children: Kaia Mary, David Burges, Kirsten Elizabeth. BA magna cum laude, Jamestown Coll., 1975; JD with distinction, U. N.D., 1978. Bar: N.D. 1978. Pvt. practice, Jamestown, ND, 1978-86; compliance officer Norwest Bank, Jamestown, ND, 1981-84; planned giving officer Jamestown Coll., Anne Carlsen Sch., Jamestown, 1984-86; asst. to pres., gen. counsel Blue Cross Blue Shield of N.D., Fargo, 1986-91, pres., chief exec. officer, 1991—, Pioneer Mutual Life Ins. Co., Fargo, 1997—99. Chmn. bd. dirs. Lincoln Mut. Life & Casualty Ins. Co., Fargo, Noridian Adminstr. Svc., LLC, Fargo, Noridian Ins. Svc., Inc., Fargo; chmn. TriWest HC All.; bd. dirs. Prime Ther, Western Conf. Prepaid Health Plans, Jamestown Coll., Cass Clay United Way, Blue Cross Blue Shield Assn. State rep. N.D. Legis. Assembly, Bismarck, 1974-86; mem. Nat. Conf. Commrs. on Uniform State Laws, Chgo., 1981—, chmn., Bismarck, 1982-86; co-chmn. Bush for Pres. Com., 1980, 88, 92; presdl. appointee Nat. Coun. on Disability, Washington, 1990. Named Outstanding Young North Dakotan, N.D. Jaycees, 1983; recipient Nat. Excellence in Leadership award State of N.D., 1988, Disting. Leadership award N.D. Psychol. Assn., 1988, Spl. Presdl. Commendation award Am. Psychiatric Assn., 1989, Toastmaster Internat. Comm. and Leadership award, 1992. Mem. ABA, N.D. Bar Assn., Cass County Bar Assn., Kiwanis, Elks, Masons, Shriners. Republican. Lutheran. Office: Blue Cross Blue Shield 4510 13th Ave S Fargo ND 58121-0002

UNIKEL, EVA TAYLOR, interior designer; b. Hungary; arrived in Can., 1956; came to U.S., 1967; d. Istvan Domolky and Lea Maria (Koszegi) Coan; m. Alan L. Unikel; 1 child, Renee Christine; m. June 26, 1993. BS, So. Ill. U., 1972. Dir. mktg. Lococo Design, St. Louis, 1982-83; project mgr., nat. dir. mktg. hosp. div. Hotel Restaurant Planners div. Profl. Interiors, St. Louis, 1983-87; founder Interior Solutions Inc., Hinsdale, Ill., 1987—. Mem. AIA (assoc.), Nat. Assn. Women Bus. Owners, Am. Soc. Interior Design (chairperson 1984-86), Interior Design Assn. Roman Catholic. Office: 500 E Ravine Rd Hinsdale IL 60521-2449 Home Phone: 630-986-4464; Office Phone: 630-464-9696.

UNSER, AL, retired professional auto racer, racing official; b. Albuquerque, May 29, 1939; s. Jerry H. and Mary C. (Craven) U.; m. Wanda Jesperson, Apr. 22, 1958 (div.); children: Mary Linda, Debra Ann, Alfred; m. Karen Barnes, Nov. 22, 1977 (div.). Auto racer U.S. Auto Club, Speedway, Ind., 1964-94. Achievements include placing 3d in nat. standings, 1968, 2d in 1969, 77, 78, 1st in 1970, 4th in 1976; winner Indpls. 500, 1970, 71, 78, 87, Pocono 500, 1976, 78, Ont. 500, 1977, 78; placed 3d in U.S. Auto Club Sports Car Club Am. Formula 5000, 1975, 2d place, 1976; Internat. Race of Champions champion, 1978; 2d pl. Indpls. Motor Speedway, 1983; CART/PPG Indy Car champion, 1983, 85. Office: IRL 4567 W 16th St Indianapolis IN 46222-2513

UPATNIEKS, JURIS, retired optical engineer; b. Riga, Latvia, May 7, 1936; arrived in U.S., 1951; s. Karlis and Eleonora (Jegers) Upatnieks; m. Ilze Induss, July 13, 1968; children: Ivars, Ansis. BSEE, U. Akron, Ohio, 1960; MSEE, U. Mich., 1965. Rsch. asst., then rsch. assoc. Willow Run Labs. U. Mich., Ann Arbor, 1960-69; rsch. engr. Inst. Sci. and Tech., U. Mich., Ann Arbor, 1969-72, Environ. Rsch. Inst. Mich., Ann Arbor, 1973-93; sr. engr. Applied Optics, Ann Arbor, 1993—2001; ret., 2001. Lectr. elec. engring. dept. U. Mich., 1971—73, adj. assoc. prof. elec. engring. and computer sci. dept., 1974—2001, adj. rsch. scientist dept. mech. engring. and applied mechanics, 1996—2001. Contbr. articles to profl. jours. 2d lt. US Army, 1961—62. Recipient Holley medal, ASME, 1976, Inventor of the Yr. award, Assn. Advancement Invention and Innovation, 1976. Fellow: Latvian Acad. Sci. (Grand medal 1999, Walter Zapp prize 2007), Acad. Soc. Austrums, Soc. Photographic Instrumentation Engrs. (Robert Gordon award 1965), Optical Soc. Am. (R. W. Wood prize 1975), Am. Latvian Assn. Achievements include patents in field. Avocations: camping, gardening, hiking. Personal E-mail: upatnks@netrek.net.

UPBIN, HAL J., consumer products company executive; b. Bronx, NY, Jan. 15, 1939; s. David and Evelyn (Sloan) U.; m. Shari Kiesler, May 29, 1960; children: Edward, Elyse, Danielle. BBA, Pace Coll., 1961. CPA, NY. Tax sr. Peat, Marwick, Mitchell & Co., NYC, 1961-65; tax mgr. Price Waterhouse & Co., NYC, 1965-71; dir. taxes Wheelabrator-Frye Inc., NYC, 1971-72, treas., 1972-74; pres. Wheelabrator Fin. Corp., NYC, 1974-75; v.p., chief fin. officer Chase Manhattan Mortgage and Realty Trust (became Triton Group Ltd. 1980), NYC, 1975-76, pres., 1976-78, pres., chmn., 1978-83, also dir.; chmn., pres., dir. Isomedics, 1983-85; chmn., pres. Fifth Ave. Cards, Inc., Fifth Retail Corp., Ashley's Stores, Ashley's Outlet Stores, 1984-88; bd. dirs. Stacy Industries, 1984-88; vice chmn. Am. Recreation Products, St. Louis, 1985-88, vice chmn., pres., 1988—, chmn., 1992—; v.p. corp. devel., chmn. acquistion com. Kellwood Co., Chesterfield, Mo., 1990—, exec. v.p. corp. devel., chmn. acquisition com., 1992—, pres., COO, 1994—, pres., COO, dir., 1995-97, pres., CEO, 1997—2005, chmn., 1999—2006, chmn. emeritus, 2006—, also bd. dirs. Bd. dirs. First Banks, Inc., Regional Bus. Coun., Coun. Nat. Trustees, Nat. Jewish Med. and Rsch. Ctr., Nat. Coun. Wash. U. Olin Sch. Bus., Brown Shoe Co.; trustee Pace U. Past pres. Jewish Temple. Mem. AICPA, NY State Soc. CPA's, Franklin Jaycees (v.p.). Home: 3740 S Ocean Blvd Apt 801 Highland Beach FL 33487-3403 Office Phone: 314-576-3100. Business E-Mail: HJU@kellwood.com.

UPHOFF, JAMES KENT, education educator; b. Hebron, Nebr., Sept. 1, 1937; s. Ernest John and Alice Marie (Dutcher) U.; m. Harriet Lucille Martin, Aug. 6, 1962; 1 child, Nicholas James. BA, Hastings Coll., 1959; MEd, U. Nebr., 1962, EdD, 1967. Tchr. Walnut Jr. H.S., Grand Island, Nebr., 1959-65, dept. chmn., 1962-65; instr. dept. edn. U. Nebr., Lincoln, 1965-66; curriculum intern Bellevue (Nebr.) Pub. Schs., 1966-67; asst. prof. edn. Wright State U., Dayton, Ohio, 1967-70, assoc. prof., 1970-75, prof. edn., 1975—, co-dir. pub. edn. religion studies ctr., 1972-75, dean br. campuses, 1974-79, dir. lab. experiences, 1982-91, chmn. dept. tchr. edn., 1994-97, dir. coll. student svcs., 1994-97, dir. profl. field experiences, prof. emeritus, 1997—, assoc. dir. Ctr. for Tchg. and Learning, 1999—. Vis. prof. U. Dayton, 1968—69, 1998, 99; adj. prof. Antioch McGregor, 2003—; mem. educator stds. bd. State of Ohio, 2004—. Author: (with others) Summer Children: Ready or Not for School, 4th edit., 1986, School Readiness and Transition Programs: Real Facts from Real Schools, 1990, 2d edit., 1995; editor: Dialogues on Development Curriculum K and I, 1987, Changing to a Developmentally Appropriate Curriculum-Successfully: 4 Case Studies, 1989; weekly columnist Oakwood Register newspapers; weekly commentator on edn. WYSO-FM Pub. Radio. Bd. dirs. pub. edn. fund Dayton Found., 1985-97; mem. Luth. Ch. coun., 1987-90, chair, 1988-90; mem. Oakwood City Schs. Bd. Edn., 1989—, v.p., 1994, 95, 03, pres., 1996, 97, 04. Phi Delta Kappa scholar, 1969; Malone fellow in Arab Islamic studies, 1989; U. Nebr. Alumni award, 2002. Mem. ASCD (dir. 1974-79, editor early childhood network 1989-98, editor and facilitator pub. edn. and religion network 1992—), Western Ohio Edn. Assn. (pres. 1974-75, exec. com. 1979-85), Ohio Assn. Supervision and Curriculum Devel. (v.p. 1972-73), Nat. Coun. Social Studies, Ohio Coun. Social Studies, Ohio Sch. Bds. Assn. (chair rules com. 1993-94, mem. policy and legislation com. 1994—. Achievement award 1995, 96, 98, 2000, 04, Master Boardsman award, 2004, trustee 1996-2002, exec. com. 1998-99, pres.-elect 2000, pres. 2001), Nat. Assn. Edn. Young Children, Dayton Area Coun. Social Studies (pres. 1970-71, 85-87), Ohio Assn. Edn. Young Children (com. chair 1992-95), Dayton Assn. for Young Children (exec. bd. 1988-94), LWV Greater Dayton (edn. dir. 1981-85), Ohio Coun. Chs. (edn. com. 1973-75), Nat. Sch. Bd. Assoc. (policy and rels. com., 2003), Ohio Dept. Edn. (gifted edn. adv. coun., 2001)Optimists Club (pres. 1983-85, sec.-treas. 1988-99), Phi Delta Kappa (chpt. pres. 1983-84, 98—, chpt. advisor 1988-94, area coord. 2001—03, chpt./mem. liaison 2004—), Kappa Delta Pi. Republican. Home: 150 Spirea Dr Dayton OH 45419-3409 Office: Wright State U CTL 023 Library Dayton OH 45435 Home Phone: 937-299-5139; Office Phone: 937-775-3651. Business E-Mail: james.uphoff@wright.edu. E-mail: jkuphoff@aol.com.

UPMEYER, LINDA, state official; b. July 1952; married. B, U. Iowa, 1997; M in Nursing, Drake U., 1999. Family nurse practitioner; state rep. Iowa, 2003—. Mem., vice-chair edn. appropriation subcom.; mem. human resources standing com.; mem. environ. protection standing com.; mem. appropriations standing com. Mem.: Iowa Nursing Assn. (chair polit. action com.), Sigma Theta Tau (mem. Gamma chpt.). Office: State Capitol E 12th and Grand Des Moines IA 50319

UPTON, FREDERICK STEPHEN, congressman; b. St. Joseph, Mich., Apr. 23, 1953; s. Stephen E. and Elizabeth Brooks (Vial) U.; m. Amey Richmond Rulon-Miller, Nov. 5, 1983; 2 children. BA in Journalism, U. Mich., 1975. Staff asst. to Congressman David A. Stockman, Washington, 1976-81; legis. asst. Office Mgmt. and Budget, Washington, 1981-83, dep. dir. legis. affairs, 1983-84, dir. legis. affairs, 1984-85; mem. US Congress from 6th Mich. dist., Washington, 1987—; mem. energy and commerce com. Field mgr. Stockman for Congress, St. Joseph, 1975; campaign mgr. Globensky for Congress, St. Joseph, 1981. Recipient Spirit Enterprise award, US C. of C., 1988—93, Legis. of Yr., Am. Ambulance Assn., 2000. Mem.: Emil Verban Soc. Republican. Congregationalist. Office: US House of Reps 2183 Rayburn House Office Bldg Washington DC 20515-2206 also: District Office 157 S Kalamazoo Mall Ste 180 Kalamazoo MI 49006 also: District Office Ste 106 800 Ship Street Saint Joseph MI 49085-2182 Office Phone: 202-225-3761, 269-385-0039, 269-982-1986. Office Fax: 269-982-0237, 202-225-4986.

URBOM, WARREN KEITH, federal judge; b. Atlanta, Nebr., Dec. 17, 1925; s. Clarence Andrew and Anna Myrl (Irelan) U.; m. Joyce Marie Crawford, Aug. 19, 1951; children: Kim Marie, Randall Crawford, Allison Lee, Joy Renee. AB with highest distinction, Nebr. Wesleyan U., 1950, LLD (hon.), 1984; JD with distinction, U. Mich., 1953. Bar: Nebr. 1953. Mem. firm Baylor, Evnen, Baylor, Urbom, & Curtiss, Lincoln, Nebr., 1953—70; judge U.S. Dist. Ct. Nebr., 1970—; chief judge U.S. Dist. Ct. Dist. Nebr., 1972—86, sr. judge, 1991—. Mem. com. on practice and procedure Nebr. Supreme Ct., 1965-95; mem. subcom. on fed. jurisdiction Jud. Conf. U.S., 1975-83; adj. instr. trial advocacy U. Nebr. Coll. Law, 1979-90; bd. dirs. Fed. Jud. Ctr., 1982-86; chmn. com. on orientation newly apptd. dist. judges Fed. Jud. Ctr., 1986-89; mem. 8th Cir. Com. on Model Criminal and Civil Jury Instrns., 1983—; mem. adv. com. on alternative sentences U.S. Sentencing Com., 1989-91. Contbr. articles to profl. jours. Trustee St. Paul Sch. Theology, Kansas City, Mo., 1986-89; active United Methodist Ch. (bd. mgrs., bd. global ministries 1972-76, gen. com. on status and role of women, 1988-96, gen. conf. 1972, 76, 80, 88, 92, 96, 2000); pres. Lincoln YMCA, 1965-67; bd. govs. Nebr. Wesleyan U., chmn. 1975-80. With AUS, 1944-46. Recipient Medal of Honor, Nebr. Wesleyan U. Alumni Assn., 1983. Fellow Am. Coll. Trial Lawyers; mem. ABA, Nebr. Bar Assn. (ho. of dels. 1966-70, Outstanding Legal Educator award 1990, Pres.'s award for Professionalism 2006), Lincoln Bar Assn. (Liberty Bell award 1993, pres. 1968-69), Kiwanis (Disting. Svc. award 1993), Masons (33 deg., Grand Master's Humanitarian award 2003), Am. Inns of Ct. (Lewis F. Powell Jr. award for Professionalism and Ethics 1995), Robert Van Pelt Am. Inn of Ct. (Lifetime Mentor award, 2002). Methodist. Home: 4421 Ridgeview Dr Lincoln NE 68516-1516 Office: US Dist Ct 586 Fed Bldg 100 Centennial Mall N Lincoln NE 68508-3859 Office Phone: 402-437-5231. Personal E-mail: urbom1@neb.rr.com. Business E-Mail: warren_urbom@ned.uscourts.gov.

URLACHER, BRIAN KEITH, professional football player; b. Pasco, Wash., May 25, 1978; s. Brad and Lavoyda Urlacher; m. Laure Urlacher (div.); 1 child, Pamela; 1 child, Riley. BA, U. N.Mex., Albuquerque, 2000. Linebacker Chgo. Bears, 2000—. Vol. United Way. Vol. Spl. Olympics, Ill., N.Mex. Named NFL Defensive Rookie of Yr., AP, 2000, NFL Defensive Player of Yr., 2005; named to Nat. Football Conf. Pro Bowl Team, 2002—07, NFL All-Pro Team, 2005—06. Office: Chgo Bears Halas Hall 1000 Football Dr Lake Forest IL 60045

URLACHER, HERBERT, state legislator; b. New England, ND, Dec. 30, 1931; m. Claire Urlacher; 5 children. Farmer, rancher; mem. N.D. State Ho. of Reps., Bismarck, 1989-91, N.D. Senate from 36th dist., Bismarck, 1992—. Pres. Stark County Sch. Officers, N.D. Water Users, West River Joint Water Resource Bd.; past pres. ch. coun. St. Mary's Ch.; bd. dirs. Water Resources Bd. N.D.; mem. Stark County Water Resource Bd.; mem. adv. bd. State Water Commn. Mem. KC, Elks. Office: ND State Capitol 600 E Boulevard Ave Bismarck ND 58505-0660 also: 3320 94th Ave SW Taylor ND 58656-9643

URNESS, KENT D., insurance company executive; b. 1948; With The St. Paul Co., Inc., 1971, v.p. comml. ins., 1985—90, sr. v.p. global splty. practices, 1999—2001, exec. v.p. internat., 2001—; sr. v.p. agy. broker svcs. St. Paul Fire and Marine Ins. Co., 1991—92; pres. St. Paul Internat. Ins. Co. Ltd., 1993—. Office: The St Paul Cos, Inc 385 Washington St Saint Paul MN 55102

USHER, PHYLLIS LAND, state official; b. Winona, Miss., Aug. 29, 1944; d. Sandy Kenneth and Ruth (Cottingham) Land; m. William A. Usher (dec. Dec. 1993). BS, U. So. Miss., 1967; MS, U. Tenn., 1969; postgrad., Purdue U., Ind. U., Utah State U. Libr. Natchez (Miss.) -Adams County Schs., 1967-68; materials specialist Fulton County Bd. Edn., Atlanta, 1969-71; cons. divsn. instructional media Ind. Dept. Pub. Instrn., Indpls., 1971-74, dir. divsn., 1974-82, dir. fed. resources and sch. improvement, 1982-85; acting assoc. supt. Ind. Dept. Edn., 1985, sr. officer Ctr. Sch. Improvement, 1985-96, asst. supt., 1996—. Pres. bd. dirs. INCOLSA, mcpl. corp., 1980-82; pres., owner Usher Funeral Home, Inc.; pres. NU Realty Corp.; mem. task force sch. Libraries Nat. Commn. Libraries and Info. Sci.; cons. in field. Bd. dirs. Hawthorne Cmty. Ctr.; mem. Gov. Inst. Conf. Children and Youth Task Force. Recipient citation Internat. Reading Assn., 1975; Title II-B fellow, U. Tenn., 1968-69. Mem. ALA, Nat. Assn. State Edn1. Media Profls., West Deanery Bd. Edn., Indpls. Archdiocese, Delta Kappa Gamma. Office: State House Rm 229 Indianapolis IN 46204-2728

USTIAN, DANIEL C., trucking executive; With Navistar Internat. Corp., 1973—, group v.p., gen. mgr. engine group, 1990—99, pres., 1999—, COO, 2002—03, CEO, 2003—, chmn., 2004—. Office: Navistar Internat Corp PO Box 1488 4201 Winfield Rd Warrenville IL 60555 Office Phone: 630-753-5000.

UTECHT, ANDREA E., lawyer; b. Olean, NY, Nov. 30, 1948; BA magna cum laude, Elmira Coll., 1970; MS, U. Pa., 1972, MBA, JD, U. Pa., 1975. Bar: Pa. 1975, NY 1976. Assoc. corp. counsel Colonial Penn Group, Inc., 1975—81; sr. v.p., gen. counsel, sec. AtoFina Chemicals, Inc., 1996—2001; v.p., gen. counsel, sec. FMC Corp., Chgo., 2001—. Mem.: Am. Corp. Counsel Assn., Phila. Bar Assn., Assn. Corp. Counsel (bd. mem.), Am. Arbitration Assn. (bd. mem.), Phi Beta Kappa. Fluent in French. Office: FMC Corp 200 E Randolph Dr Chicago IL 60601 Office Phone: 312-861-6000. Office Fax: 312-861-7127.

UTSCHIG, THOMAS S., federal judge; Bankruptcy judge U.S. Dist. Ct. (we. dist.) Wis., Eau Claire, 1986—. Office: 500 S Barstow St Eau Claire WI 54701-3657

UTT, GLENN S., JR., retired medical products executive; b. Neodesha, Kans., Aug. 7, 1926; s. Glenn S. and Reba Pauline (White) Utt; m. Mary Lou Ford, Aug. 8, 1948; 1 child, Jan A. BSEE, BSBA, Kans. State U., 1949; MBA, Harvard U., 1951. Salesman Drexel Furniture Co., NC, 1951-55; v.p. Booz Allen & Hamilton, Chgo. and Zurich, Switzerland, 1955-62; exec. v.p. Abbott Labs., North Chicago, Ill., 1962-83, also dir., ret., 1983. Chmn. bd. U.P. Hotel Group Inc., Houghton, Mich.; ret. dir. Synergen, Selectide and Sugen biotech cos. Co-author: Lalique Perfume Bottles, 1990. Alderman City of Lake Forest, Ill., 1972-76, chmn. recreational bd., 1975-78; mem. exec. com. Lake County Republican Fedn., Waukegan, Ill., 1974-83. With USN, 1944-46, USAF (res.), 1948-53. Mem.: Beta Theta Pi. Avocations: antiques, objects of art. Home: PO Box 810 Houghton MI 49931 Personal E-mail: mlbud@webtv.net.

VADNER, GREGORY A., state agency administrator; b. Indpls., Mar. 24, 1951; s. Clyde H. and Marilyn (Whickcar) V.; m. Frances A. Woods, May 21, 1983; 1 child, Ariel. BA, DePauw U., 1974; MPA, U. Mo., 1984. Mgr. A&W Root Beer Restaurant, DeSoto, Mo., 1974; photographer Chromalloy Photog. Industries, St. Louis, 1974-75; caseworker Mo. Div. Family Svcs., Hillsboro, 1975-79, income maintenance supr., 1979, county dir. I Centerville, 1979-80, county dir. II Mexico, 1980-85, county dir. IV St. Joseph, 1985-87, income maintenance supr. V Kansas City, 1987-88, dep. dir. Jefferson City, 1988; dir. Mo. Divsn. Med. Svcs., Jefferson City. Mem. Am. Pub. Welfare Assn., Nat. Eligibility Workers Assn., Reform Orgn. for Welfare. Lutheran. Avocations: photography, trout fishing, tennis. Home: 1105 Schumate Chapel Rd Jefferson City MO 65109-0585 Office: Mo Divsn Med Svcs PO Box 6500 Jefferson City MO 65102-6500

VAIL, THOMAS VAN HUSEN, retired publishing executive; b. Cleve., June 23, 1926; s. Herman Lansing and Delia (White) V.; m. Iris W. Jennings, Sept. 15, 1951; children: Siri Jennings Burki, Thomas Van Husen, Jr. AB in Politics cum laude, Princeton U., 1948; HHD (hon.), Wilberforce U., 1964; LHD, Kenyon Coll., 1969, Cleve. State U., 1973. Reporter Cleve. News, 1949-53, polit. editor, 1953-57; with Cleve. Plain Dealer, 1957-91, v.p., 1961-63, pub., editor, 1963-91, pres., 1970-91; dir. AP, 1968-74; ret., 1991. Bd. dirs. Greater Cleve. Growth Assn.; bd. dirs., past pres. Cleve. Conv. and Visitors Bur.; mem. Nat. Adv. Commn. on Health Manpower; presdl. apptd. to U.S. Adv. Commn. on Info., Pres.'s Commn. for Observance 25th Anniversary UN; trustee No. Ohio region NCCJ, Nat. Brotherhood Week chmn., 1969; trustee Cleve. Coun. World Affairs; fellow Cleve. Clinic Found.; former mem. Downtown Cleve. Corp.; former mem. distbn. com. Cleve. Found.; chmn., founder New Cleve. Campaign; trustee, founder Cleve. Tomorrow; former trustee Com. Econ. Devel.; former mem. Pres.'s Adv. Coun. on Pvt. Sector Initiatives. With USNR, 1944-46, lt. (j.g.), 1950. Recipient Nat. Human Rels. award, 1970, Cleve. Man of Year award Sales and Mktg. Execs. Cleve., 1976, Ohio Gov.'s award, 1982, Downtown Bus. Coun. recognition award Greater Cleve. Growth Assn., 1983, award NCCJ, 1970, award Mt. Vernon Adv. Com., 1994. Mem. Nat. Assn. Profl. Journalists (Lifetime Hall of Fame), Am. Newspaper Pubs. Assn., Am. Soc. Newspaper Editors, Soc. Profl. Journalists, Kirtland Country Club (Willoughby, Ohio), Sand Ridge Golf Club (Chardon, Ohio), Cypress Point Club (Pebble Beach, Calif.), Bohemian Club (San Francisco), Chagrin Valley Hunt Club (Gates Mills, Ohio), Links Club (NYC). Episcopalian. Home: L'Ecurie 14950 County Line Rd Hunting Valley Chagrin Falls OH 44022 Office: 29225 Chagrin Blvd Ste 200 Pepper Pike OH 44122-4632

VAINSCHTEIN, ARKADY, physics educator; b. Novokuznetsk, Russia, Feb. 24, 1942; MS in Physics, Novosibirsk U., 1964; Budker U., 1968. Prof. physics Novosibirsk, 1983-89; dir. theoretical physics inst. U. Minn., 1993-96, mem. theoretical physics inst., 1990—, Gloria Lubkin prof. physics, 1990—. Vis. prof. U. Minn., 1989-90. Mem. Am. Phys. Soc. Office: U Minn Sch Physics & Astronomy 116 Church St SE Minneapolis MN 55455-0149

VALADE, ALAN MICHAEL, lawyer; b. Berwyn, Ill., Jan. 26, 1952; s. Merle F. and Vera M. Valade; m. June 17, 1978. Attended, Oakland C.C., 1970—72; BA, U. Mich., 1974; JD, Wayne State U., 1977; LLM in Taxation, NYU, 1978. Bar: Mich. 1978, Fla. 1987. Assoc. Kemp, Klein, Endelman & Beer, Southfield, Mich., 1978-79; shareholder Valade, MacKinnon & Higgins, P.C., Detroit, 1979-84, Schwendener & Valade, P.C., Mason, Mich., 1985-91; ptnr. Honigman Miller Schwartz and Cohn LLP, Detroit, 1991—, chmn. tax. dept., 2002—06. Co-author: The Michigan Single Business Tax, 1991; contbr. articles to profl. jours. Fellow Mich. State Bar Found.; mem. ABA, State Bar Mich. (chmn. state and local tax com. 1991, tax. coun. 1989-92), State Bar Fla. Office: Honigman Miller Schwartz and Cohn LLP 2290 First National Bldg 660 Woodward Ave Detroit MI 48226-3506 Office Phone: 313-465-7636. Business E-Mail: avalade@honigman.com.

VALANDRA, PAUL, state legislator; m. Cheryl Valandra; four children. Student, Black Hills State U., U. S.D., Oglala Lakota Coll. Former state senator dist. 28 State of S.D., state senator dist. 27, 1993—. Mem. com. health and human svcs. S.D. State Senate; tribal adminstr. Seargant, US Marine Corps, 1972-75. Mem. Rosebud Sioux Tribal Council, 1993— Democrat. Home: PO Box 909 Mission SD 57555-0909 Office: SD State Senate State Capitol Pierre SD 57501

VALDIVIA, HECTOR HORACIO, medical educator; b. Loreto, Mex., Aug. 23, 1958; married. MD, Nat U. Mex., 1982, PhD, 1987. Teaching asst. Nat. U. Mex. Sch. Medicine, Mexico City, 1980-86; rsch. assoc. Baylor Coll. Medicine, Houston, 1986-89; assoc. scientist U. Wis. Sch. Medicine, Madison, 1989-92; rsch. asst. prof. U. Md. Med. Sch., Bapt., 1992-94; asst. prof. dept. physiology U. Wis. Med. Sch., Madison, 1994-99, assoc. prof. dept. physiology, 1999—. Lectr. and researcher in field. Contbr. articles to profl. jours., chpts. to books. Cystic Fibrosis Found. fellow, 1989-91. Mem. Am. Heart Assn. (scintific coun. 1995—), Biophys. Soc. U.S.A. Office: U Wis Med Sch Dept Physiology 1300 University Ave Madison WI 53706-1510

VALDMAN, ALBERT, language and linguistics educator; b. Paris, Feb. 15, 1931; came to U.S., 1944, naturalized, 1953; s. Jacques and Rose (Standman) V.; m. Hilde Wieners, Aug. 19, 1960; 1 child, Bertrand André. AB, U. Pa., 1953; AM, Cornell U., 1955, PhD, 1960; PhD honoris causa (hon.), U. Neuschâtel, 1991. Linguistic scientist Fgn. Service Inst., 1957-59; asst. prof. Romance langs. Pa. State U., 1959-60; mem. faculty Ind. U., Bloomington, 1960—, prof. French, Italian and linguistics, 1966—, chmn. dept. linguistics, 1963-68, Rudy prof., 1986—; vis. prof. Harvard, summer 1965. Vis. lectr. U. West Indies, 1965-66; Fulbright lectr. U. Nice, France, 1971-72, 75-76, 83-87, 89; cons. in field. Author: Applied Linguistics-French, 1960, Drillbook of French Pronunciation, 1964, 70, Trends in Language Teaching, 1966, College French in the New Key, 1965, Saint-Lucian Creole Basic Course, 1969, Basic Course in Haitian Creole, 1970, First and Second Level High School French, 1972, 2d edit., 1977, Langue et Culture, 1975, Introduction to French Phonology and Morphology, 1976, Le Creole: Structure, Statut et Origine, 1978, Haitian Creole-French English Dictionary, 1982; co-author: En Route—Introduction au français et au monde francophone, 1986; editor: Pidgin and Creole Linguistics, 1977, Le Francais hors de France, 1979; co-editor: Theoretical Orientations in Creole Studies, 1980, Historicity and Variation in Creole Studies, 1981, Issues in International Bilingual Education, 1982, Haiti Today and Tomorrow: An Interdisciplinary Study, 1984, The Evaluation of Foreign Language Proficiency, 1987, Ann pale Kreyol: Learning Haitian Creole, 1987, Dis-Moi!, Viens Voir!, C'est Ça!, 1989, Bien Entendu! Introduction á la prononciation française, 1993, Learners' Dictionary of Haitian Creole, 1996, French and Creole in Louisiana, 1997, Chez Nous, 1997, Dictionary of Louisiana Creole, 1998, 3rd edit., 2006, Etude sur les variétés du francais 2003, Le Français en Amérique du Nord, 2005, Haitian Creole-English Bilingual Dictionary, 2007. Decorated comdr. dans l'Ordre dans Palmes Académiques; recipient Florence Steiner prize, Am. Coun. Tchg. Fgn. Langs., 1998; Guggenheim fellow, 1968, Fulbright fellow, 1985. Mem. Internat. Assn. Applied Linguistics (sec.-gen. 1984-87, pres. 1987-94), Am. Assn. Tchrs. of French (v.p. 1990-94, pres. 1995-98), Comité Internat. des Créolistes (v.p. 1996-2004), Phi Beta Kappa. Office: Ind U CREDLI BH 604 Bloomington IN 47405 Office Phone: 812-855-4988. Business E-Mail: valdman@indiana.edu.

VALENTINE, LONA J., lawyer; b. Ashland, Ky., Nov. 17, 1972; BS in Math./Actuarial Sci., Bellarmine U., 1994; MBA, U. Ky., 1995, JD, 2000. Bar: Ohio 2000, Ky. 2006; cert. Arbitrator Coun. Better Bus. Bureaus. Assoc. Peck, Shaffer & Williams LLP, Cin. Named one of Ohio's Rising Stars, Super Lawyers, 2005, 2006; recipient J. Oexmann Criminal Law award, 1999. Mem.: Cin. Bar Assn., Ohio State Bar Assn., ABA, Nat. Assn. Bond Lawyers. Office: Peck Shaffer & Williams LLP 201 E 5th St Ste 900 Cincinnati OH 45202 Office Phone: 513-639-9238. Office Fax: 513-621-3813.

VALENZUELA, JULIO SAMUEL, sociologist, educator; b. Concepción, Chile, Mar. 30, 1948; came to U.S., 1970; s. Raimundo Arms and Dorothy Dueul (Bowie) V.; m. Erika Fresia Maza, Mar. 22, 1969. Licenciatura, U. Concepción, Chile, 1970; PhD, Columbia U., NYC, 1979. Asst. prof. Yale U., New Haven, 1977-80, Harvard U., Cambridge, Mass., 1980-85, assoc. prof., 1985, U. Notre Dame, Ind., 1986—89, prof. Ind., 1989—, dept. chairperson Ind., 1989—92, fellow Kellogg Inst. Ind., 1986—. Sr. assoc. fellow St. Antony's Coll., Oxford U., 1992-93, 96—; campaign adv. presidl. election, Chile, 1999; cons. labor policy Chilean Govt., 2000, 01; advisor, Chilean Govt. Pension Reform Commn., 2006. Author: Democratización vía Reforma, 1986; co-author: Chile, A Country Study, 1994; co-editor: Chile: Politics And Society, 1976, Military Rule In Chile, 1986, Issues In Democratic Consolidation, 1992, El Eslabón Perdido: Familia, Modernización y Bienestar en Chile, 2006; contbr. chpts. to books, articles to profl. jours. Pres. New Eng. Coun. of Latin Am. Studies, 1984—85. Fellow EH ind. scholarship rsch. 1983-84, conf. grant 1987; John Simon Guggenheim fellow, 1996. Mem. Am. Sociol. Assn., Internat. Sociol. Assn. (v.p. rsch. com. #44 1990-94), Latin Am. Studies Assn. (nominating com. 1987-88), Am. Polit. Sci. Assn., Soc. for the Advancement of Socio-econs., Chilean Polit. Sci. Assn. Methodist. Office: U Notre Dame Kellogg Inst Notre Dame IN 46556 Office Phone: 574-631-6410. Business E-Mail: valenzuela.1@nd.edu.

VALERIO, JOSEPH MASTRO, architectural firm executive, educator; b. Dec. 26, 1947; m. Linda A. Searl; children: Joseph Jr., Anthony. BArch, U. Mich., 1970; MArch, UCLA, 1972. Registered architect, Wis., Ill., Ind., Mo., Calif., Tex., Ariz., Minn., Ala., Iowa, Ind., Md., Mich., Okla., Ga., Mass., N.J., N.Y., N.C., Va., Utah, D.C., Wash., Oreg.; cert. Nat. Coun. Archtl. Registration Bds. Pres. Chrysalis Corp. Architects, 1970-85; assoc. prof. U. Wis., 1973-86; design dir. Swanke Hayden Connell Architects, 1985-86; v.p. architecture A. Epstein and Sons, Inc., 1986-88; pres. Valerio-Assocs. Inc., 1988-94; prin. Valerio Dewalt Train Assocs., Inc., Chgo., 1994—. Mem. nat. bd. peer reviewers GSA; spkr. Ariz. State U., UCLA, U. Ariz., U. Cin., others; cons. USG Interiors, Formica Corp., AAAS, NAS, NEA: vis. critic and lectr. in field. Prin. works include corp., high-tech. indsl., retail, instl. and residential bldgs.; author: Movie Palaces, 1983; (monograph) Joe Valerio, 1999; editor: Architectural Fabric Structures, 1985; featured in Inside Architecture, Domestic Interiors, 1997, ew Am. Apt., 1997, Internat. Interiors, 1997, Lofts/Living and Working Spaces, 1999. Mem. exec. bd. men's coun. Mus. Contemporary Art, 1989-91; mem. exec. bd. Contemporary Arts Coun., 1994-96 (pres. 1999). Recipient Honor awards Wis. Soc. Architects, 1975, 81, 84, 85, Gov.'s Award for Design Excellence, State of Mich., 1979, Gold medal Inst. Bus. Designers, 1988, Design award Progressive Architecture, 1991, Architectural Record Interiors award 1993, 95, 96, Disting. Interior award Inst. Bus. Designers, Chgo., 1993; honored by Emerging Voices series Archtl. League N.Y., 1984, Met. Home mag., Interiors mag. Fellow AIA (programs chmn. design com. Chgo. chpt. 1990, long range planning com. 1992, chair nat. com. on design 1997, Nat. Honor award 1981, 93, Interiors award Chgo. chpt. 1988, 90, 92, 95-97, 99-2002, 04, Disting. Bldg. award 1991, 93, 2004, Nat. Interior Honor award 1993, 96, 2003, Divine Detail award 1999, 2001), Chgo. Architecture Club (pres. 1994), Lambda Alpha. Office: Valerio Dewalt Train Assocs 500 N Dearborn St Fl 9 Chicago IL 60610-4900 Office Phone: 312-332-0363. Business E-Mail: jvalerio@buildordie.com.

VALERIO, MICHAEL ANTHONY, diversified financial services company executive; b. Detroit, Sept. 20, 1953; s. Anthony Rudolph and Victoria (Popoff) V.; m. Barbara Ann abozny, Oct. 8, 1983. BA, U. Mich., Dearborn, 1975. CPA, Mich. Jr. acct. Carabell, Bocknek CPA's, Southfield, Mich., 1975-76; sr. acct. Purdy, Donovan & Beal, CPA's, Detroit, 1976-77; mgr. Buctynck & Co., CPA's, Southfield, 1978-79; contr. Transcontinental Travel, Harper Woods, Mich., 1979—80; exec. v.p. Holland Cons., Inc., Detroit, 1980-85; contr., CFO SLC Recycling Industries, Inc., Warren, Mich., 1985—98; owner Pinnacle Fin. Consulting, PLLC, Livonia, Mich., 1994—. Rep. Wealth and Wisdom, Inc.; fin. cons. Am. Group Retirement Strategy Ctrs.; owner Michael Valerio, CPA/PFS, LLC, 2006—. Mem. AICPA, Mich. Soc. CPAs. Roman Catholic. Office: Pinnacle Fin Consulting PLLC Ste A 37771 Seven Mile Rd Livonia MI 48152-1003

VALINE, DELMAR EDMOND, SR., transportation executive; b. Edwardsville, Ill., May 2, 1919; s. Edward and Clara Louise (Schon) V.; m. Geraldine Goley, Aug. 26, 1939; children: Jayne M. Valine Klein, Linda L. Valine Hay, Delmar E. Jr. Student, Summer Bus. Coll., 1939. Purchasing agt. Swift and Co., Nat. Stockyards., Ill., 1937-58; asst. to pres. St. Louis Nat. Stock Yards Co., Nat. Stockyards, Ill., 1958-60; exec. v.p. St. Louis Livestock Mkt. Found., Nat. Stockyards, Ill., 1960-64; exec. sec. Nat. Museum of Transport, St. Louis, Mo.; v.p. First Ill. Bank, East St. Louis, Ill., 1967-81; bd. chairman Southwest Regional Port Dist., Ill., 1961—. Bd. dirs. First Ill. Bank, East St. Louis, 1982—, Target 2000, East St. Louis, 1977—, Inland Rivers Port and Terminals 1987—, Port of Metropolitan St. Louis, 1975—, sec., treas. Gateway Ctr. Metropolitan St. Louis, 1976—; exec. v.p. East Side Associated Industries, East St. Louis, 1990—. Mayor village of Dupo, Ill., 1945-49, mem. sch. bd. dist. 193, Dupo, 1955-56, Selective Service bd., East St. Louis, 1950-55; mem. Fed. Agy. Adv. Com., 1964-70; commr. Southwestern Ill. Planning Comm., 1976—. Recipient Medallion award, Boys Club Am., 1969. Mem. U.S. C. of C., Rotary (past pres.), Boys Club, Mo. Athletic Club, Royal Order of Jesters. Republican.

VALLIERE, ROLAND EDWARD, performing company executive; b. Pawtucket, RI, Oct. 3, 1954; s. Roland Edgar and Anita Alice (Dubois) V.; m. Stacey Lyn Rein, June 3, 1984 (separated). MusB, New England Conservatory, 1978; MFA, Brandeis U., 1984. Regional mgr. Syracuse (N.Y.) Symphony, 1984-86; gen. mgr. N.H. Symphony, Manchester, 1986-89; exec. dir. Hudson Valley Philharmonic, Poughkeepsie, N.Y., 1989-92, Omaha Symphony, Nebr., 1992-95, Kansas City Symphony, Mo., 1995—2002, dir. tech, 2002—. Presenter Am. Symphony Orchestra League, Washington, 1987, 90. Office: PO Box 22534 Kansas City MO 64113-0534

VALUKAS, ANTON RONALD, lawyer, former prosecutor; b. Chgo., June 21, 1943; s. Anton J. and Mary Ann (Giusto) Valukas; m. Janice C. Valukas (div.); children: Amy Paige, Beth Catherine; m. Maria Finitzo; children: Catherine Sara, Paul Alexander. BA in Polit. Sci., Art History, Lawrence U., 1965; JD, Northwestern U., 1968. Bar: Ill. 1968, U.S. Dist. Ct. (no. dist.) Ill. 1968, U.S. Ct. Appeals (7th cir.) 1969, U.S. Ct. Appeals (10th cir.) 1977, U.S. Ct. Appeals (3d cir.) 1982. Asst. dir. Nat. Defender Project, Chgo., 1968-70; asst. US atty. (No. dist.) Ill. US Dept. Justice, Chgo., 1970—74, chief spl. prosecutions divsn. (No. dist.) Ill., 1974, first asst. US atty (No. dist.) Ill., 1975—76, US atty. (No. dist.) Ill., 1985-89; ptnr. Jenner & Block LLP, Chgo., 1976—85, 1989—, chmn., 2007—. Instr. John Marshal Law Sch., 1972—76; adj. prof. law Northwester U. Sch. Law, 1980—82; dir., treas. Met. Fair and Exposition Authority, Chgo., 1985; spl. counsel to investigate report health care sys. City of Chgo., 1991. Bd. dirs. Boys Scouts Am., Bus. and Profl. People for Pub. Interest, 1998—, Smithsonian Inst. Librs., 2004—, mem. judicial conf. adv. com. on civil rules, 2006—; chmn. Ill. Task Force Crime and Corrections, 1992—93; mem. vis. com. Northwestern U. Sch. Law, 1992—95. Named one of Ten Outstanding Young Citizens of Chgo., Jr. C. of C., 1976; recipient Spl. Commendation award, U.S. Dept. Justice, Chgo., 1975, Disting. Grad. award, Palatine HS, Ill., 1984, Freedom award, John Marshall Sch. Law, 1985, Citizen of the Yr. award, Constn. Rights Found., 1987, Civillian of the Yr. award, Armed Forces Coun. Chgo., 1988, Man of the Yr. award, WBBM Radio, 1988, Disting. Pub. Svc. award, Anti-Defamation League B'nai B'rith, 1990, Disting. Achievement award, Lawrence U., 1990, Disting. Svc. award, Chgo. C. of C. and Industry, 1990, Alumni Merit award, Northwestern U. Alumni Assn., 1995, Richard N. Rovner award, Epilepsy Found. Greater Chgo., 2004, Judge Learned Hand award, 2005. Fellow: Am. Coll. Trial Lawyers; mem.: ABA, Chgo. Inn Ct. (pres. 2000—01), Ill. State Bar Assn., Chgo. Bar Assn., Chicagoland C. of C. (bd. dirs. 1999—), Law of Chgo. Club, Exec. Club Chgo. (bd. dirs. 1996—), Econ. Club. Chgo. (bd. dirs. 1990—). Office: Jenner & Block LLP 330 N Wabash Ave Chicago IL 60611-7603 Office Phone: 312-923-2903. Business E-Mail: avalukas@jenner.com.

VAN AKKEREN, TERRY, state official; b. Mar. 10, 1954; Student, Lakeshore Tech. Coll. Engring. technician; tool and die maker. Mem. econ. devel. com.; mem. edn. com.; mem. labor com.; mem. tourism com. Democrat. Office: State Capitol Rm 409 N PO Box 8953 Madison WI 53708-8953

VAN ANDEL, STEVE ALAN, consumer products company executive; b. Ada, Mich., Oct. 9, 1955; BLS in Econs. and Bus., Hillsdale Coll., 1978; MBA in MKtg., Miami U., Oxford, Ohio, 1979. V.p. mktg. Amway Corp., Worldwide, chmn. exec. com. policy bd. Ada; vice chmn. Amway Japan Ltd.; chmn. Amway Asia Pacific Ltd., Amway Corp., 1995—, CEO, 1995—. Dir. Met. Found., Operation Enterprise-AMA; bd. dirs. Met. Hosp. Found., Mich. Nat. Bank Corp., Ctr. for Internat. Pvt. Enterprises, Gerald Ford Found., Std. Fed. Bank, Grand Rapids John Ball Zoo Soc., Borgess Metro Health Alliance, Met. Health Corp.; mem. dean's adv. bd. Seidman Sch. of Bus.; co-CEO, Alticor Inc. Bd. dirs. Grand Rapids John Ball Soc., Amway Environmental Found. Mem. U.S. C. of C. (chmn. 2002). Office: Amway Corp 7575 Fulton St E Ada MI 49355-0001

VAN BOKKELEN, JOSEPH SCOTT, federal judge, former prosecutor; b. Chgo., June 7, 1943; s. Robert W. and W. Louise (Reynolds) Van Bokkelen; m. Sally Wardall Huey, Aug. 14, 1971; children: Brian, Kate. BA, U. ind., 1966; JD, U. Ind., 1969. Bar: Ind. 1969, US Dist. Ct. (so. dist.) Ind. 1969, US Dist. Ct. (no. dist.) Ind. 1973, US Ct. Appeals (7th cir.) 1973, US Supreme Ct. 1973. Dep. atty. gen. State of Ind., Indpls., 1969—71, asst. atty. gen., 1971—72; asst. US atty. No. Dist. Ind., Hammond, 1972—75, US atty., 2001—07; ptnr. Goldsmith, Goodman, Ball & Van Bokkelen, Highland, 1975—78, Goodman, Ball, Van Bokkelen & Leonard, 1978—2001. Recipient Outstanding Asst. US Atty. award, US Dept. Justice, 1974. Mem.: ABA, Criminal Def. Lawyers Assn., Ind. Bar Assn., Fed. Bar Assn. Office: US Dist Ct 5400 Fed Plz Ste 4200 Hammond IN 46320

VAN BRUNT, WILLIAM A., lawyer; m. Gail Van Brunt; 3 children. BS with honors, Pa. State U.; MS, MIT; JD, Boston U. Sch. Law; LLM, Harvard Sch. Law. Rschr. AVCO Rsch. and Develop.; with Kenway and Jenny, Boston, McNee, Wallace, and Nurick, Harrisburg, Pa., Hershey Foods Corp., General Mills; sr. v.p., gen. counsel Carlson Companies, Inc, Minnetonka, Minn., 2000—. Office: Carlson Companies Inc PO Box 59159 Minneapolis MN 55459 E-mail: bvanbrunt@carlson.com.

VAN BRUNT-BARTHOLOMEW, MARCIA ADELE, retired social worker; b. Chgo., Oct. 21, 1937; d. Dean Frederick and Faye Lila (Greim) Slauson; m. Orris E. Bartholomew; children: Suzanne, Christine, David. Student, Moline Pub. Hosp. Sch. Nursing, Ill., 1955—57; BA with disting. scholastic record, U. Wis., Madison, 1972, MSW, 1973. Social worker divsn. cmty. svcs. Wis. Dept. Health Social Svcs., Rheinlander, 1973, regional adoption coord., 1973—79, chief adoption and permanent planning no. region, 1979—83, asst. chief direct svcs. and regulation no. region, 1983—84; adminstr., clin. social worker No. Family Svcs., Inc., 1984—2003; ret. Counselor, psychotherapist, pub. spkr., cons. in field of clin. social work. Fed. tng. grantee, U. Wis., Madison, 1973. Home: 5264 Forest Ln Rhinelander WI 54501-7900

VAN CLEAVE, WILLIAM ROBERT, international relations educator; b. Kansas City, Mo., Aug. 27, 1935; s. Earl Jr. and Georgiana (Offutt) Van C.; children: William Robert II, Cynthia Kay. BA in Polit. Sci. summa cum laude, Calif. State U., Long Beach, 1962; MA in Govt. and Internat. Rels., Claremont Grad. Sch., Calif., 1964, PhD, 1966. Political scientist Stanford U., 1964-67; mem. faculty U. So. Calif., 1967-87, prof. internat. rels., 1974-87; prof. and dept. head Southwest Mo. State U., 1987—2005, prof. emeritus, 2005—. Sr. rsch. fellow Hoover Instn. Stanford U., 1961-1987; chmn. Strategic Alternatives Team, 1977-90; acting chmn. Pres.'s Gen. Adv. Com. on Arms Control, 1981-82; spl. asst. Office Sec. Def., mem. Strategic Arms Limitation Talks (SALT) delegation, 1969-71; dir. Def. and Strategic Studies Ctr. U. So. Calif., 1971-1987, Ctr. for Def. and Strategic Studies Southwestern Mo. State U., 1987-2005; mem. B team on Nat. Intelligence Estimates, 1976; mem. exec. panel, bd. dir. Com. Present Danger, 1980-93; dir. transition team Dept. Def., 1980-81; sr. nat. security advisor to Ronald Reagan, 1979-80; mem. nat. security affairs adv. council Republican Nat. Com., 1979-89; research council Fgn. Policy Research Inst., Inst. Fgn. Policy Analysis; co-dir. Ann. Internat. Security Summer Seminar, Fed. Republic Germany, 1981-98; trustee Am. com. Internat. Inst. Strategic Studies, 1980—; vis. prof. U.S. Army Advanced Russian Inst., Garmisch, Fed. Republic Germany, 1978-79; chmn. adv. bd. Internat. Security Coun., 1991-96; cons. in field, mem. numerous govt. adv. coms. Co-author: Strategic Options for the Early Eighties: What Can Be Done?, 1979, Tactical Nuclear Weapons, 1978, uclear Weapons, Policies, and the Test Ban Issue, 1987, Strategy and International Politics, 2000; author: Fortress USSR, 1986; mem. bd. editors Global Affairs. Co-chmn. Scholars for Reagan, 1984; mem. exec. coun., dir. NCAA rels. Haka Bowl, NCAA Postseason Football Bowl. With USMC, 1953-61. Recipient Freedom Found. award, 1976, Outstanding Contbn. award Air War Coll., 1979, award teaching excellence U. So. Calif., 1980, 86; named Outstanding Prof. U. So. Calif., 1977, Disting. Alumnus Claremont Colls., 1978; Woodrow Wilson fellow, 1962, NDEA fellow, 1963-65. Mem. Internat. Inst. Strategic Studies (U.S. com., bd. trustees). Home: 8226 E Panther Hollow Ln Rogersville MO 65742-8386 Office: Dept Def and Strategic Studies Southwest Mo State U Springfield MO 65804-0095

VAN DELLEN, H. TODD, state legislator; b. Apr. 24, 1964; m. Dana Lynn; three children. BBA, U. N.D.; JD, U. Minn. Minn. State rep. Dist. 34B, 1993—; corp. counsel EBP Health Plans, Inc. Named Best First Term Mem., State House of Reps., Politics in Minn. newsletter. Home: 14615 43rd Ave N Plymouth MN 55446-2786

VAN DEMARK, RUTH ELAINE, lawyer; b. Santa Fe, May 16, 1944; d. Robert Eugene and Bertha Marie (Thompson) Van D.; m. Leland Wilkinson, June 23, 1967; children: Anne Marie, Caroline Cook. AB, Vassar Coll., 1966; MTS, Harvard U., 1969; JD with honors, U. Conn., 1976; MDiv, Luth. Sch. Theology, Chgo., 1999. Bar: Conn. 1976, Ill. 1977, U.S. Dist. Ct. Conn. 1976, U.S. Dist. Ct. (no. dist.) Ill., U.S. Ct. Appeals (7th cir.) 1984, U.S. Supreme Ct. 1983; ordained to ministry, Luth Ch., 1999. Instr. legal rsch. and writing Loyola U. Sch. Law, Chgo., 1976-79; assoc. Wildman, Harrold, Allen & Dixon, Chgo., 1977-84, ptnr., 1985-94; prin. Law Offices of Ruth E. Van Demark, Chgo., 1995—2003; pastor Wicker Park Luth. Ch., Chgo., 1999—. Mem. rules com. Ill. Supreme Ct., 1999-2002, chair appellate rules subcom., 1996-2002; mem. dist. ct. fund adv. com. U.S. Dist. Ct. (no. dist.) Ill., 1997—. Assoc. editor Conn. Law Rev., 1975-76. Bd. dirs. Lutheran Soc. Svcs. Ill., 1998—, sec., 2000—02, chmn., 2002-; mem. adv. bd. Horizon Hospice, Chgo., 1978—, YWCA Battered Women's Shelter, Evanston, Ill., 1982-86; del.-at-large White House Conf. on Families, L.A., 1980; mem. alumni coun. Harvard Divinity Sch., 1988-91; vol. atty. Pro Bono Advs. Chgo., 1982-92, bd. dirs., 1993-99, chair devel. com., 1993; bd. dirs. Friends of Pro Bono Advs. Orgn., 1987-89, New Voice Prodns., 1984-86, Byrne Piven Theater Workshop, 1987-90, Luth. Social Svcs. Ill. (sec., 2000—), 1998—; founder, bd. dirs. Friends of Battered Women and Their Children, 1986-87; chair 175th Reunion Fund Harvard U. Div. Sch., 1992; dean Ctrl. Conf. Met. Chgo. Synod ELCA. Mem. ABA, Ill. Bar Assn., Conn. Bar Assn., Chgo. Bar Assn., Appellate Lawyers Assn. Ill. (bd. dirs. 1985-87, treas. 1989-90, sec. 1990-91, v.p. 1991-92, pres. 1992-93), Women's Bar Assn. Ill., Jr. League Evanston (chair State Pub. Affairs Com. 1987-88, Vol. of Yr. 1983-84), Chgo. Vassar Club (pres. 1979-81), Cosmopolitan Club (N.Y.C.). Home: 2046 W Pierce Ave Chicago IL 60622-1946 E-mail: revwplc@earthlink.net.

VANDENBERG, THOMAS E., lawyer, transportation services executive; BA in Bus. Adminstrn. and Fin., U. Notre Dame; JD, U. Wis., Madison. Bar: Wis. 1979. Atty. Schneider at., Inc., Green Bay, 1979, assoc. gen. counsel, gen. counsel. Mem.: Wis. Motor Carriers Assn. (dir.), Nat. Lawyers Assn., Transport Lawyers Assn. Office: Schneider Nat Inc PO Box 2545 3101 S Packerland Dr Green Bay WI 54306-2545 Office Phone: 920-592-3895. Office Fax: 920-592-3891. Business E-Mail: vandenbergt@schneider.com.

VANDENBERGHE, JAMES H., manufacturing executive; BBA, Western Mich. U., Kalamazoo; MBA, Wayne State U., Detroit. Fin. analyst Lear Siegler, Inc., 1973, v.p. fin. plastics divsn., v.p. ops. gen. seating divsn.; sr. v.p. fin., CFO, sec. Lear Corp., 1988-93, exec. v.p. fin., CFO, 1993-97, pres., COO N.Am. ops., 1997-98, vice-chmn., CFO Southfield, Mich., 1998—. Bd. dirs. DTE Energy. Bd. trustees Coll. Creative Studies; bd. visitors Wayne State U. Sch. Bus.; bd. dirs. United Way Southeastern Mich. Office: Lear Corp 21557 Telegraph Rd Southfield MI 48034-4248

VANDENBROUCKE, RUSSELL JAMES, theatre director, writer, educator; b. Chgo., Aug. 16, 1948; s. Arthur C. Sr. and Ardelle (Barker) V.; m. Mary Allison Dilg, Sept. 7, 1974; children: Aynsley Louise, Justin Arthur. BA, U. Ill., 1970; MA, U. Warwick, Coventry, Eng., 1975; MFA in Drama, Yale U., 1977, DFA in Drama, 1978. Asst. literary mgr. Yale Repertory Theatre, New Haven, 1977-78; lit. mgr., dramaturg Mark Taper Forum, Los Angeles, 1978-85; assoc. producing dir. Repertory Theatre St. Louis, 1985-87; artistic dir. Northlight Theatre, Evanston, Ill., 1987-98. Vis. prof. Yale U., 1978, La. State U., 1981, U. Calif.-San Diego, 1983, Middlebury Coll., 1985, Washington U., 1986; adj. assoc. prof. Northwestern U., 1987-2001; prof., chair theater arts U. Louisville, 2001—. Author: Truths the Hand Can Tough: The Theatre of Athol Fugard, 1985, The Theatre Quotation Book: A Treasury of Insights and Insults, 2001; editor: Contemporary Australian Plays; play adapted for radio and stage: Los Alamos Revisited, 1984, 1987, play adapted for tv: Eleanor: In Her Own Words, 1985, play adapted from Truman Capote: Holiday Memories, 1991, adapted play: Feiffer's America, An Enemy of the People, 1991, Atomic Bombers, 1997, The Trojan Women, 2004, School Play, 2004; dir.: (plays) Feiffer's America, 1988, Eleanor: In Her Own Words, Lucky Lindy, Love Letters on Blue Paper, 84 Charing Cross Rd, Three Women Talking, Smoke on the Mountain, The White Rose, Betrayal, My Other Heart, Later Life, Hedda Gabler, Bubbe Meises, Valley Song, Fires in the Mirror, The Glass House, Philoctetes, Blood Knot, Atomic Bombers, Humana Festival; dir., dir.: (plays) Proof, Christmas Carol, (play for radio): Three Women Talking; contbr. articles. Recipient L.A. Drama Critics Cir. award, 1984, Spl. Actors Equity Assn. award, 1990; Fulbright sr. scholar, Australia, 1996. Avocation: basketball. Office Phone: 502-852-8444. E-mail: russ.van@aya.yale.edu.

VAN DEN HENDE, FRED J(OSEPH), human resources executive; b. Chgo., Sept. 28, 1953; s. Maurice Everett and Alice Helen (Davey) Van Den H.; m. Sharon Joyce Kucharski, Oct. 4, 1975; children: John Michael, Karen Michelle. BA in Secondary Edn. and Social Sci., DePaul U., Chgo., 1975; grad., U. Wash. Sch. Exec. Dev., Seattle, 1981; MS in Human Resource Mgmt. and Devel., Nat. Louis U., Evanston, Ill., 1998. Cert. sr. profl. human resources. Asst. v.p. human resources Land of Lincoln Savs. and Loan, Berwyn, Ill., 1977-84; v.p. human resources Uptown Fed. Bank FSB, Niles, Ill., 1984-88; dir. human resources Archdiocese of Chgo., 1988—. Mem. Savs. Assn. Pers. Adminstrn., Berwyn, 1977-84; part-time instr. Inst. Fin. Edn., Chgo., 1984-90, Moraine Valley C.C., Palos Hills, Ill., 1984-90; adj. prof. Coll. Mgmt. and Bus., nat. Louis U., 1998-, Coll. Commerce, Dept. Mgmt., Kellstadt Graduate Sch. Bus., De Paul U., 2006-, Sch. of Leadership, Duquesne U., Pitts., Pa., 2007-; cons. in field 1990-Sch. bd. treas. St. Rene Sch., Chgo., 1981; sch. bd. mem. St. Daniel the Prophet Sch.,

Chgo., 1986-88, 93-95, sch. bd. chmn., 1988-89; boy scout leader St. Daniel Parish, Chgo., 1987-94; coach, track, St. Rene Sch., 1979-81, Vittum Park boys' baseball, 1989-92, boys' basketball, St. Daniel the Prophet Sch., 1991-95, basketball coord., 1995-96; meet official Conf. USA Indor Track and Field Championships, 2000, Conf. USA Cross-Country Championship, 2004. Recipient Oustanding Achievement in the Field of Athletics award St. Rita H.S. Alumni Assn., Chgo., 1991; Athletic scholar DePaul U., Chgo., 1971-75. Mem. Nat. Assn. Ch. Pers. Adminstrs., Soc. for Human Resource Mgmt. (mem. sch.-to-work com. 1998-2000), Ill. State C. of C. (human resources com. 1979-2003, healthcare com. 1998-2003), Inst. Internat. Human Resources, Am. Mgmt. Assn. (Chicago Area Tng. Coun. 2001—), Soc. for Human Resource Profls. (edn. adv. com. 2002—), KC (4th degree). Roman Catholic. Avocations: camping, fishing, coaching youth sports teams, horseback riding. Home: 5130 S Mulligan Ave Chicago IL 60638-1316 Office: Archdiocese of Chgo 155 E Superior St Chicago IL 60611-2911 Office Phone: 312-751-5352. Business E-Mail: fvandenhende@archchicago.org.

VANDER AARDE, STANLEY BERNARD, retired otolaryngologist; b. Orange City, Iowa, Sept. 26, 1931; s. Bernard John and Christina (Luchtenberg) Vander A.; m. Agnes Darlene De Beer, June 19, 1956; children: Paul, David, Debra, Mary. BA, Hope Coll., 1953; MD, Northwestern U., 1957. Diplomate Am. Bd. Otolaryngology. Intern Cook County Hosp., Chgo., 1957-59; resident in otolaryngology Northwestern U. Hosp., Chgo., 1966-70; mem. staff Mary Lott Lyles Hosp., Madanapalle, India, 1961-66, 71-87, Affiliated Med. Clinic, Willmar, Minn., 1987-95; ret., 1995. Served to capt., USAF, 1959-60. Fellow ACS, Am. Bd. Otolaryngology, Am. Acad. Otolaryngology. Republican. Mem. Reformed Church in America. Home: 708 2nd St SE Apt 112 Orange City IA 51041-2165

VANDERBEKE, PATRICIA K., architect; b. Detroit, Apr. 3, 1963; d. B. H. and Dolores I. VanderBeke. BS in Architecture, U. Mich., 1985, MArch, 1987. Registered arch., Ill. Archtl. intern Hobbs & Black, Assocs., Ann Arbor, Mich., 1984-86, Fry Assocs., Ann Arbor, 1988; arch. Decker & Kemp Architecture/Urban Design, Chgo., 1989-92; prin., founder P. K. VanderBeke, Arch., Chgo., 1992—. Mem. adv. com. dept. arch., Triton Coll. Contbr. photographs and articles to Inland Arch. mag.; contbr. photographs to AIA calendar. Chair recycling com. Lake Point Tower Condo. Assn., Chgo., 1990-05, chair. ops. com., 1993; mem. benefit com. The Renaissance Soc., U. Chgo., Redmoon Theater, Chgo. George S. Booth travelling fellow, 1992. Mem. AIA (participant 1st ann. leadership inst. 1997, 1st place nat. photog. contest award 1992, hon. mention 1994, Chgo. chpt. membership com., bd. dirs. 2006—), Chgo. Archl. Club, hon. mention 2000 Burnham Prize Competition, The Cliff Dwellers (mem. arts com.). Office: 155 W Burton Pl Apt 16 Chicago IL 60610-1326

VANDER LAAN, MARK ALAN, lawyer; b. Akron, Ohio, Sept. 14, 1948; s. Robert H. and Isabel R. (Bishop) Vander L.; m. Barbara Ann Ryzenga, Aug. 25, 1970; children: Aaron, Matthew. AB, Hope Coll., Holland, Mich., 1970; JD, U. Mich., Ann Arbor, 1972. Bar: Ohio 1973, U.S. Dist. Ct. (so. dist.) Ohio 1973, U.S. Ct. Appeals (6th cir.) 1978, U.S. Supreme Ct. 1981. Assoc. Dinsmore, Shohl, Coates & Deupree, Cin., 1972-79; ptnr. Dinsmore & Shohl, Cin., 1979—. Chair litig. dept., 2001—, spl. counsel Ohio Atty. Gen.'s Office, 1983-2006; spl. prosecutor State of Ohio, 1985-94; city solicitor City of Blue Ash, Ohio, 1987—, City of Silverton, Ohio, 1999-2005; trustee Cin. So. Railway, 1994—, pres., 1999—. Mem. Cin. Human Rels. Commn., 1980-86; mem. Leadership Cin. Class XIII, 1989-90; trustee Legal Aid Soc. of Cin., 1981-94, pres., 1988-90; trustee Volunteer Lawyers for the Poor Found., 2003—, pres., 2003-06. Mem. ABA, Ohio Bar Assn., Cin. Bar Assn. (ethics com. 1983—), Sixth Cir. Jud. Conf. (life), Potter Stewart Am. Inn of Ct. (master), Queen City Club. Office: Dinsmore & Shohl 1900 Chemed Ct 255 E 5th St Cincinnati OH 45202-4700 Home Phone: 513-861-8818; Office Phone: 513-977-8000. Business E-Mail: mark.vanderlaan@dinslaw.com.

VAN DER MARCK, JAN, art historian; b. Roermond, The Netherlands, Aug. 19, 1929; arrived in U.S., 1957; s. Everard and Anny (Finken) van der Marck; m. Ingeborg Lachmann, Apr. 27, 1961 (dec. 1988); m. Sheila Stamell, May 24, 1990. BA, U. Nijmegen, The Netherlands, 1952, MA, 1954, PhD in Art History, 1956; postgrad., U. Utrecht, The Netherlands, 1956-57, Columbia U., NYC, 1957-59. Curator Gemeentemuseum, Arnhem, Netherlands, 1959-61; asst. dir. fine arts Seattle World's Fair, 1961-62; curator Walker Art Ctr., Mpls., 1963-67; dir. Mus. Contemporary Art, Chgo., 1967-70; assoc. prof. art history U. Wash., Seattle, 1972-74; dir. Dartmouth Coll. Mus. and Galleries, 1974-80, Ctr. for Fine Arts, Miami, 1980-85; curator 20th century art, chief curator Detroit Inst. Arts, 1986-95. Author: (book) Romantische Boekillustratie in Belgie, 1956, Enrico Baj, 1969, Lucio Fontana, 1974, George Segal, 1975, Arman, 1984, Bernar Venet, 1988, The Art of Contemporary Bookbinding, 1997, Art and the American Experience, 1998, Lucio Pozzi, 2001, Jef Bourgeau: A User's Manual, 2007; contbr. articles to art jours., essays to catalogues. Decorated officer Order Arts and Letters, knight Order of Orange Nassau; fellow Netherlands Orgn. Pure Rsch., 1954—55, Rockefeller Found., 1957—59, Aspen Inst., 1974, 1994, Ctr. Advanced Study in Visual Arts, Nat. Gallery, Washington, 1986. Fellow: Pierpont Morgan Libr.; mem.: Les Amis de la Reliure Originale, Internat. Art Critics Assn.

VANDER MOLEN, THOMAS DALE, lawyer; b. Ann Arbor, Mich., Oct. 30, 1950; s. John and Eleanor Ruth (Driesens) Vander M.; m. Judith P. Wrahlstad, June 16, 2001; children from previous marriage: Laura, David, Eric. BA, Calvin Coll., 1972; JD magna cum laude, Harvard U., 1975. Bar: Minn. 1976, U.S. Dist. Ct. Minn. 1981, U.S. Claims Ct. 1983, U.S. Tax Ct. 1977, U.S. Ct. Appeals Fed. Cir., 1988. Law clk. to judge U.S. Ct. Appeals-First Cir., Boston, 1975-76; assoc. Dorsey & Whitney, Mpls., 1976-81; ptnr. Dorsey & Whitney LLP, Mpls., 1982—, gen. counsel, 1993—2001. Mem. editorial bd. Harvard Law Rev., 1973-75. Presbyterian. Office: Dorsey & Whitney LLP 50 South 6th St Minneapolis MN 55402-1498 Office Phone: 612-340-2934. Business E-Mail: vander.molen.tom@dorsey.com.

VAN DER VOO, ROB, geophysicist; b. Zeist, The Netherlands, Aug. 4, 1940; arrived in U.S., 1970; s. Maximiliaan and Johanna Hendrika (Baggerman) Van der V.; m. Tatiana M. C. Graafland, Mar. 26, 1966; children: Serge Nicolas, Bjorn Alexander. BS, U. Utrecht, Netherlands, 1961, MS, 1965, PhD, 1969. Rsch. asst. U. Utrecht, 1964-65, rsch. assoc., 1965-69, sr. rsch. assoc., 1969-70; vis. asst. prof. U. Mich., Ann Arbor, 1970-72, asst. prof., 1972-75, assoc. prof., 1975-79, prof. geophysics, 1979—, chmn., 1981-88, 91-95, Arthur F. Thurnau prof., 1994-97, dir. honors program Coll. Lit., Sci. and the Arts, 1998—2003. Guest prof. ETH, Zurich, Switzerland, 1978, Kuwait U., 1979, Utrecht U. and Delft U. Tech., 1997-98. Author: Paleomagnetism of the Atlantic, Tethys and Iapetus Oceans, 1993; contbr. articles to profl. jours. Recipient Russell award, U. Mich., 1976, Disting. Faculty Achievement award, 1990, Benjamin Franklin medal in Earth Scis., 2001. Mem. Geol. Soc. Am. (pres. 2004), Am. Geophys. Union, Geologische Vereinigung (Germany), Royal Acad. Scis. (Netherlands), Royal Norwegian Soc. Scis. and Letters, Sigma Xi, Phi Kappa Phi. Home: 2305 Devonshire Rd Ann Arbor MI 48104-2703 Office: U Mich 4534 CC Little Bldg Ann Arbor MI 48109-1005 Office Phone: 734-764-8322. Business E-Mail: voo@umich.edu.

VANDER WILT, CARL EUGENE, banker; b. Ottumwa, Iowa, Aug. 17, 1942; s. John Adrian and Wilma (Hulsbos) V W.; m. Carol Anne Szymanski, Jan. 29, 1977; children— Dirk Francis, Neal Adrian BS, Iowa State U., 1964, PhD, 1968; grad. Advanced Mgmt. Program, Harvard U., 1986. Research economist Fed. Res. Bank, Chgo., 1970-73, asst. v.p., 1973-74, v.p., 1974-79, sr. v.p., 1979-84, sr. v.p., CFO, 1984—2003. Adj. prof. fin. Northwestern U. Kellogg Sch. Mgmt., Ill., 2004—. Bd. dirs. Goodwill Industries of Southeastern Wis., Chgo. Bd. Roosevelt U. Capt. U.S. Army, 1968-70. Mem. Execs. Club Chgo. (dir., treas.), Banker's Club Chgo., Econ. Club Chgo. Home: 656 Locust St Winnetka IL 60093-2012

VANDERWIST, KATHRYN K., lawyer; Litig. atty. Nestle USA, 1998—99; corp. counsel Agilysys, Inc., Mayfield Heights, Ohio, 1999—2000, gen. counsel, asst. sec., 2000—01, v.p., gen. counsel, asst. sec., 2001—. Office: Agilysys, Inc 6065 Parkland Blvd Mayfield Heights OH 44124 Office Phone: 440-720-8500.

VANDEUSEN, BRUCE DUDLEY, school system administrator; b. Lorain, Ohio, Aug. 20, 1931; s. Clarence Elmer and Margaret (Richards) VanD.; m. Ann Marie Groves, Aug. 17, 1957; children: David Bruce, Elizabeth Ann. Janet Marie. BA, Ohio Wesleyan U., 1952; MS, U. Mich., 1958, PhD, 1971; MAE., Chrysler Inst. Engring., Highland Park, Mich., 1958. Registered profl. engr., Mich. Fellow Ohio State U., Columbus, 1953-54; student engr. Chrysler Corp., Highland Park, 1956-58, sr. research scientist, 1958-67; chief engr. Chrysler Def., Inc., Center Line, Mich., 1967-79, mgr. advanced devel., 1979-82; dir. advanced devel. Gen. Dynamics, Warren, Mich., 1982-87, program dir., 1987-93; pres. Edn. Svcs., Birmingham, Mich., 1994—. Contbr. numerous articles to profl. publs.; patentee electronic cirs. Trustee Birmingham Bd. Edn., Mich., 1976-88, pres., 1979-84, 87-88; trustee Birmingham Community House, 1981-87. Mem. Soc. Automotive Engrs. (chmn. sci. engring. activity 1967-69, Arch T. Colwell award 1968). Republican. Methodist. Home: 4173 Chatfield Ln Troy MI 48098-4327 Office: Edn Svcs PO Box 170 Birmingham MI 48012-0170 Office Phone: 248-269-6598. Personal E-mail: vandeus@yahoo.com.

VAN DE VYVER, SISTER MARY FRANCILENE, academic administrator; b. Detroit, Sept. 6, 1941; d. Hector Joseph and Irene Cecilia (Zygailo) V. BA, Madonna Coll., 1965; MEd, Wayne State U., 1970, PhD, 1977. Joined Sisters of St. Felix of Cantalice, Roman Cath. Ch., 1959. Tchr. Ladywood High Sch., 1967-71, Gabriel Richard H.S., 1971-74; adminstrv. asst. to pres. Madonna Coll., Livonia, Mich., 1974-75, acad. dean, 1975-76; now pres. Madonna U., Livonia, Mich. Office: Madonna U Office of President 36600 Schoolcraft Rd Livonia MI 48150-1176

VANDEWALLE, GERALD WAYNE, chief justice; b. Noonan, ND, Aug. 15, 1933; s. Jules C. and Blanche Marie (Gits) VandeW. BSc, U. N.D., 1955, JD, 1958. Bar: N.D., U.S. Dist. Ct. N.D. 1959. Spl. asst. atty. gen. State of ND, Bismarck, 1958-75, 1st asst. atty. gen., 1975-78; justice ND Supreme Ct., 1978-92, chief justice, 1993—. Mem. faculty Bismarck Jr. Coll., 1972-76; mem. Nat. Ctr. for State Cts. Rsch. adv. coun.; mem. fed.-state jurisdiction com. Jud. Conf. of the U.S. Editor-in-chief N.D. Law Rev, 1957-58. Active Bismarck Meals on Wheels Recipient Sioux award U. N.D., 1992, Ednl. Law award N.D. Coun. Sch. Attys., 1987, Love Without Fear award Abused Adult Resource Ctr., 1995, N. Dakota State Bar Assoc. Dist. Service award, 1998. Mem. ABA (co-chmn. bar admissions com. 1991-99, mem. coun. sect. legal edn. and admissions, chmn. coun. sect. legal edn. and admissions), State Bar Assn. N.D., Burleigh County Bar Assn., Conf. of Chief Justices (past pres., bd. dirs. 1996-98, chmn. fed.-state tribal rels. com.), Am. Contract Bridge League, Order of Coif, N.D. Jud. Conf. (exec. com.), Elks, KC, Phi Eta Sigma, Beta Alpha Psi (Outstanding Alumnus award Zeta chpt. 1995), Beta Gamma Sigma, Phi Alpha Delta. Roman Catholic. Office: ND Supreme Ct State Capitol 600 E Boulevard Ave Bismarck ND 58505-0530 Office Phone: 701-328-2221. Business E-Mail: gvandewalle@ndcourts.gov.

VANDE WOUDE, GEORGE FRANKLIN, molecular biologist, cancer researcher; b. Brooklyn, NY, Dec. 25, 1935; s. George Franklin Sr. and Alice Beatrice (Leudesdorff) V.W.; m. Dorothy Helen Stapel, Apr. 5, 1959; children: Susan Joan, Gail Louise, Cynthia Irene, Alice Helene. Student, Hope Coll., 1953-54; BA, Hofstra U., 1959; MS, Rutgers U., 1962, PhD, 1964. Postdoctoral rsch. assoc. USDA Plum Island, Greenport, N.Y., 1964-65, rsch. scientist, 1965-72; chief virus tumor biochemistry Nat. Cancer Inst. NIH, Bethesda, Md., 1972-81, chief lab. molecular oncology, 1981-83; dir. basic rsch. program Nat. Cancer Inst.-Frederick (Md.) Cancer R & D Ctr., 1983—98; dir., disting. scientific investigator Van Andel Rsch. Inst., Grand Rapids, Mich., 1999—. Contbr. over 100 articles and sci. papers to profl. publs., 35 book chpts. Recipient Robert J. and Claire Pasarow Found. award, 1989. Mem. AAAS, Am. Soc. for Microbiology, Am. Assn. for Cancer Rsch.; fellow Am. Acad. Arts & Sciences Achievements include research in fields of biology and cancer.

VAN DINE, HAROLD FORSTER, JR., architect, artist; b. New Haven, Aug. 28, 1930; s. Harold Forster and Marguerite Anna (Eichstedt) Van D.; m. Maureen Kallick, Mar. 1, 1983; children by previous marriage: Rebecca Van Dine, Stephanie Van Dine Natale, Gretchen Van Dine Natale. BA, Yale Coll., 1952; MArch, Yale Sch. Arch., 1958. Registered architect. Designer Minoru Yamasaki & Assocs., Detroit, 1958-60; chief designer Gunnar Birkerts & Assocs., Detroit, 1960-67; prin. Straub, Van Dine & Assocs., Troy, Mich., 1967-80; chief architecture and design officer Harley Ellis, Southfield, Mich., 1980-95; archtl. cons. Birmingham, Mich., 1995—, San Miguel de Allende, Mexico, 1995—. V.p. Fields, Devereaux, HEPY, L.A., 1984-95. Prin. works include Mcpl. Libr., Troy, Mich., campuses for Oakland CC, Mich., North Hills Ch., Troy, First Ctr. Office Plaza, chemistry bldgs at. U. Mich. and Ind. U., G.M.F. Robotics Hdqrs., Flint Ink Rsch. and Devel. Ctr., Comerica Bank Ops. Ctr., Christ the King Mausoleum, Chgo., Resurrection Mausoleum, Staten Island, Mich. Biotech Inst., Ford Sci. Rsch. Labs, Fetzer Inst. Hdqrs. and Retreat Ctr., Cen. Mich. U. Music Sch., Oakland U. Sci. Techs. Bldg., Corning Credit Union, NY. Bd. dirs. Cultural Coun. Birmingham/Bloomfield, 1990-99. Served to lt. (j.g.) USN, 1952-55 Recipient Book award AIA, 1958, Excellence in Architecture Silver medal AIA, 1958, Gold medal Detroit chpt. AIA, 1987, Mich. Soc. of Architects gold medal, 1991, over 50 major design awards; William Wirt Winchester travelling fellowship Yale U. Sch. Architecture, 1958; elect. to AIA Coll. Fellows, 1979. Mem.: Pewabic Soc. (bd. dirs. 1983—2002). Home Phone: 248-246-5814; Office Phone: 248-246-5814. Personal E-mail: mvandhv@aol.com. E-mail: artwork@harryvandine.com.

VANDIVER, DONNA, public relations executive; BJ, MBA in Mgmt. Pres. Vandiver Group, St. Louis, 1993—. Bd. dirs. Am. Heart Assn.; mem. adv. bd. Pky. Edn. Found. amed Small Bus. Person of the Yr. SBA, 1998; recipient Quest award Nat. Fedn. Press Women, 1999. Mem. Nat. Assn. Women Bus. Owners (Bd. dirs. St. Louis chpt., Disting Women Bus. Owner of the Yr. award 1999), Assn. Corp. Growth, St. Louis Press Club, Downtown St. Louis Partnership, St. Louis Regional Commerce and Growth Assn., Media Club. Office: Vandiver Group 10411 Clayton Rd Saint Louis MO 63131-2928

VANDIVER, THOMAS K., lawyer; b. Leonard, Mo., Mar. 1, 1951; BA cum laude, DePauw U., 1973; JD, Wash. U., 1977. Bar: Mo. 1977, Ill. 1978, DC 1983. Named ptnr. Armstrong, Teasdale, Kramer & Vaughan, St. Louis, 1984; now ptnr. Sonnenschein Nath & Rosenthal LLP, St. Louis. Mem.: ABA, Am. Health Lawyers Assn., Nat. Assn. Bond Attorneys, DC Bar Assn., Ill. Bar Assn., Mo. Bar Assn. Office: Sonnenschein Nath & Rosenthal LLP Ste 3000 One Met Sq Saint Louis MO 63102 Office Phone: 314-259-5829. Office Fax: 314-259-5959. Business E-Mail: tvandiver@sonnenschein.com.

VAN DUYNE, RICHARD PALMER, analytical chemistry educator, chemical physics educator; b. Orange, NJ, Oct. 28, 1945; s. John Palmer and Lorraine Montgomery (Stoller) Van D.; m. Jerilyn Elise Miripol BA, Rensselear Poly. Inst., 1967; PhD, U. N.C., 1971. Asst. prof. analytical chemistry and chem. physics Northwestern U., Evanston, Ill., 1971-76, assoc. prof., 1976-79, prof., 1979-87, Charles E. and Emma H. Morrison prof. chemistry, 1987—. Cons. Beckman Instrument Co., Fullerton, Calif., 1982-90, Eastman Kodak Co., Rochester, N.Y., 1978-91; disting. vis. prof. U. Tex., Austin, 1979; chmn. Vibrational Spectroscopy Gordon Conf., 1982; Camille and Henry Dreyfus lectr. U. Colo., Boulder, 1981; Kilpatrick lectr. Ill. Inst. Tech., 1982; O.K. Rice lectr. U. N.C., 1984; Henry Werner lectr. U. Kans., 1986; Arthur A. Vernon lectr. Northeastern U., 1992. Mem. adv. bd. Jour. Phys. Chemistry, 1983-88; contbr. chpts. to books, articles to profl. jours. Recipient Coblentz award, 1980, Fresenius award, 1981, Excellence in Surface Sci. award, 1996, Pitts. Spectroscopy award, 1991. Fellow AAAS, Am. Phys. Soc. (recipient Earle K. Plyler prize, 2004), Am. Acad. Arts & Sci.; mem. Am. Chem. Soc. Home: 1520 Washington Ave Wilmette IL 60091-2417 Office: Northwestern Univ 2145 Sheridan Rd Evanston IL 60208-0834

VAN DYK, SUZANNE B., lawyer; b. 1950; BS, U. Wis., 1971, JD, 1975. Bar: Wis. 1975, Minn. 1975. Ptnr., banking and comml. law, firm gen. counsel Dorsey & Whitney LLP, Mpls., and mem. mgmt. com., assoc., 1975—82, ptnr., 1983—. Office: Dorsey & Whitney LLP Ste 1500 50 S Sixth St Minneapolis MN 55402-1498 Office Phone: 612-340-5631. Office Fax: 613-340-2868. Business E-Mail: van.dyk.suzanne@dorsey.com.

VAN DYKE, CLIFFORD CRAIG, retired bank executive; b. Ft. Madison, Iowa, June 23, 1929; s. Charles Clifford and Frances Mary (Butterwick) Van D.; m. Edith Ellicott Powers, Aug. 4, 1951 (dec. Oct. 1980); children: Carol Elizabeth, Deborah Ellicott, Jill Anne, Lisa Ellicott. BA, Knox Coll., 1951; MBA, Harvard U., 1955. Asst. v.p. Nat. Bank of Detroit, 1962-65, v.p., 1965-76; pres. Peoples Nat. Bank & Trust Co. of Bay City, Mich., 1976-78, chmn. bd., pres. Mich., 1979-86; chmn. bd., pres., chief exec. officer New Ctr. Bank Corp., Bay City, Mich., 1986; chmn. First of Am. Bank-Bay City, N.A., 1987-89; sr. v.p. First of Am. Bank-Mid Mich. N.A., 1990-94; ret., 1994. Trustee Kantzler Found., Bay City, 1979—; chmn. bd., pres. Bay County Growth Alliance, 1987—. 1st lt. U.S. Army, 1951-53, Korea. Mem. Bay City Country Club, Saginaw Valley Torch Club, Rotary. Independent. Unitarian Universalist. Office: Bay County Growth Alliance PO Box 369 Bay City MI 48707-0369 Home Phone: 989-893-0287; Office Phone: 989-893-5596.

VAN DYKE, DANIEL L., geneticist; b. Paterson, NJ, Mar. 1, 1947; PhD, Ind. U., 1976. Cert. med. genetics and clin. cytogenetics Am. Bd. Med. Genetics. Divsn. head genetics labs. Henry Ford Hosp., Detroit, 1975—; faculty U. Mich. Med. Sch., Detroit, 1978-94, Case Western Res. U., Cleve., 1994—. Mem.: Am. Bd. Med. Genetics (pres. 1998—2000, chair dept. med. genetics 1999—). Office: Mayo Clinic 200 1st St SW Rochester MN 55902 Office Phone: 507-284-6776.

VAN DYKE, THOMAS WESLEY, lawyer; b. Kansas City, Mo., May 12, 1938; s. Harold Thomas and Elizabeth Louise (Barritt) Van D.; m. Sharon Edgar, Jan. 30, 1960; children: Jennifer Van Dyke Winters, Jeffrey. BA, U. Kans., 1960; JD, U. Mich., 1963. Bar: Mo. 1963, Kans. 1983. Atty. SEC, Washington, 1963-64; legal asst. to commr. Hamer E. Budge, Washington, 1964-65; from assoc. to ptnr. Linde Thomson Langworthy Kohn & Van Dyke, P.C., Overland Park, Kans., 1965-91. Co-chmn. ALI-ABA Tax and Bus. Planning Seminar, 1987-96, 2005-08; securities adv. panel Sec. of State of Mo., 1984-89. Mem. ABA (fed. regulation securities com. bus. law sect. 1982-2008, negotiated acquisitions com. 1989-2008), Kans. Bar Assn., Mo. Bar Assn. (corp. banking and bus. law com., chmn. full com. 1983-84, past chmn. securities law subcom.), Carriage Club (bd. dirs. 1986-89). Republican. Avocations: tennis, golf, reading. Office: Bryan Cave LLP 3500 One Kansas City Pl 1200 Main St Kansas City MO 64105 Home Phone: 913-469-8638; Office Phone: 816-374-3201. Business E-Mail: twvandyke@bryancave.com.

VAN DYKE, WILLIAM GRANT, manufacturing executive; b. Mpls., June 30, 1945; s. Russell Lawrence and Carolyn (Grant) Van D.; m. Karin Van Dyke; children: Carolyn Julie, Colin Grant, Alexander Grant, Stephanie Joyce. BA in Econs., U. Minn., 1967, MBA, 1972. V.p., CFO Northland Aluminum Co., Mpls., 1977-78; controller Donaldson Co., Inc., Mpls., 1978-80, v.p. controller, 1980-82, v.p., CFO, 1982-84, v.p., gen. mgr. indsl. group, 1984-94, pres., COO, 1994-96, pres., CEO, 1996—2004, chmn., 1996—, also bd. dirs. Bd. dirs. Graco Inc., Alliant Techsystems. Lt. U.S. Army, 1968-70, Vietnam. Mem. Kappa Sigma Alumni Assn. Avocations: running, bicycling. Office: Donaldson Co Inc 1400 W 94th St Minneapolis MN 55431-2370

VAN ENGELENHOVEN, JIM, state representative; b. Oskaloosa, Iowa, Sept. 8, 1943; m. Carol Van Engelenhoven; 1 child. Grad. H.S. Mem. Iowa Ho. Reps., DesMoines, 1999—, vice chair local govt. com., mem. health and human rights com., mem. appropriations com., mem. state govt. com., mem. transp. com. County supr. Mahaska County, 1992—98. With Iowa Air Nat. Guard, 1964—70. Mem.: Mahaska County Farm Bur., Iowa Soybean Assn., Iowa Corn Growers, Oskaloosa C. of C. Office: State Capitol East 12th and Grand Des Moines IA 50319 Home: 2309 Keokuk Dr Pella IA 50219-7823

VAN ENGEN, THOMAS LEE, state legislator; b. Sioux Center, Iowa, Mar. 28, 1953; s. Leo Herman and Dolores (Nelma) Van E.; m. Rosalyn Faye Vander Plaats, 1979; children: Matthew Thomas, David James, Jeremy Lee. BA, Dordt Coll., Sioux Center, 1979. Chair dist. 15 Minn. Ho. of Reps., St. Paul, 1992-94, mem., 1994—96; life and health ins. agt. Am. United Life Ins. Co. and Blue Cross Blue Shield Minn., St. Paul, 1997-98; devel. cons. Terwisscha Construction, Willmar, 1998—. Del. Rep. dist. and state convs., 1984-94, Minn. Rep. Ctrl. Com., 1989-94; chmn. Pipestone County Com., Minn., 1988-89, Kandiyohi County Com., 1991-93; co-chmn. dist. 15 Minn. Senate, 1990-92, chmn., 1992-94; candidate for Minn. Ho. of Reps., 1992, 2002; chmn. edn. com. Cmty. Christian Sch. Bd., 1990-94; elder Christian Reformed Ch., 1985-88, 96-99, 2001—, handicapped children and adults, 1978-82, chem. dependency counselor, 1982-94. With U.S. Army, 1972-74. Mem. CAP (mission pilot 1996—, moral leadership officer 2000—, squadron comdr. 2000—), Am. Legion, Kiwanis. Republican. E-mail: tve@tds.net.

VAN FLEET, LISA A., lawyer; BSW, Valparaiso U., 1982, JD, 1985. Bar: Ind. 1985, US Tax Ct. 1987, US Claims Ct. 1988, Mo. 1989, Ill. 1990. Ptnr., practice leader Employee Benefits and Exec. Compensation Bryan Cave LLP, St. Louis. Office: Bryan Cave LLP One Metropolitan Square 211 N Broadway, Ste 3600 Saint Louis MO 63102 Office Phone: 314-259-2326. Business E-Mail: lavanfleet@bryancave.com.

VAN FOSSEN, JAMES, state official; b. Rock Island, Ill., May 5, 1960; m. Dawn Van Fossen. AA in Bus. Adminstrn., Scott C.C.; student, St. Ambrose U. State rep., Iowa, 1995—; svc. rep. Iowa-Ill. Gas and Electric Co. Chair ways and means com.; mem. econ. devel. com.; mem. commerce and regulation com. Mem. PTA; with Ctr. for the Aging Svcs., Inc.; mem. Heritage Found., United Way, Chs. United, Quad City Arts. Mem.: Davenport C. of C., Ducks Unltd. Republican. Office: State Capitol E 12th and Grand Des Moines IA 50319

VAN FOSSEN, JIM, state representative; Police capt., Davenport, Iowa; ret.; mem. Iowa Ho. Reps., DesMoines, 2003—, mem. judiciary com., mem. natural resources com., vice chair pub. safety com. Office: State Capitol East 12th and Grand Des Moines IA 50319 Home: 13 Enchanted Island Davenport IA 52802

VAN GELDER, MARC CHRISTIAAN, retail executive; b. Amsterdam, The Netherlands, May 21, 1961; s. Bob Frits and Maria Johanna (Van Teeseling) Van G.; m. Karah L. Henry, July 7, 1990; children: Alexander F., Robert H. M of Econs., Erasmus U., Rottendam, The Netherlands, 1986; MBA, Wharton Sch., U. Pa., 1990. Asst. v.p. Drexel-Burnham Lambert, NYC, 1986-88; sr. mgr. McKinsey & Co., Amsterdam, 1990-96; dir. bus. devel. Ahold, Netherlands, 1996—98; v.p. supply chain mgmt. The Stop & Shop Supermarket Company, 1998—99, sr. v.p., logistics & supply chain mgnt., 1999-2000; pres. & CEO Peapod Inc., Skokie, IL, 2000—. Author: Venture Capital Market, 1985. Mem. Wharton Alumni Club The Netherlands (pres. 1991-98), Netherlands Am. C. of C. (bd. dirs.). Avocations: skiing, horseback riding, arts.

VAN GILDER, JOHN CORLEY, neurosurgeon, educator; b. Huntington, W.Va., Aug. 14, 1935; s. John Ray and Sarah Pool (Corley) Van G.; m. Kerstin Margarita Olesson, Mar., 1965; children: Sarah, John, Rachel, David. BA, W.Va. U., 1957, BS, 1959; MD, U. Pitts., 1961. Diplomate Am. Bd. Neurol. Surgery (examiner 1976, 79, 84). Intern Pa. Hosp., Phila., 1961, asst. resident in surgery, 1964-65, Wilkes-Barre Hosp., Pa., 1962; asst. resident neurosurgery Barnes Hosp., St. Louis, 1966-68, sr. resident, 1968-69; instr. neurosurgery Yale U. Sch. Medicine, New Haven, 1970, asst. prof., 1970-73, assoc. prof., 1973-76; prof. neurosurgery U. Iowa, Iowa City, 1976—, chmn. divsn. neurosurgery, 1976—, exec. com. dept. surgery, 1978-81. Fellow neurosurgery Washington U. Sch. Medicine, St. Louis, 1965 -66, instr., 1966; attending neurosurgeon VA Hosp., New Haven, 1970-73, cons. 1973-76; assoc. to attending neurosurgeon Yale-New Haven Med. Ctr., 1970-76; cons. VA Hosp., Iowa City, 1976—; neurol. surg. cons. Vets. Affairs Hdqrs., Washington; mem. clin. coordinating com. U. Iowa Cancer Ctr., 1979—; vis. prof. U. Tenn., 1984, Tufts U. Med. Ctr., Boston, 1986, U. Tex., San Antonio, 1987, U. Mich., Ann Arbor, 1988, People's Republic China at Hunan Med. Coll., Beijing Neurol. Inst., Tianjin Med. Coll. Hosp., Tiantan Xili, Xian Gen. Hosp., 2d Mil. Coll., Shanghai, Suzhou Med. Coll. Shanghai, 1985, USSR at Burdenk Inst., Kiev Neurol. Inst., Leningrad Neurol. Soc., 1989, Western Res. U., Cleve., 1993, Yale U., 1994, U. Wash., Seattle, 1997, Mayo Clinic, 1998, U. Calif., San Francisco, 1998, Ind. U., 1999; mem. ad. hoc rev. bd. Surg. Neurology, 2001—, Spine, 2000—, Army-Navy, Bethesda-Walter Reed, 2005; presenter in field. Author: (with others): Principles of Surgery, 2d edit., 1973, Brief Textbook of Surgery, 1976, Aneurysmal Subarachnoid Hemorrhage, 1981, Operative Neurosurgical Techniques, Indications, Methods, and Results, 1982, Sports Medicine, 1982, Neurosurgery, 1982, Clinical Neurosurgery, 1982, Operative Neurosurgical Technique, Vol. II, 1982, 88, Vol. III, 1995, Current Therapy in Neurosurgical Surgery, 1985, 2d edit., 1987, Craniovertebral Junction Abnormalities, 1987, Decision Making in Neurological Surgery, 1987, Neurological Surgery, 3d edit., 1988, Anterior Cervical Spine Surgery, 1993, Brain Surgery: Complication Avoidance and Management, 1993, Neurosurgical Emergencies, 1994, Techniques of Spinal Fusion and Instrumation, 1995, Somatic Gene Therapy, 1995, Infections in

Neurological Surgery, 1999; contbr. numerous articles and abstracts to profl. jours.; co-author teaching films; mem. editorial bd. Neurosurgery jour., 1978-84. Capt. USAF, 1962-64. Grantee NIH, 1973-78, Nat. Cancer Inst., 1980-88. Fellow: ACS (membership com. Iowa dist. #1 1983—); mem.: AMA, Am. Bd. Neurol. Surgery (dir. 1992—98, chmn. 1997—98, residency rev. com.-neurol. surgery 1995—2001, neurosurgery chmn. 1999—2001), Am. Acad. Neurol. Surgery (v.p. 1995—), Midwest Surg. Assn., Soc. Neurol. Surgeons (chmn. membership com. 1986—87, treas. 1991—, pres 1997—98, treas. 1991—96, pres. 1997, Disting. Svc. award 2004), Iowa-Midwest Neurosurg. Soc. (pres. 1978—79), Johnson County Med. Soc. (program com. 1984—88, chmn. 1985—86), Iowa Med. Soc., Neurol. Soc. Am. (long range planning com. 1984—, v.p. 1985, pres. 1998—99), Rsch. Soc. Neurol. Surgeons, Am. Assn. Neurol. Surgeons (awards com. 1986—87, bd. dirs. 1986—90, chmn. 1987—88, Disting. Svc. award 2005), Congress Neurol. Surgeons (resident placement com. 1970), Am. Physiol. Soc., Ga. Neurosurg. Soc. (hon.), Sigma Xi. Home: 330 S Summit St Iowa City IA 52240-3220 Office: U Iowa Hosps & Clinics Dept Neurosurgery 200 Hawkins Dr Iowa City IA 52242-1009 Home Phone: 319-338-9805; Office Phone: 319-356-2772. Business E-Mail: johnvangilder@uiowa.edu.

VAN GILDER, RUSSELL, food products executive; Chmn., dir. Spartan Stores, Inc., Grand Rapids, Mich.

VAN GORP, JON D., lawyer; b. Denver, Colo., June 12, 1969; BA, Calvin Coll., 1991; JD cum laude, So. Methodist Univ., 1994. Bar: Tex. 1994, Ill. 1998, NY 2004. Assoc. Thompson & Knight, Dallas, 1994—97; atty. Mayer Brown Rowe & Maw, Chgo., 1997—2003, ptnr., fin. & securitization, 2003—. Spkr. in field on fin. and securitization topics. Editor (staff): The Internat. Lawyer; contbr. articles to profl. jours. Greater Chgo. Leadership fellow, 2005. Office: Mayer Brown Rowe Maw Llp 71 S Wacker Dr Chicago IL 60606-4637 Office Phone: 312-701-7091. Office Fax: 312-706-8362. Business E-Mail: jvangorp@mayerbrownrowe.com.

VAN HAAFTEN, TRENT, lawyer; BA in Politics and Bus., Lake Forest Coll., 1987; JD with honors, Drake Law Sch., 1990. Lic. to practice law, Ind., Iowa. Chief dep. prosecuting atty., Posey County, Ind., 1991-93; prosecuting atty., 1995—. Mem. Posey County Dem. Party; pres., coach Wildcat Cub Football. Mem. Nat. Dist. Attys. Assn., Evansville Bar Assn., Posey County Bar Assn. Office: PO Box 721 Mount Vernon IN 47620-0721

VAN HANDEL, MICHAEL J., employment services executive; BS magna cum laude in Acctg., Marquette U., Milw.; MBA in Fin., U. Wis. Audit mgr. Arthur Andersen & Co.; dir. internal audit Manpower, Inc., Milw., 1989—93, v.p. internat. acctg., 1993—95, chief acctg. officer, treas., 1995—98, sr. v.p., 1998—2002, CFO, 1998—, exec. v.p., 2002—. Bd. dirs., mem. audit and risk oversight coms. Harris Bank. Bd. dirs., chmn. audit com. Milw. Pub. Mus. Named one of Best CFOs in Am., Instl. Investor, 2006. Office: Manpower Inc 5301 N Ironwood Rd Milwaukee WI 53217 Office Phone: 414-906-6305. E-mail: michael.vanhandel@manpower.com.

VAN HAREN, W(ILLIAM) MICHAEL, lawyer; b. Grand Rapids, Mich., Feb. 15, 1948; s. Adrian William and Donna Bell (Burkett) Van H.; m. Kathryn Mary Desmet, Aug. 7, 1971; children: Ryan C., Amy K., Andrew M., Megan E. BS, U. Mich., 1970; JD magna cum laude, U. Detroit, 1975. Bar: Mich. 1975, U.S. Dist. Ct. (we. dist.) Mich. 1975. Assoc. Warner, Norcross & Judd, Grand Rapids, 1975-81, ptnr., 1981—. Adj. prof. taxation Seidman Sch. Bus., Grand Valley State U., Grand Rapids, 1983-85. Assoc. editor U. Detroit Sch. Law Jour. Urban Law, 1974-75; co-editor (handbook) Probate Practice in Decedents Estates, 1985. Co-chmn. profl. divsn. Kent County United Way, Grand Rapids, 1983, 84; pres. Garfield Pk. Nature Ctr., Grand Rapids, 1977, Garfield Pk. Neighborhhod Assn., Grand Rapids, 1979; bd. dirs. Western Mich. Estate Planning Coun., 1986-89, Cath. Social Svcs., 1997-2002, Goodwill Found., 2002—; mem. fin. com. St. Robert's Ch., Ada, Mich., 1997-2002. Fellow Am. Coll. Trust and Estate Coun.; mem. Mich. Bar Assn. (probate and estate planning coun. 1981-93, treas. 1987-88, sec. 1989-90, vice chmn. 1990-91, chair 1992-93, exec. officer 1993—), Mich. Bar Found., Univ. Club. Republican. Roman Catholic. Avocations: squash, golf, hunting. Home: 3790 Bridgehampton Dr Grand Rapids MI 49546 Office: Warner Norcross & Judd 900 Fifth Third Ctr 111 Lyon St NW Ste 900 Grand Rapids MI 49503-2487 Office Phone: 616-752-2125.

VAN HARLINGEN, DALE J., physics professor; B in Physics, Ohio State U., 1972, PhD in Physics, 1977. NATO postdoctoral fellow, Cavendish Lab. U. Cambridge, England, 1977—78; postdoctoral rschr. U. Calif., Berkeley, 1978—81; asst. prof. to prof., dept. physics U. Ill., Urbana-Champaign, 1981—, head, dept. physics, 2007—. Contbr. articles to profl. jours. Recipient IBM Rsch. award, U. Ill., 1981, Xerox Faculty Rsch. award, Coll. Engring., U. Ill., 1995; fellow, John Simon Guggenheim Meml. Found., 2001; Cottrell scholar, Rsch. Corp., 1982. Fellow: Am. Phys. Soc. (Oliver E. Buckley prize in condensed matter physics 1998); mem.: NAS, Am. Acad. Arts and Scis. Office: U Ill The Materials Rsch Lab 104 S Goodwin Ave Urbana IL 61801-2902

VANHARN, GORDON LEE, academic administrator; b. Grand Rapids, Mich., Dec. 30, 1935; s. Henry and Edna (Riemersma) VanH.; m. Mary Kool, June 12, 1958; children: Pamela L., Mark L., Barbara A. BA, Calvin Coll., 1957; MS, U. Ill., 1959, PhD, 1961. Asst. prof. biology Calvin Coll., Grand Rapids, 1961-68, prof., 1970-82, acad. dean, 1982-85, provost, 1985-94, sr. v.p., provost, 1994-96, prof. interdisciplinary studies, 1996-99, prof. emeritus, 1999—; dir. Van Andel Edn. Inst., 2002—. Assoc. prof. biology Oberlin Coll., Ohio, 1968-70; assoc. physiologist Blodgett Meml. Med. Ctr., Grand Rapids, 1970-76; rsch, assoc. U. Va., Charlotteville, 1975-76. Contbr. articles to profl. jours. Mem. sci. adv. com. Gerald R. Ford, 1972-73; mem. rsch. and rev. com. Blodget Hosp., 1978-84; pres. bd. Grand Rapids Christian Sch. Assn., 1982-85; v.p. Christian Schs. Internat., 1987-93; mem Grand Rapids Pub. Sch. Bd., 1996-2002; bd. dirs. Pine Rest Found., 1997—; trustee Van Andel Edn. Inst., 2000—, dir., 2001—; exec com. Grand Rapids Edn. Reform Initiative, 2000—, Grand Rapids Student Advancement Found., 2003-2004; coord. Assn. Reformed Instns. of Higher Edn., 2001-2003. Grass Found. fellow, 1969. Mem. Phi Kappa Phi. Mem. Christian Reformed Ch. Home and Office: 1403 Cornell Dr SE Grand Rapids MI 49506

VAN HELDEN, PETE, food products executive; Sr. v.p. of oper., Jewel-Osco (subs. of Albertson's Inc.), Melrose Park, Ill.; pres., Midwest Div. Albertson's Inc., Melrose Park, Ill., 1999—, pres. & CEO, Calif. Food Div., 2004—. Office: Albertsons Inc 250 Parkcenter Blvd Boise ID 83706 Office Phone: 208-395-6200. Office Fax: 208-395-6349.

VAN HOLLEN, J(OHN) B(YRON), state attorney general, former prosecutor; b. Rice Lake, Wis., Feb. 19, 1966; s. John C. and Rosella Van Hollen; m. Lynne Pliner; children: Byron, Madelyn. BA in Polit. Sci. and Econs., St. Olaf Coll., Northfield, Minn., 1988; JD, U. Wis., Madison, 1990. Bar: Wis. 1990, US Dist. Ct. (we. dist. Wis.) 1990. Asst. state pub. defender, Spooner, Wis., 1990—91; dist. atty. Ashland County, Wis., 1993—99, Bayfield County, Wis., 1999—2002; asst. US atty. (we. dist.) Wis. US Dept. Justice, 1991—93, US atty., 2002—05; atty. Dewitt, Ross & Stevens, S.C., Madison, Wis., 2005—07; atty. gen. State of Wis., Madison, 2007—. Mem.: ABA, Dane County Bar Assn. Republican. Office: Office of Atty Gen State Capitol Ste 114E PO Box 7857 Madison WI 53707-7857

VAN HOOSER, DAVID, retired manufacturing executive; CFO, sr. v.p. Owens-Illinois Inc., Toledo. Office: Owens Ill Inc One Seagate Toledo OH 43666

VAN HOUSEN, THOMAS CORWIN, III, architect; b. Oak Park, Ill., Jan. 2, 1927; s. Thomas Corwin and Dorothea (Saunders) Van H.; children: Deborah, Victoria, Constance. BA, Lawrence U., 1951; BArch, U. Minn., Mpls., 1954; MArch in Urban Design, Harvard U., 1962. Registered architect, Minn., Wis. With Ellerbe Assocs., Inc., St. Paul, 1951-61; architect, prin. Progressive Design Assocs., Inc., St. Paul, 1961-71; architect, developer, v.p. Landmark Devel. Corp./Appletree Enterprises, Inc., Bloomington, Minn., 1971-85; architect, developer Mortenson Devel. Co., Mpls., 1985-88; architect, design, bldg. dir. D&B Collaborative, Inc., Mpls., 1989—99; mktg. cons. Horty, Elving & Assoc., Mpls., 1999—. Bldg. official City of North Oaks, Minn., 1964-78; mem. Minn. League of Municipalities-Metro, St. Paul, 1970-72, Gov.'s Open Space Adv. Com., St. Paul, 1972-74. With U.S. Air Force, 1945-47, ETO. Recipient Outstanding House award St. Paul Jaycees, 1958, 62; named finalist (team mem.) Archtl. competition Boston City Hall, 1962. Fellow AIA (nat. bd. dirs. 1985-88, v.p., pres.-elect Minn. chpt. 1994-95, pres. 1995, spl. award 1981, Presdl. citation 1988, 90, 2000); mem. N.W. YMCA. Republican. Lutheran. Avocations: tennis, swimming, music, reading. Office Phone: 612-332-4422.

VAN HOUWELING, DOUGLAS EDWARD, university administrator, educator; b. Kansas City, Mo., Sept. 20, 1943; s. Cornelius Donald and Roberta Irene (Olson) Van H.; m. Andrea Taylor Parks, Aug. 28, 1965; children: Robert Parks, Benjamin Parks BS, Iowa State U., Ames, 1965; PhD, Ind. U., 1974. Asst. prof. Cornell U., Ithaca, N.Y., 1970-81, dir. acad. computing, 1978-81; vice provost Carnegie-Mellon U., Pitts., 1981-84, adj. assoc. prof., 1981-84; vice provost, dean, prof. U. Mich., Ann Arbor, 1984-88, prof., 1984—, pres., CEO univ. corp. for advanced internet devel., 1998—. Mem. research adv. com. Online Coll. Library Consortium, Dublin, Ohio, 1984-87; trustee EDUCOM, vice chmn. bd. dirs., 1987-91; Princeton, vice chmn., 1987, council chmn., 1986-87; co-founder Interuniv. Corsortium for Ednl. Computing, 1984; chmn. bd. MERIT computer network, 1986-90, Advanced Network and Svcs., 1990—; state of Mich. del. Midwest Tech. Inst., 1986-87. Contbr. chpts. in books, articles to profl. publs. NSF fellow, 1968; Indiana U. fellow, 1969; CAUSE nat. leadership award, 1986. Mem. Simulation Symposiums (pres. 1971; grants chmn. 1972-75), N.Am. Simulation and Gaming Assn. Home: 920 Lincoln Ave Ann Arbor MI 48104-3508 Office: Univ Corp for Advanced Internet Devel 3025 Boardwalk St Ann Arbor MI 48108-3230

VAN INWAGEN, PETER JAN, philosophy educator; b. Rochester, NY, Sept. 21, 1942; s. George Butler and Mildred Gloria (Knudson) van I; m. Margery Bedford Naylor, Mar. 31, 1967 (div. Apr. 1988); 1 child, Elizabeth Core; m. Elisabeth Marie Bolduc, June 3, 1989. BS, Rensselaer Poly. Inst., 1965; PhD, U. Rochester, 1969. Vis. asst. prof. U. Rochester, NY, 1971-72; asst. prof. Syracuse U., NY, 1972-74, assoc. prof. NY, 1974-80, prof. philosophy NY, 1980-95; John Cardinal O'Hara prof. of philosophy U. Notre Dame, South Bend, Ind., 1995—. Vis. prof. U. Ariz., Tucson, 1981; lectr. U. of St. Andrews, 2003, Oxford U., 2000, U. London, 1998. Author: An Essay on Free Will, 1983, Material Beings, 1990, Metaphysics, 1993, God, Knowledge and Mystery, 1995, The Possibility of Resurrection, 1997, Ontology, Identity, and Modality, 2001, The Problem of Evil, 2006; editor: Time and Cause, 1980, Alvin Plantinga, 1985, Metaphysics: The Big Questions, 1998, Christian Faith and The Problem of Evil, 2004, Persons: Human and Divine, 2007; mem. editl. bd. Jour. Faith and Philosophy, Philos. Perspectives, Nous, Philos. Studies, Jour. of Ethics, Philosophy and Phenomenological Rsch.; contbr. articles to profl. jours. Served to capt. U.S. Army, 1969-71 NEH grantee, 1983-84, 89-90. Mem. Am. Acad. Arts and Scis., Am. Philos. Assn., Soc. Christian Philosophers. Democrat. Episcopalian. Home: 52145 Farmington Square Rd Granger IN 46530-6403 Office: U Notre Dame Dept Philosophy South Bend IN 46556-4619 Office Phone: 574-631-5910. E-mail: peter.vaninwagen.1@nd.edu.

VANLEER, JAMES G., state legislator; m. Gwendolyn Vanleer. BA, Wilberforce U.; MA, Ball State U. Benefits mgr. New Venture Gear, Inc.; mem. Ind. State Ho. of Reps. Dist. 34, mem. environ. affairs com., mem. pub. policy, ethics and vet. affairs com., mem. roads and transp. com., vice chmn. aged and aging com. Mem. Jr. Achievement Coun.; former mem. Muncie (Ind.) Housing Bd. Mem. C. of C. (mem. advocacy and local govt. com.).

VAN LUVEN, WILLIAM ROBERT, management consultant; b. Toledo, Feb. 15, 1931; s. Harold Calvin and Ruth Frick (Routson) Van L.; m. Lyda Marie Buchanan Jones, Nov. 15, 1956 (div. Sept. 1960); children: Lynn Chase, Michael Frick; m. Barbara Wilson Ehni, Aug. 17, 1968; children: Eric Finley, Jay Palmer. BBA, U. Toledo, 1957; postgrad., U. Va., 1979. Group gen. mgr. Union Camp Corp., Wayne, N.J., 1961-73, 1979-82; pres.container & carton divs. Clevepak Corp., White Plains, .Y., 1973-79; v.p., gen. mgr. Jefferson Smurfit Corp., Clayton, Mo., 1982-84; pres. Wm. R. Van Luven & Assocs. Inc., St. Louis, 1984—; exec. dir. Exec. Svcs. Corps of St. Louis. Bd. dirs. Smurfit Industries, Alton, Ill., 1982-84, O'Connor Pharm. Corp., Detroit, 1982-84; pres. Mo. Clippers, Inc. (Great Clips for Hair Franchise), 1988—. Cons. United Way of Greater St. Louis, 1987—; chair United Way Mgmt. Assistance Ctr., 1988-90; dir. Combined Health Appeal, Sherwood Forst Camp, Places for People, Inc., Christian Svc. Ctr. With USN, 1951-53. Recipient Keyman award Toledo C. of C., 1956. Mem. Fibre Box Assn., Composite Can & Tube Inst. (pres. 1979), Paperboard Packaging Council, U.S. Brewers Assn., Racquet Club (St. Louis), Univ. Club (St. Louis), Shriner, Sigma Nu. Republican. Episcopalian. Avocations: running, skiing, biking. Home: 2 Portland Ct Saint Louis MO 63108-1291 Office Phone: 314-277-7949. Personal E-mail: wrvl@aol.com.

VANMANY, SENG DAO, microbiologist; b. Vientiane, Laos, Feb. 25, 1977; arrived in US, 1980; BS in Biological Sci., So. Ill. U., Carbondale. Former prof. So. Ill. U. at Carbondale; former microbiologist Lourdes Hosp., Ky.; dir. hematology/oncology tissue bank U. Ill. Sch. of Med., Chicago, 2003—05. Former prof. bio. Paducah Community Coll.; recruiter US Air Force. Served in USAF.

VAN METER, ABRAM DEBOIS, lawyer, retired banker; b. Springfield, Ill., May 16, 1922; s. A.D. and Edith (Graham) Van M.; m. Margaret Schlipf, Dec. 1, 1956; children: Andy, Alice, Ann. BS, Kings Point Coll., 1946; JD, Northwestern U., 1948. Bar: Ill. 1949. Ptnr. Van Meter, Oxtoby & Funk, Springfield, 1949—2001; adminstrv. asst. to treas. State of Ill., Springfield, 1963; v.p. Ill. Nat. Bank, Springfield, 1964-65, pres., 1965-88, chmn. bd. dirs., 1988-90, also bd. dirs.; chmn. bd. dirs. Nat. City, Springfield, 1990-93, dir. emeritus, 1993—. Chmn. bd. dirs. Ill. Housing Devel. Authority, 1977-2003; chmn. bd. trustees So. Ill. U., 1989-2001; past bd. dirs., exec. com. Meml. Med. Ctr. Mem. ABA, Ill. Bar Assn., Sangamon Bar Assn., Chgo. Club, Chgo. Athletic Club, Sangamo Club, Island Bay Yacht Club, Cariton Club. Home: 6 Fair Oaks St Springfield IL 62704-3222 Office: Nat City 1 N Old State Capitol Plz Springfield IL 62701-1323 Personal E-mail: omvideo@aol.com.

VAN REGENMORTER, WILLIAM, state legislator; m. Cheryl; four children. Mich. jud. com., econ. devel. com., energy com.; chmn. House Rep. Caucus, 84-90. Commr. Ottawa County Bd. Commrs., 1980-82; mem. Mich. Ho. of Reps., 1982-90, Mich. Senate from 22nd dist., Lansing, 1990—. Named legis. of yr. 1985 Mich. Sheriff's Assn., Mich. Assn. Police, 1988, Police Officer's Assn. Mich., 1989; recipient Santarelli award Nat. Orgn. for Victim Assistance, 1985, justice award Found. for Improvement of Justice, 1986, leadership award Nat. Sheriff's Assn., 1987. Office: Mich Senate State Capitol PO Box 30036 Lansing MI 48909-7536 Home: 5965 16th Avenue Hudsonville MI 49426

VAN ROY, KARL, state official; b. Dec. 1, 1938; BA in Econs., St. Norbert Coll., 1961. Restaurateur; state assemblyman Wis., 2002—. Republican. Office: State Capitol Rm 8 W PO Box 8953 Madison WI 53708-8953

VAN SANT, JOANNE FRANCES, academic administrator; b. Morehead, Ky., Dec. 29, 1924; d. Lewis L. and Dorothy (Green) Van S. BA, Denison U., Granville, Ohio; MA, The Ohio State U.; postgrad., U. Colo. and The Ohio State U.; LLD (hon.), Albright Coll., 1975. Tchr., health and phys. edn. Mayfield (Ky). H.S., 1946—47; instr. Denison U., Granville, Ohio, 1948; instr. women's phys. edn. Otterbein Coll., Westerville, Ohio, 1948-52, assoc. prof., 1955-62, dept. chmn., 1950-62, chmn. div. profl. studies, 1961-65, dean of women, 1952-60, 62-64, dean of students, 1964-93, v.p. student affairs, 1968-93; v.p., dean student affairs emeritus, 1993—; cons. Instnl. Advancement, 1993—. Co-pres. Directions for Youth, 1983-84, pres., 1984-85; bd. dirs. North Area Mental Health; trustee Friendship Village of Columbus, 1996—, pres. bd., 1998—2004; trustee Westerville Civic Symphony at Otterbein Coll., 1983-88; active numerous other community orgns.; ordained elder Presbyn. Ch., 1967. Named to hon. Order of Ky. Cols., 1957; recipient Focus on Youth award Columbus Dispatch, 1983, Vol. of the Yr. award North Area Mental Health Svcs., 1982, citation Denison U., 1996. Mem. Am. Assn. Counseling and Devel., Ohio Personnel and Guidance Assn., Ohio Assn. Women Deans, Adminstrs., Counselors (treas., exec. bd. 1972-73), Nat. Assn. Student Personnel Adminstrs., Ohio Coll. Personnel Assn., Mortar Bd. (hon.), Zonta Internat. (pres. Columbus, Ohio club 1978-80, dist. gov. 1988-90, internat. svc. chmn. 1996-98, internat. found. bd. 1997-2001), Vocal Arts Resource Network (chair bd. dirs. 1994-96), Cap and Dagger Club, Torch and Key Hon., Order Omega, Alpha Lambda Delta, Theta Alpha Phi, others. Avocations: musical and children's theater production, choreography. Home: 9100 Oakwood Pt Westerville OH 43082-9643 Office: Otterbein Coll Instnl Advancement Westerville OH 43081 Business E-Mail: jvansant@otterbein.edu.

VAN SETERS, JOHN, retired biblical literature educator; b. Hamilton, Ont., Can., May 2, 1935; s. Hugo and Anne (Hubert) Van S.; m. Elizabeth Marie Malmberg, June 11, 1960; children: Peter John, Deborah Elizabeth. BA, U. Toronto, 1958; MA, Yale U., 1959, PhD, 1965; BD, Princeton Theol. Sem., 1962; ThD (hon.), U. Lausanne, Switzerland, 1999. Asst. prof. dept. Near Eastern studies Waterloo Luth. U., 1965-67; assoc. prof. Old Testament Andover Newton Theol. Sch., 1967-70; assoc. prof. dept. Near Eastern studies U. Toronto, 1970-76, prof., 1976-77; James A. Gray prof. Bibl. lit., dept. religion U. N.C., Chapel Hill, 1977-2000, chmn. dept. religious studies, 1980-88, 93-95, prof. emeritus, 2000—. Adj. prof. dept. religion and culture Wilfrid Laurier U., 2000—. Author: The Hyksos: A New Investigation, 1966, Abraham in History and Tradition, 1975, In Search of History, 1983, Der Jahwist als Historiker, 1987, Prologue to History, 1992, The Life of Moses, 1994, The Pentateuch, 1999, A Law Book for the Diaspora, 2003, The Edited Bible, 2006. Recipient James Henry Breasted prize Am. Hist. Assn., 1985, Book award Am. Acad. Religion, 1986, R.B.Y. Scott Book award Can. Soc. Bibl. Studies, 2004; Woodrow Wilson fellow, 1958; J.J. Obermann fellow, 1962-64; Guggenheim fellow, 1979-80; NEH fellow, 1985-86, Am. Coun. Learned Socs. fellow, 1991-92, sr. rsch. fellow Cath. U. Leuven, Belgium, 1998, Fgn. Rsch. fellow Nat. Rsch. Fund S.Africa, 2002. Mem. Soc. Bibl. Lit., Soc. Study Egyptian Antiquities, Cath. Bibl. Assn., Can. Soc. Bibl. Studies (pres. 1999-2000), Old Testament Soc. South Africa (hon.). Home: 70-139 Father David Bauer Dr Waterloo ON Canada N2L 6L1 E-mail: john.vanseters@sympatico.ca.

VANSKA, OSMO, music director; m. Pirkko Vanska. D (hon.), U. Glasgow. Prin. chair Turku Philharm., 1971—76; co-prin. chair Helsinki Philharm., 1977—82; music dir. Lahti Symphony Orch., 1988—96; chief condr. BBC Scottish Symphony Orch. of Glasgow, 1996—2002; music dir. Minn. Orch., 2002—. Guest condr. Boston Symphony Orch., 2002. Condr. numerous recordings with the Lahti Symphony Orch. (Gramophone award, 1996, Cannes Classical award, 2002), (recording) The Tempest (1993 Prix Academie Charles Cros.). Nominee Grammy award for Best Orchestral Performance for a recording with the BBC Scottish Symphony; named Conductor of Yr., Musical Am. Internat. Dir. Performing Arts, 2005; recipient First prize, Besancon Internat. Young Conductor's Competition, Royal Philharm. Soc. award, 2002. Achievements include led Lahti Ensemble on US tour, includign performance at Avery Fisher Hall, NYC. Avocations: sports, motorcycling. Office: Minnesota Orchestra Orchestra Hall 1111 Nicollet mall Minneapolis MN 55403

VAN SLAMBROUCK, JOHN G., lawyer; b. Toledo, Sept. 27, 1955; BA summa cum laude in Polit. Sci., Western Mich. U., 1977; JD cum laude, Thomas M. Cooley Law Sch., 1981. Bar: Mich. 1981, US Dist. Ct. (we. dist. Mich.) 1981, US Dist. Ct. (ea. dist. Mich.) 1983. Legis. aide Mich. Ho. Reps., 1978—79; law clk. State of Mich., 1979—81, asst. atty. gen., 1981—85; pvt. practice atty. The Navigators, Inc., 1985—93; shareholder Ford, Krikard, Domeny & Byrne, P.C., 1994; sr. atty. Miller, Canfield, Paddock & Stone, PLC, Kalamazoo, 1994—97, prin., 1998—, dep. leader personal svcs. grp., 2004—. Bd. dirs. Western Mich. U., 2002—. Named one of Top 100 Attys., Worth mag., 2005. Mem.: West Mich. Estate Planning Coun., Western Mich. Planned Giving Grp., Nat. Acad. Elder Law Attys., State Bar Mich. (mem. probate and estate planning sect. 1991—), ABA (real property, probate and trust law sect.), Kalamazoo County Bar Assn. (chmn. probate practice com., chmn. profl. responsibility com.). Office: Miller Canfield Paddock & Stone PLLC 444 W Michigan Ave Kalamazoo MI 49007-3751 Office Phone: 269-383-5829. Office Fax: 269-382-0244. E-mail: vanslambrouck@millercanfield.com.

VANSTROM, MARILYN JUNE CHRISTENSEN, retired elementary school educator; b. Mpls., June 10, 1924; d. Harry Clifford and Myrtle Agnes (Hagland) Christensen; m. Reginald Earl Vanstrom, Mar. 20, 1948; children: Gary Alan, Kathryn June Vanstrom Marinello. AA, U. Minn., 1943, BS, 1946. Cert. elem. tchr NY, Ill., Minn. Tchr. Pub. Sch., St. Louis Park, Minn., 1946-47, Deephaven, Minn., 1947-50, Chicago Heights, Ill., 1950-52, Steger, Ill., 1964, substitute tchr. Dobbs Ferry, N.Y., 1965-72, Yonkers, N.Y., 1965-92. Mem. Ch. Women, Christ Meml. Luth. Ch. Mem. AAUW (life, pres. So. Westchester br. 1988-90, Ednl. Found. award 1990), Evening Book Club (Met. West br. Minn., So. Westchester br. N.Y.), Yonkers Fedn. Tchrs., U. Minn. Alumni Assn. Democrat. Avocations: painting, sketching, piano, travel. Home: 12300 Marion Ln W Apt 2105 Minnetonka MN 55305-1317

VAN'T HOF, WILLIAM KEITH, lawyer; b. NYC, Feb. 18, 1930; s. William and Nell (DeValois) Van't H.; m. Barbara Marie Rogers, Oct. 6, 1961; children: Sarah Lynn, David Edward. BA, Hope Coll., 1951; LLB, U. Mich., 1954. Bar: Mich. 1954, Conn. 1955, U.S. Dist. Ct. (we. dist.) Mich. 1956, U.S. Ct. Appeals (6th cir.) 1956. Assoc. Gumbart, Corbin, Tyler & Cooper, New Haven, 1954-56; ptnr. McCobb, Heaney & Van't Hof, Grand Rapids, Mich., 1959-72, Schmidt, Howlett, Van't Hof, Smell & Vana, Grand Rapids, 1972-82, Varnum, Riddering, Schmidt & Howlett, Grand Rapids, 1983-99. Mem. faculty Inst. Continuing Legal Edn., Ann Arbor, Mich., 1974-99. Chmn. Mich. Heart Assn., 1973-75; pres. United Way Kent County, 1979-80, hon. life mem., 1986—; chmn. Am. Heart Assn., Dallas, 1989-90. Mem. ABA, State Bar Mich. (grievance and arbitration panel 1970-91, 94-, chmn. com. on coops. and condos. 1982-86), Grand Rapids Bar Assn. (trustee 1965-67), West Mich. Hort. Soc. (pres. 1992-93), Cascade Hills Country Club, Univ. Club. Home: 3508 Windshire Dr SE Grand Rapids MI 49546-3698 Office: Varnum Riddering Schmidt & Howlett 333 Bridge St NW Ste 1700 Grand Rapids MI 49504-5356 E-mail: wkvanthof@varnumlaw.com.

VAN TUYL, CECIL L., automobile dealer executive, real estate developer; Chmn., pres., CEO VT Inc., Merriam, Kans. Office: V T Inc PO Box 795 Shawnee Mission KS 66201-0795

VAN VALEN, LEIGH, biologist, educator; b. Albany, NY, Aug. 12, 1935; s. A. Donald and Eleanor (Williams) Van V.; m. Phebe May Hoff, 1959; children: Katrina, Diana; m. Virginia C. Maiorana, 1974. BA, Miami U., Ohio, 1956; MA, Columbia U., 1957, PhD, 1961. Boese fellow Columbia U., NYC, 1961-62; NATO and NIH fellow Univ. Coll. London, 1962-63; rsch. fellow Am. Mus. Natural History, NYC, 1963-66; asst. prof. anatomy U. Chgo., 1967-71, assoc. prof. evolutionary biology & conceptual founds. sci., 1971-73, assoc. prof. biology & conceptual founds. of sci., 1973-76, prof. biology and conceptual founds. of sci., 1976-88, prof. ecology, evolution, conceptual founds. sci., 1988—; rsch. assoc. dept. geology Field Mus., Chgo., 1971—. Author: Deltatheridia, A New Order of Mammals, 1966, Paleocene Dinosaurs or Cretaceous Ungulates in South America?, 1988, The Origin of the Plesiadapid Primates and the Nature of Purgatorius, 1994; editor: Evolutionary Theory, 1973—, Evolutionary Monographs, 1977—; mem. editl. bd. Jour. Molecular Evolution, 1970-76, Evolución Biológica, 1988—; mem. editl. bd. commentators Behavioral and Brain Scis., 1978—; assoc. editor Evolution, 1969-71. Nat. adv. bd. Voice of Reason, N.Y., 1981—. NIH Rsch. Career Devel. award, 1967-72; NSF grantee, 1963-71. Mem. AAUP (pres. U. Chgo. chpt.), Soc. Study Evolution (v.p. 1973, 80), Am. Soc. aturalists (v.p. 1974-75), Paleontol. Soc. (councillor 1980-82), Internat. Soc. Cryptozoology (bd. dirs.), Ecol. Soc. Am. Office: Univ Chgo Dept Ecology and Evolution 1101 E 57th St Chicago IL 60637-1503

VAN VYVEN, DALE NULSEN, retired state legislator; b. Cin., Apr. 20, 1935; s. Richard J. and Vera Nulsen Bennett (Plue) Va V.; m. Anne Saterfield, 1952; children: Pamela S. Van Vyven Seils, Stacey C. Van Vyven Petitt, Margo B. Van Vyven Johnson, Eric; m. Meredith A. Irwin; 1 child, Stuard D. Student, U. Cin., 1953-66. Packaging engr. Avco Corp., Cin., 1955-66; ins. agt. Dale N. Van Vyven, Sharonville, 1967—2004, cons., 2004—; clk. of coun. Sharonville, Ohio, 1964-65; councilman at large, 1966-75; pres. of coun. Sharonville, Ohio, 1975-78; Ohio state rep. Dist. 32, 1978—2000. Del. Rep. Nat. Conv., 1980; chmn. United Conservatives of Ohio, ALEC; mem. Ohio Retirement Study Commn., 1995—, chmn., 1996. Mem. pub. affairs com. March of Dimes, pro sr. bd. trustees. Named Outstanding Legislator Ohio, 1984, 94, Outstanding Am Lgis. Exch. Coun. leader, 1989; recipient Ohio Guardian of Small Bus. award Nat. Fedn. Ind. Bus., 1992. Mem. Sharonville C. of C., Nat. Fedn. Ind. Bus.,

Kiwanis, Jaycees. Home: 4799 Fields Ertel Rd Sharonville OH 45241-1759 Office: 11006 Reading Rd Cincinnati OH 45241-1980 also: Govtl Policy Group 17 High St Ste 245 Columbus OH 43215 Office Phone: 513-563-2542. E-mail: dvanvyven@earthlink.net.

VAN ZANDT, DAVID E., dean, law educator; b. Princeton, NJ, Feb. 17, 1953; m. Lisa A. Huestis; children: Caroline, Nicholas. AB summa cum laude, Princeton U., 1975; JD, Yale U., 1981; PhD in Sociology, U. London, 1985. Bar: Ill. Lectr. New England Coll., Arundel, England, 1977, U. London, England, 1977—78; clk. to Hon. Pierre N. Leval U.S. Dist. Ct. (so. dist.) N.Y., 1981-82; clk. to Hon. Harry A. Blackmun U.S. Supreme Ct., Washington, 1982-83; atty. Davis, Polk & Wardwell, 1984-85; spl. U.S. legal counsel Artal Grp. S.A., 1985—; asst. prof Northwestern U. Law Sch., Chgo., 1985—88, assoc. prof, 1988—91, prof., 1991—95, dean, 1995—. Mem. planning com. Northwestern U. Corporate Counsel Inst., Northwestern U. Corp. Counsel Ctr. Author: Living in the Children of God, 1991; mng. editor Yale Law Jour., 1980-81; contbr. articles to profl. jours. Recipient Isidore Brown Thesis Prize, Princeton U., 1975. Mem.: Am. Law Dean's Assn. (dir. 1998—), AMR Rsch., Inc. (dir. 1998, audit com. 2000—, compensation com. 2000—), Am. Bar Assn. (dir. 1995—, exec. com. 1998—, treas. 2000—), Phi Beta Kappa. Office: Northwestern U Sch Law Office of Dean 357 E Chicago Ave Chicago IL 60611-3059 Office Phone: 312-503-8460. Office Fax: 801-650-6873. Business E-Mail: d-van2@law.northwestern.edu.

VAN ZANTEN, DAVID THEODORE, humanities educator; b. Aug. 31, 1943; BA, Princeton U., 1965; MA, Harvard U., 1966, PhD, 1970. Asst. prof. McGill U., Montreal, 1970-71; from asst. to assoc. prof. U. Pa., Phila., 1971-79; from assoc. prof. to prof. Northwestern U., Evanston, Ill., 1979—. Office: Northwestern Univ 3-400 Kresge Hall Evanston IL 60208-2208 Office Phone: 847-491-8024. Business E-Mail: d-van@northwestern.edu.

VAN ZELST, THEODORE WILLIAM, civil engineer, engineering company executive; b. Chgo., May 11, 1923; s. Theodore Walter and Wilhelmina (Oomens) Van Z.; m. Louann Hurter, Dec. 29, 1951; children: Anne, Jean, David. BS, U. Calif., Berkeley, 1944; BS in Naval Sci., Northwestern U., 1944, BAS., 1945, MS in Civil Engring., 1948. Registered profl. engr., Ill. Pres., Soil Testing Services, Inc., Chgo., 1948-52; pres. Soiltest, Inc., Chgo., 1948-78, chmn. bd., 1978-80; sec., dir. Exploration Data Cons., Inc., 1980-82; exec. v.p. Cenco Inc., Chgo., 1962-77, vice chmn., 1975-77, also dir., 1962-77. Bd. dirs. Minann, Inc., Testing Sci., Inc., Van Zelst, Inc.; chmn. bd. dirs. Envirotech Svcs., Inc., 1983-85; sec., bd. dirs. Van Zelst, Inc. Wadsworth, Ill., 1983—; pres. Geneva-Pacific Corp., 1969-83, Geneva Resources, Inc., 1983-91. Treas. Internat. Road Fedn., 1961-64, sec., 1964-79, dir., 1973-88, vice chmn., 1980-87; pres. Internat. Road Edn. Found., 1978-80, 87-88, hon. life bd. dirs., 1988—; bd. dirs. Chgo. Acad. Scis., 1983-86, v.p., 1985-86, hon. dir., 1986-2007; bd. dirs. Pres.'s Assn., Chgo., 1985-86, Friends of Mitchell Mus., 2003-2004; Asian art coun. Art Inst. Chgo., 2004—. Lt. j.g. USNR, 1944—46. Recipient Service award orthwestern U., 1970, Merit award, 1974, Alumni medal, 1989, Svc. award U. Wis., 1971, La Sallian award, 1975; named Disting. Engring. Alumnus, U. Calif., Berkeley, 2002. Mem. ASCE (Chgo. Civil Engr. of Yr., 1988), Nat. Soc. Profl. Engrs., Western Soc. Engrs., Evanston C. of C. (v.p. 1969-73), Ovid Esbach Soc. (pres. 1968-80), Northwestern U. Alumni Assn., Tau Beta Pi, Sigma Xi. Clubs: Economic, North Shore. Achievements include invention of engring. testing equipment for soil, rock, concrete and asphalt; co-invention of Swing-wing for supersonic aircraft. Home: 1213 Wagner Rd Glenview IL 60025-3297 Office: PO Box 582 Glenview IL 60025-0582 Home Phone: 847-724-3244. Personal E-mail: tvz@earthlink.net.

VARCHMIN, THOMAS EDWARD, public health service officer; b. Chgo., Dec. 5, 1947; s. Arthur William and Laurie Eileen (Allen) V.; m. Beth Virginia Plank, Dec. 16, 1972; children: Jeffrey Thomas, Brian Arthur, Jennifer Beth, Matthew James. BA, St. Mary's Coll., Winona, Minn., 1969; MS, Western Ill. U., Macomb, 1977. Registered sanitarian Wis., lic. envirin. health practitioner Ill. Virologist, microbiologist Chgo. Dept. Health, 1974-78; environ. health and safety mgr. Great Atlantic & Pacific Tea Co., Chgo., 1978-79; adminstr. occupational safety and environ. health Nat. Safety Council, Chgo., 1979-80; mgr. environ. health Lake County Health Dept., Waukegan, Ill., 1980-84, mgr. environ. health and pub. relations, 1984-87; mgr. environ. health Cook County Dept. Pub. Health, Oak Park, Ill., 1987-89, asst. dir. environ. health, mgr. intergovtl. rels., 1989-98, dir. environ. health, 1998—. Co-chmn. West Nile Virus Com. Cook County, Ill., 2001—03; environ. health cons. Author: Final Report of West Nile Virus Committee for Cook County, 2002—03; editor: Food and Beverage ewsletter, Hospital and Health Care Newsletter, Trades and Services Newsletter, 1979—80; contbr. articles to profl. jours. NSF grantee, 1968-69 Mem.: Am. Soc. Microbiology, Nat. Safety Coun., Ill. Environ. Health Assn., Nat. Environ. Health Assn., Delta Epsilon Sigma, Phi Mu Alpha. Achievements include research on autumn food habits of game fish, behavioral and phys. devel. of barred owl nestlings in Ill. Office: Cook County Dept Pub Health 1010 Lake St Ste 300 Oak Park IL 60301-1133

VARGA, RICHARD STEVEN, retired mathematics professor; b. Cleve., Oct. 9, 1928; s. Steven and Ella (Krejcs) V.; m. Esther Marie Pfister, Sept. 22, 1951; 1 dau., Gretchen Marie. BS, Case Inst. Tech., Cleve., 1950; AM, Harvard U., Cambridge, Mass., 1951, PhD, 1954; doctorate (hon.), U. Karlsruhe, Germany, 1991, U. Lille, France, 1993. With Bettis Atomic Power Lab., Westinghouse Electric Co., 1954-60, adv. mathematician, 1959-60; prof. math. Case Inst. Tech. (now Case We. Res. U.), Cleve., 1960—69; univ. prof. math. Kent State U., Ohio, 1969—2006, dir. rsch. Inst. for Computational Math., 1980—; ret., 2006. Cons. to govt. and industry. Author: Matrix Iterative Analysis, 1962, Functional Analysis and Approximation Theory in Numerical Analysis, 1971, Topics in Polynomial and Rational Interpolation and Approximation, 1982, Zeros of Sections of Power Series, 1983, Scientific Computation on Mathematical Problems and Conjectures, 1990, Matrix Iterative Analysis, 2d revised and expanded edit., 2000, Gersgorin and his Circles, 2004; editor: Numerical Solution of Field Problems in Continuum Physics, 1970, Padé and Rational Approximations: Theory and Applications, 1977, Rational Approximations and Interpolation, 1984, Computational Methods and Function Theory, 1990, Numerical Linear Algebra, 1993; editor-in-chief. Numerische Math., 1988-2002, Electronic Transactions Numerical Analysis; mem. editl. bd. Linear Algebra and Applications, Constructive Approximation, Computational Mathematics (China), Numerical Algorithms, Analysis, Electronic Jour. Linear Algebra, Comms. in Applied Analysis. Recipient Rsch. award Sigma Xi, 1965, von Humboldt prize, 1982, Pres.' medal Kent State U., 1981, Hans Schneider prize, 2005; Guggenheim fellow, 1963; Fairchild scholar, 1974. Home: 7065 Arcadia Dr Cleveland OH 44129-6065 Office: Kent State U Inst Computational Mat Kent OH 44242-0001 Business E-Mail: varga@math.kent.edu.

VARKEY, PRATHIBHA, preventive medicine physician, medical educator; b. NY, Apr. 12, 1974; MD, Christian Med. Coll., Dr. M.G.R. Med. U., Vellore, Tamil Nadu, India, 1995; MPH in Health Care Mgmt., Harvard Sch. Pub. Health, 2001. Resident internal medicine Hosp. St. Raphael, New Haven, 1997—2000; fellow gen. preventive medicine and pub. health Mayo Clinic, Rochester, 2001—03, asst. prof. preventive medicine and internal medicine, dir. assoc. program preventive medicine fellowship. Mem.: AMA Found. (Excellence in Medicine Leadership award 2004). Office: Mayo Clinic 200 First St SW Rochester MN 55905

VARMA, ARVIND, chemical engineering educator, researcher; b. Ferozabad, India, Oct. 13, 1947; s. Hans Raj and Vijay L. (Jhanjhee) V.; m. Karen K. Guse, Aug. 7, 1971; children: Anita, Sophia. BS ChemE, Panjab U., 1966; MS ChemE, U. N.B., Fredericton, Can., 1968; PhD ChemE, U. Minn., 1972. Asst. prof. U. Minn., Mpls., 1972-73; sr. research engr. Union Carbide Corp., Tarrytown, NY, 1973-75; asst. prof. chem. engring. U. Notre Dame, Ind., 1975-77, assoc. prof., 1977-80, prof., 1980-88, Arthur J. Schmitt prof., 1988—2003, chmn. dept., 1983-88; dir. Ctr. for Molecularly Engineered Materials, 2000—03; R. Games Slayter Disting. prof., head Purdue U. Sch. Chem. Engring., 2004—. Vis. prof. U. Wis., Madison, 1981; Chevron vis. prof. Calif. Inst. Tech., Pasadena, 1982; vis. prof. Ind. Inst. Tech.-Kanpur, 1989, U. Cagliari, Italy, 1989, 92; vis. fellow Princeton U., 1996; Piercy vis. prof. U. Minn., 2001; Kane vis. prof. U. Mumbai, 2007. Co-author: Mathematical Methods in Chemical Engineering, 1997, Parametric Sensitivity in Chemical Systems, 1999, Catalyst Design, 2001; editor: (with others) The Mathematical Understanding of Chemical Engineering Systems, 1980, Chemical Reaction and Reactor Engineering, 1987; series editor: Cambridge Series in Chemical Engineering, 1996—; contbr. numerous articles to profl. jours. Recipient Tchr. of Yr. award Coll. Engring. U. Notre Dame, 1991, Spl. Presdl. award 1992, R.H. Wilhelm award AIChE, 1993, Burns Grad. Sch. award 1997, E.W. Thiele award AIChE, 1998, Chem. Engring. Lectureship award, ASEE, 2000, Rsch. Achievement award U. Notre Dame, 2001, Techs. of Yr. award Industry Week, 2005; Fulbright scholar; Indo-Am. fellow, 1988-89. Office: Purdue U Sch Chem Engring West Lafayette IN 47907 Office Phone: 765-494-4075. Business E-Mail: avarma@purdue.edu.

VARNEY, RICHARD ALAN, health facility administrator; b. Concord, NH, July 8, 1950; s. John Berry and Hattie Elizabeth (Harrington) V.; m. Suzanne Glaab, Dec. 31, 1983; stepchildren: Alysen Suzanne Bidle, Craig Judson Bidle. BS in Phys. Edn., U. N.H., 1972; MHA in Healthcare Adminstrn., Baylor U., 1984; diploma, Command and Gen. Staff Coll., 1986. Commd. 2d lt. U.S. Army, 1973, advanced through grades to lt. col., 1991; dep. asst. CEO Cutler Army Hosp., Ft. Devens, Mass., 1973—76; field med. asst. 38th ADA Bde., Osan Air Base, Republic of Korea, 1977—78; dep. asst. CEO 15th Med. Battalion, Ft. Hood, Tex., 1979—81; adminstrv. resident Ireland Army Hosp., Ft. Knox, Ky., 1982—83; COO, exec. officer U.S. Army Dental Activity, Ft. Knox, 1983—86; grad. instr. Army-Baylor Healthcare Program, San Antonio, 1986—90; project mgr. Office of the Army Surgeon Gen., Washington, 1990—93; ret. U.S. Army, 1993; office mgr. Aebi, Ginty, Romaker & Sprouse MD's, Inc., Lancaster, Ohio, 1993—2000; dir. gen. internal medicine program The Ohio State U. Med. Ctr., Columbus, 2000—04; dir. ops. Fairfield Dept. Health, Lancaster, 2005—. Mem. Source Selection Evaluation Bd.-Champus Reform, Arlington, Va., 1987; mem. adv. com. for assoc. degree program in med. assisting Ohio U., Lancaster, 1998-2000. Adult leader Boy Scouts Am., Tex., Va. and Ohio, 1988-97, 2003—; mem. Lancaster City Bd. of Health, 1996-2001, pres. pro tem, 1999-2001; mem. Fairfield County Combined Gen. Health Dist. Bd., 2002-04. Officer US Army Med. Svc. Corps, 1973—93. Decorated Legion of Merit, Order of Mil. Med. Merit award, Expert Field Med. badge; named to Hon. Order Ky. Cols., 1989, Outstanding Young Man of Am., 1982. Fellow Am. Coll. Healthcare Execs.; mem. Ctrl. Ohio Health Adminstrs. Assn., Ohio Med. Group Mgmt. Assn., Mid-Ohio Med. Mgmt. Assn., Profl. Assn. Med. Mgrs., Am. Assn. Procedural Coders, Lancaster Area Soc. for Human Resource Mrmt. (legis. rep. 1998-99, membership chair 1999—), Am. Hosp. Assn., Nat. Eagle Scout Assn., The Ret. Officers Assn., Am. Legion, Fraternal Order of Eagles, Alpha Phi Omega. Avocations: home improvement, music. Home: 1025 E 5th Ave Lancaster OH 43130-3276 Home Phone: 740-681-5665; Office Phone: 740-653-4489 x155. Personal E-mail: richvarneyosu@yahoo.com. Business E-Mail: rvarney@co.fairfield.oh.us.

VARRO, BARBARA JOAN, retired editor; b. East Chicago, Ind., Jan. 25, 1938; d. Alexander R. and Lottie R. (Bess) V. BA, Duquesne U., 1959. Feature reporter, asst. fashion editor Chgo. Sun-Times, 1959-64, fashion editor, 1964-76, feature writer, 1976-84; v.p. pub. rels. Daniel J. Edelman Inc., Chgo., 1984-85; v.p. PRB/Needham Porter Novelli, Chgo., 1985-86; editor Am. Hosp. Assn. News, Chgo., 1987-94; editor spl. sects. Chgo. Tribune, 1995-2000; ret. Recipient awards for feature writing Ill. AP, 1978, 79, 80 Mem.: PEO. Home: 219 Autumn Trail N Michigan City IN 46360

VASQUES, GARY, retail executive, marketing professional; b. 1947; With Gertz Dept. Stores, LI, NY, 1973—75; buyer domestics, blankets and bedspreads Burdines, Miami, Fla., 1975—79, divisional merchandise mgr. home textiles, 1979—83, v.p., gen. merchandise mgr. decorative home, 1983, sr. v.p., gen. merchandise mgr. domestics, home textiles and decorative home accessories, 1984, sr. v.p., gen. merchandise mgr. home store, 1985—88, group sr. v.p., 1989—90; sr. v.p., gen. mdse. mgr. Montgomery Ward, 1990—92; sr. v.p. mktg. Caldor, 1992—95; exec. v.p. mktg. Kohl's, 1995—. Office: Kohls Corp N56 W17000 Ridgewood Dr Menomonee Falls WI 53051-5660

VASSELL, GREGORY S., electric utility consultant; b. Moscow, Dec. 24, 1921; came to U.S., 1951, naturalized, 1957; s. Gregory M. and Eugenia M. Wasiljeff; m. Martha Elizabeth Williams, Apr. 26, 1957; children: Laura Kay, Thomas Gregory. Dipl. Ing. in Elec. Engring, Tech. U. Berlin, 1951; MBA in Corp. Fin., NYU, 1954. With Am. Electric Power Svc. Corp., Columbus, Ohio, 1951-88, v.p. system planning, 1973-76, dir., 1973-88, sr. v.p. system planning, 1976-88; electric utility cons. Upper Arlington, Ohio, 1988—. Bd. dirs. Columbus & Southern Ohio Electric Co., 1981-88, Cardinal Operating Co.; mem. tech. adv. com. transmission FPC, 1968-70, FERC Task Force on Power Pooling, 1980-81 Contbr. articles to profl. jours. Fellow IEEE (life); mem. NAE, Athletic Club Columbus Home and Office: 6000 Riverside Dr Dublin OH 43017

VAUGHAN, BRAD, engineering and design company executive; With Black & Veatch, Overland Park, Kans., 1974—, dir. devel. TransAmerica Generation Grid project, COO, BV Solutions Group, gen. ptnr., mgr. office ops. energy engring. and constrn. divsn., chief info. officer, 2003—. Office: Black & Veatch 11401 Lamar Overland Park KS 66211

VAUGHAN, MICHAEL RICHARD, lawyer; b. Chgo., Aug. 27, 1936; s. Michael Ambrose and Loretta M. (Parks) Vaughan; m. Therese Marie Perri, Aug. 6, 1960; children: Charles Thomas, Susan Enger. Student, U. Ill., 1954-59; LLB, U. Wis., 1962. Bar: Wis. 1962. Chief atty. bill drafting sect. Wis. Legislature, Madison, 1962-68, dir. legis. attys., 1968-72; assoc. Murphy Desmond, and predecessor, Madison, 1972-73, ptnr., 1974—. Mem. Comm. Uniform State Laws, 1966—72; cons. Nat. Commn. Marijuana and Drug Abuse, 1971—73; lectr. CLE seminars. Contbr. articles to profl. jours. Warden, vestryman St. Dunstan's Episcopal Ch., 1973—78, 1980—87; mem. Wis. Episcopal Conf., 1972—76. Mem.: ABA, Dane County Bar Assn., State Bar Wis. (dir. govtl. and adminstrv. law sect. 1971—78, mem. interprofl. and bus. rels. com. 1976—89), The Club at Olde Cypress (Naples, Fla.), Nakoma Golf Club, Madison Club, U. Wis. Law Sch. Bencher Soc., Delta Kappa Epsilon. Office: 2 E Mifflin St Ste 800 Madison WI 53701-2038 Office Phone: 608-257-7181.

VAUGHAN, THERESE MICHELE, insurance educator; b. Blair, Nebr., June 12, 1956; d. Emmett John and Lonne Kay (Smith) V.; m. Robert Allen Carber, Aug. 15, 1993; children: Kevin Leo Vaughan-Carber, Thomas S. Vaughan-Carber. BBA, U. Iowa, 1979; PhD, U. Pa., 1985. CPCU. Asst. prof. Baruch Coll., CUNY, 1986-87; cons. Tillinghast, NYC, 1987-88; dir. ins. ctr. Drake U., Des Moines, 1988-94; ins. commr. State of Iowa, Des Moines, 1994—2004; Robb B. Kelley Disting. prof. ins. and actuarial sci. Drake U., 2005—. Bd. dirs. Endurance Splty. Holdings, Prin. Fin. Group, Nat. Coun Comp. Ins. Co-editor Jour. Ins. Regulation Bd., 2005—; co-author: Fundamentals of Risk and Insurance, 1996, 99, 2003, Essentials of Insurance: A Risk Management Approach, 1995, 2001; contbr. articles to profl. jours. S.S. Huebner fellow U. Pa., 1979-82; recipient Outstanding Young Alumnus award U. Iowa, 1996; named to Iowa Ins. Hall of Fame, 2003. Mem. at. Assn. Ins. Commrs. (pres. 2002), Ins. Marketplace Stds. Assn. (bd. dirs. 2004—), Am. Risk and Ins. Assn. (v.p. 2006—), Beta Gamma Sigma, Omicron Delta Epsilon. Avocations: hiking, biking, reading. Home: 4632 Elm St West Des Moines IA 50265-2993 Office: Drake Univ 2507 University Ave Des Moines IA 50311 Business E-Mail: terri.vaughan@drake.edu.

VAUGHAN, WORTH EDWARD, retired chemistry professor; b. NYC, Feb. 1, 1936; s. Royal Worth and Sylvia Marie (Fernholz) V.; m. Diane Marilyn Mayer, Aug. 9, 1969; 1 child, Wayne John BA, Oberlin Coll., 1957; MA, Princeton U., 1959, PhD, 1960. Asst. prof. chemistry U. Wis.-Madison, 1961-66, assoc. prof., 1967-76, prof., 1977—2002, prof. emeritus, 2002—. Mem. bd. advisors Am. Exchange Bank West Br., Madison, 1983-87. Author: Dielectric Properties and Molecular Behavior, 1969; editor: Digest of Literature on Dielectrics, 1974; translation editor: Dipole Moments of Organic Compounds, 1970; contbr. articles to profl. jours. Mem. Am. Chem. Soc. (pres. Wis. sect. 1968, 1998), Phi Beta Kappa Avocations: canoeing, contract bridge. Home: 501 Ozark Trl Madison WI 53705-2538 Office: Univ Wis 1101 University Ave Madison WI 53706-1322 Office Phone: 608-262-7924. Business E-Mail: vaughan@chem.wisc.edu.

VAUGHN, EDWARD, state legislator; b. Abbeville, Ala., July 30, 1934; s. Ivory Vaughn and Posie (White) V.; m. Wilma Jean Lathion, 1957; children: Eric, Randall, Sybil, Attallah. BA, Fisk U., 1955; postgrad., U. Ill., 1955-56. Owner/founder Vaughn's Book Store, 1961—, Langston Hughes Theatre, 1975—; rep. Dist. 4 Mich. Ho. of Reps., 1995—. Contbr. articles to profl. jours. Recipient Hon. Citizenship award Republic of Uganda, East Africa, 1974, African Hist. Club award, Detroit, 1977, Great Contbrs. award Wayne County C.C., 1977, Spirit of Detroit award Detroit Common Coun., 1978. Mem. Pan-African Congress U.S., ew Directions Inst., Am. Writers league, The New Pioneers.

VAUGHN, JACKIE, III, state legislator; BA, Hillsdale Coll., Mich.; MA, Oberlin Coll., Ohio; LittB, Oxford U.; LLD (hon.), Marygrove Coll., Detroit, Shaw Coll.; HHD (hon.), Highland Park Community Coll., Mich. Tchr. U. Detroit, Wayne State U., Detroit, 1963-64; mem. Mich. Ho. of Reps., Lansing, 1966-78, Mich. Senate, Lansing, 1978—, asst. pres. pro tem, 1978-82, pres. pro tem, 1982-86, assoc. pres. pro tem, 1986—. Past pres. Mich. Young Dems.; chmn. Mich. Dr. Martin Luther King Jr. Holiday commn.; exec. bd. dirs. Detroit NAACP. With USN. Fulbright fellow; recipient Frank J. Wieting Meml. Service award, 1977, Focus and Impact award Cotillion Club, 1980, Outstanding Achievement award Booker T. Washington Bus. Assn., Outstanding Community Service award Charles Stewart Mott Community Coll. and Urban Coalition of Greater Flint, Mich., 1981; named Outstanding State Senator of Yr., Detroit Urban League Guild, 1983, Most Outstanding Legislator of Yr., Washburn-Ilene Block Club, 1983, numerous others. Mem. Am. Oxonian Assn., Fulbright Alumni Assn. Baptist. Home: 19930 Roslyn Rd Detroit MI 48221-1853 Office: Mich Senate State Capitol PO Box 30036 Lansing MI 48909-7536

VAUGHN, JEFFREY JAMES, broadcasting host, director; b. Topeka, Nov. 3, 1965; s. Leonard James and Sharon Areta (Williams) V. BS in Polit. Sci., Kans. State U., 1989. With news and sports dept. Sta. KNSS, Wichita, 1989-92, host, program dir., 1992—. Recipient Best Pub. Affairs Program award Kans. Assn. Broadcasting, 1994, 95. Office: Sfx Broadcasting 9323 E 37th St N Wichita KS 67226-2000

VAYO, DAVID JOSEPH, composer, music educator; b. New Haven, Mar. 28, 1957; s. Harold Edward and Joan Virginia (Cassidy) V.; m. Marie-Susanne Langille, 2002; children; Rebecca Lynn, Gordon Francis. MusB, Ind. U., 1980, MusM, 1982; D of Musical Arts, U. Mich., 1990. Prof. Nat. U., Heredia, Costa Rica, 1982-84, at. Symphony Youth Sch., San Jose, Costa Rica, 1982-84; asst. prof. music Conn. Coll., New London, 1988-91, Ill. Wesleyan U. Sch. Music, Bloomington, 1991-95, assoc. prof., 1995-2000, prof., 2000—. Resident artist Banff Ctr. for Arts, 1992, 94, Va. Ctr. for Creative Arts, 1994, Centrum, Port Townsend, Wash., 1996; participating composer Internat. Soc. Contemporary Music-World Music Days, Hong Kong, 2007, Yokohama, 2001, Mexico City, 1993, Internat. Double Reed Festival, Rotterdam, The Netherlands, 1995, Grand Teton Music Festival, 2006. Composer chamber composition Signals, 1997 (commd. by Koussevitzky Music Found. and Orkest de Volharding), Symphony: Blossoms and Awakenings, 1990 (performer St. Louis Symphony, Leonard Slatkin condr. 1993), Mosaics and Webs, 2003 (commd. by Nat. Assn. Coll. Wind and Percussion Instrs.), Eight Poems of William Carlos Williams for solo trombonist, 1994 (commd. by St. Louis Symphony), piano trio Awakening of the Heart (commd. Barlow Endowment for Music Composition), 1998; works pub. by Internat. Trombone Assn. Press, Berben/Italia Guitar Soc. Series and A.M. Percussion Publs. John Simon Guggenheim Meml. Found. fellow, 2001; Ill. Arts Coun. fellow, 2000. Mem. ASCAP (awards 1988—), Am. Music Ctr. (copying assistance grantee 1992), Coll. Music Soc. (presenter nat. confs.), Soc. for Electro-Acoustic Music in U.S. (presenter nat. conf.), Soc. Composers (membership chmn. 1990-2000, presenter at nat. confs.), Am. Composers Forum. Avocations: athletics, popular music, travel, reading, cooking. Office: Ill Wesleyan U Sch Music PO Box 2900 Bloomington IL 61702-2900 Home Phone: 309-828-3192; Office Phone: 309-556-3068. E-mail: dvayo@iwu.edu.

VEALE, TINKHAM, II, retired chemicals executive, engineer; b. Topeka, Dec. 26, 1914; s. George W. and Grace Elizabeth (Walworth) V.; m. Harriett Alice Ernst, Sept. 6, 1941; children: Harriett Elizabeth Veale Leedy, Tinkham III, Helen Ernst Veale Gelbach. BS in Mech. Engring., Case Inst. Tech., 1937; LLD, Kenyon Coll., 1981. Registered profl. engr. With Gen. Motors Corp., 1937-38, Avery Engring. Co., 1939, Reliance Electric Co., 1940-41; asst. to pres. Ohio Crankshaft Co., 1942-46; gen. mgr. Tocco Co., 1947-51; pres. Ric Wil Corp., 1952-53, Alco Chem. Corp., 1954-56, dir., 1954-86. Spl. ptnr. Ball Burge & Kraus, investment bankers, 1957-60; chmn. bd. V. and V. Cos., Inc. and subs., Cleve., 1960-65, Alco Standard Corp. and subs., Valley Forge, Pa., 1965-86, Horsehead Industries, Inc. and subs., N.Y.C., 1981—2001, HTV Industries Inc. and subs., Cleve., 1978—; ptnr. Fair Elm Farm, 1948-2000, Kennedy Veale Stable, 1954-2000. Trustee Veale Charitable Found., 1966—. Recipient Silver Bowl award Case Inst. Tech., 1980; recipient Gold Medal Case Inst. Tech., 1982, Univ. medal Case We. Res. U., 2003. Mem. Cleve. Engring. Soc., Nat. Soc. Registered Profl. Engrs., Newcomen Soc., Phi Kappa Psi. Home: PO Box 39 Gates Mills OH 44040-0039 Office Phone: 440-423-4144, 440-423-4473.

VEBLEN, THOMAS CLAYTON, management consultant; b. Hallock, Minn., Dec. 17, 1929; s. Edgar R. and Hattie (Lundgren) V.; m. Susan Alma Beaver, Sept. 1, 1950 (div. 1971); children: Kari Kristen, Erik Rodli, Mark Andrew, Sara Catherine; m. Linda Joyce Eaton, Aug. 30, 1975; 1 child, Kristen Kirby. Student, U. Calif., Santa Barbara, 1950—51; BS, Calif. Poly. U., 1953; MS, Oreg. State U., 1955. Corp. v.p. Cargill, Inc., Wayzata, Minn., 1955-75; spl. asst. Sec. Interior, Washington, 1965; dir. food and agr. SRI Internat., Menlo Park, Calif., 1975-80; pres. Food Sys. Assocs., Inc., Washington, 1980-94; also bd. dirs. Food System Assocs., Inc., Washington; chmn. Enterprise Cons. and Devel., Inc., Mpls., 1990—; dir. Georgetown Cons., Inc., 1993-95; convener The Superior Bus. Firm Roundtable, 1993—; chmn. Kirby Ventures LLC, Mpls., 1997—, Wyatt Ventures, LLC, Mpls., 1999—, Northshore, LLC, Mpls., 2000—. Mem. CMC Inst. Mgmt. Cons., 1988—97, pres. Washington chpt., 1991—93. Co-author: (with M. Nichols) The U.S. Food System, 1978; (with M. Abel) Creating a Superior National Food System, 1992; author: The Way of Business: An Inquiry Into Meaning and Superiority, 2006; editor Food System Update, 1986-95. Treas., bd. dirs. White House Fellows Assn., Washington, 1985; trustee Freedom from Hunger Found., Davis, Calif., 1980-99, chmn., 1986-89; bd. dirs. Patterson Sch., U. Ky., Lexington, 1976-99, Am. Near East Refugee Aid, 1994-2006. Recipient Presdl. Appointment White House Fellows Program, Washington, 1965. Mem.: Coun. on Fgn. Rels., Cato Inst., Cosmos Club. Episcopalian. Avocations: canoeing, gardening, writing. Office: Enterprise Cons and Devel Inc 2817 Lyndale Ave South Minneapolis MN 55409 Office Phone: 202-342-7640. Personal E-mail: superbizrt@aol.com.

VECCHIO, ROBERT PETER, business management educator; b. Chgo., June 29, 1950; m. Betty Ann Vecchio, Aug. 21, 1974; children: Julie, Mark. BS summa cum laude, DePaul U., 1972; MA, U. Ill., 1974, PhD, 1976. Instr. U. Ill., Urbana, 1973-76; mem. faculty dept. mgmt. U. Notre Dame, 1976—, dept. chmn., 1983-90, Franklin D. Schurz Prof. Mgmt., 1986—. Editor: Jour. of Mgmt., 1995—2000. Fellow: APA, Am. Psychol. Soc., Soc. for Indsl. and Orgnl. Psychology; mem.: Midwest Psychol. Assn., Midwest Acad. Mgmt., Acad. of Mgmt., Phi Eta Sigma, Delta Epsilon Sigma, Phi Kappa Phi. Home: 16856 Hampton Dr Granger IN 46530-6907 Office: U Notre Dame Dept Mgmt Notre Dame IN 46556

VECCHIOTTI, ROBERT ANTHONY, management and organizational consultant; b. NYC, May 21, 1941; s. R. Lucien and Louise Victoria V.; m. Dorothea Irene Hoban, Oct. 12, 1963; children: John Robert, Rachel Irene, Sara Christine. BS, St. Peter's Coll., 1962; MA, Fordham U., 1964; PhD, St. Louis U., 1973. Lic. psychologist, Mo. Psychologist Testing and Advisement Ctr., NYU, Washington Sq. campus, 1964-65; group psychologist McDonnell Douglas, St. Louis, 1967-76, sr. bus. analyst, 1976-77, mgr. bus. planning, 1977-79; pres. Orgnl. Cons. Svcs., Inc., St. Louis, 1980—. Adj. assoc. prof. mgmt. Maryville Coll., St. Louis, 1975-81. Bd. dirs. Cath. Charities St. Louis, 1981-86, Cath. Family Svc., 1986-00, Mental Health Assn. St. Louis, 1989-05, Sta. KWMU-FM, 1989-94; trustee St. Patrick;s Ctr., 2001-. With US Army, 1965-67. Fellow Soc. Indsl. and Orgnl. Psychologists; mem. APA, Rotary (past pres.). Office: Organizational Consulting Svcs Inc 230 S Bemiston Ave Ste 1107 Clayton MO 63105-1907 Home Phone: 314-991-4323; Office Phone: 314-863-1200.

VECOLI, RUDOLPH JOHN, retired history educator, director; b. Wallingford, Conn., Mar. 2, 1927; s. Giovanni Battista and Settima Maria (Palmerini) V.; m. Jill Cherrington, June 27, 1959; children: Christopher, Lisa, Jeremy. BA, U. Conn., 1950; MA, U. Pa., 1951; PhD, U. Wis., 1963. Fgn. affairs officer Dept. State, 1951-54; instr. history Ohio State U., 1957-59, Pa. State U., 1960-61; asst. prof. Rutgers U., 1961-65; assoc. prof. U. Ill., Champaign, 1965-67; prof. history, dir. Immigration History Rsch. Ctr., U. Minn., Mpls., 1967—2005; ret., 2005. Vis. prof. U. Uppsala, Sweden, 1970, U. Amsterdam, The etherlands,

1988, Maria Curie-Sklodowsk U., Lublin, Poland, 1992. Author: The People of New Jersey, 1965, Foreword to Marie Hall Ets, Rosa: The Story of an Italian Immigrant, 1970, (with J. Lintelman) A Century of American Immigration, 1884-1984, (with others) The Invention of Ethnicity, 1990; contbg. author: Gil italiani fuori d'Italia, 1983, They Chose Minnesota: A Survey of the State's Ethnic Groups, 1981, Pane e Lavoro: The Italian American Working Class, 1980, Perspectives in Italian Immigration and Ethnicity, 1977, Immigrants and Religion in Urban America, 1977, The State of American History, 1970, The Reinterpretation of American History and Culture, 1973, Failure of a Dream, Essays in the History of American Socialism, 1984, Italian Americans: New Perspectives, 1985, May Day Celebration, 1988, In the Shadow of the Statue of Liberty, 1988, From Melting Pot to Multiculturalism, 1990, Studi Sull' Emigrazione, 1991, The Lebanese in the World, 1992, Swedes in America: New Perspectives, 1993, The Statue of Liberty Revisited, 1994, La Riscoperta delle Americhe, 1994, The Encyclopedia of Twentieth Century America, 1996, The Cambridge Survey of World Migration, 1995, Print Culture in a Diverse America, 1998; editor, contbg. author: The Other Catholics, 1978, Italian Immigrants in Rural and Small Town America, 1987, The Gale Encyclopedia of Multicultural Am., 1994, Beyond the Godfather, 1997, The Lost World of Italian American Radicalism, 2003; mem. editl. bd. Jour. Am. Ethnic History, Studi Emigrazione, America: History and Life Mid-Am., Estudios Migratorios Latino Americanos, Altreitalle; co-editor (with S. Sinke) A Century of European Migrations, 1830-1930, 1991; contbr. articles to jours. Chair history com. Statue of Liberty-Ellis Island Centennial Commn. & Found., 1983-98. With USNR, 1945-46. Decorated Knight Officer, Order of Merit (Italy), 1992; recipient Campus Major honor City of Camaiore, Italy, 1996; Newberry Libr. fellow, 1964, Am.-Scandinavian Found. fellow, 1970, NEH fellow, 1985-86; Am. Philos. Soc. grantee, 1970, Fulbright-Hays sr. rsch. scholar Italy, 1973-74; Am. Coun. Learned Soc. grantee, 1974, 86, U.S. Dept. State Travel grantee, 1977, Acad. Specialist, U.S. Info. Agy., Brazil, 1993; endowed Rudolph J. Vecoli professorship Am. immigration history, 2005. Mem. Am. Italian Hist. Assn. (pres., mem. exec. coun.), Am. Hist. Assn., Orgn. Am. Historians, AAUP, Immigration History Soc. (pres., exec. coun.) Home: 2338 Chilcombe Ave Saint Paul MN 55108-1626 Business E-Mail: vecol001@tc.umn.edu.

VEDDER, JAMES J., lawyer; b. Menominee, Wis., Oct. 1, 1973; BA, U. Minn., 1995; JD, Hamline U. Sch. Law, St. Paul, 1999. Bar: Minn. 1999. Clk. Hennepin County Dist. Ct.; atty. M. Sue Wilson Law Offices; assoc. Moss & Barnett, P.A., Mpls. Contbr. articles to profl. publs. Named a Rising Star, Minn. Super Lawyers mag., 2006. Mem.: Minn. State Bar Assn., Hennepin County Bar Assn. Office: Moss & Barnett PA 4800 Wells Fargo Ctr 90 S 7th St Minneapolis MN 55402-4129 Office Phone: 612-877-5294. E-mail: vedderj@moss-barnett.com.

VEDDER, RICHARD KENT, economics professor; b. Urbana, Ill., Nov. 5, 1940; s. Byron C. and Kathleen (Fry) V.; m. Karen Pirosko, June 18, 1968; children: Virin, Vanette. BA, Northwestern U., Evanston, Ill., 1962; MA, U. Ill., 1963, PhD, 1965. Asst. prof. econs. Ohio U., Athens, 1965-69, assoc. prof. econs., 1969-74, prof. econs., 1974-85; economist Joint Econ. Com. of Congress, Washington, 1981-82; Dist. Prof. of econs. Ohio U., Athens, 1985—. Vis. prof. Claremont McKenna Coll., Calif., 1979-80, Econs. Inst. U. Colo., Boulder, 1979, 80, Washington U., St. Louis, 1995, 96; adj. scholar Am. Enterprise Inst., 2003-; dir. Ctr. for Coll. Affordability and Productivitiy, 2006; mem. Sec. of Edn.'s Commn. on Future of Edn., 2005. Author: American Economy in Historical Perspective, 1976, Can Teachers Own Their Own Schools?, 2000, Going Broke by Degree: Why College Costs Too Much, 2005; co-author: Out of Work: Unemployment and Government in Twentieth-Century America, 1993, rev. edit., 1997, The Wal-Mart Revolution. 2006. Mem. Athens Bd. Edn., 1987-91; bd. dirs. Athens Cmty. Music Sch., 1987-92, Ohio Valley Summer Theater, 2002—. Recipient rsch. grants Earhart Found., 1970, 90, Rockefeller Found., 1974, Nat. Chamber Found., 1990, fellowship Inst. for Humane Studies, Palo Alto, Calif., 1983. Mem. Am. Econ. Assn., Econ. History Assn., Rotary, U. Club. Republican. Presbyterian. Home: 7464 Ridgeview Cir Athens OH 45701-9005 Office: Ohio Univ Dept Econs Bentley Hall Annex 316 Athens OH 45701 Home Phone: 740-593-0813. Business E-Mail: vedder@ohio.edu.

VEENSTRA, KENNETH, state legislator; b. Tracy, Iowa, Apr. 19, 1939; m. Jan Veenstra; 4 children. CLU, Am. Coll., 1985. Ins. agt. State Farm Ins. Co.; mem. Iowa Ho. of Reps., Des Moines, 1994-98, Iowa Senate from 3rd dist., Des Moines, 1998—; mem. agr. com., mem. edn. com., mem. human resources com.; mem. small bus., econ. devel. and tourism com. Former mem. coun. Cavelry Christian Reformed Ch.; pres. Sioux County Assn. for Retarded Citizens; former bd. dirs. Orange City Christian Sch.; mem. Iowa Farm Bur.; founding bd. dirs. Ronald McDonald House, Iowa City. Mem. Northwestern Assn. Life Underwriters (pres. 1993-94), at. Fedn. Ind. Bus., Orange City C. of C. Republican.

VEIT, GAE, construction executive; CEO, owner Shingobee Builders, Loretto, Minn., 1980—. Recipient Contractor Yr., Am. Public Works Assn., 1994, Supplier Yr., Alliant Techsystems, 1993, Nat. Female Entrepreneur Yr., Dept. Commerce, 1991. Office: Shingobee Builders PO Box 8 Loretto MN 55357-0008 Fax: 612-479-3267.

VEITH, G. JOHN, lawyer; b. Washburn, Wis., Nov. 6, 1967; BA, SUNY, Potsdam, 1989; JD, William Mitchell Coll. Law, 1993. Bar: Minn. 1993, US Dist. Ct. (dist. Minn.) 1994, US Dist. Ct. (ctrl. dist. Ill.) 1999, US Ct. Appeals (8th cir.) 2004. Asst. city atty., St. Paul, 1992; law clk. Medicaid-Fraud Unit Minn. Atty. Gen., St. Paul, 1993; pvt. practice atty., 1993—96; atty. complex bus., probate and civil litig. Westrick & McDowall-Nix, P.L.L.P., 1996—2001; assoc. Brown & Carlson, P.A., Mpls., 2001—. Named a Rising Star, Minn. Super Lawyers mag., 2006. Mem.: Minn. Def. Lawyers Assn., ABA, Ramsey County Bar Assn., Minn. State Bar Assn., Hennepin County Bar Assn. Office: Brown & Carlson PA 5411 Circle Down Ave Ste 100 Minneapolis MN 55416 Office Phone: 763-591-9950. E-mail: jveith@brownandcarlson.com.

VELEV, MIROSLAV N., electrical and computer engineer, educator; arrived in US, 1991; BSEE, Yale U., New Haven, Conn., 1994, BS in Econs., 1994, MSEE, 1994; PhD in Elec. and Computer Engring., Carnegie Mellon U., Pitts., 2004. Tech. assoc. info. svcs. Credit Suisse First Boston Corp., NYC, 1994—95; rsch. asst. Carnegie Mellon U., Pitts., 1995—2001; vis. asst. prof. Sch. elec. and computer engring. Ga. Inst. Tech., Atlanta; pvt. practice rschr. and cons., 2003—; founder, pres., CEO, Aries Design Automation, LLC, 2005—, Self-Actualizer, LLC, 2006—. Asst. prof. Dept. Elec. and Computer Engring. U. Ill., Chgo., 2006—; mem. program coms. over 108 internat. computer sci. and computer engring. confs.; co-chair 3rd Internat. Workshop Constraints in Formal Verification, Talin, Estonia, 2005; chair 4th Internat. Workshop Constraints in Formal Verification, Bremen, Germany, 2007. Mem. editl. bd.: Jour. Universal Computer Sci., 2001—, Jour. on Satisfiability, Boolean Modeling and Computation, 2003—; contbr. over 50 papers to confs. and jours. Recipient Franz Tuteur Meml. prize, Yale U., 1994, EDAA Outstanding Dissertation award, 2005. Mem.: IEEE, Am. Assn. for Artificial Intelligence, Am. Soc. for Engring. Edn., Assn. for Computing Machinery. Achievements include development of over 1,100 formulas used in research in the computer science field of Boolean satisfiability (SAT).

VELICK, STEPHEN H., medical facility administrator; BS, Wayne State U., 1970, MS, 1980. Mgr. billing Henry Ford Hosp., Detroit, 1970-72, 72-74, mgr. patient svcs., 1974-75, asst. dir. bus., 1975-76, dir. bus. office, 1976-78, assoc. adminstr., 1978-83; exec. dir. Greenfield Health Sys. Corp., Detroit, 1983-86; chief adminstrv. officer Henry Ford Med. Group, Detroit, 1986-90; group v.p., COO Henry Ford Hosp., Detroit, 1990-95, CEO, 1995—. Adv. bd., bd. dirs. various healthcare orgns. Mem. adv. bd. Wayne State U. Coll. Pharmacy & Allied Health; active various cmty. orgns. Mem. Am. Coll. Healthcare Execs. (assoc.), Am. Hosp. Assn. Office: HFH Sys 2799 W Grand Blvd Detroit MI 48202-2608

VELLENGA, KATHLEEN OSBORNE, retired state legislator; b. Alliance, Nebr., Aug. 5, 1938; d. Howard Benson and Marjorie (Menke) Osborne; m. James Alan Vellenga, Aug. 9, 1959; children: Thomas, Charlotte Vellenga Landreau, Carolyn Vellenga Berman. BA, Macalester Coll., 1959. Tchr. St. Paul Pub. Schs., 1959-60, Children's Ctr. Montessori, St. Paul, 1973-74, Children's Ho. Montessori, St. Paul, 1974-79; mem. Minn. Ho. of Reps., St. Paul, 1980-94, mem. tax. com. and rules com., 1991—94, chmn. St. Paul del., 1987—90, chmn. criminal justice div., 1987—90, mem. Dem. steering com., 1981—94, chmn. judiciary, 1991, 92, chmn. edn. fin., 1993—94. Mem. St. Paul Family Svcs. Bd., 1994-95; exec. dir. St. Paul/Ramsey County Children's Initiative, 1994-2000. Chmn. Healthstart, St. Paul, 1987-91; mem. Children, Youth and Families Consortium, 1995-99, Macalester Coll. Bd. Alumni, 1995-2001; chair Minn. Higher Edn. Svcs. Coun., 2000—05, mem. 1995—; mem. Citizens League Bd., Minn., 1999-2002, State Commn. Cmty. Svc., 2000-04; bd. dirs. Sexual Violence Ctr., 2004-06; mem. U. Minn. Out of School Time Commn., 2004; mem. H.B. Fuller Found. Bd., 2005—. Mem. LWV (v.p. St. Paul chpt. 1979), Minn. Women Elected Ofcls. (vice chair 1994). Democrat. Presbyterian.

VENKATA, SUBRAHMANYAM SARASWATI, engineering educator, researcher; b. Nellore, Andhra Pradesh, India, June 28, 1942; came to U.S., 1968; s. Ramiah Saraswati and Lakshmi (Alladi) V.; m. Padma Subrahmanyam Mahadevan, Sept. 3, 1971; children: Sridevi Ramakumar, Harish Saraswati. BSEE, Andhra U., Waltair, India, 1963; MSEE, Indian Inst. Tech., Madras, 1965; PhD, U. S.C., 1971. Registered profl. engr., W.Va., Wash. Lectr. in elec. engring. Coimbatore (India) Inst. Tech., 1965-66; planning engr. S.C. Elec. & Gas Co., Columbia, 1969-70; postdoctoral fellow U. S.C., Columbia, 1971; instr. elec. engring. U. Mass., Lowell, 1971-72; asst. prof. W.Va. U., Morgantown, 1972-75, assoc. prof., 1975-79; prof. U. Wash., Seattle, 1979-96; prof., chmn. dept. elec. and computer engring. Iowa State U., Ames, 1996—2002, Palmer chair prof. dept. elec. and computer engring., 2003—; dean, disting. univ. prof. Wallace H. Coulter Sch. Engring., Clarkson U., Potsdam, NY, 2004—05; v.p., exec. cons. KEMA, 2005—07; prof. U. Wash, Seattle, 2008—. Cons. Puget Sound Energy Co., Bellevue, Wash., 1980-93, GEC/Alsthom, NYC, 1991-92; series editor, bd. dirs. PWS Pub. Co., 1991-98; affiliate prof. U. Wash., Seattle, 1997-07. Author: Introduction of Electrical Energy Devices, 1987; editor, IEEE Transactions on Power Systems, 1998-00, IEEE/PES Rev. Letters, 1999-03, Internat. Jour. Sys.; mem. editl. bd. IEEE/PES/Power and Energy Mag., 2003-; patentee adaptive var compensators, adaptive power quality conditioner, distribution reliability based design software. Advisor Explorers Club, Morgantown, 1976-78; sec. Hindu Temple and Cultural Ctr. Pacific N.W., Seattle, 1990, chmn., 1991, 95; founding chmn. Hindu Temple and Cultural Ctr., Ames, Iowa, 1999—. Recipient W.Va. U. Assocs. award W.Va. U. Found., 1974, 78. Fellow IEEE (editor IEEE Trans. Power Sys. 1998-00, IEEE/PES Rev. Letters 1999-03, Internat. Jour. Sys., mem. editl. bd. IEEE/PES/Power and Energy Mag., 2003-, v.p. publs., 2004-07, Best Paper award 1985, 88, 91, 2005, mem. Conf. Internat. des Grands Reseaux Electriques, IEEE Press for Power Series, 1998—, Outstanding Power Engring. Educator award 1996, chmn. power engring. edn. com. 2000—, Millenneum medal 2000, Power Edn.Com. Disting. Svc. award 2005), Power Engring. Soc. IEEE (v.p. 2004—), Sigma Xi, Tau Beta Pi, Eta Kappa Nu, Rotary. Democrat. Avocations: photography, tennis, ping pong/table tennis. Home and Office: 13224 N Risky Dr Tucson AZ 85755 Office Phone: 520-797-1161, 206-543-2386. Personal E-mail: psvenkata@comcast.net. Business E-Mail: ss.venkata@kema.com.

VENO, GLEN COREY, management consultant; b. Montreal, Que., Can., Sept. 5, 1951; came to U.S., 1953; s. Corey Elroy and Elsie Milly (Munro) V. BS in Aviation Tech. and Mgmt., Western Mich. U., 1976. Cert. mgmt. cons. Project mgr. The ASIST Corp., Oak Park, Mich., 1978-83; mgr. tech. support J.B. Systems, Inc., Woodland Hills, Calif., 1984-85; mgr. cons. svcs. Mgmt. Tech., Inc., Troy, Mich., 1985-88; v.p. Mgmt. Support Svcs., Inc., Southfield, Mich., 1989-90; owner Maintenance Mgmt. Support Svcs., Brighton, Mich., 1990—. With U.S. Army, 1969-72, Vietnam. Mem. VFW (life), Inst. Mgmt. Cons., Vietnam Helicopter Pilots Assn. Avocations: flying, boating, golf. Home: 6397 Kinyon Dr Brighton MI 48116 Office: PO Box 605 Brighton MI 48116-0605 Office Phone: 810-599-9999. E-mail: gcveno@maintenance-mgmt.com.

VENTURA, JESSE (JAMES JANOS, "THE BODY"), former governor; b. Mpls., July 15, 1951; s. George and Bernice Janos; m. Theresa Larson Masters, July 18, 1975; children: Tyrel, Jade. Student, orth Hennepin C.C., 1974—75. Profl. wrestler, 1973-84; ret.; mayor City of Brooklyn Park, Minn.; gov. State of Minn., St. Paul, 1999—2003; host The Jesse Ventura Show, 2003—. Actor: Predator, 1987, The Running Man, 1989; author: I Ain't Got Time to Bleed: Reworking the Body Politic from the Bottom Up, 1999; co-author (with Julie Mooney): Do I Stand Alone?: Going to the Mat against Political Pawns and Media Jackals, 2000; co-author: (with Dick Russell) Don't Start the Revolution Without Me!, 2008. Mayor City of Brooklyn Park, Minn., 1990-95; bd. advisors Make a Wish of Minn.; vol. football coach Champlin Park H.S.; mem. Izaak Walton League America. Mem. underwater demolition team USN, 1970—75, Vietnam. Mem. Am. Fedn. of TV and radio Announcers, Screen Actors Guild. Independent.*

VENTURINI, TISHA LEA, professional soccer player; b. Modesto, Calif., Mar. 3, 1973; Degree in phys. edn., U. N.C. Mem. U.S. Women's Nat. Soccer Team. Mem. championship team CONCACAF, Montreal, 1994. Named Player of Yr., Mo. Athletic Club, 1994; recipient Gold medal, Centennial Olympic Games, 1996, Silver medal, World Univ. Games, 1993, Hermann trophy, 1994. Achievements include 1999 World Cup Champion. Office: c/o US Soccer Fedn 1801 S Prairie Ave # 1811 Chicago IL 60616-1319

VENZAGO, MARIO, conductor, music director; b. Zurich, Switzerland, 1948; m. Marianne Venzago; children: Mario, Gabriel. Studied with, Hans Swarowsky, Vienna, 1973. Music dir. Basel Symphony Orch., 1995—2003, Heidelberg Opera, 1986—89, Deutsche Kammerphilharmonie, 1989—92, Graz Opera Ho., 1990—95, Euskadi Nat. Opera, Spain, 1998—2001, Indpls. Symphony Orch., 2002—, Swedish Nat. Orch., 2003—. Guest condr. Berlin Philharmonic, BBC, London, Leipzig Gewandhaus Orchester, London Philharmonic, City of Birmingham Symphony, Orchestre de la Suisse Romande, Phila. Orch., Tonhalle Orchestra Zurich, Tokyo's NHK Symphony, Berlin's Komische Oper, Salzburg Festival, Hannover Radio-Philharmonie, invited by Kurt Masur, Leipzig; guest condr.: Boston Symphony, Helsinki Philharmonic, Helsinki Radio; Am. debut Hollywood Bowl, 1988, appeared N.J. Symphony, Ind. Symphony, Fla. Philharmonic, 1988; dir.: Balt. Symphony, 1995 (named artistic dir. symphony's summer festival, 2000); prin. conductor Winterthur City Orch., Lucerne Opera Ho., Orchestre de la Suisse Romande. Recipient award, Diapason d'or, awards, Grand Prix du Disque, Edison prize. Office: Ind Symphony Orch 32 E Washington St Ste 600 Indianapolis IN 46204-2919 Business E-Mail: mvenvago@IndianapolisSymphony.org.

VERDOORN, D.R. (SID), retired trucking executive; b. Albert Lea, Minn., Feb. 11, 1939; s. Cornelius Emery and Gwen (Pickell) V.; m. Carol Joyce Hoekstra, July 3, 1959; children: Jay Richard, Jeffrey Lee, James Dale. Student, Cen. Coll., Pella, Iowa. With sales C.H. Robinson Worldwide, Mpls., 1963-66, mgr. San Francisco, 1966-71, pers. dir. Mpls., 1971-75, v.p., 1975-77, pres., 1977-2000, CEO, 1977—2002, chmn., 2002—06. Bd. dirs. Produce Mktg. Assocs., Newark, United Fruit and Produce, Washington. With U.S. Army, 1959-61. Republican. Avocations: hiking, water sports.

VEREEN, ROBERT CHARLES, retired trade association administrator; b. Stillwater, Minn., Sept. 8, 1924; s. George and Leona Lucille (Made) Wihren; m. Rose Catherine Blair, Nov. 5, 1945; children: Robin, Stacy, Kim. Grad. high sch. Mng. editor Comml. West Mag., Mpls., 1946-50, Bruce Pub. Co., St. Paul, 1950-53, Nat. Retail Hardware Assn., Indpls., 1953-59; mng. dir. Liberty Distbrs., Phila., 1959-63; editor Hardware Retailing, Indpls., 1963-80; assoc. pub., dir. communications Nat. Retail Hardware Assn., 1980-84, sr. v.p., 1984-87; Vereen & Assocs., Mgmt., Mktg. Cons., 1987—. Lectr. mgmt. insts.; guest lectr. on distbn. pub.; co-founder U.S.A. Direct; co-founder, ptnr. Eurotrade Mktg., 1988—; ptnr. Hardlines Pers. Finders, 1987—. Author: (with Paul M. Doane) Hunting for Profit, 1965, The Computer Age in Merchandising, 1968, Perpetuating the Family-Owned Business, 1970, The How-To of Merchandising, 1975, The How-To of Store Operations, 1976, A Guide to Financial Management, 1976, Productivity: A Crisis for Management, 1978, Hardlines Rep Report Newsletter, 1984-94, Guidelines to Improve the Rep/Factory Relationships, 1992; contbr. articles to profl. jours. and mags. Served with AUS, 1943-46. Mem. Am. Soc. Bus. Press Editors (dir., v.p. 1966-70), Soc. Nat. Assn. Publs. (dir., pres. 1970-75, chmn. journalism edn. liaison com. 1976-79), Toastmasters (v.p., treas., sec. 1955-59), Am. Hardware Mfrs. Assn. (co-founder, sec.-treas. Young Execs. Club 1958-.59, 63-65), Hardware-Housewares Packaging Expn. (founder 1960, chmn. com. packaging 1960-62, chmn. judging com. Hardware-Packaging Expn. 1975-78), Packaging Inst., Household Consumer Products Export Coun. (chmn. 1981-83), World-Wide DIY Coun. (exec. sec. 1981-99, dir. emeritus 1999-2007, newsletter editor, 2008-). Home and Office: 10769 Oriole Ct Indianapolis IN 46231-1006 Home Phone: 317-838-7632; Office Phone: 317-838-7632.

VERICH, DEMETRIO, lawyer; b. Laona, Wis., June 21, 1932; s. Peter Paul and Annetta (Mariani) V.; m. Mary Therese Rathborne, Nov. 28, 1967; children: Peter, Andrew, Nicole, Matthew, Daniel, John, Joseph. Student, St. Norbert Coll., 1951-52; BS in Engring., U.S. Naval Postgrad. Sch., 1958-60; student, U.S. aval War Coll., 1964-65; MBA, JD, U. Notre Dame, 1976. Bar: Wis. Commd. ensign USN, 1952; advanced through grades to commdr.; naval aviator USN, 1952-72; cand. for U.S. Congress 8th congl. dist. U. S. Ho. of Reps., 1976; cand. for assembly 36th assembly dist. Wis. State Legislature, 1978, 80; town atty. Laona, 1980-82; pvt. practice in law, 1980—; dist. atty. Forest County, Laona, 1990—. Pres. Laona Sch. Bd., 1989-91. Decorated DFC, 1967, Air Medal with seven stars, 1966-67, Purple Heart with two stars, 1966-67. Mem. VFW (commdr. post 6823 1990—), KC (Grand Knight 1982-83). Republican. Roman Catholic. Avocations: private pilot, aircraft homebuilder, hunting. Home: Box 137 RR 1 RR 1 Box 137 Laona WI 54541-9732 Office: Forest County Dist Atty Court House Crandon WI 54520

VERICH, MICHAEL GREGORY, state legislator; b. Warren, Ohio, Dec. 30, 1953; s. Alex and Dolores (Kudrich) V.; m. Aliza Wallace. BA magna cum laude, Bowling Green State Univ., 1976; JD, Univ. Akron, 1981; MPA, Harvard Univ., 1985. Cong. intern U.S. House Rep., Washington, 1987, cong. aide, 1976-77; State rep. Dist 59 Ohio, 1983-92, Dist 66, 1993—; chmn. aging & housing com. Ohio House Rep.; lawyer Wiener, Orkin, Abbate & Suit, 1984—. Mem. employment rels. bd. State of Ohio, Columbus; acad. hist. asst. Bowling Green State Univ., 1975-76. Named Outstanding Young Man of Yr., Edn. Excellence award, Disting. Disabled Vet. award, Legislator of Yr. award. Mem. MENSA, KC, Phi Alpha Theta, ABA, Ohio Bar Assn., Trumbull County Bar Assn. Home: 1460 Central Parkway Ave SE Warren OH 44484-4457 Office: Ohio Ho of Reps 65 E State St Ste 12 Columbus OH 43215-4259

VERING, JOHN ALBERT, lawyer; b. Marysville, Kans., Feb. 6, 1951; s. John Albert and Bernadine E. (Kieffer) V.; m. Ann E. Arman, June 28, 1980; children: Julia Ann, Catherine Ann, Mary Ann. BA summa cum laude, Harvard U., 1973; JD, U. Va., 1976. Bar: Mo. 1976, U.S. Dist. Ct. (we. dist.) Mo. 1976, U.S. Ct. Appeals (8th cir.), 1977, U.S. Ct. Appeals (10th cir.), 1980, U.S. Ct. Appeals (4th cir.) 1987, Kans. 1990, U.S. Dist. Ct. Kans. 1990; arbitrator, mediator. Assoc. Dietrich, Davis, Dicus, Rowlands, Schmitt & Gorman, Kansas City, Mo., 1976-81, ptnr., 1982—88, Armstrong Teasdale LLP, Kansas City, 1989—. Editor: U. Va. Law Rev., 1974—76. Bd. dirs. Greater Kansas City YMCA Southwest Dist., 1987. Named Best Lawyers in Am., 2008; named one of Am.'s Leading Lawyers for Bus., Chambers USA, 2007, Super Lawyers, Mo., 2007, Kans., 2007. Mem.: Kansas City Metro Bar Assn. (chmn. labor and employment law com. 2003, chmn. fed. cts. com. 2007), Harvard Club (adv. bd. schs. com. Kansas City 1977—2008, v.p. 1981—82, 1992—93, pres. 1994—96). Home: 1210 W 68th Ter Kansas City MO 64113-1904 Office: Armstrong Teasdale LLP 2345 Grand Blvd Ste 2000 Kansas City MO 64108-2617 Office Phone: 816-221-3420. Business E-Mail: jvering@armstrongteasdale.com.

VERLANDER, JUSTIN BROOKS, professional baseball player; b. Manakin Sabot, Va., Feb. 20, 1983; s. Richard Verlander. Student, Vanderbilt U., Nashville. Pitcher Detroit Tigers, 2006—. Named Am. League Rookie of Yr., Maj. League Baseball Writers Assn., 2006, Am. League Outstanding Rookie, Players Choice Awards, 2006; named to Am. League All-Star Team, 2007. Achievements include pitching in World Series during rookie season, 2006; pitched a no-hitter against the Milwaukee Brewers, June 12, 2007. Office: Detroit Tigers Comerica Park 2100 Woodward Ave Detroit MI 48201

VERRETT, SHIRLEY, soprano; b. New Orleans, May 31, 1931; d. Leon Solomon and Elvira Augustine (Harris) V.; m. Louis Frank LoMonaco, Dec. 10, 1963; 1 dau., Francesca. AA, Ventura Coll., Calif., 1951; diploma in voice (scholarship 1956-61), Juilliard Sch. Music, 1961; MusD (hon.), Coll. Holy Cross, Mass., 1978. CPA, Cert. real estate broker. Faculty U. Mich. Sch. Music, 1996—, James Earl Jones disting. univ. prof. voice, 1999—. Mem. adv. bd. Opera Ebony. Recital debut Town Hall, N.Y.C., 1958; appeared as Irina in Lost in the Stars, 1958; orchestral debut Phila. Orch., 1960; operatic debut in Carmen, Festival of Two Worlds, Spoleto, Italy, 1962; debuts with Bolshoi Opera, Moscow, 1963, N.Y.C. Opera, 1964, Royal Opera, Covent Garden, 1966, Maggio Fiorentino, Florence, 1967, Met. Opera, 1968, Teatro San Carlos, Naples, 1968, Dallas Civic Opera, 1969, La Scala, 1970, Vienna State Opera, 1970, San Francisco Opera, 1972, Paris Opera, 1973, Opera Co. Boston, 1976, Opera Bastille, Paris, 1990; guest appearances with all major U.S. symphony orchs.; toured Eastern Europe and Greece with La Scala chorus and orch., 1981; TV debut on Ed Sullivan Show, 1963; TV performances include: Great Performances series, live performance of Macbeth at La Scala, Santuzza in Cavalleria Rusticana; film debut Maggio Musicale, 1989, Macbeth, 1986; rec. artist, RCA, Columbia, ABC (Westminster), Angel Everest, Kapp, Philips Records and Deutsche Grammophon. Recipient Marian Anderson award, 1955, Nat. Fedn. Music Clubs award, 1961, Walter Naumberg award, 1958, Blanche Thebom award, 1960; named Chevalier Arts and Letters (France), 1970, Commandeur, 1984; John Hay Whitney fellow, 1959; Ford Found. fellow, 1962-63; Martha Baird Rockefeller Aid to Music Fund fellow, 1959-61; grantee William Matteus Sullivan Fund, 1959; grantee Berkshire Music Opera, 1956; recipient Achievement award Ventura Coll., 1963, Achievement award N.Y. chpt. Albert Einstein Coll. Medicine, 1975; 2 plaques Los Angeles Sentinel Newspaper, 1960; plaque Peninsula Music Festival, 1963; Los Angeles Times Woman of Yr. award, 1969 Mem. Mu Phi Epsilon. Office: U Mich Sch Music 1100 Baits Dr Ann Arbor MI 48109-2085 E-mail: verrett@umich.edu.

VERSCHOOR, CURTIS CARL, writer, consultant; b. Grand Rapids, Mich., June 7, 1931; s. Peter and Leonene (Dahlstrom) V.; m. Marie Emilie Kritschgau, June 18, 1952; children: Katherine Anne, Carolyn Marie, John Peter, Carla Michelle. BBA with distinction, U. Mich., 1951; MBA, U. Mich., Ann Arbor, 1952; EdD, No. Ill. U., DeKalb, 1977. CPA; cert. mgmt. acctg., cert. fin. planner, cert. fraud examiner, cert. internal auditor; chartered fin. cons. Pub. accountant Touche, Ross, Bailey & Smart (C.P.A.'s), 1955-63; with Singer Co., 1963-68, asst. controller, 1965-68; controller Colgate-Palmolive Co., 1968-69; asst. controller bus. products group Xerox Corp., 1969-72; controller Baxter Internat., 1972-73; CFO, v.p. fin. Altair Corp., Chgo., 1973-74; prof. DePaul U., Chgo., 1974-94, ledger and quill alumni rsch. prof., 1994—; pres. C.C. Verschoor & Assocs., Inc., 1981—. Part-time instr. Wayne State U., 1955-60. Author: Audit Committee Briefing: Understanding the 21st Century Audit Committee Governance Roles, 2000, Audit Committee Briefing: Facilitating New Audit Committee Responsibilites, 2001, Governance Update 2003, Ethics and Compliance: Challenges for Internal Auditing, 2007: Impact of the New Initiatives, 2003, Ethics and; contbg. editor: Jour. Accountancy, 1961-62, Jour. Internal Auditing, 1985—, Strategic Fin., 1999-; editl. adv. bd. Acctg. Today, 1991-2004, Internal Auditor, 1993—. Trustee Hektoen Inst. for Medicine, Chgo., 1996—. Served with AUS, 1953-55. Recipient Elijah Watts Sells award Am. Inst. C.P.A.'s, 1953; rsch. scholar Ctr. for Bus. Ethics, Bentley Coll. Mem. AICPA, Fin. Execs. Inst., Am. Acctg. Assn., Inst. Mgmt. Accts., Inst. Internal Auditors, Nat. Assn. Corp. Dirs., Assn. Cert. Fraud Examiners, Soc. for Bus. Ethics, Beta Gamma Sigma, Beta Alpha Psi, Delta Pi Epsilon, Phi Kappa Phi, Phi Eta Sigma. Home: 231 Wyngate Dr Barrington IL 60010-4840 Office: DePaul Univ One E Jackson Blvd Chicago IL 60604-2287 Personal E-mail: curtisverschoor@sbcglobal.net.

VERSYP, SHARON, women's college basketball coach; BA, Purdue U, 1989. Asst. coach U. Louisville, 1996—97; asst. coach, recruiting dir. James Madison U., Harissonburg, Va., 1997—2000; women's basektball head coach U. Maine, Orano, 2000—05, Ind. U., 2005—06, Purdue U., West Lafayette, Ind., 2006—. Recipient Coach Yr. award, America East Conf., 2003, 2005, Regional Coach Yr, NCAA, 2007. Office: Mackey Arena Rm 15 900 North University Dr West Lafayette IN 47907

VESCOVI, SELVI, pharmaceutical company executive; b. N.Y.C., June 14, 1930; s. Antonio and Desolina V.; BS, Coll. William and Mary, 1951; m. Elma Pasquinelli, Oct. 16, 1954; children: Mark, James, Anne. Salesman, Upjohn Co., N.Y.C., 1954-59, sales supr.,1959-62, product mgr. U.S. domestic pharm. dir., 1962-65, mgr. mktg. planning internat. div., 1965-71, v.p. Europe, 1971-74, group v.p. Europe, 1975-77, exec. v.p. Upjohn Internat., Inc., Kalamazoo, Mich., 1978-85, pres., gen. mgr., 1975-88, v.p. parent co., 1978-88; adj. prof. mgmt. Western Mich. U., Kalamazoo, 1988-92; chmn. bd. Carrington Labs.; bd. dirs. Centaur Corp. 2d lt. M.C., U.S. Army, 1951-53. Mem. Internat. Pharm. Mfrs. Assn., NYAC (N.Y.). Republican. Roman Catholic.

VESPER, ROSE, state legislator; m. Lee Vesper; children: Stephanie, Jennifer, Jessica. BA, Xavier U., 1960; MA, Midwestern U., 1967. Past mem. Ohio Valley Regional Devel. Commn.; Ohio Water and Sewer Rotary Commn.; pres. Ohio Clermont County Farm Bur.; rep. Ohio State Ho. Reps. Dist. 72. Mem. Nat. Fedn. Rep. Women; chmn. Clermont County Rep. Party, 1990—, Southwestern Ohio Rep. Leadership; owner, operator beef cattle/crop farm. Named Clermont County Farm Woman of Yr., 1988; recipient Disting. Svc. award Ohio Med. Polit. Action Com., 1988, Coop. Ext. Agts. Assn. award, 1990, Frances Boltom award Ohio League Young Reps., 1990. Mem. Richmond Hist. Soc., Clermont, Brown and Clinton County C. of C., State Med. Assn., Farm Bur., Farmers Union. Home: 1174 Watkins Hill Rd ew Richmond OH 45157-9504

VESPOLI, LEILA L., lawyer, energy executive; b. Akron, Ohio, 1959; BS, Miami U., Ohio, 1981; JD, Case Western Res. U., 1984. Bar: Ohio 1984. Atty. to sr. atty. Ohio Edison, Akron, 1985—97; assoc. gen. counsel FirstEnergy Corp., Akron, 1997—2000, v.p., gen. counsel, 2000—01, sr. v.p, gen. counsel, 2001—. Bd. trustees The NEOUCOM Found. Named a Women of Profl. Excellence, YWCA. Mem.: Greater Cleve. Gen. Counsel Assn., Ohio C. of C., Energy Assn. Pa. (bd. dirs.), NJ Utilities Assn. (bd. dirs.). Office: FirstEnergy Corp 76 S Main St Akron OH 44308-1890

VESTA, RICHARD V., meat packing company executive; b. Dec. 25, 1946; Pres., Green Bay, Wis.; CEO Smithfield Beef Group Inc. (formerly Packerland Packing), Green Bay, 2001—, pres. Smithfield beef divsn., 2001—. Office: Smithfield Beef Group PO Box 23000 Green Bay WI 54305-3000

VEZEAU, TIMOTHY J., lawyer; BSEE cum laude, St. Louis U., 1966; JD, Georgetown U., 1971. Bar: Ill. 1972. Patent examiner US Patent Office, 1968—70; patent advisor US Office of Navel Rsch., 1971; founding ptnr. patent practice Katten Muchin Rosenman LLP, Chgo. Mem.: ABA, Intellectual Property Law Assn. of Chgo., Ill. Bar Assn., Chgo. Bar Assn., Eta Kappa Nu, Pi Mu Epsilon. Office: Katten Muchin Rosenman LLP 525 W Monroe St Ste 1900 Chicago IL 60661-3693 Office Phone: 312-902-5516. Office Fax: 312-577-4513. Business E-Mail: timothy.vezeau@kattenlaw.com.

VIAULT, RAYMOND G., food company executive; b. NYC, Sept. 19, 1944; m. Lucille Viault; children: Lisa, Deborah, Russell. Bachelor's degree, Brown U.; MBA, Columbia U. Pres., CEO Kraft Jacobs Suchard, Zurich, Switzerland; CEO Jacobs Suchard A.G. (acquired by Kraft Gen. Foods), 1990-93; pres. Maxwell House Coffee Co. Kraft Gen. Foods, v.p., gen. mgr. desserts divsn.; with Gen. Mills, Mpls., 1996—2004, vice-chmn., 1996—2004, also bd. dirs.; responsible for meals divsn., baking divsn. Pillsbury U.S. Bakery and Food Svc. Former bd. dirs. Cereal Ptnrs. Worldwide; bd. dirs. Newell Rubbermaid, VF Corp., Safeway Inc., 2004—. Bd. overseers Columbia Grad. Sch. Bus., N.Y.C.; trustee Lawrenceville Sch., N.J.; bd. dirs. United Way Mpls., Minn. Internat. Ctr., Technoserve. Office: PO Box 1113 One General Mills Blvd Minneapolis MN 55440-1113

VICK, NICHOLAS A., neurologist; b. Chgo., Oct. 3, 1939; MD, U. Chgo., 1965. Diplomate Am. Bd. Neurology. Intern U. Chgo. Hosps., 1965, resident in neurology, 1966-68; fellow in neurology NIH, Bethesda, Md., 1968-70; staff Evanston (Ill.) Hosp., 1975—; prof. neurology Northwestern U. Med. Sch., Evanston, Ill., 1978—. Mem.: Am. Bd. Psychiatry and Neurology (past exec. dir.). Office: Evanston Hosp Dept Neurology 2650 Ridge Ave Evanston IL 60201-1781 Office Phone: 847-570-2570. Business E-Mail: nvick@enh.org.

VICKERMAN, JIM, state legislator; b. May 1, 1931; m. Wava; six children. County commr.; mem. Minn. Senate from 22nd dist., St. Paul, 1986—. Chmn. vet. and gen. legis. com.; vice-chmn. health and human svc. com., agr. and rural devel. com., local and urban govt. com, transp. com., vet. and mi. affairs com., health care com., health care and family svc. fin. divsn. com., rules and adminstrn. com., transp. com. and transp. fin. divsn. com.; farmer. Office: RR 2 Box 134 Tracy MN 56175-9430 also: Minn Senate State Capitol Building Saint Paul MN 55155-0001

VICKREY, JENE, state legislator; m. Teresa Vickrey. Kans. state rep. Dist. 6, 1993—. Carpet layer. also: Kans Ho of Reps State House Topeka KS 66612 Home: 502 S Countryside Dr Louisburg KS 66053-4024

VICTOR, MICHAEL GARY, lawyer, physician; b. Detroit, Sept. 20, 1945; s. Simon H. and Helen (Litsky) V.; children: Elise Nicole, Sara Lisabeth. Bar: Ill. 1980, U.S. Dist. Ct. (no. dist.) Ill. 1980, U.S. Ct. Appeals (7th cir.) 1981; diplomate Am. Bd. Legal Medicine, Am. Bd. Emergency Medicine, 2003. Of counsel Bollinger, Ruberry & Garvey, Chgo., 1980—99; pres. Advocate Adv. Assocs., Chgo., 1982-95; asst. prof. medicine Northwestern U. Med. Sch., Chgo., 1982—2006; lectr. U. Ill., Chgo., 1999—. Dir. emergency medicine Loretto Hosp., Chgo., 1980-85, chief. sect. of emergency medicine St. Josephs Hosp., Chgo., 1985-87; pvt. practice med. law Barrington, Ill, 1982-; v.p. Med. Emergency Svcs. Assocs., Buffalo Grove, Ill., 1989; v.p. MESA Mgmt. Corp.; exec. leadership coach Lee Hecht Harrison, Chgo. Author: Informed Consent, 1980; Brain Death, 1980; (with others) Due Process for Physicians, 1984, A Physicians Guide to the Illinois Living Will Act, The Choice is Ours!, 1989. Recipient Svc. awards Am. Coll. Emergency Medicine, 1973-83. Fellow Am. Coll. Legal Medicine (bd. govs. 1996-97, alt. del. to AMA House of Dels. 1996-97), Chgo. Acad. Legal Medicine; mem. Am. Coll. Emergency Physicians (pres. Ill. chpt. 1980, med.-legal-ins. coun. 1980-81, 83-84), ABA, Ill. State Bar Assn., Am. Soc. Law and Medicine, Chgo. Bar Assn. (med.-legal coun. 1981-83), AMA, Ill. State Med. Soc. (med.-legal coun. 1980-86, 88), Chgo. Med. Soc. Jewish. Home and Office: 153 Aberdour Ln Palatine IL 60067-8001 Office Phone: 847-934-8404. Personal E-mail: mgv@comcast.net.

VIDAVER, ANNE MARIE, plant pathology educator; b. Vienna, Mar. 29, 1938; came to U.S., 1941; d. Franz and Klara (Winter) Kopecky; children: Gordon W.F., Regina M. BA, Russell Sage Coll., 1960; MA, Ind. U., 1962, PhD, 1965. Lectr. U. Nebr., Lincoln, 1965-66, rsch. assoc., 1966-72, asst. prof., 1972-74, assoc. prof., 1974-79, prof. plant pathology, 1979—, interim dir. Ctr. Biotech., 1988-89, 97-00, head dept. plant pathology, 1984-2000, 2003—06; chief scientist USDA's RICGP, 2000—02. Contbr. articles to profl. jours. and books; patentee in field. Recipient Pub. Svc. award Nebr. Agri-Bus., 1977, Sci. award for excellence NAMA, New Orleans, 1991. Fellow AAAS, Am. Phytopath. Soc., Am. Soc. Microbiology; mem. Intersoc. Consortium for Plant Protection, Internat. Soc. Plant Pathology, Alliance for Prudent Use of Antibiotics. Avocations: indoor gardening, reading. Office: U Nebr Dept Plant Pathology Lincoln NE 68583-0722 Office Phone: 402-472-2858. E-mail: avidaver1@unl.edu.

VIDRICKSEN, BEN EUGENE, food service executive, state legislator; b. Salina, Kans., June 11, 1927; s. Henry and Ruby Mae Vidricksen; m. Lola Mae Nienke, Jan. 20, 1950 (div.); children: Nancy, Janice, Ben, Penelope, Jeffery. AB, Kans. Wesleyan U., 1951. Field supt. Harding Creamery divsn. Nat. Dairy Products, Kearney, Kans., 1951-52, plant mgr. Kraft divsn. O'Neill, Nebr., 1952-59; owner Vidricksen's Food Svc., Salina, 1959—. Cons. in field; mem. Kans. Senate, 1979—, asst. majority leader; chmn. joint bldg. constrn. com., legis. and congl. apportionment com., legis. post audit, econ. devel., transp. and utilities, pub. health and welfare, fed. and state affairs, govtl. orgn., spl. interim com. on efficiency in state govt., 1983; del. White House Conf. on Tourism and Travel, 1995, 96; mem. Hennessy/USAF Worldwide Food Svc. Evaluation Team, 1978, 79. Mem. Salina Airport Authority, 1972-84, chmn., 1976-77; chmn. Rep. Ctrl. Com., County of Saline, Kans., 1974-79; adv. coun. SBA, 1982—, chmn. adv. coun. small bus. devel. ctr.; mem. adv. bd. Salvation Army; past chmn. Salina Conv. and Tourism Bur.; vice chmn. Kans. Turnpike Authority, 1995—. Served with USN, 1945-46. Recipient Salut au Restaurateur award Fla. State U., 1974, Gov.'s Spl. award Kans. Assn. Broadcasters, Guardian award Nat. Fedn. Indep. Bus., 1989, Promotion of Tourism and Travel award Travel Ind. Assn. Kans., 1989, Support of Kans. Nat. Guard award Kans. Adjutant Gen., 1990, Good Citizenship award Kans. Engring. Soc., 1991, 92, Freedom award NRA, 1994, Kans. Nat. Guard award Excellence, 1997; named Nat. Rep. Legislator of Yr., Nat. Rep. Legislators Assn., 1991, Assoc. of Yr., Am. Womens Bus. Assn., 1992. Mem. USAF Assn., Assn. U.S. Army, Nat. Rep. Legislators Assn., Am. Legis. Exch. Coun., Pan Am. Hwy. Assn. (Internat. Achievement award 1992, Road Buiulders award 1995), North Salina Bus. Assn. (past pres.), Internat. Brdige, Tunnel and Tpke. Assn., Kans. Restaurant Assn. (past pres., Restauranteur of Yr. 1973), Kans. Tourism and Travel Commn., Kans. Film Commn., Nat. Restaurant Assn. (dir. 1977—), Travel Industry Assn. Kans. (dir.), VFW (life), Salina C. of C. (past bd. dirs.), Am. Legion, Optimists, North Salina Lions Club, Elks, Moose, Eagles, Masons (knight commdr. Scottish rite 1994), Shriners.

VIE, RICHARD CARL, insurance company executive; Student, St. Louis U., U. Mo. With Reliable Life Ins. Co., St. Louis, 1962-79; pres. Commonwealth Life Ins. Co., St. Louis, 1979-82; pres., chmn. bd. dirs. United Ins. Co. Am., Chgo., 1983—90; sr. v.p., bd. dirs. Unitrin, Inc., Chgo., 1990-92, pres., CEO, 1992—99, chmn., pres., CEO, 1999—2006, chmn., 2006—. Chmn. Life Insurers Conf., 1994; trustee Life Underwriters Tng. Coun. Bd. dirs. Concordia U. Found., 1985-94, Valparaiso U., 1995—. Lt. USN, 1958-62. Mem. The Racquet Club St. Louis, Execs. Club Chgo. Office: Unitrin Inc 1 E Wacker Dr Chicago IL 60601-1802

VIERLING, H. PHILIP, medical device company executive; With Empi, Inc., St. Paul, 1986—, v.p., officer, 1997-99, pres., COO, 1999—. Office: 599 Cardigan Rd PO Box 26500 Saint Paul MN 55126-4099

VIETOR, HAROLD DUANE, federal judge; b. Parkersburg, Iowa, Dec. 29, 1931; s. Harold Howard and Alma Johanna (Kreimeyer) V. BA, U. Iowa, 1955, JD, 1958. Bar: Iowa 1958. Law clk. U.S. Ct. Appeals 8th Circuit, 1958-59; ptnr. Bleakley Law Offices, Cedar Rapids, Iowa, 1959-65; judge Iowa Dist. Ct., Cedar Rapids, 1965-79, chief judge, 1970-79; U.S. dist. judge U.S. Dist. Ct. for So. Dist. Iowa, Des Moines, 1979-96, chief judge, 1985-92, sr. U.S. dist. judge, 1997—. Lectr. at law schs., legal seminars U.S. and Japan. Contbr. articles to profl. jours. in U.S. and Japan. Served with USN, 1952-54. Mem. Iowa Bar Assn. (pres. jr. sect. 1966-67), Iowa Judges Assn. (pres. 1975-76), 8th Cir. Dist. Judges Assn. (pres. 1986-88). Office: US Dist Ct 485 US Courthouse 123 E Walnut St Des Moines IA 50309-2035

VIETS, HERMANN, academic administrator, consultant; b. Quedlinburg, Fed. Republic Germany, Jan. 28, 1943; came to U.S., 1949, naturalized, 1961; s. Hans and Herta (Heik) V.; m. Pamela Deane, June 30, 1968; children: Danielle, Deane, Hans, Hillary BS, Polytech. U., 1965, MS, 1966, PhD, 1970. Fellow von Karman Inst., Brussels, 1969-70; group leader Wright-Patterson AFB, Dayton, Ohio, 1970-76; prof. Wright State U., Dayton, Ohio, 1976-81; assoc. dean W.Va. U., Morgantown, 1981-83; dean U. R.I., Kingston, 1983-91; pres. Milw. Sch. Engring., 1991—. Chmn. bd. dirs. Precision Stampings, Inc., Beaumont, Calif., 1977—; bd. dirs. Gehl Co., West Bend, Wis., Astro Med, Inc., West Warwick, R.I., Wenthe-Davidson Engring. Co., New Berlin, Wis., Max Kade Inst. for German-Am. Studies, Discovery World, Milw. County Rsch. Park Corp.; cons. USAF Aero Propulsion Lab., Dayton, 1976-80, Covington & Burling, Washington, 1976-77; cons. in field. Patentee in aero. field; contbr. numerous articles to profl. jours. Mem. Greater Milw. Com.; dir. Competitive Wis., Gov. Regional H.S. Excellence Co., 1994, Gov.'s Export Strategy Commn., 1994; trustee Pub. Policy Forum. Recipient Tech. Achievement award USAF, 1974, Sci. Achievement award, 1975, Gov.'s Sci. and Tech. award State of R.I., 1987, Goodrich Pub. Svc. award, 1990, Citation R.I. Legislature, 1987, 90, 91, Outstanding Alumnus award aerospace engring. dept. Poly. U., 1994; Disting. Alumnus Poly. U., 1995, Engr. of Yr. award Engrs. and Scientists of Milw., 1997; named Hon. Citizen Fachhochschule Luebeck, Germany, 1998; postdoctoral fellow NATO, 1969-70, NASA, 1965-69. Fellow AIAA (assoc., acad. affairs com. 1998—, Best Tech. Paper award Allegheny-Pitts. sect. 1982); mem. German Assn. for Luft and Raumfahrt, German-Am. Heritage Soc. (bd. dirs.), Nat. Assn. Independent Coll. and Univ. (bd. dirs.), Am. Soc. Engring. Edn., Japan-Am. Soc. (bd. dirs. 1994), Soc. Mfg. Engrs., Rotary, Sigma Xi, Phi Kappa Phi, Tau Beta Pi, Sigma Gamma Tau. Avocations: antique automobiles, beer steins, notgeld currency. Home: 4216 N Lake Dr Milwaukee WI 53211-1722 Office: Milw Sch Engring 1025 N Broadway Milwaukee WI 53202-3109

VIETS, ROBERT O., utilities executive; b. Girard, Kans., Dec. 8, 1943; s. Willard O. and Caroline L. (Bollwinkel) V.; m. Karen M. Kreiter, June 13, 1980. BA in Econs., Washburn U., 1965; JD, Washington U., 1969. Bar: Kans. 1966, Mo. 1969, Ill. 1975; CPA, Kans. Auditor Arthur Andersen & Co., St. Louis, 1969-73; mgr. spl. studies Cen. Ill. Light Co., Peoria, 1973-76, mgr. rates and regulatory affairs, 1976-80, asst. v.p., regulatory affairs, 1980-81, v.p. fin. services, 1981-83, v.p. fin. group, 1983-86, sr. v.p., 1988—, Cilcorp, Inc., Peoria, 1986-88; pres., CEO Cilcorp, Inc. and Ctrl. Ill. Light Co., Peoria, 1988—. Bd. dirs. Consumers Water Co., Lincoln Office Supply, Inc., RLI Corp.; pres., CEO, chmn. bd. QST Enterprises, Inc., 1996—. Chmn. bd. dirs. Meth. Health Svcs., Inc.; trustee Bradley U. Mem. ABA, Ill. Bar Assn., Peoria County Bar Assn., AICPA, Ill. Soc. CPAs. Lodges: Rotary (bd. dirs. 1985—, pres. 1986-87). Republican. Lutheran. Avocation: golf. Home: 11305 N Pawnee Rd Peoria IL 61615-9796

VILIM, NANCY CATHERINE, advertising executive; b. Quincy, Mass., Jan. 15, 1952; d. John Robert and Rosemary (Malpede) V.; m. Geoffrey S. Horner, Feb. 16, 1992; children: Matthew Edward Cajda, Megan Catherine Cajda, Margaret Horner. Student, Miami U., Oxford, Ohio, 1970-72. Media asst. Draper Daniels, Inc., Chgo., 1972—74; asst. buyer Campbell Mithun, Chgo., 1974—75; buyer Tatham, Laird & Kudner, Chgo., 1975—77; media buyer Adcom, Inc. div. Quaker Oats Corp., Chgo., 1977—79; media supr. G.M. Feldman, Chgo., 1979—81; v.p. media dir. Media Mgmt., 1981—83; v.p. broadcast dir. Bozell, Jacobs, Kenyon & Eckhardt, Chgo., 1983—88; v.p., media mgr. McCann-Erickson, Inc., 1989—2002; broadcast supr. OMD USA, Chgo., 2002—04; sr. media buyer GSD&M, Chgo., 2004—05; media dir. Jordan, Ross & Rose, Northfield, Ill., 2005—. Judge 27th Internat. Broadcast Awards, Chgo., 1987. Co-pres. Immaculate Conception Religious Edn. Parents Club, 1995-96. Recipient Media All Star awards Sound Mgmt. Mag., N.Y.C., 1987. Mem. Broadcast Advt. Club Chgo., Mus. Broadcast Communications, NAFE. Office: JRR Advt 790 Frontage Rd Northfield IL 60093

VILLALPANDO, JESSE MICHAEL, state legislator; b. East Chicago, Ind., July 4, 1959; s. Jesse and Rose (Oria) V.; m. Elizabeth Villalpando. BA, Ind. U., 1981, JD, 1984. Bar: Ind. 1984. Atty. Lesniak & Ruff, East Chicago; mem. from 12th dist. Ind. State Ho. of Reps., 1982—. Co-chmn. cts. com.; mem. criminal code, ins. and corps. com., judiciary com., pub. safety com., pub. policy com., ethcis com., vets. affairs com. Named to Ind. State AFL-CIO Honor Roll, 1984. Mem. Ind. State Bar Assn., Griffith Dem. Club, Hammond FDR Club, South Hammond Dem. Club, Mutualista of Gary, Phi Delta Theta. Home: 956 N Griffith Blvd Griffith IN 46319-1514 Office: Ind Ho of Reps State Capitol Indianapolis IN 46204

VILLARS, HORACE SUMNER, retired food company executive, marketing professional; b. San Francisco, Mar. 15, 1931; s. Horace Sumner and Alice Emily (Stacy) V.; m. Patricia Ann Adams, June 15, 1951; children: Rebecca, Thomas, Constance, Laura, Russell. BS, Northwestern U., 1952. With Armour Co., Chgo., 1952-54, Durkee Foods, Chgo., 1954-65; mgr. indsl. sales McCormick & Co., Balt., 1965-68; exec. v.p. Kraft Sesame Corp., Paris, Tex., 1968-71; pres. Food Ingredients, Inc., Elk Grove, Ill., 1971-99. Chmn. Sycamore Foods, Inc., Elk Grove, 1987—. Contbg. author: Encyclopedia of Food Technology, 1974, Elements of Food Technology, 1977. Mem. Inst. Food Technologists (exec. com. Chgo. sect. 1974—), Am. Assn. Cereal Chemists, Am. Oil Chemists Soc., Am. Assn. Candy Technologists (chmn. Chgo. sect. 1964-65), Am. Soc. Bakery Engrs. Republican. Avocations: golf, swimming, photography, travel. Home: 820 Acorn Dr Dundee IL 60118-2659

VILLWOCK, DON, farmer, farming association executive; m. Joyce Villwock; children: Sarah, Betsy. Degree in agrl. econs., Purdue U. Farmer; v.p. Ind. Farm Bur, 1998—, Farm Bur. Ins. Cos. Dist. dir., Knox County pres., chmn. state young farmer com., chmn. feed grains com. Ind. Farm Bur., mem. farm bill task force, farm credit task force; mem. feed grains, grain quality, farm credit coms. Am. Farm Bur. Fedn.; state exec. dir. Agrl. Stabilization and Conservation Svc., 1989—93; state agrl. liaison Sen. Richard Lugar; mem. Commn. on 21st Century Prodn. Agr., 1997. Leader 4-H; mem. Purdue Disting. Agrl. Alumnus. amed Sagamore of the Wabash, Friend of Extension. Mem.: Ind. Inst. Agr. (chmn.), Ind. Pork Producers, Ind. Soybean Growers, Ind. Corn Growers. Office: Ind Farm Bur Inc PO Box 1290 Indianapolis IN 46206

VILSACK, TOM (THOMAS JAMES), former governor; b. Pitts., Dec. 31, 1950; adopted s. Bud and Dolly Vilsack; m. Ann Christine Bell, Aug. 1973; children: Jess, Doug. BA in History, Hamilton Coll., Clinton, NY, 1972; JD, Albany Law Sch., 1975. Pvt. practice, Mt. Pleasant, Iowa, 1975—87; mayor City of Mt. Pleasant, Iowa, 1987—92; mem. Iowa State Senate, Des Moines, 1992-98; gov. State of Iowa, Des Moines, 1999—2007; announced bid for US President in 2008; dropped out of 2008 US President bid for fin. reasons on Feb. 23, 2007. Chmn. Midwest Gov. Conf., Dem. Gov. Assn.; mem. Nat. Gov. Assn. (exec. com.); vis. prof. Drake U., 2007—; bd. dir. Carnegie Learning Inc., 2007—. Founding mem. & former chmn. Governors Biotechnology Partnership; former chmn. Ethanol Coalition; bd. dir. United Way, Mt. Pleasant; former chmn. Midwest Governor's Conference. Mem. Mt. Pleasant C. of C. (pres.), Rotary (pres.). Democrat.*

VINCENT, CHARLES EAGAR, JR., sportswriter; b. Beaumont, Tex., Mar. 24, 1940; s. Charles Eagar and Hazel Ruth (Balston) V.; m. Mary Jacquelyn Bertman, Aug. 8, 1959 (div. Jan. 1969); children: Lisa Marie, Dixie Ann, Charles Joseph, John Patrick; m. Patricia Helene Skinner, Mar. 28, 1970 (div. Apr. 1985); 1 child, Susanna Lee; m. Karen Judith Peterson, Aug. 17, 1985. Student, Victoria Coll., 1958-59. Reporter Victoria (Tex.) Mirror, 1958-59, Taylor (Tex.) Daily Press, 1959-60; sports writer Beaumont (Tex.) Jour., 1960-62; sports editor Galveston (Tex.) Tribune, 1962-63; sports writer San Antonio Express-News, 1963-69, Sandusky (Ohio) Register, 1969-70, Detroit Free Press, 1970-85, sports columnist, 1985-99. Author: Welcome to My World, 1994, Broken Wings, 1998, Men of Courage; Women of Strength, 2004; co-author: (with Richard Bak) The Corner, A Century of Memories at Michigan and Trumbull, 1999. Recipient 4th Pl. award Nat. AP Sports Editors, 1981, 5th Pl., 1989, 92, Sister Mary Leila Meml. award, 1991, Mich. Columnist of Yr. award, 1991, 97; Afro-Am. Night honoree, 1991, Mich. Writer of the Yr. Nat. Sportscasters and Sportswriters, 1998. Mem.: Baseball Writers Assn. Am. Avocations: travel, cooking, genealogy. Personal E-mail: Vincentcharlie@hotmail.com.

VINCENT, FREDERICK MICHAEL, SR., neurologist, educator; b. Detroit, Nov. 19, 1948; s. George S. and Alyce M. (Borkowski) Vincent; m. Patricia Lucille Cordes, Oct. 7, 1972; children: Frederick Michael Jr., Joshua Peter, Melissa Anne. BS in Biology, Aquinas Coll., 1970; MD, Mich. State U., 1973. Cert. in neurology Am. Bd. Psychiatry and Neurology, 1979, Am. Bd. Electrodiagnostic Medicine, 1992, Am. Bd. Forensic Examiners, 1996, Am. Bd. Forensic Medicine, 1996, in neurology with subspecialty of clin. neurophysiology Am. Bd. Psychiatry and Neurology, 1996. Intern St. Luke's Hosp., Duluth, Minn., 1974; resident in neurology Dartmouth Med. Sch., Hanover, NH, 1975—77, instr. dept. medicine, chief resident neurology, 1977—78; chief neurology sect. Munson Med. Ctr., Traverse City, Mich., 1978—84; asst. clin. prof. medicine and pathology Mich. State U., East Lansing, 1978—84, chief sect. neurology Coll. Human Medicine, 1984—87, clin. prof. psychiatry and internal medicine, 1989—2004, clin. prof. medicine, 1990—, clin. prof. neurology and ophthalmology, 2001—; pvt. practice Lansing, Mich., 1987—. Clin. and rsch. fellow neuro-oncology Mass. Gen. Hosp., Boston, 1985; clin. fellow in neurology Harvard Med. Sch., Boston, 1985; cons. med. asst. program Northwestern Mich. Coll., Traverse City, 1983—84; neurology cons. radio call-in show Sta. WKAR, East Lansing, 1984—2000, Sta. WCMU-TV, 1987, 1993—. Author: (book) Neurology: Problems in Primary Care, 1987, 2d edit., 1993; contbr. articles to profl. jours. Fellow, NSF, 1969, Nat. Multiple Sclerosis Soc., 1971. Fellow: ACP, Am. Bd. Legal Medicine, Am. Assn. Neuromuscular and Electrodiagnostic Medicine (computer electronics com. 1995—98, profl. practice com. 1999—2000, practice rev. panel 2000—03), Am. Acad. Neurology (program accreditation devel. subcom. 1993—2001), Am. Bd. Forensic Examiners, Am. Heart Assn.; mem.: Am. Coll. Legal Medicine, Am. Coll. Physician Exec., Soc. for Neuro-Oncology, Movement Disorders Soc., Am. Clin. Neurophysiology Soc., Inuit Art Soc., Univ. Club, Alpha Omega Alpha. Independent. Roman Catholic. Avocations: art, fishing. Office: 1515 Lake Lansing Rd Ste F1 Lansing MI 48912-3752 Office Phone: 517-374-1055. Business E-Mail: vincen11@msu.edu.

VINCENT, JIM, performing company executive; b. NJ; m. France Nguyen; children: Lena, Claire, June. Studied at, Wash. Sch. of Ballet, Harkness House of Ballet, .C. Sch. of the Arts. Profl. dancer Jim Kylian's Nederlands Dans Theater, Nacho Duato's Compania Nacional de Danza in Spain; asst. artistic dir. Compania acional de Danza, 1990—94; concept designer, show dir. Disneyland Paris, 1997; artistic dir. Hubbard St. Dance Chgo., 2000—. Ballet master Nederlands Dans Theater II, Compa a Nacional de Danza, Opera National de Lyon. Office: Hubbard Street Dance Chgo 1147 W Jackson Blvd Chicago IL 60607

VINCI, JOHN NICHOLAS, architect, educator; b. Chgo., Feb. 6, 1937; s. Nicholas and Nicolina (Camiola) V. B.Arch., Ill. Inst. Tech., 1960. Registered architect, Ill., Mo., Mich., Pa., NCARB. Draftsman Skidmore, Owings, Merrill, Chgo., 1960-61; with City of Chgo., 1961; stencil restorer Crombie Taylor, Chgo., 1961-62; designer Brenner, Danforth, Rockwell, Chgo., 1962-68; architect Vinci, Inc., Chgo., 1977-95; ptnr. Vinci/Hamp, Architects, Inc., Chgo., 1995—; lectr. Roosevelt U., Chgo., 1969-72, Ill. Inst. Tech., Chgo., 1972-90, adj. prof., 1999. Author: (booklet) Trading Room-Art Inst. Chgo., 1977; contr. articles to profl. jours.; exhbn. designer. Bd. dirs. Music of Baroque, Chgo., 1976—87, Mies Van Der Rohe Soc., 2003—; mem. adv. com. Commn. on Chgo. Archtl. and Hist. Landmarks, 1971—83, Millennium Pk., Chgo., 2000—; exec. sec. Richard Nickel Com., Chgo., 1972—; chmn. Howard Van Doren Shaw Soc., 1994—2001; mem. Friends of the Farnsworth Ho., 2001—, Landmark Preservation of Ill. Fellow AIA; mem. Soc. Archtl. Historians, Frank Lloyd Wright Home and Studio Found., Art Inst. Chgo., The Corp. of YADDO, Chgo. Hist. Soc., Arts Club of Chgo. Roman Catholic. Home: 3152 N Cambridge Ave Chicago IL 60657-4613 Office: Vinci/Hamp Architects Inc 1147 W Ohio St Chicago IL 60622-6472

VINEYARD, JERRY D., geologist; b. Dixon, Mo., Mar. 26, 1935; s. Henry and Bessie Florence (Geisler) V.; m. Helen Louise Anderson, Nov. 24, 1960; children: Monica Lynne, Vanessa Anne. BA, U. Mo., 1960, MA, 1963. Registered profl. geologist, Ark., Mo. Lectr. in geology and geography Kansas City (Mo.) Met. Coll., 1961-63; chief publs. and info. Mo. Geol. Survey, Rolla, 1963-79; asst. state geologist Mo. Dept. Natural Resources, Rolla, 1979-89, dep. state geologist, 1989-98, interstate rivers dir., 1998—. Mem. adv. bd. U. Mo., Columbia, 1982-91. Author: Springs of Missouri, 1978; co-author: Geologic Wonders and Curiosities of Missouri, 1990, Missouri Geology, 1992. Lt. (j.g.) USN, 1958-60. Fellow Cave Rsch. Found., 1998. Fellow Geol. Soc. Am. (Disting. Hydrogeologist 1989); mem. Nat. Speleological Soc. (hon. life mem., bd. dirs., editor jour. 1973), Mo. Speleological Soc. (hon. life mem., founder 1955—), Mo. Acad. Sci. (pres. 1996), Sigma Xi (pres. Mo. chpt. 1974). Baptist. Avocations: photography, woodworking, singing. Office: 111 Fairgrounds Rd Rolla MO 65401-2909 Home: 1113 N 19th Ave Ozark MO 65721-6730 E-mail: nrvinej@mail.dnr.state.mo.us.

VINH, NGUYEN XUAN, aerospace engineering educator; b. Yen Bay, Vietnam, Jan. 3, 1930; came to U.S., 1962; s. Nguyen X. and Thao (Do) Nhien; m. Joan Cung, Aug. 15, 1955; children: Alphonse, Phuong, Phoenix, John. PhD in Aerospace Engring., U. Colo., 1965; DSc in Math., U. Paris VI, 1972. Asst. prof. aerospace engring. U. Colo., Boulder, 1965-68; assoc. prof. aerospace engring. U. Mich., Ann Arbor, 1968-72, prof. aerospace engring., 1972—. Vis. lectr. U. Calif., Berkeley, 1967; vis. prof. ecol. nat. sup. aero., France, 1974; chair prof. Nat Tsing Hua U., Taiwan, 1982. Co-author: Hypersonic and Planetary Entry Flight Mechanics, 1980; author: Optimal Trajectories in Atmospheric Flight, 1981, Flight Mechanics of High Performance Aircraft, 1993. Chief of staff Vietnam Air Force, 1957-62. Recipient Mechanics and Control of Flight award AIAA, 1994, Excellence 2000 award USPAACC, 1996. Mem. Internat. Acad. Astronautics, Nat. Acad. Air and Space (France). Achievements include research in ordinary differential equations; astrodynamics and optimization of space flight trajectories; theory of non-linear oscillations. Office: U Mich Dept Aerospace Engring 3001 FXB Bldg Ann Arbor MI 48109-2140

VINING, (GEORGE) JOSEPH, law educator; b. Fulton, Mo., Mar. 3, 1938; s. D. Rutledge and Margaret (McClanahan) V.; m. Alice Marshall Williams, Sept. 18, 1965; children: George Joseph IV, Spencer Carter. BA, Yale U., 1959, Cambridge U., 1961, MA, 1970; JD, Harvard U., 1964. Bar: DC 1965. Atty. Office Dep. Atty. Gen., Dept. Justice, Washington, 1965; asst. to exec. dir. Nat. Crime Commn., 1966; assoc. Covington and Burling, Washington, 1966-69; asst. prof. law U. Mich., 1969-72, assoc. prof., 1972-74, prof., 1974-85, Hutchins prof., 1985—. Sir Edward Youde prof., Hong Kong, 2002. Author: Legal Identity, 1978, The Authoritative and the Authoritarian, 1986, From Newton's Sleep, 1995, The Song Sparrow and the Child, 2004. NEH sr. fellow,

1982-83, Bellagio fellow Rockfeller Found., 1997. Fellow Am. Acad. Arts and Scis.; mem. ABA, D.C. Bar Assn., Am. Law Inst. (life), Century Assn., Clare Hall Cambridge U. (life). Office: U Mich 964 Legal Rsch Ann Arbor MI 48109-1215

VINSON, JAMES SPANGLER, academic administrator; b. Chambersburg, Pa., May 17, 1941; s. Wilbur S. and Anna M. (Spangler) V.; m. Susan Alexander, Apr. 8, 1967; children: Suzannah, Elizabeth. BA, Gettysburg Coll., 1963; MS, U. Va., 1965, PhD, 1967. Asst. prof. physics MacMurray Coll., Jacksonville, Ill., 1967-71; assoc. prof. physics U. N.C., Asheville, 1971-78, prof. physics, 1974-78, chmn. dept. physics, dir. acad. computing, 1974-78; prof. physics, dean Coll. Arts and Scis. U. Hartford (Conn.), 1978-83; v.p. acad. affairs Trinity U., San Antonio, 1983-87; pres. U. Evansville, Ind., 1987-2001, pres. emeritus Ind., 2001—; pres. Nat. Sci. Ctr. Found., Augusta, Ga., 2002—. Computer cons. Contbr. articles to profl. jours. Mem. Am. Phys. Soc., World Future Soc., AAAS, Am. Assn. for Advancement of Humanities, Am. Assn. for Higher Edn., Am. Assn. Physics Tchrs., Phi Beta Kappa, Sigma Xi, Phi Sigma Kappa. Methodist. Office Phone: 706-868-3600.

VIOLA, DONN J., manufacturing executive; b. Pa. BSME, Lehigh U. With Volkswagen, Masco Industries; sr. exec. v.p., COO, bd. dirs. Mack Trucks, Inc.; COO N.Am. Donnelly Corp., Holland, Mich., 1996-2001, COO, 2001—. Office: Donnelly Corp 49 W 3d St Holland MI 49423

VIRANT, PAUL, chef; b. 1970; m. Jennifer Virant; 1 child, Lincoln. Degree in Nutrition, Wesleyan Coll.; grad., Culinary Inst. Am., Hyde Park, NY. With Cascade Mountain Winery; chef March, NYC, Charlie Trotter's, Ambria, Padovani's Bistro and Wine Bar, Honolulu, Everest, Chgo., Outpost, Chgo., Blackbird, Chgo.; owner, exec. chef Vie, Western Springs, Ill. Named Best New Chef, Chgo. Mag., 2005, Rising Star Chef, Restaurant Hospitality Mag., 2005, StarChefs.com, 2005, 2006 Jean Banchet Rising Star Chef, Best New Chef, Food & Wine Mag., 2007. Office: Vie 4471 Lawn Ave Western Springs IL 60558 Office Phone: 708-246-2082. Office Fax: 708-246-2668.

VIRGO, JOHN MICHAEL, economist, researcher, educator; b. Prestbury Village, Eng., Mar. 11, 1943; s. John Joseph and Muriel Agnes (Franks) V.; m. Katherine Sue Ulmrich, Sept. 6, 1980; 1 child, Debra Marie Riekstins. BA, Calif. State U., Fullerton, 1967, MA, 1969, Claremont Grad. U., 1971, PhD, 1972. Instr. econs. Whittier (Calif.) Coll., 1970-71, Calif. State U., Fullerton and Long Beach, 1971-72, Claremont (Calif.) Grad. Sch., 1971-72; asst. prof. econs. Va. Commonwealth U., Richmond, 1972-74; assoc. prof. mgmt. So. Ill. U., Edwardsville, 1975-83, prof., 1984—. Bd. dirs., founder Internat. Health Econ. & Mgmt. Inst., Edwardsville, 1983-87. Author: Legal & Illegal California Farmworkers, 1974; author, editor: Health Care: An International Perspective, 1984, Exploring New Vistas in Health Care, 1985, Restructuring Health Policy, 1986; founder, editor-in-chief Internat. Advances in Econ. Rsch.; contbr. articles to profl. jours. Served with USN, 1965-68. Mem. AMA, Am. Econ. Assn., Am. Soc. Assn. Execs., Internat. Atlantic Econ. Soc. (founder, exec. v.p., mng. editor Atlantic Econ. jour. 1973—), European Econ. Assn., Allied Social Scis. Assn. (chmn. exec. confs. 1982-84), Western Econs. Assn., Western Econ. Assn., So. Econs. Assn., Media Club (St. Louis). Democrat. Roman Catholic. Avocations: tennis, skiing. Home: 5277 Lindell Blvd Saint Louis MO 63108-1223 Office: Internat Atlantic Econ Soc 2nd Fl 4949 W Pine Blvd Saint Louis MO 63108-1431 Office Phone: 314-454-0100. Business E-Mail: iaes@iaes.org.

VIRTEL, JAMES JOHN, lawyer; b. Joliet, Ill., May 15, 1944; BA cum laude, Loras Coll., 1966; JD cum laude, St. Louis U., 1969. Bar: Mo. 1969, Ill. 1969. Atty. Armstrong Teasdale LLP, St. Louis, 1976—. Adj. prof. law St. Louis U., 1995-99; regent Loras Coll., Dubuque, Iowa, 1996—. Editor: St. Louis U. Law Jour., 1968-69. Fellow Am. Coll. Trial Lawyers; mem. Ill. State Bar Assn., Mo. State Bar Assn. Office: Armstrong Teasdale LLP 1 Metropolitan Sq Ste 2600 Saint Louis MO 63102-2740 Office Phone: 314-342-8088. Personal E-mail: jvirtel@sbcglobal.net. E-mail: jvirtel@armstrongteasdale.com.

VISCHER, HAROLD HARRY, manufacturing executive; b. Toledo, Oct. 17, 1914; s. Harry Philip and Hazel May (Patterson) V.; m. DeNell Meyers, Feb. 18, 1938; children: Harold Harry, Robert P., Michael L. BBA, U. Toledo, 1937. With Ohio Bell Telephone Co., 1937-38; with Firestone Tire & Rubber Co., Toledo, 1948-61, nat. passenger tire sales mgr., 1953-57, dist. mgr., 1957-61; with Bandag Inc., Muscatine, Iowa, 1961-80; exec. v.p., pres. Bandag Inc. (Rubber and Equipment Sales group), 1975-80; also dir.; pres., gen. mgr. Hardline Internat., Inc., Jackson, Mich., 1980-82; chmn. Tred-X Corp., 1982—. Mem. City Council, Muscatine, 1964-76; chmn., mem. Dist. Export Council Iowa, 1964-81; chmn. Muscatine United Way, 1969-70; mem. adv. bd. Engring. Coll. Iowa State U., 1970-81; mem. Muscatine Light & Water Bd., 1979-80. Elected to Nat. Tire Dealers and Retreaders Assn. Hall of Fame, 1988, to Internat. Tire Retreading and Repairing Hall of Fame, 1990. Mem. Nat. Tire and Retreaders Suppliers Group Assn. (chmn. 1979-80, exec. com. 1977-80), Tire Retread Info. Bur. (exec. com. 1974-81), Am. Retreading Assn. (adv. bd. 1970-72), Retreading Industry Assn., Industry Man of Yr. 1979), Christian Business men's Com., Gideons. Republican. Home: 13500 Vischer Rd Brooklyn MI 49230-9022

VISCLOSKY, PETER JOHN, congressman, lawyer; b. Gary, Ind., Aug. 13, 1949; s. John and Helen (Kauzlaric) Visclosky; m. Anne Marie O'Keefe; children: John, Timothy. BS in acctg., Ind. U., Indpls., 1970; JD, U. Notre Dame, 1973; LLM in internat. and comparative law, Georgetown U., 1983. Bar: Ind., D.C., U.S. Supreme Ct. Legal asst. Dist. Atty.'s Office, NYC, 1972; assoc. Benjamin, Greco & Gouveia, Merrillville, Ind., 1973-76, Greco, Gouveia, Miller, Pera & Bishop, Merrillville, Ind., 1982-84; assoc. staff appropriations com. US Ho. Reps., Washington, 1976-80, assoc. staff budget com., 1980-82; mem. US Congress from 1st Ind. dist., 1985—; mem. appropriations com., subcoms. treasury, postal svc., gen. govt. and military constrn. Democrat. Roman Catholic. Office: US Ho Reps 2256 Rayburn Ho Office Bldg Washington DC 20515-1401 also: Dist Office Ste 9 701 E 83d Ave Merrillville IN 46410

VISEK, WILLARD JAMES, nutritionist, animal scientist, physician, educator; b. Sargent, Nebr., Sept. 19, 1922; s. James and Anna S. (Dworak) V.; m. Priscilla Flagg, Dec. 28, 1949; children: Dianna, Madeleine, Clayton Paul. B.Sc. with honors (Carl R. Gray scholar), U. Nebr., 1947; MSc (Smith fellow in agr.), Cornell U., 1949, PhD, 1951; MD (Peter Yost Fund scholar), U. Chgo., 1957; DSc (hon.), U. Nebr., 1980. Diplomate Nat. Bd. Med. Examiners. Grad. asst., lab. animal nutrition Cornell U., 1947-51; AEC postdoctoral fellow Oak Ridge, 1951-52; research assoc., 1952-53; research asst. pharmacology U. Chgo., 1953-57, asst. prof., 1957-61, assoc. prof., 1961-64; rotating med. intern U. Chgo. Clinics, 1957-58, 58-59, 59; prof. nutrition and comparative metabolism, dept. animal sci. Cornell U., Ithaca, NY, 1964-75; prof. clin. sci. (nutrition and metabolism) Coll. Medicine and dept. food sci. U. Ill. Coll. Agr., Urbana-Champaign, 1975—; prof. dept. internal medicine U. Ill. Coll. Medicine, Urbana-Champaign, 1986-93, prof. emeritus, 1993—. Bd. dirs. Coun. Agricul-ture, Sci. and Tech., 1994-97; bd. sci. advisors Coun. Sci. and Health, 1994—; Brittingham vis. prof. U. Wis. Madison, 1982-83; Hogan meml. lectr. U. Mo., 1987; mem. subcom. dog nutrition com. animal nutrition NRC-Nat. Acad. Sci., 1965-71; adv. coun. Inst. Lab. Animal Resources, NRC-Nat. Acad. Sci., 1966-69; sub-com. animal care faciltities Survey Inst. Lab. Animal Resources, 1967-70; cons., lectr. in field; mem. sci. adv. com. diet and nutrition cancer program Nat. Cancer Inst., 1976-81; mem. nutrition study sect. NIH, 1980-84; chmn. membership com. Am. Inst. Nutrition-Am. Soc. Clin. Nutrition, 1978-79, 80-83, 85; cons. VA, NSF, indsl. orgns.; Wellcome vis. prof. in basic med. scis. Oreg. State U., 1991-92; bd. sci. counselors USDA, 1989-91. Mem. editl. bd. Jour. utrition, 1980-84, editor, 1990-97; mem. editl. bd. Physiol. Rev., 1995-2001; contbr. articles to profl. jours. Bd. dirs. Coun. for Agrl. Sci. and Tech., 1994-97; active local Boy Scouts Am. Served with AUS, 1943-46. Recipient alumni award Nebr. 4-H, 1967, 97, alumni award U. Chgo., 1997, faculty merit award U. Ill. Coll. Medicine, 1988, Alumni Achievement award U. Nebr., 1997, U. Chgo., 1997; Nat. Cancer Inst. spl. fellow MIT, rsch. fellow Mass. Gen. Hosp., 1970-71; sr. scholar U. Ill., 1988. Fellow AAAS, Am. Inst. Nutrition (Osborne and Mendel award 1985), Am. Soc. Animal Sci. (chmn. subcom. antimicrobials, mem. regulatory agency com. 1973-78); mem. Am. Physiol. Soc., Soc. Pharmacology and Exptl. Therapeutics, Am. Inst. Nutrition (council 1980-83, 85-86), Soc. Exptl. Biology and Medicine, Am. Soc. Clin. Nutrition, Am. Therapeutic Soc., Am. Gastroenterol. Assn., Am. Bd. Clin. Nutrition, Innocents Soc., Fedn. Am. Socs. Exptl. Biology (sci. steering group life scis. rsch. office, adv. com. 1986-92), Am. Bd. Nutrition (bd. dirs.), Am. Soc. utritional Scis. (Conrad Elvehjem award 1996), Nat. Dairy Coun. (rsch. adv. com. 1987-91, vis. prof. nutrition program 1981-92), Gamma Alpha (pres. 1948-49), Phi Kappa Phi (pres. 1981-82), Alpha Gamma Rho (pres. 1946-47), Gamma Sigma Delta. Presbyterian (elder). Home: 1405 W William St Champaign IL 61821-4406 Office: U Ill 190 Med Sci Bldg 506 S Mathews Ave Urbana IL 61801-3618 Office Phone: 217-244-2797. Business E-Mail: wvisek@uiuc.edu.

VISKANTA, RAYMOND, mechanical engineering educator; b. Lithuania, July 16, 1931; came to U.S., 1949, naturalized, 1955; s. Vincas and Genovaite (Vinickas) V.; m. Birute Barbara Barpsys, Oct. 13, 1956; children: Renata, Vitas, Tadas. BSME, U. Ill., Champaign, 1955; MSME, Purdue U., West Lafayette, Ind., 1956, PhD, 1960, DEng (hon.), 2007, Tech. U. Munich, 1994. Registered profl. engr., Ill. Asst. mech. engr. Argonne (Ill.) Nat. Lab., 1956-59, student rsch. assoc., 1959-60, assoc. mech. engr., 1960-62; assoc. prof. mech. engring. Purdue U., West Lafayette, Ind., 1962-66, prof. mech. engring., 1966-86, Goss disting. prof. engring., 1986—. Guest prof. Tech. U. Munich, Germany, 1976-77, U. Karlsruhe, Germany, 1987; vis. prof. Tokyo Inst. Tech., 1983. Contbr. over 500 tech. articles to profl. jours. Recipient Sr. U.S. Scientist award Alexander von Humboldt Found., 1975, Sr. Rsch. award Am. Soc. Engring. Edn., 1984, usselt-Reynolds prize, 1991, Thermal Engring. award for Internat. Activity, Japan Soc. Mech. Engrs., 1994, Alumni award for Disting. Svc. U. Ill.-Urbana-Champaign, 2000, Stodola medal ETH, Zurich, 2007; Japan Soc. for Promotion of Sci. fellow, 1983. Fellow ASME (Heat Transfer Meml. award 1976, Max Jakob Meml. award 1986, Melville medal 1988), AIAA (Thermophysics award 1979); mem. AAAS, NAE, Acad. Engring. Scis. Russian Fedn. (fgn.), Lithuanian Acad. Scis. (fgn.), Sigma Xi, Pi Tau Sigma, Tau Beta Pi. Home: 3631 Chancellor Way West Lafayette IN 47906-8809 Office: Purdue Univ 585 Purdue Mall West Lafayette IN 47907-2088 Home Phone: 765-463-7816; Office Phone: 765-494-5632. Personal E-mail: rviskanta@insightbb.com. Business E-Mail: viskanta@ecn.purdue.edu.

VITITO, ROBERT J., bank executive; Mgmt. trainee Second Nat. Bank Saginaw, Mich., 1967, various Mich., 1967-86, pres. Mich., 1986; pres., chief adminstrv. officer Citizens Banking Corp., Flint, Mich., 1994-95, pres., CEO, 1995-99, chmn., 1999—. Office: Citizens Banking Corp 328 S Saginaw St Flint MI 48502-1943

VITTER, JEFFREY SCOTT, academic administrator, computer science educator, researcher; b. New Orleans, Nov. 13, 1955; s. Albert Leopold Jr. and Audrey Malvina (St. Raymond) V.; m. Sharon Louise Weaver, Aug. 14, 1982; children: Jillian St. Raymond, J. Scott Jr., Audrey Louise. BS in Math. with highest honors, U. Notre Dame, 1977; PhD in Computer Sci., Stanford U., 1980; AM (hon.), Brown U., 1986; MBA, Duke U., 2002. Asst. computer performance analyst Standard Oil Co. Calif., San Francisco, 1976—77; rsch. and tchg. asst. Stanford (Calif.) U., 1977—80, tchg. fellow, 1979; asst. prof. computer sci. Brown U., Providence, 1980—85, assoc. prof. computer sci., 1985—88, prof. computer sci., 1988—93; Gilbert, Louis and Edward Lehrman prof. computer sci. Duke U., Durham, NC, 1993—2002, chmn. dept., 1993—2001, co-dir. Ctr. for Geometric and Biol. Computing, 1997—2002; prof. computer sci. Purdue U., 2002—, Frederick L. Hovde dean Coll. of Science, 2002—. Cons. IBM, 1981-86, Inst. for Def. Analyses, 1986, Ctr. for Computing Scis., 1992—, Lucent Technologies, Bell Labs., 1997; mem. rsch. staff Math. Scis. Rsch. Inst., Berkeley, 1986, Inst. Recherche en Informatique et en Automatique, Roquencourt, France, 1986-87, Inst. Recherche en Informatique et en Automatique, Sophia Antipolis, France, 1998-1999; vis. prof. Ecole Normale Superieure, Paris, 1986-89; vis. and adj. prof. Tulane U., 1990-2006, mem. bd. advisors Sch. Sci. and Engring., 2006—; lectr. Asian Sch. on Computer Sci., Bangkok, 1987; assoc. mem. Ctr. Excellence in Space Data and Info. Scis. Author: The Design and Analysis of Coalesced Hashing, 1987, Efficient Algorithms for MPEG Video Compression, 2002; editor Algorithmica, 1994—, guest editor, 1988, 94; editor Math. Sys. Theory: Internat. Jour. on Math. Computing Theory, 1991—, Soc. for Indsl. and Applied Math. Jour. on Computing, 1989-1997, Algorithm Engineering, 1999, External Memory Algorithms, 1999; contbr. articles to profl. jours.; patentee in field. Recipient Faculty Devel. award IBM, 1984, NSF Presdl. Young Investigator award, 1985; NSF grad. fellow, 1977-80; Guggenheim fellow, N.Y.C., 1986-87. Fellow IEEE (editor Trans. on Computers 1985, 87-91), Assn. for Computing Machinery (editor Comms. 1988-95, Jour. Exptl. Algorithmics, 2000; mem.-at-large spl. interest group on automata and computability theory 1987-91, vice chair spl. interest group on algorithms and computation theory 1991-1997, chair 1997-2001, exec. com. 2001-05, Recognition of Svc. award 1997, 2001); mem. Computing Rsch. Assn. (bd. dirs. 2000-08, co-chair govt. affairs com. 2001-08), Phi Beta Kappa, Sigma Xi. Avocations: reading, golf, basketball, football, genealogy. Office: Purdue U Math Sciences Bldg 150 N University St West Lafayette IN 47907-2067 Office Phone: 765-494-1730. Business E-Mail: sciencedean@purdue.edu.

VIVERITO, LOUIS SAMUEL, state legislator; b. Chgo. m. Carolyn Strobl; children: Dean, Diane, Marianne. Mem. Ill. State Senate, 1995—. Mem. Stickney Twp. Dem. Com., 1969—; del. Dem. Nat. Conv., 1972; commr. Met. Sanitary Dist. Greater Chgo., 1980-86; mem. Cook County Zoning Bd. Appeals, 1987-95; local chmn. Chgo. Lung Assn., 1973—. Named Man of Yr., Joint Civic Com. Italian-Am., 1980; inductee Hall of Fame, Valentine Boys & Girls Club, 1987. Mem. VFW (life), Am. Legion (life), Burbank C. of C., Burbank Sertoma Club (founder).

VLCEK, DONALD JOSEPH, JR., food products executive, wholesale distribution executive, writer; b. Chgo., Oct. 30, 1949; s. Donald Joseph and Rosemarie (Krizek) V.; m. Claudia Germain Meyer, July 22, 1978 (div. 1983); 1 child, Suzanne Mae; m. Valeria Olive Russell, Nov. 11, 1989 (div. Mar. 2006); children: James Donald, Victoria Rose. BBA, U. Mich., 1971. Cert. facilitator Adizes Inst. Gen. mgr. Popps, Inc., Hamtramck, Mich., 1969-76; sr. v.p. Domino's Pizza Inc., 1978—93; pres. Domino's Pizza Distbn. Corp., Ann Arbor, Mich., 1978-93, chmn., 1993-94, also bd. dirs.; pres. Don Vlcek & Assocs., Ltd., Plymouth, Mich., 1994—; CEO Beaver Buddies, LLC, Plymouth, Mich., 2001—04; master franchisee Beaver Tails Can., Inc., Mich., Ind., Ill., Ohio, Wis.; pres. WonderPizzaUSA, 2005—07, bd. mgrs., 2005—07, COO, 2005—07; v.p. Marco's Franchising LLC, Toledo, 2007—. Profl. speaker, personal coach, seminar leader, bus. cons., workshop facilitator; trustee Domino's Pizza Ptnrs. Found.; bd. dirs. RPM Pizza Inc., Gulfport, Miss., Dimango Corp., South Lyon, Mich.; sr. v.p. distbn. and tech. Domino's Ohio Commissary, Zanesville; pres. Morel Mountain Corp.; judge 1994 Duck Stamp contest U.S. Dept. Interior, Jr. Fed. Duck Stamp Contest, 1995; bd. dirs. Beaver Tails Can. Author: The Domino Effect, 1992 (Best of Bus. award ALA 1992, Soundview's Top 30 Business books of 1993), SuperVision, 1997, Job Planning and Review System Manual, 1997, 2001; (audio cassette tape series Super Vision; contbr. articles to profl. jours. Bd. dirs. Men's Hockey League of Oak Park, Mich., 1973-78; asst. coach Redford Scorpions Jr. Travel Hockey Team. Named Person of Yr. Bd. Franchises, Boston, 1981; recipient Teal award Ducks Unltd., 1992, State Major Gifts Chmn. award, 1992, 93, State Chmn.'s award, 1992, State Major Gifts award, 1994, Russ Bengal award, 2003, Mr. Producer award, 1997, 98, 2000, others. Mem. Am. Soc. of Tng. Dirs., Mich. Steelheaders Assn. (life), Ducks Unltd. (life, Domino's Pizza chpt. treas., sponsor, chmn. 1988—, Mich. state bd. dirs., life sponsor, chmn. 1989, 91-92, state trustee 1992-98, hon. trustee 2001—, chmn. exec. com. 1992-94, major gifts chmn. 1993-98, chmn. strategic devel. com. 1994, sponsor in perpetuity Grand Slam Life, Heritage sponsor, recipient Russ Bengal award, 2003), Mich. United Conservation Club (life), Whitetails Unltd. (life), Pheasants Forever (life), Midstates Masters Bowling Assn. (bd. dirs. 1976-85), Barton Hills Country Club (golf com., capt. dist. team), U. Mich. Alumni Assn. (life), Domino's Lodge/Drummond Island Wildlife Habitat Found. (pres., chmn. bd.), Vlcek Family Wildlife Found. (pres., chmn. bd.), Elks (life), Die Hard Cubs Fan Club, Greater Detroit C. of C., Profl. Spkrs. Assn. of Mich. (bd. dirs. 1997-99), Mich. Soc. Assn. Execs., Sm. Bus. Assn. Mich., Nat. Spkrs. Assn., Profl. Spkrs. Ill. (profl.), Internat. Coaching Fedn. (cert. master), Am. Soc. Tng. Dirs., Bus. Network Profls. Republican. Roman Catholic. Avocations: hunting, fishing, hockey, art, coin collecting/numismatics. Home: 9251 Beck Rd N Plymouth MI 48170-3336 Office: Don Vlcek & Assoc Ltd PO Box 701353 Plymouth MI 48170-0963 Office Phone: 734-266-2260. Personal E-mail: vlcek2@aol.com.

VOELLGER, GARY A., business consulting executive, retired air force officer; BS in Indsl. Rels. Pers. Mgmt., San Jose State U., 1967; grad., Squadron Officer Sch., 1971; M in Psychology, Peperdine U., 1976; grad., Air Command Staff Coll., Maxwell AFB, 1979, Air War Coll., 1988; cert. in Joint Flag Officer War Fighting, Maxwell AFB, 1997; cert.in sr. mgrs. govt. seminar, Harvard U., 1997. Commd. 2d. lt. USAF, 1967, advanced through grades to maj. gen., 1996; pers. officer 379th Combat Support Grp., Wurtsmith AFB, Mich., 1967-69; undergrad. navigator trng. Mather AFB, Calif., 1969-69; weapons sys. officer 46th Tactical Fighter Squadron, MacDill AFB, Fla., 1970-70; weapons syss. officer 91st Tactical Fighter Squadron, Royal Air Force Bentwaters, Eng., 1970-72; undergrad. pilot tng. Laredo AFB, Tex., 1972; F-111 transition tng. Nellis AFB, Nev., 1973-73; F-111 pilot 428th Tactical Fighter Squadron, Takhli Royal AFB, Thailand, 1973-74; F-111 instr. pilot, flight comdr., standardization and evaluation flight examiner 523rd Tactical Fighter Squadron, 27th Tactical Fighter Wing, Cannon AFB, N.Mex., 1974-79; air ops. staff officer, politico-mil. affairs officer, asst. dep. dir. Joint Nat. Security Coun. Matters Hdqs. USAF, Washington, 1980-84; comdr. 55th Tactical Fighter Squadron, Royal Air Force, Upper Heyford, Eng., 1984-87; asst. dep. comdr. ops. 20th Tactical Fighter Wing, Royal Air Force; dep. comdr. ops. 4450th Tactical Group, Nellis AFB, Nev., 1988-89, vice comdr., 1989-90; comdr. 552nd Air Control Wing, Tinker AFB, Okla., 1990-92, Coll. Aerospace Doctrine, Rsch. and Edn., Air U., Maxwell AFB, Ala., 1992-93, 43rd Air Refueling Wing, Malmstrom AFB, Mont., 1993-94, 92nd Air Refueling Wing, Fairchild AFB, Wash., 1994-95, 437th Airlift Wing, Charleston AFB, S.C., 1995-96; dir. ops. Hdqs. Air Mobility Command, Scott AFB, Ill., 1996-98; NATO force comdr. Hdqs. NATO Airborne Early Warning Force, Mons, Belgium, 1998-2000; ret. USAF; prin. Booz Allen Hamilton, O'Fallon, Ill. Decorated D.D.S.M., Legion of Merit with oak leaf Cluster, Bronze Star medal, Meritorious Svc. medal with two oak leaf clusters, Air medal with oak leaf cluster, Armed Forces Expeditionary medal, Rep. Vietnam Gallantry Cross with Palm. Office: Booz Allen & Hamilton Inc 1728 Corporate Crossing Ste 2 O Fallon IL 62269 Office Phone: 618-622-2333. Business E-Mail: voellger_gary@bah.com.

VOGEL, ARTHUR ANTON, clergyman; b. Milw., Feb. 24, 1924; s. Arthur Louis and Gladys Eirene (Larson) V.; m. Katharine Louise Nunn, Dec. 29, 1947; children: John Nunn, Arthur Anton, Katharine Ann. Student, U. of South, 1942-43, Carroll Coll., 1943-44; B.D., Nashotah House Theol. Sem., 1946; MA, U. Chgo., 1948; PhD, Harvard, 1952; S.T.D., Gen. Theol. Sem., 1969; D.C.L., Nashotah House, 1969; D.D., U. of South, 1971. Ordained deacon Episcopal Ch., 1946, priest, 1948; teaching asst. philosophy Harvard, Cambridge, Mass., 1949-50; instr. Trinity Coll., Hartford, Conn., 1950-52; mem. faculty Nashotah House Theol. Sem., ashotah, Wis., 1952-71, asso. prof., 1954-56, William Adams prof. philosophical and systematic theology, 1956-71, sub-dean Sem., 1964-71; bishop coadjutor Diocese of West Mo., Kansas City, 1971-72, bishop, 1972-89; rector Ch. St. John Chrysostom, Delafield, Wis., 1952-56; dir. Anglican Theol. Rev., Evanston, Ill., 1964-69; mem. Internat. Anglican-Roman Cath. Consultation, 1970-90, Nat. Anglican-Roman Catholic Consultation, 1965-84, Anglican chmn., 1973-84; mem. Standing Commn. on Ecumenical Relations of Episcopal Ch., 1957-79; mem. gen. bd. examining chaplains Episcopal Ch., 1971-72. Del. Episcopal Ch., 4th Assembly World Council Chruches, Uppsala, Sweden, 1968, and others. Author: Reality, Reason and Religion, 1957, The Gift of Grace, 1958, The Christian Person, 1963, The Next Christian Epoch, 1966, Is the Last Supper Finished?, 1968, Body Theology, 1973, The Power of His Resurrection, 1976, Proclamation 2: Easter, 1980, The Jesus Prayer for Today, 1982, I Know God Better Than I Know Myself, 1989, Christ in His Time and Ours, 1982, God, Prayer and Healing, 1995, Radical Christianity and the Flesh of Jesus, 1995; editor: Theology in Anglicanism, 1985; contbr. articles to profl. jours. Vice chmn. bd. dirs. St. Luke's Hosp., Kansas City, Mo., 1971, chmn., 1973-89. Research fellow Harvard, 1950 Mem. Am. Philos. Assn., Metaphys. Soc. Am., Soc. Existential and Phenomenological Philosophy, Catholic Theol. Soc. Am. Episcopalian. Home: 720 W 44th St Apt 2005 Kansas City MO 64111-3413 E-mail: akvogel@swbell.net.

VOGEL, CARL E., communications executive; b. Oct. 18, 1957; BS in Fin. and Acctg., St. Norbert Coll., DePere, Wis. With Jones Intercable, 1983; exec. v.p. EchoStar Comm. Inc., 1994—97; CEO Star Choice Comm., 1998; chmn., CEO Primestar Inc., 1998—99; exec. v.p., COO AT&T Broadband, 1999; sr. v.p. Liberty Media Corp., 1999—2001; pres., CEO Charter Comm. Inc., 2001—05; vice chmn. EchoStar Comm. Corp., 2005—, pres., 2006—. Bd. dirs. C-SPAN, CableLabs, EchoStar Comm. Corp., 2005—. Mem.: Nat. Cable TV Assn. (bd. dirs.). Office: EchoStar Comm Corp 9601 South Meridian Blvd Englewood CO 80112 Office Phone: 303-723-1000.

VOGEL, CARL M., state legislator; Mem. Mo. Ho. of Reps. from 114th dist. Republican. Home: 311 Constitution Dr Jefferson City MO 65109-5723

VOGEL, NELSON J., JR., lawyer; b. South Bend, Ind., Oct. 13, 1946; s. Nelson J. and Carolyn B. (Drzewiecki) V.; m. Sandra L. Cudney, May 17, 1969; children: Ryan C., Justin M., Nathan J., Lindsey M. BS cum laude, Miami U., Oxford, Ohio, 1968; JD cum laude, U. Notre Dame, 1971. Bar: Ind. 1971, Mich. 1971, U.S. Dist. Ct. (no. dist.) Ind. 1971, U.S. Tax Ct. 1972, U.S. Ct. Appeals (5th cir.) 1975, U.S. Ct. Claims 1980. Acct. Coopers & Lybrand, South Bend, 1969-71; assoc. Barnes & Thornburg, South Bend, 1971-76, ptnr., 1977—. Lectr. U. Notre Dame, South Bend, 1971, 74-80; instr. Ind. U., South Bend, 1971-74; vice-chair Barnes & Thornburg, 2001—, mng. ptnr. South Bend office, 2001—. Trustee Project Future, St. Joseph Co., 2002-; pres. Big Bros./Big Sisters, South Bend, 1978-79; bd. pres. South Bend Regional Mus. Art, 1984-86; ethics com. Meml. Hosp., South Bend, 1986-94; bd. adv. Goshen Coll. Family Bus. program, 1993-99; bd. dirs. Madison Ctr., 2003-06. Mem. Nat. Employee Stock Ownership Plan Assn. (sec.-treas. Ind. chpt. 1993-95), Nat. Assn. State Bar Tax Sec. (exec. com. 1982-84), Ind. State Bar Assn. (chmn. taxation sect. 1981-82, Citation of Merit 1979), Mich. Bar Assn. (tax sect.), Ind. State HS Hockey Assn., Inc. (bd. dirs. 1998-01, treas. 1998-01), Michiana World Affairs Coun. (bd. dirs. 1992-96), Michiana World Trade Club (bd. dirs. 1992-96), Mental Health Assn. St. Joseph County (bd. dirs. 1997-01), St. Joseph County C. of C. (bd. dirs. 2005—). Home: 1146 Dunrobbin Ln South Bend IN 46614-2150 Office: Barnes & Thornburg 600 1st Source Bank 100 N Michigan St Ste 600 South Bend IN 46601-1632 Office Phone: 574-233-1171. Business E-Mail: nvogel@btlaw.com.

VOGEL, THOMAS TIMOTHY, surgeon, educator, lay worker; b. Columbus, Ohio, Feb. 1, 1934; s. Thomas A. and Charlotte A. (Hogan) V.; m. M.M. Darina Kelleher, May 29, 1965; children: Thomas T., Catherine D., Mark P., Nicola M. AB, Coll. of Holy Cross, 1955; MS, Ohio State U., 1960, PhD, 1962; MD, Georgetown U., 1965. Pvt. practice surgery, Columbus, 1971-2001; chmn. liturgy com., pres. parish coun. St. Catharine Parish, Columbus, 1971-73; chmn. diocesan adminstrn. com. Diocesan Pastoral Coun., Columbus, 1972-73, chmn., 1973-75; vice prefect Sodality of Holy Cross, 1953-55; mem. Ohio Bishop's Adv. Coun., Columbus, 1976-79. Clin. asst. prof. surgery Ohio State U., Columbus, 1974—; past trustee Peer Rev. Sys., Inc.; assoc. med. dir. United Health Care, Columbus, 1997-2000; cons. Rehabilitation Svcs.; commr., surveillance utilization rev. mem. Medicaid, State of Ohio, 1998-2000; assoc. med. dir. Palmetto GBA, 1999—. Contbr. articles to profl. jours. Chmn. coun. grad. students Ohio State U., 1961; bd. dirs. St. Vincent's Children's Ctr., 1975-83, chmn., 1981-82; past chmn. bd. trustees St. Joseph Montessori Sch. Named Knight of the Holy Sepulchre, Equestrian Order of the Holy Sepulchre of Jerusalem, 2001; recipient Layman's award, Columbus Ea. Kiwanis, 1972. Mem. ACS, Am. Physiol. Soc., Assn. for Acad. Surgery, Ohio State Med. Assn. (del. 1993—), Sigma Xi, Delta Epsilon Sigma. Roman Catholic. Home: 247 S Ardmore Rd Columbus OH 43209-1701 Office: 621 S Cassingham Rd Columbus OH 43209-2403 E-mail: vogel.3@osu.edu.

VOGT, ALBERT RALPH, forester, educator, program director; BS in Forest Mgmt., U. Mo., 1961, MS in Tree Physiology, 1962, PhD in Tree Physiology, 1966. Instr. in dendrology U. Mo., Columbia, 1965-66; asst. prof. rsch. tree physiology Ohio State U., 1966-69, assoc. prof., assoc. chmn. rsch. and adminstrn. forestry, 1969-76, prof., chmn. dept. adminstrn. and tchg. forestry, 1976-85; prof., dir. sch. natural resources U. Mo., 1985—2003, prof. emeritus, 2003—. Mem. Mo. Forest Heritage Initiative, Gov.'s Task Force Environ. Edn., Mo. Gov.'s Energy Coalition, Mo. Citizens Com. Soil, Water, and State Parks; co-chair steering com. 3d Forestry Edn. Symposium, 1991; co-chair external rev. dept. forestry So. Ill. U., Carbondale, 1993; co-chair external rev. Sch. Forest Resources Pa. State U., 1995; chair external rev.forestry U. Wis., Madison, 1997; chair on-site S.A.F. accreditation rev. dept. forest and natural resources Purdue U., 2003. Office: U Mo Sch Natural Resources 105H Natural Resources Bldg Columbia MO 65211-0001 Home Phone: 573-443-5731; Office Phone: 573-882-1627. E-mail: vogta@missouri.edu.

VOIGHT, JACK C., state official; b. New London, Wisconsin, Dec. 17, 1945; s. Oscar C. and Thelma J. (Hamm) V.; m. Martha J. (Wolfe), July 14, 1973; children: Carly and Emily. BS, U. Wis., Oshkosh, 1971. Claims adjuster U.S. F and G Ins. Co., Appleton, Wis., 1971-74; ins. agy. owner Voight Ins. Agy., Appleton, Wis., 1974—; state treas. State of Wis., 1995—2006. Bank organizer Am. Nat. Bank, Appleton, Wis. 1992-94; real estate broker Voight Realty and Ins., Appleton, 1977-92. Pres. Appleton Northside Bus. Assn., 1982; alderman city coun., City of Appleton, 1983-83, pres., 1992-93; Sgt. U.S. Army, 1968-70. Decorated Bronze Star; named Citizen of Yr. Appleton Northside Bus. Assn., 1990. Mem. Nat. Assn. State Treas., Midwest State Treas. Assn. (pres. 1996-97); Appleton Noon Optimist Club (pres. 1980). Republican. Presbyterian. Avocations: gardening, politics. Office: State Treas Wis PO Box 7871 Madison WI 53707-7871 E-mail: jack.voight@ost.state.wi.us.

VOIGTS, GENE E., lawyer; b. Kansas CIty, 1939; BA, William Jewell Coll., 1961; LLB, U. Mo., Kansas City, 1964. Mcpl. judge North Kansas City, Mo., 1965—66; pros. atty. Clay County, Mo., 1967—68; chief counsel, Criminal Div. Office of Atty. Gen., 1969; first asst. atty. gen. State of Mo., 1969—73; ptnr. litig. Shook, Hardy & Bacon LLP, Kansas City, Mo., 1976—, vice chmn., mem. Exec. Com. Mem.: ABA, Mo. Orgn. of Defense Lawyers, Lawyers Assn. Kansas City, Kansas City Met. Bar Assn., Mo. Bar Assn. Office: Shook, Hardy & Bacon LLP 2555 Grand Blvd Kansas City MO 64108 Office Phone: 816-474-6550. Office Fax: 816-421-5547. E-mail: gvoigts@shb.com.

VOINOVICH, GEORGE VICTOR, senator, former governor; b. Cleve., July 15, 1936; m. Janet (Allen) Voinovich; 3 children. BA in Govt., Ohio U., 1958; JD, Ohio State U., 1961; LLD (hon.), Ohio U., 1981. Bar: Ohio 1961, US Supreme Ct. 1968. Asst. atty. gen. State of Ohio, 1963-64; mem. Ohio Ho. of Reps., 1967-71; auditor Cuyahoga County, Ohio, 1971-76; commr., 1977-78; lt. gov. State of Ohio, Columbus, 1979, gov., 1991-98; mayor City of Cleve., 1979-89; US Senator from Ohio, 1999—; mem. fgn. rels. com., environment and pub. works com., fgn. relations com. homeland security and governmental affairs com. Pres. Nat. League Cities, 1984-85; trustee US Conf. Mayors; chmn. Midwestern Govs. Conf., 1991-92, Coun. Gt. Lakes Govs., 1992-94; chmn. Jobs for America's Graduates Program, 1995-(Nat. Leadership award 1993); mem. State and Local Govt. Coalition, 1994-Recipient Tree of Life award, Jewish Nat. Found., 1981, Cert. of Merit award Ohio U., Humanitarian award NCCJ, 1986, Disting. Urban Mayor award Nat. Urban Coalition, 1987, Nat. Public Svc. award SADD, 1991, Edn. Reform Pioneer award Nat. Bus. Roundtable, 1994, George Falcon Golden Spike award, Nat. Assn. Railroad Passengers, 2000; named one of Outstanding Young Men in Ohio Ohio Jaycees, 1970; one of Outstanding Young Men in Greater Cleve. Cleve. Jaycees; named to All-Pro City Mgmt. team City & State Mag., 1987. Mem. Rep. Govs. Assn. (vice chmn. 1991-92, chmn. 1992-93), Nat. Govs. Assn. (chmn. edn. action team on sch. readiness 1991, chmn. child support enforcement work group 1991-92, mem. strategic planning task force 1991-92, mem. human resources com., co-chmn. task force on edn. 1992-93, mem. exec. com. 1993-98, co-lead gov. on fed. mandates, chmn. 1997-98), Omicron Delta Kappa, Phi Alpha Theta, Phi Delta Phi. Republican. Roman Catholic. Office: US Senate 524 Hart Senate Office Bldg Washington DC 20510-0001 also: Central Ohio Office Rm 310 37 West Broad St Columbus OH 43215 Office Phone: 202-224-3353, 614-469-6697. Office Fax: 202-228-1382, 614-469-7733. E-mail: columbus_voinovich@voinovich.senate.gov.

VOLESKY, RON JAMES, state legislator; b. Bullhead, SD, July 13, 1954; s. Leonard and Louise (Kleinsasser) V. BA in Govt., Harvard Coll., 1976; MS in Journalism and Mass Communication, S.D. State U., 1977; postgrad., U. S.D. Sch. Law, 1980. Prodr. bicentennial programming S.D. Pub. TV, 1975; news dir., anchorman S.D. Pub. Radio Network, 1976-77; real estate salesman Montgomery Agy., 1978-79; pvt. practice as atty. Volesky Law Offices, Huron, S.D.; ptnr. Churchill, Manolis, Freeman & Volesky; mem. S.D. Ho. of Reps from 23rd dist., Pierre; majority whip S.D. Ho. of Reps, Pierre, 1983-84, mem. judiciary & transp. coms.; mem. S.D. Senate from 21st dist., Pierre, 2001—. Bd. dirs. Bank Wessington. Co-author: Who's Who Among the Sioux, 1977. Del. Rep. State Conv., 1978; chmn. Beadle County Rep. Ctrl. Com., S.D., 1979-80. Recipient Citizenship award Huron Am. Legion, 1972; scholar Harvard Club N.Y., 1972-76, Sarah and Pauline Maier scholar Harvard Coll., 1972-76. Mem. Soc. Profl. Journalists, S.D. Trial Lawyers Assn., ABA, Jaycees. Democrat. Home: 592 Dakota Ave S Huron SD 57350-2858 Office: SD House of Reps 356 Dakota Ave S Huron SD 57350-2513

VOLKEMA, MICHAEL A., office furniture manufacturer; Chmn., CEO Meridian Inc., Spring Lake, Mich.; pres., CEO Coro Inc., Zeeland, Mich., Herman Miller Inc., Zeeland, 1995—2004, chmn., 2000—. Office: Herman Miller Inc 855 E Main Ave Zeeland MI 49464-0302 Office Fax: 616-654-5234.

VOLKMER, HAROLD L., former congressman; b. Jefferson City, Mo., Apr. 4, 1931; m. Shirley Ruth Braskett; children: Jerry Wayne, John Paul, Elizabeth Ann. Student, Jefferson City Jr. Coll., 1949-51, St. Louis U. Sch. Commerce and Finance, 1951-52; LL.B., U. Mo., 1955. Bar: Mo. 1955. Individual practice law, Hannibal, 1958—; asst. atty. gen. Mo., 1955; pros. atty. Marion County, 1960-66; mem. Mo. Ho. of Reps., 1966-76; chmn. judiciary com., mem. revenue and econs. com.; mem. 95th-104th Congresses from 9th Mo. Dist., 1977-96; ranking minority mem. agr. subcom. livestock, dairy, & poultry. Served with U.S. Army, 1955-57. Recipient award for meritorious pub. service in Gen. Assembly St. Louis Globe-Democrat, 1972-74 Mem. NRA (bd. dirs., chmn. civil rights def. fund), Mo. Bar Assn., 10th Jud. Circuit Bar Assn. Clubs: KC, Hannibal Lions. Roman Catholic.

VOLLMER, DAVID L., museum director; Dir. Janice Mason Art Mus., Cadiz, Ky., Swope Art Mus., Terre Haute, Ind., 2001—. Office: Swope Art Mus 25 S 7th St Terre Haute IN 47807 Office Phone: 812-238-1676. E-mail: vollmer@swope.org.

VOLLMER, HOWARD ROBERT, artist, photographer; b. St. Paul, Dec. 16, 1930; s. Herbert Lenard and Elfreida Wilhelmena Elizabeth (Rubbert) V.; m. Velma Martin, Feb. 10, 1951; children: Mark David, Lori Lynn. BA, Hamline U., 1957; MA, Ariz. State U., 1968; postgrad., U. Minn., 1970-85. Screen print rsch. developer 3M Co., St. Paul, 1948-51; tchr. art ESL, St. Paul Pub. Schs., 1957-87; corp. product analyst, treas. Gateway Labs., Golden Valley, Minn., 1975-78; owner, photographer, artist Remember Art and Photog. Svcs., White Bear Lake, Minn., 1980—; owner, photographer, artist, writer Image Concepts, Florence, Ariz. Creator, co-presenter TV program Crafts in Edn., Sta. KTCA-TV, St. Paul, 1959. Author, illustrator: Chipmunk Children's Book, 1995, The Calling of the Way, 2003, Age of Ice, 2004. Chmn. White Bear Arts Coun., 1975-80; bd. dirs. Florence Gardens Mobile Home Assn. Sgt. USAF, 1951-52. Nat. Experienced Tchrs. Art fellow, 1967—68. Mem. Nat. Art Edn. Assn., St. Paul Fedn. Tchrs. Democrat-Farmer-Labor Party. Lutheran. Avocations: nature, hiking, woodworking, collecting stamps. Personal E-mail: hofmiler@cgmailbox.com.

VOLPI, MICHELE, chemicals executive; b. Florence, Italy; B in Bus. Adminstrn., Bocconi U., Milan, MBA. Cert. Six Sigma Green Belt. Mgmt. cons. The Boston Consulting Grp.; European mktg. dir., structured products bus. Gen. Electric Co., gen. mgr., Polymershapes Bus. Unit; global mgr., Assembly Bus. H.B. Fuller Co., 2002—04, grp. pres., gen. mgr., Global Adhesives grp., 2004—06, pres., CEO, 2006—. Office: HB Fuller Company 1200 Willow Lake Blvd Saint Paul MN 55110-5101 Office Phone: 651-236-5095. Office Fax: 651-236-5898.

VOLZ, WILLIAM HARRY, lawyer, educator; b. Sandusky, Mich., Dec. 28, 1946; s. Harry Bender and Belva Geneva (Riehl) V. BA, Mich. State U., 1968; MA, U. Mich., 1972; MBA, Harvard U., 1978; JD, Wayne State U., 1975. Bar: mich. 1975. Atty. pvt. practice, Detroit, 1975-77; mgmt. analyst Office of Gen. Counsel, HEW, Woodlawn, Md., 1977; from asst. prof. to prof. Wayne State U., Detroit, 1978—86, prof., 1986, dean, 1986—96; dir. Ctr. for Legal Studies Wayne State U. Law Sch., 1996-97; instr. Pa. State U., Coll. Sta., 1997—. Cons. Merrill Lynch, Pierce, Fenner & Smith, N.Y.C., 1980-83, City of Detroit Law Dept., 1982, Mich. Supreme Ct., Detroit, 1981; ptnr. Mich. CPA Rev., Southfield, 1983-85; expert witness in product liability, comml. law and bus. ethics; pres. Wedgewood Group. Author: Managing a Trial, 1982; contbr. articles to legal jours.; mem. editl. bds. bus. and law jours. Internat. adv. bd. Inst. Mgmt., L'viv, Ukraine, Legal counsel Free Legal Aid Clinic, Inc., Detroit 1976-96, Shared Ministries, Detroit, 1981, Sino-Am. Tech. Exch. coun., China, 1982; chair advt. rev. panel BBB, Detroit, 1988-90; pres. Mich. Acad. Sci., Arts and Letters, 1995-96, 98-2000, bd. dirs. Common Ground, Greater Detroit Alliance Bus., Olde Custodian Fund. Mem.: ABA, Players (bd. dirs.), Amateur Medicant Soc. (commissionaire 1981—85), Harvard Bus. Sch. Club Detroit, Econ. Club Detroit, Detroit Athletic Club, Beta Alpha Psi, Alpha Kappa Psi, Golden Key. Home: 3846 Wedgewood Dr Bloomfield Hills MI 48301-3949 Office: Wayne State U Sch Bus Adminstrn Cass Ave Detroit MI 48202 Home Phone: 248-644-1035; Office Phone: 313-577-4694. Business E-Mail: ab9241@wayne.edu.

VON BERNUTH, CARL W., lawyer, diversified financial services company executive; b. Feb. 2, 1944; BA, Yale U., 1966, LLB, 1969. Bar: N.Y. 1970, Pa. 1990. Corp. atty. White & Case, 1969-80; assoc. gen. counsel Union Pacific Corp., NYC, 1980-83, dep. gen. counsel fin. and adminstrn., 1984-88, v.p., gen. counsel Bethlehem, Pa., 1988-91, sr. v.p., gen. counsel, 1991-97, sr. v.p., gen. counsel and sec. Omaha, 1997—. Mem. U. Pa. Inst. for Law and Econs. Mem. Am. Corp. Counsel Assn., Practicing Law Inst. Office: Union Pacific Corp 1416 Dodge St Rm 1230 Omaha NE 68179-0001 Home: 142 Gay Bowers Rd Fairfield CT 06824-2011

VON BERNUTH, ROBERT DEAN, agricultural engineering educator, consultant; b. Del Norte, Colo., Apr. 14, 1946; s. John Daniel and Bernice H. (Dunlap) von B.; m. Judy M. Wehrman, Dec. 27, 1969; children: Jeanie, Suzie BSE, Colo. State U., 1968; MS, U. Idaho, 1970; MBA, Claremont Grad. U., Calif., 1980; PhD in Engring., U. ebr., 1982. Registered profl. engr., Calif., Nebr. Agrl. product mgr. Rain Bird Sprinkler Mfg., Glendora, Calif., 1974-80; instr. agrl. engring. U. ebr., Lincoln, 1980-82; from assoc. prof. to prof. U. Tenn., Knoxville, 1982-90; prof. Mich. State U., East Lansing, 1990—, chmn., 1992-96. V.p. Von-Sol Cons., Lincoln, 1980-82; prin. Von Bernuth Agrl. cons., Knoxville, East Lansing, 1982—. Patentee in field. With USNR, 1970—98, Vietnam. Decorated DFC (2); recipient Disting. Naval Grad. award USN Flight Program, Pensacola, Fla., 1970. Fellow Am. Soc. Agrl. Engrs.; mem. ASCE, Irrigation Assn. (Person of Yr. 1994), Naval Res. Assn. Avocations: flying, skiing, antique tractors. Office: Mich State U Sch of Planning Design & Constrn Human Ecology Bldg East Lansing MI 48824

VON FURSTENBERG, GEORGE MICHAEL, economics professor, researcher; b. Germany, Dec. 3, 1941; arrived in U.S., 1961; m. Gabrielle M. Koblitz von Willmburg, June 9, 1967; 1 child, Philip G. PhD, Princeton U., 1967. Asst. prof. Cornell U., Ithaca, NY, 1966-70; assoc. prof. Ind. U., Bloomington, 1970-73, prof., 1976-78, Rudy prof. econs., 1983—2006; sr. staff economist Coun. Econ. Advisors, Washington, 1973-76; div. chief rsch. dept. IMF, Washington, 1978-83; Robert Bendheim prof. econ. and fin. policy Fordham U., NYC, 2000—03; econ. program dir. NSF, Arlington, Va., 2006—. Project dir. Am. Coun. Life Ins., Washington, 1976—78; sr. advisor Brookings Instn., Washington, 1978—90; vis. sr. economist planning and analysis staff Dept. State, Washington, 1989—90; Bissell-Fulbright vis. prof. Can.-Am. rels. U. Toronto, 1994—95. Contbg. author, editor: The Government and Capital Formation, 1980, Capital, Efficiency and Growth, 1980, Acting Under Uncertainty: Multidisciplinary Conceptions, 1990, Regulation and Supervision of Financial Institutions in the NAFTA Countries and Beyond, 1997; editor: Internat. Money and Credit: The Policy Roles, 1983; co-author: Learning from the World's Best Central Bankers, 1998; co-editor: Monetary Unions and Hard Pegs: Effects on Trade, Financial Development, and Stability, 2004; assoc. editor: Rev. Econs. and Stats., 1987—92, Open Econs. Rev., 1997—2007, Jour. Econ. Asymmetries, 2004—; contbr. articles to profl. jours. Fulbright grantee, Poland, 1991—92. Mem.: Am. Econ. Assn., N.Am. Econs. and Fin. Assn. (pres. 2000). Roman Catholic. Avocation: tennis. Office: NSF Divsn Social and Econ Scis 995N 4201 Wilson Blvd Arlington VA 22230 Office Phone: 703-292-8202. Business E-Mail: vonfurst@indiana.edu, gvonfurs@nsf.gov.

VON KLAN, LAURENE, museum administrator; b. NY; BA in Econ., Williams Coll.; MA in Internat. Rels., U. Chgo. Tchr. Northeastern Ill. U.; dir. devel. Nature Conservancy, Ill. chpt., 1986—92; exec. dir. Friends of Chgo. River, 1992—2005; pres., CEO Peggy Notebaert Nature Mus., Chgo., 2005—. Founding mem. Coalition to Restore Urban Waters (nat. steering com.); bd. dir. River Network; steering com. Chgo. Wilderness. Founding mem., nat. steering com Coalition to Restore Urban Waters (CRUW); citizen mem. Ill. River Coordinating Coun., 1998—; bd. dir. Nat. River Network, 2002—. Named one of 100 Most Influential Women, Crain's Chgo. Bus., 2004; recipient Protector of Environment award, Chgo. Audubon, 2003. Office: Notebaert Nature Mus 2430 N Cannon Dr Chicago IL 60614 Office Phone: 773-755-5100.*

VON LEHMAN, JOHN, financial executive; BA, U. Dayton. CPA. Acct. Deloitte, Haskins & Sells; v.p., treas., chief acctg. officer The Midland Co., 1980-88, v.p., treas., CFO, 1988—. Address: 7000 Midland Blvd Amelia OH 45102-2608

VON MEHREN, GEORGE M., lawyer; b. Boston, Nov. 2, 1950; m. Barbara A. von Mehren, Dec. 20, 2003; children: Paige E., Reed C. AB, Harvard U., 1972, JD, 1977; BA, Cambridge U., Eng., 1974, MA, 1985. Bar: Ohio 1977, registered: US Supreme Ct., US Ct. Appeals (6th cir.), US Dist. Ct. (No. Dist.) Ohio. Assoc. Squire, Sanders & Dempsey LLP, Cleve., 1977-86, ptnr., 1986—, chair Internat. Dispute Resolution Practice Group, 1998—. Contbr. articles to profl. jours.; spkr. in field. Office: Squire Sanders & Dempsey 127 Public Sq Ste 4900 Cleveland OH 44114-1304 Office Phone: 216-479-8614. Office Fax: 216-479-8777. Business E-Mail: gvonmehren@ssd.com.

VON RECUM, ANDREAS F., veterinarian, bioengineer; b. Dillingen, Bavaria, Germany, July 5, 1939; arrived in U.S., 1971; s. Bogdan Freiherr and Ilse Freifrau (von Rosenberg) von R.; m. Grudrun F. Bredenbröker-Hardt, Oct. 2, 1965; children: Derik F., Vera F., Uta F., Horst F., Thomas F., Elsa F. BS, U. Giessen, 1965; DVM, Free U. Berlin, 1968, PhD, 1969; PhD in Vet. Surgery, Colo. State U., 1974. Practitioner farm animal medicine and surgery, Meitingen, Germany, 1968-69; clin. staff small animal clinic Free U. Berlin (Germany), Coll. Vet. Medicine, 1969-72; rsch. asst. surg. lab. Colo. State U., Coll. Vet. Medicine, Ft. Collins, 1972-74; dir. surg. rsch. lab. Sinai Hosp. Detroit, 1975-77; prof. dept. bioengring. Clemson (S.C.) U., 1978-93, head dept. bioengring., 1982-93; chmn. bioengring. alliance S.C. Coll. Engring., Clemson U., 1984-88; scientific staff Shriners Hosp., Greenville, SC, 1989-95; prof. Hunter endowed chair bioengring. Clemson U. Coll. Engring., 1993-97; assoc. dean rsch., prof. Coll. Vet. Medicine Ohio State U., Columbus, 1997—2004; ret., 2004; founding chmn., prof. biomed. engring. dept. Ohio State U., Columbus, 2002—. Mem. coll. exec. com. Coll. Vet. Medicine, Free U., Berlin, 1970-71; adj. assoc. prof. comparative surgery Wayne State U. Sch. Medicine, Dept. Comparative Medicine, 1975-77; adj. prof. surgery U. S.C. Sch. Medicine, 1984—, Med. U. S.C., 1987-97; adj. prof. biomaterials Coll. Dentistry, U. Nijmegen, 1993—; founding chair internat. liaison com. World's Biomaterials Socs., 1996-2000; cons. in field. Editor Jour. Investigative Surg., 1991-97; patentee in field. Recipient Fulbright Scientist award, 1990-91, Alexander von Humboldt Sr. Scientist award, 1990-91; nat. and internat. fellow Biomaterials Sci. and Engring., 1996. Fellow Am. Inst. Med. and Biol. Engring.; mem. AVMA, FBSE, Blue Ridge Vet. Med. Assn. (pres. 1984), Soc. Biomaterials (asst. editor 1986—, editl. bd. 1983, program chmn. 1990, sec.-treas. 1990-92, pres. 1993-94), Internat. Soc. Artificial Internal Organs, Am. Soc. Artificial Organs, Am. Heart Assn., Acad. Surg. Rsch. (founder 1982, pres. 1982-83, newsletter editor 1982-85, Markowitz award 2004), Biomed. Engring. Soc., Am. Soc. Engring. Edn., Assn. Advancement Med. Instrumentation. Presbyterian. Home and Office: Ohio State U Coll Engring 270 Bevis Hall 1080 Carmack Rd Columbus OH 43210-1002 Office Phone: 614-292-1285. Business E-Mail: vonrecum.1@osu.edu.

VON RHEIN, JOHN RICHARD, music critic, journalist, writer; b. Pasadena, Calif., Sept. 10, 1945; s. Hans Walter and Elsa Maryon (Brossmann) von R. AA, Pasadena City Coll., 1965; BA in Eng., UCLA, 1967; BA in Music, Calif. State U., Los Angeles, 1970. Music reviewer Hollywood (Calif.) Citizen-News, 1968-70; music editor and critic, dance critic Akron (Ohio) Beacon Jour., 1971-77; music critic Chgo. Tribune, 1977—; prof. music appreciation Rio Hondo Jr. Coll., Calif., 1970-71. Lectr., TV host, rec. annotator. Co-author (with Andrew Porter): Bravi; contbr. articles to World Book Ency., New Grove Dictionary of Music, mags. and papers. Music Critics Assn.-Kennedy Center for Performing Arts fellow, 1972, 75; recipient Peter Lisagor award Soc. Profl. Journalists, 1999. Mem. Music Critics Assn. N.Am. (edn. com., dir. 1988), Ravinia Critics Inst. (dir. 1988). Office: Chgo Tribune Co 435 N Michigan Ave Chicago IL 60611-4066 Home Phone: 773-561-2620; Office Phone: 312-222-3570. Business E-Mail: jvonrhein@tribune.com.

VON TERSCH, LAWRENCE WAYNE, engineering educator, dean; b. Waverly, Iowa, Mar. 17, 1923; s. Alfred and Martha (Emerson) Von T.; m. LaValle Sills, Dec. 17, 1948; 1 son, Richard George. BS, Iowa State U., 1943, MS, 1948, PhD, 1953. From instr. to prof. elec. engring. Iowa State U., 1946-56; dir. computer lab. Mich. State U., 1956-83, prof. elec. engring., chmn. dept., 1958-65, assoc. dean engring., 1965-68, dean, 1968-89, dean emeritus, 1989—. Author: (with A. W. Swago) Recurrent Electrical Transients, 1953. Mem. IEEE; mem. Sigma Xi, Tau Beta Pi, Eta Kappa Nu, Phi Kappa Phi, Pi Mu Epsilon Home: 4282 Tacoma Blvd Okemos MI 48864-2734 Office: Michigan State U Coll Engring East Lansing MI 48823 Personal E-mail: vontersc@egr.msu.edu. E-mail: vontersch@comcast.net.

VOOGT, JAMES LEONARD, medical educator; b. Grand Rapids, Mich., Feb. 8, 1944; married; 3 children. Student, Calvin Coll., 1962-64; BS in Biological Sci., Mich. Tech. U., 1966; MS in Physiology, Mich. State U., 1968, PhD in Physiology, 1970. Fellow, lectr. dept. physiology U. Calif., San Francisco, 1970-71; asst. prof. dept. physiology and biophysics U. Louisville Sch. Medicine, 1971-77, assoc. prof. dept. physiology and biophysics, 1977; assoc. prof. dept. physiology U. Kans. Sch. Medicine, 1977-82, prof. physiology, 1982—. Assoc. dean rsch. U. Kans. Sch. Medicine, 1982—84, chmn. dept. physiology, 1993—2001; vis. prof. Erasmus U., 1985; vice chancellor rsch. U. Kans. Med. Ctr., 2006—. Mem. editl. bd. Endocrinology, 1984-86, 89-92, Am. Jour. Physiology, 1984-88, Doody's Jour., 1995-98; ad hoc reviewer Neuroendocrinology, Sci., Biology of Reproduction, Life Scis., Jour. Endocrinology, Molecular Cellular Neuroscis., Procs. Soc. Exptl. Biology and Medicine, biochm. endocrinology study sect. NIH, 1992, reproductive endocrinology study sect., 1994-98; reviewer grants NSF; editor sci. procs. Rsch. Week, 1982-83; contbr. over 120 articles to profl. publs., 4 chpts. to books. Grantee NIH, 1972-85, 88—, NSF, 1985-86, 91-94, Ctr. on Aging, 1988, Nat. Inst. Drug Abuse, 1991-93; fellow Japan Soc. Promotion of Sci., 1993; recipient Outstanding Young Alumni award Mich. Tech. U., 1974, Honors in Edn., Med. Student Voice, 1990; inducted Mich. Tech. U. Acad. of Scis. and Arts, 2000. Mem. AAAS, Endocrine Soc., Internat. Soc. euroendocrinology (charter mem.), Am. Physiol. Soc. (pub. affairs adv. com. 1983-87) Soc. Neuroscis., Phi Kappa Phi, Sigma Xi. Office: Dept Molecular and Integrative Physiology U Kans Med Ctr 3901 Rainbow Blvd Kansas City KS 66160-0001

VOORHEES, HAROLD J., SR., state legislator; s. John and Helena V.; m. Joanne Land; children: Harold Jr., Nancy Baker Voorhees, Karla Vereecken Voorhees., Grand Rapids CC, Mich. Councilman-at-large Wyoming (Mich.) City Coun.; mayor Wyoming, Mich.; state rep. Dist. 77 Mich. Ho. of Reps., 1993—; owner, pres. Serv-U-Sweets, Inc., Grandville, Mich., 1996—. Vice chair Local Govt. Com., Mich. Ho. of Reps., 1993—; mem. Ins., Mil. & Vets. Affairs, State Affairs & Transp. Coms., 1993—. V.p. Grandville Srs. Housing Facility, 1996—. Mem. Rotary Club. Home: 5380 Kenowa Ave SW Grandville MI 49418-9507

VOORHEES, JOHN JAMES, dermatologist, department chairman; BS, Bowling Green U., 1959; MD, U. Mich., 1963. Intern U. Mich., 1963-64, resident in dermatology, 1966-69, asso. prof. dermatology Ann Arbor, 1972-74, prof., 1974—; chief dermatology service Univ. Hosp., Ann Arbor, 1975; chmn. dept. dermatology U. Mich., 1975—. Contbr. articles to profl. jours., chpts. in books. Recipient Taub Internat. Meml. award for psoriasis research, 1973, 86, Henry Russel award U. Mich., 1973; Herzog fellow Am. Dermatol. Assn., 1968-70 Mem. Am. Soc. Clin. Investigation, Am. Soc. Pharmacology and Exptl. Therapeutics, Am. Assn. Pathologists, Central Soc. Clin. Research, Soc. Investigative Dermatology, Dermatology Found., Skin Pharmacol. Soc., Assn. Profs. Dermatology, Am. Soc. Cell Biology, Am. Acad. Dermatology, Am. Dermatol. Assn., Alpha Omega Alpha. Office: U Mich Med Ctr Dept Dermatology 1910 Taubman Health Care Ctr Ann Arbor MI 48109

VORA, MANU KISHANDAS, chemical engineer, consultant; b. Bombay, Oct. 31, 1945; s. Kishandas Narandas and Shantaben K. (Valia) V., m. Nila Narotamdas Kothari, June 16, 1974; children: Ashish, Anand. BSChemE, Banaras U., India, 1968; MSChemE, Ill. Inst. Tech., Chgo., 1970, PhD in ChemE, 1975; MBA, Keller Grad. Sch. Mgmt., Chgo., 1985. Grad. asst. Ill. Inst. Tech., 1969-74; rsch. assoc. Inst. Gas Tech., Chgo., 1976-77, chem. engr., 1977-79, engring. supr., 1979-82; mem. tech. staff AT&T Bell Labs. (now Lucent Techs.), Holmdel, NJ, 1983-84, Naperville, Ill., 1984—, mgr. customer satisfaction, 1990-96, voice of the customer mgr., 1997-2000; pres., CEO Bus. Excellence, Inc., 2000—. Adj. prof. Ill. Inst. Tech., Chgo., 1993—; spkr. in field. Editor: Internat. Petroleum Encyclopedia, 1980. Chmn. Save the Children Holiday Fund Drive, 1986-99; trustee Avery Coonley Sch., Downers Grove, Ill., 1987-91; pres., dir. Blind Found. for India, Naperville, 1989—. Recipient Non-Supervisory AA award Affirmative Actions Adv. Com., 1987, 92, 97, Outstanding Contbn. award Asian Am. for Affirmative Actions, 1989, Disting. Svc. award Save the Children, 1990, Ann. Merit award Chgo. Assn. Tech. Socs., 1992. Fellow Am. Soc. for Quality (standing rev. bd. 1988—, editl. rev. bd. 1989, tech. media com. 1989, mixed media rev. bd. 1994, nat. quality month regional planning com. 1989-94, nat. cert. com. 1989-94, chmn. cert. process improvements subcom. 1990-94, testimonial awards 1995, 96, 2001, 02, exec. bd. Chgo. sect., vice chmn. sect. affairs 1993-94, sect. chmn. 1994-95, nat. dir. at large, 1996-98, nat. dir. 1998-2000, v.p. 2000-2002, vice chmn. investing in quality capital campaign, spl. award 1991, Century Club award 1992, Founders' award 1993, Joe Lisy Quality award 1994, Grant medal 2001, Lancaster medal 2005); mem. Ill. Team Excellence award (chief judge 1993-99, steering com. 1993-99, award). Hindu. Avocations: reading, photography, travel, philanthropic activities. Home: 1256 Hamilton Ln Naperville IL 60540-8373 Office: Bus Excellence Inc PO Box 5585 Naperville IL 60567-5585 Home Phone: 630-637-9301; Office Phone: 630-548-5531. Personal E-mail: manuvora@yahoo.com.

VORAN, JOEL BRUCE, lawyer; b. Kingman, Kans., Mar. 24, 1952; s. Bruce H. and Venora M. (Layman) V.; m. Marsha A. Kooser, May 26, 1979; children: Erica, Ben, Ashley. BS with honors in Bus., U. Kans., 1974; JD with distinction, U. Tex., 1977. Bar: Mo. 1977, US Dist. Ct. (we. dist. Mo.) 1977, US Tax Ct. 1986. Assoc. to ptnr. Lathrop & Gage, L.C., Kansas City, Mo., 1977—. Adv. dir. Mark Twain Bank, Kansas City, 1985-89. Bd. dirs. Kansas City YMCA, 1979—; city chmn. Prairie Village Rep. Party, Kans., 1985-88; participant Kansas City Tomorrow Project, 1989-90. Named one of Top 100 Attys., Worth mag., 2006. Fellow Am. Coll. Trust and Estate Counsel; mem. ABA, Mo. Bar Assn., Kansas City Met. Bar Assn., Kansas City Lawyers Assn., Delta Tau Delta (bd. dirs., pres. 1977-87; alumni pres. Kansas City chpt. 1989-90), Friends of Art Club, Phi Delta Phi, Order of the Coif. Republican. Roman Catholic. Avocations: tennis, golf, jogging. Office: Lathrop & Gage LC 2345 Grand Blvd Ste 2800 Kansas City MO 64108-2642 Office Phone: 816-460-5625. Office Fax: 816-292-2001. E-mail: jvoran@lathropgage.com.

VORHOLT, JEFFREY JOSEPH, lawyer, software company executive; b. Cin., Feb. 20, 1953; s. Edward C. and Rita L. (Kinross) V.; m. Marcia Anne Meyer, Apr. 30, 1976; children: Kimberly Anne, Gregory Michael, Karen Michelle. BBA cum laude, U. Cin., 1976; MBA, Xavier U., Cin., 1978; JD, Chase Law Sch., 1983. Bar: Ohio, 1983; CPA, Ohio. Sec., treas. Cin. Bell Info. Systems, Inc., 1983-84, v.p., chief fin. officer, 1984-88, also bd. dirs.; v.p., controller Cin. Bell, Inc., 1988-89; sr. v.p. Cin. Bell Info. Systems, Inc., 1989-91, Cin. Bell Telephone Co., 1991-93; CFO Structural Dynamics Rsch. Corp., Milford, Ohio, 1994—. Voting mem. Cin. Playhouse, 1986—; mem. fin. planning com. ARC, Cin., 1986-89; trustee U. Health Maintenance Orgn., Inc., 1990-93, St. Joseph Infant and Maternity Home, Inc. Mem. ABA, AICPAs, Ohio Bar Assn., Aircraft Owners and Pilots Assn., Cin. Hist. Soc., Bankers Club of Cin. (bd. govs. 1990-97). Avocations: golf, tennis, hiking, photography, running. Office: Structural Dynamics Rsch Corp 2000 Eastman Dr Milford OH 45150-2712 E-mail: jeff.vorholt@sdrc.com.

VORYS, ARTHUR ISAIAH, lawyer; b. Columbus, Ohio, June 16, 1923; s. Webb Isaiah and Adeline (Werner) V.; m. Lucia Rogers, July 16, 1949 (div. 1980); children: Caroline S., Adeline Vorys Cranson, Lucy Vorys Noll, Webb I.; m. Ann Harris, Dec. 13, 1980. BA, Williams Coll., 1945; LLB, JD, Ohio State U., 1949. Bar: Ohio 1949. From assoc. to ptnr. Vorys, Sater, Seymour & Pease LLP, Columbus, 1949-82, sr. ptnr., 1982-93, of counsel, 1993—. Supt. ins. State of Ohio, 1957-59; bd. dirs Vorys Bros., Inc., others. Trustee, past pres. Children's Hosp., Greenlawn Cemetery Found.; trustee, former chmn. Ohio State U. Hosps.; regent Capital U.; del. Rep. Nat. Conv., 1968, 72. Lt. USMCR, World War II. Decorated Purple Heart. Fellow Ohio State Bar, Columbus Bar Assn.; mem. ABA, Am. Judicature Soc., Rocky Fork Headley Hunt Club, Rocky

Fork Hunt and Country Club, Capital Club, Phi Delta Phi, Chi Psi. Home: 5826 Havens Corners Rd Columbus OH 43230-3142 Office: Vorys Sater Seymour & Pease LLP PO Box 1008 52 E Gay St Columbus OH 43216-1008

VOSS, ANNE COBLE, nutritional biochemist; b. Richmond, Ind., Aug. 22, 1946; d. James Richard and Helen Lucille (Hoyt) Coble; m. Harold Lloyd Voss, July 20, 1969; children: Daniel, Jordan Matthew, Sarah Georgette. BS, Ohio State U., 1968, PhD, 1984. Registered dietitian. Therapeutic dietitian Johns Hopkins Hosp., Balt., 1968-69; clin. instr. Ohio State U. Hosps., Columbus, 1969-70; clin. dietitian U.S. Army Med. Clinic, Rothwesten, Fed. Republic Germany, 1970-72; clin. rsch. monitor Ross Labs., Columbus, 1978-79; rsch. asst. Ohio State U., Columbus, 1979-84, rsch. assoc., lectr., 1985-91; mgr. outcomes rsch. Ross Products divsn. Abbott Labs., Columbus, Ohio, 1992—. Adj. asst. prof. Otterbein Coll., Westerville, Ohio, 1990-93; nutrition advisor Ohio Dental Assn., Columbus, 1977-93, ADA, Chgo., 1987-93; cons. Ohio Bd. Dietetics, Columbus, 1989-93; vis. scientist Rikshospitalet, Oslo, Norway, 1992. Author: Polyunsaturated Fatty Acids and Eicosanoids, 1987; author, editor: Nutrition Perspectives, 1990, 91, 2d edit., 1993; contbr. articles to profl. jours. Mem. exec. bd. Aux. to Ohio Dental Assn., Columbus, 1979-95; bd. dirs. Ohio Dental Polit. Action Com., Columbus, 1989-92, YWCA, Columbus, 1990-93; Gov.'s appointee, chmn. Ohio Bd. Dietetics. Recipient award Clement Found., Westerville, 1991, Disting. Alumni award Ohio State U., 1996; Nutrition Edn. in Tng. grant Ohio Dept. Edn., Columbus, 1978. Mem. Am. Dietetic Assn., Ohio Dietetic Assn., Med. Dietetics Assn. (founding mem., pres., v.p., sec. 1978—), Ohio Coun. Against Health Fraud (founding mem., bd. govs. 1987—), Ohio Nutrition Coun. (exec. bd. 1987-94), Columbus Dietetic Assn., Sigma Xi, Sigma Delta Epsilon (sec. 1985—). Methodist. Avocations: gardening, cooking, sewing, skiing. Home: 1526 Bridgeton Dr Columbus OH 43220-3908 Office: Abbott Labs Ross Products Divsn 625 Cleveland Ave Columbus OH 43215-1754 Office Phone: 614-624-3962. Business E-Mail: anne.voss@abbott.com.

VOSS, EDWARD WILLIAM, JR., immunologist, educator; b. Chgo., Dec. 2, 1933; s. Edward William and Lois Wilma (Graham) V.; m. Virginia Hellman, June 15, 1974; children: Cathleen, Valerie. AB, Cornell Coll., Iowa, 1955; MS, Ind. U., 1964, PhD, 1966. Asst. prof. microbiology U. Ill., Urbana, 1967-71, assoc. prof., 1971-74, prof., 1974-98, prof. emeritus, 1999—, adj. prof. dept. vet. pathobiology, 2001—, dir. cell sci. ctr. Urbana, 1988-94, Coll. Liberal Arts and Scis. Jubilee prof., 1990. Rev. panel on molecular biology-gene structure USDA, Washington, 1985-86, U.S. Dept. Energy Rsch., 1994; panel mem. in biol. scis. SF Minority Grad. Fellowships, Washington, 1986-88; sci. adv. bd. Biotech. Rsch. and Devel. Corp., 1989-1992; mem. Peer Review Com. AHA, 1993-96; study sect. innovation grant program for approaches in HIV vaccine rsch. NIH, 1997; adj. prof. U. Hawaii, Manoa, 1999-2001, Coll. Vet. Medicine, 2001—. Author, editor Fluorescein Hapten: An Immunological Probe, 1984, Anti-DNA Antibodies in SLE, 1988, adv. editor Immunochemistry, 1975—78, Molecular Immunology, 1980—2002, mem. editl. bd. Applied and Environ. Microbiology, 1979—99; contbr. articles to profl. jours. Apptd. to pres.'s coun. U. Ill. Found., 1995. Served with U.S. Army, 1956-58. NIH fellow, 1966-67, NSF fellow, 1975-77; NIH grantee, 1967—, NSF grantee, 1967—; recipient Disting. Lectr. award U. Ill., 1983; named 1st James R. Martin Univ. scholar, 1994; recipient Exemplary Contbn. award Lupus Found. Am., 1994. Ednl. Aid award E.I. DuPont, 1994, 95. Fellow Am. Inst. Chemists; mem. AAAS, Fedn. Am. Scientists, Am. Assn. Immunologists, Am. Assn. Biol. Chemists, Reticuloendothelial Soc., Am. Lupus Soc. (hon. bd. dirs. Cen. Ill. chpt. 1986—, named to Nat. Lupus Hall of Fame 1988, Cmty. Svc. award 1996), N.Y. Acad. Scis., U.S. Pharmacopeial Conv., Inc., at. Geog. Soc., Am. Chem. Soc. (tour speaker 1984-87), Protein Soc., Sigma Xi. Home: 555 Hahaione St 8H Honolulu HI 96825-1460 Office: Dept Vet Pathobiology Coll Vet Medicine 2522 VMBSB 2001 South Lincoln Ave Urbana IL 61802 E-mail: edwardv307@aol.com.

VOSS, JERROLD RICHARD, architecture educator; b. Chgo., Nov. 4, 1932; s. Peter Walter and Annis Lorraine (Hayes) V.; m. Jean Evelyn Peterson, Aug. 21, 1954; children: Cynthia Jean, Tania Hayes. B.Arch., Cornell U., 1955; M. City Planning, Harvard U., 1959; PhD (Bus. History fellow, Univ. fellow, IBM fellow), 1971. Asst. prof. U. Calif., 1960-61; asst. prof., asso. prof. U. Ill., 1961-69; asso. prof. Harvard U., 1969-71; prof. city and regional planning Ohio State U., Columbus, 1971—, chmn. dept. city and regional planning, 1971-79; dir. Ohio State U. (Knowlton Sch. Architecture), 1981-96, prof., 1996-2000, dir., prof. emeritus, 2000—. UN advisor to Govt. Indonesia, 1964-65; social affairs officer UN Secretariat, 1970-71; project mgr. UN Task Force on Human Environment, Thailand, 1975-76; dir. rsch. and devel. UN Ctr. for Human Settlements (Habitat), 1979-81; cons. Ill. Dept. Devel., J.S. Bolles & Assocs., UN Office Tech. Cooperation, UN Devel. Program, AID, Bechtel Nat. Inc., other pvt. and pub. orgns.; mem. external examiners team United Arab U., 1992—. Author: Human Settlements: Problems and Priorities; Contbr. articles to profl. jours. Mem. pub. policy com. Smithsonian Instn., 1970-73; bd. dirs. Champaign County United Community Council, 1965-69, Columbus Theatre Ballet Assn., 1972-75. Served to 1st lt. U.S. Army, 1955-57. Mem. Acad. for Contemporary Problems (asso.), Am. Am. Inst. Planners, Am. Soc. Engring. Edn., Internat. Center for Urban Land Policy (London). Office: 190 W 17th Ave Columbus OH 43210-1320

VOSS, REGIS DALE, agronomist, educator; b. Cedar Rapids, Iowa, Jan. 4, 1931; s. Francis Joseph and Mary Valeria (Womichil) V.; m. Margaret Anne Mitchell, Nov. 24, 1956; children: Lori Anne, John Patrick, David James. BS, Iowa State U., 1952, PhD, 1962. cert. profl. agronomist. Agriculturist Tenn. Valley Authority, Muscle Shoals, Ala., 1962-64; prof. Iowa State U., Ames, 1964-99, prof. emeritus, 1999—. Co-contbr. chpt. to: Fertilizer Technology and Use, 1985, Soil Testing and Plant Analysis, 1990; assoc. editor Jour. Prodn. Agr., 1988-92. Pres. FarmHouse Frat. Alumni Assn. Bd., Ames, 1990. 1st lt. USAF, 1952-56, Korea., sec. treas. Iowa State U. Retirees Assn., 2003-2004 Recipient Burlington No. Found. award Iowa State U., 1990, disting. svc. award Iowa State U. Ext., 1996, Iowa Master Farmer Exceptional Svc. award, 1998. Fellow AAAS, Am. Soc. Agronomy (bd. dirs. 1976-78, Agronomic Extension Edn. award 1984, Agronomic Achievement award 1989, Werner L. Nelson award 1992), Soil Sci. Soc. Am. (bd. dirs. 1980-83). Republican. Roman Catholic. Achievements include development of field laboratory for training of crop advisors on diagnosis of crop problems; research on effects of soil amendments on chemical indices and crop yields and economic analysis of crop yield. Business E-Mail: rvoss@iastate.edu.

VOSS, THOMAS, customer services executive; Sr. v.p. customer svcs. Ameren Corp., St. Louis, 1999—. Office: Ameren Corp One Ameren Plaza 1901 Chouteau Ave Saint Louis MO 63103-3003 Fax: 314-554-3066.

VOWELL, J. LARRY, food equipment manufacturer; With Hussmann Internat., Inc., Bridgeton, Mo., 1959-90, pres., COO, 1990—. Office: Hussmann Internat Inc 12999 Saint Charles Rock Rd Bridgeton MO 63044

VOWELL, SARAH, writer, radio personality; b. Muskogee, Okla., Dec. 27, 1969; BA, Mont. State U., Bozeman, 1993; MA, Sch. of Art. Inst. Chgo., 1996. Former columnist Time, Salon.com, San Francisco Weekly; has contbd. to magazines and newspapers including Esquire, GQ, LA Times, The Village Voice, Spin, The NY Times Book Rev., and McSweeney's; contbg. editor This Am. Life Nat. Pub. Radio, 1996—. Guest op-ed columnist NY Times, 2005. Author: Radio On: A Listener's Diary, 1997, Take the Cannoli: Stories from the New World, 2000, The Partly Cloudy Patriot, 2003, Assassination Vacation, 2005; actor(voice): (films) The Incredibles, 2004. Office: This Am Life WBEZ Radio Navy Pier 848 E Grand Ave Chicago IL 60611

VRABLIK, EDWARD ROBERT, import/export company executive; b. Chgo., June 8, 1932; s. Steven Martin and Meri (Korbel) V.; m. Bernice G. Germer, Jan. 25, 1958; children: Edward Robert, II, Scott S. BS in Chem. Engring, Northwestern U., 1956; MBA, U. Chgo., 1961; postgrad., MIT, 1970. Registered profl. engr., Ill. Dir. indsl. mktg. Eimco Corp., 1956-61; dir. indsl. mktg. and planning Swift & Co., Chgo., 1961-68; v.p., gen. mgr. Swift Chem. Co., Chgo., 1968-73; pres., chief exec. officer Estech Gen. Chems. Corp., Chgo., 1973-86; pres. Kare Internat. Inc., Chgo., 1986—. Pres. Julius and Assocs., Inc., Kare Internat., Inc.; bd dirs. Potash Phosphate Inst., Consol. Fertilizers, Ltd.; mem. mgmt. com. Esmark Inc., Korbel, Inc., Mister Lawn Care, Inc. Author; patentee in field. Bd. dirs., v.p. Northwestern U. Tech. Inst.; trustee Future Farmers Am. Mem. Internat. Superphosphate Mfrs. Assn. (dir.), Am. Inst. Chem. Engrs., Fertilizer Inst. (dir.) Clubs: Butler Nat. (Oak Brook, Ill.). Lutheran. Home: 631 Thompsons Way Palatine IL 60067-4653 Office: 141 W Jackson Blvd Chicago IL 60604-2992 Office Phone: 847-358-4948. Personal E-mail: vrabliker@aol.com.

VRAKAS, DANIEL PAUL, state legislator; b. Waukesha, Wis., Oct. 31, 1955; BA, U. Wis., Stevens Point, 1979. Wis. state assemblyman dist. 33, 1990—; chmn. Rep. Caucus. Former restaurant owner. Mem. Am. Cancer Soc.; v.p. connection bd. dirs. Waukesha County Mediation Ctr.; bd. dirs. Waukesha and Washington County Rep. Party. Named Friend of Agr., Wis. Farm Bur., 1992—, Champion of Commerce, Milw. Met. Area C. of C., 1992. Mem. Hartland, Waukesha and Delafield C. of C., Lake Country Rotary. Republican. Home: 1712 Bark River Dr Hartland WI 53029-9359

VRANA, VERLON KENNETH, retired professional society administrator, conservationist; b. Seward, Nebr., June 25, 1925; s. Anton and Florence (Walker) V.; m. Elaine Janet Flowerday, June 5, 1949; children: Verlon Rodney, Timothy James, Carolyn Elaine, Jon David. Student, U. Nebr., 1959-62; BBA, George Washington U., 1967, MBA, 1970; mgmt. course, Harvard U., 1979. Field technician Soil Conservation Svc., USDA, Seward, 1948-58, watershed planner, cons. Lincoln, Nebr., 1958-62, mem. pers. staff Washington, 1962-72, dir. pers. div., 1972-76, asst. adminstr. for mgmt., 1976-79, assoc. dep. chief for adminstrn., 1979-80; chief planning div. Nebr. Natural Resources Com., Lincoln, 1980-88; owner-farmer Blue Ridge Farm, Seward, 1980-89; exec. v.p. Soil and Water Conservation Soc., Ankeny, Iowa, 1989-91; pres. Vrana Assocs., Seward, Nebr., 1992—. Bd. dirs., sec. N.E. Natural Resources Dist., York, Nebr., 1988-89; bd. dirs. Cattle Nat. Bank and Trust, Seward; alt. dir. Renewable Natural Resources Foun., Washington, 1989-91. Contbr. articles to jours. in field. Mem. Com. on Ministry Presbyn. Ch. U.S.A., 1986-89, elder, 1970—; vice moderator Homestead Presbytery, 1989; treas. Nebr. Soil and Water Conservation Found., 1992-97; mem. Seward City Coun., 1998-2002, 04—. Recipient N.E. Centennial Grass Seeding award N.E. Centennial Commn., Lincoln, 1967, N.E. Soil Steward award N.E. atural Resources Commn., Lincoln, 1986. Fellow Soil and Water Conservation Soc. (pres. N.E. Coun. 1986, Presdl. citation 1989), Isaac Walton League (dir. Seward chpt. 1984-89), Nat. Wildlife Fedn. (soil conservationist of yr. award 1987), Seward Grange (officer 1984-89, 92-99), Shriner, Kiwanis (Disting. Pres. Seward chpt. 1996-97). Home and Office: Vrana Assocs 131 N 1st St Seward NE 68434-2130 E-mail: vv21929@alltel.net.

VRATIL, JOHN LOGAN, state legislator, lawyer; b. Great Bend, Kans., Oct. 28, 1945; s. Frank and Althea (Shuss) V.; m. Kathy Hoefer, June 21, 1971 (div. Dec. 1985); m. Anne Whitfill, Mar. 7, 1986 (div. Dec. 1992); m. Teresa Hobbs, Mar. 15, 1996; children: Alison, Andy, Kurtis, Ashley. BS in Edn., U. Kans., 1967; postgrad., U. Southampton, Eng., 1967-68; JD, U. Kans., 1971; postgrad., U. Exeter, Eng., 1972. Bar: Kans. 1971, U.S. Dist. Ct. Kans. 1971, U.S. Ct. Appeals (10th and 8th cirs.) 1975, U.S. Supreme Ct. 2005. From assoc. to ptnr. Bennett, Lytle, Wetzler & Winn, Prairie Village, Kans., 1972-83; with Lathrop & Gage, Overland Park, Kans., 1983—; mem. Kans. Senate from 11th dist., 1998—, v.p., 2003—. Contbr. articles to profl. jours. Mem. recreation commn. Prairie Village, 1982-83, mem. planning commn., 1983-84; v.p. Usher Mansion Hist. Found., Lawrence, Kans., 1990—. Fellow ABA Found.; mem. ABA, Kans. Bar Assn. (pres. 1995-96, gov. 1988-97), Kans. Bar Found. (trustee 1996-2002), Johnson County Bar Assn. (pres. 1979), Kans. Sch. Attys. Assn. (pres. 1985), Overland Park C. of C. (bd. dirs. 1985-94, pres. 1988). Republican. Avocations: sports, hunting, reading. Office: Lathrop & Gage 10851 Mastin Blvd Ste 1000 Overland Park KS 66210-2007 Address: Kansas Senate State Capitol Rm 281-E Topeka KS 66612 Home Phone: 913-341-7559; Office Phone: 913-451-5100. Business E-Mail: jvratil@lathropgage.com.

VRATIL, KATHRYN HOEFER, federal judge; b. Manhattan, Kans., 1949; BA, U. Kans., 1971, JD, 1975; postgrad., Exeter U., 1971-72. Bar: Kans. 1975, Mo. 1978, U.S. Supreme Ct., 1995. Law clk. U.S. Dist. Ct., Kansas City, Kans., 1975-78; assoc. Lathrop Koontz & Norquist, Kansas City, Mo., 1978-83; ptnr. Lathrop & Norquist, Kansas City, 1984-92; judge City of Prairie Village, Kans., 1990-92, US Dist. Ct. Kans, 1992—. Bd. dirs. Kans. Legal Bd. Svcs., 1991-92; mem. com.on admistrv. office Jud. Conf. of the U.S., 2000-06; mem. jud. coun. U.S. Ct. Appeals for the Tenth Cir., 2002-04; mem. dist. judge adv. com. Fed. Jud. Ctr., 2003—, chair, 2006—; mem. U.S. Jud. Panel on Multi Dist. Litigation, 2004—. Bd. editors Kans. Law Rev., 1974-75, Jour. Kans. Bar Assn., 1992-94. Mem. nat. adv. bd. U. Kans. Ctr. for Environ. Edn. and Tng., 1993-95. Fellow Kans. Bar Found., Am. Bar Found.; mem. ABA (editl. bd. Judges Jour. 1996-98), Am. Judicature Soc., Nat. Assn. Judges, Fed. Judges Assn., Kans. Bar Assn. (mem. bench bar com., 2000—), Mo. Bar Assn., Kansas City Met. Area Bar Assn., Johnson County Bar Assn., Assn. Women Judges, Lawyers Assn. Kansas City, Kans. State Hist. Soc., U. Kans. Law Soc. (bd. govs. 1978-81, 2005—), Kans. U. Alumni Assn. (mem. Kansas City chpt. alumni bd. 1990-92, nat. bd. dirs. 1991-96, bd. govs. Adams Alumni Ctr. 1992-95), Native Sons and Daus of Kans. (life), Jr. League Wyandotte and Johnson Counties, Order of Coif, Kans. Inn of Ct. (master 1993—, pres. 1999-2000), Phi Kappa Phi. Republican. Presbyterian. Office: Robert J Dole US Courthouse Ste 511 500 State Ave Kansas City KS 66101-2403 Office Phone: 913-551-6550.

VREE, ROGER ALLEN, lawyer; b. Chgo., Oct. 2, 1943; s. Louis Gerard and Ruby June (Boersma) V.; m. Lauren Trumbull Gartside, Mar. 29, 1969; children: Jonathan Todd, Matthew David. BA, Wheaton Coll., 1965; MA, Stanford U., 1966, JD, 1969. Bar: Ill. 1969, U.S. Dist. Ct. (no. dist.) Ill. 1969. Assoc. Sidley & Austin, Chgo., 1969—75; ptnr. Sidley Austin LLP, Chgo., 1975—. Mem.: ABA. Office: Sidley Austin LLP One South Dearborn Chicago IL 60603 E-mail: rvree@sidley.com.

VROMAN, KENDAL, investment company executive; b. 1971; BS in Applied Computer Sci., Ill. St. Univ., 1997; MBA with emphasis in Fin., Mktg., Northwestern Univ. Kellogg Sch. Mgmt., 1999. With marchFirst, Inc.; with Am. Info. Sys. Divsn. Andersen Cons. LLP; consul. Chgo. Merc. Exch. Holdings, Inc., Chgo., 2001—02, project mgr., 2002—05, dir., co-head corp. devel., 2005—. Named one of 40 Under Forty, Crain's Bus. Chgo., 2005. Office: Chgo Merc Exch Holdings Inc 20 S Wacker Dr Chicago IL 60606 Office Phone: 312-930-1000.

VROUSTOURIS, ALEXANDER, inspector general; b. Chgo., Apr. 24, 1954; BS, Loyola U., 1977; JD, John Marshall Law Sch., 1980. Bar: Ill. Asst. state atty. Cook County State Atty.'s Office, Chgo., 1980-89; inspector gen. Office of the Inspector Gen. City of Chgo., 1989—. Contbr. articles to profl. jours. Mem. Nat. Assn. Inspector Gens., Ill. Bar Assn. Office: City of Chgo Office of the Inspector Gen PO Box 2996 Chicago IL 60654-2996

VRTISKA, FLOYD P., state legislator; b. Oct. 12, 1926; m. Doris Vrtiska; children: Terri Jo, Lori Ann, Kim R. Grad., Table Rock H.S. Commr., chmn. Pawnee County, ebr., 1973-92; mem. Nebr. Legislature from 1st dist., Lincoln, 1992—; mem. agr., health and human svc. coms. Nebr. Legislature, Lincoln, vice chmn. bus. and labor com. Recipient Ak-Sar-Ben Agr. Achievement award, Outstanding Cmty. Svc. award Peru State Coll., Ak-Sar-Ben Nebr. Farm Bur. award, Appreciation award Table Rock Devel. Corp., County Ofcl. of Yr. award and Pres.'s award Nebr. Assn. County Ofcls., Spl. Svc. award Table Rock Vol. Fire Dept.

VRUWINK, AMY SUE, state legislator; b. May 22, 1975; BS, Marion Coll., Fond du Lac, Wis., 1997. Former congl. aide; mem. Wis. State Assembly, Madison, 2002—, sec. Minority Caucus, 2003—. Democrat. Office: State Capitol Rm 412N PO Box 8953 Madison WI 53708 Address: 9425 Flower Ln Milladore WI 54454

VUKMIR, LEAH, state legislator; b. Apr. 26, 1958; m. George Vukmir; children: Elena, Nicholas. BSN, Marquette U., Milw., 1980; MSN, U. Wis., 1983. Cert. pediat. nurse practitioner, RN Wis. Faculty nursing St. Mary's Med. Ctr., Children's Hosp. of Wis.; mem. Wis. State Assembly, Madison, 2002—, vice chair edn. reform com., mem. children and families com., mem. econ. devel. com., mem. criminal justice com., mem. health com. Lectr. in field; guest panelist Sunday Insight TV show; rsch. fellow Wis. Policy Rsch. Inst.; past pres. Parents Raising Ednl. Stds. in Schs. Contbr. articles to profl. jours. Vol. speedskating referee ASU; mem. stds. and assessment subcom. Gov. Tommy Thompson's Task Force on Edn. and Learning, Wis.; mem. English/lang. arts task force Coun. on Model Acad. Stds.; mem. choir Annunciation Greek Orthodox Ch. Recipient Alumni Achievement award, Brookfield East H.S., 2002, Unsung Hero award, Ctr. for Edn. Reform, Washington, 1998. Mem.: West Allis Speedskating Club. Republican. Greek Orthodox. Office: State Capitol Bldg Rm 307 N PO Box 8953 Madison WI 53708 Address: 2544 N 93d St Wauwatosa WI 53226

VUKOVICH, JOSEPH JOHN, judge; b. Youngstown, Ohio, Sept. 29, 1945; s. Joseph J. and Josephine (Kurdowski) V.; m. Patricia D. Matthews, 1988 (div.); children: Andrew Joseph, Joseph John. BA, Youngstown State U., 1968; JD, U. Akron, 1973. Bar: Ohio. Asst. atty gen. State of Ohio, 1973-77; dep. dir. law City of Youngstown, Ohio, 1978—; rep. dist. 52 Ohio Ho. Reps., Columbus, 1978-92; senator Ohio State Senate, Columbus, 1993-97; judge State of Ohio 7th Dist. Ct. Appeals, 1997—. Mem. civil and comml. law commn., 1982-84, Ohio Ho. Reps., chmn. ethics com. 1980-82, 88-92; bd. commrs. grievances and discipline Supreme Ct. Ohio, 2005—. Mem. Easter Seal Soc. Decorated Bronze star U.S. Army; recipient Meritorious Svc. award Ohio Acad. Trial Lawyers, 1981, 87, Commdrs. award Nat. Amvets 1983, Resolution of Merit, Ohio Prosecuting Attys., 1984, Meritorius Service medal U.S. Selective Svc. System, 1986. Mem. ABA, VFW (Legislator of Yr. Ohio 1982), Ohio State Bar Assn., Mahoning County Bar Assn., Cath. War Vets. Am. (Disting. Legislator Ohio 1988), Ohio Appellate Judges Assn. Office: 7th Dist Ct Appeals Mahoning County Courthouse Youngstown OH 44503

WACHTMANN, LYNN R., state legislator; m. Trudy Blue; children: Cory, Aaron. Grad., Four County Joint Vocat. Sch. Owner, pres. Maumee Valley Bottlers, Inc., apoleon, Ohio; ptnr. Culligan Water Conditioning; former councilman City of Napoleon; mem. Ho. of Reps., Ohio, 1985—98, Ohio Senate from 1st dist., Columbus, 1999—2007, chmn. health, human svcs. and aging com., mem. energy, natural resources, environment, highways and transp., ins., commerce and labor coms.; State Repr. Dist 75 Ohio State Ho. of Reps., 2007—. Vol. fundraiser Crisis Pregnancy Ctrs. of N.W. Ohio, Bryan; vol. Orphan Grain Train; mem. Rep. Ctrl. Com.; Sunday sch. tchr., usher St. Paul Luth. Ch.; bd. dirs. Ohio Water Quality Assn. Named Nat. Legislator of Yr., Am. Legis. Exch. Coun., 1994, State Legislator of Yr., Nat. Retail Fedn., 1996, Legislator of Yr., Am. Legion, 2000; recipient Bobcat Legis. award, 1993, Watchdog of the Treasury award, United Conservatives of Ohio, Oustanding Freshman Legislator of Yr. award, 2000, Grad. Wall of Fame award, Four County Joint Vocat. Sch., 1997, Legislator of Yr. Defender of Life award, Ohio Right to Life, 1997, Conservation Legis. award, League of Ohio Sportsmen Nat. Wildlife Fedn., 1997, Guardian of Small Bus. award, Nat. Fedn. Ind. Bus., 1998. Mem.: NRA, Ohio Twp. Assn., Nat. Assn. Sportsman Legislators, Am. Legis. Exch. Coun. (state chmn.), Ohio Right to Life Soc., Gideon's Internat., Ohio Farm Bur., Pheasants Forever, Ducks Unlimited. Republican. Office: 550 Euclid Ave Napoleon OH 43545-2028 Office Phone: 614-466-8150.

WACK, THOMAS E., lawyer; b. Mo., 1944; AB magna cum laude, Georgetown U., 1966; JD, Northwestern U., 1969. Bar: Mo. 1969. Ptnr., mem. exec. com. Bryan Cave LLP, St. Louis. Program dir. Fed. Practice Com. U.S. Dist. Ct. (Mo. dist.). Fellow Am. Coll. Trial Lawyers; mem. ABA, Mo. Bar Assn. (mem. bus. torts com., mem. unfair competition com. 1990-92). Office: Bryan Cave LLP One Metropolitan Square 211 North Broadway, Ste 3600 Saint Louis MO 63102 Office Phone: 314-259-2182. E-mail: tewack@bryancave.com.

WADDELL, FREDERICK H. (RICK WADDELL), finance company executive; b. June 14, 1953; BA, Dartmouth Coll., 1975; MBA, Northwestern U., 1979. Various positions Northern Trust Corp., Chgo., 1975—83, v.p., 1983—89, exec. v.p., Northern Trust Bank Calif., 1991—94, exec. v.p., wealth mgmt. group, 1994—2003, pres., corp. & instl. svc., 2003—06, pres., COO, 2006—08, pres., CEO, 2008—. Chmn. bd. trustees Kohl Children's Mus.; trustee Art Inst. Chgo., treas., mem. exec. com. Mem.: Comml. Club Chgo., Fin. Svcs. Roundtable, Exec. Club Chgo. (bd. dirs.). Avocations: reading, travel, golf. Office: Northern Trust Corp 50 S LaSalle St Chicago IL 60603 Office Phone: 312-444-3939. Office Fax: 312-444-7843.*

WADDELL, RICK See WADDELL, FREDERICK

WADDEN, RICHARD ALBERT, environmental engineer, educator, science administrator, consultant; b. Sioux City, Iowa, Oct. 3, 1936; s. Sylvester Francis and Hermina Lillian (Costello) Wadden; m. Angela Louise Trabert, Aug. 9, 1975; children: Angela Terese, Noah Albert, Nuiko Clare. Student, St. John's U., Collegeville, Minn., 1954-56; BSChemE, Iowa State U., 1959; MSChemE, N.C. State U., 1962; PhD in Chem. and Environ. Engring., Northwestern U., 1972. Registered profl. engr., Ill., cert. indsl. hygienist. Engr. Linde Co., Tonnawanda, NY, 1959-60, Humble Oil Co., Houston, 1962-65; instr. engring. Pahlavi U. Peace Corps, Shiraz, Iran, 1965-67; tech. adviser Ill. Pollution Control Bd., Chgo., 1971-72; asst. dir. Environ. Health Resource Ctr. Ill., Chgo., 1972-74; from asst. prof. to assoc. prof. environ. and occupational health scis. Sch. Pub. Health U. Ill., Chgo., 1972—79, prof., 1979—2003, dir., 1984-86, 88-92, dir. Office Tech. Transfer Ctr. Solid Waste Mgmt. and Rsch., 1987-92, dir. indsl. hygiene and hazardous waste tng. programs Occupl. Safety and Health Ctr., 1987—2002, prof. emeritus, 2003—. Vis. scientist Nat. Inst. Environ. Studies, Japan, 1978—79, invited scientist, Japan, 1983, Japan, 84, Japan, 88; cons. air pollution control, health implications energy devel., indoor air pollution. Author: (book) Energy Utilization and Environmental Health, 1978; author: (with P. A. Scheff) Indoor Air Pollution, 1983; author: Engineering Design for Control of Workplace Hazards, 1987; contbr. articles to profl. pubs. Vis. scholar, orthwestern U., Evanston, Ill., 1997; Sr. Internat. fellow, Fogarty Internat. Ctr.-NIH, 1978—79, 1983, WHO fellow, 1984. Mem.: AIChE, Am. Conf. Govtl. Indsl. Hygienists, Am. Indsl. Hygiene Assn., Air and Waste Mgmt. Assn., Am. Acad. Indsl. Hygiene (diplomate), Am. Acad. Environ. Engrs. (diplomate), Am. Chem. Soc. Address: 816 16th St Wilmette IL 60091

WADE, EDWIN LEE, lawyer, writer; b. Yonkers, NY, Jan. 26, 1932; s. James and Helen Pierce (Kinne) W.; m. Nancy Lou Sells, Mar. 23, 1957; children: James Lee, Jeffrey K. BS, Columbia U., 1954; MA, U. Chgo., 1956; JD, Georgetown U., 1965. Bar: Ill. 1965. Fgn. svc. officer U.S. Dept. State, 1956-57; mktg. analyst Chrysler Internat., S.A., Switzerland, 1957-61; intelligence officer CIA, 1961-63; industry analyst U.S. Internat. Trade Commn., 1963-65; gen. atty. Universal Oil Products Co., Des Plaines, Ill., 1965-72; atty. Amsted Industries, Inc., Chgo., 1972-73; chief counsel dept. gen. svcs. State of Ill., Springfield, 1973-75; sr. atty. U.S. Gypsum Co., Chgo., 1975-84; gen. atty. USG Corp., 1985, corp. counsel, 1986, asst. gen. counsel, 1987, corp. sec., asst. gen. counsel, 1990-93; prin. Edwin L. Wade, 1993-95; instr. Roosevelt U., Chgo., 1995-96. Author: (books) Constitution 2000: A Federalist Proposal for the New Century, 2000, Talking Sense at Century's End: A Barbarous Time.Now What?, 2000; editor: Let's Talk Sense, A Pub. Affairs ewsletter, 1994-98. Fellow Chgo. Bar Assn. (life); mem. ABA, Ill. Bar Assn., Am. Philatelic Soc. Home: 434 Mary Ln Crystal Lake IL 60014-7257 Office: Let's Talk Sense Pub Co PO Box 2195 Crystal Lake IL 60039-2195

WADE, JANICE ELIZABETH, musician, educator, conductor; b. Decorah, Iowa, May 20, 1937; d. Lloyd Edward and Vivian Lois (Caskey) Richards; children: Kendall Anne, Craig Patrick. B in Music Edn., Drake U., 1959, M in Music Edn., 1960; DMA in Violin Performance, U. Iowa, 1992. Pvt. tchr. music, freelance violinist, Des Moines, 1960-87; prof. music Wartburg Coll., Waverly, Iowa, 1987—, chair, music dept. Prin. 2d violin Des Moines Symphony, 1965—87, chmn. players com., 1978—85, mem. negotiating team, 1983—87; tchr. instrumental music Des Moines pub. schs., 1966—76; founder, music dir., condr. Des Moines Cmty. Orch., 1976—87; concertmaster Bijou Players, Des Moines, 1980—; dir., condr. Wartburg Cmty. Symphony, 1987—. Editor: Am. String Tchr. Jour., 1976—84; contbr. articles to profl. jours. Active Planned Parenthood, Mus. Panel Iowa Arts Coun., 1989—90. Mem.: AAUP, Am. Symphony Orch. League, Am. String Tchrs. Assn., Condrs'. Guild, Iowa String Tchrs. Assn. (past pres.). Avocations: sewing, jogging, home decorating, reading, woodworking. Office: Wartburg Coll Dept Music 100 Wartburg Blvd # 1003 Waverly IA 50677-2215

WADE, NIGEL, former editor in chief; b. New Zealand; Editor in chief Chgo. Times, 1996—2000. Recipient Ethics in Jour. award, 1999; grantee Nieman Fell., Harvard U. Office: Chicago Sun Times 350 N Orleans St Ste 1270 Chicago IL 60654-2148

WAGGENER, RONALD EDGAR, radiologist; b. Green River, Wyo., Oct. 6, 1926; s. Edgar Fleetwood and Mary Harlene (Hutton) W.; m. Everina Ann Stalker, Aug. 1, 1948; children: Marta, Nancy, Paul, Daphne. Student, Colo. A&M U., 1944; student, Oreg. State U., 1945; BS, U. Nebr., 1949, MS, 1952, PhD, 1957, MD cum laude, 1954, postgrad., 1955-58, St. Bartholomew's, London, 1956-57. Diplomate Am. Bd. Radiology. Intern U. Nebr. Hosp., 1954-55, resident, 1955-56, 57-58; radiation therapist Nebr. Meth. Hosp., Omaha, 1965-70, chmn. cancer com., 1964-89, dir. cancer and radiation therapy, 1964-89, dir. dept. radiology, 1970-89, dir. cancer fellowship program, 1977-89; instr. radiology U. Nebr., Omaha, 1958, asst. prof., 1959-61, radiation therapist, 1959-65, assoc. prof., 1962-80, clin. assoc. prof., 1981—. Pres. Highland Assocs. Ltd., Omaha, 1977-89; mem. cancer com. Children's Meml. Hosp., Omaha, 1970-89. Contbr. articles to profl. jours. With C.E., U.S. Army, 1944-46. Fellow AEC, 1952-53, Am. Cancer Soc., 1956-57. Fellow Am. Coll. Radiologists; mem. Nebr. Radiology Soc. (pres. 1963-64), Sigma Xi, Alpha Omega Alpha, Phi Nu. Office: 13304 W Center Rd Omaha NE 68144-3453 Home: 1227 S 109th St Omaha NE 68144-1813

WAGGONER, LAWRENCE WILLIAM, law educator; b. Sidney, Ohio, July 2, 1937; s. William J. and Gladys L. Waggoner; m. Lynne S. Applebaum, Aug. 27, 1963; children: Ellen, Diane. BBA, U. Cin., 1960; JD, U. Mich., 1963; PhD, Oxford U., Eng., 1966. Assoc. Cravath, Swaine & Moore, NYC, 1963; prof. law U. Ill., Champaign, 1968-72, U. Va., Charlottesville, 1972—74, U. Mich., Ann Arbor, 1974-84, Lewis M. Simes prof. law, 1987—. Dir. rsch., chief reporter joint editorial bd. for Uniform Trust and Estate Acts, 1986-94, dir. rsch., 1994—, mem. joint editl. bd. uniform trust and estate acts; reporter restatement (3d) of property, 1990—; adviser restatement (3d) of trusts, 1993—. Author: Family Property Law: Wills, Trusts, and Future Interests, 4th edit., 2006, Uniform Trust and Estate Statutes, 2007, California and Uniform Trust and Estate Statutes, 2007. Served to capt., U.S. Army, 1966-68. Fulbright scholar Oxford U., 1963-65; named to Sidney City Schs. Hall of Honor, Ohio, 2007. Mem. Am. Law Inst., Am. Coll. Trust and Estates Counsel, Internat. Acad. Estate and Trust Law. Office: U Mich Law Sch 625 S State St Ann Arbor MI 48109-1215 Business E-Mail: waggoner@umich.edu.

WAGGONER, SUSAN MARIE, electronics engineer; b. East Chicago, Ind., Sept. 1, 1952; d. Joseph John and Elizabeth Vasilak; m. Steven Richard Waggoner, July 31, 1976; children: Kenneth David, Michael Christopher. AS, Ind. U., 1975, BA in Journalism, 1976, BS in Physics, 1982, M in Pub. Affairs, 1991. Engring. technician aval Surface Warfare Ctr., Crane, Ind., 1978-82, electronics engr. test and measurement equipment, 1982-91, electronics engr. batteries, 1991—. Conf. chair Tri-Svc. Power Expn., 2003. Recipient Value Engring. Spl. award Dept. of Def., 2000. Mem. AIAA, Am. Soc. Naval Engrs., Fed. Mgr. Assn., Federally Employed Women, Am. Rose Soc., Am. Hort. Soc., Mensa, Theatre Circle Ind. U., Sigma Pi Sigma. Office: Naval Surface Warfare Ctr 300 Highway 361 Crane IN 47522-5001 Home: 22842 Harper Hill Rd Loogootee IN 47553-4660

WAGLE, SUSAN, state legislator, small business owner; b. Allentown, Pa., Sept. 27, 1953; m. John Thomas Wagle, Apr. 3, 1980; children: Julia Marie, Andrea Elizabeth, John Timothy, Paul Thomas. BA in Elem. Edn. cum laude, Wichita State U., 1979, post grad., 1979-82. Tchr. Chisholm Trail Elem., Kans., 1979-80; tchr. emotionally disturbed, special edn. Price Elem., Kans., 1980-82; real estate investor Kans., 1980—; prin. Wichita Bus. Inc., Kans., 1983—; mem. Kans. Ho. Reps. from 99th dist., Topeka, 1990, 92, 94-2000; speaker pro tem Kans. Ho. Reps., Topeka, 1994-2000; mem. Kans. Senate from 30th dist., Topeka, 2001—. Mem. Am. Legis. Exchange Coun. (state chmn., nat. bd. dirs., Outstanding Legis. of Yr. award 1994), Farm Bur., Nat. Fedn. Ind. Bus., Nat. Restaurant Assn., Wichita Ind. Bus. Assn. Home: 14 N Sandalwood St Wichita KS 67230-6612

WAGNER, ALEXANDER JOHANNES, physicist, educator; m. Heather Jean Ummel-Wagner, Oct. 10, 2000. Diploma in Math., U. Bielefeld, Germany, 1990, diploma in Physics, 1990; MS in Physics, U. Bielefeld, 1994; PhD in Theoretical Physics, Oxford U., Eng., 1997. Postdoctoral rsch. asst. MIT, Cambridge, Mass., 1998—99, U. Edinburgh, Scotland, 2000—02; asst. prof. N.D. State U., Fargo, 2002—. Presenter in field. Achievements include research in lattice boltzmann; spinodal decomposition; viscoelasticity. Office: ND State Univ Dept Physics Administration Dr Box 5566 Fargo ND 58105-5566 Office Phone: 701-231-9582. Business E-Mail: alexander.wagner@ndsu.edu.

WAGNER, ALYSON KAY (ALY WAGNER), professional soccer player; b. San Jose, Calif., Aug. 10, 1980; Majored in combined scis., Santa Clara U., Calif., 1999—2002. Soccer player, midfielder U.S. Women's Nat. Team, 1998—; team mem. San Diego Spirit, 2003—. No. 1 draft pick San Diego Spirit, WUSA, 2003. Finalist Hermann trophy, 2001, Mo. Athletic Club award, 2001; named second team All-Am, NSCAA, 2000, first team All-Am, 2001, first team All-Am., 2002, Offensive MVP, NCAA Final Four, 2001, Female Player of Yr., Soccer Am., 2001; recipient Top VII award, NCAA, 2002, Mo. Athletic Club Hermann trophy, 2002. Office: US Soccer Fedn 1801 S Prairie Ave Chicago IL 60616

WAGNER, BRUCE STANLEY, marketing professional; b. San Diego, Aug. 1, 1943; s. Robert Sheldon and Janet (Lowther) Wagner; m. Elizabeth Pearsall Winslow, Oct. 4, 1975; children: Sage Elizabeth, Alexander Winslow. BA, Dartmouth Coll., 1965; MBA, U. Pa., 1984. Sr. v.p. Grey Advt., Inc., NYC, 1967-81; exec. v.p., chief oper. officer Campaign '76 Media Comm., Inc., Washington, 1975-76; exec. v.p., bd. dirs. Ross Roy, Inc., Bloomfield Hills, Mich., 1981-91, Ross Roy Group, Inc., Bloomfield Hills, 1991—94; v.p. mktg. and comms. ITT Automotive Inc., Auburn Hills, Mich., 1995-99; pres. Wagner & Co., Ltd., Birmingham, Mich., 1999—2000; v.p. mktg. and corp. comms. MSX Internat. Inc., Southfield, Mich., 2001—03; pres. Wagner & Co., Ltd., Birmingham, 2004—. Mem. parents bd. Bucknell U., pres. parents bd., 1999—2000, mem. bus. adv. bd., chmn., 2003—. Mem.: Am. Assn. Advt. Agys. (chmn., bd. govs. Mich. coun. 1985—86, bd. govs. ctrl. region 1988—94), Wharton Alumni Assn. (chmn. 1983—85), Birmingham Athletic Club, Orchard Lake Country Club, Detroit Athletic Club, Wharton Club Mich. (bd. dirs. 1985—90). Office: PO Box 194 Glen Arbor MI 49636

WAGNER, BURTON ALLAN, lawyer; b. Milw., June 13, 1941; s. Irwin and Jennie (Oxman) W.; m. Georgia Olchoff, Aug. 29, 1964; children: Andrew, Laura. BBA in Acctg, U. Wis., 1963, JD, 1966, MA in Health Services Adminstrn, 1976. Bar: Wis. 1966. Assoc. legal counsel U. Wis., 1968-74; asst. to vice chancellor, legal counsel U. Wis. Hosps., 1974-77; asst. sec. Wis. Dept. Health and Social Services, 1977-83, adminstr. div. community services, 1979-83; clin. assoc. prof. health adminstrn. U. Wis.; ptnr. Thomas Harnisch & Wagner, Madison, 1983-85, Whyte & Hirschboeck, Madison, 1985-90; ptnr. (of counsel) Katten Muchin and Zavis, Madison, 1990-93; ptnr. Reinhart Boerner Van Deuren SC, Madison, 1993—. Served with USAR, 1966-68, Vietnam. Decorated Bronze Star. Mem. Soc. Law and Medicine, Wis. Bar Assn., Dane County Bar Assn. Jewish. Office: PO Box 2018 Madison WI 53701-2018 Office Phone: 608-229-2200. Business E-Mail: bwagner@reinhartlaw.com.

WAGNER, JEFF, radio personality; married. Grad., Marquette U., 1982. Head organized crime task force U.S. Atty.'s Office, 1982—93; atty. pvt. practice, 1993—98; radio host 620 WTMJ, Milw., 1998—. Rep. candidate State Atty. Gen., 1994. Avocations: golf, horse racing. Office: WTMJ 720 E Capital Dr Milwaukee WI 53212

WAGNER, JEFF, state representative; b. July 28, 1960; Grad., Mohawk H.S. Farmer, Seneca County, Ohio; state rep. dist. 81 Ohio Ho. of Reps., Columbus, 2002—, vice chair energy and environment com., mem. agr. and natural resources and conty and twp govt. coms., and regulatory reform subcom. Mem. Mohawk Bd. Edn., Ohio, 1992—94; bd. govs. North Ctrl. Ohio Ednl. Svc. Ctr., 1994—97; Seneca County commr., 1997—. Republican. Office: 77 S High St 12th fl Columbus OH 43215-6111

WAGNER, JOSEPH EDWARD, veterinarian, educator; b. Dubuque, Iowa, July 29, 1938; s. Jacob Edward and Leona (Callahan) W.; m. Kay Rose (div. Apr. 1983); children: Lucinda, Pamela, Jennifer, Douglas. DVM, Iowa State U., 1963; MPH, Tulane U., 1964; PhD, U. Ill., 1967. Asst. prof. U. Kans. Med. Ctr., Kansas City, 1967-69; assoc. prof. U. Mo. Coll. Vet. Medicine, Columbia, 1969-72, prof. vet. medicine, 1972—, Curator's prof., 1989—. Cons. Harlan Sprague Dawley, Indpls., 1984—. Author: The Biology and Medicine of Rabbits and Rodents, 1989, 4th edit., 1995. Recipient award of excellence in lab. animal medicine Charles River Found., Wilmington, Mass., 1986. Mem. AMVA, Am. Coll. Lab. Animal Medicine (pres. 1985-86), Am. Assn. Lab. Animal Scis. (pres. 1980-81). Office: U Mo-Coll of Veterinary Medicine Dept of Vet Pathobiology 1600 W Rollins Rd Columbia MO 65211-0001

WAGNER, JOSEPH M., church administrator; Exec dir. Division for Ministry of the Evangelical Lutheran Church in America, Chgo., 1987—. Office: Evangelical Lutheran Church Am 8765 W Higgins Rd Chicago IL 60631-4101

WAGNER, MARK ANTHONY, videotape editor; b. Bethlehem, Pa., Mar. 15, 1958; s. Harry Paul and Theresa Marie (Spadaccia) W.; m. Nancy Susan Davis, Sept. 8, 1984. BA in Comm., Temple U., 1980. Videotape operator Swell Pictures, Chgo., 1983-85; asst. editor Post Pro Video, Chgo., 1985-88; sr. editor Ave. Edit, Chgo., 1988-91; editor/post-prodn. supr. WMX Techs., Chgo., 1992-97; owner Spark Prodns., 1997. Recipient R.L. Jacobs Meml. award Boys' Clubs Am., 1976. Mem. at. Amusement Park Hist. Assn., Soc. Comml. Archaeology. Avocation: films.

WAGNER, MARY MARGARET, library and information scientist, educator; b. Mpls., Feb. 4, 1946; d. Harvey F.J. and Yvonne M. (Brettner) W.; m. William Moore, June 16, 1978; children: Lebohang Y.C., Nora M. BA, Coll. St. Catherine, St. Paul, 1969; MLS, U. Wash., 1973; PhD, U. Minn., 2003. Asst. libr. St. Margarets Acad., Mpls., 1969-70; libr. Derham Hall High Sch., St. Paul, 1970-71; youth worker The Bridge for Runaways, Mpls., 1971-72; libr. Guthrie Theater Reference and Rsch. Libr., Mpls., 1973-75; asst. br. libr. St. Paul Pub. Libr., 1975; prof. dept. info. mgmt. Coll. St. Catherine, St. Paul, 1975—. Del. Minn. Gov.'s Pre-White House Conf. on Librs. and Info. Svcs., 1990; mem. Minn. Pre-White House Program Com., 1989-90, Continuing Libr. Info. and Media Edn. Com. Minn. Dept. Edn., Libr. Devel. and Svcs., 1980-83, 87-2002; mem. cmty. faculty Met. State U., St. Paul, 1980—; mem. core revision com. Coll. St. Catherine, 1992-93, faculty budget adv. com., 1992-95, faculty pers. com., 1989-92, 2001-04, acad. computing com. 1991-96, ednl. policies com., 1998-01; chair curriculum subcom. Minn. Vol. Cert. Com., 1993—. Contbr. articles to profl. jours. Bd. dirs. Christian Sharing Fund, 1976-80, chair, 1977-78. Recipient Bonnie Jean Keley and Jean Kelly award Faculty Excellence, 2006; grantee U.S. Embassy, Maseru, Lesotho, Africa, Brit. Consulate, Maseru, Fed. Inst. Mus. and Libr. Scis., various founds., Upper Midwest Assn. for Intercultural Edn. travel grantee Assoc. Colls. Twin Cities. Fellow: Higher Edn Consortia for Urban Affairs (bd. dirs. 1998—2007); mem.: ALISE (chair internat. rels. com. 2001—03), ALA (libr. book fellows program 1990—91), Minn. Ednl. Media Orgn., Minn. Libr. Assn. (pres. 1981—82, chair continuing edn. com. 1987—90, steering com. Readers Adv. Roundtable 1989—91), Spl. Libr. Assn., Am. Soc. Indexers, Am. Soc. Info. Sci. Office: Coll St Catherine Dept Info Mgmt 2004 Randolph Ave Saint Paul MN 55105-1750 Office Phone: 651-690-6843. Business E-Mail: mmwagner@stkate.edu.

WAGNER, RAYMOND THOMAS, JR., lawyer, legal association administrator; b. St. Louis, June 8, 1959; s. Raymond T. and Loretto (Muenster) W.; m. Ann L. Trousdale, Feb. 20, 1987. BA, St. Louis U., 1981, MBA, 1984; JD, U. Mo., Kansas City, 1985; LLM in Taxation, Washington U., St. Louis, 1993. Bar: Mo. 1985, Ill. 1986, U.S. Supreme Ct. 1989, U.S. Tax Ct. 1989. Legal rsch. and writing instr. U. Mo., Kansas City, 1983-84; law clk. to chief justice Mo. Supreme Ct., Jefferson City, 1985-86; assoc. Gilmore & Bell, St. Louis, 1986-87, Suelthaus & Kaplan P.C., St. Louis, 1987-89; gen. counsel Mo. Dept Revenue, 1989-90; counsel to gov. State of Mo., Jefferson City, 1990-91; dir. revenue Mo. Dept. Revenue, 1991-93; counsel Armstrong Teasdale Schlafly & Davis, St. Louis, 1993; dir. revenue Ill. Dept Revenue, Springfield, 1993-95; legal and legis. v.p. Enterprise Rent-A-Car, St. Louis, 1995—; mcpl. judge City of Ballwin, Mo., 1999—2005. Adj. prof. law LLM taxation program sch. law Washington U., St. Louis, 1993—; adj. prof. tax law Fontbonne U., St. Louis, 2002-03; chmn. Gov.'s Ethics Com., 1991-92, Mo. Hwy. Reciprocity Commn., 1991-93; commr. Multistate Tax. Commn., 1991-93, Mo. Mil. Adv. Commn., 1991-93; mem. IRS Oversight Bd., 2003-, chmn., 2004-06. Precinct capt. Gravois Twp., Webster Groves, 1988; bd. dirs. Shelter the Children, St. Louis, 1988-95; bd. dirs. Foster Care Coalition St. Louis, 1995-2002, pres. 1998-2000; chmn. platform com. Mo. Rep. Conv., 1992; exec. bd. dirs. St. Louis U. Sch. Bus.; mem. chancellor's coun. U. Mo., St. Louis, 1998—. Mem. ABA, Ill. Bar Assn., Mo. Bar Assn., Bar Assn. Met. St. Louis (chmn. law student svcs. com. 1986-87, chmn. social com. 1987-88, mem. exec. com. young lawyers assn. 1988-89, co-chmn. administrv. law com., govt. liaison com. young lawyers sect. 1989-90, chmn. legis. com. 1991-2004, legal svcs. oversight commn. 2001-), Regional Commerce and Growth Assn. (vice chair pub. policy coun. 1996, chair pub. policy coun. 1998-2000, vice chair govt. affairs exec. com. 2000-02), Associated Industries Mo. (bd. dirs. 1996-2003), Mo. C.of C. (bd. dirs. 1998-2004). Republican. Roman Catholic. Home: 313 Saint Andrews Ct Ballwin MO 63011-2504 Office: Enterprise Rent-A-Car 600 Corporate Park Dr Saint Louis MO 63105-4204 Office Phone: 314-512-5000. E-mail: rwagner@erac.com.

WAGNER, ROD, library director; b. Oakland, Nebr., Sept. 14, 1948; s. Francis Lynn and Doris Jean (Egbers) W.; m. M. Diane Kennedy, June 14, 1969; children: Jennifer, Brian, James. BA Social Sci. Edn., Wayne State Coll., Nebr., 1970; MA Polit. Sci., U. Nebr. Lincoln, 1971; MA Libr. Sci., U. Mo., 1981. Rsch. coord. Nebr. Libr. Commn., Lincoln, 1972, planning, evaluation, rsch. coord., 1972-73, adminstrv. asst., 1973-74, dep. dir., 1974-87, dir., 1988—. Bd. dirs. Nebr. Universal Svcs., 1998-2006. Mem. state govt. coun. Nebr. Info. Tech. Commn., 1999—. With U.S. Army N.G., 1970-77. Mem. ALA (contbr. yearbook 1981-84), Assn. Specialized and Cooperative Libr. Agys. (bd. dirs. 1998-2000), Nebr. Libr. Assn. (pres.-elect 1993-94, pres. 1994-95), Chief Officers State Libr. Agys. (dir. 2006-08), Western Coun. State Librs. (pres. 1992-93). Presbyterian. Office: NE Libr Commn 1200 N St Ste 120 Lincoln NE 68508-2023 Office Phone: 402-471-4001. Business E-Mail: rwagner@nlc.state.ne.us.

WAGNER, WILLIAM BURDETTE, business educator; b. Oswego, NY, Apr. 27, 1941; s. Guy Wesley and Gladys M. (Redlinger) W.; divorced; 1 child, Geoffrey D. BA with highest honors, Mich. State U., 1963; MBA, Ohio State U., 1965, PhD, 1967. Research and teaching asst. Ohio State U., Columbus, 1966-68; prof. mktg. and logistics U. Mo., Columbia, 1969-2000, prof. emeritus, 2000—; internat. bus. and mgmt. cons., 1972—. Guest prof. mktg. U. Nanjing, China, 1985-87, Prince of Songla U., Hat Yai, Thailand, 1990, 92, 98, 99, Assumption U., Bangkok, 1998-99, U. of Thai C. of C., Bangkok, 1998; vis. prof. bus. Chulalongkorn U., Bangkok, 2000-03; expert witness petroleum industry, 1989—; adv. dir. Mo. State Bank, St. Louis, 1981-93. Contbr. articles to profl. jours. Univ. coordinator book procurement program for minorities McDonnell Douglas, St. Louis, 1972—; mem. St. Louis-Nanjing Sister City Com., 1985—; faculty ambassador U. Mo. Alumni Assn., 1987—; mem. speakers bur., high sch. liaison team U. Mo., 1987—; Mizzou Outreach prof., 1987—; bd. dirs. Cen. Mo. Sheltered Enterprises for Handicapped, Columbia, 1985-92. Recipient Civic Svc. award McDonnell Douglas, 1977, Educator of Yr. award Jr. C. of C., 1983, Prof. of Yr. award Coll. of Bus. and Pub. Adminstrn., 1987, Golden Key Honor Soc. Faculty Mem. of Yr. award, 1987, Faculty Mem. of Yr. award Beta Theta Pi, 1990, Prof. of Yr. award Kans. City Alumni Assn., 1990; named Mktg. Prof. of Yr., U. Mo., 1987-88, 89-91; rsch. grantee SBC, Econ. Devel. Adminstrn., U. Mo.; NDEA fellow Ohio State U., 1963-66, William T. Kemper Teaching fellow, 1991, Wakonse Teaching fellow, 1995; Fulbright scholar, Korea, 1992. Mem. Nat. Assn. Purchasing Mgmt., St. Louis Purchasing Mgmt. Assn., Coun. Logistics Mgmt., Nat. Fulbright Assn. (life), Nat. Eagle Scout Assn., Am. Soc. Transp. and Logistics (pres. Mo. chpt. 1974-75, bd. govs. 1970-74, 75-82), Delta Sigma Pi, Beta Gamma Sigma, Omicron Delta Epsilon, Rotary Internat. (Paul Harris fellow), Mo. Athletic Club (St. Louis), Jefferson Club, Troon Country Club (Scottsdale, Ariz.). Methodist. Avocations: bridge, golf, stamp collecting/philately, running, reading.

WAGNON, JOAN, state official, retired banker, retired mayor; b. Texarkana, Ark., Oct. 17, 1940; d. Jack and Louise (lucas) D.; m. William O. Wagnon Jr., June 4, 1964; children: Jack, William O. III. BA in Biology, Hendrix Coll., Conway, Ark., 1962; MEd in Guidance and Counseling, U. Mo., 1968. Sr. rsch. technician U. Ark. Med. Sch., Little Rock, 1962-64, sr. rsch. asst. Columbia, Mo., 1964-68; tchr. No. Hills Jr. HS, Topeka, 1968-69, J.S. Kendall Sch., Boston, 1970-71; counselor Neighborhood Youth Corps, Topeka, 1973-74; exec. dir. Topeka YWCA, 1977-93; mem. Kans. Legislature, 1983-94; exec. dir. Kans. Families for Kids, 1994-97; mayor City of Topeka, 1997-2001; pres. Ctrl. Nat. Bank, Topeka, 2001—03; sec. of revenue State of Kansas, 2003—. Chair Multistate Tax Commn.; v.p. Streamlined Sales Tax Governing Bd. Mem. Health Planning Rev. Commn., Topeka, 1984-85; nat. bd. Girl Scouts USA. Recipient Service to Edn. award Topeka NEA, 1979, Outstanding Achievement award, Kans. Home Econs. Assn., 1985, Equity in Action award Kans. B & PW Clubs, 1991, Disting. Svc. award Kans. Ct. Svcs. Officers, 1992, Womens Rights Star award NOW, 1994; named Woman of Yr. Mayors Council Status of Women, 1983, named one of Top Ten Legislators Kans. Mag., Wichita, 1986, Legislator of Yr., Kans. NASW, 1989. Mem. Topeka Assn. Human Svc. Execs. (pres. 1981-83), Topekans for Ednl. Involvement (pres. 1979-82), Women's Polit. Caucus (state chair). Lodges: Rotary. Democrat. Methodist. Avocations: music, swimming, boating. Office: 915 Harrison St Topeka KS 66612 Home: 4036 NE Kimball Road Topeka KS 66617 Business E-Mail: wagnon@kdor.state.ks.us.

WAGONER, RALPH HOWARD, academic administrator; b. Pitts., May 30, 1938; s. Richard Henry and Charlotte (Stevenson) W.; m. Wilma Jo Staup, Dec. 21, 1961; children: Amanda Jane, Joseph Ryan. AB in Biology, Gettysburg Coll., 1960; MS in Ednl. Adminstrn., Westminster Coll., 1963; PhD, Kent State U., 1967; postgrad., MIT, 1973, Dartmouth Coll., 1979. Prin., tchr., coach Williamsfield (Ohio) Elem. and Jr. High Sch., 1960-62; dir. elem. edn. Pymatuning Valley (Ohio) Local Schs., 1962-64, asst. supt. instrn., 1964-65; acad. counselor, asst. to dean coll. edn. Kent (Ohio) State U., 1965-66, instr. edn., 1966-67; asst. prof. Drake U., Des Moines, 1967-70, assoc. prof., 1970-71, chmn. dept. elem. edn., 1968-70, chmn. dept. tchr. edn., 1970-71, acad. adminstrn. intern Am. Council Edn., Office of Pres., 1971-72, asst. to pres., 1972-77, dir. devel., 1975-77; v.p. pub. affairs and devel., prof. Western Ill. U., Macomb, 1977-87, pres., 1987-93, Augustana Coll., Sioux Falls, SD, 1993—2000, Lutheran Ednl. Conf. of N.Am. Adj. prof. San Francisco Theol. Sem., 1971; mem. senate Drake U., 1968-77; sponsor interhall council Western Ill. U., 197893, mem. BOG/UPI task force on incentives for faculty excellence, co-chmn., faculty mentor, 1985-93; cons. in field. Co-author: (with L. Wayne Bryan) Societal Crises and Educational Response: A Book of Readings, 1969, (with Robert L. Evans) The Emerging Teacher, 1970, (with William R. Abell) The Instructional Module Package System, 1971, Writing Behavioral Objectives or How Do I Know When He Knows, 1971; contbr. articles to profl. jours. Chmn. Mid-Ill. Computer Consortium, 1980, 85, Western Ill. Corridor of Opportunity, 1987-93; mem. Pres.' Regional Adv. Coun., 1977-87; mem. investments com. McDonough County YMCA; mem. exec. com. Macomb Area Indsl. Corp.; trustee Robert Morris Coll., 1983-88, Chgo. and Carthage, Ill., 1983-88; bd. dirs. Ill. Coun. Econ. Edn., 1987-93, McDonough County United Way Dr., 1980-82; bd. trustees The Cornerstone Found. LSS of Ill., 1990-96; mem. Sioux Falls Tomorrow Task Force, 1993-94; bd. dirs. S.D. Symphony, 1993—, Edn. Telecomms. State of S.D., 1993—, Sioux Falls Devel. Found., 1993—, Children's Inn, 1993—, Sioux Valley Physicians Alliance, 1995—, LECNA, 1996—; life trustee Lutheran Social Svcs., 1996—. Recipient Man of Yr. award Andover Rotary Club, 1964, Quax Honor award, 1969-70, Disting. Alumni award Gettysburg (Pa.) Coll., 1991; named McDonough County Citizen of Yr., Elks, 1982. Fellow Am. Coun. Edn. (cons. fund raising 1984-87); mem. Am. Assn. State Colls. and Univs. (com. econ. devel. 1988, com. on athletics 1987), Ednl. Computing Network (chmn. policy bd. 1985-87), Assn. Midcontinent Univs. (coun. dels. 1987-93), Gateway Conf. (coun. dels. 1987-93), Coun. for Advancement and Support of Edn. (discussion leader, speaker, 1975, 77, 80, 84, 86, 91, 92, 93, 94, Citation award 1981, 83, Grand award 1982, Bronze award 1985, Silver award 1986), Macomb C. of C. (exec. com., bd. dirs.), Ill. Chamber Econ. Devel. Policy Task Force, Blue Key (hon.), Omicron Delta Kappa, Phi Eta Sigma (hon.), Phi Mu Alpha. Lodges: Rotary. Lutheran. Office: Augustana Coll 2001 S Summit Ave Sioux Falls SD 57197-0001 Home: 6512 Evergreen Acres Dr Wentworth SD 57075-7316

WAGONER, RICK (G. RICHARD WAGONER JR.), automotive executive; b. Wilmington, Del., Feb. 9, 1953; BS in Econs., Duke U., 1975; MBA, Harvard U., 1977. Analyst in treas.'s office, mgr. Latin Am. financing, dir. Can. and overseas borrowing, dir. capital analysis and investment GM Corp., NYC, 1977-81, treas. Sao Paulo, Brazil, 1981-84, exec. dir. fin., 1984-87, v.p., fin. mgr., 1987-88, group dir. strategic bus. planning, 1988-89, v.p. fin. Zurich, Switzerland, 1989-91, pres. Brazil, 1992-93, head Worldwide Purchasing Group, 1993-94, exec. v.p., pres. N. Am. ops., 1994-98, pres., COO, 1998—2000, pres., CEO, 2000—03, chmn., CEO, 2003—. Bd. dirs GM Corp., 1998—. Chmn. bd. visitors Fuqua Sch. Bus. Duke U.; trustee Detroit County Day Sch. Mem. Soc. Automotive Engrs. (mem. VISION 2000 exec. com.). Office: GM Corp 300 Renaissance Ctr Detroit MI 48265-0001*

WAGONER, ROBERT HALL, engineering educator; b. Columbus, Ohio, Jan. 8, 1952; s. Robert H. and Leorra (Schmucker) W.; m. Robyn K. O'Donnell, Aug. 30, 1980; children: Erin A. Wagoner Hansgen, Amy J. BS, Ohio State U., 1974, MS, 1975, PhD, 1976. NSF postdoctoral rschr. U. Oxford, Eng., 1976-77; staff rsch. scientist GM Rsch. Labs., Warren, Mich., 1977-83; assoc. prof. material sci. engring. Ohio State U., Columbus, 1983-86, prof., 1986-98, chmn. dept., 1992-96, prof. engring, 1998—. Maitre de recherche Ecole des Mines de Paris, Sophia Antipolis, France, 1990-91; dir. Ohio State U. Rsch. Found., 1991-94, Ctr. Advt. Materials Mfg. Auto Components, 1994—; trustee Orton Found., 1992-96. Co-author: Fundamentals of Metal Forming, 1997; editor: Novel Techniques in Metal Deformation, 1983, Forming Limit Diagrams, 1989. Recipient Raymond Meml. award AIME, 1981, 83; Disting. Scholar award Ohio State U., 1990, Harrison award for tchg. excellence, 1988; Presdl. Young Investigator award NSF, 1984; NSF postdoctoral fellow Oxford (Eng.) U., 1976. Fellow ASM Internat.; mem. Nat. Acad. Engring., Minerals, Metals and Materials Soc. (pres. 1997-98, dir. 1991-95, Mathewson Gold medal 1988, Hardy Gold medal 1981, v.p. 1996-97, pres. 1997—), Am. Inst. Mining, Metall., and Petroleum Engring. (trustee 1997—). TMS found. (founding mem., trustee 1997—) Achievements include developing SHEET-3 and SHEET-S, sheet forming simulation programs for indsl. use; introducing first quantitative test for plane-tensile work hardening; inventing formability test and friction test. Office: Ohio State U Dept Material Sci Engring 2041 N College Rd Columbus OH 43210-1124

WAHL, RICHARD LEO, radiologist, educator, nuclear medicine physician, researcher; b. Iowa, July 13, 1952; s. Max Henry and Josephine Elizabeth (Hogan) Wahl; m. Sandra K. Moeller, June 28, 1975; children: Daniel, Matthew, Peter, Katherine. BA in Chemistry, Wartburg Coll., 1974; MD, Washington U., St. Louis, 1978. Diplomate Am. Bd. Nuc. Medicine (pres. 1998-), Am. Bd. Radiology. Intern U. Calif., San Diego, 1978—79; resident in radiology Mallinckrodt Inst. Washington U., 1979—82, fellow in nuc. medicine and immunology, 1982—83; asst. prof. U. Mich. Med. Ctr., Ann Arbor, 1983—87, assoc. prof., 1987—90, prof., 1990—2000; dir. gen. nuc. imaging, dir. radiopharm. program U. Mich. Cancer Ctr., 1999—2003; prof., dir. nuc. medicine, vice chair tech. and new bus. devel. Johns Hopkins U., Balt., 2002—. Mem. exptl. immunology study sect. NIH, Bethesda, Md., 1990—94; sec. Am. Bd. Nuc. Medicine, 1997, chmn., 98. Editor: 2 textbooks; contbr. more than 240 articles to profl. jours., chapters to books. Named Eugene Prendegreer New Horizon lectr., RSNA, 1999; recipient Disting. Scientist award, Acad. Molecular Imaging, 2001, Jerome W. Conn rsch. award, U. Mich., 1989; grantee ACS, Dept. of Army; rsch. grantee, IH. Fellow: Am. Coll. Radiology, Am. Coll. Nuc. Physicians; mem.: AMA, Inst. for Clin. Positron Emission Tomography (bd. dirs., pres. 1996), Am. Assn. for Cancer Rsch., Am. Soc. for Clin. Investigation, Radiol. Soc. N.Am., Soc. Nuc. Medicine (Marc Tetalman award 1986, Berson and Yalow rsch. award 1992, Hounsfield rsch. award 1992). Achievements include development of the drug Bexxar, approved by US Food and Drug Adminstrn. in 2003 to treat follicular non-Hodgkin's lymphoma; 10 patents in field. Avocations: reading, sports. Office: Johns Hopkins Outpatient Ctr Divsn Nuclear Medicine 601 N Caroline St Rm 3223 Baltimore MD 21287

WAHOSKE, MICHAEL JAMES, lawyer; b. Ripon, Wis., June 4, 1953; children: Jennifer, John. BA with highest honors, U. Notre Dame, 1975, JD summa cum laude, 1978. Bar: Minn. 1978, U.S. Dist. Ct. Minn. 1979, U.S. Ct. Appeals (7th cir.) 1979, U.S. Ct. Appeals (8th and 9th cirs.) 1980, U.S. Ct. Appeals (10th cir.) 1982, U.S. Supreme Ct. 1982, U.S. Ct. Appeals (6th cir.) 1988, U.S. Ct. Appeals (fed. cir.) 1989, U.S. Ct. Appeals (D.C. cir.) 1992, U.S. Ct. Appeals (4th cir.) 1994, U.S. Ct. Appeals (11th cir.) 1996, Supreme Ct. of Winnebago Tribe of Nebr., 1996. Law clk. to judge Luther M. Swygert U.S. Ct. Appeals (7th cir.), Chgo., 1978-79; law clk. to chief justice Warren E. Burger U.S. Supreme Ct., Washington, 1979-80; assoc. Dorsey & Whitney, Mpls., 1980-85, ptnr., chmn., appellate practice, 1986—. Adj. prof. law U. Minn., Mpls., 1981-83. Exec. editor U. Notre Dame Law Rev., 1977-78; co-editor: Freedom & Education: Pierce v. Society of Sisters Reconsidered, 1978.

Recipient Vol. Recognition award Nat. Assn. Attys. Gen., 1993, Spl. Recognition award, 2003; Supreme Ct. Reception honors State and Local Legal Ctr., 1991, 92, 93, 95. Fellow: Am. Acad. Appellate Lawyers; mem.: FBA, ABA (standing com. on Amicus Briefs 1997—2002), Hennepin County Bar Assn., Minn. Bar Assn., U.S. Ct. Appeals (8th cir.) Bar Assn., Phi Beta Kappa. Office: Dorsey & Whitney LLP Ste 1500 50 S Sixth St Minneapolis MN 55402-1498 Office Phone: 612-340-8755. Office Fax: 612-340-2868. Business E-Mail: wahoske.michael@dorsey.com.

WAINSCOTT, JAMES LAWRENCE, steel industry executive; b. LaPorte, Md., Mar. 31, 1957; s. James J. and Frances J. (Cunningham) Wainscott. BS magna cum laude, Ball State U., 1979; MBA, U. Notre Dame, 1987. CPA Ind., cert. mgmt. acct., internal auditor, info. sys. auditor, chartered fin. analyst. Sr. auditor Geo. S. Olive & Co., CPAs, Indpls., 1979—82; fin. mgr. Midwest Divsn. Nat. Steel Corp., Portage, Ind., 1982—88, mgr. pension investments Pitts., 1988—90, asst. treas., asst. sec., 1991—92, treas., asst. sec. Mishawaka, Ind., 1993—95; v.p. & treas. AK Steel Holding Corp., Middletown, Ohio, 1995—98, CFO, 1998—99, sr. v.p., CFO, 1999—2003, pres., CEO, 2003—, chmn., 2006—. Instr. acctg. Purdue U., Westville, 1980—82, Valparaiso U., 1980—84; cons. Edward J. Wainscott, CPA, LaPorte, Ind., 1982. Advisor Jr. Achievement, 1984; vol. Am. Cancer Soc., Calparaiso Income Tax Assistance Program, Calparaiso Cmty./U. Campaign; pres., treas. Midwest Steel Employees Fed. Credit Union; pres. Midwest Steel Employees Assn.; mem. Ball State U. Cardinal Connection, Northwest Ind. Open Housing Coun.; chmn. dean's adv. coun. Valparaiso U.; chmn. fin. com. Good Shepherd Parish, Cin., 1999—2001; bd. dirs. Youth Svc. Bur. St. Joseph County. Mem.: U. otre Dame Exec. MBA Alumni Assn., Chgo. Soc. Fin. Analysts, Assn. for Investment Mgmt. and Rsch., Inst. Chartered Fin. Analysts, Inst. Internal Auditors, Inst. Mgmt. Acctg., Am. Inst. CPA's, Nat. Assn. Accts. (chpt. bd. dirs. 1982—86, chpt. pres. 1983—84, Past Pres. award 1984), Ind. CPA Soc. (chpt. bd. dirs. 1983—86, chpt. pres. 1984—85, chmn. chpt. activities com. 1985—86, state bd. dirs. 1987—90, chmn. chpt. task force, Pres. award 1994), Mensa, Delta Sigma Pi, Intertel, Golden Key, Blue Key. Roman Catholic. Avocations: music, chess, coin collecting/numismatics, sports, travel. Office: AK Steel Holding Corp 703 Curtis St Middletown OH 45043 Home: 8099 Carnaby Ln Cincinnati OH 45249-1567

WAINSCOTT, KENT, reporter; b. Des Plaines, Ill. Reporter, anchor WTWO-TV, Terre Haute, Ind.; bur. chief reporter WDTN-TV, Dayton, Ohio; reporter WISN, Milw., 1988—. Recipient award, Clarion, NY Festivals Internat., AP, Wis. Broadcasters Assn., Milw. Press Club, Communicator awards, 5 regional Emmy awards. Office: WISN PO Box 402 Milwaukee WI 53201-0402

WAINTROOB, ANDREA RUTH, lawyer; b. Chgo., Dec. 23, 1952; d. David Samuel and Lees (Carson) W. AB, Brown U., 1975; JD, U. Chgo., 1978. Bar: Ill. 1978, U.S. Dist. Ct. (no. dist.) Ill. 1978, U.S. Dist. Ct. (cen. dist.) Ill. 1996, U.S. Ct. Appeals (7th cir.) 1982, U.S. Supreme Ct. 1989. Assoc. Vedder, Price, Kaufman and Kammholz, Chgo., 1978-84; ptnr. Vedder, Price, Kaufman, Chgo., 1984-94, Franczek Sullivan, P.C., Chgo., 1994—. Mem. Chgo. Bar Assn., Nat. Coun. Sch. Attys. Home: 5428 S Harper Ave Chicago IL 60615-5506 Office: Franczek Sullivan 300 S Wacker Dr Ste 3400 Chicago IL 60606-6708

WAIT, RONALD A., state legislator; b. Apr. 15, 1944; BS, JD, Drake U.; MBS, No. Ill. U., MS in Spl. Edn. Farm mgr.; mem. Ill. State Ho. of Reps. Dist. 64, 1983-93, Ill. State Ho. of Reps. Dist. 68, 1995—. Bd. dirs. Highland Hosp., Boone County Housing Authority Bd., Janet Wattles Mental Health Bd., United Givers Bd.

WAITE, DENNIS VERNON, brokerage house executive, consultant; b. Chgo., Aug. 26, 1938; s. Vernon George and Marie G. Waite; m. Christine Rene Hibbs; 1 child, Kip Anthony. BA, U. Ill., 1968; MS in Journalism, Northwestern U., 1969. Fin. reporter, columnist Chgo. Sun-Times, Chgo., 1969-76; asst. prof. Northwestern U., Evanston, Ill., 1978-79; assoc. prof. Mich. State U., East Lansing, 1979-82; ptnr. Fin. Rels. Bd., Inc., Chgo., 1982-90, sr. ptnr., 1991-97, sr. counselor, 1997—. Reporter, producer econ. affairs Sta. WTTW-TV, Sta. WBBM-TV, Chgo., 1973-76; adj. faculty English, Coll. of DuPage, 1998—2004. Mem. editorial adv. bd. alumni relations U. Ill., Chgo., 1980-84, 90-94. With USAF, 1956-60, PTO. Rutgers U. fellow, 1972. Mem. Medill Alumni Assn. (bd. dirs. 1989-92). Avocations: reading, writing, history, Tae Kwon Do. E-mail: dennis_waite@yahoo.com.

WAITE, NORMAN, JR., lawyer; b. Chgo., Mar. 16, 1936; s. Norman and Lavinia (Fyke) W.; m. Jaqueline A. Hurlbutt; children: Leslie Catherine, Lindsay H., Norman III. BA, Yale U., 1958; LLB, Harvard U., 1963. Bar: Ill. 1963. Assoc. Winston & Strawn, Chgo., 1963-69, ptnr., 1969-78, capital ptnr., 1978-99, exec. com., 1978-95, vice chmn., 1989-99. Bd. dirs. Steadman/Hawkins Sports Medicine Found. Lt. (j.g.) USN, 1958-60. Mem. ABA, Chgo. Bar Assn., Cordillera Club (Vail, Colo.), Indian Hill Club (Winnetka, Ill.), Econ. Club, Eagle Springs Club (Vail, Colo.). Republican. Home: 1710 N Burling St Chicago IL 60614-5102 Office: Winston & Strawn 35 W Wacker Dr Ste 4200 Chicago IL 60601-1695

WAJER, RONALD EDWARD, management consultant; b. Chgo., Aug. 31, 1943; s. Edward Joseph and Gertrude Catherine (Rytelny) W.; m. Mary Earlene Hagan, July 5, 1969; children: Catherine, Michael. BSIE, Northwestern U., 1966; MBA, Loyola U., Chgo., 1970. Project engring. mgr. Procter & Gamble, Chgo., 1966-67; indsl. engring. mgr. Johnson & Johnson, Bedford Park, Ill., 1967-71; project mgr. Jewel Cos., Franklin Park, Ill., 1971-73; divsn. engring. mgr. Abbott Labs., orth Chicago, Ill., 1973-79; pres. bus. engring. divsn. R.E. Wajer & Assocs., Northbrook, Ill., 1979—. Contbr. articles to profl. jours. Sec. Downtown Redevel. Commn., Mt. Prospect, Ill., 1977-78; fundraising vol. Maryville Acad., Des Plaines, 1985—; bd. dirs. Lattof YMCA, Des Plaines, 1994-96; profl. advisor Sch. for New Learning, DePaul U., 1994—; mem. indsl. sector com. Lincoln Found. for Bus. Excellence, 1997-99. Recipient Cmty. Svc. award Chgo. Lighthouse for the Blind, 1989, Cert. of Merit, Village of Mt. Prospect, 1978. Mem. Inst. Indsl. Engrs. (cmty. svc. chmn. 1984), Inst. Mgmt. Cons. (cert., exec. v.p., bd. dirs. 1987-94), Assn. Mgmt. Cons. (ctrl. regional v.p. 1985-87), Midwest Soc. Profl. Cons., Northwestern Club Chgo. Roman Catholic. Office: Bus Engring 5 Revere Dr Ste 200 Northbrook IL 60062-8000 Office Phone: 847-824-0809. Business E-Mail: rewajer@busnengg.com.

WAJSGRAS, DAVID C., manufacturing executive; m. Teena Wajsgras; 3 children. BS in Acctg., U. Md., College Park; MBA in Fin., Am. U. CPA. CFO Maserati Automobile, Balt.; sr. auditor Coopers & Lybrand; contr. Contellation Investments, C.G.I.; from contr. to v.p. fin. UNC Inc., Annapolis, Md.; various sr. fin. positions AlliedSignal, Inc., Morristown, NJ, 1992—97; corp. contr. Engelhard Corp., Iselin, NJ, 1997—99; v.p. contr. Lear Corp., Southfield, Mich., 1999—2002, sr. v.p., CFO, 2002—05, exec. v.p., CFO, 2005—06; CFO, sr. v.p. Raytheon Corp., Waltham, Mass., 2006—. Mem.: Fin. Execs. Inst. Office: Raytheon Corp 870 Winter St Waltham MA 02451-1449

WAKE, MADELINE MUSANTE, academic administrator, nursing educator; Diploma, St. Francis Hosp. Sch. Nursing, 1963; BS in Nursing, Marquette U., 1968, MS in Nursing, 1971; PhD, U. Wis., Milw., 1986. Clin. nurse specialist St. Mary's Hosp., Milw., 1971-74, asst. dir. nursing, 1974-77; from dir. continuing nursing edn. to provost Marquette U., Milw., 1977—2002, provost, 2002—. Mem. devel. team Internat. Classification for Nursing Practice, Geneva, 1991-99. Chmn. bd. dirs. Trinity Meml. Hosp., Cudahy, Wis., 1991-96; bd. dirs. Blood Ctr. Wis., 2003-. Recipient Profl. Svc. award Am. Diabetes Assn.-Wis. affiliate, 1978, Excellence in Nursing Edn. award Wis. Nurses Assn., 1989; named Disting. Lectr. Sigma Theta Tau Internat., 1991. Fellow: Am. Acad. Nursing; mem.: ANA, Am. Assn. Colls. and Univs., Vis. Nurs Assn. Wis. (bd. dirs.), Am. Assn. Coll. Nursing (bd. dirs. 1999—2002). Office: Marquette Univ O'Hara Hall Milwaukee WI 53201-1881 Office Phone: 414-288-7511.

WAKE, RICHARD W., food products executive; b. 1953; BS, U of Illinois. With Aurora Eby-Brown Co., Inc., 1975—, co-pres., bd. dir. Naperville, Ill., 1983—. Office: 280 Shuman Blvd Ste 280 PO Box 3067 Naperville IL 60566-7067

WAKE, THOMAS G., food products executive; Co-pres. Eby-Brown Co., Naperville, Ill., co-chief exec., 1983—. Office: Eby Brown Co 280 Shuman Blvd Ste 280 aperville IL 60563-2578

WAKEFIELD, MARY KATHERINE, medical association administrator, medical educator; b. Aug. 12, 1954; BSN, Mary Coll., Bismarck, ND, 1976; MSN, U. Tex., Austin, 1978, PhD, 1985; grad. program for sr. mgrs. in govt., Harvard U., 1991. RN. Staff nurse ICU St. Alexius Hosp., Bismarck, ND, 1975-76; nurse United Hosp., Grand Forks, ND, 1976-77; acad. asst. sch. nursing U. Tex., Austin, 1977-78; instr. Brackenridge Sch. Nursing Austin Community Coll., 1978-79; mem. faculty U. D, Grand Forks, 1979-87, assoc. prof., chairperson, 1985-87; legis. asst. health and edn. issues Senator Q. Burdick, Washington, 1987-89; chief of staff Senator Kent Conrad, Washington, 1989—96; prof., dir. Ctr. Health Policy, Rsch. & Ethics George Mason U., Fairfax, Va., 1996—2001; prof., dir. Ctr. Rural Health U. ND Sch. Medicine & Health Sciences, Grand Forks, 2001—, assoc. dean, 2001—. Bd. dirs. AcademyHealth, ND Health Care Rev., Blue Cross Blue Shield D; mem. VA spl. med. adv. group; bd. trustees Catholic Health Initiatives; part-time staff nurse The United Hosp., Grand Forks, 1979-86; mem. faculty assoc. U. Md. Sch. of Nursing, 1990—; mem. adj. faculty George Mason U. Sch. of Nursing, Va., 1990—; selected to participate in 1991 Cong. Bundestag Staff Exchange Program, Germany; presenter in field. Editorial bd. Nursing Econs., 1990—, Jour. Rural Health, Annals of Family Medicine; contbr. articles to profl. jours. Recipient Nurse Rsch. award, Am. Orgn. Nurse Execs., 2006. Fellow Am. Acad. Nursing; mem. AAUW, ANA (coun. nursing rsch.), Inst. Medicine, D Acad. Sci., Nat. League for Nursing, Philippine Nurses Assn. of Met. Washington (hon. 1991), Sigma Theta Tau, Sigma Xi. Office: Ctr Rural Health PO Box 9037 Grand Forks ND 58202-9037 Office Phone: 701-777-3848. Office Fax: 701-777-6779.

WAKOSKI, DIANE, poet, educator; b. Whittier, Calif., Aug. 3, 1937; d. John Joseph and Marie Elvira (Mengel) W. BA in English, U. Calif., Berkeley, 1960. Writer-in-residence Mich. State U., East Lansing, 1976—, Univ. disting. prof., 1990—. Vis. writer Calif. Inst. Tech., 1972, U. Va., 1972-73, Wilamette U., 1973, Lake Forest Coll., 1974, Colo. Coll., 1974, U. Calif., Irvine, 1974, Macalester Coll., 1975, U. Wis., 1975, Hollins Coll., 1974, U. Wash., 1977, Whitman Coll., 1976, Emory U., 1980-81, U. Hawaii, 1978. Author: Coins and Coffins, 1962, Discrepancies and Apparitions, 1966, Inside The Blood Factory, 1968, The George Washington Poems, 1967, The Magellanic Clouds, 1969, The Motorcycle Betrayal Poems, 1971, Smudging, 1972, Dancing On The Grave of A Son Of A Bitch, 1973, Trilogy, 1974, Virtuoso Literature For Two and Four Hands, 1976, Waiting For the King of Spain, 1977, The Man Who Shook Hands, 1978, Cap of Darkness, 1980, The Magician's Feastletters, 1982, The Collected Greed: Parts I-XIII, 1984, The Rings of Saturn, 1986, Emerald Ice: Selected Poems 1962-87, 1988 (William Carlos Williams prize 1989), Medea The Sorceress, 1991, Jason the Sailor, 1993, The Emerald City of Las Vegas, 1995, Argonaut Rose, 1998, The Butcher's Apron: New & Selected Poems, 2000. Named Univ. Disting. Prof., Mich. State U., 1990, Author of Yr., Mich. Libr. Assn., 2003; recipient award, Mich. Arts Found., 1989, Disting. Faculty award, Mich. State U., 1989; grantee Cassandra Found., 1970, N.Y. State Cultural Coun., 1971—72, Guggenheim Found., 1972—73, Fullbright, 1984, Mich. Arts Coun., 1988. Office: Mich State U 207 Morrill Hall East Lansing MI 48824-1036 Personal E-mail: dwakoski@aol.com.

WAKSCHLAG, MILTON SAMUEL, lawyer; b. Omaha, July 4, 1955; s. Fishel and Stefa (Kleiner) W.; m. Laurie S. Weinzweig, June 15, 1980; children: Tmima, Shira, Efraim. BA, Loyola U., 1977; JD, U. Chgo., 1980; LLM in Taxation, DePaul U., 1987. Bar: Ill. 1980. Assoc. Borge and Pitt, Chgo., 1980-85, ptnr., 1986, Katten Muchin Rosenman LLP, Chgo., 1987—, chair, pub. fin. dept., chair, fin. products group, mem. pro bono com. Adv. com. on svcs. to disabled, Ill. Atty. Gen's Office; prin. faculty mem. nat. tng. seminar, Govt. Fin. Officers Assn.; co-chair Bond Buyer's Ninth Ann. Midwest Pub. Fin. Conf.; nat. conf. chmn., Ctr. Bus. Intelligence; spkr. in field. Author: Important Developments During the Year: Tax Exempt Financing, 1989; contbr. papers in field. Founder, v.p., bd. dirs., trustee Keshet: Jewish Parents of Children with Spl. Needs, 1984—2006; trustee Lincolnwood Dist. Pub. Libr., 1988-89; bd. dirs. Brisk Rabbinical Coll., 1990-2006. Recipient Pro Bono Svc. award, Katten Muchin Rosenman LLP, Guardian of Hope award, Keshet, 2006. Mem. ABA (chmn. com. on tax-exempt fin., 1999-2001), Nat. Assn. Bond Lawyers (mem. steering com. bond attys.' workshop). Office: Katten Muchin Rosenman LLP 525 W Monroe St Chicago IL 60661 Office Fax: 312-577-8897. Business E-Mail: milton.wakschlag@kattenlaw.com.

WALBERG, HERBERT JOHN, psychologist, educator, consultant; b. Chgo., Dec. 27, 1937; s. Herbert J. and Helen (Bauer) W.; m. Madoka Bessho, Aug. 20, 1965; 1 child, Herbert J. III. BE in Edn. and Psychology, Chgo. State U., 1959; ME in Counseling, U. Ill., 1960; PhD in Ednl. Psychology, U. Chgo., 1964. Instr. psychology Chgo. State U., 1962—63, asst. prof., 1964—65; lectr. edn. Rutgers U., New Brunswick, NJ, 1965—66; asst. prof. edn. Harvard U., Cambridge, Mass., 1966—69; assoc. prof. edn. U. Ill., Chgo., 1970—71, prof., 1971—84, rsch. prof., 1984—, external examiner, 1981. External examiner, 1981; ednl. cons. numerous orgns.; external examiner Monash U., 1974, 76, Australian Nat. U., 1977; speaker in field; former coord. worldwide radio broadcasts on Am. Edn. Voice of Am., USIA, Office Pres. U.S., cons. Ctr. for Disease Control U.S. Pub. Health Svcs., 1985-90. Author, editor 49 books; chmn. editl. bd. Internat. Jour. Ednl. Rsch., 1985—; contbr. over 350 articles to profl. jours., chpts. to books. Mem. Chgo. United Edn. Com., also other civic groups, 1971-86; bd. dirs. Family Study Inst., 1987; chmn. bd. dirs. Heartland Inst., 1995. Nat. Inst. Edn. rsch. grantee, 1973, NSF rsch. grantee, 1974, March of Dimes rsch. grantee, 1976, numerous others. Fellow AAAS, Am. Psychol. Assn., Royal Statis. Soc.; mem. Internat. Acad. Edn. (founding), Am. Ednl. Rsch. Assn., Assn. for Supervision and Curriculum Devel., Brit. Ednl. Rsch. Assn., Nat. Soc. for Study Edn., Evaluation Rsch. Soc., Internat. Acad. Scis., Phi Delta Kappa (Disting. Rsch. award U. Chgo. chpt. 1971, cert. of recognition 1985), Phi Kappa Phi (hon.). Lutheran. Avocation: travel. Home: 180 E Pearson St Apt 3607 Chicago IL 60611-2135 Office: U Ill 1040 W Harrison St Chicago IL 60607-7129 Office Phone: 312-505-0528. Personal E-mail: hwalberg@yahoo.com.

WALBERG, TIM (TIMOTHY LEE WALBERG), congressman, former state legislator; b. Chgo., Apr. 12, 1951; s. John Andrew and Alice (Wilcox) W.; m. Susan Gail Polensky, 1973; children: Matthew Lee, Heidi Gail, Caleb Paul. Grad., Western Ill. U., 1970; Diploma, Summit Christian Coll., 1973; BS, Ft. Wayne Bible Coll., 1975; MA with hons., Wheaton Coll. Grad. Sch., 1978. Pastor New Haven (Ind.) Bapt. Ch., 1973-77, Union Gospel Ch., Tipton, Mich., 1978-83; mem. Mich. Ho. of Reps. from 57th dist., 1983—98; pres. Warren Reuther Ctr. for Edn. & Cmty. Impact, 1999—2001; divsn. mgr. Moody Bible Inst., Chgo., 2001—06; mem. US Congress from 7th Mich. dist, Mich., 2007—, mem. agrl. com., edn. & labor com. Asst. minority whip Mich. Ho. of Reps., vice chmn. Corrections Com., mem. Agriculture, Forestry & Minerals, Edn. Econ. Devel. & Energy Coms., Prison Reform & Children at Risk Task Force. Mem. Tecumseh Kiwanis Club, Lenawee County Riding for the Handicapped, Lenawee County Basic Human Needs Task Force. Republican. Protestant. Office: 800 W Garrison Jackson MI 49202 also: 325 Cannon House Office Bldg Washington DC 20515

WALCH, TIMOTHY GEORGE, library director; b. Detroit, Dec. 6, 1947; s. George Louis Walch and Margaret Mary (Shields) DeSchryver; m. Victoria Irons, June 24, 1978; children: Thomas Emmet, Brian Edward. BA, U. Notre Dame, 1970; PhD, Northwestern U., 1975. Lectr. history Northwestern U., 1974—75; assoc. dir. Soc. Am. Archivists, Chgo., 1975-79; program analyst Nat. Hist. Publ. and Records Commn., Washington, 1979-81; budget analyst Nat. Archives and Record Svc., Washington, 1981-82; chief, publs. devel. br. Nat. Archives and Records Adminstrn., Washington, 1982-88; asst. dir. Hoover Presdl. Libr. and Mus., West Branch, Iowa, 1988-93, dir., 1993—. Co-dir. Modern Archives Inst., Nat. Archives and Records Adminstrn., 1981—88; pres. Cath. Cmty. Found. of Iowa, 2002—03; chair Iowa Ctr. Book, 2005—07, Iowa Hist. Found., 2006—07. Author: Catholicism in America, 1989, Pope John Paul II, 1989, Parish School, 1996, reprinted, 2003 and others; editor: Prologue, 1982-88, The Heritage of American Catholicism, 1988, (with Edward R. Kantowicz) European Immigrants in American Society, 1990, Herbert Hoover & Harry S Truman, 1992, Immigrant America, 1994, At the President's Side, 1997, Herbert Hoover & Franklin D. Roosevelt, 1998, Uncommon Americans, 2003, and others; assoc. editor: U.S. Cath. Historian, 1983—; guest columnist: Cedar Rapids Gazette, 1996-2006; contbr. articles to profl. jours.; guest commentator: CNN, MSNBC, Fox News, C-SPAN and others. Named to Pres.'s Club St. Ambrose U., 2005; recipient Journalism award, U.S. Cath. Press Assn., 1986, 1st place publ. award, Nat. Assn. Govt. Communicators, 1988, U.S. Archivist's award, Nat. Archives, 1993, Iowa Gov.'s Vol. award, 1995, 97, 2006, Dominican Veritas Forum award, 1996, Rogus Lecture, U. Dayton, 1999, Williams Lecture, La. State U., Shreveport, 2000, Hatfield Lecture, Oreg. Hist. Soc., 2003. Mem. Orgn. Am. Historians, US Cath. Hist. Soc., State Hist. Soc. Iowa (trustee 2005—), Rotary Internat. (Harris fellow 2005-). Office: Hoover Presdl Libr and Mus 210 Parkside Dr West Branch IA 52358 Office Phone: 319-643-6029. Personal E-mail: twalch47@aol.com. Business E-Mail: timothy.walch@nara.gov.

WALCHER, KATHLEEN, state official; b. Sept. 20, 1948; Clk. of ct. of Common Pleas, Huron County; civil sheriff deputy; deputy clk.; state rep. State of Ohio, 58th Dist., 2002—. Mem.: Juvenile and Family Law (vice-chair), Econ. Devel. and Tech., County and Twp. Govt., Agr. and Natural Resources. Republican.

WALCOTT, ROBERT, retired health facility administrator, priest; b. Boston, July 31, 1942; s. Robert and Rosamond (Pratt) W.; m. Diane Palmer, Sept. 3, 1966; 1 child, Sara. BA, Coll. of Wooster, 1964; MDiv, Ch. Div. Sch., Berkeley, Calif., 1967; M Healthcare Adminstrn., Ohio State U., 1972. Ordained Episc. priest, 1968. Planning specialist Health Planning and Devel. Coun., Wooster, Ohio, 1972—73, asst. dir., 1974—75, St. Joseph Hosp., Lorain, Ohio, 1975—78, assoc. dir., 1978—81; CEO Lakeside Meml. Hosp., Brockport, NY, 1981—85; adminstr. Dent Neurologic Inst., Buffalo, 1986—87, Oak Hills Nursing Ctr., Lorain, 1994; pastor Ch. of Transfiguration, Buffalo, 1988—91, St. Michael and All Angels Ch., Uniontown, Ohio, 1991—93; adminstr.-in-tng. Chapel Hill Cmty., Canal Fulton, Ohio, 1993; interim adminstr. Regina Health Ctr., Richfield, Ohio, 1994—95; adminstr. Ohio Pythian Sisters Home, Sophia Huntington Parker Home, Medina, 1995—2001, Homestead I and II Nursing Homes, Painesville, Ohio, 2002—02; longterm care ombudsman Luth. Met. Ministries, Cleve., 2002—05; ret. Housing com. Tremont Devel. Corp., Cleve., 1994—, bd. dirs., 1997-2002; steering com. Habitat for Humanity, Cleve., 1994-97; chair trustees Tremont West Devel. Corp., 2000-2002. Fellow Am. Coll. Healthcare Execs. Democrat. Avocations: travel, reading. Home: 2173 W 7th St Cleveland OH 44113-3621 E-mail: bobwal31@aol.com.

WALD, FRANCIS JOHN, state legislator; b. ND, Apr. 8, 1935; s. Anton S. and Magdelena (Bosch) W.; m. Sharon Kay Mischel, 1961; children: Kirk James, Mark Allen, Jo Lynn, Laura, Cara, Maria, Michael, Joe. BSBA, U. N.D., 1959. Pres., ins. broker Wald Agy. Inc., Dickinson, N.D., 1973—; mem. from dist. 37 N.D. State Ho. of Reps., Bismarck, 1979-83, 85—, chmn. appropriations, edn. and environ. coms., speaker of the ho. Commr. Midwestern Higher Education Commission, 2001—. Mem. exec. com. Conf. of Ins. Legislators. Recipient Korean Occupation award. Mem. Dickenson C. of C. (past pres.), N.D. Profl. Ins. Agts., Am. Legion, Rotary, KC, Elks, Alpha Tau Omega. Address: 433 7th St E Dickinson ND 58601-4525

WALDBAUER, GILBERT PETER, entomologist, educator; b. Bridgeport, Conn., Apr. 18, 1928; s. George Henry and Hedwig Martha (Gribisch) W.; m. Stephanie Margot Stiefel, Jan. 2, 1955; children: Gwen Ruth, Susan Martha. Student, U. Conn., 1949-50; BS, U. Mass., 1953; MS, U. Ill., Urbana, 1956, PhD, 1960. Instr. entomology U. Ill., Urbana, 1958-60, asst. prof., 1960-65, assoc. prof., 1965-71, prof., 1971—, prof. agrl. entomology Coll. Agr., 1971—, prof. emeritus, 1995—. Sr. scientist Ill. Natural History Survey; vis. scientist ICA, Palmira, Colombia, 1971; vis. sr. scientist Internat. Rice Rsch. Inst., 1978-79; cons. AID, 1985; vis. prof. U. Philippines, 1978-79. Author: Insects Through the Seasons, 1996, The Handy Bug Answer Book, 1998, The Birder's Bug Book, 1998, Millions of Monarchs, Bunches of Beetles, 2000, What Good Are Bugs?, 2003, Insights from Insects, 2005; contbg. author: Insect and Mite Nutrition, 1972, Introduction to Insect Pest Management, 1975, Evolution of Insect Migration and Diapause, 1978, Sampling Methods in Soybean Entomology, 1980, Mimicry and the Evolutionary Process, 1988, Ann. Rev. Entomology, 1991; contbr. numerous articles to profl. jours Served with AUS, 1946-47, PTO. Grantee Agrl. Rsch. Svc. USDA, 1966-71, 83-90, Nat. Geog. Soc., 1972-74, NSF, 1976-79, 82-90. Mem. AAAS, Sigma Xi, Phi Kappa Phi. Home: 807A Ramblewood Ct Savoy IL 61874-9568 Office: U Ill Dept Entomology 320 Morrill Hall Urbana IL 61801 Office Phone: 217-333-1265.

WALDBAUM, JANE COHN, art history educator; b. Jan. 28, 1940; d. Max Arthur and Sarah (Waldstein) Cohn. BA, Brandeis U., 1962; MA, Harvard U., 1964, PhD, 1968. Rsch. fellow in classical archaeology Harvard U., Cambridge, Mass., 1968-70, 72-73; from asst. prof. to assoc. prof. U. Wis., Milw., 1973-84, prof. art history, 1984—2002, chmn. dept., 1982-85, 86-89, 91-92, adj. prof. anthropology, 2002—. Dorot rsch. prof. W.F. Albright Inst. Archaeol. Rsch., Jerusalem, 1990-91; vis. scholar Hebrew U. Jerusalem, 1989-91. Author: From Bronze to Iron, 1978, Metalwork from Sardis, 1983; author (with others), co-editor: Sardis Report I, 1975; mem. editl. bd. Bull. Am. Schs. Oriental Rsch., 1994-98, Near Eastern Archaeology, 2000-2002; contbr. numerous articles to profl. jours. Woodrow Wilson Found. fellow, dissertation fellow, 1962-63, 65-66, NEH postdoctoral rsch., Jerusalem, 1989-90; grantee Am. Philos. Soc., 1972, NEH, summer 1975, U. Wis.-Milw. Found., 1983. Mem. Am. Schs. Oriental Rsch. (bd. trustees 2003—), Soc. for Archaeol. Sci., Israel Exploration Soc., Archaeol. Inst. Am. (exec. com. 1975-77, chmn. com. on membership programs 1977-81, nominating com. 1984, chmn. com. on lecture program 1985-87, acad. trustee 1993-98, 1st v.p. 1999—2002, pres. 2003-, com. profl. responsibilities 1993—, fellowships com. 1993-99, gold medal com. 1993-99, chair 1996-97, Near East Archaeology interest group 1993—, chair ann. meeting com. 1999—2002, chair regional meetings com. 1999—2002, pers. com., governance com., devel. com., fin. com.), W.F. Albright Inst. Archaeol. Rsch. (trustee 1996-2006, mem. governance com. 1996-2006), Wis. Soc. Jewish Learning (trustee 1993-99), Milw. Soc. Archaeol. Inst. (bd. dirs., pres. 1983-85, 91-95, 97-99), Phi Beta Kappa Office: U Wis Dept Anthropology PO Box 413 Milwaukee WI 53201-0413 Home Phone: 414-962-1895. Business E-Mail: JCW@uwm.edu.

WALDERA, WAYNE EUGENE, crisis management executive; b. Cayuga, ND, Mar. 23, 1930; s. Bernard Cyril and Eleanor Nee (Kugler) W.; m. Eva Jenzene Personius, Jan. 13, 1958; children: Anthony, Lori, Mia, Shauna. BSBA, N.D. State U., 1952. With Gamble-Skogmo, 1954-88; pres. Gamble div. Gamble-Skogmo, Mpls., 1972-88; pres., CEO Retail Resource Co., Mpls., 1988-89, Amdura Corp., Denver, 1989-92, also bd. dirs.; chmn. Sullivan Waldera, Inc., Mpls., 1992-93; prin., CEO Waldera & Co. Inc., Mpls., 1993—. 1st lt. USAF, 1952-54. Home: 12125 62nd St Waconia MN 55387-9411 Office: Waldera & Co Inc 700 Twelve Oaks Ctr Dr Ste 208 Wayzata MN 55391-1435 E-mail: wwaldera@uswest.net.

WALDMEIR, PETER NIELSEN, retired journalist; b. Detroit, Jan. 16, 1931; s. Joseph John and Helen Sarah (Nielsen) W.; m. Marilyn C. Choma; children—Peter William, Patti Ann, Lindsey Marilyn, Christopher Norman. Student, Wayne State U., 1949-58. From mem. staff to sports columnist Detroit News, 1949—72, gen. columnist, 1972—2004; ret., 2004. Pres. Old Newsboys Goodfellow Fund, Detroit, 1988; mem. city coun. Grosse Pointe Woods, Mich., 2005. With USMC, 1951-53. Recipient Headliners award Nat. Headliners Club, 1971, SDX Lifetime Achievement award, 2000; named Mich. Sports Writer of Yr., Nat. Sportscasters and Sportswriters, 1967, 69, 71; Heart award Variety Club Internat., 1985; inducted Mich. Journalism Hall of Fame, 2000. Mem. Sigma Delta Chi. Roman Catholic. Personal E-mail: pwaldmeir@aol.com.

WALDRON, KENNETH JOHN, mechanical engineering educator, researcher; b. Sydney, NSW, Australia, Feb. 11, 1943; came to U.S., 1965; s. Edward Walter and Maurine Florence (Barrett) W.; m. Manjula Bhushan, July 3, 1968; children: Andrew, Lalitha, Paul. BEngring., U. Sydney, 1964, M Engring. Sci., 1965, D Engring., 1999; PhD, PhD, Stanford U., 1969. Registered profl. engr., Tex. Acting asst. prof. Stanford (Calif.) U., 1968-69; lectr., sr. lectr. U. NSW, Sydney, 1969-74; assoc. prof. U. Houston, 1974-79; assoc. prof. mech. engring. Ohio State U., Columbus, 1979-81, prof., 1981—, Nordholt prof., 1984—, chmn. dept. mech. engring., 1993—. Co-author: Machines That Walk, 1988, Kinematics, Dynamic and Design of Machinery, 1999; contbr. over 215 articles to profl. jours. and conf. procs. Recipient Robotics Industries Assn. Engelberger award, 1997. Fellow ASME (tech. editor Trans. Jour. Mech. Design 1988-92, Leonardo da Vinci award 1988, Mechanisms award 1990, Machine Design award 1994); mem. Soc. Automotive Engrs. (Ralph R. Teetor award 1977), Am. Soc. for Engring. Edn. Achievements include work on adaptive suspension vehicle project. Office: Ohio State University 650 Ackerman Rd Columbus OH 43202-4500

WALENGA, JEANINE MARIE, medical educator, researcher; b. Evergreen Park, Ill., Nov. 21, 1955; d. Eugene Adam and Therese Marie Walenga. BS, U. Ill., Chgo., 1978; Diplome d'Etudes Approfondies, U. Paris VI, 1984, PhD, 1987; postgrad., Loyola U., Maywood, Ill., 1981-84. Cert. med. technologist. Med. technologist MacNeal Hosp., Berwyn, Ill., 1978-79; rsch. asst. Loyola U. Med. Ctr., Maywood, 1979-80, hemostasis rsch. lab. supr., 1980-87, co-dir. hemostasis rsch. lab., 1987—, asst. prof. thoracic/cardiovascular surgery/pathology, 1988-94, assoc. prof., 1994-2000, prof., 2000—. Mem. Cardiovascular Inst., Loyola U., 1995—; cons. in field; lectr. in field; observer Nat. Com. for Clin. Lab. Stds., 1988—; del. US Pharmacopeia, 1990—. Contbr. articles to profl. jours. amed Alumnus of Yr., U. Ill., 1990; NHLBI rsch. grantee, 1989—; recipient Investigator Recognition award, 1993. Fellow Am. Coll. Angiology; mem. Internat. Inst. for Thrombosis and Vascular (sec. 1989—), Am. Assn. Pathologists, Am. Soc. Hematology, Internat. Soc. Thrombosis and Hemostasis (sci. and standardization subcoms. control anticoagulation 1990—), Am. Soc. Clin. Pathologists, Am. Heart Assn., Am. Soc. Med. Tech. Avocations: photography, archeology, gardening, birding, travel.

WALENTIK, CORINNE ANNE, pediatrician; b. Rockville Centre, NY, Nov. 24, 1949; d. Edward Robert and Evelyn Mary (Brinskele) Finno; m. David Stephen Walentik, June 24, 1972; children: Anne, Stephen, Kristine. AB honors, St. Louis U., 1970, MD, 1974, MPH, 1992. Diplomate Am. Bd. Pediat., Am. Bd. Neonatal and Perinatal Medicine, cert. physician exec. Certifying Commn. on Med. Mgmt., Am. Coll. Physician Execs. Resident pediat. St. Louis U. Group Hosps., 1974—76, fellow neonatalogy, 1976—78; neonatalogist St. Mary's Health Ctr., St. Louis, 1978—79; from co-dir. to dir. neonatal unit St. Louis City Hosps., 1979—85; dir. neonatalogy St. Louis Regional Med. Ctr., 1985—96; asst. prof. pediat. St. Louis U., 1990—94, assoc. clin. prof., 1994—98, assoc. prof. pediat., 1998—2001, prof. pediat., 2001—. Supr. nursery follow-up program Cardinal Glennon Children's Hosp., St. Louis, 1979—, neonatologist, physician exec. for managed care and pub. policy, 1997—; dir. nurseries St. Mary's Health Ctr., Richmond Heights, Mo., 2004—; chair provider svcs. adv. bd. St. Louis Regional Health Commn. Contbr. articles to profl. jours. Mem. adv. com. Mo. Perinatal Program., 1983-86; chair cmty. adv. bd. Mo. Found. for Health. Fellow: Am. Acad. Pediat. (pres. Mo. chpt., com. on child healthcare financing); mem.: APHA, St. Louis Met. Med. Soc., Mo. State Med. Assn., Nat. Perinatal Assn. (coun. 1984—87), Mo. Perinatal Assn. (pres. 1983), Mo. Pub. Health Assn. (pres. St. Louis chpt. 1995—96). Roman Catholic. Avocations: bridge, baseball, sports. Home: 7234 Princeton Ave Saint Louis MO 63130-3027 Office: Cardinal Glennon Children's Hosp 1465 S Grand Blvd Saint Louis MO 63104-1003 Office Phone: 314-577-5642. Business E-Mail: walentca@slu.edu.

WALES, ROSS ELLIOT, lawyer; b. Youngstown, Ohio, Oct. 17, 1947; s. Craig C. and Beverly (Bromley) W.; m. Juliana Fraser, Sept. 16, 1972; children: Dod E., J. Craig. AB, Princeton U., 1969; JD, U. Va., 1974. Bar: Ohio 1974, U.S. Dist. Ct. (so. dist.) Ohio 1974, U.S. Ct. Appeals (5th cir.) 1979. Assoc. Taft, Stettinius & Hollister, Cin., 1974-81, ptnr., 1981—. Pres. US Swimming, Inc., Colorado Springs, 1979-84, US Aquatic Sports, Inc., Colorado Springs, 1984-88, 94-98, Cin. Active to Support Edn., 1987-88; chmn. sch. tax levy campaign, Cin., 1987; trustee The Childrens Home Cin., 1987—, v.p., 1995-98, pres., 1998-02; bd. dirs., sec., v.p. FINA Bur., 1988-2000; trustee Cin. State Tech. and CC, 1994—, sec. bd., 1995-98, vice-chmn., 1998-00, chair 2000-02; pres. Cin. Arts Sch., Inc., 2000-01; sec. Greater Cin. Arts and Edn. Ctr., 1996-05; mem. Anti-Doping Rev. Bd., US Anti-Doping Agy., Colo. Springs; dir. Child Welfare League Am., 2003-, treas., 2005-06, chair, 2007-. Mem. ABA, Ohio Bar Assn., Cin. Bar Assn., Internat. Swimming Fedn. of Lausanne, Switzerland (sec. 1988-92, v.p. 1992-2000). Presbyterian. Office: 425 Walnut St Ste 1800 Cincinnati OH 45202-3957 Home Phone: 513-321-8637; Office Phone: 513-357-9351. Business E-Mail: wales@taftlaw.com.

WALHOUT, JUSTINE SIMON, chemistry professor; b. Aberdeen, SD, Dec. 11, 1930; d. Otto August and Mabel Ida (Tews) S.; m. Donald Walhout, Feb. 1, 1958; children: Mark, Timothy, Lynne, Peter. BS, Wheaton Coll., 1952; PhD, Northwestern U., 1956. Instr. Wright City Community Coll., Chgo., 1955-56; asst. prof. Rockford (Ill.) Coll., 1956-59, assoc. prof., 1959-66, 81-89, prof., 1989-96, prof. emeritus, 1996—, dept. chmn., 1987-95; cons. Pierce Chem. Co., Rockford, 1968-69; trustee Rockford (Ill.) Coll., 1987-91. Contbr. articles to profl. jours. Mem. Ill. Bd. Edn., 1974-81. Mem. AAUW (Ill. bd. dirs. 1985-87), Am. Chem. Soc. (councilor 1993-99), Rockford LWV (bd. dirs. 1983-85, 2002-04), Sigma Xi. Presbyterian. Home: 3204 Wesley Way Rockford IL 61101-8803 Office: Rockford Coll 5050 E State St Rockford IL 61108-2311

WALI, MOHAN KISHEN, environmental scientist, forester, educator; b. Kashmir, India, Mar. 1, 1937; came to U.S., 1969, naturalized, 1975; s. Jagan Nath and Somavati (Wattal) W.; m. Sarla Safaya, Sept. 25, 1960; children: Pamela, Promod. BS, U. Jammu and Kashmir, 1957; MS, U. Allahabad, India, 1960; PhD, U. B.C., Can., 1970. Lectr. S.P. Coll., Srinagar, Kashmir, 1963-65; rsch. fellow U. Copenhagen, 1965-66; grad. fellow U. B.C., 1967-69; asst. prof. biology U. N.D., Grand Forks, 1969-73, assoc. prof., 1973-79, prof., 1979-83, Hill rsch. prof., 1973; dir. Forest River Biology Area Field Sta., 1970-79, Project Reclamation, 1975-83; spl. asst. to univ. pres., 1977-82; staff ecologist Grand Forks Energy Rsch. Lab. U.S. Dept. Interior, 1974-75; prof. Coll. Environ. Sci. and Forestry SUNY, Syracuse, 1983-89, dir. grad. program environ. sci., 1983-85, prof. Sch. Natural Resources, 1990—, dir. Sch. Natural Resources, assoc. dean Coll. Agr., 1990-93; dir. Environ. Sci. Grad. program Ohio State U., Columbus, 2001—06. Vice chmn. N.D. Air Pollution Adv. Coun., 1981-83; co-chair IV Internat. Congress on Ecology, 1986. Editor: Some Environmental Aspects of Strip-Mining in North Dakota, 1973, Prairie: A Multiple View, 1975, Practices and Problems of Land Reclamation in Western North America, 1975, Ecology and Coal Resource Development, 1979, Ecosystem Rehabilitation-Preamble to Sustainable Development, 1992; co-editor Agriculture and the Environment, 1993; sr. editor Reclamation Rev., 1976-80, chief editor, 1980-81; chief editor Reclamation and Revegetation Rsch., 1982-87; contbr. articles to profl. jours. Recipient B.C. Gamble Disting. Tchg. and Svc. award, U. ND, 1977. Fellow AAAS, Nat. Acad. Scis. India; mem. Ecol. Soc. Am. (chmn. sect. internat. activities 1980-84), Bot. Ecol. Soc., Can. Bot. Assn. (dir. ecology sect. 1976-79, v.p. 1982-83), Am. Soc. Agronomy, Am. Inst. Biol. Sci. (gen. chmn. 34th ann. meeting), Internat. Assn. Ecolog (co-chmn. IV Internat. Congress Ecology), Internat. Soc. Soil Sci., N.D. Acad. Sci. (chmn. editl. com. 1979-81), Sigma Xi (nat. lectr. 1983-85, pres. Ohio State chpt. 1993-94, pres. Syracuse chpt. 1984-85, Outstanding Rsch. award U. N.D. chpt. 1975). Office: Ohio State U Sch Environ and Natural Resources 2021 Coffey Rd Columbus OH 43210-1044 Business E-Mail: wali.1@osu.edu.

WALICKI, ANDRZEJ STANISLAW, philosophy educator; b. Warsaw, May 15, 1930; came to U.S., 1986, naturalized 1993. s. Michal Walicki and Anna (Szlachcinska) Chmielewska; m. Janina Derks, Mar. 10, 1953 (div. June 1970); m. Maria Wodzynska, June 17, 1972 (div. May 1985); children: Malgorzata, Adam; m. Marzena Balicka, July 27, 1985. MA, Warsaw U., 1953; PhD, Polish Acad. Scis., 1957. Asst. prof. Warsaw U., 1958-60, Polish Acad. Scis., Warsaw, 1960-64, assoc. prof., 1964-72, prof., head dept. Inst. Philosophy, 1972-81; sr. rsch. fellow Australian Nat. U., Canberra, 1981-86; O'Neill prof. history U. Notre Dame, Ind., 1986—. Vis. Kratter prof. history Stanford U., 1976. Author: The Slavophile Controversy, 1975, A History of Russian Thought, 1979, Philosophy and Romantic ationalism, 1982, Legal Philosophies of Russian Liberalism, 1987, Marxism and the Leap to the Kingdom of Freedom: The Rise and Fall of the Communist Utopia, 1995; also 13 others. Recipient award A. Jurzykowski Found., N.Y.C., 1983, Internat. Balzan prize for history Found. Internat. Premio E. Balzan, Milano, Italy, 1998; Rsch. grantee Ford Found., N.Y.C., 1960, vis. fellow All Souls Coll., U. Oxford, 1966-67, 73, Guggenheim fellow J.S. Guggenheim Meml. Found., 1991. Mem. Am. Assn. for Advancement Slavic Studies, Polish Acad. Scis. Roman Catholic. Office: U Notre Dame Dept History Notre Dame IN 46556

WALKER, BETTE, automotive executive; BS in Bus. Mgmt., U. NH; student, Bosotn U.; completed Global Leadership Executive Development Program, Harvard U. Tech. dir. Latin Am. Digital Equip. Corp.; IT exec. auto. sector safety restraint sys. AlliedSignal, Inc.; v.p., CIO, energy & chassis divsn. Delphi Corp., Troy, Mich., 1997—. Office: World Hdqrs 5725 Delphi Dr Troy MI 48098-2815

WALKER, BETTE M., information technology executive; BS in Bus. Mgmt., U. NH. Various positions most recently info. tech. dir. Latin Am. Digital Equipment Corp.; head of info. tech. automotive sector's safety restraint systems divsn. AlliedSignal Inc., head of info. tech. aerospace sector's comml. avionics divsn.; chief info. officer energy & chassis divsn. Delphi Corp., Troy, Mich., 1997, exec. dir. global bus. services and ops., now v.p., chief info. officer. amed one of Premier 100 IT Leaders, Computerworld, 2005. Office: VP & CIO Delphi Corp 5725 Delphi Dr Troy MI 48098-2815

WALKER, BRIAN C., manufacturing executive; Pres., N. Am. Herman Miller, Inc., 1999—2003, pres., COO, 2003—04, pres., CEO, 2004—, bd. dir., 2003—05. Office: Herman Miller 855 E Main Ave Zeeland MI 49464-0302 Office Phone: 616-654-3000. Office Fax: 616-654-5234.

WALKER, DUARD LEE, medical educator; b. Bishop, Calif., June 2, 1921; s. Fred H. and Anna Lee (Shumate) Walker; m. Dorothea Virginia McHenry, Aug. 11, 1945; children: Douglas Keith, Donna Judith, David Cameron, Diane Susan. AB, U. Calif., Berkeley, 1943, MA, 1947; MD, U. Calif., San Francisco, 1945. Diplomate Am. Bd. Microbiology. Intern, U.S. Naval Hosp., Shoemaker, Calif., 1945—46; asst. resident internal medicine Stanford U. Service San Francisco Hosp., 1950—52; asso. prof. med. microbiology and preventive medicine U. Wis., Madison, 1952—59, prof. med. microbiology, 1959—88, prof., chmn. med. microbiology, 1970—76, Paul F. Clark prof. med. microbiology, 1977—88, prof. emeritus, 1988—, prof., chmn. med. microbiology, 1981—88. Cons. Naval Med. Rsch. Unit, Gt. Lakes, Ill., 1958—74; mem. microbiology tng. com. Nat. Inst. Gen. Med. Scis., 1966—70; mem. nat. adv. Allergy and Infectious Diseases Coun., 1970—74; mem. adv. com. on blood program rsch. ARC, 1978—79; mem. study group on papovaviridae Internat. Com. on Taxonomy of Viruses, 1976—90; mem. vaccines and related biol. products adv. com. FDA, 1985—89; mem. rev. panel postdoct. rsch. fellowships for physicians Howard Hughes Med Inst., 1990—93. Mem. editl. bd. Infection and Immunity, 1975—83, Archives of Virology, 1981—83, Microbial Pathogenesis, 1985—90. Served to lt. (j.g.) USNR, 1943—46, served to capt. USNR, 1953—55. Fellow NRC postdoctoral virology, Rockefeller Inst. Med. Rsch., N.Y.C., 1947—49, USPHS immunology, George Williams Hooper Found., U. Calif., San Francisco, 1949—50. Fellow: Infectious Diseases Soc. Am., Am. Acad. Microbiology, Am. Pub. Health Assn.; mem.: Arts and Letters, Wis. Acad. Sics., Am. Soc. Virology, AAUP, Reticulendothelial Soc., Soc. Exptl. Biology and Medicine, AAAS, Am. Soc. Microbiology, Am. Assn. Immunologists, NAS. Home: 618 Odell St Madison WI 53711-1435 Office: U Wis Med Sch 600 Highland Ave Madison WI 53792-1510 Office Phone: 608-233-9279. Personal E-mail: dlwalke1@facstaff.wisc.edu.

WALKER, FRANK DILLING, market research executive; b. Indpls., Dec. 31, 1934; s. Frank D. and Dorothy Mae (Cole) W.; m. Jane Tatman, Aug. 25, 1979; children— Steven F., Leah R. BA, DePauw U., 1957. Chmn., CEO Walker Group, Indpls., 1960-95, Walker Clin. Evaluations, Inc., Indpls., 1986-95; chmn. Walker Info., 1995—. Bd. dirs. Am. United Life Ins. Co., NBD Ind. Nat. Bank, State Life Ins. Co.; frequent speaker on market rsch. to various groups. Contbr. articles trade publs. Past mem. Indpls. Hist. Preservation Commn.; bd. dirs. Ind. Repertory Theatre, Meth. Hosp., United Way of Greater Indpls.; adv. council Indpls. Mus. Art, Buchanan Counseling Center; former chmn. Central Ind. Better Bus. Bur.; former chmn. Indpls. Econ. Devel. Corp.; trustee Children's Mus. Indpls., Univ. Indpls.; former bd. dirs. Jr. Achievement Central Ind., mem. adv. council; trustee The Children's Mus., YMCA Found.; bd. dirs. Citizens Gas and Coke Utility. With USAF, 1958-60. Mem. Council Am. Survey Research Orgns. (past chmn. bd.), Am. Mktg. Assn. (past pres. Ind. chpt.), Indpls. Sales and Mktg. Execs. Assn. (past pres.), Indpls. C. of C. (past chmn.), Mktg. Rsch. Assn. (hon. life), Sigma Chi. Republican. Methodist. Office: Walker Info Ste 100 3939 Priority Way South Dr Indianapolis IN 46240-3833

WALKER, GEORGE HERBERT, III, former ambassador, retired investment banking company executive; b. St. Louis, Mar. 16, 1931; s. George H. and Mary (Carter) W.; m. Sandra E. Canning, Dec. 23, 1955 (div. Oct. 1962); children: Mary Elizabeth, Wendy, Isabelle; m. Kimberly Gedge, July 27, 1968 (div. Jan. 1977); children: George H. IV, Carter; m. Carol Banta, Feb. 21, 1987. BA, Yale U., 1953; LL.B., Harvard U., 1956. Bar: Conn. 1956. Gen. ptnr. G.H. Walker & Co. (later G.H. Walker, Laird Inc.), 1961-74; sr. v.p., also bd. dirs. White, Weld & Co. Inc., 1974-75; chmn. bd. dirs. G.H. Walker & Co., 1973-74; exec. v.p. Stifel Nicolaus & Co., 1976-78, pres., CEO, 1978-92, chmn., 1982—2001, chmn. emeritus, 2001—; US amb. to Hungary US Dept. State, Budapest, 2003—06. Civilian aide to sec. U.S. Army for Ea. Mo., 1973-80; bd. dirs. Laidlaw Corp., Laclede Steel Co., Eck-Adams Corp.; bd. govs. Midwest Stock Exch., 1982-88. Bd. dirs. Downtown St. Louis Inc., 1975-90, chmn., 1984-86; bd. dirs. Webster U., chmn. bd., 1987-92; trustee Mo. Hist. Soc., St. Louis Children's Hosp., 1972-92, Jefferson at. Expansion Meml. Assn., 1992; vestryman St. Ann's Ch., Kennebunkport, Maine; mem. Mo. Rep. Ctrl. Com., 1983—; adv. bd. St. Louis Area coun. Boy Scouts Am., 1989—; trustee investment trust Episcopal Diocese of Mo.; hon. bd. dirs. Anti-Drug Abuse Edn. Fund, Inc., 1990—; bd. dirs. St. Louis Zoo, 1992. With USAF, 1956-58. Mem. Rotary (St. Louis club). E-mail: walkergh@stifel.com.

WALKER, JACK L., environmental scientist; BSEE, MIT, 1962; MSEE, U. Mich., 1967, PhD in Elec. and Computer Engring., 1974. Jr. engr. GE, 1960-61; engr. Bendix Sys. Divsn., 1962-64; rsch. engr. Environ. Rsch. Inst. Mich., Ann Arbor, 1964-79, assoc. dir. radar divsn., 1979-82, dir. infrared and optics divsn., 1982-86, exec. v.p. and dir. tech. ops., 1986-95, v.p., chief scientist, 1995—. Mem. Ind. Surveillance Sci. and Engring. Group, Ballistic Missile Def. Office, Air Force Sci. Adv. Bd.; trustee Consortium for Internat. Earth Sci. Info. Network. Contbr. numerous articles to profl. publs. Recipient decoration for exceptional civilian svc. USAF, 1995. Fellow IEEE (bd. govs. Aerospace and Electronics Sys. Soc., M. Barry Carlton award 1981); mem. NAE. Office: Environ Rsch Inst Mich PO Box 134001 Ann Arbor MI 48113-4001

WALKER, JAMES S., financial executive; Grad., Miami U., Oxford, Ohio. Mgr. Ernst & Young; contr. Park-Ohio Holdings Corp., Cleve., 1983-91, v.p., treas., contr., 1991—. Office: Park-Ohio Holdings Corp 23000 Euclid Ave Cleveland OH 44117-1706

WALKER, KATHRYN A., telecommunications industry executive; B in Civil Engring., SD State U.; MS, U. Mo., degree in Engring. Asst. v.p. human resources Sprint Tech. Svcs., 1995—97; v.p. product mgmt. Sprint Bus., 1997—2002; sr. v.p. network svcs. global Markets group Sprint Corp., 2002—03, exec. v.p. network svcs., 2003—. Office: 6200 Sprint Pkwy Overland Park KS 66251

WALKER, MARTIN DEAN, specialty chemical company executive; b. 1932; married. BS, GM Inst.; MBA, Mich. State U. With GM, Detroit, 1954-70; v.p. Am. Motors Corp., Detroit, 1970-72; exec. v.p. Rockwell Internat. Corp., Pitts., 1972-86; chmn., chief exec. officer M.A. Hanna Co., Cleve., 1986—.

WALKER, PHILIP CHAMBERLAIN, II, health facility administrator; b. Big Spring, Tex., July 7, 1944; s. Philip Chamberlain and Mary Catherine (St. John) W.; m. Linda Jane Holsclaw, Jan. 21, 1978; children: Shannon M., Meghan M. BA, Cen. Wash. State Coll., 1970; MS, U. Idaho, 1971. Exec. dir. Multnomah Found. for Med. Care, Portland, Oreg., 1972-81; chief exec. officer Peer Rev. Orgn. for Wash. State, Seattle, 1981-84; dir. Preferred Provider Orgn. devel. Provident Life and Accident, Chattanooga, 1984-88; v.p. Maxicare Health Plans, LA, 1988-91; v.p., gen. mgr. Maxicare Health Plans Midwest, Chgo., 1991-92; pres. Health Plus, Peoria, Ill., 1992—2007; CEO, chmn. bd. HCH Adminstrn., Peoria, Ill., 1992-98; sr. v.p. Health Care Horizons, Albuquerque, 1992-98; exec. v.p. Proctor Health Sys., 1998—2007. Bd. dirs. RMR Group, HCH Adminstrn., Health Care Horizons; cons. in field. Contbr. articles to profl. jours. Bd. dirs. Boys and Girls Club of Greater Peoria, 2003—06; v.p. Boys and Girls Club Peoria, 2004—06; Ctrl. Ill. regional adv. bd. Multiple Sclerosis Assn., 2002—04; chmn. Hult Health Edn. Ctr., 1999—2003, bd. dirs., Cancer Ctr. for Health Living, 2001—03, Heart of Ill. United Way, 2004—07. With USAF, 1961—66, Vietnam. Mem.: Creve Coeur Club (bd. govs., pres.). Business E-Mail: plwalkerii@yahoo.com.

WALKER, RHONDA GILLUM, announcer; b. Detroit; d. Ron and Harriet Gillum; m. Derrick Walker, 1996. B of Comm., Mich. State U., 1991. Weather and traffic reporter, style trend reporter WJBK-TV, Detroit; co-host WDIV-TV, Deroit, 2003—. Office: WDIV-TV 550 W Lafayette Blvd Detroit MI 48226

WALKER, ROBERT S. (BOB), lawyer; b. Cleve., 1957; BS summa cum laude, Dyke Coll., 1979; JD summa cum laude, Cleve. State Univ., 1982. Bar: Ohio 1982. Profl. pers. ptnr. Jones Day, Cleve. Editor-in-chief Law Rev., Cleve. State Univ., 1982. Mem.: ABA, Barrister, Celebrezze Inn of Ct., Cleve., Ohio State Bar Assn. Office: Jones Day North Point 901 Lakeside Ave Cleveland OH 44114-1190 Office Fax: 216-579-0212.

WALKER, RONALD EDWARD, psychologist, educator; b. East St. Louis, Ill., Jan. 23, 1935; s. George Edward and Marnella (Altmeyer) W.; m. Aldona M. Mogenis, Oct. 4, 1958; children: Regina, Mark, Paula, Alexis. BS, St. Louis U., 1957; MS, Northwestern U., 1959, PhD, 1961. Lectr. psychology Northwestern U., 1959-61; faculty dept. psychology Loyola U., Chgo., 1961—, asst., then asso. prof., 1961-68, prof., chmn. dept., 1965—73, prof. emeritus, 1999—, acting dean Coll. Arts and Scis., 1973-74; dean Loyola U. (Coll. Arts and Scis.), 1974-80, academic v.p., 1980-81, sr. v.p., dean faculties, 1981-89, exec. v.p., 1989-99. Cons. VA, Chgo., 1965-74; Am. Psychol. Assn.-NIMH; vis. cons., 1969; vis. scientist Am. Psychol. Assn. NSF, 1968; Cook County (Ill.) rep. from Ill. Psychol. Assn., 1969-72; cons.-evaluator North Cen. Assn., 1986-99. Contbr. articles to profl. jours. Bd. trustees St. Francis Hosp., Evanston, Ill., 1986—92, Chgo. Archdiocesan Sems., 1985—97, Loyola Acad., Wilmette, Ill., 1987—93, St. Louis U., 1988—97; bd. dirs. Holy Family Villa Nursing Home, Lemont, Ill., 2002—05. Recipient Disting. Psychologist of Yr. award Ill. Psychol. Assn., 1986. Home: Unit 5I 1630 Sheridan Rd Wilmette IL 60091-1835 Business E-Mail: rwalker@luc.edu.

WALKER, SALLY M., writer; b. NJ; m. James Walker. Author: (children's books) Volcanoes, 1994, Rhinos, 1996, Earthquakes, 1996, Opossum at Sycamore Road, 1997, Hippos, 1997, The 18-Penny Goose, 1999, Dolphins, 1999, Seahorse Reef: A Story of the South Pacific, 2001, Wheels and Axles, 2001, Levers, 2001, Screws, 2001, Work, 2001, Inclined Planes and Wedges, 2001, Pulleys, 2001, Sea Horse's Surprise, 2001, Fireflies, 2001, Life in an Estuary: The Chesapeake Bay, 2002, Jackie Robinson, 2002, Fossil Fish Found Alive: Discovering the Coelacanth, 2002, Rays, 2002, Bessie Coleman: Daring to Fly, 2003, Secrets Of A Civil War Submarine: Solving The Mysteries Of The H. L. Hunley, 2005 (Am. Libr. Assn.'s Sibert Internat. Book award, 2006), Mystery Fish: Secrets Of The Coelacanth, 2005. Recipient Outstanding Trade Books for Children award (twice), Children's Choice award, 2001. Mailing: Author Mail CarolHoda Books Lerner Pub Group 1251 Washington Ave N Minneapolis MN 55401-1036

WALKER, STEVEN FRANK, management consultant; b. Indpls., Dec. 31, 1957; s. Frank Dilling and Beverly (Trudgen) W.; m. Brenda Anne Brost, July 11, 1986; children: Jack. BS, Boston U., 1980. Acct. R.A. Boston & Co., Boston, 1980-81; staff acct. NEECO, Needham, Mass., 1981-82; sr. project dir. Walker Research Inc., Phoenix, 1982-84, account exec. Walnut Creek, Calif., 1984-85, group mgr. Indpls., 1985-87, v.p. new bus., 1987-88, v.p. new ventures and corp. devel., 1988-95, CEO, 1995-98, 1999—. Bd. dirs. Walker Clin. Evaluations, Indpls., 1989—; lectr. in field. Contbr. articles to profl. ours. Bd. dirs. Boys Clubs of Indpls., 1987—; mem. mktg. com. Indpls. Zoo, 1988; capt. fund raising Indpls. C. of C., 1987-88, Children's Mus., 1986-88; charter mem. Young Leadxers for Mutz, 1988. Mem. Am. Mktg. Assn., Mktg. Research Assn., Advt. Research Found. Republican. Roman Catholic. Avocations: auto racing, golf. Office: Walker Info Inc 3939 Priority Way South Dr Indianapolis IN 46240-3834

WALKER, THOMAS RAY, city aviation commissioner; AB in Art, Dartmouth Coll., 1970; BArch, Ill. Inst. Tech., 1977. Project mgr. Lohan Assocs., 1977-86; v.p. design and constrn. The Chgo. Dock and Canal Trust, 1986-91; exec. dir. Pub. Bldg. Commn. of Chgo., 1991-95; commr. dept. transp. City of Chgo., 1995-99; commr. Chgo. Dept. of Aviation, City of Chgo., 2000—. Prin. works include Soldier Field World Cup renovation, Chgo., Wright Coll. Addition, Chgo. Pub. Schs. capital improvement program, Cityfront Ctr., Chgo., Market-Tower Officer Bldg., Indpls., Episcopal Sch. of Dallas Libr./Fine Arts addition, Frito-Lay Nat. Hdqs., Plano, Tex. Vice chmn. Chgo. Area Transp. Study; commr. State St. Commn.; mem. com. Newhouse arch. fellowship program Chgo. Arch. Found.; mem. Chgo. Planning Commn.; mem. selection com. cmty. svc. fellowship Chgo. Cmty. Trust; mem. TRB steering com. Conf. Transp. Issue in Large U.S. Cities; mem. Conf. Minority Transp. Officials; trustee Chgo. Music and Dance Theater; chmn. leadership coun. Met. Open Cmtys.; co-chmn. adv. bd./housing com. Met. Planning Coun. 1st lt. USAF, 1970-72. Mem. Intelligent Transp. Soc. of Am. (bd. dirs.), Nat. Assn. City Transp. Ofcls. (chmn.), Nat. Orgn. Minority Architects, Urban Land Inst., Lambda Alpha Internat. Office: O'Hare Internat Airport Dept of Aviation PO Box 66142 Chicago IL 60666-0142

WALKER, WALDO SYLVESTER, biologist, educator, academic administrator; b. Fayette, Iowa, June 12, 1931; s. Waldo S. and Mildred (Littelle) W.; m. Marie J. Olsen, July 27, 1952 (div.); children: Martha Lynn, Gayle Ann; m. Rita K. White, June 16, 1984. BS cum laude, Upper Iowa U., Fayette, 1953; MS, U. Iowa, 1957, PhD, 1959; D of Sci. (hon.), Upper Iowa U., 2004. Mem. faculty Grinnell (Iowa) Coll., 1958, assoc. dean coll., 1963-65, chmn. div. Natural Scis., 1968-69, dean of adminstrn., 1969-73, exec. v.p., 1973-77, dean coll., 1973-80, provost, 1977-80, exec. v.p., 1980-90, exec. v.p. and treas., 1988-90, v.p. for coll. svcs., 1990-95, prof. biology, 1968-2001, prof. emeritus, 2001—. Research assoc. U. B.C. Dept. of Botany, 1966-67. Author articles on plant physiology, ultrastructural cytology. Served with U.S. Army, 1953-55. Fellow NSF Sci. Faculty, 1966-67; recipient NSF research grants, 1960-63, 68. Mem. Am. Assn. Colls., Am. Conf. Acad. Deans (nat. chmn. 1977-78), Am. Assn. Higher Edn., Sigma Xi. Home: 1920 Country Club Dr Grinnell IA 50112-1130 Address: Grinnell Coll PO Box H2 Grinnell IA 50112-0805 E-mail: walkerws@iowatelecom.net.

WALL, CARROLL EDWARD, publishing executive; b. Cherokee, Iowa, Mar. 3, 1942; s. Clifford R. and Mabel B. (Tjossem) W.; m. Mary Ellen Stratton, Sept. 1, 1962; children: Annette, Jannette, Heather, Christopher. BA with distinction, U. Iowa, 1964; postgrad. in Chinese mil. history, U. Mich., 1964-65, MA in L.S, 1966. Reference librarian U. Mich., Dearborn, 1966-67, head librarian, 1967-84; founder, pub. Pierian Press. (pub. reference books), Ann Arbor, Mich., 1968—. Speaker, cons. in field. Editor: books, the most recent being Author Index to Public Affairs Information Service, 1965-69, 1971; author: books, the most recent being Index to A.L.A.'s Index to General Literature, 1972; contbr. articles to profl. jours.; editor Media Rev. Digest, 1970—, Reference Services Rev., 1972—, Consumers Index, 1972—, Serials Rev., 1975—, Index to Free Periodicals, 1976—, Libr. Hi Tech, 1983—, Libr. Hi Tech News, 1985—, Libr. Hi Tech. Bibliography, 1986—, Computer and Office Product Evaluations, 1989—. Mem. exec. com. Mich. region Am. Friends Service Com., 1968-73, Dearborn Hist. Commn., 1971-73; vice chmn., chmn. Fairlane Music Guild, 1971-73; trustee Pittsfield Charter Twp., 1982-89. Recipient Loleta Fyan award Mich. Library Assn., 1971; Ford Found. scholar, 1963 Mem. ALA, Mich. Library Assn. (chmn. acad. div. nominating com. 1971), Assn. Ednl. Communications and Tech., Ednl. Film Library Assn., Phi Beta Kappa, Beta Phi Mu. Office: PO Box 1808 Ann Arbor MI 48106-1808

WALL, DELLA, human resources specialist, manufacturing executive; Various positions SupeRx Drug Stores, Kroger Mfg., 1971—2000; v.p. deferred benefits Kroger Co., Cinn., 2000—01, v.p. compensation and benefits, 2001—03, corp. v.p. human resources, 2003—04, group v.p. human resources, 2004—. Bd. dirs. Profit Sharing Coun. Am. Office: Kroger Co 1014 Vine St Cincinnati OH 45202-1100 Office Phone: 513-762-4000. Office Fax: 513-762-1160.

WALL, JAMES MCKENDREE, minister, editor; b. Monroe, Ga., Oct. 27, 1928; s. Louie David and Lida (Day) W.; m. Mary Eleanor Kidder, Sept. 11, 1953; children: David McKendree, Robert Kidder, Richard James. Student, Ga. Inst. Tech., 1945-47; BA, Emory U., 1949, MDiv, 1955, LHD (hon.), 1985; MA, U. Chgo., 1960; LittD (hon.), Ohio No. U., 1969; DHL (hon.), Willamette Coll., 1978; DD (hon.), MacMurray, 1981; DHL (hon.), Coe Coll., 1987; DHL (hon.), Elmhurst Coll., 1999. Ordained to ministry United Meth. Ch., 1954. Staff writer, sports dept. Atlanta Jour., 1948-50; asst. minister East Lake Meth. Ch., Atlanta, 1953; asst. to dean students Emory U., Atlanta, 1954-55; pastor North Ga. Conf. Moreland, Luthersville Meth. Chs., Ga., 1955-57, Bethel United Meth. Ch., Chgo., 1957-59; mng. editor Christian Adv. mag., Park Ridge, Ill., 1959-63, editor, 1963-72, Christian Century mag., Chgo., 1972-99, sr. contbg. editor, 1999—. Author: Church and Cinema, 1971, Three European Directors, 1973, Winning the War, Losing Our Soul, 1991, Hidden Treasures: Searching for God in Modern Culture, 1997; author, editor: Theologians in Transition, 1981, A Century of the Century, 1987, How My Mind Has Changed, 1991. Del. Dem.

Nat. Conv., 1972, 76, 80, 92, 96, 2000; mem. Dem. Nat. Com., 1976-80, Dem. State Cen. Com., 1974-86, Pres. Commn. White House Fellowships, 1976-80. Served to 1st lt. USAF, 1950-52. Mem. Alpha Tau Omega, Omicron Delta Kappa, Sigma Delta Chi. Home: 451 S Kenilworth Ave Elmhurst IL 60126-3928 Office: Christian Century 104 S Michigan Ave Ste 700 Chicago IL 60603-5905 E-mail: jimwall65@aol.com.

WALL, ROBERT F., lawyer; b. Chgo., Jan. 7, 1952; BA with distinction, Northwestern U., 1973; JD summa cum laude, U. Santa Clara, 1977. Bar: Ill. 1977, U.S. Dist. Ct. (no. dist.) Ill. 1977. Ptnr. Winston & Strawn, Chgo. Mem. editorial bd. M&A and Corp. Control Law Reporter, 1988—. Mem. ABA. Office: Winston & Strawn 35 W Wacker Dr Chicago IL 60601-1695

WALLACE, BEN, professional basketball player; b. White Hall, Ala., Sept. 10, 1974; m. Chanda Wallace. Student, Va. Union U., Richmond, 1996. Forward-ctr. Washington Bullets, 1996—99, Orlando Magic, Fla., 1999—2000, Detroit Pistons, 2000—06, Chgo. Bulls, 2006—08, Cleve. Cavaliers, 2008—. Mem. USA Team. Named BA Defensive Player of Yr., 2002, 2003, 2005, 2006; named to NBA All-Defensive Team, 2002, 2003, 2004, 2005, 2006. Achievements include being a member of BA Champion Detroit Pistons, 2004. Office: Cleve Cavaliers One Center Ct Cleveland OH 44115

WALLACE, BOB (ROBERT EUGENE WALLACE JR.), lawyer; b. NYC, Mar. 1, 1956; s. Robert E. Wallace Sr. and Vivian A. (High) Wallace; m. Julia Wallace; children: Grant, Eric. BA in Am. Studies, Yale U., 1978; JD, Georgetown U., 1981. Bar: Mo. 1981, Pa. 1991. Legal intern NFL, NYC, 1980; assoc. Guilfoil, Petzall & Shoemake, St. Louis, 1981—91; asst. to the pres., gen. counsel Phila. Eagles, 1991—94; exec. v.p., gen. counsel St. Louis Rams, 1995—. Adj. prof. law St. Louis U., 1986-88. Bd. govs. downtown YMCA, St. Louis, 1985-88; bd. dirs. Payback, Inc., Urban League of Greater St.Louis, Operation Excel, Amateur Athletic Assn., St. Louis, 1985-88, Sports Lawyers Assn., St Louis Sports Commn. Recipient Dist. Service award St. Louis Pub. Schs., St. Louis, 1985-88. Mem. ABA (sports lawyer div.), Met. Bar Assn. (exec. com. young lawyers sect., chmn. media com. 1983-86). Democrat. Avocations: sports, reading, bike riding. Office: St Louis Rams One Rams Way Earth City MO 63045 Office Phone: 314-982-7265. Business E-Mail: bwallace@rams.nfl.com.

WALLACE, RASHEED, professional basketball player, marketing professional; b. Sept. 17, 1974; s. Jackie Wallace; m. Fatima Sanders, July 18; 3 children. Attended, U. N.C. Prof. basketball player Washington Wizards, 1995—96, Portland Trailblazers, 1996—2004, Atlanta Hawks, 2004, Detroit Pistons, 2004—; CEO Dir. Hit Studios, Phila., 2002—. Founder Rasheed A. Wallace Found., Phila., 1997. Named to NBA All-Star Team, 2000, 2001. Achievements include being a member of BA Championship Team, 2004. Office: c/o Detroit Pistons 2 Championship Dr Auburn Hills MI 48326

WALLACE, RICK, marketing professional; Dir. mktg. and procurement Alliant Foodsvc., Deerfield, Ill., to 1996, v.p. category mgmt., 1996—. Office: Alliant Food Service 9933 Woods DR Skokie IL 60077-1057

WALLACE, ROBERT B., medical educator; BSM Medicine, Northwestern U., 1964, MD, 1967; MSc Epidemiology, SUNY, 1972. Intern internal medicine Cornell U., NYC, 1967—68, resident internal medicine, 1968—69; instr. dept. medicine Emory U. Medicine, 1969—70; instr. dept. social and preventive medicine SUNY, Buffalo, 1970—72; asst. prof. preventive medicine and internal medicine Coll. Medicine U. Iowa, 1972—75; assoc. prof. preventive medicine and internal medicine Coll. Medicine U. Iowa, 1975—79, head epidemiology sect. dept. preventive medicine Coll. Medicine, 1976—85, prof. preventive medicine and internal medicine Coll. Medicine, 1979—99, head dept. preventive medicine Col. Medicine, 1986—94, dir. cancer ctr., 1994—98, prof. epidemiology Coll. Pub. Health, 1999—. Mem.: Nat. Acad. Scis., Inst. Medicine (bd. health promotion and disease prevention 1994—), Nat. Inst. Aging (nat. adv. coun. 1994—98), U.S. Preventive Svs. Task Force (sec. office assistance DHHS 1990—95), Alpha Omega Alpha.

WALLACE, SAMUEL TAYLOR, health system administrator; b. Blytheville, Ark., Sept. 2, 1943; m. Sara Billow, Apr. 30, 1992. BS, U. Mo., 1965; M.H.A., Washington U., St. Louis, 1970. Asst. adminstr. Hillcrest Med. Ctr., Tulsa, 1969-75; adminstr. St. Luke's Meth. Hosp., Cedar Rapids, Iowa, 1975-81, pres., 1981-95, Iowa Health Sys., Des Moines, 1995—. Bd. dirs. Vol. Hosp. Am., Dallas, 1982-94, Iowa Golf Charities, 2001-; chmn. bd. dirs. Vol. Hosp. Iowa, Cedar Rapids, 1983-87; bd. dirs. Greater Des Moines Partnership, 1996—, Physician Mgmt. Resources, 1996—2000, Health Enterprise of Iowa, 1995-2000; mem. Cedar Rapids coun. Boy Scouts Am., 1983, Mid-Iowa coun., 1995—. Served to capt. M.S.C. U.S. Army, 1965-68, Vietnam. Recipient Silver Beaver award Boy Scouts Am., 1980, Silver Antelope award, 1992; James E. West fellow, 1994, Dist. Eagle Scout, 2002. Fellow Am. Coll. Healthcare Execs. (Iowa bd. regents 1982-84, 88-95, interim gov. Dist. 5 1999-2000); mem. Iowa Hosp. Assn. (dir. 1982-85). Lodges: Rotary (Cedar Rapids pres. 1986-87). Republican. Methodist. Office: Iowa Health Sys 1200 Pleasant St Des Moines IA 50309-1406

WALLACH, JOHN S(IDNEY), library administrator; b. Toronto, Ohio, Jan. 6, 1939; s. Arthur M. and Alice I. (Smith) W.; children: John Michael, Wendy Anne, Bethany Lynne, Kristen Michele; m. Joyce Bapst. BS in Edn, Kent State U., 1963; M.L.S., U. R.I., 1968; M.P.A., U. Dayton, 1977. Dir. Mercer County (Ohio) Library, 1968-70, Greene County (Ohio) Library, 1970-77; assoc. dir. Dayton and Montgomery County (Ohio) Library, 1978, dir., treas., 1979—. Bd. dirs. Dayton Mus. atrual History, Family Svc. Assn., Dayton, Technology Resource Ctr. Served with USN, 1963-68, capt. ret. Mem. ALA, Ohio Libr. Assn. Office: Dayton and Montgomery County Pub Libr 215 E 3d St Dayton OH 45402-2103

WALLACH, MARK IRWIN, lawyer; b. Cleve., May 19, 1949; s. Ivan A. and Janice (Grossman) W.; m. Karla L. Wallach, 1996; children: Kerry Melissa, Philip Alexander; stepchildren: Daniel Kanter, Rachel Kanter, Adam Kanter. BA magna cum laude, Wesleyan U., 1971; JD cum laude, Harvard U., 1974. Bar: Ohio 1974, U.S. Dist. Ct. (no. dist.) Ohio, 1974, U.S. Ct. Appeals (6th cir.) 1985, U.S. Supreme Ct. 1985. Law clk. U.S. Dist. Ct., Cleve., 1974-75; assoc. Baker & Hostetler, Cleve., 1975-79; chief trial counsel City of Cleve., 1979-81; assoc. Calfee, Halter & Griswold, Cleve., 1981-82, ptnr., 1982—, co-chmn. litigation dept., 2004—. Mem. fed. ct. adv. com. U.S. Dist. Ct. (no. dist.) Ohio, 1991-95; chmn. bd. trustees Ohio Group Against Smoking Pollution, 1986-90; trustee Cleve. chpt. Am. Jewish Com., 1986—, sec. 1989-91, v.p., 1991-95, pres., 1995-97; bd. trustees Citizens League of Greater Cleve., 1978-79, 87-92. Author: Christopher Morley, 1976. Pres. Wesleyan Alumni Club, Cleve., 1983—87, 1992—2006; trustee Lyric Opera, Cleve., 1995—2006, pres., 1996—98, Ratner Schs., 1994—96, Performing Arts Together, 1997—2001; trustee The Sculpture Ctr., 2001—, pres., 2001—; trustee Bellefaire Jewish Children's Bur., 2001—06; trustee, sec. Opera Cleve., 2006—07; pres. Space Solar Power Assn., 2006—; exec. bd. Cleve. chpt. Am. Constn. Soc., 2006—. Mem.: Greater Cleve. Bar Assn., Cuyahoga County Law Dirs. Assn., Fed. Bar Assn., Ohio Bar Assn., The Club at Key Ctr., The Cleve. Racquet Club. Democrat. Jewish. Avocations: reading, bicycling, space exploration, politics. Home: 2758 Claythorne Rd Shaker Heights OH 44122-1938 Office: Calfee Halter & Griswold 1400 Key Bank Ctr 800 Superior Ave E Cleveland OH 44114-2688 Home Phone: 216-371-0287; Office Phone: 216-622-8344. Business E-Mail: mwallach@calfee.com.

WALLER, AARON BRET, III, museum director; b. Liberal, Kans., Dec. 7, 1935; s. Aaron Bret and Juanita M. (Slawson) W.; m. Mary Lou Dooley, Sept. 3, 1959; children: Bret, Mary Elizabeth. BFA, Kansas City Art Inst., 1957; MFA, U. Kans., 1958, postgrad., 1964-67; postgrad. (Fulbright grantee), U. Oslo, 1963-64. Grad. asst. U. Kans., 1957-58; dir. The Citadel Mus., Mil. Coll. S.C., 1957-58, Mus. Art, U. Kans., 1964-71; dept. head public edn. and higher edn. Met. Mus. Art, NYC, 1971-73; dir. Museum Art, U. Mich., Ann Arbor, 1973-80, Meml. Art Gallery, U. Rochester, N.Y., 1980-85, adj. assoc. prof. fine arts dept., 1980-85; assoc. dir. for edn. and pub. affairs J. Paul Getty Mus., Malibu, Calif., 1985-90; dir. Indpls. Mus. Art, 1990—. Assoc. prof. U. Mich., 1973-80; coordinator museum studies program Inst. Fine Arts, NYU, 1971-73; tchr. City Coll. N.Y., 1971-73 Mem. Assn. Art Mus. Dirs. (treas. 1980-81, trustee 1992-94), Intermuseum Conservation Assn. (pres. 1977-78), Am. Assn. Museums (nat. com. on mus. tng. 1976-78, counselor-at-large 1986-89, treas. standing com. on edn. 1990-92), Coll. Art Assn. Office: Indpls Mus Art 1200 W 38th St Ste 2X Indianapolis IN 46208-4196

WALLER, ROBERT REX, ophthalmologist, educator, foundation administrator; b. NYC, Feb. 19, 1937; s. Madison Rex and Sally Elizabeth (Pearce) W.; m. Sarah Elizabeth Pickens, Dec. 27, 1963; children: Elizabeth, Katherine, Robert Jr. BA, Duke U., 1958; MD, U. Tenn., 1963. Diplomate Am. Bd. Ophthalmology (dir. 1982—, vice chmn. 1988-89, chmn. 1989—). Intern City of Memphis Hosps., 1963-64; resident in internal medicine Mayo Grad. Sch. Medicine, Rochester, Minn., 1966-67, resident in ophthalmology, 1967-70, faculty, 1970—; assoc. prof. ophthalmology Mayo Clinic, Rochester, Minn., 1974-78, prof., 1978—; chmn. dept. ophthalmology Mayo Med. Sch., Rochester, Minn., 1974-84, cons., 1970—, bd. govs., 1978-93, chmn., 1988-93; trustee Mayo Found., Rochester, 1978—, pres., CEO, 1988-98, pres. emeritus, 1999—. Chmn. bd. trustees Healthcare Leadership Coun., Washington, 1999—2001, mem. bd. trustees, 2001—. Contbr. chpts. to books, articles to profl. jours. Elder 1st Presbyn. Ch., Rochester, 1975-78; mem. Rochester Task Force on Pub. Assembly Facilities, 1983-84. Oculoplastic Surgery fellow U. Calif. San Francisco, 1973. Mem. AMA, Minn. State Med. Assn., Zumbro Valley Med. Assn., Am. Acad. Ophthalmology, Am. Ophthalmol. Soc., Orbital Soc., Am. Soc. Ophthalmic Plastic and Reconstructive Surgery, Minn. Acad. Ophthalmology and Otolaryngology, Memphis Country Club, Old Baldy Golf Club, Augusta Nat. Golf Club, Alpha Omega Alpha, Delta Tau Delta. Presbyterian. Avocations: golf, travel, photography. Home: 199 Greenbriar Dr Memphis TN 38117-3238 E-mail: RWaller@mayo.edu.

WALLING, DONOVAN ROBERT, editor, writer; b. Kansas City, Mo., Jan. 9, 1948; s. Donovan Ernest and Dorothy Jane (Goyette) W.; m. Diana Lynn Eveland, Oct. 19, 1968 (dec. 1991); children: Katherine Anne, Donovan David, Alexander James. BS in Edn., Kans. State Tchrs. Coll., 1970; MS, U. Wis., Milw., 1975. Cert. tchr., adminstr., Wis., Ind. Tchr. Sheboygan (Wis.) Area Sch. Dist., 1970-81, 83-86, coord. lang. arts and reading, 1986-91; tchr. Dept. Def. Dependents Schs., Zweibruecken, Germany, 1981-83; dir. instrnl. svcs. Carmel (Ind.)-Clay Schs., 1991-93; dir. publs. Phi Delta Kappa Internat., Bloomington, Ind., 1993—2006; sr. cons. Ctr. for Civic Edn., Calabasas, Calif., 2007—. Mem. adj. faculty U. Wis., Oshkosh, 1986-91, Silver Lake Coll., Manitowoc, Wis., 1987-91. Author: Complete Book of School Public Relations, 1982, How To Build Staff Involvement in School Management, 1984, Teachers as Leaders, 1994, Rethinking How Art Is Taught, 2000, Visual Knowing, 2005, Teaching Writing to Visual, Auditory, and Kinesthetic Learners, 2006; also numerous articles. Mem. ASCD, Nat. Coun. Tchrs. English, Nat. Art Edn. Assn., Phi Delta Kappa (v.p. Cen. Ind. chpt. 1992-93). Avocations: writing, painting. Office: Ctr for Civic Edn 5145 Douglas Fir Rd Calabasas CA 91302-1440 Home Phone: 812-335-1456. Personal E-mail: donovanwalling@yahoo.com.

WALLIS, DEBORAH, curator; b. Salina, Kans., Mar. 17, 1971; BS, Kans. State U., Manhattan, 1993; MA in Mus. studies, U. Nebr., Lincoln, 1994. Registrar Richard ixon Libr. and Birthplace, Yorba Linda, Calif., 1995—98; dir., curator Nat. Mus. of Roller Skating, Lincoln, Nebr., 2000—. Mem.: Nebr. Mus. Assn. (bd. mem. 2002—). Office: Nat Mus Roller Skating 4730 South St Ste 2 Lincoln NE 68506

WALLWORK, WILLIAM WILSON, III, automobile executive; b. Fargo, ND, Mar. 8, 1961; s. William Wilson Jr.; m. Shannon Wallwork, July 12, 1991. AA in Automotive Mktg., Northwood U., 1981; student, San Diego State U., Moorhead State U. Lease rep. Wallwork Lease and Rental, 1984-86; sales mgr. W.W. Wallwork, Inc., Fargo, N.D., 1986-87, v.p., 1987-91, pres., 1991—; v.p. Valley Imports Inc, Fargo, N.D., 1986-91; pres. Valley Imports Inc., Fargo, N.D., 1991—. Vice chmn. Kenworth 20 Group, 1992-93, chmn., 1994-96; mem. PACCAR Chmn.'s Meeting, 1993; mem. Rockwell Internat. Dealer Adv. Bd., 1995-98. Mem. adv. bd. N.D. State U. Coll. Bus. Adminstrn., 1995-2001; mem. Civic Opera Bd., 1999-2003. Mem. Automobile Dealers Assn. N.D. (bd. dir.s), Fargo-Moorhead Automobile Dealers Assn. (v.p. 1986-88, pres. 1988-90, share house bd. 1998-2003). Avocation: skiing. Office: W W Wallwork Inc PO Box 1819 Fargo ND 58107-1819

WALMER, EDWIN FITCH, retired lawyer; b. Chgo., Mar. 24, 1930; s. Hillard Wentz and Anna C. (Fitch) W.; m. Florence Poling, June 17, 1952; children: Linda Diane Walmer Dennis, Fred Fitch. BS with distinction, Ind. U., 1952, JD with high distinction, 1957. Bar: Wis. 1957, U.S. Dist. Ct. (ea. dist.) Wis. 1957. Assoc. Foley & Lardner, Milw., 1957-65, ptnr., 1965-90, ret., 1990. Served to 1st lt. U.S. Army, 1952-54. Recipient Cal. C. Chambers award Culver (Ind.) Mil. Acad., 1948. Fellow Am. Coll. Trust and Estate Counsel; mem. Order of Coif, Dairymen's Country Club (Boulder Junction, Wis.), Vineyards Country Club (Naples, Fla.), Phi Eta Sigma, Beta Gamma Sigma. Republican. Congregationalist. Avocations: golf, fishing.

WALROD, DAVID JAMES, retail grocery chain executive; b. Toledo, Dec. 9, 1946; s. Maynard Elmer and Isabella (Soldwish) W.; m. Judith Kay Stevens, Aug. 17, 1968; children— David, Bryant, Marc Student, Michael Owens Coll.; student in food distbn. mgmt. mktg., Toledo U., 1968. With Seaway Food Town, Inc., Maumee, Ohio, 1963—, grocery merchandiser, 1971-74, v.p. supermarket ops., 1974-77, corp. v.p. ops., 1977-80, sr. v.p. ops., 1980-88, exec. v.p., chief oper. officer, 1988—. Bd. dirs. Ohio Grocers Assn. Bd. dirs. Toledo Mud Hens, Riverside Hosp., St. Francis Desales H.S., Toledo, Corp. for Effective Govt., Junior Achievement, Toledo City Parks Commn., Labor Mgmt. Coun., Bishop's Edn. Coun. Cath. Diocese of Toledo; trustee Maumee C. of C. Mem. Brandywine Country Club. Office: Seaway Food Town Inc 1020 Ford St Maumee OH 43537-1898

WALSETH, DAVID G., lawyer, insurance company executive; b. Dec. 5, 1947; BA, St. Olaf Coll.; JD, U. Minn. With Hartford Life Insurance Companies; sr. v.p., gen. counsel, corp. sec. Luth. Brotherhood Fraternal Benefit Soc.; v.p., sr. assoc. gen. counsel Thrivent Fin. for Luths.; exec. v.p., gen. counsel, corp. sec. Conseco, Inc., Carmel, Ind., 2006—. Mem.: ABA, Soc. Fin. Svc. Profls., Assn. Life Insurance Counsel, Assn. Corp. Counsel, Hennepin County Bar Assn., Minn. State Bar Assn. Office: Conseco, Inc 11825 N Pennsylvania St Carmel IN 46032

WALSH, DAVID GRAVES, lawyer; b. Madison, Wis., Jan. 7, 1943; s. John J. and Audrey B. Walsh; married; children: Michael, Katherine, Molly, John. BBA, U. Wis., 1965; JD, Harvard U., 1970. Bar: Wis. Law clk. Wis. Supreme Ct., Madison, 1970-71; ptnr. Walsh, Walsh, Sweeney & Whitney, Madison, 1971-86; ptnr.-in-charge, pres. Foley & Lardner, Madison, 1986—95. Pres., bd. regents U. Wis., 2003—; bd. dirs. Nat. Guardian Life, Madison, Thompson Investment Mgmt., Inc.; lectr. U. Wis., Madison, 1974-75, 77-78; pres. U. Wis. sys. bd. regents, 2005-. Chmn. State of Wis. Elections Bd., Madison, 1978. Lt. USN, 1965-67, Vietnam. Recipient Disting. Bus. Alumnus award U. Wis. Sch. Bus., 1997. Maple Bluff Country Club (Madison) (pres. 1987). Roman Catholic. Avocations: tennis, golf, fishing. Home: 41 Fuller Dr Madison WI 53704-5962 Office: Foley & Lardner PO Box 1497 Madison WI 53701-1497 Office Phone: 608-258-4269. Business E-Mail: dwalsh@foley.com.

WALSH, JAMES, retail supermarket executive; Sr. v.p., CFO Meijer, Grand Rapids, Mich. Office: Meijer 29129 Walker St NW Grand Rapids MI 49544 Office Fax: (616) 453-6067.

WALSH, JOHN CHARLES, investment company executive, director; b. Indpls., Sept. 8, 1924; s. John Charles; children: Michael S., Carolyn Ann, Anne D. BS, Notre Dame U., 1949. Auditor Herdrich Boggs & Co., Indpls., 1949—78; with P.R. Mallory & Co., Inc., 1978—; pres. Walgang Co. Inc., Indpls., 1970—. V.p., treas. P.R. Mallory & Co., 1971. With USMCR, 1943—45. Mem. Fin. Execs. Inst., Ind. Hist. Soc., Econ. Club, Notre Dame Club, Rotary. Home: 4974 Shadow Rock Cir Carmel IN 46033-9500 Office: 160 W Carmel Dr Ste 265 Carmel IN 46032

WALSH, JOHN E., JR., business educator, consultant; b. St. Louis, Apr. 28, 1927; s. John E. and Ann M. (Narkewicz) W. BS, U.S. Naval Acad., 1950; MBA, Washington U., St. Louis, 1957; DBA, Harvard U., 1960. Asst. prof. Washington U., St. Louis, 1959-60, assoc. prof., 1960-68, prof., 1968-2001, prof. emeritus, 2001—; vis. assoc. prof. Stanford U., 1964-65; vis. prof. INSEAD, Fontainebleau, France, 1970. Mem. exec. com. Econ. Strategy Inst. Author: Preparing Feasibility Studies in Asia, 1971, Guidelines for Management Consultants in Asia, 1973, Planning New Ventures in International Business, 1976, (with others) Strategies in Business, 1978, Management Tactics, 1980, International Business Case Studies: For the Multicultural Market Place, 1994, Joint Authoring: Managing Cultural Differences, 1994. Mem. State of Mo. leadership initiative to former Soviet Union, Poland, Hungary, 1990; mem. coun. Kearny Found. 1st lt. USAF, 1950-54. Zurn Found. fellow, 1958; Presdl. fellow Am. Grad. Sch. Internat. Mgmt. Mem. Harvard Club N.Y.C. Personal E-mail: walshjejr@aol.com.

WALSH, LAWRENCE M., state legislator; b. Joliet, Ill., Mar. 3, 1948; m. Irene; 6 children. A in Agrl. & Bus., Joliet Jr. Coll., 1968. Mem. Ill. Senate, Springfield, 1997—, mem. agrl. & conservation com., fin. insts. com. Democrat.

WALSH, MATTHEW M., construction executive; b. Chgo., Jan. 7, 1946; m. Joyce Walsh; children: Matt IV, Sean, Erin. BA in Bus., U. Notre Dame, Ind., 1968; JD, Loyola U., Chgo., 1972. CEO Walsh Group, Chgo. Bd. mem. Constrn. Industry Roundtable. Mem. bd. St. Ignatius Coll. Prep. Sch., Union League Club; mem. adv. coun. Sch. Architecture U. Notre Dame. Recipient Outstanding Achievement in Constrn. award, The Moles, 2005. Mem.: Union League Club. Office: Walsh Group 929 W Adams St Chicago IL 60607-3021 Office Phone: 312-563-5400. Office Fax: 312-563-5420.

WALSH, MICHAEL S., lawyer; b. Chgo., Sept. 29, 1951; AB, Colgate U., 1973; MBA, Cornell U., 1975; JD, So. Meth. U., 1978. Bar: Ill. 1978, U.S. Dist. Ct. (no. dist.) Ill. 1978, U.S. Ct. Appeals (fed. cir.) 1983, U.S. Ct. Appeals (9th cir.) 1985. Mem. Jenner & Block, Chgo. Mem. ABA, Ill. State Bar Assn., Chgo. Bar Assn., Computer Law Assn. Office: Jenner & Block One IBM Plz Chicago IL 60611-3608 E-mail: mwalsh@jenner.com.

WALSH, THOMAS CHARLES, lawyer; b. Mpls., July 6, 1940; s. William G. and Kathryne M. Walsh; m. Joyce Williams, Sept. 7, 1968; children: Brian Christopher, Timothy Daniel, Laura Elizabeth Smith. BS in Commerce magna cum laude, St. Louis U., 1962, LLB cum laude, 1964. Bar: Mo. 1964, U.S. Dist. Ct. (ea. dist.) Mo. 1964, U.S. Ct. Appeals (8th cir.) 1968, U.S. Supreme Ct. 1971, U.S. Ct. Appeals (6th cir.) 1972, U.S. Ct. Appeals (5th cir.) 1974, U.S. Ct. Appeals (D.C. cir.) 1980, U.S. Ct. Appeals (7th cir.) 1982, U.S. Ct. Appeals (9th cir.) 1987, U.S. Ct. Appeals (4th cir.) 1989, U.S. Ct. Appeals (11th and fed. cirs.) 1992, U.S. Ct. Appeals (2d and 10th cirs.) 1993. Jr. ptnr. Bryan, Cave, McPheeters & McRoberts, St. Louis, 1964-73; ptnr. Bryan Cave LLP, St. Louis, 1974—; mem. exec. com. Bryan Cave LLP, St. Louis, 1980-96. Mem. 8th Cir. Adv. Com., 1983-86. Bd. dirs. St. Louis Symphony Soc., 1983-95. With U.S. Army, 1965-66; lt. USNR, 1966-71. Fellow Am. Coll. Trial Lawyers, Am. Acad. Appellate Lawyers; mem. Mo. Bar Assn., St. Louis Bar Assn., Am. Law Inst., Mo. Athletic Club, Bellerive Country Club. Roman Catholic. Office: Bryan Cave LLP 1 Metropolitan Sq 211 N Broadway Saint Louis MO 63102-2750 Home Phone: 314-997-7871; Office Phone: 314-259-2284. Business E-Mail: tcwalsh@bryancave.com.

WALSH, THOMAS JAMES, state legislator; b. Chgo., July 4, 1960; s. William Dowdle and Barbara Ann (Kennedy) W. BBA, Loras Coll., 1982. Lic. real estate salesperson. From sales rep. to pub. rels. mgr.; mem. Ill. Ho. of Reps, Springfield, 1992-94, Ill. Senate from dist. 22, 1994—. Commr. Met. Water Reclamation Dist. of Greater Chgo., 1988-90, chmn. Engring. com., Health and Pub. Welfare com.; active LaGrange Park Caucus, LaGrange Park Libr., St. Francis Xavier Ch., LaGrange. Mem. Irish Fellowship Club Chgo., Phoenix Soc. of Community Family Svc. and Mental Health Assn., LaGrange Kiwanis, Loras Coll. Alumni Club Chgo. Home: 4117 Harvey Ave Western Springs IL 60558-1245

WALTER, KENNETH LUVERNE, retired agricultural facility director; b. Buffalo Lake, Minn., June 20, 1936; s. Clarence Andrew and Ruth (Schafer) W.; m. Nancy Lee Woolard, Jan. 30, 1959; children: Katrina Lynn, Matthew Thomas (dec.), Janelle Mae. BS in Agr., U. Minn., St. Paul, 1963. Sales and tech. rep. Midland Coops. Inc., Mpls., 1963-68; asst. to supt. Agr. Experiment Sta. U. Minn., Rosemount, 1968-90, acting supt. Agr. Experiment Sta., 1990-93, dir. ops. Agr. Experiment Sta., 1993-2000; ret. With USN, 1955-59. Mem. Am. Soc. Agrl. Engrs. E-mail: klwalter@tc.umn.edu.

WALTER, LYNN M., geologist, educator; PhD in Geology, U. Miami, 1983. Prof. geol. scis. U. Mich., Ann Arbor. Recipient Disting. Svc. award Geol. Soc. Am., 1999. Achievements include research on aqueous and solid phase geochemistry of sedimentary systems. Office: U Mich 2534 CC Little Bldg 425 E University Ave Ann Arbor MI 48109-1063 Fax: 734-763-4690. E-mail: lmwalter@umich.edu.

WALTER, MICHAEL D., food products executive; BS in Mgmt. and Mktg., Ea. Ill. U. Pres. ConAgra Splty. Grain Products, 1989—96, sr. v.p. trade and procurement, 1996—2000; sr. v.p. commodity procurement and econ. strategy ConAgra Foods, Omaha, 2000—. Mem., dir. Chgo. Bd. Trade. Mem.: Mpls. Grain Exch. Office: ConAgra Foods Inc 1 ConAgra Dr Omaha NE 68102-5001

WALTER, ROBERT D., health products executive; b. Columbus, OH, July 13, 1945; m. Peggy McGreevey, 1967; children: Matthew, Blane, Peter. BMechE, Ohio U., 1967; MBA, Harvard U., 1970; Ph.D (hon.), Ohio U., 1997. Engr. N. Am. Rockwell, 1968; founder Cardinal Foods Inc. (acquired by Roundy's Inc. 1988), Dublin, Ohio, 1971-88; founder, CEO Cardinal Distribution, Dublin, Ohio, 1979—94; CEO Cardinal Health, Inc. (formerly Cardinal Distribution), Dublin, 1994—2006, chmn., 2006—07. Bd. dir. Cardinal Health Inc.; bd. dirs. Viacom Inc., Am. Express; bd. trustees Battelle Meml. Inst., Ohio U. Trustee Battelle Meml. Inst. Recipient Christopher Columbus award, Greater Columbus C of C, 2001. Avocations: golf, running, skiing. Office: Cardinal Health Inc 7000 Cardinal Pl Dublin OH 43017-1092

WALTER, ROBERT IRVING, retired chemistry professor; b. Johnstown, Pa., Mar. 12, 1920; s. Charles Weller and Frances (Riethmiller) W.; m. Farideh Asghari, Oct. 17, 1973. AB, Swarthmore Coll., Pa., 1941; MA, Johns Hopkins U., Balt., 1942; PhD, U. Chgo., 1949. Instr. U. Colo., 1949-51, U. Conn., 1953-55; rsch. assoc. Rutgers U., 1951-53; assoc. physicist Brookhaven Nat. Lab., 1955-56; mem. faculty Haverford Coll., 1956-68, prof. chemistry, 1963-68; prof. U. Ill., Chgo., 1968—, prof. emeritus, 1990—. Vis. lectr. Stanford (Calif.) U., winter 1967; acad. guest U. Zurich, 1976; U.S. NAS exch. visitor to Romania, 1982, 88. Mem. Adv. Council Coll. Chemistry, 1966-70. Served with USNR, 1944-46. Grantee U.S. Army Signal Research and Devel. Lab., NIH, NSF, Dept. Energy; NSF fellow, 1960-61 Fellow AAAS; mem. Am. Chem. Soc. (vis. scientist div. chem. edn. 1964-73), Sigma Xi. Achievements include special research preparation, proof of structure, chemical and physical properties of stable aromatic free radicals, C1 reactions and mechanisms in heterogeneous catalysis, reactions of porphyrin bases. Home: 2951 Central St Unit 308 Evanston IL 60201-1284

WALTERMIRE, THOMAS ALLEN, finance company executive; b. Balt., Oct. 30, 1949; s. William Everett and Emma (Barack) W.; m. Shirley Jean Flinn, June 16, 1972; children: Todd Andrew Barack Waltermire, Kevin Adam Davis Waltermire, Heidi Alexis Nicole Waltermire. BS, Ohio State U., 1971; MBA, Harvard U., 1974. Mgr. corp. fin. B.F. Goodrich Co., Akron, Ohio, 1975-76; asst. treas., 1977-78; asst. contr., 1978-80; dir. planning, analysis chem. group B.F. Goodrich Co., Cleve, 1980, dir. purchasing div., 1981-84, v.p. comml. svcs., 1984, pres. elastomers and latex div. Cleve., 1985-89, v.p. investor rels., 1989—93; CFO Geon Co., Cleve., 1993—97, COO, 1997—99, CEO, 1999—2000, PolyOne Corp. (Geon and M.A. Hanna merger), Cleve., 2000—05. Vice chmn., bd. dirs. NorTech; mem. Ohio Third Frontier Adv. Bd.; chmn. Ohio Polymer Strategy Coun. Bd. dirs., exec. com. Ohio Bus. Roundtable; bd. dirs. Greater Cleve. Partnership, Vols. Unlimited, Cleve. Orchestra, Ohio State U. Assn., 1998—2003, Nat. Inventors Hall of Fame; chmn. Ohio State U. Assn., 1999—2001; mem. Ohio State U. Alumni Adv. Coun. Republican. Methodist.

WALTERS, GLEN ROBERT, retired banker; b. Mpls., Sept. 11, 1943; s. Sterling Thomas and Mildred Eunice (Parkinson) W.; m. Gail Elvira Engelsen, June 11, 1966; children: Nicole Marie, Brent Aaron, Hillary Renee. BA, U. Minn., Mpls., 1965, postgrad., 1965-67; banking degree, Rutgers U., New

Brunswick, NJ, 1982. Comml. banker 1st Nat. Bank, Mpls., 1967-83, sr. v.p. human resources, 1983-90; sr. v.p. Firstar Bank Minn., Mpls., 1990-2001, US Bank, Mpls., 2001—05. Served to sgt. USNG, 1967-73 Republican. Presbyterian.

WALTERS, LAWRENCE CHARLES, advertising executive; b. Cin., Apr. 1, 1948; s. Lawrence Simpson and Mary Josephine (Koerner) W.; m. Ann Morley Reifenrath, Jan. 15, 1983. Assoc. in Advt., U. Cin., 1969. Art dir. J. Walter Thompson, Chgo., 1972-78; sr. art dir. Needham Harper and Steers, Chgo., 1978-81; advt. creative dir. ACOM, Quaker, Chgo., 1981-83; co. group creative dir. Tatham, Laird, Kudner, Chgo., 1983-99; exec. creative dir. Euro R.S.C.G. Tatham, Chgo., 1996—. With the USMC, 1966-69. Democrat. Roman Catholic. Avocations: music writing, canoeing, tennis, painting. Office: Euro RSCG Tatham 36 E Grand Ave Chicago IL 60611-3506

WALTERS, MARK DOUGLAS, obstetrician, gynecologist, director; b. Toledo, July 21, 1954; s. Donald Walters; m. Virginia Walters; children: Samantha, Maxwell, Zoe. BS in biology, U. Cincinnati, 1976; MD, Ohio State U., 1980. Cert. Am. Bd. Ob-Gyn. Intern Tufts U. Sch. Medicine, Boston, 1980—81, resident in ob-gyn., 1981—84; asst. prof. dept. ob-gyn. U. Tex. Health Sci. Ctr., San Antonio, 1984—90; assoc. prof. dept. reproductive biology and ob-gyn. Case Western Reserve U. Sch. Medicine, Cleve., 1990—93; med. dir. Women's Health Ctr. U. Hospitals of Cleve., 1990—93; head sect. gen. gynecology, dir. urogynecology The Cleve. Clinic, 1993—, dir. fellowship program in urogynecology/reconstructive pelvic surgery, 1997—, vice-chair gynecology, 2006—; prof. surgery Cleve. Clinic Lerner Coll. Medicine, 2006—. Vice chair gynecology Cleve. Clinic, 2006—. Author: (book) Clinical Urogynecology, 1993, Urogynecology and Reconstructive Pelvic Surgery, 3d edit., 2006. Recipient Ann. Resident Tchg. award, MetroHealth Med. Ctr., 1996, 1999, 2000, 2002. Fellow: Am. Coll. of Obstetricians and Gynecologists; mem.: Cleve. Soc. of Ob-gyn., Soc. of Gynecologic Surgeons, Am. Urogynecology Soc., Jour. of Gynecologic Surgery (editl. bd.), Internat. Urogynecology Jour. (editl. bd.). Office: The Cleve Clinic Dept Ob-gyn 9500 Euclid Ave Desk A81 Cleveland OH 44195 Office Phone: 216-445-6586. E-mail: walterm@ccf.org.

WALTERS, RONALD OGDEN, mortgage banker; b. Holcombe, Wis., July 13, 1939; s. Ogden Eugene and Josephine Ann (Hennekens) W.; m. Margaret Ellen Weisheipl, July 14, 1962; children: Laurie, Cheryl, Michael, Patrick Student, U. Wis., 1959-62. Mgr. Thorp Fin., LaCrosse, Wis., 1962-65, regional mgr. Milw., 1965-69, ITT Consumer Fin. Corp., Milw., 1969-74, sr. v.p. Brookfield, Wis., 1974-90, exec. v.p. adminstrn., 1990-92; CEO Ideal Fin. Corp., Brookfield, 1993—, USA Funding Corp., Brookfield, Wis., 1993—. Mem. Wis. Fin. Services Assn. (pres. 1980) Republican. Roman Catholic. Avocations: boating, fishing, hunting. Home: 812 Back Bay Delafield WI 53018-1528 Office: 17035 W Wisconsin Ave Brookfield WI 53005-5734 Office Phone: 262-938-9259. Business E-Mail: rwalters@usafundingcorp.com.

WALTERS, ROSS A., federal judge; BA in History, Pa. State U., 1971; JD with high distinction, U. Iowa, 1977. Law clk. to Judge William C. Hanson US Dist. Ct. (So. Dist. Iowa), 1977—79; assoc. Herrick and Langdon, Des Moines, 1979—82, ptnr., 1982—90; judge Iowa Dist. Ct. (Jud. Dist. 5-C), 1990—94; magistrate judge US Dist. Ct. (So. Dist.) Iowa, 1994—, chief magistrate judge, 1998—2005. Chief magistrate judge US Dist. Ct. (So. Dist.) Iowa, 1998—2005. Bd. editors, contemporary studies project leader Iowa Law Rev. Legal officer, adminstrv. div. officer US Navy Reserve, 1971—74, aboard USS Oklahoma City. Office: US Courthouse Rm 440 123 E Walnut St Des Moines IA 50309-2035

WALTHIE, THEO H., chemicals executive; Grad. summa cum laude in Chem. Engring., Tech U. Delft, Netherlands. Mem. spl. assignments prog. Dow Europe, 1970—72, prodn. engr. chlorinated solvents plant Terneuzen, Netherlands, 1972—74, various purchasing positions Rotterdam, Netherlands, 1974—78; bus. mgr. Dow Chem. Iberica, 1978—82; mgr. hydrocarbon feedstock supplies Dow Europe, Horgen, Switzerland, 1982—86, bus. v.p. hydrocarbons, 1986—89, v.p. polyurethanes, 1989—91, mgr. thermosets bus. grp., 1991—92, mgr. automotive grp., 1992—95, global v.p. hydrocarbons and energy, 1995—2000; bus. grp. pres. hydrocarbons and energy Dow Chem. Co., 2000—, mem. Office of the Chief Exec., 2006—. Mem.: Assn. Petro-Chem. Producers Europe (pres. 1998, mem. steering com. 1997, pres. 1998), Internat. Isocyanate Inst. (pres.), European Isocyanate Producers Assn. (v.p.). Office: Dow Chem Co 47 Bldg Midland MI 48067

WALTMAN, ALFRED ANTHONY, state legislator; m. Sally Waltman; ten children. Grad. high sch. Former state rep. dist. 2 State of S.D., state rep. dist. 3, 1993—2000. Mem. local govt. and taxation coms. S.D. Ho. of Reps.; farmer, rancher. Democrat. Office: 12277 376th Ave Aberdeen SD 57401-8349

WALTON, ROBERT LEE, plastic surgeon; b. Lawrence, Kans., May 30, 1946; s. Robert L. and Thelma B. (Morgan) W.; m. Elisabeth K. Beahm, Oct. 7, 2000; children: Marc, Morgan, Lindsey. BA, U. Kans., 1968; MD, U. Kans., Kansas City, 1972. Diplomate Am. Bd. Surgery, Am. Bd. Plastic Surgery. Resident in surgery Johns Hopkins Hosp., Balt., 1972-74, Yale-New Haven (Conn.) Hosp., 1974-78; chief of plastic surgery San Francisco Gen. Hosp., 1979-83; prof. and chmn. dept. plastic surgery U. Mass. Med. Ctr., Worcester, 1983-94; prof., chmn dept. plastic surgery U. Chgo., 1994—2004, prof. dept. plastic surgery, 2004—. Contbr. articles to profl. jours. Founder Projecto Mira Found. for Handicapped Children, Santurce, P.R., 1990. Mem. ACS, Am. Assn. Plastic Surgeons, Am. Soc. Plastic and Reconstructive Surgery, Am. Soc. Reconstructive Microsurgery, Alpha Omega Alpha. Office: Plastic Surgery Chgo 60 East Delaware Pl Ste 1430 Chicago IL 60611 Home Phone: 312-944-0972; Office Phone: 312-337-7795. Personal E-mail: notlaw72@sbcglobal.net. Business E-Mail: drrwalton@sbcglobal.net.

WALTON, STANLEY ANTHONY, III, lawyer; b. Chgo., Dec. 10, 1939; s. Stanley Anthony and Emily Ann (Pouzar) W.; m. Karen Kayser, Aug. 10, 1963; children: Katherine, Anne, Alex. BA, Washington and Lee U., 1962, LLB, 1965. Bar: Ill. 1965, U.S. Dist. Ct. (no. dist.) Ill. 1966, U.S. Ct. Appeals (7th cir.) 1966. Ptnr. Winston & Strawn, Chgo., 1965-89, Sayfarth Shaw Fairweather, Chgo., 1989-96. Trustee Village of Hinsdale (Ill.), 1985-89; bd. dirs. Washington and Lee Law Sch., Lexington, Va., 1975-78, bd. dirs. univ. alumni, 1983-87, pres., 1986-87; bd. dirs. UNICEF, Chgo., 1983; pres. Hinsdale Hist. Soc., 1979-81, 2001—, St. Isaac Jogues PTA, 1980; sec. Hinsdale Cmty. Svc., 2000—; bd. dirs. Hinsdale Ctrl. Found., 2000—. Mem. Ill. State Bar Assn., Phi Alpha Delta, Hinsdale Golf Club. Republican. Roman Catholic. Home and Office: 6679 Snug Harbor Dr Willowbrook IL 60527 Office Phone: 630-887-9216.

WALTZ, SUSAN, political scientist, educator; Former chmn. Amnesty Internat., London, England, 1993-98; prof. internat. pub. policy Gerald Ford Sch. Pub. Policy U. Mich., Ann Arbor, 2001—. Bd. dirs. Am. Friends Svc. Com., 2000—. Office: Ford Sch Public Policy Michigan Univ 3227 Weill Hall 735 S State St Ann Arbor MI 48109 Office Phone: 734-615-8683. Business E-Mail: swaltz@umich.edu.

WALZ, TIM (TIMOTHY J. WALZ), congressman, social science educator; b. West Point, Nebr., Apr. 6, 1964; m. Gwen Whipple, 1994; children: Hope, Gus. BS in Social Sci. Edn., Chadron State Coll., Nebr., 1989; MS in Edn. Leadership, St. Mary's U., Winona, Minn., 2001. High sch. tchr. People's Rep. China, 1989—90; tchr. Alliance Pub. Schools, 1991—96, Mankato West High Sch., Mankato, Minn., 1996—2006; mem. US Congress from 1st dist. Minn., 2007—, mem. agrl. com., vets affairs com., transp. & infrastructure com. Advanced to Sgt. Major US Army Nat. Guard, 1981—2005, served in Operation Enduring Freedom, 2005. Named Neb. Citizen Soldier of Yr., 1989, Outstanding Young Nebraskan, Nebr. Junior C. of C., 1993, Mankato Tchr. of Yr., 2003, Minn. Tchr. of Excellence, 2003; recipient Minn. Ethics in Edn. award, 2002. Democrat. Lutheran. Office: 1529 Longworth House Office Bldg Washington DC 20515 also: 1134 7th St NW Rochester MN 55901

WALZER, NORMAN CHARLES, retired economics professor; b. Mendota, Ill., Mar. 17, 1943; s. Elmer J. and Anna L. Walzer; m. Dona Lee Maurer, Aug. 22, 1970; children: Steven, Mark. BS, Ill. State U., Normal, 1966; MA, U. Ill., 1969, PhD, 1970. Rsch. dir. Cities and Villages Mcpl. Problems Com., Springfield, Ill., 1974-84; vis. prof. U. Ill., Urbana, 1977-78; prof. econs. Western Ill. U., Macomb, 1978—2005, chmn. dept. econs., 1980-89, dir. Ill. Inst. Rural Affairs, 1988—2005, interim dean coll. bus. and tech., 1993-95; prof., dir. emeritus, 2005—. Author: Cities, Suburbs and Property Tax, 1981, Government Structure and Public Finance, 1984; editor: Financing State and Local Governments, 1981, Rural Community Economic Development, 1991; co-editor: Financing Local Infrastructure in Non Metro Areas, 1986, Financing Economic Development in The 1980s, 1986, Financing Rural Health Care, 1988, Rural Health Care, 1992, Rural Community Economic Development, 1992, Local Economic Development: International Trends and Issues, 1995, Community Visioning Programs: Practice and Principles, 1996, Public-Private Partnerships for Local Economic Development, 1998, Cooperative Approach to Community Economic Development, 2000, Local Government Innovations, 2000, American Midwest: Managing Change in Rural Transition, 2003, Cooperatives and Development: Applications for the 21st Century, 2003, Entrepreneurship as a Local Development Strategy, 2007. Mem. Am. Econs. Assn., Ill. Econs. Assn. (pres. 1979-80), Mid-Continent Regional Sci. Assn. (pres. 1985-86). Office: Western Ill U Ill Inst Rural Affairs 518 Stipes Hall Macomb IL 61455

WAMBERG, WARREN THOMAS, insurance company executive; b. Lakewood, Ohio, Feb. 12, 1953; s. Warren Thomas Wamberg and Janet (Fortney) Clark; m. Diane A. Ward, July 11, 1981; children: Charles, Jason, Alison, Jennifer. BA, Baldwin-Wallace Coll., 1976. CLU. Pres. Alder-Wamberg, Inc., Cleve., 1976-79; exec. v.p. Clark/Bardes Orgn., Inc., Chgo., 1978—. Bd. dirs. Alignpac, Washington. Author: articles Prospecting, 1983, Banks In Insurance, 1985, Director Benefits, 1984, Executive Benefits, 1985. Bd. dirs. Abused Children's Soc., Chgo., 1984-86; campaign mgr. Dennis Gallagher for State Rep., Cleve., 1974, John Gallagher for School Bd., 1975. Named Rookie of Yr. New England Life, 1976. Mem. Nat. Assn. Life Underwriters, Assn. Advanced Underwriters, Chgo. Commerce and Industry (pension sub-com.), Am. Soc. Assn. Execs., Million Dollar Round Table (Top of Table award 1981-86), The Forum (Internat. Forum award 1981-86) Clubs: Glenview (Golf, Ill.), Carlton (Chgo.). Republican. Presbyterian. Avocations: golf, flying. Home: 41 Sandlewood Ln Barrington IL 60010-4026 Office: Clark/Bardes Orgn Inc 815 Watertower Pl Chicago IL 60611

WAMBOLD, RICHARD LAWRENCE, manufacturing executive; b. Wilbraham, Mass., Jan. 19, 1952; s. Richard A. and Virginia M. (Reid) W.; m. Patricia Bentley, Aug. 24, 1974; children: Lauren, Carolyn, Robin. BA, U. Tex., 1974, MBA, 1977. From systems cons. to strategic planning mgr. Tenneco, Inc., Houston, 1977-81, asst. to chmn. and chief exec. officer, 1981-84, pres. Tenneco Ventures Inc., 1984-88, v.p. corp. planning and devel., 1988—; exec. v.p., gen. mgr. Internat. Bus. Group, J.I. Case Co., Racine, Wis., 1988—99; chmn. and CEO Pactiv Corp., 1999—. Mem. Nat. Venture Capital Assn., Bus. Roundtable, Comml. Club Chgo. Avocation: sailing. Office: J I Case 700 State St Racine WI 53404-3392 also: Headquaters 1900 West Field Court Lake Forest IL 60045

WANDER, HERBERT STANTON, lawyer; b. Cin., Mar. 17, 1935; s. Louis Marvin and Pauline (Schuster) W.; m. Karen Woloshin, Aug. 2004; children: Daniel Jerome, Susan Gail, Lois Marlene. AB, U. Mich., 1957; LLB, Yale U., 1960. Bar: Ill. 1960. Law clk. to judge US Dist. Ct. (no. dist.) Ill., 1960—61; ptnr. Pope Ballard Shepard & Fowle, Chgo., 1961—78, Katten Muchin Rosenman LLP, Chgo., 1978—. Chair Michael Reese Health Trust, 2006; bd. dirs. Tel. & Data Systems, Chgo.; mem. legal adv. com. to bd. govs. NY Stock Exch., 1989—92; mem. legal adv. bd. Nat. Assn. Securities Dealers, Inc., 1996—99; spkr. in field. Editor: (jour.) Bus. Law Today, 1992-93; editor-in-chief: (jour.) The Bus. Lawyer, 1993-94; contbr. numerous articles to profl. jour. Bd. dir. Jewish Fedn. Met. Chgo., 1972—, pres., 1981-83; bd. dir. Jewish United Fund, 1972—, pres., 1981-83, chmn. pub. affairs com., 1984-87, gen. campaign chmn., 1993 Mem.: ABA (sec. bus. law sect. 1992—93, vice-chair 1993—94, chair-elect 1994—95, chair 1995—96, apptd. to ABA commn. on multidisciplinary practice 1998, ABA task force on atty.-client privilege 2004, task force on fed. sentencing guidelines 2004, co-chair SEC adv. com. on smaller pub. cos. 2004), Chgo. Bar Assn., Ill. State Bar Assn., Yale Law Sch. Assn. (exec. com. 1982—86), Northmoor Country Club, Std. Club, Econ. Club, Phi Beta Kappa. Home: 70 Prospect Ave Highland Park IL 60035-3329 Office: Katten Muchin Rosenman LLP 525 W Monroe St Ste 1700 Chicago IL 60661-3693 Business E-Mail: hwander@kattenlaw.com.

WANEK, TODD, retail executive; CEO Ashley Furniture Industries, Arcadia, Wis., 2002—. Office: Ashley Furniture Industries One Ashley Way Arcadia WI 54612

WANG, ALBERT JAMES, violinist, educator; b. Ann Arbor, Mich., Nov. 19, 1958; s. James and Lydia (Ebenhoch) Wang; m. Bridget Renee Becker, June 30, 1987 (div. 2000); children: Ona Lenore, Kevin Lewis. MusB, Ind. U., 1979; MusM, U. Mich., 1981; DMA, Am. Conservatory, 1993. Prin. second violin Baton Rouge Symphony Orch., 1981-82; first violin Valcour String Quartet, Baton Rouge, 1981-82, Loyola String Quartet, 1982-83; mem. Lyric Opera Chgo. Orch., 1982—; mem. Orch. Ill., Chgo., 1982-88; prin. 2d violin Internat. Symphony Orch., Port Huron, Mich., 1984; 1st violin Internat. String Quartet, Port Huron, 1984; concertmaster, soloist Chgo. Chamber Orch., 1985-88, Chgo. Philharm., 1985—; mem. Grant Park Symphony Orch., Chgo., 1986-87; concertmaster, soloist Birch Creek Music Festival, Wis., Woodstock (Ill.) Mozart Festival Orch., 1988-90; concertmaster Rockford (Ill.) Symphony Orch., 1990-91, Northwestern Music Festival Orch., 1990—; soloist, concertmaster Pro Musica Orch. of Mauritius, 1992-93; soloist, concertmaster China tour Classical Symphony Orch., 1994, 95; soloist, concertmaster Midwest Symphony Orch., 1995-96; music dir. Baroque Masterplayers, 1994—; soloist, concertmaster Met. Arts Orch., 1995-98. Artist-in-residence St. Clair Coll., Port Huron, 1984, Elgin C.C., 1994—97; lectr. Am. Conservatory Music, Chgo., 1989—92; Fulbright lectr. Francois Mitterand Conservatory of Music, Quatre Bornes, Mauritius, 1992—93; asst. prof. violin Roosevelt U., 1993—2002; adj. prof. violin Wheaton (Ill.) Coll., 1997—2000; adj. asst. prof. violin Moody Bible Inst., Chgo., 1997—2000; v.p. sales and mktg. Music Edn. Publs., Inc., Coral Springs, Fla., 1997—98. umerous solo, recital and chamber music appearances and master classes throughout U.S., Can., France, Mauritius and China; recs. and broadcasts by Mauritian Nat. Radio and WFMT Chgo. Fine Arts Sta., PBS, Nat. Pub. Radio, and Chinese Nat. Radio and TV; numerous world premieres; recs. on New World Records and with Slavic Projection Ensemble; N.Y. recital debut at Carnegie Hall, 1998; adjudicator for state and nat. music competitions; contbr. articles and revs. to profl. jours. Vol. ARC, Literacy Vols. Am., Chgo. Pub. Librs., United Way; bd. advisors Prism Music Festival, 1984—, Am. Chamber Symphony, 1985, Symphony II, 1993-94. Fulbright grantee, 1992-93; recipient 1st prize Ann Arbor (Mich.) Symphony Competition, 1976, Soc. Am. Musicians Competition, Chgo., 1984, Internat. Concerts Atlantique Competition, N.Y.C., 1989, Chgo. Park Dist. Competition, 1991, 2nd prize Biennial Adult Artist Competition, 1992, Helmuth Fuchs Performance award 1998; selected to Arts Am. Touring Artist Roster, 1993; finalist Lilly Fellows Program in Humanities and the Arts, Valparaiso U., 1994, Harry and Sarah Zelzer Fellowship and prize; recipient Leo Sowerby medal, 1994; Christian Performing Artists' fellow. Mem. ASCAP, Am. Fedn. Musicians, Am. String Tchrs. Assn., Coll. Music Soc., Chamber Music Am., Am. Music Ctr., Music Tchrs. Nat. Assn., Christian Performing Artists' Fellowship. Avocations: powerlifting, fishing, travel, woodworking. Home: 6110 N Glenwood Ave Chicago IL 60660-1804 Office: Lyric Opera Chgo 20 N Wacker Dr Chicago IL 60606-2806 Office Phone: 312-332-2244. Personal E-mail: aw_dma@hotmail.com.

WANG, HENRY YEE-NEEN, chemical engineering educator; b. Shanghai, July 22, 1951; came to U.S., 1969; s. T. C. and Aurza Wang; m. Evangeline Yap Cesar, 1983; 1 child, Stephanie. BS, Iowa State U., 1972; MS, MIT, 1974, PhD, 1977. Rsch. asst. MIT, Cambridge, 1972-77; engring. assoc. Merckle & Co., Rahway, N.J., 1977; sr. scientist Schering-Plough, Union, N.J., 1978-79; from asst. prof. to assoc. prof. U. Mich., Ann Arbor, 1978-84, prof., 1989—. Disting. sr. scientist Mich. Biotech. Inst., Lansing, 1984—; cons. Hong Kong U. of Sci. and Tech., 1993—. Internat. editor: Jour. Ferm. Biotech., 1991—. Mem. AIChE, Am. Chem. Soc. (councilor 1984-86), Am. Soc. Microbiology, Soc. Indsl. Microbiology. Home: 1215 Bardstown Trl Ann Arbor MI 48105-2816 Office: U Mich Dept Chem Engring Ann Arbor MI 48109

WANG, SONA, venture capitalist; b. South Korea, 1958; naturalized, US; BS in Indsl. Engring., Stanford U., 1980; MBA magna cum laude, Northwestern U., 1986. Mgr., engr. Intel Corp., Calif.; investment mgr. Allstate Venture Capital; co-founder, gen. ptnr. Batterson, Johnson & Wang, Ill., 1988—2001, Inroads Capital Ptnrs., Evanston, Ill., 1995—; co-founder, mng. dir. Ceres Venture Fund, L.P., 2005—. Chmn. VIPdesk, Inc.; bd. dirs. IKOS Sys., Answer Systems (now subs. of Platinum Technologies), Sigmedics, Inc., Array Technologies, Success Lab., Inc., Ultimo Enterprises, Ltd., High Tower Software, Grand Eagle Cos., Wine.com, TrafficCast Internat., Inc., 2008—. Founding adv. coun. mem. Women's Bus. Devel. Ctr., Chgo.; mem. Coun. of 100, Northwestern U.; bd. trustees Northwestern U., Chgo. Symphony Orch.; bd. govs Met. Planning Coun.; mem. Chgo. Mayor's Coun. Tech. Adv.; bd. mem. Evanston Northwestern Healthcare & Blue Cross Blue Shield of Ill. Named one of The 100 Most Influential Women in Chgo., Crain's Chgo. Bus., 2004; recipient Leadership award for Entrepreneurship, YWCA, 2001. Office: Ceres Venture Fund LP 500 Davis St Ste 600 Evanston IL 60201 also: Inroads Capital Ptnrs Ste 2050 1603 Orrington Ave Evanston IL 60201 Office Phone: 847-864-2000. Office Fax: 847-864-9692.*

WANG, YA-HUI, conductor; b. Taiwan; arrived in U.S., 1986; Degree in Piano Performance and Conducting, Curtis Inst. Music, Peabody Conservatory. Apprentice condr. Chgo. (Ill.) Symphony Orch., 1995—96; music dir. Fort Smith (Ark.) Symphony, 1996—97; asst. condr. Detroit (Mich.) Symphony Orch., 1997—99; music dir. Akron (Ohio) Symphony Orch., 1999—2003; vice music dir. Evergreen Symphony Orch., Taipei, Taiwan, 2004—. Music dir. Omaha Nebr. Youth Orchs.; prin. condr. Chgo. (Ill.) Encore Chamber Orch.; guest condr. in field. Recipient Tokyo (Japan) Competition prize, 1994, Dimitri Mitropoulos Competition prize, Athens, Greece, 1996, Nicolai Malko Competition prize, Copenhagen, Denmark, 1998. Office: Akron Symphony Orchestra 17 N Broadway Akron OH 44308

WANKAT, PHILLIP CHARLES, chemical engineering educator; b. Oak Park, Ill., July 11, 1944; s. Charles and Grace Wankat; m. Dorothy Nel Richardson, Dec. 13, 1980; children: Charles, Jennifer. BS in Chem. Engring., Purdue U., 1966, MS in Edn., 1982; PhD, Princeton U., 1970. From asst. prof. to C.L. Lovell disting. prof. chem. engring Purdue U., West Lafayette, Ind., 1970—, head freshman engring., 1987-95, interim dir. continuing engring. edn., 1996, head interdisciplinary engring., 2000—04. Cons. pharm. firm, 1985-94. Author: Large Scale Ads and Chromatog, 1986, Equil Staged Separations, 1988, Rate Controlled Separations, 1990, Teaching Engineering, 1993, The Effective, Efficient Professor, 2002, Separation Process Engineering, 2007. With AUS, 1962-64. Recipient award in Separations Sci. and Tech., Am. Chem. Soc., 1994. Mem. AIChE, Am. Soc. Engring. Edn. (Union Carbide Lectr. award 1997), Am. Chem. Soc. Achievements include patents in field. Avocations: fishing, canoeing, camping. Office: Purdue U Dept Chem Engring 480 Stadium Mall Dr West Lafayette IN 47907-2100 Business E-Mail: wankat@ecn.purdue.edu.

WANKE, RONALD LEE, lawyer; b. Chgo., June 22, 1941; s. William F. and Lucille Wanke; m. Rose Klonowski, Oct. 23, 1987. BSEE, Northwestern U., 1964; JD, DePaul U., 1968. Bar: Ill. 1968. Assoc. Wood, Dalton, Phillips, Mason & Rowe, Chgo., 1968-71, ptnr., 1971-84, Jenner & Block, Chgo., 1984--. Lectr. John Marshall Law Sch., Chgo., 1985-94; mem. adv. com. intellectual property program, U. Fla. Coll. Law, 2001-03. Contbr. chpt. to book, articles to Software Law Jour., 1987, Internat. Legal Strategy, 1995. Office: Jenner & Block One IBM Plz Ste 4400 Chicago IL 60611-7603 Office Phone: 312-222-9350.

WANSLEY, TY, radio personality; Former news dir. Sta. WBMX-FM, Sta. WJPC-AM; former talk show host Sta. WVON-AM, Sta. WCGI-AM, Sta. WLS-AM/FM, Sta. WJJD-AM; former host, prodr. TV News Mag. Show Urban St.; radio host, info. anchor morning show Sta. WGCI-FM, Chgo. Office: Wgci Radio 233 N Michigan Ave Ste 2800 Chicago IL 60601-5704

WANTLAND, WILLIAM CHARLES, retired bishop, lawyer; b. Edmond, Okla., Apr. 14, 1934; s. William Lindsay and Edna Louise (Yost) W. BA, U. Hawaii, 1957; JD, Okla. City U., 1967; D in Religion, Geneva Theol. Coll., Knoxville, Tenn., 1976; DD (hon.), Nashotah House, Wis., 1983, Seabury-Western Sem., Evanston, Ill., 1983. With FBI, various locations, 1954-59, Ins. Co. of N.Am., Oklahoma City, 1960-62; law clk.-atty. Bishop & Wantland, Seminole, Okla., 1962-77; vicar St. Mark's Ch., Seminole, 1963-77, St. Paul's Ch., Holdenville, Okla., 1974-77; presiding judge Seminole Mcpl. Ct., 1970-77; atty. gen. Seminole Nation of Okla., 1969-72, 75-77; exec. dir. Okla. Indian Rights Assn., Norman, 1972-73; rector St. John's Ch., Oklahoma City, 1977-80; bishop Episcopal Diocese of Eau Claire, Wis., 1980-99; interim bishop of Navajoland, 1993-94; ret., 1999. Adj. prof. Law Sch. U. Okla., Norman, 1970-78; instr. canon law Nashotah House, 1983-97, 2004—; nat. coun. Evang. and Cath. Mission, Chgo., 1977-90; mem. Episcopal Commn. on Racism, 1990-92, Episcopal Coun. Indian Ministries, 1990-95, Standing Commn. on Constn. and Canons, 1992-95; assisting bishop Diocese of Dallas, 2002—04, of Ft. Worth, 2000—. Author: Foundations of the Faith, 1982, Canon Law of the Episcopal Church, 1984, The Prayer Book and the Catholic Faith, 1994; The Catholic Faith, The Episcopal Church and the Ordination of Women, 1997; co-author: Oklahoma Probate Forms, 1971; contbr. articles to profl. jours. Pres. Okla. Conf. Mcpl. Judges, 1973; v.p. South African Ch. Union, 1985-95; trustee Nashotah House, Wis., 1981—, chmn., 1992-98; bd. dirs. SPEAK, Eureka Springs, Ark., 1983-89; Wis. adv. com. US Civil Rights Commn., 1990-91; support com. Native Am. Rights Fund, 1990—; coun. mem. City of Seminole, Okla., 2002—, vice mayor, 2003—; co-chmn. Luth.-Anglican-Roman Cath. Commn. of Wis., 1989-95; pres. Wis. Episc. Conf., 1995-97, Wis. Coun. Chs., 1985-86; active Living Ch. Found., 1981-02; bd. dirs. Seminole Nation Hist. Soc., 1999—, pres., 2006—; adv. bd. Seminole Hist. Soc., 2003—. Recipient Most Outstanding Contbn. to Law and Order award Okla. Supreme Ct., 1975, Outstanding Alumnus award Okla. City U., 1980, Wis. Equal Rights Coun. award, 1986, Manitou Ikwe award Indian Alcoholism Coun., 1988, Episcopal Synod Pres.'s award, 1995, 2004. Mem. Okla. Bar Assn., Okla. Indian Bar Assn., Oklahoma City Law Sch. Alumni Assn. (pres. 1968), Ct. Indian Offenses Seminole ation Okla. (chief magistrate 2006—). Democrat. Episcopalian. Avocations: canoeing, skin-diving, cross country skiing. Personal E-mail: puca382@mbo.net.

WANZEK, TERRY MARVIN, state legislator; b. Jamestown, ND, Mar. 28, 1957; m. Janice Hoffart; 2 children. Farmer, rancher, Cleveland, N.D.; mem. N.D. Senate from 29th dist., Bismarck, 1995—; mem. edn. com. N.D. Senate, Bismarck, 1995—; vice chmn. agr. com. N.D. State Senate, Bismarck, 1995-97; chmn. agr. com., mem. edn. com. N.D. Senate, Bismarck, 1997—. Pres. Stutsman County Farm Bur. Fellow Jamestown Coll.; recipient Agriculturist award Pres.' Agr. Club N.D. State U. Mem. Stutsman County Agrl. Improvement Assn. (pres.), KC, Jamestown C. of C. Home: 404 10th St SW Jamestown ND 58401-4546

WARCH, RICHARD, former academic administrator; b. Hackensack, NJ, Aug. 4, 1939; s. George William and Helen Anna (Hansen) W.; m. Margot Lynn Moses, Sept. 8, 1962; children: Stephen Knud, David Preston, Karin Joy. BA, Williams Coll., 1961; B.D., Yale Div. Sch., 1964; PhD, Yale U., 1969; postgrad., U. Edinburgh, 1962-63; H.H.D., Ripon Coll., 1980. Asst. prof. history and Am. studies Yale U., 1968-73, asso. prof., 1973-77; asso. dean Yale Coll.; dir. summer plans Yale U., 1976-77; asso. dir. Nat. Humanities Inst., New Haven, 1975-76; v.p. acad. affairs Lawrence U., Appleton, Wis., 1977-79, pres., 1979—2004. Cons. at. Humanities Faculty; ordained to ministry United Presbyn. Ch. in U.S.A., 1968; dir. Bank One of Appleton. Author: School of the Prophets, Yale College, 1701-1740, 1973; editor: John Brown, 1973. Rockefeller Bros. Theol. fellow, 1961-62 Mem. Am. Studies Assn., Soc. for Values in Higher Edn., Winnebago Presbytery. Clubs: Rotary.

WARD, DAVID ALLEN, sociology educator; b. Dedham, Mass., June 21, 1933; s. Theodore Allen and Jessie Miller (Ketchum) W.; m. Carol Jane Barton, June 10, 1957 (div. 1964); children: Douglas Allen, Andrew Barton; m. Reneé Ellen Light, Mar. 10, 1967. BA, Colby Coll., 1955; PhD, U. Ill., 1960. Asst. prof. Wash. State U., Pullman, 1960-61; asst. research sociologist UCLA, 1961-64; assoc. prof. U. Minn., Mpls., 1965-68, prof., 1968—2002, chmn. dept. sociology, 1984-88, 92-95. Chmn. Salzburg (Austria) Seminar in Am. Studies, 1977; cons. jud. com. U.S. Ho. Reps., Washington, 1984. Co-author: Women's Prison, 1965, Prison Treatment, 1971; co-editor: Delinquency, Crime and Social Process, 1969, Confinement in Maximum Custody, 1981; editorial cons. Jour. Criminal Law and Criminology, 1968-97. Mem. Mpls. Civilian Police Rev. Bd., 1991-94. Liberal Arts fellow Harvard U. Law Sch., 1968-69; Fulbright research fellow, 1971-72; research fellow Norwegian Fgn. Office, Oslo, 1976. Mem.: Am. Soc. Criminology, Am. Sociol. Assn. (chmn. sect. criminology 1976—77). Office: Univ of Minn Dept of Sociology 909 Social Sci Bldg Minneapolis MN 55455

WARD, DAVID W., state legislator; b. Ft. Atkinson, Wis., Apr. 29, 1953; m. Jean M. Ward, 1975; 1 child, Kevin. BA, U. Wis., Platteville. Past mem. Wis. Milk Mktg. Bd., Ft. Atkinson Sch. Bd.; Wis. state assembly man dist. 37, 1992—. Farmer. Mem. Jefferson County Farm Bur., pres. Address: 3401 County Rd G Fort Atkinson WI 53538 also: Wis Assembly PO Box 8952 Madison WI 53708-8952

WARD, FRANCIS J., marketing and research executive; Founder Product and Consumer Evaluations, Inc., 1975-90; CEO MORPACE Internat. (merger Product and Consumer Evaluations, Inc. and Market Opinion Rsch.), Farmington Hills, Mich., 1990—. Office: MORPACE Internat merger Product and Consumer Evaluations Inc 31700 Middlebelt Rd Ste 0 Farmington MI 48334-2373

WARD, JONATHAN P., investment banker; b. May 6, 1954; BSChemE, U. N.H., 1976; grad. advanced mgmt. program, Harvard Bus. Sch. With R.R. Donnelley, 1977—2001, pres. Merchandise Media and Fin. Svcs. bus. units, mgr. comml. printing operation, v.p., dir. Spartanburg, S.C., mfg. divsn., exec. v.p. Comml. Print Sector, 1995—97, pres., COO, 1997—2001; pres., CEO ServiceMaster, Downers Grove, Ill., 2001—02, chmn., CEO, 2002—06; mng. dir. investment banking, chmn. Chgo. office Lazard Ltd., Chgo., 2006—. Dir. Metromail Corp., Siegwerk Inc. USA, J. Jill Group Inc., First Horizon. Trustee Goodman Theatre, Chgo.; dir. Chgo. Youth Ctrs., Evanston Northwestern Hosp. Mem.: Nat. Assn. Mfr., Direct Mktg. Assn. Office: Lazard Ltd 200 W Madison St Ste 2200 Chicago IL 60606 Office Phone: 312-407-6600. Office Fax: 312-407-6620.

WARD, LLOYD D., appliance company executive; m. Lita; 2 sons. BS Engrng, Mich. State U., 1970; MBA, Xavier U. Design engr., group leader engrng., product devel., operations, advertising Proctor & Gamble Co., 1970-88, gen. mgr. dish care products, 1988; v.p. ops. Pepsi Cola East, 1988-91; pres. Frito-Lay West PepsiCo, 1991-92, pres. Frito-Lay central divsn., 1992-96; exec. v.p., pres. Maytag Appliances, Newton, Iowa, 1996-98, COO, corp. pres., 1998—, CEO, 1999—. Special assignment PepsiCo restaurant internat. bus. Recipient Exec. Yr. award Black Enterprise mag. 1995. Office: 403 W 4th St N Newton IA 50208-3026

WARD, MICHAEL A., property company executive; Exec. v.p., COO Ramco-Gershenson Properties, Southfield, Mich., 1989—. Office: 27600 Northwestern Hwy Ste 200 Southfield MI 48034-8466 E-mail: mward@ramco.gershenson.com.

WARD, PETER ALLAN, pathologist, educator; b. Winsted, Conn., Nov. 1, 1934; s. Parker J. and Mary Alice (McEvoy) Ward. BS, U. Mich., 1958; MD, U. Mich. Med. Sch., 1960. Diplomate Am. Bd. Anatomic Pathology, 1964, Am. Bd. Immunopathology, 1983. Intern Bellevue Hosp., NYU, NYC, 1960—61; resident dept. pathology U. Mich. Med. Sch., Ann Arbor, 1961—63; postdoctoral fellow Scripps Clinic and Rsch. Found., divsn. Exptl. Pathology, La Jolla, Calif., 1963—65; chief, immunology br. Armed Forces Inst. Pathology, Wash., 1965—71; prof. dept. pathology U. Conn. Health Ctr., Farmington, 1971—80, prof. and chmn. dept. pathology, 1973—80; prof. and chmn. dept. of pathology U. Mich. Med. Sch., Ann Arbor, 1980—2005, interim dean, 1982—85. Mem. pathology study sect. NIH, Bethesda, Md., 1974—76, chmn. pathology study sect., 1976—78; mem. rsch. rev. com. NHLBI/NIH, Bethesda, Md., 1978—82; sci. adv. bd. Armed Forces Inst. Pathology, Wash., 1978—83; cons. VA Hosp., Ann Arbor, 1980—; first Godfrey D. Stobbe prof. of pathology U. Mich. Med. Sch., 1987—; bd. dir. Univs. Associated for Rsch. and Edn. in Pathology, Inc., 1988—90; disting. faculty lectr. U. Mich. Biomedical Rsch. Coun., Ann Arbor, 1989—; pres.-elect U.S./Can. Acad. Pathology, Inc., 1991—92, pres., 1992—93; past pres. and chair nominating com. U.S./Can. Acad. of Pathology, Inc., 1993—94; mem. Inst. Lab. Animal Resources, 1993—96; coun. chair Inst. Lab. Animal Rsch. Coun., 1999—; chmn. nominating com. Soc. Med. Consultants to the Armed Forces, 1989—93; mem. Inst. Medicine/NAS, 1990—; trustee Am. Bd. Pathology, 1988—97, bd. dirs., 1996—97, life trustee, 1998—; treas. Soc. Leukocyte Biology, 2000—03, pres., 2004—05; bd. dirs. Fedn. Am. Socs. for Exptl. Biology, 2004—. Capt. M.C. US Army, 1965—67, Armed Forces Inst. Pathology, Wash. Recipient R & D Achievement award, U.S. Army, 1969, Meritorious Civilian Svc. award, 1970, Parke-Davis award, Am. Soc. Exptl. Pathology, 1971, Borden Rsch. award, U. Mich. Med. Sch., 1990, Merit award, NIH, 1990-97, Nat. Pres. award in recognition of leadership as pres., Mich. State Med. Soc., 1992, Rous-Whipple award, Am. Soc. Investigative Pathology, 1996, Lifetime Nat. Assoc., Nat. Academies Sci., 2001, Gold-Headed Cane award, Am. Soc. Investigative Pathology, 2001, J. Burns Amberson Lectr., Am. Thoracic Soc., 2003, Disting. Svc. award, Assn. Pathology Chairs, 2004, Chugai award for excellence in mentoring and scholarship, Am. Soc. Investigative Pathology, 2005. Fellow: AAAS, Am. Heart Assn. (fellow, coun. on cardiopulmonary, perioperative & critical care 2003); mem.: Inst. Lab. Animal Rsch. Coun. (coun. chair 1999—), Assn. Pathology Chairmen (rsch. com. mem. 1982), Am. Soc. Investigative Pathology (rep. to faseb bd./faseb fin. com. 2004), Am. Thoracic Soc. (sci. adv. com. 1989), Am. Bd. Pathology (pres. 1996—97), Am. Assn. Immunologists (nominating com. 1992), Am. Assn. for Advancement of Sci., U.S. and Can. Acad. Pathology, Inc., NIH (mentored scientist spl. emphasis panel 2001), Nat. Heart, Lung, and Blood Inst. (com. mem. 1990, rev. com. 1990), Mich. Thoracic Soc., A. James French Soc. Pathologists (charter mem.), Am. Soc. Clin. Investigation. Achievements include patents for sulfatides as anti-inflammatory compounds, U.S. Patent No. 5, 486, 536; compositions and methods for the treatment of sepsis, U.S. Patent No. 6, 673, 346. Office: Univ Mich Med School 1301 Catherine M5240 Med Sci 1 Ann Arbor MI 48109-0602 Home Phone: 734-996-3992; Office Phone: 734-763-6384. Office Fax: 734-763-4872. Business E-Mail: pward@umich.edu.

WARD, ROSCOE FREDRICK, engineering educator; b. Boise, Idaho, Dec. 5, 1930; s. Roscoe C. W. and Alice E. (Ward); m. Julia Duffy, June 8, 1963; children: Eric R., David C. Student, U. Oreg., 1949-50; BA, Coll. of Idaho, 1953; postgrad., U. Wash., 1955-57; BS, Oreg. State U., 1959; MS, Wash. State U., 1961; Sc.D., Washington U., St. Louis, 1964. Registered profl. engr., Ohio. Asst. prof. civil engrng. U. Mo., Columbia, 1963-65, Robert Coll., Istanbul, Turkey, 1965-67; assoc. prof. civil engrng. Asian Inst. Tech., Bangkok, 1967-68; assoc. prof. civil engrng., assoc. dean Sch. Engrng. U. Mass., Amherst, 1968-75; prof. Bogazici U., Istanbul, 1974-75; br. chief biomass energy Dept. Energy, Washington, 1975-79; interregional advisor UN/World Bank, NYC, 1979-83; dean Sch. Applied Scis. Miami U., Oxford, Ohio, 1983-88, prof. paper and chem. engrng. Sch. Engrng. and Applied Scis., 1983—. Vis. scientist Csir, Republic of South Africa, 1990-91. Contbr. chapters to books, articles to profl. jours. Fellow: ASCE. Home: 4818 Bonham Rd Oxford OH 45056-1423 Business E-Mail: wardrf@muohio.edu.

WARD, SHERMAN CARL, III, (BUZZ WARD), theater manager; b. Camden, NJ, Apr. 21, 1958; s. Sherman Carl Jr. and Ann Laura (Bodie) W. BA, Princeton U., 1980; MBA, Harvard U., 1986. Contr.'s asst. McCarter Theatre Co., Princeton, N.J., 1977-80; spl. projects analyst Madison Fin. Corp., Nashville, 1980-81, dir. client svcs., 1981-83; tchr. English, vol. rschr. Nan, Thailand, 1983-84; studio ops. Walt Disney Pictures, Burbank, Calif., summer 1985; contr. Coconut Grove Playhouse, Miami, Fla., 1986-87, dir. ops., 1987-88; gen. mgr. Yale Sch. Drama, Yale Repertory Theatre, New Haven, Conn., 1988-92; exec. dir. Cin. Playhouse in the Park, 1992—. Recipient Letter of Appreciation, King of Thailand, 1984. Mem. Actor's Equity Assn. Avocations: travel, singing, dance, golf, volleyball. Office: Cin Playhouse in the Park 962 Mount Adams Cir Cincinnati OH 45202-6023

WARD, THOMAS, food products executive; b. June 9, 1958; Co-CEO, pres. Russell Stover Candies, Kansas City, Mo. Fax: 816-842-5593.

WARD-BROWN, DENISE, sculptor, educator; BFA cum laude, Temple U., 1975; MFA summa cum laude, Howard U., 1984. Assoc. prof. U. Washington, St. Louis, 1991—. One-woman shows Cinque Gallery, N.Y.C., 1984, Washington Project for the Arts, Washington, 1984, Bozeman, Mont., 1986, O St. Gallery, Washington, 1989, Montgomery Coll., Tacoma Park, Md., 1989, Fitzpatrick Gallery, Washington, 1989, U. Md., Princess Anne, Md., 1991, Pierce-Arrow Gallery, St. Louis, 1993, St. Louis Art Mus., 1995, Margaret Harwell Art Mus., Poplar Bluff, Mo., 1998; group exhbns. include Corcoran Mus. Art, Washington, 1987, George Washington U., 1987, U. Richmond, Va., 1987, Shippee Gallery, N.y.C., 1987, Strathmore Arts Ctr., Rockville, md., 1988, Rockville Arts Ctr., 1989, Notre Dame Coll., Balt., 1989, No. Va. C.C., Arlington, 1989, The Kunstrum, Washington, 1990, Montgomery Coll., Tacoma Park, Md., 1990, Smithsonian-Anacostia Mus., Washington, 1990, Art St. Louis, 1992, Lindenwood Coll., St. Louis, 1993, Murray State U. Eagle Gallery, 1993, Portfolio Gallery, St. Louis, 1994, U. Wis., Eau Claire, 1994, U. Md., College Park, 1994, St. Louis Design Ctr., 1996, Gene Pool & Assocs., N.Y.C., 1996, Smithsonian Instn., 1996, numerous others. Study grantee Penland (N.C.) Sch. Crafts, 1973, Haystack Mt. Sch. Crafts, Deer Isle, Maine, 1973, 74, Howard U./Ford Found., 1982, 83, Vt. Studio Sch., Johnson, 1986, Geog. Devel. grantee Washington D.C. Commn. on the Arts and Humanities, 1984, 85; Individual Artist grantee Washington D.C. Commn. on the Arts and Humanities, 1986, 87, 89, 91, Mbari, Ritual and Rememory, Regiona Artists' Projects grantee, 1994; Fulbright scholar African Rsch. Program, Ghana, others. Office: Dept Sculpture Sch Art Washington U Camp Box 1031 1 Brookings Dr Saint Louis MO 63130-4862 Fax: 314-935-8412. E-mail: ddwardbr@art.wustl.edu.

WARDEN, GAIL LEE, healthcare executive; b. Clarinda, Iowa, May 11, 1938; s. Lee Roy and Juanita (Haley) W.; m. Lois Jean Johnson, Oct. 9, 1965; children: Jay Christopher, Janna Lynn, Jena Marie. BA, Dartmouth Coll., 1960; MHA, U. Mich., 1962; PhD in pub. adminstrn., Cent. Mich. U., 1995. Adminstrv. asst. Blodgett Meml. Ctr., Grand Rapids, Mich., 1962; adj. Dewitt Hosp., Ft. Belvoir, Va., 1963-65; exec. v.p./COO Rush-Presbyn.-St. Luke's Med. Ctr., Chgo., 1965—76; exec. v.p. Am. Hosp. Assn., Chgo., 1976-81; pres., CEO Group Health Coop. Puget Sound, Seattle, 1981-88, Henry Ford Health Sys., Detroit, 1988—2003, pres. emeritus, 2003—. Past chmn. Am. Hosp. Assn., HRET, Steering Com. Transformational Leadership Project in Health Mgmt. Edn. and Practice; former chmn. Nat. Quality Forum; chair Nat. Ctr. Healthcare Leadership, IOM Com. on Future Emergency Medicine in US, Detroit Wayne County Health Authority; bd. dirs. Comerica Bank, Nat. Rsch. Corp.; mem. RAND Health Bd. Advisors; dir. emeritus Nat. Com. on Quality Assurance, former chmn.; former mem. Bd. Health Care Svcs., Inst. Medicine, Com. Quality Health Care in Am., Fed. Adv. Commn. Consumer Protection and Quality in Health Care Industry, at. Commn. Civic Renewal, Pew Health Professions Comms., IOM, gov. coun.; vice chair bd. dirs. Rosalind Franklin U. Medicine and Sci.; chair campaign com., mem. dean's adv. bd. U. Mich. Sch. Pub. Health. Contbr. articles to profl. jours. Former bd. dirs. Robert Wood Johnson Found., 1965; bd. dirs. Citizens Rsch. Coun. Mich.; chair Detroit Zoological Soc.; former mem. bd. dirs. Detroit Econ. Growth Corp.; former mem. Detroit Met. Wayne County Airport Commn.; former chmn. Greater Detroit Area Health Coun.; bd. dirs. Bon Secours Cottage Health Svcs., co-chair capital campaign; past mem. Fed. Adv. Commn. on Consumer Protection and Quality in the Health Care Industry. Capt. USAR. Named one of Ten Outstanding Young Men in Chgo., Jr. Assn. Commerce and Industry, 1968; named on e of 100 Most Powerfule People in Healthcare, Modern Healthcare, 2002-04; recipient Nat. Health Care award, B'nai B'rith Internat., 1992, CEO award Am. Hosp. Assn.'s Soc. for Healthcare Planning and Mktg., 1993, Gold Medal award, Am. Coll. Health Care Execs., 1999; first recipient Thompson Vis. Fellowship award, Yale, Health Quality award, Nat. Com. Quality Assurance, Disting. Svc. award, AHA, Walter J. McNerney Fellowship award for Health System Improvement, HRET. Mem. APHA, NAS Inst. Medicine (governing coun.), Am. Coll. Hosp. Adminstrs. (named Young Adminstr. of Yr. 1972), Am. Healthcare Systems, Inst. Healthcare Improvment, Nat. Resource Ctr. on Chronic Care Integration, Alpha Chi Rho. Office: Henry Ford Health System 1 Ford Pl Detroit MI 48202-3450

WARDNER, RICH, state legislator; m. Kayleen Wardner; children: Brant, Cory. Math. and chemistry tchr., football coach Dickinson (N.D.) H.S.; mem. N.D. Senate from 37th dist., Bismarck, 1991—; mem. state and fed. govt. com. N.D. Senate, Bismarck, former vice chmn., chmn. govt. and vet. affairs com., now mem. fin. and taxation com. Office: 1042 12th Ave W Dickinson ND 58601-3654 also: ND Ho of Reps State Capitol Bismarck ND 58505

WARDROP, RICHARD M., JR., former steel holding company executive; b. McKeesport, Pa. BS In Metall. Engrng., Pa. State U.; postgrad., U. Pitts. Various positions U.S. Steel Corp., 1968—92, sr. buyer raw materials Pitts., 1980—81, supt. flat-rolled products group Gary, Ind., 1981—84, divsn. mgr. for steel prodn., casting and primary rolling, 1984—86, plant mgr. for primary ops., 1986—88, gen. mgr. Mongehela Valley Works, 1988; corp. v.p. engrng. and purchasing Washington (Pa.) Steel Corp; v.p. mfg. AK Steel Holding Corp., Middletown, Ohio, 1992—95, CEO, 1995—2003, chmn., 1997—2003. Named Platinum 400 List, Forbes Mag., 1999. Mem.: Am. Iron and Steel Engrs., Am. Soc. Metals Internat. (David Ford McFarland award for achievement in metallurgy 1995), AIME.

WARE, D. CLIFTON, vocalist, educator; b. Newton, Miss., Mar. 15, 1937; s. Durward Clifton and Emma Edna (Blount) W.; m. Elizabeth Jean Oldham, June 20, 1958; children: Jon Clifton, David Michael, Stephen Alan. BA, Millsaps Coll., 1959; MusM, U. So. Miss., 1962; MusD, Northwestern U., 1970. Voice instr. U. So. Miss., Hattiesburg, 1964-69; prof. voice and pedagogy U. Minn., Mpls., 1970—2007, chmn. Roy A. Schuessler Vocal Arts Ctr., 1970—2007, prof. emeritus, 2007—. Clinician, cons., adjudicator. Author: (book, song collection and video) Voice Adventures, 1988, (text, song collection, audio cassette, CD) Adventures in Singing, 1995, 2d edit., 1998, 3rd edit., 2004, Basics of Vocal Pedagogy, 1998, The Singer's Life: Goals and Roles, 2005; made recs. St. icolas, 1977, Paul Bunyan, 1988, Vocal Explorations: The Bad, the Good, and the Other, 2003; tenor soloist opera, oratorio, recitals. Mem. Nat. Assn. Tchrs. Singing (pres. Minn. chpt. 1972-73, 81-82, found 1995-2006), Nat. Opera Assn. (pres. 1978-79), Pi Kappa Lambda, Phi Kappa Delta, Phi Mu Alpha Sinfonia, Pi Kappa Alpha. Avocations: travel, hiking, reading.

WARE, RICHARD ANDERSON, foundation executive; b. NYC, Nov. 7, 1919; s. John Sayers and Mabelle (Anderson) W.; m. Lucille Henney, Mar. 20, 1942 (div. 1972); children: Alexander W., Janet M., Bradley J., Patricia E.; m. Beverly G. Mytinger, Dec. 22, 1972. BA, Lehigh U., 1941; M in Pub. Adminstrn., Wayne State U., 1943; D in Social Sci. (honoris causa), Francisco Marroquin U., Guatemala, 1988. Research asst. Detroit Bur. Govt. Research, 1941-42; personnel technician Lend-Lease Adminstrn., Washington, 1942-43; research asso. to asst. dir. Citizens Research Council, Detroit, 1946-56; sec. Earhart and Relm Founds., Ann Arbor, Mich., 1951-70, trustee, pres., 1970-84, trustee emeritus, pres. emeritus. Prin. dep. asst. sec. def. for internat. security affairs, Washington, 1969-70; cons. Office Asst. Sec. Def., 1970-73; dir. Citizens Trust Co., 1970-87. Vice pres. Ann Arbor United Fund and Cmty. Svcs., 1968, pres., 1969; asst. dir. Mich. Joint Legis. Com. on State Reorgn., 1950-52; sec. Gov.'s Com. to Study Prisons, 1952-53; com. to chmn. Ann Arbor City Planning Commn., 1958-67; mem. Detroit Com. on Fgn. Rels., 1971-87; mem. coun. Woodrow Wilson Internat. Center for Scholars, 1977-85; vis. com. divsn. social scis. U. Chgo., 1977-85; mem. adv. com. The Citadel, 1977-85; mem. adv. coun. internat. studies program Fletcher Sch., Tufts U., 1979-85; trustee Greenhills Sch., 1973-80, Ann Arbor Area Found., 1977-83, Inst. Fgn. Policy Analysis, 1985-2003, Inst. Polit. Economy, 1985—2005, Ctr. for Study Social and Polit. Change Smith Coll., 1988—2005, Pequawket Found., 1989—, Intercollegiate Studies Inst., 1996-2004; polit. analyst Rep. Nat. Com., Washington, 1964; bd. dirs. The Liberty Fund, Inc., Indpls., 1980—2004, Bd. Fgn. Scholarships, 1984-90, chmn., 1987-89. With USAAF, 1943-46. Recipient Civilian Meritorious Service medal Dept. Def., 1970, Charles H. Hoeflich Lifetime Achievement award Intercollegiate Studies Inst., 2006; Paul Harris fellow Rotary, 1997. Fellow Mont Pelerin Soc.; mem. Govtl. Research Assoc. (trustee, v.p. 1955-56), Am. Polit. Sci. Assn., Ann Arbor Club, North Conway Country Club, Cosmos Club (Washington), Phi Beta Kappa, Phi Alpha Theta Congregationalist. Home: PO Box 310 Intervale NH 03845-0310 Office: 2200 Green Rd Ste H Ann Arbor MI 48105-1569

WAREHAM, JERROLD F., broadcast executive; b. Clinton, Iowa, 1948; s. Lyman H. and Ullainee Wareham. BS, Marquette U., 1970; student, Wharton Sch. Bus. Pres., gen. mgr. Greater Dayton Pub. TV, Ohio, 1985-93; pres., CEO Sta. WVIZ, Cleve., 1993—; chmn. Am.'s Pub. TV Stas., 1997-99. Bd. dirs. PBS. Office: WVIZ 4300 Brookpark Rd Cleveland OH 44134-1124 E-mail: jwareham@wvtl.org.

WARMBROD, JAMES ROBERT, agriculture educator, academic administrator; b. Belvidere, Tenn., Dec. 13, 1929; s. George Victor and Anna Sophia W.; m. Catharine P. Phelps, Jan. 30, 1965. BS, U. Tenn., 1952, MS, 1954; Ed.D. (Univ. fellow), U. Ill., 1962. Instr. edn. U. Tenn., Knoxville, 1956-57; tchr. high sch. Winchester, Tenn., 1957-59; asst. prof. U. Ill., Urbana, 1961-66, assoc. prof., 1966-67; prof. agrl. edn. Ohio State U., Columbus, 1968-95; ret.; Presdl. prof. Ohio State U., Columbus, 1989, Presdl. prof. emeritus, 1995, Disting. univ. prof. emeritus, 1995—, chmn. dept., 1978-86, acting assoc. dean Coll. Agr., 1989, acting v.p. agrl. adminstrn., dean Coll. Agr., 1989-91. Vis. prof. Pa. State U., 1970, U. Minn., 1971, Iowa State U., 1974, La. State U., 1986; vis. scholar Va. Poly. Inst. and State U., 1976, Univ. Coun. Vocat. Edn., 1988-89; mem. com. on agr. in secondary schs. Nat. Acad. Scis., 1985-87 Author: Review and Synthesis of Research on the Economics of Vocational Education, 1968, The Liberalization of Vocat. Education, 1974, (with others) Methods of Teaching Agriculture, 1986, 3d edit. 2004; editor: Agrl. Edn. mag., 1968-71. Served with USAF, 1954-56. Recipient Tchg. award Gamma Sigma Delta, 1977, Alumni Assn. award of merit Coll. Agrl., Consumer and Environ. Scis. U. Ill., 2004. Fellow Am. Assn. Agrl. Edn.; mem. Am. Vocat. Assn. (v.p. 1976-79, Outstanding Svc. award 1987), Am. Ednl. Rsch. Assn., Am. Vocat. Edn. Rsch. Assn. (pres. 1976), Am. Assn. Tchr. Educators in Agr. (Disting. Svc. award 1974, Disting. lectr. 1974). Office: 2120 Fyffe Rd Columbus OH 43210-1010

WARNER, CARRIE, architectural engineer; b. 1973; m. Jonathan Sladek, 2006. MArch, U. Ill., Urbana-Champaign, 1998. Sr. project engr. Halvorson & Ptnrs., Chgo. amed one of 40 Under 40, Crain's Chgo. Bus., 2006. Office: Halvorson & Ptnrs Ste 650 600 W Chgo Ave Chicago IL 60610 Office Phone: 312-274-2400. Office Fax: 312-274-2401.

WARNER, CHARLES COLLINS, lawyer; b. Cambridge, Mass., June 19, 1942; s. Hoyt Landon and Charlotte (Collins) W.; m. Elizabeth Denny, Aug. 24, 1964; children: Peter, Andrew, Elizabeth. BA, Yale U., 1964; JD cum laude, Ohio State U., 1970. Bar: Ohio 1970. Assoc. Porter, Wright, Morris & Arthur and predecessor, Columbus, 1970-76, ptnr., 1976—, also mgr. labor and employment law dept., 1988-92. Pres. Peace Corps Svc. Coun., Columbus, 1974—76, Old Worthington (Ohio) Assn., 1976—78, Worthington Ednl. Found., 1994—96, Opera Columbus, 1999—2001, Alliance for Quality Edn., Worthington, 1987—89; chmn. lawyers sect. United Way, Columbus, 1983—84; mem. alumni adv. coun. Ohio State U., 1998—2004; pres. Chamber Music Columbus, 2007—. Recipient Disting. Svc. award, Ohio State U., 2003, Cmty. Svc. award, Columbus Bar Assn., 2003. Fellow: Ohio Bar Found., Coll. Labor and Employment Lawyers, Am. Bar Found., Columbus Bar Found. (trustee 1996—, pres. 2007—); mem.: Ohio State U. Alumni Advisory Coun., Yale Club (pres. 1979—81), Lawyers Club, Capital Club, Nat. Coun. Ohio State U. Coll. Law (pres. 2002—04), Ohio State U. Law Alumni Assn. (pres. 1996—97, Disting. Svc. award 2003), FBA, Ohio Assn. Civil Trial Attys. (exec. bd. 1988—97, Frank Hurd Mem. of Yr. award 1998), Ohio Mgmt. Lawyers Assn. (chair 2004—06), Columbus Bar Assn. (bd. govs. 1982—93, pres. 1991—92, Cmty. Svc. award 2003), Ohio Met. Bar Assn. (pres. 1991—92), Ohio State Bar Assn. (chmn. fed. cts. com. 1992—94, coun. of dels. 1993—), ABA (exec. com. Met. Bar Caucus 1992—94, chmn. state and local bar ADR com. 1995—98, co-chair EEO com. 2000—02). Avocations: clarinet, singing, tennis. Home: 145 E South St Columbus OH 43085-4129 Office: Porter Wright Morris & Arthur 41 S High St Ste 2800 Columbus OH 43215-6194 Home Phone: 614-846-1160; Office Phone: 614-227-2013. E-mail: cwarner@porterwright.com.

WARNER, DON LEE, dean emeritus; b. Norfolk, NB, Jan. 4, 1934; s. Donald A. and Cleo V. (Slagel) W.; m. Patricia Ann Walker, Feb. 24, 1957; children: Mark J., Scott Lee. BS in Geol. Engrng., Colo. Sch. Mines, 1956, MSc in Geol. Engrng., 1961; PhD in Engrng. Sci., U. Calif., Berkeley, 1964. Registered profl. engr., Mo., geologist, Mo., Miss., Tex. Geol. engr. Gulf Oil Corp., Casper, Wyo., 1956, Calif. Exploration Co., Guatemala, 1957-58; civil engr. U.S. Forest Svc., Gunnison, Colo., 1958-59; teaching asst. Colo. Sch. Mines, Golden, 1959-61; rsch. asst. U. Calif., Berkeley, 1962-64; rsch. geologist and engr. U.S. Pub. Health Svc., Cin., 1964-67; chief, earth scis. Ohio Basin Region Fed. Water Pollution Control Adminstrn., 1967-69; prof. geol. engrng. U. Mo., Rolla, 1969-92, prof. emeritus geol. engrng., 1992—, dean emeritus Sch. Mines and Metallurgy, 1992—, chmn., geol. engrng., 1980-81, dean Sch. Mines and Metallurgy, 1981-93. Bd. dirs. Underground Injection Practices Coun., 1985-89; mem. adv. com. to Sec. of Interior for Mineral Resources Rsch., 1985-92; vice chmn. Mo. Bd. Geologist Registration, 2006—. Author: Subsurface Wastewater Injection, 1977. Special award scholarship Colo. Sch. Mines, 1951-56, grad. fellowship Colo. Sch. Mines, 1959-51, rsch. fellowship U. Calif., 1962-64; recipient Best Paper award Am. Water Works Assn., 1971. Fellow Geol. Soc. Am.; mem. Am. Inst. Profl. Geologists (cert.), Am. Assn. Petroleum Geologists, Geol. Soc. Am., Nat. Ground Water Assn. (sci. award 1984, disting. lectr. 1986), Blue Key, Soc. Petroleum Engrs., Scabbard and Blade, Theta Tau, Tau Beta Pi. Avocations: fishing, boating, tennis, golf. Office: Univ Mo Sch Materials Energy and Earth Resources 1870 Miner Cir Rolla MO 65409-0001 Personal E-mail: dlw@fidmail.com.

WARNER, H. TY, entrepreneur, manufacturing executive; b. Chgo., Sept. 3, 1944; s. Harold and Georgia Warner. Student, Kalamazoo Coll. Salesman Dakin Toys, Applause Inc., San Francisco; founder, owner, pres. Ty Inc., Westmont, Ill., 1985—; owner Four Seasons, NYC, 1999—, San Ysidro Ranch, 1999—, Four Seasons Biltmore, 2000—, Sandpiper Golf Course, 2003—. Founder Ty Warner Park, Ty Warner Sea Ctr. Named one of Forbes' Richest Americans, 1999—, World's Richest People, Forbes Mag., 2001—. Achievements include invention of Beanie Babies. Office: Ty Inc 280 Chestnut Ave Westmont IL 60559

WARNER, JOANNE RAINS, nursing educator, associate dean; b. Sioux Falls, SD, June 27, 1950; d. Arnold D. and Arlene M. (Lawrence) W.; children: David Warner, Isaac Daniel. BA, Augustana Coll., 1972; MA, U. Iowa, 1976; D of Nursing Sci., Ind. U., 1990. Vis. nurse Delaware County Vis. Nurse Assn., Muncie, Ind., 1976-77; cons. Ind. State Bd. Health, Indpls., 1977-78; instr. Briar Cliff Coll., Sioux Falls, 1981-82; adj. faculty Okla. Bapt. U., Shawnee, 1985; assoc. prof. Ind. U., Indpls., 1990—, assoc. dean for grad. programs, 2002—. Mem. exec. com. Friends Com. on Nat. Legis., Washington, 1992—; fellow Primary Health Care Policy, Washington, 1996; bd. trustees Earlham Coll. Campaign mgr. Doug Kinser for State Rep. Ind. House Dist. 54, 1988-94; exec. com., mem. ew Castle (Ind.) Healthy City Com., 1989-99; chair residential drive Am. Cancer Soc., New Castle, 1989. Mem. ANA, Assn. Cmty. Health Nurse Educators (bd. dirs.), Ind. Polit. Sci. Assn. (v.p. 1993-94,. pres. 1994-95). Mem. Soc. Of Friends. Office: Ind U 1111 Middle Dr Indianapolis IN 46202 Home: 3736 NE 36th Ave Portland OR 97212-1834 Office Phone: 317-274-3115.

WARNER, KENNETH E(DGAR), dean, public health educator, consultant; b. Washington, Jan. 25, 1947; s. Edgar W. Jr. and Betty (Strasburger) W.; m. Patricia A. Hilty, Oct. 1, 1977; children— Peter, Andrew AB, Dartmouth Coll., 1968; MPhil, Yale U., 1970, PhD, 1974. Lectr. dept. health mgmt. and policy Sch. Pub. Health, U. Mich., Ann Arbor, Mich., 1972—74, asst. prof., 1974—77, assoc. prof., 1977—83, prof., 1983—, chmn., 1982—88, 1992—95, Richard D. Remington Collegiate prof. pub. health, 1995—2001, dir. Tobacco Rsch. Network, Avedis Donabedian Disting. Univ. prof. pub. health, 2001—, dean, 2005—. Cons., Washington, 1976—95, Office on Smoking and Health, USPHS, Rockville, Md., 1978—, Inst. Medicine, Nat. Acad. Scis., Washington, 1984—, numerous additional pub. and pvt. orgns.; mem. bd. sci. counselors divsn. cancer prevention and control Nat. Cancer Inst., Bethesda, Md., 1985—89. Author: (with Bryan Luce) Cost-Benefit & Cost Effectiveness Analysis in Health Care, 1982; contbr. articles to profl. jours. Trustee Am. Lung Assn., Mich., Lansing, 1982; mem. subcom. on smoking Am. Heart Assn., Dallas, 1983-87; mem. com. on tobacco and cancer Am. Cancer Soc., N.Y.C., 1984-92; bd. dirs. Am. Legacy Found., 1999-2003. Hon. Woodrow Wilson fellow, 1968; W.K. Kellog Found. fellow, 1980-83; vis. scholar Nat. Bur. Econ. Research, Stanford, Calif., 1975-76; recipient Surgeon Gen.'s medallion Dr. C. Everett Koop, 1989. Fellow Assn. Health Svcs. Rsch.; mem. APHA (leadership award 1990), Inst. Medicine, Phi Beta Kappa. Office: U Mich Dept Health Sch Pub Health 109 Observatory St Ann Arbor MI 48109-2029 Office Phone: 734-763-5454. Business E-Mail: kwarner@umich.edu.

WARNER, WILLIAM HAMER, mathematician; b. Pitts., Oct. 6, 1929; s. John Christian and Louise (Hamer) W.; m. Janet Louise West, June 29, 1957; 1 dau., Katherine Patricia. Student, Haverford Coll., 1946-48; BS, Carnegie Inst. Tech., 1950, MS, 1951, PhD, 1953. Research asso. grad. div. applied math. Brown U., Providence, 1953-55; asst. prof. dept. aerospace engring. and mechanics U. Minn., Mpls., 1955-58, asso. prof., 1958-68, prof., 1968-95, prof. emeritus, 1995—. Author: (with L.E. Goodman) Statics, 1963, Dynamics, 1964; contbr. articles to profl. jours. Mem.: Soc. Natural Philosophy, Math. Assn. Am., Soc. Indsl. and Applied Math., Am. Math. Soc. E-mail: warner@aem.umn.edu.

WARNKE, AMY NICHOLLE, state legislator; BA, U. N.D. Rep. Dist. 42 N.D. Ho. of Reps., mem. appropriations com., com. on corrections, chmn. budget sect. on human svcs. Devel. dir. N.D. Cmty. Found.; bd. dirs. Protection and Advocacy Project. Mem.: Kappa Alpha Theta (pres., adv. bd. chmn.). Home: PO Box 12982 Grand Forks D 58208

WARRIOR, PADMASREE Y., computer systems network executive; b. Oct. 22, 1960; m. Mohandas A. Warrior. BSChemE, Indian Inst. Tech., New Delhi, India; MSChemE, Cornell U. Joined Motorola, Inc., Schaumburg, Ill., 1984, v.p., gen. mgr., energy sys. group, corp. v.p., chief technology officer, semiconductor products sector, v.p., 1999, corp. officer, 2000, sr. v.p., 2003—05, chief tech. officer, 2003—07, exec. v.p., 2005—07; chief tech. officer Cisco Systems, Inc., San Jose, Calif., 2007—. Gen. mgr. Thoughtbeam, Inc. (subsidiary of Motorola); mem. coun. digital economy Tex. Gov.; mem. rev. panel Tex. Higher Edn. Bd.; dir. Ferro Corp. Named one of Top 25 Chief Tech. Officers, InfoWorld mag., 2007; named to Women In Tech. Internat. Hall of Fame, 2007; recipient Women Elevating Sci. and Tech. award, Working Woman Mag., 2001. Office: Cisco Systems Inc 170 W Tasman Dr San Jose CA 95134

WARTELL, MICHAEL ALAN, academic administrator; b. Albuquerque, Nov. 4, 1946; s. Richard H. and Betty D. (Davis) Wartell; m. Ruth E. Beachy, Dec. 3, 1977; children: Justin Davis, Richard Harrison. BS, U. N.Mex., 1967; MS, Yale U., 1968, PhD, 1971. Asst. prof. chemistry Met. State Coll., 1971—75, assoc. prof., chmn. dept., 1975—78; dean sch. natural scis., prof. chemistry James Madison U., 1979—84; provost, v.p. acad. affairs Humboldt State U., Arcata, Calif., 1984—89, prof. chemistry, 1984—94; chancellor Ind U. -Purdue U., Ft. Wayne, 1994—. Mem. U.S. Army Sci. Bd., 1981—87; participant various study groups on chem. warfare, decontaminatin, biodefense; cons. U.S. Army, IRT Corp., Sandia Nat. Labs., SRI Internat., JAYCOR, HERO, Boeing Elecs., Battelle; mem. Def. Intelligence Agy. Sci. Adv. Com., 1984—; chmn. bd. visitors Def. Systems Mgmt. Coll., Ft. Belvoir, Va., 1984—, chair, 1985—. Co-author: Engineering Education and A Lifetime of Learning, 1975, Introduction to Chemistry, 1975, Fundamentals of Chemistry, 1980; contbr. articles to profl. jours. Bd. dirs. Humboldt State U. Found., 1984—. Fellow: Am. Acad. Forensic Scis.; mem.: Kappa Nu Epsilon, Am. Assn. Univ. Adminstrs. (evaluation task force 1978—79, stds. and rev. com. 1983—84), Am. Phys. Soc., Am. Chem. Soc., Phi Kappa Phi, Phi Beta Kappa, Sigma Xi. Jewish. Office: Ind U Purdue U 2101 E Coliseum Blvd Fort Wayne IN 46805-1445 E-mail: wartell@ipfw.edu.

WASAN, DARSH TILAKCHAND, academic administrator, chemical engineer, educator; b. Sarai, Salah, West Pakistan, July 15, 1938; came to U.S., 1957, naturalized, 1974; s. Tilakchand Gokalchand and Ishari Devi (Obhan) W.; m. Usha Kapur, Aug. 21, 1966; children: Ajay, Kern. BSChemE, U. Ill., 1960; PhD, U. Calif., Berkeley, 1965. Asst. prof. chem. engring. Ill. Inst. Tech., Chgo., 1964-67, assoc. prof., 1967-70, prof., 1970—, chmn. dept., 1971-77, 78-87, acting dean, 1977-78, 87-88, v.p. rsch. and tech., 1988-91, provost, 1991—, provost and sr. v.p., 1995-96, v.p., internat. and Motorola chair, 1996—. Cons. Inst. Gas Tech., 1965-70, Chgo. Bridge & Iron Co., 1967-71, Ill. EPA, 1971-72, NSF, 1971, 78-79, 87-89, Nelson Industries, 1976—, B.F. Goodrich Chem. Co., 1976-78, Exxon Rsch. & Engring. Co., 1977-89, Stauffer Chem. Co., 1980-88, ICI Ams., 1988-92, Westinghouse Savannah River Co., 1995-2004, Monsanto, 1999-2004, Dow Chem., 2006-07; Procter & Gamble lectr. U. Cin. Editor-in-chief Jour. colloid and Interface sci.; mem. publs. bd. Chem. Engring. Edn. Jour.; mem. adv. bd. Jour. Separations Tech., Current Opinion in Colloid and Interface Sci., Jour. of Dispersion Sci. and Tech.; contbr. articles to profl. jours. Recipient Donald Gage Stevens Disting. Lectureship award Syracuse U., 1991, Jakob J. Bikerman Lectureship award Case Western U., 1994, Robert Gilpin Lectr. award Clarkson U., 1995, MacMoran Disting. Lectureship award Tulane U., 1996, Sidney Ross lectr. award, 1996, Bonnet Dodge Disting. Lectureship award Yale U., 1998, Dinesh O. Shah Lectureship award U. Fla., 2004, Norman N. Li Disting. Lectureship award Wayne State U., 2005, Bird-Stewart-Lightfoot Lectureship award U. Wis., 2007; Spl. citation U.S. FDA, 2000. Fellow AIChE (Ernest Thiele award 1989, Thomas Baron award in fluid-particle systems 2002, Alpha Chi Sigma award for chem. engring. rsch. 2005); mem. AAAS, NAE, Indian NAE, Am. Chem. Soc. (award in colloid chemistry 2000, Langmuir Lectureship award 2004), Am. Soc. Engring. Edn. (Western Electric award 1972, 3M Lectureship award chem. engring. divsn. 1991), Fine Particles Soc. (pres. 1976-77, Hausner award 1982), Sigma Xi. Home: 8705 Royal Swan Ln Darien IL 60561-8433 Office: Ill Inst Tech 3300 S Federal St Chicago IL 60616-3793 Office Phone: 630-985-8180. Business E-Mail: wasan@iit.edu.

WASENDORF, RUSSELL R., SR., brokerage house executive; Dir. pub. affairs Am. Soybean Assn.; head Wasendorf & Son Co., 1980—. Wasendorf & Assoc., Inc.; chmn., CEO Peregrine Fin. Group, Inc., 1980—. Founder Stocks, Futures and Options mag., 2001, Ctr. Futures Edn.; ptnr. Allen's New Am. Cafe, Chgo. Author: (books) Commody Trading: The Essential Primer, 1985, All About Futures From The Inside Out, 1992, All About Commodities From The Inside Out, 1992, All About Options from the Inside Out, 1993, All About Managed Futures From The Inside Out, 1993, The Complete Guide To Single Stock Futures, 2003. Office: PFG Inc 190 S LaSalle St 7th Fl Chicago IL 60603 Office Phone: 800-333-5673.

WASFIE, TARIK JAWAD, surgeon, educator; b. Baghdad, Iraq, July 1, 1946; m. Barina Y. Wasfie, Mar. 11, 1975; children: Giselle, Nissan. BS, Central U., Iraq, 1964; MD, Baghdad Med. Sch., 1970. Cert. gen. surgeon. Surg. rsch. assoc. Sinai Hosp. of Detroit/Wayne State U., 1981-85; clin. fellow Coll. Phys. & Surg., Columbia U., NYC, 1985-91, postdoctoral rsch. scientist, 1987-91; attending surgeon Mich. State U./McLaren Hosp., Flint, 1991—. Contbr. articles to profl. jours. NIH grantee, 1984. Fellow ACS, Internat. Coll. Surgeons; mem. AMA, Mich. State Med. Soc., Flint Acad. Surgeons, Am. Soc. Artificial Internal Organs, Internat. Soc. Artificial Organs, Soc. Am. Gast. Endoscopic Surgeons. Achievements include production of antiidiotypic antibodies and their role in transplant immunology; development of percutenous access device. Home: 1125 Kings Carriage Rd Grand Blanc MI 48439-8715

WASHBURN, DONALD ARTHUR, retired transportation executive, investor; b. Mankato, Minn., Sept. 24, 1944; s. Donald and Geraldine Helen (Pint) W.; m. Christine Carvell, Aug. 24, 1968; children: Timothy, Abigail. BBA cum laude, Loyola U., Chgo., 1971; MBA, Northwestern U., 1973, JD cum laude, 1978. Bar: Ill. 1978. With prodn. mgmt. dept. J.T. Ryerson/Inland Steel, Chgo., 1963-68; asst. to the pres. G.B. Frank, Inc., 1969-70; cons. Intec, Inc., 1970-72; mktg. mgmt., atty. Quaker Oats, Co., 1972-79; sr. cons. Booz, Allen & Hamilton, 1979-80; from corp. v.p. to exec. v.p. Marriott Corp., Washington, 1980-90; sr. v.p. N.W. Airlines, Mpls., 1990-94, exec. v.p., 1994-98; pres. chmn. N.W. Cargo, 1997—98; chmn. N.W. Aerospace Tng. Corp., 1996—98. Bd. dirs. LaSalle Hotel Properties, Greenbrier Cos., Inc., Key Tech., Inc., Amedisys, Inc., Draper & Kramer, Inc., Victor Plastics, Inc., LAI Co., Inc.; law bd. Northwestern U., alumni adv. bd. Kellogg Grad. Sch.; adv. bd. Spell Capital Ptnrs. Fund II, LP, Fund III, LP. Contbr. articles to profl. jours. Chmn., mem. nat. bd. dirs. Friends of the Children; bd. dirs. Portland Citizens Crime Commn., Citizens Commn. on Homeless, Oreg. Bus. Assn.; dir. emeritus Childrens Cancer Rsch. Fund; chmn. nat. bd. Stand for Children. Mem.: ABA, Ill. Bar Assn., Alpha Sigma Nu, Beta Gamma Sigma. Unitarian Universalist.

WASHINGTON, CLEOPHUS (CLEO WASHINGTON), state senator; b. South Bend, Ind. BA in Polit. Sci., Wabash Coll., 1985; student, U. Iowa; JD, U. Mo., 1988. Pvt. practice; dep. pub. defender St. Joseph County, 1990-96; atty. Weisman, Kimmell & Walton, S. Bend; state senator Ind. Legislature, Indpls., 1996—. Participant Emerging Leadership Conf. Darden Sch. Bus., U. Va.; del. to tour Germany and Romania to study their polit. and econ. sys. Am. Coun. Young Polit. Leaders; founding pres. Leaders and Positive Role Models, Inc. Contbg. author: Bridging the Gaps, 1996. Mem. Ardmore LaSalle Ch. of Christ, S. Bend; 2d dist. city councilman S. Bend, 1991-95, v.p. of coun., chmn. com., city councilman at large, 1995, chmn. pub. safety, chmn. com.; mem. adv. com. Police Officers and Firefighters Pensions and Disability Fund; mem. Nat. Black Caucus Local Elected Ofcls., Minority Parenting Task Force; mem. mentor program Columbia Sch. Law, U. Mo. Fellow Coun. on Legal Edn. Opportunity. Mem. ABA, Nat. Bar Assn., Ind. State Bar Assn., Ind. Trial Lawyers Assn., St. Joseph County Bar Assn. Office: Ind State House Dist 10 200 W Washington St Indianapolis IN 46204-2728 also: 803 W Washington St Apt 3A South Bend IN 46601-1464

WASHKEWICZ, DONALD E., manufacturing executive; b. Cleve. m. Pam Washkewicz; children: Dawn, Tiffany, Bryan. BME, Cleve. State U., 1972; MBA, Case Western Res. U., Cleve., 1979. Lic. profl. engr., OH. With Parker Hannifin Corp., Cleve., 1972—, from engr. to gen. mgr. Parflex Divsn., 1972—82, v.p. ops. fluid connectors group, 1994-97, v.p., pres. hydraulics group, 1997-2000, COO, 2000—01, pres., 2000—04, 2007—, CEO, chmn., 2001—. Bd. Mfr. Alliance/MAPI. Bd. Greater Cleve. Growth Assn., Cleve. Tomorrow. Recipient George B. Davis Disting. Alumni award, Cleve. State U., 2002, Disting. Alumni award, Case Western Res. U., 2002, Ellis Island Medal of Honor, 2003. Mem.: Nat. Assn. Mfr., Nat. Soc. Profl. Engr. Office: Parker Hannifin Corp 6035 Parkland Blvd Cleveland OH 44124-4141

WASIK, JOHN FRANCIS, editor, writer, publisher; b. Chgo., July 2, 1957; s. Arthur Stanley and Virginia Frances (Gray) W.; m. Kathleen Rose. BA in Psychology, U. Ill., Chgo., 1978, MA in Communication, 1988. Sr. editor Consumers Digest Inc., Chgo., 1986—; editor, pub. Conscious Consumer and Co. Newsletters, 1986—. Author: Electronic Business Information Sourcebook, 1987, Green Company Resource Guide, 1992, The Green Supermarket Shopping Guide, 1993, The Investment Club Book, 1995. Mem. Soc. Profl. Journalists, Soc. Environ. Journalists. Office: Consumers Digest Communications 520 Lake Cook Rd Ste 500 Deerfield IL 60015-5633

WASIOLEK, EDWARD, literary critic, language and literature educator; b. Camden, NJ, Apr. 27, 1924; s. Ignac and Mary (Szczesniewska) W.; m. Emma Jones Thomson, 1948; children: Mark Allan, Karen Lee, Eric Wade. BA, Rutgers U., 1949; MA, Harvard, 1950, PhD, 1955; postgrad., U. Bordeaux, France, 1950-51. Teaching fellow Harvard U., Cambridge, Mass., 1953-54, research fellow Russian Research Ctr., 1952-54; instr. English Ohio Wesleyan U., 1954-55; asst. prof. U. Chgo., 1955-60, assoc. prof. English and Russian, 1960-64, prof. Russian and comparative lit., 1964-69, Avalon prof. comparative lit. and Russian, 1969-76, Disting. Services prof. of English, comparative lit., and Slavic studies, 1976—, chmn. comparative lit. program, 1965-83, chmn. dept. Slavic langs. and lit., 1971-77. Vis. prof. Slavic and comparative lit. Harvard, 1966-67 Author: (with R. Bauer) Nine Soviet Portraits, 1955, Crime and Punishment and the Critics, 1961, Dostoevsky: The Major Fiction, 1964, The Notebooks for Crime and Punishment, 1967, The Brothers Karamazov and the Critics, 1967, The Notebooks for the Idiot, 1968, The Notebooks for the Possessed, 1968, The Notebooks for A Raw Youth, 1969, The Notebooks for the Brothers Karamazov, 1970, The Gambler, with Paulina Suslova's Diary, 1972, Tolstoy's Major Fiction, 1978, Critical Essays on Tolstoy, 1986, Fathers and Sons: Russia at the Crossroads, 1993. Addressed UN on Tolstoy, 1988. With USNR, 1943-46. Recipient Quantrell teaching prize U. Chgo., 1961; Laing Press prize, 1972; Research fellow USSR, 1963; Guggenheim fellow, 1983-84 Mem. Modern Lang. Assn., Phi Beta Kappa, Lambda Chi Alpha. Office: Univ Chicago Dept English Chicago IL 60637 Business E-Mail: e-wasiolek@uchicago.edu.

WASS, WALLACE MILTON, veterinarian, clinical science educator; b. Lake Park, Iowa, Nov. 19, 1929; s. Authur Carl and Esther (Moberg) W.; m. Doreen McCollum, May 31, 1953; children: Karen, Kimberly, Christopher, Kirby. Student, Minn. Jr. Coll., 1947-48; BS, U. Minn., 1951, D.V.M., 1953, PhD, 1961. Diplomate: Am. Coll. Vet. Internal Medicine. Veterinarian Medford Vet. Clinic, Wis., 1953-58; instr. U. Minn. Coll. Vet. Medicine, St. Paul, 1958-63; prof. vet. medicine Iowa State U., Ames, 1964—, head dept. vet. clin. scis., 1964-83, prof., 1983-99, prof. emeritus, 1999—. Cons. U.S. AID, Bogota, Columbia, 1963, U. Yola, igeria, 1983; staff veterinarian for med. rsch. sect. Brookhaven Nat. Lab., Upton, N.Y., 1963-64; cons. investigator fur seal harvest U.S. Dept. Commerce, Pribilof Islands, 1971, South Africa, 1974; use of antibiotics in animal feed U.S. FDA, 1972; cons. Farmland Ins. Co., 1971—; spl. cons. Kasetsart U., Bangkok, Thailand, 1974, Min. of Edn., Thailand, 1994. Contbr. articles, papers in field to profl. lit. Chmn. collegiate-ch. paster parish rels. com. United Methodist Ch., 1979, chmn. stewardship and fin. com., 1982. Served to 1st lt. USAF, 1953-55. Mem. AVMA (del. 1973-88), Iowa Vet. Med. Assn., Central Iowa Vet. Med. Assn. (pres. 1977), Am. Assn. Vet. Clinicians (pres. 1971-73), Phi Kappa Phi (sec. 1984-88, Iowa State U. chpt. pres. 1989-90), Phi Zeta, Alpha Zeta, Gamma Sigma Delta Clubs: Wiltco Flying (sec. 1966-74). Home: 2166 Ashmore Dr Ames IA 50014-7840 Office: Iowa State U Dept Vet Clin Scis Ames IA 50011-0001

WASSERMAN, EDWARD ARNOLD, psychology professor; b. LA, Apr. 2, 1946; s. Albert Leonard and May (Sabin) W. BA, UCLA, 1968; PhD, Ind. U., 1972. Postdoctoral fellow U. Sussex, Brighton, Eng., 1972; from asst. prof. to prof. psychology U. Iowa, Iowa City, 1972-83, prof., 1983—, Stuit prof. exptl. psychology, 1997—. Pres. faculty senate U. Iowa, 1997-98; vis. scientist CNRS, Marseille, France, 1999. Contbr. articles to profl. jours., chpts. to books; editor several books; assoc. editor several jours. Bd. dirs. Big Bros., Big Sisters, Johnson County, Iowa, 1982-85 Ind. U. fellow, 1968, U. Iowa fellow, 1975, 82, NAS fellow, former USSR, 1976, James Van Allen Natural Scis. fellow, 1994-95. Fellow APA, Assn. Psychol. Sci.; mem. Psychonomic Soc., Midwestern Psychol. Assn., Soc. Exptl. Psychologists, Phi Beta Kappa. Office: U Iowa Dept Psychology Iowa City IA 52242

WASSERMAN, SHELDON A., state legislator; b. Milw., Aug. 15, 1961; m. Wendy Jo Wolfman; children: Joseph, Lauren, Benjamin. BS, U. Wis., 1983; MD, Med. Coll. Wis., 1987. Assemblyman Wis. State Dist. 22, 1995—. Staff physician Columbia/St. Mary's Hosp., Milw., 1991—, Sinai Hosp., Milw., 1991—. Fellow AGOG; mem. AMA, Wis. Med. Soc., Milw. County Med. Soc., Phi Beta Kappa, Phi Kappa Phi. Democrat. Address: 3487 N Lake Dr Milwaukee WI 53211-2919 also: Wis Assembly PO Box 8953 Madison WI 53708-8953

WASTAWY, SOHAIR F., library dean, consultant; b. Cairo, Nov. 7, 1954; came to U.S., 1981; s. Fahmy Elsayed Wastawy and Alia Ahmed Shaffie; children: Kareim. BA, Cairo U., 1975, MA, 1978; MLS, Cath. U., 1983; PhD, Simmons Coll., 1987. Micrographics specialist Cairo U., 1975-83; asst. prof. Inst. Pub. Administrn., Riyadh, Saudi Arabia, 1984-85; info. specialist, mktg. dir. Data Processing Services, Cairo, 1983-87; info. researcher Ill. Inst. Tech., Chgo., 1988-91, dir. libr., 1991—. Cons. UN, 1989—. Mem. Egyptian Soc. Info. Sci., Ill. Libr. Assn. Republican. Office: Illinois Inst of Tech Paul V Galvin Libr 35 W 33rd St Chicago IL 60616-3739

WATANABE, AUGUST MASARU, physician, educator, retired pharmaceutical executive; b. Portland, Oreg., Aug. 17, 1941; s. Frank H. and Mary Y. W.; m. Margaret Whildin Reese, Mar. 14, 1964; children: Nan Reiko, Todd Franklin, Scott Masaru. BS, Wheaton Coll., Ill., 1963; MD, Ind. U., 1967. Diplomate Am. Bd. Internal Medicine. Intern Ind. U. Med. Center, Indpls., 1967-68, resident, 1968-69, 71-72, fellow in cardiology, 1972-74; clin. asso. NIH, 1969-71; clin. instr. medicine Georgetown U. Med. Sch., Washington, 1970-71; mem. faculty Ind. U. Sch. Medicine, Indpls., 1972—2003, prof. medicine and pharmacology, 1978—2003, chmn. dept. medicine, 1983-90; dir. Regenstrief Inst. for Health Care Ind. U. Sch. of Medicine, Indpls., 1984-90; from v.p. to group v.p. rsch. labs. Eli Lilly & Co., Indpls., 1990-94, v.p., pres. labs, 1994-95; exec. v.p. sci. and tech. Eli Lilly and Co., Indpls., 1996—2003; chmn. bd. BioCrossroads, 2003—. Mem. pharmacology study sect. NIH, 1979-81, chmn., 1981-83; cardiovasc.-renal adv. com. FDA, 1982-85; mem. com. A, Nat. Heart, Lung and Blood Inst., 1984-88, chmn., 1986-88; bd. dir. QuatRx, Endocyte, Kalypsys, Ambrx, Marcadia Biotech; cons. in field. Contbr. articles to profl. jours.; editorial bds. sci. jours. Bd. dir. Ind. U. Found., 1989—, Indpls. Symphony Orch., 1994—, Regenstrief Found., 1995—. NIH grantee, 1972-92. Fellow ACP, Am. Coll. Cardiology, Am. Heart Assn. (councils on clin. cardiology and circulation, research rev. com. Ind. affiliate 1978-82, research and adv. com. North Central region 1978-82, adv. com. cardiovascular drugs 1976-79, chmn. com. 1979-81, chmn. program com. council on basic sci. 1982-84, chmn. com. on sci. sessions programs 1985-88, bd. dirs. 1985-88), Am. Coll. Cardiology (govt. relations com. 1979-81, trustee 1982-87); mem. Am. Fedn. Clin. Research (councilor Midwest sect. 1976-77, chmn.-elect Midwest sect. 1977-78, chmn. sect. 1978-79, chmn. sect. nominating com. 1979-80), Am. Soc. Clin. Investigation, Am. Soc. Clin. Pharmacology and Therapeutics, Am. Soc. Pharmacology and Exptl. Therapeutics (exec. com. div. clin. pharmacology 1978-81), Cardiac Muscle Soc., Central Soc. Clin. Research (councillor 1983-86, pres.-elect 1989, pres. 1990), Internat. Soc. Heart Research, Assn. Am. Physicians, Assn. Profs. of Medicine, Sigma Xi. Office: BioCrossroads Baker and Daniels Bldg 300 N Meridian St Ste 950 Indianapolis IN 46204

WATER, LINDA GAIL, public relations executive; b. Cleve., Jan. 21, 1946; d. Kenneth and Suzanne Ellen (Bergman) Water; children: Bradley Katz, Douglas Katz. BA in Mktg., John Carroll U., 1967. Feature writer, reporter Fairchild Publs., Inc., Cleve., 1963—67; asst. account exec., copywriter Dix & Eaton, Inc., Cleve., 1967—71; mgr. consumer rels. Club Products Co. div. Standex Internat., Cleve., 1971—74; mgr. advt. pub. rels. and sales promotion mgr., mktg. Hauserman, Inc., Cleve., 1974—77; comm. program mgr., mktg. comm. group Herman Miller, Inc., Zeeland, Mich., 1977—79, program mgr. market programs group, 1979—80; corp. dir. comm. and mgmt. devel. Am. Seating Co., Grand Rapids, Mich., 1980—85; dir. mktg. comm., internat. ops. and leather divs. Wolverine World Wide, Inc., Rockford, Mich., 1985—87; dir. pub. rels. and Detroit ops. Sefton Assocs. Inc., Southfield, Mich., 1988—. Mem. YWCA. Mem.: Women in Comm. (inductee Acad. Women Achievers 1986), Pub. Rels. Soc. Am., Am. Mktg. Assn.

WATERMAN, JOHN M., state legislator; b. Shelburn, Ind., May 13, 1952; m. Cheryl Lynn Waterman. Sheriff Sullivan County; mem. Ind. Senate from 39th dist., 1994—; mem. agr. and small bus. com.; mem. corrections, criminal and civil procedures com.; mem. natural resources com.; mem. pub. policy com. Mem. NRA. Office: Ind Senate State Capitol Indianapolis IN 46204

WATERS, RONALD V., III, candy company executive; m. Ann Waters. BA in History & Economics, Trinity Coll.; M in Acctg., NYU. Ptnr. KPMG Peat Marwick; v.p. fin. & adminstrn. Gillette Co., 1993—99, v.p., controller, 1999, v.p. fin. & strategic planning, Grooming & Batteries, 1998—99; sr. v.p., CFO William Wrigley Jr., Inc., Chgo., 1999—2003, COO, 2004—. Bd. dir. The Joffrey Ballet, 2003—, treas., chmn. fin. com., co-chmn., 2004; bd. dir. HNI Corp., 2002—, Greater . Mich. Ave. Assn., Goodman Theatre, Latin School of Chgo. Office: William Wrigley Jr Co 410 N Michigan Ave Chicago IL 60611

WATERS, RONALD W., theology studies educator, church administrator, pastor; b. Kokomo, Ind., July 23, 1951; s. Ronald Lee and Carolyn Elizabeth (Myers) W.; m. orma Lee Grumbling Waters, June 16, 1973; 1 child, Melinda Ronee Layman. BA magna cum laude, Ashland U., Ohio, 1973; MA in Comms. with high honors, Wheaton Coll., Ill., 1975; MDiv with high honors, Ashland Theol. Sem., Ohio, 1985; postgrad., Asbury Theol. Seminary, 1993—2002. Ordained elder Brethren Ch., 1986; lic. minister, 1985-86. Asst. to dir. Bd. of Christian Edn. The Brethren Ch., Ashland, Ohio, 1971-74; mng. editor of publs. Brethren Pub. Co., Ashland, Ohio, 1975-78, asst. to dir. and gen. mgr., 1978-80, exec. dir., 1980-82; dir. of Denom. Bus. The Brethren Ch. Nat. Office, Ashland, Ohio, 1982-84; cons. in mgmt. and computer applications, 1984-85; pastor Mt. Olive Brethren Ch., McGaheysville, Va., 1985-89; dir. Brethren Ch. Ministries The Brethren Ch. Nat. Office, Ashland, Ohio, 1989-95; asst. prof. evangelism Ashland Theol. Sem., 1996-2001; cons. for evangelism and ch. growth The Brethren Ch. Nat. Office, Ashland, 1996—2001; pastor Hammond Ave. Brethren Ch., Waterloo, Iowa, 2002—. Bd. dirs. corp. sec. Brethren Printing Co., Ashland, 1989-96; mem. mission bd. Brethren Ch. Southeastern Dist., 1987-89; mem., sec. exec. bd. Ctrl. Dist., The Brethren Ch., 2002—; mem. statement of faith task force Gen. Conf. Brethern Ch., 1981-84, polity com. 1986-91, 2004—; bd. ref. congl. adv. The Andrew Ctr., Elgin, Ill., 1994-97; founder, tchr. Young Adult Sunday Sch. class Park St Brethren Ch., Ashland, 1990-93; adv. com. Ashland Theol. Sem., 1990-95; mem. evangelism mgmt. team New Life Ministries, Mt. Joy, Pa., 1992-2001; adj. prof. Bethany Theological Seminary, 2002; spkr. in field. Author: Promise for the Future, 1993, Leader's Manual for Inviting and Welcoming New People, 1995; editor: The Brethren Evangelist mag., 1975-78, New Beginnings mag., 1995-97; contbg. editor LIFE process, 1998-99; contbr. numerous articles to religious jours.; webmaster, www.newlifeministries-nlm.org, 2000—. Mem. adv. coun. World Relief Corp., Wheaton, Ill., 1990-92; dir. vol. ministries Park St. Brethren Ch., 1998-99; sec.-treas. Ohio dist. Mission Bd., 1996-2001. Mem. Am. Soc. Ch. Growth, Nat. Assn. Brethren Ch. Elders, Black Hawk Assn. Evangelicals (pres. 2005-07). Mem. Brethren Ch. Office: Hammond Ave Brethren Ch 1604 Hammond Ave Waterloo IA 50702

WATKINS, CAROLE S., human resources specialist, medical products executive; b. 1960; BA in Bus., Franklin U., Columbus, Ohio. With O.M. Scott & Sons, Lazarus, Huntington Banks; mem. staff Ltd. Brands, Columbus, Ohio, 1989—96; v.p. human resources Pharm. Distbn. Cardinal Health, Inc., Columbus, Ohio, 1996—2000, sr. v.p. pharm. distbn. and provider svcs., 2000, exec. v.p. human resources, 2000, chief human resources officer. Office: Cardinal Health 7000 Cardinal Pl Dublin OH 43017

WATKINSON, PATRICIA GRIEVE, museum director; b. Merton, Surrey, Eng., Mar. 28, 1946; came to U.S., 1972; d. Thomas Wardle and Kathleen (Bredl) Grieve. BA in Art History and Langs. with honors, Bristol U., Eng., 1968. Sec. Mayfair Fine Arts and The Mayfair Gallery, London, 1969-71; adminstr. Bernard Jacobson, Print Pub., London, 1971-73; freelance exhbn. work, writer Kilkenny Design Ctr., Davis Gallery, Irish Arts Council in Dublin, Ireland, 1975-76; curator of art Mus. Art, Wash. State U., Pullman, 1978-83, dir., 1984-98; exec. dir. Ft. Wayne (Ind.) Mus. Art, 1998—. Asst. prof. art history Wash. State U., Pullman, 1978; mem. adv. bd. Exhibits USA, 1999—. Co-author, co-editor: Gaylen Hansen: The Paintings of a Decade, 1985. Mem. Assn. Am. Colls. and Univ. Mus. and Galleries (western regional rep. 1987-89), Art Mus. Assn. Am. (Wash. state rep. 1986-87), Internat. Coun. Mus. (modern art com. 1986-89), Wash. Mus. Assn. (bd. dirs. 1984-87), Am. Fedn. Arts (western region rep. 1987-89), Wash. Art Consortium (pres. 1993-95), Western Mus. Assn. (bd. dirs. 1996-98), ARTTABLE. Office: Ft Wayne Mus Art 311 E Main St Fort Wayne IN 46802-1997

WATNE, ALVIN L., retired surgeon, educator; b. Shabbona, Ill., Jan. 13, 1927; m. Diana Folio, Dec. 3, 1966; children: Carrie, Matthew, Andrew, Valerie. BS, U. Ill.-Chgo. Coll. Medicine, 1950, MD, 1952, MS, 1956. Diplomate: Am. Bd. Surgery. Intern Indpls. Gen. Hosp., 1952-53; resident U. Ill. Research and Edn. Hosps., Chgo., 1954-58; assoc. cancer surgeon Cancer Research, Roswell Park, Buffalo, NY, 1958, assoc. chief cancer research, 1959; assoc. prof. surgery W.Va. U., 1962-67, prof., 1967-72, acting chmn. dept. surgery, 1973-75, prof., chmn. dept. surgery, 1975-86, U. Ill., Peoria, 1986-91; dir. Cancer Ctr. of Ga., 1991-94; assoc. dir. dept. surgery Ga. Bapt. Med. Ctr., 1994-97. Cons. surgery VA, Clarksburg, W.Va., 1963-2005, vice-chmn. bd., Univ. Ill. Found., 2005 Author: Gardner's Syndrome, 1977, (2d edit.), 1979, Melanoma of Head and Neck, 1981, Polyposis Coli, 1982. Pres. W. Va. div. Am. Cancer Soc., 1967-68, 80—, v.p., 1981. Recipient Hektoen Gold medal AMA, 1958; recipient Hektoen Silver medal AMA, 1960 Mem. ACS (pres. W.Va. chpt. 1972-73, chmn. local com. 1978—, gov. 1985—), Southeastern Surg. Congress (councilor 1980—), Soc. Surg. Oncology (exec. council 1980), Soc. Head and Neck Surgeons (pres. 1982), Am. Cancer Soc. (dir.-at-large 1985—)

WATNE, DARLENE CLAIRE, county official; b. Minot, ND, Feb. 11, 1935; d. Charles A. and Anna Marie Widdel (Fjeld) W.; m. Clair A. Watne, Mar. 27, 1954; children: Carmen, Steven, Nancy, Matthew. Court reporting diploma, 1975; grad., Real Estate Inst., 1991. Cert. residential real estate specialist, N.D. Exec. sec. Grand Exalted Ruler Elks, Minot, ND, 1964-75; pres. Bus. Coll., Minot, 1974—76; ct. reporter NW Jud. Dist., Minot, 1976—90; real estate broker Watne Realtors Better Homes & Gardens, Minot, 1990—99; mem. ND Senate from 5th dist., Bismarck, 1994—2001; commr. Ward County, ND, 1994—. Active Joint Civil Svcs. to the Poor, 1995-2001. Commr. ND State Lottery, 2002—07; mem. Souris Basin Planning Coun., 2004—07, Ward County Libr. Bd., 2006—; dir. Minot Area Devel. Corp., 2006—; numerous state polit. interim senate coms.; bd. dirs. Salvation Army, Red Cross; bd. dir. ND Credit Union, 2007—. Named Minot Woman of Distinction in Bus. and Industry, 1993, Liberty award ND Bar Assn., 2000, named Citizen of Yr. ND Builders Assn., 2001. Republican. Avocations: reading, laking. Home: 520 28th Ave SW Minot ND 58701-7065

WATSON, CATHERINE ELAINE, journalist; b. Mpls., Feb. 9, 1944; d. Richard Edward and LaVonne (Slater) W.; m. Al Sicherman (div.); children: Joseph Sicherman, David Sicherman. BA in Journalism, U. Minn., 1966; MA in Teaching, Coll. of St. Thomas, 1971. Reporter Mpls. Star Tribune, 1966-72; editor Picture mag., 1972-78, Travel sect., 1978—2004; editor in chief Galena (Ill.) Gazette, 1990-91. Instr., online mentor Split Rock Arts Program, U. Minn., 1996-2006; sr. travel editor Star Tribune, 2001-04. Author: Travel Basics, 1984, Roads Less Traveled: Dispatches from the Ends of the Earth, 2005 (named Best Book Soc. Am. Travel Writers -Ctrl. States, 2001); contbr. articles to newspapers and travel mags. and books. Recipient Newspaper Mag. Picture Editor's award Pictures of Yr. Competition, 1974, awards for writing and photography Soc. Am.

Travel Writers, 1983-2004, Photographer of Yr. award, 1990, Alumna of otable Achievement award U. Minn. Coll. Liberal Arts, 1994; rsch. grant Jerome Found./Gen. Mills Found., 2004; named Lowell Thomas Travel Journalist of Yr., 1990, Lowell Thomas Bronze awards 1994, 96, 2003. Mem. Am. Newspaper Guild, Soc. Am. Travel Writers, Phi Beta Kappa, Alpha Omicron Pi.

WATSON, DENNIS WALLACE, microbiologist, educator; b. Morpeth, Ont., Can., Apr. 29, 1914; came to U.S., 1938, naturalized, 1946; s. William and Sarah (Verity) W.; m. Alicemay Whittier, June 15, 1941; children: Catherine W., William V. BSA, U. Toronto, 1934; MS, Dalhousie U., 1937; PhD, U. Wis., 1941, DSc (hon.), 1981. Rsch. assoc. U. Wis., 1942, asst. prof., 1946-49; vis. investigator Rockefeller Inst., 1942; investigator Connaught Lab. Med. Rsch. U. Toronto, 1942-44; assoc. prof. U. Minn., Mpls., 1949-52, prof., 1953-63, head dept. microbiology, 1964-84, Regents prof. microbiology, 1980-84, Regents prof. emeritus, 1984—. Vis. prof. Med. Sch. U. Wash., 1950; mem. Commn. Immunization Armed Forces Epidemiology Bd., 1946-59; bd. sci. counselors, divsn. biol. standards IH, 1957-59, allergy and immunology study sect., 1954-58; chmn. tgn. grant com. Inst. Allergy and Infectious Diseases, 1964, adv. coun., 1967-71; microbiology panel Office Naval Rsch., 1963-66 Mem. editl. bd. Infection and Immunity, 1971-72; editl. cons. Medcom Faculty Medicine, 1973— Bd. dirs. Nat. Found. Infectious Diseases, 1976-81; vice chmn. Am. Soc. Microbiology Found., 1973. With AUS, 1944-46. Recipient Rsch. Career award USPHS, 1962-64; Spl. Rsch. fellow, 1960-61. Mem. AAAS, Am. Assn. Immunologists, Am. Chem. Soc., Am. Acad. Microbiology (vice chmn. bd. govs. 1967), Am. Soc. Microbiology (pres. 1969, v.p. Found. 1972-73), Internat. Endotoxin Soc. (hon., life), Soc. Exptl. Biology and Medicine (coun. 1977-79, pres. 1976-77), Lancefield Soc., Sigma Xi, Phi Zeta. Home: 2106 Hendon Ave Saint Paul MN 55108-1419 Office: U Minn Med Sch Dept Microbiology PO Box 196 Minneapolis MN 55440-0196 Personal E-mail: watsondw651@msn.com.

WATSON, FRANK CHARLES, state legislator; b. St. Louis, July 26, 1945; s. Charles I. and Pauline (Logsdon) W.; m. Susan DeAnn Rasler, 1969; children: Charles Adam, Kathry Melissa. BPharm, Purdue U., 1968. Trustee and supr. Bond County Ctrl. Twp., Greenville, Ill., 1973-77, bd. suprs.; Ill. state rep., 1979-82; mem. Ill. State Senate, Dist. 55, 1983—, minority spokesman, mem. transp. appropriations II, elem. and secondary edn., mem. Ill. adv. coun. on alcoholism and drug abuse, legis. printing unit coms., joint com. on regulation of professions and occupation, citizens assembly coun. on energy resources, agrl. and conservations and revenue coms., asst. majority leader. Owner The Corner Clothing Store, Greenville, Ill., 1971—, Watson Drug Store, 1972—; bd. dirs. Hillview Manor Nursing Home, First Nat. Bank, Salem Nat. Bank; pharmacist. Mem. Phi Gamma Delta. Republican. Office: 950 Fairway Dr Greenville IL 62246-2336 also: Ill Senate State Capitol Springfield IL 62706-0001

WATSON, PATTY JO, anthropology educator; b. Superior, Nebr., Apr. 26, 1932; d. Ralph Clifton and Elaine Elizabeth (Lance) Andersen; m. Richard Allan Watson, July 30, 1955; 1 child, Anna Melissa MA, U. Chgo., 1956, PhD in Anthropology, 1959. Archaeologist-ethnographer Oriental Inst.-U. Chgo., 1959—60, rsch. assoc., archaeologist, 1964—70; instr. anthropology U. So. Calif., Los Angeles, 1961, UCLA, 1961, L.A. State U., 1961; asst. prof. anthropology Washington U., St. Louis, 1969—70, assoc. prof., 1970—73, prof., 1973—2004, Edward Mallinckrodt disting. univ. prof., 1993—2004, prof. emerita, 2004—; faculty affiliate anthropology U. Mont., 2003—. Mem. rev. panel NSF, Washington, 1974-76; fellow Ctr. Advanced Study in Behavioral Scis., Stanford, Calif., 1981-82, 91-92. Author: The Prehistory of Salts Cave, Kentucky, 1969, Archaeological Ethnography in Western Iran, 1979; author: (with others) Man and Nature, 1969, Explanation in Archeology, 1971, Archeological Explanation, 1984, Girikihaciyan, A Halafian Site in Southeastern Turkey; author: (editor) Archeology of the Mammoth Cave Area, 1974, Prehistoric Archeology Along the Zagros Flanks, 1983; co-editor: The Origins of Agriculture, 1992, Of Caves and Shell Mounds, 1996, Archaeology of the Middle Green River Region, Kentucky, 2005. Recipient Arthur Holly Compton Faculty Achievement award Washington U., St. Louis, 2000, Peter H. Raven award for lifetime achievement Acad. Sci. St. Louis, 2002; grantee NSF, 1959-60, 68, 70, 72-74, 78-79, NEH, 1977-78, Nat. Geog. Soc., 1969-75, Southeastern Arch. Conf. Lifetime Achievement award, 2004. Fellow Am. Anthropol. Assn. (editor archaeology 1973-77, Disting. Lectr. award 1994, Disting. Svc. award 1996), AAAS (chair sect. H 1991-92); mem. Cave Rsch. Found., Am. Acad. Arts and Scis., Am. Philos. Soc., Soc. Am. Archaeology (exec. com. 1974-76, 82-84, editor Am. Antiquity 1984-87, Fryxell medal 1990), Assn. Paleorient (sci. bd.), Nat. Speleological Soc. (hon. life, editorial bd. bull. 1979—, Sci. award), Archaeol. Inst. Am. (Gold medal Disting. Archaeol. Achievement 1999, Pomerance award 2007), Nat. Acad. Scis. Business E-Mail: pjwatson@artsci.wustl.edu.

WATSON, PAULA D., retired librarian; b. NYC, Mar. 6, 1945; d. Joseph Francis and Anna Julia (Miksza) De Simone; m. William Douglas Watson, Aug. 23, 1969; children— Lucia, Elizabeth AB, Barnard Coll., 1965; MA, Columbia U., 1966; MSLS, Syracuse U., 1972. Libr. reference U. Ill., Urbana, 1972—77, libr. city planning and landscape architecture, 1977—79, head documents libr., 1979—81; asst. dir. gen. svcs. U. Ill. Libr., Urbana, 1981—88, acting dir. gen. svcs., 1988—93, dir. ctrl. pub. svcs., 1989—93, asst. libr., 1993—95, dir. electronic info. svcs., 1995—2004, dir. scholarly comm., 2003—04; ret., 2004. Author: Electronic Journals: Acquisition and Management, 2003, E-Publishing Impact on Acquisition and Interlibrary Loan, 2004; contbr. articles to profl. jours. .Y. State Regents fellow Columbia U., N.Y.C., 1965-66; Council on Library Resources profl. edn. and tng. for librarianship grantee, 1983 Mem. ALA (sec. univ. librs. sect. ALA-Assn. Coll. and Rsch. Librs. 1989-91, com. on instnl. coop., chair pub. svcs. dirs. group, 1997-99, mem. com. inst. coop./OCLC virtual electronic libr. steering com.), Ill. Library Assn. Avocation: gardening. Home: 715 W Delaware Ave Urbana IL 61801-4806

WATSON, RALPH EDWARD, internist, educator; b. Cin., Apr. 4, 1948; s. John Sherman and Evelyn (Moore) W.; m. Demetria Rencher, Sept. 9, 1972; children: Ralph Edward, Monifa. BS, Xavier U., 1970; MD, Mich. State U., East Lansing, 1976. Diplomate Am. Bd. Internal Medicine; cert. clin. hypertension specialist. Intern U. Cin. Med. Ctr., 1976-77, resident in internal medicine, 1977-79, asst. clin. prof. internal medicine, 1980-88; asst. prof. internal medicine Mich. State U., East Lansing, 1988-94, assoc. prof., 1994—. Attending physician in hypertension clinic Mich. State U., 1988-91, assoc. dir. hypertension clinic, 1991-94, dir. hypertension clinic, 1995—, program dir. transitional yr. residency, 1990-96, assoc. program dir. internal medicine residency, 1996-2003; mem. U.S. HHS Office Minority Health Resource Person Network. Fellow ACP, Internat. Soc. Hypertension in Blacks, Am Assn. Black Cardiologists; mem. Nat. Med. Assn., Am. Soc. Internal Medicine, Lansing Area Am. Heart Assn., Am. Black Cardiologists (chair rsch. com.), Am. Soc. Hypertension, Xavier U. Alumni Assn., Alpha Omega Alpha. Office: Mich State U 338B Clinical Ctr East Lansing MI 48824-1313 Office Phone: 517-353-4811.

WATSON-BOONE, REBECCA A., dean, researcher, library and information scientist, educator; b. Springfield, Ohio, Mar. 7, 1946; d. Roger S. and Elizabeth Boone; m. Dennis David Ash, 1967 (div. 1975); m. Frederick Kellogg, 1979 (div. 1988); m. Peter G. Watson-Boone, May 26, 1989. Student, Earlham Coll., Richmond, Ind., 1964-67; BA, Case Western Res. U., Cleve., 1968; MLS, U. NC, Chapel Hill, 1971; PhD, U. Wis., Madison, 1995. Asst. reference libr. Princeton U., NJ, 1970-76; head cen. reference dept. U. Ariz., Tucson, 1976-83, assoc. dean Coll. Arts and Scis., 1984-89; co-dir. Placitas Cmty. Libr., N.Mex., 2007—. Loaned exec. Ariz. Bd. Regents, 1988-89; pres. Ctr. for Study of Info. Profls., 1995—2002. Author: Constancy and Change in the Worklife of Research University Librarians, 1998, A Good Match: Library Career Opportunities for Graduates of Liberal Arts Colleges, 2007; contbr. articles to profl. jours. Mem. ALA (div. pres. 1985-86, councilor 1988-92), Assn. Libr. and Info. Sci. Edn., N.Mex. Libr. Assn. Mem. Soc. Of Friends. Office: 30 Camino de la Vina Vieja Placitas NM 87043 Business E-Mail: rebeccawb@earthlink.net.

WATTERS, RICHARD DONALD, lawyer; b. Midland, Mich., May 3, 1951; s. Donald Wayne and Madalyn Bird (Tinetti) W.; m. Ann Elizabeth Hutchison, May 24, 1975; children: Kelly E., Nathan Paul. BS in Indsl. Engring., Bradley U., 1973; JD cum laude, St. Louis U., 1976. Bar: Mo. 1976, U.S. Dist. Ct. (we. and ea. dists.) Mo. 1976, Ill. 1977, U.S. Ct. Appeals (8th cir.) 1981; cert. healthcare mediator. Assoc. Lashly & Baer, P.C., St. Louis, 1976-81, ptnr., 1981—, dept. chmn., 1989—. Instr. St. Louis U. Sch. Law, 1977-79. Chmn., pres. United Cerebral Palsy Assn. St. Louis, 1985-88; bd. dirs. Canterbury Enterprises, sheltered workshop, St. Louis, 1988-94, participant Leadershp St. Louis, 1988-89; ethics com. DePaul Health Ctr., 1990-96. Mem. Am. Health Lawyers Assn., Mo. Soc. Hosp. Attys. (bd. dirs. 1988-94, pres. 1990-91), Mo. Bar Assn. (vice chmn. health and hosp. com. 1988-90), Bar Assn. Metro. St. Louis (co-chmn. med.-legal com. 1987). Republican. Avocation: sailing. Office: Lashly & Baer PC 714 Locust St Saint Louis MO 63101-1699 Office Phone: 314-621-2939. Business E-Mail: rdwatters@lashlybaer.com.

WATTS, EMILY STIPES, retired English language educator; b. Urbana, Ill., Mar. 16, 1936; d. Royal Arthur and Virginia Louise (Schenck) Stipes; m. Robert Allan Watts, Aug. 30, 1958; children: Benjamin, Edward, Thomas. Student, Smith Coll., 1954-56; AB, U. Ill., 1958, MA (Woodrow Wilson Nat. fellow), 1959, PhD, 1963. Instr. English U. Ill., Urbana, 1963-67, asst. prof., 1967-73, assoc. prof., 1973-77, prof., dir. grad. studies dept. English, 1977—2005, prof. emerita, 2005—; bd. dirs. U. Ill. Athletic Assn., chmn., 1981-83; mem. faculty adv. com. Ill. Bd. Higher Edn., 1984—, vice chmn., 1986-87, chmn., 1987-88. Author: Ernest Hemingway and The Arts, 1971, The Poetry of American Women from 1632 to 1945, 1977, The Businessman in American Literature, 1982; contbg. editor: English Women Writers from the Middle Ages to the Present, 1990; contbr. articles on Jonathan Edwards, Anne Bradstreet to lit. jours. John Simon Guggenheim Meml. Found. fellow, 1973-74 Mem. Am. Inst. Archaeology, Assn. Lit. Scholars Critics, Authors Guild, Ill. Hist. Soc., The Phila. Soc., Phi Beta Kappa, Phi Kappa Phi. Presbyterian. Home: 1009 W University Ave Champaign IL 61821-3317

WATTS, EUGENE J., state legislator; b. St. Louis, Oct. 17, 1942; s. Eugene H. and Norma (Shaughnessy) W.; children: Julia Brianne, Mackenzie Mulrane. AB, Knox Coll., 1964; MA, Emory U., 1965, PhD, 1969. Senator Ohio State Senate Dist. 16, 1985—, asst. pres. pro temp, chmn. reference and oversight, fin. subcom. on edn., mem. rules, edn., retirement & aging com., mem. fin. inst. and ins. com. Assoc. prof. history, rsch. asst. Ohio State U., 1972—; rsch. fellow Am. Coun. Learned Soc., 1975—. Author: The Social Basis of City Politics, 1978. Decorated Bronze star, Vietnam Campaign ribbon, Vietnam Svc. ribbon; State and Local Govt. fellow NEH, 1978; Fulbright fellow Internat. Exch. of Scholar, 1981; recipient Humanitarian Achievement award Columbia Dispatch Cmty. Svc. award, 1984; named Outstanding Legislator, Am. Legion, Amvets, Cath. War Vets., Disabled Am. Vets., Ohio State Coun. Vietnam Vets. Am., Ohio VFW, Vet. Assn. State Comdrs. and Adjutants, Ohio Assn. Chiefs of Police, Ohio Crime Prevention Assn., Ohio Prosecutors Assn. Mem. Vietnam Vet. Leadership Program (state chmn. 1982-85), Am. Legion, VFW, Fraternal Order of Police Assn., Orgn. Am. Historians, AMVETS. Home: 352 Monterey Dr Dublin OH 43017-1337

WATTS, JOHN RANSFORD, academic administrator; b. Boston, Feb. 9, 1930; s. Henry Fowler Ransford and Mary Marion (Macdonald) Watts; m. Joyce Lannom, Dec. 20, 1975; 1 child, David Allister. AB, Boston Coll., 1950, MEd, 1965; MFA, Yale U., 1953; PhD, Union Grad. Sch., 1978. Prof., asst. dean Boston U., 1958-74; prof., dean fine arts Calif. State U., Long Beach, 1974-79; dean and artistic dir. The Theatre Sch./Goodman Sch. Drama, DePaul U., Chgo., 1979-99, prof. and dean emeritus, 1999—. Mng. dir. DePaul U. Merle Reskin Theatre, 1988-99; gen. mgr. Boston Arts Festivals, 1955-64; adminstr. Arts Programs at Tanglewood, 1966-69; producing dir. Theatre Co. of Boston, 1973-75. Chmn. Mass. Coun. on Arts and Humanities, 1968-72; bd. dirs., v.p. Long Beach Pub. Cofp. for the Arts, 1975-79; mem. theatre panel Ill. Arts Coun., 1981-90. With U.S. Army, 1953-55. Recipient Lifetime Achievement award Joseph Jefferson Com., Chgo., 2000. Mem. Mass. Ednl. Comms. Commn., Am. Theatre Asasn., Nat. Coun. on Arts in Edn., Met. Cultural Alliance, U.S. Inst. Theatre Tech., League Chgo. Theatres, Chgo. Internat. Theatre Festival, St. Botolph Club (Boston), Univ. Club (Chgo.), Phi Beta Kappa, Phi Kappa Phi.

WATTS, JOHN S., JR., insurance company executive; BA in English, UCLA. Various mgmt. positions HealthNet, Northwestern Nat. Life Ins. Co.; regional dir. LA sales office Blue Cross of Calif., 1995—97, gen. mgr. large grp. svcs., 1997; acting sr. v.p. UNICARE comml. accounts large grp. divsn. ea., so. and ctrl. regions WellPoint Health Networks, Inc.; sr. v.p. large group divsn. Blue Cross and Blue Shield of Ga. (subs. WellPoint Health Networks, Inc.), 2001—03, pres., CEO, 2003—04; pres., CEO nat. accounts strategic bus. unit WellPoint, Inc, Indpls., 2004—06; pres., CEO comml. and consumer bus. strategic bus. unit WellPoint, Inc., Indpls., 2006—. Office: WellPoint Inc 120 Monument Cir Indianapolis IN 46204

WATTS, MICHAEL H., real estate company executive; b. 1967; B. in Mktg., SUNY Buffalo; MBA, U. Mich. Downtown regional leasing dir. Jones Lang LaSalle Inc., 1991—2000; sr. v.p. J.F. McKinney & Assocs., Chgo., 2000—. Named one of 40 Under 40, Crain's Chgo. Bus., 2006. Office: JF McKinney & Assocs Ste 3565 71 S Wacker Dr Chicago IL 60606 Office Phone: 312-819-4439. E-mail: mwatts@jfmckinney.com.

WATTS, RALPH, state official; b. July 1944; State rep., Iowa, 2003—. Mem. commerce, regulation and labor; mem. human resources standing com.; mem. state govt. standing com.; mem., vice-chair transp., infrastructure and capitals appropriations subcom. Office: State Capitol E 12th and Grand Des Moines IA 50319

WAXLER, BEVERLY JEAN, anesthesiologist, physician; d. Isadore and Ada Belle (Gross) Marcus; m. Richard Norman Waxler, Dec. 24, 1972; 1 child, Adam R. BS in Biology, o. Ill. U., 1971; MD, U. Ill., Chgo., 1975. Diplomate Am. Bd. Anesthesiology, Am. Bd. Pathology. Intern dept. pathology Northwestern U., Chgo., 1975—76, resident, 1976—79; instr. Rush Presbyn. St. Luke's Med. Ctr., Chgo., 1979—81; asst. prof. pathology Loyola U., Maywood, Ill., 1981—84; resident dept. anesthesiology Stroger Hosp. Cook County (formerly Cook County Hosp.), Chgo., 1984—87; attending anesthesiologist Stroger Hosp. Cook County, Chgo., 1987—; chmn. divsn. postanesthetic care Stroger Hosp. of Cook County, Chgo., 2004—; clin. asst. prof. U. Ill., Chgo., 1988—95; asst. prof. Rush Med. Coll., Chgo., 1996—. Contbr. articles to profl. jours. Grantee, Varlen Corp., 1982; Nat. Rsch. Svc. fellow, Nat. Cancer Inst., 1980. Mem.: AAAS, Ill. Soc. Anesthesiologists, Chgo. Soc. Anesthesiologists, Am. Soc. Anesthesiologists, Internat. Anesthesia Rsch. Soc. (B. B. Sankey Anesthesia Advancement award 1989), Sigma Xi. Office: Stroger Hosp Cook County Dept Anesthesiology 1901 W Harrison St Chicago IL 60612 Office Phone: 312-864-2140. Business E-Mail: bwaxler@rush.edu.

WAXSE, DAVID JOHN, judge; b. Oswego, Kans., June 29, 1945; s. I. Joseph and Mary (Poole) W.; m. Linda Schilling (div.); children: Rachel, Ryan, Rebecca; m. Judy Pfannenstiel, May 29, 1982; 1 child, Elayna. BA, U. Kans., 1967; teaching cert., Columbia U., 1968, JD, 1971. Bar: Kans. 1971, U.S. Ct. Appeals (10th cir.) 1971, U.S. Supreme Ct. 1975, U.S. Ct. Appeals (8th Cir.) 1998. Dean of students Intermediate Sch. 88, NYC, 1968-70; spl. edn. tchr. Peter Cooper Sch., NYC, 1970-71; assoc. Payne & Jones, Olathe, Kans., 1971-74, ptnr., 1974-84; of counsel Shook, Hardy & Bacon, Overland Park, Kans., 1984-86, ptnr., 1986-95; shareholder Shook, Hardy & Bacon P.C., Overland Park, 1993-95; ptnr. Shook, Hardy & Bacon L.L.P., Overland Park, Kans., 1995-99; shareholder Shook, Hardy & Bacon P.C., Overland Park, 1993-95, v.p., asst. gen. counsel, 1995-99; U.S. magistrate judge Kansas City, 1999—. Mcpl. judge City of Shawnee, Kans., 1974-80; atty. City of DeSoto, Kans., 1972-79; adj. prof. U. Kans. Sch. Law, Lawrence, 1981-82; mem. juv. code adv. com. Kans. Jud. Coun., 1979-83, guardianship adv. com., 1982-83, atty. fees adv. com., 1986-87; mem. Civil Justice Reform Act Adv. Com., U.S. Dist. Ct. for Dist. Kans., 1991-95; mem. Kans. Commn. on Jud. Qualifications, 1992-99, vice-chmn. 1994-97, chair, 1997-99; v.p. Kans. Legal Svcs., Inc., 1980-82, pres., 1985-87; bd. advisors Kans. Coll. Advocacy, 1979-80; bd. trustees, Lawyer's Com. Civil Rights Under Law, 1997-99. Author: (with others) Kansas Employment Law, 1985, Litigating Employment Law Cases, 1987, Kansas Employment Law Handbook, 1991, supplements, 1992, 95, Kansas Annual Survey, 1990-2000; contbr. articles to profl. jours. Mem. Kan. Gov.'s Adv. Com. on Criminal Justice, 1974-77; mem. Kans. Justice Commn., 1997-99; gen. counsel Western Mo. Dist. ACLU, 1976-78, 86-97, v.p., 1983-86, nat. bd. dirs., 1979-86, 91-99, chmn. children's rights com., 1980-86; mem. AIDS Pol. Network, 1987-99, med. treatment issues com., 1991-96, constn. com., 1991-99; mem. med./tech. com. AIDS Coun. Greater Kans. City, 1986-98, ethics com. consortium Midwest Bioethics Ctr., 1990-2002; bd. dirs. Parents Anonymous Kans., 1978-83, pres., 1979; bd. dirs., mem. fin. com. Kans. Com. for Prevention Child Abuse, 1980-83. Fellow Am. Bar Found., Kans. Bar Found.; mem. ABA (chmn. children's rights com. and family law sects. 1985-86, mem. ho. of dels. 2000—, professionalism com. 2000-05, bd. of editors The Profl. Lawyer, 2000-05, mem. exec. com. nat. conf. fed. trial judges 2005—), Am. Judicature Soc. (bd. dirs. 1997-2003, adv. com. for ctr. for judicial conduct 1997—), Kans. Bar Assn. (chmn. legal aid com. 1978-83, bd. govs. 1988—, v.p. 1996-97, pres.-elect 1997-98, pres. 1998-99, mem. ABA ho. dels. 2000—, Pres.' Outstanding Svc. award 1982, 2006), Kans. City Met. Bar Assn., Johnson County Bar Assn. (chmn. legal aid com. 1975-82, 92-96), Earl E. O'Connor Am. Inn of Ct. (counselor, pres.-elect 2002, pres. 2003). Office: U S Courthouse 500 State Ave Rm 219 Kansas City KS 66101-2400 E-mail: judge_waxse@ksd.uscourts.gov.

WAYNICK, CATHERINE ELIZABETH MAPLES, bishop; b. Nov. 13, 1948; d. Sevedus A. and Janet E. (Wilcox) Maples; m. Larry Wade Waynick, Nov. 28, 1968; 2 children. Student, Ctrl. Mich. U., 1966—68; BA in Religious Studies, Madonna Coll., 1981; MDiv, St. John's Provincial Sem., Plymouth, MI, 1985; DD (hon.), The Gen. Sem., NYC, 1998. Ordained deacon, 1985, priest, 1986; rector All Saints' Parish, Pontiac, Mich., 1994—97; consecrated bishop, 1997; bishop Episcopal Diocese of Indpls., 1997—. Mem. bd. Bexley Hall Sem., Rochester, NY. Office: Episcopal Diocese Indpls 1100 W 42nd St Indianapolis IN 46208 Office Phone: 317-926-5454. Office Fax: 317-926-5456.

WEAKLAND, REMBERT GEORGE, archbishop emeritus; b. Patton, Pa., Apr. 2, 1927; s. Basil and Mary (Kane) Weakland. AB, St. Vincent Coll., Latrobe, Pa., 1948, DD (hon.), 1963, LHD (hon.), 1987; MS in Piano, Juilliard Sch. Music, 1954; postgrad., Columbia U., 1954—56, PhD in Musicology, 2000; LHD (hon.), Duquesne U., 1964, Belmont Coll., 1964, Cath. U. Am., 1975, Xavier U., Cin., 1988, DePaul U., 1989, Loyola U., New Orleans, 1991, Villanova U., 1992, Dayton U., 1993, Marian Coll., Fond du Lac, Wis., 1995, St. Anselm Coll., Manchester, NH, 1996, St. Norbert Coll., De Pere, Wis., 1996, U. San Francisco, 1997, Scholastica Coll., 1998; HHD (hon.), St. Ambrose U., Davenport, 1990, Aquinas Inst. Theology, St. Louis, 1991, St Mary's Coll., Notre Dame, Ind., 1994; LLD (hon.), Cardinal Stritch Coll., Milw., 1978, Marquette U., 1981, Loyola U., Chgo., 1986, U. Notre Dame, 1987, Mt. Mary Coll., Milw., 1989, John Carroll U., Cleve., 1992; LLD (hon.), Fairfield U., 1994; D of Sacred Music (hon.), St. Joseph's Coll., Rensselaer, Ind., 1979; DST of Sacred Music (hon.), Jesuit Sch. Theology, Berkeley, Calif., 1989; DST (hon.), St. John's U., Collegeville, Minn., 1991, Santa Clara U., 1991; DST (hon.), Yale U., 1993; DD (hon.), Lakeland Coll., Sheboygan, 1991, Ill. Benedictine Coll., Lisle, Ill., 1992, Regis Coll., Toronto, 1993, Trinity Coll., Hartford, 1996, Trinity Lutheran Sem., Columbus, Ohio, 1998; D of Ministry (hon.), Catholic Theol. Union, Chgo., 1999. Professed Order of St. Benedict, 1946, ordained priest, 1951; faculty music dept. St. Vincent Coll., 1957—63, chmn., 1961—63, chancellor chmn. of bd. of Coll., 1963—67; co-adjutor archabbot St. Vincent Archabbey, 1963—67; abbot primate Benedictine Confederation, 1967—77; ordained bishop, 1977; archbishop Archdiocese of Milw., 1997—2002, archbishop emeritus, 2002—. Mem.: Ch. Music Assn. Am. (pres. 1964—66), Am. Guild Organists. Roman Catholic. Office: PO Box 070912 Milwaukee WI 53207-0912*

WEATHERWAX, THOMAS K., state legislator; b. Cedar Rapids, Iowa, Oct. 22, 1942; s. Richard G. and Alyce (Kelly) W.; m. Kay A. Weatherwax, 1972; children: Michelle, Kris Chauncey, Kevin, Steve, David, Craig. AA, Cedar Rapids Bus. Coll., 1962; student, ICS Correspondence Sch., 1963-64, U. Ky. From cost acct. to sec.-contr. Wilson & Co., Oklahoma City, 1961-78; sec.-contr. Erny's Fertilizer Svc., Walton, Ind., 1978—; bus. chmn. LEDC Indsl. Park; mem. Ind. Ho. of Reps., 1984-88, Ind. Senate from 18th dist., 1988—; chmn. transp. & interstate coop. com., local govt. financing subcom.; mem. agr. & small bus. com., commerce & consumer affairs com. Ind. State Senate. Sec. Logansport Area Devel. Corp., 1979-85; gen. chmn. United Way, 1979; mem. Hosp. Cmty. Rels. Bd., pres., 1981-83; Iron Horse Fetival gen. chmn. C. of C., 1983; mem. 21st Century com. Coun. State Govts., Nat. Conf. State Legislatures, Energy & Transp.; bd. dirs. Logansport Econ. Devel. Found., Logansport Area Devel. Corp.; mem. Grissom Cmty. Coun.; advisor Ind. Acad. Competitions Excellence; former pres. Meml. Hosp. Cmty. Rels. Bd., bd. dirs. Sangralea Valley Boys' Home; mem. steering com. Hoosier Heartland Corridor. Recipient John Tipton award Cass County Commrs., 1979, Ind. Small Bus. Champion award, Merit award Ind. Assn. Nurserymen, Guardian award Nat. Fedn. Ind. Bus., 1992, Small Bus. Champion award Ind. State C. of C., 1993, Frank M. McHale Econ. Devel. award, 1995, Nat. Rep. Legis. of Yr. award Nat. Rep. Legs. Assn., 1995, Govt. Leader of Yr. Ind. C. of C., 1995; named Outstanding Freshman Legislator, 10th Gen. Assembly, 1985. Mem. Masons (32 deg.), Shriners. Home: 3012 Woodland Dr Logansport IN 46947-1357 Office: Ind Senate State Capitol Indianapolis IN 46204

WEAVER, ARTHUR LAWRENCE, rheumatologist, consultant; b. Lincoln, Nebr., Sept. 3, 1936; s. Arthur J. and Harriet Elizabeth (Walt) Weaver; m. JoAnn Versemann, July 6, 1980; children: Arthur Jensen, Anne Christine. BS (Regents scholar) with distinction, U. Nebr., 1958; MD, Northwestern U., 1962; MS in Medicine, U. Minn., 1966. Diplomate Am. Bd. Internal Medicine, Am. Bd. Rheumatology. Intern U. Mich. Hosps., Ann Arbor, 1962-63; resident Mayo Grad. Sch. Medicine, Rochester, Minn., 1963-66; practice medicine specializing in rheumatology and internal Lincoln, 1968—2002; med. dir. Arthritis Ctr. Nebr., 1968—2002; ret., 2002. Staff mem., chmn. rheumatology dept. Bryan Meml. Hosp., 1976—78, 1982—85, 1989—91, vice-chief staff, 1984—87; chmn. fin. com. Bryancare, 1995—96; courtesy staff St. Elizabeths Hosp., Lincoln Gen. Hosp.; cons. staff VA Hosp.; chmn. Juvenile Rheumatoid Arthritis Clinic, 1970—88; asst. prof. Internal Medicine Dept. U. Nebr., Omaha, 1976—88, assoc. prof., 1988—95, clin. prof. Rheumatology divsn., 1995—; med. dir. Lincoln Benefit Life Co., 1972—90, Assurity Life Ins. Co., 1995—2003, bd. dirs., 1992—2007; adv. com. Coop. Systematic Studies in Rheumatic Diseases III; bd. dirs. M.G.I. Pharma Inc., Internat. Rheumatology Network, 2003—06, AZANO, 2007—, Corrona; cons. in field. Editl. bd. mem. Nebr. Med. Jour., 1982—96; contbr. articles to profl. jours. Mem. tech. cons. panel for rheumatology Harvard Resource Based Relative Value Study; trustee U. Nebr. Found., 1974—. Capt. med. corps US Army, 1966—68. Recipient Outstanding Nebraskan award, U. Nebr., 1958, C.W. Boucher award, 1958, Philip S. Hench Rheumatology award, Mayo Grad. Sch. Medicine, 1966, Founders award Nebr. chpt., Arthritis Found., 1997. Fellow: ACP (Nebr. coun. 1983—85, Laureate award Nebr. chpt. 1996), Am. Coll. Rheumatology (bd. dirs. 1985—96, planning com. 1987—96, sec. 1991—93, pres. rsch. and edn. found. 1991—93, exec. com. 1991—96, 2d v.p. 1993—94, 1st v.p., pres.-elect 1994—95, pres. 1995—96, chmn. nominating com. 1996—97, master 2001, 1st Paulding Phelps award 1989), Am. Rheumatism Assn. (pres.-elect Ctrl. region 1983—84, com. on rheumatologic practice 1983—87, pres. Ctrl. region 1984—85); mem.: AMA (life), Minn. Med. Assn., Midwest Coop. Rheumatic Disease Study Group (chmn. exec. com. 1986—92), Nat. Soc. Clin. Rheumatology (program chairperson 1986—87, exec. com. 1987—92, program chairperson 1988), Arthritis Found. (life; profl. del.-at-large 1987—88, 1989, 1990, 1995—96, blue ribbon rsch. com. 1995—96, bd. dirs. Nebr. chpt., Nat. Vol. Svc. citation 1988, Founder award 1997), Arthritis Health Professions Assn. (com. on practice 1984—87), Nebr. Soc. Internal Medicine (Internist of Yr. 1988), Am. Soc. Internal Medicine (coord. com. phys. payment svcs. 1988—93), U. Minn. Med. Sch. Alumni Assn., U. Mich Med. Sch. Alumni Assn., Mayo Grad. Sch. Medicine Alumni Assn., Phi Rho Sigma, Pi Kappa Epsilon, Alpha Omega Alpha, Sigma Xi, Phi Beta Kappa. Republican. Presbyterian. Home and Office: 9914 Weavers Point Rd Pequot Lakes MN 56472-6472 Office Phone: 218-562-5351. Personal E-mail: weaver2aj@tds.net.

WEAVER, DONNA RAE, winery executive; b. Chgo., Oct. 15, 1945; d. Albert Louis and Gloria Elaine (Graffis) Florence; m. Clifford L. Weaver, Aug. 20, 1966; 1 child, Megan Rae. BS in Edn., No. Ill. U., 1966, EdD, 1977; MEd, De Paul U., 1974. Tchr. H.L. Richards High Sch., Oak Lawn, Ill., 1966-71, Sawyer Coll. Bus., Evanston, Ill., 1971-72; asst. prof. Oakton Community Coll., Morton Grove, Ill., 1972-75; vis. prof. U. Ill., Chgo., 1977-78; dir. devel. Mallinckrodt Coll., Wilmette, Ill., 1978-80, dean, 1980-83; campus dir. Nat.-Louis U., Chgo., 1983-90, dean div. applied behavioral scis., 1985-89; dean Coll. Mgmt. and Bus., 1989-90; pres. The Oliver Group, Inc., Kenilworth, Ill., 1993-97; mng. ptnr. Le Miccine, Gaiole-in-Chianti, Tuscany, Italy, 1996—. Cons. Nancy Lovely and Assocs., Wilmette, 1981-84, North Ctrl. Assn., Chgo., 1982-90. Contbr. articles to Am. Vocat. Jour., Ill. Bus. Edn. Assn. Monograph, Nat. Coll. Edn.'s ABS Rev., Nat. View. Mem. Ill. Quality of Work Life Coun., 1987-90, New Trier Twp. Health and Human Svcs. Adv. Bd., Winnetka, Ill., 1985-88; bd. dirs. Open Lands Project, 1985-87, Kenilworth (Ill.) Village House, 1986-87. Recipient Achievement award Women in Mgmt., 1981, Am. Bd. Master Educators charter disting. fellow, 1986. Mem. Nat. Bus. Edn. Assn., Delta Pi

Epsilon (past pres., mem. Bears Care Gala com.). Avocations: reading, travel, decorating. Home and Office: 144 Woodstock Ave Kenilworth IL 60043-1262 Address: Azienda Agricola Le Miccine S Traversa Chiantigiana 53013 Gaiole in Chianti Italy E-mail: drw@lemiccine.com.

WEAVER, ELIZABETH A., state supreme court justice; b. New Orleans; d. Louis and Mary Weaver. BA, Newcomb Coll.; JD, Tulane U. Elem. tchr. Glen Lake Cmty. Sch., Maple City, Mich.; French tchr. Leelanau Sch., Glen Arbor, Mich.; pvt. practice Glen Arbor, Mich.; law clk. Civil Dist. Ct., New Orleans; atty. Coleman, Dutrey & Thomson, New Orleans; atty., title specialist Chevron Oil Co., New Orleans; probate and juvenile judge Leelanau County, Mich., 1975—86; judge Mich. Ct. Appeals, 1987—94; justice Mich. Supreme Ct., Lansing, 1995—. Chief justice Mich. Supreme Ct., 1999—2000, re-elected, 2002—; chief justice Peter Rellected Superior Ct. Justice, 2002—; instr. edn. dept. Ctr. Mich. U.; mem. Mich. Com. on Juvenile Justice, Nat. Conv. State Adv. Groups on Juvenile Justice for U.S.; chair Gov.'s Task Force on Children's Justice, Trial Ct. Assessment Commn., Office Juvenile Justice and Delinquency Prevention; jud. adv. bd. mem. Law and Orgnl. Econs. Ctr. U. Kans.; treas. Children's Charter of Cts. of Mich. Chairperson Western Mich. U. CLE Adv. Bd.; mem. steering com. Grand Traverse/Leelanau Commn. on Youth; mem. Glen Arbor Twp. Zoning Bd.; mem. charter arts north Leelanau County; mem. citizen's adv. coun. Arnell Engstrom Children's Ctr.; mem. cmty. adv. com. Pathfinder Sch. Treaty Law Demonstration Project; active Grand Traverse/Leelanau Mental Health Found. Named Jurist of Yr., Police Officers Assn. of Mich.; named one of five Outstanding Young Women in Mich., Mich. Jaycees; recipient Eastern award, Warren Easton Hall of Fame, Lifetime Dedication to Children award, Mich. Champions in Childhood Injury Prevention, 2000, Recognition award for outstanding svc. to Mich. children and families, Gov. Engler and Family Independence Agy., 2000, Profls. award, Mich. Assn. Drug Cts., 2002, Mary S. Coleman award, Ctr. for Civic Edn. Through Law, 2002. Fellow: Mich. State Bar Found.; mem.: ABA, Antrim County Bar Assn., Leelanau County Bar Assn., Grand Traverse County Bar Assn., La. Bar Assn., Nat. Coun. Juvenile and Family Judges, Mich. Bar Assn. (chair CLE adv. bd., chair crime prevention ctr., chair juvenile law com.), Delta Kappa Gamma (hon.). Office: Mich Supreme Ct 3300 Grandview Plz 10850 E Traverse Hwy Traverse City MI 49684-1364

WEAVER, FRANKLIN THOMAS, retired newspaper executive; b. Johnstown, NY, Oct. 11, 1932; s. Edwin K. and Bertha J. (Wendt) W.; children: Thomas, James, Michael, David, Tammy, Kelly, Anna; m. Joyce W. Phelps, Oct. 23, 1991. BA with high honors in Journalism, Mich. State U., 1954. Advt. sales rep. Grand Rapids Press, Mich., 1955-64; controller Muskegon (Mich.) Chronicle, 1964-66; mgr. Bay City (Mich.) Times, 1966-73, Jackson (Mich.) Citizen Patriot, 1973-84, pub., 1984—99; ret. Mem.: Mich. Press Assn. (pres. 1991), Newspapers Assn. Am., Greater Jackson C. of C., Ella Sharp Mus. (pres. 1995—96), Jackson Country Club.

WEAVER, JOHN H, research scientist, educator; BS, U. Mo., 1967; PhD, Iowa State U., 1972. Post doctoral fellow U. of Mo., 1973; rsch. assoc. U. of Wis., 1974—75; asst. scientist U. Wis., 1975—77; sci. assoc. Ames Lab., U.S. Dept. of Energy, Iowa, 1975—85; assoc. scientist U.of Wis., 1977—82; prof. U. of Minn., Dept. of Chem. Engring. and Materials Sci., 1982—99; prof. and head U. of Ill., Dept. of Sci. and Engring., 2000—. Adj. prof. U. Wis., 1981—82; faculty assoc. Argonne Nat. Lab., Ill., 1982—87; dir. grad. studies for materials science U. of Minn., 1982—87; faculty assoc. Argonne Nat. Lab., Ill., 1982—87; lectr. U. of Brasilia, Internat. Ctr. for Condensed Matter Physics; mem. rev. panel Dept. of Energy, 1993—; lectr., summer sch. Universidad Complutense de Madrid, 1994; u. prof. Tohoku U., Inst. for Materials Rsch., Japan, 1994; royal soc. Kan Tong Po prof. U. of Hong Kong, 1995; vis. scientist Fritz-Haber Inst. der Max Planck-Gesellschaft, Berlin, 1995; dir. grad. studies for materials science U. of Minn., 1997—99; judge Nottingham prize, 2000—, R&D 100 awards, 2000; mem. internat. adv. com. European Conf. on Surface Sci., 2001—; mem. internat. adv. bd. 6th Internat. Conf. on Atomically Controlled Surfaces, Interfaces and Nanostructures, 2000—. Reviewer, referee and arbiter Sci., Nature, Physics Today, Physics Reviews, Physics Reviews Letters, Jour. of Vacuum Sci. and Tech., Surface Sci., Jour. of Applied Physics, Applied Physics Letters, Jour. of Am. Chem. Soc., et. al., 1974—, mem. editl. bd. Jour. of Vacuum Science and Tech., 1989—93, Jour. of Materials Rsch., 1989—92, Chem. of Materials, 1991—95, Jour. of Electron Spectroscopy and Related Phenomena, 1991—2000, Fullerence Science and Tech., 1992—, Surface Science Reports, 1998—, Surface Rev. and Letters, 1998—, Royal Soc. of Chem. Electronic Jour. PhysChemComm, 1999—, R&D mag., 2000—, Surface Science, 2000—, mem. editl. adv. bd. CRC Book Series Chem. and Physics of Surfaces and Interfaces, 1993—, assoc. editor Nanostructured Materials, 1992—. Nominee outstanding rsch. award for studies of electronic interactions of hydrogen in metals, U.S. Dept. Energy, 1980; recipient G.J. Lapeyre award for synchotron radiation rsch. per Ardua ad Bremsstrahlung, 1982, spl. creativity award, at. Sci. Found., 1991—92, Nat. Science Found., 1995—96, Alexander von Humboldt sr. rsch. award, Alexander von Humboldt Found., 1995, scientist of the yr., R&D mag., 1997, disting. lectr., Am. Vacuum Soc., 1998—, Medard W. Welch award, 1999, 19th Peter. G. Winchell lectr., Purdue U., 2000. Fellow: Am. Physical Soc., Am. Vacuum Soc. (bd. dirs. 1990—91); mem.: Nat. Sci. Found. Office: Dept of Materials Sciences and Engring U of Ill at Urbana-Champaign 1304 W Green St Urbana IL 61801

WEAVER, PHILIP G., tire company executive; BS, Bowling Green State U.; degree advanced mgmt. internat. sr. mgr. program, Harvard Bus. Sch. Cert. CPA. Principal, sr. mgr. Ernst & Young; tire divsn. contr. Cooper Tire & Rubber, 1990—94; v.p. Cooper Tire & Rubber Co., Tire Divsn., 1994—98; v.p., CFO Cooper Tire & Rubber Co., Findlay, Ohio, 1998—. Mem.: Blanchard Valley Health Assn., Blanchard Valley Reg. Health Ctr., Am. Inst. of CPAs, Ohio Soc. of CPAs, Toledo Chpt. Fin. Exec. Inst. Office: Cooper Tire & Rubber Co 701 Lima Ave Findlay OH 45840

WEAVER, RICHARD L., II, writer, educator, lecturer; b. Hanover, NH, Dec. 5, 1941; s. Richard L. and Florence B. (Grow) W.; m. Andrea A. Willis; children: Richard Scott, Jacquelynn Michelle, Anthony Keith, Joanna Corinne. AB, U. Mich., 1964, MA, 1965; PhD, Ind. U., 1969. Asst. prof. U. Mass., 1968-74; assoc. prof. speech comm. Bowling Green State U., 1974-79, prof., 1979-96, dir., basic speech comm. course, 1974-96. Vis. prof. U. Hawaii-Manoa, 1981-82, Bond U., Queensland, Australia, 1990, St. Albans, Melbourne, Australia, 1990, Western Inst., Perth, Australia, 1990, pres. & CEO, And Then Some Publ. LLC. Author: (with Saundra Hybels) Speech/Communication, 1974, 2d edit., 1979, Speech/Communication: A Reader, 1975, 2d edit., 1979, Speech/Communication: A Student Manual, 1976, 2d edit., 1979, Understanding Interpersonal Communication, 1978, 7th edit., 1996, (with Raymond K. Tucker, Cynthia Berryman-Fink) Research in Speech Communication, 1981, Foundations of Speech Communication: Perspectives of a Discipline, 1982, Speech Communication Skills, 1982, Understanding Public Communication, 1983, Understanding Business Communication, 1985, Understanding Speech Communication Skills, 1985, Readings in Speech Communication, 1985, (with Saundra Hybels) Communicating Effectively, 1986, 8th edit., 2007, Skills for Communicating Effectively, 1985, 4th edit., 1993, rev. edit., 1995, (with Howard W. Cotrell) Innovative Instructional Strategies, 1987, 6th edit., 1993, (with Curt Bechler) Listen to Win: A Guide to Effective Listening, 1994, Study Guide to Accompany Communicating Effectively, 1995, 2d edit., 1998, Essentials of Public Speaking, 1996, 2d edit., 2001, (with Edgar E. Willis) How to be Funny on Purpose: Creating and Consuming Humor, 2005, And Then Some: Essays to Entertain, Motivate & Inspire, book I, 2007, Public Speaking Rules: All You Need to Give a Great Speech, 2008-. Mem. emeritus Nat. Comm. Assn., Ctrl. States Speech Assn., Ohio Speech Assn. Home and Office: 9583 Woodleigh Ct Perrysburg OH 43551-2669 Office Phone: 419-874-2124. Personal E-mail: rlweaverii@andthenworks.com.

WEAVER, ROBIN GEOFFREY, lawyer, educator; b. Columbus, Ohio, Aug. 19, 1948; BA, Ohio State U., 1970; JD, U. Mich., 1973. Bar: Ohio 1974, U.S. Dist. Ct. (no. dist.) Ohio 1974, U.S. Ct. Appeals (6th cir.) 1980, U.S. Ct. Appeals (3d cir.) 1998, U.S. Ct. Appeals (2d, 7th, and 11th cirs.) 2002, U.S. Supreme Ct., 2002, U.S. Dist. Ct. (so. dist.) Ohio 2004. Assoc. Squire, Sanders & Dempsey, Cleve., 1973-83, ptnr., 1983—; mem. faculty Nat. Inst. for Trial Adv. Northwestern U., Chgo., 1983—. Mem. Ohio Supreme Ct. Bd. of Commrs. on Grievances and Discipline, chair, 1996-97, master commr., 2002-. With U.S. Army, 1974. Fellow Am. Coll. Trial Lawyers, Internat. Soc. Barristers; mem. Cleve. Bar Assn. (pres. 2002-03); mem. ABA, Ohio Bar Assn., Cleve. Assn. Trial Attys. (life), 8th Appellate Jud. Conf., Am. Inns of Ct. (master bencher Cleve. chpt.). Office: Squire Sanders & Dempsey 4900 Key Tower Cleveland OH 44114 Office Phone: 216-479-8500. Business E-Mail: rweaver@ssd.com.

WEAVER, TIMOTHY ALLAN, lawyer; b. Elkhart, Ind., Nov. 30, 1948; s. Arthur and Joan Lucile (Yoder) W.; m. Catherine Anne Power, Nov. 23, 1974; children: Daniel Timothy, Christopher Matthew, David Colwell. AB, Brown U., 1971; JD, U. Ill., 1974. Bar: Ill. 1974, Wis. 1999, U.S. Dist. Ct. (no. dist.) Ill. 1975, U.S. Ct. Appeals (7th cir.) 1975, U.S. Dist. Ct. (no. dist. trial bar) Ill. 1982, U.S. Dist. Ct. (ea. dist.) Wis. 1999. Asst. pub. defender Cook County Pub. Defender, Chgo., 1974-75; trial atty. Chgo. Transit Authority, 1975-78; assoc. Philip E. Howard Ltd., Chgo., 1978, Pretzel & Stouffer, Chartered, Chgo., 1978-82, ptnr., 1982—. Editor: Medical Malpractice, 1989, 92, 96; contbr. chpts. to books. Mem. ABA, Ill. State Bar Assn., Ill. Assn. Def. Trial Counsel, State Bar of Wis., Civil Trial Counsel of Wis., The Lawyers Club of Chgo. Office: Pretzel & Stouffer Chartered One S Wacker Dr #2500 Chicago IL 60606 Office Phone: 312-578-7416. E-mail: tweaver@pretzel-stouffer.com.

WEAVER, W(AYNE) DOUGLAS, cardiologist, researcher, medical educator; b. Ft. Fairfield, Maine, Mar. 14, 1945; 1 child, John. BA, U. Maine, 1967; MD, Tufts U., 1971. Diplomate Am. Bd. Internal Medicine, Am. Bd. Cardiovasc. Disease. Intern, then resident U. Wash., Seattle, 1971-74, fellow in cardiology, 1974-76, prof. medicine/cardiology, 1979-96; head divsn. cardiology, dir. Henry Ford Cardiovascular Inst. Henry Ford Health Sys., Detroit, 1996—, also Darin chair cardiology; prof. medicine Wayne State U. Contbr. over 250 articles to profl. jours. (articles), assoc. editor numerous jours. Named one of Am.'s Best Cardiologists; named to Top Doctors List, Hour Mag. Fellow: Am. Coll. Cardiology (former v.p., pres. 2008—), Am. Heart Assn. Avocations: skiing, boating, golf. Office: Henry Ford Hosp 2799 W Grand Blvd Detroit MI 48202-2689 Office Phone: 313-916-4420. Business E-Mail: wweaver1@hfhs.org.*

WEAVER, WILLIAM N., JR., lawyer; AB, Oberlin Coll., 1956; JD, John Marshall Law Sch., 1964. Bar: Ill. 1964. Ptnr. Securities, Sachnoff & Weaver LLC. Co-chair S&W Bus. Group; mem. bd. dirs. Chgo. Software Assn.; mem. bd. advisors Argonne Ill. Tech. Enterprise Ctr. Former mem. bd. gov. Chgo. Symphony; bd. trustees Disciples Divinity Sch., U. Chgo.; bd. dirs. Steppenwolf Theatre Co.; mem. bd. dirs. Roger Baldwin found., Ill. Chpt. Am. Civil Liberties Union; mem. bd. advisors Michael Polsky Entrepreneurial Ctr., U. Chgo. Bus. Sch. Office: Sachnoff & Weaver Ltd 30 S Wacker Dr 29th Fl Chicago IL 60606 Office Phone: 312-207-6401.

WEAVER, WILL(IAM WELLER), language educator, writer; b. 1950; Farmer, Park Rapids, Minn., 1977-81; with Bemidji (Minn.) State U., part-time writing instr., 1979-81, assoc. prof., 1981-90, prof. English, 1990—. Author: Red Earth, White Earth, 1986, A Gravestone Made of Wheat, 1989, Striking Out, 1993; contbr. articles to profl. publs. Office: Bemidji State U Dept English Bemidji MN 56601

WEBB, B. TRENT, lawyer; b. Butler, Mo., 1967; BS, Drury Coll., 1989; JD with distinction, U. Mo., Kansas City, 1992. Bar: Mo. 1992, US Dist. Ct., We. Dist. Mo., Kans. 1993, U.S. Patent and Trademark Office, US Dist. Ct., We. Dist. Kans. Ptnr., chair intellectual property litig. practice group Shook, Hardy & Bacon LLP, Kansas City, Mo. Recipient American Jurisprudence award. Mem.: Intellectual Property Owners Assn., Beta Beta Beta, Phi Eta Sigma, Alpha Lambda Delta. Articles Editor U. Mo.-Kansas City Law Rev. Office: Shook Hardy & Bacon LLP 2555 Grand Blvd Kansas City MO 64108-2613 Office Phone: 816-559-2320. Office Fax: 816-421-5547. E-mail: bwebb@shb.com.

WEBB, DAN K., lawyer; b. Bushnell, Ill., Sept. 5, 1945; s. Keith L. and Phyllis I. (Clow) W.; student Western Ill. U., 1963-66; JD cum laude, Loyola U., 1970; m. Laura A. Buscemi, Mar. 15, 1973; children: Jeffrey, Maggie, Michael, Melanie, Megan. Bar: Ill. 1970, US Dist. Ct. (no. dist. Ill.), US Ct.Appeals (6th-8th cirs., fed. cir.), US Supreme Ct. Chief spl. prosecutions divsn. US Atty.'s Office, Chgo., 1970-76; ptnr., Cummins, Decker & Webb, Chgo., 1976-79; dir., Ill. Dept. Law Enforcement, Chgo., 1979-80; ptnr. Pierce, Webb, Lydon & Griffin, Chgo., 1980-81; US atty. (no. dist. Ill.), US Dept. Justice, Chgo., 1981-85; ptnr. Winston & Strawn LLP, Chgo., 1985—, chmn., 2006-, head litig. dept., mem. exec. com.; Iran-Contra spl. trial counsel; instr. John Marshall Law Sch., 1975—, Loyola U. Sch. Law, 1980—. Vice chmn. Met. Fair and Expn. Authority, 1978—81; bd. advs. Mercy Hosp. and Med. Ctr.; mem. Chgo. Coun. on Arson. Contbr. articles to profl. jours. Recipient spl. commendation award US Dept. Justice, 1975; named one of 10 Outstanding Young Chicagoans, Chgo. Jaycees, 1979, 100 Most Influential Lawyers, Nat. Law Jour., 2006. Fellow. Internat. Acad. Trial Lawyers, Am. Coll. of Trial Lawyers; mem. ABA, Ill. Bar Assn., Chgo. Bar Assn., Fed. Bar Assn., Legal Club Chgo., Execs. Club Chgo., at. Inst. Trial Advocacy, 1979-. Republican. Office: Winston & Strawn LLP 35 W Wacker Dr Ste 4200 Chicago IL 60601-9703 Office Phone: 312-558-5856. Office Fax: 312-558-5700. E-mail: dwebb@winston.com.

WEBB, DAVID ALLEN, writer; b. Beloit, Wis. s. Charles Webb and Marion Cecelia (Doud) Michaels. BS in Agrl. Journalism, U. Wis., 1981. Asst. mgr. Nature Food Ctrs., Eau Claire, Wis., 1993-95; mgr. Gen. Nutrition Ctr., Eau Claire, Wis., 1995-96. Cons. Tab Books, Inc., Blue Ridge Summit, Pa., 1983—85. Author: Alaskan Holiday, 2004, Friendship Lost, 2005, Growing Fruits & Berries, 1983, Practical Landscaping & Lawn Care, 1985, Making Potpourri, Colognes and Soaps-102 atural Recipies, 1988, Easy Potpourri, 1992, (novels) Kong Forest, 1999, Edwardian Summer, 1999, To The Victor, 2001, Rockstar, 2003, Alaskan Holiday, 2004, Friendship Lost, 2005. Recipient Editor's Choice award for poems, 1998-2000; Carnegie Fund for Authors grant, 1985; named to Internat. Poetry Hall of Fame, 1998. Avocations: gardening, reading, travel.

WEBB, MARTHA JEANNE, writer, educator, film producer; b. Grinnell, Iowa, Oct. 26, 1947; d. Frederick Winfield and Helen (Potter) W.; m. Bruce A. Clark; children: Marjorie, Paula, David. Student, St. Cloud State U., 1965-67, U. Minn., 1967-69, Coll. of St. Catherine, 1979-81. Personnel, pub. relations, drug abuse edn. NIH, 1967-77; account services Doremus & Co., Mpls., 1977-79; v.p. adminstrn. Webb Enterprises, Inc., Mpls., 1979-81; v.p. Russell-Manning Prodns., Mpls., 1981-86; pres. Clark Webb, Inc., Mpls., 1986-92. Pres. Minn. Film Bd., 1986-87, BCW Corp., 1988—. Author: Dress Your House for Success, 1997, Finding Home, 1998; co-prodr. Hubert H. Humphrey: A Passion for Justice, Whitney Mus., 1998. Recipient Summit awards, 1999, Distinction Communicator awards, 1998, Silver award Internat. Film and TV Festival of N.Y., 1983, 84, 85, 86, 87, Golden Eagle award CINE Festival, 1985, Gold award Telly Awards, 1987.

WEBB, O. GLENN, retired farm supplies company executive; b. 1936; married BS, U. Ill., 1957; PhD, So. Ill. U., 1973. With Growmark, Inc., Bloomington, Ill., 1966—2000, sec., 1968-72, v.p., 1972-80, pres., 1980—2000, chmn., 1980—2000; dir. Archer Daniels Midland Co., 1991—. Trustee, chmn. Am. Inst. Coop.; dir. St. Louis Farm Credit Banks, Farmers Export Co., Nat. Coop. Refinery Assn., Ill. Agr. Leadership Found.; trustee Grad. Inst. Coop. Leadership.

WEBB, PAUL, physiologist, educator, researcher, consultant; b. Cleve., Dec. 2, 1923; s. Monte F. and Barbara (Webb) Bourjaily; m. Eileen Whalen, Mar. 13, 1948; children: Shaun P., Paul S. Womacks. BA, U. Va., 1943, MD, 1946; MS in Physiol., U. Wash., 1951. Asst. prof. physiology U. Okla. Sch. Medicine, Oklahoma City, 1952—54; chief environ. sect. Aeromed. Lab., Wright-Patterson AFB, Ohio, 1954-58; prin. assoc. Webb Assocs., Yellow Springs, Ohio, 1959-82; vis. scientist INSERM, Paris, 1983; vis. prof. U. Limburg, Maastricht, The Netherlands, 1986, U. Uppsala, Sweden, 1988-89; clin. prof. cmty. health Wright State U. Sch. Medicine, Dayton, Ohio, 1980—; rsch. prof. bioengring. Wright State U., Dayton, 2005—. Cons. aerospace and undersea medicine, energy balance and thermal physiology, Yellow Springs, 1980—. Author: Human Calorimeters, 1985; contbr. articles to profl. jours. Village councilman Village of Yellow Springs, Ohio, 1969-75; mem. Air Force Scientific Adv. Bd., Washington, 1984-88. Recipient Ely award Human Factors Soc., 1972. Fellow Aerospace Med. Assn. (Aerospace Indsl. Life Scis. Assn. award 1969), Am. Inst. Med. and Biol. Engring.; mem. Am. Physiol. Soc., Am. Soc. for Clin. Nutrition, Undersea Med. Soc. (oceaneering internat. award 1979, pres. 1980-81). Home and Office: 14 Cedar Ct Yellow Springs OH 45387-1321

WEBB, RODNEY SCOTT, judge; b. Cavalier, ND, June 21, 1935; s. Chester and Aylza (Martin) W.; m. Betty M. Lykken, Aug. 31, 1957; children: Sharon, Crystal, Todd, Wade, Susan. BS, U. N.D., 1957, JD, 1959. Bar: N.D. 1959, U.S. Dist. Ct. N.D. 1965, U.S. Ct. Appeals (8th cir.) 1981. Assoc. Ringsak, Webb, Rice & Metelman, Grafton, N.D., 1959-81; state's atty. Walsh County, Grafton, 1966-74; mcpl. judge City of Grafton, 1975-81; spl. asst. atty. gen. State of N.D., 1970-81; U.S. atty. U.S. Dist. Ct. N.D., Fargo, 1981-87, judge, 1987—, chief judge, 1993—. Judge; b. Cavalier, N.D., June 21, 1935; s. Chester and Aylza (Martin) W.; m. Betty M. Lykken, Aug. 31, 1957; children: Sharon, Crystal, Todd, Wade, Susan. BS, U. N.D., 1957, JD, 1959. Bar: N.D. 1959, U.S. Dist. Ct. .D. 1965, U.S. Ct. Appeals (8th cir.) 1981. Assoc. Ringsak, Webb, Rice & Metelman, Grafton, N.D., 1959-81; state's atty. Walsh County, Grafton, 1966-74; mcpl. judge City of Grafton, 1975-81; spl. asst. atty. gen. State of N.D., 1970-81; U.S. atty. Dist. of N.D., Fargo, 1981-87, judge U.S. Dist. Ct. N.D., 1987—, Fargo, chief judge, 1996—. Col. JAG, N.D. Army N.G., ret. Mem. N.D. State Attys. Assn. (past pres.). Lutheran. Col. JAG, N.D. Army N.G., ret. Mem. .D. State Attys. Assn. (past pres.). Lutheran. Office: US Dist Ct 655 1st Ave N Ste 410 Fargo ND 58102-4952

WEBB, THOMAS EVAN, biochemistry educator; b. Edmonton, Alta., Can., Mar. 4, 1932; came to U.S., 1970, naturalized, 1978; s. Donald John and Sarah Jane (McMinis) W.; m. Ellen Adair Armstrong, Sept. 4, 1961; children: Linda Carol, Sharon Laura. BS, U. Alta., 1955, MS, 1957; PhD, U. Toronto, 1961. Rsch. assoc. Nat. Rsch. Coun., Ottawa, Can., U. Wis., Madison, 1963-65; 1961-63; asst. prof. biochemistry U. Man. (Can.), Winnipeg, 1965-66; asst. prof. McGill U., Montreal, Que., Can., 1966-70, acting dir. cancer unit., 1969-70; assoc. prof. med. biochemistry Ohio State U., Columbus, 1970-74, prof., 1974-95, prof. emeritus, 1995—. Contbr. numerous articles on biochemistry of cancer to profl. jours. Grantee NIH/Nat. Cancer Inst., 1970-95; fellow Air Force Office Sci. Rsch., 1982. Mem. Am. Soc. Biol. Scientists, Am. Assn. Cancer Research, AAAS, Sigma Xi Office: Ohio State U Dept Molecular and Cellular Biochemistry 1645 eil Ave Columbus OH 43210-1218 E-mail: TWebb74669@aol.com.

WEBB, THOMAS J., utilities executive; b. Alexandria, Va., Oct. 3, 1952; m. Donna; 3 children. B in Fin. with honors, George Mason U.; MBA. Various fin. mgmt. positions Ford Motor Co. and subs.; controller Electronics divsn., Large Front-Wheel Drive Vehicle Ctr.; CFO Visteon Corp.; chief fin. info. officer Ford Motor Co.; exec. v.p., CFO Kellogg Co., Battle Creek, Mich., 2000—02, CMS Energy, Dearborn, Mich., 2002—. Bd. dirs. Conix, Can., Hall Climate Control, Korea, Halla Electronics, Korea, Samcor, South Africa, Yan Feng, China, Toledo (Ohio) Molding and Die, Climate Sys., India, others. Office: CMS Energy 1 Energy Plaza Dr Jackson MI 49201-2357

WEBB, WILLIAM DUNCAN, lawyer, mediator; b. Dayton, Ohio, Feb. 14, 1930; s. Herbert Henry and Dorothy (Chamberlain) W.; m. Nancy Helen Regester, June 12, 1953; children: Joseph Chamberlain (dec.), Mary Helen, Nancy Katherine, Sarah Elizabeth, Lucy Ellen. AB, U. Mich., 1952, JD, 1956. Bar: Mo. 1956, Kans. 1958, U.S. Supreme Ct. 1969. Assoc. Stinson, Mag, Thomson, McEvers & Fizzell, Kansas City, Mo., 1956-58; sec. Kansas City (Mo.) Power & Light Co., 1960-78, asst. treas., 1969-78, asst. v.p. communications, 1978-79, asst. v.p. fed. affairs, 1979-84; v.p. investments Paine Webber, 1984-98. Legal counsel Fellowship of Christian Athletes. Mem. city coun. Roeland Park, Kans., 1960-62; chmn. Kansas City Myasthenia Gravis Found., 1965-67; bd. dirs. Boys Club of Kansas City, Mo., 1969-74, Greater Kansas City YMCA, Greater Kansas City chpt. ARC; chmn. bd. councilors Avila Coll., 1969-70; trustee, asst. sec., 1970-89; bd. dirs. Rural Water Dist. # 7, Johnson County, Kans., 1992-94. Mem. Internat. Maine-Anjou Assn. (dir., sec.-treas. 1969-76), Theta Delta Chi, Phi Alpha Delta. Presbyterian. Home and Office: 37000 W 155th St Gardner KS 66030-9617 E-mail: webb37ooo@aol.com.

WEBBER, E. RICHARD, JR., judge; b. Kahoka, Mo., June 4, 1942; m. Peggy Washle, July 6, 1968; children: Erin, Nicki. BS in Bus. Adminstrn., U. Mo.-Columbia, 1964, JD, 1967. Pvt. practice, Mo., 1967-79; cir. judge 1st Jud. Cir., 1979-95; judge ea. dist. Mo. U.S. Dist. Ct., Saint Louis, 1995—. Former chair Presiding Judges' Exec. Com., Supreme Ct. Coms. adopting case processing time standards & implementing family ct. Elder Memphis Presbyn. Ch.; past pres. Law Sch. Alumni Assn. U. Mo., Coun. Family & Juvenile Ct. Judges; former mem. Nat. Task Force Child Support Enforcement. Mem. ABA, Mo. Bar Assn. (former chair jud. adminstrn. divsn., co-chair gender fairness implementation com.), Mo. Trial Judges Assn. (past pres.). Office: 111 S 10th St Saint Louis MO 63102

WEBER, ARNOLD ROBERT, academic administrator; b. NYC, Sept. 20, 1929; s. Jack and Lena (Smith) W.; m. Edna M. Files, Feb. 7, 1954; children: David, Paul, Robert. BA, U. Ill., 1951; MA, MIT, 1958, PhD in Econs., 1958; DHL (hon.), U. Notre Dame, 2005, U. Ill., 2005, Northwestern U., 2005, Loyola U., 2005, Ripon Coll., 2005, U. Colo., 2005. Instr., then asst. prof. econs. MIT, 1955-58; faculty U. Chgo. Grad. Sch. Bus., 1958-69, prof. indsl. relations, 1963-69; asst. sec. for manpower Dept. Labor, 1969-70; exec. dir. Cost of Living Council; also spl. asst. to Pres. Nixon, 1971; Gladys C. and Isidore Brown prof. urban and labor econs. U. Chgo., 1971-73; former provost Carnegie-Mellon U.; dean Carnegie-Mellon U. (Grad. Sch. Indsl. Adminstrn.), prof. labor econs. and pub. policy, 1973-80; pres. U. Colo., Boulder, 1980-85, Northwestern U., Evanston, Ill., 1985-95, chancellor, 1995-98, pres. emeritus, 1998—. Cons. union, mgmt. and govt. agys., 1960—; cons. Dept. Labor, 1965; mem. Pres.'s Adv. Com. Labor Mgmt. Policy, 1964, Orgn. Econ. Coop. and Devel., 1987; vice chmn. Sec. Labor Task Force Improving Employment Svcs., 1965; chmn. rsch. adv. com. US Employment Svc., 1966; assoc. dir. OMB Exec. Office of Pres., 1970—71, spl. asst. to pres., 1971; chmn. Presdl. R.R. Emergency Bd., 1982; trustee Com. for Econ. Devel., Nat. Multiple Sclerosis Soc.; bd. dirs. Diamond Cluster Inc.; asst. sec. manpower US Dept. Labor, 1969—70. Contbr. articles to profl. jours. Lt. (j.g.) USCG, 1952—54. Laureate, Lincoln Acad. Ill.; Ford Found. Faculty Rsch. fellow, 1964-65. Mem. Am. Acad. Arts and Scis., Indsl. Rels. Rsch. Assn., Nat. Acad. Pub. Adminstrn., Comml. Club Chgo. (pres., civic com. 1995-2000), Econ. Club Chgo. (pres. 1995-97), Phi Beta Kappa. Jewish. Office: Northwestern U Office of Pres Emeritus 555 Clark St 209 Evanston IL 60208-0805 Business E-Mail: arnold-weber@northwestern.edu.

WEBER, ARTHUR, magazine executive; b. Chgo., Feb. 1, 1926; s. Philip and Mary (Arlinsky) W.; m. Sylvia Zollinger, Aug. 19, 1950; children— Randy, Lori. Student, Ill. Inst. Tech., 1943-44; BSEE, Northwestern U., 1946. Elec. design engr. Corn Products Refining Co., 1946-48, Naess & Murphy, archs. and engrs., Chgo., 1949-51, Ford Motor Co., 1952-53, Skidmore, Owings & Merill, Chgo., 1954-57, Shaw, Metz & Dolio, Chgo., 1958-59; pres. Consumers Digest mag., Chgo., 1959—; pub. Money Maker mag. (name changed to Your Money mag., 1991), 1979-97, pres., 1997—2003; pub. U. Chgo. Better Health Letter, 1995-96, pres., 1997—2003. With USN, 1944—46, with USNR, 1946—56.

WEBER, BECKY, state legislator; b. Sept. 24, 1954; Restaurant developer; ins. agt.; mem. Wis. State Assembly, Madison, 2002—, mem. budget rev. com., vice chair aging and long-term care com., mem. govt. ops. and spending limitations com., mem. ins. com., mem. rural affairs com., mem. small bus. com. Republican. Address: 2811 Antier Trail Green Bay WI 54313

WEBER, DANIEL E., association executive; b. Chgo., July 6, 1940; BS in Bus. Mgmt., DePaul U., 1962. Asst. to exec. dir. Am. Oil Chemists Soc., Chgo., 1962-67; administrv. mgr. Inst. Food Tech, Chgo., 1967-69, dir. conv. svcs., 1969-79, dir. mktg. and meetings, 1979-91; exec. dir. Inst. Food Technologists, Chgo., 1991-99, exec. v.p., CEO, 1999—. Chmn. 25th Anniversary Com. City of Rolling Meadows, 2 term ind. mem. city coun., chmn. every major com., street dedicated "Weber Drive"; officer Crusade of Mercy; bd. dirs., treas., v.p. Northwest Mental Health Assn., Disting. Svc. award. Named Meeting Planner of Yr. Assn. Conv. Ops. Mgmt., 1990. Mem. Internat. Assn. Exposition Mgrs. (charter cert. exposition mgr., v.p. 1987, pres. 1988, nat. bd. mem., chair Midwestern chpt., awards com. 1998—, chair scholarship com. 2000), Nat. Assn. Exposition Mgrs. (bd. dirs., officer, pres. 1988, v.p. 1987, cert. exposition mgr.), Am. Soc. Assn. Execs., Trade Show Bur. (bd. dirs. 1987—), Coun. Engring. and Sci. Soc. Exec. (conv. liaison coun. del. 1980-81, program chmn. meetings, expositions), Profl. Conv. Mgmt. Assn. (bd. dirs. 1992, 93), Conv. Liaison Coun. (task force on reorganization), Chgo. Soc. Assn. Execs. (chmn. directory advt., chmn. membership svcs. com., chmn. awards com.). Avocation: golf. Office: Inst of Food Techs 525 W Van Buren St Ste 1000 Chicago IL 60607-3814 E-mail: info@ift.org.

WEBER, GEORGE, oncology and pharmacology educator, researcher; b. Budapest, Hungary, Mar. 29; came to U.S., 1959; s. Salamon and Hajnalka (Arvai) W.; m. Catherine Elizabeth Forrest, June 30, 1958; children: Elizabeth Dolly Arvai, Julie Vibert Wallace, Jefferson James. BA, Queen's U., 1950, MD, 1952; MD (hon.), U. Chieti, Italy, 1979, Med. Faculty, Budapest, 1982, U. Leipzig, Fed. Republic of Germany, 1987, Tokushima U., Japan, 1988; degree, Kagawa U., Japan, 1992. Rsch. assoc. Montreal Cancer Inst., 1953-59; prof. pharmacology Ind. U. Sch. Medicine, Indpls., 1959—; dir. Lab for Exptl. Oncology Sch. Medicine, Ind. U., Indpls., 1974—; Milan Panič prof. oncology Ind. U., Indpls., 1994—, Wellcome prof., 1995—; prof. Lab. for Exptl. Oncology Sch. Medicine, Ind. U., Indpls., 1974-90, disting. prof. Lab. for Exptl. Oncology, 1990—. Chmn. study sect. USPHS, Washington, 1976-78; sci. adv. com. Am. Cancer Soc., N.Y.C., 1972-76, 94-98, Damon Runyon Fund, N.Y.C., 1971-76; mem. U.S. Nat. Com., Internat. Union Against Cancer, Washington, 1974-80, 90-94, AS, Washington, 1974-80, 90-94, U.S. Army Med. Rsch. and Breast Cancer Rsch. Program, 1996-97; prof. Brit. cancer campaign U. Oxford, Oxford, Eng., 2001; vis. prof. U. Bologna, Italy, 2001—. Editor: Advances in Enzyme Regulation, Vols. 1-48, 1962—; assoc. editor Jour. Cancer Rsch., 1969—80, 1982—89. Recipient Alecce Prize for cancer rsch. Tiberine Acad., Rome, 1971, Best Prof. award Student AMA, Indpls., 1966, 68, G.F. Gallanti prize for enzymology Internat. Soc. Clin. Chemists, 1984, Outstanding Investigator award Nat. Cancer Inst., NIH, 1986-94, Semmelweis medal & diploma Budapest, Hungary, 2001, medal Gastroenterological Soc., Aliga, Hungary, 2001, Prestigious External Award Recognition Ind. U., Indpls., Ind., 2002. Mem. Am. Soc. for Pharmacology and Exptl. Therapeutics, Am. Assn. Cancer Rsch. (G.H.A. Clowes award 1982), Russian Acad. Sci. (hon.), Hungarian Cancer Soc. (hon.), Hungarian Acad. Scis. (hon.), Acad. Scis. Bologna (Italy) (hon.). Home: 7307 Lakeside Dr Indianapolis IN 46278-1618 Office: Ind U Sch Medicine Lab Exptl Oncology 699 West Dr Indianapolis IN 46202-5119 Office Phone: 317-274-7921.

WEBER, GLORIA RICHIE, retired minister, retired state legislator; married; 4 children. BA, Washington U., St. Louis; MA, MDiv, Eden Theol. Sem., Webster Groves, Mo. Ordained to ministry Evang. Luth. Ch. Am., 1974. Family life educator Luth. Family and Children's Svcs. Mo.; mem. Mo. Ho. of Reps., 1993-94. Mo. state organizer, dir. comm. Mainstream Voters C.A.R.E., 1995. Editor: Interfaith Voices for Peace and Justice, 1996—2000. Exec. dir. Older Women's League, 1990—95. Named Woman of the Yr., Variety Club, 1978, Woman of Worth, Older Women's League, 1993; recipient Woman of Achievement award, St. Louis Globe-Dem., 1977, Unselfish Cmty. Svc. award, St. Louis Sentinel Newspaper, 1985, Faith in Action award, Luth. Svcs. St. Louis, 1994. Mem.: Older Wiser Luths. in Svc. (devotion leader), Assn. Lutheran Older Adults (mem. nat. bd. 2004—), N.Am. Interfaith Network (bd. dirs. 1993—2003), Phi Beta Kappa. Democrat. Personal E-mail: gloriaweber9@aol.com.

WEBER, H. PATRICK, lawyer; b. Cin., Jan. 25, 1949; s. Harry P. and Peggy (Sebastiani) W.; m. Marilyn Bykowski, Nov. 30, 1974; children: Kevin, Carmen, Courtney. BBA, U. Notre Dame, 1971, JD, 1974. Bar: Ohio 1974, US Dist. Ct. (so. dist. Ohio) 1974, US Tax Ct. 1975, Ky. 1990, US Claims Ct. 1991. Ptnr. Strauss & Troy, Cin., 1974-90, Barrett & Weber, Cin., 1990—. Bd. dirs. Ea. Hills Med. Billing, Inc. Trustee Med. Found. Cin., 1983—, Mercy Hosp. Anderson Found., 1990—. Named an Ohio Super Lawyer, Law & Politics Mag., 2004—06; named one of Top 100 Attys., Worth mag., 2005. Mem. ABA, Ohio Bar Assn., Cin. Bar Assn., Ky. Bar Assn., Notre Dame Alumni Assn. (trustee Cin. 1976—). Office: Barrett & Weber 500 Fourth & Walnut Ctr 105 E 4th St Cincinnati OH 45202 Office Phone: 513-721-2120. Office Fax: 513-721-2139.

WEBER, HANNO, architect; b. Barranquilla, Colombia, Sept. 24, 1937; arrived in US, 1952; s. Hans and Ester (Oks) Weber. BA magna cum laude, Princeton U., 1959, MArch, 1961. Registered arch., Ill., Fla., Mo., Pa., NJ, Va. Urban designer, rsch. assoc. Guayana project MIT and Harvard U., Caracas, Venezuela, 1961-63; project arch. Paul Schweikher Assocs., Pitts., 1963-67; asst. prof. architecture Princeton U., NJ, 1967-73; assoc. prof. Washington U., St. Louis, 1973-80; sr. design arch., studio head, assoc. Skidmore, Owings & Merrill, Chgo., 1980-83; prin. Hanno Weber & Assocs., Chgo., 1984—. Vis. lectr. Escuela Nacional de Arquitectura Universidad Nacional de Mex., 1975; rsch. assoc. Rsch. Ctr. Urban and Environ. Planning, Princeton; project dir. Cmty. Design Workshop Washington U. Sch. Architecture, St. Louis, 1973—78; prof. architecture U. Wis., Milw., 1983—. Contbr. articles to profl. jours. Mem. Pres.'s Commn. Edn. Women Princeton U., 1968—69. Finalist, Okla. City Meml. Internat. Design Competition, 1997, Green Homes for Chgo. Design Competition, 2000; recipient 1st prize winner, Flagler Dr. Waterfront Master Plan Design Competition, West Palm Beach, Fla., 1984, Mcpl. Ctr. Design Competition, Leesburg, Va., 1987, Chgo. AIA Disting. Bldg. award Citation of Merit, 1987, Urban Design award Mcpl. Govt. Ctr., Leesburg, AIA, 1992; fellow, NEH, 1970, Graham Found., 1973. Mem.: Nat. Coun. Arch. Registration Bds., Phi Beta Kappa. Office: Hanno Weber & Assocs 11 E Adams St # 702 Chicago IL 60603-6301 Home Phone: 312-664-7556; Office Phone: 312-922-5589. Business E-Mail: weber@hannoweber.com.

WEBER, HERMAN JACOB, senior district judge; b. Lima, Ohio, 1927; s. Herman Jacob and Ada Minola W.; m. Barbara L. Rice, 1948; children: Clayton, Deborah. BA, Otterbein Coll., 1949; JD summa cum laude, Ohio State U., 1951. Bar: Ohio 1952, U.S. Dist. Ct. (so. dist.) Ohio 1954. Ptnr. Weber & Hogue, Fairborn, Ohio, 1952-61; judge Fairborn Mayor's Ct., 1956-58; acting judge Fairborn Mcpl. Ct., 1958-60; judge Greene County Common Pleas Ct., Xenia, Ohio, 1961-82, Ohio Ct. Appeals (2d dist.), Dayton, 1982-85, U.S. Dist. Ct. (so. dist.) Ohio, Cin., 1985—2002, sr. judge, 2002—. Chmn. Sixth Cir. Dist. Judges Conf., 1988, Ohio Jud. Conf., Columbus, 1980-82; pres. Ohio Common Pleas Judges Assn., Columbus, 1975. Vice-mayor City of Fairborn, 1955-57, council mem., 1955-59. Served with USNR, 1945-46. Office: US Dist Ct 801 100 E 5th St Cincinnati OH 45202-3905

WEBER, JAY, radio personality; b. Wis. B English, Boradcast and Print Journalism, U. Wis., 1988. Cert. tchr. Wis. Anchor, reporter WTDY AM, Madison, Wis., 1988—90; radio host 1130 WISN, Greenfield, Wis., 1990—. Office: WISN Radio 12100 W Howard Ave Greenfield WI 53228

WEBER, KENNETH J., hotel executive; b. 1946; With Arthur Young & Co., NYC, 1968-71, ITT-Grinnell Corp., Providence, 1971-73, Farmbest Foods Internat., Jacksonville, 1973-74; regional contr. Marriott Corp., Washington, 1974-76, group contr., 1976-77, divsn. contr., 1977-79, pres., CEO Farrell's Ice Cream divsn., 1983-86; exec. v.p., CFO Isaly Co., Pitts., 1979-80; v.p., contr. Country Kitchens Internat. divsn. Carlson Cos., Inc., Mpls., 1980-81; sr. v.p. Poppin Fresh Restaurant divsn. Pillsbury Co., Mpls., 1981-83; sr. v.p., corp. contr. Red Lion Hotels Corp., Vancouver, Wash., 1987-92; sr. v.p., CFO Omni Hotels Corp., Hampton, N.H., 1992—; also v.p., treas. Omni Ctr. Corp., Richmond, Va.

WEBER, MARK R., automotive executive; B in Indsl. Engring., Kettering U.; M in Mgmt. (Sloan fellow), MIT, 1983. Various pers. and labor rels. pos. GM Fisher Body, Elyria, Ohio, 1971—78, administr. pers. svcs. Columbus, Ohio, 1978—79, pers. dir. Syracuse, NY, 1979—82; adminstr. exec. compensation GM Pers. and Devel. Staff, Detroit, 1982—83, dir., classified employee compensation, 1983—85; dir. gen. offices pers. Chevrolet-Pontiac-GM of Can. Group, Warren, Mich., 1985—88, dir. human resources, salaried pers., 1985—88, dir. indsl. rels., 1988—91; gen. dir. pers. Inland Fisher Guide, Warren, Mich., 1991—93, gen. dir. pers. and pub. affairs, 1993—98; v.p. in charge human resources Delphi Corp., Troy, Mich., 1998—2000, exec. v.p., ops., human resource mgmt. and corp. affairs, 2000—06, exec. v.p. global bus. services, 2006—. Office: World Hdqrs Delphi Corp 5725 Delphi Dr Troy MI 48098-2815

WEBER, RANDY, publishing executive; Assoc. pub. Consumers Digest and Your Money mags., pub., 1993—. Office: Consumers Digest Communications 520 Lake Cook Rd Ste 500 Deerfield IL 60015-5633

WEBER, ROBERT R., state legislator; b. Nov. 19, 1925; m. Shirley V. Roe, 1948; children: Mary, Anthony, Kathleen, William. State rep. dist. 6 State of S.D., state rep. dist. 4, 1993—. Mem. agriculture and natural resources and local govt. coms. S.D. Ho. of Reps.; farmer, rancher. Supr. Twp. Sch. Bd. Mem. S.D. Farmer's Union (state dir.), Nat. Farmers Orgn., Am. Agriculture Assn., K.C. Republican. Office: SD Ho of Reps State Capitol Pierre SD 57501 Home: 16955 US Highway 212 Clear Lake SD 57226-5141

WEBER, SHARI, state legislator; b. Owatonna, Minn., July 1, 1953; m. Marvin E. Weber. Student, St. John;s Acad. and Coll., Moorhead State U. Dir. downtown devel. Herington (Kans.) Main St. Program, Herington, Kans., 1993-97; rep. Dist. 68 Kans. State Ho. of Reps., Topeka, 1995—2003. Henry Toll fellow, 2000. Address: 405 E Lewerenz Herington KS 67449 Home Phone: 785-366-0104; Office Phone: 785-271-1404. E-mail: sjweber@kansas.net.

WEBER, SUSAN A., lawyer; b. 1958; BA, Drake U., 1984; JD, MBA, SUNY, Buffalo, 1989. Bar: Pa. 1990, D.C. 1992, Ill. 1993, U.S. Ct. Appeals (4th cir.) 1990, U.S. Ct. Appeals (3d cir.) 1991, U.S. Ct. Appeals (7th cir.) 1992. Clk. to Justice Byron White U.S. Supreme Ct.; clk. to Judge James Sprouse U.S. Ct. Appeals (4th cir.); with Sidley Austin Brown & Wood, Chgo., 1993—, ptnr., 1997—.

WEBSTER, JAMES RANDOLPH, JR., physician; b. Chgo., Aug. 25, 1931; s. James Randolph and Ruth Marian (Burtis) W.; m. Joan Burchfield, Dec. 28, 1954; children: Susan, Donovan, John. BS, U. Chgo.-Northwestern U., 1953; MD, MS, Northwestern U., 1956. Diplomate: Am. Bd. Internal Medicine (sub bd. pulmonary disease and geriatrics). Intern Phila. Gen. Hosp., 1956-57; resident in medicine Northwestern U., 1957-60, NIH fellow in pulmonary disease, 1962-64; chief medicine Northwestern Meml. Hosp., Chgo., 1976—88; prof. medicine Northwestern U. Med. Sch., 1977—, chief gen. med. sect. dept. medicine, 1987-88; chief exec. officer orthwestern Med. Group Practice, 1978-88; dir. Buehler Ctr. on Aging Northwestern U. Med. Ctr., 1988-2000. Chief staff Northwestern Meml. Hosp., 1988-90; pres. Chgo. Bd. Health, 2002—, Inst. Medicine, Chgo., Ill., 2002-04, exec. dir., 2004—; chair Ill. Ad Hoc Com. to Defend Health Care. Contbr. chpts. to books, articles to med. jours. Capt. U.S. Army, 1960-62. Recipient Outstanding Clin. tchr. award Northwestern U. Med. Sch., 1974, 77, 84, 86, Alumni Merit award Northwestern U., 1979, Henry P. Russe-Inst. of Medicine award for exemplary compassion in health care, 1997, Aeschulapian award as Physician of Yr., Anti Defamation League, 1998. Master: ACP (gov. for Ill. 1988—92, chair sub-com. on aging 1993, Clayppole award 1994); mem.: Ill. Geriatrics Soc. (pres. 1992—94), Am. Geriatrics Soc., Alpha Omega Alpha. Office: Inst Medicine Chgo Ste 525 332 S Michigan Ave Chicago IL 60604 Home: PO Box 274 Lakeside MI 49116 Office Phone: 312-663-0040. Business E-Mail: j-webster@northwestern.edu.

WEBSTER, JOHN GOODWIN, biomedical engineering educator, researcher; b. Plainfield, NJ, May 27, 1932; s. Franklin Folger and Emily Sykes (Boody) W.; m. Nancy Egan, Dec. 27, 1954; children: Paul, Robin, Mark, Lark BEE, Cornell U., 1953; MSEE, U. Rochester, 1965, PhD, 1967. Engr. North American Aviation, Downey, Calif., 1954-55; engr. Boeing Airplane Co., Seattle, 1955-59, Radiation Inc., Melbourne, Fla., 1959-61; staff engr. Mitre Corp., Bedford, Mass., 1961-62, IBM Corp., Kingston, NY, 1962-63; asst. prof. elec. engring. U. Wis., Madison, 1967-70, assoc. prof. elec. engring., 1970-73, prof. elec. and computer engring., 1973-99, prof. biomed. engring., 1999—2001, prof. emertius biomed. engring., 2001—. Author: (with others) Medicine and Clinical Engineering, 1977, Sensors and Signal Conditioning, 1991, 2d edit., 2001, Analog Signal Processing, 1999; editor: Medical Instrumentation: Application and Design, 3d edit., 1998, Clinical Engineering: Principles and Practices, 1979, Design of Microcomputer-Based Medical Instrumentation, 1981, Therapeutic Medical Devices: Application and Design, 1982; Electronic Devices for Rehabilitation, 1985; Interfacing Sensors to the IBM-PC, 1988, Encyclopedia of Medical Devices and Instrumentation, 2d edit., 2006, Tactile Sensors for Robotics and Medicine, 1988, Electrical Impedance Tomography, 1990, Teaching Design in Electrical Engineering, 1990, Prevention of Pressure Sores, 1991, Design of Cardiac Pacemakers, 1995, Design of Pulse Oximeters, 1997, The Measurement Instrumentation, and Sensors Handbook, 1999, Encyclopedia of Electrical and Electronics Engineering, 1999, Mechanical Variables Measurement, 2000, Minimally Invasive Medical Technology, 2001, Electrical Measurement, Signal Processing and Displays, 2004, Bioinstrumentation, 2004. Recipient Rsch. Career Devel. award NIH, 1971-76; NIH fellow, 1963-67; recipient Western Electric Fund award Am. Soc. Engring. Edn., 1978, Best Reference Work award, 1999, Theo C. Pilkington Outstanding Educator award, 1994. Fellow IEEE (3d Millennium medal 2000, IEEE-EMBS Career achievement award 2001), Am. Inst. Med. and Biol. Engring., Inst. Physics, Instrument Soc. Am. (Donald P. Eckman Edn. award 1974), Assn. for Advancement Med. Instrumentation (Found. Laufman-Greatbatch prize 1996). Democrat. Unitarian Universalist. Office: Univ Wis Dept Biomed Engring 1550 Engineering Dr Madison WI 53706-1609 Home Phone: 608-233-8410; Office Phone: 608-263-1574. Business E-Mail: webster@engr.wisc.edu.

WEBSTER, LESLIE TILLOTSON, JR., pharmacologist, educator; b. NYC, Mar. 31, 1926; s. Leslie Tillotson and Emily (de Forest) W.; m. Alice Katharine Holland, June 24, 1955; children: Katharine White, Susan Holland Webster Van Drie, Leslie Tillotson III, Romi Anne. BA, Amherst Coll., 1947, Sc.D. (hon.), 1982; student, Union Coll., 1944; MD, Harvard U., 1948. Diplomate: Am. Bd. Internal Medicine. Rotating intern Cleve. City Hosp., 1948-49, jr. asst. resident in medicine, 1949-50; asst. resident medicine Bellevue Hosp., NYC, 1952-53; research fellow medicine Harvard and Boston City Hosp. Thorndike Meml. Lab., 1953-55; from demonstrator to instr. medicine Sch. of Medicine Western Res. U., 1955-60; research assoc. to sr. instr. biochemistry Case Western Res. U. Sch. Medicine, 1957—60, asst. prof. medicine, 1960-70, asst. prof. biochemistry, 1960-65, asst. prof. pharmacology, 1965-67, asso. prof., 1967-70, prof. pharmacology, 1976-92, chmn. pharmacology dept., 1976-91, prof. medicine, 1980-86, prof. emeritus pharmacology dept., 1992—2007, cons., pharmacology dept., 2007—; rsch. prof. pediat., divsn. pediat. pharmacology and critical care Rainbow Babies and Children's Hosp., Case Western Res. U. Sch. Medicine, 1992—2006, cons. dept. pharmacology, 2007—. Prof., chmn. pharmacology dept. Northwestern U. Med. and Dental Sch., 1970—76; dir. med. scientist tng. program Case Western Res. U. Sch. Medicine, 1979—92; mem. gastroenterology nutritional tng. grants com. NIAMD, NIH, 1965—69; mem. sci. working group on schistosomiasis WHO, 1977—83, chmn. subsect. on chemotherapy biochemistry, 1977—83; mem. exec. com. Gt. Neglected Diseases Network, Rockefeller Found., 1978—86; mem. cellular and molecular basis of disease rev. com. NIGMS, NIH, 1984—88; cons. World Bank, Laos, 2003. Contbr. articles to sci. jour. Served to lt. med. corps. USNR, 1950-52. Russell M. Wilder fellow Nat. Vitamin Found., 1956-59; Sr. USPHS Research fellow, 1959-61; USPHS Rsch. Career Devel. awardee, 1961-69; Macy faculty scholar, 1980-81. Mem. ACP (life), Central Soc. Clin. Rsch. Coalition (emeritus), Am. Soc. Clin. Investigation (emeritus), Am. Soc. Biochemistry and Molecular Biology (emeritus), Assn. Med. Sch. Pharmacology (emeritus), Am. Soc. Pharmacology and Exptl. Therapeutics (emeritus), Alpha Omega Alpha (hon.). Home: 12546 Cedar Rd No 4 Cleveland Heights OH 44106-3294 Office: Dept Pharmacology Case We Res U 10900 Euclid Ave Cleveland OH 44106-4965 Home Phone: 216-932-6219; Office Phone: 216-368-0850. Business E-Mail: ltw2@case.edu.

WEBSTER, LOIS SHAND, association executive; b. Springfield, Ill., Sept. 25, 1929; d. Richings James and C. Odell (Gilbert) S.; m. Terrance Ellis Webster, Feb. 12, 1954 (dec. July 1985); children: Terrance Richings, Bruce Douglas, Andrew Michael. BA, Millikin U., 1951; cert. in libr. tech., Coll. Du Page County, Glen Ellyn, Ill., 1974; postgrad. libr. sci., No. Ill. U., 1977-82. Exec. asst. Am. Nuclear Soc., La Grange Park, Ill., 1973—. Contbr. articles and book chpts. to profl. publs. Field dir. Springfield coun. Girl Scouts U.S., 1951-54; libr. advisor Du Page County coun. Girl Scouts U.S., 1973-74. Recipient Octave J. Du Temple award Am. Nuclear Soc., 1989. Mem. Spl. Librs. Assn. (divsn. chmn. 1984-85, chmn. by-laws com. 1987-89, bd. dirs. 1989-92, sec. 1990-91, visioning com. 1992—), Coun. Engring. and Sci. Soc. Execs., Am. Soc. Assn. Execs., Met. Chgo. Libr. Assembly (bd. dirs. 1982-85). Avocations: travel, genealogy. Home: 5383 Newport St Lisle IL 60532-4126 Office: Am Nuclear Soc 555 N Kensington Ave La Grange Park IL 60526-5535

WEBSTER, SHAWN N., state representative, veterinarian; b. Lima, Ohio, Dec. 23, 1949; married; 3 children. DVM, Ohio State U. Rep. Ohio State Ho. Reps., Columbus, 2000—. Mem. banking, pensions and securities com. Ohio State Ho. Reps., mem. edn. com., mem. fed. grant rev. and edn. com., vice chmn. fin. and appropriations oversight subcom., vice chmn. higher edn. subcom., vice chmn. human svcs. and aging oversight subcom.; mem. gov. bd. Butler County Ednl. Svc. Ctr. Mem. governing body Butler County Ednl. Svc. Ctr., 1993—2000; bd. dir. Butler County Children Svcs., 1999—2000, Ross Local Sch., 1981—93. Mem.: AARP, Butler-Warren County Vet. Med. Assn., Cin. Vet. Med. Assn., Ohio Vet. Med. Assn., Am. Vet. Med. Assn., Ohio Farm Bur., Ohio Sch. Bds. Assn. Republican. Office: Ohio State House Reps 77 South High St 13th Floor Columbus OH 43215-6111

WEBSTER, STEPHEN BURTIS, dermatologist, educator; b. Chgo., Dec. 3, 1935; s. James Randolph Webster and Ruth Marion (Burtis) Holmes; m. Katherine Griffith Webster, Apr. 4, 1959; children: David Randolph, Margaret Elizabeth, James Lucian. BS, Northwestern U., 1957, MD, 1960. Diplomate Am. Bd. Dermatology (bd. dirs. 1992—, v.p. 1997-98, pres.). Intern Colo. Gen. Hosp., Denver, 1960-61; resident Walter Reed Gen. Hosp., Washington, 1962-65; staff physician Henry Ford Hosp., Detroit, 1969-71, Gundersen Lutheran Med. Ctr., La Crosse, 1971—; assoc. clin. prof. U. Wis., Madison, 1976—; clin. prof. U. Minn., Mpls., 1978—. Lt. col. U.S. Army, 1962-69. Fellow Am. Acad. Dermatology (sec.-treas. 1985-88, pres. 1991); mem. AMA, Am. Dermatol. Assn. (pres. 1996-97), Am. Bd. Dermatology (v.p. 1997-98, pres. 1999-2000, assoc. exec. dir. 2001—), Wis. Med. Soc., La Crosse County Med. Soc., Soc. Investigative Dermatology, Alpha Omega Alpha. Republican. Congregationalist. Avocations: bagpipes, model trains. Home: N2062 Wedgewood Dr E La Crosse WI 54601-7175 Office: Gundersen Clinic Ltd 1836 South Ave La Crosse WI 54601-5494 Business E-Mail: sbwebste@gundluth.org.

WEDL, ROBERT J., state agency commissioner; BEd, MEd, St. Cloud State U. From acting commr. to asst. commr. Minn. Dept. Children, Families, Learning, St. Paul, commr., 1996—. Address: State Dept of Chidren, Families 1500 Highway 36 W Saint Paul MN 55113-4035

WEEKS, A. RAY, real estate company executive; Co-chmn., pres., COO Duke-Weeks Realty Corp., Indpls., 1994—. Office: Duke-Weeks Realty Corp Ste 100 600 E 96th St Indianapolis IN 46240-3792

WEEKS, STEVEN WILEY, lawyer; b. Topeka, Mar. 7, 1950; s. Glen Wiley and Grace Aileen (West) W.; m. Lee Nordgren, Aug. 1, 1974 (div. 1985); 1 child, Kirstin Nordgren. BS summa cum laude, Washburn U., 1972; JD cum laude, Harvard U., 1977. Bar: Ohio. Project leader Nat. Sanitation Found., Ann Arbor, Mich., 1972; engr. Kans. Dept. Health and Environ., Topeka, 1972-74; ptnr. Taft, Stettinius & Hollister, Cin., 1977—. Dir. The Myers Y. Cooper Co., Cin.; adj. faculty Chase Coll. Law, 1987-88. Mem. adv. com. prosecuting atty., Hamilton County, Cin., 1992; mem. Hamilton County Rep. Ctrl. Com., 1994—. Mem. Ohio State Bar Assn., Cin. Bar Assn. Republican. Methodist. Avocations: computers, golf. Home: 3560 Traskwood Cir Cincinnati OH 45208

WEERTMAN, JOHANNES, materials science educator; b. Fairfield, Ala., May 11, 1925; s. Roelof and Christina (van Vlaardingen) W.; m. Julia Ann Randall, Feb. 10, 1950; children: Julia Ann, Bruce Randall. Student, Pa. State Coll., 1943-44; BS, Carnegie Mellon U., 1948, DSc, 1951; postgrad., Ecole Normale Superieure, Paris, 1951-52. Solid State physicist U.S. Naval Rsch. Lab., Washington, 1952-58, cons., 1960-67; sci. liaison officer U.S. Office Naval Rsch., Am. Embassy, London, 1958-59; faculty Northwestern U., Evanston, Ill., 1959—, prof. materials sci. dept., 1961-68, chmn. dept., 1964-68, prof. geol. scis. dept., 1963—, Walter P. Murphy prof. materials sci. and engring. emeritus, 1999—. Vis. prof. geophysics Calif. Inst. Tech., 1964, Scott Polar Rsch. Inst., Cambridge (Eng.) U., 1970-71, Swiss Fed. Inst. Reactor Rsch., 1986; cons. Cold Regions Rsch. and Engring. Lab., U.S. Army, 1960-75, Oak Ridge (Tenn.) Nat. Lab., 1963-67, Los Alamos (N.Mex.) Sci. Lab., 1967—; co-editor materials sci. books MacMillan Co., 1962-76. Author: Dislocation Based Fracture Mechanics, 1996, (with Julia Weertman) Elementary Dislocation Theory, 1964, 2d edit., 1992; mem. editorial bd. Metal. Trans., 1967-75, Jour. Glaciology, 1972—; assoc. editor Jour. Geophys. Rsch., 1973-75, 2000-01; contbr. articles to profl. jours. With USMC, 1943-46. Honored with naming of Weertman Island in Antarctica.; Fulbright fellow, 1951-52; recipient Acta Metallurgica gold medal, 1980; Guggenheim fellow, 1970-71 Fellow Am. Acad. Arts and Scis., Am. Soc. Metals, Am. Phys. Soc., Geol. Soc. Am., Am. Geophys. Union (Horton award 1972, AIME Mathewson Gold medal 1977); mem. AAAS, NAE, Am. Inst. Physics, Internat. Glaciol. Soc. (Seligman Crystal award 1983), Arctic Inst., Am. Quaternary Assn., Explorers Club, Fulbright Assn., Sigma Xi, Tau Beta Pi, Phi Kappa Phi, Alpha Sigma Mu, Pi Mu Epsilon. Home: 834 Lincoln St Evanston IL 60201-2405 Office: Northwestern U Materials Sci Dept Evanston IL 60208-0001 Home Phone: 847-328-8718; Office Phone: 847-491-3197. Business E-Mail: j-weertman2@northwestern.edu.

WEERTMAN, JULIA RANDALL, materials engineering educator; b. Muskegon, Mich., Feb. 10, 1926; BS in Physics, Carnegie-Mellon U., 1946, MS in Physics, 1947, DSc in Physics, 1951. Physicist U.S. Naval Rsch. Lab., Washington, 1952-58; vis. asst. prof. dept. materials sci. and engring. Northwestern U., Evanston, Ill., 1972-73, asst. prof., 1973-78, from asst. prof. to assoc. prof., 1973-82, prof., 1982-99, Walter P. Murphy prof., 1989, chmn. dept., 1987-92, asst. to dean grad. studies and rsch. Tech. Inst., 1973-76, Walter P. Murphy prof. emeritus, 1999—. Mem. various NRC coms. and panels. Coauthor: Elementary Dislocation Theory, 1964, 1992, also pub. in French, Japanese and Polish; contbr. numerous articles to profl. jours. Mem. Evanston Environ. Control Bd., 1972-79. Recipient Creativity award NSF, 1981, 86; Guggenheim Found. fellow, 1986-87. Fellow Am. Soc. Metals Internat. (Gold medal 2005), Minerals, Metals and Materials Soc. (leadership award 1997, Robert Mehl lectr. 2006); mem. NAE, Am. Acad. Arts and Scis., Am. Phys. Soc., Materials Rsch. Soc. (Von Hippel award 2003), Soc. Women Engrs. (Disting. Engring. Educator award 1989, Achievement award 1991). Home: 834 Lincoln St Evanston IL 60201-2405 Office: orthwestern U Dept Material Sci & Engring 2220 Campus Dr Evanston IL 60208-0876 Office Phone: 847-491-5353. Business E-Mail: jrweertman@northwestern.edu.

WEERTS, RICHARD KENNETH, music educator; b. Peoria, Ill., Oct. 7, 1928; s. Gerhard Nicholas and Ellen Marie (Lindeburg) W. BS, U. Ill., 1951; MA, Columbia U., 1956, EdD, 1960; MA, N.E. Mo. State U., 1973. Tchr. Lyndhurst (N.J.) Pub. Schs., 1956-57; dir. instrumental music Scotch Plains (N.J.) Pub. Schs., 1957-61; prof. music Truman State U., Kirksville, 1961—, chair dept. music, 1994—. Author: Handbook for Woodwinds, 1965, Developing Individual Skills for the High School Band, 1969, How to Develop and Maintain a Successful Woodwind Section, 1972, Original Manuscript Music, 1973, Handbook of Rehearsal Techniques for Band, 1976; numerous papers and monographs; nat. bd. editors The Quarterly, jour. of Ctr. for Rsch. in Music Learning and Teaching, 1989. Dir. music First United Meth. Ch., Kirksville, 1970—. Served with U.S. Army, 1951-55. Mem. Coun. for Rsch. in Music Edn., Nat. Assn. Coll. Wind and Percussion Instrs. (nat. exec. sec./treas. 1971—, editor jour. 1968—), Music Educators Nat. Conf., Phi Delta Kappa. Office: NACWPI Truman State U Divsn Fine Arts Kirksville MO 63501

WEESE, BENJAMIN HORACE, architect; b. Evanston, Ill., June 4, 1929; s. Harry Ernest and Marjorie (Mohr) W.; m. Cynthia Rogers, July 5, 1963; children: Daniel Peter, Catharine Mohr. B.Arch., Harvard U., 1951, M.Arch., 1957; cert., Ecole des Beaux Arts, Fontainebleau, France, 1956. Assoc., Harry Weese & Assocs., Architects, Chgo., 1957-77; prin. Weese Langley Weese, Chgo., 1977—. Co-founder, pres. Chgo. Arch. Found., Glessner House, Chgo., 1966. Trustee Graham Found. for Advanced Studies in Fine Arts, 1988-2006, pres. 1995-99; mem. Commn. Chgo. Landmarks, 1998—. Fellow: AIA. Home: 2133 N Hudson Ave Chicago IL 60614-4522 Office: Weese Langley Weese Ltd 9 W Hubbard St Chicago IL 60610-4630 Office Phone: 312-642-1820. Business E-Mail: bweese@wlwltd.com.

WEESE, CYNTHIA ROGERS, architect, educator; b. Des Moines, June 23, 1940; d. Gilbert Taylor and Catharine (Wingard) Rogers; m. Benjamin H. Weese, July 5, 1963; children: Daniel Peter, Catharine Mohr. BSA.S., Washington U., St. Louis, 1962; B.Arch., Washington U., 1965. Registered architect, Ill. Pvt. practice architecture, Chgo., 1965-72, 74-77; draftsperson, designer Harry Weese & Assocs., Chgo., 1972-74; prin. Weese Langley Weese Ltd., Chgo., 1977—; design critic Ball State U., Muncie, Ind., Miami U., Oxford, Ohio, 1979, U. Wis.-Milw., 1980, U. Ill.-Chgo., 1981, 85, Iowa State U., Ames, 1982, Washington U., St. Louis, 1984, U. Ill., Champaign, 1987-92, Kans. State U., 1992; dean sch. architecture Washington U., St. Louis, 1993—. Bd. regents Am. Architecture Found., 1990-93; bd. mem. Landmarks Commn. St. Louis.; mem. Mayor's Task Force Downtown Now, St. Louis, 1997—. Recipient Alpha Rho Chi award Washington U., 1965, Met. Chgo. YWCA Outstanding Achievement award, 1990. Mem. AIA (bd. dirs. Chgo. chpt. 1980-83, v.p. 1983-85, 1st v.p. 1986-87, pres. 1987-88, regional dir. 1990-92, Disting. Bldg. awards 1977, 81-83, 86, 91, 95, Interior Architecture award 1981, 90, 92, nat. v.p. 1993, chmn. urban design task force St. Louis 2004 1997—), AIA/ACSA Coun. on Archtl. Rsch. (chair 1991-92), AIA Found. (pres. Chgo. chpt. 1988-89), Soc. Archtl. Historians (bd. dirs. 1992-94), Chgo. Women in Architecture, Chgo. Network, Nat. Inst. Archtl. Edn. (bd. dirs. 1988-90), Chgo. Archtl. Club (pres. 1988-89),

Washington U. Sch. Architecture Alumni (nat. coun. 1988-93), Lambda Alpha. Clubs: Arts, Chgo. Archtl. Democrat. Office: Washington U Sch Architecture PO Box 1079 Saint Louis MO 63188-1079

WEFALD, JON, academic administrator; b. Nov. 24, 1937; s. Olav and Walma (Ovrum) W.; m. Ruth Ann; children— Skipp, Andy. BA, Pacific Lutheran U., Tacoma, 1959; MA, Wash. State U., Pullman, 1961; PhD, U. Mich., Ann Arbor, 1965. Teaching asst. Wash. State U., Pullman, 1959—61; teaching fellow U. Mich., Ann Arbor, 1961—64; assoc. prof. Gustavus Adolphus Coll., St. Peter, Minn., 1965—70; commnr. agr. State of Minn., St. Paul, 1971—77; pres. Southwest State U., Marshall, Minn., 1977—82; chancellor Minn. State Univ. System, St. Paul, 1982—86; pres. Kans. State U., Manhattan, 1986—. Author: A Voice of Protest: orwegians in American Politics 1890-1917, 1971. Mem. Mid-Am. Internat. Agri-Trade Council (pres. 1974-75), Midwest Assn. State Depts. of Agr. (sec.treas. 1976-77), U.S. Dept. Agr. Joint Council on Food and Agrl. Scis. Office: Kans State U Office of Pres 110 Anderson Hall Manhattan KS 66506-0100 Office Phone: 785-532-6221. E-mail: pres@ksu.edu.

WEFALD, SUSAN, state commissioner; m. Robert O. Wefald; children: Sarah, Kathryn, Tom. BA, U. Mich., 1969; postgrad., U. N.D. Licensed social worker; cert. consumer credit counselor. Elected mem. Bismarck Pub. Sch. Bd., pres.; commr. N.D. Pub. Svc. Commn. Mem. Energy Conservation Com., Com. Consumer Affairs at. Assn. Regulatory Utility Commrs.; sec. Mid Am. Regulatory Commn. Violinist, charter mem. Bismarck-Mandan Symphony Orch.; pres. Sakakawea Girl Scout Coun.; bd. dirs. Mo. Slope United Way. Office: ND Pub Svc Commn 600 E Boulevard Ave Bismarck ND 58505-0660 Fax: 701-328-2410.

WEG, JOHN GERARD, physician; b. NYC, Feb. 16, 1934; s. Leonard and Pauline M. (Kanzleiter) W.; m. Mary Loretta Flynn, June 2, 1956; children: Diane Marie, Kathryn Mary, Carol Ann, Loretta Louise, Veronica Susanne, Michelle Celeste. BA cum laude, Coll. Holy Cross, Worcester, Mass., 1955; MD, N.Y. Med. Coll., 1959. Diplomate: Am. Bd. Internal Medicine. Commd. 2nd lt. USAF, 1958, advanced through grades to capt., 1967; intern Walter Reed Gen. Hosp., Washington, 1959-60; resident, then chief resident in internal medicine Wilford Hall USAF Hosp., Lackland AFB, Tex., 1960-64, chief pulmonary sect., 1964-66, chief inhalation sect., 1964-66, chief pulmonary and infectious disease service, 1966-67; resigned, 1967; clin. dir. pulmonary disease div. Jefferson Davis Hosp., Houston, 1967-71; from asst. prof. to assoc. prof. medicine Baylor U. Coll. Medicine, Houston, 1967-71; assoc. prof. medicine U. Mich. Med. Sch. Univ. Hosp., Ann Arbor, 1971-74, prof., 1974—2001, prof. emeritus, 2001—. Physician-in-charge pulmonary divsn., 1971-81, physician-in-charge pulmonary and critical care med. divsn., 1981-85, co-chair instnl. review bd., 2004—; cons. Ann Arbor VA, 1971—, Wayne County Gen. Hosps., 1971-84; mem. adv. bd. Washtenaw County Health Dept., 1973—; mem. respiratory and nervous sys. panel, anesthesiology sect. Nat. Ctr. Devices and Radiol. Health, FDA, 1983—, chmn., 1985-88. Contbr. med. jours., reviewer, mem. editorial bds. Decorated Air Force Commendation medal; travelling fellow Nat. Tb and Respiratory Disease Assn., 1971; recipient Aesculpaius award Tex. Med. Assn., 1971 Master ACP (chmn. Mich. program com. 1974); fellow Am. Coll. Chest Physicians (chmn. bd. govs. 1976-79, gov. Mich. 1975-79, chmn. membership com. 1976-79, prof.-in-residence 1972—, chmn. critical care coun. 1982-85, chmn. ethics com. 1998, master fellow, 2002, master FCCP, 2002, master), Am. Coll. Chest Physicians and Internat. Acad. Chest Physicians (master, exec. council 1976-82, pres. 1980-81); mem. AAAS, Am. Fedn. Clin. Rsch., AMA, Am. Thoracic Soc. (sec.-treas. 1974-76), Am. Assn. Inhalation Therapy, Air Force Soc. Internists and Allied Specialists, Soc. Med. Consultants to Armed Forces, Internat. Union Against Tb, Mich. Thoracic Soc. (pres. 1976-78), Mich. Lung Assn. (dir., Bruce Douglas award 1981), Am. Lung Assn., Rsch. Club U. Mich., Assn. Advancement Med. Instrumentation, Central Soc. Clin. Rsch., Am. Bd. Internal Medicine (subsplty. com. on pulmonary disease 1980-86, critical care medicine test com. 1985-87, critical care medicine policy com. 1986-87), .Y. Med. Coll. Alumni Assn. (medal of honor 1990), Alpha Omega Alpha. Home: 3060 Exmoor Rd Ann Arbor MI 48104-4132 Office: B I H 245 Box 0026 1500 E Medical Center Dr Ann Arbor MI 48109-0005 Home Phone: 734-971-6156; Office Phone: 734-763-2540. Business E-Mail: jweg@umich.edu.

WEHRBEIN, ROGER RALPH, state legislator; b. Lincoln, Nebr., Aug. 18, 1938; s. Ralph Jennings and Vivian Lucille (Johns) W.; m. Jeanene Arlene Markussen, Oct. 7, 1961; children: Douglas, David. BS in Animal Scis., U. Nebr., 1960. Farmer, livestock feeder Breeze Valley Farms Inc., Plattsmouth, Nebr., 1962—; mem. Nebr. Legislature from 2nd dist., Lincoln, 1987—. Chair appropriations com. 1995—; bd. dirs. Lincoln Fed. Land Bank Assn., AG Builders of Nebr. Bd. dirs. Leadership-Edn.-Action-Devel. (LEAD), Lincoln, 1988-94. Capt. U.S. Army, 1961-62. Named to Nebr. Hall of Agrl. Achievement, 1988, honoree, 1999; U. Nebr. Block and Bridle Club honoree, 1993. Mem. Nebr. Cattlemen's Assn. (pres. 1985), Nebr. Pork Producers, Ag-Bldrs. Nebr., Toastmasters (pres. Plattsmouth chpt. 1983), Am. Legion, Nebr. Farm Bur., Rotary (pres. Plattsmouth chpt. 1983), Masons, Kiwanis (Outstanding Farmer Omaha 1985), Alpha Gamma Rho. Republican. Presbyterian. Avocations: reading, travel, agriculture. Home: 5812 Highway 66 Plattsmouth NE 68048-7488

WEHRLE, LEROY SNYDER, economist, educator; b. St. Louis, Feb. 5, 1932; s. Fred Joseph and Eleanor (Snyder) W.; m. JoAnn Griffith, Aug. 29, 1959; children— Chandra Lee, Lon Joseph. BS, Washington U., St. Louis, 1953; MA in Econs, Yale, 1956, PhD with honors, 1959. Asst. instr. Yale, 1958-59; with econ. sect. AID mission to Laos, 1960-61; sr. staff economist President's Council Econ. Advisers, 1961-62; spl. econ. adviser to U.S. Ambassador Unger, Vientiane, 1962; dep. dir. AID mission to Laos, 1963-64; asst. dir. AID mission, also econ. counsellor to U.S. ambassador, Saigon, 1964-67; asso. dir. AID Mission, Saigon, 1964-67; dept. asst. adminstr. Vietnam, AID, Dept. State, 1967-68; univ. fellow Harvard, 1968-69; sr. fellow Brookings Instn., 1969-70; dir. Ill. Inst. for Social Policy, Springfield, 1970-72; aide to Lt. Gov. Paul Simon, 1972; prof. economics Sangamon State U., 1972-88; founding ptnr., chief exec. officer Health Econs. and Mkt. Analysis Inc., Springfield, 1987-94; pres. Healthcare Cost Analysis, Inc., 1994—. Chmn. bd. Tie Collar, Ltd. Mem. spl. study group Alliance Progress, 1962; mem. Rockefeller Latin Am. Mission, 1969; chmn. study team world food and nutrition study Nat. Acad. Sci., 1976-77. Served with AUS, 1953-55. Recipient William A. Jump meml. award, 1966 Home and Office: 2001 S Bates Ave Springfield IL 62704-3304 Office Phone: 217-206-7781. Personal E-mail: wehrle@springnet1.com.

WEHRWEIN, AUSTIN CARL, freelance/self-employed reporter; b. Austin, Tex., Jan. 12, 1916; s. George S. and Anna (Ruby) W.; m. Judith Oakes, 1950; children: Sven Austin, Paul, Peter, Joanna Judith. AB, U. Wis., 1937; LL.B., Columbia U., 1940; student, London Sch. Econs., 1948. Reporter Washington Bur., UP, 1941-43, 46-48; information specialist E.C.A., London, Copenhagen, Oslo, Stockholm, 1948-51; financial writer Milw. Jour., 1951-53; staff corr. Time, Inc., Chgo., 1953-55; reporter Chgo. Sun-Times, 1955-56, fin. editor, 1956-57; chief Chgo. bur. N.Y. Times, 1957-66; editorial writer Mpls. Star, 1966-82. Editor The Observer, 1984-87. Served with USAAF, 1943-45; mem. staff Stars and Stripes 1945-46, Shanghai, China. Recipient Pulitzer prize for internat. reporting, 1953; Disting. Journalism award U. Wis., 1963; cert. of merit ABA Gavel competition, 1968, 80; Gavel award, 1969, 71 Home and Office: 2309 Carter Ave Saint Paul MN 55108-1640 E-mail: wehr2309@msn.com.

WEICHSELBAUM, RALPH R., oncologist, department chairman; BS, U. Wis., 1967; MD, U. Ill., Chgo., 1971. Intern Alameda County Hosp., Oakland, Calif., 1971-72; resident in radiation therapy Harvard Med. Sch., Boston, 1972-75; assoc. prof. radiation therapy Harvard Med. Ctr., Boston, 1980-84; assoc. prof. dept. cancer biology Harvard Sch. Public Health, Boston, 1983-84; prof., chmn. dept. radiation and cellular omcology Pritzker Sch. Medicine U. Chgo., 1984—, Harold H. Hines Jr. prof., chmn., 1990; head Michael Reese/U. Chgo. Ctr. Radiation Therapy, 1984—. Contbr. articles to profl. jours. Office: Ctr for Radiation Therapy Pritzker Sch of Medicine 5841 S Maryland Ave Chicago IL 60637-1463

WEIDENAAR, DENNIS JAY, retired economics professor; b. Grand Rapids, Mich., Oct. 4, 1936; s. John and Jennie (Beukema) W.; m. Kristin Andrews, July 14, 1943; children: Kaarin Jaye, John Andrews. AB, Calvin Coll., Grand Rapids, 1958; MA, U. Chgo., 1961; PhD, Purdue U., 1969. Asst. prof. econs. Purdue U., West Lafayette, Ind., 1966-72, assoc. prof., 1972-77, prof., 1977-83; interim dean Krannert Sch. of Mgmt., West Lafayette, 1983-84, assoc. dean, 1984-99; dean Krannert Grad. Sch. Mgmt., West Lafayette, 1990-99, prof. econs., 1999—. Cons. TRW, B.F. Goodrich, Ea. Panhandle; bd. dirs. Lafayette Ins. Co. Author: Economics. Contbr. articles to profl. jours. Bd. dirs. Ind. Coun. on Econ. Edn., Lafayette, 1974-83. Recipient The Leavey Awd for Excellence in Pvt. Enterprise Edn., Freedom's Found., Valley Forge, 1983, Distinguished Service Awd., Joint Council on Econ. Edn., N.Y., 1986, Golden Key Nat. Honor Soc., 1985. Mem. Rotary, Delta Sigma Pi, Beta Gamma Sigma (bd. dirs.), Phi Delta Kappa. Presbyterian. Home: 217 Rosebank Ln West Lafayette IN 47906-8614

WEIDENBAUM, MURRAY LEW, economist, educator; b. Bronx, NY, Feb. 10, 1927; s. David and Rose (Warshaw) Weidenbaum; m. Phyllis Green, June 13, 1954; children: Susan, James, Laurie. BBA, CCNY, 1948; MA, Columbia U., 1949; MPA, Princeton U., 1954, PhD, 1958; LLD, Baruch Coll., 1981, U. Evansville, 1983, McKendree Coll., 1993. Fiscal economist Bur. Budget, Washington, 1949—57; corp. economist Boeing Co., Seattle, 1958—62; sr. economist Stanford Rsch. Inst., Palo Alto, Calif., 1962—63; mem. faculty Washington U., St. Louis, 1964—, prof., chmn. dept. econs., 1966—69, Mallinckrodt prof., 1971—, dir. Ctr. for Study Am. Bus., 1974—81, Washington U., St. Louis, 1982—95; chmn. Ctr. for Study Am. Bus. Washington U., St. Louis, 1995—2000; asst. sec. econ. policy US Dept. Treasury, Washington, 1969—71; chmn. Coun. of Econ. Advisors The White House, Washington, 1981—82; hon. chmn. Weidenbaum Ctr. on the Economy, Govt. and Pub. Policy, St. Louis, 2001—. Chmn. rsch. adv. com. St. Louis Regional Indsl. Devel. Corp., 1965—69; exec. sec. Pres.'s Com. on Econ. Impact of Def. and Disarmament, 1964; mem. U.S. Fin. Investment Adv. Panel, 1970—72; cons. various firms and instns.; chmn. U.S. Commn. to Rev. the Trade Deficit, 1999—2000. Author: Federal Budgeting, 1964, Modern Public Sector, 1969, Economics of Peacetime Defense, 1974, Economic Impact of the Vietnam War, 1967, Government-Mandated Price Increases, 1975, The Future of Business Regulation, 1980, Rendezvous With Reality: The American Economy After Reagan, 1988, Rendezvous With Reality: The American Economy After Reagan, paperback edit., 1990, Business, Government, and the Public, 1990, Small Wars, Big Defense, 1992, The Bamboo Network, 1996, Business and Government in the Global Marketplace, 2004, One-Armed Economist, 2004, Advising Reagan: Making Economic Policy, 1981-82, 2005; mem. editl. bd.: Publius, 1971—2004, Jour. Econ. Issues, 1972—75, Challenge, 1974—81, 1983—, Business and the Contemporary World, 1997—2000. With US Army, 1945. Named Banbury fellow, Princeton U., 1952—54; named to Free Market Hall of Fame, 1983; recipient Alexander Hamilton medal, U.S. Dept. Treasury, 1971, Disting. Writer award, Georgetown U., award for disting. tchg., Freedoms Found., 1980, award for best book in econs., Assn. Am. Pubs., 1993. Fellow: Internat. Acad. Mgmt., Am. Acad. Arts & Scis., Assn. for Pvt. Enterprise Edn. (Adam Smith award 1986), City Coll. Alumni Assn. (Townsend Harris medal 1969), Soc. Tech. Comm., Nat. Assn. Bus. Economists, Cosmos. Office: Washington Univ Weidenbaum Ctr 1 Brookings Dr Saint Louis MO 63130-4899 Home Phone: 314-727-8950; Office Phone: 314-935-5662.

WEIDENTHAL, MAURICE DAVID (BUD), academic administrator, journalist; b. Cleve., Nov. 26, 1925; s. William and Evelyn Kolinsky W.; m. Grace Schwartz, Apr. 14, 1957 (dec.); 1 child, Susan Elizabeth Weldenthal Saltzman. BA, U. Mich., 1950. Mem. staff Cleve. Press, 1950-81, editl. writer, 1950-51, asst. city editor, 1956-58, edn. editor, 1958-81; v.p. pub. affairs Cuyahoga C.C. Dist., Cleve., 1981-88; dir. Urban Colls. Project, Cleve., 1989—. Editor The Urban Report, Cleve., 1989-2005; writer, cons. Ranc Inc., Georgetown, Tex., 2007-. Pub. affairs com. Greater Cleve. Growth Assn., 1981-88; bd. advisors Coun. for Advancement and Support of Edn., 1981-88, Nat. Coun. Mktg. and Pub. Rels., 1981-2005; alt. bd. dirs. St. Vincent Quadrangle, 1983-88; trustee Hebrew Free Loan Assn., 1975-86. With AUS, 1944-45. Decorated Air medal. Mem. Edn. Writers Assn., Soc. Profl. Journalists, (bd. dirs. 1996-2003), Cleve. City Club (bd. dirs. 1969-76), Cleve. Press Club. Home: 25858 Fairmount Blvd Cleveland OH 44122-2214 Office: 4250 Richmond Rd Cleveland OH 44122-6104 Personal E-mail: u2w@roadrunner.com. Business E-Mail: bud.weidenthal@tri-c.edu.

WEIGEL, RAYMOND A., manufacturing executive; b. 1917; Grad., DePaul U., Walton Sch. Commerce. Sec., treas. Lonergan Corp., 1943—46; asst. to pres. Kysor Indsl. Corp., Cadillac, Mich., 1946—48, v.p., gen. mgr., 1948—52, pres., 1952—, chmn. bd., CEO, 1962—75, CEO, dir., 1975—78. Dir. Gerber Products. Office: Kysor Industrial Corp 1 Madison Ave PO Box 579 Cadillac MI 49601-0579

WEIGERT, ANDREW JOSEPH, sociology educator; b. NYC, Apr. 8, 1934; s. Andrew Joseph and Marie Teresa (Kollmer) W.; m. Kathleen Rose Maas, Aug. 31, 1967; children: Karen Rose, Sheila Marie. BA, St. Louis U., 1958, PhL, 1959, MA, 1960; BTh, Woodstock Coll, Md., 1964; PhD, U. Minn., 1968. NIMH trainee U. Minn., Mpls., 1965-67; asst. prof. sociology U. Notre Dame, Ind., 1968-72, assoc. prof. Ind., 1972-76, prof. Ind., 1976—, chmn. dept. Ind., 1980-84, 88-89. Vis. assoc. prof. Yale U., New Haven, 1973-74. Co-author: Family Socialization, 1974, Interpretive Sociology, 1978, Society and Identity, 1986; author: Everyday Life, 1981, Social Psychology, 1983, Life and Society, 1983, Mixed Emotions, 1991, Self, Interaction, and Natural Environment, 1997, Religious and Secular Views on Endtime, 2004; adv. editor various sociology jours.; contbr. articles to profl. jours., chpts. to books. Recipient tchg. awards, 1999, 2002, 05; NSF grantee, 1969. Avocation: woodlot and prairie management. Office: U Notre Dame Dept Sociology Notre Dame IN 46556 Office Phone: 574-631-7408. Business E-Mail: aweigert@nd.edu.

WEIHING, JOHN LAWSON, plant pathologist, state legislator; b. Rocky Ford, Colo., Feb. 26, 1921; s. Henry John and Clara Adele (Krull) W.; m. Shirley Ruth Wilkerson, Aug. 18, 1948; children: Lawson James, Martin Roy, Adell Ann, Warren John. BS in Agronomy, Colo. State U., 1942; MSc in Agronomy, U. Nebr., 1949, PhD in Botany and Plant Pathology, 1954. Instr. plant pathology U. Nebr., Lincoln, 1950-54, asst. prof., 1954-56, assoc. prof., 1956-60, prof., 1960-61, 62-64, 66-71, prof., interim chmn. plant pathology dept., 1961-62, prof., dir. Panhandle Rsch. and Extension Ctr. Scottsbluff, 1971-84, with Alumni Office, Panhandle Found. Scottsbluf, 1984-86; prof., chmn. plant sci. dept. Ataturk U., Erzurum, Turkey, 1964-66; mem. dist. 48 Nebr. Legislature, Lincoln, 1987-91. Cons. Am. Hydrponics Systems, Inc., Grapevine, Tex., 1969-72. Creator U. Nebr. TV series Backyard Farmer, The Equation of Nature, 1959-60. Campaign chmn. United Way, Scottsbluff and Gering, Nebr., 1978. Lt. U.S. Army, 1942-46. Recipient Honor award Soil Conservation Soc. Am., 1982, Merit award Gamma Sigma Delta, 1977, Disting. Svc. award Nebr. Turfgrass Found., 1982, Nebr. Coop. Extension, 1970; named to Nebr. Hall Agrl. Achievement, 1987. Mem. Am. Phytopathol. Soc. (chmn. nat. extension com. 1963, pres. north cen. dir. 1971-72), AAAS, Am. Inst. Biol. Scis., Nebr. State Hist. Soc. (trustee 1992—), Scottsbluff/Gering United C. of C. (pres. 1980-81), Rotary (bd. dirs. 1977-80), Elks. Republican. Presbyterian. Avocation: archaeology. Home: 1605 Holly Dr Gering NE 69341-1954

WEIKEL, MALCOLM KEITH, healthcare company executive; b. Shamokin, Pa., Mar. 9, 1938; s. Malcolm J. and Marian Eleanor (Faust) Weikel; m. Barbara Joan Davis, Dec. 17, 1960; children: Richard, Kristin. BSc, Phila. Coll. Pharmacy and Sci., 1960; MSc, U. Wis., 1962, PhD, 1966. Mgr. Roche Labs., 1966—70; commr. health svcs. HEW, Washington, 1970—77; v.p. Am. Med. Internat., 1978—82, pres., CEO, 1982—84; exec. v.p., COO, Manor Healthcare Corp., Silver Spring, Md., 1984—86; exec. v.p. Health Care & Retirement Corp., Toledo, 1986—88, sr. exec. v.p., COO, 1988—98, sr. exec. v.p., 1998—. Recipient Sec.'s Spl. citation, HEW, 1975, 1977. Mem.: Am. Health Care Assn. (v.p. 1990—, chmn. multifacility group 1990—93). Office: Health Care & Retirement Corp PO Box 10086 Toledo OH 43699-0086

WEIL, CASS SARGENT, lawyer; b. NYC, Nov. 6, 1946; s. Theodore and Ruth Frances (Sargent) W. BA, SUNY, Stonybrook, 1968; JD cum laude, William Mitchell Coll. of Law, 1980. Bar: Minn. 1980, U.S. Dist. Ct. Minn. 1980, U.S. Ct. Appeals (8th cir.) 1980, Wis. 1984, U.S. Ct. Appeals (7th cir.) 1984; cert. bankruptcy law specialist, consumer and bus. Am. Bd. Certification. Assoc. J.R. Kotts & Assoc., Mpls., 1980-81, Wagner, Rutchick & Trojack, St. Paul, 1981-83; ptnr. Zohlmann & Weil, Wilmar, Minn., 1983, Peterson, Franke & Riach, P.A., St. Paul, 1983-91, O'Connor & Hannan, Mpls., 1991-94, Moss & Barnett, P.A., Mpls., 1994—. Editor: Minn. Legal Forms, Bankruptcy, 1983, 1987, 1991, 1992, 1993. Recipient Leading Am. Atty. award Am. Rsch. Corp., 1994, 96, 98, 2000, 02-07; named one of Minn. Top Lawyers Mpls. St. Paul Mag., 1998, 2005; named Super Lawyer Minn. Jour. Law and Politics, 2005-07. Mem. ABA (comml. fraud task force, 2006-08, mem. ctr. profl. responsibility, 2006-08) Minn. Bar Assn. (vice chmn. bankruptcy sect. 1984-88, chmn. 1988-89, profl. com., 2007-08, com. rules of profl. conduct, 2007-08), Wis. Bar Assn., Hennepin County Bar Assn. (co-chmn. debtor/creditor law sect. 2006-07), Am. Bankruptcy Inst., Turnaround Mgmt. Assn., Comml. Law League Am., Order of Barristers. Democrat. Jewish. Office: Moss & Barnett 4800 Wells Fargo Ctr 90 S Seventh St Minneapolis MN 55402 Office Phone: 612-877-5000. Business E-Mail: weilc@moss-barnett.com.

WEIL, D(ONALD) WALLACE, business administration educator; b. Cleve., July 20, 1923; s. Laurence J. and Carol S. (Wallace) W.; m. Jane A. Bittel, Dec. 29, 1947; children— John Wallace, Charles Andrew, Margaret Jane, Carol Wyn. BA, Oberlin Coll., 1947; JD, Willamette U., 1950. Pres. James Foundry Corp., Fort Atkinson, Wis., 1960-70; faculty bus. adminstrn. U. Wis., Eau Claire, 1971-74, chmn. dept. bus. adminstrn., 1974-77, prof., 1985—2003, ret., prof. emeritis, 2003—; pres. Diversified Industries, Inc., St. Louis, 1977-81, UHI Corp., Los Angeles, 1981-85. Dir. U.H.I. Corp. Diversified Industries, Inc., St. Louis, Sales Investments, Mgmt. Inc., Elmwood, Wis., Jane B. Inc., Eau Claire Served with AUS, 1942-45. Mem. Nat. SAR (life), Wis. SAR, Am. Security Council, Nat. Council Small Bus. Mgmt. Devel., Phi Kappa Phi, Beta Gamma Sigma. Republican. Congregationalist. Office: U Wis-Eau Claire Dept Bus Adminstrn Eau Claire WI 54701 Home: 11201 Fairfield Rd Apt 300A Minnetonka MN 55305

WEIL, IRWIN, literature and language professor; b. Cin., Apr. 16, 1928; s. Sidney and Florence (Levy) W.; m. Vivian Weil, Dec. 27, 1950; children: Martin, Alice, Daniel. AB, U. Chgo., 1948, MA, 1951; PhD, Harvard U., 1960; doctorate (hon.), Nevsky Inst., St. Petersburg, Russia, 1999, Russian State U. Humanities, Moscow, 2007. Sr. social sci. research analyst Library of Congress, 1951-54; teaching fellow Harvard U., 1956-58; mem. faculty Brandeis U., 1958-65; mem. faculty dept. Slavic langs. and lit. Northwestern U., Evanston, Ill., 1966—, chmn. dept., 1976-82. Vis. prof. U. Moscow, Soviet Acad. Scis.; set up series of internat. symposia between Am. scholars and USSR Acad. Scis.; founder 1st Soviet-Am. TV Student Competition in Lit., 1988-89; active in establishment of American Studies Ctr. Humanities U., Moscow, Russia. Author books and articles pub. in field; lectr. recordings, 36 Lectures on Russian Lit., 2006. Recipient Pushkin Internat. gold medal for outstanding teaching and research, 1984, Outstanding Teaching award Northwestern U. Alumni Assn., 1987, Tempo All-Professor Team, Humanities, Chicago Tribune, 1993; Ford Found. fellow, 1954-55. Mem. Am. Assn. Tchrs. Slavic and East European Langs. (exec. sec. 1962-68, Excellence in Teaching award 1993), Am. Coun. Tchrs. Russian (v.p. 1975-79, pres. 1980-84), Internat. Assn. Profs. Russian (founding U.S. mem.). Jewish. Achievements include establishing TV competition on American and Russian literature between American and Russian high schoolers. Office: Northwestern U Slavic Dept Evanston IL 60208-0001 Home Phone: 847-864-4835; Office Phone: 847-491-8254. Business E-Mail: i-weil@northwestern.edu.

WEIL, JOHN WILLIAM, technology management consultant; b. NYC, Feb. 3, 1928; s. Frank Leopold and Henrietta Amelia Weil; m. Joan Leatrice Landis, June 15, 1950; children: Nancy Ellen, Linda Jill. BS, MIT, Cambridge, 1948; PhD, Cornell U., Ithaca, NY, 1953. Various positions in nuclear reactors and computers Gen. Electric Co. (various locations), 1953-70; v.p. advanced systems and tech. Honeywell Info. Systems, Inc., Waltham, Mass., 1970-74; v.p., chief tech. officer Bendix Corp., Southfield, Mich., 1974-77, sr. v.p., chief tech. officer, 1977-83; v.p. advanced tech. and engring. Allied Corp., Southfield, 1983; pres. Modular Bio Systems, Inc., 1983-85, Weil Assocs., Inc., Bloomfield Hills, Mich., 1985-97. Founder Met. Detroit Sci. and Engring. Coalition, 1977, sec., 1977-80, pres., 1980-82; chmn. Mich. Biotech. Inst., 1981-85, trustee, 1985-92; mem. Army Sci. Bd., 1982-84. Contbr. articles to prof. jours. AEC fellow, 1950-51 Home and Office: 218 Guilford Rd Bloomfield Hills MI 48304-2737 Personal E-mail: johnww@weilhome.com.

WEIL, ROLF ALFRED, economist, retired university president; b. Pforzheim, Germany, Oct. 29, 1921; arrived in U.S., 1936, naturalized, 1944; s. Henry and Lina (Landauer) W.; m. Leni Metzger, Nov. 3, 1945; children: Susan Linda, Ronald Alan. BA, U. Chgo., 1942, PhD, 1950; D Hebrew Letters, Coll. Jewish Studies, 1967; DHL, Loyola U., 1970, Bowling Green State U., Ohio, 1986; LHD, Roosevelt U., 1988. Rsch. asst. Cowles Commn. for Rsch. in Econs., 1942-44; rsch. analyst Ill. Dept. Revenue, 1944-46; mem. faculty Roosevelt U., Chgo., 1946—, prof. fin. and econs., also chmn. dept. fin., 1954-65, dean Coll. Bus. Adminstrn., 1957-64, acting pres., 1965-66, pres., 1966-88, pres. emeritus, 1988—. Past pres. Selfhelp Home for the Aged, Chgo. Author: Through these Portals-from Immigrant to College President, 1991; contbr. articles on fin. to profl. jours. Bd. dirs. trustees Roosevelt U., Selfhelp of Chgo., Inc. Mem. Am. Econ. Assn., Cliff Dwellers Club. Office Phone: 312-341-4330. Personal E-mail: rolfleniweil@aol.com. Business E-Mail: rweil@roosevelt.edu.

WEIL, ROMAN LEE, finance educator; b. Montgomery, Ala., May 22, 1940; s. Roman L. and Charlotte (Alexander) W.; children: Alexis Cherie, Charles Alexander Roman, Lacey Lorraine. BA, Yale U., 1962; MS in Indsl. Adminstrn, Carnegie-Mellon U., 1965, PhD in Econs., 1966. CPA, CMA, Ill. From instr. to prof. U. Chgo., 1965-93, Sigmund E. Edelstone prof. acctg., 1993-97, V. Duane Rath prof. acctg., 1997—, dir. Dir.'s Coll., 1998—; dir. Chgo./Stanford/Wharton Dirs. Consortium, 2002—; Mills B. Lane prof. indsl. mgmt. Ga. Inst. Tech., 1974-76; mem. adv. com. replacement cost implementation SEC, 1976-77. Bd. dirs. NY Life Ins Mainstay VP Funds, chmn. audit com.; prof. acctg. Stanford (Calif.) U., 1984, 2004, prof. econs., 1985, prof. law, 1990-96; prof. acctg. and law YU Sch. Law, 1985; mem. adv. coun. Fin. Acctg. Stds., 1989-94; mem. task force on consolidations Fin. Acctg. Stds. Bd., 1984-89, mem. task force on discounting, 1989-99, mem. task force on fin. instruments, 1994-98, mem. adv. coun., 1989-94; dir. Dir.'s Coll., 1999-; co-founder Chgo./Stanford/Wharton Dir.'s Consortium, 2002-. Author: Fundamentals of Accounting, 1975, Financial Accounting, 10th edit., 2002, Accounting: The Language of Business, 10th edit., 1998, Inflation Accounting, 1976, Replacement Cost Accounting, 1976, Managerial Accounting, 1979, 7th edit., 2000, Litigation Svcs. Handbook, 3d edit., 2001, Litigation Services Report Writing, 2003; editor: Handbook of Modern Accounting, 1977, 3d edit., 1983, Handbook of Cost Accounting, 1980, Handbook of Cost Management, 2005, Acctg. Rev., 1974-79, Fin. Analysts Jour., 1980-88. NSF grantee, 1967-81 Mem. AICPA, Ill. Soc. CPAs, Am. Econ. Assn., Inst. Mgmt. Scis., Nat. Assn. Accts. (cert. mgmt. acct.), Am. Acctg. Assn., Inst. Managerial Acctg., Assembly Am. Collegiate Schs. Bus. (acctg. accreditation com. 1987-88), Oenonomy Soc. (co-chmn.). Home: #306 600 N Kingsbury St Chicago IL 60610 Office: U Chgo Grad Sch Bus 1101 E 58th St Chicago IL 60637-1511 E-mail: roman.weil@gsb.uchicago.edu.

WEILAND, GALEN FRANKLIN, state legislator; s. Joseph Franklin and Ida Lucille (Dunn) W.; m. Ruth Arlene Howland; children: Terry Dean, Teresa Jean. Student, Highland C.C., 1957-58. Kans. state rep. Dist. 49, 1991—. Asst. mgr. Bendena Grain Co. Mem. Elks, Masons. Address: PO Box 217 Bendena KS 66008-0217

WEILER, JEFFRY LOUIS, lawyer; b. NYC, Dec. 31, 1942; s. Kurt and Elaine (Kabb) W.; m. Susan Karen Goodman, June 8, 1964; children: Philip K., June M. BS, Miami U., Oxford, Ohio, 1964; JD, Cleve. State U., 1970. Bar: Ohio 1970, Fla. 1981; CPA, Ohio 1968; bd. cert. specialist in estate planning trust and probate law, Ohio; bd. cert. tax specialist, Fla., 1983—. Acct. Meaden & Moore, CPAs, Cleve., 1964-65; IRS agt. U.S. Dept. Treasury, Cleve., 1965-70; assoc. Ulmer & Berne, Cleve., 1970-71; ptnr. Benesch, Friedlander, Coplan & Aronoff, LLP, Cleve., 1971—. Adj. assoc. prof. Cleve.-Marshall Coll. Law, Cleve. State U., 1980-87. Contbr. to profl. pubs. Named Disting. Estate Planner, Estate Planning Coun. Cleve., 2004; named one of Top 50 in Cleve., Ohio Super Lawyers, 2004—08, Top 100 in Ohio, 2004—08. Fellow Am. Coll. Trust and Estate Counsel; mem. ABA (sect. taxation), Ohio State Bar Assn. (coun. estate planning trust and probate law sect. 1999—), Cleve. Estate Planning Inst. (chmn. 1980), Cleve. Tax Inst. (chmn. 1983), Cleve. Bar Assn. (treas. 1993-96, trustee 1988-91), Tax Club of Cleve. (sec. 1996-97, v.p. 1997-99, pres. 1999-2000). Avocations: photography, sailboat racing. Office: Benesch Friedlander Coplan & Aronoff LLP 2300 BP Tower 200 Public Sq Cleveland OH 44114-2378 Home: 451 Muirfield Dr Highland Heights OH 44143 Home Phone: 440-446-8081; Office Phone: 216-363-4551. Business E-Mail: jweiler@bfca.com.

WEINBERG, DAVID B., investor; b. Chgo., Feb. 19, 1952; s. Judd A. and Marjorie (Gottlieb) W.; m. Lynne Ellen Mesirow, July 6, 1980. AB cum laude, Harvard U., 1974; JD, Georgetown U., 1977. Bar: Ill. 1977, U.S. Dist. Ct. (no. dist.) Ill. 1977, U.S. Ct. Appeals (7th cir.) 1978. Law clerk to Hon. William G.

Clark Supreme Ct. Ill., 1977-79; assoc. Lord, Bissell & Brook, Chgo., 1979-84, ptnr., 1985-89, Mayer, Brown & Platt, Chgo., 1989-96; chmn., CEO Judd Enterprises, Inc., Chgo., 1996—; pres. Digital BandWidth LLC, Chgo., 1996—. Ill. Supreme Ct. com. Profl. Responsibility, Chgo., 1984-94, chmn. subcom. lawyers certification. Chmn. bd. trustees Ravinia Festival Assn., Highland Park, Ill., 1998—2001; vice chmn. bd. trustees Northwestern U., 1999—. Mem. Chgo. Club, Econ. Club Chgo., Lake Shore Country Club, Arts Club Chgo. Office: Judd Enterprises Bank One Plz 21 S Clark St Ste 3140 Chicago IL 60603-2090

WEINBERG, EUGENE DAVID, microbiologist, educator; b. Chgo., Mar. 4, 1922; s. Philip and Lenore (Bergman) W.; m. Frances Murl Izen, Sept. 5, 1949; children— Barbara Ann, Marjorie Jean, Geoffrey Alan, Michael Benjamin. BS, U. Chgo., 1942, MA, 1948, PhD, 1950. Instr. dept. microbiology Ind. U., Bloomington, 1950-53, asst. prof., 1953-57, asso. prof., 1957-61, prof., 1961—, head microbiology sect., med. sci. program, 1978—92. Mem. sci. adv. bd., chair publs. Iron Disorders Inst., 1998—. Served with AUS, 1942-45. Mem.: Am. Soc. Microbiology. Office: Ind U Biology Dept Jordan Hall Bloomington IN 47405 Office Phone: 812-336-5556. Fax: 812-855-6705. Business E-Mail: eweinber@indiana.edu.

WEINBERG, JUSTIN PETER, lawyer; b. 1976; married; 2 children. BA magna cum laude, St. Cloud State U., 1998; JD, William Mitchell Coll. Law, 2001. Bar: Minn. 2001, US Dist. Ct. (dist. Minn.) 2001, US Ct. Appeals (8th cir.) 2006. Assoc. Gislason & Hunter, L.L.P., New Ulm, Minn. Named a Rising Star, Minn. Super Lawyers mag., 2006. Mem.: Minn. Bar Assn. (mem. litig. and constrn. law sects.), ABA (mem. litig. and bus. sects.). Office: Gislason & Hunter LLP 2700 S Broadway PO Box 458 New Ulm MN 56073 Office Phone: 507-354-3111. E-mail: jweinberg@gislason.com.

WEINBERG, RICHARD ALAN, psychologist, educator; b. Chgo., Jan. 28, 1943; s. Meyer and Mollie I. (Soell) W.; m. Gail E. Blumberg, Aug. 25, 1964; children: Eric, Brett. BS, U. Wis., 1964; MAT, Northwestern U., 1965; PhD, U. Minn., 1968. Lic. psychologist, Minn. Asst. prof. Tchrs. Coll., Columbia U., NYC, 1968-70; prof. ednl. psychology, psychology and child psychology U. Minn., Mpls., 1970—, Birkmaier professorship, 1994-97, U. disting. tchg. prof., 1999—. Former dir. Inst. Child Devel.; former chair adv. coun. Children, Youth, and Family, chair steering com. U. Minn. Pres.'s Initiative on Children, Youth, and Family Consortium; cons. EPA; reviewer Office of Edn., NSF, NRC; guest speaker TV and radio shows. Author: (with A. Boehm) The Classroom Observer: Developing Observation Skills in Early Childhood Settings, 1997, (with Scarr and Levine) Understanding Development, 1986; former assoc. editor Contemporary Psychology; former editor: Applied Developmental Science. Bd. dirs. Children's Mus. Minn.; past pres. Am. Assn. State Psychol. Bds.; trustee Am. Assn. State Psychol. Bds. Found.; liaison Nat. Register Health Care Providers in Psychology. Grantee Bush Found., NSF, NIH. Fellow APA, Am. Psychol. Soc.; mem. Soc. Rsch. in Child Devel. (former chair pub. policy coun., chair fin. comm.), Behavior Genetics Assn., Am. Psychol. Soc. (bd. dirs.), NCAA Championship Cabinet, Phi Beta Kappa, Phi Kappa Phi. Office: U Minn 180 Child Devel 51 E River Rd Minneapolis MN 55455-0365 Business E-Mail: weinb002@umn.edu.

WEINBERG, SYLVAN LEE, cardiologist, educator, editor, writer; b. Nashville, June 14, 1923; s. Abraham J. and Beatrice (Kottler) W.; m. Joan Hutzler, Jan. 29, 1956; children: Andrew Lee, Leslie. BS, Northwestern U., 1945, MD, 1948. From intern to resident, fellow Michael Reese Hosp., Chgo., 1947—51; attending physician Good Samaritan Hosp., Dayton, Ohio, 1953—99, chief of cardiology, 1966—99, founding dir. coronary care unit, 1967—99; clin. prof. medicine Wright State U., Dayton, 1975—; dir. med. edn. Dayton Heart Hosp., 2000—. Former panelist Med. Affairs, nat. TV; pres. Weinberg Marcus Cardiomed. Group, Inc., 1970-99; pres. Arts & Comms. Internat., Inc., 1995—. Author: An Epitaph for Merlin and Perhaps for Medicine, 1983, The Golden Age of Medical Science and the Dark Age of Health Care Delivery, 2000; founding editor Dayton Medicine, 1980—, Heart & Lung, 1972-87, Am. Heart Hosp. Jour., 2002—; contbr. articles to profl. jours. Capt. U.S. Army, 1951-53, Korea. Recipient Army Commendation medal, Richard A. DeWall MD award for excellence in cardiology, Am. Heart Assn., 2001, Outstanding Pub. Svc. award, Ohio State Senate, 1980. Fellow ACP (Ohio Laureate award 1997), Am. Coll. Cardiology (editor in chief jour. ACCEL 1985-2000, pres. 1993-94), Am. Coll. Chest Physicians (pres. 1984); mem. Montgomery County Med. Soc. (pres. 1980). Avocations: writing, travel, golf. Home: 4555 Southern Blvd Dayton OH 45429-1118 Office: Dayton Heart Hosp 707 S Edwin Moses Blvd Dayton OH 45408 Personal E-mail: slwjal@aol.com.

WEINBERG, WALTER S., lawyer; b. Chgo., Sept. 12, 1956; BA in Econs., with hon., U. Chgo., 1978; JD cum laude, Northwestern U., 1981. Bar: Ill. 1981. Ptnr., Chmn. Corp. Group Katten Muchin Rosenman LLP, Chgo. Named one of Am. Leading Lawyers for Bus., Chambers USA, 2005—06, 2006—07, Ill. Super Lawyers, 2007. Mem.: ABA, Chgo. Bar Assn., Order of the Coif, Phi Beta Kappa. Office: Katten Muchin Rosenman LLP 525 W Monroe St Chicago IL 60661 Office Phone: 312-902-5405. Office Fax: 312-577-8771. Business E-Mail: walter.weinberg@kattenlaw.com.

WEINBERGER, MILES M., pediatrician, educator; b. McKeesport, Pa., June 28, 1938; divorced; 4 children; m. Leslie Kramer, Aug. 22, 1992. AB, U. Pitts., 1960, MD, 1965. Diplomate Am. Bd. Pediatrics, Am. Bd. Allergy and Immunology, Am. Bd. Pediatric Pulmonology. Intern U. Calif. Med. Ctr., San Francisco, 1965-66, pediatric resident, 1965-67; research assoc NIH, Bethesda, Md., 1967-69; allergy and pulmonary fellow U. Colo., Denver, 1969-71; staff Ross Valley Med. Clinic, Greenbrae, Calif., 1971-73; clin. pharmacology fellow U. Colo., Denver, 1973-75; divsn. dir. U. Iowa, Iowa City, 1975—. Cons. D.C.Hosp. for Sick Children, 1967-69, allergy and immunology Family Practice Program, Sonoma County Community Hosp., U. Calif. Sch. Medicine, 1972-73; clin. instr. pediatrics Georgetown U. Sch. Medicine, Washington, 1967-69; staff pediatrician part-time West Side Neighborhood Health Ctr., Denver, 1970-71; pediatric sr. staff mem. Nat.Jewish Hosp. and Research Ctr., 1973-75; clin. asst. U. Colo. Med.Ctr., 1974-75; assoc. prof. pediatrics, chmn. pediatric allergy and pulmonary div. U. Iowa Coll. Medicine, 1975-80, assoc. prof. pharmacology, 1975-79, dir. Cystic Fibrosis Ctr., 1977—, prof. pediatrics, 1980—, dir. pediatric allergy and pulmonary div., 1975—. Author: Managing Asthma, 1990; contbr. numerous articles to profl. jours., chpts. to books, also audio-visual materials, commentaries, pub. letters and presentations in field Recipient Clemens von Pirquet award Am. Coll. Allergy, 1974; grantee NIH, 1980-85, Cystic Fibrosis Ctr., Pharm. Mfrs. Assn. Fellow Am. Acad. Pediatrics (allergy sect. 1972, sect. on clin. pharmacology and therapeutics 1978, diseases of chest 1978); mem. Am. Acad. Allergy, Am. Soc. Clin. Pharmacology and Therapeutics, Soc. for Pediatric Rsch., Am. Thoracic Soc. (pres. Iowa Thoracic Soc. 1992-93), Camp Superkids of Iowa (adv. bd. 1981—), Am. Lung Assn. (pediatric pulmonbary ctr. task force com. 1984-86). Office: U Iowa Dept Pediatrics Iowa City IA 52242 Home Phone: 319-338-5807; Office Phone: 319-356-3485. Business E-Mail: miles-weinberger@uiowa.edu.

WEINBERGER, MYRON HILMAR, medical educator; b. Cin., Sept. 21, 1937; s. Samuel and Helen Eleanor (Price) W.; m. Myrna M. Rosenberg, June 12, 1960; children: Howard David, Steven Neal, Debra Ellen. BS, Ind. U., Bloomington, 1959, MD, 1963. Intern Ind. U. Med. Ctr., Indpls., 1963-64, resident in internal medicine, 1964-66, asst. prof. medicine, 1969-73, assoc. prof., 1973-76, prof., 1976—, dir. Hypertension Research Ctr., 1981—; USPHS trainee in endocrinology and metabolism Stanford U. Med. Ctr., Calif., 1966-68, USPHS spl. fellow in hypertension Calif., 1968-69. Contbr. articles to profl. jours. Recipient Tigerstedt award Am. Soc. Hypertension, 1996, Page-Bradley Lifetime Achievement award Am. Heart Assn. Coun. for High Blood Pressure Rsch., 1999. Fellow ACP, Am. Coll. Cardiology, Am. Coll. Nutrition, Am. Soc. for Clin. Pharmacology and Therapeutics; mem. AAAS, Am. Fedn. Clin. Research, AMA, Am. Heart Assn. (lifetime achievement award coun. for high blood pressure rsch. 1999), Am. Soc. Nephrology, Internat. Soc. Nephrology, Central Soc. Clin. Research, Endocrine Soc., Internat. Soc. Hypertension, Soc. for Exptl. Biology and Medicine Home: 135 Bow Ln Indianapolis IN 46220-1023 Office: Ind U Hypertension Research Ctr 541 Clinical Dr Indianapolis IN 46202-5233 Home Phone: 317-253-7927; Office Phone: 317-274-8153. Business E-Mail: mweinbe@iupui.edu.

WEINBROT, HOWARD DAVID, language educator; b. Bklyn., May 14, 1936; s. William and Rose (Shapiro) W.; m. Dawn Simon. BA, Antioch Coll., Yellow Springs, Ohio, 1958; MA with honors (Woodrow Wilson fellow 1959, grad. fellow 1959-63), U. Chgo., 1959, PhD, 1963. Tchg. fellow U. Chgo., 1962-63; instr. English Yale U., 1963-66; asst. prof., then assoc. prof. U. Calif., Riverside, 1966-69; mem. faculty U. Wis., Madison, 1969—, prof. English, 1972-84, Ricardo Quintana prof., 1984-87, Vilas prof., 1987—. Andrew W. Mellon vis. prof. Inst. Advanced Study Princeton, 1993—94. Author: The Formal Strain, 1969, Augustus Caesar in Augustan England, 1978, Alexander Pope and the Traditions of Formal Verse Satire, 1982, Essays on 18th-Century Satire, 1988, paperback, 2007, Britannia's Issue, 1993, paperback, 2007, Aspects of Samuel Johnson, 2005, Menippean Satire Reconsidered, 2005, 07; also numerous articles, revs.; editor: ew Aspects of Lexicography, 1972, Northrop Frye and 18th Century Studies; co-editor: The 18th Century: A Current Bibliography for 1973, 1975, Poetry in English, An Anthology, 1987, Eighteenth-Century Contexts, 2001. Fellow, NEH, 1975—76; Guggenheim fellow, 1988—89, Andrew Mellon fellow, Huntington Libr., 2007, Mary and Donald Rsch. fellow, 2007—, vis. mem., Inst. for Advanced Study, Princeton. Mem. Am. Soc. 18th Century Studies (mem. editl. bd. 1977-80, exec. com. 96-99), Internat. Soc. 18th Century Studies UCLA (planning com. 2003), Johnsonians, Johnson Soc. (sec.-treas. 1970-75, v.p. 2000-01, pres. 2002-03), Midwest Am. Soc. Eighteenth Century Studies, Eighteenth Century Scottish Studies. Home: 1505 Wood Ln Madison WI 53705-1456 Office: U Wis English Dept 600 N Park St Madison WI 53706-1403 Office Phone: 608-263-3819. Business E-Mail: weinbrot@wisc.edu.

WEINER, ANDREW MARC, electrical engineering educator; b. Boston, July 25, 1958; s. Jason and Geraldine Hannah (Aronson) W.; m. Brenda Joyce Garland, Apr. 1, 1989. SB in Elec. Engring., MIT, 1979, SM, 1981, ScD, 1984. Mem. tech. staff Bellcore, Red Bank, N.J., 1984-89, dist. mgr., 1989-92; prof. elec. engring. Purdue U., West Lafayette, Ind., 1992—. Assoc. editor IEEE Jour. Quantum Electronics, 1988-94; adv. editor Optics Letters, 1989-94, topical editor, 1995-98; assoc. editor: IEEE Photonics Tech. Letters, 1994-95. Fannie and John Hertz Found. grad. fellow, 1979-84. Fellow Optical Soc. Am. (tech. coun. 1988-91, Adolph Lomb award 1990), IEEE (Traveling Lectr. award Lasers and Electro-optics Soc. 1988-89, bd. Govs. Lasers and Electro-optics Soc. 1997—), Am. Soc. Engring. Edn. (Curtis W. McGraw award 1997), Internat. Commn. for Optics (ICO-97 prize). Avocations include invention of techniques for manipulating the shapes of ultrashort laser pulses; pioneering studies of ultrafast nonlinear optics. Office: Purdue U Sch Elec & Computer Engring West Lafayette IN 47907-1285

WEINER, GEORGE JAY, internist; b. Plainview, NY, Mar. 1, 1956; m. Teresa Emily Wilhelm, July 30, 1983; children: Aaron, Miriam, Nathan. BA, Johns Hopkins U., 1978; MD, Ohio State U., 1981. Cert. Am. Bd. Internal Medicine, 1985, in med. oncology Am. Bd. Internal Medicine, 1987, in hematology Am. Bd. Internal Medicine, 1988. Resident in internal medicine Med. Coll. Ohio, Toledo, 1981-85; hematology/oncology fellow U. Mich., Ann Arbor, 1985-89; asst. prof. medicine U. Iowa, Iowa City, 1989-94, assoc. prof., 1994-99, prof., 1999—, dir. Cancer Ctr., 1998—. Dir. Holden Comprehensive Cancer Ctr., U. Iowa. Contbr. articles to profl. jours. Chair subcom. A Nat. Cancer Inst., DC, 2007—; chair Iowa Consortium for Comprehensive Cancer Control, 2004—; dir. Iowa/Mayo Lymphoma Specialized Program of Rsch. Excellence. Achievements include devel. of new approaches to cancer immunotherapy. Office: Univ of Iowa 5970 JPP Iowa City IA 52242

WEINER, GERALD ARNE, stockbroker; b. Chgo., Dec. 20, 1941; s. Irwin S. and Lilyan (Stock) W.; m. Barbara I. Allen, June 18, 1967; children: Rachel Anne, Sara Naomi. BSS, Loyola U., Chgo., 1964; student, U. Vienna, 1962-63; MS, Georgetown U., 1966; postgrad., Ind. U., 1966-72, S.E. Asian Areas Cert., 1967. Pacification specialist AID, Laos, 1965; instr. polit. sci. Loyola U., Chgo., 1970-72; asst. v.p. A.G. Becker & Co., Chgo., 1973-78; sr. v.p. Oppenheimer & Co., Chgo., 1978-83, J. David Securities, Inc., Chgo., 1983-84, Morgan Stanley, Chgo., 1984—. Exec. edn. for securities industry Wharton Sch. Bus. U. Pa., 1988-90. Trustee Highland Park Police Pension Fund, 1991-2004. Mucia fellow, 1969. Mem. Midwest Bonsai Soc., Equinox Club. Republican. Jewish. Office: Morgan Stanley 70 W Madison St Ste 300 Chicago IL 60602-4278 Office Phone: 312-827-6634. Business E-Mail: gerald.weiner@morganstanley.com.

WEINER, WENDY L(OU), elementary school educator, writer; b. Milw., Jan. 2, 1961; d. Kenneth J. and Jessie M. Weiner. AA, U. Wis. Washington County, West Bend; BS, MS, U. Wis., U. Wis., Milw., 1993; prin. lic., Marian Coll. Cert. nat. cert. early childhood edn. Nat. Bd. Profl. Tchg. Standards, tchr. Wis. Tchr. Milw. Pub. Schs. Contbr. articles to profl. jours. Mem. Milw. Pub. Mus. Tchr. Adv. Coun., TV and Tech. Com., Vision and Tech. Com., Learning Mag.'s Student Best Adv. Coun. Recipient Presdl. Award in Sci. Tchg. Excellence, AT&T Recognition in Sci. Tchg. Excellence, Wis. Aerospace Educator of Yr., Milw. Tchr. of Yr., Grad. Last Decade award U. Wis. Milw. Alumni Assn., Warner Cable-Tchg. Creativity with Cable award, Excellence in Sci. Tchg. award. Wis. Elem. Sci. Tchrs. Assn., Nat. Urban Tech. in Edn. award Coun. Great City Schs., Sen. Herb Kohl Tchr. Achievement award, Ameritech-Wis. Bell Gold Tchr. Recognition award, Presdl. award for elem. sci. tchg. excellence; grantee Greater Mil. Edn. Trust, Wis. Space Grant Consortium/NASA, NSF. Mem. PTA, Wis. Aerospace Edn. Assn. (instr. mag. adviser, Sam's Club Tchr. of Yr.), YMCA-Young Astronauts, Nat. Arbor Day Assn., NSTA, Wis. Elem. Tchrs. Assn., Milw. Kindergarten Assn., Wis. Secondary Sci. Assn., Wis. Assn. Sch. Adminstrs., Milw. Reading Assn., Midwest Devel. Corp., Assn. Presdl. Awardees in Sci., Soc. for Elem. Presdl. Awardees, Coun. Elem. Sci. Internat., Civil Air Patrol (sr. officer). Avocations: crafts, walking. Office: Parkview Sch 10825 W Villard Milwaukee WI 53225 Personal E-mail: wlw23@prodigy.net.

WEINFURTER, DANIEL JOSEPH, business services executive; b. Milw., Apr. 16, 1957; s. Joseph Thomas and Betty E. (Stanton) W.; m. Martha Marie Brennan, May 14, 1983; children: Amy Jordan, Andrea Taylor. BSBA, Marquette U., Milw., 1979, MBA, 1984; postgrad., George Wash. U., Washington, DC, 1984-85. Account rep. Gen. Electric Info. Svcs., Milw., 1979-81, sr. account rep., 1982-84, project mgr. Rockville, Md., 1984-86; acting regional sales mgr. Gen. Electric Corp., Morristown, N.J., 1986, dist. sales mgr. Bensonville, Ill., 1986-87; regional sales mgr. Intelogic Trace, Inc., Schaumburg, Ill., 1987-89, area sales mgr., 1989; dir. bus. devel. Alternative Resources Corp., Lincolnshire, Ill., 1989-90, v.p. ops., 1990-93; pres. Alternative Resources Corp. Ventures, Lincolnshire, Ill., 1993—; CEO and founder Parson Group, Chgo., 1995—2002; CEO Capital H Group, Chgo., 2003—. Ad-hoc com. Riverwoods (Ill.) Village Coun., 1990—; mem. YMCA. Named number 1 of INC 500, INC Mag., 2000. Democrat. Avocations: running, raquetball, bicycling, golf, reading. Office: Capital H Group 225 W Washington St Chicago IL 60606 Home: 123 W Delaware Pl Chicago IL 60610

WEINGEIST, THOMAS ALAN, ophthalmology educator; b. NYC, Jan. 28, 1940; s. Samson and Fausta (Haim) W.; m. Carol Perera, Mar. 19, 1963 (div. Aug. 1977); children: Aaron P., Rachel; m. Catherine McGregor, Aug. 18, 1977; children: Robert M., David M. BA, Earlham Coll., 1963; PhD, Columbia U., 1969; MD, U. Iowa, 1972. Resident in ophthalmology U. Iowa, 1972-75, fellow in retina, 1976, asst. prof. ophthalmology Iowa City, 1976-80, assoc. prof., 1980-83, prof., 1983—. prof., head dept. ophthalmology, 1986—2006; Francis Heed Adler lectr. U. Pa., 2004. DeVoe lectr. Columbia U., 2001; Doheny lectr. U. S.C., 2002; vis. scientist Children's Meml. Rsch. Ctr., Chgo., 2006. Mem. editl. bd. Documenta Ophthalmologica, The Netherlands, 1989-94, Ophthalmology World News, 1994-96; med. editor Argus/Ophthalmology's World News, 1996-98; med. editor EyeNet mag., 1999-2001. Named Eye Health Advocate, Iowa Acad. Opthalmology, 2003; recipient Lifetime Achievement Award, Am. Acad. Ophthalmology, 2003. Fellow: Am. Acad. Ophthalmology (editl. bd. jour. 1982—, assoc. sec. for self-assessment 1988—93, sec. continuing edn. 1993—, trustee 1993—, sr. sec. clin. edn. 1994—, pres. 2002, Honor award 1979, Sr. Honor award 1989); mem.: Assn. Univ. Profs. Ophthalmology (pres. 1995, bd. dirs.), Am. Medico-Legal Found., Vitreous Soc., Retina Soc., Macula Soc. Avocations: photography, tennis. Home: 3 Heather Ct Iowa City IA 52245-3226 Office: U Iowa Dept Ophthalmology Iowa City IA 52242 Business E-Mail: thomas.weingeist@uiowa.edu.

WEINHAUER, BOB, professional sports team executive; b. NYC, May 23, 1939; m. Sue Robin Weinhauer; children: Jodie, Jamie, Kristen, Keri, Robert; 1 stepchild, Michelle. Diploma in phys. edn. and health, SUNY, Cortland, 1961. Coach various h.s., NYC, 1961-72; asst. coach U. Pa., Phila., 1972-77, head coach, 1977-82, Ariz. State U., 1982-85, Detroit Spirits, 1985-86; scout Phila. 76ers, 1987-88, dir. player pers., asst. coach, 1988-90, asst. gen. mgr., 1990-91; asst. coach Atlanta Hawks, 1991-93, Minn. Timberwolves, 1993-94; v.p. basketball ops. Houston Rockets, 1994-96; asst. coach Milw. Bucks, 1996-97, gen. mgr., 1997—. Named to SUNY Cortland Hall of Fame, 1995, Massapequa (N.Y.) H.S. Hall of Fame, 1997. Office: c/o Milw Bucks 1001 N 4th St Milwaukee WI 53203-1314

WEINHOLD, VIRGINIA BEAMER, interior designer; b. Elizabeth, N.J., June 21, 1932; d. Clayton Mitchell and Rosemary (Behrend) Beamer; divorced; children: Thomas Craig, Robert Scott, Amy Linette. BA, Cornell U., 1955; BFA summa cum laude, Ohio State U., 1969; MA in Design Mgmt., Ohio State U., 1982. Freelance interior designer, 1969-72; interior designer, dir. interior design Karlsberger and Assocs. Inc., Columbus, Ohio, 1972-82; assoc. prof. dept. design Ohio State U., 1982—, grad. studies chairperson, 1986-89, 1995-96; lectr. indsl. design Ohio State U., 1972, 79-80. Trustee Found. for Interior Design Edn. and Rsch., 1991-97. Mem. Inst. Bus. Designers (chpt. treas. 1977-79, nat. trustee 1979-81, nat. chmn. contract documents com. 1979-84, chpt. pres. 1981-83), Constrn. Specifications Inst., Interior Design Educator's Coun. (nat. treas. 1989-93), Interior Design Educator's Coun. Found. (nat. treas. 1992-94), Illuminating Engring. Soc. (chpt. v.p. 1997-98), AIA (assoc.), Internat. Interior Design Assn. (nat. dir. 1994-97). Prin. works include Grands Rapids (Mich.) Osteo. Hosp., Melrose (Mass.) Wakefield Hosp., Christopher Inn, Columbus, John W. Galbreath Hdqrs., Columbus, Guernsey Meml. Hosp., Cambridge, Ohio, Trinity Epis. Ch. and Parish House, Columbus, Hale Hosp., Haverhill, Mass., Ohio State U. Dept. Indsl. Design Lighting Lab., others. Author: IBD Forms and Documents Manual, Interior Finish Materials for Health Care Facilities, Subjective Impressions: Lighting Hotels and Resturants, 1989, Effects of Lighting on The Perception of Interior Spaces, 1993. Home: 112 Glen Dr Columbus OH 43085-4010 Office: Ohio State U Dept Design 128 N Oval Mall Columbus OH 43210-1318

WEINKAUF, MARY LOUISE STANLEY, retired clergywoman, educator; b. Eau Claire, Wis., Sept. 22, 1938; d. Joseph Michael and Marie Barbara (Holzinger) Stanley; m. Alan D. Weinkauf, Oct. 12, 1962 (dec. Nov. 2000); children: Stephen, Xanti. BA, Wis. State U., 1961; MA, U. Tenn., 1962, PhD, 1966; MDiv, Luth. Sch. Theology, Chgo., 1993. Grad. asst., instr. U. Tenn., 1961-66; asst. prof. English Adrian Coll., 1966-69; prof., head dept. English Dakota Wesleyan U., Mitchell, SD, 1969-89; instr. Columbia Coll., 1989-91. Pastor Calvary Evang. Luth. Ch., Siloa Luth. Ch., Ontonagon Faith, White Pine, Mich., Gowrie, Iowa, dir. Lay Sch. for Mission, Sayner Campus, 2006—. Author: Hard-Boiled Heretic, 1994, Sermons in Science Fiction, 1994, Murder Most Poetic, 1996. Trustee Ednl. Found., 1986-90; bd. dirs. Ontonagon County Habitat for Humanity, 1995-97, Luth. Campus Ministry for Wis. and Upper Mich., 1996-2002, Lakeland Area Food Pantry, 2000—, Fortune Lake Bible Camp, 2003-04, Pastime Club Adult Day Care Ctr., North Ctrl. Wis. Thrivent Fin. for Lutherans, 2006, pres., 2007. Mem. AAUW (divsn. pres. 1978-80), Nat. Coun. Tchrs. English, S.D. Coun. Tchrs. English, Sci. Fiction Rsch. Assn., Popular Culture Assn., Milton Soc., S.D. Poetry Soc. (pres. 1982-83), Delta Kappa Gamma (pres. local chpt., mem. state bd. 1972-89, state v.p. 1979-83, state pres. 1983-85), Sigma Tau Delta, Pi Kappa Delta, Phi Kappa Phi.

WEINKOPF, FRIEDRICH J., lawyer; b. Bautsch, Germany, Feb. 17, 1930; Referendar, U. Marburg, Germany, 1954; LLM, U. Pa., 1958; JD, Chgo.-Kent Coll. Law, 1967. Bar: Ill. 1967. Sr. counsel Baker & McKenzie, Chgo. Office: Baker & McKenzie 1 Prudential Plz 130 E Randolph St Fl 3600 Chicago IL 60601-6315

WEINREICH, GABRIEL, physicist, minister, educator; b. Vilnius, Lithuania, Feb. 12, 1928; came to U.S., 1941, naturalized, 1949; s. Max and Regina (Szabad) W.; m. Alisa Lourié, Apr. 19, 1951 (dec. 1970); m. Gerane Siemering Benamou, Oct. 23, 1971; children: Catherine, Marc, Daniel, Rebecca, Natalie. AB, Columbia U., 1948, MA, 1949, PhD, 1954. Ordained priest Episcopal Ch., 1986. Mem. staff Bell Telephone Labs., Murray Hill, NJ, 1953-60; mem. faculty U. Mich., Ann Arbor, 1960—, prof. physics, 1964-95; prof. emeritus, 1995—; Collegiate prof. U. Mich., 1974-76. Adj. min. St. Clare's Episcopal ch., Ann Arbor, 1985-90; rector St. Stephen's Episcopal Ch., Hamburg, Mich., 1993-96. Author: Solids: Elementary Theory for Advanced Students, 1965, Fundamental Thermodynamics, 1968, Notes for General Physics, 1972, Geometrical Vectors, 1998, Confessions of a Jewish Priest: From Secular Jewish War Refugee to Physicist and Episcopal Clergyman, 2005; editor: Mechanics of Musical Instruments, 1995. Recipient Disting. Teaching award U. Mich., 1968, Klopsteg award Am. Assn. Physics Tchrs., 1992, Internat. medal French Acoustical Soc., 1992, Hutchins Gold medal for lifetime achievement in mus. acoustics, 2002. Fellow Acoustical Soc. Am. (assoc. editor Jour. 1987-89). Home: 2116 Silver Maples Dr Chelsea MI 48118-1189 Home Phone: 734-433-1426. Business E-Mail: weinreic@umich.edu.

WEINRICH, ALAN JEFFREY, occupational hygienist; b. Passaic, NJ, Aug. 24, 1953; s. Erwin Hermann and Ann Elizabeth Weinrich; m. Nina Kathryn Hooker, Jan. 14, 1983; 1 child, Sheena Elizabeth Rochelle. BS with high honors, Rutgers U., 1975; MS, U. Iowa, 1988, postgrad., 1988-89. Cert. Am. Bd. Indsl. Hygiene, cert. environ. trainer Nat. Environ. Tng. Assn. Indsl. hygienist Tenn. Dept. Labor, Nashville, 1975-78; health info. specialist occupl. health program U. Tenn., Memphis, 1980-82; vol. tchr. Internat. Sch. Moshi, Tanzania, 1982-84; sr. rsch. asst. agrl. medicine rsch. facility U. Iowa, Iowa City, 1985-89; sr. indsl. hygienist PSI Energy, Inc., Plainfield, Ind., 1989-92; asst. dir. health & safety programs environ. mgmt. and edn. Purdue U., West Lafayette, 1992-94; assoc. dir. tech. affairs Am. Conf. Govtl. Indsl. Hygienists, Cin., 1994-97, dir. tech. affairs, 1997-99, dir. scientific affairs, 1999—. Co-editor book supplements: Documentation of the Threshold Limit Values and Biological Exposure Indices, 1996-98; editor, author ACGIH newsletter Today!; developer, editor CD-Rom publ. TLVs and Other Occupational Exposure Values. Mem. healthy cities com. Butler-Tarkington Neighborhood Assn., Indpls., 1992-94; mem. Greenways Com., City of Wyoming, Ohio. Mem. Am. Acad. Indsl. Hygiene, Am. Conf. Govtl. Indsl. Hygienists, Am. Indsl. Hygiene Assn. (v.p. Mid-South sect. 1981-82, bd. dirs. Iowa-Ill. sect. 1987-89, bd. dirs. Ind. sect. 1991-94, pres. Ind. sect. 1994-95), Internat. Occupl. Hygiene Assn., Am. Soc. Assn. Execs. Avocations: bicycling, family, reading, walking, softball. Office: Am Conf Govtl Indsl Hygienists 1330 Kemper Meadow Dr Cincinnati OH 45240-4147 E-mail: science@ACGIH.org.

WEINSHEIMER, WILLIAM CYRUS, lawyer; b. Chgo., Jan. 12, 1941; s. Alfred John and Coress (Searing) W.; m. Roberta Limarzi, June 5, 1965; children: William C. Jr., Kurt R., Robert L. BBA in Mktg., U. Notre Dame, 1962; JD, Northwestern U., 1965. Bar: Ill. 1965, U.S. Dist. Ct. (no. dist.) Ill. 1967, U.S. Tax Ct. 1968. Ptnr. Foley and Lardner LLP, Chgo., 2001—, co-chmn. estates & trusts practice group, 2001—. Lectr. continuing legal edn. programs; mem. estate planning adv. coun. Northwestern U. Author: (with others) The New Generation Skipping Tax; Analysis, Planning & Drafting, 1987; Drafting Wills and Trust Agreements, 1990; contbr. articles to profl. jours. Bd. dirs. The Ragdale Found., Lake Forest, Ill., 1987-93, Lawyers for Creative Arts, 1973-90, Winnetka United Way, 1989-92; pres. Family Svc. Winnetka-Northfield, Inc., 1978-79. Capt. U.S. Army, 1965-67. Fellow Am. Coll. Trust and Estate Coun. (bus. planning com. 1993-2002, internat. estate planning com., 1997-99, chair Ill. chpt. 1989-92, editor Actec Notes 1991-92, bd. regents 1992-96, chair edit. bd. 1993-96), chair practice com., 2004-07; mem. ABA (vice chmn. com. on generation-skipping tax 1988-92), Ill. Bar Assn., Chgo. Bar Assn. (chmn. probate practice com. 1989), Chgo. Bar Found. (bd. dirs. 1992-96), Ill. Bar Found. (bd. dirs. 1985-91), Lawyers Club, Econ. Club, Mid-Day Club, Skokie Country Club, Notre Dame Club Chgo. (bd. govs. 1984-90). Roman Catholic. Avocations: golf, visual arts, performing. Office: Foley and Lardner LLP 321 N Clark St Ste 2800 Chicago IL 60610 Office Phone: 312-832-4590. Business E-Mail: wweinsheimer@foley.com.

WEINSTEIN, JAY A., social sciences educator, researcher; b. Chgo., Feb. 23, 1942; s. Lawrence E. and Jacqueline L. (Caplan) W.; m. Diana S. Staffin, Sept. 16, 1961; m. Marilyn L. Schwartz, Nov. 25, 1972; children— Liza, Bennett. AB, U. Ill., 1963, PhD, 1973; MA, Washington U., St. Louis, 1965. Teaching fellow U. Ill., Urbana, 1963-64; teaching asst. McGill U., Montreal, Que., Canada, 1966-68; instr. Sir George Williams U., Montreal, Que., Canada, 1967-68; lectr. Simon Fraser U., Vancouver, B.C., Canada, 1968; asst. prof. North Central Coll., Naperville, Ill., 1970-71, U. Iowa, 1973-77; prof. social sci. Ga. Inst. Tech., Atlanta, 1977-86; head dept. sociology Eastern Mich. U., 1986-90, 2004—06, faculty rsch. fellow, 1990-91; grantee ednl. devel. project USIA-Soros Found., Albania, 1992—; dir. Applied Rsch. Unit, 1996—; vis. faculty, sociology U. North Fla., 2007—. Cons. World Bank Study Social and Econ. Vulnerability in

Albania, 1997, World Bank Study on Closing the Vulnerability Gap, Albania, 1997—98; project dir. Ea. Mich.-U-Ypsilanti Cmty. Outreach Partnership Ctr.; cons. pvt. and pub. agencies; rschr. in field. Author: Madras: An Analysis of Urban Ecological Structure in India, 1974, Demographic Transition and Social Change, 1976, Sociology-Technology: Foundations of Postacademic Social Science, 1982, The Grammar of Social Relations: The Major Essays of Louis Schneider, 1984; editor: Paradox and Society, 1986; (with Vinod Tewari and V.L.S. Prakash Rao) Indian Cities: Ecological Perspectives, Social and Cultural Change: Social Science for a Dynamic World, 1997, 2005, The Holocaust: A Sociological Analysis, 1997, Demography: The Science of Population, 2000; Studies in Comparative International Development, 1978-88; mem. editorial bd. Social Development Issues, 1977-85; specialized contbr. Calcutta Mcpl. Gazette, 1979—; editor: Social and Cultural Change, 1974-75; editor Mich. Soc. Rev., 1997-2003, Jour. Applied Sociology, 2004—06; Applied Social Sci., 2006-, editl. reviewer Jour. Asian Studies, Social Devel. Issues, Tech. and Culture, Am. Sociologist, Technol. Forecasting and Social Change; contbr. chpts. to book, articles to profl. jours. Recipient Charles Horton Cooley award for outstanding contbns. to sociology in Mich., 1998, Alex Boros award, 2005; Fulbright prof. Ahmedabad, India, 1975-76, Hyderabad, India, 1981-82; grantee Ga. Tech. Found., 1981-82, World Order Studies Course, 1994-97, State of Mich. Rsch. Excellence Fund; Steinberg fellow, 1967. Mem. Am. Sociol. Assn. (pres. 2002-03), Soc. for Applied Sociology (v.p. 1998-99, chair sociol. practice sect., 2004-05), mem. exec. bd. 2000, pres. 2002-03), Mich. Sociol. Assn. (pres. 1988-89, v.p. 1994-95), North Ctrl. Sociol. Assn. (pres. 2007-08, John F. Schnabel award for tchg. excellence), Sigma Xi. Jewish. Office: Eastern Mich U Sociology Dept Ypsilanti MI 48197 Home Phone: 313-563-5292; Office Phone: 734-487-0012. E-mail: weinst@aol.com, jay.weinstein@emich.edu.

WEINSTEIN, MARGO, lawyer; b. Chgo., July 25, 1960; BA with honors, Yale U., 1982; JD, Northwestern U., 1987. Bar: Ill. 1988. Law clk. US Ct. Appeals (7th cir.), Ill., 1987—88; ptnr. Sonnenschein Nath & Rosenthal, Chicago. Named one of Top 500 Leading Litigators in Am., Lawdragon mag., 2006; named to Order of the Coif, Northwestern U. Mem.: Women's Bar Assn. Ill. Office: Sonnenschein Nath & Rosenthal 7800 Sears Tower 233 S Wacker Dr Chicago IL 60606-6404 Office Phone: 312-876-3158. E-mail: mweinstein@sonnenschein.com.

WEINSTEIN, MICHAEL ALAN, political science professor; b. Bklyn., Aug. 24, 1942; s. Aaron and Grace W.; m. Deena May 31, 1964. BA summa cum laude, NYU, 1964; MA in Polit. Sci., Case Western Res. U., 1965, PhD, 1967. Asst. prof. polit. sci. Case Western Res. U., summer 1967, Va. Poly. Inst., 1967-68; asst. prof. Purdue U., 1968-70, assoc. prof., 1970-72, prof., 1972—; Milward Simpson disting. prof. polit. sci. U. Wyo., 1979; sr. conflict analyst Power and Interest ews Report, 2004—. Author: (with Deena Weinstein) Living Sociology, 1974, The Polarity of Mexican Thought, 1976, The Tragic Sense of Political Life, 1977, Meaning and Appreciation, 1978, The Structure of Human Life, 1979, The Wilderness and the City, 1982, Unity and Variety in the Philosophy of Samuel Alexander, 1984, Finite Perfection, 1985, Culture Critique: Fernand Dumont and New Quebec Sociology, 1985, (with Helmut Loiskandl and Deena Weinstein) Georg Simmel's Scopenhauer and Nietzsche, 1986; (with Deena Weinstein) Deconstruction as Cultural History/The Cultural History of Deconstruction, 1990, La Déconstruction un Jeu Symbolique, 1990, (with Deena Weinstein) Georg Simmel: Sociological Flâneur/Bricoleur, 1991, Photographic Realism as a Moral Practice, 1992, (with Deena Weinstein) Postmodern(ized) Simmel, 1993, (with Arthur Kroker) Data Trash: The Theory of the Virtual Class, 1994, Culture/Flesh: Explorations of Postcivilized Modernity, 1995, Peter Vierecki Reconciliation and Beyond, 1997, East/West: Globalizing Civilization, 2000, (with Deena Weinstein) Hail to the Shrub: Mediating the President, 2002, The Power of Silence and the Limits of Discourse at Oliver Wendell Holmes's Breakfast Table, 2005, The Imaginative Prose of Oliver Wendell Holmes, 2006; artist in residence Columbia Coll., 2002; mem. editl. bd. Humanitas, Social Philosophy Rsch. Book Series. Recipient Best Paper prize Midwest Polit. Sci. Assn., 1969; Guggenheim fellow, 1974-75; Rockefeller Found. humanities fellow, 1976; fellow Center Humanistic Studies, Purdue U., 1981, Lily Endowment Tchg. grant, 2001. Mem. Phi Beta Kappa. Home: 800 Princess Dr West Lafayette IN 47906-2038 Office: Dept Polit Sci Purdue U West Lafayette IN 47907

WEINSTOCK, JOEL VINCENT, immunologist; b. Detroit, Mar. 21, 1948; s. Herman and Esther B. (Frazein) W.; m. Allison Lee Rose, July 15, 1979; children: Lisa, Jeffrey, Andrew. BS, U. Mich., 1969; MD, Wayne State U., 1973. Diplomate Am. Bd. Internal Medicine, subspeciality gastroenterology; lic. physician, Mich., Iowa. Straight med. intern Univ. Hosp., Ann Arbor, Mich., 1973-74, resident internal medicine, 1974-76, fellow gastroenterology dept. internal medicine, 1976-78; asst. prof. internal medicine Wayne State U. Sch. Medicine, Detroit, 1978-83, assoc. prof., 1983-86, adj. assoc. prof. dept. immunology and microbiology, 1983-86, vice chief divsn. gastroenterology, 1984-86; assoc. prof., dir. gastroenterology divsn. U. Iowa, Iowa City, 1986-91, prof., dir., 1991—, dir. Ctr. Digestive Diseases, 1990—, dir. divsn. gastroenterology-hepatology, 1986—. Mem. exec. bd. Crohn's and Colitis Found. Am., N.Y.C., 1993—, mem. tng. awards rev. com., 1991-93, chmn., 1993—; chief sect. gastroenterology Hutzel Hosp., Detroit, 1978-84, dir. endoscopy unit, 1978-84, dir. nutritional support svc., 1980-84; vice chief gastroenterology dept. medicine Wayne State U. Sch. Medicine, 1984-86; dir. gastroenterology subspecialty unit Harper Hosp., Detroit, 1984-86, vice-chief gastroenterology, 1984-86; mem. sci. adv. ang grant rev. com. Crohn's and Colitis Found. Am., 1987—; mem. IH Task force for developing nat. agenda for IBD rsch., 1989; mem. Lederle award selection com., 1989; mem. study sect. NIH Core Ctr. Rev. Com., 1990, 92; mem. abstract rev. com. ASCI, 1990; vis. prof. Washington U., St. Louis, 1990, U. Tex., Houston, 1991, Cleve. Clinic, 1992, U. Md., Balt., 1993; participant various conferences and meetings; mem. Digestive Diseases Ctr. Planning Com., 19886—; mem. Adult TPN Subcom., 1986—; chmn. coord. com. Ctr. Digestive Diseases, 1986—; mem. grant rev. coms. NIH, 1980—; mem. gastroenterology subspecialty coun. CSCR, 1993—. Mem. editl. bd. Autoimmunity Forum: Gastroenterology Edit., 1989-92; mem. internat. adv. bd. Alimentary Pharmacology and Therapeutics, 1990—; sect. editor Jour. Inflammatory Bowel Disease, 1994; reviewer Am. Jour Gastroenterology, Jour. Clin. Investigation, Jour. Immunology, Jour. Clin. Immunology, Gastroenterology, Digestive Diseases and Scis.; contbr. articles to profl. jours., chpts. to books. Rsch. grantee NIH, 1982—, Sandoz Pharm., 1993, Marion Merrell Dow, 1994, Centocor, 1995. Mem. AAAS, Am. Inst. Nutrition, Am. Soc. Clin. Nutrition, Ctrl. Soc. Clin. Rsch., Am. Soc. Gastrointestinal Endoscopy, Am. Assn. Study Liver Disease, Am. Fedn. Clin. Rsch., Am. Assn. Immunologists, Ileitis and Colitis Found. Am., Am. Soc. Clin. Investigation, Clin. Immunology Soc., Am. Gastroenterological Assn. (rsch. com. 1987-90, chmn. task force rsch. fellowship awards 1989-90, program evaluation com. 1990—), Midwest Gut Club (councillor 1990—), Alpha Omega Alpha. Achievements include research in elucidaiton of immunoregulatory circuits that control granulomatous inflammation; characterization of how neurokines help control inflammatory responses. Office: U Iowa College of Med Internal Medicine 4607JCP 200 Hawkins Dr Iowa City IA 52242-1009

WEINTRAUB, JOSEPH BARTON, publishing executive; b. Phila., Dec. 2, 1945; s. George and Edith (Lubner) W.; m. Denise Waters, June 14, 1974. BA, U. Pitts., 1966; MA, U. Chgo., 1967, PhD, 1973. Assoc. faculty U. Ind., Gary, Ind., 1970-74; mktg. specialist journalism div. U. Chgo. Press, 1974-75, sr. copywriter journalism div., 1975-78; periodical specialist ABA, Chgo., 1978-80, mktg. mgr., 1980-92, dir. publ. planning, 1992-97, dir. book publ., 1997-99; mgr. dir. mktg. U. Chgo. Press, 1999—. Writer You, 2000; contbr. essays, translations, plays, poems, short fiction to lit. revs. and small press anthologies. Recipient award Literary awards, Ill. Art Coun., 1984, 2004, Barrington Art Coun., 1994. Mem. Phi Beta Kappa. Avocations: writing, language study, running. Office: U Chgo Press 1427 E 60th Street Chicago IL 60637-5418

WEINTRAUB, NEAL L., medical educator, cardiologist; Student, Tulane u., 1977-80, MD, 1984. Diplomate Am. Bd. Internal Medicine, Am. Bd. Cardiovasc. Diseases. Resident Emory U., Atlanta, 1984-86, U. Ill., Urbana-Champaign, 1986-87, clin. instr. medicine Coll. Medicine, 1987-88, asst. clin. prof. medicine Coll. Medicine, 1988-90; staff physician VA Med. Ctr., Danville, Ill., 1987-90, St. Louis, 1990-91; asst. prof. medicine Sch. Medicine St. Louis U., 1990-95, postdoctoral fellow clin. pharmacology, 1992-94; asst. cardiology divsn. U. Iowa Coll. Medicine, Iowa City, 1995-97, assoc. prof. cardiology, 1997—. Contbr. articles to profl. jours. Recipient Travel award Am. Coll. Cardiology/Bristol-Myers Squibb, 1994, Clinician Scientist award Am. Heart Assn., 1996. Mem. Alpha Omega Alpha. Achievements include research in vascular biology and physiology and lipid biochemistry. Office: U Iowa Coll Medicine CV Div Dept Internal Medicine 200 Hawkins Dr Iowa City IA 52242-1009

WEINTRAUT, STEVEN JAMES, lawyer; b. East Moline, Ill., Apr. 16, 1968; BBA in Fin., U. Iowa, 1991; JD with high distinction, U. Iowa Coll. Law, 1994. Bar: Minn. 1994. Shareholder Siegel, Brill, Greupner, Duffy & Foster, P.A., Mpls. Asst. dir. Trial Advocacy Bd. Served in USNR, 1987—92. Named a Rising Star, Minn. Super Lawyers mag., 2006; recipient Internat. Acad. Trial Lawyers award. Office: Siegel Brill Greupner Duffy & Foster PA 100 Washington Ave S Ste 1300 Minneapolis MN 55401 Office Phone: 612-337-6100. E-mail: stevenweintraut@sbgdf.com.

WEINZAPFEL, JONATHAN, public relations executive, congressional aide; b. Evansville, Ill., Nov. 16, 1965; BA, Ind. U., 1988; MA, Georgetown U., 1993. Dem. candidate 8th dist. Ind. U.S. House of Reps., 1996. Roman Catholic. Office: Weinzapfel For State Rep PO Box 6610 Evansville IN 47719-0610

WEIR, BRYCE KEITH ALEXANDER, neurosurgeon, neurologist, educator; b. Edinburgh, Apr. 29, 1936; arrived in U.S., 1992, arrived in Can., 2002; s. Ernest John and Marion Weir; m. Mary Lou Lauber, Feb. 25, 1976; children: Leanora, Glyncora, Brocke. BSc, McGill U., Montreal, Que., Can., 1958, MD, CM, 1960, MSc, 1963. Diplomate Am. Bd. Neurol. Surgery, Nat. Bd. Med. Examiners. Intern Montreal Gen. Hosp., 1960-61; resident in neurosurgery Neurological Inst., Montreal, 1962-64, 65-66, Y Neurol. Inst., NYC, 1964—65; neurosurgeon U. Alta., Edmonton, Can., 1967-92, dir. div. neurosurgery, 1982-86, Walter Anderson prof., chmn. dept. surgery, 1986-92; surgeon-in-chief U. Alta. Hosps., 1986-92; Maurice Goldblatt prof. surgery and neurology U. Chgo., 1992—2002, dir. Brain Rsch. Inst., 1993—2001, interim dean biol. scis. divsn. and Pritzker Sch. Medicine, v.p. med. affairs, 2001—02. Past pres. V Internat. Symposium on Cerebral Vasospasm; mem. neurology A study sect. NIH, 1991—93; invited speaker at over 135 profl. meetings; vis. prof. over 68 univs., including Yale U., Cornell U., Columbia U., Duke U., U. Toronto, U. Calif., San Francisco; lectr. in field. Author: Aneurysms Affecting the Nervous System, 1987, Subarachnoid Hemorrhage-Causes and Cures, 1998, Cerebral Vasospasm, 2001; co-editor: Primer on Cerebrovascular Diseases, 1997, Stroke: Pathophysiology, Diagnosis and Management, 4th edit., 2004; mem. editl. bd. Jour. Neurosurgery, chmn. bd, 1993—94, mem. editl. bd. Neurosurgery Quar., Jour. Cerebrovascular Disease, Neurosurgery; contbr. over 275 articles to profl. jours. Named Officer of the Order of Can., 1995. Fellow: ACS, Royal Coll. Surgeons Can., Royal Coll. Surgeons Edinburgh (hon.); mem.: Can. Neurosurg. Soc. (Inaugural Lifetime Achievement award 2006), Interurban Neurosurg. Soc. (chmn.), Nat. Acad. Scis., Inst. Medicine, Japan Neurosurg. Soc. (hon.), Soc. Neurol. Surgeons (Grass gold medal 1992), Am. Acad. Neurol. Surgeons, James. IV Assn. Surgeons, Am. Surg. Assn. Achievements include rsch. in cerebral vasospasm and the surgical management of intracranial aneurysms. Home: 1262 Saturna Dr Parksville BC V9P 2X6 Canada

WEIR, DAME GILLIAN CONSTANCE, musician; b. Martinborough, New Zealand, Jan. 17, 1941; d. Cecil Alexander and Clarice M. Foy (Bignell) W. Grad., Royal Coll. Music, London, 1965; Mus D (hon.), U. Victoria of Wellington, New Zealand, 1983; DLitt (hon.), Huddersfield U., 1997; Mus D (hon.), Hull U., 1999, Exeter U., 2001; Doctorate (hon.), U. Ctrl. Eng., 2001; Mus D (hon.), Leicester Univ., 2003; MusD (hon.), U. Aberdeen, Scotland, 2004. Artist-in-residence numerous univs. including Yale U, Washington U., St. Louis, U. Western Australia, Johns Hopkins U., 2005, others; vis. lectr. Royal No. Coll. Music, Manchester, Eng., 1974-89; vis. prof. organ Royal Acad. Music, London, 1997-98; Prince Consort prof. Royal Coll. of Music, London, 1999—; spkr. BBC programs on music and performance; subject of Melvyn Bragg's TV documentary South Bank Show, 2000; apptd. Disting Artist-in-residence Peabody Inst., John Hopkins U., Balt., 2005; internat. chair in organ Royal No. Coll. Music, 2006-07. Concert appearances with leading Brit. Orchs. and Boston Orch., Seattle Orch., Australian ABC Orch., Wurttemberg Chamber and other fgn. orch.; appeared in major internat. festivals including Edinburgh, Flanders, Aldeburgh, Bath, Proms, Europalia; appeared at concert halls including Royal Festival Hall, Royal Albert Hall, Lincoln Ctr., NY, Sydney Opera House; numerous radio and TV appearances in Brit. and world-wide including Royal Festival Hall Jubilee; organ cons.; adjudicator internat. competitions; contbr. The Messiaen Companion, 1995; contbr. articles to profl. jour.; recs. include complete organ works of Olivier Messiaen, others; TV documentary film on career, 1982, BBC TV programs The King of Instruments, 1989. Decorated comdr., dame comdr. Order Brit. Empire; recipient Turnovsky award 1985, Evening Std. award for outstanding solo performance, 1998-99, Lifetime Achievement award The Link Found., London, 2005; winner 1st prize St. Albans Internat. Organ Competition, 1964. Fellow Royal Coll. Organists (hon., mem. coun. 1977—, mem. exec. 1981-85, pres. 1994-96, 1st Woman pres.), Royal Can. Coll. Organists (hon.), Royal Coll. Music (London); mem. Royal Acad. Music (hon.), Inc. Soc. Musicians (1st woman pres. 1992-93), Albert Schweitzer Assn. (Silver medal 1998). Office: Karen McFarlane Artists 33563 Seneca Dr Cleveland OH 44139-5578 Office Phone: 440-542-1882. Personal E-mail: gillianweir@gillianweir.com.

WEIS, CHARLIE, college football coach; b. Trenton, NJ, Mar. 30, 1956; m. Maura Weis; 2 children. BA speech, drama, Notre Dame Univ, 1978; MA education, South Carolina Univ, 1989. Asst. coach Boonton High School, NJ, 1979, Morristown High School, NJ, 1980—84; grad. asst., defensive backs coach South Carolina U., 1985, 1986, defensive ends coach, 1987, asst. recruiting coord., 1988; head coach Franklin Township High School, 1989; def. asst., asst. special teams coach NY Giants, 1990, running backs coach, 1991—92; tight ends coach New England Patriots, 1993—94, running backs coach, 1995, wide receivers coach, 1996, NY Jets, 1997, offensive coord., wide receivers coach, 1998—99; offensive coord., running backs coach New England Patriots, 2000, offensive coord., quarterbacks coach, 2001—02, offensive coord., 2003—05; head football coach Notre Dame U., South Bend, Ind., 2005—. Co-author (with Vic Carucci): No Excuses: One Man's Incredible Rise Through the NFL to Head Coach of Notre Dame, 2006. Achievements include being a coach for Super Bowl Champion New York Giants, 1990, New England Patriots, 2000, 2003, 2004. Office: C112 Joyce Center Notre Dame IN 46556

WEIS, JODY P. (J.P. WEIS), police superintendent; b. 1957; BS in Chemistry, U. Tampa, 1979. With Houston divsn. Corpus Christi Resident Agy. FBI, investigator terrorism, narcotics and violent crimes Houston; bomb technician Houston SWAT team; with Bomb Data Ctr. FBI, 1992—94, with violent crimes/fugitive unit, 1994—96, mem. violent crimes squad Phoenix, 1996—2002, asst. spl. agent in charge Chgo. Field Office, 2002—03, dep. asst. dir. Office Profl. Responsibility, 2003—05, dep. asst. dir. for adminstrv. svcs. disvn. Office Profl. Responsibility, spl. agent in charge crime ops. LA Field Office, 2005—06, spl. agent in charge crime ops. Phila. Field Office, 2006—07; supt. Chgo. Police Dept., 2008—. 2d lt. explosive ordnance disposal US Army, ret. US Army, 1984. Office: Chgo Police Dept 3510 S Michigan Ave Chicago IL 60653 Office Phone: 312-746-6000. Business E-Mail: police@cityofchicago.com.*

WEIS, MERVYN J., physician, gastroenterologist; b. Chgo., June 9, 1940; s. Theodore A. and Anita (Stavins) W.; m. Myra Rubenstein, Nov. 26, 1966 (dec. Nov. 1990); children: Jonathan Mandel, Sari Tova; m. Anita Kaplan Sherbet, Oct. 1992. BA, Northwestern U., 1961, MD, 1965. Diplomate Am. Bd. Internal Medicine. Intern in internal medicine Michael Reese Hosp. and Med. Ctr., Chgo., 1965-66, resident in internal medicine, 1966-67, 69-70, attending physician, 1972-78; fellow in gastroenterology Northwestern U. Med. Ctr., Chgo., 1970-72; attending physician Ravenswood Hosp., Chgo., 1979-83, St. Francis Hosp., Evanston, Ill., 1984-88, Rush North Med. Ctr., Skokie, Ill., 1985-91, Louis A. Weiss Meml. Hosp., Chgo., 1972—, chmn. divsn. medicine, 1987-89, pres. med. staff, 1989-93, mem. bd. govs., 1987—. Cons. in gastroenterology VA Rsch. Hosp., Chgo., 1972-80 Contbr. articles to profl. jours. Capt. U.S. Army, 1967-69. Fellow ACP, Am. Coll. Gastroenterology, Am. Gastroenterologic Soc.; mem. AMA, Ill. State Med. Soc., Chgo. Soc. Gastroenterology, Chgo. Med. Soc., Am. Gastroenterol. Assn. (diplomate). Avocations: golf, jogging, computers. Office: 4640 N Marine Dr Ste C 6100 Chicago IL 60640-5719

WEISBACH, LOU (LOUIS E. WEISBACH), advertising executive; b. 1948; m. Ruth W. Weisbach; 4 children. Founder, pres., CEO, chmn. Ha-Lo Industries, Inc., Niles, Ill., 1972—99; CEO Stadium Capital Financing Group LLC, Chgo., 2007—. Active Ark, Chgo., Starlight Found., Misericordia, Chai Lifeline, Juvenile Diabetes Assn., RP Found.; Parkinson's Disease Found.; benefactor Keshet; active Holocaust Meml. Mus., Washington, Associated Talmud Torah; Adas Yehuda V-Shoshana Congregation; bd. dirs. Little City, Congregation B-nai Sholom; Athletes Against Drugs, Chai Lifeline, Lynn Sage Cancer Rsch. Found. Democrat. Jewish. Achievements include ranked number 14 on the Mother Jones 400, 1998. Office: Stadium Capital Financing Group LLC 190 S LaSalle St Ste 510 Chicago IL 60603 E-mail: lweisbach@seatrights.com.*

WEISBACH, LOUIS E. See WEISBACH, LOU

WEISBERG, HERBERT FRANK, political science professor; b. Mpls., Dec. 8, 1941; s. Nathan R. and Jean (Schlessinger) W.; m. Judith Ann Robinson, Dec. 16, 1979; 1 child, Bryan Bowen. BA, U. Minn., 1963; PhD, U. Mich., 1968. Asst. prof. polit. sci. U. Mich., Ann Arbor, 1967-73, assoc. prof. polit. sci., 1973-74, Ohio State U., Columbus, 1974-77, prof. polit. sci., 1977—, chmn. Dept. Polit. Sci., 2005—. Author: Central Tendency and Variation, 1992, The Total Survey Error Approach, 2005; co-author: Theory Building and Data Analysis, 1984, Controversies in Voting Behavior, 2001, Survey Research Polling and Data Analysis, 1996, Classics in Congressional Politics, 1999, The American Voter Revisited, 2008; editor: Political Science: Science of Politics, 1985, Democracy's Feast: Elections in America, 1995; co-editor Am. Jour. Polit. Sci., 1979-82, Great Theatre: The American Congress in the 1990's, 1998, Reelection 1996: How Americans Voted, 1999, Models of Voting in Presidential Elections, 2004. Mem.: Am. Polit. Sci. Assn. (program chmn. 1983), Midwest Polit. Sci. Assn. (pres. 2001—02), Phi Kappa Phi, Pi Sigma Alpha, Phi Beta Kappa. Home: 742 Gatehouse Ln Columbus OH 43235-1732 Office: Ohio State U Dept Polic Sci 2140 Derby Hall 154 N Oval Mall Columbus OH 43210-1330

WEISBERG, LOIS, arts administrator, city official; Commr. Chgo. Dept. Cultural Affairs, 1989—. Office: Chicago Cultural Center 78 E Washington St Chicago IL 60602-4816

WEISBROD, BURTON ALLEN, economist, educator; b. Chgo., Feb. 13, 1931; s. Leon H. and Idelle C. (Chernoff) W.; m. Shirley Lindsay, Dec. 23, 1951; children: Glen, Linda. BS, U. Ill., 1951; MA in Econs, Northwestern U., 1952, PhD, 1958. Lectr. econs. Northwestern U., Evanston, Ill., 1954-55; instr. econs. Carleton Coll., Minn., 1955-57, Washington U., St. Louis, 1957-58, asst. prof. econs., 1958-62, assoc. prof. econs., 1962-64; vis. assoc. prof. Princeton (N.J.) U., 1962-63; sr. staff mem. Council of Econ. Advs., Pres. U.S., 1963-64; assoc. prof. dept. econs. U. Wis., Madison, 1964-66, prof., 1966-91, Evjue-Bascom prof. econs., 1985—91; dir. Ctr. for Urban Affairs and Policy Rsch. Northwestern U., Evanston, Ill., 1990-95, John Evans prof. econs., 1990—. Vis. prof. SUNY, Binghamton, 1972; sr. Fulbright lectr. U. Autonoma de Madrid, summer, 1970; vis. prof. Yale U., 1976-77; Ziskind vis. prof. Brandeis U., 1982-83; vis. scholar, Brotman fellow J.F. Kennedy Sch., Harvard U., 1982-83; tchg. fellow Australian Nat. U., 1986; mem. rsch. adv. com. Econ. Devel. Adminstrn., U.S. Dept. Commerce, 1967-69; mem. adv. com. Commn. on Pvt. Philanthropy and Pub. Needs, 1973-75; cons. various fed. and state govt. agys., 1964—; also IBM, Econ. Coun. Can., 1969, 71, 76, 78; mem. bd. econ. advs. Public Interest Econs. Ctr., 1973-86; mem. adv. com. med. care and med. econs. to 3d Nat. Cancer Survey, 1969-71; U.S. del. UN World Population Conf., Belgrade, Yugoslavia, 1965; bd. dirs. Nat. Bur. Econ. Rsch., Inc., 1979-90; vis. scholar Phi Beta Kappa Soc., 1998-99; mem. nat. rsch. resources coun. NIH, 1999-03; mem. panel on nonmarket activity NRC, 2002-04; chair com. on philanthropy and the nonprofit sector Social Sci. Rsch. Coun., 2002-04; mem. IRS stats income divsn. Users Adv. Group, 2004-. Author: Economics of Public Health, 1961, External Benefits of Public Education, 1964, (with W. Lee Hansen) Benefits, Costs, and Finance of Public Higher Education, 1969, (with Ralph L. Andreano) American Health Policy, 1974, The Voluntary Nonprofit Sector: An Economic Analysis, 1978, (with Joel F. Handler and Neil K. Komesar) Public Interest Law: An Economic and Institutional Analysis, 1978; contbg. author: (with others) Disease and Economic Development: The Case of Parasitic Diseases in St. Lucia, West Indies, 1974, Economics and Medical Research, 1983, The Nonprofit Economy, 1988; editor (with James Worthy) The Urban Crisis, 1997; author, editor: To Profit or Not to Profit, 1998; contbr. nearly 200 articles on econs. of edn., program evaluation, health care and econs. of pvt. non-profit sector to profl. jours.; mem. editl. bd.: Jour. Human Resources, 1966-86, Internat. Jour. Social Econs, 1972—, Jour. Public Econs, 1971-87, Pub. Fin. Rev., 1990—, onprofit and Voluntary Sector Quar., 1997—; assoc. editor: Public Fin. Quar, 1972-87. Guggenheim fellow, 1969-70; Ford Faculty fellow, 1971-72; Sr. research fellow Brookdale Inst., Jerusalem, 1978—; recipient Disting. Lifetime Rsch. award Assn. Rsch. Nonprofit Orgns. and Voluntary Assns., 1997; co-recipient Carl Taube award Disting. Rsch., APHA, 1992. Fellow AAAS; mem. Am. Econ. Assn. (exec. com. 1975-77, com. status of assn. jours. 1973-74, chmn. budget com. 1977), Midwest Econs. Assn. (pres. 1980-81), Nat. Acad. Scis. Inst. Medicine, Public Choice Soc., Internat. Inst. Public Finance, AAUP (exec. com. Washington U. chpt. 1961-62). Office: Northwestern U Econs Dept 2003 Sheridan Rd Evanston IL 60208-0826 Business E-Mail: b-weisbrod@northwestern.edu.

WEISENBERGER, ANDREW, lawyer; b. Cin., Sept. 12, 1977; BS, Miami U., Ohio, 1999; JD, Louis D. Brandeis Sch. Law, U. Louisville, 2002; LLM, Georgetown U., 2003. Bar: Ohio 2002, US Dist. Ct. Southern Dist. Ohio 2003, Ky. 2004. Assoc. Santen & Hughes, Cin. Named one of Ohio's Rising Stars, Super Lawyers, 2006. Office: Santen & Hughes STE 2700 600 Vine St Cincinnati OH 45202-2409 Office Phone: 513-721-4450. Office Fax: 513-721-0109.

WEISER, IRVING, financial services company executive; b. Munich, Dec. 4, 1947; s. Siegfried and Paula (Lederman) W.; m. Marjorie Lee Dicker, Mar. 29, 1970; children: Jennifer Suh, Dana Park. BA, SUNY, Buffalo, 1969; JD cum laude, Brooklyn Law Sch., 1973. Bar: Minn., 1973. Assoc. Dorsey & Whitney, Mpls., 1973-78, ptnr., 1979-85; pres. Inter-Regional Fin. Group, Inc., Mpls., 1985-89, pres., CEO, 1990—, also bd. dirs.; pres. RBC Dain Rauscher, Mpls., 1985—89, CEO, 1990—2003, chmn., 2003—. Adj. prof. William Mitchell Coll. Law, St. Paul, 1974-81; bd. dirs. Dain Bosworth Inc., Rauscher Pierce Refsnes, Inc. Trustee Guthrie Theater Found., Mpls., 1983-90; bd. dirs. Temple Israel, 1989—, Children's Home Soc. of Minn., Mpls., 1988—, Minn. Wellspring, Mpls., 1986-88, Legal Rights Ctr., Mpls., 1978-81. Recipient Renaissance Award, Coll. of Saint Benedict, 2004. Mem. Am. Mgmt. Assn. (mem. pres. assn. 1985—), Young Pres.'s Orgn. Clubs: Mpls. Jewish. Avocations: travel, poetry, music. Office: Dain Rauscher Corp 60 S 6th St, 19th Fl Minneapolis MN 55440-1160

WEISER, MARC, venture capitalist; b. 1973; BS in Aerospace Engring., U. Mich., 1995, MBA, 1998. Mem., road show team MessageMedia, 1996; bus. devel. Dell Computer Corp.; assoc. Arbor Partners; founder QuantumShift, 1997; founder, mng. dir. RPM Ventures L.L.C., 2000—. Bd. mem. McKinley Associates, Ann Arbor Area Cmty. Found., McKinley Found., AutoTradeCenter, Oxlo Systems, Xtime, RiverGlass. Named one of 40 Under 40, Crain's Detroit Bus., 2006. Office: RPM Ventures 320 N Main St Ste 400 Ann Arbor MI 48104 Office Phone: 734-332-1700. Office Fax: 734-332-1900.

WEISMAN, ERIC, music company executive; With Premier Artists Svcs., 1985, Bassin Distbr., 1985—90, Alliance Entertainment Corp., Minnetonka, Minn., 1990, pres., CEO, 1997—2003; CEO Musicland Holding Corp., 2003—05, advisor, 2005—. Office: Musicland STE 225 1000 Skokie BLVD Wilmette IL 60091-1176

WEISMAN, GARY ANDREW, biochemist; b. Bklyn., June 18, 1951; s. Joseph Herman and Elaine (Melman) W.; m. Sandra Kay Hille, Aug. 4, 1979; children: Laura Joanne, Pamela Michelle, Veronica Evelyn. BS, Polytechnic U., 1972; postgrad., U. Bordeaux, France, 1972-74; PhD, U. Nebr., 1980. Postdoctoral rsch. assoc. Cornell U., YC, 1980-85; asst. prof. U. Mo., Columbia, 1985-92, assoc. prof., 1992-98, prof., 1998—. Spl. reviewer NIH, mem. ODCS Study Section; reviewer NSF, Am. Jour. Physiology, Jour. Biol. Chemistry, Molec. Pharmacology, Euro. Jour. Pharmacol. GLIA; editl. bd. Purinergic Signalling. Contbr. articles to profl. jours. Grantee USDA, 1987—, NIH, 1988—, CF Found., 1994-2000, Am. Diabetes, 1995-2002, Am. Heart Assn. 1994-. Mem. AAAS, Am. Chem. Soc., Am. Soc. Biochem. and Molecular Biology, Am. Diabetes Assn., Am. Heart Assn., NY Acad. Scis., Soc. for Neurosci., Am. Soc.

Nutr. Scis., Am. Soc. Pharmacol. and Exptl. Therapeut. Home: 1804 University Ave Columbia MO 65201-6004 Office: U Mo Dept Biochemistry 540E Life Scis Ctr Columbia MO 65211-7310 Home Phone: 573-443-8270. Business E-Mail: weismang@missouri.edu.

WEISMAN, JOEL, retired engineering educator; b. NYC, July 15, 1928; s. Abraham and Ethel (Marcus) W.; m. Bernice Newman, Feb. 6, 1955; 1 child, Jay (dec.) B.Ch.E., CCNY, 1948; MS, Columbia U., 1949; PhD, U. Pitts, 1968. Registered profl. engr., N.Y. Plant engr. Etched Products, NYC, 1950-51; from jr. engr. to assoc. engr. Brookhaven Nat. Lab., Upton, NY, 1951-54; from engr. to fellow engr. Westinghouse Nuclear Energy Systems, Pitts., 1954-59, from fellow engr. to mgr. thermal and hydraulic analysis, 1960-68; sr. engr. Nuclear Devel. Assocs., White Plains, NY, 1959-60; assoc. prof. nuclear engring. U. Cin., 1968—72, prof. nuclear engring., 1972-96, dir. nuclear engring. program, 1977-86, dir. lab. basic and applied nuclear research, 1984-94, prof. emeritus nuclear engring., 1996—. Co-author: Thermal Analysis of Pressurized Water Reactors, 1970, 2d edit., 1979, Chinese edit., 1981, 3rd edit., 1996, Introduction to Optimization Theory, 1973, Modern Power Plant Engineering, 1985; editor: Elements of Nuclear Reactor Design, 1977, Chinese edit., 1982, 2d edit., 1983; contbr. tech. articles to profl. jours.; patentee in field. Mem. Cin. Environ. Adv. Council, 1976-78; mem. Cin. Asian Art Soc., 1977—, v.p., 1980-82, pres., 1982-84; mem. exec. bd. Air Pollution League Greater Cin., 1980-90. Sr. NATO fellow, Winfrith Lab., U.K. Atomic Energy Authority, 1972; sr. fellow Argonne Nat. Lab., Ill., 1982; NSF research grantee, 1974-78, 82-85, 86-89; recipient Dean's award U. Cin. Coll. Engring., 1987. Fellow Am. uclear Soc. (v.p. Pitts. sect. 1957-58, mem. exec. com. thermal-hydraulics div. 1989-92); mem. Am. Inst. Chem. Engrs., Sigma Xi Democrat. Jewish. Avocation: Japanese art. Office: U Cin Dept Mech Ind & Nuclear Engr Cincinnati OH 45221-0001

WEISMANTEL, GREGORY NELSON, management consultant, computer company executive; b. Houston, Sept. 8, 1940; s. Leo Joseph and Ellen Elizabeth (Zudis) W.; m. Marilyn Ann Fanger, June 18, 1966; children: Guy Gregory, Christopher Gregory, Andrea Rose. BA in English, U. Notre Dame, 1962; MBA in Internat. Bus., Loyola U., Chgo., 1979. With mgmt. staff Gen. Foods Corp., White Plains, NY, 1966-80; pres., chief exec. officer Manor House Foods, Inc., Addison, Ill., 1980-82, Weismantel & Assocs., Downers Grove, Ill., 1982-84; v.p. perishable div. Profl. Marketers, Inc., Lombard, Ill., 1984-86, group v.p. sales and mktg. services, dir. corp. strategy, 1986-87; v.p. mng. prin. CPG Industry, Louis A. Allen Assoc. Inc., Palo Alto, Calif., 1987-88; pres., chief exec. officer The Vista Tech. Group, Ltd., St. Charles, Ill., 1989-2000, chmn. bd., 2001—02; pres. Epic Global Technol., 2002—. Bd. dirs. Epicurean Foods, Ltd., Chgo., 2004; pres. Aquitec, Inc., Chgo; pres., CEO Epic Group-Hawkeye Perfect Measure Sys., 2003-. Chmn. fin. St. Edward's High Sch. Jubilee, Elgin, Ill., 1982-85; bd. dirs. Dist. 301 Sch. Bd., Burlington, Ill., 1980-84, St. Edward's Found., Elgin, 1982—. Capt. U.S. Army, 1962-66. Recipient ICP/Chgo. Software Assoc. Re-Engring. award, 1994-96; State of Ill. grantee, 1989, Build Ill. Investment Fund, finalist KPMG Hi-tech. Entrepreneur award, Vista Technology, 2001. Mem. Grocery Mfg. Sales Execs., Chgo. Software Assn., Chg. C. of C. (small bus. com.). Clubs: Merchandising Execs., Food Products, Am. Mktg. (Chgo.), St. Charles Country Club (equity mem., fin. chmn.). Roman Catholic.

WEISS, CHARLES ANDREW, lawyer; b. Perryville, Mo., Jan. 24, 1942; s. Wallace Francis and Iola Francis Weiss; m. Marie Suzanne Desloge, June 10, 1972; children: Christopher, Robert, Julie, Anne. BJ with highest honors, U. Mo., 1964, AB with hons. in History, 1965; JD cum laude, Notre Dame U., 1968. Bar: Mo. 1968, US Dist. Ct. (ea. dist.) Mo. 1968, US Ct. Appeals (8th cir.) 1968, U.S. Supreme Ct. 1972, US Ct. Appeals (9th cir.) 1974, U.S. Ct. Appeals (2d cir.) 1977, US Ct. Appeals (1st cir.) 1987, US Ct. Appeals (5th cir.) 1992, US Ct. Appeals (fed. cir.) 2003, US Ct. Appeals (7th cir.) 2003. Law clk. to chief judge U.S. Ct. Appeals (8th cir.), 1968; ptnr. Bryan Cave LLP, St. Louis, 1969—. Lectr. St. Louis U. Law Sch., 1970-73; chmn. Legal Aid Mo. Statewide, Inc., 2003—. Supr. Red Cross Water Safety Program, Perry County, Mo., 1962-64; dir. Neighborhood Youth Corps., Perry County, 1965-66; pres. Perry County Young Dems. Club, 1965-67; committeeman Boy Scouts Am., 1982-86; mem. St. Louis Met. Sewer Dist. Civil Svc. Commn., 1999—; bd. dirs. United Way of Greater St. Louis, 1988-90. Fellow Am. Coll. Trial Lawyers; mem. ABA (ho. of dels. 1986-02, 04-, bd. govs. 2006-), Met. Bar Assn. St. Louis (pres. 1984-85), Mo. Bar Assn. (bd. govs. 1985, v.p. 1994-95, pres.-elect 1995-96, pres. 1996-97), St. Louis Bar Found. (pres. 1983), Mo. Lawyers Trust Account Found. (pres. 1992), Mo. Athletic Club (St. Louis), The Riverlands Assn., Inc. (pres. 1991-93), Jefferson Nat. Parks Assn. (chmn. 1993-2000), Notre Dame Club St. Louis (dir.), Notre Dame Law Assn. (dir., pres. 1997—). Roman Catholic. Office: Bryan Cave 211 N Broadway, Ste 3600 Saint Louis MO 63102-2733 Home Phone: 314-991-2170; Office Phone: 314-259-2215. Business E-Mail: cweiss@bryancave.com.

WEISS, ERWIN, greeting card company executive; V.p. mktg. and sales Rust Craft, Can., pres., Plus Mark, Inc., 1989; v.p. adminstrv. svcs. Carlton Cards Ltd., Can.; sales rep. Am. Greetings Corp., Cleve., 1977, sr. v.p. consumer products, 1991—. Bd. dirs. Diabetes Assn. Greater Cleve.; grad. leadership Cleve. program Greater Cleve. Growth Assn.; active various charitable orgns., Cleve. Office: Am Greetings Corp 1 American Rd Cleveland OH 44144-2301

WEISS, GERHARD HANS, German language educator; b. Berlin, Aug. 6, 1926; came to US, 1946; s. Curt Erich and Gertrud (Grothus) W.; m. Janet Marilyn Smith, Dec. 27, 1953; children: John Martin, Susan Elizabeth Weiss Spencer, James David. BA, Washington U., St. Louis, 1950, MA, 1952; PhD, U. Wis., 1956. Prof. German U. Minn., Mpls., 1956—98, assoc. dean, 1967—71, 1979, chmn. dept. German, 1987-95, prof. emeritus, 1998—, interim dir. Ctr. Austrian Studies, 1999-2001. Mem. German-Am. Textbook Commn., Braunschweig, Fed. Republic Germany, 1985-88. Author: Begegnung mit Deutschland, 1970; editor: Unterrichtspraxis, 1975-80, Minn. Monographs in the Humanities, 1964-70; contbr. articles to profl. jours. Served to lt. col. USAR, 1946-75. Recipient Cross Merit, Fed. Republic Germany, 1982, Austrian Cross of Honor 1st Class Sci. and Arts, Republic of Austria, 2004. Mem. MLA, Am. Assn. Tchrs. German (pres. 1982-83, cert. of merit 1981, Disting. German Educator award 1991, elected hon. mem. 1995), German Studies Assn. (v.p. 1997-98, pres. 1999-00), Am. Coun. Tchg. Fgn. Langs. (Nelson Brooks award 1987). Methodist. Home: 4101 Abbott Ave S Minneapolis MN 55410-1004 Business E-Mail: weiss003@umn.edu.

WEISS, JOHN ROBERT, lawyer; b. Chgo., May 7, 1961; s. Robert Gordon and Elizabeth Jean (Malecki) W.; m. Elizabeth Anne Zur, Dec. 5, 1987. BA, Northwestern U., 1982, JD, 1985. Bar: Ill. 1985, US Dist. Ct. (no. dist.) Ill. 1985, US Dist. Ct. (ctrl. dist.) Ill., 1997, US Ct. Appeals (7th cir.) 1987, US Ct. Appeals (8th cir.), 1999, US Supreme Ct. 1989. Assoc., ptnr. Chapman & Cutler, Chgo., 1985—96; ptnr. Katten Muchin Rosenman, Chgo., 1996—2006, Duane Morris LLP, Chgo., 2006—. Tchr. Chgo. Coalition for Law-Related Edn., 1985—; atty. Chgo. Vol. Legal Services, 1985—. Mem. ABA, 7th Cir. Bar Assn., Am. Judicature Soc., Ill. Bar Assn., Am. Bankruptcy Inst., Turnaround Mgmt. Assn. Roman Catholic. Avocations: golf, billiards, chess. Office: Duane Morris LLP 190 S LaSalle Dt Chicago IL 60603 Office Phone: 312-499-6700. Office Fax: 312-499-6701. Business E-Mail: jrweiss@duanemorris.com.

WEISS, JOSEPH JOEL, consulting company executive; b. Newark, July 27, 1931; s. Harry H. and Belle (Sass) W.; m. Leah Kneller, Apr. 10, 1954 (div. 1961); children: Sara, Daniel; m. Carol Lynn Seegott, Sept. 29, 1967; children: Laura, John. BSBA, Rutgers U., 1953, MBA, 1958. Dist. mgr. N.J. Bell Telephone Co., 1955-61; asst. comptroller ITT P.R. Telephone Co., San Juan, 1964-68; sr. cons. NYC, 1968-71; v.p. data services Rio De Janeiro, 1971-74; dir. ops. NYC, 1975-80; v.p. Control Data Corp., Rio De Janeiro, 1974-75; exec. v.p., chief adminstrv. officer Burger King Corp., Miami, 1980-89; chief oper. officer Goode, Olcott, Knight & Assocs., Coral Gables, Fla., 1989-90; pres. Contraband Detection Internat., Miami, Fla., 1990-92; sr. v.p. Seegott Inc., Streetsboro, Ohio, 1992—. Bd. dirs. Sta. WPB-TV. Author: How to Get from Cubicle to Corner Office, The Quotable Manager. Pres. Civic Betterment Assn., Franklin Twp., N.J., 1961; trustee U. Miami Citizens Bd., 1987—; bd. dirs. Boy Scouts Am., 1982—. Recipient Strategic Planning Achievement award Boy Scouts Am., 1985. Mem. Hist. Soc. Fla. (bd. dirs. 1986—). Clubs: Fisher Island. Republican. Presbyterian. Avocations: painting, tennis. Home: 6682 Brookside Woods Ct Se Ada MI 49301-8219

WEISS, KEVIN BARTON, epidemiologist, medical association administrator; b. Nov. 20, 1956; BA, Washington U., Mo., 1977; MS, MD, U. Chgo., 1981; MPH, Harvard U., 1985, MS, 1987. Bd. cert. internat medicine 1984. Intern internal medicine Cook County Hosp., Chgo., 1981—82, resident internal medicine, 1982—84, resident, 1984—85; tng. epidemiology US Nat. Inst. Allergy and Infectious Diseases, NIH, US Nat. Ctr. for Health Statistics, Ctrs. for Disease Control and Prevention; with Med. Ctr. George Washington U., DC, asst. prof. healthcare scis.; prof. divsn. gen. medicine, dir. Inst. for Healthcare Studies, co-dir. Inst. Health Svcs. & Policy Northwestern U.; dir. Medwest Ctr. for Health Svcs. and Policy Rsch. Hines VA Hosp. US Dept. Vets. Affairs, Ill., 2000—; pres., CEO Am. Bd. Med. Specialties, 2007—. Bd. regents ACP; initiator Nat. Cooperative Inner-City Asthma Study; prin. investigator Pediat. Asthma Care Patient Outcomes Rsch. Team Agy. for Healthcare Rsch. and Quality; prin. investigator Chgo. Initiative to Raise Asthma Health Equity Nat. Heart, Lung and Blood Inst.; mem. expert panel Asthmas Guidelines Nat. Heart, Lung and Blood Inst./Nat. Asthma Edn. and Prevention Program; chair Guideline Implementation panel Nat. Asthma Edn. and Prevention Program; chair asthma measure adv. panel NAt. Com. on Quality Assurance; chair various federally sponsored national asthma workshops. Contbr. articles to profl. pubs., chapters to books. Achievements include research in the epidemiology of asthma and asthma-related problems. Office: American Board Medical Specialties 1007 Church St Ste 404 Evanston IL 60201-5913 also: 675 N St Clair Ste 18-200 Chicago IL 60611 Office Phone: 847-491-9091. Office Fax: 847-328-3596. Business E-Mail: info@ambs.org. E-mail: k-weiss@northwestern.edu.*

WEISS, MORRY, greeting card company executive; b. Czechoslovakia, 1940; m. Judith Stone. Grad., Wayne State U. Salesman, field mgr. Am. Greetings Corp., Cleve., 1961-66, advt. mgr., 1966-68, v.p., 1969-73, group v.p. mktg. and sales, 1973-78, pres., 1978—2003, COO Cleve., 1978—87, bd. dir., chief exec. officer, 1987—2003, chmn., 1992—. Office: Am Greetings Corp 1 American Rd Cleveland OH 44144-2301

WEISS, ROBERT FRANCIS, retired academic and religious organization administrator, consultant; b. St. Louis, Aug. 27, 1924; s. Frank L.G. and Helen M. (Beck) Weiss. BA, St. Louis U., 1951, Ph.L., MA, St. Louis U., 1953, S.T.L., 1961; PhD, U. Minn., 1964. Joined Soc. of Jesus, 1946; ordained priest Roman Cath. Ch., 1959; tchr. Rockhurst HS, Kansas City, Mo., 1953—56; adminstrv. asst. to pres. St. Louis U., 1961—62; asst. dean Rockhurst Coll., Kansas City, Mo., 1964—66, dean, v.p., asst. prof. edn., 1966—72, pres., 1977—88, St. Louis U. HS, 1973—77, interim pres., 1992; asst. higher edn. and continuing formation Mo. Province S.J., St. Louis, 1989—92, treas., 1992—2003, asst. higher edn. and continuing formation, 1997—2005, asst. to treas., 2003—05, del. higher edn., 2005—; assoc. dir. Advancement Office. Mem. Commn. on Govtl. rels. Am. Coun. Edn., 1985—87; bd. dirs. Kansas City Regional Coun. for Higher Edn., 1987—88, Boys Hope Girls Hope, 1977—. Contbr. chapters to books, articles to profl. jours. Trustee St. Louis U., 1973—87, 1991—2003, Loyola U., New Orleans, 1973—82, 1985—88, United Student Aid Funds, Inc., 1977—94, U. San Francisco, 1987—99, Marymount Coll., Salina, Kans., 1986—88, St. Louis U. H.S., 1989—99, 2003—, Fontbonne Coll., St. Louis, 1973—77, Sacred Heart Program, Radio and TV Apostolate, St. Louis, 1990—96, pres., 1992—96, bd. mem., 2000—05; bd. dirs. Creighton U., Omaha, 1981—97, Our Little Haven, St. Louis, 1992—, St. Elizabeth Acad., St. Louis, 1997—2004, DeSmet Jesuit HS, 2003—, Loyola Acad., St. Louis, 2003—, chmn. bd. mems., 2005—; bd. dirs. St. John's Coll., Belize City, Belize, 2003—; bd. trustees St. Louis (Mo.) Archdiocesan Fund, 2006—; bd. regents Conception Sem. Coll., Mo., 2004—. 1st sgt. US Army, 1943—46. Decorated Bronze Star, Two Battle Stars, Combat Infantryman's Badge, Unit Presdl. Citation. Mem.: Am. Assn. for Higher Edn., Vets. Assn. Rainbow divsn. (nat. chaplain 1976—84, 1988—90, pres.-elect 1990—91, pres. 1991—92, assoc. nat. chaplain 1992—, found. pres. 2003—05), Alpha Phi Omega, Alpha Sigma Nu. Home: 3601 Lindell Blvd Saint Louis MO 63108-3393 Office: Mo Province SJ 4511 W Pine Blvd Saint Louis MO 63108-2109 Home Phone: 314-633-4425; Office Phone: 314-361-7765. Business E-Mail: rweiss@jesuits-mis.org.

WEISS, ROBERT ORR, speech educator; b. Kalamazoo, Apr. 8, 1926; s. Nicholas John and Ruth (Orr) W.; m. Ann Lenore Lawson, Sept. 16, 1951; children: Elizabeth Ann, John Lawson, James Robert, Virginia Lenore. BA, Albion Coll., 1948; MA, Northwestern U., 1949, PhD, 1954. Instr. speech Wayne State U., Detroit, 1949-51; instr. pub. speaking Northwestern U., Evanston, Ill., 1954-55; mem. faculty DePauw U., Greencastle, Ind., 1955—2002, H.B. Gough prof. speech, 1965-97, head comm. arts and scis., 1963-78, 85-86, 93. Author: Public Argument, 1995; editor: Speaker and Gavel, 1968-75, Speaking Across the Curriculum, 1990-2006; co-editor: Current Criticism, 1971; contbr. articles to profl. jours. Served with AUS, 1945-46. Recipient Fred C. Tucker Disting. Career award, 1995, Lifetime award, Nat. Ednl. Debate Assn., 1997, Presdl. citation Nat. Communication Assn., 1999. Mem. AAUP (pres. DePauw U. chpt. 1961-62), Nat. Communication Assn. (legis. assembly 1966-68), Am. Forensic Assn. (sec.-treas. 1958-59), Ctrl. States Communication Assn., Phi Beta Kappa, Delta Sigma Rho-Tau Kappa Alpha (nat. v.p. 1981-83, pres. 1983-85), Sigma Nu. Home: 210 W Poplar St Greencastle IN 46135-2638 Home Phone: 765-653-5487; Office Phone: 765-658-4490. Business E-Mail: robertweiss@depauw.edu.

WEISS, STEPHEN J., medical educator, researcher, oncologist; BA, Ohio State U., 1973, MD, 1977. E. Giffert, Love Barnett Upjohn prof. internal medicine U. Mich., Ann Arbor, 1991—, prof. cell and molecular biology divsn. Recipient Young Investigator award, Am. Fedn. Clinical Rsch., 1993, NIH Merit award, 1993—2003. Mem.: Nat Sci. Acad Inst. of Medicine. Office: Univ Mich Med Ctr Dept Medicine MSRB III 5220D 1150 LO Med Ctr Box 0640 Ann Arbor MI 48109-0640 E-mail: sjweiss@umich.edu.

WEISS, ZEV, corporate financial executive; s. Morry Weiss. BA, Yeshiva Univ.; MBA, Columbia Univ. With Am. Greetings Corp., Cleve., 1992—, exec. dir., Nat. Accounts, 1997—2000, v.p., Strategic Business Unit Division, 2000—01, sr. v.p. ventures, 2001, exec. v.p. ventures & enterprise mgmt., 2001—03, CEO, 2003—. Bd. mem. Yeshiva Univ. Office: American Greeting Corp 1 American Rd Cleveland OH 44144-2398

WEISSKOPF, THOMAS EMIL, economics educator; b. Rochester, NY, Apr. 13, 1940; s. Victor Frederick and Ellen (Tuede) W.; m. Frederique Apffel, Mar. 23, 1963 (div. June 1969); 1 child, Marc; m. Susan Contratto, Jan. 17, 1970; children: Nicholas, Jonah. BA, Harvard U., 1961; PhD, MIT, 1966. Asst. prof. econs. dept. Harvard U., Cambridge, Mass., 1968-72; prof. econs. dept. U. Mich., Ann Arbor, 1972—. Dir. residential coll. U. Mich., 1996—2001, 2002—05. Author: Beyond the Waste Land, 1983, After the Waste Land, 1991; editor: Microeconomics in Context, 2002, The Capitalist System, 1972, 1978; author: Affirmative Action in the United States and India: A Comparative Perspective, 2004; editor: The Capitalist System, 1986; author: Economics and Social Justice, 1998; contbr. articles to profl. jours. Office: Univ Mich Dept Econs 206 Lorch Hall 611 Tappan St Ann Arbor MI 48109 Business E-Mail: tomw@umich.edu.

WEISSMAN, MICHAEL LEWIS, lawyer; b. Chgo., Sept. 11, 1934; s. Maurice and Sue (Goldberg) Weissman; m. Joanne Sherwin, Dec. 19, 1961; children: Mark Douglas, Greg Steven, Scott Adam, Brett Anthony. Student White scholar, U. Chgo., 1951-52; BS in Econs, Northwestern U., 1954; MBA in Acctg., U. Pa., 1956; JD, Harvard U., 1958; postgrad. Fulbright scholar, U. Sydney, Australia, 1958-59; postgrad., Hague Acad. Internat. Law, 1959. Bar: D.C. 1958, Ill. 1959. Asst. prof. bus. law Roosevelt U., Chgo., 1959-61; pvt. practice Chgo., 1959—; mem. firm Aaron, Aaron, Schimberg & Hess, 1969-78; sr. ptnr. Boorstein & Weissman, 1978-82, Weissman, Smolev & Solow, 1982-88, Foley & Lardner, 1988-92, McBride Baker & Coles, Chgo., 1992—2001; exec. v.p., gen. counsel Bridgeview Bank Group, Chgo., 2001—04; of counsel Holland & Knight LLC, 2001—. Asst. prof. Roosevelt U., 1960—62; lectr. Lake Forest (Ill.) Coll., 1979—80; chmn. Banking Group, Union League Club Chgo.; panelist Risk Mgmt. Assn., Banking Law Inst., Midwest Fin. Conf., Greater O'Hare Assn., Miss. Law Inst., Bank Lending Inst., Chgo. Assn. Commerce and Industry, State of Art Seminars, Infocast Inc., SBA, Fed. Res. Bank Chgo., Lenders Ednl. Inst., Bank Adminstrn. Inst. Found., Lender's Forum, Clarion Legal; Fulbright sr. specialist Sch. Bus. Adminstrn., Turiba, Latvia, 2006; adj. prof. law John Marshall Law Sch., 2001—02, 2006—. Author: (book) Lender Liability, 1988, Commercial Loan Documentation and Secured Lending, 1990, How to Avoid Career-Ending Mistakes in Commercial Lending, 1996, The Lender's Edge, 1997; mem. editl. bd.: Commercial Damages, 1985—; contbr. articles to profl. jours. Mem. adv. bd. Affective Disorders Clinic, U. Ill. Med. Sch., 1979—81; instr. mentor program Risk Mgmt. Assn. Scholar, Fulbright Found., 1958—59, 2006; White scholar, U. Chgo., 1951—52. Mem.: ABA, Robert Morris Assn., Comml. Fin. Assn. Ednl. Found. (adv. bd.), Turnaround Mgmt. Assn. (steering com. Chgo. chpt.), Harvard Law Soc. Ill., Assn. Comml. Fin. Attys. (bd. dirs.), Ill. Inst. CLE (bd. dirs. 1989—2000, chmn. 2001—02), Ill. Bankers Assn. (mem. com. bank counsel 1987—88, vice chmn. 1988—89), Chgo. Bar Assn., Ill. Bar Assn., Beta Alpha Psi. Home: 2067 Old Briar Rd Highland Park IL 60035-4245 Office: Holland & Knight LLP 131 S Dearborn St 30th Fl Chicago IL 60603-5506 Office Phone: 312-715-5767. Business E-Mail: michael.weissman@hklaw.com.

WEIST, WILLIAM BERNARD, lawyer; b. Lafayette, Ind., Dec. 23, 1938; s. Bernard Francis and Frances Loretta (Doyle) W.; m. Rosemary Elaine Anderson, Apr. 30, 1963; children: Sean M., Cynthia A. BBA, U. Notre Dame, 1961; JD, U. Louisville, 1970. Bar: Ky. 1971, Ind. 1971, U.S. Dist. Ct. (no. and so. dists.) Ind. 1971. Bank examiner Fed. Res. Bank, St. Louis, 1966-67; Trust officer Citizens Fidelity Bank, Louisville, 1967-71; pvt. practice Fowler, Ind., 1971—; sr. ptnr. Dumas, Weist and Mahnesmith. Bd. dirs. Benton Fin. Corp., Fowler, Fowler State Bank; pros. atty. 76th Jud. Cir., Benton County, Ind., 1975-98. Capt. USAF, 1961-65. Fellow Ind. Bar Found. (charter mem.); mem. Ind. State Bar Assn., Ind. Pros. Attys. Assn. (pres. 1979), Ind. Pros. Attys. Coun. (chmn. 1989), at. Dist. Attys. Assn. (bd. dirs.), Columbia Club (Indpls.), Elks, KC. Avocations: golf, reading. Home: 1000 E 5th St Fowler IN 47944-1520 Office: Weist Bldg Grant Ave Fowler IN 47944-0101

WEIXLMANN, JOSEPH NORMAN, JR., language educator, academic administrator; b. Buffalo, Dec. 16, 1946; s. Joseph Norman and Mary C. (Degenhart) W.; m. Sharron Pollack, Mar. 14, 1982; children: Seth Jacob, Adira Jenna, Benjamin Ari. AB, Canisius Coll., 1968; MA, Kans. State U., 1970, PhD, 1973. Instr. U. Okla., Norman, 1973-74; asst. prof. Tex. Tech U., Lubbock, 1974-76; from asst. prof. to prof. Ind. State U., Terre Haute, 1976—2001, assoc. dean, 1987-92, acting dean, 1992-94, dean, 1994—2001; prof. St. Louis U., 2001—, dean, 2001—02, provost, 2002—. Author: John Barth, 1976, American Short-Fiction Criticism, 1982; co-editor: Black American Prose Theory, 1984, Belief vs. Theory in Black American Literary Criticism, 1986, Black Feminist Criticism, 1988, Studies in Black Am. Lit. Ann., 1984-88; editor African Am. Rev. jour., 1976-2004; contbg. editor High Plains Lit. Rev., 1987-2002; adv. editor Langston Hughes Rev., 1982—. Fellow DEA, 1970-72, NEH, 1980; Nat. Endowment for Arts grantee, 1988-95; Disting. Editor award, Conf. Editors of Learned Jours., 2005. Mem. Coll. Lang. Assn., Langston Hughes Soc., Zora Neale Hurston Soc. Office: Saint Louis U DuBourg Hall #444 Saint Louis MO 63103 Home: 6344 Wydown Blvd Saint Louis MO 63105-2213 Office Phone: 314-977-3718. Business E-Mail: weixlmj@slu.edu.

WEJCMAN, LINDA, retired state legislator; b. Dec. 1939; m. Jim. Student, Iowa State U. Minn. State rep. Dist. 61B, 1991—2000, ret., 2000. Home: 3203 5th Ave S Minneapolis MN 55408-3248

WELBURN, EDWARD T., automotive executive; b. Phila., Dec. 14, 1950; BA, Howard U., 1972. Assoc. designer GM Advanced Design Studios, 1972, Buick Exterior Studio, 1973, Oldsmobile Exterior Studio, 1975—85, chief designer, 1989—98; with Saturn global design GM, Rüsselsheim, Germany, 1996—98, exec. dir. design body-on-frame architectures, 2002, v.p. design N. Am., 2003—05, v.p. global design, 2005—; dir. GM Corp. Brand Ctr., Warren, Mich., 1998—2001. Designer Indianapolis 500 Pace Car, 1985. Recipient The Best Concept Truck, N. Am. Internat. Auto Show, 2003, Best Concept Car, Autoweek, 1995, Award of Design Excellence, Indsl. Designers Soc. Am., 1988.

WELCH, DAVID WILLIAM, lawyer; b. St. Louis, Feb. 26, 1941; s. Claude LeRoy Welch and Mary Eleanor (Peggs) Welch; m. Candace Lee Capages, June 5, 1971; children: Joseph Peggs, Heather Elizabeth, Katherine Laura. BSBA, Washington U., St. Louis, 1963; JD, U. Tulsa, 1971. Bar: Okla. 1972, Mo. 1973, U.S. Dist. Ct. (we. dist.) Mo. 1973, U.S. Dist. Ct. (ea. dist.) Mo. 1974, U.S. Ct. Appeals (8th cir.) 1977, U.S. Ct. Appeals (7th cir.) 1991. Contract adminstr. McDonnell Aircraft Corp., St. Louis, 1965-66; bus. analyst Dun & Bradstreet Inc., Los Angeles, 1967-68; atty. U.S. Dept. Labor, Washington, 1972-73; ptnr. Moller Talent, Kuelthau & Welch, St. Louis, 1973-88, Lashly & Baer, St. Louis, 1988-96, Armstrong Teasdale LLP, St. Louis, 1996—. Author: (handbook) Missouri Employment Law, 1988; contbr. book chpts. Missouri Bar Employer-Employee Law, 1985, 87, 89, 92, 94, Missouri Discrimination Law, 1999; co-editor: Occupational Safety and Health Law, 1996. Mem. City of Creve Coeur Ethics Commn., 1987-88, Planning and Zoning Commn., 1988-96; bd. dirs. Camp Wyman, Eureka, Mo., 1982—, sec., 1987-88, 2nd v.p. 1988-89, 1st v.p. 1990-92, pres., 1992-94. Mem. ABA, Fed. Bar Assn., Mo. Bar Assn., Okla. Bar Assn., St. Louis Bar Assn., Kiwanis (bd. dirs. St. Louis 1979—, sec. 1982-83, 93-94, 2003-04, v.p. 1983-84, 88-90, 92-93, 2003-04, Man of Yr. award 1985). Democrat. Mem. Christian Ch. (Disciples Of Christ). Avocations: travel, music. Office: Armstrong Teasdale 1 Metropolitan Sq Ste 2600 Saint Louis MO 63102-2740

WELCH, LYMAN W., lawyer; BA cum laude, Knox Coll., 1964; JD, Harvard Law Sch., 1967. Bar: US Tax Ct. 1976, Fla. 1978, Ill. 1968. Ptnr. Sidley Austin, LLP, Chgo. Adv. to restatement of the law of trusts project Am. Law Inst. Contbr. articles to profl. publs. Named one of Top 2 Trust and Estate Lawyers in Chgo., Town and Country mag., 1998, Best Trusts and Estates Lawyers in Am., Bloomberg Personal Fin., 1999, Top 100 Attys., Worth mag., 2005—06. Fellow: Am. Coll. Trust and Estate Counsel (mem. fiduciary litig. and estate and gift tax coms.); mem.: ABA (mem. fed. tax sect. com. on fiduciary income tax and partnerships com.). Office: Sidley Austin LLP 1 S Dearborn Chicago IL 60603 Office Phone: 312-853-4165. Office Fax: 312-853-7036. E-mail: lwelch@Sidley.com.

WELCH, MARTIN E., III, investor, retail executive; b. Detroit, June 25, 1948; m. Anne Welch; children: Michele, James, Mary Beth, Brian. BS in Acctg., U. Detroit Mercy, 1970, MBA, 1973. Audit mgr. Arthur Young & Co., Detroit, 1970-77; dir. mktg. acctg. Fruehauf divsn. Fruehauf Corp., Detroit, 1977-82; mgr. corp. acctg. Chrysler Corp., Highland Park, Mich., 1982-83, asst. contr., 1983-86, gen. auditor, 1987-88, asst. treas., 1988-91; CFO Chrysler Can., Windsor, Ont., 1986-87; sr. v.p., CFO Federal-Mogul corp., Southfield, Mich., 1991-95; exec. v.p., CFO Kmart Corp, Troy, Mich., 1995—2001; bus. advisor, dir. York Mgmt. Svcs., Somerset, NJ, 2002—; exec. v.p., CFO Oxford Automotive, Inc., Troy, Mich., 2003—04, United Rentals, Inc., Greenwich, Conn., 2005—. Mem. nat. adv. bd. JP Morgan Bank, 1997—2000; bd. dirs. No. Group Retail, Ltd., Delphi Corp. Bd. dirs. U. Detroit-Mercy. Mem.: Fin. Execs. Internat. Personal E-mail: martywelch@yahoo.com.

WELCH, MICHAEL JOHN, chemistry educator, researcher; b. Stoke-on-Trent, Staffordshire, Eng., June 28, 1939; came to U.S., 1965; s. Arthur John W. and Mary (Welch); m. Teresa Jean Conocchiolli, Apr. 22, 1967 (div. 1979); children: Colin, Lesley. BA, Cambridge U., Eng., 1961; MA, Cambridge U., 1964; PhD, London U., 1965. Asst. prof. radiation chemistry in radiology Washington U. Sch. Medicine, St. Louis, 1967-70, assoc. prof., 1970-74, assoc. prof. dept. chemistry, 1971-75, prof. dept. chemistry, 1978—, prof. radiology, 1991—, prof. molecular biology and pharmacology, 1993—; prof. biomed. engring. program Washington U., St. Louis, 1996; co-dir. Mallinckrodt Inst. Dir. radiol. scis. dept. Washington U., 1990—; mem. diagnostic radiology study sect. NIH, 1986-89, chmn., 1989-91; mem. sci. adv. com. Whitaker Found., 1995-2003. Author: Introduction to the Tracer Methods, 1972; editor: Radiopharmaceuticals and Other Compounds Labeled with Shortlived Radionuclides, 1977; assoc. editor Jour. Nuclear Medicine, 1989—2003; contbr. chpts. to books, more than 400 articles to profl. jours. Recipient Georg Charles de Hevesy Nuclear Medicine Pioneer award, 1992; scholar St. Catharine Coll. Cambridge U., 1958-61. Mem. Soc. Nuclear Medicine (trustee, pres. 1984, Paul C. Aebersold award 1980, de Hevesy Nuclear Pioneer award 1992), Radiopharm. Sci. Coun. (pres. 1980-81), Am. Chem. Soc. (St. Louis award 1988, award for nuclear chemistry 1990, Mid-West award 1991), Chem. Soc. London, Radiation Rsch. Soc., Inst. of Medicine, Sigma Xi Office: Washington U Sch Medicine Edward Mallinckrodt Inst Radiology 510 S Kingshighway Blvd Box 8225 Saint Louis MO 63110-1016 E-mail: welchm@mir.wustl.edu.

WELCH, PATRICK, state legislator; b. Chgo., Dec. 12, 1948; s. William C. and Alice W. Student, So. Ill. U., 1970; JD, Chgo. Kent Coll. Law, 1974. Bar: Ill. 1974. Pvt. practice, Peru, Ill., 1974—; mem. Ill. Senate, 1983—. Asst.

minority leader, 2003—, chmn. appropriations com.; former chmn. energy and environ. com.; nat. del., credentials com. Dem. Nat. Conv., 1976, del., 1980, 84, 88, 92, 96, 2000; del. Dem. Nat. Mid-Term Conf., 1978, 82; committeeman Ill. Dem. Cen. Com., 1978—; exec. com., 1983—; vice-chmn. Ill. Dem. Party, 1990-94, chmn. party platform com., 1994. Office: Ill State Senate State Capitol Rm 121A Springfield IL 62706-0001

WELCH, PEGGY, state representative; b. Fulton, Miss., Oct. 13, 1955; BS in Social Studies and Edn., Miss. Coll., 1977; ASN, Ivy Tech. State Coll., 1995; student, Ind. U., 1992—94. Substitute tchr. Monroe County Cmty. Sch. Corp., 1981—82, 1991; dir., probation officer Monroe County Cmty. Corrections Program, 1983—90; cert. childbirth educator Lamaze of Bloomington, Inc., 1983—94; grad. sec., dept. theater and drama Ind. U., Bloomington, 1991—94; RN, oncology Bloomington Hosp. CCU and Cancer Care Units, 1995—; state rep. dist. 60 Ind. Ho. of Reps., Indpls., 1998—, mem. human affairs, tech. R & D, and ways and means coms. Chair, nursing programs adv. bd. Ivy Tech. State Coll., Bloomington; adv. bd. Ind. U. Sch. Nursing. Named Ind. C. of C. Small Bus. Champion, 2003; recipient Heart of Ind. award, Am. Heart Assn., 2003, Child Safety Advocate award, Ind. Safe Kids Coalition, 2002, Legis. Leadership award, Ind. United Sr. Action, 2001, Meritorious Svc. award, Ind. Assn. Homes and Svcs. for the Aging, Inc., 2001, numerous other awards. Mem.: Ind. State urses Assn., Children's Organ Transplant Assn. (bd. dirs.), Fraternal Order of Police, NAACP, Women in Govt., Bloomfield C. of C., Greater Bloomington C. of C., Brown County C. of C., Local Coun. of Women, Ind. U. Theater Circle, RN Club, Monroe County Dem. Women's Club. Democrat. Office: Ind Ho of Reps 200 W Washington St Indianapolis IN 46204-2786

WELCH, ROBERT THOMAS, state legislator; b. Berlin, Wis., June 8, 1958; s. William and Betty (Baudhuin) W.; m. Jeanne M. Piechowski, Dec. 30, 1978; children: Adam, Sarah, Peter. AAS, Madison Area Tech. Coll., 1980; student, Lawrence U., 1976-78, U. Wis., Stevens Point, 1978. Surveyor Kiedrowski Engring., Stevens Point, Wis., 1981, Welch Land Surveying, Redgranite, Wis., 1982—; mem. Wis. Assembly, Madison, 1985-93, Wis. Senate from 14th dist., Madison, 1995—. Chmn. Council on Migrant Labor, Assembly Rep. Caucus; mem. assembly coms. on employment and tng., rules, elections, adminstrv. rules, orgn. Treas. Waushara County Rep., 1983-84, active State Rep. Platform Co., 1984, chmn. platform com., 1988; 4-H leader. Named one of Outstanding Young Men Am., Montgomery, Ala., 1985, 86, 87. Mem. Green Lake Ripon Area Bd. Realtors. Roman Catholic. Home: PO Box 523 Redgranite WI 54970-0523 Office: State Capitol PO Box 7882 Madison WI 53707-7882

WELGE, DONALD EDWARD, food manufacturing executive; b. St. Louis, July 11, 1935; s. William H. and Rudelle (Fritze) W.; m. Mary Alice Childers, Aug. 4, 1962; children: Robert, Tom. BS, La. State U., 1957. With Gilster-Mary Lee Corp., Chester, Ill., 1957—, pres., gen. mgr., 1965—. Dir. Buena Vista Bank of Chester; pres. Buena Vista Bankcorp. Former chmn. St. John's Luth. Bd. Edn. 1st lt. Transp. Corp, U.S. Army, 1958-63. Named So. Ill. Bus. Leader of Yr. So. Ill. U., 1988. Mem. Perryville C. of C. (pres. 1989), Chester, Ill. C. of C. (past pres.), Alpha Zeta, Phi Kappa Phi. Republican. Lutheran. Home: 5 Knollwood Dr Chester IL 62233-1416 Office: Gilster Mary Lee Co PO Box 227 Chester IL 62233-0227 Business E-Mail: dwelge@gilstermarylee.com.

WELK, THOMAS JOHN, lawyer; b. Hoven, SD, Aug. 12, 1950; s. Al John and Monica Rose (Coyle) W.; m. Genevieve T. Welk, 1975; children: Colleen, David, Kathleen. BS in Econs. with honors, U. S.D., 1972, MBA, JD, 1975. Bar: S.D. 1975, U.S. Dist. Ct. S.D. 1967, U.S. Ct. Appeals (8th cir.) 1977, U.S. Ct. Appeals (9th cir.) 1987, U.S. Tax Ct. 1981, U.S. Supreme Ct. 1981; bd. cert. civil advocacy Nat. Bd. Trial Advocacy 1995. Asst. atty. gen. State of S.D., Pierre, 1975-79, dep. atty. gen., 1979; ptnr. Boyce, Greenfield, Pashby & Welk, LLP (formerly Boyce, Murphy, McDowell & Greenfield), Sioux Falls, SD, 1979—. Mem. ABA (adminstrv. law, antitrust sect.), SD Bar Assn. (chmn., com. mem., pres. 2004-05), Am. Bd. Trial Advs., Internat. Assn. Def. Counsel, Fedn. Def. and Corp. Counsel, SD Def. Lawyers Assn. (past pres., leadership award Def. Rsch. Inst.), Westward House Country Club (pres.). Republican. Roman Catholic. Avocations: golf, hunting, travel. Office: Boyce, Greenfield, Pashby & Welk LLP 101 N Phillips Ave Ste 600 PO Box 5015 Sioux Falls SD 57117-5015 Office Phone: 605-336-2424. Office Fax: 605-334-0618. Business E-Mail: tjwelk@bgpw.com.

WELKER, WALLACE IRVING, neurophysiologist, educator; b. Batavia, NY, Dec. 17, 1926; PhD in Psychology, U. Chgo., 1954. Mem. faculty U. Wis. Med. Sch., 1957—, prof. neurophysiology, 1965-90, emeritus prof., 1990—. Served with AUS, 1945-47. Sister Kenny Found. scholar, 1957-62; recipient NIH Career Devel. award, 1962-67 Mem. Am. Anat. Soc., Neurosci. Soc. Office: 5480 Caddis Bnd Apt 202 Fitchburg WI 53711-7169

WELL, IRWIN, language educator; b. Cin., Apr. 16, 1928; s. Sidney and Florence (Levy) Well; m. Vivian Max, Dec. 27, 1950; children: Martin, Alice, Daniel. BA, U. Chgo., 1948, MA, 1951; PhD, Harvard U., 1960; D (hon.), Nevsky Inst., Petersburg, Russia, 1999. Tchg. fellow Harvard U., Cambridge, Mass., 1955-58; asst. prof. Brandeis U., Waltham, Mass., 1958-65; assoc. prof. Northwestern U., Evanston, Ill., 1966-70, prof. Russian, Russian Lit., 1970—. Pres., bd. dirs. Am. Coun. Tchrs. Russian, Washington, 1967—. Author: numerous books in field; contbr. articles to scholarly jours. Recipient Pushkin medal, Internat. Assn. Russian Profs. Jewish. Avocations: music, singing. Office: Northwestern U Slavic Dept Evanston IL 60208-2163 Home Phone: 847-864-4835; Office Phone: 847-491-8254. Business E-Mail: i-weil@northwestern.edu.

WELLER, GERALD C., congressman; b. Streator, Ill., July 7, 1957; s. LaVern and Marilyn Weller; m. Zury Rios Sosa. Degree in Agriculture, U. Ill., 1979. Aide to U.S. Congressman Tom Corcoran, 1977-78; aide to U.S. Sec. of Agriculture John R. Block, 1981-85; active family farm, 1985-88; mem. Ill. Ho. of Reps., 1987—93, U.S. Congress from 11th Ill. dist., 1995—; asst. majority whip; mem. ways and means com., 1996—; mem. Internat. Relations Com., 2003—. Rep. House Republican steering com.; mem. Newt Gingrich's policy com.; exec. com. NRCC, House Banking Com., House Veterans Affairs Com., House Transp. and Infrastructure Com. Mem. 1st Christian Ch. of Morris, Ill. Mem. Nat. Republican Legis. Assn. (nominated Legislator of Yr.). Republican. Office: US Ho Reps 1210 Longworth Ho Office Bldg Washington DC 20515-1311

WELLIN, THOMAS, music director; m. Annette Wellin; children: Claire, Christopher, Patrick. BMus summa cum laude, Ind. U.; MMus, U. Maine; postgrad., Acad. Mus. Chigiana, Siena, Italy; studied with Julius Herford, Ruggiero Ricci, Franco Rerrara, Gustav Meier. Music dir., condr. Bismarck (N.D.)-Mandan Symphony Orch., 1990—. Guest condr. Fargo-Moorhead Symphony; lectr. in field. Condr. summer concerts Pops on the Prairie, New Year's Eve Viennese Gala, Dickinson State U., I-94 Music Festival, Beulah, N.D., 4th of July Spectacular on State Capitol Mall, (CD) Vivaldi's The Four Seasons. Performing Artists fellow .D. Coun. Arts. Office: Bismarck-Mandan Symphony Orch PO Box 2031 Bismarck ND 58502-2031

WELLINGTON, JEAN SUSORNEY, librarian; b. East Chicago, Ind., Oct. 23, 1945; d. Carl Matthew and Theresa Ann Susorney; m. Donald Clifford Wellington, June 12, 1976; 1 child, Evelin Patricia. BA, Purdue U., 1967; MA in LS, Dominican U., River Forest, Ill., 1969; MA, U. Cin., 1976. Head Burnam Classical Libr. U. Cin., 1970—. Compiler Dictionary of Bibliographic Abbreviations Found in the Scholarship of Classical Studies and Related Disciplines, 1983, 2d edit., 2002, revised and expanded edit., 2003. Mem. Art. Librs. Soc. N.Am. (chair Ohio br. 1984-85). Office: U Cin Classics Libr PO Box 210191 Cincinnati OH 45221-0191

WELLINGTON, ROBERT HALL, manufacturing executive, director; b. Atlanta, July 4, 1922; s. Robert H. and Ernestine V. (Vossbrinck) W.; m. Marjorie Jarchow, Nov. 15, 1947; children: Charles R., Robert H., Christian J., Jeanne L. BS, McCormack Sch. of Engring. and Applied Scis. (formerly Northwestern Tech. Inst.), 1944; MSBA, MBA, U. Chgo., 1958. With Griffin Wheel Co., 1946-61; v.p. parent co. Amsted Industries, Inc., Chgo., 1961-74, exec. v.p., 1974-80, pres., chief exec. officer, 1981-88, chmn. bd., chief exec. officer, 1988-90. Served to lt. USN, 1943-46. Office: Amsted Industries Inc 205 N Michigan Ave Fl 44 Chicago IL 60601-5927

WELLS, JONATHAN, state legislator; m. Justina Wells. Kans. state rep. Dist. 84, 1993—. Home: PO Box 2543 Wichita KS 67201-2543

WELLS, KIMBERLY K., not-for-profit organization executive; BA in Psychology, MA in Counseling Psychology. Dir. youth svcs., dir. program svcs., assoc. exec. dir. Home Sweet Home Mission, 1987—97; exec. dir. Corp. Alliance to End Prtnr. Violence, 1997—. Mem. Workplace Com. Nat. Task Force to End Sexual and Domestic Violence Against Women; chair Promotion Com., State of Ill.; mem. Gov.'s Commn. on Status of Women in Ill. Violence Reduction Group, Ill. Corp. Citizenship Initiative; mem. steering com. Ill. Family Violence Coordinating Coun.; mem. 11th Jud. Cir. Family Violence Coordinating Coun. Planning Com.; co-chair McLean County Domestic Violence Task Force Youth and Children Work Group; treas., bd. dirs. Ill. Ctr. for Violence Prevention; grad. Leadership Am. Am. Issues Forum, 1999; guest lectr. Ill. State U., Heartland C.C. Office: 2416 E Washington St Ste E Bloomington IN 61704-4472

WELLS, LESLEY, federal judge; b. Muskegon, Mich., Oct. 6, 1937; d. James Franklin and Inez Simpson Wells; m. Charles F. Clarke, Nov. 13, 1998; children: Lauren Elizabeth, Caryn Alison, Anne Kristin, Thomas Eliot. BA, Chatham Coll., 1959; JD cum laude, Cleve. State U., 1974. Bar: Ohio 1975, US Dist. Ct. (no. dist.) Ohio 1975, US Supreme Ct. 1989. Pvt. practice, Cleve., 1975; ptnr. Brooks & Moffet, Cleve., 1975—78; dir., atty. ABAR Litig. Ctr., Cleve., 1979—80; assoc. Schneider, Smeltz, Huston & Ranney, Cleve., 1980—83; judge Ct. Common Pleas, Cleve., 1983—94, US Dist. Ct. (no. dist.) Ohio, Cleve., 1994—2006, sr. judge, 2006—. Adj. prof. law and urban policy Cleve. State U., 1980-83, 90-93. Editor, author: Litigation Manual, 1980. Past pres. Cleve. Legal Aid Soc.; legal chmn. Nat. Women's Polit. Caucus, 1981-82; chmn. Gov.'s Task Force on Family Violence, Ohio, 1983-87; mem. biomed. ethics com. Case Western Res. U. Med. Sch., 1985-94; mem. NW Ordinance US Constn. Commn., Ohio, 1986-88; master William K. Thomas Inn of Ct., 1989—, counselor, 1993, pres., 1998-99; trustee Rosemary Ctr., 1986-92, Miami U., 1988-92, Urban League Cleve., 1989-90, Chatham Coll., 1989-94. Recipient Superior Jud. award Supreme Ct. Ohio, 1983, J. Irwin award Womenspace, Ohio, 1984, award Womens City Club, 1985, Disting. Alumna award Chatham Coll., 1988, Alumni Civic Achievement award Cleve. State U., 1992, Golden Gavel award Ohio Judges Assn., 1994, Outstanding Alumni award Cleve. Marshall Law Alumni Assn., 1994, Greater Cleve. Achievement award YWCA, 1995. Mem. ABA (coun. litigation sect. 1996-99), Am. Law Inst., Ohio Bar Assn., Ohio Womens Bar Assn., Cleve. Bar Assn. (Merit Svc. award 1983), Cuyahoga County Bar Assn., Nat. Assn. Women Judges, Philos. Club Cleve. Office: 328 US Court House 201 Superior Ave Cleveland OH 44114-1234 Office Phone: 216-615-4480. Business E-Mail: lesley_wells@ohnd.uscourts.gov.

WELLS, NORMAN, JR., metal products executive; BS metallurgy, indsl. engring., U. Wash., 1971; MBA, Gonzaga U., 1980. With Castech Aluminum Group Inc., Akron, Ohio, 1989—. Office: Castech Aluminum Group Inc 753 W Waterloo Rd Akron OH 44314-1525

WELLS, RICHARD A., manufacturing executive; BSBA, U. Wis., Madison, 1960; cert. in data processing, U. Wis., Milw. CPA, Wis. With Kohler (Wis.) Co., sr. v.p. fin., CFO, 1979-1999, also mem. exec. com., pension investment com., bd. dirs. Office: Kohler Co 444 Highland Dr Kohler WI 53044-1500

WELLS, ROGER W., lawyer; b. Sioux Falls, SD, May 7, 1957; BSBA summa cum laude, Creighton U., 1979, JD summa cum laude, 1981. Bar: Nebr. 1981, U.S. Dist. Ct. ebr. 1981, U.S. Tax Ct. 1981. Gen. counsel ConAgra Foods Inc., Omaha, 2002; head, mergers and acquisitions McGrath, North, Mullin & Kratz, Omaha, 1981—. Mem. editl. staff: Creighton U. Law Rev., 1980—81. Mem.: ABA (mem. corp., banking and bus. sect., mem. taxation sect., mem. internat. law sect.), Omaha Bar Assn., Nebr. Bar Assn., Beta Gamma Sigma. Office: McGrath North Mullin and Kratz PC Ste 3700 1st Nat Tower 1601 Dodge St Omaha NE 68102 Home Phone: 402-498-0941; Office Phone: 402-341-3070. Business E-Mail: rwells@mnmk.com.

WELLS, SAMUEL ALONZO, JR., surgeon, educator; b. Cuthbert, Ga., Mar. 16, 1936; s. Samuel Alonzo and Martha Steele W.; m. Barbara Anne Atwood, Feb. 13, 1964; children: Sarah, Susan. Student, Emory U., 1954—57, MD, 1961. Intern Johns Hopkins Hosp., Balt., 1961—62, resident in internal medicine, 1962—63; asst. resident in surgery Barnes Hosp., St. Louis, 1963—64; resident in surgery Duke U., Durham, NC, 1966—70; guest investigator dept. tumor biology Karolinska Inst., Stockholm, 1967—68; asst. prof. surgery Duke U., Durham, NC, 1970—72, assoc. prof., 1972—76, prof., 1976—81; clin. assoc. surgery br. Nat. Cancer Inst., IH, Bethesda, Md., 1964—66, sr. investigator surgery br., 1970—72, cons. surgery br., 1975—; prof., chmn. dept. surgery Washington U., St. Louis, 1981—98; dir. ACS, Chgo., 1998—99, group chair, prin. investigator, oncology group, 1998—2005, exec. dir. internat. thyroid cancer study group, 2005—. Dir. Duke U. Clin. Rsch. Ctr., 1978—81; mem. Residency Rev. Com. Surgery, 1987—93, chmn., 1991—93; mem. bd. regents ACS, 1989—98, vice chmn. bd. regents, 1998—; prof. surgery Duke U. Sch. Medicine, 2001—07. Mem. editl. bd.: Annals of Surgery, 1975—93, Surgery, 1975—93, Jour. Surg. Rsch., 1981—93, editor in chief: World Jour. Surgery, 1983—92, Current Problems in Surgery, 1989—. Pres. GM Cancer Rsch. Found., 1996—2006. Lt. comdr. USPHS, 1964—66. Fellow: AAAS; mem.: ACS, Soc. Internationale de Chirurgie (pres. 2001), Soc. Surg. Oncology (pres. 1993—94), Halsted Soc. (pres. 1987), Nat. Cancer Adv. Bd., Inst. Medicine of NAS, Am. Soc. Clin. Investigation, Soc. Clin. Surgery (treas. 1980—86, v.p. 1986—88, pres. 1988—90), Soc. Univ. Surgeons (exec. coun. 1976—78), Am. Surg. Assn. (mem. coun. 1986—91, pres. 1995—96, recorder, Sci. Achievement medallion 2004), Am. Bd. Surgery (exec. com. 1986—89, vice chmn. 1987—88, chmn. 1988—89), Alpha Omega Alpha. Office: Dept Surgery Wash Univ Sch Medicine 660 S Euclid Ave Campus Box 8109 Saint Louis MO 63110 Office Phone: 919-201-0310. Business E-Mail: wellss@wudosis.wustl.edu.

WELNETZ, DAVID CHARLES, human resources executive; b. Antigo, Wis., Apr. 12, 1947; s. Francis P. and Marquette A. (Stengl) W.; m. Mary L. McCulley, Aug. 25, 1973; children: Andrew, Timothy. BS in Biology, U. Wis., Stevens Point, Wis., 1969; MS in Indsl. Rels., U. Wis. Madison, 1975. Mgr. coll. recruitment tng. Rexnord Inc., Milw., 1975-77, personnel mgr. Sarasota, Fla., 1977-80, corp. dir. employee rels. Milw., 1980-83; sr. cons. The Thompson Group, Brookfield, Wis., 1983-87, v.p., 1987-91; pres. Thompson Cons., Brookfield, 1991—. Adv. bd. SUNY, Buffalo, 1982-88; bd. dirs. Matarah Industries. Bd. dirs. Outplacement Internat., 1996—; bd. dirs. Matarah Ind., 1994—, Lutheran Social Svcs., Milw. Ctr. for Independence. Recipient Bronze Star U.S. Army, 1972. Mem. Pers. Indsl. Rels. Assn. (program com. 1988-91, chmn. pers. rsch. 1980-82), Human Resources Planning Soc., Human Resources Mgmt. Assn. Roman Catholic. Home: N54W 38928 Islandale Dr Oconomowoc WI 53066-2101 Office: The Thompson Group PO Box 756 Merton WI 53056-0756

WELSER, WILLIAM, III, military officer; B in Biology, U. Buffalo, 1971; grad., Squadron Officer Sch., 1977, Air Command and Staff Coll., 1980; M in Pers. Mgmt., Webster U., 1981; grad., Armed Forces Staff Coll., 1982, Nat. War Coll., 1988; exec. devel. program, U. N.H., 1994. Commd. 2d lt. USAF, 1971, advanced through grades to maj. gen., 1998; F-4 br. chief, job control duty officer 8th Tactical Fighter Wing, Ubon Royal Thai AFB, Thailand, 1973-74; C-141 pilot, crew contrl. 20th Mil. Airlift Squadron, Charleston AFB, S.C., 1975-79; instr. pilot, asst. chief pilot 6th Mil. Airlift Squadron Airlift Wing, McGuire AFB, N.J., 1982-83; chief airlift mgmt., chief wing current ops. 438th Mil. Airlift Wing, McGuire AFB, 1983-85; ops. officer, comdr. 6th Mil. Airlift Squadron, McGuire AFB, 1985-87; spl. asst. for gen. and flag officer matters Office of Dir., Joint Staff, Washington, 1988-90; vice comdr. 443d Airlift Wing, Altus AFB, Okla., 1990-92; comdr. 436th Airlift Wing, Dover AFB, Del., 1992-94; vice comdr. Tanker Air Lift Control Ctr., Hdqs. Air Mobility Command, Scott AFB, Ill., 1994-95, comdr., 1995-97, Air Mobility Warfare Ctr., Ft. Dix, N.J., 1997-99; dir. ops. HQ Air Edn. and Tng. Command, Randolph AFB, Tex., 1999—. Decorated Def. Superior Svc. medal, Legion of Merit with oak leaf cluster, Meritorious Svc. medal with 2 oak leaf clusters.

WELSER-MÖST, FRANZ, conductor, music director; b. Linz, Austria, Aug. 16, 1960; LHD (hon.), Case Western Reserve U., 2003. Chief condr. Sinfonieorkester Norrköping, Sweden, 1986-91, Stadtorchester Winterthur, Switzerland, 1987-90; condr. St. Louis Symphony Orch., 1989; music dir. London Philharm., 1990—96, Zurich Opera, 1995—2002, prin. condr., 2002—05, gen. music dir., 2005—; music dir. The Cleve. Orch., 2002—. Guest condr. Berlin Philharmonic, Cleveland Orch. Youth Orch., Vienna Philharm., Bavarian Radio Symphony Orch., Gustav Mahler Youth Orch. Conducting debut Salzburg Festival, Austria, 1985; Am. debut St. Louis, 1989; appearances include Vienna biennial, Lucerne Festical, Carnegie Hall. Recipient Outstanding Achievement award, Western Law Ctr. for Disability Rights, 1995, Gramophone award, 1996, Condr. of Yr. award, Musical Am. Internat. Directory of Performing Arts, 2003, Silver medal of Region of Upper Austria, 2003. Mem.: Vienna Singverein (hon.). Office: Cleve Orch Severance Hall 11001 Euclid Ave Cleveland OH 44106

WELSH, KELLY RAYMOND, lawyer, investment company executive; b. Chgo., July 6, 1952; s. Raymond J. and Mary Jane (Kelly) W.; m. Ellen S. Alberding, June 28, 1985; children: Katherine A., Julia S. AB cum laude, Harvard U., 1974; MA, Sussex U., Eng., 1975; JD magna cum laude, Harvard U., 1978. Assoc. Mayer, Brown & Platt, Chgo., 1979-85, ptnr., 1985-89; corp. counsel City of Chgo., 1989-93; v.p., assoc. gen. counsel Ameritech Corp., Chgo., 1993-96, exec. v.p., gen. counsel, 1996—2001, Northern Trust Corp., Chgo., 2001—. Chmn. Met. Pier and Exposition Authority, Chgo., 1994—. Mem. ABA, Chgo. Bar Assn., Chgo. Coun. Lawyers, Chgo. Coun. Fgn. Rels. (mem. Chgo. com.), Legal Club Chgo. Office: Northern Trust Corp 50 S LaSalle Chicago IL 60675 Office Phone: 312-630-6000.

WELSH, MICHAEL JAMES, medical educator, biophysicist, educator; b. Marshalltown, Iowa, Dec. 22, 1948; Student, Loras Coll., 1967-69; BS, U. Iowa, 1970, MD, 1974. Intern and resident internal medicine U. Iowa Coll. Medicine, Iowa City, 1974-77; clin. fellow internal medicine U. Calif. San Francisco, 1977-78; rsch. fellow cardiovasc. rsch. unit U. Calif., San Francisco, 1978-79; rsch. fellow physiology and cell biology U. Tex., Houston, 1979-80; asst. prof. medicine U. Iowa Coll. Medicine, Iowa City, 1981-84, assoc. prof. medicine, 1984-87, prof. medicine, 1987—, prof. physiology and biophysics, 1989—. Cons. VA Hosp., Iowa City, 1981—; investigator Howard Hughes Med. Inst., U. Iowa., Iowa City, 1989—. Contbr. chpts. to books and numerous articles to profl. jours. Recipient Doris F. Tulcin Cystic Fibrosis Rsch. award, 1992, Paul di Sant-Agnese Disting. Sci. Achievement award, 1993. Mem. Am. Fedn. for Clin. Rsch., Am. Physiol. Soc., Am. Thoracic Soc. (J. Burns Amberson award 1994), Iowa Thoracic Soc. Office: Howard Hughes Med Inst 500 EMRB Univ Iowa Coll Medicine Iowa City IA 52242

WELSH, ROBERT K., religious organization executive; Pres. Coun. on Christian Unity, Indpls., 1999. Office: Coun on Christian Unity PO Box 1986 Indianapolis IN 46206-1986

WELSHIMER, GWEN R., state legislator, real estate broker, appraiser; b. Poughkeepsie, NY, Nov. 5, 1935; d. Freanor Ralph and Beulah M. (Reedy) Grant; m. Billy L. Blake (div. 1979); children: Donald E., Jerry A.; m. Robert E. Welshimer (dec. 1996). Student, Kans. State U., 1953-54; cert., Jones Real Estate Coll., Colorado Springs, Colo., 1975. Cert. real estate appraiser, 1993. Exec. sec. Coll. Bd. Trustees, Bellevue, Wash., 1967-69; exec. sec. to chmn. bd. dirs. Garvey Industries, Wichita, Kans., 1969-73, adminstrv. asst. pers. and pub. affairs, 1969-73; copywriter Walter Drake & Sons, Colorado Springs, 1973-75; real estate agt. UTE Realty, Colorado Springs, 1975-76; newspaper pub., owner Black Forrest News, Colorado Springs, 1976-79; real estate broker, appraiser Gwen Welshimer Real Estate, Wichita, 1979—; coord. Epic Real Estate Sch., Wichita, 1988—; legislator Kans. Ho. of Reps., Topeka, 1990—; mem. bus., commerce and labor, ethics and elections, health and human svcs., new economy nat. conf. state legislatures cultural and econ. devel. com., 2001—; mem joint health care reform legis. oversight com., 2001—. Dem. precinct committeewoman, Wichita; bd. dirs. United Meth. Urban Ministries, Wichita, 1990—, Counseling & Mediation Ctr., Wichita, Great Plains Comprehensive Agriculture & Med. Inst. Mem.: Women Dems., Lions Club Internat. Democrat. Methodist. Home: 6103 Castle Dr Wichita KS 67218-3601

WELTERS, ANTHONY, health services executive; BA in Econs., Manhattanville Coll.; JD, NYU. Atty. SEC; exec. asst. to Sen. Jacob Javits; sr.-level positions Amtrak and US Dept. Transp.; chmn. bd., pres., CEO Americhoice (subs. of UnitedHealth Grp.), 1989—; exec. v.p. UnitedHealth Group, Mpls., 2006—07, exec. v.p., pres. pub. & sr. markets group, 2007—. Bd. trustees Healthcare Leadership Coun.; vice chmn. bd. Morehouse Sch. Medicine; mem. bd. NYU Law Sch., Wolf Trap Found. Recipient Horatio Alger award, 1998. Mailing: UnitedHealth Group PO Box 1459 Minneapolis MN 55440-1459*

WEN, SHIH-LIANG, mathematics professor; came to U.S., 1959; s. S.W. and C.F. (Hsiao) W.; m. Liang Tao; children: Dennis, Andy, Jue, Nannan. BS, Nat. Taiwan U., Taipei, 1956; MS, U. Utah, 1961; PhD, Purdue U., 1968. Assoc. research engr. The Boeing Co., Seattle, 1961-63; with dept. math. Ohio U., Athens, 1968—, successively asst. prof., assoc. prof. and prof., chmn. dept. math., 1985-93. Rsch. analyst Applied Math Rsch. Lab. USAF, Wright-Patterson AFB, Ohio, summer, 1972; vis. rsch. scientist Courant Inst. Math. Scis. NYU, 1978-79; hon. prof. Jiangxi U., People's Republic of China, 1985; disting. vis. prof. Lanzhou U., People's Republic of China, 1989. Mem. Am. Math. Soc., Soc. for Indsl. and Applied Math., Math. Assn. Am. Avocations: fishing, bridge, music. Office: Ohio Univ Dept Math Athens OH 45701 Business E-Mail: wen@math.ohiou.edu.

WENDEL, SHIRLEY ANNE, college dean; Diploma, St. Mary's Hosp. Sch. Nursing, 1970; AA, Penn Valley Cmty. Coll., 1972; BSN, Avila Coll., 1974; MN, U. Kans., 1980; PhD, Kansas State U., 1998, U. Kans., 1999. Staff nurse St. Mary's Hosp., Kans. City, Kans., 1970-74, Unity Hosp., Fridley, Minn., 1974-76; nursing instr. Kans. City Kans. Cmty. Coll., 1976-80, dean nursing edn., 1980-98, dean of nursing and allied health, 1998—. Mem. adv. com. Johnson County Cmty. Coll. nursing program, Avila Coll. nursing program, Mid Am. Nazarene Coll. nursing program; asst. Den Mother Cub Scouts, 1985-87; active Annual Health Fair. Mem. Nat. League Nursing, Kans. Assoc. Degree Nursing Educators, Collegiate Nurse Educators Greater Kans. City, Sigma Theta Tau. Home: 12100 W 141st St Shawnee Mission KS 66221-2902 Office: Kansas City Kansas Community College 7250 State Ave Kansas City KS 66112-3003 E-mail: swendel@toto.net.

WENDEL, W. HALL, JR., automotive manufacturer; b. Washington, Jan. 17, 1943; m. Deborah Wendel, 1967; 1 child, Amy. BS, U.S. Naval Acad., 1966; MBA, Harvard U., 1972. Sales adminstr. E-Z-Go Golf Carts, 1973-74, nat. sales mgr., 1974-77; v.p. sales, mktg. Polaris E-Z-Go, Medina, Minn., 1977-80, pres., 1980-81; pres., CEO Polaris Industries L.P., Medina, 1981-99, chmn., 1999—. Office: Polaris Industries Inc 2100 Hwy 55 Medina MN 55340

WENDT, ROGER, state official; b. 1933; Prin. mid. sch.; state rep. Iowa, 2003—. Mem. appropriations oversight subcom.; mem. edn. standing com.; mem. govt. oversight standing com.; mem. human resources standing comt.; mem. ways and means standing com. Office: State Capitol E 12th and Grand Des Moines IA 50319

WENGER, RONALD DAVID, surgeon; b. Phila., May 1, 1944; s. Christian Showalter and Helen Grace (Heisey) W.; m. Judith Kay Anderson, Jan. 24, 1970; children: Clayton, Lera. BA, Ohio Wesleyan U., 1966; MD, Case Western Res. U., 1970. Diplomate Am. Bd. Surgery. Intern U. Oreg. Med. Sch., Portland, 1970-71; fellow Mayo Clinic Surgery Dept., Rochester, Minn., 1973-77; clin. prof. surgery U. Wis. Med. Sch., Madison, 1977—; pvt. practice, Madison, 1977—; asst. chief surgery St. Mary's Hosp., Madison, 1980-00; chief surgery Dean Med. Ctr., Madison, 1988-93. Named one of Best Drs. in Dane County, Madison Mag., 2006. Mem. ACS (also Wis. chpt.), AMA, SAGES, Am. Assn. Endocrine Surgeons, Wis. State Med. Soc., Madison Surg. Soc., Wis. Surg. Soc. (pres. 2005—), Soc. for Surgery of Alimentary Tract. Avocations: skiing, bicycling, sailing, travel, reading. Home: 726 Farwell Dr Madison WI 53704-6032 Office: 1821 S Stoughton Rd Madison WI 53716-2257 Home Phone: 608-241-4216; Office Phone: 608-260-6853.

WENNLUND, LARRY, former state legislator, lawyer; b. DeKalb, Ill., Oct. 31, 1941; s. Donald F. and Gertrude Wennlund; m. Shirley Ann Major, 1963; children: Jayna, Donald Cass, Joelle, Kara. BA, U. Ill., 1964; JD, John Marshall Law Sch., 1968. Mem. Ill. Ho. of Reps., Springfield, 1987-97; mem. transp. and motor vehicles, jud. I, jud. II Ill. Ho. Reps., Springfield, registration and regulation, labor and commerce coms., elections com., spl. com., conflicts of interest, asst. floor leader, mem. joint com. on adminstrv. rules, asst. majority leader; pvt. practice law New Lenox, Ill. Named Legislator of Yr. Ill. State Attys. Assn., 1988, Ill. Environ. Coun., 1987-89, Ill. Hosp. Assn., 1988, Friend of Agrl. award Agrl. Assn. Activator, 1988, 89; recipient Legislative award Ill. Assn. of Ophthalmology, 1989, Legislative Leadership award Ill. Assn. Recyclers. Mem. New Lenox C. of C., Mokena C. of C., Frankfort C. of C., Lions. Home: 1234 N Cedar Rd New Lenox IL 60451-1273

WENSITS, DAVID L., aerospace transportation executive; b. Sept. 19, 1947; AAS in Aviation Maintenance, Purdue U., 1968, BS in Indsl. Supervision, 1970. Mgr. F136 reliabilioty, maintainability and safety Rolls-Royce Corp., Indpls., 1970—. With U.S. Army, 1971-73. Recipient Aerospace Maintenance award AIAA, 1996. Office: Rolls-Royce Corp SPEED Code 020 PO Box 420 Indianapolis IN 46206-0420 Home Phone: 317-486-0586; Office Phone: 317-230-4949. E-mail: david.l.wensits@rolls-royce.com, davewensits@comcast.net.

WENSITS, JAMES EMRICH, newswriter; b. South Bend, Ind., Oct. 8, 1944; s. John Andrew and Melva Mae (Betz) W.; m. Wendy Anne Reygaert, June 12, 1965; children: Cheryl Wensits Lightfoot, John, Kristin Wensits Hough, Amy; m. Catherine Marie Palmer Pope, Nov. 27, 1987 (dec. Sept. 1996); 1 stepchild, Christina Pope; m. Carol Schaal, Oct. 19, 1998. BA in Journalism, Purdue U., 1966. Reporter South Bend Tribune, 1966-92, assoc. editor, 1992—. Office: South Bend Tribune 225 W Colfax Ave South Bend IN 46626-1001

WENSTRUP, H. DANIEL, chemical company executive; b. Cin., Sept. 27, 1934; s. Carl D. and Lucille (Cahill) W.; m. Eileen O'Brien, Nov. 24, 1956; children: Gary, Julie, Patrick, Kevin, Katy, Greg. BSBA, Xavier U., 1956. Sales rep. Chemcentral Corp., Cin., 1958-66, sales mgr. Detroit, 1966-72, gen. mgr., 1972-75, v.p. regional mgr., 1975-82, v.p. dir. mktg. Chgo., 1982-86, pres., 1986—, pres., CEO, 1988-99, bd. dirs., chmn. of bd., 1998; ret., 1999. Bd. dirs. Prove Quim S.A. de C.V. Mem., supporter Mus. Sci. Industry, Chgo., 1991—, Ravinia Chgo. Symphony, 1991—, adv. com. Gov. Edgar. 1st lt. U.S. Army, 1956-58. Mem. Chem. Mfrs. Assn. (dir. 1990-92), Chem. Industry Coun. Ill. (dir. 1989-93, pres., chmn.), Nat. Paint & Coatings Assn., Nat. Petroleum Refiners Assn., Ill. Mfrs. Assn., Ill. C. of C., Medinah Country Club, Oak Brook Tennis Club, Am. Cancer Soc., NACD Edn. Found. (trustee). Republican. Roman Catholic. Avocations: golf, tennis, jogging, reading, theater.

WENTWORTH, JACK ROBERTS, business educator, consultant; b. Elgin, Ill., June 11, 1928; s. William Franklin and Elizabeth (Roberts) W.; m. Rosemary Ann Pawlak, May 30, 1956 (dec. April 29, 2006); children: William, Barbara. Student, Carleton Coll., 1946-48; BS, Ind. U., 1950, MBA, 1954, DBA, 1959. Coord. displays Cadillac divsn., Gen. Motors Corp., Detroit, 1954-56; asst. prof. bus., assoc. dir. research Sch. of Bus. Ind. U., Bloomington, 1957-60, assoc. prof., dir. rsch., 1960-70, prof., 1970-93, chmn. MBA program, 1970-76, chmn. dept., faculty rep. NCAA, 1978-85, dean Sch. of Bus., 1984-93, Arthur M. Weimer prof., 1993-97, Arthur M. Weimer prof. emeritus, 1997—. Mktg. cons., Bloomington, 1960—; bd. dirs. Kimball Internat., Jasper, Ind. Editor: (monograph) Marketing Horizons, 1965; exec. editor Bus. Horizons, 1960-70 Served to 1st lt. USAF, 1950-53. Recipient Teaching award MBA Assn., 1973, 78, 81, 84, 85, Svc. award Assn. for Bus. and Econ. Rsch., 1983; Disting. Alumni Svc. award Ind. U., 1999. Mem. Am. Mktg. Assn. (v.p. 1971-73), Grad. Mgmt. Admissions Coun. (chmn. bd. trustees 1977-78), Univ. Club, Masons, Beta Gamma Sigma (pres. Alpha of Ind. chpt. 1971-72, bd. govs. 1986-98, nat. pres. 1994-96). Republican. Methodist. Avocations: travel, bicycling, magic, model railroading, sports. Office: Indiana Univ Kelley Sch Bus Bloomington IN 47405 Personal E-mail: lurojack@yahoo.com.

WENTWORTH, RICHARD LEIGH, editor; b. Concord, NH, July 6, 1930; s. Leigh Mayhew and Yvonne Regina (Wilcott) W.; m. Marlene McClenning, June 9, 1950; children— Douglas, John, Elizabeth, James BA, U. Okla., 1956. Editorial asst. U. Okla. Press, 1957-58; asst. editor U. Wis. Press, 1958-59; mgr. sales and promotion La. State U. Press, 1959-62, asst. dir., 1962-63, dir., 1963-70; assoc. dir., editor U. Ill. Press, Urbana, 1970-79, dir. Champaign, 1979-99, editor, 1999—. Contbr. articles to pub. and sports jours. Served with USAF, 1948-52 Mem. Assn. Am. Univ. Presses (dir. 1966, 77-79), Orgn. Am. Historians, Ill. Hist. Assn., Abraham Lincoln Assn. Democrat. Home: 808 W Springfield Ave Champaign IL 61820-4725 Office: U Ill Press 1325 S Oak St Champaign IL 61820-6903

WENTZ, WILLIAM HENRY, JR., aerospace engineer, educator; b. Wichita, Kans., Dec. 18, 1933; BS in Mech. Engring. cum laude, Wichita State U., 1955, MS in Aeronautical Engring., 1961; PhD in Engring. Mechanics, U. Kans., 1969. Lic. profl. engr., Kans. Liaison engr. Beech Aircraft, 1952-53; propulsion engr. Boeing Co., Wichita, Kans., 1955; instr. mech. engring. Wichita State U., 1957-58; aerodynamicist Boeing Co., Wichita, 1958-63; from asst. prof. to assoc. prof. aeronautical engring. Wichita State U., 1963-75, prof. aeronautical engring., 1975-83, Gates-Learjet prof. aeronautical engring., 1983-86, disting. prof. aerospace engring., 1986-98, dir. Ctr. Basic and Applied Rsch. Inst. Aviation Rsch., 1986-89, exec. dir. Nat. Inst. Aviation Rsch., 1988-97; sr. fellow at. Inst. Aviation Rsch., 1997-98; disting. prof. emeritus aerospace engring., exec. dir. emer. Nat. Inst. Aviation Rsch., 1999; ret. Dir. rsch. projects Boeing Co., 1960, 61, NASA, 1964-66, 66-68, 70-71, 71-83, 86-87, 86-88, 82-87, Dept. of Def., 1986-88, Kans. Tech. Enterprise Corp., 1988-96, FAA, 1986-96. Contbr. articles to profl. jours. With USAF, 1955-57. Recipient Disting. Engr. Svc. award Wichita State U., 1999, Kans. Aviation Honors award Gov. Bill Graves, 1999; Sci. Faculty fellow NSF, 1967-68. Fellow AIAA (assoc., past chmn. Wichita sect., Outstanding advisor student chpt. 1964, 65, 70, Gen. Aviation award 1981, Engr. of Yr. award Wichita sect. 1992, Engr. of Yr. award Region V 1991-92; mem. Soc. Automotive Engrs. (Ralph R. Teeter award 1973), Sigma Gamma Tau, Tau Beta Pi. Personal E-mail: william.wentz@cox.net.

WERBA, GABRIEL, public relations consultant; b. Paris, Feb. 28, 1930; came to U.S., 1941; s. Aron and Dina (Lewin) W.; m. Barrie Celia Sakolsky, June 1, 1952; children: Dean Steffen, Annmarie Alexandra Bragdon. BA in Journalism, U. Tex., 1948; postgrad., NYU Grad. Sch. Bus., 1948-49, NYU Sch. Law, 1961-62. Account exec. Harold C. Meyers & Co., NYC, 1959-61; dir. pub. rels. and advt. Yardney Electric Corp., NYC, 1961-63, 57-59; sr. assoc. Shiefman & Assocs., Detroit, 1963-66; account exec. Merrill Lynch, Detroit, 1966-70; exec. v.p. Shiefman Werba & Assocs., Detroit, 1970-73; sr. v.p., exec. v.p., pres., chief oper. officer Anthony M. Franco, Inc., Detroit, 1973-88; pres., chief exec. officer The Werba Group, Inc. and Gabriel Werba and Assocs., Inc., Detroit, 1988-94; prin. Durocher, Dixson, Werba, L.L.C., Detroit, 1994—2003; pres. Gabriel Werba & Assoc. LLC, Farmington Hills, Mich., 2004—05, Gabriel Werba & Assocs., Farmington Hills, 2005—. Bd. dirs. Intrepid Corp., Detroit. Contbr. articles to profl. jours. Bd. dirs. Oakland Citizens League, Detroit, 1970-93, Detroit Symphony Orch. Hall, 1985—, Detroit Chamber Winds, 1985-91, The Common Ground Sanctuary, Mich., 1989-2007, vice chmn., Bloomfield Hills, 2000-06, adv. bd., 2007—; bd. dirs. The Attic Theatre, Detroit, 1989-93, The Children's Ctr., Detroit; mem. strategic planning com., chmn. comm. com., bd. dirs., 1989-95, 1996-2002, 03-05, adv. bd., 1995-96, 2002-03; bd. dirs. NATAS, Detroit, 1993-98, The Jewish Cmty. Coun. Met. Detroit, 1989-95, 2004-2007, co-chair commn. com., 2006-2007, Margaret W. Montgomery Hosp., 1993-95, adv. bd. 1988-93; bd. dirs. Lawrence P. Doss Found., 2002—, 1st vice-chmn., 2002—; staff. comm. com. Detroit Inst. Arts, 1986-92, exhibits com., 1990-2001. Named to, PRSA-Detroit Hall of Fame, 2001. Mem. Nat. Investor Rels. Inst. (past dir., pres. Detroit chpt., spkr., panelist), Pub. Rels. Soc. Am. (bd. dirs. Detroit chpt. 1988-94, pres. 1992-93, past treas. Detroit Counselors' sect., past co-chair sr. coun., past co-chair, nat. sect. coun., past nat. chmn. fin. sect., mem. bd. ethics and profl. stds. 2003-06, chair audit com. 2005-07, spkr., panelist), Fin. Analysts Soc. Detroit (past chmn. pub. info. com.), Am. Mensa (bd. dirs. 1975-91, 2003-05, nat. chmn. 1979-83), Internat. Mensa (bd. dirs. 1979-83, 85-93). Avocations: art collecting, concerts, theater. Home: 21920 River Ridge Tr Farmington Hills MI 48335 Office: Gabriel Werba & Assoc 21920 River Ridge Tr Farmington MI 48335 Office Phone: 248-478-1281. E-mail: gabewerba@sbcglobal.net.

WERGIN, GARY, radio personality; Radio host Sta. WHO-AM, Des Moines. Office: WHO Radio 1801 Grand Ave Des Moines IA 50309

WERLING, DONN PAUL, conservationist, education educator; b. Ft. Wayne, Ind., Oct. 14, 1945; s. Paul Henry and Lydia Sophia (Rebber) W.; m. Diane Mueller, July 11, 1970; 1 child, Benjamin Paul. BS, Valparaiso U., 1967; MS, Mich. State U., 1968; MEd, Loyola U., 1970; PhD, U. Mich., 1979. Dir. nature project Raymond Sch., Chgo. Bd. Edn., 1969-72; dir. Evanston (Ill.) Environ. Assn., 1973-81; dir. Henry Ford Estate U. Mich., Dearborn, 1983—2002, adj. asst. prof. edn., 1984-95, adj. assoc. prof., 1996—; exec. dir. History Ctr., Ft. Wayne, Ind., 2002—. Founder N.Am. Voyageur Conf., 1977. Author: Environmental Education and Your School Site, 1973, A School-Community Stewardship Model, 1979, Lake Michigan and Its Lighthouses, 1982, Lakes and Lighthouses, 1989, Lighthouse Library of the Great Lakes, 1993, Lore and Legacy, 1994, Keepers of Tomorrow, 1998, Henry Ford: Hearthside Perspective, 2000, Henry Ford and His Uncommon Friends, 1999, Walking the Talk of Preservation, 2003. Mem. state master plan com. on environ. edn., State of Ill, Springfield, 1970; mem. adv. com. Ill. Coastal Zone, Chgo., 1978; bd. dirs. Ill. Shore Coun. Girl Scouts U.S., 1978-82, Chgo. Maritime Soc., 1982; co-chmn. ad hoc com. estab. Nat. Auto Heritage Area, signed into law, 1998. Recipient Mayor's award City of Evanston, 1976, Russell E. Wilson award U. Mich. Sch. Edn., 1979, Svc. award Ill. Shore Coun. Girl Scouts U.S., 1978, J. Lee Barrett award Met. Detroit Tourist and Conv. Bur., 1986, award for interpretative excellence Nat. Assn. for Interpretation, 1989, 2000, Founder award Automobile Nat. Heritage Area, 2002; named to Outstanding Young Men of Am., Jaycees, 1975. Mem. Nat. Assn. Interpretation (founder), Am. Assn. Mus., Great Lakes Lighthouse Keepers Assn. (founder, pres. 1982-86), Tourist and Travel Assn. S.E. Mich. (chmn. 1984-86). Avocations: historic restoration, gardening, writing, singing, Christian and Bluewater music. Office: History Ctr 302 E Berry Fort Wayne IN 46802 E-mail: dpwerling@comcast.net.

WERNER, BILL, communication media executive; Capitol bur. chief UP Internat., Mpls., 1998—.

WERNER, CLARENCE L., transportation executive; b. 1937; Asst. mgr. Larson Grain Co., Omaha, 1958-61; with Bus. Motor Express, Inc., Omaha, 1961-62; founder Werner Enterprises, Inc., Omaha, 1956-82, pres., 1982-84, chmn., CEO, 1984—2007, chmn., 2007—. Office: Werner Enterprises Inc 14507 Frontier Rd PO Box 45308 Omaha NE 68145-0308

WERNER, LAWRENCE H., editor; BA in Journalism, Mich. State U., 1969. Reporter Courier-Jour., 1969—78; asst. features editor (Louisville) Courier-Jour., 1978—79; bus. editor Grand Rapids (Mich.) Press, 1979; consumer reporter Detroit Free Press, 1979—81; mng. editor features and sports Buffalo Courier-Express, 1981—82; features editor Dallas Times Herald, 1982—83; asst. mng. editor bus. Star Tribune, Mpls., 1983—95, reader involvement editor, 1995—. Mem.: Soc. Am. Bus. Editors and Writers (past pres.). Avocations: coaching youth soccer, travel, reading. Office: Star Tribune 425 Portland Ave Minneapolis MN 55488-0002 E-mail: werner@startribune.com.

WERNER, R(ICHARD) BUDD, retired manufacturing executive; b. Lorain, Ohio, Aug. 27, 1931; s. Paul Henry and Bessie Marie (Budd) W.; m. Janet Sue Kelsey, June 19, 1954; children: Richard Budd Jr., David Kelsey, Mary Paula. BS in Commerce, Ohio U., 1953. CPA, Ohio. Sr. auditor Arthur Andersen & Co., Cleve., 1955-59; various fin. positions Glidden Co., Cleve., 1959-65; v.p., asst. treas. Harshaw divsn. Kewanee Oil Co., Cleve., 1965-72; v.p. fin., treas. Weatherhead Co., Cleve., 1973-77, Hauserman, Inc., Cleve., 1977-81; v.p. fin., CFO SPX Corp., Muskegon, Mich., 1981-94, sr. v.p. planning and devel., 1994-95; exec. in residence coll. of bus. Ohio U., Athens, 1995—. Mem. Lakewood (Ohio) City Coun., 1972-73; mem. North Muskegon (Mich.) Sch. Bd., 1981-85; bd. mem. Appalachian Cmty. Vis. Nurse Assn., Hospice, Health Svc. Inc., 1999—. Lt. Q.M.C., U.S. Army, 1953-55. Mem. Fin. Execs. Inst. Office: Ohio U Copeland Hall Athens OH 45701

WERT, LARRY, broadcast executive; m. Julie Wert; 4 children. BA Journalism, U. Wis. With Leo Burnett Advt., ABC-TV; local sales mgr. Sta. WLS-TV, Chgo., ABC-TV Nat. Sales, NYC, Chgo., Sta. KABC-TV, LA; pres. Evergreen Media Corp., Chgo.; pres., gen. mgr. Evergreen's The Loop and AM 1000; sr. v.p. Chancellor Media Corp., Chgo.; pres., gen. mgr. Sta. WMAQ-TV, 1998—. Mem. adv. coun. Columbia Coll. Chgo. TV Dept.; elected bd. dirs. Jr. Achievement, Chgo.; bd. dirs. Children's Brittle Bone Found., Cath. League Charities, Chicagoland C. of C., Jim Shorts Children's Charities; hon. bd. dirs., mem. nominating com. RAINBOWS; bd. trustees Fenwick H.S., Oak Park, Ill. Named Hon. Chmn., 11th Ann. Have a Heart for Sickle Cell Anemia benefit, 1998; recipient Gift of Life award, 1998, Responding to Cmty. Standards of Broadcasting award, Cosmopolitan C. of C., 1998, Dante award, Joint Civic Com. Italian Ams., 2000. Office: NBC 454 N Columbus Dr Chicago IL 60611

WERTHEIM, SALLY HARRIS, director, academic administrator, dean, education educator, consultant; b. Cleve., Nov. 1, 1931; d. Arthur I. and Anne (Manheim) Harris; m. Stanley E. Wertheim, Aug. 6, 1950; children: Kathryn, Susan B., Carole J. BS, Flora Stone Mather Coll., 1953; MA, Case Western Res. U., 1967, PhD, 1970. Cert. elem. and secondary edn. tchr. Ohio. Social worker U. Hosps., Cleve., 1953-54; tchr. Fairmount Temple Religious Sch., Cleve., 1957-72; mem. faculty John Carroll U., Cleve., 1969—, chair dept. edn., 1969—86, dean Grad. Sch., 1986—99, dir. planning and assessment, 1999—2004, interim dean Coll. Arts and Scis., 2004—05, cons. Office of Acad. V.P., 2005—, interim dir. Career Ctr., 2005—06, interim dean Grad. Sch., 2007—. Cons. in field; cons. Jennings Found., Cleve.; chmn. sch. com. Cleve. Commn. on Higher Edn., 1987-99. Contbr. articles to profl. jours. Sec. Cuyahoga County Mental Health Bd., Cleve., 1978—82; pres. Montefiore Home, Cleve., 1987—90; bd. dir. Mt. Sinai Med. Ctr., Cleve., 1984—93; v.p. Mt. Sinai Health Care Found.; bd. dirs. Cleve. Edn. Fund, 1992—94, v.p., 2007; chair edn. com. Cleve. Found. Commn. on Poverty, 1988—93, Cleve. Cmty. Bldg. Initiative, 1993—95, United Way Svcs., 1994—2001; trustee Mt. Sinai Health Care Found., 1998, Gerson Found., 1998, Miller Found., 1998, Begun Found., 2001, Mandel Found., 2001; pres. Jewish Family Svc. Assn., Cleve., 1974—77; v.p. Jewish Cmty. Fedn., 1988—91, pres., 1994—97, life trustee, 1997—. Named One of 100 Most Influential Women, Cleve. mag., 1983, One of 29 Most Influential Women, Cleve. Mag., 1997; recipient award John Carroll U., Curtis Miles award for cmty. svc., 1997; grantee Jennings Found., 1984-87, Cleve. and Gund Found., 1987-90, Lilly Found., 1988; S.H. Wertheim scholarship and edn. excellence award established John Carroll U., 1997. Mem. Am. Assn. Colls. for Tchrs. Edn. (bd. dirs. 1982-85), Ohio Assn. Colls. for Tchrs. Edn. (pres. 1981-83), Coun. of Grad. Schs. Avocations: flower arranging, travel, antiques. Office: John Carroll Univ Grad Sch Cleveland OH 44118 Business E-Mail: wertheim@jcu.edu.

WERTZ, KENNETH DEAN, real estate company officer; b. Okla. City, July 14, 1946; s. Walter K. and Kathryn L. (Moore) W.; children: Adam Troy, Kirsten Paige. BS in Acctg., Okla. State U., 1968, MS in Acctg. and Econs., 1969; JD, U. San Francisco, 1978. CPA, Okla., Calif; lic. real estate broker, Okla. Sr. acct. Deloitte, Haskins & Sells, San Francisco, 1969-70, 71-75; v.p. acquisitions, mng. dir. Landsing Corp., Menlo Park, Calif., 1975-86; pres. Detrick Salsberry Mgmt. Inc., Tulsa, 1987-88; v.p. asset mgmt. Corporex Co., Cin., 1989-90; exec. v.p. real estate Brunner Cos., Dayton, Ohio, 1990-92; pres. Pillar Real Estate Advisors, Dayton, 1992—. Lt. col. Med. Svc. corps U.S. Army, 1968-98. Decorated Army Commendation medal with three oak leaf clusters, Meritorious Svc. medal. Mem. AICPA, Okla. Soc. CPAs, Calif. Soc. CPAs, Nat. Assn. Securities Dealers (fin. prin., registered sales rep.). Republican. Methodist. Avocations: bicycling, snow and water skiing, racquetball, camping, fishing. Home: 835 Huntersknoll Ln Cincinnati OH 45230-4343 Office: Pillar Real Estate Advisors 5335 Far Hills Ave Ste 318 Dayton OH 45429-2317 Home Phone: 513-232-1513; Office Phone: 937-434-4250. Personal E-mail: dw@okclighthouse.com.

WESCHCKE, CARL LLEWELLYN, publishing executive; BS, Babson Coll., 1951. Pres., publisher Llewellyn Worldwide Ltd., St. Paul, 1957—. Mem. Pub. Roundtable Minn. Office: Llewellyn Worldwide 2143 Wooddale Dr Saint Paul MN 55125-2989

WESELAK, ANNA MARIE SCHMIDT, educational association administrator, media consultant; b. Aurora, Ill., Oct. 28, 1949; d. John Joseph and Anna Florence (Sandor) Schmidt; m. Kevin John Weselak, May 20, 1972; children: Timothy Charles, Thomas John, Kristin Marie. BS, No. Ill. U., 1971, MS, 1974. Cert. early childhood edn. tchr., elem. edn. tchr. First grade tchr. Sch. Dist. 131, Aurora, 1971-75; kindergarten tchr. Pioneer Child Care Ctr., Lombard, Ill., 1987-92; sales and mktg. mgr. Minuteman Press, Addison, Ill.; owner, cons. Weselak & Assocs., 1994—; cons. Pearson Skylight, 1996—; sch. collaborative design team cons. The Ball Found., 1999—2000. Graphic media cons. Minuteman Press, Addison, Ill., 1991—; bd. dirs. DuPage regional unit Chgo. Assn. for Edn. Young Children; chmn. parent-child fair for Wk. of Young Child, 1988-89; program chmn., 1989-91, fall conf. chmn., 1991-92. Pres. Lombard PTA Coun., 1987-89, 5th dist. Gen. Fedn. Women's Clubs Ill., 1988-90, Lombard Newcomers, 1976-77, Lombard Svc. League, 1981-83; grand marshall Lombard Lilac Parade, 1993. Recipient 10 Yr. Svc. award No. Ill. U. Alumni Assn., 1980, Ill. State Bd. Edn. Those Who Excel award of merit, 1992-93; named gift AAUW, 1985, one of Outstanding Young Women Am., 1983, Lombard Woman Yr., 1989. Mem. Ill. PTA (bd. mgrs., dist. 32 dir. 1988-91, chair leadership tng. 1991-93, v.p. dist. dirs. 1993—, state conv. chmn. 1992, 93, Book of Recognition award 1990, hon. life mem.), Nat. PTA (hon. life mem., pres. elect 2003-05, pres. 2005-07), Ill. Fedn. Women's Clubs (chair budget and fin. 1990-92, editor Ill. Clubwoman mag. 1991—), Sigma Lambda Sigma (pres. 1970). Roman Catholic. Avocations: crafts, needlecrafts, sewing.

WESELI, ROGER WILLIAM, lawyer; b. Cin., Dec. 23, 1932; s. William Henry and Margaret Antoinette (Hoffman) W.; m. Sue Ann Daggett, Sept. 1, 1956; children: Erin, Stacey, Vincent. BA in Polit. Sci, U. Cin., 1955; MS in Hosp. Adminstrn, Northwestern U., 1959; D Tech. Letters (hon.), Cin. Tech. Coll., 1985; JD, No. Ky. U., 1995. Bar: Ohio 1995. Adminstrv. asst. Good Samaritan Hosp., Cin., 1959-61, asst. adminstr., 1961-70, assoc. adminstr., 1970-75, v.p., adminstr., 1975-78, exec. v.p., adminstr., 1978-79, pres., 1979-91, cons., 1991-93; cons. healthcare practice Deloitte & Touche, Cin., 1991-93; sec. Greater Cin. Hosp. Council, 1978-80, chmn. bd., 1983-84; assoc. Copeland & Brown Co., L.P.A., Cin., 1995-98, McKinney & Namei, Co., LPA, Cin., 1998—. Chmn. legis. com. health dept. Ohio Cath. Conf., 1978-83, 86; bd. dirs. Friars Boys Club, 1978-94. Recipient Praestans Inter Omnes award Purcell High Sch., 1984, Laura Jackson award Northwestrern U. Program in Health Svcs. Mgmt., 1987, Preceptor of Yr. award Xavier U. Program Hosp. and Health Svcs. Adminstrn., 1990. Fellow Am. Coll. Healthcare Execs. (regent for Ohio 1983-90, bd. govs. 1990-94); mem. ABA, Am. Hosp. Assn. (coun. on fedn. rels. 1983-84, coun. on patient svcs. 1984-86, ho. of dels. 1989-91), Ohio Bar Assn., Cin. Bar Assn., Ohio League for Nursing (v.p. 1977-79, cert. of appreciation 1978), Ohio Hosp. Assn. (chmn. govt. liaison com. 1978-83, 86, trustee 1981-83, sec.-treas. 1987, chmn.-elect 1988, chmn. 1989), Cath. Health Assn. (trustee 1983-86), Alpha Mu Sigma. Democrat. Roman Catholic. Office: 15 E 8th St Cincinnati OH 45202-2025 E-mail: healthlaw@fuse.net, rogersue@fuse.net.

WESELY, DONALD RAYMOND, state senator; b. David City, Nebr., Mar. 30, 1954; s. Raymond Ely and Irene (Sabata) W.; children: Sarah, Amanda, Andrew. BA, U. Nebr., 1977; LLD (hon.), Kirksville Coll. Osteo. Medicine, 1989. Mem. Nebr. Legislature, Lincoln, 1978-99; exec. assoc. Selection Rsch. Inst., Lincoln, 1984-86; sr. rsch. assoc. Lincoln Telephone Co., 1985—. Del., Dem. Nat. Conv., 1984, 88, 92, 96; chair Assembly on Legislature, Nat. Conf. State Legislatures., 1992-93, 96-97, exec. com., 1992-97; del. Am. Coun. Young Polit. Leaders, 1993. Recipient Friend of Edn. award Nebr. State Edn. Assn., 1982, Disting. Svc. award Nebr. Pub. Helath Assn., 1984, Disting. Alumni award Lincoln N.E. H.S., 1991, Disting. Health Care award Nebr. Nurse Anesthetists Assn., 1992, Leadership award for Quality in Health Care, Nebr. League Nursing, 1992, Pres.'s award Nebr. Acad. Physicians Assts., 1993, U. Nebr.-Lincoln Outstanding Young Alumni award 1994; named Mental Health Citizen of Yr., Nebr. Mental Health Assn., 1984, Outstanding Young Man, Nebr. Jaycees, 1985, Pub. offcl. of Yr., Nebr. assn. Retarded Citizens, 1992, Advocate of Yr., Nebr. Family Day Care Assn., 1993. Roman Catholic.

WESLEY, NORMAN H., consumer products company executive; b. Dec. 11, 1949; m. Kim Wesley; 3 children. BA, U. Utah, 1972, MBA, 1973. With Crown Zellerbach Corp., San Francisco, 1973—83; v.p. corp. devel ACCO World Corp., Wheeling, Ill., 1983—87, COO, 1987—90, pres., 1987—97, CEO, 1990—97; chmn., CEO Fortune Brands Home & Office, Inc., 1997—99; pres., COO Fortune Brands, Inc., Lincolnshire, Ill., 1999, chmn, CEO, 1999—2007, chmn., 2008—. Bd. dirs. Fortune Brands, Inc., 1999—, Pactiv Corp., 2001—, R.R. Donnelley & Sons, 2001—. Office: Fortune Brands Inc 520 Lake Cook Rd Ste 400 Deerfield IL 60015-5633*

WESLOH, STEVEN M., lawyer; b. St. Louis, Mar. 22, 1971; BA, Ind. U., 1993; JD, U. Cin. Coll. Law, 1996. Bar: Ohio 1996. Sr. assoc. Frost Brown Todd LLC, Cin. Named one of Ohio's Rising Stars, Super Lawyers, 2006. Mem.: ABA (mem., Environment, Energy and Resources Sect.), Ohio State Bar Assn. (mem., Environ. Law Com.), Cin. Bar Assn. (mem., Environ. Law Com.). Office: Frost Brown Todd LLC 2200 PNC Ctr 201 E Fifth St Cincinnati OH 45202-4182 Office Phone: 513-651-6800. Office Fax: 513-651-6981.

WESNER, PATRICIA, bank executive; m. Jim Hoffman. BA, Pa. State U.; MA Bus. Adminstrn., Marquette U. With First Wis. Nat. Bank, 1977; div. head Milw. branches Firstar Bank (now US Bank), v.p. Retail Payment Solutions. Mem. Visa USA's Deposit Products Exec. Coun., Visa's Small Bus. Exec. Coun., Visa's Internat. Adv. Coun. Bd. dirs. LSS Found., 2005—, Florentine Opera Co. Mem.: Tempo Internat. Office: US Bank 777 E Wisconsin Ave Milwaukee WI 53202

WESSELINK, DAVID DUWAYNE, finance company executive; b. Webster City, Iowa, Sept. 5, 1942; s. William David and Lavina C. (Haahr) W.; m. Linda R. DeWitt, Dec. 27, 1971; children: Catherine, Bill. BA in Bus., Ctrl. Coll., 1964; MBA, Mich. State U., 1970. Tchr. Peace Corps, Turkey, 1964-66, Karabuk Koleji, Turkey, 1967-68, Robert Koleji, Turkey, 1969-70; rsch. analyst Household Fin. Corp., Chgo., 1971-73, asst. dir. rsch., 1973-77, asst. treas. Prospect Heights, Ill., 1977, v.p., dir. rsch., 1977-82, group v.p., CFO, 1982-86, sr. v.p., CFO, 1986—; v.p., treas. Household Internat., Prospect Heights, 1988-93; sr. v.p., CFO Advanta Corp., 1993-98; exec. v.p., CFO Metris Cos., Saint Louis Park, Minn., 1998-2000, vice chmn., 2000—02, chmn., CEO, 2002—05. Bd. dirs. Flex Fund Fin. Svcs., Irvine, Calif. Bd. dirs. Ctrl. Coll., Pella, Iowa, 1990—. Mem.: Fin. Execs. Inst., Econ. Club Chgo. E-mail: lrddw@juno.com.

WESSELMANN, GLENN ALLEN, retired health facility administrator; b. Cleve., Mar. 21, 1932; s. Roy Arthur and Dorothy (Oakes) W.; m. Genevieve De Witt, Sept. 6, 1958; children: Debbie, Scott, Janet. AB, Dartmouth, 1954; MBA with distinction, Cornell U., 1959. Research aide Cornell U., Ithaca, NY, 1958-59; adminstrv. resident Meml. Hosp., NYC, 1957-58, adminstrv. asst., 1959-61, asst. adminstr., 1961-65, asst. v.p., 1965-68; v.p. for adminstrn. Meml. Hosp. for Cancer and Allied Diseases, NYC, 1968-79; exec. v.p., chief operating officer St. John Hosp., Detroit, 1979-84; pres., CEO St. John Health System, 1984-95, vice chmn., 1995-97; chmn., pres., CEO St. John Hosp. & Med. Ctr., 1984-94, ret., 1995. Mem. bus. adv. bd. City of Detroit, 1991-95, chmn., 1993-94; mem. exec. com. Greater Detroit Area Health Coun.; bd. dirs. Caymich Ins. Co. Ltd., Mich. Health Care Alliance, SelectCare, Detroit Econ. Growth Corp. Trustee Sisters of St. Joseph Health System 1981-94, Sisters of St. Joseph Health Svc., 1983-95, St. John Hosp. and Med. Ctr., 1979-95, St. John Health System, 1984-95, The Oxford Inst., 1984-95, Eastwood Clinics, 1992-95; pres. Providence Ch. Corp., Hilton Head Island, S.C., chmn. ch. fin. ocm., corp. pres. session; mem. bus. adv. bd.! City of Detroit, 1991-95, chmn. 1993-94. Served with MC AUS, 1955-57. Fellow ACHE; mem. Am. Hosp. Assn., Internat. Hosp. Fedn., Mich. Hosp. Assn. (trustee, chmn. 1994-95, mem. exec. com.), Assn. Am. Med. Colls. (Coth rep.), Am. Cancer Soc. (regional adv. bd. 1994-95), Med. Group Mgmt. Assn., Soc. Health Service Adminstrs., Sigma Phi Epsilon. Home: 63 Big Woods Dr Hilton Head Island SC 29926-2604 Personal E-mail: glengen@hargray.com.

WESSELS, BRUCE W., materials scientist, educator, department chairman; b. NYC, Oct. 18, 1946; m. Beverly T. Wessels; children: David, Kirsten. BS in Metallurgy and Materials Sci., U. Pa., 1968; PhD in Materials Sci., MIT, 1973. Tech. staff GE R&D Ctr., 1972-77, acting br. mgr., 1976; from asst. prof. to assoc. prof. orthwestern U., Evanston, Ill., 1977-83, prof. materials sci. and engring., 1984—, prof. elec. and computer engring., 1987—, Walter P. Murphy prof., 1998—, dept. chair elec. engring. and computer sci., 2005—. Vis. sci. Argonne Nat. Lab., 1978; mem. program com. Internat. Conf. Superlattices, Microdevices and Microstructures, 1987. Editor 5 books including (with G.Y. Chin) Advances in Electronic Materials, 1986; mem. editl. bd. Jour. Electronic Materials, 1982-88, 98—, Hour. Electroceramics, 2006—; contbr. articles to profl. jours.; patentee in field. Fellow ASM, Am. Phys. Soc., AIME (bd. trustees 1996-97); mem. TMS, The Minerals, Metals and Materials Soc. (chmn. electronic materials com. 1987-89, conf. program chmn. 1986-87, key reader Trans. of AIME 1985-92, bd. dirs. 1993-98, vice-chmn. exec. coun. electronic, magnetic and photonic materials divsn. 1991-92, chmn. 1993-95, v.p. 1995, pres. 1996), Electrochem. Soc. Materials Rsch. Soc. (symposium organizer 1993, 95),

Optical Soc. Am., Electroceramics (internat. program com. 2000-05), Sigma Xi, Tau Beta Pi. Office: Materials Science-Engring Northwestern U 2220 Campus Dr Evanston IL 60208-3108 E-mail: b-wessels@northwestern.edu.

WEST, CLARK DARWIN, pediatric nephrologist, educator; b. Jamestown, NY, July 4, 1918; s. Clark Darwin and Frances Isabel (Blanchard) W.; m. Ruthann Asbury, Apr. 12, 1944 (div.); children: Charles Michael, John Clark, Lucy Frances; m. Dolores Lachenman, Mar. 1, 1986. AB, Coll. of Wooster, 1940; MD, U. Mich., 1943. Intern Univ. Hosp., Ann Arbor, Mich., 1943-44, resident in pediatrics, 1944-46; fellow in pediatrics Children's Hosp. Research Found., Cin., 1948-49, research asso., 1951-89, asso. dir., 1963-89, dir. div. immunology and nephrology, 1958-89; with cardiopulmonary lab. chest service Bellevue Hosp., NYC, 1949-51; attending pediatrician Children's Hosp., 1951-89; asst. prof. pediatrics U. Cin., 1951-55, asso. prof., 1955-62, prof., 1962-89. Mem. coms. NIH, 1965-69, 1972-73 Mem. editorial bd.: Jour. Pediatrics, 1960-79, Kidney Internat., 1977-89, Clin. Nephrology, 1989-96; contbr. articles to profl. jours. Served to capt. M.C., AUS, 1946-47. Decorated Army commendation medal; recipient recognition award Cin. Pediat. Soc., 1980, Mitchell Rubin award, 1986, Henry L. Barnett award, 1995, Daniel Drake medal, 1996, John P. Peters award, 1996. Mem. Soc. Pediatric Research (sec.-treas. 1958-62, pres. 1963-64), Am. Pediatric Soc., Am. Soc. Pediatric Nephrologists (pres. 1973-74), Am. Physiol. Soc., Am. Assn. Immunologists, Am. Soc. Nephrology, Internat. Pediatric ephrology Assn., Sigma Xi, Alpha Omega Alpha. Achievements include research on immunopathogenesis and treatment of glomerulonephritides and in the complement system. Home: 11688 Aristocrat Dr Harrison OH 45030-9753 Office: Children's Hosp Med Ctr Cincinnati OH 45229 Office Phone: 513-636-4531. Personal E-mail: CWest_2865@fuse.net.

WEST, MARC, information technology executive; B in Computer ci., U. Md.; M in Human Resource Mgmt., Golden State U., San Francisco. Various positions Quick & Reilly, Move.com, Oracle and Mobil Oil; sr. v.p. and global chief info. officer Electronic Arts, Redwood City, Calif., 2000—04; sr. v.p. & chief info. officer H&R Block, Kansas City, Mo., 2004—. Named one of Premier 100 IT Leaders, Computerworld, 2006. Office: SVP & CIO H&R Block Inc One H&R Block Way Kansas City MO 64105

WEST, MICHAEL ALAN, retired hospital administrator; b. Waseca, Minn., Aug. 4, 1938; s. Ralph Leland and Elizabeth Mary (Brann) W.; m. Mary Thissen, Jan. 21, 1961; children— Anne, Nancy, Douglas. BA, U. Minn., 1961, MHA, 1963. Sales corr. Physicians and Hosps. Supply Co., Mpls., 1959-60; adminstrv. resident R.I. Hosp., Providence, 1962-63, adminstrv. asst., 1963-65, asst. dir., 1965-68; exec. asst. dir. Med. Center U. Mo., Columbia, 1968-70, assoc. dir., 1970-74, asst. prof. community health and med. practice, 1968-74; v.p. for adminstrn. Luth. Gen. Hosp., Park Ridge, Ill., 1974-80, exec. v.p., 1980-84; pres., CEO Akron Gen. Med. Ctr., Ohio, 1984-97, Akron Gen. Health Sys., 1997—2002. Bd. dirs. Vol. Hosps. Am. Inc.; chair VHA-Ctrl., Inc. Bd. dirs. Great Trails Coun. Boy Scouts Am. Mem. Am. Coll. Healthcare Execs., Akron Regional Hosp. Assn. (chmn.), Portage Country Club, Akron City Club, Catawba Island Club, Noreaster Club. Home: 495 Woodbury Dr Akron OH 44333-2780

WEST, ROBERT C., engineering company executive; b. Keytesville, Mo., 1920; married BCE, Ga. Inst. Tech., 1949. Registered profl. engr. With Sverdrup Corp., St. Louis, 1953—67, chief engr., 1967—68, v.p., 1968—69, exec. v.p., 1969—73, COO, 1973—75, pres., CEO, 1975—77, chmn. bd., pres., 1977—82, chmn. bd., 1982—88, chmn. emeritus, 1988. Bd. dirs. Centerre Bank, St. Louis, Angelica Corp.; mem. adv. com. Export-Imprt Bank U.S. Bd. dirs. St. Louis Region Commerce and Growth Assn., Laclede Sch. Law, Ranken Tech. Inst.; chmn. bd. Webster U., 1982-87; emeritus bd. dirs. Mo. Goodwill Industries; bd. dirs. St. Louis Area coun. Boy Scouts Am., now pres. North Ctrl. Region Nat. Exec. Bd.; mem. nat. adv. bd. Ga. Inst. Tech. Recipient Engr. of Yr. award, 1976, Herbert Hoover medal, 1985, Achievement award medal Engrs. Club St. Louis, 1977, Mo. Honor award for disting. svc. in engring., 1981, Silver Beaver award Boy Scouts Am., 1985. Fellow: ASCE (Profl. Recognition award 1981), Am. Cons. Engrs. Coun.; mem.: Mo. Corp. for Sci. and Tech. (chmn. bd. dirs.).

WEST, ROBERT CULBERTSON, chemistry professor; b. Glen Ridge, NJ, Mar. 18, 1928; s. Robert C. and Constance (MacKinnon) W.; children: David Russell, Arthur Scott, Derek BA, Cornell U., 1950; A.M., Harvard U., 1952, PhD, 1954; ScD (hon.), G. Asachi Tech. U., Iasi, Romania, 1995. Asst. prof. Lehigh U., 1954-56; mem. faculty U. Wis.-Madison, 1956—, prof. chemistry, 1963—, Eugene G. Rochow prof., 1980, dir. Organosilicon Rsch. Ctr., 1999—. Indsl. and govt. cons., 1961—; Fulbright lectr. Kyoto and Osaka U., 1964-65; vis. prof. U. Würzburg, 1968-69, Haile Selassie I U., 1972, U. Calif.-Santa Cruz, 1977, U. Utah, 1981, Inst. Chem. Physics Chinese Acad. Sci., 1984, Justus Liebigs U., Giessen, Fed. Republic Germany, U. Estadual de Campinas, Brazil, 1989; Abbott lectr. U. N.D., 1964, Seydel-Wooley lectr. Ga. Inst. Tech., 1970, Sun Oil lectr. Ohio U., 1971, Edgar C. Britton lectr. Dow, Midland, Mich., 1971, Jean Day Meml. lectr. Rutgers U., 1973; Japan Soc. for Promotion Sci. vis. prof. Tohoku U., 1976, Gunma U., 1987; Lady Davis vis. prof. Hebrew U., 1979; Cecil and Ida Green honors prof. Tex. Christian U., 1983; Karcher lectr. U. Okla., 1986; Broberg lectr. N.D. State U., 1986; Xerox lectr. U. B.C., 1986, McGregory lectr. Colgate U., 1988; George Watt lectr. U. Tex., 1992; David Ginsburg meml. lectr. Technion, 1993; rsch. scholar lectr. Drew U., 1995; Reed lectr. Rensselaer Poly. Inst., 1997; Lady Davis vis. prof. Technion-Israel Inst. Tech., 1990; Humboldt prof. Tech. U. Munich, 1990; vis. prof. U. Estadual de Campinas, Brazil, 1993; Dozor vis. fellow Ben Gurion U. of Negev, Israel, 1993. Co-editor: Advances in Organometallic Chemistry, Vols. I-XXXVI, 1964—, Organometallic Chemistry--A Monograph Series, 1968—; contbr. articles to profl. jours. Pres. Madison Community Sch., 1970-81; founder, bd. dirs. Women's Med. Fund, 1971—; nat. bd. dirs. Zero Population Growth, 1980-86; bd. dirs., v.p. Protect Abortion Rights Inc., 1980; lay minister Prairie Unitarian Universalist Soc., 1982. Recipient F.S. Kipling award, 1970, Outstanding Sci. Innovator award Sci. Digest, 1985, Chem. Pioneering award Am. Inst. Chemists, 1988, Wacker Silicon prize, 1989, Humboldt U.S. Scientist award, 1990. Mem. Am. Chem. Soc., Chem. Soc. (London), Japan Chem. Soc., AAAS, Wis. Acad. Sci. Home: 305 Nautilus Dr Madison WI 53705-4333

WEST, THOMAS MEADE, insurance company executive; b. Owensboro, Ky., Aug. 15, 1940; s. Frank Thomas and Vivian (Brown) W.; children: Thomas Meade, Alexandra, Theodora. BA cum laude, Vanderbilt U., 1962; MA magna cum laude, U. Mich., 1964. Various mgmt. positions Lincoln Nat. Life Ins. Co., Fort Wayne, Ind., 1981—94; pres., CEO Lincoln Nat Reins. Cos.; prin. West Cons. Corp.; chair, CEO, pres. Gen. Re Life Reins. Cos., 1999—, also bd. dirs. Bd. dirs. Union Fed. Savs. Bank of Indpls., Waterfield Mortgage Corp. Area pres. Boy Scouts Am., Ind.; dir. Jr. Achievement; trustee Am. Ballet Theatre. With U.S. Army, 1964-66. Fellow Soc. of Actuaries; mem. Am. Acad. Actuaries. Presbyterian. Home: 126 Taconic Rd Greenwich CT 06831-3113 E-mail: westconsultcorp@aol.com.

WESTBROOK, JAMES EDWIN, law educator; b. Camden, Ark., Sept. 7, 1934; s. Loy Edwin and Helen Lucille (Bethea) W.; m. Elizabeth Kay Farris, Dec. 23, 1956; children: William Michael, Robert Bruce, Matthew David. BA with high honors, Hendrix Coll., 1956; JD with distinction, Duke U., 1959; LLM, Georgetown U., 1965. Bar: Ark. 1959, Okla. 1977, Mo. 1982. Assoc. Mehaffy, Smith & Williams, Little Rock, 1959-62; asst. counsel, subcom. of U.S. Senate Jud. Com., Washington, 1963; legis. asst. U.S. Senate, Washington, 1963-65; asst. prof. law U. Mo., Columbia, 1965-68, asst. dean, 1966-68, assoc. prof., 1968-70, prof., 1970-76, 80—, James S. Rollins prof. law, 1974-76, 80—, Earl F. Nelson prof. law, 1982-99, emeritus prof., 1999—, interim dean, 1981-82; dean U. Okla. Coll. Law, Norman, 1976-80. George Allen vis. prof. law, U. Richmond, 1987; vis. prof. law Duke U., 1988, Washington U., St. Louis, 1996, 2001; reporter Mid-Am. Assembly on Role of State in Urban Crisis, 1970; dir. Summer Internship Program in Local Govt., 1968; cons. various Mo. cities on drafting home-rule charters; mem. Gov.'s Adv. Coun. on Local Govt. Law, 1967-68, Fed. Practice Com. U.S. Dist. Ct. (we. dist.) Mo., 1986-90; chmn. Columbia Charter Revision Commn., 1973-74; mem. spl. com. labor relations Mo. Dept. Labor and Indsl. Rels., 1975; mem., chmn. subcom. on domestic violence Task Force on Gender and Justice, Mo. Jud. Conf., 1990-93; mem. com. to rev. govtl. structure of Boone County, Mo., 1991. Author: (with L. Riskin) Dispute Resolution and Lawyers, 1987, supplement, 1993, 3d edit., 2005, (with L. Riskin, C. Guthrie, T. Heintz, J. Robbennolt and R. Reuben); contbr. articles to profl. jours. Chair search com. for chancellor U. Mo., Columbia, 1992, chair search com. for provost, 1998; mem. fin. com. Roman Cath. Diocese of Jefferson City, 2003—. Mem. ABA, Nat. Acad. Arbitrators, Assn. Am. Law Schs. (chmn. local govt. law round table coun. 1972), Ctrl. States Law Sch. Assn. (pres. 1982-83), Mo. Bar Assn. (vice chmn. labor law com. 1986-87, chmn. 1987-88, Spurgeon Smithton award 1995), Order of Coif, Blue Key, Alpha Chi. Roman Catholic. Home: 3609 S Woods Edge Rd Columbia MO 65203-6606 Office: U Mo Sch Law Columbia MO 65211-0001 Office Phone: 573-882-6540.

WESTERBERG, GARY W., lawyer; b. Fergus Falls, Minn., Jan. 1, 1945; BA, Cornell U., 1968; JD, So. Meth. U., 1971. Bar: Ill. 1971, US Dist. Ct. (no. dist. Ill.) 1973, US Dist. Ct. (dist. Ariz.) 1997, US Ct. Appeals (3rd cir.) 1982, US Ct. Appeals (7th cir.) 1972, US Ct. Appeals (10th cir.) 1982, US Surpeme Ct. 2007. Ptnr. Lord, Bissell & Brook, Chgo. Editor: Jour. Air Law & Commerce, 1970—71. Mem.: NTSB Bar Assn., ABA, Lawyer-Pilots Bar Assn., Internat. Assn. Def. Counsel, Internat. Bar Assn., Order of the Coif. Office: Locke Lord Bissell & Liddell LLP 111 S Wacker Dr Chicago IL 60606 Office Phone: 312-443-0245. Office Fax: 312-896-6245. E-mail: gwesterberg@lockelord.com.

WESTFALL, MORRIS, farmer, retired state legislator; b. Apr. 5, 1939; s. Raymond Earl and Ethel Faye (Neill) W.; m. Sharon Kay Douglas, Dec. 19, 1964; children: Craig Lin, Christi Dawn. BS, U. Mo., 1962. Mem. Mo. Ho. of Reps., Jefferson City, 1971-81; minority whip, 1977—80; asst. minority floor leader, 1981; mem. Mo. Senate from 28th dist., Jefferson City, 1994—2002; chmn. Senate Majority Caucus, 2001—02; operator livestock farm Halfway, Mo. State exec. dir. agrl. stabilization conservation svc. USDA, Mo., 1981-93. Mem. U. Mo. Alumni Assn., Saddle Club.

WESTLUND, MARIBETH, secondary school educator; b. Chgo., Apr. 29, 1961; d. Francis Joseph and Catherine Marie Balda. BS, Ill. State U., 1983; MEd, DePaul U., 1993. Cert. ednl. adminstr., tchr. Ill. Tchr. Our Lady of Knock Cath. Sch., Calumet City, Ill., 1985—86; dept. chair of social studies, tchr. Schaumburg H.S., Schaumburg High School, Ill., 1986—. Bd. dirs. N.W. Ctr. Against Sexual Assault. Nominee Golden Apple Educator Nominee, Golden Apple Found., 2002. Mem.: AAUW, NOW, Nat. Coun. Social Studies. Avocations: travel, hiking, bicycling, tennis. Office: Schaumburg HS 1100 W Schaumburg Rd Schaumburg IL 60194 Personal E-mail: mbwestlund@yahoo.com. E-mail: mwestlund@d211.org.

WESTMAN, JACK CONRAD, child psychiatrist, educator; b. Cadillac, Mich., Oct. 28, 1927; s. Conrad A. and Alice (Pedersen) W.; m. Nancy K. Baehre, July 17, 1953; children— Daniel P., John C., Eric C. MD, U. Mich., 1952. Diplomate Am. Bd. Psychiatry and Neurology. Intern Duke Hosp., Durham, NC, 1952-53; resident U. Mich. Med. Ctr., 1955-59; dir. outpatient svcs. Children's Psychiat. Hosp., Ann Arbor, Mich., 1961-65; assoc. prof. U. Mich. Med. Sch., 1964-65; coord. diagnostic and treatment unit Waisman Ctr., U. Wis., Madison, 1966-74, prof. psychiatry, 1965-96, prof. emeritus, 1997—. Cons. Joint Commn. on Mental Health of Children, 1967-69, Madison Pub. Schs., 1965-74, Children's Treatment Ctr., Mendota Mental Health Inst., 1965-69 Author: Individual Differences in Children, 1973, Child Advocacy, 1979, Handbook of Learning Disabilities, 1990, Who Speaks for the Children?, 1991, Licensing Parents, 1994, Born to Belong, 1997, Parenthood in America, 2001; editor Child Psychiatry and Human Devel., 1984-99; contbr. articles to profl. jours. Vice-pres. Big Bros. of Dane County, 1970-73; v.p. Wis. Assn. Mental Health, 1968-72; co-chmn. Project Understanding, 1968-75; pres. Wis. Cares, 1998—. With USNR, 1953-55. Fellow Am. Psychiat. Assn., Am. Coll. Psychiatrists, Am. Acad. Child and Adolescent Psychiatry, Am. Orthopsychiat. Assn. (bd. dirs. 1973-76); mem. Am. Assn. Psychiat. Svcs. for Children (pres. 1978-80), Multidisciplinary Acad. Clin. Edn. (pres. 1992-98). Home: 1234 Dartmouth Rd Madison WI 53705-2214 E-mail: jwestman@facstaff.wisc.edu.

WESTMAN, JUDITH ANN, clinical geneticist, dean; b. Columbus, Ohio, Nov. 7, 1957; d. Paul Marshall and Anna Marie (Stahly) Whetstone; m. David Arthur Westman, Apr. 12, 1980; children: Matthew, Joel, Rachel, Deborah. BA, Ohio No. U., 1978; MD, Ohio State U., 1981, MS, 1987. Diplomate Am. Bd. Pediatrics, Am. Bd. Med. Genetics. Resident in pediatrics Children's Hosp. Ohio State U., Columbus, 1981-84, chief resident, 1984-85, fellow clin. genetics, 1985-87, clin. asst. prof., 1987-95, clin. assoc. prof., 1995—, assoc. dean admissions and student affairs, 1996-99, assoc. dean student and med. edn., 1999—2005, assoc. dean med. edn. adminstrn., 2005—. Chair admissions com. Ohio State U. Coll. Medicine, 1990-96. Author: Medical Genetics for the Modern Clinician, 2005; contbr. articles to profl. jours. Mem. adv. bd. Coll. Arts and Scis., Ohio No. U., Ada, 1988-97, trustee, 1997—; trustee Malone Coll., Canton, Ohio, 1988-94. Grantee FDA, 1987, NCI, 2001. Fellow Am. Acad. Pediatrics, Am. Soc. Human Genetics. Republican. Mem. Ch. of God (Anderson). Avocations: music, church activities. Office: 155 Meiling Hall 370 W 9th Ave Columbus OH 43210-1238

WESTMORELAND, BARBARA FENN, neurologist, educator; b. 1940; BS in Chemistry, Mary Washington Coll., 1961; MD, U. Va., 1965. Diplomate in neurology and clin. neurophysiology Am. Bd. Psychiatry and Neurology. Intern Vanderbilt Hosp., Nashville, 1965-66; resident in neurology U. Va. Hosp., Charlottesville, 1966-70; fellow in electroencephalography Mayo Clinic, Rochester, Minn., 1970-71, assoc. cons. neurology, 1971-73; asst. prof. neurology Mayo Med. Sch., Rochester, 1973-78, assoc. prof., 1978-85, prof., 1985—. Vice chair exam. com. cert. clin. neurophysiology Am. Bd. Psychiatry and Neurology, 1998—2003, chair exam. com. cert. clin. neurophysiology, 2003—. Co-author: Medical Neurosciences, 1978, rev. edit., 1986, first author 3d edit., 1994. Recipient Herbert Jasper award, Am. Clin. Neurophysiology Soc., 2005. Mem.: Mayo History Medicine Soc. (pres. 1990—91), Am. Acad. Neurology (chair sect. clin. neurophysiology 2000—02, A.B. Baker award for lifetime achievement in edn. 2002), Ctrl. Assn. Electroencephalographers (sec.-treas. 1976—78, pres. 1979—80, chair neurology resident in-svc. tng. exam 1994—99), Am. EEG Soc. (sec. 1985—87, pres. 1991—92), Am. Epilepsy Soc. (treas. 1978—80, pres. 1987—88), Sigma Xi (pres. chpt. 1987—88).

WESTON, ARTHUR WALTER, chemist, consultant, retired chemicals executive; b. Smith Falls, Ont., Can., Feb. 13, 1914; came to U.S., 1935, naturalized, 1952; s. Herbert W. and Alice M. (Houghton) W.; m. V. Dawn Thompson, Sept. 10, 1940; children: Roger L., Randall K., Cynthia B. BA, Queen's U., Kingston, Ont., 1934, MA, 1935; PhD, Northwestern U., 1938. Postdoctoral fellow Northwestern U., Evanston, Ill., 1938-40; with Abbott Labs., North Chgo., Ill., 1940-79, dir. rsch. and devel., 1959-61, v.p. rsch. and devel., 1961-68, dir. company, 1959-68, v.p. sci. affairs, 1968-77, v.p. corp. licensing, 1977-79; v.p., dir. San-Abbott, Japan, 1976-79; cons. Abbott Labs., North Chgo., Ill., 1979-85; pres. Arthur W. Weston & Assocs., Lake Forest, Ill., 1979—. Contbr. chapters to books, articles to profl. jours. Mem. Office Sci. Rsch. and Devel., War Manpower Commn., 1942-45; mem. exec. com. indsl. chemistry, div. chemistry and chem. tech. NRC, 1961-65; mem. indsl. panel on sci. and tech. NSF, 1974-80; mem. ad hoc com. chem. agts. Dept. Def., 1961-65. Mem. Rsch. Dirs. Assn. Chgo. (pres. 1965-66), Am. Chem. Soc. (trustee Chgo. 1965-2004, dir. Chgo. sect. 1952-59, nat. com. corp. assocs. 1967-72), Dirs. Indsl. Rsch., Indsl. Rsch. Inst. (bd. dirs. 1970-73), Phi Beta Kappa, Sigma Xi, Phi Lambda Upsilon. Achievements include patents in field. Home and Office: 349 Hilldale Pl Lake Forest IL 60045-3031 Personal E-mail: awweston@aol.com.

WESTON, MICHAEL C., retired lawyer; b. Asheville, NC, Aug. 13, 1938; m. Mary Ann Damme; two children. AB in English, Brown U., 1960; JD, U. Mich., 1963. Bar: Mich. 1964, Ill. 1973. Assoc. Clark Hill, Detroit, 1963-68; from sec. to pres. corp. and indsl. consortium Econ. Devel. Corp. of Greater Detroit, 1969-73; chief staff atty. Northwestern U., Evanston, Ill., 1973-81, v.p. legal affairs, 1981-89; v.p. and gen. counsel, 1990-2001; sr. cons. Acad. Search, Inc., 2004—. Lectr. minority bus. devel. Inst. Continuing Legal Edn., conflicts of interest Nat. Coun. Univ. Rsch. Adminstrs. Contbr. articles to profl. jours. Chmn. Univ. Gallery Com., 1982-85; bd. dirs. Northwestern U. Press. Mem. ABA (sec. taxation, com. on exempt orgns., ho. of dels., lectr. Inst. on Minority Bus. Devel.), Chgo. Coun. Lawyers, Nat. Assn. Coll. and Univ. Attys. (lectr. fed. tax matters, outside activities faculty mems. univ.-cmty. rels., med. risk mgmt., bd. dirs. 1985-88, 92-97, pres. 1995-96). E-mail: m-weston@northwestern.edu.

WESTON, ROGER LANCE, banker; b. Waukegan, Ill., Mar. 2, 1943; s. Arthur Walter and Vivian Dawn Weston; children: Cynthia Page, Kent Andrew, Arthur Eladio, Rebecca Dawn, Alice Sinclair, Elliot Churchill, Evan Walter, Spencer Lance. BS, MacMurray Coll., 1965; MBA, Washington U., St. Louis, 1967. Investment adviser Harris Trust & Savs. Bank, Chgo., 1967-69; sr. investment counselor Security Suprs., Chgo., 1969-70; gen. ptnr. Sierra Capital Group, Chgo., 1970-85; exec. v.p., treas., chief fin. officer Telemed Corp., Hoffman Estates, Ill., 1971-79; vice chmn. Bank Lincolnwood, Ill., 1979-85; pres., CEO, GSC Enterprises, Lincolnwood, 1979-85; chmn. bd. dirs., pres., CEO, Great-Banc, Inc., Chgo., 1986—. Mem. Barrington Hills (Ill.) Zoning Bd. Appeals, 1987-2003, com. Asian art Art Inst. Chgo., 1987; mem. nat. coun. John M. Olin Sch. Bus., Washington U. Mem. Washington U. Eliot Soc. (Chgo. nat. com., chmn. membership com. 1996-92), Univ. Club. Republican. Presbyterian. Office: Great Banc Inc 1 N Wacker Dr Ste 4075 Chicago IL 60606

WESTPHAL, KLAUS WILHELM, university museum director; b. Berlin, Mar. 20, 1939; came to U.S., 1969; s. Wilhelm Heinrich and Irmgard (Henze) W.; m. Margaret Elisabeth Dorothea Wagner, May 16, 1969; children: Barbara, Marianne, Christine. BS in Geology, Eberhard-Karls Universität, Tübingen, Germany, 1960, MS, 1964, PhD in Paleontology, 1969. Dir. geology mus. U. Wis. Madison, 1969—. Bd. dirs. natural history coun. U. Wis. Madison, 1973—, Friends of Geology Mus., Inc., 1977—; nat. speaker on paleontology Outreach, 1977—; instr. paleontology U. Wis., 1977—; leader expeditions fossil vertebrates including dinosaurs, 1977—. Participant various tchr.-tng. projects Wis. Pub. Schs. Lutheran. Home: 3709 High Rd Middleton WI 53562-1003 Office: U Wis Geology Mus 1215 W Dayton St Madison WI 53706-1600 E-mail: westphal@geology.wisc.edu.

WEXLER, RICHARD LEWIS, lawyer; b. Chgo., June 19, 1941; s. Stanley and Lottie (Pinkert) W.; m. Roberta Seigel, June 13, 1962; children: Deborah (Mrs. Jonathan Sokobin), Joshua, Christine, Jonathan, Amie. Student, U. Mich., 1959-1962; JD cum laude, John Marshall Law Sch., 1965. Bar: Ill. 1965, U.S. Dist. Ct. (no. dist.) Ill. 1967. Gen. counsel Metro. Planning Council, Chgo., 1965-67; ptnr. Wexler, Kane, Rosenzweig & Shaw, Chgo., 1967-71, Taussig, Wexler & Shaw, Chgo., 1971-78, Wexler, Siegel & Shaw, Ltd., Chgo., 1978-83, Sachnoff & Weaver, Ltd., Chgo., 1983-91, chair real estate dept., 1985-91, mng. ptnr., 1985-90; ptnr., chmn. real estate dept. Lord Bissell & Brook, Chgo., 1991-97, mem. compensation com., 1995. Legal counsel Zoning Laws Study Commn., Ill. Gen. Assembly, Springfield, 1969-71, Urban Counties Study Commn., Springfield, 1971-72; legal counsel Ill. Coastal Zone Mgmt. Program, Springfield, 1979-81, Northeastern Ill. Planning Commn., Chgo., 1969—. Contbr. numerous articles to profl. jours. Chmn. Jewish Fedn. Met. Chgo., 1986-88, mem. numerous coms., also bd. dirs., 1978-90; chmn. Jewish United Fund, 1986-88; bd. dirs. Coun. Jewish Fedns., 1980, mem. exec. com., 1985—, v.p., 1988—, chmn. planning steering com., 1990-95, chmn. fedn./agy. rels. com., 1988-90; co-chmn. Task Force on Poverty and Low Income, 1985-87; nat. vice-chmn. United Jewish Appeal, 1988, nat. chmn., 1996-98, regional allocations chmn., 1987-88, chmn. region II, 1988-90, budget com., 1989-92, allocations com., 1990-91, campaign exec., 1991-2000; chmn. Operation Exodus II, 1993-94, chmn. nat. mktg. com., 1994-95, chmn. 1997 campaign planning and budget com., nat. chmn., 1997-98, pres. bd. trustees, 1998-2000; co-chair United Jewish Appeal Fedns. N.Am., 1998-2000; bd. dirs. Jewish Edn. Soc. N.Am., 1982-85, Hebrew Immigrant Aid Soc., 1988—, Nat. Conf. on Soviet Jewry, 1989-95, vice chmn., 1989-92, nat. chmn., 1992-94; bd. dirs. Nat. Jewish Cmty. Rels. Adv. Coun., 1988-90, vice chmn., 1988-92; chmn. Jewish Com. Rels. Coun. Chgo., 1988-89; bd. dirs Great Books Found., 2000—, chair nominating com., 2004—. Fellow Eta Lambda; mem. ABA, Ill. State Bar Assn. (Lincoln award, Legal Writing, 1966). Avocations: tennis, reading, travel. Home Phone: 847-432-1743; Office Phone: 312-443-1751. Business E-Mail: rwexler@lordbissell.com.

WEXNER, ABIGAIL, apparel executive; m. Leslie H. Wexner. Dir. Ltd. Brands, Inc., Columbus, Ohio, 1997—. Past chair governing com. Columbus Found.; chair Ctr. for Child and Family Advocacy; mem. bd. trustees Children's Hosp., Inc, The Columbus Acad., The Wexner Ctr. Found.; founder, chair Columbus Coalition Against Family Violence. Named one of Top 200 Collectors, ARTnews Mag., 2004, 2007. Avocation: Collector of Modern and Contemporary Art; British Sporting Pictures. Office: Ltd Brands Inc Three Limited Pky PO Box 16000 Columbus OH 43216

WEXNER, LESLIE HERBERT, retail executive; b. Dayton, Ohio, 1937; m. Abigail Wexner; 4 children. BSBA, Ohio State U., 1959, HHD (hon.), 1986; LLD (hon.), Hofstra U., 1987; LHD (hon.), Brandeis U., 1990; PhD (hon.), Jewish Theol. Sem. Founder, pres., chmn. bd. The Limited, Inc., fashion chain, Columbus, 1963—. Dir., mem. exec. com. Banc One Corp., Sotheby's Holdings Inc., vis. com. Grad. Sch. Design Harvard U.; mem. bus. adminstrn. adv. coun. Ohio State U.; chmn. Retail Industry Trade Action Coalition. Bd. dirs. Columbus Urban League, 1982-84, Hebrew Immigrant Aid Soc., NYC, 1982—; co-chmn. Internat. United Jewish Appeal Com.; nat. vice chmn., treas. United Jewish Appeal; bd. dirs., mem. exec. com. Am. Jewish Joint Distbn. Com., Inc.; trustee Columbus Jewish Fedn., 1972, Columbus Jewish Found., Aspen Inst., Ohio State U., Columbus Capital Corp. for Civic Improvement; former trustee Columbus Mus. Art, Columbus Symphony Orch., Whitney Mus. Am. Art, Capitol South Community Urban Redevel. Corp.; former mem. Governing Com. Columbus Found.; founding mem., first chair The Ohio State U. Found; exec. com. Am. Israel Pub. Affairs Com. Decorated cavaliere Republic of Italy; named Man of Yr., Am. Mktg. Assn., 1974; named one of Top 200 Collectors, ARTnews Mag., 2004, 2007, Forbes' Richest Americans, 1999—, Forbes' Exec. Pay, 1999—, World's Richest People, Forbes mag., 2001—. Mem. Young Presidents Orgn., Sigma Alpha Mu. Clubs: B'nai B'rith; fellow Am. Acad. Arts & Sciences Jewish. Avocation: Collector of Modern and Contemporary Art; British Sporting Pictures. Office: Limited Inc PO Box 16000 3 Limited Pkwy Columbus OH 43230-1450

WEYAND, WILLIAM J., engineering executive; BBA, Nichols Coll., 1966. Exec. v.p. Measurex Corp.; pres., CEO SDRC, Milford, Ohio, 1997—, also chmn. bd. dirs. Bd. dirs. U. Maine. Office: SDRC 2000 Eastman Dr Milford OH 45150-2740

WEYERS, LARRY LEE, energy executive; b. Nebr. BA, Doane Coll., 1967; MS, Columbia U., 1971; MBA, Harvard U., 1975. Registered profl. engr. With Babcock & Wilcox, 1971—73, Commonwealth Edison, 1975—84; mgmt. cons. Towers Perrin, 1984—85; dir. fuel svc. WPS Resources Corp., Green Bay, 1985—89, asst. v.p. energy supply, 1989—92, v.p. energy supply, 1992—94, v.p. power supply & engring., 1994—95, sr. v.p. power supply & engring., 1995, pres., COO, 1995—97, bd. dir., 1996—, pres., CEO, 1997, chmn., pres., CEO, 1998—2007; pres., CEO Integrys Energy Group (merger of WPS Resources & Peoples Energy), 2007—. Bd. dir. WS Packaging Corp., Wis. Pub. Svc. Corp., 1996—; bd. mem. Edison Elec. Inst., Am. Gas Assn., 2004, Assn. Edison Illuminating Cos., 2003. Bd. mem. Bellin Health, Green Bay Packers, Wis. Manufacturers & Comm., Competitive Wis., UTECH Ventures, Utility Bus. Edn. Coalition. Office: Integrys Energy Group PO Box 19001 Green Bay WI 54307-9001

WHALE, ARTHUR RICHARD, retired lawyer; b. Detroit, Oct. 28, 1923; s. Arthur B. and Orpha Louella (Doak) W.; m. Roberta Lou Donaldson, Oct. 29, 1949; children: Richard Donaldson, Linda Jean. BSChemE, Northwestern U., 1945; LLB, George Washington U., 1956. Bar: D.C. 1957, Mich. 1957, Ind. 1977, U.S. Patent and Trademark Office 1957. Chem. engr. Ansul Chem. Co., Marinette, Wis., 1946-47, Parke, Davis & Co., Detroit, 1947-50, writer med. lit., 1950-52; chem. engr. Bur. Ships, U.S. Dept. Navy, Washington, 1952-55, dep. sect. head, indsl. gas sect., 1954-55; patent engr. Swift & Co., Washington, 1955-56; patent atty. Upjohn Co., Kalamazoo, 1956-65; asst. mgr. organic chems. sect. patent dept. Dow Chem. Co., Midland, Mich., 1965-66, mgr., 1967-73, mng. counsel, 1973-75; asst. sec., gen. patent counsel Eli Lilly & Co., Indpls., 1975-86; of counsel Miller, Morriss & Pappas, Lansing, Mich., 1986-89, Baker & Daniels, Indpls., 1987—2003; ret., 2003. Bd. dirs. Wyckoff Chem. Co., South Haven, Mich., 1985-99; lectr. Practicing Law Inst., John Marshall Law Sch. Contbr. articles to profl. jours. Pres. Nat. Inventors Hall of Fame Found., 1978-79; bd. dirs. Holcomb Rsch. Inst., Indpls., 1982-86. Served to lt. (j.g.) USNR, 1943-46. Mem. State Bar Mich. (chmn. patent trademark copyright sect. 1967-69), D.C. Bar Assn., Midland County Bar Assn. (pres. 1974-75), Am. Bar Assn. (mem. patent trademark copyright sect.), Assn. Corp. Patent Counsel, Nat. Coun. Patent Law Assns. (chmn. 1979-80), Am. Intellectual Property Law Assn. (pres. 1974-75), Ashlar Lodge, Masons, Shriners. Republican. Presbyterian. Avocation: golf. Office: Baker & Daniels Ste 2700 300 N Meridian St Indianapolis IN 46204-1782 Office Phone: 239-262-8561. Business E-Mail: arwhale@bakerd.com.

WHALEN, SARAH EVE, professional soccer player; b. Greenlawn, NY, Apr. 28, 1976; Student in psychology, U. Conn. Mem. U.S. Nat. Women's Soccer Team, 1996—, including Nike Victory Tour, 1995, U.S. Women's Cup, 97. Named 1997 Soccer Am. Player of Yr. Achievements include holder U.Conn. career record for games played (99). Office: US Soccer Fedn 1801-1811 S Prairie Ave Chicago IL 60616

WHALEN, WAYNE W., lawyer; b. Savanna, Ill, Aug. 22, 1939; s. Leo R. and Esther M. (Yackley) W.; m. Paula Wolff, Apr. 22, 1970; children: Amanda, Clementine, Antonia, Nathaniel, Daniel. BS, U.S. Air Force Acad., 1961; JD, Northwestern U., 1967. Bar: Ill. 1967, US Ct. Appeals (7th cir.) 1968, US Supreme Ct. 1972. Commd. 1st lt. USAF, 1961, ret., 1964; assoc. Mayer, Brown & Platt, Chgo., 1967-74, ptnr., 1974, Skadden, Arps, Slate, Meagher & Flom LLP, Chgo., 1984—. Bd. dir. Van Kampen Funds, Oak Brook, Ill, Abraham Lincoln Pres. Libr., Springfield, Ill. Author: Annotated Illinois Constitution, 1972. Del. 6th Ill. Constitutional Conv., 1969-70, chmn. style drafting and submission com. Named Outstanding Young Lawyer, Chgo. Bar Found., 1970. Mem. Chgo. Club. Office: Skadden Arps 2 N La Salle St Ste 2200 Chicago IL 60602-3963

WHALEY, MARVIN, food products executive; B in polit. sci., U. Md. Mgr. trainee McDonald's Corp., 1973—80, dir. ops., 1980—83, regional v.p., Atlanta, 1983—93; pres. McDonald's China Development Co., 1994—98; sr. v.p. and internat. relationship ptnr People's Republic of China, Hong Kong, Macau, Korea and Taiwan, 1998—2000; pres., North Asia divsn. McDonald's Corp., 2000—03, pres., Asia/Middle East/Africa region, 2003—. Adv. dir. McDonald's Bd. of Dirs., 1996—97. Mem. Ronald McDonald House, Ronald McDonald's Children's Charities; Atlanta Tip Off Club. With US Army, 1967—70. Office: McDonalds Corp McDonald's Plaza Oak Brook IL 60523

WHALLON, ROBERT EDWARD, anthropology educator; b. Boston, Apr. 23, 1940; s. Robert E. and Dorothy J. (Curme) W.; m. Nadine Rose DeVries, Jan. 1, 1962 (dec.); 1 child, Saskia Olga; m. Barbara Abbott Segraves, Apr. 29, 1978 (div. May 1983); m. Nada Rakic, Jan. 16, 1990; children: Vuk Novak, Nikola Lazar. BA summa cum laude, Harvard U., 1961; MA, U. Chgo., 1963, PhD, 1966. Teaching asst. dept anthropology, Chgo., 1965; curator mediterranean prehistory, asst. prof. U. Mich., Ann Arbor, 1966-71, curator, assoc. prof., 1971-77, curator, prof., 1977—, acting dir. Mus. Anthropology, 1978—79, dir. Mus. Anthropology, 1997—2002; fellow Netherlands Inst. for Advanced Studies, 1971-72. Mem. NSF adv. panel for anthropology, 1976-77. Editor: Jour. Anthrop. Archaeology, 1981-94, Mich. Archaeologist, 1969-70; author monographs, essays; contbr. numerous articles on anthropology and archaeology to profl. jours. NSF grantee, 1967—; Woodrow Wilson fellow, 1965; NDEA fellow, 1961-64 Fellow AAAS, Current Anthrpology; mem. Soc. for Am. Archaeology (exec. com. 1981-82, com. on archaeologist-Native Am. rels. 1982), Internat. Union for Prehist. and Protohist. Scis. (Commn. 4 sec. 1976-81, pres. 1981-87, permanent coun. 1987—, exec. com. 2001--), Sigma Xi, Phi Beta Kappa. Home: 1704 Baldwin Pl Ann Arbor MI 48104-3509 Office: U Mich Mus Anthropology Ann Arbor MI 48109-1079

WHARTON, BEVERLY ANN, former utility company executive; b. St. Louis, Nov. 17, 1953; d. Lawrence A. and Helen M. Bextermueller; m. James R. Wharton, March 30, 1974; 1 child, Laura. BS, So. Ill. U., 1975; MBA, U. of S.D., 1980. Tax acct. supr. Iowa Pub. Service Co., Sioux City, Iowa, 1978-84, asst. sec., 1981-84, sec., 1984-88, v.p. staff services, 1985-88, sr. v.p. support group, 1988-91; corp. sec. Midwest Energy Co., Sioux City, 1984-88, v.p., 1986-88, sr. v.p., 1988-90; gen. mgr. Midwest Gas, Sioux City, 1991-95, group v.p., gen. mgr., 1992-95; pres. Gas divsn. Mid-American Energy Co., Sioux City, 1995-96, sr. v.p. energy delivery, 1996-98, sr. v.p., 1998-99. Bd. dirs. Security Nat. Bank, Briar Cliff Coll. Mem. Midwest Gas Assn. (bd. dirs. 1992-96), Rotary (Sioux City club). Roman Catholic. Office: Mid American Energy Co 401 Douglas St Sioux City IA 51101-1443

WHEAT, CHRISTOPHER JOHN, SR., broadcast executive; b. Boston, Dec. 22, 1950; s. Robert Haase Wheat and Florence Edith (Potter) Wiley; m. Becky Ann Renshaw, June 3, 1972; children: Christopher John Jr., Colan Michael. BE, U. Cin., 1972; postgrad., U. Pa., 1978. Account exec. Sta. WKRQ-FM, Cin., 1972-76, Sta. WKRC-AM, Cin., 1976-78, mgr. local sales, 1978-80, gen. mgr. sales, 1980-82; v.p., gen. mgr. Sta. WYNF-FM, Tampa, Fla., 1982-83, Sta. WFBQ-FM, Indpls., 1983-87, Sta. WNDE-AM, Indpls., 1987—. Mem. Little Red Door, Indpls. Cancer Soc. Named one of Outstanding Young Men of Am., 1982. Mem. Radio Broadcasters of Indpls. (v.p., pres. 1988—), U. Cin. Alumni Club, Beta Theta Pi Alumni Club, Indpls. C. of C. (ptnrs. in edn. com., Ambassadors sect.). Clubs: Indpls. Athletic. Republican. Methodist. Avocation: racquetball. Home: 10723 Seascape Ct Indianapolis IN 46256-9529 Office: Sta WFBQ-FM 6161 Fall Creek Rd Indianapolis IN 46220-5032

WHEATLEY, CHRISTINE S., lawyer; b. Pitts., Feb. 27, 1971; BA, U. Notre Dame, 1993; JD, Ohio State U., 1996. Bar: Ohio 1996. Ptnr. Porter Wright Morris & Arthur LLP, Cin. Mem., Bd. Trustees Mercy Connections Cmty. Outreach Ctr. Named one of Ohio's Rising Stars, Super Lawyers, 2006. Mem.: Ohio State Bar Assn., ABA, Cin. Bar Assn. Office: Porter Wright Morris & Arthur LLP 250 E Fifth St Ste 2200 Cincinnati OH 45202-5117 Office Phone: 513-369-4229. Office Fax: 513-421-0991.

WHEELER, DANIEL SCOTT, management executive, editor; b. Richmond, Virginia, Apr. 23, 1947; s. Arthur Bruce Jr. and Lavinia (Akers) W.; m. Kathy E. (Wheeler); children: Matthew, Beth Marie, Jennifer Lynne, Brandy, and Jennifer Ann. Attended, Va. Commonwealth U., 1966-69, Butler U., 1981, Ind. U., 1984-85. Spl. agt. orthwestern Mut. Life, Richmond, 1969-71; enlisted U.S. Navy, 1971, resigned, 1979; editor Am. Legion Mag., Indpls., 1979-85, pub., editor-in-chief, 1985-95; exec. dir. The Am. Legion, Indpls., 1995—; pub., editor in chief The Am. Legion Mag., Indpls., 2003—. Bd. dir. HPC/PM Direct. Pres. Citizen's Flag Alliance, Inc. Mem. Am. Legion, Mensa. Republican. Avocation: painting. Home: 4518 Fairhope Dr Indianapolis IN 46237-2951 Office: Am Legion PO Box 1055 Indianapolis IN 46206-1055

WHEELER, MARK C., JR., bank executive; Bachelor's, Lake Forest U.; master's, Harvard U. With Mfrs. Hanover Trust Co., NYC; mng. dir. corp. fin. Bankers Trust Co., NYC; pres., mng. dir. specialized fin. Fleet Bank, N.A. (subs. Fleet Fin. Group, Inc.), 1991-99; vice chmn. Firstar Corp., Milw., 1999—. Office: Firstar Corp 777 E Wisconsin Ave Milwaukee WI 53202-5300

WHEELER, MAURICE B., librarian; BMus, Shorter Coll.; MMus, U. Mich., MLS, 1988; PhD of Libr. Sci., U. Pitts., 1995. Dir. Detroit Pub. Libr., 1996—. Adj. prof. Emporia State U., U. Mich., Wayne State U. Mem. ALA, Nat. Opera Assn./Opera for Youth. Office: Detroit Pub Libr 5201 Woodward Ave Detroit MI 48202-4093

WHEELER, MIKE, retail food store corporate executive; CFO Hy-vec Food Stores Inc., West Des Moines, Iowa, 1998. Office: Hy-vec Food Stores Inc 5820 Westown Pkwy West Des Moines IA 50266-8223

WHEELER, PAUL JAMES, real estate executive; b. Mpls., Jan. 8, 1953; s. Philip James and Phyllis Lavonne (Holmquist) W.; m. Marianne Marie Stanton, June 3, 1978; children: Allison, Nathan, Kathryn. BA in Econs., DePauw U., 1975; MBA in Mgmt., Northwestern U., 1977. CPA, Ill. Acct. Deloitte, Haskins & Sells, Chgo., 1976-79; v.p. fin. Quinlan & Tyson, Inc., Evanston, Ill., 1979-82; sr. v.p. The Inland Real Estate Group, Inc., Oakbrook, Ill., 1982—. Bd. dirs. Westbank of Westchester, Inland Real Estate Equities. Inc., Inland Ins. Group, Inc., Oak Brook, Ill. Mem. Ill. Soc. CPA's, Nat. Assn. Real Estate Investment Trusts, Nat. Multi Housing Coun., Investment Program Assn., Libertyville Sunrise Rotary. Republican. Evangelical Free. Home: 255 Ridgeway Ln Libertyville IL 60048-2457 Office: The Inland Group Inc 2901 Butterfield Rd Oak Brook IL 60523-1190

WHEELOCK, PAM, financial executive; BA in History, Coll. St. Catherine; MA in Applied Econs., Marquette U. Exec. budget officer Minn. Dept. Fin., 1988—92; budget dir. City of St. Paul, 1992—94, dep. mayor, 1994—96, dir. dept. planning and econ. devel., 1996—99; commr. Minn. Dept. Fin., 1999—2002; sr. v.p., CFO Minn. Sports and Entertainment, 2002—. Office: Minn Wild 317 Washington St Saint Paul MN 55102

WHELAN, RICHARD J., retired academic administrator; b. Emmett, Kans, June 23, 1931; s. Richard Joseph and Margaret Alma (Cox) W.; m. Carol Ann King, Nov. 21, 1959; children— Mark Richard, Cheryl Lynne BA, Washburn U., 1955; Ed.D., U. Kans., 1966. Dir. edn. Menninger Clinic, Topeka, 1959-62; dir. edn. children's rehab. unit U. Kans. Med. Ctr., Kansas City, Kans., 1966—2000; prof. spl. edn. and pediatrics, chmn. dept. spl. edn. U. Kans., Lawrence, 1966-72, 78-80, 83-88, assoc. dean grad. studies and outreach, 1988-94, Ralph L. Smith disting. prof. child devel., 1968—2000, dean sch. edn., 1992-94, prof. emeritus, 2000—; div. dir. U.S. Office Edn., Washington, 1972-74; cons. Blue Valley Sch. Dist., Overland Park, Kans., 2000—; complaint investigator Kans. Bd. of Edn., 2000—. Cons. colls. and univs., state and fed. agys.; chmn. policy bd. Evaluation Tng., Kalamazoo, 1975-81 Author, editor: Promising Practices., 1983, Emotional and Behavioral Disorders, 1998; cons. editor Ednl. Research Ency., 1982; contbr. articles to profl. jours., chpts. to books Chmn. adv. bd. Kans. Bd. Edn., Topeka, 1982-92; mem. adv. bd. Shawnee Mission Sch. Dist., Kans., 1984-92; mem. Gov.'s Task Force on Early Childhood, 1984-92; hearing officer various sch. dists. Kans. Bd. Edn., Bur. Indian Affiars; mediator and trainer Kans. Supreme Ct Mem. Soc. for Learning Disabilities (pres. 1980-81), Council for Exceptional Children, Assn. for Persons with Severe Handicaps (bd. dirs. 1975-79), Kans. Council for Exceptional Children (pres. 1963-64, Service award 1978, award for excellence 2000), Phi Kappa Phi Avocations: reading, music, golf, flying. Home: 7400 West 148th St Overland Park KS 66223 E-mail: rwhelan@kumc.edu.

WHELPLEY, DENNIS PORTER, lawyer; b. Mpls., Feb. 16, 1951; s. John Olsen and Harriet Marie (Porter) W.; m. Patricia Jan Adamy, Nov. 27, 1976; children: Heather Nicolle, Christopher Eric. BA, U. Minn., 1973, JD magna cum laude, 1976. Bar: Minn. 1976. Assoc. Oppenheimer Wolff & Donnelly, St. Paul, 1976-83, ptnr., 1983—. Mem. Order of Coif (Minn. chpt.), Phi Beta Kappa (Alpha of Minn. chpt.), Psi Upsilon (Mu chpt.), Dellwood Hills Golf & Country Club. Avocations: golf, tennis, squash, bridge. Home: 49 Locust St Mahtomedi MN 55115-1542 Office: Oppenheimer Wolff & Donnelly 45 S 7th St Ste 3300 Minneapolis MN 55402-1614 Home Phone: 651-426-0949; Office Phone: 612-607-7397. Business E-Mail: dwhelpley@oppenheimer.com.

WHETSTONE, MATTHEW D., state representative; b. Connersville, Ind., Apr. 4, 1969; m. Deanna Whetstone. BS, Ball State U., 1992. Owner Whetstone & Assocs. Interior Design; auditor supr. State of Ind., 1993—94; comm. mgr. Ind. Telecomm. Assn., 1994—96; state rep. dist. 40 Ind. Ho. of Reps., Indpls., 1996—, ranking Rep. mem. rules and legis. procedures com., mem. ins., corps. and small bus., and pub. policy, ethics and vets. affairs coms. Mem. Brownsburg (Ind.) Town Coun., 1995—; bd. dirs. Acad. Sci., Math. and Humanities, Ball State U. Mem.: Brownsburg Kiwanis, Brownsburg Sertoma. Republican. Office: Ind Ho of Reps 200 W Washington St Indianapolis IN 46204-2786

WHIFFEN, JAMES DOUGLASS, surgeon, educator; b. NYC, Jan. 16, 1931; s. John Phillips and Lorna Elizabeth (Douglass) W.; child from a previous marriage, Gregory James; m. Sally Vilas Runge, Aug. 21, 1993. BS, U. Wis., 1952, MD, 1955. Diplomate: Am. Bd. Surgery. Intern Ohio State U. Hosp., 1955-56; resident U. Wis. Hosp., 1956-57, 59-61; instr. dept. surgery U. Wis. Med. Sch., 1962-64, asst. prof., 1964-67, asso. prof., 1967-71, prof., 1971-96, vice chmn. dept., 1970-72, acting chmn., 1972-74; asst. dean Med. Sch., 1975-96; prof. emeritus U. Wis. Med. Sch., 1996—; mem. exam. council State of Wis. Emergency Med. Services, 1974-77. Bd. dirs. Wis. Heart Assn. Served to lt. comdr. USNR, 1957-59. John and Mary R. Markle scholar in acad. medicine, also; Research Career Devel. award NIH, 1965-75 Fellow A.C.S., Am. Soc. Artificial Internal Organs. Clubs: Maple Bluff Country. Achievements include research publs. on biomaterials, thrombo-resistant surfaces and the physiology of heart-lung bypass procedures. Home: 17 Cambridge Ct Madison WI 53704-5906 Office: 600 Highland Ave Madison WI 53792-0001 E-mail: jwhiffen@wisc.edu.

WHIPPLE, DEAN, federal judge; b. 1938; BS, Drury Coll., 1961; postgrad., U. Tulsa, 1961-62; JD, postgrad., U. Mo., Kansas City, 1965. Pvt. practice, Lebanon, Mo., 1965-75; cir. judge div. II 26th Jud. Cir. Mo., 1975-87; judge US Dist. Ct. (we. dist.) Mo., Kansas City, 1987-2000, chief judge, 2000—07. Prosecuting atty. Laclede County, Mo., 1967-71. With Mo. N.G., 1956-61; USAR, 1961-66. Mem. Mo. Bar Assn. (mem. bd. govs. 1975-87, mem. exec. com. 1983-84, 86-87), Mo. Trial Judges Assn., 26th Jud. Bar Assn., Laclede County Bar Assn. (pres. 1968-69, 72-73), Kansas City Met. Bar Assn., Kansas City Inn of Ct. (instr. 1988-93), Mo. Hist. Soc., Phi Delta Phi. Office: US Courthouse 400 E 9th St Kansas City MO 64106-2607

WHIPPLE, KENNETH, utilities executive; b. 1934; BS, MIT, 1958. With Ford Motor Co., Dearborn, Mich., 1958—, systems mgr. Ford Credit, 1966-69, mgr. mgmt. svcs. dept. fin. staff, 1969-71, systems analysis mgr. fin. staff, 1971-74, asst. contr. internat. fin. staff, 1974-75, v.p. fin. Ford Credit, 1975-77, exec. v.p. Ford Credit, 1977-80, pres. Ford Credit, 1980-84, v.p. corp. strategy, 1984-86; v.p. chmn. Ford of Europe, 1986-88; exec. v.p., pres. Ford Fin. Svcs. Group, Dearborn, 1988—99; chmn., CEO CMS Energy, Dearborn, Mich., 2002—04, chmn., 2004—. Office: CMS Energy 1 Energy Plaza Drive Jackson MI 49201

WHISLER, JOE B., lawyer; b. Nevada, Mo., May 31, 1947; BA, Ctrl. Meth. Coll., 1969; JD, So. Meth. Univ., Dallas, 1972. Bar: Mo. 1972, US Ct. Appeals (8th Cir.) 1980, US Ct. Appeals (10th Cir.). Mem., atty. Cooling & Herbers PC, Kans. City, Mo. Bd. of editors: Jour. of Air Law and Commerce, 1971—72. Mem.: ABA, Lawyers Assn. of Kans. City (pres., jr. sect. 1977—78), Kans. City Met. Bar Assn., Bar Assn. of Met. St. Louis (chmn. aviatin law com. 1998, mem. planning commn. City Westwood, Kans. 1998), Barristers, Mo. Bar (bd. gov. 1979—83, 1996—, pres.-elect 2003, pres. 2004), Phi Alpha Delta. Office: Cooling & Herbers PC 2400 City Center Sq 1100 Main St Kansas City MO 64105

WHISNANT, JACK PAGE, neurologist; b. Little Rock, Oct. 26, 1924; s. John Clifton and Zula I. (Page) W.; m. Patricia Anne Rimmey, May 12, 1944; children: Elizabeth Anne, John David, James Michael. BS, U. Ark., 1948, MD, 1951; MS, U. Minn., 1955; MD (hon.), U. Edinburgh, Scotland, 1996. Intern Balt. City Hosp., 1951-52; resident in medicine and neurology Mayo Grad. Sch. Medicine, Rochester, Minn., 1952-55, instr. neurology, 1956-60, asst. prof., 1960-64, asso. prof., 1964-69, prof., 1969—; Meyer prof. neurosci. Mayo Med. Sch.; chmn. dept. neurology Mayo Clinic, Mayo Med. Sch., Mayo Grad. Sch. Medicine, 1971-81; chmn. dept. health scis. research Mayo Clinic and Mayo Med. Sch., 1987-93. Cons. neurology Mayo Clinic, 1955-96, head sect. neurology, 1963-71; dir. Mayo Cerebrovascular Clin. Rsch. Ctr., 1975-96. Contbr. articles on neurology and cerebrovascular disease to med. jours. Trustee YMCA, Rochester, pres., 1977. With USAAF, 1942-45. Decorated Air medal. NIH grantee, 1959-96. Fellow Am. Heart Assn., Am. Acad. Neurology (pres. 1993-95); mem. AMA, Am. Neurol. Assn. (pres. 1981-82), Am. Bd. Psychiatry and Neurology (bd. dirs. 1983-90, pres. 1989), Zumbro Valley Med. Soc., Minn. Med. Assn., Minn. Soc. Neurol. Scis., Ctrl. Soc. Neurol. Rsch. (pres. 1964), Alumni Assn. Mayo Found. (Disting. Alumnus award 2003). Presbyterian. Office: Mayo Clinic Dept Health Scis Rsch 200 1st St SW Rochester MN 55905-0001 Home: 211 2nd St NW Apt 716 Rochester MN 55901-2813 Personal E-mail: whisnant24@charter.net. Business E-Mail: whisnant@mayo.edu.

WHITAKER, AUDIE DALE, hospital laboratory medical technologist; b. Cin., Jan. 19, 1949; s. Audie and Wanda Edith (Weaver) W.; m. Sandra Sue McPhail, Aug. 22, 1970; children: Audie David Nathaniel, Andrea Grace, Alexandra Christine. BA, Olivet Nazarene U., 1971; Degree in Med. Tech., Silver Cross Hosp., Joliet, Ill., 1972; MS in Biology, Ball State U., 1999. Med. tech. Riverside Hosp., Kankakee, 1971-72, Silver Cross Hosp., Joliet, 1972-77; lab. mgr. Lakeshore Community Hosp., 1977-90; evening lab. supr. Community Hosp., Anderson, Ind., 1990-93; med. technologist Community Hosp. of Anderson, 1990—. Lectr. in field. Health care rep. Local Emergency Preparedness Com., Hart, Mich., 1988-90; sec., deacon, bd. dirs. West Shore Christian Fellowship, Muskegon, 1987-90, vice chmn. edn. com., 1988-90; mem. Rep. Nat. Com. S.W. Nazarene Ch. Dist. grantee, 1967, Directed Study grantee, 1970-71, rsch. grantee Sigma Xi, 1993; grad. rsch. grantee Ball State U., 1994. Mem. Am. Soc. Clin. Pathologists. Republican. Avocations: acting, poetry, astronomy. Home: 1705 N Tillotson Ave Muncie IN 47304-2601 Office: Community Hosp 1515 N Madison Ave Anderson IN 46011-3457 Personal E-mail: swhitaker778@comcast.net.

WHITAKER, CHARLES F., journalism educator; b. Chgo., Oct. 28, 1958; s. Andrew L. and Marjorie Whitaker; m. Stephanie J. Sanders, Oct. 1, 1988; children: Joshua, Christopher. BS in Journalism, Northwestern U., 1980, MS in Journalism, 1981. Suburban edn. writer N.E. Dade County Bur., Miami (Fla.) Herald, 1981-82, staff writer, 1982-84, Louisville Times, 1984-85; assoc. editor Ebony Mag., Chgo., 1985-87, sr. assoc. editor, 1987-89, sr. editor, 1989-92; mem. adj. faculty Northwestern U. Medill Sch. Journalism, Evanston, Ill., 1990-92, asst. prof. journalism, 1992—. Dir. Gertrude Johnson Williams Lit. Contest, 1989—; assoc. fellow Joint Ctr. for Polit. and Econ. Studies, Urban Policy Inst., Chgo., 1992—; advisor, faculty editor Passport Africa, 1992. Contbr. to various publs. Bd. dirs. Chocolate Chips Theatre Co., 1987—. Recipient 1st place award for mag. writing Nat. Assn. Edn. Writers, 1982; 1st place award for feature writing Louisville Assn. Black Communicators, 1984, for commentary or criticism, 1984. Mem. Nat. Assn. Black Journalists, Chgo. Assn. Black Journalists (faculty Exposure satellite program 1988—), Phi Beta Sigma (editor-in-chief Crescent 1989-93). Office: Northwestern U Medill Sch Journalism Fisk Hall 1845 Sheridan Rd Evanston IL 60208-0001

WHITAKER, FREDA N., trust company executive; BS, U. Mo., Kansas City. With Patrons Bank (now NationsBank), Olathe, Kans., Johnson County Bank (now Firstar); exec. v.p. The Midwest Trust Co., Overland Park, Kans. Mem.: Ea. Kans. Estate Planning Coun., Estate Planning Soc. Kansas City (past pres.). Office: Midwest Trust Company 5901 College Blvd Ste 100 Leawood KS 66211-1834

WHITAKER, GLENN VIRGIL, lawyer; b. Cin., July 23, 1947; s. Glenn M. and Doris (Handlon) W.; m. Jennifer Lynn Angus, Oct. 22, 1990. BA, Denison U., 1969; JD, George Washington U., 1972. Bar: Md. 1972, D.C. 1973, Ohio 1980. Law clk. to judge U.S. Dist. Ct., Balt., 1972-73; assoc. O'Donoghue and O'Donoghue, Washington, 1973-76; trial atty. civil div. U.S. Dept. Justice, Washington, 1976-78, spl. litigation counsel, 1978-80; ptnr. Graydon, Head & Ritchey, Cin., 1980-92, Voyrs, Sater, Seymour & Pease, Cin., 1992—. Emeritus master of bench Potter Stewart Inn of Ct., Cin., 1985—; adj. prof. law Coll. Law U. Cin.; mem. Am. Bd. Trial Advocates. Fellow Am. Coll. Trial Lawyers; mem. ABA, Ohio Bar Assn., D.C. Bar Assn., Md. Bar Assn., Cin. Bar Assn. Avocations: hiking, exploring. Office: Vorys Sater Seymour & Pease 221 E 4th St Ste 2100 Cincinnati OH 45202-5133 Office Phone: 513-723-4608. E-mail: gvwhitaker@vssp.com.

WHITAKER, JOHN, state official; b. Oct. 1956; State rep., Iowa, 2003—. Mem. agr. and natural resources appropriations subcom.; mem. agr. standing com.; mem. natural resources standing com.; mem. transp. standing com. Office: State Capitol E 12th and Grand Des Moines IA 50319

WHITAKER, MATTHEW GEORGE, prosecutor; JD, MBA, U. Iowa, 1995. Corp. counsel Supervalu; atty. Briggs & Morgan, Finley Alt Smith, Des Moines; US atty. (so. dist.) Iowa US Dept. Justice, Des Moines, 2004—. Office: US Courthouse Annex Ste 286 110 E Ct Ave Des Moines IA 50309

WHITBURN, GERALD, insurance company executive; b. Wakefield, Mich., July 12, 1944; s. Donald and Ruby E. (Nichols) W.; m. Charmaine M. Heise, May 3, 1969; children: Bree, Luke. BS, U. Wis., Oshkosh, 1966; MA, U. Wis., Madison, 1968; postgrad., Harvard U., 1988-00, U. Pa., 1997. Aide Gov. Warren P. Knowles, Wis., 1966-69; personal asst. USN sec. John H. Chafee, Washington, 1969-72; automoble dealer, real estate developer Merrill, Wis., 1973-80; exec. asst. to Senator Robert W. Kasten U.S. Senate, Washington, 1981-87; dep. sec. Wis. Dept. Adminstrn., Madison, 1987-89; sec. Wis. Dept. Industry, Labor and Human Rels., Madison, 1989-91, Wis. Dept. Health and Social Svcs., Madison, 1991-95; sec. exec. office of health and human svcs. Commonwealth of Mass., Boston, 1995-96; chmn., pres., CEO Ch. Mut. Ins. Co., Merrill, Wis., 1996—; dir. Property Casualty Insurers Assn. of Am., Wis. Mfrs. and Commerce, Wis. Ctr. Academically Talented Youth. Mem. U.S. Labor Sec.'s Commn. on Achieving Necessary Skills, Washington, 1990-92. Contbr. articles to newspapers. Del. Rep. at. Conv., 1988, 92, 2004. Recipient Disting. Alumni award U. Wis., Oshkosh, 1991. Office: Ch Mut Ins Co 300 Schuster Ln Merrill WI 54452 Home: 827 Parcher St Wausau WI 54403

WHITE, B. JOSEPH, former dean, business educator; BS, Georgetown U., 1969; MBA, Harvard U., 1971; PhD, U. Mich., 1975. Dean bus. adminstrn. U. Mich., Ann Arbor, 1991—2001, interim pres., 2001, Wilbur K. Pierpont Collegiate prof. leadership in mgmt. edn. and prof. bus. adminstrn. Bus. Sch., 2002—. Mng. dir. Fred Alger Mgmt., Inc., NYC. Office: Life Science Inst 210 Washtenaw Ave Rm 3407 Ann Arbor MI 48109-2216 Business E-Mail: bjwhite@umich.edu.

WHITE, DEAN, advertising executive; b. Norfolk, Nebr., 1923; m. Barbara White; 4 children. Student, U. Nebr.; grad., U.S. Merchant Marine Acad. Pres. Whiteco Industries, Inc., Merrillville, Ind., 1953-98, chmn. bd., CEO, 1998—. Chief officer Merchant Marines, Navy. Office: Whiteco Industries Inc 1000 E 700N Merrillville IN 46410-5675

WHITE, DENNIS L., transportation executive, former political organization administrator; b. 1954; Franklin County chmn. Ohio Dem. Party, 1994—2002, chmn., 2002—05; CEO Transport Consol.

WHITE, DOUG, state legislator; b. 1943; m. Shirley White; children: Steve, Jenny. BS, Ohio State U. Commr. Adams County, 1985-90; mem. Ohio Ho. of Reps from 77th & 88th dists., Columbus, 1990-96; owner, operator livestock and crop farm; mem. Ohio Senate from 14th dist., Columbus, 1996—, pres., 2002—. Mem. Ohio Cattlemen's Assn. (pres.), Ohio Beef Coun. (former treas.), Adams County Rep. Club, Ohio 4-H Found., Manchester Lions, Ohio Farm Bur. Office: Ohio Senate State House Rm 201 Columbus OH 43215

WHITE, EUGENE G., school system administrator; b. Dec. 1947; m. Jetties White; children: Reginald E., Kimberly R. BA, Ala. A&M Univ. Teacher, sch. adminstr. Wayne Cmty. Coll.; prin. Wayne High Sch., 1985—90, North Ctrl. High Sch., 1990—92; dep. supt. Indpls. Pub. Schools, 1992—94; supt. Met. Sch. Dist. Wash. Twp., 1992—2003, Indpls. Pub. Schools, 2004—. Author: Leadership Beyond Excuses: The Courage to Hold the Rope. Named Supt. of the Yr., Ind.; named to Ala. A&M Athletic Hall of Fame. Mem.: Am. Assn. Sch. Adminstr. (pres.), Ind. Assn. Pub. Sch. Supt. (past pres.), North Ctrl. Assn. (pres. commn. accreditation and sch. improvement). Office: Indianapolis Public Schools Office of the Superintendent 120 E Walnut St Indianapolis IN 46204 Office Phone: 317-226-4000.

WHITE, GREGORY A., prosecutor; b. Nov. 1949; BA in Criminal Justice and Police Adminstrn., Kent State U., 1973; JD magna cum laude, Cleveland Marshall Coll., 1976. Atty. Wilcox and White Law Firm, 1977—84; law dir. City of Elyria, 1979; prosecutor Lorain County, Ohio, 1981—2002; US atty. (no. dist.) Ohio US Dept. Justice, 2003—. With USMC, Vietnam. Office: US Attys Office 801 W Superior Ave Ste 400 Cleveland OH 44113-1852

WHITE, HAROLD F., bankruptcy judge, retired federal judge; b. Hartford, Conn., Apr. 29, 1920; s. Harry T. and Maude Evelyn (McCarthy) W.; m. Edna Jeanette Murie, 1943; children; Frances, Susan, Harold. BSc, Ohio U., 1946; JD, U. Akron, 1952. Bar: Ohio 1952. Chief police prosecutor City of Akron, Ohio, 1953; asst. prosecutor Summit County, Akron, 1957-58; bankruptcy referee, bankruptcy judge U.S. Cts., Akron, 1958-94, on recall as sr. bankruptcy judge, 1994—, on recall as bankruptcy judge, 1995-2001. Trustee Summit County Kidney Found; elder Westminster Presbyn. Ch., Akron. Named Disting. Alumni Ohio U., 1979, Outstanding Alumni U. Akron Sch. Law, 1983; recipient John Quine adj. lectr. of law award U. Akron Sch. Law, 1991. Fellow Ohio State Bar Assn. (hon. life); mem. Akron Bar Assn., Nat. Conf. Bankruptcy Judges (vice gov. 6th cir.), Commercial Law League, Am. Bankruptcy Inst. Office: Rm 455 2 S Main St Akron OH 44308-1880

WHITE, JAMES BOYD, law educator; b. Boston, July 28, 1938; s. Benjamin Vroom and Charlotte Green (Conover) W.; m. Mary Louise Fitch, Jan. 1, 1978; children: Emma Lillian, Henry Alfred; children by previous marriage: Catherine Conover, John Southworth. AB, Amherst Coll., 1960; AM, Harvard U., 1961, LLB, 1964. Assoc. Foley, Hoag & Eliot, Boston, 1964-67; asst. prof. law U. Colo., 1967-69, assoc. prof., 1969-73, prof., 1973-75; prof. law U. Chgo., 1975-83; Hart Wright prof. law and English U. Mich., Ann Arbor, 1984—. Vis.

assoc. prof. Stanford U., 1972 Author: The Legal Imagination, 1973, (with Scarboro) Constitutional Criminal Procedure, 1976, When Words Lose Their Meaning, 1981, Heracles' Bow, 1985, Justice as Translation, 1990, "This Book of Starres", 1994, Acts of Hope, 1994, From Expectation to Experience, 1999, How Should We Talk About Religion?, 2006, The Edge of Meaning, 2001, Living Speech, 2006. Sinclair Kennedy Traveling fellow, 1964-65; Nat. Endowment for Humanities fellow, 1979-80, 92; Guggenheim fellow, 1993; vis. scholar Phi Beta Kappa, 1997-98. Mem. AAAS, Am. Law Inst. Office: U Mich Law Sch 1035 Legal Research 625 S State St Ann Arbor MI 48109-1215 Office Phone: 743-936-2989. Business E-Mail: jbwhite@umich.edu.

WHITE, JAMES LINDSAY, polymer engineering educator; b. Bklyn., Jan. 3, 1938; s. Robert Lindsay and Margaret (Young) W. BS, Poly. Inst. Bklyn., 1959; MS, U. Del., 1962, PhD, 1965. Rsch. engr. Uniroyal Inc., Wayne, N.J., 1963-66, rsch. engr., group leader, 1966-67; assoc. prof. U. Tenn., Knoxville, 1967-70, prof., 1970-76, prof. in charge Polymer Sci. and Engring. Program, 1976-83; dir. Polymer Engring. Ctr. U. Akron, Ohio, 1983-89, dir. Inst. Polymer Engring. Ohio, 1989—2001, head/chmn. dept. polymer engring. Ohio, 1983-97, Harold A. Morton prof. Ohio, 1997—. Author: Principles of Polymer Engineering Rheology, 1990, Twin Screw Extrusion: Technology and Principles, 1990, Rubber Processing: Technology of Materials and Principles, 1995, (with D. Choi) Polyolefins: Processing Structure Development and Properties, 2004; editor-in-chief Internat. Polymer Processing, 1990—; contbr. over 300 articles, papers. Editor (with A.Y. Coran and A. Moet): Polymer Mixing, 2001; editor: (with H Potente) Screw Extrusion, 2003. Recipient Internat. Edn. award Soc. Plastics Engrs., 1987, Internat. Rsch. award, 1992, Extrusion Divsn. Heinz Herrmann Twin Screw Extrusion award, 2004. Mem. Polymer Processing Soc. (pres. 1985-87, editor 1987-90, editor-in-chief 1990—), Soc. Rheology (editorial bd. 1967-92, Bingham medal 1981), Soc. Rheology Japan (Yuko-sho award 1984). Office: U Akron Polymer Engring Acad Ctr Akron OH 44325-0001

WHITE, JAMES PATRICK, law educator; b. Iowa City, Sept. 29, 1931; s. Raymond Patrick and Besse (Kanak) W.; m. Anna R. Seim, July 2, 1964. BA, U. Iowa, 1953, JD, 1956; LLM, George Washington U., 1959; LLD (hon.), U. Pacific, 1984, John Marshall Law Sch., 1989, Weidner U., 1989, Campbell U., 1993; Jur D (hon.), Whittier Coll., 1992; LLD (hon.), Campbell U., 1993, Southwestern U., 1995, Quinnipiac U., 1995, Calif. Western Law Sch., 1997; LLD, Roger Williams U., 1999, New England Sch. of Law, 2001, Seattle U., 2001, We. New Eng. Coll., 2002; LHD (hon.), Barry U., 2005. Bar: Iowa 1956, D.C. 1959, U.S. Supreme Ct. 1959. Teaching fellow George Washington U. Law Sch., 1958-59; asst. prof. U. N.D. Law Sch., Grand Forks, 1959-62, asso. prof., acting dean, 1962-63, prof., asst. dean, 1963-67; dir. agrl. law rsch. program, prof. law Ind. U. Law Sch., Indpls., 1967—2002, also dir. urban legal studies program, 1971-74, prof. emeritus, 2002—; dean acad. devel. and planning, spl. asst. to chancellor Ind. U., Indpls., 1974-83. Mem. for N.D., Commn. on Uniform State Laws, 1961-66; cons. legal edn. ABA, 1974-2001, cons. emeritus, 2001—. Contbr. papers to tech. lit. Trustee Butler U., John Marshall Law Sch., Atlanta, Indpls. Mus. Art. Capt. JAGC, 1st lt. USAF, 1956—58. Recipient Thomas More award, St. Mary's U., 1965, Sagamore of the Wabash award, State of Ind.; Carnegie postdoctoral fellow, U. Mich. Ctr. for Study Higher Edn., 1964—65. Fellow: China-US Commn. Legal Edn. (commr.), Soc. for Advanced Legal Studies (Eng.) (chair Fulbright com. awards in law 1989—92), Indpls. Bar Found. (disting. fellow), Am. Bar Found. (life); mem.: ABA (Kutak award medal 2001), Indpls. Bar Assn., Am. Law Inst. (life), Am. Law Inst. (life), Iowa Bar Assn., Ind. Bar Assn., Woodstock Club (Indpls.), Order of Coif. Roman Catholic. Home: 7707 N Meridian St Indianapolis IN 46260-3651 Office: Ind U 530 W New York St Indianapolis IN 46202-3225 Home Phone: 317-253-4066; Office Phone: 317-278-9690. Business E-Mail: jwhite@iupui.edu.

WHITE, JESSE, state official; b. Alton, Ill., June 23, 1934; BS, Ala. State Coll., 1957. Profl. baseball player Chgo. Cubs; tchr., adminstr. Chgo. Pub. Sch. Sys.; mem. Ill. Gen. Assembly, Springfield, 1972—74, 1976—92, chmn. com. human svcs., mem. edn. com., mem. select com. children and aging; recorder of deeds Cook County, Chgo., 1992—98; sec. state State of Ill., Springfield, 1999—. Founder Jesse White Tumbling Team, 1959; Dem. committeeman 27th Ward, Chgo., 1996—; libr. State of Ill. State Libr.; archivist State of Ill. Served in Ill. Nat. Guard, paratrooper 101st Airborne Divsn. US Army. Recipient Archbishop Richard Chenevix Trench award, 1999; Inductee Southwestern Athletic Conf. Hall of Fame, 1995, Chgo. Pub. League Basketball Coaches Assn. Hall of Fame, 1995, Ala. State U. Sports Hall of Fame, 1999; named one of 100 Most Influential Black Americans, Ebony mag., 2006. Democrat. Office: Sec of State 213 State Capitol Springfield IL 62706 Office Phone: 217-782-2201. Office Fax: 217-785-0358. E-mail: jessewhite@ilsos.net.

WHITE, JOHN GRAHAM, science educator, research director; b. Prestatyn, Wales, Aug. 9, 1943; came to U.S., 1993; s. Bernard and Norah (Bannister) W.; m. Donna Albertson, July 26, 1980 (div. Apr. 1994); children: Phoebe, Ben, Amelia, Ruth; m. Claudia Cummins, Nov. 8, 1994. BTech, Brunel U., London, 1969; PhD, Cambridge U., Eng., 1974. Technician Med. Rsch. Coun., London, 1964-69, scientist, 1969-93; prof., dir. integrated microscopy resource U. Wis., Madison, 1993—. Cons. Bio-Rad, Herculese, Calif., 1988—. Recipient Queen's award for Tech., 1991, Mullard award Royal Soc., 1994. Achievements include two patents for confocal microscopy. Office: U Wis Lab Molecular Biology 1525 Linden Dr Madison WI 53706-1534

WHITE, JOHN HENRY, photojournalist, educator; b. Lexington, NC, Mar. 18, 1945; s. Reid R. and Ruby M. (Leverette) W.; m. Emily L. Miller, May 29, 1966 (div.); children: Deborah, Angela, Ruby, John Henry. AAS., Central Piedmont Community Coll. Photographer U.S. Marine Corps., Quantico, Va., 1966-68, Tom Walters Photograpahy, Charlotte, N.C., 1968-69; photojournalist Chgo. Daily News, 1969-78, Chgo. Sun-Times, 1978—; instr. photojournalism Columbia Coll., Chgo., 1978—. Lectr. in field Mem. Blackwell Meml. A.M.E. Zion Ch., Chgo., 1972—, steward, 1979—, supt. Sunday Sch. Recipient over 200 photography in journalism awards; recipient Pulitzer prize, 1982 Mem. Nat. Press Photograhers Assn., Ill. Press Photographers Assn. (photographer of yr. award 1971, 79, 82), Chgo. Press Photographers Assn. (pres. 1977-78 photographer of yr. award), Chgo. Assn. Black Journalists Office: Chicago Sun Times 350 N Orleans St Ste 1270 Chicago IL 60654-2148

WHITE, JOHN J., state representative, human resources specialist; b. 1959; married; 3 children. BS in Mktg., Wright State U. Rep. Ohio State Ho. Reps., Columbus, 2000—. Mem. banking, pensions and securities com. Ohio State Ho. Reps., vice chmn. health com., mem. children's healthcare and family svcs. com., mem. human svcs. and aging subcom., mem. ins. subcom., mem. pub. utilities subcom. Mem. exec. com. Montgomery County Rep. Party; vice mayor Kettering; chmn. Montgomery County Ctrl. Com.; pres. Montgomery County Young Reps. Republican. Office: Ohio State House Reps 77 South High Street 13th Floor Columbus OH 43215-6111

WHITE, JOSEPH B., reporter; b. NYC, July 7, 1958; Attended, Harvard U. Reporter The Wall St. Jour., 1998, bur. chief, 1998—. Co-author (with Paul Ingrassia): (book) Comeback: The Fall and Rise of the American Automobile Industry, 1994. Recipient Pulitzer Prize for beat reporting, 1993. Office: The Wall Street Journal Detroit Bureau 500 Woodward Ave Ste 1950 Detroit MI 48226-5497

WHITE, KATHERINE E., law educator; BSE elec. engring. and computer sci., Princeton U., 1988; JD, U. Wash., 1991; LLM in Intellectual Property, George Washington U., 1996. Bar: Mich. 1996, U.S. Supreme Ct, U.S. Ct. Appeals (fed. cir.), U.S. Ct. Appeals Armed Forces, U.S. Army Ct. Mil. Rev., U.S. Patent and Trademark Office, Wash. 1992. Intellectual property counsel U.S. Army Corps Engrs., Washington, 1992—95; jud. law clk. for Hon. Randall Rader U.S. Ct. Appeals (fed. cir.), 1995—96; assoc. prof. Wayne State U. Law Sch., Detroit, 1996—. Adj. prof. George Washington U. Law Ctr., Washington, 1994—96; regent U. Mich., Ann Arbor, 1999—; mem. patent pub. adv. com. U.S. Patent and Trademark Office, 2000—02. Actor: Intellectual Property Litigation, Pretrial Practice Guide, 1999; co-author (with Eric Dobrusin): Intellectual Property Litigation, Pretrial Practice Guide, 1999; contbr. articles to profl. publs. CPT JAG US Army, 1992—95, maj. JAG USAR, 1995—. Recipient Fulbright Sr. Scholar award, Max-Planck Inst. for Fgn. Internat. Patent, Copyright and Competition Law, 1999—2000; grantee, Max-Planck-Inst. for Fgn. Internat. Patent, Copyright and Competition Law, 2000; scholar, ROTC, Washington Law Found., 1988—91; Shaw fellow, 1994—96, White House Fellow, special coun. to the sec. of agr., 2001—02. Mem.: AAUP, ABA, Wolverine Bar Assn., Wash. State Bar Assn., Nat. Bar Assn., Mich. Patent Lawyer's Assn., Am. Intellectual Property Law Assn., Am. Assn. Law Schs., State Bar Mich. (mem. coun. intellectual property law sec., co-chmn. student liaison com., co-chmn. com. pattent issues in legislation), Princeton Club Mich. Office: Wayne U Law Sch 471 W Palmer Detroit MI 48202

WHITE, KATHY BRITTAIN, medical association executive; BS, MS, Ark. State U.; PhD in Mgmt., U. Memphis. Various sr. positions with AlliedSignal Corp., Guilford Mills, Inc.; chief info. officer Baxter Internat., 1995-96; chief info. officer, sr. v.p. Allegian Corp. (now merged with Cardinal Health), 1996-99; exec. v.p., chief info. officer Cardinal Health, Dublin, Ohio, 1999—. Bd. dirs. MECON, Inc., San Ramon, Calif., Children's Meml. Med. Ctr./Children's Meml. Hosp., Children's Meml. Found., Chgo.; former assoc. prof. info. technology U. N.C., Greensboro. Bd. dirs. Lake Forest Grad. Sch., Ill. Mem. ACHE. Office: Cardinal Health 7000 Cardinal Pl Dublin OH 43017-1091

WHITE, KEVIN M., athletic director; b. Amityville, NY, Sept. 25, 1950; m. Jane Gartland; children: Maureen, Michael, Daniel, Brian, Mariah. BBA, St. Joseph's Coll., 1972; B in Bus. Athletic Adminstrn., Ctrl. Mich. U.; PhD, So. Ill. U.; postdoctoral, Harvard U., 1985. Coach Gulf H.S., New Port Richey, Fla., Southeast Mo. State U., Ctrl. Mich. U.; athletic dir., v.p. devel. Loras Coll., Dubuque, Iowa, 1982-87; athletic dir. U. Maine, Orono, 1987-91, Tulane U., ew Orleans, 1991-96, Ariz. State U., Tempe, 1996-2000, Notre Dame (Ind.) U., 2000—. Office: Notre Dame Univ Dept Athletics Notre Dame IN 46556

WHITE, LINDA DIANE, lawyer; b. NYC, Apr. 1, 1952; d. Bernard and Elaine (Simons) Schwartz; m. Thomas M. White, Aug. 16, 1975; 1 child, Alexandra Nicole. AB, U. Pa., Phila., 1973; JD, Northwestern U., Evanston, Ill., 1976. Bar: Ill. 1976. Assoc. Walsh, Case, Coale & Brown, Chgo., 1976-77, Greenberger & Kaufmann (merged into Katten, Muchin), Chgo., 1977-82, ptnr., 1982—85, Sonnenschein Nath & Rosenthal LLP, 1985—, chair fin. com., 2007—. Mem. law bd. Northwestern U. Sch. Law; mem. trustees coun. Penn Women; mem. Samuel Zell and Robert Lurie Real Estate Ctr., Wharton Sch., U. Pa. Fellow: Am. Bar. Found.; mem.: ABA (mem. real property fin. com., mem. comml. leasing com., mem. real property, probate and trust law sect. 1987—), Practicing Law Inst. (chmn. program negotiating comml. leases 1995—99, mem. real estate law adv. com.), Chgo. Bar Assn., Ill. Bar Assn. Office: Sonnenschein Nath & Rosenthal LLP 7800 Sears Tower 233 S Wacker Dr Ste 7800 Chicago IL 60606-6491 Home Phone: 312-943-5108; Office Phone: 312-876-8950. Business E-Mail: lwhite@sonnenschein.com.

WHITE, MICHAEL REED, former mayor; b. Cleve., Aug. 13, 1951; s. Robert and Audrey (Silver) W. BA, Ohio State U., 1973, MPA, 1974. Spl. asst. Columbus (Ohio) Mayor's Office, 1974-76; adminstrv. asst. Cleve. City Coun., 1976-77; sales mgr. Burks Electric Co., Cleve., 1978-84; state senator Ohio Senate, Columbus, 1984-89; mayor Cleve., 1990—2001. Minority whip Ohio Senate Dems., 1987-89. City councilman City of Cleve., 1978-84; bd. dirs. Glenville Devel. Corp., Cleve., 1978—, Glenville Festival Found., Cleve., 1978—, United Black Fund, Cleve., 1986, Greater Cleve. Dome Corp., 1986; trustee U.S. Conf. Democratic Mayors. Named one of Outstanding Young Men Am., 1985, Outstanding Svc. award Cleve. chpt. Nat. Assn. Black Vets., 1985, Cmty. Svcs. award East Side Jaycees, Pres.'s award, 1993, named Black Profl. of Yr., 1993, Humanitarian award, 1994, Pub Svc. award Am. Pub. Power Assn., 1995. Mem. Nat. Conference Dem. Mayors. Democrat. Home: 11794 Blue Ridge Rd Newcomerstown OH 43832-9172

WHITE, MILES D., pharmaceutical executive; b. Mpls., Mar. 10, 1955; m. Kim White. BS in Mech. Engring., Stanford U., 1978, MBA, 1980. Mgmt. cons. McKinsey & Co.; with Abbott Labs., 1984—, v.p. diagnostic sys. and ops., 1993-94, sr. v.p. diagnostic ops., 1994-98, exec. v.p., 1998-99, chmn., CEO, 1999—. Bd. dirs. Abbott Labs., 1998—, Motorola Inc., 2005—, The Tribune Co., 2005—06, Fed. Res. Bank, Chgo., 2002—, chmn., 2002—04, 2005—07. Bd. trustee Field Mus., Chicago, Northwestern U., Joffrey Ballet, Chicago, Culver Ednl. Found.; mem. Stanford Grad. Sch. of Bus. Adv. Coun., Stanford Adv. Coun. on Interdisciplinary Biosciences. Mem.: Econ. Club of Chgo., Executives' Club of Chgo. (chmn.). Office: Abbott Labs 100 Abbott Park Rd Abbott Park IL 60064-6400

WHITE, ROBERT JAMES, retired columnist; b. Mpls., Nov. 6, 1927; s. Robert Howard and Claire Lillian (Horner) W.; m. Adrienne Hoffman, Sept. 24, 1955; children: Claire, Pamela, Sarah. BS, U.S. Naval Acad., 1950. V.p. White Investment Co., Mpls., 1957-67; editl. writer Mpls. Tribune, 1967-73, assoc. editor, 1973-82; editor editl. pages Mpls. Star Tribune, 1982-93, columnist, 1993-95, contbg. columnist, 1996—2006. Trustee Refugee Policy Group, Washington, 1985—95. Destroyer officer, fighter pilot, flight instr., aide and flag lt. to cmdr. Fleet Air Jacksonville USN, 1946—58. Recipient cert. of excellence Overseas Press Club, 1981. Mem. Coun. Fgn. Rels., Mpls. Club. Congregationalist. Home: Summit House 400 Groveland Ave #2212 Minneapolis MN 55403 Personal E-mail: rjw823@aol.com.

WHITE, RONNIE L., retired state supreme court justice; b. St. Louis, Mo., May 31, 1953; m. Sylvia White. AA, St. Louis C.C., 1977; BA, St. Louis U., 1979; JD, U. Mo., Kansas City, 1983. Bar: Mo. Law intern Jackson County Prosecutors Office; legal asst. U.S. Def. Mapping Agy.; trial atty. Office of Pub. Defender; mem. Mo. Ho. of Reps., 1989-93; judge Mo. Ct. Appeals, 1994; spl. judge Mo. Supreme Ct., 1994-95, justice, 1994-95, assoc. justice, 1995—2007, chief justice, 2003—05. Adj. faculty Washington U. Sch. Law, 1997—. first African-Am. Supreme Ct. justice of Mo. Office: PO Box 150 Jefferson City MO 65102-0150

WHITE, WILLIAM FREDRICK, lawyer; b. Elmhurst, Ill., Sept. 30, 1948; s. William Daniel and Carol Ruth (Laier) W.; m. Kathie Jean Nichols, May 27, 1979; children: Nicholas Roland, Andrew William. BA, U. Ill., 1970; JD, Antioch Sch. of Law, 1976. Bar: U.S. Ct. Appeals (D.C. cir.) 1976, Wis. 1982, U.S. Dist. Ct. (we. dist.) Wis. 1982, U.S. Dist. Ct. D.C. 1976, U.S. Ct. Claims 1978, U.S. Ct. Appeals (7th and 10th cirs.) 1982. With U.S. Dept. Labor, Washington, 1976; interim exec. dir. Common Cause, Washington, 1977; asst. counsel Nat. Treasury Employees Union, Washington, 1977-79, assoc. gen. counsel, 1979-81, dir. litigation, 1981-82; assoc. Michael, Best & Friedrich LLP, Madison, Wis., 1982-88, ptnr., chmn. assoc. devel. com., 1988-96, ptnr., 1988—, chair land and resources legal practice area, 1999—2002, mng. ptnr. Madison (Wis.) Office, 2002—06. Bd. dirs. Med. Physics Publ. Co.; dir. Med. Physics Found., 1988—, sec., 1994—. Chmn. Pub. Health Commn., Madison, 1983-89; bd. dirs. exec. com. Dane County Mediation Program, Madison, 1983-90, Perinatal Found., Madison, 1984-96, Arthritis Found., Madison, 1984-92, Arthritis Found., Madison, 1986-92, chmn., 1991-92; bd. dirs. Dane County Natural Heritage Found., 1988-91, Veridian Found., 2005-07; mem. Dane County Regional Airport Commn., 1991—, chmn. 1994—; chancellor Wis. Ann. Conf. United Meth. Ch., 1992—, gen. coun. Fin. and Adminstrn., 1991-2000, chmn. Legal Svcs. Com., 1992-96; bd. dirs. Downtown Madison Inc., sec. 1995-2001, chair transp. com.; mem. Dane County Transferrable Devel. Rights Task Force, Team Terrace Transp. Com., 1996-97, chair; bd. trustees Madison Mus. Contemporary Art, 1998—, dir., 2000—; co-chair Friends of Hudson Park, 1999—; Madison program chair Dane County Pub. Affairs Coun., 2000-02; dir. Capital Region Econ. Devel. Entity, Apt. Assn. South Ctrl. Wis. Mem. ABA, D.C. Bar Assn., Med. Physics Found. (bd. dirs. 1987—), Dane County Bar Assn., State Bar Assn. (sec. Health Law sect.), Transp. Devel. Assn. (dir. 1999-2003, exec. com. 1999-2003). Democrat. United Methodist. Avocations: bicycling, skiing. Office: Michael Best & Friedrich LLP Ste 700 1 S Pinckney St Madison WI 53703-2892

WHITE, WILLIAM SAMUEL, foundation executive; b. Cin., May 8, 1937; s. Nathaniel Ridgway and Mary White; m. Claire Mott, July 1, 1961; children: Tiffany, Ridgway Harding. BA, Dartmouth Coll., 1959, MBA, 1960; degree (hon.), GMI Engring. and Mgmt. Inst., 1996; LLD (hon.), Eastern Mich. U., 1975, U. Mich., 2006. With Barrett & Williams, NYC, 1961-62; sr. assoc. Bruce Payne & Assos., NYC, 1962-71; v.p. C. S. Mott Found., Flint, Mich., 1971-75, pres., 1976—, trustee, 1971—, also chmn. bd. dirs. Chmn. bd. dirs. U.S. Sugar Corp.; bd. dirs. Am. Water Works, 1999—2003. Mem. exec. com. Daycroft Sch., Greenwich, Conn., 1966-70; bd. dirs. Flint Area Conf., 1971-84, Coun. on Founds., 1985-90, Independent Sector, 1994-99, 2004—, Am. Friends Czech Republic, 1999-2004, European Found. Centre, 1994—, Civicus, 1995-2001; citizens adv. task force U. Mich., Flint, 1974-79; chmn. Coun. of Mich. Founds., 1979-81, Flint Area Focus Coun., 1988—, Afterschool Allstars, 2004-; mem. Pres.'s Task Force on Pvt. Sector Initiatives, 1982; trustee GMI Engring. and Mgmt. Inst., 1982-86, etwork European Founds., 2000—, Madriaga Found., 2004—. With U.S. Army, 1960-62. Office: C S Mott Foundation 1200 Mott Foundation Bldg Flint MI 48502-1807

WHITE, WILLIS SHERIDAN, JR., retired utilities company executive; b. nr. Portsmouth, Va., Dec. 17, 1926; s. Willis Sheridan and Carrie (Culpepper) W.; m. LaVerne Behrends, Oct. 8, 1949; children: Willis Sheridan III, Marguerite Spangler, Cynthia D.W. Haight. BS, Va. Poly. Inst., 1948; MS, Mass. Inst. Tech., 1958. With Am. Electric Power Co. Inc., 1948-91; chmn., chief exec. officer Am. Electric Power Co., Inc. and its subs., NYC, 1976-90, chmn., 1991, mem. bd. dirs., 1972-92. Pres., bd. dirs. Ohio Valley Electric Corp., Ind.-KTV Electric Corp., 1977-91. Trustee Battellle Meml. Inst., Grant/Riverside Meth. Hosp., Columbus. With USNR, 1945-46. Sloan fellow, 1957-58 Mem. IEEE, NAE, Eta Kappa Nu, Omicron Delta Kappa. Methodist.

WHITE, WILLMON LEE, magazine editor; b. Lamesa, Tex., Mar. 10, 1932; s. Aubrey F. and Jewel (Henderson) W.; m. Carol A. Nelson, Nov. 2, 1957 (div.); children: Tracy, Wrenn, Gehrig, Bob; m. Barbara K. Kelly, Sept. 16, 1977; 1 child, Theresa. BA, McMurry Coll., Abilene, Tex., 1953; MA, U. Tex., 1956. Reporter Abilene Reporter-News, 1953-54; pub. rels. writer Tex. Ins. Adv. Assn., Austin, 1955-56; asst. editor Humble Way mag. Humble Oil & Refining Co. (Exxon), Houston, 1956-65; assoc. editor, news editor Together mag. Methodist Ch., Park Ridge, Ill., 1965-69; sr. editor World Book Ency., Chgo., 1969-70; asst. editor, then asso. editor Rotarian mag. (publ. Rotary Internat.), Evanston, Ill., 1970-74, editor, 1974-95, mgr. communications and pub. rels. div., 1979-95, asst. gen. sec., editor, 1995-96; gen mgr. Rotary Found. Svcs., 1996-97, mgr. Rotary mags. and history, 1997-2000; editor-in-chief Rotarian Mag., 1996-2000; editor Rotary Centennial History, 2000—. Intern Newsweek mag., 1954 Mem. Am. Soc. Mag. Editors, Am. Soc. Assn. Execs., Soc. of Am. Archivists, Rotary, Sigma Delta Chi. Office: Rotary Internat 1560 Sherman Ave Ste 1350 Evanston IL 60201-4818 E-mail: leejeans4@yahoo.com.

WHITEAD, WESLEY, state representative; b. Sioux City, Iowa, Apr. 1933; m. Donna Whitead. Grad. h.s., Sioux City. State rep. dist. 1 Iowa Ho. of Reps., 1996—2000, 2002—; mem. labor and indsl. rels. com.; mem. local govt. state govt. appropriations com.; mem. oversight, audit and govtl. reform subcom. Mem. Riverside Project Com., Sioux City Planning and Zoning, Siouxland Met. Planning Coun. Orgn. With US Army. Democrat. Office: State Capitol East 12th and Grand Des Moines IA 50319 Address: 2108 Roosevelt Sioux City IA 51109

WHITEHOUSE, FRED WAITE, endocrinologist, researcher; b. Chgo., May 6, 1926; s. Fred Trafton Waite and Grace Caroline (Peters) W.; m. Iris Jean Dawson, June 6, 1953; children: Martha, Amy, Sarah. Student, Northwestern U., 1943-45; BS, U. Ill., Chgo., 1947, MD, 1949. Diplomate Am. Bd. Internal Medicine; cert. endocrinology and metabolism. Intern, then resident Henry Ford Hosp., Detroit, 1949-53, staff physician, 1955—, chief divsn. metabolism, 1962-88, chief divsn. endocrinology and metabolism, 1988-95; divsn. head emeritus, 1995—; fellow Joslin Clinic, Boston, 1954-55. Cons. FDA, Washington, 1980—; mem. Coalition on Diabetes Edn. and Minority Health, 1989-91. Contbr. articles to profl. jours. Bd. dirs. Wheat Ridge Found., 1984-93. Lt. USNR, 1951-53. Master ACP; mem. NIH (nat. diabetes adv. bd. 1984-88), Am. Diabetes Assn. (pres. 1978-79, Banting medal 1979, Outstanding Clinician award 1989, Outstanding Physician Educators award 1994, Best award 1994), Detroit Med. Club (pres. 1976), Detroit Acad. Medicine (pres. 1991-92). Lutheran. Avocations: bicycling, gardening. Home: 1265 Blairmoor Ct Grosse Pointe Woods MI 48236-1230 Office: Henry Ford Med Group 3031 W Grand Blvd Ste 800 Detroit MI 48202 Home Phone: 313-884-1324; Office Phone: 313-916-2131. Office Fax: 313-916-8343. Business E-Mail: fwhiteh1@hfhs.org.

WHITELEY, HERBERT E., dean; BS in Animal and Vet. Medicine, U. Maine, 1973; DVM, Purdue U., 1977; PhD in Pathology, Colo. State U., 1984. Diplomate Am. Coll. Vet. Pathologists. Dir. vet. diagnostic lab., interim dir. Office Animal Rsch. Svcs., mem. Ctr. for Biochem. Toxicology U. Conn.; prof., dept. head Conn., 1995—; faculty mem. dept. vet. pathobiology U. Ill. Coll. Vet. Medicine, Urbana, 1984—95, interim dept. head, 1994, dean, 2001—, dir., Ctr. for Zoonoses Rsch. Office: U Ill Urbana-Champaign 3505 Veterinary Medicine Basic Scis Bldg 2001 S Lincoln Ave Urbana IL 61802 Office Phone: 217-333-2760. Business E-Mail: hwhitele@uiuc.edu.

WHITEMAN, JOSEPH DAVID, retired lawyer, manufacturing company executive; b. Sioux Falls, SD, Sept. 12, 1933; s. Samuel D. and Margaret (Wallace) W.; m. Mary Kelly, Dec. 29, 1962; children: Anne Margaret, Mary Ellen, Joseph David, Sarah Kelly, Jane. BA, U. Mich., 1955, JD, 1960. Bar: D.C. 1960, Ohio 1976. Assoc. Cox, Langford, Stoddard & Cutler, Washington, 1959-64; sec., gen. counsel Studebaker group Studebaker Worthington, Inc., NYC, 1964-71; asst. gen. counsel. United Telecommunications, Inc., Kansas City, Mo., 1971-74; v.p., gen. counsel, sec. Weatherhead Co., Cleve., 1974-77, Parker Hannifin Corp., Cleve., 1977-98; ret., 1998. Immediate past chmn. bd. dirs. St. Lukes Med. Ctr. Served as lt. USNR, 1955-57. Mem. ABA, Beta Theta Pi, Phi Delta Phi. Republican. Roman Catholic. Home and Office: 2508 Robinson Springs Rd Stowe VT 05672

WHITEMAN, RICHARD FRANK, architect; b. Mankato, Minn., Mar. 24, 1925; s. Lester Raymond and Mary Grace (Dawald) W.; m. Jean Frances Waite, June 20, 1948 (dec. May 1980); children: David, Sarah, Lynn, Ann, Carol, Frank, Marie, Steven; m. Mavis Patricia Knutsen, May 30, 1982. BArch, U. Minn., 1945; MArch, Harvard U., 1948. Registered architect, Minn. Designer Ellerbe Co., St. Paul, Minn., 1946; architect Thorshov and Cerny, Mpls., 1948-53; ptnr. Jyring and Whiteman, Hibbing, Minn., 1953-62; pres. AJWM Inc., Hibbing and Duluth, Minn., 1963-72, Architects Four, Duluth, 1972-83; owner Richard Whiteman, Duluth, 1983-95; sr. architect U. Minn., Duluth. Chmn. Architect Sect. Registration Bd., Minn., 1972-80. Prin. works include Washington Sch., Hibbing, 1957 (Minn. Soc. Architects Design award 1957), Whiteman Summer Home, Pengilly, Minn. (Minn. Soc. Architects Design award 1959), Bemidji State Coll. Phys. Edn. Bldg. (Minn. Soc. Architects Design award 1960), Whiteman Residence, Griggs Hall UMD, 1990. Pres. U. for Srs., 1993-94, 2000-01; chair Duluth Housing Authority, 2001-06, vice chair, 2006—07. With USNR, 1943—45. Mem. Minn. Soc. Architects (pres. 1972), Northeast Minn. Architects (pres. 1962), Minn. Designer Selection Bd. (chmn. 1990). Clubs: Kitchi Gammi (Duluth). Lodges: Kiwanis. Democrat. Roman Catholic. Avocations: photography, fishing, cross country skiing, travel. Home: 3500 E 3rd St Duluth MN 55804-1812 E-mail: arch032425@aol.com.

WHITENER, WILLIAM GARNETT, dancer, choreographer; b. Seattle, Aug. 17, 1951; s. Warren G. and Virginia Louise (Garnett) Whitener. Student, Cornish Sch. Allied Arts, Seattle, 1958-69. Dancer NYC Opera, 1969, Joffrey Ballet, NYC, 1969-77, Twyla Tharp Dance, NYC, 1978-87; asst. to choreographer Jerome Robbins for Robbins' Broadway, NYC, 1988; artistic dir. Les Ballets Jazz de Montréal, 1991-93, Royal Winnipeg Ballet, 1993-95, Kansas City Ballet, 1996—. Coord. dance dept. Concord Acad., Mass., 1988; vis. artist U. Wash., 1989—91; dance faculty mem. Harvard U. Summer Dance, 1989—90, NYU, 1985. Dancer (Broadway plays) Dancin', 1978, choreographer Princeton Ballet, Joffrey II, John Curry Ice Theatre, Ballet Hispanico of NY, Boston Ballet Internat. Choreography Competition, Tommy Tune, Martine van Hamel/Kevin McKenzie, Ann Reinking, Seattle Repertory Theatre, Am. Ballroom Theatre, NYC, Hartford Ballet, Conn., On the Boards with Bill Irwin, PBS-TV Alive From Off Center, (Operas) A Little Night Music, Pacific Northwest Ballet, Rusalka, Seattle Opera, (Operas) Aida, Kansas City Repartory Theatre, The Pearlfishers Eugene Oreg., Lyric Opera Kans. City, dancer (films) Amadeus, Zelig, (TV films) The Catherine Wheel, Dance in America; performer: Garden of Earthly Delights, 1988. Bd. trustees DanceUSA, 2000—. Ford Found. scholar, 1963—64. Mem.: Am. Guild Musical Artists, Actor's Equity. Office: Kansas City Ballet 1616 Broadway Kansas City MO 64108-1207

WHITING, FRED C., state legislator; Mem. S.D. Ho. of Reps., Pierre, 1993-94, S.D. Senate from 32nd dist, Pierre, 1995—. Mem. judiciary state affairs and transp. coms. Republican. Home: PO Box 8187 Rapid City SD 57709-8187

WHITING, ORAN F., lawyer; b. Chgo., 1961; BS in Econs., U. Pa., 1983, BA in Internat. Bus., 1983; postgraduate student, Centro de Estudios Hispanicos, Madrid, 1984; JD, Georgetown U., 1986. Bar: Ill. 1987, US Dist. Ct. (no. dist.

Ill.) 1987, US Dist. Ct. (ctrl. dist. Ill.) 1995, US Ct. Appeals (10th cir.) 1992, US Ct. Appeals (7th cir.). Counsel to Spkr. Ill. Ho. Reps., 1995—97; spl. counsel Sedgwick, Detert, Moran & Arnold, Chgo.; ptnr. Holland & Knight, LLP, Chgo., 2006—. Commr. Ill. Ct. Claims, 1997—2006; interim gen. counsel Mercy Hosp., Chgo., 2001—02. Contbr. articles to law jours. Bd. mem. Sargent Shriver at. Ctr. Poverty Law, Evanston Symphony Orch. Mem.: Leading Lawyers Network, Ill., ABA (assoc. editor Litig. News 1996—2003, co-chmn. Electronic Pub. com., Litig. sect.), Cook County Bar Assn., Chgo. Bar Assn. Office: Holland & Knight LLP 30th Fl 131 Dearborn St Chicago IL 60603 Office Phone: 312-715-5774. E-mail: oran.whiting@hklaw.com.

WHITINGTON, PETER FRANK, pediatric hepatologist, educator; b. Memphis, May 8, 1947; s. Frank Everett and Mary Lena (Hollingsworth) Whitington; m. Susan Maurine Hoagland, June 6, 1967; children: Helen Frances Josephic, Mary Louise, Katherine Daphne, Patrick M. BA in Econs., Tulane U., 1968; MD, U. Tenn., Memphis, 1971. Diplomate Am. Bd. Pediat., Am. Bd. Pediatric Gastroenterology. Resident in pediat., then chief resident U. Tenn. Ctr. for Health Scis., 1972—74, instr., 1975, asst. prof., 1978—81, assoc. prof., 1981—84, chief divsn. pediatric gastroenterology, 1978—84; rsch. fellow in gastroenterology Johns Hopkins Hosp., Balt., 1975—77; rsch. fellow in gastroenterology dept. pediatrics U. Wis., Madison, 1977—78; assoc. prof. dept. pediat. U. Chgo. Pritzker Sch. Medicine, 1984—87, assoc. prof. depts. pediat. and medicine, 1987—92, prof., 1992—97; prof. pediat. Northwestern U. Med. Sch., 1997—, Sally Burnett Searle prof. pediat. and transplantation; dir. divsn. gastroenterology, hepatology & nutrition Children's Meml. Hosp., Chgo., 1997—, dir. organ transplantation, Siragusa Transplantation Ctr., 1997—; co-dir. Northwestern U. Affiliated Transplant Ctrs., 1997—. Chief gastroenterology LeBonheur Children's Med. Ctr., Memphis, 1978—84; numerous invited lectures and guest spkr. at profl. meetings, workshops, symposia, hosps., confs.; mem. pediatric transplantation com. United Network for Organ Sharing, Nat. Organ Procurement and Transplantation Network, 1992—94; reviewer numerous med. jours. including New Eng. Jour. Medicine, Gastroenterology, Hepatology, Jour. Pediat., Digestive Diseases and Scis., Pediat., Transplant. Editl. bd. Jour. Pediatric Gastroenterology and utrition, 1991—96, Liver Transplantation, 1994—, Pediatric Transplantation, 1997—, sect. editor Birth Defects Compendium, 1987—90, contbr. numerous articles and abstracts to med. jours. Mem. sci. adv. bd. Mid-South chpt. Nat. Found. for Ileitis and Colitis, Memphis, 1983—84; chmn. med. adv. com. Ill. chpt. Am. Liver Found., 1996—, mem., med. adv. on bd. dirs., 1993—; med. dir. The Johnny Genna Found., Chgo., 1987—; bd. dirs. Parents for Ctrl. H.S., Memphis, 1983—84, Liver/Organ Transplant Fund, Memphis, 1983—84. Recipient Cmty. Svc. award, NCCJ, Memphis, 1983; fellow postdoctoral rsch. NIH, 1977. Mem.: Am. Assn. Transplantation, N.A.m Soc. for Pediatric Gastroenterology and Nutrition, Soc. for Pediatric Rsch., Am. Gastroenterol. Assn., Gastroenterology Rsch. Group, Am. Assn. for Study of Liver Diseases. Avocations: making furniture, fly fishing. Home: 5490 S South Shore Dr Apt 8 Chicago IL 60615-5984 Office: Childrens Meml Hosp Box 57 2300 Childrens Plaza Chicago IL 60614-3394 Business E-Mail: p-whitington@northwestern.edu.

WHITLOCK, JOHN JOSEPH, museum director; b. South Bend, Ind., Jan. 7, 1935; s. Joseph Mark and Helen Marcella (Cramer) Whitlock; m. Sue Ann Kirkman, June 10, 1956; children: Kelly Ann, Michele Lynn, Mark. BS in Art, Ball State U., 1957, MA in Art, 1963; EdD, Ind. U., 1971. Tchr. art Union City (Ind.) Pub. Schs., 1957-59; tchr. art, art dir. Madison (Ind.) City Schs., 1959-64; prof. art, dir. gallery Hanover (Ind.) Coll., 1964-69; dir. Burpee Art Mus., Rockford, Ill., 1970-72; prof. arts and humanities Elgin (Ill.) Community Coll., 1970-72; dir. Brooks Meml. Art Gallery, Memphis, 1972-78; prof. mus. studies Southwestern Coll., Memphis, 1973-78; adj. asst. prof. art and museology Memphis State U., 1976-78; dir. Univ. Mus., mem. grad. faculty So. Ill. U., Carbondale, 1978-2000, emeritus dir., 2000—, also dir. mus. studies, 1978-2000, adj. assoc. prof. anthropology, 1978-2000, adj. assoc. prof. polit. sci., 1988—, adj. assoc. prof. history, 1994—, dir. mus. studies, 1989—, mem. ROTC acad. avc. coun., 1988—, mem. president's coun., 1988-93, adj. assoc. prof. art Univ. Mus., 1978-99, vis. emeritus prof., 2000—; instr. art John A. Logan Coll., 2001—. Chmn. bd. Nat. Coal Mus., 1983-85; mem. Newsfront adv. bd. NC Broadcast News, Washington, 1982-85; sr. cons. Marine Mil. Acad. Mus., 1988—, mem. bd. advisors, 1991-97. Mem. Rockford Human Rels. Commn., 1971-72; mem. pres.'s coun. Southwestern Coll., 1973-78; vol. Carbondale Police Dept., 2000—, com. resources, forensics records and acad.; bd. dirs. Carbondale Crime Stoppers, 2000—, pres., 2006—; bd. dirs. DARE, 2000—, pres., 2006—; bd. dirs. Carbondale Fire and Police Commn., 2003—; univ. club bd. So. Ill. U., 2000—, univ. mus. amb., 2000—. Mem. Am. Assn. Mus., Internat. Coun. Mus., Midwest Assn. Mus., Assn. Art Mus. Dirs., Marine Corps League (commandant Shawnee detachment 1994-96, 99-2001, comdr. USCG Aux. 1994-95), Dept. Ill. Marine Corps League (trustee rank and file 1994-99, judge advocate 1999-2005), Semper Fi Soc. (faculty adviser So. Ill. U. 1995—). Office: So Ill U 605 W Walnut St Carbondale IL 62901-2615

WHITMAN, DALE ALAN, lawyer, educator; b. Charleston, W. Va., Feb. 18, 1939; m. Marjorie Miller: 8 children. Student, Ohio State U., 1956-59; BES, Brigham Young U., 1963; LLB, Duke U., 1966. Bar: Calif. 1967, Utah 1971. Assoc. O'Melveny & Myers, Los Angeles, 1966-67; asst prof., then assoc prof. sch. law U. N.C., Chapel Hill, 1967-70; vis. prof. law UCLA, 1970-71; dep. dir. Office Housing and Urban Affairs Fed. Home Loan Bank Bd., Washington, 1971-72; sr. program analyst FHA, HUD, Washington, 1972-73; prof. law Brigham Young U., 1973—78, 1992—98, U. Wash., 1978—82; vis. prof. law U. Mo., Columbia, 1976; prof. law, dean U. Mo. Sch. Law, Columbia, 1982-88, prof., 1988—91, 1998—. Cons., lectr. in field; reporter Am. law Inst. Co-author: Cases and Materials on Real Estate Finance and Development, 1976, Real Estate Finance Law, 1979, 5th edit., 2007, Cases and Materials on Real Estate Transfer, Finance and Development. 1981, 7th edit., 2006, Land Transactions and Finance, 1983, 4d edit., 2004, The Law of Property, 1984, 3d edit., 2000, Contemporary Property, 1996, 2d edit., 2002, Restatement of Property (Mortgages), 1997; contbr. articles to profl. jours. Fellow Am. Bar Found.; mem. Am. Law Inst., Am. Coll. Real Estate Lawyers, Am. Coll. Mortgage Attys., Assn. Am. Law Schs. (pres. 2002). Avocations: piano, flying. Office: Univ Mo 216 Hulston Hall Columbia MO 65211 Office Phone: 573-884-0946. Business E-Mail: whitmand@missouri.edu.

WHITMAN, MARINA VON NEUMANN, economist, educator; b. NYC, Mar. 6, 1935; d. John and Mariette (Kovesi) von Neumann; m. Robert Freeman Whitman, June 23, 1956; children: Malcolm Russell, Laura Mariette. BA summa cum laude, Harvard U., 1956; MA, Columbia U., 1959, PhD, 1962; DHL (hon.), U. Mass., 1975; LittD (hon.), Williams Coll., 1980; LLD (hon.), Mount Holyoke Coll., 1980, Lehigh U., 1981; LHD (hon.), Clemson U., 1984; LLD (hon.), U. Notre Dame, 1984, Ea. Mich. U., 1992. Mem. faculty U. Pitts., 1962-79, prof. econs., 1971-73, disting. pub. svc. prof. econs., 1973-79; v.p., chief economist Gen. Motors Corp., NYC, 1979-85, group v.p. pub. affairs, 1985-92; disting. vis. prof. bus. adminstrn., pub. policy U. Mich., Ann Arbor, 1992-94, prof. bus. adminstrn., pub. policy, 1994—. Mem. Trilateral Commn., 1973-84, 88-95; mem. Pres. Adv. Com. on Trade Policy and Negotiations, 1987-93; mem. tech. assessment adv. coun. U.S. Congress Office of Tech. Assessment, 1990-95; mem. Consultative Group on Internat. Econs. and Monetary Affairs, 1979—; mem. U.S. Price Commn., 1971-72, Coun. Econ. Advisers, Exec. Office of Pres., 1972-73. Author: Government Risk-Sharing in Foreign Investment, 1965, International and Interregional Payments Adjustment, 1967, Economic Goals and Policy Instruments, 1970, Reflections of Interdependence: Issues for Economic Theory and U.S. Policy, 1979, New World, New Rules: The Changing Role of the American Corporation, 1999, American Capitalism and Global Convergence, 2003; bd. editors: Am. Econ. Rev., 1974-77; mem. editl. bd. Fgn. Policy; contbr. articles to profl. jours. Trustee Nat. Bur. Econ. Rsch., 1993—, Princeton U., 1980-90, Inst. Advanced Study, 1999—; bd. dirs. Peterson Inst. for Internat. Econs., 1986—, Salzburg Seminar, 1994—, Eurasia Found., 1992-95; bd. overseers Harvard U., 1972-78, mem. vis. com. Kennedy Sch., 1992-98. Fellow Earhart Found., 1959-60, AAUW, 1960-61, NSF, 1968-70, Social Security Rsch. Coun.; recipient Columbia medal for excellence, 1973, George Washington award Am. Hungarian Found., 1975. Mem. Am. Econ. Assn. (exec. com. 1977-80), Am. Acad. Arts and Scis., Coun. Fgn. Rels. (dir. 1977-87), Phi Beta Kappa. Office: U Mich Gerald Ford Sch Pub Policy Joan and Sanford Weill Hall Rm 3228 Ann Arbor MI 48109-3091 Office Phone: 734-763-4173. Business E-Mail: marinaw@umich.edu.

WHITMER, RICHARD E., insurance company executive; BS in Political Science, W. Mich. U., 1963; JD, U. Mich. Law School, 1965. Legislative counsel Gov. of Mich.; dir. Mich. Dept. of Commerce; sr. v.p., gen. counsel Blue Cross Blue Shield Mich., Detroit, 1977—87, pres., CEO, 1987—. Bd. mem. Greater Detroit Chamber of Commerce, Detroit Renaissance, United Way of Southeastern Mich., Detroit Economic Growth Corp.; chmn. New Detroit, 1991—93. Office: Blue Cross Blue Shield Mich 600 E Lafayette Blvd Detroit MI 48226-2927 Office Phone: 313-225-9000.

WHITNEY, PATRICK FOSTER, design educator; b. Edmonton, Alta., Can., Sept. 5, 1951; came to US, 1974; s. Gordon and Geraldine (Walker) W.; m. Cheryl Kent. BFA in Design with distinction, U. Alta., 1974; MFA in Design, Cranbrook Acad. Art, Bloomfield Hills, Mich., 1976. Designer RVI Corp., Chgo., 1976-79; chmn. Div. of Design Mpls. Coll. Art and Design, 1979-83; chmn. Inst. of Design, Ill. Inst. Tech., Chgo., 1983-87, dir., 1987—, Steelcase/Robert C. Pew Prof. Design. Lectr. in the field; mem., disting. advisor bd. Assn. Computing Machinery's Special Interest Group in Computer Human Interaction; chmn. US Conf. of Internat. Coun. on Graphic Design Assns., 1978; juror Presdl. Design Awards, 1995; mem. White House Council on Design; pres. Am. Ctr. for Design (ACD); principal investigator for a rsch. project called Global Companies in Local Markets. Editor Design in the Information Environment, 1984, Design Journal; author numerous published articles on design and communications. Mem. Am. Ctr. for Design (bd. dirs. 1984-86, v.p. 1986-90, pres. 1992-94), Arts Club. Office: Ill Inst Tech Inst Design 350 N LaSalle St Chicago IL 60610 Office Phone: 312-595-4900. Business E-Mail: whitney@id.iit.edu.

WHITNEY, RAY, professional hockey player; b. Saskatchewan, Alta., Can., May 8, 1972; s. Floyd and Wendy Whitney Stick boy Edmonton Oilers, 1986-87, 87-88, player, 1997, Spokane Chiefs, 1988-91, 90-91, San Jose Sharks, 1991—97, Edmonton Oilers, 1997—98, Fla. Panthers, 1998—2001, Columbus Blue Jackets, 2001—03, Detroit Red Wings, 2003—04, Carolina Hurricanes, 2005—. Named most valuable player WHL, 1988-91, 90-91, Most Valuable Player All-Star Game IHL, 1992. Achievements include being a member of Stanley Cup Champion Carolina Hurricanes, 2006. Avocation: golf. Office: Carolina Hurricanes RBC Ctr 1400 Edwards Mill Rd Raleigh NC 27607-3624

WHITNEY, RICHARD BUCKNER, lawyer; b. Corpus Christi, Tex., Mar. 1, 1948; s. Franklyn Loren and Betty Wolcott (Fish) Whitney; m. Chantal Marie Gindt, Aug. 18, 1972; children: Jennifer L, James R, Katherine E. BA in Polit. Sci., Union Coll., 1970; JD, Case Western Res. U., 1973. Bar: Ohio 1973, N.Y. 1998, US Ct Appeals (6th cir) 1974, US Ct Appeals (3d cir) 1987, US Dist Ct (so dist) NY 2000, U.S. Dist. Ct. (no. dist.) Ohio 1974. From assoc. to ptnr. Jones Day, Cleve., 1973—. Trustee Hospice of the We. Res. Mem.: Am Inns of Ct., Cleve. Bar Assn., Order of Coif. Home: 2750 Southington Rd Shaker Heights OH 44120-1603 Office: Jones Day 901 Lakeside Ave Cleveland OH 44114-1190 Business E-Mail: rbwhitney@jonesday.com.

WHITT, GREGORY SIDNEY, evolution educator; b. Detroit, June 13, 1938; s. Sidney Abram and Millicent (Ward) W.; m. Dixie Lee Dailey, Aug. 25, 1963. BS, Colo. State U., 1962, MS, 1965; PhD, Yale U., 1970. Asst. prof. zoology U. Ill., Urbana, 1969-72, asso. prof. genetics and devel., 1972-77, prof., 1977-87, prof. ecology, ethology and evolution, 1987-2000, prof. animal biology, 2000—. Affiliate Ill. Natural History Survey, 1981—; mem. NIH study sect., 1975-76 Co-editor: Isozymes: Current Topics in Biological and Medical Research, 1977-87; editor: Isozyme Bull., 1978-81; mem. editl. bd. Biochem. Genetics, 1975—, Devel. Genetics, 1978-83, Jour. Molecular Evolution, 1979-2000, Molecular Biology and Evolution, 1983-93, Molecular Phylogenetics and Evolution, 1992-2000; contbr. articles to profl. jours. Fellow AAAS; mem. Am. Soc. Microbiology, Soc. Protection Old Fishes, Archaeol. Inst. Am. Office: U Ill Dept Animal Biology 515 Morrill Hall 505 S Goodwin Ave Urbana IL 61801-3707 Home: 3108 Earle Ct Urbana IL 61802-7091

WHITTAKER, JUDITH ANN CAMERON, lawyer; b. NYC, June 12, 1938; d. Thomas Macdonald and Mindel Cameron; m. Kent E. Whittaker, Jan. 30, 1960; children: Charles Evans II, Catherine Cameron. BA, Brown U., 1959; JD, U. Mo., 1963. Bar: Mo. 1963, U.S. Dist. Ct. (we. dist.) Mo. 1963, U.S. Ct. Appeals (8th cir.) 1965, U.S. Supreme Ct. 1980, D.C. 1987. Assoc. and ptnr. Sheffrey, Ryder & Skeer, Kansas City, Mo., 1963-72; asst. and assoc. gen. coun., exec. v.p. gen. coun. Hallmark Cards, Inc., Kansas City, 1972—2004; dir., v.p., gen. coun. Univision Holdings, Inc., Kansas City, 1988-92; sec., bd. dirs. Crown Media Holdings, Inc., 2000—04; of counsel Shook, Hardy & Bacon, Kansas City, Mo., 2004—. Bd. dirs. Am. Arbitration Assn., 1997-2003. Trustee Brown U. Providence, 1977-83, U. Mo. Law Found., Kansas City, 1977-90; dir. Kansas City (Mo.) Indsl. Devel. Authority, 1981-84, Legal Aid Kansas City, 1971-77, De La Salle Sch. Episcopalian. Avocations: reading, skiing, hiking, piano, golf. Office: Shook Hardy & Bacon 2555 Grand Blvd Kansas City MO 64198-2613

WHITTEMORE, BRIAN, media consultant, advertising executive; Anchor morning news, dir. news Sta. WGY-AM, Albany, NY, 1983—86; anchor morning news WHDH Radio, Boston, 1987—90; dir. news and program WBZ Radio, Boston, 1990—95; v.p., gen. mgr. Sta. KDKA-AM, Pitts., 1996—98, Sta. WCCO-AM, Mpls., 1999—2003; pres. Best/Whittemore Prodns., LLC, Prior Lake, Minn., 2003—.

WHITTEN, MARY LOU, nursing educator; b. Vandalia, Ill., Apr. 8, 1946; d. Otto M. and Lucille (Mattes) Elam; m. Dennis L. Whitten, Aug. 27, 1966; children: Michael, Christopher, Andrew. BSN, Baylor U., 1968; MS in Nursing, So. Ill. U., 1990. RN, Ill. Instr. health occupations Okaw Vocat. Sch., Vandalia, Ill.; head nurse med.-surg. Fayette County Hosp., Vandalia; DON Kaskaskia Coll., Centralia, Ill. CPR instr. Am. Heart Assn. Vol. ARC. Mem. Am. Assn. of Women in C.C. Ill., Ill. Coun. Dirs. of Nursing, Phi Kappa Phi. Home: RR 3 Box 848 Vandalia IL 62471-9204 Office: Kaskaskia Coll 27210 College Rd Centralia IL 62801-7800 Office Phone: 618-545-3331. Business E-Mail: mwhitten@kaskaskia.edu.

WHYTE, GEORGE KENNETH, JR., lawyer; b. Waukegan, Ill., Oct. 10, 1936; s. George K. and Ella Margaret (Osgood) W.; m. Ann B. Challoner, June 20, 1964; children: Mary, Douglas. AB in Polit. Sci., Duke U., 1958; LLB, U. Wis., 1965. Bar: Wis. 1965. Law clk. to chief justice Wis. Supreme Ct., Madison, 1965-66; assoc. Quarles & Brady, Milw., 1966-73, ptnr., 1973—2004; ret., 2004. Lt. USN, 1958—62. Mem. ABA (employment law sect.), Wis. Bar Assn. (former chmn. labor and employment law sect.), Rotary (pres. 2002-03), The Town Club, Milw. Country Club. Congregationalist. Home: 1026 W Shaker Cir Mequon WI 53092-6034 E-mail: gkw@quarles.com.

WHYTE, MICHAEL P., genetics educator, researcher, director; b. NYC, Dec. 19, 1946; s. Michael Paul and Sophie (Dziuk) W.; m. Gloria Frances Golenda, Oct. 26, 1974; 1 child, Catherine Alexandra. BA in Chemistry, NYU, 1968; MD, SUNY, Bklyn., 1972. Diplomate Am. Bd. Internal Medicine, Nat. Bd. Med. Examiners. Intern, 1st yr. resident dept. medicine NYU Sch. Medicine Bellevue Hosp., NYC, 1972-74; clin. assoc. devel. and metabolic neurology br. Nat. Inst. Neurol. and Communicative Disorders and Stroke NIH, Bethesda, Md., 1974-76; fellow divsn. bone and mineral metabolism dept. medicine Washington U. Sch. Medicine, 1976-79, instr. dept. medicine, 1979-80, asst. sci. dir. Clin. Rsch. Ctr., 1979—; asst. physician Barnes Hosp., 1979—; staff physician St. Louis Children's Hosp., 1979—; NIH clin. assoc. physician Clin. Rsch. Ctr. Washington U. Sch. Medicine, 1980-82, asst. prof. medicine dept. medicine, 1980-86, assoc. prof. medicine dept. medicine, 1986-91, asst. prof. pediat. Edward Mallinckrodt dept. pediat., 1982-89, assoc. prof. pediat. Edward Mallinckrodt dept. pediat., 1989-92, prof. medicine dept. medicine, 1991—, prof. pediat. Edward Mallinckrodt dept. pediat., 1992—, prof. genetics James S. McDonell dept. genetics, 1997—; med. dir. Metabolic Rsch. Unit Shriners Hosp. for Children, St. Louis, 1982-2000, mem. staff, 1983—; assoc. attending physician Jewish Hosp., 1983—. Mem. editl. bd. Calcified Tissue Internat., 1995-2000, Jour. Bone and Mineral Rsch., 1994—; med. adv. bd. Osteogenesis Imperfecta Found., 1986—, med. adv. panel Paget's Disease Found., 1986—; chmn. med. adv. com., bd. dirs. Osteogenesis Found., 1995—; med.-sci. dir. Ctr. for Metabolic Bone Disease and Molecular Rsch. Shriners Hosp. for Children, St. Louis, 2000—. Assoc. editor: Primer on Metabolic Bone Diseases and Disorders of Mineral Metabolism, 1990, 93, 96, 99, 2003, 06; assoc. editor Calcified Tissue Internat., 1989-2000; contbr. chpts. to books, articles to profl. jours. Lt. comdr. USPHS, 1974-76. Fellow Am. Coll. Endocrinology; mem. ACP (assoc.), Assn. Am. Physicians, Am. Soc. Cell Biology, Am. Soc. Clin. Investigation, Am. Fedn. Clin. Rsch., Am. Soc. Advancement Sci., Am. Soc. Bone and Mineral Rsch. (ednl. com. 1987—, Fuller Albright award 1987, Young Investigator award 1983, Dr. Boy Frame award 1997, Frederic C. Bartter award, 2007), Am. Soc. Human Genetics, Endocrine Soc., Soc. Exptl. Biology and Medicine, Japanese Soc. Inherited Metabolic Disease (hon.), NY Acad. Scis. Office: Barnes-Jewish Hosp 216 S Kingshighway Blvd Saint Louis MO 63110-1026 Office Phone: 314-872-8305. Business E-Mail: mwhyte@shrinenet.org.

WICK, DON, radio personality; Farm broadcaster, Wabasha, Minn., 1980, Austin, Minn., Redwood Falls, Minn., Worthington, Minn., Yankton, SD; radio host Sta. WCCO Radio, Mpls., 1997—. Recipient Oscar in Agr. award excellence in agrl. journalism, 1998, 1999. Mem.: Nat. Assn. Farm Broadcasters (pres. 1997—, Farm Broadcaster of Yr. award western region 1999). Office: WCCO 625 2nd Ave S Minneapolis MN 55402

WICK, HAL GERARD, state legislator; b. New Ulm, Minn., Oct. 31, 1944; s. Roland Theodore and Esther Marie La Fontaine Wick; m. Jane Dorothy Rance, 1965; children: Anne Marie, Paula Jo, Betsey Jane, Ross Anthony. Student, Exec. Air Travel Flight Sch., Sioux Falls, SD, 1966-68; BS, S.D. State U., Brookings, 1967. Flight instr. Snediger Flying Svc., Rapid City, S.D., 1968, Airways Svc., Sioux City, Iowa, 1968-70; pilot Iowa Air Nat. Guard, Sioux City, 1970-75; chief pilot, flight instr. Soo Flying, Sioux City, 1971-72; pilot NW Airlines, Mpls., 1972—2004; mem. from Dist. 11 S.D. Ho. of Reps., 1977-80, mem. from Dist. 12, 1995-98, 2001—, majority whip, 2003—04. Chmn. Minnehaha County Rep. Party Victory Squad, S.D., 1974-76; chmn. Minnehaha County Citizens for Reagan, 1976; del. Rep. Nat. Conv., 1976; mem. Legis. Rsch. Coun., State of S.D., 1977-78, mem. Edn. and Transp. Coms.; former chmn., coord. People for Alternative to McGovern, Nat. Conservative Polit. Action Com.; state chair Am. Legis. Exch. Coun. Pilot S.D. Air Nat. Guard, 1975-94. Named Top Gun, Sioux City, 1974, Outstanding Optimist, Morning Optimist Club, 1975. Mem. Am. Legion, NG Assn., Air Line Pilots Assn., Hartford Lions. Home: 3009 W Donahue Dr Sioux Falls SD 57105-0153

WICK, SISTER MARGARET, former college administrator; b. Sibley, Iowa, June 30, 1942; BA in Sociology, Briar Cliff Coll., 1965; MA in Sociology, Loyola U., Chgo., 1971; PhD in Higher Edn., U. Denver, 1976. Instr. sociology Briar Cliff Coll., Sioux City, Iowa, 1966-71, dir. academic advising, 1971-72, v.p., acad. dean, 1972-74, 76-84, pres., 1987-99, Colls. of Mid-Am., 1985-87. Mem. adv. bd. Nations Bank, Sioux City. Bd. dirs. Mary J. Treglia Cmty. House, 1976-84, Marian Health Ctr., 1987-97, Iowa Pub. TV, 1987-95. Mem. North Ctrl. Edn. Assn. (cons.-evaluator for accrediting teams 1980-84, 89—), Siouxland Initiative (adv. bd.), Quota Internat., Rotary. Home: 3390 Windsor Ave Dubuque IA 52001-1326 Office: Briar Cliff Coll Office of the President 3303 Rebecca St Sioux City IA 51104-2324

WICKERSHAM, WILLIAM R., state legislator; b. Lusk, Wyo., Oct. 22, 1948; BSBA, Creighton U.; JD, U. Nebr. Mem. Nebr. Legislature from 49th dist., Lincoln, 1991—; mem. edn., revenue coms. Nebr. Legislature, Lincoln, 1994—, chmn. retirement sys., 1998—, chair revenue com., 1998—. Mem. ABA, Nebr. State Bar Assn., Sioux City Hist. Soc., Siouc County Agr. Soc., Elks.

WICKESBERG, ALBERT KLUMB, retired management consultant; b. Neenah, Wis., Apr. 2, 1921; s. Albert Henry and Lydia (Klumb) W.; m. Dorothy Louise Ahrensfeld, Oct. 28, 1944; children— Robert, William, James. BA, Lawrence Coll., 1943; MBA, Stanford U., 1948; PhD, Ohio State U., 1955. Staff accountant S.C. Johnson & Son, Inc., Racine, Wis., 1948-50; asst. prof. Sacramento State Coll., 1950-51; prof. U. Minn., Mpls., 1953-86, prof. emeritus, 1987—, chmn. dept. bus. adminstrn., 1959-62, dir. grad. studies, 1963-66, chmn. dept. mgmt. and transp., 1971-77. Author: Management Organization, 1966. Served with AUS, 1943-46, 51-52. Soc. Advancement Mgmt. fellow, 1972 Mem. Acad. Mgmt., Soc. Advancement Mgmt. (pres. Twin Cities chpt. 1961-62). Congregationalist. Home: 4501 Roanoke Rd Minneapolis MN 55422-5268

WICKHAM, MICHAEL W., transportation executive; b. 1946; With Roadway Express, Inc., Akron, Ohio, 1968—, terminal mgr., 1971-77, dist. mgr., 1977-81, v.p. N.E. divsn., 1981-85, v.p. western divsn., 1985-88, v.p. adminstrn. and fin., 1988-89, exec. v.p. adminstrn. and fin., 1989-90, pres., CEO, 1990-99, CEO, 1999—. Office: 1077 Gorge Blvd Akron OH 44310-2408

WICKLINE, SAMUEL ALAN, cardiologist, educator; b. Huntington, W.Va., Oct. 23, 1952; BA in Philosophy cum laude, Pomona Coll., 1974; MD, U. Hawaii, 1980. Diplomate Am. Bd. Internal Medicine, Am. Bd. Cardiology. Intern, resident in internal medicine Barnes Hosp. Barnes/Washington U. Sch. Medicine, St. Louis, 1980-83, clin. fellow in cardiology, 1983-85, rsch. fellow in cardiology, 1985-87; asst. prof. medicine Sch. Medicine Washington U. Sch. Medicine, St. Louis, 1987-93, assoc. prof., 1993—, adj. asst. prof. physics, 1990, adj. assoc. prof. physics, 1994, attending cardiologist, dir. echocardiology Jewish Hosp., 1992—, prof. medicine and physics, 1997, dir. divsn. cardiology, 1993—. Reviewer Jour. Clin. Investigation, Circulation, Arteriosclerosis and Thrombosis, Hypertension, Ultrasound in Medicine and Biology; contbr. over 100 articles to med. and sci. jours., chpts. to books on topics related to basic rsch. in cardiovascular biophysics and acoustics/ultrasonics. Grantee NIH, Am. Heart Assn., Whitaker Found. Fellow Am. Coll. Cardiology (reviewer jour.); mem. IEEE Soc. Ultrasonics, Ferroelectrics and Frequency Control, Am. Heart Assn. (coun. on radiology and clin. cardiology, Clinician-Scientist award 1988-93, Established Investigator award 1993—), Am. Soc. Clin. Investigation, Am. Inst. Ultrasound in Medicine, Acoustical Soc. Am., Alpha Omega Alpha. Home: 11211 Pointe Ct Saint Louis MO 63127-1741 Office: Jewish Hosp Cardiology 216 S Kingshighway Blvd Saint Louis MO 63110-1026

WICKLUND, DAVID WAYNE, lawyer; b. St. Paul, Aug. 7, 1949; s. Wayne Glenwood and Elna Katherine (Buresh) W.; m. Susan Marie Bubenko, Nov. 17, 1973; children: David Jr., Kurt, Edward. BA cum laude, Williams Coll., 1971; JD cum laude, U. Toledo, 1974. Bar: Ohio 1974. Assoc. Shumaker, Loop & Kendrick, Toledo, 1974-80, ptnr., 1981—. Adj. instr. law, U. Toledo, 1988. Editor-in-chief U. Toledo Law Rev. 1973-74. Mem.: ABA, Toledo Bar Assn., Ohio State Bar Assn. (bd. govs. antitrust sect. 1994—2001), U. Toledo Coll. Law Alumni Assn. (pres. 1999—2000), Inverness Club. Office: Shumaker Loop & Kendrick N Courthouse Sq 1000 Jackson St Toledo OH 43624-1573 Office Phone: 419-321-1213. Business E-Mail: dwicklund@slk-law.com.

WICKMAN, JOHN EDWARD, librarian, historian; b. Villa Park, Ill., May 24, 1929; s. John Edward and Elsie (Voss) W.; m. Shirley Jean Swanson, Mar. 17, 1951; children— Lisa Annette, Eric John. AB, Elmhurst Coll., Ill., 1953; A.M., Ind. U., 1958, PhD, 1964; LLD, Lincoln Coll., Ill., 1973. Instr. history Hanover Coll., Ind., 1959-62, Southeast Campus, Ind. U., Jeffersonville, 1962; asst. prof. history Northwest Mo. State Coll., Maryville, 1962-64; asst. to Gov. William H. Avery of Kans., Topeka, 1964-65; asst. prof. history Regional Campus, Purdue U., Fort Wayne, Ind., 1965-66; dir. Dwight D. Eisenhower Libr., Abilene, Kans., 1966-89; ret., 1989. Contbr. articles on Am. West, archival mgmt., adminstrv. history, oral history to profl. publs. Served with US Army, 1953-55. at. Ctr. for Edn. in Politics faculty fellow, 1964-65; Am. Polit. Sci. Assn. Congl. fellow, 1975-76 Mem. Oral History Assn. (v.p. 1971-72, pres. 1972-73), Western History Assn. (coun. 1972-75), Kans. Hist. Soc. (2d v.p. 1974-75, pres. 1976-77, dir.). Home: Po Box 531 Abilene KS 67410-0531

WICKS, JOHN R., lawyer; b. Ottumwa, Iowa, Dec. 8, 1937; m. Nedra Morgan, Mar. 27, 1940; children: Catherine, John. BSC, U. Iowa, 1959, JD, 1964. Bar: Iowa 1964, Minn. 1966. Assoc. Dorsey & Whitney LLP, Mpls., 1966-71, ptnr. Rochester, Minn., 1972-2000, of counsel Mpls., 2001—. Fellow: Am. Coll. Trusts and Estates Counsel; mem.: Minn. State Bar Assn. (probate and trusts law coun. 1989—92). Office: Dorsey & Whitney LLP 50 S 6th St Minneapolis MN 55402-1498 Office Phone: 612-340-8898. E-mail: wicks.john@dorsey.com.

WIDENER, CHRIS, state representative; b. Clark County, Ohio; m. Sally Widener; children: Emily, Brandon. BArch with Cert. in Historic Preservation, U. Cin., 1987. Civil svc. arch., hist. preservation officer, mem. 2003 flight com., Wright Patterson AFB; pvt. practice arch., 1989—; state rep. dist. 84 Ohio Ho. of Reps., Columbus, 1999—, vice chair, homeland security, engring. and archtl. design com., mem. agr. and natural resources, banking pensions and securities, commerce and labor, and pub. utilities coms. Seminar spkr. nat. arch. convs. Mem. Mad River-Green Local Bd. Edn., 1995—. Fellow: AIA. Republican. Office: 77 S High St 11th fl Columbus OH 43215-6111

WIDERA, GEORG ERNST OTTO, mechanical engineering educator, consultant; b. Dortmund, Germany, Feb. 16, 1938; arrived in U.S., 1950; s. Otto and Gertrude (Yzermann) Widera; m. Kristel Kornas, June 21, 1974; children: Erika, Nicholas. BS, U. Wis., 1960, MS, 1962, PhD, 1965. Asst. prof. then prof. dept. materials engring. U. Ill., Chgo., 1965-82, prof. mech. engring., 1982-91, head dept., 1983-91, acting head indsl. sys. engring. dept., 1985-86, dir off-campus engring. programs, 1987-88; prof., chmn. mech. and indsl. engring. dept. Marquette U., Milw., 1991—2002, co-dir. Ctr. Joining and Mfg. Assembly, 2002—, dir. Discovery Learning Ctr., 2000—07, sr. assoc. dean Coll. Engring., 1999—2007, interim dean Coll. Engring., 1998—99, 2003. Gastdozent U. Stuttgart, Germany, 1968; vis. prof. U. Wis.-Milw., 1973—74, Marquette U., Milw., 1979—80; cons. Ladish Co., Cudahy, Wis., 1967—76, Howmedica, Inc., Chgo., 1972—75, Sargent & Lundy, 1970—88, Nat. Bur. Stds., 1980; bd. dirs. Engrs. and Scientists Milw., 1996—98; vis. scientist Argonne Nat. Lab., Ill., 1968. Editor: Procs. Innovations in Structural Engring., 1974, Pressure Vessel Design, 1982, Jour. Pressure Vessel Tech., 1982—93, 2005—; co-editor: SME Handbook of Metalforming, 1985, 1994, Design and Analysis of Plates and Shells, 1986; assoc. editor: Pressure Vessel Tech., 1977—81, 2003—05, Applied Mechanics Revs., 1987—94, Mfg. Rev., 1991—95, mem. editl. adv. bd.: Acta Mechanica Sinica, 1990—98, mem. editl. bd.: Pressure Vessels and Piping Design Technology, 1982. Fellow Std. Oil Co. Calif., 1961—63, NASA, 1966, von Humboldt, Fed. Republic Germany, 1968—69. Fellow: WRC (chmn. subcom. design procedures for shell intersections 1983—87, chmn. com. reinforced openings and external loads 1987—91, vice chmn. com. polymer pressure components 1991—99, chmn. com. shells and ligaments 1994—97, pressure vessel rsch. coun.), ASCE (sec.-treas. structural divsn. Ill. sect. 1972—73, chmn. divsn. 1976—77, chmn. peer rev. com., tech. coun. rsch. 1984, coun. structural plastics), ASME (chmn. machine design div. Chgo. sect. 1967—68, exec. com. Chgo. sect. 1970—73, editor newsletter Chgo. sect. 1971—73, chmn. jr. awards com. applied mechanics divsn. 1973—76, chmn. design and analysis com. pressure vessel and piping divsn. 1980—83, chmn. pressure vessel rsch. com. 1982—87, bd. editors 1983—93, mem. exec. com. and program chmn. pressure vessel and piping divsn. 1985—89, vice-chmn., sec. pressure vessel and piping divsn. 1989—90, mem. bd. pressure tech. codes and stds. 1989—94, chmn. 1990—91, mem. materials and structures group 1990—91, historian, senate pressure vessel and piping divsn. 1992—93, honors and awards chmn. Milw. sect. 1992—95, mem. coun. engring. 1992—96, v.p., chair materials and structures group 1993—96, mem. tech. execs. com. 1993—96, bd. editors 2005—, Pressure Vessel and Piping medalist 1995), Wis. Mfg. Curriculum Com. (vice-chmn. exec. com. 1998—2002), 2d China Nat. Stds. Com. Pressure Vessels (hon. cons. 1989—94), Internat. Coun. Pressure Vessel Tech. (chmn. Am. regional com. 1988—, internat. chmn. 1992—96, 2003—06), Am. Soc. Engring. Edn., Soc. Mfg. Engrs. (sr.), French Pressure Vessel Assn.; mem.: Wis. Assn. Rsch. Mgmt. (v.p. 2003—04, pres. 2004—05), Tau Beta Pi. Achievements include research in mechanics of composite materials, plate and shell structures, stress analysis, pressure vessels, mechanics of deformation processing. Office: Marquette U Coll Engring PO Box 1881 Milwaukee WI 53201-1881 Home Phone: 262-789-8387; Office Phone: 414-288-4427. Business E-Mail: jpvt@marquette.edu.

WIDMAN, PAUL JOSEPH, insurance agent; b. DeSmet, SD, Dec. 18, 1936; s. Warren Clay and Lorraine (Coughlin) W.; m. Elizabeth Ann Healy, July 30, 1959; children: Cynthia, Susan, Shelly, Richard, Mark. BS, Dakota State Coll., Madison, 1959; M in Comm., S.D. State U., 1968. Tchr. Clark (S.D.) Pub. Sch., 1959-60, Henry (S.D.) Pub. Sch., 1960-64, Custer (S.D.) Pub. Sch., 1964-66; ins. agt. Horace Mann Ins., Mitchell, S.D., 1966-77, Universal Underwriters, Mitchell, S.D., 1980-87, NGM Ins. Assn., Mitchell, S.D., 1987-91, Reginald Martin Agy., Mitchell, S.D., 1991—; state rep. State of S.D., 1993—; gen. agt., ins. sales agt. Reginald Martin Agy., Mitchell, 1992—. City coun. mem. Mitchell City Coun., 1972-76; state legislator S.D. Ho. of Reps., 1993-94. Sgt. U.S. Army N.G., 1955-61. Mem. Elks, Mitchell Jaycees (pres., v.p. 1968-70, Outstanding Jaycee 1970), S.D. Jaycees (v.p., regional dir. 1969-70). Democrat. Roman Catholic. Avocations: golf, bowling, hunting. Office: Reginald Martin Agy 510 W Havens St Mitchell SD 57301-3935

WIDMAR, RUSSELL C., airport executive; V.p. airport svcs. Lockheed Air Terminal Inc., 1980-94; dir. Burbank-Glendale-Pasadena Airport, 1984; dir. ops. airport sys. divsn. Hughes Aircraft Co., Fullerton, Calif., 1994-96; exec. dir. aviation Salt Lake City Airport Authority, 1996-99; aviation dir. Kansas City Aviation Dept., 2000—. Office: Dir of Aviation 601 Brasila Ave Kansas City MO 64153

WIDMAYER, CHRISTOPHER A., legislative staff member; b. Royal Oak, Mich., Nov. 24, 1971; BA, Miami U., Oxford, Ohio, 1994. Staff asst. U.S. Rep. Bob Carr, Washington, 1994; dep. press sec. Durbin for Senate campaign, Chgo., 1995-96; Ill. press sec. Sen. Dick Durbin, Chgo., 1997—. Office: Office of Senator Dick Durbin 230 S Dearborn St Ste 3892 Chicago IL 60604-1602

WIDOWFIELD, JOHN, state legislator, state representative; b. 1964; married; 2 children. BA, Hiram Coll.; MBA, U. Akron. Rep. Ohio State Ho. Reps., Columbus, 2000—. Mem. county and township govt. com. Ohio State Ho. Reps., vice chmn. judiciary com., mem. juvenile and family law com., mem. pub. utilities com.; guard Sec. Def. The Pentagon, Washington. Mem. coun. Cuyahoga Falls. Nfantryman US Army. Decorated Commendation medal U.S. Army, Joint Svcs. Achievement medal. Mem.: Richardson (Ohio) PTA, Stow-Munroe (Ohio) Falls C. of C., Cuyahoga Falls (Ohio) C. of C., Friends Taylor Meml. Libr., Am. Legion. Republican. Office: Ohio State House Reps 77 South High Street 13th Fl Columbus OH 43215-6111

WIECEK, BARBARA HARRIET, advertising executive; b. Chgo., Mar. 30, 1956; d. Stanley Joseph and Irene (Zagajewski) W. AA, Am. Acad. of Art, Chgo., 1977. Illustrator Clinton E. Frank Advt., Chgo., 1977-78, art dir., 1978-80, assoc. creative dir., 1980-84, v.p.; instr. Am. Acad. of Art, Chgo., 1977-80; assoc. creative dir. Tatham, Laird & Kudner, 1984—, ptnr. Chgo., 1986—, creative dir., 1987—, sr. ptnr., 1995—, exec. creative dir., 1996. Recipient Silver Awd. Internat. Film Festival of N.Y., 1981, Gold Awd. Internat. Film Festival of N.Y., 1981. Roman Catholic. Avocations: painting, writing, gardening, remodeling, bicycling. Office: Tatham Euro RSCG 36 E Grand Ave Chicago IL 60611-3506

WIECK, RON, state senator, insurance agent; b. Plymouth County, Iowa, Aug. 13, 1944; Ins. agt. State Farm; state senator dist. 27 Iowa Senate, 2003—; mem. bus. and labor rels. com.; mem. govt. oversight com.; mem. local govt. com.; mem. natural resources and environment com.; vice chair commerce com. Active R.E.A.P.; pres. and dist. adminstr. Little League baseball; pres. Siouxland Sport and Cultural Congress; chair bldg. com. Woodbury County Law Enforcement Ctr.; active Washington Elem. Sch. Site Com.; citizen rep. and bd. dirs. Woodbury County Criminal Justice Com. Republican. Office: State Capitol East 12th and Grand Des Moines IA 50319

WIECZOREK, DENNIS E., lawyer; b. June 4, 1952; AB magna cum laude, Washington Univ., St. Louis, 1974; JD, Duke Univ., 1977. Bar: Ill. 1977, US Dist. Ct. (no. dist.) Ill. Ptnr., co-chair Franchise & Distribution practice group DLA Piper Rudnick Gray Cary, Chgo. Lectr.; contbr. articles to profl. jours.; co-author: Annual Franchise & Distribution Law Delelopments, 2002, Franchising: A Planning & Sales Compliance Guide; author (contributing): Fundamentals of Franchising. Mem.: ABA, Chgo. Bar Assn., Ill. Bar Assn. Office: DLA Piper Rudnick Gray Cary Ste 1900 203 N LaSalle St Chicago IL 60601-1293 Office Phone: 312-368-4087. Office Fax: 312-236-7516. Business E-Mail: dennis.wieczorek@dlapiper.com.

WIEGAND, SYLVIA MARGARET, mathematician, educator; b. Cape Town, South Africa, Mar. 8, 1945; came to U.S., 1949; d. Laurence Chisholm and Joan Elizabeth (Dunnett) Young; m. Roger Allan Wiegand, Aug. 27, 1966; children: David Chisholm, Andrea Elizabeth. AB, Bryn Mawr Coll., 1966; MA, U. Wash., 1967; PhD, U. Wis., Madison, 1972. Mem. faculty U. Nebr., Lincoln, 1967—, now prof. math.; program dir. Nat. Sci. Found., 2002—03. Vis. assoc. prof. U. Conn., Storrs, 1978-79, U. Wis., Madison, 1985-86; vis. prof. Purdue U., 1992-93, Spring 1998, Mich. State U., Fall 1997. Editor Communications in Math., 1990-2004, Rocky Mountain Jour. Math., 1991-2004; contbr. rsch. articles to profl. jours. Troop leader Lincoln area Girl Scouts U.S., 1988-92. Grantee NSF, 1985-88, 90-93, 94-96, 97-2002, NSA, 1995-97, 2002, 03-05; Vis. Professorship for Women, 1992, Nat. Security Agy., 1995-97. Mem. AAUP, Assn. Women in Math (pres.-elect 1995-96, pres. 1997-99), London Math. Soc., Math. Assn. Am., Am. Math. Soc. (mem. coun. 1994-96, chmn. policy com. on meetings and confs. 1994-96, mem. nominating com. 1997—), Can. Math. Soc. (bd. mem. at large 1997—). Avocation: running. Office: U Nebr Dept Math Lincoln NE 68588-0130 Office Phone: 402-472-7248. E-mail: swiegand@math.unl.edu.

WIEHOFF, JOHN P., trucking executive; With Arthur Anderson, 1984—92; contr., treas. C.H. Robinson Worldwide, 1992—98, sr. v.p., CFO, 1998—99, pres., 1999—2006, CEO, 2002—06, chmn., CEO, 2006—. Office: 8100 Mitchell Rd Eden Prairie MN 55344

WIEMANN, MARION RUSSELL, JR., (BARON OF CAMSTER), biologist, ambassador general; b. Sept. 7, 1929; s. Marion Russell and Verda (Peek) W.; 1 child from previous marriage, Tamara Lee (Mrs. Donald D. Kelley). BS, Ind. U., 1959; PhD (hon.), World U. Roundtable, 1991; ScD (hon.), The London Inst. Applied Rsch., 1994, ScD (hon.), 1995, World Acad., Germany, 1995. Histo-rsch. technician U. Chgo., 1959, rsch. asst., 1959-62, rsch. technician, 1962-64; tchr. sci. Westchester Twp. Sch., Chesterton, Ind., 1964-66; with U. Chgo., 1965-79, sr. rsch. technician, 1967-70, rsch. technologist, 1970-79; prin. Marion Wiemann & Assocs., cons. R&D, Chesterton, Ind., 1979-89. Advisor Porter County Health Bd., 1989-91; mem. consultive faculty World U., 1991-99, SkyWarn, Nat. Weather Svc., 1993—. Author: Tooth Decay, Its Cause and Prevention Through Controlled Soil Composition and Soil pH, 1985; contbr. articles to profl. jours. and newspapers. Vice-chmn. The Duneland 4th of July Com., 1987-91; v.p. State Microscopical Soc. Ill., 1969-70, pres., 1970-71. With USN, 1951-53. Recipient Disting. Tech. Communicator award Soc. for Tech. Communication, 1974, Internat. Order Merit (Eng.), 1991; ennobled Royal Coll. Heraldry, Australia, 1991, Highland Laird, Scotland, 1995; named Sagamore of the Wabash Gov. Ind., 1985; McCrone Rsch. Inst. scholar, 1968; named Prof. of Sci. Australian Inst. for Co-Ordinated Rsch., Australia, 1995; recipient Scouters Key award Boy Scouts Am., 1968, Arrowhead honor, 1968, Albert Einstein Silver medal, Huguenin, Le Locke, Switzerland, Henri Dunant Silver medal with silver bars, 1995, Henri Dunant Silver medal, 1995, medal of honor, England, 1996. Fellow: Australian Inst. Co-Ordinated Rsch., World Lit. Acad.; mem.: World Explorers Club, Order Internat. Fellowship, World Acad., Assn. Masters Universe, Govs. Club, Order Am. Ambassadors (sovereign ambassador 2006), VFW (post judge adv. 1986—99, apptd. post adj. 1986—99, charter mem., bd. dirs., Cross of Malta 1986). Achievements include demonstration that radiation does not produce dental caries; proved that soil calcium, magnesium, potassium and phosphorous, with soil PH, controls population size and longevity of earthworms and humans and the incidence of dental caries; demonstrated that fluoride neither reduces or prevents dental caries. Address: PO Box 1016 Chesterton IN 46304-0016 Office: Am Embassy 418 S Ninth St Chesterton IN 46304 Office Phone: 219-926-1295.

WIENEKE, DARIN SCOTT, lawyer; BA cum laude in Bus. Mgmt. and Polit. Sci., Hamline U., 1996; JD cum laude, U. Minn. Law Sch., Mpls., 2000. Bar: Minn. 2001, US Dist. Ct. (dist. Minn.) 2003. Assoc. Tewksbury, Kerfeld & Zimmer, P.A., Mpls. Named a Rising Star, Minn. Super Lawyers mag., 2006. Mem.: Minn. Trial Lawyers Assn. (co-chair new lawyers sect.), Hennepin County Bar Assn., Minn. State Bar Assn. Office: Tewksbury Kerfeld & Zimmer PA 88 S 10th St Ste 300 Minneapolis MN 55403 Office Phone: 612-334-3399. E-mail: dwieneke@tkz.com.

WIENER, DEANNA, state legislator; m. Jim Tilsen; three children. RN, St. Mary's Jr. Coll. Mem. Minn. Senate from 38th Dist., St. Paul, 1993—2002; real estate profl. Home: 7889 15th St N Saint Paul MN 55128-5604

WIENER, JOSEPH, pathologist, educator; b. Toronto, Can., Sept. 21, 1927; arrived in U.S., 1949, naturalized, 1960; s. Louis and Minnie (Salem) W.; m. Judith Hesta Ross, June 20, 1954; children: Carolyn L., Adam L. MD, U. Toronto, 1953. Intern Detroit Receiving Hosp., 1953-54; resident to chief resident pathology Mallory Inst. Pathology, 1954-55, 57-60; from asst. to assoc. prof. pathology Columbia U., NYC, 1960-68; prof. pathology N.Y. Med. Coll., NYC, 1968-78, Wayne State U., Detroit, 1978—, chmn. dept., 1978-90. Cons. NIH, 1970— Served to capt. M.C. U.S. Army, 1955-57. Grantee Heart, Lung and Blood Inst., 1971-93; fellow Coun. for High Blood Pressure Rsch., 1982. Fellow Am. Heart Assn., Am. Stroke Assn., Coll. Am. Pathologists; mem. AAAS, Am. Soc. Investigative Pathology, Am. Soc. Cell Biology, Mich. Path. Soc., Internat. Acad. Pathology, Am. Heart Assn., U.S./Can. Acad. Pathology, Mich. Heart Assn. (dir.), Internat. Soc. Hypertension. Achievements include rsch. on cellular/molecular biology of experimental hypertension. Office: 540 E Canfield St Detroit MI 48201-1928 Office Phone: 313-577-1157. Business E-Mail: j.wiener@wayne.med.edu.

WIENS, HAROLD J., electronics executive; b. Dallas, Oreg. BS in Mech. Engring., Mich. Tech. U., 1968. Exec. v.p., indsl. and consumer markets 3M Co., 1998—99, exec. v.p., indsl. and electro markets, 1999, exec. v.p., indsl. markets, 1999—2002. Mem. nat. adv. bd. Mich. Tech. U. Named to Acad. of Mech. Engring.-Engring. Mechanics, Mich. Tech. U., 1999. Mem.: QIC, Nat. Assn. of Mfrs. (bd. mem., chair, trade and tech. com.). Office: 3M Co 3M Ctr Saint Paul MN 55144

WIER, JAMES A., manufacturing executive; Exec. v.p. ops. Briggs & Stratton, 1975—91; pres., chief operating officer Simplicity Mfg. Corp., Port Washington, Wis., 1999—. Office: Simplicity Mfg Inc 500 N Spring St PO Box 997 Port Washington WI 53074-0997

WIER, PATRICIA ANN, publishing executive, consultant; b. Coal Hill, Ark., Nov. 10, 1937; d. Horace L. and Bridget B. (McMahon) Norton; m. Richard A. Wier, Feb. 24, 1962; 1 child, Rebecca Ann. BA, U. Mo., Kansas City, 1964; MBA, U. Chgo., 1978. Computer programmer AT&T, 1960-62; lead programmer City of Kansas City, Mo., 1963-65; with Playboy Enterprises, Chgo., 1965-71, mgr. systems and programming, 1971; with Ency. Britannica, Inc., Chgo., 1971—; v.p. mgmt. svcs. Ency. Britannica USA, 1975-83, exec. v.p. adminstrn., 1983-84; v.p. planning and devel. Ency. Britannica, Inc., 1985, pres. Compton's Learning Co. divsn., 1985; pres. Ency. Britannica (USA), 1986-91, Ency. Britannica N.A., 1986—94; exec. v.p. Ency. Britannica, Inc., 1986-94; pres. Ency. Britannica N.Am., 1986—94; mgmt. cons. pvt. practice, Chgo., 1994—. Cons. pvt. practice, Chgo., 1994—; bd. dirs. Alcas Corp., Mannatech Inc. Life mem. coun. Grad. Sch. Bus., U. Chgo.; mem. bd. regents Lewis U. Mem. Direct Selling Assn. (bd. dirs. 1984-93, chmn. 1987-88, named to Hall of Fame 1991), Women's Coun. U. Mo. Kansas City (hon. life) Com. 200, The Chgo. Network. Roman Catholic. Office: Patricia A Wier Inc 175 E Delaware Pl Ste 8305 Chicago IL 60611-7748 Office Phone: 312-787-4151. Personal E-mail: wier@prodigy.net.

WIERSBE, WARREN WENDELL, clergyman, writer, lecturer; b. East Chgo., May 16, 1929; s. Fred and Gladys Anna (Forsberg) W.; m. Betty Lorraine Warren, June 20, 1953; children: David, Carolyn, Robert, Judy. B.Th., No. Baptist Sem., 1953; D.D. (hon.), Temple Sem., Chattanooga, 1965, Trinity Ev-Div. Sch., 1986; LittD (hon.), Cedarville U., 1987. Ordained to ministry, Bapt. Ch., 1951. Pastor Central Bapt. Ch., East Chicago, 1951-57; editl. dir. Youth for Christ Internat., Wheaton, Ill., 1957-61; pastor Calvary Bapt. Ch., Covington, Ky., 1961-71; sr. min. Moody Ch., Chgo., 1971-78; bd. dirs. Slavic Gospel Assn., Wheaton, 1973-87; columnist Moody Monthly, Chgo., 1971-77; author, conf. minister, 1978-80; pres. ScripTex, Inc., Lincoln, Nebr., 1982—. Vis. instr. pastoral theology Trinity Div. Sch., Deerfield, Ill.; gen. dir. Back to the Bible Radio Ministries, Lincoln, Nebr., 1984-89; writer-in-residence Cornerstone Coll., Grand Rapids, Mich.; disting. prof. preaching Grand Rapids Bapt. Sem. Author: over 150 books including William Culbertson, A Man of God, 1974, Live Like a King, 1976, Walking with the Giants, 1976, Be Right, 1977, (with David Wiersbe) Making Sense of the Ministry, 1983, Why Us? Why Bad Things Happen to God's People, 1984, Real Worship: It Can Transform Your Life, 1986, The Integrity Crisis, 1988, Be What You Are, 1988, The New Pilgrim's Progress, 1989, Living With the Giants, 1993, Preaching and Teaching with Imagination, 1994, Be Myself, 1994, The Bible Exposition Commentary, 6 vols., 2004. Home and Office: 441 Lakewood Dr Lincoln NE 68510-2419

WIESNER, DALLAS CHARLES, immunologist, researcher; b. Brookings, SD, Mar. 19, 1959; s. Charles Howard Wiesner and Coleen Marie (Hendrickson) Bailey; m. Priscilla Anne Semon, 1992. BS in Microbiology with high honors, S.D. State U., 1982. HIV product devel. tech. Abbott Labs., Diagnostic Div., Abbott Park, Ill., 1985-87, HIV retrocell product mgr. North Chicago, Ill., 1987-88, sect. mgr. infectious disease and immunology Abbott Park, Ill., 1988-90; mgr. sexually transmitted diseases tech. product devel. Diagnostic div. Abbott Labs., Abbott Park, Ill., 1990-91, sect. mgr. retrovirus tech. product devel., 1991-96; with hepatitis r&d diagnostic divsn. Abbott Labs, Abbott Park, 1996—. Mem. Am. Assn. Clin. Chemistry, Am. Soc. for Microbiology, Phi Kappa Phi. Lutheran. Avocations: fishing, camping, scuba diving, photography, amateur radio. Home: 8710 Lakeshore Dr Pleasant Prairie WI 53158-4721 Office: Abbott Labs 200 Abbott Pk Rd North Chicago IL 60064-3500 Office Phone: 847-937-1873.

WIGDALE, JAMES B., bank executive; Chmn., chief exec. officer Marshall & Ilsley Bank, Milw., vice chmn. holding co., also bd. dirs. Office: Marshall & Ilsley Corp 770 N Water St Milwaukee WI 53202-3509

WIGER, CHARLES W., state legislator; b. Sept. 14, 1951; m. Christine Wiger; 5 children. BA, JD, Hamline U. Bar: Minn. Mem. Minn. Senate from 55th dist., St. Paul, 1996—. Home: 2200 Buhl Ave North Saint Paul MN 55109-1771 Office: 325 Capitol 75 Constitution Ave Saint Paul MN 55155-1601

WIGFIELD, RITA L., elementary school educator; b. Mpls., Dec. 14, 1945; d. Willard Ernest and Bernice Eleanor (Peterson) Ahlquist; m. Vernon Carter Wigfield, Oct. 9, 1982. BS, U. Minn., 1967; grad., St. Thomas Coll.; postgrad., Hamlin U. Cert. elem. educator, Minn. Tchr. Alice Smith Sch., Hopkins, Minn., 1967-80, Meadowbrook Sch., Hopkins, 1980-86, Gatewood Sch., Hopkins, 1986—. Owner Swede Country, Minnetonka, Minn., 1983—; elem. team leader Prin.'s Adv. Bd.; chmn. bldg. tech. com. Hopkins Sch. Dist., past supr. bldg. sch. patrol; coop. tchrs. Gustavus Adolphus Coll.; cons. and presenter in field. Author: We Love Literature, 1991 (Grand Prize Scholastic Inc., 1991). Mem. Wooddale Choir Evang. Christian Ch., decorating com., Mission commn., organizer fellowship dinners; mem. Loaves and Fishes, Minn. Landscape Arboretum. Recipient Hon. Mention Learning Mag., 1990, Nat. Coun Econ. edn./Internat. Paper Col. Found., 1992, 2d pl. Minn. Coun. Econ. Edn., 1992, Ashland Oil award, 1994; named Minn. Tchr. of Yr., 1992. Mem. ASCD, Nat. Assn. Miniature Enthusiasts, Am. Quilting Soc., Internat. Reading Assn., Minn. Edn. Assn., Hopins Edn. Assn. (bldg. rep., treas.), Delta Kappa Gamma (pres. Beta Beta chpt.), Kappa Delta Pi. Avocations: miniatures, quilting, flowers, cross-stitch, antiques. Office: Gatewood Elem Sch 14900 Gatewood Dr Minnetonka MN 55345-6731 Home: 7610 Smetana Ln Apt 201 Eden Prairie MN 55344-4751

WIGGINS, CANDICE DANA, professional basketball player; b. Balt., Feb. 14, 1987; d. Alan and Angela Wiggins. Grad. in Comm., Stanford U., Calif., 2008. Guard Stanford U. Cardinal, 2004—08, Minn. Lynx, 2008—. Injury replacement US Sr. Nat. Team. Finalist John R. Wooden award, 2007, 2008, Wade Trophy award, 2007, Naismith Trophy, 2008; named a Kodak/WBCA All-Am., 2004—08, First Team All-Am., AP, Sports Illustrated, ESPN.com, and CBSSportsline.com, 2008; named Player of Yr., PAC-10 Conf., 2005, 2006, 2008, US Basketball Female Athlete of Yr., 2007; named to John R. Wooden Award All-America Team, 2008; recipient Wade Trophy award, 2008. Mem.: Delta Sigma Theta. Achievements include being the third overall pick in the WNBA draft, 2008. Office: Minn Lynx 600 First Ave N Minneapolis MN 55403 Office Phone: 612-673-1600.*

WIGGINS, CHARLES HENRY, JR., lawyer; b. Balt., July 15, 1939; s. Charles Henry and Kathryn Wilson (Walker) W.; m. Wendy Jane Horn, June 20, 1964 (div. 1996); children: Charles Hunter, Rebecca Rae, Melinda Marie; m. Karen Ann Kowal, Apr. 26, 1997 (div. 2002). BSEE, U. Ill., Urbana, 1962; JD with honors, U. Ill., 1965. Bar: Ill. 1965, U.S. Dist. (no. dist.) Ill. 1970, U.S. Tax Ct. 1974, U.S. Ct. Appeals (7th cir.) 1983. Assoc. Vedder, Price, Kaufman & Kammholz, Chgo., 1969-73, ptnr., 1974—. Mem. zoning bd. appeals Village of Indian Head Pk., Ill., 1984-91. Capt. U.S. Army, 1965-68. Mem. Chgo. Bar Assn., University Club (Chgo.), Edgewood Valley Country Club (LaGrange, Ill., bd. dirs. 1991-98), SAR. Avocations: golf, tennis, bridge. Office Phone: 312-609-7525. Business E-Mail: cwiggins@vedderprice.com.

WIGGINS, DAVID STEWART, state supreme court justice; b. Chgo., Oct. 19, 1951; s. Kalman G. and Joan (Feldman) W.; m. Marsha Wiggins, Dec. 23, 1973; children: Samantha, Sydney, Taylor. BA in Philosophy, U. Ill., Chgo., 1973; JD, Drake U., 1976. Bar: Iowa 1976, U.S. Dist. Ct. (no. and so. dists.) Iowa 1976, U.S. Ct. Appeals (8th cir.) 1976, U.S. Ct. Claims, 1979, D.C. Ct. Appeals, 1979, U.S. Supreme Ct. 1979. Assoc. to ptnr. Williams, Hart, Lavorato & Kirtley, 1976—79; ptnr. Wiggins & Anderson P.C. (now Anderson & Tully), West Des Moines, 1979—2003; justice Iowa Supreme Ct., 2003—. Mem. Iowa Jud. Com. Cost of Litig., 1988, Iowa Jud. Adv. Com. Rules of Civil Procedure, 1991—97; chair Iowa Jud. Qualifications Commn., 2000—03; mem. Iowa Jud. Redistricting Commn., 2002. Fellow C. Edwin Moore Am. Inn of Ct. (master emeritus). Office: Jud Br Bldg 1111 East Ct Ave Des Moines IA 50319 Office Phone: 515-281-5175. Business E-Mail: david.wiggins@jb.state.ia.us.

WIGGINS, ROGER C., internist, educator, researcher; b. Tetbury, Eng., May 26, 1945; BA, Cambridge U., Eng., 1968; BChir, Middlesex Hosp. Med. Sch., London, 1971, MB, MA, 1972. House physician dept. medicine The Middlesex Hosp., London, 1971-72; house surgeon Ipswich (Eng.) and East Suffolk Hosps., 1972; sr. house officer Hammersmith Hosp., The Middlesex Hosp., Brompton Hosp., London, 1972-74; rsch. registrar The Middlesex Hosp. Med. Sch., London, 1975-76; postdoctoral fellow Scripps Clinic and Rsch. Found., La Jolla, Calif., 1976-78, rsch. assoc., 1978-79, asst. mem. 1, 1979-81; asst. prof. U. Mich., Ann Arbor, 1981-84, assoc. prof., 1984-90, prof., 1990—, chief nephrology, 1988—, dir. O'Brien Renal Ctr., 1988—, dir. NIH Nephrology Tng. Program, 1988-96. Lectr., speaker in field. Author chpts. to books; assoc. editor: Jour. Am. Soc. Nephrology, Clin. Sci.; contbr. articles to profl. jours. First Broderip scholar, 1971, Harold Boldero scholar, 1971, James McIntosh scholar, 1971, The Berkeley fellow Gonville and Caius Coll., 1976; recipient Leopold Hudson prize, 1971, The William Henry Rean prize, 1971, Disting. Rsch. Jerome W. Conn award, 1984. Fellow Royal Coll. Physicians (U.K.); mem. Am. Assn. Pathologists, Am. Assn. Immunologists, Am. Soc. Nephrology, Fedn. Clin. Rsch., Am. Soc. Clin. Investigation, Ctrl. Soc. Am. Fedn. Clin. Rsch., Assn. Am. Physicians. Office: U Mich Nephrology Div 3914 Taubman Ctr Ann Arbor MI 48109

WIGGINTON, ADAM, marketing professional; BSc in Zoology, U. Aberdeen; MBA in Fin., City U. With Unilever; prin. assoc. mgmt. consultancy divsn. Coopers & Lybrand; v.p. strategic planning Reed Travel Group, 1994-98, sr. v.p. of bus. devel. and circulation mktg., 1998—. Office: Oag 3025 Highland Pkwy Ste 200 Downers Grove IL 60515-5561

WIGHT, DARLENE, retired speech professional; b. Andover, Kans., Jan. 5, 1926; d. Everett John and Claudia (Jennings) Van Biber; m. Lester Delin, Jan. 21, 1950; children: Lester Delin II, Claudia Leigh. AA, Graceland Coll., 1945; BA, U. Kans., 1948, MA, 1952. Cert. tchr. Iowa, Mo. Instr. U. Kans., Lawrence, 1949-50; instr. overseas program U. Md., Munich, 1954; speech pathologist Independence (Mo.) Pub. Sch. Dist., 1958-61; assoc. prof. Graceland Coll., Lamoni, Iowa, 1961-87, prof. emeritus. Cons. Quad-County Sch. Dist., Leon, Iowa, 1966-67, Mt. Ayr (Iowa) Cmty. Sch. Dist., 1967-70; cons. Head Start program SCIAP, Leon, 1972-75, MATURA, Bedford, Iowa, 1973-75. Co-author: Speech Communication Handbook, 1979. Mem. Friends of Art, Nelson-Atkins Mus. Art, Habitat for Humanity. Recipient Award of Merit U. Kans., 1982, Award of Distinction U. Kans., 1947-48. Mem. Am. Speech, Lang. and Hearing Assn. (speech pathology clin. competency), Coun. Exceptional Children. Mem. Community Of Christ Ch. Avocations: weaving/fibers, travel, gardening, cooking. Office: Graceland U Speech Dept Lamoni IA 50140 Personal E-mail: darlene@familymatter.com.

WIGHTMAN, ALEC, lawyer; b. Cleve., Jan. 23, 1951; s. John and Betty Jane (Follis) W.; m. Kathleen A. Little, June 19, 1976; children: Nora, Emily. BA, Duke U., 1972; JD, Ohio State U., 1975. Bar: Ohio 1975, U.S. Tax Ct. 1982, U.S. Ct. Appeals (6th cir.) 1983. Assoc. Krupman, Fromson & Henson, Columbus, Ohio, 1975-77; ptnr. Krupman, Fromson, Bownas & Wightman, Columbus, 1978-82; assoc. Baker & Hostetler, Columbus, 1982-83, ptnr., 1984—, exec. ptnr., 2004—. Bd. trustees The Arthur G. James Cancer Hosp., Richard J. Solove Rsch. Inst.; bd. dirs. Cleve. Rock & Roll., Inc. Mem. ABA,

Ohio Bar Assn., Columbus Bar Assn., Ohio Oil and Gas Assn. Avocation: tennis. Office: Baker & Hostetler 65 E State St Ste 2100 Columbus OH 43215-4260 Home Phone: 614-222-0999; Office Phone: 614-462-2636. Business E-Mail: awightman@bakerlaw.com.

WIKENHAUSER, CHARLES, zoological park administrator; BS in Zoology, U. Ill., 1971. Dir. Glenn Oak Zoo, Peoria, Ill., 1973-81, John Ball Zoo, Grand Rapids, Mich., 1981-85, Pitts. Zoo, 1986-90, Milw. County Zool. Gardens, 1990—. Office: Milw County Zool Gardens 10001 W Bluemound Rd Milwaukee WI 53226-4346

WIKMAN, MICHAEL RAYMOND, advertising executive; b. Mpls., Dec. 28, 1950; s. Charles Pierce and Jeanne Elizabeth W.; m. Carrie Brandt, Feb. 7, 1981; children: Caroline Celeste, Charles Michael. B in Elected Studies, U. Minn., 1973. Analyst, supr. media services Cambell-Mithun Advt., Mpls., 1973-77, account mgr., 1977-80; pres. MWA Direct, Mpls., 1980—. Mem. Direct Mktg. Assn. (Echo award 1987), Midwest Direct Mktg. Assn. (Art, Response and Copy award 1987). Avocations: art collecting, downhill skiing, tennis, sailing. Home: 5404 Richmond Ln Minneapolis MN 55436-2437

WILANSKY, HEYWOOD, retail executive; Graduate, Canaan Coll. With May Dept. Stores Co., 1976—95, pres., CEO Filene's div., 1991—92, pres., CEO Foley's div., 1992—95; pres., CEO Bon-Ton Stores Inc., 1995—2000; prof. of mktg. Univ. Md., 2000—03; pres., CEO Filene's Basement Inc., 2003—04, Retail Ventures Inc., Columbus, Ohio, 2004—. Office: Retail Ventures Inc 3241 Westerville Rd Columbus OH 43224

WILBUR, KATHLEEN, state agency administrator; m. Tom Wilbur; children: Thomas, William, Samuel, Raymond. BA, Mich. State U. Chief staff State Senator William Sederburg, Lansing, 1983-90; dir. Mich. Dept. Licensing, Regulation, Lansing, 1991, Mich. Dept. Occupational Profl. Regulation, Lansing, 1991-95; deputy dir. Mich. Dept. Commerce, Lansing, 1991-95, acting dir., 1995-96, dir., 1996, Mich. Dept. Consumer Industry Svcs., Lansing, 1996—. Chmn. MERRA Bd. Trustees, 1996—; mem. Mich. Investment Advisory Com, 1996—; bd. dirs. Mich. State Housing Authority, Mich. Municipal Bond Authority, Mich. State Fair, Women's Caring Program, Mich. Festival. Mem. Mich. State U. Alumni Assn., East Lansing Area Zonta Club. Office: Michigan Dept Consumer & Industry Services PO Box 30004 Lansing MI 48909-7504

WILBUR, RICHARD SLOAN, medical association administrator, physician; s. Blake Colburn and Mary Caldwell (Sloan) Wilbur; m. Betty Lou Fannin, Jan. 20, 1951; children: Andrew, Peter, Thomas. BA, Stanford U., 1943, MD, 1946; JD, John Marshall, 1990. Cert. ABIM (Gastroenterology Am. Bd. Internal Medicine, 1954. Intern San Francisco County Hosp., 1946—47; resident Stanford Hosp., 1949—51, U. Pa. Hosp., 1951—52; postgrad. tng. U. Mich. Hosp., 1957, Karolinska Sjukhuset, Stockholm, 1960; staff Palo Alto (Calif.) Med. Clinic, 1952—69; dep. exec. v.p. AMA, Chgo., 1969—71, 1973—74; asst. sec. for health and environment dept. def., 1971—73; sr. v.p. Baxter Labs., Inc., Deerfield, Ill., 1974—76; exec. v.p. Council Med. Splty. Socs., 1976—91, sec. accreditation coun. for continuing med. edn., 1979—91; assoc. prof. medicine Georgetown U. Med. Sch., 1971—77, Stanford Med. Sch., 1952—69; pres. Nat. Resident Matching Plan, 1991—92. Chmn. bd., CEO Inst. Clin. Info., 1994—99; sr. v.p. healthcare Buckeye Corp. Pte, Ltd., Singapore, 1997—2000; CEO Medic Alert, 1992—94; pres. Am. Bd. Med. Mgmt., 1992; mem. Am. Bd. Electrodiagnostic Medicine, 1993—98; chmn. med. adv. bd. Med. City, Bangalore, India, 1997—2000; bd. visitors Drew U. Postgrad. Med. Sch. Contbr. articles to profl. jours. Bd. govs. ARC; chmn. Mid-Am. Blood Svcs. Bd., Lifesource Blood Bank, 1996—98; vice-chmn. Rep. Cen. Com. Santa Clara County, Calif., 1966—89; bd. dir. Nat. Adv. Cancer Coun., Nat. Health Coun., 1993—95; chmn. bd. dir. Medic Alert Found.; chmn. bd. Calif. Med. Assn., 1968—69, Calif. Blue Shield, 1966—68, Am. Med. Found., 1987—; pres. Royal Soc. Medicine Found., 1998—2004. With USNR, 1942—58. Recipient Disting. Svc. medal, Dept. Def., 1973, Scroll of merit, Nat. Med. Assn., 1971. Fellow: ACP, Am. Coll. Physician Execs. (bd. regents 1985—89, pres. 1988—89, 2006—07), Am. Coll. Legal Medicine, Internat. Coll. Dentistry (hon.); mem.: Am. Soc. Internal Medicine, Am. Gastroent. Assn., Santa Clara County Med. Soc. (hon.), Lake County Med. Soc., Ill. Med. Assn., Inst. Medicine, Union League Phila., Cedars Club, Pacific Interurban Clin. Club, Alpha Omega Alpha, Phi Beta Kappa. Home: 985 Hawthorne Pl Lake Forest IL 60045-2217 Office: APT Management Inc 736 N Western Ave #222 Lake Forest IL 60045 E-mail: aptmgmnt@aol.com.

WILCOX, JON P., state supreme court justice; b. Berlin, Wis., Sept. 5, 1936; m. Jane Ann; children: Jeffrey, Jennifer. AB in Polit. Sci., Ripon Coll., 1958; JD, U. Wis., 1965. Pvt. practice Steele, Smyth, Klos and Flynn, LaCrosse, Wis., 1965-66, Hacker and Wilcox, Wautoma, Wis., 1966-69, Wilcox, Rudolph, Kubasta & Rathjen, Wautoma, 1969-79; mem. Wis. State Legislature, 1969—75; judge Waushara County Cir. Ct., 1979-92; justice Wis. Supreme Ct., 1992—. Commr. Family Ct., Waushara County, 1977-79; del. Wis. Conservation Congress, 1975-80; vice chmn., chmn. Wis. Sentencing Commn., 1987-92; chief judge 6th Jud. Dist., 1985-92; mem. State-Fed. Jud. Coun., 1992-99, Jud. Coun. Wis., 1993-98; mem. Prison Overcrowding Task Force, 1988-90; mem. numerous coms. Wis. Judiciary; mem. faculty Wis. Jud. Coll., 1985-96; chmn. Wis. Chief Judges Com., 1990-92; co-chair comm. on judiciary as co-equal br. of govt. Wis. State Bar, 1995-97; lectr. in field. Contbr. (with others): Wisconsin News Reporters Legal Handbook: Wisconsin Courts and Court Procedures, 1987. Bd. visitors U. Wis. Law Sch., 1970—76. Lt. US Army, 1959—61. Named Outstanding Jaycee Wautoma, 1974; recipient Disting. Alumni award Ripon Coll., 1993. Fellow Am. Bar Found.; mem. ABA (com. on continuing appellate edn.), Wis. Bar Assn. (bench bar com., state bar and media law rels. com.), Wis. Law Found. (bd. dirs.), Tri-County Bar Assn., Dane County Bar Assn., Trout Unltd., Ducks Unltd., Rotary, Phi Alpha Delta. Office: Supreme Court State Capitol PO Box 1688 Madison WI 53701-1688

WILCOX, MARK DEAN, lawyer; b. May 25, 1952; s. Fabian Joseph and Zeryle Lucille (Tase) W.; m. Catherine J. Wertjes, Mar. 12, 1983; children: Glenna Lynn, Joanna Tessie, Andrew Fabian Joseph. BBA, U. Notre Dame, 1973; JD, Northwestern U., 1976; CLU, Am. Coll., 1979, ChFC, 1992. Bar: Ill. 1976, U.S. Dist. Ct. (no. dist.) Ill. 1976, Trial Bar 1982, U.S. Ct. Appeals (7th cir.) 1987, U.S. Supreme Ct. 1989. Staff asst. Nat. Dist. Attys. Assn., Chgo., 1974-75; trial asst. Cook County States Atty., Chgo., 1975; intern U.S. Atty. No. Dist. Ill., Chgo., 1975-76; assoc. Lord, Bissell & Brook, LLP, Chgo., 1976-85, ptnr., 1986—2005; founding ptnr. Walker Wilcox Matousek, LLP, Chgo., 2005—. Venue ofcl. Internat. Spl. Olympics; bd. mgrs. YMCA Met. Chgo., exec. com.; active No Bats Baseball Club Hall of Fame; past trustee Trinity United Meth. Ch.; bd. dirs., past chair Irving Park YMCA. Fellow Am. Bar Found.; mem. ABA (tort and ins. practice sect.), Am. Soc. CLU and ChFC, Chgo. Bar Assn. (ins. law com.), Am. Health Lawyers Assn., Nat. Assn. Ins. and Fin. Advisors, Def. Rsch. Inst., Soc. Fin. Svc. Profls., Trial Lawyers Club Chgo., Notre Dame Nat. Monogram Club, Union League Club, Chgo. Lions Rugby Football Club, Beta Gamma Sigma. Office Phone: 312-244-6722.

WILCOXSON, ROY DELL, plant pathologist, researcher, educator; b. Columbia, Utah, Jan. 12, 1926; m. Iva Wall, 1949; children: Bonnie, Paul, Karren, John. BS, Utah State U., 1953; MS, U. Minn., 1955, PhD in Plant Pathlogy, 1957. Asst. prof., 1957-66; prof. plant pathology U. Minn., St. Paul, 1966-91, prof. emeritus, 1991—. Spl. staff mem. Rockefeller Found.; vis. prof. Indian Agrl. Rsch. Inst., New Delhi; dir. Morocco project U. Minn., 1983-87; adj. prof. Inst. Agronomy and Vet. Medicine, Hassan II, Rabat, Morocco, 1985—. Fellow Am. Phytopath Soc., Indian NAS, Indian Phytopath Soc., AAAS. Achievements include research in diseases of forage crops and cereal crops; cereal rust diseases. Office: 1669 County Road 8230 West Plains MO 65775-5766 Address: Dept Plant Path U Minn Saint Paul MN 55101

WILD, JOHN JULIAN, surgeon, researcher, medical educator; b. Sydenham, Kent, Eng., Aug. 11, 1914; came to U.S., 1946; s. Ovid Frederick and Ellen Louise (Cuttance) W.; m. Nancy Wallace, Nov. 14, 1949 (div. 1966); children: John O., Douglas J.; m. Valerie Claudia Grosenick, Aug. 9, 1968; 1 child, Ellen Louise. BA, U. Cambridge, Eng., 1936, MA, 1940, MD, 1942, PhD, 1971. Intern, resident U. Coll. Hosp., London, 1938-42; intern U. College Hosp., London, 1938-42; staff surgeon Miller Gen., St. Charles and North Middlesex Hosps., London, 1942-44; venereologist Royal Army Med. Corps, 1944-45; rsch. fellow, instr. depts. surgery and elec. engring., prin. investigator U. Minn., Mpls., 1946-51; dir. rsch. Medico.-Technol. Rsch. Dept. St. Barnabas Hosp., Mpls., 1953-60; dir. Medico-Technol. Rsch. Unit Minn. Found., St. Paul, 1960-63; pvt. practice Mpls., 1966—90; dir. Medico-Technol. Rsch. Inst. Mpls., St. Louis Park, Minn., 1965—2006. Lectr. in field of medical instruments, ultrasound. Contbr. articles to profl. jours. Recipient Japan prize in Medical Imaging, Sci. and Tech. Found. Japan, 1991, 1st Frank Annunzio award Christopher Columbus Fellowship Found., 1998, lifetime achievement award U. Minn. Med. Sch., 2000, Ian Donald Tech. Achievement aard ISUOG, 2000. Fellow Am. Inst. Ultrasound in Medicine (Pioneer award 1978); mem. AMA, World Fedn. Ultrasound in Medicine and Biology, Minn. State Med. Assn., Hennepin County Med. Soc., N.Am. Alvis Owners Club; hon. mem. Brit. Inst. Radiology, Japan Soc. of Ultrasound in Medicine. Achievements include patents in field; origination of ultrasonic medical imaging instruments and diagnostic techniques; origination of the field of pulse-echo ultrasonic diagnostic medicine. Home and Office: Medico-Technol Rsch Inst 4262 Alabama Ave S Minneapolis MN 55416-3105

WILD, ROBERT ANTHONY, academic administrator; b. Chgo., Mar. 30, 1940; s. John Hopkins and Mary Dorothy (Colnon) Wild. BA in Latin, Loyola U., Chgo., 1962, MA in Classical Lang., 1967; STL, Jesuit Sch. Theology, Chgo., 1970; PhD in Study of Religion, Harvard U., 1977. Ordained priest 1970. From asst. to assoc. prof. Marquette U., Milw., 1975—83; vis. prof. Pont. Istituto Biblico, Rome, 1983—84; dir. Jesuit philosophate program Loyola U., Chgo., 1984—85, assoc. prof. theology, 1985—92; provincial superior Chgo. Province S.J., 1985—91; pres. Weston Jesuit Sch. Theology, Cambridge, Mass., 1992—96, Marquette U., Milw., 1996—. Trustee Jesuit Sch. Theology, Berkeley, 1985—90, Weston Sch. Theology, Cambridge, Mass., 1985—96, Marquette U., 1990—, St. Louis U., 1994—2002, Milw. Rsch. Park, 2002—05, Greater Milw. Commn., 2002—, Wis. Assn. Ind. Colls. and Univs., 1996—, chmn., 2001—07, St. Joseph's U., Pa., 2004—. Author: Water in the Cultic Worship of Isis and Sarapis, 1981; co-editor: Sentences of Sextus, 1981; contbr. articles to profl. jours. Mem.: Cath. Bibl. Soc., Soc. Bibl. Lit. Office: Marquette Univ O'Hara Hall PO Box 1881 Milwaukee WI 53201-1881 Home Phone: 414-288-5000; Office Phone: 414-288-7223. Business E-Mail: robert.wild@marquette.edu.

WILDE, HAROLD RICHARD, college president; b. Wauwatosa, Wis., May 14, 1945; s. Harold Richard and Winifred (Wiley) W.; m. Benna Brecher, Feb. 4, 1970; children: Anna, Henry, Elizabeth Ty. BA, Amherst Coll., 1967; MA, PhD, Harvard U., Cambridge, Mass., 1973. Spl. asst. to gov. Office of Gov., State of Wis., Madison, 1972-75; ins. commr. Office of Commr. of Ins., State of Wis., Madison, 1975-79; spl. asst. to pres. U. Wis. System, Madison, 1979-81; v.p. for external affairs Beloit (Wis.) Coll., 1981-91; pres. North Ctrl. Coll., Naperville, Ill., 1991—. Bd. dirs. Ctr. for Pub. Representation, Inc., Madison, 1981-87, Beloit Community Found., 1988-91, Budget Funding Corp., 1993-99, Naperville Devel. Partnership, 1996—. Mem.: Phi Beta Kappa. Home: 329 S Brainard St aperville IL 60540-5401 Office: North Ctrl Coll 30 N Brainard St Naperville IL 60540-4607 Office Phone: 630-637-5454. Business E-Mail: hrwilde@noctrl.edu.

WILDERDYKE, PAUL, state representative; b. June 1942; State rep. dist. 56 Iowa Ho. of Reps., 2003—; asst. majority leader; mem. commerce, regulation and labor com.; mem. econ. growth com.; mem. environ. protection com.; mem. human resources com.; vice chair econ. devel. com. Republican. Address: 23 Fifth St Woodbine IA 51579 Office: State Capitol East 12th and Grand Des Moines IA 50319

WILDMAN, MAX EDWARD, lawyer, director; b. Terre Haute, Ind., Dec. 4, 1919; s. Roscoe Ellsworth and Lena (Shaw) W.; m. Joyce Lenore Smith, Sept. 25, 1948; children: Leslie, William. BS, Butler U., 1941; JD, U. Mich., 1947; MBA, U. Chgo., 1952. Bar: Ill., Ind. Ptnr. Kirkland & Ellis, Chgo., 1947-67; mng. ptnr. Wildman, Harrold, Allen & Dixon, Chgo., 1967-89. Dir. Colt Industries, N.Y., Nat. Blvd. Bank, Ill. Contbr. articles to profl. jours. Trustee Butler U., Indpls., Lake Forest Hosp., Ill., Lake Bluff Library Bd., Ill.; chmn. Lake Bluff Zoning Bd. Served to lt. col. USAF, 1943-46; PTO Fellow Am. Coll. Trial Lawyers; mem. Soc. Trial Lawyers, Law Club, Legal Club, Trial Lawyers Club of Chgo. Clubs: Anglers (Chgo.), Pere Marquette Rod and Gun (Baldwin, Mich.), Shoreacres (Lake Bluff), Univ. of Chgo. Presbyterian. Office: Wildman Harrold Allen & Dixon 225 W Wacker Dr Chicago IL 60606-1224 Office Phone: 312-201-2627.

WILEY, GREGORY ROBERT, publisher; b. Sept. 21, 1951; s. William Joseph and Terese (Kunz) W.; children: Kathleen, Mary Glennon. BA in Pers. Adminstrn., U. Kans., 1974. Dist. sales mgr. Reader's Digest, St. Loius, 1976-80, regional sales dir. Chgo., 1980-82; nat. sales mgr. retail divsn. Rand McNally & Co., Chgo., 1982-83, nat. sales mgr. premium incentive divsn., 1983-86, nat. sales mgr. bookstore and mass market sales, 1986-88; book pub. The Sporting News, St. Louis, 1988-90; v.p. mktg. Marketmakers Internat., St. Louis, 1990-93, Sofsource Inc., St. Louis, 1993—96; eastern regional v.p. Handleman Co., St. Louis, 1996—2002; dir. sales and marketing, books The Sporting News, St. Louis, 2002—. Mem. Nat. Premium Sales Execs., Promotional Mktg. Assn. Am. Roman Catholic. Avocations: private pilot, historic restoration, golf. Home: 4245 Maryland Ave Saint Louis MO 63108-2905

WILEY, JOHN D., academic administrator; BS in Physics, Ind. U., 1964; MS in Physics, U. Wis., Madison, 1965, PhD in Physics, 1968. Tech. staff Bell Telephone Labs., Murray Hill, NJ, 1968—74; Alexander von Humboldt rsch. and tng. fellow Max Planck Inst., Stuttgart, Germany, 1974—75; mem. elec. and computer engring. faculty U. Wis., Madison, 1975—. co-founder Ctr. for X-Ray Lithography and Engring. Rsch. Ctr. for Plasma-Aided Mfg., chair Materials Sci. program, 1982—86, assoc. dean for rsch., Coll. Engring., 1986—89, dean, Grad. Sch., and sr. rsch. officer, 1989—94, provost & vice chancellor for acad. affairs, 1994—2000, chancellor, 2001—. Office: U Wis 161 Bascom Hall 500 Lincoln Dr Madison WI 53706

WILHELM, DAVID C., investment company executive; m. Degee Dodds; children: Luke, Logan. BA, Ohio U., 1977; MPP, Harvard U., 1990; Doctorate (hon.), U. Charleston. Rsch. dir. pub. employee dept. AFL-CIO, 1981-83; campaign mgr. Senator Paul Simon, 1984, Senator Joseph Biden for Pres., Iowa, 1985-87, Richard M. Daley for Mayor, Chgo., 1989, 91, Gov. Bill Clinton for Pres., 1991-92; exec. dir. Citizens for Tax Justice, Washington, 1985-87; pres. The Strategy Group, Chgo., 1988-91; chmn. Nat. Dem. Com., 1993-94; sr. mng. dir. investment banking Kemper Securities, Inc. (now First Union), Chgo., 1995-97; founder, sr. v.p. Wilhelm & Conlon, Inc., Chgo., 1998—2004; founder, pres. Woodland Venture Mgmt., Chgo., 2002—; founder, ptnr. Adena Ventures, 2002—, Hopewell Ventures, 2004—; founder, pres. The Strategy Group. Lectr. U. Chgo.; bd. dirs. Christian Century Mag., League of Chgo. Treasures, Children's Meml. Hosp., Chgo., Ill. Venture Capital Assocs., Chicagoland Entrepreneurial Ctr., Ill. Ventures. Bd. dirs. Chgo. Project for Violence Prevention, Ctr. for Tax and Budget Accountability. Fellow Inst. of Politics, Harvard U., 1996, recipient hon. Dr. of Public Service, Ohio Univ. Office: Woodland Venture Mgmt 20 N Wacker Dr Ste 2200 Chicago IL 60606 E-mail: wilhelm@woodlandvc.com.

WILHELM, EDWARD W., corporate financial executive; Grad., U. of Detroit. With PricewaterhouseCoopers, 1981—91; contr., v.p./contr. Kmart Corp., 1991—94; v.p. fin. Borders Group, Ann Arbor, Mich., 1994—97, v.p. planning, reporting and treasury, 1997—2000, sr. v.p., CFO, 2000—. Office: Borders Group 100 Phoenix Dr Ann Arbor MI 48108-2202

WILHIDE, STEPHEN D., medical association administrator; BA in Social Scis., Frostburg State U., Md., 1965; MSW, U. Md., 1972; MPH, U. Pitts., 1976. Exec. dir. So. Ohio Health Svcs. Network, 1976—2002, Nat. Rural Health Assn., Alexandria, Va., 2002—. Vol. VISTA, NC. With US Army, Vietnam. Named one of Most Powerful People in Healthcare, Modern Healthcare mag., 2003. Office: National Rural Health Associ 1600 Prince St Ste 100 Alexandria VA 22314-2836 Office Phone: 703-519-7910. Business E-Mail: wilhide@nrharural.com.

WILK, KENNY A., state legislator; Kans. state rep. Dist. 42, 1993—. Mgr. Hallmark Cards.

WILKE, LEROY, retired church administrator; m. Jane Wilke. Grad., Golden Valley Lutheran Coll.; MA, Minn. State U.; LittD (hon.), Concordia U., 1999. Chaplain's asst. US Army; adminstr., dir. Christian Edn., Mpls., 1969; prof. edn. Concordia Coll., St. Paul, 1976; exec. dir. dist. and congl. svcs. Luth. Ch.-Mo. Synod, St. Louis, 1985—2005. Sec. Karpenko Inst. for Nurturing and Developing Leadership Excellence, 2005—. Lutheran. Office: KINDLE c/o Emmaus Luth Ch 3120 Irving St Denver CO 80211-3632 Office Phone: 303-433-3303. Office Fax: 303-433-2280. E-mail: leroy.wilke@lcms.org.

WILKES, KENNETH G., food products company executive; BA, Cleve. State U., 1980; MBA, DePaul U., 1987. V.p., sr. corp. banker First Nat. Bank of Chgo.; v.p., treas. Libbey Inc., Toledo, Ohio, v.p., CFO, v.p., CFO, treas. Office: Libbey Inc 300 Madison Ave Toledo OH 43604

WILKINS, JEFFREY M., computer company executive; Co-founder CompuServe, 1969; founder Discovery Sys., 1985-91; pres., CEO Metatec Corp., Dublin, Ohio, 1991—, chmn. bd. dirs. Office: Metatec Internat Inc 7001 Metatec Blvd Dublin OH 43017-3219

WILKINS, JOHN WARREN, physics professor; b. Des Moines, Mar. 11, 1936; s. Carl Daniel and Ruth Elizabeth (Warren) W. BS in Engring, Northwestern U., 1959; MS, U. Ill., 1960, PhD, 1963; DTech (hon.), Chalmers Tekniska Hogskola, Göteborg, 1990. NSF fellow U. Cambridge, Eng., 1963-64; asst. prof. physics Cornell U., 1964-68, assoc. prof., 1968-74, prof., 1974-88; eminent scholar, prof. physics Ohio State U., 1988—. Vis. prof. H.C. Ørsted Inst., Copenhagen, 1968, ordita, Copenhagen, 1972-73, 75-76, 79-81; cons. Los Alamos Nat. Lab., 1984—, Lawrence Livermore Nat. Lab., 1997—; adv. com. U. Chgo. Sci. and Tech., 1990—. Assoc. editor Physica Scripta, 1977-85, Phys. Rev. Letters, 1982-85, Rev. Modern Physics, 1983-95; mem. editorial bd. Phys. Rev. B, 1991-94; coord. Comments on Condensed Matter Physics, 1985-90. Sloan fellow, 1966; Guggenheim fellow, 1985. Fellow AAAS, Am. Phys. Soc. (publs. oversight com. 1995-97, chmn. 1995-96, councillor divsn. condensed matter physics 1989-93, exec. com. divsn. biol. physics 1973-77, vice-chair through past chair divsn. condensed matter physics 2001—); mem. European Phys. Soc. Office: OSU Physics 191 W Woodruff Ave Columbus OH 43210 E-mail: wilkins@mps.ohio-state.edu.

WILKINSON, RALPH RUSSELL, retired biochemistry educator, toxicologist; b. Portland, Oreg., Feb. 20, 1930; s. Tracy Chandler and Lavern (Russell) W.; m. Evelyn Marie Wickman, Aug. 5, 1956. BA, Reed Coll., 1953; PhD, U. Oreg., 1962; MBA, U. Mo., Kansas City, 1974. Rsch. chemist VA Hosp., Kansas City, Mo., 1973-74; sr. rsch. chemist Midwest Rsch. Inst., Kansas City, 1975-84; prof. Rockhurst Coll., Kansas City, 1985-86, Cleve. Chiropractic Coll., Kansas City, 1987-99, prof. emeritus, 1999—. Cons. in biochemistry, toxicology, environ. impact, tech. assessment, Kansas City, 1984—. Author: (book) Neurotoxins and eurobiological Function, 1987; contbr. articles to profl. jours. Mem. Southtown Coun., Kansas City, Mo., 1989—, Spina Bifida Assn. Am., Kansas City, 1989—. NSF fellow, 1959-60. Mem. Am. Chem. Soc., Sigma Xi. Avocations: travel, history, biography, music, antiques. Home: 7911 Charlotte St Kansas City MO 64131-2175

WILKOWSKI, E. TODD, lawyer; b. Phillippines, June 2, 1967; BS, USAF Acad., 1989; MA, Regent U. Sch. Pub. Policy, 1998; JD, Regent U. Sch. Law, 1998. Bar: Ohio 1998, US Dist. Ct. Southern Dist. Ohio 1999, US Ct. of Appeals Sixth Cir. 2006. Counternarcotics intelligence officer Pentagon, South Am. embassies; ptnr. Keating Muething & Klekamp PLL, Cin. Dir. St. Rita Sch. for Deaf, 2000—06; dir., Alumni Bd. Regent U. Law Sch., 2000—06; dir. Friars Club, Inc., 2001—04, Cin. Teen Challenge, Inc.; mem., Bd. Trustees Coun. on Child Abuse of Southern Ohio, Inc.; mentor Help One Student to Succeed Prog., Oyler Elem. Sch.; treasurer St. Thomas More Soc. Greater Cin.; dir. Catholic Men's Fellowship, Inc.; mem., Young Exec. Com. Catholic Inner-city Schools Edn. Named one of 40 Under 40, Cin. Bus. Courier, 2004, Ohio's Rising Stars, Super Lawyers, 2005, 2006; recipient Def. Meritorious Svc. award, 1994. Mem.: Cin. Acad. Leadership for Lawyers (Class X), USAF Acad. Assn. of Graduates, Ohio State Bar Assn., Cin. Bar Assn. (vice chmn., Constrn. Law Com.). Office: Keating Muething & Klekamp PLL One E Fourth St Ste 1400 Cincinnati OH 45202 Office Phone: 513-579-6498. Office Fax: 513-579-6457.

WILL, CLIFFORD MARTIN, physicist, researcher, educator; b. Hamilton, Ont., Can., Nov. 13, 1946; m. Leslie Saxe Moser, June 26, 1970; children: Elizabeth Sue Torop, Rosalie Will Boxt. BS, McMaster U., Hamilton, 1968; PhD, Calif. Inst. Tech., 1971. Enrico Fermi fellow U. Chgo., 1972-74; asst. prof. physics Stanford U., Palo Alto, Calif., 1974-81; assoc. prof. physics Washington U., St. Louis, 1981—85, prof. physics, 1985—2005, James S. McDonnell prof. physics, 2005—, chmn. dept. physics, 1991—96, 1997—2002. Vis. assoc. physics Calif. Inst. Tech., 1976; chmn. com. on time transfer in satellite systems Air Force Studies Bd., Washington, 1984—86; rsch. assoc. Nat. Ctr. Sci. Rsch. Obs. Paris, Meudon, France, 1996; vis. prof. Hebrew U. Racah Inst. Physics, Jerusalem, 1997, U. Pierre and Marie Curie, Paris, 2006, Inst. Henri Poincare and U. Paris IX, 2006; chmn. sci. adv. com. NASA Gravity Probe B, 1998; rsch. assoc. Nat. Ctr. Sci. Rsch. Inst. Astrophysics, Paris, 2003—04, 2005, 06, 2007—. Assoc. editor Phys. Rev. Letters, 1989-92, Phys. Rev. D, 1999-2001; author: Theory and Experiment in Gravitational Physics, 1981, rev. edit., 1993, Was Einstein Right?, 1986, rev. edit., 1993. Alfred P. Sloan Found. fellow, 1975-79, McDonnell Ctr. Space Scis. fellow, 1981-, J.S. Guggenheim Found. fellow, 1996-97, J.W. Fulbright fellow, 1996-97,; recipient Sci. Writing award Am. Inst. Physics, 1987, Disting. Alumni award, McMaster U., 1996, Fellows award St. Louis Acad. Scis., 2004. Fellow Am. Phys. Soc. (exec. com. astrophysics divsn. 1988-90, vice chair, chair elect, chair topical group on gravitation 1997-2001), Am. Acad. Arts and Scis.; mem. NAS, Am. Astron. Soc., Am. Assn. Physics Tchrs. (Richtmyer Meml. Lectr. 1987), Internat. Soc. Gen. Relativity and Gravitation (pres. 2004-07). Office: Washington U Dept Physics Campus Box 1105 1 Brookings Dr Saint Louis MO 63130-4899 Office Phone: 314-935-6244. Office Fax: 314-935-6219. Business E-Mail: cmw@wuphys.wustl.edu.

WILL, ERIC JOHN, state senator; b. Omaha, Nebr., Apr. 16, 1959; s. John Babcock and Patricia Elaine (Propst) W. BA in Polit. Sci., U. So. Calif., 1981; postgrad., Creighton U., 1993—. Legis. researcher Nebr. State Legis., Omaha, 1981-90, senator, 1991—. Chmn. enrollment and rev. com., 1991-93, rules com., 1993—; vice chmn. gen. affairs com., 1991—; mem. revenue and urban affairs com., 1991—. Mem. Phi Beta Kappa. Democrat. Presbyterian. Avocations: softball, bowling, volleyball.

WILL, TREVOR JONATHAN, lawyer; b. Ashland, Wis., Aug. 11, 1953; s. William Taylor and Geraldine Sue (Trevor) W.; m. Margaret Ann Johnson, Aug. 28, 1976; children: Tyler William, Alexandra Marie, Jennifer Catherine. BA summa cum laude, Augustana Coll., 1975; JD cum laude, Harvard U., 1978. Bar: Wis. 1978, U.S. Dist. Ct. (ea. dist.) Wis. 1978, U.S. DIst. Ct. (we. dist.) Wis. 1980, U.S. Ct. Appeals (7th cir.) 1983, U.S. Supreme Ct. 1984, U.S. Dist. Ct. (ea. dist.) Mich. 1985. Assoc. Foley & Lardner LLP, Milw., 1978-87, ptnr., 1987—, chmn. product liability practice group. Adj. law prof. Marquette U. Law Sch., 1994-00. Mem. ABA, State Bar Wis., Milw. Bar Assn., Def. Rsch. Inst. Office: Foley & Lardner LLP 777 E Wisconsin Ave Ste 3800 Milwaukee WI 53202-5306 Office Phone: 414-297-5536. Office Fax: 414-297-4900. Business E-Mail: twill@foley.com.

WILLAMOWSKI, JOHN RANDALL, state representative, lawyer; b. Southbend, Ohio, July 22, 1960; married; 4 children. BA in Philosophy, U. Notre Dame, 1982; JD, Ohio Northern U., 1985. Rep. Ohio State Ho. Reps., Columbus, 1997—; ptnr. Willamowski & Willamowski, Lima, 1990—. Mem. civil and comml. law com. Ohio State Ho. Reps., mem. criminal justice com., chmn. judiciary com., mem. juvenile and family law com. Mem. ctrl. and exec. com. Allen County Rep. Party. Mem.: Allen County Bar Assn., Farm Bur., Lima/Allen County C. of C., Exchange Club, Sertoma Club. Republican. Office: Willamowski & Willamowski 730 W North St Lima OH 45801 Office Phone: 419-228-8335.

WILLARD, GREGORY DALE, lawyer; b. Pittsfield, Ill., Feb. 8, 1954; s. Wesley Dale and Rosmary (Stark) W.; m. Ann Julia Grier, June 3, 1978; children: Michael, David, John. BA summa cum laude, Westminster Coll., Fulton, Mo., 1976; JD cum laude, U. Ill., 1979. Bar: Mo., U.S. Dist. Ct. (ea. dist.) Mo., U.S. Ct. Appeals (8th Cir.). Staff asst. to Pres. Exec. Office of the Pres. The White House, Washington, 1976-77; ptnr. Bryan Cave LLP, St. Louis, 1979—, group leader Bankruptcy, Restructuring and Creditors' Rights. Co-chmn. bankruptcy com. Met. Bar Assn., St. Louis, 1983-84. Bd. Dirs. St. Louis

Children's Hosp., 1985-89, Found. for Spl. Edn., 1990—, Congress Neurol. Surgeons, 1998—. Mem. Congress of Neurol. Surgeons, Noonday Club. Office: Bryan Cave One Metropolitan Square 211 N Broadway Saint Louis MO 63102-2733 E-mail: gdwillard@bryancave.com.

WILLBORN, STEVEN L., dean, law educator; BA magna cum laude, Northland Coll., 1974; MS in Counseling, U.Wis.-Madison, 1976; JD cum laude, U. Wis. Law Sch., 1976. Asst. prof. law U. Nebr.-Lincoln Coll. Law, 1979, assoc. prof., 1982, prof., 1985, Richard C. & Catherine Stuart Schmoker Prof. Law, 1999—, dean, 2001—. Pvt. practice, 1976—79; vis. prof. University Mich. Law Sch., 1992. Co-author: Employment Law: Cases and Materials, The Statistics of Discrimination: Using Statistical Evidence in Discrimination Cases, 2002; contbr. articles to law jours. Grantee Lincoln Coll., Oxford U., 1993; vis. scholar Australian at. U., Canberra, 1988, U. Toronto, 1991; Fulbright Scholar, Inst. Advanced Legal Studies, U. London, 1985—86. Office: U Nebr-Lincoln Coll Law Ross McCollum Hall PO Box 830902 Lincoln NE 68583 E-mail: willborn@unl.edu.

WILLE, KARIN L., lawyer; b. Northfield, Minn., Dec. 14, 1949; d. James Virginia Wille. BA summa cum laude, Macalester Coll., 1971; JD cum laude, U. Minn., 1974. Bar: Minn. 1974, U.S. Dist. Ct. Minn. 1974. Atty. Dresselhuis & Assoc., Mpls., 1974-75; assoc. Dorsey & Whitney, Mpls., 1975-76; atty. Dayton-Hudson Corp., Mpls., 1976-84; gen. counsel B. Dalton Booksellers, Edina, Minn., 1985-87; assoc. Briggs & Morgan, Mpls., 1987-88; shareholder Briggs and Briggs, Mpls., 1988—2005, of counsel, 2005—. Co-chair Upper Midwest Employment Law Inst., 1983—. Named Leading Minn. Atty., Super Lawyer, Mpls.-St. Paul Mag., Twin Cities Bus. Monthly and Minn. Law and Politics; named one of Best Lawyers in Am. Mem. ABA, Minn. State Bar Assn. (labor and employment sect., corp. counsel sect., dir. 1989-91), Hennepin County Bar Assn. (labor and employment sect.), Minn. Women Lawyers, Phi Beta Kappa. Office: Briggs & Morgan 80 S 8th St Ste 2200 Minneapolis MN 55402-2157 E-mail: kwille@briggs.com.

WILLENBRINK, ROSE ANN, retired lawyer; b. Louisville, Ky., Apr. 20, 1950; d. J.L. Jr. and Mary Margaret (Williams) W.; m. William I. Cornett Jr. Student, U. Chgo., 1968-70; BA in Anthropology with highest honors, U. Louisville, 1973, JD, 1975. Bar: Ky. 1976, Ind. 1976, U.S. Dist. Ct. (we. dist.) Ky. 1976, Ohio 1999. Atty. Mapother & Mapother, Louisville, 1976-79; v.p., counsel Nat. City Bank, Louisville, 1980-99, v.p., sr. atty. Cleve., 1999—2004, Louisville, 2004—05, ret., 2005. Mem. Ky. Bar Assn., Phi Kappa Phi. Home: 6803 Chadworth Pl Prospect KY 40059 Home Phone: 502-292-2857. Personal E-mail: willenbrink@yahoo.com.

WILLETT, LANCE, orchestra executive; Exec. dir. Quad City Symphony Orch., Davenport, Iowa, 1982—. Office: Quad City Symphony Assn 327 Brady St Davenport IA 52801-1508

WILLHAM, RICHARD LEWIS, zoology educator; b. Hutchinson, Kans., May 4, 1932; s. Oliver S. and Susan E. (Hurt) W.; m. Esther B. Burkhart, June 1, 1954; children: Karen ell, Oliver Lee. BS, Okla. State U., 1954; MS, Iowa State U., 1955, PhD, 1960. Asst. prof. Iowa State U., Ames, 1959-63, assoc. prof., 1966-71, prof. dept. animal sci., 1971-78, Disting. prof., 1978—; assoc. prof. Okla. State U., Stillwater, 1963-66. Cons. in field; tchr. livestock history; guest curator exhbn. Art About Livestock, 1990. Author: A Heritage of Leadership -The First 100 Years of Animal Science at Iowa State University, 1996. Recipient Svc. award Beef Improvement Fedn., 1974, Edn. and Rsch. award Am. Polled Herefore Assn., 1979, Rsch. award Nat. Cattlemen's Assn., 1986, 91, Disting. Alumnus award Okla. State U., 1978, Regents Faculty Excellence award Iowa State U., 1993; named to Hall of Fame Am. Hereford Assn., 1982, Am. Angus Assn., 1988. Fellow Am. Soc. Animal Sci. (animal breeding and genetics award 1978, industry service award 1986), mem. Livestock Industry. Home: 2316 Hamilton Dr Ames IA 50014-8201 Office: Iowa State U Dept Animal Sci Ames IA 50011-0001 Office Phone: 515-294-3533. E-mail: rwillham@iastate.edu.

WILLIAMS, ALLEN W., JR., lawyer; b. Milw., Sept. 8, 1944; AB cum laude, Harvard U., 1966; JD cum laude, Columbia U., 1970, MBA, 1970. Bar: Wis. 1970. Legal counsel to Gov. Patrick J. Lucey State of Wis., 1971-72; ptnr. Foley & Lardner LLP, Milw. Chmn. legal com. Edison Electric Inst., 1981—. Mem. bd. editors Columbia Law Review, 1969-70. Bd. dirs. Planned Parenthood Wis., 1974-76; bd. dirs. Milw. Inst. Art and Design, 2005—, chmn., 2006. Mem. State Bar Wis., Milw. County Zool. Soc. (bd. dirs. 1977-89, pres. 1984-86), Med. Coll. Wis. (bd. dirs. 1977-97, chmn. 1984-1987). Office: Foley & Lardner LLP Firstar Ctr 777 E Wisc Ave Milwaukee WI 53202 Office Phone: 414-297-5808. Office Fax: 414-297-4900. Business E-Mail: awilliams@foley.com.

WILLIAMS, ANDY, singer, entertainer; b. Wall Lake, Iowa, Dec. 3, 1930; s. Jay Emerson and Florence (Finley) W.; m. Claudine Longet, Dec. 15, 1961 (div.); children: Noelle, Christian, Robert; m. Debbie Haas, May 3, 1991. Mem. Williams Brothers Quartet, on radio stations in Des Moines, Chgo., Cin. and Los Angeles, 1938—47, Williams Brothers, (teamed with Kay Thompson), 1947—51; solo performer, 1952—; frequent nightclub performer; performer Caesar's Palace, 1966—86. Founder, pres. Barnaby Records, 1963, Barnaby Prodns., Barnaby Sports; founder, owner Moon River Theater, Branson, Mo., 1992-, Moon River Grill, 2007-; host Andy Williams San Diego Golf Open, 1969-89. Regular performer (TV Series) Steve Allen Show, 1953-57, host & star Andy Williams Show, 1962-71 (3 Emmy awards for Best Musical/Variety Series), host Grammy Awards telecasts, 1971-77; recordings include Canadian Sunset, 1956, Butterfly, 1957, Lonely Street, 1959, The Village of St. Bernadette, 1960, I Like Your Kind of Love, Are You Sincere, Hawaiian Wedding Song, Moon River & Other Great Movie Themes, 1962, Can't Get Used to Losing You, 1963, Days of Wine and Roses, 1963, Call Me Irresponsible, 1964, Dear Heart, 1964, The Shadow of Your Smile, 1966, Born Free, 1967, Raindrops Keep Fallin' on My Head, 1970, Love Story, 1970, You've Got a Friend, 1971, Love Theme from The Godfather, 1972, The Way We Were, 1974, The Other Side of Me, 1984; film appearances include Janie, 1944, Kansas City Kitty, 1944, Something in the Wind, 1947, Ladies' Man, 1947, I'd Rather Be Rich, 1964. Named Number One Male Vocalist Top Artist on Campus Poll, 1968; recipient 17 gold albums, 3 Emmy awards, 6 Grammy awards Office: Moon River Theatre 2500 W Highway 76 Branson MO 65616-2164*

WILLIAMS, ANN CLAIRE, federal judge; b. Detroit, Aug. 16, 1949; m. David J. Stewart. BS, Wayne State U., 1970; MA, U. Mich., 1972; JD, U. Notre Dame, 1975; degree (hon.), Lake Forest Coll., 1987, U. Portland, 1993, U. Notre Dame, 1997. Law clk. to Hon. Robert A. Sprecher, 1975-76; asst. US atty. US Dist. Ct. (no. dist.) Ill., Chgo., 1976-85; faculty Nat. Inst. for Trial Advocacy, 1979—, also bd. dirs.; adj. prof., lectr. Northwestern U. Law Sch., 1979—, John Marshall Law Sch., 1979—; judge US Dist. Ct. (no. dist.) Ill., 1985-99, US Ct. Appeals (7th cir.), Chgo., 1999—. Chief Organized Crime Drug Enforcement Task Force for North Ctrl. Region, 1983-85; mem. ct. adminstrn. and case mgmt. com. Jud. Conf. US, 1990-97, chair, 1993-97. Sec. bd. trustees U. Notre Dame; founder Minority Legal Resources, Inc. Recipient Earl Burns Dickerson award, Chgo. Bar Assn., 1997, Tradition of Excellence award, Minority Legal Resources, Inc., 1997, Thurgood Marshall Jurist of Year, Legal Ministry of Second Baptist Church, 1997, Alumni of Year, Black Law Students Assn, U. Notre Dame, 1997, Morton A. Brody Disting. Jud. Svc. award, Colby Coll., 2002. Mem. FBA, Fed. Judges Assn., Ill. State Bar Assn., Ill. Jud. Coun., Cook County Bar Assn., Women's Bar Assn. Ill., Black Women's Lawyers Assn. Greater Chgo. Office: US Ct Appeals 7th Circuit 219 S Dearborn St Ste 2612 Chicago IL 60604-1803

WILLIAMS, ANNETTE POLLY, state legislator; b. Belzoni, Miss., Jan. 10, 1937; Student, Milw. Area Tech. Coll.; BS, U. Wis. Mem. Wis. State Assembly, Milw., 1980—. Attendee African-Am. Leadership summit, New Orleans; organizer Com. 21, 1985, Black Ribbon Commn. to study forced busing, Milw., 1989; panelist Nat. Conf. State Legislators, 1989; active parental sch. choice legislation; lectr. numerous colls. and univs. T.V. appearances include 60 Minutes, ABC World News, This Week with David Brinkley, McNeil Lehrer Report, The British Broadcasting Company, Great Lakes Watch on Washington, CBS This Morning, Both Sides with Rev. Jesse Jackson, CNN News; contbr. articles to profl. jours. Dem. adminstrv. and exec. com.; state chairperson Wis. Jesse Jackson for Pres. campaign; del. Nat. Dem. Conv., 1984, 88; mem. Nat. Dem. Platform Com., 1984; bd. dirs. Rainbow Coalition; founder, chmn. bd. dirs. Milw. Parental Assistance Ctr. Recipient Carrie Chapman Catt award as Nat. Women's Bus. Advocate of Yr., Outstanding Leadership award Dem. party Wis., Harambee Martin Luther King Jr. award for Outstanding Accomplishment and Svc. Am. Legis. Exchange Coun., 1991, Nat. Human Rights award Nat. Cath. Ednl. Assn., 1992, Seton award Career Youth Devel., 1992, Image award for Excellence in Community Svc. and Love of Youth Gamma Phi Delta, 1992, Community Leadership award Libertarian Party Wis., 1992, Liberty award, 1993, Martin Luther King Jr. Community Svc. award Lydell Comm., 1994; named Legislator of Yr. Freedom Mag., 1992; vis. fellow Auckland (New Zealand) Inst. Tech., 1993. Mem. Nat. Black Caucus State Legislators (bd. dirs.). Home: 3927 N 16th St Milwaukee WI 53206-2918 Office: Wis State Assembly State Capitol PO Box 8953 Madison WI 53708-8953

WILLIAMS, ARTHUR BENJAMIN, JR., bishop; b. Providence, June 25, 1935; m. Lynette Rhodes, 1985. AB, Brown U., 1957; MDiv, Gen. Theol. Sem., 1964; MA, U. Mich., 1974; DD, Gen. Theol. Sem., 1986. Clarence Horner fellow Grace Ch., Providence, 1964-65; asst. St. Mark, Riverside, R.I., 1965-67; sub-dean St. John Cathedral, Providence, 1967-68; assoc. & interim rector Grace Ch., Detroit, 1968-70; asst. to bishop Diocese of Mich., 1970-77; archdeacon Ohio Cleve., 1977-85; suffragan bishop Episcopal Diocese of Ohio, Cleve., 1986—; v.p. House of Bishops, 1995—. Chair Com. on Justice, Peace and Integrity of Creation, 1995-97; Epsicopal vis. Order of St. Benedict, 2000—. Chair editl. com. Lift Every Voice and Sing II, 1993. Episcopalian. Office: Diocese of Ohio 2230 Euclid Ave Cleveland OH 44115-2499 E-mail: bishsuff@dohio.org.

WILLIAMS, BRENT (BUZZ WILLIAMS), men's college basketball coach; b. Tex., Sept. 1, 1972; m. Corey Norman; children: Zera, Calvin, Mason. BS in Kinesiology, Okla. City U., 1994; MS in Kinesiology, Texas A&M U., Kingsville, 1999. Student asst. coach Navarro Coll. Bulldogs, 1990—92, Okla. City U. Stars, 1992—94; asst. coach U. Tex.-Arlington Mavericks, 1994—98, Tex. A&M-Kingsville Javelinas, 1998—99, Northwestern State U. Demons, 1999—2000, Colo. State U. Rams, 2000—03, assoc. head coach, 2003—04; asst. coach, recruiting coord. Tex. A&M U. Aggies, 2004—06; head coach U. New Orleans Privateers, 2006—07; asst. coach Marquette U. Golden Eagles, 2007—08, head coach, 2008—. Office: Marquette Univ c/o Dept Athletics Milwaukee WI 53201*

WILLIAMS, BRUCE, chef; Chef de cuisine Mon Ami Gabi, Chgo.; mem. staff Sherman House; apprentice too chef Larry Mason Little Corporal; with Club on 39; saute chef Zorine's and Arnie's; chef Seal Blue, Turbo, Jackie's, Bistro Zinc, Escada; chef de cuisine Mon Ami Gabi, Chgo. Office: Mon Ami Gabi 2300 N Lincoln Park W Chicago IL 60614

WILLIAMS, BRYAN C., state representative; b. 1964; married; 2 children. BS in History and Polit. Sci., Denison U. Rep. Ohio State Ho. Reps., Columbus, 1996—. Mem. commerce and labor com. Ohio State Ho. Reps., mem. edn. com., mem. health com., mem. juvenile and family law com., chmn. mcpl. govt. and urban revitalization com. Bd. govs. Orderof AHEPA, 1993—96; adminstr. Summit County Juvenile Ct., 1991—96; rsch. analyst Summit County Child Support Enforcement Agy., 1990; pres. Annunciation Greek Orthodox Ch. Bd., 1994—96; bd. trustees Porthouse Theatre, 1991—93; bd. dirs. Akron (Ohio) Civic Theater, 1994—2000. Republican. Office: Ohio State House Reps 77 South High Street 11th Floor Columbus OH 43215-6111

WILLIAMS, CAMILLA, soprano, voice educator; b. Danville, Va. d. Booker and Fannie (Cary) W.; m. Charles T. Beavers, Aug. 28, 1950. BS, Va. State Coll., 1941; postgrad., U. Pa., 1942; studies with Mme. Marian Szekely-Freschl, 1943-44, 1952, Berkowitz and Cesare Sodero, 1944-46, Rose Dirman, 1948-52, Sergius Kagen, 1958-62; MusD (hon.), Va. State U., 1986, D. (hon.), 1985. Prof. voice Bronx Coll., NYC, 1970, Bklyn. Coll., 1970-73, Queens Coll., NYC, 1974, Ind. U., Bloomington, 1977—, prof. emeritus voice. 1st black prof. voice Cen. Conservatory Music, Beijing, People's Republic China, 1983. Created role of Madame Butterfly as 1st black contract singer, N.Y.C. Ctr., 1946, 1st Aida, 1948; 1st N.Y. performance of Mozart's Idomeneo with Little Orch. Soc., 1950; 1st Viennese performance Menotti's Saint of Bleecker Street, 1955; 1st N.Y. performance of Handel's Orlando, 1971; other roles include Nedda in Pagliacci, Mimi in La Boheme, Marguerite in Faust; major tours include Alaska, 1950, London, 1954, Am. Festival in Belgium, 1955, tour of 14 African countries for U.S. Dept. State, 1958-59, Israel, 1959, concert for Crown Prince of Japan as guest of Gen. Eisenhower, 1960, tour of Formosa, Australia, New Zealand, Korea, Japan, Philippines, Laos, South Vietnam, 1971, Poland, 1974; appearances with orchs. including Royal Philharm., Vienna Symphony, Berlin Philharm., Chgo. Symphony, Phila. Orch., BBC Orch., Stuttgart Orch., many others; contract with RCA Victor as exclusive Victor Red Seal rec. artist, 1944—. Recipient Marian Anderson award (1st winner), 1943, 44, Newspaper Guild award as First Lady of Am. Opera, 1947, Va. State Coll. 75th anniv. cert. of merit, 1957, YU Presdl. Citation, 1959, Gold medal Emperor of Ethiopia and Key to City of Taiwan during Pres. Johnson's Cultural Exchange Program, 1962, Art, Culture and Civic Guild award, 1962, Negro Musician's Assn. plaque, 1963, Harlem Opera and World Fellowship Soc. award, 1963; named Disting. Virginian Gov. of Va., 1972; inducted Danville (Va.) Mus. Fine Arts and History Hall of Fame, 1974; Camilla Williams Park designated in her honor, Danville, 1974; honored by Ind. U. Sch. Music Black Music Students' Orgn., 1979; named to Hon. Order Ky. Cols., 1979; honored by Phila. Pro Arte Soc., 1982; Disting. award of Ctr. for Leadership and Devel., 1983; Taylor-Williams student residence hall at Va. State U. named in Billy Taylor's and her honor, 1985, hon. by New York Philharmonic, 1998, hon. by Amistad Rsch. Ctr., Tulane Univ., for Outstanding Contbn. to the Arts, 1998. Mem. NAACP (hon. life), Internat. Platform Assn., Alpha Kappa Alpha.

WILLIAMS, CARL CHANSON, insurance company executive; b. Cin., Oct. 16, 1937; s. Charles J. and Alcie (Brazile) W.; m. Claire Bathé, May 26, 1985; 1 child, Michelle. A.S., U. Cin., 1965; BS, SUNY-Brockport, 1974; MBA, U. Rochester, 1975. Mgr. fin. systems Xerox Corp., Rochester, N.Y., 1972-77; dir. info. mgmt. Am. Can Co., Greenwich, Conn., 1977-79, mng. dir. info. mgmt., 1979-80, mng. dir. ops. control, 1980-82; sr. v.p., dir. mgmt. info. systems DDB Needham Worldwide, YC, 1982-91; pres. The Intertechnology Group, Inc., NYC, 1990-91; v.p. infosystems and tech. Macmillan Pub. Co., NYC, 1991-93; gen. mgr. info. tech. Amoco Corp., Chgo., 1993-94, v.p. info. tech., 1994-97; sr. v.p., chief info. officer Principal Fin. Group, Des Moines, Iowa, 1997—. Cons. Stamford (Conn.) Bd. Edn., 1981-82; lectr. U. Rochester, N.Y., 1975-77; adj. prof. Fordham U., 1991—. Exec. dir. Concerned Assn. Rochester, N.Y., 1971-75; bd. dirs. Stamford Cmty. Arts Coun., 1983-84; trustee Roosevelt U., 1995-97, U. Rochester, 1999—, Exec. Leadership Found., 2000—; mem. Exec. Leadership Coun. 1993—. Mem. Soc. Info. Mgmr. (exec. coun. 1980-83, pres. 1985, pres. coun. 1986—), Exec. Leadership Coun. (found. bd. trustees). Office: Principal Fin Group 711 High St Des Moines IA 50392-0002 Home: 2420 Vintage Hill Dr Durham NC 27712-9476 E-mail: williams.carl@principal.com.

WILLIAMS, CLARENCE E., muncipal official; Student, Sinclair C.C., 1971-73, Ctrl. State U., 1973-74, Park Coll., 1986, Antioch U., 1987; BS, Wilberforce U., 1992. Housing inspector Dept. Housing & Neighborhood Affairs City of Dayton, Ohio, 1971-73, asst. coord. Neighborhood Devel. Program, 1973-75, acting supr. environ. svcs. Dept. Housing & Neighborhood, 1975-80, mgr. environ. svcs. Dept. Housing & Neighborhood Affairs, 1980, supt. waste collection Dept. Pub. Works, 1980-89, dir. Dept. Pub. Works, 1989-97, clk. of commns., 1997. Home: 1628 Kipling Dr Dayton OH 45406-4135 Office: City Commn Office 101 W 3d St City Hall Dayton OH 45402

WILLIAMS, DANIEL D., investment company executive; Sr. exec. v.p., CFO Everen Securities Inc., Chgo., until 1999. Office: Everen Securities Inc 77 W Wacker Dr Chicago IL 60601-1651

WILLIAMS, DAVID D., newspaper executive; With Chgo. Tribune, 1969—, advt. and mktg. positions, 1969-83, classified advt. dir., 1983-90; exec. v.p. Tribune Media Svcs., Chgo., 1990-91, pres., CEO, 1991—. Office: Tribune Media Svcs 435 N Michigan Ave Ste 1500 Chicago IL 60611-4012

WILLIAMS, DAVID PERRY, manufacturing executive; b. Detroit, Nov. 16, 1934; s. M.S. Perry and Virginia (Hayes) W.; m. Jill Schneider, July 27, 1972; children: Tracy, Perry, David, William, Nell. BA, Mich. State U., 1956, MBA, 1964. V.p. sales Automotive div. Kelsey Hayes Co., Romulus, Mich., 1958-71; v.p., mgr. automotive product line ITT, NYC, 1971-76; v.p., dir. Budd Co., Troy, Mich., 1976-79, sr. v.p. ops., dir., 1979-80, sr. v.p., chief ops. officer, 1980-86, pres., chief operating officer, dir., 1986—. Dir. Standard Fed. Bank, Troy, Mich., 1990—, SPX Corp., Muskegon, Mich., 1992—, Budd Canada, Inc., Kitchener, Ont., 1981—, Thyssen Budd Automotive. Served to 1st lt. USAF, 1956-58. Mem. Soc. Automotive Engrs., Bloomfield Hills Country Club, Country Club of Detroit, Yondotega, PGA Nat. Club (Fla.), Tournament Players Club (Mich.), Question Club, Royal and Ancient Golf Club of St. Andrews (Scotland), Beta Gamma Sigma. Republican. Episcopalian. Home: 333 Lincoln Rd Grosse Pointe MI 48230-1604 Office: Budd Co PO Box 2601 Troy MI 48007-2601

WILLIAMS, DELETA, state legislator; BS, Ctrl. Mo. State U. Mem. Mo. Ho. of Reps. from 121st dist., 1993—. Mem. Citizens for Drug Free Environment, Inc. Mem. Bus. and Profl. Women, C. of C., Women's Dem. Club, Mo. Fedn. Dem. Women's Club. Address: 110 E Hale Lake Rd Warrensburg MO 64093-3015

WILLIAMS, DENISE, academic administrator; b. Iowa, 1972; BBA, Detroit Coll. Bus.; M, Marygrove Coll. Assoc. dir. U. Detroit Mercy, 2001, dean of admissions, 2003—. Named one of 40 Under 40, Crain's Detroit Bus., 2006. Office: Univ Detroit Mercy FAC 100 4001 W McNichols Rd Detroit MI 48221 Office Phone: 313-993-1245. Office Fax: 313-993-3326.

WILLIAMS, EDWARD JOSEPH, banker; b. Chgo., May 5, 1942; s. Joseph and Lillian (Watkins) W.; children: Elaine, Paul; m. Ana J. Ortiz, Apr. 20, 1996. BBA, Roosevelt U., 1973. Owner Mut. Home Delivery, Chgo., 1961-63; exec. v.p. Harris Trust and Savs. Bank, Chgo., 1964—. Mem. Consumer Adv. Council, Washington, 1986—. Trustee, treas. Adler Planetarium, Chgo., 1982; trustee Roosevelt U., Chgo., Art Inst. of Chgo.; bd. dirs. Chapin-May Found., Chgo. Botanic Garden, Chgo. Capital Fund; trustee, treas. Chgo. Low Income Housing Trust Fund; dir. Leadership Coun. for Met. Open Communities; dir., former pres. Neighborhood Housing Svcs. of Chgo.; chmn. Provident Med. Ctr., Chgo., 1986; bd. dirs. Voices for Ill. Children, Chgo. Coun. on Urban Affairs; pres. Neighborhood Housing Svcs. Recipient Disting. Alumni award Clark Coll., Atlanta, 1985. Mem. Nat. Bankers Assn., Urban Bankers Forum (Pioneer award 1986, 97), Econ. Club. Chgo. Clubs: Metropolitan, Plaza (Chgo.). Office: Harris Trust & Savs Bank 111 W Monroe St Chicago IL 60603-4096

WILLIAMS, GREG, professional basketball coach; m. Suzanne Williams. Asst. coach men's basketball Rice U., Houston, 1970—75; asst. coach WBL Houston Angels, 1979—80; coach WBA Dallas Diamonds, 1981—82, WABA Dallas Diamonds, 1994; head coach women's basketball Colo. State U., 1990—97; asst. coach Detroit Shock, 1989—2000, head coach, 2000—. Named Coach of Yr., WBL, 1980—81, 1984, Southwest Conf., 1988, Western Athletic Conf., 1995—96. Office: Palace on Auburn Hills 2 Championship Dr Auburn Hills MI 48326

WILLIAMS, HAROLD ROGER, economist, educator; b. Arcade, NY, Aug. 22, 1935; s. Harry Alfred and Gertrude Anna (Scharf) W.; m. Lucia Dorothy Preuschoff, Apr. 23, 1955; children: Theresa Lynn, Mark Roger. BA, Harpur Coll., SUNY, Binghamton, 1961; MA, Pa. State U., 1963; PhD, U. Nebr., 1966; postgrad., Harvard U., 1969-70. Instr., Pa. State U., 1962-63; Instr. U. Nebr., 1965-66; mem. faculty Kent State U., Ohio, 1966—, prof. econs. and internat. bus., 1972—, chmn. dept., 1974-81, dir. Internat. Bus. Program, Grad. Sch. Mgmt., 1980-86, chmn. faculty senate, 1988-89, now prof. emeritus; assoc. dean Grad. Sch. Mgmt., 1994-96; program dir. Kent State-Geneva Program, Geneva, 1996-97. Econ. cons. and adv. to numerous govt., bus. and internat. orgns. Author over 100 books and articles in field. Served with AUS, 1954-57. Grantee NSF. Mem. Am. Econ. Assn., Internat. Econs. Assn., Acad. Internat. Bus., Midwest Econ. Assn. (v.p. 1969-70), So. Econ. Assn., Phi Gamma Mu, Omicron Delta Epsilon, Beta Gamma Sigma, Phi Beta Delta. Home: 415 Suzanne Dr Kent OH 44240-1933 Office: Rm 478 Dept Econs Kent State U Kent OH 44242-0001 Office Phone: 330-672-1085. Business E-Mail: Hwilliam@kent.edu.

WILLIAMS, J. BRYAN, lawyer; b. Detroit, July 23, 1947; s. Walter J. and Maureen June (Kay) Williams; m. Jane Elizabeth Eisele, Aug. 24, 1974; children: Kyle Joseph, Ryan Patrick. AB, U. Notre Dame, 1969; JD, U. Mich., 1972. Bar: Mich. 1972, U.S. Dist. Ct. (ea. dist.) Mich. 1972. Atty. Dickinson, Wright, PLLC (and predecessor firm), Detroit, 1972—, CEO Bloomfield Hills, Mich., 1991-2000. Pres. U.S. Law Firm Group, Inc., 2002. Mem. City of Birmingham Planning Bd., Mich. Mem.: ABA, Detroit Legal News Co. (bd. dirs. 1997—2006), Econ. Club Detroit (bd. dirs. 1996—2001), Mich. Bar Assn., Detroit Regional C. of C. (bd. dirs. 1994—2002, vice chmn. 1998—2002), Nat. Club Assn. (bd. dirs. 1994—2006, sec. 1995—97, treas. 1997—98, v.p. 1998—2002, chmn. 2002—03), Oakland Hills Country Club, Notre Dame Club Detroit (pres. 1984). Roman Catholic. Home: 993 Suffield Ave Birmingham MI 48009-1242 Office: Dickinson Wright PLLC 38525 Woodward Ave Ste 2000 Bloomfield Hills MI 48304 Office Phone: 248-433-7289. Business E-Mail: jwilliams@dickinsonwright.com.

WILLIAMS, JACK MARVIN, research chemist; b. Delta, Colo., Sept. 26, 1938; s. John Davis and Ruth Emma (Gallup) W. BS with honors, Lewis and Clark Coll., 1960; MS, Wash. State U., 1964, PhD, 1966. Postdoctoral fellow Argonne (Ill.), Nat. Lab., 1966-68, asst. chemist, 1968-70, assoc. chemist, 1970-72, chemist, 1972-77, sr. chemist, group leader, 1977—; vis. guest prof. U. Mo., Columbia, 1980, 81, 82, U. Copenhagen, 1980, 83, 85. Chair Gordon Rsch. Conf. (Inorganic Chemistry), 1980. Bd. editors: Inorganic Chemistry, 1979-96, assoc. editor, 1982-93. Crown-Zellerbach scholar, 1959-60; NDEA fellow, 1960-63; recipient Disting. Performance at Argonne Nat. Labs. award U. Chgo., 1987, Centennial Disting. Alumni award Wash. State U., 1990. Mem. AAAS, Am. Crystallographic Assn., Am. Chem. Soc. (treas. inorganic div. 1982-84), Am. Phys. Soc., Phi Beta Kappa. Office: Chemistry Div 9700 S Cass Ave Lemont IL 60439-4803

WILLIAMS, JACKIE N., law educator, former prosecutor; b. Roosevelt, Okla., Oct. 4, 1943; s. David Coleman and Grace Pearl (Southard) W.; children: Douglas Kennedy, Eric Neil. BBA, Wichita State U., 1967; JD, Washburn U. Law Sch., 1971. Bar: Kans. 1971. Asst. atty. gen. Kans. Atty. Gen.'s Office, Topeka, 1971-73; asst. dist. atty. Wichita, Kans., 1973-77; adminstrv. asst. U.S. Congressman Dan Glickman, Washington, D.C., 1977; asst. U.S. atty. Wichita, 1977-96; U.S. atty. Kans., 1996—2001; sr. fellow, criminal justice prog School of Community Affairs, Wichita State Univ, Kans., 2001—. Office: Wichita State Univ School of Community Affairs 302 Lindquist Hall, Box 135 Wichita KS 67260 E-mail: jackie.williams@wichita.edu.

WILLIAMS, JAMES CASE, metallurgist; b. Salina, Kans., Dec. 7, 1938; s. Luther Owen and Clarice (Case) W.; m. Joanne Rufener, Sept. 17, 1960; children: Teresa A., Patrick J. BS in Metall. Engring, U. Wash., Seattle, 1962, MS, 1964, PhD, 1968. Rsch. engr., lead engr. Boeing Co., Seattle, 1961-67; tech. staff N.Am. Rockwell Corp., Thousand Oaks, Calif., 1968-74; mgr. interdivisional tech. program N.Am. Aerospace group, 1974, program devel. mgr. structural materials, 1974-75; prof. metallurgy, co-dir. Ctr. for Joining of Materials, Carnegie-Mellon U., Pitts., 1975-81; pres. Mellon Inst., Pitts., 1981-83; dean Carnegie Inst. Tech., Carnegie-Mellon U., Pitts., 1983-88; gen. mgr. materials dept. GE Aircraft Engines, 1988-99; prof., Honda chair Ohio State U., Columbus, 1999—, dean engring., 2001—04. Bd. dirs. com. on engring. and tech. systems NRC, 1996-2001; chmn. Nat. Materials Adv. Bd., 1988-95, materials and structures com. NASA Aero. Adv. Com. 1992-97; mem. NASA Propulsion Rsch. and Tech. Com., 1997-99; mem. Materials Sci. and Engring. Study, 1986-88; bd. govs. Inst. for Mechs. and Materials, U. Calif., San Diego, 1989-95; trustee Min. Math. Sci. and Engring., Cin., 1988-99; mem. sci. adv. bd. USAF, 1996-2001; mem. materials rsch. com. Def. Advanced Rsch. Projects Agy., 1981-2000; adv. com. Divsn. Engring. and Phys. Sci., NRC, 2001-04, chair anotechnology Assessment com., 2005-06. Co-author: Titanium, 2003, 2d edit., 2007; co-editor: Scientific and Technological Aspects of Titanium and Titanium Alloys, 1976; contbr. numerous articles to tech. jours. Trustee Oreg. Grad. Inst. Sci. and Tech., 1988-94; cons. Cubmaster Boy Scouts Am., 1976-77. Recipient Ladd award Carnegie Inst. Tech.; Adams award Am. Welding Soc.; Boeing doctoral fellow. Fellow: TMS-AIME, Am. Soc. Metals (Disting. lectr. on materials and soc. 1997, Campbell lectr. 1999, Gold medal 1992); mem.: AIME (Leadership award 1993, App to Pract award 2002), NAE, ASM, Internat. Ti Assn. (Achievement award 2003), Alpha Sigma Mu. Republican. Episcopalian. Home: 7711 Charlotte Hull Ct New Albany OH 43054-9680 Office: Ohio State U Dept Materials Soc and Engring 143 Fontana Labs 116 W 19th Ave Columbus OH 43210 Office Phone: 614-292-7251. Business E-Mail: williams.1726@osu.edu.

WILLIAMS, JIM, newscaster; b. 1957; 1 child, Christina. BA in Media Mgmt., Columbia Coll. Writer, prodr. and reporter WGN-TV, Chgo., 1977—92; press sec. Mayor Richard M. Daley, Chgo., 1992—97; corr. ABC News, Chgo., 1997—2001; reporter WBBM-TV, Chgo., 2001—, co-anchor weekend morning news, 2003—. Office: WBBM-TV 630 N McClurg Ct Chicago IL 60601

WILLIAMS, JOHN ANDREW, physiology researcher, educator; b. Des Moines, Aug. 3, 1941; s. Harold Southall and Marjorie (Larsen) W.; m. Christa A. Smith, Dec. 26, 1965; children: Rachel Jo, Matthew Dallas. BA, Cen. Wash. State Coll., 1963; MD, PhD, U. Wash., Seattle, 1968. Staff fellow NIH, Bethesda, Md., 1969-71; research fellow U. Cambridge, Eng., 1971-72; from asst. to prof. physiology U. Calif., San Francisco, 1973-87; prof. physiology, chair dept. physiology, prof. internal medicine U. Mich., Ann Arbor, 1987—. Mem. gen. medicine study sect. NIH, Bethesda, 1985-88, NIDDK, DDK-C study sect., 1991-95. Contbr. numerous articles to profl. jours.; editor Am. Jour. Physiology: Gastrointestinal Physiology, 1985-91; assoc. editor Jour. Clin. Investigation, 1997-01; sect. editor Ann. Rev. Physiology, 2001-05. Trustee Friends Sch. in Detroit, 1992—2000. Grantee, NIH, 1973—. Fellow Am. Assn. Advancement Sci.; mem. Am. Physiol. Soc. (Hoffman LaRoche prize 1985, mem. coun. 1996-99, pres. 2003-04), Am. Soc. Cell Biology, Am. Soc. Clin. Investigation, Am. Gastroenterology Assn., Am. Pancreatic Assn. (pres. 1985-86), Assn. Am. Physicians. Democrat. Home: 1115 Woodlawn Ave Ann Arbor MI 48104-3956 Office: Dept Molecular & Intergrative Physiology Univ of Mich Med Sch Ann Arbor MI 48109 Business E-Mail: jawillms@umich.edu.

WILLIAMS, LEO V., III, career military officer; Enlisted USMC, 1970, advanced through grades to gen.; staff platoon comdr. The Basic Sch.; exec. officer Battery 1 3d Battalion 11th Marines 1st Marine Divsn.; HQ commandant 1st Battalion 11th Marines; comdg. officer Battery F 2d Battalion 3d Marine Divsn.; asst. ops. officer 2d Battalion 12th Marines 3d Marine Divsn.; officer assignments officer Manpower Personnel Br. HQ Marine Corps; transferred to USMCR, 1978; HQ commandant 1st Battalion 24th Regiment 4th Marine Divsn.; asst. ops. officer Amphibious Bridgade Support Staff; detachment commanding officer Wing HQ Squadron 4th Marine Aircraft Wing; site exec. officer Wing Support Squadron 472 4th Marine Aircraft Wing. Policy bd. mem. Marine Corps Res. Policy Bd., 1993-96; Ford Divsn. future vehicle plans mgr. sport utility vehicles Ford Motor Co., Detroit. Mem. Marine Corps Res. Officers Assn. (pres. Bates chpt. 1993-95). Office: CGMC Res Support Command 1500 E 95th St Kansas City MO 64197-0001

WILLIAMS, LOUIS CLAIR, JR., public relations executive; b. Huntington, Ind., Nov. 7, 1940; s. Louis Clair and Marian Eileen W.; children— Terri Lynn, L. Bradley, Lisa C.; m. Mary Clare Moster. B.A., Eastern Mich. U., 1963. Copywriter, Rochester (N.Y.) Gas and Electric Co., 1963-65, editor RG&E News, 1965-66; employee info. specialist Gen. Ry. Signal Co., Rochester, 1966-67, supr. employment and employee rels., 1967-69; supr. pub. rels. Heublein, Inc., Hartford, Conn., 1969-70; dir. corp. communications Jewel Cos., Inc., Chgo., 1970-71; account exec. Ruder & Finn of Mid-Am., Chgo., 1971-73, v.p., 1973-76, sr. v.p., 1976-78; cons. Towers, Perrin, Forster & Crosby, Los Angeles, 1978-79; exec. v.p., gen. mgr. Harshe-Rotman & Druck, Inc., Chgo., 1979, pres. midwest region, 1979-80; v.p. Hill & Knowlton, Inc., Chgo., 1980-81, sr. v.p., 1981-83; pres. Savlin Williams Assocs., Evanston, Ill., 1983-85, L.C. Williams & Assocs., Chgo., 1985—. Mem. Internat. Assn. Bus. Communicators (chmn. found., pres., chmn. Chgo. chpt. 1979-80), Inst. Pub. Rels. (chmn. rsch. com. 2005), Pub. Rels. Soc. Am., Publicity Club Chgo. Personal E-mail: LCWA@att.net.

WILLIAMS, LYNELL R., educational association administrator; Peer tutor, spanish Content Area Tutoring Prog., Idaho State U., 1997; dir. CAT Prog., Idaho State U., 2003; coord., tutoring & learning ctr. U. NC at Wilmington, 2003—; dir. SMART Learning Commons, U. Minn. Mem.: Assn. for Tutoring Profession (pres. 2006—07). Office: SMART Learning Commons Magrath Library 6034 1984 Buford Ave Saint Paul MN 55108

WILLIAMS, MARILYN, state legislator; Mem. 159th Dist. Mo. House of Reps., 1993—. Democrat.

WILLIAMS, MARSHA C., travel company executive; b. 1951; B in Econs., Wellesley Coll.; Masters, U. Chgo. Various positions Amoco Corp., 1989—93, treas., 1993—98, v.p., treas., 1997—98; chief adminstrv. officer Crate & Barrel, 1998—2002; exec. v.p., CFO Equity Office Properties, Chgo., 2002—07; sr. v.p., CFO Orbitz Worldwide, Inc., Chgo., 2007—. Office: Orbitz Worldwide Inc 500 W Madison Ave Ste 1000 Chicago IL 60661

WILLIAMS, MARY, state legislator; b. July 8, 1949; m. Al Williams. Grad., U. Wis., Stevens Point, 1974. Former tchr.; restaurant owner; mem. Wis. State Assembly, Madison, 2002—, vice chair agr. com., vice chair rural affairs com., mem. forestry com., mem. natural resources com., mem. small bus. com., mem. tourism com. Republican. Office: State Capitol Bldg Rm 18 W PO Box 8953 Madison WI 53708 Address: 542 Billings Ave Medford WI 54451

WILLIAMS, MELVIN DONALD, anthropologist, educator; b. Pitts., Feb. 3, 1933; s. Aaron and Gladys Virginia (Barnes) W.; m. Faye Wanda Strawder, June 20, 1958; children: Aaron Ellsworth, Steven Rodney, Craig Haywood. AB, U. Pitts., 1955, MA, 1969, PhD, 1973. Cert. in secondary edn., social sci. Pa. Dept. Edn., 1974. Owner, operator Wholesale Periodical Distbn. Co., Pitts., 1955-66; instr. dept. sociology and anthropology Carlow Coll., 1969-71, asst. prof., 1971-75, chmn. dept. sociology and anthropology, 1973-75; assoc. prof. anthropology U. Pitts., 1976-79, adj. prof., 1979-82; prof. anthropology Purdue U., 1979-83, U. Md., College Park, 1983-88, U. Mich., Ann Arbor, 1988—. Olie B. O'Connor prof. Am. instns. Colgate U., 1976-77 Author: On the Street Where I Lived, Community in a Black Pentecostal Church, The Human Dilemma, The Black Middle Class, An Academic Village, Race for Theory; editor: Selected Readings in Afro-American Anthropology; contbr. articles to profl. publs. Co-chmn. project area com. Urban Redevel. Authority, Pitts., 1972—; co-dir. interdisciplinary family community project Western Psychiat. Inst. and Clinic, 1973-76; bd. dirs. Cath. Social Svc. of Allegheny County, Pa., 1973-76; coll. ombudsman, 1991-93, faculty senate, 1993-96. Career Svc. award U. Mich., 2004; fellow NSF, 1967, NDEA, 1969; grantee NSF, 1969-72, Cmty. Action Pitts., 1969-71, Social Sci. Rsch. Coun., 1974-75, Lilly Endowment, 1980-83, 85-86, Career Achievement award U. Mich., 2004, Lifetime Svc. award U. Mich., 2004. Fellow Am. Anthrop. Assn. (long range planning com. 2005—); mem. African Studies Assn., AAAS, AAUP, Am. Sociol. Assn., Assn. Study Afro-Am. Life and History, Soc. for Psychol. Anthropology, Am. Authors Assn. (long-range planning commn. 2005—). Home: 520 W Washington St Ann Arbor MI 48103-4232 Office: University of Michigan Dept Anthropology 101 West Hall 108 S University Ave Ann Arbor MI 48109-1107 Office Phone: 734-764-7274. Business E-Mail: mddoublu@umich.edu.

WILLIAMS, MICHAEL JAMES, lawyer; b. July 13, 1954; s. Robert L. and Carol J. (Edenborg) W.; m. Sherry L. Schnieder, Oct. 27, 1984; children: Taylor Michael, Tory Lyn. AA, N.D. State Coll. Sci., 1974; Bachelor's, U. N.D., Grand Forks, 1976, JD, 1979. Bar: N.D. 1979, U.S. Dist. Ct. N.D., 1982, U.S. Dist. Ct. Minn. 1982, U.S. Ct. Appeals (8th cir.) 1982, Minn. 1985. Atty. Kapsner & Kapsner, Bismarck, N.D., 1979-82; ptnr. Miller Norman Kenney & Williams, Moorhead, Minn., 1983-89; atty. Hagen Law Office, Fargo, N.D., 1989-92; ptnr. Maring Williams Law Office, Fargo, 1992—. Mem. N.D. Bar Assn. (pres. 2005), N.D. Trial Lawyers Assn. (prers. 2004), Minn. Trial Lawyers Assn., Minn. Bar Assn. Avocation: sports. Office: Maring Williams Law Office PC 1220 Main Ave Ste 105 Fargo ND 58107-2103

WILLIAMS, PAUL STRATTON, executive recruiter; b. San Francisco, Oct. 9, 1959; s. Henry Stratton and Frances (Spurlock) W.; m. Laura Dawn Coleman, Sept. 15, 1984; children: Scott Coleman, Ryan Stratton. AB, Harvard Coll., 1981; JD, Yale U., 1984. Bar: Calif. 1984, Ohio 1987. Assoc. Gibson, Dunn & Crutcher, LA, 1984-87, Vorys, Sater, Seymour & Pease, Columbus, Ohio, 1987-90; gen. counsel Info. Dimensions, Inc., Dublin, Ohio, 1994-95; v.p., asst. gen. counsel Cardinal Health, Inc., 1995—99, sr. v.p., dep. gen. counsel, 2000—01, exec. v.p., chief legal off. and sec., 2001—05; mng. dir. Major, Lindsey and Africa, 2005—. Bd. dir. State Auto Fin. Corp.; bd. dirs. Bob Evans Farms Restaurants. Mem. Harvard Club Central Ohio. Democrat. Avocations: running, tennis. Office Phone: 312-456-1848. Business E-Mail: pwilliams@mlaglobal.com.

WILLIAMS, RICHARD DWAYNE, physician, educator, urologist; b. Wichita, Kans., Oct. 7, 1944; s. Errol Wayne and Roseanna Jane (Page) W.; m. Beverly Sue Ferguson, Aug. 29, 1964; 1 child, Wendy Elizabeth. BS, Abilene Christian U., 1966; MD, Kans. U., 1970. Diplomate Am. Bd. Urology, Nat. Bd. Med. Examiners. Intern, then resident in gen. surgery U. Minn., Mpls., 1970-72, resident in urology, 1972-76, asst. prof., 1976-79, U. Calif., San Francisco, 1979-84, assoc. prof., 1984; prof., chmn. dept. urology U. Iowa, Iowa City, 1984—. Chief urology VA Med. Ctr., San Francisco, 1979-84, VA Med. Ctr., Iowa City, 1984-88; mem. task force on bd. exams Am. Bd. Urology, 1981-85, guest examiner Oral exams, 1984-, trustee, 1994-2000; Rubin H. Flocks chair in urology U. Iowa, 1994, progress com. chair Soc. Internat. Urology (SIU), 2007-09; mem. nat. adv. coun. NIDDK, NIH. Author: (with others) Advances in Urologic Oncology, 1987, Genitourinary Cancer: Basic and Clinical Aspects, 1987, Adult and Pediatric Urology, 1987, General Urology, 1988, Textbook of Medicine, 1988, also others; editor: Advances in Urologic Oncology, 1987; guest editor Seminars in Urology, 1985, Problems in Urology: Prostate Cancer, 1989; bd. editors Jour. Urology, 1980-88; mem. editorial bd. Urology, Jour. Urology; also articles. Bd. dirs. Iowa chpt. Nat. Kidney Found., bd. sci. advisors 1989-92; pres. Am. Found. Urologic Diseases, 2003-05. Maj. USAR, 1971-77. Bordeau scholar Kans. U. Med. Ctr., 1968-69; NIH, VA, Am. Cancer Soc. grantee. Fellow ACS (chmn. urology sect. No. Calif. chpt. 1980-82, chmn. ann. meeting programs 1988, mem. residency rev. com. urology 1993-99, vice chair 1995, chair 1997); mem. AAAS, Iowa Med. Soc., Iowa Urologic Soc., Am. Urologic Assn. (dir. seminar on residency evaluation 1987, bd. editors alt. 1988-, rep. North Ctrl. sect., prodr. slide presentations 1988, recipient prizes 1982, 87, com. mem. 1987-, bd. dirs. 1994, pres.-elect 1997), Am. Assn. for Cancer Rsch., Am. Soc. Clin. Oncology, Am. Assn. GU Surgeons, Clin. Soc. Genitourinary Surgeons (sec.-treas. 1997-2000), Soc. Internat. D'Urologie (pres. US sect. 2003-06), Soc. Univ. Urologists (chmn. com. on residency evaluation 1986-88, councillor 1987-, pres. 1993), Soc. Surg. Oncology, Soc. Urologic Oncology (chmn. membership com. 1987-90, sec. 1990-94, pres.-elect 1995, pres. 1996), Johnson County Med. Soc., Flock's Soc., Western Urologic Forum, Alpha Omega Alpha. Republican. Office: U Iowa Dept Urology 200 Hawkins Dr Iowa City IA 52242-1009 Office Phone: 319-356-0760. Business E-Mail: richard-williams@uiowa.edu.

WILLIAMS, RICHARD K., police chief; b. Feb. 26, 1941; m. Deanna Williams; children: Darren, Tammi. BA of Sociology, Tenn. A&I State U., 1969; MBA, Am. U., 1976. Cpl., sgt. pers. and tng. divsn. Montgomery County Dept. Police, Rockville, Md., 1973-84, cpl., sgt., comty. rels. dir., 1975-80, lt. comty. rels./crime prevention comdr. comty. svcs., 1980-85, lt., dep. dist. comdr. Bethesda dist., 1985-88, capt., dist. comdr. Bethesda dist., 1988-92, cons. to chief of police, 1990, capt., dist. comdr. Germantown dist., 1991-92, maj., mgmt. svcs. bur. chief, 1992-93; chief of police Madison (Wis.) Police Dept., 1993—. Assoc. prof. criminal justice sect. Montgomery Coll., 1982. Bd. dirs. Comty. Action Coalition; mem. Leadership Greater Madison. Mem. Downtown Rotary of Madison, Alpha Phi Alpha. Office: Madison Police Dept 211 S Carroll St Madison WI 53703-3303 Home: 9604 Misty Mountain Rd Chattanooga TN 37421-2040

WILLIAMS, RICHARD LUCAS, III, electronics executive, director, lawyer; b. Evanston, Ill., Oct. 30, 1940; s. Richard Lucas Jr. and Ellen Gene (Munster) W.; m. Karen Louise Carmody, Nov. 11, 1967 AB, Princeton U., 1962; LLB, U. Va., 1965. Bar: Ill. 1965, D.C. 1968, U.S. Supreme Ct. 1968. Assoc. Winston & Strawn, Chgo., 1968-74, ptnr., 1974-79; sr. v.p., gen. counsel Gould Inc., Rolling Meadows, Ill., 1979-81, sr. v.p., adminstrn., gen. counsel, 1981-90, also bd. dir., 1985-88; ptnr. Smith Williams and Lodge, Chgo., 1990-95, Vedder, Price, Kaufman & Kammholz, Chgo., 1995—. Bd. dirs. GNB Batteries, Inc., 1984-86, ULINE Inc., Waukegan, Ill. Bd. dirs., 1990—, Internat. Tennis Hall of Fame, Newport, R.I., 1993-97; v.p. Chgo. Dist. Tennis Assn., 1968-70; vice chmn. Am. Cancer Soc., Chgo., 1984; bd. dirs., pres. Lake Shore Found. for Animals, Chgo., 1990-94. With JAGC USNR, 1965-68. Mem. ABA, Ill. Bar Assn., Chgo. Bar Assn., Execs. Club Chgo. (co-chmn. Western Europe internat. com. 1990-97, 2003—), The Lawyers Club (Chgo., 1997—), Meadow Club (Rolling Meadows, gov. 1979-90, chmn. 1985-90), Club Internat. Home: 1200 N Lake Shore Dr Chicago IL 60610-2370 Office: Vedder Price 222 N La Salle St Ste 2600 Chicago IL 60601-1104 Office Phone: 312-609-7588. Business E-Mail: rwilliams@vedderprice.com.

WILLIAMS, ROGER, academic administrator; Dir. Art Acad. Cin., 1977-94; dean Sch. Visual Arts, Savannah, Ga., 1994-96; acad. dean Ctr. for Creative Studies, Detroit, 1996—. Office: Ctr for Creative Studies 201 E Kirby St Detroit MI 48202-4048

WILLIAMS, SAM B., engineering executive; Chmn., CEO Williams Internat. Corp. Named to Nat. Aviation Hall of Fame, 1998; recipient Collier trophy, 1979, Wright Bros. Meml. trophy, 1988, Nat. medal of Technology, 1995. Mem.: NAE. Office: Williams Internat Corp PO Box 200 2280 W West Maple Rd Walled Lake MI 48390

WILLIAMS, STUART W., health facility administrator; b. June 11, 1943; BS, Allegheny Coll., 1954; MBA, U. Chgo., 1967. Adminstrv. resident Evanston (Ill.) Hosp., 1965-67; oper. svc. officer U.S. Naval Hosp., Quantico, Va., 1967-69; asst. dir. U. Mich. Hosp., 1969-74; adminstrv. dir. Children's Hosp., Columbus, Ohio, 1974-76, CEO, 1976—, Children's Hosp. Inc., Columbus, 1982—. Mem. Gov.'s Commn. on Ohio Health Care Costs. Mem. Am. Coll. Healthcare Execs., Am. Hosp. Assn., Assn. Am. Med. Colls., Nat. Assn. Childrens Hosps., Child Health Corp. Am., Ohio Hosp. Assn., Assn. Ohio Childrens Hosps.

WILLIAMS, THEODORE JOSEPH, engineering educator; b. Black Lick, Pa., Sept. 2, 1923; s. Theodore Finley and Mary Ellen (Shields) W.; m. Isabel Annette McAnulty, July 18, 1946; children: Theodore Joseph, Mary Margaret, Charles Augustus, Elizabeth Ann. BSCh.E., Pa. State U., 1949, MSCh.E., 1950, PhD, 1955; MS in Elec. Engring., Ohio State U., 1956. Research fellow Pa. State U., University Park, 1947-51; asst. prof. Air Force Inst. Tech., 1953-56; technologist Monsanto Co., 1956-57, sr. engring. supr., 1957-65; prof. engring. Purdue U., Lafayette, Ind., 1965-94, prof. emeritus, 1995—, dir. control and info. systems lab., 1965-66; dir. Purdue Lab. Applied Indsl. Control, 1966-94, dir. emeritus, 1995—; cons., 1964—. Vis. prof. Washington U., St. Louis, 1962-65; hon. prof. Inst. Automation, Academia Sinica, Shenyang, China, 1992. Author: Systems Engineering for the Process Industries, 1961, Automatic Control of Chemical and Petroleum Processes, 1961, Progress in Direct Digital Control, 1969, Interfaces with the Process Control Computer, 1971, Modeling and Control of Kraft Production Systems, 1975, Modelling, Estimation and Control of the Soaking Pit, 1983, The Use of Digital Computers in Process Control, 1983, Analysis and Design of Hierarchical Control Systems -With Special Reference to Steel Plant Operations, 1985, A Reference Model for Computer Integrated Manufacturing (CIM) -A Description from the Viewpoint of Industrial Automation, 1989, The Purdue Enterprise Reference Architecture, 1992; editor: Computer Applications in Shipping and Shipbuilding, 6 vols., 1973-79, Proceedings Advanced Control Confs., 19 vols., 1974-93, Architectures for Enterprise Integration, 1996. Served to 1st lt. USAAF, 1942-45; to capt. USAF, 1951-56. Decorated Air medal with 2 oak leaf clusters. Fellow AAAS, AIChE, Instrument Soc. Am. (hon. mem., pres. 1968-69, Albert F. Sperry gold medal 1990, Lifetime Achievement award 1995), Am. Inst. Chemists, Inst. Measurement and Control (London, Sr. Harold Hartley silver medal 1975), Indsl. Computing Soc.; mem. IEEE (sr.), Internat. Fedn. for Info. Processing (Silver Core award 1978), Soc. for Computer Simulation (hon.), Am. Chem. Soc., Am. Automatic Control Coun. (pres. 1965-67), Am. Fedn. Info. Processing Socs. (pres. 1976-78), Sigma Xi, Tau Beta Pi, Phi Kappa Phi, Phi Lambda Upsilon. Home: 208 Chippewa St West Lafayette IN 47906-2123 Office: Purdue U Potter Rsch Ctr Inst Interdisciplinary Engring Studies West Lafayette IN 47907-1293 Office Phone: 765-463-7828. Business E-Mail: tjwil@ecn.purdue.edu.

WILLIAMS, WALTER JOSEPH, lawyer; b. Detroit, Oct. 5, 1918; s. Joseph Louis and Emma Geraldine (Hewitt) W.; m. Maureen June Kay, Jan. 15, 1944; 1 child, John Bryan. Student, Bowling Green State U., 1935-36; BSBA, Ohio State U., 1940; JD, LL.B., U. Detroit, 1942. Bar: Mich. 1942. Title atty. Abstract & Title Guaranty Co., 1946-47; corp. atty. Ford Motor Co., 1947-51, Studebaker-Packard Corp., 1951-56; asst. sec., house counsel Am. Motors Corp., Am. Motors Sales Corp., Am. Motors Pan-Am. Corp., Evart Products Co., Ltd., 1956-65, corp. sec. house counsel, 1965-72; asst. corp. sec., dir. Am. Motors (Can.) Ltd.; dir. Evart Products Co., 1959-72; dir., corporate sec., house counsel Jeep Corp., Jeep Sales Corp., Jeep Internat. Corp., 1968-72; partner Gilman and Williams, Southfield, Mich., 1972-74; atty. Detroit Edison Co., 1974-75; asst. sec., sr. staff atty. Burroughs Corp. (and subsidiaries), 1975-84; pvt. practice, pres. Walter J. Williams P.C., Bloomfield Hills, Mich., 1984—. Charter commr. City of Dearborn Heights, Mich., 1960-63; dir. Detroit Met. Indsl. Devel. Corp., 1962-72, asst. sec. Capt. U.S. Army, 1942-46. Mem. ABA, Detroit Bar Assn. (chmn. corp. gen. counsel com. 1965-68), Fed. Bar Assn., State Bar Mich., Ohio State U. Alumni Assn. (pres. Detroit 1961-63), U. Detroit Law Alumni, Oakland Hills Country Club, Delta Theta Phi. Home and Office: 3644 Darcy Dr Bloomfield Hills MI 48301-2125

WILLIAMSON, KENT D., educational association administrator; B in Acctg., U. Ill., Urbana-Champaign, 1980, M in Polit. Sci.; student, U. Ill. Coll. Law, Salzburg Coll., Austria. Dir. mktg. and membership Nat. Coun. Tchrs. English, Urbana, Ill., assoc. exec. dir. bus., exec. dir., Am. Dairy Sci. Assn., 1999. Trainee Peace Corps, Tonga. Office: Nat Coun Tchrs English 1111 W Kenyon Rd Urbana IL 61801-1096 Office Phone: 217-328-3870. Office Fax: 217-328-0977. E-mail: kwilliamson@ncte.org.

WILLIAMSON, WAYNE C., internist, geriatrician; b. Hammond, Ind., 1952; BA, Northwestern U., 1974; MD, U. Cin., 1978. Cert. Am. Bd. Internal Medicine, 1984, in Geriatric Medicine 1992. Intern Rush Presbyn., St. Luke's Med. Ctr., Chgo., 1978—79, resident, internal medicine, 1979—81, physician; asst. prof. Rush Med. Coll.; physician Northwestern Meml. Hosp., 1999—; mem. faculty Steinberg Sch. Medicine, 1999—. Office: Northwestern Meml Hosp Galter Pavillion 201 E Huron 11-105 Chicago IL 60660 Office Phone: 312-642-7493.

WILLING, KATHERINE, former state legislator; m. Donald Willing. BS, Purdue U. Formerly tchr.; mem. from 39th dist. Ind. Ho. of Reps., 1992-97, mem. aged and aging, agr., edn., ways and means coms. Mem. Boone County Coun., 1988-92; bd. govs. Boone County Jr. Achievement; v.p. Boone County Leadership; bd. dirs., formerly treas. Witham Meml. Hosp. Found. Recipient Richard G. Lugar Excellence in Svc. award. Mem. Boone County Rep. Women's Club (pres.), Boone County and Carmel Clay County C. of C., Farm Bur., Zonta, Tri Kappa, Alpha Chi Omega. Home: 635 E Vermont St Indianapolis IN 46202-4205

WILLINGHAM, EDWARD BACON, JR., ecumenical minister, administrator; b. St. Louis, July 27, 1934; s. Edward and Harriet (Sharon) W.; m. Angeline Walton Pettit, June 14, 1957; children: Katie, Carol. BS in Physics, U. Richmond, 1956; postgrad., U. Rochester, 1958—59; MDiv., Colgate Rochester Div. Sch., 1960. Ordained to ministry Am. Bapt. Ch., 1960. Min. Christian edn. Delaware Ave. Bapt. Ch., Buffalo, 1960-62; dir. radio and TV Met. Detroit Coun. Chs., 1962-75; exec. dir. Christian Communication Coun. Met. Detroit Chs., 1976-98. Broadcast cons. Mich. Coun. Chs., 1965-75; guest cons. religious broadcasting Germany, 1968; coord. com. Mich. Ecumenical Forum, 1986, 90-92, chmn., 1991-92. Bd. mgrs. Broadcasting and Film Commn., Nat. Coun. Chs., 1965-73; mem. Muslim-Christian-Jewish Leadership Forum, 1987—; bd. deacons 1st Bapt. Ch. Birmingham, chmn., 1994-95. Recipient Gabriel award Cath. Broadcasting Assn., 1972, 1st Ann. Ecumenical award Am. Bapt. Chs. Mich., 1992, Race Rels. award Booker T. Washington Bus. Assn. Detroit, 1983, Brotherhood award Bethal AME Ch., Detroit, 2000 Mem. Assn. Regional Religious Communicators (pres. 1969-71), World Assn. Christian Comm. (cen. com. 1973-78, chmn. N.Am. Broadcast sect. 1970-71, bus. mgr., 1972-98, Pioneer in Religious Comm. award 2004), Phi Gamma Delta, Sigma Pi Sigma. Office: 21440 Lathrup St Southfield MI 48075-4218

WILLIS, BRUCE DONALD, judge; b. Mpls., Jan. 29, 1941; s. Donald Robert and Marie Evelyn (Edwards) W.; m. Elizabeth Ann Runsvold, July 17, 1971; children: Andrew John, Ellen Elizabeth. BA in English, Yale U., 1962; LLB, Harvard U., 1965. Bar: Minn., 1965, U.S. Dist. Ct. Minn. 1965, U.S. Ct. Fed. Claims 1989, U.S. Ct. Appeals (8th cir.) 1991, U.S. Supreme Ct. 1992. Assoc. Popham, Haik, Schnobrich & Kaufman, Ltd., Mpls., 1965-71, ptnr., 1971-95; judge Minn. Ct. Appeals, 1995—. Mem. jud. adv. bd. Law and Orgnl. Econs. Ctr., U. Kans., 1997—2001; adv. bd. Minn. Inst. Legal Edn., 1986—2003. Contbr. articles to profl. jours. Del. Rep. Nat. convs., 1976, 88; vice chmn. Ind.-Rep. Party Minn., 1979-81; mem. State Ethical Practices Bd., 1990-95, sec. 1990-91, vice chmn. 1991-92, chmn., 1992-93; mem. Minn. Commn. on Jud. Selection, 1991-94; mem. Minn. Bd. Jud. Stds., 1997—2005; mem. adv. com. on rules of civil appellate procedure Minn. Supreme Ct., 1997—. Named one of 1990's Lawyers of Yr., Minn. Jour. Law and Politics, 1991, one of Minn.'s Best Trial Lawyers, Minn. Lawyer, 1991. Mem.: ABA, Minn. Bar Assn. (professionalism com. 1998—). Mem. United Ch. of Christ. Home: 2940 Walnut Grove Ln N Plymouth MN 55447-1567 Office: Minn Jud Ctr 25 Rev Dr Martin Luther King Jr Blvd Saint Paul MN 55155-1500 E-mail: bruce.willis@courts.state.mn.us.

WILLIS, DONTRELLE (WAYNE), professional baseball player; b. Oakland, Calif., Jan. 12, 1982; m. Natalee Vitagliano, Dec. 8, 2006; 1 child, Adrianna Rose. Pitcher Fla. Marlins, Miami, 2003—07, Detroit Tigers, 2008—. Mem. Team USA, World Baseball Classic, 2006. Named Nat. League Rookie of Yr., 2003; named to, Nat. League All-Star Team, 2003, 2005; recipient Warren Spahn award, 2005. Achievements include being a member of the World Series Champion Florida Marlins, 2003. Mailing: c/o Detroit Tigers Comerica Pk 2100 Woodward Ave Detroit MI 48201*

WILLIS, DOUGLAS ALAN, lawyer; b. Taylorville, Ill., Feb. 22, 1963; s. Roy Willis and Sharon (Peel) Boaden. BA, Ill. Coll., 1985; JD, DePaul Coll. of Law, 1988. Bar: Ill. 1988, U.S. Dist. Ct. (no. dist.) Ill. 1988, U.S. Ct. Appeals (7th cir.) 1992, U.S. Supreme Ct. 2001. Intern BBC, Dallas, 1984, Ill. Dept. Registration/Edn., Springfield, 1983, Ill. State Senate Staff, Springfield, 1982, 84; rsch. asst. M.C. Bassiouni, Chgo., 1986-87; summer clk. Hon. Richard Mills, U.S. Dist. Judge, Springfield, 1987; asst. corp. sec. Profl. Svc. Industries, Inc., Lombard, Ill., 1991—, assoc. corp. counsel, 1989—2005, corp. counsel, 2006—. Intern U.S. House Minority Leader Robert Michel, Jacksonville, Ill., 1983. Named to Order of the Barrister, 1988, DePaul Exec. Moot Ct. Bd., 1988. Mem. Ill. State Bar Assn., Delta Theta Phi. Republican. Methodist. Home: 735 Blossom Ct Naperville IL 60540-1841 Office: Profl Svc Industries Inc 1901 S Meyers Rd Ste 400 Oakbrook Terrace IL 60181 Office Phone: 630-691-1490. Business E-Mail: doug.willis@psiusa.com.

WILLIS, JAMES R., lawyer; b. 1926; BS, W.Va. State Coll.; LLB, Case Western Reserve U., 1952. Bar: 1953. Ptnr. Willis Blackwell & Watson, Cleveland. Named one of Am. Top Black Lawyers, Black Enterprise Mag., 2003. Mem.: Nat. Assn. Criminal Def. Lawyers (pres. 1974). Office: Willis Blackwell Associates 305 S Belvoir Blvd Cleveland OH 44121-2348 Office Phone: 216-523-1100. Office Fax: 216-861-4161.

WILLIS, ROBERT ADDISON, dentist; b. Wichita, Kans., Apr. 27, 1949; s. Everett Clayton and Mary Ann (Rohlin) W.; m. Janet Sue Jones, Jan. 21, 1968 (div. Dec. 1986); children: Gregory, Jeffrey; m. Sherryl Ann Galloway, Apr. 26, 1991; children: Wes Misak, Wendy Misak. Student, Okaloosa Walton Jr. Coll., Niceville, Fla., 1970-71, Wichita State U., 1972-74; DDS, U. Mo., 1978. Dentist, Wellington, Kans., 1978—. Cons. Sumner County Regional Hosp., 1980—, Lakeside Lodge ursing Home, Wellington, 1980—. Bd. dirs. Kans. Babe Ruth Leagues, Inc., dist. commr., 1990—, mgr. Classic West team, 1990, 2005; website devel., webmaster Kansasbaberuthleagues.com, 1995—; bd. of elders Calvary Luth. Ch., 1989-94, treas., 2003—, mem. fin. com., 2003—. With USAF, 1968-71. Named to Kans. Babe Ruth Leagues Hall of Fame., 2005. Mem. ADA, Acad. Gen. Dentistry, So. Dist. Dental Soc. (pres. 1980), Kans. Dental Assn. (coun. on peer rev. 1988-89), Wellington Dental Soc. (treas. 1981—), Optimist CLub, Wellington Area C. of C. (com. on indsl. devel. 1992), Am. Legion, Xi Psi Psi. Republican. Avocations: golf, photography, jogging, collecting music records, woodworking. Home: 620 Circle Dr Wellington KS 67152-

3206 Office: 204 E Lincoln Ave Wellington KS 67152-3061 Home Phone: 320-326-2711. Business E-Mail: rwillis@sutv.com.

WILLMAN, VALLEE LOUIS, physician, surgery educator; b. Greenville, Ill., May 4, 1925; s. Philip L. and Marie A. (Dall) W.; m. Melba L. Carr, Feb. 2, 1952; children: Philip, Elizabeth, Susan, Stephen, Mark, Timothy, Jane, Vallee, Sarah. Student, U. Ill., 1942-43, 45-47; MD, St. Louis U., 1951. Diplomate Am. Bd. Surgery (sr. examiner 1976—), Am. Bd. Thoracic Surgery. Intern Phila. Gen. Hosp., 1951-52; intern, resident St. Louis U. Group Hosps., 1952-56; Ellen McBride fellow in surgery St. Louis U., 1956-57, sr. instr. surgery, 1957-58, asst. prof. surgery, 1958-61, assoc. prof., 1961-63, prof., 1963—, C. Rollins Hanlon prof. surgery, chmn. dept., 1969—, vice chmn. dept., 1967-69; attending physician St. Louis U. Hosp., 1969—; chief of surgery, 1969—; mem. staff Cardinal Glennon Children's Hosp., 1969—. Cons. St. Louis VA Hosp., 1969—. Mem. editorial bd. Jour. Thoracic and Cardiovascular Surgery, 1976-86, Archives of Surgery, 1977-87, Jour. Cardiovascular Surgery, 1982-87, N.Am. editor, 1987—; contbr. over 250 articles to profl. jours. With USN, 1943-45. Recipient Merit award St. Louis Med. Soc., 1973, Health Care Leadership award Hosp. Assn. Met. St. Louis, 1988. Fellow Am. Surg. Assn., Am. Assn. Thoracic Surgery, Cen. Surg. Assn. (pres., mem. ad hoc com. on coronary artery surgery 1971-72); mem. ACS (Disting. Svc. award 1987), Soc. for Vascular Surgery, Internat. Soc. for Cardiovascular Surgery (pres. N.Am. chpt. 1985-87), Phi Beta Kappa, Phi Eta Sigma, Alpha Omega Alpha. Roman Catholic. Office: St Louis U Hosp 3635 Vista Ave Saint Louis MO 63110-2539 Home Phone: 314-962-9413; Office Phone: 314-977-8751. Business E-Mail: willmavl@slu.edu.

WILLS, GARRY, historian; b. Atlanta, May 22, 1934; s. John and Mayno (Collins) Wills; m. Natalie Cavallo, May 30, 1959; children: John, Garry, Lydia. BA, St. Louis U., 1957; MA, Xavier U., Cin., 1958, Yale U., 1959, PhD, 1961; LittD (hon.), Coll. Holy Cross, 1982, Columbia Coll., 1982, Beloit Coll., 1988, Xavier U., 1993, St. Xavier U., 1993, Union Coll., 1993, Macalester Coll., 1995, Bates Coll., 1995, St. Ambrose, 1997, George Washington U., 1999, Spring Hill Coll., 2000, Siena Heights U., 2001, Gettysburg Coll., 2002, Am. U., 2003, Muhlenberg Coll., 2004, U. Conn., 2008. Fellow Ctr. Hellenic Studies, 1961—62; assoc. prof. classics Johns Hopkins U., 1962—67, adj. prof., 1968-80; Henry R. Luce prof. Am. culture and public policy Northwestern U., 1980—88, adj. prof., 1988—2005, prof. history emeritus, 2005—. Author: (book) Chesterton, 1961, Politics and Catholic Freedom, 1964, Roman Culture, 1966, Jack Ruby, 1967, Second Civil War, 1968, Nixon Agonistes, 1970, Bare Ruined Choirs, 1972, Inventing America, 1978, At Button's, 1979, Confessions of a Conservative, 1979, Explaining America, 1980, The Kennedy Imprisonment, 1982, Lead Time, 1983, Cincinnatus, 1984, Reagan's America, 1987, Under God, 1990, Lincoln at Gettysburg, 1992 (Pulitzer Prize for gen. non-fiction, 1993), Certain Trumpets: The Call of Leaders, 1994, Witches and Jesuits: Shakespeare's Macbeth, 1994, John Wayne's America, 1997, St. Augustine, 1999, A Necessary Evil, 1999, Papal Sin, 2000, Venice, Lion City, 2001, St. Augustine's Childhood, 2001, James Madison, 2002, Why Am I a Catholic, 2002, St. Augustine's Memory, 2002, Mr. Jefferson's University, 2002, St. Augustine's Sin, 2003, Negro President, 2003, St. Augustine's Conversion, 2004, The Rosary, 2005, Henry Adams and the Making of America, 2005, St. Augustine's Confessions, 2006, What Jesus Meant, 2006, What Paul Meant, 2006, Head and Heart, 2007, What the Gospels Meant, 2008. Recipient Merle Curti award, Orgn. Am. Historians, Nat. Book Critics Cir. award (2), Wilbur Cross medal, Yale U., Peabody award, NEH Presdl. medal, 1998, John Hope Franklin award, Chgo. Hist. Soc., First Freedom award, Coun. for the First Freedom, Lincoln Laureate, State of Ill., Lifetime Achievement award, English-Speaking Union. Mem.: AAAL, Am. Philos. Soc., Am. Antiquarian Soc., Am. Acad. Arts and Scis., Mass. Hist. Soc. Roman Catholic. Office: Northwestern U Dept History Evanston IL 60208 Business E-Mail: g-wills@northwestern.edu.

WILLS, ROBERT HAMILTON, retired publishing executive; b. Colfax, Ill., June 21, 1926; s. Robert Orson and Ressie Mae (Hamilton) W.; m. Sherilyn Lou Nierstheimer, Jan. 16, 1949; children: Robert L., Michael H., Kendall J. BS, MS, Northwestern U., 1950. Reporter Duluth (Minn.) Herald & News-Tribune, 1950-51; reporter Milw. Jour., 1951-59, asst. city editor, 1959-62; city editor Milw. Sentinel, 1962-75, editor, 1975-91; exec. v.p. Jour./Sentinel, Inc., Milw., 1991-92, pres., 1992-93; vice-chmn., 1993; also bd. dirs. Jour./Sentinel, Inc., Milw.; pub. Milw. Jour. Sr. v.p., bd. dirs. Jour. Communications; pres. Wis. Freedom of Info. Council, 1979-86, charter mem., 1979; Pulitzer Prize juror, 1982, 83, 90. Mem. media-law rels. com. State Bar Wis., 1969-99; vice chmn. privacy coun. Wis. Pub. Svc. Commn., 1996-97; mem. Wis. Privacy Coun., 1994-95. Recipient Leadership award Women's Ct. and Civic Conf. Greater Milw., 1987; inducted into Journalism Hall of Achievement Medill Sch. Northwestern U., 1997, Wis. Newspaper Assn. Found. Hall of Fame, 2001. Mem. Wis. Newspaper Assn. (pres. 1985-86, Disting. Svc. award 1992), Wis. AP (pres. 1975-76, Dion Henderson award Svc. 1993), Am. Soc. Newspaper Editors, Internat. Press Inst., Milw. Press Club (Media Hall Fame 1993), Soc. Profl. Journalists (prs. Milw. chpt. 1979-80, nat. pres. 1986-87), Sigma Delta Chi Found. (bd. dirs. 1993-96, Wis. Newsman of Yr. 1973, Freedom of Info. award Milw. chpt. 1988). Home: 2064 Tiger Links Dr Henderson NV 89012-6111 E-mail: wills2064@juno.com.

WILLSIE, SANDRA KAY, internist, educator; BS in Med. Tech., Pittsburg State U., Kans., 1975; DO, Kansas City U. Medicine and Bioscis., Mo., 1983. Diplomate in internal medicine, pulmonary diseases and critical care medicine Am. Bd. Internal Medicine, Am. Bd. Osteo. Internists, 2000. Rotating intern Univ. Hosp., Kansas City, Mo., 1983-84; resident in internal medicine U. Mo.-Kansas City Affiliated Hosps., 1984-87; fellow in pulmonary diseases and critical care medicine Truman Med. Ctr.-West, Kansas City, Mo., 1987-89; instr. medicine U. Mo.-Kansas City Sch. Medicine, 1984-89; med. dir. pulmonary clinic Truman Med. Ctr., 1991-2000; asst. prof. medicine U. Mo. Kansas City Sch. Medicine, 1989-94, assoc. prof. medicine, 1994-99, dep. asst. dean, 1994—97, asst. dean, 1997-2000, prof. medicine, 1999-2000, Kansas City U. Medicine and Bioscis., 2000—02, vice dean acad. affairs, adminstrn., med. affairs, 2002—, exec. v.p. acad. affairs, provost, dean, 2002—, exec. v.p. rsch. & med. affairs, dean Coll. Osteo. Medicine, 2007—. Invited bd. question author Am. Bd. Internal Medicine, 1995—, relevance reviewer for pulmonary disease bd. exam, 1996—; internal medicine subspecialty program pre-reviewer Accreditation Coun. for Grad. Med. Edn., 1997—2000; credentials com. Truman Med. Ctr., Inc., 1990—96, med. intensive care unit com., 1992—2000, intermediate care unit com., 1992—2000, exec. com. Truman Health Sys., 1998—2000, profl. standards com., 1998—2000. Contbr. articles to profl. jours. Bd. dirs. Girls to Women, 1995—2000, v.p. bd. dirs., 1996—2000. Fellow: Am. Coll. Physicians (state activities com. 1991—95, chair, state activities com. 1994, scientific presentations judge 1995—96, coun. mem. 1998—2004), Am. Coll. Osteo. Internists (program com. 2002—, rsch. com. 2003—, Rschr. of Yr. 2004); mem.: Met. Med. Soc. (chair women in medicine com. 1995—2000, pres. com. 1995—2000, bd. dirs. 1997—2000, exec. com. 1999—2000, chair women in medicine com. 2002—), Am. Osteo. Assn., Kans. City Pulmonary Roundtable (pres.), Soc. Critical Care Medicine, Am. Lung Assn. Mo. (bd. mem.), Jackson County Osteo. Assn., Mo. Assn. Osteo. Physicians and Surgeons, Am. Thoracic Soc., Am. Coll. Chest Physicians (chair, basic sci. com. 1995—98, scientific program com. 1995—2003, membership com. 1997—2001, gov. for Mo. 1997—2001, chair, scientific presentations and awards com. 1998—2000, vice chair, scientific program com. 1999—2000, chair, scientific program com. 2000—01, regent 2004—, Young Investigator award 1992). Office: Kansas City Univ Medicine and Bioscis 1750 Independence Ave Kansas City MO 64106-1453 Business E-Mail: swillsie@kcumb.edu.

WILLSON, MARY FRANCES, ecology researcher, educator; b. Madison, Wis., July 28, 1938; d. Gordon L. and Sarah (Loomans) W.; m. R.A. von Neumann, May 29, 1972 (dec.). BA with honors, Grinnell Coll., 1960; PhD, U. Wash., 1964. Asst. prof. U. Ill., Urbana, 1965-71, assoc. prof., 1971-76, prof. ecology, 1976-90; rsch. ecologist Forestry Scis. Lab., Juneau, Alaska, 1989-99; sci. dir. Great Lakes program Nature Conservancy, 1999-2000. Prin. rsch. scientist, affiliate prof. biology, Inst. Arctic Biology and Sch. Fisheries and Ocean Scis., U. Alaska, Fairbanks-Juneau. Author: Plant Reproductive Ecology, 1983, Vertebrate atural History, 1984; co-author: Mate Choice in Plants, 1983. Fellow Am. Ornithologists Union; mem. Brit. Ornithologists Union, Soc. for Study Evolution, Am. Soc. Naturalists (hon. mem.), Ecol. Soc. Am., Brit. Ecol. Soc. E-mail: mwillson@gci.net.

WILMOT, THOMAS RAY, medical entomologist, educator; b. Great Falls, Mont., Sept. 9, 1953; s. Donald D. and Jeanne M. W.; m. Gail A. Ballard, June 26, 1976; children: Lacey A., Eric T. BS in Entomology, Mont. State U., 1975; MS in Entomology, Oreg. State U., 1978; MPH, UCLA, 1984, PhD in Epidemiology, 1986. Inspector Cacade County Pesticide Program, Great Falls, Mont., 1970-75; mgr. Yakima County Mosquito Control, Wash., 1978-80; dir., entomologist Midland County Mosquito Control, Sanford, Mich., 1984—. Adj. instr. Saginaw Valley State U., University Center, Mich., 1988—; vector control cons., Midland, Mich., 1988—. Contbr. articles to profl. jours. Mem. Local Emergency Plan Com., Midland, Mich., 1990—; spkr. Dow Corning Spkrs. Bur., Midland, 1992-96. Pub. Health traineeship USPHS, 1980-84; recipient Achievement award Nat. Assn. Counties, 1994. Mem. Am. Mosquito Control Assn. (mem. editl. bd. 1989-92), Entomol. Soc. Am., Soc. for Vector Ecology (regional dir. 1990-99), Mich. Mosquito Control Assn. (pres. 1989, Disting. Svc. award 1994), Phi Kappa Phi. Avocation: coaching youth athletics. Office: Midland County Mosquito Control 2180 N Meridian Rd Sanford MI 48657-9200 E-mail: wilmotg@mindnet.com.

WILMOUTH, ROBERT K., commodities trader; b. Worcester, Mass., Nov. 9, 1928; s. Alfred F. and Aileen E. (Kearney) W.; m. Ellen M. Boyle, Sept. 10, 1955; children: Robert J., John J., James P., Thomas G., Anne Marie. BA, Holy Cross Coll., 1949; MA, U. Notre Dame, 1950, LLD, 1984. Exec. v.p., dir. 1st Nat. Bank Chgo., 1972-75; pres., chief adminstrv. officer Crocker Nat. Bank, San Francisco, 1975-77; pres., chief exec. officer Chgo. Bd. Trade, 1977-82; chmn. LaSalle at. Bank, 1982-99. Pres., chief exec. officer Nat. Futures Assn., 1982-2002, Spl. Policy Adv. Nat. Futures Assn., 2003-. Life trustee U. Notre Dame; mem. adv. coun. Kellogg Grad. Sch. Mgmt., Northwestern U. Mem. Chgo. Club, Barrington Hill Country Club. Office: Nat Futures Assn 200 W Madison St Ste 1600 Chicago IL 60606-3415

WILSON, AARON MARTIN, religious studies educator, college executive; b. Bazette, Tex., Sept. 30, 1926; s. John Albert and Myrtle (Hulsey) W.; m. Marthel Shoults, Jan. 31, 1947 (dec. Apr. 2001); children: Gloria Dallis, John Bert; m. Ola May Ogden, Sept. 27, 2002. BA, So. Bible Coll., 1963, DD (hon.), 1980; MA, Pitts. State U., 1972; PhD, Valley Christian U., 1980. Pastor various chs., 1947-58, Pentecostal Ch. of God, Houston, 1958-64, Modesto, Calif., 1985-88, nat. dir. Christian edn. Joplin, Mo., 1964-79, 88-93; pres. Evang. Christian Coll., Fresno, Calif., 1979-85; v.p. devel. Messenger Coll., Joplin, Mo., 1993—95; editor The Pentecostal Messenger, 1995—99, coordinating editor, 1999—2003; v.p. devel. Messenger Coll., 2005—. Treas. Evang. Curriculum Commn., 1988-93; prof. So. Bible Coll., Houston, 1962-64. Author: Basic Bible Truth, 1988, Studies on Stewardship, 1989, My Church Can Grow, 1996, Our Story, 2001. Republican. Home: 2815 Vermont Ave Joplin MO 64804 Office: Messenger Coll 300 E 50th St Joplin MO 64804 Office Phone: 417-624-7070 161. E-mail: awilson@messengercollege.edu.

WILSON, ANNE GAWTHROP, artist, educator; b. Detroit, Apr. 16, 1949; d. Gerald Shepard and Nancy Craighead (Gawthrop) Wilson; m. Michael Andreas Nagelbach. Student, U. Mich. Sch. of Art, 1967-69; BFA, Cranbrook Acad. Art, Bloomfield Hills, Mich., 1972; MFA, Calif. Coll. Arts and Crafts, 1976. Prof. Dept. Fiber & Materials Studies Sch. of the Art Inst., Chgo., 1979—. Panelist Nat. Endowment for Arts, Washington, 1986, Western States Arts Fedn./Nat. Endowment for Arts Regional Fellowships for Visual Artists, Santa Fe, 1995; co-curator Artemisia Gallery, Chgo., 1988; co-moderator Women's Caucus for Art, Chgo., 1992; panelist, workshop instr. Internat. Symposium '92, Toyama, Japan, 1992; panelist The Textile Mus., Washington, 1994; bd. trustees Haystack Sch., Deer Isle, Maine, 1990-95; lectr. Kansas City Art Inst., 1996, Australian Nat. U. Canberra Sch. Art, 1996, Textile Conservation Ctr./Courtauld Inst. Art, London, 1995, others; represented by Roy Boyd Gallery, Chgo., Revolution, Detroit and N.Y. One person shows include Chgo. Cultural Ctr., 1988, Halsey Gallery, Sch. Arts, Coll. Charleston, S.C., 1992, Madison (Wis.) Art Ctr., 1993-94, Roy Boyd Gallery, Chgo., 1994, 96, Ill. Wesleyan U., Sch. Art, Bloomington, 1995, Revolution, Detroit, 1998, Revolution, N.Y.C., 1998, Mus. for Textiles Contemporary Gallery, Toronto, Can., 1999, Mus. Contemporary Art, Chgo., 2000; exhibited in group shows Netherlands Textile Mus., 1989, Musee Cantonal des Beaux-Arts, Palais de Rumine, Lausanne, Switzerland, 1989, John Michael Kohler Arts Ctr., Sheboygan, Wis., 1992-93, 95, Mus. Contemporary Art, Chgo., 1996, 97, Ariz. State U. Art Mus., Tempe, 1997-98, Bowdoin Coll. Mus. Art, Brunswick, Maine, 1998, TBA Exhbn. Space, Chgo., 1999, Angel Row Gallery, Halifax, 1999-2000, Boulder (Colo.) Mus. Contemporary Art, 2000, Gallery 400 Sch. Art and Design Coll. Arch. and the Arts, U. Ill., Chgo., 2000, Asheville (N.C.) Mus. Art, 2000, Chgo. Cultural Ctr., 2000, Memphis Coll. Art, 2001, U. Calif. San Diego, La Jolla, 2001; represented in permanent collections Art Inst. Chgo., Met. Mus. Art, N.Y., Mus. of Contemporary Art, Chgo., Calif. Poly. State U., San Luis Obispo, Calif., M. H. De Young Meml. Mus., San Francisco, Art Inst. Chgo., Cranbrook Acad. Art Mus., Bloomfield Hills; contbr. articles and revs. to profl. jours. Recipient Louis Comfort Tiffany Found. award, 1989; Nat. Endowment for Arts curatorial fellow in decorative arts and mus. edn. Fine Arts Mus. San Francisco, 1978; Nat. Endowment for Arts Visual Artists Fellowship grantee, 1982, 88, Chgo. Artists Abroad grantee, 1988, 89, Ill. Arts Coun. Individual Artist grantee, 1983, 84, 87, 93, 99, Chgo. Artists Internat. Program grantee, 1996. Mem. Coll. Art Assn. (regional co-chair annual conf. 2001). Office: Sch of the Art Inst Fiber Dept 37 S Wabash Ave Chicago IL 60603-3002

WILSON, BRUCE G., lawyer; b. Iowa City, Dec. 17, 1949; BS, Iowa State U., 1972; MBA with distinction, U. Mich., 1974; JD with distinction, U. Iowa, 1977. Bar: Ill. 1977. Ptnr. Jenner & Block, Chgo. Mem. ABA, Ill. State Bar Assn.

WILSON, C. DANIEL, JR., library director; b. Middletown, Conn., Nov. 8, 1941; s. Clyde D. and Dorothy M. (Neal) W.; m. M. April Jackson, Apr. 1986; children: Christine, Cindy, Clyde, Ben. BA, Elmhurst Coll., 1967; MA, Dominican U., 1968; MPA, U. New Orleans, 1995. Trainee Chgo. Pub. Libr., 1967-68; instr. U. Ill., 1968-70; asst. dir. Perrot Meml. Libr., Greenwich, Conn., 1970-76; dir. Wilton Pub. Libr., Wilton, Conn., 1976-79; assoc. dir. Birmingham Pub. Libr., Birmingham, Ala., 1979-83; dir. Davenport (Iowa) Pub. Libr., 1983-85, New Orleans Pub. Libr., 1985-97, St. Louis County Libr., 1997—. With USMC, 1962-65. Mem. ALA, Internat. Assn. Met. Librs. (pres. 1998-2002), Mo. Libr. Assn., Am. Soc. Pub. Adminstrs., Rotary, Pi Gamma Mu. Episcopalian. Home: 511 W 4th St Hermann MO 65041 E-mail: dwilson@slcl.lib.mo.us.

WILSON, CHARLES A., JR., congressman, funeral director; b. Belmont, Ohio, Jan. 18, 1943; 4 children. BS, Ohio U., 1966; degree, Cin. Coll. Mortuary Sci. Mem. Ohio State Ho. Reps., Columbus, 1997—2004, Ohio State Senate, Columbus, Ohio, 2005—07, US Congress from 6th Ohio dist., 2007—, mem. sci. & tech. com., fin. svcs. com. Mem. banking, pensions and securities com. Ohio State Ho. Reps., mem. fin. and appropriations com., mem. agr. and devel. subcom., mem. rules and reference com.; vice chmn. Belmont (Ohio) Nat. Bank; bd. dirs. East Ohio Regional Hosp. Mem.: Ohio Funeral Dirs. Assn., Blue Dog Coalition, Bridgeport (Ohio) C. of C., St. Clairsville (Ohio) C. of C., Belmont (Ohio) Hills Country Club. Democrat. Roman Catholic. Office: US House Reps 226 Cannon House Office Bldg Washington DC 20515 also: 4137 Boardman Canfield Rd Canfield OH 44406-8087 Office Phone: 330-533-7250. Office Fax: 330-533-7136.

WILSON, CHARLES STEPHEN, cardiologist, educator; b. Geneva, Nebr., June 14, 1938; s. Robert Butler and Naoma Luella (Norgren) Wilson; m. Linda Stern Walt, Aug. 21, 1960; children: Michael Scott, Amy Lynn, Cynthia Lee. BA cum laude, U. Nebr., 1960; MD, Northwestern U., 1964. Diplomate Am. Bd. Internal Medicine subsplty. bd. cardiovascular disease, Nat. Bd. Med. Examiners. Intern Fitzsimons Gen. Hosp., Denver, 1964-65; fellow in internal medicine and cardiology Mayo Grad. Sch. Medicine, Rochester, Minn., 1968-72; practice medicine specializing in cardiology Lincoln, Nebr., 1972—; attending staff Bryan Meml. Hosp., 1972—, chmn. cardiology, 1976-79; clin. prof. medicine and cardiology U. Nebr. Med. Ctr., Omaha; med. dir. Bryan LGH Med. Ctr. Ultrafast CT Scanner, Lincoln, 2001—, Sch. Allied Health, Bryan LGH Coll. of Health Scis., 2002—. Mem. Mayor's Coun. on Emergency Med. Svcs., Lincoln, 1974-78; founder, chmn. Nebr. State Hypertension Screening Program; med. dir. Lincoln Mobile Heart Team, 1977-80, Lincoln Cardiac Rehab. Program, 1978-79; co-founder, pres. Nebr. Heart Inst., 1987; co-founder Lincoln Cardiac Transplant Program, 1987. Contbr. articles to profl. jours.; editorl. cons. Chest, 1975-76; assoc. editor Nebr. Med. Jour., 1981-88. Trustee U. Nebr. Found., 1983—, chmn. Nebr. Coordinating Commn. for Postsecondary Edn., 1984-88; mem. bd. regents U. Nebr., 1991—, chmn. 1994, 2001, 07. Served as maj. M.C., USAR, 1963-68. Gen. Motors Nat. scholar, 1956-60, Nat. Found. med. scholar, 1960-64, Mead Johnson scholar ACP, 1968-71. Fellow ACP, Am. Coll. Cardiology (bd. govs. 1990-93, pres. Nebr. affiliate 1992-93), Am. Coll. Chest Physicans, Am. Heart Assn. (dir. Nebr. affilate 1973-80, pres. 1976-77); mem. Mayo Cardiovascular Soc., Nebr. Cardiovascular Soc. (pres. 1989-90), Nebr. Coun. on Pub. Higher Edn. (steering com. 1991—), Lincoln Heart Assn. (dir. 1972-75, pres. 1974-75), AMA, Nebr. Med. Assn. Lancaster County Med. Soc., Am. Soc. Internal Medicine, Lincoln Found., U. Nebr. Chancellor's Club, Lincoln U. Club (dir. 1981-84), U. Nebr. Pres. Club, Phi Beta Kappa, Sigma Xi, Alpha Omega Alpha, Phi Delta Theta (pres. Nebr. Alpha chpt. 1959-60). Home: 7430 N Hampton Rd Lincoln NE 68506-1624 Office: Bryan LGH Ultrafast CT Scanner 1500 S 48th St Lincoln NE 68506

WILSON, CHRISTOPHER J., lawyer; b. Pensacola, Fla., May 25, 1965; BA cum laude, Thomas More Coll., 1988; JD cum laude, U. Notre Dame, 1991. Bar: Ohio 1991. Ptnr. Frost Brown Todd LLP; assoc. gen. counsel, asst. corp. sec. Cincinnati Bell, Inc. (formerly Broadwing, Inc.), Cincinnati, Ohio, 1999—2003, v.p., gen. counsel, 2003—. Mem. adv. coun. Nat. Assn. Minority and Women Owned Law Firms; mem. steering com. Gr. Cincinnati Minority Counsel Program. Mem.: Ohio State Bar Assn., Cincinnati Bar Assn. Office: Cincinnati Bell Inc 221 E Fourth St Cincinnati OH 45202 Business E-Mail: christopher.wilson@cinbell.com.

WILSON, CLEO FRANCINE, foundation administrator; b. Chgo., May 7, 1943; d. Cleo Antonio Chancey and Frances (Page) Watson; divorced; children: SuLyn Silbar. BA in English with distinction, U. Ill., 1976. Supr. Playboy Enterprises, Inc., Chgo., 1980-82; grants mgr. Playboy Found., Chgo., 1982-84, exec. dir., 1984—, v.p. pub. affairs, 2001—. Pres. Intuit: The Ctr. for Intuitive and Outsider Art, 1996—, 2000—. Pres. AIDS Found. Chgo., 1990-93; v.p. Donors Forum Chgo., 1986-88; sec. Chgo. Women in Philanthropy, 1986-87; advisor Chgo. Dept. Cultural Affairs, 1988-90. Recipient Kizzy Image award Black Woman Hall of Fame, 1984;, Friend for Life award Howard Brown Health Ctr, 1991, Handy L. Lindsey award for inclusiveness in philanthropy, 2004; honored by AIDS Found, Chgo, 1999; named one of Chgo's. Up and Coming by Dollars & Sense mag., 1985, Phenomenal Woman award An Expo for Today's Black Woman, 1997. Home: 6571 N Glenwood Ave Chicago IL 60626-5121 Office: Playboy Enterprises Inc 680 N Lake Shore Dr Fl 15 Chicago IL 60611-4455

WILSON, DONALD WALLIN, academic administrator, communications educator; b. Poona, India, Jan. 9, 1938; s. Nathaniel Carter and Hannah Myrtle Wilson; children: Carrie, Jennifer, Gregory, Andrew. BA, So. Missionary Coll., 1959; MA, Andrews U., 1961; PhD, Mich. State U., 1966. Dean applied arts and tech. Ont. (Can.) Colls., North Bay, 1968-73; acad. dean Olivet Coll., 1973-76; pres. Castleton State Coll., 1976-79, Southampton Coll., 1979-83, prof. communications and history, 1973-83; pres., prof. Pittsburg State U. (Kans.), 1983-95; pres. Kilang Nusantara Pacific, 1995—; exec. v.p. Shepherd of the Hills Entertainment Group, Branson, Mo., 1997—. Author: The Untapped Source of Power in the Church, 1961, Long Range Planning, 1979, The Long Road From Turmoil to Self Sufficiency, 1989, The Next Twenty-Five Years: Indonesias Journey Into The Future, 1992, The Indispensable Man: Sudomo, 1992. Mem. Kans. Adv. Coun. of C.C.'s; bd. dirs. Internat. U. Thailand; pres. Internat. Univ. Found. Named Alumnus of Achievement Andrews U., 1981; recipient Outstanding Alumni award Mich. State U., 1984. Mem. Speech Communication Assn., Assn. Asian Studies, Internat. Univ. Found. (pres.), Rotary. Methodist. Office: Kilang Nusantara Pacific Office of Pres Frontenac KS 66763 Address: 503 Ohio St Pittsburg KS 66762-6429 E-mail: wdonaldwilson@aol.com.

WILSON, DOUGLAS, genetics company executive; COO 21st Century Genetics Cooperative, 1994—. Office: 21st Century Genetics Coop 100 Mbc Dr Shawano WI 54166-6095

WILSON, EARLE LAWRENCE, church administrator; b. Rensselaer, NY, Dec. 8, 1934; s. Lawrence Wilbur Wilson and Wilhelaminia Knapp; m. Sylvia M. Beck; children: Deborah, Stephen, Colleen. B in Theology, United Wesleyan Coll., 1956, BS, 1961; M of Divinity, Evang. Sch. of Theology, 1965; M of Theology, Princeton Theol. Sem., 1967; D of Divinity, Houghton Coll., 1974. Sr. pastor Wesleyan Church, Gloversville, N.Y., 1956-61, gen. supt. Indpls., 1984—; sr. pastor First Wesleyan Church, Bethlehem, Pa., 1961-72; pres. United Wesleyan Coll., Allentown, Pa., 1972-84. Author: When You Get Where You're Going, 1966, Within a Hair's Breadth, 1989. Mem, chaplain Rotary. Republican. Home: 11697 Pompano Dr Indianapolis IN 46236-8819 Office: Wesleyan Ch PO Box 50434 Indianapolis IN 46250-0434

WILSON, EDWARD NATHAN, mathematician, educator; b. Warsaw, NY, Dec. 2, 1941; s. Hugh Monroe and Margaret Jane (Northrup) W.; m. Mary Katherine Schooling, Aug. 19, 1976; children: Nathan Edward, Emily Katherine. BA, Cornell U., 1963; MS, Stanford U., 1965; PhD, Washington U., St. Louis, 1971. Instr. Ft. Valley (Ga.) State Coll., 1965-67, Washington U., St. Louis, 1968-69, U. Calif., Irvine, 1970-71, Brandeis U., Waltham, Mass., 1971-73; asst. prof. Washington U., St. Louis, 1973-77, assoc. prof., 1977-87, dean grad. sch., 1983-93, dean univ. coll., 1986-88, prof., 1987—, chair dept. math., 1995-99. Mem. Grad. Record Exams. Bd., Princeton, N.J., 1986-90; sec.-treas. Assn. Grad. Schs. Contbr. articles to profl. jours. Mem. Brentwood Sch. Bd., Mo., 1984. Woodrow Wilson fellow, 1963; NSF fellow, 1963-65; NDEA fellow, 1967-70. Mem. Am. Math. Soc., Math. Assn. of Am. Democrat. Office: Washington U Campus Box 1146 1 Brookings Dr Saint Louis MO 63130-4899 Office Phone: 314-935-6729. Business E-Mail: enwilson@math.wustl.edu.

WILSON, EUGENE ROLLAND, retired foundation executive; b. Findlay, Ohio, Jan. 14, 1938; s. Clair and Ethel Bernice (Cryer) W.; m. Mary Ann Dalton; children: Jeff, Andy. BA, Bowling Green State U., 1960; MS, Syracuse U., 1961. Dir. devel., asst. to pres. Bowling Green (Ohio) State U., 1966-70; mgr. radio-TV advt. Columbia Gas of Ohio, Inc., Columbus, 1964-66; assoc. dir. devel. Calif. Inst. Tech., Pasadena, 1971-77, v.p. for inst. rels., 1979-80; assoc. dir. ARCO Found., LA, 1977-79, exec. dir., 1980-83, pres., 1984-94; pres. youth devel. Ewing Marion Kauffman Found., Kansas City, Mo., 1995-2000, sr. v.p., 2000—03; ret., 2003; sr. fellow Ctr. for Philanthropy and Pub. Policy, U. So. Calif.; sr. fellow Midwest Ctr. for Nonprofit Leadership, U. Mo., Kansas City. Chmn. contbns. coun. Conf. Bd.; sr. advisor Coun. of Founds. Founding trustee Arcadia (Calif.) Edn. Found.; elder trustee Presbyn. Ch. Named Outstanding Young Man Bowling Green Jaycees, 1967; recipient hon. service award Hugo Reid Sch. PTA, 1977, Corp. Social Responsibility award Mex.-Am. Legal Def. and Edn. Fund, 1989, Nat. Leadership award in edn. Inst. for Ednl. Leadership, 1992. Mem. Bowling Green State U. Alumni Assn. (pres. 1965), Gnome and Athenaeum Clubs of Caltech, Omicron Delta Kappa. Home: 14117 W 56th Ct Shawnee KS 66216-4696

WILSON, FRANKLIN D., sociology educator; b. Birmingham, Ala., Sept. 3, 1942; s. Ernest and Ollie Lee (Carter) W.; m. Marion F. Brown; children: Rachel, Chareese BA, Miles Coll., 1964; postgrad., Atlanta U., 1964-65; MA, Wash. State U., 1971, PhD, 1973. Instr. Grambling U., La., 1965-66; William H. Sewell-Bascom prof. sociology U. Wis.-Madison, 1973—, chmn. dept. Afro-Am. studies, 1984-87, chmn. dept. sociology, 1988-91, dir. Ctr. for Demography and Ecology, 1994-99. Author: Residential Consumption, Economic Opportunities and Race, 1979; deputy editor Demography, 1995-98; co-editor Am. Sociol. Rev. Bd. of Census adv. com. Profl. Assns., 1993-99. Served with U.S. Army, 1966-69; Vietnam Decorated Purple Heart, Silver Star, Vietnam medal of Valor; Census fellow Am. Statis. Assn., NSF, 1991-92, Population Coun. fellow, 1971-72. Mem. Population Assn. Am., Sociol. Rsch. Assn., Assn. Black Sociologists, Am. Sociol. Assn. (sec. 2004—). Unitarian Universalist. Avocations: swimming, reading. Office: U Wis Ctr for Demography and Ecology Social Sci Bldg Madison WI 53713 Home Phone: 608-271-8486. Business E-Mail: wilson@ssc.wisc.edu.

WILSON, FRED M., II, ophthalmologist, educator; b. Indpls., Dec. 10, 1940; s. Fred Madison and Elizabeth (Fredrick) W.; m. Karen Joy Lyman, Sept. 10, 1959 (div. June 1962); 1 child, Teresa Wilson Kulick; m. Claytonia Leigh Pemberton, Aug. 28, 1964; children: Yvonne Wilson Hacker, Jennifer Wilson DeLong, Benjamin James. AB in Med. Scis., Ind. U., 1962, MD, 1965. Diplomate Am. Bd. Ophthalmology. Intern Sacred Heart Hosp., Spokane, Wash., 1965-66; resident in ophthalmology Ind. U., Indpls., 1968-71, fellow in ophthalmology, 1971-72, F.I. Proctor Found., San Francisco, 1972-73; from asst. prof. to assoc. prof. ophthalmology Ind. U., Indpls., 1972-76, prof. ophthalmology, 1981—2005, prof. emeritus, 2005—. Med. dir. Ind. Lions Eye Bank, Inc., Indpls., 1973-99; cons. surgeon Ind. U., Indpls., 1973-2005. Contbr. articles to profl. jours., chapters to books. Lt. comdr. USNR, 1966-68, PTO. Mem. Am. Acad. Ophthalmology (assoc. sec. 1988-93, Sr. Teaching award 1989), Assn. Proctor Fellows, Soc. Heed Fellows, Am. Ophthalmol. Soc., Am. Bd. Ophthalmology (bd. dirs. 1993-2000), Ill. Soc. Ophthalmology (hon.), Mont. Acad. Ophthalmology (hon.), Pacific-Coast Ophthalmol. Soc. (hon.). Republican. Avocations: photography, guitar, history, language, natural history. Home: 12262 Crestwood Dr Carmel IN 46033-4323

WILSON, GARY LEE, airline company executive; b. Alliance, Ohio, Jan. 16, 1940; s. Elvin John and Fern Helen (Donaldson) W.; children: Derek, Christopher. BA, Duke U., 1962; MBA, U. Pa., 1963. V.p. fin., dir. Trans-Philippines Investment Co., Manila, 1964-70; exec. v.p., dir. Checchi & Co., Washington, 1971-73; exec. v.p. Marriott Corp., Washington, 1973-85; exec. v.p., chief exec. officer The Walt Disney Co., Burbank, Calif., 1985—89; co-chmn. bd. Northwest Airlines, Inc., St. Paul, 1991—97, chmn. bd., 1997—2007. Bd. of govs. Internat. Air Transport Assn.; bd. dirs. Walt Disney Co., Burbank, Calif., 1985—, Yahoo! Inc., 2001—, CB Richard Ellis, Inc. Mem. NCAA Leadership Advisory Board; bd. trustees Duke U., Keck Sch. of Medicine, U. So. Calif.

WILSON, GEORGE MACKLIN, history educator, cultural studies center administrator; b. Columbus, Ohio, Apr. 27, 1937; m. Joyce DeCoster Klain, June 11, 1960; children: George David, Elizabeth Adeline. AB in Politics and Russian Studies, Princeton U., 1958; AM in East Asian Regional Studies, Harvard U., 1960, PhD in History and Far Ea. Langs., 1965. From instr. to asst. prof. history U. Ill., Urbana-Champaign, 1964-67; assoc. prof. history Ind. U., Bloomington, 1967-76, assoc. prof. East Asian langs. and cultures, 1975-76, prof., 1976—, dir. East Asian studies program, 1970-71, 72-73, assoc. dean rsch. and advanced studies, assoc. dean internat. programs, 1972-75, dean internat. programs office of pres., 1975-78, dir. grad. studies dept. history, 1980-83, acting chair dept. history, 1983-84, summer 1981, summer 1982, dir. East Asian studies ctr., 1987—, dir. Title VI nat. resource ctr. East Asian studies, 1991-2000. Vis. lectr. Japanese history U. Mich., Ann Arbor, 1963-64, summer 1964; vist. asst. prof. history summer sch. arts and scis. Harvard U., 1966, assoc. prof. history summer sch., 1975, rsch. assoc. East Asian rsch. ctr., 1966, 75, 78-79; rsch. assoc. faculty letters Kyoto U., 1971-72, vis. prof. faculty edn., 1985; mem., chair various coms. Ind. U., mem. bd. advisors East Asian summer lang. inst., 1985—, chair Japan forum, 1990—; cons. internat. divsn. Ford Found., 1974-77, cons. history Midwest univs. consortium internat. activities, 1979-80; mem. rev. panel divsn. pub. programs NEH, 1978-80; mem. adv. screening com. Japan Coun. Internat. Exch. Scholars, 1978-81, chair, 1980-81; mem. adv. panel Annenberg Sch. Comm. and Corp. Pub. Broadcasting, 1982-84; cons. East Asian history Am. Hist. Rev., 1985-91; mem. Gov. Robert Orr's Higher Edn. Del. to Ind.'s Sister State, Zhejiang Province, China, 1988; chair I.U. Japan Forum, 1988-94; bd. dirs. Ind. Consortium Internat. Programs, 1972-78; Ind. U. mem. bd. dirs. Interuniversity Ctr. Japanese Lang. Studies in Yokohama, 1988—; presenter in field. Author: Radical Nationalist in Japan: Kita Ikki, 1883-1937, 1969, Japanese edit., 1971, Patriots and Redeemers in Japan: Motives in the Meiji Restoration, 1992; editor, contbg. author: Crisis Politics in Prewar Japan: Institutional and Ideological Problems of the 1930s, 1970; Editl. advisor for Japanese and Korean history Encyclopaedia Britannica, 1969-99; book manuscript reader U. Hawaii Press, Ind. U. Press, Princeton U. Press; article manuscript evaluator Am. Hist. Rev., Comparative Studies Soc. and History, Jour. Asian History, Jour. Asian Studies; contbr. articles and book revs. to profl. jours. Grantee U. Ill., 1965, Harvard U., 1966, 75, Ind. U., 1967, 68, 72, Am. Philos. Soc., 1968, Am. Coun. Learned Socs., 1971; Grad. Sch. Arts and Scis. fellow Harvard U., 1959-60, Fgn. Area Tng. fellow Ford Found., 1960-63, Fulbright-Hays Sr. fellow, 1971-72, Profl. fellow Japan Found., 1985. Mem. Am. Hist. Assn. (convener 1984 and 1988 ann. meetings, chair conf. Asian history 1989—), Midwest Conf. Asian Affairs (mem. nominating com. 1990-91), Midwest Univs. Consortium Internat. Activities, Inc. (liaison officer for Ind. U. 1973-78, bd. dirs. 1974-78, sec. corp. 1974-78), Assn. Asian Studies (mem. program com., Japan rep. 1985 ann. meeting), Japan-Am. Soc. Ind., Inc. (founding, mem. steering com. 1987-88, bd. dirs. 1988—), Hudson Inst. (pub.). Office: Indiana University East Asian Studies Ctr Memorial Hall W Rm 207 Bloomington IN 47405

WILSON, H. DAVID, dean; b. West Frankfort, Ill., Sept. 13, 1939; m. Jeannette Wilson; children: Jennifer, Jacqueline, Mary Jeanne. AB in Zoology, Wabash Coll., 1961; MD, St. Louis Sch. Medicine, 1966. Diplomate Nat. Bd. Med. Examiners, Am. Bd. Pediatrics. Intern pediatrics Cardinal Glennon Meml. Hosp. for Children, St. Louis U., 1966—67; resident dept. pediatrics U. Ky. Med. Ctr., Lexington, 1967—68, chief resident, 1968—69; NIH rsch. fellow U. Tex. Health Scis. Ctr., Dallas, 1971—73; fellowship Am. Coun. on Edn., 1988—89; dir. admissions Coll. of Medicine, U. Ky., 1986—88; assoc. dean for acad. affairs, prof. Coll. Medicine, U. Ky., 1989—95; dean, prof. U. N.D. Sch. of Medicine, Grand Forks, 1995—, v.p. for health affairs, 2001—. Author: (TV series) For Kids Sake, 1987-88; dir. pediatric infectious diseases U. Ky. Med. Ctr., Lexington, 1973-95, dir. cystic fibrosis care and tchg. ctr., 1975-80, med. dir., clin. virology lab., 1982-95; staff United Hosp., Grand Forks, 1995—; elected univ. senate U. Ky., 1993-96, bd. trustees Gluck Equine Rsch. Found., 1991-95, rules and elections univ. senate standing com., 1991-92, steering com. for U.K. self-study, 1990-95, co-chmn. steering com., 1990-95, chmn. review and search com. for chmn. dept. obstetrics and gynecology, 1990, chmn. curriculum com. Coll. of Medicine, 1989-95; elected acad. coun. of med. ctr. U. Ky. Med. Ctr., 1989-92; lectr. in field. Contbr. numerous articles to profl. jours. Fellow Pediatric Infectious Dieseases Soc.; mem. AMA (past mem. Coun. on Med. Edn.), Am. Soc. of Microbiology, Am. Thoracic Soc., Am. Acad. Pediatrics, Pan Am. Group for Rapid Viral Diagnosis. Home: 10 Shadyridge Estates Grand Forks ND 58201 Office: U ND Sch Medicine & Health Scis 501 North Columbia Rd Grand Forks ND 58202-9037 E-mail: hdwilson@medicine.nodak.edu.

WILSON, JACK, aeronautical engineer; b. Sheffield, Yorkshire, Jan. 5, 1933; arrived in US, 1956, naturalized, 1980; s. George and Nellie (Place) W.; m. Marjorie Reynolds, June 3, 1961 (div. Jan. 1991); children: Tanya Ruth, Cara; m. Carol Blixen, Jan. 3, 1997. BS in Aero. Engring., with 2d class hon., Imperial Coll., London, 1954; MS in Aero. Engring., Cornell U., Ithaca, NY, 1958, PhD in Aero. Engring., 1962. Cert. power pilot FAA. Sr. scientific officer Royal Aircraft Establishment, Farnborough, England, 1962-63; prin. rsch. sci. Avco-Everett Rsch. Lab., Everett, Mass., 1963-72; vis. prof. Inst. Mecanique des Fluides, Marseille, France, 1972-73; sr. scientist U. Rochester, NY, 1973-80; sr. rsch. assoc. Sohio/BP Am., Cleve., 1980-90; sr. engring. specialist Sverdrup Tech. Inc., Cleve., 1990-93, NYMA, Brook Park, 1994-98, DYNACS Engring. Co., Inc., Brook Park, 1998-2001, QSS Group Inc., Fairview Park, Ohio, 2001—06, ASRC Aerospace Corp., Fairview Park, Ohio, 2006—. Author: (chpt.) "Gas Lasers" of Applied Optics in Engineering VI, 1980, "Laser Sources" of Techniques in Chemistry XVII, 1982; contbr. articles to profl. jours. Glider pilot, instr. Thunderbirds Gliding Club, Wadsworth, Ohio, 2007—. With U. London Air Squadron, 1952—54, pilot Royal Air Force Vol. Reserve, 1950—54. Co-recipient Manly award, Soc. Automotive Engrs., 1995; recipient Soaring Gold Badge award, Fedn. Aero. Internat., Paris, 1998. Fellow AIAA (assoc.; tech. com. 1991-92). Achievements include first to demonstrate gas-dynamic laser, measurement of air ionization rate at high speeds, wave rotor performance, and unsteady ejector thrust augmentation; patents in application of high speed flow to gas laser media, devel. of antimony dopant sources. Home: 13610 Shaker Blvd Apt 202 Cleveland OH 44120-1564 Office: ASRC Aerospace Corp 21000 Brookpark Rd Cleveland OH 44135-3127 Office Phone: 216-977-8573. Business E-Mail: jack.wilson-1@nasa.gov.

WILSON, JAMES RODNEY, air equipment company executive; b. Kalamazoo, Mich., Oct. 5, 1937; s. Orton James and F. Magdalene (Critchelow) Wilson. BA in Psychology, Kalamazoo Coll., 1960. Musician, Kalamazoo, 1955-60; music tchr., 1958-60; sales rep. Wilson Air Equipment Co., Kalamazoo, 1962-70, v.p. mktg., 1970-91, pres., 1991-2000, chmn., 2001—. Cons. in field. Vol. probation officer Kalamazoo County Juvenile Ct., Kalamazoo, 1971—; vol. Big Bros. Mich. Dept. Social Svcs., Kalamazoo, 1987—; co-founder Rep. Presdl. Task Force, Washington, 1981—, life mem., 1990—; pres. bd. dirs. Kalamazoo Pub. Edn. Found., 2002—, Kalamazoo County Justees House, Dept. Corrections. Capt. US Army, 1960—68. Recipient Presdl. citation, Vols. Juvenile and Criminal Justice, 1984, cert. of Merit, Mich. Dept. Social Svcs., 1988, Points of Light award, US Pres. Bush, 1992, Disting. Svc. award, Kalamazoo Coll., 1989. Mem.: Kalamazoo Coll. Alumni Assn. (pres. 1984—86), Cathedral Canyon Country Club (pres., bd. dirs. Palm Springs, Calif. 1994—). Republican. Roman Catholic. Avocations: boating, swimming, skiing, exotic auto collecting. Office: Wilson Air Equipment Co PO Box 2620 Kalamazoo MI 49003-2620

WILSON, KAREN LEE, museum staff member, researcher; b. Somerville, NJ, Apr. 2, 1949; d. Jon Milton and Laura Virginia (Van Dyke) W.; m. Paul Ernest Walker, 1980; 1 child, Jeremy Nathaniel. AB, Harvard U., 1971; MA, NYU, 1973, PhD, 1985. Rsch. assoc., dir. excavation at Mendes, Egypt Inst. Fine Arts, NYU, 1979-81; coord. exhbn. The Jewish Mus., NYC, 1981-82, adminstrv. cataloguer, 1982-83, coord. curatorial affairs, 1984-86; curator Oriental Inst. Mus. U. Chgo., 1988-96, mus. dir., 1996—2003, rsch. assoc., 1988—; coord. Kish Project Field Mus. Natural History, Chgo., 2004—. Rsch. asso. Oriental Inst. U. Chgo. Author, editor: Mendes, 1982; contbr. articles to profl. jours. Mem.: Coll. Art Assn., Am. Oriental Soc. Office Phone: 312-665-7184, 773-702-9518. Business E-Mail: k-wilson@uchicago.edu.

WILSON, KENNETH GEDDES, physics research administrator; b. Waltham, Mass., June 8, 1936; s. E. Bright and Emily Fisher (Buckingham) Wilson; m. Alison Brown, 1982. AB, Harvard U., 1956, DSc (hon.), 1981; PhD, Calif. Tech. Inst., 1961; PhD (hon.), U. Chgo., 1976. From asst. prof. to prof. physics Cornell U., Ithaca, NY, 1963—74, James A. Weeks prof. in phys. sci., 1974—88; Hazel C. Youngberg Trustees Disting prof. Ohio State U., Columbus, 1988—. Co-author: Redesigning Education, 1974. Recipient Nobel prize in physics, 1982, Dannie Heinemann prize, 1973, Boltzmann medal, 1975, Wolf prize in physics, Wolf Found., Israel, 1980, Disting. Alumni award, Calif. Inst. Tech., 1981, A.C. Eringen medal, 1984, Franklin medal, 1982, Aneesur Rahman prize, 1993. Mem.: NAS, Am. Acad. Arts and Scis., Am. Phys. Soc., Am. Philos. Soc. Business E-Mail: wilson.9@osu.edu.

WILSON, M. ROY, academic administrator, medical educator; b. Yokohama, Japan, Nov. 28, 1953; BS, Allegheny Coll., 1976; MD, Harvard Med. Sch., 1980; MS in Epidemiology, UCLA, 1990. Diplomate Nat. Bd. Medicine, Am. Bd. Ophthalmology. Intern Harlem Hosp. Ctr., NYC, 1980-81; resident in ophthalmology Mass. Eye & Ear Infirmary/Harvard Med. Sch., Boston, 1981-84, glaucoma, 1984-85; clin. fellow in ophthalmology Harvard Med. Sch., 1980-85, clin. asst. ophthalmology, 1985-86; clin. instr. dept. surgery, Divsn. Ophthalmology Howard U. Sch. Medicine, Washington, 1985-86; asst. prof. ophthalmology UCLA, 1986-91; asst. prof., chief Divsn. Ophthalmology Charles R. Drew U. of Medicine and Sci., LA, 1986-90, assoc. prof., chief Divsn. Ophthalmology, 1991-94, acad. dean, 1993-95, dean, 1995-98, prof., 1994-98, UCLA, 1994-98; dean sch. medicine Creihton U., Omaha, 1998—, interim v.p., 1999-2000, vice pres. health scis., 2001—; pres. Tex. Tech. U. Health Sci. Ctr., Lubbock, 2003—06; chancellor U. Colo at Denver Health Scis. Ctr., 2006—. Asst. in ophthalmology Mass. Eye and Ear Infirmary, 1985-86; cons. ophthalmologist, Victoria Hosp., Castries, St. Lucia, 1985-86; hosp. appointment, UCLA; chief physician Martin Luther King, Jr. Hosp., L.A., 1986—; project dir. Internat. Eye Found., Ministry of Health, 1985-86; biology lab instr., Allegheny coll., 1975; instr. in biochemistry Harvard U. Summer Sch., 1977-78; instr. Harvard Med. Sch., 1980-85, others; cons. and presenter in field; participant comns. in field. Mem. AMA, APHA, Assn. Rsch. in Vision and Ophthalmology, Chandler-Grant Glaucoma Soc., Nat. Med. Assn., Am. Acad. Ophthalmology, Inst. Medicine (elected 2003), Soc. Eye Surgeons Internat. Eye Found., Mass. Eye and Ear Infirmary Alumni Assn., So. Calif. Glaucoma Soc., West Coast Glaucoma Study Club, Assn. Univ. Profs. in Ophthalmology, L.A. Eye Soc., Calif. Med. Assn., Am. Glaucoma Soc., Soc. Epidemiol. Rsch. Office: U Colo at Denver Health Scis Ctr 35 SYS Boulder CO 80309-0035

WILSON, MARC FRASER, art museum director; b. Akron, Ohio, Sept. 12, 1941; s. Fraser Eugene and Pauline Christine (Hoff) W.; m. Elizabeth Marie Fulder, Aug. 2, 1975. BA in European History, Yale U., 1963, MA in History of Art, 1967. Translator, project cons. Nat. Palace Mus., Taipei, Taiwan, 1968-71; assoc. curator of Chinese art Nelson Gallery-Atkins Mus., Kansas City, Mo., 1971-73, curator, Oriental art, 1973—82; Menefee D. & Mary Louise Blackwell dir., CEO elson-Atkins Mus. Art, 1982—. Mem., rapporteur Indo-US Subcom. on Edn. and Culture, Washington, 1976-79; mem. adv. com. Asia Soc. Galleries, N.Y.C., 1984—, China Inst. in Am., 1985—. Mem. adv. com. Muni-Art Commn. on Urban Sculpture, Kansas City, 1984-87; com. mem. Kansas City-Xi'an, China, Sister City program, 1986—; mem. humanities coun. Johnson County Cmty. Coll., 1976-79; commr. Japan-U.S. Friendship Commn., Washington, 1986-88; panelist Japan-U.S. Cultural and Edn. Cooperation, Washington, 1986-88; mem. mayor's task force on race relations, 1996—; mem. indemnity adv. panel, 1995—; v.p. Brush Creek Ptnrs. 1995—. Recipient William Yates Medallion Civic Svc. award William Jewell Coll., 1995, Disting. Svc. award Baker U., 1997; grantee Ford Found., Japan, Hong Kong, Taiwan, 1969-71. Mem. Assn. Art Mus. Dirs. (treas., trustee 1988-90, chmn. works of art com. 1986-90), Mo. China Coun., Fed. Coun. Arts and Humanities (chmn. arts and artifacts indemnity adv. panel 1986-89, 1995-98). Avocations: farming, auto racing. Office: Nelson-Atkins Mus Art 4525 Oak St Kansas City MO 64111-1818 E-mail: mwilson@nelson-atkins.org.

WILSON, MARGARET BUSH, lawyer; b. St. Louis, Jan. 30, 1919; married; 1 child, Robert Edmund. BA cum laude, Talladega Coll., 1940; LL.B., Lincoln U., 1943. Ptnr. Wilson & Wilson, St. Louis, 1947-65; now with firm Wilson & Assocs. Asst. dir. St. Louis Lawyers for Housing, 1969-72; asst. atty. gen. Mo., 1961-62; atty. Rural Electrification Adminstrn., Dept. Agr., St. Louis, 1943-45; instr. civil procedure St. Louis U. Sch. Law, 1971; chmn. St. Louis Land Reutilization Authority, 1975-76; mem. Mo. Coun. Criminal Justice, 1972—; chmn. Intergroup Corp., 1985-87; bd. dirs. Mut. of N.Y. Mem. gen. adv. com. ACDA, 1978-81; trustee emeritus Washington U., St. Louis; chmn. bd. trustees Talladega Coll., Ala., 1988-92; nat. bd. dirs. ARC, 1975-81, United Way, 1978-84, Police Found., 1976-93; treas. NAACP Nat. Housing Corp., 1971-84, chmn. nat. bd., 1975-84; dep. dir./acting dir. St. Louis Model City Agy., 1968-69; adminstr. Mo. Commn. Svc. and Continuing Edn., 1967-68. Recipient Bishop's award Episcopal Diocese Mo., 1962; Juliette Derricotte fellow, 1939-40, Disting. Lawyer award Bar Assn. Metro St. Louis, 1997; Margaret Bush Wilson Endowed Professorship in Arts and Scis. established at Washington U., St. Louis, 2004. Mem. ABA (chmn. youth edn. for citizenship 1991-94, chmn. Nat. Law Day 1998-2000), Nat. Bar Assn., Mo. Bar Assn., Mound City Bar Assn., St. Louis Bar Assn., Alpha Kappa Alpha. Office: Wilson & Assocs 4054 Lindell Blvd Saint Louis MO 63108-3202 Home Phone: 314-531-9276; Office Phone: 314-534-4400. Office Fax: 314-534-4403.

WILSON, MARTIN D., pharmaceutical executive; Pres., COO D & K Healthcare Resources, Inc., St. Louis.

WILSON, MICHAEL E., lawyer; b. Rantoul, Ill., Oct. 28, 1951; BA cum laude, Washington U., 1973, JD, 1977. Bar: Mo. 1977. Principal Greensfelder, Hemker & Gale, P.C., St. Louis. Instr. legal writing Washington U. Sch. Law, 1979-82; mem. nat. panel constrn. industry arbitrators and co-chmn. St. Louis Constrn. Adv. Com., 1987-97. Mem. ABA, The Mo. Bar (contbr. jour.), Bar Assn. Metro. St. Louis (contbr. jour.), Order Coif. Office: Greensfelder Hemker & Gale PC 2000 Equitable Bldg 10 S Broadway Saint Louis MO 63102-1712

WILSON, NORMAN GLENN, church administrator, writer; b. Rensselaer, NY, Nov. 3, 1936; s. Lawrence Wilbur and Wilhelmena Augusta (Knapp) W.; m. Nancy Ann Deyo, Nov. 17, 1956; children: Beth, Lawrence, Jonathan. BRE in Religious Edn., United Wesleyan Coll., 1958, DD (hon.), 1986; MA in Biblical Studies, Winona Lake Sch. Theology, 1968. Pastor The Wesleyan Ch., 1958-76, Gloversville, NY, 1963-66, North Lakeport, Mich., 1966-70, Owosso, Mich., 1970-76, dir. comm. Indpls., 1992—. Program prodr., speaker The Wesleyan Hour, Indpls., 1975—; mem. gen. adminstrn. coun. The Wesleyan Ch., Indpls., 1992—; disting. lectr. Staley Found., 1986. Author: How to Have a Happy Home, 1976, Christianity in Shoe Leather, 1978, The Constitution of the Kingdom, 1989, People Just Like Us, 1994, Follow the Leader, A Daily Spiritual Journey, 1996; editor, contbr.: Journey Into Holiness, 2000; The Call to Contentment, 2002; editor The Wesleyan Advocate, 1992-2004, Wesleyan Life, 2004-. Mem. Nat. Religious Broadcasters (bd. dirs. 1984-2005, Merit award 1984). Mem. Wesleyan Ch. Avocations: painting, antique cars. Home: 304 Scarborough Way Noblesville IN 46060-3881 Business E-Mail: wilsonn@wesleyan.org.

WILSON, PAMELA AIRD, physician; b. Milw., May 13, 1947; d. Rushen Arnold and Marianna (Dickie) W.; m. Paul Quin, June 20, 1981. BS in Zoology, U. Md., 1969; MS in Physiology, U. Wis., 1971; MD, U. Md., Balt., 1976. Diplomate Am. Bd. Internal Medicine. Asst. prof. U. Wis., Madison, 1984-91, assoc. prof., 1991—. Bd. dirs. Wis. chpt. Am. Lung Assn. past pres.; exec. com. Wis. Thoracic Soc., past pres.; mem. Gov.'s Coun. on Phys. Disabilities, 1990—. Office: U Wis Hosps & Clinics 600 Highland Ave # H6380 Madison WI 53792-0001

WILSON, RICHARD CHRISTIAN, engineering firm executive; b. Bethlehem, Pa., July 17, 1921; s. Christian and Laura Barrows (Langham) W.; m. Jean M. Avis, July 16, 1949; children— Richard A., Christy. BS, Carnegie-Mellon U., 1943; MS, Lehigh U., 1947; PhD, U. Mich., 1961. Mfg. engr. Westinghouse Electric Corp., East Pittsburgh, 1943; instr. mech. engring. Carnegie-Mellon U., Pitts., 1943-44; vacuum test engr. Kellex Corp., NYC, 1944; area supr. Carbide & Carbon Chem. Co., Oak Ridge, 1945-46; apparatus engr. Westinghouse Electric Corp., Jackson, Mich., 1947-55; instr. indsl. and operation engring. U. Mich., 1955-61, asst. prof., 1961-63, assoc. prof., 1963-66, prof., 1966-85, chmn. dept., 1973-77, assoc. dean Coll. Engring., 1968-72; pres. Techware, Inc., 1985-86, ret., 1986. Dir. Cascade Data Corp., 1969-72 Contbr. articles to profl. jours. Bd. dirs. Ecumenical Assn. Internat. Understanding, 1970-87, pres., 1975-76, 86-87; dir. Washtenaw Trombones and Jazzbones, 1995—. Mem. IEEE, Inst. Mgmt. Sci., Am. Inst. Indsl. Engrs., Ops. Research Soc. Am., Sigma Xi, Beta Theta Pi, Phi Kappa Phi. Clubs: Rotary. Home: 805 Mount Pleasant Ave Ann Arbor MI 48103-4776 Office: U Mich Dept Indsl Engring Ann Arbor MI 48109

WILSON, RICHARD EARL (DICK WILSON), media personality; b. Independence, Mo., Feb. 13, 1949; s. Paul E. and Lois P. (Chitwood) W.; m. Patricia J. Anderson, May 18, 1974; children: icole, Miranda, Spencer. BA, Ctrl. Mo. State U., 1971. Announcer Sta. WDAF-AM, Kansas City, Mo., 1971-74; host All Night Live Sta. KSHB-TV, Kansas City, 1984-85, prodr., host KC Prime, 1986; morning radio host Sta. KYYS-FM, Kansas City, 1974-84, Sta. KCMO-FM, Kansas City, 1986—; TV host talk and variety show Camp Midnite USA Network, Dick Clark Prodns., LA, 1989. Host 20 Questions pilot Buena Vista TV, Disney Studios, L.A., 1989; corp. audio and video writer and host, 1992—. Bd. mem. Leukemia Soc., Kansas City, 1987, Music Arts Inst., Independence, 1989—. Named Radio Personality of the Yr., Kansas City Media Profls., 1988, 89, named to Radio Hall of Fame, 1990. Avocations: golf, computers, broadcast prodn. Office: 4935 Belinder Rd Westwood KS 66205-1937

WILSON, RICHARD F., academic administrator; b. Point Pleasant, W.Va. m. Pat Wilson; children: Adam, Rachel. B in Math., Alderson-Broaddus Coll., 1968; MA in Higher Edn., U. Mich., 1970, PhD in Higher Edn., 1978. Math. tchr. Spencerville (Ohio) H.S., 1968—69; dir. admissions Alderson Broaddus Coll., Philippi, W.Va., 1970—74; project asst. to Dr. William Haberl, spl. asst. to the exec. officers U. Mich., Ann Arbor, 1974—75, grad. student rsch. asst. Office Acad. Planning and Analysis, 1975—76, rsch. assoc. Office Acad. Planning Analysis, 1976—78; asst. dir. Office Planning and Evaluation U. Ill., Urbana-Champaign, 1978—80, adj. asst. prof. higher edn., 1981—84, asst. vice chancellor for acad. affairs, 1981—86, assoc. chancellor, 1986—94, interim dir. corp. and found. rels., 1991, adj. prof. higher edn., 1994—2004, assoc. chancellor for devel., 1994—2004; dep. dir. U. Ill. Found., 1994—96, v.p., 1996—2004; pres. Ill. Wesleyan U., 2004—. Mem. Applie Higher Edn. Adv. Group, 1992—. Office: Ill Wesleyan Univ Pres Office Holmes Hall 204 PO Box 2900 Bloomington IL 61702

WILSON, ROGER GOODWIN, lawyer; b. Evanston, Ill., Sept. 3, 1950; s. G. Turner Jr. and Lois (Shay) W.; m. Giovinella Gonthier, Mar. 7, 1975. AB, Dartmouth Coll., 1972; JD, Harvard U., 1975. Bar: Ill. 1975, US Dist. Ct. (no. dist.) Ill. 1976, US Ct. Appeals (7th cir.) 1977, US Dist. Ct. (no. dist.) Ind. 1985, US Supreme Ct. 2006. Assoc. Kirkland & Ellis, Chgo., 1975-81, ptnr., 1981-86; sr. v.p., gen. counsel, corp. sec. Blue Cross/Blue Shield, 1986—. Speaker Nat. Healthcare Inst., U. Mich., 1987-93, Am. Law Inst.-ABA Conf. on Mng. and Resolving Domestic and Internat. Bus. Disputes, N.Y.C., 1988, Washington, 1990; cert. health cons. program Purdue U., 1993-94, Inst. for Bus. Strategy Devel., Northwestern U., 1993-94, The Health Care Antitrust Forum, Chgo., 1995, Am. Health Lawyers Assn Managed Care Law Inst., 1995, Am. Health Lawyers Assn. Conf. on Tax Issues in Healthcare Orgns., 1996. Contbg. editor: Health Care Fraud and Abuse Newsletter, 1998—2002. Advisor Constl. Rights Found., Chgo., 1982-87; mem. So. Poverty Law Ctr., Montgomery, Ala., 1981—. Mem. ABA, Am. Health Lawyers Assn. (spkr. 1984, 96), Legal Assistance Found. of Chgo. (bd. dirs., pres.), Chgo. Coun. Lawyers (bd. govs. 1988-92), Coun. Chief Legal Officers (conf. bd. 1995—), Coun. Corp. Governance (conf. bd. 1998-00), Dartmouth Lawyers Assn., Chgo. Sinfonietta (bd. dirs. 1987-05), Univ. Club, Mid-Am. Club, Phi Beta Kappa. Home: 330 N Jefferson Ct Unit2004 Chicago IL 60661 Office: Blue Cross/Blue Shield 225 N Michigan Ave Ste 200 Chicago IL 60601-7601 Office Phone: 312-297-6439. Business E-Mail: roger.wilson@bcbsa.com.

WILSON, THOMAS JOSEPH, insurance company executive; m. Jill Garling; 3 children. BSBA, U. Mich., 1979; M of Mgmt., Northwestern U., 1980. Various fin. positions Amoco Corp., Chgo., 1980-86; mng. dir. mergers and acquisitions Dean Witter Reynolds, Chgo., 1986-93; v.p. strategy and analysis Sears, Roebuck and Co., Chgo., 1993-95; sr. v.p., CFO The Allstate Corp., Northbrook, Ill., 1995-98; chmn., pres. Allstate Fin., 1999—2002; pres. Allstate Protection, 2003—05; pres., COO The Allstate Corp., Northbrook, Ill., 2005—06, pres., CEO, 2007—. Bd. dirs. Rush-Presbyn.-St. Luke's Med. Ctr. and Fed. Res. Bank Chgo. Office: The Allstate Corp 2775 Sanders Rd Northbrook IL 60062-6110

WILSON, THOMAS S., professional sports team executive; m. Linda Wilson; 3 children. BBA, Wayne State U. Dir. mktg. NBA LA Lakers and NHL LA Kings, 1974—76; sales dir. NBA Detroit Pistons, 1977, exec. dir., 1979, pres., CEO, 1993—; CEO Palace Sports & Entertainment, Inc., pres., 1992—; CEO, gov. NHL Tampa Bay Lightning, 1999—, St. Pete Times Forum, Fla., 1999—. Bd. trustees William Beaumont Hosp. Named Exec. of Yr., Oakland Execs. Assn., 1994; recipient Disting. Citizen award, Boy Scouts Am., 1988, Ernst & Young Master Entrepreneur award for State of Mich., 2002, Gerald R. Sportsperson of Yr. award, Mich. Sports Hall of Fame, 2003. Office: Detroit Pistons 5 Championship Dr Auburn Hills MI 48326-1753 also: Tampa Bay Lightning St Pete Times Forum 401 Channelside Dr Tampa FL 33602

WILSON, TOM, cartoonist, greeting card company executive; b. Grant Town, W.Va., Aug. 1, 1931; s. Charles Albert and Hazel Marie W.; m. Carol; children: Tom, Ava. Grad., Art Inst. Pitts., 1955. Advt. layout man Uniontown Newspapers Inc., Uniontown, PA, 1950-53; designer Am. Greetings Corp., Cleveland, OH, 1955-56, creative dir., 1957-78, v.p. creative devel., 1978-81; pres. Those Characters from Cleve., 1981—. Former mem. faculty Cooper Sch. Art. Cartoonist: Ziggy, 1971—, syndicated in newspapers across U.S. by Universal Press Syndicate, Kansas City; collections include: Life is Just a Bunch of Ziggys, 1973, It's a Ziggy World, 1974, Ziggy Coloring Book, 1974, Never Get Too Personally Involved with Your Own Life, 1975, Promises to Myself: Ziggy's Thirty-Day Ledger of I Owe Me's, 1975, Plants are Some of My Favorite People, 1976, Ziggys of the World Unite!, 1976, Pets Are Friends You Like Who Like You Right Back, 1977, The Ziggy Treasury, 1977, This Book is for the Birds, 1978, Encore! Encore!, 1979, Ziggy's Love Notes, 1979, Ziggy's Thinking of You otebook, 1979, Ziggy's Fleeting Thoughts Notebook, 1979, A Ziggy Christmas, 1980, Ziggy's Door Openers, 1980, Ziggy Faces Life, 1981, One Thing You Can Say About Living Alone.There's Never Any Question About Who Didn't Jiggle the Handle on the John, 1981, Short People Arise, 1981, A Word to the Wide is Sufficient, 1981, Ziggy's Sunday Funnies, 1981, Ziggy & Friends, 1982, Ziggy Faces Life.Again!, 1982, Ziggy's For You With Love, 1982, Ziggy's Gift, 1982, Ziggy's Big Little Book, 1983, Ziggy and Friends, 1983, Ziggy's Funday Sunnies, 1983, Alphabet Soup Isn't Supposed to Make Sense, 1984, Ziggy Weighs In, 1984, Ziggy's Ship Comes In, 1984, Ug! The Original Hunk, 1985, Ziggy In the Rough, 1985, Ziggy's Ins and Outs, 1985, Ziggy's Ups and Downs, 1985, Ziggy In the Fast Lane, 1987, Ziggy's Follies, 1988, Ziggy's Star Performances, 1989, Ziggy's School of Hard Knocks, 1989, Ziggy On the Outside Looking In, 1990, (also illustrator) Ziggy's Christmas Book Levels 1, 2, 1991, (also illustrator) Ziggy's Play Today Guitar Method, 1991, Look Out World.Here I Come! Ziggy's Own Down-to-Earth Humor: A Look At the Environment and Ourselves, 1991, Ziggy.A Rumor in His Own Time, 1992, The Ziggy Cookbook: Great Food From Mom's Diner, 1993, A Day in the Life of Ziggy, 1993, One-Eight Hundred-Ziggy, 1994, My Life As a Cartoon: A Ziggy Collection, 1995, Ziggy's Place. Served with U.S. Army, 1953-55. Recipient Purchase award Butler Mus. Nat. Painting Competition,

Emmy award for best animated spl., 1982. Achievements include developing Soft Touch line of greeting cards. Home: 22905 Ruple Pky Cleveland OH 44142-1100 Office: Universal Press Syndicate 4520 Main St Ste 700 Kansas City MO 64111-7701

WILSON, W. DAVID, corporate financial executive; b. 1954; At, DePauw U., 1975, Thunderbird Grad. Sch. of Intl. Mgmt., 1977. V.p. and CFO PolyOne Corp., Cleve., 2000—. Office: 33587 Walker RD Avon Lake OH 44012-1145

WILSON, WILLIAM CAMPBELL MCFARLAND, gastroenterologist; b. Pitts., Pa., June 8, 1953; s. George Lincoln and Nancy Adair (Lytle) W.; m. Marlis Howland, June 25, 1977; children: Sarah, Stephen, Corrie. BS in Biology, Va. Tech, 1975; MD, Hahnemann U., 1979. Intern, residency R.I. Hosp., Providence, 1978-82; staff internist USAF Med. Ctr., Wright-Patterson AFB, Ohio, 1982-86; fellowship Hahnemann U., Phila., 1986-88; with Digestive Care, Dayton, Ohio, 1988—. Chmn. planning com. Dayton Gastroenterology Symposium, 1990—; com. patient edn. Miami Valley Hosp., Dayton, 1990—94, quality assurance com., 1992—, vice chmn. dept. medicine, 1994—96, chmn. dept. medicine, 1996—98, chief of staff-elect, 2002—04, bd. dirs., 2002—, chief of staff, 2004—06. Bd. dirs. Fairhaven Ch., Dayton, 1990—94, 2001—, Dayton Christian Schs., Inc., 1995—, physician, 1993—2003; bd. dirs. In His Name Ministries, 2000—02. Physician USAF, 1979—86. Fellow ACP; Mem. AMA, Am. Gastroenterological Assn., Am. Coll. Gastroenterology, Am. Soc. Gastrointestinal Endoscopy, Montgomory County Med. Assn., Alpha Omega Alpha. Avocations: tennis, woodworking, bicycling, photography, computers. Office: 75 Sylvania Dr Dayton OH 45440-3237 Office Phone: 937-320-5050. E-mail: wcmw@aol.com.

WILT, JEFFREY LYNN, pulmonary and critical care physician, educator; b. Fairmont, W.Va., Nov. 15, 1963; s. Paul Lynn and Linda (Amos) W. BA, U. Mich., 1986, MD, 1988. Diplomate Am. Bd. Internal Medicine, Am. Bd. Pulmonary Diseases, Am. Bd. Critical Care Medicine, Am. Bd. Med. Examiners, Am. Bd. Nutrition Support; cert. ACLS instr. Fellow sect. pulmonary and critical care medicine W.Va. U., Morgantown, 1992-95; resident in internal medicine Blodgett-St. Mary's Hosp., Grand Rapids, Mich., 1988-91, chief med. resident in internal medicine, 1990-91; asst. dir. internal medicine residency St. Mary's Hosp., Grand Rapids, 1991-92; pvt. practice, Grand Rapids, 1995—. Asst. dir. med. ICU, Blodgett Meml. Med. Ctr., co-dir. transitional residency, 1997-98, COO internal medicine residency, 1998, program dir., 1998-99; assoc. program dir. internal medicine residency Mich. State U., Grand Rapids, 1999—, asst. prof. medicine, 1999-2003, assoc. prof., 2003—. Fellow ACP (Nat. Clin. Vignette winner 1991), Am. Coll. Chest Physicians (Young Investigators award 1993); mem. AMA, Am. Thoracic Soc., Soc. Crit. Care Medicine. Republican. Avocations: bicycling, Tae Kwon Do, magic, reading, chess. Home: 4995 Sequoia Dr SE Grand Rapids MI 49512-9622 Office: 1900 Wealthy St SE Ste 150 Grand Rapids MI 49506-2969

WINCKLER, CINDY, state representative; b. DesMoines, May 27, 1950; Educator Davenport Cmty. Sch. Dist., Pleasant Valley Sch. Dist., Calamus Sch. Dist., Davis County Sch. Dist.; mem. Iowa Ho. Reps., DesMoines, 2001—, mem. econ. devel. com., mem. appropriations com., mem. edn. com., mem. labor and indsl. rels. com., mem. ways and means com. Past nat. pres. Bus. and Profl. Women USA. Democrat. Office: State Capitol East 12th and Grand Des Moines IA 50319 also: 6 Thode Ct Davenport IA 52802

WINDHORST, JOHN WILLIAM, JR., lawyer; b. Mpls., July 6, 1940; s. John William and Ardus Ruth (Bottge) W.; divorced; 1 child, Diana Elizabeth. AB, Harvard U., 1962; LLB, U. Minn., 1965. Bar: Minn. 1965, U.S. Tax Ct., U.S. Ct. Appeals (8th cir.) 1965, U.S. Dist. Ct. Minn. 1967, U.S. Supreme Ct. 1975. Law clk. to Hon. H.A. Blackmun U.S. Cir. Ct., Rochester, Minn., 1965-66; assoc. Dorsey & Whitney, Mpls., 1966-70; with office of Revisor of Statutes State of Minn., 1967, 69; ptnr. Dorsey & Whitney, 1971-96, of counsel, 1997—. Bd. dirs. St. Paul Chamber Orch., 1980-86, Harry A. Blackmun Scholarship Found., 1996—, Minn. Taxpayers Assn., 1999—. Mem. ABA (com. on state and local taxes), Minn. Bar Assn., Hennepin County Bar Assn., Harvard Club of Minn. (pres. 1977-78). Office: 50 S 6th St Ste 1500 Minneapolis MN 55402 Home: 6566 France Ave So Apt 204 Minneapolis MN 55435 Office Phone: 612-340-2645. Business E-Mail: windhorst.john@dorsey.com.

WINE, DONALD ARTHUR, lawyer; b. Oelwein, Iowa, Oct. 8, 1922; s. George A. and Gladys E. (Lisle) W.; m. Mary L. Schneider, Dec. 27, 1947; children: Mark, Marcia, James. BA, Drake U., 1946; JD, State U. Iowa, 1949. Bar: Iowa 1949, D.C. 1968. Pvt. practice in, Newport and Wine, 1949-61; U.S. atty. So. Dist. Iowa, 1961-65; of counsel Davis, Brown, Koehn, Shors & Roberts, Des Moines. Bd. dirs. Des Moines YMCA, 1963-75; bd. dirs. Salvation Army, 1969—, chmn., 1971; bd. dirs. Davenport YMCA, 1961; bd. dirs. Internat. Assn. Y's Men, 1957-59, area v.p., 1961; bd. dirs. Polk County Assn. Retarded Persons, 1991-95; mem. internat. com. YMCA's U.S. and Can., 1961-75; v.p. Iowa Council Chs.; pres. Des Moines Area Religious Coun. Found., 1992-97; chmn. bd. trustees First Bapt. Ch., 1975; trustee U. Osteo. Medicine and Health Scis., 1980-95; Organizer Young Dems., Iowa, 1946; co-chmn. Scott County Citizens for Kennedy, 1960. Served to capt., navigator USAAF, 1943-45. Decorated D.F.C. Mem. ABA (chmn. com. jud. adminstrn. jr. bar sect. 1958), Iowa Bar Assn. (pres. jr. bar sect. 1957), Polk County Bar Assn. (sec. 1973-74), Des Moines C. of C. (chmn. city-state tax com. 1978-79, chmn. legis. com. 1979-84, bd. dirs. 1981), Des Moines Club, Masons, Kiwanis (pres. Downtown club 1969), Order of Coif, Sigma Alpha Epsilon. Office: Davis Brown Koehn Shors & Roberts 2500 Financial Ctr 666 Walnut St Des Moines IA 50309-3904

WINE-BANKS, JILL SUSAN, lawyer; b. Chgo., May 5, 1943; d. Bert S. and Sylvia Dawn (Simon) Wine; m. Ian David Volner, Aug. 21, 1965; m. Michael A. Banks, Jan. 12, 1980. BS, U. Ill., Champaign, Urbana, 1964; JD, Columbia U., 1968; LLD (hon.), Hood Coll., 1975. Bar: N.Y. 1969, U.S. Ct. Appeals (2d, 4th, 5th, 6th, 7th and 9th cirs.), U.S. Supreme Ct. 1974, D.C. 1976, Ill. 1980. Asst. press. and pub. rels. dir. Assembly of Captive European Nations, NYC, 1965-66; trial atty. criminal divsn. organized crime & racketeering U.S. Dept. Justice, 1969-73; asst. spl. prosecutor Watergate Spl. Prosecutor's Office, 1973-75; lectr. law sem. in trial practice Columbia U. Sch. Law, NYC, 1975-77; assoc. Fried, Frank, Harris, Shriver & Kampelman, Washington, 1975-77; gen. counsel Dept. Army, Pentagon, Washington, 1977-79; ptnr. Jenner & Block, Chgo., 1980-84; solicitor gen. State of Ill. Office of Atty. Gen., 1984-86, dep. atty. gen., 1986-87; exec. v.p., chief oper., officer ABA, Chgo., 1987-90; atty. pvt. practice, 1990-92; v.p., dir. transaction and govt. rels. Motorola Internat. Network Ventures, 1992-97; dir. strategic alliances Motorola Cellular Infrastructure Group, 1997—99; v.p. alliance mgmt. Maytag Corp., 1999-2001; CEO Winning Workplaces, Evanston, Ill., 2001—03; chief officer Chgo. Pub. Schs. Edn. to Careers, 2003—. Mem. EEC disting. vis. program European Parliament, 1987; chmn. bd. dirs. St. Petersburg Telecom., Russia, 1994-97, Omni Capital Ptnrs., Inc., 1994-97. Trustee Roosevelt U., 2004—; mem. adv. bd. Project Lead the Way, UIC Econ. Edn. Recipient Spl. Achievement award U.S. Dept. Justice, 1972, Meritorious award, 1973, Cert. Outstanding Svc., 1975; decorated Disting. Civilian Svc. Dept. Army, 1979; named Disting. Vis. to European Econ. Cmty. Mem.: The Chgo. Network, Internat. Women's Forum, Exec. Club (bd. dirs. 1999—2001), Econ. Club. Office: Chgo Pub Schs Edn to Careers 125 S Clark St 12th Fl Chicago IL 60603 Office Phone: 773-553-2460. Personal E-mail: jwinebanks@gmail.com.

WINEKE, JOSEPH STEVEN, political organization administrator, former state legislator; b. Madison, Wis., Jan. 5, 1957; s. Edward and Jennie Lanigan Wineke; m. Debora Howe, 1980; children: Scott, Brian, Jessica. BA, U. Wis., 1980. Alderman, Verona, Wis., 1980-83; mem. Wis. State Assembly from 79th dist., 1982—92, former mem. joint fin. com.; mem. Wis. State Senate from 27th dist., 1993—98; chmn. Wis. Dem. Party, 2006—. Rsch. assoc. Pub. Expenditure Survey of Wis., Madison, 1980-83; real estate agt; lobbyist, pub. rels. coordr., Intnat. Union Operating Engr., 1999-. Office: Wis Dem Party 222 W Washington St Ste 150 Madison WI 53703 Office Phone: 608-255-5172. Office Fax: 608-255-8919.*

WINEKE, WILLIAM ROBERT, reporter, minister; b. Madison, Wis., Apr. 4, 1942; s. Edward Ervin and Jennie Mae (Lanigan) W.; m. Susan L. Detering, Dec. 9, 1964 (div. June 1975); children: Gregory, Andrew; m. Jacqueline Cone, Mar. 18, 1990. BS, U. Wis., 1965; BDiv, chgo. Theol. Sem., 1969. Reporter Wis. State Jour., Madison, 1963-65; writer United Ch. of Christ, NYC, 1966-68; pub. rels. dir. Chgo. (Ill.) Theol. Sem., Chgo., 1968-69; reporter Wis. State Jour., Madison, 1969—; chaplain Wis. Rescue Mission, Madison, 1977—. Mem. bd. rev. Wis. Health Policy Network, Madison, 1994-2003. Fellow Religions Pub. Rels. Soc., 1974; recipient Disting. Svc. award State Med. Soc. Wis., 1992, Disting. Svc. award LWV, Madison, 1994. Democrat. Home: 1024 Ridgewood Dr Stoughton WI 53589-4125 Office: Wis State Jour 1901 Fish Hatchery Rd Madison WI 53713-1248

WINEMAN, ALAN STUART, mechanical engineering and applied mechanics educator; b. Wyandotte, Mich., Nov. 17, 1937; s. Meyer Michael and Sophia Ethel (Cohen) W.; m. Carol Sue Frank, Dec. 20, 1964; children— Lara, Daniel BSE., U. Mich., 1959; PhD, Brown U., 1964. Asst. prof. mech. engring. and applied mechanics U. Mich., Ann Arbor, 1964-69, assoc. prof. mech. engring. and applied mechanics, 1969-75, prof. mech. engring. and applied mechanics, 1975—. Contbr. articles to profl. jour. NSF grantee Mem. ASME, Soc. Rheology, Am. Acad. Mechanics, Soc. Natural Philosophy, Soc. Engring. Sci. Avocations: singing; appearing in amateur musical productions. Office: U Mich Dept Mech Engring Ann Arbor MI 48109 E-mail: lardan@umich.edu.

WINER, EDWARD L., lawyer; BA, U. Minn., Phi Beta Kappa, 1965; JD cum laude, U. Minn., 1968. Bar: Minn. 1968, Minn. (US Dist. Ct.) 1969, (US Tax Ct.) 1976, diplomate: Am. Coll. Family Trial Lawyers, cert.: (Family Law Arbitrator). Positions up to shareholder Moss & Barnett, PA, Mpls., 1968—. Law sch. mentor. Co-author: Valuation Strategies in Divorce, 2nd edit., 1992; co-editor: Premarital and Marital Agreements, 1993; contbr. articles to profl. jours. Named one of Top 100 US Attys., Worth Mag., 2006, 2007, Top 10 Divorce Lawyers in US, Best Lawyers in Am., Minn. Top 25 Litigators, Minn. Lawyer, Top 100 Super Lawyers, Minn. Law and Politics, Top 40 Vote Getters, Top Appellate Lawyers, Best Lawyers in US, Town and Country Mag., Top 100 US Family Law Trial Lawyers; named to Leading Am. Attys. Fellow: Am. Acad. Matrimonial Lawyers (past pres. Minn. Chpt.); mem.: ABA (family law sect.), Cardozo Soc. (steering com., CLE com.), Hennepin County Bar Assn. (family law sect.), Minn. State Bar Assn. (family law sect.), Phi Alpha Theta, History Hon. Soc. Avocations: physical fitness, photography. Office: Moss & Barnett Professional Association 4800 Wells Fargo Ctr 90 S 7th St Minneapolis MN 55402-4129 Office Phone: 612-877-5295. E-mail: winere@moss-barnett.com.

WINER, WARREN JAMES, insurance executive; b. Wichita, Kans., June 16, 1946; s. Henry Charles and Isabel (Ginsburg) W.; m. Mary Jean Kovacs, June 23, 1968 (div. Feb. 1973); m. Jo Lynn Sondag, May 3, 1975; children: Adam, Lauren. BS in Math., Stanford U., 1968. With Gen. Am. Life Ins. Co., St. Louis, 1968-73, dir. retirement plans, 1973-76, 2d v.p., 1976-80; v.p., sr. actuary Powers, Carpenter & Hall, St. Louis, 1980-84, sr. v.p., dir. pension div., 1984-85, pres., chief operating officer, 1985-86, lobbyist, commentator, 1985—, pres., chief exec. officer, 1986—; pres. W F Corroon, 1988-93; prin. William M. Mercer, 1993-94, mng. dir., 1994-95; exec. v.p. Gen. Am. Life Ins. Co., St. Louis, 1995—. Mem. Actuarial Exam. Com., Chgo., 1973-74. Contbr. articles to profl. jours. Bd. dirs. Lucky Lane Nursery Sch. Assn., St. Louis, 1978-93, pilot divsn. United Way, 1986-87; co-pres. Conway Sch. Parent Assn., 1986-87; bd. dirs. Paraquad, 1991—, chmn., 1994-99; bd. dirs. ATD, 1992—; chair triumph divsn. Unitd Way, 1996—. Fellow Soc. Actuaries; mem. Am. Acad. Actuaries, Enrollment of Actuaries (joint bd.), Am. Life Ins. Assn. (small case task force 1979-80), Life Office Mgmt. Assn. (ICPAC com. 1975-80), St. Louis Actuaries Club. Clubs: St. Louis, Clayton (St. Louis). Jewish. Avocations: bridge, wine tasting, swimming, weightlifting, bicycling. Office: Gen Am Benefits 13045 Tesson Ferry Rd Saint Louis MO 63128-3407

WINFIELD, MICHAEL D., engineering company executive; b. 1939; BSChemE, Ohio State U.; MBA, U. Chgo. Chem. engr. UOP, Des Plaines, Ill., 1962-74, mgr. refinery projects, 1974-76, asst. dir. tech. svcs., 1976-81, dir. bus. devel., 1981-83, v.p. tech. svcs., 1983-84, v.p. process svcs., 1984-92, pres., CEO, 1992—. Office: UOP 25 E Algonquin Rd Des Plaines IL 60016-6100

WINFREY, OPRAH, television talk show host, actress, television producer; b. Kosciusko, Miss., Jan. 29, 1954; d. Vernon Winfrey and Vernita Lee. BA in Speech Comm. and Performing Arts, Tenn. State U., 1987. News reporter Sta. WVOL Radio, Nashville, 1971-72; reporter, news anchorperson Sta. WTVF-TV, Nashville, 1973-76; news anchorperson Sta. WJZ-TV, Balt., 1976—78, host morning talk show People Are Talking, 1978—83; host talk show A.M. Chgo. Sta. WLS-TV, 1984; host The Oprah Winfrey Show, Chgo., 1985—, Oprah After the Show, Chgo., 2002—; nationally syndicated, 1986—; host series of celebrity interview spls. Oprah: Behind the Scenes; owner, prodr., chmn., CEO Harpo Prodns., 1986—. Ptnr., co-founder Oxygen Media, an Internet and cable TV co., 1998—; founder, editl. dir. O, The Oprah Magazine in conjunction with Hearst Mags., 2000; launched (mag.)first internat. edit., O, The Oprah Magazine in South Africa, 2002-, Oprah, After the Show, 2002-, O at Home, 2004-, Oprah & Friends, XM Satelite Radio Holdings, Inc., 2006-; online leader, Oprah.com, launched Live Your Best Life, 2003-; started Oprah Book Club; creator (TV series) Oprah's Big Give, 2008-Actor (films) The Color Purple, 1985 (nominated Acad. award and Golden Globe award), Native Son, 1986, There Are No Children Here, 1993, Beloved, 1998 (prodr.), Charlotte's Web (voice), 2006, Bee Movie (voice), 2007, About Us: The Dignity of Children, 1997 (TV), Before Women Had Wings, 1997; prodr. (TV series) Dr. Phil, 2002—; Listen Up: The Lives of Quincy Jones, 1990; prodr., actress (TV mini-series) The Women of Brewster Place, 1989, Brewster Place, 1990; co-prodr. The Color Purple (Broadway), 2005; exec. prodr. (ABC Movie of the Week) Overexposed, 1992; host, supervising prodr. celebrity interview series Oprah: Behind the Scenes, 1992, ABC Afterscb. Spls., 1991-93; host, exec. prodr. Michael Jackson Talks.to Oprah-90 Prime-Time Minutes with the King of Pop, 1993; exec. prodr. (TV movies) Nine, 1992, Oprah Winfrey Presents: Their Eyes Were Watching God, 2005; host Oprah Winfrey's Legends Ball (also exec. prodr.), 2006, Building a Dream: The Oprah Winfrey Leadership Acad. (also exec. prodr.), 2007, The Oprah Winfrey Oscar Special, 2007; exec. prodr. (TV miniseries) Oprah Winfrey Presents: The Wedding, 1998, David and Lisa, 1998, Tuesdays with Morrie, 1999, Amy and Isabelle, 2001, Their Eyes Were Watching God, 2005, A Dreary Date with Destiny, 2007; voice (video) Our Friend, Martin, 1999; guest appearances The Fresh Prince of Bel-Air, 1992, Ellen, 1997, Home Improvement, 1999, The Hughleys, 1999, Mad TV, 2002 and several others. Established Oprah Winfrey Found., 1987—, Oprah's Angel Network, 1997—, Christmas-Kindness South Africa, 2002—, Oprah Winfrey Scholars Program, Oprah Winfrey Leadership Academy for Girls, Henley-on-Klip, South Africa, 2006, Seven Fountains Primary Sch, South Africa, 2007. Recipient Woman of Achievement award NOW, 1986, Emmy award for Best Daytime Talk Show Host, 1987, 91, 92, 94, 95, 97, Hon. Nat. Book Award for influential contbn. to reading and books, 1999, Nat. Book Found's 50th Anniversary gold medal, 1999, America's Hope award, 1990, Industry Achievement award Broadcast Promotion Mktg. Execs./Broadcast Design Assn., 1991, Image awards NAACP, 1989, 91, 92, 94, Entertainer of Yr. award NAACP, 1989, CEBA awards, 1989, 90, 91, George Foster Peabody's 1995 Individual Achievement award, 1996, Gold Medal award IRTS, 1996, Lifetime Achievement award NATAS, 1998, People's Choice award, 1997, 98, Horatio Alger award, 1993, Bob Hope Humanitarian award, 54th Ann. Primetime Emmy Awards, 2002, Marian Anderson Award, Phila., 2003, AAP Honors award, Assn. Am. Publishers, 2003, Disting. Svc. award, Nat. Assn. Broadcasters, 2004, Global Humanitarian Action award, UN Assn. USA, 2004, Nat. Freedom award, Nat. Civil Rights Mus., 2005, Nat. Mag. award, Am. Soc. Mag. Editors, 2007, Humanitarian award, Elie Wiesel Found., 2007; ranked #1 Most Powerful In Industry, Entertainment Weekly, 1998, 200 Greatest Pop Culture Icons, VH1, 2003; named Broadcaster of Yr. Internat. Radio and TV Soc., 1988, TV Performer of Yr., TV Guide, 1997, Most Important Person in Books and Media, Newsweek, 1997; named one of 50 Most Beautiful in the World, People, 1997, America's 25 Most Influential People of the 20th Century, Time, 1998, 100 Most Powerful Women in Entertainment, Hollywood Reporter, 2004, 2006, 2007, 100 Most Influential People, TIME Mag., 2004-07, Most Powerful Women, Forbes mag., 2005-2007, 50 Women to Watch, Wall St. Journal, 2005, 100 Most Influential Black Ams., Ebony mag., 2006, 50 Most Powerful Women in Bus., Fortune mag., 1998-2007, 50 Who Matter Now, CNNMoney.com Bus. 2.0, 2006, 100 Most Powerful Celebrities, Forbes.com, 2007; named to List American Billionaires, Fortune, 2003, 400 Richest Americans, 1999-, World's Richest People, 2003-; inducted to Television Hall of Fame, 1994, Broadcasting and Cable Hall of Fame, 2002, NAACP Hall of Fame, 2005; elected to Nat. Women's Hall of Fame, Seneca Falls, Y. Initiated a campaign to establish a national database of convicted child abusers, and testified before U.S. Senate Judiciary Committee on behalf of ational Child Protection Act in 1991, as a result, President Clinton signed the "Oprah Bill" into Law on December 20, 1993, establishing the national database used by law enforcement agencies around the world; third woman in American entertainment industry to own her own studio; first African-American woman to reach billionaire status; after receiving Lifetime Acheivement Award in 1998, permanently withdrew name from Daytime Emmy Award consideration; Oprah and Oprah Winfrey Show received a total of 39 Daytime Emmy awards: seven for Outstanding Host; nine for Outstanding Talk Show; twenty-one in the Creative Arts categories; and one for supervising producer of the ABC School Special, Shades of Single Protein; celebrated the 20th year anniversary of the Oprah Winfrey Show in November, 2005. Office: Oprah Winfrey Show Harpo Studios 1058 W Washington Blvd Chicago IL 60607 Address: Harpo Prodn PO Box 909715 Chicago IL 60607 Office Phone: 312-633-0808.

WING, JOHN ADAMS, financial services executive; b. Elmira, NY, Nov. 9, 1935; s. Herbert Charles and Clara Louise (Stewart) W.; m. Joan Cook Montgomery, June 19, 1964; children: Lloyd Montgomery, Elizabeth Montgomery, Mary Ellen. BA in Econs., Union Coll., 1958; LL.B., George Washington U., 1963. Bar: Va. 1963, D.C. 1965, Ill. 1968. Fin. analyst SEC, Washington, 1960-63, trial atty., 1963-66; asst. to pres. Investors Diversified Services, Inc., Mpls., 1966-67; v.p., gen. counsel A.G. Becker & Co., Chgo., 1968-71, sr. v.p., 1971-74; pres. A.G. Becker & Co., also dir., Chgo., 1974-80; pres., then chief exec. officer & chmn. Chgo. Corp. (acquired by ABN AMRO N. Am. Inc. in 1996), 1981-98; exec. dir. Ctr. of Law and Fin. Markets Ill. Inst. of Tech., Chicago, 1998—. Bd. dirs. Chgo. Bd. Options Exch., Am. Mut. Life. Bd. dirs. Ill. Inst. Tech., Risk Mgmt. Ctr. Chgo. With U.S. Army, 1958-60. Mem. Ill. Bar Assn., Va. Bar Assn., Ill. State C. of C. (bd. dirs. capital fund). Clubs: Chgo., Economics, Civic, Mid-Day, Bond, Saddle & Cycle. Episcopalian. Office: Ctr for Law & Fin Markets Ill Inst of Tech 565 W Adams St Chicago IL 60661

WINKEL, RICHARD J., JR., state legislator; b. Kankakee, Ill., Sept. 25, 1956; m. Debra Winkel; children: Meghan, David. Of counsel Meyer Capel, P.C., Champaign, Ill.; bd. mem. Champaign County, 1992-94; Ill. state rep. Dist. 103, 1995—. Mem. Elem. and Secondary, Higher Edn., Judiciary-Criminal Law, Prosecutorial Misconduct Management Reform, Ins. and Election Reform Law Coms., Ill. House, 1995—; mem. Legis. Audit Commn.

WINKELMANN, JOHN PAUL, pharmacist; b. St. Louis, Sept. 14, 1933; s. Clarence Henry and Alyce Marie (Pierce) W.; m. Margaret (Peggy) Ann Grandy, June 16, 1967; children: John Damian and James Paul (twins), Joseph Peter, Christopher Louis, Sean Martin. BS, St. Louis U., 1955; BS in Pharmacy, St. Louis Coll. Pharmacy, 1960; ScD, London Coll. Applied Sci., 1972; EdD, Internat. Inst. for Advanced Studies, 1987. Registered pharmacist, Mo.; notary pub.; sr.cert. profl. mgr. (CM). Pres., chief pharmacist Winkelmann Apothecary, Ltd., Clayton, Mo., 1960-76; founding mem. Nat. Cath. Pharmacists Guild U.S., 1962; pres. at. Cath. Pharmacists Guild U.S. (hdqs St. Louis, 1967—), St. Louis, 1968-70, 1979—83; hon. pres. Nat. Cath. Pharmacists Guild U.S., St. Louis, 1984, co-pres., 1985—, exec. dir., 1970—, founding editor, 1967—. Distbr. pharms. and medicines to missions worldwide. Author: History of the St. Louis College of Pharmacy, 1964, Catholic Pharmacy, 1966; founding editor The Cath. Pharmacist Jour., 1967—; contbr. over 500 articles to profl. publs. Unit commr. Greater St. Louis coun. Boy Scouts Am.; charter mem. Mo. Statewide Profl. Svcs. Rev. Orgn., 1976-78; Rep. Presdl. Task Force, Washington, 1982—; trustee St. Louis Coll. Pharmacy, 1961-84, chmn. audit com., 1968-83; worker St. Louis Archdiocesan Devel. Appeal, 1969-88; bd. dirs. Missionary Sisters St. Peter Claver Adv. Bd., 1974-77; retreat capt. for parish ch., 1976-83. Capt. USAFR, ret. Decorated knight of Malta by Pope Paul VI, knight grand cross Order of the Holy Sepulchre of Jerusalem by Pope John Paul II, papal knight Assn. Pontifical Knights, knight officer Order Sts. Maurice and Lazarus, knight officer Constantinian Order St. George, knight comdr. Patriarchal Equestrian Order of Holy Cross Jerusalem, knight Order White Eagle, Poland, knight Grand Cordon of Order of St. Stanislas, Knight Grand Cordon of Order Polonia Restituta, Grant of Arms (Spain), Certification of Arms (Rep. Ireland), Gold Papal Lateran Cross (1st class), Pope Leo XIII Gold Papal Holy Land Cross of Honor, knight St. Michael of the Wing (Portugal); recipient Silver Palm of Jerusalem award medal, Confrater of the Teutonic Order, Pharm. Scholarship award Meyer Bros., 1959, Lunsford Richardson Nat. Pharmacy award, 1959, 60; 1st prize Roerig at. Pharm. Econs. Essay Contest, 1960, Medallion Cir. award Nat. Assn. Holy Name Soc., 1984, citations Govs. Mo., Ky., Tenn., Tex., Okla., Kans., Ala., Ga., Va., Nebr., Mass., Ind., W.Va., Pa., Miss., N.Mex., Ark., Ariz., SC, mayor of Paducah, Ky., Indpls., Lexington, Ky., San Antonio, New Orleans, Dodge City, Kans., County Exec. Somerset, Pulaski County, Ky; Pharmacist Yr. award, Drug Topics Publs, 2002; Commendation award Am. Inst. Hist. Pharmacy. Fellow Royal Soc. Health, Nat. Cath. Pharmacists Guild (Pharmacist of Yr. 1970), Am. Coll. Apothecaries, Am. Coll. Pharmacists, Soc. Apothecaries of London Faculty of Philosophy and History of Medicine and Pharmacy; mem. Am. Bd. Diplomates in Pharmacy (charter), Am. Inst. History Pharmacy (coun. 1977-80, state rep. 1980—, Commendation award 1966), Inst. Cert. Profl. Mgrs. (cert.), Am. Pharm. Assn., Acad. Pharm. Practice (charter 1967), St. Louis Vet. Druggists Assn., Assn. Mil. Surgeons U.S., Nat. Assn. Holy Name Soc. (v.p. 1981-91), St. Louis Archdiocesan Union Holy Name Soc. (pres. 1982-84), AMVETS, Am. Legion, Army and Navy Union, Mil. Order of World Wars, Mil. Order of Loyal Legion, Mil. Order of Foreign Wars, Order of Lafayette, Polish Legion Am. Vets., Cath. War Vets., Anchor and Caduceus Soc. of USPHS, Rho Chi.

WINKER, MARGARET A., editor; MD, U. Ill. Resident in internal medicine U. Chgo., fellowship in geriatric medicine; clin. asst. prof. geriatrics sect. U. Ill. Med. Ctr.; sr. editor Jour. of AMA. Contbr. articles to profl. jours. Mem. Am. Geriatrics Soc. (chair pub. edn. com. 1997). Office: U Chgo Graham Sch Gen Studies 5835 S Kimbark Ave Chicago IL 60637-1635 Fax: 773-702-6814.

WINKLER, CHERYL J., state legislator; m. Ralph Winkler; children: Robert C., Ralph E. Student, U. Cin. Clk. Green Twp., 1984-85, trustee, 1986-90; former rep. Ohio State Ho. Reps. Dist. 20; rep. Ohio State Ho. Reps. Dist. 34, 1993—, mem. interstate coop. com., children and youth com., mem. reference, edn. and state govt. com., mem. select com. on tech., mem. joint com. on juvenile corrections & overcrowding. Mem. Cin. Bar Assn. Aux., Green Twp. and Bridgetown Civic Clubs, Western Hamilton County Econ. Coun. Home: 5355 Boomer Rd Cincinnati OH 45247-7926

WINKLER, DONALD A., credit company executive; Former chmn., CEO Finance One (subs. Bank One Corp.); CEO, chmn. Ford Motor Credit Co., Dearborn, Mich., 1999—.

WINKLER, HENRY RALPH, retired academic administrator, historian; b. Waterbury, Conn., Oct. 27, 1916; s. Jacob and Ethel (Rieger) W.; m. Clare Sapadin, Aug. 18, 1940; children— Allan Michael, Karen Jean; m. Beatrice Ross, Jan. 28, 1973. AB, U. Cin., 1938, MA, 1940; PhD, U. Chgo., 1947; degree (hon.), Lehigh U., 1974, Rutgers U., 1977, No. Ky. U., 1978, St. Thomas Inst., 1979, Hebrew Union Coll., 1980, Xavier U., 1981, U. Akron, 1984, U. Cin., 1987, Thomas More Coll., 1989. Instr. U. Cin., 1939-40; asst. prof. Roosevelt Coll., 1946-47; mem. faculty Rutgers U., 1947-77, prof. history, 1958-77, chmn. dept., 1960-64; dean Faculty Liberal Arts, 1967, vice provost, 1968-70, acting provost, 1970, v.p. for acad. affairs, 1970-72, sr. v.p. for acad. affairs, 1972-76, exec. v.p., 1976-77, U. Cin., 1977, pres., 1977-84, pres. emeritus, 1984—, Univ. prof. history, 1977-86, prof. emeritus, 1986—. Mng. editor Am. Hist. Rev., 1964-68; vis. prof. Bryn Mawr Coll., 1959-60, Harvard, summer 1964, Columbia, summer 1967; faculty John Hay Fellows Inst. Humanities, 1960-65; bd. overseers Hebrew Union Coll., 1984—. Author: The League of Nations Movement in Great Britain, 1914-19, 1952, Great Britain in the Twentieth Century, 1960, 2d edit., 1966; editor: (with K.M. Setton) Great Problems in European Civilization, 1954, 2d edit., 1966, Twentieth-Century Britain, 1977, Paths Not Taken: British Labour and International Policy in the Nineteen Twenties, 1994, British Labour Seeks a Foreign Policy, 2004; mem. editorial bd. Historian, 1958-64, Liberal Edn., 1986—; mem. adv. bd. Partisan Rev., 1972-79; contbr. articles to jours., revs. Nat. chmn. European history advanced placement com. Coll. Entrance Exam. Bd., 1960-64; mem. Nat. Commn. on Humanities in Schs., 1967-68, Am. specialist Eastern Asia, 1968; exec. com. Conf. on Brit. Studies, 1968-75; chmn. bd. at. Humanities Faculty, 1970-73; chmn. adv. com. on history Coll. Entrance Exam. Bd., 1977-80; mem. council on acad. affairs, mem. bd. trustees, chmn., 1982-84; pres. Highland Park (N.J.) Bd. Edn., 1962-63; mem. exec. com. Nat. Assn. State Univs. and Land-Grant Colls., 1978-81, mem. Cin. Lit. Club, 1978—, pres., 1993—; bd. dirs. Am. Council on Edn., 1979-81; trustee Seasongood Good Govt. Found., 1979—, pres., 1991-93; trustee Thomas More Coll., 1986-93; mem. Ohio Indsl. Tech. and Enterprise

Bd., 1983-89; bd. dirs. Nat. Civic League, 1986—, Planning Accreditation Bd., 1988—; mem. adv coun. U. Va.'s Coll at Wise, Ohio Humanities Coun., 1994— With USNR, 1943-46. Recipient Lifetime Achievement award N.Am. Conf. on Brit. Studies, 1995, Bishop William Hughes award for disting. svc. to Cath. higher edn. Thomas More Coll., 1997, Leadership Medallion, Xavier U., 2003, Excellence award U. Cin., 2006. Mem. Am. Hist. Assn., Phi Beta Kappa, Tau Kappa Alpha, Phi Alpha Theta. Clubs: Comml., Bankers, Cin., Lit. Office: U Cin 571 Langsam Library Cincinnati OH 45221-0001 Business E-Mail: Henry.Winkler@uc.edu.

WINNECKE, JOYCELYN, editor; m. Bill Adee. Degree, U. So. Ind. Writer obituaries Evansville (Ind.) Courier and Press, 1977; reporter Wash. bur. Scripps Howard; city editor Indpls. Star; dep. metro editor, then metro news editor Chgo. Sun-Times, 1994—99; mng. editor Chgo. Sun Times, 1999—2002, Chgo. Tribune, 2002—. Office: Chgo Tribune 435 N Michigan Ave Chicago IL 60611

WINSHIP, DANIEL HOLCOMB, medical educator, dean; b. Houston, July 4, 1933; m. Winnifred Jeneanne Rowold; children: Charles Dwayne, Nancy Ellen, David Rhoads, Rebecca Susan, Molly Beth. BA, Rice U., 1954; MD, U. Tex., Galveston, 1958. Diplomate Am. Bd. Internal Medicine. Intern in internal medicine Ochsner Found. Hosp., ew Orleans, 1958-59; asst. resident U. Utah Coll. Medicine, Salt Lake City, 1959-61; fellow in gastroenterology Yale U. Sch. Medicine, New Haven, 1961-63; rsch. fellow med. ethics, fellow law, sci.-medicine program Yale U. Divinity Sch., Yale U. Law Sch., New Haven, 1977; asst. prof., then assoc. prof. medicine Marquette U. Sch. Medicine, Milw., 1963-69; assoc. prof., then prof. U. Mo. Sch. Medicine, Columbia, 1969-84, assoc. dean for VA affairs, 1982-84; prof. U. Kans. Sch. Medicine, Kansas City, 1984-87; assoc. dep. chief med. dir. dept. medicine and surgery VA Ctrl. Office, Washington, 1987-90; prof. medicine, dean Loyola U. Stritch Sch. Medicine, Maywood, Ill., 1990-99; vice chancellor health affairs U. Missouri Columbia Health Scis. Ctr., 1999—. Gastroenterologist Harry S. Truman Meml. Vets. Hosp., Columbia, 1974-79, chief med. svc., 1979-82, chief staff, 1982-84; chief staff VA Med. Ctr., Kansas City, 1984-86, dir., 1986-87; attending physician Loyola U. Med. Ctr., 1990—, Edward Hines (Ill.) Med. Ctr., 1990—; mem. adv. bd. Greater Chgo. Alliance for Mentally Ill, 1991; pres., bd. dirs. gastroenterology adv. com. VA, 1982-85, chmn. clin. and programs adv. coun., 1988-90; mem. rev. com. Mo. Dept. Mental Health, 1981-82; numerous others. Mem. editl. bd. Clin. Rsch., 1970-73, Annals Clin. Gastroenterology, 1978-83, Gastroenterology: A Weekly Update, 1978-81; assoc. editor Jour. Lab. and Clin. Medicine, 1980-83; contbr. numerous articles and abstracts to med. jours. Bd. dirs. John H. Walters Hospice Ctrl. Mo., 1982-84, chmn., 1983-84. Recipient Outstanding Clin. Tchr. in Medicine award Milwaukee County Hosp. Housestaff, 1964, Golden Apple award Student AMA, 1972, Disting. Svc. medal and award VA, 1990, Ashbel Smith Disting. Alumnus award U. Tex. Med. Br., 1992. Mem. Am. Gastroent. Assn. (com. on rsch. 1975-78, com. on tng. and edn. 1978-81, dir. clin. tchg. project 1990-82, program chmn. motility sect. 1987), Gastroenterology Rsch. Group, Ctrl. Soc. for Clin. Rsch., So. Soc. for Clin. Investigation, Am. Fedn. for Clin. Rsch., Midwest Gut Club (presiding pres. 1980-83), Soc. for Health and Human Values, Inst. Society, Ethics and Life Scis., Sigma Xi, Alpha Omega Alpha (vis. prof. U. Mo. Sch. Medicine 1991, Med. Coll. Wis. 1993). Office: U Mo Columbia Health Scis Ctr 1 Hosp Dr Columbia MO 65212-0001

WINSTEN, SAUL NATHAN, lawyer; b. Providence, Feb. 23, 1953; s. Harold H. and Anita E. Winsten; m. Patricia J. Miller, Aug. 7, 1977; children: David A., J. Benjamin, Jennifer M. BA, Beloit Coll., Wis., 1976; JD, Drake U., Des Moines, 1980. Shareholder DeWitt Ross & Stevens, Brookfield, Wis.; chmn. corp. counsel com. Wis. Mfrs. Commn., 2004—. Contbr. articles to profl. jours. Active Wis. Gov.'s Adv. Coun. on Internat. Trade, 1996-2003, co-chmn., 1999-2002; active Wis. Gov.'s Internat. Edn. Task Force, 1997-98; chmn. Wis. Mfrs. and Commerce Corp. Counsel Com., 2004-; adv. com. Great Lakes Area IRS Adv. Com. Tax Exempt Orgn./Govt. Entities Coun., 2005—. Mem. ABA (chmn. com. young lawyers divsn. 1989-90, governing coun., antitrust, bus. and internat. law sects.), Wis. Bar Assn. (chair tax exempt orgn. com. of bus law sect. 2005-06), Internat. Bar Assn., Japan-Am. Soc. Wis. (pres. 1993-94, co-founder 1990, sec. 1990-92), at. Assn. Japan-Am. Socs. (bd. dirs. 1991-97, exec. com. 1993-97), Order of Barristers, Hessen-Wisconsin, Inc. (bd. dirs.), Internat. Bar Assn. Office: DeWitt Ross & Stevens 13935 Bishops Dr Brookfield WI 53005-6605 Office Phone: 262-754-2852. Business E-Mail: snw@dewittross.com.

WINSTON, ROLAND, physicist, researcher; b. Moscow, USSR, Feb. 12, 1936; s. Joseph and Claudia (Goretskaya) W.; m. Patricia Louise LeGette, June 10, 1957; children: Joseph, John, Gregory. AB, Shimer Coll., 1953; BS, U. Chgo., 1956, MS, 1957, PhD, 1963. Asst. prof. physics U. Pa., 1963-64; mem. faculty U. Chgo., 1964—, prof. physics, 1975—, chmn. physics dept., 1989-95. Recipient Kraus medal Franklin Inst., 1996, First Solar Personality of the Yr. award, Bangalore, India, 1999. Fellow: Am. Solar Engery Soc., Am. Optical Soc., Am. Phys. Soc., AAAS; mem.: Internat. Solar Energy Soc. ((Abbot award 1987, Farrington Daniels award 2001)), Franklin Inst. (hon.). Achievements include patent for ideal light collector for solar concentrators. Office: U Calif Merced Sch Natural Sci & Engring PO Box 2039 Merced CA 95344 Home: 3384 Locksley Ct Merced CA 95340-0751 E-mail: r-winston@uchicago.edu.

WINTER, DAVID FERDINAND, electrical engineering educator, consultant; b. St. Louis, Nov. 9, 1920; s. Ferdinand Conrad and Annie (Schaffer) W.; m. Bettie Jeanne Turner; children: Suzanne, Sharie Winter Chappeau. BSEE, Washington U., St. Louis, 1942; MSEE, MIT, 1948. Registered profl. engr., Mo. Staff mem. radiation lab. MIT, Cambridge, 1942-45, rsch. assoc. electronics lab., 1945-48; prof. elec. engring. Washington U., St. Louis, 1948-55, affiliate prof. elec. engring., 1955-67; v.p. engring. and rsch. Moloney Elec. Co., St. Louis, 1955-74; v.p. rsch. and engring. Blackburn div. IT&T, St. Louis, 1974-82, dir. advanced tech. devel., 1982-86; pvt. practice cons. St. Louis, 1986—. Ct. recognized tech. expert on sources, mitigation, and effects of stray voltage on dairy cattle cons. Wis. Pub. Svc. Commn.; cons. Naval Ordanance Lab. of Ind., Indpls., 1950-53, other industries, St. Louis, 1979—. Contbr. articles to profl. jours.; holder 28 patents. Elder, pastor Maplewood Bible Chapel, St. Louis. Recipient Alumni Achievement award, Wash. U., Sch. Engring. & Applied Sci., St. Louis. Mo., 2003, Washington U., 2003. Fellow IEEE (life), Inst. Radio Engrs.; mem. NSPE, Am. Soc. Agrl. Engrs., Mo. Soc. Profl. Engrs., Sigma Xi, Tau Beta Pi, Eta Kappa Nu. Avocations: cabinet maker, photography, music instruments. Home and Office: 735 Harvard Ave University City MO 63130-3135 Office Phone: 314-727-4532. E-mail: dfwinter@hotmail.com.

WINTER, JANE, medical educator; b. NYC, 1952; MD, U. Pa., 1977; intern, U. Chgo., 1977-78, resident int. medicine, 1978-80. Fellow in hematology and oncology Columbia P&S, NYC, 1980-81, Northwestern U., 1981-83, prof., 1983—. Mem.: Ea. Coop. Oncology Group, Am. Soc. for Blood and Marrow Transplantation, Am. Assn. Cancer Rsch., Am. Soc. Clin. Oncology, Am. Soc. Hematology. Office: Divsn Hematology/Oncology 676 N St Clair St Ste 850 Chicago IL 60611-2978 Office Phone: 312-695-0990. E-mail: j-winter@northwestern.edu.

WINTER, JIMMY, entrepreneur, systems administrator; b. 1982; Web site designer Fastmusic Label, NYC, 1999; founder Music Arsenal, Omaha, 2003—. Named one of Best Entrepreneurs Under 25, BusinessWeek, 2006. Office: Music Arsenal 1909 S 61ST Ave Omaha NE 68106-2132 Office Phone: 800-231-9273. E-mail: info@musicarsenal.com.

WINTER, MILDRED M., educational administrator; BA summa cum laude, Harris Tchrs. Coll.; MEd, U. Mo.; postgrad., Harvard U., U. Cin. Exec. dir. Parents As Tchrs. at. Ctr. Inc., St. Louis. Tchr., cons., Mo., 1962-68; developer, dir. Ferguson-Florissant Parent-Child Early Edn. Program, Mo., 1969-72; first dir. early childhood edn. Mo. Dept. Elem. and Secondary Edn., 1972-84; sr. lectr. dept. elem. and early childhood edn. U. Mo., St. Louis; cons. in field. Contbr. articles to profl. jours. Named Outstanding Leader in Field of Edn., Mo. House of Reps., 1982, Outstanding Educator and Adv. for Young Children, Mo. Gov. Christopher S. Bond, 1984, Pioneer in Edn., State Bd. Edn., Mo. Dept. Edn., 1991, St. Louis Woman of Achievement in Edn., 1992; cited for Pioneering Leadership in Edn. Resolution, Mo. Senate, 1995; recipient Outstanding Svc. award Assn. Edn. of Young Children, 1984, Vol. Accreditation Leadership award, 1993, Spl. award Nat. Soc. Behavioral Pediat., 1992, Charles A. Dana Pioneering Achievements Health and Edn. Inst. Medicine award NAS, 1995. Office: Parents as Teachers Patnc 2228 Ball Dr Saint Louis MO 63146-8602

WINTER, THEODORE, state legislator; b. Slayton, Minn., Nov. 26, 1949; s. Alphonse and Josephine Schettler W.; m. Marge Meier, 1969; children: Jason, Nathan, Shannon, Brent. AA, Worthington C.C., Minn., 1970. Farmer, 1968—; Minn. State rep. Dist. 22A, 1987—. Vice-chmn. ins. and tax coms.; mem. agr. econ. develop., environ. and natural resources, govt. ops. and fin. inst. coms. Mem. Minn. Jaycees (Minn. Statesman award 1983, JCI senatorship 1983—, reg. dir. 1983, dist. dir. 1982), Fulda Area Jaycees (pres. 1981, treas. 1980), Nat. Farmer's Orgn., Fulda Area Comm. Club. Home: RR 2 Box 23 Fulda MN 56131-9503

WINTER, WILLIAM EARL, retired beverage company executive; b. Granite City, Ill., Sept. 21, 1920; s. William M. and Ada M. (Compton) W.; m. Dorothy E. Schuster, Feb. 20, 1944 (dec. 1976); children: William C., Douglas E.; m. Mildred E. Stiebel, Mar. 18, 1977. AB, U. Ill., 1942. With Seven-Up Co., St. Louis, 1946-81, v.p., dir. mktg., 1969-71, exec. v.p., 1971-74, pres., chief operating officer, 1974-76, pres., chief exec. officer, 1976-79, chmn. bd., 1979-81, also former dir., cons.; chmn. emeritus, 1996—; cons. Cadbury Beverages/Seven-Up, chmn. emeritus, 1996. Bd. dirs. YMCA Greater St. Louis, U. Ill. Found.; mem. exec. bd. St. Louis Area coun. Boy Scouts Am. Capt. U.S. Army, 1942-46. Named to Promotion Mktg. Hall of Fame, 1979, Beverage World Hall of Fame, 1986 Mem. Am. Mktg. Assn., Sales and Mktg. Execs. St. Louis, Promotion Mktg. Assn. Am. (chmn. bd. 1971-72), Phi Beta Kappa, Phi Eta Sigma, Omicron Delta Gamma. Home: 14112 Baywood Villages Dr Chesterfield MO 63017-3421 Home Phone: 314-878-9870.

WINTER, WINTON ALLEN, JR., lawyer, state senator; b. Ft. Knox, Ky., Apr. 19, 1953; s. Winton A. and Nancy (Morsbach) W.; m. Mary Boyd, July 28, 1978; children: Katie, Molly, Elizabeth. BA, U. Kans., 1975, JD, 1978. Bar: Kans. 1978. Ptnr. law firm Stevens & Brand, LLP, Lawrence, Kans., 1978—; v.p., gen. counsel Peoples, Inc., 2000-02; pres., CEO Peoples Bank, 2002—; pres. Corp. for Change; mem. Kans. Senate, 1982-92. Bd. dirs. Lawrence United Fund, Boys Club of Lawrence. Mem. ABA, Kans. Bar Assn., Douglas County Bar Assn. Kans. U. Law Soc., Rotary. Republican. Roman Catholic. Note and comment editor Kans. Law Rev., 1977-78. Office: PO Box 1795 4831 W 6th St Lawrence KS 66049 Home Phone: 785-843-4479; Office Phone: 785-842-4004. Personal E-mail: wwinter@epeoples.com. Business E-Mail: wwinter@bankingunusual1.com.

WINTERS, ANNE, poet, educator; b. St. Paul, Oct. 13, 1939; d. Warrington Woodruff and Helen Winters; 1 child, Elizabeth. BA, NYU, 1961; MA, Columbia U., 1963; Phd, U. Calif., Berkeley, 1993. Lectr. MIT, Cambridge, Mass., 1981—82, U. Calif., Davis, Calif., 1983—85; instr. St. Marys, Calif., 1985—87; asst. prof. orthwestern U., Evanston, Ill., 1991—94; mem. lit. faculty Bennington (Vt.) Coll., 1994—97; prof. English U. Ill., Chgo., 1997—. Lectr. Harvard U., Cambridge, 1995, 96; vis. assoc. prof. U. Chgo., 1997—98. Translator: Salamander: sel Poems of Robert Marteau, 1979 (Poetry prize, 1979); author: The Key to the City, 1986 (nominated Nat. Book Critics Circle prize, 1986), The Displaced of Capital, 2004 (W.C. Williams prize). Recipient Poetry award, Wellesley Coll., 1997, Lit. award, Am. Acad. Arts & Letters, 2003; grantee, NEA, 1985. Mem.: Writers Programs Am., Modern Lang. Assn. Democrat. Office: English Dept Univ Ill 601 S Morgan St Dept Mc162 Chicago IL 60607-7100

WINTERS, BRIAN JOSEPH, professional basketball coach; b. Rockaway, NY, Mar. 1, 1952; m. Julie Winters; children: Cara, Keelin, Meghan, Brendan, Kevin, Ryan. Grad., U. SC, 1974. Profl. basketball player NBA LA Lakers, 1974—75, NBA Milw. Bucks, 1975—83; asst. coach Princeton U., 1984—86, NBA Cleve. Cavaliers, 1986—93, NBA Atlanta Hawks, 1993—95, NBA Denver Nuggets, 1997—98, NBA Golden State Warriors, 1999—2001, head coach, 2001—02, NBA Vancouver Grizzlies, 1995—97, WNBA Ind. Fever, 2003—. Named to NBA All-Rookie Team, 1974, NBA All-Star Team, 1976, 1978. Office: Ind Fever Conseco Fieldhouse One Conseco Ct 125 S Pennsylvania St Indianapolis IN 46204

WINTERS, DAVID FORREST, state legislator; b. Springfield, Ill., June 30, 1952; s. Robert Winters Jr. and Helen (Steele) W.; m. Kathleen Wise, 1975; children: Colin, Theresa. BA, Dartmouth Coll., 1974; MS, U. Ill., 1976. Farmer, Winnebago County, Ill., 1976-94; commr., 1986-92; mem. Ill. State Ho. of Reps. Dist. 69, 1995—. Dir. Winnebago County Farm Bur., 1993-96.

WINTERSTEIN, JAMES FREDRICK, academic administrator; b. Copperas Cove, Tex., Apr. 8, 1943; s. Arno Fredrick Herman and Ada Amanda Johanna (Wagner) W.; m. Diane Marie Bochmann, July 13, 1963; children: Russell, Lisa, Steven, Amy. Student, U. N.M., 1962; D of Chiropractic cum laude, Nat. Coll. Chiropractic, 1968; cert., Harvard Inst. for Ednl. Mgmt., 1988. Diplomate Am. Chiropractic Bd. Radiology; lic. chiropractic, Ill., Fla., S.D., Md. Night supr. x-ray dept. DuPage Meml. Hosp., Elmhurst, Ill., 1964-66; x-ray technologist Lombard (Ill.) Chiropractic Clinic, 1966-68, asst. dir., 1968-71; chmn. dept. diagnostic imaging at. Coll. Chiropractic, Lombard, Ill., 1971-73, chief of staff, 1985-86; pres. Nat. U. Health Scis., Lombard, Ill., 1986—; pvt. practice West Chicago, Ill., 1968-73, Fla., 1973-85. Faculty Nat. Lincoln Coll. Post-Profl., Grad. and Continuing Edn., 1967—; chmn. x-ray test com. Nat. Bd. Chiropractic Examiners, 1971-73; govs. adv. panel on coal worker's pneumoconiosis and chiropractic State of Pa., 1979; v.p. Am. Chiropractic Coll. Radiology, 1981-83; mem. adv. coun. on radiation protection Dept. Health and Rehabilitative Svcs. State of Fla., 1984-85; cons. to bd. examiners State of S.C., 1983-84, State of Fla., 1980-85; cons. to peer review bd. State of Fla., 1980-84; trustee Chiropractic Centennial Found., 1989-90; mem. adv. com. Aids Alternative Health Ptnrs., 1996-2000, Consortial Ctr. for Chiropractic Rsch., 1998—; bd. dirs. Fedn. Ill. Ind. Colls. and Univs., 1995—; bd. dirs. Alternative Medicine, Inc., 1999—; spkr. in field. Pub. Outreach (Nat. Univ. Health Scis. monthly); author numerous monographs on chiropractic edn. and practice; co-inventor composite shielding and mounting means for x-ray machines; contbr. articles to profl. jours. Chmn., bd. dirs. Trinity Luth. Ch., West Chgo., 1970-72, Luth. High Sch., Pinellas County, Fla., 1979-82, St. John Luth. Ch., Lombard, 1988; chmn. bd. edn. First Luth. Sch., 1975-79; chmn. First Luth. Congregation, Clearwater, Fla., 1979-82; chmn. bldg. planning com. Grace Luth. Ch. and Sch., St. Petersburg, Fla., 1984-85; bldg. planning com. ch. expansion, new elem. sch., First Luth. Sch., 1975-79; stewardship adv. coun. Fla./Ga. dist. Luth. Ch. Mo. Synod, 1983-85; trustee West Suburban Regional Acad. Consortium, 1993-99. With U.S. Army, 1961-64. Recipient Cert. Meritorious Svc. Am. Chiropractic Registry of Radiologic Technologists, Cert. Recognition for Inspiration, Guidance, and Support Delta Tau Alpha, 1989, Cert. Appreciation Chiropractic Assn. South Africa, 1988, 1st pl. Fund Raiser Ride for Kids award Pediat. Brain Tumor Found. U.S., 1997, Cert. Appreciation Ill. Chiropractic Soc., 1997, Hope and Support award Alternative Health Ptnrs., 1998, Chiropractor of Yr., Ill. Chiropractic Soc., 2000, Person of the Yr., Alternative Medicine, Inc., 2001, NUHS Bd. Trustees Disting. Svc. award, 2002, President's citation award Maryland Chiropractic Assn., 2003. Mem. APHA, Am. Chiropractic Assn., Am. Chiropractic Coll. Radiology (pres. 1983-85, exec. com. 1985-86), Am. Chiropractic Coun. on Diagnostic Imaging, Am. Chiropractic Coun. on Diagnosis and Internal Disorders, Am. Chiropractic Coun. on Nutrition, Nat. Univ. Alumni Assn., Am. Acad. Chiropractic Physicians (sec.), Assn. Chiropractic Colls. (sec.-treas. 1986-91), Coun. Chiropractic Edn. (sec.-treas. 1988-90, v.p. 1990-92, pres. 1992-94, immediate past pres. 1994-96), Fla. Chiropractic Assn. (chmn. radiol. health com. 1977-85, Disting. Svc. award 1999). Republican. Lutheran. Avocations: reading, automobile rehabilitation, harley-davidson motorcycles, fishing.

WIOT, JEROME FRANCIS, radiologist; b. Cin., Aug. 24, 1927; s. Daniel and Elvera (Weisgerber) W.; m. Andrea Kockritz, July 29, 1972; children— J. Geoffrey, Jason. MD, U. Cin., 1953. Diplomate: Am. Bd. Radiology (trustee, pres.). Intern Cin. Gen. Hosp., 1953-54, resident, 1954-55, 58-59; gen. practice medicine Wyoming, Ohio, 1955-57; mem. faculty U. Cin., 1959-67, 68—, prof., chmn. radiology, 1973-93, acting sr. v.p., provost for med. affairs, 1985-86, prof. emeritus, 1998—; practice medicine specializing in radiology Tampa, Fla., 1967-68. Contbr. articles to med. jours. Bd. dirs. Ruth Lyons Fund, U. Cin. Found., 1997—2003, U. Cin. Hosp., 2005—. Served with USN, 1945-46. Fellow Am. Coll. Radiology (pres. 1983-84, chmn. commn. on diagnostic radiology); mem. Radiol. Soc. N.Am., Am. Roentgen Ray Soc. (pres. 1986-87), Am. Bd. Radiology (pres. 1982-84), Ohio Med. Assn., Cin. Acad. Medicine, Radiol. Soc. Greater Cin., Ohio Radiol. Soc. Office: U Cin Med Ctr Dept Radiology 234 Goodman St Cincinnati OH 45267-1000 Office Phone: 513-475-8755. E-mail: jfwiot@hotmail.com.

WIRCH, ROBERT W., state legislator; b. Nov. 16, 1943; BA, U. Wis., Parkside. Mem. Wis. Assembly from 65th dist., Madison, 1992-98, Wis. Senate from 22nd dist., Madison, 1998—. Mem. Kenosha (Wis.) County Bd. Mem. Polish Legion Am. Vets., Danish Am. Club. Address: 3007 Springbrook Rd Pleasant Prairie WI 53158-4324 Office: Wis Senate State Capitol Madison WI 53702-0001

WIRKEN, JAMES CHARLES, lawyer; b. Lansing, Mich., July 3, 1944; s. Frank and Mary (Brosnahan) W.; m. Mary Morse, June 12, 1971; children: Christopher, Erika, Kurt, Gretchen, Jeffrey, Matthew. BA in English, Rockhurst Coll., 1967; JD, St. Louis U., 1970. Bar: Mo. 1970, U.S. Dist. Ct. (we. dist.) Mo. 1970. Asst. prosecuter Jackson County, Kansas City, Mo., 1970-72; assoc. Morris, Larson, King, Stamper & Bold, Kansas City, 1972-75; dir. Spradley, Wirken, Reismeyer & King, Kansas City, 1976-88, Wirken & King, Kansas City, 1988-93; CEO The Wirken Law Group, Kansas City, 1993—. Adj. prof. U. Mo., Kansas City, 1984—89, 2001—; columnist Wirken Tips: Law Office Mktg., Mgmt. and Econ. The Daily Record, 2006, Wirkens Quips Quotes, Wit and Wisdom The Daily Record, 2003—06. Author: (books) Managing a Practice and Avoiding Malpractice, 1983; co-author: Missouri Civil Procedure Form Book, 1984; mem. editl. bd.: jours. Missouri Law Weekly, 1989—, Lender Liability News, 1990—, Emerging Trends and Theories of Lender Liability, 1991, host: Wirken on the Law KMBZ-FM, 1998—2007, Kans. City Morning News Sunday Edit. KMBZ-FM, 2007. Named Best the Bar, Kans. City Bus. Jour., 2005—07, Mo. Super Lawyer, 2006, 2007. Mem. ABA (exec. coun.), at. Conf. Bar Pres. (coun. 1992-96), Nat. Caucus of Met. Bar Leaders (exec. coun., pres. 1988-94), Am. Trial Lawyers Assn., L.P. Gas Group (founder, chair 1986-90, founder, chair lender liability group 1987-96), Mo. Bar Assn. (bd. govs. 1977-78, 2004—, chmn. econs. and methods practice com. 1982-84, quality and methods of practice com. 1989-91, vice chmn. young lawyers sect. 1976-78), Mo. Assn. Trial Attys. (bd. govs. 1983-85), Kansas City Met. Bar Assn. (pres. young lawyers sect. 1975, chair legal assistance com. 1977-78, chair tort law com. 1982, pres. 1990). Home: 47 W 53rd Kansas City MO 64112 Office: The Wirken Law Group PC 4740 Grand Blvd Ste 200 Kansas City MO 64112 Office Phone: 816-471-0330. Business E-Mail: jwirken@wirkenlaw.com.

WIRSING, DAVID A., state legislator; Commr. Coon Creek Drainage Dist. Ill.; chmn. Sycamore Youth Coun.; mem. Sycamore Sch. Bd.; chmn. Sch. Bd. LINK Advt. Com.; Ill. state rep. Dist. 70. Pres. Pork Prodrs. Exec. Bd., DeKalb Area Pork Prodrs. Bd. Mem. DeKalb County Farm Bur., Western Ill. U. Swine Rsch. Com., Sycamore Agrl. Advt. Com. Republican. Office: 225-N Stratton Off Bldg Springfield IL 62706

WIRT, FREDERICK MARSHALL, retired political scientist, educator; b. Radford, Va., July 27, 1924; s. Harry Johnson, Sr. and Goldie (Turpin) W.; m. Elizabeth Cook, Sept. 6, 1947; children: Leslie Lee, Sandra Sue, Wendy Ann. BA, DePauw U., 1948; MA, Ohio State U., 1949, PhD, 1956. Instr. to prof. polit. sci. Denison U., Granville, Ohio, 1952-66; vis. prof., lectr. U. Calif., Berkeley, 1966-68, 69-72; dir. policy scis. grad. program U. Md. Balt. County, 1972-75; prof. polit. sci. U. Ill., Urbana, 1975-2000; ret., 2000. Dir. Inst. for Desegregation Problems, U. Calif.-Berkeley, 1970-72; cons. Motion Picture Assn. Am., Rand Corp., Nat. Inst. Edn., SUNY Sch. Edn. Albany; vis. prof. U. Rochester, Nova U., U. Melbourne; acad. visitor London Sch. Econs. Author: Politics of Southern Equality, 1970 (honorable mention for best book 1972), Power in the City, 1974; (with others) School Desegregation in the North, 1967, The Polity of the School, 1975, Political Science and School Politics, 1977, Education, Recession, and the World Village, 1986, (with others) Culture and Education Policy in the American States, 1992, Ain't What We Was: Civil Rights in the New South, 1997 (Best Book on So. Politics award So. Polit. Sci. Assn., 1998), The Political Dynamics of American Education, 3d edit., 2005. Mem. Granville City Charter Commn., 1964. Grantee Am. Philos. Soc., Denison Rsch. Assn., U. Ill. Rsch. Bd., NEH, Ford Found., Ctr. Advanced Studies; fellow U. Ill., Dept. Edn., Spencer Found.; recipient Lifetime Achievement award Am. Ednl. Rsch. Assn., 1995, Am. Polit. Sci. Assn., 1994. Mem. Am. Polit. Sci. Assn. (nat. council), Midwestern Polit. Sci. Assn., Am. Ednl. Rsch. Assn., Policy Studies Orgn. Office: U Ill Dept of Polit Sci Urbana IL 61801 Home: 2340 W Seltice Way Apt 129 Coeur D' Alene ID 83814 E-mail: fmwirt@verizon.net.

WIRTZ, ELI J., lawyer, retail executive; b. West Bend, Iowa, Apr. 28, 1943; BBA, U. Iowa, 1966, JD, 1969. Assoc. to ptnr. Ahlers, Cooney, Dorweiler, Haynie Smith & Allbee, 1972—89; v.p., gen. counsel Casey's Gen. Stores, Ankeny, Iowa, 1989—. Mem.: Iowa State Bar Assn. Office: Caseys Gen Stores One Convenience Blvd PO Box 3001 Ankeny IA 50021 E-mail: legal@caseys.com.

WISE, JOHN AUGUSTUS, lawyer, director; b. Detroit, Mar. 30, 1938; s. John Augustus and Mary Blanche (Parent) W.; m. Helga M. Bessin, Nov. 27, 1965; children: Monique Elizabeth, John Eric. Student, U. Vienna, 1957—58; AB honors cum laude, Coll. Holy Cross, 1959; JD, U. Mich., 1962; postgrad., U. Munich Law Faculty, 1962—63. Bar: Mich. 1963, D.C. 1966. Assoc. Dykema, Gossett, Detroit, 1962-64; asst. to pres. Internat. Econ. Policy Assn., Washington, 1964-66; assoc. Parsons, Tennent, Hammond, Hardig & Ziegelman, Detroit, 1967-70; pres. Wise & Marsac P.C., Detroit, 1970-2001; sr. ptnr. Williams, Mullen, Clark & Dobbins, PLLC, Detroit, 2001—04; of counsel, ptnr. Howard & Howard, P.C., Detroit, 2004—. Dir. Peltzer & Ehlers Am. Corp., 1975-80, Colombian Am. Friends Inc., 1974-89. Bd. dirs. Hyde Park Coop., 1974-77; trustee Friends Sch., Detroit, 1977-81, Brighton Health Svcs. Corp., 1991-94, Providence Hosp., 2001—; mem. Fin. Adv. Com. Bd., Detroit Com. on Fgn. Rels.; chmn. bd. dirs. Brighton Hosp., 1995— Ford Found. grantee U. Munich, 1962-63. Mem. ABA, Mich. Bar Assn., Internat. Bar Assn., Detroit Athletic Club, Detroit Econ. Club. Roman Catholic. Home: 1221 Yorkshire Rd Grosse Pointe Park MI 48230-1105 Office: Pinehurst Ctr Ste 101 39400 Woodward Ave Bloomfield Hills MI 48304-5151 Office Phone: 248-723-0435. E-mail: jwise@howardandhoward.com.

WISE, KENSALL D., engineering educator; m. JoAnne Clayton, Aug. 17, 1968; children: Kevin Duane, David Andrew, Mark Alan. BSEE with highest distinction, Purdue U., 1963; MSEE, Stanford U., 1964, PhD, 1969. Mem. tech. staff Bell Telephone Labs., Murray Hill, N.J., 1963-65, Naperville, Ill., 1972-74; rsch. asst. Stanford (Calif.) U., 1965-69, rsch. assoc., lectr., 1969-72; asst. prof. elec. engring. U. Mich., Ann Arbor, 1974-78, assoc. prof. elec. engring., 1978-82, prof. elec. engring., 1982—, J. Reid and Polly Anderson prof. mfg. tech., 1993—, dir. Solid-State Electronics Lab., 1979-87, dir. Ctr. for Integrated Sensors and Circuits, 1987—, dir. SRC program in automated semiconductor mfg., 1984-98. 'rganizer, moderator panel discussion Biomed. Sensors and Assoc. Electronica Internat. Solid-State Circuits Conf., 1971, mem. program com., 1978-82, 85-86, program sec. 1990-93; mem. JTEC Study on Microelectromech. Sys. Devels. Japan, 1993; program chmn. Internat. Conf. on Solid-State Sensors and Actuators, 1985, 87, 89, 91, 93, 95; mem. program com. Symposium on VLSI Tech., 1988, 98;; mem. Internat. Steering Com. for Solid-State Sensors, 1981—; mem. Crosscut Working Group on Metrology SIA Nat. Tech. Roadmap for Semiconductors, 1996-97; cons. in field. Den leader webelos, 1980-81, 84-85, chmn. troop com. 1984-85; mem. Stake High Coun. LDS Ch., 1977-78, 83-84, 89-90, counselor to bishop, 1985-86, bishop, 1986-89, tchr. early-morning seminar, 1990-91, adult Sunday sch., 1992-98, leader HP group, 1991-92. Recipient Outstanding Paper award Internat. Solid-State Circuits Conf., 1971, 1979, Cert. of Recognition NASA, 1974, 87, Beatrice Winner award Internat. Solid-State Circuits Conf., 1986, Columbus prize Disney World-Discovery Mag. Awards for Tech. Innovation, 1997, Aristotle award Semiconductor Rsch. Corp., 1997. Fellow IEEE (vice chmn. divsn. VI instrumentation engr. in medicine and biology Southeastern Mich. sect. 1975-76, dir. 1976-77, mem. program com. internat. electron devices meeting 1977, 81-83, guest editor spl. issue Jour. Solid-State Circuits 1979, spl. issues Transactions on Electron Devices 1979-82, proceedings Integrated Sensors, Microactuators, and Microsystems, spl. issue, 1998; assoc. editor 1981-85, gen. chmn. Solid-State Sensor Conf. 1984, nat. lectr. IEEE-EDSm 1986; gen. chmn. designate Internat. Conf. on Solid-State Sensors and Actuators 1997, Paul Rappaport award Electron Devices Soc. 1990, Solid State Circuits award 1999), Am. Inst. Med. and Biol. Engring; mem. Nat. Acad. Engring. U.S.A. Achievements include development of integrated circuit process technology, solid-state sensor, design and application of custom and commercial integrated electronics; patents for method for forming regions of predetermined thickness in silicon, 1975, method for forming ICF Target Structurs using solid-state process technology, 1982, multipoint pressure-sensing catheter system, 1989, ultraminiature pressure sensor and method of making same, 1989, ultrathin-film gas detector, 1990, method of making ultraminiature pressure sensor, 1991, silicon tactile imaging array and method of making same, 1991, thermopile infrared detector and method of manufacturing same, 1991. Office: U Mich 2401 BECS Coll Engring Ann Arbor MI 48109

WISE, PHILIP LEON, state representative; b. Maryville, Mo., Sept. 5, 1946; m. Chris Burks; 1 child. BS, N.W. Mo. State U., 1969, MS, 1973; postgrad., Western Ill. U. K-12 classroom tchr., 1969—; mem. Iowa Ho. Reps., Des-Moines, 1987—, ranking mem. edn. com., mem. appropriations com., mem. commerce and regulation com. Former chair Lee County Dem. Party, 1982—86; active Dem. Leadership Coun. Legis. Advisory, 1998; asst. minority leader 75th Gen. Assembly. Mem.: NEA, Keokuk Edn. Assn., Iowa State Edn. Assn., BPO Elks. Democrat. Office: State Capitol East 12th and Grand Des Moines IA 50319 also: 503 Grand Ave Keokuk IA 52632

WISE, WILLIAM JERRARD, lawyer; b. Chgo., May 27, 1934; s. Gerald Paul and Harriet Muriel (Rosenblum) Wise; m. Peggy Spero, Sept. 3, 1959; children: Deborah, Stephen, Betsy, Lynne. BBA, U. Mich., 1955, MBA, 1958, JD with distinction, 1958. Bar: Ill. 1959. Spl. atty. Office Regional Counsel, IRS, Milw., 1959-63; with McDermott, Will & Emery, Chgo., 1963-70, Coles & Wise, Ltd., Chgo., 1971—80, Wise & Stracks, Ltd., Chgo., 1980—2000, Querrey & Harrow, Chgo., 2000—. Lectr., contbr. Ill. Inst. Continuing Legal Edn.; arbitrator Cir. Ct. Cook County Ill., 1990—. Bd. dirs. Blind Svc. Assn., Chgo., 1964—74; active Village of Winnetka, Ill., 1974—75; dir., treas. Suzuki Orff Sch. Young Musicians, Chgo., 1981—91. With US Army, 1958—59. Mem.: Chgo. Bar Assn. Home: 1401 Tower Rd Winnetka IL 60093-1628 Office: Querrey & Harrow 175 W Jackson Blvd Ste 1600 Chicago IL 60604-2827 Home Phone: 847-446-2079; Office Phone: 312-540-7104. Personal E-mail: dididoe@yahoo.com.

WISEMAN, RANDOLPH CARSON, lawyer; b. Staunton, Va., Jan. 25, 1946; s. Malcolm Bell Wiseman and Alberta Elizabeth (Forbus) Marshall; m. Patty Joanne Gray, June 28, 1969; 1 child, Michael Randolph. BS, East Tenn. State U., Johnson City, 1968; JD, Capital U., Columbus, Ohio, 1974. Bar: Ohio 1974, U.S. Dist. Ct. (so. dist.) Ohio 1974, U.S. Supreme Ct. 1977. Assoc. Tyack, Scott & Colley, Columbus, 1974-77; ptnr. Tyack, Scott, Grossman & Wiseman, Columbus, 1977-79, Tyack, Scott & Wiseman, Columbus, 1979-81, Bricker & Eckler, Columbus, 1981—2005; v.p., chief litigation counsel Nationwide Office Gen. Counsel, Columbus, Ohio, 2005—, v.p. litigation, 2005—. Contbr.: Evidence in America: The Federal Rules in the States, 1987; contbr. law articles to profl. jours. Bd. trustees Nat. Multiple Sclerosis Soc., Columbus, 1987—, chmn. 1991-93, Big Bros. Assn., Columbus, 1976-78; bd. dirs. Lifecare Alliance, Ohio Hunger Task Force. Mem.: ABA, Fed. Bar. Assn. (treas. Columbus Chpt. 1995-99, sec. 1999-00, v.p. 2000-01, pres. 2001-02), Franklin County Trial Lawyers Assn. (pres.), Columbus Bar Assn., Ohio State Bar Assn. Republican. Avocations: running, reading, auto racing. Office: VP Chief Litigation Office of General Counsel Nationwide Ins One Nationwide Plaza Columbus OH 43218 Business E-Mail: rwiseman@bricker.com.

WISHARD, DELLA MAE, former newspaper editor; b. Bison, SD, Oct. 21, 1934; d. Ervin E. and Alma J. (Albertson) Preszler; m. Glenn L. Wishard, Oct. 18, 1953; children: Glenda Lee, Pamela A., Glen Evin. Grad. HS, Bison. Mem. SD Ho. of Reps., Pierre, 1984-96; pub., editor Bison Courier, SD, 1996-2000; owner Wishards Rentals, Rapid City, SD, 2004—. Colunist: County Farm Bur., 1970—96. State comitteewoman Rep. Ctrl. Com., Perkins County, SD, 1980—84, SD, 1998—2001; Rep. precinct comitteewoman Pennington County, 2006—; chmn. Perkins County Rep., 2000—03. Mem.: SD Farm Bur. (state officer 1982), Am. Legis. Exch. Coun. (state coord. 1985—91, state chmn. 1991—96), Fed. Rep. Women (chmn. Perkins County chpt. 1978—84). Lutheran. Avocations: writing, gardening. Home and Office: 3900 S Valley Dr Rapid City SD 57703 Personal E-mail: wishd@wes.comm.com.

WISHARD, GORDON DAVIS, lawyer; b. Indpls., Jan. 7, 1945; s. William Niles Jr. and Caroline (Davis) W.; m. Anne Emison; children: Claire Wishard Hoppenworth, Gordon Davis Jr. BA, Williams Coll., 1966; JD, Ind. U., 1969. Bar: Ind. 1969, US Dist. Ct. (so. dist.) Ind. 1969, US Ct. Appeals (7th cir.) 1976, US Supreme Ct. 1980, US Tax Ct. 1983. Ptnr. Ice Miller, Indpls. Mem. Am. Coll. Trust and Estate Coun. (Ind. chmn. 1990-95). Avocations: hunting, fishing. Office: Ice Miller 1 American Sq Indianapolis IN 46282-0020 Office Phone: 317-236-2331.

WISHNER, MAYNARD IRA, retired finance company executive, lawyer; b. Chgo., Sept. 17, 1923; s. Hyman L. and Frances (Fisher) W.; m. Elaine Loewenberg, July 4, 1954; children: Ellen Kenemore, Jane Wishner, Miriam Segel. BA, U. Chgo., 1944, JD, 1947; LHD (hon.), Spertus Inst., 1998, Hebrew Union Coll., 2001, Spertus Coll. Judaica, 2001. Bar: Ill. 1947. Exec. dir. Chgo. Commn. on Human Relations, 1947-52; chief ordinance enforcement div. Law Dept., City of Chgo., 1952-55; mem. law firm Cole, Wishner, Epstein & Manilow, Chgo., 1955-63; with Walter E. Heller & Co., Chgo., 1963-86, pres., 1974-86; of counsel Rosenthal and Schanfield, Chgo., 1986-95, ret., 1995—. Dir. Walter E. Heller Internat. Corp., Am. Nat. Bank & Trust Co., and br. cos., Chgo. Pres. Jewish Fedn. Met. Chgo., 1987-89; chair Nat. Jewish Community Rels., 1992-94, pres. Coun. Jewish Fedn., 1993-96; chmn. bd. govs. Am. Jewish Com., 1977-80, nat. pres. 1980-83, hon. pres., recipient Human Rights medallion, 1975; bd. dirs. Nat. Found. for Jewish Culture; chmn. Ill. Humanities Coun.; commr. Nat. Hillel Found.; mem. vis. com. U. Chgo. Sch. Social Svc. Adminstrn. and Divsn. of the Humanities; chair Ill. Humanities Coun., 1991-93; bd. govs. Jewish Agy. for Israel. Recipient Rosenwald award Jewish Fedn. Met. Chgo., Officers Merit medal Republic of Poland, United Hellenic Leadership Coun. Frisis award, Civic Achievement award U. Chgo. Home: 1410 Sheridan Rd Wilmette IL 60091-1895 Home Phone: 847-256-5015. E-mail: maynwish@aol.com.

WISLER, DAVID CHARLES, aerospace engineer; b. Pottstown, Pa., Apr. 21, 1941; s. Lloyd William and Ruth Georgiana (Enos) W.; m. Judith Ann Caleen, Aug. 22, 1964 (dec. Mar. 1979); children: Scott David, Cheryl Lynn; m. Beth Ellen Howard, Jan. 5, 1980; 1 child, Daniel James; step children: Chad Wihtford, Christen Whitford. BS in Aero Engring., Pa. State U., 1963; MS in Aero. Engring., Cornell U., 1965; PhD in Aero. Engring., U. Colo., 1970. Rsch. engr. GE R & D Ctr., Schenectady, 1965-67; mgr. aero tech. labs. GE Aircraft Engines, Evendale, Ohio, 1985—. Mgr. univ. programs and aero tech. labs.; adj. prof. Ohio State U., U. Cin., Tsinghua U., Beijing. Editor: Jour. Turbomachinery, 2003; contbr. articles to profl. jours., chpts. to books; patentee in sloped trenches in compressors. Fellow ASME (chmn. turbomachinery com. 1993-, bd. dirs. Internat. Gas Turbine Inst. 1997-, v.p. 2003—, Melville medal for best tech. paper 1989, 98, 2003, Gas Turbine award, 1990, 92); mem. AIAA (assoc.), NAE. Achievements include patents in field. Avocation: photography. Home: 40 Trappist Walk Fairfield OH 45014-4465 Office: GE Aviation 1 Neumann Way # G407 Cincinnati OH 45215-1915 Home Phone: 513-829-2286; Office Phone: 513-243-2905. Business E-Mail: dave.wisler@ae.ge.com.

WITCHER, GARY ROYAL, minister, educator; b. Clinton, Okla., July 4, 1950; s. Alton Gale and Frances Loraine (Royal) W.; m. Victoria Amy Waddington, June 6, 1970; children: Jessica, Toni, Monica. BA in Art, Southwestern Okla. State U., 1973, BA in Art Edn., 1975, MEd in Art, 1978; MS in Bible and Min., Lubbock Christian U., 2006. Min., 1979. Tchr. Window Rock Sch. Dist., Ft. Defiance, Ariz., 1973-76, Western Heights (Okla.) Sch. Dist., Oklahoma City, 1976-77, Mustang (Okla.) Sch. Dist., 1977-79; minister Ch. of Christ, Cervignano, Italy, 1979-86, Watertown, SD, 1986—; instr. Mount Marty Coll., Watertown, 1987—. Part-time tchr. Watertown Sch. Dist., 1987—; bd. dirs. East River Bible Camp, 1988-97. Recipient 1st Place Slide Program Competition prize Am. Fedn. Mineralogical Socs., 1993, 95. Mem. Coteau des Plains Gem and Mineral Soc. (pres. 1991-92, 95, 2004-). Republican. Avocations: photography, car restoration, collecting rocks, coins and stamps. Home: 1105 4th St NE PO Box 1622 Watertown SD 57201-1202 Office: Church Of Christ PO Box 1622 Watertown SD 57201-6622

WITCOFF, SHELDON WILLIAM, lawyer; b. Washington, July 10, 1925; s. Joseph and Zina (Ceppos) W.; m. Margot Gail Hoffner, Sept. 6, 1953; children: Lauren Jill, David Lawrence, Lisa Ann, Julie Beth. BS in Elec. Engring, U. Md., 1949; JD, George Washington U., 1953. Bar: D.C. 1953, N.Y. 1955, Ill. 1956. Patent examiner Patent Office, Dept. Commerce, 1949-53; patent lawyer Bell Telephone Labs., Murray Hill, NJ, 1953-55; ptnr. Bair, Freeman & Molinare, Chgo., 1955-69, Allegretti, Newitt, Witcoff & McAndrews, Chgo., 1970-88, Allegretti & Witcoff, LTD, Chgo., 1988-95, Banner & Witcoff Ltd., Chgo., 1995—. V.p., dir. Art Splty. Co., Chgo., 1967-84; v.p. Caspian Fur Trading Co., N.Y.C.; co-founder Child Abuse Unit for Studies, Edn. and Svcs., Chgo. Fire and police commr., Skokie, Ill., 1960-63. Served with USNR, 1943-46. Mem. Am. Bar Assn., Intellectual Property Assn. of Chgo., Order of Coif, Tau Epsilon Phi, Phi Delta Phi., B'nai B'rith. Office: 10 S Wacker Dr Chicago IL 60606-7407 Personal E-mail: witcoff@hotmail.com. Business E-Mail: switcoff@bannerwitcoff.com.

WITEK, KATE, state senator, trucking company executive; b. Detroit, Oct. 22, 1954; m. Charles Wite, 1974; children: Thomas Charles, Kimberly Rose. Student, Ea. Mich. U. Owner, mgr. Witek Trucking Co.; mem. Nebr. Senate, Lincoln, 1992-98; Auditor of Pub. Accounts NE, Lincoln, 1999—. Mem. commerce and ins. com., govt., mil. and vet. affairs com. Mem. Nat. Small Bus. United, Nebr. Motor Carriers, Millard Jaycees. Republican. Home: 5179 S 147th St Omaha NE 68137-1439 Office: Auditor of Public Accounts State Capitol Suite 2303 PO Box 98917 Lincoln NE 68509-8917

WITHEM, RONALD E., state senator, trade association executive; b. Logan, Iowa, June 9, 1946; m. Diane Weinstein, 1973; children: Susanne, Justin. BA, Wayne State Coll., 1968; MS, U. Nebr., Omaha, 1975. Tchr. Papillion (Nebr.) H.S.; exec. v.p. Mech. Constructors Assn. Omaha; mem. Nebr. Senate, Lincoln, 1983—; assoc. v.p. external affairs & govtl. rels. U. Nebr., Lincoln. Chmn. edn. com., mem. rules com., revenue com., former mem. govt., mil. and vet. affairs coms. Former chmn. Edn. Commn. of States; former office mgr. U.S. Rep. John J. Cavanaugh. Mem. Papillion C. of C., LaVista C. of C., Omaha C. of C. Democrat. Home: 1104 Shady Tree Ln Papillion NE 68046-6194 Office: U Nebr Office External Affairs 3835 Holdege Lincoln NE 68583-0745

WITHERELL, DENNIS PATRICK, lawyer; b. Dec. 15, 1951; s. Thomas William and Kathryn Marie (Savage) Witherell; m. Suzanne Witherell; children: Natalie, Jay stepchildren: Jodi Brouilette, Shelby Watson, Shane Allen. AB with highest honors, U. Mich., Ann Arbor, 1973; JD summa cum laude, Ohio State U., Columbus, 1977. Bar: Ohio, US Dist. Ct. (no. dist.) Ohio, US Ct. Appeals (6th cir.). Law clk. U.S. Ct. Appeals (6th cir.), Cin., 1977—78; assoc. Shumaker, Loop & Kendrick LLP, Toledo, 1978—83, ptnr., 1983—. Exec. bd. NW Ohio chpt. March of Dimes Birth Defects Found., Toledo, 1978—91; chmn. March of Dimes Birth Defects Found., .W. Ohio chpt., 1982—84; trustee Kidney Found. of Northwest Ohio, 1988—94, pres., 1992—93; trustee Life Connection of Ohio, 1991—2004, 2006—, Vis. urse-Extra Care, 1994—99. Mem.: ABA, Nat. Multiple Sclerosis Soc. (bd. trustees Northwest Ohio chpt. 1999—, chmn. 2004—06), Soc. of Ohio Hosp. Attys., Toledo Bar Assn, Ohio State Bar Assn. (chmn. health care law com. 1988—92), Am. Health Lawyers Assn. Roman Catholic. Home: 3218 Stonegate Dr Maumee OH 43537-9476 Office Phone: 419-321-1221.

WITHERELL, MICHAEL S., physicist, educator; b. Toledo, Sept. 22, 1949; s. Thomas W. and Marie (Savage) W.; m. Elizabeth Hall. BS in Physics, U. Mich., 1968; MS, U. Wis., 1970; PhD in Physics, U. Wis., Madison, 1973. Instr. Princeton (N.J.) U., 1973-75, asst. prof., 1975-81, U. Calif., Santa Barbara, 1981-83, assoc. prof., 1983-86, prof., 1986-99, prof. physics, 2005—, vice chancellor for rsch., 2005—; dir. Fermi Nat. Accelerator Lab. (Fermilab), Batavia, Ill., 1999—2005. Guggenheim fellow John S. Guggenheim Found., 1989-90; recipient Gold award US Sec. Energy, 2004 Fellow AAAS, Am. Physical Soc. (W.K.H. Panofsky prize 1990); mem. NAS Achievements include research in application of technologies to study particle physics: silicon vertex detectors and high-speed data acquisition sys. Office: U Calif Santa Barbara Office of Rsch 3227 Cheadle Hall Santa Barbara CA 93106-2050 Office Phone: 805-893-8270. Business E-Mail: witherell@research.ucsb.edu.

WITHERS, W. RUSSELL, JR., broadcast executive; b. Cape Girardeau, Mo., Dec. 10, 1936; s. Waldo Russell Sr. and Dorothy Ruth (Harrelson) W.; 1 child, Dana Ruth. BA, S.E. Mo. State U., 1958. Disc jockey Sta. KGMO Radio, Cape Girardeau, 1955-58; account exec. Sta. WGGH Radio, Marion, Ill., 1961-62; v.p. LIN Broadcasting Corp., Nashville, 1962-69; exec. v.p., dir. Laser Link Corp., Woodbury, NY, 1970-72; owner Withers Broadcasting of Hawaii, 1975-79, Withers Broadcasting of Minn., 1974-79, Withers Broadcasting Cos., Iowa, 1981—, Mood Music Ill., Mt. Vernon, 1973—, Mood Music, Inc., Cape Girardeau, 1972—, Royal Hawaiian Radio Co., Inc., others, WROY -WRUL, 2006, WYNG, 2007. Owner various radio and TV stas. including KREX-TV, Grand Junction, Colo., KREY-TV, Montrose, Colo., KREG-TV, Glenwood Springs, Colo., Page Ins. and Real Estate, Mt. Vernon, Ill.; chmn. bd., CEO Withers Beverage Corp., Mobile, Ala., 1973—79; chmn. adv. bd. Mut. Network; bd. dirs. Theatrevision, Inc., Turneffe Island Lodge, Ltd., Belize, Sta. WDTV, Clarksburg, W.Va., WMIX-AM-TV, Mt. Vernon, KGMO-KAPE, Cape Girardeau, KOKX AM-FM, Keokuk, Iowa, KTRC, Santa Fe, KRHW and KBXB, Sikeston, Mo., WKIB Anna, Cape Girardeau, WMOK, WREZ and WZZL, Paducah, Ky., WSDR-WSSQ, WZZL, Sterling Rock Falls, Ill., WILY, WRXX (FM), Centralia, Ill., WEBQ and WEBQ-FM, Harrisburg, Ill.; pres. Ill. Pub. Airports Assn.; co-chmn. TARPAC. Bd. dir., chmn. bd. Mt. Vernon Tourism and Conv. Bur.; chmn. Mt. Vernon Airport Authority; bd. regents Lincoln Acad.; past pres. IPAA; past chmn. Conv. & Visitors, Airport Authority; bd. dir. No. Colo. C.C., Libr. Am. Broadcasters, Radio Bd., AP. With U.S. Army, 1957-58. Mem. Mt. Vernon C. of C. (bd. dir.), Nat. Assn. Broadcasters (bd. dir., exec. com.), Ill. Broadcasters Assn., Stadium Club, Mo. Athletic Club, Elks, Moose, AmVets, Masons, Shriners, Sigma Chi. Christian Scientist. Home: 16074 Hawthorne Rd Mount Vernon IL 62864-2852 Office: PO Box 1508 Mount Vernon IL 62864-0030 Home Phone: 618-244-4300; Office Phone: 618-242-3500. Personal E-mail: wrwithers@mvn.net.

WITHERS, W. WAYNE, lawyer; b. Enid, Okla., Nov. 4, 1940; s. Walter O. and Ruby (Mackey) W.; m. Patricia Ann Peppers, Dec. 12, 1974; children: Jennifer Lynn, Whitney Lee. BA, U. Okla., 1962; JD, Northwestern U., 1965. Bar: Okla. 1965, Mo. 1970, US Ct. Appeals (8th cir.), 1972, US Supreme Ct. 1972, US Ct. Appeals (fed. cir.) 1984, US Ct. Appeals (DC cir.) 1985, US Ct. Claims, 1984. Staff atty. FTC, Washington, 1965-68; co. atty. Monsanto Co., St. Louis, 1968-78, asst. gen. counsel, 1978—82; v.p., gen. counsel Monsanto Agrl. Co., St. Louis, 1978—89; exec. v.p., sec., gen. counsel Emerson Electric Co., St. Louis, 1989—. V.p. Internat. Food Biotechnology Coun., Washington, 1989-90; bd. dirs. Internat. Life Scis. Inst., Washington, 1988-89. Contbr. articles to profl. jours. Chmn. bd. Mo. Hist. Soc., 2002—04; trustee MHS, 1995—; bd. dirs. World Agrl. Forum, 1999—. Mem. ABA (sect. bus. law, com. gen. counsel, antitrust, litig.), Am. Law Inst., Bar Assn. Met. St. Louis, Am. Corp. Counsel Assn., Am. Soc. Corp. Secs., Supreme Ct. Hist. Soc., Warren E. Burger Soc., at. Ctr. State Cts., Washington Legal Found., Indsl. Biotechnology Assn. (chmn. law com. 1985-88), Environ. Law Inst. (assoc.), Nat. Agrl. Chem. Assn. (chmn. law com. 1983-85), The Conf. Bd. Coun. for Gen. Counsel (vice chmn. 1992-98), MAPI Law Coun. Office: Emerson Electric Co 8000 W Florissant Ave Saint Louis MO 63136-8506

WITHERSPOON, JOHN THOMAS, water resources consultant; b. Springfield, Mo., June 25, 1947; s. Warren Thomas and Kathryn (Corbus) w.; m. C. Frances Teter, June 12, 1971. BS, S.W. Mo. State U., 1969, MA, 1971; PhD, U. Mont., 1975. Water control inspector City of Springfield, Mo., 1976-78; dir. labs. City Utilities, Springfield, 1978-91, mgr. water treatment and supply, 1991—2001. Mem. safe drinking water commn. Mo. State Dept. Natural Resources, Jefferson City, 1992—, now chair; bd. dirs. James River Basin Partnership, Nixa, Mo., 1996; tech. advisor Watershed Com. of the Ozarks, Springfield, 1983—. Pres. Univ. Club Springfield, 1989. Mem. Am. Water Works Assn. (chair nat. and state water protection coms., Boyd Utility Mgr. award 1996, Fuller award 1999). Avocations: golf, reading, guitar, travel. Home and Office: 1248 N Yarberry Springfield MO 65802-2193 Home Phone: 417-862-1443; Office Phone: 417-861-6025. Personal E-mail: jtwithersp@aol.com.

WITKE, DAVID RODNEY, retired newspaper editor, consultant; b. Council Bluffs, Iowa, Mar. 24, 1937; s. Arnold and Rosamond Louise (Storer) W.; m. Priscilla Bill Smith, Oct. 8, 1960; 1 son, Carl. BS in Journalism, Northwestern U., 1959. Reporter, editor The Courier, Champaign-Urbana, Ill., 1962-66; copy editor The Register, Des Moines, 1966-70, city editor, 1970-73, asst. mng. editor adminstrn., 1973-74, asst. mng. editor electronics, 1974-75, mng. editor, 1975-83, dir. ops., 1983-85, dep. editor, omsbudsman, 1985-87, exec. sports editor, 1987-98, sr. editor, 1998—2002, ret., 2002; freelance cons., 2002—. Rep. Iowa Freedom of Info. Coun., Des Moines, 1973—, pres., 1986-88; vis. lectr. Drake U., 1986—, Iowa State U., 1990—; adj. faculty Simpson Coll., 2003—, adv. bd., 2007—; juror Pulitzer Prize, 1989-91; tng. cons. The Register, Des Moines, 2003—; lectr. in field Bd. dirs. Des Moines Pastoral Counseling Ctr., 2005—. Served to lt. (j.g.) USN, 1959-62, PTO. Mem. Assoc. Press Mng. Editors Assn., Mid-Am. Newspaper Assn., AP Sports Editors Assn., Iowa Newspaper Found., The Prairie Club, Sigma Delta Chi. Unitarian Universalist. Home and Office: 2521 48th Pl Des Moines IA 50310-2506 Office Phone: 515-274-0578.

WITOSKY, GARY J., retired manufacturing executive; m. Kate Witosky; 2 children. BA in Acctg. and Bus. Adminstrn., Thiel Coll., 1976. Audit mgr. Ernst & Whinney, Cleve.; treas., corp. contr. Park Corp., Cleve., until 1994; tras. Am. Axle & Mfg., Detroit, 1994-97, v.p., 1996-97, v.p. fin., CFO, 1997-99; pres., CEO Colfor Mfg. Inc., Malvern, Ohio, 1999—2001; interim v.p. fin. Thiel Coll., Greenville, Pa., 2004. Adj. prof. bus. adminstrn. Thiel Coll., Greenville, Pa., 2002—. Office: Bus Adminstrn Thiel College 75 College Ave Greenville PA 16125

WITT, GARY DEAN, former state legislator; b. Smithville, Mo., Feb. 2, 1965; s. Donald Audon and Jo Ellen Witt. BA in Comm., William Jewel Coll., 1987; JD, U. Mo., 1990. Bar: Mo. 1990, Kans. 1992. Ptnr. Witt, Hicklin & Witt, Platte City, Mo., 1990—98; assoc. cir. judge 6th Jud. Cir., Platte County, Mo., 1998—; mem. Mo. Ho. of Reps., Jefferson City, 1993-96, chmn. judiciary and ethics com., 1993-96. Named one of Ten Outstanding Young Missourians, Mo. Jaycees, 1993, Outstanding Legislator, Mo. Bar Assn., 1993; recipient Outstanding Contbn. to Adminstrn. of Justice award Mo. Jud. Conf., 1991, 92, 93, 94, 95; Walter Pope Binns pus. svc. fellow, 1993. Mem. Mo. Assn. Trial Attys. (Outstanding Legislator 1991-92, 93), Platte County Mech. and Agrl. Soc. (bd. dirs. 1992-94), Platte County Bar Assn. (pres. 2002), Mo. Assn. Probate and Assoc. Circuit Judges (pres. 2003), Platte County Hist. Soc. (treas. 1997-2001), Delta Theta Phi, Kappa Alpha Order. Democrat. Baptist. Avocation: waterskiing. Office: 428 Main St Platte City MO 64079-9438

WITTEN, LOUIS, physics professor; b. Balt., Apr. 13, 1921; s. Abraham and Bessie (Perman) W.; m. Lorraine Wollach, Mar. 27, 1949 (dec. 1987); children: Edward, Celia, Matthew, Jesse; m. Francis L. White, Jan. 2, 1992. BE, Johns Hopkins U., Balt., 1941, PhD, 1951; BS, NYU, 1944. Research assoc. Princeton U., NJ, 1951-53; research assoc. U. Md., College Park, 1953-54; staff scientist Lincoln Lab., MIT, 1954-55; assoc. dir. Martin Marietta Research Lab., Balt., 1955-68; prof. physics U. Cin., 1968-91, prof. emeritus, 1991—. Trustee Gravity Research Found. Editor: Gravitation: An Introduction to Current Research, 1962, Relativity: Procs. of Relative Conf. in Midwest of 1969, Symposium on Asymptotic Structure of Space-Time, 1976; patentee in field; contbr. numerous articles to sci. jours. First lt. Air Corps US Army, 1942—46. Fulbright lectr. Weitzmann Inst. Scis., Rehovot, Israel, 1963-64 Fellow Am. Phys. Soc.; mem. Am. Math. Soc., Internat. Astron. Union, AAAS. Office: Univ Cincinnati Dept Physics Cincinnati OH 45221-0011 Office Phone: 513-556-0532. Business E-Mail: louis.witten@uc.edu.

WITTER, RICHARD LAWRENCE, veterinarian, educator; b. Bangor, Maine, Sept. 10, 1936; s. John Franklin and Verna Harriet (Church) W.; m. Joan Elizabeth Denny, June 30, 1962; children: Jane Katherine, Steven Franklin. BS, Mich. State U., 1958, D.V.M., 1960; MS, Cornell U., 1962, PhD, 1964. Rsch. veterinarian Agrl. Rsch. Svc., USDA, East Lansing, Mich., 1964-75, dir. Avian Disease and Oncology Lab., 1975-98, veterinarian; clin. prof. pathology Mich. State U., East Lansing, 1965—. Contbr. articles to profl. jours. Recipient Disting. Alumni award Coll. Vet. Medicine, Mich. State U., 1985, Disting. Svc. award USDA, 1985, Marek Commemorative medal U. Budapest, 1997, Pfizer Excellence in Poultry Rsch. award, 1998. Mem. NAS, AVMA, Am. Assn. Avian Pathologists (P.P. Levine award 1967, 81, 88, 92, 98, Upjohn Achievement award 1992, Spl. Svc. award 1998), Poultry Sci. Assn. (CPC Internat. award 1976), World Vet. Poultry Assn. (B. Rispens rsch. award 1983). Lodges: Kiwanis. Avocations: piano, hunting, fishing, gardening. Home: 1799 Elk Ln Okemos MI 48864-5917 Office: Avian Disease and Oncology Lab 3606 E Mt Hope Rd East Lansing MI 48823-5338

WITTHUHN, BURTON ORRIN, retired university official; b. Allentown, Pa., Aug. 22, 1934; s. Ray Arthur and Mae Marcella (Kline) W.; m. Patricia King, June 24, 1961; children: Jonathan, Andrew. BS, Kutztown U., Pa., 1956; MEd, Pa. State U., 1962, PhD, 1968. Tchr. Allentown (Pa.) Pub. Schs., 1956-63; teaching asst., assoc. Pa. State U., University Park, 1963-66, rsch. asst., 1965-66; asst. prof. Ohio State U., Columbus, 1967-70; prof., chmn. dept. geography Edinboro (Pa.) State Coll., 1970-79, assoc. v.p. acad. affairs, 1980-83; provost, v.p. acad. affairs Edinboro Univ. of Pa., 1984-88, Western Ill. U., Macomb, 1988-93, acting pres., 1993, provost, v.p. acad. affairs, prof. geography, 1994—2002, ret., 2002. Vis. rsch. prof. Nat. Taiwan Normal U., 1978; cons. Project Africa/Carnegie-Mellon U., Pitts., 1967-70, 92, 87, 95; mem. mid. states periodic rev. team, Phila., 1986—; mem. mid. states evaluation team in conjunction with Am. Optometric Assn., 1987; mem. evaluation team Pa. Dept. Edn., 1988; mem. accreditation team Am. Optometric, 1990—; evaluator Higher Learning Commn. North Cen. Assn., 1994—; examiner Lincoln Found. for Bus. Excellence, 1996-2000; vice-chmn. Quad Cities Grad. Ctr., 1991-2000; mem. nat. screening com. for Africa, Inst. of Internat. Edn., 1994-96. Co-author: Discovery in Geography, 1976; co-author: So You Want to Go to College: 50 Questions to Ponder, Strategies for Timely Degree Completion: Connecting the Parts, Strategies for Timely Degree Completion: Myths and Realities, Technology: Bridge or Barrier To More Timely Degree Completion?, 1998;; mem. editl. bd. Pa. Geographer, Chronicle of CQI; contbr. chpts. to books. Mem. Edinboro Planning & Zoning Commn., 1973-77, McDonough County Tuberculosis Sanitorium Bd., 2003-; vol. Habitat Humanity, Loaves and Fishes, McDonough Dist. Hosp. Recipient Disting. Alumnus award Kutztown U., 1990; Fulbright Hays fellow, Ethiopia, Kenya, Uganda, 1965. Mem. Nat. Coun. Geog. Edn. (exec. bd. 1977-80, mem. award com. for region IV 1981), Pa. Coun. Geog. Edn. (exec. sec. 1976-79, pres. 1975-76, Outstanding Prof. award 1978), Rotary (pres. Macomb club 1998-99, Edinboro club 1972-73), State Univ. Annutants Assn. (pres. Macomb Chptr. 2003—). Methodist. Avocations: reading, golf, photography, volunteering. Home: 24 Heritage Green Hudson WI 54016 Personal E-mail: 13jose22@msn.com.

WITTLINGER, TIMOTHY DAVID, lawyer; b. Dayton, Ohio, Oct. 12, 1940; s. Charles Frederick and Dorothy Elizabeth (Golden) W.; m. Diane Cleo Dominy, May 20, 1967; children: Kristine Elizabeth, David Matthew. BS in Math., Purdue U., 1962; JD with distinction, U. Mich., 1965. Bar: Mich. 1966, U.S. Dist. Ct. (ea. dist.) Mich. 1966, U.S. Ct. Appeals (6th cir.) 1968, U.S. Supreme Ct. 1971. Assoc. Clark Hill (formerly Hill Lewis), Detroit, 1965-72, ptnr., 1973—, head litigation dept., 1976-91, gen. counsel, 1997—, chief legal officer, 1997—. Profl. assistance com. U.S. Dist. Ct. (ea. dist.) Mich., 1981-82; mem. Mich. Supreme Ct. Com. to Evaluate Mediation Ct. Rule, 1997-98; author, lectr. Ctr. for Internat. Legal Studies, 1999—; mem. coll. fellows Ctr. Internat. Legal Studies, Salzburg, Austria; vis. prof. Southern Fed. U. Rstov-un-dun, Russia. Mem. ho. of deps. Episc. Ch., NYC, 1979-2003; vice chmn. Robert Whitaker Sch. Theology, 1983-87; sec. bd. trustees Episc. Ch., Diocese of Mich., Detroit, 1983—, sec. conv. Episc. Diocese of Mich., 1990—, ch. atty., 1997—, sec. Episc. nat. econ. justice implementation com., 1988-95, Episc. nat. exec. coun., 1991-97, nat. audit com., 2000-03; mem. Nat. Standing Commn. on Ministry Devel., 2000-06; ministry com. Nat. Episc. Jubilee, Nat. Episc. Coalition for Social Witness and Justice, Fifth Province Episc. Ecclesiastical Ct. Appeal, 1997-2000; treas. Episcopal Ch. Province V, 2006-; bd. dirs. Episc. Student Found., U. Mich., 1990-93, 2000-2002; chair Grubb Inst. Behavioral Studies Ltd., Washington, 1986—, London, 1986—; bd. dirs., treas., Birmingham Village Playhouse, 2000—; bd. trustees, Michigan Interfaith Trust Fund, 2007-. Mem. ABA, Engring. Soc. Detroit, Assn. Profl. Responsibility Lawyers. Home: 736 N Glenhurst Dr Birmingham MI 48009-1143 Office: Clark Hill 500 Woodward Ave Ste 3500 Detroit MI 48226-3435

WITTMAN, RANDY SCOTT, professional basketball coach; b. Indpls., Oct. 28, 1959; m. Kathy Wittman; children: Ryan, Lauren. BS, Ind. U., 1983. Draft pick Washington Bullets, 1983; player Atlanta Hawks, 1983—88, Sacramento Kings, 1988—89, Ind. Pacers, 1989—92, asst. coach, 1992—93, Dallas Mavericks, 1993—94, Minn. Timberwolves, 1994—99, 2001—05, 2006—07, head coach, 2007—; asst. coach Orlando Magic, 2005—06; head coach Cleve. Cavaliers, 1999—2001. Named to Ind. U. Hall of Fame, 1995. Office: Minn Timberwolves Target Center 600 First Ave N Minneapolis MN 55403-1416

WIXTROM, DONALD JOSEPH, translator; b. Republic, Mich., Oct. 14, 1928; s. Joseph Albert and Edith (Johnson) W.; m. Marilyn Jean Sjoquist, Oct. 14, 1961; children: Joe Alan, Lorna Jean, Aaron Matthew. Free lance translator, Republic, 1966—. Mem. Am. Translators Assn. Baptist. Home and Office: 6035 Dogwood Rd Republic MI 49879-9214

WOBBLE, DICK, radio personality; b. St. Louis; m. Renee Wobble. Student, U. Mo. Announcer, producer Classic 99, St. Louis. Avocation: reading. Office: Classic 99 85 Founders Ln Saint Louis MO 63105

WOEHRLEN, ARTHUR EDWARD, JR., dentist; b. Detroit, Dec. 9, 1947; s. Arthur Edward and Olga (Hewka) W.; m. Sara Elizabeth Heikoff, Aug. 13, 1972; 1 child, Tess Helena. DDS, U. Mich., 1973. Resident in gen. dentistry USAF, 1973-74; gen. practice dentistry Redwood Dental Group, Warren, Mich., 1976—. Instr. Sinai Hosp., Detroit, 1977—; chief of dentistry St. John's Hosp., Macomb Ctr., Mt. Clemens, Mich., 1982—; mem. dentistry staff Hutzel Hosp., Warren; reviewer Chubb Ins. Co. (malpractice claims), 1978-89; bd. mem. Mich. Acad. Gen. Dentistry (chmn. State of Mich. Continuing Dental Edn. Accreditation). Contbr. articles on dentistry to profl. jours. Served to capt. USAF, 1973-76. Fellow Internat. Coll. of Oral Implantologists; mem. ADA, Acad. Gen. Dentistry (Master), Mich. Dental Assn., Acad. Gen. Dentistry, Am. Acad. Oral Medicine, Fedn. Dentaire Internationale, Acad. Dentistry for the Handicapped, Am. Acad. Oral Implantologists, Internat. Coll. Oral Implantologists, Macomb Dist. Dental Soc.; panel mem. Am. Arbitration Assn. Republican. Home: 25460 Dundee Rd Royal Oak MI 48067-3018 Office: 13403 E 13 Mile Rd Warren MI 48088-3188

WOELFEL, JAMES WARREN, philosophy and humanities educator; b. Galveston, Tex., Aug. 16, 1937; s. Warren Charles and Mary Frances (Washinka) W.; m. Sarah Chappell Trulove, Nov. 24, 1982; children by previous marriages: Skye Caitlin, Allegra Eve, Sarah Judith; stepchildren: Ann Marie and Paul Trulove. BA, U. Okla., 1959; MDiv, Episcopal Div. Sch., Cambridge, Mass., 1962; MA, Yale U., 1964; PhD, U. St. Andrews, Scotland, 1967. Asst. prof. philosophy and religion U. Kans., Lawrence, 1966-70, asst. prof. philosophy, 1970-71, assoc. prof. philosophy and religion, 1971-75, prof. philosophy and religious studies, 1975-88, prof. philosophy, 1988—, acting chmn. dept. religious studies, 1983-84, dir. Humanities and Western civilization program, 1985—. Manuscript reader for various presses, jours. Author: Bonhoeffer's Theology, 1970, Borderland Christianity, 1973, Camus: A Theological Perspective (republished as Albert Camus on the Sacred and the Secular, 1987), 1975, Augustinian Humanism, 1979, The Agnostic Spirit as a Common Motif in Liberal Theology and Liberal Scepticism, 1990, Portraits in Victorian Religious Thought, 1997, The Existentialist Legacy and Other Essays on Philosophy and Religion, 2006; co-editor (with Sarah Chappell Trulove): Patterns in Western Civilization, 1991, 4th edit., 2006; contbr. essays, revs. to profl. jours.; contbr. articles to profl. jours. Danforth grad. fellow Episcopal Div. Sch., Cambridge, Mass., 1959-62, U. St. Andrews, 1962-63, 65-66, Yale U., New Haven, 1963-65; Fulbright scholar U. St. Andrews, 1962-63, Pub. Scholar award Kans. Humanities Coun., 1997; grantee NEH, Exxon Found., Mellon Found., Menninger Found., Inst. for Ecumenical and Cultural Rsch. Mem. Am. Philos. Assn., Assn. for Core Texts and Courses, Phi Beta Kappa. Democrat. Avocations: piano, walking. Home: 808 Alabama St Lawrence KS 66044-3942 Office: U Kans Humanities & Western Civilization Program Bailey Hall 1440 Jayhawk Blvd Rm 308 Lawrence KS 66045-7574 Office Phone: 785-864-3011. E-mail: woelfel@ku.edu.

WOERTZ, PATRICIA ANN, agricultural company executive, retired oil company executive; b. Pitts., Mar. 17, 1953; married; 3 children. BS in Acctg., Pa. State U., 1974; grad. Internat. Exec. Devel. Program, Columbia U., 1994. Acct. Ernst & Young, Pitts., 1974—77; with Gulf Oil Corp., Pitts., 1977-81, Houston, 1981-85; with debt. reduction process, merger of Gulf and Chevron, 1985-87; fin. mgr. Chevron Info. Tech. Co., 1989-91, strategic planning mgr., 1991-93; pres. Chevron Can. Ltd., Vancouver, B.C., 1993-96, Chevron Internat. Oil Co., 1996-98; v.p. logistics and trading Chevron Products Co., Chevron Corp., 1996-98, v.p., 1998—2001; pres. Chevron Products Co., 1998—2001; exec. v.p. Global Downstream ChevronTexaco Corp, San Francisco, 2001—06; pres., CEO Archer Daniels Midland Co., Decatur, Ill., 2006—07, chmn., pres., CEO, 2007—. Bd. dirs. Archer Daniels Midland Co., 2006—, Proctor & Gamble, 2008—. Bd. trustees U. San Diego; bd. visitors Pa. State U. Named a Disting. Alumna, Pa. State U., 2005; named one of Most Powerful Women in Bus., Fortune mag., 2005, 50 Most Powerful Women in Bus., 2006, 100 Most Powerful Women, Forbes mag., 2006—07, 50 Who Matter Now, CNNMoney-.com Bus. 2.0, 2006, 50 Women to Watch, Wall St. Jour., 2006; recipient Alumni Fellow award, 2002. Mem.: Calif. C. of C. (bd. mem. 1999—), Am. Petroleum Inst. (bd. dirs.). Office: Archer Daniels Midland Co 4666 Faries Pkwy Decatur IL 62526

WOESE, CARL R., biophysicist, microbiology educator; b. Syracuse, NY, July 15, 1928; AB in Math. and Physics, Amherst Coll., 1950, DSc (hon.), 1985; PhD in Biophysics, Yale U., 1953; postgrad., U. Rochester, 1953-55; DSc (hon.), Syracuse U., 1994. Rsch. assoc. biophysics Yale U., New Haven, 1955-60; biophysicist GE Rsch. Lab., 1960-63; prof. microbiology U. Ill., Urbana-Champaign, 1964—. Stanley O. Ikenberry chair U. Ill., 1996—. Contbr. articles to profl. jours. Recipient Bergey award Bergey's Manual Trust, 1983, John D. and Catherine T. MacArthur award, 1984, Leeuwenhoek medal 1990, 1992, 23d Brown-Hazen Lctrs. award, 1992, Roger W. Stanier Meml. Lctr. award U. Calif., Berkeley, 1993, Nat. Medal Sci., 2000, Crafoord prize, 2003; Univ. Sr. scholar U. Ill., 1986. Fellow Explorer's Club, Indian NAS, Am. Acad. Arts and Scis., Am. Acad. Microbiology; mem. Deutsche Gesellschaft fur Hygiene und Mikrobiologie (corr.), Deutsche Akademie Der Naturforscher Leopoldina, Bayerische Akademie der Wissenschaften (corr.), Max-Planck Soc., NAS (Selman A. Waksman award 1997), Ctr. Advanced Study U. Ill. Office: U Ill Chem & Life Scis Lab 131 Burrill Hall 601 S Goodwin Ave Urbana IL 61801-3709

WOGAMAN, GEORGE ELSWORTH, insurance company executive, financial consultant; b. Mikado, Mich., May 29, 1937; s. Edgar R. and Leah Katherine (McGuire) W.; m. Sandra Lee Jensen, Apr. 10, 1965; children: Jennifer, Christopher. Grad. various ins. courses. CLU, registered rep.; cert. ChFc. With Blair Transit Co., Dun & Bradstreet, Chrysler Engring. Co., 1955-61; exec. chef Westward Ho!, 1961-68; owner, mgr. George Wogaman Ins. Agy., Grand Forks, N.D., 1969—. Mem. pres. coun. Farmers Ins. Group, 1988—98, 1999—2004; alderman East Grand Forks (Minn.) City Coun., 1979—2000, v.p., 1982—2000. Mem. Red River Valley Estate Planning Coun.; mem. Wesley United Meth. Ch., Grand Forks; pres. bd. dirs. Econ. Devel. and Housing Authority, East Grand Forks, Minn., 2007. Recipient Pub. Svc. award East Grand Forks City Coun., 1979. Mem. Am. Soc. CLU's, North Valley Life Underwriters Assn. (Life Underwriter of Yr. 1988), Famers Financial Solutions. Home: 1818 19 h St NW East Grand Forks MN 56721-1013 Office: 2612 Gateway Dr Grand Forks ND 58203-1406 Home Phone: 218-773-9465; Office Phone: 701-772-7108. Business E-Mail: gwogaman@farmersagent.com.

WOJCICKI, ANDREW ADALBERT, chemist, educator; b. Warsaw, May 5, 1935; s. Franciszek Wojcicki and Janina (Kozlowl) Hoskins; m. Marba L. Hart, Dec. 21, 1968; children: Katherine, Christina. BS, Brown U., 1956; PhD, Northwestern U., 1960; postdoctoral fellow, U. Nottingham, Eng., 1960-61. Asst. prof. chemistry Ohio State U., Columbus, 1961-66, assoc. prof., 1966-69, prof., 1969-2000, prof. emeritus, 2001—, acting chmn., 1981-82, assoc. chmn., 1982-83, 84-86. Vis. prof. Academia Sinica, Taipei, Taiwan, 2002-03, Case Western Res. U., 1967, U. Bologna, Italy, 1988, Nat. Sci. Council Chemistry Rsch. Promotion Ctr., Taiwan, 1994, U. Sydney, Australia, 1998; vis. researcher U. Coll. London, 1969; sr. U.S. scientist Alexander von Humboldt Found., Mulheim/Ruhr, Germany, 1975-76; vis. scholar U. Calif.-Berkeley, 1984; assoc. dean Coll. of Math. and Phys. Scis., Ohio State U., 1996-98. Contbr. articles to profl. jours. Guggenheim fellow U. Cambridge (Eng.), 1976; recipient Disting. Teaching award Ohio State U., 1968, Humboldt Sr. award Humboldt Found., 1975-76, Casimir Funk Natural Sci. award, Polish Inst. of Arts and Scis. in Am., 2001. Mem.: Am. Chem. Soc. (Columbus sect. award 1992), Phi Lambda Upsilon, Sigma Xi. Home: 825 Greenridge Rd Columbus OH 43235-3411 Office: Ohio State U 100 W 18th Ave Columbus OH 43210-1185 Office Phone: 614-292-4750, 614-292-3500.

WOLANDE, CHARLES SANFORD, former computer company executive; b. Chgo., July 25, 1954; s. Sam C. and Marie Helene (Riccio) W.; children: Eric, Jill, Patrick, Ryan, Haley. B. St. Mary's Coll., Winona, Minn., 1976. Lab. tech. Jefferson Electric, Bellwood, Ill., 1976-73; pres. Comark, Inc., Glendale Heights, Ill., 1978—2002, also CFO Bloomingdale, Ill., 1978—2002. Named High Tech. Enterpreneur of the yr., Peat, Marwick, Mitchell, Chgo., 1987; named to CRN Industry Hall of Fame, 2003. Mem. C. of C. Glendale Heights. Republican. Roman Catholic. Avocations: golf, skiing. Office: 444 Scott Dr Bloomingdale IL 60108-3111

WOLD, WILLIAM SYDNEY, molecular biology educator; b. Pine Falls, Manitoba, Can., Feb. 12, 1944; came to U.S., 1973; s. Roy and Nellie (Yurchison) W.; m. Susan Ann Lees, Dec. 30, 1967; children: Loralee Jane, William Guy, Jessica Ann, Jonathan Evered. BSc, U. Manitoba, 1965, MSc, 1968, PhD, 1973. Postdoctoral fellow St. Louis U., 1973-75, instr., 1975-76, from asst. prof. to prof. molecular virology, 1976-92, prof., chmn. dept. molecular microbiology and immunology, 1992—. Reviewer's res. NIH, Washington, 1990—; cons. Genetic Therapy, Inc., 1994. Contbr. articles to Cell Jour., Jour. Biol. Chemistry, Jour. Immunology, Jour. Virology, Virology, others; assoc. editor jour. Virology, 1990—; mem. editl. bd. Jour. Virology, 1997—. NIH grantee, 1980—. Mem. AAAS, Am. Soc. Microbiology, Am. Soc. Virology, Internat. Soc. Antiviral Rsch. Achievements include discovery and characterization of human adenovirus proteins that counteract host immunosurveillance and that either inhibit or promote cell death. Office: St Louis U Molecular Microbiology & Immunology 1402 S Grand Blvd Saint Louis MO 63104-1004

WOLF, BARTH JOEL, lawyer; Sec., mgr. legal svcs. WPS Resources Corp., Green Bay, 1999—. Office: WPS Resources Corp 700 N Adams St PO Box 19001 Green Bay WI 54307-9001 Office Phone: 920-433-4901. Office Fax: 920-433-1526.

WOLF, CHARLES BENNO, lawyer; b. Chgo., Apr. 16, 1950; s. Ludwig and Hilde (Mandelbaum) W.; m. Sarah Lloyd, Sept. 1, 1973; children: Walter Ludwig, Peter Barton. AB, Brown U., 1972; JD, U. Chgo., 1975. Bar: Ill. 1975, U.S. Dist. Ct. (no. dist.) Ill. 1975, U.S. Ct. Appeals (3rd, 4th, 5th, 6th, 7th, 8th, 9th, 10th, and 11th cirs.) 1985, U.S. Supreme Ct. 1985. Ptnr. Vedder, Price, Kaufman & Kammholz, Chgo., 1975—, exec. com., 1999—. Co-author: ERISA Claims and Litigation, 10th edit., 1995; sr. editor: Employee Benefit Law, 2007-; contbr. articles to profl. jours. Fellow Am. Coll. Employee Benefits Counsel; mem. ABA (co-chair labor sect. subcom. on collective bargaining and employee benefits, past co-chair subcom. on multi-employer plans), Internat. Found. Employee Benefit Plans. Office: Vedder Price Kaufman & Kammholz 222 N La Salle St Ste 2600 Chicago IL 60601-1100 Office Phone: 312-609-7888. Business E-Mail: cwolf@vedderprice.com.

WOLF, DON ALLEN, hardware wholesale executive; b. Allen County, Ind., June 18, 1929; s. Ellis Adolphus and Bessie Ruth (Fortman) W.; m. Virginia Ann Lunz, Oct. 8, 1949; children— Rebecca, Donna, Richard, Lisa. Student exec. course, Ind. U., 1969. With Hardware Wholesalers Inc., Fort Wayne, Ind., 1947—, purchasing mgr., 1957—92, v.p., gen. mgr., 1967—80, pres. emeritus, 1993—. Bd. dirs. Clarcor. Nat. pres. Big Brothers Soc. Am., 1977-80. Mem. Nat. Wholesale Hardware Assn. (pres. 1984-85, named Hardware Wholesaler of Year 1973, 85), Ind. State C. of C. (dir., named Ind. Businessman of Yr.). Republican. Lutheran. Office: Hardware Wholesalers Inc PO Box 868 Fort Wayne IN 46801-0868 also: 6502 Nelson Rd Fort Wayne IN 46803-1920

WOLF, KATIE LOUISE, state legislator; b. Wolcott, Ind., July 9, 1925; d. John H. and Helen Munsterman; m. Charles W. Wolf, 1945; children: Mark, Marcia. Grad., Ind. Bus. Coll., 1944. Registration officer County of White, Ind., 1960, mgr. lic. bur. Ind., 1960-68; clk. 39th Jud. Cir. Ct., 1968-78; mem. Ind. Ho. of Reps., 1985-86, Ind. State Senate, 1987—. Mem. Dem. Nat. Com., 1968-90; del. Dem. nat. convs., 1972, 76, 80, 84. Named Woman of Yr., Bus. and Profl. Women's Club, 1984, Outstanding Freshman Legislator, 1985, Legislator of Yr., Ind. Conservation Offices Assn., Ind. Trial Lawyers Assn.; recipient award, Ind. Broadcasters Assn., 1985, Athen award, Monticello Greater C. of C., 1987, award, Nat. Fedn. Ind. Bus., 1998, Lifetime Achievement award, Monticello Greater C. of C., 2000, Sagamore of the Wabash award, Gov. O'Bannon, 2000, Dir.'s award, Purdue U., 2000, 4-Way Test award, Monticello Rotary, 2001, Child Case Devel. and Step Ahead award, White County. Lutheran.

WOLF, KEN, state legislator; b. Dec. 30, 1937; m. Mary; three children. BA, U. St. Thomas. Minn. State rep. Dist. 41B, 1993—; computer cons. Home: 13617 Crosscliffe Pl Rosemount MN 55068-3558

WOLF, MICHAEL ANN, announcer; m. Kurt Wolf, 2000; 1 child. BS, Emerson Coll. Anchor WLIG-TV, LI, NY, WJAC-TV, Johnstown, Pa., WHTM-TV, Harrisburg, Pa., 1993—95; weekend morning anchor WDIV-TV, Detroit, 1995—. Office: WDIV-TV 550 W Lafayette Blvd Detroit MI 48226

WOLFE, BARBARA L., economics professor, researcher; b. Phila., Feb. 15, 1943; d. Manfred and Edith (Heimann) Kingshoff; m. Stanley R. Wolfe, Mar. 20, 1965 (div. Mar. 1978); m. Robert H. Haveman, July 29, 1983; children: Jennifer Ann Wolfe, Ari Michael Wolfe. BA, Cornell U., Ithaca, NY, 1965; MA, U. Pa., 1971; PhD, U Pa., 1973. Asst. prof. Bryn Mawr (Pa.) Coll., 1973-76; rsch. assoc. Inst. Rsch. on Poverty, Madison, Wis., 1976-77, dir., 1994—2000; from asst. prof. to assoc. prof. U. Wis., Madison, 1977-88, prof., 1988—, dir., LaFollette Sch. Pub. Affairs, 2006—. Adj. prof. Australian Nat. U., 2002-; resident scholar IAS, Wassenear, Netherlands, 1984-85, 96-97, 2007; vis. scholar Russell Sage Found., N.Y., 1991-92. Co-author: Succeeding Generations, 1994; editor: (book) Role of Budgetary Policy in Demographic Transitions, 1994, contbr. articles to profl. jours. Mem. Commn. on Children with Disabilities, Washington 1994-95, Tech. Adv. Panel Social Security, Washington, 1994-95; vice chair bd. on children, youth and families IOM and NAS, 2005; mem. adv. comm. dir., IH, 2006-. Recipient Best Article of Yr. award Rev. Income and Wealth, 1992, Fulbright award Coun. Internat. Exch. of Scholars, 1984. Mem.: Population Assn. Am., Am. Soc. for Health Econ., Internat. Health Econ. Assn., Inst. of Medicine, Assn. Pub. Policy Mgmt. (policy coun. 2001—04), Internat. Inst. Pub. Fin. (bd. mgmt. 1994—2000, v.p. 2000—03), Am. Econ. Assn. (bd. CSWEP com. 1989—92, exec. bd. 1996—99). Office: U Wis Inst Rsch on Poverty 1180 Observatory Dr Madison WI 53706-1320 Office Phone: 608-262-3581. Business E-Mail: wolfe@lafollette.wisc.edu, bwolfe@wisc.edu.

WOLFE, CHARLES MORGAN, electrical engineering educator; b. Morgantown, W.Va., Dec. 21, 1935; s. Slidell Brown and Mae Louise (Maness) W.; children— David Morgan, Diana Michele BSE.E., W.Va. U., Morgantown, 1961, MSE.E., 1962; PhD, U. Ill., 1965. Research assoc. U. Ill., Urbana, 1965; mem. staff MIT Lincoln Lab., Lexington, Mass., 1965-75; prof. elec. engring Washington U., St. Louis, 1975-97, Samuel C. Sachs prof., 1982-90, dir. semicondr. research lab., sr. prof., 1979-90. Cons. MIT Lincoln Lab., 1975-76, Fairchild Semicondr., Palo Alto, Calif., 1975-76, Air Force Avionics Lab., Dayton, Ohio, 1976-79, U. Ill., 1983-85 Author: Physical Properties of Semiconductors, 1989; editor: Gallium Arsenide and Related Compounds, 1979; contbr. articles to profl. jours., chpts. to books Served as sgt. USMC, 1955-58 Fellow: IEEE (field awards com. 1984—87, Jack A. Morton award 1990); mem.: NAE, Electrochem. Soc. (Electronics divsn. award 1978).

WOLFE, DAVID LOUIS, lawyer; b. Kankakee, Ill., July 24, 1951; s. August Christian and Irma Marie (Nordmeyer) W.; m. Gail Lauret Fritz, Aug. 25, 1972; children: Laura Beth, Brian David, Kaitlin Ann. BS, U. Ill., 1973; JD, U. Mich., 1976. Bar: Ill. 1976, U.S. Dist. Ct. (no. dist.) Ill. 1976. Assoc., Gardner, Carton & Douglas, Chgo., 1976-82, ptnr., 1983—, mem. Mgmt. Com., 2002-06, HR law dept; lectr. ABA, Estate Planning Aid Assn. for Lutherans SMART Program, Chgo., 1980-84, Ill. Inst. Continuing Legal Edn., Employee Benefits Sec. Coun., Chgo. Bar Assn., Lake Shore Nat. Bank, Ill. State Bar Assn., Daughters Charity Nat. Health Sys., Lutheran Health Sys., AM. Assn. Homes & Svcs. for Aging, Mich. Assn. Cert. Pub. Accts., Diversified Investment Advisors, Decalogue Soc., Conf Cons. Actuaries, Ind. Pension Conf., Inst Internat. Rsch., Lake Shore Bank Chgo. Contbr. articles to legal publs. Co-founder, mem. steering com. adv. bd. HR Hosp.; bd. dirs. World Law Group. Recipient Recognition award Ill. Inst. Continuing Legal Edn., 1981-84, Named to Best Lawyers Am., 1993-; named Leader in Field, Chambers USA, 2006-. Mem. ABA (sects. on taxation, corp. banking and bus. law 1981-90, lectr.), NFL Players Assn. (cert. contract advisor 1983-88), NCAA (cert. contract advisor), Ill. State Bar Assn. (employee benefits sect. council, 1986-95, past chmn., recognition award 1983), Phi Kappa Phi, Beta Alpha Psi, Beta Gamma Sigma, Sigma Iota Lambda, Phi Eta Sigma. Office: Drinker Biddle Gardner Carton 191 N Wacker Dr Ste 3700 Chicago IL 60606 Office Phone: 312-569-1313. Personal E-mail: dwolfe@gcd.com. Business E-Mail: david.wolfe@dbr.com.

WOLFE, JOHN F., publishing executive; BS in Commerce, Washington and Lee U., 1965; PhD (hon.), Ohio State U., 1999. V.p. Dispatch Printing Co., 1969, pres., 1973—99, chmn., CEO, 1994—; pub. The Columbus Dispatch, 1975—. Trustee COSI Building Devel. and Fin. Resources Corp.; minority owner Columbus Blue Jackets. Bd. mem. Columbus C. of C.; trustee Franklin County Bd. Parks and Rec. Named to Am. Acad. Achievement, 1987; recipient Disting. Svc. Award, Soc. Profl. Journalists, 1981, C. of C. Columbus Award, 1993. Office: Dispatch Printing Co 34 S 3rd St Columbus OH 43215 Office Phone: 614-461-5000. Office Fax: 614-461-6087.*

WOLFE, R. DEAN, retail executive; m. Cheryl Brecheisen, Nov. 1963; children: Craig, Bret, Ryan, Sara. BBA, U. Kans., 1966, JD, 1969. Assoc. Hoskins, King, McGannon & Hahn, Kansas City, Mo.; staff atty. legal dept. The May Dept. Stores Co., St. Louis, 1972-74, atty. real estate, 1974-75, regional mgr. real estate, 1975-78, v.p. dept. stores real estate, 1978-81, sr. v.p. real estate, 1981-86, exec. v.p. real estate, 1986-96, exec. v.p. acquisitions and real estate, 1996—; also bd. dirs. Former mem. bd. aldermen City of Clayton (Mo.), com. Recreation, Sports and Wellness Ctr., plan commn. and archtl. rev. bd., strategic planningcom., parks and recreation commn.; bd. dirs., co-chair Downtown Now. Mem. Internat. Coun. Shopping Ctrs. (past bd. trustees, exec. com.), St. Louis Regional Commerce and Growth Assn. Office: The May Dept Store Co 611 Olive St Ste 1200 Saint Louis MO 63101-1756

WOLFE, RALPH STONER, microbiology educator; b. New Windsor, Md., July 18, 1921; s. Marshall Richard and Jennie Naomi (Weybright) W.; m. Gretka Margaret Young, Sept. 9, 1950; children: Daniel Binns, Jon Marshall, Sylvia Suzanne. Mem. faculty U. Ill., Urbana, 1953—, prof. microbiology, 1961—. Cons. USPHS, Nat. Inst. Gen. Med. Scis. Contbr. microbial physiology rsch. papers to profl. jours. Guggenheim fellow, 1961, 75, USPHS spl. postdoctoral fellow, 1967; recipient Pasteur award Ill. Soc. for Microbiology, 1974, Selman A Waksman Award in Microbiology Nat. Acad. of Sciences, 1995, Applied Environ. Microbiology award Procter & Gamble, 1999. Mem. NAS (Selman Waksman award in microbiology 1995), Am. Acad. Arts and Scis., Am. Soc. Microbiology (Carski Disting. Teaching award 1971, Abbott Lifetime Achievement award 1996, Procter & Gamble award in Applied and Environ. Microbiology, 1999, hon. mem.), Am. Soc. Biol. Chemists. Office: U Ill Dept Microbiology B103 Chem & Life Scis Bldg 601 S Goodwin Ave Urbana IL 61801-3709 Office Phone: 217-333-0065.

WOLFE, SHEILA A., journalist; b. Chgo. d. Leonard M. and Rena (Karn) W. BA, Drake U. Reporter Chgo. Tribune, 1956-73, asst. city editor, 1973-75; day city editor Chgo. Tribune, 1975-79; city editor Chgo. Tribune, 1979-81, met. coordinator, 1981-83, adminstrv. asst. to mng. editor, 1983-2000. Pres. City News Bur. Chgo. 1986-88, 94-96. Recipient Beck award for outstanding profl. performance Chgo. Tribune, 1979; recipient Disting. Service award Drake U., 1982 Mem. Phi Beta Kappa.

WOLFE, STEPHEN P., manufacturing executive; V.p. fin., treas. Wheel Horse Products, Inc.; dir. ops. and adminstrn. Toro/Wheel Horse, 1986-90; pres. Toro Credit Co. (subs. Toro Co.), 1990-97; v.p., treas. Toro Co., Bloomington, Minn., 1990-97, v.p. fin., treas., CFO, 1997—. Office: Toro Co 8111 Lyndale Ave S Bloomington MN 55420-1196

WOLFERT, FREDERICK E. (RICK WOLFERT), healthcare financial services company executive; BSBA, La. State U., 1976; grad. degree in banking, U. Del. With U.S. Leasing Corp., San Francisco, 1979—88; chmn., pres., CEO KeyCorp Leasing divsn., pres., CEO KeyBank USA divsn. KeyCorp, 1988—97; pres., CEO, bd. dirs. Heller Fin., 1997—2001; pres., CEO GE Capital Healthcare Fin. Svcs., Chgo., 2001—. Bd. dirs. Jr. Achievement, Chgo., Brookfield Zoo, Chgo., St. Joseph's Carondelete Child Ctr., Chgo., La. State U. Ourso Coll. Bus. Adminstrn. Mem.: Equipment Leasing Assn. (former chmn., chmn. membership com.). Office: GE Healthcare Fin Svcs 500 W Monroe St Chicago IL 60661-3679

WOLFF, FRANK PIERCE, JR., lawyer; b. St. Louis, Feb. 27, 1946; s. Frank P. and Beatrice (Stein) W.; m. Susan Scallet, May 11, 1984; children: Elizabeth McLane, Victoria Hancox. BA, Middlebury Coll., 1968; JD, U. Va., 1971. Bar: Mo. 1971, U.S. Ct. Appeals (5th cir.) 1974, U.S. Ct. Appeals (8th cir.) 1975, U.S. Supreme Ct. 1975. Ptnr. Lewis, Rice & Fingersh, St. Louis, 1971—90; ptnr., ops. ptnr., mgmt. com. Bryan Cave LLP, St. Louis, 1997—. Bd. dirs. Misco Shawnee, Inc. Bd. dirs. Leadership St. Louis, 1985-88, Washington U. Child Guidance Clinic, St. Louis, 1976-79, Jewish Family and Children's Svc., St. Louis, 1981-83, John Burroughs Sch., 1995-2000, BJC Health Sys., Inc., 1998-2001, The Butterfly House, 2001—; gen. counsel Mo. Bot. Garden, St. Louis, 1981—, Mo. Hist. Soc., St. Louis, 1997—; trustee St. Louis Children's Hosp., 1995-2001, chairperson mission vision and values com., 1996-2001, mem. exec. com., 1997-99; co-chmn. Parks Task Force, 2004 Inc. Capt. USAR, 1968-76. Mem. ABA, Mo. Bar Assn., Bar Assn. Met. St. Louis (chmn. corp. sect. 1984-85), Noonday Club, Westwood County Club (chmn. fin. com. 1989-91, treas. 1989-91, v.p. 1991-93, pres. 1994-95, exec. com. 1989-95). Office: Bryan Cave LLP One Metropolitan Square 211 Broadway Ste 3600 Saint Louis MO 63105 Home: 30 Brighton Way Unit 2 S Saint Louis MO 63124 Office Phone: 314-259-2330. Business E-Mail: fpwolff@bryancave.com.

WOLFF, LARRY F., dental educator, researcher; b. Mankato, Minn., May 25, 1948; m. Charles Harold and Madelyn Catherine (Burns) W.; m. Elizabeth Spencer Thompson, Aug. 7, 1976; children: Adam, Ryan, Sara. BA in Biology, Mankato State U., 1970, M in Biology and Chemistry, 1971; PhD in Microbiology, Northwestern U., 1974; DDS, U. Minn., 1978; M in Periodontology, NYU, 1980; cert. in dentistry, Aarhus (Denmark) Dental Coll., 1979. Rsch. fellow Northwestern U., Chgo., 1972-74; asst. prof. dentistry U. Minn., Mpls., 1980-85, assoc. prof., 1985-96, assoc. prof. periodontology, 1985-94; prof., 1996—. Contbr. articles to profl. jours. Grantee Nat. Inst. Dental Rsch. NIH, 1982—, numerous corps., 1988—. Mem. Am. Acad. Periodontology, Am. Dental Assn., Internat. Assn. Dental Rsch., Internat. Assn. Periodontists, Minn. Dental Assn., Minn. Assn. Dental Rsch. Office: U Minn Sch Dentistry 515 Delaware St SE Minneapolis MN 55455-0348

WOLFF, MICHAEL A., state supreme court judge; Grad., Dartmouth Coll., 1967; JD, U. Minn., 1970. Lawyer Legal Svcs.; mem. faculty St. Louis U. Sch. Law, 1975-98; judge Mo. Supreme Ct., 1998—, chief justice, 2005—. Chief counsel to gov., 1993-94, spl. counsel, 1994-98. Co-author: Federal Jury Practice and Instructions, 4th edit; author monthly column Law Matters: Reflections of Chief Justice Michael A. Wolff, 2005. Chief counsel to Gov. St. Louis, 1993-94, spl. counsel, 1994-98. Office: Supreme Ct Mo PO Box 150 Jefferson City MO 65102-0150

WOLFF, RONALD KEITH, toxicologist, researcher; b. Brantford, Ont., Can., July 25, 1946; s. Roy Clifford and Agnes Audrey (Stratton) W.; m. Mary Carole Cromien Wolff, Aug. 26, 1972; children: Mark, Sarah, Andrew, Brian. BS, U. Toronto, 1964-68; MS, 1968-69, PhD, 1969-72. Diplomate Am. Bd. Toxicology, 1983. Rsch. assoc. McMaster U., Hamilton, Can., 1973-76; scientist Lovelace Inhalation Toxicology Rsch. Inst., Albuquerque, N.Mex., 1976-88; sr. rsch. scientist Eli Lilly and Co., Greenfield, Ind., 1988—2004; rsch. fellow Nektar Therapeutics, San Carlos, Calif., 2004—. Author: (book chpt.) Comprehensive Treatise on Pulmonary Toxicology, 1992, Comprehensive Toxicology, 1997; contbr. articles to profl. jours. Recipient Frank Blood award Soc. Toxicology, 1989, Thomas T. Mercer joint prize Am. Assn. for Aerosol Rsch. and Internat. Soc. Aerosols in Medicine, 2002. Mem. Am. Assn. for Aerosol Rsch., Internat. Soc. Aerosols in Medicine, Soc. Toxicology, Am. Indsl. Hygiene Assn. Avocations: camping, hiking, hockey. Office: Nektar Therapeutics 150 Industrial Rd San Carlos CA 94070 Office Phone: 650-620-6581. Business E-Mail: rwolff@nektar.com.

WOLFMAN, ALAN, medical educator, researcher; b. Bronx, NY, Mar. 12, 1956; married. Postdoctoral fellow dept. biophysics U. Rochester Med. Ctr., 1988—90; assoc. staff dept. cell biology Cleve. Clinic Found., 1990—. Adj. prof. dept. biology Cleve. State U., 1994—. Contbr. articles to profl. jours.;

periodic reviewer: Molecular Cell Biology, Jour. Biol. Chemistry, Biochemistry, BBA, ad hoc reviewer for program project: Nat. Inst. Diabetes and Digestive Kidney Diseases, 1995, invited reviewer: DRTC Pilot Project Ind. U., 1995—; presenter in field. Recipient Postdoctoral fellowship award, NIH, 1985—88, Established Investigatorship award, Am. Heart Assn., 1996—; grantee Cell Biology Tng., 1979, NIH First, 1988—93. Office: Cleve Clinic Found Rsch Inst Dept Cell Biology NC10 9500 Euclid Ave Cleveland OH 44195-0001

WOLFORD, KATHRYN FRANCES, foundation administrator; b. Reading, Pa., Dec. 12, 1957; d. Howard Francis Wolford and Katherine Eva (Auker) Carbaugh. BA in History, Gettysburg Coll., 1979; MA in Religious Studies, U. Chgo. Divinity Sch., 1980; MA in Pub. Policy, U. Chgo., 1981; PhD (hon.), Gettysburg Coll., 1995; PhD (hon.), Muhlenberg Coll., 2003. Country program rep. Ch. World Svc., Dominican Republic, 1983-85; regional rep. Nat. Coun. Chs., USA, NYC, 1985-90; program dir. for L.Am., Luth. World Relief, Balt., 1991-93, pres., 1993—2006, McKnight Found., Mpls., 2006—. Former bd. mem. Md. Assn. Nonprofit Oranizations, Gettysburg Coll., Foods Resource Bank; former bd. chair InterAction, Action by Churches Together; former bd. mem. Lutheran Cmty. Found.; mem., adv. com. Johns Hopkins U. Inst. for Policy Studies. Named Md. Top 100 Women, Md. Daily Record, 2002, 2004; recipient Young Alumni Achievement award, Gettysburg Coll., Woman of Distinction award. Democrat. Lutheran. Avocation: sailing. Office: McKnight Foundation 710 S 2nd St Ste 400 Minneapolis MN 55401 Office Phone: 612-333-4220. Office Fax: 612-332-3833.

WOLFRAM, STEPHEN, physicist, computer company executive; b. London, Aug. 29, 1959; came to U.S., 1978; Degree, Eton Coll., 1976, Oxford U., 1978; PhD in Theoretical Physics, Calif. Inst. Tech., 1979. With Calif. Inst. Tech., Pasadena, 1979-82, Inst. for Advanced Study, Princeton, NJ, 1983-86; prof. physics, math, computer sci. U. Ill., Champaign, 1986-90; founder, dir. Ctr. for Complex Sys. Rsch., 1996—98; pres., CEO Wolfram Rsch. Inc., Champaign, 1987—. Author: Theory and Applications of Cellular Automata, 1986, Mathematica: A System for Doing Mathematics by Computer, 1998, 2d edit., 1991, Mathematica Reference Guide, 1992, Mathematica: The Student Book, 1994, The Mathematica Book, 3rd edit., 1996, 5th edit., 2003, Cellular Automata and Complexity, 1994, A New Kind of Science, 2002; editor jour. Complex Systems, 1986— Fellow MacArthur Found., 1981; recipient World Leaders of Tomorrow award, World Economic Forum, 1999; named Scientist of Yr., R&D Mag., 2002. Office: Wolfram Rsch Inc 100 Trade Centre Dr Champaign IL 61820-7237 Business E-Mail: s.wolfram@wolfram.com.

WOLFRAM, THOMAS, physicist, educator; b. St. Louis, July 27, 1936; s. Ferdinand I. and Audrey H. (Calvert) W.; m. Eleanor Elaine Burger, May 22, 1965; children: Michael, Gregory, Melanie, Susan, Steven. BA, U. Calif., Riverside, 1959, PhD in Physics, 1963; MA in Physics, UCLA, 1960. Engr. Atomics Internat., Canoga Park, Calif., 1960-63; mem. tech. staff N.Am. Aviation Corp. Sci. Ctr., Thousand Oaks, Calif., 1963-68; group leader in solid state physics Rockwell Internat. Sci. Ctr., Thousand Oaks, 1968-72, dir. div. physics and chemistry, 1972-74; prof. physics, chmn. dept. physics and astronomy U. Mo., Columbia, 1974-83; dir. phys. tech. divsn. AMOCO Corp., 1983-87; v.p., gen. mgr. AMOCO Laser Co., 1987-95; bus. cons., 1995—. Cons. in field. Author: The Venture, The Dragon Tamers, Electronic and Optical Properties of d-Band Perovskites; editor: Inelastic Electron Tunneling Spectroscopy, 1978; contbr. articles to profl. jours. Recipient Disting. Prof. award Argonne Univs. Assn., 1977 Fellow: Am. Phys. Soc. Home and Office: 228 Trafalgar Ln San Clemente CA 92672 Personal E-mail: ewolfram@cox.net.

WOLIN, JEFFREY ALAN, artist; AB, Kenyon Coll., 1972; MFA, Rochester Inst. Tech., 1977. Represented by Catherine Edelman Gallery, Chgo. and Robert Mann Gallery, NYC; photographer City of Kalamazoo (Mich.) Police Dept., 1973-74; asst. prof. photography Ind. U., Bloomington, 1980-86, assoc. prof. photography, 1986-92, prof., 1993—, head art dept. Head photographics svcs. George Eastman House, Rochester, 1976-80; adj. instr. photography U. Rochester, 1978-80. Exhbns. include Ryerson Photog. Are Ctr., Toronto, Can., 1978, Northlight Gallery, Tempe, Ariz., 1980, 88, Israel Mus., Jerusalem, 1980, George Eastman House, Rochester, 1981, 82, Seattle Arts Mus., 1986, Chgo. Cultural Ctr., 1986, 87, J.B. Speed Art Mus., Louisville, 1987, Silver Image Gallery, Columbus, Ohio, 1987, Marianne Deson Gallery, Chgo., 1988, Burden Gallery, N.Y., 1988, Nexus Contemporary Art Ctr., Atlanta, 1988, 89, Images Gallery, Cin., 1989, Catherine Edelman Gallery, Chgo., 1989, 91, 92, 93, 94, San Francisco Camerawork, 1990, U. Oreg. Mus. Art, Eugene, 1990, 92, Mus. Contemporary Photography, Chgo., 1991, 92, Blue Sky Gallery, Oreg. Ctr. for Photog. Arts, Portland, 1992, Mus. Fine Arts, Houston, 1992, L.A. County Art Mus., 1992, Opsis Gallery, N.Y.C., 1992, Mus. Modern Art, N.Y.C., 1992, Ctr. Creative Photography, Tucson, 1993, Robert Klein Gallery, Boston, 1994, Nelson-Atkins Mus. Art, Kansas City, 1994, Contemporary Art Ctr., New Orleans, 1995, Mpls. Mus. Am. Art, St. Paul, 1995, Art Inst. Chgo., 1996, Internat. Ctr. Photography, 1997, others; permanent collections include Seattle Arts Mus., San Francisco Mus. Modern Art, Mus. Modern Art, N.Y., Mus. Contemporary Photography, Chgo., Mus. Fine Arts, Houston, L.A. County Art Mus., Kalamazoo (Mich.) Inst. Art, Internat. Mus. Photography at George Eastman House, Met. Mus. Art, N.Y.C., Art Inst. Chgo., Ctr. Creative Photography, Tucson, Can. Ctr. for Architecture, Montreal, others. Visual Artist fellow NEA, 1988, 92, Master Artist fellow Ind. Arts Commn., 1991, John Simon Guggenheim fellow, 1991, ArtsLink fellow to Czechoslovakia, 1994, U.S./France fellow Cité Internationale des Arts-Paris, 1994. Achievements include being subject of books and articles. Office: Catherine Edelman Gallery 300 W Superior St Chicago IL 60610-3535 Fax: 312-266-1967.

WOLLE, CHARLES ROBERT, judge; b. Sioux City, Iowa, Oct. 16, 1935; s. William Carl and Vivian (Down) W.; m. Kerstin Birgitta Wennerstrom, June 26, 1961; children: Karl Johan Knut, Erik Vernon, Thomas Dag, Aaron Charles. AB, Harvard U., 1959; JD, Iowa Law Sch., 1961. Bar: Iowa 1961. Assoc. Shull, Marshall & Marks, Sioux City, 1961-67, ptnr., 1968-80; judge Dist. Ct. Iowa, Sioux City, 1981-83; justice Iowa Supreme Ct., Sioux City and Des Moines, 1983-87; judge U.S. Dist. Ct. (so. dist.) Iowa, Des Moines, 1987-92, chief judge, 1992-99, sr. U.S. dist. judge, 2001—. Faculty Nat. Jud. Coll., Reno, 1983-2004 Editor Iowa Law Rev., 1960-61. V.p. bd. dirs. Sioux City Symphony, 1972-77; bd. dirs. Morningside Coll., Sioux City, 1977-81. Fellow Am. Coll. Trial Lawyers; mem. Sioux City C. of C. (bd. dirs. 1977-78); Iowa State Bar Assn. Avocations: sports, art, music, literature, skiing. Office: Sr US Dist Judge US Dist Ct SD IA 110 E Ct St Des Moines IA 50309 Office Phone: 775-265-3736. Business E-Mail: charles_wolle@iasd.uscourts.gov.

WOLLMAN, ROGER LELAND, federal judge; b. Frankfort, SD, May 29, 1934; s. Edwin and Katherine Wollman; m. Diane Marie Schroeder, June 21, 1959; children: Steven James, John Mark, Thomas Roger. BA, Tabor Coll., Hillsboro, Kans., 1957; JD magna cum laude, U. S.D., 1962; LLM, Harvard U., 1964. Bar: S.D. 1964. Law clerk Hon. George T. Mickleson US Dist. Ct (So. Dist, SC), 1962—63; sole practice Aberdeen, 1964—71; states atty. Brown County, Aberdeen, 1967—71; justice S.D. Supreme Ct., 1971—85, chief justice, 1978—82; judge US Ct. Appeals (8th cir.), 1985—, chief judge, 1999—2002. Mem. Jud. Conference of US, 1999—2003. With US Army, 1957—59. Mem.: Am. Jud. Soc. Office: US Ct Appeals US Courthouse & Fed Bldg 400 S Phillips Ave Rm 315 Sioux Falls SD 57104-6851

WOLMAN, J. MARTIN, retired newspaper publisher; b. Elizabeth, NJ, Mar. 8, 1919; s. Joseph D. and Dora (Baum) W.; m. Anne Paley, Sept. 12, 1943; children: Natalie, Jonathan, Ruth Ellen, Lewis Joel. Student, U. Wis., 1937-42. With Wis. State Jour., Madison, 1936-84, pub., 1968-84; pres., gen. mgr. Madison Newspaper, Inc., 1969-84, ret., 1984, dir., 1969—, Lee Enterprises, Inc., 1971-74; treas. Lee Endowment Trusts, 1988—. Sec.-treas. Madison Improvement Corp., 1958-62 Treas. Wis. State Jour. Empty Stocking Club, 1948, Children and Youth Services Inc., 1962—; mem. Mayor Madison Adv. Com., 1965; bd. dirs. United Givers Fund, 1960-64, trustee, 1980—; ex-officio Roy L. Matson Scholarship Fund, 1961, Central Madison Com., Madison Art Assn.; trustee Edgewood Coll., Madison, U. Wis. Hosp. and Clinic; chmn. Madison Area Arts Coalition, 1984-85; bd. dirs. Univ. Health Sci. Center, 1975; chmn. U.S. Savs. Bond Met. Wis., 1983; coordinator Barneveld Disaster Fund, Wis., 1985-86; mem. U. Wis. Found., 1968-95; bd. dirs., trustee Wisc. Clin. Cancer Ctr., 1986—; Dir. Wisc. Newspaper Found., 1986-88; v.p., treas. Lee Endowment Found., 1989—. Served with AUS, 1942-46. Named Advt. Man of Year Madison Advt. Club, 1969, Madison Man of Achievement, 1976, Man of Yr. Salvation Army, 1993; recipient Disting. Service award Wis. Newspaper Assn., 1982, Community Service award Inland Daily Press Assn., 1983, Ralph D. Casey Minn. award for Disting. Service in Journalism, 1987, First Ringling Bros. Silver Smile award, 1993, Outstanding Svc. for Youth award Wis. State Jour., 1995, Rounders Youth Lifetime award, 1997. Mem. Madison C. of C. (dir. 1966-70, 74-84), Inland Daily Press Assn. (dir. 1961-65), Wis. Daily Newspaper League (pres. 1961-65), Wis. Newspaper Assn. (dir. 1977-84) Clubs: B'nai B'rith.

WOLPERT, LARRY, state legislator; b. 1956; BS in Bus. Adminstrn., Ohio State U.; MBA, Capital U. Legislator Ohio State Ho. Reps., Columbus, 2000—. Chmn. county and township govt. com. Ohio State Ho. Reps., mem. econ. devel. and tech. com., mem. ins. com., mem. mcpl. govt. and urban revitalization com. Mem. Hilliard (Ohio) City Coun. Recipient William Schneider award, John M. Ashbrook award. Mem.: N.W. Franklin County Hist. Soc., Dublin (Ohio) C. of C., Hilliard (Ohio) C. of C., Farm Bur. Republican. Office: Ohio State House Reps 77 South High Street 13th Floor Columbus OH 43215-6111

WOLSTEIN, SCOTT ALAN, real estate company executive; b. Cleve., June 24, 1952; s. Bert L. and Iris (Shur) W. BS in Econs. cum laude, U. Pa., 1974; JD, U. Mich. cum laude, 1977. Assoc. Thompson, Hine & Flory, Cleve., 1977-81; co-owner, exec. v.p. Cleve. Force Soccer Team, 1979—; officer Sasson of Israel, Cleve., 1980—, also bd. dirs.; gen. ptnr. Diversified Equities, Moreland Hills, Ohio, 1981—; v.p. DE Properties Corp., Moreland Hills, 1982—, DE Transp. Co., Moreland Hills, 1983—. Participant Leadership Cleve., 1983-84; bd. trustees Men's ORT, United Cerebral Palsy, Anti-Defamation League; bd. overseers Case Western Reserve U. Athletic Dept.; alumni steering com. Leadership Cleve. Mem. ABA, Ohio Bar Assn., Cleve. Bar Assn., Maj. Indoor Soccer League (competition com., chmn. referee com. 1986—). Clubs: Wharton, U. Mich. (Cleve.). Jewish. Avocations: skiing, running, tennis, golf, bicycling. Home: 32200 Chestnut Ln Cleveland OH 44124-4328 Office: Devels Diversified Realty Corp 3300 Enterprise Pkwy Beachwood OH 44122

WOLTZ, KENNETH ALLEN, retired management consultant; b. Phila., Mar. 2, 1943; s. Herman and Florence (Varell) M.; m. Barbara Hand, June 18, 1966; children: Karyn, Diane, Kenneth. BS, U.S. Mil. Acad., 1966; MBA, Xavier U., 1971. Cert. mgmt. cons. Various mgmt. positions GE, Evansdale, Ohio and Bethesda, Md., 1968-73; mgr. systems Xerox Corp., Rochester, N.Y., 1973-75; dir. info. svcs. McGraw Edison, Des Plaines, Ill., 1975-77; mng. dir., mgmt. cons. KPMG, Chgo., 1977-80; mgmt. cons., CEO, Woltz & Assoc., Inc., Barrington, Ill., 1980—; mgmt. cons. Speaker at various Univs. With U.S. Army, 1966-68. Mem. Soc. Mgmt. Info. Systems, Inst. Mgmt. Cons., West Point Soc. (treas. 1975), Assn. Corp. Growth, Assn. Mgmt. Consulting Firms, Ind. Computer Cons. Assn. Home: 800 Ocean Dr Unit 1105 Juno Beach FL 33408-1724

WOMELDORFF, PORTER JOHN, utilities executive; b. Milw., Feb. 26, 1933; s. Virgil Leslie and Leorra (Porter) W.; m. Marilyn Sapp, Jan. 7, 1966; children: John Porter, Michael Wayne. With Ill. Power Co., Decatur, 1954-95; beginning as elec. engr., successively results supr., instrumentation engr., supr. system planning, mgr. planning, 1954-79; v.p., 1979-93; global climate program exec., 1993-95; ret., 1995; pres. Womeldorff Assocs. Ltd., 1995—97. Mem. Ill. Coal Devel. Bd., 1982-95, chair. Chair adv. bd. U. Ill. Coll. Engring., 1986-89; former chair sci. com. Global Climate Coalition. Lay mem. Central Ill. Ann. Conf., United Methodist Ch., 1968—, lay leader, 1976-79, lay mem. North Central Jurisdictional Conf., 1972—, lay mem. Gen. Conf., 1976—; lay mem. Gen. Bd. Pubs., 1992—. Served to lt. C.E., AUS, 1955-57. Decorated Army Commendation Medal. Mem. Instrument Soc. Am. (v.p. 1971-73, Power Div. Achievement award 1983), IEEE, ASME, U. Ill. Elec. Engring. Alumni Assn. (pres., dir., Outstanding Alumni award 1994), Phi Kappa Phi, Tau Beta Pi, Sigma Tau, Eta Kappa Nu, Alpha Kappa Lambda. Home: 380 W Oak Ln Decatur IL 62526-1737 E-mail: pjwom@aol.com.

WONG, DAVID T., biochemist, researcher; b. Hong Kong, Nov. 6, 1935; arrived in US, 1957; s. Chi-Keung and Pui-King Wong; m. Christina Lee, Dec. 28, 1963; children: Conrad, Melvin, Vincent. Student, Nat. Taiwan U., 1955—56; BS, Seattle Pacific U., 1961; MS, Oreg. State U., 1964; PhD, U. Oreg., 1966. Post doctoral fellow U. Pa., Phila, 1966—67; sr. biochemist Lilly Rsch. Labs., Indpls., 1968-72, rsch. biochemist, 1973-77, sr. rsch. scientist, 1978-89, rsch. advisor, 1990-97, Lilly Disting. Rsch. fellow, 1997-99, cons., 2000—. Adj. prof. biochemistry and molecular biology Ind. U. Sch. Medicine, 1986—96, adj. prof. neurobiology, 1991—. Mem. editl. bd.: Chinese Jour. Physiology, 1996—2000; contbr. articles to sci. jours. Named Alumnus of Growing Vision, Seattle Pacific U., 1991, Alumnus of Yr., 1998, Disting. Alumni Scientist award, Oreg. Health and Sci. U., 2004; recipient Scientist of Yr. Pres.' award, Chinese euroscì. Soc., 1991, Discoverers award, Pharm. Mfr. Assn., 1993, Lifetime Rsch. award, Mental Health Assn. Ind., 1996, World Difference award, Ind. Health Industry Forum, 1996, Pharm. Discoverer's award Prozac, Nat. Alliance Rsch. Schizophrenia and Depression, 1996, Outstanding Achievement in eurosci. Rsch. award, Lilly Neuroscience Eli Lilly and Co., 2000, Cornerstone award, Am. Drugstore Mus. Indpls., 2000, Excellence award, Asian Am. Alliance, Inc., 2002, Pioneer Recognition award, Com. 100, 2002, Excellence award, U.S. Pan Asian Am. C. of C., 2002, Hon. Ga. Citizen, mem. Goodwill Amb. Corp., State of Ga., 2003; Alumni fellow, Oreg. State U., 2003. Mem.: Ind. Chinese-Am. Profls. Assn. (pres. 2000), Soc. Chinese Bioscientists Am. (Disting. Scientist award for drug discovery 2004), Soc. Neurosci. (pres. Indpls. chpt. 1987, 1988), Am. Soc. Pharmacology and Exptl. Therapeutics, Am. Coll. Neuropsychopharamcology, Indpls. Assn. Chinese Ams. (pres. 1987). Achievements include patents in field; research in biochemistry and pharmacology of neurotransmission; co-inventor and developer of drugs, Prozac (Fluoxetine), Cymbalta (Duloxetine, a serotonin and norepinephrine uptake inhibitor), Strattera (Atomoxetive) for attention deficit hyperactivity disorder and dapoxetine (serotonin uptake inhibitor); research in potentially useful substances which enhance transmission of norepinephrine, dopamine, serotonin, acetylcholine, and GABA-neurons; natural products led to the discovery of caboxylic ionophores: Narasin and A204, which increase transport of cations across biomembranes. Home: 5812 E Fall Creek Parkway N D Indianapolis IN 46226-1051 Home Fax: 317-254-8288. Personal E-mail: dtwongindy@iquest.net.

WONG, VICTOR KENNETH, physics professor; b. San Francisco, Nov. 1, 1938; m. Nancy Wong; children: Cassandra, Pamela, Lianna. BS in Engring. Physics, U. Calif., Berkeley, 1960, PhD in Physics, 1966. Postdoctoral fellow Ohio State U., Columbus, 1966-68; lectr., asst. prof. U. Mich., Ann Arbor, 1968-76, adj. prof. physics, 1992-95, 96—, assoc. prof. physics Dearborn, 1976-82, prof. physics, 1982-86, chmn. dept. natural sci., 1980-83, dean Coll. Arts, Sci. and Letters, 1983-86, provost, vice chancellor acad. affairs Flint, 1986-95, prof. physics, 1986—. Adj. rsch. scientist U. Mich., 1995—, dir. info. technology for rsch., 1995-2001, dir. info. tech. campus initiatives, 2001-. Assoc. editor: Math. Revs., 1980; contbr. articles to profl. jours. Mem. AAAS, Am. Phys. Soc., Am. Assn. Higher Edn. (1st chmn. Asian caucus 1986-88), Nat. U. Continuing Edn. Assn. (mem. minority com. 1989), North Ctrl. Assn. Colls. and Schs. (cons. evaluator com. 1989—, bd. trustees higher learning commn. 2004—), Am. Coun. Edn. (mem. commn. on minorities in higher edn. 1993-96), Assn. Computing Machinery, Phi Beta Kappa, Tau Beta Pi. Office: Univ Mich Office of Provost 1071 Beal Ave Ann Arbor MI 48109-2103

WOO, BENSON, financial executive; BSEE, MIT; MBA, Harvard U. Various positions GM, 1979-94; v.p., treas. Case Corp., 1994-98; corp. v.p., CFO, York Internat. Corp., 1998—99; sr. v.p. Metris Cos., Inc., Minnetonka, Minn., 1999—2003; CFO TriMas Corp., Bloomfield Hills, Minn., 2003—.

WOO, CAROLYN YAUYAN, dean; b. Hong Kong, Apr. 19, 1954; arrived in US, 1972; m. David E. Bartkus; children: Ryan, Justin. BS in Economics, with honors and highest distinction, Purdue U., 1975, MS in Indsl. Adminstrn., 1976, PhD in Strategic Mgmt., 1979. Asst. prof. mgmt. Purdue U., 1981—85, assoc. to full prof., 1985—93, assoc. exec. v.p. acad. affairs, 1995—97; dir. profl. master's programs Purdue U. Krannert Sch. Mgmt., 1993—95; Martin J. Gillen dean Mendoza Sch. Bus., Notre Dame U., 1997—, Ray and Milann Siegfried chair entrepreneurial studies, 1997—. Bd. dirs. Aon Corp., 1998—, Nisource Industries Inc., 1998—, Circuit City Stores Inc., 2001—. Bd. dirs. Catholic Relief Services, 2004—; bd. regents U. Portland, 2004—. Recipient TIEM Found. Disting. Scholar award, Internat. Coun. Small Bus., 1987, Excellence award for edn., Asian Am. Alliance, 2002, John S. Day alumni academic svc. award, Krannert Sch. Mgmt., Purdue U., 2003. Mem.: Com. of 100, Assn. to Advance Collegiate Schools Bus. Internat. (bd. dirs. 1999—, vice chair 2002—03, chair 2003—04). Office: Notre Dame Univ 204 Mendoza College Business Notre Dame IN 46556-5646 Office Phone: 574-631-7992. Business E-Mail: Carolyn.Y.Woo.5@nd.edu.

WOOD, CORINNE GIESEKE, former lieutenant governor; b. Barrington, Ill., May 28, 1954; m. Paul R. Wood; children: Ashley, Brandon, Courtney. BS, U. Ill., 1976; JD, Loyola U., 1979. Bar: Ill. 1979. Pvt. practice; counsel Ill. Savs. and Residential Fin. Bd.; atty. Hopkins & Sutter, Chgo.; gen. counsel Ill. Commr. of Banks and trusts; state rep. 59th dist. 90th Ill. Gen. Assembly, Springfield; rep. State of Ill., 1997—99, former lt. gov. Springfield, 1999—2003. Appointed spec. asst., Ill. Atty. Gen. Former co-capt. Shields Twp. Rep. Precinct; Lake Forest chmn. John E. Porter for Congress, 1994, 96; adv. mem. Coun. of Women Advisors to U.S. Congress; past 1st v.p., bd. dirs. Women's Rep. Club, past pres., bd. mem. 10th Congl. Dist. of Lake Forest/Lake Bluff chpt.; past pres. (fin. chmn.), mem. bd. govs. Lake County Rep. Fedn.; bd. dirs. Allendale Shelter Club, Allendale Assn.; adv. bd. A Safe Place; transition bd. dirs. Anne M. Kiley Ctr. for the Developmentally Disabled; mem. LWV of Lake Forest/Lake Bluff; mem. Lake Forest Open Lands Assn.; former Lake Forest chmn., sustaining mem. Jr. League of Chgo.; former new mems. chair, membership com., Sunday sch. tchr. First Presbyn. Ch. of Lake Forest; den leader Pack 43, Boy Scouts Am.; plan commr. City of Lake Forest, 1993-97, sr. housing commr., 1993-97, ad hoc com. on sr. housing bd. mem. Recipient City of Lake Forest Spl. Recognition of Pub. Svc. award. Mem. ABA, Ill. Bar Assn., Lake County Bar Assn., Chgo. Bar Assn., House Financial Insts. Comm., Comm. on Aging, Edn. Appropriations Comm., Labor and Commerce Comm., appointed mem., Legislative Rsch. Bureau, bd. mem. Republican.

WOOD, DIANE PAMELA, federal judge; b. Plainfield, NJ, July 4, 1950; d. Kenneth Reed and Lucille (Padmore) Wood; children: Kathryn Hutchinson, David Hutchinson, Jane Hutchinson; m. Robert L. Sufit, 2006. BA, U. Tex., 1971, JD, 1975; JD (hon.), Georgetown U., 2003, Ill. Inst. Tech., 2004. Bar: Tex. 1975, DC 1978, Ill. 1993. Law clk. US Ct. Appeals (5th cir.), 1975—76, US Supreme Ct., 1976—77; atty.-adv. US Dept. State, Washington, 1977—78; assoc. Covington & Burling, Washington, 1978—80; asst. prof. law Georgetown U. Law Ctr., Washington, 1980—81, U. Chgo., 1981—88, prof. law, 1988—95, assoc. dean, 1989—92, Harold J. and Marion F. Green prof. internat. legal studies, 1990—95, sr. lectr. law, 1995—; spl. cons. antitrust divsn. internat. guide US Dept. Justice, 1986—87, dep. asst. atty. gen. antitrust divsn., 1993—95; judge US Ct. Appeals (7th cir.), 1995—. Contbr. articles to profl. jours.; bd. editors: Am. Jour. Internat. Law. Bd. dirs. Hyde Park-Kenwood Cmty. Health Ctr., 1983—85. Fellow: Am. Acad. Arts and Scis.; mem.: Am. Law Inst. (elected coun. mem. 2003), Am. Soc. Internat. Law, Phi Alpha Delta. Democrat. Office: US Courthouse 219 S Dearborn St Chicago IL 60604-1803

WOOD, HARLINGTON, JR., federal judge; b. Springfield, Ill., Apr. 17, 1920; s. Harlington and Marie (Green) W. AB, U. Ill., 1942, JD, 1948. Bar: Ill. 1948. Practiced in Springfield, 1948-69; mem. firm Wood & Wood, 1948—58, 1961—69; U.S. atty. So. Dist. Ill., 1958-61; assoc. dep. atty. gen. for U.S. attys. Justice Dept., Washington, 1969-70, assoc. dep. atty. gen., 1970-72, asst. atty. gen. civil div., 1972-73; U.S. dist. judge So. Dist. Ill., Springfield, 1973-76; circuit judge U.S. Ct. Appeals (7th cir.), Springfield, 1976—92, sr. judge, 1992—. Adj. prof. Sch. Law, U. Ill., Champaign, 1993; disting. vis. prof. St. Louis U. Law Sch., 1996-2000. Chmn. Adminstrv. Office Oversight Com., 1988-90; mem. Long Range Planning Com., 1991-96. US Army, 1942—46. Recipient Profl. Lifetime Achievement award, Inns of Ct., 2002. As rep. of US govt., his refusal to authorize use of force at Wounded Knee in 1973 is credited with helping bring a nonviolent end to the conflict. Office: US Ct Appeals PO Box 233 Petersburg IL 62675-0233

WOOD, JACKIE DALE, physiologist, educator, researcher; b. Picher, Okla., Feb. 16, 1937; s. Aubrey T. Wood and Wilma J. (Coleman) Wood Patterson. BS, Kans. State U., 1964, MS, 1966; PhD, U. Ill., 1969. Asst. prof. physiology Williams Coll., Williamstown, Mass., 1969-71; asst. prof. U. Kans. Med. Ctr., Kansas City, 1971-74, assoc. prof., 1974-78, prof., 1978-79; prof., chmn. dept. physiology Sch. Medicine, U. Nev., Reno, 1979-85; chmn. dept. physiology coll. medicine Ohio State U., Columbus, 1985-97, prof. physiology and internal medicine, 1997—. Cons. NIH, Bethesda, Md., 1982-88. Recipient Rsch. Career Devel. award IH, 1974; named Hon. Citizen City of Atzugi Japan, 1987; Alexander von Humboldt fellow, W.Ger., 1976, grantee NIH, 1971—. Fellow Am. Gastroent. Assn.; mem. AAAS, Am. Physiol. Soc. (assoc. editor 1984-96, rsch. award 1986), Soc. Neuroscience. Office: Ohio State U Dept Physiology and Cell Biology 304 Hamilton Hall 1645 Neil Ave Columbus OH 43210-1218 Home Phone: 614-457-2820; Office Phone: 614-292-5449. Business E-Mail: wood.13@osu.edu.

WOOD, JEFFREY, state official; b. Sept. 12, 1969; married; 2 children. Student, U. Wis., Eau Claire. Owner small bus.; reporter; state assemblyman Wis. Chmn. ways and means com.; mem. campaigns and election com.; mem. edn. reform com.; mem. property rights and land mgmt. com.; mem. workforce devel. com. With USN, with USNR. Republican. Office: State Capitol Rm 7 N PO Box 8953 Madison WI 53708-8953

WOOD, JOHN F., prosecutor; m. Julie Myers, 2005. Grad., U. Va.; JD, Harvard Law Sch. Staff mem. to Senator John C. Danforth US Senate, Washington; law clk. to Hon. J. Michael Luttig, US Ct. Appeals (4th Cir.), 1996—97; law clk. to Justice Clarence Thomas US Supreme Ct., 1997—98; assoc. Kirkland & Ellis LLP, 1998—2001; dep. assoc. atty. gen., counsel to assoc. atty. gen. US Dept. Justice, 2001—02; dep. gen. counsel, Office Mgmt. & Budget Exec. Office of the Pres., 2002—03; counselor to US atty. gen. US Dept. Justice, 2003—05; chief of staff to sec. US Dept. Homeland Security, 2005—07; US atty. (we. dist.) Mo. US Dept. Justice, Kans. City, 2007—. Office: US Attys Office Charles E Whittaker Courthouse 400 E 9th St Rm 5510 Kansas City MO 64106 Office Phone: 816-426-3122. Office Fax: 816-426-4210.

WOOD, JOHN FREDERICK, air transportation executive; b. NYC, Jan. 13, 1949; BA, Calif. State U., Fullerton, 1978; postgrad., No. Ariz. U., 1981. Commd. 2nd lt. USMC, 1971, pilot, 1971-79; advanced through grades to capt., 1975; resigned USMC, 1979; mgr. Winslow (Ariz.) Mcpl. Airport, 1979-81, Cheyenne (Wyo.) Airport Authority, 1981-89; dir. ops. Omaha Airport Authority, 1989-96; exec. dir. Lincoln (Nebr.) Airport Authority, 1996—. Mem. Am. Assn. Airport Execs., Airports Coun. Internat. (chmn. coms. on pub. safety and security, small airports). Office: Lincoln Airport Authority PO Box 80407 Lincoln NE 68501-0407

WOOD, KERRY, professional baseball player; b. Irving, Tex., June 17, 1977; s. Garry and Terry Wood; m. Sarah Pates. Pitcher Chgo. Cubs, 1998—. Named Nat. League Rookie of Yr., 1998; named to Nat. League All-Star Team, 2003. Achievements include most strikeouts in a 9 inning game (20); led Nat. League in strikeouts (266), 2003; over 3,000 career strikeouts; fastest to reach 1000 strikeouts in MLB history, both in appearances (134 games) and innings pitched (853). Mailing: c/o Chgo Cubs 1060 W Addison Chicago IL 60613

WOOD, MARK D., lawyer; b. Chgo., Jan. 8, 1966; BS with high honors, U. Ill., 1987; JD cum laude, U. Mich., 1990. CPA Ill., 1987; bar: Ill. 1990, US Dist. Ct., o. Dist. Ill. Ptnr., co-chair securities practice Katten Muchin Rosenman LLP, Chgo. Mem.: ABA, Am. Bar Assn. Office: Katten Muchin Rosenman LLP 525 W Monroe St Chicago IL 60661 Office Phone: 312-902-5493. Office Fax: 312-577-8858. E-mail: mark.wood@kattenlaw.com.

WOOD, MICHAEL BRUCE, orthopaedic surgeon, researcher, educator; b. Glasgow, Mont., Oct. 7, 1943; s. Benjamin Joseph and LaVaun Adele (Gray) W.; m. Mary Elizabeth Magnotto, June 17, 1967; children: Michael S., Hadley M., Benjamin D., Luke E. BA in Chemistry, Franklin and Marshall Coll., 1965; MD CM, McGill U., 1969; MS in Orthopedic Surgery, U. Minn., 1974. Diplomate Am. Bd. Orthopedic Surgery, Sub-bd. Hand Surgery. Asst. prof. Med. Coll. Ohio, Toledo, 1977-79; from asst. prof. to prof. orthopedic surgery Mayo Med. Sch., Rochester, Minn., 1979—2004. Cons. orthopedic surgery Mayo Clinic, Rochester, 1979—2004. Author: Atlas of Microsurgery, 1990, Vascularized Bone, 1996; co-editor: Jour. of Microsurgery, 1986-92; dep. editor Jour. Bone and Joint Surgery, 1996, assoc. editor, 1989-94. Trustee Mayo Found., Rochester, 1995-2003, chair exec. com., 1998-2003, pres., CEO, 1999-2003; bd. govs. Mayo Clinic, 1993-98. Maj. U.S. Army, 1974-76, Germany. NIH grantee,

1987-97; Bunnell fellow, 1986-87. Fellow Am. Assn. Orthopedic Surgery, Am. Orthopedic Assn., Am. Soc. Surgery of Hand, Am. Soc. for Reconstructive Microsurgery, Internat. Soc. for Reconstructive Microsurgery, Sigma Xi. Office: Mayo Clinic 200 1st St SW Rochester MN 55905-0002 Office Phone: 507-284-2663. Business E-Mail: wood.michael@mayo.edu.

WOOD, PAUL F., national health agency executive; b. Lockport, NY, Dec. 7, 1935; s. Dwight Edward and Frances (Fletcher) W.; m. Kathleen Frances Stretton, May 27, 1958; children: Paul S., Richard F. BA, Western Res. Univ., 1964; MA, Kent State U., 1970; PhD, Case Western Res. U., 1975. Assoc. exec. dir. United Way of Stark County, Canton, Ohio, 1967-70; owner Paul Wood Co., N. Canton, Ohio, 1970-86; dir. devel. The Salvation Army, NYC, 1986-90; pres. Nat. Coun. on Alcoholism and Drug Dependence, Inc., NYC, 1990-99; special asst. The Salvation Army, Cleve., 1999—2002; ret., 2002. Bd. dirs. Fairfield (Conn.) Chorale, 1991-94, Stepping Stones Found., 1996-99, Bedford Hills, N.Y.; fin. com. Westport United Meth. Ch., 1993-96. Mem.: Berlin Yacht Club (sec. 2006—). Avocations: sailing, computer programming. Office: The Salvation Army 2507 E 22nd St Cleveland OH 44115-3202 Personal E-mail: wood-paul@sbcglobal.net.

WOOD, ROBERT EMERSON, pediatrics educator; b. Jacksonville, Fla., Nov. 15, 1942; s. Waldo E. and Verda V. Wood. BS in Chemistry magna cum laude, Stetson U., 1963; PhD in Physiology, Vanderbilt U., 1968, MD, 1970. Bd. cert. pediatrics; bd. cert. pediatric pulmonology. Intern in pediatrics Duke U. Med. Ctr., Durham, 1970-71, resident in pediatrics, 1971-72; fellow pediatric pulmonology Case Western Res. U., Cleve., 1974-76, asst. prof. pediatrics, 1976-82, assoc. prof. pediatrics, 1982-83; assoc. prof. pediatrics, chief divsn. pediatric pulmonary medicine Dept. Pediatrics, U. N.C., Chapel Hill, 1983-88, prof. pediatrics, chief divsn. pediatric pulmonary medicine, 1988-94, dir. pediat. ICU, 1984-86, dir. Ctr. Pediat. Bronchology, 1994-99; prof. pediats. and otolaryngology Cin. Children's Hosp. Med. Ctr., U. Cin., 1999—; chief, divsn. pulmonary medicine Children's Hosp. Med. Ctr., U. Cin., 2001—05. Mem. editorial bd.: Pediatric Pulmonology, 1992—, Jour. Bronchology, 1993—; contbr. chpts. to books and articles to profl. jours. Lt. comdr. USPHS, 1972-74. amed Grad. fellow Danforth Found., 1963-68, Med. Scientist fellow Life Ins. Med. Rsch. Found., 1965-70, Clin. Rsch. fellow Cystic Fibrosis Found., 1974-76. Mem. Am. Bronchesophagological Assn., Am. Assn. for Bronchology, Soc. for Pediatric Rsch., Am. Thoracic Soc., N.C. Pediatric Soc. Office: Cin Children's Hosp Med Ctr Pediat Pulmonary Medicine 3333 Burnet Ave Cincinnati OH 45229-3039 Office Phone: 513-636-2776. Fax: 513-636-7734. Business E-Mail: rewood@cchmc.org.

WOOD, WAYNE W., state legislator; b. Janesville, Wis., Jan. 21, 1930; Grad. high sch., Stoughton, Wis. Formerly builder, contractor, factory worker; mem. Janesville City Coun., 1972-76, pres., 1974-75; mem. Wis. Ho. of Reps., Madison, 1976—. Mem. criminal justice com., rules com., ways and means com., 1985—, vice chmn., 1989-95, mem. state affairs com., 1987—. Mem. State VTAE Bd., 1975-76; mem. Coun. of State Govts. Legis. Oversight Task Force, 1983, Janesville Housing Authority, 1971-77; former mem. Children's Svc. Soc. Adv. Bd., Rock County Sr. 4-H Coun., Sinnissippi Coun. Boy Scouts Am. Mem. UAW. Home: 3822 Harvest Vw Janesville WI 53548-8302

WOOD, WILLIAM JEROME, lawyer; b. Indpls., Feb. 14, 1928; s. Joseph Gilmore and Anne Cecilia (Morris) Wood; m. Joann Janet Jones, Jan. 23, 1954; children: Steven, Matthew, Kathleen, Michael, Joseph, James, Julie, David. Student, Butler U., 1945-46; AB with honors, Ind. U., 1950, JD with distinction, 1952. Bar: Ind. 1952. Mem. firm Wood, Tuohy, Gleason, Mercer & Herrin (and predecessor), Indpls., 1952—. Bd. dirs. Grain Dealers Mut. Ins. Co., Am. Income Life Ins. Co.; gen. counsel Ind. Cath. Conf.; city atty., Indpls., 1959—60; instr. Ind. U. Sch. Law, 1960—62. Author: (book) Indiana Pastor's Legal Handbook, 3d edit., 2001, Realtors' Indiana Legal Handbook, 2d edit., 1991. Mem. Ind. Corp. Survey Commn., 1963—, chmn., 1977—86; mem. Ind. Corp. Law Study Commn., 1985—87, Ind. Non Profit Corp. Law Study Commn., 1989—91. With AUS, 1946—48. Recipient Brotherhood award, Ind. region NCCJ, 1973. Mem.: St. Thomas Moore Legal Soc. (pres. 1970), Indpls. Bar Found., Indpls. Bar Assn. (pres. 1972—73, coun. bd. mgrs. 1992—93), Ind. Bar Assn. (sec. 1977—78, award 1968), Audubon Soc., Indpls. Lit. Club (pres. 1973—74), Am. Legion. Democrat. Roman Catholic. Home: 3619 E 75th Pl Indianapolis IN 46240-3674 Office: Bank One Ctr Tower 111 Monument Cir Ste 3400 PO Box 44942 Indianapolis IN 46244-0942 E-mail: bwood@indylegal.com.

WOODARD, CLAUDETTE J., state representative, retired educational association administrator; b. 1945; married; 2 children. MEd in Curriculum and Instr. School improvement facilitator; ret.; rep. Ohio State Ho. Reps., Columbus, 2000—. Mem. edn. com. Ohio State Ho. Reps., mem. fed. grant review and edn. oversight subcom., mem. fin. and appropriations com., mem. primary and secondary edn. subcom., mem. ins. com.; adv. bd. Case Western Res. Mental Devel. Ctr. Chmn. spl. needs com. Boy Scouts Am. Spl. Projects; mem. Nat. Coun. Negro Women; treas. Coun. Exceptional Children; pres. Black Women's Polit. Action Com.; co-chmn. Women in Appt. Office Project; bd. dirs. Heights Cmty. Congress; mem. Cleve. Heights-Univ. Heights Bd. Edn., 1991—99. Mem.: Sch. Union Assn., Alpha Kappa Alpha (Meritorious Svc. award 1996). Democrat. Office: Ohio State House Reps 77 South High Street 10th Floor Columbus OH 43215-6111

WOODFORD, ARTHUR MACKINNON, library director, historian; b. Detroit, Nov. 23, 1940; s. Frank Bury and Mary-Kirk (MacKinnon) W.; m. Mary R. Woodford; children: Mark, Cristopher, Amy, Joyce, Kathleen, Lindsey. Student, U. Wis., 1958-60; BA in History, Wayne State U., 1963; AM in LS, U. Mich., 1964. Libr. Detroit Pub. Libr., 1964-74; asst. dir. Grosse Pointe (Mich.) Pub. Libr., 1974-77; dir. St. Clair Shores (Mich.) Pub. Libr., 1977—2005, Suburburn Libr. Coop., 2007. Author: All Our Yesterdays, 1969, Detroit and Its Banks, 1974, Detroit: American Urban Renaissance, 1979, Charting The Inland Seas, 1991, Tonnancour, 1994, vol. 2, 1996, This Is Detroit: 1701-2001, 2001. With USNR, 1958-64. Mem. Mich. Libr. Assn. (v.p. 1988-89), Gt. Lakes Maritime Inst., Prismatic Club Detroit (pres. 1982), Algonquin Club of Detroit and Windsor (treas. 1983-93). Avocations: tennis, bridge, reading, model ship building. Home: 3284 S Channel Dr Harsens Island MI 48028

WOODFORD, PETER C., lawyer; BA, Dartmouth Coll., 1971; JD with honors, George Washington U., 1978. Bar: Ill. 1978, US Ct. Appeals (3rd, 5th, 7th cir.), US Dist. Ct. (no. dist.) Ill., US Dist. Ct. (ea. dist.) Mich., US Tax Ct. Ptnr., gen. counsel Seyfarth Shaw LLP, Chgo. Mem.: ABA. Office: Seyfarth Shaw LLP 131 S Dearborn Ste 2400 Chicago IL 60603-5577 Office Phone: 312-460-5908. Office Fax: 312-460-7908. Business E-Mail: pwoodford@seyfarth.com.

WOODLE, ERWIN STEVE, transplant surgeon; b. Texarkana, Ark., Jan. 7, 1954; three children. BS summa cum laude, Tex. A&M U., 1976; MD magna cum laude, U. Tex. Med. Br., Galveston, 1980. Diplomate Am. Bd. Surgery, ACS. Intern, gen. surgery U. Tex. Health Sci. Ctr., Houston; resident, gen. surgery U. Calif., Davis, NIH surgical rsch. fellow; fellow, renal and pancreatic transplantation U. Chgo., fellow, hepatic transplantation and hepatobiliary surgery, NIH surgical rsch. fellow; asst. prof. surgery Washington U. Sch. Medicine, St. Louis, 1990—92; asst. prof. surgery & immunology U. Chgo., 1992—98, assoc. prof. surgery & immunology, 1998—99; prof. surgery U. Cin., 1999—, chief, divsn. transplantation, 1999—. Chmn. bd. dirs. Israel Penn Internat. Transplant Tumor Registry; com. mem. Ctr. for Biol. Evaluation and Rsch FDA, Washington, 1994—97; bd. dirs. Ohio State Consortium on Solid Organ Transplantation, 2001—, mem. liver transplantation com., 2001—, mem. pancreas/islet transplantation com., 2001—, mem. kidney transplantation com., 2001—, chmn., program review com., 2002—, vice-chmn., exec. com., 2003, chmn., exec. com., 04; pancreas/islet patient selection subcommittee Ohio Solid Organ Transplantation Consortium, 2000, mem. patient selection com., 2000—, mem. cushion fund com., 2003—; mem. scientific adv. bd. SangStat Med. Corp., Wyeth/Ayerst, Fujisawa, Medimmune, Biogen, Roche, Fujisawa Can., Immu Med, Genzyme, Novartis; several visiting professorship. Contbr. several articles to med. and sci. jours., chapters to books; abstract reviewer World Transplant Congress, 2006, Am. Transplant Congress Scientific Session, 2007, mem. editl. review bds. Clinical ephrology, Graft, Investigative Drugs, Transplantation and Lancet Oncology, ad hoc, editl. reviewer Am. Jour. Kidney Diseases, Am. Jour. Transplantation, Hepatology, Human Immunology, Internat. Immunology, Jour. Clin. Investigation, Jour. Immunology, Jour. Surgical Rsch., Jour. Vascular and Interventional Radiology, Jour. Vascular Surgery, Lancet, Liver Transplantation, Nature Biotechnology, New England Jour. Medicine, Surgery, Transplantation, Transplant Proceedings and World Jour. Surgery. Mem. med. adv. bd. Kidney Found. (Cin. Chpt.), 2001—02. Named one of America's Top Surgeons, 2004, 2006, America's Best Doctors, 2004, Health Care Heroes award, 2006; named to Paul Peters Lectureship, Tex. Transplant Soc., 2003; recipient Am. Heart Assn. Clinician Scientist award, 1992—96. Mem. AAAS, Am. Assn. for the Study of Liver Diseases, Am. Assn. Immunologists, Acad. Medicine Cin., Am. Soc. Transplant Physicians (mem. scientific studies com., 1995, chairperson, 1996-99, Kidney Pancrease Transplantation com., 1995, co-chairperson, 1996-97, program and publications com., 1996-98, 1997-2000, co-chairperson-liver/intraabdominal sect., 1996-97, chairperson 1997-99, continuing med. edn. com., 1997-2000, chairperson liver/intraabdominal subcommittee, program com., 1997-98, coun. bd. dirs., 1998, pub. policy com. 1999-2003, membership com. 2002-04), Am. Surgical Assn., Assn. for Academic Surgery, Cell Transplant Soc., Ctrl. Surgical Assn. Chgo. Assn. Immunologists, Chgo. Surgical Soc., Cin. Surgical Soc., Clin. Immunology Soc., Erlanger Soc., Ill. Surgical Soc., Internat. Coll. Surgeons, Am. Soc. Transplant Surgeons (bd. dirs., co-chmn. membership com., 2004-05), Am. Soc. Transplantation (mem. kidney pancreas com., 2006-), Internat. Liver, Transplantation Soc., Internat. Xenotransplantation Assn. Transplantation Soc., Internal Soc. for Organ Donation and Procurement, Nat. Kidney Found. (mem. med. adv. bd.), Soc. Nuclear Medicine, Soc. for Organ Sharing, St. Louis Surgical Soc., Stanley J. Dudrick Surgical Soc., Transplantation Soc., Earl. F. Wolfman Surgical Soc., Xenotransplantation Soc., Soc. Univ. Surgeons, Western Surg. Assn., Am. Diabetes Assn. (bd. pres., Cin. Cptr., 2001-2002), Mensa, Alpha Omega Alpha. Office: U Cin Dept Surgery 231 Albert Sabin Way PO Box 670558 Cincinnati OH 45267-0559 Office Phone: 513-558-6001. Business E-Mail: WOODLEES@UCMAIL.UC.EDU.

WOODMAN, HAROLD DAVID, historian, educator; b. Chgo., Apr. 21, 1928; s. Joseph Benjamin and Helen Ruth (Sollo) W.; m. Leonora Becker; children—Allan James, David Edward. BA, Roosevelt U., 1957; MA, U. Chgo., 1959, PhD, 1964. Lectr. Roosevelt U., 1962-63; asst. prof. history U. Mo., Columbia, 1963-66, assoc. prof., 1966-69, prof., 1969-71, Purdue U., West Lafayette, Ind., 1971-97, Louis Martin Sears disting. prof., 1990-97, prof. emeritus, 1997—; chmn. Com. on Am. Studies, 1981-94. Author: Conflict and Consensus in American History, 1966, 9th rev. edit., 1996, Slavery and the Southern Economy, 1966, King Cotton and His Retainers, 1968, Legacy of the American Civil War, 1973, New South-New Law, 1995; mem. editl. bd. Jour. So. History, 1972-75, Wis. Hist. Soc., 1972-76, Bus. History Rev., 1971-77, Agrl. History, 1976-82, Am. Hist. Rev., 1981-84, Jour. Am. History, 1985-88. Served with U.S. Army, 1950-52. Recipient Otto Wirth award Roosevelt U., 1990; Woodrow Wilson Internat. Center for Scholars fellow, 1977; Faculty grant Social Sci. Rsch. Coun., 1969-70; at. Humanities Ctr. fellow, 1983-84 Mem. Am. Hist. Assn., Orgn. Am. Historians, Econ. History Assn., Agrl. History Soc. (pres. 1983-84, Everett E. Edwards award 1963), Soc. Am. Historians, Bus. History Conf. (pres. 1981-82), Ind. Assn. Historians (pres. 1983-84), So. Hist. Assn. (exec. coun. 1982-85, Ramsdell award 1965, pres. 1995-96). Home: 1100 N Grant St West Lafayette IN 47906-2460 Office: Purdue U Dept History West Lafayette IN 47907 Business E-Mail: hwoodman@purdue.edu.

WOODRESS, FREDERICK ALBERT, writer; b. St. Louis, Jan. 11, 1923; s. James L. and Jessie (Smith) W.; m. Anne Loraine Blackmon, Dec. 31, 1953; 1 child, Cathy Loraine. AB, Antioch Coll., 1948; MS, U. Ky., 1971; EdD, Ball State U., 1989. Stringer, reporter various Ohio and Mo. newspapers, 1939-48; free-lance writer, 1948-49; pub. rels. asst. Meth. Div. Fgn. Missions, 1949; reporter, columnist, entertainment editor Birmingham (Ala.) Post-Herald, 1949-55; owner pub. rels., advt. consulting firm, 1955-69; asst. to chief adminstr., pub. affairs dir. U. Ala. Birmingham, 1964-69; dir. pub. rels. U. Ky., Lexington, 1969-71; pub. rels. cons. Woodress & Myers, Louisville, 1971-73; agt. Pa. Life Ins. Co., 1971-73; mktg. dir. Hunter Found. HMO, Lexington, Ky., 1973-76; instr. U. Ky. Lexington, 1977-79; nat. pub. rels. dir. Am. Legion, Indpls. and Washington, 1979-82; assoc. prof. U.S. Sports Acad., Daphne, Ala., 1982-84; asst. prof. Ball State U., Muncie, Ind., 1984-94; freelance writer, tchr., playwright, actor Muncie, 1994—. Tchr. advt. Birmingham So. Coll., 1958; instr. U.S. Sports Acad., Hong Kong, Singapore, Thailand, Malaysia, 1995-98. Co-author: 87th Infantry Div. History, 1946, Publicity Tips, 1961, Public Relations for Community/Junior Colleges, 1976, Slave or Free and 11 Other Problem-Solving Plays, 2005 (named one of 3 Best in Fiction, Ind. State Libr. Competition, 2006); author Impasse (pub. in Best One Act Plays), 1949; contbr. chpts. to books and articles to profl. mags., newspapers and jours. Information specialist, mem. staff hurricane duty U.S. Salvation Army, Haiti, 1963, New Orleans, 1965; treas. Heartland Stage Co., 2005-07. With U.S. Army, 1943-46, ETO. Recipient Best Dissertation award Ball State U., 1990, Nat. Tchr. award Soc. Profl. Journalists, 1993. Fellow Pub. Rels. Soc. Am. (v.p. Ala.-Miss. chpt., pres. Ala. chpt., chmn. nat. membership com., Presdl. Citation 1968). Episcopalian. Home and Office: 222 N Winthrop Rd Muncie IN 47304-3977

WOODRICK, ROBERT, food products executive; Chmn. D&W Food Ctrs., Grand Rapids, Mich. Emeritus trustee Aquinas Coll.; trustee Grand Rapids CC. Office: D&W Food Ctrs 3001 Orchard Vista Dr SE Grand Rapids MI 49546-7078

WOODRING, DEWAYNE STANLEY, religious organization administrator; b. Gary, Ind., Nov. 10, 1931; s. J. Stanley and Vera Luella (Brown) Woodring; m. Donna Jean Wishart, June 15, 1957; children: Judith Lynn Bigelow, Beth Ellen Carey. BS in Speech with distinction, Northwestern U., Evanston, Ill., 1954; postgrad., Northwestern U., 1954—57; MDiv, Garrett Theol. Sem., 1957; LHD, Mt. Union Coll., 1967; DD, Salem Coll., 1970. Ordained to ministry Meth. Ch., 1955. Assoc. dir. youth Gary YMCA, 1950—55; min. edn. Griffith Meth. Ch., Ind., 1955—57; min. adminstrn. and program 1st Meth. Ch., Eugene, Oreg., 1957—59; dir. pub. rels. Dakotas area Meth. Ch., 1959—60, dir. pub. rels. Ohio area, 1960—64; adminstrv. exec. to bishop Ohio East area United Meth. Ch., Canton, 1964—77, asst. gen. sec. Gen. Coun. Fin. and Adminstr. Evanston, Ill., 1977—79, assoc. gen. sec., 1979—84; exec. dir., CEO Religious Conf. Mgmt. Assn., Indpls., 1982—. Staff dept. radio svcs. 2d Assembly World Coun. Chs., Evanston, 1954; chmn. comm. commn. Ohio Coun. Chs., 1961—65; v.p. Ohio East Area United Meth. Found., 1967—76; exec. com. Nat. Assn. United Meth. Found., 1968—72, World Meth. Coun., 1986—2001; vice-chmn. commn. entertainment and program North Ctrl. Jurisdictional Conf., 1968—72, chmn., 1972—76; mem. divsn. interpretation United Meth. Ch., 1969—72, mem. commn. gen. conf., 1972—93, mgr., exec. dir., 1976—93; chmn. bd. mgrs. United Meth. Bldg., Evanston, 1977—84; mem. adv. bd. Nassau/Paradise Island, 1997—99, Red Lion Hotels and Inns, PR Conv. Ctr.; lectr., cons. in field; del. White House Travel and Tourism Conf., 1995. Creator (radio series) The Word and Music, prodr., dir. (TV series) Parables in Miniature, 1957—59. Adviser East Ohio Conf. Comm. Commn., 1968—76; bd. dirs. First Internat. Summit Edn., 1989; trustee, 1st v.p. Copeland Oaks Retirement Ctr., Sebring, Ohio, 1969—76; pres. Guild Assocs., 1971—. Named to, Ky. Cols., 1989, Hall of Leaders, Conv. Liaison Coun., 1994; recipient Cert. Meeting Profl. award, 1985, Cert. Expt. Mgr. award, 1988, Sagamore of Wabash award, State Ind., 2007. Mem.: ISAE (Meeting Planner of the Yr. award 1990), Marriott Customer Leadership Forum (mem. customer adv. bd.), Found. Internat. Meetings (bd. dirs.), Cert. Meeting Profls. (bd. dirs. 1983—92), Ind. Conv. Visitors Assn. (bd. dirs. 1996—2000), Def. Orientation Conf. Assn. (chaplain), Conv. Industry Coun. (bd. dirs., past chmn.), Meeting Profl. Internat., Am. Soc. Assn. Execs. Home: 7224 Chablis Ct Indianapolis IN 46278-1540 Office: 7702 Woodland Dr Ste 20 Indianapolis IN 46278 Office Phone: 317-632-1888.

WOODS, CURTIS E(UGENE), lawyer; b. Ft. Leavenworth, Kans., May 29, 1950; s. Cecil Eugene and Velma Marie (Storms) W.; m. Kathleen L. Kopach, June 8, 1985; children: Colin Eric, Cameron Robert, Alexandra Marie. BA, U. Mo., Kansas City, 1972; JD, Northwestern U., Chgo., 1975. Bar: Ill. 1975, Mo. 1976, U.S. Dist. Ct. (no. dist.) Ill., U.S. Dist. Ct. (we. dist.) Mo., U.S. Dist. Ct. Kans., U.S. Ct. Appeals (7th, 8th and 10th cirs.). Law clk. U.S. Ct. Appeals (7th cir.), Chgo., 1975-76; assoc. Spencer Fane Britt & Browne, Kansas City, 1976-81, ptnr., 1982-94, Sonnenschein Nath & Rosenthal, Kansas City, 1994—. Contbr. articles to profl. jours. Recipient William Jennings Bryan award Northwestern U., 1974. Mem. ABA, Mo. Bar Assn., Kansas City Bar Assn., Order of Coif. Office: Sonnenschein Nath Rosenthal 4520 Main St Ste 1100 Kansas City MO 64111-7700

WOODS, GARY V., professional football team executive, former professional basketball team executive, automotive executive; b. Nov. 9, 1943; BBA, So. West Tex. State; MBA, SMU. Pres. San Antonio Spurs, 1988—93; ceo, pres., chair. McCombs Enterprises, San Antonio, 1979—; pres., ceo Minnesota Vikings, Eden Prairie, 1998—. Office: Minnesota Vikings 9520 Viking Dr Eden Prairie MN 55344-3898 also: Mark B Woods 755 E Mulberry Ave Ste 600 San Antonio TX 78212-6013

WOODS, GEORGE EDWARD, judge; b. 1923; m. Janice Smith. Student, Ohio No. U., 1941-43, 46, Tex. A&M Coll., 1943, Ill. Inst. Tech., 1943; JD, Detroit Coll. Law, 1949. Sole practice, Pontiac, Mich., 1949-51; asst. pros. atty. Oakland County, Mich., 1951-52; chief asst. U.S. atty. Ea. Dist. Mich., 1953-60, U.S. atty., 1960-61; assoc. Honigman, Miller, Schwartz and Cohn, Detroit, 1961-62; sole practice Detroit, 1962-81; judge U.S. Bankruptcy Ct., 1981-83, U.S. Dist. Ct. (ea. dist.) Mich., Detroit, 1983-93, sr. judge, 1993—. Served with AUS, 1943-46. Fellow Internat. Acad. Trial Lawyers, Am. Coll. Trial Lawyers; mem. Fed. Bar Assn., State Bar Mich. Office: US Dist Ct 277 US Courthouse 231 W Lafayette Blvd Detroit MI 48226-2700

WOODS, JACQUELINE F., public relations executive; b. Oct. 22, 1947; BA, Muskingum Coll., 1969. Former v.p. of licensing and pricing Oracle Corp.; former pres. Ameritech Ill., Cleve., Ameritech Ohio subs. Ameritech Corp., Cleve.; sr. consultant Landau Public Relations, 2002—. Bd. dirs. Timken Co., Andersons Inc., School Specialty, Inc., 2006—. Exec. com. mem. Greater Cleve. Sports Commn.; trustee Playhouse Square, Muskingum Coll.; chair emeritus Cleve. Chapter of Am. Red Cross; bd. mem. Great Lakes Sci. Ctr., Cleve. Found., 1998—, Kent State U., 2004—, U. Hosp. Healthcare Sys., Columbus Met. Library. Named to OH Women Hall of Fame, 1998. Office: Landau Public Relations 700 W St Clair Ave Cleveland OH 44113 Fax: 312-207-1601.

WOODS, JAMES H., research scientist, consultant; b. Louisa, Ky., Sept. 18, 1937; BS, Ohio U., 1959; MA, U. Va., 1962, PhD, 1968. NDEA fellow psychology dept. U. Va., Charlottesville, Va., 1959—62; instr. psychology dept. Randolph-Macon Woman's Coll., Lynchburg, Va., 1963—64; lectr. psychology dept. U. Mich., Ann Arbor, 1965; from rsch. asst. to rsch. assoc. pharmacology dept. U. Mich. Med. Sch., Ann Arbor, 1965—70; from asst. prof. to assoc. prof. psychology dept. U. Mich., Ann Arbor, 1969—80; from asst. prof. to assoc. prof. pharmacology dept. U. Mich. Med. Sch., Ann Arbor, 1970—80; prof. psychology dept. U. Mich., Ann Arbor, 1980—; prof. pharmacology dept. U. Mich. Med. Sch., Ann Arbor, 1980—. Cons. Nat. Inst. Drug Abuse, Bethesda, Md.; cons. divsn. neuropharmacol. drug products FDA, Rockville, Md.; cons. Eli Lilly Co., Indpls., 1976—86; cons. expert adv. panel on drug dependence and alcohol problems WHO, 1983—98; cons. G.D. Searle/Monsanto, 1986—89, Nat. Inst. Drug Abuse/Nat. Adv. Coun. Alcohol, Drug Abuse and Mental Health Adminstrn., Bethesda, 1987—91, Parke Davis Rsch. Unit, Cambridge, England, 1989; cons., mem. adv. bd. Rand Corp., Drug Policy Rsch. Ctr., Santa Monica, Calif., 1990; cons. Burroughs Wellcome Co., Research Triangle Park, NC, 1990—, Eli Lilly Co., Indpls., 1991, Gliatech Corp., Cleve.; cons. expert adv. panel on drug dependence: dependence liability evaluation WHO, 1998; grant reviewer NSF, NIMH, VA, Med. Rsch. Coun. Can., others. Editl. cons.: Jour. Pharmacology and Exptl. Therapeutics, Behavioral Brain Rsch., Jour. AMA, others. Recipient rsch. grants in field. Fellow: APA, Am. Coll. Neuropsychopharmacology (mem. neuropharmacology divsn., pres. divsns. 5, 6, 25, and 28 psychopharmacology 1984); mem.: AAAS, Behavioral Pharmacology Soc., Sigma Xi, Soc. for Neuroscis., Am. Soc. for Pharmacology and Exptl. Therapeutics (mem. com. on substance abuse 1994), Collegium Internationale euro-Psychopharmacologicum, Am. Pain Soc., Assn. for Chemoreception Scis. Office: U Mich Med Sch Dept Pharmacology 1301 Med Sci Rsch Bldg 1150 W Medical Center Dr Ann Arbor MI 48109-0632

WOODS, JOHN ELMER, plastic surgeon; b. Battle Creek, Mich., July 5, 1929; m. Janet Ruth; children: Sheryl, Mark, Jeffrey, Jennifer, Judson. BA, Asbury Coll., 1949, DHL, 1999; MD, Western Res. U., 1955; PhD, U. Minn., 1966. Intern Gorgas Hosp., Panama Canal Zone, 1955-56, resident in gen. surgery, 1956-57, Mayo Grad. Sch., Rochester, Minn., 1960-65, resident in plastic surgery, 1966-67, Brigham Hosp., Boston, Mass., 1968; fellow, transplant cons. Harvard Med. Sch., Cambridge, Mass., 1969; cons. in gen. and plastic surgery Mayo Clinic, Rochester, 1969-93, vice chmn. Dept. Surgery; asst. prof. Mayo Med. Sch., Rochester, 1973-76, assoc. prof., 1976-80, prof. plastic surgery, 1980-93, Stuart W. Harrington prof. surgery. Vis. prof. Yale Sch. Medicine, New Haven, 1984, Harvard Sch. Medicine, Cambridge, 1984. Contbr. over 200 articles to profl. jours.; also 26 book chpts. and 1 film. Recipient Disting. Mayo Clinician award, 1991, Disting. Mayo Alumnus award, 1999. Mem. AMA (coun. on sci. affairs 1985-87), ACS (grad edn. com. 1985-87), Am. Bd. Med. Specialties, Am. Bd. Plastic Surgery (sec.-treas. 1985-88, chmn. 1988-89), Am. Soc. Plastic Surgeons Ednl. Fedn. (pres. 1984-85). Avocations: skiing, sailing, reading, the arts. Office: Mayo Clinic Plummer N-10 Rochester MN 55905-0001 Business E-Mail: woods.john@mayo.edu.

WOODS, NIKKI, radio personality; Former 5th grade tchr.; morning radio host, entertainment reporter Sta. WGCI-FM, Chgo. Vol. Big Sister, Little Sister Program, Chgo. Rape Crisis Ctr., Walter S. Christopher Sch. for Children. Office: Wgci Radio 233 N Michigan Ave Ste 2800 Chicago IL 60601-5704

WOODS, RICHARD DALE, lawyer; b. Kans. City, Mo., May 20, 1950; s. Willard Dale and Betty Sue (Duncan) W.; m. Cecelia Ann Thompson, Aug. 11, 1973 (div. July 1996); children: Duncan Warren, Shannon Cecelia; m. Mary Linna Lash, June 6, 1999. BA with distinction, U. Kans., Lawrence, 1972; JD, U. Mo., 1975. Bar: Mo. 1975, Kans. 2000, US Dist. Ct. (we. dist.) Mo. 1975, US Tax Ct. 1999. Assoc. Shook, Hardy & Bacon L.L.P., Kansas City, Mo., 1975-79, ptnr., 1980-2000; shareholder Kirkland & Woods, P.C., Overland Park, Kans., 2001—. Gen. chmn. Estate Planning Symposium, Kansas City, 1985-86; chair Northland Coalition, 1993. Chmn. fin. com. North Woods Ch., Kansas City, 1986-88, 93-96; mem. sch. bd. N. Kansas City Sch. Dist., 1990-97, treas., 1992-97; mem. North Kansas City Ednl. Found., 1998-2002, pres., 1999-2002; mem. devel. com. Truman Med. Ctr., 1992—, chmn., 1992-98; mem. Clay County Tax Increment Fin. Commn., 1990-99; bd. dir. Heart of Am. Family Svcs., 1998-2004, sec., 2000-01, v.p. 2003-04, The Family Conservancy, 2005-07, v.p., 2005, chmn., 2006-07, Gilda's Club Kans. City, 2003—, sec., 2005-07. Named to Best Lawyers in Am., Trusts and Estates, 1993—. Fellow Am. Coll. Trust and Estate Counsel (Kans. state chair 2006-); mem. ABA, Mo. Bar Assn., Kans. Bar Assn., Johnson County Bar Assn., Kansas City Met. Bar Assn., Lawyers Assn. Kans. City (sec., v.p., pres. young lawyers sect. 1981-84), Kans. City Estate Planning Soc. (bd. dirs. 1985-88, 93-95), Ea. Kans. Estate Planning Coun. Democrat. Office: Kirkland & Woods PC 6201 College Blvd Ste 250 Overland Park KS 66211 Office Phone: 913-469-0900. E-mail: rwoods@kcnet.com.

WOODS, ROBERT ARCHER, investment counsel; b. Princeton, Ind., Dec. 28, 1920; s. John Hall and Rose Erskine Heilman W.; m. Ruth Henrietta Diller, May 27, 1944; children: Robert Archer III (dec.), Barbara Diller (Mrs. Gregory Alan Klein), Katherine Heilman (Mrs. John E. Glennon), James Diller. AB, U. Rochester, 1942; MBA, Harvard, 1946. Account exec. Stein Roe & Farnham (investment counsel), Chgo., 1946-53, ptnr., 1954-90. Gov. Investment Co. Inst. Trustee U. Rochester; bd. dirs. Chgo. Juvenile Protective Assn., Chgo. Infant Welfare Soc., Chgo. Assn. Retarded Citizens. Served to lt. (s.g.) USNR, 1943-46. Mem. Am. Mgmt. Assn. (trustee 1973), Harvard Bus. Sch. Club Chgo. (pres. 1961), Phi Beta Kappa, Delta Upsilon. Clubs: Univ. Chgo, Chicago, Tower. Home: 470 Orchard Ln Winnetka IL 60093-4222 Office: 1 S Wacker Dr Chicago IL 60606-4614

WOODS, ROBERT EDWARD, lawyer; b. Albert Lea, Minn., Mar. 27, 1952; s. William Fabian and Maxine Elizabeth (Schmit) W.; m. Cynthia Anne Pratt, Dec. 26, 1975; children: Laura Marie Woods, Amy Elizabeth Woods. BA, U. Minn., 1974, JD, 1977; MBA, U. Pa., 1983. Bar: Minn. 1977, US Dist. Ct. Minn. 1980, US Ct. Appeals (8th cir.) 1980, Calif. 2000, US Ct. Appeals (9th cir.) 2000. Assoc. Moriarty & Janzen, Mpls., 1977-81, Berger & Montague, Phila., 1982-83, Briggs and Morgan, St. Paul and Mpls., 1983-84, ptnr., 1984-99; exec. v.p., gen. counsel InsWeb Corp., Redwood City, Calif., 1999-2000; gen. counsel BORN Info. Svcs., Inc., Mpls., 2000—04; pvt. practice Mpls., 2004—07; sr. v.p. gen. counsel Sec. Analysts Internat. Corp., Mpls., 2008—. Adj. prof. William Mitchell Coll. Law, St. Paul, 1985; exec. com., bd. dirs. LEX MUNDI, Ltd., Houston, 1989-93, chmn. bd. 1991-92; bd. dirs. Midwest Asia Ctr., 1993-95, chmn. bd., 1994-95. Co-author: (with others) Business Torts, 1989, (Carter G. Bishop) CCH Tax Research Consultant, Business Stages from Start-Up to Termination, 2005; sr. contbg. editor: Evidence in America: The Federal Rules in the States, 1987. Mem. ABA, Minn. State Bar Assn., State Bar of Calif., Hennepin County Bar Assn., Ramsey County Bar Assn. (chmn. corp., banking and bus. law sect. 1985-87), Assn. Trial Lawyers Am., Wharton Club of Minn., Phi Beta Kappa. Home: 28 Deep Lake Rd North Oaks MN 55127-6506 Office: 110 Cheshire Ln Ste 300 Minneapolis MN 55305 Office Phone: 952-838-2883. Business E-Mail: rwoods@robertewoodspa.com.

WOODSIDE, FRANK C., III, lawyer, educator, physician; b. Glen Ridge, NJ, Apr. 18, 1944; s. Frank C. and Dorothea (Poulin) W.; m. Julia K. Moses, Nov. 15, 1974; children: Patrick Michael, Christopher Ryan. BS, Ohio State U., Columbus, 1966, JD, 1969; MD, U. Cin., 1973. Diplomate Am. Bd. Legal Medicine, Am. Bd. Forensic Medicine. Mem. Dinsmore & Shohl, Cin.; clin. prof. pediats. emeritus U. Cin., 1992—. Adj. prof. law U. Cin., 1973—. Editor: Drug Product Liability, 1985—. Fellow Am. Coll. Legal Medicine, Am. Coll. Forensic Examiners, Am. Soc. Hosp. Attys., Soc. Ohio Hosp. Attys.; mem. ABA, FBA, Ohio Bar Assn., Internat. Assn. Def. Counsel, Def. Rsch. Inst. (chmn. drug and med. svc. com. 1988-91), Cin. Bar Assn. Office: Dinsmore & Shohl 1900 Chemed Ctr 255 E 5th St Cincinnati OH 45202-4700 Home Phone: 513-821-7889; Office Phone: 513-977-8266. Business E-Mail: frank.woodside@dinslaw.com.

WOODSON, GAYLE ELLEN, otolaryngologist; b. Galveston, Tex., June 9, 1950; d. Clinton Eldon and Nancy Jean (Stephens) W.; m. Kevin Thomas Robbins; children: Nicholas, Gregory, Sarah. BA, Rice U., 1972; MD, Baylor Coll. Medicine, 1975. Diplomate Am. Bd. Otolaryngology (bd. dirs., residency rev. com. for otolaryngology, exam. chair). Fellow Baylor Coll. Medicine, Houston, 1976, Inst. Laryngology & Otology, London, 1981-82; asst. prof. Baylor Coll. Medicine, 1982-87; asst. attending Harris County Hosp. Dist., Houston, 1982-86; with courtesy staff Saint Luke's Episcopal Hosp., Houston, 1982-87; assoc. attending The Methodist Hosp., Houston, 1982-87; asst. prof. U. Calif. Med. Sch., San Diego, 1987-89; chief otolaryngology VA Med. Ctr., San Diego, 1987-92; assoc. prof. U. Calif. Sch. Med., San Diego, 1989-92; prof. otolaryngology U. Tenn., Memphis, 1993—2000, So. Ill. U., 2003—. Numerous presentations and lectures in field. Contbr. numerous articles and abstracts to med. jours., also videotapes. Recipient deRoldes award, Am. Layrngol. Assn., 2003. Fellow ACS (bd. govs.), Royal Coll. Surgeons, Soc. Univ. Otolaryngologists (past pres.), Am. Soc. Head and Neck Surgery, Am. Laryngol. Assn. (pres.-elect de Roaldes award, 2003), Triological Soc.; mem. AMA, Am. Acad. Otolaryngology-Head and Neck Surgery (bd. dirs. 1993-96), Am. Med. Women's Assn. (past pres. Memphis br.), Soc. Head and Neck Oncologists Eng., Am. Physiol. Soc., Assn. Women Surgeons, Am. Soc. Head and Neck Surgeons, Johns Hopkins Soc. Scholars, Collegium OtoRhinolaryngolicum Amicus Sacrum. Office: Southern Illinois Univ PO Box 19662 Springfield IL 62794-9662 Home Phone: 217-726-0026. Business E-Mail: gwoodson@siumed.edu.

WOODWARD, FREDERICK MILLER, publisher; b. Clarksville, Tenn., Apr. 15, 1943; s. Felix Grundy and Laura Henrietta (Miller) W. m. Elizabeth Louise Smoak, Mar. 23, 1967; children: Laura Claire, Katherine Elizabeth BA cum laude, Vanderbilt U., 1965; postgrad., Tulane U., 1965-70. Manuscript editor U.S.C. Press, Columbia, 1970-73, mktg. dir., 1973-81; dir. U. Press of Kans., Lawrence, 1981—. Mem. adv. com. Kans. Ctr. for the Book, Topeka, 1987—; lectr. pub. U. Kans., Lawrence, Kans. State U., Manhattan, 1983—; book judge Western Heritage Ctr., Oklahoma City, 1988. Mem. Assn. Am. Univ. Presses (bd. dirs. 1988-91, pres. 1995-96, past pres. 1996-97), Kans. State Hist. Soc. (life), Phi Beta Kappa. Democrat. Avocations: racquetball, reading, music. Home: 2220 Vermont St Lawrence KS 66046-3066 Office: U Press Kans 2501 W 15th St Lawrence KS 66049-3905

WOODWARD, ROBERT J., JR., insurance executive; b. 1941; married. BA, Capital U., 1964, JD, 1971. With Nationwide Gen. Ins. Co., Columbus, 1964—, v.p., 1975-91, sr. v.p., 1991-95, exec. v.p., 1995—. V.p. Nationwide Life Ins. Co., Columbus, Nationwide Mut. Ins. Co., Columbus, Nationwide Mut. Fire Ins. Co., Columbus. Office: ationwide Mut Ins Co 1 Nationwide Plz Columbus OH 43215-2239

WOOLARD, LARRY, state legislator; s. Bertus and Vera Woolard; m. Mary Ann Switzer; children: Laurie Matson, Scott, Machelle, Jason. Commr. Williamson County, 1984-90; mem. Ill. Ho. Reps., Springfield, 1989—, mgm. agr. com., appropriations com., elections law com., elem. & secondary edn. com., mental health com., pub. health & infrastructure appropriations. Mem. Carterville C. of C. (chmn.), Herrin C. of C. (chmn.), Lions, Masons, Moose. Address: 840 Terminal Dr Ste 106 Marion IL 62959 Office: Ill Ho of Reps State Capitol Springfield IL 62706-0001

WOOLDREDGE, WILLIAM DUNBAR, health facility administrator; b. Salem, Mass., Oct. 27, 1937; s. John and Louise (Sigourney) W.; m. Johanna Marie; children: John, Rebecca Wistar. BA, Colby Coll., 1961; MBA, Harvard U., 1964. Staff assoc. Sun Oil Co., Phila., 1964-67; treas. Ins. Co. N.Am., Phila., 1967-72, B.F. Goodrich Co., Akron, Ohio, 1972-84, sr. v.p., 1978-79, exec. v.p., chief fin. officer, mem. mgmt. com., 1979-84; chief fin. officer, exec. v.p., dir. Belden & Blake Corp., North Canton, Ohio, 1984-89; sr. v.p., chief fin. officer, dir. Belden & Blake Oil Prodn., Inc., 1984-89; prin. dir. Carleton Group, Cleve., 1989-92; CFO, COO, v.p. King's Med. Co., Hudson, Ohio, 1993—, also bd. dirs. Pres. Hudson Econ. Devel. Corp. Bd. dirs. Salvation Army, North Park Coll. and Seminary; trustee Children's Hosp. Med. Ctr., Akron. With U.S. Army, 1956-58. Mem. Fin. Execs. Inst. Clubs: Country of Hudson. Episcopalian. Home: 100 College St Hudson OH 44236-2925 Office: King's Med Co 1920 Georgetown Rd Hudson OH 44236-4060 E-mail: wdwooldred@aol.com.

WOOLF, STEVEN MICHAEL, artistic director; b. Milw., Dec. 23, 1947; s. Raleigh and Lenore (Shurman) W. BA in Theatre, U. Wis., 1968, MFA, 1971; D of Fine Arts (hon.), U. Mo., 1993. Prodn. stage mgr. The Juilliard Sch. Drama, NYC, 1973-75; project prodr. Musical Theatre Lab., NYC, 1974-75; prodn. stage mgr. Barter Theatre, Abingdon, Va., 1976-79, Stagewest, Springfield, Mass., 1976-79; prodn. mgr. Repertory Theatre of St. Louis, 1980-83, acting artistic dir., mng. dir., 1983-85, mng. dir., 1985-86, artistic dir., 1986—. Adj. faculty Webster U., St. Louis, 1982—; mem. nat. negotiating coms. League of Resident Theatres, N.Y.C., 1986—; on-site evaluator Nat. Endowment for the Arts, 1985. Dir. plays A Life in the Theatre, 1982, the Crucible, 1986, Company, 1987, The Voice of the Prairie, 1988, 90, The Boys Next Door, 1989, Dog Logic, 1990, Born Yesterday, 1990, Terra Nova, 1991, The Diary of Anne Frank, 1991, Other Peoples Money, 1991, Six Degrees of Separation, 1992, Sight Unseen, 1993, Lion in Winter, 1993, Death and the Maiden, 1993, The Living, 1994, Wait Until Dark, 1994, The Caine Mutiny Court Martial, 1994. The Life of Galileo, 1995, Death of a Salesman, 1995, Betrayal, 1996, As Bees in Honey Drown, 1997, Who's Afraid of Virginia Woolf, 1998, Closer, 1998, Dinner With Friends, 2000, The Dresser, 2001, The Shape of Things, 2002, Copenhagen, 2003, Two Rockin' Gents, 2003, The Goat, Or Who is Sylvia, 2003, Blue/Orange, 2004, The Crucible, 2004, The Retreat From Moscow, 2004, Henry IV & Humble Boy, 2006, The History Boys, 2007, Angels in America, 2008, others. Mem. ad hoc coms. for funding Mo. Arts Coun., St. Louis, 1988; chair citizen rev. panel Reg. Arts Commn., St. Louis, 1986; bd. dirs. Mo. Citizens for the Arts, 1990—; exec. com. League of Resident Theatres, 1990—. Recipient award Mo. Citizens for the Arts, 1992, Women's Polit. Caucus, 1993, award for Individual Excellence in the Arts, Arts Edn. Coun., 1993. Mem. AFTRA, Soc. of Stage Dirs. and Choreographers, Actors Equity Assn. Office: Repertory Theatre St Louis 130 Edgar Rd Saint Louis MO 63119-3228 Home Phone: 314-367-4401; Office Phone: 314-968-7340. Personal E-mail: swoolf@repstl.org.

WOOLFORD, WARREN L., municipal official; b. Md. m. Betty Woolford; 1 child, Marcia. BS in Social Sci. and Secondary Edn., Coppin State Coll.; MA in Geography, U. Akron. Student planning intern Dept. Planning and Urban Devel., City of Akron, 1972, various planning positions, 1972-88, comprehensive planning and zoning mgr., 1988-93, dir. planning, 1993; also mem. Mayor's cabinet City of Akron. Part-time lectr. U. Akron, 1976-89. Mem. United Negro Coll. Fund Night Com.; mem. adv. com. Gt. Trail Coun. Pathfinder; bd dirs. Keep Akron Beautiful; mem. Ohio and Erie Canal Nat. Heritage Corridor Com., Akron Devel. Corp., OACA Commuter Rail Adv. Com., Dist. 8 Pub. Works Policy Com.; past mem. allocations com. United Way of Summit County, Youth Motivation Task Force. Mem. Omega Psi Phi (keeper of records and seals). Office: City of Akron Dept Planning and Urban Devel 166 S High St Fl 4 Akron OH 44308-1626

WOOLLAM, JOHN ARTHUR, electrical engineering educator, physics professor; b. Kalamazoo, Mich., Aug. 10, 1939; s. Arthur Edward and Mildred Edith (Hakes) W.; children: Catherine Jane, Susan June. BA in Physics, Kenyon Coll., 1961; MS in Physics, Mich. State U., 1963, PhD in Solid State Physics, 1967; MSEE, Case Western Res. U., 1978; Doctorate (hon.), Linköping (Sweden) U., 2004. Rsch. scientist NASA Lewis Rsch. Ctr., Cleve., 1967-80; prof. U. Nebr., Lincoln, 1979—, dir. Ctr. Microelectronic and Optical Materials Rsch., 1988—2000; pres. J.A. Woollam Co., Inc., Lincoln, 1987—. Editor Jour. Applied Physics Com., 1979-94. Trustee J.A. Woollam Found. Grantee NASA, NSF, USAF, Advanced Rsch. Projects Agy. Fellow Am. Phys. Soc., Am. Vacuum Soc. (chmn. thin film divsn. 1989-91). Office: U Nebr Dept Elec Engring 209NWSEC Lincoln NE 68588-0511 Personal E-mail: jwoollam@jawollam.com.

WOOLLEN, EVANS, retired architectural firm executive; b. Indpls., Aug. 10, 1927; s. Evans Jr. and Lydia (Jameson) Ritchey; m. Nancy Clarke Sewell, July 16, 1955 (dec. 1992); children: Ian, Malcolm Sewell. BA, MArch, Yale U., 1952. Lic. architect Ind., Ala., Conn., Del., Ill., Ky., La., Maine, Mass., N.C., Ohio, Tenn. Chmn. Woollen, Molzan & Ptnrs., Indpls., 1955—; resident Am. Acad. in Rome, spring 1996. Architect Pilot Ctr., Cin. (Nat. HUD 1975), St. Marys Coll. Libr. (Nat. AIA-ALA 1983), Grainger Libr., U. Ill., Urbana, Asbury Coll. Libr., Wilmore, Ky., Indpls. Cen. Pub. Libr. Mem. bd. Ind. State Welfare Bd., 1956-59, Art Assn., 1956-66, Indpls. Capital Improvement Bd., 1965-69. With Signal Corps U.S. Army, 1946-47. Fellow: AIA. Democrat. Address: 2801 Eagle Ridge Longmont CO 80503 E-mail: ewoollen3@indra.com.

WOOLSEY, THOMAS ALLEN, neuroscientist, biologist; b. Balt., Apr. 17, 1943; s. Clinton Nathan and Harriet (Runion) W.; m. Cynthia Tull Ward, June 8, 1969; children: Alix, Timothy. BS, U. Wis., 1965; MD, Johns Hopkins, 1969. Asst. prof. anatomy Washington U. Sch. Medicine, St. Louis, 1971-75, asst. prof. anatomy, neurobiology, 1975-77, assoc. prof. anatomy, neurobiology, 1977-80, assoc. prof. anatomy, neurobiology, physiology biophysics, 1980-83, coord. neurosci. program, 1980-84, sr. neuroscientist, 1982—, prof. neurology, neurological surgery, 1984—, dir. experimental neurology, neurological surgery, 1984—. Chmn., Washington U. Teaching Space Evaluation, 1989-90. Contbr. articles to profl. jours. NIH Rsch. grantee, 1970—; George H. and Ethel R. Bishop scholar, 1984—; recipient McKnight Neurosci. Devel. award, 1982-85, Jacob Javits award NIH, 1993-2000; fellow John Simon Guggenheim Found., 2004. Fellow AAAS; mem. Am. Assn. Anatomists, Am. Acad. Neurology, St. Louis Acad. Sci., Soc. Neurosci., Johns Hopkins Med. Surgical Assn., Cajal Club. Avocations: hiking, history, woodworking. Office: Washington U Sch Medicine 660 S Euclid Ave # 8057 Saint Louis MO 63110-1010 Home Phone: 314-495-5791; Office Phone: 314-362-3601. E-mail: tom63105@yahoo.com.

WOOTEN, JAMES H., JR., lawyer, engineering executive; BA in Criminal Justice, U. Ill., 1978; JD, U. Chgo., 1982. Assoc. Gardner, Carton & Douglas, Chgo., 1982—88; assoc. gen. counsel, asst. sec. Ill. Tool Works Inc., Glenview, Ill., 1988—2005, v.p., gen. counsel, 2005, sr. v.p., gen. counsel, corp. sec., 2005—. Mem.: ABA, Cook County Bar Assn., Exec. Leadership Coun., Minority Corp. Counsel Assn., Soc. Corp. Secs. and Governance Profls., Am. Corp. Counsel Assn., Chgo. Bar Assn., Phi Delta Phi. Office: Illinois Tool Works 3600 W Lake Ave Glenview IL 60026 E-mail: jwooten@itw.com.

WOOTEN, ROSALIE (ROSALIE O'REILLY WOOTEN), automotive company executive; Exec. v.p. O'Reilly Automotive Inc., Springfield, Mo., also bd. dir., 1993—. Office: O'Reilly Automotive Inc 233 S Patterson Ave Springfield MO 65802-2298

WORK, BRUCE VAN SYOC, small business owner, consultant; b. Monmouth, Ill., Mar. 20, 1942; s. Robert M. and Evelyn (Ruskin) W.; m. Janet Kay Brown, Nov. 12, 1966; children: Bruce, Terra. BA, Monmouth Coll., 1964; BS, U. Mo.-Rolla, 1966; postgrad., U. Chgo., 1978-79. Registered profl. engr., Ill. Various mgmt. positions Midcon Corp. (and subs.), 1966-79; pres. Indsl. Fuels Corp., Troy, Mich., 1979-85, Costain Coal Inc., Troy, Mich., 1985-89; pvt. practice small bus. cons., 1989-92; bus. cons. Wallis Oil Co., 1992-2000; small bus. cons., 2000—. Mem. various coms. Cuba United Meth. Ch. Mem. Detroit Athletic Club, Blue Key. Office: 2280 Hwy DD Cuba MO 65453-9684 Office Phone: 573-885-4724.

WORKE, GARY D., former state legislator; b. Mankato, Minn., Jan. 20, 1949; m. Kathy; four children. BS, Mankato State U.; postgrad., St. Johns Coll. Mem. Minn. Ho. of Reps., 1993-97; owner Residential Care Home. Home: 36971 Knoll Dr Waseca MN 56093-4638

WORKMAN, MICHAEL, editor-in-chief, publishing executive, art critic; Bachelor's Degree, Northwestern U., 2001. Dir. Bridge NFP, Chgo.; pub., editor-in-chief Bridge Magazine, Chgo. Lectr. Sch. Art Inst. Chgo., Northwestern U.; presenter Chgo. Mus. Contemporary Art, Chgo. Humanities Festival. Writer (column on visual art) Eye Exam, NewCity, (catalog essays) Chgo. Cultural Ctr., Chgo. corr. Flash Art, art critic and commentator WBEZ-FM; contbr. fiction, journalism and critical writing appeared in New Art Examiner, Chgo. Reader, zingmagazine, TenbyTen, Contemporary Mag. Mem.: Chgo. Art Critics Assn. Office: c/o Bridge Magazine 119 N Peoria #3D Chicago IL 60607 Office Phone: 312-421-2227. Business E-Mail: mworkman@bridgemagazine.org.

WORKMAN, ROBERT PETER, artist, cartoonist; b. Chgo., Jan. 27, 1961; s. Tom Okko and Virginia (Martin) Workman. D d'Etat, Diplome 3d Cycle, Sch. Louvre, Paris, 1997; prof. habilite, France, 1997; DEA, French U. Lumiere; D in Hieroglyphics, Nat. Inst. Lang./Civilizations, 1997; PhD, Roosevelt U.; postgrad., Sch. Art Inst. Chgo.; DSc, U. Blaise-Pascal/U. D'Auvergue, 1998. Freelance artist, Chgo.; artist Villager Newspaper, Chgo., 1991—; instr. St. Xavier Coll., Chgo., 1985; cartoonist Bridge View News, Oak Lawn, Ill., 1983—89, Village View Pubs., Oak Lawn, 1989; creator acrylic sculpture ArtStyle; adj. faculty U. Ariz., 1996. TV art dir. Media-In-Action, Oak Lawn; lectr. Oxford U., Eng., 1996; substitute tchr. Morgan Park Acad., Chgo.; artist-in-residence Chgo. Pub. Libr.; featured voice Am. Radio, 1992; maitre de confs., Paris; creator acrylic sculpture art style; creator 3-D Art Form, Tri-d' Art 21st Century; designer Oak Lawn War Meml.; prof. Nat. Mus. Natural History, France, 2001; curator Virginia I. Workman Collection, Woodson Regional Libr., Chgo. Author: (cartoon strip) Cypher, 1983-89; Sesqui Squirrel Coloring Book, 1982, Sesqui Squirrel History of Chicago, 1983, Book of Thoth, The Great Pyramid A Book in Stone, 1998, Easter Island and Egypt,(artists' books) Sesqui Squirrel History of the Constitution, Sesqui Squirrel Presents How Columbus Discovered America, The Sesqui-Squirrel Chicago Millennium Book, 1999; author: (novel) Angels of Doom, Book of THOTH, The Great Pyramid a Book in Stone, 1998, Easter Island and Egypt; contbr. to books on photography including: Wondrous Worlds, Hidden Silhouettes, Meadows of Memories, Eternal Moments; artworks and books in collections of over 120 mus. and librs. and pvt. collections, including Mus. du Louvre, Paris, Lincoln Collection, Ill., Smithsonian, Art Inst. Chgo., Daley Br. Libr., Chgo., Ill. Exec. Mansion Mus., Sesquicentennial Archives Chgo. Pub. Libr. (awards and honors), Vatican Libr., Rome, Bodleian Libr. Oxford (Eng.) U., Mt. Greenwood br. Pub. Libr. Chgo., Ill. Collection, Libr. Nat. Mus. Am. Art, Nat. Portrait Gallery, Carter Presdl. Libr., Reagan Presdl. Libr., Expo. U.S. Pavilion Lisbon, Portugal, 1998; exhibited Am. Pavilion, Expo 92, Seville, Spain, Royal Acad. Arts, 1995, Am. Pavilion, Expo 98, Lisbon, Portugal, inaugural exhbn. of the New Millennium/Chgo. Pub. Libr., 2000, online exhibitions at www.artq.net, VisualArtArray.com; featured on Sta. WBBM-TV, Chgo., 1998; contbr. poetry to books: Journey to Infinity, America at the Millennium, Treasured Poems of America; creator of Planetnet Concept; inventor Tri-CAR; inventor millenium star explorer spacecraft, Tri-CAR. Mem. nat. adv. bd. Am. Security Coun., Boston, Va.; founder Kennedy Pk. Libr., Chgo. Featured in Artist's mag., 1990; recipient Resolution City Coun. Chgo., 1992, cert. Appreciation State of Ill.; honored with Ill. House Resolution #443, 2003, Chgo. Pub. Schs. 2003 Prin. for a Day program; nominee Tchr. in Space Program, 1985. Mem. Am. Watercolor Soc., Gen. Med. Coun. (Eng.), No. Ill. Newspaper Assn., Art Inst. Chgo. (freelancer 1991), Artists' Resource Trust Ft. Wayne Mus. Art, Ridge Art Assn., VFW, S.W. Archdiocesan Singles, Friends Oxford U., Alumni Sch. Art Inst. Chgo., Alumni Sch of Louvre, KC, Mensa. Roman Catholic. Achievements include discovery of Workman's Gate 22 stones of Cydonia on Planet Mars, 2003; first Am. artist accepted into Musee du Louvre for 21st century. Home and Office: 2509 W 111th St Apt 2E Chicago IL 60655-1325 Office Phone: 773-238-5951. Personal E-mail: robertpworkman@yahoo.com.

WORMSER, ERIC SIGMUND, manufacturing executive; b. Germany, July 31, 1926; arrived in U.S., 1979, naturalized, 1944; s. Arthur and Hedie (Brettauer) Wormser; m. Dorothy M. Hendrickson, Oct. 19, 1952; children: David A., Randall J., Heidi M. BS in Chemistry, Purdue U., 1946; MBA, Ind. U., 1947. Chemist, chief chemist Lehon Co., Chgo., 1947—50; tech. dir. waterproofing divsn. Battenfeld Grease & Oil Corp., Kansas City, Mo., 1950—56; dir. rsch. Gibson-Homans Co., Cleve., 1956—61, v.p. rsch. and prodn., 1961—76, chmn. bd., 1976—. Mem.: ASTM, Am. Chem. Soc., Adhesive and Sealant Coun., Nat. Paint and Coatings Assn.

WORTH, GEORGE JOHN, retired English literature educator; b. Vienna, June 11, 1929; arrived in U.S., 1940, naturalized, 1945; s. Adolph and Theresa (Schmerzler) W.; m. Carol Laverne Dinsdale, Mar. 17, 1951; children: Theresa Jean (Wilkinson), Paul Dinsdale. AB, U. Chgo., 1948, MA, 1951; PhD, U. Ill., 1954. Instr. English U. Ill., Urbana, 1954-55; faculty U. Kans., Lawrence, 1955—, assoc. prof., 1962-65, prof. English lit., 1965-95; prof. emeritus English, 1995—; asst. chmn. dept. U. Kans., Lawrence, 1961-62, assoc. chmn., 1962-63, acting chmn., 1963-64, chmn., 1964-79. Author: James Hannay: His Life and Work, 1964, William Harrison Ainsworth, 1972, Dickensian Melodrama, 1978, Thomas Hughes, 1984, Great Expectations: An Annotated Bibliography, 1986, (book) Macmillan's Magazine, 1859-1907, 2003; editor: (with Harold Orel) Six Studies in Nineteenth Century English Literature and Thought, 1962, The Nineteenth Century Writer and His Audience, 1969, (with Edwin Eigner) Victorian Criticism of the Novel, 1985. Mem. MLA, Dickens Fellowship, Dickens Soc., Midwest Victorian Studies Assn., Rsch. Soc. for Victorian Periodicals. Office: U Kans Dept English Wescoe Hall Lawrence KS 66045-7590 E-mail: GJWorth@aol.com.

WORTHING, CAROL MARIE, retired minister; b. Duluth, Minn., Dec. 27, 1934; d. Truman James and Helga Maria (Bolander) W.; children: Gregory Alan Beatty, Graydon Ernest Beatty. BS, U. Minn., 1965; MDiv, Northwestern Theol. Seminary, 1982; DMin, Grad. Theol. Found., Notre Dame, Ind., 1988; MBA in Ch. Mgmt., Grad. Theol. Found., Donaldson, Ind., 1993; cert., Austin Presbyn. Theol. Sem., 2001; PhD, Grad. Theol. Found., 2002. Cert. Episcopal Diocese of Tex., 2003. Secondary educator Ind. (Minn.) Sch. Dist., 1965-78; teaching fellow U. Minn., 1968-70; contract counselor Luth. Social Svc., Duluth, 1976-78; media cons. Luth. Media Svcs., St. Paul, 1978-80; asst. pastor Messiah Luth. Ch., Fargo, ND, 1982-83, vice pastor, 1983-84; assoc. editor Luth. Ch. Am. Ptnrs., Phila., 1982-84; editorial assoc. Luth. Ptnrs. Evang. Luth. Ch. Am., Phila. and Mpls., 1984—2004; parish pastor Resurrection Luth. Ch., Pierre, SD, 1984-89; assoc. pastor Bethlehem Luth. Ch., Cedar Falls, Iowa, 1989-90; exec. dir. Ill. Conf. Chs., Springfield, 1990-96, Tex. Conf. of Chs., 1996—2003; ret., 2003. Asst. pastor Messiah Luth. Ch., Fargo, N.D., 1982-84; mem. pub. rels. and interpretation com. Red River Valley Synod, Fargo, 1984-86, mem. ch. devel., Pierre, 1986-87; mem. mgmt. com. office comm. Luth. Ch. in Am., N.Y.C., Phila., 1984-88; mem. mission ptnrs. S.D. Synod, 1988, chmn. assembly resolutions com., 1988; mem. pre-assembly planning com., ecumenics com., chmn. resolutions com. N.E. Iowa Synod, 1989-90; mem. ch. and society com., 1990-96; ecumenical com., 1995-96; Luth. Ecumenical Rep. Network, 1995—2003; mem. Cen. and So. Ill. Synod, 1996; mem. S.W. Tex. Synod, 1996—2003, mem. ecumenical com., 1998-2001; mem. ecumenical com. Mpls. Area synod and St. Paul Area synod ELCA, 2004—; nat. edn. cons. Am. Film Inst., Washington, 1967-70; chaplain state legis. bodies, Pierre, 1984-89; mem. exec. bd. Luth. Ecumenical Rep. Network for Region 4, Evang. Luth. Ch. in Am., 2002-03; preacher Nat. Cathedral, Washington, 2002. Author: Cinematics and English, 1967, Peer Counseling, 1977, Tischrede Lexegete, 1986, 88, 90, Way of the Cross, Way of Justice Walk, 1987, Introducing Collaboration as a Leadership Stance and Style in an Established Statewide Conference of Churches, 1993, The Anointing of Jesus--A Christological Necessity, 2001. Co-facilitator Parents of Retarded Children, 1985; bd. dirs. Countryside Hospice, 1985; cons. to adminstrv. bd. Mo. Shores Women's Ctr., 1986. Named John Macquarrie fellow, Grad. Theol. Found., 2002, homilist, Tex. Day, Washington Nat. Cathedral, 2002. Mem. NAFE, Nat. Assn. Ecumenical Staff (chair of site selection com. 1991-92, chair of scholarship com. 1993-94, mem. profl. devel. com. 1993-94, chair program planning com. 1996, bd. dirs. 1995-96), Pierre-Ft. Pierre Ministerium (v.p. 1986-87, pres. 1987-88). Democrat. Avocations: writing prose and poetry, concerts, theater, art, photography. Home: 5555 Dewey Hill Rd # 106 Edina MN 55439 Personal E-mail: cworthi@winternet.com.

WOUDSTRA, FRANK ROBERT, insurance company executive; b. Grand Rapids, Mich. BS, Ferris State Coll., 1968. CPA, Mich. Acct. Schellenber, Kregel & Kittle, CPAs, Grand Rapids, 1968-73; exec. v.p., chief exec. officer Foremost Corp. Am., Grand Rapids, 1973—, also bd. dirs. Office: Foremost Corp of Am PO Box 2450 Grand Rapids MI 49501-2450

WOYCZYNSKI, WOJBOR ANDRZEJ, mathematician, educator; b. Czestochowa, Poland, Oct. 24, 1943; came to U.S., 1970; s. Eugeniusz and Otylia Sabina (Borkiewicz) W.; m. Elizabeth W. Holbrook; children: Lauren Pike, Gregory Holbrook, Martin Wojbor. MSEE, Wroclaw Poly., 1966; PhD in Math., Wroclaw U., 1968. Asst. prof. Inst. Math. Wroclaw U., 1968-72, assoc. prof., 1972-77; prof. dept. math. Cleve. State U., 1977-82; prof., chmn. dept. math. and stats. Case Western Res. U., Cleve., 1982-91, dir. Ctr. for Stochastic and Chaotic Processes in Sci. and Tech., 1989—, chmn. dept. stats., 2002. Rsch. fellow Inst. Math. Polish Acad. Scis., Warsaw, 1969-76; postdoctoral fellow Carnegie-Mellon U., Pitts., 1970-72; vis. assoc. prof. Northwestern U., Evanston, Ill., 1976-77; vis. prof. Aarhus (Denmark) U., 1972, U. Paris, 1973, U. Wis., Madison, 1976, U. S.C., 1979, U. N.C., Chapel Hill, 1983-84, Gottingen (Germany) U., 1985, 91, 96, U. NSW, Sydney, Australia, 1988, Nagoya (Japan) U., 1992, 93, 94, U. Minn., Mpls., 1994, Tokyo U., 1997, Princeton U., 1998, U. Paris 6, 2003. Dep. editor in chief: Annals of the Polish Math. Soc., 1973-77; assoc. editor Chemometrics Jour., 1987-94, Probability and Math. Stats., 1988—, Annals of Applied Probability, 1989-96, Stochastic Processes and Their Applications, 1993-99; co-editor: Martingale Theory and Harmonic Analysis in Banach Spaces, 1982, Probability Theory and Harmonic Analysis, 1986, Nonlinear Waves and Weak Turbulence, 1993, Nonlinear Stochastic PDE's: Hydrodynamic Limit and Burgers' Turbulence, 1995, In a Reporter's Eye: The Life of Stefan Banach, 1996, Stochastic Models in Geosystems, 1997; author: (monograph) Martingales and Geometry in Banach Spaces I, 1975, part II, 1978, Burgers-KPZ Turbulence: Göttingen Lectures, 1998; co-author: Random Series and Stochastic Integrals: Single and Multiple, 1992, Distributions in the Physical and Engineering Sciences, vol. 1: Distributional and Fractal Calculus, Integral Transforms and Wavelets, 1997, Introductory Statistics and Random Phenomena. Uncertainty, Complexity and Chaotic Behavior in Engineering and Science, 1998, A First Course in Statistics for Signal Analysis, 2005. Rsch. grantee NSF, 1970, 71, 76, 77, 81, 87—, Office of Naval Rsch., 1985-96. Fellow Inst. Math. Stats.; mem. Am. Math. Soc., Am. Statis. Assn., Polish Math. Soc. (Gt. prize 1972), Polish Inst. Arts and Scis., Racquet Club East. Roman Catholic. Avocations: tennis, music, skiing, sailing, rare books collecting. Home: 3296 Grenway Rd Cleveland OH 44122-3412 Office: Case Western Res U Dept Statistics Cleveland OH 44106 E-mail: waw@po.cwru.edu.

WRAY, KENT, academic administrator; m. Wanda Wray. BS in Physics, Washburn U.; BS in Civil Engring., Kans. State U.; MS in Civil Engring., Air Force Inst. Tech.; PhD in Civil Engring., Tex. A&M U. Engr. Kans. Hwy. Dept.; chmn. dept. civil engring. Tex. Tech. U.; dean engring. and tech. Ohio U.; provost and sr. v.p. for acad. and student affairs Mich. Technol. U., Houghton, 2000—05, prof. civil engring.; provost, exec. vice chancellor academic affairs U. Mo.-Rolla, 2006—. Chair Ohio Engring. Deans Coun., 1990. Contbr. articles to profl. jours. Served in USAF, 1968—76, served in USAFR, 1976—90. Recipient Coll.-level Halliburton Outstanding Rsch. award, Halliburton Outstanding Tchr. award. Fellow: ASCE. Office: U Missouri-Rolla 204 Parker Hall 1870 Miner Cir Rolla MO 65409 Office Phone: 573-341-4138.

WRIGHT, BETTY REN, children's book writer; b. Wakefield, Mich., June 15, 1927; d. William and Revena Evelyn (Trezise) W.; m. George Albert Frederiksen, Oct. 9, 1976. BA, Milw.-Downer Coll., 1949. With Western Pub. Co., Inc., 1949-78, mng. editor Racine Editl., 1967-78. Author: The Doll House Murders, 1983, Christina's Ghost, 1985, The Summer of Mrs. MacGregor, 1986, A Ghost in the Window, 1987, The Pike River Phantom, 1988, Rosie and the Dance of the Dinosaurs, 1989, The Ghost of Ernie P., 1990, A Ghost in the House, 1991, The Scariest Night, 1991, The Ghosts of Mercy Manor, The Ghost of Popcorn Hill, 1993, The Ghost Witch, 1993, A Ghost Comes Calling, 1994, Out of the Dark, 1995, Haunted Summer, 1996, Too Many Secrets, 1997, The Ghost in Room 11, 1998, A Ghost in the Family, 1998, Pet Detectives, 1999, The Moonlight Man, 2000, The Wish Master, 2000, Crandalls' Castle, 2003, The Blizzard, 2003, Princess for a Week, 2006; contbr. articles to mags. Recipient Alumni Svc. award Lawrence U., 1973, Lynde and Harry Bradley Maj. Achievement award, 1997, numerous awards for books including Mo. Mark Twain award, 1986, 96, Tex. Bluebonnet award, 1986, 88, Young Readers award Pacific N.W. Libr. Assn., 1986, Reviewer's Choice Booklist, Ala. Young Readers award, 1987, Ga. Children's Choice award, 1988, Ind. Young Hoosier Book award, 1989, 96, Children's Choice Book/Internat. Reading Assn.—CBC, 1984, S.C. Children's Choice award, 1995, Okla. Sequoyah Children's Choice award, 1988, 95, award Fla. Sunshine State, 2001, Notable Wis. Author for Youth Lit. award, 2006. Mem.: Coun. Wis. Authors (Juvenile Book award 1985, 1996), Allied Authors, Phi Beta Kappa. Avocations: reading, travel. Home and Office: 6223 Hilltop Dr Racine WI 53406-3479

WRIGHT, CHARLES RICHARD, retired insurance executive; b. Yankton, SD, June 17, 1941; s. Ray C. and Agness (Weiland) W.; m. Mary M. Adrian; children: Charles A., Anne B., Jane E. BS, Yankton Coll., 1963. CLU. Agt. State Farm Ins., Mpls., 1963-67, agy. mgr., 1967-73, agy. dir. NYC, 1973-76, exec. asst. Bloomington, Ill., 1976-78, dep. regional v.p. Phoenix, 1978-81, v.p. agy. Bloomington, 1981-88, regional v.p., 1988-92, agy. v.p., 1992—. Mem. ins. adv. bd. Manactony Vehicle; bd. dirs. David Davis Found., Lexington Community Ctr.; bd. trustees Eureka Coll. Mem. Nat. Assn. Life Underwriters, Internat. Platform Assn., Kiwanis. Republican. Methodist. Avocations: antiques, tennis, historic restoration. Home: 10 Spencer Lexington IL 61753 Office: State Farm Ins Co One State Farm Plz Bloomington IL 61710-0001

WRIGHT, CHRIS, professional sports team executive; b. Eng. arrived in US, 1978; m. Walla Wright; children: Christy, Jeff, Ned. Grad., Carnegie Coll. Phys. Edn., Headingly Leeds, Yorkshire, Eng. Gen. mgr. Maj. Indoor Soccer League Pitts. Spirit, 1981—86, Maj. Indoor Soccer League Minn. Strikers, 1986—87; cons. State of Minn.; pres. Minn. Timberwolves, 2005—. Office: Minn Timberwolves 600 First Ave N Minneapolis MN 55403

WRIGHT, FELIX E., retired manufacturing executive; b. 1935; married Student, East Tex. State U., 1958. With Leggett & Platt, Inc., Carthage, Mo., 1959—, sr. v.p., from 1976, chief operating officer, exec. v.p., 1979, pres., COO, 1985-2000, vice chmn., 1999—2002, pres., CEO, 2000—02, chmn., CEO, 2002—06, chmn., 2006—08.

WRIGHT, FRANK GARDNER, retired newspaper editor; b. Moline, Ill., Mar. 21, 1931; s. Paul E. and Goldie (Hicks) W.; m. Barbara Lee Griffiths, Mar. 28, 1953; children: Stephen, Jeffrey, Natalie, Gregory, Sarah. BA, Augustana Coll., Rock Island, Ill., 1953; postgrad., U. Minn., 1953-54. Suburban reporter Mpls. Star, 1954-55; with Mpls. Tribune, 1955-82, N.D. corr., 1955-56, Mpls. City Hall reporter, 1956-58, asst. city editor, 1958-63, Minn. polit. reporter, 1963-68, Washington corr., 1968-72, Washington bur. chief, 1972-77, mng. editor, 1977-82; mng. editor/news Mpls. Star and Tribune, 1982-84, assoc. editor, 1984-98; ret., 1998. Juror for Pulitzer Awards, 1983-84 Chmn. Golden Valley Human Rights Commn., 1965-67; mem. exec. com. Nobel Peace Prize Forum, 2000-04; mem. faculty Augsburg Coll., 3d Age, U. St. Thomas, Ctr. for Sr. Citizens Edn., 2000-04; bd. dirs. Luth. Social Svcs., Washington. Recipient several Page 1 awards Twin Cities Newspaper Guild, 1950's, 60's, Worth Bingham prize Worth Bingham Meml. Fund, 1971; runnerup Raymond Clapper award for Washington correspondence, 1971; Outstanding Achievement award Augustana Alumni Assn., 1977; citation for excellence in internat. reporting Overseas Press Club, 1985; Minn. SPJ/SDX 1st Place Page One award for in-depth reporting, 1988, MWAP award Human Interest Reporting, 1995. Mem. Am. Newspaper Guild (chmn. Mpls. unit 1961-67, editorial v.p. Twin Cities 1963-67), Minn. AP Editors Assn. (pres. 1981), Phi Beta Kappa Home: 4912 Aldrich Ave S Minneapolis MN 55419-2353 E-mail: fgwright@aol.com.

WRIGHT, HERBERT E(DGAR), JR., geologist; b. Malden, Mass., Sept. 13, 1917; s. Herbert E. and Annie M. (Richardson) W.; m. Rhea Jane Hahn, June 21, 1943; children: Richard, Jonathan, Stephen, Andrew, Jeffrey. AB, Harvard U., 1939, MA, 1941, PhD, 1943; DSc (hon.), Trinity Coll., Dublin, Ireland, 1966, U. Minn., 1996; PhD (hon.), Lund U., Sweden, 1987. Instr. Brown U., 1946-47; asst. prof. geology U. Minn., Mpls., 1947-51, asso. prof., 1951-59, prof., 1959-74, Regents' prof. geology, ecology and botany, 1974-88, Regents' prof. geology, ecology & botany emeritus, 1988—; dir. Limnological Research Center, 1963-90. Served to maj. USAAF, 1942-45. Decorated D.F.C., Air medal with 6 oak leaf clusters; recipient Pomerance award Archeol. Inst. Am., 1985, Ann. award Sci. Mus. Minn., 1990; Guggenheim fellow, 1954-55, Wenner-Gren fellow, 1954-55. Fellow AAAS, Geol. Soc. Am. (Ann. award archeol. divsn. 1989, Disting. Career award geology and geomorphology divsn. 1992), Soc. Am. Archeology (Fryxell award 1993); mem. NAS, Ecol. Soc. Am., Internat. Quaternary Assn. (hon. pres. 16th Congress 2003), Am. Quaternary Assn. (Career award 1996). Achievements include research on Quaternary geology, paleoecology, paleolimnology and environ. archaeology in Minn., Wyo., Sweden, Yukon, Labrador, Peru, eastern Mediterranean. Home: 1426 Hythe St Saint Paul MN 55108-1423 Office: U of Minn 310 Pillsbury Dr SE Minneapolis MN 55455-0219 Business E-Mail: hew@umn.edu.

WRIGHT, JEREMIAH ALVESTA, JR., retired minister; b. Phila., Sept. 22, 1941; s. Jeremiah A. and Mary Elizabeth (Henderson) W.; m. Ramah E. Bratton, Oct. 22, 1989; 1 child, Jamila; children from previous marriage: Janet Marie Wright Hall, Jeri Lynn Wright Haynes, Nikol Reed, Nathan Reed. AB, Howard U., 1968, MA, 1969; MA in Religion, U. Chgo., 1974; D Ministry, United Theol. Sem., Dayton, Ohio, 1990. Ordained to ministry Am. Bapt. Ch., 1967. Asst. pastor Mt. Calvary Bapt. Ch., Rockville, Md., 1967-69; interim pastor Zion Bapt. Ch., Hagerstown, Md., 1969; asst. pastor Beth Eden Bapt. Ch., Chgo., 1969-71; pastor Trinity United Ch. of Christ, Chgo., 1972—2008. Rsch. asst. Am. Assn. Theol. Schs., Chgo., 1970-72; exec. dir. Chgo. Ctr. for Black Religious Studies, 1974-75; adj. prof. Chgo. Theol. Sem., 1974-75, Cath. Theol. Union, 1975; lectr. Chgo. Cluster of Theol. Schs., 1975—; mem. com. for racial justice United Ch. of Christ, 1976-80, ecumenical strategy com. Ill. Conf., 1975-76, resolutions com., 1973-74, urban mins. com. task force, 1975-76. Co-author: (with Jini Kilgore Ross) God Will Answer Prayer, 1974, What Makes You So Strong?: Sermons of Joy and Strength from Jeremiah A. Wright, Jr., 1993, Good News!: Sermons of Hope for Today's Families, 1995, (with Colleen Birchett) Africans Who Shaped Our Faith, 1995, (with Jawanza Kunjufu) Adam! Where Are You?: Why Most Black Men Don't Go to Church, 1997, (with Frank Madison Reid, III & Colleen Birchett) When Black Men Stand Up for God: Reflections on the Million Man March, 1997; author: What Can Happen When We Pray: A Daily Devotional, 2002, From One Brother To Another, Volume 2: Voices of African American Men, 2003; composer: (songs) Jesus Is His Name, 1975; contbr. articles to profl. jours. Dir. Creative Writing Workshop, Chgo., 1969-70; proposal writer, editor Dropout Prevention Program Chgo. Bd. Edn., 1971-72; bd. dirs. Malcolm X Sch. Nursing, 1974-84, Office of Ch. in Soc., United Ch. Christ, 1974-76. Recipient commendations Pres. of U.S., 1965-66; Howard U. grad. fellow, 1968-69, Rockefeller fellow, 1970-72, Carver medal, Simpson Coll, 2008 Mem. Ch. Fedn. Greater Chgo., Emergency Sch. Aid Act, Urban Ministerial Alliance, Ill. Conf. Chs., Mins. for Racial and Social Justice, United Black Christians, Omega Psi Phi, Alpha Kappa Mu. Home: 9167 S Pleasant Ave Chicago IL 60620-5512 Office: Trinity United Ch of Christ 400 W 95th St Chicago IL 60628-1120*

WRIGHT, JOHN, classics educator; b. NYC, Mar. 9, 1941; s. Henry and Dorothy (Chaya) W.; m. Ellen Faber, June 16, 1962; children: Jennifer, Emily. BA, Swarthmore Coll., 1962; MA, Ind. U., 1964, PhD, 1971. Instr. classics U. Rochester, NY, 1968—72, asst. prof., 1972—75; assoc. prof. Northwestern U., Evanston, Ill., 1975-77, prof., 1977—83, dept. chmn., 1978—97, 2000—01, John Evans prof. Latin lang. and lit., 1983—2001, prof. emeritus in svc., 2002—05, prof. emeritus, 2005—. Author: The Play of Antichrist, 1967, Dancing in Chains: The Stylistic Unity of the Comoedia Palliata, 1974, The Life of Cola de Rienzo, 1975, Essays on the Iliad: Selected Modern Criticism, 1978, Plautus: Curculio, Introduction and Notes, 1981, rev. edit., 1993, Ralph Stanley and the Clinch Mountain Boys: A Discography, 1983, The Five-String Banjo Stanley Style, 1984, rev. edit. (Clyde Pharr) Homeric Greek: A Book for Beginners, 1985, It's the Hardest Music in the World to Play: The Ralph Stanley Story in His Own Words, 1987, Traveling the High Way Home: Ralph Stanley and the World of Traditional Bluegrass Music, 1993; albums Everything She Asks For, 1993, Traveling the High Way Home, 1995, Promises, 1996, Ellen and John Wright 1, Ellen and John Wright 2, 1998, I Shook Hands with Eleanor Roosevelt, 2004; contbr. articles to profl. jours. Fellow Am. Acad. Rome, 1966-68; Nat. Endowment Humanities Younger humanist fellow, 1973-74; named to Honorable Order of Ky. Colonels; recipient songwriting prize Santa Fe Bluegrass and Old Time Music Festival, 1996. Mem.: Am. Fedn. of Musicians, Local 1000, BMI, Nat. Acad. Recording Arts and Scis., Am. Acad. in Rome Soc. of Fellows, Internat. Bluegrass Music Assn. (Print Media Personality of Yr. 1994), Chgo. Area Bluegrass Assn. Home: 1137 Noyes St Evanston IL 60201-2633 Personal E-mail: jhwright@northwestern.edu.

WRIGHT, JOHN F., state supreme court justice; BS, U. Nebr., 1967, JD, 1970. Atty. Wright & Simmons, 1970-84, Wright, Sorensen & Brower, 1984-91; mem., coord. Commn. on Post Secondary Edn., 1991-92; judge Nebr. Ct. Appeals, 1992-94; assoc. justice Nebr. Supreme Ct., 1994—. Chmn. bd. dirs. Panhandle Legal Svcs., 1970. Mem. Scottsbluff Bd. Edn., 1980-87, pres., 1984, 86. Served with U.S. Army, 1970, Nebr. N.G., 1970-76. Recipient Friend of Edn. award Scottsbluff Edn. Assn., 1992. Office: Nebr Supreme Ct 2207 State Capitol PO Box 98910 Lincoln NE 68509-8910

WRIGHT, JOSEPHINE ROSA BEATRICE, musicologist; b. Detroit, Sept. 5, 1942; d. Joseph Le Vander and Eva Lee Garrison W.; Mus.B., U. Mo., Columbia, 1963, M.A., 1967; Mus.M., Pius XII Acad., Florence, Italy, 1964; Ph.D., N.Y.U., 1975. Instr. music York Coll., CUNY, 1972-75, asst. prof., 1975; asst. prof. Afro-Am. studies in musicology Harvard U., Cambridge, Mass., 1976-81; assoc. dir. integration of Afro-Am. folk arts with music project, Nat. Endowment Humanities, 1979-82; assoc. prof. music and Black studies Coll. of Wooster, 1981-90, prof. music and Black studies, 1991-2000, prof. Music and The Josephine Lincoln Morris prof. Black studies, 2000-, chair Africana studies, 2002—; panelist, cons. on music Mass. Coun. of Arts and Humanities, 1978-80; cons. Nat. Endowment Humanities, 1982-83, 87, 89, 90, Ohio Humanities Coun., 1986; apptd. mem. Nat. Artistic Directorate, Am. Classical Music Hall of Fame, Cin. Author: Ignatius Sancho (1729-1780), An Early African Composer in England: The Collected Edition of His Music in Facsimile, 1981; editor: Am. Music, 1993-97, Music in African Am. Culture series, 1995—2000; editor of new music: The Black Perspective in Music, 1979-91, (with Sam Floyd) New Perspectives on Music: Essays in Honor of Eileen Southern, 1992; co-editor: The Bicentennial Issue of The Black Perspective in Music, 1976, (with Eileen Southern) African-American Traditions in Song, Sermon, Tale and Dance, 1991, (with Eileen Southern) Images: Iconography of Music in African-American Culture, 2000; mem. editl. bd. Jour. Am. Musicol. Soc., 2003, Am. Music, 2004, Jour. Soc. for Am. Music, 2006—; contbr. articles to profl. jours. Mem. Am. Musicol. Soc. (dir.-at-large 1998-2000), Soc. Am. Music (bd. dirs.), Nat. Coun. for black studies, U. Mo. Faculty of Arts and Sci. Alumni Assn. (trustee 1982-85), Pi Kappa Lambda. Democrat. Anglican. Office Phone: 330-263-2044. Business E-Mail: jwright@wooster.edu.

WRIGHT, JUDITH MARGARET, law librarian, educator, dean; b. Jackson, Tenn., Aug. 16, 1944; d. Joseph Clarence and Mary Catherine (Key) Wright; m. Mark A. Johnson, Apr. 17, 1976; children: Paul, Michael. BS, U. Memphis, 1966; MA, U. Chgo., 1971; JD, DePaul U., 1980. Bar: Ill. 1980. Librarian Oceanway Sch., Jacksonville, Fla., 1966-67; program dir. ARC, South Vietnam, 1967-68; documents and reference librarian D'Angelo Law Library, U. Chgo., 1970-74, reference librarian, 1974-77, dir., lectr. in law, 1980—2000, law libr., assoc. dean for libr. and info. svcs., lectr. in law, 2000—. Mem. adv. bd. Legal Reference Svcs. Quar., 1981—. Mem.: Chgo. Assn. Law Libraries, Am. Assn. Law Libraries, ABA. Democrat. Methodist. Office: U Chgo Law Sch D'Angelo Law Libr 1111 E 60th St Chicago IL 60637-2745 Home Phone: 773-947-0282; Office Phone: 773-702-9616. Office Fax: 773-702-2889. Business E-Mail: jm-wright@uchicago.edu.

WRIGHT, LLOYD JAMES, JR., broadcast executive, educator, announcer; b. San Benito, Tex., Dec. 28, 1949; s. Lloyd James Sr. and Lillian (Hemmerling) W. BA in Mass Communication, Pan Am. U., 1976; MA in Speech Communication, U. Houston, 1983. Lic. FCC restricted radiotelephone operator. Announcer Sta. KRYS, Corpus Christi, Tex., 1973-74, Sta. KZFM-FM, Corpus Christi, 1974-75, Sta. KRGV, Weslaco, Tex., 1975-76, Sta. KULF, Houston, 1976-77; instr. broadcasting Elkins Inst., Houston, 1976-77; announcer Sta. KBFM-FM, Edinburg, Tex., 1977-78; instr. radio Houston Ind. Sch. Dist., 1978-83; gen. mgr. Sta. KTAI-FM Tex. A&I U., Kingsville, 1983—; now pres., gen. mgr. WFYI-FM, Indpls. Cons. Stas. KINE, KDUV-FM, Kingsville, 1985—, weekend reporter Sta. KRIS-TV, Corpus Christi, 1987—. Producer: (documentaries) Kerrville Folk Festival, 1984, Texas Border Patrol, 1987. Served with Tex. NG, 1970-76. Mem. Nat. Assn. Broadcasters, Broadcast Edn. Assn., Tex. Assn. Broadcasters, Tex. Assn. Broadcast Educators, Tex. Speech Communication Assn. Lodges: Lions (chmn. publicity), Elks. Democrat. Methodist. Avocations: surfing, motorcycling, photography, sports cars. Office: WFYI-FM 1401 N Meridian St Indianapolis IN 46202-2304

WRIGHT, PHILIP B., lawyer; BS, U. Mo., Columbia, 1979; JD, Georgetown U., 1982; LLM, NYU, 1985. Ptnr., group co-leader Tax Advice and Controversy Bryan Cave LLP, St. Louis. Office: Bryan Cave LLP One Metropolitan Square 211 N Broadway, Ste 3600 Saint Louis MO 63102 Office Phone: 314-259-2499. Business E-Mail: pbwright@bryancave.com.

WRIGHT, SCOTT OLIN, federal judge; b. Haigler, Nebr., Jan. 15, 1923; s. Jesse H. and Martha I. Wright; m. Shirley Frances Young, Aug. 25, 1972. Student, Central Coll., Fayette, Mo., 1940-42; LLB, U. Mo., Columbia, 1950. Bar: Mo. 1950. City atty., Columbia, 1951-53; pros. atty. Boone County, Mo., 1954-58; practice of law Columbia, 1958-79; U.S. dist. judge Western Dist. Mo., Kansas City, from 1979. Pres. Young Democrats Boone County, 1950, United Fund Columbia, 1965. Served with USN, 1942-43; as aviator USMC, 1943-46. Decorated Air medal. Mem. ABA, Am. Trial Lawyers Assn., Mo. Bar Assn., Mo. Trial Lawyers Assn., Boone County Bar Assn. Clubs: Rockhill Tennis, Woodside Racquet. Lodges: Rotary (pres. Columbia 1965). Unitarian Universalist. Office: Charles E Whitaker Courthouse 400 E 9th St Ste 8662 Kansas City MO 64106-2684 Office Phone: 816-512-5700.

WRIGHT, SHARON, reporter; BA Broadcast Journalism, Mich. State U. Gen. assignment and state capitol reporter, weekend anchor Sta. WBRE-TV, Wilkes Barre, Pa., 1976—79; gen. assignment reporter, investigative reporter Sta. KMGH-TV, Denver, 1979—81; consumer investigative reporter Sta. WBZ-TV, Boston, 1981—86; gen. assignment reporter, consumer investigative reporter NBC 5, Chgo., 1986—. Recipient Outstanding Alumna award, Mich. State U., 1986, 10 Emmys. Office: BC 5 454 N Colmbus Dr Chicago IL 60611

WRIGHTON, MARK STEPHEN, academic administrator, chemistry professor; b. Jacksonville, Fla., June 11, 1949; s. Robert D. and Doris (Cutler) Wrighton; children: James Joseph, Rebecca Ann. BS, Fla. State U., 1969; PhD, Calif. Inst. Tech., 1972; DSc (hon.), U. West Fla., 1983. From asst. prof. chemistry to provost MIT, Cambridge, 1972—90, Frederick G. Keys prof in chemistry, 1981, head dept. chemistry, 1987—90, provost, 1990—95; prof., chancellor Washington U., St. Louis, 1995—. Mem. Nat. Sci. Bd., 2000—06; bd. dirs. A.G. Edwards, Inc., Brooks Automation, Danforth Plant Sci. Ctr., Nidus Ctr. for Sci. Enterprise, Barnes Jewish Hosp., BJC HealthCare, Assn. Am. Univs., St. Louis Regional Chamber and Growth Assn., Bus. Higher Edn. Forum., Univs. Rsch. Assn., Global Climate and Energy Project, Cabot Corp. Author: Organometallic Photochemistry, 1979. Trustee St. Louis Art Mus., Mo. Bot. Garden, St. Louis Symphony Orch., St. Louis Sci. Ctr.; bd. dirs. United Way Greater St. Louis; trustee St. Louis Sci. Ctr. Recipient Herbert Newby McCoy award, Calif. Inst. Tech., 1972, Disting. Alumni award, 1992, E.O. Lawrence award, Dept. Energy, 1983, Halpern award in photochemistry, N.Y. Acad. Scis., 1983, Fresenius award, Phi Lambda Upsilon, 1984, Dreyfus tchr.-scholar, 1975—80; fellow, Alfred P. Sloan, 1974—76, MacArthur fellow, 1983—88. Fellow: AAAS; mem.: Acad. of Sci. of St. Louis, Electrochem. Soc., Am. Chem. Soc. (award in pure chemistry 1981, award in inorganic chemistry 1988), Am. Philos. Soc., Am. Acad. Arts and Scis., Sigma Xi. Office: Washington Univ Office of Chancellor One Brookings Dr Campus Box 1192 Saint Louis MO 63130-4899 Office Phone: 314-935-5100. Business E-Mail: wrighton@wustl.edu.

WRIGLEY, DREW H., prosecutor, lawyer; b. Fargo, ND, Oct. 1965; BA, U. N.D., 1988; JD, Am. U., 1991. Pros. atty. City of Fargo, 1992—93; asst. dist. atty. Phila. Dist. Atty.'s Office, 1993—98; gen. counsel for pub. policy N.D. Workers Compensation Bur., 1998—99; exec. dir., legal counsel ND Rep. Party, 1999—2000; dep. chief of staff Office of Gov. of ND, 2000—01; US atty. ND US Dept. Justice, 2001—. Office: US Attys Office 655 First Ave N Ste 250 Fargo ND 58102

WRIGLEY, WILLIAM, JR., (BILL WRIGLEY JR.), candy company executive; b. 1964; s. William and Alison (Hunter) Wrigley; m. Kandis Wrigley (div.); 3 children; m. Heather Ann Rosbeck, Aug. 22, 2007. Asst. to pres. William Wrigley Jr. Co., Chgo., 1985—92, v.p., 1991—98, sr. v.p., 1999, pres., CEO, 1999—2006, exec. chmn., 2006—. Bd. dirs. William Wrigley Jr. Co., 1988—. Named one of Forbes' Richest Americans, 2006; recipient Hunt-Scanlon Human Capitol Advantage award, 2003, Golden Plate award, Acad. Achievement, 2006. Office: William Wrigley Jr Inc 410 N Michigan Ave Chicago IL 60611

WROBLEY, RALPH GENE, lawyer; b. Denver, Sept. 19, 1935; s. Matthew B. and Hedvig (Lyon) W.; m. Madeline C. Kearney, June 13, 1959; children: Kirk Lyon, Eric Lyon, Ann Lyon. BA, Yale U., 1957; JD, U. Chgo., 1962. Bar: Mo. 1962. With Bell Tel. Co., Phila., 1957-59; assoc. Stinson, Mag & Fizzell, Kansas City, Mo., 1962-65, mem., 1965-88; ptnr. Bryan, Cave, McPheeters & McRoberts, Kansas City, 1988-92, Blackwell, Sanders, Peper, Martin LLP, Kansas City, 1002—, mem. exec. com., 1992—2000. Bd. dirs. Human Resources Corp., 1971; mem. Civic Coun. Kansas City, 1986-2001; chmn. Pub. Housing Authority of Kansas City, 1971-74; vice chmn. Mayor's Adv. Commn. on Housing, Kansas City, 1971-74; bd. govs. Citizens Assn., 1965—, vice chmn., 1971-75, chmn., 1978-79; bd. dirs. Coun. on Edn., 1975-81, v.p., 1977-79; bd. dirs., pres. Sam E. and Mary F. Roberts Found., 1974-96; trustee Clearinghouse for Mid Continent Founds., 1977-96, chmn. 1987-89; bd. dirs. Bus. Innovation Ctr., 1984-91, vice-chmn. 1987-91, adv. bd. dirs., 1993-99, Midwest Regional Adv. Bd. Inst. Internat. Edn., 1989-93, Internat. Trade Assn., 1989-92, v.p., 1990; vice chmn., bd. dirs. Mid-Am. Coalition on Healthcare, 1991-2003. Mem. Mo. Bar Assn., Yale Club (pres. 1969-71, outstanding mem. award 1967). Republican. Presbyn. (elder) Home: 1015 W 67th Ter Kansas City MO 64113-1942 Office: 2300 Main St Kansas City MO 64108-2416 E-mail: rwrobley@blackwellsanders.com.

WRUBLE, BERNHARDT KARP, lawyer; b. Wilkes-Barre, Pa., Mar. 21, 1942; s. Maurice and Ruth Yvonne (Karp) W.; m. Judith Marilyn (Eyges), Nov. 16, 1968 (div. 1987); children: Justine, Vanessa, Alexis; m. Jill (Diamond), Nov. 24, 1990; children: Mattia, Austin. BA in Polit. Sci., Williams Coll., Williamstown, Mass., 1963; JD, U. Pa., 1966; postgrad., N.Y. Univ., 1972—74, Harvard U., 1978. Bar: Conn. 2003, Minn. 2000, DC 1981, NY 1968, US Supreme Ct. 1972, U.S. Dist. Ct. (so. dist.) N.Y., 1969, U.S. Dist. Ct. (ea. dist.) N.Y., 1972, U.S. Ct. Appeals (2d cir.), 1972, U.S. Supreme Ct., 1972, U.S. Ct. Appeals (7th cir.), 1974, U.S. Ct. Appeals (D.C. and 4th cir.), 1984, U.S. Ct. Appeals (5th cir.), 1985, U.S. Ct. Appeals (11th cir.) 1986. Law clk. to presiding judge U.S. Ct. Appeals (3d cir.), 1966—67; assoc. Simpson, Thacher, and Bartlet, NYC, 1968—73, ptnr., 1974—77; prin. dep. gen. counsel U.S. Dept. Army, Washington, 1977—79; dir. Office Govt. Ethics, Washington, 1979; exec. asst. to sec. and dep. sec. U.S. Dept. Energy, Washington, 1979—81; dir. President's Interagy. Coal Export Task Force, Washington, 1980—81; ptnr. Verner, Liipfert, Bernhard, McPherson, and Hand, Washington, 1981—99; sr. v.p. legal affairs N.W. Airlines, St. Paul, 1999—2001. Pres. The Bridges Resort and Tennis Club, Warren, Vt., 2007—. Bd. dir. Epilepsy Found. Am., 1983, chmn., 1991. Hartford County Pro Bono Award, 2004. Mem. ABA, D.C. Bar Assn., N.Y. State Bar Assn., Williams Coll. Alumni Assn. (pres. Washington chpt. 1986-91), Williams Coll. Soc. Alumni Assn. (exec. com. 1988-91). Democrat. Office Phone: 860-521-3543. Personal E-mail: bkwruble@yahoo.com.

WU, FRANK H., law educator, journalist; b. Cleve., Aug. 20, 1967; s. Hai and Grace (Ma) Wu. BA, Johns Hopkins U., 1988; JD, U. Mich., 1991. Bar: Calif. 1992, DC 1995. Law clerk to Honorable Frank Battisti, Cleve., 1991—92; assoc. Morrison & Foerster, San Francisco, 1992-94; fellow Stanford U. Law Sch., Palo Alto, Calif., 1994-95; asst. prof. Howard U. Law Sch., Washington, 1995—98, assoc. prof., 1998—2001, prof., 2002—04, clinic dir., 2000—02; dean, prof. law Wayne State U. Law Sch., Detroit, 2004—08. Scholar-in-residence Deep Springs Coll., 2001—03; vis. prof. U. Mich., 2002—03; adj. prof. Columbia U., 2002—04. Co-author: (book) Beyond Self Interest, 1996, Race, Rights and Reparation: Law and the Japanese American Internment, 2001; contbg. author: book The Affirmative Action Debate, 1996, Illegal Immigration Viewpoints, 1996; author: Yellow: Race in Amercia Beyond Black and White, 2001. Chmn. DC Human Rights Commn., 2001—03, DC Ct. Appeals Bd. Profl. Responsibility, 2003—04; bd. dirs. Leadership Conf. on Civil Rights Edn. Fund, 2004—; trustee Gallaudet U., 2000—. Recipient Chang-Lin Tien Edn. Leadership award, 200 Trailblazer, Nat. Asian Pacific Am. Bar Assn., 2007. Fellow: Am. Bar Found.; mem.: Com. of 100, Am. Law Inst., Asian Pacific ABA (dir. ednl. fund 1995—98). Office: Wayne State Univ Law Sch 471 W Palmer St Detroit MI 48202 Home Phone: 202-487-5775; Office Phone: 313-577-3933. Business E-Mail: frankhwu@wayne.edu.

WU, TAI TE, biological sciences and engineering educator; b. Shanghai, Aug. 2, 1935; m. Anna Fang, Apr. 16, 1966; 1 child, Richard. MB, BS, U. Hong Kong, 1956; BSMechE, U. Ill., Urbana, 1958; SM in Applied Physics, Harvard U., Cambridge, Mass., 1959; PhD in Engring. (Gordon McKay fellow), Harvard U., 1961. Rsch. fellow in structural mechanics Harvard U., 1961-63; rsch. fellow in biol. chemistry Harvard U. (Med. Sch.), 1964, rsch. assoc., 1965-66; rsch. scientist Hydronautics, Inc., Rockville, Md., 1962; asst. prof. engring. Brown U., Providence, 1963-65; asst. prof. biomath. Grad. Sch. Med. Scis., Cornell U. Med. Coll., NYC, 1967-68, assoc. prof., 1968-70; assoc. prof. physics and engring. scis. Northwestern U., Evanston, Ill., 1970-73, prof., 1973-74, prof. biochemistry and molecular biology and engring. scis., 1973-85, acting chmn. dept. engring. scis., 1974, prof. biochem., molecular biology, cell biology and biomed. engring., engring. scis., applied math., 1985-94, prof. biochemistry, molecular biology, cell biology, biomed. engring., 1994—. Author (with E.A. Kabat and others): Variable Regions of Immunoglobulin Chains, 1976, Sequences of Immunoglobulin Chains, 1979, Sequences of Proteins of Immunological Importance, 1983, Sequences of Proteins of Immunological Interest, 1987, 5th edit., 1991; editor: New Methodologies in Studies of Protein Configuration, 1985, Analytical Molecular Biology, 2001, Best Scientific Discovery or Worst Scientific Fraud of the 20th Century, 2006; contbr. articles to profl. jours. Recipient Progress award Chinese Engrs. and Scientists Assn. So. Calif., LA, 1971, Rsch. Career Devel. award NIH, 1974-79; C.T. Loo scholar, 1959-60. Mem. Am. Soc. Biochem. and Molecular Biology, Sigma Xi, Tau Beta Pi, Pi Mu Epsilon Office: Northwestern U Dept Biochem Molecular and Cell Biology Evanston IL 60208-3500 Office Phone: 847-491-7849. Business E-Mail: t-wu@northwestern.edu.

WUEST, JIM, consumer products company executive; Sr. exec. v.p. merch. and mktg. Office Max, Inc., Shaker Heights, Ohio, 1998—. Office: Office Max Inc 3605 Warrensville Center Rd Shaker Heights OH 44122-5248

WUNDER, CHARLES C(OOPER), physiologist, biophysicist, educator; b. Pitts., Oct. 2, 1928; s. Edgar Douglas and Annabel (Cooper) W.; m. Marcia Lynn Barnes, Apr. 4, 1962; children: E(dgar) Douglas, David Barnes, Donald Charles. AB in Biology, Washington and Jefferson Coll., 1949; MS in Biophysics, U. Pitts., 1952, PhD in Biophysics, 1954. Assoc. U. Iowa, Iowa City, 1954-56, asst. prof. physiology and biophysics, 1956-63, assoc. prof. physiology and biophysics, 1963-71, prof. physiology and biophysics, 1971-98, prof. emeritus, 1998—. Cons. for biol. simulation of weightlessness U.S. Air Force, 1964; vis. scientist Mayo Found., Rochester, Minn., 1966-67. Author: Life into Space: An Introduction to Space Biology, 1966; also chpts., numerous articles, abstracts Recipient Research Career Devel. award NIH, 1961-66; AEC predoctoral fellow U. Pitts., 1951-53; NIH spl. fellow, 1966-67; grantee NIH, NASA Mem. Am. Physiol. Soc., The Biophys. Soc. (charter), Aerospace Med. Assn., Iowa Acad. Sci. (chmn. physiology sect. 1971-72, 83-84, 96-97), Am. Soc. Biomechanics (founding), Aerospace Physiologist Soc., Iowa Physiol. Soc. (pres. 1996-97), Am. Soc. for Gravitational and Space Biology (Founders award 2000). Presbyterian. Achievements include the establishment of chronic centrifugation as an approach for investigating gravity's role as a biological determinant. Home: 702 W Park Rd Iowa City IA 52246-2425 Office: U Iowa BSB Iowa City IA 52242

WUNSCH, JAMES STEVENSON, political science professor; b. Detroit, Sept. 27, 1946; s. Richard Ellis and Jane Rolston (Kershaw) W.; m. Lillian C. Richards, Mar. 29, 1969 (div. Feb. 1983), 1 child, Kathryn; m. Mary Gayle Gundlach, Aug. 19, 1983; children: Hallie, Hannah. BA, Duke U., 1968; MA, Ind. U., 1971, PhD, 1974. Rsch. fellow U. Ghana, Accra, 1971-72; asst. prof. Creighton U., Omaha, 1974-78, assoc. prof., 1978-86, prof. polit. sci., 1986—, chmn. dept., 1983-93, 96—, dir. African studies program, 1998—. Social sci. analyst and cons., Ghana, Liberia, Kenya, Sudan, Thailand, Philippines, Joint African Inst., African Devel. Bank, USAID, Washington, 1978-80; vis. assoc. prof. Ind. U., Bloomington, 1985-86; sr. project mgr. Assocs. in Rural Devel., Burlington, Vt., 1987-88, cons., Bangladesh, Zambia, Nigeria, South Africa, Swaziland, Botswana, Uganda, 1985—; USIA Disting. lectr., South Africa, 1993. Author: The Failure of the Centralized State, 1990, Local Governance in Africa, 2004 (monograph) Rural Development, Decentralization and Administrative Reform, 1988; mem. bd. editors Pub. Adminstrn. and Devel., 1998—; contbr. more than 40 articles to profl. jours., chpts. to books. Bd. dirs. Omaha Symphony Chorus, 1977-78, Nebr. Choral Arts Soc., 1982-96, Voices of Omaha, 1982-85, Trinity Cathedral, Omaha, 1980-83; participant Leadership Omaha, 1982-83; mem. Omaha Com. Fgn. Rels., 1975-95; mem. govt. affairs com. Greater Omaha C. of C., 1980-85; mem. issues and interests com. Nebr. Rep. party, 1984-88. Recipient R.F. Kennedy Quality Tchg. award Creighton U., 1985, Burlington No. award, 1992, Dean's award for excellence in tchg., 1994, Dean's award for excellence in scholarship, 2000, Dean's award for excellence insvc., 2006, Student Senate award for excellence in advising, 1989; rsch. award NSF, NEH, USAID, Am. Philos. Soc., Dean's Spl. award, 2007; Fulbright-Hays fellow in Ghana, 1971-72, Internat. Affairs fellow N.Y. Coun. Fgn. Rels., 1978-79. Mem. Am. Polit. Sci. Assn., Midwest Polit. Sci. Assn., African Studies Assn., Internat. Studies Assn., Phi Beta Kappa, Pi Sigma Alpha, Phi Beta Delta. Episcopalian. Avocations: vocal music, camping, cross country skiing, bicycling. Home: 1631 N 53rd St Omaha NE 68104-4947 Office: Creighton U Dept Polit Sci 30th And California Omaha NE 68178-0001 Office Phone: 402-280-2568. Business E-Mail: jwunsch@creighton.edu.

WURTELE, CHRISTOPHER ANGUS, paint and coatings company executive; b. Mpls., Aug. 25, 1934; Valentine and Charlotte (Lindley) W.; m. Heather Campbell (div. Feb. 1977); children: Christopher, Andrew, Heidi; m. Margaret Von Blon, Aug. 21, 1977. BA, Yale U., 1956; MBA, Stanford U., 1961. V.p. Minn. Paints, Inc., Mpls., 1962—65; exec. v.p. Minn. Paints, Inc. (merged with Valspar Corp. 1970), Mpls., 1965—73, pres., CEO, 1973-96, chmn., 1973-98. With USN, 1956—59. Mem.: Mpls. Club. Episcopalian. Home: 2970 Gale Rd Wayzata MN 55391 Office: 4900 IDS Ctr 80 S 8th St Minneapolis MN 55402

WYANT, JOHN H., real estate development executive; Founder, gen. ptnr., adv. bd. Blue Chip Venture Capital Funds, Cin.; vice chmn. bd. dirs. Zaring Homes, Cin. Adj. prof. mgmt. and entrepreneurship Xavier U. Office: Zaring National Corp 625 Eden Park Dr #1250 Cincinnati OH 45202-6024

WYATT, JAMES FRANK, JR., lawyer; b. Talladega, Ala., Dec. 1, 1922; s. James Frank and Nannie Lee (Heaslett) W.; m. Rosemary Barbara Slone, Dec. 21, 1951; children: Martha Lee, James Frank III. BS, Auburn U., 1943; JD, Georgetown U., 1949, postgrad., 1950. Bar: D.C. 1949, Ala. 1950, Ill. 1953, U.S. Supreme Ct 1953. Atty. Office Chief Counsel, IRS, 1949-51; tax counsel Universal Oil Products Co., Des Plaines, Ill., 1951-63, asst. treas., 1963-66, v.p. fin., treas., 1966-75; treas. CF Industries, Inc., Long Grove, Ill., 1976-78, v.p. fin., treas., 1978-82; assoc. Tenney & Bentley, 1983-85, Arnstein, Gluck, Lehr, Barron & Milligan, 1985-88; pvt. practice, 1989—. Dir. 1st Nat. Bank, Des Plaines. Village trustee, Barrington, Ill., 1963-75; bd. dirs. Buehler YMCA, Barrington Twp. Republican Orgn., 1963—; pres. Barrington Area Rep. Workshops, 1962-63. Served to capt., Judge Adv. Gen. Corps AUS, 1944-47. Mem. Tax Execs. Inst. (v.p. 1965-66, chpt. pres. 1961-62), Fed., Am., Chgo. bar assns., Barrington Home Owners Assn. (pres. 1960-61), Newcomen Soc., Assn. U.S. Army, Scabbard and Blade, Phi Delta Phi, Sigma Chi. Clubs: Barrington Hills Country; Economics, University (Chgo.). Episcopalian. Home: 625 Concord Pl Barrington IL 60010-4508 Office: 200 Applebee St Barrington IL 60010-3060

WYATT, LANCE B., pharmaceutical executive; married. BChemE, U. Ala. Registered profl. engr. Mgr. process/project engring. Abbott Labs., Rocky Mount, NC, 1976—81, various positions hosp. products divsn., 1981—84, plant quality assurance mgr., 1984—90, dir., divisional v.p. quality assurance hosp. products divsn. Abbott Park, Ill., 1990—91, divisional v.p. quality assurance and regulatory affairs pharm. products divsn., 1991—95, corp. officer, v.p. corp. engring. divsn., 1995—2000, sr. v.p., pres. specialty products divsn., 2000—02, sr. v.p. specialty products, 2002—. Lt. U.S. Army C.E.

WYCLIFF, NOEL DON, journalist, newspaper editor; b. Liberty, Tex., Dec. 17, 1946; s. Wilbert Aaron and Emily Ann (Broussard) W.; m. Catherine Anne Erdmann, Sept. 25, 1982; children: Matthew William, Grant Erdmann. BA, U. Notre Dame, 1969. Reporter Houston Post, 1970-71, Dayton (Ohio) Daily News, 1972-73, Seattle Post-Intelligencer, 1978, Dallas Times-Herald, 1978-79, Chgo. Sun-Times, 1981-85; reporter, editor Chgo. Daily News, 1973-78; editor N.Y. Times, NYC, 1979-81, editorial writer, 1985-90; dep. editor editorial page Chgo. Tribune, 1990-91, editor editorial page, 1991-2000, pub. editor, 2000—. Occasional instr. journalism Columbia Coll., Chgo., Roosevelt U., Chgo. Finalist for Pulitzer prize in editl. writing, 1996; Woodrow Wilson fellow, 1969. Mem. Am. Soc. Newspaper Editors (Disting. Writing award for editls. 1997), Nat. Assn. Black Journalists, Nat. Assn. Minority Media Execs. Roman Catholic. Office: Chicago Tribune 435 N Michigan Ave Chicago IL 60611-4066

WYKLE, MAY L., dean, educator, researcher; BSN, Case Western Res. U., 1956, MSN Psychiat. Nursing, PhD Edn. Dean, Cellar prof. gerontological nursing Frances Payne Bolton Sch. Nursing, Ohio, 1988—; dean, dir. u. ctr. aging and health Case Western Res. U. Established ednl. programs, Europe, Africa, Asia; vis. prof. U. Mich., U. Tex.-Houston, U. Zimbabwe-Africa; del., served on planning com. White Ho. Conf. on Aging, 1993. Contbr. articles, chapters to books; author: Decision Making in Long-Term Care, Practicing Rehabilitation with Geriatric Clients, Stress and Health Among the Elderly, Family Caregiving Across the Lifespan, Service Minority Elders in the 21st Century (AJN Book of Yr. award, 2000). Dir. Robert Wood Johnson Tchg. Nursing Home Project; project dir. several tng. grants; cons. nursing homes, psychiat. hosps.; mem. bd. dirs. numerous cmty. orgns., nursing homes, profl. assns. Named first Pope Eminent scholar, Rosalynn Carter Inst. Human Devel. Southwestern State U., Americus, Ga., Outstanding Rschr. in State of Ohio, Ohio Rsch. Coun. on Aging, Ohio etwork Edn. Cons. in field of Aging, 1992; recipient Humanitarian award, Outstanding Contbns. to Nursing Profession, 1999, Acad. award, NIMH Geriatric Mental Health, Merit award, Cleve. Coun. Black Nurses, Gerontological Doris Schwartz Nursing Rsch. award, Gerontological Soc. Am., Belle Sherwin award, Cleve. Vis. Nurse Assn., Leadership award excellence in geriatric care, Midwest Alliance in Nursing, Disting. nurse-scholar lectr. award, Nat. Coun. ursing Rsch., Nursing Educator award, New Cleve. Woman mag. Fellow: Gerontological Soc. Am., Am. Acad. Nursing; mem.: NIA, NIMH, NINR, Vets Adminstrn. (geriatric/gerontology adv. com.), Sigma Theta Tau Internat. (pres.-elect 1999). Office: 10900 Euclid Ave Cleveland OH 44106

WYMAN, JAMES THOMAS, petroleum company executive; b. Mpls., Apr. 9, 1920; s. James Claire and Martha (McChesney) W.; m. Elizabeth Winston, May 6, 1950; children: Elizabeth Wyman Wilcox, James Claire, Steven McChesney. Grad., Blake Prep. Sch., Mpls., 1938; BA, Yale U., 1942. With Mpls. Star and Tribune, 1946-50; advt. mgr. Super Valu Stores, Inc., Eden Prairie, Minn., 1951-54, store devel. mgr., 1955-56, gen. sales mgr., 1956-57, sales v.p., 1957-60, dir., 1959-87, exec. v.p., 1961-64, pres., chief exec. officer, 1965-70, chmn. exec. com., 1970-76, ret., 1976. Bd. dirs. Marshall & Winston, Inc. Served to lt. (s.g.) USNR, World War II. Mem.: Minneapolis; Woodhill Country (Wayzata). Home: 2855 Woolsey Ln Wayzata MN 55391-2752 Office: 1105 Foshay Tower Minneapolis MN 55402

WYNN, NAN L., historic site administrator; b. Rock Island, Ill., Dec. 4, 1953; BA, Western Ill. U., 1975. Spl. events coord. Ill. Dept. Conservation, Springfield, 1975-77; mus. dir. Blackhawk State Hist. Site, Rock Island, 1977-81; site dir. Old State Capital Hist. Site, Vandalia, Ill., 1981-87; site mgr. Lincoln Tomb State Hist. Site, Springfield, 1986—. Office: Lincoln Tomb State Hist Site Oak Ridge Cemetery 1500 Monument Ave Springfield IL 62702-2500

WYSS, THOMAS JOHN, state legislator; b. Ft. Wayne, Ind., Oct. 24, 1942; s. John Paul and Winifred Ann (Ebersole) W.; m. Shirley Dawn Pabst, Jan. 16, 1965; children: Tamara, Angela. B in Indsl. Supervision, Purdue U., 1975. Apprentice GE, Ft. Wayne, 1961-65, mem. mfg. mgmt. staff, 1965-71, mem. mktg. mgmt. staff, 1971—2000; mem. Ind. Senate from 15th dist., 1985—. Councilman Allen County Coun., Ft. Wayne, 1976-85; chmn., founder Ind. State Crimestoppers, Indpls., 1988—. Lt. col. Ind. Air N.G., 1966—. Recipient Ind. NFIB Guardian of Small Bus. award, 1994; named Outstanding Legislator Ind. State Dental Soc., Indpls., 1987, Outstanding Legislator Ind. Dept. Bldg. Svcs., Indpls., 1987. Mem. Ind. Soc. Chgo., N.G. Assn. (Charles Dick award 1994), Ft. Wayne Jaycees (v.p. 1971-72, Key Man of Ind. and Outstanding Young Man Am. 1971), Am. Legis. Exch. Coun. (state chmn.). Avocation: politics. Home: 12133 Harvest Bay Dr Fort Wayne IN 46845-8982 Office: State Senate State Capital 200 W Washington St Ste 151 Indianapolis IN 46204-2785

XIE, YU, adult education educator; b. Zhenjiang, Jiangsu, China, Oct. 12, 1959; s. Liangyao Xie and Huazhen Zhao; m. Yijun Helen Gu, Dec. 1985; children: Raissa, Kevin. BA in Metallurgical Engring., Shanghai U. of Tech., China, 1982; MA in History of Sci., MS in Sociology, U. Wis., Madison, 1984, PhD in Sociology, 1989. From asst. to assoc. prof. U. Mich., Ann Arbor, 1989-96, John Stephenson Perrin prof. sociology, 1996, now Frederick G.L. Huetwell prof. sociology. Mem. adv. panel sociology program NSF, 1995-97; bd. dirs. Bd. Overseers of Gen. Social Survey. Dep. editor Am. Sociol. Review, 1996—; mem. editl. bd. Sociol. Methods and Rsch., 1989—, Am. Jour. Sociology, 1994-96, Sociol. Methodology, 1994-97; presenter in field; contbr. articles to profl. jours. Spencer fellow Nat. Acad. Edn., 1991-92; recipient Young Investigator award NSF, 1992-97, Faculty Scholar award William T. Grant Found., 1994-99. Fellow: Am. Acad. Arts & Sci., Academia Sinica (academician); mem. Am. Stat. Assn., Am. Sociol. Assn., Sociol. Rsch. Assn. (elected mem.), Population Assn. of Am. Office: U Mich Population Studies Ctr 426 Thompson St Ann Arbor MI 48104-2321 Business E-Mail: yuxie@umich.edu.

YABUKI, JEFFREY W., data processing company executive, former accounting company executive; BBA, Calif. State U. Cert. CPA Calif., Minn., lic. Nat. Assn. Securities Dealers. With Am. Express Co., 1987—99; v.p., mergers & acquisitions Am. Express Tax Bus. Svcs., Mpls., 1996—98, pres., CEO NYC, 1998—99; pres. H&R Block Internat., 1999—2002; exec. v.p., COO H&R Block Inc., Kans. City, 2002—05; pres., CEO Fiserv, Inc., Brookfield, Wis., 2005—. Bd. dir. PetSmart, Inc., 2004—, Fiserv Inc., 2005—, MBIA. Former mem. Minn. Bd. Accountancy. Recipient Innovator award, Bank Technology News, 2007. Office: Fiserv Inc 255 Fiserv Dr Brookfield WI 53045

YACKEL, JAMES WILLIAM, mathematician, academic administrator; b. Sanborn, Minn., Mar. 6, 1936; s. Ewald W. and Marie E. (Heydlauff) Y.; m. Erna Beth Seecamp, Aug. 20, 1960; children: Jonathan, Juliet, Carolyn. BA, U. Minn., 1958, MA, 1960, PhD, 1964. Rsch. instr. dept. math. Dartmouth Coll., Hanover, NH, 1964-66; asst. prof. dept. stats. Purdue U., West Lafayette, Ind., 1966-69, from assoc. prof. to prof., 1969-76, assoc. dean sci., 1976-87; vice chancellor acad. affairs Purdue U. Calumet, Hammond, Ind., 1987-90, chancellor, 1990-2001, chancellor emeritus, 2001—. Rsch. mathematician Inst. Def. Analysis, Washington, 1969. Author: Applicable Finite Mathematics, 1974; editor Statistical Decision Theory, 1971; contbr. articles to profl. jours. Fellow AAAS; mem. Am. Math. Soc., Math. Assn. Am., Inst. Math. Stats. Achievements include research on Ramsey's theorem and finite graphs. E-mail: yackelj@calumet.Purdue.edu.

YAFFE, STUART ALLEN, physician; b. Springfield, Ill., July 6, 1927; m. Natalie, 1952; children: Scott, Kim Yaffe Schoenburg. BS cum laude, U. Alaska, 1951; MD, St. Louis U., 1956. Diplomate Am. Bd. Family Practice. Intern St. Louis CIty Hosp., 1956-57, resident, 1957-58; physician pvt. practice, 1958—; clin. assoc. prof. So. Ill. U. Sch. Medicine., Springfield, 1971—; ptnr. Springfield Clinic, 1989—. With U.S. Army, 1945-47. Mem. AMA, Am. Acad. Family Physicians, Ill. Acad. Family Physicians, Ill. State Med. Soc., Sangamon County Med. Soc. Office: 1100 Centre West Dr Springfield IL 62704-2100 Home Phone: 217-546-3604; Office Phone: 217-793-9960.

YAGAHASHI, TAKASHI, chef; C. chef Tribute, Farmington Hills, Mich., 1996—. Named Best Restaurant in Detroit, NY Times; named one of America's Best Restaurants, Gourmet mag.; recipient award, James Beard Found., 2001. Office: Tribute 31425 W 12 Mile Rd Farmington Hills MI 48334

YAGER, VINCENT COOK, retired bank executive; b. Chgo., June 15, 1928; s. James Vincent and Juanita (Cook) Yager; m. Dorothy Marie Gallagher, Sept. 28, 1957; children: Susan Marie, Sheila Ann. BA, Grinnell Coll., 1951. V.p. comml. loan dept. Madison Bank & Trust, Chgo., 1963-68; v.p. fin. Cor-Plex Internat. Corp., Chgo., 1968-70; pres., CEO, dir. First Nat. Bank Blue Island, Ill., 1970-89; pres., CEO Great Lakes Fin. Resources, Inc., Matteson, Ill., 1982-96, bd. dirs.; ret. With US Army, 1951—53, ETO. Mem.: Econ. Club Chgo., Bankers Club Chgo., Robert Morris Assocs. (pres. chpt. 1981—82), Midlothian Country Club, Rotary. Home: 1032 S Rand Rd Villa Park IL 60181-3145 Office: Great Lakes Bank Blue Island 13057 S Western Ave Blue Island IL 60406-2418

YAMADA, TADATAKA, internist; b. Tokyo, June 5, 1945; MD, NYU, 1971. Intern Med. Coll. Va. Hosps., Richmond, 1971-72, resident in internal medicine, 1972-74; gastrointestinal fellow UCLA, 1977-79; prof. medicine U. Mich., Ann Arbor, 1996, adj. prof. internal medicine and physiology, 1996—; mem. staff U. Mich. Hosp., Ann Arbor, 1996. Adj. prof. medicine U. Mich. Hosp., Ann Arbor. Mem. AAAS, ACP, AAP, AGA, ASCI, IOM.

YAMASHINA, TADASHI (GEORGE), transportation executive; arrived in U.S., 1993; m. Hiromi Yamashina; children: Kae, Kaki. BME, Waseda U., 1977. From engr. to project mgr. Toyota Motor Corp., Aichi, Japan, 1977—93; from exec. coord. to pres. Toyota Tech. Ctr., Ann Arbor, Mich., 1993—2001, pres., 2001—. Office: Toyota Technical Ctr USA Inc 1555 Woodridge Ave RR 7 Ann Arbor MI 48105

YAMIN, JOSEPH FRANCIS, lawyer, counselor; b. Detroit, Mar. 12, 1956; s. Raymond Samuel and Sadie Ann (John) Y. 1975; BA, U. Mich., 1978; JD, London Sch. Econs., 1981; JD, Mich. State U., 1982. Bar: U.S. Ct. Appeals (6th cir.) 1982, U.S. Dist. Ct. (ea. dist.) Mich. 1982. With Allan R. Miller PC, Birmingham, Mich., 1981-93; ptnr. Beier Howlett PC, Bloomfield Hills, Mich., 1993—; instr. Detroit Coll. Law Rev., 1984-86; case evaluation Wayne County, Oakland County. Pres. Pheobe Found., 2002-04; bd. dirs. Detroit Gun Club, 2006—. Recipient Am. Jurisprudence Book award Am. Jurisprudence Soc., 1981. Mem. ABA, Oakland County Bar Assn., meditor State of Mich. Bar Assn., Law Rev., Chi Phi, Oakland County Real Property Sect. Roman Catholic. Office: Beier Howlett PC 200 E Long Lake Rd Ste 110 Bloomfield Hills MI 48304-2328 Office Phone: 248-860-1122. Business E-Mail: jyamin@beierhowlett.com.

YAMPOLSKY, VICTOR, conductor; b. Frunze, Kirgizskaj, SSR, Oct. 10, 1942; s. Vladimir and Fanny (Zaslavsky) Y. Student, Moscow Conservatory, 1961-66, Leningrad Conservatory, 1968-72. Violinist Moscow Radio Orch., 1965; violinist, asst. condr. Moscow Philharm. Orch., 1965-72; violinist Boston Symphony Orch., 1973-77; music dir. Atlantic Symphony Orch., Halifax, N.S., Can., 1977-83; condr. Tanglewood Inst., Boston U., 1977-84; prof. music Boston U., 1979-84; assoc. prof. music Northwestern U., 1984—, Carol R. and Arthur L. Rice Jr. prof. in music performance, 1993—; music dir. Peninsula Festival, Fish Creek, Wis., 1986—; hon. dir. Scotia Festival of Music, Halifax; music dir. Omaha (Nebr.) Symphony Orch., 1995—. Office: Omaha Symphony Orch 1605 Howard St Omaha E 68102-2797

YANCEY, KIM BRUCE, dermatology researcher; b. Atlanta, Nov. 25, 1952; s. Andrew Jackson and Edrie (Johnson) Yancey. BS, U. Ga., Athens, 1974; MD, Med. Coll. Ga., 1978. Diplomate Am. Bd. Dermatology. Intern dept. internal medicine Med. Coll. Ga., Augusta, 1978-79, resident dept. dermatology, 1979-81; med. staff fellow dermatology br. NIH, Bethesda, Md., 1981-84, sr. staff fellow dermatology br., 1984-85, sr. investigator dermatology br., 1993—2000; asst. prof. dept. dermatology Uniformed Svcs. U. Health Scis., Bethesda, 1985-87, assoc. prof. dept. dermatology, 1987-93, acting chmn. dept. dermatology, 1990-93; prof., chair dept. dermatology Med. Coll. Wis., Milw., 2001—. Cons. Walter Reed Army Med. Ctr., Washington, 1985—2000. Author monographs and sci. manuscripts; mem. various editl. bds.; contbr. articles to profl. jours. Grantee NIH, 1986—, NATO, 1988-93. Fellow: Am. Acad. Dermatology (editl. bd. 1986—93, 2004—); mem.: AMA, Med. Coll. Physicians (mem. exec. com. 2004—, chmn. 2004—05), Assn. Profs. Dermatology (chmn. program com. 2004), Wis. Dermatol. Assn., Dermatology Found., Am. Fedn. Med. Rsch., Soc. Investigative Dermatology (bd. dirs. 1982—84, co-chmn. ea. region 1990—92, co-chmn. program com. 2004, bd. dir. 2004—), Am. Dermatol. Assn. (Young Leadership award 1986), Am. Bd. Dermatology (v.p. 2005), Am. Soc. Clin. Investigation. Methodist. Office: Med Coll Wis Dept Dermatology 8701 Watertown Plank Rd Milwaukee WI 53226 Office Phone: 414-456-4081. Business E-Mail: kyancey@mcw.edu.

YANDELL, CATHY MARLEEN, language educator; b. Anadarko, Okla., Dec. 27, 1949; d. Lloyd O. and Maurine (Dunn) Y.; m. Mark S. McNeil, Sept. 7, 1974; children: Elizabeth Yandell McNeil, Laura Yandell McNeil. Student, Inst. des Professeurs de Français à l'Etranger U. Sorbonne, Paris, 1969—70; BA, U. N.Mex., 1971; MA, U. Calif., Berkeley, 1973, PhD, 1977. Tchg. asst. U. Calif., Berkeley, 1971, acting instr., 1976—77; asst. prof. Carleton Coll., Northfield, Minn., 1977—83, assoc. prof., 1983—89, prof. French, 1989—. Chair commn. on the status of women Carleton Coll., Northfield, 1983-85, ednl. policy com., 1985-86, 96-97, romance langs. and lits., 1990-94, chair faculty affairs com., 2000-02, pres. of faculty, 1991-94, Bryn-Jones disting. tchg. prof. humanities, 1996-99, mentor to jr. faculty, 1996—, W.I. and Hulda F. Daniell prof. French lit., lang. and culture, 1999—; dir. Paris French Studies Program, 1998, 2004. Author: Carpe Corpus: Time and Gender in Early Modern France, 2000; co-author: Vagabondages: Initiation à la litt. d'expression française, 1996, 1996; contbr. to Art & Argumentation: The Sixteenth Century Dialogue, 1993, French Texts/American Contexts: French Women Writers, 1994, Montaigne: A Collection of Essays, Vol. 4, Language and Meaning, 1995, Reflexivity in Women Writeres of the Ancien Régime, 1998, High Anxiety, 2002, Ronsard, figure de la variété, 2002, Lectrices d'Ancien Régime, 2003, Reflections on Teaching, 2004, Ecriture courante: Critical Perspectives on French and Francophone Women, 2005, Masculinites in Sixteenth-Century France, 2006, Paysage et nature a La Renaissance, 2007, Approaches to Teaching the Heptameron, 2007; editor: Pontus de Tyard's Solitaire Second, ou prose de la musique, 1980; contbr. articles to profl. jours. Active exec. com., then mem. Amnesty Internat., orthfield, 1980—. Grantee Faculty Devel., Carleton Coll., 1988, 1991; Regents' Travelling fellow, U. Calif. Berkeley, 1975—76, NEH Rsch. fellow., 1994—95, Mellon Faculty fellow, 2003, Roth Faculty Rsch. fellow, 2007, Mellon New Directions grantee, 2006. Mem.: MLA (del. 1989—92, chair exec. com. French 16th Century lit. 2001—05), Sixteenth Century Soc. (program chmn. French lit. 2007—), Phi Beta Kappa (pres. 2004—05). Democrat. Home: 514 5th St E orthfield MN 55057-2220 Office: Carleton College 1 N College St Northfield MN 55057-4044 Office Phone: 507-222-4245. Business E-Mail: cyandell@carleton.edu.

YANDERS, ARMON FREDERICK, biological sciences educator, science administrator; b. Lincoln, Nebr., Apr. 12, 1928; s. Fred W. and Beatrice (Pate) Yanders; m. Evelyn Louise Gatz, Aug. 1, 1948; children: Mark Frederick, Kent Michael. AB, Nebr. State Coll., Peru, 1948; MS, U. Nebr., 1950, PhD, 1953. Rsch. asso. Oak Ridge Nat. Lab. and Northwestern U., 1953-54; biophysicist US Naval Radiol. Def. Lab., San Francisco, 1955-58; asso. geneticist Argonne Nat. Lab., Ill., 1958-59; with dept. zoology Mich. State U., 1959-69; prof., asst. dean Mich. State U. (Coll. Natural Sci.), 1963-69; prof. biol. scis. U. Mo., Columbia, 1969—, dean Coll. Arts and Scis., 1969-82, rsch. prof., dir. Environ. Trace Substances Rsch. Ctr., 1983-93, dir. Alzheimer's Disease and Related Disorders Program, 1994—, dir. Spinal Cord Injury Rsch. Program, 2002—, rsch. prof., dir. Environ. Trace Substances Rsch. Ctr. and Sinclair Comparative Medicine Rsch. Farm, 1984-94, prof. emeritus, 1994—; dean emeritus, 2007—. Trustee Argonne Univs. Assn., 1965-77, v.p., 1969-73, pres., 1973, 76-77, chmn. bd., 1973-75; bd. dirs. Coun. Colls. Arts and Scis., 1981-82; mem. adv. com. environ. hazards VA, Washington, 1985-2002, chmn. sci. coun., 1988-2000, chmn. of com., 1990-2002. Contbr. articles to profl. jours. Trustee Peru State Coll., 1992-2001. Served from ensign to lt. USNR, 1954-58. Recipient Disting. Svc. award Peru State Coll., 1989, U. Mo., 2007. Fellow AAAS; mem. AAUP (Robert W. Martin acad. freedom award 1971), Environ. Mutagen Soc., Genetics Soc. Am., Radiation Rsch. Soc., Soc. Environ. Toxicology and Chemistry. Home: 1204 Castle Bay Pl Columbia MO 65203-6257 Office: U Mo 521 Clark Hall Columbia MO 65211-4420 Office Phone: 573-882-1640. Business E-Mail: YandersA@umsystem.edu.

YANDLE, STEPHEN THOMAS, dean; b. Oakland, Calif., Mar. 7, 1947; s. Clyde Thomas and Jane Walker (Hess) Y.; m. Martha Anne Welch, June 26, 1971. BA, U. Va., 1969, JD, 1972. Bar: Va. 1972. Asst. dir. admissions U. Va. Law Sch., Charlottesville, 1972-76; from asst. to assoc. dean Northwestern U. Sch. Law, Chgo., 1976-85; assoc. dean Yale U. Law Sch., New Haven, 1985—2002; exec. dir. Housing Authority of New Haven, 2002—04; dep. cons. on legal edn. ABA, 2004—06; v.p. global law sch. programs LexisNexis, 2007—. Bd. dirs. The Access Group, 1996-2004; lectr. in law Yale Law Sch., 2002-04; vis. scholar Am. Bar Found., 2006. Commr. New Haven Housing Authority, 1998-02; trustee Nat. Assoc. for Law Placement Found. for Rsch. and Edn., 2000-04, 07. Capt. US Army, 1972. Mem. Law Sch. Admission Coun. (programs, edn. and prelaw com. 1978-84), Assn. Am. Law Schs. (chmn. legal edn. and admissions sect. 1979, nominations com. 1987, chmn. adminstrn. of law schs. sect. 1991), Nat. Assn. for Law Placement (pres. 1984-85, co-chmn. Joint Nat. Assn. com. on placement 1986-88), New Haven Legal Assistance Assn. (bd. dirs., treas. 1992-98). Office: 70 W Madison St Ste 2200 Chicago IL 60602 Home Phone: 312-587-3147; Office Phone: 312-606-3526. Business E-Mail: stephen.yandle@lexisnexis.com.*

YARICK, PAUL E., food products executive; V.p., treas. Interstate Bakeries Corp., Kansas City, Mo. Office: Interstate Bakeries Corp PO Box 419627 Kansas City MO 64141-6627

YARRINGTON, HUGH, corporate lawyer, communications company executive; BA, Randolph-Macon Coll.; JD, George Washington U. Assoc. Wilkinson, Cragun & Barker, Washington; v.p., gen. counsel Bur. Nat. Affairs, Inc., Washington; from sr. v.p., pub. to pres., CEO, exec. com. CCH Inc., Riverwoods, Ill. Mem. Info. Industry Assn. (bd. dirs. 1988—, chmn., treas., sec.). Office: CCH Inc 2700 Lake Cook Rd Riverwoods IL 60015-3867

YASHON, DAVID, neurosurgeon, educator; b. Chgo., May 13, 1935; s. Samuel and Dorothy (Cutler) Y.; children— Jaclyn, Lisa, Steven. BS in Medicine, U. Ill., 1958, MD, 1960. Diplomate Am. Bd. Neurol. Surgery. Intern U. Ill., 1961, resident, 1961-64, asst. in neuroanatomy, 1960; clin. instr. neurosurgery U. Chgo., 1965-66; asst. prof. neurosurgery Case Western Res U., Cleve., 1966-69; assoc. prof. neurosurgery Ohio State U., Columbus, 1969-74, prof., 1974-89, prof. emeritus, 1989—; mem. staff St. Ann's Hosp., Children's Hosp., Grant Med. Ctr., Ohio State U. East Med. Ctr. Cons. Med. Research and Devel. Command, U.S. Army; mem. Neurology B Study Sect NIH. Author: Spinal Injury; contbr. articles to med. jours. Served as capt. U.S. Army, 1960-68. Fellow Royal Coll. Surgeons Can. (cert.), A.C.S.; mem. AMA, Am. Physiol. Soc., Congress Neurol. Surgeons, Am. Assn. Anatomists, Canadian, Ohio neurosurg. socs., Am. Assn. eurol. Surgeons, Research Soc. Neurol. Surgeons, Acad. Medicine Columbus and Franklin County, Soc. for Neurosci., Soc. Univ. Surgeons, Am. Acad. eurology, Assn. for Acad. Surgery, Am. Acad. Neurol. Surgery, Am. Assn. for Surgery of Trauma, Central Surg. Soc., Ohio Med. Soc., Columbus Surg. Soc., Sigma Xi, Alpha Omega Alpha. Address: 500 Columbia Pl Bexley OH 43209-1677 E-mail: dyashon@columbus.rr.com.

YASINSKY, JOHN BERNARD, nuclear scientist; b. Shenandoah, Pa., June 10, 1939; s. Joseph and Helen Y.; m. Marlene A. Tuladziecki, Apr. 28, 1962; children: Diane L., Karen A., Mark J. B.S. in Physics, Wheeling (W.Va.) Coll., 1961; M.S., U. Pitts., 1963; Ph.D. in Nuclear Sci, Carnegie Mellon U., 1966. Scientist, sr. scientist, then mgr. electric systems and plant analysis Westinghouse Bettis Lab., Pitts., 1963-71; White House fellow, spl. asst. to sec. U.S. Dept. Commerce, Washington, 1972-73; mgr. bus. devel. breeder reactor divs. Westinghouse Corp., Pitts., 1973-74, mgr. mktg. advanced reactors div., 1974-75, dir. dept. advanced coal conversion, 1975-77; pres. Westinghouse Hanford Co., Richland, Wash., 1979-80; gen. mgr. advanced power systems divs. Westinghouse Electric Corp., Pitts., after 1980, then pres. Europe, Africa and Middle East; evening instr. nuclear engring. div. Carnegie Mellon U., 1966-72; Bd. dirs. Wheeling Coll., 1981, Wash. State Council Econ. Edn., 1979-80, Tri-City Nuclear Industry Council, 1979-80, Kadlec Med. Center, 1979-80; mem. adv. com. Wash. State Joint Grad. Center, 1979-80, Hanford Energy Center, 1979-80; mem. steering com. Wash. State Energy Council, 1979-80.

Contbr. over 50 articles to profl. jours. Mem. Am. Nuclear Soc., Nat. Security Indsl. Assn., White House Fellows Assn., Atomic Indsl. Forum. Club: Pitts. Field. Office: Westinghouse Nuclear Ctr PO Box 355 Pittsburgh PA 15230-0355

YASUDA, HIROTSUGU KOGE, engineering educator, director; b. Kyoto, Mar. 24, 1930; s. Mitsuo and Kei (Niwa) Y.; m. Gerda Lisbeth Schmidtke, Apr. 6, 1968; children: Ken Eric, Werner Akira, Lisbeth Kay. BSChemE, Kyoto U., 1953; MS in Polymer Chemistry, SUNY, Syracuse, 1959, PhD in Polymer and Phys. Chemistry, 1961. Rsch. assoc. Ophthalmic Plastic Lab., Mass. Eye & Ear Infirmary, Boston, 1962-63; head biomaterial sect. eye rsch. Cedar-Sinai Med. Ctr., LA, 1963-65; vis. scientist Royal Inst. Tech., Stockholm, 1965-66; sr. chemist Rsch. Triangle Inst., Rsch. Triangle Pk., NC, 1966-72, mgr. Polymer Rsch. Lab., 1972-78; prof. chem. engring. U. Mo., Rolla, 1978-88, dir. Thin Films Inst., 1974-88, prof. chem. engring. Columbia, 1988—, chmn. dept., 1988-90, James C. Dowell rsch. prof., 1989—2003, prof. emeritus, 2003—, dir. Ctr. for Surface and Plasma Techs., 1989—. Author: Plasma Polymerization, 1985, Luminous Chemical Vaper Deposition and Interface Engineering, 2004. Home: 1004 Lake Point Ln Columbia MO 65203-2900 Office: Ctr For Surface Sci & Plasma Tech Columbia MO 65211-0001 also: Dept Chemical Engring W2033 Engineering Bldg East Columbia MO 65211 Home Phone: 573-442-9678; Office Phone: 573-882-9601. Business E-Mail: yasudah@missouri.edu.

YATES, C. DANIEL, lawyer; b. Indpls., Sept. 27, 1947; AB, Ind. U., 1969, MBA, 1973; JD, Ind. U., Bloomington, 1973. Bar: Ind. 1973. Ptnr. estate planning and bus. succession planning grp. Bose, McKinney & Evans, LLP, Indpls. Mem. adv. bd., mem. planned giving com. Indpls. Zoo; bd. trustees Children's Mus. Indpls.; chmn. asset devel. com. Ctrl. Ind. Cmty. Found., Inc.; bd. govs. Legacy Fund Cmty. Found.; mem. planned giving com. Ind. U. Sch. Medicine; mem. planned giving adv. bd. Indpls.-Marion County Pub. Libr. Found., Inc., Noble of Ind.; elder Second Presbyn. Ch.; counsel Second Presbyn. Ch. Endowment Fund; bd. dirs., chmn. planned giving coun. Eiteljorg Mus. Am. Indians and Western Art; bd. dirs., mem. planned giving com. Indpls. Symphony Orch.; bd. dirs., sec. St. Vincent Hosp. Found.; bd. dirs. D.J. Angus-Scientech Ednl. Found., Inc. Named one of Top 100 Attys., Worth mag., 2006. Fellow: Am. Coll. Trust and Estate Counsel, Ind. Bar Found.; mem.: Planned Giving Grp. Ind., Estate Planning Coun. Indpls., ABA, Ind. State Bar Assn., Indpls. Bar Assn., Hillcrest Country Club, Rotary Club Indpls., Maxinkuckee Yacht Club, Contemporary Club Indpls. (bd. dirs.), Scientech Club Indpls., Inc., Econ. Club Indpls., Ind. Soc. Chgo., Phi Alpha Delta. Office: Bose McKinney & Evans LLP 2700 First Indiana Plz 135 N Pennsylvania St Indianapolis IN 46204 Office Phone: 317-684-5143. Office Fax: 317-223-0143. E-mail: dyates@boselaw.com.

YATES, TYRONE, state representative; Grad., law sch., 1981. Lawyer Ohio Atty. Gen.'s Office, 1981—83; asst. atty. gen. State of Ohio, 1983—87; pub. defender, 1987—; state rep. dist. 33 Ohio Ho. of Reps., Columbus, 2002—, ranking minority mem., children's healthcare and family svcs. subcom., mem. criminal justice, edn., health, mcpl. govt. and urban revitalization, and ways and means coms. City councilman City of Cin., 1991—99; sr. warden St. Andrew Ch., Cin. Democrat. Office: 77 S High St 11th fl Columbus OH 43215-6111

YEAGER, DAVID P., transportation executive; b. 1953; BA, U. Dayton, 1975; MBA, Univ. Chgo., 1987. With affiliated cos. Hub Group, Inc., 1975—, vice chmn. bd. Lombard, Ill., 1992—, CEO, 1995—. Bd. dir. SPR Inc., Thrall Car Mfg. Co. Bd. dir. Children's Memorial Hospital-Chgo., Fenwick High School; mem. adv. council Univ. Dayton. Office: Hub Group 3050 Highland Pkwy Downers Grove IL 60515

YEAGER, MARK LEONARD, lawyer; b. Chgo., Apr. 7, 1950; BA, U. Mich., 1972; JD cum laude, Northwestern U., 1975. Bar: Ill. 1975, Fla. 1985, US Supreme Ct. Ptnr. McDermott, Will & Emery LLP, Chgo., 1981—; mem. Trial Dept. McDermott, Will & Emery, Chgo. Dir. Taylor Capital Group, Inc., Rosemont, Ill., 1997—. Mem. alumni adv. bd. U. Mich. Dept. Econs. Mem.: ABA. Office: McDermott Will & Emery LLP 227 W Monroe St Ste 3100 Chicago IL 60606-5096 also: Taylor Capital Group 9550 W Higgins Rd Rosemont IL 60018 Office Fax: 312-984-7700. E-mail: myeager@mwe.com.

YEAGER, PHILLIP CHARLES, transportation company executive; b. Bellevue, Ky., Nov. 15, 1927; s. Ferd A. and Helen (Koehler) Y.; m. Joyce E. Ruebusch, June 2, 1951; children: David P., Debra A. Yeager Jensen, Mark A. BA, U. Cin., 1951. Warehouse mgr. Pure Carbonic Co., Cin., 1950-52; trace clk., rate clk., asst. office mgr. Pa. R.R., Chgo., 1952-56, salesman Kansas City, Mo., 1956-59, asst. dir. Trailvan Phila., 1959-65, div. sales mgr. Milw., 1965-68; dir. Trailvan Penn-Ctrl. R.R., NYC, 1968-71; pres. Hub City Terminals, Chgo., 1971-85; chmn. The Hub Group, Chgo., 1985—; also bd. dirs. Bd. dirs. 30 Hubcity terminals. Cpl. U.S. Army, 1946-47. Recipient Achievement award Intermodal Transp. Assn., 1991, Harry E. Salzberg medallion for outstanding achievement in transp.; named Chgo. Transp. Man of Yr., Chgo. Transp. Assn., 1990. Mem. N.Y. Traffic Club, Chgo. Traffic Club. Republican. Lutheran. Avocations: golf, biking, swimming.

YEAGER, WALDO E., food company executive; CFO, treas. Seaway Food Town Inc., 1996—. Office: 1020 Ford St Maumee OH 43537-1820

YEAMANS, GEORGE THOMAS, librarian, educator; b. Nov. 7, 1929; s. James Norman and Dolphine Sophia (Manhart) Yeamans; m. Mary Ann Seng, Feb. 1, 1958; children: Debra, Susan, Julia. AB, U. Va., 1950; MLS, U. Ky., 1955; EdD, Ind. U., 1965. Asst. audio-visual dir. Ind. State U., Terre Haute, 1957—58; asst. film libr. Ball State U., Muncie, Ind., 1958—61, film libr., 1961—69, assoc. prof. libr. sci., 1969—72, prof., 1972—95, prof. emeritus, 1995—. Cons. Pendleton (Ind.) Sch. Corp., 1962, 67, Captioned Films for the Deaf Workshop, Muncie, 1963—65, Decatur (Ind.) Sch. Sys., 1978; adjudicator Ind. Media Fair, 1979—93, David Letterman Scholarship Program, 1993. Author: Projectionists' Programmed Primer, 1969, rev. edit., 1982, Mounting and Preserving Pictorial Materials, 1976, Tape Recording, 1978, Transparency Making, 1977, Photographic Principles, 1981, Computer Literacy-A Programmed Primer, 1985, Designing Dynamic Media Presentations, 1996, Robert F. Kennedy Archival Project, 1968—2004, Building Effective Creative Project Teams, 2000, Building Effective Creative Project Teams, rev. ed., 2007; songwriter: Branson Bound, 1996; contbr. articles to profl. jours. Campaign worker Wilson for Mayor, Muncie, 1979. With USMC, 1950—52. Recipient Citations of Achievement, Internat. Biog. Assn., Cambridge, Eng., 1973, Am. Biog. Assn., 1976, Mayor James P. Carey award for achievement for disting. contbns. to Ball State U. and City of Muncie, 1988; Video Info. Sys. grant, Ball State U., 1993. Mem.: ALA, NEA (del. assembly dept. audiovisual instrn. 1967), Audio-Visual Instrn. Dirs. Ind. (exec. bd. 1962—68, pres. 1966—67), Thomas Jefferson Soc. Alumni U. Va., Ind. Pub. Libr. Assn., Ind. Acad. Libr. Assn., Ind. Corp. and Network Libr. Assn., Ind. Libr. Fedn., Assn. Ednl. Comm. and Tech., Autism Soc. Am., Assn. Ind. Media Educators (chmn. auditing com. 1979—81), Ind. Assn. Ednl. Comms. and Tech. (dist. dir. 1972—76), Am. Assn. Sch. Librs., Phi Delta Kappa. Republican. Unitarian-Universalist. Avocations: photography, stamp collecting/philately, coin collecting/numismatics, genealogy. Home: 4507 W Burton Dr Muncie IN 47304-3575

YECKEL, ANITA T., state legislator; b. Salt Lake City, Nov. 12, 1942; m. Robert Yeckel; 2 children. BS in Polit. Sci., U. Mo., St. Louis, postgrad. With 1st Nat. Bank, St. Louis, 1960-68, Am. Home Savs. & Loans Assn., 1982-92; mem. Lindebergh Sch. Dist. Bd. Edn., 1990—, Mo. Senate from 1st dist., Jefferson City, 1996—. Mem. Kiwanis. Republican. Roman Catholic. Office: 8819 Gladlea Saint Louis MO 63127 Fax: 314-843-7542. E-mail: ayeckel@services.state.mo.us.

YEE, ROBERT DONALD, ophthalmologist; b. Beijing, Feb. 21, 1945; came to U.S., 1947, naturalized, 1947; s. James and Marian Y.M. (Li) Y.; m. Linda Margaret Neil, June 28, 1968; children: Jillian Neil, Allison Betram. AB in biology summa cum laude, Harvard U., 1966; MD in medicine cum laude, Harvard Med. Sch., 1970. Diplomate Am. Bd. Ophthalmology. Fullbright scholar, 1966; intern in internal medicine U. Rochester, NY, 1970-71; resident in ophthalmology Jules Stein Eye Inst. UCLA, 1971-74; fellow in neuro-ophthalmology Nat. Eye Inst., NIH, Bethesda, Md., 1974-76; chief ophthalmology Harbor-UCLA Med. Ctr., Torrance, Calif., 1976-78; asst. prof. ophthalmology Sch. Medicine UCLA, 1976-78, assoc. prof., 1978-82, prof., 1982-87; prof., dept. chmn. ophthalmology Ind. U. Sch. Medicine, Indpls., 1987—. Mem. residency rev. com. for ophthalmology Accrediation Coun. for Grad. Med. Edn., 1995-2002, vice-chmn., 1998-2000, chmn., 2000-2002. Mem. editorial bd. Investigative Ophthalmology and Visual Sci., 1982—, von Graefe's Archives of Ophthalmology, 1983-89; Feldman endowed chair ophthalmology UCLA, 1984-87; Grayson endowed chair ophthalmology Ind. U., 2003—. Author numerous med. research papers. Lt. comdr. USPHS, 1974—76. Grantee, IH, 1976—84; scholar Dolly Green Rsch. scholar, 1984—86. Fellow: ACS, Am. Acad. Ophthalmology; mem.: AMA, Accreditation Cou. for Grad. Med. Edn. (residency rev. com., chair 2000—02), Indpls. Ophthal. Soc., Ind. Med. Soc., Chinese Am. Ophthal. Soc. (pres. 1996—98), Ind. Acad. Ophthalmology, Am. Ophthal Soc., Assn. Rsch. in Vision and Ophthalmology (chmn. eye movement sect. 1981, 1987, trustee 1996—2001, v.p. 2000—01), Phi Beta Kappa, Alpha Omega Alpha. Office: Ind U Med Ctr 702 Rotary Cir Indianapolis IN 46202-5133 Office Phone: 317-274-7101. E-mail: ryee@iupui.edu.

YELLEN, DAVID N., dean, lawyer; b. 1957; BA, Princeton U.; JD, Cornell U. Bar: DC 1985. Pvt. law practice, Washington; counsel to Judiciary Com. US Ho. of Reps., Washington; prof. law Cornell U., NY Law Sch.; dean Hofstra Law Sch., Hempstead, NY, 2001—04, Max Schmertz Disting. Prof. Law; Reuschlein Disting. Visiting Prof. Villanova U. Sch. Law; dean Loyola U. Sch. Law, Chgo., 2005—. Lectr. in field of sentencing reform; adv. on white-collar crime issues Pres. Clinton's transition team. Office: Office of Dean U Loyola Chicago Law Sch 25 East Pearson St Chicago IL 60611

YEN, DAVID CHI-CHUNG, management information systems educator; b. Tai-Chung, Taiwan, Republic of China, Nov. 15, 1953; s. I-King and Chi-Ann (Ro) Y.; m. Wendy Wen-Yawn Ding, July 4, 1981; children: Keeley Ju, Caspar Lung, Christopher Jai. MBA in Gen. Bus., Cen. State U., Edmond, Okla., 1981, BS in Computer Sci., 1982; MS in Computer Sci., PhD in Mgmt. Info. Systems, U. Nebr., 1985. Asst. prof. Miami U., Oxford, Ohio, 1985-89, assoc. prof., 1989-93, prof., 1992—94, chmn. decision scis. and mgmt. info. sys., 1995—. Chmn., computer policy com. Miami U., 1991-94, computer adv. group, 1993-94, com. evaluation adminstrs., 1993, conf. chair, track chair and session chair, seminar dir., Smucker prof. internship, exec. com., 1995—, program chair; mem. Hong Kong Coun. for Acad. Accreditation, 2000—; external assessor for paculty P & T Evaluation for U.S. China U., Taiwan and Honk Kong U. Author three textbooks; editor Procs.; contbr. articles to profl. jours. External assesser Can. Rsch. and Grants Coun., Hong Kong Rsch. and Grants Coun. Served to 2d lt., Rep. China Navy. Alumni teaching scholar Miami U., 1987-88; named Prof. of Yr. Delta Sigma Pi, 1993; grantee GE, Cleve. Found., Smucker, Microsoft; recipient Sr. Faculty for Tchg. Excellence award. Mem. IEEE, Am. Chinese Mgmt. Educators Assn. (pres.-elect 1995, pres. 1996, program com. 1997—, MIS track chair 1998—), Soc. Info. Mgmt., Internat. Chinese Info. Sys. Assn., Internat. Bus. Sch. Computer User Assn., Internat. Sch. Bus. Computer User Group (chair conf., proceedings editor 1988), Assn. Computing Machinery, Ohio Mgmt. Info. System Assn., Decision Sci. Inst., Soc. Data Educators. Office: Miami U 309 Upham Hall Oxford OH 45056 E-mail: yende@muohio.edu.

YENKIN, BERNARD KALMAN, coatings and resins company executive; b. Columbus, Ohio, Dec. 2, 1930; s. Abe I. and Eleanore G. Yenkin; m. Miriam Schottenstein, Mar. 31, 1957; children: Leslie Mara, Jonathan, Allison Katsev, Amy. BA, Yale U., 1952; MBA, Harvard U., 1954. V.p. Yenkin-Majestic Paint Corp., Columbus, 1968-77, pres., 1977-85, chmn. bd., 1985—. Pres. Columbus Jewish Fedn., 1980-82, Pro Musica Chamber Orch., Columbus, 1983-85, Columbus Torah Acad., 1977-79; bd. v.p. Jewish Ednl. Svc. N.Am., N.Y.C., 1991-95. Recipient Mayor's award for Vol. Svc. City of Columbus, 1984, Young Leadership award Columbus Jewish Fedn., 1965. Mem. Yale Club of Cen. Ohio (pres. 1979-81), Yale Club of N.Y., Athletic Club (Columbus). Office: Yenkin-Majestic Industries 1920 Leonard Ave Columbus OH 43219-2514

YEUNG, EDWARD SZESHING, chemist; b. Hong Kong, Feb. 17, 1948; arrived in U.S., 1965; s. King Mai Luk and Yu Long Yeung; m. Anna Kunkwok Seto, Sept. 18, 1971; children: Rebecca Tze-Mai, Amanda Tze-Wen AB magna cum laude, Cornell U., 1968; PhD, U. Calif., Berkeley, 1972. Instr. chemistry Iowa State U., Ames, 1972-74, asst prof., 1974-77, assoc. prof. 1977-81, prof. chemistry, 1981-89, disting. prof., 1989—. Contbr. articles to profl. jours. Alfred P. Sloan fellow, 1974-76; recipient Am. Chem Soc. award in Analytical Chemistry, 1994. Fellow AAAS; mem. Soc. Applied Spectrosci. (Lester Strock award 1990), Am. Chem. Soc. (award in chem. instrumentation 1987, award in analytical chemistry 1994, award in chromatography 2002). Home: 1005 Jarrett Cir Ames IA 50014-3937 Office: Iowa State U Gilman Hall Ames IA 50011

YILEK, JOHN A., lawyer; b. Mpls., Sept. 2, 1949; BA summa cum laude, U. Minn., 1971, JD magna cum laude, 1976. Bar: Minn. 1976. Mem. Doherty, Rumble & Butler, P.A., St. Paul. Mem. ABA (com. banking law bus. law sect. 1983—), Minn. State Bar Assn. (chmn. banking law com. 1987-92, 94—), Phi Beta Kappa. Office: Doherty Rumble Butler PA 2800 Minn World Trade Ctr 100 S 5th St Ste 1200 Minneapolis MN 55402-1216

YOCKIM, JAMES CRAIG, foundation administrator; b. Williston, ND, Feb. 13, 1953; s. Daniel and Doris (Erickson) Y.; children: Jenna, Ericka. BSW, Pacific Luth. U., 1975; MSW, San Diego State U., 1979. Caseworker Dyslin Boys Ranch, Tacoma, 1975-77, head caseworker, program dir., 1979-80; landman Fayette Oil & Gas, Williston, 1980-82; owner Hy-Plains Energy, Williston, 1982-87; city fin. commr. City of Williston, 1984—88, 1998—2002; therapist Williston, 1983; senator .D. State Senate, 1986-98; owner James C. Yockim Resources, Williston, 1987—. Dir. Bethel Luth. Found., 1993—; del. N.D. Dem. Conv., 1984, 86, 88, 90, 92, 94, 96, 98, 2000, 02, 04; dist. chmn. Dem. Party, Williston, 1988; caucus chmn. Dem. Caucus N.D. State Senate; mem. N.D. Legis. Coun., 1997-98; coun. pres. 1st Luth. Ch. Recipient Ruth Meiers award N.D. Mental Health Assn., 1989, Legislator of Yr. award N.D. Children's Caucus, 1989; named Outstanding Young North Dakotan N.D. Jaycees, 1988. Mem. NASW. Avocations: racquetball, golf. Home: 1123 2nd Ave E Williston ND 58801-4302 Office: PO Box 2344 Williston ND 58802-2344 Business E-Mail: JamesYoc@dia.net.

YOCUM, CHARLES FREDRICK, biology professor; b. Storm Lake, Iowa, Oct. 31, 1941; s. Vincent Cary and Olive Lucille (Cammack) Y.; m. Patricia Joan Bury, Jan. 1, 1981; 1 son, Erik Charles. BS, Iowa State U., 1963; MS, Ill. Inst. Tech., 1968; PhD, Ind. U., 1971. Rsch. biochemist Ill. Inst. Tech. Rsch. Inst., Chgo., 1963-68; grad. fellow Ind. U., Bloomington, 1968-71; postdoctoral fellow Cornell U., Ithaca, N.Y., 1971-73; asst. prof. U. Mich., Ann Arbor, 1973-77, assoc. prof., 1978-82, prof. biol. scis. and chemistry, 1983—. Alfred S. Sussman disting. univ. prof., 2004—, chmn. dept. biology, 1985-91; vis. prof. Mich. State U., East Lansing, 1980-81; cons. NSF, Washington, 1982—. Editl. bd. Plant Physiology, Photosynthesis Rsch., Biochimica et Biophysica Acta, Jour. Biol. Chemistry; contbr. articles to various publs. Fulbright fellow, 1996; rsch. grantee NSF, 1978—, USDA, 1978—; recipient Henry Russel award U. Mich., 1977; fellow J.S. Guggenheim Found., 2002-03. Fellow AAAS; mem. Am. Chem. Soc., Am. Soc. Plant Physiologists, Am. Soc. Biol. Chemists, Am. Soc. Photobiology. Avocations: classical music, travel. Office: Dept Biology Univ of Mich Ann Arbor MI 48109-1048 E-mail: cyocum@umich.edu.

YODER, JOHN CLIFFORD, producer, consultant; b. Orrville, Ohio, Jan. 30, 1927; s. Ray Aquila Yoder and Dorothy Mildred (Hostetler) Yoder Hake; m. Alice Vigger Andersen, Mar. 2, 1963 (div. Nov. 1992); children: Gorm Clifford, Mark Edward. BA in Philosophy and Polit. Sci., Ohio Wesleyan U., 1951. Prodn. supr. Sta. WFMJ-TV, Youngstown, Ohio, 1954-62; producer Sta. NBC-TV, Chgo., 1964-72; ind. producer cons. Evanston, Ill., 1972—. Producer radio program Conversations From Wingspread, 1972-90 (George Foster Peabody Broadcasting award 1974, Ohio State award 1978, Freedoms Found. Honor medal 1978); appeared in film The Untouchables, 1994, TV program Missing Persons, 1993. Pub. rels. and pub. info. com. Chgo. Heart Assn. (Meritorious Svc. award 1978); electronic media advisor The White House, Washington, 1972; bd. dirs. Youngstown (Ohio) Symphony Soc., 1959-63, Youngstown Playhouse, 1952-63, Bensenville (Ill.) Home Soc. 1985-89. With USAF, 1945-47 PTO. Recipient Disting. Svc. award Inst. Medicine of Chgo. 1971. Mem. Am. Fedn. Television & Radio Artists,, Nat. Acad. TV Arts and Scis., Screen Actors Guild, Midwest Pioneer Broadcasters, Soc. Profl. Journalists, Mus. Broadcast Comms., Masons, Am. Legion, Chgo. Headline Club. Avocations: tennis, golf, sailing, fishing, reading. Home: 720 Noyes St Apt D 2 Evanston IL 60201-2848

YOKICH, TRACEY A., former state legislator; b. Feb. 25, 1960; BA, Mich. State U., 1982; JD, U. Detroit Law Sch., 1985. Law clk. for Hon. George Clifton Edwards, Jr., 6th Cir. U.S. Ct. Appeals, 1985-86; asst. pros. atty. Macomb County, Mich., 1986-89, asst. corp. counsel Mich., 1989-90; mem. Mich. Ho. of Reps., 1991-97. Vice chmn. election com., mem. pub. health, environ., Great Lakes, consumer, judicary and conservation coms., chmn. tourism and recreation com. Commr. Macomb County Criminal Justice Bldg. Authority. Mem. Mich. Bar Assn., Macomb County Bar Assn., Clair Shores Dem. Club. Home: 22710 Gordon Switch St Saint Clair Shores MI 48081-1308

YONTZ, KENNETH FREDRIC, medical and chemical company executive; b. Sandusky, Ohio, July 21, 1944; s. Kenneth Willard and Dorothy (Kromer) Y.; m. Jean Ann Marshall, July 21, 1962 (div. Aug. 1982); children: Terri, Christine, Michael, Jennifer; m. Karen Glojek, July 7, 1984 (wid. Dec. 1994); m. Karen Mc Diarmid, Jan. 10, 1997. BSBA, Bowling Green State U., 1971; MBA, Eastern Mich. U., 1979. Fin. planning mgr. Ford Motor Co., Rawsonville, Mich., 1970-74; fin. mgr. Chemetron Corp., Chgo., 1974-76, pres. fire systems div., 1976-80; pres. electronics div. Allen Bradley Co., Milw., 1980-83, group. pres. electronics, 1983-85, exec. v.p., 1985-86; chmn. bd. Apogent Techs., Milw., 1986—2003, Sybron Dental Specialities, Milw., 1986—2006. Bd. dirs. Rockwell Int., Milw. Founder Karen Yontz Womens Cardiac Awareness Ctr. Mem. Muirfield Village Golf Club, Vintage Club (Indian Wells, Calif.), Tradition Golf Club (La Quinta, Calif.), Chenequa Country Club (Hartford, Wis.), Flint Hills Country Club (Wichita), Milw. Country Club, Farmington Country Club (Charlottesville, Va.). Roman Catholic.

YORK, DONALD GILBERT, astronomy educator, researcher; b. Shelbyville, Ill., Oct. 28, 1944; s. Maurice Alfred and Virginia Maxine (Huntwork) Y.; m. Anna Sue Hinds, June 12, 1966; children: Sean, Maurice, Chandler, Jeremy. BS, MIT, Cambridge, 1966; PhD, U. Chgo., 1971. Rsch. asst. Princeton U., NJ, 1970-71, rsch. assoc. NJ, 1971-73, rsch. astronomer NJ, 1973-78, sr. rsch. astronomer NJ, 1978-82; assoc. prof. U. Chgo., 1982-86, prof., 1986-92, Horace B. Horton prof. astronomy and astrophysics, 1992—. Dir. Apache Point Obs., Astrophys. Rsch. Consortium, Seattle, 1984-98, Sloan Digital Sky Survey, 1990-97. Contbr. articles to profl. jours. Recipient Pub. Svc. award NASA, 1976; grantee NASA, 1978—, NSF, 1984—. Mem. Internat. Astron. Union, Am. Astron. Soc. (publs. bd. 1980-83). Democrat. Avocations: science history, religion history, swimming. Office: 5640 S Ellis Ave Chicago IL 60637-1433 Home Phone: 773-955-4961; Office Phone: 773-702-8930. Business E-Mail: don@oddjob.uchicago.edu.

YOST, LARRY D., automotive executive; Mgr. prodn. and inventory control Rockwell Internat., from 1971, pres. heavy vehicles sys. divsn., 1994-97; pres. Meritor Automotive Inc. (merger with Arvin Co.), Troy, Mich., 1997—2001, chmn., CEO, 1998—2004; ret. Office: Arvin Meritor Inc 2135 W Maple Rd Troy MI 48084-7121

YOST, WILLIAM ALBERT, psychology professor; b. Dallas, Sept. 21, 1944; s. William Jacque and Gladys (Funk) Yost; m. Lee Prater, June 15, 1969; children: Kelley Ann, Alyson Leigh. BA, Colo. Coll., Colorado Springs, 1966, DSc (hon.), 1997; PhD, Ind. U., Bloomington, 1970. Assoc. prof. psychology U. Fla., Gainesville, 1971-77; dir. sensory physiology and perception program NSF, Washington, 1982-83; prof. psychology Loyola U., Chgo., 1979—, dir. Parmly Hearing Inst., 1977—2001, dir. interdisciplinary neurosci. minor, 1977—2001, prof. hearing scis., 1990—. Prof. psychology, adj. prof. otolaryngology Loyola U., Chgo., 1990—, acting v.p. rsch., 1999—2001, assoc. v.p. rsch., dean Grad. Sch., 2001—04; individual expert bio-acoustics Am. Nat. Stds. Inst., 1983—; mem. study sect. Nat. Inst. Deafness and Other Communication Disorders, 1990—94; chair hearing bioacoustics and biomechanics com. NRC, 1992—2001, mem. bd. on behavioral cognitive and sensory scis., 1998—2004. Author: Fundamentals of Hearing, 1977, 4th edit., 2000; editor (with others) New Directions in Hearing Science, 1985, Directional Hearing, 1987, Auditory Processing of Complex Sounds, 1987, Classification of Complex Sounds, 1989, Psychoacoustics, 1993; assoc. editor Auditory Neurosci., 1994-97; ad hoc reviewer NSF, Air Force Office Sci. Rsch., Office Naval Rsch., 1981—; contbr. chpts. to books, articles to profl. jours. Pres. Evanston Tennis Assn., Ill., 1984, 90. Grantee NSF, 1974—, NIH, 1975—, AFOSR, 1983—, ONR, 1989-90. Fellow AAAS, Am. Phys. Soc., Acoustical Soc. Am. (assoc. editor jour. 1984-91, chair tech. com. 1990-94, exec. com. 1999—, v.p. 2002-04, pres. 2004—, Silver medal 2006), Am. Speech-Lang.-Hearing Assn.; mem. NAS (exec. com. on hearing bioacoustics, biomechanics 1981-87, chmn. 1993-97), Assn. Rsch. in Otolaryngology (sec.-treas. 1984-87, pres.-elect 1987-88, pres. 1988-89), Nat. Inst. Deafness and Other Comm. Disorders (task force, rev. panel 1990-94, chmn. 1994), Am. Auditory Soc. (exec. bd. 1993-98). Office Phone: 773-508-2713. Business E-Mail: wyost@luc.edu.

YOUDELMAN, ROBERT ARTHUR, financial executive, lawyer; b. L.I., NY, Mar. 28, 1942; s. Jack and Marjorie Vivian (Baer) Y.; m. Karen Leita Schneier, July 30, 1966; children: Mara, Sondra. BBA in Acctg., Case Western Res. U., 1963; LLB, NYU, 1966, LLM in Taxation, 1975. Bar: N.Y. 1969, U.S. Tax Ct. Vol. U.S. Peace Corps, Salvador, Brasil, 1966-68; mgr. Arthur Andersen & Co., NYC, 1969-77; v.p., dir. taxation The Allen Group Inc., Melville, N.Y., 1977-89, exec. v.p., CFO, 1989—. Mem. N.Y. State Hazardous Waste Task Force, Albany, 1985-87; pres. Residents for a More Beautiful Port Washington, N.Y., 1981-92; bd. dirs., treas. Transitional Housing Inc., 1997—; bd. dirs. Future Heights, 2001—. Recipient Individual Environ. Quality award for Region 2 EPA, 1992; named Citizen of Yr., Port Washington Rotary Club, 1989. Mem. ABA. Avocations: camping, hiking, environmental education and awareness. Office: Allen Telecom Inc 10500 W 153rd St Orland Park IL 60462-3071

YOUKER, JAMES EDWARD, radiologist; b. Cooperstown, NY, Nov. 13, 1928; s. Bliss Jacob and Marian (Ostrander) Y.; children— Elizabeth Ann, James David. AB, Colgate U., 1950; MD, U. Buffalo, 1954. Diplomate: Am. Bd. Radiology. Intern U. Minn., Mpls., 1954-55, resident in radiology, 1955-56, 58-60; resident in pathology Georgetown U., Washington, 1958; pvt. practice medicine, specializing in radiology Corpus Christi, Tex., 1956-58; asst. prof. radiology Med. Coll. Va., Richmond, 1961-63; research fellow U. Lund, Malmo, Sweden, 1963-64; asst. prof. radiology U. Calif., San Francisco, 1964-67; asso. prof. U. Clif., 1967-68; prof., chmn. dept. radiology Med. Coll. Wis., Milw., 1968—; dir. dept. radiology Milwaukee County Gen. Hosp., Milw., 1968-96; chmn. dept. radiology Froedtert Meml. Luth. Hosp., 1979—. Served with Project Hope, Indonesia, 1961; cons./lectr. VA Hosp., Richmond, 1961-63, San Francisco, 1964-68, Martinez, Calif., 1964-68; cons./lectr. Letterman Army Med. Center, San Francisco, 1964-68, Oakknoll Naval Hosp., Oakladn, Calif., 1964-68, VA Hosp., Milwaukee, Wis., 1968—; vis. prof. U. Calif. Sch. Medicine, San Francisco, 1974, Stanford U. Sch. Medicine, Palo Alto, Calif., 1976; vis. physician dept. cardiology St. Vincent's Hosp., Melbourne, Australia, 1974-75; mem. com. diagnosis breast cancer task force NIH, 1975-79; Head Physicians for Ford; chmn. health and med. sci. tech. com. for program planning com. North Div. High Sch., 1979; bd. dirs. Med. Coll. Wis., 1986-88, mem. residency rev. commn. for radiology, 1985-90. Contbr. numerous articles to profl. jours. Served with M.C. USN, 1956-58. N.Y. State Regents scholar, 1946; Buffalo Found. scholar, 1952; grantee USPHS; grantee Squibb Pharms.; grantee Nat. Cancer Inst.; grantee others. Fellow Am. Coll. Radiology (bd. chancellors 1978—84, vice-chmn. commn. on cancer 1972-74, chmn./mem. numerous coms., v.p. 1983-84); mem. Am. Bd. Med. Specialties (pres. 2000), AMA, Am. Roentgen Ray Soc. (adv. com. research and edn.), Assn. Univ. Radiologists (chmn. govt. affairs com. 1978-79), Med. Soc. Milwaukee County (hosp. med. staff liaison com. 1978-79), Milw. Acad. Medicine, Milw. Roentgen Ray Soc., Soc. Chairmen Acad. Radiolgy Depts. (pres. 1972, coms.), Vail Creative Concepts Conf. (co-founder), Wis. Med. Soc., Wis. Radiol. Soc., Clubs: Univ. (Milw.); Chenequa Country. Republican. Office: Froedtert Meml Luth Hosp 9200 W Wisconsin Ave Milwaukee WI 53226-3522 E-mail: jyouker@mcw.edu.

YOUNG, ANN ELIZABETH O'QUINN, historian, educator; b. Waycross, Ga. d. James Foster and Pearl Elizabeth (Sasser) O'Quinn; m. Robert William Young, Aug. 18, 1968; children: Abigail Ann, Leslie Lynn. Student, Shorter Coll.; BA, MA, U. Ga., PhD, 1965. Asst. prof. history Kearney (Nebr.) State Coll. (name changed U. ebr.-Kearney), 1965-69, assoc. prof., 1969-72, prof., 1972-00, prof. emeritus, 2000—. Participant Inst. on Islam, Middle East and World Politics, U. Mich., summer 1984, Coun. on Internat. Ednl. Exch., London, 1990, NEH Seminar NYU, 1993, faculty senate mem., 1985—, sec. 1993-94, pres., 1995-96. Conbg. author Dictionary of Georgia Biography; contbr. articles to profl. revs. Mem. NEA, PEO, Phi Alpha Theta, Delta Kappa Gamma (chpt. pres. 1978-79), Phi Mu. Republican. Presbyterian. Office: U Nebr at Kearney Dept History Kearney NE 68849-0001

YOUNG, ARTHUR PRICE, librarian, educator; b. Boston, July 29, 1940; s. Arthur Price and Marion (Freeman) Y.; m. Patricia Dorothy Foss, June 26, 1965; children: John Marshall, Christopher Price. BA, Tufts U., 1962; MA in Tchg., U. Mass., 1964; MSLS, Syracuse U., 1969; PhD, U. Ill., 1976. Head reader svcs., social sci. bibliographer SUNY-Cortland, 1969-72; rsch. assoc. U. Ill. Libr. Rsch. Ctr., Urbana, 1972-75; asst. dean pub. svcs., assoc. prof. U. Ala., Tuscaloosa, 1976-81; dean librs., prof. U. R.I., Kingston, 1981-89; dir. Thomas Cooper Libr., U. S.C., Columbia, 1989-93; sr. fellow UCLA, 1991; dean librs., mem. adj. faculty dept. history No. Ill. U., DeKalb, 1993—. Mem. adj. faculty Syracuse (N.Y.) U., 1970-71, Dominican U., River Forest, Ill., 1994-96; pres. Consortium R.I. Acad. and Rsch. Librs., 1983-85; mem. bd. govs. Univ. Press New England, 1987-89; mem. exec. bd. Ill. Libr. Computer Sys. Orgn., 1995-99; chair Coun. Dirs. State Univ. Librs., 1994-95, 2001—; sr. fellow UCLA, 1991; pres. Ill. Libr. Assn., 2002. Author: Books for Sammies: American Library Association and World War I, 1981, American Library History: A Bibliography of Dissertations and Theses, 1988, Higher Education in American Life, 1636-1986: A Bibliography of Dissertations and Theses, 1988, Cities and Towns in American History: A Bibliography of Doctoral Dissertations, 1989, Academic Libraries: Research Perspectives, 1990, Religion and the American Experience, 1620-1900: A Bibliography of Doctoral Dissertations, 1992, Religion and the American Experience, the Twentieth Century: A Bibliography of Doctoral Dissertations, 1994; The Next Library Leadership: Attributes of Academic and Public Library Directors, 2003; editl. bd. various jours. Chair Coun. of Dirs. Ill. State Univ. Librs., 1994-95, 2001-02. Served to capt. USAF, 1964-68. Recipient Berner Nash award U. Ill., 1976. Mem. ALA (chmn. editl. bd., chair Libr. Rsch. Seminar I, 1996), Assn. Coll. and Rsch. Librs. (publs. in librarianship 1982-88, chmn. Jesse H. Shera Endowment Fund com. 1991-94), Ill. Libr. Assn., S.C. Libr. Assn. (chmn. libr. adminstrn. sect. 1991-92), Assn. Rsch. Librs. (scholarly commn. com. 1991-93), Orgn. Am. Historians, Am. Hist. Assn., Horatio Alger Soc. (pres. 1999-2000), Caxton Club (Chgo.), Phi Kappa Phi, Beta Phi Mu, Phi Delta Kappa. Episcopalian. Home: 9 Sandy Brook Dr Durham NH 03824-3137 Office Phone: 815-753-9801. Business E-Mail: ayoung@niu.edu.

YOUNG, CHRISTOPHER AARON, lawyer; BA magna cum laude in Bus., Buena Vista Coll., 1995; JD with honors, U. Iowa Sch. Law, 1998. Bar: Minn. 1998, US Dist. Ct. (dist. Minn.), US Ct. Appeals (8th cir.). Sr. assoc. Fulbright & Jaworski, L.L.P., Mpls. Contbr. articles to profl. publs. Named a Rising Star, Minn. Super Lawyers mag., 2006. Mem.: Hennepin County Bar Assn., Minn. State Bar Assn. Avocations: fishing, hunting, racquetball. Office: Fulbright & Jaworski LLP 2100 IDS Ctr 80 S 8th St Minneapolis MN 55402 Office Phone: 612-321-2816. E-mail: cayoung@fulbright.com.

YOUNG, DALE LEE, banker; b. Palmyra, Nebr., Mar. 13, 1928; s. Mike P. and Grace (Clutter) Y.; m. Norma Marie Shalla, June 18, 1950; children— Shalla Ann, Philip Mike. BBA, U. Nebr., 1950. With FirsTier Bank N.A. (formerly First Nat. Bank & Trust Co.), Lincoln, Nebr., 1950-91, cashier, 1966-91, v.p., 1966-76, exec. v.p., 1976-92; sec. ISCO, Inc., Lincoln, 1991—, also bd. dirs. Bd. dirs. Lincoln Fed. Savs. Bank; sec., bd. dirs. Leasing Corp. Treas. Lincoln City Library Found.; bd. dirs., v.p. Lincoln Symphony; bd. dirs. Lincoln Community Services, ARC, Lincoln Found.; trustee Bryan Meml. Hosp., 1976-80; mem. Lincoln City Coun., 1991-98, elected mayor, 1998. Served with AUS, 1946-48, 50-51. Mem. Nebr. Art Assn., Omaha-Lincoln Soc. Fin. Analysts, Lincoln C. of C. (pres.), Theta Xi. Clubs: Nebraska, Lincoln Country. Presbyterian. Home: 3911 Firethorn Ct Lincoln NE 68520-1466 Office: PO Box 81008 Lincoln NE 68501-1008

YOUNG, DEAN A., state legislator; BA, Purdue U.; JD, Valprasio U. Mem. Ho. of Reps., Indpls., 1992—, mem. judiciary, labor & employment, pub. health coms. Pros. atty. Blackford County. Mem. Hartford City econ. devel. com., 1985—, pres. 1989-90; mem. Blackford County Cmty. Corrections Bd., 1990—. Republican. Office: Ind Ho of Reps State Capitol Indianapolis IN 46204

YOUNG, DELMON DAMARCUS, professional baseball player; b. Montgomery, Ala., Sept. 14, 1985; s. Larry and Bonnie Young. Outfielder Tampa Bay Devil Rays, 2006—07, Minn. Twins, 2008—. Named Minor League Player of Yr., Baseball Am., 2005, #1 Prospect, 2006. Achievements include being the second youngest player in the major leagues in 2006; 31 hits in his first 20 major league games, only six players in the last 50 years have matched or exceeded that total. Mailing: c/o Minn Twins Metrodome 34 Kirby Puckett Pl Minneapolis MN 55415*

YOUNG, DONALD FREDRICK, engineering educator; b. Joplin, Mo., Apr. 27, 1928; s. Oral Solomon and Blanche (Trent) Y.; m. Gertrude Ann Cooper, Apr. 15, 1950; children: Michael, Pamela, Susan, Christopher, David. BS, Iowa State U., 1951, MS, 1952, PhD, 1956. Research engr. AEC Ames Lab., 1952-55; asst. prof. Iowa State U., Ames, 1955-58, assoc. prof., 1958-61, prof. engring. sci. and mechanics, 1961-74, Anson Marston Disting. prof. engring., 1974-99, Anson Marston Disting. prof. emeritus, 1999—. Author: Introduction to Applied Mechanics, 1972, (with others) Essentials of Mechanics, 1974, (with others) Fundamentals of Fluid Mechanics, 1990, 4th edit., 2002, (with others) A Brief Introduction to Fluid Mechanics, 1997, 2d edit., 2001; contbr. articles to profl. jours. Recipient Outstanding Tchr. award Standard Oil, 1971, Faculty citation Iowa State Alumni Assn., 1972, Spl. Recognition award Iowa State U. Rsch. Found., 1988, David R. Boylan Eminent award for rsch., 1995. Fellow ASME (chmn. bioengring. div. 1973-74); mem. Am. Heart Assn., Am. Soc. Engring. Edn., Pi Tau Sigma, Pi Mu Epsilon, Phi Kappa Phi, Sigma Xi Home: 2042 Prairie Vw E Ames IA 50010-4558 Office: Iowa State U 2271 Howe Hall Ames IA 50010

YOUNG, JAMES EDWARD, lawyer; b. Painesville, Ohio, Apr. 20, 1946; s. James M. and Isabel P. (Rogers) Y. BBA, Ohio U., 1968; JD, Ohio State U., 1972. Bar: Ohio 1972. Law clk. to chief judge U.S. Ct. Appeals, Nashville, 1972-73; chief counsel City of Cleve., 1980-81, law dir., 1981-82; assoc. Jones, Day, Reavis & Pogue (now Jones Day), Cleve., 1973—79, ptnr., 1983—. Office: Jones Day 901 Lakeside Ave E Cleveland OH 44114-1190 Office Phone: 216-586-7259. Business E-Mail: jameseyoung@jonesday.com.

YOUNG, JAMES R., rail transportation executive; m. Shirley Young; 3 children. Grad., U. Nebr., Omaha. With Union Pacific Corp., 1978—, mgmt. fin. and ops., asst. v.p. re-engring. Union Pacific RR Co., 1994—95, v.p. re-engring. and design, 1995, v.p. customer svc. planning & quality, 1997, v.p. fin. & quality, sr. v.p., corp. treas., 1998—99, sr. v.p. fin., corp. contr., 1999, exec. v.p., CFO, 1999—2004, pres. & COO Union Pacific RR Co., 2004—05, bd. dirs., 2005—, pres., CEO, 2005—, chmn., 2007—. Bd. mem. Grupo Ferroviario Mexicano, Assn. Am. RRs. Bd. mem. Creighton U., Omaha, Joslyn Art Mus., U. Nebr. Med. Ctr. Office: Union Pacific Corp 1400 Douglas St Omaha NE 68179-1001 Office Phone: 402-544-5000.

YOUNG, JAY MAITLAND, health products executive, consultant; b. Louisville, Nov. 26, 1944; s. Clyde Dudley and Olive May (Tyas) Y. BA in Chemistry and Math. magna cum laude, Vanderbilt U., 1966; MS in Biochemistry, Yale U., 1967, MPhil in Phys. Chemistry, 1968, PhD in Chemistry, 1971. Cert. Am. Med. Writers Assn. Multi-disciplinary Core, 1999. Asst. prof. chemistry Bryn Mawr (Pa.) Coll., 1970-76; rsch. biochemist Abbott Labs., Ill., 1977-78, project mgr. physiol. diagnostics Abbott Park, 1978-80, project mgr. cancer product devel., 1980-82, internat. clin. specialist sci. affairs, 1982-85, clin. project mgr. physiol. diagnostic quality and sci. support, 1986-90, staff quality assurance and sci. support, 1990-93, fertility, pregnancy, thyroid mgr., quality and sci. support, 1993-95, fertility, pregnancy, thyroid, cancer mgr., product quality assurance, 1995-97, staff noninfectious disease diagnostics sci. affairs, 1997—2001; cons. and med. writer diagnostic and pharm. areas, 2002—. Cons. Inst. for Cancer Rsch., Fox Chase, Phila., 1974, vis. scientist, 1975-76; honors examiner Swarthmore Coll., 1973, 74, mem. vis. evaluation com., 1975; presenter to med. groups on cancer markers, viral hepatitis and epidemiology of AIDS, 1982-84. Contbr. articles to profl. jours. Vol. Episcopal Ch. Outreach Commn. Named to Hon. Order Ky. Cols.; predoctoral fellow NSF, Yale U., 1966-70; postdoctoral fellow, NIH, U. Oxford, 1971-72; travel grantee NATO, 1974. Mem. Am. Med. Writers Assn. (Del. Valley chpt. program chair 2002-03, treas. 2003-06, cert mem. Multi-disciplinary Core 1999). Home Phone: 773-728-1386; Office Phone: 610-322-4444. E-mail: maitland@mailbug.com.

YOUNG, JESS RAY, retired internist; b. Fairfield, Ill., Feb. 4, 1928; s. Edgar S. and Clara B. (Musgrave) Y.; m. Gloria Wynn, July 10, 1953; children— James C., Patricia A. BS, Franciscan U., 1951; MD, St. Louis U., 1955. Intern Highland Alameda County Hosp., Oakland, Calif., 1955-56; resident in internal medicine Cleve. Clinic Hosp., 1956-59, mem. staff dept. vascular medicine, 1959-97, chmn. dept., 1976-97; ret., 1998. Co-author: Leg Ulcer, 1975, Peripheral Vascular Diseases, 1991, 1996; contbr. articles to profl. jours., chpts. to books. Served with AUS, 1946-47. Mem. AMA, Am. Heart Assn. (stroke council), Am. Coll. Cardiology, Internat. Cardiovascular Soc., ACP, Am. Fedn. Clic. Research, Ohio Soc. Internal Medicine, Soc. for Vascular Medicine and Rsch., Inter-Urban Club. Methodist. Home: 1503 Burlington Rd Cleveland OH 44118-1216 Personal E-mail: jesyoung@adelphia.net.

YOUNG, JOSEPH FLOYD, JR., state legislator; b. Detroit, Nov. 4, 1950; m. Mary J. Gerbe; children: Kimberly Ann, Kerry Marie, Joe, III, Brooke Melinda., Mich. State U., Cooley Law Sch., Western Mich. U., Urban Bible Inst., Detroit. Com. analyst House Spkr. William Ryan; adminstrv. asst.; legis. asst. State Rep. Alma Stallworth; com. adminstr., legis. asst. Sen. Dale Kildee; state rep. Dist. 4 Mich. Ho. of Reps., 1978-94; mem. Mich. Senate from 1st dist., Lansing, 1994—. Chmn. State Affairs Com.; mem. Standing Coms. on Conservation, Environment & Great Lakes, Econ. Devel., Edn. & Tourism & Recreation Mich. Ho. of Reps.; mem. Families, Mental Health & Human Svc. & Judiciary Coms., Mich. State Senate, vice chmn. Local Urban & State Affairs Com. Mem. NAACP, KC, YMCA, Block Clubs. Office: Mich Senate State Capitol PO Box 30036 Lansing MI 48909-7536 Home: PO Box 32123 Detroit MI 48232-0123

YOUNG, KEVIN, literature educator, writer; b. Lincoln, Nebraska, 1970; BA, Harvard U., 1992; MFA in creative writing, Brown U., 1996. Asst. prof. English and African American studies U. Ga.; Ruth Lilly prof. of poetry Ind. U., 2001—. Vis. prof. Emory University, 2005—06. Author: (book) Most Way Home, 1995, To Repel Ghosts, 2001, Black Maria: Poems Produced and Directed by Kevin Young, 2005; editor: (anthologies) Giant Steps: The New Generation of African American Writers, 2000, Blues Poems, 2003; works have appeared in The New Yorker, The New York Times Book Review, The Paris Review, The Kenyon Review, Paideuma, and Callaloo. Finalist Nat. Book award, 2003; named one of the most powerful people under the age of 30 in the U.S., Swing Mag., 1998, a writer on the "verge", Village Voice, 2001; Guggenheim Found. fellowship, 2003—04. Office: Dept of English Indiana U 442 Ballantine Hall Bloomington IN 47405

YOUNG, LEON D., state legislator; b. July 4, 1957; Degree in police sci., Milw. Area Tech. Coll.; student, U. Wis., Milw. Police officer; mem. Social Devel. Commn. Minority Male Forum on Corrections. Mem. NAACP, Urban League. Home: 2224 N 17th St Milwaukee WI 53205-1220 Office: Wis Assembly PO Box 8952 Madison WI 53708-8952

YOUNG, MARVIN OSCAR, lawyer; b. Union, Mo., Apr. 4, 1929; s. Otto Christopher and Irene Adelheide (Barlage) Y.; m. Sue Carol Mathews, Aug. 23, 1952; children: Victoria Leigh, Kendall Marvin. AB, Westminster Coll., 1951; JD, U. Mich., 1954, LLD, 1989. Bar: Mo. 1954. Practice law firm Thompson, Mitchell, Thompson Douglas, St. Louis, 1954-55, 57-58; atty. Mo. Farmers Assn., Columbia, 1958-67; exec. v.p. First Mo. Corp., Columbia, 1965-68; v.p. ops. MFA-Central Coop., Columbia, 1967-68; v.p., gen. counsel, sec. Peabody Coal Co., St. Louis, 1968-82; gen. counsel Peabody Holding Co., Inc., St. Louis, 1983-85; also dir., sec. subs. and affiliates Peabody Coal Co.; ptnr. Gallop, Johnson & Neuman, St. Louis, 1986—, chmn. corp. dept., 1988-90, chmn. energy dept., 1990—. City atty., Warson Woods, Mo., 1990—; spkr. in field. Contbr. articles to profl. jours. Pres. Warson Woods PTA, 1974-75; trustee Met. Sewer Dist. St. Louis, 1974-80, chmn. 1978-80; mem. Mo. Energy Coun., 1973-77, Mo. Environ. Improvement and Energy Resources Authority, 1983-87, vice-chmn. 1986-87; trustee Eastern Mineral Law Found., 1983-98; pres. Alumni Assn. Westminster Coll., Fulton, Mo., 1978-80, trustee coll., 1977—, exec. com., 1978-2003, chmn. 1986-90, chmn. investment com., 1998-2002; chmn. Churchill Meml. and Libr., Fulton, 1992-2000; mem. chancellor's coun. adv. bd. U. Mo., St. Louis, 1992—; trustee Stages—St. Louis, 2001—; lawyers adv. coun. Gt. Plains Legal Found., Kansas City, Mo., 1976-84; mem. Rep. Com. Boone County, Mo., 1962-68, chmn. legis. dist. com., 1962-64, 66-68; alt. del. Rep. Nat. Conv., 1968; pres. Clayton Twp. Rep. Club, 1973-77; mem. St. Lucas United Ch. of Christ, 2004—. Capt. USAF, 1955-57. Churchill fellow Churchill Meml. and Libr., Fulton, Mo.; recipient Alumni Merit award Westminster Coll., 1972; named Coal Lawyer of Yr., Nat. Coal Assn., 1994 Mem. ABA, Mo. Bar Assn., Bar Assn. Met. St. Louis, Round Table Club St. Louis, John Marshall Rep. Lawyers Club (pres. 1977), Mo. Athletic Club, Shamrock Club St. Louis County, Rotary (bd. dirs. St. Louis club 1993-95), Barristers Soc. (life), Order of Coif (life), Masons, Shriners. Home: 555 Flanders Dr Saint Louis MO 63122-1617 Office: Gallop Johnson & Neuman LC 101 S Hanley Rd Ste 1700 Saint Louis MO 63105-3489 Office Phone: 314-615-6210. E-mail: moyoung@gjn.com.

YOUNG, MARY ANN, lawyer; b. Alton, Ill., May 1, 1952; d. William Jerome and Barbara Ann (Blocher) Y. Student, St. Mary of the Plains Coll., 1970-71; BA in Econs., Washburn (Kans.) U., 1974; JD, U. Mo., 1976. Bar: Mo. 1977. Pvt. practice, Holden, Mo., 1977-84, Warrensburg, Mo., 1984—. Atty. City of Holden, 1978-80; asst. prosecutor Johnson County, Mo., 1978-80, 83-88; bd. dirs. Indsl. Svc. Contactors Sheltered Workshop, Warrensburg. Mem. Rep. Women, Johnson County, 1988-89, CLIMB, Johnson County, 1989—, Task Force for Drug Free Mo., Johnson County, 1989—; 2d. v.p. Johnson County Rep. Women, 1989—. Mem. Mo. Bar Assn., Johnson County Bar Assn., Johnson County C. of C., Mo. Farm Bur. Roman Catholic. Avocations: antique collecting, gardening. Office: 307 N Holden St Warrensburg MO 64093-1705

YOUNG, PAUL ANDREW, anatomist; b. St. Louis, Oct. 3, 1926; s. Nicholas A. and Olive A. (Langford) Y.; m. Catherine Ann Hofmeister, May 14, 1949; children— Paul, Robert, David, Ann, Carol, Richard, James, Steven, Kevin, Michael. BS, St. Louis U., 1947, MS, 1953; PhD, U. Buffalo, 1957. Asst. in anatomy U. Buffalo, 1953, instr. anatomy, 1957; asst. prof. anatomy St. Louis U., 1957, assoc. prof., 1966, prof., 1972—, chmn. dept., 1973—2004, prof. anatomy in surgery, 2004, prof. and chair emeritus, dept. anatomy and neurobiology, 2006. Author: (with B.D. Bhagat and D.E. Biggerstaff) Fundamentals of Visceral Innervation, 1977, (with P.H. Young) Basic Clinical Neuroanatomy, 1996, (with P.H.Young and D.L.Tolbert) Basic Clinical Neuroscience, 2007, also computer assisted neurological anatomy tutorials; contbr. articles to profl. publs. Recipient Preclinical Golden Apple Tchg. award, St. Louis U. Sch. Medicine, 1974, 2000, Outstanding Preclinical, 1981, 1985, 1986, 1991, 1992, tchg. award, St. Louis Acad. Sci., 1993, Emerson Excellence for St. Louis U. faculty, 2001, Acad. Sci. Outstanding Sr. Louis Scientist award, 2008. Mem. Am. Assn. Anatomists, Am. Assn. Clin. Anatomists, Soc. Neurosci., Sigma Xi, Alpha Omega Alpha. Office: St Louis Univ Ctr for Anatomical Science and Education 1402 S Grand Blvd Saint Louis MO 63104-1004 Home Phone: 636-225-1437; Office Phone: 314-977-8025. Personal E-mail: pay10326@gmail.com. Business E-Mail: youngpa@slu.edu.

YOUNG, PHILIP HOWARD, library director; b. Ithaca, NY, Oct. 7, 1953; s. Charles Robert and Betty Irene (Osborne) Young; m. Nancy Ann Stutsman, Aug. 18, 1979. BA, U. Va., 1975; PhD, U. Pa., 1980; MLS, Ind. U., 1983. Asst. prof. history Appalachian State U., Boone, NC, 1980-82; reference asst. Lilly Libr. Ind. U., Bloomington, 1982-83; adminstr., info. specialist Ind. Corp. Sci. & Tech., Indpls., 1983-85; dir. Krannert Meml. Libr. U. Indpls., 1985—. Mem.: Archeol. Inst. Am., Am. Libr. Assn., Phi Beta Kappa, Beta Phi Mu, Phi Alpha Theta. Democrat. Home: 4332 Silver Springs Dr Greenwood IN 46142-9623 Office: U Indpls Krannert Meml Libr 1400 E Hanna Ave Indianapolis IN 46227-3630 Office Phone: 317-788-3399. E-mail: pyoung@uindy.edu.

YOUNG, R. JAMES, insurance company executive; V.p. fin. and planning The Allstate Corp., Northbrook, Ill., 1997-2000, v.p. property and casualty ops., 2000—. Office: The Allstate Corp 2775 Sanders Rd # F6 Northbrook IL 60062-6110

YOUNG, R. MICHAEL, state legislator; b. May 14, 1951; BA, Ind. U. Mem. Ind. Ho. of Reps. from 92nd dist., Indpls., 1986-2000; mem. ins. corps. and small bus. com., govt. affairs com.; mem. Ind. Senate from 35th dist., 2001—. Real estate developer; polit. cons.; mng. ptnr. Phoenix Devel. Mem. Marion County Bd. Zoning Appeals, Wayne Twp. Rep. Com., Pike Twp. Rep. Com., Eagle Creek Rep. Com.; precinct committeeman. Republican. Home: 3102 Columbine Ct Indianapolis IN 46224-2021 Office: Ind Senator 200 W Washington St Indianapolis IN 46204

YOUNG, RAY G., automotive executive; B in Bus. Adminstrn., U. Western Ontario, 1984; M Bus. Adminstrn., U. Chgo., 1986. Joined GM Can., 1986, dir. capital markets and fgn. exchange, 1988—93; regional treas. GM Europe, Brussels, 1993—96; v.p. fin. CAMI Automotive, 1996—2001; v.p., CFO GM N. Am., Detroit, 2001—04; pres., mng. dir. GM do Brasil, 2004—07; group v.p. fin. GM Corp., Detroit, 2007—08, exec. v.p., CFO, 2008—. Office: GM Corp 300 Renaissance Ctr Detroit MI 48265-3000*

YOUNG, RAYMOND ALLEN, chemist, educator; BS in Wood Products Engring., SUNY, Syracuse, 1966, MS in Paper Chemistry, 1968; PhD in Wood and Polymer Chemistry, U. Wash., 1973. Process supr. Kimberly-Clark Corp., Niagara Falls, N.Y., 1968-69; vis. scientist Swedish Forest Products Lab., Stockholm, 1972-73; postdoctoral fellow, staff scientist Textile Rsch. Inst., Princeton, N.J., 1973-74; prof. wood and polymer chemistry dept. forestry U. Wis., Madison, 1975—. Cons. UN, USAID, NATO, Rome, Shell Oil, London, Kimbely-Clark Corp., Union Carbide Corp., Grain Processing Corp., Stone & Webster Engrings. Cons., Mead Corp., Biodyne Chems., Resource Mgmt. Assocs.; expert witness various law firms. Author: Cellulose: Structure, Modification and Hydrolysis, 1986, Modified Cellulosics, 1978, Introduction to Forest Science, 2d edit., 1990, Paper and Composites from Agro-Based Resources, 1996, Environmentally Friendly Technologies in the Pulp and Paper Industry, 1998; contbr. chpts. to books, articles to profl. jours.; patentee infield. Fulbright scholar Royal Inst. Tech., Stockholm, 1972; recipient Sr. Fulbright Rsch. award Aristotelian U., Thessaloniki, Greece, 1989, Sci. Exchange award to Romania Nat. Acad. Sci., 1990. Mem. Am. Chem. Soc. (publicity chmn. Cellulose Paper and Textile divsn. 1980-82, student coord. 1992-95), Internat. Acad. Wood Sci. Office: Dept Forest Ecology Mgmt U Wis Madison WI 53706

YOUNG, REBECCA MARY CONRAD, retired state legislator; b. Clairton, Pa., Feb. 28, 1934; d. Walter Emerson and Harriet Averill (Colcord) Conrad; m. Merwin Crawford Young, Aug. 17, 1957; children: Eve, Louise, Estelle, Emily. BA, U. Mich., 1955; MA in Teaching, Harvard U., 1963; JD, U. Wis., 1983. Bar: Wis. 1983. Commr. State Hwy. Commn., Madison, Wis., 1974-76; dep. sec. Wis. Dept. of Adminstrn., Madison, 1976-77; assoc. Wadsack, Julian & Lawton, Madison, 1983-84; elected rep. Wis. State Assembly, Madison, 1985-99. Translator: Katanga Secession, 1966. Supr. Dane County Bd., Madison, 1970-74; mem. Madison Sch. Bd., 1979-85. Recipient Wis. NOW Feminist of Yr. award, 1996, Eunice Zoghlin Edgar Lifetime Achievement award ACLU, 1997, Outstanding Legislator award Wis. Counties Assn., 1998, Voice for Choice award Planned Parenthood Wis., 1998, Luan Gilbert award for outstanding activities in domestic violence intervention and prevention Domestic Violence Intervention Svc., 1998. Mem. LWV. Democrat. Avocations: board games, hiking. Home: 639 Crandall St Madison WI 53711-1836

YOUNG, RICHARD D., state legislator; b. Dec. 2, 1942; m. Ashira Wendler Young; 5 children. AA, Vincennes U., 1992. Mem. Ind. Senate from 47th dist., 1988—; mem. agr., small bus., edn., fin. and natural resource coms.; minority leader, 1996—. Farmer. Mem. Farm Bur., Crawford County C. of C., Lions.' Democrat. Home: 10347 E Daugherty Ln Milltown IN 47145-9801 Office: Ind Senate State Capitol 200 W Washington St Indianapolis IN 46204-2728

YOUNG, ROBERT P., JR., state supreme court justice; B cum laude, Harvard U., 1974, JD, 1977. Atty. Dickinson, Wright, Moon, Van Dusen & Freeman, 1977-1992; v.p., corp. sec., gen. counsel AAA Mich., 1992; judge Mich. Ct. Appeals 1st Dist., 1995—98; justice Mich. Supreme Ct., 1999—. Mem. Mich. Civil Svc. Commn.; bd. trustees Cen. Mich. U. Mem.: ABA, Mich. State Bar Assn., Mich. Supreme Ct. Historical Soc. Office: Mich Supreme Ct PO Box 30052 Lansing MI 48909-7552

YOUNG, RON, state representative; b. Canton, Ohio, Sept. 27, 1946; 5 children. Degree in Psychology, Kent State U.; degree in Edn., Cleve. State U. Rep. Ohio Ho. Reps., Columbus, Ohio, 1996—. Chmn. commerce and labor com. Ohio Ho. Reps., mem. homeland security, engring. and arch. design com. With US Army. Mem.: Nat. Fedn. Ind. Bus. Republican.

YOUNG, RONALD FARIS, commodities trader; b. Schenectady, Dec. 17, 1939; s. James Vernon and Dorothy (Girod) Y.; m. Anne Randolph Kendig, Feb. 23, 1963; children: Margaret Randolph Reynolds, Anne Corbin Gray. BA, U. Va., 1962; MBA, Harvard U., 1966. Grain trader Continental Grain Co., 1966-70; pres. Conti-Commodities, Chgo., 1970; v.p. commodity sales DuPont, Glore Forgan, Chgo., 1971-72; self-employed commodity trader Chgo. Bd. Trade, 1972-78; ind. trader Va. Trading Co., 1978-90, pres., 1978-84, dep. chmn., 1984-89; pres. Randolph Ptnrs., Ltd., 1983-91. Chmn. bd. Chgo. Bd. Trade, 1978, dir., 1975—77, 1980, 2003. Bd. dirs. Princeton Fund, 1981-82, Lake Forest Hosp., 1981-84, Lake Forest Country Day Sch., 1981-86. Served with USMCR, 1959-65. Mem. Racquet Club (bd. dirs. 1989-97), Onwentsia Club (Lake Forest, Ill., bd. dirs. 1981-90, pres. 1991-93), Everglades Club (Palm Beach, Fla.), Bath and Tennis Club of Palm Beach (bd. dirs. 2007—). Republican. Episcopalian. Home: 531 N Mayflower Rd Lake Forest IL 60045

YOUNG, WALTER R., JR., manufacturing executive; Former pres. Wheelabrator Corp., Atlanta; chmn., pres., CEO Champion Enterprises, Auburn Hills, Mich., 1990—. Office: Champion Enterprises 2701 Cambridge Ct Ste 300 Auburn Hills MI 48326

YOUNGBLOOD, BETTY J., academic administrator; b. Detroit; m. Ralph P. Youngblood; 1 child. BA in Political Sci., Oakland U., Rochester, Mich.; MA in South Asian Studies, U. Minn., PhD in Political Sci. Formerly mem. faculty State U. West Ga., Tex. Tech. U.; various adminstrv. positions Kennesaw State U., Marietta, Ga.; v.p. acad. affairs MacMurray Coll., Jacksonville, Ill., Wesley Coll., Dover, Del.; vice chancellor acad. affairs, dean faculty, prof. polit. sci. U. Wis.-Superior, 1990-91, acting chancellor, 1991-92, chancellor, 1992—95; pres. We. Oreg. U., 1995—2002, Lake Superior State U., Mich., 2002—. Cons., evaluator North Ctrl. Assn. Colls. and Schs. Contbr. articles to profl. jours. Bd. dirs. United Way, Sault Ste. Marie. Rsch. grantee for study in N.W. India. Mem. Sault Ste. Marie C. of C., War Meml. Hosp., Rotary. Office: Lake Superior State Univ 650 W Easterday Ave Sault Sainte Marie MI 49783

YOUNGBLOOD, RICHARD NEIL, columnist; b. Minot, ND, May 9, 1936; s. Edward Anthony and Helen (Condo) Y.; m. Adele Henley, May 4, 1957 (div. 1983); children: Kent Jay, Ruth Adele, Beth Alise; m. Mary Dinneen, July 14, 1984. BA, U. N.D., 1958. Reporter Grand Forks (N.D.) Herald, 1955-63, Mpls. Star Tribune, 1963-67, asst. city editor, 1967-69, bus./fin. editor, 1969-84, columnist, 1984-98, freelance writer, 98—. Recipient Excellence award in bus. and fin. journalism John Handcock Mut. Life, 1974; named Newspaper Farm Editor of Yr. Newspaper Farm Editors of Am., 1965. Avocations: reading, crossword puzzles, boating. Office: Mpls Star Tribune 425 Portland Ave Minneapolis MN 55488-1511

YOUNGE, WYVETTER HOOVER, state legislator; b. St. Louis, Aug. 23, 1930; s. Ernest Jack and Annie (Jordan) H.; m. Richard G. Younge, 1958; children: Ruth F., Torque E., Margrett H. BS, Hampton Inst., 1951; JD, St. Louis U., 1955; LLM, Wash. U., 1972. Ill. state rep. Dist. 114, 1975—; mem. appropriation II com., chmn. urban redevel. com. Ill. Ho. Reps., labor and com., vice chmn. energy, environ. and natural resources com., aging, edn. appropriations, human svc., reappointment coms., chmn. higher edn. com.; asst. circuit atty. City of St. Louis; pvt. practice, 1955—; exec. dir. Neighborhood Ctrs. War on Poverty, 1965-68; East St. Louis adv. and devel. nonprofit housing corp., 1968—. Author: The Implementation of Old Man River, 1972. Recipient Humanity award Project Upgrade, 1969, Citizen of Yr. award Monitor Newspaper, Cert. of Recognition Black Heritage Com. Mem. Alpha Kappa Alpha. Democrat. Address: 1617 N 46th St East Saint Louis IL 62204-1919 also: Ill Ho of Reps State Capitol Springfield IL 62706-0001

YOUNGER, JENNIFER A., university librarian; BA in history, U. Wis.-Madison, MLA, PhD in info. studies. Various positions in libr. sys. U. Wis.-Madison, 1977—91; asst. dir. tech. svc. Ohio State U. libr., 1991—97; Edward H. Arnold dir. univ. libraries U. Notre Dame, 1997—. Editor: (jour.) Library Resources & Technical Services. Mem.: ALA, Assn. Libr. Collections & Tech. Svc. (pres. 1993—94), Beta Phi Mu. Office: Univ Notre Dame 221 Hesburgh Library Notre Dame IN 46556 Office Phone: 574-631-7790. Office Fax: 574-631-6772. E-mail: Jennifer.A.Younger@nd.edu.

YOUNGER, JUDITH TESS, law educator; b. NYC, Dec. 20, 1933; d. Sidney and Kate (Greenbaum) Weintraub; m. Irving Younger, Jan. 21, 1955; children: Rebecca, Abigail M. BS, Cornell U., 1954; JD, NYU, 1958; LLD (hon.), Hofstra U., 1974. Bar: N.Y. 1958, U.S. Supreme Ct 1962, D.C. 1983, Minn. 1985. Law clk. to judge U.S. Dist. Ct., 1958-60; assoc. firm Chadbourne, Parke, Whiteside & Wolff, NYC, 1960-62; mem. firm Younger and Younger, and (successors), 1962-67; adj. asst. prof. NYU Sch. Law, 1967-69; asst. atty. gen. State of N.Y., 1969-70; assoc. prof. Hofstra U. Sch. Law, 1970-72, prof., assoc. dean, 1972-74; dean, prof. Syracuse Coll. Law, 1974-75; dep. dean, prof. law Cornell Law Sch., 1975-78, prof. law, 1975-85; vis. prof. U. Minn. Law Sch., Mpls., 1984-85, prof., 1985-91, Joseph E. Wargo Anoka County Bar Assn. prof. family law, 1991—. Of counsel Popham, Haik, Schnobrich & Kaufman, Ltd., Mpls., 1989-95; cons. NOW, 1972-74, Suffolk County for Revision of Its Real Property Tax Act, 1972-73; mem. N.Y. Gov.'s Panel To Screen Candidates of Ct. of Claims Judges, 1973-74; mem. Minn. Lawyers' Profl. Responsibility Bd., 1991-93. Contbr. articles to profl. jours. Trustee Cornell U., 1973-78. Mem.: AAUP (v.p. Cornell U. chpt. 1978—79), ABA (council legal edn. 1975—79), Minn. Bar Assn., Assn. of Bar of City of N.Y., Am. Law Inst. (adv. restatement property 1982—84). Home: 3520 W Calhoun Pkwy Minneapolis MN 55416-4657 Office: U Minn Law Sch Minneapolis MN 55455 Home Phone: 612-925-5894; Office Phone: 612-625-5844. Business E-Mail: young001@umn.edu.

YOUNGMAN, OWEN RALPH, newspaper executive; b. Chgo., Apr. 24, 1953; s. Ralph Elmer and Charlotte Earldine (Ottoson) Y.; m. Linda Ann Erlandson, Aug. 24, 1975. DSc, LHD, North Park U., 2005. Sportswriter Ashtabula (Ohio) Star-Beacon, 1969-71; office clk. Chgo. Tribune, 1971-73, transcriber, 1973-75, copy editor, slotman, 1976-79, copy chief, news editor, 1979-83, dep. sports editor, 1984-86, assoc. met. editor, 1986-88, assoc. features editor, 1988-90, dep. fin. editor, 1990-91, assoc. mng. editor, 1991-93, features editor, 1993-95, mng. editor, features, 1995, dir. interactive media, 1996-99, dir. planning and devel., 1999, v.p. devel., 2000—06, sr. v.p. strategy and devel., 2007—. Bd. dirs. Swedish Covenant Hosp., Legacy, Inc. Web site, Solti Found. USA; nat. exec. bd. Evang. Covenant Ch. Named to Ashtabula HS Alumni Hall of Fame, Ohio, 2005. Mem. Newspaper Assn. Am. New Media Fedn., Am. Soc. Newspaper Editors, Presidents Club North Park U., Arts Club Chgo. Avocation: vocal and instrumental music. Home: 40 Kenmore Ave Deerfield IL 60015-4750 Office: Chicago Tribune 435 N Michigan Ave Chicago IL 60611-4066 Home Phone: 847-940-1191; Office Phone: 312-222-4179. Business E-Mail: oyoungman@tribune.com.

YOUNGQUIST, WAYNE, reporter; PhB, U. Wis., Milw.; M Sociology, Rutgers U. Polit. analyst, now sr. polit. analyst WISN, Milw., 1978—. Instr. sociology U. Wis., Milw., Ithaca Coll., No. Ill. U., Marquette U., 1974—78, U. Wis., Whitewater; host seminars TV and Radio News Dirs. Found. Recipient Rockefeller Found. fellow, Princeton U.; fellow, NIMH. Office: WISN PO Box 402 Milwaukee WI 53201-0402

YOURZAK, ROBERT JOSEPH, management consultant, educator, engineer; b. Mpls., Aug. 27, 1947; s. Ruth Phyllis Sorenson. BCE, U. Minn., 1969; MSCE, U. Wash., 1971, MBA, 1975. Registered profl. engr., Wash., Minn. Surveyor N.C. Hoium & Assocs., Mpls., 1965-68, Lot Surveys Co., Mpls., 1968-69; site layout engr. Sheehy Constrn. Co., St. Paul, 1968; structural engring. aide Dunham Assocs., Mpls., 1969; aircraft and aerospace structural engr., program rep. Boeing Co., Seattle, 1969-75; engr., estimator Howard S. Wright Constrn. Co., Seattle, 1976-77; dir. project devel. and adminstrn. DeLeuw Cather & Co., Seattle, 1977-78; sr. mgmt. cons. Alexander Grant & Co., Mpls., 1978-79; mgr. project sys. dept., project mgr. Henningson, Durham & Richardson, Mpls., 1979-80; dir. project mgmt., regional offices Ellerbe Assocs., Inc., Mpls., 1980-81; pres. Robert Yourzak & Assocs., Inc., Mpls., 1982—. Lectr. engring. mgmt. U. Wash., 1977-78; lectr., adj. asst. prof. dept. civil and mineral engring. and mech./indsl. engring. Ctr. for Devel. of Tech. Leadership, Inst. Tech.; mem. strategic mgmt. and orgn. dept., mgmt. scis. dept. Sch. Mgmt., U. Minn., 1979-90, 96—; bd. adv. inst. tech., 1989-93; founding mem., membership com., mem. U. of Minn. com. Minn. High Tech. Coun., 1983-95; instr. principles mgmt. dept. bus. and pub. policy Concordia U., 1997, instr. constrn. mgmt., constrn. estimating and scheduling, bldg. orgn. and tech., project mgmt. and planning skills, project mgmt. software, supervision and applied leadership, and supervisory techniques for bus. Inver Hills C.C., 1998—; instr. introduction to engring. and design, statics, mechanics of materials, ops. mgmt. North Hennepin C.C., 2002—; adj. instr. ops. mgmt. Hamline U., St. Paul, 2001; spkr. in field. Author: Project Management and Motivating and Managing the Project Team, 1984, (with others) Field Guide to Project Management, 1998, 2004 (sec. edition). Chmn. regional art group experience Seattle Art Mus., 1975-78; mem. Pacific N.W. Arts Coun., 1977-78, ex-officio adviser Mus. Week, 1976; bd. dirs. Friends of the Rep. Seattle Repertory Theatre, 1973-77; mem. Symphonics Seattle Symphony Orch., 1975-78. Named Outstanding Young Man of Am., U.S. Jaycees, 1978; scholar Boeing Co., 1967-68, Sheehy Constrn. Co., summer 1967. Fellow ASCE (chmn. continuing edn. subcom. Seattle chpt. 1976-79, chmn. program com. 1978, mem. transp. and urban planning tech. group 1978, Edmund Friedman Young Engr. award 1979, chmn. continuing edn. subcom. 1979-80, chmn. energy com. Minn. chpt. 1980-81, bd. dirs. 1981-89, sec. 1981-83, v.p. profl. svcs. 1983-84, v.p. info. svcs. 1984-85, pres. 1986-87, past pres. 1987-89, spkr.), PMI Project Mgmt. Inst. (cert. project mgmt. prof., spkr., founding pres. 1985, chmn., adv. com. 1987-89, bd. dirs. 1984-86, program com. chmn. and organizing com. mem. Minn. chpt. 1984, spkr., project mgr. internat. mktg. program 1985-86, chmn. internat. mktg. standing com. 1986, long range and strategic planning com. 1988-93, chmn. 1992, v.p. pub. rels. 1987-88, ex-officio dir. 1989, 92, internat. pres. 1990, chmn. bd. 1991, ex-officio chmn. 1992, internat. bd. dirs., chmn. nominating com. 1992, PMI fellow 1995, chmn. exec. dir. selection com. 1996-97, Robert J. Yourzak Scholarship Award established Minn. chpt. 1998—), Inst. Indsl. Engrs. (pres. Twin Cities chpt. 1985-86, chmn. program com. 1983-84, bd. dirs. 1985-88, awards com., chmn. 1984-89, fellow 1999, spkr.); mem. ASTD (So. Minn. chpt.), Am. Cons. Engrs. Coun. (peer reviewer 1986-89), Am. Arbitration Assn. (mem. Mpls. panel of constrn. arbitrators), Minn. Surveyors and Engrs. Soc., Cons. Engrs. Coun. Minn. (chmn. pub. rels. com. 1983-85, vice chmn. 1988, chmn. 1989, program com. chmn. Midwest engrs. conf. and exposition 1985-90, spkr., Honor award 1992), Inst. Mgmt. Cons. (cert. mgmt. cons.), Mpls. Soc. Fine Arts, Internat. Facility Mgmt. Assn., Am. Soc. Engring. Edn., Rainer Club (co-chmn. Oktoberfest), Sierra club, Chowder Soc., Mountaineers, North Star Ski Touring, Chi Epsilon (life). Office: 7320 Gallagher Dr Ste 325 Minneapolis MN 55435-4510

YOVICH, DANIEL JOHN, chemist, educator; b. Chgo., Mar. 5, 1930; s. Milan D. and Sophie (Dorociak) Y.; m. Anita Barbara Moreland, Feb. 7, 1959; children: Daniel, Amy, David, Julie Ann. Ph.B., DePaul U., 1952; MA, Governors State U., 1975, MS, 1976. Cert. reality therapist, profl. mgr. Formulator Nat. Lead Co., 1950-52, 56-59; researcher Montgomery Ward, Chgo., 1959-62; tech. dir. Riley Bros., Inc., Burlington, Iowa, 1962-66, Mortell Co., Kankakee, Ill., 1966-70; exec. dir. Dan Yovich Assos., 1970-79; asst. prof. Purdue U., Hammond, Ind., 1979-84, assoc. prof., 1984-90, prof., 1990-2000, prof. emeritus, 2000—. Instr. Army Security Agy. Sch., 1954—56, Napoleon Hill Acad., 1965—66; cons. Learning House, 1964—; assoc. Hill, Zediker & Assocs. Psychologists, Kankakee, 1975—79; mem. adv. bd. Nat. Congress Inventor Orgns., 1984; vis. prof. Grand Valley State U., 2000—, Northwood U., 2001—. Author: Applied Creativity; prdr., moderator: (program) Careers Unlimited, Sta. WCIU-TV, Chgo., 1967; contbr. articles to profl. jours.; patentee game Krypto, coating Sanitane. Mem. cmty. adv. coun. Governors State U., 1978; mem. Hammond (Ind.) Hist. Soc. Served to 1st lt. AUS, 1952-56. Recipient Outstanding Citizen Award News Pub. Co. Am., 1971, Outstanding Tchr. award Purdue U., 1980, 82, 83, Faculty Service award Nat. U. Continuing Edn. Assn., 1984, Disting. Service award Purdue U.-Calumet Alumni Assn., 1988, Arthur Young award Venture Mag., 1988, Entrepreneurial Edn. award Inc. Mag., 1990, Indiana Spirit of Innovation award, 1996. Mem. World Future Soc., Am. Soc. Profl. Supervision (exec. sec. 1986), Inventors and Entrepreneurs Soc. Am. (founder, exec. dir. 1984, prodr. Salute Vet. Recognition Programs 1999—), Global Intuition Network, Internat. Creativity Network, Infantry Officer Cand. Sch. Alumni Assn. (life), Napoleon Hill Found., Inst. Reality Therapy, Inst. Contemporary Living, Soc. Am. Inventors (life), Am. Legion, Vets. of the Battle of the Bulge (historian), Army and avy Club of Grand Rapids Home: 3527 Whispering Brook Dr SE Kentwood MI 49508-3733 E-mail: danyovich@sbcglobal.net.

YSSELDYKE, JAMES EDWARD, psychology professor; b. Grand Rapids, Mich., Jan. 1, 1944; 2 children. Student in psychology, Calvin Coll., 1962-65; BA in Psychology and Biology, Western Mich. U., 1966; MA in Sch. Psychology, U. Ill., 1968, PhD, 1971. Lic. cons. psychologist, Minn. Tchr. spl. edn. Kent County Juvenile Ct. Ctr., Grand Rapids, 1966-67; rsch. asst. U. Ill. Inst. Rsch. on Exceptional Children, 1969-70, tchg. asst. dept. ednl. psychology, 1970; sch. psychology intern Oakland County Schs., Pontiac, Mich., 1970-71; asst. prof. sch. psychology Pa. State U., 1971-75, assoc. prof., 1975, U. Minn., Mpls., 1975-79, prof., 1979-91, dir. Inst. Rsch. on Learning Disabilities, 1977-83, dir. Nat. Sch. Psychology Insvc. Tng. Network, 1977-83, dir. sch. psychology program, 1987-93, dir. Nat. Ctr. on Ednl. Outcomes, 1991-99, assoc. dean for rsch., 2000—05. Emma Birkmaier endowed prof. U. Minn., 1998-2000; advisor, cons. and researcher in field. Author: (with J. Salvia) Assessment in Special and Remedial Education, 2007, 10th edit., (with B. Algozzine and M. Thurlow) Critical Issues in Special and Remedial Education, 1992, 3d edit., 2000, Strategies and Tactics for Effective Instruction, 1997, (with S.L. Christenson) Functional Assessment of Academic Behavior, 2003, (with B. Algozzine) Every Teachers Guide to Special Education, 2007; editor: Exceptional Children, 1984-90; assoc. editor: The School Psychologist, 1972-75, mem. editorial bd., cons. editor numerous jours.; contbr. chpts. to books and articles to jours. Recipient Disting. Tchg. award U. Minn., 1988, Disting. Alumni award U. Ill. Coll. Edn., 1998; fellow NIMH, 1967-69; grantee in field. Fellow APA (Lightner Witmer award 1973); mem. APA, NASP, Am. Ednl. Rsch. Assn., Coun. for Exceptional Children (Rsch. award 1995), Coun. for Ednl. Diagnostic Svcs. Office: Univ Minn Coll Edn Human Devel 350 Elliott Hall 75 E River Rd Minneapolis MN 55455-0296 Business E-Mail: jim@umn.edu.

YU, ANTHONY C., religion and literature educator; b. Hong Kong, Oct. 6, 1938; came to U.S., 1956, naturalized, 1976; s. P.C. and Norma (Au) Y.; m. Priscilla Tang, Sept. 18, 1963; 1 son, Christopher Dietrich. BA, Houghton Coll., 1960; STB, Fuller Theol. Sem., 1963; PhD, U. Chgo., 1969, DLitt, 1996. Instr. U. Ill., Chgo., 1967-68; asst. prof. U. Chgo., 1968-74, assoc. prof., 1974-78, prof., 1978—2005, prof. emeritus, 2005—. Assoc. vis. prof. Ind. U., Bloomington, 1975; Whitney J. Oates short-term vis. fellow Princeton U., 1986; disting. vis. prof. Faculty of Arts, U. Alta., Can., 1992; mem. joint com. on study Chinese civilization Am. Coun. Learned Socs., 1980-86, bd. dirs., 1986-94; regional chmn. Mellon Fellowship in Humanities, 1982-92; bd. dirs. Ill. Humanities Coun., 1995-97; vis. prof. dept. religion Chinese U. Hong Kong, 1997; mem. com. social thought U. Chgo., 2004—. Asst. editor Jour. Asian Studies, 1975-78; co-editor Jour. Religion, 1980—; author, editor: Parnassus Revisited, 1973; editor, translator: The Journey to the West, 4 vols., 1977-83, Essays on The Journey to the West and Other Studies (in Chinese), 1989, The Monkey and the Monk, An Abridgment of the Journey to the West, 2006; co-editor (with Mary Gerhart) Morphologies of Faith: Essays on Religion and Culture in Honor of Nathan A. Scott, Jr., 1990, Rereading the Stone: Desire and the Making of Fiction in Dream of the Red Chamber, 1997, State and Religion in China: Historical and Textual Perspectives, 2005, Dream of the Red Chamber, Journey to the West, and Other Studies, Chinese edit., 2006. Recipient Gordon J. Laing prize, 1983; Danforth fellow, 1960-67; Guggenheim fellow, 1976-77; NEH translation grantee, 1977-82; Am. Coun. Learned Socs. sr. fellow, 1986-87, Mellon Emeriti fellow, 2006—; Masterworks Study grant NEH Seminar for Pub. Sch. Tchrs., 1992; elected academician Academia Sinica, 1998; Phi Beta Kappa vis. scholar 2001-02. Fellow Am. Acad. Arts and Scis.; mem. MLA (exec. coun. 1998—2001), Assn. for Asian Studies, Am. Acad. Religion (bd. dirs. 1995-97), Am. Comparative Lit. Assn., Milton Soc. Am., Arts Club. Home: 950 N Clark St Unit G Chicago IL 60610-8702 Office: U Chicago 1025 E 58th St Chicago IL 60637-1509 Office Phone: 773-702-8245. Business E-Mail: acyu@midway.uchicago.edu.

YU, GEORGE TZUCHIAO, political science professor; b. London, May 16, 1931; s. Wangteh and Ying (Ho) Y.; m. Priscilla Chang, Aug. 11, 1957; children: Anthony, Phillip. AB, U. Calif., Berkeley, 1954, MA, 1957, PhD, 1961. Asst. prof. polit. sci. U. N.C., Chapel Hill, 1961-65; assoc. prof. polit. sci. U. Ill., Urbana, 1965-70, prof., 1970—, head dept., 1987-92, dir. Ctr. for East Asian and Pacific Studies, 1992—, dir. grad. studies, 1981-85, chair Asian Am. studies com., 1997—2002. Vis. sr. lectr. polit. sci. Univ. Coll., Nairobi, 1968. Author: The Chinese Anarchist Movement, 1961, 65, Party Politics in Republican China, 1966, China and Tanzania, 1970, China's African Policy, 1975, Intra-Asian International Relations, 1977, Modern China and Its Revolutionary Process, 1985, American Studies in China, 1993, China in Transition, 1994, Asia's New World Order, 1997, Mongolia and Northeast Asia, 1999. Grantee, Social Sci. Rsch. Coun., 1967—68, 1970—71, NEH, 1978—81, 1984—86, Earhart Found., 1976—77, 1981—83, 1988, Ford Found., 1985—87, 1989, 1992, Freeman Found., 1996, 1997, 1999, 2001—03. Mem. Assn. Asian Studies. Office: 702 S Wright St Urbana IL 61801-3631 Business E-Mail: g-yu@uiuc.edu.

YU, HYUK, chemist, educator; b. Kapsan, Korea, Jan. 20, 1933; s. Namjik and Keedong (Shin) Y.; m. Gail Emmens, Jan. 20, 1964; children: Jeffrey, Steven, Douglas. BSChemE, Seoul Nat. U., 1955; MS in Organic Chemistry, U. So. Calif., 1958; PhD in Phys. Chemistry, Princeton U., 1962. Rsch. assoc. Dartmouth Coll., Hanover, NH, 1962-63; rsch. chemist Nat. Inst. Sci. and Tech., Washington, 1963-67; asst. prof. U. Wis., Madison, 1967-69, assoc. prof., 1969-78, prof. chemistry, 1978—, Evan P. Helfaer chair chemistry, 1991—95, Eastman-Kodak prof. emeritus, W.H. Stockmayer prof. emeritus. Fulbright-Hays lectr. Inha U., Inchon, Korea,1972; chmn. Gordon Rsch. Conf. Polymer Physics, 1986, 93; cons. LG Chem., Daejeon. Contbr. articles to profl. jours. John Simon Guggenheim Found. fellow, 1984; recipient Alexander von Humboldt award Humboldt Found., 1992. Fellow Am. Phys. Soc. (High-Polymer Physics prize, 1994); mem. Am. Chem. Soc. (exec. com. polymer chemistry divsn., editorial adv. bd. 1988-91, Ho-Am Basic Sci. prize, 1997, Colloid and Surface Chemistry Langmuir Lectr. award 1999), N.Y. Acad. Scis., Biophys. Soc., Materials Rsch. Soc., Korean Chem. Soc. (life), Polymer Soc. Korea (life), Sigma Xi (chpt. pres. 1987-88). Office: Univ Wis 1101 University Ave Madison WI 53706-1396 Home Phone: 608-437-4862. Business E-Mail: yu@chem.wisc.edu.

YU, JIU-KANG, mathematics professor; BS in Math., Nat. Taiwan Univ., Taipei, 1989; PhD, Harvard Univ., 1994. Instr. Princeton Univ., 1994—96, asst. prof., 1996—2000; assoc. prof. Purdue Univ., 2003—; asst. prof. Univ. Md., 2000—03, assoc. prof., 2003—. Recipient Chern prize, Internat. Congress of Chinese Mathematicians, 2001; fellow, Alfred P. Sloan Found., 1994, 2001—03. Achievements include being one of 18 top mathematicians and computer scientists (Atlas of Lie Groups Project) from the US to successfully map E8, one of the largest and most complicated structures in mathematics. Office: Dept Math Purdue Univ West Lafayette IN 47907 Office Phone: 765-494-1946. Business E-Mail: jyu@math.purdue.edu.

YU, LINDA, newswoman, television anchorwoman; b. Xian, China, Dec. 1, 1946; BA in Journalism, U. So. Calif., 1968. With Sta. KTLA-TV, Los Angeles, Sta. KABC-TV, Los Angeles; news anchor, reporter Sta. KATU-TV, Portland, Oreg.; gen. assignment reporter Sta. KGO-TV, San Francisco; with Sta. WMAQ-TV, Chgo., 1979-84, gen. assignment reporter, weekend anchor, 1979-80, co-anchor Monday-Friday edit. NEWSCENTERS, 4:30 PM, 1980-81, co-anchor NEWSCENTER5, 10:00 PM, 1981-84; co-anchor Eyewitness News, WLS-TV, Chgo., 1984—; spl.: Linda Yu in China, 1980; anchor WLS-TV, Chgo., 1984—. Recipient Chgo. Emmy award, 1981, 82, 87. Office: Sta WLS-TV 190 N State St Chicago IL 60601-3302

YUILL, THOMAS MACKAY, academic administrator, microbiology educator; b. Berkeley, Calif., June 14, 1937; s. Joseph Stuart and Louise (Dunlop) Y.; m. Ann Warnes, Aug. 24, 1960; children: Eileen, Gwen. BS, Utah State U., 1959; MS, U. Wis., 1962, PhD, 1964. Lab. officer Walter Reed Army Inst. Rsch., Washington, 1964-66; med. biologist SEATO Med. Rsch. Lab., Bangkok, 1966-68; asst. prof. U. Wis., Madison, 1968-72, assoc. prof., 1972-76, prof., 1976—2003, dept. chmn., 1979-82, assoc. dean, 1982-93, dir. Gaylord Nelson Inst. Environ. Studies, 1993—2003, emeritus prof. and dir., 2003—. Cons. NIH, Bethesda, 1976-86, CDC, 2005-; chmn. Viral Diseases Panel, U.S.-Japan Biomed. Scis. Program, 1979-86, Am. Com. Arbovirology, 1982—; bd. dirs. Cen. Tropical Agrl. Res. Teaching, Turrialba, Costa Rica, 1988-96. Contbr. chpts. to books, articles to profl. jours. Served to capt. U.S. Army, 1964-66. Recipient grants state and fed. govts., 1968—. Mem. Orgn. Tropical Studies (pres. 1979-85), Wildlife Disease Assn. (treas. 19880-85, pres. 1985-87, editl. bd. 1989-2003), Am. Soc. Tropical Medicine and Hygiene (editl. bd. 1984-96), Nat. Assn. State Univ. Land Grant Colls., EPA Task Force (co-chair 1994-2002), Sigma Xi. Avocations: flying, cross country skiing, music. Office Phone: 801-491-3226. Business E-Mail: tmyuill@wisc.edu.

YUNE, HEUN YUNG, retired radiologist; b. Seoul, Feb. 1, 1929; arrived in US, 1966; s. Sun Wook and Won Eun (Lee) Y.; m. Kay Kim, Apr. 12, 1956; children: Jeanny Kim, Helen Kay, Marc Eany. MD, Severance Med. Coll., Seoul, 1956. Lic. physician, Republic of Korea, Ind.; diplomate Am. Bd. Radiology, Korean Bd. Radiology. Intern Presbyn. Med. Ctr., Chonju, Korea, 1956-57, resident in surgery, 1957-60; resident in radiology Vanderbilt U. Hosp., Nashville, 1960-63, instr. radiology, 1962-64; chief radiology Presbyn. Med. Ctr., Chonju, Korea, 1964-66; from asst. to assoc. prof. radiology Vanderbilt U. Med. Sch., ashville, 1966-71; prof. radiology Ind. U. Sch. Medicine, Indpls., 1971-91, John A. Campbell prof. radiology, 1991-94, John A. Campbell prof. radiology emeritus, 1994—, dir. residency program, 1985-94, prof. otolaryngology, head and neck surgery, 1992-94, prof. otolaryngology, head and neck surgery emeritus, 1994—, ret., 2007. Vis. prof. Yonsei U. Coll. Medicine, Seoul, 1985, Ajou U. Coll. Medicine, Suwon, 1995-96; active staff Ind. U. Hosps., 1971-2006, Indpls. VA Hosp., 1971-99, 2000-06, Wishard Meml. Hosp., 1971-99, 2000-06. Editl. reviewer Am. Jour. Roentgenology, 1975—, Radiology, 1985—, Jour. Vascular and Interventional Radiology, 1989—; mem. editl. adv. bd. Yonsei Med. Jour., 2003—,; contbr. articles to profl. jours. Ordained elder Presbyn. Ch. Capt. Rep. of Korea Army, 1951-55. Decorated Bronze Star, U.S. Army, Wharang medal for meritorious mil. svc., Rep. of Korea Army. Fellow Am. Coll. Radiology; mem Assn. Univ. Radiologists, Radiol. Soc. N.Am., Am. Roentgen Ray Soc., Alpha Omega Alpha, others. Avocations: painting, photography, music appreciation, golf, travel. Home: 2887 Brook Vista Carmel IN 46032-4096 Personal E-mail: hyune@iupui.edu.

YURCHUCK, ROGER ALEXANDER, retired lawyer; b. Amityville, NY, June 9, 1938; s. Alexander and Ella Marie (Munley) Y.; m. Sally Ward, Apr. 14, 1961 (div. 1972); children: Scott, Lauren; m. Susan Holland, June 1, 1985 (div. 2005). AB cum laude, Northwestern U., 1959; LLB, Harvard U., 1962. Bar: Ohio 1962. Assoc. Vorys, Sater Seymour and Pease, Columbus, Ohio, 1962-68, ptnr., 1969—71, 1973—2002, ptnr. Cin. office, 1984—2002; v.p., gen. counsel Fed. Home Loan Mortgage Corp., Washington, 1971-73. Vice chmn., bd. dirs. Securities Investors Protection Corp., Washington, 1982-88. Del. Rep. Nat. Conv., 1980, 84. Mem. Ohio Bar Assn., Queen City Club (Cin.), Phi Beta Kappa. Republican. Episcopalian. Home Phone: 513-421-1481; Office Phone: 202-467-8805. Business E-Mail: rayurchuck@vssp.com.

YZERMAN, STEVE (STEPHEN GREGORY YZERMAN), professional sports team executive, retired professional hockey player; b. Cranbrook, BC, Can., May 9, 1965; m. Lisa Brennan; children: Isabella Katherine, Maria Charlotte, Sophia Rose. Center Detroit Red Wings, 1983—2006, captain, 1986—2006, v.p., 2006—; gen. mgr. Team Can., IIHF World Championship, Moscow, 2007. Player NHL All-Star Game, 1984, 1988—93, 1997, 99, 2000; mem. Team Can., Olympic Games, Nagano, Japan, 1998, Salt Lake City, 2002. Named Sporting News NHL Rookie of Yr., 1984; named to All-Rookie Team, NHL, 1984, First All-Star Team, 2000; recipient Lester B. Pearson award, 1989, Conn Smythe Trophy, 1998, Frank J. Selke Trophy, 2000, Bill Masterton Trophy, 2003, Lester Patrick Award, 2006. Achievements include being the youngest person ever to play in the NHL All-Star game, 1984; being a member of Stanley Cup Champion Detroit Red Wings, 1997, 1998, 2002; being a member of gold medal Canadian Hockey team, Salt Lake City Olympic Games, 2002; being the longest serving captain in NHL history; having his number, 19, retired by Detroit Red Wings, 2007. Office: Detroit Red Wings Joe Louis Arena 600 Civic Center Dr Detroit MI 48226-4419

ZABEL, SHELDON ALTER, lawyer, educator; b. Omaha, Apr. 25, 1941; s. Louis Julius and Anne (Rothenberg) Z.; m. Roberta Jean Butz, May 10, 1975; children: Andrew Louis, Douglas Patrick, Robert Stewart Warren. AB cum laude, Princeton U., 1963; JD cum laude, Northwestern U., 1966. Bar: Ill. 1966, U.S. Supreme Ct. 1976. Law clk. to presiding justice Ill. Supreme Ct., 1966-67; assoc. Schiff, Hardin LLP, Chgo., 1967-73, ptnr., 1973—. Instr. environ. law Loyola U., Chgo. Mem. ABA, Chgo. Bar Assn., Chgo. Coun. Lawyers, Order of Coif, Union League Club, Met. Club (Chgo.) Jewish. Avocations: skiing, bicycling. Office: Schiff Hardin LLP Sears Tower 233 S Wacker Dr Ste 6600 Chicago IL 60606-6473 Home Phone: 312-642-7824; Office Phone: 312-258-5540. Business E-Mail: szabel@schiffhardin.com.

ZACK, DANIEL GERARD, library consultant; b. Waukegan, Ill., Oct. 1, 1943; s. Raymond Gerard and Rosanna Marie (Atkinson) Z.; m. Mary Frances Anthony, Aug. 25, 1966; children: Jennifer Lee, Rebecca Jane. BA in Psychology, Western Ill. U., 1967; MS in Libr. Sci., U. Ill., 1975. Editor IBM Corp., Rochester, Minn., 1968-70, Memorex Corp., Mpls., 1970-74; rsch. assoc. Libr. Rsch. Ctr. U. Ill., Urbana, 1974-75; asst. dir. Portage County Pub. Libr., Stevens Point, Wis., 1976-78; dir. Burlington Pub. Libr., Iowa, 1978-87, Gail Borden Pub. Libr., Elgin, Ill., 1987—2004, Beloit Pub. Libr., Wis., 2007—; with Libr. Cons. Svcs., 2004—. Trustee Batavia Pub. Libr., Ill., 1997-2003; founder Friends of Ill. Libr., 1990, bd. dirs. 1990-97. Mem. ALA, ACLU, Ill. Libr. Assn. (mgr. pub. libr. forum 1991-92, 2002-03, exec. bd. dirs. 1992-95, pub. policy com. 1995-98), Pub. Libr. Assn. (intellectual freedom com. 1993-96), Kiwanis.

ZACKS, GORDON BENJAMIN, manufacturing executive; b. Terre Haute, Ind., Mar. 11, 1933; s. Aaron and Florence Melton (Spurgeon) Z.; married; children: Catherine E., Kimberly A. BA, Coll. Commerce, Ohio State U. With R.G. Barry Corp., Pickerington, Ohio, 1955—, exec. v.p., 1964-65, pres., 1965—, chmn. bd., 1979—, now also chief exec. officer, chmn., 1992—. Mem. Nat. Republican Senatorial Com.; hon. chmn. United Jewish Appeal; bd. dirs. numerous Jewish orgns., locally and nationally. Mem. Chief Exec. Officer Orgn., Am. Mgmt. Assn. Republican. Home: 140 N Parkview Ave Columbus OH 43209-1436 Office: R G Barry Corp 13405 Yarmouth Dr NW Pickerington OH 43147-8493 also: R G Barry Corp PO Box 129 Columbus OH 43216-0129

ZAGEL, JAMES BLOCK, federal judge; b. Chgo., Mar. 4, 1941; s. Samuel and Ethel (Samuels) Z.; m. Margaret Maxwell, May 27, 1979. BA, U. Chgo., 1962, MA in Philosophy, 1962; JD, Harvard U., 1965. Bar: Ill. 1965, U.S. Dist. Ct. (no. dist.) Ill. 1965, U.S. Supreme Ct. 1970, U.S. Ct. Appeals (7th cir.) 1972. Asst. state atty. Cook County, 1965—69; asst. atty. gen. criminal justice divsn. State of Ill., Springfield, 1970-77; chief prosecuting atty. Ill. Jud. Inquiry Bd., Springfield, 1973-75; exec. dir. Ill. Law Enforcement Commn., Springfield, 1977-79; dir. Ill. Dept. Revenue, Springfield, 1979-80, Ill. Dept. State Police, Springfield, 1980-87; judge U.S. Dist. Ct. (no. dist.) Ill., Chgo., 1987—. Co-author: Criminal Law and Its Administration, 1989, Cases and Comments on Criminal Procedure, 1992, Author's Money to Burn, 2002. Named Outstanding Young Citizen, Chgo. Jaycees, 1977; recipient Disting. Svc. Merit award Assn. Commerce and Industry, 1983. Mem. Chgo. Bar Assn., Jud. Conf. of U.S. (codes of conduct com. 1987-92). Office: US Dist Ct 219 S Dearborn St Ste 2588 Chicago IL 60604-1801

ZAGEL, MARGARET MAXWELL, lawyer; b. Centralia, Ill., Jan. 17, 1949; d. Francis Edgar and Joan (Beckmeyer) Maxwell; m. James Block Zagel, May 27, 1979. BA, Tulane U., 1970; JD, U. Ill., 1973. Bar: Ill. 1973, U.S. Ct. Appeals (7th cir.), U.S. Supreme Ct. Atty. Ill. Appellate Defender's Office, Chgo., 1973-75, law clk. to Hon. Seymour Simon, 1975-76; assoc., then ptnr. Schuyler Roche & Zwirner, Chgo., 1976-84; gen. counsel Grant Thornton LLP, Chgo., 1984-98, mng. prin. risk, regulatory & legal affairs, gen counsel, 2003; v.p., gen. counsel Tellabs, Inc., Lisle, Ill., 1998—99; sr. v.p., chief legal and admin. officer Organic, Inc., San Francisco, 1999—2001; spec. coun. litigation transactions Arthur Andersen LLP, 2002; practice lead, corp. governance, risk and crisis mgmt., co-gen. coun. Altheimer & Gray, 2002—03. Mem. planning com. Securities Inst. Northwestern U., Chgo., 1993—, mem. corp. counsel planning com., 1994-2000; mem. civil justice reform adv. com. U.S. Cir. Ct. (no. dist.) Ill., Chgo., 1994-95; mem. Ill. Commn. Regulatory Issues, mem. ACCA 1986, Nat. Assoc. Corp. Dir., 2002-2004, Economic Club Chgo. 2003-, Women Corp. Dirs. 2003-; mem. vis. com. Coll. Law U. Ill., 1997-2001; bd. dirs. Atrion Corp. 2002-2003. Bd. trustees Court Theatre. Mem.: Econ. Club Chgo. Office: Grant Thornton LLP 175 W Jackson 20th Fl Chicago IL 60604

ZAHNEIS, LEONA BETH, lawyer; b. Louisville, Ky., Oct. 22, 1971; BS in Nursing, Eastern Ky. U., 1993; JD, Salmon P. Chase Coll. Law, 2001. Bar: Ohio 2001; lic. Ky., 1993. Assoc. White, Getgey & Meyer Co., LPA, Cin. Named one of Ohio's Rising Stars, Super Lawyers, 2006. Mem.: Northern Ky. Bar Assn. (Judge West award), Ohio State Bar Assn., Cin. Bar Assn., Order of Curia. Office: White Getgey & Meyer Co LPA 1700 Fourth & Vine Tower 1 W Fourth St Cincinnati OH 45202-3621 Office Phone: 513-241-3685. Office Fax: 513-241-2399.

ZAHNISER, RACHEL S., lawyer; b. Campbellsville, Ky., Dec. 12, 1972; BA in Eng., Centre Coll. Ky, 1994; MSLS, U. Ky., 1995, JD, 1999. Bar: Ky. 1999, Ohio 2003. Law clerk Chief US Dist. Judge, Eastern Dist. Ky., US Cir. Judge, Sixth Cir. Ct. of Appeals; assoc. Taft, Stettinius & Hollister LLP, Cin., mem., Profl. Women's Resource Grp. Named one of Ohio's Rising Stars, Super Lawyers, 2006. Mem.: Order of Coif. Office: Taft Stettinius & Hollister LLP 425 Walnut St Ste 1800 Cincinnati OH 45202-3957 Office Phone: 513-381-2838. Office Fax: 513-381-0205.

ZAIMAN, K(OICHI) ROBERT, dentist; b. Cin., Oct. 19, 1944; s. Noboru Gary and Toshiko (Matsuyama) Zaiman; m. Kimberly Ann Sass, Nov. 6, 1976; children: Kara Jean, Matthew Robert. Student, Creighton U., Omaha, 1962-64, DDS, 1968. Asst. prof. Creighton U. Sch. Dentistry, Omaha, 1971-73, assoc. prof., 1973-75; pvt. practice dentistry Omaha, 1971—. Dir. Chicano and Native-Am. Free Clinic Creighton U., Omaha, 1970—75. Mem. bd. elders King of Kings Luth. Ch., 1990—95, deacon, 1995—; past v.p., bd. dirs. Japanese-Am. Citizens League, Omaha, 1977—86. Fellow: Internat. Coll. Dentistry, Acad. Continuing Edn., Acad. Gen. Dentistry (nat. del. 1971—76, pres. 1976—77), Pierre Fauchard Internat. Hon. Acad.; mem.: ADA, Omaha Dental Study Club (pres. 1999—2001), Nebr. Dental Assn. (del. 1971—94, 1996—), Omaha Dist. Dental Soc. (bd. dirs. 1968, treas. 1980—85, peer rev. 1996—), Delta Sigma Delta (pres. 1973—74). Office: 10841 Q St Ste 109 Omaha NE 68137-3741 Office Phone: 402-339-4999.

ZAKAS, JOSEPH C., state legislator; b. Chgo., Nov. 4, 1950; s, Anthony and Ann (Phillips) Z.; m. Margaret Anne Kaiser, 1978; children: Mary Sarah, Katherine Grace, Stephen John. BA, U. Ill., 1972; JD, MBA, U. Notre Dame, 1980. Mem. Ind. Senate from 11th dist., 1982—; majority whip Ind. Senate; assoc. Thorne, Grodnik & Ransel, South Bend, Ind., 1980—. Chmn. admin. rules oversight commn., govt. affairs and transactions com., chmn. civil law divsn. judiciary com.; mem. natural resources com., ethics com. taxation divsn., finance and public policy com., govt. and regulatory affairs coms. Bd. dirs. REAL Serv, Michiana Arts & Sci. Coun.; active Blue Ribbon Commn. Against Domestic Violence. Mem. Am. Bar Assn., Ind. Bar. Assn., St. Joseph County Bar Assn., Knights of Columbus. Republican. Office: Ind Senate 200 W Washington St Indianapolis IN 46204 also: Ind State Senate State Capital Indianapolis IN 46204

ZAKIN, JACQUES LOUIS, chemical engineering educator; b. NYC, Jan. 28, 1927; s. Mordecai and Ada Davies (Fishbein) Z.; m. Laura Pienkny, June 11, 1950; children: Richard Joseph, David Fredric, Barbara Ellen, Emily Anne, Susan Beth. BSChemE, Cornell U., 1949; MChemE, Columbia U., 1950; DEng. Sci., NYU, 1959. Chem. engr. Flintkote Research Labs., Whippany, NJ, 1950-51; research technologist, research dept. Socony-Mobil, Bklyn., 1951-53, sr. research technologist, 1953-56, supervising technologist, 1959-62; assoc. prof. chem. engring. U. Mo., Rolla, 1962-65, prof., 1965-77, dir. minority engring. program, 1974-77, dir. women in engring. program, 1975-77; chmn. dept. chem. engring. Ohio State U., Columbus, 1977-94, Helen C. Kurtz prof. chem. engring., 1994-2000, Helen C. Kurtz prof. emeritus, 2000—. Chmn. sci. manpower and resources com. Coun. Chem. Rsch., 1984-86, governing bd., 1986-89; exec. com., 1988-89; adv. bd. State of Ohio Alternative Fuels, 1992-93; vis. prof. Technion, 1968-69, 94-95, Hebrew U., 1987; disting. vis. prof. Mex. Acad. Scis. and Mex.-USA Found. for Scis., 1999. Co-editor: Proc. Turbulence Symposium, 1969, 71, 73, 75, 77, 79, 81, 83; contbr. articles to profl. jours Bd. dirs. Rolla Cmty. Concert Assn., 1966-77, 2d v.p., 1975-77; bd. dirs. Ozark Mental Health Assn., 1976-77; trustee Ohio State Hillel Found., 1981-84, treas., 1984-89, pres., 1989-92; trustee Congregation Beth Tikvah, 1983; bd. trustees Columbus Jewish Fedn., 1989-92; co-chmn. Academics and Scientists for Soviet Refuseniks. With USNR, 1945-46. Recipient Outstanding Rsch. award U. Mo., 1970, U. Mo. Rolla Acad. Chem. Engrs., 2007, Josef Hlavka Meml. medal Czechoslovakian Acad. Sci., 1992, Clara M. and Peter L. Scott Faculty award, 1996, Rsch. award Japanese Govt., 2001; named Outstanding Educator of Yr., Ohio Soc. Profl. Engrs., 1994, Tech. Person of Yr., Columbus Tech. Coun., 1987; Am. Chem. Soc. Petroleum Rsch. Fund Internat. fellow, 1968-69, Socony-Mobil Employee Incentive fellow NYU, 1956-59, Sr. Fulbright Rsch. fellow Technion, 1994-95. Fellow Am. Inst. Chem. Engrs.; mem. Am. Chem. Soc., Soc. of Rheology, Am. Soc. Engring. Edn., U. Mo. Acad. Chem. Engrs., Sigma Xi, Phi Lambda Upsilon, Phi Eta Sigma, Alpha Chi Sigma, Tau Beta Pi, Phi Kappa Phi. Jewish. Achievements include patents in field. Office: Ohio State U 140 W 19th Ave Columbus OH 43210-1110 Office Phone: 614-688-4113. Business E-Mail: zakin.1@osu.edu.

ZALK, ROBERT H., retired lawyer; b. Albert Lea, Minn., Dec. 1, 1944; s. Donald B. and Juliette J. (Erickson) Z.; m. Ann Lee Anderson, June 21, 1969; children: Amy, Jenna. BA, Carleton Coll., 1966; JD, U. Minn., 1969. Bar: Minn. 1969, U.S. Dist. Ct. Minn. 1969. Assoc. Popham, Haik, Schnobrich, Kaufman & Doty, Mpls., 1969-72; atty. No. States Power Co., Mpls., 1972-73, Wright, West & Diessner, Mpls., 1973-84, Fredrikson & Byron P.A., Mpls., 1984-94, Zalk & Assocs., Mpls., 1994-95; ptnr. Zalk & Eayrs, Mpls., 1995-98, Zalk & Wood, Mpls., 1999, Zalk & Bryant, Mpls., 2000—06, ret., 2006. Fellow Am. Acad. Matrimonial Lawyers (pres. Minn. chpt. 2000-01), Minn. Bar Assn. (co-chmn. maintenance guideline com. 1991-94), Hennepin County Bar Assn. (co-chmn. family law sect. 1990-91). Office: Zalk & Bryant 5861 Cedar Lake Rd Minneapolis MN 55416-1481 Office Phone: 952-545-3392. Business E-Mail: rzalk@zalkbryant.com.

ZAMBIE, ALLAN JOHN, lawyer; b. Cleve., June 9, 1935; s. Anton J. and Martha (Adamski) Z.; m. Nancy Hall, Sept. 22, 1973. Student, Ohio U., 1953-54; BA, Denison U., 1957; LL.B., Western Res. U. (now Case Western Res. U.), 1960. Bar: Ohio 1960. Asso. firm Hribar and Conway, Euclid, Ohio, 1961-63; staff atty. The Higbee Co., Cleve., 1963-67, asst. sec., 1967-69, sec., 1969-74, v.p.-sec., 1974-88, gen. counsel, 1978-88; v.p., sec., gen. counsel The Lamson & Sessions Co., Cleve., 1989-94; of counsel Conway, Marken, Wyner, Kurant & Kern Co., LPA, Cleve., 1994-95; v.p.-sec. John P. Murphy Found., Cleve., 1996-2000, exec. v.p., 2001—. V.p., sec. Kulas Found., 2001—06, v.p., sec., treas. Kulas Found., 2006-. Trustee Cleve. Music Sch. Settlement, pres. bd. trustees, 1980—82, treas., 1996—2001; trustee N.E. Ohio affiliate Am. Heart Assn., 1989—96. With US Army, 1960—61. Mem.: Am. Soc. Corporate Secs. (nat. v.p. 1977—), Cleve. Bar Assn., Ohio Bar Assn. Office: 50 Pub Sq Ste 924 Cleveland OH 44113-2203 Home: 25243 Bryden Rd Beachwood OH 44122 Office Phone: 216-623-4772. Business E-Mail: azambie@murphykulas.org.

ZAMBRANO, CARLOS ALBERTO, professional baseball player; b. Puerto Cabello, Venezuela, June 1, 1981; m. Ismary Zambrano; 2 children. Pitcher Chgo. Cubs, 2001—. Named to at. League All-Star Game, 2004, 2006; recipient Silver Slugger award, 2006. Achievements include allowing only 9 home runs in the 2003 season, making him the second big league starter since Pedro Martinez to allow fewer than 10 home runs in a full season; becoming the youngest Cub in franchise history to start on Opening Day and pitch in an All-Star game, 2004. Mailing: Wrigley Field 1060 W Addison Chicago IL 60613-4397 Office Phone: 773-404-2827.*

ZAMOYSKI, JAMES J., corporate lawyer; JD, Wayne State U., LLM in Taxation. CPA, Mich. Various positions to v.p., gen. mgr. of aftermarket opers. Federal-Mogul Corp., Geneva, 1976-97, sr. v.p., gen. counsel Southfield, Mich., 1997—. Office: Federal-Mogul Corp 26555 Northwestern Hwy Southfield MI 48034-2146

ZANDER, EDWARD J., communications executive; b. Bklyn., Jan. 12, 1947; m. Mona Zander; 2 children. BSEE, Rensselaer Poly. Inst., 1968; MBA, Boston U., 1975. Formerly with Apollo Computer, Data Gen., Raytheon; with Sun Microsystems Inc., Palo Alto, Calif., 1987—2002, COO, 1998—2002, pres., COO, 1999—2002; mng. dir. Silver Lake Ptnrs., 2002—03; CEO Motorola Inc., Schaumburg, Ill., 2004—08, chmn., 2004—. Bd. dirs. Documentum, Inc., Portal Software, Inc., Rhythms etconnections, inc., Seagate Tech., Time Warner Inc., 2007—. Mem. sci. adv. bd. Rensselaer Poly. Inst., Troy, NY, presdl. advisor; mem. dean's adv. bd., sch. of mgmt. Boston U.; bd. dirs. Jason Found. for Edn.; mem. Economics Club Chgo., Exec. Club Chgo.; mem. civic com. Comml. Club Chgo. Named one of 50 Who Matter Now, CNNMoney.com Bus. 2.0, 2006. Office: Motorola Inc 1303 E Algonquin Rd Schaumburg IL 60196

ZANDER, JANET ADELE, psychiatrist; b. Miles City, Mont., Feb. 19, 1950; d. Adelbert William and Valborg Constance (Buckneberg) Z.; m. Mark Richard Ellenberger, Sept. 16, 1979; 1 child, Evan David Zander Ellenberger. BA, St. Olaf Coll., 1972; MD, U. Minn., 1976. Diplomate Am. Bd. Psychiatry and Neurology. Resident in psychiatry U. Minn., Mpls., 1976-79, fellow in psychiatry, 1979-80, asst. prof. psychiatry, 1981—; staff psychiatrist St. Paul Regions Hosp., 1980—, dir. edn. in psychiatry, 1980-94, dir. inpatient psychiatry, 1986—2005, vice chair dept. psychiatry, 1991-96, divsn. head behavioral health, 2002. Bd. dirs. Perry Assurance. Contbr. research articles to sci. jours. Sec. Concentus Musicus Bd. Dirs., St. Paul, 1981-89; mem. property com. St. Clement's Episcopal Ch., St. Paul, 1985. Mem. Am. Psychiat. Assn., Am. Med. Women's Assn., Minn. Psychiat. Soc. (ethics com. 1985-87, women's com. 1985-87, coun. 1994-96), Minn. Med. Assn., Ramsey County Med. Soc. (bd. dirs. 1994-96). Democrat. Avocations: singing, skiing. Home: 230 Crestway Ln West Saint Paul MN 55118-4424 Office: Regions Hosp 640 Jackson St Saint Paul MN 55101-2502 Office Phone: 651-254-2777. E-mail: janet.a.zander@healthpartners.com.

ZANGERLE, JOHN A., lawyer; b. Lakewood, Ohio, Jan. 24, 1942; BA, Haverford Coll., 1964; JD, Case Western Res. U., 1967. Bar: Ohio 1967. Ptnr. Baker & Hostetler, Cleve. Office: Baker & Hostetler LLP 3200 Nat City Ctr 1900 E 9th St Ste 3200 Cleveland OH 44114-3475

ZANOT, CRAIG ALLEN, lawyer; b. Wyandotte, Mich., Nov. 15, 1955; s. Thomas and Faye Blanch (Sperry) Zanot. AB with distinction, U. Mich., 1977; JD cum laude, Ind. U., 1980. U.S. Ct. Appeals (6th cir.) 1985, U.S. Dist. Ct. (ea. dist.) Mich. 1987, U.S. Dist. Ct. (we. dist.) Mich. 1990. Law clk. to presiding justice Allen County Superior Ct, Ft. Wayne, 1980-81; ptnr. Davidson, Breen & Doud P.C., Saginaw, Mich., 1981—. Mem.: ABA, Genesee County Bar Assn., Bay County Bar Assn., Saginaw County Bar Assn., Mich. Bar Assn. Roman Catholic. Home: 547 S Linwood Beach Rd Linwood MI 48634-9432 Office: Davidson Breen & Doud PC 1121 N Michigan Ave Saginaw MI 48602-4762 Office Phone: 989-752-9595. E-mail: umchiphi@aol.com.

ZARDETTO-SMITH, ANDREA, medical educator; BS in Biology, Coll. of St. Elizabeth, 1978; MS in Physiology, Loyola U. of Chgo., 1983, PhD, 1990. Rsch. biologist G.D. Searle, Skokie, Ill., 1978—83; postdoctoral fellow dept. internal medicine U. Iowa, 1990—91; postdoctoral rschr. NIH, 1990—92; assoc. dept. anatomy U. Iowa, 1993—96; prof. phys. and occupl. therapy and pharm. sci. Creighton U., Omaha, 1996—2002; prof. biology and neuroscience U. Nebr., Omaha, 2002—. Prin. investigator Brains Rule! Nat. Neurosci. Expositions, a Sci. Edn. Drug Abuse Partnership Award Nat. Inst. on Drug Abuse. Grantee NSF, 1996—98. Mem.: AAAS, Assn. of Women in Sci. (pres. ea. Iowa chpt. 1994—96), Women in Neurosci. (past pres.), Am. Assn. Clin. Anatomists, Am. Assn. Anatomists, Soc. for eurosci. (com. neuroscience literacy). Achievements include research in on the role of various neurotransmitters in brainstem and forebrain circuits that modulate body fluid balance and how they affect overall control of blood pressure; development of model program for improving neuroscience literacy. Office: Univ Nebraska ASH 347 3001 Dodge St Omaha NE 68182

ZAREFSKY, DAVID HARRIS, academic administrator, communication editor; b. Washington, June 20, 1946; s. Joseph Leon and Miriam Ethel (Lewis) Z.; m. Nikki Sheryl Martin, Dec. 23. 1970; children: Beth Ellen, Marc Philip. BS, Northwestern U., 1968, MA, 1969, PhD, 1974. Instr. communication studies Northwestern U., Evanston, Ill., 1968-73, asst. prof., 1974-77, assoc. prof., 1977-82, prof., 1982—, chmn. dept., 1975-83, assoc. dean Sch. Speech, 1983-88, dean, 1988-2000. Author: President Johnson's War on Poverty, 1986 (Winans-Wichelns award 1986), Lincoln, Douglas and Slavery, 1990 (Winans-Wichelns award 1991), Public Speaking: Strategies for Success, 1996, 5th edit., 2007; co-author: Contemporary Debate, 1983, Fundamentals of Argumentation Theory, 1996; editor: Rhetorical Movement, 1993; co-editor: American Voices, 1989, Contemporary American Voices, 1992, Fundamentals of Argumentation Theory, 1996; contbr. articles to profl. jours. Recipient Best Article award So. Speech Communication Assn., 1985, 98, Midwest Forensic Assn., 1988; named Debate Coach of the Year Georgetown U., 1973, Emory U., 1972. Mem. AAUP, Nat. Comm. Assn. (pres. 1993, dist. scholar award 1994, disting. svc. award 2001, mem. award 2002), Ctrl. States Comm. Assn. (pres. 1986-87), Rhetoric Soc. Am. (pres. 2006—), Am. Forensic Assn. (Svc. award 1989, Dist. Scholar award 1999), Delta Sigma Rho-Tau Kappa Alpha (Svc. award 1986), others. Democrat. Jewish. Avocations: stamp collecting/philately, reading, travel. Office: Northwestern U 1815 Chicago Ave Evanston IL 60208-1340 Office Phone: 847-491-5850.

ZAREMSKI, MILES JAY, lawyer; b. Chgo., Aug. 16, 1948; s. Samuel and Ann (Levine) Z.; m. Elena Cinthia Resnik, July 19, 1970; children: Jason Lane, Lauren Devra. BS, U. Ill., 1970; JD, Case Western Res. U., 1973. Bar: Ill. 1973, Pa. 2000, Ind. 2000, U.S. Dist. Ct. (no. dist.) Ill. 1973, U.S. Dist. Ct. Nebr. 1996, U.S. Dist. Ct. (ea. dist.) Tenn. 1997, U.S. Dist. Ct. (no. dist.) Ind. 2005, U.S. Ct. Appeals (7th cir.) 1973, U.S. Ct. Appeals (8th cir.) 1988, U.S. Ct. Appeals (6th cir.) 1998, U.S. Ct. Appeals (9th cir.) 2002, U.S. Supreme Ct. 1977. Spl. asst. state's atty. Lake County, Ill., 1980-82; ptnr. Kamensky, Rubinstein, Hochman, & DeLott, Lincolnwood, Chgo., Ill., 2000—06; ptnr., founder Kamensky Law Group, Northbrook, Ill., 2007—. Arbitrator, mandatory arbitration programs Cook and Lake Counties, Ill., 1990—; asst. prof. med. jurisprudence Rosalind Franklin U. Medicine and Sci., 1991—; adj. faculty U. Chgo. Law Sch., 1999—2001; advisor to congressman and staffs on patient rights, 1999—2003; adj. prof. Case We. Res. Law Sch., 2002—03; vis. prof. divsn. of law Macquarie U., Sydney, 2004; cons. Gerson-Lehmon, Washington, NY, 2005—; clin. advisors, NYC, 2007—; lectr. nat. and internat. healthcare, medical jurisprudence. Editor: Medical and Hospital Negligence, 4 vols., 1988, supplement, 1993, 95-99; contbr. chpts. in books and articles to profl. jours.; author: Reengineering Healthcare Liability Litigation, 1997, supplement, 1999; mem. editl. bd. Medicine and Law, Haita, Israel, 2004—; patentee in field Oversight com. law sch. Case Western Res. U., Cleve., 1999, alumni bd. dirs., 1996-99; mem. exec. com. law sch. ctr for health care Loyola U., Chgo., 1987-89; mem. lakefront commn. City of Highland Park, Ill., 1982-84; bd. dirs., coun., officer Regional Organ Bank Ill., Chgo., 1986-91, The Lambs, Libertyville, Ill., 1982-84, Jocelyn Ctr. for Mental Health, 1994-96; field play marshall U.S. Olympics Baseball, Atlanta, 1996. Named one of Outstanding Young Men in Am., U.S. Jaycees, 1979; named Superlawyer, Health Care-Ill., 2005, 06, Leading Lawyer, 2005, 06. Fellow: Am. Bar Found., Am. Coll. Legal Medicine (assoc. in law 1973—91, editl. bd. Jour. Legal Medicine 1981—, chair legal com. 1996—98. chair Amicus com. 1997—, bd. govs., sec. 1999—2000, treas. 2000—01, pres.-elect 2001—02, pres. 2002—03); mem.: ABA (editor-in-chief Forum 1979—81, vice chmn. 1979—90, chmn. med. and law com. 1984—85, editl. bd. Forum on Health Law 1989—91, spl. com. on med. profl. liability 1991—95, 1998—, chmn. spl. com. on med. profl. liability 2000—03, chmn. std. com. med. profl. liability 2003—05, chmn. emeritus std. commn. on med. profl. liability 2005—, chmn. med. and law com. 2005—, various coms. tort, trial and ins. practice sect.), Medicine and Law (mem. editl. bd.), Am. Arbitration Assn. (arbitrator 2002—, comml. arbitration panel 2006—), World Congress Med. Law (mem. editl. bd. Medicine and Law 2004—), Ill. Assn. Healthcare Attys., Quality Mgmt. Health Care (editl. bd.), Am. Soc. Writers on Legal Subjects (scribes), Am. Health Law Assn. (vice chair hosp. liability com. 1999—2001), Am. Soc. Law and Medicine (editor-in-chief 1981—83, bd. editors 1983—86), Lake County Bar Assn., Ill. Bar Assn. (1st and 3d prizes 1978—79). Jewish. Avocations: baseball, soccer, coaching athletic teams. Office: Kamensky Rubinstein Hochman DeLott 7250 N Cicero Ave Ste 200 Lincolnwood IL 60712 Office Phone: 847-982-1776, 847-418-3830. Business E-Mail: mzaremski@kr-law.com.

ZARING, ALLEN G., homebuilding company executive; Student, Babson Coll. Founder, chmn., CEO Zaring Homes, 1964—. With U.S. Army. Recipient High Achievement award Profl. Builders Mag.; named Builder of Yr., Home Builders Assn. Greater Cin., 1995, Ams. Best Builder. Office: 625 Eden Park Dr #1250 Cincinnati OH 45202-6024 Fax: 513-247-2667.

ZARLE, THOMAS HERBERT, academic administrator; b. Akron, Ohio, Oct. 11, 1939; BS, Springfield Coll., 1963; MA, Ohio U., 1965; PhD, Mich. State U., 1970; MPH, Harvard U., 1978. V.p. instl. advancement Bentley Coll., Waltham, Mass., until 1988; pres. Aurora U., Ill., 1988—2000. Office: Aurora U Office of Pres 347 S Gladstone Ave Aurora IL 60506-4892

ZARTMAN, DAVID LESTER, retired zoology educator, researcher; b. Albuquerque, July 6, 1940; s. Lester Grant and Mary Elizabeth (Kitchel) Z.; m. Micheal Aline Plemmons, July 6, 1963; children: Kami Renee, Dalan Lee. BS cum laude in Dairy Husbandry, N.Mex. State U., 1962; MS in Genetics, Ohio State U., 1966, PhD in Genetics, 1968. Cert. dairy cattle specialist, Am. Registry Profl. Animal Scientists. Jr. ptnr. Marlea Guernsey Farm, Albuquerque, 1962-64; grad. rsch. assoc. Ohio State U., Columbus, 1964-68; asst. prof. dairy sci. N.Mex. State U., Las Cruces, 1968-71, assoc. prof., 1971-79, prof., 1979-84, Ohio State U., Columbus, 1984—2006, emeritus prof., 2006—. Chmn. dept. Ohio State U., Columbus, 1984-99; pres. Mary K. Zartman, Inc., Albuquerque, 1976-84; cons. Bio-Med. Electronics, Inc., San Diego, 1984-89, Zartemp, Inc., Northbrook, Ill., 1990, Recom Applied Solutions, 1993-2000, Am. Registry of Profl. Animal Scientists, 1996—, Midwest Univs. Consortium for Internat. Assistance, 2004. Contbr. articles to profl. jours.; patentee in field. Recipient State Regional Outstanding Young Farmer award Jaycees, 1963, Disting. Rsch. award N.Mex. State U. Coll. Agr. and Home Econs., 1983, Outstanding Svc. award Ohio Forage and Grassland Coun., 1999, Grazier of Yr. award Gt. Lakes Internat. Grazing Conf., 2001, hon. state degree Ohio FFA, 2000, The Jack Tucker Disting. Svc. award Ohio Forage and Grassland Coun., 2004; course acclaimed by Humane Soc. of U.S.; named one of Top 100 Agr. Alumni, N.Mex. State U. Centennial, 1987; spl. postdoctoral fellow NIH, New Zealand, 1973; Fulbright-Hayes lectr., Malaysia, 1976. Fellow AAAS; mem. Am. Dairy Sci. Assn., Am. Soc. Animal Sci., Dairy Shrine Club, Ohio Farm Bur., Sigma Xi, Gamma Sigma Delta, Alpha Gamma Rho (1st Outstanding Alumnus N.Mex. chpt. 1985), Alpha Zeta, Phi Kappa Phi. Home: 7671 Deer Creek Dr Worthington OH 43085-1551 Office: Ohio State U 2027 Coffey Rd Columbus OH 43210-1043 Home Phone: 614-431-3479; Office Phone: 614-292-1387. Business E-Mail: zartman.3@osu.edu.

ZATKOFF, LAWRENCE P., federal judge; b. 1939; m. Nancy L. Chenhall; four children. BSBA, U. Detroit, 1962; JD cum laude, Detroit Coll. Law, 1966. Bar: Mich., U.S. Supreme Ct. Mem. corp. personnel staff Chrysler Corp., 1962-66; asst. prosecuting atty. Macomb County, Mich.; with Moll, Desenberg, Purdy, Glover & Bayer, Detroit, 1966-68; ptnr. LaBarge, Zatkoff & Dinning, Roseville, 1968-78; probate judge Macomb County, 1978-82; judge Macomb County Cir. Ct., 1982-87; chief judge U.S. Dist. Ct. (ea. dist.) Mich., 1986—. Part-time faculty Detroit Coll. Law; mem. rep. assembly Mich. State Bar, mem. spl. com. on grievances; appointed assoc. govt. appeal agt. SSS, 1969-72. Guest lectr., past mem. scholarship ball com. Macomb County Community Coll.; citizen's adv. bd. Macomb-Oakland Regional Ctr., 1978-79; ex officio mem. Macomb County Youthscope; adv. bd. Met. Detroit chpt. March of Dimes; trustee St. Joseph Hosp. of Mt. Clemens; mem. Selfridge Air NG Base Community Council; Rep. candidate 12th dist. U.S. Congress Mich., 1976, party treas. 12 dist. 1975, exec. com., 1975, chmn. Macomb County exec. com., 1976, del. several nat. and regional Rep. Convs., Macomb County campaign coordinator for U.S. Sen. candidate Marvin Esch, 1976. Mem. ABA, Fed. Bar Assn., Mich. Bar. Assn., Macomb County Bar. Assn. (dir., treas. Young Lawyers sect., past probate ct. liason to bd. dirs., mem. cir. ct. liason com.), Detroit Bar Assn., Am. Judicare Soc., Am. Arbitration Assn., Nat. Orgn. Legal Problems of Edn., Nat. Council Juvenile and Family Ct. Judges, Mich. Probate and Juvenile Ct. Judges Assn. (mental health com.), Nat. Coll. Probate Judges, Mich. Judges Assn., VFW (legal case rep. 1976, spokesman Vietnamese Embassy Paris 1976, judge Voice of Democracy programs 1975, state wide scholarships judge, Voice of Democracy awards 1975, 76, Americanism award 1976, Spl. Recognition award 1978). Clubs: 100, Macomb County 300, Rep. Majority (charter). Office: US Dist Ct US Courthouse Rm 730 231 W Lafayette Blvd Detroit MI 48226-2700

ZAVATSKY, MICHAEL JOSEPH, lawyer; b. Wheeling, W.Va., Dec. 15, 1948; s. Mike and Mary (Mirich) Z.; m. Kathleen Hanson, May 28, 1983; children: David, Emily. BA in Internat. Studies, Ohio State U., 1970; MA in Polit. Sci., U. Hawaii, 1972; JD, U. Cin., 1980. Bar: Ohio 1980, U.S. Dist. Ct. (so. dist.) Ohio 1981, U.S. Ct. Appeals (6th cir.) 1985, U.S. Supreme Ct. 1989. Ptnr. Taft, Stettinius & Hollister, Cin., 1980—. Adj. prof. in trial practice and immigration law U. Cin., 1986— Trustee Internat. Visitors Ctr., Cin., 1984-86; bd. dirs. Cin. Charter Com., 1988-91; bd. dirs., mem. steering com. Leadership Cin., 1994-96. Capt. USAF, 1973-77. William Graham fellow U. Cin., 1979, East West Ctr. fellow U. Hawaii, 1970; named Best Lawyers in Am., 1995—, Ohio Super Lawyers, 2003—, Cin. Leading Lawyers, 2004—. Mem ABA, Ohio Bar Assn., Cin. Bar Assn., Am. Immigration Lawyers Assn. (chmn. Ohio chpt. 1987-88, 90-93), Potter Stewart Inn of Ct., Order of Coif. Home: 3820 Eileen Dr Cincinnati OH 45209-2013 Office: 1800 US Bank Tower Cincinnati OH 45202 Office Phone: 513-357-9393.

ZAVIS, MICHAEL WILLIAM, lawyer; b. Chgo., Apr. 19, 1937; s. Herbert and Ruth (Kanes) Z.; m. Joan Gordon, June 1960; children: Amy Zavis Perlmutter, Cathy. BS, U. Pa., Wharton, 1958; JD, U. Chgo., 1961. Bar. Ill., U.S. Dist. (no. dist.) Ill., U.S. Ct. Appeals (7th cir.). Assoc. Peebles, Greenberg & Keele, Chgo., 1961-63, Greenberger, Krauss & Jacobs, Chgo., 1964-69; ptnr. Goldberg, Weigle, Mallin & Gitles, Chgo., 1969-74, Katten, Muchin & Zavis, Chgo., 1974—. Bd. dirs. Ill. Devel. Fin. Authority; mem. adv. com. Sch. Social Svcs. U. Chgo. Editor U. Chgo. Law Rev., 1960-61. Fellow ABA, Ill. State Bar Assn., Chgo. Bar Assn.; mem. Bryn Mawr Country Club (Lincolnwood, Ill.) (past pres.), Standard Club, Boca Rio Country Club. Office: Katten Muchin & Zavis 525 W Monroe St Ste 1600 Chicago IL 60661-3693

ZAWADA, EDWARD THADDEUS, JR., physician, educator; b. Chgo., Oct. 3, 1947; s. Edward Thaddeus and Evelyn Mary (Kovarek) Z.; m. Nancy Ann Stephen, Mar. 26, 1977; children: Elizabeth, Nicholas, Victoria, Alexandra. BS summa cum laude, Loyola U., Chgo., 1969; MD summa cum laude, Loyola-Stritch Sch. Medicine, 1973. Diplomate Am. Bd. Internal Medicine, Am. Bd. Nephrology, Am. Bd. Nutrition, Am. Bd. Critical Care, Am. Bd. Geriatrics, Am. Bd. Clin. Pharm., Am. Bd. Forensic Examiners, Am. Bd. Forensic Medicine; specialist Hypertension, Am. Soc. Hypertension. Intern UCLA Hosp., 1973, resident, 1974-76; asst. prof. medicine UCLA, 1978-79, U. Utah, Salt Lake City, 1979-81; assoc. prof. medicine Med. Coll. Va., Richmond, 1981-83; assoc. prof. medicine, physiology & pharmacology U. SD Sch. Medicine, Sioux Falls, 1983-86, Freeman prof., chmn. dept. Internal Medicine, 1987—2002, prof. emeritus, 2002—, chief div. nephrology and hypertension, 1983-88, pres. univ. physician's practice plan, 1992—95; v.p. sci. affairs, dir. dialysis, critical care Avera Health Sys., 2002—04, dir. e-icu, 2004—. Chief renal sect. Salt Lake VA Med. Ctr., 1980-81; asst. chief med. service McGuire VA Med. Ctr., Richmond, 1981-83. Editor: Geriatric ephrology and Urology, 1984; contbr. articles to profl. publs. Pres. Minnehaha div. Am. Heart Assn., 1984-87, pres. Dakota affiliate Am. Heart Assn., 1989-91. VA Hosp. System grantee, 1981-85, 85-88; Health and Human Svcs. grantee Pub. Health Scvs. Rsch. Adminstrn. Bureau Health Profl., 1993—. Master ACP; fellow Am. Coll. Chest Physicians, Am. Coll. Nutrition, Am. Coll. Clin. Pharmacology, Internat. Coll. Angiology, Am. Coll. Angiology, Am. Coll. Clin. Pharmacology, Am. Coll. Forensic Examiners, Royal Soc. Medicine, Soc. for Vascular Medicine and Biology, Am. Soc. Nephrology, Am. Geriatric Soc.; mem. Internat. Soc. Nephrology, Am. Soc. Pharmacology and Exptl. Therapeutics, Am. Physiol. Soc., Am. Inst. Nutrition, Am. Soc. Clin. Nutrition, Am. Soc. Transplant Physicians, Westward Ho Country Club. Democrat. Roman Catholic. Avocations: golf, tennis, skiing, cinema, music. Home: 2908 S Duchess Ave Sioux Falls SD 57103-4826 Office: North Central Kidney Inst 1001 E 21st St Ste 300 Sioux Falls SD 57105-1017 Office Phone: 605-322-5800. E-mail: ezawada@sio.micko.net, edward.zawada@mckennan.org.

ZDUN, JAMES J., finance executive; V.p. fin. adminstrn. Holophane a divsn. of Nat. Svc. Industries, 1999—. Office: 250 E Broad St Ste 1400 Columbus OH 43215-3775

ZEALEY, SHARON JANINE, lawyer; b. St. Paul, Aug. 30, 1959; d. Marion Edward and Freddie Zealey. BS, Xavier U. of La., 1981; JD, U. Cin., 1984. Bar: Ohio 1984; U.S. Dist. Ct. (so. dist.) Ohio 1985; U.S. Ct. Appeals (6th cir.) 1990; U.S. Supreme Ct. 1990. Law clk. US Atty. S. Dist. Ohio, Cin., 1982; trust adminstr. US Bank (formerly First Nat. Bank), Cin., 1984-86; atty. UAW Legal Svcs., Cin., 1986-88; assoc. Manley, Burke, Lipton & Fischer, Cin., 1988-91; mng. atty. and dep. atty. gen. Ohio Atty. Gen. Office, Cin., 1991-95; asst. US atty. criminal div. for So. Dist. Ohio US Attys. Office, Cin., 1995-97; United States atty. So. Dist. Ohio, Cin., 1997—2001; ptnr. Blank Rome LLP, 2001—06; sr. litig. counsel Coca-Cola Co., Atlanta, 2006—. Adj. instr. Coll. Law U. Cin., 1997—; mem. U.S. Atty. Gen.'s Adv. Com., 1999—2001, chair civil rights subcom., 2001; mem. merit selection com. Sixth Cir. Ct. of Appeals Bankruptcy Ct., 1992—96, 2003. Mem. commn. Cin. Cmty. Action Now, 2001—; commr. Tall Stacks Commn., City of Cin., 1990—94, Mayor's Commn. on Children,

City of Cin., 1992—94; mem. equal employment adv. rev. panel City of Cin., 1989—91; trustee, bd. visitors U. Cin. Coll. Law, 1992—2006; trustee Legal Aid Soc. Cin., 1987—92; bd. dirs. Freestore Foodbank, 2003—, Playhouse in the Park, 2002—06, Nat. Inst. for Law and Equity, 2002—; co-chair Greater Cin. Minority Counsel Program, 2005—06; mem. exec. bd. Cin. Youth Collaborative, 2005—06. Named Career Woman of Achievement, Cin. YWCA, 1988; named one of Top Ten Women Attys., Women's Bus. Cin., 2005; named to Super Lawyers, Ohio, 2006; recipient Disting. Alumni award, Friends of Women's Studies, U. Cin., 2001, Theodore M. Berry award for outstanding achievement in politics and in svc. to cmty., Cin. chpt. NACCP, 1998, Nicholas Longworth III Alumni Achievement award for disting. pub. svc., U. Cin. Coll. Law, 1997. Mem. Black Lawyers Assn. of Cin. (pres. 1989-91, round table 1988-), Legal Aid Soc. (sec. 1991-92), ABA, Fed. Bar Assn., Ohio Bar Assn., Nat. Bar Assn. (bd. govs. 1988-1990, Mem. of Yr. region VI 1990), Cin. Bar Assn. (trustee 1989-94), Cin. CAN Commn. Democrat. Episcopalian. Office: Coca-Cola Co One Coca-Cola Plz NAT 2062 PO Box 1734 Atlanta GA 30301 Office Phone: 404-676-2121. Business E-Mail: zealey@blankRome.com.

ZECK, VAN, federal agency administrator; b. Morgantown, W.Va. BS, W.Va. U., 1970. With U.S. Dept. Treas., 1971—, various positions in data processing, marketable securities ops., adminstrn., with bur. internal audit staff; asst. commr. financing Bur. Pub. Debt U.S. Dept. Treas., 1982—87, dep. commr., 1987—98, commr., 1998—. Office: US Dept Treas Bur Pub Debt PO Box 7015 Parkersburg WV 26106

ZEDLER, JOY BUSWELL, ecological sciences educator; b. Sioux Falls, SD, Oct. 15, 1943; d. Francis H. and Charlotte (Johnson) Buswell; m. Paul H. Zedler, June 26, 1965; children: Emily and Sarah (twins). BS, Augustana Coll., 1964; MS, U. Wis., 1966, PhD, 1968. Instr. U. Mo., Columbia, 1968-69; prof. San Diego State U., 1969-97; Aldo Leopold prof. restoration ecology, arboretum, botany U. Wis., Madison, 1998—. Mem. Nat. Wetland Tech. Com., Water Sci. Tech. Bd. Nat. Rsch. Coun., 1991-94; dir. Pacific Estuarine Rsch. Lab., 1985—, Coastal and Marine Inst., 1991-93; gov. bd. The Nature Conservancy, 1995—; trustee Environ. Def. Fund, 1998—. Author: Ecology of Southern California Coastal Wetlands, 1982, Salt Marsh Restoration, 1984; co-author: A Manual for Assessing atural and Restored Wetlands, 1990, Ecology of Tijuana Estuary, 1992, Tidal Wetland Restoration, 1996; editor: Handbook for Restoring Tidal Wetlands, 2000. Fellow San Diego Natural History Mus.; mem. Ecol. Soc. Am. (mem. pub. affairs com. 1988-90), Soc. Wetlands Scientists, Soc. Ecol. Restoration. Achievements include pioneering studies of impacts of freshwater inflows to coastal wetlands in southwestern U.S. and Australia; contributions to understanding of coastal wetland functioning; development of methods for improving restoration projects in wetlands; identification of shortcomings of wetland restoration projects; role of diversity in the function restored ecosystems, improving the science of restoration ecology. Office: U Wis Botany Dept Madison WI 53706

ZEFFREN, EUGENE, cosmetics executive; b. St. Louis, Nov. 21, 1941; s. Harry Morris and Bess (Dennis) Z.; m. Steccia Leigh Stern, Feb. 2, 1964; children: Maryl Renee, Bradley Cruvant. AB, Washington U., 1963; MS, U. Chgo., 1965, PhD, 1967. Research chemist Procter & Gamble Co., Cin., 1967-75, sect. head, 1975-77, assoc. dir., 1977-79; v.p. R & D, Helene Curtis, Inc., Chgo., 1979-95; pres. Helene Curtis USA, Chgo., 1995-96; sr. v.p. Helene Curtis bus. unit Unilever Home and Personal Care USA, Chgo., 1996-98, exec. v.p., COO hair and deodorant bus. unit, 1998-2000; sr. v.p. brand devel. Unilever Home and Personal Care .Am., 2000—02; chmn. NFG Stuff, LLC, 2002—07; CEO AG Brands, LLC, 2005—. Mem. vis. com. for phys. scis. U. Chgo., 1997-06; active Wash. U. Nat. Coun. for Arts and Scis., 1997—; pres. bd. dirs. River North Dance Co., 1998-2000, chmn. 2000-04. Co-author: The Study of Enzyme Mechanisms, 1973; contbr. articles to profl. jours. Bd. dirs. Goodman Theatre, 1999—, Children's Meml. Rsch. Ctr., 2002—05; trustee Spertus Inst. Jewish Studies, 2002—. Recipient award, Cosmetic Ingredient Buyers and Suppliers, 1990. Mem. AAAS, Am. Chem. Soc., Soc. Cosmetic Chemists, Cosmetic Toiletry and Fragrance Assn. (sci. adv. com. 1979-95, vice chmn. 1984-88, chmn. 1988-90, bd. dirs. 1996-02), Soap and Detergent Assn. (bd. dirs., exec. com. bd. 2000-02), Indsl. Rsch. Inst., Omicron Delta Kappa. Democrat. Jewish. Achievements include patents in field of enzymes and hair care. Avocations: tennis, skiing, reading adventure and espionage novels.

ZEIKUS, J. GREGORY, microbiologist, educator; BA, U. S.Fla., 1967; MS, Indiana U., 1968, PhD, 1970; D of Honoris Causa in Applied Biol. Scis. (hon.), U. Gent, Belgium, 1992. Postdoctoral fellow Lab. Thermal Biology USPHS, W. Yellowstone, Mont., 1970; NIH postdoctoral fellow dept. microbiology U. Ill., Urbana-Champaign; from asst. to assoc. prof. dept. bacteriology U. Wis., Madison, 1972—80, prof. dept. bacteriology, 1980—84; prof. biochemistry Mich. State U., E. Lansing, 1984—86, prof. microbiology and biochemistry, 1986—; exec. dir. Mich. Biotechnology Inst., E. Lansing, 1984—86; pres. MBI Internat., E. Lansing, 1986—2002, v.p. tech. acquisition and pres. emeritus, 2002—. Grantee, U.S. Dept. Energy, 1980—, U.S. Dept. Agr., 1989—, 1996—99, NSF, 1995—98. Office: Dept Microbiology and Molecular Genetics Mich State U 410 Biochemistry East Lansing MI 48824

ZEILSTRA, DAVID C., lawyer, transportation executive; BA, Wheaton Coll., 1990; JD, Duke U., 1994. Assoc. Mayer, Brown & Platt, 1994—96; asst. gen. counsel Hub Group, Inc., Downers Grove, Ill., 1996—99, v.p., gen. counsel, sec., 1999—. Office: Hub Group Inc 3050 Highland Parkway, Ste 100 Downers Grove IL 60515-5543 Office Phone: 630-271-3600. E-mail: dzeilstra@hubgroup.com.

ZEKMAN, PAMELA LOIS, reporter; b. Chgo., Oct. 22, 1944; d. Theodore Nathan and Lois Jane (Bernstein) Z.; m. Fredric Soll, Nov. 29, 1975. BA, U. Calif., Berkeley, 1965. Social worker Dept. Public Aid Cook County, Chgo., 1965-66; reporter City News Bur., Chgo., 1966-70, Chgo. Tribune, 1970-75, Chgo. Sun-Times, 1975-81; investigative reporter Sta. WBBM-TV, Chgo., 1981—. Recipient Pulitzer Prize awarded to Chicago Tribune for gen. local reporting on vote fraud series, 1973; Community Service award for vote fraud series UPI, 1972; Feature Series award for nursing home abuses series AP, 1971; Pub. Service award for slumlord series UPI, 1973; Newswriting award AP, 1973; In Depth Reporting award for police brutality series AP, 1974; Investigative Reporting awards Inland Daily Press Assn., 1974, 78; Investigative Reporting award for series on city waste AP, 1975; Pulitzer Prize for pub. service for series on hosp. abuses, 1976; Investigative Reporting award for series on baby selling, 1976; Pub. Service award for series on currency exchange abuses UPI, 1976; Investigative Reporting award for series on abuses in home for retarded children AP, 1977; Soc. Midland Authors Golden Rake award; UPI Public Service award; Ill. AP award; Nat. Headliners Club award; Sweepstakes award for Mirage Tavern investigative project, 1978; Nat. Disting. Service award for series on med. abuses in abortion clinics Sigma Delta Chi, 1979; named Journalist of Yr. No. Ill. U., 1979; recipient George Foster Peabody Broadcasting award, 1982, 85, RTNDA Investigative Reporting award, 1983, DuPont Columbia award 1982, 87. Office: WBBM-TV 630 N McClurg Ct Chicago IL 60611-4495

ZELICKSON, SUE, newspaper and cookbook editor, television reporter and host, food consultant; b. Mpls., Sept. 13, 1934; d. Harry M. and Bernice (Gross) Zipperman; m. Alvin S. Zelickson, Aug. 21, 1956; children— Barry M., Brian D. B.S. in Edn., U. Minn., 1956. Cert. elem. tchr., S.C., Minn. Tchr. various schs. Mpls., S.C., Golden Valley, Minn., 1956-79; writer, editor, columnist Mpls.-St. Paul Mag., 1980—, Buylines, Mpls., 1984—; TV-radio reporter Sta. WCCO-KSTP, Mpls, 1980—, Lifestyles with Sue Zelickson Sta. WCCO cable; restaurant developer, cons. Mpls., 1978—; v.p. Passage Tours, Mpls., 1984-88. Coordinator, editor: Much Ado About Food, 1978; Minnesota Heritage Cookbook, 1979; Lee Ann Chin's Chinese Cuisine, 1981; Collins Back Room Cooking Secrets, 1981; The Governor's Table Cookbook, 1981; Chocolate Days & Chocolate ights, 1982; Food for Show, Food on the Go, 1983; Wild Rice Star of The North, 1985; Look What's Cooking Now, 1985. Contbr. articles to Sun Newspaper, Post Publs., Mpls., Tribune. Public relations, promoter, fundraiser Mpls. Boys & Girls Club, Mpls. Inst. Arts, Hennepin County Med. Soc. Aux., Ronald McDonald House, Bonaventure Mall, Women's Assn. Minn. Symphony Orchestra, Council Jewish Women, Mt. Sinai Hosp., Brandeis U. Women, Minn. Opera Assn., Guthrie Theatre, Sholom Home, Am. Cancer Soc., M.S. Soc., March of Dimes, Am. Heart Assn.; bd. dirs. U. Minn. Alumni Bd., Golden Valley State Bank. Recipient Outstanding Achievement award There's Living Proof Am. Cancer Soc., Duluth, Minn., 1984; Outstanding Achievement award Boys & Girls Club Minn., 1984. Mem. Nat. Council Jewish Women, Women's Assn. Minn. Orch., numerous others. Avocations: reading, travel; writing; painting. Home and Office: 101 Ardmore Dr Minneapolis MN 55422-5209

ZELINSKY, DANIEL, mathematics professor; b. Chgo., Nov. 22, 1922; s. Isaac and Ann (Ruttenberg) Z.; m. Zelda Oser, Sept. 23, 1945; children: Mara Sachs, Paul O., David. BS, U. Chgo., 1941, MS, 1943, PhD, 1946. Rsch. mathematician applied math group Columbia U., NYC, 1944-45; instr. U. Chgo., 1943-44, 46-47; Nat. Rsch. Coun. fellow Inst. Advanced Study, Princeton, NJ, 1947-49; from asst. to assoc. prof. dept. math. Northwestern U., Evanston, Ill., 1949-60, prof., 1960-93, prof. emeritus, 1993—, acting chmn. math. dept., 1959-60, chmn., 1975-78. Vis. prof. U. Calif. Berkeley, 1960, Fla. State U., Tallahassee, 1963, Hebrew U., Jerusalem, 1970-71, 85, others; vis. scholar Tata Inst., 1979; mem. various coms. Northwestern U.; lectr. in field. Author: A First Course in Linear Algebra, 1968, rev. edit., 1973; contbr. articles to profl. jours. Fulbright grantee Kyoto U., 1955-56, grantee NSF, 1958-80; Guggenheim fellow Inst. Advanced Study, 1956-57, Indo-Am. fellow, 1978-79. Fellow AAAS (mem. nominating com. sect. A 1977-80, chmn. elect sect. A 1984-85, chmn. 1985-86, retiring chmn. 1986-87), Am. Math. Soc. (mem. coun. 1961-67, editor Transactions of A.M.S. 1961-67, mem. various coms., mem. editorial bd. Notices of A.M.S. 1983-86, chmn. editorial bds. com. 1989, chmn. ad hoc com. 1991-92). Jewish. Home: 613 Hunter Rd Wilmette IL 60091-2213 Office: Northwestern U Dept Math Evanston IL 60208-0001 Business E-Mail: dz@northwestern.edu.

ZELL, SAMUEL, real estate company executive, publishing executive; b. Chgo., Sept. 28, 1941; s. Bernard Zell; m. Helen Zell; 3 children. BA, U. Mich., 1963, JD, 1966, LLD (hon.), 2005. With Yates Holleb and Michelson, 1966-68; co-founder, pres. Equity Fin. & Mgmt. Co., Chgo., 1968—76; chmn., pres. Equity Group Investments, LLC (formerly Equity Fin. & Mgmt. Co.), Chgo., 1976—; chmn. Great Am. Mgmt. and Investment Inc., 1981—; co-chmn. Revco D.S.; owner Chgo. Cubs, 2007—; chmn., CEO Tribune Co., 2007—. Chmn. Delta Queen Steamboat Co., New Orleans, 1984—, Eagle Industries Inc.; chmn. Itel Corp., 1985—, Nat. Assn. Real Estate Investment Trusts, 1998-2000; bd. dirs. The Tribune Co., 2007-Named one of Forbes' Richest Americans, 2006, World's Richest People, Forbes Mag., 2005—, 50 Who Matter Now, Business 2.0, 2007. Republican. Avocations: racquetball, skiing. Office: Equity International Two N Riverside Plz Ste 700 Chicago IL 60606 also: Tribune Co 435 N Mich Ave Chicago IL 60611

ZELLER, JOSEPH PAUL, advertising executive; b. Crestline, Ohio, Mar. 19, 1940; s. Paul Edward and Grace Beatrice (Kinstle) Z.; m. Nancy Jane Schmidt, June 17, 1961; children: Laurie, Joe. BA, U. Notre Dame, 1962; MFA, Ohio U., 1963. Mgr.radio/television Drewrys Ltd. USA, Inc., South Bend, Ind., 1963-64; media supr. Tatham-Laird & Kudner, Chgo., 1964-67; v.p. assoc. media dir. J. Walter Thompson Co., Chgo., 1967-77; v.p. media dir, v.p. Campbell-Mithun, Chgo., 1977-80; sr. v.p., dir. media, fin., chmn. media coun. D'Arcy Masius Benton & Bowles, Chgo., 1980-96, sr. v.p., 1996-2000; pres. Fox River Trading Co., East Dundee, Ill., 2000—. Chmn. Z Prop, 1986—; dir. circle Desert Caballeros Mus., 1994-96; founder Native Am. Images web mag., 1999. Pres. Amateur Hockey Assn. Ill., 1985. Named to Ill. Hockey Hall of Fame, 2005. Mem. Broadcast Pioneers, Chgo. Advt. Club, Moose. Roman Catholic. Avocations: hockey, photography, music. Business E-Mail: trader@rivertradingpost.com.

ZELLER, MARILYNN KAY, retired librarian; b. Scottsbluff, Nebr., Mar. 1, 1940; d. William Harold and Dorothy Elizabeth (Wilkins) Richards; m. Robert Jerome Zeller, May 21, 1966; children: Kevin Jerome and Renae Kay. BS, Calvary Bible Coll., 1985; MLS, U. Mo., Columbia, 1989. Cert. libr. File clk. Waddell & Reed, Kansas City, Mo., 1962-65; payroll clk. Century Fin. Co., Kansas City, Mo., 1965-67, Percy Kent Bag Co., Independence, Mo., 1968-70; accounts receivable Swansons on the Plaza, Kansas City, 1971-73; clk. casualty ins. Mill Mutuals, Kansas City, 1977-80; registrar's asst. Calvary Bible Coll., Kansas City, 1980-85, libr. asst., 1985-88, asst. libr., 1988-89, head libr., 1990—96. Chairperson libr. com. Calvary Bible Coll., Kansas City, 1990-96; libr. rep. Friends of the Hilda Kroeker Libr., Kansas City, 1990-96. Author: History of the Christian Librarian's Association, 1989. Mem. Christian Librs. Assn. Avocations: walking, reading, crocheting, sewing, swimming. Home: 401 13th Ave N Greenwood MO 64034-9750

ZELLNER, ARNOLD, economics, econometrics and statistics professor; b. Bklyn., Jan. 2, 1927; s. Israel and Doris (Kleiman) Z.; m. Agnes Marie Sumares, June 20, 1953; children— David S., Philip A., Samuel N., Daniel A., Michael A. AB in Physics, Harvard U., Cambridge, Mass., 1949; PhD in Econs., U. Calif., Berkeley, 1957; D (hon.), U. Autonoma de Madrid, 1986, Tecnia de Lisboa, Portugal, 1991, U. Kiel, Germany, 1998, Erasmus U., Rotterdam, Netherlands, 2006. Asst., then assoc. prof. econs. U. Wash., 1955-60; Fulbright vis. prof. Netherlands Sch. Econs., Rotterdam, 1960-61; assoc. prof., then prof. econs. U. Wis., 1961-66; H.G.B. Alexander disting. service prof. econs. and statistics U. Chgo., 1966-96, prof. emeritus, 1996—; dir. H.G.B. Alexander Rsch. Found., 1973—. Cons. Battelle Meml. Inst., 1964—71; vis. rsch. prof. U. Calif., Berkeley, 1971, vis. prof., 1997—2007, Am. U., Cairo, 1997, Hebrew U., 1997; trustee Nat. Opinion Rsch. Corp., 1973—80; bd. dirs. Nat. Bur. Econ. Rsch., 1980—; seminar leader NSF-NBER Seminar on Bayesian Inference in Econometrics and Stats., 1970—95. Co-author: Systems Simulation for Regional Analysis, 1969, Estimating the Parameters of the Markov Probability Model, 1970; author: Bayesian Inference in Econometrics, 1971, Basic Issues in Econometrics, 1984, Bayesian Analysis in Econometrics and Statistics: The Zellner View and Papers, 1997, Statistics, Econometrics and Forecasting, 2004; editor: Economic Statistics and Econometrics, 1968, Seasonal Analysis of Economic Time Series, 1978, Simplicity, Inference and Modelling, 2001; assoc. editor: Econometrica, 1962-68; founding co-editor: Jour. Econometrics, 1972—; co-editor Studies in Bayesian Econometrics and Statistics, 1975, The Economics of Marine Resources, 2001, The Structural Econometrics, Time Series Analysis Approach, 2004; founding editor ASA Jour. Bus. and Econ. Stats., 1983; contbr. articles to profl. jours. Pres. Leonard J. Savage Meml. Trust Fund, Chgo., 1977-2000. Fellow AAAS, Am. Acad. Arts and Scis., Am. Econ. Assn., Internat. Inst. Forecasters, Econometric Soc., Am. Statis. Assn. (pres. elect 1990—, pres. 1991—, chmn. bus. and econs. sect. 1980, chmn. Bayesian statis. sci. sect. 1993); mem. Internat. Statis. Inst., Internat. Soc. Bayesian Analysis (co-pres. 1993, pres. 1994-96, Founders award 1998), Soc. Actuaries (trustee, rsch. found., 1994-98). Avocations: golf, tennis, travel, theater, music. Home: 5628 S Dorchester Ave Chicago IL 60637-1722 Office: U Chgo Grad Sch Bus 5807 S Woodlawn Ave Chicago IL 60637-1511 Business E-Mail: arnold.zellner@chicagogsb.edu.

ZELMAN, SUSAN TAVE, school system administrator; m. Allan Zelman; 3 children. DEd, U. Mich.; D in Pub. Edn. (hon.), U. Rio Grande, Ohio; D in Humanities (hon.), Youngstown U. Assoc. prof. edn. Emmanuel Coll., Boston, chair dept. edn.; assoc. commr. ednl. dept. personnel Mass. Dept. Edn., 1988—94; dep. commr. Mo. Dept. Elem. and Secondary Edn., Jefferson City, 1994—99; supt. pub. instrn. Ohio Dept Edn., Columbus, 1999—. Rschr. Edn. Tech. Ctr. Harvard Grad. Sch. Edn. Recipient Nat. Sci. Rsch. Opportunity award, Columbus Tchrs. Coll. Office: Ohio Dept Edn 25 S Front St Columbus OH 43215-4183

ZEMM, SANDRA PHYLLIS, lawyer; b. Chgo., Aug. 18, 1947; d. Walter Stanley and Bernice Phyllis (Churas) Z. BS, U. Ill., 1969; JD, Fla. State U., Tallahassee, 1974. Bar: Fla. 74, Ill. 75. With fin. dept. Sinclair Oil, Chgo., 1969-70; indsl. rels. advisor Conco Inc., Mendota, Ill., 1970-72; assoc. Seyfarth, Shaw, Fairweather & Geraldson, Chgo., 1975-82, ptnr., 1982—. Mem. Art Inst. Alliance, Chgo., 1993—97, 2006—; bd. dirs. Chgo. Residential Inc., 1995—97, pres., 1995—97. Mem. Ill. State Bar Assn., Fla. State Bar Assn., Univ. Club Chgo. (bd. dirs. 1991-94); Nat. Coll. of Labor and Employment Lawyers. Office: Seyfarth Shaw LLP 831 S Dearborn St Ste 2400 Chicago IL 60603-5577

ZENNER, SHELDON TOBY, lawyer; b. Chgo., Jan. 11, 1953; s. Max and Clara (Goldner) Z.; m. Ellen June Morgan, Sept. 2, 1984; children: Elie, Nathaniel. BA, Northwestern U., 1974, JD, 1978. Bar: U.S. Dist. Ct. (no. dist.) Ill. 1978. Assoc. Shadur, Krupp & Miller, Chgo., 1978-80; law clk. to judge U.S. Dist. Ct. (no. dist.) Ill., Chgo., 1980-81; asst. U.S. atty., dep. chief spl. prosecutions div. No. Dist. of Ill., Chgo., 1981-89; ptnr. Katten Muchin Rosenman LLP, Chgo., 1989—. Adj. faculty Medill Sch. Journalism, Northwestern U., 1982-89, Sch. of Law, 1986—; mem. practitioners adv. com. U.S. Sentencing Commn.; mem. editl. adv. bd. Northwestern U. Magazine. Mem. Phi Beta Kappa. Office: Katten Muchin Rosenman LLP 525 W Monroe St Chicago IL 60661-3693 Office Phone: 312-902-5476. Business E-Mail: sheldon.zenner@kattenlaw.com.

ZEPF, THOMAS HERMAN, retired physics professor; b. Cin., Feb. 13, 1935; s. Paul A. and Agnes J. (Schulz) Z. BS summa cum laude, Xavier U., 1957; MS, St. Louis U., 1960, PhD, 1963. Asst. prof. physics Creighton U., Omaha, 1962-67, assoc. prof., 1967-75, prof., 1975—2002, prof. emeritus, 2002—, acting chmn. dept. physics, 1963-66, chmn., 1966-73, 81-93, coord. allied health programs, 1975-76, coord. pre-health scis. advising, 1976-81. Cons. physicist VA Hosp., Omaha, 1966-71; vis. prof. physics St. Louis U., 1973-74; program evaluator Am. Coun. on Edn., 1988-2002. Contbr. articles and abstracts to Surface Sci., Bull. Am. Phys. Soc., Proceedings Nebr. Acad. Sci., The Physics Tchr. Jour., others. Recipient Cert. Recognition award, Phi Beta Kappa U. Cin. chpt., 1953. Mem. Am. Phys. Soc., Am. Assn. Physics Tchrs. (pres. Nebr. sect. 1978), Nebr. Acad. Sci. (life, chmn. physics sect. 1985-05), Internat. Brotherhood Magicians, Soc. Am. Magicians (pres. assembly #7, 1964-65), KC, Sigma Xi (Achievement award for rsch. St. Louis chpt. 1963, pres. Omaha chpt. 1993-94), Sigma Pi Sigma. Roman Catholic. Office: Creighton U Dept Physics Omaha NE 68178-0001 Home Phone: 402-558-3125. Business E-Mail: thzepf@creighton.edu.

ZEPNICK, JOSH, state official; b. Mar. 21, 1968; married. MA, U. Minn., 1998. Congl. and legis. aide; mem. Wis. State Assembly, Madison, 2002—, mem. fin. instns. com., govt. ops. and spending limitations com., energy and utilities com., workforce devel. com. Democrat. Office: State Capitol Rm 418 North PO Box 8953 Madison WI 53708-8953

ZHANG, YOUXUE, geology educator; b. Huarong County, Hunan, China, Sept. 17, 1957; came to U.S., 1983; s. Zaiyi Zhang and Dezhen Wu; m. Zhengjiu Xu; children: Dan, Ray. BS in Geol. Scis., Peking U., Beijing, 1982; MA in Geol. Scis., Columbia U., 1985, MPhil, 1987, PhD in Geol. Scis., 1989. Grad. rsch. asst. Columbia U., NYC, 1983-88; postdoctoral fellow Calif. Inst. Tech., 1988-91; asst. prof. geology U. Mich., Ann Arbor, 1991-97, assoc. prof., 1997—2004, prof., 2004—. Contbr. articles to profl. jours. Named Young Investigator, NSF, 1994. Fellow: AAAS, Geol. Soc. Am.; mem.: Am. Geophys. Union, Geochem. Soc. (F.W. Clarke medal 1993), Mineral. Soc. Am., Sigma Xi. Office: Dept Geol Sci U Mich Ann Arbor MI 48109-1005 E-mail: youxue@umich.edu.

ZHAO, JIA, lawyer; b. Shanghai, Sept. 23, 1940; came to U.S., 1980; BA, Beijing Fgn. Studies U., 1963; JD, Harvard U., 1983. Bar: Ill. 1985, D.C. 1986. U.S. desk officer dept. Am. and Oceanic Affairs, Fgn. Ministry People's Republic of China, 1972; atty. Arnold & Porter, Washington, Covington & Burling, Washington, Pillsbury, Madison & Sutro, San Francisco; 1st sec. dept. treaty and law, Am. and oceanic affairs Chinese Fgn. Ministry, 1986—88; with Baker & McKenzie, Chgo., 1988—, ptnr., 1994—. Mem. ABA, D.C. Bar, Chgo. Bar Assn., Beijing Fgn. Econ. Law Assn. Office: Baker and McKenzie One Prudential Plz 130 E Randolph Dr Chicago IL 60601

ZICHEK, SHANNON ELAINE, retired secondary school educator; b. Lincoln, Nebr., May 29, 1944; d. Melvin Eddie and Dorothy Virginia (Patrick) Zichek. AA, York Coll., ebr., 1965; BA, U. Nebr., Kearney, 1968, postgrad., 1980—82, U. Nebr., 1989, postgrad., 1992, U. Okla., Edmond, 1970—75. Tchr. history and English, N.W. H.S., Grand Island, Nebr., 1968—99, ret., 1999. Republican. Home: 2730 N North Rd Grand Island NE 68803-1143

ZICKUS, ANNE, state legislator; b. Apr. 6, 1939; m. Charles Zickus, 1958; children: Kathy, Chuck. Alderman City of Palos Hills, Ill., 1973-75; state rep. Dist. 47, Ill., 1989-90, Dist. 48, Ill., 1993—; dir. Ill. State Crime Commn., 1997. Dir. Helping Hand Rehab. Ctr., 1995—. Mem. Suburban Assn. Realtors, at. Assn. Realtors. Republican. Home: 7909 W 112th St Palos Hills IL 60465-2731

ZIEGELBAUER, ROBERT F., state legislator; b. Aug. 26, 1951; BA, Notre Dame; MS, U. Pa. Mem. Manitowoc County Bd., City Coun., fin. dir.; now mem. dist. 25 Wis. State Assembly, 1992—; owner of retail music shop. Democrat. Home: 1213 S 8th St Manitowoc WI 54220-5311 Office: Wis Assembly PO Box 8952 Madison WI 53708-8952

ZIEGENHAGEN, DAVID MACKENZIE, retired health facility administrator, not-for-profit developer; b. Mpls., May 25, 1936; s. Elmer Herbert Ziegenhagen and Margaret Ruth (Mackenzie) Kruger; m. Mary Ange Kinsella, Nov. 26, 1966 (div. Dec. 1982); children: Marc, Eric; m. Mary Kinsella, Feb. 7, 2002. BA in Mass. Comm., Political Sci., U. Minn, 1961. Reporter WCCO-TV, Mpls., 1956—61; assoc. dir. Thailand Peace Corps, Bangkok, 1963-65, Thailand program officer Washington, 1965—67, dir. Western Samoa Apia, 1967-70; exec. dir. Mental Health Assn. Minn., 1970-76; co-founder, pres. Current Newspapers, Inc., Burnsville, Minn., 1975-84; sr. program officer The St. Paul Found., 1982—85; pres. DMZ Assocs., Cloverdale, Calif., 2000—; exec. dir. Minn. Bd. Med. Practice, St. Paul, 1985-88; CEO, pres. Stratis Health, Bloomington, Minn., 1988-2000. Democrat. Avocations: travel, international development, arts.

ZIEGLER, ANN E., retail executive; b. 1958; BA, Coll. William and Mary; JD, U. Chgo. With Skadden, Arps, Slate, Meagher & Flom; asst. counsel Sara Lee Corp., 1993—94, exec. dir. corp. devel., 1994—2000, v.p., 1997—2000, sr. v.p. corp. devel., 2000—01, sr. v.p. mergers and acquisitions, 2001—, CFO bakery group, 2003—, sr. v.p. adminstrn. bakery group. Bd. dirs. Unitrin, Inc. Office: Sara Lee Corp 3 First Nat Plaza Chicago IL 60602-4260

ZIEGLER, DEWEY KIPER, neurologist, educator; b. Omaha, May 31, 1920; s. Isidor and Pearl (Kiper) Z.; m. Mar. 30, 1954; children: Amy, Laura, Sara. BA, Harvard U., 1941, MD, 1945. Diplomate Am. Bd. Psychiatry and Neurology (bd. dirs. 1974-83, exec. com. 1978-82). Intern in medicine Boston City Hosp., 1945-46; asst. resident then chief resident in neurology N.Y. Neurol. Inst.-Columbia U. Coll. Physicians and Surgeons, 1948-51; resident in psychiatry Boston Psychopathic Hosp., 1951-53; asst. chief neurol. service Montefiore Hosp., NYC; and asst. prof. neurology Columbia U., 1953-55; asst. prof. U. Minn., 1955-56; asso. clin. prof. U. Kans. Med. Sch., 1956-64, chief dept. neurology, 1968-85; prof. U. Kans. Med. Center, 1964-89, prof. emeritus, 1989—. Cons. Social Security Adminstrn., 1975—; mem. com. on certification and co-certification Am. Bd. Med. Specialties, 1979-82 Author: In Divided and Distinguished Worlds, 1942; Contbr. numerous articles to profl. jours. Served to lt., j.g., M.C. USNR, 1946-48. Fellow Am. Acad. Neurology (pres. 1979-81); mem. AMA, Am. Neurol. Assn. (v.p. 1972-73), Am. Headache Assn. Jewish. Home: 8347 Delmar Ln Shawnee Mission KS 66207-1821 Office: Kans U Med Ctr 3900 Rainbow Blvd Kansas City KS 66103-2918 Home Phone: 913-648-7244.

ZIEGLER, DONALD N., state senator; b. Mar. 6, 1949; m. Joyce Ziegler; 2 children. Mem. dist. 26 Minn. Senate, St. Paul, 1999—. Republican. Home: 4915 400th Ave Blue Earth MN 56013-6204

ZIEGLER, EKHARD ERICH, pediatrics educator; b. Saalfelden, Austria, Apr. 12, 1940; children: Stefan, Gabriele, Lena. MD, U. Innsbruck, Austria, 1964. Diplomate: Am. Bd. Pediatrics. Intern U. Innsbruck, 1966-67, resident in pediatrics, 1967-68 70-71, resident in pharmacology, 1964-66, asst. dept. pediatrics, 1970-73; vis. instr. pediatrics U. Iowa, Iowa City, 1968-70, asst. prof. pediatrics, 1973-76, assoc. prof., 1976-81, prof., 1981—. Mem. nutrition study sect. NIH, 1988-92. Recipient Nutrition award Am. Acad. Pediatrics, 1988. Mem. Am. Soc. Clin. Nutrition, Soc. Pediatric Research, Soc. Exptl. Biology and Medicine, .Am. Soc. Pediatric Gastroenterology, Midwest Soc. Pediatric Research, Am. Pediatric Soc., The Nutrition Soc., N.Y. Acad. Scis., Am. Acad. Pediatrics., Am. Dietetic Assn. (hon.). Clubs: Univ. Athletic (Iowa City). Office: U Iowa Dept Pediatrics Iowa City IA 52242 Office Phone: 319-335-4570. Business E-Mail: ekhard-ziegler@uiowa.edu.

ZIEGLER, RICHARD J., dean, educator; BS in biology, Muhlenberg Coll., 1965; PhD in microbiology, Temple U., 1970. Rsch. assoc. in microbiology Rockefeller U., 1970—71; asst. prof. microbiology U. Minn.-Duluth, 1971—77, assoc. prof. microbiology, 1977—89; prof. microbiology Sch. Medicine, U. Minn.-Duluth, 1989—, interim dean, 1997—98, dean, 1998—. Recipient James

H. Sova award, Minn. Med. Found., 2000. Office: UMD Sch Medicine 1035 Univ Dr Duluth MN 55812 Office Phone: 218-726-7572. Fax: 218-726-7383. Business E-Mail: rziegler@d.umn.edu.

ZIEMAN, MARK, editor, publishing executive; b. El Dorado, Kan., Jan. 17, 1945; m. Kristi Zieman (div.); m. Rhonda Chriss Lokeman; 4 children. Degree in Journalism, Kans. U., 1983. Mem. staff Houston bur. The Wall St. Jour., 1984—86; columnist Kans. City Star, 1986—89, editor projects desk, 1989—92, mng. editor, 1992—97, v.p, editor, 1997—, interim pub., 2008—. Recipient Pulitzer prize, 1992. Office: The Kansas City Star 1729 Grand Blvd Kansas City MO 64108-1458 Office Phone: 816-234-4878. E-mail: zieman@kcstar.com.*

ZIEMAN, MARK L., state senator, small business owner, farmer; b. Postville, Iowa, Jan. 17, 1945; m. Jennifer Zieman; 4 children. Student, Iowa State U., 1963—64. Owner and farmer, 1965—2000; owner and operator Cherry Valley Ent Inc., 1983—2000; pres. Lowells Electric, 1993—2000; state senator dist. 8 Iowa Senate, 2001—; mem. adminstrn. and regulation com.; mem. appropriations com.; mem. agr. com.; mem. local govt. com.; mem. transp. com.; vice chair small bus., econ., devel., and tourism com. Voice Postville H.S. basketball; mem. New H.S., 1983—84; treas. Allamakee Farm Bur.; mem. Call Com. for New Pastor; pres. Iowa Future Farmers Am., 1964; chair Mem. Allamakee County Farm Bur.; active Good Samaritan Adv. Bd., 1998—2000; chair Allamakee County Zoning Bd., 2000; chmn. Allamakee County Reps., 1988—96; mem. Allamakee Ctrl. Com., 1988—2000; county chair Nassle for Congress, 1990—92. Mem.: Iowa Motor Truck Assn. (bd. dirs. 1998—2000), Tri-City Golf Course (pres. 1996). Republican. Lutheran. Address: 284 Luana Rd Postville IA 52162 Office: State Capitol East 12th and Grand Des Moines IA 50319

ZIEMER, JAMES L., motorcycle company executive; BBA, MBA, U. Wis., Milw. CPA Wis. With Harley-Davidson, Inc., Milw., 1969—, v.p., CFO, 1990—2005, pres., CEO, 2005—; pres. Harley-Davidson Found., 1993—. Bd. dirs. Harley-Davidson, Inc. Office: Harley-Davidson Inc PO Box 653 3700 W Juneau Ave Milwaukee WI 53201-0653

ZIEMER, PAUL D., utility company executive; b. Manitowoc, Wis., 1922; married. BBA, U. Wis., 1948. With Wis. Pub. Svc. Corp., Greenbay, Wis., 1948—, divsn. acct., 1958—61, adminstrn. acct., 1961—64, treas., 1964—66, v.p., treas., 1966—69, v.p. fin. adminstrn., 1969—71, pres., CEO, 1971—, also chmn., bd. dirs. Bd. dirs. Larsen Co., Competitive Wis., Edison Electric Inst., First Wis. Corp., Krueger, Inc., Wis., Green Bay Packers, Inc., Forward Wis., Electric Power Rsch. Inst. Mem.: Wis. Utilities Assn. (bd. dirs.), Wis. Assn. Mfrs. and Commerce (bd. dirs.).

ZIEN, DAVID ALLEN, state legislator; b. Chippewa Falls, Wis., Mar. 15, 1950; s. Allen Roy Zien and Orpha Mattix; m. Suzanne Eleanor Bowe, Sept. 8, 1992; children: Travis, Aryan, Kurt, Amber, Lori, Angel-Sky, Rebecca. BS in Geography and Bus. cum laude, U. Wis., Eau Claire, 1974; MS in Guidance and Counseling summa cum laude, U. Wis. Stout, Menomonie, 1975; postgrad., U. Wis., Superior, 1975-80; doctoral studies, U. Wis., 1980-84. Roofer pvt. practice, Chippewa Falls, Wis., 1970-75; longshoreman Superior, Wis., 1975-79; vet. outreach counselor State of Wis., Superior, 1975-79, job svc. counselor Medford, Wis., 1980-83; campus adminstr. Northcentral Tech. Coll., Medford, Wis., 1983-88; mem. Wis. Assembly, Eau Claire, Wis., 1988-93, Wis. Senate from 23rd dist., Madison, 1993—. Wis. vets. outreach dir. VFW, Madison, Wis., 1975-84. Contbr. articles to profl. jours. Speaker, presenter Rep. Party of Wis., 1984—; advisor Wis. Cmty. Edn. Assn., 1983-89. Sgt. USMC, Vietnam, 1968-70. Named Legislator of Yr. ABATE of Wis., 1990, VFW, 1990, 92-93, State of Wis., 1991, Am. Legion, 1993, Wis. Assn. Concerned Vets., 1993, Wis. Farm Bur. Friend of Agr., 1991-94, NFIB Guardian of Small Bus., 1992; recipient Wis. Counties Assn. Cert. Appreciation 1993-94, Hmong Stout Student Assn. Outstanding Good Friend award, 1993-94, State Hist. Soc. Cert. Appreciation, 1994. Mem. VFW, RA, DAV, WVV (Vet. of Yr. 1992), VEC (Damn Fine Legislator 1992), VVA (Disting. Achievement award 1993), WACVO, HOG, ALEC, NCSL, AFA, CMA, AMA, BOLT, ABATE, ANY, WVT, Northland VV, USMC League & Club, Eagles, Nat. Motorcycle Hall of Fame, Grandma's Marathon, Christian Outdoorsmen, Nat. Rep. Legislators, Am. Life League, Am. Legion, Iron Bde., Internat. Assn. Employment Security, Am. Legis. Exch., Wis. Wildlife Fedn., Highground Vets. Meml. Project, Wis. Vets. Tribute Com., Elks, Masons. Lutheran. Avocations: motorcycling, hunting, running. Home: 1716 63rd St Eau Claire WI 54703-6857

ZIERDEN, DON, professional basketball coach; m. Anne Zierden; children: Isaiah, Rachel. Student, Mt. Senario Coll. Coach De La Salle HS, U. Tulsa, 1986—88, Continental Basketball Assn. La Crosse Catbirds, 1990—94; head coach Continental Basketball Assn. Pitts. Piranhas, 1995, Continental Basketball Assn. La Crosse Bobcats, 1996; video coord. NBA Minn. Timberwolves, 1999—2000, asst. coach, dir. player devel., 2000—05; asst. coach NBA Detroit Pistons, 2005—07; head coach WNBA Minn. Lynx, 2007—. Office: Minn Lynx 600 First Ave N Minneapolis MN 55403

ZIETLOW, RUTH ANN, reference librarian; b. Richland Center, Wis., Apr. 5, 1960; d. James Eldon and Dixie Ann (Doudna) Z.; m. David Robert Voigt, Aug. 22, 1992; children: Eleanor Ruth, Isabel Anna, Carl James. BA in English, U. Nebr., 1987; MA in Libr. Studies, U. Wis., 1990; cert. in info. sys., U. St. Thomas, St. Paul, 1995. English instr. Guangzhou (China) English Lang. Ctr. Zhongshan U., 1987-88; adminstrv. asst. Helm Group, Lincoln, Nebr., 1988-89; circulatio supr. Sch. Edn. U. Wis., Madison, 1990-91; libr. specialist St. Paul Pub. Libr., 1991-92; reference librarian coordinator extention library svcs. U. St. Thomas, 1991—. Author manual: Electronic Communication and Information Resources Manual, 1995. Mem. Minn. Libr. Assn. (chair Distance Learning Roundtable 1999-2000). Avocations: gardening, reading. Office: U St Thomas O'Shaughnessey-Frey Libr 2115 Summit Ave Saint Paul MN 55105-1048 E-mail: razietlow@stthomas.edu.

ZIMMERMAN, DORIS LUCILE, chemist; b. LA, July 30, 1942; d. Walter Merritt and Letta Minnie (Reese) Briggs; m. Christopher Scott Zimmerman, June 5, 1964; children: Susan Christina, David Scott, Brian Allan. BS in Chemistry, Carnegie Mellon U., 1964; MS in Chemistry, Youngstown State U., 1989, MS in Materials Engring., 1992; PhD in Chemistry, Kent State U., 2004. High sch. tchr. Ohio County Schs., Vienna and Campbell, 1983-87; sr. chemist Konwal, Warren, Ohio, 1988-91; adj. faculty mem. Kent State U., Ohio, 1991—; temp. full-time instr. dept. chemistry Edinboro U. Pa., 1995-97, 2000. Substitute tchr. County Schs. of Ohio, Warren, 1972-82; tutor, 1965—; vis. prof. Case Western Res. U., Cleve., 2000-01, Thiel Coll., Pa., 2006-; vis. faculty Pa. State, 2001-03. Instr. water safety ARC, Warren, 1965-2002; chmn. Trumbull Mobile Meals, Warren, 1977-92, Pink Thumb Garden Club, Warren, 1965—. Recipient Svc. award ARC, 1981, Trumbull Mobile Meals, 1985. Mem. Am. Inst. Chemists, Materials Info. Soc., Soc. for the Advancement Material and Process Engring. (treas. 2002-2007), Am. Chem. Soc. (sec. 1985-90, chmn. elect 1990, 2004, chmn. 1991, 2005, alt. councilor 1992—2004, 2005, counselor 2005-2007, Commendation award 1990), Carnegie Mellon Alumni Assn. (admissions councilor, Svc. award 1981), Phi Lambda Upsilon, Phi Kappa Phi, Sigma Xi. Republican. Methodist. Avocations: masters' swimming, sailboat racing, tennis, bridge. Home and Office: 1390 Waverly Dr NW Warren OH 44483-1718 Home Phone: 330-847-2283. Personal E-mail: zimdoris@aol.com.

ZIMMERMAN, HOWARD ELLIOT, chemist, educator; b. NYC, July 5, 1926; s. Charles and May (Cohen) Zimmerman; m. Jane Kirschenheiter, June 3, 1950 (dec. Jan. 1975); children: Robert, Steven, James; m. Martha L. Bailey Kaufman, Nov. 7, 1975 (div. Oct. 1990); stepchildren: Peter B. Kaufman, Tanya Kaufman; m. Peggy J. Vick, Oct. 1991. BS, Yale U., 1950, PhD, 1953. NRC fellow Harvard U., 1953-54; faculty Northwestern U., 1954-60, asst. prof., 1955-60; assoc. prof. U. Wis., Madison, 1960-61, prof. chemistry, 1961—, Arthur C. Cope and Hilldale prof. chemistry, 1975—. Chmn. 4th Internat. Union Pure and Applied Chemistry Symposium on Photochemistry, 1972; organizer, chmn. Organic Photochemistry Symposium at Pacifchem, Honolulu, 1972, Honolulu, 95, Honolulu, 2000, Honolulu, 05. Author: (book) Quantum Mechanics for Organic Chemists, 1975; mem. editl. bd.: Jour. Organic Chemistry, 1967—71, Molecular Photochemistry, 1969—75, Jour. Am. Chem. Soc., 1982—85, Revs. Reactive Intermediates, 1984—89; contbr. articles to profl. jours. and chpts. to profl. texts. Recipient Halpern award for photochemistry, N.Y. Acad. Scis., 1979, Chem. Pioneer award, Am. Inst. Chemists, 1986, Sr. Alexander vonHumboldt award, 1988, Hilldale award, U. Wis., 1988—89, 1990, Porter medal, IUPAC, 2006. Mem.: NAS, Inter-Am. Photochemistry Assn. (co-chmn. orgnic divsn. 1977—79, exec. com. 1979—86), German Chem. Soc., Chem. Soc. London, Am. Chem. Soc. (James Flack Norris award 1976, Arthur C. Cope Scholar award 1991, XXI IUPAC Porter medal 2006), Phi Beta Kappa, Sigma Xi. Home: 7813 Westchester Dr Middleton WI 53562-3671 Office: U Wis Chemistry Dept 1101 University Ave Madison WI 53706-1322 Business E-Mail: Zimmerman@chem.wisc.edu.

ZIMMERMAN, JAMES M., retail company executive; b. 1944; Chmn. Rich's Dept. Store div. Federated Dept. Stores, 1984-88; pres., COO Federated and Allied Dept. Stores, Cin., 1988-97; CEO Federated Dept. Stores, Cin., 1997—2003, chmn., 1997—. Office: Federated Department Stores Inc 7 W 7th St Cincinnati OH 45202-2424

ZIMMERMAN, JAMES M., lawyer; b. Cin., Apr. 7, 1974; BA, Vanderbilt U., 1996, JD, 1999. Bar: Ohio 1999. Ptnr. Taft, Stettinius & Hollister LLP, Cin., 1999—. Mem., oper. bd. Main St. Ventures, Cin. Mem., Bd. of Trustee Cin. County Day Sch. Named one of Ohio's Rising Stars, Super Lawyers, 2005, 2006, 2007. Mem.: Ohio State Bar Assn., Cin. Bar Assn., Order of Coif. Office: Taft Stettinius & Hollister LLP 425 Walnut St Ste 1800 Cincinnati OH 45202-3957 Office Phone: 513-381-2838. Office Fax: 513-381-0205. E-mail: zimmerman@taftlaw.com.

ZIMMERMAN, JAY, secondary school educator; Tchr. Physics Brookfield Ctrl. High Sch., Wis., 1980—. Recipient Disting. Svc. Citation, 1993. Office: Brookfield Ctrl High Sch 16900 Gebhardt Rd Brookfield WI 53005-5138

ZIMMERMAN, JO ANN, retired health science association administrator, educator, retired lieutenant governor; b. Van Buren County, Iowa, Dec. 24, 1936; d. Russell and Hazel (Ward) McIntosh; m. A. Tom Zimmerman, Aug. 26, 1956; children: Andrew, Lisa, Don and Ron (twins), Beth. Diploma, Broadlawns Sch. of Nursing, Des Moines, 1958; BA with honors, Drake U., 1973; postgrad., Iowa State U., 1973—75. RN, Iowa. Asst. head nurse maternity dept. Broadlawns Med. Ctr., Des Moines, 1958—59, weekend supr. nursing svcs., 1960—61, supr. maternity dept., 1966—68; instr. maternity nursing Broadlawns Sch. Nursing, 1968—71; health planner, community rels. assoc. Iowa Health Systems Agy., Des Moines, 1978—82; mem. Iowa Ho. Reps., 1982—86; lt. gov., pres. of Senate, State of Iowa, 1987—91; cons. health svcs., grant writing and continuing edn. Zimmerman & Assocs., Des Moines, 1991—2000; dir. patient care svcs. Nursing Svcs. Iowa, 1996—98; nurse case mgr. Olsten Health Svcs. (now Gentiva Health Svcs.), 1998—2004; founder JAZ Tours, 2002—04, ret., 2004, 2004. Ops. dir. Medlink Svcs., Inc., Des Moines, 1992-96. Contbr. articles to profl. jours. Mem. advanced registered nurse practioner task force on cert. nurse mid-wives Iowa Bd. ursing, 1980-81, Waukee, Polk County, Iowa Health Edn. Coord. Coun., Iowa Women's Polit. Caucus, Dallas County Women's Polit. Caucus; chmn. Des Moines Area Maternity Nursing Conf. Group. 1969-70, task force on sch. health svcs. Iowa Dept. Health, 1982, task force health edn. Iowa Dept. Pub. Instruction, 1979, adv. com. health edn. assessment tool, 1980-81, Nat. Lt. Govs., chair com. on Agrl. and Rural Devel., 1989; Dallas County Dem. Ctrl. Com., 1972-84, 98—; bd. dirs. Waukee Cmty. Sch. Bd., 1976-79, pres. 1978-79; bd. dirs. Iowa PTA, 1979-83, chair Health Com., 1980-84; mem. steering com. ERA, Iowa, 1991-92; founder Dem. Activist Women's Network (DAWN), 1992; mem. Disciples of Christ Mission Group to El Salvadore, 2003, 04; founder health ministry First Christian Ch., Des Moines, Iowa, 2004. Named to Iowa Women's Hall of Fame, 2005; recipient Woman Achievement award, YWCA Greater Des Moines, 2005, Search Your Heart award, Am. Heart Assn., 2007. Mem. ANA, LWV (health chmn. met. Des Moines chpt.), Iowa Nurses Assn., Iowa League for Nursing (bd. dirs. 1979-83), Family Centered Childbirth Edn. Assn. (childbirth instr., advisor), Iowa Cattleman's Assn., Am. Lung Assn. (bd. dirs. Iowa 1988-92), Dem. Activist Women's Network (founder 1992), State Hist. Soc. Iowa (bd. mem. 2007-), First Christian Ch. Des Moines (pres. elect 2008), Dallas County Master Gardeners (pres. 2008). Mem. Christian Ch. Avocations: gardening, sewing, reading, bridge.

ZIMMERMAN, JOHN, public relations executive; Dir. pub. and consumer affairs Meijer, Inc., Grand Rapids, Mich., 1994—. Office: Meijer Inc 2929 Walker Ave NW Grand Rapids MI 49544-9428

ZIMMERMAN, MARTIN B., automotive executive; b. New York City, June 19, 1946; B (hon.), Dartsmouth Coll.; D in Econ., Mass. Inst. of Tech. Faculty mem. Sloan Sch. of Mgmt., Mass. Inst. of Tech.; prof. bus. econ. dept. Univ. Mich. Grad. Sch. Bus. Admin., 1983—85, prof. and chmn. bus. econ. dept., 1985; co. chief economist Ford Motor Co., Dearborn, Mich., 1987—94, exec. dir. govtl. rels. and corp. econ., 1994—99, v.p. govtl. affairs, 1999—2001, group v.p., corp. affairs, 2001—. Sr. economist President's Coun. of Econ. Advisors, Washington, 1985—86; adv. coun. Nat. Aeronautic and Space Admin., 1988—92. Serves on bd. of the Citizens Rsch Coun. of Mich., Cmty. Found. of S.E. Mich. and Detroit Met. Visitors and Conv. Bur. Recipient Blue Chip Econ. Forecasting Award. Mem.: Citizens Rsch. Coun. of Mich., Bus. for Soc. Responsibility (bd. dir.), The Panel of Econ. Advisors to the Congl. Budget Office, Com. for Econ. Devel. (bd. of trustees), Nat. Assn. Bus. Economists, Phi Betta Kappa. Office: Ford Motor Co One American Rd Dearborn MI 48123-1899

ZIMMERMAN, MARTIN E., financial executive; b. Chgo., Jan. 28, 1938; s. Joseph and Sylvea Zimmerman; m. Rita Kalifon, June 20, 1961 (div. 1992); children: Jacqueline, Adam. BSEE, MIT, 1955-59; MBA in Fin., Columbia U., 1961. Dir. market research Nuclear-Chgo., Inc. div. G.D. Searle & Co., 1964-67; pres. Telco Mktg. Services, Inc., Chgo., 1967-74; chmn., chief exec. officer Linc Capital, Inc., Chgo., 1975-2000; chmn. Linc Capital, 1975-2000; chmn., CEO LFC Capital, Inc., 2000—. Contbr. numerous articles on leasing to profl. mags. Bd. overseers Columbia U. Grad. Sch. Bus.; trustee Mus. Contemporary Art, Chgo. Capt. U.S. Army, 1961-63. McKinsey scholar, Kennecott Copper fellow Columbia U., 1959-61. Mem. Equipment Lessors Assn. (bd. dirs.). Clubs: University, Mid-Am. (Chgo.). Avocations: fishing, hunting, skiing, amateur radio. Home: 100 E Bellevue Pl Chicago IL 60611-1157 Office: LFC Capital Inc Ste 207 303 E Wacker Dr Chicago IL 60601-5298

ZIMMERMAN, MARY ALICE, performing arts educator, director, playwright; BA, MA, PhD, Northwestern U. Asst. prof. performance studies Northwestern U., Evanston, Ill.; artistic assoc. Goodman and Seattle Repertory Theater; mem. Lookingglass Theater Company, Chicago. Writer, dir. (plays) The Notebooks of Leonardo da Vinci, Secret in the Wings, 1991, Arabian Nights, 1992, Journey to the West, 1995, Mirror of the Invisible World, 1997, Eleven Rooms of Proust, 1998, The Odyssey, 1999, Metamorphoses, 2001 (Best Dir., Tony Awards, 2002, Best Dir., Best New Play, Drama Desk Awards, 2002), Silk, 2005, Argonautika, 2006; dir.: (plays) All's Well That Ends Well, 1995, Henry VIII, 1997, A Midsummer Night's Dream, 2000, Measure for Measure, 2001, Trojan Women, 2003, Pericles, 2004; dir., co-librettist (Operas) Galileo Galilei, 2002. Active Lookingglass Theatre Co. Recipient MacArthur Fellowship, 1998, 20 Joseph Jefferson Awards for best direction. Fellow: Am. Acad. Arts & Sci. Office: Northwestern U Sch Communication 1800 Sherman Ave Rm 401 Evanston IL 60201 Office Phone: 847-491-3623.*

ZIMMERMAN, STEVEN CHARLES, chemistry professor; b. Chgo., Oct. 8, 1957; s. Howard Elliot and Jane (Kirschenheiter) Z.; m. Sharon Shavitt, Aug. 5, 1990; 2 children, Arielle Reneé, Elena Michelle. BS, U. Wis., 1979; MA, MPhil, Columbia U., PhD, 1983. Asst. prof. chemistry U. Ill., Urbana, 1985-91, assoc. prof. chemistry, 1991-94, prof. chemistry, 1994—, Roger Adams prof. chem., interim chem. dept. head; affiliate faculty mem. Beckman Inst. Mem. bioorganic natural products study sect. NIH, 1994—98. Contbr. articles to profl. publs. Recipient Presdl. Young Investigator award NSF, 1988-93, Buck-Whitney award Am. Chem. Soc., 1995, Arthur C. Cope Scholar award, 1997; Alfred P. Sloan fellow, 1992-93. Fellow: AAAS. Home: 55 Chestnut Ct Champaign IL 61822-7121 Office: U Ill 345B Roger Adams Lab 600 S Mathews Ave Urbana IL 61801 Office Phone: 217-333-6655. Office Fax: 217-244-9919. Business E-Mail: sczimmer@uiuc.edu.

ZIMMERMAN, WILLIAM, political science educator; b. Washington, Dec. 26, 1936; s. William III and Isabel Edith (Ryan) Z.; m. Barbara Lamar; children: W. Frederick, Carl L., Alice R.; m. Susan McClanahan, Dec. 10, 1989; 1 child, Rachel Thompson. BA with honors, Swarthmore Coll., 1958; MA, George Washington U., 1959; PhD, Columbia U., 1965. Lectr. dept. polit. sci. U. Mich., 1963-64, from asst. to assoc. prof. dept. polit. sci., 1964-74, assoc. chmn. dept. polit. sci., 1971, dir. Ctr. for Russian and East European studies, 1972-78, 91-92, prof. dept. polit. sci., 1974—, assoc. dean for faculty Coll. of Lit., Sci. and Arts, 1981-84. Vis. asst. prof. Columbia U., summer 1966; rsch. assoc. IPPS, 1978—; co-dir. Program for Internat. Peace and Security Rsch., 1983—; program dir. Ctr. for Polit. Studies, 1989—, dir., 1997—; vis. prof. Harvard U., winter 1988; sr. rsch. assoc. Soviet Interview Project, prin. investigator for various confs. and studies; program chmn. comparative communist studies Am. Polit. Sci. Assn. meetings, 1973; mem. adv. coun. Ctr. for Advanced Russian Studies, Woodrow Wilson Ctr., Smithsonian Instn., 1975-84; exec. com., trustee Nat. Coun. Soviet and East European Rsch., 1978-81. Recipient Helen Dwight Reid award Am. Polit. Sci. Assn., 1965; Fgn. Area tng. fellow Ford Found., 1961-62, William Bayard Cutting traveling fellow Columbia U., 1962-63; rsch. grantee Inst. for War and Peace Studies and Russian Inst., Columbia U., 1965, Inter-univ. com. travel grantee Am./Soviet exch. of young faculty, 1956-66, rsch. grantee Program on Internat. Orgn., U. Mich., 1967, 68, 72, Fulbright-Hays grantee for rsch. in Yugoslavia, 1970, IREX travel grantee to Romania, 1975. Mem. Am. Assn. for Advancement of Slavic Studies (co-chmn. planning com. on Soviet fgn. policy, chmn. Shulman prize com.), Nat. Coun. on Soviet and East European Rsch. (exec. com., bd. trustees 1978-81), Coun. on Fgn. Rels., Phi Kappa Phi. Avocation: stamp collecting/philately. Office: U Mich 426 Thompson St Ann Arbor MI 48104-2321

ZIMOV, BRUCE STEVEN, software engineer; b. Cin., Oct. 16, 1953; s. Sherman and Sylvia Zimov; m. Cathy Lynn Zimov, July 24, 1999. BS in Physics, U. Cin., 1975, MA in Philosophy, 1979. Physicist Kornylak Corp., Hamilton, Ohio, 1982-83; software engr. Entek Sci. Corp., Cin., 1983-89, project mgr., 1989-95, systems mgr., 1995-2000, AOL sr. tech. mgr., 2000—07, K12 sr dir., 2007—. Inventor chess variants, table tennis variant. Mem. IEEE, Internat. Neural Network Soc., Tri-State Online Philosophy SIG (founder). Avocations: philosophy, chess, Web surfing, computers, economics. E-mail: mindnova@aol.com.

ZIMPHER, NANCY LUSK, academic administrator; b. Gallipolis, Ohio, Oct. 29, 1946; d. Aven Denzle and Elsie Gordon (Hammond) L.; 1 child from a previous marriage, William Fletcher Zimpher; m. Kenneth R. Howey, May 8, 1987. BS, Ohio State U., 1968, MA, 1971, PhD, 1976. Cert. K-12 Tchr., Ohio. English tchr. Montgomery County Schs., Md., 1968, Reynoldsburg (Ohio) Schs., 1970; substitute tchr. Rolla (Mo.) City Schs., 1970-71; tchr. Phelps County Schs., Mo., 1971-72; grad. teaching assoc. Coll. Edn. Ohio State U., Columbus, 1972-73; dir. Coll. of Edn. Ohio State U., Columbus, 1973-74, grad. adminstrn. asst. to dean, 1974-76, dir. field experiences alumni rels., 1976-80, coord. undergraduate programs, 1980-84; asst. prof. Ednl. Policy and Leadership Ohio State U., 1984-86, assoc. prof., 1986-91, full prof., 1991-98, assoc. dean, 1992, dean, 1993, exec. dean, 1994; chancellor, prof. curriculum and instrn. U. Wis., Milw., 1998—2003; pres. U. Cin., 2003—. Prin. investigator U.S. Office Edn. Field Devel. Grant, 1981-83, 85-88; co-principal investigator Metro. Life Found. Grant. 1989—, 1992—; cons. The Holmes Group, Lansing, Mich., 1991—. Book rev., editor: Journal of Teacher Education, 1986-89; co-author: Book Profiles of Preservice Teacher Education, 1989, RATE Profiles, 1987-92, A Time for Boldness: A Case Story of Institutional Change, 2002; co-editor: University Leadership in Urban School Renewal: The President's Role, 2004, Boundary Spanners: A Key to Success in Urban Partnerships, 2006, Recruiting, Preparing and Retaining Teachers for Urban Schools, 2006, Creating a New Kind of University, 2006. Chair Faculty Compensation and Benefits Commn., 1989-90, Fiscal Com., 1991-92, Spousal Equivalency Com., 1990-91, Search Com., v.p. for Fin., 1992, Ohio State U; pres., chair bd. dirs. Holmes Partnership, 1997; chair edn. vision coun. United Way Franklin County, 1997; chair bd. dirs. United Way Franklin County, 1998; chair bd. dirs. Nat. Assn. State Univs. and Land-Grant Colls., 2007; chair Urban Serving Univs., 2005—. Fellow Com. for Instnl. Coop., Acad. Leadership Program. 1989-90; recipient Disting. Rsch. award, Disting. Teacher Educator award Assn. Tchr. Educators, 1990, Adams Professorshi Coll. Edn. Ind. State U., 1990—. Alumni Disting. Tchg. award, The Ohio State U., 1992, Chief Exec. Leadership award Coun. for the Advancement and Support Edn., 2003, Career Woman of Achievement award YWCA, 2004, Profl. Achievement award Ohio State U., 2004; named YWCA Woman of Achievement, 1997. Mem. Am. Edn. Rsch. Assn., Am. Assn. Coll. Teacher Edn. Rsch. Comm., Assn. Tchr. Educators, ASCD, Phi Delta Kappa. Episcopalian. Avocations: watercolorist, golf, sewing. Office: Univ Cin 625 Univ Pavilion PO Box 210063 Cincinnati OH 45221-0063

ZINN, GROVER ALFONSO, JR., retired religion educator; b. El Dorado, Ark., June 18, 1937; s. Grover Alfonso and Cora Edith (Saucke) Z.; m. Mary Farris, July 28, 1962; children: Jennifer Anne, Grover Andrew. BA, Rice U., 1959; BD, Duke U., 1962, PhD, 1969; spl. student, U. Glasgow, Scotland, 1962-63. Asst. minister The Barony Ch., Glasgow, 1962-63; instr. in religion Oberlin Coll., Ohio, 1966-68, asst. prof., 1968-74, assoc. prof., 1974-79, prof., 1979—2006, Danforth prof. religion, 1986—2006, Danforth prof. religion emeritus, 2006—, chmn. dept. religion, 1980-84, 85-86, 1993-94, 98-00, assoc. dean coll. arts and scis., 2001—05. Translator: Richard of St. Victor: The Twelve Patriarchs, The Mystical Ark, and Book Three of the Trinity, 1979; co-editor: Medieval France: An Encyclopedia, 1995; mem. editl. bd. Dictionary of Biblical Interpretation; contbr. articles to profl. jours. H.H. Powers Travel grantee Oberlin Coll., 1969, 85; Dempster fellow United Meth. Ch., 1965-66, NEH Younger Humanist fellow, 1972-73, Research Status fellow Oberlin Coll., 1972-73, 97-98, Faculty Devel. fellow Oberlin Coll. 1985, Lilly Endowment fellow U. Pa., 1981-82; recipient ACLS Travel award, 1982. Mem.: Ecclesiastical History Soc., Am. Soc. Ch. History (coun. mem. 1989—92, 1995—98), Medieval Acad. Am. (councillor 1983—86, 2003—06). Democrat. Methodist. Achievements include research in medieval Christian mysticism, theology, and iconography. Avocations: photography, electronics. Home: 61 Glenhurst Dr Oberlin OH 44074-1423 Office: Oberlin Coll Dept Religion Rice Hall Oberlin OH 44074 Office Phone: 440-775-5027. Business E-Mail: grover.zinn@oberlin.edu.

ZINNER, ERNST K., physics educator, earth and planetary science educator, researcher; b. Steyr, Austria, Jan. 30, 1937; MS, Tech. U., Vienna, Austria, 1960; PhD in Physics, Wash. U., Mo., 1972. Instr. physics Coll. Vet. Medicine, Vienna, 1963-64; program and calculation magnetic field distbr. Brown-Boveri Co., Switzerland, 1964-65, rsch. assoc., 1972-74, sr. rsch. scientist, 1974-89; rsch. prof. physics Wash. U., St. Louis, 1989—. Vis. scientist Max-Planck Inst. Physics, Germany, 1980, Max-Planck Inst. Chemistry, Germany, 1980, U. Pavia, Italy, 1989. Recipient J. Lawrence Smith medal NAS, 1997. Fellow Am. Physics Soc., Meteoritical Soc.; mem. AAAS, Am. Geophysics Union, Sigma Xi. Office: Wash U Campus Box 1169 1 Brookings Dr Saint Louis MO 63130-4862

ZINTER, STEVEN L., state supreme court justice; m. Sandra Zinter; 2 children. Doctorate, Univ. So. Dakota, 1975, BS, 1972. Pvt. practice, 1978—86; state atty. Hughes County; cir. judge State of So. Dakota, 1987—97; presiding judge Sixth Judicial Cir., 1997—2002; judge SD Supreme Court, 2002—. Mem. Harry S Truman Found.; trustee So. Dakota Retirement Sys.; elect. pres. So. Dakota Corrections Commn. Mem.: ABA, S.D. Judges Assn. (past pres.), S.D. Bar Assn. Office: SD Supreme Ct 500 E Capital Ave Pierre SD 57501-5070

ZIOMEK, JONATHAN S., journalist, educator; b. Newport News, Va., July 28, 1947; s. Stanley Walter and Joy Carmen (Schmidt) Z.; m. Rosalie Ziomek, Aug. 14, 1977; children: Joseph, Jennifer; 1 stepchild, Daniel. BA in Sociology, U. Ill., 1970, MS in Journalism, 1982. Reporter, labor writer, feature writer, Sun. fin. editor Chgo. Sun-Times, 1970-78; press sec. for U.S. Senate campaign, Chgo., 1979-80; asst. prof. Medill Sch. Journalism, Northwestern U., Evanston, Ill., 1983-88; dir. grad. editl. programs Medill Sch. Journalism/Northwestern U., Evanston, Ill., 1988—2004, asst. dean, 1994—2004, assoc. prof., 1994—. Rapporteur Aspen Inst., Journalism and Soc. Seminar, 2004, McCormick Found. Mil. and Media Conf., 2005-06; presenter, cons. in field. Contbr. articles to popular mags.; editor: Chgo. Journalist Newsletter, 1991-93. Participant Internat. Visitors Ctr., Chgo., 1988—; fact-finder USIA, Bulgaria and Yugoslavia, 1990. Mem. Assn. for Edn. in Journalism and Mass Communications, Soc. Profl. Journalists, Nat. Assn. Sci. Writers, Chgo. Headline Club. Home: 2149 Hartrey Ave Evanston IL 60201-2571 Office: Northwestern Univ Medill Sch Journalism Evanston IL 60208-0001

ZIPES, DOUGLAS PETER, cardiologist, researcher; b. White Plains, NY, Feb. 27, 1939; s. Robert Samuel Zipes and Josephine Helen Weber; m. Marilyn Joan Jacobus, Feb. 18, 1961; children: Debra, Jeffrey, David. BA cum laude,

Dartmouth Coll., 1961, B of Med. Sci., 1962; MD cum laude, Harvard Med. Sch., 1964. Diplomate Am. Bd. Internal Medicine. Intern, resident, fellow in cardiology Duke U. Med. Ctr., Durham, NC, 1964-68; vis. scientist Masonic Med. Rsch. Lab., Utica, NY, 1970-71; from asst. prof. medicine to disting. prof. emeritus Ind. U., Indpls., 1970—2004, disting. prof. emeritus, 2004—, Medtronic Zipes chair cardiology Sch. Medicine, 2004—, Zipes vis. prof., 2005. Bd. dirs. Inst. for Clin. Evaluation; cardiology adv. com NIH, 1991—94; mem. med. adv. bd. ABCNews.com, 2000—; mem. dean's coun. Dartmouth Med. Sch., Ind. Med. Sch. Contbr. articles to profl. jours., chapters to books in medicine. Pres., bd. dir. Indpls. Opera Co., 1983-85; mem. study sect. NIH, Washington, 1977-81; mem. nat. merit rev. bd. VA, 1982-85, Cardiology Adv. Com. NHLBL, 1991-98, chmn. steering com. AVID; chmn. Data and Safety Monitoring Bd. AFFIRM, 1996-2002; bd. dir. Am. Bd. Internal Medicine Found., 2002-04; chmn. Am. Bd. Internal Medicine, 2002-03. Named Sagamore of Wabash, Gov. of Ind., 2001; recipient Disting. Achievement award, Am. Heart Assn., 1989, Disting. Alumnus award, Duke U. Med. Ctr., 2007. Master Am. Coll. Cardiology (chmn. ACC/AHA subcom. to assess EP studies, chmn. young investigators award com. 1988-94, trustee 1992-97, 2002-05, chair nominating com. 2003, chmn. devel. com. 1996-2001, sci. sessions program com. 1996-98, v.p. 1999-2000, pres. 2001-02, co-chair ventricular arrhythmias guidelines 2003—, Bethesda (Md.) conf. guidelines athletes with heart disease, chair campaign the future, endowed lectr. 2005, Disting. Scientist award 1996, endowed Douglas P. Zipes Disting. Young Scientist award 2005); fellow ACP, Am. Heart Assn. (exec. com. 1980-88, sci. sessions program 1983-86, chmn. various coms., chmn. 1995, bd. dir. Internat. Cardiology Found. 1993-98, bd. dir. 1994-96, chmn. emergency cardiac care com. 1995-96, Herrick award 1997, Cor Vitae award 2004); mem. Am. Soc. Clin. Investigation, Assn. Univ. Cardiologists (v.p. 1994, pres. 1995), Assn. Am. Physicians, Am. Physiol. Soc., Cardiac Electrophysiology Soc. (pres. 1985-86), Heart Rhythm Soc. (pres. 1988-90, trustee 1990-2000, lectr. 2005, Disting. Scientist award 1995), InterAm. Soc. Cardiology (1st v.p. 1995-98), Ind. Cardiac Electrophysiology Soc. (founder), Argentine Soc. Cardiology (hon. fgn. mem., 2007). Home: 10614 Winterwood Carmel IN 46032-9688 Office: Ind U Sch Medicine 1100 W Michigan St Indianapolis IN 46202-5208 Home Phone: 317-962-0556; Office Phone: 317-697-2406. Business E-Mail: dzipes@iupui.edu.

ZIPFEL, PAUL ALBERT, bishop; b. St. Louis; s. Albert and Leona (Rau) Zipfel. BST, Cath. U. Am., 1961; MA in Edn., St. Louis U., 1965. Ordained priest Archdiocese of Saint Louis, 1961, aux. bishop, 1989—96; ordained bishop, 1989; bishop Diocese of Bismarck, ND, 1996—. Roman Catholic. Office: Diocese of Bismarck PO Box 1575 420 Raymond St Bismarck ND 58502-1575 Office Phone: 701-223-1347. Office Fax: 701-223-3693.*

ZIRBES, MARY KENNETH, retired minister; b. Melrose, Minn., Sept. 4, 1926; d. Joseph Louis and Clara Bernadine (Petermeier) Z. BA in History and Edn., Coll. St. Catherine, 1960; MA in Applied Theology, Sch. Applied Theology, Berkeley, Calif., 1976. Joined Order of St. Francis, Roman Cath. Ch., 1945. Tchr. Pub. Grade Sch., St. Nicholas, Minn., 1947-52; prin. Holy Spirit Grade Sch., St. Cloud, Minn., 1953-59, St. Mary's Jr. HS, Morris, Minn., 1960-62; coord. Franciscan Mission Team, Peru, South America, 1962-67, Franciscan Missions, Little Falls, Minn., 1967-70; dir. St. Richard's Social Justice Ministry, Richfield, Minn., 1971-80, Parish Community Devel., St. Paul, Mpls., Minn., 1980-85; councillor gen. Franciscan Sisters of Little Falls, 1960-62, 67-70; asst. dir. Renew-Archdiocese of St. Paul-Mpls., 1986-89; coord. Parish Social Justice Ministry-Archdiocese of St. Paul-Mpls., 1990-93; min. Franciscan Assocs., 1993—2003; leader of team on evangelical life Franciscan Sisters of Little Falls, 1994-96; ret., 2003. Co-developer Assn. of Pastoral Ministers, Mpls., St. Paul, 1979-81, Compañeros/Sister Parishes-Minn. and Nicaragua, 1984-89, Minn. Interfaith Ecology Coalition, 1989-92. Author: Parish Social Ministry, 1985, (manual) Acting for Justice, 1992. Organizer Twin Cities Orgn., Mpls., 1979-80; bd. dirs. Franciscan Sisters Health Care, Inc., Little Falls, 1990-93, Rice-Marion Residents Assn., St. Paul, 1991-92. Named Outstanding chair Assn. Pastoral Ministers, 1981; recipient Five Yrs. of Outstanding Svc. award Companeros, 1989. Mem. Assn. Pastoral Ministers (chair 1979), Voices for Justice-Legis. Lobby, Audubon Soc., Network, Minn. Call to Action, Com. on Peace, Justice and Integrity of Creation, Joint Religious Legis. Coalition. Avocations: painting, birding, golf, reading. Personal E-mail: sebri02@charter.net.

ZLATOFF-MIRSKY, EVERETT IGOR, violinist; b. Evanston, Ill., Dec. 29, 1937; s. Alexander Igor and Evelyn Ola (Hill) Z.-M.; m. Janet Dalbey, Jan. 28, 1976; children from previous marriage— Tania, Laura. B.Mus., Chgo. Mus. Coll., Roosevelt U., 1960, M.Mus., 1961. Mem. faculty dept. music Roosevelt U., Chgo., 1961-66. Founding mem., violinist, violist Music of the Baroque, 1971-2003. Violinist orch. Lyric Opera of Chgo., 1974-2003; concert master, pers. mgr., 1974-2003, violinist, violist, Contemporary Chamber Players U. Chog., 1964-82, solo violinist, Bach Soc., 1966-83; violist, violinist, Lexington String Quartet, 1966-81; rec. artist numerous recs., radio-TV and films; solo violinist appearing throughout U.S. Recipient Olive Ditson award Franklin Honor Soc., 1961 Mem. Nat. Acad. Rec. Arts and Scis. Republican. Roman Catholic. Home: 1600 Old Pecos Trail Santa Fe NM 87505 E-mail: jdzm@aol.com.

ZOBRIST, GEORGE WINSTON, computer scientist, educator; b. Highland, Ill., Feb. 13, 1934; s. George H. and Lillie C. (Augustin) Z.; m. Freida Groverlyn Rich, Mar. 29, 1955; children: Barbara Jayne, George William, Jean Anne. BS, U. Mo., 1958, PhD, 1965; MS, Wichita State U., 1961. Registered profl. engr., Mo., Fla. Electronic scientist U.S. Naval Ordnance Test Sta., China Lake, Calif., 1958-59; rsch. engr. Boeing Co., Wichita, 1959-60; instr. Wichita State U., 1960-61; assoc. prof. U. Mo., Columbia, 1961-69, U. So. Fla., Tampa, 1969-70; chmn. elec. engring. dept. U. Miami, Coral Gables, Fla., 1970-71; prof. U. South Fla., Tampa, 1971-72, 73-76; prof., chmn. dept. elec. engring. U. Toledo, 1976-79; dir. computer sci. and engring. Samborn, Steketee, Otis, Evans, Inc., Toledo, 1979-82; prof. computer sci. Grad. Engring. Ctr. U. Mo., St. Louis, 1982-85, prof. computer sci. Rolla, 1985-99, chmn. dept., 1994-99, prof. emeritus, 1999—. Rsch. prof. U. Edinburgh, Scotland, 1972-73; lectr. U. Western Cape, South Africa, 1995 summer; cons. Wilcox Electric Co., Bendix Corp., both Kansas City, Mo., 1966-68, ICC, Miami, 1970-71, Def. Comm. Agy., Washington, 1971, 72, U.S. Naval Rsch. Labs., Washington, 1971, Med. Svc. Bur., Miami, 1970-71, NASA, Kennedy Space Ctr., Fla., 1973-76, 88, 89, 93, 94, Prestolite Corp., Toledo, 1977-79, IBM, Lexington, Ky., 1983-86, Wright-Patterson AFB, Ohio, 1986, PAFB, Fla., 1987, McDonnell Douglas, Mo., 1989, Digital Systems Cons., Mo., 1989, Oak Ridge Nat. Labs., 1992. Author: Network Computer Analysis, 1969, Progress in Computer Aided VLSI Design, 1988-90; editor Internat. Jour. Computer Aided VLSI Design, 1989-91, Object Oriented Simulation IEEE Press, 1996, Computer Sci. and Computer Engring. Monograph series, 1989-91, Internat. Jour. Computer Simulation, 1990-96, VLSI Design, 1992-2002; editor IEEE Potentials Mag., 1996-99, 2003; assoc. editor, 1984-96, 99—; contbr. articles to profl. jours. Served with USAF, 1951-55. Named Young Engr. of Yr. ctrl. chpt. Mo. Soc. Profl. Engrs., 1967; NSF summer fellow, 1962, 64; NASA, IBM, DOE, UES/AFOSR, McDonnell Douglas rsch. grantee, 1967-88. Fellow IEEE (life, mem. IEEE Press editl. bd. 1998—); mem. Am. Legion, Rotary, Sigma Xi, Tau Beta Pi, Phi Eta Sigma, Eta Kappa Nu, Pi Mu Epsilon, Upsilon Pi Epsilon. Home: 12030 Country Club Dr Rolla MO 65401-7469 Office: U Mo Rolla Dept Computer Sci 1870 Miner Cir Rolla MO 65409-0001 Business E-Mail: zobrist@umr.edu.

ZOELLER, DAVID LOUIS, lawyer, bank executive; b. Indpls., Nov. 26, 1949; s. John Louis and M. Maxine (Snoderly) Z.; m. Wesley Anne Carlton, Aug. 14, 1971; children: Laura Anne, David Carlton. BA, So. Meth. U., Dallas, 1971; JD, Ind. U., 1974. Bar: Ind. 1974, US Dist. Ct. (so. dist. Ind.) 1974. Asst. sec., legal counsel Stokely-Van Camp Inc., 1974-83; legal mgmt. positions through exec. v.p., sec., gen. counsel Nat. City Corp., Cleve., 1983—. Mem. ABA, Ind. Bar Assn., Indpls. Bar Assn., Ohio Bar Assn., Cleve. Bar Assn., Am. Soc. Corp. Secs., Lawyers Coun. Fin. Svcs. Roundtable. Republican. Presbyterian. Office: at City Corp Nat City Ctr 1900 E 9th St Cleveland OH 44114-3484 Office Phone: 216-222-2000.

ZOLA, GARY PHILLIP, rabbi, historian; b. Chgo., Feb. 17, 1952; m. Stefani Paula Rothberg; children: Amanda Roi, Jorin Benjamin, Jeremy Micah, Samantha Leigh. BA in Am. History with distinction, U. Mich., 1973; MA in Counseling Psychology, Northwestern U., 1976; PhD in Am. Jewish History, Hebrew Union Coll., Cin., 1991. Ordained rabbi, 1982. Dir. informal edn. and youth activities Temple Israel, Mpls., 1973-74; regional youth dir., asst. camp dir. Olin-Sang-Ruby Union Inst., UAHC, Chgo., 1974-77; student pulpit B'nai Israel Congregation, Williamson, W.Va., 1978-79; mem. student pulpit Anshe Sholom Congregation, Olympia Fields, Ill., 1979-80, Columbus Hebrew Congregation, Columbus, Ind., 1981-82; rabbi for high holy days Chgo. Jewish Experience, Chgo., 1982-94; nat. dir. admissions Hebrew Union Coll.-Jewish Inst. Religion, Cin., 1982-89, nat. dean admissions and student affairs, 1989-91, nat. dean admissions, student affairs and alumni rels., 1991-98; exec. dir. Jacob Rader Marcus Ctr. Am. Jewish Archives at Hebrew Union Coll., Cin., 1998—; assoc. prof. Am. Jewish Experience Hebrew Union Coll. Jewish Inst. of Religion. Del. Emerging Leaders Conf., Am. Coun. for Internat. Leadership, 1989, 91; bd. dirs. Am. Jewish Com., Cin., 1982—, mem. exec. com., 1984—; bd. dirs. Hillel U. Cin., 1991-94, Jewish Fedn., Cin., 1993-95; pres. Greater Cin. Bd. Rabbis, 1993-95, Jewish Cmty. Rels. Coun., (bd. dir.,1994—); founding mem. Kehillah of Cin., Jewish Think Tank; pres. Martin Luther King Jr. Coalition Cin., 2003-05; chair Commn. for Commemorating 350 Years of Am. Jewish History. Author: Isaac Harby of Charleston, 1994; editor: Hebrew Union College--Jewish Institute of Religion--A Centennial History, 1875-1975, (Michael A. Meyer), 1992, Women Rabbis: Exploration and Celebration, 1996, The Dynamics of American Jewish History, 2003, A Place of Our Own: The Rise of Reform Jewish Camping, 2006; editor: The American Jewish Archives Jour., 1998—; contbr. numerous scholarly articles to profl. jours.; mem. editl. bd. Reform Judaism. Bd. dirs. ethics com. Jewish Hosp., Cin.; life mem. N.Am. Fedn. Temple Youth; active NCCJ. Mem. Ctrl. Conf. Am. Rabbis, Orgn. Am. Historians, Assn. Jewish Studies, So. Jewish Hist. Soc., Am. Jewish Hist. Soc., N.Am. Fedn. Temple Youth (life), Abraham Lincoln Bicentennial Commn. Academic Coun. Office: Hebrew Union Coll Jewish Inst Religion 3101 Clifton Ave Cincinnati OH 45220-2404

ZOLLARS, WILLIAM D., freight company executive; b. 1947; BA, U. Minn., 1969. Various exec. positions with Eastman Kodak, 1970—94; sr. v.p. Ryder Integrated Logistics Ryder Sys., Inc., 1994—96; pres. Yellow Freight Sys., 1996-99; chmn., pres., CEO YRC Worldwide, Inc. (formerly Yellow Roadway Corp.), Overland Park, Kans., 1999—. Bd. dirs. Cigna Corp., Cerner Corp., Butler Mfg. Co. Trustee ProLogis Trust, Midwest Rsch. Inst.; bd. mem. Heart of Am. United Way, Civic Council of Greater Kans. City, Carlson Sch. Mgmt., Univ. Minn., NAM. Mem.: Am. Trucking Assn. (bd. mem.), Phi Beta Kappa. Office: YRC Worldwide Inc 10990 Roe Ave Overland Park KS 66211-1213

ZOLNO, MARK S., lawyer; BA Polit. Sci., No. Ill. Univ., 1965; JD, John Marshall Law Sch., 1978; MA cum laude Internat. Rels., Universidad de las Américas, Mexico, 1974. Bar: Ill. 1978, U.S. Dist. Ct. (no. dist.) Ill. 1979, U.S. Ct. Internat. Trade 1979, U.S. Ct. Appeals (fed. cir.) 1979. With U.S. Customs Svc., Dept. Commerce, U.S. Trade Rep's. Office, Internat. Trade Commn., Fed. Trade Commn., FDA; ptnr. Katten, Muchin, Rosenman, Chgo., 1988—. Past chmn. Chgo. Bar Assn. Customs and U.S. Trade Law Com.; lectr. in field. Contbr. articles to profl. jours. Office: Katten Muchin Rosenman 525 W Monroe St Ste 1900 Chicago IL 60661-3693 Office Phone: 312-902-5436. Business E-Mail: mark.zolno@kattelaw.com.

ZOLOMIJ, ROBERT WILLIAM, landscape architect, consultant; b. Phila., Oct. 13, 1942; s. William and Anna (Sikacz) Z.; m. Joanne M. Volk, Oct. 2, 1965; children: Nancy Lyn, Christopher John; m. Nancy S. Helfferich, Nov. 21, 1992. BS in Landscape Architecture, Pa. State U., 1965; M Landscape Architecture, U. Ill., 1971. Lic. landscape arch., Ill. Site planner Bucks County Planning Commn., Doylestown, Pa., 1965-67; assoc. prof. U. Ill., Urbana, 1968-78; sr. landscape arch. Skidmore Owings & Merrill, Chgo., 1978-79; sr. assoc. Barton-Aschman Assocs., Evanston, Ill., 1979-84; v.p. Harland Bartholomew Assocs., Northbrook, Ill., 1984-86, Land Design Collaborative, Inc., Evanston, 1986—. Co-author: Time Saver Standards for Landscape Architects, 1988. Univ. fellow U. Ill., 1967. Fellow Am. Soc. Landscape Archs. (chpt. treas. 1986-88, v.p. 1988-90, pres. 1990-92). Avocations: golf, travel, reading, woodworking. Home: 3429 Harrison St Evanston IL 60201-4953 Office: 5142 Main St Skokie IL 60077-2102

ZONA, LOUIS ALBERT, museum director; s. Patricia Zona; 1 child, Tace. BS in Edn. magna cum laude, Youngstown U., Ohio, 1966; MS in Edn., U. Pitts., 1969; DFA, Carnegie Mellon U., 1973. Asst. to dir. The Butler Inst. of Am. Art, Youngstown, 1980—81, exec. dir., 1981—, also chief curator; prof. art history Youngstown State U., 1970—, chmn. art dept., 1978-82. Adj. prof. art and museology Westminster Coll., 1976-80. Contbr. numerous articles to profl. publs. Recipient Gari Melchers medla Artists' Fellowship, NYC, 1996, Gov.'s award for the Arts in Ohio, 1990, Disting. Profl. Svc. award Ohio Steel Valley Art Tchrs. Assn., 1982. Office: Butler Inst Am Art Beecher Ctr 524 Wick Ave Youngstown OH 44502 Office Phone: 330-743-1711. E-mail: l_zona@butlerart.com.

ZONIS, MARVIN, political scientist, educator; b. Boston, Sept. 18, 1936; s. Leonard and Clara (Barenberg) Z.; m. Lucy Salenger, Jan. 3, 1976; children by previous marriage-Nadia E. Leah; 1 stepdaugher, Brix E. Smith. AB, Yale U., 1958; postgrad., Harvard Grad. Sch. Bus., 1958-59; PhD, M.I.T., 1968; candidate, Inst. for Psychoanalysis, Chgo., 1977-85. Mem. faculty U. Chgo., 1966—, assoc. prof. and prof. behavioral scis., 1973-89—, prof. Grad. Sch. Bus., 1989—; dir. U. Chgo. (Center for Middle Eastern Studies), 1976-79; pres. Marvin Zonis and Assocs., Internat. Cons., 1991—. Cons. in field; chmn. com. on Middle East Am. Coun. Learned Socs.-Social Sci. Rsch. Coun., 1970-76; pres. Am. Inst. Iranian Studies, 1969-71; bd. dirs. CNA Fin. Corp. Author: The Political Elite of Iran, 1971, Khomeini, The Islamic Republic of Iran, and the Arab World, 1987, Majestic Failure: The Fall of the Shah, 1991, The East European Opportunity: The Complete Business Guide and Source Book, 1992; co-author The Kimchi Matters: Global Business and Local Politics in a Crisis Driven World, 2002; contbr. articles to profl. jours. Served with USAF, 1959-60. Recipient Quantrell award for excellence in teaching U. Chgo., 1979 Home: 4950 Chicago Beach Dr Chicago IL 60615 Office: U Chgo 5807 S Woodlawn Ave Chicago IL 60637-1515 Office Phone: 773-702-8753. Business E-Mail: marvin.zonis@chicagogsb.edu.

ZOOK, ELVIN GLENN, plastic surgeon, educator; b. Huntington County, Ind., Mar. 21, 1937; s. Glenn Hardman and Ruth (Barton) Z.; m. Sharon Kay Neher, Dec. 11, 1960; children— Tara E., Leigh A., Nicole L. BA, Manchester Coll., 1959; MD, Ind. U., 1963. Diplomate Am. Bd. Surgery, Am. Bd. Thoracic Surgery, Am. Bd. Plastic Surgery. Intern Meth. Hosp., Indpls., 1963-64; resident in gen. and thoracic surgery Ind. U. Med. Center, Indpls., 1964-69; resident in plastic surgery Ind. U. Hosp., Indpls., 1969-71, asst. prof. plastic surgery, 1971-73; asso. prof. surgery So. Ill. U., Springfield, 1973-75, prof., 1975—, chmn. div. plastic surgery, 1973—. Mem. staff Meml. Med. Center, St. Johns Hosp., Springfield. Contbr. articles to med. jours. Mem. Assn. Acad. Surgery, Am. Soc. Plastic Surgery (sec. 1988-91, v.p. 1991-92, pres.-elect 1992-93, pres. 1993-94), Midwestern Soc. Plastic Surgery (pres. 1986-87), ACS, Sangamon County Med. Soc. (pres. 1987), Am. Cleft Palate Assn., Am. Assn. Plastic Surgery (trustee 1987-90), Plastic Surgery Rsch. Coun. (chmn. 1981), Am. Burn Assn., Ill. Surg. Soc., Am. Soc. Surgery Hand (coun.), Am. Bd. of Plastic Surgery (sec.-treas. 1988-91, chmn. 1991-92), Am. Soc. Aesthetic Plastic Surgery, Am. Soc. Surgery of Trauma, Assn. Acad. Chmn. Plastic Surgery (pes. 1986-87), Am. Surg. Assn., RRC for Plastic Surgery, Sangamo Club, Springfield Med. Club, Island Bay Yacht Club. Clubs: Sangamo, Springfield Med, Island Bay Yacht. Presbyterian. Home: 7235 Mansion Rd Chatham IL 62629-8763 Office: 747 N Rutledge St Springfield IL 62702-6700 E-mail: ezook@siumed.edu.

ZOPP, ANDREA LYNNE, energy company executive; b. Rochester, NY, Jan. 25, 1957; d. Reuben K. and P. Greta (Hurst) Davis; m. William E. Zopp, Jr., Oct. 7, 1989; children: Alyssa, Kelsey, William. BA cum laude, Harvard Coll., 1978; JD, Harvard U., 1981. Bar: Ill. 1981, U.S. Dist. Ct. (no. dist.) Ill. 1981, U.S. Ct. Appeals (7th cir.) 1982. Law clk. Hon. George N. Leighton, U.S. Dist. Ct., Chgo., 1981-83; asst. U.S. atty. U.S. Atty.'s Office, Chgo., 1983-86, dept. chief OCDETF, 1986-88, dep. chief criminal lit., 1988-90; ptnr. McDermott, Will & Emery, Chgo., 1990-91; chief narcotics prosecutions bur. Cook County State's Attys. Office, Chgo., 1991-92, first asst. state's atty., 1992—96; ptnr. Sonnenschein Nath & Rosenthal, 1997—2000; v.p., dep. gen. counsel Sara Lee Corp., 2000—03; sr. v.p., gen. counsel Sears, Roebuck & Co., Hoffman Estates, Ill., 2003—06; exec. v.p., chief human resources officer Exelon Corp., 2006—. Mem. Gov.'s Commn. on Capital Punishment, State of Illinois, 2000—; bd. dirs. Andrew Corp., 2005—07. Bd. dirs. Aux. Bd., Art Inst. Chgo., 1987-2000, Chgo. Regional Bd. of Jr. Achievement, 1991-95, Chgo. Area Project, 1992—. Fellow Leadership Greater Chgo., 1989-90; Kizzy Scholarship Fund award, 1991-92; named a Women of Achievement, The Anti-Defamation League, 2008 Fellow Am. Bar Found., Am. Coll. Trial Lawyers; Mem. ABA, Chgo. Bar Assn., Chgo. Inn of Ct., Cook County Bar Assn., Black Women Lawyers Assn., Leadership Greater Chgo. (bd. dirs.). Avocations: running, music, theater. Office: Exelon Corp 10 S Dearborn St 48th Fl PO Box 805398 Chicago IL 60680*

ZORE, EDWARD JOHN, financial services executive; b. Milw., July 5, 1945; s. Joseph F. and Marie A. Z.; m. Diane Widemshek, Aug. 19, 1967; children: Annemarie, Kathryn. BS in Econs., U. Wis., Milw., 1968, MS in Econs., 1970. With investment dept. Northwestern Mut. Fin. Network, Milw., 1969—, chief investment officer, 1990—98, CFO, 1995—98, exec. v.p. life and disability income ins., 1998—2000, pres., 2000—, CEO, 2001—. Bd. trustees Northwestern Mut. Fin. etwork, 2000—; bd. dirs. Manpower, Inc., 2000—. Republican. Roman Catholic. Office: Northwestern Mutual 720 E Wisconsin Ave Milwaukee WI 53202-4797

ZORN, ERIC JOHN, newspaper columnist; b. New Haven, Jan. 6, 1958; s. Jens Christian and Frances (Barnhart) Z.; m. Johanna Wolken, Nov. 2, 1985; children: Alexander, Anna Lise, Benjamin. BA, U. Mich., 1980. With Chgo. Tribune, 1980—, met. reporter, 1985-86, columnist, 1986—. Instr. Northwestern U. Medill Sch. Journalism, Evanston, Ill., 1985-89. Co-author: Murder of Innocence, 1990. Avocation: old-time square dance caller. Office: Chgo Tribune PO Box 25340 435 N Michigan Ave Chicago IL 60611-4066

ZOUHARY, JACK, federal judge; b. Toledo, Dec. 18, 1951; BA cum laude, Dartmouth Coll., 1973; Rufus Choate scholar; JD, U. Toledo Coll. Law, 1976. Atty. Robison, Curphey & O'Connell, Toledo, 1976—99, Fulley & Henry, Ltd., Toledo, 2004—05; sr. v.p. & gen. counsel S.E. Johnson Companies, Maumee, Ohio, 2000—03; judge Lucas County Common Pleas Ct., 2005—06, US Dist. Ct. (No. dist.) Ohio, 2006—. Mem.: ABA, Inns of Ct. -Morrison Waite ch., Am. Assn. Trial Lawyers, Toledo Bar Assn., Ohio Bar Assn. Office: 203 US Ct House 1716 Spielbusch Ave Toledo OH 43604-1363 Office Phone: 419-213-5675. Office Fax: 419-213-5680.

ZUCARO, ALDO CHARLES, insurance company executive; b. Grenoble, France, Apr. 2, 1939; s. Louis and Lucy Zucaro; m. Gloria J. Ward, Oct. 12, 1963; children: Lucy, Louis, Faye. BS in Acctg, Queens Coll., NYC, 1962. C.P.A., N.Y., Ill. Ptnr. Coopers & Lybrand (and predecessor), Chgo. and NYC, 1962-76; exec. v.p., chief fin. officer Old Republic Internat. Corp., Chgo., 1976-81, pres., 1981—, CEO, 1990—93, chmn., CEO, 1993—. Pres., bd. dirs. Old Republic Life Ins. Co., Old Republic Life of N.Y., Old Republic Ins. Co., Internat. Bus. and Merc. Reassurance Co., Republic Mortgage Ins. Co., Old Republic Nat. Title Ins. Co., Home Owners Life Ins. Co. Editor: Financial Accounting Practices of the Insurance Industry, 1975, 76. Mem. AICPAs. Roman Catholic. Office: Old Republic Internat Corp 307 N Michigan Ave Chicago IL 60601-5311

ZUCKER, DAVID F., former information technology executive; b. Wichita Falls, Tex., Aug. 8, 1962; s. Paul Zucker and Margaret Anne (Keating) Chisholm. BA in Econ., Princeton U., 1984; MBA, Harvard, 1988. Fin. analyst Goldman, Sachs & Co., NYC, 1984-86; exec. pub. ABC, Inc., Travel Agent Mag., NYC, 1988-90; mgr. current series programming ABC Entertainment, LA, 1991; dir. programming Eurosport, London, Paris, 1992-93; v.p. programming to exec. v.p. ESPN, Inc., Bristol, Conn., 1993-94; sr. v.p., managing dir. ESPN Internat., NYC, 1995—99; pres., CEO Diva Systems Corp., 1999—2000, Skillgames LLC, 2000—02; mng. dir. Walker Digital LLC, 2000—02; pres., COO Playboy Enterprises, Inc., 2002—03; pres., CEO Midway Games, Inc., 2003—08.*

ZUCKER, ROBERT A(LPERT), psychologist; b. NYC, Dec. 9, 1935; s. Morris and Sophie (Alpert) Z.; m. Martine Latil; children: Lisa, Alex, Eleanor; m. Kristine Ellen Freeark, Mar. 10, 1979; 1 child, Katherine. B.C.E., CCNY, 1956; postgrad., UCLA, 1956-58; PhD, Harvard U., 1966. Diplomate Am. Bd. Profl. Psychology (clin.); lic. psychologist, Mich. From instr. to asst. prof. psychology Rutgers U., 1963-68; from asst. prof. to assoc. prof. to prof. Mich. State U., 1968-94; prof. psychology in psychiatry and psychology U. Mich., 1994—, dir. Addiction Rsch. Ctr., 1994—, dir. substance abuse sect. Dept. Psychiatry, 1994—, faculty assoc. RCGD Inst. for Social Rsch., 1996—. Vis. prof. U. Tex., Austin, 1975; vis. rsch. prof. psychology in psychiatry U. Mich., 1990-91; vis. scholar Nat. Inst. Alcohol Abuse and Alcoholism, 1980; dir. clin. tng. Mich. State U., 1982-94; lectr. Nebr. Symposium on Motivation, 1986; cons. in field. Co-author, editor: Further Explorations in Personality, 1981, Personality and the Prediction of Behavior, 1984, The Emergence of Personality, 1987, Studying Persons and Lives, 1990, Personality Structure in the Life Course, 1992, The Development of Alcohol Problems: Exploring the Biopsychosocial Matrix of Risk, 1994, Alcohol Problems Among Adolescents: Current Directions in Prevention Research, 1995, Alcohol Problems and Aging, 1998, Multiproblem Youth: Intervention and Treatment, 2004; contbr. chpts. and articles to profl. publs. Bd. dirs. Nat. Coun. on Alcoholism-Mich., 1978-82; mem. Psychosocial Initial Rev. Group, Nat. Inst. Alcohol Abuse and Alcoholism, 1989-92; mem. HPRB study sect. Ctr. for Sci. Rev., NIH, 1998-2000. Recipient Fellow's award, Inst. Children Youth and Families, Mich. State U., 1993, Excellence in Clin. Rsch. award, Blue Cross-Blue Shield Mich. Found., 1997; Method for External Rsch. in Time (MERIT) grantee, NIH, 2003—. Fellow AAAS, APA (pres. addictions divsn. 50 1997-98), APS, Am. Orthopsychiat. Assn.; mem. Midwestern Psychol. Assn., Rsch. Soc. on Alcoholism (sec., bd. dirs. 2000-03, bd. dirs. 2007—), Polish Soc. Rsch. Addictions, Polish Soc. Psychiatrists (hon., named to Hall Fame 2007). Office: Univ Mich Addiction Rsch Ctr 4250 Plymouth Rd Ann Arbor MI 48109-5740 Office Phone: 734-232-0280. Business E-Mail: zuckerra@umich.edu.

ZUERN, ROSEMARY LUCILE, manufacturing executive, treasurer; b. Eureka, Wis., May 28, 1934; d. Kenneth Arthur and Vera Christine (Barnett) George; m. David Lee Zuern, June 30, 1956. Student, U. Wis., 1954-56. With Kimberly-Clark Corp., Neenah, Wis., 1956-78, sales promotion specialist, 1969—78, trade show adminstr., 1978—79; conv. mgr. Smith Bucklin & Assocs., Chgo., 1979-84, account exec., 1984-96; exec. dir. Bakery Equipment Mfrs. Assn., Chgo., 1984-96, Soc. Gynecologic Oncologists, Chgo., 1984-96; assoc. sec., treas. Internat. Baking Industry Exposition, Chgo., 1986-98; ret., 1998. Consumer cons. Kimberly-Clark Corp., Neenah, 1969. Recipient Lifetime Achievement award, Bakery Equipment Mfrs. Assn., 2007. Mem. World Airlines Hist. Soc., Exptl. Aircraft Assn., Charles A. Lindbergh Collectors Soc. (past pres.). Avocations: stamp collecting/philately, philography, music, antiques, historic firehouse restoration. Home and Office: 913 Wylde Oak Dr Oshkosh WI 54904-7633 Personal E-mail: rosyposy@charter.net.

ZUKOSKI, CHARLES FREDERICK, IV, chemical engineering educator, academic administrator; b. Birmingham, Ala., Aug. 17, 1955; BA in Physics, Reed Coll., 1977; PhD in Chem. Engring., Princeton U., 1984. Asst. prof. dept. chem. engring U. Ill., Urbana, 1985-90, assoc. prof., 1990-93, prof., 1994—, alumni prof. chem. engring., 1994—, head chem. engring., 1995—, vice chancellor rsch., William H. and Janet G. Lycan prof. Contbr. articles to profl. jours. Fulbright scholar, Dept. Applied Math., U. Melbourne, 1992; recipient NSF Presdl. Young Investigator award, 1986, Everitt Tchg. award, 1992, Ralph K. Iler award, Am. Chem. Soc., 1997, Alpha Chi Sigma award, AIChE, 2002. Mem.: NAE. Office: U Ill Dept Chem Engring 109 Roger Adams Lab MC-712 Box C-3 600 S Mathews Ave Urbana IL 61801 Office Phone: 217-333-0034. Office Fax: 217-333-5052. E-mail: czukoski@uiuc.edu.

ZUKOWSKY, JOHN ROBERT, curator, museum director; b. NYC, Apr. 21, 1948; s. John and Mary (Charchan) Z. BA, Hunter Coll., CUNY, 1971; MA, SUNY, Binghamton, 1974, PhD, 1977. Archtl. archivist Hudson River Mus., Yonkers, N.Y., 1974-76, Art Inst. Chgo., 1978-81, architecture curator, 1981—2004; dir. Westcott House Found., Springfield, Ohio, 2004—05; chief curator Intrepid Sea, Air and Space Mus., NYC, 2005—. Mem. Historic Sites Adv. Council, Springfield, Ill., 1982-83, Landmarks Preservation Council, Chgo., 1982-83; jury mem. Honor awards AIA, Washington, 1987. Co-author: Hudson River Villas, 1985, The Sky's the Limit Chicago Skyscrapers, 1990, Austrian Architecture and Design, 1991; co-author, editor: Mies Reconsidered, 1986, Chicago Architecture: 1872-1922, 1987, Chicago Architecture and Design, 1923-93, 1993, The Many Faces of Modern Architecture, 1994, Karl Friedrich Schinkel, 1781-1841: The Drama of Architecture, 1994, Building for Air Travel: Architecture and Design for Commercial Aviation, 1996, Japan 2000,

1998, Skyscrapers: The New Millennium, 2000, 2001, Building for Space Travel, 2001; editor: A System of Architectural Ornament (Louis H. Sullivan), 1990; author: Space Architecture: The Work by John Frassanito and Associates for NASA, 1999; contbr. articles to profl. jours. Decorated Chevalier des arts and lettres (France), Verdienst/Ehren Kreuz, Austria; recipient Honig award Chgo. chpt. Am. Soc. Appraisers, 1989; postdoctoral rsch. fellow NEH, 1977-78, Rsch. fellow, NEA, 1991. Mem. AIA (hon., Disting. Svc. award Chgo. chpt. 1986), Arts Club Chgo. Business E-Mail: jzukowsky@westcotthouse.org.

ZUNG, THOMAS TSE-KWAI, architect; b. Shanghai, Feb. 8, 1933; came to the U.S., 1937, naturalized, 1954; 1 child, Thomas Bates. Student, Drew U., 1950-51, Va. Poly. Inst., 1951-53, Columbia U., 1955-57; BArch, U. Mich., 1960; MS in Design Sci., Internat. Coll., 1982. Project arch. Edward Durell Stone, Arch., NYC, 1958, 60-65; arch. Cleve., 1967—. Pres. Buckminster Fuller, Sadao and Zung, Archs., 1979—; disting. sr. fellow Stanford U. Librs.; John Denver Windstar Found. Symposium spkr., Aspen, Colo., 2004. Author-editor: Buckminster Fuller, Anthology for the New Millennium; prin. works include City Cleve. Pub. Utilities Bldg., Cleve. State U. Geodesic Elongated Dome, Mayfran, Inc., Sawmill Creek Lodge, U. Akron Guzzetta Hall, Music, Speech and Theater Arts Ctr., Alumni Ctr. Bowling Green State U., U. Akron Master Plan-West, City of East Cleveland, Superior Euclid beautification plan, student recreation ctr. Bowling Green State U., Glenville Pub. Libr., campus bldg. Tex. Wesleyan Coll., recreation, health and phys. edn. bldg. Wittenberg U., Medina Res. Park Office, arena, health, phys. edn. complex U. Akron, Dyke Coll., Lima State Prison, Cleve. Children's Christian Home, State of Ohio Pre-Release Ctr. Cleve., Lorain-Grafton State Prison, Mayfield H.S., Asian Village Project, Cleve. Metroparks Tropical Rainforest Bldg., Student Union Wittenberg U., YWCA, Salem, Ohio, China Internat. Trade Ctr., People's Rep. China, additions to Cleve. Hopkins Internat. Airport, Ohio State U. Coll. of Dentistry-Postle Hall and Hist. Costume and Textile Mus., Master Plan Schreiner Coll. and Cailloux Student Ctr., Griffin Welcome Ctr., Master Plan Walsh Univ., Walsh Student Union, Columbus, Western Res. Psychiat. Hosp., Ohio, Trumbull State Prison, Ohio Dept. Transp. Prototypical Rest Stop Design; patentee in field. Trustee Pace Assn., 1970-73, Karamu House, 1974-80, Cleve. Inst. Music, 1979-86, Chinese Cultural Assn., 1980-84, Ohio Arts Coun., 1982-84; task force chmn. Greater Cleve. Growth Assn., 1970; mem. Coun. Human Rels., 1972, Leadership Cleve. Class '77; cubmaster local Boy Scouts Am., 1977-79; vestryman St. Christopher-by-River, 1980-83; bd. dirs. Buckminster Fuller Inst., 1983—, Pearl S. Buck Found., 1989-98, cons. arch. hist. house com.; mem. Adv. Coun. Aging, State of Ohio, 1997—; founder, pres. Bratenahl 100, 2006-. With Signal Corps, U.S. Army, 1953-55. Decorated 5 medals; recipient Pub. Works award, State of Ohio, 1971, Design award, Korean Inst. Constrn. Tech., 1984, Ohio Valley ABC Design Excellence award, Wittenberg U. Student Union, 1989, Synergeticists N.E. Corridor award, 2005, Buckminster Fuller SNEC award, 2005, others; Disting. sr. fellow, Stanford U. Librs. Mem. AIA (dir. Cleve. chpt. 1980, Design award Cleve. chpt. 1972, Design award 1989), Am. Soc. Planning Ofcls., English Speaking Union (trustee 1972-75), Ohio Soc. Archs., Ohio Assn. Minority Archs. and Engrs. (trustee 1982-90), Hermit Club, City Club (dir. 1972-74, v.p. 1974), Rotary; Buckminster Fuller Inst. (bd. mem.). Office: Buckminster Fuller Sadao & Zung 1 Bratenahl Pl Cleveland OH 44108-1181

ZUNICH, JANICE, pediatrician, geneticist, educator, health facility administrator; b. New Kensington, Pa., Sept. 2, 1953; d. Nick and Mary (Zivkovich) Z.; m. Milan Katic, June 20, 1981; children: Nikola Ilija, Milana. BS, Ohio State U., 1974, MD, 1978. Diplomate Am. Bd. Pediat., Nat. Bd. Med. Examiners, Am. Bd. Med. Genetics (clin. genetics, clin. cytogenetics). Intern, then resident in pediat. Columbus Children's Hosp., Ohio, 1978-81; genetics fellow Luth. Gen. Hosp., Park Ridge, Ill., 1981-83; asst. prof. pediat. W.Va. U. Med. Ctr., Morgantown, 1983-85, assoc. dir. cytogenetics, 1984-85; clin. assoc. prof. med. genetics, dir. Genetics Ctr. Ind. U. Sch. Medicine NW, Gary, 1985—. Genetics cons. Cmty. Hosp., Munster, Ind., Porter Meml. Hosp., Valparaiso, Ind., St. Anthony Med. Ctr., Crown Point, Ind., Meth. Hosp., Gary and Merrillville, Ind., St. Margaret Hosp., Hammond, Ind., St. Mary Med. Ctr., Hobart, Ind., LaPorte (Ind.) Hosp., Meml. Hosp., South Bend, Ind. Contbr. articles to profl. jours. Mem. med. com. Planned Parenthood, N.W.-N.E. Ind., Merrillville, 1987-99; mem. med. adv. com. Svcs. for Children with Spl. Health Care Needs, Indpls., 1989-92; chmn. Lake County Task Force on Teen Pregnancy, 1998-2000; mem. Lake County Child Fatality Rev. Com., 2003-; mem. Lake County Fetal and Infant Mortality Rev. Com., 2004—; mem. Lake County Child Protection Team, 2000—; treas. Mental Health Assn. Lake County, 1995-99, bd. dirs., 1991—. Named Person of Yr. Down Syndrome Assn. N.W. Ind., Highland, 1988; Charles F. Whitten fellow Sickle Cell Found. N.W. Ind., 1990. Fellow: AMA, Am. Coll. Med. Genetics (founding fellow), Am. Acad. Pediat.; mem.: Lake County Med. Soc., Ind. State Med. Assn., Am. Soc. Human Genetics, Great Lakes Regional Genetics Group (financing genetics svcs. sub-com. 1988—99), Alpha Epsilon Delta, Phi Beta Kappa. Eastern Orthodox. Avocations: piano, folk dancing, choral singing, travel. Office: Ind U Sch Medicine NW 3400 Broadway Gary IN 46408-1101 Home Phone: 219-322-7740; Office Phone: 219-980-6560. Business E-Mail: jzunich@iun.edu.

ZURAITIS, MARITA, insurance company executive; V.p. ceded-reins. USF&G Comml. Ins. Group, br. v.p., regional v.p., sr. v.p.; sr. v.p. U.S. ins. ops. The St. Paul Co., Inc., St. Paul, 1998—2001, exec. v.p. Comml. Lines Group, 2001—02, CEO Comml. Lines Group, 2003—. Office: The Saint Paul Cos Inc 385 Washington St Saint Paul MN 55102

ZURHEIDE, CHARLES HENRY, consulting electrical engineer; b. St. Louis, May 9, 1923; s. Charles Henry and Ollie C. Z.; m. Ruth M. Plueck, June 25, 1949; children— Barbara Anne, Pamela S BS in Elec. Engring, U. Mo., Columbia, 1944. Registered profl. engr., Mo. Distbn. engr. Laclede Power & Light Co., St. Louis, 1944-45; sub-sta. engr., then indsl. engr. Union Electric Co., St. Louis, 1945-51; chief elec. engr. Fruin-Colnon Contracting Co., St. Louis, 1951-54; a founder, treas., v.p. Smith-Zurheide, Inc., St. Louis, 1954-65; pres. Zurheide-Herrmann, Inc., St. Louis, 1965—, chmn. bd., 1988—2002; ret. Chmn. Elec. Code Rev. Commn., St. Louis, 1965-, Mo. Bd. Profl. Engrs., 1977-82, St. Louis Indsl. Devel. Commn., 1965-67; mem. adv. panel region 6 GSA, 1977—; plan commn., City of Ferguson, Mo., 1968-73; tech. adv. com. St. Louis C. of C., 1977; mem. Mo. Pub. Svc. Commn. Task Force on Retail Wheeling of Electricity, 1998 Recipient Dist. Svc. in Engring. award, U. Mo., 1976. Fellow Am. Cons. Engrs. Council; mem. Mo. Soc. Profl. Engrs. (Engr. of Year award 1970), Cons. Engrs. Council Mo., IEEE, Illuminating Engring. Soc., Engrs. Club St. Louis (Achievement award 2003), Tau Alpha Pi. Clubs: Norwood Hills Country, Mo. Athletic Home: 14336 Spyglass Rdg Chesterfield MO 63017-2140 Office: Zurheide-Herrmann Inc 4333 Clayton Ave Saint Louis MO 63110-1684 Business E-Mail: czurheide@zhideas.com.

ZURIER, REBECCA, art history educator; AB, Harvard U., 1978; PhD, Yale U., 1988. Assoc. prof. U. Mich., Ann Arbor; Schragis fellow in modern arts Syracuse U., 1990—92. Guest curator Metropolitan Lives: The Ashcan Artists and Their New York Nat. Mus. Am. Art, Smithsonian Instn., 1995; guest curator Yale U. Art Gallery, 1986; vis. appts. U. So. Calif., Emory U., U. Pa., George Washington U., 1988—90. Author: The American Firehouse: An Architectural and Social History, 1982, Art for the Masses (1911-1917): A Radical Magazine and Its Graphics, 1988 (Alfred H. Barr award Coll. Art Assn., 1996); co-author (with Robert W. Snyder and Virginia Mecklenburg): Metropolitan Lives, 1995. Charles Warren Ctr. for Studies in Am. History, Harvard U. fellow, 1999, Getty Postdoctoral grantee, 1993. Office: Univ Mich Art History Dept 519 S State St Ann Arbor MI 48109-1357

ZURKOWSKI, ROY, health club chain executive; b. 1931; married. With Vic Tanny, 1952—62, now pres. Birmingham, Mich.; with Health & Tennis Corp Am. (parent), Chgo., 1962—72, v.p. from 1972, now pres. Office: Vic Tanny 6420 Telegraph Rd Bloomfield Hills MI 48301-1758 also: Bally's Health & Tennis Corp 2029 Century Park E Los Angeles CA 90067-2901

ZVARA, CHRISTINE C., middle school education educator; BS in Physical Edn. and Adaptive Physical Edn., U. Wis. Mid. and secondary physical edn. specialist grades 6-12 Gibraltar Schs., Fish Creek, Wis. Coord. Dance for Heart Event; mem. swim team bd. Door County YMCA, 1991-95; vol. Sister Bay Fall Classic Run, 1988-91; mem. Sturgeon Bay Sch. Booster Club, 1992—, Sturgeon Bay Band Parents Club, 1991—, Friends of Gibraltar PTO, 1982—. Named Coord. of Yr. Wis. ortheast Dist. Jump Rope for Heart, 1993. Home: 205 S 10th Ave Sturgeon Bay WI 54235-1803 Office: Gibraltar Sch RR 1 Box 205-g Fish Creek WI 54212-9801

ZWEBEN, STUART HARVEY, information scientist, educator, dean; b. Bronx, NY, Apr. 21, 1948; s. Max D. and Ruth (Schwartz) Z.; m. Rochelle T. Small, June 13, 1971; 1 child, Naomi. BS, CUNY, 1968; MS, Purdue U., 1971, PhD, 1974. Sys. analyst IBM Corp., Kingston, NY, 1969-70; asst. prof. Ohio State U., Columbus, 1974-80, from vice chmn. to acting chmn. computer sci. dept., 1982-84, assoc. prof., 1980-92, prof., 1992—, chmn., 1994—2005, assoc. dean academic affairs and adminstrn. Coll. Engring., 2006—. Pres. Computing Scis. Accreditation Bd., Stamford, Conn., 1989-91, v.p. 1987-89, sec., treas. 1986-87; sec.-treas. Fedn. on Computing in the U.S., Washington, 1992. Contbr. articles to profl. jours. Rsch. grantee NSF, 1981-83, 88-97, 2005-06, Army Rsch. Office, 1980-83, Dept. Edn., 1983-85, Applied Info. Tech. Rsch. Ctr., 1990-91, Honda R&D, 1998-2006, Dayton, Ohio, 2003-; Equipment grant AT&T Bell Labs, 1984, 86-88. Fellow Accreditation Bd. Engring. and Tech., Inc. (computing accreditation commn. exec. com. 2001—, vice chmn. ops., 2005-06, chair-elect, 2006-07, chmn., 2007—), Assn. for Computing Machinery (pres. 1994-96, v.p. 1992-94, coun. mem. 1982-88, chpt. bd. chmn. 1982-85, publications bd. 1988-92, fin. com. 1990-92, nominating com. chmn. 1999-2000, fellows com. chmn. 2003, constn. and bylaws chmn. 1988-92, Recognition of Svc. award 1980, 85, 87-88, Outstanding Contbn. award 1997); mem. AAUP, IEEE Computer Soc. (assoc. editor 1990-98), Computing Rsch. Assn. (bd. dirs. 1997-2004, Spl. Svc. award 2006), Coun. Sci. Soc. Presidents (sec. 1998), Columbus Tech. Coun. (Tech. Person of Yr. award 2000). Avocations: sports, stamp collecting/philately. Office: Ohio State U Computer Scis 2015 Neil Ave Columbus OH 43210-1210 Office Phone: 614-292-9526. Business E-Mail: zweben@cse.ohio-state.edu.

ZWEIFEL, DAVID ALAN, newspaper editor; b. Monroe, Wis., May 19, 1940; s. Cloyence John and Uva Lorraine (Skinner) Z.; m. Sandra Louise Holz, Sept. 7, 1968; children: Daniel Mark, Kristin Lynn. BJ, U. Wis., 1962. Reporter The Capital Times, Madison, Wis., 1962-71, city editor, 1971-78, mng. editor, 1978-83, editor, 1983—. V.p. Simpson St. Free Press, 2001—; bd. dirs. Swiss Am. Ctr., Friends of Monona Terrace, Capital Times Co., Madison Newspapers Inc., William T. Evjue Charitable Trust. V.p. Alliance for Children and Youth, Madison, 1983—; bd. dirs. United Cerebral Palsy Dane County, Madison, 1984-91. Lt. U.S. Army, 1963-65; col. USNG, ret. Named Investigative Reporter of Yr. Madison Press Club, 1972; Disting. Journalism grad., U. Wis., 2003 Mem.: Soc. Profl. Journalists (Spl. Achievement award 1992, 1996), Wis. Freedom of Info. Coun. (pres. 1986—2000), Wis. AP (pres. 1987—88), Am. Soc. Newspaper Editors (com. freedom of info., Pulitzer Prize juror 2000, 2001), U. Wis. Alumni Assn., Wis. N.G. Assn. (trustee 1975—81), Elks. Avocations: running, bowling, book collecting. Home: 5714 Tecumseh Ave Monona WI 53716-2964 Office: The Capital Times PO Box 8060 Madison WI 53708-8060

ZWICK, GARY ALAN, lawyer; b. Cleve., July 7, 1954; s. Coleman David and Eleanor Elaine (Brodsky) Z.; m. Linda Hollander, June 29, 1980; children: Melissa Ann, Daniel Benjamin. BBA in Acctg. and Fin., Kent State U., 1976; JD, Cleve.-Marshall Coll. Law, 1980; LLM in Taxation, Georgetown U., 1982. CPA Ohio, 1981; bar: Ohio 1980, US Tax Ct. Staff acct. Coleman D. Zwick, Cleve., 1976-80; shareholder, dir. tax Cohen & Co., Cleve., 1982-97; tax atty., dir. Walter & Haverfield, LLP, Cleve., 1997—, head tax & wealth mgmt. sect., chair fed. tax grp. Adj. prof. tax law Cleve. State U. Coll. Law. Named an Ohio Super Lawyer, Law & Politics Mag., 2004—07; named one of Top 100 Attys., Worth mag., 2005—06. Office: Walter & Haverfield LLP The Tower at Erieview 1301 E 9th St Ste 3500 Cleveland OH 44114-1821 Office Phone: 216-928-2902. Office Fax: 216-916-2340. E-mail: gzwick@walterhav.com.

ZWICKEY, SHEILA KAYE, lawyer; b. Chgo., July 9, 1951; d. Ewald Arthur Zwickey and Kathryn Allene (Hurst) Zaiden. BS, U. Wis., 1973; MSW, U. Ind., 1975, JD, 1981. Social worker Dept. of Corrections/State of Ind., Indpls., 1975-81; dep. pub. defender State of Ind., Indpls., 1981-85; pub. defender Rush County, Rushville, Ind., 1985-90, Wayne County, Richmond, Ind., 1986-90; prosecuting atty. Rush County/State of Ill., Rushville, 1991—; pvt. practice Batesville, Ind., 1991—. Bd. dirs. Ind. Pub. Defender's Coun., Indpls. Bd. dirs. Rush City Humane Soc., 1988-89; officer Rush County/Ind. Dem. Women's Club, 1991—. Mem. Kiwanis, Rush City Bar Assn. (pres. 1988-89). Democrat. Roman Catholic. Office: Prosecutors Office Rush County Ct House Rushville IN 46173

ZWIER, TIMOTHY S., chemistry professor; married. BS in Chemistry, Calvin Coll., 1977; PhD Chem. Physics, U. Colo., Boulder, 1981. Postdoctoral rsch. assoc. U. Chgo. James Franck Inst., 1981—83; asst. to assoc. prof. chemistry Calvin Coll., 1983—88; asst. prof. chemistry Purdue U., West Lafayette, Ind., 1988—93, assoc. prof. chemistry, 1993—97, prof. chemistry, 1997—. JILA vis. fellow, 1994—95; mem. planetary atmosphere review panel NASA, 2000, 03, 04; assoc. head dept. chemistry Purdue U., 2001—03, head dept. chemistry, 2004—; mem. combustion rsch. facility adv. bd. Sandia Nat. Labs., 2004—; mem. external adv. com. for rsch. corp. evaluation James Madison U., 2005—; lectr. in field. Co-editor: Internat. Revs. in Phys. Chemistry, 1998—2003; sr. editor: Jour. Phys. Chemistry, 2003—; mem. editl. bd. Molecular Physics, 2001—; contbr. articles to profl. jours. Named Faculty Scholar, Purdue U., 1999—2004; Alfred P. Sloan Rsch. fellow, 1989—91. Fellow: Am. Phys. Soc. (councilor-at-large divn. chem. physics 2002—05, Earle K. Plyler prize for Molecular Spectroscopy 2007); mem.: AAAS, Am. Astron. Soc., Am. Chem. Soc. Office: Purdue U Rm B155 Dept Chemistry 560 Oval Dr West Lafayette IN 47907-2084 E-mail: zwier@purdue.edu.

ZYWICKI, ROBERT ALBERT, retired electric power industry executive; b. Chgo., Sept. 23, 1930; s. Martin Albert and Margaret Irene (Mackowski) Z.; m. Barbara Joan Hagerty; children: Robert, Cheryl, Cindy, Carrie. B in Commerce, Northwestern U., 1966. Teller Chgo. Title and Trust Bank, Chgo., 1949-50; painter Getz Molding Co., Chgo., 1950-51; purchasing agt. Woodworker's Tool Works, Chgo., 1953-54; serviceman Addressograph Multigraph, Chgo., 1954-55; mem. Chgo. Fire Dept., 1955-62; v.p. Anixter Bros. Inc., Skokie, Ill., 1955-87; co-owner A-Z Industries, Northbrook, Ill., 1987—2003; ret., 2003. Served as cpl. U.S. Army, 1951-53. Mem. Am. Legion (comdr.). Republican. Roman Catholic. Avocations: thoroughbred horse racing, classical music, baseball card collecting, tennis. Home: 1330 Sprucewood Ln Deerfield IL 60015-4771 Personal E-mail: peter1330@comcast.net.

Professional Index

AGRICULTURE

UNITED STATES

COLORADO

Montrose
Kontny, Vincent L. *rancher, retired engineering executive*

ILLINOIS

East Peoria
Frison, Rick *agricultural company executive*

Kenilworth
Clary, Rosalie Brandon Stanton *timber farm executive, civic worker*

Pleasant Plains
Thomas, Evelyn B. *agricultural products supplier*

Quincy
Finlay, Timothy *agricultural products supplier*
Foster, Michael *agricultural products supplier*

Urbana
Cheryan, Munir *agricultural and biochemical engineering educator*
Hoeft, Robert Gene *agricultural studies educator*
Spitze, Robert George Frederick *agricultural studies educator*

INDIANA

Fort Wayne
Marine, Clyde Lockwood *agricultural products supplier, consultant*

Indianapolis
Hegel, Carolyn Marie *farm owner and organization executive*
Kron, Randy *farmer, agricultural association administrator*
Villwock, Don *farmer, farming association executive*

West Lafayette
Lechtenberg, Victor L. *agricultural studies educator*

IOWA

Ames
Mullen, Russell Edward *agricultural studies educator*
Topel, David Glen *agricultural studies educator*

Des Moines
Mertz, Dolores Mary *farmer, state legislator*

Mason City
Kuhlman, James Weldon *retired county extension education director*

West Des Moines
Lang, Craig *farmer, farm association officer*

KANSAS

Claflin
Burmeister, Paul Frederick *farmer*

Garden City
Reeve, Lee M. *farmer*

Iola
Strickler, Ivan K. *dairy farmer*

Manhattan
Ahlerich, Stan *farmer, farm association administrator*
McKee, Richard Miles *retired agricultural studies educator*

MICHIGAN

Howell
Cotton, Larry *ranching executive*

Pigeon
Maust, Joseph J. *agricultural products supplier*

MINNESOTA

Saint Paul
Christopherson, Al *farm association executive*
Sviggum, Steven Arthur *farmer, state representative*

MISSOURI

Jefferson City
Boatright, Matt *agricultural products supplier, state agency administrator, director*

Nixa
Kreider, Jim *farmer, former state legislator*

NEBRASKA

Lincoln
Neidig, Bryce P. *farmer, farm association administrator*

NORTH DAKOTA

Pettibone
DeKrey, Duane Lee *farmer, rancher*

OHIO

Columbus
Ockerman, Herbert W. *agricultural studies educator*

SOUTH DAKOTA

Elk Point
Chicoine, Roland Alvin *farmer, former state legislator*

Saint Lawrence
Lockner, Vera Joanne *farmer, rancher, state legislator*

ADDRESS UNPUBLISHED

Brooks, Kenneth N. *forestry educator*
Durnell, Earl *rancher*
Jacobson, Norman L. *retired agricultural educator, researcher*
Joseph, Chris *business services executive*
Luening, Robert Adami *retired agricultural studies educator*
Walter, Kenneth Luverne *retired agricultural facility director*
Webb, O. Glenn *retired farm supplies company executive*
Westfall, Morris *farmer, retired state legislator*

ARCHITECTURE & DESIGN

UNITED STATES

CALIFORNIA

Newport Beach
Blankenship, Edward G. *architect*

COLORADO

Longmont
Woollen, Evans *retired architectural firm executive*

FLORIDA

Naples
Lickhalter, Merlin *architect*

ILLINOIS

Bloomington
Switzer, Jon Rex *architect*

Champaign
Baker, Jack Sherman *retired architect*
Boubekri, Mohamed *architecture educator*
Hopkins, Lewis Dean *architecture educator*
Riley, Robert Bartlett *landscape architect*

Chicago
Balasi, Mark Geoffrey *architect*
Barney, Carol Ross *architect*
Beeby, Thomas H. *architect*
Belluschi, Anthony C. *architect*
Cook, Richard Borreson *architect*
Epstein, Sidney *architect, civil engineer*
Gardunio, Joseph *landscaping company executive*
Hackl, Donald John *architect*
Holabird, John Augur, Jr. *retired architect*
Jahn, Helmut *architect*
Kerbis, Gertrude Lempp *architect*
Kirkegaard, R. Lawrence *architect, acoustical engineer*
Legge Kemp, Diane *architect, landscape consultant*
Matthei, Edward Hodge *architect*
McCullagh, Grant Gibson *retired architect*
Phillips, Frederick Falley *architect*
Schirn, Janet Sugerman *interior designer*
Simovic, Laszlo *architect*
Smith, Adrian Devaun *architect*
Terp, Dana George *architect*
Tigerman, Stanley *architect, educator*
Torgersen, Torwald Harold *architect, consultant*
Valerio, Joseph Mastro *architectural firm executive, educator*
VanderBeke, Patricia K. *architect*
Vinci, John Nicholas *architect, educator*
Weber, Hanno *architect*
Weese, Benjamin Horace *architect*
Whitney, Patrick Foster *design educator*

Evanston
Grunsfeld, Ernest Alton III *architect*

Glenview
Bradtke, Philip Joseph *architect*

Highland Park
Dirsmith, Ronald *architect*

Hinsdale
Anderson, Harry Frederick, Jr. *architect*
Unikel, Eva Taylor *interior designer*

Kenilworth
Schneider-Criezis, Susan Marie *architect*

Schaumburg
Otis, James, Jr. *architect*

Skokie
Siegal, Burton Lee *product designer, consultant, inventor*
Zolomij, Robert William *landscape architect, consultant*

Winnetka
Schlossman, John Isaac *architect*

INDIANA

Carmel
Eden, Barbara Janiece *commercial and residential interior designer*
McLaughlin, Harry Roll *architect*

Michigan City
Brockway, Lee J. *architect*

Mishawaka
Ponko, William Reuben *architect*
Troyer, LeRoy Seth *architect*

Muncie
Ernstberger, Eric *landplanning architectural company executive*

New Haven
Cole, Kenneth Duane *architect*

South Bend
Smith, Thomas Gordon *architect*

IOWA

Ames
Lewis, Calvin Fred *architect, educator*
Palermo, Gregory Sebastian *architect*

Cedar Rapids
Stone, Herbert Marshall *architect*

Iowa City
Neumann, Roy Covert *architect*

KANSAS

Lawrence
Alstrom, Sven Erik *architect*
Grabow, Stephen Harris *architecture educator*

Manhattan
Kremer, Eugene R. *architecture educator*

Overland Park
Conrad, William Merrill *architect*

MICHIGAN

Ann Arbor
Beckley, Robert Mark *architect, educator*
Benford, Harry Bell *naval architect*
Marans, Robert Warren *planning consultant, architect, educator*
Metcalf, Robert Clarence *architect, educator*

Bloomfield Hills
Allen, Maurice Bartelle, Jr. *architect*
Brown, Jack Wyman *architect*

Chelsea
Fry, Richard E. *architectural firm executive*

Detroit
Francis, Edward D. *architect*
Frank, Richard Calhoun *architect*
Roehling, Carl David *architect*

Flint
Tomblinson, James Edmond *architect*

MINNESOTA

Duluth
Salmela, David Daniel *architect*
Whiteman, Richard Frank *architect*

Minneapolis
Clemence, Roger Davidson *landscape architect, educator*
Faricy, Richard Thomas *architect*
Jacob, Bernard Michel *architect*
Martin, Roger Bond *landscape architect*
Parker, Leonard S. *architect, educator*
Rand, Peter Anders *architect*
Tollefson, Lee *architect*

MISSOURI

Branson
Ownby, Jerry Steve *landscape architect, educator*

Clayton
Christner, Theodore Carroll *architect*

Kansas City
Seligson, Theodore H. *architect, interior designer, urban planner*

Saint Louis
Chivetta, Anthony Joseph *architect*
Cotton, W(illiam) Philip, Jr. *architect*
Michaelides, Constantine Evangelos *architect, educator*
Obata, Gyo *architect*
Thalden, Barry *architect*
Weese, Cynthia Rogers *architect, educator*

Springfield
Liu, Yuan Hsiung *drafting and design educator*

NEBRASKA

Lincoln
Morrow, Andrew Nesbit *interior designer, business owner*
Stange, James Henry *architect*
Steward, Weldon Cecil *architecture educator, architect, consultant*

Omaha
Bowen, Gary Roger *architect*
Polsky, Donald Perry *architect*
Ryan, Mark Anthony *architect, lawyer*

OHIO

Cincinnati
Chatterjee, Jayanta *architecture and planning educator*
Fitzgerald, James T. *architect*
Glendening, Everett Austin *architect*
Goetzman, Bruce Edgar *architecture educator*
Meisner, Gary Wayne *landscape architect*
Nielsen, George Lee *architect*
Senhauser, John Crater *architect*

Cleveland
Behnke, William Alfred *retired landscape architect*
Eberhard, William Thomas *architect*
Gibans, James David *architect, consultant*
Hancock, James Beaty *interior designer*
Kelly, John Terence *architect*
Madison, Robert Prince *architect*
Melsop, James William *architect*
Zung, Thomas Tse-Kwai *architect*

Columbus
Bohm, Friedrich (Friedl) K. M. *architectural firm executive*
Kirk, Ballard Harry Thurston *architect*
Voss, Jerrold Richard *architecture educator*
Weinhold, Virginia Beamer *interior designer*

Kent
Sommers, David Lynn *architect*

Painesville
Filson, Ronald Coulter *architect, educator, dean*

Toledo
Hills, Arthur W. *architectural firm executive*

WISCONSIN

Eau Claire
Larson, Brian Foix *architect*

Madison
Nisbet, Thomas K. *architect*
Tishler, William Henry *landscape architect, educator*

Milwaukee
Greenstreet, Robert Charles *architect, educator*

Soldiers Grove
Quebe, Jerry Lee *retired architect*

Waukesha
Schwartz, Robert Terry *industrial designer, director*

ADDRESS UNPUBLISHED

Degenhardt, Robert Allan *architectural firm executive, engineering executive*
Ellington, Howard Wesley *architect*
Flowers, Damon Bryant *architect*
Hutchins, Robert Ayer *architectural consultant*
Keeley, Larry *innovation strategist*

Molnar, Donald Joseph *landscape architecture educator*
Pettitt, Jay S. *architect, consultant*
Poor, Janet Meakin III *landscape designer*
Preiser, Wolfgang Friedrich Ernst *architect, educator, consultant, researcher*
Ryan, John Michael *landscape architect*
Salzman, Arthur George *retired architect*
Sims, Howard F. *architectural firm executive*
Thorland, Timothy *architectural firm executive*
Van Dine, Harold Forster, Jr. *architect, artist*
Van Housen, Thomas Corwin III *architect*

ARTS: LITERARY *See also* COMMUNICATIONS MEDIA

UNITED STATES

ILLINOIS

Chicago
Camper, John Jacob *writer, academic administrator*
Hoover, Paul *poet*
Plotnik, Arthur *writer, columnist*
Terkel, Studs (Louis Terkel) *writer, journalist*
Turow, Scott F. *writer, lawyer*
Verschoor, Curtis Carl *writer, consultant*
Vowell, Sarah *writer, radio personality*
Winters, Anne *poet, educator*

Evanston
Gibbons, William Reginald, Jr. *poet, writer, translator, editor*
Kertész, Imre *writer*

Lake Forest
Swanton, Virginia Lee *writer, publisher*

Northfield
Mamet, David Alan *playwright, scriptwriter*

Urbana
Lieberman, Laurence *poet, educator*

INDIANA

Bloomington
Mitchell, Bert Breon *literary translator*

Indianapolis
Gregory, Valiska *writer*

Muncie
Woodress, Frederick Albert *writer*

IOWA

Iowa City
Bell, Marvin Hartley *poet, language educator*
Johnson, Nicholas *writer, lawyer, educator*
Merrill, Christopher Lyall *writer*
Stern, Gerald Daniel *poet*
Swensen, Cole *poet, educator*

KANSAS

Leawood
Garwood, Julie *writer*

MICHIGAN

Ann Arbor
Gregerson, Linda Karen *poet, language educator, critic*

Detroit
Madgett, Naomi Long *poet, editor, publisher, educator*

East Lansing
Wakoski, Diane *poet, educator*

Kalamazoo
Light, Christopher Upjohn *freelance/self-employed writer, photographer*

Republic
Wixtrom, Donald Joseph *translator*

West Bloomfield
Brin, David *writer, astronomer*

MINNESOTA

Anoka
Lindbergh, Reeve *writer, poet*

Minneapolis
Walker, Sally M. *writer*

Saint Paul
Doermann, Humphrey *writer, consultant*

MISSOURI

Saint Louis
Gass, William H. *writer, educator*
Phillips, Carl *poet, educator*
Schlafly, Phyllis Stewart *writer*

NEBRASKA

Lincoln
Magorian, James *poet, writer*

NEW YORK

New York
Castro, Jan Garden *writer, art educator, consultant*
Eisenberg, Lee B. *writer*
Paretsky, Sara N. *writer*

OHIO

Cleveland
Kovel, Ralph Mallory *writer, antique expert*
Kovel, Terry Horvitz *writer, antiques authority*

Perrysburg
Weaver, Richard L., II, *writer, educator, lecturer*

WASHINGTON

Port Townsend
Kooser, Ted (Theodore J. Kooser) *poet*

WISCONSIN

Janesville
Axtell, Roger E. *writer, retired marketing professional*

Madison
Moore, Lorrie *writer, English professor*

Racine
Wright, Betty Ren *children's book writer*

ADDRESS UNPUBLISHED

Anshaw, Carol *writer*
Ashley, Renee *writer, creative writing educator, consultant*
Fuller, Jack William *writer, retired publishing executive*
Hautman, Pete (Peter Murray) *writer*
Hornbaker, Alice Joy *writer*
Jerome, Kathleen A. *writer, retired publishing executive*
Kotlowitz, Alex *writer, journalist*
Marks, Martha Alford *writer*
Masek, Mark Joseph *writer*
Stern, Richard Gustave *writer*
Stone, John Timothy, Jr. *writer*
Webb, David Allen *writer*
Webb, Martha Jeanne *writer, educator, film producer*

ARTS: PERFORMING

UNITED STATES

ARIZONA

Flagstaff
Schellen, Nando *opera director*

CALIFORNIA

San Jose
Nahat, Dennis F. *performing company executive, choreographer*

ILLINOIS

Bloomington
Brown, Jared *theater director, educator, writer*
Vayo, David Joseph *composer, music educator*

Chicago
Aitay, Victor *concert violinist, music educator*
Arpino, Gerald Peter *performing company executive*
Basden, Cameron *dancer*
Berryman, Diana (Kapnas) *radio personality*
Boynton, Rick *performing company executive*
Conte, Lou *choreographer, director*
Daniel, T. *mime performer, theater director, choreographer*
Elfstrand, Mark *radio personality*
Farina, Dennis *actor*
Gaines, Barbara *theater director*
Garcia, Gerson *radio personality*
Gueno, Barbara *radio personality*
Haney, Tracy *radio personality*
Hayden, John *radio director*
Herseth, Adolph Sylvester (Bud Herseth) *classical musician*
Higgins, Ruth Ellen *theatre producer*
Hiller, Steve *radio personality*
Jean, Kenneth *conductor*
Jeff, Kevin Iega *choreographer, performing company executive*
Kalver, Gail Ellen *dance company executive, musician*
Larrick, Monte *radio personality*
Lavey, Martha *performing company executive*
Letts, Tracy *actor, playwright*
Lustrea, Anita *radio personality*
Mach, Elyse *musician, music educator, writer*
Markey, Judy *radio personality, writer*
Mason, William *opera company director*
McGee, Howard *radio personality*
O'Malley, Kathy *radio personality*
Ran, Shulamit *composer*
Robinson, Reginald R. *musician*
Rosenberg, Thomas B. *film producer, real estate company executive*
Ross, Lori *radio personality*
Savage, Terry *television personality, journalist, stockbroker*
Schulfer, Roche Edward *theater executive director*
Shepherd, Wayne *radio personality*
Shoss, Deanna *theatre executive*
Springer, Jerry (Gerald Norman Springer) *television talk show host, radio personality*
Stifler, Venetia Chakos *dancer, educator, choreographer*
Tallchief, Maria *former ballerina*
Taylor, Koko *singer*
Trogani, Monica *ballet dancer*
Vincent, Jim *performing company executive*
Wang, Albert James *violinist, educator*
Wansley, Ty *radio personality*
Winfrey, Oprah *television talk show host, actress, television producer*
Woods, Nikki *radio personality*
Yu, Linda *newswoman, television anchorwoman*

Evanston
Eberley, Helen-Kay *opera singer, recording industry executive, poet*
Galati, Frank Joseph *stage and opera director, educator, screenwriter, actor*
Hemke, Frederick L. *music educator*
Kujala, Walfrid Eugene *musician, educator*
McDonough, Bridget Ann *music theatre company director*
Peters, Gordon Benes *retired musician*
Reimer, Bennett *music educator, writer*
Yoder, John Clifford *producer, consultant*
Zimmerman, Mary Alice *performing arts educator, director, playwright*

Galesburg
Polay, Bruce *musician, conductor, educator*

Geneva
Klenke, Deborah Ann *band and choral director, department chairman*

Park Forest
Billig, Etel Jewel *theater director, actress*

Rockford
Larsen, Steven *orchestra conductor*

Springfield
Deal, Karen Lynne *conductor*

Urbana
Hedlund, Ronald *baritone*
Taylor, Stephen Andrew *composer, music educator*

INDIANA

Bloomington
Effron, David Louis *conductor, performing company executive*
Mac Watters, Virginia Elizabeth *singer, music educator, actress*
Michael, R. Keith *theatre and dance educator*
Phillips, Harvey G. *musician, performing arts educator*
Svetlova, Marina *ballerina, retired choreographer*

Evansville
Savia, Alfred *conductor*

Fort Wayne
Franklin, Al *artistic director*
Sack, James McDonald, Jr. *radio and television producer, marketing executive*

Indianapolis
Everly, Jack *conductor*
Griswold, Tom *radio personality*
Ilgen, Dorothy L. *arts foundation executive*
Johnson, David Allen *vocalist, minister, lyricist, investment advisor*
Kevoian, Bob *radio personality*
Matis, Jimmy *radio personality*
McGee, Chick *radio personality*
Metcalf, Dean *radio personality*
Venzago, Mario *conductor, music director*

Kokomo
Highlen, Larry Wade *music educator, piano rebuilder, tuner*

Richmond
Bordo, Guy Victor *conductor*

Warsaw
Cleveland, Ashley *musician*

IOWA

Cedar Rapids
Hall, Kathy L. *orchestra executive*
Tiemeyer, Christian *conductor*

Davenport
Schleicher, Donald *music director*
Willett, Lance *orchestra executive*

Des Moines
Giunta, Joseph *conductor, music director*
Harden, Van *radio personality*
Mickelson, Jan *radio personality*
Mill, Jeth *performing company executive*
Mill, Seth *orchestra executive*
Pearson, Mark *radio personality*
Wergin, Gary *radio personality*

Dubuque
Hemmer, Paul Edward *musician, communications executive, composer*

Indianola
Larsen, Robert LeRoy *artistic director*
Mace, Jerilee Marie *performing arts association administrator*

Iowa City
Hovland, Jody *theater director*

Orange City
Barker, Jeff *theater and speech educator*

Waverly
Wade, Janice Elizabeth *musician, educator, conductor*

KANSAS

Emporia
DeBauge, Janice B. *musician*

Lawrence
Hilding, Jerel Lee *music and dance educator, retired dancer*
Tsubaki, Andrew Takahisa *theater director, educator*

Manhattan
Mortenson, Kristin Oppenheim *musician*

Mission
Day, Bobby *radio personality*
Knight, Charlie *radio personality*
McKay, Mark *radio personality*
Munday, Dave *radio personality*

Shawnee Mission
Taylor, Scott *radio personality*

Westwood
Abbott, Bill *radio personality*
Bryan, David *radio personality*
Carson, Roger *radio personality*
Cramer, Ted *radio personality*
Cunningham, Wes *radio personality*
Edwards, Jay *radio personality*
Efron, Bruce *radio personality*
Hurst, Dan *radio personality*
Lawrence, David *radio personality*
Michaels, Dinah *radio personality*
Morelack, Mike *radio personality*
Railsback, Mike *radio personality*
Wilson, Richard Earl (Dick Wilson) *media personality*

Wichita
Berman, Mitchell A. *orchestra executive*
Bryan, Wayne *producer*
Johnson, C. Nicholas *dance company executive*
Sewell, Andrew *music director*

KENTUCKY

Frankfort
Fletcher, Winona Lee *theater educator*

MICHIGAN

Ann Arbor
Bolcom, William Elden *composer, educator, musician*
Kunzel, Erich, Jr. *conductor, arranger, educator*
Scharp-Radovic, Carol Ann *choreographer, classical ballet educator*
Sparling, Peter David *dancer, educator*
Verrett, Shirley *soprano*

Benton Harbor
Schults-Berndt, Elfie *music educator*

Bloomfield Hills
Haidostian, Alice Berberian *concert pianist, volunteer, not-for-profit fundraiser*

Detroit
Clark-Cole, Dorinda Grace *singer, evangelist*
Clark-Sheard, Karen Valencia *gospel singer, evangelist*
DiChiera, David *opera company director*
Dworkin, Aaron P. *violinist, educator*
Harlan, Carmen *television journalist*
Kang, Emil J. *orchestra executive*

Grand Rapids
Allen, Gary *radio personality*
Dionne, Neal *radio personality*
Kaser, Bob *radio personality*
Lockington, David *conductor*
Matlak, John *radio personality*
Schmidt, Gordon Peirce *artistic director*

Kalamazoo
Harvey, Raymond Curtis *conductor*
Ratner, Carl Joseph *opera stage director, baritone*

Midland
Brooks, Peter *radio director*
Diehl, Ann *radio personality*
Hutchinson, Dennis *radio director*
Johnson, Steve *radio personality*
Kirkpatrick, Larry *radio personality*
LaHaie, Perry *radio director*
Lawrence, Jeremy *radio director*

Rochester Hills
Daniels, David Wilder *conductor, author, music educator*
Eisenhower, Laurie *performing company executive*

Saline
Gannett, Diana Ruth *musician, educator*

Southfield
Okun, Maury *dance company executive*

MINNESOTA

Bloomington
Smith, Henry Charles III *symphony orchestra conductor*

Chanhassen
Prince, (Prince Rogers Nelson) *musician, actor*

Duluth
Fields, Allen *artistic director*

Minneapolis
Barnard, Tom *radio personality*
Bundy, Bill *radio personality*
Carter, Adam *radio personality*
Eskola, Eric *radio personality*
Fetler, Paul *retired composer*
Filloon, Karen *radio personality*
Fleezanis, Jorja Kay *musician, educator*
Hagevik, Bruce *radio personality*
Houlton, Lise *performing company executive*
Hyslop, David Johnson *retired arts administrator*
Jeffries, Kim *radio personality*
Jones, Susie *radio personality*
Lee, Dave *radio personality*
Malmberg, Al *radio personality*
Maloney, Rita *radio personality*

Mamayek, Telly *radio personality*
McKinney, Jeff *radio personality*
Miller, John William, Jr. *bassoonist*
Murphy, Steve *radio personality*
Oakes, Laura *radio personality*
Peterson, Patty *radio personality*
Russell, Tim *radio personality*
Severinsen, Doc (Carl H. Severinsen) *conductor, musician*
Sewell, James *artistic director*
Shelby, Don *radio personality*
Stanfield, Rebecca *radio personality*
Strom, Roger *radio personality*
Thomson, Steve *radio personality*
Vanska, Osmo *music director*
Wick, Don *radio personality*

Minnetonka
Jarvis, Linda Marie *music director, educator*

Moorhead
Revzen, Joel *conductor*

Saint Paul
Coppock, Bruce *orchestra executive*
McGegan, Nicholas *music director*

Wayzata
Skrowaczewski, Stanislaw *conductor, composer*

MISSOURI

Branson
Williams, Andy *singer, entertainer*

Kansas City
Bentley, Jeffrey *performing company executive*
Tyler, Sean *radio personality*
Valliere, Roland Edward *performing company executive*
Whitener, William Garnett *dancer, choreographer*

Kirksville
Weerts, Richard Kenneth *music educator*

Saint Louis
Armbruster, Bob *radio personality*
Bernstein, Mark D. *theater director*
Briccetti, Joan Therese *theater manager, arts management consultant*
Connett, Jim *radio director*
Elliot, Bill *radio personality*
Frier, Chuck *radio personality*
Klemm, Ron *radio producer*
Roberts, John *radio personality*
Stewart, John Harger *music educator*
Sudholt, Tom *radio personality*
Wobble, Dick *radio personality*
Woolf, Steven Michael *artistic director*

Springfield
Spicer, Holt Vandercook *retired theater educator*

Wentzville
Berry, Chuck (Charles Edward Anderson Berry) *musician, composer*

NEBRASKA

Lincoln
Dixon, Wheeler Winston *film and video studies educator, writer*
Fawcett-Yeske, Maxine Ann *music educator*
Miller, Tice Lewis *theater educator*

Omaha
Cleary, Pamela Ann *symphony executive*
Johnson, James David *concert pianist, organist, educator*
Yampolsky, Victor *conductor*

NEW MEXICO

Santa Fe
Zlatoff-Mirsky, Everett Igor *violinist*

NEW YORK

New York
Fogel, Henry *orchestra administrator*
Leppard, Raymond John *conductor, musician*
Nelly, (Cornell Haynes Jr.) *rap artist*

NORTH DAKOTA

Bismarck
Lundberg, Susan Ona *musical organization administrator*
Wellin, Thomas *music director*

Fargo
Harris, Bob *radio personality*
Schultz, Ed (Edward Andrew Schultz) *radio personality*
Sunday, Jack *radio personality*

OHIO

Akron
Wang, Ya-Hui *conductor*

Canton
Moorhouse, Linda Virginia *symphony orchestra administrator*

Cincinnati
Alexander, Jeffrey *performing company executive*
Beggs, Patricia Kirk *performing company executive*
Garrett, Bob *radio personality*
Gilbert, Jay *radio personality*
Hills, Alan *performing company executive*
Hoffman, Joel Harvey *composer, educator*
James, Jefferson Ann *performing company executive, choreographer*
Jarvi, Paavo *conductor, music director*
Monder, Steven I. *orchestra executive*
Morgan, Victoria *performing company executive, choreographer*
Paavo, Jarvi *conductor*
Scott, Jim *radio personality*
Stern, Edward *performing company executive*
Tocco, James *pianist*
Ward, Sherman Carl, III, (Buzz Ward) *theater manager*

Cleveland
Albrecht, Chris *talent agency executive, former broadcast executive*
Bamberger, David *opera company executive*
Bishop, Mark *radio personality*
Ivers, Mike *radio personality*
Jackson, Don *radio personality*
Kallik, Chip *radio director*
Morris, Thomas William *symphony orchestra administrator*
Topilow, Carl S. *symphony conductor*
Weir, Dame Gillian Constance *musician*
Welser-Möst, Franz *conductor, music director*

Columbus
Charles, Gerard *performing company executive, choreographer*
Hart, Daniel *orchestra executive*
Rosenstock, Susan Lynn *orchestra administrator*

Dayton
Burke, Dermot *choreographer*
Gittleman, Neal *orchestra conductor*
Hanna, Marsha L. *artistic director*

Elyria
Greer, Richard *radio personality*
Kimble, Bernie *radio director*
Murphy, Tom *radio personality*
Ribbins, Mark *radio personality*

Holland
Conlin, Thomas *conductor*

Independence
Lanigan, John *radio personality*
Malone, Jimmy *radio personality*

Oregon
Knorr, John Christian *entertainment executive, bandleader, producer*

Strongsville
Oltman, C. Dwight *conductor, educator*

Toledo
Bell, Robert *orchestra executive*

Yorkville
Estrada, Erik (Henry Enrique Estrada) *actor*

SOUTH DAKOTA

Sioux Falls
Bennett, Thomas *orchestra executive*

WISCONSIN

Eau Claire
House, George *radio personality*

Greenfield
Dolan, Bob *radio personality*
True, Steve *radio personality*
Weber, Jay *radio personality*

Madison
DeMain, John *opera company director*
Dembski, Stephen Michael *composer, music educator*
Mackie, Richard H. *orchestra executive*

Milwaukee
Belling, Mark *radio personality*
Delfs, Andreas *conductor, musical director*
Hanreddy, Joseph *stage director*
Harris, Christine *dance company executive*
Howard, Clark *radio personality*
Pink, Michael *performing company executive*
Reardon, Mark *radio personality*
Samson, Richard Max *theater director, investment company executive*
Sykes, Charlie *radio personality*
Uecker, Bob *actor, radio announcer, former baseball player, television personality*
Wagner, Jeff *radio personality*

CANADA

MANITOBA

Winnipeg
Lewis, André Leon *performing company executive*

ONTARIO

Callander
Haig, Susan *conductor*

Kitchener
Coles, Graham *conductor, composer*

AUSTRALIA

Perth
Dow, Simon *artistic director, choreographer*

ENGLAND

Leeds
Ichino, Yoko *ballerina*
Nixon, David *dancer*

GERMANY

Berlin
Barenboim, Daniel *conductor, pianist, music director*

ADDRESS UNPUBLISHED

Akos, Francis *retired violinist, conductor*
Aliev, Eldar *former artistic director, choreographer, educator*
Bach, Jan Morris *composer, educator*
Bassett, Leslie Raymond *composer, educator*
Belew, Adrian *guitarist, singer, songwriter, producer*
Blake, Darcie Kay *radio news director, anchor*
Boardman, Eunice *retired music educator*
Boe, David Stephen *musician, educator, dean*
Burbank, Gary *radio personality*
Chisholm, Jacky Clark *singer, evangelist*
Claver, Robert Earl *television producer, director*
Cunningham, Bill *radio personality*
de Blasis, James Michael *performing company executive, theater producer*
Fuerstner, Fiona Margaret Anne *ballet company executive, educator*
Furman, Andy *radio personality*
Hall, Tom T. *retired country singer, songwriter*
Horisberger, Don Hans *conductor, musician*
Järvi, Neeme *conductor, music director*
Klotman, Robert Howard *retired music educator*
Moffatt, Joyce Anne *performing company executive*
Moss, Joel Charles *radio production director*
Palermo, James W. *artistic director*
Reams, Michael Thomas *director, singer, actor*
Rosenthal, Arnold H. *film director, producer, writer, graphic designer, calligrapher*
Rousseau, Eugene Ellsworth *musician, educator, consultant*
Sculfield, Tony *radio personality, comedian*
Sedelmaier, John Josef *filmmaker*
Siciliani, Alessandro Domenico *conductor*
Sloan, Scott *radio personality*
Suzuki, Hidetaro *violinist*
Vandenbroucke, Russell James *theatre director, writer, educator*
Wagner, Mark Anthony *videotape editor*
Ware, D. Clifton *vocalist, educator*
Williams, Camilla *soprano, voice educator*

ARTS: VISUAL

UNITED STATES

DISTRICT OF COLUMBIA

Washington
Jecklin, Lois Underwood *art corporation executive, consultant*

FLORIDA

Clearwater
Slade, Roy *artist, college president, museum director*

ILLINOIS

Chicago
Bowman, Leah *fashion designer, consultant, photographer, educator*
Burroughs, Margaret Taylor Goss *artist*
Coffey, Susanna Jean *artist, educator*
Edelstein, Teri J. *art educator, director, consultant*
Fotopoulos, James *artist*
Gray, Richard *art dealer, consultant, holding company executive*
Gunning, Tom *art educator*
Hannum, Terence J. *artist, director, art critic*
Heller, Reinhold August *art educator, consultant*
Hill, Gary *video artist*
Hindman, Leslie Susan *auction company executive*
King, Andre Richardson *architectural graphic designer*
Kolkey, Gilda *artist*
Look, Dona Jean *artist*
Postiglione, Corey M. *artist, critic, educator*
Thall, Robert *photographer, educator*
Wilson, Anne Gawthrop *artist, educator*
Wolin, Jeffrey Alan *artist*
Workman, Robert Peter *artist, cartoonist*

Edwardsville
Malone, Robert Roy *artist, educator*

Evanston
Conger, William Frame *artist, educator*

Oak Lawn
Jachna, Joseph David *photographer, educator*

South Holland
Fota, Frank George *artist*

Winnetka
Plowden, David *photographer*

INDIANA

Bloomington
Lowe, Marvin *artist, educator*

West Lafayette
Ichiyama, Dennis Yoshihide *art educator, educational association administrator*

IOWA

Des Moines
Messer, Randy Keith *graphics designer, illustrator*
Reece, Maynard Fred *artist, writer*

Iowa City
Lasansky, Mauricio *artist*
Scott, John Beldon *art history educator, writer*

KANSAS

Lawrence
Hermes, Marjory Ruth *machine embroidery and arts educator*

Topeka
Lee, Karen *art appraiser*

MARYLAND

Annapolis
Markman, Ronald *artist, educator*

MICHIGAN

Ann Arbor
Eisenberg, Marvin Julius *retired art history educator*
Zurier, Rebecca *art history educator*

Dearborn
Cape, James Odies E. *fashion designer*

Detroit
Abt, Jeffrey *art educator, art historian, artist, writer*
DuMouchelle, Ernest J. *art appraiser*
DuMouchelle, Lawrence F. *art appraiser*
Johnson, Lester Larue, Jr. *artist, educator*
Moldenhauer, Judith A. *graphic design educator*
Sousanis, Nick *art web site designer*

Grand Blanc
Thompson, Thomas Adrian *sculptor*

Hillsdale
Frudakis, Anthony Parker *sculptor, educator*

Mount Pleasant
Born, James E. *art educator, sculptor*

Port Huron
Rowark, Maureen *fine arts photographer*

MINNESOTA

Duluth
Chee, Cheng-Khee *artist, educator*

Frazee
Ulmer, James Howard *potter*

Mankato
Frink, Brian Lee *artist, educator*

Minneapolis
Asher, Frederick M. *art educator, art historian*
Hallman, Gary L. *photographer, educator*
Marling, Karal Ann *art history educator, social sciences educator, curator*
Rose, Thomas Albert *artist, educator*

Saint Paul
Lasansky, Leonardo *artist, educator*
Tylevich, Alexander V. *sculptor, architect*

MISSOURI

Bolivar
Gott, Wesley Atlas *art educator*

Columbia
Larson, Sidney *art educator, artist, writer, conservator*

Saint Louis
Burkett, Randy James *lighting designer*
Colangelo, Carmon *artist, printmaker, educator*
Essman, Alyn V. *photographic studios company executive*
Fondaw, Ronald Edward *artist, educator*
Greenblatt, William *photographer*
Hansman, Robert G. *artist, educator*
Ward-Brown, Denise *sculptor, educator*

NEBRASKA

Lincoln
Kunc, Karen *artist, educator*
Neal, Mo (P. Maureen Neal) *sculptor*

NEW YORK

New York
Brychtova, Jaroslava *sculptor*
Cucullu, Santiago *artist*

OHIO

Athens
Lazuka, Robert *artist, art educator*

Aurora
Lawton, Florian Kenneth *artist, educator*

Bowling Green
Ocvirk, Otto George *artist*

Cincinnati
Brod, Stanford *graphics designer, educator*
Rexroth, Nancy Louise *photographer*

Cleveland
Adams, Henry *art educator*
Deming, David Lawson *art educator*

Columbus
Goff, Wilmer Scott *retired photographer*

Georgetown
Ruthven, John A. *wildlife artist*

Hilliard
Cupp, David Foster *photographer, journalist*

Oxford
Ewing, Susan R. *artist, educator*

Toledo
McGlauchlin, Tom *artist*

SOUTH DAKOTA

Vermillion
Freeman, Jeffrey Vaughn (Jeff Freeman) *artist, educator*

Yankton
Clatworthy, Catherine Lynn *educational trainer, graphics designer*

WISCONSIN

Hollandale
Colescott, Warrington Wickham *artist, printmaker, educator*

Madison
Myers, Frances J. *artist*
Nice, Don *artist*

Milwaukee
Waldbaum, Jane Cohn *art history educator*

Mount Horeb
Becker, David *artist, retired educator*

ADDRESS UNPUBLISHED

Boynton, Sandra Keith *illustrator, cartoonist, stationery products executive*
Herzberg, Thomas *artist, educator, illustrator*
Kwong, Eva *artist, educator*
Martin, Noel *graphics designer, educator*
Ortman, George Earl *artist*
Rankin, Scott David *artist, educator*
Reinoehl, Richard Louis *artist, scholar*
Stokstad, Marilyn Jane *art history educator, curator*
Sumichrast, Jozef *illustrator, designer*
Trainor, Jim *animator, filmmaker*
Vollmer, Howard Robert *artist, photographer*

ASSOCIATIONS AND ORGANIZATIONS *See also specific fields*

UNITED STATES

ARIZONA

Phoenix
Swartz, Jack *retired chamber of commerce executive*

DISTRICT OF COLUMBIA

Washington
Linehan, Lou Ann *political organization worker*
Portnoy, Elliott Ivan *lobbyist, lawyer*

GEORGIA

Athens
Algeo, John Thomas *association executive, retired educator*

ILLINOIS

Chicago
Blackshere, Margaret *labor union administrator*
Bloch, Ralph Jay *professional association executive, marketing consultant*
Bourdon, Cathleen Jane *professional society administrator*
Cassens Weiss, Debra Sue *professional association administrator, publishing executive*
Crow, Steven D. *educational association administrator*
Davis, Mary Ellen K. *educational association administrator*
Dolan, Thomas Christopher *professional society administrator*
Franke, Richard James *art association administrator, retired investment banker*
Gary, Warlene D. *educational association administrator*
Hunter, Mattie *human services executive*
Jackson, Jesse Louis *civil rights activist, clergyman*
Johnson, Gary Thomas *cultural organization administrator, museum administrator*
Jones, Mary Laura *not-for-profit developer*
Keenan, Barbara Byrd *professional society administrator*
Knapp, Paul Raymond *think-tank executive*
Kolata, David *advocate*
Kudo, Irma Setsuko *not-for-profit executive director*
Lurie, Ann LaSalle *foundation administrator*
MacDougal, Gary Edward *corporate board member, foundation trustee*
Mazany, Terry *foundation administrator*
Mercer, David Robinson *cultural organization administrator*
Minow, Josephine Baskin *civic volunteer*
Olsen, Rex Norman *trade association executive*
Parker, Bonita M. *civil rights organization executive*
Richman, Harold Alan *social welfare policy educator*
Schiele, Michele M. *not-for-profit fundraiser, medical association administrator*
Serrano, Justin Forbes *education executive*
Shanahan, Betty *professional society administrator*
Sigmon, Joyce Elizabeth *professional society administrator*
Simmons, Adele Smith *foundation executive, former educator*
So, Frank S. *educational association administrator*
Tarlov, Alvin Richard *foundation administrator, physician, educator*
Weber, Daniel E. *association executive*
Wilson, Cleo Francine *foundation administrator*

Evanston
Arrington, Michael Browne *foundation administrator*
Gordon, Julie Peyton *foundation administrator*
Lewis, Charles A. *foundation administrator*
Rielly, John Edward *educational association administrator*
Thrash, Patricia Ann *retired educational association administrator*

La Grange Park
Webster, Lois Shand *association executive*

Morton Grove
McKenna, Andrew, Jr. *political organization administrator, printing company executive*

River Forest
Eisel, Jean Ellen *educational association administrator*

Rosemont
Good, William Allen *professional society executive*

Schaumburg
Little, Bruce Washington *professional society administrator*
Tompson, Marian Leonard *professional society administrator*

Skokie
Gleason, John Patrick, Jr. *trade association executive*

Urbana
Williamson, Kent D. *educational association administrator*

Wilmette
Brink, Marion Francis *trade association administrator*

INDIANA

Bloomington
Joekel, Ronald G. *fraternal organization administrator*
Mobley, Tony Allen *foundation administrator, former dean, recreation educator*
Wells, Kimberly K. *not-for-profit organization executive*

Evansville
Early, Judith K. *social services director*

Friendship
Miller, John *foundation administrator*

Indianapolis
Braun, Robert Clare *retired association and advertising executive*
Buckley, Pamela Kay *educational association administrator*
Clark, J. Murray (Murray Clark) *political organization administrator, lawyer*
Finley, Katherine Mandusic *professional society administrator*
Harper, Terrance G. *journalism organization administrator*
McLaughlin, Sherry *association administrator*
Parker, Dan J. *political organization administrator*
Quarles, Beth *civil rights administrator*
Recker, Thomas Edward *fraternal organization executive*
Robbins, N. Clay *foundation administrator*
Santos, Richard J. *association administrator*
Sparks, Donald Eugene *interscholastic activities association executive*
Vereen, Robert Charles *retired trade association administrator*

Muncie
Bakken, Douglas Adair *foundation executive*
Stanley, Kelly N. *foundation administrator*

North Manchester
Myers, Anne M. *developer*

Terre Haute
Aldridge, Sandra *civic volunteer*

West Lafayette
Baumgardt, Billy Ray *professional society administrator, agriculturist*

IOWA

Ames
Ahoy, Christopher Keen *educational association administrator, architect*

Clive
Tank, Alan *trade association administrator*

Des Moines
McGuire-Riggs, Sheila *Democratic party chairman*
Peterson, Michael K. *political organization administrator*

Fairfield
Hagelin, John Samuel *political organization administrator, theoretical physicist*

Iowa City
Ferguson, Richard L. *educational association administrator*

KANSAS

Fort Riley
Spurrier-Bright, Patricia Ann *professional society administrator*

Kansas City
Benjamin, Janice Yukon *development executive*
Campbell, Joseph Leonard *trade association executive*
Jones, Charles W. *labor union executive*

Lawrence
Mona, Stephen Francis *golf association executive*

Shawnee
Wilson, Eugene Rolland *retired foundation executive*

Shawnee Mission
Gates, Lawrence C. *political organization worker, lawyer*

Topeka
Frahm, Sheila *association executive, academic administrator, former government official*
Freden, Sharon Elsie Christman *state education official*
Perry, Nancy *foundation administrator*

KENTUCKY

Louisville
Early, Jack Jones *foundation executive*

MICHIGAN

Ann Arbor
Ware, Richard Anderson *foundation executive*

Battle Creek
Mawby, Russell George *retired foundation executive*
Overton-Adkins, Betty Jean *foundation administrator*

Belmont
Powers, Linda S. *art association administrator*

Detroit
Gettelfinger, Ron *labor union administrator*
Noland, Mariam Charl *foundation executive*

East Lansing
Mitstifer, Dorothy Irwin *honor society administrator*

Flint
Maynard, Olivia P. *foundation administrator*
White, William Samuel *foundation executive*

Gaylord
Smith, Frank Earl *retired trade association administrator*

Kalamazoo
Petersen, Anne C. (Cheryl Petersen) *foundation administrator, educator*

Lansing
Anuzis, Saulius (Saul Anuzis) *political organization administrator*
Brewer, Mark Courtland *political organization administrator, lawyer*
Stein, Trisha *advocate*

Sterling Heights
Fleming, Mac Arthur *retired labor union administrator*

Troy
Hodges, Michele *chamber of commerce executive*
Hunia, Edward Mark *foundation executive*

MINNESOTA

Chaska
Burke, Steven Francis *organization executive*

Lake Lillian
Marquardt, Steve Robert *advocate*

Minneapolis
Isaak, Larry A. *educational association administrator*
Johnson, John Warren *retired professional society administrator*
King, Reatha Clark *community foundation executive*
Wolford, Kathryn Frances *foundation administrator*

Rochester
Frerichs, Donald L. *foundation administrator, retired state legislator*
Shulman, Carole Karen *professional society administrator*

Saint Paul
Carey, Ron *political organization administrator*
Eibensteiner, Ron *political organization administrator, venture capitalist*
Kolehmainen, Jan Waldroy *professional association administrator*
Pampusch, Anita Marie *foundation administrator*
Williams, Lynell R. *educational association administrator*

MISSOURI

Branson
Bowers, John C. *association executive*

Bridgeton
Kenison, Raymond Robert *fraternal organization administrator*

Chesterfield
Diamandis, Peter H. *foundation administrator, entrepreneur*

Columbia
Palo, Nicholas Edwin *professional society administrator*

Earth City
Anderhalter, Oliver Frank *educational organization executive*

Jefferson City
Temporiti, John J. *political organization administrator, lawyer*

Kansas City
Bugher, Robert Dean *professional society administrator*

Saint Louis
Bascom, C. Perry *retired foundation administrator, lawyer*
Breckenridge, Joanne *political organization administrator*
Horn, Joan Kelly *political research and consulting firm executive*
Kimmey, James Richard, Jr. *foundation administrator*
Pope, Robert E(ugene) *fraternal organization administrator*
Winter, Mildred M. *educational administrator*

Springfield
O'Block, Robert *association, publishing executive*

NEBRASKA

Lincoln
Rosenow, John Edward *foundation executive*

Lyons
Hassebrook, Chuck *not-for-profit developer*

Omaha
Bell, C(lyde) R(oberts) (Bob Bell) *foundation administrator*
Flickinger, Thomas Leslie *hospital alliance executive*
Manna, John S. *fraternal organization administrator*

Seward
Vrana, Verlon Kenneth *retired professional society administrator, conservationist*

NORTH DAKOTA

Bismarck
Emineth, Gary *political organization administrator*
Haugland, Erling *political organization executive*
Karls, Ken *foundation executive, former political organization administrator*
Kleingartner, Larry *agricultural association executive*
Strauss, David *political organization administrator, former federal official*

Fargo
Thompson, Vern *political organization executive*

Williston
Yockim, James Craig *foundation administrator*

OHIO

Akron
Martino, Frank Dominic *union executive*

Cincinnati
Parker, Linda Bates *professional development organization administrator*
Ray, Glenn *art association administrator*

Cleveland
Bergholz, David *foundation administrator*
Boyd, Byron A. *labor union administrator*
Calkins, Hugh *foundation executive*
Cleary, Michael J. *educational administrator*
Distelhorst, Garis Fred *trade association administrator*
Pike, Kermit Jerome *cultural organization administrator*
Thompson, Paul C. *labor union administrator*

Columbus
Bennett, Robert Thomas *political organization administrator, lawyer, accountant*
De Maria, Paolo *policy advisor*
Franano, Susan Margaret Ketteman *art association administrator, musician*
Leland, David J. *political association executive*
Newman, Diana S. *foundation administrator, consultant, writer*
Selby, Diane Ray Miller *retired fraternal organization administrator*

Dayton
Daley, Robert Emmett *retired foundation executive*
Mathews, David (Forrest David Mathews) *foundation executive, former secretary of health education and welfare*
Schwartzhoff, James Paul *foundation executive*

Dublin
Needham, George Michael *association executive*

Lewis Center
Heinlen, Daniel Lee *alumni organization administrator, consultant*

North Canton
Fernandez, Kathleen M. *cultural organization administrator*

Oxford
Miller, Robert James *educational association administrator*

Worthington
Luck, James I. *foundation executive*

Youngstown
Redfern, Chris *political organization administrator, former state representative*

OKLAHOMA

Norman
Mooneyham, Bobby R. *educational association administrator*

SOUTH DAKOTA

Hayti
Frederick, Randall Davis *former political organization administrator, former state legislator*

Pierre
Adam, Karl *political organization administrator, bank executive*

Rapid City
Erickson, John Duff *retired educational association administrator*

Sioux Falls
Billion, Jack (John Joseph Billion) *political organization administrator, retired orthopedic surgeon, former state representative*
Piper, Kathleen *former political organization administrator*

TENNESSEE

Athens
Brown, Sandra Lee *art association administrator, consultant, artist*

TEXAS

Fort Worth
Haw, Bill *association executive*

Houston
Menninger, Roy Wright *medical foundation executive, psychiatrist*

WISCONSIN

Appleton
Hinkens, Kay L. *social services association executive*
Jodarski, Richard R. *social services association executive*
Krueger, James H. *social service association executive*
Lapacz, Steven P. *social services association executive*
Rugland, Walter S. *fraternal benefit society executive*

Madison
Brennan, Robert Walter *association executive*
Higby, Gregory James *historical association administrator, historian*
Olson, Norman Fredrick *not-for-profit developer, retired food science educator*
Wineke, Joseph Steven *political organization administrator, former state legislator*

Milwaukee
Boese, Gil Karyle *cultural organization administrator*
Gracz, Gregory L. *labor union administrator*
Randall, Gerard *foundation administrator*
Schneider, Thomas Paul *non-profit agency administrator*
Taylor, Allen M. *community foundation executive*

Shawano
Lyon, Thomas L. *agricultural organization administrator*

ADDRESS UNPUBLISHED

Abnee, A. Victor *trade association executive*
DeVos, Elisabeth (Betsy) *political association executive*
DeVries, Robert Allen *foundation administrator*
Dickeson, Robert Celmer *retired foundation administrator, management consultant*
Donnell, Harold Eugene, Jr. *retired professional society administrator*
Gilchrest, Thornton Charles *retired association executive*
Harwick, Dennis Patrick *insurance association administrator, lawyer*
Hogsett, Joseph H. *political organization worker, former state official*
Jondahl, Lynn *foundation administrator*
Kabat, Linda Georgette *civic leader*
Klarich, David John *lobbyist, lawyer*
Kreer, Irene Overman *association and meeting management executive*
Kruesi, Frank Eugene *lobbyist, former government executive*
Langer, Edward L. *trade association administrator*
Liljegren, Frank Sigfrid *art association administrator, artist, educator*
McCormack, Michael Joseph *foundation administrator*
McDaniel, Mike *former political association executive*
McFate, Kenneth Leverne *trade association administrator*
Palmer, Robert Erwin *association executive*
Porter, John Wilson *educational association administrator, director*
Pullen, Penny Lynne *non-profit organization administrator, retired state legislator*
Richardson, William Chase *retired foundation executive*
Sanford, Sarah J. *healthcare executive*
Schuster, Elaine *retired civil rights professional*
Smith, Margaret Taylor *volunteer*
Spring, Terri *political organization executive*
Weselak, Anna Marie Schmidt *educational association administrator, media consultant*

ATHLETICS

UNITED STATES

ARIZONA

Phoenix
Agler, Brian *professional basketball coach*

CALIFORNIA

Anaheim
Hunter, Torii Kedar *professional baseball player*
Schneider, Mathieu *professional hockey player*

Jamul
Smith, Akili *professional football player*

La Mirada
Razov, Ante *professional soccer player*

Los Angeles
Garciaparra, Nomar (Anthony Nomar Garciaparra) *professional baseball player*

San Diego
Edmonds, Jim (James Patrick Edmonds) *professional baseball player*
Maddux, Gregory Alan *professional baseball player*

San Francisco
Durham, Ray *professional baseball player*
Policy, Carmen A. *professional sports team executive*

Stanford
Bowlsby, Bob *athletic director*

COLORADO

Colorado Springs
Schultz, Richard Dale *national athletic organization executive*

CONNECTICUT

New Haven
Brand, Myles *sports association and former academic administrator*

DISTRICT OF COLUMBIA

Washington
Cruz, Deivi *professional baseball player*

ILLINOIS

Bridgeview
Guppy, John *professional sports team executive*

Carbondale
Lowery, Christopher M. *men's college basketball coach*

Chicago
Agoos, Jeff *professional soccer player*
Akers, Michelle Anne *professional soccer player*
Bondra, Peter *professional hockey player*
Buehrle, Mark (Alan) *professional baseball player*
Burnitz, Jeromy *professional baseball player*
Cabrera, Orlando (Luis) *professional baseball player*
Cromwell, Amanda Caryl *former soccer player, coach*
Daze, Eric *professional hockey player*
Dempster, Ryan Scott *professional baseball player*
Ducar, Tracy *former soccer player*
Dudley, Rick (Richard C. Dudley) *professional sports team executive*
Dye, Jermaine *professional baseball player*
Einhorn, Edward Martin (Eddie Einhorn) *professional baseball team executive*
Fawcett, Joy Lynn *retired professional soccer player*
Fotopoulos, Danielle *former soccer player*
Foudy, Julie Maurine *retired professional soccer player, Olympic athlete*
Fukudome, Kosuke *professional baseball player*
Gabarra, Carin Leslie *professional soccer player, professional soccer coach*
Gaters, Dorothy *basketball coach*
Gregg, Lauren *women's soccer coach*
Guillen, Ozzie (Oswaldo Jose Barrios Guillen) *professionall baseball manager*
Hamm, Mia (Mariel Margaret Hamm) *retired professional soccer player*
Heinrichs, April *soccer coach*
Hucles, Angela Khalia *professional soccer player*
Jones, Cobi *professional soccer player*
Keller, Deborah Kim *former soccer player*
Khabibulin, Nikolai *professional hockey player*
Konerko, Paul *professional baseball player*
Kreis, Jason *professional soccer coach, retired professional soccer player*
Lilly, Kristine Marie (Kristine Lilly Heavey) *professional soccer player*
Lynch, Edward Francis *professional sports team executive*
MacMillan, Shannon Ann *professional soccer player*
Mercer, Ron *professional basketball player*
Milbrett, Tiffeny Carleen *professional soccer player*
Overton, Bo *professional basketball coach*
Parlow, Cynthia Maria *professional soccer player*
Paxson, John *professional sports team executive, retired professional basketball player*
Piniella, Lou (Louis Victor Piniella) *professional baseball team manager*
Pizer, Howard Charles *sports and entertainment executive*
Ralph, Damani *professional soccer player*
Ramirez, Aramis *professional baseball player*
Reddick, Catherine Anne (Cat Reddick) *Olympic athlete*
Reinsdorf, Jerry Michael *professional sports team owner, real estate company executive, accountant, lawyer*
Reyna, Claudio *professional soccer player*
Savard, Denis Joseph *professional hockey coach, former professional hockey player*
Schanwald, Steve *professional sports team executive*
Schwartz, Alan Gifford *sport company executive*
Schwoy, Laurie Annette *professional soccer player*
Scurry, Briana Collette *professional soccer player*
Selolwane, Diphetogo (Dipsy Selolwane) *professional soccer player*
Sirotka, Mike *professional baseball player*
Slaton, Danielle Victoria *professional soccer player*
Sobrero, Kate (Kathryn Michele Sobrero) *professional soccer player*
Soriano, Alfonso Guilleard *professional baseball player*
Staples, Thori Yvette *former soccer player*
Streiffer, Jenny *former soccer player*
Tallon, Dale *professional sports team executive*
Thome, Jim *professional baseball player*
Trammell, Alan Stuart *professional baseball coach, retired professional baseball player*
Venturini, Tisha Lea *professional soccer player*
Wagner, Alyson Kay (Aly Wagner) *professional soccer player*
Whalen, Sarah Eve *professional soccer player*
Wood, Kerry *professional baseball player*
Zambrano, Carlos Alberto *professional baseball player*

Lake Forest
Angelo, Jerry *professional sports team executive*
Grossman, Rex *professional football player*
Jaeger, Jeff Todd *professional football player*
McCaskey, Michael B. *professional football team executive*
Murphy, Karen *sports association executive*
Phillips, Ted *professional sports team executive*
Smith, Lovie *professional football coach*
Urlacher, Brian Keith *professional football player*

Mahomet
Thompson, Margaret M. *physical education educator*

Park Ridge
Delany, Jim (James Edward Delany) *sports association administrator, lawyer*

Westmont
Tricase, Elizabeth *gymnast*

INDIANA

Bloomington
Crean, Tom (Thomas Aaron Crean) *men's college basketball coach*

Indianapolis
Addai, Joseph *professional football player*
Bird, Larry Joe *professional sports team executive, retired professional basketball player*
Catchings, Tamika Devonne *professional basketball player*
Croshere, Austin *professional basketball player*
Dungy, Tony *professional football coach*
Faulk, Marshall Williams *retired professional football player*
Ganassi, Chip *professional race car executive, owner*
Harrison, Marvin *professional football player*
Irsay, James Steven *professional football team owner*
Manning, Peyton *professional football player*
Morway, David S. *professional sports team executive*
O'Neal, Jermaine *professional basketball player*
Patrick, Danica Sue *race car driver*
Polian, Bill *professional football team executive*
Stevens, Brad K. *men's college basketball coach*
Unser, Al *retired professional auto racer, racing official*
Winters, Brian Joseph *professional basketball coach*

Notre Dame
Weis, Charlie *college football coach*
White, Kevin M. *athletic director*

West Lafayette
Sims-Curry, Kristy *women's college basketball coach*
Versyp, Sharon *women's college basketball coach*

IOWA

Ames
Fennelly, William *basketball coach*

Iowa City
Lickliter, Todd *men's college basketball coach*

KANSAS

Lawrence
Henrickson, Bonnie *women's college basketball coach*
Self, Bill *men's college basketball coach*

Manhattan
Martin, Frank (Francisco J. Martin) *men's college basketball coach*
Patterson, Deb *women's college basketball coach*
Snyder, Bill *football coach*

Wichita
Marshall, Gregg *men's college basketball coach*

MASSACHUSETTS

Boston
Cassell, Samuel James *professional basketball player*
Fernandez, Manny (Emmanuel Fernandez-Lemaire) *professional hockey player*
Gonzalez, Juan (Alberto Vazquez) *professional baseball player*

MICHIGAN

Allen Park
Kitna, Jon *professional football player*
Marinelli, Rod *professional football coach*
Millen, Matt *professional sports team executive*
Pritchett, Kelvin *professional football player*
Schmidt, Chuck *professional football team executive*

Ann Arbor
Beilein, John Patrick *men's college basketball coach*
Berenson, Red (Gordon A. Berenson) *hockey coach, retired professional hockey player*
Rodriguez, Rich *college football coach*

Auburn Hills
Billups, Chauncey *professional basketball player*
Dumars, Joe III *professional sports team executive, retired professional basketball player*
Hamilton, Richard Clay *professional basketball player*
Johnson, Shannon *professional basketball player*
Laimbeer, Bill *professional basketball coach, retired professional basketball player*
McDyess, Antonio *professional basketball player*
Montross, Eric Scott *professional basketball player*
Ostfield, Alan *professional sports team executive*
Saunders, Flip (Philip D. Saunders) *professional basketball coach*
Wallace, Rasheed *professional basketball player, marketing professional*
Williams, Greg *professional basketball coach*
Wilson, Thomas S. *professional sports team executive*

Canton
Finnerty, Bryan *sports association executive*

Detroit
Bing, David *retired professional basketball player, metal products executive*
Bowman, William Scott (Scotty Bowman) *professional hockey coach*
Cabrera, Miguel (Jose Miguel Cabrera) *professional baseball player*
Chelios, Chris (Christos K. Chelios) *professional hockey player*
Datsyuk, Pavel *professional hockey player*
Devellano, James Charles *professional hockey manager, baseball executive*
Dombrowski, David *baseball team executive*
Higginson, Bobby *professional baseball player*
Holland, Ken *professional sports team executive*
Ilitch, Marian *professional hockey team and food service executive*
Ilitch, Michael *professional hockey team and food products executive*
Leyland, Jim (James Richard Leyland) *professional baseball manager*
Lidstrom, Nicklas *professional hockey player*
Mclendon, Lloyd *professional baseball coach, retired baseball player*
Nabozny, Heather *professional sports team groundskeeper*
Ordonez, Magglio Jose *professional baseball player*
Osgood, Chris *professional hockey player*
Polanco, Placido Enrique *professional baseball player*
Rodriguez, Ivan Torres *professional baseball player*
Rogers, Kenny (Kenneth Scott Rogers) *professional baseball player*
Sheffield, Gary Antonian *professional baseball player*
Verlander, Justin Brooks *professional baseball player*
Willis, Dontrelle (Wayne) *professional baseball player*
Yzerman, Steve (Stephen Gregory Yzerman) *professional sports team executive, retired professional hockey player*

East Lansing
Izzo, Thomas *college basketball coach*

Livonia
Gilbert, Daniel *professional sports team owner, mortgage company executive*

Mount Pleasant
Deromedi, Herb William *athletic director*

MINNESOTA

Eden Prairie
Allen, Jared Scot *professional football player*
Brzezinski, Rob *professional sports team executive*
Childress, Brad *professional football coach*
Hoard, Leroy *professional football player*
Johnson, Brad *professional football player*
McCombs, Billy Joe (Red McCombs) *professional football team executive*
McCombs, Charline *professional sports team executive*
Poppen, Steve *professional sports team executive*
Woods, Gary V. *professional football team executive, former professional basketball team executive, automotive executive*

Minneapolis
Gardenhire, Ronald Clyde *professional athletics manager*
Garrett, Dean *professional basketball player*
Griffith, Roger *professional sports team executive*
Kelly, Tom (Jay Thomas Kelly) *retired professional sports team manager*
McHale, Kevin Edward *professional sports team executive, retired professional basketball player*
Monroe, Craig (Keystone) *professional baseball player*
Moor, Rob *professional sports team executive*
Morneau, Justin Ernest George *professional baseball player*
Nanne, Louis Vincent *professional hockey team executive*
Olowokandi, Michael *professional basketball player*
Peterson, Adrian Lewis *professional football player*
Ryan, Terry *professional sports team executive*
Smith, Katie (Katherine May Smith) *professional basketball player*
Smith, Tubby *men's college basketball coach*
Sprewell, Latrell Fontaine *professional basketball player*
Stack, Jim *professional sports team executive*
Wiggins, Candice Dana *professional basketball player*
Wittman, Randy Scott *professional basketball coach*
Wright, Chris *professional sports team executive*
Young, Delmon Damarcus *professional baseball player*
Zierden, Don *professional basketball coach*

Saint Paul
Backstrom, Niklas *professional hockey player*
Bombardir, Brad *professional hockey player*
Demitra, Pavol *professional hockey player*
Lemaire, Jacques *professional hockey coach*
Naegele, Robert O., Jr. *professional sports team executive*
Sperling, Jac *professional sports team executive*

MISSOURI

Columbia
Pinkel, Gary *college football coach*

Earth City
Chandler, Christopher Mark (Chris Chandler) *professional football player*
Shaw, John *sports association administrator*

Kansas City
Allen, Marcus *retired professional football player*
Brett, George Howard *baseball executive, former professional baseball player*
Cunningham, Gunther *professional football coach*
Gansler, Robert *professional soccer coach*
Gonzalez, Tony *professional football player*
Johnson, Larry (Larry Alphonso Johnson Jr.) *professional football player*
McGuff, Joseph Thomas *professional sports team executive*
Peterson, Carl V. *professional football team executive*
Robinson, Spencer T. (Herk Robinson) *professional baseball team executive*
Smith, Louis *sports association administrator*
Steadman, Jack W. *professional football team executive*
Sweeney, Mike (Michael John Sweeney) *professional baseball player*

Saint Louis
Benes, Andrew Charles *retired professional baseball player*
Brewer, Eric *professional hockey player*
Brooks, Richard L. *professional football coach*
Carpenter, Chris *professional baseball player*
Checketts, Dave (David Wayne Checketts) *professional sports team executive*
DeWitt, William O., Jr. *professional sports team executive*
Hanser, Frederick Otto *professional sports team executive*
Haslett, Jim *professional football coach*
Jasiek, Jerry *professional sports team executive*
Lalime, Patrick *professional hockey player*
La Russa, Tony, Jr., (Anthony La Russa Jr.) *professional baseball manager*
Laurie, William *sports team executive*
Linehan, Scott *professional football coach*
MacInnis, Al *professional sports team executive, retired professional hockey player*
Morris, Matthew Christian *professional baseball player*
Murray, Andy *professional hockey coach*
Pace, Orlando Lamar *professional football player*
Pleau, Larry (Lawrence Winslow Pleau) *professional sports team executive*
Pujols, Albert (Jose Alberto Pujols) *professional baseball player*
Sauer, Mark *professional sports team executive*
Schoendienst, Albert Fred (Red Schoendienst) *professional baseball coach, former baseball player*
Tkachuk, Keith *professional hockey player*

St. Louis
Long, Christopher Howard *professional football player*

NEBRASKA

Lincoln
Collier, Barry S. *coach*
Osborne, Tom (Thomas William Osborne) *college athletic director, former congressman, retired college football coach*
Pelini, Bo *college football coach*
Solich, Frank *coach*

NEW JERSEY

East Rutherford
Cartwright, James William (Bill Cartwright) *professional basketball coach, retired professional basketball player*

Secaucus
Bradley, Bob *professional soccer coach*
Meola, Tony *professional soccer player, actor*

NEW YORK

Bronx
Peña, Tony (Antonio Francisco Peña) *professional baseball coach, retired professional baseball player*

Flushing
Hernandez, Roberto *professional baseball player*
Santana, Johan (Johan Alexander Santana Araque) *professional baseball player*

New York
McHale, John Joseph, Jr. *major league baseball executive, former professional sports team executive*
Shanahan, Brendan Frederick *professional hockey player*

NORTH CAROLINA

Raleigh
Irbe, Arturs *professional hockey player*
Whitney, Ray *professional hockey player*

OHIO

Berea
Clark, Dwight Edward *sports team executive, former professional football player*
Crennel, Romeo *professional football coach*
Jacobs, Douglas C. *professional sports team executive*
Lewis, Jamal *professional football player*

Canton
Elliott, Peter R. *retired athletic organization executive*
Mack, Tom *retired professional football player*

Cincinnati
Baker, Dusty (Johnnie B. Baker Jr.) *professional baseball team manager, retired professional baseball player*
Cordero, Francisco Javier *professional baseball player*
Griffey, Ken, Jr., (George Kenneth Griffey Jr.) *professional baseball player*
Jocketty, Walt (Walter J. Jocketty) *professional baseball team manager, professional sports team executive*
Johnson, Chad *professional football player*
Neagle, Dennis Edward (Denny Neagle) *professional baseball player*
Palmer, Carson *professional football player*
Santiago, Benito Rivera *professional baseball player*
Sawyer, John *professional football team executive*

Cleveland
Boland, James C. *sports association executive*
Brown, Mike *professional basketball coach*
Ferry, Danny *professional sports team executive, retired professional basketball player*
Gardocki, Christopher *professional football player*
Hill, Tyrone *professional basketball player*
Ilgauskas, Zydrunas *professional basketball player*
James, LeBron Raymone *professional basketball player*
Kirby, Terry *professional football player*
Komoroski, Len *professional sports team executive*
Riggleman, James David *former professional baseball team manager*
Sabathia, C.C. (Carsten Charles Sabathia) *professional baseball player*
Stornes, Mark *professional sports team executive*
Wallace, Ben *professional basketball player*

Columbus
Agnew, Gary *professional hockey coach*
Foster, Jim (James S. Foster) *women's college basketball coach*
Hitchcock, Ken *professional hockey coach*
Matta, Thad Michael *men's college basketball coach*
Modin, Fredrik *professional hockey player*
Nash, Rick *professional hockey player*
Pastore, Donna Lee *physical education educator*
Tressel, Jim (James Patrick Tressel) *college football coach*

Fairfield
Robertson, Oscar Palmer (Big O Robertson) *chemical company executive, former professional basketball player*
Sheehan, Samantha *gymnast*

PENNSYLVANIA

Philadelphia
Sanderson, Geoff *professional hockey player*

RHODE ISLAND

Providence
Davis, Keno *men's college basketball coach*

TEXAS

Dallas
Nelson, Donnie *professional sports team executive*

VIRGINIA

Roanoke
Carr, Bonnie Jean *professional ice skater*

WASHINGTON

Kirkland
Leiweke, Tod *professional sports team executive*

Pullman
Bennett, Dick *college basketball coach*

Seattle
Lawton, Matt *professional baseball player*

WISCONSIN

Green Bay
Jones, John *professional sports team executive*
McCarthy, Mike *professional football coach*

Greendale
Kuhn, Roseann *sports association administrator*

Madison
Bielema, Bret *university football coach*
Ryan, Bo (William F. Ryan Jr.) *men's college basketball coach*
Sauer, Jeff *university hockey coach*

Milwaukee
Bogut, Andrew *professional basketball player*
Hammond, John R. *professional sports team executive*
Manning, Daniel Ricardo *professional basketball player*
Selig-Prieb, Wendy *sports team executive*
Skiles, Scott Allen *professional basketball coach*
Steinmiller, John F. *professional sports team executive*
Weinhauer, Bob *professional sports team executive*
Williams, Brent (Buzz Williams) *men's college basketball coach*

CANADA

ALBERTA

Calgary
Joseph, Curtis Shayne *professional hockey player*

ONTARIO

Toronto
Thomas, Frank Edward *professional baseball player*
Eckstein, David Mark *professional baseball player*
Rolen, Scott Bruce *professional baseball player*

ADDRESS UNPUBLISHED

Arena, Bruce *professional soccer coach*
Baylor, Don Edward *former professional baseball manager, retired professional baseball player*
Bruce, Isaac Isidore *professional football player*
Carlisle, Rick (Richard Preston Carlisle) *former professional basketball coach, retired professional basketball player*
Carr, Lloyd H. *retired college football coach*
Culpepper, Daunte *professional football player*
Edwards, Michelle Denise *professional basketball player*
Eldredge, Todd *figure skater*
Fick, Robert *professional baseball player*
Fijalkowski, Isabelle *professional basketball player*
Grissom, Marquis Deon *professional baseball player*
Hargrove, Mike (Dudley Michael Hargrove) *former professional baseball team manager*
Harlan, Robert Ernest *retired professional football team executive*
Harris, Larry *professional sports team executive*
Hart, James Warren *retired athletic administrator, professional football player*
Krause, Jerry (Jerome Richard Krause) *former professional basketball team executive*
Krystkowiak, Larry Brett *former professional basketball coach*
Lynch, Bill *university football coach*
MacLean, Doug *former professional hockey coach, former sports team executive*
Manuel, Jerry *former professional sports team manager*
Mariucci, Steve *professional football coach, former college football coach*
McCarney, Dan *former college football coach*
McGwire, Mark David *retired professional baseball player*
Nemcova, Eva *professional basketball player*
Parins, Robert James *professional football team executive, judge*
Pirtle, Laurie Lee *retired women's college basketball coach*
Rampone, Christie P. *professional soccer player*
Rison, Andre *retired professional football player*
Sampson, Kelvin Dale *former college basketball coach*
Sanders, Barry *retired professional football player*
Segui, David *professional baseball player*
Smith, Ozzie (Osborne Earl Smith) *retired professional baseball player*
Tice, Mike (Michael P. Tice) *former professional football coach*

BUSINESS *See* FINANCE: INDUSTRY

COMMUNICATIONS *See* COMMUNICATIONS MEDIA; INDUSTRY: SERVICE

COMMUNICATIONS MEDIA *See also* ARTS: LITERARY

UNITED STATES

CALIFORNIA

Calabasas
Walling, Donovan Robert *editor, writer*

Del Mar
Marcus, Larry David *broadcast executive*

Los Angeles
Larson, Gary *cartoonist*

San Diego
Kyle, Robert Campbell, II, *publishing executive*

COLORADO

Denver
Clark, Gary R. *newspaper editor*

DISTRICT OF COLUMBIA

Washington
King, Emery Clarence *TV news correspondent*
McPherson, Peter (M. Peter McPherson) *publishing executive, educational association administrator*

FLORIDA

Naples
Moore, Oliver Semon III *publishing executive, consultant*
Penniman, Nicholas Griffith, IV, *retired newspaper publisher*

GEORGIA

Athens
Soloski, John *journalism and communications educator*

IDAHO

Boise
Gowler, Vicki Sue *editor-in-chief*

ILLINOIS

Arlington Heights
Baumann, Daniel E. *publishing executive*
Lampinen, John A. *newspaper editor*
Ray, Douglas Kent *newspaper executive*

Bartlett
Markle, Sandra *publishing company executive*

Belleville
Richmond, Richard Thomas *journalist*

Bloomington
Merwin, Davis Underwood *newspaper executive*

Buffalo Grove
Kuennen, Thomas Gerard *journalist*

Champaign
Dulany, Elizabeth Gjelsness *editor*
McCulloh, Judith Marie *editor*
Meyer, August Christopher, Jr. *broadcast executive, lawyer*
Wentworth, Richard Leigh *editor*

Chicago
Adamle, Mike *sports commentator*
Agema, Gerald Walton *publishing executive*
Ahern, Mary Ann *reporter*
Anderson, Karl Stephen *editor*
Artner, Alan Gustav *art critic, journalist*
Baca, Stacey *newscaster*
Barr, Emily L. *broadcast executive*
Barron, John *editor*
Bell, Clark Wayne *business editor, educator*
Bigelow, Chandler III *publishing executive*
Blakley, Derrick *newscaster*
Bleifuss, Joel *journalist*
Boers, Terry John *sportswriter, radio and television personality*
Brewster, Gregory Bush *telecommunications educator*
Brock, Kathy *newscaster*
Brooks, Marion *newscaster*
Brotman, Barbara Louise *journalist, writer*
Burns, Diann *newscaster*
Burton, Cheryl *newscaster*
Callaway, Karen A(lice) *journalist*
Cappo, Joseph C. *journalist, writer*
Chapman, Darrian *sportscaster*
Chapman, Stephen James *columnist*
Childers, Mary Ann *newscaster*
Ciezadlo, Janina A. *art critic, educator*
Cooke, Michael *editor-in-chief, publishing executive*
Cooper, Ilene Linda *magazine editor, author*
Cowen, Stephen *editor-in-chief*
Cross, Robert Clark *journalist*
Curwen, Randall William *journalist, editor*
Davlantes, Anna *newscaster*
DeBat, Donald Joseph *media consultant, columnist*
Dee, Ivan Richard *book publisher*
DeLong, Ray *editor*
Dold, Robert Bruce *journalist*
Dowdle, James C. *cable television executive*
Duncanson, Jon *newscaster*
Dyson, Marv *broadcast executive*
Ebert, Roger Joseph *film critic*
Essex, Joseph Michael *visual communication planner*
Everhart, Bruce *radio station executive*
Feder, Robert *columnist*
Ferguson, Renee *news correspondent, reporter*
Ferrara, Annette *editor, educator*
Fetridge, Clark Worthington *publishing executive*
Flanagan, Sylvia *editor*
Flanagin, John Mead *publishing executive*
Flock, Jeffrey Charles *news bureau chief*
Fontanarosa, Phil Bernard *medical journal executive editor, emergency physician, educator*
Francuch, Paul Charles *broadcast journalist*
Freidheim, Cyrus F., Jr. *publishing executive*
Freidheim, Cyrus F., Jr. *publishing and former food products executive*
Giangreco, Mark *sportscaster, director*
Gomez, Sylvia *newscaster*
Gremillion, Robert *publishing executive*
Guillen, Alita (Alita Haytayan) *newscaster*
Hallinan, Joseph Thomas *journalist*
Hardin, Terrence Armstrong *former radio broadcasting manager*
Harlan, Byron *newscaster*
Harvey, Paul *commentator, writer, columnist*
Hefner, Christie Ann *publishing executive*
Higgins, Jack *editorial cartoonist*
Hill, Darlene *newscaster*
Hirt, Jane *editor*
Hlavacek, Roy George *publishing executive*
Hong, Ellee Pai *newscaster*
Hsu, Judy *newscaster*
Huntley, Robert Stephen *newspaper editor*
Idol, Anna Catherine *magazine editor*
Iglauer, Bruce *record company executive*
Jacobson, Walter (Skippy Jacobson) *newscaster, journalist*
Johnson, Dick *newscaster*
Johnson, Rob *newscaster*
Jones, Linda *communications educator*
Jordan, Karen *newscaster*
Judge, Bernard Martin *retired editor, publishing executive*
Kamyszew, Christopher D. *film executive, educator, curator*
Kay, Dick *news correspondent*
King, Jennifer Elizabeth *editor*
Klaviter, Helen Lothrop *magazine editor*
Klemens, Thomas Lloyd *editor*
Kotulak, Ronald *newspaper science writer*
Kramer, Darren *newscaster*
Kramer, Weezie Crawford *former broadcast executive*
Krashesky, Alan *newscaster*
Krueger, Bonnie Lee *editor, writer*
Kwan, Nesita *newscaster*
Larson, Roy *journalist, publishing executive*
Leckey, Andrew A. *financial columnist*
Lemon, Don *newscaster*
Levine, Jay *newscaster*
Lipinski, Ann Marie *publishing executive*
Loesch, Katharine Taylor *communications educator, theater educator*
Longworth, Richard Cole *journalist, writer*
Loo, Nancy *newscaster*
Lyon, Jeffrey *journalist, author*
Lythcott, Marcia A. *newspaper editor*
Madigan, John William *publishing executive*
Magers, Ron *newscaster*
Martinez, Natalie *newscaster*
McDaniel, Charles-Gene *journalism educator, writer*
McDougal, Alfred Leroy *publishing executive*

McNally, Andrew, IV, *publishing executive, director*
Nash, Jessie Madeleine *journalist, science writer*
Nault, William Henry *publishing executive*
Needleman, Barbara *newspaper executive*
Neubauer, Charles Frederick *investigative reporter*
Norman, Art *newscaster*
Odelbo, Catherine G. *publishing executive*
O'Dell, James E. *newspaper publishing executive*
Parisi, Joseph (Anthony) *magazine editor, writer, consultant, educator*
Peerman, Dean Gordon *magazine editor*
Pender, Nancy *newscaster*
Peres, Judith May *journalist*
Perez, Sylvia *newscaster, reporter*
Pilchen, Ira A. *editor*
Pope, Kerig Rodgers *retired magazine executive*
Primm, Earl Russell III *publishing executive*
Reardon, John E. *broadcast executive*
Reindl, James *newspaper editor*
Rice, Linda Johnson *publishing executive*
Rice, William Edward *journalist*
Robinson, Robin *newscaster*
Roeper, Richard *columnist*
Rogers, Phil *reporter*
Rosati, Allison *newscaster*
Roy, Kevin *newscaster*
Rynkiewicz, Stephen Michael *journalist*
Sabin, Neal F. *broadcast executive*
Sambolin, Zoraida *newscaster*
Saunders, Hosea *newscaster*
Saunders, Warner *newscaster*
Savini, Dave *reporter*
Saxenmeyer, Mark Harold *television news reporter*
Scanlan, Thomas Cleary *publishing executive, editor*
Scherb, Jeff R. *publishing executive*
Shaw, William *broadcast executive*
Smith, Sam *columnist, writer*
Smith, Scott Clybourn *publishing executive*
Sneed, Michael (Michele Sneed) *columnist*
Stoklosa, Gregory A. *publishing executive*
Stone, Steven Michael *sports announcer, former baseball player*
Suchomel, Mark *publishing executive*
Suppelsa, Mark *newscaster, reporter*
von Rhein, John Richard *music critic, journalist, writer*
Wade, Nigel *former editor in chief*
Wasiolek, Edward *literary critic, language and literature educator*
Weintraub, Joseph Barton *publishing executive*
Wert, Larry *broadcast executive*
White, John Henry *photojournalist, educator*
Wier, Patricia Ann *publishing executive, consultant*
Williams, David D. *newspaper executive*
Williams, Jim *newscaster*
Winker, Margaret A. *editor*
Winnecke, Joycelyn *editor*
Workman, Michael *editor-in-chief, publishing executive, art critic*
Wright, Sharon *reporter*
Wycliff, Noel Don *journalist, newspaper editor*
Youngman, Owen Ralph *newspaper executive*
Zekman, Pamela Lois *reporter*
Zorn, Eric John *newspaper columnist*

Countryside
Daly, Joel T. *newscaster*

Crystal Lake
Keller, William Francis *publishing consultant*

Deerfield
Wasik, John Francis *editor, writer, publisher*
Weber, Randy *publishing executive*

Des Plaines
Clapper, Marie Anne *magazine publisher*

Evanston
Borcover, Alfred Seymour *journalist*
Felknor, Bruce Lester *publishing executive, consultant, writer*
Galvin, Kathleen Malone *communications educator*
Ghiglione, Loren Frank *journalism professor*
Jacobs, Norman Joseph *publishing executive*
Kuenster, John Joseph *editor*
McCarron, John Francis *editor*
Peck, Abraham *editor, writer, educator, media consultant*
Whitaker, Charles F. *journalism educator*
White, Willmon Lee *magazine editor*
Ziomek, Jonathan S. *journalist, educator*

Glen Ellyn
Beers, V(ictor) Gilbert *publishing executive*

Highland Park
Johnson, Curtis Lee *publishing executive, editor, writer*
Pattis, Mark R. *publishing company executive*
Rutenberg-Rosenberg, Sharon Leslie *retired journalist*

Kenilworth
Cook, Stanton R. *media company executive*

Lake Forest
Schulze, Franz, Jr. *critic, educator*

Lincolnshire
Strother, Jay D. *legal editor*

Mount Vernon
Withers, W. Russell, Jr. *broadcast executive*

Oak Brook
Biedron, Theodore John *publishing and advertising executive*

Peoria
McConnell, John Thomas *publishing executive*
Murphy, Sharon Margaret *retired communications educator*

Peru
Carus, Andre Wolfgang *educational publishing firm executive*
Carus, Milton Blouke *children's periodicals publisher*

Rockford
Fleming, Thomas J. *editor, publishing executive*
Jacobi, Fredrick Thomas *newspaper publisher*

Skokie
Feinberg, Henry J. *publishing executive*

Springfield
Harper, William Wayne *broadcast executive*

Tinley Park
Flanagan, John F. *publishing executive*

Urbana
Andersen, Kenneth Eldon *speech communication educator, consultant*
Christians, Clifford Glenn *communications educator*
Dash, Leon DeCosta, Jr. *journalist*
Ono, Kent Alan *communications educator*

Wauconda
Bolchazy, Ladislaus Joseph *publishing company executive*

Wheaton
Hollingsworth, Pierce *publishing executive*
Taylor, Mark Douglas *publishing executive*

Wilmette
Weisman, Eric *music company executive*

Winnetka
Quaal, Ward Louis *broadcast executive*

INDIANA

Bloomington
Cookman, Claude *journalist, educator*
Jacobi, Peter Paul *journalism educator, writer*
Schurz, Scott Clark *journalist*

Fort Wayne
Klugman, Stephan Craig *newspaper editor*
Pellegrene, Thomas James, Jr. *editor, researcher*

Indianapolis
Adamak, M. Jeanelle *broadcast executive*
Ahern, Mike *newscaster*
Carlini, Pat *newscaster*
Chase, Alyssa Ann *editor*
Comiskey, Nancy *newspaper editor*
Dumandan, Joy *newscaster*
Fine, Pamela B. *newspaper editor*
Fleming, Marcella *journalist*
Garmel, Marion Bess Simon *retired arts journalist*
Graves, Sam *communications media executive*
Harlan, Kohr *newscaster*
Henry, Barbara Ann *publishing executive*
Knox, Debby *newscaster*
Kopp, Bruce *newscaster*
Lee, Kristi *broadcast executive, reporter*
Lyst, John Henry *former newspaper editor*
Morehead, Andrea *newscaster*
Natz, Jacques *news director*
Robinson, Keith *newspaper editor*
Russell, Frank Eli *retired newspaper publishing executive*
Ryder, Anne *newscaster*
Ryerson, Dennis *editor*
Schilling, Emily Born *editor, professional society administrator*
SerVaas, Cory *editor-in-chief*
Smiley, Wynn Ray *nonprofit corporation executive*
Stehr, John *newscaster*
Swan, Scott *newscaster*
Wheat, Christopher John, Sr. *broadcast executive*
Wheeler, Daniel Scott *management executive, editor*
Wright, Lloyd James, Jr. *broadcast executive, educator, announcer*

Inglefield
James, Marion Ray *retired publishing executive, editor*

Knightstown
Richardson, Shirley Maxine *editor*

Michigan City
Varro, Barbara Joan *retired editor*

Muncie
Bell, Stephen Scott (Steve Bell) *journalist, educator*

Munster
Colander, Patricia Marie *newspaper editor*

South Bend
Schurz, Franklin Dunn, Jr. *media executive*
Wensits, James Emrich *newswriter*

IOWA

Ames
Alumbaugh, JoAnn McCalla *magazine editor*

Cedar Rapids
Keller, Eliot Aaron *broadcast executive*

Davenport
Brocka, Bruce *editor, educator, application developer*
Gottlieb, Richard Douglas *media executive*
Schermer, Lloyd G. *publishing and broadcasting company executive*

Des Moines
Burnett, Robert A. *retired publisher*
Byal, Nancy Louise *food editor*
DeWulf Nickell, Karol *editor-in-chief*
Gartner, Michael Gay *editor, baseball and television executive*
Graham, Diane E. *newspaper editor*
Hollingsworth, Laura L. *publishing executive*
Kerr, William T. *publishing and broadcast executive*
Lacy, Stephen M. *publishing and broadcasting executive*
Little, Christopher Mark *publishing company executive, lawyer*
Myers, Mary Kathleen *publishing executive*
Peterson, David Charles *photojournalist*
Rehm, Jack Daniel *publishing executive*
Rhein, Dave *newspaper editor*
Sheehan, Carol Sama *magazine editor*
Stier, Mary P. *publishing executive*
Witke, David Rodney *retired newspaper editor, consultant*

Iowa City
Duck, Steve Weatherill *communications educator*

Mason City
Collison, Jim *publishing executive*

Waterloo
Green, Nancy Loughridge *publishing executive*

West Des Moines
Dooley, Donald John *retired publishing executive*

KANSAS

Hutchinson
Buchanan, Bruce *publishing executive*

Lawrence
Dickinson, William Boyd, Jr. *media consultant*
Simons, Dolph Collins, Jr. *publishing executive, editor*

Manhattan
Seaton, Edward Lee *editor, publishing executive*

Olathe
Dodd, James B. *Internet executive*

Salina
Entriken, Robert Kersey, Jr. *editor, writer*

Topeka
Cornish, Kent M. *broadcast executive*

Wichita
Dill, Sheri *publishing executive*
Hatteberg, Larry Merle *photojournalist*
Vaughn, Jeffrey James *broadcasting host, director*

KENTUCKY

Fort Mitchell
Silvers, Gerald Thomas *retired publishing executive*

MARYLAND

Baltimore
Donovan, Dianne Francys *journalist*

MASSACHUSETTS

South Hadley
Elleman, Barbara *editor*

MICHIGAN

Ann Arbor
Beaver, Frank Eugene *critic, historian*
Bedard, Patrick Joseph *editor, writer, consultant*
Csere, Csaba *editor-in-chief*
Hessler, David William *information and multimedia systems educator*
Lewis, Robert Enzer *editor, educator*
Martin, Bruce James *newspaper editor*
Wall, Carroll Edward *publishing executive*

Birmingham
Berman, Laura *journalist, writer*

Dearborn
Hogan, Brian Joseph *editor*
Kiska, Timothy Olin *communications educator, radio producer*

Detroit
Andrews, Caesar *editor*
Anger, Paul *newspaper editor*
Ashenfelter, David Louis *reporter*
Bennett, Grace *publishing executive*
Blomquist, David Wels *journalist*
Bullard, George *newspaper editor*
Burzynski, Susan Marie *newspaper editor*
Cantor, George Nathan *journalist*
Colby, Joy Hakanson *critic*
DeRamus, Betty Jean *columnist*
Diebolt, Judith *newspaper editor*
Falls, Joseph Francis *sportswriter, editor*
Garagiola, Steve *announcer*
Henderson, Angelo B. *journalist*
Hill, Charles *newspaper editor*
Hunke, David L. *publishing executive*
Laughlin, Nancy *newspaper editor*
Lazarus, Lila *announcer*
Lee, Marcella *announcer*
Parry, Dale D. *publisher, editor*
Scillian, Devin *announcer*
Smyntek, John Eugene, Jr. *editor*
Spencer, Ruth *announcer*
Stark, Susan R. *film critic*
Taylor, Jeff *reporter, editor*
Walker, Rhonda Gillum *announcer*
White, Joseph B. *reporter*
Wolf, Michael Ann *announcer*

East Lansing
Freedman, Eric *journalist, educator, writer*
Greenberg, Bradley Sander *communications educator*

Ferndale
Haberman, Jeremy *music venue executive*

Flint
Samuel, Roger D. *newspaper publishing executive*

Grand Rapids
Baker, Richard Lee *book publishing company executive*
Bolinder, Scott W. *publishing company executive*
Gundry, Stanley N. *publishing company executive*
Kaczmarczyk, Jeffrey Allen *journalist, music and dance critic*
Kregel, James R. *publishing executive*

Grosse Pointe
Bryfonski, Dedria Anne *publishing executive*

Grosse Pointe Farms
Christian, Edward Kieren *broadcasting station executive*

Jackson
Goldsen, Bruce I. *radio executive*

Lansing
Brown, Nancy Field *editor*

Saginaw
Chaffee, Paul Charles *newspaper editor, publisher*

Southfield
Ali, Sandra *announcer*
Carman, Kam *announcer*
Catallo, Heather *newscaster*
Centofanti, Deena *announcer*
Clifford, Carolyn *news correspondent, reporter*
Dickerson, Brian *columnist*
Dunlop, Michael *broadcast executive*
Feldman, Murray *announcer*
Gayle, Monica *broadcast journalist*
Gilchrist, Grace *broadcast executive*
Hupe, Pallas *announcer*
Lee, Alan *announcer*
LewAllen, Dave *announcer*
Lewis, Diane *announcer*
Makupson, Amyre Porter *broadcast executive*
Margolis, Sherry *newscaster*
McDonald, Christy *newscaster*
Perkins, Huel *newscaster*
Purtan, JoAnne *announcer*
Smith, Erik *announcer*
Stinger, Fanchon *newscaster*
Timmons, Robbie *news anchor*
Turner, Frank *announcer*

Troy
Brumfield, Jim *news executive*
Hucal, Michelle *editor*

Waterford
James, William Ramsay *broadcast executive*

Wixom
Alpert, Daniel *broadcast executive*

MINNESOTA

Duluth
Gruver, Nancy *publishing executive*
Latto, Lewis M. *broadcast executive*

Eagan
Collier, Ken O. *editor*

Eden Prairie
Spendlove, Steve Dale *broadcast executive*

Edina
Bisping, Bruce Henry *photojournalist*

Minneapolis
Blanchard, J. A. III *publishing executive*
Boyd, Belvel James *newspaper editor*
Buoen, Roger *newspaper editor*
Carter, Roy Ernest, Jr. *retired journalist, educator*
Cowles, John, Jr. *publishing executive, women's sports promoter, philanthropist*
Crosby, Jacqueline Garton *newspaper editor, journalist*
Flanagan, Barbara *journalist*
Harte, Christopher M. *publishing executive, investment manager*
Haverkamp, Judson *editor*
Ison, Christopher John *investigative reporter*
Johnson, Cheryl (C.J. Johnson) *newspaper columnist*
Johnson, Gary L. *publishing executive*
Kramer, Joel Roy *journalist, newspaper executive*
Laing, Karel Ann *publishing executive*
Lerner, Harry Jonas *publishing executive*
Marshall, Sherrie *newspaper editor*
McDaniel, Jan *broadcast executive*
McEnroe, Paul *reporter*
McGuire, Tim *editor*
Meador, Ron *newspaper editor, writer*
Mohr, L. Thomas *newspaper executive*
Pyle, Dave *newspaper editor*
Reichgott Junge, Ember Darlene *broadcast commentator, retired state senator, lawyer, writer, radio personality, communications executive*
Roloff, Marvin L. *publishing executive*
Scallen, Thomas Kaine *broadcast executive*
Slovut, Gordon *reporter*
Smetanka, Mary Jane *reporter*
Werner, Lawrence H. *editor*
White, Robert James *retired columnist*
Wright, Frank Gardner *retired newspaper editor*
Youngblood, Richard Neil *columnist*
Zelickson, Sue *newspaper and cookbook editor, television reporter and host, food consultant*

Minnetonka
Swartz, Donald Everett *broadcast executive*

Saint Louis Park
Kalman, Marc *radio station executive*

Saint Paul
Amidon, Paul Charles *publishing executive*
Bree, Marlin Duane *publisher, author*
Feinberg, David Erwin *retired publishing executive*
Fladung, Thom *editor-in-chief*
Fruehling, Rosemary Therese *publishing executive, author*
Gilmore, Guy L. *publishing executive*
Henry, John Thomas *retired newspaper executive*
Higgins, Harold K. *retired publishing executive*
Hubbard, Stanley Stub *broadcast executive*
Kling, William Hugh *broadcast executive*
Meers, Bill M. *news executive*
Sadowski, Richard J. *former publishing executive*
Straight, Cathy *editor*
Tyner, Howard A. *retired publishing executive, newspaper editor, journalist*
Wehrwein, Austin Carl *freelance/self-employed reporter*
Weschcke, Carl Llewellyn *publishing executive*

MISSOURI

Columbia
Loory, Stuart Hugh *journalist*
Sanders, Keith Page *journalism educator*

Jefferson City
Benson, Joseph Fred *journalist, legal historian*

Kansas City
Allen, John L., Jr. *journalist, writer*
Batiuk, Thomas Martin *cartoonist*
Cahill, Patricia Deal *radio station executive*
Davis, James Robert *cartoonist*
Gray, Helen Theresa Gott *editor*
Guisewite, Cathy Lee *cartoonist*
Gusewelle, Charles Wesley *journalist, writer*
Lindenbaum, Sharon *publishing executive*
McDermott, Alan *newspaper editor*
Mc Meel, John Paul *newspaper syndicate and publishing executive*
Oliphant, Patrick *cartoonist*
Palmer, Cruise *newspaper editor*
Reed, William T. *broadcast executive*
Roush, Sue *newspaper editor*
Stevens, Paul *newspaper editor*
Wilson, Tom *cartoonist, greeting card company executive*
Zieman, Mark *editor, publishing executive*

Saint Louis
Bennett, Patricia Ann *radio executive*
Clayton, John Anthony *radio broadcast executive*
Ehrlich, Ava *broadcast executive*
Elkins, Ken Joe *retired broadcast executive*
Engelhardt, Thomas Alexander *editorial cartoonist*
Freeland, A. Jerome *publishing executive*
Gauen, Patrick Emil *news correspondent*
Holt, Glen Edward *editor*
Kanne, Marvin George *newspaper publishing executive*
Korando, Donna Kay *journalist*
Mette, Virgil Louis *publishing executive, biology educator*
Mowbray, Kevin D. *publishing executive*
Norman, Charles Henry *broadcast executive*
Pulitzer, Michael Edgar *publishing executive*
Randolph, Jennings, Jr., (Jay Randolph) *sportscaster*
Regnell, Barbara Caramella *retired media educator*
Robbins, Arnie *editor*

Smithville
Johnson, Darryl Thomas *communications educator*

Springfield
Champion, Norma Jean *communications educator, state legislator*
Glazier, Robert Carl *publishing executive*
Sylvester, Ronald Charles *newspaper writer*
Van Cleave, William Robert *international relations educator*

Town And Country
Stoeffler, David Bruce *publishing executive*

NEBRASKA

Lincoln
Dyer, William Earl, Jr. *retired newspaper editor*
Raz, Hilda *editor-in-chief, educator*

Omaha
Gottschalk, John E. *newspaper publishing executive*
King, Larry *editor*
Nicol, Brian *publishing executive*
Sands, Deanna *editor*
Simon, Paul H. *newspaper editor*

NEVADA

Henderson
Wills, Robert Hamilton *retired publishing executive*

NEW YORK

New York
Lagani, Daniel *publishing executive*

NORTH CAROLINA

Winston Salem
Price, Henry Escoe *broadcast executive*

NORTH DAKOTA

Fargo
DeVine, Terry Michael *newspaper editor*
Littlefield, Robert Stephen *communications educator, training consultant*
Marcil, William Christ, Sr. *publisher, broadcast executive*

Grand Forks
Glassheim, Eliot Alan *editor, state legislator*

OHIO

Akron
Burbach, Mike *editor*
Stewart, Mizell III *editor*

Athens
Metters, Thomas Waddell *sportswriter*
Sanders, David *university press administrator*
Stempel, Guido Hermann III *journalism educator*

Bowling Green
Clark, Robert King *communications educator, consultant, actor, model*

Chagrin Falls
Lange, David Charles *journalist*

Cincinnati
Beckwith, Barbara Jean *journalist*
Boehne, Richard *newspaper company executive*
Borgman, James Mark *editorial cartoonist*
Buchanan, Margaret E. *publishing executive*
Burleigh, William Robert *media executive*
Callinan, Tom *editor-in-chief*
Flanagan, Martha Lang *publishing executive*
Knue, Paul Frederick *newspaper editor*
Lapin, Jeffry Mark *magazine publisher*
Lowe, Kenneth W. *multimedia executive*
McMullin, Ruth Roney *retired publishing executive*
Mechem, Charles Stanley, Jr. *retired broadcast executive*
Moll, William Gene *broadcasting company executive*
Standen, Craig Clayton *newspaper executive*

Cleveland
Bauer, Alan R. *internet company executive*
Brandt, John Reynold *editor, journalist*
Davis, David Aaron *journalist*
Egger, Terrance C.Z. *publishing executive*
Fabris, James A. *journalist*
Giannetti, Louis Daniel *film critic, educator*
Goldberg, Susan *editor*
Greer, Thomas H. *newspaper executive*
Jensen, Kathryn Patricia (Kit) *broadcast executive*
Jindra, Christine *editor*
Kanzeg, David George *radio station executive*
Kovacs, Rosemary *newpaper editor*
Long, Robert M. *newspaper publishing executive*
Machaskee, Alex *retired newspaper publishing company executive*
Molyneaux, David Glenn *newspaper travel editor*
Santisi, Terri M. (Theresa M. Santisi) *multi-media company executive*
Shaw, Scott Alan *photojournalist*
Strang, James Dennis *editor*
Wareham, Jerrold F. *broadcast executive*

Columbus
Altman, Jim *newscaster*
Cambern, Andrea *newscaster, reporter*
Cox, Mitchel Neal *editor*
Curtin, Michael Francis *publishing executive, writer*
Dervin, Brenda Louise *communications educator*
Fiorile, Michael J. *publishing executive*
Grossberg, Michael Lee *theater critic, writer*
Hamper, Anietra *news anchor*
Harris, Yolanda *newscaster*
Headrick, Mike *newscaster*
Hollingsworth, Holly *newscaster*
Jackson, Mike *newscaster*
Johnston, Jeffery W. *publishing executive*
Kaylor, Dave *newscaster*
Kefauver, Weldon Addison *publishing executive*
Kiefer, Gary *newspaper editor*
Marrison, Benjamin J. *editor-in-chief*
Marshall, Colleen *newscaster*
Massie, Robert Joseph *publishing company executive*
Murphy, Andrew J. *managing news editor*
Ouzts, Dale Keith *broadcast executive*
Pave, Angela *newscaster*
Pick, Heather *newscaster*
Rea, Cabot *newscaster*
Revish, Jerry *newscaster, reporter*
Sherrill, Thomas Boykin III *retired newspaper publishing executive*
Spiegel, Gabe *newscaster*
Stallworth, Sam *broadcast executive*
Strickler, Chuck *newscaster*
Strode, George K. *sports editor*
Sullivan, Terri *newscaster, reporter*
Wolfe, John F. *publishing executive*

Dayton
Carollo, Russell *journalist*
Franklin, Douglas E. *publishing executive*
Matheny, Ruth Ann *editor*

Lyndhurst
Kastner, Christine Kriha *newspaper correspondent*

Mason
Smith, C. LeMoyne *retired publishing executive*

Painesville
Modic, Stanley John *business editor, publisher, retired columnist*

Pepper Pike
Vail, Thomas Van Husen *retired publishing executive*

Sidney
Stevens, Robert Jay *magazine editor*

Toledo
Block, John Robinson *newspaper publisher, editor-in-chief*
Block, William K., Jr. *media executive*
Brickey, Suzanne M. *editor*
Royhab, Ronald *journalist, editor*

SOUTH DAKOTA

Pierre
Callahan, Patrick *communication media executive*

Rapid City
Wishard, Della Mae *former newspaper editor*

Sioux Falls
Garson, Arnold Hugh *publishing executive*

TEXAS

Dallas
Brown, Colleen *broadcast executive*

VIRGINIA

Arlington
Holovaty, Adrian *editor, web site designer*

WISCONSIN

Appleton
Oppmann, Andrew James *newspaper editor*

Eau Claire
Clark, Judy *newscaster*
Gallagher, Bob *newscaster*
Kreitlow, Pat *newscaster*
Rupnor, Jennifer *journalist*
Tuckner, Michelle *newscaster*

Greendale
Kaiser, Ann Christine *magazine editor*
Pohl, Kathleen Sharon *editor*
Reiman, Roy J. *publishing executive*

Hales Corners
Enk, Scott *editor, researcher, activist*

Iola
Krause, Chester Lee *publishing executive*

Janesville
Fitzgerald, James Francis *broadcast executive*

Madison
Burgess, James Edward *publishing executive*
Burns, Elizabeth Murphy *media executive*
Drechsel, Robert Edward *journalism educator*
Dunwoody, Sharon Lee *journalism and communications educator*
Foley, Ellen Madaline *journalist*
Gruber, John Edward *editor, historian, photographer*
Haslanger, Philip Charles *journalist*
Hastings, Joyce R. *editor*
Hopson, James Warren *publishing executive*
Hoyt, James Lawrence *journalism educator, writer*
Rothschild, Matthew *editor*
Wineke, William Robert *reporter, minister*
Zweifel, David Alan *newspaper editor*

Milwaukee
Anderson, Mike *newscaster*
Atwater, John *news correspondent*
Behrendt, David Frogner *retired journalist*
Bohr, Nick *reporter*
Brenner, Elizabeth (Betsy Brenner) *publishing executive*
Davis, David *newscaster*
Dawson, Kim *reporter*
DeRusha, Jason *reporter*
Elliot, Tammy *newscaster*
Farris, Trueman Earl, Jr. *retired newspaper editor*
Foster, Richard *journalist*
Garcia, Astrid J. *newspaper executive*
Gay, Duane *reporter*
Henry, Colleen *reporter*
Henry, Rick *broadcast executive*
Hinkley, Gerry *newspaper editor*
Hughes, T. Lee *newspaper editor*
Jallings, Jessica *reporter, newscaster*
Jaques, Damien Paul *theater critic*
Kaiser, Martin *editor-in-chief*
Kleefisch, Rebecca *reporter*
Kritzer, Paul Eric *publishing executive, lawyer*
Lee, Jack (Jim Sanders Beasley) *broadcast executive*
McCann, Dennis John *columnist*
Mykleby, Kathy *newscaster, reporter*
Salamme, Matt *reporter*
Spore, Keith Kent *newspaper executive*
Stafford, Lori *reporter*
Sullivan, Edward *periodical editor*
Taff, Gerry *reporter*
Wainscott, Kent *reporter*
Youngquist, Wayne *reporter*

Superior
Billig, Thomas Clifford *publishing executive, marketing professional*

Wausau
Baker, Mark *television newscaster*

West Bend
Fraedrich, Royal Louis *magazine editor, publisher*

CANADA

ONTARIO

London
McLeod, Philip Robert *publishing executive*

ADDRESS UNPUBLISHED

Adams, Cheryl *newscaster*
Agarwal, Suman Kumar *editor*
Anderson, Jon Stephen *newswriter*
Armstrong, Douglas Dean *journalist*
Ayala, Michael *newscaster*
Barnes, Harper Henderson *critic, editor, writer*
Brisbane, Arthur Seward *newspaper publisher*
Brown, Paul *former publishing executive*
Brumback, Charles Tiedtke *retired newspaper executive*
Christiansen, Richard Dean *retired newspaper editor*
Clapper, Lyle Nielsen *magazine publisher*
Clifton, Douglas C. *retired newspaper editor*
Cohen, Allan Richard *broadcast executive*
Crutchfield, James N. *publishing executive*
Dawson, Virginia Sue *retired editor*
Donaldson, Bob *newscaster*
Dubin, Stacia *newscaster*
Fair, Hudson Randolph *recording company executive*
FitzSimons, Dennis Joseph *former broadcast and publishing executive*
Forner, Tracy *newscaster*
Gaines, William Chester *journalist*
Goldsborough, Robert Gerald *publishing executive, author*
Greene, Robert (Bob) Bernard, Jr. *news correspondent, journalist, writer*
Hedberg, Paul Clifford *broadcast executive*
James, Sheryl Teresa *journalist*
Kamin, Blair Douglass *architecture critic*
Kelleher, Timothy John *retired publishing company executive*
Kisor, Henry Du Bois *retired editor, columnist, critic, writer*
Krulitz, Leo Morrion *retired business executive, director*
Laurence, Michael Marshall *editor*
Leach, Janet C. *publishing executive*
Lipman, David *retired journalist, multi-media consultant*
Manos, John *editor-in-chief*
McHenry, Robert (Dale) *editor*
Meriwether, Heath J. *newspaper consultant, retired publisher, educator*
Mora, Antonio Gonzalez III *broadcast journalist*
Moyer, J. Keith *former publishing executive*
Palmer, Bradley Beran *sportscaster*
Pepper, Jonathon L. *media executive*
Plotnick, Harvey Barry *publishing executive*
Quade, Vicki *editor, writer, playwright, theater producer*
Sanger, Lawrence Mark *editor-in-chief*
Seaman, William Casper *retired news photographer*
Sedgwick, Sally Belle *publishing company executive*
Shapiro, Richard Charles *publishing executive, sales executive, marketing professional*
Skinner, Thomas *broadcast executive*
Snader, Jack Ross *retired publishing company executive*
Soeteber, Ellen *journalist, editor*
Stevens, Tony *broadcast executive, radio personality*
Sund, Jeffrey Owen *retired publishing company executive*
Tammeus, William David *journalist, columnist*
Teagan, John Gerard *publishing executive*
Thornton, Thomas Noel *former publishing executive*
Torgerson, Katherine P. *media consultant, corporate communications specialist*
Trudeau, Garretson Beekman (Garry Trudeau) *cartoonist*
Vincent, Charles Eagar, Jr. *sportswriter*
Waldmeir, Peter Nielsen *retired journalist*
Watson, Catherine Elaine *journalist*
Weaver, Franklin Thomas *retired newspaper executive*
Weber, Arthur *magazine executive*
Werner, Bill *communication media executive*
Whittemore, Brian *media consultant, advertising executive*
Wolfe, Sheila A. *journalist*
Wolman, J. Martin *retired newspaper publisher*

EDUCATION *See also* specific fields for postsecondary education

UNITED STATES

ARIZONA

Green Valley
Turner, Harold Edward *retired education educator*

Scottsdale
Stone, Alan Jay *retired academic administrator*

CALIFORNIA

Irvine
Policano, Andrew J. *dean, finance educator*

Orange
Kraft, Arthur *dean*

San Luis Obispo
Gardebring, Sandra S. *academic administrator*

COLORADO

Boulder
Wilson, M. Roy *academic administrator, medical educator*

CONNECTICUT

New Britain
Miller, John Winston *academic administrator*

Storrs Mansfield
Hogan, Michael J. *academic administrator*

FLORIDA

Destin
O'Brien, Gregory Michael St. Lawrence *academic administrator*

Fort Myers
Crowe, James Wilson *university administrator, educator*
Drushal, Mary Ellen *retired education educator*

Miami
Fish, Stanley Eugene *dean, language educator*

Pensacola
Surles, Carol D. *academic administrator*

Sarasota
Miller, Peggy Gordon Elliott *retired academic administrator*

The Villages
Behrendt, Richard Louis *academic administrator*

Winter Garden
Gillet, Pamela Kipping *special education educator*

GEORGIA

Atlanta
Benveniste, Lawrence M. *dean*
Mahaley-Johnson, Hosanna *school system administrator*

ILLINOIS

Alton
Boyle, Ann M. *dean, dental educator*

Aurora
Zarle, Thomas Herbert *academic administrator*

Bloomington
Wilson, Richard F. *academic administrator*

Carbondale
Dixon, Billy Gene *academic administrator, educator*

Mead, John Stanley *university administrator*
Poshard, Glenn (Glendal W. Poshard) *academic administrator, former congressman*
Scott, Shirley Clay *dean*
Snyder, Carolyn Ann *education educator, librarian, director*

Carlinville
Pride, Miriam R. *college president*

Champaign
Ghosh, Avijit *dean*
Gomez, Terrine *school director*
Harris, Zelema M. *academic administrator*
Herman, Richard H. *academic administrator*
Hurd, Heidi M. *dean, humanities and law educator*
Ikenberry, Stanley Oliver *education educator, director, former university president*
Loeb, Jane Rupley *academic administrator, educator*
McConkie, George Wilson *education educator*
Spodek, Bernard *early childhood educator*

Charleston
Rives, Stanley Gene *retired academic administrator*

Chicago
Beane, Marjorie Noterman *academic administrator*
Bindenagel, James Dale *university executive*
Bouton, Marshall Melvin *academic administrator*
Bowman, Barbara Taylor *early childhood educator*
Cafferty, Pastora San Juan *education educator*
Culp, Kristine Ann *dean, theology studies educator*
Daniel, Elnora D. *academic administrator*
Duncan, Arne *school system administrator*
Felton, Cynthia *educational director*
Garanzini, Michael J. *academic administrator, priest*
Getz, Godfrey Shalom *dean, pathologist, educator*
Gold, Carol R. *dean, nursing educator*
Graham, Bruce S. *dean, educator*
Gross, Theodore Lawrence *university administrator, author*
Holtschneider, Dennis H. *academic administrator, priest*
Johnson, Mary Ann *vocational school owner*
Jones, Tony *academic administrator*
Keiderling, Timothy Allen *chemistry educator, researcher*
Kim, Mi Ja *dean, academic administrator*
King, Tim *charter school administrator*
Krent, Harold J. *dean, law educator*
Landsberg, Lewis *dean, endocrinologist, medical researcher*
Levmore, Saul *dean, law educator*
Madara, James Lee *dean, pathologist, educator, epitheliologist*
Malcolm, Christine Anne *university hospital administrator*
McCray, Curtis Lee *academic administrator*
McPherson, Michael Steven *academic administrator, economist*
Mell, Patricia *dean*
Minogue, John P. *academic administrator, educator, priest*
O'Reilly, Charles Terrance *university dean*
Panko, Jessie Symington *education educator*
Piderit, John J. *university educator*
Restivo, Charles L. *academic administrator*
Richardson, John Thomas *academic administrator, clergyman*
Rothman-Denes, Lucia Beatriz *biology educator*
Schieser, Hans Alois *education educator*
Schubert, William Henry *curriculum studies educator*
Shaver, Joan Louise Fowler *dean, women's health nurse*
Snyder, Edward Adams *dean, economics professor*
Steinberg, Salme Elizabeth Harju *academic administrator, historian*
Stowell, Joseph III *academic administrator*
Sulkin, Howard Allen *academic administrator*
Swanson, Don Richard *university dean*
Van Zandt, David E. *dean, law educator*
Wasan, Darsh Tilakchand *academic administrator, chemical engineer, educator*
Yandle, Stephen Thomas *dean*
Yellen, David N. *dean, lawyer*

Danville
Mervis, Louis *school system administrator*

Dekalb
Legg, J. Ivan *academic administrator*
Peters, John G. *academic administrator, political scientist*

Des Plaines
Lee, Margaret Burke *college president, language educator*

Downers Grove
LaRocca, Patricia Darlene McAleer *middle school educator*
Nichols, Karen J. *dean*

Elgin
Puotinen, Arthur Edwin *college president, minister*

Eureka
Hearne, George Archer *academic administrator*

Evanston
Bienen, Henry Samuel *academic administrator, political scientist, educator*
Boye, Roger Carl *academic administrator, journalism educator*
Christian, Richard Carlton *dean, former advertising agency executive*
Dumas, Lawrence B. *academic administrator*
Jain, Dipak Chand *dean, marketing educator, consultant*
Lewis, Dan Albert *education educator*
McCoy, Marilyn *director*
Miller, Thomas Williams *former university dean*
Peterson, Penelope Loraine *dean, education educator*
Weber, Arnold Robert *academic administrator*
Zarefsky, David Harris *academic administrator, communication editor*

Galesburg
Taylor, Roger Lee *academic administrator, lawyer*

Glen Carbon
Lazerson, Earl Edwin *retired academic administrator*

Itasca
Bufe, Noel Carl *program director*

Lake Forest
Bransfield, Joan *principal*

Libertyville
Kremkau, Paul *principal*

Lincolnwood
Greenblatt, Deana Charlene *elementary school educator*

Lombard
Benning, Joseph Raymond *principal*

Macomb
Goehner, Donna Marie *retired university dean*

Mattoon
Luther, Robert K. *college president*

Maywood
Slogoff, Stephen *dean, anesthesiologist, educator*

Naperville
Wilde, Harold Richard *college president*

Normal
Presley, John Woodrow *educator, dean*

Oak Park
Adelman, William John *retired academic administrator, industrial relations specialist*

Oakbrook Terrace
Cason, Marilynn Jean *academic administrator, lawyer*
Levine, Norman M. *academic administrator*
Taylor, Ronald Lee *academic administrator*

Palatine
Bassi, Suzanne Howard *retired secondary school educator, volunteer*

Palos Hills
Crawley, Vernon Obadiah *academic administrator*

Park Ridge
Culverwell, Rosemary Jean *retired principal, elementary school educator*

Plainfield
Diercks, Eileen Kay *educational media coordinator, elementary school educator*

Quincy
Simpson, William Marshall *academic administrator*

River Forest
Carroll, Donna M. *academic administrator*

Rock Island
Bahls, Steven Carl *academic administrator, educator*
Horstmann, James Douglas *retired academic administrator*
Tredway, Thomas *college president*

Rockford
Chapdelaine, Roland Joseph *academic administrator*

Rolling Meadows
Peekel, Arthur K. *secondary school educator*

Schaumburg
Westlund, Maribeth *secondary school educator*

Skokie
Sloan, Judi C. *former physical education educator*

Springfield
Bretz, William Franklin *retired elementary and secondary education educator*
Koch, Christopher A. *school system administrator*
Poorman, Robert Lewis *retired academic administrator*
Stephens, Norman L. *former academic administrator*

University Park
Maimon, Elaine Plaskow *academic administrator*

Urbana
Stukel, James Joseph *academic administrator, mechanical engineer, educator*
Whiteley, Herbert E. *dean*

Wheaton
Ford, Andrew Thomas *former academic administrator*
Litfin, A. Duane *academic administrator*

Wilmette
McNeill, Thomas B. *director, retired lawyer*

INDIANA

Angola
Reynolds, R. John *academic administrator, educator*

Bloomington
Arnove, Robert Frederick *education educator*
Barnes, A. James *dean*
Bertenthal, Bennett Ira *dean, psychologist, educator*
Brown, Trevor *dean*
Louis, Kenneth R.R. Gross *academic administrator*
McRobbie, Michael Alexander *academic administrator, computer scientist, educator*
Robel, Lauren *dean, law educator*
Ryan, John William *academic administrator*
Smith, Carl Bernard *education educator*
Smith, Daniel C. *dean, finance educator*
Sullivan, Michael Francis III *educational consultant*

Carmel
Rand, Leon *academic administrator*

Evansville
Hoops, H. Ray *college president*
Jennings, Stephen Grant *academic administrator*

Fishers
Shults, Anna *elementary school educator*

Fort Wayne
Hamrick, Linda L. *secondary school educator*
Robinson, Wendy Y. *school system administrator*
Snyder, Arthur E. *academic administrator*
Wartell, Michael Alan *academic administrator*

Franklin
Martin, William Bryan *chancellor, lawyer, minister*

Gary
Smith, Vernon G. *education educator, state legislator*

Greencastle
Bottoms, Robert Garvin *academic administrator*

Hammond
Delph, Donna Jean (Maroc) *education educator, consultant, academic administrator*
Fehring, Mary Ann *secondary school educator*

Indianapolis
Bepko, Gerald Lewis *retired academic administrator, law educator*
Boyd, Rozelle *retired academic administrator*
Brater, Donald Craig *dean, educator*
Brenner, Mark Lee *academic administrator, physiologist, educator*
Broome, Marion *dean*
Clark, Charles M., Jr. *medical school administrator*
Goldblatt, Lawrence I. *dean, educator, researcher*
Gooldy, Patricia Alice *retired elementary school educator*
Pitts, Beverley J. *academic administrator*
Reed, Suellen Kinder *school system administrator*
Stookey, George Kenneth *retired director, retired dental educator*
White, Eugene G. *school system administrator*

Lafayette
Jischke, Martin C. *retired academic administrator*

Marion
Barnes, James Byron *university president*

Muncie
Gora, JoAnn M. *academic administrator*
Linson, Robert Edward *retired academic administrator*

Munster
Fies, James David *elementary school educator*

New Harmony
Rice, David Lee *university president emeritus*

North Manchester
Switzer, Jo Young *college president*

Notre Dame
Burish, Thomas Gerard *academic administrator, psychology professor*
Burke, Leo *dean, director*
Castellino, Francis Joseph *university dean*
Crosson, Frederick James *retired dean, humanities educator*
Helquist, Paul M. *chemistry educator, researcher*
Hyder, Anthony K. *academic administrator, science educator*
Jenkins, John I. *academic administrator*
Malloy, Edward Aloysius *academic administrator*
Maziar, Christine M. *academic administrator*
O'Hara, Patricia Anne *dean, law educator*
O'Meara, Onorato Timothy *academic administrator, mathematician*
Scheidt, W. Robert *chemistry educator, researcher*
Woo, Carolyn Yauyan *dean*
Younger, Jennifer A. *university librarian*

Pendleton
Phenis-Bourke, Nancy Sue *educational administrator*

Richmond
Bennett, Douglas Carleton *academic administrator*

Roanoke
Cutshall-Hayes, Diane Marion *elementary school educator*

South Bend
Harriman, Gerald Eugene *retired business administrator, economics professor*
Perrin, Kenneth Lynn *university chancellor*

Terre Haute
Benjamin, Lloyd William III *academic administrator*
Hunt, Effie Neva *retired dean, literature educator*
Leach, Ronald George *education educator, librarian*
Moore, John William *former university president*

Upland
Kesler, Jay Lewis *retired academic administrator*

Valparaiso
Harre, Alan Frederick *academic administrator*
Miller, John Albert *university educator, consultant*
Scales, Freda S. *dean, nursing educator*
Schnabel, Robert Victor *retired academic administrator*

West Lafayette
Beering, Steven Claus *academic administrator, medical educator*
Córdova, France Anne-Dominic *academic administrator, astrophysicist*
Cosier, Richard A. *dean, finance educator*
Feinberg, Richard Alan *consumer science educator, consultant*
Ford, Frederick Ross *retired university official*
Gappa, Judith M. *academic administrator*
Gentry, Don Kenneth *academic dean*
Moore, David Sheldon *statistics educator, researcher*
Rebar, Alan H. *dean*
Shertzer, Bruce Eldon *education educator*
Vitter, Jeffrey Scott *academic administrator, computer science educator, researcher*

IOWA

Ames
Allen, Benjamin J. *academic administrator*
Ebbers, Larry Harold *education educator*
Geoffroy, Gregory L. *academic administrator, educator*

Hoffman, Elizabeth *academic administrator, economics professor*

Ankeny
Keese, Jan *elementary school educator*

Cedar Falls
Lundy, Sherman Perry *secondary school educator*

Cedar Rapids
Brighi, Robert J. *principal*
Plagman, Ralph *principal*

Davenport
Rogalski, Edward J. *university administrator*

Des Moines
Gaines, Ruth Ann *secondary school educator*
Jeffrey, Judy *school system administrator*
Jeschke, Thomas *gifted education educator*
Maxwell, David E. *academic executive, educator*

Dubuque
Dunn, M. Catherine *college administrator, educator*
Toale, Thomas Edward *school system administrator, minister*

Grinnell
Osgood, Russell King *academic administrator*

Iowa City
Boyd, Willard Lee *academic administrator, educator, lawyer, museum director*
Brennan, Robert Lawrence *educational director, psychometrician*
Buckwalter, Kathleen C. *academic administrator, educator*
Dreher, Melanie Creagan *dean, nursing educator*
Feldt, Leonard Samuel *academic administrator, educator*
Johnsen, David C. *dean, dental educator*
Jones, Carolyn *dean, law educator*
Mason, Sally Kay Frost *academic administrator, biology professor*
Plapp, Bryce Vernon *biochemistry educator*
Robillard, Jean Eugene *dean, educator*
Saterfiel, Thomas Horne *education researcher, administrator*
Spriestersbach, Duane Caryl *academic administrator, speech pathology/audiology services professional, educator*

Marshalltown
Tambrino, Paul August *college president*

Pacific Junction
Krogstad, Jack Lynn *associate dean, accounting educator*

Sioux City
Rants, Carolyn Jean *academic administrator, educator*
Wick, Sister Margaret *former college administrator*

Urbandale
Hoyt, Kenneth Boyd *education educator, writer*

Waverly
Menzel, Ferol Schricker *academic administrator*

KANSAS

Carbondale
McCollum, Susan *elementary school educator*

Emporia
Schallenkamp, Kay *academic administrator*

Frontenac
Wilson, Donald Wallin *academic administrator, communications educator*

Great Bend
Law, Veldon Lee *college administrator*

Hays
Hammond, Edward H. *university president*

Kansas City
Atkinson, Barbara F. *dean, medical educator, executive vice chancellor*
Burke, Thomas Richard *community college administrator*
Clifton, Thomas E. *academic administrator, minister*
Miller, Karen L. *dean, nursing educator*
Wendel, Shirley Anne *college dean*

Lawrence
Frederickson, Horace George *retired academic administrator, humanities educator*
Hemenway, Robert E. *academic administrator, language educator*
Lariviere, Richard Wilfred *academic administrator, educator*
Locke, Carl Edwin, Jr. *academic administrator, engineer, educator*
McAllister, Stephen Robert *dean, law educator*
Peterson, Nancy *special education educator*
Turnbull, Ann Patterson *special education educator, consultant, research director*

Leawood
Talley, Melvin Gary *academic administrator*

Lindsborg
Humphrey, Karen Ann *college director*

Manhattan
Coffman, James Richard *academic administrator, veterinarian, educator*
Higgins, James Jacob *statistics educator*
Richardson, Ralph C. *dean*
Wefald, Jon *academic administrator*

Overland Park
Whelan, Richard J. *retired academic administrator*

Sublette
Swinney, Carol Joyce *secondary school educator*

Topeka
Dennis, Dale M. *school system administrator*

Farley, Jerry B. *academic administrator*

Uniontown
Conard, Norman Dale *secondary school educator*

Wichita
Beggs, Donald Lee *academic administrator*

KENTUCKY

Bellevue
Nester, William Raymond, Jr. *retired academic administrator*

MAINE

Newfield
Patten, Ronald James *university dean*

MASSACHUSETTS

Ashfield
Bannister, Geoffrey *academic administrator, geographer*

Boston
Scrimshaw, Susan Crosby *academic administrator*

Cambridge
Dye, Nancy Schrom *academic administrator, historian, educator*

Wellesley
Schlesinger, Leonard Arthur *academic administrator*

MICHIGAN

Adrian
Caine, Stanley Paul *college administrator*

Allendale
Niemeyer, Glenn Alan *academic administrator, history professor*

Alma
Tracy, Saundra J. *academic administrator*

Ann Arbor
Ball, Deborah Loewenberg *dean, education educator*
Bryant, Barbara Everitt *academic administrator, researcher, retired marketing professional, federal agency administrator*
Caminker, Evan H. *dean, law educator*
Courant, Paul Noah *university librarian, economist, educator*
Dobranski, Bernard *dean, law educator*
Dolan, Robert J. *dean*
Fleming, Suzanne Marie *academic administrator, freelance/self-employed writer*
Hilton, James L. *university librarian*
Kalbfleisch, John David *statistics educator*
Kelch, Robert Paul *former dean, pediatric endocrinologist*
Matthews, Rowena Green *biological chemistry educator*
Omenn, Gilbert Stanley *academic administrator, internist, scientist*
Paul, Ara Garo *university dean*
Polverini, Peter J. *dean, dental educator*
Robbins, Jerry Hal *educational administration educator*
Rogers, Bryan L. *dean*
Rogers, Bryan Leigh *dean, artist, educator*
Schacht, Jochen Heinrich *biochemistry educator*
Sullivan, Thomas Patrick *academic administrator*
Tice, Carol Hoff *intergenerational specialist, consultant*
Ulaby, Fawwaz Tayssir *academic administrator, engineering educator*
Van Houweling, Douglas Edward *university administrator, educator*
Warner, Kenneth E(dgar) *dean, public health educator, consultant*
White, B. Joseph *former dean, business educator*
Xie, Yu *adult education educator*

Armada
Kummerow, Arnold A. *superintendent of schools*

Big Rapids
Ryan, Ray Darl, Jr. *academic administrator*

Birmingham
VanDeusen, Bruce Dudley *school system administrator*

Bloomfield Hills
Doyle, Jill J. *elementary school principal*

Brighton
Jensen, Baiba *school system administrator*

Clarkston
Mousseau, Doris Naomi Barton *retired elementary school principal*

Commerce Township
Boynton, Irvin Parker *retired assistant principal*

Dearborn Heights
Johns, Diana *secondary school educator*

Detroit
Barrett, Nancy Smith *academic administrator*
Edelstein, Tilden Gerald *academic administrator, historian, educator*
Fay, Sister Maureen A. *university president*
Kyff, Kimberly *elementary school educator*
Mitchell, Connie *director*
Reid, Irvin D. *academic administrator*
Rogers, Richard Lee *academic administrator, educator*
Steiman, H. Robert *dean, dental educator*
Williams, Denise *academic administrator*
Williams, Roger *academic administrator*

East Lansing
Abbett, William S. *former dean*
Brophy, Jere Edward *education educator, researcher*
Harrison, Jeremy Thomas *dean, law educator*
Honhart, Frederick Lewis III *academic director*
Mackey, Maurice Cecil *university president, economist, lawyer*
Rothert, Marilyn L. *dean, nursing educator*
Simon, Lou Anna Kimsey *academic administrator*
Snoddy, James Ernest *education educator*
Strampel, William Derkey *dean, medical educator*

Elk Rapids
Thompson, Richard Thomas *academic administrator*

Farmington Hills
Hagerty, Robert E. *academic administrator*

Flint
Arnold, Allen D. *academic administrator*
Lorenz, John Douglas *college official*

Grand Rapids
Calkins, Richard W. *former college president*
Diekema, Anthony J. *college president, consultant*
Evans, Oliver H. *college administrator*
Lubbers, Arend Donselaar *retired academic administrator*
VanHarn, Gordon Lee *academic administrator*

Grosse Pointe Woods
Robie, Joan *elementary school principal*

Holland
Nyenhuis, Jacob Eugene *academic administrator*

Interlochen
Kimpton, Jeffrey S. *academic administrator*

Kalamazoo
Bailey, Judith Irene *academic administrator, educator, consultant*
Haenicke, Diether Hans *academic administrator emeritus, educator*
Palchick, Bernard S. *academic administrator, painter, educator*
Showalter, Shirley H. *former academic administrator*
Stufflebeam, Daniel LeRoy *education educator*

Lansing
Piveronus, Peter John, Jr. *education educator*
Straus, Kathleen Nagler *academic administrator, educator*

Livonia
Kujawa, Sister Rose Marie *academic administrator*
McDowell, Richard William *academic administrator*
Van de Vyver, Sister Mary Francilene *academic administrator*

Ludington
Puffer, Richard Judson *retired college chancellor*

Macomb
Farmakis, George Leonard *retired education educator*

Midland
Barker, Nancy Lepard *university official*
Grzesiak, Katherine Ann *primary school educator*

Rochester
Packard, Sandra Podolin *education educator, consultant*
Russi, Gary D. *academic administrator*

Saginaw
Scharffe, William Granville *academic administrator, educator*

Sault Sainte Marie
Youngblood, Betty J. *academic administrator*

Southfield
Chambers, Charles MacKay *academic administrator, lawyer, consultant*

University Center
Boyse, Peter Dent *academic administrator*
Gilbertson, Eric Raymond *academic administrator, lawyer*

Utica
Olman, Gloria G. *secondary school educator*

Warren
Lorenzo, Albert L. *academic administrator*

Williamston
Johnson, Tom Milroy *dean, physician, educator*

Ypsilanti
Lewis-White, Linda Beth *elementary school educator*

MINNESOTA

Albert Lea
Rechtzigel, Sue Marie (Suzanne Rechtzigel) *child care center executive*

Alexandria
Lillestol, Jane Brush *educational consultant*

Austin
Schmid, Harald Heinrich Otto *biochemistry educator, academic administrator*

Bird Island
Cooper, Roger *secondary school educator, former state legislator*

Burnsville
Freeburg, Richard L. *primary education educator*

Collegeville
Reinhart, Dietrich Thomas *academic administrator, social studies educator*

Duluth
Martin, Kathryn A. *academic administrator*
Ziegler, Richard J. *dean, educator*

Falcon Heights
Kreuter, Gretchen V. *academic administrator*

Long Lake
Lowthian, Petrena *academic administrator*

Mankato
Nickerson, James Findley *retired education educator*

Marine On Saint Croix
Gavin, Robert Michael, Jr. *educational consultant*

Minneapolis
Atwood, John Brian *dean*
Bowie, Norman Ernest *university official, educator*
Bruininks, Robert H. *academic administrator, psychologist, educator*
Cerra, Frank Bernard *dean*
DiGangi, Frank Edward *academic administrator*
Dooley, David J. *elementary school principal*
Edwardson, Sandra *dean, nursing educator*
Fruen, Lois *secondary school educator*
Houston, Michael J. *dean, management educator*
Johnson, Alex Moore *dean, law educator*
Johnson, David Chester *academic administrator, sociologist, educator*
Lindell, Edward Albert *academic and religious organization administrator*
Lloyd, Patrick M. *dean, dental educator*
Mengler, Thomas M. *dean*
O'Keefe, Michael *academic administrator, physicist*
O'Keefe, Thomas Michael *academic administrator*
Schuh, G(eorge) Edward *dean, agricultural economist*
Stephens, Lee-Ann Williams *elementary school educator, educator*
Sullivan, Alfred Dewitt *academic administrator*

Minnetonka
Vanstrom, Marilyn June Christensen *retired elementary school educator*
Wigfield, Rita L. *elementary school educator*

Moorhead
Barden, Roland Eugene *university administrator*
Dille, Roland Paul *college president*
Treumann, William Borgen *university dean*

Northfield
Oden, Robert A., Jr. *academic administrator*

Richfield
Devlin, Barbara Jo *school district administrator*

Roseville
Seagren, Alice *school system administrator, former state legislator*

Saint Paul
Brushaber, George Karl *academic administrator, minister*
Dykstra, Robert *retired education educator*
Harvey, Patricia A. *school system administrator*
Klausner, Jeffrey S. *dean*
Lee, Andrea Jane *academic administrator, nun*
McCormick, James Harold *academic administrator*
Muscoplat, Charles *dean*
Osnes, Larry G. *academic administrator*
Rochon, Thomas Richard *academic administrator*
Rosenberg, Brian C *academic administrator*
Stroud, Rhoda M. *elementary school educator*
Vecoli, Rudolph John *retired history educator, director*

Waseca
Frederick, Edward Charles *university official*

Winona
DeThomasis, Brother Louis *academic administrator*
Franz, Craig Joseph *academic administrator, biology professor*
Krueger, Darrell William *academic administrator*

MISSISSIPPI

Hattiesburg
Saunders, Martha Dunagin *academic administrator*

MISSOURI

Clayton
Mach, Ruth *principal*

Columbia
Brouder, Gerald T. *academic administrator*
Crist, William Miles *dean, pediatrician, educator*
Deaton, Brady J. *academic administrator*
Dessem, R. Lawrence *dean, law educator*
Forsee, Gary D. *academic administrator, former telecommunications industry executive*
Lamb, Gordon Howard *academic administrator*
Libby, Wendy B. *academic administrator*
Payne, Thomas L. *university official*

Fayette
Inman, Marianne Elizabeth *academic administrator*

Forsyth
Klinefelter, Sarah Stephens *retired dean, broadcast executive*

Fulton
Lamkin, Fletcher M., Jr. *academic administrator*

Hillsboro
Adkins, Gregory D. *higher education administrator*

Independence
Franklin, J. Richard *principal*

Jefferson City
King, D. Kent *school system administrator*
Mahoney, Carolyn Ray *academic administrator*
Novotney, Donald Francis *superintendent of schools*

Kansas City
Byers-Pevitts, Beverley *college administrator, educator*
Collins, Kathleen *academic administrator, art educator*
Drees, Betty *dean, educator*
Eubanks, Eugene Emerson *education educator, consultant*
Guilliland, Martha W. *academic administrator*
Jonas, Harry S. *medical education consultant*
Sizemore, William Christian *retired academic administrator, county official*
Suni, Ellen Y. *dean, law educator*
Willsie, Sandra Kay *internist, educator*

Kirksville
Dixon, Barbara Bruinekool *academic administrator*

Lees Summit
Reynolds, Tommy *secondary school educator*

Liberty
Tanner, Jimmie Eugene *retired dean*

Maryville
Hubbard, Dean Leon *academic administrator*
Strating, Sharon L. *elementary school educator, professional staff developer, educational consultant*

Parkville
Breckon, Donald John *academic administrator*

Raymore
Spainhower, James Ivan *retired college president*

Rolla
Carney, John F. III *academic administrator*
Warner, Don Lee *dean emeritus*
Wray, Kent *academic administrator*

Saint Joseph
Murphy, Janet Gorman *college president*

Saint Louis
Allen, Renee *principal*
Baker, Shirley Kistler *academic administrator, university librarian*
Biondi, Lawrence *academic administrator, priest*
Blankenship, Robert Eugene *biochemistry educator*
Danforth, William Henry *retired academic administrator, physician*
Dodge, Paul Cecil *academic administrator*
George, Thomas Frederick *academic administrator*
Gilligan, Sandra Kaye *private school director*
Givens, Henry, Jr. *academic administrator*
Gupta, Mahendra R. *dean*
Hrubetz, Joan *retired dean, nursing educator*
Koff, Robert Hess *academic administrator, adult education educator*
Lewis, Jeffrey E. *dean, law educator*
Marsh, James C., Jr. *secondary school principal*
Monteleone, Patricia L. *dean*
O'Neill, Sheila *principal*
Thomas, Pamela Adrienne *special education educator*
Weiss, Robert Francis *retired academic and religious organization administrator, consultant*
Welch, Michael John *chemistry educator, researcher*
Wrighton, Mark Stephen *academic administrator, chemistry professor*

Springfield
Moore, John Edwin, Jr. *academic administrator*
Toste, Anthony Paim *chemistry educator, researcher*

Warrensburg
Limback, E(dna) Rebecca *vocational education educator*

Webster Groves
Schenkenberg, Mary Martin *principal*

Wildwood
Truitt, William Harvey *private school educator*

Windyville
Condron, Daniel Ralph *academic administrator, metaphysics educator*

NEBRASKA

Bellevue
Muller, John Bartlett *university president*

Grand Island
Zichek, Shannon Elaine *retired secondary school educator*

Hastings
Kort, Betty *secondary school educator*

Kearney
Johnston, Gladys Styles *university official*

Lincoln
Bradley, Richard Edwin *retired academic administrator*
Christensen, Douglas D. *school system administrator*
Grew, Priscilla Croswell *academic administrator, geologist, educator, museum director*
Nelson, Darrell Wayne *retired academic administrator, research scientist*
Owens, John C. *academic administrator*
Perlman, Harvey Stuart *academic administrator*
Reinhardt, John W. *dean, dental educator*
Tonack, DeLoris *elementary school educator*
Willborn, Steven L. *dean, law educator*

Omaha
Belck, Nancy Garrison *dean, educator*
Bruckner, Martha *academic administrator*
Fjell, Mick *principal*
Haselwood, Eldon LaVerne *retired education educator*
Ho, David Kim Hong *education educator*
Newton, John Milton *academic administrator, psychologist, educator*
Tucker, Michael *elementary school principal*

NEVADA

Las Vegas
Shuman, R. Baird *academic administrator, consultant, language educator, writer*

NEW HAMPSHIRE

Durham
Huddleston, Mark Wayne *academic administrator, political scientist, educator*

NEW JERSEY

Camden
Solomon, Rayman Louis *dean, law educator*

West Orange
Thomas, Gary L. *retired academic administrator*

NEW MEXICO

Placitas
Watson-Boone, Rebecca A. *dean, researcher, library and information scientist, educator*

NORTH DAKOTA

Bismarck
Evanson, Barbara Jean *middle school education educator*
Joersz, Fran Woodmansee *secondary school educator*
Potts, Robert Leslie *academic administrator*
Sanstead, Wayne Godfrey *school system administrator*

Ellendale
Schlieve, Hy C. J. *school administrator*

Fargo
Chapman, Joseph Alan *academic administrator*
Lardy, Sister Susan Marie *academic administrator*

Grand Forks
Kupchella, Charles Edward *academic administrator, writer, educator*
Mondry, Diane *secondary school educator*
Nordlie, Robert Conrad *biochemistry educator*
Wilson, H. David *dean*

Minot
Shaar, H. Erik *academic administrator*

West Fargo
Boutiette, Vickie Lynn *elementary school educator, reading specialist*

OHIO

Ada
Baker, Kendall L. *academic administrator*

Akron
Barker, Harold Kenneth *former university dean*
Capers, Cynthia Flynn *dean, nursing educator*
Kelley, Frank Nicholas *dean*
Martin, Jack *educational services company executive, former federal agency administrator*
Ruebel, Marion A. *university president*

Athens
Bruning, James Leon *academic administrator, educator*
Crowl, Samuel Renninger *retired dean, language educator*
Krendl, Kathy *dean*
McDavis, Roderick J. *academic administrator*

Berea
Malicky, Neal *academic administrator*

Bowling Green
Heckman, Carol A. *biology educator*
Ribeau, Sidney A. *academic administrator*

Chagrin Falls
Brown, Jeanette Grasselli *retired director*

Chillicothe
Basil, Brad L. *technology education educator*

Cincinnati
Greengus, Samuel *academic administrator, theology studies educator*
Harrison, Donald Carey *academic administrator, cardiologist, educator*
Kohl, David *dean, emeritus librarian*
Lindell, Andrea Regina *dean, nurse*
Martin, William Joseph, II, *dean, educator*
Smith, Gregory Allgire *academic administrator*
Stern, David Mark *dean, educator*
Sublett, Roger H. *academic administrator*
Thompson, Adrienne *secondary school educator*
Winkler, Henry Ralph *retired academic administrator, historian*
Zimpher, Nancy Lusk *academic administrator*

Cleveland
Byrd-Bennett, Barbara *school system administrator*
Cerone, David *academic administrator*
Cullis, Christopher Ashley *dean, biology educator*
Eastwood, Gregory Lindsay *former academic administrator*
Eustis, Joanne D. *university librarian*
Goldberg, Jerold S. *academic administrator*
Grossman, Mary Margaret *retired elementary school educator*
Hundert, Edward M. *former academic administrator, educator*
McArdle, Richard Joseph *retired academic administrator*
Parker, Robert Frederic *university dean emeritus*
Queen, Joyce *elementary school educator*
Schwartz, Michael *academic administrator, sociology educator*
Snyder, Barbara Rook *academic administrator*
Thornton, Jerry Sue *community college president*
Topol, Eric Jeffrey *academic administrator, cardiologist, educator*
Weidenthal, Maurice David (Bud) *academic administrator, journalist*
Wertheim, Sally Harris *director, academic administrator, dean, education educator, consultant*
Wykle, May L. *dean, educator, researcher*

Columbus
Beck, Paul Allen *dean, political science professor*
Bell, Karen A. *dean*
Cottrell, David Alton *school system administrator*
de la Chapelle, Albert *education educator*
Fields, Henry William *college dean*
Fingerhut, Eric D. *academic administrator, former state legislator and congressman, lawyer*
Griffith, Dennison W. *academic administrator, artist, educator*
Harris, Gene T. *school system administrator*
Jackson, John Charles *retired secondary school educator, writer*
Koenigsknecht, Roy A. *dean*
Kronmiller, Jan E. *dean, academic administrator*
Oates, Thomas R. *former university executive*
Otte, Paul John *academic administrator, consultant*
Oxley, Margaret Carolyn Stewart *elementary school educator*
Rogers, Nancy Hardin *dean, law educator*
Sanfilippo, Alfred Paul *dean, medical educator, pathologist*
Sedmak, Daniel D. *academic administrator*
Stephens, Thomas M(aron) *education educator*
Zelman, Susan Tave *school system administrator*

Dayton
Calico, Robert A. *dean*
Curran, Daniel J. *academic administrator, sociologist, educator*
Fitz, Brother Raymond L. *university president*
Heft, James Lewis *academic administrator, theology studies educator*
Martin, Patricia *dean, nursing educator*
Part, Howard Mitchell *dean*
Pestello, Fred P. *academic administrator*
Sifferlen, Ned *academic administrator*
Uphoff, James Kent *education educator*

Delta
Miller, Beverly White *former college president, educational consultant*

Dublin
Meek, Violet Imhof *retired dean*

Eastlake
Kerata, Joseph J. *secondary school educator*

Euclid
Miller, Demetra Fay Pelat *elementary school educator, city official*

Fairborn
Combs, Eric A. *social studies educator*

Findlay
Freed, DeBow *academic administrator*

Gambier
Nugent, S. Georgia *academic administrator*
Spaid, Gregory P. *academic administrator, art educator*

Harrison
Stoll, Robert W. *principal*

Hilliard
Lowery, Doug *principal*

Hudson
Hallenbeck, Linda S. *elementary school educator*

Kent
Cartwright, Carol Ann *retired academic administrator*
Gaston, Paul Lee *academic administrator, language educator*
Gosnell, Davina J. *dean, nursing educator*

Kettering
Hoffman, Sue Ellen *retired elementary school educator*

Mansfield
Riedl, John Orth *retired university dean*

New Albany
Partlow, Madeline *principal*

Oberlin
Koppes, Clayton R. *academic administrator*
Krislov, Marvin *academic administrator, lawyer, educator*
MacKay, Alfred F. *dean, philosophy educator*

Oxford
Hodge, David Charles *academic administrator, geography professor*
Sessions, Judith Ann *dean, university librarian*
Shriver, Phillip Raymond *academic administrator*
Thompson, Bertha Boya *retired education educator*

Painesville
Davis, Barbara Snell *education educator*

Patriot
Riggle, Patricia Carol *special education educator*

Pepper Pike
Stano, Sister Diana *academic administrator*

Rio Grande
Evans, Clyde Merrill *academic administrator, state representative*

Sagamore Hills
Miller, Susan Ann *retired school system administrator*

Springfield
Kinnison, William Andrew *retired university president*

Toledo
Closius, Phillip J. *dean, law educator*

University Heights
Niehoff, Robert L. *academic administrator*

Westerville
DeVore, C. Brent *college president, educator*
Husarik, Ernest Alfred *educational administrator*
Van Sant, Joanne Frances *academic administrator*

Wilberforce
Henderson, John L. *academic administrator*

Youngstown
Sweet, David Charles *academic administrator*

PENNSYLVANIA

York
Rodney, Joel Morris *university chancellor*

SOUTH DAKOTA

Aberdeen
Fouberg, Glenna M. *career planning administrator*

Brookings
Chicoine, David Lyle *academic administrator*

Pierre
Melmer, Rick *school system administrator*

Selby
Akre, Donald J. *school system administrator*

Sioux Falls
Ashworth, Julie *elementary school educator*
Talley, Robert Cochran *academic administrator, cardiologist*
Wagoner, Ralph Howard *academic administrator*

Vermillion
Dahlin, Donald C(lifford) *academic administrator*

Wessington Springs
Mohling, Charlotte *middle school educator*

Yankton
Foster, James Caldwell *dean, historian*

TEXAS

College Station
Byrne, C. William, Jr. *athletics program director*

Georgetown
Lovin, Keith Harold *retired academic administrator, philosopher, educator*

Richardson
Daniel, David Edwin *academic administrator, civil engineer*

The Woodlands
Beller, Stephen Mark *retired academic administrator*

UTAH

Orem
Sederburg, William Albert *academic administrator, former state senator*

VIRGINIA

Rockbridge Baths
Glidden, Robert Burr *academic administrator, consultant, music educator*

Springfield
Kurth, Ronald James *retired academic administrator, military officer*

WASHINGTON

Clinton
Powers, David Richard *educational administrator*

Richland
Glennen, Robert Eugene, Jr. *retired academic administrator*

WISCONSIN

Appleton
Beck, Jill *academic administrator, dancer, educator*

Beloit
Burris, John Edward *academic administrator, biologist, educator*
Ferrall, Victor Eugene, Jr. *academic administrator, lawyer*

Brookfield
Zimmerman, Jay *secondary school educator*

De Forest
O'Neil, J. Peter (James Peter O'Neil) *elementary school educator, computer scientist*

De Pere
Manion, Thomas A. *chancellor*

Eau Claire
Richards, Jerry Lee *academic administrator, religious studies educator*

Fish Creek
Zvara, Christine C. *middle school education educator*

Genesee Depot
Kaldhusdal, Terry Lee *elementary school educator*

Glendale
Moeser, Elliott *principal*

Green Bay
Hardy, Deborah Lewis *dean, educator, dental hygienist*
Shepard, W. Bruce *academic administrator*

Hudson
Witthuhn, Burton Orrin *retired university official*

Kenosha
Campbell, F(enton) Gregory *academic administrator, historian*

La Crosse
Gow, Joe *academic administrator*
Hitch, Elizabeth *academic administrator*

Madison
Aberle, Elton David *retired dean*
Burmaster, Elizabeth *school system administrator*
Davis, Kenneth Boone, Jr. *dean, law educator*
Frazier, Kenneth L. *university librarian*
Grobschmidt, Richard A. *school system administrator*
Hamers, Robert J. *chemistry educator, researcher*
Johnson, Richard Arnold *statistics educator, consultant*
Knetter, Michael Mark *dean*
Ladson-Billings, Gloria J. *education educator*
Mash, Donald J. *college president*
Odden, Allan Robert *education educator*
Reilly, Kevin P. *academic administrator*
Skochelak, Susan E. *dean*
Underwood, Julie K. *dean, former law educator*
Wiley, John D. *academic administrator*

Menomonie
Furst-Bowe, Julie *academic administrator*
Lee, Howard D. *academic administrator*
Sedlak, Robert *academic administrator*
Sorensen, Charles W. *academic administrator*

Merrill
Gravelle, John David *secondary school educator*

Milwaukee
Aman, Mohammed Mohammed *dean, library and information science professor*
Andrekopoulos, William *school system administrator*
Coffman, Terrence J. *retired academic administrator*
Dunn, Michael J. *dean*
Feinsilver, Donald Lee *psychiatry professor*
Fuller, Howard *education educator, academic administrator*
Hatton, Janie R. Hill *principal*
Kearney, Joseph D. *dean, law educator*
Lobb, William K. *dean, dental educator*
Rindler, Robert *academic administrator*
Schneider, Mary Lea *college administrator*
Schroeder, John H. *university chancellor*
Viets, Hermann *academic administrator, consultant*
Wake, Madeline Musante *academic administrator, nursing educator*
Weiner, Wendy L(ou) *elementary school educator, writer*
Wild, Robert Anthony *academic administrator*

Pewaukee
Anderson, Richard Todd *college president*

Platteville
Markee, David James *academic administrator, education educator*

River Falls
Thibodeau, Gary A. *academic administrator*

Sheboygan
Fritz, Kristine Rae *retired secondary school educator*

Stevens Point
Bunnell, Linda Hunt *academic administrator*

Washburn
Krutsch, Phyllis *academic administrator*

Waukesha
Falcone, Frank S. *former academic administrator*
Hastad, Douglas Noel *academic administrator, physical education educator*

Whitewater
Greenhill, H. Gaylon *retired academic administrator*
Prior, David James *college dean*

ADDRESS UNPUBLISHED

Aiken, Michael Thomas *former academic administrator*
Allen, Charles Eugene *university administrator, agriculturist, educator*
Alutto, Joseph Anthony *academic administrator, former dean, management educator*
Banaszynski, Carol Jean *secondary school educator*
Barrett, Janet Tidd *academic administrator*
Bauer, Otto Frank *academic administrator, communications executive, educator*
Benedict, Barry Arden *university administrator*
Billups, Norman Fredrick *college dean, pharmacist, educator*
Bowling, John C. *academic administrator*
Bryan, Lawrence Dow *retired college president, consultant*
Chafel, Judith Ann *education educator*
Christopherson, Myrvin Frederick *college president*
Coleman, Mary Sue *academic administrator*
Collens, Lewis Morton *retired academic administrator, law educator*
Copeland, Henry Jefferson, Jr. *former college president*
Corey, Judith Ann *retired elementary school educator*
Corkins, Bob *school system administrator*
Dohmen, Mary Holgate *retired primary school educator*
Dorsey, John Kevin *dean*
Drake, George Albert *retired academic administrator, historian, educator*
Duderstadt, James Johnson *academic administrator, engineering educator*
Duncan, Robert Bannerman *dean, strategy and organizations educator*
Edwards, Mark U., Jr. *academic administrator, history professor, writer*
Felicetti, Daniel A. *academic administrator*
Fodrea, Carolyn Wrobel *adult education educator, reading researcher*
Garland, James C. *retired academic administrator*
Glynn, Edward *retired academic administrator*
Goldenberg, Kim *retired academic administrator, internist, consultant*
Graves, Wallace Billingsley *retired university executive*
Habecker, Eugene Brubaker *academic administrator*
Hart, Katherine Miller *college dean*

Henikoff, Leo M., Jr. *academic administrator, medical educator*
Hepner, James O. *medical school director*
Herbert, Adam William, Jr. *former academic administrator, educator*
Herron, Orley R. *college president*
Hill, Emita Brady *academic administrator, consultant*
Hoffman, Sharon Lynn *adult education educator*
Hoffsis, Glen F. *dean*
Holbrook, Karen Ann *retired academic administrator, biologist*
Hotchkiss, Eugene III *retired academic administrator*
Hulbert, Samuel Foster *college president*
Jakubauskas, Edward Benedict *college president*
Jorns, David Lee *retired university president*
Kerrigan, John E. *academic administrator*
Kinney, Thomas J. John *adult education educator*
Kliebhan, Sister M(ary) Camille *academic administrator*
Koleson, Donald Ralph *retired college dean, educator*
Lambert, Daniel Michael *retired academic administrator*
Lantz, Joanne Baldwin *retired academic administrator*
Larson, John M. *retired educational consultant*
Larson, Vicki Lord *academic administrator, communication disorders educator*
Lex, William Joseph *college official*
Link, David Thomas *dean, lawyer*
Lyall, Katharine Culbert *former academic administrator, economist, educator*
Lynn, Naomi B. *academic administrator*
Magruder, Jack *retired academic administrator*
Manuel, Ralph Nixon *retired private school executive*
Matasar, Ann B. *retired dean, finance educator*
Matsler, Franklin Giles *retired education educator*
Mayer, Robert Anthony *retired college president*
McCann, Diana Rae *secondary school educator*
Monson, David Carl *school system administrator, state legislator, farmer*
Nagy, Donna M. *dean, law educator*
Nelsen, William Cameron *educational consultant*
New, Rosetta Holbrock *retired secondary school educator, retired department chairman, retired nutrition consultant*
Pacheco, Manuel Trinidad *retired academic administrator*
Park, John Thornton *retired academic administrator*
Ponitz, David H. *former academic administrator*
Preusser, Joseph William *academic administrator*
Read, Sister Joel *retired academic administrator*
Riendeau, Diane *secondary school educator*
Schiller, Robert E. *former school system administrator*
Schlegel, John P. *academic administrator*
Schwartz, Eleanor Brantley *academic administrator*
Shah, Y. T. *academic administrator*
Slorp, John S. *retired academic administrator*
Sonnenschein, Hugo Freund *academic administrator, writer, economist, educator*
Spear, Peter D. *retired academic administrator*
Stark, Joan Scism *education educator*
Stellar, Arthur Wayne *school system administrator*
Straumanis, Joan *academic administrator, consultant*
Swanson, Patricia Klick *retired academic administrator, retired foundation administrator*
Touhill, Blanche Marie *retired academic administrator, historian, educator*
Tunheim, Jerald Arden *academic administrator, physicist, educator*
Vinson, James Spangler *academic administrator*
Warch, Richard *former academic administrator*
Watts, John Ransford *academic administrator*
Winterstein, James Fredrick *academic administrator*
Yuill, Thomas MacKay *academic administrator, microbiology educator*

ENGINEERING

UNITED STATES

ARIZONA

Tucson
Venkata, Subrahmanyam Saraswati *engineering educator, researcher*

CALIFORNIA

Walnut Creek
Hanson, Robert Duane *engineering educator*

COLORADO

Boulder
Murnane, Margaret Mary *engineering and physics educator*

Denver
Reshotko, Eli *aerospace engineer, educator*

Fort Collins
Matthies, Frederick John *civil and environmental engineer*

Vail
Brown, William Milton *retired electrical engineering educator, emeritus chief scientist*

ILLINOIS

Argonne
Chang, Yoon Il *nuclear engineer*
Kumar, Romesh *chemical engineer*
Till, Charles Edgar *nuclear engineer*

Belleville
Thien-Stasko, Vicki Lynn *civil engineer*

Carbondale
Chugh, Yoginder Paul *mining engineering educator*

Champaign
Katehi, Linda P.B. *engineering educator*

Chicago
Agarwal, Gyan Chand *engineering educator*
Babcock, Lyndon Ross, Jr. *environmental engineer, educator*
Banerjee, Prashant *industrial engineer, computer scientist, educator*
Chung, Paul Myungha *mechanical engineer, educator*
Davis, DeForest P. *architectural engineer*
DeSantiago, Michael Francis *mechanical engineer*
Dix, Rollin C(umming) *mechanical engineering educator, consultant*
Dutta, Mitra *engineer, educator*
Epstein, Raymond *engineering and architectural executive*
Graupe, Daniel *engineering educator*
Gupta, Krishna Chandra *mechanical engineering educator*
Guralnick, Sidney Aaron *engineering educator*
Hartnett, James Patrick *engineering educator*
Lin, James Chih-I *biomedical and electrical engineer, educator*
Lue-Hing, Cecil *civil engineer*
Mansoori, G. Ali *chemical engineer, educator*
Miller, Irving Franklin *chemical, biomedical engineer, academic administrator, educator*
Minkowycz, W. J. *mechanical engineering educator*
Minneste, Viktor, Jr. *retired engineering executive*
Murata, Tadao *engineering and computer science educator*
Stark, Henry *technology educator*
Warner, Carrie *architectural engineer*

Clarendon Hills
Moritz, Donald Brooks *mechanical engineer, consultant*

Decatur
Koucky, John Richard *metallurgical engineer, manufacturing executive*

Des Plaines
Anthony, Donald Barrett *engineering executive*
Relwani, Nirmal Murlidhar (Nick Relwani) *mechanical engineer*
Winfield, Michael D. *engineering company executive*

Evanston
Achenbach, Jan Drewes *engineering scientist*
Backman, Vadim *biomedical engineer, educator*
Bankoff, Seymour George *chemical engineer, educator*
Bazant, Zdenek Pavel *engineering educator*
Belytschko, Ted *engineering educator*
Brazelton, William Thomas *chemical engineer, educator, dean*
Carr, Stephen Howard *materials engineer, educator*
Cheng, Herbert Su-Yuen *mechanical engineering educator*
Chung, Yip-Wah *engineering educator*
Colgate, J. Edward *mechanical engineering educator*
Daniel, Isaac Mordochai *mechanical engineering educator*
Daskin, Mark Stephen *engineering educator*
Fine, Morris Eugene *materials engineer, educator*
Finno, Richard J. *engineering educator*
Fourer, Robert Harold *industrial engineering educator, consultant*
Frey, Donald Nelson *industrial engineer, educator, retired manufacturing executive*
Goldstick, Thomas Karl *biomedical engineering educator*
Haddad, Abraham Herzl *electrical engineering educator, researcher*
Keer, Leon Morris *engineering educator*
Kliphardt, Raymond A. *engineering educator*
Krizek, Raymond John *engineering educator, consultant*
Kung, Harold Hing-Chuen *engineering educator*
Liu, Wing Kam *mechanical engineering educator, civil engineer, educator*
Murphy, Gordon John *electrical engineer, educator*
Ottino, Julio Mario *engineering educator*
Plonus, Martin Algirdas *electrical engineering educator*
Shah, Surendra Poonamchand *engineering educator*
Taflove, Allen *electrical engineer, educator, researcher, consultant*
Weertman, Julia Randall *materials engineering educator*

Glenview
Flaum, Russell M. *engineering executive*
Gerstner, Robert William *structural engineering educator, consultant*
Hansen, Thomas J. *engineering executive*
Van Zelst, Theodore William *civil engineer, engineering company executive*

Lake Forest
Lambert, John Boyd *chemical engineer, consultant*

Mount Prospect
Scott, Norman Laurence *engineering consultant*

Naperville
Joyce, William H. *retired engineering company executive, chemical engineer*
Vora, Manu Kishandas *chemical engineer, consultant*

Oakbrook Terrace
Savage, Murray *engineering executive*

Park Ridge
Bridges, Jack Edgar *electronics engineer*

Peoria
Rainson, Ronald Lee *engineering executive, consultant*

Plainfield
Chakrabarti, Subrata Kumar *marine research engineer*

Quincy
Centanni, Ross J. *engineering executive*

Saint Charles
De Lerno, Manuel Joseph *retired electrical engineer*

Skokie
Corley, William Gene *engineering research executive*

Urbana
Basar, Tamer *electrical engineer, educator*
Bergeron, Clifton George *engineer, educator*
Blahut, Richard Edward *electrical and computer engineering educator*
Bragg, Michael B. *engineering educator*
Chao, Bei Tse *mechanical engineering educator*
Chato, John Clark *mechanical and bioengineering educator*
Coleman, Paul Dare *physics and electrical engineering educator*
Conry, Thomas Francis *mechanical engineering educator*
Cook, Harry Edgar *engineering educator*
Eden, James Gary *electrical engineer, physicist, educator, researcher*
Feng, Milton *engineering educator*
Garcia, Marcelo Horacio *engineering educator, consultant*
Gardner, Chester Stone *electrical and computer engineering educator, consultant*
Hajek, Bruce E. *electrical engineer, educator*
Hall, William Joel *retired civil engineer, educator*
Hannon, Bruce Michael *engineering educator*
Hanratty, Thomas Joseph *chemical engineer, educator*
Herrin, Moreland *retired engineering educator*
Hess, Karl *engineering and science educator*
Holonyak, Nick, Jr. *electrical engineering educator*
Huang, Thomas Shi-Tao *electrical engineering educator, researcher*
Jacobson, Sheldon Howard *engineering educator*
Jones, Benjamin Angus, Jr. *retired agricultural engineering educator, science administrator*
Krier, Herman *mechanical and industrial engineering educator*
Kumar, Panganamala Ramana *electrical and computer engineering educator*
Makela, Jonathan James *engineering educator*
Maxwell, William Hall Christie *civil and environmental engineer, educator*
May, Walter Grant *chemical engineer, educator*
Mayes, Paul Eugene *engineering educator, consultant*
Miley, George H. *nuclear and electrical engineering educator, plasma engineer, energy conversion scientist*
Miller, Robert Earl *engineering educator*
Rao, Nannapaneni Narayana *electrical engineer*
Snoeyink, Vernon L. *civil engineer, educator*
Solomon, Wayne C. *aerospace engineer, educator*
Stallmeyer, James Edward *engineering educator*
Swenson, George Warner, Jr. *engineering educator*
Trick, Timothy Noel *electrical and computer engineering educator, researcher*
Zukoski, Charles Frederick, IV, *chemical engineering educator, academic administrator*

Wilmette
Wadden, Richard Albert *environmental engineer, educator, science administrator, consultant*

INDIANA

Crane
Waggoner, Susan Marie *electronics engineer*

Evansville
Blandford, Dick *electrical engineering and communications educator*
Gerhart, Philip Mark *engineering educator*

Fort Wayne
Shoemaker, John Calvin *aeronautical engineer, engineering company executive*

Hammond
Pierson, Edward Samuel *engineering educator, consultant*

Indianapolis
Dillon, Howard Burton *retired civil engineer*

Kokomo
Nierste, Joseph Paul *software engineer*

Lafayette
Bernhard, Robert James *mechanical engineer, educator*
Fox, Robert William *mechanical engineering educator*
Gustafson, Winthrop Adolph *retired engineering educator*
Liley, Peter Edward *retired engineering educator*
Lindenlaub, John Charles *electrical engineer, educator*

Noblesville
Monical, Robert Duane *engineering company executive*

Notre Dame
Gray, William Guerin *engineering educator*
Incropera, Frank Paul *mechanical engineering educator*
Liu, Ruey-Wen *electrical engineering educator*
Merz, James Logan *electrical and materials engineering educator, researcher*
Ovaert, Timothy Christopher *mechanical engineering educator*
Sain, Michael Kent *electrical engineering educator*
Schmitz, Roger Anthony *chemical engineer, educator, academic administrator*
Stadtherr, Mark A. *chemical engineer, educator*
Sweeney, Thomas Leonard *chemical engineering educator, researcher*
Szewczyk, Albin Anthony *engineering educator*

West Lafayette
Albright, Lyle Frederick *chemical engineering educator*
Andres, Ronald Paul *chemical engineer, educator*
Barany, James Walter *industrial engineering educator*
Cohen, Raymond *retired mechanical engineer, educator*
Cooper, James Albert, Jr. *electrical engineering educator*
Delleur, Jacques William *retired engineering educator*
Drnevich, Vincent Paul *engineering educator*
Farris, Thomas N. *engineering educator*
Friedlaender, Fritz Josef *electrical engineering educator*
Grace, Richard Edward *engineering educator*
Harr, Milton Edward *engineering educator, consultant*
Koivo, Antti Jaakko *electrical engineering educator, researcher*
Landgrebe, David Allen *electrical engineer*
Lin, Pen-Min *electrical engineer, educator*
Marshall, Francis Joseph *aerospace engineer*
Ong, Chee-Mun *engineering educator*
Reklaitis, Gintaras Victor *chemical engineer, educator*
Salvendy, Gavriel *industrial engineer, educator*
Schneider, Steven Philip *aeronautical engineer, educator*
Schwartz, Richard John *electrical engineering educator, researcher*
Sinha, Kumares Chandra *engineering educator, consultant*
Solberg, James Joseph *industrial engineering educator*
Sozen, Mete Avni *engineering educator*
Taber, Margaret Ruth *retired engineering technology educator*
Thomas, Marlin Uluess *industrial engineer, academic administrator, educator*
Tsao, George T. *chemical engineer, educator*
Varma, Arvind *chemical engineering educator, researcher*
Viskanta, Raymond *mechanical engineering educator*
Wankat, Phillip Charles *chemical engineering educator*
Weiner, Andrew Marc *electrical engineering educator*
Williams, Theodore Joseph *engineering educator*

IOWA

Ames
Anderson, Robert Morris, Jr. *electrical engineer*
Basart, John Philip *electrical engineering and remote sensing researcher*
Baumann, Edward Robert *environmental engineering educator*
Buchele, Wesley Fisher *retired agricultural engineering educator*
Cleasby, John LeRoy *civil engineer, educator*
Glatz, Charles E. *engineering educator*
Kushner, Mark Jay *engineering and physics educator, dean*
Larsen, William Lawrence *engineering educator*
Melvin, Stewart Wayne *engineering educator*
Mischke, Charles Russell *mechanical engineering educator*
Okiishi, Theodore Hisao *mechanical engineering educator*
Sanders, Wallace Wolfred, Jr. *civil engineer*
Young, Donald Fredrick *engineering educator*

Cambridge
Colvin, Thomas Stuart *agricultural engineer, farmer*

Clear Lake
Brown, Robert Grover *engineering educator*

Iowa City
Arora, Jasbir Singh *engineering educator*
Lonngren, Karl Erik *electrical and computer engineering educator*
Patel, Virendra Chaturbhai *mechanical engineer, educator*

Madrid
Handy, Richard Lincoln *civil engineer, educator*

Muscatine
Stanley, Richard Holt *consulting engineer*
Thomopulos, Gregs G. *consulting engineering company executive*

KANSAS

Lawrence
Benjamin, Bezaleel Solomon *structural engineer, educator*
Darwin, David *engineering educator, consultant*
Green, Don Wesley *chemical and petroleum engineering educator*
Moore, Richard Kerr *electrical engineering educator*
Muirhead, Vincent Uriel *retired aerospace engineer*
Rolfe, Stanley Theodore *civil engineer, educator*
Roskam, Jan *aerospace engineer*
Rowland, James Richard *electrical engineering educator*

Leawood
Karmeier, Delbert Fred *engineer, consultant, realtor*

Manhattan
Chung, Do Sup *agricultural engineering educator*
Erickson, Larry Eugene *chemical engineering educator*
Hagen, Lawrence Jacob *agricultural engineer*
Johnson, William Howard *retired agricultural engineer, educator*
Lee, E(ugene) Stanley *engineering educator*
Simons, Gale Gene *nuclear and electrical engineer, educator*

Mcpherson
Grauer, Douglas Dale *civil engineer*

Overland Park
Daniel, Karen *engineering and design company executive*
Rodman, Leonard C. *engineering and construction executive*
Vaughan, Brad *engineering and design company executive*

Salina
Crawford, Lewis Cleaver *engineering executive, researcher*

Shawnee Mission
Gaboury, David *engineering company executive*

Wichita
Hansen, Ole Viggo *chemical engineer*

MARYLAND

College Park
Skibniewski, Miroslaw Jan *engineering educator*

Hagerstown
Ksienski, Aharon Arthur *retired electrical engineer*

MASSACHUSETTS

Nantucket
Saperstein, Lee Waldo *mining engineering educator*

MICHIGAN

Ann Arbor
Akcasu, Ahmet Ziyaeddin *nuclear engineer, educator*
Assanis, Dennis N. (Dionissios) *mechanical engineering educator*
Aupperle, Eric Max *engineering educator, research scientist*
Becher, William Don *retired electrical engineer, educator, writer*
Bhattacharya, Pallab Kumar *electrical engineering educator, researcher*
Bilello, John Charles *engineering educator, director*
Bitondo, Domenic *engineering executive*
Bonder, Seth *mechanical engineer*
Bunch, Howard McRaven *engineering educator, researcher*
Calahan, Donald Albert *electrical engineering educator*
Chaffin, Don Brian *industrial engineering educator, research director*
Chen, Michael Ming *mechanical engineering educator*
England, Anthony Wayne *engineering and science educator, dean*
Friedmann, Peretz Peter *aerospace engineer, educator*
Gibala, Ronald *metallurgical engineering educator*
Gilbert, Elmer Grant *engineering educator, control theorist*
Haddad, George Ilyas *engineering educator, director*
Hayes, John Patrick *electrical engineering and computer science educator, consultant*
Kammash, Terry *nuclear engineering educator*
Kearfott, Kimberlee Jane *nuclear engineer, educator, health physicist*
Knoll, Glenn Frederick *nuclear engineering educator*
Koren, Yoram *mechanical engineering educator*
Kozma, Adam *electrical engineer*
Ludema, Kenneth C. *mechanical engineer, educator*
Martin, William Russell *nuclear engineering educator*
McClamroch, N. Harris *aerospace engineering educator, consultant, researcher*
Merte, Herman, Jr. *mechanical engineering educator*
Meyer, John Frederick *engineering educator*
O'Brien, William Joseph *materials engineer, educator, consultant*
Pehlke, Robert Donald *materials and metallurgical engineering educator*
Petrick, Ernest Nicholas *mechanical engineer, researcher*
Pollock, Stephen Michael *operations research engineer, educator, consultant*
Powell, Kenneth Grant *aerospace engineering educator*
Rumman, Wadi (Saliba Rumman) *civil engineer, consultant*
Schwank, Johannes Walter *chemical engineering educator*
Scott, Norman Ross *electrical engineering educator*
Sengupta, Dipak Lal *engineering educator*
Senior, Thomas Bryan A. *electrical engineering educator, researcher, consultant*
Sobel, Alan *electrical engineer, physicist*
Solomon, David Eugene *engineering company executive*
Steel, Duncan Gregory *engineering educator*
Tai, Chen-To *electrical engineering educator*
Vinh, Nguyen Xuan *aerospace engineering educator*
Wang, Henry Yee-Neen *chemical engineering educator*
Wilson, Richard Christian *engineering firm executive*
Wineman, Alan Stuart *mechanical engineering and applied mechanics educator*
Wise, Kensall D. *engineering educator*

Carleton
Rancourt, James Daniel *optical engineer*

Commerce Township
Benson, Jack Duane *mechanical engineer, research scientist*

Dearborn
Cairns, James Robert *mechanical engineering educator*
Gandhi, Haren S. *chemical engineer*
Kim, Byung Ro *environmental engineer*
Little, Robert Eugene *engineering educator*
Thai-Tang, Hau *automotive engineer*

Detroit
Chou, Clifford Chi Fong *research engineering executive*
King, Albert I. *engineering educator*
Kline, Kenneth Alan *mechanical engineering educator*
Kummler, Ralph H. *chemical engineer, educator, dean*
Putatunda, Susil Kumar *metallurgy educator*
Rathod, Mulchand *mechanical engineering educator*

East Lansing
Andersland, Orlando Baldwin *retired engineering educator*
Beck, James V. *mechanical engineering educator*
Chen, Kun-Mu *electrical engineering educator*
Cutts, Charles Eugene *retired engineering educator*
Foss, John Frank *mechanical engineering educator*
Goodman, Erik David *engineering educator*
Lloyd, John Raymond *mechanical engineering educator*
Pierre, Percy Anthony *engineering educator*
Saul, William Edward *engineering educator*
Segerlind, Larry J. *agricultural engineering educator*
von Bernuth, Robert Dean *agricultural engineering educator, consultant*
Von Tersch, Lawrence Wayne *engineering educator, dean*

Farmington
Neyer, Jerome Charles *consulting civil engineer*

Flint
John, James Edward Albert *mechanical engineer, educator*

Greenbush
Simpkin, Lawrence James *engineering company executive*

Grosse Pointe Shores
Holness, Gordon Victor Rix *engineering executive, mechanical engineer*

Harrison Township
Rivard, Jerome G. *engineering executive*

Holland
Stynes, Stanley Kenneth *retired chemical engineer, educator*

Houghton
Crittenden, John Charles *engineering educator*
Heckel, Richard Wayne *metallurgical engineering educator*
Lumsdaine, Edward *mechanical engineering educator, dean*

Leland
Soutas-Little, Robert William *mechanical engineer, educator*

Midland
Meister, Bernard John *retired chemical engineer*

Niles
Marshall, Gerald Francis *optical engineer, consultant, physicist*

Pontiac
Hampton, Philip Michael *consulting engineering company executive*

Rochester
Loh, Robert N. K. *engineering educator*
Polis, Michael Philip *engineering educator*

Rochester Hills
DiCosmo, Nino *engineering company executive*

Shelby Township
Jacovides, Linos Jacovou *electrical engineer, researcher*
Nagy, Louis Leonard *engineering executive, researcher*
Osuch, Debra K. *environmental engineer*

Southfield
McKeen, Alexander C. *retired engineering executive, foundation administrator*
Peterson, Voleen Brianne *chemical engineer*

Troy
Taylor, Bill *manufacturing engineer*

Walled Lake
Williams, Sam B. *engineering executive*

Warren
Bolander, William J. *mechanical engineer*
Lett, Philip W. *engineering executive*
Pawlak, Andrzej M. *electrical engineer*

MINNESOTA

Albert Lea
Christianson, Darcey K. *broadcast engineer*

Chanhassen
Thorson, John Martin, Jr. *electrical engineer, consultant*

Grand Marais
Napadensky, Hyla Sarane *engineering consultant*

Madison
Husby, Donald Evans *engineering company executive*

Minneapolis
Bakken, Earl Elmer *electrical engineer, bioengineering company executive*
Crouch, Steven L. *mining engineer, dean*
Cunningham, Thomas B. *aerospace engineer*
Cussler, Edward Lansing, Jr. *chemical engineer, educator*
Davis, Howard Ted *engineering educator*
French, Catherine E. Wolfgram *engineering educator, researcher*
Galambos, Theodore Victor *civil engineer, educator*
Gerberich, William Warren *engineering educator*
Goldstein, Richard Jay *mechanical engineer, educator*
Joseph, Daniel Donald *aeronautical engineer, educator*
Kvalseth, Tarald Oddvar *mechanical engineer, educator*
Lambert, Robert Frank *electrical engineer, educator, consultant*
Leger, James Robert *engineering educator*
Liu, Benjamin Young-hwai *engineering educator*
Oriani, Richard Anthony *metallurgical engineer, educator*
Persson, Erland Karl *electrical engineer, executive*
Pfender, Emil *mechanical engineering educator*
Ramalingam, Subbiah *mechanical engineer, educator*
Rauenhorst, Gerald *architectural engineer, construction executive*
Sparrow, Ephraim Maurice *mechanical engineering scientist, educator*
Svärd, N. Trygve *electrical engineer*

Oak Park Heights
Jones, Edwin Channing, Jr. *retired electrical and computer engineering educator*

Saint Paul
Lampert, Leonard Franklin *mechanical engineer*
Maze, Thomas H. *engineering educator*

South Saint Paul
Fairhurst, Charles *engineering educator*

MISSOURI

Ballwin
Cornell, William Daniel *mechanical engineer*

Columbia
Pringle, Oran Allan *mechanical and aerospace engineering educator*
Yasuda, Hirotsugu Koge *engineering educator, director*

Ferguson
Bruns, Billy Lee *electrical engineer, consultant*

Kansas City
Davis, (Francis) Keith *civil engineer*
Robinson, John Hamilton *civil engineer*

Lake Lotawana
Heineman, Paul Lowe *consulting civil engineer*

Rolla
Barr, David John *engineering educator*
Crosbie, Alfred Linden *mechanical engineering educator*
Day, Delbert Edwin *ceramic engineering educator*
O'Keefe, Thomas Joseph *metallurgical engineer*
Rao, Vittal Srirangam *electrical engineering educator*
Schonberg, William Peter *engineering educator, department chairman*
Sheffield, John William *mechanical engineering educator*
Summers, David Archibald *research mining engineer, educator, director*

Saint Charles
Harmon, Robert Wayne *electrical engineering executive*

Saint Louis
Byrnes, Christopher Ian *engineering educator*
Cox, Jerome Rockhold, Jr. *electrical engineer*
Dudukovic, Milorad P. *chemical engineering educator, consultant*
Gould, Phillip Louis *engineering educator*
Husar, Rudolf Bertalan *mechanical engineering educator*
Peters, David Allen *mechanical engineering educator, consultant*
Ross, Monte *electrical engineer, researcher*
Shrauner, Barbara Wayne Abraham *electrical engineer, educator*
Staley, Robert W. *mechanical engineer, utilities executive*
Sutera, Salvatore Philip *mechanical engineer, educator*
Szabo, Barna Aladar *engineering educator*
Zurheide, Charles Henry *consulting electrical engineer*

Springfield
Rogers, Roddy Jack *civil, geotechnical and water engineer*

University City
Winter, David Ferdinand *electrical engineering educator, consultant*

NEBRASKA

Clay Center
Hahn, George LeRoy *agricultural engineer, biometeorologist*

Lincoln
Bahar, Ezekiel *electrical engineering educator*
Edwards, Donald Mervin *systems engineer, educator, dean*
Hanna, Milford A. *agricultural engineering educator*
Nelson, Don Jerome *electrical engineering and computer science educator*
Rajurkar, Kamlakar Purushottam *mechanical engineering educator*
Splinter, William Eldon *agricultural engineering educator*
Woollam, John Arthur *electrical engineering educator, physics professor*

Omaha
Durham, Charles William *civil engineer, director*

NEVADA

Reno
Tsoulfanidis, Nicholas *engineering educator, dean*

NEW YORK

Syosset
Kazanowski, Larry *engineer*

NORTH DAKOTA

Grand Forks
Bandyopadhyay, Biswanath Prasad *manufacturing engineer, educator, consultant*

Minot AFB
Atkinson, Thomas P. *environmental engineer*

OHIO

Akron
White, James Lindsay *polymer engineering educator*

Athens
Dinos, Nicholas *engineering educator, administrator*

Barberton
Kitto, John Buck, Jr. *mechanical engineer*

Canton
Hoecker, David *engineering executive*

Cincinnati
Agrawal, Dharma Prakash *engineering educator*
Cabezas, Heriberto *chemical engineer, researcher*
Ghia, Kirti N. *fluid mechanics engineer, aerospace educator*
Greenberg, David Bernard *chemical engineering educator*
Halstead, David E. *aeronautical engineer*
Hodge, Bobby Lynn *mechanical engineer, manufacturing executive*
Kowel, Stephen Thomas *electrical engineer, educator*
Kreitzer, Melvyn, II, *optical engineer*
Manwaring, Steve R. *mechanical engineer*
Rubin, Stanley Gerald *aerospace engineering educator*
Shin, Hyŏun-Woo *aircraft engineer*
Smith, Leroy Harrington, Jr. *mechanical engineer, consultant*
Weisman, Joel *retired engineering educator*
Wisler, David Charles *aerospace engineer*

Cleveland
Angus, John Cotton *chemical engineering educator*
Baer, Eric *engineering and science educator*
Burghart, James Henry *electrical engineer, educator*
Coulman, George Albert *chemical engineer, educator*
Deissler, Robert George *fluid dynamics researcher*
DellaCorte, Christopher *engineer*
Hardy, Richard Allen *mechanical engineer, engineering executive*
Heuer, Arthur Harold *ceramics engineer, educator*
Ko, Wen-Hsiung *electrical engineering educator*
Lefkowitz, Irving *engineering educator*
Liu, Chung-Chiun *chemical engineering educator*
Olson, Sandra *aerospace engineer*
Ostrach, Simon *engineering educator*
Povinelli, Louis A. *aeronautical engineer*
Prahl, Joseph Markel *mechanical engineering educator*
Saada, Adel Selim *civil engineer, educator*
Savinell, Robert Francis *engineering educator*
Wilson, Jack *aeronautical engineer*

Columbus
Altan, Taylan *engineering educator, director*
Bhushan, Bharat *mechanical engineer*
Brodkey, Robert Stanley *chemical engineering educator*
Davis, James Frederick *chemical engineer, researcher, educator, consultant*
Fan, Liang-Shih *chemical engineering educator*
Feinberg, Martin Robert *chemical engineering educator*
Fenton, Robert Earl *electrical engineering educator*
Houser, Donald Russell *mechanical engineering educator, consultant*
Keaney, William Regis *engineering and construction services executive, consultant*
Kennedy, Lawrence Allan *mechanical engineering educator*
Kouyoumjian, Robert G. *electrical engineering educator*
Liu, Ming-Tsan *computer engineering educator*
Miller, Don Wilson *nuclear engineering educator*
Ozkan, Umit Sivrioglu *chemical engineering professor*
Peters, Leon, Jr. *retired engineering educator*
Rapp, Robert Anthony *metallurgical engineering educator*
Redmond, Robert Francis *nuclear engineering educator*
Rubin, Alan J. *engineering educator*
Sebo, Stephen Andrew *electrical engineer, educator, researcher, consultant*
Singh, Rajendra *mechanical engineering educator, director*
Wagoner, Robert Hall *engineering educator*
Waldron, Kenneth John *mechanical engineering educator, researcher*
Zakin, Jacques Louis *chemical engineering educator*

Dayton
Ballal, Dilip Ramchandra *mechanical engineering educator*
Kazimierczuk, Marian Kazimierczuk *electrical engineer, educator*
Schmitt, George Frederick, Jr. *materials engineer*
Sturgess, Geoffrey J. *aeronautical research engineer*

East Liverpool
Beals, Robert J. *ceramics engineer*

Gates Mills
Enyedy, Gustav, Jr. *chemical engineer*

Lakeside Marblehead
Haering, Edwin Raymond *chemical engineering educator, consultant*

Medina
Lahey, Joseph Patrick *engineering executive*
Rog, Joseph W. *engineering company executive*

Middletown
Gilby, Steve *metallurgical engineering researcher*

Milford
Weyand, William J. *engineering executive*

North Olmsted
Bluford, Guion Stewart, Jr. *engineering company executive*

Oxford
Ward, Roscoe Fredrick *engineering educator*

Rossford
Salmon, Stuart Clive *manufacturing engineer*

Shaker Heights
Siegel, Robert *heat transfer engineer*

Worthington
Compton, Ralph Theodore, Jr. *electrical engineering educator*

Wright Patterson AFB
Chelette, Tamara Lynne *biomedical engineer*

Yellow Springs
Trolander, Hardy Wilcox *engineering executive, consultant*

Youngstown
Fok, Thomas Dso Yun *civil engineer*

OREGON

Portland
Clausing, Arthur Marvin *mechanical engineering educator*

PENNSYLVANIA

Pittsburgh
Nielsen, Paul Douglas *engineering executive, retired military officer*

SOUTH CAROLINA

Bluffton
Jerger, Edward William *engineering educator, dean*

SOUTH DAKOTA

Rapid City
Gowen, Richard Joseph *electrical engineer, educator, retired academic administrator*

Spearfish
Addy, Alva Leroy *mechanical engineer*

WISCONSIN

Brookfield
Curfman, Floyd Edwin *retired engineering educator*
Thomas, John *mechanical engineer, artist*

Frederic
Rudell, Milton Wesley *aerospace engineer*

Madison
Beachley, Norman Henry *mechanical engineer, educator*
Berthouex, Paul Mac *civil and environmental engineer, educator*
Bird, Robert Byron *chemical engineering educator, author*
Bohnhoff, David Roy *agricultural engineer, educator*
Boyle, William Charles *engineering educator*
Chang, Y. Austin *materials engineer, educator*
Converse, James Clarence *agricultural engineering educator*
Corradini, Michael L. *engineering educator*
DeVries, Marvin Frank *mechanical engineering educator*
Dietmeyer, Donald Leo *retired electrical engineering educator*
Dumesic, James A. *chemical engineer*
Emmert, Gilbert Arthur *retired engineering educator*
Gustafson, David Harold *industrial engineering and preventive medicine educator*
Hill, Charles Graham, Jr. *chemical engineering educator*
Kulcinski, Gerald LaVerne *nuclear engineer, educator, dean*
Lasseter, Robert Haygood *electrical engineering educator, consultant*
Lightfoot, Edwin Niblock, Jr. *retired chemical engineering educator*
Lillesand, Thomas Martin *engineer, educator*
Lipo, Thomas A. *electrical engineer, educator*
Long, Willis Franklin *electrical engineering educator, researcher*
Lovell, Edward George *mechanical engineering educator*
Novotny, Donald Wayne *electrical engineer, educator*
Peercy, Paul Stuart *engineering educator*
Ray, Willis Harmon *chemical engineer*
Russell, Jeffrey Scott *engineering educator*
Shohet, Juda Leon *electrical and computer engineering educator, researcher, information technology executive*
Skiles, James Jean *electrical and computer engineer, educator*
Smith, Michael James *industrial engineering educator*
Webster, John Goodwin *biomedical engineering educator, researcher*

Milwaukee
Demerdash, Nabeel Aly Omar *electrical engineer*
Fournelle, Raymond Albert *engineering educator*
Gaggioli, Richard Arnold *mechanical engineering educator*
Heinen, James Albin *electrical engineering educator*
Widera, Georg Ernst Otto *mechanical engineering educator, consultant*

New Glarus
Bubenzer, Gary Dean *agricultural engineering educator, researcher*

Racine
Meissner, Alan Paul *research engineer*

WYOMING

Worland
DeGroat, Paul Percy *electrical engineer, consultant*

CANADA

MANITOBA

Winnipeg
Bateman, Leonard Arthur *engineering executive*
Kuffel, Edmund *electrical engineering educator*

ADDRESS UNPUBLISHED

Altschaeffl, Adolph George *retired civil engineering educator*
Amann, Charles Albert *mechanical engineer, researcher*
Bechtel, Stephen E. *mechanical engineer, educator*
Beumer, Richard Eugene *retired engineering executive*
Bierley, Paul Edmund *aeronautical engineer, musician, author, publisher*
Borroni-Bird, Christopher E. *transportation engineer*
Carnahan, Brice *chemical engineer, educator*
Chen, Shoei-Sheng *retired mechanical engineer*
Dull, William Martin *retired engineering executive*
Egbert, Robert Iman *electrical engineer, educator, academic administrator*
Eyman, Earl Duane *electrical science educator, consultant*
Halpin, Daniel William *engineering educator, consultant*
James, Charles Franklin, Jr. *retired engineering educator*
Johnson, Howard Paul *retired agricultural engineering educator*
Loper, Carl Richard, Jr. *metallurgical engineer, educator*
Muller, Marcel W(ettstein) *electrical engineering educator*
Munger, Paul R. *engineering educator*
Nichols, Robert Leighton *civil engineer*
Ogata, Katsuhiko *engineering educator*
Ott, Karl Otto *nuclear engineer, consultant*
Pedersen, Karen Sue *electrical engineer*
Ramer, James LeRoy *civil engineer*
Raven, Francis Harvey *mechanical engineer, educator*
Reid, Robert Lelon *engineering educator, dean*
Robe, Thurlow Richard *retired engineering educator, dean*
Rolewicz, Robert John *estimating engineer*
Ryan, Carl Ray *electrical engineer, educator*
Shulman, Yechiel *engineering educator*
Siegal, Rita Goran *engineering company executive*
Stewart, Albert Elisha *safety engineer, engineering executive*
Strano, Michael *chemical engineer*
Taiganides, E. Paul *agricultural and environmental engineer, consultant*
Upatnieks, Juris *retired optical engineer*
Velev, Miroslav N. *electrical and computer engineer, educator*
Wentz, William Henry, Jr. *aerospace engineer, educator*
West, Robert C. *engineering company executive*
Wolfe, Charles Morgan *electrical engineering educator*

FINANCE: BANKING SERVICES
See also FINANCE: INVESTMENT SERVICES

UNITED STATES

DISTRICT OF COLUMBIA

Washington
Poole, William *retired bank executive*

FLORIDA

Fort Lauderdale
Leach, Ralph F. *banker*

ILLINOIS

Blue Island
Yager, Vincent Cook *retired bank executive*

Burr Ridge
McCormack, Robert Cornelius *investment banker*

Chicago
Adams, Austin A. *bank executive*
Blair, Edward McCormick *investment banker*
Bynoe, Peter Charles Bernard *investment banker, lawyer*
Daley, William M. *bank executive, former secretary of commerce*
Dancewicz, John Edward *investment banker*
Eddy, David Latimer *banker*
Fenton, Clifton Lucien *investment banker*
Freehling, Stanley Maxwell *investment banker*
Freund, Kristen P. *bank executive*
Glickman, Robert Jeffrey *bank executive*
Grzywinski, Ron *bank executive*
Hasten, Joseph Erwin *bank executive*
Hastings, Barry G. *trust company executive*
Haydock, Walter James *banker*
Heagy, Thomas Charles *banker*
Houghton, Mary *bank executive*
Lorenz, Katherine Mary *bank executive*
McNally, Alan G. *bank executive*
Mitchell, Lee Mark *private equity investor, executive*
Montoya, Carlos *bank executive*
Reilly, Robert Frederick *investment banker*
Roberts, Theodore Harris *banker*
Schulte, David Michael *investment banker*
Socolofsky, Jon Edward *banker*
Stevens, Mark *banker*
Stirling, James Paulman *investment banker*
Tescher, Jennifer *bank executive*
Theobald, Thomas Charles *banker*
Thomas, Richard Lee *banker*
Ward, Jonathan P. *investment banker*
Weston, Roger Lance *banker*
Williams, Edward Joseph *banker*

Fox River Grove
Abboud, Alfred Robert *banker, investor, consultant, director*

Lake Forest
Kuhn, Ryan Anthony *investment banker*
Ross, Robert Evan *bank executive*
Seaman, Irving, Jr. *banker*
Swift, Edward Foster III *investment banker*

Melrose Park
Giancola, James J. *bank executive*

Northbrook
Keehn, Silas *retired bank executive*
Sewright, Charles William, Jr. *mortgage banking advisory services company executive*

Oak Park
McLaren, Ruth *bank executive*

Palatine
Fitzgerald, Gerald Francis *retired banker*

Rockford
Meuleman, Robert Joseph *banker*

Rosemont
Hoppe, Mark A. *bank executive*

Skokie
Griffiths, Robert Pennell *banker*

Winnetka
Klapperich, Frank Lawrence, Jr. *investment banker*
Vander Wilt, Carl Eugene *banker*

INDIANA

Indianapolis
Heger, Martin L. *bank executive*
Melton, Owen B., Jr. *banking company executive*
Paine, Andrew J., Jr. *bank executive*

La Porte
Bakwin, Edward Morris *banker*

Muncie
Anderson, Stefan Stolen *retired banker*
Sursa, Charles David *banker*

South Bend
Jones, Wellington Downing III *banker*

Terre Haute
Smith, Donald E. *banker, director*

IOWA

Mason City
Rodamaker, Marti Tomson *bank executive*

KANSAS

Leawood
Allison, Mark S. *trust company executive*
Kleinman, Michael A. *trust company executive*
Lang, Daniel W. *trust company executive*
Whitaker, Freda N. *trust company executive*

Manhattan
Stolzer, Leo William *bank executive*

Olathe
Roby, Brian L. *bank executive*

Overland Park
De Vries, Robert John *investment banker*

Shawnee Mission
Bergman, Bradley Anthony *trust company executive*
McEachen, Richard Edward *banker, lawyer*

Topeka
Dicus, John Carmack *savings bank executive*

KENTUCKY

Louisville
Griffith, Mary H. *bank executive*

MARYLAND

Chevy Chase
Gibbons, John *mortgage company executive*

MICHIGAN

Bay City
Van Dyke, Clifford Craig *retired bank executive*

Bloomfield Hills
Colladay, Robert S. *trust company executive, consultant*
McQueen, Patrick M. *bank executive*
Miller, Eugene Albert *retired bank executive*

Detroit
Babb, Ralph W., Jr. *bank executive*
Beran, John R. *banker*
Jeffs, Thomas Hamilton, II, *retired bank executive*
Lewis, John D. *banking official*

Farmington Hills
Heiss, Richard Walter *retired bank executive, consultant, lawyer*

Flint
Vitito, Robert J. *bank executive*

Grand Rapids
Canepa, John Charles *banking consultant*

Ionia
Kohls, William Richard *bank executive*

Lansing
Cunningham, Paula Diane *bank executive, former academic administrator*

Southfield
Shields, Robert Emmet *merchant banker, lawyer*

MINNESOTA

Eden Prairie
Hanson, Dale S. *retired bank executive*

Minneapolis
Beechem, Kathleen *bank executive*
Carlson, Jennie Peaslack *bank executive*
Cecere, Andrew *bank executive*
Cooper, William Allen *bank executive*
Davis, Richard K. *bank executive*
Griffith, Sima Lynn *investment banker, consultant*
Grundhofer, John F. *bank executive*
Morrison, Clinton *banker*
Pohlad, Carl R. *bank and professional sports team executive*
Stern, Gary Hilton *bank executive*
Thormodsgard, Diane L. *bank executive*

Wayzata
Berg, John A. *banker*
Brown, Neil W. *bank executive*
Nagorske, Lynn A. *bank executive*

MISSOURI

Bridgeton
Brunngraber, Eric Henry *banker*

Cameron
Just, David Glen *savings and loan association executive*

Clayton
Kemper, David Woods, II, *banker*
Schepman, Steven F. *bank executive*

Kansas City
Hoenig, Thomas M. *bank executive*
Kemper, Jonathan McBride *banker*
Kemper, Rufus Crosby, Jr. *retired bank executive*
Reiter, Robert Edward *banker*

Saint Louis
Barksdale, Clarence Caulfield *retired banker*
Bealke, Linn Hemingway *banker*
Blake, Allen H. *bank executive*
Bullard, James B. *bank executive*
Costigan, Edward John *retired investment banker*
Dierberg, James F. *bank executive*
Edwards, Benjamin Franklin III *investment banker*
Leonard, Eugene Albert *banker*
Rasche, Robert Harold *banker, retired economics educator*
Stoecker, David Thomas *retired banker*

Springfield
McCartney, N. L. *investment banker*
Turner, William V. *bank executive*

NEBRASKA

Lincoln
Stuart, James *bank executive, advertising executive, announcer*
Young, Dale Lee *banker*

Omaha
Harvey, Jack K. *holding company executive*
Lauritzen, Bruce Ronnow *banker*

Waterloo
O'Brien, Nancy Lynn *bank executive*

NEW YORK

New York
Gorter, James Polk *investment banker*
Scharf, Charles W. *bank executive*

NORTH DAKOTA

Cando
Jorde, Terry J. *bank executive*

Fargo
Mengedoth, Donald Roy *commercial banker*

OHIO

Akron
Brecht, Robert P. *bank executive*
Cochran, John R. *bank executive*

Canton
Carpenter, Noble Olds *retired bank executive*

Cincinnati
Schaefer, George A., Jr. *bank executive*
Thiemann, Charles Lee *banker*

Cleveland
Bibb, Paul E., Jr., (Buck Bibb) *bank executive*
Bingay, James S. *bank executive*
Gillespie, Robert Wayne *banker*
Glickman, Carl David *banker*
Gorney, Jon L. *bank executive*
Hamilton Brown, Terri *bank executive*
Irving, Lee G. *bank executive*
Kelly, Jeffrey D. *bank executive*
Lenn, Stephen Andrew *investment banker*
Mooney, Beth *bank executive*
Pianalto, Sandra *bank executive*
Potter, Susan Kuniholm *bank executive*
Seifert, Shelley Jane *bank executive*

Columbus
Arvia, Anne L. *bank executive*
Geier, Peter E. *bank executive, health facility executive*
Glaser, Gary A. *bank executive*
Hoaglin, Thomas E. *savings and loan association executive*
Johnson, Julia F. *bank executive*
McCoy, John Bonnet *retired bank executive*

Hamilton
Immelt, Mark W. *bank executive*

New Albany
Page, Linda Kay *bank executive*

Newark
De Lawder, C. Daniel *bank executive*
Kozak, John W. *bank executive*
McConnell, William Thompson *bank executive*

Pepper Pike
Mc Call, Julien Lachicotte *banker*

Rocky River
O'Brien, John Feighan *investment banker*

Toledo
Carson, Samuel Goodman *retired bank executive*
Kunze, Ralph Carl *retired savings and loan association executive*

Wooster
Christopher, David L. *bank executive*

SOUTH DAKOTA

Sioux Falls
Sanford, T(homas) Denny *bank executive*

TENNESSEE

Nashville
Shell, Owen Gladstone, Jr. *retired bank executive*

TEXAS

Dallas
Buttigieg, Joseph J. *bank executive*

VIRGINIA

Ashburn
Pavsek, Daniel Allan *banker, educator*

WISCONSIN

Brookfield
Bauer, Chris Michael *banker*
Walters, Ronald Ogden *mortgage banker*

Milwaukee
Chenevich, William L. *bank executive*
Murphy, Judith Chisholm *trust company executive*
Wesner, Patricia *bank executive*
Wheeler, Mark C., Jr. *bank executive*
Wigdale, James B. *bank executive*

Pewaukee
Long, Robert Eugene *retired banker*

Sauk City
Lins, Debra R. *bank executive*

WYOMING

Cheyenne
Knight, Robert Edward *bank executive, educator*

CANADA

ONTARIO

Toronto
Techar, Frank J. *bank executive*

ADDRESS UNPUBLISHED

Andreas, David Lowell *retired banker*
Becker, John Alphonsis *retired bank executive*
Bobins, Norman R. *retired bank executive*
Christenson, Gregg Andrew *bank executive*
Conlon, Harry B., Jr. *banking company executive*
Daberko, David A. *retired bank executive*
Darr, Milton Freeman, Jr. *retired banker*
Ennest, John William *bank executive*
Fanning, Edward J. *bank executive*
Fitzgerald, William Allingham *savings and loan association executive, director*
Hetland, James Lyman, Jr. *banker, lawyer, educator*
Istock, Verne George *retired bank executive*
Moffett, David McKenzie *bank executive*
Moriarty, Donald William, Jr. *bank executive*
Morrison, John M. *bank executive*
Moskow, Michael H. *retired bank executive*
Nash, John Arthur *bank executive*
O'Malley, Robert C. *bank executive*
Pontius, Stanley N. *bank holding company executive*
Schutter, David John *banker*
Siefers, Robert George *banker*
Smith, Edward Byron, Jr. *bank executive*
Thomas, J. Mikesell (Mike Thomas) *former bank executive*
Walters, Glen Robert *retired banker*

FINANCE: FINANCIAL SERVICES

UNITED STATES

ARIZONA

Goodyear
Eppen, Gary Dean *business educator*

CALIFORNIA

El Segundo
Rotherham, Thomas G. *diversified financial services company executive*

Larkspur
Hanna, Nessim *marketing educator*

San Francisco
James, George Barker, II, *financial executive*

FLORIDA

Bradenton
Hashmi, Sajjad Ahmad *finance educator, dean*

Naples
Hansen, Claire V. *financial executive*

GEORGIA

Alpharetta
Corby, Francis Michael, Jr. *business executive*

ILLINOIS

Buffalo Grove
McConville, Rita Jean *finance executive*

Champaign
Brighton, Gerald David *retired finance educator*
Perry, Kenneth Wilbur *finance educator*
Schoenfeld, Hanns-Martin Walter *finance educator*

Chicago
Baniak, Sheila Mary *accountant, educator*
Barré, Laura *finance company executive*
Burack, Elmer Howard *management educator*
Chapman, Alger Baldwin *financial services company executive, lawyer*
Chookaszian, Dennis Haig *retired financial executive*
Christianson, Stanley David *finance company executive*
Chromizky, William Rudolph *accountant*
Cotter, Daniel A. *diversified financial services company executive*
Fensin, Daniel *diversified financial service company executive*
Fitzgerald, Robert Maurice *financial and retired bank executive*
Fleming, Richard H. *finance executive*
Garrigan, Richard Thomas *finance educator, consultant, editor*
Gluth, Robert C. *management company executive*
Goss, Howard S(imon) *financial executive*
Hicks, Cadmus Metcalf, Jr. *financial analyst*
Hoenig, Jonathan *financial analyst, investment company executive, television personality*
Jaffe, Howard Allen *financial company executive*
Kalt, David *diversified financial services company executive*
Kamerick, Eileen Ann *corporate financial executive, lawyer*
Kenney, Brian A. *financial services executive*
Kudish, David J. *financial executive*
Kullberg, Duane Reuben *accounting firm executive*
Lorch, Robert K. *corporate financial executive*
Mallory, Robert Mark *controller, finance company executive*
Mayer, Raymond Richard *business administration educator*
Medvin, Harvey Norman *retired diversified financial services company executive*
Mendenhall, Candice *former finance company executive*
Navratil, Robert J. *financial executive*
O'Connell, Edward Joseph III *financial executive, accountant*
Pavelich, Daniel L. *retired account and tax management consulting executive*
Pritzker, Nicholas J. *diversified financial services company executive*
Rasin, Rudolph Stephen *corporate financial executive*
Reed, M. Scott *accounting company executive*
Rodgers, Cynthia *anchor, correspondent*
Schornack, John James *accountant*
Schueppert, George Louis *financial executive*
Schumann, William Henry III *corporate financial executive*
Sullivan, Bernard James *accountant*
Szypulski, Wayne R. *controller, food products executive*
Tyler, W(illiam) Ed *finance company executive*
Waddell, Frederick H. (Rick Waddell) *finance company executive*
Weil, Roman Lee *finance educator*
Wing, John Adams *financial services executive*
Zimmerman, Martin E. *financial executive*

Deerfield
Boyd, Joseph Don *diversified financial services company executive*
Serwy, Robert Anthony *accountant*

Elgin
FitzGerald, Timothy J. *corporate financial executive*

Evanston
Jacobs, Donald P. *finance educator*
Kotler, Philip *marketing educator, writer*
Powers, Marian *finance educator*
Prince, Thomas Richard *accountant, educator*
Sawhney, Mohanbir S. *finance educator*
Scott, Walter Dill *management educator*
Stern, Louis William *marketing educator, consultant*

Glen Ellyn
Holman, James Lewis *financial consultant, management consultant*

Glendale Heights
Cook, Doris Marie *retired accountant, educator*

Glenview
Mack, Stephen W. *financial planner*

Gurnee
Hall, Terry *accountant*

Kenilworth
Bott, Harold Sheldon *accountant, management consultant*

La Grange Park
Perkins, William H., Jr. *retired finance company executive*

Lake Forest
Bielinski, Donald Edward *financial executive*
Pappano, Robert Daniel *financial company executive*

Lincolnshire
Ludes, John T. *financial executive*

Northbrook
Newman, Lawrence William *financial executive*
Pilch, Samuel H. *controller, corporate financial executive*

Oak Brook
Bossmann, Laurie *controller, hardware company executive*
Grimes, Steven P. *corporate financial executive*

Oakbrook Terrace
Catalano, Gerald *accountant*
Keller, Dennis James *management educator*
Spinell, Richard E. *financial services company executive*

Orland Park
Youdelman, Robert Arthur *financial executive, lawyer*

Park Ridge
Russell, William Steven *treasurer*

Prospect Heights
Aldinger, William F. III *diversified financial services company executive*
Gilmer, Gary D. *credit services company executive*

Riverdale
Hoekwater, James Warren *treasurer*

Riverwoods
Guthrie, Roy A. *financial company executive*
Hochschild, Roger C. *finance company executive*

Rockford
McManaman, William Robert *diversified financial services company executive*

Westchester
Kastory, Bernard H. *finance educator, former food products executive*
Nelson, Thomas George *retired consulting actuary*

Westmont
Moor, Roy Edward *finance educator*

Wilmette
Wishner, Maynard Ira *retired finance company executive, lawyer*

Winnetka
Toll, Daniel Roger *corporate financial executive, volunteer*

INDIANA

Bloomington
Dalton, Dan R. *finance educator, former dean*
DeHayes, Daniel Wesley *business educator*
Wentworth, Jack Roberts *business educator, consultant*

Carmel
Goodwin, William Maxwell *financial executive, retired*

Fort Wayne
Owen, Dave A. *finance executive*

Hobart
Arand, Frederick Francis *accountant, finance company executive*

Indianapolis
Carlock, Mahlon Waldo *financial planner, consultant, retired school system administrator*
Israelov, Rhoda *financial planner, entrepreneur*
Long, Clarence William *accountant*

Jasper
Schneider, Robert F. *treasurer*

Notre Dame
Shannon, William Norman III *finance educator, food service executive*
Vecchio, Robert Peter *business management educator*

South Bend
Cohen, Ronald S. *accountant*

West Lafayette
Cooper, Arnold Cook *management educator, researcher*
Lewellen, Wilbur Garrett *management educator, consultant*
Moskowitz, Herbert *management educator*

IOWA

Des Moines
Vaughan, Therese Michele *insurance educator*

Fonda
Tamm, Eleanor Ruth *retired accountant, writer*

Iowa City
Collins, Daniel W. *accountant, educator*
Lie, Erik *finance educator*
Riesz, Peter Charles *marketing educator, consultant*

West Des Moines
McNamara, David Joseph *financial and tax planning executive*

KANSAS

Fort Scott
Mann, Henry Dean *accountant, bank executive*

Lawrence
Beedles, William LeRoy *finance educator, consultant*

Leawood
Dykes, Archie Reece *finance company executive*

Overland Park
Stem, Carl Herbert *business educator*

Pittsburg
Bicknell, O. Gene *financial executive*

Topeka
Fink, Ruth Garvey *diversified financial services company executive*
Reser, Elizabeth May (Betty Reser) *bookkeeper*

Wichita
Redman, Peter *finance company executive*
Scott, Tillian Peter *corporate financial executive*

MICHIGAN

Ann Arbor
Cornelius, Kenneth Cremer, Jr. *finance executive*
Huntington, Curtis Edward *actuary*
Seyhun, Hasan Nejat *finance educator, department chairman*
Wilhelm, Edward W. *corporate financial executive*

Auburn Hills
Drexler, Mary Sanford *financial executive*
Knight, Jeffrey Alan *corporate financial executive*

Detroit
Acton, Elizabeth S. *corporate financial executive*
de Molina, Alvaro G. *finance company executive, former bank executive*
Kahalas, Harvey *business educator*

East Lansing
Arens, Alvin Armond *accountant, educator*
Miracle, Gordon Eldon *advertising educator*

Farmington Hills
Kern, Michael L. III *corporate financial executive*

Grand Rapids
Staples, David M. *corporate financial executive*

Livonia
Valerio, Michael Anthony *diversified financial services company executive*

Marquette
Larson, Larry Gene *financial planner*

Midland
Merszei, Geoffrey E. *corporate financial executive*

Monroe
Mlocek, Sister Frances Angeline *financial executive*

Oxford
Smith, Jay Lawrence *financial planning company executive*

Plymouth
Longhofer, Ronald Stephen *financial consultant*

Southfield
Rawden, David *financial services company executive*
Thornton, John T. *corporate financial executive*

Troy
Dellinger, Robert J. *corporate financial executive*
Gerber, William Kenton *financial executive*
Rappleye, Richard Kent *financial executive, consultant, educator*

West Bloomfield
Meyers, Gerald Carl *finance educator, writer, expert witness, consultant*

MINNESOTA

Golden Valley
Harrison, David D. *corporate financial executive*

Hopkins
Measelle, Richard Leland *accountant*

Minneapolis
Avella, Joseph Ralph *university professor*
Berry, David J. *former financial services company executive*
Berryman, Robert Glen *accounting educator, consultant*
Campbell, Jon R. *diversified financial services company executive*
Cracchiolo, James M. *diversified financial services company executive*
Doyle, Michael J. *corporate financial executive*
Duff, Andrew S. *corporate financial executive*
Hoffmann, Thomas Russell *business management educator*
Hubers, David Ray *financial services company executive*
James, J. Bradford *financial officer*
Kinney, Earl Robert *mutual funds company executive*
Moller, Andrew K. *finance company executive*
Petersen, Douglas Arndt *financial consultant*
Prange, Michael J. *finance company executive*
Rudelius, William *marketing educator*
Weiser, Irving *financial services company executive*

Minnetonka
Morisato, Susan Cay *actuary*

Plymouth
Hauser, Elloyd *finance company executive*

Saint Paul
Baukol, Ronald Oliver *retired finance company executive*
Bessette, Andy F. *diversified financial services company executive*
Crittenden, Bruce A. *finance company executive*
Heyman, William Herbert *financial services executive*
Wheelock, Pam *financial executive*

MISSOURI

Bridgeton
Collett, Lawrence *diversified financial service company executive*

Chesterfield
Driscoll, Charles Francis *financial planner*

Columbia
Nikolai, Loren Alfred *accounting educator*

De Soto
Kostecki, Mary Ann *financial tax consultant, small business consultant*

Fenton
Powers, James G. *corporate financial executive*

Jefferson City
Liese, Christopher A. *benefits and financial consulting company owner, state legislator*

Kansas City
Bloch, Henry Wollman *diversified financial services company executive*
Brandmaier, Jeff *diversified financial services company executive*
Garrison, Larry Richard *accounting educator*
Graebner, Carol F. *diversified financial services company executive, lawyer*
Ingraham, James H. *diversified financial services company executive*
Kemper, Alexander C. *finance company executive*
Rozell, Joseph Gerard *accountant*
Salizzoni, Frank L. *finance company executive*
Thome, James J. *financial executive*

Maryland Heights
Stiften, Edward J. *corporate financial executive*

O Fallon
McElhatton, Jerry *credit card company executive*

Saint Louis
Armstrong, Theodore Morelock *corporate financial executive*
Badalamenti, Anthony *financial planner*
Brown, Melvin F. *finance company executive*
Burch, Stephen Kenneth *finance company executive, real estate investor*
Eichholz, Dennis R. *controller, treasurer*
Green, Darlene *controller, municipal official*
James, William W. *financial consultant*
Kniffen, Jan Rogers *finance company executive*
Liggett, Hiram Shaw, Jr. *retired diversified financial services company executive*
Novik, Steve *finance company executive*
Rich, Harry Earl *corporate financial executive*
Snyder, William W. *corporate financial executive*

Springfield
Denton, D. Keith *management educator*

MONTANA

Rollins
Greer, Willis Roswell, Jr. *finance educator*

NEBRASKA

Fremont
Dunklau, Rupert Louis *financial planner, consultant*

Lincoln
Byrd, Lorelee *state treasurer*
Digman, Lester Aloysius *management educator*
Lienemann, Delmar Arthur, Sr. *accountant, real estate developer*

Omaha
Fairfield, Bill L. *finance company executive*
Munger, Charles T. *diversified company executive*

Papillion
Miller, Drew *financial management company executive*

NEW YORK

New York
Miller, Heidi G. *diversified financial company executive*

OHIO

Amelia
Hayden, Joseph Page, Jr. *finance company executive*
Von Lehman, John *financial executive*

Avon Lake
Wilson, W. David *corporate financial executive*

Bowling Green
Lunde, Harold Irving *retired management educator*

Cambridge
Baylor, Richard C. *financial company executive*
Crane, Gary E. *financial executive*

Cincinnati
Anderson, Jerry William, Jr. *diversified financial services company executive, educator*
Arnold, Neal E. *corporate financial executive*
Bell, Sandra Elizabeth *corporate financial executive*
Carey, Christopher L. *financial company executive*
Conaton, Michael Joseph *diversified financial services company executive*
Hoverson, Robert L. *finance company executive*
Lindner, Craig *financial services company executive*
Lindner, Robert David *finance company executive*
Lintz, Robert Carroll *retired diversified financial services company executive*
Magee, Mark E. *lawyer, financial executive*
Schiff, John Jefferson, Jr. *finance company executive*
Siekmann, Donald Charles *accountant*

Cleveland
Boyle, Kammer *financial planner, investment advisor, research analyst, options trader*
Grisko, Jerome P., Jr. *diversified financial services company executive*
Hawkinson, Gary Michael *financial services company executive*
Hennessy, Sean P. *corporate financial executive*
Koch, Charles John *credit agency executive*
Lerner, Randolph D. *finance company executive*
Mayne, Lucille Stringer *finance educator*
Neu, Richard W. *credit agency executive*
Quinlan, Mark *credit agency executive*
Robertson, William Richard *diversified financial services company executive, retired banker*
Skolnik, David Erwin *financial analyst*
Stratton-Crooke, Thomas Edward *financial consultant*
Walker, James S. *financial executive*
Weiss, Zev *corporate financial executive*

Columbus
Adams, Marty E. *diversified financial services company executive*
Bailey, Robert L. *finance company executive*
Berry, William Lee *business administration educator*
Boylan, John Lester *financial executive, accountant*
Cruz-Myers, Theresa *finance company executive*
Headley, Richard D. *corporate financial executive*
Hill, Terri *diversified financial services company executive*
James, Donna A. *diversified financial services company executive*
Keller, Michael C. *diversified financial services company executive*
Kidder, C. Robert *finance company executive*
Kontos, Mark *treasurer*
LaLonde, Bernard Joseph *finance educator*
Raabe, William Alan *tax writer, business educator*
Ricord, Kathy *diversified financial services company executive*
Zdun, James J. *finance executive*

Cuyahoga Falls
Moses, Abe Joseph *financial planner, consultant*

Dayton
Cronin, Patrick G. *financial executive*
Reading, Anthony John *accountant*
Singhvi, Surendra Singh *financial consultant*

Dublin
Pollner, Julia A. *financial executive*

East Liverpool
Baumgardner, Edward *financial company executive*

Fairfield
Stecher, Kenneth W. *financial corporation executive*

Hamilton
O'Dell, Michael Ray *accountant, bank executive*

Harrison
Kocher, Juanita Fay *retired auditor*

North Olmsted
McCafferty, Owen Edward *accountant, dental-veterinary consultant*

Solon
Plush, Mark J. *finance company executive*

Toledo
Hiltz, Kenneth A. *corporate financial executive*

SOUTH DAKOTA

Sioux Falls
Rogers, David Hughes *banking and financial service professor, dean, real estate company executive*

TEXAS

San Marcos
Palmer, Roger Raymond *finance educator*

WISCONSIN

Appleton
Hilker, Lyle J. *financial services organization executive*
Stellmacher, Jon Michael *corporate financial executive*

Beloit
Rodeman, Frederick Ernest *accountant*

Brookfield
Breu, George *accountant*

De Pere
Rueden, Henry Anthony *accountant*

Eau Claire
Weil, D(onald) Wallace *business administration educator*

Green Bay
Lempke, Michael R. *treasurer*

Madison
Aldag, Ramon John *management and organization educator*
Nevin, John Robert *business educator, consultant*

Milwaukee
Culver, Curt S. *diversified financial services company executive*
Furlong, Mark Francis *diversified financial services company executive, bank executive*
Kendall, Leon Thomas *finance and real estate educator, retired insurance company executive*
Kuester, Dennis J. *diversified financial services company and bank executive*
Schnoll, Howard Manuel *financial consultant, investment company executive*
Zore, Edward John *financial services executive*

Racine
Lamb, Steven G. *financial executive*

ADDRESS UNPUBLISHED

Almeida, Richard Joseph *finance company administrator*
Bennett, James E. *finance company executive*
Benson, Donald Erick *finance company executive*
Benson, Jim *finance company executive*
Butler, John Musgrave *financial consultant*
Castellina, Daniel J. *financial executive*
Chelberg, Bruce Stanley *holding company executive*
Cooper, Ken Errol *retired management educator*
Culp, Mildred Louise *corporate financial executive*
Edwards, James D. *accounting company executive*
Ernst, Mark A. *diversified financial services company executive*
Fleming, Cecil *retired finance company executive*
Friedman, Joan M. *retired accountant, educator*
Gaines, Brenda J. *retired financial services company executive*
Geissinger, Frederick Wallace *finance company executive*
Gleijeses, Mario *holding company executive*
Harper, W(alter) Joseph *financial consultant*
Hill, Lowell Dean *agricultural marketing educator*
Holloran, Thomas Edward *business educator*
Horwitz, Ronald M. *business administration educator*
Hunter, Buddy D. *holding company executive*
McMains, Melvin L(ee) *administrative executive*
Mednick, Robert *accountant*
Mosner, Lawrence J. *retired financial administration company executive*
Nair, Raghavan D. *accountant, educator*
Nelson, Mary Ellen Dickson *retired actuary*
Rosenberg, Sheli Zysman *retired finance company executive*
Sandor, Richard Laurence *financial company executive*
Sexton, Carol Burke *finance company executive, consultant*
Sheridan, Patrick Michael *retired finance company executive*
Smart, Jill Bellavia *financial consultant*
Steinberg, Gregg Martin *financial and management consultant, investment banker*
Wagner, William Burdette *business educator*
Walsh, John E., Jr. *business educator, consultant*
Waltermire, Thomas Allen *finance company executive*
Wesselink, David Duwayne *finance company executive*
Winkler, Donald A. *credit company executive*
Woo, Benson *financial executive*

FINANCE: INSURANCE

UNITED STATES

ARIZONA

Sun City
Reynolds, John Francis *insurance company executive*

CALIFORNIA

Oakland
Halvorson, George Charles *healthcare insurance company executive*

CONNECTICUT

Greenwich
West, Thomas Meade *insurance company executive*

GEORGIA

Atlanta
Hilliard, Robert Glenn *insurance company executive, lawyer*

ILLINOIS

Bloomington
Axley, Dixie L. *insurance company executive*
Blackburn, John D. *insurance company executive*
Brunner, Kim M. *insurance company executive, lawyer*
Rust, Edward Barry, Jr. *insurance company executive, lawyer*
Tipsord, Michael L. *insurance company executive*
Wright, Charles Richard *retired insurance executive*

Chicago
Adams, John S. *insurance company executive*
Bartholomay, William C. *insurance brokerage company and professional sports team executive*
Bradley, Thomas A. *insurance company executive*
Case, Gregory C. *insurance company executive*
Davies, Christa *insurance company executive*
DeMoss, Jon W. *insurance company executive, lawyer*
Fernandez, Geno *insurance company executive*
Hinkelman, Ruth Amidon *insurance company executive*
Jerome, Jerrold V. *retired insurance company executive*
McCaskey, Raymond F. *insurance company executive*
Rodgers, James Foster *insurance research executive, economist*
Ryan, Patrick G. *insurance company executive*
Toft, Richard P(aul) *title insurance executive*
Tyree, James C. *insurance company executive*
Vie, Richard Carl *insurance company executive*
Wamberg, Warren Thomas *insurance company executive*
Zucaro, Aldo Charles *insurance company executive*

Decatur
Braun, William Joseph *life insurance underwriter*

Itasca
Gallagher, J. Patrick, Jr. *insurance company executive*
Gallgher, J. Patrick, Jr. *risk management marketing company executive*
Lishka, Edward Joseph *underwriter, consultant*
McClure, Walter F. *risk management marketing company executive*

Lake Forest
Eckert, Ralph John *insurance company executive*
Peterson, Donald Matthew *insurance company executive*

Long Grove
Mathis, David B. *insurance company executive*

Naperville
Dombeck, Harold Arthur *insurance company executive*

Northbrook
Cruikshank, John W. III *insurance agent*
Liddy, Edward M. *insurance company executive*
Pike, Robert William *insurance company executive, lawyer*
Wilson, Thomas Joseph *insurance company executive*
Young, R. James *insurance company executive*

Oak Brook
Davis, Thomas William *insurance company executive*
Muschler, Audrey Lorraine *insurance broker*

Peoria
Michael, Jonathan Edward *insurance company executive*

Skokie
Hedien, Wayne Evans *retired insurance company executive*

Springfield
Simpson, William Arthur *insurance company executive*
Stooksbury, Walter Elbert *insurance company executive*

Wheaton
Hamilton, Robert Appleby, Jr. *insurance company executive*

INDIANA

Carmel
Dick, Rollin Merle *former insurance company executive*
Husman, Catherine Bigot *retired insurance company executive, consultant*

Fort Wayne
Clarke, Kenneth Stevens *insurance company executive*
Robertson, Richard Stuart *insurance holding company executive*

Greenwood
Daniel, Michael Edwin *insurance agency executive*

Indianapolis
Braly, Angela Fick *health insurance company executive, lawyer*
Glasscock, Larry Claborn *health insurance company executive*
Lytle, L(arry) Ben *insurance company executive, lawyer*
McKinney, E. Kirk, Jr. *retired insurance company executive*
Norman, LaLander Stadig *retired insurance company executive*
Robinson, Larry Robert *insurance company executive*
Watts, John S., Jr. *insurance company executive*

Pendleton
Kischuk, Richard Karl *insurance company executive*

Portage
Collie, John, Jr. *insurance agent*

IOWA

Council Bluffs
Nelson, H. H. Red *insurance company executive*

Des Moines
Brooks, Roger Kay *insurance company executive*
Evans, John Erik *insurance company executive*
Gersie, Michael H. *insurance company executive*
Griswell, J. Barry *insurance company executive*
Kalainov, Sam Charles *insurance company executive*
Kelley, Bruce Gunn *insurance company executive, lawyer*
Williams, Carl Chanson *insurance company executive*

KANSAS

Eudora
Miller, David Groff *insurance agent*

Lenexa
Grant, W. Thomas, II, *insurance company executive*

MARYLAND

Reisterstown
Tirone, Barbara Jean *retired health insurance administrator*

MICHIGAN

Detroit
Whitmer, Richard E. *insurance company executive*

Grand Haven
Horning, Daniel D. *underwriter*

Grand Rapids
Woudstra, Frank Robert *insurance company executive*

Lansing
Arends, Herman Joseph *former insurance company executive*
Fisher, John W. *insurance company executive*
Looyenga, Roger L. *insurance company executive*

MINNESOTA

Minneapolis
Feldman, Nancy Jane insurance company executive
Mikan, G. Mike healthcare services company executive
Nicholson, Bruce J. insurance company executive
Tuckson, Reed V. physician, health insurance company executive
Turner, John Gosney insurance company executive, director

Minnetonka
Rivet, Jeannine M. health insurance company executive
Robbins, Orem Olford insurance company executive

Owatonna
Annexstad, Albert T. insurance company executive

Saint Paul
Lipp, Robert I. insurance company executive
Senkler, Robert L. insurance company executive
Treacy, John C. insurance company executive
Urness, Kent D. insurance company executive
Zuraitis, Marita insurance company executive

Wayzata
McGuire, William W. retired insurance company executive

MISSOURI

Kansas City
Lakin, Scott Bradley insurance agent
Malacarne, C. John insurance company executive, lawyer

Maryland Heights
Buselmeier, Bernard Joseph insurance company executive

Saint Louis
Bryant, Donald L., Jr. insurance and benefits company executive
Ott, David T. insurance company executive
Winer, Warren James insurance executive

Springfield
Ostergren, Gregory Victor insurance company executive

NEBRASKA

Holdrege
Hendrickson, Bruce Carl life insurance company executive

Lincoln
Arth, Lawrence Joseph insurance executive

Omaha
Conley, Eugene Allen retired insurance company executive
Jay, Burton Dean insurance actuary
Neary, Daniel P. insurance company executive
Sigerson, Charles Willard, Jr. insurance agency executive
Strevey, Guy Donald insurance company executive

NORTH DAKOTA

Grand Forks
Wogaman, George Elsworth insurance company executive, financial consultant

OHIO

Amelia
Hayden, Robert W. insurance company executive

Cincinnati
Barrett, John F. insurance company executive
Clark, James Norman insurance executive
Hardy, Thomas Cresson insurance company executive
Horrell, Karen Holley insurance company executive, lawyer
Lindner, Carl H. III insurance company executive
Lindner, Carl Henry, Jr. insurance company executive, professional sports team owner
Lindner, S(tephen) Craig insurance company executive
Runk, Fred J. retired insurance company executive

Cleveland
Clapp, Kent W. insurance company executive
Lewis, Peter Benjamin insurance company executive
Renwick, Glenn M. insurance company executive

Columbus
Barnes, Galen R. insurance company executive
Duryee, Harold Taylor insurance consultant
Gasper, Joseph J. insurance company executive
Jurgensen, William G. insurance company executive
Oakley, Robert Alan insurance executive
Rasmussen, Stephen S. insurance company executive
Woodward, Robert J., Jr. insurance executive

Hamilton
Marcum, Joseph LaRue insurance company executive

Rocky River
Riedthaler, William Allen risk management professional

SOUTH DAKOTA

Mitchell
Widman, Paul Joseph insurance agent

WISCONSIN

Kenosha
DeSimone, Alfred S. insurance agent

Madison
Anderson, David R. insurance company executive
Johnson, J. Brent insurance company executive
Larson, John David insurance company executive, lawyer
Post, Jeffrey H. insurance company executive
Spencer, C. Stanley insurance company executive

Merrill
Whitburn, Gerald insurance company executive

Milwaukee
Granoff, Mark Howard insurance company executive
Hefty, Thomas R. insurance company executive
Long, Gary former insurance company executive

Neenah
Rudolph, Carl J. insurance company executive

Stevens Point
Schuh, Dale R. insurance company executive

ADDRESS UNPUBLISHED

Becker, JoAnn Elizabeth retired insurance company executive
Blair, Cary insurance company executive
Bolger, David P. former insurance company executive
Bolnick, Howard Jeffrey insurance company executive, educator, investor
Cooper, Charles Gordon retired insurance company executive
Crockett, Joan M. retired insurance company executive
Engel, Philip L. retired insurance company executive
Grover, Charles W. insurance company executive
Kardos, Paul James insurance company executive
Kirsch, William S. former insurance company executive, lawyer
Lardakis, Moira Gambrill insurance executive, lawyer
Maatman, Gerald Leonard insurance company executive
McCarthy, Harold Charles retired insurance company executive
Moone, Robert H. retired insurance company executive
Pierce, Harvey R. retired insurance company executive
Rockwood, Frederick Whitney insurance company executive
Schroeder, Kenneth Louis reinsurance company executive
Sollars, Frank B. automobile insurance company executive
Strong, John David insurance company executive

FINANCE: INVESTMENT SERVICES

UNITED STATES

ILLINOIS

Broadview
Smerz, Nancy entrepreneur

Chicago
Amboian, John Peter, Jr. investment company executive
Beeson, Gerald A. investment company executive
Bergonia, Raymond David venture capitalist
Block, Philip Dee III retired investment company executive
Brodsky, William J. investment company executive
Carey, Charles P. mercantile exchange executive
Carnahan, Ellen venture capitalist
Case, Donni Marie investment company executive, consultant
Chaleff, Carl Thomas investment company executive
Claeys, Jerome Joseph III investment company executive
Cloonan, James Brian investment company executive
Collins, Michelle L. venture capitalist
Cronin, Kathleen M. mercantile exchange executive, lawyer
Crown, James Schine investment company executive
Dan, Bernard W. former commodities exchange executive
Desmond, Bevin investment research company executive
Donohue, Craig S. mercantile exchange executive
Duffy, Terrence A. mercantile exchange executive
Gelber, Brian commodities trader
Gordon, James A. investment company executive
Greenberg, Steve brokerage house executive
Griffin, Kenneth C. investment company executive
Herron, David A. stock exchange executive
Hobson, Mellody investment company executive
Kelly, Arthur Lloyd investment company executive
Leszinske, William O. investment company executive
Levenson, Carol A. corporate bond research company executive
Marcovici, Michael investment company executive
Miner, Thomas Hawley entrepreneur
Neubauer, Nickolas J. brokerage house executive
Osborn, William A. investment company executive
Pero, Perry R. investment company executive
Pritzker, Penny investor
Rogers, John W., Jr. investment company executive
Schwertfeger, Timothy R. investment company executive
Slansky, Jerry William investment company executive
Stearns, Neele Edward, Jr. investment company executive
Underwood, Robert Leigh venture capitalist
Vroman, Kendal investment company executive
Wasendorf, Russell R., Sr. brokerage house executive
Weinberg, David B. investor
Weiner, Gerald Arne stockbroker
Wilhelm, David C. investment company executive
Williams, Daniel D. investment company executive
Wilmouth, Robert K. commodities trader
Woods, Robert Archer investment counsel

Deerfield
Howell, George Bedell investment company executive
Jordan, John W., II, holding company executive

Downers Grove
Smith, James C. entrepreneur

Evanston
Wang, Sona venture capitalist

Highland Park
Uhlmann, Frederick Godfrey securities trader

Lake Forest
Young, Ronald Faris commodities trader

Naperville
Calamos, John Peter, Sr. brokerage house executive
Penisten, Gary Dean entrepreneur

Northbrook
Edelson, Ira J. venture capitalist

Oak Brook
Kelly, Donald Philip entrepreneur
Peckenpaugh, Robert Earl investment advisor

Vernon Hills
Krasny, Michael P. investment company executive

Westmont
Warner, H. Ty entrepreneur, manufacturing executive

INDIANA

Carmel
Walsh, John Charles investment company executive, director

Indianapolis
Cohen, Morton A. venture capitalist
Sheehan, Kevin Edward venture capitalist

KANSAS

Lenexa
Hunter, Robert Tyler brokerage house executive

Shawnee Mission
Morford, John A. investment company executive

MASSACHUSETTS

Cambridge
Leiden, Jeffrey Marc venture capitalist, molecular biologist, cardiologist

MICHIGAN

Ann Arbor
Weiser, Marc venture capitalist

Birmingham
Kothari, Rajesh Ujamlal investment company executive

Detroit
Blaszkiewicz, David investment company executive
Porcher, Robert III entrepreneur, retired professional football player

Grand Blanc
Serra, Joe investment company executive

Livonia
Katzman, David investment company and professional sports team executive

Southfield
Prokop, Kevin investment company executive

Trenton
Tang, Cyrus investment company executive

MINNESOTA

Minneapolis
Cowles, John Jay III investment company executive, entrepreneur
Falker, John Richard investment advisor
Fauth, John J. venture capitalist
Gallagher, Gerald Raphael venture capitalist
Lindau, Philip commodities trader
Piper, Addison Lewis securities executive
Quam, Lois investment company executive, former health insurance company executive
Schreck, Robert commodities trader

Minnetonka
Anderson, David Wayne entrepreneur, former federal agency administrator

Saint Paul
Rothmeier, Steven George investment company executive

Stillwater
Horsch, Lawrence Leonard venture capitalist, corporate financial executive

Waubun
Christensen, Marvin Nelson venture capitalist

MISSOURI

Kansas City
Latshaw, John entrepreneur, director
Petersen, Robert R. brokerage house executive
Stowers, James Evans, Jr. investment company executive

Lees Summit
Korschot, Benjamin Calvin retired investment company executive

Saint Louis
Avis, Robert Grier investment company executive, civil engineer
Foster, Scarlett Lee investor relations executive
Skrainka, Alan Frederick securities analyst

Springfield
Cavner, Nadia investment company executive

NEBRASKA

Lincoln
Laphen, James A. investment company executive

Omaha
Buffett, Warren Edward entrepreneur, investment company executive
Hamburg, Marc D. investment company executive
Moglia, Joseph H. brokerage house executive
Ricketts, John Joe brokerage house executive
Winter, Jimmy entrepreneur, systems administrator

NEW JERSEY

Princeton
Gund, Gordon venture capitalist, investment company executive

NEW YORK

New York
Kraemer, Harry M. Jansen, Jr. investment and former medical products executive

OHIO

Alpha
James, Francis Edward, Jr. investment advisor

Bay Village
Hook, John Burney investment company executive

Cincinnati
Lucke, Robert Vito investment company executive

Cleveland
Brentlinger, Paul Smith venture capital executive
Charnas, Michael (Mannie) investment company executive
Feuer, Michael venture capitalist, former office products executive
Morgenthaler, David Turner venture capitalist
Shepard, Ivan Albert securities and insurance broker
Summers, William B., Jr. brokerage house executive

Columbus
Pointer, Peter Leon investment executive
Turnbull, Cheryl Lankard investment company executive

Lancaster
Hurley, Samuel Clay III investment management company executive

TEXAS

Dallas
Tucker, Keith A. investment company executive

WISCONSIN

Milwaukee
Kasten, G. Frederick, Jr. investment company executive
Pollack, Mark Brian investment company executive
Samson, Allen Lawrence investor, bank executive

ADDRESS UNPUBLISHED

Aurin, Robert James entrepreneur
Bowles, Barbara Landers investment company executive
Colker, David A. former stock exchange executive
Doherty, Charles Vincent investment advisor
Engelbreit, Mary art licensing entrepreneur
Goel, Karan entrepreneur
Horsager, Kent R. former grain exchange executive
Jewell, Joseph entrepreneur
Knox, Lance Lethbridge venture capitalist
Luthringshausen, Wayne brokerage house executive
Maguire, John Patrick investment company executive
McCausland, Thomas James, Jr. retired brokerage house executive
McNeill, Robert Patrick investment advisor
Palumbo, Michael investment company executive
Sallen, Marvin Seymour investment company executive
Shuman, Ann investment company executive
Stevens, Paul G., Jr. brokerage house executive
Strong, Richard S. investment company executive
Waite, Dennis Vernon brokerage house executive, consultant
Welch, Martin E. III investor, retail executive

GOVERNMENT: AGENCY ADMINISTRATION

UNITED STATES

COLORADO

Denver
Maurstad, David Ingolf federal agency administrator, insurance company executive

DISTRICT OF COLUMBIA

Washington
Paulose, Rachel Kunjummen *federal agency administrator, former prosecutor*

ILLINOIS

Chicago
Casillas, Frank C. *former state agency administrator*
Coyle, Dorothy *government agency administrator*
Dickman, Martin J. *federal agency administrator*
Henderson, William J. *former postmaster general*
Hillard, Terry G. *retired protective services official*
Jibben, Laura Ann *state agency administrator*
Jones, Stephanie J. *federal agency administrator*
Nash, Donald Gene *federal investigator, economist*
Padron, D. Lorenzo *state agency administrator*
Ruder, David Sturtevant *government official, lawyer, educator*
Thomas, Cherryl T. *former federal agency administrator*
Weis, Jody P. (J.P. Weis) *police superintendent*

Oak Brook
Garrigan, William Henry III *protective services official*

Springfield
Beverline, Jerry *state agency administrator*
Brown, Kirk *secretary of transportation*
Doyle, Rebecca Carlisle *state agency administrator*
Mogerman, Susan *state agency administrator*
Moore, Robert *protective services official*
Phelps, David Dwain *state agency administrator, former congressman*

INDIANA

Indianapolis
Baker, Jerry L. *police chief*
Boehm, Peggy *state agency administrator*
Carraway, Melvin J. *protective services official*
Feldman, Richard David *health commissioner*
Gerdes, Ralph Donald *fire safety consultant*
Masback, Craig *executive director United States track and field*
Pagac, Gerald J. *state agency administrator*
Phillips, Charles W. *state agency administrator*
Ripley, Judith G. *state agency administrator*

La Porte
Hiler, John Patrick *former government official, former congressman, business executive*

Lafayette
Geddes, Leslie Alexander *forensic engineer, educator, physiologist*

IOWA

Ankeny
Goodin, Julia C. *forensic specialist, state official*

Des Moines
Bair, Gerald D. *state government official*
Brickman, Kenneth Alan *state agency administrator*
Gronstal, Thomas B. *state agency administrator*
Henry, Phylliss Jeanette *marshal*
Moulder, William H. *police chief*
Nelson, Charlotte Bowers *retired public administrator*

Iowa City
Atchison, Christopher George *public health director*

KANSAS

Colby
Finley, Philip Bruce *retired state adjutant general*

Lawrence
Burke, Paul E., Jr. *government agency administrator, consultant*

Overland Park
McCann, Vonya B. *federal agency administrator, telecommunications industry executive*

Pratt
Hover, Gerald R. *state agency administrator*

Topeka
Parks, Blanche Cecile *public administrator*
Rock, Richard Rand, II, *protective services official*
Thull, Tom (John Thomas Thull) *state agency administrator*
Tomkins, Andy *state commissioner education*

MARYLAND

Bethesda
Niederhuber, John Edward *federal agency administrator, oncologist, surgeon, immunologist*

MASSACHUSETTS

Watertown
Tompkins, Curtis Johnston *government agency administrator*

MICHIGAN

Ann Arbor
Bierbaum, Rosina M. *federal agency administrator*

Detroit
Bully-Cummings, Ella M. *police chief*

Lansing
Stokes, Rodney *state agency administrator*
Wilbur, Kathleen *state agency administrator*

MINNESOTA

Bloomington
Aljets, Curtis J. *federal agency administrator*

Saint Paul
Beers, Anne *protective services official*
Boudreau, Lynda L. *state agency administrator*
Finney, William K. *police chief*
Morrissey, Bill *state agency administrator*
Wedl, Robert J. *state agency commissioner*

MISSOURI

Jefferson City
Eiken, Doug K. *state agency administrator*
Saunders, John L. *state agency administrator*
Vadner, Gregory A. *state agency administrator*

Kansas City
Bartch, Floyd O. *police chief*
English, Robert Bradford *marshal*
Hainje, Dick G. *FEMA administrator, former fire fighter*

Saint Louis
Henderson, Ronald *police chief*

NEBRASKA

Lincoln
Amack, Rex *state agency administrator*
Baird, Samuel P. *state finance director*
Kilgarin, Karen *state official, public relations consultant*

Omaha
Hansen, James Allen *state agency administrator*

NORTH DAKOTA

Bismarck
Dwelle, Terry *state agency administrator*
Johnson, Roger *state agency administrator*
Karsky, Timothy J. *state agency administrator*

OHIO

Akron
Shane, Sandra Kuli *postal service administrator*

Canal Winchester
Flowers, Larry Lee *protective services official*

Cleveland
Jettke, Harry Jerome *retired government official*
Jones, Thomas Franklin *protective services official*

Columbus
Cicchino, Samuel *deputy marshal*
Jackson, G. James *protective services official*
Jackson, James G. *police chief*
Taylor, Joel Sanford *government agency administrator, retired lawyer*

Hiram
Chema, Thomas V. *government official, consultant, academic administrator, lawyer*

Montpelier
Deckrosh, Hazen Douglas *retired state agency educator and administrator*

Reynoldsburg
Dailey, Fred L. *state agency administrator*

Youngstown
Gransee, Marsha L. *federal agency executive*

SOUTH DAKOTA

Pierre
Duncan, Dick *former state agency administrator*
Healy, Bryce *state agency administrator*
Johnson, Curtis J. *state agency administrator*

Rapid City
Duhamel, Judith Reedy Olson *public information officer, former state senator*

Sioux Falls
Swenson, Lyle W. *protective services official*

WEST VIRGINIA

Parkersburg
Zeck, Van *federal agency administrator*

WISCONSIN

Madison
Brancel, Ben *state agency administrator*
Cronin, Patti Adrienne Wright *state agency administrator*
Mach, Michael J. *state agency administrator*
Neville, Dallas S. *protective services official*
Williams, Richard K. *police chief*

Milwaukee
Hegerty, Nannette H. *police chief*

ADDRESS UNPUBLISHED

Booker, Joseph W., Jr. *warden*
Burns, Larry Wayne *marshall*
Cochran, Dale M. *former state agency administrator*
Gerry, Martin Hughes, IV, *federal agency administrator, lawyer*
Gillmor, Karen Lako *state agency administrator*
Grandguist, Betty L. *former director elder affairs*
Guttau, Michael K. *state agency administrator, banker*
Kearns, Merle Grace *state agency administrator*
Norris, Clarence W. (Clancy Norris) *former state agency administrator*
O'Donnell, F. Scott *former state agency administrator*
Oliver, Jerry Alton *former police chief*
Parrino, Cheryl Lynn *federal agency administrator*
Sahr, Bob *former state agency administrator*
Schulz, Michael John *fire and explosion analyst, consultant*
Smith, Roy Allen *United States marshal*
Steffy, Marion Nancy *state agency administrator*

GOVERNMENT: EXECUTIVE ADMINISTRATION

UNITED STATES

DISTRICT OF COLUMBIA

Washington
Graber, Richard William *ambassador, lawyer*
Green, Mark Andrew *ambassador, former congressman*
Olson, Allen Ingvar *former governor of North Dakota*

ILLINOIS

Champaign
Semonin, Richard Gerard *retired state official*

Chicago
Athas, Rita Reagen *municipal official*
Balanoff, Clem *county election director*
Craig, John Bruce *former ambassador, air transportation executive*
Daley, Richard Michael *mayor*
Dempsey, Mary A. *library commissioner, lawyer*
Enenbach, Mark Henry *community action agency executive, educator*
Frias, Rafael *city official*
Hoffman, David H. *city manager*
Madigan, Lisa *state attorney general*
Quinn, Patrick *lieutenant governor*
Rothstein, Ruth M. *county health official*
Sledge, Carla Elissa *county official*
Stone, Bernard Leonard *vice mayor, alderman, lawyer*
Suarez, Ray *city official*
Topinka, Judy Baar *state official, political organization worker*
Trotter, Cortez *city official, former fire commissioner*
Vroustouris, Alexander *inspector general*
Walker, Thomas Ray *city aviation commissioner*

Evanston
Ingersoll, Robert Stephen *former diplomat, federal agency administrator*

Lake Zurich
Dixon, John Fulton *village manager*

Quincy
Points, Roy Wilson *municipal official*

Springfield
Blagojevich, Rod R. *governor, former congressman*
Boozell, Mark Eldon *state official*
Curry, Julie A. *state official*
Darr, William A. *commissioner*
Giannoulias, Alexi *state official*
Hasara, Karen A. *mayor*
McDonald, Jess *state official*
White, Jesse *state official*

Urbana
Edgar, Jim *former governor*
Prussing, Laurel Lunt *mayor, economist*

Vernon Hills
Ryg, Kathleen Schultz *municipal government official*

INDIANA

Columbus
Carter, Pamela Lynn *former state attorney general*

Indianapolis
Ballard, Gregory A. *mayor, retired military officer*
Carter, Steve *state attorney general*
Cohen, Edward *state official*
Cohn, Edward L. *commissioner corrections department*
Daniels, Mitchell Elias, Jr. *governor, former federal official*
Klika, Cristine M. *state official*
Mourdock, Richard E. *state official*
Nass, Connie Kay *state auditor*
Rokita, Todd *state official*
Skillman, Becky Sue *lieutenant governor, former state legislator*
Usher, Phyllis Land *state official*

South Bend
Davis, Katherine Lyon *former lieutenant governor*

IOWA

Des Moines
Arnold, Richard *state official*
Bergman, Bruce E. *municipal official*
Boal, Carmine *state official*
Buhr, Florence D. *county official*
Chambers, Royd *state official*
Corning, Joy Cole *retired state official*
Culver, Chet (Chester John Culver) *governor*
Daniels, Preston A. *mayor*
Deluhery, Patrick John *retired state official*
Fitzgerald, Michael Lee *state official*
Gaskill, Mary *state official*
Gipp, Chuck *state official*
Hahn, James *state official*
Heaton, Dave *state official*
Heddens, Lisa *state official*
Horbach, Lance *state official*
Huseman, Dan *state official*
Huser, Geri D. *state official*
Jacobs, Libby Swanson *state official*
Judge, Patty Jean *lieutenant governor, nurse*
Mauro, Michael Anthony *state official*
Miller, Thomas J. *state attorney general*
Struyk, Doug *state official*
Tymeson, Jodi *state official*
Upmeyer, Linda *state official*
Van Fossen, James *state official*
Watts, Ralph *state official*
Wendt, Roger *state official*
Whitaker, John *state official*

Marion
Pate, Paul Danny *mayor*

KANSAS

Coffeyville
Garner, Jim D. *state official, lawyer*

Garden Plain
Stovall, Carla Jo *former state attorney general*

Hutchinson
Kerr, Dave *state official, marketing professional*

Pittsburg
Trent, Darrell M. *ambassador, academic administrator, transportation executive*

Pratt
Hayden, (John) Michael *state official, former governor*

Topeka
Jenkins, Lynn M. *state official, former state legislator*
McClinton, James Alexander *mayor, former state agency administrator*
Mitchell, Gary R. *former state official*
Parkinson, Mark Vincent *lieutenant governor, former state legislator*
Sebelius, Kathleen Gilligan *governor*
Shallenburger, Tim *state official*
Simmons, Charles E. *state official*
Six, Stephen N. *state attorney general, former judge*
Thornburgh, Ron E. *state official*
Wagnon, Joan *state official, retired banker, retired mayor*

Wichita
Knight, Robert G. *mayor, investment banker*
Mayans, Carlos *former mayor*

MICHIGAN

Ann Arbor
Sheldon, Ingrid Kristina *retired mayor, controller*

Detroit
Kilpatrick, Kwame Malik *mayor*
Maseru, Noble A.W. *city health department administrator*

Grand Rapids
Logie, John Hoult, Sr. *former mayor, lawyer*
Posthumus, Richard Earl *former lieutenant governor, farmer*

Lansing
Cannon, Patrick D. *federal offical, broadcaster*
Cherry, John D., Jr. *lieutenant governor, former state senator*
Cox, Mike (Michael A. Cox) *state attorney general*
Granholm, Jennifer Mulhern *governor*
Kleine, Robert J. *state official*
Land, Terri Lynn *state official*
McGinnis, Kenneth L. *former state official*
Roberts, Douglas B. *state official*

Negaunee
Friggens, Thomas George *state official, historian*

Taylor
Pitoniak, Gregory Edward *mayor*

Troy
Pappageorge, John *state official*

Warren
Kolakowski, Diana Jean *economic development director*

MINNESOTA

Burnsville
Hatch, Mike *former state attorney general*

Golden Valley
Leppik, Margaret White *municipal official*

Minneapolis
Carlson, Arne Helge *former governor*
Mondale, Joan Adams *wife of former Vice President of United States*
Rybak, R. T. *mayor*

Northfield
Levin, Burton *diplomat*

Saint Paul
Hanson, Tom *state official*
Kessler, Robert W. *municipal official*
Molnau, Carol L. *lieutenant governor, former state legislator*
Pawlenty, Timothy James *governor*
Ritchie, Mark *state official*
Riveness, Phillip J. *city manager, retired state legislator*
Roberts, A(rthur) Wayne *organization administrator*
Swanson, Lori A. *state attorney general, lawyer*

MISSOURI

Jefferson City
Blunt, Matt (Matthew Roy Blunt) *governor, former state official*

Carnahan, Robin *state official*
Clayton, Robert Morrison III *commissioner*
Farmer, Nancy *state official*
Kinder, Peter D. *lieutenant governor, former state senator*
Lumpe, Sheila *commissioner, retired state legislator*
Nixon, Jeremiah W. (Jay) *state attorney general*
Steelman, Sarah *state official*

Kansas City
Archer, J(ohn) Barry *municipal official*
Barnes, Kay *former mayor*
Danner, Kathleen Frances Steele *federal official*
Davis, Richard Francis *city government official*
Levi, Peter Steven *municipal official, lawyer*
Price, Charles H., II, *former ambassador*
Rocha, Catherine Tomasa *municipal official*

Kennett
Thomason, Larry *state official*

Saint Charles
Gross, Charles Robert *county official, former state senator, former bank executive*

Saint Louis
Carpenter, Sharon Quigley *municipal official*
Harmon, Clarence *former mayor, law educator*
Slay, Francis G. *mayor*

NEBRASKA

Lincoln
Beermann, Allen J. *former state official*
Boyle, Anne C. *state commissioner*
Bruning, Jon Cumberland *state attorney general*
Foley, Mike *state official*
Gale, John A. *state official*
Heineman, David Eugene *governor*
Moul, Maxine Burnett *state official*
Osborn, Shane *state official*
Seng, Coleen Joy *director*
Sheehy, Rick *lieutenant governor, former mayor*

Omaha
Fahey, Mike *mayor*
Moore, Scott *former state official*

NEW YORK

New York
Curiel, Carolyn *former ambassador*

NORTH DAKOTA

Bismarck
Clark, Tony *state commissioner*
Dalrymple, Jack *lieutenant governor, former state legislator*
Hoeven, John *governor*
Jaeger, Al (Alvin A. Jaeger) *state official*
Poolman, Jim *commissioner*
Preszler, Gary *state commissioner*
Schmidt, Kelly *state official*
Stenehjem, Wayne Kevin *state attorney general, lawyer*
Wefald, Susan *state commissioner*

Edinburg
Myrdal, Rosemarie Caryle *state official, former state legislator*

Mandan
Paul, Jack Davis *retired state official, addictions consultant*

Minot
Watne, Darlene Claire *county official*

OHIO

Akron
Doty, Karen M. *county official, lawyer*
Kidder, Joseph P. *city service director*
Plusquellic, Donald L. *mayor*
Rothal, Max *city manager, lawyer*
Woolford, Warren L. *municipal official*

Canton
Healy, William J., II, *mayor, former state legislator*

Cincinnati
Mallory, Mark L. *mayor, former state legislator*

Cleveland
Campbell, Jane Louise *former mayor*
Konicek, Michael *city official*

Columbus
Bonini, James *federal official*
Brunner, Jennifer Lee *state official, lawyer*
Carter, Melinda *municipal official*
Chandler, Kathleen Leone *mayor, educator, state representative*
Coleman, Michael Bennett *mayor*
Dann, Marc *state attorney general, former state senator*
Fisher, Lee I. *lieutenant governor, former state attorney general*
Lashutka, Gregory S. *mayor, lawyer*
McGrath, Barbara Gates *city manager*
O'Brien, Ronald Joseph *lawyer*
Strickland, Ted *governor, former congressman*
Thompson, William Edward *state official*

Dayton
McLin, Rhine Lana *mayor, former state legislator*
Taft, Bob (Robert Alphonso Taft II) *former governor, educator*
Williams, Clarence E. *muncipal official*

Lakewood
Cain, Madeline Ann *mayor*

Newcomerstown
White, Michael Reed *former mayor*

Toledo
Carroll, William J. *municipal official*
Finkbeiner, Carlton S. (Carty Finkbeiner) *mayor*
Kovacik, Thomas L. *chief operating officer and safety director*

Uniontown
Taylor, Mary *state official*

Wellston
Carey, John Allen *mayor*

Worthington
Speck, Samuel Wallace, Jr. *state official*

SOUTH DAKOTA

Pierre
Butler, Richard D. *state treasurer*
Daugaard, Dennis M. *lieutenant governor, former state senator*
Everson, Curt *state commissioner*
Larson, Vernon LeRoy *state official*
Long, Larry *state attorney general*
Nelson, Chris A. *state official*
Rounds, Mike (Marion Michael Rounds) *governor*

Rapid City
Eccarius, Scott *state official, eye surgeon*

VIRGINIA

Alexandria
Freeman-Wilson, Karen *retired state attorney general, prosecutor, educational association administrator*

WISCONSIN

Madison
Bauman, Susan Joan Mayer *mayor, lawyer, commissioner*
Deer, Ada E. *former federal agency official, social worker, educator*
Doyle, Jim (James Edward) *governor, former state attorney general*
Earl, Anthony Scully *retired governor, lawyer*
Friske, Donald *state official*
Gielow, Curt *state official*
Gottlieb, Mark *state official*
Hines, J. A. *state official*
La Follette, Douglas J. *state official*
Lautenschlager, Peggy A. *former state attorney general*
Lawton, Barbara *lieutenant governor*
LeMahieu, Daniel R. *state official*
Lothian, Thomas A. *state official*
Sass, Dawn Marie *state official*
Shilling, Jennifer *state official*
Sinicki, Christine *state official*
Steinbrink, John P. *state official*
Stone, Jeffrey *state official*
Suder, Scott *state official*
Thompson, Barbara Storck *state official*
Townsend, John F. *state official*
Van Akkeren, Terry *state official*
Van Hollen, J(ohn) B(yron) *state attorney general, former prosecutor*
Van Roy, Karl *state official*
Voight, Jack C. *state official*
Wood, Jeffrey *state official*
Zepnick, Josh *state official*

Milwaukee
Barrett, Thomas M. *mayor, former congressman*
Edwards, Horace Burton *former state official, oil pipeline company executive, management consultant*

Pewaukee
Farrow, Margaret Ann *former lieutenant governor*

CANADA

MANITOBA

Winnipeg
Curtis, Charles Edward *Canadian government official*

FRANCE

Paris
Lagarde, Christine *French government official, lawyer*

ADDRESS UNPUBLISHED

Barnett, Mark William *former state attorney general*
Benson, Joanne E. *retired lieutenant governor*
Bernstein, James C. *retired commissioner*
Binsfeld, Connie Berube *former state official*
Blackwell, Ken (John Kenneth Blackwell) *former state official, former mayor*
Boddicker, Dan *state official*
Bradley, Jennette B. *former state official, lieutenant governor*
Carlson, E. Dean *state official*
Cleveland, Clyde *retired city official*
Dyrstad, Joanell M. *former lieutenant governor, consultant*
Ebert, Dorothy Elizabeth *retired county clerk*
Fraser, Donald MacKay *retired mayor, congressman*
Gilmore, Kathi *former state treasurer*
Growe, Joan Anderson *former state official*
Harder, Robert Clarence *state official*
Hazeltine, Joyce *former state official*
Johnson, Bruce E. *former lieutenant governor, state legislator*
Johnson, Rick *state official*
Kelly, Randy C. *former mayor St. Paul*
Kiffmeyer, Mary *former state official*
Kramer, Mary Elizabeth *ambassador, former state legislator*
Montgomery, Betty Dee *former state attorney general, retired state legislator*
Moore, John Eddy *former lieutenant governor*
Morrison, Paul J. *former state attorney general, former prosecutor*
Norquist, John Olaf *former mayor*
O'Connell, James Joseph *port official*
Ong, John Doyle *former ambassador, retired manufacturing executive*
Orr, Kay A. *former governor of Nebraska*
Pederson, Sally J. *former lieutenant governor*
Peterson, Bart (Barton R. Peterson) *former mayor*
Petro, Jim (James Michael) *former state attorney general*
Pirsch, Carol McBride *retired county official, state senator, community relations manager*
Qualls, Roxanne *mayor*
Ryan, James E. *former state attorney general*
Sayles Belton, Sharon *former mayor*
Schunk, Mae Gasparac *former state official*
Sherrer, Gary *former state lieutenant governor, bank executive*
Stevens, Greg *state official*
Stroup, Kala Mays *former education commissioner, educational alliance administrator*
Ventura, Jesse (James Janos, "The Body") *former governor*
Vilsack, Tom (Thomas James) *former governor*
Walcher, Kathleen *state official*
Walker, George Herbert III *former ambassador, retired investment banking company executive*
Wood, Corinne Gieseke *former lieutenant governor*

GOVERNMENT: LEGISLATIVE ADMINISTRATION

UNITED STATES

ARIZONA

Tucson
Hodges, Richard *former state legislator*

CALIFORNIA

Stockton
Singleton, Marvin Ayers *state legislator, otolaryngologist*

DISTRICT OF COLUMBIA

Washington
Akin, Todd (William Todd Akin) *congressman, former state legislator*
Bachmann, Michele *congresswoman, former state legislator*
Baldwin, Tammy *congresswoman, lawyer*
Bayh, Evan (Birch Evan Bayh III) *senator, former governor*
Bean, Melissa *congresswoman*
Biggert, Judith Borg *congresswoman, lawyer*
Blunt, Roy D. *congressman*
Boehner, John Andrew *congressman*
Bond, Christopher Samuel (Kit Bond) *senator, lawyer*
Boswell, Leonard L. *congressman*
Boyda, Nancy *congresswoman*
Braley, Bruce *congressman*
Brown, Sherrod Campbell *senator, former congressman, former state official*
Brownback, Sam Dale *senator, lawyer*
Bruce, Terry Lee *congressman*
Burton, Dan L. *congressman*
Buyer, Steven Earle *congressman, lawyer*
Camp, David Lee *congressman, lawyer*
Carnahan, Russ (John Russell Carnahan) *congressman, lawyer*
Carson, André D. *congressman, marketing specialist*
Chabot, Steven Joseph *congressman, lawyer*
Clay, William Lacy, Jr. *congressman*
Cleaver, Emanuel, II, *congressman, former mayor, minister*
Coleman, Norman, Jr. *senator, former mayor*
Conrad, Kent (Gaylord Kent Conrad) *senator*
Conyers, John, Jr. *congressman*
Costello, Jerry F., Jr. *congressman, former county official*
Davis, Danny K. *congressman*
Dingell, John David *congressman*
Donnelly, Joseph *congressman, lawyer*
Dorgan, Byron Leslie *senator*
Durbin, Dick (Richard Joseph Durbin) *senator*
Ehlers, Vernon James *congressman*
Ellsworth, Brad (Bradley Ellsworth) *congressman, former police officer*
Emanuel, Rahm *congressman*
Emerson, Jo Ann H. *congresswoman*
Feingold, Russell Dana *senator, lawyer*
Fortenberry, Jeffrey Lane *congressman*
Foster, Bill (George William Foster) *congressman, physicist*
Grassley, Chuck (Charles Ernest Grassley) *senator*
Graves, Samuel B., Jr. *congressman, retired state legislator*
Gutierrez, Luis V. *congressman, elementary education educator*
Hagel, Chuck (Charles Timothy Hagel) *senator*
Hare, Phil (Philip G. Hare) *congressman*
Harkin, Thomas Richard *senator*
Hill, Baron Paul *congressman*
Hoekstra, Peter *congressman, manufacturing executive*
Hulshof, Kenny Charles *congressman*
Jackson, Jesse Louis, Jr. *congressman*
Johnson, Timothy Peter *senator*
Johnson, Timothy Vincent *congressman, lawyer*
Jones, Stephanie Tubbs *congresswoman, lawyer, prosecutor*
Jordan, Jim (James D. Jordan) *congressman, former state legislator*
Kagen, Steven L. *congressman, physician*
Kildee, Dale Edward *congressman*
Kilpatrick, Carolyn Cheeks *congresswoman*
Kind, Ronald James *congressman, lawyer*
King, Steve *congressman*
Kirk, Mark Steven *congressman*
Kline, John *congressman*
Klobuchar, Amy Jean *senator, lawyer*
Knollenberg, Joseph Castl (Joe Knollenberg) *congressman*
Kohl, Herbert H. *senator, professional sports team owner*
LaHood, Ray H. *congressman*
Latham, Tom *congressman*
Latta, Robert Edward (Bob Latta) *congressman, former state legislator*
Levin, Carl Milton *senator*
Levin, Sander Martin *congressman, lawyer*
Lipinski, Daniel *congressman*
Loebsack, Dave *congressman, former political science professor*
Lugar, Dick (Richard Green Lugar) *senator*
Manzullo, Donald A. *congressman, lawyer*
McCaskill, Claire C. *senator, former auditor*
McCollum, Betty *congresswoman*
McIntosh, David M. *former congressman*
Miller, Candice S. *congresswoman*
Moore, Dennis *congressman*
Moore, Gwendolynne S. (Gwen Moore) *congresswoman*
Moran, Jerry *congressman*
Nelson, (Earl) Ben(jamin) *senator, former governor, lawyer*
Obama, Barack Hussein, Jr. *senator, former state legislator*
Oberstar, James L. *congressman*
Obey, David Ross *congressman*
Pence, Michael Richard *congressman*
Peterson, Collin C. *congressman*
Petri, Thomas Evert *congressman*
Pomeroy, Earl Ralph *congressman, retired commissioner*
Ramstad, James *congressman, lawyer*
Regula, Ralph Straus *congressman, lawyer*
Roberts, Charles Patrick (Pat Roberts) *senator*
Rogers, Mike (Michael J. Rogers) *congressman*
Rush, Bobby L. *congressman*
Ryan, Paul *congressman*
Sandlin, Stephanie Herseth *congresswoman, lawyer*
Schakowsky, Janice *congresswoman*
Schmidt, Jean *congresswoman*
Sensenbrenner, F(rank) James, Jr. *congressman*
Shimkus, John Mondy *congressman*
Skelton, Ike (Isaac Newton Skelton IV) *congressman*
Smith, Adrian M. *congressman, real estate agent*
Souder, Mark Edward *congressman*
Space, Zack (Zachary T. Space) *congressman*
Stabenow, Deborah Ann *senator, former congresswoman*
Stupak, Bart (Bartholomew Thomas Stupak) *congressman, lawyer*
Sutton, Betty *congresswoman, lawyer*
Terry, Lee Raymond *congressman, lawyer*
Thune, John Randolph *senator*
Tiahrt, Todd (W. Todd Tiahrt) *congressman, former state senator*
Turner, Michael R. *congressman*
Upton, Frederick Stephen *congressman*
Visclosky, Peter John *congressman, lawyer*
Voinovich, George Victor *senator, former governor*
Walz, Tim (Timothy J. Walz) *congressman, social science educator*
Weller, Gerald C. *congressman*
Wilson, Charles A., Jr. *congressman, funeral director*

FLORIDA

Leesburg
Mares, Harry *state legislator*

Venice
Dorso, John *state legislator*

ILLINOIS

Alton
Bowles, Evelyn Margaret *state legislator*

Belleville
Holbrook, Thomas Aldredge *state legislator*

Bloomingdale
Roskam, Peter James *congressman, former state legislator, lawyer*

Bloomington
Brady, William E. *state legislator*
Maitland, John W., Jr. *state legislator*

Blue Mound
Noland, N. Duane *state legislator*

Carbondale
Bost, Mike *state legislator*

Chicago
Berman, Arthur Leonard *retired state legislator*
Bugielski, Robert Joseph *state legislator*
Burke, Daniel J. *state legislator*
Burke, Edward Michael *alderman*
Capparelli, Ralph C. *state legislator*
Cohen, Ira *legislative staff member*
Colom, Vilma *alderman*
DeLeo, James A. *state legislator*
Dillard, Kirk Whitfield *state legislator, lawyer*
Doherty, Brian Gerard *alderman*
Dudycz, Walter W. *state legislator*
Feigenholtz, Sara *state legislator*
Harris, Gregory Scott *state representative*
Jones, Emil, Jr. *state legislator*
Jones, Shirley M. *state legislator*
Molaro, Robert S. *state legislator, lawyer*
Shaw, William *state legislator*
Stroger, Todd H. *former state legislator*
Widmayer, Christopher A. *legislative staff member*

Christopher
Mitchell, Ned *state legislator*

Coal City
O'Brien, Mary Kathleen *state legislator, lawyer*

Collinsville
Hoffman, Jay C. *state legislator*

Crystal Lake
Skinner, Calvin L., Jr. *state legislator*

East Alton
Davis, Steve *state legislator*

East Moline
Jacobs, Denny *state legislator*

East Saint Louis
Clayborne, James F., Jr. *state legislator*
Younge, Wyvetter Hoover *state legislator*

Elmhurst
Biggins, Robert A. *state legislator*

Galesburg
Hawkinson, Carl E. *state legislator*

Gilson
Moffitt, Donald L. *state legislator*

Greenville
Watson, Frank Charles *state legislator*

Hillside
Turner, John W. *state legislator*

Jacksonville
Findley, Paul *former congressman, author, educator*

Joliet
McGuire, John C. *state legislator*

Lombard
Cronin, Dan *state legislator*

Macomb
Myers, Richard P. *state legislator*

Mahomet
Greene, Terry J. *legislative staff member*

Milan
Brunsvold, Joel Dean *state legislator, educator*

Mount Prospect
Sullivan, Dave *state legislator*

Mount Vernon
Jones, John O. *state legislator*
O'Daniel, William L. *state legislator*

New Lenox
Wennlund, Larry *former state legislator, lawyer*

Northbrook
Parker, Kathleen Kappel *state legislator*

Palos Hills
Zickus, Anne *state legislator*

Palos Park
O'Malley, Patrick J. *state legislator*

Peoria
Leitch, David R. *state legislator*

Pontiac
Ewing, Thomas William *congressman, lawyer*

Quincy
Donahue, Laura Kent *former state senator*
Tenhouse, Art *state representative, farmer*

Romeoville
Hassert, Brent *state legislator*

Roselle
Karpiel, Doris Catherine *state legislator*

Skokie
Lang, Louis I. *state legislator, lawyer*

Springfield
Black, William B. *state legislator*
Boland, Michael Joseph *state legislator*
Bomke, Larry K. *state legislator*
Collins, Jacqueline Y *state senator*
Currie, Barbara Flynn *state legislator*
Daniels, Lee Albert *state legislator*
Davis, Jack *congressman*
Davis, Monique D. (Deon Davis) *state legislator*
Del Valle, Miguel *state legislator*
Flowers, Mary E. *state legislator*
Granberg, Kurt *state legislator, lawyer*
Halvorson, Debbie DeFrancesco *state legislator*
Hannig, Gary L. *state representative*
Jones, Wendell E. *state legislator*
Klingler, Gwendolyn Walbolt *state representative*
Krause, Carolyn H. *state legislator, lawyer*
Lauzen, Christopher J. *state legislator*
Link, Terry *state legislator*
Luechtefeld, David *state legislator*
Madigan, Michael Joseph *state legislator, political organization administrator*
Mahar, William F., Jr. *state legislator*
Maloney, Edward Dennis *state senator, assistant principal*
Mitchell, Gerald Lee *state legislator*
Moore, Andrea S. *state legislator*
Mulligan, Rosemary Elizabeth *legislator*
Munoz, Antonio *state legislator*
Pankau, Carole *state senator*
Parke, Terry Richard *state legislator*
Persico, Vincent Anthony *state legislator*
Peterson, William E. *state legislator*
Petka, Ed (Edward F.) *state legislator*
Pugh, Coy *state legislator*
Radogno, Christine *state legislator*
Rauschenberger, Steven J. *state legislator*
Ronen, Carol *state legislator*
Rutherford, Dan *state legislator*
Ryder, Tom *state legislator*
Santiago, Miguel A. *state legislator*
Saviano, Angelo *state legislator*
Schoenberg, Jeffrey M. *state legislator*
Shadid, George P. *state legislator*
Sieben, Todd *state legislator*
Silverstein, Ira I. *state legislator*
Smith, Michael Kent *state legislator*
Stephens, Ronald Earl *state legislator*
Syverson, Dave *state legislator*
Trotter, Donne E. *state legislator, hospital administrator*
Turner, Arthur L. *state legislator*
Welch, Patrick *state legislator*
Wirsing, David A. *state legislator*
Woolard, Larry *state legislator*

Stockton
Lawfer, I. Ronald *state legislator*

Sycamore
Burzynski, James Bradley *state legislator*

Teutopolis
Hartke, Charles A. *state legislator*

Westchester
Lightford, Kimberly A. *state legislator*

Western Springs
Durkin, James B. *state legislator*
Walsh, Thomas James *state legislator*

Westmont
Bellock, Patricia Rigney *state legislator*

INDIANA

Attica
Harrison, Joseph William *state legislator*

Bloomington
Kruzan, Mark R. *state legislator*

Chesterton
Ayres, Ralph Donald *state legislator*

Columbus
Hayes, Robert E. *former state legislator*

Covington
Grubb, Floyd Dale *state legislator*

Crawfordsville
Brown, Timothy N. *state legislator*

Crown Point
Conlon, James Charles *former state legislator*

East Chicago
Harris, Earl L. *state legislator*

Evansville
Avery, Dennis Theodore *state legislator*
Lutz, Larry Edward *state legislator*

Fort Wayne
Alderman, Robert K. *state legislator*
Moses, Winfield Carroll, Jr. *state legislator, construction company executive*

Fowler
Leuck, Claire M. *state legislator*

Gary
Borst, Lawrence Marion *state legislator*
Brown, Charlie *state representative*

Hartford City
Ford, David Clayton *state senator, lawyer*

Indianapolis
Adams, R. Tiny *state representative*
Aguilera, John *state representative*
Alting, Ronnie Joe *state legislator, restaurateur*
Antich-Carr, Rose Ann *state legislator*
Austin, Terri Jo *state representative*
Bardon, Jeb *state representative*
Becker, Vaneta G. *state representative*
Behning, Robert W. *state legislator*
Blade, Mark J. *state legislator*
Bodiker, Richard William, Sr. *state legislator*
Borror, Randy L. *state representative*
Bosma, Brian Charles *state legislator*
Breaux, Billie J. *state legislator*
Budak, Mary Kay *state legislator*
Cheney, Duane *state representative*
Cherry, Robert W. *state representative*
Chowning, Alan B. *state representative*
Day, John J. *state representative*
Dembrowski, Nancy J. *state senator*
Dickinson, Mae *state legislator*
Dillon, Gary (Doc) *state senator*
Dvorak, Ryan M. *state representative*
Frizzell, David Nason *state legislator*
Gard, Beverly J. *state legislator*
GiaQuinta, Benjamin E. *state representative*
Goodin, Terry A. *state representative*
Gutwein, Eric A. *state representative*
Hasler, Brian K. *state representative*
Heim, Steven *state representative*
Herrell, Ron *state representative*
Hinkle, Phillip D. *state representative*
Hoffman, Robert A. *state representative*
Howard, Glenn L. *state legislator*
Hume, Lindel O. *state legislator*
Jackman, Robert N. *state legislator, veterinarian*
Jacobs, Andrew, Jr. *former congressman, educator*
Johnson, Steven R. *state legislator*
Kenley, Howard *state legislator*
Kersey, Clyde R. *state representative*
Kittle, Jim, Jr. *state representative, political party administrator*
Klinker, Sheila Ann J. *state legislator, middle school educator*
Koch, Eric Allan *state representative*
Kuzman, Robert Daniel *state representative*
Lanane, Timothy S. *state legislator, lawyer*
Landske, Dorothy Suzanne (Sue Landske) *state legislator*
Lawson, Connie *state legislator*
Lawson, Linda *state senator*
Lehe, Donald J. *state representative*
Leonard, Daniel J. *state representative*
Long, David C. *state legislator, lawyer*
Lubbers, Teresa S. *state legislator, public relations executive*
Mahern, Edmund M. *state representative*
Marendt, Candace L. *state legislator*
Mays, Carolene *state representative*
Merritt, James W., Jr. *state legislator, real estate developer*
Mills, Morris Hadley *state senator, farmer*
Mrvan, Frank, Jr. *state legislator*
Neese, Timothy *state representative*
Noe, Cindy J. *state representative*
Nugent, Johnny Wesley *state legislator, tractor company executive*
Oxley, Dennie R., II, *state representative*
Paul, Allen E. *state legislator*
Pelath, Scott D. *state representative*
Pflum, Phillip *state representative*
Pierce, Matt *state representative*
Porter, Gregory W. *state legislator*
Reske, Scott E. *state representative*
Richardson, Kathy Kreag *state legislator*
Ripley, Michael A. *state representative*
Robertson, Paul Joseph *state legislator*
Rogers, Earline S. *state legislator*
Ruppel, William J. *state legislator*
Saunders, Thomas E. *state representative*
Server, Gregory Dale *state legislator, counseling administrator*
Simpson, Vi *state senator*
Sipes, Connie W. *state legislator, educator*
Skinner, Timothy D. *state senator*
Smith, Samuel, Jr. *state legislator*
Steele, Brent E. *state legislator*
Stevenson, Dan Charles *state legislator*
Stilwell, Russell *state representative*
Sturtz, W. Dale *state legislator*
Stutzman, Marlin *state representative*
Summers, Vanessa *state legislator*
Tabaczynski, Ron *state legislator*
Thomas, Andrew P. *state representative*
Thompson, Jeff *state representative*
Torr, Gerald R. *state representative*
Turner, Paul Eric *state legislator*
Ulmer, John D. *state representative*
Villalpando, Jesse Michael *state legislator*
Washington, Cleophus (Cleo Washington) *state senator*
Waterman, John M. *state legislator*
Weatherwax, Thomas K. *state legislator*
Welch, Peggy *state representative*
Whetstone, Matthew D. *state representative*
Willing, Katherine *former state legislator*
Wyss, Thomas John *state legislator*
Young, Dean A. *state legislator*
Young, R. Michael *state legislator*
Young, Richard D. *state legislator*
Zakas, Joseph C. *state legislator*

Kokomo
Buck, James Russell *state legislator*

Lagrange
Meeks, Robert L. *state legislator*

Macy
Friend, William C. *state legislator*

Madison
Lytle, Markt L. *state legislator*

Martinsville
Bray, Richard D. *state legislator*

Merrillville
Dobis, Chester F. *state legislator*

Mishawaka
Fry, Craig R. *state legislator*

Muncie
Munson, Bruce N. *state legislator*

New Albany
Cochran, William C. *state legislator*

Plymouth
Cook, Gary L. *state legislator*

Redkey
Liggett, Ronald David *state legislator*

Selma
Craycraft, Allie V., Jr. *state legislator*

Seymour
Bailey, William W. *state legislator, realtor*

South Bend
Bauer, Burnett Patrick *state legislator*

Terre Haute
LaPlante, R. Brooks *state representative*

Uniondale
Espich, Jeffrey K. *state legislator*

Valparaiso
Alexa, William E. *state legislator*

Warsaw
Adams, Kent J. *state legislator*

West Lafayette
Scholer, Sue Wyant *retired state legislator*

IOWA

Ames
Hammond, Johnie *state legislator*
Kurtenbach, James *state representative, finance educator*
Rosenberg, Ralph *retired state legislator, lawyer, non-profit administrator, educator*

Carlisle
Fink, Bill A. *state legislator*

Cascade
Hosch, Julie *state senator*

Cedar Rapids
Fiegen, Thomas L. *state legislator, lawyer, economics educator*

Davenport
Tinsman, Margaret Neir *state legislator*

Des Moines
Alons, Dwayne *state representative*
Angelo, Jeff M. *state legislator*
Behn, Jerry *state legislator*
Berry, Deborah *state representative*
Black, Dennis H. *state legislator*
Boettger, Nancy J. *state legislator*
Bolkcom, Joe L. *state legislator*
Bukta, Polly *state representative*
Carroll, Danny *state representative*
Cohoon, Dennis *state representative*
Connolly, Mike W. *state legislator*
Connors, John *state representative*
Courtney, Thomas *state senator*
Dandekar, Swati *state representative*
Davitt, Mark *state representative*
Dearden, Dick L. *state legislator*
DeBoef, Betty *state representative*
Dix, Bill *state representative*
Dolecheck, Cecil *state representative*
Dotzler, Bill *state senator*
Drake, Jack E. *state representative*
Dvorsky, Robert E. *state senator*
Eichhorn, George *state representative*
Elgin, Jeff *state representative*
Fallon, Ed *state representative*
Foege, Ro *state representative*
Ford, Wayne *state representative*
Fraise, Eugene S. *state legislator*
Frevert, Marcella R. *state representative, elementary school educator*
Garman, Teresa Agnes *state legislator*
Gaskill, E. Thurman *state legislator*
Granzow, Polly *state representative, language educator*
Gronstal, Michael E. *state legislator*
Grundberg, Betty *state legislator, property manager*
Hoffman, Clarence *state representative*
Hogg, Robert *state representative*
Horn, Wally E. *state legislator*
Houser, Hubert *state representative*
Hunter, Bruce *state representative, customer service administrator*
Hutter, Joe *state representative, retired protective services official*
Iverson, Stewart E., Jr. *state legislator, political organization administrator*
Jenkins, G. Willard *state representative*
Jochum, Pam *state representative*
Johnson, David *state senator*
Kettering, Steve *state senator*
Kibbie, John *state legislator*
Kreiman, Keith *state senator, lawyer*
Kuhn, Mark A. *state representative, farmer*
Lalk, David *state representative, farmer*
Lamberti, Jeff *state legislator, lawyer*
Lensing, Vicki *state representative, funeral home business owner*
Lukan, Steven *state representative*
Lundby, Mary A. *state legislator*
Lykam, Jim *state representative*
Maddox, O. Gene *state legislator, lawyer*
McCarthy, Kevin *state representative, lawyer*
McKibben, Larry *state legislator, lawyer*
Miller, David Paul *state legislator, lawyer*
Miller, Helen *state representative, lawyer*
Murphy, Patrick Joseph *state representative*
Oldson, Jo *state representative, lawyer*
Olson, Donovan *state representative*
Olson, Steven *state representative, farmer*
Paulsen, Kraig *state representative, military officer*
Petersen, Janet *state representative*
Putney, John *state senator, farmer*
Quirk, Brian *state representative*
Raecker, Scott *state representative, educational association administrator*
Ragan, Amanda *state senator*
Rants, Christopher C. *state representative*
Rasmussen, Dan *state representative, contractor*
Rayhons, Henry V. *state representative*
Reasoner, Michael J. *state representative, small business owner*
Rittmer, Sheldon *state senator, farmer*
Roberts, Rod *state representative*
Sands, Thomas *state representative, banker*
Schickel, Bill *state senator, broadcast executive*
Schrader, David Floyd *state legislator*
Seng, Joe *state senator, veterinarian*
Seymour, James *state senator, retired health facility administrator*
Shoultz, Donald L. *state representative*
Shull, Doug *state senator*
Smith, Mark D. *state representative*
Smith, Neal Edward *congressman*
Stewart, Roger *state senator*
Szymoniak, Elaine Eisfelder *retired state senator*
Taylor, Todd *state representative*
Thomas, Roger D. *state representative*
Tjepkes, David A. *state representative, protective services official*
Van Engelenhoven, Jim *state representative*
Van Fossen, Jim *state representative*
Whitead, Wesley *state representative*
Wieck, Ron *state senator, insurance agent*
Wilderdyke, Paul *state representative*
Winckler, Cindy *state representative*
Wise, Philip Leon *state representative*
Zieman, Mark L. *state senator, small business owner, farmer*

Epworth
Flynn, Thomas L. (Tom Flynn) *state legislator*

Fremont
Hedge, H. Kay *state senator*

Grafton
Bartz, Merlin E. *state legislator*

Greenfield
Baudler, Clel *state representative*

Le Mars
Klemme, Ralph F. *state representative*

New Liberty
Sievers, Bryan *state senator, farmer*

Plainfield
Jensen, John W. *state legislator*

Sioux City
Hansen, Steven D. *state legislator*

Steamboat Rock
Taylor, Ray *state senator*

Storm Lake
Eddie, Russell James *state legislator, sales executive*

West Des Moines
Churchill, Steven Wayne *former state legislator, marketing professional*

KANSAS

Arcadia
McKechnie, Ed *state legislator*

Atchison
Henry, Gerald T. *state legislator*

Bendena
Weiland, Galen Franklin *state legislator*

Brookville
Kejr, Joseph *former state legislator*

Carbondale
Howell, Andrew *state legislator*

Clay Center
Braden, James Dale *former state legislator*

Clifton
Taddiken, Mark *state legislator*

Concordia
Freeborn, Joann Lee *state legislator, farmer, former educator*

Derby
Myers, Don V. *state legislator*

Eastborough
Helgerson, Henry *state legislator*

Emporia
Barnett, James A. *state legislator*

Garnett
Feuerborn, Bill *state legislator*

Great Bend
Edmonds, John *state legislator*

Greensburg
McKinney, Dennis *state legislator*

Haddam
Hardenburger, Janice *state legislator*

Harper
Alldritt, Richard *state legislator*

Herington
Weber, Shari *state legislator*

Holton
Hutchins, Becky J. *state legislator*

Hutchinson
Kerr, David Mills *state legislator*
O'Neal, Michael Ralph *state legislator, lawyer*

Ingalls
Neufeld, Melvin J. *state legislator*

Inman
Downey, Christine *state legislator*

Junction City
Geringer, Gerald Gene *state legislator*

Kansas City
Haley, David *state legislator*
Henderson, Broderick *state legislator*

Lawrence
Ballard, Barbara W. *state legislator*
Brady, William Robert *state senator*
Praeger, Sandy *state legislator*
Ryun, Jim (James Ronald Ryun) *former congressman*

Leavenworth
Graeber, Clyde D. *former state legislator*

Manhattan
Glasscock, Kenton *state legislator*

Mcpherson
Emler, Jay Scott *state senator, lawyer*
Nichols, Richard Dale *former congressman, banker*

Neodesha
Chronister, Rochelle Beach *former state legislator*

Olathe
O'Connor, Kay F. *state legislator*
Toplikar, John M. *state legislator*

Osage City
Humerickhouse, Joe D. *state legislator*

Overland Park
Vratil, John Logan *state legislator, lawyer*

Prairie Village
Langworthy, Audrey Hansen *state legislator*

Roeland Park
Tomlinson, Robert Mark *state legislator*

Salina
Brungardt, Pete *state legislator*
Horst, Deena Louise *state legislator*

Shawnee
Jordan, Nick M. *state legislator, hotel recreational facility executive*

Shawnee Mission
Lane, Al *state legislator*

Topeka
Allen, Barbara *state legislator*
Barone, James L. *state legislator*
Brownlee, Karin S. *state legislator*
Carlin, Sydney *state representative*
Findley, Troy Ray *former state legislator, bank officer*
Gilmore, Phyllis *state legislator*
Gilstrap, Mark *state legislator*
Goodwin, Greta Hall *state legislator*
Heinemann, David J. *state legislator*
Hensley, Anthony M. *state legislator*
Holmes, Carl Dean *state representative, landsman*
Huelskamp, Tim *state legislator*
Jackson, David D. *state legislator*
Jones, Dennis C. *state representative, lawyer*
Kirk, Nancy A. *state legislator, nursing home administrator*
Lee, Janis K. *state legislator*
Mays, Doug *state representative, lawyer*
Mays, M. Douglas *state legislator, financial consultant*
McClure, Laura *state legislator*
Merrick, Raymond F. *state representative*
Morris, Stephen R. *state legislator*
Nichols, Rocky *state representative, non-profit consultant*
Oleen, Lana *state legislator*
Pauls, Janice Long *state legislator*
Petty, Marge D. *state senator*
Powell, Anthony J. *state legislator, lawyer*
Powers, Bruce Theodore (Ted Powers) *state legislator*
Ruff, L. Candy *state legislator*
Salisbury, Alicia Laing *state senator*
Saville, Pat *state senate official*
Schmidt, Derek *state legislator*
Schodorf, Jean *state legislator*
Spangler, Douglas Frank *state legislator*
Steinger, Chris *state legislator*
Swenson, Dale *state legislator*
Tanner, Ralph M. *state legislator*
Thimesch, Daniel J. *state legislator*
Toelkes, Dixie E. *state legislator*
Umbarger, Dwayne *state legislator*
Vickrey, Jene *state legislator*

Towanda
Corbin, David R. *state legislator*

Wamego
Pugh, Edward W. *state legislator*

Wichita
Dean, George R. *state legislator*
Donovan, Leslie D., Sr. *state legislator*
Feleciano, Paul, Jr. *state legislator*
Gilbert, Ruby *state legislator*
Gooch, U. L. *state legislator*
Harrington, Nancey *state senator*
Jennison, Robin L. *former state legislator, lobbyist*
Landwehr, Brenda *state legislator, corporate financial executive*
Ott, Belva Joleen *former state legislator*
Pottorff, Jo Ann *state legislator*
Wagle, Susan *state legislator, small business owner*
Wells, Jonathan *state legislator*
Welshimer, Gwen R. *state legislator, real estate broker, appraiser*

MICHIGAN

Adrian
Berryman, James *state legislator*

Allendale
Jellema, Jon *state legislator, educator*

Detroit
Bennane, Michael J. *former state legislator*
Bonior, David Edward *former congressman, educator*
Stallworth, Alma Grace *former state legislator*

Dewitt
Cropsey, Alan Lee *state legislator, lawyer*

Farmington Hills
Dolan, Jan Clark *former state legislator*

Fenton
Conroy, Joe *former state legislator*

Flint
Clack, Floyd *former state legislator*

Grandville
Voorhees, Harold J., Sr. *state legislator*

Grayling
Lowe, Allen *state legislator*

Grosse Ile
Palamara, Joseph *state legislator*

Huntington Woods
Gubow, David M. *state legislator*

Jackson
Griffin, Michael J. *former state legislator*
Letarte, Clyde *state legislator*
Walberg, Tim (Timothy Lee Walberg) *congressman, former state legislator*

Kentwood
DeLange, Walter J. *former state legislator*

Lansing
Barcia, James A. *state senator, former congressman*
Bennett, Loren *state legislator*
Bouchard, Michael J. *state legislator*
Byrum, Dianne *state legislator, small business owner*
DeBeaussaert, Kenneth Joseph *state legislator*
DeGrow, Dan L. *state legislator*
Dingell, Christopher Dennis *state legislator*
Dunaskiss, Mat J. *state legislator*
Emerson, Robert *state legislator*
Emmons, Joanne *state legislator*
Gast, Harry T., Jr. *state legislator*
Goschka, Michael John *state legislator*
Gougeon, Joel *state legislator*
Green, Mike *state legislator*
Gustafson, Dan *state legislator*
Hammerstrom, Beverly Swoish *state legislator*
Hart, George Zaven *state legislator*
Hoffman, Philip Edward *legislative consultant*
Koivisto, Don *state legislator*
Leland, Burton *state legislator*
Llewellyn, John T. *state legislator*
McManus, George Alvin, Jr. *state legislator, cherry farmer*
Miller, Arthur J., Jr. *state legislator*
Murphy, Raymond *state legislator*
North, Walter *state legislator*
Owen, Lynn *state legislator*
Profit, Kirk A. *former state legislator*
Schuette, Bill *state legislator*
Scott, Martha G. *state legislator*
Shugars, Dale L. *state legislator*
Sikkema, Kenneth R. *state legislator*
Smith, Virgil Clark *state legislator*
Steil, Glenn *state legislator*
Stille, Leon E. *state legislator*
Van Regenmorter, William *state legislator*
Vaughn, Jackie III *state legislator*
Young, Joseph Floyd, Jr. *state legislator*

Litchfield
Nye, Michael Earl *former state legislator*

Livonia
McCotter, Thaddeus George *congressman*

Marysville
London, Terry *former state legislator*

Mount Clemens
Rocca, Sue *state legislator*

Mount Pleasant
Randall, Gary Lee *former state legislator*

Paw Paw
Middaugh, James (Mike) *former state legislator*

Rochester
Crissman, Penny M. *state legislator*
Peters, Gary Charles *state legislator, lawyer, educator*

Saint Clair Shores
Yokich, Tracey A. *former state legislator*

Sturgis
Oxender, Glenn S. *state legislator*

Troy
Hillegonds, Paul *former state legislator*

Washington
Jaye, Dave *state legislator*

MINNESOTA

Albert Lea
Schwab, Grace S. *state legislator*

Andover
Hanson, Paula E. *state legislator*

Apple Valley
Knutson, David Lee *state legislator, lawyer*

Bloomington
Belanger, William V., Jr. *state legislator*

Blue Earth
Ziegler, Donald N. *state senator*

Brainerd
Samuelson, Donald B. *former state legislator*

Brandon
Bettermann, Hilda *state legislator*

Burnsville
McElroy, Dan *state legislator*

Center City
Swenson, Douglas *state legislator*

Chokio
Berg, Charles A. *state legislator*

Circle Pines
Runbeck, Linda C. *state legislator*

Coon Rapids
Foley, Leo Thomas *state legislator, lawyer*

Crookston
Lieder, Bernard L. *state legislator, civil engineer*

Dassel
Ness, Robert *state legislator, educational consultant*

Duluth
Huntley, Thomas *state legislator, science educator*

Eden Prairie
Luther, William P. *former congressman*
Paulsen, Erik *state legislator*

Erskine
Moe, Roger Deane *former state legislator, secondary education educator*

Excelsior
Johnson, Dave *state legislator*
Oliver, Edward Carl *retired state legislator, insurance company executive, small business owner*

Fairmont
Fowler, Chuck *former state legislator*

Forest Lake
Broecker, Sherry *state legislator*

Fulda
Winter, Theodore *state legislator*

Glyndon
Langseth, Keith *state legislator, farmer*

Ivanhoe
Mulder, Richard Dean *state legislator*

Lakeland
Larsen, Peg *state legislator*

Madison
Peterson, Doug *state legislator*

Mankato
Dorn, John *state legislator*
Hottinger, John Creighton *state legislator, lawyer*

Maple Grove
Girard, Jim *former state legislator*
Limmer, Warren E. *state legislator, real estate broker*

Marshall
Lesewski, Arlene *state legislator, insurance agent*

Minneapolis
Greenfield, Lee *state legislator*
Johnson, Alice M. *state legislator*
Mickelson, Stacey *state legislator*
Spear, Allan Henry *state legislator, historian, educator*
Wejcman, Linda *retired state legislator*

North Branch
Ring, Twyla L. *state legislator, newspaper editor*

Northfield
Neuville, Thomas M. *state legislator, lawyer*

Plymouth
Van Dellen, H. Todd *state legislator*

Preston
Davids, Gregory M. *state legislator*
Scheevel, Kenric James *state legislator*

Red Wing
Dempsey, Jerry *state legislator*

Rogers
Lindner, Arlon *state legislator*

Rosemount
Wolf, Ken *state legislator*

Rush City
Jennings, Loren G. *state legislator, business owner*

Saint Louis Park
Mondale, Theodore Adams *former state senator*

Saint Paul
Abrams, Ronald Lawrence *state legislator*
Anderson, Ellen Ruth *state legislator*
Bakk, Thomas *state legislator*
Beckman, Tracy *state legislator*
Berglin, Linda *state legislator*
Betzold, Donald Richard *state legislator*
Bishop, David T. *state legislator*
Bradley, Fran *state legislator*
Carlson, Lyndon Richard Selvig *state legislator, secondary school educator*
Chaudhary, Satveer *state senator*
Clark, Karen *state legislator*
Cohen, Richard J. *state legislator*
Day, Richard H. *state legislator*
Dehler, Steve *state legislator*
Dille, Stephen Everett *state legislator, veterinarian, farmer*
Erhardt, Ron *state legislator*
Fischbach, Michelle L. *state legislator*
Flynn, Carol *state legislator*
Frederickson, Dennis Russel *state legislator, farmer*
Goodno, Kevin P. *state legislator*
Greiling, Mindy *state legislator*
Hackbarth, Tom *former state legislator*
Harder, Elaine Rene *state legislator*
Hasskamp, Kris *state legislator*
Hausman, Alice *state legislator*
Higgins, Linda I. *state legislator*
Hugoson, Gene *state legislator, farmer*
Jacobs, Joel *former state legislator, municipal official*
Jaros, Mike *state legislator, administrative assistant*
Kahn, Phyllis *state legislator*
Kelley, Steve *state legislator, lawyer*
Kierlin, Bob *state legislator*
Kiscaden, Sheila M. *state legislator*
Kleis, David *state legislator*
Krinkie, Philip B. *state legislator*
Laidig, Gary W. *state legislator*
Larson, Cal *state legislator*
Mariani, Carlos *state legislator*
Marty, John *state legislator, writer*
McGuire, Mary Jo *state legislator*
Minge, David *former congressman, lawyer, law educator*
Murphy, Mary C. *state legislator*
Murphy, Steven Leslie *state legislator, utilities company official*
Novak, Steven G. *state legislator*
Olson, Edgar *state legislator*
Olson, Gen *state legislator*
Olson, Mark *state legislator*
Opatz, Joe *state legislator*
Osskopp, Mike *state legislator*
Otremba, Ken *state legislator*
Ourada, Mark *state legislator*
Ozment, Dennis Dean *state legislator*
Pappas, Sandra Lee *state senator*
Pariseau, Patricia *state legislator*
Pellow, Richard Maurice *former state legislator*
Pelowski, Gene P., Jr. *state legislator*
Pogemiller, Lawrence J. *state legislator*
Price, Leonard Russell (Len Price) *state legislator*
Ranum, Jane Barnhardt *state senator, lawyer*
Robling, Claire A. *state legislator*
Rostbert, Jim *state legislator*
Rukavina, Tom *state legislator*
Scheid, Linda J. *state legislator*
Solberg, Loren Albin *state legislator, secondary education educator*
Stevens, Dan *state legislator*
Terwilliger, Roy W. *state legislator*
Wiener, Deanna *state legislator*
Wiger, Charles W. *state legislator*

Shakopee
Kelso, Becky *former state legislator*

Side Lake
Janezich, Jerry R. *state legislator, small business owner*

South Saint Paul
Metzen, James P. *state legislator, bank executive*

Stillwater
Holsten, Mark *state legislator*
Krentz, Jane *former state legislator, elementary school educator*

Tower
Johnson, Douglas J. *state legislator, secondary education counselor*

Tracy
Vickerman, Jim *state legislator*

Walters
Kalis, Henry J. *state legislator, farmer*

Waseca
Worke, Gary D. *former state legislator*

White Bear Lake
Chandler, Kevin *former state legislator*

Willmar
Johnson, Dean Elton *state legislator, Lutheran pastor*

MISSOURI

Ballwin
Secrest, Patricia K. *state legislator*

Chesterfield
Hale, David Clovis *former state representative*

Edgar Springs
McBride, Jerry E. *state legislator*

Eureka
May, Brian Henry *state legislator*

Festus
Stoll, Steve M. *state legislator*

Florissant
Schneider, John Durbin *state legislator*

Gerald
Froelker, Jim *state legislator*

Half Way
Legan, Kenneth *state legislator, farmer*

Harrisonville
Hartzler, Vicky J. *state legislator*

High Ridge
Alter, William *state legislator*

Huggins
Lybyer, Mike Joseph *former state legislator, farmer*

Independence
Mays, Carol Jean *state legislator*

Jefferson City
Backer, Gracia Yancey *state legislator*
Barnett, Rex *state legislator*
Bland, Mary Groves *state legislator*
Boucher, Bill *state legislator*
Caskey, Harold Leroy *state legislator*
Childers, L. Doyle *state legislator*
Days, Rita Denise *state legislator*
Goode, Wayne *state legislator*
Graham, James *state legislator*
Green, Timothy P. *state legislator*
Griesheimer, John Elmer *state representative*
Harlan, Timothy *state legislator*
Hartzler, Ed *state legislator*
Hosmer, Craig William *state legislator*
Kauffman, Sandra Daley *state legislator*
Koller, Don *state legislator*
Linton, William Carl *state legislator*
Lograsso, Don *state legislator, lawyer*
Long, Elizabeth L. *state legislator, small business owner*
Luetkenhaus, William Joseph *state legislator*
Marble, Gary *state legislator*
Mathewson, James L. *state legislator*
Prost, Donald *former state legislator*
Rizzo, Henry *state legislator*
Rohrbach, Larry *state legislator*
Ross, Carson *state legislator*
Russell, John Thomas *state legislator*
Sallee, Mary Lou *state legislator*
Scheve, May E. *state legislator, political organization worker*
Schilling, Mike *state legislator*
Schwab, David *state legislator*
Scott, Delbert Lee *state legislator*
Scott, John E. *state legislator*
Sims, Betty *state legislator*
Skaggs, Bill *state legislator*
Stokan, Lana J. Ladd *state legislator*
Surface, Chuck L. *state legislator*
Tate, Phil *state legislator*
Vogel, Carl M. *state legislator*

Joplin
Burton, Gary L. *state legislator*

Kansas City
Lyon, Bob *state legislator*

Kirkwood
Gibbons, Michael Randolph *state legislator, lawyer*

Lees Summit
Bonner, Dennis *state legislator*
Kenney, William Patrick *state legislator*

Liberty
Quick, Edward E. *state legislator*

O Fallon
Kissell, Don R. *state legislator*

Perryville
Naeger, Patrick A. *state legislator*

Platte City
Witt, Gary Dean *former state legislator*

Saint Ann
Foley, James M. *state legislator*

Saint Charles
House, Ted C. *state legislator*

Saint Joseph
Shields, Charles W. *state legislator*

Saint Louis
Auer, Ron *state legislator*
Bray, Joan *state legislator*
Davis, Dorathea *state legislator*
Dixon, Alan John *former senator, lawyer*
Dougherty, J. Patrick *state legislator*
Ford, Louis H. *state legislator*
Mueller, Walt *state legislator*
Murphy, Jim *state legislator*
O'Toole, James *state legislator*
Shelton, O. L. *state legislator*
Treadway, Joseph L. *state legislator*
Troupe, Charles Quincy *state legislator*
Yeckel, Anita T. *state legislator*

Saint Peters
Donovan, Laurie B. *former state legislator*
Ostmann, Cindy *state legislator*

Smithville
Ridgeway, Luann *state legislator*

Springfield
Hancock, Mel *former congressman*

Theodosia
Robirds, Estel *state legislator*

Union
Overschmidt, Francis S. *state legislator*

Unionville
Summers, Don *state legislator*

Versailles
Pryor, Chuck *state legislator*

Warrensburg
Williams, Deleta *state legislator*

Warrenton
Nordwald, Charles *state legislator*

Webb City
Elliott, Mark T. *state legislator*

Webster Groves
McClelland, Emma L. *state legislator*

West Plains
Garnett, Jess *former state legislator*

NEBRASKA

Bellevue
Hartnett, D. Paul *state legislator*

Eddyville
Jones, James E. *state legislator*

Hastings
Bohlke, Ardyce *state legislator*

Lincoln
Aguilar, Raymond M. *state legislator*
Baker, Thomas C. *state legislator*
Beutler, Christopher John *state legislator*
Bourne, Patrick J. *state legislator*
Bromm, Curt *state legislator*
Brown, Pam *state legislator*
Byars, Dennis M. *state legislator*
Chambers, Ernest *state legislator*
Connealy, Matt J. *state legislator*
Crosby, LaVon Kehoe Stuart *state legislator, civic leader*
Cudaback, Jim D. *state legislator*
Cunningham, Douglas D. *state legislator*
Dickey, L. Robert *state senator*
Engel, Leo Patrick *state legislator*
Erdman, Philip *state legislator, farmer*
Janssen, Ramon E. *state legislator*
Kramer, David J. *state representative, lawyer*
Kremer, Robert M. *state legislator*
Kristensen, Douglas Allan *former state legislator*
Kruse, Lowen V. *state legislator*
Landis, David Morrison *state legislator*
Maxwell, Chip *state legislator*
Pedersen, Dwite A. *state legislator*
Pederson, Donald W. *state legislator*
Preister, Donald George *state legislator, greeting card manufacturer*
Price, Marian L. *state legislator*
Raikes, Ronald E. *state legislator*
Schimek, DiAnna Ruth Rebman *state legislator*
Suttle, Deborah S. *state legislator*
Thompson, Nancy P. *state legislator*
Tyson, Eugene *state legislator*
Witek, Kate *state senator, trucking company executive*
Withem, Ronald E. *state senator, trade association executive*

Omaha
Lindsay, John Conal *state legislator*
Lynch, Daniel C. *state legislator*
Quandahl, Mark C. *former state legislator, lawyer, political organization administrator*

Plattsmouth
Wehrbein, Roger Ralph *state legislator*

NORTH DAKOTA

Arnegard
Drovdal, David (Skip Drovdal) *state legislator*

Ashley
Kretschmar, William Edward *state legislator, lawyer*

Belcourt
Bercier, Dennis *state legislator*

Bismarck
Boucher, Merle *state legislator*
Clayburgh, Richard Scott *state tax commissioner*
Coats, James O. *state legislator*
Delzer, Jeff W. *state legislator*
Dever, Dick *state legislator*
Dickson, Thomas (Tom) A. *state representative, lawyer*
Freier, Tom D. *state legislator*
Goetz, William G. *state legislator*
Gulleson, Pam *state legislator*
Heigaard, William Steven *state senator*
Kelsch, RaeAnn *state legislator*
Kilzer, Ralph *state legislator*
Mutzenberger, Marv *state legislator*
Nelson, Carolyn *state legislator*
O'Connell, David Paul *state legislator*
Price, Clara Sue *state legislator*
Robinson, Larry J. *state legislator*
Sand, Harvey *state legislator*
Sandvig, Sally *state legislator*
Schmidt, Arlo E. *state legislator*
Schobinger, Randy Arthur *state legislator*
Solberg, Kenneth R. *state legislator*
Stenehjem, Bob *state legislator*
Svedjan, Ken *state legislator*
Sveen, Gerald O. *state legislator*
Thoreson, Laurel *state legislator*
Tomac, Steven Wayne *state legislator, farmer*
Traynor, Daniel M. *state representative*
Urlacher, Herbert *state legislator*

Bowman
Bowman, Bill *state legislator*
Kempenich, Keith *state legislator*

Braddock
Naaden, Pete *former state legislator*

Casselton
Nelson, Gary J. *state legislator*

Cavalier
Trenbeath, Thomas L. *state legislator, lawyer*

Center
Mahoney, John Jeremy *former state legislator*

Crosby
Andrist, John M. *state senator*

Devils Lake
Kunkel, Richard W. *state legislator*
Traynor, John Thomas, Jr. *state legislator, lawyer*

Dickinson
Wald, Francis John *state legislator*
Wardner, Rich *state legislator*

Dunn Center
Brown, Grant Claude *retired state legislator*

Edgeley
Schimke, Dennis J. *former state legislator*

Fargo
Berg, Rick Alan *state legislator, real estate investor*
Bernstein, LeRoy George *state legislator*
Fischer, Tom *state legislator*
Flakoll, Timothy John *state legislator, animal scientist*
Gorman, Stephen Thomas *former state legislator*
Grindberg, Tony *state legislator*
Lee, Judith *state legislator*
Mathern, Deb *state legislator*
Mathern, Tim *state senator*
Tennefos, Jens Junior *retired state senator*

Fessenden
Klein, Jerry *state legislator*

Fullerton
Kelsh, Jerome *state legislator*

Grafton
Gorder, William E. *state legislator*
Tallackson, Harvey Dean *state legislator, real estate and insurance salesman*

Grand Forks
Christenson, Linda *state legislator*
Delmore, Lois M. *state legislator*
DeMers, Judy Lee *retired state legislator, dean*
Espegard, Duaine C. *state legislator*
Nottestad, Darrell *state legislator*
Polovitz, Michael *state legislator*
Warnke, Amy Nicholle *state legislator*

Hankinson
Heitkamp, Joel C. *state legislator*

Hazen
Christmann, Randel Darvin *state legislator*
Galvin, Pat G. *state legislator*

Hope
Kroeplin, Kenneth *state legislator*

Jamestown
Hanson, Lyle *state legislator*
Nething, David E. *state legislator*
Wanzek, Terry Marvin *state legislator*

Kenmare
Froseth, Glen *state legislator*

Larimore
Mutch, Duane *state legislator*

Lehr
Erbele, Robert S. *state legislator*

Leonard
Belter, Wesley R. *state legislator*

Lidgerwood
Grumbo, Howard *state legislator*

Lisbon
Huether, Robert *state legislator*

Mandan
Boehm, James *state legislator*
Cook, Dwight C. *state legislator*

Minnewaukan
Every, Michael A. *state legislator*

Minot
Klein, Matthew M. *state legislator*
Krebsbach, Karen K. *state legislator*
Redlin, Rolland W. *state legislator*
Timm, Mike *state legislator*
Tollefson, Ben C. *state legislator, retired utilities executive*

Palermo
Kinnoin, Meyer D. *state legislator*
Nichols, Ronald *state legislator*

Ray
Torgerson, Jim *state legislator*

Regent
Krauter, Aaron Joseph *state legislator, farmer*

Towner
Gunter, G. Jane *state legislator*

Underwood
Freborg, Layton W. *state legislator*

Wahpeton
Thane, Russell T. *state legislator*

Williston
Byerly, Rex R. *state legislator*
Lyson, Stanley W. *state legislator*
Rennerfeldt, Earl Ronald *state legislator, farmer, rancher*

OHIO

Aurora
Herington, Leigh Ellsworth *state legislator, lawyer*

Avon
Bender, John R. *retired state legislator*

Bourneville
Shoemaker, Michael C. *state legislator*

Bowling Green
Gardner, Randall *state legislator, realtor*

Brookpark
Colonna, Rocco J. *state legislator*

Canfield
Gerberry, Ronald Vincent *state legislator*

Chesterland
Grendell, Diane V. *state legislator, nurse*

Cincinnati
Blessing, Louis W., Jr. *state legislator, lawyer*
Luebbers, Jerome F. *state legislator*
Van Vyven, Dale Nulsen *retired state legislator*
Winkler, Cheryl J. *state legislator*

Cleveland
Drake, Grace L. *retired state senator, cultural organization administrator*
Jerse, Edward *state representative*
Oakar, Mary Rose *congresswoman*
Pringle, Barbara Carroll *state legislator*
Suster, Ronald *judge, former state legislator*

Columbus
Allen, Dixie J. *state representative*
Armbruster, Jeffry J. *state legislator*
Aslanides, James *state representative*
Austria, Steve *state legislator*
Barrett, Catherine L. *state representative*
Beatty, Joyce *state representative*
Beatty, Otto, Jr. *former state legislator, lawyer*
Benjamin, Ann Womer *former state legislator, lawyer*
Blasdel, Charles R. *state representative*
Boccieri, John A. *state representative*
Book, Thomas Todd *state representative*
Brady, Daniel R. *state legislator*
Brinkman, Tom, Jr. *state representative*
Britton, Sam *state legislator*
Brown, Edna *state representative*
Buehrer, Stephen *state senator*
Calvert, Charles *state representative*
Carano, Kenneth A. *state representative*
Carmichael, Jim *state representative*
Cates, Gary *state representative*
Cirelli, Mary M. *state representative*
Clancy, Patricia *state representative*
Collier, Thom *state representative*
Core, Anthony E. *state representative*
Coughlin, Kevin *state senator*
Daniels, David T. *state representative*
DeBose, Michael *state representative*
DeWine, Kevin *state representative*
DiDonato, Gregory L. *state legislator*
Distel, L. George *state representative*
Domenick, John *state representative*
Driehaus, Steve *state representative*
Espy, Ben *state legislator, lawyer*
Evans, David R. *state representative*
Faber, Keith L. *state representative*
Fedor, Teresa *state senator*
Fessler, Diana M. *state representative*
Furney, Linda Jeanne *state legislator*
Gardner, Robert A. *state legislator*
Gibbs, Bob *state representative*
Gilb, Mike *state representative*
Glenn, John Herschel, Jr. *former senator, retired astronaut*
Goodman, David *state senator*
Hagan, John P. *state representative*
Hagan, Robert F. *state legislator*
Hartley, David *state legislator, lawyer*
Hartnett, William J. *state representative*
Hollister, Nancy *state legislator*
Hoops, James M. *state representative*
Hughes, Jim *state representative*
Husted, Jon *state representative*
Key, Annie L. *state representative*
Krebs, Eugene Kehm, II, *state legislator*
Lawrence, Joan Wipf *former state legislator*
Martin, Earl J. *state representative*
Mason, Lance T. *state representative*
McGregor, Jim *state representative*
Mead, Priscilla *state legislator*
Miller, Ray *state senator*
Mottley, James Donald *state legislator, lawyer*
Oelslager, W. Scott *state legislator*
Otterman, Robert J. *state representative*
Patton, Sylvester *state representative*
Patton, Thomas *state representative*
Perry, Jeanine *state representative*
Peterson, Jon M. *state representative*
Prentiss, C. J. *state legislator*
Pryce, Deborah Denine *congresswoman*
Raga, Tom *state representative*
Raussen, Jim *state representative*
Ray, Roy Lee *state legislator, public finance consultant*
Reidelbach, Linda *state representative*
Reinhard, Steve *state representative*

Roberts, Thomas Michael *state legislator*
Roberts, Tom *state senator*
Schaffer, Tim *state representative*
Schlichter, John M. *state representative*
Schneider, Michelle G. *state representative*
Schuck, William *state legislator*
Seaver, Derrick *state representative*
Seitz, Bill *state representative*
Setzer, Arlene J. *state representative, retired secondary school educator*
Smith, Geoffrey C. *state legislator, state representative*
Smith, Shirley A. *state legislator, state representative*
Spada, Robert F. *state legislator*
Stewart, Dan *state representative*
Stewart, Jimmy *state representative*
Stivers, Steve *state senator*
Strahorn, Fred *state representative*
Sykes, Barbara *state legislator, state representative*
Sykes, Vernon L. *state legislator*
Taylor, William *state legislator*
Terwilleger, George E. *state legislator*
Tiberi, Patrick Joseph *congressman, former state legislator*
Trakas, James Peter *state legislator, state representative*
Ujvagi, Peter *state representative, manufacturing executive*
Verich, Michael Gregory *state legislator*
Wagner, Jeff *state representative*
Webster, Shawn N. *state representative, veterinarian*
White, Doug *state legislator*
White, John J. *state representative, human resources specialist*
Widener, Chris *state representative*
Widowfield, John *state legislator, state representative*
Williams, Bryan C. *state representative*
Wolpert, Larry *state legislator*
Woodard, Claudette J. *state representative, retired educational association administrator*
Yates, Tyrone *state representative*

Dayton
Corbin, Robert L. *state legislator*
Reid, Marilyn Joanne *state legislator, lawyer*

Dublin
Watts, Eugene J. *state legislator*

Fremont
Damschroder, Rex *state legislator*

Girard
Latell, Anthony A., Jr. *state legislator*

Hamilton
Fox, Michael *former state legislator, underwriting consultant*

Hillsboro
Snyder, Harry Cooper *retired state legislator*

Jefferson
Boggs, Robert J. *former state senator*

Kettering
Horn, Charles F. *state senator, lawyer, electrical engineer*

Lakewood
Kucinich, Dennis John *congressman*

Lima
Willamowski, John Randall *state representative, lawyer*

Lisbon
Logan, Sean D. *state legislator*

Maumee
Olman, Lynn *state legislator*

Mineral Ridge
Ferderber, June H. *state legislator*

Napoleon
Wachtmann, Lynn R. *state legislator*

New Philadelphia
Metzger, Kerry R. *state legislator*

New Richmond
Vesper, Rose *state legislator*

Oak Harbor
Opfer, Darrell Williams *state representative, educator*

Painesville
LaTourette, Steven C. *congressman*
Sines, Raymond E. *former state legislator*

Saint Clairsville
Carnes, James Edward *state legislator*

Springfield
Hobson, David Lee *congressman, lawyer*

Toledo
Greenwood, Tim *former state legislator, lawyer*
Kaptur, Marcia Carolyn (Marcy Kaptur) *congresswoman*

Wapakoneta
Brading, Charles Richard *state representative*

Warren
Ryan, Timothy J. *congressman*

Wheelersburg
Ogg, William L. *state legislator*

Willowick
Troy, Daniel Patrick *former state legislator, county official*

Wooster
Amstutz, Ronald *state legislator*

SOUTH DAKOTA

Aberdeen
Waltman, Alfred Anthony *state legislator*

Armour
Putnam, J. E. (Jim) *state legislator*

Brookings
Brown, Arnold M. *state legislator*

Burke
Cerny, William F. *state legislator*

Claremont
Cutler, Steve Keith *state legislator*

Cottonwood
Gabriel, Larry Edward *state legislator*

Garretson
Rogen, Mark Endre *former state senator, farmer*

Gettysburg
Schreiber, Lola F. *former state legislator*

Huron
Haley, Pat *state legislator*
Volesky, Ron James *state legislator*

Iroquois
Flowers, Charles Edward *state legislator*

Madison
Belatti, Richard G. *state legislator*
Lange, Gerald F. *state legislator*

Miller
Morford, JoAnn (JoAnn Morford-Burg) *state senator, investment company executive*

Mission
Lucas, Larry James *state legislator*

Mud Butte
Ingalls, Marie Cecelie *former state legislator, retail executive*

Philip
Porch, Roger A. *former state legislator*

Pierre
Adam, Patricia Ann *legislative aide*
Dennert, H. Paul *state legislator*
Everist, Barbara *state legislator*
Fiegen, Kristie K. *state legislator*
Ham, Arlene H. *state legislator*
Koskan, John M. *state legislator*
Lawler, James F. *state senator*
Monroe, Jeff *state legislator*
Nelson, Pamela A. *state legislator*
Olson, Kevin Mel *state legislator*
Pederson, Gordon Roy *state legislator, retired military officer*
Reedy, John J. *state legislator*
Richter, Mitch *state legislator*
Roe, Robert A. *state legislator*
Shoener, Jerry James *state legislator*
Symens, Paul N. *state legislator, farmer*
Valandra, Paul *state legislator*
Weber, Robert R. *state legislator*

Pine Ridge
Hagen, Richard E. (Dick) *state legislator*

Rapid City
Fitzgerald, Carol E. *state legislator*
Napoli, William Bill *state legislator*
Whiting, Fred C. *state legislator*

Scotland
Kloucek, Frank John *state legislator*

Sioux Falls
Dunn, Rebecca Jo *state legislator*
Koetzle, Gil *state legislator, fire fighter, professional association administrator*
Munson, David Roy *state legislator*
Wick, Hal Gerard *state legislator*

Watertown
Drake, Robert Alan *state legislator, animal nutritionist, mayor*
Ries, Thomas G. (Torchy) *former state legislator*

Wentworth
Kringen, Dale Eldon *state legislator, transportation executive*

Wessington
Duxbury, Robert Neil *retired state legislator*

Yankton
Hunhoff, Bernie P. *state legislator*
Michels, Matthew *state representative, lawyer*
Moore, Garry Allen *state legislator*
Munson, Donald E. *state legislator*

VIRGINIA

Alexandria
Chrismer, Rich *state legislator*
Collins, Cardiss *retired congresswoman*

WISCONSIN

Albany
Powers, Mike *state legislator*

Beloit
Schooff, Dan *state legislator*

Black Earth
Klug, Scott Leo *former congressman*

Black River Falls
Musser, Terry M. *state legislator*

Burlington
Porter, Cloyd Allen *former state representative*

De Pere
Lasee, Alan J. *state legislator*

Eastman
Johnsrud, DuWayne *state legislator*

Eau Claire
Kreibich, Robin G. *state legislator*
Zien, David Allen *state legislator*

Forest Junction
Ott, Alvin R. *state legislator*

Fort Atkinson
Ward, David W. *state legislator*

Green Bay
Cowles, Robert L. *state legislator*
Kelso, Carol *state legislator*
Weber, Becky *state legislator*

Greenfield
Rutkowski, James Anthony *former state legislator*

Hartland
Vrakas, Daniel Paul *state legislator*

Janesville
Wood, Wayne W. *state legislator*

Juneau
Fitzgerald, Scott *state legislator*

Ladysmith
Reynolds, Martin L. *state legislator*

Luck
Dueholm, Robert M. *state legislator*

Luxemburg
Hutchison, Dave *state legislator*
Swoboda, Lary Joseph *state legislator*

Madison
Albers, Sheryl Kay *state legislator*
Berceau, Terese L. *state representative*
Bies, Garey D. *state representative*
Black, Spencer *state legislator*
Bock, Peter Ernest *state legislator*
Breske, Roger M. *state legislator*
Chvala, Charles Joseph *state legislator*
Coggs, G. Spencer *state legislator*
Colon, Pedro A. *state representative*
Cullen, David A. *state legislator*
Darling, Alberta Helen *state legislator, art gallery director, marketing professional*
Duff, Marc Charles *state legislator*
Erpenbach, Jon *state legislator*
Fitzgerald, Jeff *state representative*
Goetsch, Robert George *state legislator*
Gronemus, Barbara *state legislator*
Gunderson, Scott Lee *state legislator*
Gundrum, Mark *state representative*
Hahn, Eugene Herman *state legislator*
Hansen, Dave *state senator*
Hasenohrl, Donald W. *state legislator*
Hundertmark, Jean L. *state representative*
Jeskewitz, Suzanne E. *state representative*
Kanavas, Theodore J. *state senator*
Kedzie, Neal J. *state senator*
Kerkman, Samantha *state representative*
Kestell, Steven G. *state representative*
Krawczyk, Judy *state representative*
Kreuser, James E. *state legislator*
Krug, Shirley *state legislator*
Krusick, Margaret Ann *state legislator*
Lasee, Frank G. *state legislator*
Lassa, Julie M. *state representative*
Lehman, John W. *state representative*
Lehman, Michael A. *state legislator*
Leibham, Joseph K. *state senator*
Loeffelholz, Gabe *state representative*
McCormick, Terri *state legislator*
Meyer, Dan *state legislator*
Miller, Mark F. *state legislator*
Moen, Rodney Charles *state legislator, retired naval officer*
Montgomery, Phil *state legislator*
Nischke, Ann M. *state legislator*
Olsen, Luther S. *state legislator*
Owens, Carol *state legislator*
Petrowski, Jerry J. *state legislator*
Pettis, Mark L. *state legislator*
Plache, Kimberly Marie *state legislator*
Plale, Jeffrey T. *state legislator*
Pocan, Mark *state legislator*
Pope-Roberts, Sondy *state legislator*
Reynolds, Tom G. *state senator*
Rhoades, Kitty *state legislator*
Richards, Jon *state legislator*
Riley, Antonio *state legislator*
Risser, Fred A. *state legislator*
Robson, Judith Biros *state legislator*
Roessler, Carol Ann *state legislator*
Rosenzweig, Peggy A. *state legislator*
Ryba, John J. *state legislator*
Schultz, Dale Walter *state legislator*
Seratti, Lorraine M. *state legislator*
Skindrud, Rick *state legislator*
Stepp, Cathy *state senator*
Towns, Debi *state legislator*
Turner, Robert Lloyd *state legislator*
Underheim, Gregg *state legislator*
Vruwink, Amy Sue *state legislator*
Vukmir, Leah *state legislator*
Welch, Robert Thomas *state legislator*
Williams, Annette Polly *state legislator*
Williams, Mary *state legislator*
Wirch, Robert W. *state legislator*
Young, Leon D. *state legislator*
Young, Rebecca Mary Conrad *retired state legislator*
Ziegelbauer, Robert F. *state legislator*

Menomonie
Clausing, Alice *state legislator*
Plouff, Joe *state legislator*

Milwaukee
Carpenter, Timothy W. *state legislator*
George, Gary Raymond *former state legislator*
LaFave, John *state legislator*
Morris-Tatum, Johnnie *state legislator*
Potter, Rosemary *state legislator*
Wasserman, Sheldon A. *state legislator*

Minocqua
Handrick, Joseph W. *state legislator*

Nashotah
Neumann, Mark W. *former congressman, real estate developer*

Neenah
Ellis, Michael G. *state legislator*
Kaufert, Dean R. *state legislator*

Peshtigo
Gard, John *state legislator*

Port Washington
Hoven, Tim *state legislator*

Pulaski
Drzewiecki, Gary Francis *state legislator*

Racine
Ladwig, Bonnie L. *state legislator*

Rice Lake
Hubler, Mary *state legislator*

River Falls
Harsdorf, Sheila Eloise *state legislator, farmer*

Schofield
Decker, Russell S. *state legislator*

Shawano
Ainsworth, John Henry *state legislator*

Sheboygan
Baumgart, James Raymond *state legislator*

Superior
Boyle, Frank James *state legislator*

Waukesha
Huelsman, Joanne B. *state legislator*

Waunakee
Travis, David M. *state legislator*

Wausau
Huber, Gregory B. *state legislator*

West Allis
Bell, Jeanette Lois *former state legislator*

West Bend
Grothman, Glenn *state legislator*
Panzer, Mary E. *state legislator*

West Salem
Huebsch, Michael D. *state legislator*

Wisconsin Rapids
Schneider, Marlin Dale *state legislator*

WYOMING

Buffalo
Madden, Cheryl Beth *state legislator*

ADDRESS UNPUBLISHED

Aarsvold, Ole *state legislator*
Aker, Alan D. *state legislator*
Ballard, Charlie *state legislator*
Ballou, John Dennis *state legislator*
Balow, Larry C. *state representative*
Barrett, William E. *former congressman*
Becker, Rich *state legislator*
Beggs, Carol Edward *state legislator*
Bennett, Jon *state legislator*
Bodem, Beverly A. *state legislator*
Bogina, August, Jr. *former state official*
Bogue, Eric H. *state legislator, lawyer*
Boyd, Barbara *state legislator*
Brashear, Kermit Allen *state legislator, lawyer*
Broderick, B. Michael, Jr. *state legislator, banker*
Brooks, Roger *state legislator*
Brosz, Don *retired state legislator*
Brown, Richard Ellsworth *state legislator*
Burke, Brian B. *former state legislator, lobbyist*
Burton, Woody *state legislator*
Carpenter, Dorothy Fulton *retired state legislator*
Chocola, Chris (Joseph Christopher Chocola) *former congressman, lawyer*
Chrysler, Richard R. *former congressman*
Churchill, Robert Wilson *state legislator, lawyer*
Cierpiot, Connie *former state legislator*
Clay, William Lacy *former congressman*
Crane, Philip Miller *former congressman*
Crump, Wayne F. *state legislator*
Curtis, Candace A. *former state legislator*
Daggett, Roxann *state legislator*
Danner, Patsy Ann *former congresswoman*
Daschle, Thomas Andrew *former senator*
Davis, Kay *state legislator*
Dayton, Mark Brandt *former senator*
DePiero, Dean E. *state representative*
DeWine, Mike (Richard Michael DeWine) *former senator, lawyer*
Drake, Richard Francis *state legislator*
Duncan, Cleo *state legislator*
Duniphan, J. P. *state legislator, small business owner*
Dvorak, Michael A. *state legislator*
Entenza, Matt *state legislator*
Enz, Catherine S. *state legislator*
Erlandson, Mike *legislative staff member*
Erwin, Judy *state legislator*
Evans, Brent *state legislator*
Evans, Lane Allen *retired congressman*
Fantin, Arline Marie *state legislator*
Farmer, Mike *state legislator*
Fitzgerald, Peter Gosselin *banker former senator, lawyer*
Fitzwater, Rodger L. *state legislator*
Flora, Vaughn Leonard *state legislator*
Ford, Jack *state legislator*
Frederick, Virginia Fiester *state legislator*
Freese, Stephen J. *state legislator*
Frenz, John Gregory *state representative*
Ganske, J. Greg *former congressman, plastic surgeon*
Garton, Robert Dean *state legislator*
Gaskill, Sam *state legislator*
Grams, Rodney D. *former senator, former congressman*
Gratz, William W. *state legislator*

Gutknecht, Gil (Gilbert William Gutknecht Jr) *former congressman, former state legislator*
Haas, Bill *state legislator*
Hagan-Harrell, Mary M. *state legislator*
Haines, Joseph E. *state legislator*
Hanson, Dell *state representative, farmer*
Harris, Bill *state legislator*
Hastert, Dennis (John Dennis Hastert) *retired congressman*
Hegeman, Daniel Jay *state legislator*
Hendrickson, Carl H. *state legislator*
Hickey, John Joseph *state legislator*
Hilgert, John A. *state legislator*
Hohulin, Martin *state legislator*
Hoppe, Thomas J. *state legislator*
Hostettler, John Nathan *former congressman*
Hottinger, Jay *state legislator*
Howard, Janet C. *former state legislator*
Howard, Jerry Thomas *former state legislator*
Howerton, Jim *state legislator*
Hudkins, Carol L. *state legislator*
Hutmacher, James K. *state legislator, water drilling contractor*
Jacob, Ken *state legislator*
Jacobs, Leonard J. *state legislator*
Jacobson, Jeff *state legislator*
James, Troy Lee *state legislator*
Jensen, Jim *state legislator*
Johnson, Jay Withington *former congressman*
Johnson, Sidney B. *state legislator*
Johnson, Thomas Lee *state legislator*
Jolivette, Gregory *state representative*
Judge, John *state legislator*
Kasich, John R. *former congressman*
Kasten, Mary Alice C. *state legislator*
Keiser, George J. *state legislator*
Kennedy, Mark Raymond *former congressman*
Kenner, Howard A. *state legislator*
Kerns, Brian D. *former congressman*
Kiel, Shelley *state senator*
Kleczka, Gerald Daniel *former congressman*
Klemm, Richard O. *state legislator*
Kleven, Marguerite *state legislator*
Klusman, Judith Anderson *state legislator*
Koziura, Joseph Frank *state representative*
Kramer, Kent *state representative, finance company executive*
Kringstad, Edroy *state legislator*
Kromkowski, Thomas S. *state legislator*
Krupinski, Jerry W. *state legislator*
Kruse, Dennis K. *state legislator*
Lewis, James A. *state legislator*
Lindaas, Elroy Neil *state legislator*
Lipinski, William Oliver *former congressman*
Manternach, Gene *state representative, farmer*
Mautino, Frank J. *state legislator*
McCarthy, Karen P. *former congresswoman, former state legislator*
McClain, Richard Warner *state legislator*
McCoy, Matthew William *state legislator*
McKean, Andy *state legislator*
McLaren, Derryl *state legislator*
Meshel, Harry *former state senator, political party official*
Miller, Dale Andrew *city councilman*
Miller, Patricia Louise *state legislator, nurse*
Minor, Melvin G. *state legislator*
Mitchell, James W. *state official, former state legislator*
Moseley-Braun, Carol *former senator, former ambassador*
Murat, William M. *legislative staff member*
Murphy, Harold *state legislator*
Murphy, Michael B. *state legislator*
Murray, Connie Wible *state official, former state legislator*
Myers, Jon D. *state legislator*
Myers, Richard E. *state representative, trucking executive*
Nein, Scott R. *state legislator*
Netzley, Robert Elmer *state legislator*
Novak, John Philip *state legislator*
O'Connor, Patrick J. *state legislator*
Orfield, Myron Willard, Jr. *state legislator, educator*
Osterhaus, Robert *state representative, pharmacist*
Ourada, Thomas D. *former state legislator*
Perricone, Charles *former state legislator*
Philip, James (Pate Philip) *retired state legislator*
Poe, Donald Raymond *state legislator*
Pond, Phyllis Joan Ruble *state legislator, educator*
Pouche, Fredrick *state legislator*
Price, Larry *state representative*
Redfern, Donald B. *state legislator, lawyer*
Redfield, Pamela A. *state legislator*
Redwine, John Newland *state legislator, physician*
Rehberg, Kitty *state legislator*
Rest, Ann H. *state legislator*
Rhodes, Jim *state legislator*
Rife, Jack *state legislator*
Rivers, Lynn N. *former congresswoman*
Robertson, Martha Rappaport *state legislator, consultant*
Roman, Twyla I. *state legislator*
Sabo, Martin Olav *former congressman*
Salerno, Amy *state legislator*
Salmans, Larry D. *state legislator*
Sawyer, Thomas C. *former congressman*
Schrock, Edward J. *state legislator*
Schuerer, Neal *state legislator*
Schwarz, Joe (John J.H. Schwarz) *former congressman, physician*
Sexton, Mike W. *state legislator*
Sferra, Daniel J. *state legislator, state representative*
Shearer, Mark Smith *state legislator*
Shibilski, Kevin W. *state legislator*
Shriver, Joseph Duane *state legislator*
Smith, Alma Wheeler *state legislator*
Smith, Nick H. *former congressman, archivist, farmer*
Sodrel, Michael Eugene *former congressman, small business owner*
Soukup, Betty A. *state legislator*
Stuhr, Elaine Ruth *state legislator*
Swenson, Howard *state legislator, farmer*
Sykora, Barbara Zwach *state legislator*
Talent, James Matthes *former senator, congressman, lawyer*
Tavares, Charleta B. *former state legislator*
Taylor, Richard D. *state representative*
Treppler, Irene Esther *retired state senator*
Tuma, John *former state legislator, lawyer*
Tunheim, James Ronald *state legislator, farmer*
Tyson, Robert *state legislator*
Van Engen, Thomas Lee *state legislator*
Vanleer, James G. *state legislator*
Vaughn, Edward *state legislator*
Veenstra, Kenneth *state legislator*
Vellenga, Kathleen Osborne *retired state legislator*
Viverito, Louis Samuel *state legislator*
Volkmer, Harold L. *former congressman*
Vrtiska, Floyd P. *state legislator*
Wait, Ronald A. *state legislator*
Walsh, Lawrence M. *state legislator*
Wesely, Donald Raymond *state senator*
Wickersham, William R. *state legislator*
Wilk, Kenny A. *state legislator*
Will, Eric John *state senator*
Williams, Marilyn *state legislator*
Winkel, Richard J., Jr. *state legislator*
Winters, David Forrest *state legislator*
Wolf, Katie Louise *state legislator*
Young, Ron *state representative*

HEALTHCARE: DENTISTRY

UNITED STATES

ILLINOIS

Chicago
Bramson, James B. *dentist, dental association administrator*
Graber, Thomas M. *orthodontist, researcher*
Jackson, Gregory Wayne *orthodontist*

Geneva
Lazzara, Dennis Joseph *orthodontist*

Naperville
Grimley, Jeffrey Michael *dentist*

Westmont
Schefdore, Ronald L. *dentist*

INDIANA

Elkhart
Bryan, Norman E. *dentist*

Indianapolis
Hartsfield, James Kennedy, Jr. *orthodontist, geneticist*

IOWA

Iowa City
Bishara, Samir Edward *orthodontist*
Olin, William Harold *orthodontist, educator*

KANSAS

Wellington
Willis, Robert Addison *dentist*

MICHIGAN

Dearborn Heights
Abramson, Marc A. *dentist*

Warren
Woehrlen, Arthur Edward, Jr. *dentist*

MINNESOTA

Minneapolis
Douglas, William *dental educator, biomedical research administrator*
Shapiro, Burton Leonard *dentist, geneticist, educator*
Wolff, Larry F. *dental educator, researcher*

MISSOURI

Kansas City
Moore, Dorsey Jerome *dentistry educator, maxillofacial prosthetist*
Reed, Michael John *dentist, dean, educator*

NEBRASKA

Fremont
Roesch, Robert Eugene *dentist*

Mc Cook
Blank, Don Sargent *dentist*

Omaha
Zaiman, K(oichi) Robert *dentist*

NORTH CAROLINA

Charlotte
Chadwick, Gregory D. *endodontist*

OHIO

Cleveland
De Marco, Thomas Joseph *periodontist, educator*

Columbus
Buchsieb, Walter Charles *orthodontist, director*
Goorey, Nancy Jane *dentist*
Stevenson, Robert Benjamin III *prosthodontist, writer*

Hilliard
Relle, Attila Tibor *dentist, geriatrics services professional*

Uniontown
Naugle, Robert Paul *dentist*

WISCONSIN

Beloit
Green, Harold Daniel *dentist*

Racine
Sikora, Suzanne Marie *dentist*

ADDRESS UNPUBLISHED

Barkmeier, Wayne W. *dentist, researcher, educator*
Christiansen, Richard Louis *orthodontist, educator, dean*
Hoffman, Jerry Irwin *retired dental educator*
Kotowicz, William Edward *dental educator*

HEALTHCARE: HEALTH SERVICES

UNITED STATES

ALABAMA

Hoover
Kennon, Rozmond Herron *retired physical therapist*

ARIZONA

Scottsdale
Brown, Frederick Lee *health facility administrator*
Pelham, Judith *health system administrator*

CALIFORNIA

San Francisco
Rosenheim, Margaret Keeney *social welfare policy educator*

DISTRICT OF COLUMBIA

Washington
Bailar, John Christian III *retired public health educator, physician, statistician*

FLORIDA

Jacksonville
Harmon, Robert Gerald *public health executive*

GEORGIA

Augusta
Narsavage, Georgia Roberts *nursing educator, researcher*

ILLINOIS

Arlington Heights
Baptist, Allwyn J. *healthcare consultant*

Bloomington
Hunt, Roger Schermerhorn *healthcare administrator*

Bolingbrook
Price, Theodora Hadzisteliou *mental health services professional*

Centralia
Whitten, Mary Lou *nursing educator*

Chicago
Andreoli, Kathleen Gainor *nurse, educator, dean*
Berman, Laura *sex therapist*
Bristo, Marca *human services administrator*
Brown, Charles Eric *health facility administrator, biochemist*
Cox-Hayley, Deon Melayne *geriatrics services professional*
Giachello, Aida L. *social worker*
Goldsmith, Ethel Frank *medical social worker*
Gonzalez, William G. *healthcare advisor*
Hefner, David Stuart *health facility administrator, consultant*
Heltne, Paul Gregory *researcher, museum director*
Lerner, Wayne M. *healthcare executive*
Logemann, Jerilyn Ann *speech pathologist, educator*
Magoon, Patrick Michael *hospital administrator*
McDermott, Mary Ann *nursing educator*
Obama, Michelle (Michelle LaVaughn Robinson Obama) *hospital administrator, lawyer*
Riordan, Michael C. *hospital administrator*
Rojek, Kenneth John *health facility administrator*
Rudnick, Ellen Ava *health facility administrator*
Schwartz, John Norman *human services administrator*

Deerfield
Hicks, Judith Eileen *nursing administrator*
Shakno, Robert Julian *hospital and social services administrator*

Dekalb
Frank-Stromborg, Marilyn Laura *nursing educator*

Downers Grove
Thomas, Daniel J. *health services executive*

Evanston
Hughes, Edward F. X. *healthcare educator, preventive medicine physician*
Neaman, Mark Robert *hospital administrator*

Galesburg
Kowalski, Richard Sheldon *hospital administrator*

Glen Ellyn
Cummings, Joan E. *health facility administrator, educator*

Glenview
Coulson, Elizabeth Anne *physical therapist, educator, state representative*

Godfrey
Kessler, William Eugene *healthcare executive*
Smith, Linda Jeane *allied health educator*

Joliet
Lynch, Priscilla A. *nursing educator, psychotherapist*

Macomb
Hopper, Stephen Rodger *hospital administrator*

Manteno
Balgeman, Richard Vernon *radiology administrator, alcoholism counselor*

Maywood
Barbato, Anthony L. *hospital administrator, medical educator*

Moline
Larson, Sandra B. *nursing educator*

Mount Prospect
Catizone, Carmen A. *health science association administrator, secretary*

Northbrook
Betz, Ronald Philip *pharmacist*
Lever, Alvin *health science association administrator*

Northfield
Lubawski, James Lawrence *healthcare consultant*

Oak Brook
Baker, Robert J(ohn) *hospital administrator*
Risk, Richard Robert *health care executive*
Skogsbergh, James H. *health facility administrator*

Oak Park
Varchmin, Thomas Edward *public health service officer*

Park Forest
Steinmetz, Jon David *health facility administrator, psychologist*

Park Ridge
Boe, Gerard Patrick *health science association administrator, educator*
Campbell, Bruce Crichton *hospital administrator*

Rockford
Maysent, Harold Wayne *hospital administrator*

Skokie
McCarthy, Michael Shawn *health care company executive, lawyer*

Springfield
Hundley, Elaine E. *retired nursing education administrator*
Schmidt, Mark James *state public health official*

University Park
Samson, Linda Forrest *nursing educator, dean*

Urbana
Baker, David Hiram *nutritionist, educator*
Chow, Poo *wood technologist*
Erdman, John W. *nutritionist, educator*
Siedler, Arthur James *nutrition and food science educator*
Tripp, April *special education services professional*
Visek, Willard James *nutritionist, animal scientist, physician, educator*

Westchester
Clarke, Richard Lewis *health science association administrator*

Westmont
Tieken, Robert W. *relocation services company executive, retired tire manufacturing company executive*

INDIANA

Anderson
Whitaker, Audie Dale *hospital laboratory medical technologist*

Bloomington
Austin, Joan Kessner *mental health nurse*

Bluffton
Brockmann, William Frank *retired health facility administrator*

Hammond
Chandler, Melanie Lynn *surgical technologist, paralegal*
Smokvina, Gloria Jacqueline *nursing educator*

Indianapolis
Corley, William Edward *hospital administrator*
Davis, Edgar Glenn *healthcare executive, educator*
Dickenson-Hazard, Nancy Ann *pediatric nurse practitioner, consultant*
Gilroy, Sue Anne *hospital administrator, former state official*
Handel, David Jonathan *health facility administrator*
Humphreys, Katie *health agency administrator*
Loveday, William John *hospital administrator*
Riegsecker, Marvin Dean *pharmacist, state senator*
Warner, Joanne Rains *nursing educator, associate dean*

Lafayette
Geddes, LaNelle Evelyn *nurse, physiologist*
McBride, Angela Barron *nursing educator*

Mishawaka
Haley, David Alan *healthcare executive*

Muncie
Irvine, Phyllis Eleanor *nursing educator, administrator*

New Haven
Frantz, Dean Leslie *psychotherapist*

Valparaiso
Carr, Wiley Nelson *hospital administrator*

West Lafayette
Belcastro, Patrick Frank *pharmacist, researcher*
Christian, John Edward *health science association administrator, educator*
Kirksey, Avanelle *nutrition educator*
Peck, Garnet Edward *pharmacist, educator*
Shaw, Stanley Miner *pharmacist, educator*

IOWA

Des Moines
Inman, Lorinda K. *nursing administrator*
Jessen, Lloyd K. *pharmacist, lawyer*
Wallace, Samuel Taylor *health system administrator*

Glenwood
Campbell, William Edward *mental hospital administrator*

Jesup
Loeb, DeAnn Jean *nurse*

Lamoni
Kirkpatrick, Sharon Minton *nursing educator, academic administrator*

KANSAS

Colby
Morrison, James Frank *optometrist, state legislator*

Kansas City
Godwin, Harold Norman *pharmacist, educator*
Jerome, Norge Winifred *nutritionist, anthropologist, educator*

Lenexa
Mangun, Clarke Wilson, Jr. *public health physician, consultant*

Manhattan
Shanklin, Carol W. *dietician, educator*
Steele, James L. *researcher*

Oskaloosa
Flower, Joann *nurse, former state legislator*

Overland Park
Jones, George Humphrey *retired healthcare executive, hospital facilities and communications consultant*

Topeka
Bauman-Bork, Marceil *health services administrator*
Sheffel, Irving Eugene *health facility administrator*

Wichita
Guthrie, Diana Fern *nursing educator*

MICHIGAN

Allen Park
Kirby, Dorothy Manville *social worker*

Ann Arbor
Griffith, John Randall *health facility administrator, educator*
Hinshaw, Ada Sue *nursing educator, former dean*
Kalisch, Beatrice Jean *nursing educator, consultant*
Ketefian, Shaké *nursing educator*
McLaughlin, Catherine G. *healthcare educator*
Mosberg, Henry I. *pharmacist, educator, medicinal chemist*
Oakley, Deborah Jane *public health service officer, nursing educator*
Reame, Nancy King *nursing educator*
Romani, John Henry *health science association administrator, educator*

Bloomfield Hills
Mack, Robert Emmet *retired hospital administrator*
Zurkowski, Roy *health club chain executive*

Detroit
Berke, Amy Turner *health science association administrator*
Duggan, Michael E. *health facility administrator*
Hanks, Robin *rehabilitation nurse*
Heppner, Gloria Hill *health facility administrator, educator*
Jacox, Ada Kathryn *nurse, educator*
Moses, Gregory H., Jr. *health services administrator*
Redman, Barbara Klug *nursing educator*
Schlichting, Nancy Margaret *hospital administrator*
Velick, Stephen H. *medical facility administrator*
Warden, Gail Lee *healthcare executive*

Farmington
Burns, Sister Elizabeth Mary *retired hospital administrator*

Grand Rapids
Brent, Helen Teressa *school nurse*
Kranz, Kenneth Louis *human resources company executive*

Ionia
Ulmer, Evonne Gail *health science association administrator*

Kalamazoo
Lander, Joyce Ann *retired nursing educator, retired medical/surgical nurse*

Plainwell
Tiefenthal, Marguerite Aurand *school social worker*

Royal Oak
Matzick, Kenneth John *hospital administrator*

Troy
Potts, Anthony Vincent *optometrist, orthokeratologist*

MINNESOTA

Cottage Grove
Glazebrook, Rita Susan *nursing educator*

Eden Prairie
Petersen, Maureen Jeanette Miller *management information technology director, retired nurse*

Hastings
Blackie, Spencer David *physical therapist, administrator*

Minneapolis
Ackerman, F. Kenneth, Jr. *health facility administrator*
Farr, Leonard Alfred *hospital administrator*
Hemsley, Stephen J. *healthcare company executive*
Kane, Robert Lewis *public health service officer, educator*
Kralewski, John Edward *health service research educator*
Page, David Randall *hospital administrator*
Sprenger, Gordon M. *hospital administrator*
Suryanarayanan, Raj Gopalan *pharmacist, researcher, consultant, educator*
Welters, Anthony *health services executive*

Minnetonka
Coyle, Michael J. *medical administrator*

New Brighton
Appel, William Frank *pharmacist*

Robbinsdale
Anderson, Scott Robbins *hospital administrator*

Rochester
Cortese, Denis A. *healthcare executive, medical educator*
Frusti, Doreen Kaye *nursing administrator*
Mrazek, David Allen *child and adolescent psychiatrist*
Prendergast, Franklyn G. *health facility administrator, medical educator*

Saint Paul
Barry, Anne M. *public health officer*
Shepherd, Terry L. *health facility administrator*

MISSOURI

Branson West
McCall, Charles Barnard *retired health facility administrator*

Chesterfield
Ashworth, Ronald Broughton *health facility executive, accountant*

Columbia
Gysbers, Norman Charles *counselor, educator*

Kansas City
Devanny, E. H. (Trace) III *healthcare informatics executive*
Eddy, Charles Alan *chiropractor*
McKelvey, John Clifford *mental health services professional*
Oliver, Thornal Goodloe *retired health facility administrator*

Kirksville
Schwend, Michael T. *hospital administrator*

Macon
Maddox, Wilma *health facility administrator*

Maryland Heights
Cacchione, Patrick Joseph *health association executive*

Saint Charles
Eggleston, Harry *optometrist*

Saint Louis
French, Douglas Dewitt *medical facility administrator*
Ryan, Sister Mary Jean *health facility executive*
Schoenhard, William Charles, Jr. *health system executive*
Stretch, John Joseph *social worker, educator, management consultant*

NEBRASKA

Omaha
Hachten, Richard Arthur, II, *healthcare system executive*

NEW YORK

Buffalo
Nielsen, Nancy H. *health organization executive*

New York
Donald, Arnold W. *health science association administrator, former food products executive*

NORTH DAKOTA

Fargo
Rice, Jon Richard *health facility administrator, physician*

Grand Forks
Nielsen, Forrest Harold *research nutritionist*

OHIO

Akron
West, Michael Alan *retired hospital administrator*

Bath
Hoffer, Alma Jeanne *nursing educator*

Cincinnati
Cook, Jack McPherson *hospital administrator*
Derstadt, Ronald Theodore *health facility administrator*
Goldstein, Sidney *pharmacist*
Schubert, William Kuenneth *hospital medical center executive*
Weinrich, Alan Jeffrey *occupational hygienist*

Cleveland
Altose, Murray David *critical care physician, educator*
Blum, Arthur *social worker, educator*
Cosgrove, Delos M. (Toby Cosgrove) *health facility administrator, surgeon*
Rothstein, Fred C. *health facility administrator*
Stark, George Robert *health science association administrator*
Walcott, Robert *retired health facility administrator, priest*
Wood, Paul F. *national health agency executive*

Columbus
Anderson, Carole Ann *nursing educator, academic administrator*
Bachman, Sister Janice *healthcare executive, religious order administrator*
Beckholt, Alice *clinical nurse specialist*
Blom, Dave *healthcare industry executive*
Fawcett, Sherwood Luther *lab administrator*
Schuller, David Edward *cancer center administrator, otolaryngologist*

Dayton
Nixon, Charles William *retired acoustician*

Dublin
White, Kathy Brittain *medical association executive*

Gallipolis
Niehm, Bernard Frank *retired health facility administrator*

Hudson
Wooldredge, William Dunbar *health facility administrator*

Kettering
Peres, Frank J. *healthcare administrator*

Lancaster
Varney, Richard Alan *health facility administrator*

Saint Clairsville
Hahn, David Bennett *health facility administrator, consultant, marketing professional*

Sidney
Leffler, Carole Elizabeth *retired women's and mental health nurse*

Toledo
Brass, Alan W. *healthcare executive*
Cavanaugh, Steven M. *healthcare company executive*
Kneen, James Russell *health care administrator*
Ormond, Paul A. *healthcare company executive*
Weikel, Malcolm Keith *healthcare company executive*

Westlake
Coeling, Harriet Van Ess *nursing educator, editor*

PENNSYLVANIA

Philadelphia
Cooper, Richard Alan *health policy consultant*

SOUTH CAROLINA

Hilton Head Island
Wesselmann, Glenn Allen *retired health facility administrator*

TEXAS

Houston
Bleiberg, Efrain *medical clinic executive*

VIRGINIA

Charlottesville
Howell, Robert Edward *hospital administrator*

WASHINGTON

Seattle
Hansen, Thomas Nanastad *hospital administrator, pediatrician*

WISCONSIN

Green Bay
McIntosh, Elaine Virginia *nutrition educator*

Madison
Baton, Mary Rose Gallagher *medical technician, entertainer*
Brennan, Patricia Flatley *nursing and systems engineering educator*
Derzon, Gordon M. *hospital administrator*
Fryback, Dennis G. *health services research educator*
Littlefield, Vivian Moore *nursing educator, administrator*
Marlett, Judith Ann *nutritional sciences educator, researcher*
Neumann, Thomas Alan *educational administrator*
Schoeller, Dale Alan *nutrition research educator*

Menasha
Mahnke, Kurt Luther *psychotherapist, clergyman*

Milwaukee
Howe, G. Edwin *healthcare executive*
Lange, Marilyn *social worker*
Neumann, Donald A. *physical therapist, educator*

Rhinelander
Van Brunt-Bartholomew, Marcia Adele *retired social worker*

Shawano
Wilson, Douglas *genetics company executive*

ENGLAND

Grantham
Kingsley, James Gordon *college administrator*

ADDRESS UNPUBLISHED

Austin, James H(oward), Jr. *healthcare executive*
Ball, John Robert *healthcare executive*
Biegel, David Eli *social worker, educator*
Branstad, Terry Edward *healthcare facility executive, former governor*
Couch, Daniel Michael *healthcare executive*
Douglas, Janice Green *physician, educator*
Duerksen, George Louis *music therapist, educator*
Edelsberg, Sally Comins *retired physical therapist, educator*
Flynn, Pauline T. *retired speech pathologist, educator*
Frobenius, John Renan *hospital administrator*
Gavin, Mary Jane *retired medical/surgical nurse*
Goodman, Julie *retired nurse midwife*
Graham, Jewel Freeman *social worker, lawyer, educator*
Gregg, Robert Lee *retired pharmacist*
Harms, Nancy Ann *nursing educator*
Headlee, Raymond *retired psychotherapist*
John, Gerald Warren *pharmacist, educator*
Juenemann, Sister Jean *hospital executive*
Kane, John C. *retired health care products company executive*
Katen-Bahensky, Donna *health facility administrator*
Koebel, Sister Celestia *health care system executive*
Kuhler, Deborah Gail *grief therapist, retired state legislator*
Lanphear, Bruce Perrin *health facility administrator, educator*
Leininger, Madeleine Monica *nursing educator, consultant, retired anthropologist, editor, writer, theorist*
Levin, Arnold Murray *social worker, psychotherapist, educator*
Lund, Doris Hibbs *retired dietitian*
McCall-Rodriguez, Leonor *healthcare services company executive, entrepreneur*
Mecklenburg, Gary Alan *retired hospital administrator*
Milewski, Barbara Anne *pediatrics nurse, neonatal/perinatal nurse practitioner, critical care nurse*
Moon, John C. *healthcare company executive*
Nesbitt, John Arthur *recreational therapist, writer, educator, researcher*
Nichols, Elizabeth Grace *nursing educator, dean*
Parham, Ellen Speiden *nutrition educator*
Redburn, Amber Lynne *nursing educator*
Reeves, Bruce *social worker*
Scherer, Ronald Callaway *voice scientist, educator*
Searles, Lynn Marie *community health nurse*
Sierra-Amor, Rosa Isabel *health facility administrator*
Simon, Bernece Kern *retired social worker*
Simpson, Jack Benjamin *medical technologist, business executive*
Smith, Gloria Richardson *nursing educator*
Walker, Philip Chamberlain, II, *health facility administrator*
Williams, Stuart W. *health facility administrator*
Winkelmann, John Paul *pharmacist*
Ziegenhagen, David Mackenzie *retired health facility administrator, not-for-profit developer*
Zimmerman, Jo Ann *retired health science association administrator, educator, retired lieutenant governor*

HEALTHCARE: MEDICINE

UNITED STATES

ARIZONA

Tucson
Hattery, Robert Ralph *radiologist, educator*

CALIFORNIA

Los Angeles
Gewertz, Bruce Labe *surgeon, educator*

San Diego
Roizen, Michael F. *anesthesiologist, medical educator, writer*

Santa Barbara
Marcus, Joseph *child psychiatrist*

Stanford
Horwitz, Ralph Irving *internist, epidemiologist, educator, dean*

COLORADO

Denver
Gravlee, Glenn P(age) *anesthesiologist, educator, director*
Langsley, Pauline Royal *psychiatrist*
Shindell, Sidney *preventive medicine physician, educator, department chairman*

FLORIDA

Bonita Springs
Kopf, George Michael *retired ophthalmologist*

Jacksonville
Mooradian, Arshag Dertad *internist, educator*

Marco Island
Krause, Charles Joseph *otolaryngologist*

Placida
Prabhudesai, Mukund M. *pathology educator, health facility and academic administrator, researcher*

Tampa
Smith, David John, Jr. *plastic surgeon*

IDAHO

Sandpoint
Bird, Forrest M. *retired medical inventor*

ILLINOIS

Arlington Heights
DeDonato, Donald Michael *obstetrician, gynecologist*
Jensen, Lynn Edward *retired medical association administrator, economist*
Pochyly, Donald Frederick *physician, hospital administrator*

Belleville
Franks, David Bryan *internist, emergency physician*

Champaign
Gold, Paul Ernest *psychology and behavioral neuroscience educator*
Rosenblatt, Karin Ann *cancer epidemiologist*

Chicago
Abcarian, Herand *surgeon, educator*
Abelson, Herbert Traub *pediatrician, educator*
Albrecht, Ronald Frank *anesthesiologist*
Andersen, Burton Robert *immunologist, educator, medical historian*
Astrachan, Boris Morton *psychiatry educator, consultant*
Baldwin, DeWitt Clair, Jr. *pediatrician, educator*
Balk, Robert A. *medical educator*
Balsam, Theodore *physician*
Baron, Joseph Mandel *hematologist*
Barton, John Joseph *obstetrician, gynecologist, administrator, educator, researcher*
Bassiouny, Hisham Sallah *surgeon, educator*
Beck, Robert N. *nuclear medicine educator*
Becker, Michael Allen *internist, rheumatologist, educator*
Benson, Al Bowen III *oncologist, educator*
Betts, Henry Brognard *physiatrist, educator, health facility administrator*
Bonow, Robert Ogden *cardiologist, educator*
Bowman, James Edward *pathologist, educator*
Brasitus, Thomas Albert *gastroenterologist, educator*
Bunn, William Bernice III *occupational health and environmental medicine executive, epidemiologist, lawyer*
Caro, William Allan *physician, educator*
Cavallino, Robert P. *radiologist*
Celesia, Gastone Guglielmo *neurologist*
Chambers, Donald Arthur *biochemistry and molecular medicine educator*
Champagne, Ronald Oscar *medical association administrator*
Charles, Allan G. *obstetrician, educator*
Charrow, Joel *pediatrician, geneticist, educator, director*
Chatterton, Robert Treat, Jr. *reproductive endocrinology educator*
Chen, David *spinal cord injury physician*
Cho, Wonhwa *biomedical researcher*
Christoffel, Katherine Kaufer *pediatrician, epidemiologist, educator*
Coe, Fredric L. *internist, educator, researcher*
Cohen, Edward Philip *microbiology and immunology educator*
Colley, Karen J. *medical educator, researcher*
Conway, James Joseph *radiologist, educator*
Corlin, Richard F. *gastroenterologist*
Costa, Erminio *pharmacologist, cell biologist, educator*
Cummins, Thomas Kenneth *psychiatrist*
Davison, Richard *internist, educator*
Deutsch, Thomas Alan *ophthalmologist, educator, dean*
Deutsch, William Emil *ophthalmology professor*
Diamond, Seymour *physician*
Dooley, Sharon L. *obstetrician, gynecologist*
Dunea, George *nephrologist, educator*
Elias, Sherman *obstetrician, gynecologist, clinical geneticist, educator*
Faxon, David Parker *cardiologist*
Feldman, Ted *cardiologist*
Fennessy, John James *radiologist, educator*
Ferguson, Mark Kendric *surgeon, educator*
Flaherty, Emalee Gottbrath *pediatrician*
Flaherty, Timothy Thomas *radiologist*
Frederiksen, Marilynn C. *physician*
Frohman, Lawrence Asher *endocrinology educator, scientist*
Gapstur, Susan Mary *cancer epidemiologist, educator, researcher*
Gewurz, Anita Tartell *physician, medical educator*
Glass, Richard McLean *psychiatry educator, medical editor*
Glassroth, Jeffrey *internist, educator*
Goldberg, Arnold Irving *psychoanalyst, educator*
Golomb, Harvey Morris *hematologist, oncologist, educator*
Gorbien, Martin John *medical educator, geriatrician*
Gordon, Leo I. *hematologist, oncologist, educator*
Grammer, Leslie Carroll *allergist*
Grayhack, John Thomas *urologist, educator*
Greenberger, Paul Allen *allergist, immunologist, educator, medical researcher*
Gregory, Stephanie Ann *hematologist, educator*
Hambrick, Ernestine *retired colon and rectal surgeon*
Harris, Jules Eli *medical educator, physician, clinical scientist, administrator*
Hellman, Samuel *radiologist, educator*
Herbst, Arthur Lee *obstetrician, gynecologist*
Hinojosa, Raul *physician, ear pathology researcher, educator*
Honig, George Raymond *pediatrician*
Hughes, John Russell *neurologist, educator*
Jameson, James Larry *medical educator, endocrinologist, internist*
Jeevanandam, Valluvan *surgeon, educator*
Jensen, Harold Leroy *medical liability insurance administrator, physician*
Johnson, Timothy Patrick *health and social researcher*
Kahrilas, Peter James *medical educator, researcher*
Katz, Adrian Izhack *medical educator, physician*
Katz, Robert Stephen *rheumatologist, educator*
Kennett, Robert L. *medical organization executive*
Kirschner, Barbara Starrels *gastroenterologist*
Kirsner, Joseph Barnett *physician, educator*
Kloss, Linda L. *medical association administrator*
Knote, John A. *diagnostic radiologist*
Leff, Alan Richard *medical educator, researcher*
Leventhal, Bennett Lee *psychiatry and pediatrics educator, academic administrator*
Lopez, Carolyn Catherine *physician*
Luchins, Daniel Jonathan *psychiatrist*
Lurain, John Robert III *gynecologist*
Malkinson, Frederick David *dermatologist, educator*
Martin, Gary Joseph *medical educator*
McGee, Edwin C., Jr. *surgeon*
Mehlman, David Joel *cardiologist, educator*
Meltzer, David Owen *internist, educator, economist*
Mendelson, Ellen B. *radiologist, educator*
Metz, Charles Edgar *radiology educator*
Miller, Richard J. *pharmacologist, educator*
Millichap, Joseph Gordon *neurologist, educator*
Moawad, Atef *obstetrician, gynecologist, educator*
Moss, Gerald S. *medical educator*
Musacchio, Robert A. *medical association administrator*
Naclerio, Robert Michael *otolaryngologist, educator*
Nahrwold, David Lange *surgeon, educator*
Nakajima, Yasuko *medical educator*
Narahashi, Toshio *pharmacology educator*
Nyhus, Lloyd Milton *retired surgeon, educator*
Olson, Jack Conrad, Jr. *geriatrician*
Olson, Sandra Forbes *neurologist*
Palmisano, Donald J. *surgeon, medical educator*
Pappas, George Demetrios *anatomist, cell biologist, educator*
Pergament, Eugene *medical geneticist*
Plested, William G. III *surgeon*
Pope, Richard M. *rheumatologist*
Poznanski, Andrew Karol *pediatric radiologist*
Prinz, Richard Allen *surgeon*
Ramsey-Goldman, Rosalind *physician*
Reardon, Thomas R. *physician, medical association administrator*
Reddy, Janardan K. *medical educator*
Ridenour, Joey *medical association administrator, operations research specialist*
Robertson, William Wright, Jr. *orthopedist, educator*
Robinson, June Kerswell *dermatologist, educator*
Rogers, Eugene Jack *retired medical educator*
Roizen, Nancy J. *physician, educator*
Rosen, Steven Terry *oncologist, hematologist*
Rosenfield, Robert Lee *pediatric endocrinologist, educator*
Rotman, Carlotta H. *physician*
Rowley, Janet Davison *physician*
Sabbagha, Rudy Elias *obstetrician, gynecologist, educator*
Sachs, Greg Alan *preventive medicine physician*
Sandler, Richard H. *pediatric gastroenterologist*
Sandlow, Leslie Jordan *gastroenterologist, educator*
Scarse, Olivia Marie *cardiologist, consultant*
Schade, Stanley Greinert, Jr. *hematologist, educator*
Schafer, Michael Frederick *orthopedic surgeon*
Schilsky, Richard Lewis *oncologist, researcher*
Schuler, James Joseph *vascular surgeon*
Sciarra, John J. *obstetrician, gynecologist, educator*
Scommegna, Antonio *obstetrician, gynecologist, educator*
Seeler, Ruth Andrea *pediatrician, educator*
Serota, Scott *medical association administrator*
Shields, Thomas William *surgeon, educator*
Short, Marion Priscilla *neurogenetics educator*
Siegler, Mark *internist, educator*
Smith, David Waldo Edward *pathology and gerontology educator, physician*
Socol, Michael Lee *obstetrician, gynecologist, educator*
Song, David *plastic surgeon, medical educator*
Southgate, Marie Therese *physician, editor*
Sparberg, Marshall Stuart *gastroenterologist, educator*
Steinhorn, Robin H. *neonatologist, educator*
Strassner, Howard Taft, Jr. *obstetrician, educator*
Taraszkiewicz, Waldemar *physician*
Telfer, Margaret Clare *internist, hematologist, oncologist*
Tomar, Russell Herman *pathologist, educator, researcher*
Toriumi, Dean Michael *facial, plastic and reconstructive surgeon, educator*
Umbdenstock, Richard J. *medical association administrator*
Walton, Robert Lee *plastic surgeon*
Waxler, Beverly Jean *anesthesiologist, physician*
Webster, James Randolph, Jr. *physician*
Weichselbaum, Ralph R. *oncologist, department chairman*
Weis, Mervyn J. *physician, gastroenterologist*
Whitington, Peter Frank *pediatric hepatologist, educator*
Williamson, Wayne C. *internist, geriatrician*
Winter, Jane *medical educator*

Decatur
Requarth, William Henry *surgeon*

Deerfield
Faulkner, Larry R. *medical association administrator, former dean, educator, researcher, writer*
Sanner, John Harper *retired pharmacologist*

Downers Grove
Bastian, Robert W. *otolaryngologist*
Richardson, Brent Earl *otolaryngologist*

Elmhurst
Blain, Charlotte Marie *internist, educator*

Evanston
Bloomer, William David *radiologist, oncologist, educator*
Crawford, James Weldon *psychiatrist, educator, administrator*
Kentor, Paul Martin *allergist*
Khandekar, Janardan Dinkar *oncologist, educator*
Mustoe, Thomas Anthony *physician, plastic surgeon*
Nelson, Richard Lawrence, Jr. *surgeon, educator*
Peterson, Lance Robert *physician*
Sprang, Milton LeRoy *obstetrician, gynecologist, educator*
Stumpf, David Allen *pediatric neurologist*
Traisman, Howard Sevin *retired pediatrician*
Vick, Nicholas A. *neurologist*
Weiss, Kevin Barton *epidemiologist, medical association administrator*

Galesburg
Tourlentes, Thomas Theodore *retired psychiatrist*

Glen Ellyn
Agruss, Neil Stuart *cardiologist*
Dieter, Raymond Andrew, Jr. *physician, thoracic and vascular surgeon*

Godfrey
King, Ordie Herbert, Jr. *oral pathologist*

Highland Park
Kaplan, Mark E. *allergist*

Hillsboro
Mulch, Robert F., Jr. *physician*

Hines
Best, William Robert *internist, educator, dean*

Hinsdale
Brueschke, Erich Edward *physician, researcher, educator*

Joliet
Layman, Dale Pierre *retired medical educator, researcher, writer*
Ring, Alvin Manuel *pathologist, educator*

Lake Barrington
Morris, Ralph William *chronopharmacologist*

Lake Forest
Levy, Nelson Louis *immunologist, educator, surgeon*
Wilbur, Richard Sloan *medical association administrator, physician*

Lombard
Henkin, Robert Elliott *nuclear medicine physician*
Kasprow, Barbara Anne *biomedical researcher, writer*

Long Grove
Ausman, Robert K. *surgeon, research and development company executive*

Maywood
Albain, Kathy S. *oncologist*
Biller, Jose *neurologist, educator*
Canning, John Rafton *urologist*
Gamelli, Richard Louis *surgeon, educator*
Gianopoulos, John George *obstetrician*
Light, Terry Richard *orthopedic hand surgeon*
Moran, John Francis *cardiologist*
Nand, Sucha *medical educator*
Pickleman, Jack R. *surgeon*
Stiff, Patrick Joseph *internist, hematologist, oncologist, educator*

Melrose Park
Klein, Lloyd William *cardiologist, researcher*

Naperville
Bufalino, Vincent John *cardiologist, medical administrator*
Folk, Frank Anton *surgeon, educator*
Ozog, Diane L. *allergist*
Pollak, Raymond *general and transplant surgeon*

North Chicago
Barsano, Charles Paul *medical educator, dean*
Freese, Uwe Ernest *physician, educator*
Gall, Eric Papineau *internist, educator*
Hawkins, Richard Albert *medical educator, administrator*
Nair, Velayudhan *pharmacologist, educator, academic administrator*
Schneider, Arthur Sanford *medical educator*
Sierles, Frederick Stephen *psychiatrist, educator*
Taylor, Michael Alan *psychiatrist*
Wiesner, Dallas Charles *immunologist, researcher*

Northbrook
Cucco, Ulisse P. *retired obstetrician, gynecologist*

Oak Brook
Fritzsche, Peggy J. *medical association administrator, radiologist*
Rathi, Manohar Lal *pediatrician, neonatologist*

Peoria
Meriden, Terry *physician*
Miller, Rick Frey *emergency physician*

River Grove
Hillert, Gloria Bonnin *anatomist, educator*

Rock Island
Bradley, Walter James *emergency physician*

Rockford
Frakes, James Terry *gastroenterologist, educator*

Skokie
Horwitz, Irwin Daniel *otolaryngologist, educator*

Springfield
Frank, Stuart *cardiologist*
Holland, John Madison *retired family practice physician*
Myers, Phillip Ward *otolaryngologist*
Rabinovich, Sergio *physician, educator*
Sumner, David Spurgeon *surgeon, educator*
Woodson, Gayle Ellen *otolaryngologist*
Yaffe, Stuart Allen *physician*
Zook, Elvin Glenn *plastic surgeon, educator*

Urbana
Krock, Curtis Josselyn *pulmonologist*
Nelson, Ralph Alfred *physician*
O'Morchoe, Charles Christopher Creagh *anatomist, surgeon, educator*
Voss, Edward William, Jr. *immunologist, educator*

Washington
Stine, Robert Howard *retired pediatrician, allergist*

Wilmette
Hier, Daniel Barnet *neurologist*

Winfield
Loughead, Jeffrey Lee *physician*

Winnetka
Rubnitz, Myron Ethan *pathologist, educator*

INDIANA

Alexandria
Irwin, Gerald Port *physician*

Anderson
King, Charles Ross *physician*

Bedford
Hunter, Harlen Charles *orthopedic surgeon*

Bloomington
Bishop, Michael D. *emergency physician*
Moore, Ward Wilfred *medical educator*
Rink, Lawrence Donald *cardiologist*

Carmel
Cohen, Marlene Lois *pharmacologist*
Wilson, Fred M., II, *ophthalmologist, educator*
Yune, Heun Yung *retired radiologist*

Chesterton
Martino, Robert Salvatore *orthopedic surgeon*

Fishers
Thomas, John Arlen *pharmacologist, educator, science administrator*

Fort Wayne
Lee, Shuishih Sage *pathologist*

Gary
Iatridis, Panayotis George *medical educator*
Zunich, Janice *pediatrician, geneticist, educator, health facility administrator*

Indianapolis
Allen, Stephen D(ean) *pathologist, microbiologist*
Aprison, Morris Herman *retired experimental and theoretical neurobiology educator*
Bergstein, Jerry Michael *nephrologist*
Besch, Henry Roland, Jr. *pharmacologist, educator*
Brandt, Ira Kive *pediatrician, geneticist*
Broadie, Thomas Allen *surgeon, educator*
Brown, Edwin Wilson, Jr. *preventive medicine physician, educator*
Broxmeyer, Hal Edward *medical educator*
Coleman, John Joseph III *surgery educator*
Daly, Walter Joseph *medical educator*
Dyken, Mark Lewis, Jr. *neurologist, educator*
Eigen, Howard *pediatrician, educator*
Einhorn, Lawrence Henry *oncologist, medical educator*
Ghetti, Bernardino Francesco *neuropathologist, educator*
Grosfeld, Jay Lazar *surgeon, educator*
Hansell, Richard Stanley *obstetrician, gynecologist, educator*
Helveston, Eugene McGillis *pediatric ophthalmologist, educator*
Holden, Robert Watson *radiologist, educator, dean*
Inui, Thomas Spencer *physician, educator*
Irwin, Glenn Ward, Jr. *medical educator, physician, academic administrator*
Jackson, Valerie Pascuzzi *radiologist, educator*
Johnston, Cyrus Conrad, Jr. *medical educator*
Justice, Brady Richmond, Jr. *medical services executive*
Knoebel, Suzanne Buckner *cardiologist, educator*
Lemberger, Louis *pharmacologist*
Lumeng, Lawrence *physician, educator*
Madura, James Anthony *surgeon, educator*
Miyamoto, Richard Takashi *otolaryngologist*
Norins, Arthur Leonard *dermatologist, educator*
Nurnberger, John I., Jr. *psychiatrist, educator*
Rex, Douglas Kevin *gastroenterologist, educator*
Richter, Judith Anne *pharmacologist, educator*
Rogers, Robert Ernest *medical educator*
Ross, Edward *cardiologist*
Roth, Lawrence Max *pathologist, educator*
Sherman, Stuart *internist, gastroenterologist*
Smith, James Warren *pathologist, educator, microbiologist, parasitologist*
Stehman, Frederick Bates *obstetrician, gynecologist, educator*
Sutton, Gregory Paul *obstetrician, gynecologist*
Watanabe, August Masaru *physician, educator, retired pharmaceutical executive*
Weber, George *oncology and pharmacology educator, researcher*
Weinberger, Myron Hilmar *medical educator*
Yee, Robert Donald *ophthalmologist*
Zipes, Douglas Peter *cardiologist, researcher*

Lafayette
Langston, Edward Lee *physician, pharmacist*

Logansport
Brewer, Robert Allen *physician*

Marion
Fisher, Pierre James, Jr. *physician*

Walton
Chu, Johnson Chin Sheng *retired physician*

West Lafayette
Borch, Richard Frederic *pharmacology and chemistry educator*
Borowitz, Joseph Leo *pharmacologist, educator*
Cramer, William Anthony *biochemistry and biophysics researcher, educator*
Johns, Janet Susan *physician*
Nichols, David Earl *pharmacy educator, researcher, consultant*
Rutledge, Charles Ozwin *pharmacologist, educator*
Tacker, Willis Arnold, Jr. *medical educator, researcher*

IOWA

Burlington
Paragas, Rolando G. *physician*

Cedar Rapids
Krivit, Jeffrey Scot *surgeon*
Norris, Albert Stanley *psychiatrist, educator*

Davenport
Edgerton, Winfield Dow *retired gynecologist*

Des Moines
Ely, Lawrence Orlo *retired surgeon*
Olds, John Ward *internist*

Iowa City
Abboud, Francois Mitry *physician, educator*
Afifi, Adel Kassim *physician*
Andreasen, Nancy Coover *psychiatrist, educator, neuroscientist*
Banker, Gilbert Stephen *industrial and physical pharmacy educator, academic administrator*
Buckwalter, Joseph Addison *orthopedic surgeon, educator*
Burns, C(harles) Patrick *hematologist, oncologist*
Clifton, James Albert *physician, educator*
Cooper, Reginald Rudyard *orthopedic surgeon, educator*
Eckstein, John William *internist, educator, retired dean*
Fellows, Robert Ellis *medical educator, researcher*
Galask, Rudolph Peter *obstetrician, gynecologist*
Gantz, Bruce Jay *otolaryngologist, educator*
Grose, Charles Frederick *pediatrician, epidemiologist*
Hammond, Harold Logan *oral and maxillofacial pathologist, retired educator*
Heistad, Donald Dean *cardiologist*
Hussey, David Holbert *physician*
Kerber, Richard E. *cardiologist*
Lamping, Kathryn G. *medical educator, medical researcher*
Lauer, Ronald Martin *pediatric cardiologist, researcher*
LeBlond, Richard Foard *internist, educator*
Lynch, Richard Gregory *medical educator*
Mason, Edward Eaton *surgeon*
Medh, Jheem D. *medical educator, biochemist, researcher*
Merchant, James A. *medical educator*
Morriss, Frank Howard, Jr. *pediatrics educator*
Nelson, Herbert Leroy *psychiatrist*
Niebyl, Jennifer Robinson *obstetrician, gynecologist, educator*
Noyes, Russell, Jr. *psychiatrist*
Ponseti, Ignacio Vives *orthopaedic surgery educator*
Richerson, Hal Bates *internist, allergist, immunologist, educator*
Robinson, Robert George *psychiatry educator*
Snyder, Peter M. *medical educator, medical researcher*
Strauss, John Steinert *dermatologist, educator*
Tephly, Thomas Robert *pharmacologist, educator, toxicologist*
Thompson, Herbert Stanley *neuro-ophthalmologist*
Tsalikian, Eva *physician, educator*
Van Gilder, John Corley *neurosurgeon, educator*
Weinberger, Miles M. *pediatrician, educator*
Weiner, George Jay *internist*
Weingeist, Thomas Alan *ophthalmology educator*
Weinstock, Joel Vincent *immunologist*
Weintraub, Neal L. *medical educator, cardiologist*
Welsh, Michael James *medical educator, biophysicist, educator*
Williams, Richard Dwayne *physician, educator, urologist*
Ziegler, Ekhard Erich *pediatrics educator*

Orange City
Vander Aarde, Stanley Bernard *retired otolaryngologist*

KANSAS

Coffeyville
Hawley, Raymond Glen *pathologist*

Kansas City
Anderson, Harrison Clarke *pathologist, educator, biomedical researcher*
Arakawa, Kasumi *physician, educator*
Damjanov, Ivan *pathologist, educator*
Dunn, Marvin Irvin *physician*
Godfrey, William Ashley *ophthalmologist*
Grantham, Jared James *nephrologist, educator*
Hudson, Robert Paul *medical educator*
Johnson, Joy Ann *diagnostic radiologist*
Lawrence, Walter Thomas *plastic surgeon*
McCallum, Richard Warwick *medical researcher, clinician, educator*
Mohn, Melvin Paul *anatomist, educator*
Schloerb, Paul Richard *surgeon, educator*
Suzuki, Tsuneo *molecular immunologist*
Voogt, James Leonard *medical educator*
Ziegler, Dewey Kiper *neurologist, educator*

Lenexa
Kagan, Stuart Michael *pediatrician*

Manhattan
Oehme, Frederick Wolfgang *medical researcher, educator*

Olathe
Monzon, Carlos Manuel *physician*

Shawnee Mission
Bell, Deloris Wiley *physician*
Fleming, Michael O. *physician*
Henley, Douglas E. *medical association administrator*

Topeka
Johnson, Patsy *nursing association administrator*
Menninger, William Walter *psychiatrist*

Wichita
Guthrie, Richard Alan *physician*
Oxley, Dwight K(ahala) *pathologist*

KENTUCKY

Lexington
Moser, Debra Kay *medical educator*

MARYLAND

Baltimore
Wahl, Richard Leo *radiologist, educator, nuclear medicine physician, researcher*

MASSACHUSETTS

Worcester
Menon, Mani *urological surgeon, educator*

MICHIGAN

Ann Arbor
Abrams, Gerald David *pathologist, educator*
Albers, James Wilson *neurologist*
Alderman, Amy Kathleen *plastic surgeon, educator*
Ansbacher, Rudi *physician*
Bacon, George Edgar *pediatrician*
Baker, Laurence Howard *oncology educator*
Bates, Eric Randolph *physician*
Bloom, Jane Maginnis *emergency physician*
Bodmer, Rolf A. *medical educator*
Bole, Giles G. *physician, researcher, medical educator*
Burdi, Alphonse Rocco *anatomist*
Cameron, Oliver Gene *psychiatrist, educator, psychobiology researcher*
Carlson, Bruce Martin *anatomist*
Casey, Kenneth Lyman *neurologist*
Coran, Arnold Gerald *pediatrician, surgeon*
Craig, Clifford Lindley *orthopaedic pediatric surgery educator*
Davis, Wayne Kay *medical educator*
De La Iglesia, Felix Alberto *pathologist, toxicologist*
Donabedian, Avedis *physician, educator*
Fajans, Stefan Stanislaus *retired internist*
Fekety, Robert *physician, educator*
Fox, David Alan *rheumatologist, immunologist*
Frueh, Bartley Richard *surgeon*
Galea, Sandro *epidemiologist*
Gelehrter, Thomas David *medical educator, geneticist*
Gilman, Sid *neurologist*
Goldstein, Steven Alan *medical and engineering educator*
Greden, John Francis *psychiatrist, educator*
Greenfield, Lazar John *surgeon, educator*
Halter, Jeffrey Brian *internal medicine educator, geriatrician*
Hiss, Roland Graham *retired internist, educator*
Hogikyan, Norman Dertad *otolaryngologist*
Hollenberg, Paul Frederick *pharmacology educator*
Horowitz, Samuel Boris *biomedical researcher, educational consultant*
Hu, Howard *occupational medicine physician, educator*
Julius, Stevo *internist, physiologist, educator*
Kaplan, George A. *medical educator*
Kuhl, David Edmund *nuclear medicine physician, educator*
Kunkel, Steven *pathologist, educator*
Lee, Marie Catherine *medical educator*
Lichter, Allen S. *oncologist, educator, dean*
Lichter, Paul Richard *ophthalmology educator*
Lopatin, Dennis Edward *immunologist, educator*
Lozoff, Betsy *pediatrician, educator*
Margolis, Philip Marcus *psychiatrist, educator*
Markel, Howard *physician, educator*
Martel, William *radiologist, educator*
Maxwell, Donald Robert *pharmacologist*
Midgley, A(lvin) Rees, Jr. *reproductive endocrinology educator, researcher*
Miller, Josef M. *otolaryngologist, educator*
Monto, Arnold Simon *epidemiology educator*
Morgenstern, Lewis B. *medical educator*
Owyang, Chung *gastroenterologist, researcher*
Pitt, Bertram *cardiologist, educator, consultant*
Platt, Jeffrey Louis *experimental surgeon, immunologist, pediatric nephrologist, educator*
Powsner, Edward Raphael *physician*
Quint, Douglas Joseph *neuroradiology educator*
Reddy, Venkat Narsimha *ophthalmologist, researcher*
Rosenthal, Amnon *pediatric cardiologist*
Schottenfeld, David *retired epidemiologist, educator*
Schteingart, David Eduardo *internist*
Strang, Ruth Hancock *pediatrician, educator, cardiologist, priest*
Stross, Jeoffrey Knight *internist, educator*
Thompson, Norman Winslow *surgeon, educator*
Todd, Robert Franklin III *oncologist, educator*
Voorhees, John James *dermatologist, department chairman*
Ward, Peter Allan *pathologist, educator*
Weg, John Gerard *physician*
Weiss, Stephen J. *medical educator, researcher, oncologist*
Wiggins, Roger C. *internist, educator, researcher*

Bloomfield Hills
Ball, Patricia Ann *physician*
Mathog, Robert Henry *otolaryngologist, educator*

Dearborn
Fordyce, James George *physician*

Detroit
Abramson, Hanley Norman *pharmacy educator*
Amirikia, Hassan *obstetrician, gynecologist*
Bock, Brooks Frederick *emergency physician*
Cohen, Sanford Ned *pediatrician, educator, academic administrator*
Davis, Ronald Mark *preventive medicine physician*
Fromm, David *surgeon*
Hashimoto, Ken *dermatologist, educator*
Jampel, Robert Steven *ophthalmologist, educator*
Kantrowitz, Adrian *surgeon, educator*
Kaplan, Joseph *pediatrician*
Kelley, Mark Albert *physician, educator, health products executive*
Lim, Henry Wan-Peng *dermatologist*
Lisak, Robert Philip *neurologist, researcher, educator*
Lupulescu, Aurel Peter *medical educator, researcher, physician*
Lusher, Jeanne Marie *pediatric hematologist, educator*
Maiese, Kenneth *neurologist, neuroscientist*
Miller, Orlando Jack *obstetrician, gynecologist, educator, geneticist*
Nathanson, Saul David *oncologist, surgeon, educator*
Prasad, Ananda Shiva *medical educator*
Silverman, Norman Alan *cardiac surgeon*
Smith, Wilbur Lazar *radiologist, educator*
Sokol, Robert James *obstetrician, gynecologist, educator*
Weaver, W(ayne) Douglas *cardiologist, researcher, medical educator*
Whitehouse, Fred Waite *endocrinologist, researcher*
Wiener, Joseph *pathologist, educator*

East Lansing
Beckmeyer, Henry Ernest *anesthesiologist, pain management specialist, educator*
Brody, Howard *medical educator*
Gottschalk, Alexander *radiologist, educator*
Moore, Kenneth Edwin *pharmacology educator*
Potchen, E. James *radiology educator*
Ristow, George Edward *neurologist, educator*
Rosenman, Kenneth D. *medical educator*
Watson, Ralph Edward *internist, educator*

Farmington Hills
Blum, Jon H. *dermatologist*
Luby, Elliot Donald *psychiatrist, educator*

Fife Lake
Knecht, Richard Arden *family practitioner*

Flint
Jayabalan, Vemblaserry *nuclear medicine physician, radiologist*

Frankenmuth
Shetlar, James Francis *physician*

Grand Blanc
Wasfie, Tarik Jawad *surgeon, educator*

Grand Rapids
Hammond, Dennis Clyde *plastic surgeon, educator*
Swanson, Alfred Bertil *orthopaedic and hand surgeon, educator*
Wilt, Jeffrey Lynn *pulmonary and critical care physician, educator*

Kalamazoo
Toledo-Pereyra, Luis Horacio *transplant surgeon, researcher, historian educator*

Lansing
Vincent, Frederick Michael, Sr. *neurologist, educator*

Marine City
Brown, Ronald Delano *endocrinologist*

Northport
Schultz, Richard Carlton *plastic surgeon*

Oak Park
Kaplan, Randy Kaye *podiatrist*

Rochester Hills
Badalament, Robert Anthony *urologist, oncologist*

Royal Oak
Dworkin, Howard Jerry *retired nuclear medicine physician, educator*
LaBan, Myron Miles *physician, hospital administrator*
Ryan, Jack *physician, retired hospital corporation executive*

Saginaw
Ferlinz, Jack *cardiologist, educator*

Traverse City
Tobin, Patrick John *dermatologist*

Troy
Schafer, Sharon Marie *anesthesiologist*

West Bloomfield
Sawyer, Howard Jerome *physician*
Sobel, Howard Bernard *osteopath, educator*

MINNESOTA

Burnsville
Lakin, James Dennis *allergist, immunologist, director*

Duluth
Aufderheide, Arthur Carl *pathologist*
Eisenberg, Richard Martin *pharmacology educator*

Edina
Tagatz, George Elmo *retired obstetrician, gynecologist, educator*

Minneapolis
Aamoth, Gordon M. *medical association administrator*
Bache, Robert James *physician, educator*
Blackburn, Henry Webster, Jr. *retired epidemiologist*
Brown, David Mitchell *pediatrician, educator, dean*
Buchwald, Henry *surgeon, educator, researcher*
Charnas, Lawrence *neurologist*
Chavers, Blanche Marie *pediatrician, educator, researcher*
Craig, James Lynn *physician, health services administrator*
Dykstra, Dennis Dale *physiatrist*
Fisch, Robert Otto *medical educator*
Haines, Stephen John *neurosurgeon*
Hanson, Arthur Stuart *physician, consultant*
Harper, Patricia Nelsen *psychiatrist*
Hays, Thomas S. *medical educator, researcher*
Ingbar, David H. *physician, researcher*
Joseph, Marilyn Susan *gynecologist*
Kaplan, Manuel E. *physician, educator*
Keane, William Francis *nephrology educator, research foundation executive*
Leon, Arthur Sol *research cardiologist, exercise physiologist*
Loh, Horace H. *pharmacology educator*
Luepker, Russell Vincent *epidemiology educator*
Mandel, Sheldon Lloyd *dermatologist, educator*
Mazze, Roger Steven *medical educator, researcher*
Moller, James Herman *pediatrician, educator*
Najarian, John Sarkis *surgeon, educator*
Palahniuk, Richard John *anesthesiology educator, researcher*
Phibbs, Clifford Matthew *surgeon, educator*
Powell, Deborah Elizabeth *pathologist, dean*
Quie, Paul Gerhardt *pediatrician, educator*
Rothenberger, David Albert *surgeon*
Sabath, Leon David *internist, educator*
Thompson, Roby Calvin, Jr. *orthopedic surgeon, educator, department chairman*
Thompson, Theodore Robert *pediatric educator*
Toscano, James Vincent *medical foundation president*
Wild, John Julian *surgeon, researcher, medical educator*

Olivia
Cosgriff, James Arthur *physician*

Pequot Lakes
Weaver, Arthur Lawrence *rheumatologist, consultant*

Rochester
Bartholomew, Lloyd Gibson *physician*
Bowie, E(dward) J(ohn) Walter *hematologist, researcher*
Brimijoin, William Stephen *pharmacologist, neuroscientist, educator, researcher*
Brown, Arnold Lanehart, Jr. *pathologist, educator, dean*
Cofield, Robert Hahn *orthopedic surgeon, educator*
Danielson, Gordon Kenneth, Jr. *cardiovascular surgeon, educator*
Dickson, Edgar Rolland *gastroenterologist*
Douglass, Bruce E. *physician*
Engel, Andrew George *neurologist*
Feldt, Robert Hewitt *pediatric cardiologist, educator*
Fye, W. Bruce III *cardiologist*
Gibbons, Raymond John *cardiologist*
Gracey, Douglas Robert *internist, educator, pulmonologist, physiologist*
Hauser, Stephen Crane *gastroenterologist*
Knopman, David S. *neurologist*
Kyle, Robert Arthur *medical educator, oncologist*
LaRusso, Nicholas F. *gastroenterologist, educator, scientist*
Lofgren, Karl Adolph *retired surgeon, educator*
Lucas, Alexander Ralph *child psychiatrist, educator, writer*
Mackenzie, Ronald Alexander *anesthesiologist*
Malkasian, George Durand, Jr. *obstetrician, educator*
Mulder, Donald William *physician, educator*
Neel, Harry Bryan III *surgeon, scientist, educator*
Pairolero, Peter Charles *surgeon, educator*
Perry, Harold Otto *dermatologist*
Phillips, Sidney Frederick *gastroenterologist, educator*
Piepgras, David G. *neurosurgeon, educator*
Pittelkow, Mark Robert *physician, dermatologist, educator, researcher*
Prakash, Udaya B.S. *internist, educator*
Pulido, Jose S. *physician*
Rogers, Roy Steele III *dermatologist, educator, dean*
Rosenow, Edward Carl III *medical educator*
Siekert, Robert George *retired neurologist, educator*
Stegall, Mark D. *surgeon, medical educator*
Symmonds, Richard Earl *gynecologist*
Tarvestad, Anthony M. *psychiatrist*
Varkey, Prathibha *preventive medicine physician, medical educator*
Whisnant, Jack Page *neurologist*
Wood, Michael Bruce *orthopaedic surgeon, researcher, educator*
Woods, John Elmer *plastic surgeon*

Saint Paul
Burton, Charles Victor *neurosurgeon*
Edwards, Jesse Efrem *pathologist, educator*
Michael, Alfred Frederick, Jr. *physician, medical educator*
Rydell, Catherine M. *medical association administrator, former state legislator*
Swaiman, Kenneth Fred *pediatric neurologist, educator*
Titus, Jack L. *pathologist, educator*
Zander, Janet Adele *psychiatrist*

Stillwater
Asch, Susan McClellan *pediatrician*

Virginia
Knabe, George William, Jr. *pathologist, educator*

MISSOURI

Cape Girardeau
Sacha, Robert Frank *osteopath, educator*

Columbia
Colwill, Jack Marshall *physician, educator*
Cunningham, Milamari Antoinella *retired anesthesiologist*
Eggers, George William Nordholtz, Jr. *anesthesiologist, educator*
Hardin, Christopher Demarest *medical educator*
Hillman, Richard Ephraim *pediatrician, educator*
James, Elizabeth Joan Plogsted *pediatrician, educator*
König, Peter *pediatrician, educator*
Nolph, Georgia Bower *physician*
Perkoff, Gerald Thomas *physician, educator*
Perry, Michael Clinton *internist, academic administrator, educator*
Stephenson, Hugh Edward, Jr. *retired surgeon*
Tarnove, Lorraine *medical association executive*
Winship, Daniel Holcomb *medical educator, dean*

Kansas City
Abdou, Nabih I. *physician, educator*
Ardinger, Robert Hall, Jr. *physician, educator*
Butler, Merlin Gene *physician, medical geneticist, educator*
Dimond, Edmunds Grey *medical educator*
Hagan, John Charles III *ophthalmologist*
Long, Edwin Tutt *surgeon*
McGregor, Douglas Hugh *pathologist, educator*
McPhee, Mark Steven *gastroenterologist, educator*
Molteni, Agostino *pathology educator*
Piepho, Robert Walter *pharmacy educator, researcher*
Poston, Walker Seward, II, *medical educator, researcher*
Salomone, Joseph Anthony III *emergency medicine physician*

Maryland Heights
Miller, Steven *medical administrator*

Pilot Knob
deCastro, Fernando Jose *pediatrics educator*

Saint Louis
Alpers, David Hershel *gastroenterologist, educator*
Bacon, Bruce Raymond *physician*
Berland, David I. *psychiatrist, educator*
Brodeur, Armand Edward *pediatric radiologist*
Case-Schmidt, Mary E. *pathologist, educator*

Chaplin, David Dunbar *medical research specialist, educator*
Chaplin, Hugh, Jr. *preventive medicine physician, educator*
Chole, Richard Arthur *otolaryngologist, department chairman*
Cloninger, Claude Robert *psychiatrist, epidemiologist, educator, researcher*
Cryer, Philip Eugene *endocrinologist*
Dewald, Paul Adolph *psychiatrist, educator*
DiPersio, John F. *oncologist*
Dodge, Philip Rogers *neurologist, educator*
Dougherty, Charles Hamilton *pediatrician*
Eberlein, Timothy J. *surgeon*
Fitch, Coy Dean *internist, educator*
Flye, M. Wayne *surgeon, immunologist, educator, writer*
Fredrickson, John Murray *otolaryngologist*
Friedman, William Hersh *otolaryngologist, educator*
Gay, William Arthur, Jr. *thoracic surgeon*
Gelberman, Richard H. *orthopedist, surgeon*
Goldberg, Anne Carol *physician, educator*
Gordon, Jeffrey Ivan *gastroenterologist, educator, molecular biologist, researcher*
Grossberg, George Thomas *psychiatrist, educator*
Grubb, Robert L., Jr. *neurosurgeon*
Hammerman, Marc Randall *nephrologist, educator*
Holmes, Nancy Elizabeth *pediatrician*
Holtzman, David Michael *neurologist*
Hyers, Thomas Morgan *internist, biomedical researcher*
Johnson, Eugene M. *neurologist, molecular biologist, pharmacologist, educator*
Johnson, Robert Graham *surgeon, educator, researcher*
Kaminski, Donald Leon *surgeon, gastroenterologist, educator*
Kelly, Daniel P. *cardiologist, molecular biologist*
Kipnis, David Morris *physician, educator*
Klahr, Saulo *nephrologist, educator*
Knutsen, Alan Paul *pediatrician, immunologist, allergist*
Kolker, Allan Erwin *ophthalmologist*
Kornfeld, Stuart A. *hematology educator*
Kouchoukos, Nicholas Thomas *surgeon*
Landau, William Milton *neurologist, department chairman*
Ludmerer, Kenneth Marc *medical educator*
Majerus, Philip Warren *physician*
Manske, Paul Robert *orthopedic hand surgeon, educator*
Martin, Kevin John *nephrologist, educator*
Middelkamp, John Neal *pediatrician, educator*
Morley, John Edward *physician*
Myerson, Robert J. *radiologist, educator*
Owens, William Don *anesthesiology educator*
Peck, William Arno *internist, educator, dean, academic administrator*
Perez, Carlos A. *radiation oncologist, educator*
Prensky, Arthur Lawrence *pediatric neurologist, educator*
Purkerson, Mabel Louise *physician, physiologist, educator*
Rao, Dabeeru C. (D.C. Rao) *epidemiologist, educator*
Reh, Thomas Edward *radiologist, educator*
Robins, Lee Nelken *medical educator*
Royal, Henry Duval *nuclear medicine physician, educator, director*
Ryall, Jo-Ellyn M. *psychiatrist*
Schonfeld, Gustav *medical educator, researcher, administrator*
Schreiber, James Ralph *obstetrician, researcher*
Schwartz, Alan Leigh *pediatrician, educator*
Shapiro, Larry J. *pediatrician, scientist, dean, educator*
Siegel, Barry Alan *radiologist*
Slatopolsky, Eduardo *nephrologist, educator*
Slavin, Raymond Granam *allergist, immunologist*
Smith, Morton Edward *ophthalmology educator, dean*
Spector, Gershon Jerry *otolaryngologist, educator, researcher*
States, David Johnson *biomedical scientist, physician*
Strunk, Robert Charles *physician*
Sweet, Stuart C. *pediatrician*
Teitelbaum, Steven Lazarus *pathology educator*
Ternberg, Jessie Lamoin *pediatric surgeon, educator*
Thach, William Thomas, Jr. *neurologist, educator*
Ulett, George Andrew *psychiatrist*
Unanue, Emil Raphael *immunopathologist*
Walentik, Corinne Anne *pediatrician*
Wells, Samuel Alonzo, Jr. *surgeon, educator*
Whyte, Michael P. *genetics educator, researcher, director*
Wickline, Samuel Alan *cardiologist, educator*
Willman, Vallee Louis *physician, surgery educator*
Young, Paul Andrew *anatomist*

Springfield
Hackett, Earl Randolph *neurologist*

Town And Country
Levin, Marvin Edgar *physician*

MONTANA

Billings
Knapp, Howard Raymond *internist, clinical pharmacologist*

NEBRASKA

Hastings
Pankratz, Todd Alan *obstetrician, gynecologist*

Lincoln
Wilson, Charles Stephen *cardiologist, educator*

Omaha
Armitage, James O. *medical educator*
Benson, John Alexander, Jr. *internist, educator*
Casale, Thomas Bruce *medical educator*
Ferlic, Randolph *medical educator*
Fusaro, Ramon Michael *dermatologist, preventive medicine physician, researcher*
Godfrey, Maurice *biomedical scientist*
Hodgson, Paul Edmund *surgeon, department chairman*
Imray, Thomas John *radiologist, educator*
Kessinger, Margaret Anne *medical educator*
Klassen, Lynell W. *rheumatologist, transplant immunologist*
Lynch, Henry Thomson *medical educator*
Maurer, Harold Maurice *pediatrician*
Mohiuddin, Syed Maqdoom *cardiologist, educator*
Nairn, Roderick *immunologist, educator, biochemist*
O'Brien, Richard L(ee) *physician, educator, academic administrator*
Quigley, Herbert Joseph, Jr. *pathologist, educator*
Rogan, Eleanor Groeniger *oncologist, educator*
Tinker, John Heath *anesthesiologist, educator*
Waggener, Ronald Edgar *radiologist*
Zardetto-Smith, Andrea *medical educator*

Papillion
Dvorak, Allen Dale *radiologist*

NEVADA

Las Vegas
Goodenberger, Daniel Marvin *medical educator*
Noback, Richardson Kilbourne *medical educator*

NEW JERSEY

Hackensack
Gardin, Julius Markus *cardiologist, educator*

NEW MEXICO

Santa Fe
Schiller, William Richard *surgeon*

NORTH CAROLINA

Durham
James, Sherman Athonia *epidemiologist, educator*
Silver, Donald *surgeon, educator*

NORTH DAKOTA

Fargo
Mitchell, James Edward *physician, educator*

Grand Forks
Sobus, Kerstin MaryLouise *physician, physical therapist*
Wakefield, Mary Katherine *medical association administrator, medical educator*

Williston
Adducci, Joseph Edward *obstetrician, gynecologist*

OHIO

Akron
Emmett, John Colin *retired inventor, consultant*
Evans, Douglas McCullough *surgeon, educator*
Milsted, Amy *biomedical educator*

Aurora
Allen, Marc Kevin *emergency physician, educator*

Beachwood
Katzman, Richard A. *cardiologist, internist, consultant*
Moskowitz, Roland Wallace *internist*

Bexley
Yashon, David *neurosurgeon, educator*

Bratenahl
Jones, Trevor Owen *biomedical industry executive, management consultant*

Bryan
Carrico, Virgil Norman *physician*

Canton
Howland, Willard J. *radiologist, educator*
Kellermeyer, Robert William *physician, educator*
Rubin, Patricia *internist*

Cincinnati
Adolph, Robert J. *medical educator*
Alexander, James Wesley *surgeon, educator*
Balistreri, William Francis *pediatric gastroenterologist*
Bellet, Paul Sanders *pediatrician, educator*
Boat, Thomas Frederick *pediatrician, pulmonologist, researcher, educator*
Boyd, Deborah Ann *pediatrician*
Bridenbaugh, Phillip Owen *anesthesiologist*
Buncher, Charles Ralph *epidemiologist, educator, biostatistician*
Coberly, LeAnn *internist*
Cole, Theodore John *osteopathic and naturopathic physician*
Creaghead, Nancy A. *medical association administrator*
de Courten-Myers, Gabrielle Marguerite *retired neuropathologist*
DeWitt, Thomas *pediatrician, educator*
Finkelman, Fred D. *medical educator*
Gelfand, Michael Joseph *radiologist, educator*
Griffith, John Francis *pediatrician, administrator, educator*
Heimlich, Henry J. *physician, surgeon, educator*
Hess, Evelyn Victorine *medical educator*
Holland, Edward J. *ophthalmologist, surgeon*
Hutton, John James *medical researcher, educator, retired dean*
Kleindorfer, Dawn Olson *medical educator, neurologist*
Loggie, Jennifer Mary Hildreth *retired physician, educator*
Lucky, Anne Weissman *dermatologist*
Nasrallah, Henry Ata *psychiatry researcher, educator*
Neale, Henry Whitehead *plastic surgery educator*
Rapoport, Robert Morton *medical educator*
Rashkin, Mitchell Carl *internist, pulmonary medicine specialist*
Sarembock, Ian Joseph *internist, cardiologist*
Schreiner, Albert William *internist, educator*
West, Clark Darwin *pediatric nephrologist, educator*
Wiot, Jerome Francis *radiologist*
Wood, Robert Emerson *pediatrics educator*
Woodle, Erwin Steve *transplant surgeon*

Cleveland
Awais, George Musa *obstetrician, gynecologist*
Berger, Melvin *allergist, immunologist*
Berger, Nathan Allen *medical educator, academic administrator*
Bronson, David Leigh *physician, educator*
Cascorbi, Helmut Freimund *anesthesiologist, educator*
Castele, Theodore John *radiologist*
Cole, Monroe *neurologist, educator*
Daroff, Robert Barry *neurologist, educator*
Davis, Pamela Bowes *pediatric pulmonologist*
Doershuk, Carl Frederick *physician, educator*
Eiben, Robert Michael *pediatric neurologist, educator*
Ellis, Lloyd H., Jr. *emergency physician, art historian*
Elston, Robert C. *medical educator*
Fazio, Victor Warren *physician, colon and rectal surgeon*
Geho, Walter Blair *biomedical research executive*
Holzbach, Raymond Thomas *gastroenterologist, educator, writer*
Iannotti, Joseph Patrick *orthopedic surgeon*
Jackson, Edgar B., Jr. *medical educator*
Kass, Lawrence *hematologist, oncologist, educator*
Lamm, Michael Emanuel *pathologist, immunologist, educator*
Lefferts, William Geoffrey *internist, educator*
Lenkoski, Leo Douglas *retired psychiatrist, educator*
Lowe, John Burton *medical association administrator, molecular biologist, educator, pathologist*
Malangoni, Mark Alan *surgeon, educator*
McCrae, Keith R. *medical educator, researcher*
McHenry, Martin Christopher *physician, educator*
Montague, Drogo K. *urologist*
Moravec, Christine D. Schomis *medical educator*
Neuhauser, Duncan vonBriesen *medical educator*
Nissen, Steven E. *cardiologist, researcher*
Novick, Andrew Carl *urologist*
Olness, Karen Norma *medical educator*
Pretlow, Thomas Garrett *physician, pathology educator, researcher*
Rehm, Susan *physician*
Shuck, Jerry Mark *surgeon, educator*
Stange, Kurt C. *medical educator*
Stavitsky, Abram Benjamin *immunologist, educator*
Walters, Mark Douglas *obstetrician, gynecologist, director*
Webster, Leslie Tillotson, Jr. *pharmacologist, educator*
Wolfman, Alan *medical educator, researcher*
Young, Jess Ray *retired internist*

Columbus
Balcerzak, Stanley Paul *retired hematologist, oncologist, director, medical educator*
Barth, Rolf Frederick *pathologist, educator*
Berntson, Gary Glen *psychiatry, psychology and pediatrics educator*
Billings, Charles Edgar *physician*
Bloomfield, Clara Derber *oncologist, educator, medical institute administrator*
Bowman, Louis L. *emergency physician*
Bullock, Joseph Daniel *pediatrician, educator*
Capen, Charles Chabert *veterinary pathology educator*
Christoforidis, A. John *radiologist, educator*
Cramblett, Henry Gaylord *pediatrician, virologist, educator*
Ellison, Edwin Christopher *surgeon, educator*
Fass, Robert J. *epidemiologist, academic administrator*
Ferguson, Ronald Morris *surgeon, educator*
Goldschmidt, Pascal Joseph *medical educator, cardiologist*
Huheey, Marilyn Jane *ophthalmologist, educator*
Kakos, Gerard Stephen *thoracic and cardiovascular surgeon*
Laufman, Leslie Rodgers *hematologist, oncologist*
Leier, Carl Victor *internist, cardiologist*
Lewis, Richard Phelps *cardiologist, educator*
Long, Sarah Elizabeth Brackney *physician*
Morrow, Grant III *medical research director, pediatrician*
Mueller, Charles Frederick *radiologist, educator*
Needham, Glen Ray *entomology and acarology educator, researcher*
Newton, William Allen, Jr. *pediatrician, pathologist*
Ruberg, Robert Lionel *surgery educator*
Rund, Douglas Andrew *emergency physician*
Sayers, Martin Peter *pediatric neurosurgeon*
Sommer, Annemarie *pediatrician*
Stoner, Gary David *cancer researcher*
Vogel, Thomas Timothy *surgeon, educator, lay worker*

Dayton
Abromowitz, Herman I. *family physician, occupational medicine physician*
Dunn, Margaret M. *general surgeon, educator, university official*
Heller, Abraham *psychiatrist, educator*
Mohler, Stanley Ross *preventive medicine physician, educator*
Monk, Susan Marie *pediatrician, educator*
Nanagas, Maria Teresita Cruz *pediatrician, educator*
Ruegsegger, Donald Ray, Jr. *radiological physicist, educator*
Weinberg, Sylvan Lee *cardiologist, educator, editor, writer*
Wilson, William Campbell McFarland *gastroenterologist*

Fairfield
Chin, Nee Oo Wong *reproductive endocrinologist*

Gahanna
Robbins, Darryl Andrew *pediatrician*

Galena
Berggren, Ronald Bernard *surgeon, retired educator*

Grove City
Kilman, James William *surgeon, educator*

Hilliard
Skillman, Thomas Grant *endocrinology consultant, former educator*

Kettering
Mantil, Joseph Chacko *nuclear medicine physician, researcher*

Lyndhurst
Guyuron, Bahman *plastic surgeon, educator*

Madison
Stafford, Arthur Charles *medical association administrator*

Mason
Beary, John Francis III *rheumatologist, pharmaceutical executive, medical researcher*
Nordlund, James John *dermatologist*

North Canton
Di Simone, Robert Nicholas *radiologist, educator*

Norwalk
Gutowicz, Matthew Francis, Jr. *radiologist*

Parma
Lazo, John, Jr. *physician*

Rootstown
Brodell, Robert Thomas *internal medicine educator*
Campbell, Colin *obstetrician, gynecologist, dean*
Nora, Lois Margaret *neurologist, educator, academic administrator, dean*

South Euclid
Macklin, Martin Rodbell *psychiatrist*

Sylvania
Burkhart, Craig Garrett *dermatologist, researcher*

Toledo
Comerota, Anthony James *vascular surgeon, biomedical researcher*
Howard, John Malone *surgeon, educator*
Jacobs, Lloyd A. *vascular surgeon*
Knotts, Frank Barry *physician, surgeon*
Mulrow, Patrick Joseph *medical educator*
Shelley, Walter Brown *dermatologist, educator*
Talmage, Lance Allen *obstetrician, gynecologist, military officer*

Westerville
St. Pierre, Ronald Leslie *public health and medical educator, academic administrator*

Wooster
Kuffner, George Henry *dermatologist, educator*

PENNSYLVANIA

Newtown Square
Cordes, Eugene Harold *retired pharmacy and chemistry educator*

Philadelphia
Davis, Glenn Craig *psychiatrist*
Lewis, Frank Russell, Jr. *surgeon*

Upper Saint Clair
Raymond, Bruce Allen *retired surgeon, medical association administrator*

SOUTH DAKOTA

Sioux Falls
Fenton, Lawrence Jules *medical educator*
Jaqua, Richard Allen *pathologist*
Morse, Peter Hodges *ophthalmologist, educator*
Zawada, Edward Thaddeus, Jr. *physician, educator*

TENNESSEE

Memphis
Waller, Robert Rex *ophthalmologist, educator, foundation administrator*

TEXAS

Houston
Batsakis, John George *pathology educator*
Gabbard, Glen Owens *psychiatrist, psychotherapist*

VIRGINIA

Alexandria
Wilhide, Stephen D. *medical association administrator*

Norfolk
Hood, Antoinette Foote *dermatologist*

WASHINGTON

Port Orchard
Thoman, Mark Edward *pediatrician*

WISCONSIN

Appleton
Boren, Clark Henry, Jr. *general and vascular surgeon*

Baileys Harbor
Schultz, Richard Otto *ophthalmologist, educator*

Eagle River
Agre, James Courtland *physiatrist*

Fond Du Lac
Treffert, Darold Allen *psychiatrist, writer, hospital administrator*

Hales Corners
Kuwayama, S. Paul *physician, immunologist, allergist*

Janesville
Gianitsos, Anestis Nicholas *surgeon*

La Crosse
Newcomer, Kermit Lee *retired internist, kidney specialist*
Webster, Stephen Burtis *dermatologist, educator*

Madison
Albert, Daniel Myron *ophthalmologist, educator*
Bass, Paul *retired medical educator*
Boutwell, Roswell Knight *oncology educator*

Brooks, Benjamin Rix *neurologist, educator*
Burgess, Richard Ray *oncologist, molecular biologist, biotechnologist, educator, researcher, consultant*
Connors, Kenneth Antonio *retired pharmacy educator*
DeMets, David L. *medical educator, biomedical researcher*
Dodson, Vernon Nathan *preventive medicine physician, educator*
Fahien, Leonard August *physician, educator*
Farrell, Philip M. *physician, dean, educator, researcher*
Ford, Charles Nathaniel *otolaryngologist, educator*
Graziano, Frank Michael *medical educator, researcher*
Hetsko, Cyril Michael *internist*
Jefferson, James Walter *psychiatrist, educator*
Johnson, Maryl Rae *cardiologist*
Laessig, Ronald Harold *preventive medicine and pathology educator, state official*
Leavitt, Lewis A. *pediatrician, educator*
Lemanske, Robert F., Jr. *allergist, immunologist*
MacKinney, Archie Allen *physician*
Maki, Dennis G. *epidemiology educator*
Malter, James Samuel *pathologist, educator*
Nordby, Eugene Jorgen *orthopedic surgeon*
Peters, Henry Augustus *neurologist*
Pickhardt, Perry J. *radiology educator, researcher*
Pitot, Henry Clement III *pathologist, educator*
Reynolds, Ernest West *retired internist, educator*
Robins, H(enry) Ian *medical oncologist*
Schutta, Henry Szczesny *neurologist, educator*
Sondel, Paul Mark *pediatric oncologist, educator*
Valdivia, Hector Horacio *medical educator*
Walker, Duard Lee *medical educator*
Wenger, Ronald David *surgeon*
Westman, Jack Conrad *child psychiatrist, educator*
Whiffen, James Douglass *surgeon, educator*
Wilson, Pamela Aird *physician*

Manitowoc
Trader, Joseph Edgar *orthopedic surgeon*

Mequon
Terry, Leon Cass *neurologist, educator*

Milton
Enlow, Donald Hugh *retired anatomist, dean*

Milwaukee
Fink, Jordan Norman *allergist, educator*
Foldy, Seth Leonard *physician, educator*
Kochar, Mahendr Singh *physician, health facility administrator, research scientist, educator, writer, consultant*
Larson, David Lee *surgeon*
Montgomery, Robert Renwick *medical association administrator, educator*
Olinger, Gordon Nordell *surgeon*
Soergel, Konrad Hermann *physician*
Stokes, Kathleen Sarah *dermatologist, educator*
Towne, Jonathan Baker *vascular surgeon*
Yancey, Kim Bruce *dermatology researcher*
Youker, James Edward *radiologist*

Nashotah
Hollister, Winston Ned *pathologist*

Racine
Stewart, Richard Donald *internist, educator, writer*

CANADA

BRITISH COLUMBIA

Parksville
Weir, Bryce Keith Alexander *neurosurgeon, neurologist, educator*

MANITOBA

Winnipeg
Friesen, Henry George *endocrinologist, educator*
Haworth, James Chilton *pediatrics educator*

ADDRESS UNPUBLISHED

Ackerman, John Henry *health services consultant, physician*
Adamson, John William *hematologist*
Adler, Solomon Stanley *internist, hematologist, oncologist*
Anderson, Dyke A. *former medical association administrator*
Applebaum, Edward Leon *otolaryngologist, educator*
Bahl, Tracy L. *healthcare executive*
Bar, Robert S. *endocrinologist, educator*
Baron, Jeffrey *retired pharmacologist*
Bashook, Philip G. *medical association executive, educator*
Beckett, Victoria Ling *physician*
Bernstein, Jay *pathologist, researcher, educator*
Bonaventura, Leo Mark *gynecologist, educator*
Borden, Ernest Carleton *oncologist, educator*
Boudreau, Robert James *nuclear medicine physician, researcher*
Bubrick, Melvin Phillip *surgeon*
Caston, J(esse) Douglas *retired medical educator*
Dubin, Howard Victor *dermatologist*
Eaton, Merrill Thomas *psychiatrist, educator*
Erkonen, William Edward *radiologist, medical educator*
Esterly, Nancy Burton *retired physician*
Feldman, Eva Lucille *neurology educator*
Fenoglio-Preiser, Cecilia Mettler *retired pathologist, educator*
Fitch, Frank Wesley *pathologist, immunologist, dean, educator*
Fletcher, James Warren *physician*
Gajl-Peczalska, Kazimiera J. *retired surgical pathologist, immunopathologist, educator*
Geha, Alexander Salim *cardiothoracic surgeon, educator*
Gilchrist, Gerald Seymour *pediatric hematologist, oncologist, educator*
Goldmann, Morton Aaron *cardiologist, educator*
Green, David *hematologist*
Green, Morris *retired pediatrician, educator*
Gullickson, Glenn, Jr. *physician, educator*
Hand, Roger *physician, educator*
H'Doubler, Francis Todd, Jr. *surgeon*
Heidelberger, Kathleen Patricia *physician*
Higginbotham, Edith Arleane *radiologist, researcher*
Himes, John Harter *medical researcher, educator*
Hirsch, Lawrence Leonard *physician, retired educator*
Howell, Joel DuBose *internist, educator*
Jacobs, Danny O. *surgeon, medical educator*
Janicak, Philip Gregory *psychiatrist, educator*
Jensen, Erik Hugo *pharmaceutical quality control consultant*
Jones, Edward *retired pathologist*
Judge, Nancy Elizabeth *obstetrician, gynecologist*
Kabara, Jon Joseph *biochemical pharmacology educator*
Kaye, Gordon Israel *pathologist, anatomist, educator*
Kisker, Carl Thomas *pediatrician, educator*
Kohrman, Arthur Fisher *pediatrics educator*
Lagunoff, David *pathologist, educator*
Levitt, Seymour Herbert *radiologist, educator*
Mahoney, Mary C. *radiologist, educator*
Mair, Douglas Dean *pediatrician, educator, consultant*
Manning, John Warren III *retired surgeon, medical educator*
Marcdante, Karen Jean *medical educator*
Mathewson, John Jacob *emergency and family practice physician*
Matzke, Jay *internist*
Maves, Michael Donald *medical association executive*
McCoy, Frederick John *retired plastic surgeon*
McKinney, William T. *psychiatrist, educator*
Mead, Beverley Tupper *physician, educator*
Meerschaert, Joseph Richard *retired physician*
Meyer, Paul Reims, Jr. *orthopedic surgeon*
Moore, Emily Allyn *pharmacologist*
Mullan, John Francis (Sean Mullan) *neurosurgeon, educator*
Murray, Raymond Harold *physician*
Nelson, Virginia Simson *pediatrician, educator, physiatrist*
O'Leary, Dennis Sophian *accrediting body executive*
Osborn, Gerald Guy *dean, psychiatrist, educator*
Palmer, Raymond Alfred *administrator, librarian, consultant*
Pearson, Paul Hammond *physician*
Penkava, Robert Ray *radiologist, educator*
Perez, Dianne M. *medical researcher*
Perlmutter, David H. *physician, educator*
Perry, Burton Lars *retired pediatrician*
Peters, William P. *oncologist, science administrator, dean, educator*
Peterson, Ann Sullivan *physician, consultant*
Pflum, Barbara Ann *retired allergist*
Pujana, Maria Jose *neurologist*
Ragland, Terry Eugene *emergency physician*
Raichle, Marcus Edward *radiology and neurology educator*
Reid, Orien *former medical association administrator*
Rodriguez, Manuel Alvarez *pathologist*
Rollins, Arlen Jeffery *osteopathic physician*
Ruoho, Arnold Eino *pharmacology educator*
St. Cyr, John Albert, II, *cardiovascular surgeon, thoracic surgeon*
Sanders, Joe Maxwell, Jr. *pediatrician*
Sato, Paul Hisashi *pharmacologist*
Scheiber, Stephen Carl *psychiatrist*
Schulman, Sidney *neurologist, educator*
Schwartz, Judy Ellen *thoracic surgeon*
Scott, Bruce A. *otolaryngologist*
Shayman, James Alan *nephrologist, educator*
Small, Joyce Graham *psychiatrist, educator*
Sobkowicz, Hanna Maria *retired neurologist*
Speicher, Carl Eugene *pathologist*
Stoneman, William III *plastic surgeon, educator*
Stueland, Dean Theodore *emergency physician*
Swerdlow, Martin Abraham *pathologist, educator*
Tandon, Rajiv *psychiatrist, educator*
Tardy, Medney Eugene, Jr. *retired otolaryngologist, facial plastic surgeon*
Thorsen, Marie Kristin *radiologist, educator*
Tolia, Vasundhara K. *pediatric gastroenterologist, educator*
Trujillo, Angelina *endocrinologist*
Walenga, Jeanine Marie *medical educator, researcher*
Wallace, Robert B. *medical educator*
Watne, Alvin L. *retired surgeon, educator*
Westmoreland, Barbara Fenn *neurologist, educator*
Yamada, Tadataka *internist*

HUMANITIES: LIBERAL STUDIES

UNITED STATES

CALIFORNIA

Stanford
Saller, Richard Paul *classics educator*

GEORGIA

Atlanta
Gilman, Sander Lawrence *liberal arts and sciences professor, historian, writer*

ILLINOIS

Bloomington
Bridges, Roger Dean *historian*

Carbondale
Ammon, Harry *history professor*
Dettmar, Kevin John Hoffmann *literature and language professor*
Fladeland, Betty *historian, educator*

Champaign
Antonsen, Elmer Harold *Germanic languages and linguistics educator*
Douglas, George Halsey *language educator, writer*
O'Neill, John Joseph *speech educator*
Smith, Ralph Alexander *cultural and educational policy educator*
Watts, Emily Stipes *retired English language educator*

Chicago
Aronson, Howard Isaac *linguist, educator*
Bevington, David Martin *English literature educator*
Biggs, Robert Dale *Near Eastern studies educator*
Boyer, John William *history professor, dean*
Brinkman, John Anthony *historian, educator*
Bruegmann, Robert *architectural historian, educator*
Chakrabarty, Dipesh *history professor*
Cohen, Charles Emil *art historian, educator*
Cohen, Ted *philosopher, educator*
Cullen, Charles Thomas *historian, librarian*
Debus, Allen George *historian, educator*
Dembowski, Peter Florian *foreign language educator*
Erlebacher, Albert *historian, educator*
Fleischer, Cornell Hugh *history educator*
Geyer, Michael *history professor*
Goldsmith, John Anton *linguist, educator*
Gray, Hanna Holborn *historian, educator*
Haley, George *Romance languages educator*
Harris, Neil *historian, educator*
Hast, Adele *historian, editor, writer*
Haugeland, John *philosophy educator*
Headrick, Daniel Richard *history and social sciences educator*
Hellie, Richard *historian, educator*
Johnson, Janet Helen *literature educator*
Keenan, James George *classics educator*
Lawler, James Ronald *French language educator*
Lieb, Michael *English educator, humanities educator*
Manning, Sylvia *language educator*
Najita, Tetsuo *history professor*
Nussbaum, Martha Craven *philosophy and classics educator*
Pollock, Sheldon Ivan *language educator*
Roy, David Tod *literature educator*
Sewell, William Hamilton, Jr. *historian*
Shaughnessy, Edward Louis *language educator*
Sochen, June *history professor*
Thaden, Edward Carl *history professor*

Elgin
Parks, Patrick *English language educator, humanities educator*

Evanston
Belting, Hans *art historian, educator, writer*
McCurry, Stephanie *historian, educator*
Pierrehumbert, Janet Breckenridge *language educator*
Sheridan, James Edward *history professor*
Sundquist, Eric John *American studies educator*
Van Zanten, David Theodore *humanities educator*
Weil, Irwin *literature and language professor*
Weil, Irwin *language educator*
Wills, Garry *historian*
Wright, John *classics educator*

Homewood
Schillings, Denny Lynn *retired history professor, educational and grants consultant*

Macomb
Hallwas, John Edward *retired English language educator*

Palatine
Hull, Elizabeth Anne *retired English language educator*

Park Ridge
O'Connell, Laurence J. *bioethics research administrator*

River Forest
Jackson, William Vernon *Latin American studies and library science educator*

Springfield
Davis, George Cullom *historian*
Temple, Wayne Calhoun *historian, writer*

Urbana
Arnstein, Walter Leonard *retired historian*
Haile, H. G. *German language and literature educator*
Hoxie, Frederick Eugene *history professor*
Jacobson, Howard *classics educator*
Kim, Chin-Woo *linguist, educator*
Koenker, Diane P. *history professor*
Love, Joseph LeRoy *history professor, former cultural studies center administrator*
McColley, Robert McNair *historian, educator*
Newman, John Kevin *classics educator*
Scanlan, Richard Thomas *classics educator*
Schacht, Richard Lawrence *philosopher, educator*
Solberg, Winton Udell *historian, educator*
Spence, Mary Lee *historian, educator*
Talbot, Emile Joseph *French language educator*

INDIANA

Bloomington
Anderson, Judith Helena *English language educator*
Dunn, Jon Michael *logician, dean emeritus, consultant*
Gros Louis, Kenneth Richard Russell *humanities educator*
Johnson, Owen Verne *historian, educator*
Juergens, George Ivar *history professor*
Lebano, Edoardo Antonio *foreign language educator*
Martins, Heitor Miranda *foreign language educator*
Mickel, Emanuel John *foreign language educator*
Peterson, M. Jeanne *historian, educator*
Ransel, David Lorimer *history professor*
Rosenberg, Samuel Nathan *French and Italian language educator*
Sinor, Denis *history professor, linguist*
Valdman, Albert *language and linguistics educator*
Wilson, George Macklin *history educator, cultural studies center administrator*
Young, Kevin *literature educator, writer*

Crawfordsville
Barnes, James John *historian, educator*

Fort Wayne
Scheetz, Sister Mary JoEllen *English language educator*

Greencastle
Dittmer, John Avery *history professor*
Weiss, Robert Orr *speech educator*

Indianapolis
Bodenhamer, David Jackson *historian, educator*
Davis, Kenneth Wayne *language educator, business communication consultant*

Notre Dame
Appleby, R(obert) Scott *history educator*
Delaney, Cornelius Francis *philosophy educator*
Doody, Margaret Anne *English language educator*
Jemielity, Thomas John *language educator*
Lanzinger, Klaus *language educator*
Marsden, George M. *history professor, writer*
Matthias, John Edward *English literature educator*
McInerny, Ralph Matthew *philosopher, educator, writer*
Noll, Mark A. *history professor*
O'Rourke, William Andrew *literature and language professor, writer*
Rosenberg, Charles Michael *art historian, educator*
Sayre, Kenneth Malcolm *philosophy educator*
Walicki, Andrzej Stanislaw *philosophy educator*

South Bend
van Inwagen, Peter Jan *philosophy educator*

Terre Haute
Baker, Ronald Lee *folklore educator*

Valparaiso
Peters, Howard Nevin *foreign language educator*

West Lafayette
Bertolet, Rodney Jay *philosophy educator*
Broden, Thomas Francis III *French language educator*
Contreni, John Joseph, Jr. *humanities educator*
Mc Bride, William Leon *philosopher, educator*
Mork, Gordon Robert *historian, educator*
Roberts, Randy W. *history professor*
Woodman, Harold David *historian, educator*

IOWA

Cedar Falls
Maier, Donna Jane-Ellen *history professor*
Schnucker, Robert Victor *historian, educator*
Sweet, Cynthia R. *historian, genealogist, historic museum director*

Grinnell
Kaiser, Daniel Hugh *historian, educator*
Kintner, Philip L. *history professor*
Michaels, Jennifer Tonks *foreign language educator*

Iowa City
Addis, Laird Clark, Jr. *philosopher, educator, musician*
Dettmer, Helena R. *classics educator*
DiPardo, Anne *English language educator*
Ertl, Wolfgang *German language and literature educator, artist*
Folsom, Lowell Edwin *language educator*
Green, Peter Morris *classics educator, writer, translator*
Hawley, Ellis Wayne *historian, educator*
Kerber, Linda Kaufman *historian, educator*
McKee, Christopher Fulton *historian, educator*
Raeburn, John Hay *language educator*
Ringen, Catherine Oleson *linguistics educator*
Scullion, Rosemarie *literature educator*

Lamoni
Wight, Darlene *retired speech professional*

Oskaloosa
Porter, David Lindsey *history and political science professor, writer*

KANSAS

Dighton
Stanley, Ellen May *historian, consultant*

Great Bend
Gunn, Mary Elizabeth *retired language educator*

Lawrence
Alexander, John Thorndike *historian, educator*
Eldredge, Charles Child III *art history educator*
Gunn, James Edwin *language educator*
Johnson, Wallace Stephen, Jr. *Asian languages educator*
Kuznesof, Elizabeth Anne *history educator*
Li, Chu-Tsing *art historian, educator*
Quinn, Dennis B. *English language and literature educator*
Saul, Norman Eugene *historian, educator*
Spires, Robert Cecil *foreign language educator*
Tuttle, William McCullough, Jr. *history professor*
Woelfel, James Warren *philosophy and humanities educator*
Worth, George John *retired English literature educator*

North Newton
Sprunger, Keith L. *historian, educator*

Olathe
Anderson, Joshua M. *speech educator*

Topeka
Powers, Ramon Sidney *historian, society administrator*

MASSACHUSETTS

Granby
Ingham, Norman William *literature educator, genealogist*

Revere
Paananen, Victor Niles *language educator*

MICHIGAN

Ann Arbor
Alexander, Buzz (William) *literature and language professor*
Blouin, Francis Xavier, Jr. *history professor*

Bornstein, George Jay *literary educator*
Cowen, Roy Chadwell, Jr. *language educator*
Curley, Edwin Munson *philosophy educator*
Delbanco, Nicholas Franklin *language educator, writer*
Dunnigan, Brian Leigh *historian, curator*
Eisenstein, Elizabeth Lewisohn *historian, educator*
Ferrell, Robert Hugh *historian, educator*
Feuerwerker, Albert *historian, educator*
Forsyth, Ilene Haering *art historian*
Hackett, Roger Fleming *historian, educator*
Knott, John Ray, Jr. *language educator*
Mersereau, John, Jr. *literature and language professor*
Mizruchi, Mark Sheldon *sociology professor, business administration professor*
Munro, Donald Jacques *philosopher, educator*
Nelson, Roy Jay *retired French educator*
Pernick, Martin Steven *history professor*
Railton, Peter Albert *philosophy educator*
Scodel, Ruth *humanities educator*
Smith, Sidonie *literature educator*
Stolz, Benjamin Armond *foreign language educator*
Trautmann, Thomas Roger *history professor, anthropology educator*

Beulah
Tanner, Helen Hornbeck *historian, consultant*

Big Rapids
Mehler, Barry Alan *humanities educator, journalist, consultant*

Dearborn
Little, Daniel Eastman *philosopher, educator, director*
Papazian, Dennis Richard *retired historian, educator, commentator*

Detroit
Brill, Lesley *literature and film studies educator*
Small, Melvin *historian, educator*

East Lansing
Fisher, Alan Washburn *historian, educator*
Mansour, George P. *Spanish language and literature educator*
Natoli, Joseph *language educator*
Silverman, Henry Jacob *history professor*

Farmington
Ellens, J(ay) Harold *philosopher, educator, psychotherapist, minister*

Grand Rapids
Hoekema, David Andrew *philosophy educator, academic administrator*
Schmidt, Gary David *language educator*

Jerome
Dillon, Merton Lynn *historian, educator*

Kalamazoo
Breisach, Ernst A. *historian, educator*
Dybek, Stuart *language educator, writer*
Julien, Catherine *history professor*

Livonia
Holtzman, Roberta Lee *French and Spanish language educator*

Portage
Jones, Leander Corbin *history professor, media specialist*

MINNESOTA

Bemidji
Weaver, Will(iam Weller) *language educator, writer*

Forest Lake
Marchese, Ronald Thomas *ancient history and archaeology educator*

Mankato
Preska, Margaret Louise Robinson *historian, educational association administrator*

Minneapolis
Bales, Kent Roslyn *language educator*
Browne, Donald Roger *speech communication educator*
Campbell, Karlyn Kohrs *speech educator*
Erickson, Gerald Meyer *classical studies educator*
Farah, Caesar Elie *language educator, historian*
Firchow, Evelyn Scherabon *German language and literature educator, writer*
Firchow, Peter Edgerly *language professional, educator, writer*
Garner, Shirley Nelson *language educator*
Kohlstedt, Sally Gregory *historian, educator*
Pazandak, Carol Hendrickson *liberal arts educator*
Ross, Donald, Jr. *language educator, academic administrator*
Scott, Robert Lee *speech educator*
Tracy, James Donald *historian, educator*
Weiss, Gerhard Hans *German language educator*

Northfield
Clark, Clifford Edward, Jr. *history professor*
Iseminger, Gary Hudson *philosophy educator*
Mason, Perry Carter *philosophy educator*
McKinsey, Elizabeth *humanities educator, consultant*
Soule, George Alan *literature educator*
Yandell, Cathy Marleen *language educator*

Saint Cloud
Hofsommer, Donovan Lowell *history professor*

Saint Paul
Stewart, James Brewer *historian, writer, college administrator*

Vadnais Heights
Polakiewicz, Leonard Anthony *foreign language and literature educator*

MISSOURI

Branson
Ford, Jean Elizabeth *retired language educator*

Columbia
Bien, Joseph Julius *philosophy educator*
Mullen, Edward John, Jr. *Spanish language educator*
Overby, Osmund Rudolf *art historian, educator*
Schwartz, Richard Brenton *English language educator, dean, writer*
Strickland, Arvarh Eunice *history professor*
Timberlake, Charles Edward *historian, educator*

Kirksville
Rose, (M.) Lynn *history professor*

Liberty
Howell, Thomas *history professor*

Saint Louis
Barmann, Lawrence Francis *historian, educator*
Krukowski, Lucian *philosopher, educator, artist*
Perry, Lewis Curtis *historian, educator*
Ruland, Richard Eugene *literature educator, critic, historian*
Schwarz, Egon *language educator, writer, critic*
Shea, Daniel Bartholomew, Jr. *literature and language professor, educator*
Ullian, Joseph Silbert *philosophy educator*
Weixlmann, Joseph Norman, Jr. *language educator, academic administrator*

NEBRASKA

Kearney
Young, Ann Elizabeth O'Quinn *historian, educator*

Lincoln
Leinieks, Valdis *classicist, educator*
Sawyer, Robert McLaran *historian, educator*

NEW MEXICO

Taos
Bolls, Imogene Lamb *English language educator, poet*

NORTH CAROLINA

Pinehurst
Nordloh, David Joseph *literature and language professor, dean*

NORTH DAKOTA

Bismarck
Newborg, Gerald Gordon *retired state archives administrator*

OHIO

Akron
Knepper, George W. *historian, educator*

Athens
Borchert, Donald Marvin *philosopher, educator*
Matthews, Jack (John Harold Matthews) *language educator, writer*
Ping, Charles Jackson *philosophy educator, retired university president*

Bowling Green
Browne, Ray Broadus *popular culture educator*

Cincinnati
Bleznick, Donald William *Romance languages educator*
Ciani, Alfred Joseph *dean*
Harmon, Patrick *historian, retired editor, commentator*
Lewis, Gene Dale *historian, educator*
Schrier, Arnold *historian, educator*

Cleveland
Anderson, David Gaskill, Jr. *Spanish language educator*
Friedman, Barton Robert *language educator*
Greppin, John Aird Coutts *philologist, editor, educator*
Salomon, Roger Blaine *retired language educator*

Columbus
Anderson, Donald Kennedy, Jr. *language educator*
Babcock, Charles Luther *classics educator*
Battersby, James Lyons, Jr. *language educator*
Beja, Morris *English literature educator*
Boh, Ivan *philosophy educator*
Boyle, Kevin Gerard *historian, educator, writer*
Brooke, John L. *history professor*
Hahm, David Edgar *classics educator*
Hare, Robert Yates *musicologist, educator*
Hoffmann, Charles Wesley *retired foreign language educator*
Jarvis, Gilbert Andrew *humanities educator, writer*
Jebsen, Harry Alfred Arthur, Jr. *history professor*
Joseph, Brian Daniel *language educator*
Kasulis, Thomas Patrick *humanities educator*
Peterson, Gale Eugene *historian*
Rule, John Corwin *history professor*
Scanlan, James Patrick *philosophy and Slavic studies educator*
Stephan, Alexander Friedrich *German language and literature educator*

Dayton
Alexander, Roberta Sue *history professor*
Harden, Oleta Elizabeth *literature educator, academic administrator*

Granville
Knobel, Dale Thomas *historian, educator, university president*
Lisska, Anthony Joseph *humanities educator, philosopher*

Kent
Beer, Barrett Lynn *historian*
Marovitz, Sanford Earl *English language and literature educator*
Reid, S.W. *language educator*

Solon
Gallo, Donald Robert *retired literature educator*

Toledo
Smith, Robert Freeman *history professor*

Wooster
Schilling, W. A. Hayden *history professor*

Yellow Springs
Fogarty, Robert Stephen *historian, educator, editor*

Youngstown
Bowers, Bege Kaye *literature and communications educator, academic administrator*

SOUTH DAKOTA

Sioux Falls
Huseboe, Arthur Robert *American literature educator*
Staggers, Kermit LeMoyne, II, *history and political science professor, state legislator, municipal official*

TEXAS

Bryan
Bryant, Keith Lynn, Jr. *history professor*

VIRGINIA

Williamsburg
Spencer, Donald Spurgeon *historian, academic administrator*

WASHINGTON

Mercer Island
Dawn, Clarence Ernest *historian, educator*

WISCONSIN

Appleton
Chaney, William Albert *retired history professor*
Goldgar, Bertrand Alvin *historian, educator*

Madison
Berg, William James *language educator, writer, translator*
Bogue, Allan George *historian, educator*
Brandt, Deborah *English educator*
Ciplijauskaite, Birute *humanities educator*
Cronon, William *history professor*
Dubrow, Heather *literature educator*
Fowler, Barbara Hughes *classics educator*
Frykenberg, Robert Eric *historian, educator*
Hamerow, Theodore Stephen *historian, educator*
Kleinhenz, Christopher *foreign language educator, researcher, director*
Knowles, Richard Alan John *language educator*
Kutler, Stanley Ira *historian, lawyer, educator*
Leavitt, Judith Walzer *history of medicine educator*
Powell, Barry Bruce *classicist, educator*
Sewell, Richard Herbert *retired historian, educator*
Sonnedecker, Glenn Allen *pharmaceutical historian, educator*
Spear, Thomas Turner *history educator*
Weinbrot, Howard David *language educator*

Middleton
O'Brien, James Aloysius *foreign language educator*

Milwaukee
Bicha, Karel Denis *historian, educator*
De Rosa, Rey Charles *history professor, dean*
Gallop, Jane (Jane Anne Gallop) *women's studies educator, writer*
Hribal, C. J. *language educator*
McCanles, Michael Frederick *retired English language educator*
Siegel, Robert Harold *English literature educator, writer*

ADDRESS UNPUBLISHED

Bateman, John Jay *classics educator*
Baym (Stillinger), Nina *literature educator, researcher, writer*
Benseler, David P. *foreign language educator*
Butchvarov, Panayot Krustev *philosophy educator*
Collins, Martha *English language educator, writer*
Cooper, John Milton, Jr. *history educator, author*
Dyson, Anne Haas *English language educator*
Eadie, John William *historian, educator*
Hunter, J(ames) Paul *literature and language professor, literary critic*
Jones, Peter d'Alroy *historian, writer, retired educator*
Kastor, Frank Sullivan *language educator*
Kramer, Dale Vernon *retired language educator*
Lifka, Mary Lauranne *history professor*
Lisio, Donald John *historian, educator*
Longsworth, Robert Morrow *language educator*
Norberg, Arthur Lawrence, Jr. *historian, physicist, educator*
Pursell, Carroll Wirth *history educator*
Reeves, Kathleen Walker *English language educator*
Schumacher, Julie Alison *literature and language professor*
Shillingsburg, Miriam Jones *literature educator, academic administrator*
van der Marck, Jan *art historian*
Wright, Josephine Rosa Beatrice *musicologist, educator*

HUMANITIES: LIBRARIES

UNITED STATES

FLORIDA

Jacksonville
Lee, Hwa-Wei *librarian, educator, consultant*

Venice
Asp, William George *librarian*

ILLINOIS

Buffalo
Coss, John Edward *retired archivist*

Carbondale
Bauner, Ruth Elizabeth *library director*
Koch, David Victor *librarian, administrator*
Koch, Loretta Peterson *librarian, educator*

Champaign
Krummel, Donald William *librarian, educator*

Chicago
Brown, Richard Holbrook *library director, historian, researcher*
Choldin, Marianna Tax *librarian, educator*
Funk, Carla Jean *library association director*
Gerdes, Neil Wayne *library director, educator*
Hanrath, Linda Carol *librarian, archivist*
Nadler, Judith *library director*
Sullivan, Peggy *librarian, consultant*
Wastawy, Sohair F. *library dean, consultant*

Deerfield
Fry, Roy H(enry) *librarian, educator*

Downers Grove
Saricks, Joyce Goering *librarian*

Evanston
Pritchard, Sarah Margaret *library director*

Joliet
Johnston, James Robert *library director*

Kaneville
Christiansen, Raymond Stephan *librarian, educator*

Lake Forest
Miller, Arthur Hawks, Jr. *librarian, archivist*

Quincy
Tyer, Travis Earl *librarian, consultant*

Skokie
Anthony, Carolyn Additon *librarian*

Springfield
Smith, Richard Norton *library director*

Urbana
Brichford, Maynard Jay *archivist*
O'Brien, Nancy Patricia *librarian, educator*
Shtohryn, Dmytro Michael *librarian, educator*
Watson, Paula D. *retired librarian*

Wheeling
Long, Sarah Ann *librarian*
Mc Clarren, Robert Royce *librarian*

Woodstock
Koehler, Jane Ellen *librarian*

INDIANA

Bloomington
Chitwood, Julius Richard *retired librarian*
Pauwels, Colleen Kristl *library director, educator*
Rudolph, Lavere Christian *library director*

Bluffton
Elliott, Barbara Jean *librarian*

Fort Wayne
Krull, Jeffrey Robert *library director*

Gary
Moran, Robert Francis, Jr. *library director*

Indianapolis
Bundy, David Dale *librarian, educator*
Ewick, Ray (Charles Ray Ewick) *librarian*
Fischler, Barbara Brand *librarian*
Gnat, Raymond Earl *librarian*
Young, Philip Howard *library director*

Lafayette
Mobley, Emily Ruth *library director, educator, dean*

Muncie
Yeamans, George Thomas *librarian, educator*

Notre Dame
Hayes, Stephen Matthew *librarian*

Richmond
Farber, Evan Ira *librarian*
Kirk, Thomas Garrett, Jr. *librarian*

West Lafayette
Nixon, Judith May *librarian*

IOWA

Cedar Rapids
Armitage, Thomas Edward *library director*

Davenport
Runge, Kay Kretschmar *library consultant*

Des Moines
Isenstein, Laura *library director*

Iowa City
Bentz, Dale Monroe *retired librarian*
Huttner, Sidney Frederick *librarian*

West Branch
Walch, Timothy George *library director*

KANSAS

Abilene
Wickman, John Edward *librarian, historian*

Lawrence
Crowe, William Joseph *librarian*

Topeka
Marvin, James Conway *librarian, consultant*

MICHIGAN

Allendale
Murray, Diane Elizabeth *librarian*

Ann Arbor
Beaubien, Anne Kathleen *librarian*
Daub, Peggy Ellen *library administrator*
Dougherty, Richard Martin *library and information science professor*

Bloomfield Hills
Papai, Beverly Daffern *retired library director*

Detroit
Mika, Joseph John *library and information scientist, educator*
Spyers-Duran, Peter *librarian, educator*
Wheeler, Maurice B. *librarian*

Harsens Island
Woodford, Arthur MacKinnon *library director, historian*

Kalamazoo
Amdursky, Saul Jack *library director*
Grotzinger, Laurel Ann *librarian, educator*

West Bloomfield
Morgan, Jane Hale *retired library director*

MINNESOTA

Minneapolis
Johnson, Donald Clay *librarian, curator*
Johnson, Margaret Ann (Peggy) *library administrator*
Shaughnessy, Thomas William *retired librarian*

Northfield
Hong, Howard Vincent *library administrator, philosophy educator, editor, translator*

Rochester
Key, Jack Dayton *librarian*

Roseville
Miller, Suzanne Marie *library director, educator*

Saint Paul
Wagner, Mary Margaret *library and information scientist, educator*
Zietlow, Ruth Ann *reference librarian*

Saint Peter
Haeuser, Michael John *library administrator*

MISSOURI

Columbia
Alexander, Martha Sue *retired librarian*
Almony, Robert Allen, Jr. *librarian*

Greenwood
Zeller, Marilynn Kay *retired librarian*

Hermann
Wilson, C. Daniel, Jr. *library director*

Independence
Ferguson, John Wayne, Sr. *librarian*
Johnson, Niel Melvin *archivist, historian*

Kansas City
Bradbury, Daniel Joseph *library administrator*
Sheldon, Ted Preston *library dean*

Saint Louis
Holt, Leslie Edmonds *librarian*

Springfield
Busch, Annie *library director*

NEBRASKA

Lincoln
Connor, Carol J. *library director*
Montag, John Joseph, II, *librarian*
Wagner, Rod *library director*

NEW HAMPSHIRE

Durham
Young, Arthur Price *librarian, educator*

NORTH CAROLINA

Winston Salem
Sutton, Lynn Sorensen *librarian*

NORTH DAKOTA

Bismarck
Ott, Doris Ann *librarian*

OHIO

Bluffton
Dudley, Durand Stowell *retired librarian*

Cincinnati
Brestel, Mary Beth *librarian*
Everson, Jean Watkins Dolores *librarian, media consultant, educator*
Proffitt, Kevin *archivist*
Schutzius, Lucy Jean *retired librarian*
Wellington, Jean Susorney *librarian*

Columbus
Black, Larry David *library director*
Brown, Rowland Chauncey Widrig *library and information scientist, consultant*
Studer, William Joseph *library director*

Dayton
Klinck, Cynthia Anne *library director*
Wallach, John S(idney) *library administrator*

Delaware
Schlichting, Catherine Fletcher Nicholson *librarian, educator*

Hubbard
Trucksis, Theresa A. *retired library director*

Middleburg Heights
Maciuszko, Kathleen Lynn *librarian, educator*

Oberlin
English, Ray *library administrator*

Toledo
Scoles, Clyde Sheldon *library director*

Wooster
Hickey, Damon Douglas *library director*

SOUTH DAKOTA

Sioux Falls
Dertien, James LeRoy *librarian*
Thompson, Ronelle Kay Hildebrandt *library director*

WISCONSIN

Bloomer
Kane, Lucile M. *retired archivist, historian*

Kenosha
Baker, Douglas Finley *library director*

Madison
Bunge, Charles Albert *library science educator*

Milwaukee
Herrera, Alberto, Jr. *librarian*
Huston, Kathleen Marie *library administrator*

Sheboygan Falls
Potter, Calvin J. *retired library director*

ADDRESS UNPUBLISHED

Abid, Ann B. *art librarian*
deBear, Richard Stephen *library planning consultant*
Estes, Elaine Rose Graham *retired librarian*
Everett, Karen Joan *retired librarian, genealogist, educator*
Ford, Barbara Jean *librarian, educator*
Jenkins, Darrell Lee *librarian*
Korenic, Lynette Marie *librarian*
Leary, Margaret A. *law library director*
Parker, Sara Ann *librarian, consultant*
Rayward, Warden Boyd *librarian, educator*
Runkle, Martin Davey *library director*
Sager, Donald Jack *librarian, consultant, retired publishing executive*
Sawyers, Elizabeth Joan *retired librarian, director*
Shedlock, James *library director, consultant*
Slavens, Thomas Paul *library science educator*
Sparks, William Sheral *retired librarian*
Zack, Daniel Gerard *library consultant*

HUMANITIES: MUSEUMS

UNITED STATES

ARIZONA

Tucson
King, James Edward *retired museum director, consultant*

CALIFORNIA

Palm Springs
Stearns, Robert Leland *curator*

COLORADO

Grand Junction
Bradley, William Steven *art museum director*

FLORIDA

Saint Petersburg
Schloder, John E. *museum director*

ILLINOIS

Bolingbrook
Madori, Jan *art gallery director*

Carbondale
Whitlock, John Joseph *museum director*

Champaign
Nevling, Lorin Ives, Jr. *museum administrator*

Chicago
Alexander, Karen *museum staff member*
Balzekas, Stanley, Jr. *museum director*
Cuno, James *museum director*
Czestochowski, Joseph Stephen *administrator, publisher, investor*
Knappenberger, Paul Henry, Jr. *science museum director*
Kubida, Judith Ann *museum administrator*
Mc Carter, John Wilbur, Jr. *museum executive*
Mosena, David R. *museum administrator*
Nordland, Gerald *museum administrator, historian, consultant*
Rabineau, Phyllis *museum administrator*
Slemmons, Rod *museum director, art educator, curator*
Smith, Elizabeth Angele Taft *curator*
Von Klan, Laurene *museum administrator*
Weisberg, Lois *arts administrator, city official*

Evanston
Lewis, Phillip Harold *museum curator*
Robertson, David Alan *museum director, educator*

Springfield
Hallmark, Donald Parker *museum director, educator*
Mc Millan, R(obert) Bruce *retired museum director, anthropologist*
Styles, Bonnie W. *museum director, archaeologist*
Wynn, Nan L. *historic site administrator*

INDIANA

Bloomington
Calinescu, Adriana Gabriela *curator, art historian*
Gealt, Adelheid Maria *museum director*

Evansville
Streetman, John William III *museum director*

Fort Wayne
Watkinson, Patricia Grieve *museum director*

Indianapolis
Waller, Aaron Bret III *museum director*

Notre Dame
Loving, Charles Roy *museum director, curator*

Terre Haute
Vollmer, David L. *museum director*

IOWA

Ames
Pohlman, Lynette *museum director, curator*

Cedar Rapids
Pitts, Terence Randolph *museum director, consultant*

Iowa City
Smothers, Ann Elizabeth *museum director*

KANSAS

Chanute
Froehlich, Conrad Gerald *museum director, researcher*

Dodge City
Clifton-Smith, Rhonda Darleen *art educator, art center administrator*

Lawrence
Hardy, Saralyn Reece *museum director*
Norris, Andrea Spaulding *art museum director*

Manhattan
Render, Lorne *museum director*

Pratt
Shrack, Christopher George *curator*

Wichita
Steiner, Charles K. *museum director, painter*

MASSACHUSETTS

Boston
Nold, Carl Richard *museum administrator*

MICHIGAN

Ann Arbor
Bailey, Reeve Maclaren *museum curator*
Steward, James *museum director, art history educator*

Dearborn
Ameri, Anan *museum director*

Detroit
Beal, Graham William John *museum director*
Darr, Alan Phipps *curator, historian*
Parrish, Maurice Drue *museum executive*
Peck, William Henry *curator, archaeologist, educator, art historian*
Terry, Robin *museum director*

East Lansing
Bandes, Susan Jane *museum director, educator*
Dewhurst, Charles Kurt *museum director, curator, language educator*

Flint
Germann, Steven James *museum director*

Kalamazoo
Norris, Richard Patrick *museum director, historian, educator*

MINNESOTA

Minneapolis
Feldman, Kaywin *museum director, curator*
King, Lyndel Irene Saunders *museum director*
Steglich, David M. *museum administrator, lawyer*

Saint Paul
Archabal, Nina M(archetti) *historic site director*

MISSOURI

Columbia
Goodrich, James William *retired historian executive*

Hannibal
Sweets, Henry Hayes III *curator*

Independence
Hackman, Larry J. *program director, consulant*

Kansas City
Cozad, Rachael Blackburn *museum director*
McKenna, George LaVerne *art museum curator*
Scott, Deborah Emont *curator*
Wilson, Marc Fraser *art museum director*

Rolla
Combs, Robert Kimbal *museum director*

Saint Joseph
Chilcote, Gary M. *museum director, reporter*
Oldman, Terry L. *museum director*

Saint Louis
Burke, James Donald *museum administrator*

Springfield
Berger, Jerry Allen *museum director*

NEBRASKA

Boys Town
Lynch, Thomas Joseph *museum director*

Lincoln
Wallis, Deborah *curator*

Omaha
Joyner, John Brooks *museum director*

NEW YORK

Hamilton
Moynihan, William J. *museum executive*

New York
Halbreich, Kathy *museum director*

NORTH DAKOTA

Fargo
Pauley, Edward E. *museum administrator*

OHIO

Akron
Kahan, Mitchell Douglas *museum director*

Cincinnati
Crew, Spencer *museum administrator*
DeWitt, Katharine Cramer *museum administrator*
Long, Phillip Clifford *retired museum director*

Cleveland
Rub, Timothy F. *museum director*
Snyder, Jill *museum director*

Dayton
Meister, Mark Jay *museum director, professional society administrator*

Mentor
Miller, Frances Suzanne *historic site curator*

Toledo
Bacigalupi, Don *museum director*

Wright Patterson AFB
Metcalf, Charles David *museum director, retired military officer*

Youngstown
Ruffer, David Gray *museum director, former college president*
Zona, Louis Albert *museum director*

OREGON

Portland
Taylor, J. Mary (Jocelyn Mary Taylor) *museum director, educator, zoologist*

PENNSYLVANIA

Philadelphia
Turner, Evan Hopkins *retired art museum director*

SOUTH DAKOTA

Lake City
Daberkow, Dave *historic site director*

TEXAS

Houston
Shearer, Linda *museum director*

VIRGINIA

Richmond
Nyerges, Alexander Lee *museum director*

WISCONSIN

Green Bay
Justen, Ralph *museum director*

Madison
Fleischman, Stephen *museum director*
Garver, Thomas Haskell *curator, consultant, writer*
Pillaert, E(dna) Elizabeth *museum director*
Westphal, Klaus Wilhelm *university museum director*

Milwaukee
Bowman, Russell *museum director*
Carter, Curtis Lloyd *museum director*
Green, Edward Anthony *museum director*
Keegan, Daniel T. *museum director*
Temmer, James Donald *museum director*

ADDRESS UNPUBLISHED

Ahrens, Kent *museum director, art historian*
Harrington, Beverly *museum director*
Hellmers, Norman Donald *retired historic site director*
Kahn, James Steven *retired museum director*
Mercuri, Joan B. *museum administrator*
Narkiewicz-Laine, Christian K. *museum director, painter, poet*
Rigaud, Edwin Joseph *museum administrator*
Steadman, David Wilton *retired museum director, deacon*
Terrassa, Jacqueline *museum director*
Wilson, Karen Lee *museum staff member, researcher*
Zukowsky, John Robert *curator, museum director*

INDUSTRY: MANUFACTURING
See also FINANCE: FINANCIAL SERVICES

UNITED STATES

ALABAMA

Foley
Dudley, Kenneth Eugene *manufacturing executive*

ARKANSAS

Springdale
Bond, Richard L. *food products executive*
Lochner, James V. *food products executive*

CALIFORNIA

Belvedere Tiburon
Thompson, Morley Punshon *textile company executive*

Fremont
Rusch, Thomas William *manufacturing executive*

Irvine
Mussallem, Michael A. *healthcare company executive*

Newport Beach
Bennett, Bruce W. *retired construction executive, civil engineer*

Rancho Santa Fe
Step, Eugene Lee *retired pharmaceutical executive*

San Francisco
Martin, Terence D. *food products executive*

Sunnyvale
Barnes, W. Michael *electronics executive*

CONNECTICUT

Waterbury
Bulriss, Mark *chemicals executive*

DISTRICT OF COLUMBIA

Washington
Cole, Kenneth W. *automotive executive*
Lorell, Beverly H. *medical products executive, consultant*

FLORIDA

Boca Grande
Hayes, Scott Birchard *retired raw materials company executive*

Cape Coral
Stuart, Robert *container manufacturing executive*

Fort Lauderdale
Dawes, Alan S. *automotive company executive*

Lake Mary
Bindley, William Edward *pharmaceutical executive*

Naples
Flaten, Alfred N. *retired food and consumer products executive*
Nugent, Daniel Eugene *agricultural products executive, director*
Salentine, Thomas James *pharmaceutical executive*
Sampson, John Eugene *food products executive, consultant*
Swanson, Donald Frederick *retired food company executive*

Palm Beach
Karman, James Anthony *manufacturing executive*
Pearlman, Jerry Kent *electronics company executive*

Venice
Lanford, Luke Dean *retired electronics company executive*

Wesley Chapel
Revelle, Donald Gene *manufacturing and health care company executive, consultant*

GEORGIA

Atlanta
Dobson, Rick *metals company executive*
Francis, Julie *beverage company executive*

Braselton
Copper, James Robert *manufacturing executive*

Duluth
Belle, Gerald *pharmaceutical executive*

Sea Island
Mc Swiney, James Wilmer *retired pulp and paper manufacturing company executive*

IDAHO

Boise
Markuson, Richard K. *former pharmaceutical association executive*
Van Helden, Pete *food products executive*

ILLINOIS

Abbott Park
Aruffo, Alejandro *pharmaceutical executive*
Brown, Thomas D. *pharmaceutical executive*
Dempsey, William G. *pharmaceutical executive*
Flynn, Gary L. *pharmaceutical executive*
Freyman, Thomas C. *pharmaceutical executive*
Gonzalez, Richard A. *pharmaceutical executive*
Lussen, John Frederick *pharmaceutical laboratory executive*
Nemmers, Joseph M., Jr. *pharmaceutical executive*
White, Miles D. *pharmaceutical executive*

Arlington Heights
Bifulco, Frank *toy company executive*
Hughes, John *chemical company executive*
Li, Norman N. *chemicals executive*

Aurora
Cano, Juventino *manufacturing company executive*

Barrington
Burrows, Brian William *retired research and development company executive*

Bedford Park
Courtney, David W. *chemical company executive*

Blue Island
Hackenast, Sherri *race track owner, former race car driver*

Champaign
Richards, Daniel Wells *manufacturing executive*

Chester
Welge, Donald Edward *food manufacturing executive*

Chicago
Adelson, Lawrence Seth *electronics executive, lawyer*
Barnes, Brenda C. *food products executive*
Bergere, Carleton Mallory *contractor*
Bernick, Howard Barry *manufacturing executive*
Brake, Cecil Clifford *retired diversified manufacturing executive*
Bryan, John Henry *food and consumer products company executive*
Burdiss, James E. *paper company executive*
Carlson, James R. *food products executive*
Conant, Howard Rosset *steel company executive*
Cooper, Charles Gilbert *cosmetics executive*
Covalt, Robert Byron *chemicals executive*
Crown, Lester *manufacturing executive*
Curran, Raymond M. *paper-based packaging company executive*
Cygan, Thomas S. *metal products executive*
Dages, Peter F. *manufacturing executive*
deKool, L.M. (Theo DeKool) *food products executive*
Delaney, James M. *metal products executive*
Ferguson, Diana S. *food products executive*
Gamoran, Reuben *candy company executive*
Gidwitz, Ronald J. *personal care products company executive*
Giesen, Richard Allyn *business executive*
Goetschel, Arthur W. *industrial manufacturing executive*
Gordon, Ellen Rubin *candy company executive*
Gordon, Melvin Jay *food products executive*
Greenfield, Roger Alan *restaurant company executive*
Haben, Mary Kay *candy company executive*
Heisley, Michael E., Sr. *manufacturing executive, professional sports team owner*
Hinrichs, Charles A. *paper company executive*
Jartz, John G. *food company executive*
Jezuit, Leslie James *manufacturing executive*
Klinger, Steven J. *paper company executive*
Koeliner, Laurette *manufacturing executive, human resources specialist*
Kopriva, Robert S. *food products executive*
Lazarus, Steven *technology company exective*
Little, William G. *manufacturing executive*
Losh, J. Michael *former automotive company executive*
Luster, Jory F. *president of manufacturing company*
McCallum, J. D. *manufacturing executive*
McKee, Keith Earl *manufacturing technology executive*
McMillan, Cary D. *food products executive*
Meysman, Frank L. *food and consumer products executive*
Miglin, Marilyn *cosmetics executive*
Mohr, Terrence B. *food company executive*
Montgomery, Gary B. *manufacturing executive*
Moore, Patrick J. *paper company executive*
Murphy, Michael Emmett *retired food company executive*
Novich, Neil S. *metals distribution company executive*
Nühn, Adriaan *food products executive*
Owen, Clarence B. *construction materials manufacturing executive*
Parrish, Overton Burgin, Jr. *pharmaceutical corporation executive*
Patel, Homi Burjor *apparel executive*
Pearson, Ford G. *manufacturing executive*
Perez, William D. (Bill Perez) *candy company executive, former sports apparel company executive*
Ptak, Frank Stanley *manufacturing executive*
Reum, W. Robert *manufacturing executive*
Rosenberg, Gary Aron *real estate development executive, lawyer*
Rubin, Stephen D. *food products executive*
Skyes, Gregory *food products executive*
Stack, Stephen S. *manufacturing executive*
Stone, Alan *container company executive*
Sykes, Gregory *food products executive*
Tryloff, Robin S. *food products executive*
Umans, Alvin Robert *manufacturing executive*
Walsh, Matthew M. *construction executive*
Waters, Ronald V. III *candy company executive*
Wellington, Robert Hall *manufacturing executive, director*
Williams, Richard Lucas III *electronics executive, director, lawyer*
Wolfert, Frederick E. (Rick Wolfert) *healthcare financial services company executive*
Wrigley, William, Jr., (Bill Wrigley Jr.) *candy company executive*

Crystal Lake
Anderson, Lyle Arthur *retired manufacturing executive*

Decatur
Bayless, Charles T. *agricultural products executive*
Kraft, Burnell D. *agricultural products company executive*
Mills, Steven R. *agricultural company executive, accountant*
Staley, Henry Mueller *manufacturing executive*
Woertz, Patricia Ann *agricultural company executive, retired oil company executive*

Deerfield
Del Salto, Carlos *pharmaceutical executive*
Parkinson, Robert L., Jr. *medical products executive, health facility administrator*
Reid-Anderson, James *diagnostic equipment company executive*

Des Plaines
Frank, James S. *automotive executive*
O'Dwyer, Mary Ann *automotive executive*
Schwarz, Steven R. *stationary company executive*

Downers Grove
Porter, Chris *food products executive*
Stevenson, Judy G. *instrument manufacturing executive*

Dundee
Villars, Horace Sumner *retired food company executive, marketing professional*

Elk Grove Village
Field, Larry *paper company executive*

Elmhurst
Duchossois, Craig J. *manufacturing executive*
Duchossois, Richard Louis *manufacturing and racetrack executive*
Fealy, Robert S. *manufacturing executive*
Garvin, Thomas Michael *food products company executive*

Frankfort
Burhoe, Brian Walter *automotive executive*

Franklin Park
Caruso, Fred *plastics manufacturing company executive*
Dean, Howard M., Jr. *food company executive*
Greisinger, James *food products executive*
Simpson, Michael *retired metals service center executive*

Freeport
Alldredge, William T. *metal products executive*
McDonough, John J. *household products company executive*

Glenview
Smith, Harold B. *manufacturing executive*
Speer, David Blakeney *chemicals executive*

Highland Park
Hulseman, Robert L. *manufacturing executive*

Hoffman Estates
Nicholas, Arthur Soterios *manufacturing executive*

Itasca
Boler, John M. *manufacturing executive*
Fellowes, James *manufacturing executive*
Garratt, Reginald George *electronics executive*

Lake Forest
Begley, Christopher B. *pharmaceutical executive*
Campbell, Andrew *manufacturing executive*
Carroll, Barry Joseph *manufacturing and real estate executive*
Dreimann, Leonhard *manufacturing executive*
Hamilton, Peter Bannerman *retired manufacturing executive, lawyer*
Haser, William H. *automotive executive*
Keyser, Richard Lee *distribution company executive*
Larson, Peter N. *manufacturing executive*
Leemputte, Peter G. *manufacturing executive*
Lenon, Richard Allen *chemical corporation executive*
Lyons, Dudley E. *manufacturing executive*
O'Mara, Thomas Patrick *manufacturing executive*
Sherrill, Gregg M. *automotive executive*
Trammell, Kenneth R. *automotive executive*

Lake Villa
Anderson, Milton Andrew *chemicals executive*

Lanark
Abbott, David Henry *manufacturing executive*

Lisle
King, J. Joseph *electronics executive*
Krehbiel, Frederick August, II, *electronics executive*

Mahomet
Bosworth, Douglas LeRoy *manufacturing executive, educator*

Melrose Park
Boswell, Gina R. *cosmetics executive*

Moline
England, Joseph Walker *heavy equipment manufacturing company executive*
Hanson, Robert Arthur *retired agricultural equipment executive*
Henderson, Donald L. *agricultural products executive, landscape company executive*
Jones, Nathan Jerome *farm machinery manufacturing company executive*
Lane, Robert W. *farm equipment manufacturing executive*

Mundelein
Mills, James Stephen *medical supply company executive*

Naperville
Rao, Prasad *electronics executive*
Smetana, Mark *food products executive*
Wake, Richard W. *food products executive*
Wake, Thomas G. *food products executive*

Niles
Herb, Marvin J. *food products executive*
Schyvinck, Christine *electronics executive*

Northbrook
Sayatovic, Wayne Peter *manufacturing executive*

Northfield
Carlin, Donald Walter *retired food products executive, consultant*
Hadley, Stanton Thomas *manufacturing executive, director, lawyer*
Lynch, Kirsten *food products executive*
McLevish, Timothy R. *food products executive*
Rosenfeld, Irene B. *food products company executive*
Stepan, Frank Quinn, Jr., (F. Quinn Stepan Jr.) *chemical company executive*

Oak Brook
Alvarez, Ralph *food products executive*
Armario, Jose M. *food products executive*
Onstead, R. Randall, Jr. *food products executive*
Skinner, James A. *food products executive*
Thompson, Don *food products executive*
Whaley, Marvin *food products executive*

Orland Park
Gittelman, Marc Jeffrey *manufacturing and financial executive*

Peoria
Burritt, David B. *manufacturing executive*
McPheeters, F. Lynn *retired manufacturing executive*
Oberhelman, Douglas R. *tractor company executive*
Owens, James W. *manufacturing executive*
Shaheen, Gerald L. *manufacturing executive*

Quincy
Cornell, Helen W. *manufacturing executive*
Roth, Philip R. *manufacturing executive*

River Forest
Douglas, Kenneth Jay *food products executive*

Rolling Meadows
Brennan, Charles Martin III *construction company executive*
Hill, David K., Jr. *construction executive*

Rosemont
Isenberg, Howard Lee *manufacturing executive*
Meinert, John Raymond *apparel executive, investment banker*
Reyes, J. Christopher *food products distribution executive*

Schaumburg
Delaney, Eugene A. *electronics executive*
Desai, Samir T. *electronics executive*
Galvin, Robert W. *electronics executive*
Morrison, Patricia B. *electronics executive*
Nemcek, Adrian R. *electronics executive*

Skokie
Mason, Earl Leonard *retired food products executive*

Trenton
Barnett, Thomas Glen *manufacturing executive*

Warrenville
Horne, John R. *farm equipment company executive*
Lannert, Robert Cornelius *manufacturing executive*
Lennes, Gregory *manufacturing and financing company executive*

Westchester
Faison, Ralph E. *communications equipment manufacturing executive*
Scott, Samuel C. *food products executive*

Westmont
Kuhn, Robert Mitchell *retired rubber company executive*

Wheeling
Rogers, Richard F. *construction company executive, architect, engineer*

Wilmette
Coughlan, Gary Patrick *pharmaceutical executive*
Egloff, Fred Robert *manufacturers representative, writer, historian*

Winnetka
Kennedy, George Danner *chemical company executive*
Markey, Maurice *food products executive*
Puth, John Wells *manufacturing executive, consultant*

INDIANA

Anderson
Snyder, Thomas J. *automotive company executive*

Batesville
Classon, Rolf Allan *pharmaceutical company executive*

Bluffton
Lawson, William Hogan III *electrical motor manufacturing executive*

Carmel
Stauder, Alfred Max *wire products company executive*

Chesterton
Brown, Gene W. *steel company executive*

Columbus
Blackwell, Jean Stuart *manufacturing executive*
Loughrey, F. Joseph *manufacturing executive*
Solso, Theodore M. *manufacturing executive*

Elkhart
Corson, Keith Daniel *manufacturing executive*
Kloska, Ronald Frank *manufacturing executive*
Ladehoff, Leo William *metal products manufacturing executive*
Martin, Rex *manufacturing executive*
Powell, Michael N. *metal products executive*
Shuey, John Henry *manufacturing executive*

Evansville
Koch, Robert Louis, II, *manufacturing company executive, mechanical engineer*
Muehlbauer, James Herman *manufacturing and distribution executive*

Fort Wayne
Burns, Thagrus Asher *manufacturing company executive, former life insurance company executive*
Busse, Keith E. *manufacturing executive*
Rifkin, Leonard *metals company executive*

Franklin
Janis, F. Timothy *technology company executive*

Goshen
Davis, Cole (Coleman Davis III) *recreational vehicle manufacturing executive*
Schrock, Harold Arthur *manufacturing executive*

Indianapolis
Andretti, Michael Mario *racing company executive, retired professional race car driver*
Atkins, Steven *construction executive, contractor*
Burks, Keith W. *pharmaceutical executive*
Connelly, Deirdre P. *pharmaceutical executive*
Doney, Bart J. *manufacturing executive*
Dunn, Steven M. *construction executive*
Foxworthy, James C. *manufacturing executive*
Goodman, Dwight *manufacturing executive*
Hunt, Robert Chester *construction company executive*
Hunt, Robert G. *construction company executive*
King, J. B. *medical device company executive, lawyer*
Lacy, Andre Balz *industrial executive*
Lechleiter, John C. *pharmaceutical executive*
Lugar, Thomas R. *manufacturing executive*
Mays, William G. *chemical company executive*
Rice, Derica W. *pharmaceutical executive*
Santini, Gino *pharmaceutical executive*
SerVaas, Beurt Richard *manufacturing executive*
Taurel, Sidney *pharmaceutical executive*

Jasper
Thyen, James C. *furniture company executive*

Lafayette
Meyer, Brud Richard *retired pharmaceutical executive*

Loogootee
Burcham, Eva Helen (Pat) *retired electronics technician*

Middlebury
Corson, Thomas Harold *retired manufacturing executive*
Guequierre, John Phillip *manufacturing executive*

Mishawaka
Merryman, George *automotive executive*
Rubenstein, Pamela Silver *manufacturing executive*

Munster
Corsiglia, Robert Joseph *retired electrical construction company executive*

Nappanee
Shea, James F. *manufacturing executive*

Plainfield
Bounsall, Phillip A. *electronics company executive*
Howell, J. Mark *electronics company executive*
Laikin, Robert J. *electronics executive*

Seymour
Rust, Lois *food company executive*

Valparaiso
McGill, James C. *manufacturing executive, director*

Warsaw
Dvorak, David C. *medical products executive, lawyer*
Noblitt, Niles L. *medical products executive*

IOWA

Ames
Abbott, David L. *agricultural products executive*

Cedar Rapids
Jones, Clayton M. *electronics company executive*

Dubuque
Crahan, Jack Bertsch *retired manufacturing executive*
Tully, Thomas Alois *building materials executive, consultant, educator*

Muscatine
Askren, Stan A. *manufacturing executive*
Howe, Stanley Merrill *manufacturing executive*

Newton
Beer, William L. *appliance company executive*
Blanford, Lawrence J. *appliance company executive*
Moore, George C. *manufacturing executive*
Ward, Lloyd D. *appliance company executive*

Okoboji
Pearson, Gerald Leon *food products executive*

Pella
Dout, Anne Jacqueline *manufacturing and sales company executive*

Saint Ansgar
Kleinworth, Edward J. *agricultural company executive*

West Des Moines
Pomerantz, Marvin Alvin *manufacturing executive*

KANSAS

Dodge City
Chaffin, Gary Roger *business executive*

Hutchinson
Dick, Harold Latham *manufacturing executive*

Leawood
Terry, Robert Brooks *food products executive, lawyer*

Lenexa
Pierson, John Theodore, Jr. *manufacturing executive*

Mission
Schmitt, Andrew B. *manufacturing executive*

Olathe
Burrell, Gary *retired manufacturing executive*
Kao, Min H. *manufacturing executive*

Scott City
Duff, Craig *agricultural products executive*

Shawnee Mission
Steer, Robert L. *food products executive*

Silver Lake
Rueck, Jon Michael *manufacturing executive*

Topeka
Etzel, Timothy *manufacturing executive*

Wichita
Eby, Martin Keller, Jr. *construction company executive*
Nienke, Steven A. *construction company executive*

MASSACHUSETTS

Natick
McConnell, William F., Jr. *medical products executive*

Waltham
Wajsgras, David C. *manufacturing executive*

Westwood
Kushner, Jeffrey L. *manufacturing executive*

MICHIGAN

Ann Arbor
Cole, David Edward *automotive executive, educator*
Decaire, John *electronics executive, aerospace engineer*
Decker, Raymond Frank *chemicals and metal products executive*
Herzig, David Jacob *retired pharmaceutical company executive, consultant*
Motawi, Karim *textiles executive*
Robertson, David Wayne *pharmaceutical executive*

Auburn Hills
Betts, Douglas D. *automotive executive*
Boag, Simon *automotive executive*
Campi, John Paul *automotive executive*
Davidson, William M. *manufacturing executive, professional sports team owner*
Farrar, Stephen Prescott *glass products manufacturing executive*
Fiedler, John F. *automotive executive*
Gerson, Ralph Joseph *manufacturing executive*
Gilles, Ralph Victor *automotive designer*
Kalina, John *auto parts company executive*
LaSorda, Tom (Thomas W. LaSorda) *automotive executive*
Manganello, Timothy M. *auto parts company executive*
Nardelli, Robert Louis *automotive executive, former consumer home products company executive*
Press, Jim (James E. Press) *automotive executive*
Sidlik, Thomas W. *automotive executive*
Unger, Susan J. *automotive executive*
Young, Walter R., Jr. *manufacturing executive*

Battle Creek
Banks, Donna Jo *food products executive*
Bryant, John A. *food products executive*
Jenness, James M. *food products executive*
Mackay, David (A.D. David Mackay) *food products executive*
Pilnick, Gary H. *food products executive, lawyer*
Shei, H. Ray *food products executive*

Belleville
Stebbins, Donald J. *car parts manufacturing company executive*

Benton Harbor
Brown, Mark E. *manufacturing executive*
Fettig, Jeff M. *manufacturing executive*

Beulah
Edwards, Wallace Winfield *retired automotive executive*

Birmingham
Sharf, Stephan *automotive executive*

Bloomfield Hills
DiFeo, Samuel X. *automotive executive*
Dugas, Richard J., Jr. *construction executive*
Pickard, William Frank *plastics company executive*
Pietrowski, Anthony *research and development company executive*
Pulte, William J. *construction executive*

Brooklyn
Vischer, Harold Harry *manufacturing executive*

Cadillac
Weigel, Raymond A. *manufacturing executive*

Cass City
Althaver, Lambert Ewing *manufacturing executive*

Dearborn
Bannister, Michael E. *automotive executive*
Brown, Thomas K. *automotive executive*
Cischke, Susan Mary *automotive executive*
Corlett, Ed *automotive executive*
Farley, James D. (Jim Farley) *automotive executive*
Fields, Mark *automotive executive*
Ford, Bill (William Clay Ford Jr.) *automotive company executive*
Ford, William Clay *automotive and professional sports team executive*
Johnston, Michael Francis *auto parts company executive*
Leclair, Don (Donat R. Leclair Jr.) *automotive executive*
Leitch, David G. *automotive executive, lawyer*
Marcin, Robert H. *automotive executive*
Mays, J. C. *automotive executive*
Parry-Jones, Richard *automotive executive*
Pestillo, Peter John *auto parts company executive, lawyer*
Rintamaki, John M. *automotive executive*
Zimmerman, Martin B. *automotive executive*

Deckerville
Smith, Wayne Arthur *export company executive*

Detroit
Barclay, Kathleen S. *automotive executive*
Cyprus, Nicholas Stanley *automotive executive, accountant*
Dauch, Richard E. *automotive executive*
Guthrie, Carlton L. *automotive manufacturing company executive*
Henderson, Fritz A. (Frederick A. Henderson) *automotive executive*
Kalman, Andrew *manufacturing executive, director*
Kantrowitz, Jean *health products executive*
Kempston Darkes, V. Maureen *automotive executive*
LaNeve, Mark R. *automotive executive*
Levy, Edward Charles, Jr. *manufacturing executive*
Lowery, Elizabeth *automotive executive*
Lutz, Robert Anthony (Bob Lutz) *automotive executive*
Middlebrook, John G. *automotive executive*
Nicholson, James M. *chemicals executive*
Rakolta, John, Jr. *construction executive*
Robinson, Joel D. *manufacturing executive*
Soave, Anthony *manufacturing executive*
Szygenda, Ralph J. *automotive executive*
Wagoner, Rick (G. Richard Wagoner Jr.) *automotive executive*
Young, Ray G. *automotive executive*

Farmington
Badawy, Aly Ahmed *automotive parts manufacturing company executive*

Ferndale
Dodd, Geralda *metal products executive*

Flint
Goodstein, Sanders Abraham *scrap iron company executive*

Fraser
Butler, James E. *automotive executive*

Grand Rapids
Baker, Hollis MacLure *furniture manufacturing company executive*
Currie, William G. *forest products executive*
Glenn, Michael B. *forest products executive*
Hackett, James P. *manufacturing executive*
Helder, Bruce Alan *metal products executive*
Keane, James P. *manufacturing executive*
Sadler, David G(ary) *manufacturing executive*
Secchia, Peter F. *forest products executive, former United States ambassador to Italy*
Woodrick, Robert *food products executive*

Grosse Pointe
Manetta, Richard L. *chemicals executive, lawyer*

Holland
Donnelly, John F. *automotive part company executive*
Haworth, Richard G. (Dick Haworth) *office furniture manufacturer*
Reed, Scott *automotive parts company executive*
Viola, Donn J. *manufacturing executive*

Houghton
Utt, Glenn S., Jr. *retired medical products executive*

Howell
Tupper, Leon F. *manufacturing executive*

Kalamazoo
Bergy, Dean H. *health products executive*
Edmondson, Keith Henry *retired chemical company executive*
MacMillan, Stephen P. *health products executive*
Markin, David Robert *motor company executive*
Wilson, James Rodney *air equipment company executive*

Lansing
Hines, Marshall *construction engineering company executive*

Livonia
Cantie, Joseph S. *automotive executive*
Drouin, Joe *automotive executive*
Plant, John Charles *automotive executive*

Madison Heights
Kafarski, Mitchell I. *chemical processing company executive*

Mason
Dart, Kenneth Bryan *manufacturing executive*
Myers, William *food container manufacturing executive*

Midland
Burns, Stephanie A. *chemicals executive*
Carbone, Anthony J. *chemicals executive*
Gross, Richard M. *chemicals executive*
Kepler, David E., II, *chemicals executive*
Kresge, Charles T. *chemicals executive*
Liveris, Andrew N. *chemical company executive*
Walthie, Theo H. *chemicals executive*

Monroe
Darrow, Kurt L. *manufacturing executive*
Kiser, Gerald L. *furniture company executive*

Muskegon
Blystone, John B. *manufacturing executive*

Northville
Clawson, Curtis J. *manufacturing executive*

Novi
Johnson, S.A. (Tony Johnson) *automotive executive*
Mallak, James A. *auto parts company executive*

Plymouth
Massey, Donald E. *automotive executive*
Navarre, Robert Ward *manufacturing executive, director*
Vlcek, Donald Joseph, Jr. *food products executive, wholesale distribution executive, writer*

Portage
Brown, John Wilford *health products executive*

Rochester
Baker, Kenneth R. *energy company executive*
Stempl, Robert C. *energy company executive*

Rochester Hills
Akeel, Hadi Abu *robotics executive*
Stempel, Robert C. *automobile manufacturing company executive*

Royal Oak
DeMaria, Mark *construction executive*

Saranac
Herbrucks, Stephen *food products executive*

Southfield
Alapont, José Maria *automotive executive*
DelGrosso, Douglas G. *manufacturing executive*
Kamsickas, James *automotive executive*
Lynch, George Michael *auto parts manufacturing executive*
Maibach, Ben C. III *construction company executive*
Rossiter, Robert E. *manufacturing executive*
Schmelzer, Wilhelm A. *manufacturing executive*
Shilts, Nancy S. *automotive executive, lawyer*
Snell, Richard A. *equipment manufacturing company executive*
Vandenberghe, James H. *manufacturing executive*

Taylor
Gardner, Lee M. *automotive parts executive*
Rosowski, Robert Bernard *manufacturing executive*

Tecumseh
Herrick, Todd W. *manufacturing executive*

Troy
Arle, John P. *electronics executive*
Barth, Volker J. *electronics executive*
Battenberg, J. T. III *automotive company executive*
Bertrand, James A. *electronics executive*
Blahnik, John G. *electronics executive*
Buschmann, Siegfried *retired manufacturing executive*
Butler, Kevin M. *electronics executive*
De La Riva, Juan L. *automotive company executive*
Eggert, Glenn J. *manufacturing executive*
Hachey, Guy C. *electronics executive*
Hirsch, Joachim V. (Jake) *aeronautics company executive*
Lorenz, Mark C. *automotive executive*
Mahone, Barbara Jean *automotive executive*
McClure, Charles G. *automotive executive*
Miller, Robert Stevens, Jr., (Steve Miller) *automotive parts company executive*
Nelson, R. David *electronics executive*
O'Neal, Rodney *automotive company executive*
Ordonez, Francisco A. (Frank) *automotive executive*
Owens, Jeffrey J. *electronics executive*
Runkle, Donald L. *electronics executive*
Serafyn, Alexander Jaroslav *retired automotive executive*
Sloan, Hugh Walter, Jr. *automotive executive*
Walker, Bette *automotive executive*
Weber, Mark R. *automotive executive*
Williams, David Perry *manufacturing executive*
Yost, Larry D. *automotive executive*

Ypsilanti
Edwards, Gerald *plastics company executive*

Zeeland
Bauer, Fred T. *technology products executive*
Jen, Enoch *electro-optical technology products executive*
LaGrand, Kenneth *technology products company executive*
Nickels, Elizabeth Anne *office furniture manufacturing executive*
Ruch, Richard Hurley *manufacturing executive*
Volkema, Michael A. *office furniture manufacturer*
Walker, Brian C. *manufacturing executive*

MINNESOTA

Austin
Brown, Eric A. *food products executive*
Fielding, Ronald *food products executive*

Hodapp, Don Joseph *food company executive*
Johnson, Joel W. *food products executive*
McCoy, Michael J. *food products company executive*
Ray, Gary J. *food products executive*

Bayport
Garofalo, Donald R. *window manufacturing executive*
Johnson, Michael O. *window manufacturing executive*

Biwabik
Anderson, Davin Charles *business representative, labor consultant*

Bloomington
Buhrmaster, Robert C. *manufacturing executive*
Wolfe, Stephen P. *manufacturing executive*

Brooklyn Park
Rogers, David *apparel executive*

Chanhassen
Palmberg, Paul W. *retired electronics executive*

Eden Prairie
Bolton, William J. *food products executive*
Henningsen, Peter, Jr. *manufacturing executive*

Fairmont
Rosen, Thomas J. *food and agricultural products executive*

Golden Valley
Hogan, Randall J. *manufacturing and electronics executive*

Hopkins
Rappaport, Gary Burton *defense equipment executive*

La Crescent
Gelatt, Charles Daniel *manufacturing executive*

Lindstrom
Messin, Marlene Ann *plastics company executive*

Loretto
Veit, Gae *construction executive*

Maple Plain
Haley, Thomas William *manufacturing executive*

Marshall
Burr, Tracy L. *food products executive*
Herrmann, Dan *food products executive*
Miller, Donald *food products executive*
Pippin, M. Lenny *food products executive*

Medina
Malone, Michael W. *manufacturing executive*
Tiller, Thomas C. *manufacturing executive*
Wendel, W. Hall, Jr. *automotive manufacturer*

Mendota Heights
Frechette, Peter Loren *dental products executive*

Minneapolis
Bader, Kathleen M. *chemicals executive*
Belton, Y. Marc *food products executive*
Bonsignore, Michael Robert *former electronics and computer company executive*
Buxton, Winslow Hurlbert *paper company executive*
Campbell, Dugald K. *automotive company executive*
Cathcart, Richard J. *technology company executive*
Collins, Arthur D., Jr. *medical products executive*
Cook, William M. *manufacturing executive*
Curler, Jeffrey H. *packaging manufacturing executive*
Dallas, H. James *medical products executive*
Demeritt, Stephen R. *food products executive*
Dimond, Robert B. *food products executive*
Durkin, G. Michael *food products executive*
Ferrari, Giannantonio *electronics executive*
Field, Benjamin R. III *packaging manufacturing executive*
Fowler, Robert Edward, Jr. *former agricultural products company executive*
George, William Wallace *former manufacturing executive*
Goldberger, Robert D. *food products company executive*
Hawkins, William A. III *medical products executive*
Hoffman, Michael J. *manufacturing executive*
Jacobs, Irwin Lawrence *diversified corporate executive*
Johnson, Dale *contractor equipment company executive*
Keiser, Kenneth E. *food products executive*
Lumpkins, Robert L. *food products executive*
Melrose, Kendrick Bascom *manufacturing executive*
Merrigan, William A. *food services company executive*
Mortenson, M. A., Jr. *construction executive*
Murphy, Daniel J., Jr. *aerospace and defense manufacturing company executive, military officer*
Page, Gregory R. *agricultural products and diversified services company executive*
Reyelts, Paul C. *chemical company executive*
Roe, John H. *manufacturing executive*
Rompala, Richard M. *chemical company executive*
Spoor, William Howard *food products executive*
Van Dyke, William Grant *manufacturing executive*
Wurtele, Christopher Angus *paint and coatings company executive*

Minnetonka
Erlandson, Patrick J. *health products executive*
Leach, Michael *financial executive*
Moore, Terry L. *financial executive*

Plymouth
Friswold, Fred Ravndal *manufacturing executive*
Kahler, Herbert Frederick *manufacturing executive*
Nagler, Lorna E. *apparel executive*
Prokopanko, James T. *agricultural products executive*

Rochester
Mayr, James Jerome *fertilizer company executive*

Saint Paul
Buckley, George W. *manufacturing executive*
Campbell, Patrick D. *manufacturing executive*
Critzer, Susan L. *health products company executive*
DeSimone, Livio Diego *retired diversified manufacturing company executive*
Ihlenfeld, Jay V. *manufacturing executive*
Johnson, John D. *energy and food products executive*
Kuhrmeyer, Carl Albert *manufacturing executive*
Landwehr, Steven J. *manufacturing executive*
Laptewicz, Joseph E., Jr. *medical products executive*
Mahan, James T. *manufacturing executive*
Nozari, Moe S. *manufacturing executive*
Palensky, Frederick J. *manufacturing executive*
Palmquist, Mark L. *energy and food products executive*
Powell, David W. *manufacturing executive*
Reich, Charles *manufacturing executive, research scientist*
Sauer, Brad T. *manufacturing executive, mechanical engineer*
Schmitz, John *energy and food products executive*
Schuman, Allan L. *chemicals executive*
Stake, James B. *manufacturing executive*
Starks, Daniel J. *medical technology and services executive*
Thulin, Inge G. *manufacturing executive*
Tucker, Raymond A. *chemical company executive*
Vierling, H. Philip *medical device company executive*
Volpi, Michele *chemicals executive*
Wiens, Harold J. *electronics executive*

Wayzata
Hoffman, Gene D. *food company executive, consultant*
Johnson, Sankey Anton *manufacturing executive*
Luthringshauser, Daniel Rene *manufacturing executive*
Sullivan, Austin Padraic, Jr. *retired diversified food company executive*

MISSOURI

Bridgeton
Vowell, J. Larry *food equipment manufacturer*

Carthage
Cornell, Harry M., Jr. *furnishings company executive*
Flanigan, Matthew C. *manufacturing executive*
Haffner, David S. *manufacturing executive*
Jett, Ernest Carroll, Jr. *paper company executive, lawyer*

Chesterfield
Carpenter, Will Dockery *chemicals executive*
Jones, Robert E. *construction executive*
Winter, William Earl *retired beverage company executive*

Clayton
Ball, Kenneth Leon *manufacturing company executive, organizational development consultant*
Buechler, Bradley Bruce *plastics company executive, accountant*
Rupp, Joseph D. *metal products executive*

Excelsior Springs
Schroeder, Horst Wilhelm *food products executive*

Grain Valley
Olsson, Björn Eskil *railroad supply company executive*

Kansas City
Bartlett, Paul Dana, Jr. *agribusiness executive*
Bass, Lee Marshall *food products company executive*
Berkley, Eugene Bertram (Bert) *envelope company executive*
Bezner, Jody *agricultural products company executive*
Campbell, Terry M. *food products executive*
Dees, Stephen Phillip *agricultural products executive, lawyer*
Hebenstreit, James Bryant *agricultural products executive, venture capitalist*
Kafoure, Michael D. *food products executive*
O'Dell, Jane *automotive company executive*
Yarick, Paul E. *food products executive*

Lebanon
Russell, Doug *manufacturing executive, political organization administrator*

Maryland Heights
Lowenberg, David A. *pharmaceutical executive*
Paz, George *health products executive*
Steward, David L. *technology company executive*
Tenholder, Edward J. *pharmaceutical executive*

Saint Louis
Adams, Albert Willie, Jr. *lubrication company executive*
Armstrong, J. Hord III *pharmaceutical company executive*
Baker, W. Randolph *brewery company executive*
Brown, JoBeth Goode *food products executive, lawyer*
Busch, August Adolphus, IV, *brewery company executive*
Clausen, Robert A. *chemicals executive*
Collins, Michael J. *medical company executive*
Crews, Terrell K. *agricultural products executive*
Dean, Warren Michael *design and construction company executive*
Dill, Charles Anthony *manufacturing and computer company executive*
Edison, Bernard Alan *retired apparel executive*
Farr, David N. *electronics executive*
Faught, Harold Franklin *retired electrical equipment manufacturing company executive*
Fox, Sam *manufacturing executive*
Fromm, Ronald A. *apparel executive*
Galvin, Walter J. *electrical equipment manufacturing executive*
Grant, Hugh *agricultural products executive*
Gupta, Surendra Kumar *chemicals executive*
Harrington, Michael Francis *paper and packaging company executive*
Harvey, David R. *chemical company executive*
Hirsch, Raymond Robert *chemicals executive, lawyer*
Holliman, W. G. (Mickey), Jr. *furniture manufacturing executive*
Hunt, Kevin J. *food products executive*
Jacob, John Edward *corporate executive, communications executive*
Kretschmer, Charles J. *electronics executive*
Kummer, Fred S. *construction company executive*
Lambright, Stephen Kirk *brewing company executive, lawyer*
Mannix, Patrick C. *manufacturing executive*
McCarthy, Michael M. *construction executive*
McCoole, Robert F. *construction company executive*
McGinnis, W. Patrick *diversified company executive*
Monroe, Thomas Edward *business and financial executive*
Moore, Dennis J. *electronics executive*
Quinn, Jeffry N. *chemicals executive, lawyer*
Reynolds, Robert A., Jr. *electric distributor executive*
Sathe, Sharad Somnath *chemical company executive*
Scherer, George F. *construction executive*
Shanahan, Michael Francis *retired manufacturing executive, former hockey team executive*
Snively, David Frederick *agricultural products company executive, lawyer*
Stokes, Patrick T. *brewery company executive*
Suter, Albert Edward *manufacturing executive*

Springfield
O'Reilly, David E. *auto parts company executive*
O'Reilly, Lawrence P. *auto parts company executive*
Wooten, Rosalie (Rosalie O'Reilly Wooten) *automotive company executive*

Washington
Stelzner, Paul Burke *textile company executive*

Wentzville
Cowger, Gary L. *automotive executive*

NEBRASKA

Elkhorn
Regan, Timothy James *grain company executive*

Lincoln
Fisher, Calvin David *food products executive*

Lindsay
Parker, Gary Dean *manufacturing executive*

Omaha
Barber, Roger L. *grain marketing company executive*
Bolding, Jay D. *food products executive*
Bragg, Russell J. *food products executive*
Chow, Joan K. *food products executive*
DiFonzo, Kenneth W. *financial officer*
Faith, Marshall E. *grain company executive*
Gerhardt, Kenneth W. *retired agricultural products executive*
Goslee, Dwight J. *agricultural products executive*
Johnson, Owen C. *food products executive*
Norton, Robert R., Jr. *former food products executive*
Pieshoski, Michael J. *construction executive*
Stinson, Kenneth E. *construction and mining company executive*
Walter, Michael D. *food products executive*

NEW HAMPSHIRE

New Castle
Baker, Robert I. *manufacturing executive*

NEW JERSEY

Camden
Reardon, Nancy Anne *food products executive*

Englewood Cliffs
Lawrence, James A. *food products executive*

Park Ridge
Frissora, Mark P. *automobile rental and leasing company executive*

NEW YORK

Melville
Duval, Daniel Webster *electronics executive*

New York
Becherer, Hans Walter *retired agricultural equipment executive*
Koch, David Hamilton *chemical company executive*

NORTH CAROLINA

Arden
Stackhouse, David William, Jr. *retired furniture systems installation contractor*

Charlotte
Thompson, Ronald L. *manufacturing executive*

Hertford
Johnson, Donald Lee *retired agricultural materials processing company executive*

Wilmington
Tomlinson, Joseph Ernest *manufacturing executive*

Winston Salem
Chaden, Lee A. *apparel and former food products executive*

OHIO

Akron
Gingo, Joseph Michael *chemicals company executive*
Kaufman, Donald Leroy *building products executive*
Keegan, Robert J. *manufacturing executive*
Kramer, Richard J. *manufacturing executive*
Tyrrell, Thomas Neil *former metal processing executive*
Wells, Norman, Jr. *metal products executive*

Athens
Werner, R(ichard) Budd *retired manufacturing executive*

Avon Lake
Kent, Deborah *automotive executive*
Patient, William F. *chemicals executive*

Canton
Birkholz, Raymond James *metal products manufacturing company executive*
Griffith, James W. *manufacturing executive*

Chagrin Falls
Brophy, Jere Hall *manufacturing executive*

Cincinnati
Aguirre, Fernando *food products executive*
Christie, James R. *technology company executive*
Coombe, V. Anderson *retired valve manufacturing company executive*
Farmer, Richard T. *uniform rental and sales executive*
Farmer, Scott D. *apparel executive*
Griffin, Mark W. *paper company executive*
Heschel, Michael Shane *retail food products executive*
Hutton, Edward Luke *retired medical products executive*
Jones, Daniel W. *construction executive*
Meyer, Daniel Joseph *machinery company executive*
Pichler, Joseph Anton *food products executive*
Schlotman, J. Michael *food products executive*
Smale, John Gray *diversified industry executive*

Cleveland
Ault, John L. *manufacturing executive, accountant*
Collins, Duane E. *manufacturing executive*
Connor, Christopher M. *manufacturing executive*
Cutler, Alexander MacDonald *manufacturing executive*
Elliott, Daniel Robert, Jr. *manufacturing executive, lawyer*
Fruchtenbaum, Edward *greeting card company executive*
Haeck, James F. *manufacturing executive*
Holmes, Arthur S. *manufacturing executive*
Hwang, Jennie S. *electronics executive, writer*
Jameson, J(ames) Larry *chemical company executive*
Jenson, Jon Eberdt *metal products executive*
Kissel, Edward W. *metal products executive*
Luke, Randall Dan *retired manufacturing executive, lawyer*
Mandel, Jack N. *manufacturing executive*
McFadden, John Volney *retired manufacturing company executive*
Moll, Curtis E. *manufacturing executive*
Pugh, David L. *manufacturing executive*
Ratner, Albert B. *building products company executive, land developer*
Reid, James Sims, Jr. *former automobile parts manufacturer*
Schulze, John B. *manufacturing executive*
Sullivan, Dennis W. *power systems company executive*
Tomsich, Robert J. *heavy machinery manufacturing executive*
Washkewicz, Donald E. *manufacturing executive*
Weiss, Erwin *greeting card company executive*
Weiss, Morry *greeting card company executive*

Columbus
Carter, William H. *chemicals executive*
Evans, Daniel E. *manufacturing executive, restaurant chain company executive*
Kohrt, Carl Fredrick *research and development company executive*
Maher, Frank Aloysius *research and development company executive*
Margolis, Jay M. *clothing executive*
McConnell, John P. *metal products executive*
Morrison, Craig O. *chemicals executive*
Pfening, Frederic Denver III *manufacturing executive*
Radkoski, Donald J. *food products company executive*
Ricart, Fred *automotive company executive*
Schottenstein, Robert H. *construction executive*
Spoerry, Robert F. *manufacturing executive*
Wexner, Abigail *apparel executive*
Yenkin, Bernard Kalman *coatings and resins company executive*

Dayton
Caspar, John M. *manufacturing executive*
Ciccarelli, John A. *manufacturing executive*
Diggs, Matthew O'Brien, Jr. *air conditioning and refrigeration manufacturing executive*
Harlan, Norman Ralph *construction executive*
Hedeen, Rodney A. *manufacturing executive*
Isaacson, Milton Stanley (Jim) *research and development company executive, engineer*
Kerley, James J. *manufacturing executive*
Mathile, Clayton Lee *pet food company executive*
Nyberg, Lars *former electronics company executive*
Perkins, Stephen J. *manufacturing executive*

Delaware
Huml, Donald Scott *manufacturing executive*

Dublin
Borror, Douglas G. *construction company executive*
Clark, R. Kerry (Kerry Clark) *health products executive*
Clement, Henry Joseph, Jr. *diversified building products executive*
Dolch, Gary D. *health products executive*
Henderson, Jeffrey W. *health products executive*
Lamp, Benson J. *tractor company executive*
Millar, James F. *pharmaceutical executive*
Walter, Robert D. *health products executive*

Elyria
Mixon, Aaron Malachi III *medical products executive*
Spitzer, Alan *automotive executive*

Findlay
Armes, Roy V. *manufacturing executive*
Stephens, D. Richard *manufacturing executive*
Weaver, Philip G. *tire company executive*

Gates Mills
Veale, Tinkham, II, *retired chemicals executive, engineer*

Greenville
Buchy, Jim *food products executive*

Hilliard
Baker, John *electronics executive*
Koehler, Jim *electronics executive*

Hudson
Reynolds, A. William *retired manufacturing company executive*

Jackson Center
Thompson, Wade Francis Bruce *manufacturing executive*

Lorain
Bado, Kenneth Steve *automotive company administrator*

Mansfield
Gorman, James Carvill *manufacturing executive*

Mason
Kohlhepp, Robert J. *apparel executive*

Maumee
Anderson, Richard Paul *agricultural company executive*
Yeager, Waldo E. *food company executive*

Mayfield Heights
Baines, Don A. *manufacturing executive*
Rankin, Alfred Marshall, Jr. *manufacturing executive*

Medina
Evans, Kenneth M. *manufacturing executive*
Morris, John H. *manufacturing executive*
Smith, Richey *manufacturing executive*
Sullivan, Frank C. *manufacturing executive*
Sullivan, Thomas Christopher *coatings company executive*

Mentor
Callsen, Christian Edward *health products executive*
Sanford, Bill R. *medical products executive*

Middletown
Wainscott, James Lawrence *steel industry executive*

Milford
Klosterman, Albert Leonard *technical development business executive, mechanical engineer*

New Albany
Jeffries, Michael S. (Mike Jeffries) *apparel executive*

New Bremen
Dicke, James Frederick, II, *manufacturing executive*

New Philadelphia
Jonker, Bruce A. *manufacturing executive*
Phillips, Barry L. *manufacturing executive*

Niles
Odle, John H. *metal products executive*
Rupert, Timothy G. *metal products executive*

North Canton
Lynham, C(harles) Richard *manufacturing executive*

Orrville
Byom, John E. *food company executive*
Byrd, Vincent C. *food products company executive*
Duncan, Fred A. *food products company executive*
Mackus, Eloise L. *food products company executive*
Smucker, Richard K. *food products executive*
Smucker, Timothy P. *food products executive*

Pickerington
Zacks, Gordon Benjamin *manufacturing executive*

Randolph
Pecano, Donald Carl *automotive manufacturing executive*

Richfield
Anthony, Leonard Morris *steel company administrator, consultant*

Seven Hills
Turner, John *manufacturing executive*

Solon
Rosica, Gabriel Adam *retired manufacturing executive, electrical engineer*

Toledo
Convis, Gary L. *automotive parts company executive*
DeBacker, Michael Lee *automotive executive, lawyer*
Devine, John Martin *automotive parts company executive*
Lemieux, Joseph Henry *manufacturing executive, researcher*
Lonergan, Robert C. *financial executive*
Reynolds, Richard I. *food products company executive*
Romanoff, Milford Martin *retired building contractor*
Thaman, Michael H. *building material systems executive*
Van Hooser, David *retired manufacturing executive*
Wilkes, Kenneth G. *food products company executive*

Westerville
Krueger-Horn, Cheryl *apparel executive*

Westlake
Hellman, Peter Stuart *technical manufacturing executive*

Wickliffe
Cooley, Charles P. *chemicals executive*
Hambrick, James L. *chemicals executive*

Youngstown
Marks, Esther L. *metals company executive*
Powers, Paul J. *manufacturing executive*

PENNSYLVANIA

Greenville
Witosky, Gary J. *retired manufacturing executive*

SOUTH DAKOTA

Dakota Dunes
Leman, Eugene D. *meat industry executive*
Peterson, Robert L. *meat processing executive*

Sioux Falls
Christensen, David Allen *retired manufacturing executive*
Rosenthal, Joel *manufacturing executive*

TEXAS

Houston
Netherland, Joseph H. *manufacturing executive*

Richardson
Thompson, Richard L. *retired manufacturing executive*

VIRGINIA

Roanoke
Jackson, Darren Richard *automotive parts company executive*

WISCONSIN

Appleton
Boldt, Oscar Charles *construction executive, director*
Seifert, Kathi P. *manufacturing executive*

Clintonville
Simpson, Vinson Raleigh *manufacturing executive, director*

Eau Claire
Cohen, Maryjo R. *manufacturing executive*
Cohen, Melvin Samuel *manufacturing executive*
Rasmussen, Earl R. *lumber company and home improvement retail executive*
Soper, LaVern G. *appliance and houseware manufacturer*

Germantown
Dohmen, John F. *pharmaceutical executive*

Green Bay
Ferguson, Larry P. *food products executive*
Kress, William F. *manufacturing executive*
Kuehne, Carl W. *food products executive*
Liddy, Brian *food products executive*
Liegel, Craig A. *meat packing company executive*
Marsh, Miles L. *paper company executive*
McGarr, Joseph W. *paper company executive*
Vesta, Richard V. *meat packing company executive*

Kenosha
Emma, Edward C. *apparel executive*

Kohler
Cheney, Jeffrey Paul *manufacturing executive*
Kohler, Herbert Vollrath, Jr. *diversified manufacturing company executive*
Wells, Richard A. *manufacturing executive*

Madison
Carlson, Chris *lumber company executive*
Macfarlane, Alastair Iain Robert *manufacturing executive, consultant*
Shain, Irving *retired chemicals executive, academic administrator*

Manitowoc
Growcock, Terry D. *manufacturing executive*

Marathon
Menzner, Donald *food products executive*

Merrill
Bierman, Jane *wood products company executive*

Milwaukee
Beals, Vaughn Le Roy, Jr. *retired motorcycle manufacturing executive*
Bleustein, Jeffrey L. *motorcycle company executive*
Bomba, Steven J. *controls company executive*
Carter, Valerie *food products executive*
Colbert, Virgis W. *food products executive*
Daniels-Carter, Valerie *food franchise executive*
Davis, Don H., Jr. *multi-industry high-technology company executive*
Frenette, Charles S. *food products executive*
Grade, Jeffery T. *manufacturing executive*
Hanson, John Nils *industrial high technology manufacturing company executive*
Honold, Linda Kaye *human resources development executive*
Keyes, James Henry *manufacturing executive*
Koss, John Charles *consumer electronics products manufacturing company executive*
Long, Tom *brewery executive*
Manning, Kenneth Paul *specialty chemical company executive*
Martin, Vincent Lionel *retired manufacturing executive*
Nosbusch, Keith D. *multi-industry high-technology company executive*
O'Toole, Robert Joseph *retired manufacturing executive*
Parker, Charles Walter, Jr. *retired manufacturing executive*
Roell, Stephen A. *manufacturing executive*
Shiely, John Stephen *manufacturing executive, lawyer*
Sterner, Frank Maurice *manufacturing executive*
Ziemer, James L. *motorcycle company executive*

Neenah
Theisen, Henry J. *manufacturing executive*

Oshkosh
Zuern, Rosemary Lucile *manufacturing executive, treasurer*

Pleasant Prairie
Cherry, Peter Ballard *electrical products corporation executive*
Morrone, Frank *electronics executive*

Port Washington
Wier, James A. *manufacturing executive*

Racine
Burke, Thomas A. *manufacturing executive*
Campbell, Edward Joseph *retired machinery company executive*
Christman, Richard M. *manufacturing executive*
Johnson, H(erbert) Fisk *manufacturing executive*
Konz, Gerald Keith *retired manufacturing executive*
McCollum, W. Lee *chemical company executive*
Rosso, Jean-Pierre *electronics executive*
Wambold, Richard Lawrence *manufacturing executive*

South Milwaukee
Kitzke, Eugene David *research and development company executive*

Sturtevant
Bailey, Michael J. *manufacturing executive*
Johnson, S. Curtis *chemicals executive*

Sussex
Losee, John Frederick, Jr. *manufacturing executive*

Waukesha
Hogan, Joseph M. *health products executive*
Maas, Duane Harris *distilling company executive*
Nigl, Jeffrey M. *telecommunications company executive*

West Bend
Gehl, William D. *manufacturing executive*
Hahn, Kenneth P. *manufacturing executive*
Mulcahy, Michael J. *light contruction and agricultural manfucturing*

Wisconsin Rapids
Evans, Gorton M. *paper products executive*
Gottschalk, Guy *agricultural products executive*

CANADA

MANITOBA

Winnipeg
MacKenzie, George Allan *company director*

ADDRESS UNPUBLISHED

Adams, Jennifer *medical products executive*
Allemang, Arnold A. *chemicals executive*
Anderson, Timothy *pharmaceutical executive*
Andreas, Dwayne Orville *agricultural products executive*
Andreas, G(lenn) Allen, Jr. *former agricultural company executive*
Aschauer, Charles Joseph, Jr. *retired health products executive*
Barlow, John F. *automotive glass products company executive*
Barry, Jonathan B. *chemicals and communications executive*
Barth, John M. *retired manufacturing executive*
Barton, Robert H. III *automotive executive*
Bayly, George V. *manufacturing executive*
Beard, Eric A. *pharmaceutical executive*
Belz, Raymond T. *manufacturing executive*
Beracha, Barry Harris *retired food products executive*
Bernthal, Harold George *health products executive, director*
Bishop, Charles Joseph *retired manufacturing executive*
Bixby, Harold Glenn *manufacturing executive, director*
Bollenbacher, Herbert Kenneth *steel company official*
Brauer, Keith E. *medical products executive*
Brightfelt, Robert *diagnostic company executive*
Burns, Michael J. *former automotive parts company executive*
Busch, August Adolphus III *retired brewery company executive*
Calcaterra, Edward Lee *construction company executive*
Chen, Di *electronics executive, optical engineer, consultant*
Christensen, Gary M. *building materials company executive*
Clark, Wesley M. *manufacturing executive*
Conte, Richard R. *homebuilding and mortgage banking company executive*
Craft, Edmund Coleman *retired manufacturing executive*
Cull, Robert Robinette *manufacturing executive*
Dattilo, Thomas A. *retired manufacturing executive*
DeBruce, Paul *agricultural food products company executive*
Dohrmann, Russell William *retired manufacturing executive*
Dollens, Ronald W. *pharmaceutical executive*
Dougherty, Robert Anthony *retired manufacturing company executive*
Drexler, Richard Allan *manufacturing executive*
Drohan, David F. *medical products company executive*
Evans, Thomas E. *autoparts company executive*
Farrell, W. James *retired metal products manufacturing company executive*
Foote, William Chapin *manufacturing executive*
Gilbert, Allan Arthur *retired manufacturing executive*
Gilmour, Allan Dana *retired automotive company executive*
Glanzmann, Thomas H. *healthcare company executive*
Glover, James Todd *manufacturing executive*
Gloyd, Lawrence Eugene *retired diversified manufacturing company executive*
Golden, Charles Edward *retired pharmaceutical company executive*
Graham, Allister P. *food products executive*
Green, Sonia Maria *automotive executive*
Greenberg, Jack M. *former food products executive*
Haas, Howard Green *retired bedding manufacturing company executive*
Hagenlocker, Edward E. *retired automobile company executive*
Hake, Ralph F. *former appliance manufacturing executive*
Hamp, Steven K. *automotive executive*
Hann, Daniel P. *former medical products executive, lawyer*
Hardis, Stephen Roger *retired manufacturing company executive*
Harshman, Richard R. *manufacturing executive*
Hazleton, Richard A. *chemicals executive*
Henning, George Thomas, Jr. *retired steel company executive*
Holden, Betsy D. *former food products company executive*
Hudson, Katherine Mary *manufacturing executive*
Hunt, V. William (Bill) *automotive supplier executive*
Hurd, Richard Nelson *pharmaceutical executive*
Hushen, John Wallace *manufacturing executive*
Janak, Peter Harold *retired automotive company executive*
Jantz, Kenneth M. *construction executive*
Jones, David D., Jr. *marine engine equipment executive*
Juhl, Daniel Leo *manufacturing and marketing firm executive*
Kampouris, Emmanuel Andrew *retired corporate executive*
Kaplan, Arnold *health service organization executive*
Karter, Elias M. *paper products company executive*
Kelley, James *automotive sales executive*
Kelley, Thomas William *automotive sales executive*
Keough, Michael J. *paper manufacturing executive*
Kerber, Ronald Lee *industrial corporation executive*
Kerr, Michael D. *construction company executive*
Koenemann, Carl F. *retired electronics company executive*
Krygier, Roman J. *automotive executive*
Kurnick, Robert H., Jr. *automotive executive, lawyer*
Landon, Robert Gray *retired manufacturing company executive*
Lane, Michael Harry *steel company executive*
Langbo, Arnold Gordon *retired food products company executive*
Lapinsky, Joseph F. *manufacturing executive*
Liebler, Arthur C. *automotive executive*
Ligocki, Kathleen A. *former auto parts company executive*
Linville, Randal L. *agricultural company executive*
Lock, Richard William *packaging company executive*
Macher, Frank E. *automotive executive*
Mahoney, Robert William *electronic and security systems manufacturing executive*
Manning, William Dudley, Jr. *retired specialty chemical company executive*
Marcantonio, Richard L. *uniform company executive*
McGillivray, Donald Dean *seed company executive, agronomist*
McIlroy, Alan F. *manufacturing executive*
McKenna, William John *retired textile products executive*
Michaels, Jack D. *manufacturing executive*
Milberg, Joachim *retired automotive executive*
Millard, Charles Phillip *manufacturing executive*
Miller, Harold Edward *retired manufacturing conglomerate executive, consultant*
Mills, Charles N. *healthcare supplies and products company executive*
Miskowski, Lee R. *retired automotive executive*
Molfenter, David P. *former electronics executive*
Moore, John Ronald *manufacturing executive*
Morris, G. Ronald *automotive executive*
Mullens, Delbert W. *automotive executive*
Nelson, Glen David *health products executive, physician*
O'Connor, Kevin *construction materials manufacturing executive*
O'Donnell, Kevin *retired metal products executive*
Oesterling, Thomas Ovid *retired pharmaceutical executive*
Olson, Tharlie Earl *paper company executive*
Oster, Lewis Henry *manufacturing executive, industrial engineer, consultant*
Padilla, James Jerome (Jim Padilla) *retired automotive executive*
Petyo, Michael Edward *construction company owner*
Pond, Byron O., Jr. *retired manufacturing executive*
Quinn, Donal *diagnostic equipment company executive*
Rayburn, David B. *retired manufacturing executive*
Reinhard, Joao Pedro *chemicals company executive*
Richter, Robert C. *retired automotive executive*
Roberts, Michael J. *former food products executive*
Ross, Dennis E. *retired automotive executive, lawyer*
Rougier-Chapman, Alwyn Spencer Douglas *furniture manufacturing company executive*
Sabo, Richard Steven *retired electronics executive*
Sante, William Arthur, II, *electronics manufacturing executive*
Schmalz, Douglas J. *retired agricultural company executive*
Shaffer, Alan Lee *manufacturing systems company executive*
Shah, Rajesh K. *auto parts manufacturing executive*
Shapira, David S. *food products and retail grocery executive*
Sharkey, Leonard Arthur *automobile company executive*
Smith, F. Alan *automobile manufacturing company executive*
Smith, Frederick Coe *retired manufacturing executive*
Smith, John Francis, Jr., (Jack Smith) *retired automotive executive*
Smith, Robert Hugh *retired engineering construction company executive*
Soderberg, Leif G. *electronics company executive*
Sopranos, Orpheus Javaras *manufacturing executive*
Spertus, Eugene *frame manufacturing company executive*
Springer, Neil Allen *manufacturing executive*
Staley, Warren R. *agricultural products and diversified services company executive*
Stephens, Thomas G. *automotive executive*
Stiritz, William P. *food products executive*
Templin, Kenneth Elwood *paper company executive*
Thursfield, David W. *automotive executive*
Tinker, H(arold) Burnham *chemical company executive*
Toan, Barrett A. *former health products executive*
Uchida, Hiroshi *diagnostic equipment company executive*
Van Gilder, Russell *food products executive*
Vescovi, Selvi *pharmaceutical executive*
Walker, Martin Dean *specialty chemical company executive*
Ward, Thomas *food products executive*
Wardrop, Richard M., Jr. *former steel holding company executive*
Welburn, Edward T. *automotive executive*
Wenstrup, H. Daniel *chemical company executive*
Wilson, Martin D. *pharmaceutical executive*
Wormser, Eric Sigmund *manufacturing executive*
Wright, Felix E. *retired manufacturing executive*
Wyatt, Lance B. *pharmaceutical executive*
Yontz, Kenneth Fredric *medical and chemical company executive*
Young, Jay Maitland *health products executive, consultant*

Zeffren, Eugene *cosmetics executive*

INDUSTRY: SERVICE

UNITED STATES

ARIZONA

Tucson
Cooper, Corinne *communications consultant, lawyer*

CALIFORNIA

Los Angeles
Cecere, Domenico *homebuilding company executive*
Schultz, Louis Michael *advertising agency executive*

Rutherford
Staglin, Garen Kent *computer company executive, venture capitalist*

San Diego
Dammeyer, Rodney Foster *distribution company executive*

Santa Barbara
Scheinfeld, James David *retired travel company executive*

COLORADO

Boulder
Langer, Steven *human resources specialist, consultant, psychologist*

Englewood
Vogel, Carl E. *communications executive*

Monument
De Francesco, John Blaze, Jr. *public relations consultant, writer*

DISTRICT OF COLUMBIA

Washington
Clifton, James K. *market research company executive*

FLORIDA

Boca Raton
Rhein, Arthur *computer company executive*

Bonita Springs
Hauserman, Jacquita Knight *management consultant*

Destin
Ferner, David Charles *non-profit management and development consultant*

Highland Beach
Upbin, Hal J. *consumer products company executive*

Juno Beach
Woltz, Kenneth Allen *retired management consultant*

Jupiter
Fried, Herbert Daniel *advertising executive*

Key Biscayne
Cardozo, Richard Nunez *marketing professional, educator, entrepreneur*

Naples
Bileydi, Sumer *advertising agency executive*
Meyers, Christine Laine *marketing and media executive, consultant*

Singer Island
Dixson, J. B. *communications executive*

ILLINOIS

Addison
Christopher, Doris K. *consumer products company executive*

Arlington Heights
Fields, Sara A. *travel company executive*
Holtz, Michael P. *hotel executive*

Aurora
Hopp, Nancy Smith *marketing executive*
Michelsen, John Ernest *software and internet services company executive*

Bannockburn
Slavin, Craig Steven *management and franchising consultant*

Barrington
Koten, John A. *retired communications executive*
Lee, Catherine M. *business owner, educator*
Ross, Frank Howard III *management consultant*
Sweet, Charles Wheeler *retired executive recruiter*

Batavia
Mann, Phillip Lynn *data processing company executive*

Bensenville
Kolkey, Eric Samuel *customer communications specialist*
Oates, Zehavah Whitney *data processing executive*

Bloomingdale
Flaherty, John Joseph *quality assurance company executive*
Wolande, Charles Sanford *former computer company executive*

Bloomington
Dietz, William Ronald *corporate management professional*

Bolingbrook
Alvarado, Serafin *wine connoisseur*
Sheehan, James Patrick *printing company executive, former media company executive*

Broadview
Lazar, Jill Sue *home healthcare company executive*

Buffalo Grove
Tracy, Allen Wayne *management consultant*

Burr Ridge
Bernatowicz, Frank Allen *management consultant*
Bottom, Dale Coyle *marketing executive, director, management consultant*

Carol Stream
Gale, Neil Jan *Internet company executive, computer scientist, consultant*

Chicago
Akins, Cindy S. *human resources professional*
Allen, Belle *management consulting firm and communications executive*
Amberg, Thomas L. *public relations executive*
Bailey, Robert, Jr. *advertising executive*
Baker, Mark *food service executive*
Bard, John Franklin *consumer products executive*
Bayer, Gary Richard *advertising executive*
Bayless, Rick *chef*
Bensinger, Peter Benjamin *consulting firm executive*
Bernardin, Thomas L. *advertising executive*
Be Sant, Craig *marketing executive*
Bess, Ronald W. *advertising executive*
Beugen, Joan Beth *communications executive*
Bonaparte, William *communications company executive*
Bowen, William Joseph *management consultant*
Brashears, Donald Robert *advertising agency executive*
Briand, Michael *chef*
Bubula, John *chef*
Burrell, Thomas J. *marketing communication executive*
Campbell, Alex *mobile marketing executive*
Carlson, Michael *chef*
Carr, Steve *public relations executive*
Cass, Edward Roberts (Peter Cass) *hotel and travel marketing professional*
Castorino, Sue *communications executive*
Cesario, Robert Charles *marketing executive*
Chipparoni, Guy *communications company executive*
Coletta, John *chef*
Conidi, Daniel Joseph *private investigation agency executive*
Cornell, Rob *hotel executive*
Cox, Allan James *management consultant*
DeHart, Jacob *Internet company executive*
Donnelley, James Russell *printing company executive*
Draft, Howard Craig *advertising executive*
Dragonette, Rita Hoey *public relations executive*
Englehart, Hud *communications company executive*
Fisher, John James *advertising executive*
Frankel, Bernard *advertising executive*
Furth, Yvonne *advertising executive*
Gadsby, Monica M. *marketing executive*
Gardner, Howard Alan *travel company executive, writer, editor*
Gerber, Phillip *advertising executive*
Gilbert, David R. *public relations executive*
Glasser, James J. *retired leasing company executive*
Golding, Norman Max *marketing professional*
Golin, Alvin *public relations company executive*
Gordon, Edward Earl *management consultant, educator*
Gray, Dawn Plambeck *work-family consultant, publishing executive*
Grieveson, Koren *chef*
Growney, Robert L. *former communications company professional, venture capitalist*
Haffner, Charles Christian III *retired printing company executive*
Hansen, Carl R. *management consultant*
Harkna, Eric *advertising executive*
Healy, Sondra Anita *consumer products company executive*
Hewitt, Pamela S. *human resources specialist*
Hollis, Donald Roger *management consultant*
Hoplamazian, Mark Samuel *hotel executive*
Huggins, Lois M. *human resources specialist, consumer products company executive*
Husting, Peter Marden *advertising consultant*
Joho, Jean *chef*
Kahan, Paul *chef*
Klues, Jack *communications executive*
Kobs, James Fred *direct marketing consultant*
Kokonas, Nick J. *restaurant owner*
Kornick, Michael *chef*
Krivkovich, Peter George *advertising executive*
Krupnick, Elizabeth Rachel *human resources consulting firm and former insurance company executive*
Lane, Kenneth Edwin *retired advertising agency executive*
LaVelle, Avis *consulting firm executive*
Leadbetter, Tiffany *hotel executive*
Leigh, Sherren *communications and publishing executive, editor*
Levy, Deborah *security company executive*
Lynnes, R. Milton *advertising executive*
Mackiewicz, Laura *advertising agency executive*
Martinez, Jim *communications executive*
McCann, Renetta *advertising executive*
McConnell, E. Hoy, II, *advertising and public policy executive*
McCullough, Richard Lawrence *advertising executive*
Melamed, Leo *global consulting firm executive*
Miller, Ellen *advertising executive*
Mityas, Sherif *management consultant*
Morley, Michael B. *public relations executive*
Moster, Mary Clare *public relations executive*
Mulqueen, Michael Patrick *food service executive, retired military officer*
Nelson, Harry Donald *telecommunications executive*
Noonan, Jack *analytics software and solutions company executive*
Ormesher, David T. *advertising executive*
Paul, Ronald Neale *management consultant*
Payne, Thomas H. *market research company executive*
Petrillo, Nancy *public relations executive*
Philbin, Jack *communications executive*
Pincus, Theodore Henry *public relations executive*
Plotkin, Manuel D. *management consultant, educator, former corporate executive, government official*
Posner, Kathy Robin *retired communications executive*
Posner, Kenneth Robert *former hotel corporation executive*
Prather, Susan Lynn *public relations executive*
Pritzker, Thomas Jay *hotel executive*
Quinlan, Thomas J. III *printing company executive*
Rabin, Joseph Harry *marketing research company executive*
Radomski, Robyn L. *marketing executive*
Redmond, Andrea *executive recruiter*
Reid, Daniel James *public relations executive*
Reitman, Jerry Irving *advertising agency executive*
Rich, S. Judith *public relations executive*
Rooney, John Edward *communications company executive*
Rooney, Phillip Bernard *service company executive*
Rosenberg, Robin *executive chef*
Sampanthavivat, Arun *chef*
Sampson, Ronald Alvin *advertising executive*
Seebert, Kathleen Anne *international sales and marketing executive*
Segal, Mindy *chef*
Serlin, Marsha *waste management service administrator*
Shepherd, Daniel Marston *executive recruiter*
Shirley, Virginia Lee *advertising executive*
Sive, Rebecca Anne *public relations executive*
Sotelino, Gabino *chef*
Stead, James Joseph, Jr. *security firm executive*
Stern, Carl William, Jr. *management consultant*
Stocklosa, Gregory A. *printing company executive*
Stratton, Steven F. *real estate executive*
Strubel, Ella Doyle *advertising executive, public relations executive*
Strubel, Richard Perry *Internet company executive*
Swinand, Andrew *advertising executive*
Talbot, Pamela *public relations executive*
Taylor, Collette *public relations executive*
Teichner, Lester *general management executive*
Tentori, Giuseppe *chef*
Tobaccowala, Rishad *marketing professional*
Tribbett, Charles *executive recruiter*
Trotter, Charlie *chef*
Tyson, Kirk W. M. *management consultant*
Van Den Hende, Fred J(oseph) *human resources executive*
Walters, Lawrence Charles *advertising executive*
Weinfurter, Daniel Joseph *business services executive*
Weisbach, Lou (Louis E. Weisbach) *advertising executive*
Wiecek, Barbara Harriet *advertising executive*
Williams, Bruce *chef*
Williams, Marsha C. *travel company executive*

Deerfield
Brunner, Vernon Anthony *marketing executive*
Carbonari, Bruce A. *consumer products company executive*
Omtvedt, Craig P. *consumer products executive*
Reich, Victoria J. *consumer products company executive*
Wesley, Norman H. *consumer products company executive*

Des Plaines
Baerenklau, Alan H. *hotel executive*
Mueller, Kurt M. *hotel executive*

Downers Grove
Duffield, Michael O. *data processing executive*
Mrozek, Ernest J. *customer service administrator*
Schwemm, John Butler *printing company executive, lawyer*
Soenen, Michael J. *consumer products company executive*
Spainhour, J. Patrick (James Patrick Spainhour) *outsourcing company executive, former apparel executive*
Stair, Charles William *former service company executive*
Wigginton, Adam *marketing professional*

Edwardsville
Dietrich, Suzanne Claire *communications consultant, researcher, museum director*
Suhre, Richard L. *transportation company executive*

Elburn
Hansen, H. Jack *management consultant*

Evanston
Larson, Paul William *public relations executive*
Robbins, Henry Zane *public relations and marketing executive*

Flossmoor
Crum, James Francis *waste recycling company executive*

Franklin Park
Bailey, Richard *food company executive*
Ravencroft, Thomas A. *food company executive*

Galena
Fullmer, Paul *public relations counselor*

Glen Ellyn
Conti, Paul Louis *management consulting company executive*

Glencoe
Isaacs, Roger David *public relations executive*

Glenview
Franklin, Lynne *corporate communications specialist, writer*
Grubbs, Robert W. *computer services company executive*
Turner, Lee *travel company executive*

Glenwood
Latta, Brent *consumer products company executive*

Highland Park
Cohen, Burton David *food service executive, lawyer*
Harris, Thomas L. *public relations executive*
Rodriguez, Ramiro *chef*

Hinsdale
Amsler, Jana *chef*
League, David *hardware company executive*
Rodriguez, Edgar *chef*

Hoffman Estates
Lee, Gregory A. *human resources specialist*

Kenilworth
Guelich, Robert Vernon *retired management consultant*
Steingraber, Frederick George *management consultant*
Weaver, Donna Rae *winery executive*

Lake Bluff
Scott, Karen Bondurant *consumer catalog company executive*

Lake Forest
Brewer, Paul Huie *advertising executive, artist, portrait painter*
Chieger, Kathryn Jean *consumer products company executive*
Crawford, Robert W., Jr. *furniture rental company executive*
Fluno, Jere David *consumer products company executive*
Miller, Mark C. *waste management administrator*
Rand, Kathy Sue *public relations executive, consultant*
Stecko, Paul T. *packaging company executive*

Lake In The Hills
Kacek, Don J. *management consultant*

Libertyville
Conklin, Mara Loraine *public relations executive*

Lincolnshire
DeCanniere, Dan *human resources executive*

Lincolnwood
Lebedow, Aaron Louis *consulting company executive*

Lisle
Donnelly, Gerard Thomas *arboretum director*

Melrose Park
Bernick, Carol Lavin *consumer products company executive*
Cernugel, William John *consumer products company executive, distributor*

Morton Grove
Smolyansky, Julie *consumer products company executive*

Mount Prospect
Gerlitz, Curtis Neal *purchasing agent*
Sayers, Gale *computer company executive, retired professional football player*

Mundelein
Eastham, Dennis Michael *advertising executive*

Naperville
Bell, Bradley J. *water treatment company executive*
Fritz, Roger Jay *management consultant*
Shanine, George *sales executive, information technology executive*

Northbrook
Clarey, John Robert *executive recruiter, consultant*
Ehrenberg, Maureen *management consultant*
Lesnik, Steven Harris *public relations and sports marketing executive*
Marshall, Irl Houston, Jr. *franchise consultant*
Sprieser, Judith A. *former software company executive*
Sudbrink, Jane Marie *sales and marketing executive*
Wajer, Ronald Edward *management consultant*

Northfield
Grimes, Sally *marketing professional*
Vilim, Nancy Catherine *advertising executive*

Oak Brook
DeLorey, John Alfred *printing company executive*
Fenton, Tim *food service executive*
Fields, Janice L. *food service executive*
Glenn, J. Thomas *consumer products company executive*
Golden, Neil B. *marketing executive*
Nelson, Robert Eddinger *retired management consultant*
Paull, Matthew H. *food service executive*
Turner, Fred L. *retired fast food company executive*

Oak Park
Barry, Richard A. *public relations executive*
Cannon, Patrick Francis *public relations executive*
Devereux, Timothy Edward *advertising executive*

Oakbrook Terrace
Hegenderfer, Jonita Susan *public relations executive*

Park Ridge
Campbell, Dorothy May *management consultant*
Matthews, Roy S. *management consultant*

Peoria
Banwart, Sidney C. *human resources executive*

Plainfield
Hofer, Thomas W. *landscape company executive*

Prospect Heights
Lynch, William Thomas, Jr. *advertising executive*

Riverwoods
Hebda, Lawrence John *data processing executive, consultant*

Rockford
Morrissey, Mary F. (Fran) *human resource consulting company executive*

Rolling Meadows
Cain, R. Wayne *sales, finance and leasing company executive*

Rosemont
Barlett, James Edward *data processing executive*
Blake, Norman Perkins, Jr. *computer company executive*
Le Menager, Lois M. *incentive merchandise and travel company executive*

Saint Charles
Nellemann, Lynne O'Shea *management consultant*

Schaumburg
Brown, Gregory Q. *communications executive*
Cataldo, C. A. *hotel executive*
Cataldo, Robert J. *hotel executive*
Fox, Thomas J. *communications executive*
Liska, Paul J. *communications executive, former insurance compny executive*
Roman, Ray *communications executive*
Tandy, Karen Pomerantz *communications executive, former federal agency administrator*
Zander, Edward J. *communications executive*

Skokie
Brennan, William P. (Bill Brennan) *computer company executive*
Karp, Gary *marketing and public relations executive*
Sperzel, George E., Jr. *former personal care industry executive*
Wallace, Rick *marketing professional*

Westchester
Carroll, Thomas John *retired advertising executive*

Western Springs
Virant, Paul *chef*

Wheeling
Banchet, Jean *chef*

Willowbrook
Foley, Joseph Lawrence *sales executive*
Mathisen-Reid, Rhoda Sharon *international communications consultant*

Winnetka
Thomas, John Thieme *management consultant*

INDIANA

Auburn
Kempf, Jane Elmira *marketing executive*

Bloomington
Patterson, James Milton *marketing specialist, educator*

Columbus
Tucker, Thomas Randall *public relations executive*

Evansville
Kitch, Frederick David *advertising executive*
Weinzapfel, Jonathan *public relations executive, congressional aide*

Fort Wayne
Schweickart, Jim *advertising executive, broadcast executive, consultant*
Wolf, Don Allen *hardware wholesale executive*

Indianapolis
Ayars, Patti *human resources specialist, health products executive*
Gilman, Alan B. *restaurant company executive*
Quiring, Patti Lee *human resource consulting company executive*
Ruben, Gary A. *marketing and communications consultant*
Simmons, Roberta Johnson *public relations firm executive*
Slaymaker, Gene Arthur *public relations executive*
Spanogle, Robert William *marketing and advertising company executive, association administrator*
Walker, Frank Dilling *market research executive*
Walker, Steven Frank *management consultant*

Liberty
Pringle, Lewis Gordon *marketing professional, educator*

Merrillville
White, Dean *advertising executive*

Mishawaka
Dooley, Roger *Internet company executive*

Muncie
Norris, Tracy Hopkins *retired public relations executive*

West Lafayette
Schendel, Dan Eldon *management consultant, finance educator*

Zionsville
Brown, Zak *marketing executive*

IOWA

Ames
Rizai, Matthew M. *marketing and finance professional*

Ankeny
Lamberti, Donald *convenience store executive*

Cedar Rapids
Cardella, Tom *sales executive*

Davenport
Monty, Mitchell *landscape company executive*

Fairfield
Hawthorne, Timothy Robert *direct response advertising and communications company executive*
Kelly, Thomas *advertising executive*

KANSAS

New Century
Huber, Dennis G. *communications executive*

Overland Park
Campbell, Harry *communications executive*
Fuller, Michael B. *communications executive*
Green, John Lafayette, Jr. *strategic planning executive, former educational association administrator*
Hill, Lloyd Lester *food service executive*
Hodge, Ralph J. *communications executive*
Kissinger, Jim *communications executive*
McEvoy, Thomas J. *communications executive*
Meyer, John P. *communications executive*
Stout, Michael W. *communications executive*

Shawnee Mission
Mealman, Glenn *corporate marketing executive*

Topeka
Sipes, Karen Kay *communications executive*

Wichita
Koch, Charles de Ganahl *industrial company executive*
Menefee, Frederick Lewis *advertising executive*

MARYLAND

Silver Spring
Bissell, John Howard *marketing executive*

MICHIGAN

Ada
Lyall, Lynn *consumer products company executive*
Van Andel, Steve Alan *consumer products company executive*
Weiss, Joseph Joel *consulting company executive*

Ann Arbor
Belcher, Louis David *marketing professional, retired mayor*
Brandon, David A. *food service executive*
Foley, Daniel Ronald *personnel director, lawyer*

Auburn Hills
Rae, Nancy A. *human resources specialist, automotive executive*

Benton Harbor
Binkley, David A. *human resources specialist*

Birmingham
Hill, Richard A. *advertising executive*
Smith, Todd P. *marketing executive*

Bloomfield Hills
Berline, James H. *advertising and public relations executive*
Czarnecki, Walter P. *truck rental company executive*

Brighton
Veno, Glen Corey *management consultant*

Detroit
Bassett, Tina *communications executive*
Demos, Dave *marketing executive*
Go, Robert A. *management consultant*
Ilitch, Denise *food services executive*
Lowell, Scott *restaurant manager, real estate developer*
Novak, Raymond Francis *environmental services administrator, pharmacology educator*
Ponder, Dan *public relations executive*
Rosenau, Pete *public relations executive*
Schweitzer, Peter *advertising agency executive*
Stern, Todd *restaurant manager*
Topacio, Angela *marketing executive*

Farmington
Ward, Francis J. *marketing and research executive*
Werba, Gabriel *public relations consultant*

Farmington Hills
Benedict, Elise *moving company executive*
Manna, Martin *public relations executive, marketing executive*
Yagahashi, Takashi *chef*

Ferndale
Huvaere, Jason *production company executive*

Franklin
Prentice, Matthew *food service executive*

Freeland
Bailey, William L. *communications executive*

Glen Arbor
Wagner, Bruce Stanley *marketing professional*

Grand Rapids
Baker, Frank C. (Buzz Baker) *advertising executive*
Bruyn, Kimberly Ann *public relations executive, consultant*
DeVos, Richard Marvin, Jr., (Dick DeVos) *retired direct sales company and sports team executive*
Gordon, Dan A. *food service executive*
Messner, James W. *advertising executive*
Seyferth, Virginia M. *public relations executive*
Smith, Bill *advertising and marketing executive*
Spaulding, Dan *public relations executive*
Zimmerman, John *public relations executive*

Grosse Pointe Park
Krebs, William Hoyt *industrial hygienist, health science association administrator*

Grosse Pointe Woods
Cusmano, J. Joyce *public relations executive*

Hillsdale
Bachelder, Cheryl Anne *former food service company executive*

Kalamazoo
Gershon, Richard A. *commmunications educator*
Gilchrist, James A. *communication educator*

Livonia
Barfield, Jon E. *employment company executive*
Maibach, Ben C., Jr. *consumer products company executive*
Morrison, Andrew J. *marketing professional*

Midland
Sosville, Dick *sales and marketing executive*

Novi
Flinchbaugh, Jamie *training services executive*

Royal Oak
Stanalajczo, Greg Charles *computer company executive*

Southfield
Barnett, Marilyn *advertising executive*
Caponigro, Jeffrey Ralph *public relations counselor*
Hudson, Cheryl L. *communications executive*
Jackson, Michael B. *service company executive*
Jackson, Roger A. *human resources specialist, automotive executive*
Kalter, Alan *advertising agency executive*
Randazzo, Richard P. *human resources professional*

Taylor
Manoogian, Richard Alexander *consumer products company executive*

Troy
Adderley, Terence Edward *human resources executive*
Camden, Carl T. *human resources company executive*
McLaren, Karen Lynn *advertising executive*

Warren
Gervason, Robert J. *advertising executive*
Gilbert, Suzanne Harris *advertising executive*
Hopp, Anthony James *advertising agency executive*
Ludwig, William John *advertising executive*

West Bloomfield
Amladi, Prasad Ganesh *management consulting executive, health care consultant, researcher*
Smith, Nancy Hohendorf *sales executive, marketing professional*

MINNESOTA

Bloomington
Mona, David L. *public relations executive*
Taylor, Susan S. *performance consultant*

Eagan
Hatlen, Roe Harold *restaurant executive*

Eden Prairie
Harmel, Paul *photography company executive*

Hastings
Avent, Sharon L. Hoffman *manufacturing company executive*

Hopkins
Dunlap, William DeWayne, Jr. *advertising agency executive*

Mankato
Schreier, Bradley *management executive*

Minneapolis
Beardsley, John Ray *public relations firm executive*
Blackwell, Todd V. *human resources specialist*
Bonner, Brigid Ann *marketing professional*
Cameron, Patricia *advertising executive*
Cross, Bruce A. *food service company executive*
deBruin Sample, Anne *human resources specialist*
Doherty, Valerie *employment services professional, lawyer*
Eich, Susan *public relations executive*
Eickhoff, John R. *information services company executive*
Fallon, Patrick R. *advertising executive*
Gage, Edwin C., III, (Skip Gage) *travel and marketing services executive*
Grimes, David Lynn *communications executive*
Hill, Tessa *non profit environmental group executive*
Kelly, Charles Harold *advertising executive*
Koutsky, Dean Roger *advertising executive*
Krueger, Richard Arnold *technology executive*
Lehodey, John Francois *hotel company executive*
Lenzmeier, Allen U. *consumer products company executive*
Lynch, Leland T. *advertising executive*
Mouser, Les (Lyman Mouser) *advertising executive*
Owens, Scott Andrew *sales executive*
Palmore, Rick (Roderick A. Palmore) *consumer products company executive, lawyer*
Pohlad, Robert C. *consumer products company executive*
Powell, Ken (Kendall J. Powell) *consumer products company executive*
Roth, Thomas *marketing executive*
Sanger, Stephen W. *consumer products company executive*
Scoville, James Griffin *industrial relations professor*
Spong, Douglas K. *public relations executive*
Sullivan, Michael Patrick *food service executive*
Tunheim, Kathryn H. *public relations executive*
Turner, Ronald L. *information services executive*
Veblen, Thomas Clayton *management consultant*
Viault, Raymond G. *food company executive*
Wickesberg, Albert Klumb *retired management consultant*
Wikman, Michael Raymond *advertising executive*
Yourzak, Robert Joseph *management consultant, educator, engineer*

Minnetonka
Berman, Lyle *recreational facility executive*
Gillies, Donald Richard *marketing and advertising consultant, educator*
Joly, Hubert Bernard *hotel and travel company executive*
Nelson, Marilyn Carlson *hotel and travel company executive*
Porter, Jim *human resources specialist*

New Brighton
Grieman, John Joseph *communications executive*

North Mankato
Taylor, Glen A. *printing, direct mail and technology executive, professional sports team owner*

Plymouth
Evans, David *communications executive*

Saint Paul
Axelrod, Leonard *management consultant*
Baker, Douglas M., Jr. *service industry executive*
Brooks, Phillip *advertising executive*
Courtney, Eugene Whitmal *computer company executive*
Fritze, Steven L. *service industry executive*

South Saint Paul
Olen, Gary *marketing company executive*

Wayzata
Waldera, Wayne Eugene *crisis management executive*

Willmar
Norling, Rayburn *food service executive*

MISSOURI

Ballwin
Macauley, Edward C. *retired company executive*

Chesterfield
Stork, Donald Arthur *advertising executive*

Clayton
Vecchiotti, Robert Anthony *management and organizational consultant*

Columbia
Helvey, William Charles, Jr. *communications specialist*

Fenton
Lipovsky, Robert P. *marketing executive*
Maritz, W. Stephen *marketing professional, service executive*

Kansas City
Bartlett, Sherie *printing company executive*
Benner, Richard Edward, Jr. *marketing consultant, volunteer, investor*
Bernstein, Robert *advertising executive*
Brown, Peter C. *movie theater company executive*
Druten, Robert J. *greeting card company executive*
Hall, Donald Joyce, Sr. *greeting card company executive*
Kovac, F. Peter *advertising executive*
Kuhn, Whitey *advertising executive*
Robertson, Leon H. *management consultant, educator*
Solberg, Elizabeth Transou *public relations executive*
Stevens, Jane *advertising executive*
Stowers, James W. III *data processing executive*

Liberty
McCaslin, W. C. *products and packaging executive*

Monett
Henry, Michael E. *computer company executive*

O Fallon
Ractliffe, Robert Edward George *management executive*

Saint Louis
Adams, W. Randolph, Jr. *retired management consultant, performing company executive*
Bachmann, John William *security firm executive*
Bellville, Margaret (Maggie Bellville) *communications executive*
Black, Dale R. *hotel and gaming company executive*
Blake, William Henry *credit and public relations consultant*
Craft, Gerard Ford *chef*
Curran, Michael Walter *management scientist*
Davis, Irvin *advertising, public relations and broadcast executive*
Drury, Charles Louis, Jr. *hotel executive*
Graham, John Dalby *public relations executive*
Kennedy, Craig *rental company executive*
Kent, Jerald L. *communications company executive*
Khoury, George Gilbert *printing company executive, sports association executive*
Klein, Ward M. *consumer products company executive*
Kornblet, Donald Ross *communications company executive*
Loynd, Richard Birkett *consumer products company executive*
Lyons, Gordon *marketing executive*
Musial, Stan(ley) (Frank Musial) *hotel and restaurant executive, former baseball team executive, former baseball player*
Newman, Andrew Edison *restaurant manager*
Pillai, Pragash *communications executive*
Riley, Michael Robert *marketing and business development executive*
Schnuck, Scott C. *grocery store executive*
Sibbald, John Ristow *management consultant*
Siemer, Paul Jennings *public relations executive*
Taylor, Andrew C. *rental and leasing company executive*
Taylor, Jack Crawford *rental and leasing company executive*
Tyler, William Howard, Jr. *advertising executive, educator*
Vandiver, Donna *public relations executive*
Van Luven, William Robert *management consultant*
Voss, Thomas *customer services executive*

Springfield
Hammons, John Q. *hotel executive*
Noble, Robert B. *advertising executive*
Witherspoon, John Thomas *water resources consultant*

NEBRASKA

Omaha
Gupta, Vinod *business lists company executive*
Hedren, Paul Leslie *retired parks director, historian*
Phares, Lynn Levisay *public relations communications executive*
Roskens, Ronald William *management consultant, retired academic administrator*
Stubblefield, Robert F. *travel agency executive*

NEW JERSEY

Short Hills
Quinlan, Michael Robert *retired fast food franchise company executive*

NEW YORK

New York
Bloom, Stephen Joel *distribution company executive*
Brandt, William Arthur, Jr. *consulting executive*
Fine, Deborah *Internet company executive, former apparel executive*
Truwit, Mitchell *private equity*

NORTH DAKOTA

Fargo
Tharaldson, Gary Dean *hotel developer, owner*
Wallwork, William Wilson III *automobile executive*

Grand Forks
Rolshoven, Ross William *legal investigator, artist*

OHIO

Akron
Geier, Kathleen T. *human resources specialist*

Canton
Suarez, Benjamin *consumer products company executive*

Cincinnati
Antoine, Richard L. *human resources specialist, consumer products company executive*
Arnold, Susan E. *consumer products company executive*
Artzt, Edwin Lewis *consumer products company executive*
Bateman, Sharon Louise *public relations executive*
Baumgardner, Michael H. *marketing professional*
Bouquin, Bertrand *chef*
Brooks, Randy *research company executive*
Brunner, Gordon F(rancis) *household products company executive*
Byrnes, Bruce L. *consumer products company executive*
Comisar, Michael E. *restaurant manager*
Daley, Clayton Carl, Jr. *consumer products company executive*
deCavel, Jean-Robert *chef*
Dillon, David Brian *retail grocery executive*
Dougherty, David Francis *business process outsourcing executive*
Ellenberger, Richard G. *telecommunications executive*
Goodwin, John P. *consumer products company executive*
Hicks, Irle Raymond *food service executive*
Lafley, A.G. (Alan George Lafley) *consumer products company executive*
Lockhart, John Mallery *management consultant*
McDonald, Robert Alan (Bob McDonald) *consumer products company executive*
Mooney, Kevin W. *telecommunications executive*
Otto, Charlotte R. *consumer products company executive*
Pepper, John Ennis, Jr. *former consumer products company, historical museum executive*
Schorr, Roger J. *employee and customer care company executive*
Shipley, Tony L(ee) *software company executive*
Stengel, James R. *marketing executive*
Tatham, Ron *marketing executive*
Wall, Della *human resources specialist, manufacturing executive*
Zaring, Allen G. *homebuilding company executive*

Cleveland
Cook, Susan J. *human resources specialist, manufacturing executive*
Crawford, Edward E. *consumer products company executive*
Danco, Léon Antoine *management consultant, educator*
DeGroote, Michael G. *management consulting company executive*
Dunbar, Mary Asmundson *retired communications executive, investor relations and public relations consultant*
Fountain, Ronald Glenn *management consultant, corporate financial executive, entrepreneur, educator*
Gallagher, Patrick Francis Xavier *public relations executive*
Johnson, John Frank *professional recruitment executive*
Mabee, Keith V. *communications and investor relations executive*
Perkovic, Robert Branko *retired international management consultant*
Roop, James John *public relations executive*
Scaminace, Joseph M. *paint store executive*
Stashower, David L. *advertising executive*
Thompson, Stephen Arthur *sales consultant*
Woods, Jacqueline F. *public relations executive*

Columbus
Burke, Kenneth Andrew *advertising executive*
Drongowski, Steve *advertising executive*
Iammartino, Nicholas R. *corporate communications executive*
Jacobs, Alexis A. *automobile company executive*
Kirkwood, William Thomas *corporate professional*
Milenthal, David *advertising executive*
Mitchell, Cameron M. *restaurant executive*

Dayton
Brown, Craig J. *printing company executive*
Davis, Robert A. *data storing company executive*
Dorsman, Peter A. *printing company executive*
Geswein, Gregory T. *software company executive*
Nuti, William R. *computer services company executive*
Ringler, James M. *computer services company executive*
Tatar, Jerome F. *business products executive*

Delaware
Sparks, William B., Jr. *consumer products company executive*

Dublin
Anderson, Kerrii B. *food service executive*
Freytag, Donald Ashe *management consultant*
Pickett, James V. *food service executive*
Smith, K(ermit) Wayne *computer company executive*
Watkins, Carole S. *human resources specialist, medical products executive*
Wilkins, Jeffrey M. *computer company executive*

Elyria
Pucko, Diane Bowles *public relations executive*

Galion
Cobey, Ralph *industrialist*

Gates Mills
Reitman, Robert Stanley *management consultant, not-for-profit advisor*

Lancaster
Phillips, Edward John *consulting firm executive*

Loveland
Jackson, Eric C. *Internet company executive*

Marysville
Hagedorn, James *landscape company executive*

Maumee
Konopinski, Virgil James *retired industrial hygienist, consultant*

Mayfield Heights
Newman, Joseph Herzl *advertising executive, consultant*

Oberlin
Cartier, Brian Evans *consumer products company executive*

Oxford
Yen, David Chi-Chung *management information systems educator*

Salem
Fehr, Kenneth Manbeck *retired computer company executive*

Shaker Heights
Cornell, Edward L. *consumer products company executive*
Wuest, Jim *consumer products company executive*

Sylvania
Block, Allan James *communications executive*
Ring, Herbert Everett *retired management executive*

Toledo
Meier, John F. *consumer products company executive*
Paquette, Jack Kenneth *management consultant, author, historian*
Stroucken, Albert P. L. *consumer products company executive, former chemical company executive*

West Chester
End, William Thomas *marketing executive*

Westlake
Doane, Tim *travel company executive*
George, James W. *travel company executive*
Kuhn, Edwin P. *travel company executive*

Wooster
Schmitt, Wolf Rudolf *consumer products executive*

Worthington
Bender, Bob *advertising executive*

Youngstown
Estrin, Melvyn J. *computer products company executive*

TENNESSEE

Brentwood
Byars, Leisa *marketing professional, music company executive*

TEXAS

Lubbock
Jugenheimer, Donald Wayne *advertising executive, communications educator, academic administrator*

VIRGINIA

Alexandria
Nelson, David Leonard *data processing executive*

Reston
Fulgoni, Gian Marc *Internet company executive*
Maher, David Willard *Internet company executive*

WASHINGTON

Seattle
Bocian, Peter *beverage service company executive*

WISCONSIN

Algoma
Golomski, William Arthur Joseph *consulting company executive*

Appleton
Hasselbacher, Darlene M. *human resources executive*
McManus, John Francis *association executive, writer*
Mischka, Thomas *marketing professional*

Brookfield
Bader, Ronald L. *advertising executive*
Jensen, Kenneth R. *data processing executive*
Nickerson, Greg *public relations executive*
Yabuki, Jeffrey W. *data processing company executive, former accounting company executive*

Grafton
Schneider, Carol Ann *staffing services company executive*

Green Bay
Bender, Brian *consumer products executive*
Meng, John C. *food service executive*

Hartford
Fowler, John *printing company executive*

Kohler
Kohler, Laura E. *human resources executive*

Madison
Bishop, Carolyn Benkert *public relations counselor*
Piper, Odessa *chef*
Pyle, Thomas F., Jr. *consumer products company executive*

Mequon
Elias, Paul S. *retired marketing executive*

Merton
Welnetz, David Charles *human resources executive*

Middleton
Knapstein, Michael *advertising executive*

Milwaukee
Arbit, Bruce *direct marketing executive, consultant*
Beck, Barbara J. *employment services executive*
Counsell, Paul S. *retired advertising executive*
Davis, Susan F. *human resources specialist*
Hagerman, Douglas M. *consumer products company executive, lawyer*
Hunter, Victor Lee *marketing executive, consultant*
Jacobs, Bruce Edward *management consultant*
Joerres, Jeffrey A. *employment services executive*
Joseph, Jules K. *retired public relations executive*
Laughlin, Steven L. *advertising executive*
Marcus, Stephen Howard *hospitality and entertainment company executive*
Mueller, Marylin *graphic supply company executive*
Randall, William Seymour *leasing company executive*
Ransom, Randy *marketing executive*
Schoenfeld, Howard Allen *management consultant, lawyer*
Van Handel, Michael J. *employment services executive*

Plymouth
Gentine, Lee Michael *marketing professional*

Racine
Johnson-Leipold, Helen P. *outdoor recreation company executive*
Klein, Gabriella Sonja *retired communications executive*

Waterford
Karraker, Louis Rendleman *retired corporate executive*

Waukesha
Myers, Gary *public relations executive*

ADDRESS UNPUBLISHED

Boehnen, David Leo *food service executive, lawyer*
Chait, Jon Frederick *human resources specialist, lawyer*
Chlebowski, John Francis, Jr. *leasing company executive*
Chorengel, Bernd *international hotel corporation executive*
Corwell, Ann Elizabeth *public relations executive*
Diederichs, Janet Wood *public relations executive*
Duarte, Gloria *chef*
Dvorak, Kathleen S. *former consumer products company executive*
Echols, Mary Evelyn *motivational speaker and business consultant, writer*
Engels, Thomas Joseph *sales executive*
Farr, Mel *automotive sales executive, former professional football player*
Feller, Robert William Andrew *public relations executive, retired professional baseball player*
Fleming, Thomas A. *retired administrative assistant*
Francis, Philip Hamilton *management consultant*
Gasser, Michael J. *consumer products company executive*
Glahn, Jeffrey *communications executive*
Glass, Kenneth Edward *management consultant*
Goldstein, Alfred George *consumer products company executive*
Gorsline, Stephen Paul *security specialist*
Guarascio, Philip *advertising executive*
Hall, Hansel Crimiel *communications executive*
Harr, Lucy Loraine *public relations executive*
Haupt, Roger A. *advertising executive*
Heise, Marilyn Beardsley *public relations and publishing company executive*
Hersher, Richard Donald *management consultant*
Hewes, Philip A. *computer company executive*
Holzer, Edwin *advertising executive*
Jackson, Monica Denee *purchasing agent*
Jernstedt, Richard Don *public relations executive*
Johnson, Steven M. *food service executive*
Jones, David A. *former consumer products company executive*
Kegerreis, Robert James *management consultant, marketing professional, educator*
Kupper, Bruce David *advertising executive*
Linda, Gerald *advertising and marketing executive*
Longaberger, Tami *home decor accessories company executive*
MacDonald, John *marketing executive*
Mack, Jim *advertising executive*
Marsh, Don Ermal *supermarket executive*
McCracken, Steven R. *former consumer products company executive*
McElwreath, Sally Chin *corporate communications executive*
McGee, Patrick Edgar *postal service clerk*
McKay, Melinda *hotel executive*
Metty, Theresa M. *communications executive*
Miller, Bernard Joseph, Jr. *advertising executive*
Moeller, Robert John *management consultant*
Moog, Matthew *Internet company executive*
Muma, Leslie M. *former data processing company executive*
Nevin, Robert Charles *information systems executive*
Olins, Robert Abbot *communications research executive*
Orr, James Francis *retired business process outsourcing executive*
Parker, Lee Fischer *sales executive*
Peppel, Michael E. *computer company executive*
Perry, Chris Nicholas *retired advertising executive*
Plakmeyer, Steve *food service executive*
Plank, Betsy (Mrs. Sherman V. Rosenfield) *public relations counsel*
Pollard, C. William *environmental services executive*
Proctor, Barbara Gardner *advertising agency executive, writer*
Roemer, James Paul *data processing executive, writer*
Ryan, Thomas *food service executive*
Saligman, Harvey *retired consumer products and services company executive*
Schlensker, Gary Chris *landscape company executive*
Schonberg, Alan Robert *personnel director*
Schubert, Helen Celia *public relations executive*
Schuessler, John T. (Jack Schuessler) *retired food service executive*
Schultz, Louis Edwin *management consultant*
Schwartz, Michael Robinson *management consultant*
Sease, Gene Elwood *communications executive*
Shevitz, Mark H. *sales promotion and marketing executive*
Simecka, Betty Jean *marketing executive*
Sincoff, Michael Z. *human resources and marketing executive, educator*
Smith, Donald Nickerson *food service executive*
Smith, Steven J. *communications company executive*
Sotir, Mark *automotive rental executive*
Stage, Brian *hotel executive*
Sternlieb, Lawrence Jay *marketing professional, writer*
Stone, James Howard *management consultant*
Streeter, Stephanie Anne *former printing company executive*
Tramonto, Rick *chef*
Tripp, Marian Barlow Loofe *retired public relations executive*
Vidricksen, Ben Eugene *food service executive, state legislator*
Water, Linda Gail *public relations executive*
Weber, Kenneth J. *hotel executive*
Weismantel, Gregory Nelson *management consultant, computer company executive*
Williams, Louis Clair, Jr. *public relations executive*
Williams, Paul Stratton *executive recruiter*
Zeller, Joseph Paul *advertising executive*

INDUSTRY: TRADE

UNITED STATES

ARIZONA

Scottsdale
Dauphinais, George Arthur *import company executive*

Tempe
Corcoran, Philip E. *wholesale distribution executive*

COLORADO

Vail
Jones, Jeffrey W. *retail executive*

FLORIDA

Naples
Ludwig, Richard Joseph *small business owner*

ILLINOIS

Chicago
Blagg, Joe W. *retail executive*
Doolittle, Sidney Newing *retail executive*
Field, Marshall *retail executive*
Gin, Sue Ling *retail executive*
Goltz, Jay *small business owner*
Hoye, Donald J. *hardware distribution company executive*
Hunt, Holly *small business owner*
Nickell, Jake *internet retail executive, apparel designer*
Robins, Joel *import/export company executive*
Vrablik, Edward Robert *import/export company executive*
Ziegler, Ann E. *retail executive*

Decatur
Bradshaw, Billy Dean *retired retail executive*

Deerfield
Ferkenhoff, Robert J. *retail executive*
Karlin, Jerome B. *retail executive*
Rein, Jeffrey A. *retail executive*
Rudolphsen, William M. *retail executive*

Des Plaines
Gochnauer, Richard Wallis *wholesale distribution executive*

Glenview
Letham, Dennis J. *wholesale company executive*

Hoffman Estates
Barraza, Lupe *retail executive*
Bousquette, Janine M. *retail executive*
Crowley, William C. *retail executive*
Johnson, W. Bruce *retail executive*
O'Leary, Robert J. *retail executive*

Itasca
Duncan, Sam K. *retail executive*

Lake Forest
Loux, P. Ogden *distribution company executive*
Ryan, James T. *wholesale distribution executive*
Stirling, Ellen Adair *retail executive*

Lisle
Reese, Howard Fred *wholesale distribution executive*

Lombard
Barnholt, Brandon K. *retail executive*

Melrose Park
Kloster, Carol Good *wholesale distribution executive*

Milan
Kelly, Robert J. *supermarket executive*
Plumley, S. Patric *retail executive*

Morton Grove
McKenna, Andrew James *wholesale distribution, printing company executive, sports association executive*

Oak Brook
Hanner, John *retail executive*
Hodnik, David F. *retail company executive*
Jung, Howard J. *retail executive*

Quincy
Niemann, Richard Henry *retail executive*

River Grove
Litzsinger, Richard Mark *retail executive*
Stanton, Kathryn *retail executive*

Round Lake
Laskowski, Richard E. *retail hardware company executive*

Schaumburg
Richter, Glenn *retail executive*

Steger
Carpenter, Kenneth Russell *international trading executive*

INDIANA

Elkhart
Drexler, Rudy Matthew, Jr. *professional law enforcement dog trainer*

Fort Wayne
Curtis, Douglas Homer *small business owner*

Indianapolis
Beekman, Philip E. *retail company executive*
Cohen, Alan H. *retail executive*
LaCrosse, James *retail executive*
Marsh, Charles Alan *retail executive*
Marsh, William Lynn *retail executive*

Yorktown
Smith, Hartman William *supermarket executive*

IOWA

Boone
Cramer, Robert *retail executive*

West Des Moines
Pearson, Ronald Dale *retail food stores corporation executive*
Wheeler, Mike *retail food store corporate executive*

KANSAS

Kansas City
Baska, James Louis *wholesale grocery company executive*

Shawnee Mission
Van Tuyl, Cecil L. *automobile dealer executive, real estate developer*

Topeka
Cantrell, Duane L. *retail executive*
Hicks, Ken Carlyle *retail executive*
Porzig, Ullrich E. *retail executive*
Rubel, Matthew Evan *retail executive*

Wichita
Gates, Walter Edward *small business owner*

MICHIGAN

Bad Axe
Sullivan, James Gerald *small business owner*

Belleville
Bailey, Glenn E. *wholesale distribution executive*

Birmingham
Glassman, Eric I. *retail executive*

Bloomfield Hills
Robinson, Jack Albert *retail executive*

Dearborn
Adray, Deborah *retail executive*

Detroit
McGee, Sherry *retail executive*
Tushman, J. Lawrence *wholesale distribution executive*

Grand Rapids
Kolk, Fritz D. *retail executive*
Meijer, Douglas *retail company executive*
Meijer, Hank *retail company executive*
Meijer, Mark *retail executive*
Meyer, James B. *retail executive*
Sturken, Craig C. *retail executive*
Walsh, James *retail supermarket executive*

Lansing
LaHaine, Gilbert Eugene *retail lumber company executive*

Muskegon
McKitrick, James Thomas *retired retail executive*

Redford
Barnaby, Alan *retail executive*

Three Rivers
Lewis, Darrell L. *retail executive*

Troy
Elder, Irma *retail executive*
Koch, Albert Acheson *music distribution company executive, management consultant*
Strome, Stephen *former music distribution company executive*

MINNESOTA

Eden Prairie
Engel, Susan E. *retail executive*
Knous, Pamela K. *wholesale distribution executive*
Noddle, Jeffrey *retail and food distribution executive*

Edina
Emmerich, Karol Denise *foundation executive, daylily hybridizer, former retail executive*
Finkelstein, Phil *retail executive*

Minneapolis
Ahlers, Linda L. *retail executive*
Erickson, Ronald A. *retail executive*
Hale, James Thomas *retail executive, lawyer*
Mammel, Russell Norman *retired food distribution company executive*
Schulze, Richard M. *retail executive*
Scovanner, Douglas A. *retail executive*
Steinhafel, Gregg W. *retail executive*
Stephenson, Vivian M. *former retail executive*
Trestman, Frank D. *distribution company executive, director*
Ulrich, Robert J. *retail executive*

Minnetonka
Benson, Keith A. *retail executive*
Kriegel, David L. *retail executive*

Richfield
Anderson, Bradbury H. *retail executive*
Muehlbauer, James L. *retail executive*

Saint Paul
Lindahl, Dennis *retail executive*
Nash, Nicholas David *retail executive*

MISSOURI

Chesterfield
Kleffner, Gregory William *retail executive, accountant*

Cuba
Work, Bruce Van Syoc *small business owner, consultant*

Kansas City
Stueck, William Noble *small business owner*

Maryland Heights
Marcus, John *wholesale distribution executive*

Saint Louis
Bennet, Richard W. III *retail executive*
Berger, Wayne C. *retail executive*
Bridgewater, Bernard Adolphus, Jr. *retired retail executive*
Hinshaw, Juanita *electric distributor executive*
Schnuck, Craig D. *grocery store company executive*
Wolfe, R. Dean *retail executive*

NEBRASKA

Sidney
Cabela, Richard N. *retail executive*

NEW JERSEY

Wayne
Babrowski, Claire Harbeck *retail executive*

NORTH DAKOTA

Grand Forks
Kiesau, Jean *retail executive*

OHIO

Cincinnati
Clark, David W. *retail executive*
Cody, Thomas Gerald *retail executive, lawyer*
Cole, Tom *retail executive*
Grove, Janet E. *retail executive*
Hodge, Robert Joseph *retail executive*
Hoguet, David Dilworth *rental furniture executive*
Hoguet, Karen M. *retail executive*
Javosky, Rudolph V. *retail executive*
Kronick, Susan D. *retail executive*
Lundgren, Terry J. *retail company executive*
Miller, Robert G. *retail executive*
Tysor, Ronald W. *retail executive*
Zimmerman, James M. *retail company executive*

Cleveland
Anderson, Warren *distribution company executive*
Crosby, Fred McClellan *retail executive*
Stone, Harry H. *retail executive*

Columbus
Biresi, Mark A. *retail executive*
Burgdoerfer, Stuart *retail executive*
Faber, Timothy *retail executive*
Finkelman, Daniel P. *retail executive*
Hailey, V. Ann *retail executive*
Hollis-Allbritton, Cheryl Dawn *retail paper supply store executive*
Kaufman, Barry D. *retail executive*
Kelley, William G. *retail stores executive*
Ketteler, Thomas R. *retail executive*
Killion, Theo *retail executive*
Potter, Michael J. *retail stores executive*
Razek, Edward G. *retail executive*
Redgrave, Martyn Robert *retail executive*
Ricart, Rhett C. *retail automotive executive*
Ricker, Jon *retail executive*
Schottenstein, Jay L. *retail executive*
Shapiro, Mark D. *retail executive*
Soll, Bruce A. *retail executive*
Travis, Tracey Thomas *retail executive*
Turney, Sharen Jester *retail executive, cosmetics executive*
Wexner, Leslie Herbert *retail executive*
Wilansky, Heywood *retail executive*

Dayton
Jenefsky, Jack *wholesale company executive*
Mershad, Frederick J. *retail executive*
Rose, Stuart *retail executive*

Galion
Butterfield, James T. *small business owner*

Hudson
Carney, Brian P. *retail executive*

Maumee
Walrod, David James *retail grocery chain executive*

New Albany
Riley, Susan Jean *retail executive*
Stevens, Kenneth T. *retail executive*

Pickerington
Callander, Kay Eileen Paisley *business owner, retired education educator, writer*

Reynoldsburg
Neal, Diane L. *retail executive*

Shaker Heights
Killeen, Michael F. *retail executive*
O'Donnell, Gene *retail executive*

Youngstown
Gottron, Francis Robert III *small business owner*

WASHINGTON

Redmond
Fiske, Neil S. *retail executive*

WISCONSIN

Arcadia
Wanek, Todd *retail executive*

Beloit
Story, Kendra *wholesale distribution executive*

Eau Claire
Helland, Mark Duane *small business owner*
Menard, John R., Jr. *home improvement retail executive*

Green Bay
Bettiga, Michael J. *retail executive*
Eugster, Jack Wilson *retail executive*

Menomonee Falls
Blanc, Caryn *retail executive*
Jeffries, Telvin *retail executive*
Kellogg, William S. *retail executive*
Mansell, Kevin B. *retail executive*
McDonald, Wesley S. *retail executive*
Meier, Arlene *retail executive*
Montgomery, Larry (R. Lawrence Montgomery) *retail executive*
Vasques, Gary *retail executive, marketing professional*

Milwaukee
Mariano, Robert A. *retail executive*

ADDRESS UNPUBLISHED

Arnold, Gary L. *retail executive*
Barth, David Keck *retired wholesale distribution executive, consultant*
Bernauer, David W. *retired retail executive*
Carolan, Douglas *wholesale company executive*
Conaway, Charles C. *former retail company executive*
Fenn, Wade R. *retail executive*
Goddu, Roger *former retail executive*
Goldstein, Norman Ray *international trading company executive, consultant*
Huntress, Betty Ann *retired small business owner, secondary school educator*
Jorndt, Louis Daniel *former retail drug store chain executive*
Kahn, Eugene S. *former department store chain executive*
Kelly, Gerald F, Jr. *retail executive*
Kipper, Barbara Levy *wholesale distribution executive*
Kogut, John Anthony *wholesale distribution executive*
Lacy, Alan Jasper *retired retail executive*
Lewis, Aylwin B. *former retail executive, former food service company executive*
Lueken, Harold W. *retail executive*
Marshall, Ron *retail executive*
Nichols, Grace A. *retired retail executive*
Peterson, Gary J *retail executive*
Quinnell, Bruce Andrew *retail book chain executive*
Sunderland, Henry D. *retail company executive*
Sweeney, Thomas Bell III *retail company executive*
Van Gelder, Marc Christiaan *retail executive*

INDUSTRY: TRANSPORTATION

UNITED STATES

CALIFORNIA

Los Angeles
Palmer, James F. *aerospace transportation executive*

San Francisco
Foret, Mickey Phillip *retired air transportation executive*

FLORIDA

Satellite Beach
Loney, Mary Rose *former airport administrator, aviation industry consultant*

Venice
Barney, Charles Richard *retired transportation executive*

GEORGIA

Atlanta
Anderson, Richard H. *air transportation executive*

ILLINOIS

Chicago
Andolino, Rosemarie S. *airport terminal executive*
Apelbaum, Phyllis L. *delivery messenger service executive*
Bell, James A. *aerospace transportation executive*
Burkhardt, Edward Arnold *rail transportation executive*
Foland, Jeffrey T. *air transportation sales executive*
Gibson, Roger *air transportation executive*
Koellner, Laurette *aerospace transportation executive*
Luttig, J(ohn) Michael (John Michael Luttig) *aerospace transportation executive, former federal judge*
McNerney, James, Jr., (W. James McNerney) *aerospace transportation executive, former manufacturing executive*
Nord, Henry J. *transportation executive*
Stephens, Richard *aerospace transportation executive*
Studdert, Andrew Paul *air transportation executive*
Tilton, Glenn F. *air transportation executive*

Downers Grove
Yeager, David P. *transportation executive*

Elk Grove Village
Brace, Frederic F. (Jake Brace) *air transportation executive*
Hacker, Douglas A. *air transportation executive*
Puma, Grace M. *air transportation executive*

Hillside
Marzullo, Larry A. *transportation executive*

Lake Forest
Krasnewich, Kathryn *water transportation executive*

Mahomet
Roberson, Roger T. *transportation executive*

Naperville
Benson, Kevin E. *transportation executive*
Stangl, Peter E. *transportation executive*

Oak Brook
Duerinck, Louis T. *retired rail transportation executive, lawyer*
Goodwin, James E. (Jim Goodwin) *retired air transportation executive*

Warrenville
Ustian, Daniel C. *trucking executive*

INDIANA

Evansville
Shaffer, Michael L. *transportation company executive*

Fort Wayne
Uber, Larry R. *transportation executive*

Indianapolis
Roberts, David *airport executive*
Wensits, David L. *aerospace transportation executive*

Jeffersonville
Hagan, Michael Charles *transporation executive*

Noblesville
Morrison, Joseph Young *transportation executive, consultant*

IOWA

Cedar Rapids
Smith, Herald Alvin, Jr. *transportation executive*
Smith, John M. *trucking executive*

Coralville
Gerdin, Russell A. *transportation executive*

Des Moines
Ruan, John *transportation executive*

Fort Dodge
Smith, William G. *transportation executive*

KANSAS

Lenexa
Taggart, David D. *trucking executive*

Overland Park
Zollars, William D. *freight company executive*

Wichita
Bell, Baillis F. *airport terminal executive*
Meyer, Russell William, Jr. *air transportation executive*

KENTUCKY

Erlanger
Siebenburgen, David A. *airline company executive*

MICHIGAN

Ann Arbor
Drake, John Warren *aviation consultant*
Yamashina, Tadashi (George) *transportation executive*

Detroit
Feldhouse, Lynn *automotive company executive*
Newman, Andrea Fischer *air transportation executive*
Robinson, Lester W. *airport executive*

Flint
Trout, Michael Gerald *airport administrator*

Grand Rapids
Auwers, Stanley John *motor carrier executive*
Gainey, Harvey Nueton *transportation executive*

Lansing
Schmidt, Thomas Walter *airport executive*

Waterford
Randall, Karl W. *air transportation executive, lawyer*

Ypsilanti
Snoddy, Anthony L. *manufacturing executive*

MINNESOTA

Eagan
Griffin, J. Timothy *air transportation executive*
Haan, Philip C. *air transportation executive*
Hirst, Richard B. *air transportation executive, lawyer*
Oren, Donald G. *transportation executive*
Steenland, Douglas M. *air transportation executive*

Eden Prairie
Lindbloom, Chad M. *transportation executive*
Radunz, Paul A. *transportation executive*
Wiehoff, John P. *trucking executive*

Minneapolis
Anderson, Tim *airport terminal executive*
Hamiel, Jeff *airport executive*
Harper, Donald Victor *retired transportation and logistics educator, consultant*
Oppegaard, Grant E. *water transportation executive*

North Oaks
Engle, Donald Edward *retired rail transportation executive, lawyer*

Saint Cloud
Anderson, Harold E. *trucking company executive*

Saint Paul
Birdsall, Doug *airline company executive*

Warba
Currie, Earl James *transportation executive*

MISSOURI

Chesterfield
Baer, Robert J. *retired transportation company executive*

Fenton
Ellington, Donald E. *transportation company executive*
Huber, Scott *transportation services executive*
Stadler, Gerald P. *transportation executive*

Joplin
Brown, Glenn F. *transportation executive, department chairman*

Kansas City
Cooper, Thom R. *transportation executive*
Widmar, Russell C. *airport executive*

Saint Louis
Griggs, Leonard LeRoy, Jr. *air transportation executive, consultant*
McDonnell, Sanford Noyes *air transportation executive*

Springfield
Low, Robert E. *transportation executive*

NEBRASKA

Lincoln
Acklie, Duane William *transportation company executive*
Wood, John Frederick *air transportation executive*

Omaha
Evans, Ivor J. (Ike) *railroad executive*
Smithey, Donald Leon *airport authority director*
Starzel, Robert F. *rail transportation executive*
Werner, Clarence L. *transportation executive*
Young, James R. *rail transportation executive*

NEW YORK

New York
Armstrong, Neil Alden *retired astronaut*

NORTH CAROLINA

Charlotte
Handy, John W. *shipping company executive, retired military officer*

OHIO

Akron
Wickham, Michael W. *transportation executive*

Cincinnati
Holscher, Robert F. *airport terminal executive*

Cleveland
Dannemiller, John C. *transportation company executive*

Rocky River
Shively, Daniel Jerome *retired transportation executive*

Toledo
Hartung, James H. *airport authority executive*

Xenia
Bigelow, Daniel James *aerospace executive*

SOUTH DAKOTA

Sioux Falls
Smith, Murray Thomas *transportation company executive*

WISCONSIN

Appleton
Crowley, Geoffrey Thomas *airline executive*

Green Bay
Lofgren, Christopher B. *trucking executive*
Schneider, Donald J. *trucking company executive*

Marshfield
Roehl, Everett *transportation executive*

Milwaukee
Bateman, C. Barry *airport terminal executive*

Mondovi
Marten, Randolph L. *transportation executive*

Oshkosh
Bohn, Robert G. *transportation company executive*
Schoenrock, Tracy Allen *airline pilot, aviation consultant*
Szews, Charles *transportation executive*

ADDRESS UNPUBLISHED

Bain, Douglas G. *retired aerospace transportation executive, lawyer*
Burton, Raymond Charles, Jr. *retired transportation company executive*
Checchi, Alfred A. *air transportation executive, financial consultant*
Compton, William F. *retired air transportation executive*
Davidson, Richard K. *retired rail transportation executive*
Gitner, Gerald L. *air transportation executive, investment banker*
Goldstein, Bernard *transportation and hotel executive*
Hannemann, Timothy W. *aerospace transportation executive*
Heckel, John Louis (Jack Heckel) *aerospace management executive*
Hedrick, Larry Willis *retired airport executive*
Johnson, William S. *transportation executive*
Kaczka, Jeff *trucking and relocation services executive*
Martin, William F. *retired transportation executive*
Matthews, L. White III *railroad executive*
McCarthy, Paul Fenton *aerospace transportation executive, retired military officer*
McDonald, Peter D. *air transportation executive*
Miller, Paul David *aerospace transportation executive, retired admiral*
Saubert, Walter E. (Wally Saubert) *trucking and transportation company executive*
Stonecipher, Harry Curtis *former aerospace transportation executive*
Tague, John Patrick *air transportation executive*
Valine, Delmar Edmond, Sr. *transportation executive*
Verdoorn, D.R. (Sid) *retired trucking executive*
Washburn, Donald Arthur *retired transportation executive, investor*
White, Dennis L. *transportation executive, former political organization administrator*
Wilson, Gary Lee *airline company executive*
Yeager, Phillip Charles *transportation company executive*

INDUSTRY: UTILITIES, ENERGY, RESOURCES

UNITED STATES

ILLINOIS

Argonne
Ban, Stephen Dennis *gas industry executive*

Chicago
Carlson, LeRoy Theodore, Jr. *telecommunications industry executive*
Clark, Frank M. *utilities executive*
Gillis, Ruth Ann M. *utilities executive*
Henry, Brian C. *telephone company executive*
Hightman, Carrie J. *telecommunications industry executive, lawyer*
Moeller, William E. *cement, oil and gas company executive*
Morrow, Richard Martin *retired oil company executive*
Niederpruem, Gary J. *metal company executive*
Perez, David *utilities executive*
Rogers, Desiree Glapion *utilities executive*
Rowe, John William *utilities executive*
Zopp, Andrea Lynne *energy company executive*

Decatur
Womeldorff, Porter John *utilities executive*

Deerfield
Zywicki, Robert Albert *retired electric power industry executive*

Naperville
Birck, Michael John *telecommunications industry executive*
Pullen, Robert W. *telecommunications industry executive*
Strobel, Russ M. *gas industry executive, lawyer*

Peoria
Viets, Robert O. *utilities executive*

Schaumburg
Mark, Kelly S. *telecommunications industry executive, investment advisor*
O'Connor, James, Jr., (Jim O'Connor) *telecommunications industry executive*

INDIANA

Columbus
Able, Warren Walter *natural resource company executive, physician*

Evansville
Ellerbrook, Niel Cochran *gas industry executive*
Reherman, Ronald Gilbert *gas and electric company executive*

Highland
Purcell, James Francis *former utility executive, consultant*

Indianapolis
Bell, William Vernon *utility executive*
Griffiths, David Neal *utilities executive*

Merrillville
Skaggs, Robert C., Jr. *utilities executive, lawyer*

IOWA

Des Moines
Abel, Gregory E. *utilities company executive*
Sokol, David Lee *utilities company executive*

Sioux City
Wharton, Beverly Ann *former utility company executive*

KANSAS

Overland Park
Betts, Gene M. *telecommunications industry executive*
Ferrell, James Edwin *nuclear energy industry executive*
Gerke, Thomas A. *telecommunications industry executive, lawyer*
Krause, Arthur B. *retired telecommunications industry executive*
LeMay, Ronald T. *telecommunications industry executive*
Strandjord, M. Jeannine *telecommunications industry executive*
Walker, Kathryn A. *telecommunications industry executive*

Pittsburg
Nettels, George Edward, Jr. *retired mining executive*

Shawnee Mission
Pressman, Ronald R. *utilities executive*

Topeka
Chandler, Charles Q., IV, *energy executive*

MICHIGAN

Detroit
Anderson, Gerard M. *energy executive*
Beale, Susan M. *electric power industry executive*
Buckler, Robert J. *energy distribution company executive*
Champley, Michael E. *electric power industry executive*
Earley, Anthony Francis, Jr. *utilities company executive, lawyer*
Taylor, S. Martin *utilities executive*

Fraser
Cattaneo, Michael S. *heating and cooling company executive*

Jackson
Harris, Patti B. *telecommunications executive*
Joos, David W. *energy executive*
Webb, Thomas J. *utilities executive*
Whipple, Kenneth *utilities executive*

Saint Clair Shores
Glancy, Alfred Robinson III *retired public utility company executive*

MINNESOTA

Eden Prairie
Switz, Robert E. *telecommunications executive*

Minneapolis
Cadogan, William J. *telecommunications company executive*
Gogel, Raymond E. *energy executive*
Kelly, Richard C. *energy executive*
Wyman, James Thomas *petroleum company executive*

Saint Paul
Robertson, Jerry Earl *retired manufacturing company executive*

MISSOURI

Joplin
McKinney, Myron W. *electronic company executive*

Kansas City
Baker, John Russell *utilities executive*
Chesser, Michael J. *gas and electric power industry executive*
Empson, Jon R. *utilities executive*
Green, Richard Calvin, Jr. *electric power and gas industry executive*
Jackson, Marcus *electric power industry executive*
Mackenzie, Nanci *gas company executive*
Riggins, William G. *electric power industry executive*
Stamm, Keith G. *energy executive*

Saint Louis
Baxter, Warner L. *electric power industry executive*
Boyce, Gregory H. *energy executive*
Brandt, Donald Edward *utilities company executive*
Hilton, Thomas Scott *coal company executive*
Leer, Steven F. *mining executive*
Monser, Edward L. *electric power industry executive*
Navarre, Richard A. *mining executive*
Quenon, Robert Hagerty *retired mining consultant and holding company executive*
Rainwater, Gary L. *electric power industry executive*
Smit, Neil *telecommunications industry executive*
Stroup, John S. *high speed electronic industry executive*

Springfield
Jura, James J. *electric utility executive*

NEBRASKA

Omaha
Crouse, Jerry K. *energy company executive*
Grewcock, William L. *mining company executive*
Scott, Walter, Jr. *telecommunications industry executive*

NORTH CAROLINA

Charlotte
Rogers, James Eugene *energy executive*

OHIO

Akron
Alexander, Anthony J. *electric power industry executive*
Marsh, Richard H. *energy executive*
Smart, George M. *energy executive, former packaging company executive*

Avon
Connelly, John James *retired oil company technical specialist*

Chagrin Falls
Miller, John Robert *oil industry executive*

Cincinnati
Aumiller, Wendy L. *utilities executive*
Braunstein, Mary *energy consulting company executive*
Bryant, John *utilities executive*
Cyrus, Michael J. *electric power industry executive*
Duncan, R. Foster *utilities company executive*
Esamann, Douglas F. *utilities executive*
Ficke, Gregory C. *utilities executive*
Foley, Cheryl M. *electric power industry executive*
Gaines, Bennett L. *utilities executive*
Murphy, Theodore R., II, *utilities executive*
Newton, Frederick J. III *utilities executive*
Noonan, Sheila M. *energy consulting company executive*
Randolph, Jackson Harold *utility company executive*

Cleveland
Ginn, Robert Martin *retired utility company executive*
Lucking, Paul *telecommunications executive*
O'Neil, Thomas J. *mining company executive*
Stropki, John M., Jr. *electric power industry executive*

Columbus
Addis, Paul D. *utilities executive*
Clements, Donald M. *utilities executive*
Fayne, Henry W. *electric power industry executive*
Grossman, Jeffrey W. *utilities company professional*
Koeppel, Holly Keller *electric power industry executive*
Lhota, William J. *electric company executive*
Markowsky, James J. *retired utilities executive*
Massey, Robert John *telecommunications executive*
Morris, Michael G. *electric power industry executive*
Powers, Robert P. *electric power industry executive*
Tomasky, Susan *electric power industry executive*

Dayton
Lansaw, Judy W. *public utility executive*

Dublin
Vassell, Gregory S. *electric utility consultant*

Newark
DallePezze, John Raymond *lighting company executive*

Westerville
Feck, Luke Matthew *retired utility executive*

SOUTH DAKOTA

Pierre
Dunn, James Bernard *mining company executive, state legislator*

Rapid City
Korpan, Richard *retired energy executive*
Lien, Bruce Hawkins *minerals and oil company executive*

Sioux Falls
Bradley, Walter A. III *utilities company executive*

TEXAS

Dallas
Harless, Katherine J. *telecommunications industry executive*

Houston
Kelly, Janet Langford *oil industry executive, lawyer*

WISCONSIN

Green Bay
Weyers, Larry Lee *energy executive*

La Crosse
Rude, Brian David *utilities executive*

Madison
Harvey, William D. *utilities executive, lawyer*
Liu, Lee *utility company executive*
Protsch, Eliot G. *utilities and corporate financial executive*

Milwaukee
Klappa, Gale E. *energy executive*
Leverett, Allen L. *energy executive*

CANADA

MANITOBA

Saint Andrews
Lang, Otto *retired gas industry executive, former Canadian cabinet minister*

ADDRESS UNPUBLISHED

Barr, James III *telecommunications company executive*
Baumgartner, John H. *gas industry executive*
Boulanger, Rodney Edmund *energy company executive*
Brinzo, John S. *mining executive*
Brown, Stephen S. *telecommunications industry executive*
Chelle, Robert Frederick *electric power industry executive, educator*
Draper, E(rnest) Linn, Jr. *retired electric utility executive*
Engelhardt, Irl F. *coal company executive*
English, Floyd Leroy *telecommunications industry executive*
Esrey, William Todd *telecommunications company executive*
Ewing, Stephen E. *natural gas company executive*
Ferger, Lawrence A. *gas distribution utility executive*
Forster, Peter Hans *utility company executive*
Garberding, Larry Gilbert *retired utilities companies executive*
Greer, Carl Crawford *petroleum company executive*
Guy, William Lewis *retired energy consultant, former governor*
Haines, James S., Jr. *retired energy executive*
Halloran, Kathleen L. *retired gas industry executive, accountant*
Helton, Sandra Lynn *telecommunications industry executive*
Howard, James Joseph III *utility company executive*
Humke, Ramon Lyle *utilities executive*
Kaufman, Raymond L. *energy company executive*
Lobbia, John E. *retired utility company executive*
Lowrie, William G. *former oil company executive*
MacFarlane, John Charles *utilities executive*
Mc Carthy, Walter John, Jr. *retired utilities executive*
Mueller, Charles William *electric utility executive*
Neale, Gary Lee *utilities executive*
O'Malley, Thomas D. *petroleum industry executive*
Prabhu, Krish Anant *former telecommunications industry executive, educator*
Rogers, Justin Towner, Jr. *retired utility company executive*
Sim, Richard Guild *utilities executive*
Strobel, Pamela B. *former energy executive*
Torgerson, James Paul *energy company executive*
White, Willis Sheridan, Jr. *retired utilities company executive*
Ziemer, Paul D. *utility company executive*

INFORMATION TECHNOLOGY *See also* SCIENCE: MATHEMATICS AND COMPUTER SCIENCE

UNITED STATES

CALIFORNIA

San Jose
Warrior, Padmasree Y. *computer systems network executive*

San Rafael
Hughes, Louis Ralph *information technology executive*

FLORIDA

Sanibel
Trevor, Alexander Bruen *information technology consultant*

ILLINOIS

Burr Ridge
Rosenberg, Robert Brinkmann *information technology executive*

Chicago
Bariff, Martin Louis *information systems educator, consultant*
Bergstein, Melvyn *information technology executive*
Drewry, June E. *information technology executive*
Fried, Jason *software development company executive*
Hansson, David Heinemeier *application developer*

Effingham
Fatheree, Joseph G. *informaation technology educator*

Skokie
Seeder, Richard Owen *infosystems specialist*

Vernon Hills
Edwardson, John Albert *information technology executive*
Klein, Barbara A. *information technology executive*

Warrenville
Data, Art J. *information technology executive*

INDIANA

Carmel
Bostick, Russell M. *information technology executive*

IOWA

Waverly
Brunkhorst, Robert John *computer programmer, analyst*

MICHIGAN

Bloomfield Hills
Weil, John William *technology management consultant*

Detroit
Kruse, Ronia *information technology executive*

Highland Park
Henry, William Lockwood *information technology executive*

Troy
Walker, Bette M. *information technology executive*

Ypsilanti
Boone, Morell Douglas *information technology educator*

MINNESOTA

Buffalo
Moon, James Russell *retired technology education educator*

Elk River
McClure, Alvin Bruce *watchmaker*

Excelsior
Henke, Janice Carine *educational software developer, marketing professional*

Minneapolis
Perlman, Lawrence *retired information technology executive*

MISSOURI

Fenton
Hoffman, Gilbert L. *information technology executive*

Kansas City
Amigoni, Michael *information technology executive*
McDonnell, Thomas A. *information technology executive*
Patterson, Neal L. *information systems company executive*
West, Marc *information technology executive*

Saint Louis
Elliott, Susan Spoehrer *information technology executive*
Hassell, Stephen C. *information technology executive*
Pollack, Seymour Victor *computer science educator*

OHIO

Cincinnati
Cloyd, G. Gil *information technology executive*
Laney, Sandra Eileen *information technology executive*

Columbus
Adams, Richard C. *information technology executive*

Dublin
Davids, Jody R. *information technology executive*

Maineville
Collins, Larry Wayne *computer technician, small business owner*

Marion
Rowe, Lisa Dawn *computer programmer, analyst, consultant*

SOUTH DAKOTA

Spearfish
Ellis, Mary Louise Helgeson *retired healthcare technology company executive*

TEXAS

Denton
Garcia, Oscar Nicolas *computer science educator*

Plano
Musser, Cherri M. *information technology executive*

WISCONSIN

Green Bay
Lynch, Matthew J. *information technology executive, retail executive*

ADDRESS UNPUBLISHED

Bass, Steven Craig *computer science educator*
Buckley, Joseph Paul III *computer technician*
Govern, Maureen *information technology executive*
Johansson, Nils A. *information services executive*
Niederberger, Jane *information technology executive*
Toirac, S(eth) Thomas *software engineering executive, consultant*
Tolva, John *information technology manager*
Treinavicz, Kathryn Mary *application developer*
Zimov, Bruce Steven *software engineer*
Zucker, David F. *former information technology executive*

INTERNET *See* INFORMATION TECHNOLOGY

LAW: JUDICIAL ADMINISTRATION

UNITED STATES

CALIFORNIA

Rancho Mirage
Gordon, Myron L. *federal judge*

ILLINOIS

Benton
Gilbert, J. Phil *federal judge*

Chicago
Andersen, Wayne R. *federal judge*
Ashman, Martin C. *federal judge*
Aspen, Marvin Edward *federal judge*
Bauer, William Joseph *federal judge*
Bobrick, Edward Allen *retired judge*
Bower, Glen Landis *judge, lawyer*
Bucklo, Elaine Edwards *United States district court judge*
Burke, Anne M. *state supreme court justice*
Castillo, Ruben *federal judge*
Coar, David H. *federal judge*
Conlon, Suzanne B. *federal judge*
Cousins, William, Jr. *retired judge*
Cudahy, Richard D. *federal judge*
Denlow, Morton *federal magistrate judge*
Easterbrook, Frank Hoover *federal judge*
Fitzgerald, Thomas Robert *state supreme court justice*
Flaum, Joel Martin *federal judge*
Funderburk, Raymond *judge*
Garman, Rita B. *state supreme court justice*
Gettleman, Robert William *judge*
Gottschall, Joan B. *judge*
Grady, John F. *federal judge*
Hart, William Thomas *federal judge*
Holderman, James F., Jr. *federal judge*
Keys, Arlander *federal judge*
Kilbride, Thomas L. *state supreme court justice*
Kocoras, Charles Petros *federal judge*
Lefkow, Joan Humphrey *federal judge*
Leighton, George Neves *retired judge*
Leinenweber, Harry D. *federal judge*
Lindberg, George W. *federal judge*
Manning, Blanche M. *federal judge*
Marovich, George M. *federal judge*
Miller, Benjamin K. *retired state supreme court justice*
Moran, James Byron *federal judge*
Nordberg, John Albert *federal judge*
Norgle, Charles Ronald, Sr. *federal judge*
Pallmeyer, Rebecca Ruth *judge*
Plunkett, Paul Edmund *federal judge*
Posner, Richard Allen *federal judge*
Rovner, Ilana Kara Diamond *federal judge*
St. Eve, Amy J. *federal judge*
Schmetterer, Jack Baer *federal judge*
Shadur, Milton Irving *judge*
Sonderby, Susan Pierson *federal bankruptcy judge*
Stamos, John James *judge*
Thomas, Robert R. *state supreme court justice*
Williams, Ann Claire *federal judge*
Wood, Diane Pamela *federal judge*
Zagel, James Block *federal judge*

Downers Grove
McGarr, Frank James *retired federal judge, consultant*

East Saint Louis
Cohn, Gerald B. *federal judge*
Stiehl, William D. *federal judge*

Maple Park
Nickels, John L. *retired state supreme court justice*

Nashville
Karmeier, Lloyd A. *state supreme court justice*

Peoria
Heiple, James Dee *retired state supreme court justice*
McDade, Joe Billy *federal judge*
Mihm, Michael Martin *federal judge*

Petersburg
Wood, Harlington, Jr. *federal judge*

Rock Island
Darrow, Clarence Allison *judge*

Rockford
Mahoney, Patrick Michael *federal judge*
Reinhard, Philip Godfrey *federal judge*

Rolling Meadows
Roti, Thomas David *judge*

Skokie
Fein, Roger Gary *judge*

Springfield
Evans, Charles H. *federal judge*
Lessen, Larry Lee *federal judge*
Mills, Richard Henry *federal judge*

Urbana
Baker, Harold Albert *federal judge*
Bernthal, David Gary *judge*
McCuskey, Michael Patrick *federal judge*

Wheaton
Leston, Patrick John *judge*

INDIANA

Fort Wayne
Cosbey, Roger B. *federal magistrate judge*
Lee, William Charles *judge*

Hammond
Lozano, Rudolpho *federal judge*
Moody, James T(yne) *federal judge*
Rodovich, Andrew Paul *magistrate judge*
Van Bokkelen, Joseph Scott *federal judge, former prosecutor*

Indianapolis
Barker, Sarah Evans *judge*
Barnes, Michael Phillip *judge*
Boehm, Theodore Reed *state supreme court justice*
Dickson, Brent E. *state supreme court justice*
Foster, Kennard P. *magistrate judge*
Givan, Richard Martin *retired judge*
Hamilton, David F. *judge*
McKinney, Larry J. *federal judge*
Metz, Anthony J. III *federal judge*
Otte, Frank J. *federal judge*
Rucker, Robert D. *state supreme court justice*
Shepard, Randall Terry *state supreme court chief justice*
Shields, V. Sue *federal magistrate judge*
Sullivan, Frank, Jr. *state supreme court justice*

Lafayette
Kanne, Michael Stephen *federal judge*

South Bend
Manion, Daniel Anthony *federal judge*
Miller, Robert L., Jr., (Bob Miller) *federal judge*
Ripple, Kenneth Francis *federal judge*
Sharp, Allen *federal judge*
Tinder, John Daniel *federal judge*

Terre Haute
Lewis, Jordan D. *federal judge*

IOWA

Algona
Andreasen, James Hallis *retired state supreme court judge*

Cedar Rapids
Hansen, David Rasmussen *federal judge*
Kilburg, Paul J. *federal judge*
Mc Manus, Edward Joseph *federal judge*
Melloy, Michael J. *federal judge*

Chariton
Stuart, William Corwin *judge*

Council Bluffs
Peterson, Richard William *retired judge, lawyer*

Des Moines
Bremer, Celeste F. *judge*
Cady, Mark S. *state supreme court justice*
Carter, James Harvey *retired state supreme court justice*
Colloton, Steven M. *federal judge*
Fagg, George Gardner *federal judge*
Harris, K. David *senior state supreme court justice*
Hecht, Daryl L. *state supreme court justice*
Jackwig, Lee M. *federal judge*
Jarvey, John Alfred *federal judge*
Larson, Jerry Leroy *state supreme court justice*
Lavorato, Louis A. *retired state supreme court justice*
Longstaff, Ronald Earl *federal judge*
McGiverin, Arthur A. *former state supreme court chief justice*
Streit, Michael J. *state supreme court justice*
Ternus, Marsha K. *state supreme court chief justice*
Vietor, Harold Duane *federal judge*
Walters, Ross A. *federal judge*
Wiggins, David Stewart *state supreme court justice*
Wolle, Charles Robert *judge*

Ida Grove
Snell, Bruce M., Jr. *judge*

Osceola
Reynoldson, Walter Ward *retired judge, lawyer*

Sioux City
Bennett, Mark Warren *federal judge, lawyer, educator*
Edmonds, William L. *federal judge*
O'Brien, Donald Eugene *federal judge*

KANSAS

Kansas City
Lungstrum, John W. *federal judge*
Rushfelt, Gerald Lloyd *magistrate judge*
Vratil, Kathryn Hoefer *federal judge*
Waxse, David John *judge*

Lawrence
Briscoe, Mary Beck *federal judge*
Six, Fred N. *retired state supreme court justice*
Tacha, Deanell Reece *federal judge*

Topeka
Allegrucci, Donald Lee *state supreme court justice*
Beier, Carol Ann *state supreme court justice*
Crow, Sam Alfred *judge*
Davis, Robert Edward *state supreme court justice*
Larson, Edward *retired state supreme court justice*
Luckert, Marla Jo *state supreme court justice*
Marquardt, Christel Elisabeth *judge*
McFarland, Kay Eleanor *state supreme court chief justice*
Nuss, Lawton R. *state supreme court justice*
Robinson, Julie Ann *judge*
Rogers, Richard Dean *federal judge*
Rosen, Eric S. *state supreme court justice*

Wichita
Belot, Monti L. III *federal judge*
Brown, Wesley Ernest *federal judge*
Marten, J. Thomas *judge*

KENTUCKY

Paducah
Foreman, James Louis *retired judge*

MICHIGAN

Ann Arbor
Guy, Ralph B., Jr. *federal judge*
O'Meara, John Corbett *federal judge*
Pepe, Steven Douglas *federal magistrate judge*

Bay City
Binder, Charles E. *magistrate judge*
Ludington, Thomas Lamson *federal judge*

Birmingham
La Plata, George *federal judge*

Detroit
Borman, Paul David *judge*
Callahan, J(ohn) William (Bill Callahan) *judge*
Cleland, Robert Hardy *federal judge*
Corrigan, Maura Denise *state supreme court justice*
Cox, Sean F. *federal judge*
Duggan, Patrick James *federal judge*
Edmunds, Nancy Garlock *federal judge*
Feikens, John *federal judge*
Friedman, Bernard Alvin *federal judge*
Hood, Denise Page *federal judge*
Keith, Damon Jerome *federal judge*
Kelly, Marilyn *state supreme court justice*
Kennedy, Cornelia Groefsema *federal judge*
Komives, Paul J. *federal judge*
Levin, Charles Leonard *state supreme court justice*
Lombard, Arthur J. *judge*
Mallett, Conrad LeRoy, Jr. *former state supreme court chief justice, hospital administrator*
Mathis, Greg *judge, radio personality*
Morgan, Virginia Mattison *judge*
Rosen, Gerald Ellis *federal judge*
Ryan, James Leo *federal judge*
Taylor, Anna Diggs *federal judge*
Woods, George Edward *judge*
Zatkoff, Lawrence P. *federal judge*

Grand Rapids
Bell, Robert Holmes *federal judge*
Brenneman, Hugh Warren, Jr. *judge*
Miles, Wendell A. *federal judge*
Quist, Gordon Jay *federal judge*
Scoville, Joseph Giacomo *federal magistrate, judge*
Stevenson, Jo Ann C. *federal bankruptcy judge*

Kalamazoo
Enslen, Richard Alan *federal judge*

Kentwood
Kelly, William Garrett *judge*

Lansing
Cavanagh, Michael Francis *state supreme court justice*
Harrison, Michael Gregory *judge*
Markman, Stephen J. *state supreme court justice*
McKeague, David William *federal judge*
Suhrheinrich, Richard Fred *federal judge*
Taylor, Clifford Woodworth *state supreme court justice*
Young, Robert P., Jr. *state supreme court justice*

Marquette
Greeley, Timothy P. *federal judge*

Traverse City
Weaver, Elizabeth A. *state supreme court justice*

White Lake
Boyle, Patricia Jean *retired state supreme court justice*

MINNESOTA

Anoka
Quinn, R. Joseph *district judge*

Lake Elmo
Tomljanovich, Esther M. *retired judge*

Minneapolis
Davis, Michael J. *judge*
Doty, David Singleton *federal judge*
Kishel, Gregory Francis *federal judge*
Lebedoff, Jonathan Galanter *retired judge, mediator*
Loken, James Burton *federal judge*
MacLaughlin, Harry Hunter *retired judge*
Montgomery, Ann D. *federal judge, educator*
Murphy, Diana E. *federal judge*
Noel, Franklin Linwood *judge*
Rosenbaum, James Michael *federal judge*

Minnetonka
Rogers, James Devitt *judge*

Saint Paul
Alsop, Donald Douglas *federal judge*
Anderson, G. Barry *state supreme court justice*
Anderson, Paul Holden *state supreme court justice*
Anderson, Russell A. *state supreme court chief justice*
Bastian, Gary Warren *judge*
Gildea, Lorie Skjerven *state supreme court justice*
Hanson, Samuel Lee *state supreme court justice*
Kyle, Richard House *federal judge*
Lancaster, Joan Ericksen *judge*
Meyer, Helen M. *state supreme court justice*
Page, Alan C. *state supreme court justice*
Schiltz, Patrick Joseph *federal judge*
Stringer, Edward Charles *judge, lawyer*
Willis, Bruce Donald *judge*

MISSOURI

Benton
Heckemeyer, Anthony Joseph *circuit court judge*

Cape Girardeau
Blanton, Lewis M. *federal judge*

High Ridge
Karll, Jo Ann *retired judge, lawyer*

Jefferson City
Knox, William Arthur *judge*
Limbaugh, Stephen Nathaniel, Jr. *state supreme court judge*
Price, William Ray, Jr. *state supreme court justice*
Stith, Laura Denvir *state supreme court justice*
Teitelman, Richard B. *state supreme court judge*
White, Ronnie L. *retired state supreme court justice*
Wolff, Michael A. *state supreme court judge*

Kansas City
Benton, William Duane *federal judge*
Bowman, Pasco Middleton, II, *judge*
Federman, Arthur *federal judge*
Gaitan, Fernando J., Jr. *federal judge*
Gibson, John Robert *federal judge*
Larsen, Robert Emmett *federal judge*
Laughrey, Nanette Kay *federal judge*
Sachs, Howard F(rederic) *federal judge*
Smith, Ortrie D. *judge*
Ulrich, Robert Gene *judge*
Whipple, Dean *federal judge*
Wright, Scott Olin *federal judge*

Saint Louis
Filippine, Edward Louis *federal judge*
Gruender, Raymond W. *federal judge, former prosecutor*
Hamilton, Jean Constance *judge*
Limbaugh, Stephen Nathaniel *federal judge*
Medler, Mary Ann L. *federal judge*
Noce, David D. *judge*
Shaw, Charles Alexander *judge*
Stohr, Donald J. *federal judge*
Webber, E. Richard, Jr. *judge*

Springfield
Holstein, John Charles *former state supreme court judge*

NEBRASKA

Lincoln
Beam, Clarence Arlen *federal judge*
Connolly, William M. *state supreme court justice*
Gerrard, John M. *state supreme court justice*
Hastings, William Charles *retired state supreme court chief justice*
Heavican, Michael G. *state supreme court justice*
Hendry, John V. *retired state supreme court justice*
Kopf, Richard G. *federal judge*
McCormack, Michael *state supreme court justice*
Miller-Lerman, Lindsey *state supreme court justice*
Piester, David L(ee) *magistrate judge*
Stephan, Kenneth C. *state supreme court justice*
Urbom, Warren Keith *federal judge*
Wright, John F. *state supreme court justice*

Omaha
Bataillon, Joseph Francis *chief federal judge*
Riley, William Jay *federal judge*
Ross, Donald Roe *federal judge*
Shanahan, Thomas M. *judge*
Strom, Lyle Elmer *judge*

NORTH DAKOTA

Bismarck
Conmy, Patrick A. *federal judge*
Crothers, Daniel J. *state supreme court justice*
Kapsner, Carol Ronning *state supreme court justice*
Kautzmann, Dwight C. H. *federal magistrate judge*
Maring, Mary Muehlen *state supreme court justice*
Neumann, William Allen *retired state supreme court justice*
Sandstrom, Dale Vernon *state supreme court justice*
VandeWalle, Gerald Wayne *chief justice*

Fargo
Bright, Myron H. *federal judge*
Bye, Kermit Edward *federal judge, lawyer*
Hill, William A(lexander) *judge*
Klein, Karen K. *federal judge*
Webb, Rodney Scott *judge*

Minot
Kerian, Jon Robert *retired judge*

OHIO

Akron
Bell, Samuel H. *federal judge, educator*
Dowd, David D., Jr. *federal judge*
Shea-Stonum, Marilyn *federal bankruptcy judge*
White, Harold F. *bankruptcy judge, retired federal judge*

Bowling Green
Mayberry, Alan Reed *judge*

Cincinnati
Barrett, Michael Ryan *federal judge*
Beckwith, Sandra Shank *federal judge*
Clay, Eric L. *federal judge*
Cook, Deborah L. *federal judge, former state supreme court justice*
Dlott, Susan Judy *judge, lawyer*
Hopkins, Jeffery P. *federal judge*
Perlman, Burton *judge*
Rogers, John Marshall *judge, educator*
Spiegel, S. Arthur *federal judge*
Sutton, Jeffrey S. *federal judge*
Weber, Herman Jacob *senior district judge*

Circleville
Long, Jan Michael *judge*

Cleveland
Aldrich, Ann *judge*
Baxter, Randolph *judge*
Boyko, Christopher Allan *federal judge*
Hemann, Patricia Alice *federal judge*
Markus, Richard M. *judge, arbitrator*
Moore, Karen Nelson *judge*
Morgenstern-Clarren, Pat *federal judge*
Nugent, Donald Clark *judge*
Oliver, Solomon, Jr. *judge*
O'Malley, Kathleen M. *federal judge*
Perelman, David S. *federal judge*
Wells, Lesley *federal judge*

Columbus
Abel, Mark Rogers *federal judge*
Caldwell, Charles M. *federal judge*
Cole, Ransey Guy, Jr. *federal judge*
Cupp, Robert Richard *state supreme court justice, former state senator, attorney*
Graham, James Lowell *federal judge*
Holschuh, John David *federal judge*
King, Norah McCann *federal judge*
Lanzinger, Judith Ann *state supreme court justice*
Moyer, Thomas J. *state supreme court chief justice*
Norris, Alan Eugene *federal judge*
O'Connor, Maureen *state supreme court justice*
O'Donnell, Terrence *state supreme court justice*
Pfeifer, Paul E. *state supreme court justice*
Sargus, Edmund A., Jr. *judge*
Sellers, Barbara Jackson *federal judge*
Smith, George Curtis *judge*
Stratton, Evelyn Lundberg *state supreme court justice*

Dayton
Clark, William Alfred *federal judge*
Knapp, James Ian Keith *judge*
Merz, Michael *federal judge*
Petzold, John Paul *judge*

Toledo
Carr, James Gray *federal judge*
Katz, David Allan *federal judge*
Potter, John William *federal judge*
Zouhary, Jack *federal judge*

Warren
Nader, Robert Alexander *judge, lawyer*

Youngstown
Economus, Peter Constantine *judge*
Vukovich, Joseph John *judge*

SOUTH DAKOTA

Aberdeen
Kornmann, Charles Bruno *judge*

Pierre
Gilbertson, David *state supreme court justice*
Konenkamp, John K. *state supreme court justice*
Meierhenry, Judith Knittel *state supreme court justice*
Miller, Robert Arthur *former state supreme court chief justice*
Sabers, Richard Wayne *state supreme court justice*
Zinter, Steven L. *state supreme court justice*

Rapid City
Battey, Richard Howard *judge*
Bogue, Andrew Wendell *federal judge*
Schreier, Karen Elizabeth *judge*

Sioux Falls
Jones, John Bailey *federal judge*
Piersol, Lawrence L. *federal judge*
Wollman, Roger Leland *federal judge*

TENNESSEE

Nashville
Merritt, Gilbert Stroud *federal judge*

WISCONSIN

Appleton
Froehlich, Harold Vernon *judge, retired congressman*

Eau Claire
Utschig, Thomas S. *federal judge*

Madison
Abrahamson, Shirley Schlanger *state supreme court chief justice*
Bradley, Ann Walsh *state supreme court justice*
Butler, Louis Bennett, Jr. *state supreme court justice*
Crabb, Barbara Brandriff *federal judge*
Crocker, Stephen L. *federal magistrate judge*
Crooks, Neil Patrick *state supreme court justice*
Deininger, David George *judge*
Foust, Charles William *judge*
Martin, Robert David *judge, educator*
Prosser, David Thomas, Jr. *state supreme court justice and former legislator*
Roggensack, Patience Drake *state supreme court justice*
Shabaz, John C. *judge*
Wilcox, Jon P. *state supreme court justice*

Milwaukee
Adelman, Lynn *federal judge*
Callahan, William E., Jr. *federal judge*
Clevert, Charles Nelson, Jr. *federal judge*
Curran, Thomas J. *federal judge*
Evans, Terence Thomas *federal judge*
Goodstein, Aaron E. *federal magistrate judge*
Kessler, Joan F. *judge, lawyer*
McGarity, Margaret Dee *federal judge*
Randa, Rudolph Thomas *federal judge*
Shapiro, James Edward *judge*
Stadtmueller, Joseph Peter *federal judge*
Sykes, Diane S. *federal judge, former state supreme court justice*

ADDRESS UNPUBLISHED

Amundson, Robert A. *state supreme court justice*
Barbosa, Manuel *judge*
Barliant, Ronald *federal judge*
Barta, James Joseph *retired federal judge*
Batchelder, Alice M. *federal judge*
Blatz, Kathleen Anne *former state supreme court justice*
Bowman, John J. *judge*
Boylan, Arthur J. *judge*
Burg, Randall K. *federal judge*
Callow, William Grant *retired judge*
Coffey, John Louis *federal appellate judge*
Cohn, Avern Levin *district judge*
Cook, Julian Abele, Jr. *federal judge*
Douglas, Andrew *retired state supreme court justice*
Duff, Brian Barnett *federal judge*
Engel, Albert Joseph *retired federal judge*
Freeman, Charles E. *state supreme court justice*
Gilmore, Horace Weldon *former federal judge*
Goldman, Marc L. *federal judge*
Gorence, Patricia Josetta *judge*
Graves, Ray Reynolds *retired judge*
Harrison, Moses W., II, *state supreme court chief justice*
Heaney, Gerald William *retired federal judge*
Hyman, Michael Bruce *judge*
Jordan, Michelle Denise *judge*
Kunkle, William Joseph *judge, lawyer*
Lioi, Sara Elizabeth *judge*
Magill, Frank John *federal judge*
Magnuson, Paul Arthur *federal judge*
McMorrow, Mary Ann Grohwin *retired state supreme court justice*
Meschke, Herbert Leonard *retired state supreme court justice*
Nelson, David Aldrich *former federal judge*
Neuman, Linda Kinney *retired state supreme court justice, lawyer*
Newblatt, Stewart Albert *federal judge*
Polster, Dan Aaron *judge*
Pusateri, James Anthony *judge*
Renner, Robert George *federal judge*
Resnick, Alice Robie *retired state supreme court justice*
Rice, Walter Herbert *federal judge*
Schultz, Louis William *retired judge*
Senechal, Alice R. *federal magistrate judge, lawyer*
Sheedy, Patrick Thomas *judge*
Sinclair, Virgil Lee, Jr. *judge, writer*
Squires, John Henry *judge*

LAW: LAW PRACTICE AND ADMINISTRATION

UNITED STATES

ARIZONA

Carefree
Putney, Mark William *lawyer, utilities executive*

Phoenix
Donovan, Timothy R. *lawyer*

CALIFORNIA

Claremont
Kury, Bernard Edward *lawyer*

Los Angeles
Shiba, Wendy C. *lawyer*

San Francisco
Tarun, Robert Walter *lawyer*

Santa Monica
Modisett, Jeffrey A. *lawyer, former state attorney general*

Torrance
Carlson, Terrance L. *lawyer, aerospace transportation executive*

COLORADO

Denver
Bartlit, Fred Holcomb, Jr. *lawyer*

Lafayette
Manka, Ronald Eugene *lawyer*

CONNECTICUT

Hartford
Kelly, Peter Galbraith *lawyer*

New Haven
Cole, Elsa Kircher *lawyer*

Stamford
Krutter, Forrest Nathan *lawyer*

Waterbury
Lipshaw, Jeffrey Marc *lawyer, chemicals executive, educator*

DISTRICT OF COLUMBIA

Washington
McClure, James A. *lawyer, former senator*
Sevart, Daniel Joseph *lawyer*
Smith, Tefft Weldon *lawyer*
Taronji, Jaime, Jr. *lawyer*

FLORIDA

Delray Beach
Garcia D., Elisa Dolores *lawyer*

Destin
Estes, Royce Joe *lawyer*

Jacksonville
Sadowski, Peter T. *lawyer*

Lecanto
Goss, Richard Henry *lawyer*

Naples
Adams, John Marshall *lawyer*
McSwiney, Charles Ronald *lawyer*

Port Saint Lucie
Lambert, George Robert *lawyer, realtor*

Village Of Golf
Sutter, William Paul *lawyer*

GEORGIA

Atlanta
Zealey, Sharon Janine *lawyer*

ILLINOIS

Barrington
Lee, William Marshall *lawyer*
Wyatt, James Frank, Jr. *lawyer*

Belleville
Bauman, John Duane *lawyer*
Hess, Frederick J. *lawyer*
Ripplinger, George Raymond, Jr. *lawyer*

Bloomington
Kennett, Christie Shih *lawyer*
Reynard, Charles G. *lawyer, educator*
Sullivan, Laura Patricia *lawyer, insurance company executive*

Burr Ridge
Decker, Richard Knore *lawyer*
Richmond, William Patrick *lawyer*

Carbondale
Clemons, John Robert *lawyer*

Carrollton
Strickland, Hugh Alfred *lawyer*

Carthage
Glidden, John Redmond *lawyer*

Champaign
Cribbet, John Edward *law educator, former university chancellor*
Johnson, Lawrence Eugene *lawyer*
Johnston, Janis L. *law librarian, educator*
Kindt, John Warren *lawyer, educator*
Krause, Harry Dieter *law educator*
Maggs, Peter Blount *lawyer, educator*
Mamer, Stuart Mies *lawyer*
Pope, Daniel James *lawyer*

Chicago
Abrams, Lee Norman *lawyer*
Acker, Ann E. *lawyer*
Acker, Frederick George *lawyer*
Adelman, Stanley Joseph *lawyer*
Adelman, Steven Herbert *lawyer*
Adess, Melvin Sidney *lawyer*
Agnello, Gino J. *federal court administrator*
Alberts, Barry S. *lawyer*
Albrecht, Thomas W. *lawyer*
Albright, Christine L. *lawyer*
Allen, Gemma B. *lawyer*
Allen, Henry Sermones, Jr. *lawyer*
Allen, Julie O'Donnell *lawyer*
Allen, Ronald Jay *law educator*
Allen, Thomas Draper *lawyer*
Alschuler, Albert W. *law educator*
Amend, James Michael *lawyer*
Anderson, Cathy C. *lawyer*
Anderson, J. Trent *lawyer*
Anderson, Kimball Richard *lawyer*
Anderson, William Cornelius III *lawyer*
Andreozzi, Bradley Joseph *lawyer*
Angst, Gerald L. *lawyer*
Anthony, Michael Francis *lawyer*
Anvaripour, M. A. *lawyer*
Appel, Nina Schick *law educator, dean, academic administrator*
Armstrong, Edwin Richard *lawyer*
Aronson, Virginia L. *lawyer*
Athas, Gus James *lawyer*
Avery, Robert Dean *lawyer*
Axley, Frederick William *lawyer*
Babcock, Sandra L. *lawyer, educator*
Badel, Julie *lawyer*
Baird, Douglas Gordon *law educator, dean*
Baker, Pamela *lawyer*
Baldwin, Shaun McParland *lawyer*
Bannon, John A. *lawyer*
Banoff, Sheldon Irwin *lawyer*
Barden, Larry A. *lawyer*
Barker, William Thomas *lawyer*
Barner, Sharon R. *lawyer*
Barnes, James Garland, Jr. *lawyer*
Barr, John Robert *retired lawyer*
Barrett, Roger Watson *lawyer*
Barron, Harold Sheldon *lawyer*
Barron, Howard Robert *lawyer*
Barry, Norman J., Jr. *lawyer*
Bart, Susan Therese *lawyer*
Bashwiner, Steven Lacelle *lawyer*
Bauer, Julie A. *lawyer*
Baugher, Peter V. *lawyer*
Baumgartner, William Hans, Jr. *lawyer*
Beck, Philip S. *lawyer*
Becker, Scott *lawyer*
Beem, Jack Darrel *retired lawyer*
Bellows, Laurel Gordon *lawyer*
Bennett, Robert William *law educator*
Berens, Mark Harry *lawyer*
Berenzweig, Jack Charles *lawyer*
Berger, Robert Michael *lawyer*
Berkoff, Adam T. *lawyer*
Berkoff, Mark Andrew *lawyer*
Berkowitz, Sean M. *lawyer*
Berkson, Stuart M *lawyer*
Berman, Debbie L. *lawyer*
Bernardini, Charles *lawyer, alderman*
Bernick, David M. *lawyer*
Bernstein, H. Bruce *lawyer*
Berolzheimer, Karl *retired lawyer*
Bertagnolli, Leslie A. *lawyer*
Bettman, Suzanne (Sue Bettman) *lawyer*
Biebel, Paul Philip, Jr. *lawyer*
Biederman, Jerry H. *lawyer*
Bitner, John Howard *lawyer*
Bixby, Frank Lyman *retired lawyer*
Block, Neal Jay *lawyer*
Blount, Michael Eugene *lawyer*
Blust, Larry D. *lawyer*
Boberg, Wayne D. *lawyer*
Bodenstein, Ira *lawyer*
Boehnen, Daniel A. *lawyer*
Bogaard, Jonathan Harvey *lawyer*
Boggs, Catherine J. *lawyer*
Boho, Dan L. *lawyer*
Boies, Wilber H. *lawyer*
Bomchill, Fern Cheryl *lawyer*
Bostwick, Jarrett T. *lawyer*
Bouma, Robert Edwin *lawyer*
Bowe, William J(ohn) *lawyer*
Bowen, Stephen Stewart *lawyer*
Boykin, Richard Renarda *lawyer, former legislative staff member*
Boykins, Michael L. *lawyer*
Bramnik, Robert Paul *lawyer*
Braun, Bruce *lawyer*
Brennan, Joseph *lawyer*
Brennan, Noelle C. *lawyer*
Brice, Roger Thomas *lawyer*
Bridgman, Thomas Francis *retired lawyer*
Brizzolara, Charles Anthony *lawyer, director*
Bro, Ruth Hill *lawyer*
Brogan, Lisa S. *lawyer*
Bromley, Richard *lawyer*
Brown, Alan Crawford *lawyer*
Brown, Donald James, Jr. *lawyer*
Brown, Gregory K. *lawyer*
Brown, Matthew S. *lawyer*
Bruner, Philip Lane *arbitrator*
Bruner, Stephen C. *lawyer*
Bryant, David J. *lawyer*
Bryant, L. Edward *lawyer*
Buck, Willis R., Jr. *lawyer*
Bulger, Brian Wegg *lawyer*
Burke, Thomas Joseph, Jr. *lawyer*
Burns, Daniel T. *corporate lawyer*
Burns, James B. *prosecutor*
Burns, Robert Patrick *law educator*
Burns, Terrence Michael *lawyer*
Busey, Roxane C. *lawyer*
Bussman, Donald Herbert *lawyer*
Butler, John William, Jr. *lawyer*
Caisman, Saul *lawyer*
Callahan, Michael R. *lawyer*
Campbell, William J., Jr. *lawyer*
Canty, Dawn M. *lawyer*
Carlin, Dennis J. *lawyer*
Carlson, Stephen Curtis *lawyer*
Carlson, Walter Carl *lawyer*
Carpenter, David William *lawyer*
Carr, Jeffrey W. *lawyer, manufacturing executive*
Carr, Walter Stanley *lawyer*
Carren, Jeffrey P. *lawyer*
Carroll, James J. *lawyer*
Carroll, William Kenneth *lawyer, educator, psychologist, theologian*
Ceko, Theresa C. *lawyer, educator*
Chandler, Kent, Jr. *lawyer*
Cheely, Daniel Joseph *lawyer*
Chemers, Robert Marc *lawyer*
Cherney, James Alan *lawyer*
Cherry, Daniel Ronald *lawyer*
Chico, Gery J. *lawyer, school system administrator*
Chizewer, David J. *lawyer*
Ciancio, Ronlad J. *lawyer*
Cicero, Frank, Jr. *lawyer*
Clark, James Allen *lawyer, educator*
Clark, James E. *lawyer*
Clarke, Peter D. *lawyer*
Clemens, Richard Glenn *lawyer*
Clifford, Robert A. *lawyer*
Cohen, Frederick H. *lawyer*
Cohen, Melanie Rovner *lawyer*
Cole, Thomas Amor *lawyer*
Collen, John *lawyer, educator*
Comella, Phillip L. *lawyer*
Comiskey, Michael Peter *lawyer*
Conklin, Thomas William *lawyer*
Conlon, William F. *lawyer*
Conroy, John J., Jr. *lawyer*
Conviser, Richard James *lawyer, educator, publications company executive*
Conway, Michael Maurice *lawyer*
Copeland, Edward Jerome *lawyer*
Corwin, Sherman Phillip *lawyer*
Costello, John William *lawyer*
Coward, Nicholas F. *lawyer*
Crane, Charlotte *law educator*
Crane, Edward M. *lawyer*
Crane, Mark *lawyer*
Craven, George W. *lawyer*
Crawford, Dewey Byers *lawyer*
Cremin, Susan Elizabeth *lawyer*
Crihfield, Philip J. *lawyer*
Crisham, Thomas Michael *lawyer*
Crossan, John Robert *lawyer*
Csar, Michael F. *lawyer*
Cummings, Andrea J. *lawyer*
Cunningham, Robert James *lawyer*
Curran, Barbara Adell *retired law foundation administrator, lawyer, writer*
Curtis, James L. *lawyer*
Cusack, John Thomas *lawyer*
Custer, Charles Francis *lawyer*
Daley, Susan Jean *lawyer*
Dam, Kenneth W. *law educator, former federal agency administrator*
D'Amato, Anthony *law educator*
Dasso, James Daniel *lawyer*
Davidson, Stanley J. *lawyer*
Davis, Michael W. *lawyer*
Davis, Muller *lawyer*
Davis, Scott Jonathan *lawyer*
Dechene, James Charles *lawyer*
Dees, Richard Lee *lawyer*
de Hoyos, Debora M. *lawyer*
Deitrick, William Edgar *lawyer*
Delp, Wilbur Charles, Jr. *lawyer*
Dent, Thomas G. *lawyer*
Denvir, Robert F. *lawyer*
Desideri, Lawrence R. *lawyer*
D'Esposito, Julian C., Jr. *lawyer*
Despres, Leon Mathis *lawyer, former city official*
Devine, Richard A. (Dick DeVine) *lawyer*
Diamond, Shari Seidman *law and psychology professor*
Dickstein, Beth J. *lawyer, accountant*
Dixon, Stewart Strawn *lawyer, consultant*
Dockterman, Michael *lawyer*
Dohrn, Bernardine *law educator, advocate*
Dolan, Michael F. *lawyer*
Donlevy, John Dearden *lawyer*
Dorman, Gregg M. *lawyer*
Dorman, Jeffrey Lawrence *lawyer*
Douglas, Charles W. *lawyer*
Downing, Robert Allan *lawyer*
Downs, Robert K. *lawyer*
Doyle, John Robert *lawyer*
Drymalski, Raymond Hibner *lawyer, banker*
Dube, Monte I. *lawyer*
Duhl, Michael Foster *lawyer*
Dunlop, Karen Owen *lawyer*
Dunn, Edwin Rydell *lawyer*
Durchslag, Stephen P. *lawyer*
Durkin, Kevin P. *lawyer*
Dykstra, Paul Hopkins *lawyer*
Eaton, Maja Campbell *lawyer*
Edwards, Charles Lloyd *lawyer*
Edwards, Christine Annette *lawyer*
Egan, Kevin James *lawyer*
Eggert, Russell Raymond *lawyer*
Eimer, Nathan Philip *lawyer*
Eisner, Rebecca Suzanne *lawyer*
Ekdahl, Jon Nels *lawyer*
Elden, Gary Michael *lawyer*
Elrod, Steven M. *lawyer*
English, John Dwight *lawyer*
Entin, Frederic J. *lawyer*
Epstein, Bennett L. (Buzz Epstein) *lawyer*
Epstein, Richard A. *law educator*
Erens, Jay Allan *lawyer*
Esrick, Jerald Paul *lawyer*
Evanich, Kevin Reese *lawyer*
Even, Francis Alphonse *lawyer*
Fahner, Tyrone C. *lawyer, former state attorney general*
Fayhee, Michael R. *lawyer*
Fazio, Peter Victor, Jr. *lawyer*
Feagley, Michael Rowe *lawyer*
Feinstein, Fred Ira *lawyer*
Feldman, Mark I. *lawyer*
Fellows, Jerry Kenneth *lawyer*
Ferber, Leonard *lawyer*
Ferencz, Robert Arnold *lawyer*
Ferguson, Stanley Lewis *lawyer*
Ferrini, James Thomas *lawyer*
Fields, Barry E. *lawyer*
Findlay, Donald Cameron *lawyer, former federal agency administrator, insurance company executive*
Finke, Robert Forge *lawyer*
Fitzgerald, Patrick J., Jr. *prosecutor*
Fontaine, Mary C. *lawyer*
Formeller, Daniel Richard *lawyer*
Fort, Jeffrey C. *lawyer*
Foudree, Bruce William *lawyer*
Fowler, Don Wall *lawyer*
Fox, Elaine Saphier *lawyer*
Fox, Paul T. *lawyer*
Franch, Richard Thomas *lawyer*
Franklin, Richard Mark *lawyer*
Fraumann, Willard George *lawyer*
Frederick, Thomas James *lawyer*
Freeborn, Michael D. *lawyer*
Freed, Mayer Goodman *law educator*
Freehling, Daniel Joseph *lawyer, consultant*
Freeman, Lee Allen, Jr. *lawyer*
Friedli, Helen Russell *lawyer*
Friedman, Lawrence Milton *lawyer, finance company executive*
Friedman, Roselyn L. *lawyer, mediator*
Fross, Roger Raymond *lawyer*
Furlane, Mark Elliott *lawyer*
Gaggini, John Edmund *lawyer*
Galainena, M. David *lawyer*
Gallopoulos, Gregory Stratis *lawyer*
Gangemi, Columbus Rudolph, Jr. *lawyer, educator*
Garber, Samuel B. *lawyer, retail executive*
Garcia, Paul R. *lawyer*
Gavin, John Neal *lawyer*
Gavin, Steven J. *lawyer*
Gearen, John Joseph *lawyer*
Gecker, James M. *lawyer*
Geiman, J. Robert *lawyer*
Gelman, Andrew Richard *lawyer*
George, John Martin, Jr. *lawyer*
Georges, Mara Stacy *lawyer*
Geraghty, Diane C. *law educator*
Gerber, David Joseph *lawyer, educator*
Gerber, Dean N. *lawyer*
Gerber, Lawrence *lawyer*
Gerlits, Francis Joseph *lawyer*
Gern, Ronald L. *lawyer, real estate company executive*
Gersh, Deborah Louise *lawyer*
Gerstein, Mark Douglas *lawyer*
Gianos, Diane E. *lawyer*
Gibbons, William John *lawyer*
Gilbert, Howard N(orman) *lawyer, director*
Gilford, Steven Ross *lawyer*
Gladden, James Walter, Jr. *lawyer*
Godfrey, Richard Cartier *lawyer*
Golan, Stephen Leonard *lawyer*
Goldblatt, Stanford Jay *lawyer*
Golden, Bruce Paul *lawyer*
Golden, William C. *lawyer*
Good, Steven Loren *real estate consultant*
Gordon, Phillip *lawyer*
Goroff, David B. *lawyer*
Gottlieb, Gidon Alain Guy *law educator*
Graham, Robert L. *lawyer*
Gralen, Donald John *lawyer*
Grant, Robert Nathan *lawyer*
Graves, Robert J. *lawyer*
Greenbaum, Lewis *lawyer*
Greenberg, Richard T. *lawyer*
Griffith, Donald Kendall *lawyer*
Grimm, Terry M. *lawyer*
Gullikson, Rosemary *lawyer*
Guthman, Jack *lawyer*
Hahn, Arthur W. *lawyer*
Hahn, Frederic Louis *lawyer*
Hall, Jeffrey A. *lawyer*
Hall, Joan M. *lawyer*
Halperin, Errol R. *lawyer*
Hammes, Jeffrey C. *lawyer*
Hammond, Celeste M. *law educator*
Hannah, Wayne Robertson, Jr. *lawyer*
Hannay, William Mouat III *lawyer*
Hanson, Ronald William *lawyer*
Hanzlik, Paul F. *lawyer*
Hardgrove, James Alan *lawyer*
Harmon, Teresa Wilton *lawyer*
Harper, Steven James *lawyer*
Harrington, Carol A. *lawyer*
Harrington, James Timothy *lawyer*
Harris, Donald Ray *lawyer*
Harris, Phillip H. *lawyer*
Harris, Susan V. *lawyer*
Harrison, Holly A. *lawyer*
Harrison, Joseph Horatio, Jr. *lawyer*
Harrison, Louis S. *lawyer*
Harrold, Bernard *lawyer*
Hartz, Michael O. *lawyer*
Hayes, David John Arthur, Jr. *legal association executive*
Hayward, Thomas Zander, Jr. *lawyer*
Heatwole, Mark M. *lawyer, director*
Heinz, John Peter *lawyer, educator*
Heinz, William Denby *lawyer*
Heisler, Quentin George, Jr. *lawyer*
Heller, David S. *lawyer*
Heller, Stanley J. *lawyer, physician, educator*
Helman, Robert Alan *lawyer*
Helmholz, R(ichard) H(enry) *law educator*
Henderson, Janet E. E. *lawyer*
Hendrickson, John P. *lawyer*
Henning, Joel Frank *lawyer, writer*
Henry, Frederick Edward *lawyer*
Hensel, Paul H. *lawyer*
Herald, J. Patrick *lawyer*
Herbert, William Carlisle *lawyer*
Herman, Sidney N. *lawyer*
Herpe, David A. *lawyer*
Hess, Sidney J., Jr. *lawyer*
Hesse, Carolyn Sue *lawyer*
Hickey, John Thomas, Jr. *lawyer*
Hilliker, Donald Beckstett *lawyer*
Hillman, Jordan Jay *law educator*
Hitselberger, Carol A. *lawyer*
Hochberg, Kevin J. *lawyer*
Hodes, Scott *lawyer*
Hodgman, David Renwick *lawyer*
Hofer, Roy Ellis *lawyer*
Hoff, John Scott *lawyer*
Hoffman, Richard Bruce *lawyer*
Homburger, Thomas Charles *lawyer*
Horwich, Allan *lawyer*
Horwood, Richard M. *lawyer*
Hoskins, Richard Jerold *lawyer*
Howe, Jonathan Thomas *lawyer*
Howell, R(obert) Thomas, Jr. *lawyer, former food company executive*
Hugi, Robert F. *lawyer*
Hummel, Gregory William *lawyer*
Hunt, Lawrence Halley, Jr. *lawyer*
Hunter, James Galbraith, Jr. *lawyer*
Isaacson, Samuel B. *lawyer*
Ismail, Tarek *lawyer*
Jacobs, Caryn Leslie *lawyer, former prosecutor*
Jacobson, Marian Slutz *lawyer*
Jacobson, Richard Joseph *lawyer*
Jacover, Jerold Alan *lawyer*
Jager, Melvin Francis *lawyer*
Jahns, Jeffrey *lawyer*
Jast, Raymond Joseph *lawyer*
Johnson, Garrett Bruce *lawyer*
Johnson, Richard Fred *lawyer*
Joseph, Robert Thomas *lawyer*
Junewicz, James J. *lawyer*
Kallick, David A. *lawyer*
Kamin, Chester Thomas *lawyer*
Kaplan, Joel H. *lawyer*
Kaplan, Sidney Mountbatten *lawyer*
Karlin, Edward J. *lawyer*
Kastel, Howard L. *lawyer, business executive*
Katten, Melvin L. *lawyer*
Katz, Stuart Charles *lawyer, musician*
Kauffman, Peter H. *lawyer, energy executive*
Kaufman, Andrew Michael *lawyer*
Kelley, Lydia R.B. *lawyer*
Kellman, Sandra Y. *lawyer*
Kelly, Charles Arthur *lawyer*
Kelly, Raymond J., Jr. *lawyer*
Kenney, Colleen M. *lawyer*
Kenney, Crane H. *lawyer*
Kenney, Frank Deming *lawyer*
Kikoler, Stephen Philip *lawyer*
Kim, Michael Charles *lawyer*
King, Sharon Louise *retired lawyer*
Kins, Juris *lawyer*
Kipperman, Lawrence I. *lawyer*
Kirchhoefer, Gregg G. *lawyer*
Kirkpatrick, John Everett *lawyer*
Kissel, Richard John *lawyer*
Kistenbroker, David H. *lawyer*
Kitch, Paul R. *lawyer*
Kite, Steven B. *lawyer*
Klenk, James Andrew *lawyer*
Klenk, Timothy Carver *lawyer*
Knight, Christopher Nichols *lawyer*
Koch, Steven *lawyer, investment banker, finance company executive*
Kohn, Shalom L. *lawyer*
Kolek, Robert Edward *lawyer*
Kopelman, Ian Stuart *lawyer*
Koppelman, Andrew Martin Mayer *law educator*
Kramer, Andrea S. *lawyer*
Krasny, Paula J. *lawyer*
Kravitt, Jason Harris Paperno *lawyer*
Kriss, Robert J. *lawyer*
Kroll, Barry Lewis *retired lawyer*
Kurtz, David S. *lawyer*
Kuta, Jeffrey Theodore *lawyer*
Ladd, Jeffrey Raymond *lawyer*
Laidlaw, Andrew R. *lawyer*
Lampert, Steven A. *lawyer*

Landes, Stephen J. *lawyer*
Landes, William M. *law educator*
Landow-Esser, Janine Marise *lawyer*
Landsman, Stephen A. *lawyer*
Lane, Ronald Alan *lawyer*
Laner, Richard Warren *lawyer*
Lanznar, Howard S. *lawyer*
Lassar, Scott R. *lawyer, former prosecutor*
Latimer, Kenneth Alan *lawyer*
Learner, Howard Alan *lawyer*
Leisten, Arthur Gaynor *lawyer*
Leonard, Laura L. *lawyer*
LeRoy, Spencer III *lawyer*
Levi, John G. *lawyer*
Levin, Charles Edward *lawyer*
Levin, Jack S. *lawyer*
Levin, Lawrence Daniel *lawyer*
Levin, Michael David *lawyer*
Levine, Laurence Harvey *lawyer*
Levy, Peter A. *lawyer*
Levy, Susan C. *lawyer*
Lien, John Donovan *lawyer*
Liggio, Carl Donald *lawyer*
Lind, Jon Robert *lawyer*
Linklater, William J. *lawyer*
Lipton, Lois Jean *lawyer*
Lipton, Richard M. *lawyer*
Litwin, Burton Howard *lawyer*
Litwin, Stuart M. *lawyer*
Lockwood, Gary Lee *lawyer*
Looman, James R. *lawyer*
Lorch, Kenneth F. *lawyer*
Loughnane, David J. *lawyer*
Lovejoy, Paul Robert *lawyer, air transportation executive*
Lowinger, Frederick Charles *lawyer*
Lubin, Donald G. *lawyer*
Luning, Thomas P. *lawyer*
Luscombe, George A., II, *lawyer*
Lutter, Paul Allen *lawyer*
Lynch, John Peter *lawyer*
MacCarthy, Terence Francis *lawyer*
Malkin, Cary Jay *lawyer*
Malovany, Howard *lawyer*
Mancoff, Neal Alan *lawyer*
Mandell, Floyd A. *lawyer*
Marshall, Juli Wilson *lawyer*
Martin, Arthur Mead *lawyer*
Martin, Laura Keidan *lawyer*
Marwedel, Warren John *lawyer*
Marx, David, Jr. *lawyer*
Mason, Richard J. *lawyer*
Matis, Nina B. *lawyer*
Matsakis, Elias N. *lawyer*
Mayer, Frank D., Jr. *retired lawyer*
McBreen, Maura Ann *lawyer*
McCaleb, Malcolm, Jr. *lawyer*
McCloy, Elizabeth K. *lawyer*
McClure, James Julius, Jr. *lawyer, former city official*
McCormick, Steven D. *lawyer*
McCracken, Thomas James, Jr. *lawyer*
McCue, Judith W. *lawyer*
McDermott, John H. *lawyer*
McDonald, Sally J. *lawyer*
McDonald, Thomas Alexander *lawyer*
McDonough, John Michael *lawyer*
McGaan, Andrew Raymond *lawyer*
McGrath, William Joseph *lawyer*
McKenzie, Robert Ernest *lawyer*
McKinley, Anne C. *lawyer*
McLaren, Richard Wellington, Jr. *lawyer*
McLaughlin, T. Mark *lawyer*
McMahon, Daniel John *lawyer*
McMasters, James *law librarian, educator*
McMenamin, John Robert *lawyer*
McVisk, William Kilburn *lawyer*
Mehlman, Mark Franklin *lawyer*
Mehrberg, Randall Eric *lawyer, utilities executive*
Melbinger, Michael S. *lawyer*
Melton, David Reuben *lawyer*
Mensik, Michael *lawyer*
Meyer, Michael Louis *lawyer*
Michalak, Edward Francis *lawyer*
Mihelic, Tracey L. *lawyer*
Miller, Kenneth W. *lawyer*
Miller, Lee I. *lawyer*
Miller, Paul J. *lawyer*
Miller, Peter C. *lawyer*
Miller, Stephen Ralph *lawyer*
Millner, Robert B. *lawyer*
Minichello, Dennis *lawyer*
Minow, Newton Norman *lawyer, educator*
Montgomery, Charles Barry *lawyer*
Montgomery, William Adam *lawyer*
Morency, Paula J. *lawyer*
Morgan, Betsy Stelle *lawyer*
Morgan, Donna Evensen *lawyer*
Morrison, Kenneth P. *lawyer*
Morrison, Portia Owen *lawyer*
Morsch, Thomas Harvey *lawyer, educator*
Muchin, Allan B. *lawyer*
Mudd, Anne Chestney *mediator, law educator, real estate broker*
Mullen, J. Thomas *lawyer*
Murdock, Charles William *lawyer, educator*
Murray, Daniel Richard *lawyer*
Murtaugh, Christopher David *lawyer*
Myers, Lonn William *lawyer*
Nash, Gordon Bernard, Jr. *lawyer*
Neal, Langdon D. *lawyer*
Neely, Ellen J. *lawyer*
Neff, David M. *lawyer*
Neumer, Stephen M. *lawyer*
Newlin, Charles Fremont *lawyer*
Newman, Terry E. *lawyer*
Nicastro, Tracey A. *lawyer*
Nicklin, Emily *lawyer*
Niehaus, Mary C. *lawyer*
Nijman, Jennifer T. *lawyer*
Niro, Cheryl *lawyer*
Nitikman, Franklin W. *lawyer*
Nord, Robert Eamor *lawyer*
Notz, John Kranz, Jr. *arbitrator, mediator, retired lawyer*
Novak, Theodore J. *lawyer*
Nowacki, James Nelson *lawyer*
Nussbaum, Bernard J. *lawyer*
Nyhan, Lawrence J. (Larry) *lawyer*
O'Brien, James Phillip *lawyer*
Oesterle, Eric Adam *lawyer*
O'Hagan, James Joseph *lawyer*
O'Leary, Daniel Vincent, Jr. *lawyer*
Olian, Robert Martin *lawyer*
Olson, Steven R. *lawyer*
O'Malley, John Daniel *lawyer, educator, banker*
O'Neil, Michael C. *lawyer*
O'Neill, Bridget R. *lawyer*
Pagano, Richard C. *lawyer, trucking executive*
Pallasch, B. Michael *lawyer, director*
Palmer, John Bernard III *lawyer*
Panich, Danuta Bembenista *lawyer*
Parkhurst, Beverly Susler *lawyer, judge*
Parkhurst, Todd Sheldon *lawyer*
Partridge, Mark Van Buren *lawyer, educator, mediator, writer*
Parzen, Stanley Julius *lawyer*
Pascal, Roger *lawyer*
Pavalon, Eugene Irving *lawyer*
Pecoulas, George A. *lawyer*
Pedersen, Peer *lawyer*
Pengra, R. Rene *lawyer*
Perrelli, Thomas J. *lawyer*
Peters, Charles H.R. *lawyer*
Petersen, Donald Sondergaard *lawyer*
Peterson, Bradley Laurits *lawyer*
Peterson, Randall Theodore *law librarian, educator*
Peterson, Ronald Roger *lawyer*
Piekarski, Victor J. *lawyer*
Pinsky, Michael S. *lawyer*
Piskorski, Thomas James *lawyer*
Polaski, Anne Spencer *lawyer*
Pollock, Earl Edward *lawyer*
Ponder, Anita J. *lawyer*
Poor, J. Stephen *lawyer*
Pope, Michael Arthur *lawyer*
Prager, Mark L. *lawyer*
Preece, Lynn Sylvia *lawyer*
Presser, Stephen Bruce *lawyer, educator*
Price, Charles T. *lawyer*
Price, Paul L. *lawyer*
Price, William S. *lawyer*
Prior, Gary L. *lawyer*
Pritikin, David T. *lawyer*
Prochnow, Douglas Lee *lawyer*
Qasim, Imad Isa *lawyer*
Quaini, Duane C. *lawyer*
Rankin, James Winton *lawyer*
Rappaport, Richard J. *lawyer*
Ratner, Gerald *lawyer*
Raynal, Lazar Pol *lawyer*
Read, Sarah J. *lawyer*
Reagan, Paul V. *lawyer*
Reategui, Lisa J. *lawyer*
Redish, Martin Harris *law educator*
Reed, Keith Allen *lawyer*
Reich, Allan J. *lawyer*
Reicin, Ronald Ian *lawyer*
Reidy, Daniel Edward *lawyer*
Reis, Leslie Ann *lawyer, educator*
Reiter, Michael A. *lawyer, educator*
Relias, John Alexis *lawyer*
Renwick, Scott *lawyer*
Resnick, Donald Ira *lawyer*
Reum, James Michael *lawyer*
Reyes, Victor H. *lawyer*
Reynolds, Thomas A. III *lawyer*
Rhind, James Thomas *lawyer*
Rhodes, Charles Harker, Jr. *lawyer*
Rich, Nancy Jean *lawyer*
Richard, Howard M. *lawyer*
Richards, Brian F. *lawyer*
Richardson-Lowry, Mary *lawyer*
Richman, Joan M. *lawyer*
Richman, John Marshall *lawyer, food products executive*
Richman, Lawrence I. *lawyer*
Richmond, James Glidden *lawyer*
Rieger, Mitchell Sheridan *lawyer*
Riley, James B., Jr. *lawyer*
Riley, Robert H. *lawyer*
Ritchie, William Paul *lawyer*
Roberts, John Charles *law educator*
Robin, Richard C. *lawyer*
Roche, James McMillan *lawyer*
Rooney, Matthew A. *lawyer*
Ropski, Gary Melchior *lawyer*
Rosen, Barry S. *lawyer*
Rosenbloom, Lewis Stanley *lawyer*
Rosenfield, Andrew M. *lawyer, educator*
Ross, Nancy G. *lawyer*
Rotner, Philip R. *lawyer*
Roy, Paul J.N. *lawyer*
Rudnick, Lewis G. *lawyer*
Rudnick, Paul David *lawyer*
Rudnick, William Alan *lawyer*
Rudoy, Herbert L. *lawyer*
Rudstein, David Stewart *law educator*
Rundio, Louis Michael, Jr. *lawyer*
Russell, Paul Frederick *lawyer*
Rutkoff, Alan Stuart *lawyer*
Ruxin, Paul Theodore *lawyer*
Ryan, Edward F. *lawyer*
Ryan, Priscilla E. *lawyer*
Ryan, Thomas F. *lawyer*
Sabl, John J. *lawyer*
Salpeter, Alan N. *lawyer*
Salzman, Jerrold E. *lawyer*
Sanchez, Manuel (Manny Sanchez) *lawyer*
Sanchez, Vincent A. *lawyer*
Sanders, David P. *lawyer*
Sanders, Richard Henry *lawyer*
Sathy, Anup *lawyer*
Saunders, George Lawton, Jr. *lawyer*
Sawyier, David R. *lawyer*
Schaffer, Henry M. *lawyer*
Scharf, Stephanie A. *lawyer*
Schiller, Donald Charles *lawyer*
Schimberg, A(rmand) Bruce *retired lawyer*
Schink, James Harvey *lawyer*
Schlitter, Stanley Allen *lawyer*
Schmidt, John R. *lawyer*
Schneider, Dan W. *lawyer, consultant*
Schneider, Robert Jerome *lawyer*
Schoonhoven, Ray James *retired lawyer*
Schopf, William Grant *lawyer*
Schorer, Joseph U. *lawyer*
Schoumacher, Bruce Herbert *lawyer*
Schreck, Robert A., Jr. *lawyer*
Schriver, John T. III *lawyer*
Schulte, Stephen Charles *lawyer*
Schultz, Kurt Lee *lawyer*
Schulz, Keith Donald *corporate lawyer, writer*
Schuman, William Paul *lawyer*
Schwab, Stephen Wayne *lawyer*
Schwartz, Donald Lee *lawyer*
Scogland, William Lee *lawyer*
Seegers, Lori C. *lawyer*
Selman, Russell Bertram *lawyer, department chairman*
Sennet, Charles Joseph *lawyer*
Sergi, Vincent A.F. *lawyer*
Serritella, James Anthony *lawyer*
Serritella, William David *lawyer*
Serwer, Alan Michael *lawyer*
Sessions, Barbara C. *lawyer*
Sfikas, Peter Michael *lawyer, educator*
Shadur, Robert H. *lawyer*
Shapiro, Keith J. *lawyer*
Shapiro, Stephen Michael *lawyer*
Shapiro, Steven A. *lawyer*
Shapo, Marshall Schambelan *lawyer, educator*
Sheffield, Jeffrey T. *lawyer*
Sher, Susan *lawyer*
Sherman, Jeremy P. *lawyer*
Shields, Thomas Charles *lawyer*
Shindler, Donald A. *lawyer*
Shulruff, Stuart P. *lawyer*
Siegel, Howard Jerome *lawyer*
Silberman, Alan Harvey *lawyer*
Silverman, Gary R. *lawyer*
Silverman, Ross O. *lawyer*
Simon, Arthur Joseph *lawyer*
Simon, George T. *lawyer*
Simon, John Bern *lawyer*
Singer, William S. *lawyer*
Skilling, Raymond Inwood *lawyer*
Skinner, Mary Jacobs *lawyer*
Sklarsky, Charles B. *lawyer*
Smedinghoff, Thomas J. *lawyer*
Smith, Arthur B., Jr. *lawyer*
Smith, Todd A. *lawyer*
Smolen, Lee M. *lawyer*
Solovy, Jerold Sherwin *lawyer*
Solow, Michael Barry *lawyer*
Spector, David M. *lawyer*
Spellmire, George W. *lawyer*
Spiegler, Joseph Andrew *lawyer*
Spindler, George S. *lawyer, retired oil industry executive*
Spiotto, James Ernest *lawyer*
Sproger, Charles Edmund *retired lawyer*
Stack, John Wallace *lawyer*
Stallworth, Stanley B. *lawyer*
Stanhaus, James Steven *lawyer*
Starkman, Gary Lee *lawyer*
Stassen, John Henry *lawyer*
Steinberg, Morton M. *lawyer*
Stern, Gary B. *lawyer*
Sternstein, Allan J. *lawyer*
Stetler, David J. *lawyer*
Stevens, Linda K. *lawyer*
Stevens, Stanley M. *lawyer*
Stevenson, Adlai Ewing III *lawyer, retired senator*
Stiegel, Michael Allen *lawyer*
Stillman, Nina Gidden *lawyer*
Stoll, John Robert *lawyer, educator*
Stone, Geoffrey Richard *lawyer, educator*
Stone, Randolph Noel *law educator*
Stone, Susan A. *lawyer*
Streff, William Albert, Jr. *lawyer*
Strohm, Bruce C. *lawyer, real estate company executive*
Such, Domingo P. III *lawyer*
Sullivan, Barry *lawyer*
Sullivan, Marcia Waite *lawyer*
Sullivan, Thomas Patrick *lawyer*
Sunstein, Cass Robert *law educator*
Sussman, Arthur Melvin *law educator, foundation administrator*
Swibel, Howard Jay *lawyer*
Swibel, Steven Warren *lawyer*
Swiger, Elinor Porter *lawyer*
Sykes, Alan O'Neil *lawyer, educator*
Tabin, Julius *lawyer, physicist*
Tetzlaff, Theodore R. *lawyer*
Thies, Richard Brian *lawyer*
Thomas, Frederick Bradley *lawyer*
Thomas, Stephen Paul *lawyer*
Thompson, James Robert, Jr. *lawyer, former governor*
Thorne-Thomsen, Thomas *lawyer*
Thurston, James Kendall *lawyer*
Toohey, James Kevin *lawyer*
Toth, Bruce A. *lawyer*
Trapp, James McCreery *lawyer*
Treston, Sherry S. *lawyer*
Trost, Eileen Bannon *lawyer*
Truskowski, John Budd *lawyer*
Turilli, M. Louise *lawyer*
Ungaretti, Richard Anthony *lawyer*
Utecht, Andrea E. *lawyer*
Valukas, Anton Ronald *lawyer, former prosecutor*
Van Demark, Ruth Elaine *lawyer*
Van Gorp, Jon D. *lawyer*
Vezeau, Timothy J. *lawyer*
Vree, Roger Allen *lawyer*
Waintroob, Andrea Ruth *lawyer*
Waite, Norman, Jr. *lawyer*
Wakschlag, Milton Samuel *lawyer*
Wall, Robert F. *lawyer*
Walsh, Michael S. *lawyer*
Wander, Herbert Stanton *lawyer*
Wanke, Ronald Lee *lawyer*
Weaver, Timothy Allan *lawyer*
Weaver, William N., Jr. *lawyer*
Webb, Dan K. *lawyer*
Weinberg, Walter S. *lawyer*
Weinkopf, Friedrich J. *lawyer*
Weinsheimer, William Cyrus *lawyer*
Weinstein, Margo *lawyer*
Weiss, John Robert *lawyer*
Weissman, Michael Lewis *lawyer*
Welch, Lyman W. *lawyer*
Welsh, Kelly Raymond *lawyer, investment company executive*
Westerberg, Gary W. *lawyer*
Whalen, Wayne W. *lawyer*
White, Linda Diane *lawyer*
Whiting, Oran F. *lawyer*
Wieczorek, Dennis E. *lawyer*
Wildman, Max Edward *lawyer, director*
Wilson, Roger Goodwin *lawyer*
Wine-Banks, Jill Susan *lawyer*
Wise, William Jerrard *lawyer*
Witcoff, Sheldon William *lawyer*
Wolf, Charles Benno *lawyer*
Wolfe, David Louis *lawyer*
Wood, Mark D. *lawyer*
Woodford, Peter C. *lawyer*
Wright, Judith Margaret *law librarian, educator, dean*
Yeager, Mark Leonard *lawyer*
Zabel, Sheldon Alter *lawyer, educator*
Zagel, Margaret Maxwell *lawyer*
Zavis, Michael William *lawyer*
Zemm, Sandra Phyllis *lawyer*
Zenner, Sheldon Toby *lawyer*
Zhao, Jia *lawyer*
Zolno, Mark S. *lawyer*

Chicago Heights
Cifelli, John Louis *lawyer*

Crystal Lake
Shank, William O. *lawyer*
Wade, Edwin Lee *lawyer, writer*

Decatur
Dunn, John Francis *lawyer, state representative*
Reising, Richard P. *lawyer*
Smith, David James *lawyer*

Deerfield
Blanchard, Eric Alan *lawyer*
Montgomery, William A. *lawyer*
Pearson, Louise S. *lawyer*
Persky, Marla Susan *lawyer*
Roche, Mark A. *lawyer, consumer products company executive*
Roisman, Peter Scott *lawyer*
Scott, John Joseph *lawyer*

Des Plaines
Meyer, Susan M. *lawyer*

Downers Grove
Kaput, Jim L. *lawyer*
Moran, Michael Robert *corporate lawyer*
Myers, Daniel N. *lawyer, association executive*
Siedlecki, Nancy Therese *lawyer, funeral director*
Zeilstra, David C. *lawyer, transportation executive*

Edwardsville
Rikli, Donald Carl *lawyer*

Elgin
Akemann, David R. *lawyer*
Golden, Loren S. *lawyer*

Evanston
Dana, David *law educator*
Nechin, Herbert Benjamin *lawyer*
Shefsky, Lloyd Edward *lawyer*

Galesburg
Mangieri, Paul L. *lawyer*

Galva
Massie, Michael Earl *lawyer*

Glen Ellyn
Conti, Lee Ann *lawyer*
Sandrok, Richard William *lawyer*

Glencoe
Berland, Abel Edward *lawyer, real estate agent*

Glenview
Baetz, W. Timothy *lawyer*
Berkman, Michael G. *lawyer*
Dul, John A. *lawyer, electronics executive*
Hagy, James C. *lawyer*
Knox, James Edwin *lawyer*
Wooten, James H., Jr. *lawyer, engineering executive*

Granite City
Rarick, Philip Joseph *lawyer, retired state supreme court justice*

Hanover
Bleveans, John *lawyer*

Highland Park
Gash, Lauren Beth *lawyer, state legislator*
Karol, Nathaniel H. *lawyer, consultant*
Lieberman, Myron *lawyer*
Nelson, Richard David *lawyer*
Reed, Jan Stern *lawyer*
Schar, Stephen L. *lawyer*
Schindel, Donald Marvin *retired lawyer*

Hinsdale
Botti, Aldo E. *lawyer*

Hoffman Estates
Block, Janice L. *lawyer*

Itasca
Rosengren, John Charles *lawyer*

La Grange
Kerr, Alexander Duncan, Jr. *lawyer*

Lafox
Seils, William George *lawyer*

Lake Bluff
Nissen, William John *lawyer*

Lake Forest
Covington, George Morse *lawyer*
Doyle, Joseph E. *lawyer, manufacturing executive*
Howard, John Lawrence *lawyer*
Smith, Brian J. *lawyer*

Lincolnshire
Michalik, John James *legal association administrator*
Ryan, John *lawyer*

Lincolnwood
Carroll, Howard William *state legislator*
Zaremski, Miles Jay *lawyer*

Lisle
Butt, Edward Thomas, Jr. *lawyer*
Hecht, Louis Alan *lawyer*

Long Grove
Conway, John K. *lawyer*
Obert, Paul Richard *lawyer, manufacturing executive*

Mc Gaw Park
Feather, William L. *corporate lawyer*

Melrose Park
Schmidt, Gary P. *lawyer, personal care industry executive*

Moline
Jenkins, James Robert *lawyer, manufacturing executive*
Morrison, Deborah Jean *lawyer*

Morrison
Spencer, Gary L. *state government lawyer*

Naperville
Broad, Matthew *lawyer*
Corvino, Beth Byster *lawyer*
Gracey, Paul C., Jr. *lawyer, utilities executive*

Landsman, Stephen N. *lawyer*
Shaw, Michael Allan *lawyer*
Tibble, Douglas Clair *lawyer*

Northbrook
Abbey, G(eorge) Marshall *lawyer, retired health facility administrator*
Lapin, Harvey I. *lawyer*
Levenfeld, Milton Arthur *lawyer*
McGinn, Mary J. *lawyer, insurance company executive*
Rosemarin, Carey Stephen *lawyer*
Teichner, Bruce A. *lawyer*

Oak Brook
Barnes, Karen Kay *lawyer*
Congalton, Susan Tichenor *lawyer*
Hollins, Mitchell Leslie *lawyer*
Ring, Leonard M. *lawyer, writer*
Santona, Gloria *lawyer, food products executive*
Sherman, Jennifer L. *lawyer*

Oakbrook Terrace
Willis, Douglas Alan *lawyer*

Oregon
Floski, Doug *lawyer*

Palatine
Victor, Michael Gary *lawyer, physician*

Park Forest
Goodrich, John Bernard *lawyer, consultant*

Park Ridge
Hegarty, Mary Frances *lawyer*
LaRue, Paul Hubert *retired lawyer*
Naker, Mary Leslie *legal firm executive*

Peoria
Allen, Lyle Wallace *lawyer*
Buda, James B. *lawyer, manufacturing executive*
Strodel, Robert Carl *lawyer*

Princeton
Bernabei, Marc P. *lawyer*

Riverwoods
Gold, Deidra D. *lawyer*
Yarrington, Hugh *corporate lawyer, communications company executive*

Rock Island
Lousberg, Peter Herman *former lawyer*

Rockford
Cyrs, Michael Thomas *lawyer*
Reno, Roger *lawyer*

Rosemont
Fitzgerald, Jeremiah Michael *lawyer*

Schaumburg
Lawson, A. Peter *lawyer*
Marshall, John David *lawyer*
Meltzer, Brian *lawyer*
Nehs, (William) Scott *lawyer*

Shorewood
Heaphy, John Merrill *lawyer*

Springfield
Heaton, Rodger A. *prosecutor*
Kelley, Patrick Wayne *prosecutor*
Mathewson, Mark Stuart *lawyer, editor*
Quinlan, William J. *lawyer*
Van Meter, Abram DeBois *lawyer, retired banker*

Sterling
Pace, Ole Bly III *lawyer*

Streamwood
Bailey, Robert Short *retired lawyer*

Urbana
Balbach, Stanley Byron *lawyer*
Kearns, James Cannon *lawyer*
Piland, John Charles *lawyer*
Thies, Richard Leon *lawyer, director*

Vernon Hills
Leahy, Christine A. *lawyer, information technology executive*

Vienna
Trambley, Donald Brian *lawyer*

Villa Park
Lubin, Peter Scott *lawyer*

Warrenville
Boardman, Robert A. *retired lawyer*
Covey, Steven K. *lawyer*

Waukegan
Henrick, Michael Francis *lawyer*
Leibowitz, David Perry *lawyer*

Western Springs
Hanson, Heidi Elizabeth *lawyer*
Rhoads, Paul Kelly *lawyer*

Wheaton
Birkett, Joseph E. *lawyer*
Kincaid, John Bruce *lawyer*

Willowbrook
Walton, Stanley Anthony III *lawyer*

Wilmette
Baisley, James Mahoney *retired lawyer*

Winnetka
Abell, David Robert *lawyer*
Berner, Robert Lee, Jr. *lawyer*
Crowe, Robert William *lawyer, mediator*
Ellwood, Scott *lawyer*
Hales, Daniel B. *lawyer*
Hickman, Frederic W. *retired lawyer*
McWhirter, Bruce J. *retired lawyer*

INDIANA

Angola
Cain, Tim J. *lawyer*

Batesville
de Maynadier, Patrick D. *lawyer*

Bloomington
Aman, Alfred Charles, Jr. *law educator*

Boonville
Corne, Todd *lawyer*

Carmel
Stein, Richard Paul *lawyer*
Walseth, David G. *lawyer, insurance company executive*

Columbus
Harrison, Patrick Woods *lawyer*
Rose, Marya Mernitz *lawyer*

Danville
Baldwin, Patricia Ann *lawyer*

East Chicago
Jeske, Marc R. *lawyer*

Elkhart
Gassere, Eugene Arthur *lawyer, investment company executive*
Harman, John Royden *retired lawyer*
Treckelo, Richard M. *lawyer*

Evansville
Heidorn, Robert E. *lawyer*
Levco, Stanley M. *lawyer*

Fort Wayne
Baker, Carl Leroy *lawyer*
Colvin, Sherrill William *lawyer*
Helmke, Paul (Walter Paul Helmke Jr.) *lawyer, former mayor*
Pope, Mark Andrew *lawyer, academic administrator*
Shoaff, Thomas Mitchell *lawyer*

Fowler
Weist, William Bernard *lawyer*

Franklin
Hamner, Lance Dalton *prosecutor*

Hammond
Capp, David A. *prosecutor*
DeGuilio, Jon E. *lawyer*
Diamond, Eugene Christopher *lawyer, health facility administrator*

Indianapolis
Albright, Terrill D. *lawyer*
Allen, David James *lawyer*
Armitage, Robert Allen *lawyer, pharmaceutical executive*
Badger, David Harry *lawyer*
Barkley, James M. *lawyer, real estate company executive*
Beckwith, Lewis Daniel *lawyer*
Beeler, Virgil L. *lawyer*
Boldt, Michael Herbert *lawyer*
Born, Samuel Roydon, II, *retired lawyer, mediator*
Bowman, Frank O. *law educator*
Brooks, Susan W. *prosecutor*
Butt, P. Lawrence *lawyer*
Carney, Joseph Buckingham *lawyer*
Choplin, John M., II, *lawyer*
Clark, James Murray *lawyer, former state legislator*
Deer, Richard Elliott *lawyer*
Downs, Thomas K. *lawyer*
Drentlicher, David *lawyer, educator, physician*
Dutton, Stephen James *lawyer*
Elberger, Ronald Edward *lawyer*
Evans, Daniel Fraley, Jr. *lawyer*
Fisher, James R. *lawyer*
FitzGibbon, Daniel Harvey *lawyer*
Fruehwald, Kristin Gail *lawyer*
Huston, Michael Joe *lawyer*
Jegen, Lawrence A. III *law educator*
Johnstone, Robert Philip *retired lawyer*
Kashani, Hamid Reza *lawyer, computer consultant*
Kemper, James Dee *lawyer*
Kerr, William Andrew *lawyer, educator*
Kinney, Eleanor De Arman *law educator*
Kirk, Carol *lawyer*
Kleiman, David Harold *lawyer*
Knebel, Donald Earl *lawyer*
Kuntz, William Henry *lawyer, mediator*
Lee, Stephen W. *lawyer*
Lisher, John Leonard *lawyer*
Lofton, Thomas Milton *lawyer*
Maine, Michael Roland *lawyer*
McKeon, Thomas Joseph *lawyer*
McKinney, Dennis Keith *lawyer*
Mc Kinney, Robert Hurley *lawyer, corporate financial executive*
Miller, David W. *lawyer*
Neff, Robert Matthew *lawyer, finance company executive*
Nolan, Alan Tucker *lawyer, writer, arbitrator*
Paul, Stephen Howard *lawyer*
Petersen, James L. *lawyer*
Pilgrim, Jill *lawyer, consultant*
Reynolds, Robert Hugh *lawyer*
Roberts, William Everett *lawyer*
Rusthoven, Peter James *lawyer*
Ryder, Henry Clay *lawyer*
Scaletta, Phillip Ralph III *lawyer*
Schlegel, Fred Eugene *lawyer*
Scism, Daniel Reed *lawyer*
Shula, Robert Joseph *lawyer*
Slaughter Andrew, Anne *lawyer*
Stayton, Thomas George *lawyer*
Steger, Evan Evans III *retired lawyer*
Stieff, John Joseph *lawyer*
Strain, James Arthur *lawyer*
Sutherland, Donald Gray *retired lawyer*
Tabler, Bryan G. *lawyer*
Tabler, Norman Gardner, Jr. *lawyer*
Thompson, William Harkins *lawyer*
Whale, Arthur Richard *retired lawyer*
White, James Patrick *law educator*
Wishard, Gordon Davis *lawyer*
Wood, William Jerome *lawyer*
Yates, C. Daniel *lawyer*

Kokomo
Fleming, James Richard *lawyer*

Lafayette
Bean, Jerry Joe *lawyer*
Hart, Russell Holiday *retired lawyer*

Merrillville
Compton, Clyde D. *lawyer*
Manous, Peter J. *lawyer*
Smith, Arthur Edward, Jr. *lawyer*

Mount Vernon
Van Haaften, Trent *lawyer*

New Albany
Bourne, James E. *lawyer*

Noblesville
Church, Douglas D. *lawyer*

Notre Dame
Edmonds, Edmund P. *law librarian, educator, dean*
Gunn, Alan *retired law educator*
Robinson, John Hayes *law educator*

Plainfield
Fivel, Steven Edward *lawyer, communications executive*

Rushville
Zwickey, Sheila Kaye *lawyer*

Sandborn
Gregg, John Richard *lawyer*

Shelbyville
McNeely, James Lee *lawyer*

South Bend
Carey, John Leo *lawyer*
Reinke, William John *lawyer*
Seall, Stephen Albert *lawyer*
Shaffer, Thomas Lindsay *lawyer, educator*
Vogel, Nelson J., Jr. *lawyer*

Terre Haute
Bopp, James, Jr. *lawyer*

Valparaiso
Gaffney, Edward McGlynn *law educator, dean*
Koeppen, Raymond Bradley *lawyer*
Persyn, Mary Geraldine *law librarian, educator*

Vernon
Smith, Gary Lee *lawyer*

Vincennes
Emison, Ewing Rabb, Jr. *lawyer*

Wabash
Plummer, Alfred Harvey III *lawyer*

IOWA

Ankeny
Wirtz, Eli J. *lawyer, retail executive*

Atlantic
Barry, James Patrick *lawyer*

Burlington
Beckman, David *lawyer*
Hoth, Steven Sergey *lawyer, educator*

Cedar Rapids
Chadick, Gary Robert *lawyer*
Collins, Kevin Heath *lawyer*

Coralville
Coulter, Charles Roy *lawyer*

Davenport
Dettmann, David Allen *lawyer*

Decorah
Belay, Stephen Joseph *lawyer*

Des Moines
Begleiter, Martin David *law educator, consultant*
Brauch, William Leland *lawyer*
Brennan, Scott M. *lawyer, political organization administrator*
Campbell, Bruce Irving *lawyer*
Carroll, Frank James *lawyer, educator*
Claypool, David L. *lawyer*
Conlin, Roxanne Barton *lawyer*
Critelli, Nicholas *lawyer, barrister*
Eaton, Jay *lawyer*
Fisher, Gordon R., Jr. *lawyer*
Fisher, Thomas George *lawyer, retired media company executive*
Fisher, Thomas George, Jr. *lawyer*
Haggerty, Joseph K. *lawyer, insurance company executive*
Hansell, Edgar Frank *lawyer*
Harris, Charles Elmer *retired lawyer*
Hill, Luther Lyons, Jr. *lawyer*
Jensen, Dick Leroy *lawyer*
Narber, Gregg Ross *lawyer*
Nickerson, Don C. *lawyer, retired prosecutor, judge*
Shaff, Karen E. *lawyer, insurance company executive*
Shors, John Dennis *lawyer*
Whitaker, Matthew George *prosecutor*
Wine, Donald Arthur *lawyer*

Dubuque
Hammer, David Lindley *lawyer, writer, investor*

Garner
Hovda, Theodore James *lawyer*

Grundy Center
Kliebenstein, Don *retired lawyer*

Harlan
Salvo, J. C. *lawyer*

Holstein
Goettsch, Kirk E. *lawyer*

Iowa City
Bonfield, Arthur Earl *law educator*
Hines, Norman William *law educator, retired dean*
Holland, Charles Joseph *lawyer*
Kurtz, Sheldon Francis *lawyer, educator*
Tomkovicz, James Joseph *law educator*

Marshalltown
Brennecke, Allen Eugene *lawyer*

Muscatine
Nepple, James Anthony *lawyer*

Nevada
Countryman, Dayton Wendell *lawyer*

Newton
Scholten, Roger Keith *lawyer*

Northwood
Krull, Douglas Arthur *lawyer*

Sioux City
Fredregill, Alan *lawyer*
Kalafut, Mark A. *lawyer*

Waterloo
Ferguson, Thomas Joseph *lawyer*

West Des Moines
Hockenberg, Harlan David *lawyer*
Houser, Thomas J. *lawyer*
Power, Joseph Edward *lawyer*
Tully, Robert Gerard *lawyer*

KANSAS

Fort Scott
Reynolds, Zackery E. *lawyer*

Garden City
Loyd, Ward Eugene *lawyer*

Gardner
Webb, William Duncan *lawyer, mediator*

Hutchinson
Hayes, John Francis *lawyer*
Swearer, William Brooks *lawyer*

Iola
Toland, Clyde William *lawyer*

Kansas City
Sutherland, John Stephen *lawyer*

Lawrence
Casad, Robert Clair *legal educator*
Smith, Glee Sidney, Jr. *lawyer*
Turnbull, H. Rutherford III *lawyer, educator*
Winter, Winton Allen, Jr. *lawyer, state legislator*

Leavenworth
Crow, Martha Ellen *lawyer*
Crow, Michael P. *lawyer*

Leawood
Devlin, James Richard *lawyer*

Lincoln
Crangle, Robert D. *lawyer, management consultant, entrepreneur*

Oberlin
Hirsch, Steven W. *lawyer*

Olathe
Erker, Thomas J. *lawyer*
Kline, Phillip D. *prosecutor, former state attorney general*

Overland Park
Churay, Daniel J. *lawyer*
Ellis, Jeffrey Orville *lawyer*
Martin, Alson Robert *lawyer*
O'Brien, Timothy Michael *lawyer*
Stanton, Roger D. *lawyer*
Woods, Richard Dale *lawyer*

Shawnee Mission
Badgerow, John Nicholas *lawyer*
Becker, David M. *lawyer*
Bond, Richard Lee *lawyer, state senator*
Keim, Robert Bruce *lawyer*
Starrett, Frederick Kent *lawyer*

Topeka
Concannon, James M. *lawyer, educator, dean*
Elrod, Linda Diane Henry *lawyer, educator*
Engel, Charles T. *lawyer*
Hayse, Richard Franklin *lawyer*
Irick, Larry D. *lawyer, energy executive*
Keefer, J(ames) Michael *lawyer*
Kobach, Kris William *law educator, political organization administrator*
Massey, Michael J. *lawyer, retail executive*
Rock, Richard Rand *lawyer, former state senator*

Wichita
Docking, Thomas Robert *lawyer, former state lieutenant governor*
Foulston, Nola Tedesco *lawyer*
Melgren, Eric Franklin *prosecutor, lawyer*
Moore, Tim J. *lawyer*
Parks, Linda S. *lawyer*
Rathbun, Randall Keith *lawyer*
Roth, James R. *lawyer*
Thompson, Lee (Morris Thompson) *lawyer*
Williams, Jackie N. *law educator, former prosecutor*

KENTUCKY

Covington
Land, Suzanne Prieur *lawyer*
Schaeffer, Andrew *lawyer*
Smith, Pete A. *lawyer*

Lakeside Park
Schmidt, Thomas Joseph, Jr. *lawyer*

Prospect
Willenbrink, Rose Ann *retired lawyer*

LOUISIANA

Shreveport
Nelson, Ralph Stanley *lawyer*

MICHIGAN

Ann Arbor
Allen, Layman Edward *law educator, research scientist*
Anderson, Austin Gothard *lawyer, consultant, academic administrator*
Carney, Thomas Daly *lawyer*
Cooper, Edward Hayes *lawyer, educator*
Darlow, Julia Donovan *lawyer*
DeVine, Edmond Francis *retired lawyer*
Duquette, Donald Norman *law educator*
Frier, Bruce Woodward *law educator*
Gray, Whitmore *lawyer, educator*
Joscelyn, Kent Buckley *lawyer*
Kahn, Douglas Allen *law educator*
Kamisar, Yale *lawyer, educator*
Krier, James Edward *law educator, writer*
Kuehn, George E. *lawyer*
MacKinnon, Catharine Alice *lawyer, educator, writer*
Miller, William Ian *law educator*
Payton, Sallyanne *law educator*
Reed, John Wesley *lawyer, educator*
Roach, Thomas Adair *lawyer, mediator*
St. Antoine, Theodore Joseph *retired law educator, arbitrator*
Sandalow, Terrance *law educator*
Simpson, A.W. Brian *law educator*
Stein, Eric *retired law educator*
Sullivan, Teresa Ann *law and sociology educator, academic administrator*
Vining, (George) Joseph *law educator*
Waggoner, Lawrence William *law educator*
White, James Boyd *law educator*

Auburn Hills
Gasparovic, John J. *lawyer*
Greenfield, Susan L. *lawyer*
Horiszny, Laurene Helen *lawyer*

Benton Harbor
Hopp, Daniel Frederick *lawyer, manufacturing company executive*

Birmingham
Elsman, James Leonard, Jr. *lawyer*
Kienbaum, Thomas Gerd *lawyer*
Polzin, Charles Henry *lawyer*
Schaefer, John Frederick *lawyer*
Thorpe, Norman Ralph *lawyer, automotive executive, retired military officer*

Bloomfield Hills
Banas, C(hristine) Leslie *lawyer*
Berlow, Robert Alan *lawyer*
Birnkrant, Sherwin Maurice *lawyer*
Bogas, Kathleen Laura *lawyer*
Burstein, Richard Joel *lawyer*
Charla, Leonard Francis *lawyer, publishing executive*
Clippert, Charles Frederick *lawyer*
Cook, Steven M. *lawyer, construction executive*
Dawson, Stephen Everette *lawyer*
Devaney, Dennis Martin *lawyer, educator*
Gold, Edward David *lawyer*
Googasian, George Ara *lawyer*
Kasischke, Louis Walter *lawyer*
Ledwidge, Patrick Joseph *lawyer*
LoPrete, James Hugh *lawyer*
Martin, J(oseph) Patrick *lawyer, judge*
McCuen, John Francis, Jr. *lawyer*
McDonald, Patrick Allen *lawyer, educator, arbitrator*
Norris, John Hart *lawyer, director*
Rader, Ralph Terrance *lawyer*
Simon, Evelyn *lawyer*
Snyder, George Edward *lawyer*
Williams, J. Bryan *lawyer*
Williams, Walter Joseph *lawyer*
Wise, John Augustus *lawyer, director*
Yamin, Joseph Francis *lawyer*

Dearborn
Taub, Robert Allan *lawyer*

Detroit
Archer, Dennis Wayne *lawyer, former mayor*
Ash, George W. *lawyer*
Bilstrom, Jon Wayne *lawyer*
Brustad, Orin Daniel *lawyer*
Calkins, Stephen *lawyer, educator*
Candler, James Nall, Jr. *lawyer*
Charfoos, Lawrence Selig *lawyer*
Cohan, Leon Sumner *lawyer, retired electric company executive*
Cohen, Norton Jacob *lawyer*
Collier, James Warren *retired lawyer*
Costello, Thomas, Jr. *lawyer, computer company executive*
Cothorn, John Arthur *lawyer*
Cranmer, Thomas William *lawyer*
Deason, Herold McClure *lawyer*
Deitch, Laurence B. *lawyer*
Diehl, Nancy J. *lawyer*
Draper, James Wilson *lawyer*
Drutchas, Gregory G. *lawyer*
Dudley, John Henry, Jr. *lawyer*
Dunn, William Bradley *lawyer*
Faison, W. Mack *lawyer*
Felt, Julia Kay *lawyer*
Gershel, Alan M. *prosecutor*
Green, Saul A. *lawyer*
Hall, Elliott Sawyer *lawyer*
Hampton, Verne Churchill, II, *lawyer*
Herstein, Carl William *lawyer*
Hughes, Thomas A. *lawyer, utilities executive*
Kamins, John Mark *lawyer*
Katz, Donald L. *lawyer*
Kessler, Philip Joel *lawyer*
Krsul, John Aloysius, Jr. *lawyer*
Lewand, F. Thomas *lawyer*
Lewis, David Baker *lawyer*
Lockman, Stuart M. *lawyer*
Mahoney, Joan *law educator*
Mamat, Frank Trustick *lawyer*
McIntyre, Michael John *lawyer, educator*
Mitseff, Carl *lawyer*
Murphy, Stephen Joseph III *prosecutor*
Nadeau, Steven C. *lawyer*
O'Hair, John D. *lawyer*
Oldford, Floyd Mark *legal association administrator*
Parker, George Edward III *lawyer*
Rassel, Richard Edward *lawyer*
Raymond, Richard Gerard, Jr. *lawyer*
Rozof, Phyllis Claire *lawyer*
Saxton, William Marvin *lawyer*
Schwartz, Alan Earl *lawyer, director*
Semple, Lloyd Ashby *lawyer*
Shannon, Margaret Anne *lawyer*
Shapiro, Michael Bruce *lawyer*
Sherrick, Daniel William *lawyer*
Smith, James Albert *lawyer*
Smith, S. Kinnie, Jr. *lawyer*
Sparrow, Herbert George III *lawyer, educator*
Thelen, Bruce Cyril *lawyer*
Timm, Roger K. *lawyer*
Turner, Reginald Maurice, Jr. *lawyer*
Valade, Alan Michael *lawyer*
Volz, William Harry *lawyer, educator*
White, Katherine E. *law educator*
Wittlinger, Timothy David *lawyer*
Wu, Frank H. *law educator, journalist*

Dexter
McHugh, Richard Walker *lawyer*

East Lansing
Lashbrooke, Elvin Carroll, Jr. *law educator, consultant*

Farmington
Shaevsky, Mark *lawyer*

Farmington Hills
Bernstein, Richard *lawyer*
Brodhead, William McNulty *lawyer, retired congressman*
Mall, Sanford J. *lawyer*

Grand Rapids
Barnes, Thomas John *lawyer*
Blackwell, Thomas Francis *lawyer*
Botsford, Jon Douglas *lawyer*
Bradshaw, Conrad Allan *retired lawyer*
Brady, James S. *lawyer*
Brinkmeyer, Scott S. *lawyer*
Curtin, Timothy John *lawyer*
Davis, Henry Barnard, Jr. *lawyer*
DeBoer, James N. *lawyer*
Deems, Nyal David *lawyer, mayor*
DeYonker, Alex J. *lawyer, food products executive*
McNeil, John W. *lawyer*
Mears, Patrick Edward *lawyer*
Missad, Matthew J. *lawyer*
Sytsma, Fredric A. *lawyer*
Titley, Larry J. *lawyer*
Van Haren, W(illiam) Michael *lawyer*
Van't Hof, William Keith *lawyer*

Grosse Pointe
Amsden, Ted Thomas *lawyer*
Maurer, David Leo *lawyer*

Grosse Pointe Farms
Axe, John Randolph *lawyer, finance company executive*
Thurber, Peter Palms *lawyer*

Grosse Pointe Park
Brand, George Edward, Jr. *retired lawyer*
Mogk, John Edward *law educator, association executive, consultant*

Hastings
Crowley, Dale Alan *prosecutor*

Hickory Corners
Bristol, Norman *lawyer, arbitrator, retired food products executive*

Highland
Bullard, Willis Clare, Jr. *lawyer*

Holland
Murphy, Max Ray *lawyer*

Inkster
Bullock, Steven Carl *lawyer*

Ionia
Palmer, Charles A. *lawyer, educator*

Iron Mountain
Paupore, Jeffrey George *lawyer*

Jackson
Marcoux, William Joseph *lawyer*
Smith, Stanton Kinnie, Jr. *lawyer*

Kalamazoo
Hall, Curtis E. *lawyer*
Marquardt, Michele C. *lawyer*
Van Slambrouck, John G. *lawyer*

Lansing
Baker, Frederick Milton, Jr. *lawyer*
Demlow, Daniel J. *lawyer*
Fink, Joseph Allen *lawyer*
Foster, Joe C., Jr. *lawyer*
Hollowell, Melvin J, Jr. *lawyer*

Leland
Jetton, Girard Reuel, Jr. *lawyer, retired oil industry executive*

Livonia
Bialosky, David L. *lawyer, automotive executive*
Hoffman, Barry Paul *lawyer*

Manistee
Swain, Dennis Michael *lawyer*

Midland
Donker, Norman Wayne *prosecutor*
Kalil, Charles James *lawyer, chemicals executive*
Scriven, John G. *retired lawyer, retired chemical company executive*

Monroe
Lipford, Rocque Edward *lawyer*

Mount Clemens
Ciaramitaro, Nick *prosecutor*

Muskegon
McKendry, John H., Jr. *lawyer*
Nehra, Gerald Peter *lawyer*

Niles
Pasula, Angela Marie *lawyer*

Northville
Cauley, Patrick C. *lawyer*

Novi
DiRita, David M. *lawyer, manufacturing executive*

Pinckney
Britton, Clarold Lawrence *lawyer, consultant*

Plymouth
Robinson, Logan Gilmore *lawyer*

Pontiac
Gorcyca, David G. *lawyer*

Saginaw
Zanot, Craig Allen *lawyer*

Saint Joseph
Butzbaugh, Alfred M. *lawyer*

Sault Sainte Marie
Morello, Steven John *lawyer*

Southfield
Brooks, Ernie L. *lawyer*
Darling, Robert Howard *lawyer*
Dawson, Dennis Ray *lawyer, manufacturing executive*
Fieger, Geoffrey Nels *lawyer*
Fox, Stacy L. *lawyer*
Jacobson, Michael F. *lawyer*
Katz, Robert L. *lawyer*
Ninivaggi, Daniel A. *lawyer, manufacturing executive*
Ponitz, John Allan *lawyer*
Rochkind, Louis Philipp *lawyer*
Thurswell, Gerald Elliott *lawyer*
Toll, Sheldon Samuel *lawyer*
Zamoyski, James J. *corporate lawyer*

Sterling Heights
Markey, James Kevin *lawyer*

Taylor
Hirsch, David L. *lawyer*
Leekley, John Robert *lawyer, consumer products company executive*

Traverse City
Dettmer, Michael Hayes *lawyer, former prosecutor*
Quick, Albert Thomas *lawyer, educator*

Troy
Alterman, Irwin Michael *lawyer*
Baker, Vernon G., II, *lawyer, automotive executive*
Bishop, Michael *lawyer, state senator*
Cantor, Bernard Jack *lawyer*
Gelder, John William *lawyer*
Hirschhorn, Austin *lawyer*
Knoll, Jay B. *lawyer*
Kruse, John Alphonse *lawyer*
May, Alan Alfred *lawyer*
Navarro, Monica *lawyer*
Nolte, Henry R., Jr. *lawyer, former automobile company executive*
Peters, Thomas M. *lawyer*
Sherbin, David M. *lawyer*
Thurber, John Alexander *lawyer*

Van Buren Township
Donofrio, John *lawyer*

Washington
Levine, Peter S. *corporate lawyer*

Wixom
Darke, Richard Francis *lawyer*

Ypsilanti
Eggertsen, John Hale *lawyer*

Zeeland
Christenson, James E. *lawyer*

MINNESOTA

Austin
Cavanaugh, James W. *lawyer*

Bloomington
Broeker, John Milton *lawyer*
Mooty, John William *lawyer*
Nelson, Eric John *lawyer*
O'Keefe, Daniel P. *lawyer*

Brooklyn Park
Landry, Paul Leonard *lawyer*

Center City
Bernhardson, Ivy Schutz *lawyer*

Chatfield
Opat, Matthew John *lawyer*

Crookston
Swanson, Wayne Harold *lawyer*

Detroit Lakes
Stowman, David L. *lawyer*

Duluth
Amberg, Deborah Ann *lawyer*
Burns, Richard Ramsey *lawyer*

Eagan
Dulas, DeAnne L. *lawyer*
Schwartz, Arthur *lawyer*

Eden Prairie
Carlson, Jeffrey *lawyer*
Feuss, Linda Anne Upsall *lawyer*
Gernander, Barton Carl *lawyer*
Gilbert, James H. *lawyer, former state supreme court justice*
Hansen, Erik Frederick *lawyer*

Edina
Bakken, Eric Allen *lawyer*
Davidson, Ann D. *lawyer, aerospace transportation executive*
Drewes, Matthew A. *lawyer*
Renz, Christopher P. *lawyer*
Schaibley, Ann M. *lawyer*
Schulze, Chad William *lawyer*
Towey, Anne C. *lawyer*

Glencoe
Junge, Michael Keith *lawyer*

Golden Valley
Ainsworth, Louis Lynde *lawyer, manufacturing executive*
Breimayer, Joseph Frederick *patent lawyer*

Grand Marais
Hennessy, William Joseph *prosecutor*

Hastings
May, Nicholas G.B. *lawyer*

Hopkins
Hoard, Heidi Marie *lawyer*

Jackson
Steffan, Mark Thiel *lawyer*

Mankato
Gage, Fred Kelton *lawyer*
Kohlmeyer, Jason C. *lawyer*
Rosengren, Christopher Paul *lawyer*

Marshall
Paskach, David M. *lawyer, food products executive*

Medina
McConnell, Mary Patricia *lawyer*

Mendota Heights
Cotter, Patrick Linnae *lawyer*

Minneapolis
Abramson, Norman M. *lawyer*
Ali, Jeffer *lawyer*
Anderson, Eric Scott *lawyer*
Anderson, Leslie J. *lawyer*
Anderson, Richard J. *lawyer*
Baillie, James Leonard *lawyer*
Ballintine, Daniel John *lawyer*
Beekman, Marvin Lee *lawyer*
Berens, William Joseph *lawyer*
Berg, Thomas Kenneth *lawyer*
Bergerson, David Raymond *lawyer*
Borger, John Philip *lawyer*
Brand, Steve Aaron *lawyer*
Branson, Timothy E. *lawyer*
Breyer, K. Jon *lawyer*
Brink, David Ryrie *lawyer*
Buckingham, Elizabeth C. *lawyer*
Buratti, Dennis P. *lawyer*
Burns, Robert Arthur *lawyer*
Busdicker, Gordon Gene *retired lawyer*
Camarotto, David Earle *lawyer*
Caplan, Allan Hart *lawyer*
Carlson, Thomas David *lawyer*
Cattanach, Robert Edward, Jr. *lawyer*
Chadwick, Eric Hugh *lawyer*
Champlin, Steven Kirk *lawyer*
Christiansen, Jay David *lawyer*
Cialkowski, David Michael *lawyer*
Ciresi, Michael Vincent *lawyer*
Clary, Bradley G. *lawyer, educator*
Conn, Gordon Brainard, Jr. *lawyer*
Constantine, Katherine A. *lawyer*
Crosby, Thomas Manville, Jr. *lawyer*
Davis, Aaron W. *lawyer*
Deach, Jana Aune *lawyer*
DeVries Smith, Kate *lawyer*
Diviney, Craig David *lawyer*
Durocher, Vernle C. (Skip), Jr. *lawyer*
Eck, George Gregory *lawyer*
Eng, Holly S.A. *lawyer*
Engh, N. Rolf (Rolf Engh) *lawyer*
Fabel, Thomas Lincoln *lawyer*
Finzen, Bruce Arthur *lawyer*
Fisher, Michele Renee *lawyer*
Flom, Gerald Trossen *lawyer*
Forneris, Jeanne M. *lawyer*
Frase, Richard S. *law educator*
Freeman, Michael O. *lawyer*
Freeman, Todd Ira *lawyer*
French, John Dwyer *retired lawyer*
Gagnon, Craig William *lawyer*
Gallagher, Patrick J. *lawyer*
Garon, Philip Stephen *lawyer*
Garton, Thomas William *lawyer*
Genereux, L. Joseph *lawyer*
Gill, Richard Lawrence *lawyer*
Goldsmith, Scott K. *lawyer*
Goodman, Christopher Lawrence *lawyer*
Gordon, John Bennett *lawyer*
Gottschalk, Stephen Elmer *retired lawyer*
Greener, Ralph Bertram *lawyer*
Gross, David J.F. *lawyer*
Hamel, Mark Edwin *lawyer*
Hansen, Robyn L. *lawyer*
Harris, John Edward *lawyer*
Haynsworth, Harry Jay, IV, *law educator*
Hayward, Edward Joseph *lawyer*
Heffelfinger, Thomas Backer *lawyer, former prosecutor*
Heiberg, Robert Alan *lawyer*
Helsene, Amy L. *lawyer*
Hendrixson, Peter S. *lawyer*
Herr, David Fulton *lawyer, educator*
Hibbs, John Stanley *lawyer*
Hinderaker, John Hadley *lawyer, political blogger*
Hippee, William H., Jr. *lawyer*
Hobbins, Robert Leo *lawyer*
Holden, Susan M. *lawyer*
Howland, Joan Sidney *law librarian, educator*
Jackson, J. David *lawyer*
Jacobson, Carrie Isabelle *lawyer*
Jameson, Jennifer A. *lawyer*
Jarboe, Mark Alan *lawyer*
Johnson, G. Robert *lawyer*
Johnson, Gary M. *lawyer*
Johnson, Larry Walter *lawyer*

Jonason, William A. *lawyer*
Jones, B. Todd *lawyer, former prosecutor*
Jones, Jeffrey A. *lawyer*
Joyce, Joseph M. *lawyer, retail executive*
Kalinsky, Robert A. *lawyer*
Kaplan, Sheldon *lawyer, director*
Kelly, A. David *lawyer*
Keyes, Jeffrey J. *lawyer*
Klaas, Paul Barry *lawyer*
Knopf, Matthew J. *lawyer*
Koneck, John Michael *lawyer*
Lancaster, Peter McCreery *lawyer*
Lavik, Bricker L. *lawyer*
Lazar, Raymond Michael *lawyer, educator*
Lebedoff, David Miller *lawyer, writer*
Lillehaug, David Lee *lawyer*
Lindsay, Michael Anthony *lawyer*
Linnell, Norman C. *lawyer*
Loucks, Kathleen Margaret *lawyer*
Lucke, Stephen P. *lawyer*
Lueck, Martin R. *lawyer*
Magid, Creighton (Chip) Reid *lawyer*
Magnuson, Roger James *lawyer*
Manning, William Henry *lawyer*
Manthey, Thomas Richard *lawyer*
Martin, Phillip Hammond *lawyer*
Matson, Timothy C. *lawyer*
Matthews, James Shadley *lawyer*
Mayerle, Thomas Michael *lawyer*
McDonald, John J., Jr. *lawyer*
McGunnigle, George Francis *lawyer, judge*
McIntyre, John Lawrence *lawyer*
McLaughlin, Patrick J. *lawyer*
Meier, Lisa M. *lawyer*
Melendez, Brian *lawyer, political organization administrator*
Mellum, Gale Robert *lawyer*
Meshbesher, Ronald I. *lawyer*
Minish, Robert Arthur *lawyer*
Mitau, Lee R. *lawyer, bank executive*
Moe, Thomas O. *lawyer*
Mondale, Walter Frederick *lawyer, former Vice President of United States*
Montpetit, Jeffrey M. *lawyer*
Mooty, Bruce Wilson *lawyer*
Morrison, Fred LaMont *law educator, dean*
Nelson, Gary Michael *lawyer*
Nelson, Julie Loftus *lawyer*
Nelson, Richard Arthur *lawyer*
Ness, David Michael *lawyer*
Novak, Leslie Howard *lawyer*
O'Neill, Brian Boru *lawyer*
O'Neill Moreland, Tamara *lawyer*
Ort, Shannon *lawyer*
Paar, Christopher R. *lawyer*
Palmer, Deborah Jean *lawyer*
Parsons, Charles Allan, Jr. *lawyer*
Payne, William Bruce *lawyer, director*
Pentelovitch, William Zane *lawyer*
Peterson, David C. *lawyer*
Peterson, Neal N. *lawyer*
Pluimer, Edward J. *lawyer*
Potter, David B. *lawyer*
Pratte, Robert John *lawyer*
Price, Joseph Michael *lawyer*
Radmer, Michael John *lawyer, educator*
Raskind, Leo Joseph *law educator*
Ratchye, Boyd Havens *lawyer*
Reinhart, Robert Rountree, Jr. *lawyer*
Reuter, James William *lawyer*
Revnew, Thomas Richard *lawyer*
Rockenstein, Walter Harrison, II, *lawyer*
Rockwell, Winthrop Adams *lawyer*
Roe, Roger Rolland, Jr. *lawyer*
Rosenbaum, Robert A. *lawyer*
Rothenberg, Elliot Calvin *lawyer, writer*
Safley, James Robert *lawyer*
Saksena, Marian E. *lawyer*
Sand, David Byron *lawyer*
Sanner, Royce Norman *lawyer*
Santana, Lymari Jeanette *lawyer*
Sawyer, Charles F. *lawyer*
Schmaltz, David G. *lawyer*
Schnell, Robert Lee, Jr. *lawyer*
Schulkers, Joan M. *lawyer*
Scouton, David Earl *lawyer*
Seibert, Troy J. *lawyer*
Seifert, James J. *lawyer*
Shaheen, Christopher T. *lawyer*
Shnider, Bruce Jay *lawyer*
Short, Marianne Dolores *lawyer*
Sieben, Jeffrey Scott *lawyer*
Silver, Alan Irving *lawyer*
Silverman, Robert Joseph *lawyer*
Sipkins, Peter W. *lawyer*
Soland, Norman R. *corporate lawyer*
Sorenson, Christopher J. *lawyer*
Stageberg, Roger V. *lawyer*
Stein, Robert Allen *lawyer, educator, former legal association administrator*
Stern, Leo G. *lawyer*
Stoeri, William R. *lawyer*
Struthers, Margo S. *lawyer*
Struyk, Robert John *lawyer*
Sullivan, E. Thomas *law educator*
Swanson, David P. *lawyer*
Tinkham, Thomas W. *lawyer*
Trucano, Michael *lawyer*
Van Brunt, William A. *lawyer*
Vander Molen, Thomas Dale *lawyer*
Van Dyk, Suzanne B. *lawyer*
Vedder, James J. *lawyer*
Veith, G. John *lawyer*
Wahoske, Michael James *lawyer*
Weil, Cass Sargent *lawyer*
Weintraut, Steven James *lawyer*
Whelpley, Dennis Porter *lawyer*
Wicks, John R. *lawyer*
Wieneke, Darin Scott *lawyer*
Wille, Karin L. *lawyer*
Windhorst, John William, Jr. *lawyer*
Winer, Edward L. *lawyer*
Woods, Robert Edward *lawyer*
Yilek, John A. *lawyer*
Young, Christopher Aaron *lawyer*
Younger, Judith Tess *law educator*
Zalk, Robert H. *retired lawyer*

New Ulm
Weinberg, Justin Peter *lawyer*

North Saint Paul
O'Brien, Daniel William *lawyer, lumber company executive*

Northfield
Lundergan, Barbara Keough *lawyer*

Owatonna
Birk, Peg J. *lawyer*

Plymouth
Mack, Richard L. *lawyer, software company executive*

Rochester
Orwoll, Gregg S.K. *lawyer*
Schneider, Mahlon C. *lawyer*
Seeger, Ronald L. *lawyer*
Stevens, Jeremy R. *lawyer*

Roseville
Fisher, Rebecca Rhoda *lawyer*
Fullerton, Denise S.S. *lawyer*

Saint Paul
Allison, John Robert *lawyer*
Arnold, Valerie Downing *lawyer*
Bell, Lawrence T. *lawyer*
Carruthers, Philip Charles *lawyer, prosecutor, former state legislator*
Cyr, Lisa Watson *lawyer*
Fisk, Martin H. *lawyer*
Fitzgerald, Kelly Patrick *lawyer*
Galvin, Michael John, Jr. *lawyer*
Gehan, Mark William *lawyer*
Geis, Jerome Arthur *lawyer, educator*
Hintz, Chad Jason *lawyer*
Janzen, Peter S. *lawyer, food products executive*
Johnson, Paul Oren *lawyer*
Jones, C. Paul *lawyer, educator*
Jones, Patricia L. *lawyer*
Kastelic, David Allen *lawyer, energy and food products executive*
Kirwin, Kenneth Francis *law educator*
Lebedoff, Randy Miller *lawyer*
Leighton, Robert Joseph *lawyer*
Lillie, John Canfield III *lawyer*
McNeely, John J. *lawyer*
Micallef, Joseph Stephen *retired lawyer*
O'Malley, Kevin Thomas *lawyer*
Prohofsky, Dennis E. *lawyer, insurance company executive*
Pugh, Thomas Wilfred *lawyer*
Seymour, McNeil Vernam *lawyer*
Smith, Marschall Imboden *lawyer*
Smith, Steve C. *lawyer, state legislator*
Spence, Kenneth F. III *lawyer, insurance company executive*
Thompson, Mark K. *lawyer*
Todd, John Joseph *lawyer*

Shoreview
Scarfone, Anthony C. *lawyer*

Waite Park
Pearson, Andrew R. *lawyer*

Wayzata
Palmer, Brian Eugene *retired lawyer*
Schnobrich, Roger William *lawyer*

Winona
Brosnahan, Roger Paul *retired lawyer*

Woodbury
Spencer, David James *lawyer*

Worthington
Kohler, Kenneth James *lawyer*

MISSOURI

Ballwin
Banton, Stephen Chandler *lawyer*

Cassville
Melton, Emory Leon *lawyer, state legislator, publisher*

Chesterfield
Gerard, Jules Bernard *law educator*
Hier, Marshall David *lawyer*
Pollihan, Thomas Henry *lawyer*

Clayton
Mohan, John J. *lawyer*

Columbia
Bunn, Ronald Freeze *retired lawyer, academic administrator, political scientist*
Fisch, William Bales *law educator*
Moore, Mitchell Jay *lawyer, educator*
Westbrook, James Edwin *law educator*
Whitman, Dale Alan *lawyer, educator*

Earth City
Wallace, Bob (Robert Eugene Wallace Jr.) *lawyer*

Fenton
Stolar, Henry Samuel *lawyer*

Hollister
Lowther, Gerald Halbert *lawyer*

Independence
Albano, Michael Santo John *lawyer*

Jackson
Swingle, Harry Morley, Jr. *prosecutor*

Jefferson City
Bartlett, Alex *lawyer*
Callahan, Richard G. *prosecutor*
Deutsch, James Bernard *lawyer*
Tettlebaum, Harvey M. *lawyer*

Kansas City
Adams, Robert T. *lawyer*
Anderson, Christopher James *lawyer*
Bacon, Jennifer Gille *lawyer*
Bates, William Hubert *lawyer*
Beck, James M. *lawyer*
Beck, William G. *lawyer*
Becker, Thomas Bain *lawyer*
Beckett, Theodore Charles *lawyer*
Beihl, Frederick *retired lawyer*
Belzer, Irvin V. *lawyer*
Berkowitz, Lawrence M. *lawyer*
Blanton, W. C. *lawyer*
Bradshaw, Jean Paul, II, *lawyer*
Brous, Thomas Richard *lawyer*
Brown, Peter W. *lawyer*
Bruening, Richard P(atrick) *lawyer*
Canfield, Robert Cleo *lawyer*
Clarke, Milton Charles *lawyer*
Clegg, Karen Kohler *lawyer*
Connor, Kevin M. *lawyer*
Crawford, Howard Allen *lawyer*
Cross, William Dennis *lawyer*
Culp, Donald Allen *lawyer*
Daley, Matthew James *lawyer*
Davis, John Charles *lawyer*
Davis, Stanley D. *lawyer*
Deacy, Thomas Edward, Jr. *lawyer*
Dietrich, William Gale *lawyer, real estate developer, consultant*
Donnelly, Paul E. *lawyer*
Dover, Mark A. *lawyer*
Dreyer, Leo Philip *lawyer*
Edgar, John M. *lawyer*
Egan, Charles Joseph, Jr. *lawyer, consumer products company executive*
Eldridge, Truman Kermit, Jr. *lawyer*
Epps, Mischa Buford *lawyer*
Erickson, David R. *lawyer*
Evans, Craig L. *lawyer*
Foster, Mark Stephen *lawyer*
Gardner, Brian E. *lawyer*
Graves, Todd Peterson *lawyer, former prosecutor*
Green, Robert K. *lawyer, former energy executive*
Greer, Norris E. *lawyer*
Gross, Michael J. *lawyer*
Grossman, Robert D. *lawyer*
Hargrave, Mark William *lawyer*
Harris, Charlie J., Jr. *lawyer*
Heeter, James A. *lawyer*
Hill, Stephen L., Jr. *lawyer, former prosecutor*
Hindman, Larrie C. *lawyer*
Holt, Ronald Lee *lawyer*
Johnson, Mark Eugene *lawyer*
Johnson, Mark P. *lawyer*
Kaplan, Harvey L. *lawyer*
Kilroy, John Muir *lawyer*
Kilroy, William Terrence *lawyer*
Langworthy, Robert Burton *lawyer*
Levings, Theresa Lawrence *lawyer*
Lindsey, David Hosford *lawyer*
Litan, Robert Eli *lawyer, economist*
Lombardi, Cornelius Ennis, Jr. *lawyer*
Long, Gary R. *lawyer*
Magill, Kent B. *lawyer*
Marquette, I. Edward *lawyer*
Martucci, William Christopher *lawyer*
Matheny, Edward Taylor, Jr. *lawyer*
McCandless, Jeffry Scott *lawyer*
McLarney, Charles Patrick *lawyer*
McManus, James William *lawyer*
Mick, Howard Harold *lawyer*
Milton, Chad Earl *lawyer*
Moedritzer, Mark *lawyer*
Mordy, James Calvin *retired lawyer*
Murphy, John F. *lawyer*
Newsom, James Thomas *lawyer*
Northrip, Robert Earl *lawyer*
O'Dear, Craig Steven *lawyer*
Owens, Stephen J. *lawyer*
Palmer, Dennis Dale *lawyer*
Pelofsky, Joel *lawyer*
Price, James Tucker *lawyer*
Prugh, William Byron *lawyer*
Reardon, Michael Edward *lawyer*
Rebein, Joseph M. *lawyer*
Reitz, Christopher M. *lawyer, gas industry executive*
Roush, Nancy Schmidt *lawyer*
Sampson, William Roth *lawyer*
Satterlee, Terry Jean *lawyer*
Schult, Thomas P. *lawyer*
Sexton, J. Stan *lawyer*
Shaw, John W. *lawyer*
Shughart, Donald Louis *retired lawyer*
Simpson, John W. *lawyer*
Spaeth, Nicholas John *lawyer, former state attorney general*
Spalty, Edward Robert *lawyer*
Spencer, Richard Henry *lawyer*
Sutton, Ray Sandy *lawyer, food products executive*
Toll, Perry Mark *lawyer, educator*
Van Dyke, Thomas Wesley *lawyer*
Vering, John Albert *lawyer*
Voigts, Gene E. *lawyer*
Voran, Joel Bruce *lawyer*
Webb, B. Trent *lawyer*
Whisler, Joe B. *lawyer*
Whittaker, Judith Ann Cameron *lawyer*
Wirken, James Charles *lawyer*
Wood, John F. *prosecutor*
Woods, Curtis E(ugene) *lawyer*
Wrobley, Ralph Gene *lawyer*

Kennett
Sokoloff, Stephen Paul *lawyer*

Liberty
Hampton, Trenton D. *lawyer*

Louisiana
Smith, Philip G. *lawyer*

Maryland Heights
Boudreau, Thomas M. *lawyer, health products executive*

Mount Vernon
Stemmons, Randee Smith *lawyer*

Nevada
Ewing, Lynn Moore, Jr. *lawyer*

New London
Briscoe, John W. *lawyer*

Olivette
DePew, Shawna Cecila *lawyer*

Platte City
Cozad, John Condon *lawyer*

Saint Joseph
Kranitz, Theodore Mitchell *lawyer*

Saint Louis
Alber, John I. *lawyer*
Appleton, R. O., Jr. *lawyer*
Arnold, John Fox *lawyer*
Atwood, Hollye Stolz *lawyer*
Aylward, Ronald Lee *lawyer*
Babington, Charles Martin III *lawyer*
Baker, Nannette A. *lawyer, city official*
Baldwin, Edwin Steedman *lawyer*
Ball, Dan H. *lawyer*
Banstetter, Robert J. *lawyer*
Becker, David Mandel *law educator, author, consultant*
Belz, Mark *lawyer*
Berger, John Torrey, Jr. *lawyer*
Berwick, Philip *law librarian, director, dean*
Bobak, Mark T. *lawyer*
Bonacorsi, Ellen E. *lawyer*
Bonacorsi, Mary Catherine *lawyer*
Brickey, Kathleen Fitzgerald *law educator*
Brickler, John Weise *lawyer*
Brickson, Richard Alan *lawyer*
Brody, Lawrence *lawyer, educator*
Brownlee, Robert Hammel *lawyer*
Burroughs, Harold R. *lawyer*
Burson, Charles W. *lawyer, retired agricultural products executive*
Carp, Larry *lawyer*
Carr, Gary Thomas *lawyer*
Clark, Stephen Robert *lawyer*
Clear, John Michael *lawyer*
Conran, Joseph Palmer *lawyer*
Copeland, Douglas Allen *lawyer*
Cornfeld, Dave Louis *lawyer*
Cornfeld, Richard Steven *lawyer*
Corrigan, William M. *lawyer*
Cousins, Steven *lawyer*
Covington, Ann K. *lawyer, former state supreme court justice*
Cupples, Stephen Elliot *lawyer*
Danforth, John Claggett *lawyer, former ambassador, senator*
Dorwart, Donald Bruce *lawyer*
Dowd, Edward L., Jr. *lawyer, former prosecutor*
Dowd, Thomas F. *lawyer*
Duesenberg, Richard William *lawyer*
Ellis, Dorsey Daniel, Jr. *lawyer, educator*
Erlinger, James H. III *lawyer*
Falk, William James *lawyer*
Farris, Clyde C. *lawyer*
Fogle, James Lee *lawyer*
Fournie, Raymond Richard *lawyer*
Frank, Michael M. *lawyer*
Godiner, Donald Leonard *lawyer*
Goebel, John J. *lawyer*
Goldstein, Steven *lawyer*
Goran, Mark H. *lawyer*
Greaney, Thomas L. *lawyer, educator*
Grebel, Lawrence Bovard *lawyer*
Green, Dennis Joseph *retired lawyer*
Guarigila, Dale A. *lawyer*
Guerri, William Grant *lawyer*
Gunn, Michael Peter *lawyer*
Hanaway, Catherine Lucille *prosecutor*
Hansen, Charles *lawyer*
Hays, Ruth *lawyer*
Hellmuth, Theodore Henning *lawyer*
Hermeling, Caroline L. *lawyer*
Hiles, Bradley Stephen *lawyer*
Huber, Charles G., Jr. *lawyer*
Inkley, John James, Jr. *lawyer*
Jackson, Rebecca R. *lawyer*
Jaudes, Richard Edward *lawyer*
Jayne, Thomas R. *lawyer*
Johnson, E. Perry *lawyer*
Johnson, Sandra Hanneken *law educator*
Joley, Lisa Annette *lawyer, brewery company executive*
Jones, Robert Gerard *lawyer*
Joyce-Hayes, Dee Leigh *lawyer*
Keffer, Richard *lawyer*
Keller, Juan Dane *retired lawyer*
Kelly, Douglas Laird *lawyer, investment company executive*
King, Douglas Willard *lawyer*
Klobasa, John Anthony *lawyer*
Kuhlmann, Fred Mark *lawyer*
Lause, Michael Francis *lawyer*
Lebowitz, Albert *lawyer, writer*
Lents, Don Glaude *lawyer*
Lieberman, Edward Jay *lawyer*
Lonsberg, John V. *lawyer*
Lybarger, Jerry *lawyer*
Madsen, Matthew J. *lawyer*
Mandelstamm, Jerome Robert *lawyer*
Martin, Lisa Demet *lawyer*
Massey, Raymond Lee *lawyer*
McCarter, Charles Chase *lawyer*
McCarter, W. Dudley *lawyer*
McCauley, Matthew D. *lawyer*
McDaniel, James Edwin *lawyer*
McKinnis, Michael Bayard *lawyer*
Meisel, George Vincent *lawyer*
Merrill, Charles Eugene *lawyer*
Metcalfe, Walter Lee, Jr. *lawyer*
Miller, Jan Paul *lawyer, former prosecutor*
Moore, McPherson Dorsett *lawyer*
Mulligan, Michael Dennis *lawyer*
Murray, George E. *lawyer*
Neville, James Morton *retired lawyer, consumer products company executive*
Newman, Charles Andrew *lawyer*
Noel, Edwin Lawrence *lawyer*
Nouss, James L., Jr. *lawyer*
Oberlander, Michael I. *lawyer, consumer products company executive*
O'Keefe, Michael Daniel *lawyer*
Olson, Robert Grant *lawyer*
O'Malley, Kevin Francis *lawyer, educator, writer*
Palans, Lloyd Alex *lawyer*
Palmer, Fredrick D. *lawyer, energy executive*
Phoenix, G. Keith *lawyer*
Pickle, Robert Douglas *lawyer, apparel executive*
Poscover, Maury B. *lawyer*
Raclin, Grier C. *lawyer*
Rataj, Edward William *lawyer*
Redd, Charles Appleton *lawyer*
Rice, Charles Marcus, II, *lawyer*
Ritter, Robert Forcier *lawyer*
Ritterskamp, Douglas Dolvin *lawyer*
Roodman, David A. *lawyer*
Rose, Albert Schoenburg *lawyer, educator*
Rubenstein, Jerome Max *lawyer*
Sachs, Alan Arthur *lawyer*
Sale, Llewellyn III *lawyer*
Sandberg, John Steven *lawyer*
Sant, John Talbot *lawyer*
Schnuck, Terry Edward *lawyer*
Schoch, Alexander C. *lawyer, energy executive*
Seabaugh, William F. *lawyer*
Searls, Eileen Haughey *retired lawyer, law librarian, educator*
Shands, Courtney, Jr. *lawyer*
Shostak, Burton H. *lawyer*

Smith, Arthur Lee *lawyer*
Sobol, Lawrence Raymond *lawyer*
Stratmann, Gayle G. *lawyer, consumer products company executive*
Sugg, Reed Waller *lawyer*
Sullivan, Steven R. *lawyer*
Teasdale, Kenneth Fulbright *lawyer*
Terry, Nicholas P. *law educator*
Turley, Michael Roy *lawyer*
Vandiver, Thomas K. *lawyer*
Van Fleet, Lisa A. *lawyer*
Virtel, James John *lawyer*
Wack, Thomas E. *lawyer*
Wagner, Raymond Thomas, Jr. *lawyer, legal association administrator*
Walsh, Thomas Charles *lawyer*
Watters, Richard Donald *lawyer*
Weiss, Charles Andrew *lawyer*
Welch, David William *lawyer*
Willard, Gregory Dale *lawyer*
Wilson, Margaret Bush *lawyer*
Wilson, Michael E. *lawyer*
Withers, W. Wayne *lawyer*
Wolff, Frank Pierce, Jr. *lawyer*
Wright, Philip B. *lawyer*
Young, Marvin Oscar *lawyer*

Springfield
Roberts, Patrick Kent *lawyer*
Shantz, Debra Mallonee *lawyer*

Stockton
Hammons, Brian Kent *lawyer*

Trenton
Hudson, Steven Daniel *lawyer, judge*

Warrensburg
Young, Mary Ann *lawyer*

NEBRASKA

Benkelman
Owens, Judith L(ynn) *lawyer*

Broken Bow
Sennett, John O. *lawyer*

Chadron
Bump, Bevin B. *lawyer*

Columbus
Hart, Carl Kiser, Jr. *lawyer*

Kearney
Schroeder, Kent A. *lawyer*

Lincoln
Crump, Linda R. *lawyer*
Frobom, LeAnn Larson *lawyer*
Guthery, John M. *lawyer*
Lacey, Gary Eugene *lawyer*
Perry, Edwin Charles *lawyer*
Rembolt, James Earl *lawyer*
Robak, Kim M. *lawyer*
Schizas, Jennifer Anne *law association administrator*

Omaha
Achelpohl, Steven Edward *lawyer*
Bailis, David Paul *lawyer*
Barrett, Frank Joseph *lawyer, insurance company executive*
Brownrigg, John Clinton *lawyer*
Caporale, D. Nick *lawyer*
Daub, Hal (Harold John Daub Jr.) *lawyer*
Dittrick, William G. *lawyer*
Dolan, James Vincent *lawyer*
Fitzgerald, James Patrick *lawyer*
Grant, John P. *lawyer*
Hamann, Deryl Frederick *lawyer, bank executive*
Hemmer, J. Michael *lawyer, rail transportation executive*
Jansen, James Steven *lawyer*
Jenkins, Melvin Lemuel *lawyer*
Jensen, Sam *lawyer*
Longo, Amy L. *lawyer*
McCusker, Thomas J. *lawyer, insurance company executive*
Miller, Roger James *lawyer*
Monaghan, Thomas Justin *former prosecutor*
Reiser, Richard Scott *lawyer*
Rock, Harold L. *lawyer*
Schilken, Michael C. *lawyer*
Schropp, Tobin *lawyer*
Sharpe, Robert Francis, Jr. *lawyer, food products executive*
Stenberg, Donald B. *lawyer*
von Bernuth, Carl W. *lawyer, diversified financial services company executive*
Wells, Roger W. *lawyer*

Sidney
Schaub, Paul B. *lawyer*

West Point
Donner, Thomas Benjamin *lawyer*

NEVADA

Las Vegas
James, Phyllis A. *lawyer*

Reno
Kaleta, Paul J. *lawyer, utilities executive*

NEW JERSEY

Lebanon
Sabatino, Thomas Joseph, Jr. *lawyer, pharmaceutical executive*

NEW YORK

New York
Collins, Joseph P. *lawyer*
Cusack, John T. *lawyer*
de Lasa, José M. *lawyer*
Ford, Ralph A. *lawyer, moving and relocation company executive*
Goldman, Louis B. *lawyer*
Kelly, Christopher M. *lawyer*
Li, Tze-chung *lawyer, educator*
Merrill, Thomas Wendell *lawyer, educator*
Napolitano, Steven V. *lawyer*

NORTH CAROLINA

Kitty Hawk
Tucker, Don Eugene *retired lawyer*

NORTH DAKOTA

Beulah
Quast, Larry Wayne *lawyer*

Bismarck
Gilbertson, Joel Warren *lawyer*
King, Lawrence Edmund *lawyer*
Moore, Sherry Mills *lawyer*
Murry, Charles Emerson *lawyer, federal official*
Olson, John Michael *lawyer*

Dickinson
Greenwood, Dann Edward *lawyer*

Fargo
Herman, Sarah Andrews *lawyer*
Holman, Maureen *lawyer*
Unhjem, Michael Bruce *lawyer*
Williams, Michael James *lawyer*
Wrigley, Drew H. *prosecutor, lawyer*

Grand Forks
Davis, W. Jeremy *retired lawyer, dean*

OHIO

Akron
Bartlo, Sam D. *lawyer*
Belsky, Martin Henry *law educator, dean*
Briggs, Robert W. *lawyer*
Fisher, James Lee *lawyer*
Harvie, Crawford Thomas *lawyer*
Lee, Brant Thomas *lawyer, educator, federal official*
Lombardi, Frederick McKean *lawyer*
Richert, Paul *law educator*
Taylor, E. Jane *lawyer*
Trotter, Thomas Robert *lawyer*
Vespoli, Leila L. *lawyer, energy executive*

Avon Lake
Pyke, John Secrest, Jr. *lawyer, polymers company executive*

Bay Village
Kapp, C. Terrence *lawyer*

Beachwood
Clegg, Christopher R. *lawyer*
Sullivan, John E. III *lawyer*

Bellefontaine
Heaton, Gerald Lee *lawyer*

Bellevue
Meyers, John Edward *prosecutor*

Bowling Green
Hanna, Martin Shad *lawyer*

Canton
Bennington, Ronald Kent *lawyer*
Burkhart, William R. *lawyer*

Cardington
Hall, Howard Ernest *lawyer*

Chagrin Falls
Smith, Barbara Jean *lawyer*

Cincinnati
Adams, Edmund John *lawyer*
Allison, Jon B. *lawyer*
Anderson, James Milton *lawyer, hospital administrator*
Anderson, William Hopple *lawyer*
Anstaett, Jennifer Griffin *lawyer*
Anthony, Thomas Dale *lawyer*
Auttonberry, Sheri E. *lawyer*
Bahlman, William Thorne, Jr. *retired lawyer*
Baldwin, William D.G. *lawyer*
Bell, Ronald A. *lawyer*
Bergeron, Pierre H. *lawyer*
Bishop, Jerome C. *lawyer*
Black, Stephen L. *lawyer*
Blandford, Colleen M. *lawyer*
Blaske, Nathan H. *lawyer*
Blickensderfer, Matthew C. *lawyer*
Braun, Joseph J. *lawyer*
Bride, Nancy J. *lawyer*
Bridgeland, James Ralph, Jr. *lawyer*
Britt, Kent A. *lawyer*
Broderick, Dennis John *lawyer, retail executive*
Bronson, Michael J. *lawyer*
Bruvold, Kathleen Parker *retired lawyer*
Burke, Rachel E. *lawyer*
Cappel, Harry W. *lawyer*
Carr, George Francis, Jr. *retired lawyer*
Cathey, Christopher D. *lawyer*
Cawood, James M. III *lawyer*
Chesley, Stanley Morris *lawyer*
Childs, Erin C. *lawyer*
Christenson, Gordon A. *law educator*
Christopher, John E. *lawyer*
Cioffi, Michael Lawrence *lawyer*
Cissell, James Charles *lawyer*
Coffaro, Steven C. *lawyer*
Combs, Eric K. *lawyer*
Cooney, Kevin L. *lawyer*
Cors, Jeanne Marie *lawyer*
Craig, L. Clifford *lawyer*
Cruz, A. B., III, (Anatolio Benedicto Cruz III) *lawyer*
Dehner, Joseph Julnes *lawyer*
DeLong, Deborah *lawyer*
Denton, D. Brock *lawyer*
Desai, Deepak K. *lawyer*
Diller, Edward Dietrich *lawyer*
Dornette, W(illiam) Stuart *lawyer, educator*
Eckner, Shannon F. *lawyer*
Ellerman, Paige L. *lawyer*
Erhart, Sue A. *lawyer*
Evans, James E. *lawyer*
Faller, Susan Grogan *lawyer*
Faulkner, Laura R. *lawyer*
Feichtner, Douglas J. *lawyer*
Finan, Richard H. *lawyer*
Fink, Jerold Albert *lawyer*
Fitzsimmons, Becky Barlow *lawyer*
Flamm, Justin D. *lawyer*
Flanagan, John Anthony *lawyer, educator*
Freedman, William Mark *lawyer, educator*
Fronduti, John S. *lawyer*
Frooman, Thomas E. *lawyer*
Garfinkel, Jane E. *lawyer*
Garretson, Matthew Lee *lawyer*
Gaunt, Karen Kreider *lawyer*
Geoppinger, Jeffrey D. *lawyer*
Gettler, Benjamin *lawyer, manufacturing company executive*
Ghassomian, Kevin R. *lawyer*
Giannella, Andrew R. *lawyer*
Giles, Brian T. *lawyer*
Glass, Joanne Wissman *lawyer*
Goodman, Stanley *lawyer*
Greenberg, Gerald Stephen *lawyer*
Habel, Christopher S. *lawyer*
Hardy, William Robinson *lawyer*
Harris, Irving *lawyer*
Hastings, Kerry P. *lawyer*
Hawkins, William H., II, *lawyer*
Hayden, Jeremy A. *lawyer*
Heinlen, Ronald Eugene *lawyer*
Heldman, James Gardner *lawyer*
Heldman, Paul W. *lawyer, food service executive*
Hess, Ashley W. *lawyer*
Hicks, Drew M. *lawyer*
Hicks, Sarah Ellington *lawyer*
Hill, Thomas Clark *lawyer*
Hinegardner, Laura A. *lawyer*
Hoffman, Bridget C. *lawyer*
Hylander, Jessica S. *lawyer*
Jackson, Kory A. *lawyer*
Johnson, James J. *lawyer*
Jones, Nathaniel Raphael *lawyer, retired federal judge*
Jurs, Peter B. *lawyer*
Kallas, Hani R. *lawyer*
Kane, Scott A. *lawyer*
Katz, Reuven J. *lawyer*
Kelley, John Joseph, Jr. *lawyer*
Kern, David Graham *lawyer*
Kindt, Monica V. *lawyer*
Kordons, Uldis *lawyer*
Kyle, Kimberly *lawyer*
Langston, Malinda L. *lawyer*
Lauer, Richard T. *lawyer*
Lawrence, James Kaufman Lebensburger *lawyer*
Lawrence, Jennifer L. *lawyer*
Liss, William J. *lawyer*
Lockwood, Bert Berkley, Jr. *law educator*
Longenecker, Mark Hershey, Jr. *lawyer*
Lorentz, Joshua A. *lawyer*
Love, Lisa A. *lawyer*
Lundrigan, Nicole M. *lawyer*
Malof, Kevin K. *lawyer*
Manley, Robert Edward *lawyer, economist*
Mann, David Scott *lawyer, former congressman*
Mason, Jeremy R. *lawyer*
Mason, Rachel J. *lawyer*
Maxwell, Robert Wallace, II, *lawyer*
McClain, William Andrew *lawyer*
McCluskey, Laurie A. *lawyer*
McGavran, Frederick Jaeger *lawyer*
McHenry, Powell *lawyer*
McKay, Bernard L. *lawyer*
McPeek, Bradley *lawyer*
Meister, Julia B. *lawyer*
Meranus, Leonard Stanley *lawyer*
Meyers, Pamela Sue *lawyer*
Miller, Robert Judd *lawyer*
Miller, W. Timothy *lawyer*
Moeddel, Michael J. *lawyer*
Mordino, Joseph T. *lawyer*
Nalbandian, John B. *lawyer*
Nechemias, Stephen Murray *lawyer*
Newman, Danny Merril *lawyer*
Oberhaus, Geoffrey Luther *lawyer*
O'Grady, Michael J. *lawyer*
O'Guinn, M. Dave III *lawyer*
O'Reilly, James Thomas *lawyer, educator, writer*
Pacheco, Bryan E. *lawyer*
Parker, R. Joseph *lawyer*
Petrie, Bruce Inglis *lawyer*
Phillips, T. Stephen *lawyer*
Porotsky, Richard D., Jr. *lawyer*
Rammes, Lisa M. *lawyer*
Ramsey, Jamie M. *lawyer*
Ramundo, Kimberly E. *lawyer*
Reichert, David *lawyer*
Reuter, Mark F. *lawyer*
Reynolds, Paul L. *lawyer, bank executive*
Rich, Robert Edward *lawyer*
Richardson, Eric W. *lawyer*
Roach, Adrienne J. *lawyer*
Rogers, Brie S. *lawyer*
Rohner, Nicholas K. *lawyer*
Rose, Donald McGregor *retired lawyer*
Ross, Lori A. *lawyer*
Rowe, Rachael A. *lawyer*
Rucker, Fanon A. *lawyer*
Ruehlmann, Mark John *lawyer*
Ruh, Michael A., Jr. *lawyer*
Schatz, Brett A. *lawyer*
Schmit, David E. *lawyer*
Schuck, Thomas Robert *lawyer, farmer*
Shaffer, Robert M.M. *lawyer*
Shearer, David A., Jr. *lawyer*
Shore, Thomas Spencer, Jr. *retired lawyer*
Silbersack, Mark Louis *lawyer*
Smyth, Robery M. *lawyer*
Sprecher, Christina M. *lawyer*
Sprecher, Kevin S. *lawyer*
Stern, Noah J. *lawyer*
Strauss, William Victor *lawyer*
Swigert, James Mack *lawyer*
Teeters, Jeffrey R. *lawyer*
Tepe, Thomas M., Jr. *lawyer*
Tobias, Charles Harrison, Jr. *lawyer*
Tobias, Paul Henry *lawyer*
Tomain, Joseph Patrick *law educator, retired dean*
Townsend, Robert J. *lawyer*
Trauth, Joseph Louis, Jr. *lawyer*
Uhi, Judd R. *lawyer*
Valentine, Lona J. *lawyer*
Vander Laan, Mark Alan *lawyer*
Wales, Ross Elliot *lawyer*
Weber, H. Patrick *lawyer*
Weeks, Steven Wiley *lawyer*
Weisenberger, Andrew *lawyer*
Weseli, Roger William *lawyer*
Wesloh, Steven M. *lawyer*
Wheatley, Christine S. *lawyer*
Whitaker, Glenn Virgil *lawyer*
Wilkowski, E. Todd *lawyer*
Wilson, Christopher J. *lawyer*
Woodside, Frank C. III *lawyer, educator, physician*
Zahneis, Leona Beth *lawyer*
Zahniser, Rachel S. *lawyer*
Zavatsky, Michael Joseph *lawyer*
Zimmerman, James M. *lawyer*

Cleveland
Adamo, Kenneth Robert *lawyer*
Adams, Albert T. *lawyer*
Andorka, Frank Henry *lawyer*
Andrews, Oakley V. *lawyer*
Ashmus, Keith Allen *lawyer*
Austin, Arthur Donald, II, *lawyer, educator*
Bacon, Brett Kermit *lawyer*
Bamberger, Richard H. *lawyer*
Bauer, Fred D. *lawyer*
Bays, James C. *lawyer*
Berick, James Herschel *lawyer*
Bilchik, Gary B. *lawyer*
Binford, Gregory Glenn *lawyer*
Blattner, Robert A. *lawyer*
Braverman, Herbert Leslie *lawyer*
Bravo, Kenneth Allan *lawyer*
Brennan, Maureen *lawyer*
Brucken, Robert Matthew *lawyer*
Bryenton, Gary Lynn *lawyer*
Burke, Kathleen B. *lawyer*
Cain, J. Matthew *prosecutor*
Cairns, James Donald *lawyer*
Carrick, Kathleen Michele *law librarian*
Carson, Van *lawyer*
Clarke, Charles Fenton *lawyer*
Collin, Thomas James *lawyer*
Coquillette, William Hollis *lawyer*
Crist, Paul Grant *lawyer*
Cudak, Gail Linda *lawyer*
Currivan, John Daniel *lawyer*
Cyphert, Michael A. *lawyer*
Demitrack, Thomas *lawyer*
DiVenere, Anthony Joseph *lawyer*
Doris, Alan S(anford) *lawyer*
Dorrell, John S. *lawyer, insurance company executive*
Dugan, Patrick J. *lawyer*
Duncan, Ed Eugene *lawyer*
Duvin, Robert Phillip *lawyer*
Emrick, Charles Robert, Jr. *lawyer*
Fabens, Andrew Lawrie III *lawyer*
Falsgraf, William Wendell *retired lawyer*
Fay, Regan Joseph *lawyer*
Feinberg, Paul H. *retired lawyer*
Fischer, Michelle K. *lawyer*
Friedman, Harold Edward *lawyer*
Friedman, James Moss *lawyer*
Gabriel, D. Bruce *lawyer*
Ganske, Lyle G. *lawyer*
Gentile Sachs, Valerie Ann *lawyer*
Gerhart, Peter Milton *law educator*
Glaser, Robert Edward *lawyer*
Goins, Frances Floriano *lawyer*
Gold, Gerald Seymour *lawyer*
Goldfarb, Bernard Sanford *lawyer*
Goler, Michael David *lawyer*
Goodman, David S. *lawyer*
Grossman, Theodore Martin *lawyer*
Hagen, Daniel C. *lawyer*
Haiman, Irwin Sanford *lawyer*
Hamilton, J. Richard *lawyer*
Hardy, Michael Lynn *lawyer*
Harris, Paul N. *lawyer*
Hastings, Susan C. *lawyer*
Heiman, David Gilbert *lawyer*
Hewitt, Christopher J. *lawyer*
Hochman, Kenneth George *lawyer*
Hollington, Richard Rings, Jr. *lawyer*
Horst, J. Robert *lawyer*
Horvitz, Michael John *lawyer*
Jacobs, Leslie William *lawyer*
Janke, Ronald Robert *lawyer*
Jeavons, Norman Stone *lawyer*
Jenks, Carl M. *lawyer*
Jorgenson, Mary Ann *lawyer*
Kahrl, Robert Conley *lawyer*
Kaiser, Gordon S., Jr. *lawyer*
Katcher, Richard *lawyer*
Katz, Lewis Robert *law educator*
Kelly, Dennis Michael *lawyer*
Kestner, Robert Steven *lawyer*
Kilbane, Catherine M. *lawyer*
Kilbane, Thomas Stanton *lawyer*
Kirchick, Calvin B. *lawyer*
Knerly, Stephen John, Jr. *lawyer*
Kohn, William Irwin *lawyer*
Korngold, Gerald *law educator, former dean*
Kramer, Eugene Leo *lawyer*
Kundtz, John Andrew *lawyer*
Kurit, Neil *lawyer*
Lawniczak, James Michael *lawyer*
Lease, Robert K. *lawyer*
Leavitt, Jeffrey Stuart *lawyer*
Leiken, Earl Murray *lawyer*
Lennox, Heather *lawyer*
Lewis, John Bruce *lawyer*
Lewis, John Francis *lawyer*
Maloney, Mary D. *lawyer*
Marting, Michael G. *lawyer*
Mason, Thomas Albert *retired lawyer*
Mast, Bernadette Mihalic *lawyer*
Matia, Paul Ramon *lawyer*
Mc Cartan, Patrick Francis *lawyer*
McCarthy, Mark Francis *lawyer*
McKee, Thomas Frederick *lawyer*
McLaughlin, Patrick Michael *lawyer*
Mehlman, Maxwell Jonathan *law educator*
Melsher, Gary William *lawyer*
Messinger, Donald Hathaway *lawyer*
Meyer, G. Christopher *lawyer*
Millstone, David Jeffrey *lawyer*
Moore, Kenneth Cameron *lawyer*
Nance, Frederick *lawyer*
Newman, John M., Jr. *lawyer*
Nicols, Howard J.C. *lawyer*
Okada, Ronald Shig *lawyer*
O'Keefe, Francis Ronald *lawyer*
Ollinger, W. James *lawyer*
Owendoff, Stephen Peter *lawyer*
Ozanne, Dominic Laurant *lawyer, construction company executive*
Perris, Terrence George *lawyer*
Piraino, Thomas Anthony, Jr. *lawyer*
Plant, Thomas A. *lawyer*
Pollock, R. Jeffrey *lawyer*
Putka, Andrew Charles *lawyer*

Rains, M. Neal *lawyer*
Rapp, Robert Neil *lawyer*
Rawson, Rachel L. *lawyer*
Rawson, Robert H., Jr. *lawyer*
Rekstis, Walter J. III *lawyer*
Reppert, Richard Levi *lawyer*
Rickert, Jeanne Martin M. *lawyer*
Roberts-Mamone, Lisa A. *lawyer*
Rosenbaum, Jacob I. *retired lawyer*
Ruben, Alan Miles *law educator*
Rydzel, James A. *lawyer*
Sawyer, Raymond Terry *lawyer, consultant, theater producer*
Schaefer, David Arnold *lawyer*
Schneider, David Miller *lawyer*
Shumaker, Roger Lee *lawyer*
Sicherman, Marvin Allen *lawyer*
Slinger, Michael Jeffery *law librarian, director*
Sloan, David W. *lawyer*
Smith, N. Lindsey *lawyer*
Sogg, Wilton Sherman *lawyer*
Solomon, Randall Lee *lawyer*
Stanley, Hugh Monroe, Jr. *lawyer*
Stanton, R. Thomas *lawyer*
Steindler, Howard Allen *lawyer*
Stellato, Louis Eugene *lawyer*
Stevens, Thomas Charles *lawyer*
Strauch, John L. *lawyer*
Striefsky, Linda A(nn) *lawyer*
Strimbu, Victor, Jr. *lawyer*
Stuhan, Richard George *lawyer*
Swartzbaugh, Marc L. *lawyer*
Swift, Christopher J. *lawyer*
Thimmig, Diana Marie *lawyer*
Thomas, Dynda A. *lawyer*
Toohey, Brian Frederick *lawyer*
Toomajian, William Martin *lawyer*
von Mehren, George M. *lawyer*
Walker, Robert S. (Bob) *lawyer*
Wallach, Mark Irwin *lawyer*
Weaver, Robin Geoffrey *lawyer, educator*
Weiler, Jeffry Louis *lawyer*
White, Gregory A. *prosecutor*
Whitney, Richard Buckner *lawyer*
Willis, James R. *lawyer*
Young, James Edward *lawyer*
Zambie, Allan John *lawyer*
Zangerle, John A. *lawyer*
Zoeller, David Louis *lawyer, bank executive*
Zwick, Gary Alan *lawyer*

Cleveland Heights
Chilcote, Lee A. *lawyer*

Columbus
Acker, Alan Scott *lawyer*
Bailey, Daniel Allen *lawyer*
Berndt, Ellen German *lawyer*
Bibart, Richard L. *lawyer*
Bridgman, G(eorge) Ross *lawyer*
Brooks, Richard Dickinson *lawyer*
Brown, Philip Albert *lawyer*
Brubaker, Robert Loring *lawyer*
Buchenroth, Stephen Richard *lawyer*
Carnahan, John Anderson *retired lawyer*
Carpenter, Michael H. *lawyer*
Chappelear, Stephen Eric *lawyer*
Cheap, Richard A. *lawyer, bank executive*
Chester, John Jonas *lawyer, educator*
Cross, Jeffrey D. *lawyer, electric power industry executive*
Crowder, Marjorie Briggs *lawyer*
Cvetanovich, Dan L. *lawyer*
Davis, Julia A. *lawyer, retail executive*
DeRousie, Charles Stuart *lawyer*
Dietrich, Thomas W. *corporate lawyer, insurance company executive*
Di Lorenzo, John Florio, Jr. *retired lawyer*
Dreher, Darrell L. *lawyer*
Fahey, Richard Paul *lawyer*
Fay, Terrence Michael *lawyer*
Feheley, Lawrence Francis *lawyer*
Fisher, Lawrence L. *lawyer*
Fisher, Lloyd Edison, Jr. *lawyer*
Fried, Samuel P. *lawyer*
Fu, Paul Shan *law librarian, consultant*
Gall, John Ryan *lawyer*
Grauer, David W. *lawyer*
Grendell, Timothy Joseph *lawyer*
Gross, James Howard *lawyer*
Gunsett, Daniel J. *lawyer*
Hairston, George W. *lawyer*
Hardymon, David Wayne *lawyer*
Harwood, Sandra Stabile *lawyer, state representative*
Hatler, Patricia Ruth *lawyer*
Haubiel, Charles W., II, *lawyer*
Hollenbaugh, H(enry) Ritchey *lawyer*
Huffman, Fordham E. *lawyer*
Jackson, Janet Elizabeth *city attorney, association executive*
Jackson, Reginald W. *lawyer*
Jenkins, George L. *lawyer, entrepreneur*
Jenkins, John Anthony *lawyer*
Johnson, Bruce S. *law librarian, educator*
Johnson, Mark Alan *lawyer*
Keane, John B. *lawyer, electric power industry executive*
King, G. Roger *lawyer*
King, James R. *lawyer*
Kirila, Jill S. *lawyer*
Kurtz, Charles Jewett III *lawyer*
Lehman, Harry Jac *lawyer*
Linville, Ronald G. *lawyer*
Long, Thomas Leslie *lawyer*
Markus, Kent Richard *lawyer*
Martin, William Giese *lawyer*
McAlister, Robert Beaton *lawyer*
McConnaughey, George Carlton, Jr. *retired lawyer*
McCutchan, Gordon Eugene *retired lawyer, insurance company executive*
McDermott, Kevin R. *lawyer*
McKenna, Alvin James *lawyer*
McNealey, J. Jeffrey *lawyer, corporate executive*
Miller, Terry Morrow *lawyer*
Minor, Charles Daniel *lawyer, director*
Minor, Robert Allen *lawyer*
Moloney, Thomas E. *lawyer*
Mone, Robert Paul *lawyer*
Moul, William Charles *lawyer*
Nissl, Colleen Kaye *lawyer*
Oman, Richard Heer *retired lawyer*
Petricoff, M. Howard *lawyer, educator*
Phillips, James Edgar *lawyer*
Pigman, Jack Richard *lawyer*
Pressley, Fred G., Jr. *lawyer*
Quigley, John Bernard *law educator*
Radnor, Alan T. *lawyer*
Ramey, Denny L. *bar association executive director*
Ray, Frank Allen *lawyer*
Reasoner, Willis Irl III *lawyer*
Ridgley, Thomas Brennan *lawyer*
Robinson, Barry R. *lawyer*
Robol, Richard Thomas *lawyer*
Ryan, Joseph W., Jr. *lawyer*
Saad, Michael D. *lawyer*
Saxbe, William Bart *former United States attorney general, senator, lawyer*
Schrag, Edward A., Jr. *lawyer*
Sheward, Richard S. *lawyer*
Shumate, Alex *lawyer*
Sidman, Robert John *lawyer*
Sowald, Heather Gay *lawyer*
Stern, Geoffrey *lawyer*
Stinehart, Roger Ray *lawyer*
Taggart, Thomas Michael *lawyer*
Tait, Robert E. *lawyer*
Tarpy, Thomas Michael *lawyer*
Thomas, Duke Winston *lawyer*
Todd, William Michael *lawyer*
Turano, David A. *lawyer*
Vorys, Arthur Isaiah *lawyer*
Warner, Charles Collins *lawyer*
Wightman, Alec *lawyer*
Wiseman, Randolph Carson *lawyer*

Dayton
Burick, Lawrence T. *lawyer*
Cramblit, Miggie E. *lawyer*
Faruki, Charles Joseph *lawyer*
Gottschlich, Gary William *lawyer*
Hadley, Robert James *lawyer*
Heyman, Ralph Edmond *lawyer*
Jenks, Thomas Edward *lawyer*
Johnson, C. Terry *lawyer*
Kinlin, Donald James *lawyer*
Lieb, Peter *lawyer*
Lockhart, Gregory Gordon *prosecutor*
Macklin, Crofford Johnson, Jr. *lawyer*
Rion, John Hayes *lawyer*
Rogers, Richard Hunter *lawyer*

Defiance
Strausbaugh, Jeffrey Alan *lawyer*

Delaware
Martz, Gary R. *lawyer*

Dublin
Bennett, George H., Jr. *lawyer, healthcare company executive*
Borror, David S. *lawyer*
McCorkle, Leon Marshall, Jr. *lawyer, educator*

Eastlake
Callender, James Sutton, Jr. *lawyer, state legislator*

Elyria
Miller, Bridget A. *lawyer*

Fairfield
Crane, Debra K. *lawyer*

Findlay
Kline, James Edward *lawyer*

Galena
Greek, Darold I. *lawyer*

Hillsboro
Coss, Rocky Alan *lawyer*

Holland
Machin, Barbara E. *lawyer*

Howard
Lee, William Johnson *lawyer*

Independence
Kola, Arthur Anthony *lawyer*

Jefferson
Eckart, Dennis Edward *lawyer, former congressman*

Lakewood
Skindell, Michael J. *lawyer*

Lancaster
Libert, Donald Joseph *lawyer*

Lebanon
Oliver, Timothy Allen *lawyer*

Marietta
Fields, William Albert *lawyer*

Marysville
Aronowitz, David M. *lawyer, chemicals executive*
Hamilton, Robert Otte *lawyer*

Maumee
Burchinow, Naran U. *lawyer*
Marsh, Benjamin Franklin *lawyer*
Witherell, Dennis Patrick *lawyer*

Mayfield
Jarrett, Charles Elwood *lawyer, insurance company executive*

Mayfield Heights
Bittenbender, Charles A. *lawyer*
Vanderwist, Kathryn K. *lawyer*

Mc Connelsville
Ross, Richard Lee *lawyer*

Medina
Tompkins, P. Kelly *lawyer, manufacturing executive*

Miamisburg
Battles, John Martin *lawyer*
Byrd, James Everett *lawyer*

Middletown
Horn, David C. *lawyer*

Milford
Mongelluzzo, John Andrew *lawyer*
Vorholt, Jeffrey Joseph *lawyer, software company executive*

Moreland Hills
Groetzinger, Jon, Jr. *lawyer, pharmaceutical executive, educator*

Newark
Mantonya, John Butcher *lawyer*
Mencer, Jetta *lawyer*
Reidy, Thomas Anthony *lawyer*

North Canton
Dettinger, Warren Walter *lawyer*

Orrville
Harlan, Mary Ann *lawyer*

Pepper Pike
Schnell, Carlton Bryce *lawyer*

Perrysburg
Baehren, James W. *lawyer*

Portsmouth
Grimshaw, Lynn Alan *lawyer*
Horr, William Henry *retired lawyer*

Seven Hills
Moran, Glenn J. *corporate lawyer*

Shaker Heights
Bixenstine, Kim Fenton *lawyer*

Toledo
Bixler, R. Jeffrey *lawyer*
Krull, Stephen Keith *lawyer*
McBride, Beverly Jean *lawyer*
McWeeny, Philip *corporate lawyer*
O'Connell, Maurice Daniel *lawyer*
Pletz, Thomas Gregory *lawyer*
Spitzer, John Brumback *lawyer*
Strobel, Martin Jack *lawyer, manufacturing and distribution company executive*
Wicklund, David Wayne *lawyer*

Warren
Rossi, Anthony Gerald *lawyer*

Westlake
Skulina, Thomas Raymond *lawyer*

Wickliffe
Bauer, Joseph W. *lawyer, chemicals executive*
Kidder, Fred Dockstater *retired lawyer*

Willoughby
Coulson, Charles Ernest *lawyer*
Driggs, Charles Mulford *lawyer*

Wooster
Kennedy, Charles Allen *lawyer*

Worthington
Brinkman, Dale Thomas *lawyer*

Youngstown
Roth, Daniel Benjamin *lawyer, company executive*

Zanesville
Micheli, Frank James *lawyer*

SOUTH DAKOTA

Aberdeen
Richards, Carlyle Edward *lawyer*

Dakota Dunes
Hagan, Sheila B. *corporate lawyer*

Ipswich
Beck, Vaughn Peter *lawyer*

Madison
Ericsson, Richard L. *lawyer*

Philip
Kemnitz, Ralph A. *lawyer*

Pierre
Gerdes, David Alan *lawyer*
Johnson, Julie Marie *lawyer, lobbyist, judge*
Riter, Robert C., Jr. *lawyer*
Rogers, Darla Pollman *lawyer*
Thompson, Charles Murray *lawyer*

Rapid City
Foye, Thomas Harold *lawyer*
Goodsell, G. Verne *lawyer*
Hagg, Rexford A. *lawyer, former state legislator*
Helmers, Steven J. *lawyer, energy executive*
Palmer, J. Crisman *lawyer*

Sioux Falls
Jackley, Martin J. (Marty Jackley) *prosecutor*
Knapp, Thomas Joseph *lawyer*
Luce, Michael Leigh *lawyer*
Marshall, Mark F. *lawyer*
McBride, Ted *prosecutor*
Tapken, Michelle G. *prosecutor*
Travis, Richard L. *lawyer*
Welk, Thomas John *lawyer*

Yankton
McGovern, Peter John *law educator*

UTAH

Provo
Staheli, Kory D. *law librarian*

Salt Lake City
McDermott, Kathleen E. *lawyer, corporate executive*

VERMONT

Stowe
Whiteman, Joseph David *retired lawyer, manufacturing company executive*

VIRGINIA

Virginia Beach
Hall, Glenn Allen *lawyer, state representative*

WISCONSIN

Barron
Babler, James Carl *lawyer*

Brookfield
Sprague, Charles W. *lawyer, finance company executive*
Winsten, Saul Nathan *lawyer*

Chippewa Falls
Scobie, Timothy Franklin *lawyer*

Crandon
Verich, Demetrio *lawyer*

Grafton
Maynard, John Ralph *lawyer*

Green Bay
Andrews, Steven R. *lawyer*
Burnett, Ralph George *lawyer*
Vandenberg, Thomas E. *lawyer, transportation services executive*
Wolf, Barth Joel *lawyer*

Hales Corners
Case, Karen Ann *lawyer*

Janesville
Steil, George Kenneth, Sr. *lawyer*

Kenosha
Marrinan, Susan Faye *lawyer*

Kohler
Black, Natalie A. *lawyer*

La Crosse
Sleik, Thomas Scott *lawyer*

Lake Geneva
Braden, Berwyn Bartow *lawyer*

Madison
Bablitch, William A. *lawyer, retired state supreme court justice*
Barkan, Steven M. *law librarian, educator*
Barnhill, Charles Joseph, Jr. *lawyer*
Barnick, Helen *retired judicial clerk*
Bartell, Jeffrey Bruce *lawyer*
Behnke, Michelle A. *lawyer*
Bochert, Linda H. *lawyer*
Bugge, Lawrence John *lawyer, educator*
Chandler, Richard Gates *lawyer*
Charo, Robin Alta *law educator*
Curtis, Charles G., Jr. *lawyer*
Eldridge, James Francis *lawyer, insurance company executive*
Field, Henry Augustus, Jr. *lawyer*
Hanson, David James *lawyer*
Heymann, S. Richard *lawyer*
Hildebrand, Daniel Walter *lawyer*
Holbrook, John Scott, Jr. *lawyer*
Klauser, James Roland *lawyer*
Langer, Richard J. *lawyer*
Lavers, Richard Marshall *lawyer*
Linstroth, Tod Brian *lawyer*
Marshall, Kathryn Sue *lawyer*
McCallum, Laurie Riach *state government lawyer*
Melli, Marygold Shire *law educator*
Mohs, Frederic Edward *lawyer*
Monaghan, David A. *corporate lawyer*
Mowris, Gerald William *lawyer*
Peterson, Erik Charles *prosecutor*
Potter, Kevin *lawyer*
Prange, Roy Leonard, Jr. *lawyer*
Ragatz, Thomas George *lawyer*
Skilton, John Singleton *lawyer*
Steingass, Susan R. *lawyer*
Swan, Barbara J. *lawyer, utilities executive*
Temkin, Harvey L. *lawyer*
Vaughan, Michael Richard *lawyer*
Wagner, Burton Allan *lawyer*
Walsh, David Graves *lawyer*
White, William Fredrick *lawyer*

Manitowoc
Jones, Maurice D. *lawyer*

Menasha
Kneezel, Ronald D. *lawyer*

Menomonee Falls
Dynek, Sigrid *corporate lawyer, retail executive*
Schepp, Richard D. *lawyer, retail executive*

Mequon
Burroughs, Charles Edward *lawyer*
O'Shaughnessy, James Patrick *lawyer, consultant*
Richman, Stephen Erik *retired lawyer, consultant*
Whyte, George Kenneth, Jr. *lawyer*

Milwaukee
Abraham, William John, Jr. *lawyer*
Alverson, William H. *lawyer*
Babler, Wayne E., Jr. *lawyer*
Ballman, Patricia Kling *lawyer*
Bannen, John Thomas *lawyer*
Barnes, Paul McClung *lawyer*
Beckwith, David E. *lawyer*
Benfield, Linda E. *lawyer*
Berdan, Robert J. *lawyer, insurance company executive*
Berkoff, Marshall Richard *lawyer*
Biehl, Michael Melvin *lawyer, writer*
Biller, Joel Wilson *lawyer, retired diplomat*
Biskupic, Steven M. *prosecutor, lawyer*
Boer, Ralf Reinhard *lawyer*
Bowen, Michael Anthony *lawyer, writer*
Branch, Joseph C. *lawyer*
Bremer, John M. *lawyer*
Bruce, Peter Wayne *lawyer, insurance company executive*
Busch, John Arthur *lawyer, business executive*
Cannon, David Joseph *lawyer*
Casey, John Alexander *lawyer*
Casper, Richard Henry *lawyer*

Chokey, James A. *lawyer*
Christiansen, Keith Allan *lawyer*
Clark, James Richard *lawyer*
Connolly, Gerald Edward *lawyer*
Cutler, Richard W. *lawyer*
Daily, Frank J(erome) *lawyer*
Dallman, Robert Edward *lawyer*
Dionisopoulos, George Allan *lawyer*
Drummond, Robert Kendig *lawyer*
Duback, Steven Rahr *lawyer*
Emanuel, John F. *lawyer*
Erickson, Randall J. *lawyer*
Florsheim, Richard Steven *lawyer*
Flynn, William Frederick *lawyer*
Frautschi, Timothy Clark *lawyer*
Friedman, James Dennis *lawyer*
Galanis, John William *lawyer*
Gallagher, Richard Sidney *lawyer*
Gefke, Henry Jerome *lawyer*
Geilfuss, C. Frederick, II, *lawyer*
Gemignani, Joseph Adolph *lawyer*
Geske, Janine Patricia *law educator*
Ghiardi, James Domenic *lawyer, educator*
Goodkind, Conrad George *lawyer*
Groethe, Reed *lawyer*
Guerin, D. Michael *lawyer*
Haberman, F. William *lawyer*
Harrington, John Timothy *retired lawyer*
Hase, David John *lawyer*
Hatch, Michael Ward *lawyer*
Hoffman, Nathaniel A. *lawyer*
Huff, Marsha Elkins *lawyer*
Ireland, Emory *lawyer*
Jaspan, Stanley S. *lawyer*
Johannes, Robert J. *lawyer*
Jost, Lawrence John *lawyer*
Kamps, Charles Q. *retired lawyer*
Kennedy, John Patrick *lawyer, corporate financial executive*
Kircher, John Joseph *law educator*
Kringel, Jerome Howard *lawyer*
Krueger, Raymond Robert *lawyer*
Kubale, Bernard Stephen *lawyer*
Kurtz, Harvey A. *lawyer*
LaBudde, Roy Christian *lawyer*
Lane, Jeffrey H. *lawyer*
Langley, Grant F. *municipal lawyer*
Levit, William Harold, Jr. *lawyer*
Lione, Gail Ann *lawyer*
Lueders, Wayne Richard *lawyer*
Lynch, Michael *lawyer, staffing company executive*
Marcus, Richard Steven *lawyer*
Martin, Quinn William *lawyer*
McCann, E. Michael *lawyer*
McGaffey, Jere D. *retired lawyer*
McGinnity, Maureen Annell *lawyer*
McGrath, Brian W. *lawyer*
McKeown, James T. *lawyer*
McSweeney, Maurice J. (Marc McSweeney) *lawyer*
Medved, Paul Stanley *lawyer*
Melin, Robert Arthur *lawyer*
Mitten, Matthew John *law educator, lawyer*
Mulcahy, Robert William *lawyer*
Neubauer, Lisa S. *lawyer*
Obenberger, Thomas E. *lawyer*
Okarma, Jerome D. *lawyer, manufacturing executive*
Olivieri, José Alberto *lawyer*
Pence, Thomas C. *lawyer*
Phillips, Thomas John *lawyer*
Pindyck, Bruce Eben *lawyer, corporate financial executive*
Priebus, Reince *lawyer, political organization administrator*
Renz, Greg W. *lawyer*
Romoser, W. David *lawyer*
Rothman, Jay O. *lawyer*
Santelle, James Lewis *prosecutor*
Schnur, Robert Arnold *lawyer, educator*
Scrivner, Thomas William *lawyer*
Sennett, Nancy J. *lawyer*
Shapiro, Robyn Sue *lawyer, educator*
Shriner, Thomas L., Jr. *lawyer*
Smith, David Bruce *lawyer*
Terschan, Frank Robert *lawyer*
Titley, Robert L. *lawyer*
Tyson, Joseph B., Jr. *lawyer*
Will, Trevor Jonathan *lawyer*
Williams, Allen W., Jr. *lawyer*

Monroe
Luhman, Gary Lee *lawyer*

Oshkosh
Blankfield, Bryan J. *lawyer, automotive executive, accountant*
Kelly, John Martin *lawyer*

Prairie Du Chien
Baxter, Timothy C. *prosecutor*

Shawano
Bruno, Gary Robert *lawyer*

Siren
Kutz, Kenneth L. *district attorney*

Stevens Point
O'Reilly, William M. *lawyer, insurance company executive*

Sturtevant
Brandes, JoAnne *lawyer*

Superior
Marcovich, Toby *lawyer*

Waukesha
Macy, John Patrick *lawyer*
McCoy, John V. *lawyer*

Wausau
Drengler, William Allan John *lawyer*
Orr, San Watterson, Jr. *lawyer*

Wauwatosa
Heath, Robert F. *lawyer*
Savage, Thomas Ryan *lawyer*

CANADA

MANITOBA

Winnipeg
Schnoor, Jeffrey Arnold *lawyer*

CHINA

Hong Kong
Nelson, Steven Craig *lawyer*

ADDRESS UNPUBLISHED

Alberty, William Edwin *lawyer*
Andreozzi, Louis Joseph *lawyer*
Andrews, Frank Lewis *lawyer*
Arnold, Jerome Gilbert *lawyer*
Aune, Debra Bjurquist *lawyer*
Bagan, Grant Alan *lawyer*
Bearmon, Lee *lawyer*
Bell, Albert Jerome *lawyer*
Bell, John William *lawyer*
Berger, Sanford Jason *retired lawyer, securities dealer, real estate broker*
Bernstein, Merton Clay *law educator, arbitrator*
Beukema, John Frederick *lawyer*
Beyer, Marcus Paul *lawyer*
Bierig, Jack R. *lawyer, educator*
Blakey, G. Robert (George Robert Blakey) *law educator*
Blatt, Harold Geller *lawyer*
Brady, Edmund Matthew, Jr. *lawyer*
Brady, Terrence Joseph *mediator, arbitrator, retired judge*
Branagan, James Joseph *lawyer*
Breece, Robert William, Jr. *lawyer, investment company executive*
Brehl, James William *lawyer*
Brennan, James Joseph *lawyer, bank executive*
Brown, B. Andrew *lawyer*
Brown, Herbert Russell *lawyer, writer*
Bujold, Tyrone Patrick *lawyer*
Burk, Robert S. *lawyer*
Burke, Carol A. *lawyer*
Busch, Arthur Allen *lawyer*
Buttrey, Donald Wayne *lawyer*
Calise, William Joseph, Jr. *lawyer*
Carmichael, Lloyd Joseph *lawyer*
Carpenter, Susan Karen *defender*
Cassidy, John Harold *lawyer*
Chefitz, Joel Gerald *lawyer*
Chiara, Margaret Mary *former prosecutor, lawyer*
Chiles, Stephen Michael *retired lawyer*
Christian, John M. *lawyer*
Clark, Beverly Ann *retired lawyer*
Closen, Michael Lee *retired law educator*
Cohen, Christopher B. *lawyer*
Coleman, Robert Lee *retired lawyer*
Collins, Jeffrey G. *lawyer, former prosecutor*
Connolly, C. Lawrence *lawyer*
Connor, Laurence Davis *retired lawyer*
Coolley, Ronald B. *lawyer*
Cooper, Hal Dean *lawyer*
Cottrell, Frank Stewart *former lawyer, manufacturing executive*
Coughlan, Kenneth L. *lawyer*
Daugerdas, Paul M. *lawyer*
Dawson, Suzanne Stockus *lawyer*
Denneen, John Paul *lawyer*
DeVylder, Edgar Paul, Jr. *lawyer*
Doane, Marcia E. *lawyer, retired food products executive*
Donohoe, Jerome Francis *lawyer*
Draper, Gerald Linden *retired lawyer*
Dutile, Fernand Neville *law educator*
Eaton, Larry Ralph *lawyer*
Emert, Timothy Ray *lawyer*
Erlebacher, Arlene Cernik *retired lawyer*
Faulkner, James Vincent, Jr. *lawyer*
Feldman, Scott Milton *lawyer*
Ferguson, Bradford Lee *lawyer*
Ford, George Burt *retired lawyer*
Francois, William Armand *lawyer*
Frantz, Martin H. *prosecutor*
Frasier, Ralph Kennedy *lawyer, bank executive*
Freed, Michael J. *lawyer*
Frick, David Rhoads *lawyer, retired insurance company executive*
Fuller, Samuel Ashby *retired lawyer, mining executive*
Gamble, E. James *lawyer, accountant*
Garth, Bryant Geoffrey *lawyer, educator*
Gentner, Joshua D. *lawyer*
George, Joyce Jackson *lawyer, writer, retired judge*
Getzendanner, Susan *lawyer*
Giampietro, Wayne Bruce *lawyer*
Gilbert, Ronald Rhea *lawyer*
Gleeson, Paul Francis *retired lawyer*
Goldschmidt, Lynn Harvey *lawyer*
Goodman, Elizabeth Ann *retired lawyer*
Gourley, Sara J. *lawyer*
Grace, Walter Charles *retired prosecutor*
Graham, David F. *lawyer*
Grazin, Igor Nikolai *law educator, state official*
Hackett, Wesley Phelps, Jr. *lawyer*
Hanket, Mark John *lawyer*
Hemmer, James Paul *lawyer*
Henry, Robert John *lawyer*
Henson, Robert Frank *retired lawyer*
Hester, Thomas Patrick *lawyer*
Huston, Steven Craig *lawyer*
Jacobs, John Patrick *lawyer*
Jambor, Robert Vernon *lawyer*
Johnson, Eugene Laurence *lawyer*
Johnson, James I. *lawyer*
Johnson, Lael Frederic *lawyer*
Kapnick, Richard Bradshaw *lawyer*
Keating, Daniel Louis *law educator*
Kempf, Donald G., Jr. *retired lawyer*
Kenrich, John Lewis *retired lawyer*
King, Michael Howard *lawyer*
Kirschner, William Steven *lawyer*
Kohlstedt, James August *lawyer*
Kratt, Peter George *lawyer*
Krehbiel, Robert John *lawyer*
Kreindler, Marla J. *lawyer*
Kroenert, Robert Morgan *retired lawyer*
Krohnke, Duane W. *retired lawyer*
Kroll, Steven L. *lawyer*
Lamborn, LeRoy Leslie *law educator*
Larson, Charles W., Sr. *retired prosecutor*
Larson, Gregory Dane *lawyer*
Lavey, Warren G. *lawyer*
Lawson, Kenneth L. *lawyer*
Lazar, Kathy Pittak *lawyer*
Lea, Lorenzo Bates *lawyer*
Lempert, Richard Owen *lawyer, educator*
Licata, Anthony R. *lawyer, real estate developer*
Linde, Maxine Helen *lawyer, corporate financial executive, investor*
Logan, James Kenneth *lawyer, retired judge*
Logstrom, Bridget A. *lawyer*
Lubben, David J. *retired lawyer*
MacCarthy, John L. *lawyer*
MacKinnon, Kevin Scott *lawyer*
Maclin, Alan Hall *lawyer*
Madsen, H(enry) Stephen *retired lawyer*
Maher, Francesca Marciniak *lawyer, former air transportation executive*
Mangler, Robert James *lawyer, judge*
Marovitz, James Lee *retired lawyer*
Marshall, Siri Swenson *lawyer, retired consumer products company executive*
Martineau, Robert John *retired law educator*
Masters, David Allen *lawyer*
Mattson, Stephen Joseph *retired lawyer*
Maule, Theresa Moore *lawyer*
Maynard, Robert Howell *retired lawyer*
McCormick, Michael D. *lawyer*
McCoy, John Joseph *lawyer*
McCracken, Ellis W., Jr. *retired lawyer, corporation executive*
McCue, Howard McDowell III *lawyer, educator*
McMahon, James E. *lawyer, former prosecutor*
Meldman, Robert Edward *lawyer*
Moford, Craig S. *prosecutor*
Morof, Jeffrey W. *lawyer*
Morrison, Donald William *lawyer*
Moustakis, Albert D. *prosecutor*
Mulaney, Charles W. *lawyer*
Mulroy, Thomas Robert, Jr. *lawyer*
Murphy, Kathleen M. *lawyer*
Murphy, Sandra Robison *lawyer*
Newman, Joan Meskiel *lawyer*
Nix, Edmund Alfred *lawyer*
North, John E., Jr. *lawyer*
O'Flaherty, Paul Benedict *lawyer*
Olson, Robert Wyrick *lawyer*
Palizzi, Anthony N. *retired lawyer, retail corporation executive*
Parrette, Leslie Jackson *lawyer*
Pesch, Ellen P. *lawyer*
Peterson, Bruce D. *lawyer, energy executive*
Pratt, Robert Windsor *lawyer*
Pytell, Robert Henry *retired lawyer, judge*
Ralston, Richard H. *lawyer*
Rawlins, Randa *lawyer*
Rea, Anne E. *lawyer*
Redman, Clarence Owen *lawyer*
Rice, Leonard S. *lawyer*
Rissman, Burton Richard *lawyer*
Rose, Michael Dean *retired lawyer, educator*
Roston, David Charles *lawyer*
Saliterman, Richard Arlen *lawyer*
Sapp, John Raymond *lawyer*
Saunders, Terry Rose *lawyer*
Schlozman, Bradley J. *former prosecutor*
Schneider, Carl Edward *law educator*
Schultz, Dennis Bernard *lawyer*
Shepard, Michael J. *prosecutor*
Shepherd, Stewart Robert *lawyer*
Shere, Dennis *lawyer, writer, retired publishing executive*
Shirley, Bryan Douglas *lawyer*
Simon, Barry Philip *lawyer, retired air transportation executive*
Smith, Carole Dianne *retired lawyer, editor, writer, product developer*
Smith, Gordon Howell *lawyer*
Snider, Lawrence K. *lawyer*
Snyder, Jean Maclean *lawyer*
Somer, Thomas Joseph (T.J. Somer) *lawyer*
Spicer, S(amuel) Gary *lawyer, writer, educator*
Squires, Vernon T. *lawyer*
Stinnett, J. Daniel *lawyer*
Stoller, John R. *lawyer*
Streicher, James Franklin *retired lawyer*
Swaney, Thomas Edward *lawyer*
Sweeney, James Raymond *retired lawyer*
Taft, Sheldon Ashley *retired lawyer*
Terp, Thomas Thomsen *lawyer*
Thoman, Henry Nixon *lawyer*
Torf, Philip R. *lawyer, pharmacist*
Torgerson, Larry Keith *lawyer*
Tucker, Watson Billopp *lawyer*
Ulrich, Werner
Walmer, Edwin Fitch *retired lawyer*
Weber, Susan A. *lawyer*
Weston, Michael C. *retired lawyer*
Wexler, Richard Lewis *lawyer*
Wiggins, Charles Henry, Jr. *lawyer*
Wilcox, Mark Dean *lawyer*
Wilson, Bruce G. *lawyer*
Wruble, Bernhardt Karp *lawyer*
Yurchuck, Roger Alexander *retired lawyer*

MEDICINE *See* HEALTHCARE: MEDICINE

MILITARY

UNITED STATES

ILLINOIS

Mattoon
Phipps, John Randolph *retired army officer*

O Fallon
Voellger, Gary A. *business consulting executive, retired air force officer*

Rockford
Borling, John Lorin *military officer*

Scott Air Force Base
Hogle, Walter S. *career officer*
Regan, Gilbert J. *retired career officer*

INDIANA

Indianapolis
Poel, Robert Walter *military officer, physician*

KANSAS

Fort Leavenworth
O'Neill, Mark E. *military officer*
Steele, William M. *career military officer*

MICHIGAN

Warren
Beauchamp, Roy E. *career officer*

MINNESOTA

Red Wing
Plehal, James Burton *career officer*

MISSOURI

Kansas City
Williams, Leo V. III *career military officer*

Saint Louis
Strevey, Tracy Elmer, Jr. *army officer, surgeon, health facility administrator*

OHIO

Brookpark
Heil, Michael Lloyd *military officer, academic administrator*

Columbus
Saunders, Mary L. *career officer*

Dayton
Raggio, Robert Frank *career officer*

Wright Patterson AFB
Amend, Joseph H. III *military officer*
Cranston, Stewart E. *career officer*
Mushala, Michael C. *career officer*
Pearson, Wilbert D. *career officer*
Samic, Dennis R. *retired career officer*
Sieg, Stanley A. *military official*
Stewart, J. Daniel *air force official*
Stewart, Todd I. *military officer*
Stubbs, Jerald D. *career military officer*

ADDRESS UNPUBLISHED

Aldridge, Donald O'Neal *military officer*
Anderson, Edgar Ratcliffe, Jr. *career officer, physician, health facility administrator*
Arbuckle, Joseph W. *military officer*
Bartrem, Duane Harvey *retired military officer, residential designer, consultant*
Bongiovi, Robert P. *career officer*
Goslin, Thomas B. *career officer*
Heng, Stanley Mark *national guard officer*
Herriford, Robert Levi, Sr. *retired military officer*
Kloeppel, Daniel L. *career officer*
Palmer, Dave Richard *retired military officer, academic administrator*
Sullivan, Paul F. *career officer*
Welser, William III *military officer*

REAL ESTATE

UNITED STATES

FLORIDA

Fort Lauderdale
Markos, Chris *retired real estate company executive*

ILLINOIS

Champaign
Guttenberg, Albert Ziskind *planning educator*

Chicago
Beban, Gary Joseph *real estate corporation officer*
Berger, Miles Lee *land economist*
Bluhm, Neil Gary *real estate company executive*
Bucksbaum, John *real estate company executive*
Bucksbaum, Matthew *real estate investment trust company executive*
Crocker, Douglas, II, *real estate executive*
DeWoskin, Margaret Fogarty *real estate company executive*
Dominski, Matthew S. *property manager*
Durburg, Jack E. *real estate company executive*
Eubanks-Pope, Sharon G. *real estate company executive, entrepreneur*
Ezgur, Michael H. *real estate company executive*
Freibaum, Bernard *real estate development company executive*
Galowich, Ronald Howard *real estate company executive, venture capitalist, pilot*
Geleerd, James D. (Jake Geleerd) *property manager*
Jarrett, Valerie Bowman *real estate company executive, former stock exchange executive*
Kincaid, Richard D. *real estate company executive*
King, Donald A., Jr. *real estate company executive*
Klebba, Raymond Allen *property manager*
Michaels, Robert A. *real estate development company executive*
Morrill, R. Layne *real estate broker, executive, professional association administrator*
Neithercut, David J. *real estate company officer*
Pacher, Nancy A. *real estate company executive*
Primo, Quintin E. III *real estate company executive*
Scott, Stuart L. *real estate company executive*
Tanguay, Mark H. *real estate company executive*
Travis, Dempsey Jerome *real estate company executive*
Watts, Michael H. *real estate company executive*
Zell, Samuel *real estate company executive, publishing executive*

Evanston
Perlmutter, Robert *land company executive*

Lake Zurich
Schultz, Carl Herbert *real estate developer*

Northbrook
Metz, Adam S. *real estate company executive*

Northfield
Kleinman, Burton Howard *real estate investor*

Oak Brook
Goodwin, Daniel L. *real estate company executive*
Parks, Robert D. *real estate company executive*
Wheeler, Paul James *real estate executive*

Rosemont
Skoien, Gary *real estate company executive*

Westmont
Harten, Ann M. *relocation services executive*

Wheaton
Strobeck, Charles LeRoy *real estate company executive*

INDIANA

Evansville
Matthews, Charles David *real estate appraiser, consultant*

Fort Wayne
Werling, Donn Paul *conservationist, education educator*

Indianapolis
Crosser, Richard H. *real estate company executive*
Holihen, Jennifer A. *real estate development company executive*
Jewett, John Rhodes *real estate executive*
Kohart, Mary Beth *real estate company executive*
McKenzie, Lloyd W. *real estate development executive*
Simon, Herbert *real estate developer, professional sports team owner*
Simon, Melvin *real estate developer, professional sports team owner*
Sokolov, Richard Saul *real estate company executive*
Weeks, A. Ray *real estate company executive*

Terre Haute
Perry, Eston Lee *real estate and equipment leasing company executive*

KANSAS

Topeka
Blair, Ben *real estate company executive*

MICHIGAN

Ann Arbor
Rycus, Mitchell Julian *urban security and energy planning educator, consultant*

Bingham Farms
Robinson, Steve *real estate company executive*

Bloomfield Hills
Larson, Robert Craig *real estate company officer*
Taubman, Robert S. *real estate developer*

Detroit
Grabowski, Jon *real estate company executive*

Farmington Hills
Gershenson, Joel *property company executive*
Rose, Sheldon *property manager*

Grosse Ile
Smith, Veronica Latta *real estate company officer*

Royal Oak
Atchison, Steven *real estate company executive*

Saginaw
Cline, Thomas William *real estate leasing company executive, management consultant*

Southfield
Gershenson, Dennis *property company executive*
Ward, Michael A. *property company executive*

MINNESOTA

Duluth
Bowman, Roger Manwaring *real estate company officer*

Minneapolis
Boelter, Philip Floyd *real estate company officer, construction executive*

Minnetonka
Karlen, Greg T. *real estate executive*

MISSOURI

Chesterfield
Morley, Harry Thomas, Jr. *real estate executive*

Dunnegan
Harman, Mike *real estate broker, small business owner*

Kansas City
Dumovich, Loretta *retired real estate company and transportation executive*
Shutz, Byron Christopher *real estate company officer*

Saint Louis
Meissner, Edwin Benjamin, Jr. *retired real estate broker*

Springfield
Carlson, Thomas Joseph *real estate developer, lawyer*

NEBRASKA

Lincoln
Tavlin, Michael John *real estate company and manufacturing executive*

NORTH DAKOTA

Bismarck
Christianson, James D. *real estate developer*

OHIO

Amelia
Hayden, John W. *real estate company executive*

Beachwood
Wolstein, Scott Alan *real estate company executive*

Chagrin Falls
Stec, John Zygmunt *retired real estate company officer*

Cincinnati
Gratz, Ronald G. *real estate development executive*
Wyant, John H. *real estate development executive*

Cleveland
Carney, Tana *real estate company executive*
Jacobs, Richard E. *real estate company executive, sports team owner*
Miller, Samuel H. *real estate company executive*
Ratner, Charles A. *real estate executive*
Ratner, James *real estate developer*

Columbus
Pizzuti, Ronald A. *real estate developer*
Schuler, Robert Leo *appraiser, consultant*

Dayton
Wertz, Kenneth Dean *real estate company officer*

Dublin
Donnell, Jon M. *real estate executive*

Gates Mills
Schanfarber, Richard Carl *real estate broker*

New Albany
Kessler, John Whitaker *real estate developer*

Richmond Heights
Friedman, Jeffrey I. *real estate company executive*

Shaker Heights
Solganik, Marvin *real estate executive*

Youngstown
Cafaro, Anthony M. *real estate developer, retail executive*
DeBartolo, Edward John, Jr. *real estate developer, former professional football team owner*

WISCONSIN

Beaver Dam
Butterbrodt, John Ervin *real estate company officer*

Madison
Ring, Gerald J. *real estate developer, insurance company executive*

Milwaukee
Stein, Gerald *real estate and diversified holding company executive*

ADDRESS UNPUBLISHED

Bednarowski, Keith *construction, design and real estate executive*
Beitler, J. Paul *real estate developer*
Corey, Kenneth Edward *urban planning and geography educator, researcher*
Frankel, Stuart *real estate company executive*
Peacock, Christopher A. *former real estate company executive*
Reschke, Michael W. *real estate company officer*
Spehr, Steven *real estate company executive*
Taubman, A. Alfred *real estate developer*
Toshach, Clarice Oversby *real estate developer, retired computer company executive*

RELIGION

UNITED STATES

COLORADO

Denver
Wilke, LeRoy *retired church administrator*

FLORIDA

Bartow
Meuser, Fredrick William *retired church administrator, historian*

IDAHO

Nampa
Bowers, Curtis Ray, Jr. *chaplain*

ILLINOIS

Belleville
Braxton, Edward Kenneth *bishop*
Schlarman, Stanley Girard *bishop emeritus*

Bloomington
Skillrud, Harold Clayton *minister, retired bishop*

Carol Stream
Myra, Harold Lawrence *publisher*

Chicago
Almen, Lowell Gordon *church official*
Bacher, Robert Newell *church official*
Betz, Hans Dieter *theology studies educator*
Browning, Don Spencer *religious educator*
Brummel, Mark Joseph *religious organization administrator*
Doherty, Sister Barbara *religious institution administrator*
Doniger, Wendy *history of religions educator*
Farrakhan, Louis (Louis Eugene Walcott) *religious organization administrator*
George, Francis Eugene Cardinal *cardinal, archbishop*
Goedert, Raymond Emil *bisphop emeritus*
Hanson, Mark S. *bishop*
Jakubowski, Thaddeus Joseph *bishop emeritus*
Jegen, Sister Carol Frances *religious studies educator*
Kane, Francis Joseph *bishop*
Larsen, Paul Emanuel *religious organization administrator*
Lotocky, Innocent Hilarion *bishop emeritus*
Lyne, Timothy Joseph *bishop emeritus*
Magnus, Kathy Jo *religious organization executive*
Mansueto, Joseph Daniel *publisher*
Manz, John R. *bishop*
Margolis, Rob *publisher*
Marshall, Cody *bishop*
McAuliffe, Richard L. *church official*
McGinn, Bernard John *theologian, educator*
Miller, Charles S. *clergy member, church administrator*
Muhammad, Ava *minister and national spokesperson for the Nation of Islam*
Rajan, Fred E. N. *clergy member, church administrator*
Shafer, Eric Christopher *minister*
Sherwin, Byron Lee *religion educator, college official*
Thistlethwaite, Susan Brooks *religious organization administrator*
Thurston, Stephen John *pastor*
Wagner, Joseph M. *church administrator*
Wall, James McKendree *minister, editor*
Wright, Jeremiah Alvesta, Jr. *retired minister*
Yu, Anthony C. *religion and literature educator*

Decatur
Morgan, E. A. *church administrator*

Elgin
Nolen, Wilfred E. *church administrator*
Reimer, Judy Mills *pastor, religious executive*

Elmhurst
Angadiath, Jacob *bishop*

Galva
Swatos, William Henry, Jr. *priest, sociologist*

Itasca
Constant, Anita Aurelia *publisher*

Joliet
Imesch, Joseph Leopold *bishop emeritus*
Kaffer, Roger Louis *bishop emeritus*

Naperville
Raccah, Dominique Marcelle *publisher*

Orland Park
Gorman, John Robert *bishop emeritus*

Peoria
Duncan, Royal Robert *publisher*

River Forest
O'Meara, Thomas Franklin *priest, educator*

Rockford
Doran, Thomas George *bishop*

South Holland
Perry, Joseph Nathaniel *bishop*

Springfield
Lucas, George J. *bishop*
Ryan, Daniel Leo *bishop emeritus*

Villa Park
Pittelko, Roger Dean *clergyman, theology studies educator*

Wheaton
Schwanda, Tom *religious studies educator*

INDIANA

Anderson
Grubbs, J. Perry *church administrator*

Bloomington
Gallman, John Gerry *publisher*

Demotte
Huff, John David *church administrator*

Evansville
Gettelfinger, Gerald Andrew *bishop*

Fishers
Christenson, Le Roy Howard *missions mobilizer*

Fort Wayne
D'Arcy, John Michael *bishop*
Mann, David William *minister*

Indianapolis
Bray, Donald Lawrence *religious organization executive, minister*
Hamm, Richard L. *church administrator*
Johnson, James P. *religious organization executive*
Marshall, Carolyn Ann M. *church official*
Polston, Mark Franklin *minister*
Sindlinger, Verne E. *bishop*
Waynick, Catherine Elizabeth Maples *bishop*
Welsh, Robert K. *religious organization executive*
Wilson, Earle Lawrence *church administrator*
Woodring, DeWayne Stanley *religious organization administrator*

Lafayette
Higi, William Leo *bishop*
Minor, Ronald Ray *minister*
O'Callaghan, Patti Louise *urban ministry administrator*

Noblesville
Wilson, Norman Glenn *church administrator, writer*

Notre Dame
Blenkinsopp, Joseph *biblical studies educator*
Hesburgh, Theodore Martin *clergyman, former university president*
McBrien, Richard Peter *theology educator*

Winona Lake
Ashman, Charles H. *retired minister*
Davis, John James *religion educator*
Julien, Thomas Theodore *religious denomination administrator*
Lewis, Edward Alan *religious organization adminstrator*

IOWA

Ankeny
Hartog, John, II, *theology educator, librarian*

Cedar Falls
Lindberg, Duane R. *bishop, historian*

Davenport
Amos, Martin John *bishop*
Franklin, William Edwin *bishop emeritus*

Des Moines
Charron, Joseph Leo *bishop emeritus*
Epting, C. Christopher *bishop*
Feld, Thomas Robert *religious organization administrator*

Dubuque
Barta, James Omer *priest, psychology educator, church administrator*
Hanus, Jerome George *archbishop*

Grinnell
Mitchell, Orlan E. *clergyman, academic administrator*

Iowa City
Bozeman, Theodore D. *religion educator*

Orange City
Scorza, Sylvio Joseph *religion educator*

Sioux City
Nickless, Ralph Walter *bishop*
Soens, Lawrence Donald *bishop emeritus*

Storm Lake
Miller, Curtis Herman *bishop*

Waterloo
Waters, Ronald W. *theology studies educator, church administrator, pastor*

West Des Moines
Stines, Fred, Jr. *publisher*

KANSAS

Copeland
Birney, Walter Leroy *religious administrator*

Dodge City
Gilmore, Ronald Michael *bishop*

Kansas City
Keleher, James P. *archbishop emeritus*
Naumann, Joseph Fred *archbishop*

Lawrence
Woodward, Frederick Miller *publisher*

North Newton
Fast, Darrell Wayne *minister*

Salina
Fitzsimons, George Kinzie *bishop emeritus*

Topeka
Eichhorn, Arthur David *minister of religion*
Smalley, William Edward *bishop*

Wichita
Essey, Basil *bishop*
Gerber, Eugene John *bishop emeritus*
Jackels, Michael Owen *bishop*

MASSACHUSETTS

Cambridge
Adams, Charles Gilchrist *theology studies educator, pastor*

Squantum
Robertson, Michael Swing *minister*

MICHIGAN

Ann Arbor
Day, Colin Leslie *publisher*
Gomez, Luis Oscar *Asian and religious studies educator, clinical psychology educator*

Berrien Springs
Andreasen, Niels-Erik Albinus *religious educator*

Bloomfield Hills
Mc Gehee, H. Coleman, Jr., (Harry Coleman McGhhe) *retired bishop*
Randall, Chandler Corydon *theologian*

Dearborn
Hess, Margaret Johnston *religious writer, educator*

Detroit
Anderson, Moses Bosco *bishop emeritus*
Gumbleton, Thomas John *bishop emeritus*
Maida, Adam Joseph Cardinal *cardinal, archbishop*
Quinn, John Michael *bishop*

Farmington Hills
Plaut, Jonathan Victor *rabbi*

Gaylord
Cooney, Patrick Ronald *bishop*

Grand Rapids
Anderson, Roger Gordon *minister*
Barnes, Rosemary Lois *minister*
Borgdorff, Peter *church administrator*
Breitenbeck, Joseph M. *retired bishop*
DeVries, Robert K. *retired publisher, consultant*
Hofman, Leonard John *minister*
Hurley, Walter Allison *bishop*
Rozeboom, John A. *religious organization administrator*

Jackson
Popp, Nathaniel *archbishop*

Kalamazoo
Badra, Robert George *theology studies and humanities educator*
Donovan, Paul V. *bishop emeritus*
Murray, James A. *bishop*

Lansing
Boyea, Earl Alfred, Jr. *bishop*
Mengeling, Carl Frederick *bishop emeritus*

Marquette
Garland, James Henry *bishop emeritus*
Schmitt, Mark Francis *bishop emeritus*

Northville
Davis, Lawrence Edward *church official*

Portage
Lee, Edward L. *retired bishop*

Saginaw
Carlson, Robert James *bishop*

Southfield
Ibrahim, Ibrahim Namo *bishop*
Willingham, Edward Bacon, Jr. *ecumenical minister, administrator*

Spring Arbor
Thompson, Stanley B. *church administrator*

Warren
Samra, Nicholas James *bishop emeritus*

MINNESOTA

Bloomington
McDill, Thomas Allison *minister*
Sawatsky, Ben *church administrator*

Crookston
Balke, Victor Herman *bishop emeritus*

Edina
Brown, Laurence David *retired bishop*
Worthing, Carol Marie *retired minister*

Fergus Falls
Egge, Joel *clergy member, academic administrator*
Jahr, Armin N., II, *clergy member, church administrator*
Overgaard, Robert Milton *retired religious organization administrator*

Mankato
Orvick, George Myron *religious organization administrator, minister*

Minneapolis
Chemberlin, Peg *minister, religious organization administrator*
Corts, John Ronald *minister, religious organization executive*
Hamel, William John *church administrator, minister*
Lee, Robert Lloyd *pastor, religious association executive*
Moraczewski, Robert Leo *publisher*
Olson, David Wendell *bishop*

Northfield
Crouter, Richard Earl *religion educator*
Dudley, Paul V. *retired bishop*

Rochester
Rinden, David Lee *clergyman*

Rosemount
Kaufman, Jeffrey Allen *publisher*

Saint Cloud
Kinney, John Francis *bishop*

Saint Paul
Hopper, David Henry *theologian, educator*
Jaberg, Eugene Carl *theology educator, administrator*
Kennelly, Sister Karen Margaret *church administrator, nun, retired academic administrator*
Nienstedt, John Clayton *archbishop*
Thomas, Margaret Jean *clergywoman, religious research consultant*

Saint Peter
Jodock, Darrell Harland *minister, educator*

Winona
Harrington, Bernard Joseph *bishop*

MISSOURI

Excelsior Springs
Mitchell, Earl Wesley *clergyman*

Fayette
Keeling, Joe Keith *religious studies educator, retired dean*

Hazelwood
Rose, Joseph Hugh *clergyman*

Independence
Lindgren, A(lan) Bruce *church administrator*
Tyree, Alan Dean *clergyman*

Jefferson City
Gaydos, John Raymond *bishop*
Kelley, Patrick Michael *minister, state legislator*
King, Robert Henry *minister, religious organization administrator, former education educator*

Joplin
Wilson, Aaron Martin *religious studies educator, college executive*

Kansas City
Boland, Raymond James *bishop emeritus*
Cunningham, Paul George *minister*
Diehl, James Harvey *church administrator*
Finn, Robert William *bishop*
Knight, John Allan *clergyman, theology studies educator*
Petosa, Jason Joseph *publisher*
Stone, Jack *religious organization administrator*
Sullivan, Bill M. *church administrator*
Vogel, Arthur Anton *clergyman*

Poplar Bluff
Black, Ronnie Delane *religious organization administrator, mayor*

Saint Louis
Baumer, Martha Ann *minister*
Burke, Raymond Leo *archbishop*
Gaulke, Earl H. *publisher, clergyman, editor*
Hermann, Robert Joseph *bishop*
Kieschnick, Gerald B. *religious organization administrator*
Mahsman, David Lawrence *writer, church administrator*
O'Shoney, Glenn *church administrator*
Rosin, Walter L. *retired religious organization administrator*
Wiley, Gregory Robert *publisher*

Springfield
Baird, Robert Dean *mission director*
Leibrecht, John Joseph *bishop emeritus*

NEBRASKA

Bellevue
Milone, Anthony Michael *bishop emeritus*

Grand Island
Dendinger, William Joseph *bishop, former career officer*

Lincoln
Bruskewitz, Fabian Wendelin *bishop*
Wiersbe, Warren Wendell *clergyman, writer, lecturer*

Omaha
Curtiss, Elden Francis *archbishop*

NEVADA

Henderson
Luckett, Byron Edward, Jr. *chaplain, retired military officer*

NEW JERSEY

Newark
Myers, John Joseph *archbishop*

NEW YORK

Cambridge
Kriss, Gary W(ayne) *priest*

New York
Hirschfield, Bradley *rabbi*

NORTH DAKOTA

Bismarck
Zipfel, Paul Albert *bishop*

Fargo
Foss, Richard John *bishop*

OHIO

Beavercreek
Clarke, Cornelius Wilder *religious organization administrator, minister*

Cincinnati
Harrington, Jeremy Thomas *priest, publishing executive*
Hoffman, Lawrence A. *rabbi*
Moeddel, Carl Kevin *bishop emeritus*
Pilarczyk, Daniel Edward *archbishop*
Zola, Gary Phillip *rabbi, historian*

Circleville
Norman, Jack Lee *church administrator, consultant*
Tipton, Daniel L. *religious organization executive*

Cleveland
Abrams, Sylvia Fleck *religious studies educator*
Buhrow, William Carl *religious organization administrator*
Guffey, Edith Ann *religious organization administrator*
Lennon, Richard Gerard *bishop*
Williams, Arthur Benjamin, Jr. *bishop*

Columbus
Griffin, James Anthony *bishop, academic administrator*

Lakewood
Sherry, Paul Henry *minister, religious organization administrator*

London
Hughes, Clyde Matthew *religious denomination executive*

Lorain
Quinn, Alexander James *bishop*

Oberlin
Zinn, Grover Alfonso, Jr. *retired religion educator*

Parma
Moskal, Robert M. *bishop*

Sidney
Lawrence, Wayne Allen *publisher*

Steubenville
Scanlan, Michael *priest, academic administrator*
Sheldon, Gilbert Ignatius *bishop emeritus*

Struthers
Sugden, Richard Lee *pastor*

Toledo
Blair, Leonard Paul *bishop*
Donnelly, Robert *bishop*
Donnelly, Robert William *bishop emeritus*
James, William Morgan *bishop*

Westlake
Loehr, Marla *chaplain*

Wickliffe
Pevec, Anthony Edward *bishop emeritus*

PENNSYLVANIA

Beyer
Cornell, William Harvey *clergyman*

Pittsburgh
Miller, William Charles *theological educator, minister*

Selinsgrove
Thomforde, Christopher Meredith *minister*

SOUTH DAKOTA

Rapid City
Cupich, Blasé J. *bishop*

Sioux Falls
Swain, Paul Joseph *bishop*

Watertown
Witcher, Gary Royal *minister, educator*

VERMONT

Wolcott
Fisher, Neal Floyd *religious organization administrator*

WISCONSIN

Cottage Grove
Baird, Robert Dahlen *retired theology studies educator*

Green Bay
Banks, Robert J. *bishop emeritus*
Morneau, Robert Fealey *bishop*

Iola
Mishler, Clifford Leslie *publisher*

La Crosse
Listecki, Jerome Edward *bishop*

Madison
Bullock, William Henry *bishop emeritus*
Enslin, Jon S. *bishop*
Fox, Michael Vass *theology studies educator*

Milwaukee
Callahan, William Patrick *bishop*
Dolan, Timothy Michael *archbishop*
Seiberlich, June Schaut *chaplain*
Sklba, Richard John *bishop*
Weakland, Rembert George *archbishop emeritus*

Superior
Fliss, Raphael Michael *bishop emeritus*

CANADA

ONTARIO

Waterloo
Van Seters, John *retired biblical literature educator*

ADDRESS UNPUBLISHED

Anderson, Hugh George *bishop*
Baumhart, Raymond Charles *religious organization administrator*
Bayne, David Cowan *priest, educator, lawyer*
Be Vier, William A. *retired religious studies educator*
Bunkowske, Eugene Walter *religious studies educator*
Castle, Howard Blaine *retired religious organization administrator*
Christopher, Sharon A. Brown *bishop*
Craig, Judith *bishop*
Dimond, Robert Edward *publisher*
Dipko, Thomas Earl *retired minister, religious organization administrator*
Duecker, Robert Sheldon *retired bishop*
Eitrheim, Norman Duane *retired bishop*
Frankson-Kendrick, Sarah Jane *publisher*
Hernandez, Ramon Robert *retired minister, school librarian*
Holle, Reginald Henry *retired bishop*
Hudnut, Robert Kilborne *clergyman, writer*
Huras, William David *retired bishop*
Jones, William Augustus, Jr. *retired bishop*
Kucera, Daniel William *archbishop emeritus*
Lucas, Bert Albert *pastor, social services administrator, consultant*
Marty, Martin Emil *theology studies educator*
McClellan, Larry Allen *minister, educator*
Miller, Vernon Dallace *minister*
Mischke, Carl Herbert *retired religious association executive*
Moran, John *religious organization administrator*
Muckerman, Norman James *priest, writer*
Mutti, Albert Frederick *retired minister*
Nycklemoe, Glenn Winston *bishop*
Place, Michael D. *priest, former health association administrator*
Preus, David Walter *bishop, minister*
Rose, Robert John *bishop emeritus*
Schmitt, Howard Stanley *minister*
Schultz, Clarence John *minister*
Shotwell, Malcolm Green *minister*
Simms, Lowelle *synod executive*
Thompson, Richard Lloyd *retired pastor*
Trask, Thomas Edward *religious organization administrator*
Wantland, William Charles *retired bishop, lawyer*
Weber, Gloria Richie *retired minister, retired state legislator*
Weinkauf, Mary Louise Stanley *retired clergywoman, educator*
Zirbes, Mary Kenneth *retired minister*

SCIENCE: LIFE SCIENCE

UNITED STATES

CALIFORNIA

La Jolla
Rahman, Yueh-Erh *biologist*

San Carlos
Wolff, Ronald Keith *toxicologist, researcher*

COLORADO

Fort Collins
Paul, Eldor Alvin *agriculture, ecology educator*

DISTRICT OF COLUMBIA

Washington
Milkman, Roger Dawson *genetics educator, molecular biologist, researcher*
Ucko, David Alan *science foundation official*

ILLINOIS

Argonne
Schriesheim, Alan *science administrator*

Berwyn
Parker, Alan John *veterinary neurologist, educator, researcher*

Brookfield
Rabb, George Bernard *zoologist, conservationist*

Carbondale
Burr, Brooks Milo *zoology educator*
Renzaglia, Karen A. *biologist, educator*

Champaign
Batzli, George Oliver *ecology educator*
Hager, Lowell Paul *biochemistry educator*
Levin, Geoffrey Arthur *botanist*
Sanderson, Glen Charles *science director*

Chicago
Arzbaecher, Robert C(harles) *research institute executive, electrical engineer, researcher*
Beattie, Ted Arthur *zoological gardens and aquarium administrator*
Bell, Graeme I. *biochemistry and molecular biology educator*
Bell, Kevin J. *zoological park administrator*
Brown, Joel S. *evolutionary ecologist, educator*
Carlstrom, John E. *astronomy educator*
Chakrabarty, Ananda Mohan *microbiologist*
Charlesworth, Brian *biologist, genetics and evolution educator*
Davidson, Richard Laurence *geneticist, educator*
Desjardins, Claude *physiologist, dean*
Ernest, J. Terry *ocular physiologist, educator*
Fisher, Lester Emil *retired zoo administrator*
Greenberg, Bernard *retired entomologist*
Haselkorn, Robert *virology educator*
Houk, James Charles *physiologist, educator*
Li, Wen-Hsiung *geneticist*
Mahowald, Anthony Peter *geneticist, developmental biologist, educator*
Mateles, Richard Isaac *biotechnologist*
McClintock, Martha K. *biologist, educator*
Mugnaini, Enrico *neuroscience educator*

Olopade, Olufunmilayo Falusi (Funmi Olopade) *geneticist, educator, oncologist, hematologist*
Preuss, Daphne *geneticist, biology professor*
Pritchard, Jonathan K. *geneticist, educator*
Provus, Barbara Lee *retired executive search consultant*
Roizman, Bernard *virologist, educator*
Rymer, William Zev *research scientist, administrator*
Shirbroun, Richard Elmer *veterinarian, cattleman*
Solaro, Ross John *physiologist, biophysicist*
Steck, Theodore Lyle *biochemistry and molecular biology educator, physician*
Storb, Ursula Beate *molecular genetics and cell biology educator*
Straus, Lorna Puttkammer *biology professor*
Van Valen, Leigh *biologist, educator*
York, Donald Gilbert *astronomy educator, researcher*

Des Plaines
Lee, Bernard Shing-Shu *research company executive*

Evanston
Dallos, Peter John *neurobiologist, educator*
Enroth-Cugell, Christina Alma Elisabeth *neurophysiologist, educator*
Taam, Ronald Everett *physics and astronomy educator*
Takahashi, Joseph S. *neuroscientist, educator*
Weertman, Johannes *materials science educator*
Wu, Tai Te *biological sciences and engineering educator*

Havana
Sparks, Richard Edward *aquatic ecologist*

Homewood
Pumper, Robert William *microbiologist, educator*

Macomb
Anderson, Richard Vernon *ecology educator, researcher*
Barclay, Martha Jane *science educator, research scientist*

Maywood
Schultz, Richard Michael *biochemistry educator, researcher*

Mount Prospect
Garvin, Paul Joseph, Jr. *toxicologist*

Normal
Stevenson, Cheryl D. *science educator, researcher*

Northbrook
King, Robert Charles *biologist, educator*

Peoria
Kurtzman, Cletus Paul *microbiologist, researcher*

Rock Island
Anderson, Richard Charles *geology educator*

Savoy
Hoffmeister, Donald Frederick *zoologist, educator*
Stout, Glenn Emanuel *retired science administrator*

Springfield
Munyer, Edward Arnold *zoologist*

Urbana
Banwart, Wayne Lee *agronomy, environmental science educator*
Berenbaum, May Roberta *entomology educator*
Buetow, Dennis Edward *physiologist, educator*
Crang, Richard Francis Earl *botanist, writer, research scientist*
Crofts, Antony Richard *biochemistry and biophysics educator*
Ehrlich, Gert *science educator, researcher*
Endress, Anton G. *horticulturist, educator*
Frazzetta, Thomas Henry *evolutionary biologist, educator*
Friedman, Stanley *insect physiologist, educator*
Greenough, William Tallant *psychobiologist, educator*
Heichel, Gary Harold *agronomist, educator*
Holt, Donald A. *agronomist, consultant, researcher, retired academic administrator*
Hymowitz, Theodore *plant geneticist, educator*
Mc Glamery, Marshal Dean *agronomist, educator, weed scientist*
Meyer, Richard Charles *microbiologist, educator*
Nanney, David Ledbetter *geneticist, educator*
Nickell, Cecil D. *agronomy educator*
Robinson, Gene Ezia *biologist, educator*
Seigler, David Stanley *botanist, educator, chemist*
Waldbauer, Gilbert Peter *entomologist, educator*
Weaver, John H *research scientist, educator*
Whitt, Gregory Sidney *evolution educator*
Wolfe, Ralph Stoner *microbiology educator*

INDIANA

Bloomington
DeVoe, Robert Donald *visual physiologist*
Gest, Howard *microbiologist, educator*
Ketterson, Ellen D. *biologist, educator*
Nolan, Val, Jr. *retired biologist, lawyer*
Preer, John Randolph, Jr. *biology professor*
Raff, Rudolf A. *science educator, researcher*
Rieseberg, Loren *botanist, educator*
Ruesink, Albert William *biologist, plant sciences educator*
Steinmetz, Joseph Edward *neuroscience and psychology educator*
Weinberg, Eugene David *microbiologist, educator*

Chesterton
Wiemann, Marion Russell, Jr., (Baron of Camster) *biologist, ambassador general*

Crawfordsville
Simmons, Emory G. *mycologist, microbiologist, botanist, educator*

Indianapolis
Borst, Philip Craig *veterinarian, councilman*
Burr, David Bentley *anatomy educator*
Christian, Joe Clark *medical genetics researcher, educator*
Fibiger, Hans Christian *science administrator*
Follas, William Daniel *science administrator*
Jones, Robert Brooke *microbiologist, educator, associate dean*
Ochs, Sidney *neurophysiology researcher, educator*
Rhoades, Rodney Allen *physiologist, educator*

Lafayette
Hasegawa, Paul M. *horticulturist, educator*
Nicholson, Ralph Lester *botanist, educator*
Rao, Palakurthi S.C. *soil science educator*

Muncie
Hendrix, Jon Richard *biology professor*
Henzlik, Raymond Eugene *zoophysiologist, educator*
Mertens, Thomas Robert *biology professor*

Notre Dame
Bender, Harvey A. *biology professor*
Burns, Peter C. *science and engineering educator*
Jensen, Richard Jorg *biologist, educator*
Pollard, Morris *microbiologist, educator*
Shrader-Frechette, Kristin *science educator*

Valparaiso
Schlender, William Elmer *management sciences educator*

West Lafayette
Albright, Jack Lawrence *animal science and veterinary educator*
Amstutz, Harold Emerson *veterinarian, educator*
Axtell, John David *genetics educator, researcher, agronomist*
Borgens, Richard *biologist*
Bracker, Charles E. *plant pathologist, educator, researcher*
Edwards, Charles Richard *entomology and pest management educator*
Harmon, Bud Gene *animal sciences educator, consultant*
Hoover, William Leichliter *forestry and natural resources educator, financial consultant*
Hunt, Michael O'Leary *wood science and engineering educator*
Janick, Jules *horticultural scientist, educator*
Johannsen, Chris Jakob *agronomist, educator, administrator*
Le Master, Dennis Clyde *retired forester, economist, educator*
McFee, William Warren *soil scientist*
Nelson, Philip Edwin *food scientist, educator*
Norton, Lloyd Darrell *research soil scientist*
Ohm, Herbert Willis *agronomy educator, agriculturist*
Ortman, Eldon E. *retired entomologist, educator*
Sherman, Louis Allen *biology professor, department chairman*

IOWA

Ames
Beran, George Wesley *veterinary microbiology educator*
Berger, P(hilip) Jeffrey *animal science educator, geneticist*
Bolin, Steven Robert *veterinarian researcher*
Burris, Joseph Stephen *agronomy educator*
Clark, Lynn G. *botanist, educator*
Fehr, Walter Ronald *agronomist, researcher, educator*
Freeman, Albert E. *agricultural science educator, dairy cattle geneticist*
Ghoshal, Nani Gopal *veterinarian, educator*
Greve, John Henry *veterinary parasitologist, educator*
Hallauer, Arnel Roy *geneticist*
Hatfield, Jerry Lee *plant physiologist, agricultural meteorologist*
Johnson, Lawrence Alan *cereal technologist, educator, administrator*
Karlen, Douglas Lawrence *soil scientist, researcher*
Mertins, James Walter *entomologist*
Moon, Harley William *veterinarian*
Moore, Kenneth James *agronomist, educator*
Munkvold, Gary P. *plant pathologist, educator*
Nutter, Forrest *plant pathologist*
O'Berry, Phillip Aaron *retired veterinarian*
Owen, Micheal *agronomist, educator*
Ross, Richard Francis *veterinarian, microbiologist, dean, educator*
Seaton, Vaughn Allen *retired veterinary pathology educator*
Tylka, Gregory L. *plant pathologist, educator*
Wass, Wallace Milton *veterinarian, clinical science educator*
Willham, Richard Lewis *zoology educator*

Eldora
Kerns, Steve *geneticist*

Grinnell
Walker, Waldo Sylvester *biologist, educator, academic administrator*

Iowa City
Apicella, Michael Allen *microbiologist, educator*
Campbell, Kevin Peter *physiology and biophysics educator*
Gibson, David Thomas *microbiology educator*
Hausler, William John, Jr. *microbiologist, educator, public health service officer*
Husted, Russell Forest *research scientist*
Kessel, Richard Glen *zoology educator*
Koontz, Frank P. *microbiology educator, research administrator*
Maxson, Linda Ellen *biologist, educator*
Pessin, Jeffrey E. *physiology educator*
Stay, Barbara *zoologist, educator*
Wunder, Charles C(ooper) *physiologist, biophysicist, educator*

West Des Moines
Rosen, Matthew Stephen *retired botanist*

KANSAS

Emporia
Sundberg, Marshall David *biology professor*

Hays
Coyne, Patrick Ivan *physiological ecologist*

Kansas City
Behbehani, Abbas M. *clinical virologist, educator*
Cheney, Paul D. *physiologist, educator*
Doull, John *toxicologist, pharmacologist*
Ebner, Kurt Ewald *biochemistry educator*
Klaassen, Curtis D. *toxicologist, educator*
Noelken, Milton Edward *biochemistry educator, researcher*

Lawrence
Angino, Ernest Edward *retired geology and engineering educator*
Armitage, Kenneth Barclay *retired biology professor*
Byers, George William *retired entomology educator*
Downing, David *science administrator*
Haufler, Christopher Hardin *botany educator*
Johnston, Richard Fourness *biologist, educator*
Lichtwardt, Robert William *mycologist*
Michener, Charles Duncan *entomologist, researcher, educator*
Shankel, Delbert Merrill *microbiologist, biologist, educator*

Manhattan
Erickson, Howard Hugh *veterinarian, physiology educator*
Kaufman, Donald Wayne *research ecologist*
Kirkham, M. B. *plant physiologist, educator*
Mengel, David Bruce *agronomy and soil science educator*
Posler, Gerry Lynn *agronomist, educator*
Richard, Patrick *science research administrator, nuclear scientist*

Olathe
Goodwin, Becky K. *educational technology resource educator*

Parsons
Lomas, Lyle Wayne *agricultural research administrator, educator*

MARYLAND

Bethesda
Nabel, Gary Jan *virologist*

MASSACHUSETTS

Cambridge
Lindquist, Susan Lee *biology and microbiology professor*

MICHIGAN

Ann Arbor
Akil, Huda *neuroscientist, educator, researcher*
Alexander, Richard Dale *zoology educator*
Anderson, William R. *botanist, educator, curator*
Atreya, Sushil Kumar *planetary-space science educator, astrophysicist*
Christensen, A(lbert) Kent *anatomy educator*
Clark, Noreen Morrison *behavioral science educator, researcher*
Dawson, William Ryan *zoology educator*
Drach, John Charles *research scientist, educator*
Easter, Stephen Sherman, Jr. *biology professor*
Farrand, William Richard *retired geology educator*
Faulkner, John Arthur *physiologist, educator*
Ginsburg, David *genetics educator, researcher*
Hawkins, Joseph Elmer, Jr. *physiologist, educator*
Kaufman, Peter Bishop *biological sciences educator*
Moore, Thomas Edwin *biologist, educator, museum director*
Mourou, Gerard A. *research administrator*
Neidhardt, Frederick Carl *microbiologist, educator*
Pascual, Mercedes *biology professor*
Petty, Elizabeth Marie *geneticist*
Shappirio, David Gordon *biologist, educator*
Stoermer, Eugene Filmore *biologist, educator*
Williams, John Andrew *physiology researcher, educator*
Woods, James H. *research scientist, consultant*
Yocum, Charles Fredrick *biology professor*
Zhang, Youxue *geology educator*

Augusta
Johnson, Wilbur Corneal (Joe Johnson) *wildlife biologist*

Dearborn
Schneider, Michael Joseph *biologist*

Detroit
Beierwaltes, William Howard *physiologist, educator*

East Lansing
Bukovac, Martin John *horticulturist, educator*
Cross, Aureal Theophilus *geology and botany educator*
Dennis, Frank George, Jr. *retired horticulture educator*
Fischer, Lawrence Joseph *toxicologist, educator, science administrator*
Fluck, Michele M(arguerite) *biology professor*
Hackel, Emanuel *science educator*
Hollingworth, Robert Michael *toxicology researcher*
Johnson, John Irwin, Jr. *neuroscientist*
Keegstra, Kenneth G. *plant biochemistry administrator*
Lenski, Richard Eimer *evolutionary biologist, educator*
Lucas, Robert Elmer *soil scientist, researcher*
McMeekin, Dorothy *botanist, plant pathologist, educator*
Patterson, Maria Jevitz *microbiology/pediatric infectious disease professor*
Petrides, George Athan *ecologist, educator*
Root-Bernstein, Robert Scott *biologist, educator*
Sharkey, Thomas David *botanist, educator*
Tiedje, James Michael *microbiologist, ecologist, educator*
Tien, H. Ti *biophysics and physiology educator, researcher*
Tolbert, Nathan Edward *biochemistry educator, plant pathologist*
Witter, Richard Lawrence *veterinarian, educator*
Zeikus, J. Gregory *microbiologist, educator*

Edwardsburg
Floyd, Alton David *cell biologist, consultant*

Grand Rapids
Carlotti, Ronald John *food scientist*

Hickory Corners
Lauff, George Howard *biologist*

Kalamazoo
Marshall, Vincent de Paul *industrial microbiologist, researcher*

Midland
Bus, James Stanley *toxicologist*

Okemos
Lockwood, John LeBaron *plant pathologist, educator*

Rochester Hills
Unakar, Nalin Jayantilal *biological sciences educator*

Saline
Cruden, Robert William *botany educator*

Sanford
Wilmot, Thomas Ray *medical entomologist, educator*

MINNESOTA

Duluth
Heller, Lois Jane *physiologist, educator, researcher*
Johnson, Arthur Gilbert *microbiology educator*

Minneapolis
Adams, John Stephen *geography educator*
Dworkin, Martin *microbiologist, educator*
Georgopoulos, Apostolos P. *neuroscientist, neurologist, educator*
Gorham, Eville *retired ecologist*
Haase, Ashley Thomson *microbiology professor, researcher*
Hart, John Fraser *geography educator*
Huang, Victor Tsangmin *food scientist, researcher*
Johnson, Kenneth Harvey *veterinary pathologist*
Jones, Thomas Walter *astrophysics educator, researcher*
Knuth, Russ *histologist, radio personality*
Magee, Paul Terry *geneticist and molecular biologist, educator*
Meyer, Maurice Wesley *retired physiologist, dentist, neurologist*
Moore, Randall Charles *biology professor*
Porter, Philip Wayland *geography educator*
Taylor, Doris Anita *molecular biology educator*
Watson, Dennis Wallace *microbiologist, educator*

Moorhead
Gee, Robert LeRoy *agriculturist, dairy farmer*

Morris
Ordway, Ellen *biologist, educator, entomologist, researcher*

Rochester
Maher, L. James III *molecular biologist*
Shepherd, John Thompson *physiologist*
Van Dyke, Daniel L. *geneticist*

Saint Paul
Barnwell, Franklin Hershel *zoology educator*
Busch, Robert Henry *geneticist, researcher*
Bushnell, William Rodgers *agricultural research scientist*
Davis, Margaret Bryan *paleoecology researcher, educator*
Diesch, Stanley La Verne *veterinarian, educator*
Ehlke, Nancy Jo *agronomist*
Ek, Alan Ryan *forester, educator*
Hornbach, Daniel J. *biologist, educator*
Kerr, Sylvia Joann *science educator*
Kommedahl, Thor *plant pathology educator*
Leonard, Kurt John *retired plant pathologist, director*
May, Georgiana *biologist, educator*
McKinnell, Robert Gilmore *retired zoologist, biology professor, geneticist*
Phillips, Ronald Lewis *plant geneticist, educator*
Roy, Robert Russell *toxicologist*
Sadowsky, Michael J. *microbiologist, educator*
Tordoff, Harrison Bruce *retired zoologist, educator*

MISSOURI

Columbia
Blevins, Dale Glenn *agronomy educator*
Brown, Olen Ray *microbiologist, biomedical researcher, educator*
Eisenstark, Abraham *research director, microbiologist*
Finkelstein, Richard Alan *retired microbiology educator, consultant*
Ignoffo, Carlo Michael *insect pathologist-virologist*
Morehouse, Lawrence Glen *veterinarian, educator, academic administrator*
Poehlmann, Carl John *agricultural researcher*
Roberts, R. Michael *animal scientist, biochemist, educator*
Vogt, Albert Ralph *forester, educator, program director*
Wagner, Joseph Edward *veterinarian, educator*
Yanders, Armon Frederick *biological sciences educator, science administrator*

Eureka
Lindsey, Susan Lyndaker *zoologist*
Sexton, Owen James *vertebrate ecology educator, conservationist*

Jefferson City
Reidinger, Russell Frederick, Jr. *fish and wildlife scientist*

Kansas City
Krumlauf, Robert Eugene *neuroscientist, educator*
Neaves, William Barlow *cell biologist, educator*
Spigarelli, James L. *science administrator*

Maryland Heights
Gillette, Richard Gareth *neurophysiology educator, researcher*

Saint Charles
Radke, Rodney Owen *agricultural research executive, consultant*

Saint Louis
Ackers, Gary Keith *biophysical chemistry educator, researcher*
Allen, Garland Edward *biologist, professor, writer*
Beachy, Roger *biologist, plant pathologist, researcher*

Elgin, Sarah Carlisle Roberts *biology professor, researcher*
Fraley, Robert T. *biotechnologist*
Green, Maurice *molecular biologist, educator, virologist*
Hoessle, Charles Herman *zoological park administrator, director*
Hogan, Michael Ray *life science executive*
Hultgren, Scott J. *microbiologist educator*
Miller, James Gegan *research scientist*
Petersen, Steven E. *neuroscientist, health facility administrator, educator*
Raven, Peter Hamilton *botanist, director*
Schlesinger, Milton J. *virology educator, researcher*
Templeton, Alan Robert *biology professor*
Wold, William Sydney *molecular biology educator*
Woolsey, Thomas Allen *neuroscientist, biologist*

Springfield
Steffen, Alan Leslie *entomologist*

Villa Ridge
Laskowski, Leonard Francis, Jr. *microbiologist*

Wentzville
Garrett, Dwayne Everett *veterinary clinic executive*

West Plains
Wilcoxson, Roy Dell *plant pathologist, researcher, educator*

NEBRASKA

Ewing
Dierks, Merton Lyle *veterinarian*

Gering
Weihing, John Lawson *plant pathologist, state legislator*

Lincoln
Francis, Charles Andrew *agronomy educator, consultant*
Gardner, Charles Olda *botanist, researcher, financial analyst*
Genoways, Hugh Howard *systematic biologist, educator*
Massengale, Martin Andrew *agronomist, educator, university president*
McClurg, James Edward *research laboratory executive*
Sander, Donald Henry *retired soil scientist*
Specht, James E. *agronomist, educator*
Stoddard, Robert H. *geography educator*
Taylor, Stephen Lloyd *toxicologist, educator, food scientist*
Vidaver, Anne Marie *plant pathology educator*

Omaha
Badeer, Henry Sarkis *physiology educator*
Bowen, Brent *aviation educator*
Simmons, Lee Guyton, Jr. *zoological park director*

NEW YORK

New York
Fuchs, Elaine V. *molecular biologist, educator*

NORTH DAKOTA

Bisbee
Keller, Michelle R. *science educator*

Bismarck
Carlisle, Ronald Dwight *nursery owner*

Grand Forks
Carlson, Edward C. *anatomy educator, cell biologist, department chairman*
Crawford, Richard Dwight *biology professor, researcher*
Fox, Carl Alan *research executive*

OHIO

Akron
Millman, Irving *microbiologist, educator, retired inventor*

Bowling Green
Clark, Eloise Elizabeth *biologist, educator*

Cincinnati
Maruska, Edward Joseph *zoological park administrator*
Saal, Howard Max *clinical geneticist, pediatrician, educator*
Safferman, Robert Samuel *microbiologist, researcher*
Schaefer, Frank William III *microbiologist, researcher*
Schiff, Gilbert Martin *virologist, microbiologist, educator*
Silberstein, Edward Bernard *nuclear medicine educator, oncologist, researcher*

Cleveland
Blackwell, John *science educator*
Caplan, Arnold I. *biology professor*
Dell'Osso, Louis Frank *neuroscience educator*
Herrup, Karl *neurobiologist*
Lando, Jerome Burton *macromolecular science educator*
Luck, Richard Earle *astronomy educator*
Suri, Jasjit S. *research scientist*
Taylor, Steve Henry *zoologist*

Columbus
Corbato, Charles Edward *geology educator, academic administrator*
Crawford, Daniel J. *biologist, educator*
Croce, Carlo M. *research scientist*
Floyd, Gary Leon *plant cell biologist*
Foland, Kenneth A. *geological sciences educator*
Foster, Woodbridge A. *medical entomologist, educator*
Fry, Donald Lewis *physiologist, educator*
Glaser, Ronald *microbiologist, educator*
Haury, David Leroy *science education specialist*
Kapral, Frank Albert *microbiologist and immunology educator*
Marzluf, George Austin *biochemistry educator*
Newsom, Gerald Higley *astronomy educator*
Peterle, Tony John *zoologist, educator*
Reeve, John Newton *molecular biology and microbiology educator*
Roth, Robert Earl *ecologist, educator*
Triplehorn, Charles A. *entomologist, educator*
von Recum, Andreas F. *veterinarian, bioengineer*
Warmbrod, James Robert *agriculture educator, academic administrator*
Webb, Thomas Evan *biochemistry educator*
Westman, Judith Ann *clinical geneticist, dean*
Wood, Jackie Dale *physiologist, educator, researcher*
Zartman, David Lester *retired zoology educator, researcher*

Cumberland
Reece, Robert William *zoological park administrator*

Dayton
Gregor, Clunie Bryan *geology educator*

Delaware
Fry, Anne Evans *zoology educator*

Hamilton
Munson, Richard Howard *horticulturist*

Milford
Gascoigne, William M. *research executive*

Newark
Greenstein, Julius Sydney *zoology educator*

Oxford
Eshbaugh, W(illiam) Hardy *botanist, educator*
Rypstra, Ann *zoology educator*

Powell
Borin, Gerald W. *zoological park administrator*

Wooster
Cooper, Richard Lee *agronomist, educator*
Ferree, David Curtis *horticultural researcher*
Hall, Franklin R. *entomology researcher, educator*
Hoitink, Henricus A. *plant pathology educator*
Madden, Laurence Vincent *plant pathology educator*

Wyoming
Cooley, William Edward *research scientist, consultant*

Yellow Springs
Webb, Paul *physiologist, educator, researcher, consultant*

SOUTH DAKOTA

Brookings
Krishnan, Padmanaban *food scientist, educator*
Moldenhauer, William Calvin *soil scientist*

TEXAS

Burkburnett
Estes, James Russell *botanist, educator*

San Antonio
Perry, George *neuroscientist, educator*

VIRGINIA

Blacksburg
Kelly, James Michael *plant and soil scientist*

WISCONSIN

Cottage Grove
Lund, Daryl Bert *retired food science educator*

Fitchburg
Welker, Wallace Irving *neurophysiologist, educator*

Madison
Anderson, Christopher *astronomy educator*
Bisgard, Gerald Edwin *biosciences educator, researcher*
Brock, Thomas Dale *retired microbiology professor*
Burkholder, Wendell Eugene *retired entomology educator, researcher*
Buss, Daryl *veterinarian, dean*
Cassinelli, Joseph Patrick *astronomy educator*
Dolan, Terrence Raymond *neurophysiology educator*
Easterday, Bernard Carlyle *veterinary medicine educator*
Ensign, Jerald C. *bacteriology educator*
Evert, Ray Franklin *botany educator*
Greaser, Marion Lewis *science educator*
Guillery, Rainer Walter *anatomy educator*
Handelsman, Jo *plant pathologist, educator*
Hopen, Herbert John *horticulture educator*
Iltis, Hugh Hellmut *botanist, educator, environmental advocate*
Ives, Anthony Ragnar *ecologist*
Jeanne, Robert Lawrence *entomologist, educator*
Kaesberg, Paul Joseph *virology researcher*
Kawaoka, Yoshihiro *virologist, educator*
Kemnitz, Joseph William *physiologist, researcher*
Kimble, Judith E. *molecular biologist, cell biologist*
Magnuson, John Joseph *zoology educator*
Marrett, Cora B. *science educator*
Miller, Paul Dean *breeding consultant, geneticist, educator*
Moss, Richard L. *physiology educator*
Sheffield, Lewis Glosson *physiologist*
Susman, Millard *geneticist, educator*
Szybalski, Waclaw *geneticist, educator*
Thomson, James Alexander *molecular biologist, educator*
Turner, Monica Goigel *ecologist*
White, John Graham *science educator, research director*
Zedler, Joy Buswell *ecological sciences educator*

Merrimac
Hall, David Charles *retired zoological park administrator, veterinarian*

Middleton
Horsch, Robert B. *biotechnologist*

Milwaukee
Besharse, Joseph Culp *cell biologist, researcher*
Cowley, Allen Wilson, Jr. *physiologist*
Kampine, John P. *anesthesiology and physiology educator*
Wikenhauser, Charles *zoological park administrator*

Shawano
Heikes, Keith *science administrator*

Sheboygan
Abler, Ronald Francis *geography educator*

CANADA

MANITOBA

Winnipeg
Persaud, Trivedi Vidhya Nandan *anatomy educator, researcher, consultant*

ADDRESS UNPUBLISHED

Achgill, Ralph Kenneth *retired research scientist*
Ahlquist, Paul Gerald *molecular biology researcher, educator*
Ahrens, Franklin Alfred *veterinary pharmacology educator*
Andrews, Richard Vincent *physiologist, educator*
Barnes, Robert F *agronomist*
Bentley, Charles Raymond *geophysics educator*
Bers, Donald Martin *physiology educator*
Boerner, Ralph E. J. *forest soil ecologist, plant biology educator*
Borisy, Gary G. *science administrator, researcher, molecular biology professor*
Decker, Walter Johns *toxicologist*
Grunder, Hermann A. *science administrator, director, research scientist*
Helgeson, John Paul *plant pathology and botany educator*
Karr, Gerald Lee *agricultural economist, state senator*
Laster, Danny Bruce *animal scientist*
LaVelle, Arthur *anatomy educator*
Lippincott, James Andrew *retired biochemistry and biological sciences educator*
Michaelis, Elias K. *neurochemist*
Miller, Patrick William *research scientist, educator*
Mitchell, John Laurin Amos *biological science educator*
Moll, Russell Addison *aquatic ecologist, science administrator*
Peterson, David Maurice *retired physiologist*
Reetz, Harold Frank, Jr. *agronomist*
Richardson, Rudy James *toxicology and neurosciences educator*
Salkind, Michael Jay *science administrator, metallurgical engineer*
Setser, Carole Sue *food scientist, educator*
Smarr, Larry Lee *science administrator, astrophysicist, educator*
Sperelakis, Nicholas, Sr. *retired physiology and biophysics educator, researcher*
Vande Woude, George Franklin *molecular biologist, cancer researcher*
VanMany, Seng Dao *microbiologist*
Voss, Regis Dale *agronomist, educator*
Willson, Mary Frances *ecology researcher, educator*
Wilson, Kenneth Geddes *physics research administrator*

SCIENCE: MATHEMATICS AND COMPUTER SCIENCE *See also* INFORMATION TECHNOLOGY

UNITED STATES

COLORADO

Lafayette
Dowling, Thomas Allan *retired mathematics professor*

ILLINOIS

Chicago
Ash, J. Marshall *mathematician, educator*
Bona, Jerry Lloyd *mathematician, educator*
Bookstein, Abraham *information science educator*
Drinfeld, Vladimir Gershonovich *mathematician, educator*
Dupont, Todd F. *mathematics professor*
Erber, Thomas *mathematics and physics professor*
Foster, Ian Tremere *computer scientist*
Gibbons, Robert D. *biostatistics educator*
Hanson, Floyd Bliss *mathematician*
Kirkpatrick, Anne Saunders *systems analyst*
Lawler, Gregory Francis *mathematics professor*
Madansky, Albert *statistics educator*
May, J. Peter *mathematics professor*
Stigler, Stephen Mack *statistician, educator*
Thisted, Ronald Aaron *statistician, educator, consultant*

Dekalb
Sons, Linda Ruth *mathematician, educator*

Evanston
Davis, Stephen Howard *applied mathematics professor*
Devinatz, Allen *retired mathematician, educator*
Jerome, Joseph Walter *mathematics professor*
Manin, Yuri Ivanovich *mathematician*
Matkowsky, Bernard Judah *mathematician, educator*
Olmstead, William Edward *mathematics professor*
Tanner, Martin Abba *statistician, educator*
Zelinsky, Daniel *mathematics professor*

La Grange Park
Butler, Margaret Kampschaefer *retired computer scientist*

Urbana
Burkholder, Donald Lyman *mathematician, educator*
Carroll, Robert Wayne *mathematics professor*
Gray, John Walker *mathematician, educator*
Henson, C. Ward *mathematician, educator*
Jockusch, Carl Groos, Jr. *mathematics professor*
Tondeur, Philippe Maurice *mathematician, educator*

INDIANA

Bloomington
Prosser, Franklin Pierce *computer scientist*
Purdom, Paul Walton, Jr. *computer scientist*
Puri, Madan Lal *mathematics professor*

Fort Wayne
Beineke, Lowell Wayne *mathematics professor*
Stoll, Wilhelm *mathematics professor*

Greencastle
Anderson, John Robert *retired mathematics professor*

Indianapolis
Reid, William Hill *mathematics professor*

Lafayette
de Branges de Bourcia, Louis *mathematics professor*

Muncie
Ali, Mir Masoom *retired statistician, educator*

Notre Dame
Kogge, Peter Michael *computer scientist, educator*
Pollak, Barth *mathematics professor*
Sommese, Andrew John *mathematics professor*

West Lafayette
Abhyankar, Shreeram Shankar *mathematics professor*
Rice, John Rischard *computer scientist, researcher, educator*
Yu, Jiu-Kang *mathematics professor*

IOWA

Ames
Fuller, Wayne Arthur *statistics educator*
Isaacson, Dean Leroy *statistician*

Cedar Rapids
Bahadur, Birendra *displays research specialist*

Grinnell
Adelberg, Arnold Melvin *mathematics professor, researcher*

Iowa City
Hogg, Robert Vincent, Jr. *mathematical statistician, educator*
Robertson, Timothy Joel *statistician, educator*

KANSAS

Lawrence
Himmelberg, Charles John III *mathematics professor, researcher*

Shawnee Mission
Flora, Jairus Dale, Jr. *statistician*

MARYLAND

Laurel
Teeters, Joseph Lee *mathematician, consultant*

MICHIGAN

Ann Arbor
Beutler, Frederick Joseph *information scientist*
Brown, Morton B. *biostatistics educator*
Conway, Lynn *computer scientist, electrical engineer, educator*
Hochster, Melvin *mathematician, educator*
Larsen, Edward William *mathematician, nuclear engineering educator*
Lewis, Donald John *mathematics professor*
Stembridge, John Reese *mathematics professor*

Dearborn
Brown, James Ward *mathematician, educator, author*

Detroit
Schreiber, Bertram Manuel *mathematics professor*

East Lansing
Moran, Daniel Austin *mathematician, educator*
Stapleton, James Hall *retired statistician, educator*

Kalamazoo
Paul, Annegret *mathematics professor*

MINNESOTA

Minneapolis
Bingham, Christopher *statistics educator*
Markus, Lawrence *retired mathematics professor*
Miller, Willard, Jr. *mathematician, educator*
Pour-El, Marian Boykan *mathematician, educator*
Serrin, James Burton *mathematics professor*

Moorhead
Heuer, Gerald Arthur *mathematician, educator*

Northfield
Appleyard, David Frank *retired mathematics professor*
Steen, Lynn Arthur *mathematician, educator*

MISSOURI

Columbia
Flournoy, Nancy *statistician, educator*
Schrader, Keith William *mathematician*

Rolla
Grimm, Louis John *mathematician, educator*
Ingram, William Thomas III *mathematics professor*
Zobrist, George Winston *computer scientist, educator*

Saint Louis
Baernstein, Albert, II, *mathematician, educator*
Boothby, William Munger *retired mathematics professor*
Epner, Steven Arthur *computer consultant*
Nussbaum, A(dolf) Edward *mathematician, educator*
Turner, Jonathan Shields *computer science educator, researcher*
Wilson, Edward Nathan *mathematician, educator*

NEBRASKA

Lincoln
Wiegand, Sylvia Margaret *mathematician, educator*

NEVADA

Reno
Kleinfeld, Erwin *mathematician, educator*

NORTH CAROLINA

Cape Carteret
Mullikin, Thomas Wilson *mathematics professor*

OHIO

Athens
Wen, Shih-Liang *mathematics professor*

Cleveland
Clark, Robert Arthur *mathematician, educator*
de Acosta, Alejandro Daniel *mathematician, educator*
Goffman, William *mathematician, educator*
Szarek, Stanislaw Jerzy *mathematics professor*
Woyczynski, Wojbor Andrzej *mathematician, educator*

Columbus
Chandrasekaran, Balakrishnan *computer scientist, educator*
Friedman, Avner *mathematician, educator*
Muller, Mervin Edgar *computer scientist, consultant, statistician, educator*
Santner, Thomas *statistician, educator*
Zweben, Stuart Harvey *information scientist, educator, dean*

Dayton
Rucker, Richard S. *information systems executive*

Kent
Varga, Richard Steven *retired mathematics professor*

Westerville
Brombacher, Bruce E. *mathematics educator*

Wooster
Hales, Raleigh Stanton, Jr. *retired mathematics professor, academic administrator*

PENNSYLVANIA

Phoenixville
Koenig, Michael Edward Davison *information science educator*

WISCONSIN

Chetek
Fossum, Robert Merle *mathematician, educator*

La Crosse
Matchett, Andrew James *mathematics professor*

Madison
Askey, Richard Allen *mathematician, educator*
Beck, Anatole *mathematician, educator*
DeWitt, David J. *computer scientist*
Draper, Norman Richard *statistician, educator*
Johnson, Millard Wallace, Jr. *mathematics and engineering professor*
Malkus, David Starr *mathematician*
Ono, Ken *mathematician, educator*
Rabinowitz, Paul H. *mathematics educator*
Robinson, Stephen Michael *mathematician, educator*

Pleasant Prairie
Biland, Alan Thomas *computer integrated manufacturing executive*

ADDRESS UNPUBLISHED

Bailar, Barbara Ann *retired statistician*
Boardman, Elizabeth Drake *computer security professional*
Downey, Deborah Ann *systems specialist*
Fulton, William *mathematics professor*
Gehring, Frederick William *mathematician, educator*
Halberstam, Heini *mathematics professor*
Krantz, Steven George *mathematics professor, writer*
Pollock, Karen Anne *computer analyst*
Roitman, Judith *mathematician, educator*
Simon, Janos *computer science educator*
Tan, Hui Qian *computer science, civil engineering educator*
Ullman, Nelly Szabo *statistician, educator*
Warner, William Hamer *mathematician*
Yackel, James William *mathematician, academic administrator*

SCIENCE: PHYSICAL SCIENCE

UNITED STATES

ARIZONA

Tucson
Dunn, Floyd *biophysics and biomedical engineering professor*

CALIFORNIA

Berkeley
Moore, C. Bradley *chemistry professor*

La Jolla
Dixon, Jack Edward *biological chemistry professor, consultant*

Merced
Winston, Roland *physicist, researcher*

Sacramento
Purdy, James Aaron *medical physics professor*

San Clemente
Wolfram, Thomas *physicist, educator*

Santa Barbara
Witherell, Michael S. *physicist, educator*

COLORADO

Boulder
Truce, William Everett *chemist, educator*

Windsor
Mayer, Victor James *geologist, educator*

FLORIDA

Bonita Springs
Brown, Theodore Lawrence *chemistry professor*

Venice
Peterson, Francis *retired physicist, educator*

ILLINOIS

Argonne
Abrikosov, Alexei Alexeyevich *physicist*
Bader, Samuel David *physicist*
Carpenter, John Marland *engineer, physicist*
Crabtree, George *physicist*
Derrick, Malcolm *physicist*
Dyrkacz, Gary R. *chemist, researcher*
Katz, Joseph Jacob *retired chemist, educator*
Lawson, Robert Davis *theoretical nuclear physicist*
Peshkin, Murray *physicist*
Schiffer, John Paul *physicist, educator*
Steindler, Martin Joseph *chemist*
Stock, Leon Milo *chemist, educator*

Batavia
Bardeen, William Allan *research physicist*
Chrisman, Bruce Lowell *physicist, administrator*
Jonckheere, Alan Mathew *physicist*
Lach, Joseph Theodore *physicist*
Peoples, John, Jr. *physicist, researcher*
Tollestrup, Alvin Virgil *physicist*

Champaign
Buschbach, Thomas Charles *geologist, consultant*
Gross, David Lee *geologist*
Rebeiz, Constantin Anis *plant biochemist, lab and foundation administrator, educator*
Slichter, Charles Pence *physicist, researcher*
Wolfram, Stephen *physicist, computer company executive*

Chicago
Beckers, Jacques Maurice *astrophysicist*
Berry, Richard Stephen *chemist*
Blumberg, Avrom Aaron *physical chemistry professor*
Bonham, Russell Aubrey *chemistry professor*
Bosnich, Brice *chemistry professor*
Chin, Cheng *physicist, educator*
Cronin, James Watson *physicist, researcher*
Curran, Ed *meteorologist, reporter*
Eastman, Dean Eric *physicist, researcher*
Epstein, Wolfgang *retired biochemist, educator*
Erdös, Ervin George *pharmacology and biochemistry professor*
Freed, Karl Frederick *chemistry professor*
Gislason, Eric Arni *chemistry professor*
Gomer, Robert *chemistry professor*
Halpern, Jack *chemist, educator*
Harvey, Jeffrey A. *physics professor*
Harvey, Ronald Gilbert *research chemist*
Hast, Malcolm Howard *biomedical scientist, educator*
Herzenberg, Caroline Stuart Littlejohn *physicist*
Hildebrand, Roger Henry *astrophysicist, physicist*
Iqbal, Zafar Mohd *biochemist, molecular biologist, pharmacologist, cancer researcher, toxicologist, consultant*
Kadanoff, Leo Philip *physicist, educator*
Kouvel, James Spyros *physicist, educator*
Levi-Setti, Riccardo *physicist, director*
Levy, Donald Harris *chemistry professor*
Liao, Shutsung *biochemist, molecular oncologist*
Makinen, Marvin William *biophysicist, educator*
Miller, Brant *meteorologist*
Nambu, Yoichiro *physics professor*
Newcomb, Martin Eugene, Jr. *chemistry professor*
Norris, James Rufus, Jr. *chemist, educator*
Oehme, Reinhard *physicist, researcher*
Olsen, Edward John *geologist, educator, curator*
Palmer, Patrick Edward *radio astronomer, educator*
Pilcher, James Eric *physicist*
Rosner, Jonathan Lincoln *physicist, researcher*
Rosner, Robert *astrophysicist, educator*
Schug, Kenneth Robert *chemistry professor*
Skilling, Thomas Ethelbert III *meteorologist, educator*
Srivastava, Anurag K. *research scientist*
Stroscio, Michael Anthony *physicist, researcher*
Truran, James Wellington, Jr. *astrophysicist, educator*
Turner, Michael Stanley *astrophysics professor, researcher, science administrator*

Dekalb
Kimball, Clyde William *physicist, researcher*

Downers Grove
Green, David William *chemist, educator*
Hubbard, Lincoln Beals *medical physicist, consultant*

Evanston
Chang, R. P. H. *materials science educator*
Freeman, Arthur J. *physics educator*
Godwin, Hilary A. *chemistry professor, research scientist*
Ibers, James Arthur *chemist, educator*
Johnson, David Lynn *retired materials scientist, educator*
Lambert, Joseph Buckley *chemistry professor*
Margoliash, Emanuel *biochemist, educator*
Mirkin, Chad A. *chemistry professor*
Oakes, Robert James *physics and astronomy professor*
Odom, Teri Wang *chemist*
Olson, Gregory Bruce *materials science and engineering educator, academic director*
Sachtler, Wolfgang Max Hugo *chemistry professor*
Seidman, David N(athaniel) *materials scientist, engineer, educator*
Shriver, Duward Felix *chemistry professor, researcher, consultant*
Silverman, Richard Bruce *chemist, biochemist, educator*
Spears, Kenneth George *chemistry professor*
Stoddart, J(ames) Fraser *chemistry professor, researcher*
Ulmer, Melville Paul *physics and astronomy educator*
Van Duyne, Richard Palmer *analytical chemistry educator, chemical physics educator*
Walter, Robert Irving *retired chemistry professor*
Wessels, Bruce W. *materials scientist, educator, department chairman*

Glenview
Rorig, Kurt Joachim *chemist, science association director*

Hinsdale
Kaminsky, Manfred Stephan *physicist*

Lake Forest
Weston, Arthur Walter *chemist, consultant, retired chemicals executive*

Lemont
Williams, Jack Marvin *research chemist*

Naperville
Sherren, Anne Terry *chemistry professor*

North Chicago
Loga, Sanda *physicist, researcher*

Northfield
Shabica, Charles Wright *retired geologist, earth science educator*

Oak Park
Fanta, Paul Edward *chemist, educator*

Peoria
Cunningham, Raymond Leo *retired research chemist*

Rock Island
Hammer, William Roy *paleontologist, educator*

Rockford
Walhout, Justine Simon *chemistry professor*

Round Lake
Breillatt, Julian Paul, Jr. *biochemist, biomedical engineer*

Urbana
Beak, Peter Andrew *chemistry professor*
Bishop, Stephen Gray *physicist*
Cahill, David G. *materials scientist, engineer, educator*
Ceperley, David Matthew *physics professor*
Crutcher, Richard Metcalf *astronomer, educator*
Goldwasser, Edwin Leo *physicist*
Greene, Joseph E. *material science researcher*
Greene, Laura Helen *physicist*
Gruebele, Martin *chemistry and biophysicist professor*
Iben, Icko, Jr. *astrophysicist, educator*
Jonas, Jiri *chemist, educator*
Katzenellenbogen, John Albert *chemistry professor*
Kelleher, Neil L. *chemist, educator*
Kieffer, Susan Werner *geologist, educator, media consultant*
Klein, Miles Vincent *physics professor*
Leggett, Anthony James *physics professor, researcher*
Lu, Yi *chemistry professor*
Makri, Nancy *chemistry professor*
Mantulin, William W. *biophysicist, lab administrator*
Mapother, Dillon Edward *physicist, academic administrator*
Martinez, Todd J. *chemistry professor*
Pirkle, William H. *chemistry professor*
Rowland, Theodore Justin *physicist, researcher*
Schweizer, Kenneth Steven *physics professor*
Snyder, Lewis Emil *astrophysicist, educator*
Suslick, Kenneth Sanders *chemistry professor*
Switzer, Robert Lee *biochemistry professor*
Van Harlingen, Dale J. *physics professor*
Woese, Carl R. *biophysicist, microbiology educator*
Zimmerman, Steven Charles *chemistry professor*

Winfield
Morss, Lester Robert *chemist*

Woodridge
Shen, Sin-Yan *physicist, acoustical engineer, musicologist*

INDIANA

Bloomington
Cameron, John M. *nuclear scientist, educator, administator*
Clemmer, David E. *chemistry professor, researcher*
Edmondson, Frank Kelley *retired astronomer*
Hanson, Gail G. *physicist, researcher*
Hattin, Donald Edward *geologist, educator*
Hites, Ronald Atlee *chemist, educator*
Kauffman, Erle Galen *geologist, paleontologist*
Lane, N. Gary *retired paleontologist*
Letsinger, Robert Lewis *chemistry professor*
Macfarlane, Malcolm Harris *physicist, educator*
Mufson, Stuart Lee *astronomer, educator*
Novotny, Milos Vlastislav *chemistry professor*
Parmenter, Charles Stedman *chemistry professor*
Peters, Dennis Gail *chemist*
Pollock, Robert Elwood *nuclear scientist*

Elkhart
Free, Helen Murray *chemist, consultant*

Fort Wayne
Stevenson, Kenneth Lee *chemist, educator*

Indianapolis
Fife, Wilmer Krafft *retired chemistry professor*
Lau, Pauline Young *chemist*
Mirsky, Arthur *retired geologist, educator*
Pearlstein, Robert M. *physics educator*
Wong, David T. *biochemist, researcher*

Lafayette
Brewster, James Henry *retired chemistry professor*
Feuer, Henry *retired chemist*
Gartenhaus, Solomon *physicist, educator*
Loeffler, Frank Joseph *physicist, educator*
Pardue, Harry L. *chemist, educator*
Porile, Norbert Thomas *chemistry professor*

Muncie
Harris, Joseph McAllister *retired chemist*

Notre Dame
Fehlner, Thomas Patrick *chemistry professor*
Feigl, Dorothy Marie *chemistry professor, academic administrator*
Marshalek, Eugene Richard *retired physics educator, researcher*
Meisel, Dan *chemist*
Schuler, Robert Hugo *chemist, educator*
Thomas, John Kerry *chemistry professor*
Trozzolo, Anthony Marion *chemistry professor*

West Lafayette
Adelman, Steven Allen *chemist, educator*
Barnes, Virgil Everett, II, *physics professor*
Cooks, R(obert) Graham *chemist, educator*
Diamond, Sidney *chemist, educator*
Judd, William Robert *engineering geologist, educator*
Laskowski, Michael, Jr. *chemist, educator*
Lipschutz, Michael Elazar *chemistry professor, consultant, researcher*
Margerum, Dale William *chemistry professor*
McMillin, David Robert *chemistry professor*
Morrison, Harry *chemistry professor*
Negishi, Ei-ichi *chemistry professor*
Overhauser, Albert Warner *physicist*
Ramdas, Anant Krishna *physicist, optics scientist*
Rossmann, Michael George *biochemist, educator*
Zwier, Timothy S. *chemistry professor*

IOWA

Ames
Armstrong, Daniel Wayne *chemist, educator*
Barnes, Richard George *physicist, researcher*
Barton, Thomas J. *chemistry professor, researcher*
Bowen, George Hamilton, Jr. *astrophysicist, educator*
Clem, John Richard *physicist, educator*
Fritz, James Sherwood *chemist, educator*
Gordon, Mark S. *chemist, educator*
Gschneidner, Karl Albert, Jr. *metallurgist, educator, editor, consultant*
Hong, Mei *chemistry professor*
Horowitz, Jack *biochemistry educator*
Houk, Robert Samuel *chemistry professor*
Jacobson, Robert Andrew *chemistry professor*
Ruedenberg, Klaus *theoretical chemist, educator*
Tabatabai, M. Ali *chemist, biochemist*
Yeung, Edward Szeshing *chemist*

Cedar Falls
Koob, Robert Duane *chemistry professor, academic administrator*

Cedar Rapids
Feller, Steven Allen *physics educator*

Grinnell
Swartz, James Edward *chemistry professor, educator, dean*

Iowa City
Burton, Donald Joseph *chemistry professor*
Donelson, John Everett *biochemistry professor, molecular biologist*
Glenister, Brian Frederick *geologist, educator*
Gurnett, Donald Alfred *physics professor*
Koch, Donald LeRoy *retired geologist, state agency administrator*
Montgomery, Rex *biochemist, educator*
Titze, Ingo Roland *physics professor*

Spencer
Lemke, Alan James *environmental specialist*

West Des Moines
Lynch, David William *physicist, retired educator*

KANSAS

Lawrence
Ammar, Raymond George *physicist, researcher*
Dreschhoff, Gisela Auguste Marie *physicist, researcher*
Enos, Paul *geologist, educator*
Gerhard, Lee Clarence *geologist, educator*
Harmony, Marlin Dale *chemistry professor*
Landgrebe, John Allan *chemistry professor*
Mitscher, Lester Allen *chemist, educator*

Stella, Valentino John *chemistry professor*

Manhattan
Setser, Donald Wayne *chemistry professor*

Pittsburg
Foresman, James Buckey *geologist, industrial hygienist, geochemist*

Topeka
Barton, Janice Sweeny *chemistry professor*

MICHIGAN

Ann Arbor
Agranoff, Bernard William *biochemist, educator*
Akerlof, Carl William *physics professor*
Aller, Hugh Duncan *astronomer, educator*
Ashe, Arthur James III *chemistry professor*
Bartell, Lawrence Sims *chemist, educator*
Blinder, Seymour Michael *chemistry and physics professor, researcher*
Chupp, Timothy Edward *physicist, educator, academic administrator*
Clarke, Roy *physicist, researcher*
Dekker, Eugene Earl *biochemistry educator*
Filisko, Frank Edward *physicist, researcher*
Fisk, Lennard Ayres *physicist, researcher*
Gingerich, Philip Derstine *paleontologist, evolutionary biologist, educator*
Griffin, Henry Claude *retired chemistry professor*
Guan, Kun-Liang *biochemist, educator*
Jones, Lawrence William *retired physicist*
Kesler, Stephen Edward *geology educator*
Krimm, Samuel *physicist, researcher, educator, administrator*
Krisch, Alan David *physics professor*
Lahann, Joerg *chemist*
Longone, Daniel Thomas *chemistry professor*
Morris, Michael David *chemistry professor*
Neal, Homer Alfred *physics professor, researcher, academic administrator*
Nordman, Christer Eric *chemistry professor*
Nriagu, Jerome Okon *environmental geochemist*
Parkinson, William Charles *physics professor, researcher*
Pollack, Henry Nathan *geophysics educator*
Robertson, Richard Earl *physical chemist, educator*
Roe, Byron Paul *physics professor*
Roush, William R. *chemistry professor*
Savit, Robert Steven *physics professor, consultant*
Townsend, LeRoy B. *chemistry professor, researcher, academic administrator*
Van der Voo, Rob *geophysicist*
Walker, Jack L. *environmental scientist*
Walter, Lynn M. *geologist, educator*
Wong, Victor Kenneth *physics professor*

Big Rapids
Mathison, Ian William *chemistry professor, dean, consultant*

Chelsea
Weinreich, Gabriel *physicist, minister, educator*

Detroit
Frade, Peter Daniel *chemist, educator, administrator*
Gupta, Suraj Narayan *physicist, researcher*
Kirschner, Stanley *chemist*
Oliver, John Preston *chemistry professor*
Stewart, Melbourne George, Jr. *physicist, researcher*
Thomas, Robert Leighton *physicist, researcher*

East Lansing
Abolins, Maris Arvids *physicist, educator*
Austin, Sam M. *physicist, educator*
Blosser, Henry Gabriel *physicist*
Brown, Boyd Alex *physicist, researcher*
D'Itri, Frank Michael *environmental research chemist*
Dye, James Louis *retired chemistry professor*
Gelbke, Claus-Konrad *nuclear physics educator*
Gottfried, Michael D. *paleontologist, educator*
Harrison, Michael Jay *physicist, researcher*
Kaplan, Thomas Abraham *physicist, educator*
Kirkpatrick, R(obert) James *geologist, educator*
Preiss, Jack *biochemistry professor*

Grand Rapids
Greenfield, John Charles *biochemist, professional society administrator*

Grosse Pointe Park
Orton, Colin George *medical physicist*

Houghton
McGinnis, Gary David *chemist, science educator*

Kentwood
Yovich, Daniel John *chemist, educator*

Midland
Chao, Marshall *chemist*
Nowak, Robert Michael *chemist*

Mount Pleasant
Dietrich, Richard Vincent *geologist, educator*

Okemos
Burnett, Jean B. *biochemist, educator*

Rochester
Ovshinsky, Stanford Robert *physicist, inventor, energy executive, information company executive*

Shelby Township
Smith, John Robert *physicist, department chairman*

Troy
Fritzsche, Hellmut *physics professor*

Warren
Herbst, Jan Francis *physicist, researcher*

West Bloomfield
Harwood, Julius J. *metallurgist, educator*

Ypsilanti
Barnes, James Milton *retired physics and astronomy professor*
Jones, Frank N. *chemist, researcher, educator, consultant*

MINNESOTA

Austin
Holman, Ralph Theodore *retired biochemistry professor, nutritionist*

Lakeville
Phinney, William Charles *retired geologist*

Minneapolis
Ackerman, Eugene *biophysics professor*
Carr, Peter William *chemistry professor*
Edwards, Richard Lawrence *geology educator*
Goldman, Allen Marshall *physics professor*
Halley, James Woods *physics professor*
Hogenkamp, Henricus Petrus Cornelis *biochemistry researcher, educator*
Kuhi, Leonard Vello *astronomer, academic administrator*
Lynch, Mike *meteorologist, radio personality*
Marshak, Marvin Lloyd *physicist, researcher*
Portoghese, Philip Salvatore *medicinal chemist, educator*
Shifman, Mikhail *physicist*
Siepmann, Joern Ilja *chemistry professor*
Tran, Nang Tri *research scientist, electrical engineer, entrepreneur*
Truhlar, Donald Gene *chemist, educator*
Vainschtein, Arkady *physics educator*
Wright, Herbert E(dgar), Jr. *geologist*

Northfield
Cederberg, James *retired physics professor*
Noer, Richard J. *physics professor, researcher*

Rochester
Kao, Pai Chih *clinical chemist*

Saint Paul
Perry, James Alfred *environmental scientist, academic administrator, educator, consultant*
Prager, Stephen *chemistry professor*
Rubens, Sidney Michel *physicist, consultant*

MISSOURI

Columbia
Bauman, John E., Jr. *chemistry professor*
Decker, Wayne Leroy *meteorologist, educator*
Ethington, Raymond Lindsay *geology educator, researcher*
Gehrke, Charles William *biochemistry professor*
Hawthorne, Marion Frederick *chemistry professor*
Johns, Williams Davis, Jr. *geologist, educator*
Plummer, Patricia Lynne Moore *chemist, educator*
Randall, Douglas D. *biochemist, educator*
Randall, Linda Lea *biochemist, educator*
Shelton, Kevin L. *geology educator*
Weisman, Gary Andrew *biochemist*

Creve Coeur
Bockserman, Robert Julian *chemist*

Kansas City
Ching, Wai Yim *physics professor, researcher*
Durig, James Robert *chemistry professor*
Parizek, Eldon Joseph *geologist, educator, dean*
Rodenhuis, David Roy *meteorologist, educator*
Rost, William Joseph *chemist*
Wilkinson, Ralph Russell *retired biochemistry educator, toxicologist*

Kirksville
Festa, Roger Reginald *chemist, educator*

Maryland Heights
Chinn, Rex Arlyn *chemist*

Rolla
Adawi, Ibrahim Hasan *physics professor*
Alexander, Ralph William, Jr. *physics professor*
Mc Farland, Robert Harold *retired physicist*
Vineyard, Jerry D. *geologist*

Saint Louis
Agarwal, Ramesh Kumar *aeronautical scientist, researcher, educator*
Bender, Carl Martin *physics professor, consultant*
Burgess, James Harland *physics professor, researcher*
Cowsik, Ramanath *physics professor*
Fitzpatrick, Susan *biochemist, neurologist, foundation administrator*
Friedlander, Michael Wulf *physicist, researcher*
Gibbons, Patrick Chandler *physicist, researcher*
Gross, Michael Lawrence *chemistry professor*
Israel, Martin Henry *astrophysicist, educator, academic administrator*
Macias, Edward S. *chemistry professor, dean, academic administrator*
Marshall, Garland Ross *biochemist, biophysicist, medical educator*
Murray, Robert Wallace *chemistry professor*
Norberg, Richard Edwin *physicist, researcher*
Sly, William S. *biochemist, educator*
Will, Clifford Martin *physicist, researcher, educator*
Zinner, Ernst K. *physics educator, earth and planetary science educator, researcher*

Springfield
Thompson, Clifton C. *retired chemistry professor, academic administrator*

NEBRASKA

Lincoln
Blad, Blaine L. *agricultural meteorology educator, consultant*
Eckhardt, Craig Jon *chemistry professor*
Jones, Lee Bennett *chemistry professor, academic administrator*
Treves, Samuel Blain *geologist, educator*

Omaha
Zepf, Thomas Herman *retired physics professor*

NEW YORK

Troy
Linhardt, Robert John *chemistry professor*

NORTH DAKOTA

Fargo
Wagner, Alexander Johannes *physicist, educator*

Grand Forks
Jacobs, Francis Albin *biochemist, educator*

OHIO

Akron
Bohm, Georg G. A. *physicist*
Cheng, Stephen Zheng Di *chemistry professor, polymer engineer*
Gent, Alan Neville *physicist, researcher*
Kennedy, Joseph Paul *chemist, researcher*
Piirma, Irja *chemist, educator*

Beachwood
Krieger, Irvin Mitchell *retired chemistry professor*

Cincinnati
Ford, Emory A. *chemist, researcher*
Francis, Marion David *consulting chemist*
Goodman, Bernard *physics professor*
Heineman, William Richard *chemistry professor*
Jensen, Elwood Vernon *biochemist*
Mark, James Edward *physical chemist, department chairman*
Merchant, Mylon Eugene *physicist, engineer*
Witten, Louis *physics professor*

Cleveland
Bidelman, William Pendry *astronomer, educator*
Carey, Paul Richard *biophysicist*
Goldstein, Marvin Emanuel *aerospace scientist*
Hanson, Richard Winfield *biochemist, educator*
Klopman, Gilles *chemistry professor*
Koenig, Jack Leonard *chemist, educator*
Kowalski, Kenneth Lawrence *physicist, researcher*
Krauss, Lawrence Maxwell *physicist, astronomy educator, researcher, author*
Mawardi, Osman Kamel *retired plasma physicist*
Rogers, Charles Edwin *physical chemistry and polymer science professor*
Schuele, Donald Edward *retired physics professor, dean*

Columbus
Behrman, Edward Joseph *biochemistry educator*
Bergstrom, Stig Magnus *geology educator*
Chisholm, Malcolm Harold *chemistry professor*
Daehn, Glenn Steven *materials scientist*
De Lucia, Frank Charles *physicist, researcher*
Elliot, David Hawksley *geologist, educator*
Epstein, Arthur Joseph *physics and chemistry educator*
Herbst, Eric *physicist, astronomer, chemist*
Jezek, Kenneth Charles *geophysicist, educator, researcher*
Ling, Ta-Yung *physicist*
Madia, William Juul *chemist*
Miller, Terry Alan *chemistry professor*
Reibel, Kurt *physicist, researcher*
St. Pierre, George Roland, Jr. *materials scientist, engineering executive, educator*
Shore, Sheldon G. *chemist, educator*
Soloway, Albert Herman *medicinal chemist*
Sugarbaker, Evan R. *nuclear science research administrator*
Voss, Anne Coble *nutritional biochemist*
Wali, Mohan Kishen *environmental scientist, forester, educator*
Wilkins, John Warren *physics professor*
Williams, James Case *metallurgist*
Wojcicki, Andrew Adalbert *chemist, educator*

Dayton
Battino, Rubin *retired chemistry professor*
Spokane, Robert Bruce *biophysical chemist*

Euclid
Dowell, Michael Brendan *chemist*

Highland Hills
Brathwaite, Ormond Dennis *chemistry professor*

Kent
Doane, J. William *physics educator and researcher, science administrator*
Tuan, Debbie Fu-Tai *chemist, educator*

Marietta
Jache, Albert William *retired chemistry professor, academic administrator, research scientist*

Oberlin
Carlton, Terry Scott *retired chemist, educator*
Simonson, Bruce Miller *geologist, educator*

Ottawa Hills
Goodridge, Alan Gardner *research biochemist, educator*

Oxford
Cox, James Allan *chemistry professor*
Gordon, Gilbert *chemist, educator*
Macklin, Philip Alan *retired physics professor*

Painesville
Dietrich, Joseph Jacob *retired chemist, research and development company executive*
Scozzie, James Anthony *chemist*

Sheffield Lake
Friend, Helen Margaret *chemist*

Toledo
Averill, Bruce Alan *chemistry professor*
Bagley, Brian G. *materials science educator, researcher*

Upper Arlington
Relle, Ferenc Matyas *chemist*

Warren
Zimmerman, Doris Lucile *chemist*

Wright Patterson AFB
Garscadden, Alan *physicist*

PENNSYLVANIA

Pine Grove Mills
Lundberg, Joe *meteorologist, radio personality*

Pittsburgh
Yasinsky, John Bernard *nuclear scientist*

SOUTH DAKOTA

Rapid City
Smith, Paul Letton, Jr. *geophysicist*

TEXAS

Richardson
Salamon, Myron Ben *physicist, educator, dean*

VIRGINIA

Hartfield
Johnson, Carl Randolph *chemist, educator*

WASHINGTON

Bellingham
Cox, David Jackson *biochemistry professor*

Redmond
Meshii, Masahiro *materials science educator*

WISCONSIN

Eau Claire
Dawkins, Rusty *meteorologist*
Dusk, Brooke *meteorologist*
Jedda, John *meteorologist*

Kenosha
Kolb, Vera M. *chemist, educator*

Madison
Adler, Julius *biochemist, educator, biologist*
Anderson, Louis Wilmer, Jr. *physicist, researcher*
Barger, Amy J. *astronomer, educator*
Barger, Vernon Duane *physicist, educator*
Beinert, Helmut *biochemist*
Blackwell, Helen E. *chemistry professor*
Botez, Dan *physicist*
Bretherton, Francis P. *atmospheric and oceanic sciences educator*
Callen, James Donald *plasma physicist, nuclear engineer*
Christensen, Nikolas Ivan *geophysicist, educator*
Churchwell, Edward Bruce *astronomer, educator*
Clay, Clarence Samuel *acoustical oceanographer*
Cleland, W(illiam) Wallace *biochemistry educator*
Coppersmith, Susan Nan *physicist*
Crim, Forrest Fleming, Jr. *chemist, educator*
Dahl, Lawrence Frederick *chemistry professor*
DeWerd, Larry Albert *medical physicist, educator*
Dott, Robert Henry, Jr. *geologist, educator*
Ediger, Mark D. *chemistry professor*
Ellis, Arthur Baron *chemist, educator*
Evenson, Merle Armin *chemist, educator*
Farrar, Thomas C. *chemist, educator*
Gallagher, John Sill III *astronomer*
Gellman, Samuel Helmer *chemist, educator*
Himpsel, Franz Josef *physicist, researcher*
Hokin, Lowell Edward *biochemist, educator*
Kiessling, Laura Lee *chemist, researcher*
Lagally, Max Gunter *physics professor*
Larbalestier, David Chistopher *materials scientist, educator*
Lardy, Henry A(rnold) *biochemistry professor*
Lawler, James Edward *physics professor*
Lin, Chun Chia *research physicist, educator*
Maher, Louis James, Jr. *geologist, educator*
Mukerjee, Pasupati *chemistry professor*
Pondrom, Lee Girard *physicist, researcher*
Pray, Lloyd Charles *geologist, educator*
Rich, Daniel Hulbert *retired chemistry professor*
Robertson, James Magruder *geological research administrator*
Savage, Blair deWillis *astronomer, educator*
Scherer, Victor Richard *physicist, computer scientist, musician, consultant*
Sih, Charles John *pharmaceutical chemistry professor*
Skinner, James Lauriston *chemist, educator*
Vaughan, Worth Edward *retired chemistry professor*
West, Robert Culbertson *chemistry professor*
Young, Raymond Allen *chemist, educator*
Yu, Hyuk *chemist, educator*
Zimmerman, Howard Elliot *chemist, educator*

Middleton
Ferry, James Allen *physicist, electrostatics company executive*

Milwaukee
Baden, Mark *meteorologist*
Bader, Alfred Robert *chemist*
Burch, Thaddeus Joseph, Jr. *physics professor, priest*
Buss, Daniel Frank *environmental scientist*
Griffith, Owen Wendell *biochemistry professor*
Haworth, Daniel Thomas *chemistry professor*
Hill, Lance *meteorologist*
Karkheck, John Peter *physics professor, researcher*
Severson, Sally *meteorologist*

Stoughton
Huber, David Lawrence *physicist, researcher*

Whitefish Bay
Hendee, William Richard *medical physics educator, academic administrator, radiologist*

Williams Bay
Hobbs, Lewis Mankin *astronomer*

CANADA

MANITOBA

Winnipeg
Smith, Ian Cormack Palmer biophysicist

ADDRESS UNPUBLISHED

Ames, Donald Paul retired air research director
Amy, Jonathan Weekes chemist, educator
Baym, Gordon Alan physicist, researcher
Blander, Milton chemist
Bohm, Henry Victor physicist
Carlson, Janet Lynn chemistry professor
Edwards, Helen Thom physicist
Einhorn, Martin B. physicist, educator
Goldwasser, Eugene biochemist, educator
Govindjee, biophysics, biochemistry, and biology professor
Hanks, Alan R. retired chemistry professor
Hoeg, Donald Francis chemist, consultant, research and development company executive
Jackson, Edwin Atlee retired physicist, educator
Jordan, Thomas Fredrick physics professor
Krawetz, Stephen Andrew molecular medicine and genetics scientist, educator
Lederman, Leon Max physicist, researcher
Nagel, Sidney Robert physics professor
Nair, Vasu chemist, educator
Oka, Takeshi physicist, physical chemist, astronomer, educator
Pollack, Gerald Leslie physicist, researcher, educator
Pytte, Agnar physicist, retired academic administrator
Qutub, Musa Yacub hydrogeologist, educator, consultant
Rozelle, Lee Theodore physical chemist, researcher
Scherer, Norbert Franz chemistry professor
Schwartz, Shirley E. retired chemist, researcher
Shaw, Melvin Phillip physicist, engineering educator, psychologist
Sikorski, James Alan research chemist
Sullivan, Kathryn D. geologist, former astronaut, former science association executive
Sunderman, Duane Neuman chemist, research and development company executive
Suttie, John Weston biochemist
Taylor, Kathleen (Christine Taylor) physical chemist, researcher
Thompson, Mary Eileen chemistry professor

SOCIAL SCIENCE

UNITED STATES

ARIZONA

Scottsdale
Baker, Edward Martin engineering and industrial psychologist

Tempe
Prescott, Edward C. economist, educator

Tucson
Axinn, George Harold rural sociology educator

ARKANSAS

Little Rock
Kaza, Greg John economist, educator

CALIFORNIA

Santa Monica
Moskos, Charles C. social studies educator

COLORADO

Fort Collins
Ahmann, John Stanley retired psychologist

FLORIDA

Port Saint Lucie
Augelli, John Pat geographer, educator, writer, consultant, rancher

ILLINOIS

Arlington Heights
Griffin, Jean Latz political strategist, writer, publisher

Carbondale
Bozzola, John Joseph botany educator, researcher
Kapusta, George botany educator, agronomist, researcher

Champaign
Arnould, Richard Julius economist, educator, consultant, dean
Eriksen, Charles Walter psychologist, educator
Kanfer, Frederick H. psychologist, educator
Triandis, Harry Charalambos psychologist, educator

Chicago
Baum, Bernard Helmut sociologist, educator
Becker, Gary Stanley economist, educator
Ben-Yoseph, Miriam social sciences educator
Bidwell, Charles Edward sociologist, educator
Carlton, Dennis William economics professor
Coase, Ronald Harry economist, educator
Cohler, Bertram Joseph psychologist, educator
Cox, Charles C. economist
Cropsey, Joseph retired political science professor
Dawson, Michael C. political science professor
Depoy, Phil E. special studies think-tank executive
Drezner, Daniel William political scientist, educator
Fernandez, James anthropology educator
Fogel, Robert William economist, educator, historian
Freeman, Leslie Gordon anthropologist, educator
Freeman, Susan Tax anthropologist, educator, culinary historian
Gannon, Sister Ann Ida retired philosophy educator
Gardiner, John Andrew political science educator
Gibson, McGuire archaeologist, educator
Gould, John Philip economist, educator
Graber, Doris Appel political scientist, writer, editor
Grossman, Lisa Robbin clinical psychologist, lawyer
Heckman, James Joseph economist, educator
Kaye, Richard William labor economist
Larson, Allan Louis political scientist, educator, lay worker
Laumann, Edward Otto sociology educator
Levine, Donald Nathan sociologist, educator
Liu, Ben-chieh economist
Lucas, Robert Emerson, Jr. economist, educator
McNeill, G. David psychologist, educator
Mikesell, Marvin Wray geography educator
Mufson, Elliott J. psychologist, director, neurologist, educator
Murphy, Kevin M. economics professor
Myerson, Roger Bruce economist, educator
Nicholas, Ralph Wallace anthropologist, educator
Peltzman, Sam economics professor
Pugh, Roderick Wellington retired psychologist
Rosen, George economist, educator
Sanders, Jacquelyn Seevak psychologist, educator
Smith, Raymond Thomas anthropology educator
Smith, Stan Vladimir economist, finance company executive
Stocking, George Ward, Jr. anthropology educator
Taub, Richard Paul social sciences educator
Walberg, Herbert John psychologist, educator, consultant
Zellner, Arnold economics, econometrics and statistics professor
Zonis, Marvin political scientist, educator

Dekalb
Smith, Harvey social science research administrator

Evanston
Braeutigam, Ronald Ray economics professor, educational association administrator
Gentner, Dedre psychology professor
Gordon, Robert James economics professor
Hurter, Arthur Patrick economist, educator
Irons, William George anthropology educator
Kalai, Ehud economist, researcher, educator
Mills, Edwin Smith economics professor
Porter, Robert Hugh economics educator
Reiter, Stanley economist, educator
Satterthwaite, Mark A. economics professor
Weisbrod, Burton Allen economist, educator

Hinsdale
Dederick, Robert Gogan economist

Macomb
Walzer, Norman Charles retired economics professor

Maryville
Stark, Patricia Ann psychologist

Moline
Penn, J. B. economist, former federal agency administrator

Naperville
Cowlishaw, Mary Lou government educator

Springfield
Wehrle, Leroy Snyder economist, educator

Urbana
Baer, Werner economist, educator
Carmen, Ira Harris political scientist, educator
Gabriel, Michael psychology professor
Giertz, J. Fred economics professor
Giles, Eugene anthropology educator
Gove, Samuel Kimball retired political science professor
Kolodziej, Edward Albert political scientist, educator
Leuthold, Raymond Martin agricultural economics professor
Nettl, Bruno anthropologist, musicologist, educator
Resek, Robert William economist
Schmidt, Stephen Christopher agricultural economist, educator
Wirt, Frederick Marshall retired political scientist, educator
Yu, George Tzuchiao political science professor

Wilmette
Walker, Ronald Edward psychologist, educator

INDIANA

Bloomington
Brehm, Sharon Stephens psychology professor, former academic administrator
Conrad, Geoffrey Wentworth archaeologist, educator
DeWeese, Devin A. history educator
Estes, William Kaye psychologist, educator
Goldstone, Robert L. psychologist, educator
Guth, Sherman Leon (S. Lee) psychologist, educator
Hofstadter, Douglas Richard cognitive scientist, educator, writer
Nosofsky, Robert M. psychology educator
O'Meara, Patrick O. political science professor
Ostrom, Elinor political science professor, researcher
Ostrom, Vincent A(lfred) political science professor
Patrick, John Joseph social sciences educator
Peebles, Christopher Spalding anthropologist, educator, dean, academic administrator
Saunders, W(arren) Phillip, Jr. economics professor, consultant, writer
Smith, Frederick Robert, Jr. social studies educator, educator

Carmel
Rychlak, Joseph Frank psychologist, educator

Granger
Craypo, Charles labor economics professor

Lafayette
Hardin, Lowell Stewart retired economics professor
Schönemann, Peter Hans psychologist, educator

Muncie
Swartz, B. K., Jr., (Benjamin Kinsell Swartz Jr.) archaeologist, educator

New Albany
Crump, Claudia geographer, educator

Notre Dame
Arnold, Peri Ethan political scientist
Bartell, Ernest economist, educator, priest
Despres, Leo Arthur sociologist, anthropologist, educator, academic administrator
Hallinan, Maureen Theresa sociologist, educator
Mirowski, Philip Edward economics professor
Swartz, Thomas R. economist, educator
Valenzuela, Julio Samuel sociologist, educator
Weigert, Andrew Joseph sociology educator

South Bend
Carrington, Michael Davis criminal justice and security consultant
Dowty, Alan Kent political scientist, educator

West Lafayette
Cicirelli, Victor George psychologist
Farris, Paul Leonard agricultural economist
Gruen, Gerald Elmer psychologist, educator
Horwich, George economist, educator
Perrucci, Robert sociologist, educator
Theen, Rolf Heinz-Wilhelm political science educator
Tyner, Wallace Edward agricultural economics educator
Weidenaar, Dennis Jay retired economics professor
Weinstein, Michael Alan political science professor

IOWA

Ames
Flora, Cornelia Butler sociologist, educator
Fox, Karl August retired economist, educator, eco-behavioral scientist
Gradwohl, David Mayer anthropology educator
Harl, Neil Eugene economist, educator, lawyer, writer
Johnson, Stanley R. economist, educator
Klonglan, Gerald Edward sociology educator
Roskey, Carol Boyd social studies educator, dean, director

Des Moines
Demorest, Allan Frederick retired psychologist

Iowa City
Albrecht, William Price economist, educator, government official
Fethke, Gary C. economics professor, former dean
Fuller, John Williams economics professor
Geweke, John Frederick economics professor
Kim, Chong Lim political science professor
Loewenberg, Gerhard political science professor
Nathan, Peter E. psychologist, educator
Siebert, Calvin D. economist, educator
Wasserman, Edward Arnold psychology professor

KANSAS

Fort Leavenworth
Schneider, James Joseph military theory educator, consultant

Lawrence
Barnett, William Arnold economics professor
Heller, Francis Howard retired law and political science educator
Lane, Meredith Anne botany educator, museum director
Schroeder, Stephen Robert psychology researcher
Shaffer, Harry George economics professor

Manhattan
Barkley, Andrew Paul economics professor
Murray, John Patrick psychologist, educator, researcher
Nafziger, Estel Wayne economics professor
Phares, E. Jerry retired psychology professor
Prins, Harald Edward Lambert anthropologist, educator
Roper, Donna C. archaeologist
Thomas, Lloyd Brewster economics professor

Topeka
Spohn, Herbert Emil psychologist

Winfield
Schul, Bill Dean psychological administrator, author

MARYLAND

Baltimore
Grossman, Joel B(arry) political science educator

MICHIGAN

Ann Arbor
Bornstein, Morris economist, educator
Brace, C. Loring anthropologist, educator
Cain, Albert Clifford psychologist, educator
Campbell, John Creighton political science educator
Cohen, Malcolm Stuart economist
Dominguez, Kathryn Mary economist, educator
Ellsworth, Phoebe Clemencia psychology professor
Gruppen, Larry Dale psychologist, educational researcher
Hagen, John William psychology professor
House, James Stephen social psychologist, educator
Jackson, James Sidney psychologist, educator
Johnston, Lloyd Douglas social sciences educator
Kim, E. Han financial economist, educator
Kingdon, John Wells political science professor
Kmenta, Jan retired economics professor
Marcus, Joyce (Joyce Marcus Flannery) anthropology educator
McKeachie, Wilbert James psychologist, educator
Mitchell, Edward John economist, retired educator
Nisbett, Richard Eugene psychology professor
Paige, Jeffery Mayland sociologist, educator
Parsons, Jeffrey Robinson anthropologist, educator
Pedley, John Griffiths archaeologist, educator
Schwarz, Norbert psychology professor
Shapiro, Matthew David economist, educator
Singer, Eleanor sociologist, editor
Singer, J. David political science professor
Stafford, Frank Peter, Jr. economics professor, consultant
Tropman, John Elmer social sciences educator
Waltz, Susan political scientist, educator
Weisskopf, Thomas Emil economics educator
Whallon, Robert Edward anthropology educator
Whitman, Marina von Neumann economist, educator
Williams, Melvin Donald anthropologist, educator
Zimmerman, William political science educator
Zucker, Robert A(lpert) psychologist

Detroit
Goodman, Allen Charles economist, educator
Pietrofesa, John Joseph psychologist, educator

East Lansing
Abeles, Norman psychologist, educator
Abramson, Paul Robert political scientist, educator
Ballbach, Philip Thornton political consultant, investor
Fisher, Ronald C. economics educator
Ilgen, Daniel Richard psychology professor
Kreinin, Mordecha Eliahu economics professor
Lang, Marvel urban affairs educator
Manderscheid, Lester Vincent agricultural economics educator
Menchik, Paul Leonard economist, educator
Press, Charles retired political science professor
Robbins, Lawrence Harry anthropologist, educator
Schlesinger, Joseph Abraham political scientist
Strassmann, W. Paul economics professor

Grand Haven
Parmelee, Walker Michael psychologist

Northport
Thomas, Philip Stanley economist, educator

Saugatuck
Genetski, Robert James economist

Southfield
Hotelling, Harold economics professor, lawyer

West Bloomfield
Marx, Thomas George economist

Ypsilanti
Weinstein, Jay A. social sciences educator, researcher

MINNESOTA

Duluth
Hoffman, Richard George psychologist
Rapp, George Robert (Rip) geology and archeology educator

Minneapolis
Berscheid, Ellen S. psychology professor, writer, researcher
Bouchard, Thomas Joseph, Jr. psychology professor, researcher
Chipman, John Somerset retired economist, educator
Erickson, W(alter) Bruce business and economics educator, entrepreneur
Gudeman, Stephen Frederick anthropology educator
Hansen, Jo-Ida Charlotte psychology professor, researcher
Holt, Robert Theodore political science professor, educator, dean
Hurwicz, Leonid economist, educator
Knoke, David Harmon sociology educator
Kudrle, Robert Thomas economist, educator
Lewis, Stephen Richmond, Jr. economist, educator
Ostrom, Don political science professor
Shively, William Phillips political scientist, educator
Ward, David Allen sociology educator
Weinberg, Richard Alan psychologist, educator
Ysseldyke, James Edward psychology professor

Richfield
Gallagher, Shawna Barbara psychologist, educator

Saint Paul
Dahl, Reynold Paul economics professor
D'Aurora, James Joseph psychologist, consultant
Jessup, Paul Frederick financial economist, educator
Rossmann, Jack Eugene psychologist, educator
Ruttan, Vernon Wesley agricultural economist, educator

Upsala
Piasecki, David Alan social studies educator

MISSOURI

Columbia
Biddle, Bruce Jesse social psychologist, educator
Dolliver, Robert Henry psychology professor
LoPiccolo, Joseph psychologist, educator, author
Rowlett, Ralph Morgan archaeologist, educator
Salter, Christopher Lord geography educator

Kansas City
Graham, Charles research psychologist
Lubin, Bernard psychologist, educator

Saint Louis
Beck, Lois Grant anthropologist, educator, author
Browman, David L(udvig) archaeologist
Cosmopoulos, Michael archaeologist, educator
Etzkorn, K. Peter sociology educator, administrator, consultant, writer
Greenbaum, Stuart I. economist, educator
Holden, Robert (Bob Holden) political science professor, former governor
Leven, Charles Louis economics professor
Le Vine, Victor Theodore retired political science professor
Miller, Gary J. political economist
Neuefeind, Wilhelm economics professor, university administrator
North, Douglass Cecil economist, educator
O'Connell, Daniel Craig retired psychologist, educator
Olney, John William psychiatry professor
Ozawa, Martha Naoko social work educator
Salisbury, Robert Holt political science professor

Storandt, Martha *psychologist*
Virgo, John Michael *economist, researcher, educator*
Weidenbaum, Murray Lew *economist, educator*

NEBRASKA

Lincoln
MacPhee, Craig Robert *economist, educator*

Omaha
Wunsch, James Stevenson *political science professor*

NEW HAMPSHIRE

Keene
Hackett, John Thomas *retired economist and financial executive*

NEW JERSEY

Princeton
Allen, Danielle S. *political science and classics educator*

NORTH DAKOTA

Fargo
Gustafson, Cole Richard *agricultural economics educator*

Grand Forks
Penland, James Granville *psychologist*

OHIO

Akron
Franck, Ardath Amond *psychologist, educator*

Ashland
Ford, Lucille Garber *economist, educator*

Athens
Ungar, Irwin Allan *botany educator*
Vedder, Richard Kent *economics professor*

Bowling Green
Hakel, Milton Daniel, Jr. *psychologist, educator, writer, consultant*

Cedarville
Firmin, Michael Wayne *psychology professor*

Chillicothe
Smith, Ralph Edward *psychology assistant*

Cincinnati
Bieliauskas, Vytautas Joseph *psychologist, educator*
Bishop, George Franklin *political scientist, educator*
Bluestein, Venus Weller *retired psychologist, educator*
Scherer, Anita (Anita Stock) *gerontologist, marketing consultant*

Cleveland
Beall, Cynthia *anthropologist, educator*
Binstock, Robert Henry *public policy educator, writer*
Carlsson, Bo Axel Vilhelm *economics professor*
Deal, William Thomas *retired school psychologist*
Grundy, Kenneth William *political science professor*
Hokenstad, Merl Clifford, Jr. *social work educator*
Kilbane, Sally Conway *economics professor*
Kolb, David Allen *psychologist, educator*
Lewine, Mark Saul *anthropology professor*
Mayland, Kenneth Theodore *economist*
McHale, Vincent Edward *political science professor*
Sibley, Willis Elbridge *anthropology educator, consultant*

Columbus
Alger, Chadwick Fairfax *political scientist, educator*
Brewer, Marilynn B. *psychology professor*
Coons, James William *economist*
Huber, Joan Althaus *sociology educator*
Kiecolt-Glaser, Janice Kay *psychologist*
Mueller, John Ernest *political science professor, dance critic*
Naylor, James Charles *psychologist, educator*
Peterson, Ruth D. *sociologist*
Tuckman, Bruce Wayne *educational psychologist, educator, researcher*
Weisberg, Herbert Frank *political science professor*

Dayton
Rowell, Katherine Renee *sociologist, educator*

Kent
Feinberg, Richard *anthropologist, educator*
Williams, Harold Roger *economist, educator*

Moreland Hills
Tolchinsky, Paul Dean *organization design psychologist*

Oberlin
Friedman, William John *psychology professor*

Oxford
Rejai, Mostafa *political science professor*

SOUTH DAKOTA

Lennox
Brendtro, Larry Kay *psychologist*

Vermillion
Clem, Alan Leland *retired political scientist, educator*

TEXAS

Houston
Allen, Jon G. *psychologist*
Lewis, Lisa *psychologist, administrator*

VERMONT

Wallingford
Gutmann, David Leo *psychology professor*

VIRGINIA

Arlington
von Furstenberg, George Michael *economics professor, researcher*

Fredericksburg
Rampersad, Peggy A. Snellings *sociologist, consultant*

Harrisonburg
Kreider, Leonard Emil *retired economics professor*

WISCONSIN

Beloit
Davis, Harry Rex *political science professor*
Green, William *archaeologist*

Madison
Brock, William Allen III *economist, educator*
Chapman, Loren J. *psychology professor*
Goldberger, Arthur Stanley *economics professor*
Graf, Truman Frederick *agricultural economist, educator*
Greenfield, Norman Samuel *psychologist, educator*
Hansen, W. Lee *economics professor*
Hester, Donald Denison *economics professor*
Kluender, Keith R. *psychology educator*
Mueller, Willard Fritz *economics professor*
Nichols, Donald Arthur *economist, educator*
Rice, Joy Katharine *psychologist, education educator*
Strier, Karen Barbara *anthropologist, educator*
Wilson, Franklin D. *sociology educator*
Wolfe, Barbara L. *economics professor, researcher*

Middleton
Dorner, Peter Paul *retired economist, educator*

Milwaukee
Handelman, Howard *political scientist, educator*
Kupst, Mary Jo *psychologist, researcher*
Moberg, David Oscar *sociology educator*

New Berlin
Bielke, Patricia Ann *psychologist*

Oshkosh
Gruberg, Martin *political science professor*

Whitefish Bay
Hawkins, Brett William *retired political science professor*

CANADA

ONTARIO

London
Davenport, Paul *economics professor*

ADDRESS UNPUBLISHED

Adelman, Richard Charles *gerontologist, educator*
Aliber, Robert Z. *economist, educator*
Allen, Bruce Templeton *retired economics professor*
Allen, Leatrice Delorice *psychologist*
Anderson, James George *sociologist, educator, communications educator*
Blank, Rebecca Margaret *economist*
Boff, Kenneth Richard *engineering research psychologist*
Bourguignon, Erika Eichhorn *anthropologist, educator*
Boyce, David Edward *transportation and regional science educator*
Brandl, John Edward *public affairs educator*
Cacioppo, John Terrance *psychologist, educator, researcher*
Chase, Clinton Irvin *psychologist, educator*
Cohen, Jerome *psychology educator, electrophysiologist*
Denevan, William Maxfield *geographer, historical ecologist, educator*
Earle, Timothy Keese *anthropology educator*
Garn, Stanley Marion *physical anthropologist, educator*
Geake, Raymond Robert *psychologist*
Greeley, Andrew Moran *sociologist, writer*
Howrey, Eugene Philip *retired economics and statistics professor*
Kahana, Eva Frost *sociology educator*
Karim, Muhammad Bazlul *political scientist, educator*
Lee, Mordecai *political scientist, educator*
Lucas, Wayne Lee *sociologist, educator*
Lundstedt, Sven Bertil *behavioral and social scientist, educator*
Maehr, Martin Louis *psychology professor*
Richardson, Laurel Walum *sociology educator*
Sameroff, Arnold Joshua *developmental psychologist, educator, research scientist*
Shapiro, Leo J. *social researcher*
Stokey, Nancy L. *economist, educator*
Sumner, William Marvin *anthropology and archaeology educator*
Swanstrom, Thomas Evan *economist*
Watson, Patty Jo *anthropology educator*
Weil, Rolf Alfred *economist, retired university president*
Yost, William Albert *psychology professor*